TWENTIETH CENTURY
AUTHORS

THE AUTHORS SERIES

TWENTIETH CENTURY AUTHORS

A Biographical Dictionary of Modern Literature

Edited by

STANLEY J. KUNITZ

and

HOWARD HAYCRAFT

COMPLETE IN ONE VOLUME WITH
1850 BIOGRAPHIES AND
1700 PORTRAITS

NEW YORK
THE H. W. WILSON COMPANY
NINETEEN HUNDRED FORTY-TWO

Preface

THIS work, which has been in preparation for more than four years, aims to provide a foundation-volume of authentic biographical information on the writers of this century, of all nations, whose books are familiar to readers of English. No attempt has been made to include foreign authors on the basis of their reputation in their native lands or tongues: the criterion, in general, has been the degree of acceptance of their translated works in the United States and England. *Twentieth Century Authors* supersedes two out-of-print preliminary volumes, *Living Authors* (1931) and *Authors Today and Yesterday* (1933), which together contained sketches of approximately 800 authors. The present volume includes biographies of more than 1850 authors, illustrated by more than 1700 portraits. Each sketch is newly written.

Primary emphasis has been on professional men and women of letters whose vocation is the writing of books of fiction, poetry, history, biography, criticism, etc. When a biography is included of a man or woman who is only secondarily a writer of books, the reason for the exception is given in the text. The sketches range, in assigned length, from 300 to 1500 words, roughly in proportion to the importance of the subject, but frequently influenced by extraneous considerations, such as term of career and amount of available data. By and large, in the selection of authors the editors have been guided less by their personal critical preferences than by an effort to satisfy the general taste. *Twentieth Century Authors* is a reference work, not a judgment-seat. Its ideal realization would be to contain the lives of all modern writers in whom all readers are interested. This is manifestly impossible, and no doubt every reader who consults this volume will be disappointed at the omission of some authors and surprised at the inclusion of some others. The editors, however, are sanguine enough to hope that most readers will find herein most of the modern authors whose names they know or whose books they enjoy. Future supplementary volumes will be able to rectify the omissions and to include, as well, the names of newcomers to the literary scene, some of whom have already gained prominence since the closing of the alphabetical lists for the present volume.

Despite the inconvenience to the editors of this volume, some authors have persisted in living and working well into the twentieth century after beginning their careers in the nineteenth. With respect to such border-line cases, the editors' policy has been to include only those authors who, in the literary sense, have flourished since 1900. Sketches of others of the same generation who flourished earlier may be found in two previous biographical dictionaries by the same editors: *British Authors of the Nineteenth Century* (1936) and *American Authors: 1600-1900* (1938), both likewise published by The H. W. Wilson Company. The names of such authors have been entered in the present alphabet, with cross-references to the pertinent volume. For a more complete listing of writers of books for children, the reader is advised to consult *The Junior Book of Authors* (Wilson, 1934).

Every living author in this volume who could be reached was invited to write his own sketch. As can be seen, the response to this request was more than gratifying. Many who did not contribute autobiographies were extremely helpful in supplying needed biographical and bibliographical data. The immense job of assembling more than 1700 portraits could not have been accomplished without the generous cooperation of the publicity departments of dozens of publishing houses. It needs to be said, however, that where portraits are poor, out-of-date, or lacking entirely, the blame must be ascribed either to the curious photo-phobia of a handful of otherwise enterprising firms or the fantastic ideas held by some publishers (and photographers!) as to what constitutes a reproducible photograph.

In accordance with general library practice, the editors have conformed to Library of Congress name forms and pseudonym policy, except when modification has seemed imperative. (The Library of Congress, for example, persists in listing the works of the late B. M. Bower under "B. M. Sinclair," the *second* of her three marriage names!) Cross-references have been provided whenever they seemed helpful. With respect to Russian names, the transliterative system now used by the Library of Congress has been abandoned in favor of simpler forms which, if frequently inconsistent one with the other, will at least not confound the average reader.

Each biographical sketch is followed by a list of the principal works of the author in question, with original dates of publication. A list of biographical and critical sources about each author is also given as a guide to further study. Although the bibliographical entries have been checked many times and brought up-to-date at every proof-reading, they are selective and practical, not definitive in nature, nor should they be cited in determining debatable "firsts" or obscure bibliographical points.

In this project the editors have had the pleasure of working with an unusually capable staff of research specialists and writers, including Betty Alsterlund, Miriam Allen deFord, Angel Flores, Herbert B. Grimsditch, Wilbur C. Hadden, and Earle F. Walbridge. The major contribution of Miss deFord merits special acknowledgment. We wish also to express our appreciation of the courteous helpfulness of the staff of the New York Public Library, particularly in the Picture Collection, Reference, and Photostat departments.

––––––––––

In earlier reprintings of this volume (1944, 1950, 1956) two steps were taken to increase the usefulness of the work to the reader and librarian: (1) death dates of all authors who died since 1942 were added in footnotes; (2) certain corrections of fact, brought to our attention by the subjects themselves or by readers, were made in the text.

In the fifth printing in 1961, a necrology was added on pages viii-ix listing the authors who had died since the fourth printing of the book in 1956 or whose deaths at earlier dates had not been previously noted. Each subsequent printing brings this necrology up to date.

Additional material supplementing many of the sketches in the foundation volume and new biographical sketches of authors who have become prominent since 1942 will be found in *Twentieth Century Authors: First Supplement* (1955).

THE EDITORS

NECROLOGY

Adams, F. P. Mar. 23, 1960
Adams, S. H. Nov. 16, 1958
Akins, Z. Oct. 29, 1958
Aldanov, M. A. Feb. 25, 1956
Aldington, R. July 28, 1962
Allingham, M. June 30, 1966
Anderson, M. Feb. 28, 1959
Andrews, R. C. Mar. 11, 1960
Angell, N. Oct. 7, 1967
Anthony, K. S. Nov. 20, 1965
Arlen, M. June 23, 1956
Arvin, N. Mar. 22, 1963
Asbury, H. Feb. 24, 1963
Asch, N. Dec. 23, 1964
Asch, S. July 10, 1957
Ashton, H. R. June 27, 1958
Auslander, J. June 22, 1965

Babel, I. E. 1938
Bacon, J. D. D. July 29, 1961
Baker, D. June 17, 1968
Barnes, M. A. Oct. 25, 1967
Baroja y Nessi, P. Oct. 30, 1956
Barretto, L. Dec. 30, 1971
Basso, H. May 13, 1964
Baum, V. Aug. 29, 1960
Beard, M. R. Aug. 14, 1958
Becker, M. L. Apr. 27, 1958
Beebe, W. June 4, 1962
Beerbohm, M. May 20, 1956
Bell, C. Sept. 17, 1964
Bemelmans, L. Oct. 1, 1962
Benda, J. June 7, 1956
Benoit, P. Mar. 3, 1962
Bentley, E. C. Mar. 30, 1956
Bercovici, K. Dec. 27, 1961
Berenson, B. Oct. 6, 1959
Blackmur, R. P. Feb. 2, 1965
Beston, H. Apr. 15, 1968
Blake, G. Aug. 29, 1961
Blixen, K. D. Sept. 7, 1962
Bogan, L. Feb. 4, 1970
Bojer, J. July 3, 1959
Bone, D. W. May 17, 1959
Bordeaux, H. Mar. 29 (?), 1963
Borden, M. Dec. 2, 1968
Bottome, P. Aug. 23, 1963
Bowers, C. G. Jan. 21, 1958
Bradley, J. H. Jr. Aug. 18, 1962
Brailsford, H. N. Mar. 23, 1958
Braithwaite, W. S. B. June 8, 1962
Brecht, B. Aug. 14, 1956
Brighouse, H. July 25, 1958
Brinton, C. C. Sept. 7, 1968
Brittain, V. M. Mar. 29, 1970
Bromfield, L. Mar. 18, 1956
Brooks, V. May 2, 1963
Brophy, J. Nov. 13, 1965
Brown, J. M. Mar. 16, 1969
Bullett, G. Jan. 3, 1958

Burlingame, R. Mar. 19, 1967
Bynner, W. June 1, 1968
Byrd, R. E. Mar. 11, 1957

Cabell, J. B. May 5, 1958
Campbell, R. Apr. 23, 1957
Campbell, W. S. Dec. 25, 1957
Canby, H. S. Apr. 5, 1961
Cannan, G. June 30, 1955
Cannan, J. Apr. 22, 1961
Carco, F. May 26, 1958
Carossa, H. Sept. 12, 1956
Carroll, P. V. Oct. 20, 1968
Cendrars, B. Jan. 21, 1961
Cestre, C. Nov. 16, 1958
Chamberlin, W. H. Sept. 12, 1969
Church, R. Mar. 4, 1972
Churchill, W. L. S. Jan. 24, 1965
Cleghorn, S. N. Apr. 4, 1959
Cocteau, J. Oct. 11, 1963
Cohen, O. R. Jan. 6, 1959
Cole, G. D. H. Jan. 14, 1959
Colum, M. G. M. Oct. 22, 1957
Colum, P. Jan. 11, 1972
Conkling, G. W. H. Nov. 15, 1958
Connolly, J. B. Jan. 20, 1957
Coppard, A. E. Jan. 13, 1957
Cournos, J. Aug. 27, 1966
Craig, G. July 29, 1966
Crichton, K. S. Nov. 24, 1960
Crofts, F. W. Apr. 11, 1957
Crothers, R. July 5, 1958
Croy, H. May 24, 1965
Cummings, E. E. Sept. 3, 1962

Dane, C. Mar. 28, 1965
Dargan, O. T. Jan. 22, 1968
Davis, C. B. July 19, 1962
Davis, E. H. May 18, 1958
Davis, H. L. Oct. 31, 1960
Davis, O. Oct. 14, 1956
Dawson, C. W. Aug. 10, 1959
Day Lewis, C. May 22, 1972
De la Mare, W. J. June 22, 1956
De la Roche, M. July 12, 1961
Dell, F. July 23, 1969
Derleth, A. W. July 4, 1971
Destouches, L. F. July 1, 1961
Dillon, G. May 9, 1968
Döblin, A. June 26, 1957
Doolittle, H. Sept. 27, 1961
Dos Passos, J. R. Sept. 28, 1970
Du Bois, W. E. B. Aug. 27, 1963
Duhamel, G. Apr. 13, 1966
Dunsany, E. J. M. D. P. Oct. 25, 1957
Duranty, W. Oct. 3, 1957

Eastman, M. Mar. 25, 1969
Eaton, W. P. Feb. 26, 1957
Eddy, G. S. Mar. 4, 1963
Ehrenbourg, I. Sept. 1, 1967
Eliot, G. F. Apr. 21, 1971
Eliot, T. S. Jan. 4, 1965
Ervine, J. G. Jan. 24, 1971

Fabricius, J. W. Nov. 23, 1964
Farjeon, E. June 5, 1965
Farson, N. Dec. 12, 1960
Faulkner, W. July 6, 1962
Fauset, J. R. Apr. 30, 1961
Fay, S. B. Aug. 29, 1967
Fearing, K. June 26, 1961
Ferber, E. Apr. 16, 1968
Feuchtwanger, L. Dec. 21, 1958
Fisher, D. F. C. Nov. 9, 1958
Fisher, V. July 9, 1968
Flavin, M. Dec. 27, 1967
Fleming, P. Aug. 18, 1971
Flexner, A. Sept. 21, 1959
Flynn, J. T. Apr. 13, 1964
Forbes, E. Aug. 12, 1967
Forester, C. S. Apr. 2, 1966
Forster, E. M. June 7, 1970
Fowler, G. July 2, 1960
Franck, H. A. Apr. 17, 1962
Frank, L. Aug. 18, 1961
Frank, W. D. Jan. 9, 1967
Frankau, P. June 8, 1967
Freeman, Joseph Aug. 9, 1965
Freuchen, P. Sept. 2, 1957
Frost, R. Jan. 29, 1963
Fuess, C. M. Sept. 9, 1963
Fülöp-Müller, R. May 7, 1963
Fyleman, R. Aug. 1, 1957

Gannett, L. Feb. 3, 1966
Gardner, E. S. Mar. 11, 1970
Gibbs, A. H. May 24, 1964
Gibbs, P. H. Mar. 10, 1962
Gibson, W. W. May 26, 1962
Giono, J. Oct. 8, 1970
Giovannitti, A. Dec. 31, 1959
Gladkov, F. V. Dec. 20 (?), 1958
Gogarty, O. St. J. Sept. 22, 1957
Gold, M. May 14, 1967
Golding, L. Aug. 9, 1958
Graf, O. M. June 28, 1967
Graham, D. June 22, 1959
Greene, A. B. July 25, 1961
Greene, W. Jan. 23, 1956
Grierson, H. J. C. Feb. 19, 1960
Guérard, A. L. Nov. 12, 1960
Guitry, S. July 24, 1957
Gulbranssen, T. Oct. 10, 1962
Gunther, J. May 29, 1970

Hackett, F. Apr. 24, 1962
Hagedorn, H. July 27, 1964
Haldane, J. B. S. Dec. 1, 1964
Hall, J. W. Nov. 13, 1960
Hallgren, M. A. Nov. 10, 1956
Hamilton, E. May 31, 1963
Hammett, D. Jan. 10, 1961
Harriman, J. Jan. 1, 1961
Hart, M. Dec. 20, 1961
Hauser, H. Apr. 1955
Heard, G. Aug. 18, 1971
Hecht, B. Apr. 18, 1964
Hemingway, E. July 2, 1961
Henderson, A. Dec. 6, 1963
Herbert, A. P. Nov. 11, 1971
Herbst, J. Jan. 28, 1969
Hesse, H. Aug. 9, 1962
Hillyer, R. S. Dec. 24, 1961
Hindus, M. G. July 18, 1969
Hobart, A. T. Mar. 14, 1967
Hodgson, R. Nov. 3, 1962
Holden, R. P. June 26, 1972
Housman, L. Feb. 20, 1959
Howe, M. A. De W. Dec. 6, 1960
Hughes, L. May 22, 1967
Hughes, Rupert, Sept. 9, 1956
Hull, H. R. July 15, 1971
Hume, C. Mar. 26, 1966
Humphries, R. Apr. 22, 1969
Hurst, F. Feb. 23, 1968
Hurston, Z. N. Jan. 28, 1960
Hutchinson, A. S. M. Mar. 14, 1971
Huxley, A. L. Nov. 23, 1963

Irwin, W. A. Feb. 14, 1959

Jacks, L. P. Feb. 17, 1956
Jacob, N. E. Aug. 27, 1964
Jeffers, R. Jan. 20, 1961
Jesse, F. T. Aug. 6, 1958
Jung, C. G. June 6, 1961

Kagawa, T. Apr. 23, 1960
Kallas, A. J. M. K. 1956
Kaufman, G. S. June 2, 1961
Kelland, C. B. Feb. 18, 1964
Keller, A. G. Oct. 31, 1956
Kennedy, M. July 31, 1967
Kerr, S. Feb. 6, 1965
Keyes, F. P. July 3, 1970
Knox, R. A. Aug. 24, 1957
Kreymborg, A. Aug. 14, 1966
Krutch, J. W. May 22, 1970
Kyne, P. B. Nov. 25, 1957

Lane, R. W. Oct. 31, 1968
La Farge, O. Aug. 2, 1963
Lamb, H. Apr. 9, 1962

Lancaster, B. June 20, 1963
Langner, L. Dec. 26, 1962
Larbaud, V. Feb. 2, 1957
Lee, M. Apr. 3, 1971
Lewis, D. B. W. Nov. 23, 1969
Lewis, W. Mar. 7, 1957
Liddell Hart, B. H. Jan. 29, 1970
Liepmann, H. June, 6, 1966
Lockridge, F. L. D. Feb. 17, 1963
Long, H. Oct. 17, 1956
Lovelace, D. W. Jan. 17, 1967
Lowenthal, M. Mar. 15, 1969
Luhan, M. G. D. Aug. 13, 1962
Lynd, R. S. Nov. 1, 1970

Mabbott, T. O. May 15, 1968
Macaulay, R. Oct. 30, 1958
McCullers, C. S. Sept. 29, 1967
McFee, W. July 2, 1966
Mackaye, P. Aug. 31, 1956
McKenny, R. July 25, 1972
Mackenzie, C. Nov. 30, 1972
MacManus, S. Oct. 23, 1960
MacNeice, L. Sept. 3, 1963
Mac Orlan, P. June 27, 1970
Mann, E. Aug. 27, 1969
Marks, J. A. Mar. 15, 1964
Marks, P. Dec. 27, 1956
Marquand, J. P. July 16, 1960
Marriott, C. July 16, 1957
Martin du Gard, R. Aug. 22, 1958
Martínez Ruiz, J. Mar. 2, 1967
Masefield, J. May 12, 1967
Matson, N. H. Oct. 18, 1965
Maugham, W. S. Dec. 16, 1965
Mauriac, F. Sept. 1, 1970
Maurois, A. Oct. 9, 1967
Mercer, C. W. Mar. 4, 1960
Middleton, G. Dec. 23, 1967
Miller, M. Dec. 27, 1967
Millis, W. Mar. 17, 1968
Moore, M. C. Feb. 5, 1972
Morgan, C. Feb. 6, 1958
Morley, C. D. Mar. 28, 1957
Muir, E. Jan. 3, 1959
Mulford, C. E. May 10, 1956
Murray, G. May 20, 1957
Murry, J. M. Mar. 13, 1957
Muzzey, D. S. Apr. 14, 1965

Nash, O. May 19, 1971
Nathan, G. J. Apr. 8, 1958
Nevins, A. Mar. 5, 1971
Newman, E. July 7, 1959
Nicolson, H. G. May 1, 1968
Niebuhr, R. June 1, 1971
Niles, B. R. Apr. 13, 1959

Norris, K. T. Jan. 18, 1966
Norway, N. S. Jan. 12, 1960
Noyes, A. June 28, 1958

O'Casey, S. Sept. 18, 1964
Odets, C. Aug. 14, 1963
O'Hara, J. Apr. 11, 1970
Onions, O. Apr. 9, 1961
Ostenso, M. Nov. 24, 1963
O'Sullivan, V. July 18, 1940
Overstreet, H. A. Aug. 17, 1970

Pach, W. Nov. 27, 1958
Palmer, F. Sept. 2, 1958
Papini, G. July 8, 1956
Parker, D. June 7, 1967
Parrish, A. Sept. 5, 1957
Parsons, G. Dec. 8, 1956
Parsons, W. Oct. 28, 1958
Partridge, B. July 5, 1960
Patchen, K. Jan. 8, 1972
Paterson, I. M. B. Jan. 10, 1961
Paul, E. H. Apr. 7, 1958
Paul, L. Feb. 13, 1970
Peattie, D. C. Nov. 16, 1964
Peffer, N. Apr. 12, 1964
Pérez de Ayala, R. Aug. 5, 1962
Perry, R. B. Jan. 22, 1957
Pertwee, R. Apr. 26, 1963
Peterkin, J. M. Aug. 10, 1961
Phillpotts, E. Dec. 29, 1960
Pilnyak, B. 1937 (?)
Pinski, D. Aug. 11, 1959
Postgate, R. W. Mar. 30, 1971
Pound, E. L. Nov. 1, 1972
Powell, D. Nov. 14, 1965
Powys, J. G. June 17, 1963
Pringle, H. F. Apr. 7, 1958
Putnam, N. W. Mar. 8, 1962

Quinn, A. H. Oct. 16, 1960

Ransome, A. June 3, 1967
Rascoe, B. Mar. 19, 1957
Raynolds, R. Oct. 24, 1965
Read, H. E. June 12, 1968
Regler, G. Jan. 14, 1963
Remarque, E. M. Sept. 25, 1970
Remizov, A. M. Nov. 26, 1957
Rice, E. L. May 8, 1967
Richardson, D. M. June 17, 1957
Richmond, G. L. S. Nov. 26, 1959
Richter, C. Oct. 30, 1968
Rinehart, M. R. Sept. 22, 1958

Twentieth Century Authors

ABBOTT, ELEANOR HALLOWELL
(September 22, 1872-   ), American short
story writer and novelist, writes: "1872 was

S. W. Woodward

the year of my birth,
a n d C a m b r i d g e,
Mass., the site and
scene of it, at that
particular era of the
city's intellectual and
historical e x i s t e n c e
which I have tried to
revisualize in *Being
Little in Cambridge
When Everyone Else
Was Big.* Between
the time of living that little life and the time
of telling about it, I have had fifteen other
books published, the most widely known of
them perhaps being *Molly Make-Believe,* and
have also contributed about seventy-five short
stories and an occasional bit of verse to most
of the current magazines. In the vista of my
childhood was our grandfather Jacob Abbott
who wrote the *Rollo Books,* great-uncle Gorham who founded the 'Spingler Institute
for Young Females' out of which enterprise Vassar College was later evolved, the
younger uncle, Lyman Abbott,[qv] who succeeded Henry Ward Beecher as pastor of
Plymouth Church in Brooklyn, and Cousin
Arthur who helped to engineer the building
of the Brooklyn Bridge. Most certainly it
looked like a very 'Abbott-y' world.

"Educated for the most part in the private
schools of Cambridge, with occasional sorties
into the realms of Higher Education as evidenced by special courses at Radcliffe College, honor compels me to state that I have
never been a real scholar, nor often a very
enthusiastic student. Only by literature as
it expresses itself through fiction, poetry, or
essay, and by psychology in so far as it concerns itself with the human emotions, has
my imagination ever been truly fired or my
interest unflaggingly sustained.

"Having been, as I have every reason to
believe, weaned on a bottle of ink, it was
only to be expected that I should take the
earliest possible opportunity to try my hand
at the various forms of imaginative writing
—including even advertising. Eventually I
became secretary and teacher of English
composition at the Lowell State Normal
School. Here, though I kept on persistently
with my own writing, the accruing discour-
agements so heavily outweighed the occa-

sional successes that I was just on the verge
of abandoning all hope of a literary career,
when suddenly *Harper's Magazine* accepted
two long poems and I won three of the short
story prizes which *Collier's* and the *Delineator* were offering. Then the struggle was
over.

"In 1908, shortly subsequent to this, I
married Dr. Fordyce Coburn, and after a
few years' residence in Lowell we removed
for sheer love of country-living to an old
farm in Wilton, N.H., where we have lived
ever since except for intermittent ventures
into Florida, the mid-South, or even just
New York. In all fairness I cannot close
this without acknowledging that my husband's unfailing interest in my work, his
criticisms and cordial helpfulness, have made
him infinitely more than just a 'silent partner' in my chosen profession."

PRINCIPAL WORKS: Sick-Abed Lady and Other
Stories, 1911; Molly Make-Believe, 1912; White
Linen Nurse, 1913; Little Eve Edgerton, 1914; The
Indiscreet Letter, 1915; Stingy Receiver, 1917;
Ne'er-Do-Much, 1918; Old Dad, 1919; Peace on
Earth, 1920; Rainy Week, 1921; Fairy Prince and
Other Stories, 1922; Silver Moon, 1923; Love and
the Ladies, 1928; But Once a Year, 1930; The
Minister Who Kicked the Cat and Other Stories,
1932; Being Little in Cambridge When Everybody
Else Was Big, 1936.

ABOUT: Abbott, E. H. Being Little In Cambridge When Everybody Else Was Big; Woman's
Home Companion October 1918.

ABBOTT, LYMAN (December 18, 1835-
October 22, 1922), American editor, clergy-
man, and publicist, was born in Roxbury,
Mass., the third son
of the Rev. Jacob
Abbott, noted pioneer
educator and juvenile
writer (the *Rollo
Books,* etc.), and
Harriet (V a u g h a n)
Abbott. He was edu-
cated p r i v a t e l y in
Maine and in New
York City and en-
tered New York Uni-

versity at the age of fourteen. After his
graduation he practiced law briefly with two
brothers. In 1857 he married his cousin
Abby Frances Hamlin and in 1859 he left
the legal profession to prepare for the Congregational ministry under the tutelage of
his uncle, the writer and clergyman J. S. C.
Abbott. Ordained in 1860, he held a pastorate in Terre Haute, Ind., through the Civil

War years, resigning in 1865 to become corresponding secretary of the American Union Commission, a ministerial organization for healing the wounds of conflict. Book-reviewing for *Harper's,* to provide a necessary supplementary income for his growing family, led to a series of editorial associations. In 1881 he succeeded Henry Ward Beecher as editor of the *Christian Union* and in 1888 he was made permanent pastor of Beecher's famous Plymouth Congregational Church in Brooklyn, N.Y. He resigned the pastorate in 1899 to give his full time to journalism.

In 1893 the *Christian Union* shed its clericals to become the *Outlook* with Abbott as editor, a post he held to the end of his days; and the most influential period of his life began. As might be expected from its background, the *Outlook* was inevitably moralistic, but it was never smugly so. In its own time and place it was outstanding, distinguished alike for its editorial vigor and literary excellence, and in political philosophy closely alligned with the "progressivism" of Theodore Roosevelt, who became Abbott's warm personal friend. In 1912, in fact, Abbott courageously sacrificed a substantial portion of his magazine's circulation to support Roosevelt's candidacy for President on the "Bull Moose" ticket.

Energetic, sincere, public-spirited—though an unfortunate chauvinism sometimes clouded his liberal tendencies—Abbott in his latter days became something of a minor national patriarch, with a flowing white beard and wrinkled visage. He died in his eighty-seventh year, active to the last. A prolific writer, he published a number of books on religious theory and practice, a biography of his friend Henry Ward Beecher, and two readable volumes of recollections (*Reminiscences* and *Silhouettes of My Contemporaries,* the latter completed at eighty-five), in addition to a long list of topical and inspirational ephemera. His chief assets in his original works were his spontaneity and clarity. But it is for his long and effective editorship of the *Outlook* that he is best remembered. Though the unusual span of his life and the period of his greatest influence make him indisputably a twentieth century figure, in spirit he was the last of the potent nineteenth century churchmen-journalists. He was a unique link between two epochs.

PRINCIPAL WORKS: The Theology of an Evolutionist, 1897; The Life and Literature of the Ancient Hebrews, 1901; The Other Room, 1903; Henry Ward Beecher, 1903; The Great Companion, 1904;

The Spirit of Democracy, 1910; America in the Making, 1911; Letters to Unknown Friends, 1913; Reminiscences, 1915, 1923; The Twentieth Century Crusade, 1918; What Christianity Means to Me, 1921; Silhouettes of My Contemporaries, 1921.

ABOUT: Abbott, L. Reminiscences; Outlook November 8, 1922; the Abbott manuscript collection at Bowdoin College, Brunswick, Maine.

*ABDULLAH, ACHMED (1881-), novelist and adventurer, writes: "I am British, though born at Yalta, in the Crimea, of mixed Russian-Afghan ancestry, a Russian-Orthodox father, a Moslem mother. I am myself a devout Roman Catholic. I was educated at Eton, Oxford, by French Jesuit fathers, and at the University of Paris. I spent long years

Oggiano

in the British army, cavalry, 'regulars.' I saw service in India, China, Tibet, France, Mesopotamia, West Africa, East Africa, Egypt. I have a number of decorations. I have written for a number of English, American, and French magazines, and also a number of books (twenty-seven at last count), a number of plays, amongst them being the hits *Toto* [with Leo Ditrichstein] and *The Grand Duke* [with Lionel Atwill]; and a number of motion pictures, the best known being *The Thief of Bagdad* and *The Lives of a Bengal Lancer.* I was, formerly, a well known polo player."

* * *

Achmed Abdullah is an adopted name; the author never reveals the name to which he was born. A certain aura of personal mystery, in fact, is part of his stock-in-trade. His racy "autobiography," *The Cat Had Nine Lives,* revels in vivid anecdote and picaresque incident but is vague as to names and dates. His mother's uncle, he says, was the Amir of Afghanistan; and he relates that his mother attempted to poison her second husband, an Indian border chief. The book is crammed with similar spectacular material, which is also characteristic of his out-and-out fiction. Captain Abdullah, as he is usually addressed, is a short, stocky, baldish man who customarily wears a monocle. For the last several years he has lived in New York, surrounded by what interviewers have described as "oriental splendor," and he has a summer cottage in Maine. He was married to Rosemary A. Dolan in 1940. Among the honors ascribed to him

* Died May 12, 1945.

are a doctorate of "Koranic Law" from the College of El-Azar, Cairo, and membership in the French Academy. His highly colored stories of romance, intrigue, and adventure appear constantly in the popular magazines. He makes no claim to profundity, but even his critics admit that his lively fiction has genuine pace and verve.

PRINCIPAL WORKS: *Fiction*—The Red Stain, 1915; The Blue-Eyed Manchu, 1917; The Trail of the Beast, 1919; Wings, 1920; Alien Souls, 1921; Shackled, 1924; The Swinging Caravan, 1925; The Wild Goose of Limerick, 1926; Steel and Jade, 1927; Broadway Interlude (with F. Baldwin) 1929; Black Tents, 1930; The Romantic Young Man, 1932; Never Without You, 1934; Flower of the Gods (with F. Oursler) 1936; Deliver Us From Evil, 1939; The Shadow of the Master (with F. Oursler) 1940. *Plays*—Toto (with L. Ditrichstein) 1920; The Grand Duke (with L. Atwill) 1921. *Miscellaneous*—Chanson Coleur Puce (poems) 1900; A Grammar of Little Known Bantu Dialects, 1902; Lute and Scimitar (translated verse) 1928; Dreamers of Empire (with T. C. Pakenham) 1929; The Cat Had Nine Lives (autobiography) 1933; For Men Only: A Cook Book (with J. Kenny) 1937.

ABOUT: Abdullah, A. The Cat Had Nine Lives; Wilson Library Bulletin October 1929.

ABERCROMBIE, LASCELLES (January 9, 1881-October 27, 1938), English poet, critic, and scholar, sometimes called "the

Georgian laureate," was born at Ashton-on-Mersey, Cheshire, the eighth of nine children of William Abercrombie, stockbroker, and Sarah Ann (Heron) Abercrombie. Patrick Abercrombie, the architect and authority on regional planning, was an older brother. From a preparatory school, Locker's Park, Hemel Hempstead, Hertfordshire, Lascelles Abercrombie went in 1895 to Malvern College, whence he passed in 1900 to Owens College (now the University of Manchester). There he studied in the honors school of chemistry; but in 1902 he found the appeal of letters stronger than that of science, and left without a degree. The Boer War had greatly reduced the family resources, so Lascelles had to cast about for a livelihood. He worked first as a quantity surveyor, living frugally with a brother in Birkenhead, but soon turned to journalism. From 1907 to 1909 he had a staff post on the Liverpool *Daily Courier,* writing leading articles and literary and musical criticism. Night work and the general pace of a daily sheet proved, however, too much for his delicate constitu-

tion, so he entered the free-lance field. For some time he was play reader to the Liverpool Playhouse. His first book, *Interludes and Poems,* came out in 1908, and in 1909 he married Catherine Gwatkin, a Liverpool art student.

Late in 1910 Abercrombie and his wife moved from Birkenhead to Much Marcle, Herefordshire; and the next year to Ryton, near Dymock, Gloucestershire, where they lived economically but happily until 1914. Several volumes appeared during this time, including the authoritative *Thomas Hardy: A Critical Study* (1912), and the four issues of *New Numbers* (1914), in which Abercrombie was associated with "the Georgians" Rupert Brooke, John Drinkwater, and Wilfrid Gibson. Unfit for war service, he entered the inspection department of a Liverpool shell factory in May 1915 and remained there until the Armistice, publishing nothing during these years. He had meantime acquired some more or less regular revenues as one of three joint-beneficiaries under Rupert Brooke's will (the other two were Wilfrid Gibson and Walter de la Mare).

In 1919 Abercrombie was invited to become the first holder of a new lectureship in poetry at the University of Liverpool. As deeply learned in theory as he was skilled in practice, he took naturally to the academic life; and honors students greatly benefited from his lectures on Aristotle, Longinus, Lessing, and other great esthetic philosophers—during which he paced the rostrum from side to side. In 1922 he became full Professor of English at the University of Leeds, where, according to Sir Michael Sadler, then vice-chancellor, he exerted a "wide and winning influence." He remained there seven years, producing more poetry and some of his most important critical works, despite the pressure of a rigorous climate and the onset of chronic diabetes, which thenceforward demanded constant treatment and eventually stopped his writing altogether, though he continued to teach and lecture until his last months.

Bedford College for Women, in the University of London, called him to its chair of English Literature in 1929. In the following year he received an unusual honor in the publication of his collected *Poems* in the Oxford Poets Series, being one of only two poets (Robert Bridges, the laureate, was the other) to be included in this notable series in their own lifetimes. The same year brought an invitation to deliver the British Academy's annual Shakespeare Lecture, which he published as *A Plea for the Liberty of Interpreting.* Abercrombie was happy to be in London. Living in Notting Hill, he moved out into the country for vacations, and was often in the provinces lecturing, at Malvern, Manchester, Cambridge, and elsewhere. A voyage to the Canary Islands in 1933 gave a temporary fillip to his health. In April 1935 he lectured on Wordsworth at Johns Hopkins University, Baltimore, Md.; and on his return to England accepted an invitation to be Goldsmiths' Reader at Oxford, and Fellow of Merton College.

Election to the British Academy crowned Abercrombie's career as a scholar in 1937. He had never taken a degree by examination, but held honorary awards, of M.A. (Liverpool, 1920), Litt.D. (Cambridge, 1930, and Manchester, 1935) and D.Lit. (Belfast, 1933). From May 1938 his health became seriously impaired, and he died in October of that year, at fifty-seven, at the Hospital of St. John and St. Elizabeth, London, leaving his wife and four children, three sons and one daughter, the eldest twenty-nine and the youngest seventeen. His last published works had appeared in 1932.

The ancient classics and the grimmer Elizabethan dramatists contributed to Abercrombie's mental furniture, and his early scientific training left frequent marks on his vocabulary. Little known to the general public in comparison with his talent, rather forbidding in style, he was forced by circumstance as well as by temperament into the ivory tower of the learned prosodist. From his book-lined study he sent forth until his last years, almost annual volumes of verse-plays, poems, poetic theory, and forthright criticism. Most influential of the latter were his *The Theory of Poetry* and *The Idea of Great Poetry,* together with his critical study of Hardy. Believing that the chief function of dialogue is "to be, not imitative, but expressive; and [that] language finds its most expressive use in poetry," he wrote many poetic dramas, some of which were staged, though without notable success. This circumstance failed to disturb him, and he considered the six-act *The Sale of St. Thomas* (1911-1931) to be his *magnum opus.*

As a poet, apart from the dramatist, his attitude is epitomized in his "Indignation Ode," directed against machine civilization, which he detested in all its manifestations. His poetic style is "difficult," abstract, and intellectual, and it has repelled many readers on first introduction to his work; but persistence is rewarding, revealing what one commentator calls "unusual force, original-

ity, and power to excite . . . terror." Neither as a man nor as a writer does Lascelles Abercrombie appeal to those whom William James called the tenderminded. He was essentially shy, and in consequence his manner seemed to strangers abrupt and unreceptive; and the same characteristics appear in his closely-knit, profoundly reasoned critical works and in his deeply thoughtful, unemotional poetry. Among his few close friends he was known as a man of simple tastes, gay, modest, an enthusiastic praiser of other men's work. He excelled in informal discussion, and had special merits as a reader-aloud, using ordinary diction rather than the formal intonations so beloved of the average reciter.

PRINCIPAL WORKS: *Poetry and Drama*—Interludes and Poems, 1908; Mary and the Bramble, 1910; The Sale of St. Thomas (Act I only) 1911; Emblems of Love, 1912; Deborah, 1912; Four Short Plays, 1922; Phoenix, 1923; Twelve Idyls and Other Poems, 1928; The Poems of Lascelles Abercrombie (Oxford Poets Series) 1930; The Sale of St. Thomas (all six acts) 1931. *Critical Works*—Thomas Hardy: A Critical Study, 1912; Speculative Dialogues, 1913; The Epic, 1914; An Essay Toward a Theory of Art, 1922; Principles of English Prosody, 1923; Stratford-on-Avon: Report on Future Development (with P. Abercrombie) 1923; The Theory of Poetry, 1924; The Idea of Great Poetry, 1924; Romanticism, 1926; Progress in Literature, 1929; A Plea for the Liberty of Interpreting (British Academy Shakespeare Lecture) 1930; Principles of Literary Criticism, 1932; Poetry: Its Music and Meaning, 1932.

ABOUT: Cumberland, G. Set Down in Malice; Elton, O. Lascelles Abercrombie: 1881-1938 (reprint from *Proceedings of the British Academy*; full bibliography); Jones, L. First Impressions; Maynard, T. Our Best Poets; Monro, H. Some Contemporary Poets; Morgan, A. E. Tendencies of Modern English Drama; Thouless, P. Modern Poetic Drama; Untermeyer, L. Modern British Poetry; Walkley, A. B. More Prejudices; The Times (London) October 28, 1938.

ACTON, JOHN EMERICH EDWARD DALBERG, 1st Baron Acton. See "BRITISH AUTHORS OF THE 19TH CENTURY"

*ADAMIC, LOUIS (March 23, 1899-   ), American sociological writer and novelist, writes: "I was born of peasant parents, in the village of Blato, in Carniola or Slovenia, then a part of Austria, at this writing still a part of Yugoslavia. My formal education in the old country included second gymnasium. I emigrated to the United States late in 1913, when I was not quite 15. My motives in this move, and the circumstances which contributed to it, are more or less explained in my second book, *Laughing in the Jungle,* published in 1932. The same book contains

* Died September 4, 1951.

also an informal account of my early years as an immigrant in this country. I have been a foreign-language newspaper man, a soldier in the United States Army, a worker, a rover, a pilots' secretary in Los Angeles harbor. When I was 12 or 13, in my native country, I wrote something in the Slovenian language which found its way into a juvenile magazine. I suppose I always wanted to write. I scribbled while in the American army; also I recall that I modeled in clay while in the trenches. In the early 1920's while bumming around the country, I began to translate Slovenian, Croatian, and Serbian stories into English; most of these translations appeared in the *Living Age,* then published in Boston.

Oggiano

"In 1928 H. L. Mencken took my first story or article for the *American Mercury.* Then came the idea for the book *Dynamite,* which brought me to New York in 1929. The book was published in 1931. The same year I married Stella Sanders, a native of New York. In 1932 I received a Guggenheim Fellowship. This took me to Yugoslavia for a year, which resulted in *The Native's Return,* in 1934, a Book-of-the-Month Club selection. Then I wrote two novels: *Grandsons* and *Cradle of Life.* In 1936 I took a trip to Guatemala and wrote, in 1937, *The House in Antigua. My America* appeared in 1938.

"My chief literary influence has been Ivan Cankar, a Slovenian novelist, one of whose stories (*Yerney's Justice*) I translated into English; it was published in book form by the Vanguard Press in 1926.

"In 1937 I bought a small old farm near Milford, N.J., where I now live. I like to live in the country, where I can take walks, have dogs, saw wood. I read a great deal, but not so much as I used to: no time."

* * *

Louis Adamic's position in American letters is unique. He is peculiarly fitted for the vast project on which he is engaged at present—an attempt to evaluate America in terms of the immigrants and the varying racial factors which have coalesced to form a nation. He is frank and boyish in appearance, looking younger than his years, engagingly shy. Burton Rascoe said of *My America,* which in a sense is Adamic's credo: "It takes its place with the great autobiographical

stories, . . . a grand book." In 1941 he received the John Anisfield Award and an honorary Litt.D. from Temple University. He is also editor of *Common Ground,* a magazine of inter-racial American culture.

PRINCIPAL WORKS: Dynamite, 1931; Laughing in the Jungle, 1932; The Native's Return, 1934; Grandsons, 1935; Cradle of Life, 1936; The House in Antigua, 1937; My America, 1938; From Many Lands, 1940.

ABOUT: Literary Digest April 7, 1934; New York Times Book Review December 29, 1940, February 23, 1941; Newsweek May 16, 1938; Rotarian February 1939; Saturday Review of Literature February 15, 1941; Scholastic April 4, 1934; Wilson Library Bulletin September 1934.

ADAMS, FRANKLIN PIERCE

("F.P.A.") (November 15, 1881-   ), American journalist, wit, and poet, was born in Chicago, the son of Moses Adams and Clara (Schlossberg) Adams. After being graduated from the Armour Scientific Academy in 1899, he spent a year at the University of Michigan, to which he has remained humorously devoted ever since. A

NBC

brief attempt at selling insurance turned him to journalism and he began his first column on the Chicago *Journal* in 1903, then moved it to New York, where it appeared in the *Evening Mail* from 1904 to 1913, in the *Tribune* until 1921 (where it first appeared under the famous name of "The Conning Tower"), in the *World* until 1931, and then with that paper's death back in the *Herald Tribune* until 1937. A disagreement over salary which went back to more fundamental differences caused a rupture between this paper and Mr. Adams, who took "The Conning Tower" a little later to the New York *Post,* where it appeared until September 1941.

Since 1938 also Mr. Adams has become known to an even wider public as one of the permanent "board of experts" of the radio program "Information, Please." His interest in quizzes and questionnaires goes back all the way to 1927, when he and Harry Hansen published a book of questions and answers called *Answer This One.*

But it is as "F.P.A.," the conductor, versifier, wit, and sometimes scholar of "The Conning Tower," that he remains best known. In this, long our senior and most respected newspaper "column," appeared the early contributions of many of the

5

celebrated American writers of today, including Edna St. Vincent Millay, Dorothy Parker, Sarah Cleghorn, Arthur Guiterman, Sinclair Lewis, the late Ring Lardner, George Kaufman, Moss Hart, John Erskine, Edna Ferber, Deems Taylor, and a host of others. Mr. Adams is also no mean classical scholar, and his translations of Horace, Propertius, and other Latin poets, though lighthearted, are among the best of their kind. In occasional serious vein, he is also a genuine poet. As Robert H. ("Bob") Davis remarked, he "swings a rhythmic, wicked pen at the foibles of the day. . . . F.P.A. tells the truth about everybody but himself."

He has been twice married, in 1904 to Minna Schwartze, and in 1925 to Esther Sayles Root, and he has four children. With them he lives in New York in the winter and in Westport, Conn., in the summer. During the First World War he served as a captain in the United States Intelligence Service, in France, and ran a column in the A.E.F.'s *Stars and Stripes,* the brilliantly conducted magazine which was among other things the first cradle of the *New Yorker.*

"Attractively ugly," with the long features of an intelligent horse, a bushy moustache, large bright eyes, and a certain general facial resemblance to the comedian Groucho Marx, "F.P.A." is a sort of epitome of the best in current American journalistic comment. His "sane and salty" paragraphs and verses would make excellent material to be buried in a time capsule to show the essential spirit of our time. His outlook has become increasingly liberal in recent years. He is not the father of columnists, the late Bert Leston Taylor and others having preceded him, but he is the godfather at least of most of the contemporary newspaper columns. His long-continued modernized version of Pepys' diary has given birth, rather unfortunately in some cases, to an entire literary *genre,* but in his own hands remains delightfully fresh. His wit is so keen that it often hides the substrata of real erudition and sound common sense. He professes to hate writing; is devoted to his family, tennis, and poker.

In addition to the published books made up of gleanings from his columns and more serious verses, he collaborated with O. Henry, in 1909, in writing a musical comedy, *Lo.*

PRINCIPAL WORKS: Tobogganing on Parnassus, 1910; In Other Words, 1912; By and Large, 1914; Weights and Measures, 1917; Something Else Again, 1920; Overset, 1922; So There! 1922; So Much Velvet, 1924; Half a Loaf, 1927; Christopher Columbus, 1931; The Diary of Our Own Samuel Pepys, 1935; The Melancholy Lute, 1936; The Week-End Companion (with D. Taylor) 1942.

ABOUT: Case, F. Do Not Disturb; Masson, T. L. Our American Humorists; Christian Science Monitor Magazine December 21, 1938; Harper's Magazine February 1942; Nation's Business July 1939; Newsweek March 13, 1937; Poetry July 1937; Time March 15, 1937, August 25, 1941.

ADAMS, HENRY. See "AMERICAN AUTHORS: 1600-1900"

*ADAMS, JAMES TRUSLOW (October 18, 1878-), American historian, writes: "I was born in Brooklyn, N.Y., the son of William Newton Adams and Elizabeth Harper (Truslow) Adams. On the Adams side I am descended from Francis Adams, who settled in Maryland in 1658 and soon moved to Virginia. My great and great-great Adams grandfathers

P. MacDonald

lived on the next plantation to George Washington at Mt. Vernon, and are frequently mentioned in Washington's diary as friends. My great-grandfather became a shipping merchant in Alexandria and lost his fortune by having his ships captured by the British. He later became United States Consul in Austria and afterwards bought a coffee estate in Cuba, where he died. My grandfather went to Venezuela, and there married Carmen de Michelena, a member of a distinguished family whose ancestors had been prominent in Spanish America from 1585. I was educated at various preparatory schools in Brooklyn, including the Brooklyn Polytechnic, and as the Polytechnic had just been extended into a college, I continued there and took my B.A. degree in 1898. I then went to Yale with the intention of studying to become a professor of philosophy, but decided I did not wish to continue and received my degree of M.A. for the work I had done.

"Meanwhile I had accepted a position in a bond office in Wall Street and also one as secretary of the small Jamestown and Chautauqua Railway. Changing my positions from time to time, I worked up to partnership in a stock exchange firm; I was also vice-president and director of a small national bank and treasurer and director of a manufacturing company, thus having had practical experience in manufacturing, finance, and transportation. Retiring on a small income later, I went to live in a farm-

* Died May 18, 1949.

ing community and acquired some knowledge of agriculture. While in Wall Street I visited and worked in forty-three of the forty-eight states. In the First World War I was on the House Commission to prepare data for the Peace Conference, and a captain in the Military Intelligence Division of the General Staff. I was detailed for special duty at the Peace Conference, having charge of the confidential maps on which the new boundaries were being drawn. On my return from France in 1919 I began writing history, following two small privately printed local histories written before I entered the army. In 1927 I married Kathryn M. Seely. We have no children.

"By request of a group of Senators I appeared before the Senate Judiciary Committee in opposition to the President's Supreme Court Plan in 1937. I was a member of the Pulitzer Prize Jury on history 1924-32, chairman 1930-32. For ten years, until I resigned in 1937, I was a member of the Advisory Council of the *Yale Review*. I was awarded the Pulitzer Prize of $2000 for history for *The Founding of New England*, in 1921, and in 1932 was awarded a prize of $1000 by the *Yale Review* for the best article on public affairs. I am a member of many historical societies and of the National Institute of Arts and Letters and the American Academy of Arts and Letters, and a Fellow of the Royal Society of Literature (England). I have honorary doctorates from Columbia, Rhode Island State College, Wesleyan University, Lehigh University, and the University of Pittsburgh."

* * *

Mr. Adams is the greatest authority on the New England Adamses, though he is not related to them. He says his aim in writing history is "to make people think, and to relieve a certain pressure on my own mind." He lives in Southport, Conn., very quietly, since he detests "society." Physically, with his high forehead and *pince-nez,* but with a bristly moustache over a full mouth, he appears to be what some of his critics have called him—a cross between the creative historian and the conservative capitalist.

PRINCIPAL WORKS: Memorials of Old Bridgehampton, 1916; History of the Town of Southampton, 1918; The Founding of New England, 1921; Revolutionary New England: 1691-1776, 1923; New England in the Republic: 1776-1850, 1926; Provincial Society: 1690-1763, 1927; Hamiltonian Principles, 1928; Jeffersonian Principles, 1928; Our Business Civilization (in England: A Searchlight on America) 1929; The Adams Family, 1930; The Epic of America, 1931; The Tempo of Modern Life, 1931; The March of Democracy, 1932-33; Henry Adams, 1933; America's Tragedy, 1935; The Record

of America (with C. G. Vannest) 1935; The Living Jefferson, 1936; Building the British Empire, 1938; Dictionary of American History (editor) 1940; America's Progress in Civilization (with G. E. Freeland) 1940; Empire on the Seven Seas, 1940; America Looks at the British Empire, 1941; The Record of America (with C. G. Vannest) 1941.

ABOUT: New York Times Book Review October 9, 1932; Rotarian August 1940; Time September 16, 1940; Wilson Library Bulletin April 1933.

ADAMS, SAMUEL HOPKINS (January 26, 1871-), American novelist, writes: "Presbyterianism of a liberal, even heretical, brand enveloped my childhood. After a public and high school education in Rochester, N.Y., I went, as by foreordination, to Hamilton College, whither my father, grandfather, five uncles, and numerous cousins had preceded me. Although I de-

voted more industry to writing than to study, no prizes ever came my way except for the fact that my name is dubiously immortalized in a collection of collegiate poetry, appended to a charming little fantasy—which happens to have been written by Clinton Scollard! From college I went to the New York *Sun,* traditionally the sternest training-school of ambitious young journalists. Nine years of reporting was enough; in fact, too much. I jumped at the chance to leave Park Row and join the staff of *McClure's Magazine.* Having become interested in medical science, I made public health my specialty, being, I believe, the first American writer to attempt to popularize it. My subsequent series in *Collier's Weekly,* exposing patent medicine quackery, was credited with furthering the passage of the first Pure Food and Drug Act.

"Meantime I had been contributing short stories and serials to the magazines. That became my principal professional interest, with subsequent incursions into editorial writing and biography. Some fifteen or sixteen of my stories have been done into movies; some with a result so painful that I have been unable to sit through the presentation; one, at least, *It Happened One Night* (1934), improved in the adaptation, and was directed and acted with such artistry and verve that I should like to see it again.

"If I were to repeat my career, I could ask nothing better than the life of a professional writer. It permits freedom of thought, action, and mode of existence, and this in an era when individual choice, threatened as it is throughout an imperiled world, has never been so precious."

* * *

Samuel Hopkins Adams was born in Dunkirk, N.Y., the son of Myron and Hester Rose (Hopkins) Adams. Besides his B.A., he has an L.H.D. degree from Hamilton, and studied medicine as well; he was, though a layman, made an associate member of the American Medical Association in 1913. He married Elizabeth R. Noyes in 1898; they had two daughters. In 1915 he married Jane Peyton Van Norman. He lives now in the summer in Auburn, N.Y., and in the winter in Beaufort, S.C. He keeps fit by playing tennis daily, and collects early American prints and other antiques. He says his "vices" are "fishing and antiquing." The names of his characters he frequently gets from country churchyards.

His best known novel is *Revelry*, based on the scandals of the Harding administration. It was suppressed in Washington, condemned by various state legislatures, and a dramatization was banned in Philadelphia, but it sold 100,000 copies; his subsequent biography of Harding shows how accurate it was. In his early years, as a by-product of his food and drug investigations, he wrote a number of unusual detective stories centered around a character named Average Jones. They were praised by connoisseurs and are still found in anthologies; but now, the author says, Average Jones is "long since dead," because "there are no more mystery plots left where he came from." Some of his later novels have been historical; others, like *Siege, The Clarion*, and *Success*, have been exposés of current civic evils. In nearly half a century of writing, he has only two stories unsold.

PRINCIPAL WORKS: The Mystery (with S. E. White) 1905; The Great American Fraud, 1906; The Flying Death, 1906; Average Jones, 1911; The Secret of Lonesome Cove, 1913; The Clarion, 1914; Little Miss Grouch, 1915; The Unspeakable Perk, 1916; Our Square and the People in It, 1917; Common Cause, 1918; Wanted: A Husband, 1919; Success, 1921; From a Bench in Our Square, 1922; Siege, 1924; The Piper's Fee, 1925; Revelry, 1926; The Flagrant Years, 1929; The Godlike Daniel (biography of Daniel Webster) 1930; The Gorgeous Hussy, 1934; The President's Mystery Story (with others) 1935; Perfect Specimen, 1936; Maiden Effort, 1937; The World Goes Smash, 1938; The Incredible Era: The Life and Times of Warren G. Harding, 1939; Both Over Twenty-One, 1940; Whispers, 1940.

ABOUT: Filler, L. Crusaders for American Liberalism; Bookman March 1927, November 1929; New Yorker June 22, 1940; Saturday Review of Literature December 18, 1926; Wilson Library Bulletin May 1934.

*ADE, GEORGE (February 9, 1866-   ), American humorist and playwright, writes: "My father was John Ade, born in England; my mother was Adaline (Bush) Ade, of Scotch-Irish descent. I came on the scene as a Hoosier, at Kentland, Ind. From the time I could read I had my nose in a book, and I lacked enthusiasm for manual labor. After high school I attended  Purdue University, taking the scientific course because I had no ambition to be an engineer or an agriculturalist; a star student as a freshman but wobbly later on and a total loss in mathematics. I received my B.S. in 1887; later I had honorary L.H.D. degrees from Purdue and Indiana University.

"Between 1887 and 1890 I did all sorts of work for two Lafayette newspapers and rather enjoyed a brief experience with a company making patent medicines and developing a health resort. Went to Chicago in 1890 and found a job as reporter on the *Morning News*, later known as the *Record*. From 1893 to 1900 I had charge of a two-column story department. In 1900 I did my last newspaper work and went out to China, Japan, and the Philippines on a visit. Before that I had been to Europe twice and had published five books.

"My early story stuff was intended to be 'realistic' and I believed firmly in short words and short sentences. By a queer twist of circumstances I have been known to the general public as a humorist and a writer of slang. I never wanted to be a comic or tried to be one. Always I wrote for the 'family trade' and I used no word or phrase which might give offense to mother and the girls or to a professor of English.

"Having been absurdly in love with the theatre for years, I found time, after I began syndicating my *Fables* in 1900, to make a shy attempt at writing for the stage. I wrote the book and verses for an operetta, *The Sultan of Sulu*, first written for amateur production, and later for other musical pieces. The plays without music which might be worth remembering include *The County*

* Died May 16, 1944.

Chairman and *The College Widow.* I had three failures.

"In 1915 I took up a permanent residence at Hazelden Farm, near Brook, Ind., within fifteen miles of my birthplace. I am a bachelor, but prefer to live in my own home. In the winter I go to Miami Beach, Fla., or travel farther afield—I have looped the globe twice and made many journeys to Europe, the Orient, and the West Indies. Ever since I settled down in the country I have been involved in activities which did not call my name to the attention of the general public but which have been an interesting part of my career. For quite a number of years I have paid more attention to these activities than I have to writing.

"I have done a number of short plays and several motion pictures, including *Our Leading Citizen* and *Woman Proof.* My enthusiasms include golf, travel, horse-racing, and the spoken drama. My antipathies are social show-offs, bigots on religion, fanatics on total abstinence, and all persons who take themselves seriously. I won't let myself become a mossback or a has-been, so I keep the old bean in touch with the latest news, the latest plays, the latest movies, and the latest books. I have a card-index memory for the words and music of old songs. I love to put on big parties or celebrations and see a throng of people having a good time. I do not choose to make speeches or listen to speeches.

"I am a member of the National Institute of Arts and Letters and am on the executive committee of the Authors' Guild."

* * *

Mr. Ade is now a semi-invalid because of a bad heart, but his mind is still keen and his nature as sociable as ever. Carl Van Doren gave him a place among the "American vernacular philosophers" as "a continuer of the old wisdom and the inventor of a new idiom." Though the slang of the early 1900's is now a dead language, there remains in his work a residue of freshness which still makes much of it highly readable and humanly amusing.

PRINCIPAL WORKS: Artie, 1896; Pink Marsh, 1897; Doc Horne, 1899; Fables in Slang, 1900; More Fables, 1900; Forty Modern Fables, 1901; The Girl Proposition, 1902; People You Know, 1903; In Babel, 1903; Breaking Into Society, 1903; True Bills, 1904; In Pastures New, 1906; The Slim Princess, 1907; Knocking the Neighbors, 1912; Ade's Fables, 1914; Hand-Made Fables, 1920; Single Blessedness, 1922; Bang! Bang! 1928; The Old-Time Saloon, 1931; Thirty Fables, 1933.

ABOUT: Hind, C. L. More Authors and I; Masson, T. L. Our American Humorists; Mencken, H. L. Prejudices: First Series; Van Doren, C.

Many Minds; American Magazine July 1920; Bookman October 1921; Century Magazine January 1923; Saturday Review of Literature February 27, 1937.

ADLER, ALFRED (February 7, 1870-May 28, 1937), Austrian neurologist and psychoanalyst, was born in Penzig, Austria, near Vienna. His father was a grain merchant, and the family background was a cultured one. There were few other Jews in the countryside near them. Adler's mother was Hungarian. His father was born in Burgenland, then

part of Hungary, in the same village as the violinist Joachim, and became a Protestant Christian early in life. The boy had a siege with pneumonia at five, and decided to become a doctor. The family moved to a farm at Währingerstrasse, and young Adler spent his boyhood and youth in or near Vienna, then at the peak of European civilization. His friendships with other boys were notable for their number and variety. Adler's famous theory of the inferiority complex as the key to human neuroses (opposed to Freud, who believed that psychic problems grew out of sex suppression) had its genesis, Adler explained, in "early organic inferiority that I struggled hard to overcome. Just as nature affords compensation to injured organs, so the spirit of man can also be trained to compensate him for all psychic disturbances produced by defective organs." In 1895 Adler received a degree from the medical school of the University of Vienna, which, however, refused him his Dozentur for a thesis on "The Nervous Character." (His Ph.D. came later from the Long Island College of Medicine in New York.) In 1897 he began general practice as an eye-specialist. Adler met Sigmund Freud in 1906—he had defended Freud's theories in the *Neue Freie Presse*—and two years later they attended together the first International Congress of Psychoanalysis. They parted finally in 1911. Adler encouraged his followers to read Freud and attend his lectures; Freud, regarding Adler as a renegade in a rival camp, made an "almost scurrilous attack" on him in his *History of Psychoanalysis.* In his insistence on the ego as the great driving force in mankind, Adler tended to neglect or belittle Freud's theory of the importance of the subconscious. Although refused permission to lecture at the University of Vienna, Adler established guidance clinics in the schools, sponsored by the Board of Education, and in 1932 received official recognition as an honored citizen of Vienna.

Adler's marriage to Raissa Timofejewña, a Moscow-born student in Vienna, and the birth of three daughters and a son who found some difficulty in asserting himself against the competition of his elder sisters, gave him plenty of clinical material. Family life went more smoothly after the First World War, during which Adler served two years as a military doctor near the Russian front at Cracow and Brunn. Before the war he had founded his school of psychoanalysis, The Free Psychoanalysts and his journal *Internationale Zeitschrift für Individual-Psychologie,* which was revived after the war under his editorial guidance. Adler lectured at Columbia University in 1927, going in 1932 to the Long Island College of Medicine to occupy the first chair in medical psychology in the United States. In 1930 he published an important study of homosexuality. His clinics for the prevention of neurosis and psychosis, crime, and other life failures were very popular. He fell dead at sixty-seven of a heart attack on Union Street in Aberdeen, Scotland, and was cremated at Edinburgh. Alexandra Adler, a research fellow in neurology at Harvard, finished her father's lecture tour. Adler was a short, stocky man with fine eyes and a beautiful tenor voice, a fiery temper under excellent control, and a sympathetic manner with his patients. Phyllis Bottome, Adler's biographer, whose husband was his secretary, calls Adler "at once the easiest of men to know and the most difficult, the frankest and most subtle, the most conciliatory and the most ruthless." He loved music, drama, the cinema, cafés, country walks, and swimming.

PRINCIPAL WORKS: Organ Inferiority and Its Physical Compensation (Studie über Minderwertigkeit von Organen) 1907; The Neurotic Constitution (Über den Nervosen Charakter) 1921; The Practice and Theory of Individual Psychologie (Praxis und Theorie der Individual-Psychologie) 1924; Understanding Human Nature (Menschenkenntnis) 1927; The Case of Miss R, 1928; Problems of Neurosis, 1929; The Case of Miss A, 1931; The Pattern of Life, 1931; What Life Should Mean to You, 1931; Social Interest: A Challenge to Mankind, 1939.

ABOUT: Bottome, P. Alfred Adler: A Biography; Ganz, U. La Psychologie d'Alfred Adler; Mairet, P. A B C of Adler's Psychology; Orgler, H. Alfred Adler: The Man and His Work; New York Times May 29, 1937; Psychoanalytic Review April 1916.

ADLER, FELIX (August 13, 1851-April 24, 1933), Jewish-American philosopher and university professor, founder of the Ethical Culture movement, was born at Alzey, Germany, coming to the United States at sixteen when his father, Samuel A. Adler, was called to the ministry of the Temple Emanu-El in New York City. Graduating from Columbia in 1870,  young Adler studied philosophy and economics at universities in Berlin and Heidelberg, obtaining his Ph.D. degree in 1873. Although he could have succeeded his father in the rabbinate, Adler preferred to accept an appointment at Cornell as professor of Hebrew and Oriental literature from 1874 to 1876, when he organized the Society for Ethical Culture, with which his name was identified for the rest of his life. He wrote, lectured, and edited the *International Journal of Ethics.* In 1902 a chair of social and political ethics was especially created for him at Columbia. In 1908-09 he was an exchange professor at the University of Berlin, appointed by Theodore Roosevelt.

While still a student abroad, Adler explains in his *An Ethical Philosophy of Life,* he read Friedrich Albert Lange's *Die Arbeitfrage* (The Labor Question), which proved epoch-making in his life. "I would go out as the minister of a new religious evangelicism. Instead of preaching the individual God, I was to stir men up to enact the Moral Law." He advocated (as does the Oxford Group) sex purity; as well as continued intellectual development and, especially, devoting surplus income beyond one's genuine needs to the elevation of the working class. With the profoundest reverence for Hebrew prophets and for Christ, he thought Hebraism circumscribed by the monotheistic idea and Christianity by the centrality of Christ. (The *Outlook* dismissed *An Ethical Philosophy of Life* as "sheer polytheism, however sublimated.") Professor Adler was an effective agitator against child labor, tenement congestion, and other social abuses. His Ethical Culture schools have spread from New York to Chicago, Philadelphia, St. Louis, San Francisco, England, Germany, Austria, Italy, and Japan. Adler married Helen Goldmark of Brooklyn in 1880; they had two sons and three daughters. He died just past his eighty-second birthday.

PRINCIPAL WORKS: Creed and Deed, 1877; The Ethics of the Political Situation, 1884; The Moral Instruction of Children, 1892; Marriage and Divorce, 1905; Life and Destiny: or, Thoughts From the Ethical Lectures of Felix Adler, 1905; The Religion of Duty (with W. H. Maxwell) 1905; What the Ethical Culture School Stands For, 1910; The World Crisis and Its Meaning, 1915; An Ethical Philosophy of Life, 1918; The Reconstruction of the Spiritual Ideal (Hibbert lectures at Oxford) 1923.

ABOUT: Adler, F. An Ethical Philosophy of Life; New York Times April 26, 1933.

"A.E." See RUSSELL, G. W.

AGAR, HERBERT (September 29, 1897-), American editor, poet, and critic, winner of the Pulitzer Prize for history,

Pinchot

was born in New Rochelle, N.Y., and educated at the Newman School, Newark, N.J., Columbia (B.A. 1919), and Princeton (M.A. 1920, Ph.D. 1922). He also received an honorary Litt.D. degree from Southwestern University, Memphis, Tenn., in 1936. From 1929 to 1934 he was London correspondent for two Louisville, Ky., papers, the *Courier-Journal* and the *Times*. For the next four years he edited a syndicated newspaper column called "Time and Tide." In 1940 he returned to the *Courier-Journal* as its editor. From 1930 to 1934 he was literary editor of the *English Review*, London, an unusual post for an American. During the First World War he served as seaman and then as chief quartermaster in the United States Naval Reserve. He was married in 1918 to Adeline Scott; they had a son and a daughter. After a divorce, he was married in 1933 to Eleanor Carroll Chilton,[qv] the novelist, and they live in Louisville. In 1941 he received an honorary LL.D. from Boston University.

In spite of his Northern birth and rearing, Dr. Agar is considered one of the so-called Southern Agrarian Group, and was joint editor with Allen Tate of the symposium, *Who Owns America?* (1936). In 1933 he won the Pulitzer Prize for history with *The People's Choice.* His early work was in poetry and poetic criticism, but of recent years, both in books and magazine articles, he has confined himself almost exclusively to political, economic, social, and historical

questions. He did, however, bring out a translation from the French, *The Defeat of Baudelaire,* in 1932. His articles appear frequently in the scholarly reviews. In 1940 he brought out, in collaboration with Helen Hill, *Beyond German Victory,* his view of America's position in a world dominated by Hitler. He was an early and ardent disciple of American intervention in the Second World War.

PRINCIPAL WORKS: Fire and Sleet and Candlelight (poems, with W. Fisher and E. C. Chilton) 1928; Milton and Plato, 1928; The Garment of Praise (with E. C. Chilton) 1929; Bread and Circuses, 1930; The People's Choice, 1933; Land of the Free, 1935; What Is America? 1936; Pursuit of Happiness: The Story of American Democracy, 1938; Beyond German Victory, 1940; The City of Man (with others) 1940.

*AGATE, JAMES EVERSHED (September 9, 1877-), English dramatic critic and novelist, was born in Pendleton, near Manchester, and was edu-

cated at the Giggleswick Grammar School. He also studied music from childhood, and is an accomplished pianist. After leaving school he went to London and became a freelance journalist. In 1905 he was made dramatic critic of the *Daily Dispatch.* After a year he returned to Manchester, where he was dramatic critic of the *Guardian* until the outbreak of the First World War. He served throughout as an officer, in France from 1916 to the end of the war. In 1918 he married Sidonie Joséphine Edmée Mourret-Castillon, a Frenchwoman. From 1921 to 1923 he was dramatic critic of the *Saturday Review,* then took the same post, which he still holds, on the *Sunday Times.* He was also dramatic critic of the British Broadcasting Corporation from 1925 to 1932, and for several years film critic of the *Tatler.* In 1932 he edited an anthology, *English Dramatic Critics.* He visited the United States for the first time in 1937, spending his entire visit in New York.

His avocation is the breeding and exhibition of show harness ponies; his favorite horse he named "Ego," and the four volumes of his autobiography are dedicated to it! This in a way is a revelation of Mr. Agate's personality; in temperament, if not in his criticisms (which are usually more or less conventional) he is the *enfant terrible* of British dramatic criticism. Bald and florid, he looks and dresses more like a sportsman than a literary figure. He is genial, outspoken, and engagingly self-centered. "I have never," he has remarked, "written anything but autobiography." All his writing he calls "monologue with digressions," and he says frankly that all his novels are about himself and that he is the hero of them all. He has published four volumes of autobiography, mostly merely transcripts of his diaries, and full of detail of his daily living. He says unabashedly that he has been in debt ever since 1917, and he has even been arrested for debt. Yet in 1926 he sued a religious journal for libel because of an unfriendly review. He won the suit technically, but was awarded damages of one farthing.

Most of Mr. Agate's writing is ephemeral, a fact he would be the last to deny. There is, however, a solid residuum of useful and observant, if not startlingly original, comment on the theatre of his day, which few men have known more intimately; he is shrewd, friendly, and has immense enthusiasm. Unlike most dramatic critics, he has never been tempted to write a play of his own. Indeed, his three novels all belong to one decade of his middle life, and for some years he has confined himself to comment either upon the theatre or, less frequently, upon life as he sees it about him.

PRINCIPAL WORKS: L. of C. [Lines of Communication] 1917; Buzz, Buzz, 1918; Responsibility (novel) 1919; At Half-Past Eight, 1921-22; Alarums and Excursions, 1922; The Contemporary Theatre, 1923, 1924, 1925, 1926; Fantasies and Impromptus, 1923; On an English Screen, 1924; White Horse and Red Lion: Essays in Gusto, 1924; Blessed Are the Rich (novel) 1924; The Common Touch, 1926; Agate's Folly, 1926; A Short View of the English Stage, 1926; Playgoing, 1927; Rachel: A Biography, 1928; Gemel in London (novel) 1928; Their Hour Upon the Stage, 1930; My Theatre Talks, 1933; First Nights, 1934; Ego (autobiography) 1935; Ego 2: More Autobiography, 1936; More First Nights, 1937; Ego 3: Still More Autobiography, 1938; Bad Manners, 1938; The Amazing Theatre, 1939; Speak for England (anthology) 1939; Ego 4: Yet More Autobiography, 1940.

ABOUT: Agate, J. Ego, Ego 2, Ego 3, Ego 4.

AIKEN, CONRAD POTTER (August 5, 1889-), American poet, novelist, and short story writer, was born in Savannah, Ga., of old New England stock, the eldest of three sons and his attractive mother's favorite. His father was a brilliant but erratic physician who took him at the age of nine to witness an eye operation. The boy was profoundly affected, and has since often reverted to medical themes. He wrote his first poem at nine. In 1900 he was taken to New Bedford, Mass., to live

with a great-great-aunt, his home having been broken up when his father killed his mother and then committed suicide. His aunt's mansion and New Bedford harbor are described in *Blue Voyage*. At thirteen Conrad began memorizing a pocket edition of Poe's poems, basis of his first literary period. Poe influenced his rhythms and his quest for musical "symphonies."

After attending Middlesex School, Concord, Aiken entered Harvard with the famous class of 1911, his classmates including a number of men who made their mark in later years—John Reed, Heywood Broun, Alan Seeger, Robert Edmond Jones, and Walter Lippmann. Aiken wrote for the *Harvard Monthly* and *Advocate,* and was president of the latter and class poet. In his senior year he was placed on probation for cutting classes for ten days in order to make an English poem out of Gautier's short story "La Morte Amoureuse." In protest Aiken resigned and went to Italy for six months, returning in the fall of 1911. A few weeks after the June commencement he married Miss Jessie McDonald of Montreal, who became the mother of his three children, John, Jane, and Joan. After a year's honeymoon in Italy, France, and England he settled in Cambridge, Mass. Made independent by a small income, Aiken chose literature as a profession, beginning his career at the very dawn of America's poetry renaissance with *Earth Triumphant and Other Tales in Verse* (1914). Aiken's poetic influences have been many, his early poems in particular being obviously derivative, showing traces of Masefield, Keats, Browning, and Pater. Unlike Eliot, however, he is only indirectly indebted to the French Symbolists, owing partly to his difficulty with French, although he did try Verlaine, Rimbaud, Baudelaire, Mallarmé, Vildrac, and Laforgue somewhat later. In 1915 Aiken fell under the influence of the Imagists, and he moved with his family to Boston in order to be near John Gould Fletcher, his poetic mentor. *Turns and Movies* (1916) recalls the *Spoon River Anthology* of Masters, but *The Jig of Forslin* (1915) evidenced already, years before MacLeish, Tate, and Aldous Huxley, the all-powerful Eliot influence. *Nocturne of Remembered Spring* (1916) was so Eliot-ish that Aiken himself wrote a savage anonymous review for a Chicago paper. However *The House of Dust* (1920), "a poem of the soul of a city," preceded and possibly influenced *The Waste Land*.

"Conrad Aiken's early association with the Imagists," writes Fred B. Millett, "obscures rather than clarifies the basic movement of his spirit. He was never in any real sense an Imagist, although certain early poems have a harsh reality that made them seem fresh and novel. But he turned quickly away from such external realism to a solitary devotion to the creation of poetry that should come as close as possible to the art of music. To this end, he cultivated the flowing repetitive movement of symphonic music . . . encouraged in this direction by his enthusiastic conversion to the doctrines of psychoanalysis."

Steeped from his college days in Freud, Ellis, James, and Bergson, Aiken in his remarkable but comparatively rare short stories and novels as well as in his poetry utilizes the resources of psychoanalytical theory as foundations for intensely subjective and subtle character revelation. In such novels as *Blue Voyage* (1927) and *Great Circle* (1933) the subjective emphasis of Joyce is clearly perceptible; the structure as well as the content of the former recalls *Ulysses*.

Aiken's *Selected Poems* won the Pulitzer Prize for 1929, and the Shelley Memorial Award. In 1934 he received a Guggenheim fellowship. Most of his recent years were spent in England, at Rye, Sussex, where with his present wife, Mary (Hoover) Aiken, he conducted Jeake's House Summer School for "informal study in writing and painting," confined to six students. Because of the war, the school was removed to South Dennis, Cape Cod.

In the First World War Aiken refused to serve on the grounds that as a poet he was engaged in an "essential industry" not to be classed with billiard-marking, setting up candlepins, and speculation in theatre tickets. He has the distinction of being the first American poet to be excused from war duty in order to write poetry.

Aiken enjoys sports, especially tennis, and is an ardent movie fan. He is "passionately fond of music (Bach and Beethoven my chief happiness, Haydn and Mozart almost as good)." He reads very little, and poetry scarcely at all. Lately he has become increasingly interested in painting. His friends are mostly doctors, psychoanalysts, and painters.

Houston Peterson in *The Melody of Chaos* describes Aiken as "an epitome of disillusioned modernity, a romanticist without hope, a realist steeped in speculative psychology," and he disagrees with Aldous Huxley, who once wrote: "Mr. Aiken . . . has a flow of language that is refreshing in this age of meagerly trickling springs. . . . But . . . his facility is his undoing; for he is content to go on pouring out melodious language . . . almost indefinitely. . . . If Mr. Aiken is to be more than an agreeable maker of coloured mists he will have to find some new intellectual formula into which to concentrate the shapelessness of his vague emotion." To which Peterson replies: "Along with melody and colored mists and psychological complexity, the outstanding merit of Aiken's poetry is its intellectual formula, which no other author has elaborated so rigorously or so effectively."

PRINCIPAL WORKS: *Poetry*—Earth Triumphant, 1914; The Jig of Forslin, 1916; Turns and Movies, 1916; Nocturne of Remembered Spring, 1917; The Charnel Rose, 1918; The House of Dust, 1920; Punch: The Immortal Liar, 1921; Priapus and the Pool, 1922; The Pilgrimage of Festus, 1923; Senlin, 1925; Prelude, 1929; Selected Poems, 1929; John Deth, 1930; The Coming Forth by Day of Osiris Jones, 1931; Preludes to Memnon, 1931; Prelude, 1932; And in the Hanging Gardens, 1933; Landscape West of Eden, 1934; Time in the Rock, 1936; And in the Human Heart, 1940. *Fiction*—Bring! Bring! and Other Stories, 1925; Blue Voyage, 1927; Costumes by Eros (short stories); Among the Lost People (short stories) 1934; King Coffin, 1935; A Heart for the Gods of Mexico, 1939; Conversation, 1939. *Criticism*—Scepticisms, 1919; Gehenna, 1930.

ABOUT: Hatcher, H. H. Creating the Modern American Novel; Kreymborg, A. Our Singing Strength; Loggins, V. I Hear America; Millet, F. B. Contemporary American Authors; Monroe, H. A Poet's Life; Peterson, H. The Melody of Chaos; Untermeyer, L. American Poetry Since 1900, The New Era in American Poetry; Dial May 31, 1919; Hound and Horn January-March 1932; Poetry January 1931, April 1932, June 1935, May 1937; University of California Chronicle January 1932.

AKINS, ZOË (October 30, 1886-), American poet and playwright, was born in Humansville, Mo., the daughter of Thomas J. Akins and Elizabeth (Green) Akins. She was educated at home, at Monticello Seminary, Godfrey, Ill., and at Hosmer Hall, St. Louis, Mo. From early childhood the theatre fascinated her; her colored nurse took her when she was hardly more than a baby to every "road show" that came to the little town, and she had a toy theatre with which she played indefatigably and for which she made up dramas of her own. She went to New York with the hope of becoming an actress, but she was dissuaded as not having sufficient talent, and easily deflected into writing for the stage instead. She had already turned her hand to writing, having had poems and essays published in Reedy's famous *Mirror*. Her first published volume was poems, and she will occasionally publishes poetry in the magazines. The vast bulk of her work, however, is dramatic in nature. It includes a number of film plays, perhaps the best known of which was the screen version of Edna Ferber's *Show Boat*.

In 1932 Miss Akins married Captain Hugo Cecil Levinge Rumbold. He has died since. For some years she has lived in Pasadena, Calif., which is now her permanent home. She continues to write frequently for the motion pictures, and says she enjoys doing so more than she does writing plays for stage production. In 1941 she published her first novel, *Forever Young*.

Her dramatization of Edith Wharton's *The Old Maid* won the Pulitzer Prize for drama in 1935. There was at first some protest, since it was not an original play, but it was pointed out that Marc Connelly had previously won the prize for *The Green Pastures*, which was an adaptation of Roark Bradford's *Ol' Man Adam and His Chillun*. Perhaps the best known of her own plays are *Déclassée* and *Daddy's Gone a-Hunting*.

Though Miss Akins has made occasional sorties into the field of serious drama, notably in *The Furies*, she is essentially a light comedian. George Jean Nathan, never an easily pleased critic, granted her "grace and humor and droll insight." He deplored, however, the pretentiousness of the plays of her middle period, and called her "a horrible example of what affectation can do to a real talent." In her later work she has shed this false glamor and piling up of excrescent ornament, and the chief complaint to be made at present of her work is that she is devoting her time almost entirely to the motion pictures and has had no play, except for one adaptation, produced since 1936. There are few contemporary playwrights with Miss Akins' light touch at her best, and her wit is free from the mordant cynicism which marks the comedy of Clare Boothe, who is perhaps nearest her in tone. Her poetry, without being "im-portant," has lyric quality and genuine emotion pictorially expressed.

PRINCIPAL WORKS: *Poetry*—Interpretations, 1911; The Little Miracle (verse play) 1936; The Hills Grow Smaller, 1937. *Plays (date of production)*—Papa, 1919 (published 1914); The Magical City, 1919; Déclassée, 1919 (published 1923); Footloose, 1920; Daddy's Gone a-Hunting, 1921 (published 1923); The Varying Shore, 1921; Greatness, 1922 (published as The Texas Nightingale, 1923); A Royal Fandango, 1924; First Love (adaptation) 1926; Thou Desperate Pilot, 1927; The Furies, 1928; The Love Duel (adaptation) 1929; The Greeks Had a Word For It, 1929; The Old Maid (adaptation) 1935; O Evening Star, 1936; The Human Element (adaptation) 1939. *Novel*—Forever Young, 1941.

ABOUT: American Mercury May 1928; Saturday Review of Literature May 11, 1935; Wilson Library Bulletin June 1935.

ALAIN-FOURNIER. See FOURNIER

ALDANOV, M. A. (1888-   ) is the writing-name of Mark Aleksandrovich Landau-Aldanov, Russian novelist and essayist, who was born and educated in Russia but has been an *emigré* in France since 1919. In his book on Lenin (1922) Aldanov described himself as a socialist who is, at the same time, a counter-revolutionist and an anti-militarist, belonging to the labor party led by Miakotine and Pechekhonof. Aldanov is a member of the French Physico-Chemical Society and the Russian Chemical Association. His most recent address was given as 11 Rue Gudin, Paris. Mme. Tatiana Landau, his wife, has translated some of his books, written in Russian, into French; others were written originally in that language. His trilogy of novels about the French Revolution and after, 1793-1821, "The Thinker," has been translated into English. The general title was taken from the chimera or gargoyle, "Le Penseur" (otherwise called "Le Diable Penseur") which is on the summit of the Cathedral of Notre Dame de Paris. Parts of the work appeared serially in *Annales Contemporaines*, 1921-22. The material for the first volume, which Isabel Paterson called a magnificent effort, if not absolutely a great novel, was derived from the state libraries, chiefly in Paris, and the Museums—Carnavalet, Hôtel des Invalides, Malmaison, and Conciergerie—as well as from family archives and traditions, opened to the novelist by persons in political and official positions. *The Ninth Thermidor*, this first novel of the trilogy, culminates with the execution of Robespierre on July 27, 1794 (the Ninth Thermidor in the Revolutionary calendar).

The Devil's Bridge, the second novel, was published in Russian as *Chortov Most. Saint Helena: Little Island,* the concluding part, was also translated into Polish. *The Devil's Bridge* had a less favorable reception than its predecessor, V. Sackville-West calling it untidy in design, and Clifton Fadiman summing it up as the manufacture of a frigid and clever dilettante. The London *Times* commented on Aldanov's "gift of mordant irony." He once stated that the First World War and the Russian Revolution had rejuvenated civilization much as the earthquake rejuvenated Messina.

WORKS AVAILABLE IN ENGLISH TRANSLATION: Lenin, 1922; Saint Helena: Little Island, 1924; The Ninth Thermidor, 1926; The Devil's Bridge, 1928; The Key, 1931.

ABOUT: Aldanov, M. A. Lenin; International Who's Who.

ALDEN, HENRY MILLS. See "AMER- ICAN AUTHORS: 1600-1900"

ALDINGTON, RICHARD (1892-), English novelist and poet, was born in Hampshire. He was educated at Dover Col-

Blackstone

lege and the University of London, but was not graduated from the university. He had been writing (chiefly verse) from about the age of fifteen, and never considered any profession except writing. In 1913 he was literary editor of the *Egoist,* whose sponsors were the same group that later introduced Imagism with its attendant free verse, in England—the cult that later was "kidnaped" for America by Amy Lowell. Indeed, in this same year, 1913, Mr. Aldington was married to Hilda Doolittle,[qv] the American poet who writes as "H.D." and who with Ezra Pound was the focus of this group of literary pioneers. They were divorced later, but during their marriage Aldington was primarily a poet. In later years he almost abandoned poetry for fiction.

In 1916, at twenty-four, he entered the First World War as a private in the infantry, later becoming an officer. Violet Hunt described him, on leave and in uniform, at some of the meetings of the *Egoist* group at the time, and said that his outdoor air made him resemble a young farmer. The net result of his war experiences, however,

was to leave him demobilized, soon after the Armistice, with a bad case of shell shock. He was penniless as well so in spite of the condition of his nerves he was obliged to find work at once. He became a member of the staff of the London *Times* literary supplement, reviewing French books. A few months of this was all he could stand; he was ordered to the country as his only hope of recovery, and in 1919 he moved to a workman's cottage in Berkshire.

It was eight years before his shattered nerves recovered. During this time he published four volumes of poems, but made his living by free-lance criticism and by translations from the French, Italian, and Latin. A rich American paid him a large sum for an anthology of Romance poems, and with this money he was able to give up hack work and gain the leisure for creative writing. But his new work was no longer in verse, but in prose. He had lived for varying periods in Italy, France, and Switzerland, and later settled on the Riviera, where he lived until the outbreak of the Second World War. He is now in America.

His war experiences had given him an immense store of psychological hatred and anger, which were spilled out freely in his early novels. Because he loved his native country so deeply, he chastised it bitterly. Few novels are more cruel in their analysis or more indignant in their presentation than *Death of a Hero* and *The Colonel's Daughter.* When he was being openly angry he was strong and powerful; but when, as in some of his novelettes and short stories, he became ironic, his irony was heavy and dull. Indirection is not his forte. As John Wheelwright remarked (of his poetry, but it is equally true of his prose): "Agnostic whimsey is his weakness; but, by way of compensation, material honesty is his strength." The same critic added that "his poetry splits into fully truthful but not fully conscious records set down in sombre numbers."

Aldington has finally cleansed himself of all the accumulated resentment of one war just in time to re-accumulate it in another. What will the effect will be on his work cannot yet be told. But it may be significant that his best and strongest work appeared when his hatred and wrath were newest. His later books have been progressively less alive and more labored. He may be one of those writers who can reach their heights only under the stimulus of personal emotion.

In early middle life he is still (as Derek Patmore described him) "a handsome, ath-

letic man with fair hair and clear blue eyes."
He may be now at the beginning of a third
period, the form of which is yet undetermined. He published his most recent volume
of poetry in 1938; in 1936, in collaboration,
he wrote his only play. Either of these may
be the mode of his future writing, or he may
recapture the tone of his first and best
novels. In any event, he is one of the most
interesting of contemporary writers, and
one of the few whose potentialities are not
yet crystallized and from whom surprises
are not yet impossible.

PRINCIPAL WORKS: *Poetry*—Images Old and
New, 1915; War and Love, 1918; Images of Desire, 1919; Exile and Other Poems, 1923; A Fool
i' the Forest, 1925; Collected Poems, 1928; Love
and the Luxembourg, 1930; The Eaten Heart,
1931; Poems, 1934; Crystal World, 1938. *Prose*—
Death of a Hero, 1929; Roads to Glory (short
stories) 1930; The Colonel's Daughter, 1931; Last
Straws (short stories) 1931; Soft Answers (novelettes) 1932; All Men Are Enemies, 1933; Women
Must Work, 1934; Artifex: Sketches and Ideas,
1935; Life of a Lady (play, with D. Patmore)
1936; Very Heaven, 1937; Seven Against Reeves,
1938; Rejected Guest, 1939; Life for Life's Sake:
A Book of Reminiscences, 1941. *Edited*—The Viking Book of Poetry of the English Speaking World,
1941.

ABOUT: Aldington, R. Life for Life's Sake;
Bookman October 1931, September 1932; Nation
May 30, 1934; Nuova Antologia August 16, 1931,
March 16, 1937; Poetry October 1934, June 1938;
Saturday Review of Literature April 28, 1934;
South Atlantic Quarterly April 1939.

*ALDRICH, Mrs. BESS (STREETER)
(February 17, 1881-   ), American novelist,
writes: "I was born in Cedar Falls, Iowa.

My parents were
James and Mary
(Anderson) Streeter,
pioneer settlers in
eastern Iowa. My
grandfather, Zimri
Streeter, his wife,
three sons, and seven
daughters, came into
the state in 1852,
traveling by ox team,
the trip from Illinois
Blackstone
taking three weeks. There were no bridges
then, and the caravan was brought across
the river by ferry. My mother's family
came two years later, also by ox team,
and purchased land from the government
for $1.25 an acre. Grandfather Streeter
represented Black Hawk County in the first
Iowa State Legislature, where his reputation
for joking gave him the title of 'the Wag
of the House.' Father and mother were
married in a log cabin in 1855. They lived
to see Cedar Falls and Waterloo grow from

a few cabins to prosperous cities, one a
college town, one an industrial center. Authentic history of this growth is in my novel,
Song of Years.

"Because I was born at the tag-end of a
large family I never experienced any of the
pioneer hardships of which I wrote, for by
that time my parents were living in a growing town with its (for the times) convenien-
ces. But from this early association with
many relatives who did live through the
settling of the Midwest, I gained much first-
hand information concerning that period and
have made use of it in many books.

"Graduating from the Cedar Falls High
School and then from State Teachers' College, I taught for six years before my marriage, one year in Boone, Iowa, three years
in Marshalltown, Iowa, one in Salt Lake
City, Utah, and one in the primary training
school at my old college. In 1907 I married
Charles S. Aldrich, who had been the youngest captain in the Spanish-American War,
and had been later in Alaska as United
States Commissioner. We lived first in Tip-
ton, Iowa, and then moved to Elmwood,
Neb., where my husband was a banker and
attorney, and where I still retain my home.
Mr. Aldrich died in 1925, when our daughter
and three sons were small.

"My published output consists of about
150 short stories in various leading magazines, and nine books, which have all been
translated into various foreign languages."

* * *

Mrs. Aldrich travels a great deal, but always returns to her roomy, typically Middle
Western house in Elmwood, for to her, as
Annie Russell Marble said, "the small town
is a microcosm of the world." If nothing
else brought her back, her garden would do
so, for she is a devoted and ardent gardener.
Her long oval face, framed by soft grey
hair, shows thoughtfulness, gentleness, and
the pawky humor she inherited and which
has saved her admittedly sentimental and
"wholesome" novels from mawkishness. She
is from and of the Middle West; its history
is in her blood and she can write of no other
place. *A Lantern in Her Hand*, which became a best seller, she wrote as a tribute to
the pioneer mother, and she says she would
have written it had she known that not a
single copy would be sold.

Until 1918, Mrs. Aldrich wrote under the
pseudonym of "Margaret Dean Stevens."
Since then she has used her own name. One
of her stories, which later gave its title to
a short story collection, "The Man Who
Caught the Weather," was in the O. Henry

Memorial Volume for 1931. She received
an honorary Litt.D. from the University of
Nebraska in 1934. Her first short story won
a prize when she was seventeen, but she
published nothing more until after her marriage. Her typical book covers the entire
life, from youth to age, of a Middle Western
woman, and her thesis is that love, marriage,
and children are the most important things
in life. Her intense feeling for nature, a
natural gift for characterization, and her
humor place her work in a rather higher
category than its philosophy might indicate.

PRINCIPAL WORKS: Mother Mason (short sto-
ries) 1924; The Rim of the Prairie, 1925; The
Cutters, 1926; A Lantern in Her Hand, 1928; A
White Bird Flying, 1931; Miss Bishop, 1933;
Spring Came On Forever, 1935; The Man Who
Caught the Weather (short stories) 1936; Song
of Years, 1939; The Drum Goes Dead, 1941.

ABOUT: Good Housekeeping May 1938; Ladies'
Home Journal June 1933.

"ALEICHEM, SHALOM." See RABI-
NOWITZ, S. J.

*ALLEN, FREDERICK LEWIS (July 5,
1890-), American historian and editor,
writes: "Frederick Lewis Allen was born in
Boston. His father
was the Rev. Fred-
erick Baylies Allen,
who at that time was
Phillips Brooks' as-
sistant at Trinity
Church, Boston, and
later became the Sup-
erintendent of the
Boston Episcopal
City Mission. His
mother, before her
marriage was Alberta Hildegarde Lewis, of
Philadelphia. Mr. Allen spent five years at
Groton School, graduating in 1908; and then
four years at Harvard, graduating in 1912
(and completing, during his senior year, the
advanced work for an M.A. degree which
he was granted in 1913). After graduation
he taught English at Harvard during the
years 1912-14. Then he went into magazine
editing, first as an assistant editor of the
Atlantic Monthly (1914-16) and then as
managing editor of the Century (1916-17).
He left the Century when the United States
entered the war, and for two years was with
the Council of National Defense in Washington; then he spent the four years 1919-23
as Secretary to the Corporation at Harvard.
In 1923 he returned to editorial work, this
time on Harper's Magazine in New York;

this connection he has kept ever since. In
1931 he was promoted to the associate editorship of Harper's, in 1941 to the chief
editorship.

"He was married in 1918 to Dorothy
Penrose Cobb, and by this marriage had a
daughter and a son. In 1928 his daughter
died, and in 1930 Mrs. Allen died. Two
years later, he was married to Mrs. Agnes
(Rogers) Hyde. From 1923 to 1937 Mr.
Allen lived in Scarsdale, N.Y., and commuted to his editorial job. Since then he
has been living in a house near his New
York office.

"Shortly after his graduation from Harvard he began writing short humorous and
satirical articles and sketches—first for
Punch (London) and other magazines, later
mostly for Harper's (they appeared in its
'Lion's Mouth' department). Except for
scattered short stories and serious articles,
these light brief sketches, of which several
were published every year, were his chief
literary product until 1930, when he wrote
an informal history of the United States in
the 1920's, entitled Only Yesterday. This
became one of the best-selling books of 1932.
He followed it with two books of pictures
and text produced in collaboration with his
wife, and with a history of the financial era
1900-35 in America—The Lords of Creation.
Early in 1940 he brought out Since Yesterday, a companion volume to Only Yesterday,
covering the 1930's."

* * *

At the death of Lee Foster Hartman, in
1941, Frederick Lewis Allen became the
sixth editor-in-chief of Harper's since the
magazine's founding in 1850.

Mr. Allen, who may be described as a sort
of contemporary historian, is markedly long-
headed, with a high forehead and a rather
saturine expression which is belied by his
actually alert and sociable nature. In spite
of the years he has spent in New York, he
is still essentially a New Englander; his
interest in his native section is evidenced by
his trusteeship of Bennington College in
Vermont. His work is journalistic, but in
the best sense of that word.

PRINCIPAL WORKS: Only Yesterday, 1931; The
American Procession (with A. Rogers) 1933;
Metropolis (with A. Rogers) 1934; The Lords
of Creation, 1935; Since Yesterday, 1940.

ABOUT: New York Herald Tribune October 8,
1941; New York Times February 18, 1940; Saturday Review of Literature June 29, 1940; Writer's
Journal November 1941.

*ALLEN. HERVEY (December 8, 1889-   ), American novelist, poet, and biographer, was originally named William Hervey Allen, Jr. His mother's maiden name was Helen Eby Myers. He was born in Pittsburgh. He attended the U.S. Naval Academy of Annapolis, but overstrained himself in athletics and received an honorable discharge. He then entered the University of Pittsburgh, graduating with honors in 1915. After a short time in the employ of the Bell Telephone Co., he joined the Pennsylvania National Guard, and after strike duty in the steel country was sent to the Mexican border in 1916. During the World War he was a First Lieutenant of Infantry, was badly wounded, and was twice invalided. Before returning to America he was instructor in English in the French Military Mission at Favernay.

Pinchot

In 1919 he settled in Charleston, S.C., where he met Du Bose Heyward, with whom he collaborated on a volume of poems and in founding the Poetry Society of South Carolina. He went North again in 1920 to do graduate work at Harvard, but returned to Charleston in 1922 and for two years taught English in the Charleston High School. He was then for a year a lecturer at Columbia, and next taught American literature at Vassar. It was there that he met Ann Hyde Andrews, whom he married in 1927. They have two daughters and a son. In 1930 and 1931 he was a lecturer on modern poetry at the Bread Loaf, Vt., summer school for writers. He was one of the original staff of the *Saturday Review of Literature.*

Anthony Adverse, his best known book, took five years in the writing, while Mr. Allen was living in Bermuda. When it was finished, it had consumed his entire bank account except $30, for it was impossible to do any other work during its preparation. From the royalties of that tremendous best seller, he bought Bonfield Manor, on the Eastern Shore of Maryland, where he now lives. He believes that every human being should be self-sustaining, and therefore farms his estate, which is his chief interest aside from literature. A tall, florid, blond man, partly bald, he resembles (in spite of his horn-rimmed spectacles) an English country gentleman rather than a poet or a novelist.

Of his method of composition he says: "I simply seem to remember, to recall completely as if it had actually happened, what I write about. When I can't 'recall' it, I can't write. It is a kind of imaginative reporting. I work slowly, a few paragraphs a day." *Action at Aquila,* another historical novel, published five years after *Anthony,* failed signally to repeat the popular success of the earlier book.

Until *Gone with the Wind* appeared as its rival in length and popularity, *Anthony Adverse* was the best-selling and most discussed novel of its generation. To readers who wondered at his apparent first-hand acquaintance with the varied scenes of that picaresque romance, he acknowledged that most of these places had never been known to him except through the printed word; as with the historical details, he had simply absorbed an immense amount of information and then set his "imaginative reporting" to work.

Though he is thought of primarily as a novelist, Mr. Allen is a not inconsiderable poet. His war ballad, "The Blindman," which first appeared in *Wampum and Old Gold* (a volume in the Yale Series of Younger Poets), gave its name to the Blindman Prize for Poetry, which the Poetry Society of South Carolina offered for five years. His 1927 biography of Poe, *Israfel* (revised and republished in 1934), shares with those by Joseph Wood Krutch and Arthur Hobson Quinn a preeminent place in contemporary books on the subject.

PRINCIPAL WORKS: *Poetry*—Ballads of the Border, 1916; Wampum and Old Gold, 1921; The Bride of Huitzal, 1922; Carolina Chansons (with Du B. Heyward) 1922; The Blindman, 1923; Earth Moods, 1925; New Legends, 1929; Sarah Simon, 1929. *Fiction*—Anthony Adverse, 1933; Action at Aquila, 1938; It Was Like This, 1940. *Miscellaneous*—Towards the Flame, 1926; Israfel: The Life and Times of Edgar Allan Poe, 1927; Poe's Brother (with T. O. Mabbott) 1927.

ABOUT: Literary Digest August 11, 1934; New York Times Book Review July 6, 1941; Publishers' Weekly August 24, 1935; Saturday Review of Literature December 9, 1933, January 13, 1934, March 5, 1938; Time March 7, 1938.

ALLEN, JAMES LANE. See "AMERICAN AUTHORS: 1600-1900"

ALLINGHAM, MARGERY (1904-   ), English detective story writer, writes: "I was born in London in 1904, the eldest child of my father, H. J. Allingham, the *feuilleton* writer, whose serials appeared in all the popular weeklies of the day.

* Died December 28, 1949.

"My father and mother were first cousins and I came of a family of 'blood' writers; among them John Till Allingham, who wrote melodramas in the early 19th century, and a later John Allingham, who was a very popular writer of boys' school stories in the '90s. My grandfather was the proprietor of a religious newspaper and I was brought up from babyhood in an atmosphere of ink and paper.

"Soon after I was born the family removed to Layer Breton, a little village in Norman Essex five miles from Tolleshunt D'Arcy, where I now live.

"When I was seven years old my father began to train me to become a writer like himself. I was given a study of my own and a plot for a fairy story. Under his supervision I wrote and rewrote this story for nearly a year, at which time I began another. Between this time and my sixteenth year, when I produced my first published novel, my education proceeded on more or less orthodox lines. I was a boarder at the Perse Girls' School in Cambridge, keeping up my efforts toward authorship in the holidays.

"About this time I became a student of dramatic art with a view to becoming a playwright, and in 1927 I married Philip Youngman Carter, an artist of my own age whom I had known for many years. The following year I wrote *The Crime at Black Dudley*, the first of my detective stories about Mr. Albert Campion.

"After a few years in London my husband and I returned to the country to live in a Queen Anne house which I had known since a child. Here in Tolleshunt D'Arcy our life is typical of the English countryside. Horses, dogs, our garden, and village activities take up most of our leisure time. I am a domesticated person, with democratic principles and very few unorthodox convictions. Apart from my books I write a great many short stories, serials, and book reviews, and in my spare time I write letters. I have no particular axe to grind and I belong to no rigid school of thought but am content to hold with the poet that the proper study of mankind is man.

"Don Marquis is my favorite American author and the writers who have influenced me most in my life are, I should say, Shakespeare, Sterne, and the elder Dumas."

* * *

Margery Allingham's detective novels featuring mild, bespectacled, engaging Albert Campion fall into two periods: those written before 1934, of a light, picaresque nature, purely as entertainment; and those written since, which have made her a recognized leader of the new generation of English detection writers who are attempting to fuse the *roman policier* with the "legitimate" novel of character and psychology. John Strachey calls her "one of three white hopes" of the modern detective story, the other two in his opinion being "Nicholas Blake" and "Michael Innes." She is noted particularly for her deft handling of character and her highly literate style.

PRINCIPAL WORKS: Blackerchief Dick, 1923; The Black Dudley Murder (in England: The Crime at Black Dudley) 1929; Look to the Lady, 1930; Mystery Mile, 1931; Police at the Funeral, 1932; Sweet Danger, 1933; Death of a Ghost, 1934; Flowers for the Judge, 1936; Dancers in Mourning, 1937; Mr. Campion: Criminologist (short stories) 1937; The Fashion in Shrouds, 1938; Black Plumes, 1940; Traitor's Purse, 1941; The Oaken Heart, 1941.

ABOUT: Haycraft, H. Murder for Pleasure: The Life and Times of the Detective Story; Saturday Review of Literature January 7, 1939; Wilson Library Bulletin March 1939.

ALTSHELER, JOSEPH ALEXANDER (April 29, 1862 - June 5, 1919), juvenile writer, was born in Three Springs, Ky., the son of Joseph Altsheler and Louise (Snoddy) Altsheler. He was educated at Liberty College (Glasgow, Ky.) and Vanderbilt University. He worked briefly on the Louisville *Evening Post*, and then in 1885, became a reporter on

the *Courier-Journal*. In 1892 he left this paper to go to New York as a feature writer for the *World*; for it he covered the Chicago World's Fair in 1893 and went to Hawaii to report the attempts to re-establish the monarchy after annexation. Before the turn of the century he became editor of the *World's* tri-weekly magazine edition. This indirectly led to his real career as an author, for being in need of a story for boys, and no satisfactory one being available, he decided to write one himself. Thus began a long list of juvenile stories, interspersed with a few accepted for adult reading also. Most of them are included in one of six series, dealing with the Frontier and the Indian Wars, the Great West, the Young Trailers, Texas, the Civil War, and the First World War. In 1918, by vote of the public libraries, Altsheler was found to be the most popular boys' writer in America.

As the subjects of his series would indicate, he was greatly interested in American history, Francis Parkman being his particular idol; and he went to great pains to insure authentic historical facts in his books. Some of them are, indeed, a bit top-heavy with history. But he had a natural gift for writing, a liking for the young (though he had no children of his own), much fresh humor, and ability in characterization. Nothing could better indicate the improvement in juvenile literary taste in the past fifty years than the contrast between Altsheler's vivid, individualized, coherent stories and the pale, rambling, prosperity-centered preachments of Horatio Alger a generation earlier.

In 1888 Altsheler had married Sarah Boles, whom he had met when he was in Liberty College. They had a son, Sidney. Together with his wife he was traveling in Europe during the summer of 1914, and they were caught in Germany when the World War broke out. The hardships they endured in getting back to America broke Altsheler's health, and for his five remaining years he was a semi-invalid, dying in New York at the age of fifty-seven.

He was a handsome man, with broad shoulders and a square, clean-shaven jaw. Though the list of Altsheler's books did not equal the incredible number poured out by Horatio Alger, there were nevertheless more of them than it would be profitable to catalogue. A representative selection, however, gives their flavor and perhaps explains, through their variety of subject, why he so captivated the imagination and held the loyalty of his boy readers from the '90's of one century to the '20's of the next. Some of these books, such as *A Herald of the West* or *Circling Campfires,* are indeed not unworthy of adult reading, for they are first-rate historical romances. The only novel Altsheler wrote directly intended for adult consumption was *The Candidate,* based on his experiences gained while a newspaper reporter; but it had small success and he turned back to his immensely popular juvenile stories.

PRINCIPAL WORKS: The Sun of Saratoga, 1897; A Soldier of Manhattan, 1898; A Herald of the West, 1898; The Last Rebel, 1900; In Circling Camps, 1900; The Wilderness Road, 1901; Before

the Dawn, 1903; The Candidate, 1905; The Young Trailers, 1907; The Forest Runners, 1908; The Free Rangers, 1909; The Horsemen of the Plains, 1910; The Riflemen of the Ohio, 1910; The Scouts of the Valley, 1911; The Border Watch, 1912; The Texan Star, 1912; Apache Gold, 1913; The Texan Scouts, 1913; The Guns of Bull Run, 1914; The Guns of Shiloh, 1914; The Scouts of Stonewall, 1914; The Sword of Antietam, 1914; The Star of Gettysburg, 1915; The Hunters of the Hills, 1916; The Shades of the Wilderness, 1916; The Tree of Appomattox, 1916; The Keepers of the Trail, 1916; The Shadow of the North, 1917; The Eyes of the Woods, 1917.

ABOUT: Kunitz, S. J. & Haycraft, H. (eds.). The Junior Book of Authors; Moore, A. C. Joseph A. Altsheler and American History; Bookman April 1899, February 1903; New York Times June 7, 1919.

ALVÁREZ QUINTERO, SERAFÍN (March 1871-April 12, 1938) and his brother ***JOAQUIN*** (January 1873-), Spanish playwrights, were born at Utrera and educated at Seville. They began writing in their school days and by the time they were seventeen and fifteen they had dozens of plays in their closet. In January 1888 the Teatro Cervantes of Seville  produced their one-act skit *Esgrima y Amor* and soon agreed to put on another of their one-acters, *Belén, 12, Principal.* The brothers worked for nine years as clerks in the Treasury Department in Madrid, writing after hours their plays and sketches, many of which were performed in leading Madrid theatres. But it was not until the late nineties that they won recognition. In 1896 they contributed to the Madrid periodical *Nuevo Mundo* under the pseudonym "Diablo Cojuelo" (Limping Devil), and published their first book of verse. From 1897 on without interruption they wrote short comedies for several playhouses. Like the old Spanish dramatists Lope de Vega and Lope de Rueda, whom they resembled in many ways, they saw material for their plays everywhere around them and promptly dramatized every little incident. It was, however, at the beginning of the century, with *El Patio* (1900) and *Las Flores* (1901), that their best poetical qualities and sustained inspiration were revealed—these comedies pictured their native Andalusia in all its radiance. From the earliest, they excelled in depicting background as well as in handling dialogue, which is always gay and vivacious and redeems the decidedly superficial presentation

* Died June 15, 1944.

of character; analysis and depth of characterization are never found in their work.

By October 1908 the Quintero *genre*—which is in the old Spanish tradition of the "theatrical" theatre and the *commedia dell' arte*—had become so popular that their comedy *Las de Caín* was produced the same evening in Madrid, Barcelona, Vigo, and Seville.

The brothers continued to write charming plays such as *A Sunny Morning* (1905), *Doña Clarines* (1908), *A Hundred Years Old* (1909), *The Fountain of Youth,* and *Malvaloca* (1912). In 1915 the town of Utrera in honor of her native sons placed a memorial stone on the house of their birth. In 1920 Serafín was elected to the Spanish Royal Academy and five years later Joaquín was similarly honored.

When in 1928 the city of Seville erected a monument in one of its public parks in honor of the brothers Quintero, Seville was speaking for the whole of Andalusia: the Quinteros, with their gay spontaneity and brisk dialogue, had translated, to a certain extent, a part of Andalusian life. Of course the Quinteros overlooked the less sparkling aspects of Spanish life, and in the hundreds of pieces contained in the fifty-odd volumes of their *Teatro Completo,* there is a wearying sameness. Over and over again come the admonitions: keep away from physical and moral distress; avoid poverty, crime, and squalor; don't marry a sinful woman; rich folks marry poor folks if the latter are virtuous, humble, and Catholic; women talk a lot but often they know when to keep quiet. Such is the content of the brothers Quintero theatre. Their sole purpose was to entertain, and they achieved unprecedented popularity. Professor L. A. Warren says: "The existence which the Quinteros most enjoy presenting is the pleasant life of the comfortable in a delightful, conventionalized setting of flowers and oranges, gaiety and charm, the traditional, old-fashioned Andalusia with just a dash of smart modern manners. So with the characters; there are no deep conflicts of the passions of love, hate, and jealousy; instead there is wit and chatter round the minor social disharmonies of life. . . . Clear, bright, light, and gay are their pieces, sparkling with a keen wit and with a delicate touch for which Seville is famous."

Joaquín Alvárez Quintero, the surviving brother, has sent the editors of this volume through his secretary the following explanation of the brothers' attitude toward the Spanish Revolution and of Serafín's death: "The authors took no active part in politics; but nevertheless their aspirations made them sympathetic to anything which would aggrandize Spain. The inception of the National Movement in 1936—with which they were heartily in accord—found them in the Escorial, shut up in the Red zone, but on the side of Franco, for whose victory, with so many other oppressed Spaniards, they fervently prayed; and it was in the hope of that victory—maintained with unconquerable faith—that Serafín was surprised by death."

Since the older brother's death, the younger brother continues to write under the same dual name: Serafín and Joaquín Alvárez Quintero.

Works Available in English Translation: A Sunny Morning, 1914 (later published under the title A Bright Morning); Malvaloca, 1916; By Their Words Ye Shall Know Them, 1917; Fortunato, 1918; Papa Juan: or, The Centenarian, 1918; The Fountain of Youth, 1922; Four Plays: The Women Have Their Way, A Hundred Years Old, Fortunato, and The Lady from Alfaqueque, 1927; The Widow's Eyes, 1929; Grief, 1930; Four Comedies: Love Passes By, Don Abel Wrote a Tragedy, Peace and Quiet, Doña Clarines, 1932.

About: Martínez Ruiz, J. Los Quinteros y Otras Páginas; Bell, A. F. G. Contemporary Spanish Literature; Bueno, M. Teatro Español Contemporáneo; Martín Caballero, F. Vidas Ajenas; Pérez de Ayala, R. Las Máscaras; Warren, L. A. Modern Spanish Literature; Zurita, M. Historia del Genero Chico; Bulletin Hispanique January 1926; Nueva Cultura June-July 1935; New Republic February 7, 1923; New York Times April 14, 1938; Nuova Antologia May 1, 1938; Quarterly Review April 1919.

ALVERDES, PAUL (May 6, 1897-), German novelist, was born in Strassburg, the son of an insurance manager. He was educated at the Universities of Jena and Munich, receiving a Ph.D. degree from the latter. In spite of his youth he served in the First World War, and was severely wounded in France in 1915. From his hospital experiences he drew the moving story of *The Whistlers' Room,* both his best known and his best novel. He has also published much poetry (none of it translated into English), and is considered an authority on the newer German poetry. He has translated James Fenimore Cooper into German. In 1925 he married Rose Weidner. On the most recent information concerning him, he was living in Munich. What part, if any, he is playing in the Second World War is unknown. However, his work has always been non-political and non-controversial, a fact which has probably enabled him to be among the very few reputable German authors who have found it possible to continue to live in Germany since the Hitler régime began.

Alverdes' early writing was strongly influenced by that of Hans Carossa. As P. Beaumont Wadsworth remarked, "He came to maturity [as a writer] very slowly." His work is characterized by "a quiet, lyrical quality, a poetic vein and an interest in the individual soul and faith in the eternal verities." There is in him none of the bitterness which marks most post-war novels in Germany as elsewhere. His books are all short, his style muted, tender without being sentimental, full of compassionate understanding.

Neither of his two later novels translated into English gained even the limited public won by *The Whistlers' Room*, which Alexander Woollcott tried in vain to boost into a best-seller. This is a study of a hospital ward where soldiers are confined who were wounded in the throat, so that they can talk only through silver pipes, in a sort of whistle. It follows the lives of these men, drawn from every stratum of society and of the most varied backgrounds and natures, for several months, while some of them die and some of them are cured, and to most of them "nothing happens." Nothing, in the sense of anything strenuous or dramatic, ever "happens" to any of Alverdes' characters. He is distinctly a minor novelist, but none the less a gifted and sympathetic one.

WORKS AVAILABLE IN ENGLISH: The Whistlers' Room, 1929; Reinhold: or, The Transformed, 1932; Changed Men, 1933.

ABOUT: Bookman June-July 1932.

AMMERS-KÜLLER, Mrs. JO VAN

(August 13, 1884-), Dutch novelist, writes: "I was born and spent my youth in the little old town of Delft, where several generations of Küllers lived as doctors or lawyers. I was an only child and had a dog as a beloved playmate. As a child of about ten or twelve, I wrote stories and plays which were performed by myself and my friends; I remember that they had a beautiful beginning, but were always muddled up towards the end. As a girl of 14, I had, to my great surprise and satisfaction, a short story printed in a magazine. Serious work began, however, many

years later, for I married young and spent several years in household duties and the upbringing of two sons. But as soon as they went to school I turned to my old hobby of writing, and produced a play that was put upon the stage and a novel that was printed, both in 1919. My work (plays and novels) had considerable success from the beginning; I was already one of the most-read authors in Holland when I published in 1925 *The Rebel Generation*, which was not a great success and a best-seller in Holland, but brought me international fame, as it was translated and published successively in ten languages.

"Since then all my books have been translated and are regularly published in many countries. This brings me in contact with foreign readers, and as I speak (as do most Dutch people) French, German, and English fluently, I have traveled and lectured in Germany, Denmark, Finland, Poland, Hungary, and Switzerland. I have been in America twice, in 1926 and in 1936; the last time I stayed with my friend Hendrik Willem Van Loon and his wife and visited President Roosevelt with him. In the summer of 1938, after having finished my historical trilogy, *The House of Tavelinck*, I made a trip to the Dutch East Indies, anticipating the writing of an historical novel about the first colonization.

"I was for many years the secretary of the P.E.N. Club in Holland, and the organizer of the congress that took place in The Hague and Amsterdam in 1931. Twice I was a guest of honor in Great Britain, once in London, I think in 1928, and once in Edinburgh, in 1932. Many friendships arose from contact with P.E.N. members. I loved and admired John Galsworthy, and I was a great friend of Mrs. Dawson Scott. During the last few years, having traveled in so many countries, I have been out of touch with many of my English friends.

"In April 1939 it was twenty-five years since I published my first novel. I have written since then about thirteen novels, which have appeared in twelve different languages"

* * *

Esther Forbes has said of Jo van Ammers-Küller: "She is too good a realist to be cynical. . . . She has a strong hold on life, and for that reason a strong hold on her art." As almost the only contemporary novelist of Holland well known to readers of English, her intimate "family" pictures of Dutch life, detailed and realistic, have a special interest; and she is above all an excellent story-teller.

WORKS AVAILABLE IN ENGLISH: The Rebel Generation, 1928; The House of Joy, 1929; Jenny Heysten's Career, 1930; Tantalus, 1930; No Surrender, 1931; Masquerade, 1932; The House of Tavelinck, 1938.

ABOUT: Hansen, A. C. Twentieth Century Forces in European Fiction; Bookman November 1930.

ANDERSEN NEXØ. See NEXØ

*ANDERSON, FREDERICK IRVING (November 14, 1877-), American short-story writer, notes:  "Born Aurora, Ill., son of Andrew and Elizabeth (Adling) Anderson. Educated in public schools and Wharton School, University of Pennsylvania ('99). Married Emma Helen de Zouche of New York (born Montreal, Canada, 1908; died July 1937). Newspaper work, Aurora News 1895-96; on staff New York World 1898-1908, contemporary with David Graham Phillips, Irvin Cobb, Samuel G. Blythe, Reginald de Koven, James Huneker, Irving Bacheller, Theodore Dreiser, O. Henry, Robert H. Davis, etc. Wrote on agricultural economics, 1910-14; published The Farmer of Tomorrow (1914); wrote and spoke on farm water power and electricity; published Electricity for the Farm (1915), which was published also in Spanish for Latin America. Published short stories and novelettes in the Saturday Evening Post, under editorship of George Horace Lorimer, for twenty consecutive years, 1913-33; also many short stories in other American and English periodicals. Published three short story collections and selected stories in various anthologies. Stories are of New York or New England setting. Those of New York deal with the scene between Van Bibber and the night club era; those of New England with archaic hill regions. The Berkshires are the actual setting, but they are characteristic of any of the remote regions. Present address, East Jamaica, Vt."

* * *

The greater number of Frederick Irving Anderson's stories deal with crime and detection, and they are highly regarded by serious students of that genre. In originality, command of plot, and rich American

flavor, his work is frequently compared with Melville Davisson Post's.[qv] Several of his stories of Sophie Lang and Deputy Parr have been filmed.

PRINCIPAL WORKS: The Farmer of Tomorrow, 1913; The Adventures of the Infallible Godahl, 1914; Electricity for the Farm, 1915; The Notorious Sophie Lang (published in England only) 1925; The Book of Murder, 1930.

ABOUT: Haycraft, H. Murder for Pleasure: The Life and Times of the Detective Story; Honce, C. Mark Twain's Associated Press Speech.

ANDERSON, MAXWELL (December 15, 1888-), American dramatist and poet, was born in Atlantic, Pa., the son of the Rev. William Lincoln Anderson and Premely (Stevenson) Anderson. He was reared in various parts of the Middle West, as his father was appointed to different churches, and received his B.A. from the University  Vandamm of North Dakota in 1911. He then went to Stanford University, where he received an M.A. degree in 1914. He had previously taught school in North Dakota and California, and while at Stanford acted as instructor in English. On leaving Stanford he entered journalism, and was successively with the Grand Forks (N.D.) Herald and the San Francisco Chronicle and Bulletin until 1918, when he went to New York and was an editorial writer on the Evening Globe and the Morning World, and on the editorial staff of the New Republic, until 1928. Since that time he has devoted himself entirely to authorship. He had already gained sufficient attention as a poet to join with Padraic Colum, Genevieve Taggard, and others in founding Measure, a magazine of poetry, in 1920.

Because Mr. Anderson's first great success was in his collaboration with Laurence Stallings in What Price Glory, it is usually thought that he, like Stallings, served in the First World War. The first-hand experience from which that play was drawn was, however, entirely contributed by its other author. His next two plays were also written with Mr. Stallings, and the next after that, Outside Looking In, was an adaptation of Jim Tully's Beggars of Life. By this time Mr. Anderson was firmly established as one of the leading American playwrights, and (with the exception of Gods of the Lightning, based more or less on the Sacco-

* Died December 24, 1947.

Vanzetti case, the details of which were furnished by Harold Hickerson), he has done no further work in collaboration.

In 1911 Mr. Anderson married Margaret Haskett, who died in 1931, leaving three sons. In 1933 he married Gertrude Maynard, by whom he has a daughter. They live in New York in the winter, and on a farm thirty miles from the city in the summer. There Mr. Anderson, six feet tall, heavily built, with a massive head, full face, dark wavy hair, and earnest eyes behind spectacles, writes, walks, drives, and collects old American songs. He is no sportsman and plays no games; indeed he has little leisure for recreation, for he is a hard and continuous worker. With Elmer Rice, Robert Sherwood, S. N. Behrman, and, originally, the late Sidney Howard, he is a member of the Playwrights' Group, which produces the plays written by its members.

He won the Pulitzer Prize for drama in 1933 with *Both Your Houses,* and the Drama Critics' Award twice, in 1936 with *Winterset* and in 1937 with *High Tor.* To the increasing regret of his admirers, he has become apparently wedded to the idea of writing his plays in verse—and frequently in blank verse, which with its archaic air makes realism in a contemporary play seem absurd, and fails to redeem even non-contemporary plays—as witness the flat failure of *Journey to Jerusalem* in 1940. Without going so far as to agree with Edmund Wilson that Anderson is "at his worst in verse," since he is in the non-dramatic field an authentic poet, it is true that his later plays would have been stronger had they been written in forthright prose. They have sometimes read better than they acted, never a compliment to a play written to be performed on the stage; and they have sometimes been strained and dull. Nevertheless in all of them there have been passages of great beauty and poignancy.

It may well be that Mr. Anderson's own ambition is to produce plays primarily for the library rather than for the theatre. Even in this he has not always been entirely successful, but it is an ambition more lofty and more solid than that of most modern dramatists. Dramatic intensity he has always had, even when it is half-stifled by rhetoric.

Mr. Anderson has in other words been a playwright markedly uneven in attainment, but one to be criticized only on a level of high seriousness. He has written nothing trivial, even in his one-act plays, *The Feast of Ortolans* and *Second Overture;* and the worst that can be said of him is that sometimes his reach has exceeded his grasp—as what writer's has not? At his best, he is among the half dozen most considerable dramatists of our time. There are faults in all his plays, but *Elizabeth the Queen, Valley Forge, Winterset,* and *High Tor* at least will not soon be forgotten.

PRINCIPAL WORKS: White Desert, 1923; What Price Glory (with L. Stallings) 1924; The Buccaneer (with L. Stallings) 1925; First Flight (with L. Stallings) 1925; Outside Looking In, 1925; You Who Have Dreams (poems) 1925; Saturday's Children, 1927; Gypsy, 1928; Gods of the Lighting (with H. Hickerson) 1928; Elizabeth the Queen, 1930; Night Over Taos, 1932; Both Your Houses, 1933; Valley Forge, 1934; Winterset, 1935; The Essence of Tragedy (essays) 1935; The Masque of Kings, 1936; The Wingless Victory, 1936; High Tor, 1936; Star-Wagon, 1937; Knickerbocker Holiday, 1938; Journey to Jerusalem, 1940; Eleven Verse Plays, 1940; Candle in the Wind, 1941.

ABOUT: Magazine of Art April 1937; New Republic June 23, 1937; Poetry January 1941; Saturday Review of Literature January 30, 1937; Theatre Arts Monthly June 1933, August 1934, May 1936.

ANDERSON, SHERWOOD (September 13, 1876-March 8, 1941), American novelist and short story writer, was born in Camden, Ohio, the son of Irwin and Emma (Smith) Anderson. His mother was partly of Italian descent. His father was the prototype of the son's fictional character, "Windy McPherson" —a roaming, improvident, easy-going man, a teller of tall stories.

Anderson said that his first exercises in fiction came from imaginative reconstructions of his father's unlikely tales of his apocryphal experiences. The family moved aimlessly about Ohio, and each of the seven children was born in a different town. Most of Anderson's boyhood was spent in Clyde, Ohio. His schooling was spotty, since he had to leave school frequently to take odd jobs to help out, and he seems to have had no formal education after fourteen, when his mother died, though for a short time he attended Wittenberg College. He served in Cuba during the Spanish-American War, and finally became manager of a paint factory in Elyria, Ohio. It was from this factory that he walked out suddenly one day, deliberately leaving behind the impression that he had lost his mind. As Clifton Fadiman remarked, in an article on Anderson in the *Nation,* "the dramatization of this moment is his major contribution to the interpretation of American life. . . . He is obsessed with the experience of sudden self-discovery."

He did not, however, immediately take to creative writing, but went to Chicago to live with his brother Karl, later a well known painter, and became an advertising copy writer. Publishers were secured for his first books with great difficulty, chiefly through the efforts of the "Chicago Group"—including Theodore Dreiser, Floyd Dell, and Carl Sandburg—then emerging as a literary force in America. *Winesburg, Ohio* first brought him into wide public notice, though the only one of his books to approach the "best-seller" class was one of the poorest of them, *Dark Laughter.* For many years Anderson was thought of primarily as a writer on sex, the focal theme of most of his stories. This reputation was as untrue of him as it was of D. H. Lawrence, who also acquired it. Both men were rebels against industrial civilization with all of its implications, including the suppression and crippling of the natural exercise of sexual and all other emotions.

In 1921 Anderson went to Europe for a year, then for another year lived in New Orleans. For a while that city and New York were his stopping places; then in 1924 he moved to Marion, Va., and became editor simultaneously of the town's two papers—one Republican and one Democratic. It was freely predicted at the time that this would be merely a passing phase; on the contrary it became his established way of life. For a long time he even lived over the printshop, so as to be handy to the pressroom. Later, however, he had a stone and log house on Ripshin Creek, twenty-two miles from Marion near the North Carolina border. There a separate cabin served as a study; this originally was built on a hill, but the beauty of the scenery distracted him from his work, so he moved it down by the creek. A few years before his death he announced that writing as an art had ceased to have validity in America, and that the new and living form of expression was in the motion pictures to which he would devote himself in the future. But he made no actual move in that direction.

Anderson was married four times, and had two sons and a daughter. His second wife, from whom he was divorced, was Tennessee Mitchell, the sculptor. The day of their divorce in 1924 he married his third wife, Elizabeth Prall, of Berkeley, Calif. His fourth wife was Eleanor G. Anderson.

In appearance, Sherwood Anderson could never be mistaken for anything except what he was—a Middle Western American. His leonine head, with its masses of wavy hair, his heavy-set figure, ill at ease except in loose, informal clothing, had in them a hint of a beardless Whitman, transferred in time to the twentieth century and in place to the fertile plains. William Allen White called him, half-facetiously, "the Dostoievsky of Winesburg, Ohio, the mid-American Chekhov," but actually he had little in common with either of these great Russians except a preoccupation with interior mental processes and an absence of sharply defined plot. Fadiman came much nearer to the truth in denominating him a "re-emergent adolescent," with "the bewilderment of a mature man who has suddenly been forced to think." His gloom and his rebellion were those of adolescence, but his softness and sentimentality those of late middle age.

It was the fashion to speak of Sherwood Anderson as "confused," and he himself perpetuated that epithet by a half-childlike, half-Socratic habit of asking questions about fundamentals, of acknowledging that he had not yet made up his mind about life and settled down to see it grimly out. The main characters of his novels and stories were all "split-off sections of himself," and he was happiest in his reconstructions of his own boyhood. It was here, in the race-track stories especially and in the studies of thwarted personalities in *Winesburg, Ohio* and *The Triumph of the Egg,* that he wrote his finest tales.

His autobiography, *A Story Teller's Story,* was half fiction, his fiction nearly all autobiography. He was an American phenomenon which could have occurred nowhere else. Robert Morss Lovett well said of him: "It is in thus seizing on scraps of reality and projecting them beyond the small range controlled by the senses that Sherwood Anderson's imagination brings fiction to the enhancement of life, and enlarges his art beyond the limits of naturalism into expressionism."

In February 1941, Sherwood Anderson left for South America as a sort of unofficial ambassador of good will. He was taken from his ship at Colon, Panama, suffering from an intestinal obstruction. There he died of peritonitis a few days later, at the age of sixty-four. His body was returned to the United States.

PRINCIPAL WORKS: Windy McPherson's Son, 1916; Marching Men, 1917; Mid-American Chants (poems in prose) 1918; Winesburg, Ohio, 1919; Poor White, 1920; The Triumph of the Egg,

1921; Many Marriages, 1922; Horses and Men, 1923; A Story Teller's Story, 1924; Dark Laughter, 1925; Sherwood Anderson's Notebook, 1926; Tar; Middle West Childhood, 1927; Hello Towns, 1929; Perhaps Women, 1931; Beyond Desire, 1933; Death in the Woods, 1933; No Swank, 1934; Puzzled America, 1935; Kit Brandon, 1936; Plays, 1937; Home Town (Face of America Series) 1940; Memoirs, 1942.

ABOUT: Anderson, S. A Story Teller's Story, Tar: Middle West Childhood, Memoirs; Hansen, H. Mid-West Portraits; Canadian Forum August 1937; Catholic World November 1929; Dial January 1922; Nation June 12, 1929, November 9, 1932; New York Times March 9, 1941; New Republic November 25, 1936; Saturday Review of Literature March 22, 1941.

ANDREEV. See ANDREYEV

*ANDREWS, CHARLES MC LEAN
(February 22, 1863-   ), American historian and Pulitzer Prize winner, writes: "Born in

Bachrach

Wethersfield, Conn., son of a minister. At the age of seventeen entered Trinity College, Hartford, graduating 1884, winning Oratorical Prize, editor of the *Tablet*. After two years' teaching in the West Hartford High School, entered Johns Hopkins University, scholar and fellow in history, and Ph.D. in 1889. Then to Bryn Mawr College, as associate, associate professor, and professor of history, 1889-1907. Called back to Johns Hopkins as professor of history, 1907-10, and then to Yale as Farnam Professor of American History, 1910-31, Director of Historical Publications, 1931-33, now emeritus. Married, 1895, Evangeline H. Walker; daughter and son (now assistant in history at Yale). At Yale edited Historical Publications, 1912-33 [fifty volumes], lectured in the Graduate School only, and took part in the administration of the school. During these years lectured at the University of Helsingfors, Finland, 1911; at the Universities of Iowa, Wisconsin, Chicago, Michigan, New York University, and College of William and Mary. Acting president, American Historical Association, 1924, and president, 1925. Member of many historical societies, here and abroad. Received honorary degrees from Trinity, Lehigh, Yale, Harvard, and Johns Hopkins. Fellow of American Academy of Arts and Sciences, member National Institute of Arts and Letters (gold medalist, 1937), American Academy of Arts and Letters, American Philosophical Society, Phi Beta Kappa.

"Have written on English history and history of the nineteenth century, but for many years have devoted attention to American Colonial history. Spent parts of ten years in England preparing a *Guide to the British Archives* relating to Colonial history to 1783, published by the Carnegie Institution of Washington, 1908-14 (seven volumes). Have contributed volumes to the *Home University Library*, the *American Nation* series, the *Original Narratives of Early American History*, the *Chronicles of America,* and *American Legal Records Publications.* The first volume of *The Colonial Period of American History* received the Pulitzer Prize in history for 1935. In collaboration with my wife brought out in 1921 *Journal of a Lady of Quality,* and Dickinson's *God's Protecting Providence.* With Mrs. E. P. Trowbridge prepared *Old Houses of Connecticut,* 1923.

"With Mrs. Andrews have traveled widely in this country, Europe, and the Far East. Trip around the world, fifteen months, 1926-27. Residence in New Haven."

PRINCIPAL WORKS: The River Towns of Connecticut, 1889; The Old English Manor, 1892; The Historical Development of Modern Europe (2 vols.) 1896-98; Contemporary Europe, Asia, and Africa, 1902; A History of England, 1903; Colonial Self-Government: 1632-1689, 1904; British Commissions, Councils, and Committees: 1622-1675, 1908; A Bibliography of History (with J. L. Gambrell & L. L. Tall) 1912; A Short History of England, 1912; Guide to the Manuscript Material for the History of the United States in the Public Record Office (2 vols.) 1912-14; The Boston Merchants and the Non-Importation Movement, 1917; Fathers of New England and Colonial Folk-Ways, 1919; The Colonial Background of the American Revolution, 1924; Our Earliest Colonial Settlements, 1933; The Colonial Period of American History (4 vols.) 1934-38.

ABOUT: Essays in Colonial History Presented to Charles McLean Andrews by His Students; Kraus, M. A History of American History; Pennsylvania Magazine of History and Biography July 1935; Time December 28, 1936.

ANDREWS, Mrs. MARY RAYMOND (SHIPMAN) (186?-August 2, 1936), American novelist and short story writer, was born in Mobile, Ala., in a year which she always refused to disclose, but which—judging from her marriage in 1884—probably fell somewhere in the 1860's. Her father, the Rt. Rev. Jacob Shaw Shipman, was rector of Christ Church in Mobile; her mother was Ann Louise Shipman. Bishop Shipman of New York was a brother. She passed her girlhood at Lexington, Ky., graduated from a "now extinct school" at seventeen, and studied with her father, also studying law with her husband, William Shankland Andrews, later a justice of the

* Died September 9, 1943.

New York State Court of Appeals. With their son, Paul Shipman Andrews, now dean of the Syracuse (N.Y.) University College of Law, the Andrews family spent thirty summers at a camp a hundred miles from Quebec. Mrs. Andrews did much of her writing there, also qualifying as a good sportswoman by shooting seven deer, three caribou, and two moose in 1926. "The Sabine Maiden," a story published in *Ainslee's Magazine*, derived the same humor from masculine undress that Mary Roberts Rinehart found in her "Twenty-Three-and-One-Half-Hours' Leave," and was reprinted with several other magazine stories in *The Eternal Masculine*, which sold very well. *The Perfect Tribute* was based on an apocryphal episode connected with Lincoln's Gettysburg Address, a story reported to Mrs. Andrews by her son, who had it from Walter Burlingame, whose father heard it from Edward Everett. Published in *Scribner's Magazine* in 1905, this sentimental footnote to history sold over 600,000 copies in book form. The New York *Times* spoke of Mrs. Andrews' fiction as possessing "saccharine and mystic tendencies relieved by a certain mild and harmless humor," while the *Nation* called her "an accomplished story-teller, writing at times with a rhythm and dignity which place her quite above the average." She traveled extensively. Three days after her death, presumably in her seventies, following an operation, Judge Andrews died at seventy-eight as the result of a fall.

PRINCIPAL WORKS: Bob and the Guides, 1906; A Good Samaritan, 1906; The Perfect Tribute, 1906; The Militants, 1907; Better Treasure, 1908; The Enchanted Forest, 1909; The Lifted Bandage, 1910; Counsel Assigned, 1912; Marshall, 1912; The Eternal Masculine, 1913; August First (with R. I. Murray) 1915; Three Things, 1915; The Eternal Feminine, 1916; Crosses of War, 1918; Joy in the Morning, 1919; His Soul Goes Marching, 1922; Yellow Butterflies, 1922; A Lost Commander: Florence Nightingale, 1929.

ABOUT: Baright, L. B. An Appreciation of Mary Raymond Shipman Andrews; Kunitz, S. J. & Haycraft, H. (eds.). The Junior Book of Authors; Newsweek August 15, October 17, 1936; New York Times August 3, 1936.

ANDREWS, ROY CHAPMAN (January 26, 1884-), American zoologist and explorer, writes: "Roy Chapman Andrews was born in Beloit, Wis. His life as a naturalist and explorer began when as a boy he made his earliest observations of bird and animal life in the woods and streams near his home. In 1906 he graduated from Beloit College, and immediately came to New York and the American Museum of Natural History. The early years of his scientific career and explorations, beginning in 1908, to Vancouver Island and Alaska, and later as a special naturalist aboard the U.S.S. 'Albatross' to the Dutch East Indies, Borneo, and the Celebes, were devoted to a specialized study of the life and habits of whales. His subsequent explorations and research have carried him to practically every land and sea.

"In 1914 he felt that he had done his duty by whales and turned his attention to land explorations. His first important expedition was in the unexplored forests of Northern Korea and the Manchurian border. Prof. Henry Fairfield Osborn's prophecy that Central Asia would prove to be the incubating center for Northern mammalian life focused his attention on the possibilities of exploration on this grim plateau. He conceived the idea of a series of expeditions extending over a period of ten years, embracing every field of science that would further the reconstruction of the complete past history of the Central Asian plateau. As leader of the Central Asian Expeditions, Mr. Andrews took his first expedition into the field in 1916 to work in the territory of Tibet, Southwest China, and Burma. His second expedition went into North China and Outer Mongolia in 1919, and the third worked in Central Asia, especially in Mongolia, from 1921 to 1930. It was the largest land exploring expedition that has ever been sent out from America, comprising forty men, 150 camels, and eight motor cars. The cost of the work was $700,000. In the Gobi Desert it discovered some of the richest fossil fields in the world. It discovered the first known dinosaur eggs; skeletons of the oldest, as well as the largest known land mammals; geological strata previously unknown; and evidences of primitive human life. It mapped many regions previously unknown and brought out the largest collection of recent mammals ever taken from Asia."

* * *

Dr. Andrews (he has honorary Sc.D. degrees. from Beloit and from Brown University, as well as an M.A. from Columbia) has been awarded the Elisha Kent Kane Gold Medal of the Philadelphia Society (for distinguished geographical research); the

Hubbard Medal of the National Geographic Society, the ninth awarded in forty-five years; the Vega Gold Medal of the Swedish Geographical Society; the Loczy Medal of the Hungarian Geographical Society; the Explorers' Club Medal; and the Charles P. Daly Gold Medal of the American Geographical Society. He was president of the Explorers' Club from 1931 to 1935, and in 1935 became director of the American Museum of Natural History. He is widely known as a lecturer and radio speaker. His writing has grown directly out of his scientific and exploratory work, and is subsidiary to it, but he commands an easy flowing style and his non-technical books and articles make absorbing reading.

He was married in Paris in 1914 to Yvette Borup, by whom he had two sons, and from whom he was divorced in 1930. In 1935 he married Wilhelmina Christmas. He is unassuming in appearance, his most notable characteristic being his keen blue eyes. He is known as an explorer "who refuses to have adventures," since adventures in his eyes are the mark of a badly prepared expedition. His salient trait, Fitzhugh Green remarked, is his "absolute, direct naturalness"—which appears in his writing as much as it does in his personality.

In November, 1941 Dr. Andrews submitted his resignation of the directorship of the Museum of Natural History, on the ground that world conditions had narrowed the field of exploration and that the problems consequently confronting the Museum were not those for which he was fitted "either by inclination, temperament, or training. I shall hope to continue close relations with the Museum and continue to serve it in other ways as long as I live."

PRINCIPAL WORKS: The California Gray Whale, 1914; The Sei Whale (with H. von W. Schulte) 1916; Whale Hunting With Gun and Camera, 1916; Camps and Trails in China (with Y. Andrews) 1918; Across Mongolian Plains, 1921; On the Trail of Ancient Man, 1926; Ends of the Earth, 1929; The New Conquest of Central Asia, 1932; This Business of Exploring, 1935; Exploring With Andrews, 1938; This Amazing Planet, 1940.

ABOUT: Andrews, R. C. Ends of the Earth; American Magazine May 1929; Asia August 1924; Natural History December 1937; Popular Science February 1941; Science June 2, 1922.

ANDREYEV, LEONID NIKOLAE-VICH (June 18?, 1871-September 12, 1919), Russian novelist, dramatist, and short story writer, was born in Orel, central Russia, the son of Nikolai Andreyev, a surveyor. His father died early of cerebral hemorrhage, the same disease that was to kill the son. Although Leonid was a precocious child, he was a lagging student, and just barely managed to pass the law course in the University of St. Petersburg (Leningrad). He was besides by this time in extreme poverty, and already the victim of his life-long depression. A suicide attempt, his third, in 1894, led to his restraint by the authorities, and the reaction from this brought on a plunge into debauchery. He pulled himself together, transferred to the University of Moscow, and managed to achieve a law degree. As an attorney, however, Andreyev was a rank failure. He turned to painting, with some success; then abruptly he became a police reporter for the Moscow *Courier*.

This was the beginning of his career as a writer, for the essays he wrote for his paper as a side-line soon attracted attention. In 1898 he published his first short story, "Bargamot and Garaska," which attracted the attention of Gorky. Gorky, only three years Andreyev's senior but already nationally known, poured himself out in generous encouragement, and Andreyev flourished under his praise. His first book of stories was published in 1901, but it was a year later, with *In the Fog,* that he attained real recognition. For a while he was enormously popular; then, led by Countess Tolstoy, the legions of convention were on him, attacking him for his frankness and "filth." Morbidly sensitive to criticism, Andreyev withdrew into himself. It was at this period that he built the villa in Finland, at Kuokkala, in which his last years were spent.

He was too anti-social ever to follow Gorky into his revolutionary beliefs, though he did spend a short term in prison with his friend after the abortive revolution of 1905. He became increasingly conservative until it was not surprising that he espoused the World War whole heartedly, supported Kerensky, and turned violently against the Soviet government. In the end he retired to Finland, from which he sent out impassioned protests against the Bolshevik régime.

As a writer, Andreyev gradually shook off the early influence of Chekhov and became increasingly symbolic in style. Chief example of this is his play, *The Life of Man,* which when produced by the Moscow

Art Theater was so ridiculed that a burlesque of it was almost immediately offered at a comedy theatre. As his stories, novels, and plays sank ever more deeply into the abyss of horror which was his milieu, he grew to be accepted as "the apostle of gloom," the master of chaos. Yet he wanted fame, and he wanted power: "happiest of all," he told Gorky, "are those who are loved with fear." He stood all his life on the edge of madness, if never completely over the boundary.

In many ways Andreyev's was a contradictory nature. This dark, heavy-set man was a bit of a dandy. He was brutal and graceless in his relations with his friends, yet he was as dependent on them as a child, and suffered acutely from loneliness. He was twice married—in 1902 to Alexandra Veligorsky, who died of puerperal fever in Berlin in 1906, and in 1908 to Anna Denisevich, who survived him. He adored and clung to them and his children, but he must have been a painful companion, especially in his last days—poor, angry, suffering, and obsessed by death. In his character, if not in his work, Andreyev was a sort of Russian Strindberg minus the misogyny of the Swede.

In his work, if he resembles any other author, it is Poe—but a Poe who has crossed the border of fantasy into the realm of absolute blackness. "His chaos, his terrible pet," says Alexander Blok, "is only more gruesome because one feels and does not see it." And he adds: "He insistently asks the senseless, irritating question asked by children: 'Why?'" Alexander Kaun touches the same note: "He does not solve problems, he only raises questions." The one exception to this is the magnificently affirmative story written in white heat, the invective against capital punishment called *The Seven Who Were Hanged*. It is a revelation of the Andreyev who might have been. In his other most celebrated plays and novels—in *The Life of Man, King Hunger, He Who Gets Slapped, The Red Laugh*, and the rest—he twangs on our nerves but seldom moves our hearts.

The fact is that Andreyev was written out, burnt out, before the World War started, which is one reason he so welcomed it. He had forced the depths of his subconscious mind until they could no longer respond. He pronounced his own obituary in his words to Gorky: "I must write a story about a man who all his life, suffering madly, sought the truth. And behold, truth appeared to him, but he shut his eyes stopped his ears, and said: 'I do not want thee, however fair thou mayst be, for my life, my torments have kindled in my soul a hatred of thee!'"

PRINCIPAL WORKS AVAILABLE IN ENGLISH TRANSLATION: *Plays*—Savva, 1906; The Life of Man, 1907; Anathema, 1909; A Dilemma, 1910; He Who Gets Slapped, 1916; The Waltz of the Dogs, 1922. *Fiction*—The Red Laugh, 1904; The Seven Who Were Hanged, 1909; Silence and Other Stories, 1910; Judas Iscariot and Others, 1910; The Crushed Flower and Other Stories, 1916; Confessions of a Little Man During Great Days, 1917; When the King Loses His Head and Other Stories, 1920; Satan's Diary, 1920; The Abyss 1929.

ABOUT: Gorky, M. Reminiscences of Leonid Andreyev; Kaun, A. Leonid Andreyev: A Critical Study; Persky, S. M. Contemporary Russian Novelists; Phelps, W. L. Essays on Russian Novelists; Current Literature September 1908; Dial November 15, 1919; Living Age June 16, 1923; New Republic December 24, 1919, June 28, 1922.

"ANET, CLAUDE." See SCHOPFER, J.

ANGELL, Sir NORMAN (December 26, 1874-), English economist and peace advocate, writes: "Childhood in England, boyhood at a French *lycée*, adolescence at Geneva University, early manhood as a cowboy and prospector in Western America and Mexico; then work on American papers, then on French, and then for ten years with the late Lord Northcliffe  as newspaper manager, constituted the beginnings of Norman Angell's career. Since about 1910 authorship and peace agitation; *The Great Illusion* (twenty-five foreign editions), popular books on economics, particularly on money; the invention of card games which reveal the intricacies of currency; Parliament; Nobel Peace Prize [1933]; membership of the Council of the Royal Institute of International Affairs; executive of the League of Nations Union; and in his leisure moments farming a little island off the coast of Essex and sailing a little yacht in the North Sea."

* * *

Sir Norman's name originally was Ralph Norman Angell Lane; he was born at Holbeach, the son of Thomas Angell Lane, a justice of the peace. He was created a knight in 1931. He is unmarried. He was a Labor M.P. from North Bradford from 1929 to 1931. His Nobel Prize was shared with Arthur Henderson. He was editor of *Foreign Affairs* from 1928 to 1931. Besides the offices he mentions, he was co-president of the *Comité Mondial Contre la Guerre et le Fascisme. The Great Illusion,* his best known work, was published in eleven countries and in fifteen languages. Critics have remarked on the logic and conviction of his approach, and the clarity and simplicity of his style. Though his lifework may seem at the present moment to have been a failure, if the world ever achieves lasting peace he will have made an important contribution to that end.

PRINCIPAL WORKS: Patriotism Under Three Flags, 1903; Europe's Optical Illusion, 1909; The Great Illusion, 1910; Peace Theories and the Balkan War, 1912; War and the Essential Realities, 1913; The Foundations of International Polity, 1914; Prussianism and Its Destruction, 1914; The World's Highway, 1915; The Dangers of Half-Preparedness, 1916; Why Freedom Matters, 1916; War Aims, 1917; The Political Conditions of Allied Success, 1918; The Economic Chaos and the Peace Treaty, 1919; The Fruits of Victory, 1921; If Britain Is To Live, 1923; Must Britain Travel the Moscow Road? 1926; The Public Mind: Its Disorders, Its Exploitation, 1926; The Money Game, 1928; The Story of Money, 1930; Can Governments Cure Unemployment? (with H. Wright) 1931; The Unseen Assassins, 1932; The Press and the Organization of Society, 1933; The Great Illusion in 1933, 1933; From Chaos to Control, 1933; For What Do We Fight? 1939; America's Dilemma, 1940; What Kind of Peace? 1941.

ABOUT: Christian Century December 19, 1934; Contemporary Review August 1936; Independent Woman January 1936; Nation (London) March 29, 1930; Nineteenth Century March 1941; Saturday Review of Literature June 10, 1933, December 29, 1934; Spectator March 29, 1930; Survey Graphic December 1940.

ANKER LARSEN, JOHANNES (September 18, 1874-   ), Danish novelist, writes: "I was born on the little Danish island

Langeland. My father was a sailor; my mother, daughter of a farmer. I lived on the farm among Danish peasants the first sixteen years of my life, became a student in the high school, studied theology at the University of Copenhagen, as well as a little law and religious philosophy; left the university and became an actor and writer of plays and short stories, was a producer of plays (*régisseur*) at the great theatres in Copenhagen. After the issue of *The Philosopher's Stone* [which won the Gyldendal Prize of 70,000 kroner in 1923] I left the stage, but returned later to the Royal Theatre in Copenhagen as literary censor. I have been married twice, first to Bodil Lindegaard, then to Gudrun Lendrop, both daughters of well known Danish physicians.

"I left theology deprived of all belief in Christianity. Still there was that religious feeling that seemed inherent in my nature and not to be eradicated as long as life was in me; so I studied as a layman the other great religions of the world, had even a look into theosophy and occultism, till at last I gave up every attempt to find in religion or *isms* a substitute for the Christianity of my childhood and nourishment for my religious feeling. Then life began to show me a little more of itself. Glimpses of a deeper reality came to me, and led me, in the course of some years, into an experience of eternity, not an ecstatic rapture, but an experience as simple and natural as seeing and feeling the sunshine. Since then I find my ordinary daily life placed in the very middle of eternity; this is not caused by the process of reasoning, it is a simple unquestionable fact, I sense life in that way.

"When I began to write novels I naturally tried to express life as I saw it, especially the so-called 'mystical' side of it. I confess it has been more important to me to strengthen such presentments than to show artistic skill. I do not read much; I am interested in life, this strange living life that will reveal to a living man anything of its deep reality that he is able to *live up to,* not intellectually reason out.

"I am very fond of outdoor life; have for many years lived in the woods near a beautiful lake in the environs of Copenhagen. My favorite sport has been boxing, and even when nearly sixty I could take my four rounds with younger adversaries. Of this I am very proud."

* * *

The "quest of a living faith" has been the mainspring of all Anker Larsen's novels. One character, the *Kandidaten* (graduate or professor), his ideal man, appears "openly or incognito" in all his books; of this character another says: "He's jumped head first into religion and come out safely on the other side."

There was great astonishment in Denmark when, in competition with its most celebrated novelists, the Gyldendal Prize "for a novel of Scandinavian life written in the traditions of Dostoievsky and Dickens" was won by "a retired journalist, mediocre actor and manager, author of a few popular theatrical plays, and some unsuccessful novels." The book (*The Philosopher's Stone*) appeared simultaneously in half a dozen languages and made its author internationally famous. He has never repeated this success; the mysticism in his later books has outweighed the story. However, one of Anker Larsen's severest critics, W. W. Worster, was obliged to note the "scenes of idyllic beauty" that came "as a respite" to the strained idealism and arbitrary tragedy of much of his work.

No word concerning Anker Larsen has come out of Denmark since the Nazi invasion.

WORKS AVAILABLE IN ENGLISH: The Philosopher's Stone, 1924; Martha and Mary, 1926; A Stranger in Paradise, 1929; With the Door Open, 1931.

ABOUT: Hoffding, H. Religiøse Tanketyper; Fortnightly Review December 1925; Living Age December 8, 1923; Neue Literatur January 1932; New York Times Book Review May 4, 1924.

ANNUNZIO, GABRIELE D' (March 12, 1863-March 1, 1938), Italian poet, playwright, novelist, propagandist, military leader, and eccentric, was born in Pescara (Abruzzi). His father was Francesco Rapagnetta, a rich landowner and mayor of Pescara, who had legally added the name of d'Annunzio; his mother had been Luisa de Beneditis. The boy was educated at the College of Prato, in Tuscany, and at the University of Rome. He began writing early, poetry being his first love, and he published a volume of poems *Prima Vere* (with a play on the Italian words of "spring" and "first truths") while he was still in school, in 1879. Before his majority he was the author of five published volumes of poetry, and was a scandalous public figure. For a while he was on the staff of the Rome *Tribuna*, where under the pseudonym of "Duca Minimo" ("the least of the dukes," another revelation of his abounding arrogance) he published a series of brilliant *feuilletons*. Soon novels and plays as well as poems were streaming from his pen, and it was not long before he was able to leave his first and only regular journalistic position. By the time his best known novel, *Il Trionfo della Morte* (*The Triumph of Death*), appeared in 1894 he was known, at thirty-one, as Italy's most popular author.

Until the World War, d'Annunzio's career was solely that of a highly successful author, who wrote incessantly, made money easily and spent it even more easily, and built up a reputation for glittering eccen-

tricity. He can hardly be said to have had a private life, since all his personal affairs, most of all his long liaison with the great actress Eleonora Duse, were conducted in public, or immediately afterwards subjected to the most open description, in the manner of George Sand and her books concerning her lovers.

In 1912, swamped by debt and bankrupt, d'Annunzio abruptly quitted Italy for France, and announced that henceforth he would write in French and make Paris his permanent home. At the first declaration of war, he offered his "sword" to France. The French government had much more need for so powerful a propagandist as a speechmaker than as a soldier; it paid his 25,000 francs of debts and sent him home to urge Italy to join the Allies. Once he had succeeded, he forgot his expatriate pronouncements. Suddenly the super-esthete became a warrior and a leader of men. He served successively in the Italian cavalry, infantry, and navy, on one occasion invading an Austrian port in a small motor-boat, and escaping unharmed. His greatest glory, however, was as an aviator. He flew over Vienna dropping leaflets against the Central Powers; he flew his plane wherever danger was thickest; he was shot through the wrist and another bullet ended the sight of one eye and for a time blinded him completely. (This experience, too, he turned to literature, in *Notturno*.) When the war ended, he was commander of the air squad at Venice.

In September 1919 came the spectacular adventure at Fiume. Dalmatia, of which Fiume is the capital, had been taken from Austria by the Versailles Treaty and made a ward of the League of Nations. Many Italians felt strongly that it should be, as it had once been, Italian; d'Annunzio acted on the opinion. With 12,000 "Arditi," he made what he called a "holy entrance" into the city, occupied it, and ruled it as an absolute dictator until the beginning of 1921. He defied the Rapallo Treaty of 1920, which gave Dalmatia its independence, and at the end of the year actually declared war on Italy! His attitude toward "self-determination" was expressed in his boast: "Even if the citizens of Fiume do not desire annexation, I desire it even against their wishes." And when he finally surrendered and marched out, he was received as a conqueror, not a rebel. His proclamation said simply: "Citizens, Gabriele d'Annunzio is here. Not a word. Continue to weep for joy." As a matter of practical politics, Fiume became Italian in 1924.

D'Annunzio retired to his home, "Vittoriale," on the Lake of Garda, in the foothills of the Alps—Catullus' laughing and beloved lake. He turned his house into a war museum, with even his war-plane grounded on the estate, and willed it to Italy after his death. He had written nothing since the war except addresses and essays on it and on the peace, but now he began his long-projected autobiography (*Le Faville del Maglio*, 1924-1928). In 1922 he fell from a window, and injured himself severely. He recovered to find Fascism in control.

In spite of one enigmatic quarrel with Mussolini, d'Annunzio was an ardent Fascist from the first. In fact, he was inclined to think of himself as a precursor of Fascism, and certainly its salute and its war-cry are those of his "Arditi." He helped to organize the Fascist Seamen's Federation, and in every respect he stood behind Mussolini and approved every suppression, brutality, and excess of the régime. In gratitude Mussolini had him created Prince of Monte Nevoso, an hereditary title, in 1924. Also, in 1927, the Fascist régime sponsored an "official" collected edition of all his works.

After 1936 this voluptuary and hedonist lived the life of a recluse at Vittoriale—but a recluse in the grand style. He spent his life in a cell, but a staff of a hundred servants waited on him. Egocentric and flamboyant as ever, he prepared to make his death as sensational as his life had been. He would like to be blown from a cannon, he said, or perhaps he would find a chemical which would dissolve his living body into its elements. He furnished a strange "room of the leper," replete with the paraphernalia of witchcraft and black magic, in which he would go to die when his time came. But he never had the opportunity. He died of a cerebral hemorrhage, sitting at his desk, with his archaic quill pen between his fingers, eleven days before his seventy-fifth birthday.

This thin little man with his strange pale eyes and immense bald dome of a head had some unexplained fascination for women. Duse in her later years devoted all her great art to forcing the public to accept his plays, since she would act in virtually no others. Even after he cast her off and broke her heart by exposing all their inmost secrets in *Il Fuoco* (*The Flame of Life*), which William Drake calls "the most swinish novel ever written," she labored for years to build a theatre which should be a sort

of d'Annunzio Bayreuth. Luisa Baccara, a distinguished pianist, gave up her career to live with d'Annunzio and minister to him in a long illness in 1937. She was assisted by his wife, who had been long estranged from him but returned now to help care for him. His minor affairs of the heart were innumerable and frequently unsavory. He was twice married, to Maria Hardouin, and after her death to the Duchess of Galese. By his two wives he had three sons, the oldest of whom inherited his title.

Megalomaniac and eccentric to the point of insanity though he was, there is no doubt of d'Annunzio's exceeding talent, which had at least the effrontery of genius. He was one of the founders of realism in Italian fiction; many of his poems are magnificent, though they translate badly; and his plays, though marred by floridity and a cold deliberate sensuality, have a sort of decadent grandeur. President of the Royal Academy of Italy, he was called by the French critic Crémieux "the great national poet of imperialist Italy." He was a man who wrote always in a fever, and the cream of his work has the nightmare-splendor of a half-delirious dream.

His best writing was over and done before the turn of the century, but he lived on for almost four decades to become perhaps the greatest modern eccentric.

PRINCIPAL WORKS AVAILABLE IN ENGLISH TRANSLATION: *Fiction*—Episcopo & Company, 1896; The Triumph of Death, 1896; The Intruder, 1898; The Maidens of the Rocks, 1898; The Child of Pleasure, 1898; The Flame of Life, 1900; Tales of My Native Town, 1920. *Plays*—The Dead City, 1902; Francesca da Rimini, 1902; Gioconda, 1902; The Daughter of Jorio, 1907; The Honeysuckle, 1915.

ABOUT: Annunzio, G. de. Le Faville del Maglio (autobiography); Antongini, T. d'Annunzio; Griffin, G. Gabriel d'Annunzio; Kennard, J. S. Italian Romance Writers; Macdonald, J. N. A Political Escapade: The Story of Fiume; Nardelli, F. & Livingston, A. Gabriel the Archangel; Passini, F. d'Annunzio; Zaldumbide, G. La Evolucion de Gabriele d'Annunzio; Mercure de France April 1, 1938, April 15, 1938, June 1, 1938, February 1, 1939; New Republic September 28, 1938; Saturday Review of Literature June 11, 1938.

"ANSTEY, F." See GUTHRIE, T. A.

ANTHONY, KATHARINE SUSAN (November 27, 1877-), American biographer, writes: "My birthplace was Roseville, Ark. This is one of those lost frontier towns, traces of which remain in so many parts of the country. Later my family removed to Fort Smith, Ark., where I received a public school education. My parents were Ernest Augustus Anthony and Susan Jane (Cathey) Anthony. My grandfather, Henry Augustus Anthony, came from Providence, R.I., and married south of the Mason and Dixon Line. All the rest of my family were of unmixed Southern lineage, most of which can be traced back to colonial settlers in the North Carolina uplands.

Dexter

"I had two years in the Peabody College for Teachers (Nashville, Tenn.), followed by a bachelor's degree at the University of Chicago, and one year of study abroad at the Universities of Freiburg and Heidelberg. I was first a teacher in public schools, later at Wellesley College. Then, feeling the urge to write, I removed to New York and engaged in sporadic teaching and social work. I did social research and editorial work for the Russell Sage Foundation, and found it excellent training to put the data and statistics secured by others into readable form. My first independent writing was done along this line.

"My parents stimulated my ambition in the early years. The personal influence of teachers strengthened tendencies no doubt already formed in the home. From this it was but a step to the personal influence of favorite authors. From the time I learned to read, books were my intimate companions. At a very early age I became interested in the woman movement from having had a mother who was a pioneer worker for woman's suffrage. Later I traveled a great deal and did research work in foreign countries, and also in this country, using the materials thus gained in articles for periodicals. In reading I prefer historical works that are written primarily from the human, economic, and social point of view. In fiction I admire very much the works of Thomas Mann, Somerset Maugham, John Steinbeck, and Virginia Woolf. I have always been a great admirer of Freud's writings, not only for their scientific contribution but for their clear literary style.

"In my social preferences I believe I prefer the contacts of home life and friends to those of more casual society, but this is probably only because I find the latter more time-consuming. I believe in democracy and the power of the vote. Though not fond of political activity I am always ready to ally myself with that political party which seems

at the moment in the most practical way to be serving the cause of a civilized life for most of the people. At the moment I admire very much Mayor La Guardia of New York, Eleanor Roosevelt, Senator Norris, Justice Brandeis, Bernard Shaw, and Jacqueline Cochran.

"I live in New York in the winter and in summer at Gaylordsville, Conn."

* * *

Miss Anthony is unmarried. Brown haired and blue eyed, she impresses people by her quiet, self-possessed, unharried manner. "She is not," said Grenville Vernon, "one of the 'new' biographers. . . . If she has preconceptions she does not fashion them into a Procrustean bed and stretch her victim upon it." Herbert Gorman remarked that her books are "'portraits' with biographical digressions rather than full-length biography."

PRINCIPAL WORKS: Mothers Who Must Earn, 1914; Feminism in Germany and Scandinavia, 1915; Margaret Fuller: A Psychological Biography, 1920; Catherine the Great, 1925; Queen Elizabeth, 1929; Marie Antoinette, 1933; Louisa May Alcott, 1937.

ABOUT: Bookman March 1933; Boston Evening Transcript Book Section May 23, 1931; New York Herald Tribune "Books" December 15, 1929.

*ANTIN, MARY (1881-), American sociological writer, writes: "One of the best novels I never wrote is called *The Unwilling Celebrity*. It deals with the embarrassment of a woman who never succeeded in reconciling a large measure of public recognition with her insufficient achievement. My only friend and critic who would have spontaneously honored the sincerity  of my complaint is long since dead: Josephine Lazarus, to whom I had to dedicate 'my book'—it is very nearly an only book!—because she foretold years ahead that I would write such a chronicle and that it would make a stir. She also said, with equal conviction, that I was not a literary person.

"I have been bored and bothered informing editors, at frequent intervals during twenty-eight years, that I'm still the author of *The Promised Land*. The books I haven't written mean much more to me, but not being a literary person I have allowed other things first calls on my time and energy. My loving friends offer a long string of alibis for my unproductivity—indisputable alibis; but to admit alibis is only to restate the point that I am not primarily an author. In the development of a true artist hindrances only intensify the drive to create and deepen and refine the expression, though at the cost, sometimes, of the warping of the artist's personality.

"The more noisy phases of my life were forced on me by a sense of duty, but I freed myself, every time, by the strength of my need for what the psalmist calls 'truth in the inward parts.' Thus a combination of shock and reverence drove me into the bypath of public life: shock of the revelation, through the immense acclaim accorded *The Promised Land,* that Americans were so little aware of the unique spiritual mission of America; and reverence for the few who did exemplify prophetic citizenship—such as Jane Addams, Booker T. Washington, Lillian Wald, Jacob Riis. My resistance to the ordeal of the lecture platform broke down when contemporary heroes of the battles of democracy pressed it on me. So for a period of years (1913-18) I crisscrossed the United States as an itinerant preacher, playing homely but passionate variations on one master theme, the spiritual meaning of America, before audiences ranging from university forum to state prison. In spite of major handicaps, such as an inexpert use of the voice, I was a success. But applause and fat fees and return engagements were unconvincing in absence of a sense of vocation. I got out of the business as soon as I could, by the back door of a nervous breakdown, but glad of any kind of exit from what I considered a false position. I felt I had not *earned* the authority the public allowed me.

"I had previously unloaded the pyramid of honors, civic and literary, which had been heaped on me by the usual headlong process of rewarding a popular success. One day I sat down and wrote a wholesale lot of letters of resignation. When I finished, I didn't belong to a single author's club or patriotic society. I was myself again, whatever that was. Josephine Lazarus would have understood. My husband understood. It was all the understanding I needed.

"One current of continuity runs underneath all the abortive phases of my life, and that is nothing that ranks as a calling in our Western civilization. You couldn't make a career of it, but it sometimes makes a character, and it has made—is making—my life. From childhood on I have been obliged to drop anything I was doing to run after any man who seemed to know a little more than I did about God. In this pursuit, to which indeed I have given the right of way over other interests, can be found the meaning of the voluntary deviations and realignments of my nearly sixty years. If any literary faculty has survived in me after some three decades—the best creative decades—of almost total disuse (and at this moment I am setting up to explore that possibility), that is what I most want to write about: how a modern woman has sought the face of God—not the name nor the fame but the *face* of God—and what adventures came to meet her on this most ancient human path."

* * *

Mary Antin was born in Polotzk, Russia, in the "Pale of Settlement," of middle-class Jewish parents. Her father lost his position, came to America, and sent for his wife and family in 1894. He had become a grocer in Chelsea, Mass., where his thirteen-year-old daughter went from first to fifth grade in half a school year, and saw her first poem published in the Boston *Herald.* After the Girls' Latin School she went to New York, where she studied from 1901 to 1904 at Teachers' College, Columbia, and Barnard College, without taking a degree. In 1901 she married Amadeus W. Grabau, then professor of palaeontology at Columbia, and they have one daughter. After some years of residence in Great Barrington, Mass., they live now on a farm in Spring Valley, N.Y. *The Promised Land,* first serialized in the *Atlantic Monthly,* had as its implicit thesis the same statement made explicitly in her later book, *They Who Knock at Our Gates*: "What we get in the steerage is not the refuse, but the sinew and bone of all the nations."

PRINCIPAL WORKS: From Polotzk to Boston, 1899; The Promised Land, 1912; They Who Knock at Our Gates, 1914.

ABOUT: Antin, M. From Polotzk to Boston, The Promised Land; Beard, A. E. S. Our Foreign-Born Citizens; Parkman, M. R. Heroines of Service; Wade, M. H. Pilgrims of Today; Common Ground March 1941.

APOLLINAIRE, GUILLAUME (Wilhelm Kostrowitzki) (August 26, 1880-November 10, 1918), French poet, novelist, and essayist, was the illegitimate son of a father of unknown nationality, probably a Church dignitary, and a Polish adventuress supposedly of aristocratic birth. From the fanciful "autobiographical facts" furnished by himself, it seems probable that he was born in Monte Carlo. His childhood and youth were spent in constant traveling from one international resort to another, though he had several years at school in Germany. At twenty he appeared in Paris, changed his name, and before long became the type and incarnation of the Left Bank Bohemian. His associates were mostly painters, and he is credited with the "discovery" of Picasso, "Douanier" Rousseau, Braque, Marie Laurencin, and many others of the extreme moderns.

His own writing, first in verse, then in prose, like the painting of the time went through "Impressionist" and "Cubist" phases. Truculent, reckless, and bombastic, he liked to think of himself as the apotheosis of the vagabond poet, a sort of twentieth century Villon; actually he was a great deal of a bookworm, haunting the *Bibliothèque Nationale* and making up for a lack of creative power by a combination of "ribald exuberance, genial madness, grotesque inspiration, and pure impudence" (William A. Drake). A big, burly man, somewhat resembling Mussolini in countenance, Apollinaire had also the appearance of a Roman emperor of the decadent period. He was married, his wife's name being Jacqueline, though he called her Ruby.

His career as jester and playboy of the "advanced" art groups was permanently interrupted by the World War. He went to the front as an artillery officer in the French army, but soon transferred to the air force. He continued to write, bringing out a mimeographed volume of war poems from the front itself. Three times he was seriously wounded, the last injury being a bullet through his head which necessitated trepanning. He recovered from the wound, but his constitution was so weakened that he succumbed to influenza, a day before the Armistice.

How much of Apollinaire's buffoonery was a mask for deliberate satire only the future can determine. There is more than a touch in him of the erotic pedantry of the Alexandrian Greek writers—even to the production of poems grotesquely printed to become physical word-drawings of their subjects. His best known book, a semi-autobiographical, semi-fantastic novel called *Le Poète Assassiné* (1916), has been characterized as "sheer premeditated insanity." Matthew Josephson praised his "great energy, curiosity, and disrespect." Jean Cocteau, one of his earliest and most celebrated associates, twenty years after his death summed up Apollinaire in the ambiguous statement: "He had a great drop of glory on the end of his pen." He has been called "the Helio-

gabolus of the Intellect, the Marco Polo of the new spirit in art." Perhaps what will be left of his memory in the end is his rôle as a stimulator of others. His own work will for the most part perish, slain by its mixture of over-cerebralism and unintelligibility.

Apollinaire's only book to achieve English translation was *Le Poète Assassiné*, which was published in 1923 as *The Poet Assassinated*. A few of his late-period poems were included in *The European Caravan*, edited by Samuel Putnam (1931). Otherwise the interested reader must go to the original French. Of his poetical works *Alcools* (1913), *Case D'Armons* (1915), *Vitam Impendere Amori* (1917), and *Calligrammes* (1918) have been most widely discussed. *L'Hérèsiarque et Cie.* (1910), a collection of tales, is considered by some critics his prose masterpiece. His single play, *Les Mammelles de Tieresias* (1918), anticipated surrealism.

ABOUT: Billy, A. Guillaume Apollinaire; Drake, W. A. Contemporary European Writers; Rosenfeld, P. Men Seen; Current Opinion February 1919; Dial March 1922; Mercure de France January 1, 1939.

APPEL, BENJAMIN (September 13, 1907-), American novelist, writes: "I grew up in the West Side of Manhattan, in the neighborhood known as 'Hell's Kitchen,' now almost a ghost town in the great city. The 'original settlers,' the people of the tenements, were mostly of Irish Catholic stock, with a minority of Italians, Greeks, French, Germans, Jews, Poles, etc. Both of my parents had come from

Pinchot

fairly wealthy families in Poland, families that had begun to lose their money when my parents were still young. Through my boyhood they attempted to shield me as best they could from the casual ordinary day-to-day terror of a poor neighborhood, with its crime, drunkenness, vice, corruption, suffering, ignorance.

"Later on in life, after getting out of Lafayette College in 1929, it never occurred to me to write of what I had known as a child and as a young man. Without having read a line of Proust or Joyce at the time, I spent my early years as a struggling writer in an effort to master style and form, and was little concerned with content. These works remain unpublished with the exception of *Four Roads to Death,* a metaphysical examination of values, set in the Taklamakan Desert in Asia, an area I had never visited.

"With my first published novel, *Brain Guy,* I began to put down on paper all I knew of crime, poverty, politics, etc.—the world of the poor, the world of the factory and the saloon and the ward-heeler club and the railroad flat. *Runaround* concerned itself with politics; *The Power-House* with labor racketeering and the struggle of plain folk for a meaning in life. *The People Talk,* begun in 1939, was a non-fiction book about America, its people and problems in the last (speaking relatively) summer of peace, before the outbreak of war between England and Germany. This book complemented the three novels mentioned above. It was mainly about plain people, their hopes, aspirations, jobs. These books as well as half of my sixty or seventy published stories marked my first phase as a writer of a certain material, of people not usually represented in books or stories. Now I expect to do several books dealing with the relations of middle class people to the society we live in. I believe in the people with all truth and sincerity. I believe in these United States and the people of these states. I don't believe in slick or hoke writing or any writing that writes down to people.

"I've been married since 1936 to Sophie Marshak. I didn't work my way through college, as my father hit a wealthy period at that time. But I have worked, for short periods mainly, as a bank clerk, factory worker, real estate collector and agent, clerk; and for still shorter periods as a lumberjack and farmer. Mainly, I have written. I played football, rowed crew, threw discus and javelin in high school. I worked at football and crew in college and got sick of it when I was a junior, which marked the end of me as a serious athlete. I have fished since I was ten, spending most of my summers, as far as I can remember, on lakes and in the woods.

"I began writing as a little-magaziner, published in nineteen little magazines in one twelve-month period. O'Brien reprinted stories of mine in his 1934 and 1935 anthologies, also in his *Best Short Stories 1915-1939*; other reprints 1934 and 1937.

"I feel that 1939 forever ended not only the first phase of my own work as a writer, but also a definite period in American history. I look forward with hope to the future both for myself as a writer and for the country—and this from no Pollyanna make-up, but simply because I have faith in the ordinary folk of America."

* * *

Mr. Appel was born in New York and still lives there. Besides Lafayette, he spent a year at the University of Pennsylvania and a year at New York University. He is a member of the national board of the League of American Writers.

PRINCIPAL WORKS: Mixed Vintage (poems) 1929; Brain Guy, 1934; Four Roads to Death, 1935; Runaround, 1937; The Power-House, 1939; The People Talk (non-fiction) 1940.

ABOUT: New York Times June 16, 1940; Publishers' Weekly June 29, 1940.

ARAGON, LOUIS (1897-), French poet and novelist, has already had (and he is still only in early middle age) two distinct

careers. Very little is known of his early history or his personal life. He first came into public attention as one of the founders and leaders of the Surrealist school of art and writing. Surrealism, which succeeded Dadaism, was of course characterized both in theory and practice by deliberate unintelligibility, or by intelligibility only to the subconscious mind; and Aragon was one of its high priests in the field of letters. His Surrealist period, in Paris, followed immediately after his service in the First World War; because of his youth, he served only in the last year. Following his Surrealist productions (which may be classified either as prose or verse, according to the reader's understanding of them), for a brief period he wrote poetry in a rather more orthodox vein. According to D. S. Mirsky, however, Aragon "was never primarily a poet, and should not be judged by his poetic compositions."

His complete rightabout, not only of style but also of life, beliefs, and even temperament, followed soon after. He became as a writer a leader in the "Socialistic Realism Movement," as an individual an active Communist. Whether his marriage about this time to "a beautiful Russian" helped bring about the change or was an effect of it is not known. In any event, he became a member of the Communist Party, secretary of the French section of a "popular front" organization, the International Association of Writers for the Defense of Culture," a member of the editorial staff of the Communist newspaper, *L'Humanité,* and later managing editor of the Communist evening paper, published in Paris, *Ce Soir.* He was also on the board of directors of the review, *Europe,* and at some time during this period received a suspended sentence of five years for a poem which was thought to have insulted the French flag. This did not prevent him from receiving, in 1936, the *Prix Renaudot* —which was given, however, not for his poetry but for the novels which have been the characteristic work of his second period, after (to quote Mirsky once more) he "killed one artist within himself and found another."

A week before the outbreak of the Second World War, *Ce Soir* was suppressed by the government. Conflicting reports were issued concerning Aragon. The actual details of his subsequent war service are revealed in Aragon's letter (March 31, 1941) to an American friend, from Nice, in the Free Zone:

"As for me, I was evacuated from Dunkirk to England, returned to France at the port of Brest on June 4 (1940). . . ; from the Seine to the Dordogne, we were in contact with the German troops, hand to hand fighting, and that made three very incredible weeks, during which . . . I found myself almost each day behind the enemy lines. I was actually taken prisoner at Angoulême on June 24, but only for half an hour, and I managed to get out of it . . . with six vehicles and thirty men, right under the nose of two mounted machine-guns guarding the entrance to the city. When we met in the shop in Brest, I was buying some ribbon for the *croix de guerre* of my first citation. I have received a second (with palm) and I was awarded the *medaille militaire.* I look very respectable indeed with all my decorations and my hair whitened by age. . . ."

Malcolm Cowley described Aragon, in 1936, with his "proud head and ingratiating white-toothed smile, . . . an amazing combination of fancy, of quick, cruel wit, and literary erudition." He has never been a Bohemian, but is noted for his personal abstemiousness. In complete contrast to the style of his Surrealist period, his novels are characterized by simplicity, by the use of ordinary, everyday spoken language, and by "the almost complete absence of so-called picturesqueness." Yet, said Cowley, "in spite of his new life he has remained . . . a sharp, engaging writer . . . whose personality as revealed in his books is more brilliant and coherent than the books themselves."

Aragon's wife is Elsa Triolet, author of a biography of the Russian poet Mayakovsky which the French authorities seized and destroyed during the war.

The official translator of Aragon's work is Professor Haakon Chevalier of the University of California. Aragon's current series of novels, pictures of Europe before and after 1914, bears the general title *The Real World.*

WORKS AVAILABLE IN ENGLISH: Red Front (poem, translated by E. E. Cummings) 1933; The Bells of Basel, 1936; Residential Quarter, 1938; The Century Was Young, 1941.

ABOUT: Annales Politiques et Littéraires December 25, 1936; Clipper [Hollywood, Calif.] June 1941; Living Age March 1935; New Republic October 7, 1936; Saturday Review of Literature September 6, 1941; Time January 13, 1941.

ARCHER, WILLIAM (September 23, 1856-December 27, 1924), British dramatist and critic, had rather an unusual family background. He was born in Perth, Scotland, the eldest of nine children of Thomas and Grace (Morison) Archer, but his ancestors had been a roving lot, his grandparents had settled in Norway, and his father had lived in Australia and had  been a '49er in the California gold rush. While he was still in college his parents moved permanently to Australia. He himself hated to stay "put." He traveled extensively on the Continent and made numerous trips to the United States, besides one journey around the world.

He was educated at George Watson's College, Edinburgh, and at the University of Edinburgh (M.A. 1876). Immediately following his graduation he made his round-the-world trip. After 1873 he did occasional journalistic work, and on his return to Europe he became Paris correspondent of the San Francisco *Chronicle,* then spent a year on the Edinburgh *Evening News,* at the same time contributing articles to the *Globe Encyclopaedia.* In 1878 he moved to London as dramatic critic of the *Figaro,* with which he remained for five years, except for one year spent in Italy. To please his father he read law in the Middle Temple and was admitted to the bar, but never practiced. He then went to the London *World,* with which his name was chiefly identified. He was dramatic critic of this paper from 1884 to 1905, and published five annual volumes of criticisms first appearing there. Until 1920 he continued as dramatic critic on other periodicals—the *Tribune,* the *Nation,* and the *Star,* all of London. He did not retire until the tremendous success of *The Green Goddess* made him financially independent. He was a public-spirited man and wrote largely on social as well as dramatic topics.

In 1884 Archer married Frances Elizabeth Trickett. They had one son. During the World War he was connected with the Censorship Division of the Intelligence Department. He was secretary of the Simplified Spelling Board (as a reward, he said, for always having been a bad speller), and spoke at its first meeting in New York. He was the recipient of the Norwegian Knighthood of the Order of St. Olav, bestowed in recognition of his almost lifelong campaign for the work of Henrik Ibsen. He died in consequence of an operation which had been found necessary after a year of increasingly severe illness.

Archer was a Free Thinker, a member of the Rationalist Press Association; but like many Free Thinkers of his period, he was also a convinced Spiritualist. He was an early student of psycho-analysis and the Freudian theory of dreams, and his phenomenally successful melodrama, *The Green Goddess,* had its inception in a dream. The play was written for George Arliss, and was something of a *tour de force.* By definition a critic is supposed to be "one who criticizes because he cannot write," but here was a sixty-five-year-old man and a forty-three-year-long critic whose only important play (a war drama was never produced, and three one-acters were not even published until after his death) was the hit of two continents and has become a permanent part of the English drama.

Until this play was produced, Archer to the general public was the man who made English and American audiences accept Ibsen. He was also the dramatic godfather of Shaw and Granville-Barker, but Ibsen was his first love and dearest *protégé.* As a child, in Norway, Archer had unlearned English; then he forgot his Norwegian, but later relearned the language—or, rather, the Danish which is Norway's literary tongue. He discovered Ibsen when he was only seventeen, and he was twenty-four when by his translation of *Pillars of Society* he brought about the great Norseman's first ap-

pearance on the English stage. His is the definitive translation of Ibsen's collected plays. The names of Ibsen and Archer are inseparable in the history of English literature.

As a critic Archer was esteemed for his independence of judgment and integrity. He considered good criticism "the faculty for making the best of the actual without losing sight of the ideal." He never ceased to stress the importance of natural speech cadence in the drama. Among performers Bernhardt and Duse gave him particular pleasure. Of his absorbing passion for literature and the theatre he said, "These two things have I loved, sometimes blindly and foolishly, sometimes, I hope, with understanding; and it has been the instinctive, inevitable effort of my life to make these two one flesh."

Archer was very British in appearance, tall, robust, red-cheeked, with a long, thin, black moustache, and a pronounced Scottish burr which he never lost. Everyone who counted for anything in the English stage of his lifetime was his friend, his disciple, or (in the case of Sir Henry Irving at least) his enemy. Wilde and Pinero as well as Shaw sat at his feet, and he actually collaborated with Shaw in the first version of *Widowers' Houses.* A valuable book was lost to posterity when William Archer died without writing his memoirs.

PRINCIPAL WORKS: The Fashionable Tragedian (with R. W. Lowe) 1877; English Dramatists of Today, 1882; Henry Irving, 1883; About the Theater, 1886; Masks or Faces? 1888; William Charles Macready, 1890; The Theatrical "World," 1894-98; Study and Stage, 1899; America Today, 1900; Poets of the Younger Generation, 1902; Real Conversations, 1904; Let Youth But Know, 1905; A National Theater (with H. Granville-Barker) 1907; Thro' Afro-America, 1910; The Life, Trial, and Death of Francisco Ferrer, 1911; Art and the Commonweal, 1912; Playmaking, 1912; The Great Analysis: A Plea for a Rational World-Order (anonymous) 1912; The Thirteen Days: July 23-August 4, 1914, 1915; Knowledge and Character, 1916; India and the Future, 1917; God and Mr. Wells, 1917; War Is War (play) 1919; The Green Goddess (play) 1921; The Old Drama and the New, 1923; William Archer as Rationalist (collection, ed. by J. M. Robertson) 1925; The Religion of Tomorrow, 1925; Three Plays, 1927.

ABOUT: Archer, C. William Archer: Life, Work, and Friendships; Murry, J. M. Things to Come; American Scandinavian Review April 1925; Bookman (London) February 1925; Century June 1923; Drama November 1926; Outlook January 7, 1925; Saturday Review of Literature October 17, 1931.

"A. RIPOSTE." See MORDAUNT, E. M. C.

ARLEN, MICHAEL (November 16, 1895-), English novelist, was born Dikrān Kuyumjian, at Rustchuk, Bulgaria, of Armenian parents. He  changed his name by deed poll, for obvious reasons, after he began his career as a writer in English. He first went to England as a boy, and was naturalized as a British subject in 1922. He was educated at Malvern College, and for three months was a student of medicine at the University of Edinburgh. In 1928 he married the Countess Atalanta Mercati, and they have one son and one daughter. For a number of years, until the outbreak of the Second World War, they lived at Cannes, on the Riviera.

Arlen's first encouragement as a writer came from the late A. R. Orage, then editor of the *New Age*. His first book, however, had been published when he was only eighteen. Besides his novels and short stories, he has written several plays, including a dramatization of *These Charming People*, with Walter Hackett, and the dramatization of *The Green Hat* in which Katharine Cornell appeared in the character of Iris March. Later the novel became a motion picture starring Greta Garbo.

It was with *The Green Hat,* in 1924, that Arlen sprang into sudden celebrity. The book made him half a million dollars in royalties, and was for a while the most talked of novel in English. He never repeated its startling success, largely because that success depended on the exact era of the book's appearance. History moved on past Arlen, but he did not move with it. Fame, however, did not spoil him; he remained exactly what he had always been personally, an alert, boyishly vain, friendly man who frankly gloried in the spotlight and in the acquisition of wealth, and prided himself on a sophistication which covered considerable naiveté. A friend has described him as "immaculate." "His slim, perfectly proportioned figure is the joy of his tailor. His ties and socks are a gracefully subdued symphony. His barber is the best in town. His Rolls Royce is at least six inches longer than any other Rolls Royce." He has thick, wavy, dark hair and a bristly light red moustache.

It cannot be denied that Michael Arlen is a superficial writer, and now one badly dated.

His books are out of Bulwer and Disraeli by Wilde and Ouida. He has been always an "explorer in Mayfair," and the only world he knows is the artificial world of a society now in its death-throes. Gorham B. Munson called his "an opium dream style," yet added that "if he has no standards he is shrewdly civilized." Robert Morss Lovett called Arlen's style "the summary of his qualities and the epitome of his world. Piquant if concentrated, it becomes vulgar when diluted." His *genre* is "a combination of sexual farce and melodrama." Claude C. Washburne remarked that "he knows how a sophisticated novel should be written: to wit, in a baroque and decorative prose"; but not infrequently he betrays by some grammatical howler the fact that English is not his native tongue. George Jean Nathan, who called him "a purveyor of . . . rented dress suit literature" which "apes literature to the manor born," nevertheless acknowledged that "he knows how to tell a story, has a measure of humor, and even an occasionally nice wit."

PRINCIPAL WORKS: The London Venture, 1913; The Romantic Lady (short stories) 1915; Piracy, 1918; These Charming People (short stories) 1920; The Green Hat, 1924; Mayfair (short stories) 1925; Young Men in Love, 1927; Lily Christine, 1928; Babes in the Wood (short stories) 1929; Men Dislike Women, 1931; Man's Mortality, 1933; Hell! Said the Duchess, 1934; The Crooked Coronet, 1937; The Flying Dutchman, 1939.

ABOUT: American Mercury November 1925; Arts and Decoration May 1925; Bookman January 1929, August 1932; Living Age April 10, 1926; New Republic December 10, 1924; Nineteenth Century October 1925; Saturday Review of Literature July 22, 1939.

ARMSTRONG, HAMILTON FISH (April 7, 1893-), American editor and writer on international affairs, was born in New York City. His  father was D. Maitland Armstrong, artist and American Consul General to Italy; Margaret Armstrong,*qv* the biographer and novelist, and Helen Maitland Armstrong, the artist, are his sisters. He was educated at Princeton

Kazanjian

(B.A. 1916). During the First World War he was a lieutenant in the American army, and was military attaché to the Serbian War Mission in the United States and then acting military attaché of the American legation in Belgrade. He was on the editorial staff of the New York *Evening Post* from 1919 to 1921, then for a year its special correspondent in Eastern Europe. He became managing editor of the quarterly review, *Foreign Affairs,* in 1922, and has been its editor since 1928. He is a director of the Council on Foreign Relations, past president of the Woodrow Wilson Foundation, and a corresponding member of the School of Slavonic Studies, in London. He has received decorations from Serbia, Rumania, and Czechoslovakia, and is an officer of the Legion of Honor. At present he is a member of the President's Advisory Committee on Political Refugees. He was three times a delegate to the International Studies Conference. In 1918 he married Helen MacGregor Byrne, and they had one daughter. They were divorced in 1938. Mr. Armstrong lives in New York City. He is a frequent contributor to the more serious reviews, and is regarded as one of the leading contemporary American authorities on foreign affairs and international relations. In earlier years he published a number of poems; at present he confines himself to prose works which, to quote one commentator, are "respectfully reviewed, learned, but never best-sellers." He is a serious-looking man with a small moustache; *Time* called him "thick-thatched, sobersided."

PRINCIPAL WORKS: Book of New York Verse (ed.) 1918; The New Balkans, 1926; Where the East Begins, 1929; Hitler's Reich: The First Phase, 1933; Foreign Affairs Bibliography (ed., with W. L. Langer) 1933; Europe Between Wars? 1934; The Foreign Policy of the Powers (ed.) 1935; Can We Be Neutral? (with A. W. Dulles) 1936; We or They, 1937; When There Is No Peace, 1939; Can America Stay Neutral? (with A. W. Dulles) 1939; Chronology of Failure: The Last Days of the French Republic, 1940.

ABOUT: Time May 17, 1937.

*ARMSTRONG, MARGARET NEIL-SON (September 24, 1867-), American biographer and painter, was born in New York

City, the daughter of David Maitland Armstrong, an artist, maker of stained-glass windows, and diplomatic consul, and Helen Neilson Armstrong, a descendant of the famous wooden-legged Dutch governor of New York, Peter Stuyvesant. Helen Maitland Armstrong, painter and stained-glass craftsman, is her sister; and Hamilton Fish Armstrong,[qv] twenty-five years younger, author, specialist in European

politics, and editor of *Foreign Affairs,* is her brother.

At the age of two, when her father was appointed United States Consul to the Papal State, she was taken to Italy. After the Italian seizure of Rome, Maitland Armstrong became Consul General to Italy; and since there was at this time no Minister, his duties were to a large extent diplomatic. Margaret's only memory of this period was a Papal procession in which she distinguished herself by hand-clapping, shouting, and running toward the Pope while everyone else was kneeling devoutly. On their return to New York they divided their time between an old estate overlooking Newburgh Bay ("Danskammer," a shortened form of an old Dutch name which Henry Hudson is believed to have given it) and a handsome house on West Tenth Street, for a while occupied by the famous Tile Club. During a summer at Curson's Mills, near Newburyport, Mass., Susan Hale, letter-writer, traveler, and sister of Edward Everett Hale and Lucretia Peabody Hale, gave young Margaret her first painting lessons. Miss Armstrong has today considerable interest and ability in this art, but refuses to give up her "amateur standing."

She had long been a trowel gardener and in 1915 made a name for herself as a botanist. At the end of a camping trip through Grand Canyon and the Yosemite Valley, she assembled, with the aid of J. J. Thornber, a *Field Book of Western Wild Flowers,* a kind of classic in its own province. When her father died in 1918, his memoirs were incomplete; she finished and published them, two years later, as *Day Before Yesterday.* In 1923 she edited a book of Jacob Abbott's delightful *Franconia Stories;* and in 1930 came her first-person story of an American family's life and letters through *Five Generations.* In 1938 her study of the "passionate Victorian" *Fanny Kemble* was a Book-of-the-Month Club choice; so also was her *Trelawny* (1940), portrait of another picturesque Victorian, who was a friend of Byron and Shelley and a champion of freedom for the Greeks. Her interest in Trelawny was the outgrowth of the Kemble biography.

It is said that Miss Armstrong is a woman of few prejudices and is an intelligent listener. She neither over-writes nor condescends to her material. Her mystery story, *Murder in Stained Glass,* makes use of the

* Died July 18, 1944.

background of artistic craftsmanship in which she grew up.

PRINCIPAL WORKS: Field Book of Western Wild Flowers (ed.) 1915; Day Before Yesterday, 1920; Franconia Stories (ed.) 1923; Five Generations, 1930; Fanny Kemble: A Passionate Victorian, 1938; Murder in Stained Glass, 1939; Trelawny: A Man's Life, 1940; The Man With No Face, 1941.

ABOUT: Armstrong, D. M. Day Before Yesterday; Armstrong, M. Five Generations; Book-of-the-Month Club News June 1938, September 1940; Christian Science Monitor Magazine November 9, 1940; New York Herald Tribune "Books" October 20, 1940.

ARMSTRONG, MARTIN DONIS-THORPE (October 2, 1882-), English novelist and poet, writes: "Martin Armstrong was born near Newcastle-on-Tyne. On his father's side he comes of a Border family; his maternal grandmother was Elizabeth Wordsworth, cousin to the poet. He was educated at Charterhouse School and Pembroke College, Cambridge, where he took a B.A. degree in mechanical science, a subject which he disliked intensely. His chief interests were classical and modern literature and music. After two years in an architect's office he went to Italy, where he lived for a year. During this time and on subsequent visits he made a close study, with no definite object but his own satisfaction, of pre-Renaissance and Renaissance Italian art.

"When the [First] World War broke out he joined the Artists' Rifles as a private, obtained a commission in 1915 in the 8th Middlesex Regiment, and in 1917 went to France and stayed at the front there till the Armistice. On returning to England he obtained a post in the Ministry of Pensions which he resigned a year later to take up free-lance journalism and other more serious literary work. From 1922 to 1924 he was associate literary editor of the *Spectator*. In 1930 he married Jessie (McDonald) Aiken, a Canadian, previously the wife of Conrad Aiken, and they have one son.

"His chief hobbies are walking, gardening (which includes growing vegetables for the house), music, wine, painting (especially modern), and English, French, Italian, and Spanish literature. His knowledge of these four languages is unsystematic: there is no period in any of them of which he has an exhaustive knowledge; of many he has no knowledge at all.

"He cannot say which writers have influenced him most, but certainly French novelists more than English novelists. An early enthusiasm for R. L. Stevenson has long since vanished. He has always disliked Tennyson and Browning and now dislikes most of Shelley. A few of his favorites nowadays (after Shakespeare, Milton, Wordsworth, Dante, and the Cervantes of *Don Quixote*) are John Donne and the Metaphysical Poets, Racine, Balzac, and Paul Valéry. The musicians he prefers are William Byrd and others of the old Englishmen, Bach, Haydn, Mozart, Beethoven, some of Brahms, and Sibelius."

* * *

Mr. Armstrong's stories usually appear in English magazines, and in general he is better known in England than in America. He is unusually versatile, and has written in many unrelated fields. Louis Untermeyer called him "a prose writer of delicate nuances," while rather deprecating his "crocus-crowded lyrics." Llewellyn Jones spoke of his "interest in the quality of human life as it is lived moment by moment," and John Freeman of his outlook as "sane and humorous, avoiding tragedy as far as he possibly can. . . He has preserved the English tradition of reticence and restraint."

PRINCIPAL WORKS: *Novels*—The Goat and Compasses (in America: At the Sign of the Goat and Compasses) 1925; Desert, 1926; The Stepson (in America: The Water Is Wide) 1927; St. Christopher's Day (in America: All in a Day) 1928; The Sleepy Fury, 1929; Adrian Glynde, 1930; Mr. Darby, 1931; Lover's Leap, 1932; General Buntop's Miracle, 1934; Venus Over Lannery, 1935; A Case of Conscience, 1936; Spanish Circus (1788-1808) 1937; The Snake in the Grass, 1938. *Short Stories*—The Puppet Show, 1922; The Bazaar, 1924; Sir Pompey and Madame June, 1927; The Fiery Dive, 1929; The Paint Box (juvenile) 1931; The Foster Mother and Fifty-Four Conceits, 1933; Bazaar and Other Stories, 1939; Simplicity Jones and Other Stories, 1940. *Miscellaneous*—Exodus (poetry) 1912; Thirty New Poems, 1918; Lady Hester Stanhope, 1920; The Buzzards (poetry) 1921; The Birdcatcher (poetry) 1929; Collected Poems, 1931; The Major Pleasures of Life (edited) 1934; What Is Happiness? (with others) 1938; Victorian Peepshow, 1939.

ABOUT: Armstrong, M. D. Victorian Peepshow; Untermeyer, L. Modern British Poetry; Bookman (London) September 1929.

ARMSTRONG, PAUL (April 25, 1869-August 30, 1915), American playwright and adapter, was born in Kidder, Mo., the son of Richard Armstrong, who later engaged in the steamship business, and Harriet (Scott) Armstrong. He attended public schools in Bay City, Mich. At twenty-one he was licensed as a master of steam-vessels and for a while was a

purser on a river boat before setting out for Buffalo, N.Y., where he joined successively the *Express,* the *Courier,* and the *News.*

He had meanwhile been trying his hand at short stories, but with small encouragement from any publishers. After two years (1896-98) on the Chicago *Times Herald* and the *Inter-Ocean* he went to New York, and over the signature "Right Cross" did some sporting articles for several metropolitan dailies. Almost immediately he began writing for the theatre. *Just a Day Dream,* his first attempt, made only Boston stock; and *The Superstition of Sue, St. Ann,* and the early version of *Society and the Bull Dog* were almost unnoticed by the critics; but *The Heir to the Hoorah,* a tremendous success, marked the beginning of a prodigious ten years of play-writing in which he turned out nearly twenty farces, vaudeville skits, and folk comedies.

In 1907 he adapted Bret Harte's story, "Salomy Jane's Kiss," and in the year following he collaborated with Rex Beach on a farce called *Going Some.* For *Alias Jimmy Valentine* (1909), his most complete hit, he was indebted to O. Henry ("A Retrieved Reformation") ; it was written in one week, inspired numerous imitations on the "crook" theme, and was revived in 1921. A few years before his death he formed the Paul Armstrong Company, producers, but accomplished nothing notable.

Armstrong was married in London in 1899 to a Kansas City girl, Rella Abell, by whom he had three daughters. When she divorced him fourteen years later he married Kittie Cassidy, of Baltimore, an actress who afterwards, as Catharine Calvert, gained considerable prominence on the screen; and by her had one son.

PRINCIPAL WORKS: The Superstition of Sue, 1904 (?) ; St. Ann, 1904 (?) ; Society and the Bull Dog, 1904 (?) ; The Heir to the Hoorah, 1905 ; Ann Lamont, 1905 (revision of St. Ann) ; In a Blaze of Glory, 1906 ; Salomy Jane, 1907 ; Society and the Bull Dog (revised) 1908 ; Via Wireless, 1908 ; Blue Grass, 1908 ; The Renegade, 1909 ; For a Woman, 1909 ; Alias Jimmy Valentine, 1909 ; The Deep Purple, 1910 ; A Romance of the Underworld, 1911 ; The Greyhound, 1912 ; (in collaboration with W. Mizner) ; The Escape, 1912 ;

A Love Story, 1913 ; Woman Proposes, 1913 ; To Save One Girl, 1913 ; The Bludgeon, 1914 ; The Heart of a Thief, 1914 ; Mr. Lorelei, 1916.

ABOUT: Mantle, B. & Sherwood, G. P. The Best Plays of 1909-1919 ; New York Dramatic Mirror September 8, 1915 ; New York Times August 31, 1915.

ARTSYBASHEV, MIKHAIL PETRO-VICH (October 18, 1878-March 3, 1927), Russian novelist and dramatist, was born in southern Russia, in the province of Kharkov. His father was a retired army officer and small land-owner, Peter Artsybashev ; his mother, a lady of Polish blood and a great-niece of the famous Kosciusko. She inherited not only glory, but

also a tendency to tuberculosis, of which she died when Mikhail was three years old, and which she passed on to her only son.

The first talent displayed by Artsybashev was for painting, but it was only after a long and bitter struggle with his father, who wished him to follow his own military career, that he was allowed to study art. At the same time he began writing, though at this time chiefly poetry. His reconciliation with his father was short-lived, since at twenty, against his family's wishes, he married Anna Koboushko, the daughter of a neighbor of slightly lower social class and equal genteel impoverishment. Their only child, Boris (who spells his name "Artzybasheff"), became a well known illustrator and writer of juvenile books, and is a resident of the United States.

Artsybashev went in 1899 to St. Petersburg (Leningrad) to study at the Imperial Academy of Fine Arts, from which he was graduated in 1904. Since he received no financial help from his father, he was obliged to earn his and his little family's living by drawing cartoons and writing articles for the newspapers. It was 1902 before he attained any recognition as a writer, with *Ivan Lande,* which first struck his prevailing note of overhanging death though not yet its companion note of sex. The unsuccessful revolution of 1905 found him sympathetic, and resulted in a volume of stories called *Tales of the Revolution.*

It was in 1907 that Artsybashev achieved fame and immense popularity with his *magnum opus, Sanine.* This apologia for unrestrained sexual expression and revolt against all authority appeared just at a period of world history when a rebellious generation was peculiarly susceptible to its teachings. Banned everywhere, it was yet translated into all major languages, including the Japanese. *Sanine* cults arose, chiefly appealing to the young, and his disciples conscientiously gave themselves over to lives of "self-expression" not infrequently culminating in suicide.

To Artsybashev himself, by inclination and conviction an Anarchist, this gospel was the natural consequence of his revolt and despair of humanity. His later novels preached the same sermon, for his harp had only two strings. The Czarist government sensed an enemy in this outspoken and immensely popular novelist, and in 1912 he underwent a few months of imprisonment. When he emerged from prison there was no change in his theme, since his experience had only confirmed his bitterness; but now he began to give form to it in the drama as well as in fiction. He established a weekly magazine, entitled *Svoboda* (Liberty), which became his personal organ and the outlet for his opinions. With the beginning of the First World War, the paper was sternly suppressed.

Like most of the Anarchists of Russia, Artsybashev became completely estranged from the revolutionary movement with the triumph of the Bolsheviks. He did not, however, immediately join the dissidents in emigrating from the country, nor was he ever exiled. But his paper, which he had revived, was again interdicted; he was several times arrested and released; his books were put on the "forbidden list"; and he who had been with Andreyev the highest paid author in Russia became actually destitute. Finally he went to Poland, his mother's fatherland, and from Warsaw for the third time published *Svoboda*. In it he poured forth incessant invective against the Soviet government, which tried in vain to have him extradited and silenced. By this time, however, he was far gone in tuberculosis, and he died soon after, at only forty-eight.

Artsybashev was a minor Andreyev, without that great pessimist's gloom and near-madness. An individualist in appearance as in everything else, he refused to wear "Western" clothes, but dressed in colored silk and velvet blouses which contrasted strangely with his full beard and his nose-glasses. Though he had long abandoned painting, he resembled the Bohemian artist of tradition far more than he did the successful author.

To Artsybashev there were only two realities—sex and death. Life to him, as Alexander Nazarov remarks, was "a procession of human bodies filled with animal desire and slowly moving to the grave." He is usually linked by critics with Andreyev and with Ivan Bunin, but actually he is much closer to Maupassant. For, in strange contrast to his subjects, his style was never incoherent, but laconic, fresh, and even bright with a sort of Gallic clarity. His plays are superior, as literature, to his fiction, though they too are marred by a tendency to clichés of which Maupassant would never have been guilty. Even had the war and the revolution never taken place, it is unlikely that his rather hysterical popularity would have lasted his lifetime. By the time of his death, he had been almost forgotten by a reading public to which *Sanine* had once been a household word and "the schoolboys' Bible."

PRINCIPAL WORKS AVAILABLE IN ENGLISH TRANSLATION: *Fiction*—The Breaking Point, 1915; Ivan Lande, 1915; The Millionaire, 1915; Sanine, 1915; Tales of the Revolution, 1917; The Savage, 1924. *Plays*—War, 1916; Jealousy, 1917; The Law of the Savage, 1923; Lovers and Enemies (produced) 1927.

ABOUT: Huneker, J. G. Unicorns; Olgin, M. J. Guide to Russian Literature; Phelps, W. L. Essays on Russian Novelists; Saturday Review of Literature April 9, 1927.

ARVIN, NEWTON (August 23, 1900-   ), American biographer and critic, writes: "I was born [Frederic Newton Arvin, Jr.] in Valparaiso, Ind., of typical Middle Western middle class stock. I spent my boyhood more or less in the typical village way of Indiana, though I was of course more of a book-worm than was at all normal; my chief friendship in  childhood, and later, was with David Lilienthal, who has since made so honorable a name for himself on the T.V.A. My schooling was entirely in the public schools and the high school of Valparaiso, and then —for no very clear reason except that my brother had done graduate work there—I was sent to Harvard. There I learned a great deal from the books at Widener, a good deal from my classmates, and a little (but that is saying much) from my teachers.

"For a few months after graduating, in 1921, with no serious intentions on my part as a teacher, I taught a lot of Detroit small boys in a private school; though this half-hearted experiment was a signal failure, I somehow—still without any clear designs on an academic career—became a member, the next fall, of the English department at Smith; and here I have been ever since. The one exception is the year I spent (1925-26) very inefficiently assisting Dr. Victor S. Clark in editing the *Living Age,* when it was still under the aegis of Ellery Sedgwick and the *Atlantic Monthly.*

"While I was still in college, thanks to the delicate generosity of Van Wyck Brooks toward young writers, I had begun to write reviews for the *Freeman;* and throughout the 1920's I continued to do a certain amount of journalistic writing in addition to teaching. I have managed somehow to edit one book and (at great intervals) to write two others, and to contribute occasional articles to reviews during the 1930's."

* * *

Mr. Arvin, the son of Frederic Newton Arvin and Jessie (Hawkins) Arvin, married Mary J. Garrison in 1932. He is now associate professor of English at Smith College. In 1935 and 1936 he was awarded a Guggenheim Fellowship. He is a serious-looking, youngish, spectacled man with straight brown hair. With what has been called "his habitual under-statement about himself," he omits to mention that he was graduated from Harvard with a Sheldon traveling fellowship, *summa cum laude,* and with a Phi Beta Kappa key. Seward Collins, an unfriendly critic, nevertheless speaks of "his high abilities as a clear, forceful, and orderly writer," and another commentator has praised "the subtle critical formulations worked unobtrusively into his smooth and scholarly prose." He is liberal in his political beliefs.

PRINCIPAL WORKS: Hawthorne, 1929; The Heart of Hawthorne's Journals (ed.) 1929; Whitman, 1938.

ABOUT: Bookman October 1930; Time October 31, 1938; Wilson Library Bulletin January 1939.

ASBURY, HERBERT (September 1, 1891-), American biographer and historian, was born in Farmington, Mo., the fifteenth of sixteen children of Samuel L. Asbury, himself the son and grandson of Methodist ministers and a collateral descendant of Francis Asbury, first Methodist Bishop ordained in America, and Ellen N. (Prichard) Asbury. Both parents were descendants of Roger Williams. His father, a Confederate veteran, was one of the founders of the original Ku Klux Klan. He

was reared in the strictest Puritanism, from which he reacted violently in adolescence. He was educated at Elmwood Seminary, Baptist College, and Carleton College, all in Farmington. He began his newspaper career on the Quincy, Ill., *Journal,* 1910-12, and continued it on the Peoria *Journal,* the Atlanta *Georgian,* and the New York *Press, Tribune, Sun, Herald,* and *Herald Tribune.* Among newspaper men he is considered "one of the fastest and most capable rewrite men in the business." He left the *Herald Tribune* in 1928 to devote himself entirely to his own writing. His newspaper career was interrupted by war service from 1917 to 1919; he entered the army as a private and left it as a second lieutenant of infantry, served in France, was badly gassed, and still suffers from the effects.

"A good showman," Asbury made his literary reputation with "Hatrack," a story (really a chapter from his *Up From Methodism*) which appeared in the *American Mercury.* H. L. Mencken was arrested in Boston on orders of the Watch and Ward Society for selling copies of this number of the magazine, and editors began to ask for more of Asbury's work. In 1928 Mr. Asbury married Helen Hahn, also a writer, who was on the staff of the *Herald Tribune* with him. Since then, all his books have been dedicated "to Helen." They live in Canada Lake, N.Y., in the Adirondacks. Aside from writing, he worked in his boyhood as a printer's devil and a freight loader on Mississippi boats. He has also played professional baseball. But he says of himself: "I have always written, ever since I can remember. And I always have [written] and always shall write the sort of thing I want to write, regardless of how much or how little money I get doing it."

Mr. Asbury's special field is the portrayal of the shadier side of the past of great American cities. As one critic remarked, "he writes readable yet straightforward prose; he selects effective stories and details that make them real; finally, he knows his subjects thoroughly as a scholar, and is not content with lurid generalizations." Another called him "a practised hand at ferreting out crime and one who, at the same time, has the artistic ability to recapture meretricious glamour."

He describes himself as an "infidel," and once planned to spend his years from fifty to sixty in writing a history of religion. The nearest he has come so far to fulfilling this intension is in his biography of his ancestor, Bishop Asbury.

PRINCIPAL WORKS: Up From Methodism, 1926; The Devil of Pei-Ling, 1927; A Methodist Saint: The Life of Bishop Asbury, 1927; The Gangs of New York, 1928; The Bon Vivant's Companion (ed., with J. Thomas) 1928; Carry Nation, 1929; Ye Olde Fire Laddies, 1930; The Barbary Coast, 1933; All Around the Town, 1934; The Breathless Moment (ed., with P. V. D. Stern) 1935; The French Quarter, 1936; Sucker's Progress, 1938; Not at Night! (ed.) 1939; Gem of the Prairie, 1940; Golden Flood, 1942.

ABOUT: Asbury, H. Up From Methodism; Bookman October 1926; Literary Digest August 26, 1933; Newsweek August 12, 1933, October 10, 1936.

ASCH, NATHAN (July 10, 1902-),

American novelist, writes: "I was born in Warsaw, Poland, the son of Sholem Asch,[qv]

the novelist, and Mathilda (Spira) Asch. By the time I was thirteen and had come to America, my family had lived in Switzerland, Germany, and France; and I went to school in all these countries. Later I went to school in Brooklyn, and attended Syracuse and Columbia Universities. After that, Wall Street, from which I broke away, and went back to Europe and began to write. I was in Paris during the days when the Lost Generation was trying to find itself, but I probably was too young to be considered part of it. Ford Madox Ford published my first story in the *Transatlantic Review*, and was instrumental in having my first book, *The Office*, published in 1925.

"My third novel, *Pay Day*, was suppressed. I have written reviews for the *Nation*, the *New Republic*, and the *Dial*, and short stories for many magazines. Before the present situation developed in Germany, all of my work was published there, as well as in several other European countries. It was partly as a result of my foreign income's being altogether cut off that I went to Hollywood, where I worked for three large motion picture companies. I have also worked for the Government in Washington, having been Special Assistant in the Works Progress Administration for more than two

years [1937-39]. I have traveled much through America, and have been in every state but two (Iowa and Nebraska); have also lived for longer periods in many parts of the country."

* * *

The result of Mr. Asch's intensive travels through the United States was his survey of what Americans are thinking which he called *The Road*. He is unmarried, and is now living in New York. *Pay Day* was suppressed because of the frankness of its description of the "recreation" hours of a small clerk; it is in a way a continuation of the realism, the dreary and deadening monotony of "white collar" workers' lives, depicted in *The Office*.

PRINCIPAL WORKS: The Office, 1925; Love in Chartres, 1927; Pay Day, 1930; The Valley, 1935; The Road: In Search of America (non-fiction) 1937.

ASCH, SHOLEM (November 1, 1880-),

Yiddish novelist and dramatist, was born in Kutno (or Kutnia), Poland, the son of

poor Jewish parents, Moishe and Malka (Wydawski) Asch. He has in the past spelled his given name "Shalom" and has occasionally omitted the "c" from his last name. He had no education but that in Rabbinical theology given in the Hebrew

school of his village, until in 1899 he went to Warsaw. He had earned his own living from the age of sixteen. In Warsaw he first came into contact with "European," especially German, literature and culture. Within a year he had published his first book, a volume of novelettes written in Hebrew. He turned then to the writing of plays in Yiddish, which is essentially a mixed German-Hebrew dialect with some Russian and Polish elements. It is in this tongue that he has written nearly all his novels, plays, and poems since that time. Gradually he acquired a wide reputation among Yiddish-speaking Jews in Europe and America; he was introduced to this public in America in 1908, when Abraham Cahan published some of his short stories in the *Jewish Morning Journal*, New York.

At this time Asch was living in Switzerland. He had been married to Mathilda Spira in 1901, and they have had a daughter and three sons, one of whom, Nathan Asch,[qv] is a novelist in English. The play, *The God of Vengeance,* which Asch wrote during his Swiss residence, secured him his first non-Yiddish audience. Translated into German, it was produced by Max Reinhardt in Berlin in 1910. In Paris, London, and New York, its sordid realism gave rise to much controversy. Asch made his first visit to the United States in this same year, staying six months and then going to Paris. On the outbreak of the First World War he brought his family to New York, where he was naturalized in 1920. In 1925 he returned to Europe, to France, where he wrote his trilogy, *Three Cities,* his first book dealing with a wider world than that of his own people. In 1924 his collected works appeared in Warsaw in eighteen volumes—though he has of course continued to write since that time.

Early in the 1930's Asch returned permanently to America. However, he made frequent trips to Europe until the outbreak of the present war, and paid a long visit to the new Jewish colonies in Palestine, which were the theme of *Song of the Valley.* In *The Nazarene* he gave a Jewish portrait of Jesus. He has written regularly for *Forward,* the Yiddish paper of which Cahan has been editor for many years, and several of his novels first appeared there as serials. Best known of these to English and American readers, besides those already mentioned, are *Mottke the Thief* and *Uncle Moses.* Asch has also been the author of numerous plays, which have been produced with success by the Yiddish Theatre in New York. He lives in Stamford, Conn. He is president of the Jewish section of the P.E.N. Club, and received an honorary Doctorate of Jewish Letters from the New York Jewish Seminary in 1937.

Though he speaks English fluently and has occasionally written in it, Sholem Asch remains essentially a Yiddish writer whose works appear in translation. He is tall and heavy-set, with a small moustache. "It is when his face lights up," said Herbert S. Gorman, "and he smiles agreeably albeit a bit shyly, that his features take on an intellectual aspect. His shyness is somewhat accentuated by the care he takes in selecting his English words. One must grasp at half-finished sentences to follow him with any degree of success."

Padraic Colum has given another description of him, as a "bulky man with a strong forehead and thick hair," and with "trusting eyes." "He is not a prophet; he is a seeker after revelation. His sympathy is finally with the patient things, the patient people." Franz Werfel wrote of him: "In him re-sides a great seer of reality and a true *advocatus dei.* . . . He is a realist and an epic writer. . . . The farther he moves from Judaism, the more his soul grows in Biblical power."

WORKS AVAILABLE IN ENGLISH: Mottke the Thief, 1917; America, 1918; The God of Vengeance, 1918; Uncle Moses, 1920; Kiddush-Ha-Shem: An Epic of 1648, 1926; The Mother, 1930; Sabbatai Zevi, 1930; Three Cities (trilogy: Petersburg, Warsaw, Moscow) 1933; Salvation, 1934; In the Beginning, 1935; The War Goes On, 1937; Three Novels, 1938; Song of the Valley, 1939; The Nazarene, 1939; What I Believe, 1941; Children of Abraham, 1942.

ABOUT: Gorman, H. S. Procession of Masks; Atlantic Monthly December 1940; Bookman February 1918, June 1923; Living Age February 1931; Menorah Journal January 1937; Nation February 14 and 28, 1923; New York Times April 28, 1940.

ASHTON, HELEN ROSALINE (October 18, 1891-), English novelist and literary biographer, was born in London, the daughter of the late Arthur J. Ashton, King's Counsel, Recorder of Manchester, Judge of Appeal in the Isle of Man, and the author of some legal reminiscences. His daughter was educated at London University, obtaining the degrees of  M.B. and B.Ch., and qualifying for the practice of medicine, although she did not avail herself of the privilege. She was also a nurse in the First World War. Helen Ashton's first book, *A Lot of Talk,* was a medicated novel, in the well-known phrase of Oliver Wendell Holmes; the fourth, *Doctor Serocold,* an account of one day in the life of an English country doctor, was made a choice of the Book-of-the-Month Club in New York. Her husband, Arthur Edward North Jordan, barrister-at-law of Gray's Inn and the Oxford Circuit, whom she married in 1927, had stated that such a *tour-de-force* was impossible. Mrs. Jordan, who had learned during her medical studies how much emotional experience can be squeezed into a doctor's day, grants that her success in achieving it was hardly fair, considering her previous experience.

For a change of pace, her next novel but one, *Bricks and Mortar,* dealt with the experiences of an architect. *Belinda Grove,* the history of a Regency house in the suburbs of London, whose inhabitants felt the influence of a kindly ghost, was the result of an idea given the novelist by a stranger at a dinner party. Miss Ashton explored the northern suburbs of London, especially Islington, to find such a house. Belinda Grove, however, is an entirely imaginary place, relieving the minds of her publishers, who had feared a suit for libel. Miss Ashton has never attempted historical fiction in the ordinary sense, she once stated, although allowing her imagination free play over the Wordsworths in the *William and Dorothy* of 1938. With her husband, she lives at 13 South Square, Gray's Inn, London, in paneled rooms looking out on the hall where Queen Elizabeth dined. Their country house is at Pinchards, an old Queen Anne house at Stockton, Wiltshire, and for recreation the Jordans spend holidays trout-fishing in Ireland, where the novelist takes notes for new books in her tiny handwriting.

PRINCIPAL WORKS: A Lot of Talk, 1927; Far Enough, 1928; A Background For Caroline, 1929; Doctor Serocold, 1930; Mackerel Sky, 1930; Bricks and Mortar, 1932; Belinda Grove, 1932; Family Cruise, 1934; Hornet's Nest, 1934; Dust Over the Ruins, 1935; People in Cages, 1937; William and Dorothy, 1938; The Swan of Usk, 1939; Tadpole Hall, 1941

ASHTON, WINIFRED. See DANE, C.

*ATHERTON, Mrs. GERTRUDE FRANKLIN (HORN) (October 30, 1857-   ), American novelist, writes. "I was

born in San Francisco. My father, Thomas Lodowick Horn, came from Stonington, Conn., to California in the 1850's and was a member of the famous Vigilance Committee. My mother was Gertrude Franklin, whose father, Stephen Franklin, also came to San Francisco in the 1850's. My mother and father separated when I was two years old, and he brought me up, and inculcated in me a taste for serious literature, although as he began when I was fourteen I was rather rebellious at the time.

"I was educated at various private schools, the last being Sayre Institute, Lexington, Ky. I was threatened with consumption and my grandfather sent me there, as the doctor recommended a severe climate. I should have remained two years, but absentmindedly got engaged to two young men at once and thought California was the safest place for me. Soon after my arrival at home I married (February 14, 1876) George Henry

Bowen Atherton, son of Faxon D. Atherton, whose family came from England to Dedham, Mass., in Colonial days. He built us a house on his Fair Oaks estate (now known as Atherton) and I spent my married life there. Had two children, George Goñi, who died at the age of six, and Muriel, now Mrs. Atherton Russell.

"I began to write very early, first at school; and soon after I was married I published articles and a novelette in the San Francisco *Argonaut*, also articles and stories in the *News Letter*. I wrote a novel, *What Dreams May Come*, and was four years finding a publisher. Collectors pay a high price for this little book, on account of its rarity, although the content is worthless. After my husband's death in the late 1880's, I went to New York, and was soon launched on my writing career; all this I have described in my autobiography, *Adventures of a Novelist*. I shall remark here only that any career is a fight from start to finish, and needs as much will-power and courage as talent. But it would not be half so interesting otherwise. As to development, that goes on insensibly from year to year; otherwise, literary careers are brief, however sensational.

"All social strata interest me. Am a great newspaper reader, as I am interested in politics and world affairs, although when writing a book I never open a newspaper or a letter until after luncheon. Am also somewhat interested in civic affairs and am a member of the San Francisco Art Commission and have served on the Public Library Board of Directors.

"As to honors, have received the degree of Litt.D. from Mills College and LL.D. from the University of California. A 'Gertrude Atherton Day' was held at the International Golden Gate Exposition shortly after it opened, and a beautiful illuminated scroll of honor presented to me by the director of the fair. Am a life member of the American Historical Society.

"As to political convictions, I was brought up in a family of Democrats, but would certainly vote for a Republican president if I thought him a better man for the country. Abominate such 'isms' as Communism, Fascism, Nazism, Socialism. Am quite willing to admit that our form of government is far from perfect, but want something better, not worse.

"Have never married a second time, as I prize liberty and freedom too much to sacrifice either to any man—and men, husbands, have their rights. Husbands are a great responsibility, and dependent upon

* Died June 14, 1948.

wives for comfort; it is hardly fair to desert them for months at a time when a book is in process of delivery (I always hide myself in some country-town hotel when writing a book), or if it is necessary to go suddenly on a long voyage in search of material.

"I change my mind too often about public figures and authors to risk making a statement of preferences, but am faithful to the Greek tragic poets.

"My home is in San Francisco, but there are times when I conclude it is a good place to get away from, and leave for New York or Europe. Lived for seven or eight years in England, six years in Munich, months at a time in other cities of Europe and the United States.

"The most popular of my books have been *The Conqueror,* just brought out in a new format, after passing the half million mark, *The Immortal Marriage, Dido, Rezánov, The Splendid Idle Forties* (short stories of Old California), *Adventures of a Novelist, California: An Intimate History,* and *Black Oxen.* My own favorite is *Tower of Ivory.*"

* * *

No one who sees Gertrude Atherton, a distinguished statuesque blonde, can believe that the author of these words, and of some forty books, is actually at this writing (1941) nearly eighty-four years old. Her remarkable youthfulness is due in part, as she has made public, to glandular therapy, but mostly to her own indomitable spirit. *Newsweek* has remarked on her "brilliant, supple brain," and her "enormous capacity for work." She has conducted a "fifty-year war against Mrs. Grundy."

PRINCIPAL WORKS: The Doomswoman, 1892; A Whirl Asunder, 1895; Patience Sparhawk and Her Times, 1897; His Fortunate Grace, 1897; The Californians, 1898; A Daughter of the Vine, 1899; Senator North, 1900; The Aristocrats, 1901; The Conqueror, 1902; A Few of Hamilton's Letters, 1903; Rulers of Kings, 1904; The Bell in the Fog, 1905; The Travelling Thirds, 1905; Rezánov, 1906; Ancestors, 1907; The Gorgeous Isle, 1908; Tower of Ivory, 1910; Julia France and Her Times, 1912; Perch of the Devil, 1914; California: An Intimate History, 1914; Before the Gringo Came, 1915; Mrs. Belfame, 1916; The Living Present, 1917; The White Morning, 1918; The Avalanche, 1919; Sisters-in-Law, 1921; Sleeping Fires, 1922; Black Oxen, 1923; The Crystal Cup, 1925; The Immortal Marriage, 1927; The Jealous Gods, 1928; Dido, Queen of Hearts, 1929; The Sophisticates, 1931; The Adventures of a Novelist, 1932; Golden Peacock, 1936; Can Women Be Gentlemen, 1938; The House of Lee, 1940.

ABOUT: Bookman July 1929, Sepetmber 1930; Newsweek December 14, 1935, September 5, 1938; Saturday Review of Literature May 28, 1932; Wilson Library Bulletin March 1931.

ATKINSON, BROOKS. See ATKINSON, J. B.

*ATKINSON, Mrs. ELEANOR (STACKHOUSE) (1863-), American novelist, writes: "My first bit of luck was to be born in Rens-selaer, in northwestern Indiana. It had been settled late, and largely by people of old American stock from the Eastern seaboard and, southern Ohio. So it had, from pioneer days, many people of superior education and public spirit.  My father, of Philadelphia Quaker parentage, and my mother, of Colonial ancestry in Connecticut, were typical. One of the memories of a happy childhood in Rensselaer was the early discovery of books. Before I could read, my mother read to me her favorite poets: Scott, Burns, and Tennyson. Soon I was exploring our own and other people's bookshelves, and finding whatever was there for me. And I was scribbling industriously on any topic that kindled the imagination. With that good start I should have gone faster and farther; and might reasonably have been expected to find literary material in my own experience. Instead, I went as far afield as Edinburgh, French Flanders, the Island of Martinique, and the Ohio wilderness of a century before. I think I had nothing to say about that. It appears to me that a creative writer's choice of subject must be governed by his mental limitations and emotional responses. I know what mine are.

"I had been graduated from the Indianapolis Normal Training School before breaking into print; and it took a lot of experimental writing, during four years of teaching, there and in Chicago, and then a fortunate circumstance for me to get into newspaper work. My career as a special writer on the Chicago *Tribune,* over the pen name of 'Nora Marks,' came to an end with my marriage in 1891 to Francis Blake Atkinson, a news editor with ideas, initiative, and energy. Our talents being in the same field and complementary, we presently launched a publishing venture: *The Little Chronicle,* a current events weekly for grammar and high school grades. Unable to find suitable serials, I wrote two myself, and was surprised when both of them were brought out in book form. Thus I became an author by accident, not intention. Most of my books happened more or less in this way, as the by-product of much anonymous literary work.

"As many women have proved, professional writing can be successfully combined with home making. When our paper was sold we went on the staff of the F.E. Compton Co., publishers of students' encyclopedias, my husband as managing editor. As an associate editor, researcher, and writer, I worked on contract, doing my writing at home and on my own time. Books, and some magazine articles, were written in the intervals between contracts. Both my daughters caught the matrimonial bug and scribbler's itch early. As 'Dorothy Blake' and 'Eleanor Blake' they are today professional writers and home-makers.

"Only two of my books can be said to have been premeditated and long prepared for: *Greyfriars Bobby* and *Johnny Appleseed*. They are the two that have had the widest appeal and have survived the longest. So there, perhaps, is an argument for the greater offense for anyone who thinks of committing the crime of writing a book."

* * *

Mrs. Atkinson today makes her home in Manhasset, Long Island, a suburb of New York City. She has published no new books for more than two decades, but in her late seventies she is the same intelligent, kindly, and humanitarian woman whose sincere and unpretentious stories have given wholesome enjoyment to readers of all ages for more than two generations. Perhaps *Greyfriars Bobby*, a true classic wherever dog stories are read and loved, will live longest of her books; it has already been continuously in print for more than a quarter-century. It is an interesting circumstance that though nearly all of Mrs. Atkinson's books were originally written for (and read by) adults, their greatest and continuing popularity has been with younger readers. "I think it was fortunate," she says, "that I did not know that young people were going to care for my stories. I might have made the mistake of writing down to them. An author never knows his luck!"

PRINCIPAL WORKS: Mamzelle Fifine, 1903; The Boyhood of Lincoln, 1908; Lincoln's Love Story, 1909; The Story of Chicago, 1910; Greyfriars Bobby, 1912; A Loyal Love, 1912; The How and Why Library, 1913; Johnny Appleseed, 1915; Hearts Undaunted, 1917; Poilu, 1918; Pictured Knowledge (with others) 1918.

ABOUT: Kunitz, S. J. & Haycraft, H. (eds.). The Junior Book of Authors.

ATKINSON, JUSTIN BROOKS (November 28, 1894-), American dramatic critic, essayist, and traveler who signs himself Brooks Atkinson, was born in Melrose, Mass., the son of Jonathan Henry Atkinson and Garafelia (Taylor) Atkinson. He plunged into publishing at the age of eight, and printed (rubber type) his own paper, *The Watchout.* When he was twelve he joined the National Amateur Press Association and printed (lead type) *The Puritan.* The last words he set for this journal were: "This age is dedicated to the flapper, the salamander, Charlie Chaplin, and F. P. A."

Oggiano

He went to Harvard, was graduated in 1917, and for the last three months of the year following, served at Camp Upton (N.Y.) as a corporal in the army. Meanwhile he had done some news-gathering for the Springfield (Mass.) *Daily News.* After a brief instructorship at Dartmouth he began four years of reporting and reviewing for the Boston *Transcript.* (In one of his columns he mentioned a poor young actor who had "spluttered and spurted" his way through a Harvard theatrical, and who happened to be John Mason Brown, now Atkinson's friend and colleague.) During these same years Atkinson was editing the *Harvard Alumni Bulletin.*

In 1922 he came to New York as book reviewer for the *Times.* He took a small dusty room overlooking Washington Square. By 1925 Atkinson had transferred his whole allegiance to the drama and for fifteen years has been a sensitive and scholarly critic of the stage. He was married, in 1926, to Oriana Torrey, of New York City.

Skyline Promenades (1925), reflections on mountain climbing and kindred interests, was his first book. Two years later he published a study of a long-revered hero, *Henry Thoreau: The Cosmic Yankee*; and in 1931 came *East of the Hudson*, a collection of rural delights. In 1934 he wrote the story of a "round-the-world journey in a five-passenger freighter," the "Cingalese Prince." His *Cleo for Short*, a 2000-word tribute to his much-loved police dog who died in 1940, first appeared in the *Atlantic Monthly.* It was with her that Atkinson used to roam the Twelfth Street waterfront or take long bird-walks—he is a first-rate ornithologist—in the country.

The commercial influence of newspaper reviews makes Atkinson's business no "idyllic profession of theatre-going and scribbling on yellow pads." When a curtain goes down on an opening performance he leaps into the aisle, dashes over to his coop at the *Times,* and gets to work on a review for a morning paper which, for the most part, is already in type. If the opening line comes easily ("Praise God from whom first sentences flow!") the battle is virtually won.

Atkinson has occasionally been charged with spreading undue gloom along Broadway —whether by a grim three-word-verdict or by the spirit of his note on *Thanks for Tomorrow:* "Thanks for tomorrow, thanks for last week, thanks for next Friday—in fact, thanks for everything except last night." His opinions, however, provide a kind of middle-of-the-road gauge, and have a measurable influence on box-office returns.

PRINCIPAL WORKS: Skyline Promenades, 1925; Henry Thoreau: The Cosmic Yankee, 1927; East of the Hudson, 1931; The Cingalese Prince, 1934; Ralph Waldo Emerson's Complete Essays and Other Writings (ed.) 1940; Cleo For Short, 1940.

ABOUT: Atkinson, B. East of the Hudson; Atkinson, B. Skyline Promenades; Atkinson, B. The Cingalese Prince; Carnegie Magazine November 1934; New York Times Magazine March 24, 1940; Nation March 8, 1941; Reader's Digest November 1937; Saturday Review of Literature November 12, 1938; Theatre Arts June 1936; Time November 14, 1938, May 1, 1939.

*AUBRY, OCTAVE (September 1, 1881-), French novelist and historian, was born in Paris of a well-to-do bourgeois family. Hav-ing the advantages of a fine education, he crowned his academic career with two doctorates from the University of Paris: one in literature, his chosen vocation, the other in law, to ease the minds of his parents. The first two decades of the century revealed Aubry as a fanciful young writer, somewhat sentimental, but quite promising: *De l'Amour, l'Ironie, et de la Pitié* (1904) which came out with a charming introductory letter by Madame Severine, was followed two years later by *La Face d'Airain,* "the novel of individual energy," as he subtitled it. Then in the Pinchon Series of Law and Jurisprudence he published *L'Indulgence et la Loi* (1908), prefaced by Alexandre Ribot and with hitherto unpublished letters by Henri Barboux and others.

In his next few works Aubry returned to fiction. While the critics commended *Soeur Anne* (1912), the *Nouvelle Revue* beginning May 1912 serialized *L'Homme Dans la Cime* (1913), a novel with Scandinavian background and characters—the hero was named Harold Frijtsen. In 1913 Aubry travelled in Spain, which can be called his second fatherland: in June 1913 the *Nouvelle Revue* published a deeply felt descriptive sketch of Avila, "the mystic city of Saint Theresa," and years later he returned to his Spanish theme in *Couleur de Sang* (1926), intimate portraits of Granada, Seville, Toledo, and Madrid; *Visions d'Espagne* (1927); *L'Espagne: Les Provinces du Sud de Seville à Cordove* (1929); and *L'Espagne: Les Provinces du Nord de Tolede à Burgos* (1930).

However, the works which made Aubry's name world-famous are those in which he combined his fictional talent with his historical erudition (he has been called the leading living authority on the Napoleonic period). His re-creative work as historical romancer began in 1924 and has not ended yet. *The Lost King* (1924), dealing with Louis XVII, was followed by: *The Empress Might-Have-Been: The Love Story of Marie Valevska and Napoleon* (1925); *On the King's Couch* (1926), dramatic sketches of Casanova, Louis XV, and Mlle. Anne de Romans; *Brelan de Femmes ou le Coup d'Etat de Brumaire* (1927); *The Emperor Falls in Love: The Romance of Josephine and Napoleon* (1927). With these fictionalized slices of history, Aubry's name became known outside France. By 1928 four of these works were available in English.

In 1929 Aubry presented a vivid picture of Napoleon III, *The Phantom Emperor,* towards whom he is extremely indulgent, followed by one of *Eugenie: Empress of the French* (1931), and, after a long sojourn in Vienna, of Napoleon II, the Aiglon, *The King of Rome* (1932). In the wake of his slight *La Trahison de Marie Louise* (1933), and following a period of intensive study in English archives and in Napoleon's island of captivity, Aubry produced one of his greatest works—Maurois called it "the most impartial and best documented"—*Saint Helena* (1935), a height which he did not abandon in his two other most significant achievements: *Napoleon: Soldier and Emperor* (1936) and *The Second Empire* (1938). Gilbert Chase has said that in his full-length portrait-biography of Napoleon, Aubry "sheds light on every phase of this extraordinary career and illumines the entire man in a steady glow of intelligent and sympathetic appraisal"; while of *The Second Empire* the historian Maurice Reclus declares: "All the qualities are found here which have made Octave Aubry one of the unquestioned leaders of our most recent historical school, chiefly that mastery of the reconstruction of the past, that gift for making it live again *within* . . . by which from the mass of dead things which constitute the matter of history there emerges, under the pen of the exact scholar transformed into subtle magician, the feeling and experience of *presence.*"

Aubry has filled posts in the Ministries of Justice, Public Instruction, and Interior. He is an officer of the Legion of Honor. During the Second World War he was war correspondent for a Paris newspaper, and at the date of this writing is reported living in occupied France. He owns a magnificent mansion on the Rue de Lille in Paris, which was built in 1749 for the Princess de Lamballe, the friend of Mme de Pompadour. Among his most prized possessions is a death mask of Napoleon, the most beautiful of the three impressions made by Altommarchi from the original mask.

WORKS AVAILABLE IN TRANSLATION: The Empress Might-Have-Been, 1927; On the King's Couch, 1927; The Lost King, 1927; The Emperor Falls in Love, 1928; The Phantom Emperor, 1929; Gaspard Hauser: The Orphan of Europe, 1930; Eugenie: Empress of the French, 1931; The King of Rome, 1932; Saint Helena, 1936; Napoleon: Soldier and Emperor, 1938; The Second Empire, 1940.

ABOUT: Boston Transcript November 16, 1929, November 12, 1932, December 12, 1936, January 7, 1939; Christian Science Monitor April 8, 1933; New Republic January 6, 1937; New York Herald Tribune "Books" August 14, 1927, January 15, 1928, March 25, 1928, December 29, 1929, January 10, 1932, December 11, 1932, December 20, 1936, November 13, 1938; New York Times May 8, 1927, December 20, 1936, October 27, 1940; Saturday Review of Literature January 21, 1927, August 4, 1928, December 26, 1931, October 19, 1940; Time November 30, 1936; Times (London) Literary Supplement March 30, 1933.

AUDEN, WYSTAN HUGH (February 21, 1907-), English poet, was born in York, the son of George Augustus Auden, a retired medical officer, and Constance Rosalie (Bicknell) Auden. He was educated at Gresham's School, Holt, and at Christ Church College, Oxford. For a short time after leaving the university he was a schoolmaster. Very soon however, he became associated with the small group of very young poets in London who (partly by constantly bringing one another into public attention) became recognized as the most promising of the new generation in English poetry. They were all strongly oriented to the left, some of them being orthodox Communists. Auden's close friend, Stephen Spender, says, however, that Auden was never in complete agreement with Communist doctrine. He continues, however, to feel himself (to quote Malcolm Cowley) "a class traitor, a spy, a Copperhead"—in other words, he is in open rebellion against the

mores and opinions of the upper bourgeoisie into which he was born. In 1937 he was an ambulance driver for the Loyalists during the Spanish Revolution, and he is married to Erika Mann [w] (herself a writer), the daughter of the great German refugee novelist, Thomas Mann.

On his return from Spain in 1937, Auden was the recipient of the King's Poetry medal, the second to be awarded—a sufficient indication of his position among contemporary British poets. He was then living in Birmingham, but in 1939 he came to the United States as a permanent resident. He has taken out his first papers, and his latest volume was published in America before publication in England. In the course of his Americanization he wrote an unpublished operetta on Paul Bunyan, the mythical American lumberman. Brooklyn is his residence.

A good deal of Auden's work has been written in collaboration with Christopher Isherwood; his *Letters From Iceland,* written with Louis MacNeice, grew from a visit to that country the two writers made together in 1936. He edited the English Number of *Poetry* in 1937, has translated from the German the poems of the late Ernst Toller, and has edited three anthologies—*Oxford Poetry 1926* with Charles Plumb; *The Poet's Tongue* (1935) with John Garrett, and the *Oxford Book of Light Verse* in 1938. In this last field he is himself the master of a pungent satirical style that is openly reminiscent of the Byron of *Don Juan.*

He is five feet eleven inches in height, with long, straight, very fair hair and hazel eyes. He confesses to a harmless youthful exhibitionism, and says he would like to be a first-class diver, because it would be "such a marvelous way of showing off." It is perhaps partly this love of "showing off" that manifests itself in his verbal pyrotechnics. As Cowley remarked, "he suggests

E. E. Cummings, has the same crazy wit, the same delight in playing with words, and the same indifference as to whether he is being understood." "His attitudes and symbols are Janus-faced," said David Daiches, who thought Auden a poet still "in the wilderness, wondering whom he should talk to." His earlier work was much influenced by the Jesuit poet, Gerard Manley Hopkins.

He is extremely versatile. William Troy called him "a satirist of . . . vigor, freshness, and ingenuity, . . . but his satire is strongest on the purely negative side." James Burnham thought that he "has written more successful prose than verse, a prose that at its best is colorful, swift, and flexible." Spender, his nearest rival and greatest admirer, has granted that he is "sometimes overloaded with his material," but he insists that Auden's poetry has "a vitality, an explosive violence, that leaves his contemporaries dazed." Even his detractors, who complain of the "obscurity" of his work, admit that it is "always interesting." The final word on a poet who after all is still very young and only at the beginning of what should be a long career has yet to be uttered.

Auden's most recent work has less superficial sparkle than before, but shows a deepening of theme and the signs of an awakening religious sensibility.

PRINCIPAL WORKS: Poems, 1930; The Orators (prose and verse) 1932; The Dance of Death, 1933; The Dog Beneath the Skin: or, Where Is Francis? (play, with C. Isherwood) 1935; Look, Stranger (in America: On This Island) 1936; The Ascent of F.6 (play, with C. Isherwood) 1936; Letters From Iceland (with L. MacNeice) 1937; Spain, 1937; On the Frontier (with C. Isherwood) 1938; The Oxford Book of Light Verse (ed.) 1938; Journey to a War (prose, with C. Isherwood) 1939; Another Time, 1940; The Double Man, 1941.

ABOUT: Leavis, F. R. New Bearings in English Poetry; American Review May 1934; Bookman (London) March 1934; Commonweal December 28, 1934, August 2, 1935; Harper's Magazine October 1940; London Mercury April 1939; Nation August 8, 1934, March 27, 1937, February 1, 1941; New Republic September 26, 1934; Poetry May 1931, May 1933, June 1939, April 1940; Saturday Review of Literature November 10 and December 5, 1934, February 13 and October 19, 1937; Sewanee Review April 1938; Time August 7, 1939; Virginia Quarterly Review #3 1937, #4 1938.

AUMONIER, STACY (1887-December 21, 1928), English novelist and short story writer, was the son of William Aumonier, an architectural sculptor. He was educated at Cranleigh, and began his career as a decorative designer and landscape painter, exhibiting frequently at the Royal Academy, the Royal Institute, and the In-

ternational. In 1908 Aumonier launched out as a society entertainer, giving recitals of his own original character sketches at the Comedy, Criterion, and the other theatres. Aumonier began writing in 1913. During the First World War, he served as a private, afterwards working as a maker of charts at the Ministry of National Service. The first of Aumonier's  literary work to attract notice was "The Friends," a short story concerning two furniture salesmen who drank themselves to death. His literary agent refused it, but somehow it appeared in the English Review, with American publication in the Century Magazine. Boston Transcript readers voted it one of the fifteen best stories of the year; clergymen made it a theme for sermons. The Querrils, his best known novel, is a sympathetic and observant study of a wartime family.

Aumonier died in Switzerland at forty-one after a long illness. The London Mercury described him as "a picturesque-looking man, handsome in an aquiline way, with piercing eyes, a black stock, and a great wave of hair tumbling over his forehead. He was a writer who only just fell short of doing something very good." Three Bars' Interval (which includes "The Friends") "never had the notice to which its candor, economy, and constructive power entitled it." The short stories reflected the charm and humor of a many-sided person, who had been a painter, entertainer, and journalist. Rebecca West said of Heartbeat, "Mr. Aumonier's creations are dyed in the fast dyes of the authentic imagination. Casually, indolently as Mr. Aumonier invents them, he achieves that confusion between the real and the imagined world which is the envy of all artists." Katherine Mansfield strikes the familiar dissident note in her Athenaeum notice of One After Another: "It is rich and poor, cold and hot, dull and deeply interesting, but the impression of the whole is of something which has just not succeeded." Aumonier married Gertrude Peppercorn, a concert pianist who appeared in the United States.

PRINCIPAL WORKS: Three Bars' Interval, 1917; The Querrils, 1919; One After Another, 1920; Heartbeat, 1922; Miss Bracegirdle and Others, 1923; Odd Fish: Being a Casual Selection of London Residents (with George Belcher) 1923;

Overheard: Fifteen Tales, 1924; Little Windows, 1931.

ABOUT: Bookman March 1929; Bookman (London) February 1929; London Mercury February 1929.

AUSLANDER, JOSEPH (October 11, 1897-), American poet and anthologist, was born in Philadelphia, the son of Louis

Auslander and Martha (Asyueck) Auslander. He entered Columbia University at sixteen, spending the year 1914-15 there, and received his B.A. degree from Harvard University in 1917. From 1919 to 1923 he was an instructor in English at Harvard, continuing graduate study there until 1924 and taking a leave of absence in 1921-22 to attend the Sorbonne in Paris on a Parker fellowship. In 1929 he returned to Columbia as lecturer in poetry, remaining until 1937 when he assumed his present post as consultant in English poetry at the Library of Congress, Washington, D.C. In May 1930 he married Svanhild Kreutz, who died the following January, leaving a daughter, Svanhild Frances Martha. The present Mrs. Auslander, fourteen years his junior, is Audrey Wurdemann *qv* who won the 1935 Pulitzer poetry prize for her first book of poems, *Bright Ambush*. Auslander was poetry editor of the *North American Review* from 1936 until its publication was discontinued. He is a member of P.E.N. and the Poetry Society of America, and is a corresponding member of the Hispanic Society of America.

Pinchot

Joseph Auslander's first book of poems, *Sunrise Trumpets*, was published in 1924, with an introduction by Padraic Colum calling attention to its felicities. *Cyclops' Eye* was Auslander's second book. In this he essayed some stark narrative, as in *Steel*, *Two That Unlatched Heaven*, and *Knockabout*. *The Winged Horse*, a history of poetry intended primarily for young readers, with its supplementary anthology, *The Winged Horse Anthology*, was written in collaboration with a Columbia colleague, Frank Ernest Hill. *Letters to Women* (1929), addressed to Elinor Wylie, Fanny Brawne, and other unusual women, and Auslander's translations of Petrarch's Sonnets, are others of his books that have enjoyed wider reading than most volumes of poetry achieve. Auslander's recent work has fre-

quently been criticized as being too facile and superficial.

PRINCIPAL WORKS: Sunrise Trumpets, 1924; Cyclops' Eye, 1926; The Winged Horse (with F. E. Hill) 1927; Hell in Harness, 1929; Letters to Women, 1929; No Traveler Returns, 1933; Will Shakespeare, 1934; Prose Cavalcade, 1934; More Than Bread, 1936; Riders at the Gate, 1939. *Editor*—The Winged Horse Anthology (with F. E. Hill) 1928; Shakespeare's Sonnets, 1931. *Translator*—The Fables of La Fontaine: Books 1-6, 1930; The Vigil of Venus, 1931; The Sonnets of Petrarch, 1931.

ABOUT: Drinkwater, J. & others. Twentieth-Century Poetry; Boston Transcript August 3, 1929; Harvard College, Class of 1917: Quindecennial Report.

AUSTIN, ALFRED. See "BRITISH AUTHORS OF THE 19TH CENTURY"

AUSTIN, Mrs. MARY (HUNTER) (September 9, 1868-August 13, 1934), American novelist and essayist, was born in Carlinville, Ill., the daughter of George and Savilla (Graham) Hunter. Her father was a Civil War captain turned farmer, her mother a feminist but a rigid Puritan. They made it plain that she was an unwanted child. A born rebel, she was

also a born writer and a born mystic. She was graduated from Blackburn College in 1888. The same year her father died and her mother moved to southwestern California, in the desert, her final home being on a ranch near Bakersfield. In 1891 Mary Hunter married Stafford Austin, a rancher and teacher. They settled at Lone Pine, Inyo County. He had never told her of the taint in his family, and their only child, a daughter, was born an imbecile. Grimly the mother put her in an institution, and when her feckless husband made a failure of teaching as he had of farming, she gave him the housework to do and took his place in school. The desert and the Indians fascinated her; she steeped herself in Indian legends and customs, and began to write of them. *Overland Monthly* took two stories from her, but it was not until 1900 that she began to make a living by writing, when the *Atlantic Monthly* opened its doors to her and she also began to sell stories for children to the juvenile magazines. She was utterly out of tune with all the conventions of her time and place, and her neighbors hated her. She was always what she called herself, "Woman Alone."

In 1896 she separated from her husband, and in 1900, with her first chance as a free lance writer, she settled in Carmel, then a tiny village, and was one of the founders of the literary colony which included George Sterling, Jack London, and many others later famous. Her first book, *The Land of Little Rain*, made enough to send her to Europe in 1903, and much of her time for several years was spent there or in New York. Finally in 1918 she settled permanently in Santa Fé, N.M., where she died sixteen years later of a heart attack at nearly sixty-six. In Santa Fé she conducted "an austere rule as a kind of uncrowned empress." The Indians were her special care, and as she became increasingly mystical she seemed removed from ordinary life. No one was indifferent to her; people either detested and feared her formidable personality, or they worshiped and obeyed. Carl Van Doren described her, with her "grave dignity that was somehow larger than pride," her ability to remain motionless like an Indian, her brown face and beautiful hands. She was short and dumpy, but she wore her hair piled high and carried herself like a queen.

Van Doren was right in saying that as a personality she was greater than as a writer. A thoroughgoing feminist, she interpreted all life in terms of herself, and she could never forget herself. She did much to preserve folklore of the Indians otherwise lost (she wrote the chapter on Aboriginal Literature in the *Cambridge History of American Literature*); her mysticism, if muddled, was always desperately sincere; but her writing was symbolistic, abstruse, and often confused. Yet occasionally there are beautiful and passionate pages that show what she might have been had not all her strength been spent in fighting life. She seems to have possessed genius without possessing talent. She was a pathetic, even a tragic, figure, who found peace only in a mystical fusion with nature and primitive humanity.

PRINCIPAL WORKS: *Fiction*—The Basket Woman (juvenile short stories) 1904; Isidro, 1904; Santa Lucia, 1908; Lost Borders (short stories) 1909; Green Bough, 1913; The Lovely Lady, 1913; Love and the Soul Market, 1914; A Woman of Genius, 1917; The Ford, 1917; The Trail Book (juvenile) 1918; Outland (as "Gordon Stairs") 1919; No. 26 Jayne Street, 1920; Starry Adventure, 1931; One Smoke Stories, 1934. *Miscellaneous*—The Land of Little Rain, 1903; The Flock, 1906; Christ in Italy, 1911; The Arrow Maker (play) 1911; California: Land of the Sun, 1914 (as Lands of the Sun, 1927); The Man Jesus, 1915 (as A Small Town Man, 1925); American Rhythm (essays and poems) 1923; Land of the Journey's Ending, 1924; Everyman's Genius, 1925; The Children Sing in the Far West (poems) 1828; Amerindian Songs, 1930; Experiences Facing Death, 1931; Earth Horizon (autobiography) 1932; Can Prayer Be Answered? 1934.

ABOUT: Austin, M. Earth Horizon; Calverton, V. F. The Liberation of American Literature; Doyle, H. McK. Mary Austin: Woman of Genius; Farrar, J. The Literary Spotlight; Overton, G. M. The Women Who Make Our Novels; Pattee, F. L. The New American Literature; Pearse, T. M. The Beloved House; Van Doren, C. Contemporary American Novelists, Many Minds; American Mercury June 1911; Bookman December 1932; Commonweal August 24, 1934, December 29, 1939; Nation August 29 and October 10, 1934; New Republic December 21, 1932; Saturday Review of Literature November 12, 1932, September 8, 1934; Sunset Magazine September 1919; Survey September 1934; Virginia Quarterly Review April 1937; Wilson Library Bulletin June 1940.

AYALA. See PÉREZ DE AYALA

*AYSCOUGH, Mrs. FLORENCE (WHEELOCK) (1878-), American poet and authority on Chinese literature, was born in Shanghai, China, the daughter of Thomas Reed Wheelock, a Canadian, and Edith Haswell (Clarke) Wheelock. Florence Wheelock had private tutors, and also attended Mrs. Quincy Shaw's School in Boston. During the  years in Boston she struck up a schoolgirl friendship with Amy Lowell which endured through succeeding years and eventually became a collaboration. In November 1917 she visited Miss Lowell at the latter's Brookline home, Sevenels, and for four years they worked over translations of the poems of Li T'ai Po and Tu Fu, chiefly by mail, though with occasional meetings. For many years Mrs. Ayscough—she still uses for literary purposes the name of her first husband, Francis Ayscough Ayscough of Leicestershire and Shanghai, who died in 1933 leaving no children—was honorary librarian of the North China Branch of the Royal Asiatic Society in Shanghai. She is one of the eight honorary members of the Society, being the first woman to receive the honor. One of her young associates, Nung Chu, who knew no English, furnished her with all the apparatus of the *scholia* of the poetry to be translated, as well as an analysis of the written characters. Her prose versions were worked over into free verse renderings

* Died April 24, 1942.

by Miss Lowell. The resultant *Fir-Flower Tablets* (1922) are, says Foster Damon in his *Amy Lowell,* the climax of a literary trend of the times. In 1852, a year before Perry's great expedition, Richard Henry Stoddard included some Chinese subjects in his *Poems,* and Thomas Holley Chivers published his *Chinese Serenade.* Ezra Pound, in the twenties, was writing his *Cathay,* based on the notes of Ernest Fenollosa of Salem, and Arthur Waley and Witter Bynner were also translating or adapting from the Chinese. "The modern attitude of mind was closely akin to that of the ancient Chinese," remarks Mr. Damon. Arthur Waley's review of *Fir-Flower Tablets* in the New York *Evening Post,* on February 4, 1922, was not so "violent" as Miss Lowell had expected, but she did not relish some reviewers' advice to Mrs. Ayscough to get rid of Miss Lowell and to Miss Lowell to learn Chinese before she ventured on any more similar work.

Mrs. Ayscough, whom Damon calls an expert Sinologue, has lectured on Chinese art, literature, and society in London, Paris, Berlin, New York, and many other cities. She wrote articles for the *Encyclopedia Sinica,* and her papers have appeared in the *Proceedings* of learned societies. The Ayscoughs lived for many years at Shanghai in Wild Goose Happiness House. *A Chinese Mirror,* dedicated to Amy Lowell, who died before the book appeared, was dated from the Bay of Plentiful Fish, New Brunswick, Canada. In September 1935 Mrs. Ayscough was married to Professor Harley Farnsworth MacNair, also on outstanding Sinologue, at Guernsey, the Channel Islands. Their present home is the House of the Wutung Trees, Woodlawn Avenue, Chicago. For recreation, Mrs. Ayscough MacNair prefers sailing, swimming, riding, the theatre and music. Since 1938 she has lectured on Chinese literature at the University of Chicago.

PRINCIPAL WORKS: Fir-Flower Tablets (with A. Lowell) 1922; A Chinese Mirror: Being Reflections of the Reality Behind Appearance, 1925; The Autobiography of a Chinese Dog, 1926; Tu Fu: The Autobiography of a Chinese Poet, 1929-34; Pictures of the Chinese World, 1931; Firecracker Land, 1932; Travels of a Chinese Poet, 1934; Chinese Women: Yesterday and Today, 1937.

ABOUT: Damon, S. F. Amy Lowell.

"AYSCOUGH, JOHN." See BICKER-STAFFE-DREW, F. B. D.

"AZORÍN." See MARTÍNEZ RUIZ, J.

BABBITT, IRVING (August 2, 1865-July 15, 1933), American scholar and "Humanist," was born in Dayton, Ohio, the son of Dr. Edwin Dwight Babbitt and Augusta (Darling) Babbitt. His father was a romantic, whose associates were largely of the "lunatic fringe" that gathers on the edge of liberal groups, and as the family moved gradually from Ohio to California the  boy found himself surrounded by people whose fuzzy minds and loose outlook on life he detested. Most of his later reactionary dogmatism was a revolt from the conditions of his boyhood. By the help of an uncle, he was able to go to Harvard, from which he received his B.A. in 1889 and his M.A. in 1893, then studied for a year in Paris. From an early interest in Greek and Latin he turned to French, though it was the French intellect, rather than the French character, which he admired.

For a year he was instructor in Romance languages at Williams College, then returned to Harvard and remained on its faculty the rest of his life, starting as instructor in French and in 1912 becoming full professor. He was a frequent exchange lecturer, at Yale, Amherst, Stanford, the University of Toronto, and Kenyon College; he was exchange professor at the Sorbonne in 1923, and was a correspondent of the Institute de France. In 1900 he married Dora Mary Drew, and they had a son and a daughter.

In his professional capacity he edited works by Racine, Voltaire, Taine, and Renan, but outside his domestic life and his teaching—which was marked by a fantastic range of allusion and an impersonally brusque authority that commanded respect and attention—his only interest was in the promulgation of the system of philosophy and ethics known as "Humanism"—rather unfortunately so, since the name had already been pre-empted by a Rationalistic religious group. Even in this field, he left most of the public pleading to Paul Elmer More, while he himself (though the subject was apt to become the "King Charles' head" even of his lectures on French literature) devoted his energies to the production of scholarly treatises. Only once did he appear on the platform, in New York, to defend his system, and then, being unaccustomed to any but a student audience, he did not give a very good account of himself.

Babbitt's "Humanism" is difficult to define except in negative terms. Its mottoes were "nothing too much—decorum—restraint—the will to refrain." It was violently opposed to romanticism and naturalism in any field of thought, and Rousseau was its devil. It was in essence a sort of latter-day Calvinism, anti-sentimentalist and obscurantist. The past tense is used because, though for a short time it became a matter for public discussion, it has now few advocates, Seward Collins being almost the only prominent spokesman it still possesses. Fundamentally it was a sort of non-violent intellectual fascism, classical and Puritanical at once, and extended to every province from religion to literature. As Russell Wilbur said of Babbitt, he took "his own New England conscience, his Puritan and bourgeois prejudices, to be 'the higher will in man.'"

Babbitt was a genuine scholar, with (to quote the *Nation*) "a prodigious familiarity with international literature, which he seemed sometimes to read chiefly in order to denounce it." Although arbitrary and dogmatic in his convictions, he was personally sympathetic and kindly, single-minded in the honesty of his belief, faithful to his creed, personally not at all ambitious, and modest concerning his own literary powers, which indeed were not great, his style as a writer being far from graceful. "His mind set early into its permanent position," remarked Austin Warren. "He seems, indeed, to have been born full-grown." Harry Salpeter described him as he was on his New York lecture appearance, tall and powerfully built but stooped, with a massive head, a long and concave face, a strong jaw, thin, set lips, eyes piercing, cold, and clear. "The heir of intellectual Puritanism," Mary M. Colum called him, "made very scholarly and given a tinge of internationalism, . . . a powerful analytical mind . . . perpetually confusing the aim of literature and the aim of philosophy."

PRINCIPAL WORKS: Literature and the American College, 1908; The New Laokoön, 1910; The Masters of Modern French Criticism, 1912; Rousseau and Romanticism, 1919; Democracy and Leadership, 1924; French Literature, 1928; On Being Creative and Other Essays, 1932; The Dhammapada: With an Essay on Buddha and the Occident, 1936; Spanish Character and Other Essays, 1940.

ABOUT: Humanism and America (symposium); Leander, F. Humanized Naturalism; Mercier, L. J. A. The Challenge of Humanism; Shepard, O. & Manchester, F. A. Irving Babbitt; American Review February and April 1934, December 1935, May, September and November 1936, May 1937;

Canadian Forum October 1933, January to April 1931; Catholic World October 1938; Commonweal January 25, 1935, June 26, 1936; Nation July 26, 1933; Outlook July 16, 1930, Saturday Review of Literature December 17, 1932, October 19, 1940; Scribner's Magazine February and June 1930.

BABEL, ISAAK EMMANUILOVICH

(1894-   ), Russian short story writer, was born in the Moldavanka district of Odessa, a picturesque "kingdom within a kingdom, steeped in poverty and crime, and defiant of police and sanitary regulations." When Isaak was three, his family moved to Nikolaiev, but the pogroms of 1905 forced them to flee for their lives and they returned to Odessa. Babel declares: "My father, a Jewish business man, made me study Yiddish, the Bible, and the Talmud. I had to study many branches of learning from morning to night. I would rest from all this at school—the Nicholas I Commercial Institute, a jolly, noisy, dissolute, polyglot establishment attended by the sons of foreign merchants, of Jewish brokers, Poles of noble extraction, Old-Believers, and a host of overgrown billiard players. During vacations we would spend our time at the harbor or playing billiards in Greek cafés, or drinking cheap Bessarabian beer in the Moldavanka. French was taught best of all. The teacher was a native of Brittany, and like all Frenchmen he had a gift for literature. From him I learned the classics by heart. I came in close touch with the French colony and at the age of fifteen began to write stories in French." By "classics" was meant above all Flaubert and Maupassant, and for two years the Russian boy wrote stories in French, *à la* Maupassant.

Babel studied social sciences in the Kiev gymnasium, and was graduated from the University of Saratov. "In 1915 I settled down in St. Petersburg. Here I had a tough time, for like all Jews I did not have the 'right of residence.' [All Jews were banned from the city.] I dodged the police and lived on Pushkin Street, in a cellar with a waiter who was always drunk. In 1916 I started making the rounds of editorial offices but was always turned away with the advice to become a shop assistant, to which I paid no heed. In 1916 I met Maxim Gorky. I owe everything to this meeting. Gorky printed my first stories in his magazine *Letopis* [*Annals*], November 1916 (for which I was arrested), and he taught me a number of important things. It turned out that these tolerable youthful essays owed their success merely to good luck. My further attempts met with failure and in general my writing was surprisingly poor. Gorky then sent me out among living people. From 1917 to 1924 it was my fortune to learn a lot. I was a soldier on the Roumanian front, afterwards worked in the Cheka and in the Commissariat for Education, served in the Northern Army against Yudenich and in the First Cavalry Army, worked in the Odessa Provincial Committee, as a reporter in Petersburg and Tiflis, and in an Odessa printing shop. Only by 1923 did I learn to express my thoughts clearly and concisely. I therefore set 1924 as the beginning of my literary career. That year, the magazine *Left* published my stories 'Salt,' 'The Letter,' 'Dolgushov's Death,' 'The King,' and others. Two years later I wrote my *Red Cavalry* and *Odessa Tales*." Since then Babel has written a few brilliant stories: "The Road" (1933), "Guy de Maupassant" (1934), "Awakening" (1934), and "Oil" (1935). His literary output has been small, yet extremely significant for its touching beauty and technical virtuosity. John Cournos finds in Babel's prose "the quality of pure poetry," and Mirsky says that many Russians know such stories as "The Letter" and "Salt" by heart and love to recite them aloud.

Babel's finest tales remain the *Story of My Dove-cote* (1925) and *Red Cavalry* (1926), thirty-four sketches depicting incidents in Budenny's Volhynia campaign in 1920. Babel, who served with Budenny's Red Cavalry, renders vivid, often violent, first-hand scenes of bravery and suffering. Babette Deutsch claims that "none of his contemporaries can match Babel for vigor, for speed, for the taut, strained character of his prose, for its lyricism. His style is as terse as algebra, and yet packed with poetry."

WORKS AVAILABLE IN ENGLISH TRANSLATION: Red Cavalry, 1929; Benia Krik, 1935.

ABOUT: Cournos, J. Short Stories Out of Soviet Russia; Kunitz, J. Azure Cities; London, K. The Seven Soviet Arts; Pozner, V. Panorama de la Littérature Russe Contemporaine; Reavey, G. & Slonim, M. Soviet Literature; Struve, G. Soviet Russian Literature; Books October 27, 1929; International Literature January 1933; Menorah Journal November 1928, March 1931; Saturday Review of Literature April 27, 1929.

*BACHELLER, IRVING (September 26, 1859-   ), American novelist, writes: "I was born Irving Addison Bacheller in Pierpont, N.Y., a few miles from the St. Lawrence River and the edge of the Adirondack wilderness. It was a year of remarkable arrivals. Among them were Darwin's *Origin of Species* and spectrum analysis. Samuel L. Clemens began his work as 'Mark Twain' that year. Washington Irving passed away about the time of my birth and they seem to have thought that his name would be a help to me. For fear that it might not be enough, they coupled it with Addison.

Blackstone

"It was soon discovered that farm work and I had no high opinion of each other, and that I enjoyed reading and could learn rather easily. Some thought I would have to be a minister or a lawyer. All through my boyhood the curious characters of the countryside amused and interested me. I was immensely delighted with Dickens' *Great Expectations* when nearing my twelfth year.

"When I was thirteen I became the telegraph operator and kerosene clerk in a country store. We moved to the village for better schools. When they took me in at St. Lawrence University, I discovered that the Civil War was, in our countryside, being perpetuated by uncivil thinking. For that reason I founded the first chapter in the North of a firmly established Southern fraternity. It helped to wash the bloody shirt and was one of the best acts of my inglorious career.

"I graduated in 1882 and went to New York. To my surprise I learned that Mr. Dana did not need my help on the editorial page of the *Sun,* so I became a reporter. It was not a job I liked, but I got along with it. Late in 1884 I founded the first newspaper syndicate in America. I kept at it for twelve years with Kipling, Doyle, Anthony Hope, Stanley J. Weyman, Conrad, and many others contributing.

"In 1896 I sold out and began to write. My job was interrupted by a call from Joseph Pulitzer to join the editorial staff of the *World.* After a year and four months I got a leave of absence to finish *Eben Holden.*"

* * *

Mr. Bacheller is the son of Sanford Paul Bacheller and Achsa Ann (Buckland) Bacheller. In 1883 he married Anna Detmar Schultz. He received his M.S. degree from St. Lawrence in 1892 (honorary M.A. 1901), and has honorary doctor's degrees from his alma mater and from Middlebury College. He is a trustee of St. Lawrence and of Rollins College. In 1937 he received the medal for art from the Grand Masonic Lodge of New York State. He lives now in Winter Park, Fla., with a summer home in Riverside, Conn. He is a large, heavy man, still unbent by age, and still athletic in his eighties. He has a heavy white moustache and his white hair is still abundant. He is well known as an after-dinner speaker and orator, and is fond of singing old-fashioned ballads.

Eben Holden, the best known of his novels, was a best seller in its day. His work is full of humor and of keen observation, especially of rural types. He appears frequently in the magazines with humorous or semi-philosophical articles.

PRINCIPAL WORKS: *Novels*—The Master of Silence, 1890; The Still House of O'Darrow, 1894; Eben Holden, 1900; D'ri and I, 1901; Darrel of the Blessed Isles, 1903; Vergilius, 1904; Silas Strong, 1906; The Hand-Made Gentleman, 1909; The Master, 1910; Keeping Up With Lizzie, 1911; Charge It, 1912; The Turning of Griggsby, 1913; Marryers, 1914; The Light in the Clearing, 1917; Keeping Up With William, 1918; The Prodigal Village, 1920; In the Days of Poor Richard, 1922; The Scudders, 1923; Father Abraham, 1925; Dawn —A Lost Romance of the Time of Christ, 1927; The House of the Three Ganders, 1929; A Candle in the Wilderness, 1930; Uncle Peel, 1933; The Harvesting, 1934; The Oxen of the Sun, 1935; The Winds of God, 1941. *Biography and Autobiography*—A Man for the Ages, 1919; Opinions of a Cheerful Yankee, 1926; Coming Up the Road, 1928; A Boy for the Ages, 1937; From Stores of Memory, 1938.

ABOUT: Bacheller, I. Opinions of a Cheerful Yankee, Coming Up the Road, From Stores of Memory; Hanna, A. J. A Bibliography of the Writings of Irving Bacheller; American Magazine July 1925.

BACON, Mrs. JOSEPHINE DODGE (DASKAM) (February 17, 1876-), American novelist and juvenile writer, was born

in Stamford, Conn., the daughter of H. Sawyer Daskam and Anne (Loring) Daskam. She was graduated from Smith College in 1898. In 1903 she married Selden Bacon; they have two daughters and a son. Many of her early stories were written

Kesslere

under her maiden name. She lives now in New York, spending the winters in Florida. For ten years she was an active member of the National Girl Scout Executive Committee, edited the *Girl Scout Magazine* (now the *American Girl*), and also edited the official handbook publications of the Girl Scouts. Her twin interests, she writes the editors of this volume, are public health service and amateur theatricals; the latter she engages in during the summer at the Onteora Club in the Catskills. In 1935 she won the League of Nations Association prize for an international hymn by an American poet written to the first sixteen bars of Beethoven's "Ode to Joy"; her song was entitled "Hymn for the Nations."

The Madness of Philip, a story about a discontented Fresh Air Fund street urchin who returned to the city with a thankful, "Gee! N'Yawk's the place!" written shortly after her graduation from college, made her known as the creator of a new satirical style and of a humorous treatment of the child in fiction. *Smith College Stories,* is still being read year after year by enthusiastic freshmen. *The Memoirs of a Baby,* a satire on modern methods of child training, became a best seller and is on the shelves of many young parents today. A recent novel for adults, *The Root and the Flower,* is a three-generation novel of American women. In 1901 she compiled an anthology of nonsense verse.

PRINCIPAL WORKS: *Adult Fiction*—The Imp and the Angel, 1901; Fables for the Fair, 1901; The Madness of Philip, 1902; Whom the Gods Destroyed, 1902; Middle Aged Love Stories, 1903; Poems, 1903; Memoirs of a Baby, 1904; Her Fiancé, 1904; The Domestic Adventurers, 1907; An Idyll of All Fools' Day, 1908; In the Border Country, 1909; Margarita's Soul (as "Ingraham Lovell") 1909; Biography of a Boy, 1910; The Inheritance, 1912; The Strange Cases of Dr. Stanchon, 1913; The Luck o' Lady Joan, 1913; Today's Daughter, 1914; Open Market, 1915; On Our Hill, 1918; Square Peggy, 1919; Blind Cupid, 1923; Truth o' Women, 1923; Medusa's Head, 1926; Counterpoint, 1927; Kathy, 1933; Cassie-on-the-Job, 1936; The House by the Road, 1937; The Root and the Flower, 1939; Down in the Closet, 1940; The World in His Heart, 1941. *Juvenile*—Sister's Vocation and Other Girls' Stories, 1900; Ten to Seventeen, 1908; While Caroline Was Growing, 1911; Luck of Lowry, 1931; The Girl in the Window, 1932; The Room on the Roof, 1934; Girl Wanted! 1938.

ABOUT: Delineator November 1921.

*BACON, LEONARD (May 26, 1887-),

American poet and critic, Pulitzer Prize winner in poetry, was born in Solvay, N.Y., of a family long distinguished in American history. Delia Bacon, who founded the Bacon-Shakespeare theory, was his great-aunt; the family is not, however,

* Died January 1, 1954.

related to Francis Bacon himself. Mr. Bacon was educated at St. George's school, Newport, R.I., and at Yale (B.A. 1900).

He became instructor in English at the University of California in 1910, and resigned as full professor in 1923. (There was an interruption in 1917 and 1918 when he was a second lieutenant assigned to duty in San Diego and Washington, and another when a nervous breakdown forced his retirement for a year.) He has spent much of his life in Europe, and has lived all over the United States, but has finally returned to his ancestral home, in Peace Dale, R.I. In 1912 he married Martha Sherman Stringham, and they have three daughters. Since 1923 he has done no teaching, but has devoted his time entirely to writing.

Lean and blond, he looks like a cross between a champion tennis player and a college professor. John P. Marquand has remarked on his "positive personality," which is another way of saying that Mr. Bacon is highly opinionated, and occasionally wrongheaded. On the other hand, he is occasionally brilliant, and always full of vigorous life. As Marquand said, he is "a man of the so-called 'privileged' class who has dealt cheerfully and sensibly with his life." Another critic, who noted his "wit, learning, and nimbleness of mind," called him "the man of letters in the truest sense of the words."

This characterization is applicable to him both as poet and prose writer. (He is a constant book reviewer and essayist on literary topics, principally for the *Saturday Review of Literature.*) He describes himself as "a comic poet." This must be taken in the classical sense; he is not a humorist, but a satirist, an enemy of his time, though more in a nagging than in a grand manner. He was awarded the Pulitzer Prize in 1941 for *Sunderland Capture,* one of his least considerable accomplishments.

PRINCIPAL WORKS: Ulug Beg, 1923; Ph.D.'s, 1925; Animula Vagula, 1926; Guinea Fowl and Other Poetry, 1927; The Legend of Quincibald, 1928; Lost Buffalo, 1930; The Furioso, 1932; Dream and Action, 1934; The Voyage of Autoleon, 1935; The Goose on the Capitol, 1936; Rhyme and Punishment, 1936; Bullinger Bound, 1938; Semi-Centennial, 1939; Sunderland Capture, 1940.

ABOUT: Bacon, L. Semi-Centennial; Poetry July 1937; Current Biography June 1941; Publishers' Weekly May 10, 1941; Saturday Review of Literature March 25, 1939, May 10, 1941.

BAGNOLD, ENID, English novelist, writes: "I am the only daughter of Col. Arthur Henry Bagnold, C.B., C.M.G., and of Ethel (Alger) Bagnold. My brother, Major Ralph Bagnold, who won the Royal Geographical Society's Gold Medal for his expeditions across the sand sea in the Libyan Desert, has written a book called *Libyan Sands,*

and is a world authority on sand particles and dune formation. We two children were taken to Jamaica for some years in our childhood, when my father was Commanding Royal Engineer there, and my childhood up to the age of twelve was passed in garrison towns. At twelve I went to school at Priors Field, Godalming, a school owned by the mother of Julian and Aldous Huxley, and there I stayed till seventeen, when I went to Switzerland (a school from which I ran away), to Paris, and to Marburg. At nineteen I went to Walter (now Richard) Sickert's school of drawing and painting, and later etched with him alone for a year. At this period I made a number of friends whose names have since become known: Gaudier-Brzeska, Lovat Fraser, Katherine Mansfield, Ralph Hodgson.

"When the war broke out in 1914 I went as a V.A.D. into the Royal Herbert Hospital, Woolwich, and at the end of the two years' work there I wrote what does not now seem a very critical little book, *A Diary Without Dates.* I was immediately sent away from the hospital for a breach of military discipline. Later I joined the F.A.N.Y. (a romantic organization which first came to life in the Boer War), and with a small unit I was sent to join the French Army as a driver. Attached to a garage of a hundred French men drivers, our unit led the isolated and rather fantastic life of a dozen men in a boat. With this unit as the war ceased (and it ceased almost as I was crossing to France), I was swept up with the French armies as the Germans rolled back, and joined in the wild moments of the entry into Metz of General Pétain. A very short time later I was the first woman to be sent as driver to Verdun, and stayed two nights in a cubicle in the subterranean passages. It took me the following year to write a novel of my experience, *The Happy Foreigner.*

"In the spring of 1920 I met my future husband, Sir Roderick Jones, chairman of

Reuter's News Agency. I met him, but was then on the point of leaving for Vienna with the Society of Friends. I went to Vienna but he characteristically continued by cable conversations already begun in London; I returned, and we were married in the early summer, and went to Canada for our honeymoon, to the Imperial Press Conference held there that year.

"We now have a daughter and three sons. My daughter, Laurian Jones, illustrated *Alice and Thomas and Jane* when she was eight, and *National Velvet* when she was thirteen. When not at our London house, we live in the village of Rottingdean, near Brighton, in a house that used to belong to Sir Edward Burne-Jones, and we own a second house just across the road in which Rudyard Kipling lived and wrote for twenty years."

* * *

Though she has never acknowledged it, it has been an open secret almost from the beginning that Lady Jones was the author of *Serena Blandish,* by 'A Lady of Quality,' which sprightly narrative was a great success in 1925, and three years later was dramatized by S. N. Behrman and became a hit on Broadway. In fact, as late as 1929, Ernest Boyd thought 'Enid Bagnold' was still another pseudonym of this versatile author! *National Velvet,* her best known novel, is the story of a race horse, and *The Door of Life* a revealing but never mawkish tale of approaching motherhood. Her recreations, she says, are riding and "showing children's ponies." She is noted in London society for her classic beauty.

PRINCIPAL WORKS: A Diary Without Dates, 1917; Sailing Ships (poems) 1918; The Happy Foreigner, 1920; Serena Blandish: or, The Difficulties of Getting Married (anonymous) 1925; Alice and Thomas and Jane (juvenile) 1930; National Velvet, 1935; The Squire (in America: The Door of Life) 1937.

ABOUT: Behrman, S. N. Three Plays (see Preface); Ede, H. S. Savage Messiah; Mansfield, K. Novels and Novelists; Newsweek May 4, 1935, October 3, 1938; Revue Politique et Littéraire August 1939.

BAILEY, HENRY CHRISTOPHER (February 1, 1878-   ), English detective story writer, writes: "I am a Londoner born and bred and by habit; the only son of Henry and Jane (Dillon) Bailey. I married in 1908 Lydia Haden Janet, daughter of Alexander Haden and Catherine Guest, Manchester; we have two daughters. I went to school in London, to University College, Oxford, and was a classical scholar at Corpus Christi College, Oxford,

winning First Class Classical Honours and also being coxswain of the college boat.

"While at Oxford—or, rather, on a vaca-tion—I wrote my first novel, *My Lady of Orange*, which, falling into the hands of the late Andrew Lang, got published in England and the United States of America while the author was still an undergraduate. This was historical, and a series of historical novels followed, among them *Springtime, The Sea Captain, The Fool,* and *Knight at Arms.*

"On leaving Oxford I joined the staff of the *Daily Telegraph,* London, and at various times have been its dramatic critic, one of its war correspondents, and (now) leader writer.

"During the war, as a relief, I began to write detective stories and created Mr. Fortune, now well known on both sides of the Atlantic, in half a dozen languages besides English, and recognized as one of the few immortals of crime and detection. Mr. Fortune's cases are now not only in many anthologies but even in school books.

"In 1930 I produced another expert in crime, Joshua Clunk, who has now almost equal fame."   * * *

Bailey is generally named as one of the "Big Five," the mythical "inner circle" of British detection writers. Plump, drawling Reggie Fortune leaped into popularity as one of the leading sleuths of the "naturalistic" school of detective fiction which followed the close of the World War, and has retained his position for nearly two decades. *Cognoscenti* have pointed out that many of his mannerisms crop up again in "S.S. Van Dine's" more austere Philo Vance. Contrary to the general trend away from the short story in detective fiction, most of the Fortune cases have appeared in that form. Clunk, however, has so far appeared only in novels.

Stephen Vincent Benét has said: "Of all the fictional detectives, perhaps Mr. Reginald Fortune comes nearest to the dream of all good detective story readers."

PRINCIPAL WORKS: Karl of Erbach, 1902; Gentleman of Fortune, 1907; Colonel Greatheart, 1908; God of Clay, 1908; Storm and Treasure, 1910; The Lonely Queen, 1912; The Sea Captain, 1913; Forty Years After; The Story of the Franco-German War, 1914; Gentleman Adventurer, 1915; The Highwayman, 1916; Call Mr. Fortune, 1920; Mr. Fortune's Practice, 1922;

Knight at Arms, 1925; Mr. Fortune's Trials, 1926; Mr. Fortune, Please, 1926; The Fool, 1927; The Young Lovers, 1929; The Merchant Prince, 1929; The Garston Murder Case, 1930; Mr. Fortune Speaking, 1930; Judy Bovenden, 1930; Mr. Fortune Explains, 1931; Mr. Cardonnel, 1932; The Red Castle Mystery, 1932; A Case for Mr. Fortune, 1932; The Shadow on the Wall, 1934; The Sullen Sky Mystery, 1935; Mr. Fortune Objects, 1935; A Clue for Mr. Fortune, 1936; Mr. Fortune's Case Book, 1936; The Twittering Bird Mystery (in England: Chunk's Claimant) 1937; Black Land, White Land, 1937; This Is Mr. Fortune, 1938; The Great Game, 1939; Mr. Clunk's Text, 1939; Mr. Fortune Here, 1940; The Bishop's Crime, 1941; Orphan Ann, 1941; The Apprehensive Dog, 1942; Meet Mr. Fortune: A Reggie Fortune Omnibus, 1942.

ABOUT: Haycraft, H. Murder for Pleasure: The Life and Times of the Detective Story; Thompson, H. D. Masters of Mystery; Literary Digest April 20, 1935.

*BAILEY, TEMPLE (188?-), American

popular novelist and writer of short stories, was born in Petersburg, Va., of Massachu-

setts ancestry, the daughter of Milo Varnum Bailey and Emma (Sprague) Bailey. She was christened Irene Temple Bailey. Her childhood was spent in Washington, D.C., where she now makes her home at the Wardman Park Hotel, and which is the scene of one of her better novels, *Fair As the Moon.* She was educated at private schools in Richmond, Va., and also took some special collegiate courses. *Judy,* her first book, published in 1907, was a book for girls, and these young women and their daughters constitute her principal reading public. Miss Temple's novels are frequently serialized in women's magazines of large national circulation, and she has been called the highest-paid writer in the world. In 1933 *McCall's Magazine* paid her $60,000 for a serial, and *Cosmopolitan Magazine* commissioned three serials and from five to ten short stories, paying $325,000 for the lot. Miss Bailey is unmarried; a Republican; a Presbyterian; and a member of the Chevy Chase and Arts clubs in Washington, as well as of the Authors' Club in Boston. She seldom grants interviews.

Harris C. Ewing

Of Miss Bailey's work in general, the New York *Times* once commented: "Whatever may be the secret of the popularity of these innocuous, virginal novels, the fact of their popularity is unquestioned." It is esti-

mated that at least three million of her books, including reprints, have been sold, and her readers must be reckoned at many millions more, since nearly half these sales are made to circulating libraries. Temple Bailey was John Wanamaker's favorite author; whenever a new novel was published he always ordered 150 to 200 copies to give to friends. The Wanamaker stores are the best single outlet for the Temple books, which also sell well in Boston, and in the South and Far West. Miss Bailey writes her serials as they are published, though she confesses that she disapproves of the method. She prefers to write short stories, considering them her most artistic work. She has always wanted to write a sequel to *Contrary Mary,* but is afraid that stories of young married people are out of her *métier,* which is the idealistic presentation of young love.

PRINCIPAL WORKS: Judy, 1907; Glory of Youth, 1913; Contrary Mary, 1915; Mistress Anne, 1917; Adventures in Girlhood, 1917; The Tin Soldier, 1919; The Trumpeter Swan, 1920; The Gay Cockade, 1921; The Dim Lantern, 1923; Peacock Feathers, 1924; The Holly Hedge, 1925; The Blue Window, 1926; Wallflowers, 1927; Silver Slippers, 1928; Burning Beauty, 1929; Wild Wind, 1930; So This Is Christmas, 1931; Little Girl Lost, 1932; Enchanted Ground, 1933; The Radiant Tree, 1934; Fair As the Moon, 1935; I've Been to London, 1937; Tomorrow's Promise, 1938; The Glory of Youth, 1938; The Blue Cloak, 1941.

ABOUT: Overton, G. M. The Women Who Make Our Novels; Publishers' Weekly June 24, 1933; Saturday Evening Post November 15, 1919; Saturday Review of Literature April 11, 1936.

BAKELESS, JOHN EDWIN (December 30, 1894-), American editor and biog-

rapher, was born at Carlisle, Pa., the son of Oscar H. and Sara (Harvey) Bakeless. After attending the State Normal School at Bloomsburg, Pa., he proceeded to Williams College, receiving the degree of B.A. in 1918. In June 1920 Mr. Bakeless was granted a master's degree by Har-

vard University and was married to Katherine Little of Bloomsburg. During the First World War he was commissioned a second lieutenant of infantry, in 1918, and was assigned as instructor to the Central Officers' Training School at Camp Lee. Making the best of both wars, *in esse* and *in posse,* Mr. Bakeless's first two books were *The Economic Causes of Modern War* (1921) and *The Origin of the Next War* (1926). *Maga-*

zine Making, the third, was written out of practical experience primarily for his classes in journalism at New York University, where he has been lecturer, 1927-28, instructor, 1929-30, and assistant professor since 1930. Mr. Bakeless edited the *Living Age* in 1928-29 after an apprenticeship of five years (1921-25) as literary editor and managing editor. He also was managing editor of the *Forum* in 1926-28, and literary adviser to the *Independent,* now deceased, for a year.

Christopher Marlowe: The Man in His Time, which the *Saturday Review of Literature* called a full-blooded book, useful, important, and almost exemplary, was the result of years of study at Harvard as a graduate student (1919-26) and trips abroad to examine all other existing documentary evidence concerning the Elizabethan playwright whose short, full life and mysterious death have fascinated so many investigators. Seven months in England, in 1936-37, on a Guggenheim Fellowship, enabled Mr. Bakeless to turn up seven new documents relating to Marlowe or his immediate family. (At Harvard he was the only man since the Bowdoin Prizes were established over a century ago to take the Graduate Bowdoin Prize in two successive years, one year in literature, the next in biology. Other men have won the prize twice, but the joker in the successive-years' feat is that the prize is awarded one year in humanities, the next in science.)

The same freshness of data and interpretation is evident in *Daniel Boone: Master of the Wilderness,* which in large measure supplants the hitherto standard study by Reuben Gold Thwaites.

Mr. Bakeless, who writes in a brisk, breezy style, is physically also an alert, rapidly-moving person, with thick hair and a moustache, a distinctive voice, and a long-established habit of seeking surcease from his own investigations in the doings of Colonel Gore, Roger Sheringham, Lord Peter Wimsey, and Hercule Poirot.

PRINCIPAL WORKS: The Economic Causes of Modern War, 1921; The Origin of the Next War, 1926; Magazine Making, 1931; Christopher Marlowe: The Man in His Time, 1937; Daniel Boone: Master of the Wilderness, 1939.

ABOUT: Christian Science Monitor November 3, 1937; London News-Chronicle, January 26, 1937; Key Reporter (Phi Beta Kappa Society) Autumn 1938; N.Y.U. Alumnus April 1938; Scholastic January 8, 1940; Wilson Library Bulletin April 1940.

BAKER, Mrs. DOROTHY (DODDS) (April 21, 1907-   ), American novelist, writes: "I was born in Missoula, Mont.

My father, Raymond Dodds, was chief division dispatcher for the Northern Pacific Railroad, and my mother, Alice Dodds, was very good at dry fly casting. So I went around with my mother and caught a lot of trout. And then, though I was against it, we moved to California and my father went into the oil business and my mother took up fancywork and I went to school, through grammar school, high school, and parts of three colleges. I was good in grammar school, very good in high school, but practically worthless in college. After it was over I went to France. This was in the days when practically everybody was either a writer or going to be. We took a ninety-nine-year lease on a very fine apartment and I started a novel; but I wasn't too sure what the novel was going to be about and it didn't get any clearer as it progressed, and so I finally convinced myself that it might be better just to call the whole thing off. And then after a while we came back to the United States, ninety-nine-year lease notwithstanding, and settled down in Berkeley, Calif., where my husband (Howard Baker) got a job teaching English in the university. I went back to school out of force of habit and got myself an M.A. in the French department, and then worked for three years in a private school teaching Latin. I liked the Latin and the students, and there was a new magazine just starting up in California, so I wrote a story about teaching Latin in a private school, and sent it off, and after some hesitation the magazine took the story and published it. This slight encouragement was all it took to make me write another story, and when I very unexpectedly sold that too, I began to think of myself as a writer, and after that happened it was no time at all until I quit my job and took to writing in what must be called dead earnest.

"My first novel was published in 1938. A couple of Broadway producers thought it would make a good play and got me to try my hand at adapting it for the stage. I spent more than a year working on some six versions, but I never quite wrote what was wanted, and so the play was never produced.

But the time wasn't wasted, exactly, because I learned some things about how not to write a play. Some time I would like to try another one, but at the moment I feel safer with fiction.

"When I first began to write I was seriously hampered by an abject admiration for Ernest Hemingway, and I found that the only way I could grow up and get over it was simply to quit writing any direct discourse. I didn't allow myself any quotation marks until I felt confident that I could write, for good or ill, my own stuff. On the other hand I have very deliberately studied and have been influenced by the non-fiction method of Otis Ferguson. In fiction I admire above all else simplicity and clarity in both phrase and story. My greatest advantage as a writer has been the constant chastening criticism of two very strict poets, Howard Baker and Yvor Winters."

* * *

Mrs. Baker is now living in Cambridge, Mass., where her husband teaches at Harvard University. They were married in 1930, and have one child, born in 1940. In 1935 she won a Houghton Mifflin Fellowship for creative writing. Her undergraduate college work was done at Whittier College, University of California at Los Angeles (B.A. 1928), and Occidental College (B.E. 1930). Her highly praised first novel, *Young Man With a Horn* is based on the life of Leon (Bix) Beiderbecke, the swing musician.

PRINCIPAL WORK: Young Man With a Horn, 1938.

ABOUT: Life August 8, 1938.

BAKER, GEORGE PIERCE (April 4, 1866-January 6, 1935), American university professor and writer on drama and the

D. Keller

theatre, was born in Providence, R.I., the son of Dr. George Pierce Baker and Lucy Daily (Cady) Baker. Graduating from Harvard College in 1887, he stayed on to teach English next year, forensic from 1889 to 1892, and English again from 1892 to 1895. He was made a full professor in 1905 and remained till 1924, giving his celebrated courses, English

47 and 47a. The 47a Workshop attracted fledgling playwrights from all over the country, finding here the instructor of their most ambitious dreams and an opportunity to try out experimental plays which no commercial manager would consider. These plays, presented, mounted, staged, and acted by Baker's students, were given at Agassiz House, Radcliffe College, the feminine annex to Harvard. Edward Sheldon's *Salvation Nell,* produced and successfully played by Mrs. Minnie Maddern Fiske, was the first important boxoffice success to emerge from Professor Baker's play-writing course. His many students included, among others, Eugene O'Neill, Philip Barry, S. N. Behrman, Sidney Howard, Robert Edmond Jones, John V. A. Weaver, John Mason Brown, Rachel Field, and Thomas Wolfe—who put him into *Of Time and the River* as Professor Hatcher. The school, always a more or less unwanted stepchild at Harvard, moved in 1925 to vastly superior quarters at Yale University. Professor Baker became professor of the history and technique of the drama at the newly organized department of drama, and director of the University Theatre donated by Edwin S. Harkness, which was formally opened December 10, 1926. With a fully equipped plant and a staff of competent assistants Baker gave courses in play writing, stage designing, costuming, lighting, criticism and pageantry—he wrote and directed *The Pilgrim Spirit* in July-August, 1921, for the Massachusetts Tercentenary Pageant at Plymouth. Baker retired in 1933 as head of the department and was succeeded by Walter Prichard Eaton. In 1893 he married Christina Hopkinson of Cambridge, and they had four sons. Professor Baker received honorary degrees from Williams, Yale, and Delaware. He was a man of patrician appearance, but had warmth, humor, and some New England idiosyncrasies. *Dramatic Technique* is his best-known book.

PRINCIPAL WORKS: The Principles of Argumentation, 1895; The Development of Shakespeare as a Dramatist, 1907; Dramatic Technique, 1919; Specimens of Argumentation (ed.) 1893; Forms of Public Address, 1904; Some Unpublished Correspondence of David Garrick, 1907; Charles Dickens and Maria Beadnell: Private Correspondence, 1908; Plays of the 47 Workshop: I-IV, 1918-1925; Modern American Plays, 1920; Yale One-Act Plays, 1930.

ABOUT: Brown, J. M. & others. George Pierce Baker; Brown, J. M. Broadway in Review; New York Times January 7, 1935; Scholastic January 26, 1935; Theatre Arts Monthly July 1933, February 1935.

*BAKER, RAY STANNARD (April 17, 1870-), American journalist, Pulitzer Prize winning biographer, and essayist, who

writes both under his own name and as "David Grayson," was born in Lansing, Mich., the son of Joseph Stannard Baker and Alice (Potter) Baker. When he was still a child, Baker's family moved to the border-line of northern Wisconsin, at a time when Indians still scoured the plains. The boy became familiar with the rough life of the pioneer, and acquired the rudiments of his education at a back-woods school. At nineteen he received a B.S. degree from Michigan State College (augmented by an honorary LL.D. in 1917). After leaving college in 1889, he took a partial law course and studied literature at the University of Michigan. From 1892 to 1897 he was a reporter and sub-editor of the Chicago *Record,* where he became interested in the life and problems of the under dog. In January 1896 he married Jessie I. Beal; they have two sons and two daughters. For relief from the newspaper grind, Baker took solitary walks in the country, where he made "casual contacts with unvarnished strangers." His imaginative writing was done at night, and the consequent stories in *Century* and the *Youth's Companion* attracted the attention of John S. Phillips, editor of *McClure's Magazine.* He wrote to Baker to come to New York, and there Baker remained from 1898 on, managing the McClure Syndicate and for six years serving as associate editor of the magazine. For it Baker wrote crusading articles which investigated railroad management, the Negro problem, and the "Spiritual Unrest." McClure sent him around the world by way of the Trans-Siberian Railway; he was halted at Vienna, however, and sent to Constantinople to assist in the rescue of an American woman held by bandits.

Blackstone

In 1906 Baker joined in the purchase of the *American Magazine,* and was one of its editors until 1915. In 1910 he made the acquaintance of Woodrow Wilson, then governor of New Jersey, which resulted in his later designation by the World War President to be the posthumous editor of his papers. The monumental *Woodrow Wilson: Life and Letters* appeared in eight volumes from 1927 to 1939 and received, as an entity,

the Pulitzer Prize for biography in 1940, less than a month after its editor's seventieth birthday.

Soon after going to the *American,* Baker began his double life as himself and as "David Grayson," keeping the secret of the authorship of *Adventures in Contentment* (1907) and subsequent books intact not only from his reading public but even from the illustrator of the books, Thomas Fogarty, for almost a decade. "It is difficult to think of any precise precedent for this mixture of essay, philosophy, homely observation and quiet humor with its essentially American pattern of thought," wrote Grant Overton. "The febrile character of much American life was already marked, and the remedy of an equally feverish optimism had yet to be widely prescribed. The time was propitious, the sentiment of David Grayson had an ingratiation." Baker himself has said: "I have written more than one book and many an article that was pure toil, but every word of the Grayson books was written for the sheer sense of release and joy which the writing gave me." The secret of their authorship was revealed in the *Bookman* in its issue for March 1916 after Baker had been amused and annoyed by impostors who had claimed to have written the books, and who had even lectured under the Grayson name. The essays and sketches have been translated into several foreign languages, so that Horace and his Harriet and the Scotch Preacher have sown their wholesome platitudes widespread.

Mr. Baker today makes his home at Amherst, Mass., where he is a trustee of the Jones Library. He is also a member of the National Institute of Arts and Letters, the American Historical Association, Phi Beta Kappa, and the Century Club in New York City.

PRINCIPAL WORKS: Seen in Germany, 1901; Following the Color Line, 1908; The Spiritual Unrest, 1910; What Wilson Did at Paris, 1919; The New Industrial Unrest, 1920; Woodrow Wilson and World Settlement: A History of the Peace Conference, 1922; Woodrow Wilson: Life and Letters, 1927-39. *Editor*—The Public Papers of Woodrow Wilson (with W. E. Dodd) 1925-6; Native American: The Book of My Youth (autobiography) 1941. *As "David Grayson"*—Adventures in Contentment, 1907; Adventures in Friendship, 1910; The Friendly Road, 1913; Hempfield, 1915; Great Possessions, 1917; Adventures in Understanding, 1925; Adventures in Solitude, 1931; The Countryman's Year, 1936.

ABOUT: Baker, R. S. Native American; Overton, G. M. American Nights Entertainment; Bookman March 1916; Mentor October 1925; Publishers' Weekly May 11, 1940; Saturday Evening Post January 13, 1940; Saturday Review of Literature May 11, 1940.

* Died July 12, 1946.

BALDWIN, FAITH (October 1, 1893-), American novelist, writes: "Was born in New Rochelle, N.Y.  My father, Stephen C. Baldwin, a well-known trial lawyer, was born in China, where his parents had been missionaries for twenty-six years. Much of my family history I've told in *American Family*. We moved to Brooklyn when I was seven and there I lived mostly until a few years ago. Was educated at various schools in Brooklyn and at Mrs. Dow's in Briarcliff. Was in Germany from 1914 to 1916. Came home and did War Camp Community Service work at Camp Upton. Was married to Hugh H. Cuthrell in 1920 and have four children: two boys and two girls, including boy and girl twins. Some years ago decided I wanted to live in the country, bought a farm in Connecticut which has plenty of ancient elm and apple trees, and an old white farmhouse which had to be comfortably modernized—named the place Fable Farm.

"Have traveled a good bit—been in almost every state in the Union, in Hollywood often on business, and in 1939 made my second visit to Hawaii and my first to Australia and New Zealand. Like to spend my summer vacations along the St. Lawrence. Loathe all violent exercise except swimming and love to explore the woods. Also love gardens, flowers, sunshine, other people's books, book-collecting, beautiful Chinese things, and people. Am a constant reader of all kinds of books. Books have been meat and drink to me, they have been comfort and help, stimulus and narcotic. Would rather read than eat or sleep; and, confidentially, I'd much rather read books than write them.

"Have had sixty books published, besides many articles, stories, poems, and what not in various magazines and newspapers. I began to write (a drama, *The Deserted Wife*, which still exists in a copybook) at the age of six, my first poems appeared in the *Christian Advocate* when I was eleven, and I wrote my first novel, *Alimony*, while doing war work."

* * *

Faith Baldwin is small, blue-eyed, and vivacious. She is distinctly a "circulating library" novelist, writing light sophistication mixed with "sugary sentimentality," but she has a story-telling gift which keeps her work

interesting. She types her own manuscripts, fast but inaccurately, and "slaves and suffers over her work." She now ranks next to Kathleen Norris in her field, both in prolificness and in financial returns. She says she "would rather be a biologist, an obscure scientist, an actress, a doctor, an explorer" than a novelist. Nevertheless, though her work may be ephemeral, its present popularity is assured.

PRINCIPAL WORKS: Mavis of Green Hill, 1921; Laurel of Stony Stream, 1923; Sign Posts (verse) 1924; Magic and Mary Rose, 1924; Thresholds, 1925; Those Difficult Years, 1925; Three Women, 1926; Departing Wings, 1927; Alimony, 1928; Garden Oats, 1929; Broadway Interlude (with A. Abdullah) 1929; The Office Wife, 1930; Make-Believe, 1930; Skyscraper, 1931; Today's Virtue, 1931; Judy, 1931; Babs and Mary Lou, 1931; Myra, 1932; Week-End Marriage, 1932; District Nurse, 1932; Self-Made Woman, 1932; Girl-on-the-Make (with A. Abdullah) 1932; White-Collar Girl, 1933; Beauty, 1933; Love's A Puzzle, 1933; Honor Bound, 1934; Innocent Bystander, 1934; American Family, 1935; The Puritan Strain, 1935; The Moon's Our Home, 1935; Private Duty, 1936; Men Are Such Fools! 1936; This Man Is Mine, 1936; The Heart Has Wings, 1937; Twenty-Four Hours a Day, 1937; Manhattan Nights, 1937; The High Road, 1937; Enchanted Oasis, 1938; Rich Girl, Poor Girl, 1938; Hotel Hostess, 1938; Career by Proxy, 1939; White Magic, 1939; Station Wagon Set, 1939; Rehearsal for Love, 1940; "Something Special," 1940; Medical Center, 1940; And New Stars Burn, 1941; Two Different People, 1941; Temporary Address: Reno, 1941; The Heart Remembers, 1941; Blue Horizons, 1942; Breath of Life, 1942.

ABOUT: Time July 8, 1935; Writer May 1940.

BALFOUR, ARTHUR JAMES, 1st Earl (August 25, 1848-March 19, 1930), English philosophic and political writer and statesman, was born in Scotland but of English parents—James Maitland Balfour and Lady Blanche Cecil, daughter of the Marquess of Salisbury. From Eton, where his lifelong dilettante attitude gave him the nickname of "Nancy," he went to Trinity

Underwood

College, Cambridge; he was the later recipient of numerous honorary degrees. He entered politics in 1868, as Member of Parliament from Hartford, and continued in the House of Commons from one constituency or another until he was created Earl of Balfour in 1922. In spite of his apparent indolence he speedily became, first a leader, and then *the* leader of the Conservative Party. In the course of his long career he was Chief Secretary for Ireland (where his land policy caused him to be known as "Bloody Balfour"), First Lord of the Treasury, First Lord of the Admiralty, Foreign Secretary, Lord President of the Council, and, from 1902 to 1905, Prime Minister. He headed the British Mission to the United States in 1917, and the British Mission to the Washington Conference in 1921. He was the author of the policy by which the Jews obtained (at least the promise of) a "national home" in Palestine, and he was a powerful influence at the Versailles Conference.

In all these activities he remained a diehard Tory, the last of the old aristocratic "gentlemen in politics." His indecision and apparent indolence, and his unshakeable conviction that his class was foreordained to govern the world, earned him many enemies. Opposed to them he had many admirers, but few warm friends. He never married. His avocations were impersonal—music and tennis, which he played assiduously at eighty.

It is as a philosopher that he is of chief interest in the history of literature. His mind was original if not profound, and he had enormous skill at dialectic. His magnetism and brilliance are reflected in his books, which are never dull though they are now neglected. In philosophy he was opposed to the doctrine of Naturalism, and held that man is differentiated from other animals, not by his possession of reason, but by his submission to authority. As Lord Ponsonby said, he was "quite unable to master the fact that character in the long run tells more than brains. His standard was intellectual." But Algernon Cecil is kinder, if no less just, in saying that than Balfour's there was "no mind more subtle, no manner with greater charm, no learning more lightly carried."

More even than the Order of Merit, Balfour valued his election to the presidency of the British Academy. It was the crowning honor of one who had been the chief spirit half a century before of the "Souls," that coterie of aristocrats who cultivated the garden of their minds and never allowed the weeds of later-day thought to threaten the fine flower of their culture.

PRINCIPAL WORKS: A Defense of Philosophic Doubt, 1879; Essays and Addresses, 1893; The Foundations of Belief, 1895; Economic Notes on Insular Free Trade, 1903; Reflections Suggested by the New Theory of Matter, 1908; Speeches on Fiscal Reform, 1906; Criticism and Beauty, 1909; Theism and Humanism, 1915; Essays, Speculative and Political, 1920; Theism and Thought, 1923; Opinions and Argument, 1927.

ABOUT: Dugdale, B. E. C. Arthur James Balfour; Hapgood, N. Literary Statesmen; Malcolm,

I. Z. Lord Balfour: A Memory; Rayleigh, R. J. S. Lord Balfour in His Relation to Science; Raymond, E. T. Mr. Balfour; Ward, W. D. Ten Personal Studies; Christian Century April 9, 1930; Current History April 1930; Literary Digest April 5, 1930; Nation April 2, 1930; Nation (London) March 29, 1930; Saturday Review March 22, 1930; Saturday Review of Literature December 6, 1930.

BANG, HERMAN JOACHIM (April 20, 1857-January 29, 1912), Danish novelist, poet and critic, was born on the island of

Zealand near Schleswig, the son of a pastor. His parents, of a noble and ancient Danish family, were obliged to leave home during the Danish-German war of 1864. Recollections of his childhood played a large part in Bang's early work. He was educated at the Academy of Sorö and at Copenhagen, becoming a journalist. From 1884 on he was chief correspondent of the newspaper *National-Tidende*. A burst of literary activity four years before, when he was twenty-three, produced two volumes of criticism (essays on the realistic movement in literature), and a first novel, *Haablöse Slaegter* (Families Without Hope). The novel showed the first manifestations of a vigorous and original talent for studying the everyday life of ordinary people in remote corners of his country. Bang often returned to this theme, to show behind the peaceful events of daily life the tragedy of existence. *Stuk* (Stucco) in 1887, was a satire on the speculation and chicanery rife in great cities (one is reminded of Gilbert Cannan's *The Stucco House*), and rather scandalized the citizenry of Copenhagen. *Tine*, two years later, sketched with delicate psychology the story of a village girl, against a powerfully imagined succession of battle scenes of the Danish-German war. Bang's passionate women are always more convincing than his men, who show only halfhearted desire or a sullen resignation. *Tine* won Bang the friendship of Ibsen, as well as the enthusiastic admiration of Jonas Lie, whom Bang had also admired and to some extent imitated, and gave him a place in the front rank of Scandinavian novelists. His second novel, *Faedra* (1883) revived the ancient tragic legend against a modern setting, employing the same theme that inspired Racine and gave Sarah Bernhardt her most famous role in classic French tragedy,

Phèdre. These first novels displayed ardent sensuality and a supersensitive contemplation of self; Bang frequently selected as his protagonist a young man of distinguished family who was tired of the pleasures of life. He himself had a face of romantic interest in young manhood, with a large nose, chiseled mouth and thick hair cut straight across his forehead. Emil Ludwig calls him, in *Genie und Charakter* (the essay does not appear in the English translation, *Genius and Character*) "Schauspieler und Regisseur, Journalist und Rezitator, Kosmopolit und Abenteurer," and farther on, "Weltmann und Aristokrat." His poetry displayed sympathy, occasional morbidity, but humor and bohemian gayety. Bang died suddenly while on an American lecture tour. His own most picturesque imaginings probably did not envisage a death in Ogden, Utah, at sixty-four.

WORKS AVAILABLE IN ENGLISH TRANSLATION: Denied a Country (De Uden Faedreland) 1927; Ida Brandt (Ludrigsbakke) 1928.

ABOUT: Bang, H. K. Ti Aar (recollections); Fog, F. Les Littératures Danoise et Norvegienne d'Aujourd'hui; Ludwig, E. Genie und Charakter; Rosenberg, P. A., Hermann Bang, Nordische Portraits.

BANGS, JOHN KENDRICK (May 27, 1862-January 21, 1922), American humorist,

was born, lived all his life, and died in Yonkers, N.Y. He was the son of Francis N. Bangs, president of the New York City Bar Association, and Amelia (Bull) Bangs, and his paternal grandfather had been the president of Wesleyan University.

He was graduated from Columbia (Ph.B. 1883), and for a year studied law, but instead of being admitted to the bar he became in 1884 associate editor of *Life.* In 1888 he joined the staff of *Harper's Monthly* and remained with it until 1899, when he became editor of another Harper magazine, *Literature.* During his last years he spent most of his time in traveling through the country as a humorous lecturer. He was an active Democrat, unsuccessful candidate for mayor of Yonkers in 1894, president of the Halsted School in Yonkers, vice-president of the town's Board of Education, a vestryman of the Episcopal Church, and, rather incongruously, director of a gas company. In 1886 he married Agnes Lawson; three of their children survived infancy.

This is the record of a typical small town American of the latter half of the nineteenth century, and that, despite his long years in New York during office hours, was just what Bangs was. He belonged to a period later than that of "Artemus Ward" and "Josh Billings," and he outlived his own period—that of James Whitcomb Riley—and saw his reputation eclipsed by the rising George Ade and the young Ring Lardner. The little wizened, bald-headed man who made fun of his own appearance was a very popular lecturer, but in retrospect his lectures were not very funny, and they were almost offensively "moral." "Genial" is the damning word most frequently applied to him.

Yet Bangs was a genuine humorist, who merely wrote too much, so that his more solid performances are hidden by the mass of trivialities. At his best he was really amusing—who can forget, for example, the man who far from being afraid of ghosts frightened *to life* the specter which came to haunt him, so that a large heavy man took the place of the sheeted apparition? The "Idiot," the dead celebrities of the house boat, and the enchanted typewriter had their moments, too.

It is easier to say what Bangs was not, as a humorist, than what he was. He was not a parodist, or a nonsense-writer, or a delver into the psyche of the illiterate as was "Josh Billings," for example. His was the wit of the lecture room and the croquet-ground. His best known character was the "Idiot," who is merely all of us in our absent-minded moments. The "House Boat" books were lighthearted burlesques on history, somewhat in the vein of Mark Twain's "diaries" of Adam and Eve. His books pretend only to be entertaining, and they are. Nothing of his work will live, but it was harmless, and had a good deal more point than much that passed for humor in one of the dreariest eras of American comic writing.

PRINCIPAL WORKS: Katharine: A Travesty, 1887; Mephistopheles, 1888; Tiddledywink Tales, 1891; In Camp With a Tin Soldier, 1892; Coffee and Repartee, 1893; Toppleton's Client, 1893; The Water Ghost, 1894; Mr. Bonaparte of Corsica, 1895; The Idiot, 1895; A House Boat on the Styx, 1895; The Pursuit of the House Boat, 1897; Ghosts I Have Met, 1898; The Enchanted Typewriter, 1899; Echoes of Cheer (verse) 1912; Foothills of Parnassus (verse) 1914; From Pillar to Post, 1914; Half Hours With the Idiot, 1917; The Cheery Way (verse) 1920.

ABOUT: Bangs, F. H. John Kendrick Bangs: Humorist of the Nineties; Review of Reviews March 1922; National Education Association Journal March 1925.

BANNING, Mrs. MARGARET (CULKIN) (March 18, 1891-   ), American novelist, writes: "I was born in Buffalo, Minn.,

the daughter of William Edgar Culkin and Hannah Alice (Young) Culkin. I received my B.A. at Vassar in 1912, a certificate from the Chicago School of Civics and Philanthropy in 1913, and in the same year was

Pinchot

a Research Fellow of the Russell Sage Foundation. I am a member of Phi Beta Kappa. I was married in 1914 to Archibald Tanner Banning, of Duluth, Minn. We had two daughters (one deceased) and two sons (one deceased). I am a trustee of the St. Paul Institute of Science, of Vassar College, and of the Duluth Public Library. I am ex-president of the Duluth Branch of the American Association of University Women. I am a Republican and a Catholic. I live and vote in Duluth, but have a cottage in the woods of Wisconsin and a house in Tryon, N.C. I write everywhere, but my office overlooks Lake Superior, and there I work on a schedule of seven hours a day. I am widely traveled and have had the unusual experience of being abroad at the outbreak of three wars—in London in 1914, in San Sebastian at the commencement of the Spanish Revolution, and in Paris at the time of the first mobilization in 1939."

* * *

Mrs. Banning is a markedly pretty woman, with a broad intellectual forehead and the wavy dark hair and blue eyes of her Irish ancestry. Though she is classed by Katharine Fullerton Gerould among the writers of "fiction created by woman writers for women readers," she is a cut above the usual run of this variety. She has wit and she has a genuine interest in social problems which gives substance to her novels. She is a frequent contributor of stories and serials to the women's and the general magazines, also writes articles and reviews for the *Saturday Review of Literature,* and is frequently heard on broadcast programs.

PRINCIPAL WORKS: Half Loaves, 1921; Spellbinders, 1922; Country Club People, 1923; Handmaid of the Lord, 1924; Women of the Family, 1926; Pressure, 1927; Money of Her Own, 1928; Prelude to Love, 1929; Mixed Marriage, 1930; The First Woman, 1932; The Third Son, 1933; The Iron Will, 1935; Letters to Susan, 1936; Too Young To Marry, 1938; You Haven't Changed, 1938; Out in Society, 1940; Enough To Live On, 1940; Salud! A South American Journal, 1941; A Week in New York, 1941; Women for Defense, 1942.

ABOUT: Writer March 1940.

"BARBELLION, W. N. P." See CUMMINGS, B.

BARBER, MARGARET FAIRLESS ("Michael Fairless") (May 7, 1869-August 24, 1901), English nature-writer and mysticist, was born at Castle Hill, Rastrick, in the West Riding of Yorkshire, the daughter of Fairless Barber and Maria (Musgrave) Barber. She read Scott and Dickens before twelve and fraternized with frogs; later pets in-

cluded Jacob, a French bulldog, Phoebe, a magnificent orange Persian, and Trilby, another cat who looked like "a depressed charwoman." For a time she was a nurse, known as The Fighting Sister, in one of London's worst slums, the Jago [*cf.* Arthur Morrison's *A Child of the Jago*]. A spinal weakness had developed in her girlhood and she became a semi-invalid in a roadside country cottage, the lodge of an empty and decaying house and park, with a decrepit old woman and a mentally deficient girl for maids. She gave food, patches, and thread to tramps, who marked her gateposts with safety signs against other tramps. She also lived in an old Georgian house on the Chelsea Embankment in London, where she made a crucifix (in 14th century style) which is in St. John the Baptist's Church in Pimlico Road.

The Roadmender, "Michael Fairless's" famous devotional book, was written during the twenty months in bed that preceded her death at thirty-two; it was serialized in *The Pilot.* Her pen-name was derived from a childhood friend, later Sir Michael McDonnell, Chief Justice of Palestine, and from her father. The fresh beauty and mystical tone of the book appealed to workmen and queens alike. Posthumously published, as were all her books, it went through thirty-one impressions in its first decade; a first edition now fetches ten pounds. The last chapter was dictated on her deathbed, after nine days of starvation. Her body was taken from Mock Bridge, a Sussex farmhouse near Henfield, to the little churchyard at Ashurst near Steyning. "Michael Fairless" was very tall, witty, with a fair complexion, much brown hair and very large eyes. She never married.

PRINCIPAL WORKS: The Gathering of Brother Hilarius, 1901; The Roadmender, 1902; The Grey Brethren, 1905; Complete Works, 1932.

ABOUT: Barber, M. F. Complete Works (see Biographical Note by M. E. Dowson); Palmer, W. S. & Haggard, A. M. Michael Fairless: Her Life and Writings.

BARBUSSE, HENRI (May 17, 1874-August 30, 1935), French novelist and essayist, was born in Asnières (Seine) but  was only half French, his mother being an Englishwoman. His father was a journalist and dramatist, a political liberal and a Free Thinker. In early childhood Barbusse was taken to England for several years, but so young that he soon forgot all the English he had learned. His formal education was at the Collège Rollin in Paris. He began his writing career as a journalist on the *Petit Parisien* and the *Écho de Paris,* where his early essays and a youthful volume of verse (*Fleureuses,* 1895) attracted the attention of the French-Jewish writer Catulle Mendès. Barbusse became Mendès's literary protégé, and in time his son-in-law. By 1910 Barbusse was editor of the magazine, *Je Sais Tout.*

The gentle, idealistic young man, full of a rather vague pacifism, author of three tragic novels (notably *L'Enfer,* 1908), was completely transformed by the World War. At the time he subscribed to all the dogmas of his time and place; he believed sincerely that the war was a struggle of democracy against militarism, and he was eager to take his part. He was none too strong physically, however, this tall, rangy, English-looking Frenchman, and at first he was put into the auxiliary forces. He persisted until he was sent to the front as a private in the Territorial Army.

Barbusse saw service in some of the heaviest fighting of the early part of the war. He was never wounded—though a bullet once went through his cap—but he was three times invalided out for dysentery, the third time permanently. He received three citations for bravery, specifically for saving wounded comrades under fire. After his third illness he stayed in Paris working in the censorship department.

Out of his war experience came his best known novel, the tremendous indictment of war named *Le Feu* (known in English as *Under Fire*) which received the Prix Goncourt in 1917, just when it was being refused publication in America (a decision that was hurriedly reversed!). Gradually Barbusse's mild pacifism hardened into political and economic radicalism. With the Russian Revolution and the formation of the Third International he became a Communist, and so remained, through all developments and vicissitudes, for the remainder of his life. Though he wrote other novels and stories, he became increasingly engrossed in the production of propagandistic books and manifestoes. At the time of his death he was planning a huge "collective novel" which was to demonstrate a new type of fiction appropriate to a revolutionary milieu.

Barbusse organized in 1932 the first World Congress against War and Fascism, and the next year he spoke in New York at the second Congress. He served for fifteen years or more as correspondent of *L'Humanité,* the French organ first of the Socialist and then of the Communist movement.

Utterly fearless, he ran every risk with intrepidity in his revulsion against war, which to him was the mainspring of his radical beliefs. He was no mere dreamer, but essentially a practical organizer, who not only wrote books but also formed associations like the Republican Association of Ex-Service Men in France and its international counterpart elsewhere in Europe, with the avowed aim of "making war on war." Only once was he brought before a criminal court, and that was in 1923 on a charge of having urged French soldiers not to march against the German people; he was acquitted because the speech had been made not in France but in Germany!

Barbusse died where he would have wished—in Moscow, in the Kremlin Hospital. He had gone as a delegate to the seventh Congress of the Third International, and had there contracted pneumonia.

With the possible exception of *All Quiet on the Western Front, Under Fire* is the most powerfully realistic of the novels to come out of the World War, among those written by contemporaries and combatants. It has had a tremendous effect in the past and its influence is not yet spent. Though its author grew to be less and less of a "literary man" in the "ivory tower" sense, still even the most special of his pleadings are written with grace and persuasiveness. He was not perhaps among the first rank of writers of his era, but he was unmistakably gifted. Whether Barbusse wrote of Jesus, Zola, or Stalin, no reader could mistake the fact that he was reading the work of a man of letters in the best traditions of French culture. Henri Barbusse will be remembered primarily, however, as one of "the terrible meek" whose impassioned protests against brutality and injustice may some day help to civilize warring humanity.

PRINCIPAL WORKS AVAILABLE IN ENGLISH TRANSLATION: Meissonier, 1912; Under Fire, 1917; We Others, 1918; The Inferno, 1918; Light, 1919; Creed of a Fighter, 1920; Chains, 1925; Jesus, 1927; I Saw It Myself, 1928; One Looks at Russia, 1931; Zola, 1933; Stalin, 1935.

ABOUTS Living Age November 1935; Nation September 3, 1938; Saturday Review of Literature September 23, 1939.

BARCLAY, Mrs. FLORENCE LOUISA (CHARLESWORTH) (December 2, 1862-March 10, 1921), English novelist, was

born in the rectory at Limpsfield, Surrey, the daughter of the Rev. Samuel Charlesworth, a reserved man who had been married late in life. He moved his family to a parish in the Limehouse district of London when Florence was seven. At seventeen she went to Belstead to visit friends, and there met the Rev. Charles W. Barclay. They were married in March 1881 at St. Anne's Church, Limehouse, and spent a honeymoon of four months in Palestine. Mrs. Barclay was kept busy with parish duties and with bearing and raising two sons and six daughters at Little Amwell Vicarage, Hertford-Heath, Hertford, Hertfordshire. In 1909 she toured the Chautauqua circuit in the United States with her sister, Mrs. Ballington Booth, lecturing on "Palestine and the Bible." In 1905 she had been laid up for nine months with an overstrained heart, caused by an overlong bicycle ride, and to while away the time wrote her second and sensationally successful romance, *The Rosary. The Wheels of Time,* her first book, was published in September 1908. Mrs. Booth offered the manuscript of *The Rosary* to Putnam's, and the novel appeared simul-

taneously in London and New York in 1909. By the time of Mrs. Barclay's death in 1921 it had sold over a million copies. She came again to the United States in 1910 to receive a royal welcome and witness the publication of *The Mistress of Shenstone,* which was filmed with Pauline Frederick. In 1912 Mrs. Barclay received a blow on the head; a cerebral hemorrhage threatened to put an end to her writing, but another opportune accident, when she was hit on the head by an oar while boating on the lake at Keswick, restored her productivity. Much of her royalties went to support her numerous charities. Her later years were spent at the Corner House, Overstrand, Norfolk. Her husband resigned the living after Mrs. Barclay had died at fifty-eight under an anesthetic, preparatory to an operation which it was hoped would relieve the continuous internal pain she had suffered for some years. She was an attractive woman, with masses of dark brown, later silvered, hair and a rich contralto voice. One of her daughters wrote her biography, in which she said that her mother "wrote for ordinary readers who asked merely to be pleased, rested, interested, and amused."

She had skill, J. C. Squire once admitted. "Nobody else can write a silly story half so well as she. Her English is fluent and vivid, although loose; her humor is genuine if not subtle; and she handles dialogue, such as it is, very cleverly. But above all, she knows how to serve out the glamour and the pathos with a ladle." "Though on all sides the blood rains down in torrents," he concluded, "love's interests still are in safe hands with Florence." *The Broken Halo,* recommended to Norman Douglas as "the worst novel ever written," concerns, as he says, "a penniless agnostic youth who marries a bewitching and pious creature on the wrong side of sixty." The situation is chastely handled, for Mrs. Barclay could "damp the glowing embers of the flesh with an aptly-chosen quotation from Nehemiah or Habakkuk."

PRINCIPAL WORKS: The Wheels of Time, 1908; The Rosary, 1909; The Mistress of Shenstone, 1910; The Following of the Star, 1911; Through the Postern Gate, 1912; The Upas Tree, 1912; The Broken Halo, 1913; The Wall of Partition, 1914; My Heart's Right There, 1914; In Hoc Vince, 1915; The White Ladies of Worcester, 1917.

ABOUT: Douglas, N. Experiments; Florence L. Barclay: By One of Her Daughters; Squire, J. C. Books in General: First Series.

*BARING, MAURICE (April 27, 1874-), English novelist, essayist, and poet, writes: "I was born in London in 1874. I went first

to two preparatory schools and then to Eton College, which I left when I was seventeen. I then went abroad to study languages, to Germany first and then to Italy. In 1893 I went to Trinity College, Cambridge University, for a year, and after that I again went abroad and studied languages. I passed the examination into His Majesty's Diplomatic Service in 1898 and was appointed *attaché* to the British Embassy in Paris in 1899. While I was at Paris I published a book in French of parodies of French authors, called *Hildesheim*. In 1900 I was transferred as Third Secretary to Copenhagen and in 1902 to Rome. I stayed there a year and was then transferred to the Foreign Office in London.

"In 1904 I decided to abandon the diplomatic career and to take up journalism. I had by that time published only two books of verse, *The Black Prince* and *Gaston de Foix*, in 1902 and 1903. I had spent some time in Russia and had learned the Russian language well enough to speak it, so that when the Russo-Japanese War broke out in 1904 and I proposed to the editor of the *Morning Post* that I should go out as their correspondent he accepted me. I went out in 1904 and stayed in Manchuria till the winter of 1905. I went back again in 1905 just before peace was concluded, and when I returned from the front to Moscow a general strike had broken out all over the country. From that time until 1912 I spent most of my time in Russia, writing a weekly article for the *Morning Post* on Russian affairs for the first three years. In 1909 I went as special correspondent for the *Morning Post* to Turkey. In 1912 I went round the world and in October I went as *Times* special correspondent for the Balkan War.

"In 1914 when the World War broke out I was given a commission in the Intelligence Corps and transferred to the Royal Flying Corps, where I was on the staff of the first Little Flying Corps which went out to France from England, consisting of four squadrons. I remained in the Flying Corps till the end of the war, and from 1915 to 1918 I acted as personal secretary to General Trenchard.

"In 1919, when the war was over, I began to write novels. Before this I wrote a volume of reminiscences called *The Puppet Show of Memory*. My best known novels are *C, Cat's Cradle, Daphne Adeane,* and *Tinker's Leave*. Besides novels, I have written books on Russia, plays, short stories, fairy tales, and books of verse, serious and light. The novels have been translated into many languages, *Daphne Adeane* into nearly every European language, including Catalan, Czech, and Hungarian."

* * *

Mr. Baring's modest account of himself omits much. He is the fourth son of the first Lord Ravelstoke, and is a devout convert to the Roman Catholic Church. In the Air Force in the First World War he was a major and wing commander. He is a Chevalier of the French Legion of Honor. With Hilaire Belloc he edited the *North Street Gazette*, which ran to only one, but that one a distinguished, issue. He is a man of immense erudition; his style is sober and leisurely. His novels for the most part treat of the diplomatic and social circles with which he has been most familiar. William Lyon Phelps said of him: "He is one of the most brilliant of contemporary men of letters; original, learned, wise, witty, humorous, tender, sympathetic, whose published works show an extraordinary versatility. . . He combines honor with reverence, passionate loyalty with outrageous mirth."

PRINCIPAL WORKS: *Novels*—A Triangle, 1923; C, 1924; Cat's Cradle, 1925; Daphne Adeane, 1926; Tinker's Leave, 1927; The Coat Without Seam, 1929; Roger Peckham, 1930; In My End Is My Beginning, 1931; Friday's Business, 1933; The Lonely Lady of Dulwich, 1934; Darby and Joan, 1936. *Poetry*—The Black Prince, 1902; Gaston de Foix, 1903; Collected Poems, 1918 and 1920; Selected Poems, 1930. *Miscellaneous*—The Russian People, 1911; Diminutive Dramas, 1911; The Mainsprings of Russia, 1914; The Puppet Show of Memory, 1922; Half a Minute's Silence, 1925; Comfortless Memory, 1928; Algae: Anthology of Phrases, 1928; Lost Lectures: or, The Fruits of Experience, 1932; Sarah Bernhardt, 1934; Unreliable History, 1934; Have You Anything To Declare? 1936.

ABOUT: Baring, M. The Puppet Show of Memory; Chaundy, L. Bibliography of First Editions of the Works of Maurice Baring; Los Vergnas, R. Chesterton, Belloc, Baring; Smyth, E. M. Maurice Baring; Bookman August 1932, November 1932; Catholic World November 1939; Commonweal August 14, 1929, August 30, 1935; Harper's Magazine May 1939.

BARING-GOULD, SABINE. See "BRITISH AUTHORS OF THE 19TH CENTURY"

* Died December 14, 1945.

BARKER, GRANVILLE-. See GRAN-VILLE-BARKER

BARLOW, JANE (1857-April 17, 1917), Irish poet, critic, and chronicler of peasant life, was born at the sea village of Clontarf, County Dublin, the daughter of the Rev. James William Barlow, Vice Provost of Trinity College, Dublin, and Mary Louisa (Barlow) Barlow. Her whole life was spent in the environs of Dublin. The excellence of her later scholarship was good evidence of the thoroughness with which she had been educated at home; and she received an honorary degree from Trinity College.

Thomas William Rolleston, who in the new *Dublin University Review* gave W. B. Yeats his first appearance (1884) in print, "discovered" Jane Barlow two years later and issued the first of her *Bogland Studies,* published in book form in 1892. In this collection of tales-in-verse she had full command of the idiom of the Irish peasant, who as narrator served a function similar to that of the chorus in the old Greek plays.

Sir William Robertson Nicoll believed that Jane Barlow had genuinely captured the pathos of poverty and suggested that as a creative artist she might be able to do for Ireland what Barrie had done for Scotland. She welcomed his advice, and the first of the *Irish Idylls* ("One Too Many") appeared in the *British Weekly.* Through the book ran a quiet and steady humor, but the portraiture was less satisfying, less earth-sprung than that of her Scottish model. She published more than a dozen titles—largely tales and verse in the Irish vein—during twenty years of writing; and her very last sketch, "Rescues," appeared in the *Saturday Review* only ten days before her death, at sixty.

Miss Barlow was slight of build; although never strong physically, she delighted in long tramps through the Dublin and Wicklow Mountains. She died of an illness which had developed during an extremely cold winter.

She appears to have had no alliance with the bolder and more realistic Irish writers of her day: her work, as Lord Morley suggested, lacked "the sullen and harsh element that always strikes one as a substratum in so much of Irish life and character." Swinburne praised her *Ghost Bereft,* a book of poems, and contended, moreover, that one of her tales outdid Victor Hugo. Stephen Gwynn finds a diffuseness in her verse, but credits her with a learned mind and predicts that her poetry will "not always be neglected."

PRINCIPAL WORKS: Bogland Studies, 1892; Irish Idylls, 1892; Kerrigan's Quality, 1893; Maureen's Fairing, 1895; Strangers at Lisconnel, 1895; Ghost-Bereft, 1901; By Beach and Bog Land, 1905.

ABOUT: Gwynn, S. Irish Literature and Drama; Irish Book Lover June, July 1917.

BARNES, DJUNA, American poet, playwright, and miscellaneous author, was born in Cornwall-on-the-Hudson, N.Y., the daughter of Wald and Elizabeth (Chappell) Barnes. She was educated at home and received some of her first pay-checks from New York newspapers. Djuna Barnes was one of the original members of the Theatre Guild; for a while wrote a column

for its *Magazine*; and was briefly associated with the *Little Review.* She was among those lesser-known playwrights for whom the famous Provincetown Players provided an extraordinary kind of market: during the fall of 1919 and the spring of 1920 they produced her "Three From the Earth," "An Irish Triangle," and "Kurzy of the Sea."

One of her earliest appearances in print was *The Book of Repulsive Women,* issued in November 1915 as a Bruno Chap Book (small fifteen-cent monthlies edited by Guido Bruno "in his garret on Washington Square, New York"). Shortly afterward several of her pieces were accepted by *All-Story Weekly* and the *Dial*; and somewhat later, by *Smart Set.* In 1923 came *A Book,* a potpourri of stories, plays, and verse; and in 1925 she was represented in the *Contact Collection of Contemporary Writers,* a sampling of "works in progress," published in Paris by the Three Mountains Press. *Ryder,* a volume of explosive prose, appeared in 1928 in a heavily expurgated American edition. Djuna Barnes is also the author of the anonymous and privately published *Ladies' Almanack.* In 1936 she published a psychological study (*Nightwood*) of five fantastic people living in Paris. It is ostensibly a novel, but one of her critics referred

to it as a kind of "vicarious confession."
It has a "decay," some said, that is reminiscent of Oscar Wilde or Walter Pater
(with "due modern improvements in frankness"), but almost every reviewer acknowledged Miss Barnes' uncommon skill in the
manipulation of words.

Miss Barnes has always been a writer for
"advanced" and special groups, a person
about whom legends are told but who has
been little known to the general reading
public. She is averse to publicity and says,
"my memory is as bad as Montaigne's."
Alfred Kreymborg has referred to her as
the "Junoesque Djuna Barnes." She draws
well, has illustrated several books, including
a number of her own, and has a great fondness for horses. In her twenties she went
to Europe and until recent years has spent
most of her life in Paris, where she became
a friend of Gertrude Stein, and in the south
of France. She is living currently in New
York, but expects some day to return to
Europe; she has a house on Old Church
Street, Chelsea, and considers London her
permanent home.

T. S. Eliot, in his introduction to the
American edition of *Nightwood*, credited her
with "the great achievement of a style, the
beauty of phrasing, the brilliance of wit and
characterization, and a quality of horror and
doom very nearly related to that of Elizabethan tragedy." With this estimate Edwin
Muir agrees, asserting that her writing is
"more felicitous, the more painful the theme
she is dealing with.... Her vision is purely
tragic, with that leavening of sardonic wit
which comes from long familiarity with
tragedy.... Hers is the only prose by a living
author which can be compared with that of
Joyce, and in one point it is superior to his:
in its richness in exact and vivid imagery,
... inevitable and inventive at the same
time.... Her imagination is sensuous and
intellectual; drawn from the hidden, and reinforced by worldly knowledge.... Her
prose has the closeness and precision of poetry yet is a workable prose medium."

In spite of such encomiums, most of her
books have had no popularity, and reviewers
have tended either to ignore them or to rate
them as showy, obscure, and eccentric *tours
de force*.

PRINCIPAL WORKS: The Book of Repulsive
Women, 1915; A Book, 1923 (reprint, with additions, as A Night Among the Horses, 1929);
Contact Collection of Contemporary Writers, 1925;
Ryder, 1928; Nightwood, 1936.

ABOUT: Barnes, D. Nightwood (see Introduction by T. S. Eliot); Deutsch, H. & Hanau, S.
The Provincetown: A Story of the Theatre;
Kreymborg, A. Troubadour; Muir, E. The
Present Age From 1914; Stein, G. The Autobiography of Alice B. Toklas.

BARNES, HARRY ELMER (June 15,
1889-   ), American historian and sociologist,
writes: "I was born on a farm near Auburn,
N.Y. My father was
a prison official and
later superintendent
of a boys' school near
Erie, Pa. After graduating from Port Byron High School in
1906, I studied engineering by correspondence and
worked two years as
a bridge engineer.
The next year I taught school at Montezuma,
N.Y. I then entered Syracuse University,
working my way through college in a drug
store, and as shipping master for a cannery
in summer. I graduated from Syracuse in
1913 at the head of my class, and continued
to study and teach there until 1915, getting
my M.A. in 1914. I received a Ph.D. in history from Columbia in 1918, spending the
previous year in research work at Harvard.
I became a lecturer in history at Columbia
in 1917, professor of history at Clark University in 1920, professor of historical sociology at Smith College in 1923 (at the same
time being professor of economics and sociology *ad interim* at Amherst from 1923
to 1925). I was lecturer in education at
Teachers' College, Columbia, in 1937-38.

"My writings have been mainly in the
fields of cultural history, criminology and
penology, and the history of sociology. In
cultural history I was mainly influenced by
James Harvey Robinson, and edited a posthumous volume of his best essays. In 1917-
18 Dwight Morrow engaged me to investigate New Jersey penal institutions. Probably
the book which stirred most interest here
and abroad was my *Genesis of the World
War*, which destroyed the myth of sole German guilt. But my critical writings against
Hitler have ended my former popularity in
Germany. Much excitement was stirred by
my address as vice-president of the American Association for the Advancement of
Science in 1928, on "Science vs. Religion."
My *Twilight of Christianity* was not 'a defense of atheism' but has been called the
most important critical appraisal of religion
since Paine's *Age of Reason*.

"In 1929 I resigned from Smith College
to enter the editorial department of the

Scripps-Howard newspapers. I remained in this work until 1940. While my experience in journalism was interesting and illuminating it was also disillusioning.

"In politics, I have been a liberal, but I have recently been disillusioned by the stupidity of the liberals in repeating their folly of 1917 by supporting war. My current political philosophy is very fluid and uncertain, but I am sure I shall never again espouse the liberal cause. For that matter, the war is likely to end all liberalism."

* * *

Dr. Barnes married L. Grace Stone in 1910; they had one son. After a divorce he married Jean Hutchison Newman in 1935. Besides his own works, he has edited numerous volumes of history and sociology. He has been called "a dynamo of intellectual energy," and the late Ernest Sutherland Bates said of him: "His very name arouses violent emotions of attraction or repulsion. . . . He is undoubtedly a fundamentally irreverent person. . . . There is something almost appalling in his omnivorous digestion of facts. No one, it is urged, could really have such encyclopedic knowledge, there must be a catch in it somewhere."

PRINCIPAL WORKS: Sociology Before Comte, 1917; Social History of the Western World, 1921; Progress of American Penology, 1922; Sociology and Political Theory, 1923; The New History and Social Studies, 1924; The Genesis of the World War, 1926; The Repression of Crime, 1926; History and Social Intelligence, 1927; An Economic and Social History of Europe (with M. M. Knight & F. Fluegel) 1927; Living in the Twentieth Century, 1928; In Quest of Truth and Justice, 1928; The Twilight of Christianity, 1929; The Making of a Civilization (with E. A. Dexter & M. G. Walker) 1929; World Politics in Modern Civilization, 1930; The Story of Punishment, 1930; Battling the Crime Wave, 1931; Can Man Be Civilized? 1932; Prohibition Versus Civilization, 1932; The Money Changers Versus the New Deal, 1934; History of Western Civilization (2 vols.) 1935; Intellectual and Cultural History of the Western World, 1937; A History of Historical Writing, 1937; Social Thought From Lore to Science (2 vols., with H. Becker) 1938; Society in Transition, 1939; Contemporary Social Theory (with H. Becker) 1940; Social Institutions, 1942.

ABOUT: American Mercury November 1939; Commonweal November 16, 1929, February 28 and March 6, 1936; Scholastic January 26, 1935; Virginia Quarterly Review October 1940.

BARNES, Mrs. MARGARET (AYER)
(April 8, 1886-), American novelist, writes: "I was born in Chicago. My father, Benjamin F. Ayer, was the General Counsel of the Illinois Central Railroad, and my mother, Janet (Hopkins) Ayer, was the daughter of James Hopkins, a judge on the Federal bench in Madison, Wis. Both my parents were born in the East, my father in Kingston, N.H.—he was a graduate of Dartmouth and of the Harvard Law School—and my mother in Granville, N.Y. They were both descendants of the English settlers who came to this country in the middle 1600's. My mother was a Colonial Dame. The youngest of five children, I had two older  brothers and two older sisters. My sister Janet is now the novelist, Janet Ayer Fairbank.[iv] I prepared for Bryn Mawr College at the University School for Girls in Chicago, concentrated in college in English and philosophy, and graduated with my class in 1907. Having returned to Chicago to live with my family, in 1910 I married Cecil Barnes, a lawyer, a graduate of Harvard College and of the Northwestern Law School. We have three sons. The two older boys are graduates of Harvard and the youngest is a junior there at this time.

"I began to write in 1926, after a motor accident in France, in which I broke my back. Up to that time it had never occurred to me to try to write professionally, and I wrote my first short stories merely to amuse myself in the long months I spent in plaster casts and spine braces. When I had recovered—for I did recover completely—a friend suggested that I try to sell one, and I offered a story to *Pictorial Review.* To my great surprise the editor bought it, and then, of course, I began to take my scribbling more seriously. I sold the other stories I had written eight of them in all, to various magazines, and in 1928 they were published in book form under the title *Prevailing Winds.*

"All my life I had been very much interested in the theatre, and about this time I tried my hand at three plays. The first was a dramatization of Edith Wharton's novel, *The Age of Innocence,* and it was produced by Katharine Cornell in 1928. The other two plays I wrote in collaboration with the experienced dramatist, Edward Sheldon: *Jenny,* which was produced by Jane Cowl in 1929, and *Dishonored Lady,* which was produced by Katharine Cornell in 1930.

"My first novel, *Years of Grace,* was published in 1930, and it was awarded the Pulitzer Prize in Letters for that year. Since then I have written four more novels, have contributed short stories to magazines, and done quite a little lecturing.

"I have lived in Chicago all my life, except for my four years as an undergraduate at Bryn Mawr College and the two years of the last war which I spent in Washington, D.C., but I spend my summers on Mt. Desert Island, in Maine. I think that the greatest influences in my life have been extensive reading, my college education, and love of nature, friends, and family—to which might be added the accident in France that turned me into a writer. I vote for the man in any party that seems to me the best candidate and consider myself a liberal but am not a New Dealer. I would also describe myself at the moment [1939] as a puzzled pacifist and certainly a determined isolationist. I did not think that we should enter the World War in 1917 and nothing that has happened since has led me to alter that opinion. My principal interests, in more normal times when the tragedy of war does not engulf our thoughts, are reading and writing, music and the theatre, and hill-climbing, camping, and cruising with my husband and our sons. I do not play games and I do not like night clubs and I have very little interest in formal social life. But friends mean a great deal to me and so does lively conversation."

* * *

Mrs. Barnes is a pretty, brown-eyed woman with clear skin and abundant dark hair. Though her novels are distinctly of the "woman's magazine" type, they are unpretentious, have charm and persuasiveness, and are among the best of their *genre*.

PRINCIPAL WORKS: Prevailing Winds (short stories) 1928; Jenny (play, with Edward Sheldon) 1929; Dishonored Lady (play, with Edward Sheldon) 1930; Years of Grace, 1930; Westward Passage, 1931; Within This Present, 1933; Edna His Wife, 1935; Wisdom's Gate, 1938.

ABOUT: Bookman February 1930; Literary Digest December 15, 1928; Pictorial Review August 1931.

BAROJA Y NESSI, PÍO (December 28, 1872-), Spanish novelist, writes: "I was born in San Sebastian, province of Guipuzcua. My father's name was Serafín Baroja y Zornoza. He was a mining engineer who had done some writing in Castilian and Basque. My mother's name was Carmen Nessi y Goñi; she came from Madrid. My father's family were originally noblemen; my mother's name is Italian, from Como in Lombardy. The earliest recollection of my life is the ineffectual bombardment of San Sebastian by the Carlists in 1875 or 1876. I have a faint recollection of

having been taken up from my bed one night in a blanket and carried to a châlet next to the shore. We went to live in the basement of the châlet. Upon this house fell three shells that smashed the ceilings and made a hole in our garden wall through which my brothers and I used to pass.

"From San Sebastian I went with my family to Madrid, where my father was attached to the Institute of Geography and Statistics; then he was transferred to Pamplona, within whose walls we lived as in time of war— but it was a very diverting town for a boy. This part of my life served as the background for several semi-autobiographical novels. From Pamplona I later returned to Madrid, where I began to study medicine; then, after five years, I followed my family to Valencia, where I finished my course. In 1893 I received my doctor's degree in Madrid. At that time I began to write articles in various periodicals.

"The municipal doctor's post in Cestona (Guipuzcua) was vacant; I was the only applicant for it and was given the post. I began to feel myself a Basque, and to pick up the thread of the race which was lost to me. After a year and a half of rural medicine I moved to San Sebastian with the intention of practicing there, but it was not profitable and I returned to Madrid, where I had the opportunity of renting a bakery with my brother. I was a baker for seven or eight years, struggling against economic difficulties. Later I tried a few other industrial and commercial ventures, and also a little journalism, without success. At twenty-six I went to Paris, and thence to Italy, Switzerland, Germany, and Holland, looking for work, but could find none. Finally I returned to my mother in Madrid and decided to dedicate myself to literature—which was like dedicating myself to fantasy, since I knew that literature was in Spain 'a means of living without a livelihood.'

"At the time I was a baker I knew and mingled with workers and poor people who lived miserably and frequented taverns and dives. It is from my knowledge of the low life of Madrid that I wrote the trilogy, *The Struggle for Life*.

"I have never married. For many years I lived in the winter in Madrid and in the summer in Vera de Bidasoa (Navarre), where I owned an old house that belonged to the family of Alzate. All my book collections and my own records are there now. I had never mixed in politics except for a few months in 1910, when I belonged to the republican party. I was in Vera de Bidasoa when I was surprised by the revolution of 1936. Out of foolish curiosity I went to see the rebel Carlist and Falangist troops enter Pamplona. They arrested me, were on the point of shooting me, imprisoned me at Santesteban, then freed me, and I was able to escape to France. I am living now in Paris.

"As an author I am not spacious, but I am original. My favorite modern authors have been Dickens, Poe, Balzac, Stendhal, and Dostoievsky. Of all these the one who influenced me most was Dostoievsky. I have not had great sales either in or outside of Spain."

* * *

For some time following the end of the Franco revolution, Señor Baroja's fate and whereabouts were unknown, until, in 1940, he wrote the preceding sketch from Paris. (His fortunes since the Nazi conquest are not known.) His exile seems to have been, as he describes it, purely due to an accident, since in 1937 he had published in the *Nación*, Buenos Aires, an article unstintingly condemning the Spanish Republic and expressing his hope for a Fascist dictatorship, as "the lesser of two evils." Yet he also says: "I am a man of liberal tendencies who believes always that everything of value in a country comes only from the obscure and despised masses." In any event, it is not likely that his books are now permitted circulation in Spain, since his unsparing picture of the wretchedness of the workers and peasants is an implicit condemnation of their exploitation, whatever personal views he may express in articles.

He has had many enemies among critics and writers in Spain—partly because he has been a Freethinker and anti-clerical, but mainly because of his literary style, which has been condemned as harsh and clumsy. It is so with deliberate intent: W. A. Drake has called it "acrid, economical to rigidity, almost brusquely direct. . . . His concern is ever with the idiom, never with the phrase. . . . Baroja does not know how to see, how to think, how to write, except honestly and sincerely." Perhaps he wrote his own epitaph when he said: "I pour out my spirit continually into the eternal molds without expecting that anything will result from it."

When José Ortega y Gasset wrote that Baroja "would never amount to anything," Baroja accepted the accusation calmly, saying that this was just what he had been told by everyone since he first went to school at the Institute of Pamplona!

He is a strange man, cynical, pessimistic, outspoken, almost alarmingly frank, "an unabashed reporter of depravity, corruption, and misery," with a *penchant* for characters drawn from "the lower depths." Yet under his profound pessimism is an idealization of "the divine element of humanity," a softness hidden beneath the crusty exterior. He himself remarked: "If Mephistopheles wanted to buy my soul, he could not buy it with a decoration or a title, but only if he promised me effusive sympathy and something sentimental." In appearance he is almost insignificant—small, bald, with a drooping moustache and a close-cropped gray (once yellowish) beard. He disarms his attackers by mildly accepting all their attacks and then stubbornly proceeding on his own way, just as he did before.

James Fitzmaurice-Kelly called Baroja "a deep-rooted pessimist," with "a strain of intense energy. . . He has much of Dickens' power of observation and gift of visualizing, but all of Dickens' blemishes: use of neologisms, . . . exaggerated vision." Ernest Boyd too called him "Dickens grown sardonic." Despite the discontinuity of his work, his love of melodrama, his "bad humor," his obsession for depicting the depths of human degradation, he remains nevertheless a great realist—"the best known, the most translated, and the least read novelist of contemporary Spain." Perhaps his greatest work is in the trilogy translated into English as *The Struggle for Life* (*La Lucha por la Vida*). (Nearly all his novels have been written in the trilogy form.) He has written twenty whole volumes also about one of his own ancestors, Eugenio de Aviraneta, a nineteenth century revolutionary and adventurer, under the general title of *Memorias de un Hombre de Acción* (*Memories of a Man of Action*). He has written a number of essays, many of them loosely autobiographical in tone; only one of these, *Youth and Egolatry* (*Juventud, Egolatría*), has been translated into English.

Some critics have attempted to evaluate Baroja in terms of his Basque ancestry. Samuel Putnam said of him: "He is frank, misanthropic, pessimistic, passionate, capricious—in other words, he is a Basque." But by his own statement his mother was a Madrileña and partly of Italian descent. It seems much more nearly accurate to say that he is, as he himself proclaims, an "original."

WORKS AVAILABLE IN ENGLISH: The City of the Discreet, 1917; Caesar or Nothing, 1919; Youth and Egolatry (non-fiction) 1920; The Struggle for Life (The Quest, 1922; Weeds, 1923; Red Dawn, 1924); The Lord of Labraz, 1926; The Tree of Knowledge, 1928; Paradox King, 1931.

ABOUT: Baroja y Nessi, P. Youth and Egolatry (see Introduction by H. L. Mencken), Rapsodías; Bell, A. F. G. Contemporary Spanish Literature; Boyd, E. Studies in Ten Literatures; de Casson, F. Panorame de la Littérature Espagnole; Dos Passos, J. Rosinante to the Road Again; Drake, W. A. Contemporary European Writers; Madariaga, S. de. The Genius of Spain; Pino, F. Pío Baroja (in Spanish); Reid, J. T. Modern Spain and Liberalism; Trend, J. B. A Picture of Modern Spain; Bookman (London) September 1931; Living Age September 15, 1929; Nineteenth Century September 1925; Revue Politique et Littéraire December 19, 1936.

BARR, Mrs. AMELIA EDITH (HUDDLESTON). See "AMERICAN AUTHORS: 1600-1900"

BARR, ROBERT (September 16, 1850-October 21, 1912), British-American novelist, journalist, detective story writer, and

wit, was born in Glasgow, came to Canada when he was four, and was eventually enrolled in the Normal School, Toronto. Until 1876, the year of his marriage to Eva Bennett, he served as headmaster at a public school in Windsor. Shortly afterwards he entered the States and became a reporter on the Detroit *Free Press*, and is said to have rifled mail bags, crossed a river on ice floes, and run a revolver gauntlet—all in pursuit of news.

In 1881 he sailed for England and edited a British edition of the *Press*. By 1892 he was anxious to start something of his own, and took on Jerome K. Jerome (instead of Kipling, believing that Jerome would be easier to "manage") as a partner. The *Idler* (1892-97) was a boon to the reading public, and, until a libel suit brought against Jerome's weekly *To-day* washed him out financially, proved a godsend to its owners. To the famous *Idler* "at-homes" came Ramsay MacDonald, Gilbert Parker, Anthony Hope, Arthur Conan Doyle, and many others.

Barr's published volumes (almost a score) were largely light tales and extravagant ro-

mances. He was "a born story teller," and the public eagerly gobbled his ephemeral works—only to forget them almost immediately. He would be virtually unknown today except for the presence in detective story anthologies of some of the adventures from his *Triumphs of Eugène Valmont*. In this lone excursion into the field of detective writing he created for his central character a slightly ludicrous Gallic detective to whom Agatha Christie's currently popular Hercule Poirot seems to bear more than an accidental resemblance. In his own lifetime, Barr was better known as a magazine than as a book author, his work appearing prolifically on both sides of the Atlantic. He sometimes used the pseudonym "Luke Sharp."

Early in 1905 he was in Paris for a short time; and from some "unfashionable Italian town" he sent back, in the spring of 1912, comments-with-a-perspective on the British political scene.

During Barr's residence in Canada an Iroquois tribe had made him a chief. Years later he reciprocated: an Iroquois chief, dressed in a white-man's suit and straw hat, came to London seeking redress of grievances, and Barr, after insisting that he change to his native regalia, took him to Commons where he cut such a figure that "Mr. Gladstone and Sir William Harcourt sought an introduction to him. . . ." Barr's health failed steadily in the months before his death, which occurred at Woldingham, Surrey.

PRINCIPAL WORKS: In a Steamer Chair, 1892; From Whose Bourn, 1893; The Face and the Mask, 1894; In the Midst of Alarms, 1894; A Woman Intervenes, 1896; The Mutable Many, 1897; The Countess Tekla, 1899; The Unchanging East, 1900; The Victors, 1901; Over the Border, 1902; The Tempestuous Petticoat, 1905; A Rock in the Baltic, 1906; The Triumphs of Eugène Valmont, 1906; The Measures of the Rule, 1907; Stranleigh's Millions, 1908; Cardillac, 1909; The Sword Maker, 1910.

ABOUT: Doyle, A. C. Memories and Adventures; Haycraft, H. Murder for Pleasure: The Life and Times of the Detective Story; Jerome, J. K. My Life and Times; Bookman December 1912; Critic November 1903; Technical World Magazine April 1912; London Times October 22, 1912.

BARRÈS, MAURICE (September 22, 1862-December 5, 1923), French novelist and essayist, was born in Charmes-sur-Moselle, in Lorraine, eight years before it and Alsace became German provinces. His grandfather had died a hostage in Germany during the Napoleonic wars. The intense nationalism, his most prominent characteristic, was well come by.

He was educated at the Lycée in Nancy, and in 1883 went to Paris to study law, at his father's wish. Soon, however, he drifted into journalism. Anatole France and Leconte de Lisle praised  his magazine articles and encouraged him to turn author. Two magazines which he founded and edited were exceedingly short-lived, but served to keep his name before the public. In 1888 his first book appeared, *Sous l'Oeil des Barbares,* the first of a trilogy devoted to the "culte de moi," an anarchistic exaltation of the ego. In 1889 he was elected deputy from Nancy, as a follower of the nationalist general Boulanger, who by a narrow margin escaped becoming dictator of France. Failing reelection, he spent a year abroad, chiefly in Venice and Toledo. He returned to found, with Charles Maurras, a nationalist paper called *La Cocarde.* Two more novel trilogies followed, one devoted to "the romance of national energy," the other to a similar theme, "the bastions of the east." These, with several very subjective travel books, and two pastoral novels (his best work), *Colette Baudoche* and *La Colline Inspirée,* made up the sum total of his books—though for four years he wrote a daily article for the *Echo de Paris,* and these essays were later collected in a volume.

From 1906, when Barrès was elected deputy from Paris, a post he held for the remainder of his life, his career was divided between politics and literature. He seldom spoke in the Chamber of Deputies, however, but confined his political activities to written propaganda. He lived as if within a mask, the man himself unknown. His nature was centripedal—its focus was first his own ego, then the glory of France. Always highstrung and frail, he succumbed suddenly to a heart attack on the very day of publication of his book, *Une Enquête aux Pays au Levant,* leaving behind him an unfinished autobiography and a mass of still unpublished correspondence.

"The art of writing," said Barrès, "must satisfy these two requirements—it must be musical and meet the demands for mathematical precision, which exists among the French in every well-regulated soul."

Acquaintances spoke often of Barrès' "Roman profile and manner." His characteristic expression was "a dreamy gaze under half-closed eyelids, the mouth in its almost voluptuous curve recalling a face of Rossetti's."

He was a hero worshiper, blind to the faults of his idols, and he loved France "like a lover." His plotless novels and the prose poems of his travel books are rather reminiscent of Chateaubriand, though in his earliest style he caught the ironic inflexion of his enemy, Ernest Renan. Barrès considered his lifework to be the defense of the eastern frontier and the stimulation of the "collective egotism" called nationalism, which absorbed his energies as president of the *Ligue des Patriotes.*

PRINCIPAL WORKS AVAILABLE IN ENGLISH TRANSLATION: The Undying Spirit of France, 1917; The Faith of France, 1918; Colette Baudoche, 1918; The Sacred Hill, 1929.

ABOUT: Drake, W. A. Contemporary European Writers; Guérard, A. L. Five Masters of French Romance; Huneker, J. G. Egoists; Thibaudet, M. Les Princes Lorrains; Annales Politiques et Littéraires October 19, 1924; Freeman January 16, 1924; Literary Review March 22 and April 5, 1924; Living Age November 25, 1922, February 9, 1924; London Mercury October 1925; London Quarterly Review December 1924; Sewanee Review October 1924.

BARRETTO, LARRY (May 30, 1890-   ), American novelist, was born Laurence Brevoort Barretto in Larchmont, N.Y., the son of Gerard Morris Barretto and Laura (Brevoort) Barretto, a descendant of Hendrick Brevoort, the early New Yorker whose farm became Greenwich Village. Young Larry read practically every Henty book available  and was sent to a private school (Hoosac) in Hoosick, N.Y. After his graduation he got a newspaper job in Plainfield, N.J. It lasted just one week. On new advice he went to work in Wall Street. He found no "romance in debentures" and within the next five years ran through about a dozen jobs, including the writing of advertising copy for cast-iron pipes.

The First World War found him opening packing-cases in a publishing house, where he could "at least *smell* the new-bound books" even though he couldn't write them. (He had suddenly realized that he had nothing to say and had stopped sending out stories.) By the spring of 1917 he had enlisted in the U.S. ambulance corps and remained as a private for the duration. He served with the French, and on his discharge was awarded a Croix de Guerre, merely, he says, because "there was an extra one to be given."

He admits that the war, for him, was an escape. But what was much more significant, it convinced him that he had something to say: ". . . the whole pageant of living and dying compressed into a matter of minutes had made me articulate at last." His first novel, *A Conqueror Passes*, one of the earliest books to tell the story of the returned soldiers, was published in 1925. It was written at night; refused by two agents; and then accepted by the first publisher who saw it. Soon afterwards came *To Babylon* and *Walls of Glass*. In 1928 he wrote a tale of conflict between the new modernism and the disintegrating aristocracy; and in the year following, his autobiographical novel, *Horses in the Sky*. Meanwhile he had been an assistant editor of *Adventure Magazine*. He had a tremendous fondness for the theatre and, 1926-27, served as dramatic critic for the *Bookman*.

He was married in 1923 to Anna Appleton Flichtner, first cousin of the wife of Louis Bromfield. The romance, says Barretto, would probably never have taken place had not his own ambulance crashed headlong into Mr. Bromfield's one dark night in France during the war. The Barrettos spend their winters in New York and their summers—"theoretically"—in an old upstate farmhouse. They have no children, but they keep a tailless mongrel cat whose one failing is sea-sickness.

During the 1930's Barretto published four more novels and in 1940 came a fictional study (*Journey Through Time*) of the gulf that lies beween the generation which fought the First World War and that destined to fight the Second.

Larry Barretto believes that writing is, among other things, good hard work. As he acquires vision enough to see his inadequacies and "ambition enough to try to overcome them," it gets, he says, just a little bit harder.

PRINCIPAL WORKS: A Conqueror Passes, 1924; To Babylon, 1925; Walls of Glass, 1926; Old Enchantment, 1928; Horses in the Sky, 1929; The Indiscreet Years, 1931; Three Roads From Paradise, 1933; Bright Mexico, 1935; Tomorrow Will Be Different, 1936; Hawaiian Holiday (with B. Cooper) 1938; Journey Through Time, 1940.

ABOUT: Bookman January and September 1926; Ladies' Home Journal January 1927; Wilson Library Bulletin March 1930.

BARRIE, Sir JAMES MATTHEW, Bart.

(May 9, 1860-June 19, 1937), British dramatist and novelist, was born in a Lowland Scotch village named Kirriemuir, in Forfarshire, a village later to be made famous under the name of Thrums. His mother, born Margaret Ogilvy, has been celebrated almost too much by her adoring son, whereas he has only a word of kindly condenscension for his father. Nevertheless,  David Barrie, the weaver, a stout Chartist but also a devout Presbyterian, deserved more recognition than he received. There were ten children, only a few of whom survived infancy.

Margaret Ogilvy undoubtedly was a superior woman. Unwittingly she ruined her son as an adult human being, but she made him a man of culture and a writer. In spite of the poverty of the home she saw to it that he was educated—rather against his will, for he was an utterly idle pupil at Dumfries Academy, with his head on nothing but cricket, and he had a hard pull to secure his M.A. at Edinburgh in 1882. In later years both Edinburgh and St. Andrews (of which he was rector from 1919 to 1922) conferred an LL.D. on him, and both Oxford and Cambridge a D.Litt., but there is no disguising the fact that James Barrie was anything but a student in his youth.

He was a reader, however, passionately devoted to James Fenimore Cooper and, later on, to Robert Louis Stevenson, a rather incongruous combination which is revelatory of the nature of the devoté. At Dumfries also he beheld Thomas Carlyle, who disdained to speak to any of the awe-struck small fry. With Stevenson, Barrie began a correspondence that ripened into long-distance friendship, and might have led him to Samoa had Stevenson not died. Barrie's only serious poem was on his friend's death.

In 1883 Barrie made his first essay in journalism, on the Nottingham *Journal*. He applied for and just missed a job on a Liverpool paper, and then, on the strength of one published and one accepted article in London magazines, he set out, in 1885, for the metropolis, which was to be his home ever after. He had asked the first editor who accepted his work for advice on this move, and was told to stay away—so he left for London at once. For five or six years he supported himself precariously by innumerable anonymous free-lance essays, some of them purporting to be the autobiographical experiences of engineers or explorers, but most of them whimsically humorous, now with a rather stale *fin-de-siècle* flavor. The immense field open for exploitation in his native village remained undiscovered for a long time, in spite of the success of *Auld Licht Idylls.*

Until about 1900 Barrie was primarily a novelist and essayist who occasionally wrote plays; after that time he became a dramatist who very infrequently wrote in non-dramatic form. His first plays, three one-acters, were produced in 1891, and his first full-length play, *Walker, London,* in 1892. He even collaborated with A. Conan Doyle on the libretto of a comic opera, *Jane Annie,* produced by D'Oyly Carte—about as odd a collaboration as has yet been seen on the English stage. With *Quality Street* and *The Admirable Crichton* in 1903, and above all with *Peter Pan* in 1904, Barrie the playwright had come to stay, and he never wrote a major work of fiction thereafter. He had become closely associated with Charles Frohman, the manager, and with Frohman's principal star, Maude Adams, coming to the United States in 1896 to see Miss Adams through the drama version of *The Little Minister.* Her name is inseparably connected also with *Quality Street,* and to thousands of Americans she *was* Peter Pan.

On this American visit Barrie disclaimed several volumes purporting to be his work and passing in the United States under his name. One of these, however, *A Tillyloss Scandal,* several times republished in this country, is known to be by him.

This journey took place during Barrie's little-known and unsuccessful marriage, which lasted from 1894 to 1909. His wife was Mary Ansall, an actress. After their divorce, the Barrie of legend emerged—the pipe-smoking tutelary deity of Adelphi Terrace across the street from Shaw; the friend of George Meredith, of Thomas Hardy, of W. E. Henley. (Wendy, in *Peter Pan,* is a memory of Henley's beloved little daughter who died as a child.) He was created a baronet in 1913, and the Order of Merit was conferred on him in 1922, in recognition of his war plays, best known of which was *The Old Lady Shows Her Medals.*

The little left-handed man with the bulging dome of forehead had an obvious touch of the elfin in him. The myth that grew up of the shy, taciturn, shrinking Barrie, a sort of aging Peter Pan, was not unfostered

by its object. As a matter of fact, Barrie was a canny Scot, an excellent man of business, who left a tidy fortune; and also, as a matter of fact, he adored being in the public eye, loved to make speeches, and would have been acutely unhappy had he really been condemned to be the recluse of the Barrie tradition.

He did not even really like children or get on well with them, though he had loved little Margaret Henley, and though he cared tenderly for the little son of Captain Robert Scott, who left his wife and child in his friend's charge in the tragic letter he wrote as he lay dying in the Antarctic waste.

No, the key to Barrie the man and very largely to Barrie the writer lies in his own words: "Nothing that happens after we are twelve matters very much," and in his lament, "Oh, that we were boys and girls all our lives!" He knew the psychological danger of that clinging to youth—see *Sentimental Tommy* and, still more, *Tommy and Grizel,* where Tommy's incapacity for adult responsibility drives Grizel to insanity and in the end causes his own abruptly accidental death. But he could not wholly avoid it.

It is a commonplace and a *cliché* nowadays to say that a man has a mother-fixation. Nevertheless Margaret Ogilvy conditioned the entire existence of her favorite child. He was arrested, not in childhood, but in adolescence. His Scotch ancestry, and primarily his mother, kept him in bondage always to a rather misty, fairy world, where there was neither time nor death, where anything might happen and the dead were the most expected of visitors. It is because of her too that he could write of love only in terms of mother-love—all his women mother their men. Probably it was the inability of his wife to live up to that specification which was the ultimate cause of their separation. Babbie and Gavin, Tommy and Grizel, Peter and Wendy—the pattern repeats itself endlessly.

What saved him for a later age was the pawky humor which also came from Margaret Ogilvy, that and her forthright independence of spirit which lifted its head in her son's play, *The Twelve Pound Look,* the real hero of which is a typewriting machine. Trivial he might be sometimes, foggily nebulous he was often, but there was still something tough in the core of J. M. Barrie which kept him from the mere whimsicality of an A. A. Milne. The admirers of his early Scottish stories might bewail his increasing Anglicization, forgetting how overweighted with dialect those early stories were, but actually Barrie grew in stature up to *Dear Brutus* and *Mary Rose*. He juggled with time as John Balderston did in *Berkeley Square;* he was an alien to the scientific spirit of his age, but his phantoms have wit and the light touch and even, so to speak, body.

After a long pause of fourteen years without writing, his two last Biblical plays appeared, utterly unlike any of his previous work. Perhaps they foreshadowed a new phase, but it was too late. After all, he was seventy-seven when he died, and could hardly be expected to launch on a new career.

Barrie has been likened to Dickens and to Hans Christian Andersen. In his earlier novels there was an echo of Stevenson, and one may even catch an occasional note of W. S. Gilbert and of Wilde! But all in all, Barrie is Barrie. He never grew up completely, and his inner life became arid and stunted; but we are the gainers by his loss.

PRINCIPAL WORKS: *Fiction*—Better Dead, 1887; Auld Licht Idylls, 1888; An Edinburgh Eleven, 1888; When a Man's Single, 1888; A Window in Thrums, 1889; The Little Minister, 1891; Sentimental Tommy, 1895; Tommy and Grizel, 1900; The Little White Bird, 1902; Peter Pan in Kensington Gardens, 1906. *Plays*—The Professor's Love Story, 1895; The Wedding Guest, 1900; Quality Street, 1903; Little Mary, 1903; The Admirable Crichton, 1903; Peter Pan, 1904; Alice Sit-by-the-Fire, 1905; What Every Woman Knows, 1908; The Legend of Leonora, 1910; The Will, 1913; Der Tag, 1914; A Kiss for Cinderella, 1916; The Old Lady Shows Her Medals, 1916; Dear Brutus, 1917; Echoes of the War, 1918; The Truth About the Russian Dancers, 1920; Mary Rose, 1920; Shall We Join the Ladies? 1922; The Two Shepherds, 1936; The Boy David, 1936. *Non-Fiction*—My Lady Nicotine, 1890; Margaret Ogilvy, 1896; Courage, 1922.

ABOUT: Braybrooke, P. J. M. Barrie; Chalmers, P. R. The Barrie Inspiration; Darton, F. J. H. J. M. Barrie; Darlington, W. A. J. M. Barrie; Kennedy, J. Thrums and the Barrie Country; Mackail, D. Barrie; Moult, T. Barrie; Roy, J. A. James Matthew Barrie; Catholic World October 1937; Christian Century July 14, 1937; Christian Science Monitor May 18, 1938; January 6, 1940, November 16, 1940; Dial August 1923; National Review January 1938; New Statesman and Nation June 26, 1937.

"BARRINGTON, E." See BECK, L. M. A.

*BARRY, PHILIP (June 18, 1896-   ), American playwright, was born in Rochester, N.Y., the son of James Corbett Barry and Mary Agnes (Quinn) Barry. His father and grandfather were born in Ireland near Dublin, and migrated to the United States when James Barry was a boy of ten. Very evident traces of Celticism are discernible in Philip Barry's work, from

Joseph, the horse, in *White Wings* (1926), who is related to the animals of James Stephens, down to the mysticism of *Hotel Universe* (1930) and *The Joyous Season* (1933), which deals with a second-generation Irish family living in Boston and has a nun for its motivating figure. "I was only bright in spots, and was expelled once for being a general nuisance," was  Barry's description of his education in a letter to Barrett H. Clark, who says that the dramatist is usually "uncompromisingly reticent in talking about his career and achievements." It is known, however, that Barry attended the public schools of Rochester, began to write at nine, and in 1919 received his B. A. degree from Yale, and wrote his only one-act play, produced that year by the Yale Dramatic Club but never published. As a clerk in the Department of State at Washington and an *attaché* in the American Embassy in London from May 1918 to February 1919, he found a diplomatic career "very dull indeed." From 1919 to 1922 Barry was a student at Harvard, chiefly in the 47 Workshop of Professor George Pierce Baker, where he learned the fundamentals of his future profession. Here "he wrote some, acted hard, and shifted scenery brilliantly." *A Punch For Judy,* written during the course for Workshop production, was revived by Knowles Entrikin at his semi-experimental theatre at Scarborough-on-Hudson in 1927.

Barry was married to Ellen Semple in 1922. They have two sons, Philip Semple Barry and Jonathan Peter Barry. In 1922, also, Barry saw the New York production of his first play, *You and I,* a three-act comedy. It ran six months; *The Youngest,* a comedy of youth, ran three months in 1924; *In a Garden,* a rather esoteric play with Laurette Taylor as a novelist's wife, continued two months; and *White Wings,* though one of his gayest and most appealing comedies, achieved only three weeks in 1926. *John,* a five-act play about John the Baptist, was produced by the Actors Theatre in 1927 and was withdrawn after ten performances. *Paris Bound,* that same year, was the first of Barry's several boxoffice successes, and established him as a "dashing, debonair, sophisticated author of smart plays," with dialogue distinguished by biting wit. Richard Watts disliked their occasional "meretricious smartness and hollow glibness," preferring the "deep sensitivity and brooding compassion" of *Here Come the Clowns* (1938) dramatized from Barry's own fantastic novel, *War in Heaven.*

Barry is a member of the National Institute of Arts and Letters as well as of the American Society of Dramatists and the Authors' League of America. His college fraternity was Alpha Delta Phi, and his clubs include the Yale, University, Century, Players and Coffee House clubs in New York City. He has written scenarios in Hollywood, going there in 1934. On his return from a sojourn in France in June 1939, he reported things "very dull across the water" and expressed his belief that there is more inspiration for a creative writer in the United States. Barry is a cleanshaven, dark man with keen eyes behind his glasses. The Barry family lives on Jupiter Island, Hobe Sound, Fla. They are Roman Catholics.

PRINCIPAL WORKS: *Plays*—You and I, 1922; The Youngest, 1924; In a Garden, 1925; White Wings, 1926; John, 1927; Paris Bound, 1927; Cock Robin (with E. L. Rice) 1928; Holiday, 1929; Hotel Universe, 1930; Tomorrow and Tomorrow, 1931; The Animal Kingdom, 1932; The Joyous Season, 1933; Bright Star, 1935; Spring Dance, 1936; Here Come the Clowns, 1938; The Philadelphia Story, 1939; Liberty Jones, 1941. *Novel*—War in Heaven, 1938.

ABOUT: Brown, J. M. Upstage; Skinner, R. D. Our Changing Theatre; Boston Transcript October 26, 1929; Catholic World March 1935; Theatre Arts Monthly November 1929; Theatre Guild Magazine May 1930; Wilson Library Bulletin April 1930.

BARTLETT, VERNON (April 30, 1894-), English journalist, novelist, and radio commentaor, was born in Westbury,

Wiltshire, the son of T. O. Bartlett of Swanage. He attended Blundell's, Tiverton, a school made famous in R. D. Blackmore's *Lorna Doone,* left school at sixteen, and traveled abroad to study for the consular service. Time spent with a German family in Bromberg laid the foundation for his later novel of adolescence, the *Calf Love* of 1929. His travels took him also to Florence, Madrid, and Paris, where he had begun to study at the Sorbonne in 1914 when the First World War broke out. Made a second lieutenant early the next year,

Bartlett spent five months at the front, much of the time in command of his company; spent his twenty-first birthday in a hospital train with a slight wound; and was invalided home.

Recovering from two years' illness, Bartlett entered journalism, first with the London *Daily Mail* and then Reuter's news agency, covering the Paris Peace Conference for the latter. For three weeks he was the first Paris correspondent of the *Daily Herald.* Returning to London, he was private secretary for the editor of the *Times* for a while, until his paper sent him to Europe as special correspondent to cover revolutions and insurrections. In 1920 Barlett was with the Polish army in its war against the Bolshevists, and witnessed various upheavals in Germany. As representative of the *Times* in Rome, he left a few days after Mussolini came into power. Next Bartlett was director of the London office of the League of Nations secretariat, where, as he plaintively observes in his engaging autobiography, *This Is My Life,* he was the civil servant of over fifty governments, none of whom he dared offend.

For six years Bartlett was the most popular and practically the only British radio broadcaster on international affairs, leaving in October 1933 after one of his talks had ruffled the feelings of the Foreign Office. Bartlett became diplomatic correspondent of the *News Chronicle,* was founder and editor of the *World Review,* broadcast the Dollfuss funeral from Vienna, and spent two months in war-torn Spain. He has been an Independent Progressive member of Parliament from the Bridgewater Division of Somerset since 1938. With R. C. Sheriff, he turned the latter's war-play, *Journey's End,* into a novel. A robust, jovial individual, Bartlett considers his favorite recreations walking, swimming, and talking in country inns. His clear, forceful books are chiefly derived from his journalistic experiences. Mrs. Bartlett was Marguerite van den Bemden of Antwerp; they have two sons.

PRINCIPAL WORK: Mud and Khaki, 1916; Behind the Scenes at the Peace Conference, 1919; The Brighter Side of European Chaos, 1925; Topsy Turvy, 1927; Calf Love, 1929; No Man's Land, 1930; The World: Our Neighbor, 1931; Nazi Germany Explained, 1933; If I Were Dictator, 1935; This Is My Life (U.S. title: International Europe) 1938.

ABOUT: Bartlett, V. This Is My Life; Current History January, August 1940.

BARZUN, JACQUES MARTIN (November 30, 1907-), American historian of French birth, was born at Créteil, France,  the son of Henri Martin Barzun (a writer, and a member of the so-called "Abbaye" group which included Duhamel, Vildrac, and Romains) and of Anne Rosa Barzun. His youth was thus passed in a circle of artistic and intellectual activity and of "concentrated innovation." The First World War interrupted this extra-curricular education—as well as the more formal one of the Lycée Janson de Sailly—and paved the way for Mr. Barzun's transplantation to America. His father had been sent on an official mission to the United States, and after the peace the family followed him. In 1923 he entered Columbia College, and was graduated at the head of his class in 1927. For three years he was on the staff of the University daily as dramatic critic, and also served as "campus correspondent" for city newspapers. He wrote the book and lyrics of the annual musical show, and, under various pen names, contributed "light literature" to *Vanity Fair*.

At the same time, and for a year after graduation, he did historical research as apprentice-assistant to several co-operative projects. He finally gave over the possibilities of law and diplomacy in favor of historical and critical writing. Two research fellowships and an appointment as lecturer in history at the Columbia University summer session of 1928 clinched the matter.

From that time on, his life has been devoted to lecturing, writing, and foreign travel anchored in research. A remnant of his old interest in the law led him to study Montesquieu and so to come upon the traces of an old controversy waged in France about the hereditary rights of nobles and commoners. The history of this idea and its entanglements he began to describe in *The French Race*, which was published as his doctoral dissertation in 1932. The following year he became an American citizen and went abroad on a fellowship from the Council of Learned Societies to pursue the subject into its contemporary ramifications. The result appeared under the title of *Race*. In his later books he has rounded out the history of those ideas in science, social science, and art which he feels to be dominant in the modern world.

In addition to frequent publication in the learned journals in his field, he has contributed critical (and sometimes polemic) articles to the New York *Herald Tribune "Books,"* the *Atlantic Monthly*, the *Nation*, and the *Saturday Review of Literature*. At the time of this writing he is assistant professor of history at Columbia. He is married and lives in New York, with a summer home in Concord, Mass.

PRINCIPAL WORKS: The French Race: Theories of Its Origins and Their Social and Political Implications Prior to the Revolution, 1932; Visual Outline of English History, 1933; Race: A Study in Modern Superstition, 1937; Of Human Freedom, 1939; Culture in the Democracy, 1940; Darwin, Marx, Wagner: Critique of a Heritage, 1941.

BASSETT, JOHN SPENCER (September 10, 1867-January 27, 1928), American historian and educator, was born in Tarboro, N.C., the son of Richard Baxter, a passive opponent of slavery (he himself owned several Negro mechanics), and Mary Jane (Wilson) Bassett. He prepared at the Graded School of Goldsboro (N.C.) and at the Davis Military School for Trinity College (now Duke University), from which he was graduated in 1888. He received his Ph.D. from Johns Hopkins University in 1891 and in the year following he married Jessie Lewellin.

Meanwhile he had been an instructor at Trinity, and had organized the "9019," the college's first scholarship society; he was shortly made professor of history. In twelve years of able teaching he laid the groundwork for an excellent collection of books on the South; published a number of his own North Carolina researches; and in 1902 became the first editor of the *South Atlantic Quarterly*, founded at his suggestion by the "9019." The October 1903 issue, in which he sounded a note of hope for the Negro's future, led to a factional request for his resignation. The trustees, fortunately, voted it down, and answered their opponents with a statement in defense of academic liberty.

Bassett was called to Smith College in 1906 and remained there until the time of his death. During these years he founded the *Smith College Studies in History* and wrote a vast amount of historical and biographical works, including the first really adequate biography of Andrew Jackson and chronicles of international as well as domestic relations; moreover he edited several volumes of significant letters. In 1919 he was elected secretary of the American Historical Association, an unpaid office to which he devoted a considerable amount of time and strength, despite the fact that he was an active professor and was frequently absorbed in some public enterprise. He was greatly interested in the Northampton Historical Society, and gave the first check towards the establishment of its endowment fund. It is said that he rarely became tired, and when he did, a short relaxation gave him prodigious new energy.

Bassett's last night in Northampton was spent in reading the proofs of a new book. Only a day or so later he was run down in Washington by a trolley car; and he died in his sixty-first year. Perhaps his most significant achievement as an historian was the soundness with which he criticized a very complex contemporary society.

PRINCIPAL WORKS: The Constitutional Beginnings of North Carolina (Johns Hopkins Studies) 1894; Slavery and Servitude in the Colony of North Carolina (Ibid.) 1896; Anti-Slavery Leaders in North Carolina (Ibid.) 1898; The Writings of Colonel William Byrd, 1901; The Federalist System, 1906; The Life of Andrew Jackson (2 vols.) 1911; Short History of the United States, 1913; The Middle Group of American Historians, 1917; Correspondence of George Bancroft and Jared Sparks, 1917; Our War With Germany, 1919; The Westover Journal of John Selden, Esq., 1921; Major Howell Tatum's Journal, 1922; Expansion and Reform, 1926; Correspondence of Andrew Jackson (ed., 3 vols.) 1926-31; The Writing of History (ed.) 1926.

ABOUT: Adams, H. B. Tribute of Friends: With a Bibliography (Johns Hopkins Studies, 1902); Nation February 8, 1928; Smith Alumnae Quarterly May 1928.

BASSHE, EMJO (1900-October 28, 1939), Russian-American dramatist, was born Emanuel Jo Basshe in Vilna, Russia, coming to the United States as a boy in 1912. He worked as a cub reporter on the Boston *Globe* and the Boston *Journal,* and helped out backstage with the Provincetown Theatre, both in the original house in the Massachusetts town, and in the small experimental theatre on MacDougal Street in Greenwich Village, New York City, where his symbolical play, *Adam Solitaire,* was produced November 7, 1925. This sketchily written drama of the transmogrification of a young man's soul, shown against a background of triangular, unbalanced buildings, to the accompaniment of the chants of fiends and demoniacs, was described by Alexander Woollcott as a tragedy in fourteen intermissions.

Basshe was associated with the Provincetown Theatre from 1919 to 1926, when he left to become one of the five founders of the New Playwrights Theatre, which began producing at the Fifty-Second Theatre in February 1927. His play, *Earth,* done by an all-Negro cast, was one of their first productions. In Boston, Basshe had "rubbed elbows with the plaintive souls of the Negro Ghetto on Tremont Street," as Eric Walrond expresses it; and he spent the winter of 1921 in Harlem, New York City, where he filled prescriptions for Negroes in a Lenox Avenue drugstore, and studied the even more variegated colored types in this great metropolitan center, which draws its population from the British West Indies as well as the American South.

Basshe spent six months in Virginia, Georgia, Kentucky and Florida, bunking with the colored farming folk, swapping yarns with them, and absorbing their traditions and manner of speech. This experience proved useful in the latter years of Basshe's life, when he directed Paul Green's *Roll, Sweet Chariot* and *Turpentine* at the Lafayette Theatre in Harlem, for the Negro Theatre Division of the W.P.A. Federal Theatre. In 1931 he obtained a Guggenheim fellowship for creative work in the theatre, and later won first prize in the University of Chicago competition for the best unproduced long play of 1935. On October 11, 1939, Basshe was brought from his home at Rock Tavern, Orange County, N.Y., to Bellevue Hospital in New York City, and died there a little more than two weeks later of an unannounced ailment. He wrote several one-act plays which expressed the same spirit of revolt as his longer productions. "Futility, energy and variety are what we mostly feel," wrote Stark Young of Basshe's *Centuries,* "with stretches of platitude. Now and then the invention is remarkable."

PRINCIPAL WORKS: Earth, 1927; Centuries: Portrait of a Tenement House, 1928; Doomsday Circus, 1938.

ABOUT: Basshe, E. Earth (see Introduction by E. Walrond); New Republic December 21, 1927; New York Times October 29, 1939.

BASSO, HAMILTON (September 5, 1904-), American novelist and biographer, writes: "First he was born. That happened in New Orleans. His parents were honest, not particularly poor. His grandfather, Joseph Basso, established one of the first shoe factories in the South, about ten years after the Civil War. Then, after a proper amount of time had passed, our subject went to school, and finally to Tulane University where he studied law for four years but did not take a degree. (He could have gotten one, too. Honest.) When he first started wanting to write, our subject cannot remember. Sometimes, when he is in the middle of a book and it looks as if  he'll never finish it, he thinks he has been writing forever. He was first published, however, in the old *Double-Dealer,* and is sometimes called a member of the *Double-Dealer* group —Sherwood Anderson, William Faulkner, Roark Bradford, Lyle Saxon, Oliver LaFarge; occasional visiting Elks like Eugène Jolas, Edmund Wilson, John Dos Passos. A good time was had by all, including our subject, and then he wrote a very, very bad first novel (the first of two very bad novels that have got into print). It was the beginning of a long process of learning to write at the expense of the public, and the process was to continue for a long time—and still does, but with more charity and mercy.

"That was in 1929, and the subject was earning a living by working as a reporter on the New Orleans *Item.* Then he moved to the *Times-Picayune,* where he had a brief moment of being night city editor when the regular editor got sick, and then in a moment of extraordinary folly he became an advertising copy-writer. The crash put an end to that piece of nonsense, and, in 1933, the subject's biography of General P.G.T. Beauregard was published on the very day Mr. Roosevelt closed all the banks. So the life of a writer, said the subject's wife, is like the perils of Pauline. (Wife's maiden name, Etolia Moore Simmons; married in 1930; one son.)

"Then some wandering: mountains of Western North Carolina, New York, the low country of South Carolina, Europe, New England, back to North Carolina where the subject now lives four miles from a mountain hamlet called Pisgah Forest. After *Beauregard* came four novels, of which *Days Before Lent* was given the Southern Authors' Award for 1940. There has been a good bit of magazine writing, also, and inclusion in various anthologies: short story and essay, even school-books. So it all boils down to the not very interesting fact that the subject is a man who likes to write and writes for a living and thinks of himself more as a craftsman than as an artist. He

is now writing another novel and hopes, God willing, to write many more."

* * *

For a short time about 1935, Mr. Basso was on the staff of the *New Republic.* He spent the winter of 1940-41 in Charlottesville, Va., "because our house in the mountains is pretty uninhabitable in the winter and also because my son has to have little people to play with to make up for the squirrels, chipmunks, frogs, etc., that he associates with in the summer. The idea is to try to get him to understand that there are people in the world—even though the things people are now doing make chipmunks and squirrels seem nicer."

PRINCIPAL WORKS: Relics and Angels, 1929; Beauregard: The Great Creole, 1933; Cinnamon Seed, 1934; In Their Own Image, 1935; Courthouse Square, 1936; Days Before Lent, 1939; Wine of the Country, 1941.

ABOUT: Publishers' Weekly February 3, 1940; Wilson Library Bulletin October 1939.

BATES, ARLO. See "AMERICAN AUTHORS: 1600-1900"

BATES, ERNEST SUTHERLAND (October 14, 1879-December 4, 1939), American biographer, historian, and educator, was born at Gambier, Ohio, the son of Cyrus Stearns Bates and Laverna (Sutherland) Bates. He received a B.A. degree from the University of Michigan in 1902, his master's degree the next year, and a Ph.D. in 1908 from Columbia University,  where he was also a tutor in English.

Seventeen years of teaching followed the doctorate. From 1908 until 1915 he was professor of English at the University of Arizona, and for the next ten years he taught English and philosophy at the University of Oregon. In 1925 he courageously resigned his Oregon post as a protest against restraint of free speech by the university authorities, and moved with his family to New York to make his living by his pen. From 1926 to 1929 he was literary editor of the great *Dictionary of American Biography;* from 1933 to 1936, associate editor of the *Modern Monthly.* He also became a highly respected critic, specializing in religious and historical subjects. His criticisms, like his own books, were lucid, readable, and soundly considered.

His philosophic studies were largely responsible for Bates' not becoming a clergyman, as he planned at one time, but he retained a lifelong interest in religion and in the Bible, which in his hands became a best-seller of an unusual type. *The Bible Designed To Be Read As Living Literature*, as respectfully edited by Bates, rearranged the King James and revised versions, omitted many of the repetitions and genealogies, and had a merited success. He also wrote a *Biography of the Bible*, an account of its derivation and authorship; another "biography," of Judas Iscariot; and edited *The Four Gospels* for the Limited Editions Club. The religious theme was varied somewhat in *Mary Baker Eddy: The Truth and the Tradition*, a closely documented biography of the founder of Christian Science written in collaboration with J. V. Dittemore, a former director of the sect's Mother Church. Bates' later works showed an increasing interest in the American tradition, always from the liberal point of view, including a critical study of William Randolph Hearst, (with Oliver Carlson) and histories of Congress and the Supreme Court. Nearly all his books were published in the last ten years of his life.

Ernest Sutherland Bates died at sixty of a sudden heart attack at his home in New York City, a few minutes after writing the last page of *American Faith*, a brilliant and significant interpretation of American democracy in terms of the nation's religious evolution. Published posthumously, it was hailed by critics as the author's "monument." Surviving Bates at his death were his third wife, Gladys (Graham) Bates, also a writer, whom he married in 1920, and a son by his divorced second wife, Rosalind (Boido) Bates, whom he wed in 1913. He was first married in 1902 to Florence (Fisher) Bates, who died.

Bates had smiling eyes and an intelligent, "almost Slavic face," according to the New York *Herald Tribune*, which also said: "The list of his achievements reads as if it must be the work of a *dilettante*; but Mr. Bates was rather the encyclopedist." Henry Seidel Canby called him "courageous, indomitable, and extraordinarily versatile." Essentially a "scholarly popularizer," Bates was an indefatigable worker and a sound and conscientious craftsman.

PRINCIPAL WORKS: A Study of Shelley's Drama, 1908; The Friend of Jesus (in England: The Gospel According to Judas Iscariot) 1928; This Land of Liberty, 1930; Mary Baker Eddy: The Truth and the Tradition (with J. V. Dittemore) 1932; The Bible Designed To Be Read As Living Literature, 1936; Hearst: Lord of San Simeon (with O. Carlson) 1936; The Story of Congress: 1789-1935, 1936; The Story of the Supreme Court, 1936; American Hurly-Burly (with A. Williams) 1937; Biography of the Bible, 1937; The Pageant of the States (with H. S. Schiff) 1938; American Faith, 1940.

ABOUT: New York Herald Tribune December 5, 6, 1939; New York Times December 5, 1939; Saturday Review of Literature December 16, 1939.

BATES, HERBERT ERNEST (May 16, 1905-), English story writer, was born in Rushden, Northampton, the son of Albert Ernest Bates and Lucy Elizabeth (Lucas) Bates. He was educated at the Grammar School, in Kettering, then worked for a while on a local newspaper. Disliking the drudgery of journalism, he became a clerk in a leather warehouse.  This may have seemed worse, but at least it gave him leisure to write first a play and then a novel. At the same time he was engaged in a series of theological controversies with the local dignitaries of the church; he was at once prodigy and *enfant terrible*, and was regarded with apprehension by nearly everyone he knew except his mother's father, a salty old farmer, full of stories and of reminiscences of gypsies and prize-fighters. It was an unorthodox but valuable training for a precocious young writer.

Bates attained his majority and publication of his first novel together. He is still young, but he has already published eighteen volumes of fiction, besides innumerable uncollected stories and two volumes of rural essays. He is a prolific and widely anthologized story writer—he has appeared more often than any other author in Edward J. O'Brien's annual *Best British Short Stories*. In addition he has written several plays. In 1931 he married Marjorie Helen Cox, and they have a son and two daughters. He lives now at Little Chart, Kent. He is a fair-haired, smooth-shaven young man, with something Puckish and faintly Celtic in his expression. He is a thorough countryman, who understands every aspect of rural life and labors incessantly to present it beautifully. Characteristically, his chief recreation is gardening.

Mr. Bates owes much to the early encouragement given him by Edward Garnett, and by that critic's son, the novelist David Garnett. The latter, though noting that his early sketches were "lyrical but slight," and that "his great merit is not originality, but sensibility," has nevertheless said, "there is no living English writer of whose future work I feel more confident." After working out from under the influence of Joseph Conrad, whose indirect method of narrative he imitated without much success, he has grown constantly in clarity and vigor. Conrad's influence was followed by that of Stephen Crane, and English critics frequently comment on the "American" tone of Bates' work. Without being in any sense "proletarian" in approach, his stories are nearly all concerned with the working class, and particularly with agricultural laborers or with those in small towns whose real background is of the country. They are simple people, whose small tragedies he has universalized. Fred Urquhart noted his "nostalgia for strange countries, and his preoccupation with madness"—and, it may be added, with death. Yet he is no minor Hardy; side by side with these tragic themes run the stories concerning "my uncle Silas," lustily Rabelaisian, full of earthy humor. His work is not nearly so well known in America as it is in England (perhaps because, however "American" his style, his subject-matter is so indigenously English).

In 1941 Bates joined the R.A.F., giving up for the duration his weekly "Country Life" column in the *Spectator*.

PRINCIPAL WORKS: The Two Sisters, 1926; Day's End and Other Stories, 1927; Catherine Foster, 1929; Seven Tales and Alexander, 1929; The Hessian Prisoner, 1930; Charlotte's Row, 1931; The Fallow Land, 1932; The House With the Apricot and Twenty Tales, 1933; The Woman Who Had Imagination and Other Stories, 1934; Thirty Tales, 1934; The Poacher, 1935; Cut and Come Again (short stories) 1935; Duet, 1935; Through the Woods (essays) 1936; A House of Women, 1936; Down the River (essays) 1937; Something Short and Sweet (short stories) 1937; Spella Ho, 1938; The Flying Goat (short stories) 1939; The English Countryside (with others) 1939; My Uncle Silas (short stories) 1940; Carrie and Cleopatra (play) 1940; Country Tales, 1940; The Beauty of the Dead and Other Stories, 1941; Seasons and the Gardener, 1942.

ABOUT: Bookman (London) September 1930; Life and Letters Today December 1939.

BATES, KATHARINE LEE (August 12, 1859 March 28, 1929), American poet, juvenile writer, and author of the famous hymn "America the Beautiful," was the youngest of five children. She was born in Falmouth, Mass., the daughter of Rev. William Bates, a Congregationalist minister who died less than a month after Katharine's birth, and Cornelia Frances (Lee) Bates, a woman of such intellectual

energy that she learned Spanish when she was over seventy. While still a small child living on Cape Cod, Katharine Bates wrote an abundance of stories and verses. In 1871 her family removed to Wellesley Hills; she later entered Wellesley College, at a time, she afterwards recalled, when the proposal of an athletic program that included tennis was fiercely voted

down as "boisterous and unladylike"; and was graduated in 1880. She received an M.A. degree in 1891.

Meanwhile she had taught first one year at Natick High School and then four at Dana Hall, Wellesley, Mass. She was appointed instructor in English literature at Wellesley College in 1885; and in 1891, following graduate study at Oxford, she was awarded a full professorship, which she retained until the time of her retirement as professor emeritus in 1925. During the summer holidays and four sabbatical years she made several journeys abroad, one of which followed the receipt of a $700 prize for "Rose and Thorn," a short story written while she served a precautionary quarantine in a Boston attic.

The verses of "America the Beautiful," said to have been inspired by the view from the top of Pike's Peak and by some of the pageantry of the Chicago World's Fair of 1893, appeared in the *Congregationalist* for July 4, 1895. It has been perennially suggested that this be adopted as the national anthem; and several years after her death, when "The Star-Spangled Banner" was referred to by some as a "hymn of hate," the newer anthem gained in favor.

A few years later she published a Spanish travel book, edited a volume on American literature and a collection of ballads. In 1906 the *Chautauquan,* an educational monthly which had begun to cater to more lively reading interests, sent her to England to do a series of articles ("A Reading Journey in English Counties") which were afterwards enlarged and published in book form (*From Gretna Green to Lands End*).

As a tribute to the memory of her closest friend, Katharine Coman, who died in 1915, Miss Bates wrote "In Bohemia: A Corona of Sonnets," which appeared in a posthumous volume of *Selected Poems.* Her verse is generally fluent, simple, optimistic, unspectacular.

She spent her last years at her Wellesley home, the "Scarab," including among her guests William Butler Yeats, Bliss Carman, Robert Frost, Anna Hempstead Branch, and other literary friends. Although she had a real love for solitude, at the same time she had much of the great-hearted "charm of quiet talk." As a poet she left a fragile, joyful, though somewhat conventional kind of beauty.

PRINCIPAL WORKS: English Religious Drama, 1893; English Drama, 1896; Spanish Highways and Byways, 1900; From Gretna Green to Lands End, 1907; American Literature, 1911; America the Beautiful and Other Poems, 1911; Fairy Gold, 1916; Ballad Book, 1917; The Retinue, 1918; Sigurd: Our Golden Collie, 1919; Pilgrim Ship, 1926; Selected Poems of Katharine Lee Bates, 1930.

ABOUT: Bates, K. L. Selected Poems . . . (see Foreword); Bradford, G. Letters: 1918-1931; Kunitz, S. J. & Haycraft, H. (eds.). The Junior Book of Authors; St. Nicholas January 1931.

BATES, RALPH (1899-   ), English novelist, comes of a working-class family from Northern England, had only an elementary  education, and went to work in a factory at sixteen. At eighteen he enlisted in the First World War, and served in France as a private until its end. In 1923 he went to Spain, and lived there until the end of the Spanish Revolution. Spain was the subject of all his earlier novels. He settled in a fishing village, worked in a fish cannery, and organized the fishermen's union. To the villagers he was known as "El Fantastico." They were overcome by his enormous energy —by the way he worked, spent his leisure hours in swimming or wrestling, and slept only three or four hours a night. He had lived in the Pyrenees on first coming to Spain, and is an expert mountain-climber. When the Franco revolt broke out, he organized the mountaineers into scouting parties. He served at the front from the very beginning, and helped to organize the International Brigade, of which he was a commissar. The only interruption to his activities was when he was sent to the United States for a few months on a military mission for the Loyalists.

After Franco's victory, Bates escaped from Spain and came back to the United States. He has since divided his time between this country and Mexico, the latter being the scene of his latest novel. It is not surprising that he stands out as perhaps the best informed—not even excepting André Malraux or Ernest Hemingway—of the chroniclers of the preceding disturbed decade in Spain. He knows thoroughly the country, its people, and the working-class radical movement. As one critic remarked: "He lived revolution; when it came, he could almost write it with his eyes shut." "No writer now at work," said the *Literary Digest* in 1936, "is better equipped to peer into the dogged bitterness of civil strife and report it without a stuffy intellectual approach."

Mr. Bates is, however, much more than a labor organizer who knows Spain. He is also a born writer with a gift for narrative and a brilliant style. His first interest was in music, and he wrote a biography of Schubert which has been reprinted several times. But his real talent is for stripped, athletic fiction. Fred T. Marsh said that "his novels show the fusion of the intellect with the artist by which the front rank may be gained. The well from which he draws is one of compassion for all men and profound faith in mankind as its own master, so that his novels of violence, suffering, and death and a pervading sadness are yet on the side of optimism. . . . His outlook is more that of a modern Rousseauist than of any other kind of Socialist."

He looks like a country schoolmaster or a small-town business man, rather stocky, with light brown hair, a clipped moustache, and spectacles. His voice is low and rather monotonous, and he is not an accomplished speaker, being personally a shy and reticent man who hates crowds and formal gatherings. He is unmarried. A member of the P.E.N. Club and of the League of American Writers, he has addressed conventions of both societies. He is still relatively young, but his reputation thus far depends on his novels and stories of Spain, in which (to quote Mr. Marsh again) "his finely wrought, hammered-out prose came as a shock and a delight after the cast metal of much and often excellent journalism in the field." Politically he is a Leftist, but the Soviet-Nazi pact of 1939 led him to make an open break with the Communists.

PRINCIPAL WORKS: Sierra, 1933; Franz Schubert, 1934; Lean Men, 1935; The Olive Field, 1936; Rainbow Fish, 1937; Sirocco (short stories) 1939; The Fields of Paradise, 1940; The Undiscoverables and Other Stories, 1942.

ABOUT: Colophon #3 1939; Literary Digest September 5, 1936; New York Herald Tribune "Books" October 20, 1940; Saturday Review of Literature October 19, 1940.

BAUM, LYMAN FRANK (May 15, 1856-
May 6, 1919), American fantasist, dramatist, and juvenile writer, was born at Chit-

tenango, N.Y., the
son of Benjamin
Ward Baum and
Cynthia (Stanton)
Baum. His only for-
mal education was at
Peekskill Military
Academy. From 1888
to 1890 Baum was
editor of *Saturday
Pioneer* at Aberdeen,
S.D.; from 1897 to
1902 editor of a Chicago magazine for window decorators, *The Show Window.* The
needs of a growing family (he had married
Maude Gage of Fayettesville, N.Y., in
1882) made Baum cast about for other
sources of income. *Father Goose: His Book*
turned out to be a best seller in 1899. In
ninety days 90,000 copies, illustrated by W.
W. Denslow, were called for. Maxfield
Parrish had contributed characteristic pictures to the preceding *Mother Goose in
Prose* (1897). *The Wonderful Wizard of
Oz* ("the first distinctive attempt to construct a fairyland out of American materials," to quote Edward Wagenknecht) was
published in 1900, and the sensationally successful musical extravaganza, *The Wizard
of Oz,* was produced in Chicago the next
year, starring David Montgomery and Fred
Stone. In 1939, twenty years after Baum's
death at the age of sixty-three, Hollywood
produced an ornate Technicolor film version,
with Broadway comedians and Hollywood
stars cavorting in the rôles of the Scarecrow,
the Tin Woodman, the Cowardly Lion, the
Wizard, and Glinda the Good. Other of
Baum's inventions—Jack Pumpkinhead, the
Sawhorse, the Woggle Bug, the Gump, Tik-
Tok, Woozy, and Teddy Bear—did not appear in this film.

Baum wrote twenty-four books for girls
as "Edith Van Dyne" and others as "Schuyler Stanton" and "Floyd Akers." The children of America, however, clamored for
more and still more Oz books; the series
was continued after Baum's death, in Hollywood, by Ruth Plumley Thompson. Several
Oz episodes were dramatized, and Baum
wrote two unimportant adult plays, *The
Maid of Arran* (1881) and *The Queen of
Killarney* (1885).

Oz was a Utopian place, with no disease
and no poverty, and no political dissension
except in the outlying regions. The books
were lacking in style and in imaginative

distinction, but they did induce American
children to look for the element of wonder
in the world around them, and were decidedly American in their employment of the
forces of nature—tidal waves, earthquakes,
and Kansas cyclones—and in their reliance
on mechanical gadgets for magical effects.
Baum, rebelling against writing more Oz
books in 1910, declared in *The Emerald City
of Oz* that it had been permanently cut off
from communication with the rest of the
world. It was a simple matter for him to
state that the country had developed wireless telegraphy, when he decided to resume
with *The Patchwork Girl of Oz,* one of the
best of the series, in 1913.

Baum's photographs show a tired, thoughtful, quizzical face, with eyeglasses and a
heavy moustache. He was always punctilious about answering the hundreds of letters
he received from children, and was also
pleased when a Church of England clergyman wrote him that the Oz books had proved
a great solace in war-time. For recreation
Baum raised fine varieties of chrysanthe-
mums.

PRINCIPAL WORKS: Mother Goose in Prose,
1897; Father Goose: His Book, 1899; The Wonderful Wizard of Oz, 1900; The Master Key, 1901;
The New Wizard of Oz, 1903; The Land of Oz,
1904; Queen Zixi of Ix, 1905; Ozma of Oz, 1907;
Baum's Fairy Tales, 1908; Dorothy and the Wizard
of Oz, 1908; The Road to Oz, 1909; The Emerald
City of Oz, 1910; Sky Island, 1912; The Patchwork Girl of Oz, 1913.

ABOUT: Wagenknecht, E. Utopia Americana;
Chicago Tribune May 18, 1919.

BAUM, VICKI (January 24, 1888-),
Austrian novelist now living in America,
writes: "I was born in Vienna, the single
child of a good fam-
ily in very bourgeois
surroundings. As a
rather dreamy a n d
romantic child I was
always in opposition
to the very dry and
strict education my
parents thought to be
the right thing for
my sort of character.
At the age of eight I

started studying the harp, and three years
later I made my first appearance on the
lecture platform. Although I was devoted
to music, I always used the nights for writing and reading secretly. I was fourteen
when the first of my short stories appeared
in print.

"At eighteen I married. My first husband
was a writer and as unsuited for practical

life as myself. We parted friends before long, and remained friends till he died. After my divorce I went to Germany, and for three years played the harp in the orchestra and was professor of the musical high school in Darmstadt. My time was shared between music, writing, and (during the war) nursing. I got married in 1916 to my best friend since childhood, Richard Lert, who happened to be the conductor of the orchestra I was playing in.

"By sheer accident one of our young actors, who was the brother of Jakob Wassermann, discovered that my writing desk was filled up with stories and novels I had written just for the fun of it. He sent one of them to a publisher and this man to my big surprise printed my work. After two of my books had been published, I got two baby sons and completely forgot about being a promising young writer. It was six years later that I took up writing again.

"All this time I was moving from one town to another, accompanying my husband. In 1926 I went to Berlin and took a job editing some of the magazines published by the then biggest German publishers (and also mine), Ullstein. I gave up music as a profession after marriage, but I felt and still feel that a writer should always have some profession which brings him into close contact with the realities of life.

"I would still be an editor if a clever young writer, Dr. Erdei, had not come along and bothered me to dramatize my novel, *Grand Hotel.* I did it against my own convictions and it turned out to be surprisingly successful. I got an invitation to come to New York to see it performed, and the country just got me. I came to America in 1931 and my visit was supposed to last two weeks. I am still here, and was naturalized in 1938. I brought my family over and we are living in Los Angeles.

"I like books, music, children, trees, and bad people. I dislike high society, politics, bridge, and important people—if they know they are important. I don't smoke or drink —not as a principle, but because I don't like to. My main vice is dancing, whenever I get a chance. The writers I like best are Thomas Mann, Ernest Hemingway, Sinclair Lewis, Knut Hamsun, Dostoievsky, Colette, and Herman Bang."

* * *

Since 1932 Vicki Baum has been writing for the movies. Her novels, however, are still written in German and then translated. She is a slender blonde with "blue eyes which seem a little tired," and a manner "both concentrated and abstracted." She speaks an excellent English (as her autobiographical sketch indicates), though vocally with a slight German accent, and her voice is "a soft, slow, faintly melancholy monotone" which does not in the least accord with her animated and energetic nature. The usual date given for her birth is 1888, though in *Who's Who in America* she gives it as 1896. Her special gift is for the "group novel," which brings together in one place many varied personalities and describes their interrelations.

WORKS AVAILABLE IN ENGLISH: Grand Hotel, 1931; Martin's Summer, 1931; And Life Goes On, 1932; Helene, 1932; Secret Sentence, 1932; Falling Star, 1934; Men Never Know, 1935; Sing, Sister, Sing, 1936; Tale of Bali (non-fiction) 1937; Shanghai, 1937, 1938; Saturday Night (play) 1939; Central Stores, 1940; The Ship and the Shore, 1941; The Christmas Carp, 1941; Marion Alive, 1942.

ABOUT: Annales Politiques et Littéraires April 7, 1933; Pictorial Review September 1931; Saturday Review of Literature January 1, 1938.

BAZIN, RENÉ (December 26, 1853-July 21. 1932), French novelist, was born René François Nicolas Marie Bazin on a farm in the province of Anjou. He was a delicate but an extremely happy child and many of the joys of his early youth were afterwards recorded in *Contes de Bonne Perrette.* He attended the lycée and studied for the priesthood at the petit séminaire Mongazon at Angers;  took up law, practicing for a short time only; and then began the teaching of criminal law in the Roman Catholic University of Angers. He was later awarded a doctor of laws degree by the University of Paris. He was writing all the time, and little by little his literary pursuits gained complete precedence.

Stephanette, his first novel, appeared when he was thirty-one; *Une Tache d'Encre,* his third novel and the first of his works to be translated into English, and *Sicile,* his first travel book, received awards from the French Academy. In 1896 his collective works were crowned by this same body. He traveled extensively during the 'nineties, and in 1899 and 1901 appeared his two best known works, *La Terre Qui Meurt,* the story of a family of farmers in the Vendean marshes, and *Les Oberlé,* a novel about an Alsatian who deserts from the German army to cross into France; *Le Blé qui Lève*

(1907) was projected as an illustration of the tyranny of trade unions. But the theme with which he was chiefly preoccupied, in his novels—a protest against the prevailing type of sex fiction, against Zola and the "naturalistic school"—was the love of the peasant for his native soil. He had a Catholic point of view about poverty ("a blessing in disguise") ; and he handled his peasants with the utmost tenderness.

In 1903 (inducted 1904) he was elected to the French Academy. He was married to Aline Bricard, by whom he had eight children ; his eldest daughter, Elizabeth (Madame Sainte-Marie Perrin), was the author of *Pèrelins d'Emmaüs* and *Images.* Bazin never lost his love of the country, where he could "see the infinite in things, and . . . listen to its life . . ." and he was an ardent huntsman.

He was a frail man with a love for simplicity in all things and a violent hatred for insincerity and pretence. He had a natural calmness of manner but he could speak out and speak loudly to those who listened to the defeatist prophecies of a French decadence—"Don't accept those words. Protest. Be indignant."

In all he was the author of about fifty volumes of fiction, travel, biography, and essays. His books, said Edmund Gosse, could be recommended to the English people "without the possibility of a blush." Bazin's unreserved Catholicism played a strong part in shaping his literary convictions.

PRINCIPAL WORKS AVAILABLE IN ENGLISH TRANSLATION : A Blot of Ink, 1892; Autumn Glory, 1901 ; Redemption, 1908 ; The Coming Harvest, 1908 ; The Barrier, 1910 ; The Children of Alsace, 1912 ; Those of His Own Household, 1914.

ABOUT : Gosse, E. W. French Profiles; Stephens, W. French Novelists of Today; Talbot, F. S. (ed.). Fiction by Its Makers; Revue des Deux Mondes July 1, 1929, August 1, 1932; Catholic World September 1932.

*BEACH, REX ELLINGWOOD (September 1, 1877-).

American novelist and miscellaneous writer, was born in Atwood,

Mich., a younger son of Henry Walter Beach and Eva Eunice (Canfield) Beach, and was named Rex Ellingwood Beach. In his own phrasing, Beach was born in a log house on a stumpy farm in Michigan along about milking time. Atwood is not far from the home of

the late James Oliver Curwood, another popular novelist of the "he-man" school. Beach's father ran a fruit farm. Determining to seek a warmer climate, he put his family on the schooner "Fair Play" and made his way south to Florida, where they settled at Tampa. Rex was sent to boarding school at fourteen. He attended Rollins College, Winter Park, Fla., from 1891 to 1896 ; went to Chicago for a year at the College of Law and disliked it, and joined the Chicago Athletic Association to play professional football. Transferring to the swimming team, he broke an indoor record at water polo in the winter of 1897. Returning to the study of law at the Kent College of Law in 1899, he left in 1900 to join the gold rush to the Klondike, which he never reached. With his two partners, Beach was dumped off a boat one rainy night at Rampart City, where they spent a long hard winter. In June 1900 he was in Nome. Returning twice to the United States, he resumed law study; tried zinc mining in Missouri ; then made a disastrous attempt to work the beach sands at Nome with machinery. Meeting two of his former associates who had sold a story or two, Beach determined to attempt to write. "On the credit side was a fair knowledge of Alaska and the placer mining game, a wide acquaintance of rough and ready people, and their methods of life, and a certain amount of mining property which was almost valueless." *Pardners* appeared in 1905, and his first best-seller and second novel, *The Spoilers,* in 1906. "The Victor Hugo of the North," as some reviewers dubbed him, was prompt to follow up his advantage with two more popular favorites, *The Barrier* and *The Silver Horde,* the first a romance of half-breeds, and the second a genuinely interesting novel about salmon fishing and breeding which has been filmed. *The Spoilers, The Barrier,* and *The Silver Horde* were collected in an omnibus, *Alaskan Adventures,* in 1935.

Beach married Edith Crater in 1907, and they have lived in New York State in a house named Topside, at Ardsley-on-Hudson, and at Sebring, Fla. Cosmo Hamilton, who had been charmed by Beach's tales of "strong hairy men and strong hairy deeds," found the author to be "a man standing six-feet-one in his socks, [with] a back as broad as a door, a hand like a leg of mutton, a deep, vibrating voice, soft blue eyes with a twinkle." "There is no repose in him," commented C. C. Baldwin. "To him a tree is not a tree unless it is one of the monster

* Died December 7, 1949.

redwoods of California; a man is not a man until he has attained he-manhood." Baldwin is also of the opinion that Beach's northern stories lack the sincerity and depth of Jack London's. Beach was president of the Author's League of America from 1917 to 1921. His New York clubs are the Players, Lambs, New York Athletic, and Coffee House, and he is a member of several country clubs, including the Sleepy Hollow Country Club.

PRINCIPAL WORKS: Pardners, 1905; The Spoilers, 1906; The Barrier, 1907; The Silver Horde, 1909; Going Some, 1910; The Ne'er-do-well, 1911; The Net, 1912; The Iron Trail, 1913; The Auction Block, 1914; Heart of the Sunset, 1915; Rainbow's End, 1916; The Crimson Gardenia, 1916; Laughing Bill Hyde, 1917; The Winds of Chance, 1918; Oh, Shoot! Confessions of an Agitated Sportsman, 1921; Flowing Gold, 1922; Big Brother, 1923; The Goose Woman, 1925; Padlocked, 1926; The Mating Call, 1927; Don Careless, 1928; Son of the Gods, 1929; Money Mad, 1931; Men of the Outer Islands, 1932; Beyond Control, 1932; Alaskan Adventures (omnibus) 1933; Hands of Dr. Locke, 1934; Masked Women, 1934; Wild Pastures, 1935; Jungle Gold, 1935; Valley of Thunder, 1939; Personal Exposures (autobiography) 1941.

ABOUT: Baldwin, C. C. The Men Who Make Our Novels; Beach, R. E. Personal Exposures; Hamilton, C. People Worth Talking About; Rinehart, M. R. My Story; American Magazine August 1924; New York Times Book Review August 17, 1941.

BEALS, CARLETON (November 13, 1893-), American political and sociological writer, writes: "I was born in Medicine  Lodge, Kansas; my father, Leon Eli Beals, a l a w y e r and journalist, moved from Kansas to California when I w a s three years old. My m o t h e r was Elvina Sybilla Blickensderfer. I attended grammar and high school in Pasadena, then worked my way through the University of California, graduating in 1916. After my freshman year I had to stay out for a year because of lack of funds. Among the occupations I had in those years were those of carpenter, foundryman, mechanic's helper, waiter, teacher and tutor, grocery clerk, bookseller, cashier, fruit-picker, harvest hand, cowboy, teamster, shoe salesman, and paid chess player for a retired banker. While in the university I twice won the Bonnheim Essay Prize and the Bryce History Essay Prize, and was awarded a graduate scholarship at Columbia.

"After graduating I tried writing short stories but had no success in getting any published, and finally took a job with the Standard Oil Company of California, working in their export department in Richmond, Calif. Soon enough bored at punching an adding machine, I decided to see the world, and left for Mexico in a second-hand Ford. It had to be abandoned, and I continued the journey with wild burros rounded up in the hills. After going broke and suffering considerable hardship, I reached Mexico City. There I founded the English Preparatory Institute, taught at the American High School, and became principal, and was also an instructor on the personal staff of President Carranza. In addition to these activities, I continued writing, and had a number of magazine articles accepted, the first two by *Current History* and the *North American Review*. (I am now a contributing editor of *Current History*.) I also started to write a book on Mexico.

"In 1920 I went to Spain, where I lived for about a year, traveling widely and continuing to write. The following year I went to Italy, where I watched the development of the Fascist movement, witnessed the march on Rome, and interviewed Mussolini.

"In 1922 I returned to Mexico and a year later went back to the United States, living in New York for over a year. My first two books, one on Mexico and one on Italy, were published almost simultaneously in 1923. My third book, *Brimstone and Chili*, was written partly in New York City and partly on Prince Edward's Island, in Canada, and completed in Tioga, Pa., but I read the proof in Mexico, where I stayed for some years, doing journalistic work.

"In 1926 I toured Central America, and in 1927 I was sent by the *Nation* to write a series of articles on Nicaragua. I crossed the jungles of Honduras and Nicaragua on horseback and succeeded in locating the rebel general, Augusto Sandino, who was combating the American invasion—a scoop that had international repercussions. The articles were published in every European language, and even in Chinese and Japanese.

"In 1929 I returned to the United States to lecture and continued on to Europe, revisiting Spain, where I met most of the leaders of the later Republican government and became a close friend of Manual Azaña, who was later president. I went on to North Africa, Spanish and French Morocco, Algiers, and Tunisia, and horsebacked into the Rif country. I investigated Mussolini's Italy, went on to Greece and Turkey, and went into the Soviet Union via the Black Sea. I also spent some time in Germany.

"After another short trip to Mexico, I returned to live in New York. In 1930 I was awarded a Guggenheim Fellowship to complete my study of Porfirio Diaz.

"In 1932 I went to Cuba, which I had visited briefly many times, in order to investigate conditions under the dictatorship of Gerardo Machado, the result being the book, *The Crime of Cuba.*

"In 1933 I lived in New York, but that summer went out on a sheep ranch in Wyoming and also lectured at the University of California. (I had previously in 1927 lectured at the University of Mexico, giving a course on Central America.) Toward the end of the year I returned to Cuba and toured South America, although most of my time was spent in Peru.

"In March 1934 the North American Newspaper Alliance sent me to Cuba to cover a general strike that threatened to become a revolution, and from there I went to Louisiana, to investigate the kingdom of Huey P. Long. The following year I was sent by the New York *Post* to cover the Scottsboro trial in Alabama, and I continued there investigating the conditions of share-croppers.

"The years following I lived mostly in Branford, Conn., on the Long Island Sound, but in 1937 drove across the country and down to Mexico, where I participated in the 'trial' of Leon Trotsky. Convinced that this trial was merely a farce being conducted by his intimate friends, I resigned from the so-called 'impartial' jury, and returned to the United States.

"Among other things, I am on the Board of Governors of the Academy of Foreign Relations, a sponsor of the National Gallery of the American Indian, and a member of the Society of American Historians. I have been a contributor to the *Encyclopaedia of Social Sciences,* published by Columbia University. Although I have lent my name to various organizations and committees which have espoused causes I have felt to be admirable, I have no political affiliations, because I feel that a free-lance writer should not be obligated to remain silent when he desires to be critical. Like most contemporary Americans, I am hostile to all foreign 'isms' that advocate systems which would abridge political and personal liberties.

"My literary tastes are varied, and my favorite authors at present are John Dos Passos, John Steinbeck, James Farrell, Robinson Jeffers, Ellen Glasgow, Eugene O'Neill, William Faulkner, Katherine Anne Porter.

Among writers who have most influenced me at some time or other I would name particularly Cervantes, Papini, Darwin, Zimmern, Tenney Frank (*Roman Imperialism*), Marx, Shelley, Keats, Shakespeare, Emerson, Whitman, Turner (*American Frontier*), Gustavus Myers, Veblen, Freud, Peréz Galdos, Voltaire, and many others."

* * *

To this autobiographical account, there need be added only the summing up of Carleton Beals' work by Harold DeWolf Fuller: "He has pronounced views, but presents a documented picture." Keen observation, wide interest, and a sort of taciturn geniality are his outstanding personal characteristics.

PRINCIPAL WORKS: Mexico: An Interpretation, 1923; Rome or Death: The Story of Fascism, 1923; Brimstone and Chili, 1927; Destroying Victor, 1929; Mexican Maze, 1930; Banana Gold, 1932; Porfirio Diaz: Dictator of Mexico, 1932; The Crime of Cuba, 1933; Black River, 1933; Fire on the Andes, 1934; The Story of Huey P. Long, 1935; The Stones Awake, 1936; America South, 1937; Glass Houses: Ten Years of Free-Lancing, 1938; The Coming Struggle for Latin America, 1938; American Earth, 1939; The Great Circle: Further Adventures in Free-Lancing, 1940; Pan America, 1941.

ABOUT: Current History January 1940; Literary Digest October 7, 1933; Saturday Review of Literature August 26, 1933, November 26, 1938; Travel September 1940; Wilson Library Bulletin November 1932.

*BEARD, CHARLES AUSTIN (November 27, 1874-), American historian and political scientist, was born in Knightstown, Ind., the son of William Henry Beard and Mary (Payne) Beard. He was educated at De Pauw University (Ph.B. 1898), Oxford, Cornell, and Columbia (M.A. 1903, Ph.D. 1904). On his graduation from high school, his father bought for him and  his brother a country weekly, the Knightstown *Sun,* and they ran it with success for four years. In his years at De Pauw he also acted as a reporter for the Henry County *Republican.* His father was a building contractor and banker, with a keen interest in politics and social questions. In the son these turned to an interest in labor, and at Oxford he was one of the founders of Ruskin College, the first labor college in an English university.

He began teaching in Columbia in 1904, and by 1915 was professor of politics. In 1917, though he was in favor of America's participation in the First World War, he resigned in protest against the dismissal of J. McKeen Cattell and H. W. L. Dana because of their anti-war stand. Dr. Beard had already been in trouble with the Columbia authorities through his book, *An Economic Interpretation of the Constitution*— one of the earliest books to point out the economic interests and bias of the Founding Fathers. After his resignation he was for five years director of the Training School for Public Service, in New York. In 1922 he was adviser to the Institute of Municipal Research in Tokyo, and was called back to Japan as an adviser after the earthquake the next year. With Thorstein Veblen, John Dewey, and James Harvey Robinson he founded the New School of Social Research, in New York, and for four years he was head of the New York Bureau of Municipal Research. In 1927 and 1928 he was an adviser to the Jugoslav government, in Belgrade. He is a past president of the American Historical Association, the American Political Science Association, and the National Association for Adult Education.

In 1900 Dr. Beard married Mary Ritter, and they have a son and a daughter. The daughter, Miriam Beard (Mrs. Alfred Vagts, wife of the refugee German historian) is well known as an author in her own right, as is Mrs. Beard.*qv* The Beards live in New Milford, Conn., in a big house, formerly a boys' school, overlooking the Housatonic River. They run a successful farm, and Dr. Beard sells 300,000 quarts of milk a year. As Hubert Herring remarked, "he combines the zeal of a crusader with the sound instincts of a good horse trader." He has been described as "wiry, white-haired, amiably skeptical." His amiability, however, can be interrupted by what the late Randolph Bourne called his "Olympian anger," when he confronts a situation arousing his righteous indignation. He has always been a doughty fighter for academic freedom, and "the one thing he hates above everything else is imperialism." Part of every winter he spends in Washington, so as to keep in closer touch with the nation's business. He has been called everything from a Communist (which he is not: he himself says he is "not Marxian but Madisonian") to an Isolationist—which, technically, he also is

not. He has been a storm center among his own colleagues for years, the historians calling him a political scientist, the political scientists an historian. Hubert Herring's conclusion is that "he is not quite so good an economic henchman as he is an historian." As a teacher his motto was: "Let us examine the assumptions," and that is what he is still doing as a writer. "Democracy," he has said, "is a cause that is never won, but I believe it will never be lost."

Perhaps his best known book to the general public is *The Rise of American Civilization*, written with his wife—a collaboration which he describes as "a division of argument." Besides his own books, he has edited a number of anthologies, including *Whither Mankind?* (1930), and *America Faces the Future* (1932). His chief defect as a writer for the layman is that he is somewhat ponderous; one critic said of his *Economic Interpretation of the Constitution* that no such sensational work was ever so dully written! Nevertheless, his books are well worth the labor required to master their contents. And in spite of the *furore* which every new publication of his arouses in academic circles, he received in 1940 the first annual award of the New York City Association of Teachers of Social Studies.

PRINCIPAL WORKS: The Office of Justice of the Peace, 1904; Introduction to the English Historians, 1906; Development of Modern Europe (with J. H. Robinson, 2 vols.) 1907; Readings in Modern European History (with J. H. Robinson, 2 vols.) 1908-09; Readings in American Government, 1909; American Government and Politics, 1910; American City Government, 1912; An Economic Interpretation of the Constitution, 1913; American Citizenship (with M. R. Beard) 1913; Contemporary American History, 1914; The Economic Origins of Jeffersonian Democracy, 1915; History of the American People (with W. C. Bagley) 1918; History of the United States (with M. R. Beard) 1921; Our Old World Backgrounds (with W. C. Bagley) 1922; Cross-Currents in Europe Today, 1922; The Economic Basis of Politics, 1922; Administration and Politics of Tokyo, 1923; The Rise of American Civilization (with M. R. Beard) 1927; The American Party Battle, 1928; The Balkan Pivot—Yugoslavia (with G. Radin) 1929; Towards Civilization, 1930; The Nature of the Social Sciences, 1934; The Idea of National Interest, 1934; The Open Door at Home, 1934; The Discussion of Human Affairs, 1936; America in Mid-Passage (with M. R. Beard) 1939; Foreign Policy for America, 1940; Public Policy and the General Welfare, 1941.

ABOUT: American Review January 1935; Harper's Magazine May 1939; Journal of Political Economy December 1935; Nation April 8, 1936; New Republic January 2, 1935, October 4, 1939; School and Society July 13, 1940, October 19, 1940; Time May 22, 1939, May 20, 1940.

BEARD, DANIEL CARTER (June 21, 1850-June 11, 1941), American Boy Scout founder and writer for boys, who was better  known as "Dan" Beard, wrote the editor of this volume not long before his death at ninety: "I come of a family of artists and authors. My father, four brothers, two sisters, an uncle, a cousin, and a niece were all artists of note. I was born in Cincinnati, Ohio, and spent my early life in that city and in Covington, Ky., just across the Ohio River. As a boy, I took a great interest in the pioneers of Kentucky, and became possessed with the idea of living as nearly like them as possible. Before reaching manhood I was a true Scout and knew how to live the life of the wilderness. I was educated in the schools of Covington. At nineteen I was graduated as a civil engineer and entered the office of the city engineer of Cincinnati. Later, because of the opportunity which it offered for travel, I became a map maker for a map publishing company. (I had early shown an aptitude for drawing.) A chance visit to New York settled my vocation. I had made some sketches of animals and these attracted the attention of a magazine editor and led to the beginning of my career as an illustrator. Many of Mark Twain's books were illustrated by me.

"When I was thirty-two I began writing books for boys. The phenomenal success of my first book lured me from the career of an artist to that of a writer. I was for seven years, however, an instructor in the Woman's School of Applied Design, inaugurating the first class in animal drawing in the world. Also, for a time, I was editor of *Recreation Magazine*. My mail from boy readers became so large that I had to employ several secretaries to assist me in handling it. Boys came by the hundred to my private camp on Lake Teedyuskung, in Pike County, Pa., and this led to the establishing of the Dan Beard Outdoor School, which still operates each summer for instruction in woodcraft under my direction.

"Readers of my books formed a group known as the Sons of Daniel Boone. This was the forerunner of the Boy Scouts of America, a movement which I have served as National Scout Commissioner since its beginning.

"I was married in 1894 to Beatrice Alice Jackson, and we have a son and daughter. For many years we lived in Flushing, N.Y. Our home is now located in Suffern, N.Y. At the age of ninety, though in poor health, I still maintain my active work as an author and illustrator, and each month I contribute a page to the magazine, *Boy's Life*.

* * *

"Uncle Dan" Beard, dressed in buckskin, with his snowy Vandyke beard and his bronzed face was a familiar figure at Boy Scout gatherings for thirty years, where as chairman of the National Court of Honor he made the awards to the Boy Scout heroes of the year. He himself received innumerable medals and awards, including the Roosevelt Distinguished Service Gold Medal. "All my life," he once said, "I've been doing just what I wanted to do." As one friendly critic remarked, he "made the old frontier a living thing in the lives of boys, and taught them to uphold the sturdy virtues of the pioneers." He died of the infirmities of age at his home, "Brooklands," at Suffern, N.Y., just ten days before his ninety-first birthday.

PRINCIPAL WORKS: American Boys' Handy Book, 1882; Moonlight and Six Feet of Romance (novel) 1890; Outdoor Handy Book, 1900; Jack of All Trades, 1900; Boy Pioneers and Sons of Daniel Boone, 1909; The Buckskin Book and Buckskin Calendar, 1911; Boat Building and Boating, 1911; Shelters, Shacks, and Shanties, 1914; Bugs, Butterflies, and Beetles, 1915; Signs, Signals, and Symbols, 1918; Field and Forest Handy Book, 1920 (as The Book of Camp-Lore and Woodcraft, 1936); American Boys' Book of Wild Animals, 1921; The Black Wolf Pack, 1922; American Boys' Book of Birds and Brownies of the Woods, 1923; Do It Yourself, 1925; Wisdom of the Woods, 1927; Buckskin Book for Buckskin Men and Boys, 1929; Boy Heroes of Today, 1932; Hardly a Man Is Now Alive (autobiography) 1939.

ABOUT: Beard, D. C. Hardly a Man Is Now Alive; Clemens, C. & Sibley, C. Uncle Dan; Kunitz, S. J. & Haycraft, H. (eds.). The Junior Book of Authors; American Magazine May 1924; Nature Magazine June 1937; New York Herald Tribune June 12, 1941; New York Times June 12, 1941; Newsweek July 4, 1938; Pictorial Review February 1927; Publishers' Weekly October 26, 1929.

BEARD, Mrs. MARY (RITTER) (August 5, 1876-), American sociologist, was born in Indianapolis, her maiden name being Ritter. She received a Ph.B. from De Pauw University in 1897, and has done graduate work at Columbia University. She was married in 1900 to Charles A. Beard,[qv] the historian, and they have a son and a daughter. She has traveled and studied widely in Europe and the Orient, and has long been active in the labor movement. Before granting of the vote to women she was also a leading suffragette. In 1937 she organized the World Center for Women's Archives, feeling that the contributions of women had

never received sufficient attention from historians of civilization. She has also shown a particular interest in the improvement of nursing and the welfare of nurses. Besides her own books, she has collaborated with her hus-

Underwood

band in several others, and has been editor or co-editor of a number of volumes, including *America Through Women's Eyes* (1934) and *Laughing Their Way* (1934). She is a plump, wholesome-looking woman whose succinct style and sense of humor have lightened the serious subjects with which she deals. Her home is in New Milford, Conn., on the Housatonic River, but she usually spends the winters in Washington with her husband. She is a member of the scholars' fraternity, Phi Beta Kappa. Her daughter is also well known as a writer and translator. "By Charles and Mary Beard" has become a sort of trade-mark in contemporary American historical writing.

PRINCIPAL WORKS: American Citizenship (with C. A. Beard) 1913; A Short History of the American Labor Movement, 1920; History of the United States (with C. A. Beard) 1921; The Rise of American Civilization (with C. A. Beard) 1929; On Understanding Women, 1931; The Making of American Civilization (with C. A. Beard) 1937; America in Mid-Passage (with C. A. Beard) 1939.

ABOUT: American Nursing Journal October 1938; Christian Science Monitor Monthly July 27, 1939; New York Times December 1, 1940; Scholastic May 15, 1937.

BEARDSLEY, AUBREY. See "BRITISH AUTHORS OF THE 19TH CENTURY"

BEAUCHAMP, MARY ANNETTE. See RUSSELL, M. A. B. R.

BEAUCHAMP, KATHLEEN MANSFIELD. See MANSFIELD, K.

BEAUCLERK, HELEN DE VERE (September 20, 1892-), English novelist, writes: "Helen Beauclerk, formerly Helen Mary Dorothea Bellingham, was born in Cambridge. On her father's side she is of a North of England family settled in Ireland (Castle Bellingham); on her mother's side, Lowland Scottish (Dunlop, of Keppoch

in Ayrshire). She was adopted at an early age by a relative and changed her name to Beauclerk. [Since Beauclerk and De Vere are family names of the Dukes of St. Albans, the detective-minded reader will have a fair idea of the author's family connections.]

"No schooling. At the age of seven went to live in France. Studied music—for six hours a day, hence the absence of other education—not very successfully, at Paris Conservatoire. Read every available book at every available opportunity. Worked a little as piano teacher and accompanist, but had no real taste for anything but writing. From the age of thirteen to twenty, wrote, in French, stories and novels that were all firmly destroyed by her strong critical sense. Published first story, in French, in Paris *Figaro*, 1914. Worked as translator and secretary in London during 1914-1918 war, eventually as journalist, having learned to write easily in English. In 1919 joined staff of *Evening Standard*, later of Birmingham *Post*. Has published four novels, also articles, short stories, and translations from the French, notably the first two-thirds of Amedée Ozenfant's *Journey Through Life*, 1939. The first three novels were historical or in an historical setting.

"Has always regretted that circumstances forbade a university education and career such as was followed by her mother's family. Love of music, however, very strong, also of early Christian history and religious history generally. Attracted to, but not convinced by, astrology, palmistry, and the so-called occult sciences. Decided, on the approach of the 1939 war, that a love of the past was a form of escapism and that a novelist's job was to write of contemporary life. Proposes in the future to continue doing so.

"Chief interests: reading French books, writing English books, and wearing good-looking clothes."

* * *

Miss Beauclerk is unmarried. Her father was a brigadier general and baronet, her mother of a family prominent in church and university circles. She is a "typical" English blonde in appearance, tall and slender, with delicately aquiline features. *The Love of the Foolish Angel* was first choice of the British Book Society in 1929 and was also a selection of the American Book Guild. Of her work Miss Beauclerk says: "Writing is a queer business. Everything goes into it, yet nothing comes out precisely in the form it was experienced. You take, you do not copy, from Nature; you transpose, and always indirectly. That at least is my method."

PRINCIPAL WORKS: The Green Lacquer Pavilion, 1926; The Love of the Foolish Angel, 1929; The Mountain and the Tree, 1935; So Frail a Thing, 1940.

ABOUT: Wilson Library Bulletin March 1930.

BECK, Mrs. LILY (MORESBY) ADAMS ("E. Barrington," "Louis Moresby," pseuds.) (?-January 3, 1931),

English novelist and mystic, was the daughter of Admiral John Moresby and the grand-daughter of Admiral-of-the-Fleet Sir Fairfax Moresby. Her first acquaintance with the Orient came when her father was stationed there; she visited India, Ceylon, China, Java, Egypt, Burma, Japan; crossed the great Himalayan Pass, and sojourned in Little Tibet among the Mongolian people, studying their manners and customs. Mrs. Beck made a trip through Canada after the First World War and decided to make her home in British Columbia. Her house in Victoria was a museum of Orientalia set in a secluded and lovely English garden. The idea for her first short story, a tale of the Orient included in *The Ninth Vibration* (1922) came to her in 1919 in the lobby of a Victoria hotel. This was published under the name of L. Adams Beck. Mrs. Beck's grandfather, Admiral Moresby, had been a midshipman in Nelson's fleet, and her grandmother, as a girl, had known Byron. From this juxtaposition emerged two bestsellers of 1924 and 1925, *The Divine Lady,* about Nelson and Lady Hamilton, and *Glorious Apollo,* a fictional study of Byron with a bias in favor of Anne Milbank, his wife. Both historical romances were published as the work of "E. Barrington," leading critics this time to confuse them with the work of Emilie Isabel Barrington (Mrs. Russell Barrington). Mrs. Beck continued to travel most of the time, British Columbia still serving as her base; she died in 1931 at an undetermined age in Kyoto, Japan. Thoroughly versed in Oriental doctrine, she claimed never to know weariness of mind or body. Small, frail and ageless, with restless eyes and

hands, she looked worn and faded at times, while continuing to speak with youthful zest. One of her publishers, George Doran, speaks impatiently of her as not only an ascetic but a martinet, imposing her habits and beliefs on her immediate circle, and a most difficult person to deal with in business relations. Her reconstructions of the period of *The Beggar's Opera* (*The Chaste Diana*) and the times of Perdita Robinson, the mistress of George IV and Charles Fox, still have their interest and values, although their lush romanticism is no longer in fashion.

PRINCIPAL WORKS: *As "E. Barrington"*—"The Ladies!" 1922; The Chaste Diana, 1923; The Gallants, 1924; The Divine Lady, 1924; Glorious Apollo, 1925; The Exquisite Perdita, 1926; The Thunderer, 1927; The Empress of Hearts, 1928; The Laughing Queen, 1929; The Duel of the Queens, 1930; The Irish Beauties, 1931; Anne Boleyn, 1932; The Crowned Lovers, 1935. *As "L. Adams Beck"*—The Ninth Vibration and Other Stories, 1922; The Key of Dreams, 1922; The Perfume of the Rainbow, 1923; The Way of Stars, 1925; Dreams and Delights, 1926; The House of Fulfilment, 1927; The Story of Oriental Philosophy, 1928; The Way of Power, 1928; The Garden of Vision, 1929; The Openers of the Gate, 1930; The Joyous Story of Astrid, 1931; A Beginner's Book of Yoga (ed. by D. M. Bramble), 1937. *As "Louis Moresby"*—The Treasure of Ho, 1924; The Glory of Egypt, 1926; Rubies, 1927; Captain Java, 1928.

ABOUT: Doran, G. H. Chronicles of Barabbas; Canadian Bookman December 1929; Publishers' Weekly January 10, 1931; Wilson Library Bulletin November 1930, February 1931.

BECKER, Mrs. MAY (LAMBERTON) (August 26, 1873-), American editor and critic, writes: "My family is unmitigated New England on both sides as far back as they go, but I was born in New York. My mother taught me till I went to high school, where the teachers were so amazed to find somebody who enjoyed study that they shoved me on with

Oggiano

speed and glory. Before graduation I was working on a newspaper as musical and dramatic critic because the editor thought I had a good vocabulary and the staff was running out of synonyms. At twenty I married a gentleman who took me abroad for a long honeymoon and brought me back into the heart of professional musical society in New York. Beginning as a lecturer on musical history, I used the same technique later for lectures on contemporary literature, especially of other countries. In 1915 the New

York *Evening Post* asked me to create a department for its book section and gave me a free hand to do so. As at the close of practically every lecture I had been asked about a book for some specific purpose about which I had not been lecturing, I knew that a department answering such questions on a personal, individual basis, as one reader to another, would have human interest. Readers thought so too, and 'The Reader's Guide' has not missed a beat since it began, though it moved to the *Saturday Review of Literature* in 1924 and to the New York *Herald Tribune* "*Books*" in 1933. The number of letters it has received has reached astronomical figures.

"As a result of writing *Adventures in Reading*, for young people beginning to read adult literature, I found myself successively (and simultaneously with the 'Guide') book-editor of *American Girl, Youth's Companion,* and *Scholastic,* and, for two glorious years of struggle, editor of *St. Nicholas.* When that had to be sold down the river in 1932 I went to "*Books*" as editor of the page of 'Books for Young People,' and soon after brought over the 'Guide' to the same review, where I have conducted both departments ever since. I have the most fascinating job, for which I trained chiefly by learning to read at an early age and by taking unfeigned delight in listening to shop talk of every kind, especially of trades and professions I know nothing about. My vicarious interests have thus been wide; I grew up in a family that never stopped arguing politics and theology, and my daughter, Beatrice Warde, is a typographical expert who lives in London and is internationally known under her professional name of 'Paul Beaujon.' Running the 'Reader's Guide' sounds difficult when you try to explain it; I therefore do not try any longer, because when I do I scare myself.

"For many years I have spent my summers and some midwinters with my daughter in London, carrying on the 'Guide' from her roof-garden on Pimlico Wharf, an address for which my correspondents have a personal affection. In New York I live at the apartment of my Siamese cats on Morningside Drive."

* * *

This sketch gives a bit of the flavor of Mrs. Becker's inimitable style. She has been called "a reference librarian at large" and one who "keeps more facts stored in her head than any other woman alive." Her maiden name was Lamberton; she was married to Gustave L. Becker in 1894 and divorced in 1911. She attends to her enormous correspondence personally, without even a secretary. In her late sixties she is still young looking, with lively dark eyes and a refreshing zest for life. The *Publishers' Weekly* well called her "unique and irreplaceable."

In 1940 Mrs. Becker contributed the full royalties from her *Introducing Charles Dickens* to the purchase of an ambulance which was sent to London for war relief work; and her contributions of time and energy to the cause of the United Nations were tireless and endless.

PRINCIPAL WORKS: A Reader's Guide Book, 1923; Adventures in Reading, 1927; Golden Tales of Our America, 1929; Books As Windows, 1929; Golden Tales of the Old South, 1930; Golden Tales of New England, 1931; Golden Tales of the Prairie States, 1932; Under Twenty, 1932; Golden Tales of the Far West, 1935; First Adventures in Reading, 1936; Choosing Books for Children, 1937; Golden Tales of Canada, 1938; Golden Tales of the Southwest, 1939; Introducing Charles Dickens, 1940; Growing Up With America: An Anthology, 1941; The Home Book of Christmas, 1941.

ABOUT: Ferris, H. & Moore, V. Girls Who Did; Bookman May 1925; Boston Evening Transcript August 5, 1933; Publishers' Weekly October 10, 1931, September 30, 1939; Scholastic October 14, November 4, 1940; Wilson Library Bulletin March 1933.

*BEDEL, MAURICE (December 30, 1884-   ), French novelist and miscellaneous writer, was born in Paris, of an old Parisian family. In his childhood the family spent summers in a small house of romantic setting, La Vallée aux Loups, on the outskirts of Paris, near the spot where Chateaubriand wrote his *Memoires d'Outre Tombe.* Rabelais and Montaigne, however,  are Bedel's acknowledged masters, and from 1908 to 1928 he passed many summers in a house of his own in Touraine where Rabelais was born. Bedel studied at the College Sainte-Croix, not at Montherlant, but in the annex at Vésinet. On graduation, he was "seized by a passion to know. All knowledge attracted me, especially scientific knowledge. I had a horror of illness, but I was obstinate enough to study theoretical medicine—I was eighteen then, and it became my introduction to the study of man." Distaste for hospital atmosphere turned him to study of mental diseases, and he handed in a thesis for a degree on "Obsessions." In the evenings Bedel studied painting at the Académie Julien. He also gained some fame as an entomologist. Occasionally he contributed poems to little reviews, most often to *Schcherazade,* edited by Jean Cocteau. Bedel's first volume of verse, *Le Cahier de Phane,* was published in 1913. The First World War now intervened, and he served as an adjutant in the French army, receiving a wound in 1915. As an army doctor, he had occasion to attend Alpine troops in the Vosges, and here he met forty Norwegians attached to the troops as skiers. He became interested in their psychology and their matter-of-fact attitude towards divorce. The Scandinavian countries seemed to him abodes of sanity. Bedel also visited Morocco with French sharpshooters, becoming acquainted with the Foreign Legion and the native tribes of Africa.

After the war, Bedel obtained a post as secretary to a Norwegian collector of modern art, and extended his investigations into Norwegian psychology. *Jerôme: 60 Latitude Nord,* the resultant novel, won the Goncourt Prize in 1927, being the twenty-fifth novel to receive the award. The vote of the committee stood 6 to 3. It would also have won the Prix Renaudot, which went instead to Bernard Nabonne's *Maitena* after the Goncourt jury's decision was announced. In its unexpected metaphor, spirit of modernity, somewhat cynical outlook on life, and swift characterization it resembled the novels of Paul Morand and Jean Giraudoux. *Molinoff: or, The Count in the Kitchen,* like the later *Tovarich* of Jacques Deval, made sport of the old theme of impoverished aristocrats in domestic service. Others of Bedel's books are *Philippine* (1930), *Zulfu* (1932), *La Nouvelle Arcadie* (1934), *L'Alouette aux Nuages* (1935), *Le Laurier d'Apollon* (1936), and *Bengali* (1937). His home is in Paris.

WORKS AVAILABLE IN ENGLISH TRANSLATION: Jerôme: or, The Latitude of Love, 1928; Molinoff: or, The Count in the Kitchen, 1928; The New Arcadia, 1935.

ABOUT: Boston Evening Transcript February 11, 1928.

*BEDFORD-JONES, HENRY (April 29, 1887-), American novelist and translator, writes: "Born [Henry James O'Brien Bedford-Jones] in Napanee, Ont., Canada, Henry Bedford-Jones has lived the greater part of his life in the United States and is a citizen thereof. Since 1908 he has been a

prolific writer, and it is estimated that he has earned via the typewriter between a half-million and a million dollars within this period. His product has appeared in virtually all the better-class magazines here and in England, and he has published between sixty and seventy books of all natures. While he is best known as a writer for the fiction magazines, his output has comprised historical, juvenile, and other branches of writing.  Much of his early life was spent in Michigan and he is still a legal resident of Conway, in that state, although southern California claims him as a part-year resident. He has lived much abroad, being foreign correspondent for the Boston *Globe.* He has done a number of translations, notably the unpublished letters of Maurice and Eugénie de Guerin.

"Known for some years as a philatelic writer and a collector of stamps and historical letters, as well as an authority upon Oriental rugs, he has largely given up his collecting activities. A good deal of his time is spent motoring about this country and Canada. His wife, the former Mary McNally Bernardin, is associated with him in most of his work, and her name appears with his on numerous books and stories, as co-author.

* * *

Mr. Bedford-Jones was married in 1914 to Helen Swing Williamson, by whom he had two daughters and a son; later they were divorced and he remarried. He has published two books of technical advice to what he frankly calls "fictioneers," including himself in this category. He is one of the best known of "pulp paper magazine" story writers, and one of the better of its men in that medium.

PRINCIPAL WORKS: The Cross and the Hammer, 1912; Flamehair the Skald, 1913; Conquest, 1914; Under Fire, 1915; Against the Tide, 1924; Star Woman, 1924; Son of Cincinnati, 1925; Rodomont, 1925; St. Michael's Gold, 1926; Breeze in the Moonlight (trans.) 1926; King's Passport, 1927; Black Bull, 1927; Passion of Yang Kwei-fei (trans.) 1928; This Fiction Business, 1929; Cyrano, 1930; D'Artagnan's Letter (with M.McN. Bedford-Jones) 1931; Drums of Dambala, 1932; Graduate Fictioneer, 1932; King's Pardon, 1933; The Mission and the Man, 1939.

ABOUT: Nation September 11, 1935.

BEEBE, WILLIAM (July 29, 1877-),
American naturalist and writer, was born
in Brooklyn, N.Y., the son of Charles Beebe

H. Mitchell

and Henrietta Maria
Beebe, and was chris-
tened Charles Wil-
liam. He received
a B.S. degree from
Columbia University
in 1898; remained
another year doing
postgraduate study;
and in 1899 became
curator of ornithol-
ogy at the New York
Zoological Society, known in the city as the
Bronx Zoo, and director of its Department
of Scientific Research. As a boy Beebe was
fond of reading Jules Verne and G. A.
Henty, and later read Kipling, Buchan, and
Wells. A taste for adventure and exploration so fostered was not long in seeking
expression in deeds. His first expedition
was made into the heart of Mexico, with
his first wife, Mary Blair (otherwise Blair
Niles,[qv] the writer), and his first book was
Two Bird-Lovers in Mexico (1905). His
wife collaborated with him on *Our Search
For a Wilderness* (1910). The present
Mrs. Beebe, whom he married in 1927, was
Elswyth Thane, author of *The Tudor
Wench* and other books. His experiences
at the Zoological Society's research station
at Kartabo, British Guiana, yielded *Tropical
Wild Life,* written in collaboration with G. I.
Hartley and P. G. Howes, and the beautiful
series of *Monographs of the Pheasants,* pub-
lished from 1918 to 1922.

During the First World War Beebe saw
service as an aviator. Somewhat depressed
in mind, he returned to Guiana for peace
and solace, and wrote the papers originally
published in the *Atlantic Monthly* and elsewhere which were collected in *Jungle Peace*
(1918), heartily praised by Theodore Roosevelt in what was probably one of his last
book reviews. Its sequel, *Edge of the
Jungle,* was also well received. "The magic
of creating romance from the tiny event is
Beebe's," commented John Farrar in the
Bookman. Walter Prichard Eaton and some
other literary naturalists occasionally complained mildly that Beebe's style was a trifle
too portentous, and that he strove a little
too evidently to create literature in everything he wrote. The *Dial* termed his style
"sonorous and imaginative rather than nervous." "The *Isness* of facts is boring and
futile, the *Whyness* is the chief reason for

going on living," according to the scientist
himself.

Beebe was the first man to descend so far
in the ocean's depths as 3,028 feet, in his
especially constructed "bathysphere," and
his *Half Mile Down* (1934) had an exciting
story to tell. These experiments were made
in the waters at Nonsuch, Bermuda, hence
Nonsuch: Land of Water (1932) and the
Field Book of the Shore Fishes of Bermuda,
written with J. Tee-Van, artist of the expedition. *The Arcturus Adventure* (1926) had
described the Society's first oceanographic
expedition. *Zaca Venture* (1938) recorded
its twenty-fourth expedition, this time on
the schooner *Zaca* in the Gulf of California,
from March to May of 1936. Beebe is a
Fellow of the New York Academy of Sciences, a member of the Linnaean Society,
the Society of Mammalogists, the Audubon
Society, and numerous others, and holds the
Elliott and John Burroughs medals. For
his studies of pheasants he lay for hours in
the thick grass of Sarawak jungles to watch
their mating dance, though tortured by an
army of ants and in momentary danger of
discovery by head-hunting Dyaks. *Galapagos: World's End* (1923) was a fully
illustrated account of those strange reptiles,
iguanas.

The naturalist is tall and thin, and in 1930
had his only illness in thirty years. His
home is in New York City, a few doors from
Central Park.

PRINCIPAL WORKS: Two Bird-Lovers in Mexi-
co, 1905; The Bird: Its Form and Function, 1906;
Log of the Sun, 1906; Our Search for a Wilder-
ness (with M. B. Beebe) 1910; Tropical Wild Life
in British Guiana (with G. T. Hartley & P. G.
Howes) 1917; Monographs of the Pheasants, 1918-
22; Jungle Peace, 1918; Edge of the Jungle, 1921;
Galapagos, World's End, 1923; Jungle Days, 1925;
The Arcturus Adventure, 1926; Pheasants: Their
Lives and Homes, 1926; Pheasant Jungles, 1927;
Beneath Tropic Seas, 1928; Nonsuch: Land of
Water, 1932; Exploring With Beebe, 1932; Field
Book of the Shore Fishes of Bermuda (with J.
Tee-Van) 1933; Half Mile Down, 1934; Zaca
Venture, 1938; A Book of Bays, 1942.

ABOUT: University of California. Publications
in English: 1929.

*BEEDING, FRANCIS (pseudonym of
John Leslie Palmer and Hilary Aidan St.
George Saunders), was born, in a manner
of speaking, soon after 1920, when Mr.
Palmer, a graduate of Balliol College, Oxford University, dramatic critic and assistant editor of the *Saturday Review* from
1910 to 1915, and dramatic critic of the
Evening Standard from 1916, joined the
Permanent Secretariat of the League of Nations at Geneva. Mr. Saunders, also an

* J. L. Palmer died August 5, 1944; Hilary
Saunders died December 16, 1951.

Oxford man and a former officer in the Welsh Guards, was another member of the Secretariat, and was famous for his knowledge of the best wining and dining places in Europe.

Both men resigned from the League in 1939, by which time they had, as "Francis Beeding," published a score of "full-blooded, high-sounding and richly melodramatic carryings-on most excellently told," in the words of the New York *Herald Tribune "Books."* The adventures of Colonel Alastair Granby, secret-service agent extraordinary, alternated with *romans policiers* of unusual excellence, such as *Death Walks in Eastrepps.*

In a statement issued by Palmer (who was born in 1885, married Mildred Hodson Woodfield in 1911, has a son and daughter, and is the author of *The Comedy of Manners, Peter Paragon, Jennifer, Molière,* and other novels and books on the theatre), the aim of the writers of the Beeding books was described as "taking a situation as contemporary as possible and dealing with it in a way which does not run absolutely counter to fact. . . . They preserve their anonymity in order to be able to be just as extravagant as they please in the invention of incident and the presentation of the issues." This enforced anonymity has made the ordinary methods of publicity difficult; however, in the summer of 1925 Saunders appeared at Norwich (scene of *The Norwich Victims,* filmed as a typical Emlyn Williams chiller under the title *Dead Men Tell No Tales*) and gave a talk, as Francis Beeding, on "his" method of work. Palmer heckled him from the audience until Saunders, in seeming desperation, invited him to the platform, where the twain were revealed to be one.

After the outbreak of the Second World War, Saunders went to work for the Air Ministry, and was the anonymous author of *The Battle of Britain,* a Ministry pamphlet (1941) which sold three million copies in England alone and was translated into twenty-five languages, and of its almost equally popular successor, *Bomber Command.* Palmer is the author of a number of mystery novels of his own, both over his own signature and as "Christopher Haddon."

PRINCIPAL WORKS: The Seven Sleepers, 1925; The Little White Hag, 1926; The Hidden Kingdom, 1927; The House of Dr. Edwardes, 1928; The Six Proud Walkers, 1928; The Five Flamboys, 1929; Pretty Sinister, 1929; The Four Armourers, 1930; The League of Discontent, 1930; Take It Crooked, 1931; The Three Fishers, 1931; Death Walks in Eastrepps, 1931; Murder Intended, 1932; The Norwich Victims, 1935; The Nine Waxed Faces, 1936; The Eight Crooked Trenches, 1936; No Fury (U.S. title: Murdered, One By One) 1937; The Black Arrows, 1938; Big Fish (U.S. title: Heads Off at Midnight) 1938; He Could Not Have Slipped, 1939; The Ten Holy Horrors, 1939; Not a Bad Show (U.S. title: Secret Weapon) 1940; Eleven Were Brave, 1941; Twelve Disguises, 1942.

ABOUT: Life May 26, 1941.

BEER, THOMAS (November 22, 1889-April 18, 1940), American essayist and novelist, was born in Council Bluffs, Iowa, the son of William Collins Beer and Martha Ann Alice (Baldwin) Beer. He was reared in Bucyrus, Ohio, and while he was still a boy the family moved to Yonkers, N.Y. He received his B.A. at Yale in 1911, and then studied law at  Columbia, the sixth generation of his family to become a lawyer. From 1913 to 1917 he practiced in the office of his father, an attorney and a friend and associate of Marcus A. Hanna, whose biographer the son was to become. When the United States entered the First World War he served in France as a First Lieutenant of Field Artillery. It was on his return to America that he began to write seriously, though he had been class poet in Yale and had been active in student publications. Soon his writing was sufficiently successful to enable him to drop the law altogether. He never married, but lived alone in winter in his old-fashioned house in Yonkers, and in summer in an equally large and Victorian house at Nantucket.

Beer wrote remarkably few books in view of the solid reputation he built up by his writing. For the last seven years of his life he had been in ill health and was able to write little, though at the time of his death he was working on a new novel, to be called *The Wall and the Arrow,* and also on a critical work named *Form, Color, and Design.* Much of his energy was given to stories for the popular magazines, which, in spite of the praise given them by Elmira F. Groggin ("surface immobility and unawareness, behind which plays lightning thought, communicated in brief and stubborn words") were not of the superb quality of his critical work or even of his novels. He was found dead in bed of a heart attack.

Beer's was an arresting personality. "An aristocrat of letters," Lewis Mumford called him; Emily Clark said he was "a gentleman of the old school"; Waldo Frank spoke of his "adverse sociability." He lived a divided life, his eyes on the present but his heart in the past. Extremely shy, fastidiously dignified, amazingly generous, he was, as Miss Clark said, "sensitive to every shift of feeling in the [few] people he bothered to see." He was plump, short, broad-shouldered, with a powerful head, intensely pale skin, determined chin and jaw, and alert brown eyes. At home he did his writing in pajamas, often lying flat on his stomach on a bed. Mumford called him "a combination of extreme sophistication and elementalness, of cool intellectual appraisal and extreme tenderness." Similarly, Waldo Frank said: "His destructive books have an appeal profound beyond cleverness, and bitter-sweet, because it is a tender boy who does the destroying."

No one who has read *Stephen Crane* and *The Mauve Decade* needs to be told that Thomas Beer could write. What James W. Lane called (with a remarkable mixture of metaphors) "the tart yet purple music of his prose" was in every line. Joseph Henry Jackson marked "his passion for the exact word, . . . his careful, often precious, but usually singularly effective style." He shares with Lytton Strachey the real fatherhood of the "new biography," and his brilliance was comparable, though less biting. In contrast with the English biographer, he infused into his writing a nostalgic warmth which the cold and glittering Strachey lacked.

PRINCIPAL WORKS: The Fair Rewards (novel) 1922; Stephen Crane, 1923; Sandoval (novel) 1924; The Mauve Decade, 1926; The Road to Heaven (novel) 1928; Hanna, 1929; Mrs. Egg and Other Barbarians (short stories) 1933.

ABOUT: Arts and Decoration June 1926; Bookman May 1924, June 1928, November 1931; New Republic June 9, 1926; New York Herald Tribune "Books" August 24, 1941; Publishers' Weekly April 27, 1940; Saturday Review of Literature May 12, 1934, May 4, 1940, September 13, 1941; Time April 29, 1940.

BEERBOHM, Sir MAX (August 24, 1872-   ), English caricaturist, essayist, novelist, and parodist, was born in London, the son of Julius E. Beerbohm and Eliza (Draper) Beerbohm and a younger half-brother of the celebrated actor-manager Sir Herbert Beerbohm-Tree (1853-1917). He was educated at the Charterhouse and at Merton College, Oxford, and before

leaving the university was already known as an essayist, a wit, and a gifted cartoonist. He burst upon *fin de siècle* London and was soon one of the brilliant lights of the famous *Yellow Book*. In 1898, following a visit to the United States, he succeeded George Bernard Shaw as dramatic critic of the *Saturday Review*. It is difficult to describe his position in London at that period; he was a sort of institution, an emblem and epitome of "the irrepressible, the light of touch, the inimitable, the insouciant, and the impertinent." He knew everybody and caricatured everybody, in seemingly careless drawings which exposed the naked souls of their unhappy subjects. He parodied every well known writer of the time—and he is one of the greatest parodists who ever lived. In a word, he was "Max," the name signed in infinitesimal letters to all his caricatures. (His earliest drawings had been signed "H. Maxwell Beerbohm," but most people have forgotten long ago that he was ever anything but "Max.") When he was knighted in 1939, it was like giving an extra title to a fact of nature. He himself, with sly modesty, has remarked: "My gifts are small, I've used them very well and discreetly, never straining them, and the result is that I've made a charming little reputation."

In 1910 he married Florence Kahn, an American from Memphis, Tenn., but long a well known actress on the English stage. They made their home in Rapallo, Italy, together with Gordon Craig, and, later, Ezra Pound. Although Sir Max has had ten one-man exhibitions in London, he did not revisit his native city until 1936, when he was much saddened by its commercialization—in other words, by the disappearance of his ebullient youth. At the outbreak of the Second World War he came back to England "for the duration."

Sir Max is an honorary LL.D. of Edinburgh University, but there has never been any taint of seriousness in his writing, any more than in his drawing. Stark Young called his essays "grace and leisure themselves," though he added that "the light touch grows into boredom all too soon when it comes to dealing with art." There has certainly never been any touch of boredom in his verses or stories. *Zuleika Dobson*, published in 1911, has become a sort of classic in its author's lifetime; its deft irony has embalmed an entire period in its brief pages. "Few writers have given more exquisite pleasure," said Christopher Morley, lamenting that Sir Max must be "growing old in the shatter of a civilization that he was one of the few to illuminate with suffused lightning." The late E. F. Benson said that he has "the quality of sympathetic ridicule," and "purifies the mind not by pity and terror, but by laughter." If the 'Nineties ever merited the epithet of Gay, it is thanks to Max Beerbohm.

A. S. Frere-Reeves remarked that Sir Max "has all the innocent happiness of disposition of the good." He has, however, his prejudices, which include formidable women writers and large parties where he cannot rivet attention on his own witty conversation. He is a little man, partly bald, with a cavalry-moustache that cannot hide his look of the cherub. Rebecca West has described him as looking "extraordinarily like a little Chinese dragon in white porcelain. . . . Like them he has a perfectly round forehead and blue eyes that press forward in their eagerness; and his small hands and feet have the neat compactness of paws."

Essentially, he is still a citizen of the era of his youth; his sophistication, his wicked brilliance, and his wit are of the turn of the century. Gradually, however, he has grown up a little, especially as a caricaturist; his latest drawings have a broader sweep, are apt to pick out "the weakness of strength" not so much in a celebrated individual as in a group or a class. Critics were quick to say that he had lived abroad too long; they meant only that they wanted him as he had always been, at once bubbling and caustic, a licensed pricker of the great. He has published numerous collections of his caricatures; as a writer he has been more economical, and the relatively little he has had printed holds always to his highest standard of achievement.

PRINCIPAL WORKS: A Christmas Garland (parodies) 1895; The Works of Max Beerbohm, 1896; The Happy Hypocrite, 1897; More, 1899; Yet Again, 1907; Zuleika Dobson, 1911; And Even Now, 1920; Defense of Cosmetics, 1922; A Variety of Things, 1928; Around Theatres, 1930; The Dreadful Dragon of Hay Hill, 1931.

ABOUT: Lynch, J. G. B. Max Beerbohm in Perspective; Bookman June 1929; New Republic December 31, 1930; Saturday Review December 25, 1926; Saturday Review of Literature September 7, 1940; Spectator January 31, 1931; South Atlantic Quarterly April 1931.

BEHRMAN, SAMUEL NATHANIEL (June 9, 1893-), American dramatist, writes: "S. N. Behrman was born in Worcester, Mass., the son of Joseph and Zelda (Feingold) Behrman. The isolation of a Worcester boyhood had the advantage of an immersion in assorted literature: Horatio Alger and Shakespeare in equal parts.

After graduating from high school Mr. Behrman attended Clark College and met the venerable G. Stanley Hall, who later became the prototype of a professorial liberal in *Meteor*. George Pierce Baker was at Harvard giving his '47 Workshop' course, and Mr. Behrman went there to study in 1916; Sidney Howard was a fellow-student. Then came New York and long years of unemployment. Unable to get a job, he took a Master's degree in English at Columbia, studying with Brander Matthews and John Erskine.

"It took him exactly eleven years to sell his first play, The Second Man, and as he looks back, the mystery of his persistence during those years of rejection seems insoluble. Besides his plays, he has had several Hollywood engagements.

"Like the traditional comedian who hopes to play tragedy, Mr. Behrman hopes one day to write a novel."

* * *

To this brief and modest sketch it may be added that before he went to college Mr. Behrman had a brief experience on Broadway playing in a vaudeville sketch he himself had written. Production of his first play by the Theatre Guild in 1927 was preceded by two collaborations, with J. Kenyon Nicholson and Owen Davis, and he also was a book reviewer for the New York Times and the New Republic, and for a while was a theatrical press agent. From the time of his first production he has been outstandingly successful, nearly every one of his plays being a hit. Among his motion pictures may be mentioned Queen Christina, starring Greta Garbo, and the adaptation of A Tale of Two Cities, starring Ronald Colman. He lives in New York.

Joseph Wood Krutch said that Behrman had emerged from obscurity "with both attitude and technical skill fully formed." He spoke of his "persistent anti-heroicism, . . .

comic wisdom,... gift for the phrase,... intelligence, wit, tolerance, and grace." Stark Young also called him "one of those rare authors in the theatre who do not mistrust civilized society, and do not think that Times Square must understand or no tickets will be sold." From the beginning, though he has been primarily a comedian, there has been an element of solid thought in all his plays, and he has never been superficial or merely "smart."

Though he has not yet written the novel to which he looks forward, he does frequently write short stories (and occasionally articles), which appear in the literary periodicals. He is a hard-working playwright who keeps his private life to himself, and much less is known of him by the general public than of many dramatists of lesser reputation.

PRINCIPAL WORKS (DATE OF PRODUCTION): The Second Man, 1927; Serena Blandish, 1928; Meteor, 1929; Brief Moment, 1932; Biography, 1933; Love Story, 1934; Rain From Heaven, 1935; End of Summer, 1936; Amphytrion 38 (adaptation from French) 1937; Wine of Choice, 1938; No Time for Comedy, 1939; The Tally Method, 1942.

ABOUT: American Mercury June 1927; Nation February 13, 1929, July 19, 1933; New Republic December 28, 1932; Theatre Arts Monthly February 1933, June 1934, April 1941.

*BEITH, Sir JOHN HAY ("Ian Hay")

(April 17, 1876-   ), English novelist and dramatist, is the son of the late John A. Beith of Manchester and Altnacraig, Oban. He attended Fettes College, preparatory to going to St. John's College, Cambridge University, where he received a Second Class in the Classical Tripos in 1898. Beith served with the rank of captain in the Argyll and Sutherland Highlanders, Ninth Division, British Expeditionary Force, during the First World War, and his war book, The First Hundred Thousand, first published under the pseudonym "K(1)," was one of the first of its sort to sell in large quantities in the United States. The tone was distinctly cheerful. Beith, by the time of the war, was the author of half-a-dozen novels as "Ian Hay," and the book appeared as the work of "K(1), The Junior Subaltern," because, he explained, "I didn't want my reputation as a novelist to be spoiled!"

He was mentioned in despatches, won the Military Cross, and was made a C.B.E. in 1918. Since seniority in the Army was ranked by length of service, he was actually the junior subaltern in his regiment. In 1915, the year the book was published, Beith married Helen Margaret Speirs of Polmont Park, Stirlingshire. They have (or did have at last report) a pleasant house on Charles Street in London off Berkeley Square. (Janet Beith, who won a $20,000 prize for her novel, No Second Spring, in 1933, is a niece, not a daughter of "Ian Hay.") Beith served as Director of Public Relations at the War Office, 1938-41. He ranks among the three finest bow-shots in England, and is a member of the Royal Company of Archers, the ancient bodyguard headed by the Duke of Connaught, which always attends the King when he goes into residence at the Palace of Holyrood in Edinburgh. In pre-war days Beith also boated and golfed with his long-time friend, P. G. Wodehouse, whose Damsel In Distress and Baa, Baa, Black Sheep Beith dramatized in 1929. He wrote Good Luck (1923) with Seymour Hicks; The Midshipmaid (1931) with S. K. Hall; Orders Are Orders (1932) with Anthony Armstrong; A Present From Margate (1933) with A. E. W. Mason; and numerous other comedies, of which his own favorite is Admirals All (1934), written in collaboration with S. K. Hall. Tilly of Bloomsbury (1919) and Housemaster (1936) were pleasantly received in the United States. His novels are slight, romantic, and frequently amusing. He is an Officer of the Order of St. John of Jerusalem, a Governor of Guy's Hospital, and President of the Dramatists' Club; and his clubs are the Beefsteak, Garrick, Caledonian, and Bath. "Ian Hay" is tall, dark, and tanned, with a soldierly figure and a little military moustache. He writes in longhand; a secretary types his manuscripts.

PRINCIPAL WORKS: Pip, 1907; The Right Stuff, 1908; A Man's Man, 1909; A Safety Match, 1911; Happy-Go-Lucky, 1913; A Knight on Wheels, 1914; The Lighter Side of School Life, 1914; The First Hundred Thousand, 1915; Carrying On, 1917; The Last Million, 1918; The Willing Horse, 1921; The Lucky Number, 1923; The Shallow End, 1924; Paid, With Thanks, 1925; Half-a-Sovereign, 1926; The Poor Gentlemen, 1928; Their Name Liveth, 1931; The Middle Watch, 1930; The Midshipmaid, 1932; The Great Wall of India, 1933; David and Destiny, 1934; Lucky Dog, 1934; Housemaster, 1936; The King's Service, 1938; Stand At Ease, 1940.

ABOUT: Braybrooke, P. Novelists, We Are Seven; Windsor Magazine March 1935.

* Died September 22, 1952.

BELASCO, DAVID (July 25, 1859-May 14, 1931), American playwright and theatrical producer, was born in San Francisco,

Abbe

the son of Humphrey Belasco and Reina (Martin) Belasco, in the cellar of a house in Howard Street. His father, of an old Portuguese Hebrew family, was born in London in 1830, and worked for a time as a circus clown ("the first Harlequin of London," his son David called him in some highly embroidered and unreliable memoirs). David Belasco's uncle David James (1839-93) was a fairly well-known English actor. The boy attended a monastery in Victoria, B.C., where his father was a storekeeper, ran away to join a traveling circus, and at eleven appeared at the Victoria Theatre as the Duke of York in Charles Kean's production of *Richard III*. Back in San Francisco, he received instruction in elocution, left school in 1871, and in 1873 married Cecilia Loverich. His wife went with him on barnstorming tours and bore him two daughters, one of whom, Reina, married Morris Gest, the theatrical producer. A Belasco melodrama, *La Belle Russe,* partly based on Wilkie Collins's *The New Magdalen,* was produced at Wallack's, New York City, in May 1882. In October he produced his first play at the Madison Square Theatre on the south side of Twenty-Fourth street.

Belasco met Mrs. Leslie Carter, just emerged from a sensational divorce suit, when he was running the Lyceum School of Acting, and molded her undisciplined talents into those of a creditable melodramatic actress, presenting her, from 1889 to 1906, in *The Heart of Maryland, Du Barry, Zaza, Adrea,* and other plays. In September 1902 he opened the remodeled Republic Theatre on Forty-Second Street as the Belasco; the Stuyvesant Theatre, built and opened in 1907, was renamed the Belasco in 1910, and still stands on Forty-Fourth street. It embodied innovations such as footlights sunk below the level of the stage. Belasco's productions were also notable for minutely realistic stage settings and properties. Their literary content was small. A firm believer in the star system, he managed Frances Starr, Lionel Atwill, David Warfield, Mrs. Fiske, Lenore Ulric, Ina Claire, Fanny Brice, Helen Gahagan and Katherine Cornell (but not for long). Blanche Bates starred in

two immensely successful plays, *Madame Butterfly,* written with John Luther Long, and *The Girl of the Golden West,* both made into operas with scores by Giacomo Puccini. Geraldine Farrar was long identified with *Madame Butterfly.* Belasco produced 374 plays in all.

He had "a short, bent, robust, big-boned body, with forward-pointing shoulders, a big head, and thick, silky, glistening white hair." For the greater part of his life Belasco affected semi-clerical dress. He died in a New York hotel in his seventy-second year.

PRINCIPAL WORKS: La Belle Russe, 1881; Madame Butterfly (with John Luther Long); Sweet Kitty Bellairs, 1903; The Music Master (with Charles Klein) 1904; The Girl of the Golden West, 1905; The Rose of the Rancho (with Richard Walton Tully) 1906; The Return of Peter Grimm, 1911.

ABOUT: Brown, J. M. Upstage; Busch, N. Twenty-One Americans; Edgett, E. F. I Speak for Myself; Lewisohn, L. The Drama and the Stage; Winter, W. The Life of David Belasco; New York Times May 15, 1931; Theatre Guild Magazine November 1929.

BELFRAGE, CEDRIC (1904-), British journalist and adventurer, was born in London, descendant of a long line of clergymen

and brewers. He was brought up "on the comfortable side of the fence in a comfortable country" and it was almost inevitable, he says, that he should be nourished on escapology. He was sent to carefully selected public schools, among them

Greshams and Holt, and was cautiously protected from everything practical. After two years at Cambridge he left without a degree. In his teens he had answered an advertisement for atheistic tracts and had thereby "lost faith in the magical aspects of Christianity" and taken refuge in "dream islands."

These, however, were only a temporary drug. A fascination with the whole idea of the cinema drove him eventually into its innermost temples: from press agent at three pounds a week; to scenario reader, for Universal Pictures, in New York; and finally, movie critic—for a variety of papers that included the London *Picturegoer* and *Film Weekly,* the New York *Sun* and *Herald Tribune,* and a number of American "fan magazines."

But by 1930 he had exhausted stardom's interview prospects and had been thrown out of four major studios. Moreover, he had adopted a policy of such complete candor as a critic that on one occasion the entire film industry withdrew advertising from Belfrage's paper. He wanted to let the whole affair blow over, and so quit reviewing for a while.

With about half the necessary funds for a round-the-world journey he sailed for Spain early in 1934. Proceeds from copy, he believed, would tide him over. The cruise lasted eleven months and took him from the Holy Land to Persia, India, Australia, Bali, and the South Sea Islands. During a stay in California on his return he reiterated his earlier conviction that Hollywood's intelligent people were all "harnessed to the business of doping the world with false values." And then back to England: he had had his "little flutter" in his "escape to end escape," and regarded himself, once more, as just another Fleet Street devil. In 1937 he published notebook impressions of this whole adventure, *Away From It All.* About a year later came *Promised Land: Notes For a History,* pruned from his own feature-article reserves and the loan of a massive collection of Hollywoodiana.

His wife, Molly Castle, is a journalist in her own right. They have one daughter.

Belfrage has made, in all, at least a half-dozen visits to the United States. He believes that America is endowed with a spirit that is "fundamentally democratic."

PRINCIPAL WORKS: Away From It All: An Escapologist's Notebook, 1937; Promised Land: Notes For a History, 1938; Let My People Go, 1940; South of God, 1941; They All Hold Swords, 1941.

ABOUT: Belfrage, C. Away From It All; Harper's September 1936.

BELL, ADRIAN (October 4, 1901-), English novelist, poet, and nature-writer, is the eldest son of Robert Bell and Frances (Hanbury) Bell. He was named Adrian Hanbury Bell and was educated at Uppingham. After leaving school, he went as a pupil on a Suffolk farm; farmed there for nine years; and has lived and written there ever since. In 1931 he married Marjorie Gibson, and they have a son and two daughters. These short and simple annals are expanded in Mr. Bell's distinguished agrarian novels. The preface to *Silver Ley,* the narrative of a young gentleman-farmer who had had previous experience with a practical farm, states, as usual, that "None of the characters in this book is to be regarded as the portrait of a living person."

Mr. Bell, nevertheless, has evidently had close acquaintance with the thatchers, hedgers, harvesters and change-ringers, whom he describes. *Men and the Fields* is a recent non-fictional study of agriculture, in depressed areas and elsewhere in England. An extract from *Silver Ley* may illustrate Mr. Bell's style and his slant on life: "My work was arduous, but my mind was easy. My hours were long, but I was master of them and did not have to live as a city man, tethered to nine-thirty a.m. like a goat to a tree. I had got the first taste of that fierce and stubborn independence of the farmer which is both the wonder of others and their parrot cry against him when his trade is adverse." Mr. Bell's apparently simple style is an effective medium for close observation of natural phenomena, and his humorous observation cordially embraces both Suffolk farming types and the individualities of barnyard inhabitants—notably the teeming cats.

PRINCIPAL WORKS: Corduroy, 1930; Silver Ley, 1931; The Cherry Tree, 1932; Folly Field, 1933; The Balcony, 1934; Poems, 1935; By-Road, 1937; Men and the Fields, 1939; Shepherd's Farm, 1939; Open Air (ed.) 1940.

BELL, CLIVE (September 16, 1881-), English art critic, writes: "I was born into a county family, in which money, respectability, correct ways of thinking and feeling, conventional success, hunting, shooting, and fishing counted for much; and the things for which I care most counted for nothing. This is of some importance, because reaction against the conditions in which I was reared has made of me as mild and  conservative a rebel as you could wish to meet. At my preparatory school, where I learned a good deal, I was not very happy; at Malborough, where I unlearned all that I had been taught, I was miserable. In 1899 I went to Cambridge (Trinity), and there my real life began. There I made lifelong friends, and there—thanks partly to those friends—I found myself. For five-and-twenty years and more, from the time I went to Cambridge, my life—the great war to end war notwithstanding—was exquisitely happy. The arts, especially the visual arts and literature, are what I have depended on to give point to existence. I have not been obliged to earn my living. Time has never hung heavy on my hands. I have never felt the slightest inclination to play cards or solve crossword puzzles. The fact that I am as much at home in French as in English civilization has precisely doubled the pleasures of my life.

"I am extremely sociable—not to say convivial: I love my friends and I love the good things of life. Mildly liberal, I have never been a politician, but I hope I have taken an intelligent interest in economics and contemporary statesmanship. At some personal inconvenience I have been a consistent advocate of peace. I am intensively sensitive to the charms of femininity. This has been a cause of great happiness. Were I to live much longer doubtless it would become a source of misery. But of this I have little fear; for I have a notion that I am the sort of person for whom the future will find no place."

* * *

Mr. Bell was married in 1907 to Vanessa Stephen, sister of Virginia Woolf. He is a Chevalier of the Legion of Honor (1936). His critical articles are a regular feature of the *New Statesman and Nation*. It is his theory that art should be pure, isolated aestheticism, or, to quote Henry Ladd, "the doctrine of the complete separation of Art from Life, of the artist from the social man." Gilbert Seldes called him "witty and intelligent and obstinate and tolerant at once." With his "notoriously agile mind," Burton Rascoe said he was "the curious combination of a critic who obviously feels art emotionally and who writes in terms of intellectual or objective criticism. He has intellectualized his passion, his sensitivity, and his taste too much. . . . [But] he writes in vigorous but cadenced, easy, lucid, and charming manner." To the aesthetic vocabulary Mr. Bell has contributed the now familiar phrase, "significant form," as a criterion of value in art.

PRINCIPAL WORKS: Art, 1914; Peace at Once, 1915; Pot Boilers, 1918; The Legend of Monte della Sibilla, 1920; Poems, 1921; Since Cézanne, 1922; On British Freedom, 1923; Landmarks in Nineteenth Century Painting, 1927; Civilization, 1928; Proust, 1929; An Account of French Painting, 1931; Enjoying Pictures, 1934.

ABOUT: Bookman September 1922, October 1928; Nation January 4, 1928.

BELL, MACKENZIE (March 2, 1856-December 13, 1930), English poet, biographer, traveler, and imperialist, was born Henry Thomas Mackenzie Bell in Liverpool, the youngest child of Thomas Bell and Margaret (Mackenzie) Bell. He was educated privately in the expectation of preparing for a law career; but instead of proceeding to Cambridge he did some

rather extensive studying in Spain, Portugal, Italy, and France. About this time he began to acquire a tremendous interest in imperialism, and from the formation of W. E. Forster's Imperial Federation Committee until its dissolution he was a member.

In 1884 he published a critical monograph of a figure who, he contended, had been most unwarrantably neglected—*A Forgotten Genius: Charles Whitehead*. Almost fifteen years later he wrote the somewhat more authoritative *Christina Rossetti: A Biographical and Critical Study*, for which he had not only the advantage of personal acquaintance with his subject but also first-hand information from Christina Rossetti's literary executor, William Michael Rossetti. The impressiveness of his documentation, however, was sometimes eclipsed by a too obvious kind of hero-worship.

Miscellaneous verse which had appeared, during the 'eighties and 'nineties, in the *Churchman*, the *Literary World*, and the *Pall Mall Magazine*, was gathered in *Pictures of Travel and Other Poems*. Most of it now seems particularly lacking in originality of motivation and skill of execution.

He spent the year 1905-06 in Madeira. In 1910 he was the unsuccessful liberal candidate for parliament in the Borough of St. George, Hanover Square, London; during the same year he ran as a Progressive candidate for London County Council. Bell was largely responsible for the establishing, in Liverpool, of a memorial to the poet Felicia Hemans.

At the time of the First World War he issued a series of ballads, burdened with the conventional sentiment of the hour—off-to-the-front courage, "no man's land" terror, heroic glory, etc. Many of them were set to music.

Bell died at Bayswater in his seventy-seventh year. His interests both literary and political, appear to have been too much scattered to have had any very lasting significance.

PRINCIPAL WORK: A Forgotten Genius: Charles Whitehead, 1884; Christina Rossetti: A Biographical and Critical Study, 1898; Pictures of Travel and Other Poems, 1898; Poems: With Dedicatory Essay to Theodore Watts-Dunton, 1909; Poetical Pictures of the Great War, 1917.

ABOUT: London Times December 15, 1930; prefatory notes in the works.

"BELL, NEIL." See SOUTHWOLD, S.

BELLAH, JAMES WARNER (September 14, 1899-   ), American novelist, writes: "James Warner Bellah was born in New

Pinchot

York City, the son of the late James Warner Bellah and Harriet Louise (Johnson) Bellah. He was educated at Wesleyan (Middletown, Conn.) and Columbia Universities, B.A. Columbia 1923. He was a member and vice-president of the undergraduate Philolexian Society, founded by Alexander Hamilton. He served during the First World War as a Second Lieutenant (pilot) 117th Squadron, Royal Air Force, and after the Armistice in General Haller's Expedition for the Relief of Poland, with the rank of Captain. He was in the advertising business in New York City from 1923 to 1925, and instructor in English at Columbia in the same years. He returned to the university to give Dorothy Scarborough's course in short story writing, after her death, in 1936-37. He was special correspondent in China during the last of the Chang Tso-Ling campaigns, 1927-28, in Europe in 1928 for *Aero Digest,* and special correspondent for the *Saturday Evening Post* on all the initial Pan American Airways flights through the West Indies and Central America in 1929. The same year he was a member of the crew of the first plane carrying mail from Miami to Panama and return. He has been a contributor to many general and air magazines in America, to practically every English magazine, and, in translation, to Swedish, French, German, Dutch, and Turkish periodicals. His stories are included in thirty American-European anthologies. By request of Millington-Drake, late first secretary of the British Legation at Copenhagen, *The Gods of Yesterday* has been specially bound and placed in the Eton Memorial Library. It is in the library of the Imperial War Museum in London, under letters and by request of the Duke of Windsor when Prince of Wales, then chairman of the Museum, and also in the *Musée de la Guerre* in Paris, by request of the French Ministry of War.

"Mr. Bellah has traveled extensively and incessantly for twenty-two years in upward of fifty countries, has lived for periods of time in England and France, and has lectured and written extensively on his travels.

His sports are deep sea fishing, ocean racing, and, until recently, fencing; he is vice-president of the Amateur Fencers' Club of America. He belongs to the Society of Colonial Wars, Sons of the Revolution (Fraunce's Tavern), and Loyal Legion. He lives now in New York City."

* * *

Mr. Bellah was married in 1937 to Ruth Yeaton Power-O'Malley. He has one son by a previous marriage. His light hair is worn brushed back in a pompadour, and he wears a clipped moustache. Most of his work has been uncollected from magazines, since he publishes only a small proportion of his serials in book form. Donald Gordon said of him that he writes "a crack modern love story intelligently handled. . . . He is a sprint starter and plot and characters are developed with fast strokes. . . . It is prime entertainment."

PRINCIPAL WORKS: Sketch Book of a Cadet from Gascony, 1923; Frantic Years, 1927; Gods of Yesterday, 1928; Sons of Cain, 1929; Dancing Lady, 1932; White Piracy, 1933; The Brass Gong Tree, 1936; South by East a Half East, 1936; This Is the Town, 1937; Seven Must Die, 1938; The Bones of Napoleon, 1940.

ABOUT: New York Times July 7, 1940. Saturday Evening Post January 28, 1928.

*BELLAMANN, HENRY (April 28, 1882-   ), American novelist, musician, and poet, was born in Fulton Mo., the son of George Heinrich and Caroline (Krähenbühle) Bellamann. He was, presumably, christened "Heinrich Hauer" but appears to have replaced this with "Henry" about the time he began to publish verse. From secondary schools he went to the local

M. Horowitz

Westminster College; then to the University of Denver; and during the years 1898-1900 he pursued special studies in New York, London, and Paris. In France he was a student of Charles M. Widor, famous French organist, composer, and teacher, and Isidor Philipp of the Conservatoire National.

In September 1907 he was married to Katherine Jones of Cathage, Miss., who in 1931 published a novel called *My Husband's Friends.* For the next seventeen years he was Dean of the School of Fine Arts at Chicora College for Women, Columbia, S.C.

He served two years as chairman of the examining board of Juilliard Musical Foun-

* Died June 16, 1945.

dation and then two more years (1926-28) with the Rockefeller Foundation. For a short time he was acting professor of music at Vassar and then accepted a deanship at the Curtis Institute of Music, where he edited *Overtones.* He resigned from this post in the very early 'thirties.

Bellamann's first book, a slim volume of verse called *A Music Teacher's Note Book,* appeared in 1920. Three years later, after his poems had begun to work their way into a variety of magazines, he published a larger and more pretentious selection under the title, *Cups of Illusion.* In 1926 came his first novel, *Petenera's Daughter,* and another in 1928 (*Crescendo*). Between these came a book of poems, *The Upward Pass.* He wrote another novel in the early 'thirties, and then a "murder and macabre mystery on an eerie island off the Carolina coast"—*The Gray Man Walks. Kings Row* (1940), a many-charactered, intense novel, of a realistic and psycho-analytical nature, showing the distortions of life in a small Midwest town, was a surprise best-seller that was made into a motion picture and has kept on selling. *Floods of Spring,* is the story of a Pennsylvania Dutch farmer and his wife who emigrate to Missouri to a little town near "Kings Row," after the close of the Civil War; the family's story is continued through the turn of the century.

France made Bellamann a Chevalier of the Legion of Honor in 1931; he is a member of numerous musical and literary organizations. Bellamann's career is particularly interesting in that he was a musician before he began to write; his first novel did not appear until he was forty-four, and he was fifty-eight when he achieved his first real popular success with *Kings Row.*

PRINCIPAL WORKS: A Music Teacher's Note Book, 1920; Cups of Illusion, 1923; Petenera's Daughter, 1926; The Upward Pass, 1927; Crescendo, 1928; The Richest Woman in Town, 1932; The Gray Man Walks, 1936; King's Row, 1940; Floods of Spring, 1942.

ABOUT: Commonweal October 26, 1934; Music Quarterly January 1933; Overtones October 1926; Time April 15, 1940.

*BELLOC, HILAIRE (July 27, 1870-   ), Anglo-French historian, essayist, novelist, poet, and miscellaneous writer, was born at Saint-Cloud, Paris, the son of Louis Swanton Belloc, a French barrister, and his English wife, Bessie Rayner Parkes. He was christened Joseph Hilaire Pierre. Educated at the Oratory School, Birmingham, he afterwards served for a year or so in the 8th regiment of French artillary at Toul, Meurthe-et-Moselle, as a

driver. In January 1893 he went up to Balliol College, Oxford, where he read history and became president of the Union (the University debating society). He won the Brackenbury History Scholarship, and was graduated with first-class honors in 1895, after an unusually short period of study.

On coming down from college Belloc at once began to write, winning repute by newspaper and magazine work and very quickly starting his remarkably versatile and prolific career as an author of books. His first published volume was *Verses and Sonnets,* in 1895. A year later *The Bad Child's Book of Beasts* came out, as the precursor of some of the most delightful children's books in the language. *Danton* (1899) and *Robespierre* (1901) were the first fruits of his historical learning; while in *The Path to Rome* (1902) he showed those qualities of humor, pious Roman Catholicism, and love of traveling that have remained prime concomitants of his work.

Early in the century he became the devoted friend of the late G. K. Chesterton, an author who shared his opposition to free thought and socialism, his love of the medieval period, and his extreme political individualism. The two men, jointly with the late Cecil Chesterton, founded the *New Witness,* a weekly paper devoted to the exposition of their political views and the exposure of political irregularities. Until the death of Chesterton these two writers were associated with unusual closeness in idea, so that Mr. Bernard Shaw christened the combination "the Chesterbelloc."

From 1906 to 1910 Belloc was a Liberal Member of Parliament for South Salford (which stands to Manchester much as Brooklyn does to New York); but he conceived a poor opinion of the House of Commons and the party system and so did not stand again, feeling that he could exercise more influence by his writings than as a member of the legislature. It was 1912, however, before he brought out a political book, *The Servile State.* The interim period had been filled chiefly with children's books and essays. Of the first group the *Cautionary Tales* (1907) proved to be a priceless feast of humor, representing the utterly English side of a writer whose French side appears strongly in his historical and polemical writings. These verse tales are in the nature of parodies of Jane and Ann Taylor, and relate with zest and glee the fearful after careers of children who Chew String, who Tell Lies, and who Bang Doors. A further series came out later. Of the essays, *On Nothing* (1908) and *On Everything* (1909) are typical examples. Belloc is one of those essayists of genius who really can write entertainingly and often profoundly "on nothing." In other words, he can take his text from some most trivial happening or phenomenon and weave around it a rich garment of wit and philosophy.

Belloc's historical writings include *A General Sketch of the European War*, a four-volume *History of England* and a study of *The Jews*. The whole of his historical thought is colored by his intense Catholicism, which leads him to look back (not wistfully, for one cannot imagine Belloc's being wistful) to what we call the Dark Ages as being really ages of light in which the Pope's spiritual and temporal ascendancy was unchallenged. He is a vigorous, not to say truculent, controversialist, and has in his day drawn swords with such a doughty opponent as Mr. H. G. Wells, to whose *Outline of History* he wrote a "Companion," which provoked the reply: *Mr. Belloc Objects.*

Other sides of Belloc's vast productivity are represented by light novels like *The Missing Masterpiece* (a skit on detective fiction), by narrations of travel like *The Cruise of the Nona* and by politico-sociological studies such as *The Crisis of Our Civilization.* Travel (especially under the aspect of pilgrimage) has inspired much of his writing; and since the death of E. V. Lucas, in June 1938, he has conducted the column called "A Wanderer's Note-Book" in the London *Sunday Times.* His native Sussex has often moved him to enthusiastic praise in prose and verse, and he has written much on The Road, for its extreme antiquity and social significance have profoundly impressed him. He has a deep "sense of the past," and on the whole tends to look backward rather than forward.

Belloc received in 1934 the Papal honor of Knight Commander with Star of the Order of St. Gregory the Great. In 1896 he married an American, Elodie Agnes Hogan, of Napa, Calif., who died in 1914, leaving him three sons and two daughters. The eldest son, Louis, died in the First World War; the youngest, Peter, lost his life in the Second World War. In personal appearance Belloc is massive and stocky, with keen eyes, a belligerent jaw, and a square head.

PRINCIPAL WORKS: Verses and Sonnets, 1895; The Bad Child's Book of Beasts, 1896; The Path to Rome, 1902; On Nothing, 1908; On Everything, 1909; On Anything, 1910; On Something, 1911; The Jews, 1922; On, 1923; History of England (4 vols.) 1925-27; Richelieu; 1929; Wolsey, 1930; The Man Who Made Gold, 1931; Oliver Cromwell, 1931; Napoleon, 1932; The Crisis of Civilization, 1937; Charles II: The Last Rally, 1939; The Silence of the Sea and Other Essays, 1940; Cautionary Verses, 1941; Places, 1942; Elizabeth: Creature of Circumstance, 1942.

ABOUT: Belloc, H. Why I Am a Catholic; Braybrooke, P. Some Catholic Novelists; Braybrooke, P. Some Thoughts on Hilaire Belloc; Las Vergnas, R. Chesterton, Belloc, Baring; Catholic World May, June 1940; Irish Monthly May 1940; Living Age December 1940; London Mercury September 1921.

BELLOC LOWNDES. See LOWNDES

BEMELMANS, LUDWIG (April 27, 1898-   ), Austro-American essayist and illustrator, was born at Beran, in the Tyrol, in territory that was then Austrian and is now Italian. His father, Lambert Bemelmans, was a Belgian, a rather ne'er-do-well painter; his mother, Frances (Fisher) Bemelmans, was the daughter of a prosperous Bavarian brewer. Owing to his  father's frequent absences from home, he was reared under the influence of his mother's family. They found the spirited boy hard to manage; after two rebellious years at the Lyceum in Regensburg, he was sent to a private academy at Rothenburg (both towns are in Bavaria), with no more satisfactory results   Finally his family in despair took him out of school and apprenticed him to his uncle, who owned a string of resort hotels in the Tyrolean Alps. There he managed to be such a problem that he was finally given his choice of a reform school or immigration to America. He chose America, and arrived in New York in 1914. He had letters to the managers of various large hotels, and after two disastrous experiences, secured a minor position in the large and exclusive dining-room of what he has called, in his autobiographical books, the "Hotel Splendide." There he remained for three years, gradually working up to a position as a waiter, but meanwhile drawing constantly. He took a few art lessons, but found they injured his spontaneity and taught him nothing; the charm of his drawing lies in its "natural naïveté of line."

When the United States entered the First World War, Bemelmans enlisted, and was sent to Camp Gordon, in Georgia—an experience inimitably described in *My War With the United States*. When he was demobilized (he had been naturalized in 1918), he returned to New York. For some time he worked again in hotels and restaurants, but gradually won some success as an artist. He decorated Jascha Heifitz's studio, illustrated books, and (though not until 1935) did the settings for a Broadway play. In 1933 he opened his own restaurant; it ran for several years. For a while he did a comic strip, with verses for the New York *World*, but it failed to catch the public eye, and he was let out. In 1935 he married Madeline Freund; they have one daughter.

Bemelmans' first books were made of pictures and verses for children. *Hansi* was a success, and enabled him to devote most of his time to drawing and writing. In 1937 he made a long trip to Ecuador (he made a second one in 1940), and his book *Quito Express* grew out of his South American experiences. He lives now at Mt. Kisco, N.Y., where he writes on a silver-plated typewriter which is his dearest possession. He does most of his writing and drawing in the bath tub, saying that his mind works best when his body is immersed in hot water. He claims that he took to writing only because he had insomnia, and that if he could sleep well he would never write again. He is stocky, almost totally bald, with a round, amiable face.

It is almost impossible to describe Bemelmans' work; its flavor is purely his own. He is a genuine humorist, a master of sly under-statement. His books for children are of the type which adults enjoy just as greatly. He always illustrates his own works, as well as his magazine articles. How accurate in detail his autobiographical confidences may be, no one can say; but the word which most nearly describes them and his other writings is "delightful."

PRINCIPAL WORKS: Hansi (juvenile) 1934; Golden Basket (juvenile) 1935; Castle Number Nine (juvenile) 1936; Quito Express, 1937; My War With the United States, 1937; Life Class, 1938; Madeline (juvenile) 1939; Small Beer, 1939; Fifi (juvenile) 1940; The Donkey Inside, 1941; At Your Service, 1941; Hotel Splendide, 1941.

ABOUT: Bemelmans, L. My War With the United States, Life Class; Current Biography 1941; New York Times January 26, 1941; Newsweek July 24, 1937, January 20, 1941; Publishers' Weekly October 22, 1938; Saturday Review of Literature November 12, 1938, January 18, 1941; Time January 2, 1941; Wilson Library Bulletin April 1939.

BEMIS, SAMUEL FLAGG (October 20, 1891-), American historian and winner of the Pulitzer Prize, was born in Worcester, Mass., and educated at Clark University (B.A. 1912, M.A. 1913) and Harvard (M.A. 1915, Ph.D. 1916). He also did graduate study in history in France and England. Clark conferred a D.H.L. degree on him in 1937. He was at Colorado College, Colorado Springs, from 1917 to 1920, first as instructor and then as associate professor of history. From 1920 to 1923 he was professor of history at Whitman College, Walla Walla, Wash. After a year as research associate of the Carnegie Institute of Washington, he served a year as professor of history at George Washington University. In 1935 he became Farnam Professor of Diplomatic History at Yale, a position he still holds. In 1937 and 1938 he was Carnegie visiting professor to several Latin-American universities (he speaks Spanish fluently and has published a book in Spanish); and he has taught in the summer schools of Harvard, Stanford, and the Universities of Washington and Minnesota. He was also a lecturer at Harvard just before going to Yale. In 1919 he married Ruth M. Steele. They have one daughter, and live in New Haven, Conn.

Professor Bemis was the editor and part-author of the ten-volume *American Secretaries of States and Their Diplomacy* (1927-29). In 1927 he received the Pulitzer history prize for his *Pinckney's Treaty: A Study of America's Advantage From Europe's Distress*. He is also a frequent contributor of articles on history to the scholarly reviews. His work is almost all too technical for the lay reader.

PRINCIPAL WORKS: Jay's Treaty: A Study in Commerce and Diplomacy, 1923; Pinckney's Treaty, 1926; The Hussey-Cumberland Mission and American Independence, 1931; The Diplomacy of the American Revolution, 1935; A Guide to the Diplomatic History of the United States (with G. G. Griffin) 1935; A Diplomatic History of the United States, 1936; La Politica Internacional de las Estados Unidos: Interpretaciones (The International Politics of the United States: Interpretations) 1939.

ABOUT: School and Society May 14, 1927.

*BENAVENTE Y MARTINEZ, JACINTO (August 12, 1866-), Spanish playwright, Nobel Prize winner, was born in Madrid of a wealthy middle-class family. His father, Dr. Mariano Benavente, was an eminent specialist in children's diseases to whose memory a statue was erected in Madrid's Buen Retiro gardens. Jacinto

was educated at the famous San Isidro Institute, where he showed astounding precocity; but his best teachers, he declared later, were "a book read, the street, a walk." From the earliest he liked to stay home putting up marionette shows. He preferred directing his playlets to writing them, and at the end of his career maintained that he would rather have been a great actor than a playwright. In order to please the family he entered the University of Madrid Law School, but dropped out at the age of nineteen, when his father died, and devoted himself exclusively to literature. His earliest plays, published under the title *Teatro Fantástico* (1892) marked a reaction against the realism then in vogue; these four plays are all, as the title indicates, of a romantic, fantastic character, strongly reminiscent of Shakespeare's comedies and of Musset. *Teatro Fantástico* was soon followed by other collections of skits, sketches, and dialogues of Madrilenian life, and by *Cartas de Mujeres*, letters by imaginary women, which evidenced the young writer's keen insight into the feminine world.

All these works were mere exercises in composition, a forging of tools. Benavente's career as a playwright actually began with *El Nido Ajeno*, produced October 6, 1894. From 1894 to 1901 eighteen of his plays found their way to the boards, all satirizing the Spanish aristocracy and exposing their foibles with merciless precision. Benavente then moved from satire to a broader depiction of the international scene, and tried his hand at pageants and comedies of middle-class life. In December 1907 he attained the pinnacle of his fame with *The Bonds of Interest*, a charming comedy combining the satiric and the humorous with a higher if vapid idealist philosophy. Benavente wrote over fifty plays afterward, but never surpassed this comedy.

Benavente translated Shakespeare and Molière, edited a literary magazine, *La Vida Literaria*, and in 1909 founded with the actor Porredon a children's theatre, writing for it such delightful fairy plays as *The Prince Who Learned Everything Out of*

Books (1909). From 1910 until the First World War Benavente devoted most of his time to his weekly column in *El Imparcial*, dealing with all manner of subjects, later collected in his five-volume *De Sobremesa*—"after-dinner conversation." Just as the public was beginning to say that Benavente had run dry—his admission into the Royal Spanish Academy (1913) was to them symptomatic of death—Benavente scored his greatest popular success with *La Malquerida* (December 1913). This tragedy of peasant life was liked both because of its conventionality of form and its melodramatic content, handled with utmost realism and local color. During the war Benavente ranged himself on the side of Germany; his pro-German propaganda culminated in *El Año Germanófilo*, a symposium which he edited in 1916. In 1922 he was awarded the Nobel Prize. Spain's younger generation objected strenuously, but the aristocracy he once chastised came to his defense. Later his friends and enemies were reversed, when during the Franco rebellion Don Jacinto stood by the Loyalists and refused to leave Madrid.

Professor Northrup has called Benavente "the one outstanding figure, the king of the Spanish drama... His methods are modern ... He studiously avoids threadbare theatrical conventionalities. Action is slighted. Interest depends upon character. He is not without technique, but it is a new technique, in some respects analogous to Shaw's."

WORKS AVAILABLE IN ENGLISH TRANSLATION: The Smile of Mona Lisa, 1915; Plays: 1st Series (His Widow's Husband, The Bonds of Interest, The Evil Doers of Good, La Malquerida) 1917; Plays: 2nd Series (No Smoking, Princess Bebé, The Governor's Wife, Autumnal Roses) 1919; Plays: 3rd Series (The Prince Who Learned Everything Out of Books, Saturday Night, In the Clouds, The Truth) 1923; Plays: 4th Series (The School of Princesses, A Lady, The Magic of an Hour, Field of Ermine) 1924; Brute Force, 1935; At Close Range, 1936.

ABOUT: Bell, A. F. G. Contemporary Spanish Literature; Boyd, E. Studies From Ten Literatures; Bueno, M. Teatro Español Contemporáneo; Cienfuegos, C. Benavente y la Crítica; Clark, B. H. The Continental Drama of Today; Dos Passos, J. Rosinante to the Road Again; Dukes, A. The Youngest Drama; Goldberg, I. The Drama of Transition; Jameson, S. Modern Drama in Europe; Lázaro, A. Jacinto Benavente: De Su Vida y De Su Obra; Onís, F. de. Jacinto Benavente; Starkie, W. Jacinto Benavente; Warren, L. A. Modern Spanish Literature; Criterion April 1923; Drama November 1915; Mercure de France December 1, 1922; Times Literary Supplement January 11, 1923, September 18, 1924; Yale Review October 1923

*BENCHLEY, ROBERT CHARLES

(September 15, 1889-   ), American humorist, was born in Worcester, Mass., the son of Charles Henry Benchley and Jane (Moran) Benchley. He received his B.A. from Harvard in 1912. After a brief experience translating French catalogs for the Boston Museum of Fine Arts, he went to New York to the branch advertising office of the Curtis Publishing Co. In 1914 he returned to Boston and for a year did personnel work for a large paper company. In 1916 and 1917 he was again in New York on the staff of the *Tribune*, first as associate editor of its Sunday magazine, then as editor of the *Tribune Graphic*. He lost his position because of a story indicating that Americans did not want to enter the war. The next year he was secretary of the Aircraft Board in Washington. After the war he became managing editor of *Vanity Fair*, with Robert E. Sherwood and Dorothy Parker among his colleagues. In 1920 and 1921 he conducted a column, "Books and Other Things," in the New York *World*. At the same time he was made dramatic editor of *Life,* and continued with that magazine (he became editor in 1924) until 1929, when he went to the *New Yorker,* whose dramatic editor he still is. He also conducts, under the pseudonym of "Guy Fawkes," an occasional department in the *New Yorker* analyzing the New York press.

Mr. Benchley's career on the stage began in 1923 with the Music Box Revue. His *Treasurer's Report,* given first in that medium, later became the first all-talking motion picture ever made. In all, he has since then made over twenty-five motion picture one-reelers. "How to Sleep" won the award of the Academy of Motion Picture Arts and Sciences in 1936. Since 1937 he has at various times appeared or acted as master of ceremony on radio broadcasts, both on sustaining and sponsored programs.

In 1914 he married Gertrude Darling, and they have two sons. Their home is in Scarsdale, N.Y., but actually Mr. Benchley spends about half the year in Hollywood.

Here is a triple career in each department of which Mr. Benchley rates at the very top; and yet he considers himself a frustrated failure. J. Bryan III called him "the most versatile humorist in America"; Stephen

Leacock said that no one exceeded him "in the ingenious technique of verbal humor. As a writer of nonesense for nonesense's sake, he is unsurpassed." But what he wanted in life was to be a social service worker and to write a history of the period of Queen Anne! He is quite sincere in his absurd modesty, and in an awkward shyness which he hides by "bluster and specious joviality." The vagueness, the gaucheries, the petty humiliations which are so funny on the screen, over the radio, or on the printed page are all straight out of Mr. Benchley's own unfortunate experiences; as Mr. Bryan said, "he is misfortune's fool, and makes capital of a handicap." His is a "character where anomaly is the norm and inconsistency the standard." The soul of kindness and courtesy, immensely beloved by his friends, extravagantly generous, he nevertheless thinks of himself as a miserable man who has wasted his opportunities and talents. Nothing can arouse him to anger except the spectacle of injustice, and then he becomes an implacable fighter. This engaging personality is housed in a bulky and carelessly dressed form (he has been described as an "unstylish stout"), topped by a sober face with owlish spectacles. In other words, Mr. Benchley looks exactly like the unhappy persons he writes about and portrays (and who are portrayed in the Gluyas Williams drawings which illustrate his books), whose neckties always slip over to their ears and who constantly stumble over chairs or bump into doors. Luckily for the public, he has been able to capitalize his defects with a fresh, naïve humor which possesses much point but no sting.

PRINCIPAL WORKS: Of All Things, 1921; Love Conquers All, 1922; Pluck and Luck, 1925; The Early Worm, 1927; 20,000 Leagues Under the Sea: or, David Copperfield, 1928; The Treasurer's Report, 1930; No Poems, 1932; From Bed to Worse, 1934; My Ten Years in a Quandary, 1936; After 1903—What? 1938; Inside Benchley, 1942.

ABOUT: Current Biography 1941; Saturday Evening Post September 23 and October 7, 1939; Saturday Review of Literature May 19 and December 26, 1936, January 8, 1938.

BENDA, JULIEN

(December 28, 1867-   ), French essayist, writes: "The enemy of Bergsonism, Julien Benda, was born in Paris. He was a pupil at the Central School. Having as little taste for applied science as for pure mathematics, he left this school, attended the course of the Faculty of Letters at the University of Paris, and received his bachelor's degree in history, with first honors, in 1894.

"At the time of 'the affair,' [the Dreyfus case], we find him at the *Revue Blanche,* where he contributed articles which were later collected in a volume now out of print, *Dialogues à Byzance* [*Dialogues at Byzantium*] (1900). In 1907, his friend Charles Péguy got him to write the introduction to the pamphlet of Georges Sorel on *The Metaphysical Preoccupations of Modern Physicists.* It was also to Péguy's *Cahiers de la Quinzaine* [a series of bi-weekly pamphlets] that the essayist was to contribute his first novel, *L'Ordination* (1910), which was to obtain a vote of five against five for the Goncourt Prize. 1910 marks the year when M. Benda, emerging from the studious meditation in which he had been bound, really commenced his career as a writer. He was then forty-three years old. After *Mon Premier Testament* [*My First Testament*], he wrote, in 1912, *Le Bergsonism,* which he followed, in 1913, by a work entitled *Sur le Succès de Bergsonism* [*On the Success of Bergsonism*]. In these books, wrote M. René Lalou, he opposed Sorel and Bergson as a pamphleteer; fighting hand to hand against 'the gratuitous assumptions of the new dogma,' he outlined the confusions of Bergsonism on the meaning of the word

'intuition,' and victoriously demonstrated that 'what Bergson calls intuition is only the intelligence, as against a sort of bureaucratic function of the spirit, to which he arbitrarily reserves that name.' For Julien Benda, 'intelligence is not an attribute of dead matter,' but only 'of thought in action, of living cerebration, of passionate intelligence.'

"During the war [1914-18], M. Benda took up again the journalist's pen and contributed to *Figaro* articles which were collected into volumes under the titles of *Les Sentiments de Critias* [*The Sentiments of Critias*] and *Billets de Sirius* [*Letters From Sirius*]. After the war, he wrote, among other works, *Belphégor: Essai sur l'Aesthétique de la Presente Societé* [*Belphegor: An Essay on the Aesthetics of Present-Day French Society*], in which he denounced the tendency of his contemporaries to 'make the exercise of the spirit a matter of emotion.' Two novels and another book of essays followed. In 1927 appeared *La Trahison des Clercs* [*The Treason of the Intellectuals*], a book which had a sensational success, but was very badly understood by most of its readers; an honest book which tries to restore the primacy of the spiritual and to break the thousand threads which attach the intellect to power and falsify its judgment. For the author, the writer fails in his function when, face to face with political developments, he abandons the contemplative and the eternal for the sake of the partial and the provisional. He himself wrote: 'Once the moralist gave lessons to actuality. Now he takes his hat off to it.'

"He has written numerous books of historical and philosophical essays since, and two autobiographical works, *La Jeunesse d'un Clerc* [*The Youth of an Intellectual*] (1937) and *Un Régulier dans le Siècle* [*A Regulator in His Century*]. It cannot be denied that these two books, which complete and clarify *La Trahison des Clercs,* constitute a psychological document of an unusual, stirring, and disturbing nature.

"M. Benda is a commander of the Legion of Honor. He is a regular contributor to *Temps, Nouvelles Littéraires,* the *Dépêche* (Toulouse), the *Revue de Paris,* and the *Nouvelle Revue Française.* In the last named, he frequently publishes his notes on 'the atmosphere of the month.' Some people see in these a political flavor, but the author of *Belphégor* confines himself to exposing the mysticism of the 'intellectual.' In 1936, 1937, and 1938 he lectured in the United States, particularly at Harvard and Princeton, and he has taken part in the work of the 'House of Culture' and in the movement of the anti-Fascist intellectuals."

* * *

Philosophically, M. Benda is a classicist and opposed to the whole school of intuition and "nature" which stems from Rousseau, but he is not a reactionary economically or politically. Irving Babbitt, though deploring Benda's "drift toward fatalism and occasional misanthropy," called him "an acute diagnostician of the modern mind and its maladies, ... a combination of keen analysis with honesty and courage."

Benda's autobiographical sketch was written in 1939. Since the fall of France, he has been permitted, as an anti-Fascist and a Jew, to exist on sufferance; but he has demonstrated his courage by refusing to keep silent.

WORKS AVAILABLE IN ENGLISH: The Treason of the Intellectuals (in England: The Great Betrayal) 1928; Belphegor, 1929; Living Thoughts of Kant, 1940.

ABOUT: Benda, J. La Jeunesse d'un Clerc, Un Régulier dans le Siècle; Read, H. E. Julien Benda and the New Humanism; Talvart, H. Bibliographie de Julien Benda; Europe Nouvelle September 7, 1935; Hibbert Journal April 1935; Journal of Philosophy May 26, 1932; Mercure de France August 15, 1930; Revue des Deux Mondes October 1, 1925; Revue Politique et Littéraire November 2, 1929; Saturday Review of Literature October 27, 1928, March 23, 1929.

BENEFIELD, BARRY (1880*-), American novelist, writes:

Bachrach

"Barry Benefield was born [John Barry Benefield] and, as the saying is, brought up in Jefferson, in the Northeastern corner of Texas and almost on the border of Louisiana. Though a small city now, Jefferson was in the 1860's the second commercial city of the state. The coming of the railroads in the '70's broke up Jefferson's close connection with New Orleans, but it was and still is more of Louisiana than of Texas in its way of life. Young Benefield did not escape the influence of the bayou country. After graduation from the state university at Austin [B.Litt., 1902], he ran away from the principalship of a city school with which a benevolently dictatorial university employment committee was threatening him, and found asylum with the Dallas *Morning News* as a cub reporter. Police headquarters, where he spent most of his time, seemed to be a promising sort of place to young Benefield, but after a few months New York seemed more promising. And so to New York, and to six or seven years on the city staff of the *Times*.

"Banished by a dictatorial doctor to the New Jersey countryside to catch up on his sleep, he began writing short fiction to pass the time left over from sleeping. Magazines printed it—*Scribner's, Collier's, Smart Set* (at the time when it was belligerently smart), and others. Then he married, and income from short stories being on the chancy side he once more sought a job. A book-publishing house this time, and he has been more or less in the book-publishing business ever since, as often as not a part-time worker. The full-time literary life, which he has tried several times, is to him a mortal bore.

"Mr. Benefield wrote his first novel, *The Chicken-Wagon Family,* while doing a full-time publishing job, to prove to himself that he could write one. A friend showed it to several editors; Mr. Benefield then hid it in the drawer of his desk reserved for papers which are to be first neglected and presently forgotten. It was resurrected and published more or less by accident, and was a so-called best seller.

"Mr. Benefield has had one period in Hollywood (the customary six weeks), and came away with liking and admiration for the creative movie workers and with the conviction that they are unconscious victims of a pervasive, unjustified, vicious inferiority complex as to their robust and splendidly promising young art. Promising provided they strangle their self-imposed censors and throw them into the Pacific.

"Mr. Benefield is at present (1940) a half-time editor of a New York publishing house and lives in Peekskill, N.Y. Commuting up and down the Hudson, with a seat always on the river side, is to him one of life's keenest delights. There's that boyhood on the bayous showing up again."

* * *

Barry Benefield is the son of Benjamin Jefferson Benefield and Adelaide (Barry) Benefield. He was married in 1913 to Lucille Stallcup, also a Texan. He might be taken rather for a teacher or a minister than for a writer, with his spectacles, his rather severe mouth, and his high, bulging forehead. Nevertheless warmth and sympathy are prominent in his very popular novels—indeed, their weakness lies in the ever-present danger of sentimentality. His short stories are much more realistic; Edward J. O'Brien said of them: "Those who are dumb have never had their feelings and experience interpreted so clearly before.... His restrained quiet is the outward and visible sign of a profound interior drama."

PRINCIPAL WORKS: The Chicken-Wagon Family, 1925; Short Turns (short stories) 1926; Bugles in the Night, 1927; A Little Clown Lost, 1928; Valiant Is the Word for Carrie, 1935; April Was When It Began, 1939.

ABOUT: Benefield, B. Short Turns (see Introduction by E. J. O'Brien); Mentor September 1926.

*BENÉT, STEPHEN VINCENT (July 22, 1898-), American poet and story writer,

Pulitzer Prize winner, was born in Bethlehem, Pa., the son of Colonel J. Walker Benét and Frances Neill (Rose) Benét. It was a writing family; the father loved and knew poetry, and Stephen Benét is the brother of William Rose Benét *qv* and Laura Benét and the uncle of James Benét. Until her death he was also the brother-in-law of Elinor Wylie; and his wife, who was Rosemary Carr (they were married in 1921 and have two daughters and a son), is also a writer. The Benéts and the Van Dorens are New York's first writing families.

Mr. Benét's grandfather and great-grandfather as well as his father, were army officers. He was reared in various army posts to which his father was assigned, but most of his boyhood was spent in Benicia, Calif., on San Francisco Bay. He went to school  there, and later in Georgia, and then to Yale, where he received his B.A. in 1919 and his M.A. in 1920 (honorary Litt.D. 1937). He then went to France to do graduate work at the Sorbonne. It was there that he met Mrs. Benét, who was on the staff of the Paris edition of the Chicago *Tribune*.

He has never followed any profession except writing. His first volume, six dramatic monologues in verse, was published when he was only seventeen. For his living, in his earlier years, he depended on his stories and novels; they were rather lean years, and he was dissatisfied with his accomplishment and obsessed by the desire to write a long narrative poem drawn from the military records which he had pored over as a boy in his father's library. A Guggenheim Fellowship in 1926 enabled him to take his family to Paris and get to work on this poem, which eventually appeared as *John Brown's Body*. Into it he poured all his talent for the ballad form, his emotional patriotism, and his unusually minute knowledge of the period. It is not surprising that it won the Pulitzer Prize for poetry in 1929. His next great success was the prose story, *The Devil and Daniel Webster*, which in a few years has become a minor American classic and has even been turned into a grand opera. He himself wrote an operetta based on Washington Irving's *Legend of Sleepy Hollow*, which was performed over the radio in a national broadcast in 1937.

Mr. Benét also is one of the staff reviewers of the *Saturday Review of Literature* and a member of the American Academy of Arts and Letters. On his return from Paris in 1927, he went to live in Rhode Island, but in 1930 moved to New York, which is his present home. He is tall and dark and wears glasses.

His brother has said that "poetry was from the first a bright valor in his blood." Nevertheless, his achievement as a poet has been singularly uneven. He ranges from the fusion of feeling and intellect at a high level predominant in *John Brown's Body* and in many of his shorter narrative poems and ballads to a jingling verse on the level of Eugene Field or James Whitcomb Riley. One of his finest performances is a startling series of fantastic poems about a nightmare New York of the future where termites destroy the city silently, or where the machines revolt and become the masters. Lately he has become exceedingly agitated by the current international situation, and his *Nightmare at Noon* is a powerful though almost hysterical warning of America's danger. One critic remarked that "his heavily emotional approach to national concerns is slightly pre-war, like his verse forms." Nevertheless, at his best he is a poet of almost the first rank. His novels have been his least successful work; but his short stories in the folk-lore vein are perfect of their kind—indigenously American, stamped with authenticity, and wholly delightful. Mr. Benét is at his best either in the ballad or in stories which might be called ballads in prose.

PRINCIPAL WORKS: *Poetry*—Five Men and Pompey, 1915; Young Adventure, 1918; Heavens and Earth, 1920; Ballad of William Sycamore, 1790-1880, 1923; Tiger Joy, 1925; John Brown's Body, 1928; Ballads and Poems, 1931; Burning City, 1936; Johnny Pye and the Fool-Killer, 1938; Nightmare at Noon, 1940; Selected Verse (2 vols.) 1942. *Prose*—The Beginning of Wisdom, 1921; Young People's Pride, 1922; Jean Huguenot, 1923; Spanish Bayonet, 1926; Jane Shore's Daughter, 1934; The Devil and Daniel Webster, 1937; Thirteen O'Clock, 1937; Tales Before Midnight, 1939; Zero Hour, 1940; Summons to the Free, 1941; Selected Works, 1942.

ABOUT: Delineator September 1930; New York Times April 21, 1940; Poetry August 1936; Saturday Review of Literature December 27, 1930, April 7, 1934, July 20, 1939, November 15, 1941; Time June 22, 1936, August 30, 1937; Yale Review Spring 1941.

*BENÉT, WILLIAM ROSE (February 2, 1886-   ), American poet and novelist, writes: "The subject of this sketch at one time had his birth celebrated by his friend, Christopher Morley, in the following verse:

> Old Bill Benét, Old Bill Benét,
> Born in a Fort on Ground-Hog Day!

(the fort being Fort Hamilton, New York Harbor). This incidentally gives one a clue to the pronunciation of the *celebrité's* last name. When W. R. B.'s grandfather, Stephen Vincent Benét (the elder), entered West Point, in 1845, the accent was pre-

* Died May 4, 1950.

sumed to be French and the French pronunciation attached to it. The family, whose name was originally pronounced Ba-na-te, came from Catalonia. The subject of this memoir had a great-great-grandfather, Esteban Benét, who be-

Delar

came a master mariner in the Spanish Merchant Marine and settled in St. Augustine in 1785. He married Catalina Hernandez, and in 1812 he was lost at sea with his ship. His brother was a Post-Captain in the Spanish Navy and was assassinated in Havana. This fact pleases the more brutal instinct of his descendant.

"The grandfather of William Rose Benét and Stephen Vincent Benét,^{qv} the first Stephen Vincent, was a Brigadier General in the United States Army and at one time Chief of Ordnance. Their father, James Walker Benét, was retired as Colonel of Ordnance. Both were West Pointers. On the other hand, both the Benét brothers went to Yale University. William Rose Benét, twelve years older than Stephen, graduated there from the Sheffield Scientific School in 1907. He had previously graduated from the Albany Academy in 1904

"It will be sufficiently clear that at his present advanced age this writer concerns himself with the past, allowing his children to concern themselves with the future. His son, James Walker Benét, spent two and a half years in Spain, driving ambulance and truck for the Loyalist cause, which Mr. Benét and his brother supported in this country. His older daughter recently made him a grandfather; his younger daughter was recently married in California, and resides there. The above are children of Mr. Benét's first marriage to Teresa Frances Thompson, a sister of Kathleen Norris, the novelist. The first Mrs. Benét died in the post-war influenza epidemic which so shadowed the east. Mr. Benét's second wife was Elinor Wylie,^{qv} the poet and novelist, whose collected poetry and prose he edited posthumously. A third time (1932) he married Lora Baxter, well known in the theatre. They were amicably divorced and Miss Baxter has married again.

"The most earnest desire of this writer's life has been to write poetry. He has spent his lifetime in trying, with mixed results. He has published a number of books of poems, one novel, a book of fugitive pieces chiefly contributed to the *Literary Review* and the *Saturday Review of Literature,* has written a few short stories, some light verse, some verse and prose for children, a one-act fantasia which in 1939 was produced at the famous Dock Street Theatre in Charleston, S.C., and has edited several anthologies, the best of which is the *Oxford Anthology of American Literature,* in collaboration with Norman Holmes Pearson. He is at work at present upon a long semi-autobiographical poem, having recently completed a rhymed narrative for children and a book in rhyme celebrating the chief flights of international aviation. He feels least dissatisfaction with a handful of poems he has written over a long period of years. Among these are several inspired by Elinor Wylie, one called 'Man Possessed' inspired by his first wife, and several ballads, notably one paying homage to Jesse James, the great American outlaw. Perhaps his most popular poem has been 'Whale,' a fantastic ballad of the higher mammalia. He cherishes a sneaking fondness himself for a long poem concerned with the ancient Tartar invasion of China, called 'The Great White Wall.' He feels it to contain certain passages that may please later readers now in the limbo of time.

"This writer has also amused himself with a slight gift for eccentric draughtmanship, and once produced a series of fantastic animals painted upon the cardboards which accompany men's shirts home from the laundry. A recent illness has made an abstinent of an inveterate cigarette smoker and cramped his style of drinking and spending evenings in ornate bars. He is rather skeptical about the future of the world, though in his youth he used to enjoy getting a poem into the old *Masses.* He was once a shavetail in the Air Service and a ki-wi (which means non-flying). That was in the last war. In the present one, which may either remake or end the world, he does not anticipate any very important part. His general thesis is that the acquisition of power ruins any fine altruistic dream. Nevertheless he believes that the world will get better and that, eventually it will even outlaw war.

"He does not believe in writers' becoming propagandists for any political system, but in their writing the truth that is in them as they see it. He does not believe in people's being told what to think. In fact, all his life, he has been fighting that idea. He believes that half the time people take

117

themselves much too seriously—present-day radicals for a vital instance—and would rather enjoy the many delightful absurdities of life with the generous and kindly than carry a torch with the zealots. This will get him nowhere in the end, except before the firing-squad. He hates and abhors all secret police and that whole manner of running a country. He thinks the United States has more virtues than the present hot-heads admit, and way and above any other country gives people a chance to be most hot-headed, which they promptly accept with screams of joy. He says, of course democracy is an imperfect system, but he vastly prefers it to any other. Above all, he thinks trying to write poetry is the best kind of life in the world—not trying to tell people about it, which he has also tried [as instructor at Mills College, Oakland, Calif., in 1936]. He knows it is a world full of man-made horror, but he has retained his own kind of faith, which is no more ridiculous than anyone's else. He thinks he has known some of the finest people who ever existed, and that does not incline him to pessimism. He hates tyranny and cruelty. All the above does not make him a good writer, but it makes him a fairly good average example of human being."

* * *

Mr. Benét was on the staff of *Century Magazine* from 1911 to 1918. He has been the poetry critic of the *Saturday Review of Literature* from its beginning. In 1919 and 1920 he was assistant editor of the *Nation's Business,* and went from there to the *Literary Review* of the New York *Evening Post,* from which the *Saturday Review of Literature* grew. Besides his brother Stephen, his sister Laura is also known as a poet. In 1941 Mr. Benét married a fourth time; his bride was Marjorie Flack, author and illustrator of children's books.

Louis Untermeyer has described him as "tall, lean, with a curiously hesitant step, a low and almost deprecating voice, his face continually wrinkling with warmth and pleasure." His poetry is colorful and romantic. Rolfe Humphries called him "a journeyman of letters," but Marguerite Wilkinson said he was "a builder. . . . His strongest rhythms have the certitude of an arch. . . ." In 1942 he received the Pulitzer Prize for poetry for *The Dust Which Is God,* an autobiographical verse narrative.

PRINCIPAL WORKS: *Poetry*—Merchants From Cathay, 1913; The Falconer of God, 1914; The Great White Wall, 1916; The Burglar of the Zodiac, 1918; Perpetual Light, 1919; Moons of Grandeur, 1920; Man Possessed, 1927; Rip Tide (novel in verse) 1932; Starry Harness, 1933; Golden Fleece, 1935; With Wings As Eagles, 1940; The Dust Which Is God, 1941. *Prose*—The First Person Singular (novel) 1922; The Flying King of Kurio (juvenile) 1926; Wild Goslings, 1927; Adolphus the Adopted Dolphin (juvenile) 1941.

ABOUT: Benét, W. R. The Dust Which Is God; Bookman April 1921, October 1923; Poetry April 1934; Saturday Review of Literature July 27, 1936.

BENNETT, ARNOLD (May 27, 1867-March 27, 1931), English novelist and playwright, was originally named Enoch Arnold, after his father — a  curious person who failed as a pottery manufacturer, became a pawnbroker, and at thirty-four emerged as a solicitor! He was also a household martinet, and it was not until his death that Arnold Bennett's mother developed a personality of her own. All in all, they were a large and salty family, flesh-and-bone genuine citizens of the immortal Five Towns which are really six. Bennett was born near Hanley, North Staffordshire, and from infancy he soaked in every detail of that hard, obstinate country whose inhabitants had been making pottery when the Romans invaded England.

The mere facts of his life are quickly told; it is the man himself and his work that are interesting. His father wanted him to follow in his footsteps as a solicitor. He sent him to Newcastle Middle School, then on his graduation had him matriculate by non-resident examination in London University, meanwhile putting him in his own office to act as law student and unpaid clerk. The boy had played about a bit with writing for local papers, but had never thought of a literary career. In 1885 he quarreled politely with his father and went to London where he got a job as cost clerk in a solicitor's office. Then, on the strength of one accepted story in the famous *Yellow Book,* and a twenty guinea prize from *Tit Bits,* he threw up the job and took one at a smaller salary with a "ladies' magazine" named *Woman.* There, under the name of "Gwendolyn," he wrote beauty hints and advised the lovelorn! The experience was a good one: it gave him an extraordinary insight into the mental and emotional workings of some types of women.

In 1896 he cut loose from this and began to free-lance, writing book and play reviews, stories, articles, anything he could sell. All his life he was "not an author, but a writing man." As supremely confident as his own "Denry the Audacious," he began keeping a journal ostensibly for posterity, and long before he could afford it moved to Bedfordshire in the anticipation of a large income. In 1900 he went even farther; he moved to France and for eight years lived near Fontainebleau. He worked indefatigably, writing some half million words per year, and carefully noting down their number and the exact amount he received for them. He always drove a sharp bargain, and when he sold material by the word, he demanded payment for every "the" and "and." Without being a miser—he was always a free spender —he had the passion for concrete coin in his hands which he gave to his "Earlforward" in *Riceyman Steps.* He had become a popular run-of-the-mill novelist, but he had not yet produced any of his best books. He was still enthralled by the French authors, Flaubert, the Goncourts, Zola, and the Russians, especially Dostoievsky, who were to make him, at his best, a really great novelist of the naturalistic school.

He was a bad man to marry—undomestic, tyrannical, a charmer of women and charmed by them—but a French actress, Marguerite Hebrard, took the chance in 1907. She herself has written of their life together, terminated by their separation in 1921. They seem never to have been divorced—at any rate there was considerable legal doubt as to the validity of any decree. His last years with the actress Dorothy Cheston (Bennett), were described by the latter in another book about him. During their married life Arnold and Marguerite lived in France and in England, for some years in a house in Essex. But he died of typhoid fever in a luxury hotel, like the one he had celebrated in *Imperial Palace.*

Bennett was obsessed by a sort of bachelor finickiness. He carried demands for punctuality and neatness to an absurd degree. He was easily bored—he tired of his home, his car, his yacht, and apparently of his wife. Behind all this, behind his heavy-set figure with its flamboyant clothes, his drooping eyelids over dark eyes, his half-open mouth, his crest of gray hair, his speech impediment (softened into a mere stammer in later life), was a shy man who, as Rebecca West says, "converted the oddities of which he was sensitive into a baroque exterior behind which he could hide."

He professed to be a radical in both religion and politics; but in his true philosophy —industry, patriotism, thrift—he was bourgeois to the core; and he is the laureate of the lower middle class of provincial England. He never thought of himself as a "literary" person; he was far more interested in financial returns than in artistic acclaim. He might have been the character in one of his plays who said: "I'm not a blooming reformer, I'm a merchant." He ascribed his success to a tenacious memory, a sound taste in literature and a journalistic flair for "seeming to know more than one does know" —to which might be added a genius for observation. The people in his handful of really first-class novels are all real, three-dimensional, solid human beings, but their emotions are muted; they are inarticulate when we try to penetrate their surface. As Dorothy Van Doren puts it, "he will tell anything, but he will not raise his voice." Constance and Sophia Baines, Clayhanger, Hilda Lessways, "Denry"—they are all, unlike as they are to one another, built of the tough, impenetrable clay of Staffordshire.

Arnold Bennett wrote far too much for the good of his ultimate reputation. His literary history is a succession of waves— one leading up to the high mark of *The Old Wives' Tale* and *Clayhanger,* then a gradual descent (at first very gradual), then a lesser crest in *Riceyman Steps* and *Elsie and the Child,* and then back again to the merely competent and popular. Whether he might have risen once more had he lived, no one can know. He was like Antaeus—his power was that of a giant while he kept his feet rooted in his native earth. In more ways than a mere accident of similar subject, his career resembles that of a contemporary American, Sinclair Lewis.

The "Five Towns" stories, all of them— but *The Old Wives' Tale* and *Clayhanger* most of all—are in the first rank of English novels. They are compact of realism—and a genuinely English realism, not the Frenchified realism of George Moore. He did almost the same thing, later, for the same class of people in London, but others have done as much. No others have ever done what he did for the shopkeepers and potters and other "middle class Anglo-Saxons under a high standard of living" in the Five Towns. Staffordshire belongs to him as Wessex belongs to Thomas Hardy, or as Yorkshire once belonged to Emily Brontë.

He himself would have made a splendid novel. He had more than a bit of vulgarity, details of illness and death fascinated him morbidly, he was rather a hypochondriac, he was obstinate and arbitrary, he never admitted himself wrong even in trifles, he was not far from mercenary. But he was also a passionate hater of injustice, an *arrivé* who regarded the splendid world about him with "the unenvious wonder of a child," a man of genuine and (quite unwittingly) pathetic charm. He was a middle-class neurotic who transmuted his neuroses to something very near genius—while all the time he disclaimed any ambition or ability beyond those of any other man who could and would work unceasingly and "live on twenty-four hours a day."

Nobody has ever succeeded better in making dull people interesting. That is his supreme achievement. There are no dull passages in even the least of his novels and stories, any more than in his shrewdly theatrical plays. The less interesting intrinsically his characters, the more interesting he makes them. When the twentieth century is over, Arnold Bennett will be somewhere near the top of its list of novelists—a great writer who spent most of his time doing pot-boilers, but who, in spite of himself, half a dozen times produced books which were foreordained classics.

PRINCIPAL WORKS: *Fiction*—A Man From the North, 1898; The Grand Babylon Hotel, 1902; Anna of the Five Towns, 1902; Leonora, 1903; A Great Man, 1904; Tales of the Five Towns, 1905; The Book of Carlotta (in England, Sacred and Profane Love) 1905; Whom God Hath Joined, 1906; The Grim Smile of the Five Towns, 1907; Buried Alive, 1908; The Old Wives' Tale, 1908; Helen With the High Hand, 1910; Clayhanger, 1910; Hilda Lessways, 1911; Denry the Audacious (in England, The Card) 1911; The Matador of the Five Towns and Other Stories, 1912; The Old Adam (in England, The Regent) 1913; The Price of Love, 1914; These Twain, 1916; The Lion's Share, 1916; The Pretty Lady, 1918; Our Women, 1920; Mr. Prohack, 1922; Lilian, 1923; Riceyman Steps, 1923; Elsie and the Child, 1925; Lord Raingo, 1926; The Woman Who Stole Everything and Other Stories, 1927; The Vanguard (in England, The Strange Vanguard) 1928; Accident, 1929; Imperial Palace, 1930; The Night Visitor and Other Stories, 1931; Stroke of Love and Dream of Destiny, 1932. *Plays (besides dramatized novels)*—What the Public Wants, 1909; The Honeymoon, 1911; Milestones (with Edward Knoblock) 1912; The Title, 1918; Judith, 1919; The Love Match, 1922; Body and Soul, 1922; The Return Journey, 1928. *Miscellaneous*—The Truth About an Author, 1903; How to Live on Twenty-four Hours a Day, 1907; Your United States (in England, Those United States) 1912; Books and Persons, 1917; From the Log of the Velsa, 1920; Things That Have Interested Me, 1921, 1923, 1925; The Savour of Life, 1928; Mediterranean Scenes, 1928.

ABOUT: Bennett, A. The Truth About an Author; Journal of Arnold Bennett: 1896-1929; Bennett, D. C. Arnold Bennett: A Portrait Done at Home; Bennett, M. My Arnold Bennett; Cross, W. L. Four Contemporary Novelists; Darton, F. J. H. Arnold Bennett; Simons, J. B. Arnold Bennett and His Novels; Nation April 8 and 15, 1931; New Republic April 8, 1931; Nineteenth Century May 1931; Saturday Review of Literature April 4, 1931, May 2, 1931, September 5, 1931; Yale Review December 1928.

BENOîT, PIERRE (July 6, 1886-), French novelist, was a vivacious but studious youngster who followed his father into the army. He was stationed in Tunis, source of his later romances that evoke visions of palm trees and sands and the fierce African sun. He also studied at the University of Paris. *Diadumène* (1914) was Benoît's first novel. *Koenigsmarck*,  the next, was serialized in the *Mercure de France* and showed its author to be one of the long line of story-tellers which had begun in the seventeenth century and culminated in Dumas. *L'Atlantide* (1919) won Benoît the Grand Prix de Roman of the Académie Française, and in English translation was widely read. It also caused some critics to draw a "deadly parallel" between *L'Atlantide* and Rider Haggard's *She*, which it resembled in theme and even in characters. Antinéa suggested She, or Ayesha; and the Captain Morhange of Benoît's romance called up memories of the Leo Vincey of the Haggard novel. Benoît studied African monographs and geographical bulletins to insure the authencity of his backgrounds; he even found the details of the costume of Clementine in the novel in *Moniteur des Dames et des Demoiselles* for February 1863. His romances have animation and color. They are generally of exactly the same length, and usually have heroines whose names begin with A. Benoît's style is simple and bare, but nevertheless rich. Each book has for its basis one strong and simple feeling; the development of the story is furnished by the repercussions on one character or another of the original force. Love of power and usurpation is the theme of *Koenigsmarck*; horror of tedium of life and death in *Atlantide*; religious and racial sentiment in *Le Puits de Jacob* (1925), violence of passion in *Alberte* (1926) and horror of compromise and jealousy in *Le Lac Salé* (1921). *Mademoiselle de la Ferté* (1923) is a medical novel. Benoît's later works include *Le Dé-*

jeuner de Sousceyrac (1931); *L'Ile Verte,* 1932; and *Fort de France* (1933). He has been a member of the Académie Française since 1931, and is a former president of the Société des Gens de Lettres. His latest recorded address was in Paris. Benoît's books are written on large white sheets of paper, in a small, somewhat tremulous, but regular handwriting. In the days of his greatest prosperity he was an inveterate traveler and cosmopolite, traversing North Africa, Syria, and other countries. He has treated his subjects from the point of view of his own country, having particular respect and veneration for those who had served France. His chief admiration among French writers is Balzac.

WORKS AVAILABLE IN ENGLISH TRANSLATION: Atlantida, 1920; Secret Spring, 1920; Salt Lake, 1922; Jacob's Well, 1926; The Lady of Lebanon, 1930; Alberte, 1930; Axelle, 1930; Mademoiselle de la Ferté, 1930.

ABOUT: Le Correspondant February 25, 1920; La Minerve Française March 1920; Revue des Deux Mondes November 15, 1932.

BENSON, ARTHUR CHRISTOPHER
(April 24, 1862-June 17, 1925), English essayist, poet, and scholar, was the oldest

surviving son of Edward White Benson, Archbishop of Canterbury, and his second cousin Mary (Sidgwick) Benson. He was born at Wellington College, where his father was then headmaster, and passed his entire life in a scholastic atmosphere. From Eton he went to King's College, Cambridge, with a scholarship, and took a first class in the classical tripos in 1884. He returned to Eton as master, becoming house master in 1892. He wrote a book on teaching, yet as a matter of fact he disliked his profession, cared only for a few of his bookishly minded pupils, and found his only happiness in the leisure hours he could give to writing. In 1903 he resigned and went to Cambridge to live, his primary task at the time being the editing, with Viscount Esher, of the letters of Queen Victoria—who had shown him much personal favor. He was sufficiently prosperous by then to be able to accept a fellowship of Magdalene College though no stipend was connected with it, and at Magdalene he lived for the remainder of his life. In 1915 he was elected a master, but even before that

he had grown to be "the strongest cultural influence at Cambridge." He wrote constantly—poems, essays, and biographies—almost a hundred volumes in all, some of them very popular, especially in America.

Yet this tall, heavy-set, blond, ruddy man, a keen mountain-climber, was actually a nervous invalid for much of his life. He had two severe attacks of melancholia, one in 1907 and another, lasting five years, in 1917. When he died (of pleurisy followed by heart trouble), and his friends read the 180 volumes of his diary, they found a different Benson from the hearty, liberal-minded, genial, industrious man they had known. Here Benson, who had never married and who had spent all his years in the shades of the classical grove, lamented that life had let him be "neither soldier nor lover."

Benson could not bear an idle moment. He continued to write in after-school hours, explored the countryside on a bicycle, and made hurried trips to London to attend meetings of various educational committees or the Modern Languages Association (of which he was at one time president) or to examine naval candidates at the Admiralty. He carried on a voluminous correspondence with his readers, many of them feminine admirers. One American lady, whom he had never met, but with whom he became friendly through letters, left him a gift of a considerable fortune. The money he used for the benefit of his college.

As a poet, Benson was surprisingly colorless and conventional; probably the only verse of his that will be remembered is his lyric, "Land of Hope and Glory," to Elgar's "Pomp and Circumstance." As a biographer—he wrote the lives of Fitz Gerald, D. G. Rossetti, and Pater for the *English Men of Letters* series—he is competent, but no more. His novels are far behind those of his brother E. F. Benson, or even his brother Robert Hugh Benson. But where A. C. Benson excels is in a mode now out of fashion, the meditative literary and philosophical essay. His essays are not personal or familiar but they have the charm of a pleasant conversation in a library; and many of them belong in any collection of the best of their *genre* in the language.

PRINCIPAL WORKS: *Essays and Biography*—Archbishop Laud, 1887; Men of Might (with H. F. W. Tatham) 1890; Essays, 1896; Fasti Etonenses, 1899; Life of Archbishop Benson, 1899; The Schoolmaster, 1902; Tennyson, 1904; Rossetti, 1904; Edward Fitzgerald, 1905; Walter Pater, 1906; From a College Window, 1906; The Thread of Gold, 1906; The Gate of Death, 1906; Beside Still Waters, 1907; The Altar Fire, 1907; At Large, 1908; The Silent Isle, 1910; Ruskin, 1911;

121

Leaves of the Tree, 1911; Thy Rod and Thy Staff, 1912; Along the Road, 1913; Joyous Gard, 1913; Where No Fear Was, 1914; The Orchard Pavilion, 1914; Escape and Other Essays, 1915; Hugh: Memoirs of a Brother, 1915; Memories and Friends, 1924; Rambles and Reflections, 1926. *Poetry*—Poems, 1893; Lyrics, 1895; Lord Vyet and Other Poems, 1896; The Professor and Other Poems, 1900; Peace and Other Poems, 1905. *Novels*—Memoirs of Arthur Hamilton, 1886; The Hill of Trouble, 1903; The Isles of Sunset, 1904; The Child of the Dawn, 1912; Watersprings, 1913; Father Payne, 1916; The House of Menerdue, 1925.

ABOUT: Benson, A. C. Selections From Diary (ed. by P. Lubbock); Leaves of the Tree; Thy Rod and Thy Staff; Memories and Friends; James, H. Letters to A. C. Benson; Ryle, E. H. (ed) A. C. Benson As Seen by Some Friends; Williams, H. Modern English Writers; Bookman (London) August 1925; Independent January 8, 1927; Spectator June 27, 1925.

BENSON, EDWARD FREDERIC (July 24, 1867-February 29, 1940), English novelist, essayist, and biographer, was born at

Wellington College, of which his father, Edward White Benson, who afterwards became Archbishop of Canterbury, was then headmaster. His mother, Mary (Sidgwick) Benson, was a daughter of his father's cousin; and of her six children two besides Edward rose to considerable distinction: the Very Reverend Monsignor Robert Hugh Benson, a priest in the Catholic Arch-Diocese of Westminster and a religious writer; and Arthur Christopher Benson,*qqv* Master of Magdalene College, Cambridge.

The Bensons moved to Lincoln for a while and then to Truro, and as Edward afterwards said of his earlier years, "We were all of us draughtsmen, ornithologists, conchologists, geologists, poets, and literary folk." And each member of the family contributed his quota—"at least four pages of prose or one page of verse"—to the intramural *Saturday Magazine.*

At Marlborough he sat "solid and immovable"—academically—until A. H. Beesley, one of the masters and a scholar in his own right, succeeded in introducing him to the perenially new and human quality in the classics. He became editor of the *Marlburian* and wrote imitations of Addison and Tennyson. While he was at King's College, Cambridge, he published, with a decidedly wavering confidence, *Sketches From Marlborough.*

Like many another English youth Benson had done some fruitful digging for relics of the Roman occupation. It was William Gladstone who taught him how to make blotting-paper squeezes of the inscriptions he had unearthed in the wall of the city of Chester. During his last year at Cambridge he combined his classical research with his talent for archaeological grubbing; and from 1892 to 1895 he was studying and working at the British School of Archaeology in Athens.

Meanwhile his first real book, *Dodo*, reduced to hardly more than a fragment of his first draft (which Henry James and Lucas Malet had heartlessly but helpfully dissected), had occasioned an actual "boom" in the publishing world. The fact that a son of the Archbishop of Canterbury should have written a book so candidly unepiscopal and that like other ruthless novelists he should have put so many of his own loving townspeople into such unpleasantly identifiable rôles was reason enough for a record-breaking sale—irrespective of *Dodo's* own particular merit. Unfortunately the "successor to that abhorred comet" happened to be what Benson himself admitted was a "poor book," *The Rubicon.* The Grub Street reviewing guns did their best to annihilate him.

During the 'nineties and early 1900's Benson wrote an incredible amount of light fiction, including a series devoted to Lucia Pillson, the first of which was *Queen Lucia* (1920) and the last *Trouble for Lucia* (1939). Some years later his *forte* was biography (Alcibiades, King Edward VII, Charlotte Brontë, Sir Francis Drake) written largely in the essay manner. Among the best known of his more personal and reflective contemporary histories was *As We Were,* subtitled "A Victorian Peep-Show." In his study of the Kaiser, published in 1936, he scored something of a "scoop" on the cause of William II's withered arm. For the preparation of *Queen Victoria's Daughters* the Royal Family had turned over to Benson a considerable amount of unpublished material.

From 1934 to 1937 Benson was mayor of Rye, and his home there was the famous Lamb House, which for eighteen years was the residence of the ex-American Henry James. He was made a Member of the Order of the British Empire, for literary achievement, and was an honorary fellow of Magdalene College, Cambridge. He died in England in his seventy-third year. The fact that he published about eighty volumes and had numerous non-literary interests as well is sufficient evidence of the ease and pleasure with which he wrote. His urbanity and Victorianism as a writer have suggested a likeness to Anthony Hope; his irony is only occasional, suave, and gentle, and appears sometimes to be made of "silks and satins still fragrant with crumpled roses that recall what can never be again."

PRINCIPAL WORKS: Dodo, 1893; The Rubicon, 1894; The Babe, B. A., 1897; Mammon & Co., 1900; The Relentless City, 1903; Account Rendered, 1911; David Blaize, 1916; Queen Lucia, 1920; Colin, 1923; Paying Guests, 1929; Life of Alcibiades, 1929; Ferdinand Magellan; As We Were, 1930; Henry James: Letters to A. C. Benson and Auguste Monod, 1930; Charlotte Brontë, 1932; As We Are, 1932; Ravens' Brood, 1934; Queen Victoria, 1935; The Kaiser and English Relations, 1936; Queen Victoria's Daughters, 1938; Trouble for Lucia, 1939; Final Edition, 1940.

ABOUT: Benson, E. F. As We Are, As We Were, Our Family Affairs, Final Edition; New York Herald Tribune March 1, 1940; New York Times March 1, 1940; Saturday Review of Literature August 3, October 19, 1940.

BENSON, GODFREY RATHBONE.
See CHARNWOOD, G. R. B.

BENSON, ROBERT HUGH (November 18, 1871-October 19, 1914), English novelist and Catholic apologist, was the fourth

son and youngest child of Edward White Benson and Mary (Sidgwick) Benson, his second cousin. Two of his brothers, Edward Frederic and Arthur Christopher Benson,[qqv] also became prominent literary figures. Robert Hugh was born at Wellington College, where his father, later Archbishop of Canterbury, was the school's first headmaster. In 1872 the elder Benson became chancellor of Lincoln Cathedral, in 1877 bishop of the new diocese at Truro, and in 1882, when he became archbishop, the family lived at Lambeth Palace and Addington Court near Croydon. In 1882 Hugh attended preparatory school at Clevedon, Somerset; in 1885 he won a scholarship to Eton. He soon showed himself a high-strung, romantic youth; ecclesiastical surroundings and the reading of J. Henry Shorthouse's theological romance *John Inglesant* made a deep impression on Benson. After an unsuccessful try at the Indian service Benson entered Trinity College, Cambridge University, in October 1890, where he began the study of theology. He was ordained deacon in 1894, with some private misgivings; at a retreat he received help from Father Basil Maturin.[qv] Ordained a priest of the Church of England in 1895, Benson spent the autumn of 1896 at Hackney Wick, among poor people. A stay (for discipline) at the Community of the Resurrection at Mirfield, Yorkshire, and lectures by Canon (later Bishop) Gore further unsettled his religious convictions, and in September 1903 Benson was received into the Roman Catholic Church. At Llandaff House, Cambridge, he read theology and began to write intense and febrile historical fiction, followed by novels of modern life. *The Sentimentalists* utilized as a character his sometime friend "Baron Corvo" (Frederick Rolfe [qv]), with whom he collaborated on a life of Archbishop Becket. Most of his writing was done at an old house on Hare Street, Buntingford, Hertfordshire, which he "quaintly adorned." His recreations were embroidering, gardening, and entertaining friends. Benson was popular as man and preacher in spite of his stammer and shrill voice. "Feverish and systematic overwork" soon undermined his nervous system, and he died at forty-three of pneumonia supervening on false angina. Death occurred at Salford, in the presence of his brother Arthur, to whom he was much attached. *Come Rack! Come Rope!* with its vividly described scenes of torture, and *Oddsfish*, a romance of Charles II, are perhaps his best known work in America.

PRINCIPAL WORKS: The Light Invisible, 1903; By What Authority? 1904; The King's Achievement, 1905; The Queen's Tragedy, 1905; The Sentimentalists, 1906; The Conventionalists, 1908; The Necromancers, 1909; None Other Gods, 1910; A Winnowing, 1910; The Coward, 1912; Come Rack! Come Rope! 1912; An Average Man, 1913; Paradoxes of Catholicism, 1913; Oddsfish, 1914; Initiation, 1914; Loneliness, 1915.

ABOUT: Benson, A. C. Hugh; Benson, E. F. Our Family Affairs, Final Edition; Braybrooke, P. Some Catholic Novelists; Martindale, C. C. The Life of Monsignor Robert Hugh Benson; Rolfe, F. The Desire and Pursuit of the Whole.

BENSON, STELLA (1892-December 6, 1933), English novelist, was born at Lutwyche Hall, Muchwenlock, Shropshire, the daughter of Ralph Beaumont Benson and Caroline (Cholmondeley) Benson, daughter of the Rev. R. H. Cholmondeley. Mary Cholmondeley, the novelist, was her aunt.

Stella was a delicate child, and so was educated privately, at home, on the French Riviera, in Germany and in Switzerland.

A lifelong love of travel early declared itself. Just before the war she took an interest in woman suffrage and worked for a time in  the East End of London for the Charity Organization Society. Dissatisfied with the Society's methods, she felt that the best way to see the life of the poor was to share it. She therefore opened a small general shop in the depressed district of Hoxton, taking a local woman as partner. There she remained until 1917, writing her first two novels, *I Pose* and *This Is the End* during that period. *I Pose* was sent to the great publishing house of Macmillan, with a request for a decision in a week's time, and accepted by them. Miss Benson then became a land worker, but owing to the weakness of her lungs left for America in June 1918.

She was under doctor's orders for California, but spent some time (and all her money) in New York and New England, so that when she arrived in California she had to take menial employment on a ranch. Just before Christmas, 1918, she arrived in San Francisco with five dollars in her pocket, and on Christmas day she finished her third novel, *Living Alone*. She passed eighteen months living in a tiny room in Berkeley, working first as lady's maid, bill collector, and book agent, but later securing more suitable posts, first as tutor in the University of California and next as editorial reader for the University Press.

In January 1920, she set off for England again by way of the Far East. She took eighteen months on the journey and had all manner of adventures, including tiger shooting in India, teaching fifty Chinese boys in a mission school, and working in the X-ray department of an American hospital at Peking. In China, too, she met the man she was to marry—John O'Gorman Anderson, of the Customs service. The wedding took place in London in 1921 and the honeymoon was spent in traveling the American continent from East to West in a Ford car, a journey described in *The Little World*.

Back in China, the Andersons were stationed first at the remote village of Mengtse, in the Yunnan, next in the bitterly cold Kirin province of Manchuria, and later in an up-country town in South China, whence they escaped with difficulty from a dangerous situation caused by the internecine wars. Stella Benson's later books included *Goodbye, Stranger*, a retelling of familiar myths and stories, *The Man Who Missed the 'Bus*, an exercise in the uncanny, and *Tobit Transplanted* (American title: *The Far-Away Bride*), the book which established her reputation. It relates with intricate detail and considerable insight the life of a White Russian community in Manchuria. *Worlds Within Worlds* was a collection of travel articles from magazines. Two collections of short stories, *Hope Against Hope* and *Christmas Formula* were also made. Her last place of residence was Hongay, in the province of Tongking. There she died of pneumonia a month before her forty-first birthday.

"My first book, *I Pose*," wrote Stella Benson in the last year of her life, "was written in order to Show Off. . . . *Living Alone* was the first of my books the writing of which interested me impersonally—the first, in fact, that was in some measure a book about *other people*, not only about myself in different masochistic or romantic or inverted guises. . . . *The Poor Man* was written in a mood of revulsion against visions, and for this reason was a very formless and—in a sense—an even more immature book than its predecessors. . . . My last novel, *Tobit Transplanted*, being written within a fixed frame (the frame provided by the apocryphal story), allowed me greater scope than usual for detachment of outlook. It is my first really consistent effort to record, as honestly as was possible to me, the point of view of people *as other people*—not as people seen by me or seen through myself, but people *seeing* by themselves—each from the vantage point of his own identity."

Stella Benson was recognized by the few from her beginnings as a wit and an original, but it was only with the publication of *Tobit Transplanted* that she reached high circulation figures. Frail, diffident, and modest, she wrote anywhere and at any time, using a pencil and working in an exercise book. Tolstoy was her most admired author. She was devoted to dogs, which figured largely both in her books and her life, was a fine horseman, and made competent drawings in pen-and-ink.

PRINCIPAL WORKS: I Pose, 1915; This Is the End, 1917; Twenty (poems) 1918; Living Alone, 1919; Kwan-Yin, 1922; The Poor Man, 1922; Pipers and a Dancer, 1924; The Little World, 1925; The Awakening, 1925; Goodbye, Stranger, 1926; Worlds Within Worlds, 1928; The Man Who Missed the 'Bus, 1928; The Far-Away Bride (English title: Tobit Transplanted) 1930; Hope Against Hope and Other Stories, 1931; Christmas

Formula and Other Stories, 1932; Pull Devil—Pull Baker, 1933; Mundos: An Unfinished Novel, 1935; Poems, 1935; Collected Short Stories, 1936.

ABOUT: Benson, C. Mainly Players; Collins, J. The Doctor Looks at Literature; Gawsworth, J. Ten Contemporaries (2d series) [contains personal note by Stella Benson]; Mais, S. P. B. Some Modern Authors; Roberts, R. E. Portrait of Stella Benson; Wylie, I. A. R. My Life With George; The Bookman (London) May, 1932; The Times (London) December 8, 1933.

*BENT, SILAS (May 9, 1882-), American publicist, writes: "Silas Bent was born in Millersburg, Ky. His father was the

Rev. Dr. James Mc-Clelland Bent, a Baptist clergyman; his mother was born Sallie Burnam. One was of settler New England stock, the other of settler Virginia stock. The son, reared at Bowling Green, Ky., was a student at Ogden College, the president of which, Major William A. Obenchain, was the last surviving member of Robert E. Lee's personal staff. It was a rebel college. When Silas Bent was eleven, his father died; his mother lived to eighty-seven, and died unreconstructed. After receiving a B.A. at Ogden in 1902, Bent went into newspaper work in Louisville at nothing a week, but in the course of time was put on the payroll at $8. In three and a half years, having achieved $20 a week, he realized that he was at the reportorial apex, so far as salary went, and moved on to the St. Louis Post-Dispatch, where he served six years, but not continuously; he taught during the first term of the School of Journalism at Missouri University in 1908.

"Bent went next to the Chicago American, but had worked there only a few months when he had an opportunity to take charge of publicity for a banking reform organization, prior to the passage of the Federal Reserve Act. When the league was dissolved he went to New York, where he worked successively for the Herald, the World, and the Times. He quit newspaper work in 1920 to free-lance, he hoped, but could not resist an offer from William J. Cochran to take charge of newspaper and magazine publicity for the Democratic National Committee. The upshot was that he press-agented Governor James M. Cox of Ohio into complete obscurity.

"Thereafter Bent served for eighteen months as associate editor of the Nation's

Business in Washington. His resignation left him free to follow his bent toward free-lancing, which he has done ever since. His first book was a by-product of a series of lectures at the New York School for Social Research, and he signed a contract for it before it was written. His other books have been written on assignment. He is currently at work on a biography of a Kentucky judge, which will be his first output strictly on his own initiative. His magazine contributions range from Liberty up to the Virginia Quarterly Review. He has written mostly personality sketches, political and economic articles.

"In 1916 he married Elizabeth Chism Sims. They live in Old Greenwich, Conn. By tradition and preference he is a Democrat, but voted in 1936 for Norman Thomas. Although a devout man, he is not a church member."

PRINCIPAL WORKS: Ballyhoo, 1927; Strange Bedfellows, 1928; Machine-Made Man, 1929; Justice Oliver Wendell Holmes: A Biography, 1932; Buchanan of the Press (novel) 1932; Slaves by the Billion, 1938; Newspaper Crusaders, 1939; Old Rough and Ready: Zachary Taylor (with S. B. McKinley) 1941.

BENTLEY, EDMUND CLERIHEW (July 10, 1875-), English journalist, humorist, and writer of detective fiction, author of the epochal Trent's Last Case, writes: "I was born in Shepherd's Bush, a suburb of London; son of an official in the Lord Chancellor's Department, which corresponds to the Ministry of Justice in other European countries. Paternal

ancestry, wholly English; maternal, wholly Scottish; result, pure British. My school was St. Paul's, the London school founded by Colet, Dean of St. Paul's, in the reign of Henry VIII. Here it was that I met G. K. Chesterton, my lifelong and closest friend: see his Autobiography; see also my memoirs (1940). I won in 1894 a history scholarship at Merton College in Oxford. At the University I did as many things as possible, this being my idea of what a University meant. I became President of the Oxford Union in 1896. At Oxford I discovered the fascination of the sport of rowing; was captain one year of the University boat club; and failed to become a member of the University crew. After leaving Oxford I lived in London and studied law;

was called to the bar in 1902. About the same time I was called to journalism, in which most of my subsequent life has been passed. From that year until 1912 I was on the editorial staff at the *Daily News,* which I preferred because it was the English paper most bitterly opposed to the South African war. I believed earnestly in liberty and equality; I do still. In 1912 I joined the staff of the *Daily Telegraph,* which was independent Conservative in opinion; for over twenty years I wrote editorials for this paper, mainly about foreign affairs, which was my favorite political study. During my service on this paper and the *News* I wrote constantly for other journals as well; my output ranged from the most responsible sort of political writing in the *Fortnightly Review* to the least responsible kind of light verse in *Punch.*

"In 1905 I published a volume of nonsense verse called *Biography for Beginners,* illustrated by the fantastic pencil of G. K. Chesterton. It originated a sort of formless four-line verse which has been called a 'clerihew' ever since then, because the book was published under my baptismal name. This was followed many years later by *More Biography* (1929) and *Baseless Biography* (1939). In 1913 I published *Trent's Last Case,* which was intended to be a new sort of detective story, and is still selling quite well. In 1936 Warner Allen collaborated with me in *Trent's Own Case.* In 1938 appeared a book of short stories called *Trent Intervenes.* In that year I began the book of memoirs already mentioned, which is by far the best thing I have produced—according to me.

"All my life I have been a writer by vocation, having begun in a school magazine and gone on in a student one which, with some friends, I founded at Oxford. The main influence in my life has been my association with G. K. Chesterton; for the rest, my outlook was established by the great Victorians, who passed on to me the ideas of the Greeks about essential values, namely, physical health, freedom of mind, care for the truth, justice, and beauty. Things I dislike: most of them can be reduced to one thing—sloppiness.

"In 1902 I married Violet Boileau, who has survived that event until now. We have two sons, an engineer and an artist, both successful."

* * *

Mr. Bentley's diffident reference above to *Trent's Last Case* is a testimony to his inherent modesty; for this novel has been hailed by critics of the detective story all over the world as one of the true masterpieces of the *genre.* Urbanely written, with humor, ingenuity, and deft characterization, it has been credited with changing the whole course of crime fiction. Chesterton called it "the finest detective story of modern times." John Carter found that it marked the end of the romantic, or Sherlock Holmes, period in the detective novel and the beginning of the naturalistic era. Dorothy Sayers has pronounced it "an acknowledged masterpiece." Almost a quarter-century elapsed between the first and second Trent books. While the second, perhaps only naturally, failed to attain the unusual prominence of the first, it was well received and the London *Spectator* discovered in it "the same leisurely Edwardian wit, the same bouquet" of its predecessor.

Today Mr. Bentley lives modestly and quietly with his wife in Paddington; a large, graying, genial, essentially simple, idealistic, generous man. Of the two Bentley sons, the younger, Nicolas Clerihew, is known not only as an artist and illustrator, but also as a humorous writer; thus following in the footsteps of his father, who began his career by contributing light verse and parodies to *Punch* and similar periodicals while he was yet at Oxford. The elder Bentley has a particular fondness for the stories of Damon Runyon, and his attempt on one occasion to write a preface in that author's Americanese amused reviewers in the United States for reasons that he could scarcely have intended. For the same reason—the difficulty of transmitting topical or colloquial humor from one nation to another—his own lighter works are little known outside his native land. But as a writer of detective fiction he is indisputably an international figure; in John Carter's words: "the father of the contemporary detective novel."

After six years of retirement from active journalism, E. C. Bentley returned to the *Daily Telegraph* in 1940 as chief literary critic, replacing Harold Nicolson, called into war service by the government.

PRINCIPAL WORKS: Biography for Beginners (by "E. Clerihew") 1905; Trent's Last Case, 1913; More Biography, 1929; Trent's Own Case (with H. W. Allen) 1936; Trent Intervenes, 1938; A Second Century of Detective Stories (ed.) 1938; Baseless Biography, 1939; Those Days: An Autobiography, 1940.

ABOUT: Bentley, E. C. Those Days; Chesterton, G. K. Autobiography, Come to Think of It; Haycraft, H. Murder for Pleasure: The Life and Times of the Detective Story; Thomson, H. D. Masters of Mystery; Saturday Review of Literature January 7, 1939.

BENTLEY, PHYLLIS (November 19, 1894-), English novelist, writes: "I was born in Halifax, a cloth-manufacturing town  of about 95,000 population in the West Riding of Yorkshire. I was the daughter of Joseph Edwin and Eleanor Bentley. My father was a cloth manufacturer of great skill and reputation; my mother's father and relatives were also engaged in this local textile trade. (My parents' portraits, though not their circumstances, may be found in my novel *Carr*; my mother's great-uncle, a great educationist in his day—a school in Bradford is called after him—was the original of the character of Joth in *Inheritance*.) Halifax, situated in the heart of the Pennine chain, is a very hilly, bleak, windy place. These climatic conditions nearly robbed me of life a few hours after I had received it, for the chimney of the room in which I lay was blown down, and its stones, mingled with the flaming coals, rolled out of the hearth and across the floor. (I used this incident in *Sleep in Peace*.) Wild moor-clad hills, and storms of wind and rain, were among the earliest of my recollections; mingled with these was the forest of mill chimneys, belching black smoke, which rose from every level of the steep slopes of Halifax.

"From my earliest days I was a book-lover, for I always meant to be a novelist and a learned person; I fear I was a very self-righteous, solemn, bespectacled child. I was educated at the Halifax High School and the Cheltenham Ladies' College, and took a B.A. degree (London) in 1914. During the last war I first taught in the local Boys' Grammar School, and then became a secretary in the Ministry of Munitions headquarters in London. Throughout the war period I was writing my first novel, *Environment*, the story—need it be said?—of a Yorkshire girl rather like myself; but this went through many vicissitudes of rejection, enlargement, compression, and modification, before it finally achieved publication, together with its sequel *Cat-in-the-Manger*, in 1922 and 1923.

"After the war I dropped by chance into the job of cataloging various local libraries. I say 'by chance,' for my family were very much opposed to my doing any work at all; it was only the post-war slump and my own persistent longing which finally made me a wage-earner. In the 1920's I classified and cataloged, single-handed, three West Riding libraries, amounting in all to about 90,000 volumes. I loved this work, and the classifying of so many diverse books, which necessitated a slight knowledge of them all, or at least an understanding of their subject, was I think very profitable to me.

"It was about this time (1925-26) that I was first asked to lecture, to an English Association in a West Riding town. For my subject I choose "The Regional Novel." I had no idea then that this was, in fact, my own line in fiction; it is only recently that I have understood that what Henry James calls 'the pattern in the carpet' of my work is the presentation of my native county. My first novels all had Yorkshire backgrounds and characters, but their themes were not Yorkshire; they dealt merely with private lives. But in 1931 I was moved to a deep sympathy with the West Riding by its stoic endurance of suffering during the post-war slump, and began to investigate its economic history. The result was first *Inheritance*, the story of the coming of the industrial revolution to Yorkshire, and then *A Modern Tragedy*, a record of the effect on a linked group of people of the hardships of the slump.

"The rise of dictatorships in Europe moved me to write *Freedom, Farewell!* which is a study of how and why the dictatorship of the Caesars supplanted the old republican ideals of Rome. *Sleep in Peace* and *Take Courage* are both pieces of Yorkshire history again; it seems that I have now written of Yorkshire history from 1625 to 1672, and from 1812 to the present day. It would please me to write a Yorkshire novel of the eighteenth century, just to fill the gap, but whether that will be granted me or not I do not know.

"Besides writing fiction, I review it and lecture on it (I toured Holland in 1935, and the United States in 1934, 1936, and 1939) and broadcast on it. My recreations are walking and the amateur drama—for thirteen years I have been an executive member of a local society devoted to the production of the more permanent and intelligent forms of dramatic art. I think I may say that I have two great interests—humanity, and the enrichment of human life by culture; and I am especially eager that the little unit of earth I call my native county shall be thus enriched."

* * *

Miss Bentley, who is unmarried, is still bespectacled, but no longer "self-righteous and solemn"—humor and sympathy are apparent in her expressive face. Although her work is so localized, it is not provincial, for the problems of which she treats are world-wide, and her pictures of industrial life have a large American as well as an English public.

PRINCIPAL WORKS: The World's Bane (non-fiction) 1918; Pedagomania (non-fiction) 1918; Environment, 1922; Cat-in-the-Manger, 1923; The Spinner of the Years, 1928; The Partnership, 1928; Carr, 1929; Trio, 1930; Inheritance, 1932; A Modern Tragedy, 1934; The Whole of the Story, 1935; Freedom, Farewell! 1936; Sleep in Peace, 1938; Take Courage, 1940; The Power and the Glory, 1940; Manhole, 1941.

ABOUT: Bookman (London) July 1931; New York Times February 2, 1941.

BERCOVICI, KONRAD (June 22, 1882-   ), Rumanian-American novelist, dramatist, short-story and miscellaneous writer, was born in Braila, Rumania, the son of Jackot Bercovici and Mirel Bercovici. He was educated privately, and spent much of his youth among the tents of gypsies who poured into Rumania from the borders of Hungary, listening to their songs, learning their language, and being accepted into their ranks, so that Bercovici has been able to say: "There is not a gypsy in the world who cannot tell you who I am. I am a gypsy by choice and not by blood, by temperament and not race." At forty-six he published his highly colored Story of the Gypsies (1928). Previously he had studied the organ in Paris, and had played the organ at Grace Episcopal Church in New York City after coming to the United States in 1916. In preparation for speaking English he had memorized Samuel Butler's The Way of All Flesh word for word, but had so much difficulty in making himself understood that he pretended to be a mute. He now speaks English, Rumanian, French, German, Greek, Yiddish, Italian, and Spanish. Bercovici's first book, Crimes of Charity, an indictment of the callousness and indifference of organized charity, as he had seen it in New York, was refused by several publishers as being a one-sided picture. It finally appeared with an introduction by John Reed, who praised its "style of bald narration which carries absolute conviction of human character, in simple words packed with atmos-

Oggiano

phere." Bercovici married Naomi Librescu in 1902, and has four children, Hyperion (author, as Rion Bercovici, of a satirical novel about a publicity agent, For Immediate Release, published in 1937), Gordon, Rada, and Mirel. Rada Bercovici has been a concert singer; her father wrote several gypsy songs for her début, and has also experimented in symphonic composition. Bercovici was on the staff of the New York World from 1917 to 1920, and spent a year (1920-21) on the New York Evening Post. He has traveled in Greece and Italy, Palestine, Egypt, Persia, and India. That Royal Lover (1931) and The Incredible Balkans (1933) were written from his intimate acquaintance with the Rumanian scene, and were spiced with sufficient intrigue, scandal, and inside gossip to insure a large sale. In Russia, one of the few countries where Bercovici has never lived, some of his books sell by thousands. He now makes his home in Ridgefield, Conn., where several other writers live, is up at 6 A.M., writes till noon, and never sets a sentence down on paper until it is so clear in his mind that no potential reader can mistake its meaning. The Survey once said: "Konrad Bercovici is too thorough-going a gypsy to write an empty or a dull book. Gypsy entertainers never cheat a friendly public." An occasional critic finds an occasional book rather superficial or incompletely developed.

Bercovici has edited Best Short Stories of the World (1935) for the Star Books series. Edward O'Brien included "Ghitza" in The Best Short Stories of 1920. The collection of that name (Ghitza and Other Romances of Gypsy Blood) presents tales of gypsies in Carpathia, Normandy, Spain and Sicily, the Italian quarter of New York, and the Finnish colony in Minnesota. Bercovici has something of the "Romany rye" in his physical appearance; he would doubtless meet a warm welcome from the characters who people the George Borrow gypsy romance of that name.

PRINCIPAL WORKS: Crimes of Charity, 1917; Dust of New York, 1918; Ghitza and Other Romances of Gypsy Blood, 1919; Murdo, 1921; Costa's Daughter (play) 1923; Ileana: The Marriage Guest, 1924; Around the World in New York, 1924; On New Shores, 1925; Singing Winds, 1926; Volga Boatman, 1926; The Story of the Gypsies, 1928; Peasants (short stories) 1928; Nights Abroad, 1928; The Crusades, 1929; Alexander: A Romantic Biography, 1929; Between Earth and Sky, 1929; For a Song, 1931; That Royal Lover, 1931; Against the Sky, 1932; Main Entrance, 1932; The Incredible Balkans, 1933; It's the Gypsy in Me, 1941.

ABOUT: Bercovici, K. It's the Gypsy in Me; Wilson Library Bulletin May 1929.

*BERDYAEV, NIKOLAI ALEKSAN-
DROVICH (1874-), Russian writer,
was born at Kiev, the "God-protected mother
of Russian cities,"
and published his first
book, *Subjectivism
and Individualism in
Social Philosophy*, at
twenty-six, since
when he has become
one of the most pro-
lific and widely read
of contemporary Rus-
sian writers.

Berdyaev suffered
exile for a time during youth, and was again
threatened with banishment just before the
fall of the imperial government for having
criticized the Erastianism of the governing
Synod of the Orthodox Church in his country. After the Revolution he received the
chair of philosophy in the University of
Moscow, but after two years of imprisonment was expelled by the Bolshevists in 1922
as an upholder of religion. In 1934 Berdyaev
was living in Paris, where he directed the
Academy of the Philosophy of Religion,
which he founded in Germany, and edited a
review called *Putj* ("The Way").

"Dostoievsky has played a decisive part
in my spiritual life," Berdyaev has said.
"While I was still a youth a slip of him, so
to say, was grafted upon me. He stirred
and lifted up my soul more than any other
writer or philosopher has done, and for me
people are always divided into 'dostoievsky-
ites' and those to whom his spirit is foreign.
It is undoubtedly due to his 'cursed questioning' that philosophical problems were
present to my consciousness at so early an
age." Berdyaev's *Dostoievsky: An Interpretation* originated in a series of seminar
lectures at the University of Moscow in the
winter of 1920-21.

Berdyaev first became interested in idealistic philosophy when he was exiled at twenty-
five from Kiev to Vologda, in North Russia,
directly east of the present Leningrad, and
began to study Schopenhauer, Kant and
Fichte. After his expulsion in 1922 from
Russia he was associated in France with a
group of scholars interested in the philosophy
of the spirit, *une philosophie pneumatique*.
Berdyaev still speaks of himself as being a
member of the Russian Orthodox Church,
although he emphasizes the fact that his
allegiance is inward rather than outward.
His methods are those of intuition, and he
is impatient with what he looks upon as the

formalism of Roman Catholicism. Catholics
are interested in his work, and most of the
translations of his books and essays have
been published in New York by a firm specializing in Catholic literature.

Berdyaev is reluctant to be classified with
other outstanding philosophers of past or
present, regarding his philosophy as essentially "prophetic," according to Vernon J.
Bourke, writing on "The Gnosticism of M.
Berdyaev" in *Thought*. His opposition to
metaphysics arises out of his intense anti-
intellectualism. "Spirit alone can defeat the
bourgeois condition; no material means will
avail," he writes in *The Bourgeois Mind*.
His book on *The Origin of Russian Communism* emphasizes its national and Russian
character. "A knowledge of Marxism will
not help to understand the national roots
of Russian Communism." His first book,
Subjectivism, which has not been translated,
endeavored to describe the tendencies in
Marxism which are idealistic. "To assert
that Christianity is hostile to man's activity
contradicts, in the first place, history," he
contends. "Mechanical civilization endang-
ers the heart." Bourke calls him an example
of a very complex mentality. "For Berdyaev
there exists an aristocracy of the spirit."

Works Available in English Translation:
The Russian Revolution: Two Essays on Its
Implication in Religion and Psychology, 1931;
The End of Our Time, Together with an Essay on
the General Line of Soviet Philosophy, 1933;
The Bourgeois Mind, and Other Essays, 1934;
Dostoievsky: An Interpretation, 1934; The Fate
of Man in the Modern World, 1935; Freedom
and the Spirit, 1935; The Meaning of History,
1936; The Origin of Russian Communism, 1937;
War and the Christian Conscience, 1938; Leon-
tiev, 1940.

About: Berdyaev, N. A. Dostoievsky (see
Translator's Note by D. Attwater); Schultze, B.
Die Schau der Kirche bei Nikolai Berdiajew;
Journal of Social Philosophy July 1939; Thought
December 1936.

BERENSON, BERNHARD (June 26,
1865-), American art critic, was born in
Lithuania of a poor Jewish family, but
brought to Boston in early childhood. He
was educated at the Boston Latin School
and at Boston University; he then became a protégé of Mrs. Jack Gardner, a
wealthy art patron, and she put him through
Harvard, where he received his B.A. in 1887.
While at Harvard he was baptized as an
Episcopalian. A poor boy who nevertheless
said he had been "brought up almost exclusively on words," he went from Harvard
to Oxford. There he met Logan Pearsall
Smith, the essayist, whose sister, Mary
Logan Whitall (Smith) Costelloe, he mar-

ried in 1900. (The Smiths were Philadelphians living in England.)

Before this, however, Mr. Berenson had discovered his  spiritual home and his lifework. He had gone to Florence, where while he studied the paintings in the galleries he earned his way by competing, at a lower price, with the regular gallery guides. By 1900 he had already published four small volumes of Italian painting, had begun to formulate his critical beliefs, and had achieved recognition as an expert on the authenticity of paintings—the means by which he has built up a fortune. It was in the year of his marriage that he bought Villa Tatti, in Settignano, near Florence, with its forty acres of fir, cypress, and formal gardens, which became his permanent home.

For many years Mr. Berenson has been recognized as the greatest living connoisseur of Italian art, particularly of the period of the Renaissance. Beginning with Mrs. Gardner, collectors and dealers alike have grown to rely implicitly on his judgment, until his authority now is unassailable. His critical theory of tactile values—that form is the pre-eminent criterion of the worth of a painting—has influenced greatly the development of art in this century. He is besides a classical scholar, who converses easily in ancient Greek. He is a member of the American Academy of Arts and Letters and a foreign associate of the Royal Academies of Belgium and Norway.

Whether Mr. Berenson has been able to retain his Italian residence during the Second World War is not known at this writing; on the latest information, he was still at Settignano. There, "a frail, spirited, punctilious graybeard," he has reigned for more than a generation as (to quote the late J. G. Huneker) "a benevolent tyrant." He is a celebrated host, but only to those who interest him; he has no patience with bores or dilettantes, whom he can treat with brusqueness. Among his friends he is noted as a brilliant conversationalist and a caustic wit. Dignified and reserved, he has his idiosyncrasies; he never touches a typewriter, he refuses to use a telephone, he retires every night at eleven and gets up promptly at half-past seven. He has been

for years at work on a monumental study of "the rediscovery of the lost arts of design." His *Drawings of the Florentine Painters*, published in 1903, was reissued in 1938 as practically a new work, including a thousand illustrations as against 190 in the earlier edition. Four of his earlier volumes were also reissued in 1932 under the general title of *Italian Pictures of the Renaissance*. In his earlier years he tried his hand at both poetry and novels, but made no mark with either; and only his writings on art survive. Among painters, dealers, and collectors he is an almost mythical figure, the last word on genuineness, period, and value in Italian painting.

PRINCIPAL WORKS: Venetian Painters of the Renaissance, 1894; Lorenzo Lotto, 1895; Florentine Painters of the Renaissance, 1896 (revised edition 1938); Central Italian Painters of the Renaissance, 1897; The Study and Criticism of Italian Art (three series) 1901-15; The Drawings of the Florentine Painters, 1903; The North Italian Painters of the Renaissance, 1907; A Sienese Painter of the Franciscan Legend, 1909; Catalogue of the Italian Paintings in the J. G. Johnson Collection, 1913; Venetian Painting in America—the Fifteenth Century, 1916; Essays on Sienese Paintings, 1918; Catalogue of Italian Paintings in the Widener and Friedsam Collections, 1926; Three Essays in Method, 1927; Introductory Essay to the Speculum Humanae Salvationis, 1927; Essays in Mediaeval Art, 1930; Italian Pictures of the Renaissance, 1932.

ABOUT: Living Age November 1, 1926, June 1929; Magazine of Art April 1940; Time April 10, 1939.

*BERESFORD, JOHN DAVYS (March 7, 1873-), English novelist who signs his works J. D. Beresford, writes: "I was born at Castor, a small village in Northamptonshire, of which my father, the Rev. J. J. Beresford, was Rector. He was born in 1822 and my grandfather, also a clergyman, in 1774, so these three generations have covered, up to now, a period of 166  years, a record that may be beaten by my youngest child, a daughter, who was born in 1926. Owing to the carlessness of a nurse, I contracted a form of infantile paralysis when I was three years old, and have been lame ever since, a factor that helped to decide my choice of careers. I was educated at Oundle and Peterborough, but left school at seventeen to be articled first to a local and then to a London architect, afterwards

* Died February 2, 1947.

finding a place as draughtsman in the offices of another London architect with a very large practice, mainly in the building of hospitals. I remained there for eight years, and then deciding that there was no future for me in that profession, tried my hand at various jobs, including advertising, with rather indifferent success.

"In those years I made various attempts to write, beginning no fewer than four novels and finishing one (unpublished), but my first real start in the world of letters was through my association with the *Westminster Gazette,* then a thriving evening paper with a great reputation for its literary articles and reviews. This was at the beginning of 1907, from which time I have lived entirely by writing, though my first novel, *Jacob Stahl* (the first volume of a trilogy), was not published until 1911.

"After my marriage to Beatrice Roskams, I lived for a time in North Cornwall, later in Buckinghamshire, coming up to London for the winter. From 1918 to 1923 I acted as literary adviser to the firm of Collins & Sons, and then took my wife and family (we had three boys at that time) to live in France, where we stayed for four years.

"I may say that I have no political convictions. My youth was spent under a strong Conservative influence, but as I began to think for myself I moved continually further to the left. Now I feel that there is so little honesty and sincerity in English politics, so little difference in effect between a Conservative and a Labour Government, that I do not trouble to vote. As to literary and social preference, in both cases my inclination is towards the books and company of independent thinkers. My favorite authors are Shaw, Aldous Huxley, H. G. Wells, Sinclair Lewis, and Upton Sinclair, all of them determined critics of our present social system.

"I am currently writing in collaboration with Esmé Wynne-Tyson, as sincere and genuine a pacifist as I am myself, a novel to be called *Peace Island,* in which we hope to elucidate the reasons for the failure of pacifism up to date. I am also writing a novel to be called *Quiet Corner.*"

* * *

Mr. Beresford has the face of a seeker and a questioner—of one who refuses to take life at its face value. He is interested in theosophy and is a student of the occult; his hobby is carpentering. To quote Charles Hanson Towne, he has "quiet tastes and an instinct for contemplation." He has been a prolific novelist, though his first books were perforce written after long hours as a publisher's reader. Now he spends most of the day in regular hours for writing. Besides his novels and several books of nonfiction, he has written three one-act plays, in collaboration with Arthur Scott Craven and Kenneth Richmond. *Jacob Stahl* was as essential a part of the social education of the young generation of the early 1900's as were the novels of H. G. Wells. Like their author, his novels are quiet and slow-moving, but, as Towne remarked, "he has a genius for the apt and telling phrase." He has written one mystery novel, *The Instrument of Destiny.*

PRINCIPAL WORKS: *Novels*—Jacob Stahl, 1911; The Hampdenshire Wonder, 1911; A Candidate for Truth, 1912; Goslings, 1913; The House in Demetrius Road, 1914; The Invisible Event, 1915; The Mountains of the Moon, 1915; These Lynnekers, 1916; God's Counterpoint, 1918; House Mates, 1917; The Jervaise Comedy, 1919; An Imperfect Mother, 1920; Revolution, 1921; The Prisoners of Hartling, 1922; Love's Pilgrim, 1923; Unity, 1924; The Monkey Puzzle, 1925; That Kind of Man (American title: Almost Pagan) 1926; The Tapestry, 1927; The Instrument of Destiny, 1928; All or Nothing, 1928; Real People, 1929; Love's Illusion, 1930; An Innocent Criminal, 1931; The Old People, 1931; The Middle Generation, 1932; The Next Generation, 1932; The Young People, 1933; The Inheritor, 1933; The Camberwell Miracle, 1933; Peckover, 1934; On a Huge Hill, 1935; The Faithful Lovers, 1936; Cleo, 1937; Snell's Folly (with E. Wynne-Tyson) 1939; Strange Rival, 1940. *Short Stories*—Nine Impressions, 1918; Signs and Wonders, 1921; The Imperturbable Duchess and Other Stories, 1923; The Meeting Place, 1929; Blackthorn Winter, 1936. *Non-Fiction*—H. G. Wells, 1915; W. E. Ford: A Biography (with K. Richmond) 1917; Taken From Life (with E. O. Hoppé) 1922; Writing Aloud, 1928; Seven Bobsworth, 1930; The Case for Faith Healing, 1934; What I Believe, 1938.

ABOUT: Bookman October 1924.

BERGSON, HENRI (October 12, 1859-January 4, 1941), French philosopher, winner of the Nobel Prize, was born in the heart of Paris, in the rue Lamartine, Montmartre. He derived from an Irish-Jewish family of Polish extraction. At the age of nine he entered the Lycée Fontane (now Lycée Condorcet), only a few blocks from his home. An extremely brilliant  student, he showed special gifts in science, literature and mathematics, although he had some difficulty with his geography. Before leaving the *lycée* at eighteen he won a prize for solving a mathematical problem; his paper was published in full in the *Annales de Mathématiques*. At first Henri had contemplated following mathematics as his life work; later, on obtaining his *baccalauréat*, he hesitated between literature and science, but finally he preferred, he said, the harder road—philosophy.

Bergson entered the École Normale Supérieure where he fell under the influence of his philosophy professors, the idealists Ravaisson, Lachelier, and Boutroux, and distinguished himself as a Hellenist: Professor Tournier honored him by recording his name among the rare students who had proposed decisive emendations and corrections of Greek texts supposed to be corrupt. After three years at the École Normale (1878-1881), Bergson was given a teaching position at the *lycée* in Angers, where he remained two years.

In 1883 Bergson was promoted and taught philosophy in the Lycée Blaise Pascal of Clermont-Ferrand till 1888. The old town of Clermont was conducive to study because of its quietude and its pleasant *milieu*: the *lycée's* rector, the father of the famous novelist Paul Bourget, was extremely fond of Bergson, and, besides, the young philosopher had become quite popular as a lecturer. On February 21, 1884, for instance, he delivered a lecture on "Laughter." The local paper reported: "What do we laugh at? Why do we laugh? Many people did not know; some had never thought about it, although they had lived happily and well. . . . The audience, much interested, had assembled in such numbers that many could not obtain admission and were obliged to return home grumbling at the luck of their fellows. But all those who had found room on the benches left the place delighted, nay charmed, with what they had heard." Sixteen years later the ideas expressed at this meeting, grown and matured, appeared in book form under the title *Laughter*. In 1884 Bergson sent to press an edition of Lucretius, with his notes, commentaries, and a long introduction on the relation between poetry and philosophy; because of its sterling qualities this textbook still holds its own, after more than fifty years of school use. Two years later Bergson wrote an article, "De la Simulation Inconsciente dans l'État d'Hypnotisme," showing how the hypnotized subject, unable to disobey instructions, resorts to any possible device in order to obey, with the result that he seems expert in deception, but the deception is unconscious. This provocative study appeared in the *Revue Philosophique* for November 1886 and shows the new interest which Dr. Montin's performances in Clermont had aroused in him.

In 1889 Bergson submitted to the University of Paris the two theses for his doctorate: one in Latin, *Quid Aristoteles de Loco Senserit*, and the other in French, *Essai sur les Données Immediates de la Conscience*, the first draft of his epoch-making *Time and Free Will*; after a brilliant defense in public, he obtained his *docteur-ès-lettres*. He moved immediately to Paris and taught philosophy at the Collège Rollin and soon after at the Lycée Henri IV where he carried on preparatory studies for his work *Matter and Memory*, the cornerstone of his philosophical system. Bergson said:

I set myself the following problem: What is it that modern physiology and pathology can teach with regard to the time-honored question of the relation between matter and mind, when the learner is without prejudice and is determined to forget every speculation that he has already entertained on the subject, and is also determined to set aside, in the pronouncements of scientific men, all that is not purely and simply a statement of facts? When I began to study the subject I soon discovered that the problem could not be solved, even provisionally, unless it were narrowed down to that of memory. And in memory itself I was led to mark out a field which I had more and more to restrict. After having fixed on the memory of words I saw that the problem thus formulated was still too great, and that it is the memory of the *sound* of words which puts the question in its most precise and most interesting form. The literature of aphasia is enormous; I took five years to consider it. And then I arrived at this conclusion: that between the psychological fact and its substratum in the brain there must be a relation answering to no one of the ready-made concepts offered by philosophy for our use.

Passages from this provocative work appeared in 1896 in the *Revue de Philosophie* ("Mémoire et Reconnaissance") and in the *Revue de Métaphysique* ("Perception et Matière"). Bergson's reputation was growing by leaps and bounds and in 1898 he was promoted to the École Normale Supérieure and two years later to the Collège de France, where he occupied first the chair of Greek philosophy and afterwards, as successor to Gabriel Tarde, the chair of modern philosophy. With his wife (he married Marcel Proust's cousin, Mlle. Neuberger) and daughter he lived at his Villa Montmorency, in Auteuil, a quiet quarter near Paris, and spent his summers at his Villa Bois-Gentil, near Geneva, in the mountains of Saint Cergue, overlooking Mont Blanc. In 1900 he read before the International Congress of Philosophy a short paper, "Notes sur les Origines Psychologiques de Notre Croyance à la Lois de Causalité," showing that belief in the law of causality is based upon the coordination of tactile impressions and visual impressions.

Bergson contributed papers on dreams to the Psychological Institute, and on psychophysical parallelism to the Société Française de Philosophie (1901), and in 1903 he joined the Academy of Moral and Political Sciences where he introduced new authors, chose candidates for prize awards, and performed other administrative functions. His short article on "Les Courbes Respiratoires Pendant l'Hypnose" (1904) came to the attention of the Society for Physical Research of London and was very favorably discussed there (nine years later Bergson became the President of this Society).

However it was not till after 1907 that Bergson's name became truly international: his *Creative Evolution,* considered by some his greatest work, was translated into numerous languages and widely discussed in foreign countries. Bergson delivered lectures at Bologna, Oxford and Birmingham (1911), at the University of London (1912) and at Columbia University (1913). Finally in 1914 he was elected to the French Academy and in 1927 he was awarded the Nobel Prize "in recognition of his rich and life-giving ideas and resplendent art with which they are presented."

Bergson became more popular than he ever cared to: his lectures at the Collège de France were included as one of Paris' attractions, his fan mail surpassed that of movie stars, impertinent visitors forced him to change his residence frequently (so that he was called the Wandering Jew). Exasperated, he resigned his position in 1921. From that date until shortly before his death he devoted most of his energies to the writing of his books and to sundry activities in committees for international cooperation. In his latter years he lived quietly at Passy and his name was not in the telephone book. An octogenarian, he still dressed fastidiously as in his younger days when he wore a close-buttoned cutaway, derby hat and straight standing collar with cushion cravat, round cuffs, the white *passe poil* and congress gaiters. His eyes did not lose their penetrative and pensive brilliance and there was in him something of a Greek jurist.

Despite his later works, *Mind Energy* (1919) and *The Two Sources of Morality and Religion* (1932), Bergson's claim to fame rests on his early *Time and Free Will*

(1889), *Matter and Memory* (1896), and *Creative Evolution* (1907). These three works synthesize the best in Bergson and the best features of the intuitionist school.

It is in the field of literature that Bergson's influence is most evident; in the novels of Proust, the poetry of Claudel, the essays of Péguy and Thibaudet. Philosophers like Cunningham, Solomon, etc. admit that "the philosophical consequences of Bergson's doctrines have been various, running all the way from a general skepticism to a reassertion of religion, while literary historians like Thibaudet and Mornet claim that "whatever the fate of its message, *Creative Evolution* will remain a literary landmark because of the fascinating and poetic power of its style. . . . It is a style of elaborate harmonies, but of comparative clearness. . . . It contains, like that of Pascal, the *frisson métaphysique*, the sense of vastness and soul-yearning. . . . Although Bergson has formulated no system of aesthetics, his influence upon recent aesthetic currents and criticism is indisputable."

Although it is said that Bergson became a convert to Catholicism in his last years, he was extremely proud of his Jewish blood, and in December 1940, only a month before his death, refused the Vichy government's offer to exempt him from the post-conquest decrees requiring the resignation of Jewish employees from state positions. On December 9, he voluntarily gave up his honorary chair at the Collège de France, although the government had asked him to remain because of his "artistic and literary services to the nation." He also declined exemption from the public registration demanded of all Jews in occupied France. Eighty-one and feeble, he rose from his sick bed and in dressing gown and slippers, supported by his valet and nurse, stood in line before the registration offices. As the New York *Herald Tribune* said: "It was a brave and supremely tragic termination to a great career." The effort may well have hastened his death, which occurred shortly afterwards from pulmonary congestion.

WORKS AVAILABLE IN ENGLISH TRANSLATION: Time and Free Will, 1910; Matter and Memory, 1911; Laughter, 1911; Creative Evolution, 1911; Introduction to Metaphysics, 1912; Dreams, 1914; The Meaning of the War, 1915; Mind-Energy, 1920; The Two Sources of Morality and Religion, 1935.

ABOUT: Bernstein, H. With Master Minds; Björkman, E. A. Voices of Tomorrow; Carr H. W. The Philosophy of Change; Chevalier, J. H. Bergson; Cunningham, G. W. A Study in the Philosophy of Bergson; James, W. Pluralistic Universe; Loomba, R. M. Bradley and Bergson; Moore, J. M. Theories of Religious Experience; Ruhe, A. & Paul, N. M. H. Bergson: An Account of His Life and Philosophy; Santayana, G. Wings of Doctrine; Slosson, E. E. Major Prophets of To-day; Solomon, J. Bergson; Williamson, C. C. H. Writers of Three Centuries; Commonweal January 17, 1941; Nation March 22, 29, 1941; New York Herald Tribune January 6, 7, 1941; Nineteenth Century February 1941.

"BERKELEY, ANTHONY." See COX, A. B.

*BERNANOS, GEORGES (1888-),

French writer, was born in Paris and was educated at the University of Paris and the Institut Catholique. He was a "discovery" of Léon Daudet's, and his first work was published by Daudet. Like him, Bernanos is a devout Catholic and a Royalist, and he was long active in the *Action Française,* a pre-war political party which was affiliated with Fascist groups. However, in 1936 he went to live in Palma, in the Balearic Islands, and what he saw there during the Spanish Civil War turned him into an anti-clerical, dissociated from reactionary intransigence, but still devoted to Catholicism. His *Grands Cimitières Sous la Lune,* translated into English as *A Diary of My Times,* aroused severe criticism from those who had formerly been his most ardent advocates.

Bernanos is more than novelist; he is an essayist and publicist, and a prolific and vigorous pamphleteer. John Charpentier called him "a moralist rather than a disinterested observer, but above all a controversialist, furious and unappeasable." His novels, however, are not mere fictionalized tracts, but have much high-pitched eloquence and melodramatic power. He is magniloquent and prolix, but he has force. In 1936 he won the Grand Novel Prize of the French Academy for his *Diary of a Country Priest.* In 1937 he left Palma and returned to France, to live at La Bayorre, near Hyères. He is married, and has "a numerous family." Dark, with a big moustache and a gray pompadour, he has the fixed gaze of a fighter, a mystic, or a fanatic. Ben Ray Redman said that he was "often breathless and even incoherent, but always on the side of the angels." *The Star of Satan,* in two parts, dealing with a girl and her fall, and with the life and death of a country priest, has been described as "a storehouse of . . . sublimity and neuroticism."

In a recent utterance, Bernanos said that world events had reduced him to a state of despair, to a feeling that there was neither a creed nor a party to which "men of good will" could now belong, but that even so it was these "men of good will" with whom he aligned himself.

After the fall of France in 1940, Bernanos took up residence in Brazil.

WORKS AVAILABLE IN ENGLISH: A Crime, 1936; The Diary of a Country Priest, 1937; A Diary of My Times (non-fiction) 1938; The Star of Satan, 1939.

ABOUT: Annales Politiques et Littéraires January 1, 1930; Commonweal March 3, 1939; Illustration July 18, 1936; Mercure de France June 15, 1931; New Statesman and Nation September 17, 1938; Saturday Review of Literature November 26, 1938, June 22, 1940.

*BERNSTEIN, HENRY (1876-),

French dramatist, was born Henry Léon Gustav Charles Bernstein in Paris. His

father, a business man of Polish stock, died when his son was twenty. Ida Seligman Bernstein, his mother, was a daughter of William Seligman, the American banker and member of the Wall Street firm of J. & W. Seligman, hence the English spelling of Henry Bernstein's name. The boy was painted at six by the famous painter Manet, the Bernsteins' summer neighbor at Versailles, who also painted battledores for young Henry's amusement. Henry Bernstein left the army four months before the expiration of his term of military service in 1899, and returned the next year from Brussels, where he had been conducting an affair of the heart, to join a light-duty corps; he was exempted even from this service through the interest of Mme. Simone le Bargy. Bernstein also attended Cambridge University in England, where he established a racing stable and once won a race at Cottenham. A celebrated boulevardier who owned 147 pairs of trousers and expended much of his inheritance on gambling operations, he turned to the theatre to make another fortune, to such good effect that from February 1904 through June 1914 there was never a night when a Bernstein play was not being performed somewhere in Paris.

Bernstein's *Le Voleur* (1906) was played in America as *The Thief* by Margaret Illington, late wife of Major Edward Bowes of

* Died July 5, 1948.   * Died November 27, 1953.

radio fame. William Gillette played in *Samson* next year; David Belasco produced *The Secret* in 1913 for Frances Starr; and Ralph Richardson, now better-known as an actor in moving pictures, appeared in London in *Promise,* an adaptation of Bernstein's *Espoir* (1934). *Après Moi* (1911), the first play of Bernstein's to attain the Comédie Française, was the occasion of an anti-Semitic riot led by Léon Daudet and his group, the Camelots du Roi. Bernstein fought one of his thirteen duels with Daudet. In May 1938 he also quarreled and dueled with Édouard Bourdet, director of the Comédie, and took back *Judith,* written in 1922, *La Rafale* (1905), and *Le Secret* (1913) from the theatre. Bernstein's plays are "violent, realistic melodramas of everyday life." He is "a child of Scribe, with something of the striking craftsmanship of Sardou."

During the First World War Bernstein was a military observer in the aviation service in Macedonia; was wounded and sent to Iraq; and wrote in hospital *L'Eléva tion,* a drama of more depth and feeling than usual. In 1915 he married Antoinette Martin in Flanders. For twenty years he owned his own theatre, the Gymnase, in Paris; later he rented Les Ambassadeurs. In 1939 Bernstein represented the French Dramatists Society at the New York World's Fair, and in July 1940 he arrived on the "Samaria" as a refugee from the Germans, who had threatened to horsewhip him when they arrived in Paris, where his play *Elvire* was running. In 1941 the Vichy government ordered him deprived of his French citizenship. Bernstein is six feet three in height, with blue eyes.

WORKS AVAILABLE IN ENGLISH TRANSLATION: The Thief, 1907; Samson, 1907; The Secret, 1913; Promise, 1934.

ABOUT: Benoist, H. Le Théâtre d'Aujourd'hui; Clark, B. H. Contemporary French Dramatists; Hamilton, C. M. Seen on the Stage; Smith, H. A. Main Currents of Modern French Drama; New York Times November 18, 1917; January 17, 1937; New Yorker August 31, 1940; Theatre Magazine May 1909; Time February 19, 1940.

BESANT, Mrs. ANNIE (WOOD) (October 1, 1847-September 20, 1933), English writer on social and religious topics, was born in London the only daughter of William B. P. Wood, a half-Irishman who had studied medicine but never practised it, and Emily (Morris) Wood, an Anglo-Irish lady. Her father died when she was five, and her mother, sacrificing everything to put her son through Harrow and Cambridge, allowed the girl to be educated by Miss Marryat, sister of the novelist Frederick Marryat. She was away from home from eight to fifteen.

Much of her later career may be traced to the hurt her pride received in childhood; much more to her unhappy marriage. A beautiful, dark girl, her head full of theology and her heart of religious ecstasy, she drifted into marriage in 1867 with a narrow, hide-bound clergyman, Frank Besant, brother of Walter Besant the essayist. She bore him a son and a daughter, but their miserable life together was ended in 1873, after a growing skepticism had forced her to refuse further participation in church ritual. She was given custody of their daughter, but a few years later lost her as well as the son to her husband, since she had become an active Free Thinker, co-editor with Charles Bradlaugh of the *National Reformer,* and co-speaker with him on every platform. After she was tried and convicted (though the indictments were quashed later) of circulating a pamphlet on birth control, even a recital of the physical cruelty she had suffered failed to win her a divorce. Besant died in 1917.

All Mrs. Besant's lightning changes of belief were conditioned by her emotional nature. Her next move was to Socialism, under the influence of Edward Aveling, who later married Karl Marx's daughter. She became less and less interested in pure Rationalism, and resigned from the *National Reformer* in 1883. In the next phase she edited a magazine, *Our Corner,* established the Law and Liberty League, and helped to win a celebrated strike, that of the exploited girls in the Bryant & May match factory. She served on the London School Board and the London County Council, and did much for wayward children and homeless girls.

Then W. T. Stead introduced her to the writings of Helena Blavatsky, and she suddenly became an avowed Theosophist. She was Mme. Blavatsky's right-hand helper until her death in 1891 and became her successor as head of the Esoteric School, though not until after a bitter struggle which lost the Theosophists nearly all their American adherents, who formed a rival group. In 1894 she went to India, her home thenceforth. She became president of the Theosophical Society in 1907, and remained so until her death. From 1914 on she interested herself in Indian politics as an extreme nationalist, and was interned by the British government during the war. Soon after, she discovered in a young Hindu, Krishnamurti, the "new Messiah" (a role disclaimed by himself), and toured the world with him. Always interested in education, she was the founder of the Central Hindu College at Benares. She died at Madras at nearly eighty-six.

Though Annie Besant always wrote voluminously, and was the author of some hundred books and pamphlets, she was primarily a propagandist, whatever her cause. She has no particular standing as a writer, but in herself was one of the most interesting personages of her time, worthy of intensive psychological study.

PRINCIPAL WORKS: On the Deity of Jesus of Nazareth, 1873; On the Nature and Existence of God, 1875; Marriage, 1879; Auguste Comte, 1885; Reincarnation, 1892; Autobiography, 1893; Death and After, 1893; The Self and Its Sheaths, 1895; Path of Discipleship, 1895; Four Great Religions, 1897; Esoteric Christianity, 1901; Theosophy and the New Psychology, 1904; Thought Power, 1911; The Ideals of Theosophy, 1912; Lectures on Political Science, 1919; Theosophy and World Problems, 1922; Shall India Live or Die? 1925.

ABOUT: Besant, A. Autobiographical Sketches; Autobiography; Besterman, T. Annie Besant; The Mind of Annie Besant; Wells, G. H. Life of Annie Besant; West, G. Mrs. Annie Besant; Williams, G. L. The Passionate Pilgrim; Christian Century October 4, 1933; Newsweek September 30, 1933.

BESANT, Sir WALTER. See "BRITISH AUTHORS OF THE 19TH CENTURY"

BESIER, RUDOLF (July 1878-June 15, 1942), English dramatist, of Dutch-English extraction, was born in Java. He was edu-

cated at Elizabeth College, Guernsey, and at Heidelberg University in Germany. He worked for several years in London in various journalistic capacities, chiefly for the firm of C. Arthur Pearson, Ltd. He was once called upon to take around the world two youths who had won prizes in a contest conducted by a Pearson's boys' paper, and in New York City made several acquaintances who were later to acclaim his most successful play, *The Barretts*

of Wimpole Street. Besier's first play, *The Virgin Goddess* (1908), written during his American visit, was a classic tragedy produced at the Adelphi Theatre in London. In *Olive Latimer's Husband*, next year, the late Mrs. Patrick Campbell "complained for two hours against fate in that cushioned voice of hers." *Don*, produced at the New Theatre in New York City in 1909, was one of the few comedies to be produced at that imposing institution. Mrs. Minnie Maddern Fiske scored a personal triumph in *Lady Patricia* (1912), a satire on an English *précieuse*. Kenneth Macgowan, the new assistant dramatic critic on the Boston *Transcript*, commented on the "polished, finished English" of Besier's dialogue.

Besier married Charlotte Woodward, daughter of the Rev. P. S. Woodward of Plumpton, Sussex. He collaborated with Hugh Walpole in writing *Robin's Father*; with H. G. Wells made a dramatization of the latter's novel, *Kipps*; and, with May Edginton, the novelist, wrote *Secrets,* a chronicle play in which Margaret Lawrence played in New York. Besier also made several translations and adaptations from the French.

The Barretts of Wimpole Street, after being declined by two London producers, reached production at the Malvern Festival in August 1930. Refused by twenty-seven New York producers, the play was read by Katherine Cornell and eagerly accepted by her. She staged it at the Hanna Theatre in Cleveland on the evening of January 29, 1931; gave it 370 New York performances, and more than 700 performances in all. The play has also been produced in Canada, Australia, Paris, Rome, Milan, Florence, Budapest, Prague, Copenhagen and Oslo. A literate, tensely interesting play, it aroused some indignant response from the Barrett family, who objected to the Freudian implications in the characterization of Edward Moulton-Barrett, Elizabeth's father. Mr. Besier, a handsome dark man with an aquiline nose, died at his home in Surrey at sixty-three.

PRINCIPAL WORKS: Don, 1910; Lady Patricia, 1912; The Barretts of Wimpole Street, 1931.

ABOUT: Cornell, K. I Wanted To Be an Actress; New York Times June 16, 1942.

BESSIE, ALVAH CECIL (June 4, 1904-), American story-writer, novelist, and essayist, writes: "I was born in New York City, the son of Daniel N. Bessie and Adeline (Schlesinger) Bessie. I was graduated from DeWitt Clinton High School

in 1921 and from Columbia (B.A.) in 1924. I worked as actor and stage manager, 1924-28, with the Provincetown Playhouse, the Theatre Guild, and Walter Hampden. I went to Paris in December 1928 and worked as a rewrite man with the *Paris-Times* that winter. I published my first short story in *transition* in 1929. I have held a variety of jobs since then: book-store manager, office manager, lecturer on natural history to Boy Scouts, editor in a publishing house, researcher, on the staffs of the New York *Herald Tribune* and the *New Yorker*, as Sunday magazine editor, also drama, literary, and motion picture editor of the Brooklyn *Daily Eagle*, as drama critic of the *New Masses*, and as free-lance editorial consultant for publishers and magazines.

"I have translated from the French works by Pierre Loüys, Gautier, Octave Mirbeau, and others. My short stories and articles have appeared in many magazines and have been reprinted in O'Brien's *Best Stories of 1931, 1932, 1933,* and *1934,* in the O. Henry Memorial volume for 1936, in Uzzell's *Short Story Hits* (1932), and in *A Preface to College Prose* (1935). I received a Guggenheim Fellowship for creative writing in 1935-36. I was married in 1930 to Mary Burnett. We had two sons. We were divorced in 1938."

* * *

In 1931 Mr. Bessie and his wife went to Vermont as servants to an architect. After four months they bought an old farmhouse and lived in the Green Mountains for four years. It was there that Mr. Bessie, then bearded and romantic-looking, wrote a novel—not his first, for he had already written and destroyed two. On his return to New York he learned to fly. In 1937 he went to Spain to offer his services to the Loyalists as a pilot. Finding that only native Spaniards were wanted, he enlisted in the Lincoln Battalion. He remained until the end of the war, continuously at the front; he was front-line correspondent for the Battalion's official paper, *Volunteer for Liberty.* He has told the story of his experience in *Men in Battle.* "The example of Madrid has not been lost on the world," he says, "and every advance of Fascism must and will be met by the increasing and ultimately overpowering determination to resist of all men of good will."

As indicated in his autobiographical sketch, Bessie is at present living in New York, where he is the hard-hitting drama reviewer of the *New Masses* and does free-lance editorial work.

PRINCIPAL WORKS: Dwell in the Wilderness (novel) 1935; Men in Battle, 1939; Bread and a Stone (novel), 1941.

ABOUT: Literary Digest September 7, 1935; Scholastic March 12, 1938; Wilson Library Bulletin January 1940.

BESTON, HENRY (June 1, 1888-), American naturalist and miscellaneous author, writes: "I was born [Henry Beston Sheahan: his name has been legally changed for twenty-five years] in Quincy, Mass., the son of a physician who had studied medicine in France and of a Frenchwoman of old military and Bonapartist family. I had a New England boyhood of sea and shore enriched with a good deal of the French spirit, for I spoke French as easily as English. My most important teacher was William Everett, headmaster of Adams Academy. Superb scholar and Victorian eccentric all in one, he upheld in that forlorn school and in a commercial town an arrogant integrity of the things of the mind and a fierce belief in their importance. After the Academy came Harvard, and then a year in France teaching English at the University of Lyons. The First World War found me a part of 'the long, murderous years and the terrible, murderous days,' and my land service was followed by an interlude with the American Navy and the curious world of the submarines. After the war came Spain, and some returning of spiritual peace. A year later began the adventure of the solitary year on the great outer dunes of Cape Cod, that year of contemplation and observation of nature recorded in *The Outermost House.*

Bachrach

"In 1930, I married Elizabeth Coatsworth, poet and writer for children. We have two daughters of our own, and have been making our home in Nobleboro, Maine, calling our house Chimney Farm. My interest in America is constantly deepening; in Europe they would call me an 'Americanist.' My *American Memory* is the first study of our history to give a proper perspective to the role of the American Indian. *Herbs and the Earth* is a study of the relation of man to the green world. I still write children's books, and my old *Firelight Fairy Book* is still thoroughly alive. I am author of *The St. Lawrence* in the Rivers of America series. The snow is deep as I write, but our snowshoes are waiting for us at the door, and from the great chimneys a smoky fragrance of yellow birch blows off into the bright and living air."

* * *

Mr. Beston, who describes himself "sometimes as vague as a Dunsany figure in the mist," received his B.A. at Harvard in 1909, M.A. 1911. From 1919 to 1923 he was editor of the *Living Age*. In whatever field he undertakes he is the most conscientious and sensitive of craftsmen.

PRINCIPAL WORKS: Full Speed Ahead, 1919; Firelight Fairy Book, 1919; Starlight Wonder Book, 1923; The Book of Gallant Vagabonds, 1925; The Sons of Kai, 1926; The Outermost House, 1928; London, 1929; Herbs and the Earth, 1935; American Memory, 1937; The St. Lawrence River, 1941; The Tree That Ran Away, 1941.

ABOUT: Harvard University, Class of 1909: Twenty-Fifth and Thirtieth Annual Reports; Kunitz, S. J. & Haycraft, H. (eds.). The Junior Book of Authors.

BEVERIDGE, ALBERT JEREMIAH
(October 6, 1862-April 27, 1927), American historian and statesman, was born on a

farm on the border of Adams and Highland counties, Ohio, the son of Thomas H. Beveridge and Francis (Parkinson) Beveridge, both of whom had migrated west from the Piedmont region of Virginia. At twelve he was a plowboy, two years later a railroad laborer, and at fifteen a logger and teamster. From high school he went to De Pauw University (then Indiana Asbury, whose president in answer to one of Beveridge's penny-postal inquiries, had sent him a cordial note). He received a Ph.B. degree in 1885, having paid his own way by capturing almost every possible cash award; an M.A. in 1888; and an LL.D. in 1902.

Beveridge "read law" in a law office (the customary legal training of his day), was admitted to the bar in 1887, and had twelve years' practice in Indianapolis. Before taking his seat (for Indiana) in the U.S. Senate chamber, in December 1899, he made a jour-

ney for his own enlightenment to the newly acquired Philippines. He advocated a politics purge in tariff-law administration and the passage of child-labor amendments; and he was long remembered as an eloquent (sometimes *too* eloquent) speaker. His military carriage added to the handsomeness of his well-formed head, lean face, blue-gray eyes, and mobile mouth. Beveridge was re-elected in 1905, but the Old Guard never completely "accepted" him; he was defeated for a third term in 1911. In the Republican split of 1912 he went with Theodore Roosevelt and became temporary chairman of the Progressive National Convention at Chicago.

His first wife, Katherine Langsdale, whom he had married in 1887, died in 1900. In 1907 he married Catherine Eddy, and by her had two children.

Following a trip to Siberia and Russia he published *The Russian Advance* (1903) which, however, was soon discredited by the events of the Russo-Japanese war; between 1905 and 1908 he brought out four volumes —on the Bible, current events, jobs, personal habits, etc. As a correspondent in Germany he wrote *What Is Back of the War*, regarded in the United States as decidedly pro-German.

Meanwhile he had done the thorough-going spade-work for his *Life of John Marshall* (4 vols.), an exhaustive political interpretation of the Supreme Court in the light of Chief Justice Marshall's influence. This 1920 Pulitzer Prize winner was referred to as "easily the most acceptable thing of its kind . . . in the wide field of jurisprudence." Beveridge was not only a careful writer but he had the will-to-pursue of the scholarly researcher: ". . . the little fact is as important as what is called the big fact. The picture may be well-nigh finished but it remains vague for want of one more fact."

After his senatorial defeat of 1922 he began careful work on his *Abraham Lincoln*. No editor, at first, had shown the slightest sign of sympathy for the idea. But when high praise for his manuscript began to pour in from Oliver Wendell Holmes, Lord Haldane of England, and J. Franklin Jameson, Beveridge became reassured that his patient study of the Herndon-Weik papers (heretofore inaccessible) and the eight closely-printed volumes of the Journal of the Illinois Legislature had been far from futile. Of the contemplated four volumes he lived to finish only two, bringing the narrative down to August 1858. (A survey of 1858-61 was appended, by the editors, to the second volume.)

Even after continued absorption in his writing and his own declaration that politics had become, in his mind, "child's play and women's needle work,'" he appears to have been momentarily tempted once more, in 1926, by the political overtures of some of his confrères. But in the years since his death Beveridge the historical biographer has thrown Beveridge the statesman into relative obscurity.

PRINCIPAL WORKS: The Russian Advance, 1903; The Young Man and the World, 1905; The Bible as Good Reading, 1906; The Meaning of the Times, 1907; Work and Habits, 1908; Americans of To-day and Tomorrow, 1908; What Is Back of the War, 1915; The Life of John Marshall (Vols. 1 and 2) 1916; (Vols. 3 and 4) 1919; Abraham Lincoln, 1928.

ABOUT: Beveridge, A. J. Abraham Lincoln (see Preface); Bowers, C. G. Beveridge and the Progressive Era; American Magazine October 1910; Outlook July 18, 1917; New York Times April 28, 1927; Indianapolis Star April 28, 1927.

BIBESCO, MARTHE LUCIE (LAHOVARY), Princesse (1887-), Rumanian novelist and essayist who writes in French,

was born Marthe Lucile Lahovary, in Rumania, but was brought up in France from the age of five, and has lived most of her life in Paris. She is the daughter of Jean Lahovary, former Minister for Foreign Affairs and President of the Senate, and of Princess Smaranda (Emma) Mavrocordato, a collateral descendant of Prince Mavrocordato who was the friend of Byron and Shelley. At sixteen she married her cousin, Prince George Bibesco, grandson of the Prince of Wallachia (now Rumania). He is now president of the International Aeronautical Federation. She must not be confused with Princesse Elizabeth Bibesco, who is an Englishwoman.

Princesse Bibesco published her first travel book (*The Eight Paradises*) at eighteen, after a visit to Persia and the Near East. It was crowned by the French Academy. Besides the books written under her own name, many of which have been translated into various European languages, she has written six historical novels under the pseudonym of "Lucile Decaux." The only one of these to be translated into English was *Katia*, and authorship of the six was not acknowledged until this book was made into a movie.

Until war broke out, she stayed in Paris only during the winter, and spent the rest of the year in Rumania, either in her husband's ancestral Palace of Mogosoëa or in their summer home at Posada, in the Carpathians. Her hobbies are gardening and aviation. She is a devout and somewhat mystical Catholic. Her work as a novelist and travel writer has been highly praised by such critics as Anatole France and Marcel Proust. Jean Moreas called her style "the severe architecture of the rose." She is best known in America and England for her reminiscences of the titled and diplomatic worlds; one critic remarked that "she is related to most of the Almanach de Gotha, but her interest in royalty is that of a commoner.... Unlike most aristocratic authors, Princesse Bibesco writes well."

WORKS AVAILABLE IN ENGLISH: *Novels*—Catherine-Paris, 1928; The Green Parrot, 1929; Balloons, 1929; Worlds Apart, 1935; Katia, 1939. *Non-Fiction*—The Eight Paradises, 1923; Isvor: The Country of Willows, 1924; Royal Portraits, 1928; Egyptian Day, 1930; Some Royalties and a Prime Minister, 1930; Lord Thomson of Cardington, 1932; Crusade for the Anemone: Letters From the Holy Land, 1932; Alexander of Asia, 1935; A Daughter of Napoleon, 1937; Flowers: Tulips, Hyacinths, Narcissi, 1940.

ABOUT: Bookman May 1932; Illustration February 9, 1935; Pictorial Review May 1932; Woman's Journal March 1928.

BICKERSTAFFE-DREW, FRANCIS BROWNING DREW, Count (February 11, 1858-July 3, 1928) English priest, novelist, and essayist, who

wrote over the signature "John Ayscough," was born at Headingly, Leeds, the son of the Rev. Harry Lloyd Bickerstaffe, clergyman of the Church of England, and Mona Brougham (Drew) Bickerstaffe. From a Lichfield grammar school he went to St. Chad's College, Denstone, and then to Oxford; and while still an undergraduate, in his twenty-first year, he was received into the Roman Catholic Church. About this time, moreover, he added his mother's name to his surname.

Meanwhile he had completed some studies at Hammersmith for the priesthood; was ordained in 1884; and was shortly made Assistant Priest of the Pro-Cathedral, Kensington, remaining two years. After serving as Acting Chaplain to the Forces he was fully commissioned at Plymouth in 1892 and later went in this capacity to Malta and Salisbury Plain.

By the time he was fifty he had attained a certain ecclesiastical precision of expression and had acquired not only some well-founded literary tastes, but a strange love of military life—all of which set the stage for fifteen years of writing. *Dromina* (1909), a glowing Romany saga in which medieval traditions and graces are, with passionate fidelity, carried over into the 19th century, was followed by *Mezzogiorno,* the tale of how a soul was granted to the heroine through the ministrations of the Roman Church. In 1914 he published *Monksbridge,* a rather sportive indictment of the great Anglican educational foundations; and in somewhat the same spirit of good-natured abuse he wrote a tender comedy, *The Foundress,* based on his American tour in 1917— but spoiled, said some critics, by melodrama.

His *San Celestino,* a full account of the life and papal elevation of St. Celestine V, has been cited by some critics as his best book.

Pope Pius X (as did Leo XIII) made Bickerstaffe-Drew private chamberlain, later adding the dignity of Domestic Prelate. In 1909 he became a Papal Count. In addition to further religious and military honors he was awarded honorary Litt.D. degrees by two American universities, Marquette and Notre Dame. His manners were said to have been fastidious but undeniably impressive. Although his elaborate tales have not survived contemporary criticism very well, there are, among his writings, pieces of autobiography and comment which have not lost their significance.

PRINCIPAL WORKS: Dromina, 1909; San Celestino, 1909; Mezzogiorno, 1910; Faustula, 1912; Monksbridge, 1914; The Foundress, 1921; Dobachi, 1922; Pages from the Past, 1922; Brogmersfield, 1924.

ABOUT: Bickerstaffe-Drew, F. B. D. Pages From the Past; London Times July 5, 1928.

BIERCE, AMBROSE GWINNETT. See "AMERICAN AUTHORS: 1600-1900"

BIGGERS, EARL DERR (August 26, 1884-April 5, 1933), American novelist and writer of detective fiction, the inventor of Charlie Chan, was born in Warren, Ohio, the son of Robert J. Biggers and Emma E. (Derr) Biggers. He graduated from Harvard in 1907 and began newspaper work on the Boston *Traveler* where he ran a humorous column and wrote occasional dramatic criticism. A sample of his characteristically American wit was his comment

on this experience in later years; writing a humorous column in Boston—he said—was a good deal like making faces in church it offended a lot of nice people, and it wasn't much fun. A play, *If You're Only Human,* produced in 1912 was unprofitable, but a novel published the next year, *The Seven Keys to Baldpate,* yielded a dramatization by George M. Cohan that was sensationally successful.

Produced by Cohan who played the leading rôle in the original Broadway production, this melodrama of a writer who shut himself up in a deserted hotel to write a novel against time (the play had a trick ending) ran for years on the legitimate stage, was played by innumerable stock companies, was filmed in the silent and talking moving pictures, and was even revived with an all-star cast by the Players Club.

Charlie Chan, Biggers' patient, likeable aphoristic Chinese detective came along a dozen years later in *The House Without a Key* (1925). He was not drawn directly from life, although Chang Apana, a Chinese Hawaiian detective, who called on Biggers at his Honolulu home, thought differently. "Sinister and wicked Chinese are old stuff," Biggers once explained, "but an amiable Chinese on the side of law and order had never been used. . . . If I understand Charlie Chan correctly, he has an idea that if you understand a man's character you can nearly predict what he is apt to do in any set of circumstances." Chan (who never appeared in a short story, to the perennial regret of anthologists) continued to dog Biggers for the rest of his life, as Sherlock Holmes dominated Conan Doyle. Like Holmes, too, he is one of those rare fictional characters who have transcended and outlived the stories in which they appeared, as well as their authors. Chan figured in six full novels, five of them collected in the 1,600-page omnibus, *The Celebrated Cases of Charlie Chan,* published during Biggers' lifetime. The last Chan story was *The Keeper of the Keys* (1932). (Biggers had a predilection—rather confusing to his readers—for titles with the word "key.") All the novels were serialized in the *Saturday Evening Post* before book publication. Some of them were translated into as many as ten different foreign languages. The actor Warner Oland embodied the character to perfection in a long series of talking pictures, though not all of the scenarios (after the original stories had been used up) were worthy of the talents either of the detective or his personifier. (J. P. Marquand's[qv] later Japanese detective, Mr. Moto, hero of a similar cinematic sequence, seems more than accidentally related.) Charlie has also figured in several radio scripts and even in a newspaper comic-strip: Biggers would scarcely have been pleased by some of the transformations his originally simple and dignified character has undergone at the hands of others since his creator's death.

As the *Nation* said in an obituary editorial, Biggers' detective fiction was also good literature, and Chan symbolized the sagacity, kindliness, and charm of the Chinese people: his epigrams "redistilled the wisdom of the ages in a new and captivating fashion." It must be admitted, however, that the stories have become a shade old-fashioned by later standards, and are remembered today less for themselves than for the wise, smiling, pudgy little Chinese they introduced.

Biggers was short, round, dark, with twinkling eyes and a friendly manner; he was a skilled and kindly craftsman who knew his audience and his *métier*. He died of heart disease at Pasadena, Calif., in his forty-ninth year, leaving his wife, Eleanor (Ladd) Biggers, whom he had married in 1912, and a son.

PRINCIPAL WORKS: *Charlie Chan Stories*—The House Without a Key, 1925; The Chinese Parrot, 1926; Behind That Curtain, 1928; The Black Camel, 1929; Charlie Chan Carries On, 1930; The Keeper of the Keys, 1932. *Other Fiction*—Seven Keys to Baldpate, 1913; Love Insurance, 1914; The Agony Column, 1916; Fifty Candles, 1926. *Plays*—If You're Only Human, 1912; Inside the Lines, 1915; A Cure for Curables, 1917; See-Saw (musical comedy based on Love Insurance) 1919; Three's a Crowd, 1919.

ABOUT: Harvard College, Class of 1907: Twenty-Fifth Anniversary Report; Haycraft, H. Murder for Pleasure: The Life and Times of the Detective Story; Mantle, B. American Playwrights of Today; Canadian Bookman June 1933; Nation April 19, 1933; New York Herald Tribune April 6, 1933.

*BINDLOSS, HAROLD (1866-), English novelist, was born in Liverpool, and after leaving school spent a number of years at sea and in various British colonies, chiefly Africa and Western Canada. He returned to England in 1896, and entered journalism. After several years on London newspapers he began writing stories of colonial life, and this has been almost without exception his theme ever since. He is little known in America, though several of his books have been published in this country; but he is a remarkably prolific author of books of romantic adventure which have found a wide audience in England. Little is known of his private life, except that he is married and lives now in Carlisle, Cumberland, in the extreme North of England. In spite of his seventy-five years, he is still hard at work, and though he no longer publishes two or three novels a year, he still manages to spin out of his seemingly inexhaustible memories of youth at least one volume annually. The only non-fiction book he has written is his first published volume, an account of the Niger territory at the end of the nineteenth century. His books have no particular depth, but they are lively and entertaining, and he has a gift for racy narrative and for convincing background. Formerly his stories appeared in many British magazines, but in recent years he has confined himself entirely to the novel form.

PRINCIPAL WORKS: In the Niger Country (non-fiction) 1898; A Wide Dominion, 1899; Ainslie's Ju-Ju, 1900; A Sower of Wheat, 1902; The Concession Hunters, 1903; The Mistress of Bonaventure, 1904; The League of the Leopard, 1904; Daventry's Daughter, 1904; Alton of Somasco, 1905; The Impostor, 1905; Beneath Her Station, 1906; The Cattle Baron's Daughter, 1906; A Damaged Reputation, 1906; The Dust of Conflict, 1907; His Lady's Pleasure, 1907; By Right of Purchase, 1907; The Liberationist, 1908; Thrice Armed, 1908; The Greater Power, 1909; The Gold Trail, 1910; Rancher Carteret, 1910; Alison's Adventure, 1911; The Pioneer, 1912; The Wastrel, 1913; The Allinson Honour, 1914; Blake's Burden, 1914; The Secret of the Reef, 1915; The Borderer, 1916; Carmen's Messenger, 1917; Sadie's Conquest, 1917; Agatha's Fortune, 1918; Askew's Victory (in America: The Buccaneer Farmer) 1918; Wyndham's Partner, 1919; Dearham's Inheritance, 1919; Stayward's Vindication, 1920; The Head of the House, 1920; Musgrave's Luck, 1921; The Man From the Wilds, 1922; The Keystone Block, 1923; The Boys of Wildcat Ranch (juvenile) 1924; Andrew's Folly, 1924; Carson of Red River, 1924; Helen: The Conqueror (in America: Pine Creek Ranch) 1925; A Debt of Honour, 1925; The Broken Net, 1926; Footsteps, 1927; The Dark Road, 1927; Halford's Adventure, 1928; The Firm Hand (in America: The Lone Hand) 1928; Frontiersmen (in America: The Frontiersman) 1929; Harden's Escapade (in America: The Man at Willow Ranch) 1930; The Harder Way, 1930; A Moorside Feud, 1930; Carter's Triumph, 1931; Right of Way, 1932; The Loser Pays, 1933; The Stain of the Forge, 1933; Sonalta Gold, 1934; The Lady of the Plain, 1935; The Forbidden River, 1936; Fellside Folk, 1937; Posted Missing, 1938; Valeria Goes West, 1939; What's Mine I Hold, 1940.

BINGHAM, ALFRED MITCHELL

(February 20, 1905-), American economist and journalist, writes: "Born in Cambridge, Mass. Father, Hiram Bingham, then teaching history at Harvard, later at Princeton and Yale; Lieutenant-Governor and Governor of Connecticut, United States Senator 1924-32. Ancestors included three

colonial governors of Connecticut, also pioneer missionaries to Hawaii. Married, 1934, Sylvia Doughty Knox; two sons and a daughter. Educated at Groton School, Yale College, Yale Law School. Editor *Yale Law Journal* and received De Forest Medal for public speaking; Phi Beta Kappa. Admitted to Connecticut bar 1930, but never practiced law. Traveled and studied abroad, 1930-32, in principal European countries, Soviet Union, Near East, India, Far East; as occasional correspondent for Hartford *Times* and other New England papers interviewed Mussolini, Venizelos, Gandhi, Chiang Kai-shek and other prominent figures. Founded, in 1932, with Selden Rodman, *Common Sense,* a monthly journal of progressive opinion and comment, and have edited it with him up to the present. Co-editor, with Selden Rodman, of *Challenge to the New Deal,* 1934, a symposium on economic and social problems, with an introduction by John Dewey.

"Registered as a Republican when made a voter in Salem, Conn., in 1926, active in Republican campaigns and as delegate to Republican conventions in Connecticut in 1928 and 1930. Joined League for Independent Political Action in 1932, active in efforts to launch a third party as executive secretary of Farmer Labor Political Federation and American Commonwealth Federation, 1932-36. Supported New Deal after 1936. Changed registration to Democratic 1939. Elected to Connecticut State Senate for term 1941-42; chairman of Senate Agriculture Committee. Home, Colchester, near Salem, Conn."

PRINCIPAL WORKS: Insurgent America: Revolt of the Middle Classes, 1935; Man's Estate: Adventures in Economic Discovery, 1939; The United States of Europe, 1940.

ABOUT: Literary Digest February 10, 1934.

BINNS, ARCHIE (July 30, 1899-), American novelist and historian of the Northwest, was born Archie Fred Binns in Port Ludlow, Wash., the son of Frank Binns and Atlanta Sarah (McQuah) Binns. His father was one of the pioneers of Western Washington; his mother was born aboard the

S.S. "Atlantic," commanded by her father just outside New York near Ambrose Light. Archie Binns' grandfather was a cotton

Pinchot

blockade runner during the Civil War who was killed at sea at thirty-one and buried off the Cape of Good Hope. A second cousin, Jack Binns, was radio operator on the S.S. "Republic" at the time of its collision with the S.S. "Florida" off Nantucket Lightship. At eighteen Archie Binns joined a lightship crew off Umatilla Reef near Cape Flattery, Wash. for nine months, putting in one stretch of 160 days without going ashore. His service as fireman and the conversations he held with his mates, of varying life-experiences and philosophies, are recorded in the novel *Lightship* (1934). Binns enlisted in the U.S. Army in 1918, and was commissioned a second lieutenant in the Field Artillery Reserve in 1923. He took a B.A. degree in 1922 from Stanford University, where he studied philosophy, and in September 1923 married Mollie Windish. They have two daughters, Jacqueline and Georgia.

In 1923 Binns left the S.S. "Ecuador" in New York (being then a sailor) and went to Washington, D.C., as correspondent for Scripps-Howard newspapers. For a time he was editor of the Leonard Scott Publication Company. In 1931 he collaborated with Felix Riesenberg on the latter's *The Maiden Voyage. Esquire* and *Yachting* published his stories. *Lightship* was rejected by several publishers before it was finally accepted. *The Laurels Are Cut Down* ranges from the Pacific Northwest to Siberia, and concerns two young Americans, bewildered and hurt by fate, who must go on living in their native woods even after the "laurels are cut down." *The Land Is Bright* deals with the migration to Oregon in the early 'fifties. Mr. Binns, it is said, "writes always of simple people in the grip of fundamental emotion"; he is excellent at large canvases, but is regarded by some critics as weak in structural sense. For recreation he travels in his own sailboat. He is dark in complexion, with a small moustache.

PRINCIPAL WORKS: Lightship, 1934; Backwater Voyage, 1936; The Laurels Are Cut Down, 1937; The Land Is Bright, 1939; Mighty Mountain, 1940; Northwest Gateway: The Story of the Port of Seattle, 1941; The Roaring Land, 1942.

ABOUT: Wilson Library Bulletin February 1935.

BINYON, LAURENCE (August 10, 869-), English poet, dramatist, and art critic, writes: "I was born at Lancaster, and have lived most of my life in London. From St. Paul's School, London, I got a scholarship at Trinity College, Oxford. On leaving Oxford I entered the service of the British Museum, first in the Department of Printed Books, then in the Department of Prints and Drawings. From about 1900 I began to take a special interest in Oriental art, and in 1908 published *Painting in the Far East,* the first book on the subject in a European language. From 1913 to 1933 I was in charge of the Oriental Paintings and Prints in the Museum. In 1894 I published my first book, *Lyric Poems,* followed soon by several other volumes at intervals. During the last war I published a number of poems collected as *The Four Years.* One of these poems, 'For the Fallen,' has been engraved on war-memorials all over the British Empire. It was set to music by Elgar. My *Collected Poems* (two volumes) were published in 1931.

"My first play, *Paris and Oenone,* was acted at the Haymarket Theatre in 1906. In 1907 *Attila* was produced at His Majesty's Theatre, in 1923 *Arthur* at 'the Old Vic.' One-act plays of mine are performed fairly frequently by amateur or semi-amateur companies in the country.

"I have published several works on Oriental painting, especially Chinese, also on English drawings and water-colors; but my heart is in poetry. I am now translating Dante in triple rhyme. Have published *Inferno* and *Purgatorio* and am half-way through *Paradiso.* Also still work at my own poetry.

"I have lectured in Britain, Paris, Berlin, Holland, Scandinavia, Vienna, Rome, Japan, and many places in the United States. Have been four times to America and enjoyed each trip. Was Norton Professor of Poetry at Harvard, 1933-34.

"Since 1934 I live in the country, and now much prefer country life to London. I married Cicely Margaret Powell in 1904; have three daughters and five grandchildren."

* * *

Laurence Binyon is the son of the Rev. F. Binyon and Mary (Dockray) Binyon.

* Died March 11, 1943.

He is a cousin of Stephen Phillips. He has an honorary Litt.D. from Oxford, LL.D. from Glasgow, and is a Fellow of the Royal Society of Literature. He has been president of the English Association and the English Verse-Speaking Association. He now lives in Streatley, Berkshire.

He looks the scholar he is, serious, conservative, and bookish. His "infinite patience" and "kindly courtesy" are proverbial among research workers who have come to him for information and assistance. As a poet and a dramatist he is distinguished and finished in style rather than emotional, though some of his shorter lyrics have a touching melancholy. Harold Laski said of him that he is "part of the great tradition of English poetry, with a rare power of imaginative reflection," and called his work "grave, finely carved, and profoundly thoughtful."

PRINCIPAL WORKS: *Poetry*—Lyric Poems, 1894; Poems, 1895; London Visions: Book I, 1895, Book II, 1898; The Praise of Life, 1896; Porphyrion, 1898; Primavera (with A. S. Cripps, M. Ghose, S. Phillips) 1900; Odes, 1900; The Death of Adam and Other Poems, 1903; Penthesilea, 1905; England and Other Poems, 1909; Auguries, 1913; The Winnowing Fox, 1915; Bombastes in the Shades, 1915; The Anvil, 1916; The Cause, 1917; The New World, 1918; The Four Years, 1919; The Secret, 1920; Selected Poems, 1922; The Sirens, 1924; Poems, 1926; The Idols, 1928; Collected Poems, 1931; Akbar, 1932. *Plays*—Attila, 1907; Arthur, 1923; Ayuli, 1923; Boadicea, 1927; Sophro the Wise, 1927; Three Short Plays (Godstow Nunnery, Love in a Desert, Memnon) 1930; The Young King, 1935; Brief Candles, 1938. *Art Criticism and Essays*—Dutch Etchers of the Seventeenth Century, 1895; John Crome and John Sell Cotman, 1897; Western Flanders, 1898; Thomas Girton: His Life and Work, 1900; Painting in the Far East, 1908; Japanese Art, 1909; The Flight of the Dragon, 1911; Botticelli, 1913; English Poetry in Its Relation to Poetry and Other Arts, 1919; The Court Painters of the Grand Moguls, 1921; The Drawings and Engravings of W. Blake, 1922; Japanese Colour Prints, 1923; The Followers of William Blake, 1925; Tradition and Reaction in Modern Poetry, 1926; The Engraved Designs of William Blake, 1926; The Poems of Nizami, 1928; Landscape in English Painting and Poetry, 1929; English Water Colours, 1933; Persian Miniature Painting (with J. B. Wilkinson & Basil Gray) 1933; The Spirit of Man in Asian Art, 1935; Art and Freedom, 1939.

ABOUT: Literary Digest November 4, 1933; London Mercury September 1930; Saturday Review of Literature January 9, 1932; Sewanee Review July 1935.

"BIRMINGHAM, GEORGE A." See HANNAY, J. O.

BIRRELL, AUGUSTINE (January 19, 1850-November 20, 1933), English essayist and statesman, was born near Liverpool, the youngest son of Charles Birrell, a well known Baptist minister, and Harriet Jane (Grey) Birrell. He was educated at Trinity College, Cambridge, and was called

to the bar in 1875. He "took silk" in 1893, and from 1896 to 1899 was professor of law at University College. His chief interest was in politics, and from 1889 to 1918, except for the "khaki election" during the Boer War when all Liberals lost their seats, he was constantly in the House of Commons. He married young, but his first wife died soon after their marriage. In 1888 he married the daughter of the poet Frederick Locker-Lampson; she was at the time the widow of Tennyson's son Lionel. They had two sons.

Birrell's political career came to its culmination and its downfall in his appointment in 1907 as chief secretary for Ireland. He had previously been minister of education. When growing unrest brought on the Easter Rebellion of the Sinn Feiners in 1916, Birrell took on his own shoulders all the blame, though it seems evident that the *laissez faire* policy which allowed the rebellion to take place had been the political "line" of his own dominant party, the Liberals, and that no other course would have been open to him. He resigned under fire. Fortunately for him he outlived the opprobrium, and had fifteen years of a peaceful old age.

His literary career was in his own mind always subsidiary to law and politics. When commiserated for not being able to continue in the path of literature, he replied: "I never went very far along that path." Nevertheless, his earliest books are his best. Best of all is *Obiter Dicta,* a collection of essays "by the way" (from the legal phrase of that meaning). They served to introduce a new word into the language—a term already applied to him as a trial court lawyer and a parliamentary speaker. This word is "to birrell," which means, according to one authority, "to comment on life in a combination of irony and kindly mordancy, with apparent irrelevance, but with actual point." In all his essays, outside his rather perfunctory biographies and his editing of Boswell, John Wesley, and Locker-Lampson, the outstanding characteristic is a sort of side-long humor. Unlike many humorists, Birrell had wit as well; and on occasion he could be a hard hitter. As Edward Shillito says, his

is "the talk of a wise man who treated the world as he would his friends by his own fireside." He never quite recovered the freshness of his first writing, but to the end of his life he never wrote a dull word.

Though he "outlived his career," both politically and as a writer, Birrell remained to the end alert, interested, and alive. He was a handsome old man, with fresh skin, a shock of white hair, and clean-cut features, whose springy walk and easy flow of conversation were the stand-by of a score of London drawing rooms. He is too much neglected now, and well deserves to have the dust blown off his half-dozen best volumes.

PRINCIPAL WORKS: Obiter Dicta, 1884; Life of Charlotte Brontë, 1885; Obiter Dicta: Second Series, 1887; Res Judicatae, 1892; Essays and Addresses, 1901; William Hazlitt, 1902; Andrew Marvell, 1905; In the Name of the Bodleian and Other Essays, 1905; Collected Essays and Addresses, 1922; More Obiter Dicta, 1924; Et Cetera, 1930; Things Past Redress, 1937.

ABOUT: Birrell, A. Things Past Redress; Gosse, E. W. Books on the Table; Christian Century December 13, 1933; Contemporary Review January 1934; Fortnightly Review January 1934; Literary Digest December 30, 1933.

*BJÖRKMAN, EDWIN AUGUST (October 19, 1866-), Swedish-American novelist and critic, was born in Stockholm, Sweden, the son of Anders August Björkman and Johanna Elizabeth (Anderson) Björkman. He dedicated his first book to be published in America, *Is There Anything New?,* "To the memory of my father, whose loving sacrifices opened me

a way toward self-expressive work." Edwin Björkman was educated at the South-End Higher Latin School, Stockholm, and from fifteen on was a clerk, actor, and journalist in Sweden, coming to the United States in 1891. His two novels, *The Soul of a Child* (1922) and its next-year's sequel, *Gates of Life,* are largely autobiographical, and were frank in tone. Joining the Scandinavian colony in Minnesota, Björkman edited the Minnesota *Posten,* published in St. Paul, from 1892 to 1894; was a reporter and music critic on the *Times,* Minneapolis, from 1894 to 1897; and in the latter year came East to work as a reporter on the New York *Sun* and *Times.* He was a member of the 23d Regiment, New York Militia, during the Spanish-American War, 1898. In 1906

* Died November 16, 1951.

he joined the editorial staff of the New York *Evening Post,* and was a department editor of the *World's Work,* a political and historical monthly, in 1909. As editor of the Modern Drama Series, 1912-15, Björkman introduced Strindberg, Björnson, and Schnitzler to an American audience. The First World War found him back in Sweden as representative of the British Department of Information, 1915-17, and for the next two years he was director of the Scandinavian bureau of the American Committee on Public Information. From 1920 to 1922 Björkman was an associate director of the League of Nations News Bureau. For three years he was literary editor of the Asheville (N.C.) *Times,* from 1926 to 1929, an experience leading to his appointment as state director for the North Carolina Federal Writers Project, beginning in 1935. Mr. and Mrs. Björkman (she was Lucy Millender of Asheville) live at Biltmore, N.C. He is a member of the Pen and Plate Club, a Democrat, and was made a Knight of the Order of the Dannebrog in 1919. "A man begins only then to live in the full sense of the term [at forty-five]," Björkman declared in 1911; he is still active in his seventies. Besides his pioneer work in the drama—done against American indifference, as he testifies in his dedication to *Voices of Tomorrow* —Björkman has translated novels by Gustaf af Geijerstam, Frank Heller, Harry Soiberg, and Olav Duun. He also translated Georg Brandes' *Jesus: A Myth* (1926).

PRINCIPAL WORKS: Is There Anything New Under the Sun? 1911; Gleams: A Fragmentary Interpretation of Man and His World, 1912; Voices of Tomorrow, 1913; Scandinavia and the War, 1914; The Cry of Ukraine, 1915; The Soul of a Child (novel) 1922; Gates of Life (novel) 1923; The Search for Atlantis, 1927; The Wings of Azrael (poem) 1934.

ABOUT: Century Magazine December 1925; April 1926.

BLACKMUR, RICHARD P. (1904-), American poet and literary critic, is reticent both with his own publishers and the pub-lishers of biographical dictionaries. It is probable that he was born in Massachusetts and attended the public schools of Boston. The Blackmur family, which is Scotch in origin, dropped the "i" from Blackmuir sometime in the past. Richard Blackmur

w. Pierce

did not attend any institution of higher learning, but after working as a clerk in the Dunster House Bookshop in Cambridge, Mass., was associated with Lincoln Kirstein in editing the *Hound and Horn,* a periodical concerned with modern arts and letters and largely staffed by graduates from Harvard. He has also been advisory editor of the *Kenyon Review,* and himself was appointed to assist in the newly created course in Creative English at Princeton in September 1940. It was established by a two-year grant from the Carnegie Foundation and organized by Allen Tate, who was familiar with Blackmur's "vigorous, tough-minded" literary criticism and invited him to join him in the enterprise. The course is not given as part of the usual curriculum of the English Department.

Blackmur obtained grants from the Guggenheim Foundation in 1937 and 1938, and devoted the time to writing a work of large scope on Henry Adams. He was married in 1930 to Helen Dickson, an artist, of Harrington, Maine, where they have lived from time to time; the Blackmurs have no children. Mrs. Blackmur designed the jacket for his book of literary critiques, *The Expense of Greatness* (1940).

Commenting on T. E. Lawrence's remark that "the everlasting effort to write is like trying to fight a feather-bed," Blackmur observes: "You meet a serious writer today, and you ask him where he teaches. If he doesn't teach, the chances are he does something else," such as "working for Mr. Luce [of *Time, Fortune,* and *Life* magazines] . . . which appears to be a kind of fur-lined purgatory."

Blackmur has discussed, with especial particularity, the work of T. E. Lawrence and D. H. Lawrence, and such other moderns as E. E. Cummings, Ezra Pound, Hart Crane, Marianne Moore, T. S. Eliot, and Yvor Winters. His Introduction to the critical prefaces written by Henry James for the New York edition of James' novels first appeared in *Hound and Horn,* next as a foreword to James' *The Art of the Novel,* and latterly in Blackmur's *The Double Agent* (1935). *From Jordan's Delight* (1937), his volume of poems, struck William Rose Benét as showing "an imperfect ear for accent . . . and sometimes a jarring and uncouth use of words. But there is also undeniable distinction to his mind." Blackmur is described as being slight, of medium height, with bushy brown hair streaked with gray, and sharp, grayish-blue eyes.

PRINCIPAL WORKS: Dirty Hands: or, The True-Born Censor, 1932; The Double Agent: Essays in Craft and Education, 1935; From Jordan's Delight (poems) 1937; The Expense of Greatness (essays) 1940; Henry James, 1941.

ABOUT: Williams, O. (ed.). New Poems: 1940; Winters, Y. Primitivism and Decadence: A Study of American Experimental Poetry; Poetry (magazine) October 1938.

*BLACKWELL, ALICE STONE (September 14, 1857-), American translator, publicist, and biographer, writes:

"Alice Stone Blackwell was born at East Orange, N.J., the daughter of Henry B. Blackwell and Lucy Stone. She was reared in an atmosphere of progress. Her aunt, Dr. Elizabeth Blackwell, was the first woman in modern times to take a medical degree. Her aunt by marriage, the Rev. Antoinette Brown Blackwell, was the first woman in the world to be ordained as a minister. Her father had a reward of $10,000 offered for his head at a great public meeting in the South, because of his active part in the rescue of a young slave-girl. Her mother, Lucy Stone, was called the morning star of the woman's rights movement. Susan B. Anthony, Julia Ward Howe, and Frances E. Willard all declared themselves her converts. [She refused to change her name on marriage, and the Lucy Stone League is named in her honor.]

"Alice Stone Blackwell took her B.A. at Boston University, C.L.A. in 1881, and later was received into Phi Beta Kappa. Even before leaving college, she had begun to help her parents in their work on woman suffrage. She wrote or edited most of the controversial literature of the movement. She was an editor of the *Woman's Journal* from 1833 to 1917, first as assistant to her parents and after their death as editor-in-chief. In 1917 the *Woman's Journal* was consolidated with two other papers to form the *Woman Citizen,* and she continued as contributing editor.

"Chiefly through her efforts, the National and the American Woman Suffrage Associations, which had long worked separately, were induced to come together as the National American Woman Suffrage Association, and she was secretary of the united society for almost twenty years. She was president of the New England and the Massachusetts Woman Suffrage Associations. She is Honorary President of the Massachusetts League of Women Voters, an Honorary

Trustee of Boston University, Vice President of the Boston Evening Clinic and Hospital, and was President of the Massachusetts Branch of the American Association of University Women (then called the Association of Collegiate Alumnae). She was a Presidential Elector for LaFollette in 1924. She was awarded the Ford Hall Forum medal for 'service to humanity,' the Order of Melusine for her services to the Armenians (she had been secretary of the first society of Friends of Armenia), and the Jewish Rose by the *Jewish Advocate.*

"She has found recreation in putting foreign poetry into English verse, and has translated poems from the Armenian, Russian, Yiddish, Hungarian, and Spanish. She is a Socialist in principle though not a party member. She has written many letters to the press on the unpopular side of various controverted questions. She says that in old age it adds much to the interest of life to have a whole stableful of hobbies."

* * *

Miss Blackwell has never married. She has lived for many years in Cambridge, Mass., revered as the last of the leaders of the great days of militant feminism in America.

PRINCIPAL WORKS: The Little Grandmother of the Russian Revolution—Catherine Breshkovsky's Own Story, 1917; Lucy Stone: Pioneer of Woman's Rights, 1930.

ABOUT: Woman Citizen January 1926; Woman's Journal December 1929.

*BLACKWOOD, ALGERNON (1869-), English mystic, novelist, and short story writer, writes: "I was brought up in an extremely narrow Evangelical atmosphere where most natural impulses were repressed: dancing, theatres, cards, gambling, alcohol, etc., were 'of the devil.'

Moody and Sankey, revivalists of that day, stayed at our country house. Being of an emotional nature, I was frequently 'converted,' and always afraid of hell.

"Since I betrayed no particular talent, I was sent out to Canada, aged 20, and in Toronto I got a job on the *Canadian Methodist Magazine,* whose editor told me I wrote his children's articles 'easily.' A small capital from home tempted me to go shares in a dairy farm—a failure in six months.

* Died March 15, 1950.   * Died December 10, 1951.

With the small amount saved from a forced sale of my Jersey cattle I bought a small hotel in Toronto. It also failed in six months. I fled to the backwoods of Ontario, then drifted to New York City, and by the merest luck got a job as reporter on the *Evening Sun,* where I was a third-rate reporter. I learned much of life on its seamy side. But gold had been found on Rainy River, and I raced out there, found nothing but experience, and returned to New York and got a job on the *Times,* where I did well. I went through, meanwhile, prolonged periods of semi-starvation, till one day, through the kindness of William E. Dodge, a friend of my father's (now dead), I became private secretary to James Speyer, the millionaire banker, and lived happily, running his household, till he married and I returned to England, aged 30. My 'lean years' in New York, meanwhile, had included various means of livelihood; posing as artist's model (to Charles Dana Gibson, among others), actor in a touring troupe, making eau de cologne soap, and several other things.

"During these years my one and only passion was—Nature. I read, of course (from free libraries), with a starving hunger to learn and know. Imaginative literature in French, German, English crammed me; scientific reading came much later. But no desire to write lay in me; in my years of newspaper reporting I betrayed no talent; I had one yearning only, intense and passionate: to get away into the woods or forests by myself. Nature, apparently, gave me something that human nature could not give. I had tried poetry now and again, but realized I was a poet in feeling only, not in expression, and gave it up. Meanwhile, fed by my few possible excursions into wild nature, and by tasting something of the bitter dregs of life in the raw as well, I was—presumably—developing. My intense interest in the so-called 'psychic' region rushed uppermost. Most of my books deal with imaginative speculation in this debatable region. I have been called the 'Ghost Man,' so that when I broadcast it must preferably be a 'ghost story' of sorts. My real interest here, however, lay always and still lies in the question of a possible *extension of human faculty* and the suggestion that the Man in the Street possesses strange powers which never manifest normally.

"I was 36 when I began to write—due entirely to chance: a friend carried off a number of stories I had laid aside in a cupboard as of interest only to myself. He sent them, without my knowledge, to a pub-

lisher and they were accepted. Until then no idea of trying to get published had seriously occurred to me. These stories, I think, were the accumulated repressed results of dreams, yearnings, hopes, and fears due to early Evangelical upbringing, ecstasies tasted in wild nature, draughts of bitter kind in New York's underworld life, and a wild certainty, if still half a dream, that human consciousness holds illimitable possibilities now only latent. They provided the raw material. Writing, I incline to think, is chiefly functional: the mind *must,* in one way or another, express—get rid of—what it has taken in."

* * *

Mr. Blackwood was born in Kent, the second son of Sir Arthur Blackwood, K.C.B., Financial Secretary to the Post Office, and of Sydney, widow of the fifth Duke of Manchester. He was educated at Wellington College, Edinburgh University, a Moravian School in the Black Forest (Germany), and by tutors in France and Switzerland. He is unmarried, and in times of peace lives for the most part on the Continent. In 1941, at seventy-two, he narrowly escaped death when a Nazi bomb destroyed his London flat and all his effects.

PRINCIPAL WORKS: The Empty House, 1906; The Listener, 1907; John Silence, 1908; Jimbo, 1909; The Education of Uncle Paul, 1909; The Human Chord, 1910; Lost Valley and Other Stories, 1910; The Centaur, 1911; Pan's Garden, 1912; A Prisoner in Fairyland, 1913; Incredible Adventures, 1914; The Extra Day, 1915; Julius Le Vallon, 1916; The Wave: An Egyptian Aftermath, 1916; Day and Night Stories, 1917; Promise of Air, 1918; The Garden of Survival, 1918; The Bright Messenger, 1921; The Wolves of God and Other Fey Stories (with Wilfred Wilson) 1921; Episodes Before Thirty (autobiography) 1923; Tongues of Fire and Other Sketches, 1924; Sambo and Snitch, 1927; The Dance of Death and Other Tales, 1928; Dudley and Gilderoy: A Nonsense, 1929; Full Circle, 1929; The Fruit Stoners, 1934; Shocks, 1935; Tales, 1939; The Adventures of Dudley and Gilderoy, 1941.

ABOUT: Blackwood, A. Episodes Before Thirty; Saturday Review of Literature February 15, 1936, May 31, 1941.

BLAKE, GEORGE (October 28, 1893-   ), Scottish novelist, was born in Greenock, a Clyde seaport which has formed the background for many of his books. He was educated in a local day school, and then started to read law. When the First World War broke out, he enlisted, served at Gallipoli, was wounded, and invalided home. He did not return to the law, but entered journalism, writing weekly articles on books for the Glasgow *Evening News.* In 1923 he married Ellie Malcolm Lawson; they have two sons and a daughter. In 1924 he went to London as acting editor of *John o' London's Weekly*; in 1928 he became editor of the *Strand Magazine,* and from 1930 to 1932 he was director of a publishing house. He then returned to Scotland, living in Helensbury, Dumbartonshire, and devoted himself entirely to writing. With the beginning of the present war, he came back to London and is now engaged in the Ministry of Information. While he was recovering from his war wounds he spent a winter in the Hebrides, which has also furnished background materials for his novels. Several of his plays were produced by the Scottish National Players, in Glasgow. Besides his novels and his travel books, he writes articles frequently for the reviews, and in 1936 edited a book on the steamship "Queen Mary." Much of his early work was written under the pseudonym "Vagabond." He is rather fair, with "rebellious hair and a pugnacious mouth," one eyebrow higher than the other, heavyset, with "a frown on his face but a twinkle in his eye."

Mr. Blake's chosen field has been industrial, middle-class Scotland. He has done much to end the reign of sentimental romanticism in writing about Scotland, his influence being analogous to that of the realistic Southern writers in this country. His earlier novels were marred by melodrama and occasional stridency, but with the years his work has grown more mellow and more assured. His *Down to the Sea,* partly autobiographical is a moving account of the ships that were built at Clydeside and the men who built them. The *Spectator* commented on "the infectious enthusiasm" of the Clydeside novelist. He is a sociable man, very musical, whose manner is described as being "as downright and emphatic as his prose."

PRINCIPAL WORKS: *Novels*—Mince Collop Close, 1923; The Wild Men, 1925; Young Malcolm, 1926; Paper Money, 1928; The Path of Glory, 1929; The Seas Between, 1930; Returned Empty, 1931; Gettin' in Society, 1931; Sea Tangle, 1932; The Valiant Heart, 1933; The Shipbuilders, 1935; David and Joanna, 1936; Down to the Sea, 1937; Late Harvest, 1938. *Non-Fiction*—Scotland of the Scots, 1918; Vagabond Papers, 1922; Coasts of Normandy, 1929; The Press and the Public, 1930; The Heart of Scotland, 1934; Rest and Be Thankful, 1934.

ABOUT: Bookman (London) July 1928.

"BLAKE, NICHOLAS." See D A Y LEWIS, C.

BLAKER, RICHARD (March 4, 1893-February 19, 1940), English novelist, was born in India, the son of R. H. Blaker, I.S.O. (Imperial Service Order), Keeper of the Records, Government of India, and Assistant Secretary of the Department of Education, retired in 1921. Richard Blaker attended Queen's College, Oxford University, where he received his M.A. degree in the classics. On the outbreak of the First World War in 1914 he enlisted in the Royal Field Artillery, and saw active service in France, Egypt, and Palestine. Blaker's seventh novel, *Medal Without Bar* (1930) was a 663-page account of the war, a solidly realistic, unsensational story describing the work of the big guns and the subalterns who manned and directed them.

After demobilization he began a steadily successful career in novel-writing, beginning with *The Voice in the Wilderness* (1925), about a man who, though living in his own family circle, is estranged from all its members, wife, daughter, and son. The romantic and adventurous novel, *Here Lies a Most Beautiful Lady* (1935), and its next-year's sequel, *But Beauty Vanishes,* had excellent sales in America. They were followed by *David and Judah,* a Biblical novel published in the United States under the title *Thou Art the Man.*

The permanent residence of the Blakers was at Bovingdon, Hertfordshire, but he died in Santa Monica, Calif., two weeks before his forty-seventh birthday. His wife, Mayo Blaker, survived. Blaker left unfinished a novel which had been scheduled for publication by a New York firm. The cause of his death was stated by Blaker's friend, Louis Golding, the writer, to have been the infections and gas poisoning he suffered during the war. Blaker's ability in structure and characterization and his finish of style won him the commendation of critics in general, if not reaching the positiveness of Golding's declaration that "his sense of people ranks him with Arnold Bennett and [his] sense of things is as consummate as Rudyard Kipling's." *Medal Without Bar* has solid claims to rank among the best British novels of the First World War, and the other novels rise well above the level of popular entertainment. His inspired sense of "gadgetry" caused Blaker to be called by some reviewers a man's novelist, although he was unusually gifted at portraying female characters. Blaker had a deft hand with a plane and chisel; friends in his English cottage sat on chairs and dined from sideboards built by their host. The novelist was a man of prepossessing appearance, "a most winning amalgam of strength and sweetness," according to Golding, with a clean-shaven face, thin lips, large nose and curling hair. A dramatization of his novel, *The Voice in the Wilderness,* was produced at the Q Theatre, London, in November 1938.

PRINCIPAL WORKS: The Voice in the Wilderness, 1922; Geoffrey Castleton, Passenger, 1923; Oh! the Brave Music, 1925; Enter a Messenger, 1926; Scabby Dickson, 1927; The Umpire's Game, 1929; Medal Without Bar, 1930; The Needle-Watcher, 1932; Night-Shift, 1934; Here Lies a Most Beautiful Lady, 1935; But Beauty Vanishes, 1936; David of Judah (U.S. title: Thou Art the Man) 1937; Love Went A-Riding (U.S. title: On Pegasus He Rode) 1938.

ABOUT: London Times February 21, 27, 1940; Publishers' Weekly February 24, 1940.

BLAND, Mrs. EDITH (NESBIT). See NESBIT, E.

BLASCO IBÁÑEZ, VICENTE (January 1867-January 28, 1928), Spanish novelist, was born in Valencia—a very important point, for all his life

he was a typical son of that warm, braggart, energetic Mediterranean city. At seventeen he went to Madrid to study law, and together with his degree collected a six-months' prison sentence (the first of more than thirty) for a republican sonnet. All his life he was a republican and a liberal—though, with strange inconsistency, an anti-feminist as well. He was married twice and had several children by his first wife. But women concerned him only emotionally, not intellectually. His feminine characters are nearly all two-dimensional.

He returned to Valencia after his years in Madrid and a short stay in Paris, and, neglecting the law, plunged at once into journalism. In 1891 he founded a republican paper, *El Pueblo* (The People). From the beginning he was constantly in hot water, and in 1896 he received a sentence of exile for advocating the cause of the Cuban revolutionists. Between his return and the voluntary exile which he imposed upon himself at the beginning of the Primo Rivera regime, he was six times a legislative delegate. He fought many duels, was badly wounded more than once, and, as said, spent much of his time in prison, sometimes at hard labor.

All the time, he was writing the regional novels of his first and best period, instinct with feeling for his native province and its country people. Zola was his chief model, and these realistic studies of fisherman and peasants are by far the finest of his work. From them he proceeded to the "city" novels —modeled in part again on Zola—in which his protagonists became city workers and bull fighters. Ironically, in translation at least Blasco Ibáñez is best known by his poorest books, the grandiose "international" volumes inspired by the World War and its aftermath. *The Four Horsemen of the Apocalypse* was at the time of its publication the world's record-breaker for book sales. It made him a rich man, especially after it and *Mare Notrum* were filmed. Rudolph Valentino was the appropriate star of these pictures.

Blasco Ibáñez's removal to the Riviera came after he had challenged both Alfonso XII and Primo Rivera to duels. He built himself a palace at Mentône, rather too reminiscent of that of another *grand poseur,* d'Annunzio, and it was there that he died while at work on a "peace novel" to be called *The Fifth Horseman of the Apocalypse.* He had previously made two long tours—one in 1909 to South America, where he attempted to colonize Patagonia and actually founded two short-lived towns, and another, some fifteen years later, around the world with a party of millionaires.

There was always something meretricious about the man, though there was never the slightest doubt of the fervor and sincerity of his republican sentiments. He was hated and vilified in Spain in the last years of the monarchy, and he was in actual danger (though not so great as he pretended) of being kidnapped to Fascist Italy and made away with. An Italian publisher with whom he had a contract printed his books with a label regretting that he was obliged to carry out the agreement and publish the works of "that anti-Fascist swine."

Blasco Ibáñez was large, heavy, and rugged in appearance; partly bald; and, except for the moustache which he sometimes wore and his thick Catalan lips, had features not unlike those of the late Edgar Wallace. In manner he was said to give an impression of coldness at the first instant, followed by quick warmth when his sonorous voice boomed forth. He was at all times impatient and impulsive. In his later years, he conceived a passion for boastfulness, publicity, and the bizarre, and was given to such affectations as receiving interviewers while attired in flowered silk pajamas. More than one critic lamented his abandonment of "literature for advertisement."

He asked to be buried in France, but at the birth of the Spanish republic his remains were taken home with military honors to Valencia. His ornate palace he bequeathed to "writers of all nations," though not until the death of his widow (his second wife) who is still alive. His has been a queer fate; primarily he was a man of action, voluble, boastful, posturing every minute; yet this "untidy genius," who wrote carelessly, who was superficial and sloppy in his style, whose basic culture was sufficiently indicated by the fact that in his study he had portraits of Zola, Anatole France, and Pearl White (the movie heroine of *The Perils of Pauline*), was still, as E. Allison Peers says, "a regionalist of exquisite sensibility." The same critic has pronounced his final estimate: "He erected on the ruins of a solid literary reputation a pretentious edifice of none but financial value."

Nevertheless, when *The Four Horsemen* and *Blood and Sand* are forgotten, there will still remain the author of *The Mayflower* (*Flor de Mayo*), *The Cabin* (*La Barranca*), and *Reeds and Mud* (*Canas y Barro*), vivid re-creations of life among the rural poor of Spain. Profuse and spontaneous he always was, in his most inconsiderable work; in the early regional novels he comes very near to being great.

PRINCIPAL WORKS AVAILABLE IN ENGLISH: *Novels*—The Blood of the Arena, 1911 (as Blood and Sand, 1919) ; Sónnica, 1912; The Cabin, 1917; The Four Horsemen of the Apocalypse, 1918; The Fruit of the Vine, 1919; The Dead Command, 1919; Mare Nostrum (Our Sea) 1919; The Shadow of the Cathedral, 1919; Luna Benamor, 1919; The Last Lion and Other Tales, 1919; The Enemies of Women, 1920; Woman Triumphant, 1920; The Torrent, 1921; The Mayflower, 1921; The Temptress, 1923; Queen Calafia, 1924; The Mob, 1927; The Intruder, 1928; Reeds and Mud, 1928; The Phantom With Wings of Gold, 1931; The Three Roses, 1932. *Travel and History*—Mexico in Revolution, 1920; In the Land of Art, 1923; A Novelist's Tour of the World, 1926; The Pope of the Sea, 1927; Unknown Lands, 1929; The Borgias: or, At the Feet of Venus, 1930.

ABOUT: Bell, A. F. G. Contemporary Spanish Literature; Swain, J. O. Vicente Blasco Ibáñez;

Catholic World February 1925; Contemporary Review May 1928; Current History September 1926 Literary Digest February 25, 1928; Living Age May 9, 1925; March 1, 1928; Nation April 15 1925, February 8, 1928; Nineteenth Century and After April 1928; Saturday Review of Literature February 11, 1928.

BLIVEN, BRUCE ORMSBY (July 27 1889-), American editor and critic, was born in Emmetsburg, Iowa, the son of Charles F. Bliven and Lilla C. (Ormsby) Bliven. He received his B.A. from Stanford University in 1911. In 1913 he married Rose Emery; his only son is now also a writer and journalist.

Associated News

Mr. Bliven was a reporter for the San Francisco *Bulletin* from 1909 to 1912. He then did advertising copy writing for two years, and then went to Los Angeles a director of the department of journalism of the University of Southern California fo two years more. From 1916 to 1918 he was on the staff of *Printer's Ink*. From 1919 to 1923 he was on the New York *Globe*, as chief editorial writer, managing editor, and associate editor successively. In 1923 he joined the staff of the *New Republic* a managing editor, and has been president and editor since 1930. Since 1927 he has also been the New York correspondent of the Manchester *Guardian*. He has lectured on journalism at Columbia and New York Universities and elsewhere, and in the course of his journalistic work has traveled much in America and abroad. He is a director of the Foreign Policy Association of the United States, of the American Council of the Institute of Pacific Relations, and of the Twentieth Century Fund, and a member of the Committee on Cultural Relations With Latin America. He is also a member of the Descendants of the American Revolution.

He contributes frequently to magazines of opinion, besides his weekly articles and editorials in the *New Republic*. He lives in downtown New York.

Mr. Bliven may be described as a liberal rather than a radical. He is a sociable, approachable man, despite his everlasting race with the deadline. He is heavy set, with thick dark hair now graying, a clipped moustache, and recently acquired spectacles

His style is persuasive and easy. As George Soule said of him: "Bruce Bliven knows his United States from side to side and from top to bottom. . . . There are few who can observe more closely what goes on in America, interpret it more accurately, or write about it more cogently." His only published volume outlines the major problems of contemporary science and the efforts being made to solve them.

WORKS: The Men Who Make the Future, 1942.

ABOUT: Current Biography 1941; New Republic October 18, 1939, March 10, 1941.

BLIXEN, KAREN (DINESEN), Baronesse (1885-), Danish story and travel writer who is known as "Isak Dinesen," reports: "I grew up near the sea in the country. I studied painting in Copenhagen and later in Paris and Rome, and had much fun. I had a few short stories and a little marionette comedy published. In 1914 I married my cousin, Baron Blixen, and went with him to British East Africa, now the Kenya Colony, where my family bought a· big coffee plantation for us. In 1921 I got a divorce from my husband, and took over the management of the farm myself. To my mind the life of a farmer in the East African highlands is near to an ideal existence.

"I began to write there to amuse myself in the rainy season. My native servants took a great interest in my work, believing that I was attempting to write a sort of new Koran, and used to come and ask me what God had now inspired me to write.

"Unfortunately, when coffee p r i c e s dropped I had to give up my farm, in 1931. This was a very hard blow to me, and it caused me distress to leave my people. I hope I shall go back there some time. I have been living now for some time with my mother in my old home, Rungstledlund, Denmark."

* * *

Baronesse Blixen's father, Captain A. W. Dinesen, was an adventurous naval officer who lived for three years as a trapper with the Indians in Minnesota and wrote a series of letters on hunting, under the pseudonym of "Boganis," his Indian name. Her brother served with distinction in the First World War with the Royal Canadian Highlanders, and wrote a book on his experiences. Her husband, now married to an Englishwoman, is a well-known big game hunter, who has also written several books on this subject; he is a cousin of King Christian of Denmark.

Seven Gothic Tales, the best-seller which first brought Baronesse Blixen to general attention, was written in English. "Eerie" and "distinguished" have been the critics' names for it. Severe illness delayed publication of her second book, translated from the Danish as *Out of Africa.* It is a fascinating account of her years in Kenya, where her Kikuyu servants were most of the time her only companions. She is still in poor health, thin to the point of emaciation, with deep-set eyes and a thoughtful, finely cut face. Julius Clausen called her "a women of the world in the best sense of the term." When she is well her favorite recreation is sailing; she could manage a boat almost before she could walk. Her seventeen years in Africa she considers the high point of her life; she was doctor, judge, teacher, and counsellor as well as employer to the natives, and grew to know them intimately. She does not think of herself as primarily a writer, but she has a true gift for narrative and for historical evocation. Her home is in extreme Northeastern Denmark, near Elsinore, and the ancient ancestral house in which she lives is described in one of the *Seven Gothic Tales.*

PRINCIPAL WORKS: Seven Gothic Tales, 1934; Out of Africa, 1938: Winter Tales, 1942.

ABOUT: Dinesen, I. Out of Africa; American Scandinavian Review March 1938; Wilson Library Bulletin January 1936.

*BLOCH, JEAN-RICHARD (May 25, 1884-), French novelist, playwright, poet, critic, and social thinker, was born in Paris of a family of Alsatian Jews closely related to the Shopfers from whom André Maurois derives. His student days in the French capital were exceedingly uneventful. Although from the earliest he had shown talent for literature and the sciences—writing poems in the Musset tradition, Molièresque plays, and a zoology treatise inspired by Buffon—he never attended literary or scientific coteries. After

finishing his compulsory service in the army, he entered the Sorbonne for advanced work in history and geography. Shortly thereafter he moved to Poitiers where he has resided up to this day and carried on his literary work. In 1910 he wrote many short stories and essays and a play, *L'Inquiète*, which he sent to the great Antoine, then Director of the Odéon. In the summer of 1910, after months of waiting, letters of congratulation began to pour in from friends and relatives, much to Bloch's bewilderment. Finally he learned from a *Le Matin* clipping that *L'Inquiète* had been included in the Odéon repertoire for that season, together with plays of other little known young writers: Duhamel, Romains, and Marie Leneru.

In the same year Bloch founded a "technical review of art and humanity" called *L'Effort*, which soon developed into *L'Effort Libre*, "a journal of revolutionary civilization," showing him to be "less sympathetic than combative." An acrimonious comment on Romain Rolland's *Le Théâtre du Peuple* was not overlooked by the old veteran, who answered Bloch's arguments point by point. A fruitful and lasting friendship resulted. In *L'Effort Libre* Bloch voiced his social concerns, influenced by Rolland, Élie Faure, and the anarcho-syndicalist Georges Sorel.

On the advice of Bachelin, Bloch sent a collection of short stories, *Levy,* to the publishing house of the *Nouvelle Revue Française* which, after a warm endorsement from Gide, published it in 1912. Encouraged, Bloch applied himself to writing down the experiences of a veteran of the war of 1870 with whom he went boating near Poitiers in the spring of 1911; the narrative thread developed in the course of the years into the magnificent novel, *& Co.* Bloch corrected proofs in a hospital bed during the First World War, having been seriously wounded at the Marne, Champagne, and Verdun. *& Co.* (1918) reminded Romain Rolland of the genius of Balzac: "I make bold to say, without any reservations, that here is the only French novel I know which is worthy to take its place among the masterpieces of the *Human Comedy.*"

In July 1920 Bloch noticed a small item in a provincial paper, *L'Avenir de Vienne,* telling how a Kurdistan tribe had attacked and pillaged a Greek village in Anatolia and this piece of news haunted him until it became in his fertile imagination *A Night in Kurdistan* (1925), a social novel peppered with love and adventure against an exotic background.

With *Carnaval est Mort* (1920) Bloch began a series of essays "for the better understanding of my epoch" which he has continued in his provocative *Destin du Siècle* (1930) and *Offrande à la Politique* (1933). But he was not through with the theatre. On November 17, 1926, the Odéon presented his mature play *Le Dernier Empereur,* a tremendous success in Paris, Berlin, Geneva and Stockholm. After other minor theatrical works: *Forces du Monde* (1927), a ballet for the composer Daniel Lazarus, based on Gobineau's story *L'Illustre Magicien,* and a dramatization of his tender novellette *Dix Filles dans un Pré* (1927) and of *A Night in Kurdistan,* done for the composer Alex Tansman, Bloch translated Leonhard Frank's play *Karl and Anna,* which was a Paris hit in 1929.

In 1932 Bloch returned to fiction: *Sybille* (translated into English as *Ganymede and the Serpent*) deals with the life of a dancer strikingly resembling Isadora Duncan.

To find Bloch in the rôle of active social thinker one must turn to his periodical contributions to *Europe* and *Commune,* to his activities in writers' congresses and the Workers' University, as well as to those impassioned articles in defense of the Loyalist Spanish, in *Espagne, Espagne!* (1936), and in defense of a proletarian culture, in *Naissance d'une Culture* (1937).

Before the Second World War Bloch was living on his estate, La Mérigote, a few miles from Poitiers. His beautiful hanging garden on a rugged cliff overlooked the valley of the Clain. On his walls hung reproductions of his favorite painters: Van Gogh and Titian. When tired of writing he played (on the piano or the phonograph) his favorite composer, Mozart. Bloch often went to Paris on business: "I like the city and the revolt against the city; I like to see my friends and to refrain from seeing them; I dislike work and I work enormously. I live in the country for most of the year, where my favorite sports are bicycling, motorcycling, motoring, and all other modes of transportation, including walking and cargo-boating." Bloch has a kind smiling face; his gestures are nervous and awkward, there is in him something of the man of action and, paradoxically enough, something of the Oriental dreamer.

Since the fall of France in 1940, Jean-Richard Bloch has to all intents and purposes disappeared. Neither his publishers nor his friends in this country have received word from him.

WORKS AVAILABLE IN ENGLISH TRANSLATION:
& Co, 1929; A Night in Kurdistan, 1931.

ABOUT: Bloch, J. R. & Co (see Introduction
by R. Rolland); Czerzefkow, S. & Lalou, R. Les
Écrivains chez Eux; Ehrhard, J. E. Le Roman
Français depuis Marcel Proust; Kohn, H. L'Hu-
manisme Juif; Lefèvre, R. Une Heure Avec;
Lalou, R. Contemporary French Literature; Mi-
chaud, R. Modern Thought and Literature in
France; Commune November 1933, January and
February 1937; La Grande Revue September 1924;
Left Review August 1935; Nouvelle Revue Decem-
ber 15, 1926; Revue Bleue June 19, 1926.

BLOK, ALEXANDR ALEXANDRO-VICH (1880-August 9, 1921), Russian poet, was born in St. Petersburg (Lenin-

grad), the son of a professor in the University of Warsaw. The family was of Holstein descent. When he was a baby his parents were separated, and he was reared by his mother's family, the Beketovs, his grandfather being a well known scientist. He received his degree in philology at the University of St. Petersburg in 1906, having previously studied law. He had then already been married for three years, to the daughter of the famous chemist Mendeleev. He had been publishing poems from the age of twenty, and in 1904 his first volume was brought out, *Songs to the Beautiful Lady.* The "beautiful lady" is no individual, but an abstract ideal of spiritual beauty. Blok was at this time strongly influenced by Verlaine, and was a thorough Symbolist.

The abortive revolution of 1905 engaged his enthusiasm, though reality was always difficult for Blok. It did at least have the effect of changing his style with his viewpoint, and losing him his early admirers. In the First World War he announced himself a pacifist, though later he reluctantly served in the army. With the revolution of 1917, he became affiliated with the Left Socialist Revolutionary Party, which later joined the Communist Party. It is to this period that Blok's most famous poems, outside Russia at least, belong—chiefly *The Twelve,* a powerful mystical presentation of the Bolshevist movement, with "the old, worn world" depicted as "a homeless hound, too weak to bark." The same theme appears in *The Scythians* (translated by Babette Deutsch and Abraham Yarmolinsky):

For the last time, old world, we bid you come,
Feast brotherly within our walls.
To share our peace and glowing toil
Once only the barbarian lyre calls.

However, Blok's personal participation in any practical movement was necessarily tenuous. His was the temperament of an "ivory tower" poet fallen on days of action—he remained largely unintelligible to the average reader, wallowed in the most extreme pessimism, and had the fanaticism of the excessively emotional. His long, brooding face with its mass of black hair sufficiently proclaims the hyperthyroid type. Gorky called him "a man who feels very deeply and destructively." It is probable that if he had not died suddenly of heart failure (brought on largely by malnutrition, for he had no popular appeal in most of his work, and his last days were destitute), he would have ended his own life. He was rapidly tending toward absolute despair, in spite of his profound belief in the Soviet state, which he amalgamated with his personal brand of "vague and practically irreligious mysticism." He remains one of the great post-revolutionary Russian poets, a writer, as Agnes C. Hansen says, "of undeniable power and poignancy."

PRINCIPAL WORKS AVAILABLE IN ENGLISH:
The Twelve, 1920; Poems in Deutsch, B. & Yar-
molinsky, A. Modern Russian Poetry; Selver, P.
Modern Russian Poetry.

ABOUT: Mirsky, D. S. Contemporary Russian
Literature; Olgin, M. J. Guide to Russian Literature; Living Age November 19, 1921; November
10, 1923; Poetry: A Magazine of Verse December
1921.

BLUNDEN, EDMUND CHARLES (November 1, 1896-), English poet, critic, and editor, was born in Yalding, Kent, near

Maidstone. He went from Cleave's Grammar School, Yalding, to Christ's Hospital, London, leaving school to enter the army in 1916. He served as a lieutenant with the Royal Sussex Regiment in France and Belgium, was gassed, and re-

ceived the Military Cross. Like many young English soldiers, his university education was received after the war; he is a Master of Arts of Oxford. In the interim he became a journalist in London, was associated with J. Middleton Murry on the *Athenaeum,* and became its sub-editor. In 1921 illness compelled him to leave England and he went to South America on a tramp steamer, the result being his first prose book. It was followed immediately by the volume of poems, *The Shepherd,* which won him the Hawthornden Prize in 1922. From 1924 to 1927 he was Professor of English Literature at the University of Tokyo, the chair created for Lafcadio Hearn and which has had several distinguished writers as occupants since that time. Since 1931 he has been Fellow and Tutor at Merton College, Oxford.

Mr. Blunden has been married twice: in 1918 to Mary Davies, by whom he had a son and a daughter; and in 1933 to Sylva Norman, also a writer, with whom he collaborated on his only novel. He is a Fellow of the Royal Society of Literature, and received its Arthur Benson Medal in 1930. In 1932 he delivered the Clark Lecture at Trinity College, Cambridge, his subject being Charles Lamb, a writer on whom he is one of the greatest living authorities.

Edmund Gosse described Blunden's appearance in youth—"like a chinchilla, with his gray clothes, sharp nose, and wonderful eyes. What eyes! Those of Keats must have held that expression. I thought him perfectly charming, so simple and ardent and responsive." In early middle life, he still fits that description; his is unmistakably a poet's face. His interests are primarily scholarly and literary, and his only hobby is fishing; he is an ardent angler.

Both as essayist and poet, he is essentially a nature writer. He is a realist of nature, an accurate observer who keeps his eye on the object and transforms the commonplace as does Robert Frost in America. Stephen Gwynn spoke of his "close and loving observation" and called him "especially a poet of the countryside and most intimately English. . . . His stanzas are packed with native stuff, none the less original because they carry everywhere the impress of discipleship. . . . Sober steadfastness and temperance inform his work."

This critic, however, spoke also of his "loyalty to tradition," and Francis E. Barker noted a tendency in his work to "become increasingly literary." He is as much the scholar as the poet. He has edited, with critical introductions, the works of many English authors, among them John Clare, Henry Vaughan, William Collins, Lamb, Coleridge, the later James Thomson ("B.V."), and Wilfred Owen, the war poet. His special interests are in seventeenth and eighteenth century poetry, particularly in the metaphysical and the nature poets of those periods.

The other influence on his work has been his war experiences. A friend of Siegfried Sassoon, he too has spoken out in condemnation of war, but in a far gentler tone. He was never one of the bitter and impassioned group represented by Sassoon. He is in this as in all things a gentle and kindly man who believes that even irony should be clothed in beauty. In his farewell address to his pupils in Tokyo he called himself "a frail guide," and asked his students to forgive him if he had spoiled any of their dreams. But he is no weakling; he is a finely tuned instrument which vibrates in undertones—a word which significantly is one of his own favorites.

PRINCIPAL WORKS: *Poetry*—Pastorals, 1916; The Harbingers, 1916; The Waggoner and Other Poems, 1920; The Shepherd and Other Poems of Peace and War, 1922; To Nature, 1923; Masks of Time, 1925; English Poems (two series) 1925-26; Japanese Garland, 1927; Retreat, 1928; Near and Far, 1929; Poems, 1930; Halfway House, 1932; An Elegy and Other Poems, 1937; Poems: 1930-1940, 1941. *Prose*—The Bonadventure: A Random Journal of an Atlantic Holiday, 1922; Christ's Hospital: A Retrospect, 1923; On the Poems of Henry Vaughan, 1927; Leigh Hunt's "Examiner" Examined, 1928; Undertones of War (prose and verse) 1929; Nature in Literature, 1929; An Essay on English Literature in Japan, 1929; Shakespeare's Significances, 1929; Life of Leigh Hunt, 1930; Leigh Hunt and His Circle, 1930; Votive Tablets, 1931; The Face of England, 1932; Fall In, Ghosts! 1932; Charles Lamb and His Contemporaries, 1932; We'll Change Our Ground: or, Two on a Tour (novel, with S. Norman) 1932; The Mind's Eye, 1933; On Shelley (with others) 1938; Undertones of War, 1940; Keats' Publisher: A Memoir of John Taylor, 1940.

ABOUT: Newbolt, H. New Paths on Helicon; Squire, J. C. Essays on Poetry; Freeman August 3, 1921; Fortnightly January 1931; October 1940; London Mercury September 1920, July 1922, October 1926; London Quarterly Review July 1928; New Statesman October 30, 1920; Nineteenth Century January 1931; Poetry Review July-August 1932; Revue Anglo-Americaine August, 1931; Saturday Review May 27, 1922.

BLUNT, WILFRED SCAWEN. See "BRITISH AUTHORS OF THE 19TH CENTURY"

*BODENHEIM, MAXWELL (May 26, 1893-), American poet and novelist, was born in Hermanville, Miss. He had no formal schooling, but is entirely self-educated. From 1910 to 1913 he served a full enlistment in the U.S. Army. He was first published by Harriet Monroe in *Poetry,* and in 1939 received that magazine's Oscar Blumenthal Prize. He was married in 1918 (the year in which his first book of poems appeared) to

* Died February 6, 1954.

Minna Schein. They had one son. They were divorced in 1938, and in 1939 he married Grace (Fawcett) Finan, widow of a painter who died in 1934. He lives in Brooklyn in the winter and in Catskill, N.Y., in the summer. He has lived in or near New York since his youth, and was one of the early residents of Greenwich Village in the old Bohemian days. His long feud with Ben Hecht was one of the prime sources of literary gossip in the pre-war years. He was connected with the Federal Writers' Project in New York in 1938 and 1939, and early in 1940 became a researcher with the Bibliographies and Indices Project. In August 1940 he was suspended on the ground that his affidavit, required of all WPA workers, that he was not a Communist was false. He stated that he had been a member of the Communist Party in the past, but had left it some time ago.

Pinchot

His present wife writes: "It's fun to watch him in the country. He enjoys every leaf and twig. We plan to make our permanent home in Catskill, one of these days. He likes to roam the hills and raid the orchards.... Within the past year [1939-40] Mr. Bodenheim has completed a book of verse entitled *One Generation* and a critique of the child prodigy entitled *The Lyrical Child*. Both are ready for the publisher. At present, he is gathering material for a novel dealing with the underprivileged class of a large city (New York, really)."

This bucolic picture of Mr. Bodenheim is in startling contrast to his stormy literary history. His novels are savagely realistic, revealing him as "an impassioned and bitter critic of current institutions." Several have as background the small Southern towns he knew as a boy, the same country which is William Faulkner's *milieu*, but they are strictly urban and lower-class. Most of them are laid in New York. They are exceedingly "frank," and one at least, *Replenishing Jessica*, was suppressed. But Bodenheim is no pornographer; he is in deadly earnest, and there is an evangelistic tone to all his novels, in spite of their wild humor. The keynote of all his work is hatred, hatred for meanness and dirt and cruelty, and sometimes, it seems, hatred for humanity itself. He has

fallen into neglect and the stream of fiction has run past him, but he was one of the pioneers in bringing naturalism of the French school into American writing.

He himself considers *Blackguard, Crazy Man, Georgie May,* and *Sixty Seconds* his best novels. It is as a poet, however, that he has done his most brilliant and valuable work, characterized by a mastery of metaphor and an incorrigible sense of the grotesque.

PRINCIPAL WORKS: *Poetry*—Minna and Myself, 1918; Advice, 1920; Introducing Irony, 1922; The Sardonic Arm, 1923; The King of Spain, 1924; Against This Age, 1925; Returning to Emotion, 1926; Bringing Jazz, 1930. *Novels*—Blackguard, 1923; Crazy Man, 1924; Replenishing Jessica, 1925; Ninth Avenue, 1926; Georgie May, 1927; Sixty Seconds, 1929; A Virtuous Girl, 1930; Naked on Roller Skates, 1931; Duke Herring, 1931; Run, Sheep, Run, 1932; Six A.M., 1932; New York Madness, 1933; Slow Vision, 1934; Lights in the Valley, 1942.

ABOUT: Arts & Decoration March 1924; Bookman September 1928; Poetry March 1925.

BOGAN, LOUISE (August 11, 1897-), American poet, was born at Livermore Falls, Maine, the daughter of Daniel Joseph Bogan and Mary Helen (Shields) Bogan. Her parents were both of Irish descent. Her paternal grandfather was a sea-captain out of Portland Harbor. She was educated at Mount St. Mary's Academy, Manchester, N.H., the Boston Girls' Latin School, and for a year at Boston University. In 1916 she married Curt Alexander, who died in 1920, leaving his widow with a daughter. In 1925 she married Raymond Holden, also a poet; they were divorced in 1937. For the past seventeen years she has lived for the most part in New York, though she spent a year in Santa Fé, N.M., another in Vienna (in 1922), and in 1933 and 1937 was abroad on a Guggenheim Fellowship.

Miss Bogan's poems were first published in the *New Republic*, to which she still contributes. Besides poetry, she writes some fiction and a great deal of criticism, most of which has appeared in the *Nation, Poetry: A Magazine of Verse, Scribner's* and the *Atlantic Monthly*; since 1931 she has been regular reviewer of poetry for the *New Yorker*. In 1938 she received the Helen Haire Levinson Prize given annually by *Poetry*. In 1930 she had won the John Reed Memorial Prize from the same magazine.

She writes: "I am a person who cares a great deal for privacy and anonymity in my life. On the whole, I prefer to have the main facts put down, without any dressing of literary color."

From the beginning of her career, Louise Bogan has received the acclaim of critics. Ford Madox Ford placed her "in a quiet landscape that contains George Herbert, and Donne and Vaughan." Allen Tate called her "the most accomplished woman poet of our time." Yvor Winters, who thinks Miss Bogan "suffers no diminution by comparison with the best of the English lyricists," has pointed out that her work shows "intricacy of feeling, and hence of style, rather than of idea. Each poem is an insulated unit, . . . a sharply defined segment of experience, raised to something very near major power by the sheer brilliance of the craftsmanship. . . . She is beyond any doubt one of the principal ornaments of contemporary American poetry."

Because of Miss Bogan's dislike of publicity, few personal facts concerning her are available. In appearance she is slender, with thick dark hair, delicately aquiline features, and deep-set, brooding eyes.

PRINCIPAL WORKS: Body of This Death, 1923; Dark Summer, 1929; The Sleeping Fury, 1937; Poems and New Poems, 1941.

ABOUT: Nation April 13, 1940; New Republic October 16, 1929; Poetry April 1942; Wilson Library Bulletin March 1930.

BOILEAU, ETHEL (YOUNG), Lady

(1882?-January 16, 1942), English novelist, was born in London, the daughter of the

Rev. James Foster Young, and was christened Ethel Mary Young. She was privately educated, and took some courses in Dresden, Germany, as well. Some time prior to 1914, when her first book, *The Fire of Spring*, was published, Ethel Young married Lieutenant-Colonel Raymond Frederic Boileau, later Sir Raymond Boileau. The baronetcy was created in 1838, and he was the fourth to hold the title. The Boileaus lived at Ketteringham Park, Wymondham, Norfolk; they had no children. Sir Raymond was a Deputy-Lieutenant and Justice of the Peace in Norfolk. His wife's preferred recreations were hunting, deer stalking, and fishing. Her clubs were the International Sportsman, An Comunn Gaidhealach, and the Incorporated Society of Authors. Ethel Boileau's first pronounced American success was *Hippy Buchan*, a romantic tale of a returned soldier who found himself at cross-purposes with the girl he had left behind and whose difficulties were not lessened when he suddenly became the Marquess of Fort George. Florence Haxten Britten spoke of Ethel Boileau's "imaginative vivacity, literary skill and sophistication, tinctured with a frank zest for the romantic glamour attaching to fine things, fine people, and a noble history." Her fondness for lost causes led her to compose a brochure on Bonnie Prince Charlie entitled *The Fair Prince: The Story of the Forty-Five*, which was "the result of a demand from visitors to Glenfinnan for a short explanatory pamphlet." In 1936, also, she published another American best-seller, *Clansmen*, dedicated to "Scots in Exile." This long romance recounting the present-day adventures of Captain Alan Breck Stewart seemed to Lewis Gannett "pure unadulterated hooey of the Walter Scott tradition, lushly written with gay asides on the Scotch character, and lilting episodes in the Romeo-and-Juliet mood. Unfortunately she insists on introducing solemn asides, preaching little Tory sermons." Ethel Boileau's books were particularly popular in the Dominion of Canada.

PRINCIPAL WORKS: The Fire of Spring, 1914; The Box of Spikenard, 1922; Hippy Buchan, 1925; The Arches of the Years, 1930; Turnip-Tops (U.S. title: The Gay Family) 1932; When Yellow Leaves . . . , 1934; Clansmen, 1936; Ballade in G Minor, 1938.

ABOUT: The Author's and Writer's Who's Who 1934; New York Times January 17, 1942; Saturday Review of Literature March 5, 1938.

BOJER, JOHAN

(March 6, 1872-), Norwegian novelist, writes: "The fisherman's hut where I grew up was gray like the sea and the sand on the beach—like the rocks around. But if I kneeled upon the wooden seat under the window I saw far away the red, yellow, and white painted houses of the well-to-do. It was like a bit of Paradise to stare at, and it was

evident to my mind that the people living in those bright houses must be bright and beautiful and that I must have a house like that when I grew up. Out there near the sea the soil was poor, few families possessed more than a cow or two, and milk was a costly thing. But from the window seat I saw large farms in front of the forest, and there would be flocks of cattle and sheep and horses. There the people would drink milk with their porridge, not water sweetened with treacle, they would have enough wool to weave good clothes for themselves, and need not shiver with cold. And just imagine the quantities of meat and bacon and real butter there must be—these people surely did not eat fish and fish and fish again every day of their lives as we did.

"I began my life as a literary tramp. I lived for five years in Paris as a correspondent for Norwegian newspapers, three years were spent in Italy, two years in Germany. I have frequently visited England, wandered through Holland and Belgium, and tried everywhere to profit by what I saw. The time in Paris from 1902 to 1907 appears to me the richest. I was at an age when there is no limit to one's activity. I wrote newspaper articles and books, read incredible amounts in various languages, at the same time leading a merry Bohemian life with artist friends. There were so many hours in a day and a night, and everything which made an impression is so easily recalled; my heart was still full of dreams and of youth.

"At the moment I recall the first half-century of my life with gratitude, because the kindly fates have filled my life with so many varied experiences, and have little by little given me what I glimpsed, far, far away, standing at the window of a gray cottage. In the course of forty-five years I have written novels, plays, short stories, and a lot of articles in the press, amongst which I want to mention a series of letters from the front in France.

"My novels describe the lives of plain Norwegian people (*The Last Viking, The Emigrants*), they contain psychological studies (*The Power of a Lie, Our Kingdom*) or lyrical pictures of youth and outdoor life (*Life, The Eyes of Love*). I have sometimes been called a writer of 'ideas,' because I have often placed my characters in relation to some social or religious idea (*The Great Hunger, The New Temple*). I have been much interested in politics, but have never belonged to any political party, having always wanted to be free to see things with my own sound eyes, and have consequently been called a reactionary by Communists and a radical by conservatives. The greatest misfortune of mankind is that objective truth no longer exists. This state of things can be mended only through a religious re-vival over the whole world. That is why I have been for some time pondering on this one question: Is Christianity in its present form able to unite and to lead modern minds toward new aims? If not, where then is salvation to be found?"

* * *

In 1899, when he was twenty-three, Bojer married Ellen Lange. They have three daughters and one son. In 1907 he returned with his family to Norway, and has since lived there almost continuously, bringing up his children, and striking roots deep into the native soil. The novel by which the name of Johan Bojer became established in this country was *The Great Hunger*, published in English in 1919. His French biographer, P. G. la Chesnais, said of him: "Bojer is of the family of great writer-philosophers." His interest is in the psychology of his characters, their social and religious outlook, not, like Hamsun's, primarily in their material life.

WORKS AVAILABLE IN ENGLISH: The Power of a Lie, 1909; The Great Hunger, 1919; The Face of the World, 1919; Life, 1920; Treacherous Ground, 1920; The Last of the Vikings, 1923; A Pilgrimage, 1924; The Prisoner Who Sang, 1924; The Emigrants, 1925; The New Temple (sequel to The Great Hunger) 1928; The Everlasting Struggle, 1931; The House and the Sea, 1934; By Day and Night, 1937; The King's Men, 1940.

ABOUT: Chesnais, P. G. la Johan Bojer; Gad, C. Johan Bojer: The Man and His Works; American-Scandinavian Review June 1934; Journal des Débats September 9, 1932.

BOK, EDWARD WILLIAM (October 9, 1863-January 9, 1930), Dutch-American editor, essayist, and winner of the Pulitzer Prize for biography, was born in Helder, Holland, but was brought to the United States at the age of six. He was educated in the public schools of Brooklyn, N.Y., but at thirteen had to leave school and go to work—at first as a night office

Chandler

boy with the Brooklyn *Eagle*, then as a telegraph company office boy. He went to night school and studied typewriting and shorthand, eventually becoming a stenographer in two successive publishing houses. From this position he became head of the advertising department of *Scribner's Magazine* and the *Presbyterian Review*. He founded and from

1882 to 1884 edited the *Brooklyn Magazine,* which finally became the *Cosmopolitan.* In 1886 he founded the Bok Syndicate Press; in consequence of the success of this enterprise he was asked to edit the *Ladies' Home Journal.* From 1889 to 1919, when he resigned, he was most closely identified in the public mind with this magazine, which he made into a leader in its class, paying well for the work of distinguished authors, and introducing departments and features which had an appreciable influence on the outlook and ways of thinking of the women of that period. He also married the daughter of the publisher, Mary Louise Curtis.

Bok introduced many new ideas into American journalism, including the women's page in newspapers and the weekly literary review. His two greatest interests were in the peace movement and in music. In 1923 he offered $100,000 as an American Peace Award for the best plan for cooperation between the United States and other countries to prevent war; only half the award was paid, however, as by the rules the remaining half was to be paid on acceptance of the idea by the United States Senate, and this never happened. On his death Bok left an endowment to broadcast concerts of the Philadelphia Orchestra to the public schools of the United States and Canada, and provided for a memorial in Florida which includes one of the greatest of the world's carillons.

E. W. Bok was an Alger story come true; he was so typical of its stock hero that he became almost a living caricature of him. Even in his boyhood, with sublime self-assurance, he built up a large and valuable autograph collection by merely writing to every famous man and woman he could reach and asking for their philosophy and advice. He believed in all the copy-book rules and made them work. His naïveté and innocent self-confidence were stupendous. He was a sort of sincere Elbert Hubbard, and his books of essays are trite assemblies of platitudes. But he was a really first-class editor, and he had an unfailing feeling for the public attitude. He was a born advertising man. One critic said he had "a genius for banality." His philanthropy, however, was real, and such legacies as the annual Bok Award in Philadelphia for service to humanity evince the worthy use to which he put the wealth he eventually acquired. The award of the Pulitzer Prize in biography in 1920 to his autobiography was less a recognition of Bok as an author

than a tribute to the American hero-tale of the Poor Boy Who Makes Good.

PRINCIPAL WORKS: Successward, 1895; The Young Man in Business, 1900; The Americanization of Edward Bok, 1920; Two Persons, 1922; A Man From Maine, 1923; Twice Thirty, 1925.; You: A Personal Message, 1926; Dollars Only, 1926; Perhaps I Am, 1928.

ABOUT: Bok, E. W. The Americanization of Edward Bok, Twice Thirty; Etude March 1931; Ladies' Home Journal March 1930; Publishers' Weekly January 18, 1930.

BOLITHO, HECTOR (1898-   ), New Zealand novelist, historian, and biographer, writes: "Hector Bolitho spent a happy, healthy, but hampered childhood in New Zealand. [He was born Henry Hector Bolitho.] Reporter on New Zealand newspaper at seventeen years. In uniform, on Home Service, during last war to end wars, at eighteen years.  Toured Antipodes with then Prince of Wales (now Duke of Windsor) at twenty-one years. Editor *Shakespearian Quarterly* and literary editor *Sunday News*, Sydney, Australia, at twenty-three years. Came to England at twenty-four. First novel published at twenty-five. Since then, twenty-seven books of history, biography, and fiction. Most important of these, *Albert the Good, Victoria and Albert, Victoria the Widow and Her Son,* and reminiscences, entitled *Older People.* Most successful book, *Edward VIII: His Life and Reign,* published after abdication. Hector Bolitho declares himself free from ambition, reconciled to being a second-rate writer because *life* interests him more than any record he can make of it with his pen. Has traveled vastly, in Germany, Italy, Palestine, Egypt, Australia, Africa, Canada, and United States. Lives in Essex, nine miles from a railway station, and enjoys quiet. For eight years lived in cloisters of Windsor Castle, where he wrote his historical works. Declares that his ambition now is to escape from Europe, with its sourness, and live on a few acres, with a small white house, in California, because he feels that the old world is tired and sick with history. Wishes to dig down into the earth and not find a Romain coin or an Elizabethan ornament; wishes to live on new, clean earth, for the last stretch of his life. Prefers California of all the United States and prefers the United States of all countries, because the people are honest and comparatively true."

* * *

Hector Bolitho is a sort of unofficial court biographer and historian to the English royal family. His closeness of feeling with them is evidenced by the abrupt change from the adulation of his early writing about the Duke of Windsor to the highly critical frankness of the book written after Edward had ceased to be king. *Albert the Good* has been called "the best Royal Family book since Strachey's *Queen Victoria*"—though it is decidedly not in Strachey's satirical vein. Nevertheless, Bolitho, though sympathetic, is no mere amanuensis, but treats his subjects as human beings. He was born in Auckland, the son of Henry and Ethelred Frances Bolitho, and is unmarried. Besides his original work, he has edited the letters of Queen Victoria and Prince Albert and of Lady Augusta Stanley.

PRINCIPAL WORKS: *Fiction*—Solemn Boy, 1927; Judith Silver, 1929; The House in Half Moon Street (short stories) 1936. *Non-Fiction*—The Islands of Wonder, 1920; With the Prince in New Zealand, 1920; The New Zealanders, 1928; Thistledown and Thunder, 1928; The New Countries, 1929; The Glorious Oyster, 1929; A Victorian Dean: A Memoir of Arthur Stanley (with Very Rev. A. V. Baillie) 1930; The Flame on Ethirdova, 1930; Albert the Good and the Victorian Reign, 1932; Alfred Mond, First Lord Melchett, 1933; Beside Galilee: A Diary in Palestine, 1933; The Prince Consort and His Brother, 1934; Twelve Jews, 1934; Victoria the Widow and Her Son, 1934; Older People, 1935; Marie Tempest, 1936; James Lyle Mackay, First Earl of Inchcape, 1936; Edward VIII: His Life and Reign (in America: King Edward VIII: An Intimate Biography) 1937; King George VI: A Character Study, 1937; Royal Progress: One Hundred Years of British Monarchy, 1937; Victoria and Albert, 1938; Victoria and Disraeli (radio play) 1938; The Emigrants, Early Travelers to the Antipodes (with J. Mulgan) 1939; Haywire: An American Travel Diary, 1939.

ABOUT: Bolitho, H. Older People; Time March 29, 1937.

BOLITHO, WILLIAM (1890-June 2, 1930), English journalist and miscellaneous writer, was born William Bolitho Ryall at Cape Town, South Africa, of Dutch-English parentage. His father was an impecunious Plymouth Brother preacher; his mother, a harried nagging woman. After the British had burnt their farm (the family had fought on the side of the Boers) the Ryalls lived for a while in a tank, then in mean streets in Cape Town. William sold newspapers; worked under a Negro foreman on the scaffolding of Cape Town

Cathedral; read the Elizabethan dramatists; and taught himself to read Cicero and Racine. From a school in Rondebosch, a suburb, he went to South African University in Cape Town, where he played rugger football for South Africa. Working his way to England as stoker on a British liner, Bolitho found himself in London, in a shabby duck suit, standing by the Marble Arch. A woman passerby gave him a white feather—a superfluous gesture, since he had already decided to fight in the First World War. The war, as his wife Sybil wrote in her poignant biographical novel, *My Shadow As I Pass*, tortured and all but broke him. Bolitho was the only man to escape when he and fifteen others were buried alive in a trench cave-in, following the explosion of a mine on the

Somme front in 1916. A passing Tommy pulled him out by the feet.

Contacts made in hospital gave him entrée into the newspaper world. Bolitho acted as Paris correspondent for the Manchester *Guardian,* and as special European correspondent sent dispatches to the New York *World,* which brought him to New York in 1928-29 to write a tri-weekly column for the newspaper's then famous "opposite editorial" page. The *Literary Review* called him "a man of sinewy mind who writes upon current topics with a depth of insight and vigor of intellect that combine to make his articles literature instead of merely ephemeral journalism." One of the very few writers who could retell the story of a famous crime with accuracy, clarity, and real psychological intelligence, Bolitho wrote a study of five mass-murderers—Burke, Troppmann, George Joseph Smith, Landru, and Fritz Haarmann—in his *Murder for Profit,* which ranks in quality with similar works by William Roughead, Tennyson Jesse, H. B. Irving, and Edmund Pearson. *Leviathan (England-France)* and *Italy Under Mussolini* proved his quality as a political commentator; his *Twelve Against the Gods* is a collection of unusual biographical studies. Most of his writing was done on the Bolitho estate, La Prefête, near Avignon at Montfavet in southern France, which his wife, who came of an old Viennese family living in London, helped to make an English garden oasis. His eyes, writes Mrs.

Bolitho, were his only beauty, with their metallic, jewel-like blue; his hair was "neither quite gold nor quite red"; he had a strong Afrikaans accent; and "a biggish nose," says Noel Coward, "which he had a trick of whacking with his finger when he wished to emphasize some particular point." Bolitho died at Avignon in his fortieth year of peritonitis following an operation for appendicitis; his body was cremated. A posthumous play, *Overture,* was produced in New York in December 1930, and a final gleaning of his articles, *Camera Obscura,* had a preface by Coward. The beginnings of a novel, published in Mrs. Bolitho's book, show distinct promise.

PRINCIPAL WORKS: Leviathan (England-France) 1924; Italy Under Mussolini, 1926; Murder for Profit, 1926; Twelve Against the Gods, 1929; Camera Obscura, 1931.

ABOUT: Bolitho, S. My Shadow As I Pass, Twelve Against the Gods (see Introduction by A. Woollcott to 1941 ed.); Broun, H. C. Collected Edition; Coward, N. Present Indicative; Slocombe, G. The Tumult and the Shouting; London Mercury July 1930; New York Times June 4, 5, 1930; Saturday Review of Literature July 12, 1930.

BONE, DAVID WILLIAM (1874-), Scottish naval officer and writer on the sea, was born in Partick, near Glasgow, Scotland, a son of David Drummond Bone, a well-known Glasgow journalist, whose great-grandfather was a boyhood companion of Robert Burns. Muirhead Bone, the famous etcher, is David Bone's brother, and illustrated his *Merchantmen-at-Arms* (1919), a history of the British Merchants' Service during the First World War, which appeared in a revised edition ten years later. David Bone went to sea at fifteen as an apprentice in the "City of Florence," an old-time square rigger, and has been at sea ever since. After seven years under sail, he joined the Anchor Line in 1899 and was promoted to a command in 1915. He was master of the S.S. "Columbia," which carried passengers between the Clyde and the Hudson rivers for twenty years. Bone began contributing articles on seafaring life to journals in 1900. In 1910 he published *The Brassbounder,* which his close friend Christopher Morley has called "a classic of the square-sail era." *Broken Stowage,* five years later, is a collection of sea sketches. Bone also wrote a preface to a book by another friend and fellow-mariner, Felix Riesenberg, *Under Sail.* In 1902 he married Mary Helen Bell Cameron of Edinburgh; they have a son and daughter and live at Athole Gardens in Glasgow. At sixty-six Captain Bone lists his recreations as yacht-

ing, golf, and country life. Morley, who calls *Merchantmen-at-Arms* "a book of enthralling power and truth," ends his essay on David Bone's work with the conclusion that "in the long roll of great writers who have reflected the simplicity and severity of sea life, Captain Bone will take a permanent and honorable place."

PRINCIPAL WORKS: The Brassbounder, 1910; Broken Stowage, 1915; Merchantmen-at-Arms, 1919; The Lookoutman, 1923; Capstan Bars, 1931.

ABOUT: Morley, C. Modern Essays: First Series.

*BONSELS, WALDEMAR (February 21, 1881-), German nature writer, reports: "My ancestry is mixed Norman French, Dutch, German, and Frisian. My mother came from Denmark. I was born in Ahrensburg, near Hamburg. My childhood and early youth I passed in the country. My father's restless life made us change our residence often, wandering from one city  to another. Even when I was already going to school, my father went back to the university to study for a new profession. I studied at the gymnasium at Kiel, but mostly managed to stay away from classes and ramble around in the country without being caught. I held out until the end of my junior year, an effort due mostly to my father's insistence. All in all, the recollections of my childhood and youth are full of pleasant memories and happy days. This was entirely due to my mother, who seemed to think that the whole aim of her life was centered in me.

"After school I was sent out to learn a number of trades. These apprenticeships taught me at least one good thing, the ability to keep away from all such occupation as I could not bring into harmony with my disposition and destiny. My father did his best to suppress these qualities in me, so much so that on a night in 1898, at seventeen, I left home and started on a tramping career. Out of my restless and sometimes dangerous journeys through Germany, I remember only a few faces. I remember best that I read Dostoievsky and the Gospels, Schiller, and a tremendous lot of poor fiction which, happily, I have since forgotten.

"By means which I had better not mention, I managed to leave Europe for Asia. When

* Died August 1, 1952.

I was in India, where I spent a long time, just as I had previously spent considerable time in Egypt, I pondered on many things, but I never once thought of becoming a writer. My verses, written in this period, I hated heartily, and none of them has survived.

"I married very early, and the marriage did not last long. I returned to Germany in 1905. And then, as I found myself alone again in the world, I decided to write. My first story was privately printed in 1906. I married again, and from my two marriages I have four sons."

* * *

Where Waldemar Bonsels is now, or what has been his fate since the present war began, is unknown. When the above sketch was written he was living in Ambach, in Bavaria, on the Starnberger See. He was immensely popular in pre-Nazi Germany, so much so that an anthology of his best passages was published in 1924. No work by him has been translated into English since 1931.

Bonsels' travels took him all over Europe, and to the United States, Turkey, and Ceylon as well as to India and Egypt. He is a poet in prose, a highly mystical nature-lover, who does not always avoid sentimentality. The finest of his work, however, has given him a secure niche in his small and special field. Some of his works, such as *Indian Journey* and *The Adventures of Maya the Bee*, have become minor classics in their own time.

WORKS AVAILABLE IN ENGLISH: The Adventures of Maya the Bee, 1922; Heaven Folk, 1922; Indian Journey, 1928; The Adventures of Mario, 1930; Notes of a Vagabond, 1931.

ABOUT: Adler, F. Waldemar Bonsels (in German); Eloesser, A. Modern German Literature; Rheinfurth, K. Der Neue Mythus: Waldemar Bonsels und Sein Werk; Saturday Review of Literature July 7, 1928.

BOOTHE, CLARE (April 10, 1903-   ), American playwright, was born in New York, her name originally being Ann Clare Booth. Her childhood was spent in Memphis, where her father, William F. Booth owned a soft drink factory; in Chicago; and, after her parents were divorced and her mother, Ann (Snyder) Booth, was married again to Dr. A. E. Austin, in Greenwich, Conn. She was educated at private schools. In her girlhood she ran away from home and got a job with a New York company manufacturing paper novelties; an attack of appendicitis ended the experience. In 1923 she married George

Tuttle Brokaw, a wealthy New Yorker. They had one daughter, Ann. In 1929 they were divorced. Mrs. Brokaw was dissatisfied with a purely social life, and succeeded in securing a position on *Vanity Fair*; by 1932 she was managing editor. It was at this time that she published her only novel, a satire on the New York society which she had known during her marriage. She  wrote during this period under the name of Clare Boothe Brokaw.

From childhood, when she "produced" her first play at the age of ten, the theatre had interested her. The first play of her mature years, *Abide With Me*, a study of a sadistic psychopath, was produced in 1935, by which time she had left *Vanity Fair* and had held her only public position, on the N.R.A. Theatre Code. The play was a failure and her next one, which was to make her famous, was in a very different vein. In this same year she was married to Henry R. Luce, editor-in-chief of *Time, Life,* and *Fortune*. They live in New York in the winter, but she does her writing mostly in the summer, on their 7,000-acre ranch in South California, where she has erected a startlingly modern but beautiful house.

In 1937 *The Women*, which had 657 performances in New York, showed that Clare Boothe had at last found her own *métier*. Since she is independently wealthy, the critical success of the play meant more to her than the financial returns, and she donated the first six months' royalties to the Dramatists' Guild. In 1938-39 *Kiss the Boys Goodbye* was taken by audiences to be a travesty on the search for a movie Scarlett O'Hara to play in *Gone With the Wind*, but was surprisingly announced by Miss Boothe in the preface to the printed edition to be really a warning of the imminence of Fascism in America. (The fact that the play had mercilessly pilloried the well-loved liberal columnist Heywood Broun made Miss Boothe's assertion doubly baffling.) *Margin for Error*, produced in 1939, was a mystery melodrama with some contemporary political overtones.

Clare Boothe has been called "the most beautiful living playwright." She is a blonde, with a high, musical voice. She is temperamentally a strange mixture—ambitious, executive, with a genius for organization, ultra-sophisticated, yet calm, patient, and oddly unsure of herself and dependent on approval of her work by others. She has made many and vindictive enemies, especially among those who feel she has caricatured them and their friends. That is to be expected, in view of the nature of her work. She is lacking in plot sense or inventiveness, but her dialogue, with its "undeviating malice, snap, and brutality," is unerring, and if her characters are mere figures in a cartoon, it is a brilliant cartoon. Milton Mackaye remarked of her: "She writes of the rich and for the rich—but she always gives them hell. . . . Her women are sluts, backbiters, or dumb-bells, her men are androgynes, lechers, or sots." This is her chosen *milieu,* and no one could move about in it with more accomplished grace or with more deadly perception.

PRINCIPAL WORKS: Stuffed Shirts (novel) 1931; The Women, 1937; Kiss the Boys Goodbye, 1939; Margin for Error, 1940; Europe in the Spring (non-fiction) 1940.

ABOUT: Ladies' Home Journal November 1938; Life May 27, June 3, 1940; New York Times October 13, 1940; New Yorker January 4, 11, 1941; Scribner's Magazine March 1939; Time November 13, 1939.

BORDEAUX, HENRY (January 29, 1870-), French novelist, was born at Thonon-les-Bains, Haute-Savoie. It is to be noted that he spells his first name in the E n g l i s h, not the French, manner. He began his career as an attorney, and practi c e d from 1890 to 1900, at Paris. He was married in 1901, and has three daughters. He served in the First World War

from the beginning, becoming the equivalent of a major, and receiving two citations for bravery, Commandership of the Legion of Honor, and decorations from Greece, Italy, Sweden, Belgium, and Rumania. He has been a member of the French Academy since 1919, and has been given an honorary doctorate by the University of Montreal. He received the Bordin and Monyon prizes of the French Institute. He has traveled a good deal, notably on a long tour of the Orient, which gave rise to three books. Besides his novels, he has published travel books, biographies, and works of dramatic criticism—a hundred volumes in all. For many years he was a regular contributor to the *Echo de Paris.* In time of peace he has spent his summers in his native Savoy, where his chief recreations, even at seventy, are motoring and mountain-climbing. His seventieth birthday was marked by a national observance and the publication of a book containing eulogies on his work contributed by many of the most noted critics of France, and by his old neighbors in his native province.

As a novelist, M. Bordeaux has been immensely popular both in France and abroad, as much for his subject-matter and viewpoint as for his style. He is not a great artist, but he has the art of reaching and pleasing the great mass of serious-minded middle-class readers. Deeply religious and ethical, he is, as Frederick L. Green remarked, "social and didactic. . . . His favorite theme is the solidarity of the family, regarded as the social unit." He is noted for his devotion to his own three daughters, and is personally a man of great charm and sweetness of nature. His novels are sometimes heavy-handed and moralistic, but they contain also passages of real beauty; he is at his best when he deals with nature or with his travels. At his reception into the Academy, Henri de Régnier rightly called him "a moralist-novelist," and he himself has given as his literary creed: "One serves one's family, one's country, God, art, science, an ideal. Shame to him who serves only himself."

Since the fall of France in 1940, Bordeaux' moralistic attribution of blame for the debacle has led him into close association with French writers of Fascist tendencies.

WORKS AVAILABLE IN ENGLISH: *Novels*—The Parting of the Ways, 1911; The Woollen Dress, 1912; Footprints Beneath the Snow, 1913; The Fear of Living, 1913; The Awakening (in another translation: The Mind Awakened) 1914; The House, 1914; The Will To Live, 1914; The House That Died, 1922; The Gardens of Omar, 1924; Which Was the Greater Love? 1930; Annette and Philibert: The New Children's Crusade, 1932. *Miscellaneous*—Georges Guynemer: Knight of the Air, 1918; Saint Francis de Sales: Theologian of Love, 1929; Shattered (play, in Best One-Act Plays of 1933) 1934; Palestine, 1939.

ABOUT: Bordeaux, H. Le Calvaire de Cimiez (see Foreword by L. Descavez); Bordeaux, P., M., & C. (ed.). Hommage à Henry Bordeaux; Annales Poltiques et Littéraires June 1, 1929; Catholic World January 1920; Nuova Antologia June 16, 1929.

BORDEN, MARY (1886-), Anglo-American novelist, was born in Chicago, the daughter of William Borden. She was graduated from Vassar College in 1908, and was married soon after, the marriage later ending in divorce. She then made a tour around the world, ending in England and France, and she has never since lived in the United States, though she has since visited her native country occasionally. At the outbreak of the First World War she was in France, and she remained there from 1915 to 1918, equipping and directing a mobile hospital at the front. In recognition of her services to the French Army, she received medals from both France and England, including the Croix de Guerre and was made a member of the Legion of Honor. In 1918 she was married to Brigadier-General Edward Louis Spears, of the British Army, and since then has lived in London, all her books being first published there. There are four children in the Spears family. She is a British subject, and by now is more

English than American; she is an adherent of the Church of England, takes an interest in English politics, and is one of the best known and most brilliant of London hostesses. Nevertheless, she has not forgotten her childhood in America, and the old family homestead in Indiana appears in more than one of her novels.

Mary Borden did not begin her career as a novelist until after the war, her first book, *The Romantic Woman*, appearing in 1919. In addition to her novels, she writes frequently for the magazines in England and the United States, contributing both stories and articles. The latter often deal with the social and temperamental differences and likenesses between the people of her old country and her new, a theme which she is unusually well fitted to handle.

Very distinguished in appearance, with clear-cut, delicate features, Mary Borden has the characteristics of her present *milieu* rather than of the roaring Chicago of the 1880's. She is conservative, retiring, and extremely reserved. Her novels, however, reveal perspicuity, keen observation, and a quiet but devastating wit. They reveal also a warm sympathy which underlies their cleverness. She has, both in life and in her writing, a distaste for emotionalism and for lack of self-control—bred by her early experiences with the more excitable evangelical religious sects, which inspired her with a life-long horror of violent emotion. She is, however, deeply religious on another plane, and several of her books have had backgrounds drawn from the history of Christianity. Others deal with the two societies she

has known best—that of the Middle West of yesterday, and of the British and French aristocracy of today. A favorite subject, as in her articles, is the impact of Old World civilization on a woman of the New World, a theme dear also to Henry James, whom Miss Borden resembles often in outlook—though never in her style, which is subtle but direct. Among her books is a volume of essays and poems arising from her experiences in the war.

PRINCIPAL WORKS: The Romantic Woman, 1919; Jane, Our Stranger, 1922; Three Pilgrims and a Tinker, 1924; Jericho Sands, 1925; Four O'Clock, 1926; Flamingo, 1927; Jehovah's Day, 1928; The Forbidden Zone (essays and poems) 1929; A Woman With White Eyes, 1930; Sarah Gay, 1931; Mary of Nazareth, 1933; The Technique of Marriage, 1933; The King of the Jews, 1935; Action for Slander, 1936; Strange Week-End (in England: The Black Virgin) 1938; Passport for a Girl, 1939.

ABOUT: Saturday Review of Literature January 29, 1938.

*BORGESE, GIUSEPPE ANTONIO

(November 12, 1882-   ), Italian-American novelist, scholar, and critic, writes: "I was born in Polizzi Gene-

Moffet

rosa, a little town in the mountains of Sicily, the third child of a provincial lawyer and humanist and of his humble wife. Necessity separated me from my parents soon; I lived in Palermo with uncles and aunts from 1888 to 1900; the regular studies were completed in Florence (Ph.D. 1903). Years of unplanned apprenticeship took me to Naples, the Lombard Lakes, Berlin, and Turin. In Turin I was appointed literary editor of the daily *La Stampa,* and married a Florentine poetess, Maria Freschi, by whom I had two children. The elder, Leonardo, is a painter and writer in Italy. Tolstoy and De Sanctis, the great liberal historian of literature, had been the masters of my Sicilian adolescence. D'Annunzio and Croce took their place for a short while in Florence. Goethe became the constant companion of my maturer youth and of later years. In politics, after a brief spell of reactionary nationalism (1904-08), I returned to liberal and markedly progressive convictions, from which I was not to deflect any more. Likewise, sentimental inclinations toward the Catholicism of my ancestry were held in check and finally over-

* Died December 4, 1952.

come by the desire for a rational and universal religion.

"Criticism and aesthetics, however, were the main concerns of my youth until the World War. A *History of Romantic Criticism in Italy* (1905) was my first book, published by Croce. It was followed by hundreds of essays and articles on Italian and European literatures. Many of them, after having appeared in the *Corriere della Sera* of Milan or in other periodicals, were collected in volumes. A book on d'Annunzio (1909) put an end to the short-lived cult for the alluring *mauvais maître*. An essay on *Faust* tried to give evidence of the intellectual and structural unity in Goethe's capital work. The essays in which I opposed the fragmentism and intuitionalism of Croce's philosophy were collected much later (1934), together with a more recent outline of aesthetics and a summary of history of criticism, under the title of *A Poetics of Unity*.

"The World War, which I could observe closely as an officer on the fronts and as a diplomat in France and Switzerland, released the long suppressed urge toward imagination and poetry. Novels, plays, short stories, poems, appeared in the following decade, together with work in criticism, in aesthetics, in politics, with translations from Goethe and Chamisso, and with an historical reconstruction of the *Tragedy of Mayerling*. But the war and its aftermath also brought me to a direct contact with politics. As head of the Press and Propaganda Bureau under Orlando's premiership, as organizer of the Roman Congress in April 1918, as chief delegate of the Italian Government to the Interallied Conference in London, in August 1918, and finally as foreign editor of the *Corriere dell Sera*, I developed whatever action I could in favor of a unified and democratic Europe on a parallel line with Wilson's intention. This record and the general trend of my thought were not apt to make of me a *persona grata* to the Fascist régime.

"I had been professor of German literature at the University of Rome (1910-17), and taught German literature and later aesthetics at the University of Milan. I lived in Milan from 1919 to 1931, in circumstances which the growth of Fascism made increasingly difficult. In 1931 I came to America, at first as visiting professor at the University of California. The Fascist oath which was soon after forced on all Italian professors and which I refused, changed my temporary residence in the United States into a permanent allegiance. In the years following I taught at Dr. Johnson's New School in New

York and as Neilson professor at Smith College; since 1936 I have been professor of Italian literature at the University of Chicago, giving also courses in the department of political science. My work, essays or books, is now written in English. *Goliath: The March of Fascism,* published in 1937, has been translated into several languages, although not yet into Italian. In 1938 I became an American citizen. At the end of 1939 I married Elizabeth, daughter of Thomas Mann. I am writing now a drama in verse on the conquest of Mexico for the American composer, Roger Sessions.

"Unity, across all separations, has been the leading inspiration of my life and work —beyond and against the disintegration, ethical, aesthetic, and social, of contemporary man. To this inspiration I hope to devote whatever is left of time and vigor to me."

* * *

This autobiographical sketch is sufficient evidence of Professor Borgese's command of English. W. Y. Elliott called him "a master of literary style, balanced, profound, . . . with the subtlety of the best Italian scholarship, and prose astonishingly crisp and beautiful. An exile, unlike Dante in many ways, he yet savors the bitter bread and has been nourished to a great work."

Works Available in English: Rubè (novel) 1923; On Dante Criticism, 1936; Goliath: or, The March of Fascism, 1937.

About: Boyd, E. Studies From Ten Literatures; Drake, W. A. Contemporary European Writers; Palmieri, E. G. A. Borgese (in Italian); American Scholar Spring 1938, Winter 1940; Nation October 13, 1928; Nuova Antologia April 16, 1930; Revue des Deux Mondes September 1, 1921; Vital Speeches June 15, 1940; Yale Review Winter 1938.

BOTTOME, PHYLLIS (May 31, 1884-), English novelist, was born in Rochester, Kent, the daughter of the Rev. William Macdonald Bottome, an American clergyman from New York, and Mary (Leatham) Bottome, from a village named for her family, Leatham, Yorkshire. From nine to sixteen she lived in America, while her father was minister of Grace  Church, in Jamaica, Long Island. As a girl she had stage ambitions, and was studying in a dramatic school when she contracted tuberculosis. A cure at Davos, Switzerland, was successful, but ended any hope of becoming an actress. Instead, she took to writing, and her first novel, written when she was only seventeen, was promptly accepted by Andrew Lang, then a publisher's reader. Until the World War, she spent her winters in England, her summers in Italy.

In 1914 and 1915 she was a relief worker in Belgium, and in 1916 she wrote special articles under the direction of the Ministry of Munitions. Before her illness she had been engaged to marry A. E. Forbes-Dennis, but had broken the engagement because of her health. Now, fully recovered, she met him again, and in 1917 they were married. He was then an officer at the front, and before the war was over he was severely wounded. When he was well again he was appointed Intelligence Officer at Marseilles, and after the Armistice became Passport Control Officer in Vienna. This was invaluable experience for a novelist, for Miss Bottome was brought into contact with almost every sort of human being in those moments of stress when character reveals itself. In Vienna, in the terrible days following the war, she organized food depots for relief of the starving people. Whenever possible she went to Italy for a few months of recuperation and rest, and when the emergency was over she and her husband made their permanent home in a châlet in the Austrian Tyrol, where, surrounded by her dogs, and in what was then the peace of a beautiful valley, she was able to concentrate on her writing. In Italy also they owned a house on Lago d'Orta, in Novara.

Now Miss Bottome's official home is in London, though she has lately been in Hollywood, supervising production of the filming of one of her novels. Although she had not visited America for nearly forty years, she had always felt close to it, and as if she "had never altogether left it." In recent years, she has become very much interested in psychology and in the modified psychoanalytic system of Dr. Alfred Adler, whose biography she wrote; *Private Worlds* is an outgrowth of that interest. A liberal and anti-Fascist, she has written in *The Mortal Storm* one of the strongest of many novels exposing the working of the Nazi régime.

Phyllis Bottome's work is uneven, but at its best it merits the praise of Clarice Lorenz Aiken, who spoke of her "subtlety, brilliant force, exquisite grace and impeccable taste, and calm astuteness." She is especially successful in short stories, written with what another critic called "masculine vigor and directness." She herself has expressed her literary creed in these words: "If a writer is true to his characters they will give him his plot. . . . Observation must play second fiddle to integrity. . . . The mind of the artist should shine out at us, without the blur of personal proclivities."

Miss Bottome is a distinguished looking woman, with beautiful white hair, thick black eyebrows, and vivid dark eyes. She is slender, with an oval face expressing both delicacy and forcefulness.

PRINCIPAL WORKS: Raw Material, 1905; Broken Music, 1907; The Dark Tower, 1909; The Crystal Heart, 1911; Old Wine, 1920; Belated Reckoning, 1925; Plain Case, 1928; Strange Fruit (short stories) 1928; Windlestraws, 1929; Tatter'd Loving, 1929; Wind in His Fists, 1931; Devil's Due, 1931; The Advances of Harriet, 1933; Private Worlds, 1934; Innocence and Experience, 1935; Level Crossing, 1936; The Mortal Storm, 1937; Danger Signal (in America: Murder in the Bud) 1939; Alfred Adler: Apostle of Freedom (in America: Alfred Adler) 1939; The Heart of a Child, 1940; Masks and Faces, 1940; The Mansion House of Liberty, 1941; London Pride, 1941.

ABOUT: Bookman October 1932; Publishers' Weekly June 23, 1934.

*BOTTOMLEY, GORDON (February 20, 1874-), English poet, was born at the manufacturing town of Keighley, Yorkshire, the son of Alfred Bottomley and his wife Maria (Gordon) Bottomley, and educated at the Keighley Grammar School. From the age of nineteen his health was poor. He did not pass on to a university, but soon began to write poetry and has devoted the whole of his life to this art. "I have no biography," he once told R. L. Mégroz; "there is nothing that ever happened to me." Quite early in life he settled in the North Lancashire region, not far from the Scottish border and the Lake District, at Silverdale; and it was from a printing house at Kendal, in Lakeland, that he privately issued his first volume, *The Mickle Drede and Other Verses*, in 1896. Only 150 copies of this book were run off; and only 500 of a second book of verses, in 1899— a publication which he later thought immature and withdrew as far as possible.

With *The Crier by Night* (1902) and *The Riding to Lithend* (1909) Bottomley began what has been perhaps the main task of his life, namely the revival of English verse drama. He has never lost sight of the fact that verse was originally written for declamation, and has always striven to produce metrical work lending itself to such treatment. Some of his short verse dramas, like *The Singing Sands, The Widow,* and *Ardvorlich's Wife* are specifically designed for performance in ordinary small rooms without any scenery.

Bottomley has drawn much of his inspiration from Scandinavian and Scottish sources. He is president of the Scottish Community Drama Association and is highly interested in the work of the Scottish Association for the Speaking of Verse. In 1915 he dared greatly by producing *King Lear's Wife,* a prelude to Shakespeare's play, and followed it in 1921 with *Gruach,* which was a similar treatment of *Macbeth.* This latter won him the Femina-Vie Heureuse Prize in 1923. So sound and sober a judge as the late Lascelles Abercrombie hailed these venturesome pieces with enthusiasm, saying: ". . . it has become clear now that at no time in the history of English poetry since the seventeenth century has the requisite combination of dramatic and poetic talents existed until now in the person of Mr. Bottomley."

In 1925 Bottomley was awarded the Arthur Benson Medal of the Royal Society of Literature. A year later he became a Fellow of that Society, and witnessed a very successful performance of *King Lear's Wife* at the Festival Theatre, Cambridge. In 1930 the University of Aberdeen conferred on him an honorary Doctorate in Laws.

Bottomley is a skilled metrist, ringing the changes on a large variety of forms. A solemn or tragic note runs through a great deal of his work, and he has produced few "songs of joy." Opportunity for the recital of many of his works has been provided by the Oxford Recitations. In his poetic dramas he has sometimes turned for technical devices to the Japanese Nō theatre.

Bottomley is a heavily bearded figure who lives remotely in his country home and takes no part in social life. All observers speak of his great personal charm, his courage under disability, and his all-pervasive love of literature. In 1905 he married Emily, youngest daughter of Mr. Matthew Burton, of Arnside, a village near his Silverdale home.

PRINCIPAL WORKS: *Poems*—The Mickle Drede, 1896; Poems at White-Nights, 1899; The Gate of Smaragdus, 1904; Chambers of Imagery (2 series) 1907, 1912; A Vision of Giorgione, 1910; Poems of Thirty Years, 1925; Festival Preludes, 1930. *Verse Dramas*—The Crier by Night, 1902; Midsummer Eve, 1905; The Riding to Lithend, 1909; Laodice and Danaë, 1909; King Lear's Wife, 1915; (all foregoing in one volume, 1920); Gruach, and

Britain's Daughter, 1921; Scenes and Plays, 1929; Lyric Plays, 1932; The Acts of Saint Peter, 1933; Choric Plays and a Comedy, 1939.

ABOUT: Agate, J. The Contemporary Theatre; Bush, D. Mythology and the Romantic Tradition in English Poetry; Lucas, F. L. Authors, Dead and Living; Monro, H. Some Contemporary Poets; Morgan, A. E. Tendencies of Modern English Drama; Newbolt, H. New Paths on Helicon; Thouless, P. Modern Poetic Drama; Williams-Ellis, A. An Anatomy of Poetry.

BOURGET, PAUL CHARLES JO-SEPH (September 2, 1852-December 25, 1935), French novelist, dramatist, and essayist, was born in Amiens, son of a mathematics instructor.
When seven he decided to write a work on entomology, having inherited from his father, he believed, his scientific bent, and from his mother, of German descent, his poetic and metaphysical leanings. His first reading matter was a  two-volume Shakespeare in French, the only literary material in the household, which served to raise little Paul to table. The boy learned his first letters at Strasbourg, began his classical studies at Clermont, and finished them in Paris. In 1867, upon reading *Père Goriot,* Bourget decided to emulate Balzac. After completing his studies at the Lycée Louis le Grand he took his licenciate degree in 1872, tried Greek philology at the École des Hautes Études and briefly attended the Hôtel Dieu medical school clinic.

His allowance cut off because he refused to continue preparing for the teaching profession, Bourget worked as tutor first at Reusse's school and in 1874 at Lelarge's, where his colleagues included Brunetière. Worshipping Musset, Victor Hugo and Sully Prudhomme, the young man numbered mostly poets among his friends—Coppée, Richepin, Barbey d'Aurevilly. In 1875 his first volume of poems appeared: *La Vie Inquiète.* Three years later he published a novel in verse, *Edel,* so highly praised by the critics, especially Jules Lemaître, that the *Revue des Deux Mondes* asked Bourget for an article on the younger poets.

From his twenty-seventh year Bourget began to contribute regularly to *Le Journal des Débats,* and to *Le Globe* and *Revue des Deux Mondes* as dramatic critic. At the salons of Madam Adam he met Alexandre Dumas *fils,* Leconte de Lisle, Turgenev, and

Taine (whose lectures had thrilled him as a boy). By 1880 he had arrived; everything he wrote went to press. He gave up tutoring, traveled in Italy, Spain and England from 1880 to 1884, writing popular travel sketches along the way.

Turning gradually from poetry to criticism, Bourget from 1880 on wrote his famous essays on Baudelaire, Flaubert, Renan, and Stendhal which appeared in *La Nouvelle Revue Française* and later in his book *Essais de Psychologie Contemporaine,* described by Abbé Dimnet as "a satisfactory picture of the French mind under the Second Empire."

In May 1883, "in a small room at Oxford, a few steps from the old Worcester College haunted by Thomas de Quincey's ghost," says Bourget, "I began my first novel, *L'Irreparable.*" *L'Irreparable* was rather a long short story. His first real novel, *A Cruel Enigma* (1885) was the success of the year, and from it Bourget's reputation dates. Thenceforth he wrote novels in the same vein year after year until *The Disciple,* which "marked a change in the author's point of view from detached psychologist to convinced moralist." *The Disciple* has been said to mark an important date in the intellectual and moral history of France. The book caused a sensation, battles raged over it, the most celebrated of which was the debate between Anatole France and Brunetière.

In 1890, Bourget married a Mlle. David of Antwerp and left for Italy. A prolific writer, Bourget produced one novel after another; and his "naturalism in fine clothes," as Lemaître called it, became all the rage. In 1895 he visited the United States, to be lampooned by Mark Twain in the *North American Review* ("What Paul Bourget Thinks of Us") and defended by Max O'Reall in the same magazine ("Mark Twain and Paul Bourget").

After 1902, the year of his much discussed novel *L'Étape,* Bourget tried his hand at the drama and had a great success in 1910 with *La Barricade* and in 1911 with *Le Tribun.*

Bourget's last really important work (begun 1916) was *Nos Actes Nous Suivent* (1927). After 1927 he wrote several novels showing his preoccupation with the contemporary scene, especially as it concerns the modern young woman. *Agnès Délas* (1928), for instance, deals with a woman bank employee, *La Rechute* (1929) with the relations between an aviator and a girl law student; *Le Louveteau* (1931) analyzes the mentality of a boy scout, and *Une Laboran-*

tine takes up the women who work in medical laboratories. *L'Adoptée* describes the life of two girl students at the School of Political Science.

Bourget was admitted to the French Academy in 1895 (occupying the famous thirty-third *fauteuil,* previously occupied by Voiture, Voltaire, and Maxime du Champ) and was an Officer of the Legion of Honor. In 1923 his friends gathered in Balzac's house on the Rue Raynouard to offer him a beautiful plaquette of himself by Paul Roussel. The grand prix Orisis was awarded him in 1930, and two years later literary France celebrated his eightieth birthday.

Poor health prevented Bourget from completing the novel which might have been the crowning achievement of his life—*Croire.* Early Christmas morning, 1935, he died of pneumonia, at eighty-three. He was buried in Montparnasse Cemetery, not far from his friend Guy de Maupassant, simply, as he had requested, without flowers or flowery speeches.

Most of Bourget's best work was completed before the turn of the century. Had he died in middle age, he would doubtless be classified in fact—as he is in spirit—as a nineteenth century man-of-letters. It is chiefly the circumstance of his long life which gives him place in a volume devoted to twentieth century authors.

PRINCIPAL WORKS AVAILABLE IN ENGLISH TRANSLATION: A Cruel Enigma, 1887 (also as Love's Cruel Enigma, 1891); A Love Crime, 1887 (also as Was It Love? 1891); André Cornelis, 1887 (also as The Son, 1893; as The Story of André Cornelis, 1914; as Sins of Desire, 1930); Lies, 1892 (also as A Living Lie, 1896; as Our Lady of Lies, 1910); The Disciple, 1898; A Woman's Heart, 1891; Pastels of Men, 1891 (also as A Saint, 1895); Impressions of Italy, 1892; Cosmopolis, 1893; Outre Mer: Impressions of America, 1895; The Land of Promise, 1895; A Tragic Idyll, 1896; Antigone and Other Portraits of Women, 1898 (also as Some Portraits of Women, 1898); Domestic Dramas, 1900; The Screen, 1901; The Blue Duchess, 1902; Monica and Other Stories, 1902; Divorce: A Domestic Tragedy of Modern France, 1904; The Weight of a Name, 1908; Two Sisters, 1912; The Night Cometh, 1916; The Gaol, 1924.

ABOUT: Bacourt, P. de & Cunliffe, J. W. French Literature During the Last Half Century; Bowman, E. M. The Early Novels of Paul Bourget; Dimnet, E. Paul Bourget (Modern Biographies); Drake, W. A. Contemporary European Literature; Ellis, H. Views and Previews; Feuillerat, A. Paul Bourget; Gosse, E. French Profiles; Guerard, A. L. Five Masters of French Romance; La Due, W. C. Paul Bourget and the French Roman à Thèse; Ross, F. E. Goethe in Modern France; Saueracken, J. Bourget und der Naturalismus; Stephens, W. French Novelists of Today; Turquet-Milnes, G. Some Modern French Writers; Bookman May 1931; Contemporary Review December 1927; Living Age September 4, 1926.

BOURNE, RANDOLPH SILLIMAN

(May 30, 1886-December 22, 1918), American essayist, was born in Bloomfield, New

Jersey, the son of Charles and Sara Randolph (Barrett) Bourne. An accident in childhood left him badly deformed; he never appeared in public unless wrapped in a large cape, and was barely able to get about. His spirit was

Bloomfield Public Library

unbroken, however, and within his three decades he accomplished more than many who lacked his handicap.

After a year as a proof-reader of music, he entered Columbia (B.A. 1912, M.A. 1913), and then on a scholarship spent a year in London and Paris. He had been a contributor to the *Atlantic Monthly* from 1911, and in 1913 his first volume, a book of essays called *Youth and Life,* was published. He was on the staff of the *New Republic* from its inception, in 1914, and was a contributing editor also of the *Dial* and the *Seven Arts,* until the latter was suppressed by the government during the First World War because of its pacifist tendencies.

Bourne's first interest was in progressive education, on which he wrote two books, under the influence of John Dewey. The war found in him a voice of protest, one of the most powerful of the time, though his disabilities might have provided an easy excuse for his remaining aloof from so dangerous a position. He was the spokesman in chief of the young anti-war radicals of 1914 to 1918. At the time of his death, during the great influenza epidemic of 1918, he was engaged in writing a history of conscientious objection to war in the United States. In 1916 he had compiled a symposium, *Towards a Lasting Peace.*

Bourne was a seminal influence. His conversation is said to have been even more stimulating than his written words. Men of his own generation, young with him, who came under his influence (*e.g.,* Van Wyck Brooks, Bruce Bliven) were profoundly affected by him. His personal misfortunes directed all his energies into intellectual channels, to the enrichment of his associates. It was as if he realized how short a time he had, and poured himself out eagerly. His deformity, which saved him from both draft and imprisonment, gave him freedom to speak out. Survival of the war would have enlarged and perhaps deflected his interests,

but no one can doubt his would have been always a voice for freedom—lonely but finding here and there an echo to carry on his message.

Randolph Bourne never let unhappiness interfere with his life. He was keenly sensitive, and suffered both because of the broken, repulsive body which was his outward form, and because intellectually he was out of tune with almost all the thinkers of his own era. He had dedicated himself, as he himself says, to the bringing of a "fuller, richer life to more people on this earth." As Floyd Dell remarks, in a touching tribute in the *New Republic,* Bourne's outstanding characteristics were "restless and relentless curiosity, . . . the mood of perpetual inquiry, and the courage to go down unfamiliar ways in search of truth." He was a war casualty as surely as, in another way, were Rupert Brooke, Alan Seeger, and Joyce Kilmer.

Considering that he died at thirty-two, Bourne left a full book-shelf to posterity—six finished volumes, besides the compilation, and sufficient material for two more posthumous collections of essays. His was a first-rate mind, triumphing over double and almost insuperable difficulties. American culture lost much when this unhappy, celibate little hunchback was stricken by a disease brought from the very battlefields against which he had raised his lonely rebellious voice.

With the advent of the Second World War, the League of American Writers—then strongly pacifist and non-interventionist—established the Randolph Bourne Memorial Award, to be presented biennially to the American writer who had performed "the most distinguished service for culture and peace." The first award was presented to Theodore Dreiser in 1941.

PRINCIPAL WORKS: Youth and Life, 1913; Arbitration and International Politics, 1913; Impression of Europe: 1913-14, 1914; The Gary Schools, 1916; Education and Living, 1917; Untimely Papers (ed. by J. Oppenheim) 1919; The History of a Literary Radical and other Essays (ed. by Van W. Brooks) 1920.

ABOUT: Bourne, R. History of a Literary Radical; Rosenfeld, P. Port of New York; Bookman October 1922; Dial January 11, 1919, January 1920; New Republic January 4, 1919; Yale Review April 1919.

BOWEN, ELIZABETH

(June 7, 1899-), Anglo-Irish novelist, was born, as Elizabeth Dorothea Cole Bowen, in Dublin, the only child of Henry Cole Bowen and Isabella Pomeroy (Colley) Bowen. On both sides she was of Anglo-Irish descent, the family estate, Bowen's Court, Kilrrery, County Cork, which she still owns, ving been given by Cromwell to one of r ancestors. At seven she was taken to e in the South of England. When she was

twelve her mother died, later her father remarried, and she left home at nineteen. Until, in 1923, she was married to Alan Cameron, she lived alone in London and on the Continent. She describes her youth and her beginnings as a writer:

"When I was fourteen I was sent to arding school at Downe House, in Kent, rmerly Charles Darwin's home [and now e Darwin Memorial Museum]. When I 't school I went to live in Ireland. For e last year of the war I worked in a shell-ock hospital near Dublin. When I was neteen my father let me go back to Eng-nd, or travel, or do—within accepted limits whatever I liked. When I was twenty-one very generously gave me my own money. was not much money, though more than could afford, and I soon found my own st ideas of life had been immoderate. I ed from hand to mouth; I was extravagant, d had to sell or pawn many things I lued. For months together I had to live ry quietly—but this was a good thing, as made me begin to write. I wrote my first ort stories when I was twenty. From the ment that my pen touched paper, I thought nothing but writing, and since then I have ught of practically nothing else. I have en idle for months, or even for a year, at ime; but when I have nothing to write, I l only half alive. I lived in London. pent winters in Italy. One rather awful nter in a hotel at Bordighera—where a oved aunt of mine was wintering and ere I had gone to teach her children— oduced, later, The Hotel."

After her marriage Miss Bowen lived first ar Northampton; in 1926 her husband was pointed to a teaching position at Oxford, I they live now in near-by Old Heading-, in a cottage that was once the stable the village manor house. In times of ce she spends part of every week in a elsea flat in London, and visits Italy yearly. 1931 she inherited the family home in land, and spends part of every summer re. "Very blonde, very near-sighted, tall, unhandsome in a gaunt Anglo-Irish man-," Miss Bowen likes life orderly, loves

small gay parties, enjoys the movies, detective stories, music, and long walks, and is inordinately shy about her own work. She shares with the late Virginia Woolf a position as the most distinguished of contemporary woman novelists in England. Her theme is invariably the upper middle class which she knows best. As Phyllis Bentley has remarked, "her short stories and novels are limited in range, . . . but as regards human emotion they are both deep and wide; there is a poignancy, an intensity, in her presentation of experience."

PRINCIPAL WORKS: Encounters (short stories) 1923; The Hotel, 1927; Ann Lee's and Other Stories, 1928; Joining Charles and Other Stories, 1929; Friends and Relations, 1931; To the North, 1932; The Cat Jumps (short stories) 1934; The House in Paris, 1935; The Death of the Heart, 1938; Bowen's Court, 1941; Look at All These Roses, 1941.

ABOUT: Bowen, E. Bowen's Court; Saturday Review of Literature January 28, 1939; Time March 2, 1936, January 30, 1939.

"BOWEN, MARJORIE." See LONG, G. M. V. C.

BOWER, B. M. (November 15, 1871-July 23, 1940), American woman writer of Western stories—the vast majority of whose readers believed her to be a man—was born Bertha Muzzy in Cleveland, Minn., the daughter of Washington Muzzy and Eunice A. (Miner) Muzzy. She was educated in public schools and under private teachers in Montana, where she

had been taken as a small child by her parents and where she was permitted to roam the Montana ranges and fraternize with cowboys. In 1890, at nineteen, she was married to Clayton J. Bower, and brought up a family of two sons and a daughter.

In 1904 "B. M. Bower" published her first and still one of her best-liked Western romances, Chip of the Flying U, which had less solidity and fewer overtones than Owen Wister's contemporary The Virginian, but had a cheerful humor, lifelike characters, and amusing complications to recommend it. A talking-picture version released in 1939 preserved few of its values. Chip and the Flying U outfit figured in more than one sequel. Its sixty-odd companions were praiseworthy for a good, clear English style, authentic backgrounds, and rapid adventure.

Critics were generally kind to Mrs. Bower. The New York *Herald Tribune*, editorializing on her death, commented: "For all its concessions to unreality, the 'Western' retains its millions of fans throughout the years, and, oddly, the bulk of the market is in the West. These fans are quick to spot a bogus story. . . . This is the reason some of the most successful writers of Western sagas have been men (and a few women) who actually had some first-hand knowledge of what they were writing about. Some of them are former ranch hands. The *aficionados* of sagebrush literature swear by these writers. Mrs. Bower herself passed her early years in Montana, and so was able to give her output a certain authenticity. [Her] death will cause no great upheaval in the steady flow of American literature, but it does remove one of the most successful practitioners of a curious art—an art which is considerably more difficult than most persons imagine."

Mrs. Bower was married twice more; in 1906 to Bertrand W. Sinclair of Edinburgh, Scotland, by whom she had a daughter, Dele Frances Sinclair; and lastly to Robert Ellsworth Cowan of Texas. For some unfathomable reason, the Library of Congress persists in listing her work under "B. M. Sinclair." She lived for a time at De Poe Bay, Ore., but spent the last twenty years of her life at Los Angeles, where she died at nearly sixty-nine. She was a Democrat. One son and two daughters, one in Australia, survived.

PRINCIPAL WORKS: Chip of the Flying U, 1904; The Lure of the Dim Trails, 1907; Her Prairie Knight, 1908; The Lonesome Trail, 1909; The Long Shadow, 1909; The Happy Family, 1910; The Range Dwellers, 1910; Good Indian, 1912; Lonesome Land, 1912; The Uphill Climb, 1913; The Gringos, 1913; The Ranch at the Wolverine, 1914; Flying U Ranch, 1914; Flying U's Last Stand, 1915; Jean of the Lazy A, 1915; The Phantom Herd, 1916; Heritage of the Sioux, 1916; The Lookout Man, 1917; Starr of the Desert, 1917; Cabin Fever, 1918; Skyrider, 1918; The Thunder Bird, 1919; Rim o' the World, 1920; The Quirt, 1920; Cow Country, 1921; Casey Ryan, 1921; Trail of the White Mule, 1922; The Voice at Johnnywater, 1923; The Parowan Bonanza, 1923; The Bellehelen Mine, 1924; Desert Brew; 1924; Meadowlark Basin, 1925; Black Thunder, 1925; White Wolves, 1926; Van Patten, 1926; The Adam Chasers, 1927; Points West, 1928; The Swallowfork Bulls, 1928; Rodeo, 1929; Fool's Goal, 1930; Tiger Eye, 1930; The Long Loop, 1931; Dark Horse, 1931; Laughing Water, 1932; Rocking Arrow, 1932; Trails Meet, 1933; Open Land, 1933; The Flying U Strikes, 1934; The Haunted Hills, 1934; The Dry Ridge Gang, 1935; Trouble Rides the Wind, 1935; The Five Furies of Leaning Ladder, 1935; Shadow Mountain, 1936; The North Wind Do Blow, 1936; Pirates of the Range, 1937; The Wind Blows West, 1938; Starry Night, 1938; The Singing Hill, 1939; The M on Horseback, 1940; Sweet Grass, 1940; The Sp of the Range, 1940; The Family Failing, 1941.

ABOUT: New York Times July 24, 1940; New week August 5, 1940; Publishers' Weekly Aug 3, 1940.

BOWERS, CLAUDE GERNADE (November 20, 1879-), American journali historian, and diplomat, was born in We field, Ind., the son of Lewis Bowers and Juliet Bowers, and was educated in Indianapolis. Taking part in a state oratorical contest, young Bowers chose Alexander Hamilton as his subject, reading up on Jefferson also as a natural corollary.

Harris & Ewi

He won the contest. In 1901-02 he subtuted as editorial writer—he was study law at the time—for a friend on the India apolis *Sentinel* who wanted to go fishing a appealed to Bowers to take his place. Nev paper work proving congenial, he was on Terre Haute *Star* from 1903 to 1906; edi the Fort Wayne *Journal Gazette* from 19 and was editorial writer on the New Y *Evening World* from 1923 to 1931, wl both morning and evening *Worlds* came an end. Bowers transferred to Hear New York *Journal* to write a daily colu

In the interim between Terre Haute : Fort Wayne, Bowers was secretary to U Senator John W. Kern from 1911 to 19 writing a campaign life of the latter in 19 He had himself been an unsuccessful can date for Congress from the Terre Ha District in 1904; attended the Democr National Convention in 1908 as a delega delivered the keynote address to the Del cratic State Convention in 1920; and in 1 acted in a similar capacity at the Natic Convention at Houston, which respon enthusiastically to his spellbinding, ea screaming address of the old-fashioned ty His book, *The Party Battles of the Jack Period* (1925) had led to an invitation speak at the Jackson Day dinner at Wa ington in January 1927. Two years la the Literary Guild made his *The Tragic* one of their 1929 selections. The "pai taking and profuse" documentation of book had been largely procured dur Bowers' lunch hour, when he would d uptown from Park Row to examine ne papers of the 1865-77 period in a spe room at the New York Public Library.

rson and Hamilton (1925) had a sequel, *Jefferson in Power*, eleven years later; H. S. Commager called the latter a brilliant piece [of] special pleading. Of *Beveridge and the Progressive Era* Oswald Garrison Villard [w]rote: "If it is not definitive history but the [ve]ry highest grade of journalistic-historical [wr]iting that Mr. Bowers has given us, it [is] none the less most welcome."

His services to the party have been rec[og]nized by ambassadorships to Spain and [to] Chile, his present post. The Spanish [re]volution gave Ambassador Bowers some [thr]illing times, evacuating Americans from [Sa]n Sebastian; visiting danger spots on the [no]rthern coast on a ship which served as a [flo]ating embassy; setting up a temporary [em]bassy at Hendaye; and searching for [Am]ericans of the Abraham Lincoln Battal[io]n who were lost or killed in action. A [tal]l, thin man with mournful eyes, Mr. Bow[er]s smokes thick black cigars. He married [Si]bil McCaslin in 1911; they have a daugh[ter], Patricia.

PRINCIPAL WORKS: Irish Orators, 1916; Life [of] John Worth Kern, 1918; The Party Battles [of] the Jackson Period, 1922; Jefferson and Hamil[ton], 1925; The Tragic Era, 1929; Beveridge and [the] Progressive Era, 1932; Jefferson in Power, [193]6; The Spanish Adventures of Washington [Irv]ing, 1940.

ABOUT: Literary Digest June 24, 1933; Nation [No]vember 26, 1939; New Outlook May 1934; [Ne]wsweek August 21, 1939; Wilson Library Bul[leti]n October 1936.

[B]OYD, ERNEST AUGUSTUS (June 28, [18]87-), Irish-American critic, was born [in] Dublin, of Scottish, Irish, and Spanish

ancestry. He was privately educated by a French tutor and then went to school in Switzerland and Germany. He is a thorough linguist, speaking fluent French, German, Italian, Spanish, modern Greek and several other tongues. From [191]0 to 1913 he was on the staff of the [Iris]h *Times*, Dublin; then he passed the [com]petitive examinations for the British [Co]nsular Service and served as vice-consul [in] Baltimore, Barcelona, and Copenhagen. [Th]e same year he entered the service, he [ma]rried a Frenchwoman, Madeleine Rey[nie]r; they were divorced later and she pub[lish]ed a novel, a thinly veiled *roman à clef* [dea]ling with their life together.

[Ba]chot

* Died December 30, 1946.

In 1920 Mr. Boyd resigned from the Consular Service and settled permanently in New York, where he now lives. During the First World War he had been accused of being a Sinn Feiner (he was not, though he was sympathetic to the Nationalist cause), and had considerable difficulty in retaining his post.

It was H. L. Mencken, in Baltimore, who first encouraged Mr. Boyd to write. He began by doing translations and critical articles. For two years after his coming to New York he wrote the editorials on foreign politics for the *Evening Post* and also contributed to its *Literary Review*, then edited by Henry Seidel Canby, which grew into the present *Saturday Review of Literature*. He was then for a year a reader and adviser on foreign literature for Alfred A. Knopf, the publisher; for another year read plays for the Theatre Guild; and was literary editor first of the *Independent* and then of the *New Freeman* until both these magazines expired. Since then he has been entirely a free-lance writer and translator.

He is also noted as a *raconteur* and has long been prominent in the social world of literary New York. In his boyhood he was the model for Christ in the Stations of the Cross in the Dublin Cathedral, and he still retains not only his coppery beard, but also his benign and saintly expression—which is belied by his explosive, electric speech and his heavy baritone voice. Benjamin De Casseres, who called him "a fine type of the cultivated, civilized Irish gentleman," described him as sometimes looking "like a pre-Raphaelite Parnell, sometimes like the Victorian Shaw, sometimes like a Titian Nazarene." He always dresses in brown, even in evening clothes. De Casseres added: "His mind is a kind of melting-pot for all the books contained in the world. . . . His style is not the man. It is a style that is deft, sure, studied, low-spoken. His irony is coy. It is even shy at times. But it is always effective in entertaining value."

His scholarship, attested by numerous critical works and many translations from the French (some with his former wife), is undoubted, but he is also an unpredictable, erratic, and emotional critic. As L. B. Hessler remarked of him, "he has no sense of humor and takes his pleasures sadly, even that of fighting. He has a grudge to satisfy." He has immovable prejudices— e.g., that against Milton—and allows no facts to stand in the way of them. However, he is a stimulating and provocative essayist, able to turn his enormous fund of

BOYD

information into sharp and colorful prose.
He is an associate member of the Irish
Academy of Letters. He has translated and
edited all of Maupassant's works in eighteen
volumes.

PRINCIPAL WORKS: Contemporary Drama of
Ireland, 1917; Appreciations and Depreciations,
1917; Ireland's Literary Renaissance, 1922; Por-
traits: Real and Imaginary, 1924; Studies in Ten
Literatures, 1925; H. L. Mencken, 1925; Guy de
Maupassant: A Biographical Study, 1926; Literary
Blasphemies, 1927; After the Fireworks: A
Comedy (with M. Davidson) 1930; The Pretty
Lady, 1934.

ABOUT: Arts and Decoration January 1929;
Bookman July 1931; North American Review
September 1935; Saturday Evening Post March
23, 1940.

*BOYD, JAMES (July 2, 1888-   ), American novelist, was born in Dauphin County,
Pa., the son of John Yeomans Boyd and

Eleanor Gilmore
(Herr) Boyd. He
was educated at the
Hill School, Potts-
town, Pa., Princeton
(B.A. 1910), and
Trinity College, Cam-
bridge. When he was
thirteen the family
moved to North Caro-
lina, the home of his
ancestors, and he has
lived for many years in Southern Pines.
Between Princeton and Cambridge, he
worked for one summer on the Harrisburg,
Pa., *Patriot*. He says of this experience:
"I was dramatic critic one week, sporting
editor another, then human interest writer,
and finally I drew the cartoons." In 1917
he married Katharine Lamont, and they have
two sons and a daughter. He was at this
time on the staff of Doubleday, Page & Co.,
the publishers. During the First World War
he served as first lieutenant in the American Expeditionary Force in France, and
participated in the St. Mihiel and the first
and second Meuse-Argonne offensives. He
returned with shattered health, and was
ordered by his doctors to go South at once.

"I had to do something," he says, "so I
decided to try writing short stories. I tried
all kinds. I believe that imagination has to
be born, but that style is pure craftsmanship.
I decided to give five years to apprenticeship before I either succeeded or gave up.
Then the trial balloons I sent out started
selling."

At this time he met the late John Galsworthy, who was traveling in America.
Galsworthy became interested in his work,

Pinchot

helped him with advice, and made the re
ommendation that American publishers "ke
their eye on James Boyd." His first nov
appeared in 1926. His novels are all h
torical, covering different periods of Ame
can history, and they are notable for th
naturalness and careful realism. They a
solid reconstructions of the past, delineat
with loving fidelity to fact.

In Southern Pines, however, Mr. Bo
is known not as an author but as the Mas
of Hounds and an ardent fox-hunter. I
has built a house patterned after the fame
"Westover," William Byrd's Virginia ma
sion, and lives there all the year round. I
suffers from sinus trouble, and has had th
operations, but in appearance he is bro
and muscular, and full of enthusiasm a
energy. He was a popular army officer, a
is popular now among his rural neighbo
he has even been asked to conduct a Ne
funeral. He dictates his books; reads noth
much but history and books about railroa
mining, and hunting; draws well, writes g
comic verse, and hates all games but pol
He has the faculty of complete absorpt
in what he is doing, and in consequence
notoriously unpunctual. The late Julian
Meade said of him: "He knows as m
about narrative technique as about f
hunting. . . . He has the kind of optim
which comes from the complete lack of f
a fundamental and genuine belief in
greatness of life and people, and an irrepr
sible feeling for the varied adventures
living."

PRINCIPAL WORKS: Drums, 1925; Marching
1927; Long Hunt, 1930; Roll River, 1935; Bi
Creek, 1939.

ABOUT: Publishers' Weekly April 15, 19
Saturday Review of Literature June 29, 1935.

BOYD, THOMAS (July 3, 1898-Janu
27, 1935), American novelist and short-st
writer, was born Thomas Alexander B
at Defiance, Ohio, the
day after an Ameri-
can army fighting in
Cuba captured San-
tiago from Spanish
troops. His parents
were Thomas Alex-
ander Boyd and Alice
(Dunbar) Boyd.
Young Boyd left high
school at eighteen to
enlist in the Marine
Corps, May 14, 1917, trained at Pa
Island, S.C., and joined the Sixth Regim
at Quantico in August. Going to Fra

Bachr

th the Second Division of the American
xpeditionary Force, he was in the trenches
: miles from Verdun in March of 1918.
yd fought at Belleau Wood, Soissons, and
. Mihiel until put out of action by a gas
ell at Blanc Mont in October, and was
arded a Croix de Guerre. After his dis-
arge from the army in July 1919, he went
work on a newspaper in St. Paul, Minn.,
ere Sinclair Lewis, Scott Fitzgerald,
oodward Boyd, and the Flandraus, made
a literary colony to which Thomas Boyd
came more than eligible with his *Through
e Wheat*, which the New York *Times*
led the least partisan and most brilliant of
ughboy reminiscences. As objective and
otionless as Stephen Crane's *The Red
dge of Courage*, the novel shared the in-
rest of a post-war reading public with John
s Passos' *Three Soldiers*, although less
de in range and variegated in types than
e latter. Battle, in the Boyd novel, is seen
rough the eyes and felt with the senses of
rgeant William Hicks, both dulled and
adened by incessant bombardment and an
cumulation of horrors. (*In Time of Peace*
esents ex-Sergeant Hicks as a heavy-
inking and unhappily married newspaper
porter. It is a novel which is "for all its
ietness a jeremiad and almost untouched
th happiness.")
Through the Wheat appeared when Boyd
as twenty-five and was literary critic
the St. Paul *News*. He married Margaret
oodward Smith of Chicago, and they had
daughter, Elizabeth Grace Boyd. In 1929
married Ruth Fitch Bartlett of Milwau-
e, and they made their home in Woodstock,
.., where several of his American historical
d biographical studies were written. Boyd
ed suddenly at thirty-six of a cerebral
morrhage at Ridgefield, Conn., at the
me of friends. He had come there to
nearer his New York publishers, and had
ffered an earlier stroke in a taxicab two
eeks previously. His last novel and a biog-
phy of John Fitch, inventor of the steam-
at, were published after his death.

Boyd's birthplace was on historic ground,
d his interest in local history was
nuine and far-reaching. *Shadows of the
ng Knives* concerns Angus McDermott,
frontiersman and scout for the British
d Indians in Ohio, just before the Revolu-
on. *Simon Girty, The White Savage*, is an
teresting biographical study of the rene-
de who led the British and Indians against
e whites. War stories which Boyd wrote
r magazines were collected in *Points of*
Honor, on which the moving picture "Blaze
of Glory" was based.

PRINCIPAL WORKS: *Fiction*—Through the
Wheat, 1923; The Dark Cloud, 1924; Points of
Honor, 1925; Shadow of the Long Knives, 1925;
In Time of Peace, 1928. *Biography*—Samuel
Drummond, 1925; Simon Girty, The White Savage,
1928; Mad Anthony Wayne, 1929; Lighthorse
Harry Lee, 1931; Poor John Fitch, 1935.

ABOUT: New York Times January 28, 1935;
Wilson Library Bulletin November 1935.

BOYLE, KAY (February 19, 1903-),
American novelist and poet, writes: "I was
born in St. Paul, Minn., and was educated
rather sketchily in
Philadelphia, Atlantic
City, and Cincinnati.
In the last named city
I also attended the
Conservatory of Mu-
sic. In 1921 I mar-
ried a Frenchman,
Richard Brault, in
New York, and came
to Europe in 1922. I
have never returned
to America since that time [see below], but
have lived among French people in France,
Austrians in Austria, and spent two years in
England.

"My first poems were published in *Broom*
and *Poetry*, and Lola Ridge, with whom I
worked on *Broom* in New York after my
marriage, was one of the greatest influences
in my life. Later, Ernest Walsh's *This
Quarter* and Eugene Jolas' *transition* published my stories and poems. I should say
that it was largely due to the encouragement
of these two editors that I went on with my
writing, as making a living for myself and
daughter took the greater part of my time
and strength for several years. In 1931 I
divorced my husband and married Laurence
Vail, an American artist and writer. We
now live in our own home in Mégève, Haute
Savoie, with our six children, (four of whom
are mine, and two Laurence Vail's from his
former marriage). We are both radical-
minded, socially and politically.

"I was awarded a Guggenheim Fellowship
in 1934 for the study required on an epic
poem on aviation, which work is still in progress. I was also awarded the O. Henry
Memorial Prize in 1935 for the short story
entitled 'The White Horses of Vienna.'"

* * *

Kay Boyle was first taken to Europe when
she was six months old, and has passed more
of her life abroad than in America. Of
delicate health, and threatened by tubercu-

losis, she has had to spend much of her time in warm climates or on mountain-tops—she is an enthusiastic mountaineer as well as a good horsewoman. She says she likes "to be cool, to travel to strange places, meet odd people, play chess," and that her favorite reading is of "poetry, and accounts of flying, Arctic or undersea exploration." Tall, slender, and dark-haired, she possesses distinction if not beauty. As a writer, she has been strongly influenced by the so-called "*transition* school," and her pitfall is, like theirs, a private vocabulary which sometimes baffles the reader. Intellectuality is the note of her work, and she has been called "one of the more uncomfortably brilliant of our short story writers and novelists," while her poetry has been spoken of as "wayward" and suggestive. Her recurrent theme is that of youth faced with disease or death, and her presentation is brief and stark, with little background or preparation. But, to quote Evelyn Harter, "her intellectual varietism has never obscured her fundamental tenderness, humor, and spirit, and her native sense of obligation in craftsmanship." She is a bold experimenter in technique, and as one critic put it, "she is bound to be interesting —even her failures are spectacular." She herself says: "I should like my prose to be lucid, direct, and clean." In her successes, which are no less spectacular than her failures, that is the effect she achieves.

Kay Boyle's autobiographical sketch was written in 1939. The Vails were unable to leave France after the conquest, until the summer of 1941 when, with their six children, they returned to the United States by Clipper plane. It was the largest family unit that had ever made the trans-Atlantic flight. The Vails now live at Nyack, N.Y. where Kay Boyle gives an adult education course in writing at the local high school.

PRINCIPAL WORKS: Wedding Day and Other Stories, 1929; Plagued by the Nightingale, 1930; Year Before Last, 1931; The First Lover and Other Stories, 1932; Gentlemen, I Address You Privately, 1933; My Next Bride, 1934; The White Horses of Vienna and Other Stories, 1935; Death of a Man, 1936; Monday Night, 1937; Glad Day (poems) 1938; The Youngest Camel (juvenile) 1939; The Crazy Hunter (novelettes) 1940; Armistice Diary, 1942.

ABOUT: Bookman June 1932; New York Times Book Review August 3, 1941; Newsweek August 1, 1938; Poetry September 1939; Reader's Digest September 1940; Time December 26, 1938.

BOYLESVE, RENÉ (1867-January 15, 1926), French novelist, was born René Marie Auguste Tardiveau at La Haye-

Descartes (Indre-et-Loire). "Over all work the serene atmosphere of th Loire country, the limpid clearness of rivers, the subtle irony united to wh has been called *le bons sens libre et ra leur*, of those who dwell upon its ban shed a vague but irresistible charm," accor ing to Winifred Stephens. At home t young Tardiveau read Lamàrtine and illu trated magazines with absorption. He w educated at the Jesuit College of Poitie Tours, and studied at the Facultés des Lettr et de Droit in Paris, as well as the Éco Libre des Sciences Politiques. His traini at the latter institution did not persuade h to try for a diplomatic post; the writ Boylesve began to contribute to the Rev Bleue and other periodicals. Le Médec des Dames de Néans (1896), his first nov with its story of a youthful pupil of an abl sacrificed by a doctor to the erotic whin of the bored wife of a lawyer, sounded the outset Boylesve's favorite theme of t triumph of the strong over the weak and common sense over poetry. His most important novels, in fact, are those concerning provincial life — *Mademoiselle Cloque* (1899), *La Becquée* (1901), *L'Enfant à la Balustrade* (1903), and *La Jeune Fille Bien Élevée* (1909) and its sequel, *Madeleine Jeune Femme* (translat as *A Gentlewoman of France*).

Boylesve's deep affection for the pa made him one of the first to recognize Ma cel Proust and his importance. He was fervent advocate of social order and d cipline, like Barrès; also like Barrès, he h a tenderness for the Catholic Church, though an agnostic. He was a master irony. Boylesve was elected to the Académ Française in 1919. Fragments of his p vate diary, published after his death Charles Du Bos as *Feuilles Tombées*, d played "critical and introspective gifts of t rarest kind." Photographs show a man i maculately dressed, with a large nose a Dickensian beard and whiskers.

WORKS AVAILABLE IN ENGLISH TRANSLATIO A Gentlewoman of France, 1916; You No Long Count (Tu n'es Plus Rien) 1918; Young Vigilan (Daily Bread and The Child at the Balustrad 1929.

ABOUT: Bertaut, J. Les Romanciers du No veau Siècle; Gosse, E. Leaves and Fruit; Reve M. René Boylesve; Stephens, W. French Nov ists of Today.

OYNTON, PERCY HOLMES (Octo-
- 30, 1875-), American scholar and critic,
ites: "I was born in Newark, N.J., my

father, George Mills
Boynton, a Presby-
terian clergyman, pas-
tor of the Broad
Street Church. In the
spring of 1889 he was
called to be pastor of
the Congregational
Church in Jamaica
Plain, Boston, and
was in this pulpit un-

▸derwood   til he become Execu-
e Secretary of the Congregational Sunday
▸hool and Publishing Society. My school-
▸ was broken by the fact that in 1888 we
▸ved to Newton Center, Mass., so that I
nt successively to the grammar school in
▸naica Plain, to the Roxbury Latin School,
▸d then to the public schools in Newton,
▸duating from high school in 1893 and
▸sequently from Amherst College in 1897,
▸d from Harvard with an M.A. degree in
▸98. I hold also the degree of Litt.D. from
▸nherst, 1939. After graduation from Har-
▸rd I taught for four years at Smith
▸ademy, St. Louis, a boys' school connected
▸th Washington University. In 1902 I came
▸ the University of Chicago as a graduate
▸dent, became a member of the department
▸ English within three months, and have
▸en at the university ever since.

▸'At the time I came here there was ex-
▸mely little formal work offered anywhere
▸ American literature. Since that time,
▸der my direction, the work has expanded
▸til now there are four men giving instruc-
▸n in this field here, with the use of a li-
▸ry equipment which surpasses all except
▸at of three or four places in the East.
▸ere is a substantial group of graduate
▸dents here always, and past graduates
▸ doing distinguished work at scores of
▸iversities and colleges in the country. I
▸ve been associate editor of our special
▸urnal, *American Literature,* and chairman
▸ the American literature section of the
▸odern Language Association. I was dean
▸ the college of Arts, Literature, and Sci-
▸ce of the university from 1912 to 1923.
▸y output on American literature has been
▸pplemented by a rather wide experience as
▸lecturer and broadcaster and by a dozen
▸ars of work (1904-16) as Principal of
▸struction (in charge of the public pro-
▸ms and summer schools) at the original
▸autauqua Institution, Chautauqua, N.Y."

* * *

* Died July 8, 1946.

Professor Boynton was married in 1902
to Lois Damon, and they have two sons.
His hobby is yachting at his summer home
at Mystic, Conn. In addition to his own
books he has edited a number of texts, including works by Benjamin Franklin, Fenimore Cooper, and Mark Twain. He also
contributes reviews and articles frequently to
the leading American magazines and scholarly journals. In 1941, a few weeks before
his retirement as professor of English at
the close of the academic year, he received
the tenth annual award of the Chicago
Foundation for Literature, for "distinguished
service to literature as exemplified by the
excellence of his work as teacher and critic,
the high standard of his scholarship, and his
notable contributions to the literary life of
our day." The New York *Times* called his
America in Contemporary Fiction (1940)
"tolerant and open-minded. . . . It is a pleasant surprise to find one of the older academic
critics of literature giving serious attention
to contemporary American fiction."

PRINCIPAL WORKS: First View of English and
American Literature (with others) 1909; London
in English Literature, 1913; Principles of Composition, 1915; History of American Literature,
1919 (college textbook; as school textbook, 1923);
Some Contemporary Americans, 1924; More Contemporary Americans, 1927; The Rediscovery of
the Frontier, 1931; The Challenge of Modern
Criticism, 1931; Literature and American Life,
1936; America in Contemporary Fiction, 1940.

BRADFORD, GAMALIEL (October 9,
1863-April 11, 1932), American "psychogra-
pher," was born in Boston and lived there

or near there all his
life, dying at his home
in Wellesley Hills. He
belonged by ancestry
to the Boston "Brah-
min caste," being
eighth in descent
from Governor Wil-
liam Bradford of the
Plymouth Colony.
His father was Ga-
maliel Bradford, a   D. Ullman
banker; his mother Clara Crowninshield
(Kinsman) Bradford.

All his nearly seventy years Bradford
was a semi-invalid. The nature of his illness is unknown, and it was probably largely
hypochondriacal, though it caused him periods of intense suffering, subjective or not.
He entered Harvard in 1882, but found it
necessary to leave again almost immediately.
For an invalid he was certainly a copious
writer; however, he lived a most retired life,
seldom emerging from his home except to

frequent the library of the Athenaeum society in Boston. He had an honorary Litt.D. degree from Washington and Lee University, and was a member of the American Academy of Arts and Letters. In 1886 he married Helen Hubbard Ford.

Bradford deliberately made himself into a biographer, after having failed as poet, novelist, and playwright. He believed he had invented the word "psychograph" to describe his peculiar *genre* of "condensed, essentially artistic presentations of character," though (strangely unknown to him) the term was applied by Taine to Sainte-Beuve—who was confessedly Bradford's model. He did, however, devote several volumes to individual celebrities treated at greater length, though his characteristic form is the brief "soul picture." He said: "As a portrait-painter I could present a man at only one moment of his career, and depict his character in only one phase, one situation, one set of conditions and circumstances. Now the aim of psychography is precisely the opposite to this. Out of the perpetual flux of actions and circumstances that constitutes a man's whole life, it seeks to extract what is essential, what is permanent and so vitally characteristic."

Bradford's journal, which he started in early youth and which was published posthumously, is not the least interesting of his works. Though it was apparently always written with publication in mind, it is as self-revelatory as *The Education of Henry Adams*. Its self-pity is repellent, and so is its naïve snobbery, reminiscent of John P. Marquand's "George Apley." But it, like his letters (like most house-bound intellectuals, he was an indefatigable letter-writer), reveals also the extraordinarily wide range of his reading. Practically all his time was spent, like a bee's, in ingesting nectar and producing honey—though honey with sometimes an acrid flavor. His is a prime example of the mind wholly given over to investigation into and reporting of the minds and personalities of other men. His interest is in motives—in what made the wheels go round; he is the anatomist always, whether his subject be another or himself. It is a bent which deprived his novels and plays of life, but gave it to his psychographs.

He himself was a "damaged soul"—as Newton Arvin acutely remarks, "a quite recognizable younger contemporary of Henry Adams." He was exaggeratedly modest, and was quite frank about his search for a medium of literary expression which might gain him a place in public notice. There is something hollow about all his work; the impression he gives is that here was a man dogged set upon becoming an author who had particular talent and no vital message to deliver. In consequence, critical opinion has been most contradictory, ranging from Henry Hazlitt's "less brilliance than simple competence, . . . industry, patience, persistence careful and conscientious workmanship," to John Macy's "truly balanced mind and rich generous nature." His individualism and isolation were at once his strength and his weakness. He wrote like what he was—little, gray-bearded, bald-headed recluse with a large inherited income, no health, bad nerves, and an inquiring mind. Perhaps the best picture of Gamaliel Bradford, the man and the writer, is given by himself, in verse:

My prose is decorous,
Or strips other men,
Discreetly sonorous
On things that have been.
My verse tears the curtain
From shuddering me,
Pale, haggard, uncertain,
As souls should not be.

PRINCIPAL WORKS: *Biography*—Types of American Character, 1895; Lee: The American, 191 Confederate Portraits, 1914; Union Portraits, 191 Portraits of Women, 1916; A Naturalist of Soul 1917; Portraits of American Women, 1919; American Portraits, 1922; Damaged Souls, 1923; Bare Souls, 1924; Soul of Samuel Pepys, 1924; Wives 1925; Darwin, 1926; D. L. Moody: A Worker Souls, 1927; The Haunted Biographer, 1927; God Made Them, 1929; Daughters of Eve, 19; The Quick and the Dead, 1931; Saints and Sinners, 1932; Biography and the Human Heart 1932; Elizabethan Women, 1936. *Novels*—The Private Tutor, 1904; Between Two Masters, 190 Matthew Porter, 1908. *Verse*—A Pageant of Life 1904; A Prophet of Joy, 1920; Shadow Verse 1920. *Miscellaneous*—Life and I, 1928; Unmade in Heaven (play) 1917; Journal, 1933; Letters 1934.

ABOUT: Bacon, L. Semicentennial; Bradford G. Life and I, Journal, Letters; Bookman May 1932; Nation April 27, 1932, September 27, 19; New Republic October 18, 1933; Saturday Review of Literature September 23, 1933; Scholastic February 10, 1941.

*BRADFORD, ROARK (August 1896-   ), American novelist and short story writer, was born in Lauderdale County Tenn., near the Mississippi but fifteen miles from a railroad. He is the eighth eleven children of Richard Clarence Bradford and Patricia Adelaide (Tillman Bradford; his full name is Roark Whitney Wickliffe Bradford. Although he is a direct descendent of Gov. William Bradford of Massachusetts, his family has been resident in the South since colonial days.

* Died November 13, 1948.

Aside from country schools in Tennessee and Arkansas, his only education has been in the Artillery Schools of the Army. He was a First Lieutenant of Artillery during the World War, but never got to France.

Instead he served in various capacities, chiefly as ballistics instructor, until 1920, when he was demobilized in Atlanta, and went to work on the Atlanta *Georgian*. In 1922 he moved to the New Orleans *Times-Picayune*, where he was night city editor

Pinchot

and later Sunday editor. He is still a resident of New Orleans.

His first published fiction was about Negroes—a series of stories for the New York *World*—and that has been his main subject ever since. The second story he ever sold won the O. Henry Prize for the best short story of 1927. The *World* series eventually became his first book, *Ol' Man Adam an' His Chillun*, which was made by Marc Connelly into the immensely successful play (later also a motion picture), *Green Pastures*, winner of the Pulitzer Prize in 1930. *John Henry*, published in 1931, was a Literary Guild selection, and in 1939 Mr. Bradford rewrote this story of the mythical Negro hero (analogy of the lumbermen's Paul Bunyan) as a play, set to music by Jacques Wolfe.

In New Orleans Mr. Bradford lives with his wife and son in "the earliest apartment house in the United States," the old Pontalba Building in the French Quarter. Mrs. Bradford was Mary Rose (Sciarra) Hinler, of Indianapolis. They travel a great deal, spending most summers in Santa Fé, N.M., and some time every year in Florida and in New York. They also own a plantation near Shreveport, La., which they visit several times a year.

While Mr. Bradford is writing a story he paints pictures of Negro cabins and churches, and "though he may paint badly he paints very enthusiastically indeed." He has a remarkable collection of phonograph records of Negro songs, and loves to sing them and cowboy songs. He is a genial and hospitable host, a good cook, an ardent fisherman, and a really expert horseman. He renews his source-material constantly, both by visits to his Little Bee Bend Plantation in Louisiana, by attending Negro churches "to hear sermons by illiterate

preachers," and by inviting in for impromptu performances "strolling street bands of Negro musicians who may know nothing of music but who can sing and play the traditional songs of the black man."

In appearance he is stocky, gray-eyed, and slightly bald. He is a major in the Artillery Reserve and hopes his small son may grow up to be a soldier, though he himself says he "wouldn't be anything but a writer—even though it took ten years to find my *métier*."

PRINCIPAL WORKS: Ol' Man Adam an' His Chillun, 1928; This Side of Jordan, 1929; Ol' King David an' the Philistine Boys, 1930; How Come Christmas, 1930; John Henry, 1931; Kingdom Coming, 1933; Let the Band Play Dixie (short stories), 1934; The Three Headed Angel, 1937; John Henry (play, with J. Wolfe) 1939.

ABOUT: Collier's January 1940; Reader's Digest July 1940; Theatre Arts March 1940; Wilson Library Bulletin June 1930.

BRADLEY, ANDREW CECIL (March 26, 1851-September 2, 1935), English university professor and writer on poetry, was born at Cheltenham, the son of the Rev. Charles Bradley, first incumbent of St. James's Chapel, Clapham, headquarters since 1829 of the evangelical "Clapham Sect," and Emma (Linton) Bradley. The Bradleys were an old Yorkshire family,

but his branch had been in the south of England since the early eighteenth century. Andrew was a day boy at Cheltenham School, where he was "a neat and steady bat" (at cricket), and arrived at Balliol College, Oxford, in 1869; its golden age began next year with the advent of Benjamin Jowett. Escaped from an atmosphere of rigid evangelicalism, young Bradley plunged headlong into the world of poetry. He also was an ardent worshiper of Mazzini, the Italian patriot. Bradley was a Fellow of Balliol in 1874; lectured there from 1876 to 1881; was Professor of Modern Literature, University College, Liverpool, from 1881 to 1889; and Professor of English Language and Literature at Glasgow University from 1889 to 1900. After living a year at Kensington Bradley was unanimously elected Professor of Poetry at Oxford. He was one of the first college dons to lecture on English literature to women. He was not in the first flight as a classical scholar, and his undergraduate students at Balliol found him rather enigmatic. But his *Shakesperean*

Tragedy has been a standby in college Shakespeare courses since its publication, and his commentary on Tennyson's *In Memoriam* is well known. Bradley had a gentle face and voice, and was of slight build. His autumn holidays were spent mountain-climbing in Switzerland. Bradley was greatly distressed by the First World War; his powers of concentration began to fail, and the latter years were "a long gradual decay," his final release a source of relief and gratitude to the sister who had been burdened with his care. Bradley never married.

PRINCIPAL WORKS: A Commentary on Tennyson's *In Memoriam*, 1901; Shakesperean Tragedy, 1904; Oxford Lectures on Poetry, 1909; A Miscellany, 1929; Ideals of Religion, 1940.

ABOUT: British Academy Proceedings 1935.

BRADLEY, FRANCIS HERBERT. See "BRITISH AUTHORS OF THE 19TH CENTURY"

BRADLEY, JOHN HODGDON, Jr. (September 17, 1898-), American geologist, writes: "It has never been certainly established whether I am a scientist or a writer. Real scientists have called me a writer and real writers have called me a scientist. The disadvantage of this confusion is that people do not take me as seriously as they otherwise might. The advantage is that neither do I.

"In remaining an amateur I have not been without a certain consistency of purpose. As a boy in the upper Mississippi Valley the grand passions of my life were fishing and hunting fossils. I have been fishing and hunting fossils ever since. Though my fishing is still pure fishing, my fossil hunting has become adulterated with what for lack of a better term might be called philosophizing. After years of collecting fossils it seemed reasonable enough that I should attempt to formulate a coherent picture of the societies they represented and the world they inhabited. Most of my writing has developed as a result of that attempt.

"Most of my life, however, has been spent as a teaching geologist, and I can honestly include teaching among my particular likes. In this I suspect I am fortunate because I have not known many university teachers who enjoyed teaching. On the other hand, I must include among my particular dislikes

the attempt to teach and to think simultaneously. I know it is heresy to say so, but I have not found a university environment notably conducive to thought. Whenever the morbid desire to think has taken hold of me I have run away. I am a runaway at present —and I like it so well that I doubt whether I'll ever return to the barn."

* * *

This sketch will give an indication of the delightful style which has made Professor Bradley's popular books on geology exactly what the adjective implies. He writes from Lowell, Mass., but unless he makes good his threat "never to return to the barn," he is professor of geology at the University of Southern California, in Los Angeles, and has been since 1929. He was born in Dubuque, Iowa, educated at Phillips Exeter Academy, Harvard (B.A., *magna cum laude*, 1921), and the University of Chicago (Ph.D., *magna cum laude*, 1924). He taught geology in Harvard, the University of North Carolina, and the University of Montana, before going to his present post. During the First World War he was a private in the Marines. He is a Fellow of the American Association for the Advancement of Science, the Geological Society of America, and the Paleontological Society of America. In geology his specialty is invertebrate paleontology. In 1922 he married Katharine Leighton Hilton, and they have one daughter.

PRINCIPAL WORKS: The Earth and Its History, 1928; Parade of the Living, 1930; Fauna of the Kimmswick Limestone, 1930; Autobiography of the Earth, 1935; Farewell Thou Busy World, 1935; Patterns of Survival: An Anatomy of Life, 1938.

BRADLEY, KATHERINE HARRIS. See "BRITISH AUTHORS OF THE 19TH CENTURY"

BRAILSFORD, HENRY NOEL, (1873-), British journalist, was born at Mirfield, Yorkshire, the son of the Rev E. J. Brailsford. He obtained his M.A. degree at Glasgow University, with philosophical and classical honors, and in 1895 was assistant to the Professor of Logic there and lecturer in Queen Margaret College. He soon left teaching for journalism, however, serving as leader-writer on the Manchester *Guardian,* and the London *Tribune, Daily News,* and *Nation* successive-

ly. He joined the Independent Labor Party in 1907; next year he was a volunteer in the Greek Foreign Legion. From 1910 to 1912 Brailsford was Honorary Secretary to the Conciliation Committee for Women's Suffrage; was a member of the Carnegie International Commission in the Balkans in 1913—he had published a book about Macedonia in 1906—and in 1918 contested the Montrose Burghs as a Labor candidate.

Brailsford's first book was a novel, *The Broom of the War-God* (1898). His other books in the field of *belles-lettres* are *Adventures in Prose: A Book of Essays* (1911), and *Shelley, Godwin, and Their Circle* (1913), contributed to the Home University Library. *The War of Steel and Gold: A Study of Armed Peace,* published in the year of the outbreak of the First World War, went through several editions.

During 1919 Brailsford traveled through the blockaded areas of Europe as correspondent for the *Daily Herald*, the Manchester *Guardian*, the *Nation*, and the (New York) *New Republic*. He edited the *New Leader* from 1922 to 1926. Since 1937 Brailsford has contributed regularly to the *New Republic*. He is also well known as a pamphleteer: *If We Want Peace* (1933) is one of the Day to Day Pamphlets; *Why Capitalism Means War* (1939) was contributed to the New People's Library; and *Democracy for India* (1940) is a Fabian pamphlet sold for twopence. *Olives of Endless Age: Being a Study of This Distracted World and Its Need for Unity* (1927) was also published in the United States.

S. K. Ratcliffe writes: "In a fuller degree perhaps than any English writer of his kind, he combines a power of lucid and trenchant exposition with a gift of irony." The London *Times* commented that "he commands a fluent and attractive style which temps him to expound in detail every idea which crosses his mind." Brailsford lives in London.

PRINCIPAL WORKS: The Broom of the War-God (novel) 1898; Adventures in Prose, 1911; Shelley, Godwin, and Their Circle, 1913; The War of Steel and Gold, 1914; A League of Nations, 1917; Across the Blockade: A Record of Travels in Enemy Europe, 1919; Socialism for To-Day, 1925; How the Soviet Works, 1927; Olives of Endless Age, 1927; Rebel India, 1932; Property or Peace, 1934; Why Capitalism Means War, 1939; America Our Ally, 1940.

ABOUT: Nevinson, H. W. Fire of Life; Time September 23, 1940.

BRAITHWAITE, WILLIAM STANLEY BEAUMONT (December 6, 1878-), American Negro poet and an-

thologist, was born in Boston, the son of William Smith Braithwaite and Emma (De Wolfe) Braithwaite. He is mainly self-educated, but was given an honorary master's degree in 1918 from Atlanta University and an honorary LL.D. from Talladega College the same year, in recognition of his labors in the field of poetry. His *Anthology of Magazine Verse and Year Book of American Poetry* was begun in 1913 and continued in seventeen volumes, ceasing publication in 1929. Braithwaite made these anthologies something of a vested interest, similar to the work of Edward J. O'Brien in the field of the short story. It occurred to O'Brien and Braithwaite to found a Poetry Society a short while before Harriet Monroe launched the magazine *Poetry*, but even Miss Monroe, who acidly called Braithwaite "Sir Oracle," was willing to admit in her posthumous autobiography that this was a coincidence.

Braithwaite married Emma Kelly of Montross, Va., in June 1903, and their first daughter, now Mrs. Merrill Carter, was named Fiona Lydia Rossetti. Katharine Keats Braithwaite, Edith Carman Braithwaite, and Francis Robinson Braithwaite also bear poetical names. In all, there are four sons and three daughters. Braithwaite is a member of the Poetry Society of America, the New England Poetry Society, and the Authors Club, and in 1918 was given the Spingarn Medal, awarded to members of the colored race for outstanding achievements.

Conrad Aiken observed that Braithwaite's selections in anthologies favored poets who "observe toward life an attitude of chaste, romantic awe, and it is this attitude, particularly when it approaches the sweetly ecstatic or appears to be barely concealing a sob, that most delights Mr. Braithwaite. Must poetry be all marshmallows and tears? . . . Mr. Braithwaite's cloudy inaccuracy of style [conveys] vaguely interpretative rather than judicial criticism." Many librarians, however, have reason to be grateful to Braithwaite for his industry and skill in editing. His present home is in New York City.

PRINCIPAL WORKS: Lyrics of Life and Love, 1904; The House of Falling Leaves, 1908; The Poetic Year for 1916, 1916; The Story of the

Great War, 1919; Our Essayists and Critics of Today, 1920; Sandy Star (verse) 1926; Going Over Tindal: A Fragment Wrenched From the Life of Titus Jabson (novel) 1927; Frost on the Green Leaf (short stories) 1928. *Editor or Compiler*—The Book of Elizabethan Verse, 1906; The Book of Georgian Verse, 1908; The Book of Restoration Verse, 1909; Anthology of Magazine Verse and Year Book of American Poetry, 1913-29; Golden Treasury of Magazine Verse, 1918; The Book of Modern British Verse, 1919; Victory! Contributed by 38 American Poets, 1919; Anthology of Massachusetts Poets, 1922; Our Lady's Choir: A Contemporary Anthology of Verse by Catholic Sisters, 1931; The Story of the Years Between, 1918-39, 1940; Poems, New and Selected, 1940.

ABOUT: Aiken, C. P. Scepticisms; Monroe, H. A Poet's Life; New England Magazine December 1905; Poetry January 1917.

"BRAMAH, ERNEST." See SMITH, E. B.

BRANCH, ANNA HEMPSTEAD (March 18, 1875-September 8, 1937), American poet, wrote the compilers of this volume before her death: "I

was born in New London, Connecticut. My childhood and school days were spent in New York and Brooklyn. I went to the Froebel Academy in Brooklyn and then to the Adelphi Academy in Brooklyn where I graduated in 1893. These were private schools.

"My father was a lawyer, John Lock Branch, son of Judge William Branch, of Lake County, Ohio. He practiced law for many years in New York City. My mother was Mary Lydia Bolles, daughter of Mary Hempstead and John Roger Bolles of New London. Her mother wrote and illustrated children's poems and little tales, which were published in a book called *Casket of Toys*. My grandfather, John Roger Bolles, was a poet, author of several books, as well as a lawyer.

"My mother, after graduating from the Young Ladies High School in New London, studied at the school of Dr. Emerson in Boston. She wrote several well known poems, among them "The Petrified Fern." She wrote stories for children which have retained their popularity to this day: *Kanter Girls* and *Guld the Cavern King*.

"After graduating from the Adelphi in Brooklyn, I went to Smith College, graduating in 1897, having been the editor-in-chief of the college monthly and Ivy Orator.

"After that I went to the American Academy of Dramatic Arts in New York, where I graduated. Meanwhile the family went to live in New London after my father retired from his law business in New York City. We inherited the old Hempstead house, where my grandmother Mary Hempstead spent her girlhood. It was built by Robert Hempstead about 1640 and has been the home of the Hempstead family for ten generations, if we include my own.

"For many years I have spent a large part of every year at Christadora House in New York City, one of our oldest and most celebrated settlement houses. I have given volunteer service along social lines, especially the dramatic and literary. Here I direct the work of the Poets' Guild and am much interested in friendship among nations through the medium of poetry. . . .

"I was the founder of the International Poetry Society. Interested in social service, I pioneered the playground movement in New London and was for several years closely associated with its progress. . . .

"With the exception of a few trips abroad and up to Newfoundland and Canada, I spend my summers quietly at Hempstead House in New London, where I greatly enjoy the swimming and boating; or in a little house at Bethlehem, New Hampshire."

* * *

Miss Branch never married, but lived a quiet, retired life except for her reading tours. Her chief interest outside her work was in Christadora House, a low-cost home for working women in New York. During the Century of Progress Fair at Chicago, 1933, she served as chairman of poetry for the National Council of Women.

Anna Hempstead Branch was a genuine mystic (see such poems as "Divinity"), and was the possessor of an authentic lyric gift. She had force and power on occasion too—as witness "Nimrod," which Alfred Kreymborg called "the greatest single narrative in the whole length of American poetry." In general, however, her work is delicate rather than strong; no one would doubt its having been written by a woman, and a woman born in the last quarter of the nineteenth century. There is a long silent period in her life, between the publication of *Rose of the Wind* in 1910 and of *Sonnets From a Lock Box* in 1929.

She was almost a beautiful woman, with classic features and heavy dark hair, and her portrait is that of a belated pre-Raphaelite maiden. Her poems too have a tang of the pre-Raphaelite about them; she has the mystical approach and, at her best, some of the exquisite lyricism of a minor Christina Rossetti.

PRINCIPAL WORKS: The Heart of the Road and Other Poems, 1901; The Shoes That Danced and Other Poems, 1905; Rose of the Wind, Nimrod and Other Poems, 1910; Sonnets From a Lock Box and Other Poems, 1929.

ABOUT: Bolles, J. K. Father Was an Editor; Publishers' Weekly September 18, 1937; New York Times September 9, 1937.

*BRAND, MAX (May 29, 1892-), American writer of Western stories, is the pseudonym of Frederick Faust, who also writes

under a number of other names and in other *genres*. (He is, for example, the author of the motion pictures centering around "Dr. Kildare.") However, the greater part of his immense output is under the name of Brand and is made up of books about the traditional West. He has been called "King of the Pulp Writers," and it is estimated that in twenty years he has written and published some twenty-five million words, in books, stories, and scenarios.

He averages a wordage equal to a full-length book every three weeks. He is immensely popular abroad, and has been translated into every European language. His books appear constantly in reprints, and before the war his sales in England were almost as large as in America. Yet he started his literary career as a verse writer and has published (under his own name) two volumes of poems!

Mr. Faust was born in Seattle, the son of Gilbert Leander Faust and Elizabeth (Uriel) Faust. He went to high school in Modesto, Calif., and attended the University of California, though he was not graduated. In 1917 he married Dorothy Schillig, and they have a son and a daughter. For many years he lived in New York, then moved to Northern Italy, where until the Second World War he and his family lived in a villa in the mountains.

Edward H. Dodd, Jr. has described him as "a tall fellow, six feet two, with broad shoulders and a massive head, . . . a resonant, cultured voice, . . . the predilection of a gourmet for rare wines and fine victuals,

. . . a dreamy talker of boundless imagination, who could hold you spellbound by the hour as he discoursed on anything from Omar Khayyam to China Clippers." He dictates to "relays" of stenographers, working intensively while he subsists on "an incredible amount of black coffee." He is one of the few men who regularly gets the top rate of four cents a word for his stories from the pulp magazines—and, to quote Dodd again, "in the pulps you have to deliver the goods. No attitudes or affectations get by."

Some eighty-five books have appeared under the name of Max Brand, only a few of which can be listed here.

PRINCIPAL WORKS: The Untamed, 1918; The Night Horseman, 1920; Trailin'! 1920; The Seventh Man, 1921; The Village Street (as Frederick Faust) 1922; Alcatraz, 1923; Dan Barry's Daughter, 1924; Fire Brain, 1926; Blue Jay, 1927; White Wolf, 1928; Pleasant Jim, 1928; Pillar Mountain, 1928; Gun Tamer, 1929; Mistral, 1929; Destry Rides Again, 1930; Mystery Ranch (in England: Mystery Valley) 1930; The Happy Valley, 1931; Smiling Charlie, 1931; The Jackson Trail, 1932; Valley Vultures, 1932; Twenty Notches, 1932; Longhorn Feud, 1933; The Outlaw, 1933; Slow Joe, 1933; Brothers on the Trail, 1934; Crooked Horn, 1934; Rancher's Revenge, 1934; Timbal Gulch Trail, 1934; The Hunted Riders, 1935; The Rustlers of Beacon Creek, 1935; The Seven of Diamonds, 1935; Clung, 1935; Tiger, 1935; Happy Jack, 1936; The King Bird Rides, 1936; Harrigan, 1936; South of Rio Grande, 1936; The Streak, 1937; Trouble Trail, 1937; The Iron Trail, 1938; Dead or Alive, 1938; Singing Guns, 1938; Lanky for Luck, 1939; Fightin' Fool, 1939; Gunman's Gold, 1939; Marbleface (in England: Poker Face) 1939; Six Golden Angels, 1939; The Dude, 1940; The Secret of Dr. Kildare, 1940; Young Dr. Kildare, 1941; Dr. Kildare Takes Charge, 1941; Long Chance, 1941; Silver Tip, 1942; Dr. Kildare's Crisis, 1942.

ABOUT: Publishers' Weekly March 26, 1938.

BRAND, MILLEN (January 19, 1906-), American novelist, writes: "I was born in Jersey City, in the shadow of the People's

Palace on Bergen Avenue—nearby was the Jersey Central Railroad cut that ran through the city from the meadows to New York Harbor. We played along it and went to school on Union Street; on my street were the Swensons, the Sultzes, the

Hoaglands, the Van Ambergs, the Fredericks, the Fraleys, and around the corner the Wests. It's all changed now, began changing in my grandparents' time. We lived in my grandparents' house, part of which we rented. My father was an electrician working on contract jobs, my mother was a nurse. Albert Myers, my grandfather, was a carpenter and rode to his shop, even as an old man, on a bicycle, his pants legs clipped in with shiny black metal clips. I guess a good many people in Jersey City remember him.

"My father had a nostalgic longing for the farm; his father was a farmer. Around 1912 his father helped him get a farm near Long Branch or Eatontown and we farmed there for a few years. I rode the plough horse, helped dig grubs out of the peach trees and fight blight in the quinces, raised a half acre of potatoes, went to a little cross-roads school, and finally didn't go to school at all. It was a good life. Farming didn't pay and we had to come back to the city.

"In the city I got sick and nearly died. That quieted me down and maybe started me on a bent for writing. I decided I was going to live by my head when I grew up, that being the way writing was looked at in a family of working people. But now I think the mechanic's turn comes out in me, even if I write. In our family it comes out in different ways—sometimes makes surgeons. My brother is a wireless operator.

"I like to write about common people. A lot of it shows in The Outward Room—John Kohler, his friend Meyer, and the other men from the machine shop, Anna in the dress shop. I believe common working people think better than any other people. I was in a shop in Allentown the other day and heard the men talking. They said the truck factory was on one shift and so-and-so was working two days a week. They said it was hard to get by. The thinking of people like that is what's eventually back of government. Other people think about shifts in factories too, but not as well or seriously.

"Here are some of the formal things the publishers of this book want me to tell about. B.A. and B. Litt. at Columbia, worked for eight years after graduation for the New York Telephone Company, published The Outward Room in 1937 and left the job to write. Published The Heroes in 1939. Winter of 1939-40 Sidney Kingsley's dramatization of The Outward Room [as The World We Make] was produced on Broadway. Now teach short-story writing at New York University. Belong to the Authors' League, the League of American Writers, and the Teachers' Union. Have a small farm in Pennsylvania where I live most of the time. Like the largo movement of Beethoven's Sonata Opus 10, No. 3, and the

second movement of the Quartet, Opus 127. Will play chess if necessary. Would like to write better than I do."

* * *

Mr. Brand modestly omits to mention that he was graduated from Columbia with honors, and that while there he was managing editor of the Varsity, wrote about half a year's contributions under various pseudonyms, won $125 in literary prizes, and while a student lectured on the French symbolist poets, using his own translations. In 1931 he married Pauline Leader, author of And No Birds Sing. They had two daughters (one deceased) and two sons, but are now separated. He is his own severest critic; he wrote the first draft of The Outward Room (which sold 110,000 copies) in two and a half months, laid it aside six months to cool, spent eight months rewriting it, and finally kept just one paragraph of the original unchanged. At that time he would get up at five o'clock, make his and his children's breakfast, be at the office by seven, type his novel till nine, then after work barricade himself behind books in the Public Library and write some more. His quiet, sober treatment, whether of a psychopathic problem in The Outward Room or of the neglected inmates of a home for old soldiers in The Heroes, makes for deep pathos; he is like a kind and understanding physician to his characters, without ever falling into sentimentality.

PRINCIPAL WORKS: The Outward Room, 1937; The Heroes, 1939.

ABOUT: Newsweek May 1, 1937; Wilson Library Bulletin June 1937; Writer August 1940.

*BRANDE, Mrs. DOROTHEA (THOMPSON) (January 12, 1893-), American novelist and miscellaneous writer, was

born in Chicago, the daughter of Frederic Shepard Thompson and Alice (Prescott) Thompson. She was educated privately and at Mrs. Sarrett's school for girls, also attending the University of Chicago, Lewis Institute, and the University of Michi-

Pinchot

gan. After holding editorial and reportorial positions on the Journal of the American Medical Association, the Chicago Record-Herald, and the Chicago Tribune, she came east to take a job as circulation manager of the American Mercury, then edited by H. L.

* Died December 17, 1948.

Mencken, from 1923 to 1926, and the next year became an associate editor of the *Bookman*, edited by Seward Collins. Mrs. Brande, who has a son, Justin Herbert Brande, by her first marriage, is now Mrs. Seward Collins. She was associate editor of the *American Review*, successor to the *Bookman*, in 1933-34. She lives at New Canaan, Conn. Besides lecturing, she has conducted classes in short-story writing. Mrs. Brande's chief diversions are reading philosophy, travel by sea, and watching cats, of which she has five.

Reading philosophy, or psychology, sent Mrs. Brande into the best-seller ranks with her inspirational book, *Wake Up and Live*, which sold quantities in the trade edition and as a Pocket Book. She had begun to read *Human Personality*, by F. W. H. Myers, when she recognized that the book was proving an eye-opener. She stopped reading for a time to meditate, and "When I picked up the book again I was a different person."

According to Mrs. Brande, most of us are victims to a Will to Fail; she has worked out "The Twelve Disciplines" to counteract this tendency. Twenty years before she found the formula, she had written seventeen short stories and twenty book reviews, and one attempt at a novel, abandoned less than a third of the way through. Two years after her enlightenment, she had written three books, twenty-four articles, four short stories, made seventy-two lectures, erected the scaffolding of three more books, and written innumerable letters of consultation and professional advice. One of these novels, *Most Beautiful Lady* (1935) a detective story, was published in England under the title *Beauty Vanishes*. *Letters to Philippa* (1937), chiefly commentary on current literature, is published by a firm specializing in Catholic books.

PRINCIPAL WORKS: Becoming a Writer, 1934; Most Beautiful Lady, 1935; Wake Up and Live, 1936; Letters to Philippa, 1937; My Invincible Aunt, 1938.

ABOUT: Brande, D. Wake Up and Live (see "About the Author").

BRANDES, GEORG MORRIS COHEN

(February 4, 1842-February 19, 1927), Danish literary critic, was born in Copenhagen, the son of a merchant of Jewish descent. Through the family name was originally Cohen, the critic's father used the name of Brandes. Georg Brandes' younger brother Edvard also became a critic, novelist, and playwright.

Brandes' precocious genius won him a gold medal for a critical essay while he was still a student in the University of Copenhagen. He was graduated in 1864, *cum praecipua laude*, and for the next six years taught Danish classes in a normal school, frequently interrupting his teaching to travel in France and Germany. In 1870 he received his Ph.D. degree, and the next year he became reader in *belles lettres* at the university. The professor of aesthetics had promised that Brandes should be his successor, but when the chair became vacant in 1872, the young critic, already the author of two volumes, was denied it, on the incontrovertible but irrelevant grounds that he was a Jew, a radical, and an atheist. He remained all three throughout his long life, gradually winning his way to literary canonization, then deliberately sacrificing his popularity in old age for the sake of his principles. The idea of his destiny, expressed in his youth, remained always with him: "The Powers have designated me the champion of great ideas against great talents, unfortunately greater than I."

From 1877 to 1883 Brandes lived in Berlin. It was not until 1902 that he finally secured the professorship promised him in 1870. He was by that time the author of nearly all the most important books to issue from his pen, and his works had already been published in a collected edition. In 1912, when he was seventy, his birthday was the occasion of a great official celebration. Two years later he was anathematized because he could not follow the pro-Ally "neutrality" of most of his colleagues, but remained really neutral in the World War. His French friends, particularly Clemenceau, deserted and reviled him, and meanly accused him of being arrogant and a lover of flattery. He bore their attacks with dignity hiding an obvious wound. He died, following an operation, two weeks after his eighty-fifth birthday, and even posthumously he was assailed because the obituary notices called him "professor"—"like a German."

Brandes' whole life was a crusade, and he had little leisure for personal affairs. However, in 1876 he married the widow of his first German translator, and he was devoted to his wife, his children, and later to his two granddaughters. He was a square-headed, small man, red-haired in youth, with a beautiful voice and mild manner. He thought of himself always as the voice of European, as opposed to national, literature, yet to the end there remained something local and even provincial about his personality. But the scope of his interests and achievements was as large as the intellectual world. He wrote with equal ease in Danish, English, French, and German, and read Polish and Russian as well. He traveled in all these countries, and lectured in English in both England and the United States—which he left hastily in 1914 because New York was too strenuous for him! He was the champion of every forward-looking movement. He translated Mill's *Subjection of Women* and introduced feminism into Denmark. He pushed and publicized Ibsen and Nietzsche until they entered the consciousness of every educated Scandinavian. He was the chief Scandinavian protagonist of the non-historicity theory of Jesus. And even in old age his mind was open—as when after years of attack he met Freud and became convinced of the value of psychoanalysis. He is generally conceded to have been the greatest literary critic since his master Taine. As an editorial writer remarked in the *Nation*, he was "a living refutation of the theory that it is no longer possible for a single man to take all literary knowledge as his province"—adding shrewdly that essentially Brandes was "a fighter for liberty, reason, and nature who only by chance, perhaps, found his issues in the field of literature." Even the Catholic *Commonweal*, which might be expected to be violently in disagreement with Brandes, spoke of the range of his mind as being "very nearly the range of the modern European mind," and of his masterpiece, *Main Currents of the Nineteenth Century Literature*, as being "as vast in scope as anything the mind of a writer has ever grappled with."

Brandes outlived his age, the scientific, rationalist, naturalistic age of Darwin. But he himself was one of the great triumphs of that age, and his work will have a value to posterity that outweighs its demoded air now. He estimated his own place very truly: "I am called a critic; that term is too small for me. I am called a philosopher; that term is too big. . . . I have the reward of having helped to make an epoch."

PRINCIPAL WORKS AVAILABLE IN ENGLISH: Lord Beaconsfield, 1880; Impressions of Russia, 1890; William Shakespeare, 1898; Ibsen and Björnson, 1899; Main Currents of Nineteenth Century Literature, 1901-05; Reminiscences of My Childhood and Youth, 1906; Anatole France, 1908; Friedrich Nietzsche, 1909; Ferdinand Lassalle, 1911; Aristotle, 1912; The World at War, 1917; Julius Caesar, 1918; The World Tragedy, 1920; Goethe, 1924; The Jesus Myth, 1926; Hellas, 1926; Voltaire, 1930.

ABOUT: Boyd, E. A. Studies From Ten Literatures; Brandes, G. Reminiscences of My Childhood and Youth; Moritzen, J. Georg Brandes in Life and Letters; Nathansen, H. Georg Brandes (in Danish); Bookman (London) April 1927; Contemporary Review September 1930; Living Age April 1, 1927; Mercure de France March 15, 1927; Nation March 2, 1927; New Republic March 23, 1927.

BRAWLEY, BENJAMIN GRIFFITH (April 22, 1882-February 1, 1939), American Negro educator and miscellaneous writer, was born in Columbia, S.C., the son of Edward MacKnight and Margaret Sophronia (Dickerson) Brawley. He received a B.A. degree at nineteen from Atlantic Baptist College, now Morehouse College, in 1901, and a similar degree from  the University of Chicago in 1906. His second book was a history of Morehouse College; his first, *A Short History of the American Negro* (1913) had reached a fourth edition a quarter-century later, in 1939, the year of Brawley's death at fifty-six. His text-books on English literature, Freshman English, English drama, and English literature are widely used in Negro colleges, and his *The Negro Genius: A New Appraisal of the Achievement of the American Negro in Literature and the Fine Arts* (1937) is the standard work in its field, with its dispassionate consideration of the work of such Negro writers as Charles Waddell Chesnutt, Countee Cullen, Jessie Fauset, and others.

Brawley obtained his M.A. degree from Harvard University in 1908; was pastor of a Baptist Church in Brockton, Mass., for some years, and in 1912 married Hilda Damaris Prowd, of Kingston, Jamaica, B.W.I. John Farrar included him in the *Bookman Anthology of Essays: 1923*.

Of his own people Brawley says: "The Negro himself as the irony of American civilization is the supreme challenge to American literature. Like Banquo's ghost he will not down. All faith and hope, all love and longing, all rapture and despair, look out from the eyes of this man who is ever with us and whom we never understand."

Brawley was dean and professor of English at Morehouse College from 1912 to 1920; professor of English at Shaw College from 1923 to 1931; and from then until his death in Washington, D.C., a week after suffering a stroke, he was professor of English at Howard University. He wrote a life of the Negro poet, Paul Laurence Dunbar, and edited a collection of Dunbar's *Best Stories.* Anson Phelps Stokes contributed an introduction to Brawley's *Doctor Dillard of the Jeanes Fund.* Brawley was also president of the Association of Colleges for Negro Youth in 1919-20.

PRINCIPAL WORKS: A Short History of the American Negro, 1913; History of Morehouse College, 1917; The Negro in Literature and Art; 1918; A Social History of the American Negro, 1921; A Short History of English Drama, 1921; A New Survey of English Literature, 1926; Freshman Year English, 1929; Doctor Dillard of the Jeanes Fund, 1930; Negro Builders and Heroes, 1937; The Negro Genius, 1937; Paul Laurence Dunbar, 1937.

ABOUT: Farrar, J. (ed.). Bookman Anthology of Essays, 1923; Nation October 23, 1937; New York Times February 7, 1939.

BREASTED, JAMES HENRY (August 27, 1865-December 2, 1935), American historian, Orientalist and university professor,

was born in Rockford, Ill., the son of Charles Breasted and Harriet N. (Garrison) Breasted. The family was Dutch and Danish. Breasted's first American ancestor, Jan van Breestede, arrived in New Amsterdam in 1647. Breasted attended North Central College, then North-Western College, at Napierville, Ill., leaving in 1888 with a B.A. degree to study two years at the Chicago Theological Seminary, his first intention being to enter the Congregational ministry. His interest aroused by the renascence of Semitic studies at Yale under William Rainey Harper, Breasted went to New Haven for graduate study in Hebrew, receiving his M.A. degree in 1892. Harper, already planning for a new University of Chicago, and knowing Breasted's interest in archaeology, urged him to study in Europe, promising him a position in Chicago on his return. Breasted obtained his Ph.D. at the University of Berlin in 1894 and married Frances Hart of Oakland, Calif., in the same year; they had two sons and a daughter. (The year after her death in 1934 he mar-

ried his sister-in-law, Imogen Hart Richmond.) Scientific excavation had just begun at this time, and there were no textbooks available for the study of hieroglyphics or cuneiform writing. After publication of a Latin dissertation on certain hymns of Akhenaton, the heretic pharaoh, Breasted was commissioned by royal academies of Berlin, Leipzig, Munich and Göttingen to copy and arrange Egyptian inscriptions preserved in museums of Europe, for the *Berlin Egyptian Dictionary*—not published until the 1920's and then by grace of a grant from John D. Rockefeller, Jr. He led his first archaeological expedition into Egypt in 1894, then took up the promised position at the University of Chicago, where he was appointed assistant director of the Haskell Oriental Museum. His classes in Egyptology were so small that he went on lecture tours to supplement his income. From 1905 to 1933 Breasted was professor of Egyptology and Oriental History, marking his promotion by publication of *A History of Egypt* (1905), which with *A History of the Ancient Egyptians* (1908) exhibited Egyptians as an admirable people with a romantic history.

Breasted's lucid, attractive style was marked by an infectious verve and enthusiasm. He emphasized the development of moral thought in Egypt as a contribution to modern ethics, and was apt to slur over the later degradation and decline of Egyptian civilization. *Ancient Times: A History of the Early World* (1916) elicited an enthusiastic review from Theodore Roosevelt, and the book and its later editions had a large popular sale. Various ancient and medieval histories written in collaboration with James Harvey Robinson were widely used in colleges and universities. In 1905-06 and again in 1906-07 Breasted with his wife and son, aided by a photographer and copyist, made a record of the historical monuments of pharaonic times along 1200 miles of the Nile.

In 1919 Breasted became director of the New Oriental Institute at the University of Chicago, being relieved of other duties as teacher to devote all his attention to the work of the Institute in Chicago and in the Near East. He termed the search for all existing remains of Oriental civilization a "New Crusade." Breasted "brought to America the realization that our cultural ancestry is rooted in the distant past and made European scholars aware of the peculiar contribution which American scholarship might make to humanistic research." A man of gentle manners, with white hair and moustache, Breasted died at seventy of a hemolytic streptococcic infection contracted as he returned from a trip to the Near East.

PRINCIPAL WORKS: A History of Egypt: From the Earliest Times to the Persian Conquest, 1905; A History of Ancient Egyptians, 1908; Development of Religion and Thought in Ancient Egypt, 1912; Outlines of European History (with J. H. Robinson) 1914; Ancient Times, 1916; Survey of the Ancient World, 1916; History of Europe: Ancient and Medieval (with J. H. Robinson) 1921; General History of Europe (with J. H. Robinson & E. P. Smith) 1921; The Conquest of Civilization (revision of Ancient Times) 1926; The Dawn of Conscience, 1933; The Oriental Institute, 1933.

ABOUT: National Academy of Sciences: Biographical Memoirs. Vol. 18, no. 5, 1936; American Historical Review January 1936; Christian Century December 11, 1935; Newsweek, December 7, 1935; Publishers' Weekly December 7, 1935; School and Society December 7, 1935; Time December 9, 1935.

BRECHT, BERTOLT (February 10, 1898-   ), German poet, playwright and novelist, familiarly known as "Bert Brecht" throughout Germany-in-Exile, was born in Augsburg, the capital of Bavarian Swabia. "As a boy I was mobilized in the war and placed in a hospital. I dressed wounds, applied iodine, gave enemas, performed bloodtransfusions. If the doctor ordered me: 'Amputate a leg, Brecht,' I would answer: 'Yes, your Excellency,' and cut off the leg." Becht's *Ballad of the Dead Soldier*, describing how they dug up a soldier, patched him up, and sent him back to the front, circulated by word of mouth throughout Germany, winning its author the undying hatred of the military. His writings and unremitting political activities—he was a member of the Augsburg Revolutionary Committee—earned him the honor of being fifth on the Nazi murder list when Hitler's Beer Hall Putsch (November 1923) failed.

Brecht studied natural sciences and medicine at the universities of Munich and Berlin. His major interest, however, was literature, especially the theatre: he wrote dramatic sketches and produced plays at the Kammerspiele. In 1922 his five-act drama, *Trommeln in der Nacht*, about a returned artilleryman who finds his wife living with a soldier, scored a tremendous success, was played in 120 theatres, and brought him the Kleist prize. Shortly thereafter Reinhardt appointed him to the staff of the Deutsche Theater where Brecht adapted Elizabethan, Chinese, and Spanish dramas, and produced some of his own plays: *Im Dickicht der Stadt* (1922), a cinematographic picture of Chicago; *Baal* (1924), the biography of a Don Juanesque chauffeur; *Edward II*

(1924), an adaptation, with Lion Feuchtwanger, of Marlowe's historical drama; and *Mann ist Mann* (1926), a Kiplingesque comedy about an Irish packer who goes to buy a fish for his wife and disappears as a machine gunner in an English colonial army.

After the Schiffbauerdam Theater of Berlin was offered to Brecht for his productions, he trained actors who later became some of the finest in the world—among them, Oskar Homolka, Peter Lorre, Helene Weigel, Lotta Lenia, Alexander Granach, Ernst Busch—and developed his theory of a non-Aristotelian or "Epic" drama, adumbrated already in *Mann ist Mann*. Brecht wished both actor and audience "to stand outside the character and incidents portrayed on the stage. The actor is to feel himself not overflowing with the real emotions of a Hamlet or a Lear, but reproducing them, portraying them, while retaining his own independence as commentator and observer. Similarly [according to this theory] the spectator retains his right to criticize Hamlet or Lear, and not to be swept away in the flood of emotions which the poet has generated around those characters." Invited by Erwin Piscator, whom Brecht considers "one of the most important theatre men of all times," he wrote for the Piscatorbühne an adaptation of Jaroslav Hasek's novel *The Good Soldier Schweik*, which had a continuous run of more than six months. For the Music Festival of 1927 Brecht wrote the libretto *Das Kleine Mahagonny,* a biting expressionistic satire with music by Kurt Weill. *Dreigroschenoper* (1928), based on John Gay's *The Beggar's Opera* and with music by Weill, played continuously for more than a year and with over four hundred performances in Berlin alone. It was staged in English in New York by Gifford Cochran and Jerry Krimsky in April 1933 as *The Three-Penny Opera* and was also filmed.

For the Baden-Baden Music Festival of 1929 Brecht experimented with a radio play, *Der Flug der Lindberghs,* music by Hindemith and Weill, and for the Music Week in Berlin (1930) he wrote *Der Jasager,* a short opera for children, with music by Weill. *Die Massnahme* (1930), music by Hans Eisler, a "Lehrstück" for working-class audiences, met with brilliant success in Berlin. After exciting radio adaptations of *Hamlet* and *Macbeth,* and a radio parody of Schiller's *Maid of Orleans, Die Heilige Johanna der Schlachthöfe,* which when produced in Darmstadt ended in a Fascist brawl, Brecht wrote *Kuhle Wampe,* a scenario for a proletarian film produced by S. T. Dudow and shown widely in the United States.

In 1933, when Brecht's dramatic version of Gorky's *Mother* was in its sixty-first performance in Berlin, the police mounted the stage and arrested the actors. The play, translated by Paul Peters, was staged by the Theatre Union of New York in December 1935. After Hitler's rise to power Brecht was expelled from the Third Reich and has since lived in France, Norway, the Soviet Union, and now the United States.

In exile Berthold Brecht has written a novel, *A Penny for the Poor* (1934), an amplification of his *Dreigroschenoper*, mercilessly exposing with mordant wit the faults and failures of the present age. For the theatre he has created the vitriolic anti-Nazi satire, *Round Heads, Peak Heads* (1937), and an equally pungent sequence of plays on life in the Third Reich, the best of which are perhaps *The Informer* (1938) and *The Jewish Wife* (1938). The most significant of his short dramas, however, is the one-act *Señora Carrar's Rifles* (1938), dealing with the Spanish war.

"Physically," Sergei Tretyakov remarked, "[Brecht] resembles a note blown through a very slender clarinet. His hooked-nosed face recalls that of Voltaire and Rameses. He is indeed a strange fellow, who appears at brilliant first nights, where everyone is in evening clothes, unshaven and wearing a rumpled black shirt without a tie." His nose supports a pair of old-fashioned rimmed spectacles "such as nobody else wears." And he is a good chauffeur: "He can assemble a machine or take it apart. The scar on his cheek he received in an automobile accident. Read Feuchtwanger's novel *Success*. His engineer Prechl is patterned on Brecht."

Hated by the Nazis, Brecht was fortunate to escape with his life and arrive in this country safely at last in 1941. He is living now in Los Angeles. *Mother Courage*, an historical play of the Thirty Years War has been tentatively announced for publication here.

WORKS AVAILABLE IN TRANSLATION: A Penny for the Poor, 1937.

ABOUT: Bithell, J. Modern German Literature; Eloesser, A. Modern German Literature; Boston Transcript November 5, 1938; International Literature May 1937; Internationale Literatur July 1935; International Theatre No.2, 1934; Left Review July 1936; Nation November 26, 1938; New York Times November 20, 1938; Partisan Review March-April 1941; Times (London) Literary Supplement July 17, 1937.

BRETT YOUNG. See YOUNG.

BREUER, ELIZABETH (October 18, 1892-), American novelist who writes as Bessie Breuer, writes: "I was born in Cleveland, Ohio (father a composer, Samuel Aaron Freedman, and mother Julia Bindley) and went to the Missouri State University in the School of Journalism, and to be a reporter was to me the nearest approach to literature, which I thought  came full-fledged from the brain with attendant fires of inspiration. That is the provincial's idea of creation as gleaned from worship of the dead in all the arts, the dead and safe and sure; and this fixed formula remained with me, rendering me mute, incapable, and miserable, until after successive years as a reporter on the St. Louis *Times,* the New York *Tribune* (where I was editor of the women's department and for six months Sunday editor—twenty-two years old then), as national director of magazine publicity for the American Red Cross the closing years of the war, and on the staff of the *Ladies' Home Journal.* At long last, courage in hand, I wrote many articles on feminism, etc., for *Harper's Magazine,* and then, migrating with all the others at the time, I went to France and there got the courage to write the things that belonged to me, through the friendship and encouragement of Kay Boyle, Laurence Vail, and others. My first short stories were accepted simultaneously by *Story* in Vienna and by *Harper's Magazine* in the United States. After that came my two novels, both published in London, Austria (for Germany), Czechoslovakia, and France.

"Somewhere Freud has said that psychologists have frank records of the male, but the female is shrouded and secreted and known to no man. That has been to me our great sin as writers, those of us who are women: that nowhere in our history as artists have we been the earth-shakers because we *dared* not. So I try, oh, just a tiny bit, to write of what I truly see and have known; and not being a member of some powerful literary clan, am scolded for my lack of morality, or ignored. Also, I am concerned greatly with economic position of what we call the 'modern' writers—hardly any of them can make their livings with their art. None of the many leagues of writers, concerning themselves with political and other liberties, have ever concerned themselves with this real liberty of an artist to be truly entitled to even the lowest living wage, or his true liberty to be heard.

"I am married to Henry Varnum Poor, the painter, and have a son and daughter; live in the country near New York; swim, ride, walk, make preserves just to touch the wonderful fruits, cook—and write also."

* * *

Miss Breuer, dark and intense-looking, has been called "post-Marx, post-Freud, post-D. H. Lawrence, post-Joyce." The undeserved neglect accorded her work comes as much from her experimental style as from any alleged obscenity in it. She says: "Experimental writing is always right, . . . even when it cannot be understood by others."

Breuer was her name in her first marriage; her second marriage was to Carl Kahler. Besides her living children, she has had a daughter who died in childhood. Her story, "Birthday," was included in the *Story Anthology* (1931). Dorothy Dunbar Bromley called *Memory of Love* "the American *Anna Karenina*." In both her novels Miss Breuer has undoubtedly come near to realizing her ambition to "look the sexual nature, the animal which women are basically and first, mammals and their young, directly in the face." The result is not "pleasant," but it is powerful.

PRINCIPAL WORKS: Memory of Love, 1934; The Daughter, 1938.

ABOUT: Wilson Library Bulletin October 1938.

BREWSTER, WILLIAM. See "AMERICAN AUTHORS: 1600-1900"

BRIDGE, ANN,* is the carefully guarded pseudonym of an English novelist who is also the wife of an important official of the British Foreign Office,  formerly a diplomat in China, Yugoslavia, and Hungary. She is always aware of censorship, and says it is "enjoined" on her to keep her pseudonymity as strict as possible. She visited the United States in the summer of 1941, arriving from Budapest via Russia and Japan, but though she granted an interview and the publication of her photograph, her name was still suppressed.

All that is known of her personally is that her mother was American, her father

English; that she was born in Bridgend, Surrey, from the name of which she adopted her *nom de plume*; that she spent much of her girlhood visiting relatives in Northern Italy (the scene of *Enchanter's Nightshade*); that she was educated at home and at the London School of Economics; that she spent many years with her husband in North China, and then in Dalmatia; and that she has two sons, one currently in the R.A.F., the other in the British Navy.

She is a tall, brown-haired woman who says she is "very strong, physically and nervously," and whose personality is positive, energetic, and self-confident. She is immensely interested in people, talks to everyone from cab drivers to waiters, and is constantly on the go. She is a devotee of sailing, skiing, and swimming; speaks fluent French, German, Italian, and Chinese, and a smattering of other languages, including Mongolian; and habitually sends telegrams in Latin. During her trip to America she worked on a novel dealing with the Spanish Civil War as seen from the French frontier, doing about a thousand words a day, which she considers "capital progress."

"I don't in the least mind work," she says, "and get on with it rapidly enough, but writing has been my third job for so long that I'm accustomed to pushing it aside. I am wife and mother first, and a writer only afterwards. I'm extremely conscientious, write with care and rewrite with even greater care, so that each book takes me months if not years and is as good as I possibly can make it, but it is definitely spare-time work. . . . I'm saved from turning in on myself as so many full-time writers do." Actually she has so little leisure that most of her writing is done between 7 and 9 A. M., before breakfast.

Her first novel, *Peking Picnic*, won the *Atlantic Monthly* prize in 1932. The China Ann Bridge knows is that of extraterritorial society, not Pearl Buck's China of the Chinese. Nevertheless, of this and her other novels with foreign setting Amy Loveman said truly that she renders "the distinctive characteristics of a foreign society without making that society strange or alien to the pattern of our own."

To quote Miss Loveman further, her chief characteristic is "a sophistication that is made mellow by understanding." She is most at home in the half-lights and pastel colors, in the borderland between thought and reverie, between inclination and emotion. This gives to her writing a Jamesian note, without the involution of style which ac-

* Pseudonym of Mary Dolling (Sanders) O'Malley, Lady O'Malley (1889-).

companied Henry James' subtlety. Her own style is direct and delicate, full of what Margaret Mackprang Mackay called "fluid, luminous images." Her weakness is a detachment which sometimes dissolves her characters into shadows—or even into caricatures. The unevenness of her work doubtless springs from the limitations of the conditions under which it is done. That she has a great natural gift is evidenced by the fact that despite these limitations she has found it possible and necessary to keep on writing.

PRINCIPAL WORKS: Peking Picnic, 1932; Ginger Griffin, 1934; Illyrian Spring, 1935; The Song in the House (short stories) 1936; Enchanter's Nightshade, 1937; Four-Part Setting, 1939.

ABOUT: Journal des Débats August 18, 1933; New York Times Book Review July 27, 1941; Saturday Review of Literature October 23, 1937, October 28, 1939.

BRIDGES, ROBERT (October 23, 1844-April 21, 1930), English poet and Poet Laureate, was born at Walmer, Isle of  Thanet, County of Kent, the son of John Thomas Bridges, landowner, who died when the boy was nine, and Harriett Elizabeth (Affleck) Bridges, daughter of a baronet. He was educated at Eton and at Corpus Christi College, Oxford, from which he received degrees of M.A., M.B., and, later, honorary D. Litt. After leaving the university he traveled on the Continent, then studied medicine at St. Bartholemew's Hospital (the famous "Bart's") in London. He became casualty physician at St. Bartholemew's, assistant physician at the Children's Hospital, and physician at the Great Northern Hospital. He had, however, no real interest in medicine, and as soon as he felt financially able to do so he retired from practice and went to live at Yattendon. For the remainder of his life poetry was his chief concern. In 1884 he married Monica Waterhouse, daughter of a Royal Academician. They had one son and one daughter.

Though he had published many volumes of poems and a few of criticism, Bridges was little known except to an esoteric group when he was appointed Poet Laureate in 1913 to succeed Alfred Austin. He was never a popular writer, and because he refused to write to governmental order became known as "the Silent Laureate." This was hardly fair, for during his years of silence he was preparing his most ambitious work, *The Testament of Beauty*, the embodiment of his life's philosophy. As laureate he received honorary degrees from St. Andrews, Harvard, and the University of Michigan, and in 1929 the Order of Merit. But he led a life essentially retired and secluded, his only public interest being the Society for Pure English, which he ran practically single-handed. He was deeply interested in prosody, and was an authority on French verse forms. He did one great literary service in editing, and rescuing from utterly unmerited obscurity, the poems of Gerard Manley Hopkins (1844-89), a converted Catholic and a priest, whose "modern metaphysical" poetry is the forerunner of much of the most "advanced" verse of today. Hopkins' long correspondence with Bridges has been published.

The laureate's home in later years was at Chilswell, Boar's Hill, Oxford, where he was the friend of many of the university's most eminent men, including George Santayana, the American-Spanish philosopher. Only the year before his death (at eighty-five) Bridges had published his last and most ambitious poem, an unusual prolongation of poetic productivity. To the end he was physically strong and active. In his youth he had been an athlete, and he was a great walker, a tall, lean, strong, sturdy old man, with deep, burning eyes, thick white hair, and a little white beard. He was fond of music, and played the harpsichord well; at Yattendon he trained the village choir. Among his friends he was noted for his sense of humor and robust outspokenness, characteristics undiscoverable in his work. He himself must have enjoyed the newspaper headline which, on his American tour in 1924, on behalf of the Society for Pure English, greeted his refusal to lecture— "King's Canary Won't Chirp!"

Essentially, however, Bridges was an aristocrat, and this characteristic was so prominent in his writing as to obscure other sides of his personality. He never speaks in his poetry of workers or the common people without a tinge of contempt. Though he has been called "the poet of the English landscape," the effect he gives is of coldness, frigid nobility, and intellectual aloofness. Passion he had, and deep passion, but it was always controlled; he believed that art was a thing aside from emotion. Technically he was an innovator, developing a sort of free verse based on natural accent, almost without punctuation.

The fact is that Bridges' poetry is a curious combination of consummate style, pure formal beauty, and a complete lack of profundity of thought. This is most obvious in the long philosophical poem, *The Testament of Beauty,* which was his *magnum opus.* Enthusiastic admirers compared it to Lucretius, and yet it is hackneyed and often prosy. Sometimes it is worse—it becomes rhetorical and garrulous. It is his shorter lyrics, condensed, powerful, and often austerely beautiful, that give him his claim, not to the immortality predicted for him by his worshipers, but to a substantial place among the minor poets of England.

Bridges desired that no biography of him should be written, and himself destroyed the documents which could be used for one. He considered his *Three Friends* to contain everything about himself that he wished the public to know.

When he died he was succeeded in the laureateship by John Masefield.

PRINCIPAL WORKS: *Prose*—Milton's Prosody, 1893; John Keats: A Critical Essay, 1895; The Necessity of Poetry, 1918; Three Friends, 1932. *Poetry*—The Growth of Love, 1876; Eros and Psyche, 1885; Shorter Poems, 1890; Ibant Obscuri, 1917; October and Other Poems, 1920; New Verse 1925; The Testament of Beauty, 1929. *Plays (in verse)*—Prometheus the Firegiver, 1884; The Feast of Bacchus, 1889; Nero, 1890; Palicio, 1890; Ulysses, 1890; The Christian Captives, 1890; Achilles in Scyros, 1890; Humours of the Court, 1893; Demeter: A Masque, 1905. *Anthologies*—The Spirit of Man (in English and French) 1916; Yattendon Hymnal, 1917; Chilswell Book of English Poetry, 1924.

ABOUT: Davis, E. L. Some Modern Poets; Dowden, E. New Studies in Literature; Garrod, H. W. Poetry and the Criticism of Life; Guerard, A. Robert Bridges; Young, F. B. Robert Bridges; Bookman April 1930; London Mercury June 1930; New Statesman April 26, 1930; Saturday Review of Literature April 12, 1930.

BRIEUX, EUGÈNE (January 19, 1858-December 6, 1932), French dramatist, was the son of a poor carpenter living in the working-class Temple District in Paris. He went as far as the intermediate school but then had to leave and go to work, at fifteen, as a clerk. In his off hours the boy read intensively, even teaching himself Latin. He planned vaguely to become a missionary. Actually, however, he was a foreordained playwright, for he had written his first play at the age of twelve. At twenty-one he was

married, and in the same year his first play, *Bernard Palissy* (written with Gaston Salandri), was produced. He had to wait eleven years for his next production. Meanwhile he became a journalist at Dieppe and Rouen, finally rising to the editorship of *La Nouvelliste,* in the latter city. The paper died, and Brieux went back to Paris, freelancing for various newspapers and magazines. His first success was *Blanchette,* produced by Antoine in 1892. For twenty years thereafter, Brieux wrote a play a year. He was primarily a teacher and a crusader, and the controversial nature of the subjects of many of his dramas subjected him to official censorship—particularly in the case of *Les Avariés,* famous in America and England as *Damaged Goods.* Bernard Shaw became his sponsor in England, and hailed him as the greatest French dramatist since Molière. That he certainly was not.

This big, handsome man, rather "English" and athletic in appearance, was actually a semi-invalid for the latter part of his life, and lived in strict seclusion on the Riviera. He died at Nice of pleurisy. He had attained recognition before his death—was a Commander of the Legion of Honor and a member of the French Academy, in fact the only representative it ever sent to a foreign institute (to the American Academy of Arts and Letters in 1914). At the same time he was derided as "the Tolstoy of the Temple District" and "honest Brieux."

The fact is, Brieux was always didactic, always in deadly earnest though his plays were labeled comedies, for he knew people would rather laugh than be instructed. He himself knew very well that it was the causes to which his plays were dedicated—the welfare of the poor, of women, of children—that meant more to him than dramatic style or substance, though he had these too in full measure. He said of himself: "I have wished that the amount of suffering upon the earth might be diminished a little because I have lived. . . . The sight of suffering in others has always been unbearable to me." The present realistic public approach to many social questions, including those of illegitimacy and venereal disease, is in part at least due to that ambition of Eugène Brieux's.

PRINCIPAL WORKS AVAILABLE IN ENGLISH: The June Bugs, 1907; Three Plays (Maternity, The Three Daughters of M. Dupont, Damaged Goods) 1911; The School for Mothers-in-Law, 1911; The Philanthropists, 1913; Two Plays (Blanchette, The Escape) 1913; Three Plays (The Red Robe, False Gods, Woman on Her Own) 1916; The Deserter, 1917; Artists' Families, 1918; The Americans in

France, 1920; The Cradle, 1922; The Advocate, 1923.

ABOUT: Bennett, A. Books and Persons; Clark, B. H. Contemporary French Dramatists; Dukes, A. Modern Dramatists; Scheifley, W. H. Brieux and Contemporary French Society; Thomas, P. V. The Plays of Eugène Brieux; Forum December 1921; North American Review March 1915; Revue des Deux Mondes December 15, 1932; Saturday Review (London) December 10, 1932.

*BRIFFAULT, ROBERT (1876-), English anthropologist, philosopher of history, and novelist, was born in London, the son

of Frederic Briffault, a Frenchman in the diplomatic service in Spain and Italy, and Margaret M. (Stewart) Briffault, a Scotswoman. Briffault père became involved in the plots centering around Louis Napoleon, resigned from the diplomatic corps, and became naturalized as a British subject. The son was educated privately, chiefly in Florence. He studied medicine in London, and at the extremely early age of eighteen received the degrees of Bachelor of Medicine and of Surgery. He went to New Zealand in 1894, and at once started practice there. He was also president of the Auckland Branch of the New Zealand Institute, in whose *Transactions* he published a series of medical articles.

When the First World War began, he volunteered, and served with the Fifth Yorkshire and Lancashire Regiment in France, Flanders, and Gallipoli. He was gassed and disabled for active duty at Nieuport, and was demobilized with the Military Cross (awarded him twice for conspicuous bravery). After the war he returned to England, but retired from his profession, and until economic and sociologic questions became his chief concern, his work was in the field of social anthropology. His first articles in this province appeared in the *English Review* in 1907, but he was forty-three before his first book was published. Always inclined to the Left, about 1930 he became an avowed Communist. In recent years he has tended to disagree with doctrinaire Communist tactics and trends, and on latest information he was doing war work in England. Until the outbreak of the Hitler War he had lived for the most part in Paris.

Mr. Briffault has been married twice: first to Anna Clarke, who died in 1919, leaving a son and a daughter; and secondly to Herma Hoyt, an American from Ohio, who is well known as a translator, chiefly from the Italian.

He is dark, with strongly marked, aquiline features. He loves animals, especially cats, and usually owns a Siamese. He is fond of Italian art, particularly of the Venetian and Florentine schools of the Renaissance, and is devoted to opera, both Italian and Wagnerian. Among his literary preferences he lists Shakespeare, Dante, Shelley, Montaigne James Joyce, Voltaire, Victor Hugo, Anatole France, and Goethe; among his literary dislikes, Racine, Pope, Dryden, Schiller, Paul Valéry, and Gertrude Stein. In religion he is an agnostic and materialist.

Mr. Briffault's earlier books, culminating in *The Mothers,* and including *Rational Evolution,* were masterly summaries of his theories of anthropology from the psychological approach. *The Mothers* was probably the most notable work in its field since *The Golden Bough,* Sir James Frazer's epochal work. His more purely economic and political works have been too angry and controversial to be very convincing. Of late years he has become a novelist, rather unfortunately so—although *Europa* was widely read. His novels are merely vehicles for his social ideas, rather than solid pictures of the pre-war Europe which is their scene, and they are written in a stilted, unreal language which makes it impossible to think of their characters as living beings. The objection to them on the ground of undue frankness is less tenable. It is obvious, however, that Mr. Briffault is not a born novelist, and it is to be hoped that after the war he will revert to the style of his earlier books.

PRINCIPAL WORKS: The Making of Humanity, 1919; Psyche's Lamp: A Revaluation of Psychological Principles, 1921; The Mothers: A Study of the Origins of Sentiments and Institutions (3 vols.) 1927; Rational Evolution (a rewriting of The Making of Humanity) 1930; Sin and Sex, 1931; Breakdown: The Collapse of Traditional Civilization, 1932; Europa: The Days of Ignorance (novel) 1935; Reasons for Anger, 1936; Europa in Limbo (novel) 1937; Decline and Fall of the British Empire, 1938; The Ambassadress (novel) 1939; Fandango (novel) 1940.

ABOUT: Westermarck, E. A. Three Essays on Sex and Marriage; Nation September 2, 1931; Saturday Review of Literature March 18, 1940; Wilson Library Bulletin January 1936.

BRIGHOUSE, HAROLD (July 26, 1882-), English novelist and dramatist, was born in Eccles, Lancashire, and for several years engaged in the cotton trade.

---

* Died December 11, 1948.

During the First World War, Brighouse was a member of the Royal Air Force, and was attached to the Intelligence Staff of the Air Ministry. As member of the literary staff of the Manchester *Guardian* he put in some time as dramatic critic of the paper, and became well acquainted with Miss Annie Elizabeth Horniman and her repertory theatre in Manchester. His first play, *Dealing in Futures*, a study of the relations between capital and labor, was produced by the Glasgow Repertory Theatre in 1909. *Garside's Career*, a comedy of politics, written in 1914, was produced at the Copley Theatre, Boston, Mass., in February 1919. *Hobson's Choice*, first produced by Miss Horniman in 1916, reached the Comedy Theatre in New York City later. Brighouse, who has written fully fifty one-act plays, was represented by two at a time in April 1918, when Whitford Kane was playing

Lonesome Like at the Comedy Theatre with the Washington Square Players, and *Maid of France*, a war sketch, was being performed at the Greenwich Theatre. In 1930-31 he was chairman of the dramatic committee of the Authors' Society. Brighouse lives in London; his recreations are play-going and fell-walking.

Harold Brighouse has been called the last survivor of the "Manchester School" of playwrights, which was launched when Stanley Houghton's play *Hindle Wakes* (which Brighouse novelized in 1927) was produced. The success of the Irish Players before the First World War had given a stimulus to folk drama, and Brighouse has an excellent sense of the homeliness, humor, and sense of character of the Lancashire folk. He is not, however, an exclusively Lancashire dramatist; only five of his plays have Lancashire backgrounds. Six plays in all were produced by Miss Horniman's company. Brighouse also adapted Molnar's *Mr. Somebody* for production in the United States, in 1936. His novels are less well known here.

PRINCIPAL WORKS: *Novels*—Fossie For Short, 1917; Hobson's Choice (with C. Forrest) 1917; The Silver Lining, 1918; The Marbeck Inn, 1920; Hepplestalls, 1922; The Wrong Shadow, 1923; Captain Shapely, 1923; Hindle Wakes (from play by S. Houghton) 1927. *Plays*—Dealing in Futures, 1909; Graft, 1911; The Odd Man Out, 1912; The Game, 1913; Garside's Career, 1914; The Road to Raebury, 1915; The Hillarys (with S. Houghton) 1915; Hobson's Choice and The Clock Goes Round,

1916; Other Times: A Volume of Three Lancashire Plays, 1920; Mary's John, 1924; What's Bred in the Bone, 1927; Safe Amongst the Pigs, 1929; In America, 1936; London Front, 1941. *One-Act Plays*—Plays For the Meadow and the Lawn, 1921; Open-Air Plays, 1927; Four Fantasies, 1931; The Funk-Hole, 1938; Under the Pylon, British Passport, 1938.

ABOUT: Brighouse, H. Hobson's Choice (see Preface by B. I. Payne).

*BRIGHT, Mrs. MARY CHAVELITA (DUNNE) ("George Egerton") (December 14, 1860-   ), English novelist, dramatist, and translator, was born in Melbourne, Australia, a daughter of Captain John J. Dunne of Queen's County and Isabel George (Bynon) Dunne of Glamorganshire. The girl was educated privately, and had an exciting series of experiences outside school. She was in camp at Tauranga during the Maori War; went in a sailing vessel to Valparaiso to see her mother's uncle, Admiral Don George Bynon, arriving during a bombardment; then traveled to Wales and Ireland. Mary Dunne's first marriage, to H. H. W. Melville, in 1888, ended next year with his death. In 1891 she married Egerton Clairmonte, who died ten years later—he was the author of a novel, *The Africander*. In 1901 she became the wife of Reginald Golding Bright. Intending at first to be an artist, she became a writer as an afterthought when "family affairs" prevented the necessary course of study.

"George Egerton's" *Keynotes* (1893) describes the intimacies of married life; it is the book of a devoted wife inseparable from a stupid husband. The next-year's *Discords* voiced the thoughts of a woman "conscious of being ill-treated and driven to despair." Aside from these and other novels also somewhat in the vein of "Elizabeth," "George Egerton" made an English adaptation from Henry Bernstein's play *La Rafale (The Whirlwind,* 1911) and translated Knut Hamsun's novel, *Hunger,* in 1926.

An original founder of the Irish Genealogical Research Society, Mrs. Bright, with her eightieth year behind her, makes her home in London and continues to list her recreations as languages, dialects, and needlework. She has traveled extensively in Europe, has been to South America, and has visited the United States four times.

* Died August 13, 1945.

She is described as having an attractive, delicate face with a decided chin.

PRINCIPAL WORKS: Keynotes, 1893; Discords, 1894; Young Ofeg's Ditties, 1895; Symphonies, 1897; Fantasia, 1898; The Wheel of God, 1898; Rosa Amorosa, 1901; Flies in Amber, 1905; His Wife's Family, (play) 1908; The Backsliders (play) 1910; The Rafale (adaptation) 1911; The Daughter of Heaven (adaptation) 1912; The Attack (adaptation) 1912; Wild Thyme (adaptation) 1914; Camilla States Her Case, 1925.

ABOUT: Hansson, L. M. Six Modern Women.

BRINIG, MYRON (December 22, 1900-), American novelist, was born in Minneapolis, the son of Maurice and Rebecca (Coin) Brinig. He  was a student at New York University from 1917 to 1919, and at Columbia from 1919 to 1921, but did not graduate. He was reared in Butte, Mont., the "Silver Bow" of his novels, and he knew that section of the Northwest

Disraeli

at just the right period—when pioneers were still living from whom he could hear stories of the old days, and yet in the midst of the changes of a later period. As the son of a Jewish storekeeper, he gained insight into another aspect of life which has been a constituent part of the building of the West, and yet which has seldom been considered by authors in this field. Mr. Brinig made good use of it in *Singermann*, the story of a Jewish immigrant who became a Western merchant.

Perhaps the most successful of his novels was *The Sisters*, which later became a popular motion picture. This was an epitome of the evolution from pioneer days to modern urbanization in Montana in terms of the experiences and lives of a family. *May Flavin*, somewhat in the same mode, followed it but was less successful. *Wide Open Town* is a flamboyant picture of Butte in the great years of copper-mining, when it was the only town of any size in a vast area, and hence the Mecca of miners and lumbermen in their leisure hours, and of the gamblers, saloon-keepers, and light ladies who catered to them.

Mr. Brinig is a dark, stocky man, still youthful in appearance. He is unmarried; recent addresses are New York and New Mexico. He has not forgotten Montana, though he has visited it seldom of late, and he can still write about it with loving, nostalgic detail, but he is beginning to paint in other backgrounds more recent in his experience, a change which his admirers find cause to lament. Fred T. Marsh, in reviewing one of his novels, remarked: "Without being a sentimentalist, he loves lingering over old times and old characters. His prose is distinctive, even powerful. He approaches his work with seriousness, which is not to say that it lacks humor or sentiment." The chief exception to this judgment might be *Madonna Without Child*, which is both humorless and sentimental; however, as a first novel these faults of youth can be excused. Mr. Brinig's most recent books have been less favorably received than the best of his early work. He does his writing in regular hours. Unlike most novelists, he seldom writes short stories, but confines himself almost entirely to the more expansive full-length narrative mode.

PRINCIPAL WORKS: Madonna Without Child, 1929; Singermann, 1929; Anthony in the Nude, 1930; Wide Open Town, 1931; This Man Is My Brother, 1932; The Flutter of an Eyelid, 1933; Out of Life, 1934; The Sun Sets in the West, 1935; The Sisters, 1937; May Flavin, 1938; Anne Minton's Life, 1939; All of Their Lives, 1941.

ABOUT: Bookman April 1931; Time June 13, 1939.

BRINTON, CLARENCE CRANE (February 2, 1898-), American historian who signs his works as Crane Brinton. writes: "I was born in Winsted, Conn. I was graduated from Harvard, *summa cum laude,* in 1919, having just got in on the fringe of the war of 1914-18 by serving in the Students' Army Training Corps. After a year's travel on a Harvard fellowship

Bachrach

in a post-war Europe that now seems in retrospect amazingly cheerful, I spent three years on a Rhodes Scholarship at New College, Oxford, where I got my university teacher's license—the Ph.D.—in 1923. Since then I have had a sober and orthodox career as a teacher of history at Harvard, attaining as associate professor in 1935 the serenity of academic tenure. My interests as reflected in the courses I teach and in my books have been centered on France, England, and Germany in the eighteenth and nineteenth centuries, and more especially on the French revolutionary period as a focus.

"The history of my mind is hardly more lively than that of my career as student and teacher. As an undergraduate I came under the rather fantastically contradictory influences of Irving Babbitt and Harold Laski. At Oxford, like many American Rhodes Scholars, I found a romantic atmosphere, but no creed and in my particular field no great man. Since my return to teaching and writing I should suppose I have proved my orthodoxy by following the usual pattern from youthful radicalism to middle-aged moderation. Or perhaps the Babbitt influence proved stronger than the Laski influence. Like many of my generation I consider myself 'anti-intellectual,' not in the wildly romantic sense of disliking reason, but in the skeptical sense of doubting from actual experience the extent to which reason, as intellectuals commonly use the term, affects the actions of men in societies. If sectarian names may be used, I suppose I may at this stage be considered a Paretan.

"Since my writing is so closely related to my teaching, and since I have hitherto managed to avoid the miscellaneous public speaking which drains off so much academic energy, I have managed to write quantitatively a good deal, at least for a professor. Especially with the *Saturday Review of Literature* and with the *Southern Review* I have had most agreeable relations. I am sorry not to be able to report any hobbies or avocations beyond gardening, walking, and a vulgar and unintellectual pleasure in motoring. I believe I can balance these tastes by confessing that I have been for the past ten years a devout summer resident of the latest haven of the American intellectual—Vermont. I am unmarried."

* * *

Professor Brinton is editor of the *American Oxonian,* and serves on the editorial boards of the *American Scholar* and the *Journal of the History of Ideas.* Albert Guerard called him "a civilized man, a disciple of the Enlightenment." Jacques Barzun remarked that his books "prove, among other things, that a gifted teacher and writer can modulate from the monographic study of records to the composition of entertaining biography without losing, at either end, his scholarship or his chosen public."

PRINCIPAL WORKS: The Political Ideas of the English Romanticists, 1936; The Jacobins: An Essay in the New History, 1930; English Political Thought in the Nineteenth Century, 1933; A Decade of Revolution: 1789-99, 1934; French Revolutionary Legislation on Illegitimacy, 1936; The Lives of Talleyrand, 1936; The Anatomy of Revolution, 1938; Nietzsche, 1941.

ABOUT: Christian Science Monitor Magazine September 21, 1940; Saturday Review of Literature March 22, 1941.

BRISBANE, ARTHUR (December 12, 1864-December 25, 1936), American journalist, was the son of the radical economist Albert Brisbane, a Fourierist and member of the Brook Farm colony, and his wife Sarah (White) Brisbane. He was born in Buffalo, and after a public school education spent five years of travel and study in France and Germany. In 1882 he

International

went to work as a reporter for the New York *Sun* ("inducted into daily journalism by that renegade from his Brook Farm ideals, Charles A. Dana," as the *Christian Century* puts it), and then became first London correspondent, then editor of the *Evening Sun.* From 1890 to 1897 he was managing editor of Pulitzer's *World,* first of the "yellow journals." In the latter year he went to the *Evening Journal* and to Hearst, with whom he was closely associated thereafter. He bought papers in Washington and Milwaukee and then sold them to Hearst; in 1918 he edited the Chicago *Herald and Examiner* and helped to found the Chicago *American;* and in his last years he was editor of the tabloid New York *Daily Mirror..* He was the highest paid newspaper man in the world, receiving $260,000 a year for his columns, "Today" and "This Week" (he owned the copyright of the titles), which reached an estimated audience of 30,000,000. In 1912 he married Phoebe Cary. He died of a heart attack, on Christmas day, just past his seventy-second birthday. His large fortune was partly the result of immense real estate holdings in the United States and Mexico.

For nearly forty years Brisbane was Hearst's mouthpiece and the public's "daily mental Santa Claus" (*Literary Digest*). He subordinated whatever beliefs he himself held to those of the Lord of San Simeon. He contradicted himself glibly, and participated in activities (such as prize fights and horse races) which he excoriated in his columns. He was an outstanding example of the complete cynic. It is difficult to recall that he was his idealistic father's son. His editorials, as *Newsweek* remarks, were "written for and believed by the uneducated," and it was the uneducated who made him rich and temporarily famous.

Yet Brisbane had much natural talent. As the *New Republic* says, he was "a master of the stripped reportorial style, . . . also a master of the commonplace." *Time* notes that he "possessed a great stock of odds and ends of information, like the hodge-podge of an almanac, which was mightily impressive to his readers." Oswald Garrison Villard has probably said the final and kindest word on this mild-looking man who turned out daily enormous masses of copy and had practically no private life of his own:

"A man with an extraordinary range of knowledge, with unquestioned writing ability, . . . [who] wrote down to the mass mind. He made the widest possible appeal by reducing things to their simplest form. . . . A hired man who bartered his beliefs and rejoiced in his shame because thereby he made great sums of money."

PRINCIPAL WORKS: Editorials From the Hearst Newspapers, 1906; Mary Baker G. Eddy, 1908; Today and the Future Day, 1925.

ABOUT: Gauvreau, E. My Last Million Readers; Christian Century January 6, 1937; Nation January 2, 9, 1937; New Republic January 6, 1937; Newsweek January 2, 1937; Time January 4, 1937, March 18, 1940.

BRISTOW, GWEN (September 16, 1903-), American novelist, writes: "I was born in Marion, S.C., the daughter of Louis

Judson Bristow and Caroline Cornelia (Winkler) Bristow, and was educated at Judson College, Marion, Ala., and in the School of Journalism of Columbia University. I was a reporter on the New Orleans *Times-Picayune* from 1925 to 1933. Since then I have given all my time to writing fiction. I was married in 1929 to Bruce Manning, at that time a newspaper reporter, now a motion picture producer. We live in Beverly Hills, Calif. My mystery novel, *The Invisible Host,* written with my husband, was dramatized in 1930 by Owen Davis under the title of *The Ninth Guest,* and later made into a motion picture.

"I don't remember when I first decided I was going to be a writer; it simply never occurred to me that I was going to be anything else. From the time when I first discovered the use of a pencil I have never been able to see a pile of white paper without wanting to scribble on it. My father, a minister, had been a newspaper correspondent before ordination, while he served in the army during the Spanish-American

war. My own first appearance in print occurred when I was twelve. When I was graduated from high school I wrote a two-act play that was presented by the graduating class. In college I wrote several other plays, and also wrote anything assigned by any teacher to anybody, with a price-range of from twenty-five cents to three dollars. In New York, when I attended the Pulitzer School of Journalism at Columbia, I earned my way, among other methods, by writing rags-to-riches biographies of successful business men and selling them to trade journals. As a newspaper reporter, I had the time of my life. My husband was a reporter on a rival newspaper to the *Times-Picayune,* the *Item,* and our marriage made us grimmer professional rivals than ever, doing our best to beat each other on exclusive stories. Meanwhile we were both doing a lot of private scribbling between assignments. I had written two novels by this time, which were so awful that even in my exuberance I knew they were not fit to print. Our mystery novel grew out of schemes we concocted to murder our next-door neighbor, who had a raucous radio!

"It was in Hollywood that I began writing my trilogy of Louisiana novels, taking the same family from pre-Revolutionary days to the World War. The first, *Deep Summer*— the fifth novel I had written besides mystery stories—was a success. In between novels I have gone on strenuous lecture tours. In 1939 we bought a house in Beverly Hills, where I have the two unnecessary luxuries I have dreamed of all my life—a swimming pool and a private study with a really big desk, and even bigger sofa, and plenty of windows.

"People ask us how we manage with two writers in the same family. It's really very simple. He never sees anything I write until it is printed and I never see anything he writes until the picture is on the screen. So, as that leaves us nothing to argue about, we can spend our leisure time outdoors playing games, which is what we both like to do anyway."

PRINCIPAL WORKS: The Invisible Host (with B. Manning) 1930; Deep Summer, 1937; The Handsome Road, 1938; This Side of Glory, 1940.

ABOUT: New York Post April 17, 1940; Publishers' Weekly March 16, 1940; Saturday Review of Literature February 22, 1941.

BRITTAIN, VERA MARY (1896?-), English essayist and novelist, writes: "My family came from Staffordshire and had lived for about two centuries in the neighborhood of the Potteries up to the time of my birth. We moved, however, when I was very young, and my childhood was spent in the pleasant English countryside of Cheshire and Derbyshire. I was educated at a private school—St. Monica's, Kingswood—and went up to Somerville College, Oxford, with an exhibition in 1914. This inauspicious year made my stay there a short one. So many of my friends were serving at the front that the life of a student became intolerable, and in 1915 I became a Red Cross nurse and served for four adventurous years in army hospitals in London, Malta, and France. This period is described in *Testament of Youth.*

My work and experiences during the war turned me from an ordinary patriotic young woman into a convinced pacifist, and I have been closely associated with the work of Peace Movements in both England and the United States, particularly since the appearance of *Testament of Youth.*

"In 1919 I went back to Oxford and finished the remaining two years of my course in the Honours School of Modern History. During those two years one of my contemporaries at Oxford was Winifred Holtby, who had also served during the war in the Women's Army Auxiliary Corps. We went down from Oxford together, and in 1922 settled in a flat in London and set to work to bombard publishers and editors with our early efforts. Publishers proved more accessible than editors, and I published two early novels in 1923 and 1924. My life with Winifred Holtby, both then and later, is described in *Testament of Friendship.*

"Between 1921 and 1925 I traveled extensively in Europe, and my journeys included a visit to the Rhineland, the Ruhr, and Cologne, during the post-war occupation of Germany.

"In 1925 I was married to George E. G. Catlin, then Assistant Professor, and afterwards Professor of Politics, in Cornell University. My husband and I had been at Oxford together, as he too had served in the war, but we did not meet at that time, and I came to know him through a 'fan-mail' letter he wrote me about my novel, *The Dark Tide.* Soon after our marriage I went out to America with my husband and lived for a year in Ithaca, N.Y., and New York City. In 1927 I had a son, and in 1930 a daughter.

During the babyhood of the children, I made my home in England, but have always spent long intervals in the United States, and in 1934 came over for the first time on a lecture tour. I did a second tour in 1937 and a third in 1940. Our London home is now in Chelsea, and we have a country cottage at Allum Green in the New Forest."

* * *

Vera Brittain is a handsome woman, with wavy dark hair and chiseled features. In Chelsea she lives on Cheyne Walk, made famous by Carlyle, Whistler, and others. She was born in Newcastle, the daughter of Thomas Arthur Brittain and Edith Mary (Bervon) Brittain. Her little daughter, at ten, says, "I seem to be good at writing, so I suppose I'll have to be a writer too."

In an interview during a recent lecture tour, Miss Brittain said: "It took me four years to write *Testament of Youth*—one of the babies was born in the middle. Otherwise, I think I might have written it in two years. But life, either personal or artistic, is much more complete with children. I used to give only two hours a day to my book. But if I had given it up entirely, some day I would have found domestic life intolerable. My husband wouldn't have liked the kind of woman who hung around the house all day waiting for him to take her out at night." She and Dr. Catlin have separate workrooms, but similar working habits, both preferring to write at night. Her advice to writers is: "Start writing young, simply because you can stand the knocks much better. The only way to write is to write. Don't study too much how to do it. You have to find your own technique. You can't find that in any text-book."

PRINCIPAL WORKS: Verses of a V.A.D., 1918; The Dark Tide (novel) 1923; Not Without Honour (novel) 1924; Women's Work in Modern England, 1928; Halcyon: or, The Future of Monogamy, 1929; Testament of Youth, 1933; Poems of the War and After, 1934; Honourable Estate (novel) 1936; Thrice a Stranger, 1938; Testament of Friendship, 1940; England's Hour, 1940.

ABOUT: Christian Science Monitor Magazine February 17, 1940; March 1, 1941; Literary Digest October 14, 1933; Saturday Review of Literature January 13, 1940; Wilson Library Bulletin March 1934.

BRIUSOV. See BRYUSOV

*BROADHURST, GEORGE H. (1866-), Anglo-American dramatist, was born in Walsall, Staffordshire, England, in the heart of the "Black Country," the youngest child of a poor family. When he received a prize for knowledge of theology and the cate-

* Died January 31, 1952.

chism, and was praised by the future Archbishop of York, his mother hoped that George might have a clerical career. Instead he ran away from home at sixteen and came to the United States by steerage. Going directly to Chicago, young Broadhurst obtained a job with the Board of Trade at $5 a week and held it seven years. To relieve the tediousness of this vocation, he went

regularly to Hooley's (later Powers') Theatre and saw the first acts of plays from the gallery, went home to figure out what the playwright would do with his theme and characters in the second and third acts, and then went back to the gallery subsequently to see how his findings compared with the dramatist's.

Later he became manager of several traveling theatrical companies; in the off season he worked in a Minnesota grain house, and while a bookkeeper there wrote his first play, *The Speculator,* which made some money. His first farce, *What Happened to Jones,* was refused by several managers because it had only one scene, but this farce and its successor, *The Wrong Mr. Wright,* were successfully produced. Broadhurst also managed the Academy of Music, Baltimore; the Lyceum in Minneapolis; the Harris House in Grand Forks, N.D., and the Bush Theatre in San Francisco. In course of time he had his own theatre, the Broadhurst, now operating on West 44th Street in New York City.

The Man of the Hour (1907) was Broadhurst's first pronounced New York success; it was a play of political corruption in which the central figure, Richard Horrigan, the Boss, was supposed to have been derived from New York City's Tammany leader, the late Charles F. Murphy. *Bought and Paid For* (1913), his best-known play, which has also been filmed, was a drama depicting the struggle between a noble telephone operator and her financier husband. It struck George Jean Nathan as possessing "one exceedingly well-drawn character, a terse editorial technic, and a rather nicely perceived and executed sense of dramatic balance." Broadhurst wrote several other well-carpentered plays, and occasionally collaborated in writing musical comedies. In 1926 he returned to live permanently in England, and has since written no plays, although

he has contributed short stories to magazines in both countries. From 1908 to 1915 Broadhurst made a fortune of $342,514. Disputes with his first wife, Mrs. Ida Raymond Broadhurst, at one time made it necessary to conduct his business from the state of New Jersey. Later he married Lillian Trimble Bradley, herself a playwright.

PRINCIPAL WORKS: What Happened to Jones, 1910; Why Smith Left Home, 1912; The Law of the Land, 1914; Bought and Paid For, 1916; The Man of the Hour, 1916.

ABOUT: New York Sun August 3, 1919; Theatre Magazine May 1907; October 1917.

*BROCH, HERMANN** (November 1, 1886-), German novelist, spent his childhood in Austria, where he pursued mathematical and philosophical studies. Becoming director of a textile concern in Vienna, he frequented the company of writers who considered themselves the advanced guard of Austrian literature, and met in the Rotundensaal of the

Café Zentral to smoke and play chess. Broch's company was pleasantly tolerated, but he was not considered one of their number; not "a man of the guild." One *littérateur* even included one of Broch's stories in a work of his own without acknowledgment, and without remonstrance on Broch's part. But he was biding his time, and with the *Schlafwaendler (The Sleepwalkers)* of 1931 became an outstanding writer who eclipsed his erstwhile companions, although he broke silence only when he had something of importance to say. Three years later *Die Unbekannte Grosse* was translated into English as *The Unknown Quantity.* In a paper on James Joyce contributed to *Neue Rundschau,* Broch indicated that he believed abstract thinking combined with the pictorial a requirement of the modern novel.

Broch was living in Berlin at the time that *The Unknown Quantity* was translated. He is and will be known, however, for his first novel—actually his first, not merely the first to be translated—the trilogy *The Sleep Walkers,* in three volumes, turned into English by Willa and Edwin Muir. This involved and powerful work deals in each volume with a different class and a different period: "Pasenow: or, Romanticism," is laid in 1888; "Esch: or, Anarchism," in 1903; "Huguenau: or, Realism," in 1918, at the end of the First World War. In the last volume all three titular heroes are brought together, and Huguenau, the symbol of single-minded business and profit, triumphs. The theme in general is the disintegration of social values through the differentiation of men's objectives into separate categories, stripping humanity bare of its interrelations which provide the essential materials of a real civilization. Broch, however, is no cynic and no pessimist; he believes that this is an historical process which will in time reverse itself, that man will again become unified and a new civilization will arise from the dry-rot of the old.

Edwin Muir, writing in the *Bookman* in 1932, said of *The Sleep Walkers* that it was "a work of great beauty," and of Broch that he was "an exquisite artist, a psychologist of astonishing depth and originality, a thinker of sweeping range." He spoke of the complex nature of the trilogy, through which is scattered a series of essay-chapters on the philosophical theme of the book, and also (in the third volume) an unconnected story acting as a sort of counterpoint to the major *motif,* some of it, in the original, written in verse as a sonnet sequence ("The Adventures of a Salvation Army Girl in Berlin"). Broch's clarion cry throughout is: "The unity of humanity must be restored." Summing up the book, Mr. Muir said: "It is a work of formal elaboration and harmonious balance, done with consummate skill and exquisite finish."

Hermann Broch has lived in the United States in recent years—a refugee from Hitlerism, though he is impeccably Aryan and Teutonic—and was awarded a Guggenheim fellowship in 1941.

WORKS AVAILABLE IN ENGLISH: The Sleep Walkers, 1932; The Unknown Quantity, 1935.

ABOUT: Bookman November 1932; Life and Letters To-Day Winter 1936; Neue Rundschau January 1933, May 1934; Saturday Review of Literature October 19, 1940.

BROCK, CLUTTON-. See CLUTTON-BROCK

BROD, MAX (May 27, 1884-), German novelist, poet, dramatist, and essayist, was born in Prague, then part of the Austro-Hungarian Empire. His father, Adolf Brod, was a Jewish banker. He was educated at the Prague Grammar School and University, receiving the D.Jur. degree. (Later the university conferred an honorary LL.D. degree upon him.) In 1907 he began the practice of law in Prague, and became a minor government official. Later he also entered journalism, being for a number of years edi-

tor of the *Prager Tagblatt,* a daily newspaper. In 1912 he began his activities as a Zionist, and he was the founder and vice-president of the National Jewish Council of Austro-Hungary. He was a lifelong friend of Franz Kafka, and on Kafka's death he rescued his manuscripts and published them —although against the author's express orders that all his literary remains should be destroyed. Dr. Brod also wrote a biography of Kafka, as well as one of Heine. He was interested in the stage from his youth, and among his plays (not translated into English) is one on Byron.

After the Nazi conquest of Austria, Dr. Brod went to Palestine, where he now lives permanently in Tel Aviv. He is the director there of the Habima Theatre. He is unmarried. Four of his novels have been translated into English, but his work in other fields is not known to the English-speaking public. His novels are for the most part historical, and deal particularly with the Jews of the Middle Ages. However, his best known novel, *The Redemption of Tycho Brahe,* is a psychological study of that great astronomer of the sixteenth century. He has also published, in German, several volumes of essays, including a scholarly work on Paganism, Judaism, and Christianity. He is the author of several volumes of poems as well, and his plays were produced regularly in Austria and Germany before the Hitler regime.

One critic has said of him: "Brod's work is strongly steeped in a peculiar compound of the Jewish, Czech, and German national spirits, . . . fantastic, mystic, with flashes of violent realism, strongly erotic, intellectually acute, and abnormally sensitive to atmosphere. It is further characterized by exceptional narrative skill and limpidity of style."

His novels for some reason were not very successful in English, and nothing of his has been translated since 1930.

WORKS AVAILABLE IN ENGLISH: The Redemption of Tycho Brahe, 1928; Reubeni: Prince of the Jews, 1928; Three Loves, 1929; The Kingdom of Love, 1930.

BROMFIELD, LOUIS (December 27, 1896-), American novelist, was born in Mansfield, Ohio, the son of Charles and Annette Maria (Coulter) Bromfield. His father was a farmer, the descendant of Ohio pioneers of the eighteenth century, and Louis expected to follow him on the ancestral farm. With this in mind he spent a year in the Cornell University Agricultural College, but he was already in revolt against the poverty, hard work, and narrow

environment of his childhood, and instead of going on with his course he transferred to an arts course at Columbia. When the First World War broke out, he left college and joined the French army as an ambulance driver. In two years he saw service on every sector of the front, and he was awarded the *Croix de Guerre*. Columbia gave him an honorary B.A. because of his war service, though he never returned to college.

Instead he worked with the City News Association in New York, then with the Associated Press, and then with the *Musical Courier*. (Later, when he lived in France, he was foreign correspondent of *Musical America*.) Subsequently he was on the staff of Putnam's, assisted a theatrical producer, was a private tutor, did theatre, music, and art criticism for the *Bookman*, and was one of the original staff of *Time*.

Bromfield had already written four novels, later destroyed, before he published *The Green Bay Tree* in 1924. In 1921 he had married Mary Appleton Wood, and they had three daughters. Largely to give them a European education, he moved to France. The 1926 Pulitzer Prize was awarded to him for *Early Autumn*. In 1933 he bought a 1000-acre farm near his birthplace and announced that he would thenceforth devote himself to the American scene in his writing —a promise he has not kept.

Bromfield's friends have often wondered when he writes, for he seems always to have time for gardening—he is a passionate gardener—for swimming, skiing, painting, or social gatherings. As a matter of fact he writes only two hours a day, from 9.30 to 11.30 A.M., but he works intensively in that time, as his eleven books and two plays testify. As the *Saturday Review of Literature* said, he is "restless, gregarious, apparently lazy and easy-going, . . . with abundant versatility and crowding powers of invention."

Bromfield's interest centers around his women characters, who are always the central or at least the strongest figures in his novels. His own favorites among his books are *The Farm* and *The Strange Case of Miss Annie Spragg*. Louise Maunsell Field has noted his "respect for the rich traditions of the Anglo-Saxon novel, . . . balanced by a fondness for experiment," and the late

Stuart P. Sherman said Bromfield's "glamorous flowing movement" affected him "like the cantabile style in music."

Bromfield's recent books have been strongly criticised for false glitter and Hollywood sensationalism, and it is true that his new novels are snatched up, on publication, for the movies. Bromfield resents being asked to duplicate the quality of his earliest volumes.

Physically he is tall and spare, with a loose-knit body and a leisurely manner which is belied by his actual vivacity and energy. Recently he was made a Chevalier of the Legion of Honor for his services in repatriating the International Brigade in Spain, and he has even been mentioned as a possible candidate for Governor of Ohio on the Democratic ticket. He admits that he would some day like to be Secretary of Agriculture.

PRINCIPAL WORKS: The Green Bay Tree, 1924; Possession, 1925; Early Autumn, 1926; The House of Women (play) 1927; The Strange Case of Miss Annie Spragg, 1928; Awake and Rehearse (short stories) 1929; Twenty Four Hours, 1930; A Modern Hero, 1932; The Farm, 1933; Here Today and Gone Tomorrow (includes No. 55, The Listener, Fourteen Years After, and Miss Mehaffy) 1934; The Man Who Had Everything, 1935; DeLuxe (play) 1935; The Rains Came, 1937; It Takes All Kinds, 1939; Night in Bombay, 1940; Wild Is the River, 1941; Until the Day Break, 1942

ABOUT: Bookman April 1932; Canadian Forum July 1931; Nation October 23, 1935; New York Times Book Review March 29, 1942; Saturday Review of Literature April 14, 1934, October 23, 1937; Time October 25, 1937, May 11, 1940, December 28, 1940.

BROOKE, RUPERT (August 3, 1887-April 23, 1915), English poet, was born at Rugby, the second son of William Parker Brooke and Mary Ruth (Cotterill) Brooke. The boy was named Rupert Chawner Brooke. His father was a housemaster at Rugby School, and Rupert was educated in his house. A schoolmate wrote years afterwards: "Rupert had

an extraordinary vitality at school, which showed itself in a glorious enthusiasm and an almost boisterous sense of fun." He was happy there, and though he wrote verse, won the school English prize for verse, and helped to edit a magazine, he was not backward in outdoor pursuits, playing for the school both at football and at cricket.

In 1906 he went up to King's College, Cambridge, where he read classics officially but spent most of his time devouring English literature. He soon made his mark socially, as a handsome, charming personality. His radical views on religion and politics were underlined by his membership in the Heretics and the University Fabian Society (of which he became the president). He also joined the Carbonari, helped to found the Marlowe Society, and acted in several of its productions. He won the Harness Prize with an essay on "Puritanism in the Early English Drama" and took a second in the classical tripos in 1909. A. C. Benson, Master of Magdalene College at that time, has left an impression of the young undergraduate: "He was far more striking in appearance than exactly handsome in outline. His eyes were small or rather deeply set, his features healthily rounded, his lips frank and expressive. It was the coloring of his face and hair which gave a special character to his look. The hair rose very thickly from his forehead, and fell in rather stiff arched locks on either side—he grew it full and over-long; it was of a beautiful dark auburn tint inclining to red, but with an underlying golden gleam in it. . . . He was strongly built, but inclined to be sturdy, and even clumsy, rather than graceful or lithe. . ."

Brooke's father died suddenly in 1910, and for a term Rupert deputized as head of the house. He now settled in the Cambridgeshire village of Grantchester, reading, writing, bathing, and frequently running up to London, where he met (Sir) Edward Marsh, to whose friendship and hospitality he owed much. Other friends were Edmund Gosse, John Drinkwater, Walter de la Mare, Wilfrid Gibson, W. H. Davies, and the Asquiths. The year 1911 was divided between a journey to Germany and Italy and hard work on a thesis on John Webster and the Elizabethan drama, which gained him a fellowship at King's. A small volume of *Poems*, published at the end of 1911, had excited some favorable comment. At Christmas of that year Brooke had a nervous breakdown, but a spring and early summer in Berlin restored him. It was during this visit that his memorable poem, "Grantchester," was written. Later in the year he returned to England and planned, with Drinkwater, Wilfrid Gibson, and Harold Monro, the volume called *Georgian Poetry: 1911-1912*, which appeared in December.

After having been admitted to his fellowship in May 1913, Brooke set out on a long period of travel, going first to New York, and thence to Boston, through Canada, down to San Francisco, out to Hawaii, Samoa, Fiji, New Zealand, and Tahiti, where he spent several months. From the United States he sent home travel letters to the *Westminster Gazette* and from Tahiti various poems, some of which appeared in a quarterly called *New Numbers*. In June 1914 he returned home by way of the United States.

The outbreak of the war seemed to him to demand instant action. In September 1914 he obtained a commission in the Royal Naval Division and was present the following month at the Antwerp engagement. After the failure of that diversion the troops were brought back to Blandford for training, and on February 28, 1915, Brooke was sent out to the Dardanelles. But he never saw active service there. Refusing the offer of a staff post by Sir Ian Hamilton, he found himself on April 17 at the island of Scyros. He was in low health after an attack of sunstroke at Port Said. He now contracted an infection of the lip, which quickly turned to septicemia, and on April 23 he died. He was buried the same day at Scyros, and left a will directing that any royalties accruing from his works should be equally divided between three poet friends—Walter de la Mare, Wilfrid Gibson, and Lascelles Abercrombie.

The popularity of Brooke's poetry may be largely attributable to the conventional simplicity of his concepts and the romantic appeal of his life. His work, nevertheless, combines a vivid, sensuous delight in everyday things with humor, a wan nostalgic pathos, and a strongly evocative imagination. Metrically it is resourceful, musical, and often original. The octosyllabic couplet and the sonnet were forms of which Brooke had special mastery. "Grantchester," and his sonnets, "Peace," "The Dead," and "The Soldier" are familiar to even casual readers of modern English poetry. By his Apollonian beauty, his personal charm, his generous and graceful spirit—to which must be added the timeliness of his appearance and the mode of his death—Brooke has become a legend which, after a quarter-century, has hardly yet begun to grow dim.

PRINCIPAL WORKS: The Bastille, 1905; Puritanism . . . in the Early English Drama . . ., 1910; Poems, 1911; 1914 and Other Poems, 1915; John Webster and the Elizabethan Drama, 1916; Letters From America, 1916; Selected Poems, 1917; The Collected Poems: with a Memoir [by Edward Marsh] 1918; Lithuania: A Drama in one act, 1922.

ABOUT: Adcock, A. St. J. For Remembrance; Benson, A. C. Memories and Friends; Brooke, R.

Letters From America (see Introduction by Henry James); Browne, M. Recollections of Rupert Brooke; Collins, H. P. Modern Poetry; De la Mare, W. Rupert Brooke and the Intellectual Imagination; Douglas, N. Looking Back; Drinkwater, J. Rupert Brooke: An Essay; Garrod, H. W. The Profession of Poetry; Guibert, A. Rupert Brooke; Marsh, E. H. Rupert Brooke: A Memoir; Phelps, W. L. The Advance of English Poetry in the Twentieth Century; Squire, J. C. Books in General.

BROOKE, STOPFORD AUGUSTUS.
See "BRITISH AUTHORS OF THE 19TH CENTURY."

BROOKS, CHARLES STEPHEN (June 25, 1878-June 29, 1934), American essayist and writer of travel books,

was born and died at Cleveland, Ohio. His parents, of old New England stock, were Stephen Edmund Brooks and Mary Elizabeth (Coffinberry) Brooks. Graduating from Yale in 1900 with a B.A. degree, he returned to Cleveland and the printing business of Brooks Company, staying for fifteen years and becoming vice-president of the company. Even after resigning to devote himself to writing, Brooks retained a directorate in the firm. But he was more interested in traveling abroad by bicycle, writing little plays for little theatres (he was founder and later president of the Playhouse, Cleveland's little theatre, and vice-president of the Playhouse Foundation), and "carrying on the essay tradition of Hazlitt and Lamb with that studied artlessness whose other name is charm," as the *Dial* phrased it. His subjects ranged over toy-shops, lawn-mowers, leather suspenders, going to the movies, and the asperities of the early British reviewers. *Wappin' Wharf*, a burlesque of a child's idea of pirate life, and reprinted with other playlets in *Frightful Plays!*, was written in 1921; a decade later it had undergone more than a hundred and fifty performances. When the United States entered the First World War, Brooks was associated with the labor employment division of the Emergency Fleet Corporation of Washington, and studied and drafted material for use in President Wilson's peace negotiations in Paris. The first Mrs. Brooks was Minerva Cozens Kline; the second, Mary Seymour Curtis-Brown, was an artist who illustrated a number of his books, notably *English Spring*,

which laid as much stress on the discomfitures and disappointments of travel in England as on its charms. *An Italian Winter* is chiefly concerned with Taormina. Brooks made one *sortie* into the field of the historical novel with *Luca Sarto*. In 1922-24 he lectured on English literature at the College for Women of Western Reserve University. In F. H. Law's *Modern Essays and Stories* Brooks disclosed some of the tricks of the trade of writing essays.

PRINCIPAL WORKS: *Essays*—There's Pippins and Cheese to Come, 1917; Chimney-Pot Papers, 1919; Hints to Pilgrims, 1921. *Travel Books*—Journeys to Bagdad, 1915, Roundabout to Canterbury, 1926; Roads to the North, 1928; English Spring, 1932; An Italian Winter, 1933. *Little Theatre Plays*—Frightful Plays! 1922; The Tragedy of Josephine Maria, 1931; A Window at the Inn, 1934. *Novel:* Luca Sarto, 1920. *Autobiography*—Prologue, 1931.

ABOUT: New York Times June 30, 1934; Publishers' Weekly July 21, 1934; Scholastic March 16, 1935.

BROOKS, VAN WYCK (February 16, 1886-   ), American critic and biographer,
writes: "Van Wyck Brooks was born in Plainfield, N.J. He was educated in the Plainfield public schools. At the age of twelve, he went abroad with his family and spent a year in Germany, France, and England. He entered Harvard in 1904 and belonged to the class of 1908, but

V. Semler

he took his degree in 1907. He was one of the editors of the *Harvard Advocate* and a member of Phi Beta Kappa. Leaving college, he went to England and lived there as a journalist for a year and a half. During this time he made several visits to Paris. He was connected for a year with Curtis-Brown & Co., literary agents. He wrote articles for two or three London and Manchester newspapers and magazines and published in London his first book, *The Wine of the Puritans*, 1908. Returning to America, he lived in New York, 1908-1911, working on the *Standard Dictionary* and *Collier's Encyclopaedia*. For one year he was an editorial assistant on the *World's Work* under Walter H. Page.

"In 1911, he went to California, and he was married at Carmel (where he lived at various times in later years) to Eleanor Kenyon. He wrote there his books on Mark Twain and Henry James. His first son was born in California in 1912; since then he and his wife have had another son. He was instructor in English at Leland Stanford University, 1911-1913, and he wrote at Palo Alto his life of John Addington Symonds.

"In 1913 he returned to England with his wife and son. He had been asked to teach in the Workers' Educational Association, and he conducted a class at South Norwood, near Croydon. He wrote *America's Coming of Age* in England and published there *The Malady of the Ideal*, and he finished *The World of H. G. Wells* during a summer in Brittany.

"Three months after the war began, he returned to New York and, shortly afterwards, entered the Century Co. It was then that he began translating French books. As one of a household of translators, he has had more or less of a hand in the translation of thirty-one French books. During the year of its existence, 1917-1918, he was an associate editor of *The Seven Arts,* and he wrote *Letters and Leadership* in New York. In 1921, he contributed to Harold Stearns' symposium, *Civilization in the United States,* the paper called 'The Literary Life in America.'

"In 1920, he settled in Westport, Conn., which has since remained his home; and for the four years 1920-1924 he was literary editor of the *Freeman*. In this he wrote a weekly page called 'A Reviewer's Notebook.' About one-fourth of the papers written for this were later collected in *Sketches in Criticism*. Of the rest, a few were included in *Emerson and Others*, a book that preceded his *Life of Emerson*. His *Three Essays on America, 1934,* was a revised collection of earlier writings.

"He was ill from 1926 to 1931, and was able to do little work. However, he wrote two articles for the *Encyclopaedia Britannica* and one for the *Dictionary of American Biography*, and for about a year he contributed a weekly paper, discussing new books, to the *Independent*.

"In *The Flowering of New England*, he published the first volume—first in point of composition but not in the ultimate order of sequence—of a long-projected history of literature in America. He has also edited, more or less, with or without prefaces, works by Columbus (or Las Casas), William Godwin, Washington Irving, Gamaliel Bradford, Randolph Bourne, and Llewelyn Powys. He received the Dial Award and, in 1937, the Pulitzer Prize in history. He has also received the degree of Litt.D. from Columbia University and from Tufts and Bowdoin

Colleges. He is a member of the American Academy of Arts and Letters, is one of six vice-presidents of the League of American Writers, and is a Socialist."

* * *

Bernard Smith has called Brooks "the most influential critic of the past twenty years. His early work was a principal factor in the erection of the lofty cultural standards which have encouraged the rise of a mature, philosophic criticism in America." Recently Brooks' basically conservative taste has asserted itself, and he has condemned Joyce, Eliot, Henry James, Proust, etc., as mere "coterie writers" who have "conspired to destroy tradition."

PRINCIPAL WORKS: The Wine of the Puritans, 1909; The Malady of the Ideal, 1913; John Addington Symonds, 1914; The World of H. G. Wells, 1915; America's Coming-of-Age, 1915; Letters and Leadership, 1918; The Ordeal of Mark Twain, 1920 (revised edition 1933); The Pilgrimage of Henry James, 1925; Emerson and Others, 1927; The Life of Emerson, 1932; Sketches in Criticism, 1932, Three Essays on America, 1934; The Flowering of New England, 1936; New England: Indian Summer, 1940; On Literature Today, 1941; The Opinions of Oliver Allston, 1941.

ABOUT: Brooks, V. W. The Opinions of Oliver Allston; Bookman June 1930, September 1930; Catholic World January 1935; Dial January 1925; New Freeman June 11, 1930; New Republic August 26, 1936; New York Herald Tribune October 6, 1940; New York Times October 6, 1940; Sewanee Review March 1935.

BROPHY, JOHN (December 6, 1899-   ), English novelist, writes: "I was born in Liverpool, both my parents, John and Agnes (Bodell) Brophy, being Protestant Irish. I reckon myself a Londoner now, and I have also lived in Egypt and in various parts of Europe. I was taken away from Liverpool very young and did not return until a few years before the Great War  began, but the early impressions of the great seaport, built on sandstone, swept by wet winds, full of bitter religious and political controversies, have always remained with me. I drew very much on my Liverpool experiences in two novels, *The Bitter End* and *Waterfront*. My home life had the traditionally Irish feckless air: sometimes money was plentiful, sometimes unobtainable. I often went to stay for six months at a time in Dublin. Before I was twelve I took an emotional, partisan interest in politics, and, revolting against the tenets of my home, I was all for Women's Suffrage and Home Rule.

"In November 1914 I thought it romantic to run away from school (a co-educational school where I was perfectly happy), give a false age, and enlist in the British Army. Four years soldiering, some of it with the infantry in France and Belgium, shook me up a good deal but did not altogether cure me of romantic idealism. When the Armistice came I was still not nineteen, and lame from trench-foot complicated by blood-poisoning. I took a degree, on a government grant, at Liverpool University and spent a year at Durham University, mostly studying the then new psychoanalysis. Jobs were hard to get, and in 1924 I married Charis Weare Grundy (born in Chicago) and went to Cairo, in the Egyptian Civil Service, as a teacher. After two years my wife fell ill, and we had to return. I talked myself into a job I had no qualifications for—on the advertising staff of a big store—and later moved to London, where I became chief copywriter to the biggest British advertising agency. But these were only means of making a living: I wanted to write, I intended to write, and after I had published my fourth novel I found myself able to live by authorship. Such business ability as I have acquired has been forced out of me by circumstance, although I do not regret the widening of my experience.

"I am healthy, not unduly neurotic, and perfectly happy in my home life: to that extent, perhaps, I am not in tune with the age I live in. I write journalism off the surface of my mind, and keep its depths for gestating and producing novels. For some time I was, subconsciously, unable to trust myself to embark on big schemes in fiction, but I had long made up my mind to write one longish and, I hoped, profound novel, in effect a life of Shakespeare. That was Gentleman of Stratford. I rather think it marks the beginning of my real writing career.

"I am still married to the same wife, and the longer that goes on the better for me. I have one daughter, ten years old [1940], who excels me in everything, even in writing."

* * *

Mr. Brophy's first novel was written in the evenings, after ten or more hours' work at the store. He is a heavy-set, dark-haired man, with a moustache and tortoise-shell spectacles, who lists among his recreations "watching people." Among his more athletic pursuits are cricket, hockey, and lawn tennis, and he is an excellent cook, though he says "I don't really like work of any kind." He is ambitious to write plays, and thinks Bernard Shaw "the greatest influence on our generation." He says he likes literary people "if they look on writing as a job and not a branch of mysticism."

He is more widely known at home than in America, Gentleman of Stratford being his first generally read novel here. Of one of his early novels of the First World War a critic remarked that "the sincerity of the author is apparent, but the naïveté of his characters is occasionally disconcerting." He is probably right in thinking that his best work is still before him, since even today he is only in early middle age.

His activity in the Home Guard during the Second World War led to his writing of several popular manuals on civilian defense.

PRINCIPAL WORKS: The Bitter End, 1928; Fanfare (in America: Peter Lavelle) 1930; Songs and Slang of the British Soldier, 1914-18 (with Eric Partridge) 1930; Flesh and Blood, 1931; English Prose (non-fiction) 1932; The Rocky Road, 1932; Waterfront, 1934; The World Went Mad, 1934; I Let Him Go, 1935; The Ramparts of Virtue, 1936; Ilonka Speaks of Hungary, 1936; Felicity Greene, 1937; Behold the Judge, 1937; Man, Woman, and Child, 1938; The Ridiculous Hat, 1939; The Queer Fellow, 1939; Gentleman of Stratford, 1939; The Home Guard, 1940; Immortal Sergeant, 1942.

ABOUT: Bookman October 1928; Wilson Library Bulletin June 1935.

BROUN, HEYWOOD CAMPBELL (December 7, 1888-December 18, 1939), American journalist, essayist, and novelist, was born in Brooklyn, N.Y., the son of Heywood Cox Broun, who was of English birth and owner of a large printing plant, and Henriette (Brose) Broun. His first writing was done in the Horace Mann School, New York, where he edited the  school paper. He spent four years at Harvard, from 1906 to 1910, but never received his degree because he could not work off a "condition" in elementary French. Instead he went to work in the sports department of the New York Morning Telegraph. It was there that he first wrote the baseball stories which made him known to a wider public than usually is familiar with sports writers. From the Telegraph he went in 1912 to the Tribune, where after doing sports and general rewrite he began his famous column, "It Seems to Me." In 1921 he took the column to the *World.* He left there in 1928, after trouble with the publisher over his indignant championship of Sacco and Vanzetti, followed by a criticism of his own paper in the department which at the same time he was conducting in the *Nation.* He appeared next in the *Telegram,* a Scripps-Howard paper which on the death of the *World* became the *World-Telegram.* The increasing conservatism of the Scripps papers caused a severance of relations with this paper late in 1939; his column had been appearing in syndicated form in Scripps papers all over the country. He accepted an offer to take his column to the *Post,* but had written only one contribution when he was seized by his last illness. His department in the *Nation* ran from 1925 to 1931, was resumed in 1935, but a few months later he left the staff and began an irregularly appearing column in the *New Republic,* called "Shoot the Works." This was still appearing at the time of his death. For a while also he had a column in the *CIO News* (Washington, D.C.), and for his last several years had published and edited in Stamford, Conn., his home, *Broun's Nutmeg,* a weekly paper which he made into a national periodical.

Mr. Broun was married in 1917 to Ruth Hale, writer and founder of the Lucy Stone League, and they had one son, who is also a journalist. They were amicably divorced in 1933, and she died the following year. In 1935 he married Constantina (Connie) Madison (Mrs. Johnny Dooley, widow of a vaudeville actor), a stage dancer and singer of Spanish descent. It was partly by her influence that a few months before he died he was received into the Roman Catholic Church, though he had been reared as an Episcopalian and for many years had been a freethinker.

During the First World War Mr. Broun was in France as a correspondent with the American army. He was stagestruck all his life, and in 1931 he produced and acted in his own musical comedy, also called *Shoot the Works.* He also lectured on drama at Columbia and at the Rand School of Social Science, in New York. He was for a short time a member of the Socialist Party, and ran for Congress on that ticket in 1930. Later he became attracted to Communism, but was never affiliated with the Communist Party. In 1933 he founded the American Newspaper Guild, which later became affiliated with the American Federation of Labor and still later with the Congress of Industrial Organizations, and he was its president and guiding spirit to the time of his death. Another of his interests was painting, to which he took in middle age, and though without instruction he had several interesting one-man shows in New York. For many years he was a member of the board of the Book-of-the-Month Club.

It is difficult to describe Heywood Broun briefly, for his was a far more complex nature than what Christopher Morley called "his apparently naïf exhibitionism" indicated. Huge, disheveled, like an amiable bear, with his kind brown eyes and his deep voice with its unexplained Southern drawl, he appeared to be what he was on the surface —sociable, tolerant, lazy, unpunctual, a good mixer, a *bon vivant,* a wit. Beneath this exterior there was a perplexed, humble, seeking human being, easily roused to implacable fury at injustice or cruelty, faithful, sensitive, and inherently unhappy. Those who knew this Heywood Broun were not surprised by the apparent reversal of all his previous beliefs in middle life. Morley has remarked that he seemed to him "a kind of mediaeval figure, a strolling friar," who "took his simplicity and kindliness" out into a sophisticated world "and was everywhere beloved for his drollery and devotion, his generosity, and his hatred of oppression." He died of pneumonia, in Stamford, a short time after his fifty-fifth birthday. The grief at his passing was of a depth and sincerity seldom occasioned by the death of a public figure.

As a writer, much of his work was ephemeral, and all of it was startlingly uneven. But at his best, there was a depth, a warmth, and a power in his writing that were the outward expression of the man himself.

PRINCIPAL WORKS: A.E.F.: With General Pershing and the American Forces, 1918; Seeing Things at Night, 1921; Nonsensorship (with others) 1922; Pieces of Hate, 1922; The Boy Grew Older (novel) 1922; The Sun Field (novel) 1923; Sitting on the World, 1924; Anthony Comstock: Roundsman of the Lord (with M. Leech) 1927; Christians Only: A Study in Prejudice (with G. Britt) 1931; It Seems to Me, 1935; Collected Edition (ed. by H. H. Broun) 1941.

ABOUT: Broun, H. It Seems To Me; Newspaper Guild of N.Y. Heywood Broun As He Seemed to Us; Bookman March 1928, July 1931; Canadian Forum February 1940; Christian Century January 3, 1940; Commonweal July 1, 1938; Living Age February 1940; Nation September 3 and October 1, 1930, March 21, 1938, December 30, 1939; New Republic December 25, 1939; Outlook October 30, 1929, August 13, 1930; Saturday Review of Literature December 30, 1939; Time December 25, 1939; Wilson Library Bulletin December 1936.

BROWN, ABBIE FARWELL (1872-

March 4, 1927), American writer of children's books, was born of an old New England family in a small  house on Beacon Street, Boston, where she died some fifty-five years later. Her parents were Benjamin F. Brown and Clara (Neal) Brown. The family library was stocked with Shakespeare, Scott, George Eliot, Dickens and Thackeray. At eleven the girl wrote and illustrated a magazine, *The Catkin*, with her mother and sister Ethel, who later illustrated Abbie's child verses in *St. Nicholas*. Attending the Girls' Latin School, she showed her fondness for Lewis Carroll by editing *The Jabberwock*. In 1894 Abbie Brown graduated from Radcliffe College, visiting England five years later and assembling the material for her first book, *The Book of Saints and Friendly Beasts* (1900). The carvings on the choir stalls of the Chester Cathedral had particularly captivated her, as well as the story of St. Werburgh and the goose. In 1902, with a successful book, *The Lonesomest Doll* behind her, she helped edit a Young Folks' Library and published her own *In The Days of the Giants* and a book of verse, *A Pocketful of Posies*. All her books show charm and delicate style; she believed that "there can never be too careful writing for children" and lived up to her principles. Two of her short stories won prizes, and she was the author of many song-texts and choruses as well as the cantatas *Rock of Liberty* and *The Guardian Angel*. Miss Brown, who never married, traveled abroad again in 1906, 1910 and 1913, and after the establishment of the MacDowell Colony in Peterboro, N.H., spent several summers there, writing *The Boyhood of Edward MacDowell* (1924). She was president of the New England Poetry Club, and was a frequent lecturer. Her personality was buoyant and attractive. A collection of fossils, shells and stones which she assembled in her childhood is now in the Children's Museum at Boston.

PRINCIPAL WORKS: The Book of Saints and Friendly Beasts, 1900; The Lonesomest Doll, 1901; In the Days of the Giants, 1902; A Pocketful of Posies (verse) 1902; The Curious Book of Birds, 1903; The Flower Princess, 1904; The Star Jewels and Other Wonders, 1905; The Story of St. Christopher, 1905; Brothers and Sisters, 1906; Friends and Cousins, 1907; Fresh Posies (verse) 1908; John of the Woods, 1909; Tales of the Red Children (with J. M. Bell) 1909; The Christmas Angel, 1910; Their City Christmas, 1912; Swapping Day (play) 1912; The Lucky Stone, 1914; Songs of Sixpence (verse) 1914; Kisingtown Town, 1915; Surprise House, 1917; Heart of New England (poems) 1920; Round Robin, 1921; The Lights of Beacon Hill, 1922; The Boyhood of Edward MacDowell, 1924; Our Christmas Tree, 1925.

ABOUT: Kunitz, S. J. & Haycraft, H. (eds.). The Junior Book of Authors; Libraries April 1927.

*BROWN, ALICE (December 5, 1857-),

American novelist and dramatist, writes: "Life has been so crowded that it's rather  like the old geography picture of the Russian family fleeing across the steppes and throwing out the children to the pursuing wolves. There's been nothing in it—nothing that could be told—of any interest to anybody. I have been abroad several times, for five or six months at a time, chiefly in England, and once had a walking trip of five months in England, with Louise Imogen Guiney. I am chiefly interested in the theatre, and in 1914 got Winthrop Ames' prize of $10,000 for a play, *Children of Earth*. And now I am watching the screen with an expectant interest because it has opened a new door in the house of life. And I am, like all right-minded people at present, rebellious and amazed at the human animal, who has taken the good gifts of God in scientific discovery for use in havoc and ruin, and, in lesser ways, has not hesitated in degrading the English language by a careless freedom of innovation from which it may not recover. And thus you may see that, having no unfounded optimism, I cannot find that everything is for the best 'in this best of all possible worlds.'"

* * *

No one would imagine from this modest apologia that Alice Brown has been for more than fifty years the last New England story writer in the tradition of Sarah Orne Jewett and Mary E. Wilkins Freeman, and a distinguished biographer, poet, and playwright as well. In her eighties, she is a most remarkable person, full of verve and humor. She has published nothing since 1935, but she is still alive to the world and at work recording her impressions of it. She was born in Hampton Falls, N.H., the daughter of Levi and Elizabeth (Lucas) Brown, and has never married. She was educated at Robinson Seminary, Exeter, N.H., and for a number of years was a teacher, first in New Hampshire and then in Boston. She hated teaching, and was glad to escape from it permanently in 1885, when she became a member of the staff of the *Youth's Companion*. Her first novel, *My Love and I*, was published under the pseudonym of "Martin Redfield," because it was told in the first person from a man's standpoint. She has written almost every kind of novel, even a detective novel, *The Mysteries of Ann*, but her real forte is the short story, and she has taken for her own the New England village of "Tiverton," which is probably Hampton Falls or Exeter. She lives now on Beacon Hill, in Boston, spending her summers in New Hampshire, on her ancestral farm near the sea.

PRINCIPAL WORKS: *Fiction*—My Love and I, 1886; Fools of Nature, 1887; Three Heroines of English Romance (with L. I. Guiney & H. P. Spofford) 1894; Meadow Grass, 1895; The Day of His Youth, 1897; Tiverton Tales, 1899; The King's End, 1901; Margaret Warrener, 1901; The Mannerings, 1903; Judgment, 1903; High Noon, 1904; Paradise, 1905; The Court of Love, 1906; The Country Road, 1906; Rose MacLeod, 1908; The Story of Thyrza, 1909; John Winterbourne's Family, 1910; Country Neighbors, 1910; The One-Footed Fairy, 1911; The Secret of the Clan, 1912; Robin Hood's Barn, 1913; Vanishing Points, 1913; The Prisoner, 1916; Bromley Neighborhood, 1917; The Flying Teuton, 1918; The Black Drop, 1919; The Wind Between the Worlds, 1920; Homespun and Gold, 1920; Old Crow, 1922; Ellen Prior, 1923; The Mysteries of Ann, 1925; Dear Old Templeton, 1927; The Diary of a Dryad, 1932; Jeremy Hamlin, 1934; The Willoughbys, 1935. *Plays*—Joint Owners in Spain, 1914; Children of Earth, 1915; One Act Plays, 1921; Charles Lamb, 1924; The Golden Ball, 1929; The Marriage Feast, 1931; The Kingdom in the Sky, 1932. *Poems*—The Road to Castalay, 1896 (with additional poems, 1917); Ellen Prior, 1923. *Miscellaneous*—Robert Louis Stevenson: A Study (with L. I. Guiney) 1895; By Oak and Thorn, 1896; Life of Mercy Otis Warren, 1896; Louise Imogen Guiney: A Study, 1921.

ABOUT: Overton, G. The Women Who Make Our Novels; Pattee, F. L. The Development of the American Short Story; Rittenhouse, J. B. The Younger American Poets; Williams, B. C. Our Short Story Writers; Atlantic Monthly July 1906; Current Opinion July 1914; Mentor September 1927; Outlook December 17, 1919; Spectator May 15, 1909.

BROWN, GEORGE DOUGLAS. See "BRITISH AUTHORS OF THE 19TH CENTURY"

B R O W N, JOHN MASON (July 3, 1900-   ), American dramatic critic and writer on the theatre, was born in Louisville, Ky., the son of John Mason Brown and Carrie (Ferguson) Brown. He was a reporter on the staff of the Louisville *Cour-*

ier-Journal at seventeen, and had already determined that he was going to be a dramatic critic in the not-too-distant future. When he arrived at Harvard in 1919 Brown was well versed in Aristotle, Schlegel, Hazlitt, and the other heavy cannon of a critic's battery. At Harvard, besides taking the usual academic courses, he studied in Professor George Pierce Baker's "47 Workshop," wrote the plays required by the course, and even did a little acting.

Oggiano

After receiving his B.A. in 1923 Brown was a teacher of the history of the theatre, Shakespeare, and allied subjects at the summer session of the University of Montana, returning there in 1929 and 1931. After a year on the Boston *Transcript* as assistant to the eccentric and prodigiously learned H. T. Parker, he was invited to New York City by Mrs. Edith Isaacs to join the staff of *Theatre Arts Monthly*, now *Theatre Arts*. In addition to routine editorial duties he wrote a monthly article on the current theatre, usually scholarly in tone, but less exuberant than his later daily journalism on the New York *Post*. Brown stayed on the magazine from 1924 to 1928, and in 1929 went to the *Post*, where he proved that a critic who leaned towards academicism could still be an acute judge of the commercial possibilities of the play under review; his acumen in picking winners or predicting failures gave him the leading position for several years at the head of the table of critical batting averages figured out by the hard-boiled editors of *Variety*, the weekly organ of show-business. For a time Brown shared an apartment with Donald Oenslager, the scenic designer, and Marshall Best, editor of the Viking Press. He married Catherine Screven Meredith of Harrisburg, Pa., in 1933, and they have two sons, Preston and Meredith. Their home is in New York City.

Brown was staff lecturer at the American Laboratory Theatre from 1925 to 1931; gave a course on the history of theatrical criticism at Yale in 1932; lectured on play-writing and the history of dramatic criticism at the Harvard summer school from 1937 to 1939; and in the summer of 1935 gave a course on play-writing at the Middlebury College-Breadloaf Writers' Conference. He has returned to this Vermont college as a lecturer in the course of his lecture tours about the country, during which, as Walter Prichard

Eaton has remarked, he often puts on a better show than is afforded by some of the plays he discusses. His delivery is of machine-gun velocity; every sweeping period is crowned by a wise-crack which delightfully titillates clubwomen and Junior Leaguers; and he is almost as physically active on the rostrum as Dimitri Mitropoulos on the conductor's stand. From time to time his reviews and periodical articles are collected in volumes which are useful for reference and diverting to read. *Letters From Greenroom Ghosts* (1934) is a successful *tour-de-force*. Brown has china-blue eyes, curling blond hair, and a candid, innocent expression which is traditionally part of a dramatic critic's stock in trade.

In September 1941 Brown left the *Post* to become dramatic critic for the New York *World-Telegram*.

PRINCIPAL WORKS: The Modern Theatre in Revolt, 1929; Upstage: The American Theatre in Performance, 1930; Letters From Greenroom Ghosts, 1934; The American Theatre As Seen By Its Critics (with M. J. Moses) 1934; The Art of Playgoing, 1936; Two on the Aisle, 1938; Broadway in Review, 1940; Accustomed As I Am, 1942.

ABOUT: Brown, J. M. Accustomed As I Am; Morehouse, W. Forty-Five Minutes Past Eight; Rice, A. H. The Inky Way; Saturday Review of Literature November 9, 1940; Theatre Arts February 1941.

BROWN, ROLLO WALTER (March 15, 1880-), American novelist and essayist, writes: "Rollo Walter Brown was born

near Crooksville, in the hills of Southeastern Ohio, the youngest of three sons of Alexander and Rosalba (Search) Brown. His father's family came from England and Scotland by way of Virginia and Maryland, and his mother's from England by way of New Jersey and Pennsylvania. As a boy he worked on a hill farm, in a clay mine and a log pottery, and occasionally in a coal mine. By the time he was seventeen he had stumbled upon Victor Hugo, Defoe, and Byron, and decided to go to high school—in the county seat, New Lexington. Then he had an opportunity to study law in an office in Zanesville. But he discovered that what he was interested in was the drama of the courtroom. So he went to Ohio Northern University (1899-

1903) and to Harvard (1903-05) to explore the field of literature. Then he taught—at Wabash College, Carleton, and Harvard. But throughout what one college president called 'his disturbingly vivid career' as a teacher, his great interest remained in the drama of America that he saw all about him, and in 1924 he turned exclusively to writing.

"He has done much of his writing in Peterboro, N.H., either in the MacDowell Colony or at a made-over farmhouse called Schwab Cottage, across the river from the Colony. He is much interested in architecture, and probably would have been an architect if he had grown up where such people existed. He likes the French, and gets on well with them."

* * *

Mr. Brown has M.A. degrees from Ohio Northern and Harvard, as well as honorary doctorates from Lawrence, Wabash, and Marietta Colleges. In 1905 he married Ella A. Brocklesby; they have no children. As a boy, until deflected by literature, he wanted to be an inventor. His biographies, Marston Balch said, are distinguished by being "at once a character analysis and a narrative." Another critic remarked of them that "he approaches his subject with knowledge, spirit, and intimate sympathy." As a novelist he has sometimes been thought to be more nearly related to some of the Northern Europeans than to contemporary Americans. He himself says that most of his work as a writer "seems to center round the struggle of the individual to kick loose and be the most of himself possible."

He is a corporate member of the Edward MacDowell Association, and in 1912 and 1917 made extended tours in France, studying methods of teaching, and speaking on Franco-American relations. He has traveled everywhere in America as a lecturer. In appearance he is serious-looking and bespectacled, with grizzled, curly hair above a high forehead.

PRINCIPAL WORKS: The Art of Writing English (with N. W. Barnes) 1913; How the French Boy Learns to Write, 1915; The Creative Spirit, 1925; Dean Briggs, 1926; Lonely Americans, 1929; The Firemakers (novel) 1931; Toward Romance (novel) 1932; The Hillikin (novel) 1935; On Writing the Biography of a Modest Man, 1935; As of the Gods (novel) 1937; Next Door to a Poet, 1937; I Travel by Train, 1939; There Must Be a New Song, 1942.

BROWN, YEATS-. See YEATS-BROWN

B R O W N, Mrs. ZENITH (JONES)
("Leslie Ford," "David Frome," pseuds.)
(1898-   ), American writer of detective fic-

tion, was born in Smith River, Del Norte County, Calif., the daughter of the Rev. Minor Jones and Mary Francis (Watkins) Jones. Her father was an Episcopal clergyman who was born at Chestertown on Maryland's Eastern Shore, where
the family had settled in the eighteenth century; his father was rector of Emmanuel Church at Chestertown for twenty years. Mrs. Jones was descended from the Calvert family who founded Maryland in 1634. Zenith Jones had ten brothers and sisters. She claims to have been brought up in a papoose basket by a squaw. After attending high school in Tacoma, Wash., she was student assistant in Philosophy, Greek Civilization, and Freshman 1 at the University of Washington, marrying Ford K. Brown in 1918 and receiving a B.A. degree in 1921.

When Mr. Brown went to England to study, preparatory to becoming a member of the faculty of St. John's College (Md.), his wife absorbed local color and English idiom and idiosyncrasies so successfully that few readers identified the resulting *Mr. Pinkerton* detective stories by "David Frome" as the work of an American woman. *The Hammersmith Murders* (1930) marked the first appearance of Evan Pinkerton, a shy, rabitty, and sentimental little Welshman, and his burly Scotland Yard crony, Inspector Bull; and a long list of Pinkerton-Bull cases has followed from the "Frome" pen. The popular American Colonel Primrose and his "functotum" Sergeant Buck came on the stage in 1934 in a "Leslie Ford" story, *The Strangled Witness*; their numerous later adventures are mostly narrated in the approved manner of Mary Roberts Rinehart by Grace Latham, a sprightly widow.

Mrs. Brown's novels, notable under either of her pen-names for intelligence and skill, have been translated into nine languages and have enjoyed unusual sales. Those written as "Frome" adhere closely to the accepted standards of detective fiction and are highly regarded by connoisseurs; the "Ford" *opera* are looser in construction but have brought their author greater financial returns through serialization in the popular magazines, where they appeal particularly to women readers.

Mrs. Brown has a teen-age daughter, Janet; two dogs, Dr. Watson and Mr. Moto; and a farm near Chestertown, Md., which her ancestors owned in 1800. Writing in the *Saturday Review of Literature* in 1939, Jane Shore described Mrs. Brown as "tall, slender, vivid, smartly dressed, *soignée*. She dislikes beaches, water, sun, sports, and the household arts, refuses to be ill, and hates ineptitude. She likes dogs, gardening, Negroes, and the land."

PRINCIPAL WORKS: *As "David Frome"*—Murder of an Old Man, 1929; In at the Death, 1929; The Hammersmith Murders, 1930; The Strange Death of Martin Green, 1931; The Man From Scotland Yard, 1932; Two Against Scotland Yard, 1933; The Eel Pie Murders, 1933; Scotland Yard Can Wait! 1933; Mr. Pinkerton Goes to Scotland Yard, 1934; Mr. Pinkerton Finds a Body, 1934; Mr. Pinkerton Grows a Beard, 1935; Mr. Pinkerton Has the Clue, 1936; Mr. Pinkerton at the Old Angel, 1939. *As "Leslie Ford"*—The Sound of Footsteps, 1932; By the Watchman's Clock, 1932; Murder in Maryland, 1933; The Clue of the Judas Tree, 1933; The Strangled Witness, 1934; Burn Forever, 1935; Ill Met by Moonlight, 1936; The Simple Way of Poison, 1937; Three Bright Pebbles, 1938; False to Any Man, 1939; Reno Rendezvous, 1939; The Town Cried Murder, 1939; Road to Folly, 1940; The Murder of a Fifth Columnist, 1941; Murder With Southern Hospitality, 1942.

ABOUT: Haycraft, H. Murder for Pleasure: The Life and Times of the Detective Story; Saturday Review of Literature September 9, 1939.

*BROWNE, LEWIS (June 24, 1897-   ). Anglo-American historian and biographer, writes: "I was born in London, of poor

but Jewish parents [Harry A. and Stessa (Fiesta) Browne]. I seem to have been a bright but highly undependable pupil, and though I was able to enter secondary school as a 'scholarship boy' when not yet eleven, my career there was altogether

disappointing. Almost my only interest was in 'composition' and drawing, and by the time I was thirteen I was already making abortive attempts at writing 'books.' When I was fourteen my mother's ill health compelled the family to move to a more clement place. By fortuitous circumstances we were drawn to Portland, Ore., where my father, an optician, became the proprietor of a jewelry store. I found employment in a large department store, where I fell into the habit of stealing off to read Gibbon and other of my favorite authors. I was firmly commanded to attend to business or get out. So I got out.

"At the suggestion of the local rabbi, I decided to prepare for the Jewish ministry. After returning to high school for the final semester, I entered the Hebrew Union College in Cincinnati, and was there six years in all, simultaneously taking my B.A. degree at the neighboring University of Cincinnati. I spent most of my time writing stories and articles for magazines which obdurately refused to publish them. Not until my last years at college did I at last succeed in penetrating the editorial boycott—in the *Smart Set* and the *North American Review*. In 1920 I became the minister of Temple Israel in Waterbury, Conn. Thereafter I was kept too busy preaching and agitating—I had been converted to Socialism while at college—to find time for *belles lettres*. Three years later I met Sinclair Lewis, and under his influence I wrote a lengthy apologia for religious and social heresy which no publisher wanted. I had become involved in a 'free speech fight' which led to my resignation as rabbi. The congregation presented me with a portable typewriter—an appropriate if not too tactful gift.

"I went to New York, then back to Portland, and toiled on a long autobiographical novel. But this time too I had missed the mark. In desperation I set to work on a popular history of the Jews, which I had long cherished the thought of writing. I buried myself in Westport, Conn., and for eleven months did a daily stint of five hours' research and five hours' writing. When the work was finished, I was down to my last fourteen dollars in cash, so I looked about for a job. I was offered the pastorate of the Free Synagogue in Newark, and the day after I had accepted, I learned that the first publisher to whom my book had been submitted had eagerly snapped it up!

"I remained in Newark two years, then resigned to write. While my second book was sky-rocketing its way to success I was in Soviet Russia, studying the anti-religious movement there. The offer of an American lecture tour brought me back. I have been sedulously writing and lecturing ever since. Since 1929 I have lived in Southern California, where I met my wife, Myna Eisner Lissner, whom I married in 1930. Most recently I have lectured on Modern Civilization at the University of California, University of Hawaii, and Columbia. I doubt whether I can possibly live long enough to write all the books for which I already have titles."

* * *

Mr. Browne's books, some of them modeled on the style (and illustrations) of his friend Hendrik Willem van Loon, have been exceedingly popular. As Joseph J. Reilly said, "He has learned to handle masses of history with a deft hand and with a sense of the drama of the past." Of late years he has been crippled from arthritis, from which he has suffered since boyhood, but has gone on indomitably both writing and lecturing. He is a dark, short, slender man, whom illness has made look older than his years, but whose mellow voice and eager mind are still young and very much alive.

PRINCIPAL WORKS: Stranger Than Fiction: A Short History of the Jews, 1925; This Believing World: A Simple Account of the Religions of Mankind, 1926; That Man Heine (with E. Weihl) 1927; The Graphic Bible, 1928; Why Are Jews Like That? 1929; The Final Stanza, 1930; Since Calvary: An Interpretation of Christian History, 1931; Blessed Spinoza, 1932; How Odd of God, 1934; All Things Are Possible (novel) 1935; Oh, Say, Can You See! (novel) 1937; The Graphic Bible (ed.) 1941; Something Went Wrong, 1942.

ABOUT: Wickham, H. The Misbehaviorists, American Magazine January 1929; Bookman November 1931; Wilson Library Bulletin February 1933.

BROWNELL, WILLIAM CRARY (August 30, 1851-July 22, 1928), American literary critic, was the son of Isaac Wilbour Brownell and Lucia Emilie (Brown) Brownell. He graduated from Amherst College in 1871, at twenty, with the degree of B.A. The same institution gave him two honorary degrees, an L.II.D., in 1896, and an LL.D. twenty years later.

P. MacDonald

Columbia made him an honorary Litt.D. in 1910, by which time Brownell was generally recognized as the foremost "critical representative of our literary aristocracy," in the words, some years later, of Stuart P. Sherman (this by way of reproof of H. L. Mencken, who had called Brownell a "worthy if somewhat gummy man"). He was on the staff of the *Nation* from 1879 to 1881, before beginning a forty-year connection with the solid publishing firm of Charles Scribner's Sons as literary adviser. *French Traits*, his first book, was adopted by the Chautauqua Reading Circle and gained the cordial approval of Edith Wharton, who sometimes called on Brownell in his cramped and crowded office at Scribner's, but found it easier to approach his aloof, shy, and elusive personality by correspondence. His *Victorian Prose Masters* in 1901, followed by *American Prose Masters* next year, with their blue binding and gold stamping bore "the very insignia of discipline and good taste." They were (also in the words of Robert Morss Lovett) influenced in their view of the function, methods, standards, and ethos of criticism, by Matthew Arnold, whose name frequently appeared by citation and reference in the first book. Brownell's style, according to G. M. Harper, rarely appeals to the eye and never to the ear; he had no instinct for metaphor.

Brownell always inveighed against extravagance of personal expression, believing that the objective of criticism is to "discern and characterize the abstract qualities informing the concrete expression of the artist." James Russell Lowell, in Brownell's opinion, was in this respect "reflectively indolent." Hawthorne rather exasperated him; Poe he regarded as the "solitary artist of our elder literature"; in fact he found all his Americans except Cooper and Henry James somewhat thin and poverty-stricken. In his last years Brownell led the life of a recluse, and as Lovett puts it, failed in urbanity. He was married twice, first in 1878 to Virginia S. Swinburne of Newport, and ten years after her death to Anna Gertrude Hall (Gertrude Hall, the poet, novelist, and translator of Rostand). Brownell, it goes without saying, was a member of the American Academy of Arts and Letters.

PRINCIPAL WORKS: French Traits, 1889; French Art, 1892; Victorian Prose Masters, 1901; American Prose Masters, 1902; Criticism, 1914; Standards, 1917; The Genius of Style, 1924; Democratic Distinction in America, 1927.

ABOUT: Harper, G. M. John Morley and Other Essays; Sherman, S. P. Critical Woodcuts, Points of View; Wharton, E. A Backward Glance; Bookman January 1925; New Republic October 10, 1928; New York Times July 23, 1928; Saturday Review of Literature August 4, 1928; Scribner's Magazine November 1928.

*BRUCE, WILLIAM CABELL (March 12, 1860-), American biographer and Pulitzer Prize winner, writes: "William Cabell Bruce was born in Charlotte County, Va., at Staunton Hall. He was educated by private tutors and at Pampatike Academy and Norwood High School and College, in Virginia. In 1879-80 he attended the Law School at the University of Virginia, and from 1880 to 1882 the Law School of the University of Maryland. In college he received essay and oratorical medals, and he was one of the editors of the *University of Virginia Magazine*. He entered on the

* Died May 9, 1946.

practice of law in Baltimore, and continued until his retirement in 1940. In 1893 he was elected to the Maryland State Senate from Baltimore, and was, by a practically unanimous vote, later elected president of that body.

In 1903 he was appointed head of the Baltimore City Law Department, and in 1910 was appointed chief counsel of the Public Service Commission of Maryland. In 1916 he was an unsuccessful aspirant to nomination as United States Senator, but was elected, as a Democrat, in 1922. In 1928 he was nominated again but was defeated because of his opposition to

Salisbury

extreme soldier bonus measures, anti-Catholic bigotry, and Prohibition.

"His *Benjamin Franklin Self-Revealed* was awarded the Pulitzer Prize for biography in 1919. Besides his other books, he has had privately printed three separate compilations of selections from his speeches, addresses, and occasional writings. Home, Ruxton, Md. Wife, Louise Este Fisher, daughter of his law partner; two sons, one (David K. E. Bruce), author of *Revolution to Reconstruction.*"

* * *

A third son is now deceased. Senator Bruce has honorary LL.D. degrees from Hampden-Sydney College and Loyola College, Baltimore. He is a brother-in-law of the late Thomas Nelson Page and is related to James Branch Cabell. At the University of Virginia he received a medal as the best debater of the Jefferson Literary Society, defeating Woodrow Wilson.

PRINCIPAL WORKS: Below the James, 1918; Benjamin Franklin Self-Revealed, 1918; John Randolph of Roanoke, 1923; Seven Great Baltimore Lawyers, 1931; Recollections, 1931; Imaginary Conversations With Franklin, 1933.

ABOUT: Bruce, W. C. Recollections.

BRUNNGRABER, RUDOLF (1900-), Austrian novelist, writes: "I am descended from an Austrian peasant family, which has lived for centuries in the same village. My grandfather had eight sons and four daughters. My father left for the city, for Vienna, where he married a country girl and lived as a mason. He was killed in the World War, which also cast me out on my destined path. I could not stay longer in the Teachers' College where I was a student, and in the post-war years I wandered all over Europe. At different times I was a tutor, a fiddler in a movie house, a dishwasher in a hotel, a stonebreaker, an ivory  engraver, a longshoreman, a woodcutter, a newsboy, a copyist of the Old Masters, and in other occupations. In 1922, when the effects of the first world-wide depression reached me, on the shores of the Lapland Sea, I came back to Vienna, where I underwent the most extreme poverty.

"I lived two years without work, on nothing, like a Robinson Crusoe in the great city. Then one of the last ministers of the Austro-Hungarian monarchy, who had seen my sketches, took me under his protection, so that I could become a painter. So I went for four years to art school, where at first I believed I was going to be the successor of Tintoretto, and later realized that I barely possessed, up to a certain grade, the mechanical skill for this art, and not at all the genius.

"Therefore at this time I studied economics also, and in my twenty-ninth year wrote *Karl and the Twentieth Century.* The book appeared in 1932, and represented an experiment in showing the dependence of the fate of the individual on the great connections of politics, industry, and technology. It was translated into many languages, including the Japanese, and won a literary prize in Austria. In 1936 there followed the novel *Radium,* which described the rôle of the elements in medicine, science, and industry, and was translated into thirteen languages. The success of these factual books, in which the author is more of an activist than an aesthete, may be considered a logical outcome, since there is no solution for the catastrophic artistic problems of modern prose.

"Then for a long time I dwelt in the realm of pure poetry, and so produced the Biblical-mythological novel, *Die Engel in Atlantis* (*The Angel in Atlantis*) (published in 1938), in which I undertook to portray that part of the world's history which ended with the Flood. In 1939 there appeared—though written in 1937—an historical novel, *Opium-krieg* (*Opium War*), in which I treated much less of the war itself than of the contrasts between the Occident and the Orient."

* * *

Karl, in *Karl and the Twentieth Century,* is the author himself, suddenly becoming aware that his problems are not individual ones, but that he is part of a world-wide order and a world-wide movement of history. It has been called "a work of economic fatalism," with all "the force and power of the twentieth century." It received the Julius Reich Prize, and was translated into English at the insistence of Dorothy Thompson, then still a foreign correspondent. No politician, Herr Brunngraber is still living in Germany, as far as can be learned. His activities since the Second World War began are not known.

WORKS AVAILABLE IN ENGLISH: Karl and the Twentieth Century (in England: Twentieth Century Tragedy) 1933; Radium, 1937.

ABOUT: Wilson Library Bulletin April 1934.

*BRUSH, Mrs. KATHARINE (ING-HAM) (August 15, 1902   ), American novelist, was born in Middletown, Conn., the daughter of Charles Samuel Ingham, headmaster of a private school for boys, and Clara Louise (Northrop) Ingham. She was reared in Washington, Baltimore, and Newbury, Mass., and was graduated from the Centenary Collegiate Institute, Hackettstown, N.J.  She wrote voluminously from childhood, keeping a diary which she drew on later, together with her letters, for her quasi-autobiography. At sixteen she became a minor member of the staff of the Boston *Traveler,* eventually conducting a motion picture column and doing some dramatic criticism. In 1920 she married Thomas Stewart Brush, a newspaperman, and went to live in East Liverpool, Ohio, where his father owned a paper. They had one son. From 1923 she began to write again, her first published work being light verse. Then she began doing short stories, her first sales being to *College Humor,* which for a long time was her main outlet. In 1927 she and her husband moved to New York, and at the end of 1928 they were divorced. The following year she married Hubert Charles Winans, a banker and economist. Her third and fourth novels were bestsellers, and the resultant period of great prosperity, she acknowledges, turned her head, so that her life became so full of clothes, a huge duplex apartment, and trips to Europe that for several years she was scarcely able to write. In her diverting and disarming book, *This Is On Me,* a combination of autobiography and professional record, she tells frankly of her fallow periods as well as her successes—one of the former giving rise to this very book. Besides her novels and short stories, she has done a great deal of motion picture writing in Hollywood and has been a sort of glorified sports reporter. In 1941 she obtained a divorce from Winans in Reno.

Essentially Katharine Brush is a disciple of Scott Fitzgerald, and belongs as much as he to the post-war days, the "jazz age." Like him, however, she is capable of far more "important" writing than most of her work indicates. "Night Club" is one of the most frequently reprinted of American short stories. There is wholesome acid in her pen, and it seldom drips molasses. She is a tiny woman, with dark red hair and an aquiline nose which she deplores. She loves clothes and jewelry, dancing and the theatre, ocean voyages, and football; she does interior decorating and collects antique jewelry. Her daily program is to work five hours (she is currently conducting a syndicated weekly column called "Out of My Mind"), read and study for three, and devote the rest of her time to her family and to recreation. She is a constant reviser, and it takes her a year, on the average, to write a novel and a month for a short story, with rests between. She is an immensely hard worker and a hard player, full of verve and persistence, and at her best she is, as Margaret Culkin Banning remarked, "one of the people . . . who proved that popular prose need not be sloppy or sentimental or untrue to life."

PRINCIPAL WORKS: Glitter, 1926; Little Sins, 1927; Night Club (short stories) 1929; Young Man of Manhattan, 1930; Red Headed Woman, 1931; Other Women (short stories) 1932; Don't Ever Leave Me, 1933; This Is on Me, 1940; You Go Your Way, 1941; The Boy From Maine, 1942.

ABOUT: Brush, K. This Is on Me; Publishers' Weekly February 23, 1935; Saturday Evening Post September 26, 1931; Saturday Review of Literature May 18, 1940; Time May 13, 1940.

BRYCE, JAMES, Viscount. See "BRITISH AUTHORS OF THE 19TH CENTURY."

BRYUSOV, VALERY YAKOVLEVICH (December 13, 1873-October 9, 1924), Russian poet and short-story writer, was born and died in Moscow. He was, wrote Stephen Graham in 1918, "a Russian of strong Euro-

pean tastes and temperament, a sort of Mediterraneanized Russian, with greater affinities in France and Italy than in his native land. A hard, polished, and even merciless personality, he has little in common with the compassionate spirits of Russia." With Konstantin Balmont, he helped found the modernist school. His first poems, *Tertia Vigilia* (1901), *Urbi et Orbi* (1903), and *Stephanos* (1905), showed an affinity to the French Symbolists. Émile Verhaeren, whom Bryusov translated (he also translated Paul Verlaine, Maurice Maeterlinck, Gabriele d'Annunzio, and Oscar Wilde) had an especial influence on his poems of the town and of revolt against social evils. Alexander Pushkin was, however, his special admiration and object of study; like Pushkin, he chose to treat of the bizarre and horrible. Poe was another influence, and Graham remarks that the theme of the stories in *The Republic of the Southern Cross and Other Stories,* might have been worked out by Algernon Blackwood. (The title-story describes a community of millions of workers living at the South Pole.) The Russian short story, as Graham points out, was supposed to possess some particular idea and conception; one told only for the sake of plot was almost unknown. Bryusov's "fine virile style" was admired by his Russian readers for its brevity and directness. He edited *The Scales* and the literary section of *Russkaja Myslj*; his complete works were published in twenty-five volumes in 1912. *The Flaming Angel* (1909) is an historical novel of Germany in the sixteenth century. After the October revolution of 1917 Bryusov joined the Communist party. Not much of his work has been translated into English— *The Republic of the Southern Cross* includes six tales from the Russian of *The Axis of the Globe,* a collection of the early 1900's—but readers with a fair knowledge of Russian will find his poetry rewarding and not too difficult. *Dalekie i Bliskie* (The Far and Near) comprises two volumes of essays on Russian poets. Bryusov is "not an hysterical type of writer and not emotionally convinced of the truth of his writing," states Graham, "but wilfully persistent, affirming unreality intellectually and defending his conception with a sort of masculine impressionism." His early verse was somewhat decadent in style, but his later poetry was more classical, scholarly, and rhetorical.

WORKS AVAILABLE IN ENGLISH TRANSLATION: The Republic of the Southern Cross and Other Stories, 1918.

ABOUT: Bryusov, V. Y. The Republic of the Southern Cross (see Introduction by S. Graham).

BUCHAN, JOHN, 1st Baron Tweedsmuir

(August 26, 1875-February 11, 1940), Scottish novelist, biographer, historian, publisher,

lawyer, and diplomat, was one of a large family born to a Free Church minister of the same name at Perth. In a boyhood he has described as "one of the idlest on record" he attended several humble schools at Perth and later a grammar school at Glasgow, whither the family had removed. At the age of seventeen he commenced study at Glasgow University, reading Classics under the young Gilbert Murray. After graduation he thought of various occupations, and decided he must contrive to go to Oxford. This he did by way of a scholarship at Brasenose College. He had a distinguished career there, carrying off the Stanhope Essay Prize, the Newdigate Prize for verse, and a first in *literae humaniores*, and in his last year acting as President of the Union.

Deciding to take up advocacy as a profession, Buchan went to London in 1900, and after groundwork studies in a solicitor's office was called to the Bar by the Middle Temple in 1901. He helped the *Spectator* editorially, but later in the same year he was invited by Lord Milner to become a member of his staff in South Africa.

Returning in 1903, Buchan began in earnest that full and brilliant career which was to embrace literature, publishing, soldiering, and politics, and was to be crowned by his appointment as representative of the King in Canada. A long series of breathless stories of adventure, including *Prester John, Greenmantle,* and *The Thirty-Nine Steps* (which became an especially effective film under Alfred Hitchcock's direction), endeared him to a huge public. The law was abandoned (though never forgotten); a partnership in the publishing house of Thomas Nelson & Sons, Ltd., came in 1907; and later Buchan became a director of the great Reuter press agency. In the spring of 1915 he went to France as a war correspondent. He was shortly placed in charge of news services at G.H.Q., and in 1917 was brought home as Director of Information. Notwithstanding all these activities (in the course of which Buchan rose to the rank of colonel) he found time to edit Nelson's popular history of the war in twenty-four volumes and to accumu-

late material for his own four-volume *History of the War* (1921-22).

From 1921 to 1930 Buchan was Curator of the Oxford University Chest. He kept up his prolific output of fiction, adding to it excellent biographies of *Montrose, Cromwell, Julius Caesar,* and other worthies, although only his week-ends and two summer months in Scotland were available for writing. Business and politics occupied the bulk of each week. It was not until 1927 that Buchan entered Parliament, as a Conservative member for the Scottish Universities, winning a by-election by more than 14,000 votes. He was an elder of the Church of Scotland in London for thirty years; so he was an appropriate choice for the office of Lord High Commissioner to that Church in 1933-34. In 1935 came the final honor, in his nomination as Governor-General of Canada. A peerage and a G.C.M.G. were natural accompaniments. Lord Tweedsmuir (as he now became) had been many times to Canada, and now showed the liveliest interest in her aspirations and the widest knowledge of her people. He paid an official visit to the President of the United States during his term of office. His death, early in 1940, following a fall which injured the skull, was deeply mourned by Canadians, Scots, and English alike.

The honors, political and academic, that came to Buchan, make an imposing list. He was created a Companion of Honor in 1932 and a Privy Councillor in 1937. Glasgow University made him LL.D. in 1919, St. Andrews likewise in 1930, while Oxford awarded him her D.C.L. in 1934. He was an honorary Fellow of his old college, Brasenose; and during a leave period in 1938 was made Chancellor of Edinburgh University. Honorary doctorates were conferred on him by Edinburgh, McGill, Toronto, Queen's, Manitoba, Harvard, Yale, and Columbia.

The general public will probably remember Buchan the romancer longer than Tweedsmuir the proconsul. Improbable though his plots were in the highest degree, he had the knack of claiming the reader's absolute absorption, and (partly by geographical exactitude) creating an extraordinary sense of actuality. Clean, often too-noble idealism suffused his work, which frequently reflected his own favored pursuits, like fishing, riding, mountaineering, and deer-stalking. His stories made ideal moving picture material and many of these have been filmed. His historical work, though semi-popular, was sound and informed with imagination; and Professor G. M. Trevelyan said that his *Cromwell* "seems to me the best thing ever written about the personal character, the soul of Oliver Cromwell."

Buchan married in 1907 Susan Charlotte, daughter of the late Hon. Norman Grosvenor, and had three sons and one daughter. He was, said Henry Seidel Canby, "a phenomenon more Scotch than English, and, one might say, as American as Scotch. A spare figure, a kindly face, a gentle voice, and a warm nature, were inspired by a kind of driving, restless energy."

PRINCIPAL WORKS: *Fiction*—John Burnet of Barns, 1898; Grey Weather: Moorland Tales of My Own People, 1899; A Lost Lady of Old Years, 1899; The Half-Hearted, 1900; The Watcher by the Threshold and Other Tales, 1902; A Lodge in the Wilderness, 1906; Prester John, 1910; The Moon Endureth (tales) 1912; Salute to Adventurers, 1915; The Thirty-Nine Steps, 1915; Greenmantle, 1916; The Power-House, 1916; Mr. Standfast, 1919; The Path of the King, 1921; Huntingtower, 1922; Midwinter, 1923; The Three Hostages, 1924; John Macnab, 1925; The Dancing Floor, 1926; Witch Wood, 1927; The Runagates' Club, 1928; The Courts of the Morning, 1929; Castle Gay, 1930; The Blanket of the Dark, 1931; The Gap in the Curtain, 1932; The Magic Walking-Stick, 1932; A Prince of the Captivity, 1933; The Free Fishers, 1934; The House of the Four Winds, 1935; The Island of Sheep, 1936; Mountain Meadow, 1941. *Biography*—Sir Quixote of the Moors, 1895; Sir Walter Raleigh, 1911; Andrew Jameson, Lord Ardwall, 1913; The Marquis of Montrose, 1913; Francis and Riversdale Grenfell, 1920; Lord Minto: A Memoir, 1924; The Man and the Book: Sir Walter Scott, 1925; Montrose, 1928; Julius Caesar, 1932; Sir Walter Scott, 1932; Oliver Cromwell, 1934. *History*—Brasenose College, 1898; The Battle of Jutland, 1917; The Battle of the Somme, 1917; A History of the South African Forces in France, 1920; A History of the Great War (4 vols.) 1921-22; A Book of Escapes and Hurried Journeys, 1922; Days to Remember: The British Empire in the Great War, 1923; A History of the Royal Scots Fusiliers, 1925; The Causal and the Casual in History (Rede Lecture) 1929; The Kirk in Scotland: 1560-1929 (with G. A. Smith) 1930; The Massacre of Glencoe, 1933; Gordon at Khartoum, 1934; The King's Grace: 1910-1935, 1935; Men and Deeds (essays) 1935. *Miscellaneous*—Scholar Gipsies (essays) 1896; The African Colony: Studies in the Reconstruction, 1903; The Law Relating to the Taxation of Foreign Income, 1905; Some Eighteenth Century Byways and Other Essays, 1908; Poems: Scots and English, 1917; The Last Secrets, 1923; Homilies and Recreations, 1926; Andrew Lang and the Border, 1932; Pilgrim's Way: An Essay in Autobiography, 1940.

ABOUT: Adcock, A. St. J. Gods of Modern Grub Street; Buchan, J. Pilgrim's Way; Johnson, R. B. Some Contemporary Novelists; Pilgrims of the United States: Speeches at a Dinner in Honor of John Buchan; Atlantic Monthly May-July 1940; Canadian Magazine May 1935; Canadian Forum October 1936; Saturday Review of Literature October 30, 1937; February 17, 1940; Spectator February 16, 1940; Time October 21, 1935, February 19, 1940, September 2, 1940; The Times (London) February 12, 13, 14, 15, 1940.

*BUCHHOLTZ, JOHANNES (1882-   ), Danish novelist, writes: "I was born in Odense, the largest town on the island of Fyn, Denmark, the last of a row of children. (Well . . . a little boy came later, but he died soon.) When I now look back on my rather distant childhood, it does not seem at all strange that I have become an author. For that calling one

must first and foremost have feeling and fancy, and both were found in my parents to an extraordinary degree. They were entirely different, but suited each other well. The home was poor, very poor. Some money came in, of course, but it was spent on father's inventions, which were many and diverse. He was a gifted man and had received a good schooling. The neighbors sought his advice in many matters. Every day he went out to a woods at the beach and offered shiny white stones to God. I was along many times; and he took me to Communion in raspberry juice in a metal goblet. This happened before the grand drawings in the lottery.

"Mother was in close contact with nature —with animals, birds, and flowers. (Here I received my best inheritance!) Also, she had an almost incomprehensible respect for learning. With her poor pennies she let me subscribe for a large encyclopaedia—it came in separate numbers, and I read them one after the other, from A to Z. That may be why I sometimes have the feeling that I know everything: at other times, however, the opposite feeling.

"After I finished school I was in a lawyer's office for a short time, and later with the Danish State Railways. But there were others who were better than I was at conducting lawsuits and at getting the trains to run on the stroke of the clock. Then I began to write novels. Now, if anyone should maintain that there are those who write better novels than I do, I am not impressed. *My* books could have been written only by me. Perhaps they have their spots, but they belong there, just like spots on certain birds' eggs.

"To date I have written about thirty books, among them a few plays, and many of them have gone out beyond Denmark's boundaries. If you should ask what the aim of my writing is, I can only say that just as the finch and the nightingale sing so well, I too do as well as I can to make my eggs nicely oval. I like people in spite of their many and big faults, and I think my life is worth living. My books can scarcely be said to be without *Tendenz*. My convictions necessarily stamp my writings and give them purpose. One thing more: I like to write about odd people, and it is my experience that when types are accurately described, they operate as solutions for the complexes of those readers who recognize themselves in the book's characters.

"America has swallowed up many of my friends and relatives as an oven consumes wood, and I hated that country heartily. But now that Europe more and more behaves like a delirious man, I have come to the conclusion that America is perhaps not so crazy!"

* * *

Buchholz lived, at last reports, in Struer, Denmark. Of fair complexion, with a lined, tanned face, he looks not unlike a western American rancher. In 1932 *Susanne* won the Danish prize in the Inter-Scandinavian Contest. His work is noted for its broad humor. Julius Clausen has called him "a skilled and practiced writer."

WORKS AVAILABLE IN ENGLISH: Egholm and His God, 1922; The Miracles of Clara van Haag, 1922; Susanne, 1933; Secret Arrows, 1934; The Saga of Frank Dover, 1938.

ABOUT: American-Scandinavian Review May 1932.

BUCK, PAUL HERMAN (August 25, 1899-), American historian and university professor, winner of the Pulitzer Prize, was

born in Columbus, Ohio, the son of Henry John Buck and Adele (Kreppelt) Buck, and received his B.A. degree from Ohio State University two months before his twenty-second birthday. He stayed on at Ohio State to get his master's de-

Bachrach

gree, and was granted another from Harvard in 1924, his Ph.D. following in 1935. The year 1925-26 was spent on a Sheldon Traveling Fellowship in London and Paris, and in December 1927 he was married to Sally Burwell Botts.

On his return from abroad, Buck became an instructor in history at Harvard for the next decade, receiving his promotion to an assistant professorship in 1936. He was made an associate professor in 1939, the year after he received the Pulitzer Prize for his book on post-Civil War reconstruction and reconciliation, *The Road to Reunion: 1865-1900*. Harvard, with its well-known insistence on its faculty's writing and publishing extended works of research, put its *imprimatur* on this book, the "original complete bibliography" of which contained 1600 items of manuscripts, Federal and state documents, books, pamphlets, periodical articles, and newspapers. It was dedicated to Arthur Meier Schlesinger, another Harvard historian, "without whose constant criticism and stimulating advice this book would not have been possible."

"The history of how two bitter foes were reconciled, two rival societies harmonized, therefore, leads to the core of American life since the Civil War," states the preface. The writer's endeavor, fulfilled in a readable and well-rounded as well as painstakingly documented book, was "to describe and correlate the many themes, political, social, economic, cultural, and emotional, which figured in the complexity of postwar life." "Americans registered one of their noblest achievements when within a single generation true peace had come to those who had been at war," concludes Dr. Buck. He has been Associate Dean of the Faculty at Harvard since 1938, and is a member of the Faculty Club. His fraternities, social and honorary, are Kappa Sigma and Phi Beta Kappa; he is an Episcopalian; and a member of the American Historical Association, the Mississippi Valley Historical Association, and the Southern Historical Association.

PRINCIPAL WORK: The Road to Reunion, 1937.

ABOUT: Publishers' Weekly May 7, 1938; Saturday Review of Literature May 7, 1938; Scholastic May 21, 1938.

BUCK, Mrs. PEARL (SYDENSTRICKER) (June 26, 1892-), American novelist and winner of the Nobel Prize

for Literature, writes to the editors of this volume of her background and early life: "I am the daughter of American missionaries, Absalom and Caroline (Stulting) Sydenstricker, whose families lived in Virginia and West Virginia. I was born in

Hillsboro, W.Va., but was taken to China at an early age. The exigencies of difficult early years, when my parents lived in the far interior of China, resulted in the death

of all the children older than myself except one brother who left home to be educated in America before I can remember. My parents lived in many places but when I was a child moved to a city on the Yangtse River called Chinkiang. My mother taught me and fitted me for college and gave me all that I have. Most of all did she teach me the beauty that lies in words and in what words will say."

When I was fifteen I was sent to boarding school in Shanghai. By this time I had almost ceased to think of myself as different, if indeed I had ever thought so, from the Chinese. I must not forget another chief figure in my childhood, and that is my old Chinese nurse, who took care of us all for eighteen years, and told me tales of her youth. When I was seventeen I was taken to Europe and England and then home to America, where I completed my education at Randolph-Macon College in Virginia. At the end of my college life I went to my home in China to find my mother seriously ill. Two years I spent in taking care of her. Then I married a young American, Dr. John Lossing Buck, an 'agricultural missionary,' and my mother being recovered we went to a town in North China where his work was and there we lived for five years, when we came to Nanking.

"Part of my life in Nanking was spent in teaching English literature in the University of Nanking and in the Southeastern University. We had two daughters. In 1932 we came to America, where Dr. Buck went to Cornell for a year's research."

* * *

The remainder, and the most important part, of Pearl Buck's story she modestly omits. She had wanted to write ever since, as a child, she was a consistent prizewinner in the juvenile weekly edition of the *Shanghai Mercury*. Her first book, *East Wind, West Wind*, though it received critical recognition, did not make much of a stir. But the publication of *The Good Earth*, in 1931, made literary history. It won the Pulitzer Prize, it became a successful motion picture, it gave its author the Howells Medal of the American Academy of Arts and Letters in 1935, and with her subsequent work it led to her becoming the Nobel Prizewinner in 1938.

Meanwhile, in 1932, a speech and a magazine article in which Mrs. Buck, who had been a missionary since girlhood, criticized the personnel of foreign missions led to a heated controversy with the Presbyterian Board of Foreign Missions. Eventually,

she resigned as a missionary, and one of her supporters on the Board resigned with her, in protest. The next year the Bucks returned to China. But in 1934 Mrs. Buck came back to New York alone, joined the editorial staff of the John Day Co., her publishers, and secured a divorce. In 1935 she married Richard J. Walsh, president of the publishing company and editor of *Asia*. They live on a farm at Perkasie, Pa., with her two daughters and four adopted children —three boys and a girl.

In 1925 Mrs. Buck (under which name she still writes) had come to America on furlough and secured her M.A. at Cornell. She is also an honorary M.A. of Yale. In 1936 she was made a member of the National Institute of Arts and Letters.

After eight Chinese novels, besides a translation of the classic *Shui Hu Chuan* (*All Men Are Brothers*), and two remarkable biographies of her father and mother, Mrs. Buck has turned to writing of the contemporary American scene. But she cannot escape the public identification of her with the Chinese background which she is so peculiarly fitted to depict: to the world she will always be the author of *The Good Earth*, which still remains the best of her Chinese novels.

"The truth is," she told the Columbia School of Journalism, "I cannot be happy without writing novels, quite irrespective of whether they are read or not. I am one of those unfortunate creatures who cannot function completely unless he is writing, has written, or is about to write, a novel."

Mrs. Buck is a tall, rather severely handsome "demi-blonde." She is a liberal both in religion and in politics, and has emerged, during the Second World War, as a passionate spokesman for economic and political equality for the "colored" peoples of the world.

PRINCIPAL WORKS: East Wind, West Wind, 1929; The Good Earth, 1931; The Young Revolutionist, 1931; Sons, 1932; The First Wife and Other Stories, 1933; The Mother, 1934; A House Divided, 1935; The Exile, 1936; Fighting Angel, 1936 (these two biographies together as The Spirit and the Flesh, 1937); The Patriot, 1937; This Proud Heart, 1938; The Chinese Novel (Nobel Prize Lecture) 1939; Today and Forever, 1941; Of Men and Women, 1941; Dragon Seed, 1942; American Unity and Asia, 1942.

ABOUT: Kirkland, W. M. Girls Who Became Writers; Canadian Bookman June 1939; Christian Century April 26, 1933; Christian Science Monitor Monthly January 29, 1936; Illustration December 31, 1938; Library Journal December 1, 1938; Mercure de France January 1, 1939; Nation May 17, 1933; New York Herald Tribune "Books" January 18, 1942; New York Times March 10, 1940; Pictorial Review January 1932; Saturday Review of Literature August 20, 1932, November 19, 1938.

BULLEN, ARTHUR HENRY. See "BRITISH AUTHORS OF THE 19TH CENTURY"

BULLEN, FRANK THOMAS (April 5, 1857-February 26, 1915), English writer of sea stories, was born at Paddington, London,

son of a workingman who drank, gambled, and quarreled with his wife. Frank and his elder sister went to live with an aunt who supported them and several of her own family by dress-making. Frank attended a dame school, but had learned to read before that. The death of the aunt threw him on the streets at the tender age of nine. After three years' experience as errand boy and street arab he shipped as cabin boy on his uncle's *Arabella,* which was lying at the West Indian Docks. At eighteen Bullen found himself in the famous whaling center, New Bedford, Mass., and signed on the *Cachalot.* Bullen's best-known book, *The Cruise of the "Cachalot,"* emerged from this experience in 1898, and Rudyard Kipling wrote to him: "It's immense—I've never read anything that equals it in its deep-sea wonder and mystery, nor do I think that any book before has so completely covered the business of whale-fishing, and at the same time given such real and new sea pictures." Bullen was a junior clerk at twenty-seven in the Meteorological Office in London, and cordially disliked it. A chance to contribute to the *Morning Leader* at two pounds a week, and the encouragement of St. Loe Strachey, famous editor of the *Spectator,* enabled him to leave the office. Bullen removed his wife, Amelia Grimwood Bullen, and their three daughters to a country house at Millfield, fifty miles from London. He wrote thirty-six books in his seventeen years of authorship and supplemented his income by giving well-received courses of lectures throughout the British Isles. *Recollections,* one of Bullen's several autobiographical books, is almost entirely given up to these lecturing experiences. He died at Madeira before his fifty-eighth birthday, after some years of precarious health, his life not having been an easy one. Bullen had a ruddy face, quizzical smile, short beard and mustaches curled to a point; he was born in the same year as Joseph Conrad and somewhat resembled him in physical appearance.

PRINCIPAL WORKS: The Cruise of the "Cachalot," 1898; Idylls of the Sea, 1899; The Log of a Sea Waif, 1899; With Christ at Sea, 1900; The Men of the Merchant Service, 1900; Deep-Sea Plunderings, 1901; The Apostles of the South East, 1901; Sea-Wrack, 1903; Our Heritage the Sea, 1906; Frank Brown, Sea Apprentice, 1906; The Call of the Deep, 1907; Young Nemesis, 1909; Fighting the Icebergs, 1910; A Beauty Boy, 1912; From Wheel and Outlook, 1913.

ABOUT: Bullen, F. The Log of a Sea Waif; Recollections.

BULLETT, GERALD WILLIAM (December 30, 1893-), English novelist, writes: "I was born at Forest Hill, a Southeastern suburb of London. When I was between two and three we moved to Muswell Hill (North London), which was then little more than a village but was soon to become a large suburb, and a monument of the respectabilities which in my

intolerant teens I enjoyed despising. We belonged to the middle middle-class, keeping up appearances on a small income. We were never well off, nor did we experience real poverty. Though I am a Cockney by birth, and a man of Sussex (where I lived for many years) by adoption, I feel it is to the Midlands, where both my parents were born and bred, that I spiritually belong. In rural Leicestershire, my mother's county, I spent perhaps the most blissful hours of my early childhood, in a series of never-to-be-forgotten visits to aunts, cousins, and a grandmother. My mind is permanently dyed in the color of those memories, and the concept *England,* for me, has at its core the rich, green, quiet complacency of rural Leicestershire.

"My father could not afford to have me expensively educated: I acquired the elements at a small private day-school of a kind which I imagine no longer exists. There, with two friends (both brilliant boys, and both killed in the war of 1914-18), I ran a highly unofficial school magazine, to which I contributed almost my first attempt at fiction. At the age of sixteen I was put, willy-nilly, into a bank: which, by the way, was at least a less unpropitious prelude to authorship than daily journalism (my own wish) would have been. My mother died when I was ten, my father when I was twenty. I wrote my first full-length novel (never published and long since destroyed) at the age of eighteen. My first published novel was written in my twenty-first year (while I was still a bank clerk) and published in 1916 by the first and only publisher who had seen it. By that time I was serving (not in the air) with the Royal Flying Corps in France. I read my first press notices in a barrack-room at Boulogne. At the end of the war I got an Ex-Servicemen's Government Grant to enable me to read for the English Tripos at Cambridge University; this I owed largely (I suspect) to the recommendation of Sir Arthur Quiller-Couch, who had read my one published novel and some unpublished poems. After graduating from Jesus College in 1921, I began reviewing for the *Times Literary Supplement* and other literary journals, and began writing short stories, novels, and an occasional critical or general essay. I married Rosalind Gould at the end of 1921, and have one daughter.

"I belong to no church and to no political party. I believe that no culture, no real civilization, is possible without freedom of thought and expression; but I do not believe in economic *laissez-faire,* the doctrine that every man has a right to beggar his neighbor if he can: I suppose the phrase 'liberal Socialism' would about cover my political creed. I believe that world peace can be secured only by federation; but I do not imagine that there is any virtue in the mere repetition of that blessed word. My attitude to religion is shown in an anthology, *The Testament of Light,* and more precisely defined in a little book entitled *Problems of Religion.* The book of my own by which I privately set most store is a sheaf of lyrics entitled *Poems in Pencil.* Among the novels, the following, in order of writing, are the best known: *The History of Egg Pandervil* (with its sequel, *Nicky Son of Egg*), *The Jury* (which has been copiously imitated and stolen from), *The Snare of the Fowler, The Bending Sickle, A Man of Forty,* and (the latest and lightest) *When the Cat's Away.*"

* * *

Mr. Bullett gives as his favorite recreation "staring at rural England." He says he detests "prudery, prohibition, 'blood sports,' central heating, and literary tea parties." He does not like to be interviewed, and cannot understand "why readers should wish to know the details of a writer's personal life." He has now left Sussex for Petersfield, Hampshire. Of his work the late T. Earle Welby said that it contains "such things as the mind can brood upon indefinitely, finding and losing meaning after meaning. They are the creations of a poet."

PRINCIPAL WORKS: *Fiction*—The Progress of Kay, 1916; The Street of the Eye (short stories) 1923; Mr. Godley Beside Himself, 1924; The Baker's Cart (short stories) 1925; The Panther, 1926; The Spanish Caravel (juvenile) 1927; The History of Egg Pandervil, 1928; The World in Bud (short stories) 1928; Nicky Son of Egg, 1929; Marden Fee, 1931; Remember Mrs. Munch (juvenile) 1931; I'll Tell You Everything (with J. B. Priestley) 1932; Helen's Lovers (short stories) 1932; The Quick and the Dead, 1933; Eden River, 1934; The Jury, 1935; The Happy Mariners (juvenile) 1935; The Snare of the Fowler, 1936; The Bending Sickle, 1938; Twenty-Four Tales (short stories) 1938; A Man of Forty, 1939; When the Cat's Away, 1940. *Miscellaneous*—The Innocence of G. K. Chesterton, 1923; Walt Whitman, 1924; Modern English Fiction, 1926; Germany, 1930; The Testament of Light (ed.: second series, 1934) 1932; The English Galaxy (ed.) 1933; The Bubble (poems) 1934; The Story of English Literature, 1935; Poems in Pencil, 1937; Problems of Religion, 1938; The Jackdaw's Nest (ed.) 1939.

*BUNIN, IVAN ALEXEYEVICH (October 22, 1870-   ), Russian poet and novelist, winner of the Nobel Prize, was born in Voronezh, of a family "noble though impoverished" whose origins were "lost in the mists of time." Up to the age of seven he lived on his father's estate in the Yelets district and studied at home with a tutor, "an excellent story teller," who  taught him to read and write "with the aid of a Russian translation of Don Quixote," and nurtured his young mind with Russian folk-epics and fairy-tales, with Gogol and *Robinson Crusoe.* The tutor painted in water-colors "and for a long time captivated me by a passionate dream of becoming a painter." In the evening Ivan's mother used to recite Pushkin. All these influences were partly responsible for Bunin's precocious literary awakening: at the age of eight, while a student at the Yelets Gymnasium, he had written his first poems. By the time he completed his secondary education he had decided to become a writer.

After a year or so at the University of Moscow his travels and literary adventures began: Kharkov, Crimea, journalist on the *Orlovsky Vietsnik,* librarian and district court statistician at Poltava, discovery of Tolstoy. The sensitive poet, whose work, strongly influenced by Lermontov and Pushkin, delighted the readers of the *Novoe Slovo* and the *Russkoye Bogatsvo,* wanted to follow Tolstoy's teachings, but on his return to Moscow he met the Greek refugee Sakni and married his daughter (1898).

Bunin's collected verse had begun to appear as early as 1891; however it was not until 1901, with the publication of *Listopod* (meaning "falling of the leaves," a popular expression signifying autumn), that he was hailed as a major writer. His orthodox poetry and translations of Byron's *Cain* and Longfellow's *Hiawatha* earned him, in 1903, the Pushkin Prize, the highest literary award given by the Russian Academy. His stories which had begun to appear in 1897, had also attracted wide attention. In 1909 he was elected to the literary section of the Academy and, as if to prove his worth, wrote *The Village,* published in 1910, a novel which made his name internationally famous. *The Village* depicted, without flattery the Russian people of Czarist times, their complexity and tragedy, a theme which he used soon after (1912) in his other masterpieces, *Sukhodol* (translated into English as "Dry Valley" in *The Elaghin Affair*), which, together with Goncharov's *Oblomov* and Saltykov's *The Golovlev Family,* stands out, according to D. S. Mirsky, as "the greatest *monumentum odiosum* erected to the memory of the Russian provincial gentry."

In the years preceding the first World War, Bunin traveled widely: Italy, Turkey, Palestine, Egypt, Greece, Algeria, Tunisia. At the time of the Russian Revolution Bunin sided with the reactionary groups. He left Moscow in May 1918; stayed in the South of Russia until the following February; and then fled the country. Meanwhile he has lived, for the most part, in France, spending his summers in Grasse. In the late 'twenties he gave up his little attic room in Paris and went to live on the Riviera. He is a tall slender man with gray hair. Life, he admits, has served him up "much honey and still more bitterness," but he has denied the charge that he is "cruel and gloomy." It is said that when he won the Nobel Prize for Literature (1933) he asked the amount of the prize, was told that it was 600,000 francs (about $37,980), and then smiled and said "I'm very lucky, but, of course, there is the Tarascon barber who won 5,000,000."

His literary output has been somewhat scant, but his autobiographical novel, *The Well of Days* (1930), shows that his gifts as a story-teller have not been impaired. Koulmann claims that Bunin "surpasses all Russian writers in artistic talent, clearness and elegance of style, power of description and variety of themes," and Mirsky says

that his language is "classical, sober, concrete. Its only expressive means is exact notation of things; it is objective because its effect depends entirely on the 'objects' spoken of. Bunin is probably the only modern writer whose language would have been admired by the 'classics,' by Turgenev and Goncharov."

* * *

In 1941 the Tolstoy Foundation, of New York, reported through the New York *Times* that it had received word that Bunin and his wife Vera Nikolaevna were destitute in Grasse in Unoccupied France, whither they had escaped from Paris after the Nazi conquest; and solicited funds for their relief. Bunin, at seventy, had lost all his funds and belongings, and his wife was suffering from anemia.

WORKS AVAILABLE IN ENGLISH TRANSLATION: The Gentleman From San Francisco, 1922; The Dreams of Chang, 1923; The Village, 1923; Fifteen Tales, 1923; Mitya's Love, 1926; The Well of Days, 1933; Grammar of Love, 1934; The Elaghin Affair, 1935.

ABOUT: Mirsky, D. S. Contemporary Russian Literature; Olgin, M. J. Guide to Russian Litterature; Pozner, V. Panorama de la Littérature Russe Contemporaine; Literary Digest May 23, 1925; Monde Slave April 1928; Nuova Antologia January 1934; Revue de France December 15, 1933; Revue de Paris December 1, 1933; Slavonic Review January 1933.

*BURGESS, GELETT (January 30, 1866-   ), American humorist, novelist, and short-story writer, was born in Boston, Mass., the son of Thomas H. Burgess and Caroline (Brooks) Burgess, and was named Frank Gelett Burgess. At twenty-one he received a B.S. degree from the Massachusetts Institute of Technology, which "gave him precision  of thought, if not direction," and where he edited the *Tech,* the student magazine. After graduation Burgess went to work as a draughtsman with the Southern Pacific Railway for three years. In 1891 he was instructor in topographical drawing at the University of California, leaving in 1894 as the result of an escapade involving the pulling-down of a cast-iron statue of the famous Dr. Cogswell, which Burgess regarded as one of the aesthetic scandals of San Francisco. For the next year he was designer and associate editor of a little magazine called the *Wave;* from 1895 to 1897 he was associated with Bruce Porter in a similar venture called the *Lark*. One quatrain appearing in the first issue, "The Purple Cow," has followed Burgess all the days of his life since its appearance; years later he was impelled to write a sequel threatening instant death to anybody who dared quote it to him. Burgess often wrote entire numbers of the magazine, "from cover design to jocose advertisements." *Goops and How To Be Them* (1900) introduced a queer new race of beings, ill-behaved children whose atrocious manners were warning to youngsters in real life. With Porter Garnett, Burgess also edited *Le Petit Journal des Refusées*, every copy of which was printed on a different pattern of wallpaper. Burgess' "Experiments in Symbolic Psychology," thirty water-colours, have been exhibited in a Fifth Avenue art gallery.

Vivette (1897) dedicated to Fanny Van de Grift Stevenson, the wife of R. L. S., was Burgess' first piece of fiction. With Will Irwin, he wrote *The Picaroons* (1903), picaresque tales of San Francisco told with the technique and framework of the *Arabian Nights*. Its successor, *The Reign of Queen Isyl*, was also written in collaboration with Irwin. *Are You a Bromide?* (1907) dealt a devastating blow to "chestnuts" and platitudes, and *Burgess Unabridged* added dozens of neologisms coined by Burgess for special emergencies. One of them, "blurb" ("self-praise; to make a noise like a publisher,") has actually been adopted into dictionaries. In 1906 Burgess was associate editor of another magazine, *Ridgeway's*. In his fiction, he "loves machinery and the intricacies of technique; loves the extravagant, the outrageous," according to Vincent Starrett, who finds it irritating that Burgess, with "the ability to do fine things, persists in writing quickly, carelessly, at times almost slovenly." He was married to Estelle Loomis in 1914; his present address is the Players Club in New York City. His books in recent years have been principally repetitions of his early vein, varied by occasional mystery stories.

PRINCIPAL WORKS: Vivette, 1897; The Lively City o' Ligg, 1898; Goops and How To Be Them, 1900; A Gage of Youth, 1901; A Nonsense Book, 1901; The Romance of the Commonplace, 1902; More Goops, 1903; The Picaroons (with W. Irwin) 1903; The Reign of Queen Isyl (with W. Irwin) 1903; The Rubáiyát of Omar Cayenne, 1904; A Little Sister of Destiny, 1906; Are You a Bromide? 1907; The White Cat, 1907; The Heart Line, 1907; The Maxims of Methuselah, 1907; Blue Goops and Red, 1909; Lady Méchante, 1909; Find the Woman, 1910; The Cave Man (play) 1911; The Master of Mysteries, 1912; The Goop Directory, 1913; The Maxims of Noah, 1913; Love in a Hurry, 1913; Burgess Unabridged, 1914; The Goop Encyclopedia, 1915; War: The Creator, 1916; Mrs.

Hope's Husband, 1917; Ain't Angie Awful, 1919; Have You an Educated Heart? 1923; Why Men Hate Women, 1927; The Bromide and Other Theories, 1933; Two O'Clock Courage, 1934; Too Good Looking, 1936; Look Eleven Years Younger, 1937; Short Words Are Words of Might, 1939; New Goops, 1940; Ladies in Boxes, 1942.

ABOUT: Masson, T. L. Our American Humorists; Starrett, V. Buried Caesars. Christian Science Monitor Magazine July 13, 1940; New York Times Book Review June 8, 1941; New York Times Magazine January 26, 1941.

"BURKE, FIELDING." See DARGAN, O. T.

BURKE, KENNETH (May 5, 1897-), American critic, was born in Pittsburgh and educated at Ohio State and Columbia Universities. In 1926 and 1927 he did research for the Laura Spelman Rockefeller Foundation; from 1927 to 1929 he was music critic of the *Dial,* and during the latter of these two years also did editorial work for the Bureau of Social Hygiene.  From 1934 to 1936 he was music critic of the *Nation.* He has lectured on literary criticism at the University of Chicago, Syracuse University, and the New School for Social Research. In 1928 he won the *Dial* award of $2000 for distinguished service to American literature. He was awarded a Guggenheim Fellowship in 1935. He was married in 1919 to Lily Mary Batterham, by whom he had two daughters; after a divorce, he was married in 1933 to her sister, Elizabeth Batterham, by whom he has two sons. He lives in Andover, N.J. He has been the translator of many noted contemporary German authors, including Thomas Mann, Arthur Schnitzler, Hugo von Hofmannsthal, Otto Spengler, and Emil Ludwig. He is a medium-sized man with a tense face, a wavy dark pompadour over a high forehead, a small moustache, and glasses. The keenness of his perception and the scholarliness of his mind are unmistakable; but a rather involved and exotic style has kept him largely what C. L. Glicksberg called "the critic's critic." He began writing as a poet, and has, in prose, written with approximately equal frequency as a critic of music and of literature. He belongs to the most "advanced" school of literary theory, and has tended to become more and more a critical philosopher rather than a mere commentator on contemporary literature. Crane Brinton perhaps best summed him up in a phrase, as "a literary critic of high rank, a discerning and widely read student of human cultures, an admirable stylist."

PRINCIPAL WORKS: The White Oxen, 1924; Counter-Statement, 1931; Towards a Better Life: A Series of Declamations or Epistles, 1932; Permanence of Change: Anatomy of Purpose, 1935; Attitudes Toward History (2 vols.) 1937; The Philosophy of Literary Form, 1941.

ABOUT: Dial January 1929; Sewanee Review April-July 1933, July 1937; South Atlantic Quarterly January 1937.

*BURKE, THOMAS (1886-), English novelist and essayist, writes: "Thomas Burke was born in London. His father died when

the son was a few months old, and the family had some years of struggle. He left school at fifteen and entered a commercial office. Hated it. His interest was centered in the arts. Began writing. Sold his first story when sixteen. Left commercial office at nineteen, and became assistant to second-hand bookseller. Later, entered the office of a literary agency, where he stayed for seven years. During that time issued privately two volumes of verse and published some anthologies. Was then commissioned by a publisher to do his first book —a series of London sketches, *Nights in Town,* and followed it with a volume of short stories, *Limehouse Nights,* which brought commissions from English and American editors, and enabled him to devote himself to literary work.

"Married, 1918, Winifred Wells, who, under the pen-name of 'Clare Cameron,' has published *Rustle of Spring* and *Green Fields of England,* and now edits a Buddhist quarterly, *Buddhism in England.*

"Interests: books, music, curios, friends (one at a time), wandering in London and country. Hates parties, functions, and any crowd-gathering."

* * *

Until Thomas Burke was nine he lived with his uncle in the London district of Poplar. He was occasionally given a gallery seat at Covent Garden, and for a long time indulged in the dream that he might become and opera singer. For four years he was cooped up in an orphanage. And when "the mess of the Boer War was still being cleared

up . . . and the House of Commons was still a career for the more lazy members of the Great Families" he found himself obliged to earn his own living. The moods of London streets were already getting into his marrow, and a few years later he sent off a dozen atmosphere sketches to Frank Cazenove, who ran a literary agency. Burke's manuscript was no flashy "find," but it led to seven years' experience working under Cazenove, whose professional judgment was acute. The agency was "killed by the war" (1914), and Burke went off to work in the American division of the Ministry of Information.

Burke lacked no inclination to write. At the age of twenty he coddled his vanity and had printed twenty-five copies of his own *Verses.* A little later the *English Review* began to take his short stories and poems. His early pieces about London's Chinatown (*Limehouse Nights*), "admittedly violent stuff written hastily," was in no way deserving of a broadside charge that he had given a "falsely melodramatic picture of Limehouse life," for as he himself said, he was "simply telling tales." Between this book and his 1937 *Dinner Is Served* came a succession of short stories, four novels with scatterings of autobiography, his fine-comb descriptions of London, and a number of ballads.

Burke is a small, neat, sharp-featured, spectacled man who looks more like the city clerk he once was, for a while, than like a romantic and sometimes melodramatic writer. Of this tendency to deal with the more lurid aspects of the London slums—a sort of compensation for his own retiring nature and love of solitude—A. St. John Adcock remarked that Burke's work was "more truthful for being melodramatic, for there is always more melodrama than tragedy in human life."

PRINCIPAL WORKS: *Short Stories*—Limehouse Nights, 1916; Twinkletoes, 1917; More Limehouse Nights (English title: Whispering Windows) 1920; East of Mansion House, 1926; A Tea-Shop in Limehouse (English title: Pleasantries of Old Quong) 1931; Night Pieces, 1935; *Novels*—The Wind and the Rain; The Sun in Splendour, 1926; The Flower of Life, 1929; Murder at Elstree, 1936; Abduction: A Story of Limehouse, 1939; *Poetry*—Verses, 1906; London Lamps, 1917; The Song Book of Quong Lee of Limehouse, 1920. *Essays*—Nights in London (English title: Nights in Town) 1915; Out and About London, 1919; The Outer Circle: Rambles in Remote London, 1921; The London Spy, 1922; The English Inn, 1930; City of Encounters, 1932; The Real East End, 1932; The Beauty of England, 1933; London in My Times, 1934; Will Someone Lead Me to a Pub? 1936; Dinner Is Served, 1937; Living in Bloomsbury, 1939; Streets of London Through the Centuries, 1941.

* Died September 22, 1945.

ABOUT: Adcock, A. St. J. The Glory That Was Grub Street; Björkman, E. Thomas Burke: A Critical Appreciation of the Man of Limehouse; Burke, T. City of Encounters; Burke, T. The Wind and the Rain (autobiographical novel); Bookman September 1917; January 1927; Dial July 19, 1917; Time March 31, 1941; Wilson Library Bulletin May 1933.

BURLINGAME, ROGER

(May 7, 1889-), American novelist and miscellaneous writer, is the son of Edward Livermore Burlingame, editor for a time of *Scribner's Magazine,* and Ella Frances (Badger) Burlingame, and grandson of Anson Burlingame, U. S. Minister to China. He was named William Roger Burlingame. He attended Morristown School in New Jersey, and after receiving his B.A. degree from Harvard College in 1913 was handyman on the old *Independent* in New York and advertising manager for a publishing house. "I was a pacifist but I had a swell time in the war. It took about ten years to disillusion me and make me understand that I was not fighting for democracy or anything else." Burlingame took some courses at the Sorbonne; came home in the summer of 1919 to work at Charles Scribner's Sons as book editor, which "is what they call office boys in publishing houses," and had a novel, *Susan Shane,* accepted as a serial by *Pictorial Review.* This feminist novel was followed by a novel about artists, *High Thursday* (the first, *You Too,* was a satire on the advertising game), and Burlingame went abroad for four years. News of the stock-market crash reached him while rowing on the gulf of Genoa; he turned his ready cash of $500 into lire and came back to New York. In 1933 Burlingame married Angeline Whiton of New York, director of the literary agency of Ann Watkins, Inc. *Three Bags Full,* Burlingame's chronicle-novel of 1936, sold well, and he bought a farm in West Redding, Conn., where he raises chickens and tomatoes, and ministers to fourteen dogs. Two factual books, *March of the Iron Men* (1938) and its sequel, *Engines of Democracy,* were written to develop the thesis that "the history of invention in America is virtually a history of the United States in terms of its technology." *Whittling Boy* is a life of Eli Whitney.

Burlingame has edited a selection of the stories of Richard Harding Davis (*From Gallegher to The Deserter,* 1927) and in 1932 published *Peace Veterans* as a member of the Veterans Justice Committee, who raised money on their bonuses to combat the growing demands made on the government by organized veterans.

PRINCIPAL WORKS: *Novels*—You Too, 1924; Susan Shane, 1926; High Thursday, 1928; The Heir, 1930; Cartwheels, 1934; Three Bags Full, 1936. *Miscellaneous*—Peace Veterans, 1932; March of the Iron Men, 1938; Engines of Democracy, 1940; Whittling Boy, 1941.

ABOUT: Harvard University, Class of 1913; Twenty-Fifth Anniversay Report.

BURMAN, BEN LUCIEN

(December 12, 1895-), American novelist, was born in Covington, Ky., the son of Sam and Minna Burman. He started writing in childhood, and in high school was editor of a school paper. He went to Harvard, but left in his senior year to enlist in the World War. He was seriously wounded at Belleau Woods, but even under fire and

Oggiano

in the hospital he kept on writing. He returned to Harvard to finish his course, receiving his B.A. in 1920, and then became a reporter on the Boston *Herald.* In 1921 he was assistant city editor of the Cincinnati *Times Star,* and in 1922 a special writer for the New York *Sunday World.* For a short time he worked with the Newspaper Enterprise Association and the Scripps Howard organization, then returned to Covington to devote himself to fiction.

Covington being a river town, Burman had been familiar with the river and its life from his earliest days. After floundering around for subjects it suddenly struck him that the Mississippi was his predestined background. At first, however, he could not interest editors in river stories, and for several years he made his way by writing detective stories under a pseudonym. At that time his only work published under his own name was a series of Kentucky mountain ballads which appeared in the *Century Magazine.* He also reviewed books for the *Nation.* Another hard period began when the detective magazine for which he had done most of his work changed its policy, and he refused to change his style to suit. Once he was down to his last cent when he received a check for a story lost three years before—from a magazine to which he had never sent it! It was not until 1926 that the first of his river stories was published, in the *Pictorial Review,* and reprinted in the O'Brien collection. From that time on it was easy sailing; he became "the man who made America river-conscious."

In 1927 Mr. Burman married Alice Caddy; they have no children. In 1930 his war injuries returned, and he was very ill and traveling from place to place to find relief when he wrote his second novel; it took three years to complete, and half way through he tore it up and started again. His third novel also took three years to write, not because of ill health this time but because again dissatisfied, he destroyed the manuscript and started over. All his novels have been filmed, *Steamboat Round the Bend* starring Will Rogers.

Mr. Burman knows the Mississippi not only from observation; he has been a cub pilot, a sailor, and even an amateur "hoodoo doctor" in order to get close to his Negro characters. He has been in innumerable floods, in tornadoes and hurricanes. He is a convinced realist, who believes that a writer must be "a disciplined rebel." Joseph Henry Jackson called him "an authentic voice among those who are telling America what she is really like." In 1938 the Southern Authors Award Committee awarded him its annual prize, and in 1939 the United States Government named a Mississippi lighthouse after him. He is a member of P.E.N., and on the Board of Directors of the Authors' League of America.

PRINCIPAL WORKS: Mississippi, 1929; Steamboat Round the Bend, 1933; Blow for a Landing, 1938; Big River to Cross, 1940.

ABOUT: New York Times Book Review March 23, 1941; Saturday Evening Post October 7, 1939; Wilson Library Bulletin November 1939.

BURNETT, Mrs. FRANCES ELIZA (HODGSON) (November 24, 1849-October 29, 1924), Anglo-American novelist

and writer for children, was born in Manchester, England, the eldest daughter of Edwin Hodgson, a prosperous hardware wholesaler, and Eliza (B o o n d) Hodgson. The Civil War ruined business in the "cotton shires" of England and the father had died in 1854, leaving his business to his wife's management. By 1865 the family was poverty-stricken and glad to join Mrs. Hodgson's brother in Knoxville, Tennessee—though in a log cabin.

"Fanny" Hodgson started writing stories, modeled on those in English magazines, when she was seventeen, after a small private school had proved a failure. Almost from the first she was successful; in later years she said she had never written an unaccepted manuscript.

In 1873 she married Dr. Swan M. Burnett, of Knoxville, and in 1877 they moved to Washington, where her two sons were born. The older died at sixteen, a lasting grief to her. Gradually her success as a writer conflicted with Dr. Burnett's career as a physician, and they drifted apart. She went to Europe and they were divorced in 1898. He remarried later and died in 1906. Meanwhile Mrs. Burnett had married, apparently on an impulse, a young physician who wanted to be an actor, Stephen Townesend. The couple were obviously badly mated, and after a second divorce in 1901, Mrs. Burnett resumed the name under which she had become celebrated. She moved frequently from one country to another, for some time maintaining a residence in Kent, England. Finally she settled down in Long Island, where gardening became her passion. She died there just before her seventy-fifth birthday.

"A late Victorian Titaness," someone has called her. The adjective is apt, but not the noun. She was, rather, the last representative of the "lady novelist." Her nickname among her intimates was "Fluffy," and in old age she was given to titian wigs and frilly clothing. She lived always in a sort of dream-world, where all was sweetness and light; but she could be ruthless to those who crossed her will, and a despot to her family. She was given to lavish endearments and was a devotee of various semi-mystic cults. She was an indubitable snob, and she shut her eyes deliberately to reality. Nevertheless, she cannot be held entirely accountable for what after all was the pattern of her environment in the 1880's and 1890's when she came to fame. Children loved her, as she them, and she was kind and generous to need she could understand.

Her great achievement, of course, was *Little Lord Fauntleroy,* for which a generation of small boys arose to call her cursed—and which virtually ruined her own son's life. But she was a born story-teller, of genuine talent. Her first novel, *That Lass o' Lowrie's,* was her best. An anonymous writer in the *Bookman* remarks rather cruelly that "she has written her one book more times than it need have been written." But that "one book" in many guises made her rich, kept her happy, and brought joy to millions of simple souls. Oversweetened with nineteenth century romanticism, her girl's mind never entirely grew up.

PRINCIPAL WORKS: That Lass o'Lowrie's 1877; Surly Tim and Other Stories, 1877; Haworth's, 1879; Louisiana, 1880; A Fair Barbarian, 1881; Through One Administration, 1883; Little Lord Fauntleroy, 1886; Editha's Burglar, 1886; Sara Crewe, 1888; Little Saint Elizabeth, 1889; The One I Knew Best of All, 1893; A Lady of Quality, 1896; In Connection with the De Willoughby Claim, 1899; The Making of a Marchioness, 1901; In the Closed Room, 1904; Miss Crespigny, 1907; The Secret Garden, 1909; T. Tembaron, 1913; The Head of the House of Coombe, 1922; Robin, 1922.

ABOUT: Burnett, F. H. The One I Knew Best of All; Burnett, V. The Romantick Lady; Machara, W. B. The Young Heart; Overton, G. The Women Who Make Our Novels; Bookman October 1922, February 1925, April 1927; Good Housekeeping February 1922, July, 1925, Outlook November 12, 1924; Saint Nicholas January 1925.

BURNETT, WHIT (August 14, 1899-), American editor and short story writer, writes: "I was born in Salt Lake City, Utah, of English, Welsh, Danish, and German descent. On both sides my ancestors tried on and off to be Mormons, but finally relaxed. My wife, Martha Foley, is Irish (born in Boston), and our son was born in Vienna, where a few months earlier in the same year we founded the magazine *Story,* devoted exclusively to short stories of literary significance.

Pinchot

"From sixteen to thirty-two, with lapses of academic educational years (no degrees) at the Universities of Utah and California and one outright loafing year in Europe (1925-26), I was in newspaper editorial work in Salt Lake City, Los Angeles, Santa Barbara, San Francisco, and New York: at eighteen assistant city editor of the Salt Lake *Telegram,* at twenty-one night city editor of the Associated Press in San Francisco, and at twenty-four on the then combined telegraph and cable copy desk of the New York *Times.* In 1927 I was assistant city editor of the Associated Press in New York. My first fiction was published in the old *Smart Set,* then edited by Mencken and Nathan.

"I was in Paris for the next two years, as city editor of the New York *Herald's* European edition. Eugene Jolas and Elliott Paul, then editing *transition,* published

others of my stories. After a short trip to Russia, I went to Vienna as foreign correspondent for the New York *Sun,* covering the Balkans. In Vienna, then quiet, peaceful, static, social democratic, I married Martha Foley, who was also a foreign correspondent at the time. We took a small cottage on the edge of the Vienna Woods, and in our spare time we began the periodical assembling of short stories in an attempt to bring out regularly in some form such an impressive group that, upon proper presentation in America, these writers would be taken into the quality magazines with their short stories—an art form at that time decidedly out of favor in the American quality periodicals. Among the earliest stories assembled was included work by Kay Boyle, James Farrell, Erskine Caldwell, etc. The first issue of *Story* was mimeographed. When the *Sun's* Foreign Service collapsed in the depression, just after I had covered the first Geneva disarmament conference (which also collapsed) the magazine was transferred to a cheaper printing-ground, Palma, in Majorca, where it continued bi-monthly as usual until, in the middle of the depression, it was 'imported' into America through the instrumentation of Manuel Komroff and others. Its first American issue appeared the day the banks closed, just after Roosevelt's first inauguration. It has appeared ever since. High premiums have been paid for the scarce first mimeographed issue, and early numbers are also collectors' items.

"With the exception of a little time out for writing two books, my life has been tied up with *Story* since its founding. At some periods of its career the magazine has received as many as 350 story manuscripts a day, and a general average of more than a hundred daily, usually from unknown authors. Its 'discoveries' have been numerous, including William Saroyan, Tess Slesinger, Allan Seager, Dorothy McCleary, Richard Wright, Eric Knight, and scores of others. In 1935, when the magazine's stock other than that held by the editors was purchased by Dr. Kurt Semon, a kind of spiritual circle was completed for the magazine. Founded in Vienna, by Americans resident in Europe, it is now supported by a German (long part owner and editor of the *Frankfurter-Zeitung*), now resident and citizen of America. In 1935 the Story Press imprint was founded, by which *Story* discoveries of book length were published under the joint imprint of the Story Press and Harper & Bros. In 1939 this imprint was transferred to J. B. Lippincott & Co. For several years the magazine has conducted an annual college contest, and it conducted a contest for the best writing in the WPA Writers' Project which uncovered the Negro artist Richard Wright. We have printed about a thousand stories in ten years. We have steered clear of schools, axes, etc., and have been guided solely by the feeling for literary merit, artistry, and originality.

"So far as I personally am concerned, editing has sadly sidetracked the original writing urge. There is very little time left. We still read everything that comes in; there is no 'first' reader. Even so, we get time for trout-fishing when they're biting. This is accomplished by living in the country, at Croton-on-Hudson. It also leaves time for chamber music: none any more for tennis, or big game hunting, or skiing, or travel. For a couple of years now we have striven toward that impossible perfectionist aim, a well-balanced string quartette. I am librarian and play the viola. I frequently receive mail designed for W. R. Burnett, but no royalty checks: no relative.

"I have had stories in *The Fifty Best American Short Stories, The Short Story Case Book,* and the O'Brien anthologies of 1931, 1932, 1933, 1934, and 1935."

PRINCIPAL WORKS: A Story Anthology (ed., with M. Foley) 1933; Story in America (ed.) 1934; The Maker of Signs (short stories) 1934; The Flying Yorkshireman and Other Novellas (ed.) 1938; The Literary Life and the Hell With It, 1939.

ABOUT: Burnett, W. The Literary Life and the Hell With It; American Mercury January 1931, September 1933, November 1933; Newsweek January 23, 1939.

BURNETT, WILLIAM RILEY (November 25, 1899-), American novelist, writes: "I was born in Springfield, Ohio, of old American stock; my father Theodore Addison Burnett, my mother Emily Upson Colwell Morgan. I went to grammar school in Springfield, then Dayton, high school in Columbus. Later I graduated from Miami Military Institute, Germantown, Ohio. I enrolled in the College of Journalism of Ohio State University, but attended for only one semester. I married Marjorie Louise Bartow when I was twenty-one. Up until marriage my chief preoccupation was athletics: I played basketball, boxed, played football and baseball in prep school. After marriage, I began to

read extensively and soon began to have literary ambitions. I knocked around at various jobs, all in Ohio, till finally I got a job as statistician for the State of Ohio, Bureau of Labor Statistics, a political job, by the way, which enabled me to make enough to live on and left me enough time to do my writing. By this time I had definitely settled on a literary career. I wrote without the slightest encouragement (except for my wife, who entirely sympathized with my ambitions and helped me in every way) for nearly eight years. I never sold a line. I persisted, either through stupidity or determination, I've never been able to decide which. By this time I had accumulated five novels, several plays, a hundred short stories; I'd tried everything but verse.

"Disgusted, I threw up my job and went to Chicago. Unwittingly I'd done the very thing I should have done. The city made a terrific impact on me. The result: *Little Caesar,* my first published work. The Literary Guild brought it out as its June choice in 1929. It sold in the hundred thousands. A smash-hit movie was made from it, making a star of Edward G. Robinson, and starting a new trend in the picture business. It was translated into six languages, including Dutch and Portuguese, and now, eleven years later, it still sells and is mentioned almost every week in some publication or other.

"There's hardly anything else to tell. Over half of my later books have been made into movies, and two of them have been book club choices. I'm still happily married and live in Glendale, Calif., ten miles from Hollywood. In 1930 I won the O. Henry Memorial Award for the best short story of the year, 'Dressing Up,' which has been reprinted in anthologies and has been translated into several languages.

"Although a cry of 'Hemingway' was raised when my books began to appear, I was but little influenced by him. I was influenced mostly by European writers, by way of translation—I can read no languages easily except English, though I can make a stab at French. I formed my present style after a long study of Merimée, Flaubert, and Maupassant; also Pió Baroja, an unappreciated (in this country) Spanish writer, and Giovanni Verga, a little-known Italian author, who to me, in *Maestro Don Guesaldo,* has written the greatest of all realistic novels, and whose short stories are better than those of Chekhov or Maupassant.

"My hobbies are badminton, table tennis, and raising and racing greyhounds."

* * *

Elsewhere Mr. Burnett said that he likes biography, home-cooked food, music, dogs, and cats. He is heavy-set, dark-haired, long-headed, with heavy eyebrows and moustache He writes his first drafts quickly, then spends months in revision and polishing. Jonathan Daniels said the "unquestionably can write fast-paced, reader-holding fiction," though he added that "a good deal of his writing is as vivid and as superficial as lacquer." T. S. Matthews spoke of his "mature and keen technique," and noted that he "gives the impression of never interfering—either with us or with his characters."

PRINCIPAL WORKS: Little Caesar, 1929; Iron Man, 1930; Saint Johnson, 1930; The Silver Eagle, 1931; The Giant Swing, 1932; Dark Hazard, 1933; Goodbye to the Past, 1934; The Goodhues of Sinking Creek, 1934; King Cole, 1936; The Dark Command, 1938; High Sierra, 1940; The Quick Brown Fox, 1942.

ABOUT: Arts and Decoration June 1929; Outlook January 15, 1930.

BURNHAM, Mrs. CLARA LOUISE (ROOT) (May 26, 1854-June 20, 1927), American novelist, was born at Newton,

Mass., the daughter of George F. Root, composer of "The Battle Cry of Freedom," a Civil War marching song, and Mary (Woodman) Root, a musician. Her father was descended from a Puritan settler of Connecticut in 1640. After childhood years in Newton and North Reading, Mass., the girl went to Chicago at nine and attended public and private schools, with the intention of becoming a musician. She married Walter Burnham, a lawyer, before she was twenty. Mrs. Burnham spent most of her life in Chicago, with three months every summer in a Maine cottage on Bailey's Island, well out from the mainland and reached from Portland. Her writing, begun after her brother had once playfully locked her in a room with the command to produce a poem, was done at a desk in a hotel apartment overlooking Lake Michigan. After some creditable short stories and *Dr. Latimer,* a novel of Maine, inspiration descended on her one evening when she was dressed for the theatre, and Mrs. Burnham sat down to write her first Christian Science novel, *The Right Princess.* These cheery, optimistic books, well-laden with propaganda for the faith, appealed to Scientists and to admirers of the *Pollyanna* type of romance.

Jewel: A Chapter in Her Life, was a best-seller of 1903. "I like *Jewel* best," Mrs. Burnham once declared. "I think she is my high-water mark. It is a Christian Science book and without the Christian Science terminology that is used in the story—well, it would be a kind of *Little Lord Fauntleroy;* it wouldn't be *Jewel.*" No one disputed Mrs. Burnham's mastery in her chosen field, and she had a devoted following. Tall, slender, blonde and with blue eyes, she had marked vivacity and enjoyed meeting people. Her plot structure was admirable, her style generally free from mannerisms. Her characters developed the plot, she declared. She wrote from 9 A. M. till noon, rarely making changes in the first copy. Death came at seventy-three at her summer home, "The Mooring," Bailey's Island, Casco Bay, Maine.

PRINCIPAL WORKS: "No Gentlemen," 1881; A Sane Lunatic, 1882; Dr. Latimer: A Story of Casco Bay, 1893; Miss Pritchard's Wedding Trip, 1901; The Right Princess, 1902; Jewel: A Chapter in Her Life, 1903; Jewel's Story Book, 1904; The Opened Shutters, 1906; The Leaven of Love, 1908; Clever Betsy, 1910; The Inner Flame, 1912; The Right Track, 1914; Instead of the Thorn, 1916; In Apple-Blossom Time, 1919; The Queen of Farrandale, 1923; The Lavarons, 1925; Tobey's First Case, 1926.

ABOUT: Overton, G. M. The Women Who Make Our Novels; Boston Herald June 22, 1927; Boston Transcript June 22, 1927; New York Times June 22, 1927.

BURR, Mrs. ANNA ROBESON (BROWN) (May 26, 1873-September 10, 1941), American essayist, biographer, and novelist, wrote to the compilers of this book shortly before her death: "Anna Robeson Burr was born a Philadelphian in 1873 and thus somewhat escaped the formative influences of the twentieth century. Her first quarter-century

saw her happy and ambitious, and terminated in a marriage which made her the more value her fondness for study. She tried to write first while still almost a child, and after the usual beginners' experiences found success in a book about books, *The Autobiography: A Critical and Comparative Study,* which cost her several years of work and won a marked success among literary people. The pathway thus was cut for her later books when, with her husband and two little girls, she stayed in England during the war. From her life there she produced a group of novels, which deal with the effect of English life on an American in a romantic, picturesque, and perhaps even humorous manner. Since 1925, four later stories have carried this romantic mood into new places, and have been followed by two biographies; while in editing Alice James' *Journal*, Mrs. Burr has brought it into the attention it deserves. Meanwhile, she lives in a new home in Bryn Mawr, Pa., surrounded by books and friends."

* * *

Mrs. Burr was born Anna Robeson Brown, the daughter of Henry Armitt Brown and Josephine Lea (Baker) Brown, and was educated in private schools. In 1899 she married Dr. Charles H. Burr. Both her biographies, of the banker James Stillman, and of the celebrated physician and novelist, S. Weir Mitchell, were based on long personal acquaintance. Her house, called "Scrivens," was near Bryn Mawr College and within easy commuting distance of Philadelphia, the region which, except for her years in England, was always her home. It was there that she died at the age of sixty-eight.

PRINCIPAL WORKS: *Novels*—The House on Charles Street, 1921; The House on Smith Square, 1923; The Wrong Move, 1923; The Great House in the Park, 1924; St. Hellus, 1925, West of the Moon, 1926; Palludia, 1928; The Same Person, 1931; Wind in the East, 1933; The Bottom of the Matter, 1935; The Golden Quicksand, 1936. *Biographies*—Portrait of a Banker, 1927; Weir Mitchell: Life and Letters, 1931; Alice James—Her Journal, 1935. *Miscellaneous*—The Autobiography, 1909; The Religious Confession, 1914.

ABOUT: New York Times September 11, 1941.

*BURROUGHS, EDGAR RICE (September 1, 1875-), American novelist, creator of the "Tarzan" stories, was born in Chicago.

In his childhood his family was wealthy, and he was sent to a succession of private schools, ending at the Michigan Military Academy. He then enlisted in the army, but was soon discharged as under age. Fifteen years or more followed during which he was a cattle drover in Idaho, a worker on an Oregon gold dredge, a railroad policeman in Salt Lake City, and attempted a confusing number of minor business ventures, sometimes for others, sometimes for himself, and always unsuccessfully. In 1900

he married Emma Centennia Hulbert, and they had two sons and a daughter. In 1935 he married Florence Gilbert, who divorced him seven years later.

At thirty-six he was as complete a failure as could have been located among the "John Does" of any large city. The only recreation he could afford was a habit of daydreaming wild adventures, on other planets or in wild places of the earth. Happening on some pulp magazines, he, who had never written a word, decided he could do better than the stories he read there, by merely verbalizing his reveries. The result was a serial on life in Mars, which he sold to the Munsey publications. In 1912 he wrote his first "Tarzan" story, and his first book appeared in 1914.

The rest is history. Mr. Burroughs is not so much a writer as an institution. He has sold twenty-five million copies of Tarzan books in fifty-six languages. Tarzan is in the movies, the comic strips, on the radio, and has passed into the English language. Mr. Burroughs lives on a ranch in Southern California where the post office is called Tarzana. He dictates to a staff of secretaries, and he has incorporated himself. He has not yet seen Africa, where most of the Tarzan stories take place. The story of the English boy adopted and reared by apes—Tarzan himself is by now a grandfather—has some of the universality of folk-lore (and is more than a little reminiscent of Kipling). An editorial in *Commonweal* aptly called the stories "somewhat below Rider Haggard, somewhat above Trader Horn." Alva Johnston has called Mr. Burroughs "a master of the slaughter house branches of fiction," with "a certain galloping commonplaceness as one of his assets, but . . . pages of his books have the authentic flash and sting of story-telling genius." A big, bullet-headed man who looks like an army officer, he rides and golfs when he is not working on his giant industry. Probably few literate adults could read a Tarzan story with pleasure—but probably few of them failed to devour Tarzan stories in their earlier years. Burroughs' continuing series of books on Mars has never found the same vast public.

PRINCIPAL WORKS: Tarzan of the Apes, 1914; The Return of Tarzan, 1915; The Beasts of Tarzan, 1916; The Son of Tarzan, 1917; A Princess of Mars, 1917; Tarzan and the Jewels of Opar, 1918; The Gods of Mars, 1918; Jungle Tales of Tarzan, 1919; The Warlord of Mars, 1919; Tarzan the Untamed, 1920; Thuvia, Maid of Mars, 1920; Tarzan the Terrible, 1921; The Mucker, 1921; The Chessmen of Mars, 1922; At the Earth's Core, 1922; Tarzan and the Golden Lion, 1923; Pellucidar, 1923; The Girl From Hollywood, 1923;

* Died March 19, 1950.

The Land That Time Forgot, 1924; The Cave Girl, 1924; Tarzan and the Ant Men, 1925; The Bandit of Hell's Bend, 1925; The Eternal Lover, 1925; The Moon Maid, 1926; The Mad King, 1926; The Outlaw of Torn, 1927; The War Chief, 1927; The Tarzan Twins, 1927; The Master Mind of Mars, 1928; Tarzan, Lord of the Jungle, 1928; The Monster Men, 1929; Tarzan and the Lost Empire, 1929; Tanar of Pellucidar, 1930; Tarzan at the Earth's Core, 1930; A Fighting Man of Mars, 1931; Tarzan the Invincible, 1931; Jungle Girl, 1932; Tarzan Triumphant, 1932; Apache Devil, 1933; Tarzan and the City of Gold, 1933; Pirates of Venus, 1934; Tarzan and the Lion Man, 1934; Lost on Venus, 1935; Tarzan and the Leopard Men, 1935; Swords of Mars, 1936; Tarzan's Quest, 1936; The Oakdale Affair, 1937; Back to the Stone Age, 1937; Thebad and the Lion, 1938; Tarzan the Magnificent, 1939; Synthetic Men of Mars, 1940.

ABOUT: Commonweal November 6, 1929; Literary Digest November 30, 1929; Saturday Evening Post July 29, 1939.

BURROUGHS, JOHN. See "AMERICAN AUTHORS: 1600-1900"

BURT, Mrs. KATHARINE (NEWLIN) (September 6, 1882-   ), American novelist, writes: "I was born at Fishkill-on-Hudson,

N.Y., in 1882, which means that I have survived, with considerable nonchalance, several major depressions and two wars. My father's name was Thomas Shipley Newlin, my mother's Julia Onderdonck. I was educated by governesses and a private school, Miss Mackie's, at Newburgh, N.Y. I ferried across the Hudson River daily, being driven by a team and carriage to the ferry. I 'graduated' at the age of seventeen and had no further formal education. I was considered 'finished.' Later I took a course in kindergarten in Munich, Germany, and had a diploma. Began writing children's stories, which were published in England. Met my husband, Maxwell Struthers Burt,^{qv} at Oxford, and was married to him in 1913. We have a son and a daughter, both born on the Bar BC Ranch in Wyoming, where my husband and I homesteaded and later had one of the first 'dude' ranches in the West. We had cattle and a boys' ranch too.

"Wrote and published my first novel, *The Branding Iron,* during a winter when we were literally buried in snow in our one-story log cabin. It was a best seller and was sold to the movies. Many of my novels have been published serially and several have

been filmed. Also wrote many short stories and a little verse. After success with our books, my husband and myself sold out from dude ranching and now have a smaller ranch of our own in the same country, Jackson Hole, Wyo., where we spend our summers. Winters at 'Hibernia,' Southern Pines, N.C. Was fiction editor of the *Ladies' Home Journal* during 1928-30.''

* * *

Mrs. Burt first took to writing novels at her husband's urging. Most of her books have been "Westerns," but more sober and realistic than the word usually implies, and with a strongly feminine viewpoint. She and her husband work in separate studies, never collaborate, but are valued critics of each other's work.

PRINCIPAL WORKS: The Branding Iron, 1919; Hidden Creek, 1920; The Red Lady, 1920; Snow Blind, 1921; "Q," 1922; Quest, 1925; Cock's Feather, 1928; A Man's Own Country, 1931; The Tall Ladder, 1932; Beggars All, 1933; This Woman and This Man, 1934; Rapture Beyond, 1935; The Monkey's Tail (as "Rebecca Scarlet") 1936; When Beggars Choose, 1937; Safe Road, 1938; If Love I Must, 1939; No Surrender, 1940; Fatal Gift, 1941.

ABOUT: Arts & Decoration November 1938; Good Housekeeping May 1938; Sunset April 1921.

*BURT, MAXWELL STRUTHERS (October 18, 1882-   ), American novelist who signs his books as Struthers Burt, writes: "I was born in Baltimore, but I am tired of calling attention to the fact that my parents were both Philadelphians, in Baltimore only temporarily, and that I was taken away from Baltimore and brought home to Philadelphia when I

Allied News-Photo

was six months old. My father was Horace Brooke Burt, a lawyer, my mother, Hester Ann Jones. My original Burt ancestor in this country, Nathaniel, was an Irish rebel who fled from Ireland around 1790; on my mother's side I had six generations of American-Welsh Baptist ministers. Both of which facts make me, I hope, both rebellious and tolerant. I was educated in private schools in Philadelphia and entered Princeton University, from which I was graduated in 1904. In Princeton I was editor-in-chief of the *Tiger,* on various other undergraduate papers, and wrote two Triangle Club shows. After Princeton, I went to the University of Munich for a year, and then for a year and a half to Oxford University—Merton

* Died August 28, 1954.

College. I was called back to an instructorship in English at Princeton, which position I held for two years.

"Before going to Princeton, between school and college, I was a reporter on the old Philadelphia *Times,* for two years, under Col. A. K. McClure, a famous editor of those days. I was sixteen when I started and still hold the record, I think, of the youngest reporter on any Philadelphia city-desk. Why I am still alive, I don't know.

"After teaching for two years at Princeton, I drifted west permanently. I had been going west every chance I got ever since I was eighteen. I had it very much in my blood. The Burt great-grandfather to whom I have referred was a fur trader for a while when he first came to this country, and my uncle was a cattleman, so I spent most of my holidays in the West, in various states, working on ranches.

"In 1908 I settled in Jackson Hole, Wyo., and in 1912 I homesteaded and desert-claimed with a partner and started the Bar BC Ranches, of which until two years ago, when I sold out my interests, I was president. I now have a small ranch of my own in the same country, and spend as much time there as I can. I have been a citizen of Wyoming since 1908 and regard it as my home. [Mr. Burt's winter home is in Southern Pines, N.C.]

"In 1918 I married Katharine Newlin, herself a very well-known writer [under the name of Katharine Newlin Burt *qv*] and at one time fiction editor of the *Ladies' Home Journal.* We have a son, who is now in the music department of Princeton, and a daughter. During the First World War I was in the Air Service, but never got abroad.

"As to my writing, like most writers, I started when I was about eight. I have written a lot and, fortunately or unfortunately, a great many different things: novels, verse, many articles. I've been the parent of a long list of titles.

"I am an Episcopalian, I suppose. I am an admirer of President Roosevelt. I have a good many dislikes, but have forgotten them in my present [1940] dislike of Hitler and Stalin; but I have even more likings. I like tennis, fly-fishing, riding, and exploring; but above all I like writing, and actually running a ranch. I don't like much modern prose; but I like a great deal of poetry. The only good short stories I know at present, except every now and then, are being published in the *New Yorker.* The rest, for the most part, aren't short stories at all, but that curious bastard American form, the condensed novel."

* * *

Mr. Burt's thin face, deep-set quizzical eyes, sharp features, and tight mouth seem to belong more to the ex-college professor than to the Wyoming rancher. He was first encouraged to write by Philip Keats Speed, grand-nephew of John Keats, who was his city editor on the Philadelphia *Times.* A critic has called him "a good workman with words, who writes fine pages of description and some really witty dialogue." Richmond P. Bond remarked: "His prose is smart and not precious, biting and not bitter, polished and not glossy."

PRINCIPAL WORKS: In the High Hills, 1914; John O'May and Other Stories, 1918; Songs and Portraits (verse) 1921; Chance Encounters, 1921; The Interpreter's House, 1924; The Diary of a Dude Wrangler, 1924; When I Grow Up to Middle Age (verse) 1925; The Delectable Mountains, 1926; They Could Not Sleep, 1928; The Other Side, 1929; Festival, 1931; Entertaining the Islanders, 1933; Escape from America, 1936; Powder River, 1939; Along These Streets, 1942.

ABOUT: Arts and Decoration November 1938; Bookman April 1931; New York Times Book Review December 28, 1941; Saturday Review (London) November 14, 1931; Scholastic April 29, 1939.

BURY, JOHN BAGNELL (October 16, 1861-June 1, 1927), Irish classical scholar and historian, was born at Monaghan, the eldest son of the Rev. Edward John Bury, successively curate, rector, and canon, and Anna (Rogers) Bury, "a clever woman and a great reader." He was first taught Greek and Latin by his father, attended Foyle College, Londonderry, where, at the age of  ten he amazed his examiner; entered Trinity College, Dublin, in 1878; and was graduated four years later with a top place in classics and a fourth in mental and moral philosophy. He was made a fellow of Trinity College, Dublin, in 1885, and in the same year married his second cousin Jane Bury, by whom he had one son. After serving a number of important professorships he was chosen regius professor of modern history in the University of Cambridge, succeeding Lord Acton; this post he held until his death.

As an undergraduate Bury had prepared, with Sir John Pentland Mahaffy, an edition of *The Hippolytus of Euripides* (1881) and had written four papers which appeared in the *English Historical Review* in 1886. *The Nemean Odes of Pindar* and *The Isthmian Odes of Pindar,* his most valuable contributions to classical scholarship, followed shortly. From 1888 to 1891 he edited *Kottabos,* and for this magazine did Greek translations of Latin verse.

Bury learned Russian and Hungarian (he had pursued Sanskrit, Hebrew, and Syriac several years before) and in 1889 he published two remarkably astute volumes of *History of the Later Roman Empire From Arcadius to Irene.* Between 1896 and 1900 he produced a long-needed seven-volume edition of Gibbon's *Decline and Fall,* with full notes and appendices. A history of Greece and a life of St. Patrick were followed by a monumental series on public law. His lectures delivered at Harvard in 1908 appeared as *The Ancient Greek Historians.* Bury's philosophy was perhaps best embodied in *The Idea of Progress*: wherein the theory of human progress emerges from an interpretation of history which regards men as slowly advancing in a definite and desirable direction. On the assumption (unverifiable) that "we shall not soon reach a point in our knowledge of nature beyond which the human intellect is unqualified to pass," this progress will continue indefinitely. The process itself must be the necessary outcome of the psychical and social nature of man, and not at the mercy of any external will.

Bury wrote almost nothing that could be called light; his humor was largely irony. He had a certain austerity of manner which appeared to leave him with little of the ever-needed patience and sympathy of the university leader. From 1910 on, his health declined noticeably but he remained intellectually alert to the day of his death. His influence on his own students was relatively slight, but his achievements in research were outstanding: of this his own writings are the best evidence.

PRINCIPAL WORKS: History of the Later Roman Empire From Arcadius to Irene, 1889; The Nemean Odes of Pindar, 1890; The Isthmian Odes of Pindar, 1893; History of the Roman Empire From Its Foundation to the Death of Marcus Aurelius, 1893; History of Greece to the Death of Alexander the Great, 1900; The Life of St. Patrick and His Place in History, 1905; The Ancient Greek Historians, 1909; A History of the Freedom of Thought, 1914; The Idea of Progress: An Inquiry Into Its Origin and Growth, 1920; History of the Later Roman Empire From the Death of Theodosius I to the Death of Justinian, 1923.

ABOUT: Baynes, N. H. A Bibliography of the Works of J. B. Bury. . . . With a Memoir; Temperley, H. Selected Essays of J. B. Bury (see Introduction).

BUTLER, ELLIS PARKER (December 5, 1869-September 13, 1937), American humorist, wrote to the editors of this volume shortly before his death: "I was born at Muscatine, Iowa, on the Mississippi River, my father then being in the pork-packing business with my grandfather. The business failed and my father became a bookkeeper and as he was poor and had  eight children, of which I was the eldest, I lived most of my youth with my aunt Lizzie, a cultured spinster who gave me a liking for literature and my early education.

"Because I had to go to work I had but one year in high school, and from 1886 to 1897 I worked as bill-clerk and salesman in several local concerns, the last eight years in a wholesale grocery where my father was bookkeeper. All this time I was writing verses and short humor, and in 1897 on the advice of three New York editors I went to New York. Here I continued writing humor and did editorial work on two trade papers and in 1899 with Thomas A. Cawthra established the *Decorative Furnisher* magazine.

"In 1899 I married Ida A. Zipser, of Muscatine, and we have had five children, of whom four are living. In 1905 my best known story, *Pigs Is Pigs,* was published in the *American Magazine* and as a book in 1906 and had a remarkable success. A year or so earlier I had moved to Flushing, on Long Island, and I now sold my interest in our magazine, and with my wife and daughter spent about a year in Paris and doing some sight-seeing in England and on the Continent, after which we returned to Flushing where we have lived in the same house ever since.

"While continuously writing I have taken much interest in local matters in Flushing, making that my principal recreation. I was a founder of the Dutch Treat Club, of the Authors' League, of the Authors' League Fund, etc., and am now president of the Tuscarora (fishing) Club, and so on. My other recreations have been trout fishing and stamp collecting.

"The three greatest influences in my work were my aunt Lizzie Butler and my high school English teacher, who gave me an admiration and appreciation of literature, and my father, who was an enthusiastic admirer of Mark Twain and the other humorists of that day. Mark Twain was close to us, having lived in Muscatine awhile, and Bob Burdette was but sixty miles down the river.

"My writing has been voluminous but for the most part fiction stories and articles for the magazines, my books being selections from these, with but two or three exceptions. I have tried writing novels but never with much success."

* * *

Ellis Parker Butler died at Williamsville, Mass., in his sixty-eighth year. Although his name is one of the best known in the annals of American humor, he really had no significant style or *métier,* and his reputation rests almost solely on one slight but hilarious contribution, *Pigs Is Pigs.*

PRINCIPAL WORKS: Pigs Is Pigs, 1906; The Jack-Knife Man, 1913; Philo Gubb: Correspondence School Detective, 1918; Swatty, 1920; In Pawn, 1921; Jibby Jones, 1923; Butler Readings, 1925; The Behind Legs of the 'Orse, 1927; Dollarature, 1929.

ABOUT: Masson, T. L. Our American Humorists; Boston Evening Transcript May 1, 1926; New York Times September 13, 1937; St. Nicholas November 1935.

BUTLER, SAMUEL. See "BRITISH AUTHORS OF THE 19TH CENTURY"

BYNNER, WITTER (August 10, 1881-), American poet, was born in Brooklyn, N.Y., the son of Thomas Edgarton Bynner and Annie Louise (Brewer)  Bynner. His paternal grandfather was editor of a newspaper in Worcester, Mass., and his uncle, Edwin Lasseter Bynner, was a novelist. He was graduated from Harvard in 1902, and had been on the staff of the *Advocate.* He became assistant editor of *McClure's Magazine,* and at the same time literary advisor for McClure, Phillips & Co. Later he held the same position with Small, Maynard & Co. From 1908 to 1918 he lived in Cornish, N.H., writing and publishing poetry; then for a year he conducted a class in verse-writing at the University of California. After this he traveled extensively in the Orient, particularly in China, and Chinese poetry became the second great

literary influence in his life. It was followed by American Indian poetry, when he took up his residence in Santa Fé, N.M., where he now lives. He is unmarried.

Harriet Monroe called Bynner "a transplanted product of down-east culture. He has broken away from the Harvard tradition which threatened at one time to enslave him . . . has traveled, mind and body, in the Orient, and has made . . . our Southwest wonderland his permanent home, not only in terms of real estate and residence, but in the loyalties and wistful ardors of his spirit."

Though Bynner's poetry was successful from the first, he became widely known to the general public through a hoax perpetrated by him and Arthur Davison Ficke, who, under the respective pseudonyms of "Emanuel Morgan" and "Anne Knish" published a book called *Spectra,* supposedly the work of two new adherents to the free verse, Imagist school then (1916) at its apogee. Later he brought out another similar volume, *Pins for Wings.* Bynner's translation, with Dr. Kiang Kang-hu, of the poems included in *The Jade Mountain* (1929) was the first volume of Chinese verse to be translated in full by an American poet.

Witter Bynner is a pianist as well as a poet. Louis Untermeyer described him as "tall, immaculate, and aloof," but among his friends he is noted for his booming laugh and his geniality. To the editors of this volume he wrote: "I may add these comments, if they make for fun, that I first loathed and then loved Walt Whitman as a person, and now regard him as a first-rate artist; that my favorite political personages in American history are Thomas Paine, Thomas Jefferson, Wendell Phillips, and Grover Cleveland; and that I still, from the lyrical point of view, have a great deal of confidence."

Louis Untermeyer remarked of Bynner: "His work is definite in its values, straightforward in speech, clean-cut in technique, undeviatingly sincere in the expression of his convictions."

PRINCIPAL WORKS: Young Harvard, 1907; Tiger (play) 1913; The Little King (play) 1914; The New World, 1915; Iphigenia in Tauris (play) 1915; Spectra (with A. D. Ficke, as "Emanuel Morgan") 1916; Grenstone Poems, 1917; A Canticle of Praise, 1919; Pins for Wings (as "Emanuel Morgan") 1920; Caravan, 1925; Cake (play) 1926; The Persistence of Poetry (prose) 1929; Indian Earth, 1929; Eden Tree, 1931; Guest Book, 1935; Selected Poems, 1936; Against the Cold, 1940.

ABOUT: Starrett, V. Books Alive; Poetry August 1930; December 1940; Scholastic November 14, 1936; Sunset Magazine March 1929.

BYRD, RICHARD EVELYN (October 25, 1888-), American naval officer and polar explorer, was born at Winchester, Va.,  the second of three sons of Richard Evelyn Byrd and Eleanor B o l l i n g (Flood) Byrd, who traces her lineage to Henry of Navarre. The Byrds have been prominent figures in Virginia for three centuries; Admiral Byrd's brother, Harry Flood Byrd, is U. S. Senator from Virginia and a former governor of the state. Westover, the family seat, was begun in 1690, took forty-five years to complete, and has twice been ravaged by fire. Richard Byrd was fifteen years old when the Wright brothers flew at Kittyhawk; twenty-one when Bleriot flew the Channel; was past twenty-five when he took his first airplane ride; and nearly thirty before he qualified as an aviator. At twelve he made a trip around the world alone, sailing from San Francisco to call on Judge Adam C. Carson in the Philippines. Young Byrd attended Shenandoah Valley Academy; was the youngest boy in Virginia Military Institute; attended the University of Virginia; and in 1908 was appointed a midshipman at Annapolis, graduating in 1912; he served as an ensign in 1913-14, and was retired for physical disability (a broken foot) in 1916. In January 1915 he married Marie D. Ames of Boston; they have three children, two girls and a son.

During the First World War Byrd was Lieutenant Commander of the U. S. air forces in Canada from July 1918 to the Armistice; his first air training was obtained at the Naval Flying School at Pensacola, Fla. He was commander of the aviation unit of the Navy-MacMillan Polar Expedition from June to October 1925. On May 9, 1926, Byrd made the first airplane flight over the North Pole, accompanied by Floyd Bennett, and returned to his base at King's Bay, Spitzbergen. For this exploit he was promoted to Commander. Next year he made a rather bungled flight with three companions across the Atlantic, covering 1,360 miles in fifteen and a half hours from New York to France, June 29-July 1, 1927. The South Pole was his next aerial conquest, on November 29, 1929; in 1930 he was made a Rear Admiral. *Little America* (1930) contains the detailed record of this flight, written with fullness of detail and some modest literary skill, following *Skyward* (1928),

which chronicled the North Pole flight. A second expedition was made in 1933, under variegated auspices. *Discovery* (1935), written for popular, non-scientific consumption, and Byrd's most notable and self-revelatory piece of writing, *Alone,* were literary by-products. A third trip to the Antarctic regions, beginning in November 1939, was made as Commanding Officer of the United States Antarctic Service. Admiral Byrd holds the Congressional Medal of Honor, has twenty-odd citations from the Navy Department, numerous honorary degrees, is a Commander of the Legion of Honor, and is a member of more than fifty organizations. He is small, compact, with a high, slightly sloping forehead, hair rippling in wavelets, and a serene manner which masks iron self-control. He is an extremely popular lecturer.

PRINCIPAL WORKS: Skyward, 1928; Little America, 1930; Discovery, 1935; Alone, 1938.

ABOUT: Foster, C. Rear Admiral Byrd; Green, F. Dick Byrd—Air Explorer; Murphy, C. J. V. Struggle: The Life and Exploits of Commander Richard E. Byrd; Riotor, L. Byrd au Pôle Sud; Life July 8, 1940; Reader's Digest January 1940; Time July 17, 1939.

BYRNE, DONN (November 20, 1889-June 18, 1928), Irish-American novelist, whose name was originally Brian Oswald Donn-Byrne and then Brian O'Beirne, was born (though he was ashamed to admit it) in Brooklyn, where his father, Thomas Donn-Byrne, an architect, and his mother Jane (McParlane) Donn-Byrne, had gone to see the completion of some  architectural enterprise. They returned to Ireland in a few months, and the boy grew up in County Antrim. He received his M.A. from University College, Dublin, and then studied at the Sorbonne and in Leipzig. To escape his parents' plans for his future, he ran away to South America, where for a while he punched cows and wrote verses, with some idea of becoming "a cowboy poet." Instead he emigrated next to New York, where, when literature proved unproductive, he worked in a garage. He was discharged from three New York papers, but finally found a means of livelihood on the staff of first the *New Standard* and then the *Century Dictionary.* In 1911 he married Dorothea Cadogan, co-author of the successful play, *Enter Madame.* They had two sons and two daughters.

Byrne's first books were a *succès d'estime* without making much money, but with *Messer Marco Polo,* in 1920, he burst into fame and fortune. Unfortunately he was extravagant by nature, and soon was living so far beyond even a large new income that he and his family had their Connecticut home attached and were forced to leave hurriedly for Ireland. For several years they traveled restlessly from place to place, Byrne all the time writing, sometimes combining business and pleasure by traveling for local color— as when they went to Syria for the background for *Brother Saul.* In 1928, on a night's gambling winnings at Cannes, he bought Castle Coolmaine, in County Cork. He had hardly been settled there when his automobile broke through a sea-wall into the ocean and he was killed.

A thin, nervous, excitable young man, Byrne made enemies wherever he went. He was an Orangeman and at outs with the Sinn Feiners, he despised America and proclaimed himself "last of the Irish story tellers"; in Ireland and England, on the other hand, he was derided as a "synthetic" and "professional" Irishman. When he died the *Outlook* remarked justly that he was still only a promising young writer. Yet he had an exquisite ear for language (he who had once been fired from a newspaper for "bad English"!) and he was in his work as in his life a true romantic. His novels, and the posthumous collections of his short stories which continued to come out in book form for some years after his death, will probably for some time to come continue to delight readers. There was a fiery innocence even in his quarrelsomeness, and for a brief youthful period in New York he was heart and soul of the young writers who were creating among them an American literary renaissance.

PRINCIPAL WORKS: Stories Without Women, 1915; The Stranger's Banquet, 1919; The Foolish Matrons, 1920; Messer Marco Polo, 1920; The Wind Bloweth, 1922; Changeling and Other Stories, 1923; Blind Raftery, 1924; O'Malley of Shanganagh, 1925; Hangman's House, 1926; Brother Saul, 1927; Crusade, 1927; Destiny Bay, 1928; Field of Honor, 1929; Ireland: The Rock Whence I Was Hewn, 1929; A Party of Baccarat, 1930; Rivers of Damascus and Other Stories, 1931; The Woman of the Shee and Other Stories, 1932; The Island of Youth, 1933.

ABOUT: Adcock, St. J. Gods of Modern Grub Street; Macauley, T. Donn Byrne: Bard of Armagh; Mellon, P. Donn Byrne: His Place in Literature; Bookman April 1929; Catholic World February 1929; North American Review November 1930; Outlook July 4, 1928.

CABELL, JAMES BRANCH (April 14, 1879-), American novelist, was born in Richmond, Va., the son of Robert Gamble Cabell and Anne (Branch) Cabell. He is F.F.V. of the F.F.V.'s, and has written a number of genealogical works bearing on his ancestry and that of other Virginia families. He was educated at William and Mary College (B.A. 1898), and  while he was still a student there was also instructor in Greek and French. Then, after a short experience in the pressroom of the Richmond *Times,* he went to New York, where he was a reporter on the *Herald* for two years. In 1901 he held a similar position on the Richmond *News.* For ten years thereafter he was a free lance writer; then (after a rather surprising two years in the West Virginia coal mines) he was appointed Genealogist of the Virginia Chapter of the Sons of the Revolution, and subsequently has held similar posts for several other societies. In 1913 he married Priscilla Bradley, also of an old Virginia family; they have one son.

Since then he has lived very quietly in Richmond, with a reputation for aloofness and hauteur that is actually due to extreme shyness. He differentiates sharply between his life as a writer (during the hullabaloo about *Jurgen,* in 1919, a writer very much in the limelight) and his life as a Virginia gentleman. It is said that one of his cousins, returning from a visit to New York, telephoned Mrs. Cabell and told her with excitement that she had seen James' name in a New York newspaper! He did consent to be first president of the Virginia Writers' Club, but seldom came to meetings and resigned as soon as possible. In 1932 he joined with five other well known writers to found and edit the short-lived *American Spectator,* but he seldom leaves Richmond (except for his summer home in Ophelia, Va.) and is never seen at the usual literary gatherings.

A good-looking, serious-faced man with eyeglasses, Cabell seems much more like a college professor than like the creator of the mythical country of Poictesme. He writes all his books directly on the typewriter, without carbons, so there is always only one draft of each. By a railroad accident, the only copy of *The Silver Stallion* lay for thirty-six hours in a ditch! He likes to spend his Sundays alone, pasting up clip-

pings for his big collection of scrapbooks.
There is something boyish in all this; and
there is something adolescent in Cabell's
entire philosophy and in the romances which
grew from it. It is not by accident that
during his greatest vogue, in the 1920's, his
chief admirers were college students.

He is a pure escapist; to whom reality is
both unpleasant and unimportant. He loves
cryptograms and anagrams; his style, which
occasionally is capable of real nobility and
beauty, often degenerates into what Peter
Monro Jack called "a curious mode out of
a dozen archiac styles from the Bible to
Irish poetic drama, by way of Malory and
Hewlett"; his constant preoccupation with
sex, which led to the attempt to censor *Jurgen*
and a notable victory for freedom of speech
in America, too often becomes mere
naughtiness.

He has been so extravagantly praised—
Benjamin De Casseres called him "the
Watteau of ironists, the Debussy of prose,
Spinoza of word-magic, the Prometheus of
an American Renaissance," and this was only
one of many similar ecstatic descriptions—
that the greatest genius could not live up
to the praise heaped upon him. On the
other hand, he has been unfairly attacked
by indignant realists who deprecate his cloudy
romances. As Jack remarked, he "has carried the novel of escape, pretence, and sophisticated grandeur to the point at which
it becomes a composed philosophy of life,"
and Maxwell Anderson added temperately
that "his unsoundness as a critic of literature is only the corollary of his fundamental
failure as a critic of life." He is the un-
touchable resident of the ivory tower, the
dauntless champion of pure romance and
roseate dream, the indefatigable spokesman
of "art for art's sake." His appeal is only
to a certain type of mind in a certain era,
and the rude facts of life in the past decade
have caused him to be unjustifiably neglected.
About 1930 he announced that James Branch
Cabell would never write again; "Branch"
Cabell, however, without the "James," soon
began a series of books of semi-philosophical,
semi-critical essays.

His survival, however, must stand or fall
with the novels which are a chronicle of
Manuel of Poictesme, from *The Eagle's
Shadow* to *The Way of Ecben.* Clifton
Fadiman has said judiciously of these novels:
"The world in which he lives is one built up
out of his own preferences. . . It has the
beauty and formal perfection of a well-
known soap-bubble." The bubble may perhaps have burst, but while it lasted it was
often beautifully iridescent.

234

PRINCIPAL WORKS: *Novels*—The Eagle's
Shadow, 1904; The Line of Love, 1905; Gallantry,
1907; The Cords of Vanity, 1909; Chivalry, 1909;
The Soul of Melicent, 1913 (as Domnei, 1920);
The Rivet in Grandfather's Neck, 1915; The Cer-
tain Hour, 1916; The Cream of the Jest, 1917; Beyond Life, 1919; Jurgen, 1919; Figures of Earth,
1921; The Jewel Merchants, 1921; The Lineage
of Lichfield, 1922; The High Place, 1923; The
Silver Stallion, 1926; The Music From Behind the
Moon, 1926; Something About Eve, 1927; The
White Robe, 1928; The Way of Ecben, 1929;
Townsend of Lichfield, 1930. *Miscellaneous*—From
the Hidden Way (verse) 1916; Straws and Prayer-
Books, 1924; Some of Us, 1930. Between Dawn
and Sunrise (with John Macy) 1930; These Restless Heads, 1932; Special Delivery, 1933; Smirt,
1934; Ladies and Gentlemen, 1934; Smith, 1935;
Preface to the Past, 1936; Smire, 1937; The King
Was in His Counting House, 1938; Hamlet Had
an Uncle, 1940; The First Gentleman of America,
1942.

ABOUT: Boynton, P. H. Some Contemporary
Americans; Holt, G. A Bibliography of the Writ-
ings of James Branch Cabell; Van Doren, C. James
Branch Cabell; American Mercury December 1926,
January 1928; March 1940; Bookman October 1927,
December 1928, February 1931; Englische Studien
#3, 1938; Nation April 12, 1933; New Republic
January 13, 1937; Saturday Review of Literature
October 29, 1927, February 29, 1936, January 27,
1940; Sewanee Review April 1929, July 1930,
October 1931, January 1934; Time March 31, 1941;
Virginia Quarterly Review April 1926, July 1929.

CABLE, GEORGE WASHINGTON. See
"AMERICAN AUTHORS: 1600-1900"

*CAHAN, ABRAHAM (July 7, 1860-   ),
Russian-American novelist and editor, was
born in Vilna, and educated at the Teachers'
Institute there. Later
he attended a law
school in New York,
but was never ad-
mitted to the bar. He
came to the United
States in 1882, and is
a naturalized citizen.
In 1887 he married
Anna Braunstein. Af-
ter editing a weekly
paper and a monthly

magazine in Yiddish, he became editor-in-
chief of the New York *Jewish Daily Forward,* and still held that post at past eighty.
Since 1887 he has also been contributing
stories and articles to American magazines.
Some of his books have been written in
Yiddish, others—including his best known
novel, *The Rise of David Levinsky,* the
story of another Russian Jewish immigrant
—in English. He is an old-time Social Democrat, far to the right of any existing Socialist parties, and is bitterly anti-Communist.
In earlier years he was active in trade union
organization, particularly in the clothing

* Died August 31, 1951.

field; but the union labor movement has also gone beyond his nineteenth century craft unionism. Nevertheless, he is still, at eighty, active, wide-awake, and he says "still learning." To a symposium on how it feels to be eighty years old, he wrote: "This old man *knows* that the end of his world is near at hand and that he is liable to sing his swan song any day; but he is scarcely aware of it. . . . Life is full of content. . . . But I sometimes feel like the reader of a thrilling novel who is not sure of being able to finish it."

Cahan's own contribution to literature, aside from his realistic novel and some accurate pictures of New York East Side life, has not been important; most of his energies have gone to his editorial work. But he has for many years been the guardian angel of young Jewish writers; Sholem Asch is perhaps the best known of those whose careers he has fostered and encouraged, but he is only one of many. Besides his books in English, he is the author of a novel in Yiddish, *Raphael Naarizoch* (1907), and of a five-volume autobiography in the same language.

WORKS AVAILABLE IN ENGLISH: The White Terror and the Red (non-fiction) 1905; The Imported Bridegroom and Other Stories of the New York Ghetto, 1906; Yekl: A Tale of the New York Ghetto, 1910; The Rise of David Levinsky, 1917.

ABOUT: Cahan, A. Bletter von Mein Leben (5 vols. in Yiddish); American Mercury October 1939.

CAIN, JAMES MALLAHAN (July 1, 1892-), American novelist, was born in Annapolis, Md., and educated at Washing-

ton College, of which his father, James W. Cain, was president. He received his B.A. there in 1910, at the early age of eighteen, his M.A. in 1917. He was a reporter on the Baltimore *American* in 1917 and 1918. It was at this time that he met H. L. Mencken, who encouraged him to write. He enlisted when America entered the First World War, and served in France; during this period he was editor of the *Lorraine Cross,* the official newspaper of the 79th Division, American Expeditionary Force. Returning to Baltimore in 1919, he went to work for the Baltimore *Sun,* and remained with it until 1923, when he went to St. John's College, Annapolis, for a year as professor of journalism. He then joined the staff of the New York *World,* and wrote editorials under Walter Lippmann. Later he conducted a weekly column of political dialogues in this paper, afterwards collected into a volume. Mencken, who had been urging him to try his hand at fiction, published his first story in the *American Mercury.* With the publication of *The Postman Always Rings Twice,* a best-seller, Mr. Cain abandoned journalism for good. He went to Hollywood to help in the filming of that novel, and Los Angeles is now his permanent address, though he visits New York frequently. He has been married twice: to Mary Rebecca Clough in 1920, and to Elina Sjosted Tyszecka, of Helsingfors, Finland, in 1927.

Besides his novels, short stories, and motion pictures, Mr. Cain has written several full-length magazine serials which have not been published in book form. He has also written a number of one-act plays. His earliest ambition was to be a professional singer, like his mother, and he studied musical theory assiduously, only to be told in the end that his voice was not sufficiently good to justify singing as a career. Music, however, remains his favorite recreation. He is a dark, burly man, with black hair worn in a pompadour and heavy black eyebrows, who looks more like a schoolmaster or an amiable priest than a sophisticated novelist. His work is all of the "hard-boiled" school fathered by Ernest Hemingway, but rather superficially tougher and faster-moving than his master's. One critic detected "philosophic overtones . . . above the rattling melodrama of the plot."

PRINCIPAL WORKS: Our Government (non-fiction) 1930; The Postman Always Rings Twice, 1934; Serenade, 1937; Mildred Pierce, 1941.

ABOUT: American Magazine April 1938; New Republic November 11, 1940; Saturday Review of Literature December 4, 1937.

CAINE, Sir HALL (May 14, 1853- August 31, 1931), English novelist and playwright, was born Thomas Henry Hall Caine at Runcorn, Cheshire,

the son of a Manx blacksmith and a Cumbrian mother. He had no more than a brief primary schooling (part of it in the Isle of Man and part in Liverpool) and at fourteen became a clerk to a Liverpool architect. He had no

special aptitude for this profession, and his leisure was largely spent in the local free library. Subject to attacks of nervous depression, he went during one of these to the Isle of Man, where he assisted a schoolteacher uncle and eventually succeeded him, running the school for about a year. Called back to Liverpool by his architect employer, he resumed his old work, but still had his heart in books and writing. He began to contribute to professional journals like *The Builder,* helped in the organization of literary societies, and did a certain amount of lecturing. In due course he left his architect for service with a builder, and in this post began to come into contact with the manual worker. His journalistic writings in spare time provoked some correspondence from Ruskin (for he was a vigorous Christian Socialist) and procured him the friendship of the poet, William Watson.

The turning point in Caine's career came at the age of twenty-five. He gave a lecture in Liverpool defending D. G. Rossetti against the moral strictures of Robert Buchanan, and forwarded a copy of it to the poet, who was sufficiently grateful to send a letter, under date July 29, 1879, inviting the obscure Liverpudlian to call on him at any time when he might be in town. A voluminous correspondence followed, over a period of some three years, and in 1881 Caine went into residence at Cheyne Walk, Chelsea, as a kind of secretary to Rossetti. He was witness of the final pathetic drug-ridden stage, and a few months after the poet's death, in 1882, published his *Recollections* of those days.

Soon after this event, Caine sent an article on the poet-painter William Bell Scott to the *Liverpool Mercury.* The editor John Lovell not only printed it but invited Caine to be a regular outside contributor on a retaining fee of £100 a year. He accepted, and, taking rooms in Clement's Inn, London, sent out book reviews, police-court reports, dramatic criticisms, and stock obituaries. This poorly paid but freely exercised journalistic work greatly enlarged his knowledge of human nature, gave him ample practice in writing, and procured him some slight acquaintance with celebrities like Theodore Watts-Dunton, Algernon Swinburne, Matthew Arnold, and Robert Browning. Robert Buchanan took pains to atone for what he now realized to have been an unfair criticism of Rossetti, and for some two years was Caine's friend. The *Athenaeum* and the *Academy* provided some additional revenue, and before beginning his novel-writing Caine was making about 300 pounds a year.

Deciding at length to stake all on the novel, Caine retired to the Isle of Wight, and after terrific strivings and extensive rewriting, produced a novel in a Cumbrian setting called *The Shadow of a Crime.* This he followed with *A Son of Hagar.* In 1887, remembering advice from Rossetti to write about the Isle of Man, he brought out *The Deemster,* which was the first of a series of novels which carried him to the highest pinnacle of popular favor. This book was sold outright for 150 pounds, and Caine had to write for ten years before he earned more than a modest competence; but in the long run he attained to colossal sales comparable with those of Marie Corelli. He bought Greeba Castle, a fine house in the Isle of Man, for some time sat in the House of Keys (the parliament of that island) and when he died at seventy-eight left the very considerable fortune of 250,000 pounds. Not all this accrued from novels. Several of his books he turned into plays with great success, and in later years his film rights were eagerly sought after.

Always an ardent propagandist, Caine investigated the Russo-Polish persecutions of the Jews in 1892-93 and wrote a series of articles thereon in the London *Times.* Two years later he went to Canada at the request of the Incorporated Society of Authors and successfully acted against the proposed Canadian Copyright Bill. During the War of 1914-18 he edited *King Albert's Book,* for which he was made an Officer of the Order of Leopold. Thereafter he conducted a vigorous propaganda directed towards American participation in the war, for which he was created K.B.E. in 1918. Four years afterwards he was named a Companion of Honor.

Caine's special blend of robust morality, social reformism, and sentiment, assisted by the regional setting of his books, commended his work to a huge public, but because of his crudity in plot and characterization and his lack of depth he is not considered to be more than a minor popular writer. He was none the less a most careful and conscientious craftsman, writing slowly and revising much, and he took great pains in studying sites beforehand. He traveled a good deal, and paid several visits to the United States. He was an excellent man of business, and made substantial sums by operating in Manx real estate.

Concurrently with his other work Caine was engaged from 1893 onward on a *Life of Christ,* and at his death left a manuscript of three million words. Collated by secretaries and edited by his two sons over a period of seven years, this book appeared in 1938.

Caine had a domed head, wide-open eyes, and a small pointed beard, and in general appearance was not unlike certain portraits of Shakespeare. He married, in 1882, Mary Chandler, of Walthmstow, Essex, and had two sons. Both have been for long periods Members of Parliament, Gordon Ralph Hall in the Conservative interest and Derwent Hall in that of Labor.

PRINCIPAL WORKS: *Fiction*—The Shadow of a Crime, 1885; A Son of Hagar, 1887; The Deemster, 1887; The Bondman, 1890; The Scapegoat, 1891; Cap'n Davy's Honeymoon—The Last Confession—The Blind Mother, 1893; The Manxman, 1894; The Christian, 1897; The Eternal City, 1901; The Prodigal Son, 1904; Doña Roma, 1905; The White Prophet, 1909; The Woman Thou Gavest Me, 1913; The Master of Man, 1921; The Woman of Knockaloe, 1923. *Miscellaneous*—Sonnets of Three Centuries, 1882; Recollections of D. G. Rossetti, 1882; Cobwebs of Criticism, 1883; The Little Manx Nation, 1891; The Little Man Island, 1894; My Story, 1908; King Edward: A Great Prince and a Great Man, 1910; The Drama of Three-Hundred and Sixty-Five Days: Scenes in the War, 1915; Our Girls: Their Work for the War, 1916; The Life of Christ, 1938. *Plays*—The Bondman Play, 1906; The Eternal Question, 1910.

ABOUT: Bernstein, H. The Road to Peace; Caine, T. H. H. My Story; Cumberland, G. Set Down in Malice; Essays of the Year: 1930-31 (see Essay by E. Shanks); MacCarthy, D. Portraits; Pearson, H. Modern Men and Mummers; The Times (London) September 1, 1931; The Bookman (London) December 1931.

CALDWELL, ERSKINE (December 17, 1903-   ), American novelist, writes: "From the day of my birth until I reached the age

M. Bourke-White

of twenty years, I rarely lived longer than six months in the same place. My home was the entire South, from Virginia to Florida, from the Atlantic to the Mississippi. My father, a Presbyterian minister, in his official capacity as secretary of his denomination was required to visit and reside several months at each church. Life was a constant change of faces and surroundings. My father owned one of the first automobiles to be seen in the South, and traveling from one state to another in those days was an adventure never to be forgotten. Our troubles ranged from arrests for frightening horses in Mississippi to being held captive by moonshiners in the mountains of Virginia. I became so filled with wanderlust that at the age of fourteen I began

sleeping in my clothes in order to be ready to leave home at a moment's notice. It was several months before my mother discovered what I was doing and put a stop to it.

"I was born in the country many miles from railroad or post office. The place where I was born was so remote it had no name. It was in Coweta County, Georgia. The nearest landmark was a church several miles away. It was called White Oak.

"I was the only child of Ira S. and Caroline Prestone (Bell) Caldwell. I attended primary school in Virginia for a year, grammar school in Tennessee for a year, and high school in Georgia for a year. These were the only three occasions when we were in one place long enough for me to enter school. My mother taught me the remainder of the time.

"When I was eighteen, I enrolled at Erskine College, Due West, S.C., but remained only a short time. I went to sea on a boat that was running guns for a revolt in a Central American republic, and ended up several months later in Mexico. My next attempt to complete my education was when I entered the University of Virginia after having won a scholarship offered by the United Daughters of the Confederacy. I remained there almost a year, working nights in a poolroom for room and board. I had begun to write short stories, though, before I left, and continued writing while working in a variety store in Pennsylvania, playing professional football, managing a lecture tour for a British soldier of fortune, and selling building lots in Alabama under three feet of water. I attended the University of Pennsylvania for a short time, making my expenses, and more, as a bodyguard for a Chinaman, and then returned to the University of Virginia.

"Before the year was out I was working as a cub reporter on the Atlanta *Journal*. The stories I was writing were still not good enough to suit me and I made no attempt to get them published. I gave up my newspaper job after a year and went to Maine, where I remained for five years, vowing not to come out until I had succeeded in writing a good short story. At the end of four years I sent to various magazines a story called "Country Full of Swedes." It was the story I had been trying to write for seven or eight years. After a year the story turned up at the *Yale Review*. It was given the Yale Review $1,000 Award for Fiction in 1933. During those five years in Maine I had also written two novels, *Tobacco Road* and *God's Little Acre*.

"Several times during the next two years I went to Hollywood and wrote motion picture scripts. The dramatization of *Tobacco Road* was settling down to a good long run of six or seven years in New York. I went back to the South with the idea of writing a book to be called *You Have Seen Their Faces.* Margaret Bourke-White wanted to take the photographs for it. The result was a work of two years' collaboration.

"I am married to Margaret Bourke-White now (1937), and we have a home in the woods at Darien, Conn."

* * *

In 1925 Mr. Caldwell married Helen Lannigan, and they had two sons and a daughter. Later they were divorced.

Anyone who doubts Mr. Caldwell's close personal knowledge of the underdogs of whom he writes should note that in addition to the jobs he mentions he has also been a cotton-picker, a lumber-mill hand, a hackdriver, a stagehand in a burlesque theater, a soda-jerker, and a cook and waiter. Exactly six feet high, with hair so red that his friends call it pink, he has the physique of the football player he has been, and a round, candid, innocent face which has confounded judges on the numerous occasions his work has been sued for obscenity—and cleared. Of late years he has become consciously leftist in his economic views, but he still writes with complete frankness and macabre humor, "as well as he can," to quote Carl Van Doren, "about as much as he knows and feels." *Tobacco Road*, made into a play by James Kirkland, had the longest run in the history of the American theatre, surpassing even the fabulous *Abie's Irish Rose.*

In 1941 the Caldwells were in Russia when the German invasion began. They remained for a while in Moscow, he as correspondent to *PM* and she as photographer for *Life*; both were frequently heard in America by short-wave broadcast. On their return here he published a book on his experiences.

PRINCIPAL WORKS: The Bastard, 1929; Poor Fool, 1930; American Earth (non-fiction) 1931; Tobacco Road, 1932; God's Little Acre, 1933; We Are the Living (non-fiction) 1933; Journeyman, 1935; Kneel to the Rising Sun (short stories) 1935; Some American People (non-fiction) 1935; You Have Seen Their Faces (with M. Bourke-White, non-fiction) 1937; Southways (non-fiction) 1938; North of the Danube (with M. Bourke-White, non-fiction) 1939; Jackpot, 1940; Trouble in July, 1940; Say, Is This the U. S. A.? (with M. Bourke-White) 1941; All-Out on the Road to Smolensk, 1942.

ABOUT: American Mercury April 1940; Christian Century February 16, 1938; Nation October 18, 1933; New Republic April 10, 1935; New York Times March 31, 1940; Scholastic May 28, 1938; Time March 11, 1940.

CALDWELL, JANET TAYLOR (September 7, 1900-), American novelist who signs her works as Taylor Caldwell, writes: "Born in Manchester, England, of Scottish parents, Arthur Francis Caldwell and Anna Marks. Family *alleged* to go back to Mary, Queen of Scots, but think this pure egotism. Family belongs to clan of MacTavish, and has a coat-of-arms, a  fountain, a 'cauld well' or 'caulder,' from which the family name was finally corrupted into Caldwell. Tincture of Irish blood from maternal grandmother's side, but not enough to matter. William Taylor, a maternal great-uncle, once owned all the railroads in Scotland, and others were distillers to the King of England, and teetotalers. Family half Roman Catholic, half Presbyterian, with the Presbyterian running well in front. Brought to America with my brother because my father's profession (commercial artist) was 'overrun' with Germans, for which our family has a deep and passionate aversion. Father found himself in the midst of them, in Buffalo, and it literally broke his heart, so that he died at the age of fifty-two. Landed in America on March 7, 1907, and have been here ever since. I married William F. Combs in 1919, and have one daughter by that marriage. Divorced in 1931 and married present husband, Marcus Reback. Have another daughter by this marriage. Husband officer in the Department of Justice, Buffalo. Am a graduate of the University of Buffalo. Started to write at the age of eight, and have continued to do so, with more or less success. Novels all best sellers. Have three more novels underway, writing them simultaneously. Only hobbies: reading, parties, and keeping house."

* * *

Dynasty of Death was written in nine months, between one and five o'clock in the morning, typed at a kitchen table. The book, strident and rhetorical, created a sensation; it was generally supposed to have been written under a pseudonym by some well-known author, preferably a man with first-hand experience of the great munition manufacturing families. There was great astonishment when it was discovered that the author was really a "tall, nervous, blonde housewife" from Eggertsville, N.Y, a suburb of Buffalo. The author's only previously published writing had been confession stories! Mrs. Reback was a yeomanette in the First World War, and met her husband when she was a stenographer in the Immigration Service in Buffalo.

PRINCIPAL WORKS: Dynasty of Death, 1938; The Eagles Gather, 1940; The Earth Is the Lord's: A Tale of the Rise of Genghis Khan, 1941; The Strong City, 1942.

ABOUT: Newsweek October 3, 1938; Publishers' Weekly October 15, 1938; Wilson Library Bulletin February 1940.

CALLAGHAN, MORLEY (1903-), Canadian novelist, was born in Toronto, the son of Thomas and Mary (Dewan) Callaghan. On both sides he is of Irish descent. He was educated at St. Michael's College of the University of Toronto (B.A. 1925) and at the Osgoode Hall Law School. Between college and law school he was first a reporter on the Toronto *Daily Star* and then for a while ran a circulating library. While on the *Star* he met Ernest Hemingway, who became interested in his work and encouraged him. From 1926 he began to write seriously, and in 1929, in Paris, he met through Hemingway most of the "expatriate" writers and editors then living there, and saw his first stories published in *This Quarter, transition,* Ezra Pound's *The Exile,* and later in the first *American Caravan.* Mr. Callaghan was then on his honeymoon, having married Florence Loretta Dee in 1929. They now have one son.

Two stories published in *Scribner's Magazine* first brought him to the attention of the general reading public. He was by this time back in Canada, and now lives permanently in Toronto. He knows all Eastern Canada well, however, for he spent his college vacations as a traveling subscription agent for magazines. He is a short, stocky man, with black, curly hair, a small moustache, and bright blue eyes. In school he was an athlete, a good boxer, a football player, and pitcher on the baseball team; in college he turned from athletics to public speaking, once winning a debate on free speech. He still practices law, though for the past ten years most of his time has gone to writing.

He has the distinction of having had stories of his published for nine successive years in Edward J. O'Brien's annual anthologies of *The Best Short Stories.*

Although in a sense Mr. Callaghan is a disciple of Hemingway's, with the same detailed realism and the same bare, clipped speech, he is, as the New York *Times* remarked, "never as emotionally blunt and harsh and violent" as is Hemingway or Erskine Caldwell. In his stories there are "lyrical inferences and sympathy" which appear rarely in writing of this school. This difference may arise from his religious feeling; he is a devout Catholic. In general, however, his books belong to the same *genre* as Hemingway's, Caldwell's, William Faulkner's, and even James Cain's—stripped, spare, and intense in their style, coldly observational in their matter. But, whether in novel or short story form, Morley Callaghan's writing is unmistakably his own; as another critic said, "he plows sturdily ahead, following his own furrow." He can be considered one of the most genuinely promising of the younger group of Canadian writers. *They Shall Inherit the Earth* is perhaps his best work to date.

PRINCIPAL WORKS: Strange Fugitive, 1928; A Native Argosy (short stories) 1929; It's Never Over, 1930; No Man's Meat (novelettes) 1931; Broken Journey, 1932; Such Is My Beloved, 1934; They Shall Inherit the Earth, 1935; Now That April's Here and Other Stories, 1936; More Joy in Heaven, 1937.

ABOUT: Canadian Forum February 1932; Literary Digest September 28, 1935; Scholastic March 13, 1937.

CALVERTON, VICTOR FRANCIS (June 25, 1900-November 20, 1940), American critic and editor, wrote to the editors of this volume a few months before his untimely death at the age of forty: "I was born in Baltimore at the turn of the century, of German-American parents whose main pride was in their revolutionary ancestry. My first political recollection was of hearing my father denounce the Spanish-American War. His words had a profound influence upon me and led me, no doubt, to view society from the radical point of view which has dominated all my literary work. My teens were torn with conflict: should I become a professional baseball player or a writer? I got a job as time-

Pach

keeper with the Bethlehem Steel Co., stole enough time from the company to read a book a day, and saved enough money to go to Johns Hopkins University, where I was miseducated by the professors but succeeded in educating myself by reading twelve books a week for several years. Seven books were most influential in shaping my thought during that period: Buckle's *History of Civilization in England,* Darwin's *Origin of Species,* Kropotkin's *Mutual Aid,* Bagehot's *Physics and Politics,* Lester Ward's *Applied Sociology,* Sumner's *Folkways,* Marx's *Capital.* Almost equal in importance were Dostoievsky's *The Brothers Karamazov,* Tolstoy's *War and Peace,* Goncharov's *Oblomov,* Flaubert's *Madame Bovary,* Shaw's *An Unsocial Socialist,* Hardy's *Jude the Obscure,* Andreyev's *The Red Laugh,* Melville's *Moby Dick,* Thomson's *City of Dreadful Night,* Shakespeare's sonnets and at least half a dozen of his plays, Ibsen's and Strindberg's dramas, Landor's poetry, and also the poems of Shelley, Keats, Burns, and, in America, of Whitman, Poe, and William Ellery Leonard, especially the latter's *Two Lives.*

"I founded the *Modern Quarterly* in 1923 because I believed it important to have a magazine where writers with radical vision but literary interests could find a voice. The magazine always strove to adhere to that ideal. In its pages appeared almost every left-wing liberal and radical who had artistic aspirations. In 1933 the magazine was converted into the *Modern Monthly* and continued as such until 1938; since then it has reverted to its original quarterly form, in which it still appears.

"My books have all been attempts to amplify and extend what I was doing with the magazine. My first book, *The Newer Spirit,* aimed to establish the bases for a sociological criticism of literature. Other books ventured into the fields of morality and marriage, the history of culture, and religion. My latest interest has been in American history interpreted from a left-wing point of view, and *The Awakening of America* is the first volume of a projected three-volume study of the theme. My interest in fiction, I might add, antedated my concern for things historical, political, economic. Each of my novels has been bound up with the psycho-sociological approach dominant in all my critical and historical studies. In a sentence, what I have tried to do has been to find a lowest common denominator from which all work, creative, as well as critical, can be judged, because I am convinced such a dis-

covery can result in better creation and better criticism."

* * *

Victor Francis Calverton's name was originally George Goetz. He was married, and considered Baltimore his home. Although a Marxist, he was for many years at war with the Communists, and they with him. Van Wyck Brooks praised his "suppleness and authority, fairness of spirit and feeling for motives," and Henry Seidel Canby called him "careful and often most illuminating, scholarly, and documented." Besides his own books, he was editor or co-editor of six anthologies (four with Samuel D. Schmalhausen). He was American editor of *La Paix Mondiale,* and long conducted a department in *Current History.* The cause of his early death was pernicious anemia. He was survived by his wife, Nina Melville. He had just finished work on his final volume, *Where Angels Dared to Tread,* a history of Utopian colonies in America, which was published posthumously.

PRINCIPAL WORKS: The Newer Spirit, 1925; Sex Expression in Literature, 1926; The Bankruptcy of Marriage, 1928; Three Strange Lovers (stories) 1929; The New Ground of Criticism, 1930; American Literature at the Cross Roads, 1931; The Liberation of American Literature, 1931; For Revolution, 1932; The Passing of the Gods, 1934; The Man Inside (novel) 1935; The Making of America, 1938; The Awakening of America, 1939; Where Angels Dared to Tread, 1941.

ABOUT: American Journal of Sociology January 1941; Saturday Review of Literature September 17, 1932; May 11, November 30, 1940; Sewanee Review July 1938.

"CAMBRIDGE, ELIZABETH." See HODGES, B. K. W.

CAMPBELL, ROY (October 2, 1901-), South African poet, writes: "Born [Ignatius Roy Dunnachie Campbell] in Durban, Natal, the son of Dr. Samuel George Campbell and Margaret (Dunnachie) Campbell. Was brought up when not at school in the wilds of Natal and Rhodesia. Joined up in the Sixth South African Infantry at the age of fifteen, but was arrested and sent back  to the Durban High School from Potchefstroom. Was later sent to Oxford, but, failing to pass exams, I came down through France, walking from Lyons to Marseilles, and lived for some time among the fishermen.

Returning to England, I met Mary Margaret Gorman and we married at once [1922]. Having no money, we retired to wild Wales and lived in a fishermen's cabin, where I wrote *The Flaming Terrapin* and worked at odd jobs among the fishermen. [He also taught Shakespeare to a class of working-men, and acknowledges he eked out his living by some poaching!] Returned to South Africa with my wife and daughter, where I edited *Voorslag,* which caused a great furore and from which I was sacked. I returned with my wife and two daughters steerage to England, where I collected the material for *The Georgiad.* After which I returned to my original haunts on the Mediterranean, running two fishing boats and jousting [also steer-throwing and bull fighting] professionally for the town of Martigues from 1928 to 1931. I won the steer-throwing championship of Provence in 1932 and 1933. I also bred and sold horses. I served with Franco's forces throughout the Spanish Revolution, besides being war correspondent of the *Tablet* (London), and was cited for saving the Carmelite archives at Toledo in 1937. I now live in Toledo."

* * *

About 1935 Mr. Campbell became a convert to the Roman Catholic Church; he had formerly been an aggressive Freethinker. Soon after, he announced himself as a Fascist. In *Who's Who* he lists himself as a "horse merchant," with poetry given merely as his "recreation." Ever since the sensational appearance of *The Flaming Terrapin,* he has been hailed as "the Byron of our time." Edith Sitwell called him "a poetic tornado"; Arthur Colton, "reckless, violent, and congested, . . . the first figure of distinction in South African letters since Olive Schreiner"; and Geoffrey Stone, "distressingly uneven, . . . a careless but naturally gifted craftsman." He is a self-conscious romantic, dark, intense, and fiery; yet his intellectual approach is that of conservative classicism, and his satirical verse is in the eighteenth century tradition. He has a tremendous appetite for words, with which he stuns the reader. Much of his poetry is more accurately rhetoric. He is a violent throw-back to two disparate eras—the classical and the neo-romantic—combined in the different modes of his own writing. None of his later work has had the impact of his first youthful volume, which apparently will remain his masterpiece.

PRINCIPAL WORKS: The Flaming Terrapin, 1924; The Wayzgoose, 1928; Adamastor, 1930; The Gum Trees, 1930; Poems, 1930; The Georgiad, 1931; Choosing a Mast, 1931; Taurine Provence (prose) 1932; Mithraic Emblems, 1932; Flowering Reeds, 1933; Broken Record (autobiography) 1934; Flowering Rifle, 1939

ABOUT: Campbell, R. Broken Record; Lewis, W. Blasting and Bombardiering; Untermeyer, L. Modern British Poetry; American Review December 1936; Bookman December 1932; New Republic March 18, 1931; Poetry May 1931.

CAMPBELL, WALTER STANLEY (August 15, 1887-), American miscellaneous author who signs his books with his original name of Stanley Vestal, writes: "Walter Stanley Campbell was born of parents of old American stock (Massachusetts and Virginia) near Sevry, Kansas, son of Walter Mallory Vestal and Isabella Louise (Wood) Vestal. His  father died soon after, and his mother became a teacher, a profession which she followed with enthusiasm for considerable portions of her life. He was educated at the public schools in Fredonia, Kans.; Guthrie, Okla.; and at Southwestern State Normal School, Weatherford, Okla., of which his stepfather, J. R. Campbell, was first president. In 1908 he went to Oxford University, as first Rhodes Scholar from the new State of Oklahoma. There he became a member of Merton College, and read for Honours in English Language and Literature, taking his B.A. in 1911, M.A. in 1915. During boyhood he had been led to read good literature, and had become acquainted with the Cheyenne Indians and acquired a keen interest in their ways and history. His stepfather had been one of Bancroft's men, and the history of the West was a familiar subject in the family. On returning to the States from Oxford, these interests persisted. His work was teaching: first in the Male High School, Louisville, Ky.; later at the University of Oklahoma. When the United States entered the World War, he enlisted in the first Officers' Training Camp, Fort Logan H. Roots, and three months later, on his birthday, 1917, was commissioned a Captain of Field Artillery. After graduating from the School of Fire (First War Class), Fort Sill, he rejoined his regiment and served until March 1919 (six months in France). He found the war a stimulating experience, but the army rather a bore.

"Back in the States, he pursued his hobbies, read widely, traveled during his summer vacations over most of the Plains and Rocky Mountain States, and began to feel the inconvenience of living in a region which, though possessing a colorful past, had comparatively little literature of its own. He decided to try to create something to satisfy this craving. His first attempts were published in the *American Mercury,* the *Southwest Review,* and *Poetry,* and led to the publication of a book, *Fandango: Ballads of the Old West,* 1927. Since that time he has published twelve more books, edited three, and appeared in various magazines, his work including poetry, biography, history, juvenile and adult fiction, a murder mystery, and two textbooks. At present, Professor Campbell is Director of Courses in Professional Writing at the University of Oklahoma, and conducts courses in professional and creative writing both on the campus and by correspondence.

"He was at Yaddo, 1927; Fellow Guggenheim Memorial Foundation, 1930. Member of Authors' Club (London), Association of University Professors, Phi Beta Kappa, Authors' League of America. Favorite sports: polo and chess. Taste in literature: good work of any kind. Can eat anything but tapicoa, mashed potatoes, whipped cream. Summer home: Cerro Pajarito, near Santa Fé, N.M."

* * *

In 1917 Professor Campbell married Isabel Jones, who has also published some poetry. They have two daughters. An outdoor-looking man, whose chief recreation is horseback riding and who also plays polo, "Stanley Vestal" looks far more like a Western author than like a college professor. He is not, however, a "Western author" in the blood-and-thunder, "pulp magazine" tradition. His work includes ballads, novels, biography, and history, but all of it is factual in background and carefully documented It makes no less absorbing reading for being reliable. He is considered a leading authority on the old Southwest, particularly Oklahoma and New Mexico, and especially on the Indians of that territory. As a writer he is competent rather than highly gifted, but he has a good story sense, he knows his technique thoroughly, and he is always accurate and never dull. His one mystery story was excellent.

PRINCIPAL WORKS: Fandango: Ballads of the Old West, 1927; Kit Carson, 1928; Happy Hunting Grounds, 1928; 'Dobe Walls, 1929; Sitting Bull, 1932; Warpath, 1934; New Sources of Indian History, 1934; The Wine Room Murder, 1935; Mountain Men (novel) 1936; Revolt on the Border, 1938; Professional Writing, 1938; The Old Santa Fé Trail, 1939; Writing Magazine Fiction, 1940; King of the Fur Traders, 1940; Short Grass Country, 1941; Bigfoot Wallace, 1942.

ABOUT: Rotarian November 1940; Writer September, November 1940, January 1941.

CANBY, HENRY SEIDEL (September 6, 1878-), American critic, writes: "Henry Seidel Canby was born of Quaker stock in Wilmington, Del., where his family have lived for many generations. He was brought up an Episcopalian but educated at a Quaker school which left definite marks on his thinking and on his temperament. He began amateur writing while at school, taking a prize in his sixteenth year for a little tale of the Revolution which has been frequently reprinted since. He went to Yale in 1896, taking a degree of Ph.B. in 1899, and while there was an editor of two college magazines but achieved no other university distinction.

Oggiano

"After graduation he continued in the Graduate School, becoming more and more interested in criticism and teaching. His first teaching was as an assistant in composition, and shortly after taking his doctor's degree in 1905 he was put in charge of the reorganization of Freshman English in Sheffield Scientific School (Yale) and became intensely interested in the problem of teaching literature to young men.

"At this time his first books, textbooks on composition and results of his research in fiction, were published. *The Short Story in English* (1909) is a history of that literary form and is still a standard text. He continued with writing of a more literary nature, including a number of short stories for magazines, and later published a number of essays which ranged all the way from discussions of the undergraduate and the professor to articles in pure literary criticism. In 1915 and 1920 his *College Sons and College Fathers* and his *Everyday Americans,* which brought together many of these essays, were published.

"In 1918, having in the meantime married Marion Ponsonby Gauze and acquired two sons, he got the better part of the year free for war work and was sent abroad to serve under the British Committee of Information. His work there developed into a general liaison service which took him to Ireland and Paris and to three of the western fronts. His *Education by Violence,* published in 1919, summed up the result of this work and his reflections thereon. It was in 1919 also that he published his first and last novel, *Our House,* which had a good beginning but a bad end.

"Shortly after his return he was invited to become literary editor of the New York *Evening Post* and was given an opportunity to organize a new type of critical review. The result was the *Literary Review,* first added to the *Post* in 1920. In 1924, shortly after a change of ownership in the *Post,* he with a number of his associates founded the *Saturday Review of Literature,* of which he was editor until 1936. He is now a contributing editor. He had not, however, severed his connection with Yale, although on a complete leave of absence for much of this period. In 1911, while at Yale, he helped to organize the *Yale Review,* serving under Governor Wilbur Cross, and was an assistant editor until he came to New York in 1920. Since 1920, he has given an occasional course at Yale in literary criticism and in literary writing, and is now acting as adviser to seniors preparing to write books.

"His more recent books have been in the field of literary and social criticism and the study of American literature, and in biography. *Definitions: First and Second Series,* and *American Estimates* brought together essays and studies that had been published in various magazines, especially in the *Saturday Review. Classic Americans* (1931) was a more ambitious work, a study of the great American writers up to Whitman viewed against the social and intellectual background of a developing America. In 1934 he published *The Age of Confidence,* a study of the 1890's, a more personal, more literary, and less documentary work than his preceding books. In 1936 he published *Alma Mater,* a critical reminiscence of American college life. *Seven Years' Harvest,* in the same year, was an essay collection. In 1937 he edited the works of Henry D. Thoreau, and in 1939 published *Thoreau: A Biography,* for which he had been preparing for many years.

"Ever since its founding he has been the chairman of the board of judges of the Book-of-the-Month Club. He has been once president of, and four times a delegate abroad for, the American P.E.N. Club. He holds an honorary degree of Litt.D. from Knox College, is an Honorary Fellow in Letters of Union College, and Associate Fellow of Silliman College, Yale University. He is secretary of the National Institute of Arts and Letters. His home is Killingworth, Clinton, Conn."

* * *

Norman Foerster called Canby "a typical scouting reporter of the movements of the stream of literature. . . . In command of the history of literature, . . . in knowledge of contemporary letters, . . . he has perhaps no equal in America today." H. L. Mencken called him "an idealist, but of the type which remembers that there is such a thing as reality." In his writing, Mencken added, "there is never any strain, never any sacrifice of simplicity to effect, but all the same it shows hard and honest effort."

PRINCIPAL WORKS: The Short Story, 1902; The Short Story in English, 1909; A Study of the Short Story, 1913; College Sons and College Fathers, 1915; Education by Violence, 1919; Our House, 1919; Everyday Americans, 1920; Definitions, 1922-24; Better Writing, 1926; American Estimates, 1929; Classic Americans, 1931; The Age of Confidence, 1934; Alma Mater: The Gothic Age of the American College, 1936; Seven Years' Harvest, 1936; Thoreau: A Biography, 1939; The Brandywine, 1941.

ABOUT: Canby, H. S. The Age of Confidence; Bookman July 1930; Readers' Digest March 1941; Saturday Review of Literature April 6, 1929, December 7, 1940.

CANFIELD, DOROTHY. See FISHER, D. F. C.

CANNAN, GILBERT (June 25, 1884-), English novelist, dramatist, and critic, was born in Manchester, the son of Henry and Violet (Wright) Cannan. His paternal uncle is the well-known economist, Edwin Cannan. He was educated at the University of Manchester and at King's College, Cambridge, then read for the law and was admitted to the bar in 1908. He never practised, however, though he sometimes used his legal knowledge in his novels. He was keenly interested in the theatre from his youth, and in 1909 and 1910 was drama critic of the London *Star.* With John Drinkwater and others he founded the famous Manchester Repertory Theatre, and he has himself appeared on the stage: in 1918 he acted in Congreve's *Way of the World.* But, though he has written many plays, and one novel of theatrical life (*Mummery*), Cannan is immeasurably better as a novelist than as a dramatist.

But he first came to wide public attention as neither. Though he had published two novels and had had two plays produced in 1911, he was little known until his translation of Romain Rolland's *Jean Christophe* began to appear in that year. His translation in four volumes (1911-13) is no longer the standard one, but it served to introduce the translator as well as the French novelist to the English book world. Cannan's own first success was with *Round the Corner*— a *succès de scandale* at first, since it was suppressed by the censor because of its frankness. It was strongly influenced by Artsybashev's *Sanine*. Incidentally, it is probably Cannan's best novel.

For a writer of pure English stock, the influences on Cannan's work have been varied and rather unusual. They include not only Rolland and Artsybashev (and Gorky as well), but also the later Samuel Butler, George Meredith, Joseph Conrad, and Laurence Sterne—a rather mixed bag; and the results are equally diverse. Another interest which constantly crops up in his work is Jewish life and the delineation of Jewish character—notable in *Mendel* and *Sembal*. Through much of his work Cannan gives the impression of feeling his way, trying to find his final *forte*. He has written a *roman à clef, Pugs and Peacocks* (laid in Cambridge at the time of the First World War), a propaganda novel, *Devious Ways* (a type of fiction which he has elsewhere unsparingly condemned), and half a dozen other kinds of fiction. Although he was once considered one of the most "daring" of the younger novelists, it is now impossible to catalog him in any group or category.

Yet the real love of his life has been the drama, in which he has been relatively unsuccessful. His first plays belong to the period of the Irish literary renaissance, and were more or less consciously modeled on those of Synge and Lady Gregory. Cannan had not their mastery of the spoken tongue, and his plays are stilted and unreal. Still, he once stated that he had "never been really interested in anything else" except the drama, that he considered his work as a novelist merely a preparation for a greater career as a playwright, and that very soon he intended to stop writing anything except plays. At the same time he resumed his old place as a dramatic critic, this time on the *Nation* (London). The actual fact was that he soon ceased to write anything whatever. His last book was published in 1924, when he was only forty. As early as 1931 one critic referred to him in the past tense, as if he were dead. But he is still alive, in middle age, and living in London. His silence, according to Richard Aldington, is due to the fact that he was certified as insane in 1919. His only book since that time may have been written some years earlier.

Cannan was married to Mary Ansell, the actress, who had previously been the wife of James M. Barrie. Her second marriage also ended in divorce after a few years, and Cannan has not remarried. During the years they were together, he and his wife lived in a picturesque transformed windmill in Buckinghamshire, with D. H. Lawrence and J. Middleton Murry as their neighbors. He made one trip to the United States, in 1919, and another to Africa. Formerly he was fond of motoring and swimming, and of travel when possible, and listed "journalism" not among his pursuits but among his recreations! He is thin, with aquiline features, brooding eyes, and thick white hair.

To sum up his place as a novelist (his only important place in literature), he is a master ironist, anti-sentimental, forthright, and with an easy command of characterization. He is far from a great writer, but at his best he is a very good one.

PRINCIPAL WORKS: *Novels*—Peter Homonculus, 1909; Devious Ways, 1910; Little Brother, 1912; Round the Corner, 1913; Old Mole, 1914; Old Mole's Novel, 1914; Young Earnest, 1915; Mendel, 1916; Three Pretty Men (in America: Three Sons and a Mother) 1916; The Stucco House, 1918; Mummery, 1918; Pink Roses, 1919; Time and Eternity, 1919; Pugs and Peacocks, 1920; Sembal, 1922; Annette and Bennett, 1922; The House of Prophecy (sequel to Sembal) 1924. *Plays*—Miles Dixon, 1910; James and John, 1911; Mary's Wedding, 1912; Wedding Presents, 1912; The Perfect Widow, 1912; The Arbour of Refuge, 1913; A Short Way With Authors, 1913; Four Plays, 1913; Three, 1913; The Right to Kill (with F. Keyzer) 1915; Everybody's Husband, 1917; The Release of the Soul, 1920; Seven Plays, 1923. *Miscellaneous*—The Joy of the Theatre, 1913; Satire, 1914; Samuel Butler, 1915; Adventurous Love and Other Verses. 1915; Windmills: A Book of Fables (verse) 1915; The Anatomy of Society, 1919; Letters From a Distance, 1924.

ABOUT: Aldington, R. Life For Life's Sake; Cunliffe, J. W. English Literature During the Last Half-Century; George, W. L. A Novelist on Novels; Goldring, D. Reputations; Gould, G. The English Novel of Today; James, H. Notes on Novelists; Williams, H. Modern English Writers; Current Opinion July 1920; Dial February 1920; Freeman August 22, 1923; Literary Digest International Book Review July 23, 1923.

CANNAN, JOANNA (1898-), English novelist, was born in Oxford, her father, Charles Cannan, being secretary to the delegates of the Oxford University Press and a Fellow of Trinity College. She is a first cousin of the novelist Gilbert Cannan[qv] and a niece of Edwin Cannan, the economist. She was educated at Wychwood School, Oxford, and in Paris, and her first ambition was to be an artist—not because she had any particular talent, but because an older sister wrote verses and she thought one writer in the family was enough. However, she had written stories from childhood, and she published stories and articles all through her girlhood. In 1921 she married Captain H. J. Pullein-Thompson, who retired from the army to enter business. Their first home  was in Wimbledon, then they moved to the Chiltern Hills, and now live in Oxford. They have a son and three daughters, the youngest of whom are twins.

It was not until after she had married and started raising her family that Miss Cannan turned to novel-writing. Her first novel appeared in 1923, and she has averaged about one a year ever since. She has also written a number of juvenile stories, originally written for her own children. Several of her novels have been mysteries, but her usual *genre* is the novel of manners, informed with wit and irony and what one critic called "delicate malice." She is shy and retiring, has never known many other writers or moved in literary circles, and aside from her writing and her family her chief interests are in fox-hunting and mountaineering. She is a slender blonde, very feminine in appearance (she loves furs and jewelry) but with rather angular face and figure. She is a dog-lover, and always owns at least one dog. She says she dislikes games and all kinds of machinery, prefers horses to motors, and describes herself as "a hopeless reactionary."

Rebecca West admired Miss Cannan's "power to create a piteous and lovable character"; P. S. Forman praised her "economy in words, and penetrating, nearly cruel, analysis of character." Her work is not cold, however; nearly always there is one sympathetic character on whom the author dwells with affectionate warmth. She considers her first three novels very bad, and wishes they could be removed from circulation—though two of them have been reprinted in cheaper editions. Her best books to date are *High Table,* the study of a prig (which she modestly says was based on her own nature in youth), and *Ithuriel's Hour,* a devastating analysis of arrogance and the will to power. They are evidence that her *métier* is not so much narrative as characterization. Not all her books have been published in America, and she was well known at home before her work attracted any wide attention here. But it has gradually won its way, until today she has a waiting public on both sides of the Atlantic for each new novel as it appears.

Like almost everyone in England, she is now busy with war work.

PRINCIPAL WORKS: Misty Valley, 1923; Wild Berry Wine, 1925; The Lady of the Heights, 1926; Sheila Both-Ways, 1928; The Simple Pass On (in America: Orphan of Mars) 1929; No Walls of Jasper (mystery) 1930; High Table, 1931; Ithuriel's Hour, 1931; Snow in Harvest, 1932; North Wall, 1933; Under Proof (mystery) 1934; The Hills Sleep On, 1935; Frightened Angels, 1936; Hand to Burn (mystery) 1936; A Pony For Jean (juvenile) 1937; Another Pony For Jean (juvenile) 1938; We Met Our Cousins (juvenile) 1938; Princes in the Land, 1938; They Rang Up the Police (mystery) 1939; London Pride, 1939; The Idle Apprentice, 1940; Death at the Dog (mystery) 1941.

ABOUT: Bookman (London) September 1931, December 1933.

CANNON, Mrs. CORNELIA (JAMES)

November 17, 1876-   ), American novelist, essayist, and writer for children, writes: "I was born a hundred years after the signing of the Declaration of Independence, in St. Paul, Minn., a city and a state whose existence was not even imagined at that time. During my childhood life was simpler than today and we were comfortably unaware  of a world outside of our national boundaries. I went to the public schools and prepared for college there. Radcliffe College gave me a B.A. and later in life Wheaton College conferred upon me the degree of Doctor of Humane Letters. In 1901 I married Dr. Walter B. Cannon, the physiologist, and went to Cambridge, Mass., to live. I began writing inspired by moral indignation at the wrongs of the world and enthusiasm at human achievements, which I voiced in the *Atlantic Monthly, Harper's* the *North American Review,* etc. This was followed by two novels and by a series of four children's books concerned with the early Spanish explorations in our Southwest, the country of the Pueblo Indians.

"Five children have shared what time was left from my literary labors and served as remorseless critics during the production of the children's books. One of them, Marian Cannon, illustrated the last two of the Pueblo books and has now embarked on writing and illustrating her own books.

"Travel has ever been a ruling passion with me. On our wedding trip my husband and I were the first known persons to climb a certain mountain in what is now Glacier

Park, and it was named Cannon Mountain for us. Being arrested in Russia by the G.P.U. during a trip round the world has left me with a combined martyr complex and a conviction of the menace secret police are to innocent people the world over. The working of democracy, which with all its faults seems to me the best form of society yet devised by man, the public education which is basic to it, and the preservation of civil rights which alone makes it workable have long been and still are my dominating interests."

* * *

Mrs. Cannon is a tall, slender, white-haired woman with aquiline features. She is the daughter of Henry Clay James and Francis Linda (Haynes) James. Her two novels for adults concern themselves respectively with wheat farmers in the Middle West and a New Hampshire mill town. Her juveniles have been called "exciting and good."

PRINCIPAL WORKS: *Novels*—Red Rust, 1928; Heirs, 1930. *Juveniles*—The Pueblo Boy, 1926; The Pueblo Girl, 1929; Lazaro in the Pueblos, 1931; The Fight for the Pueblo, 1934.

ABOUT: Kunitz, S. J. & Haycraft, H. (eds.). The Junior Book of Authors.

CANTWELL, ROBERT (January 31, 1908-), American novelist, writes: "I was born [Robert Emmett Cantwell] in Little

Pinchot

Falls, Wash. My great-grandfather, from Kentucky, was the first American settler in western Washington (1844), and founded the town of Tumwater on the site of Olympia. I lived in the small mill towns of Onalaska and Carlisle, went to high school in Aberdeen and Chehalis, and attended the University of Washington for one barren and miserable year. Then I worked for four years in a veneer factory at Hoquiam. I had part-time jobs also in a print shop, as a section hand on the Northern Pacific Railroad, in a wholesale hardware house in San Francisco, in a drafting office, and in restaurants in Seattle and Phoenix, Ariz. In 1929 I got a job on a pipe-line construction crew in the desert Northeast of El Paso, Tex. About that time my first story was published in the *American Caravan* and I took a bus to New York. I got a contract for a novel, and after learning that I could not finish one to my own satisfaction, took another bus back west. The

book was finished in 1931. Meanwhile I did free-lancing, book reviews, articles, and stories, and wrote the literary comment for the *New Outlook*. I have worked on the staffs of the *New Republic, Time,* and *Fortune.*

"I married Betsy Chambers in 1931, and we have had two daughters (one deceased). We now live in New York, but have lived in Baton Rouge, La., my wife's home town, in Boston, and in Carmel and Oakland, Calif. I like to travel, especially to drive, around this country, and wish I could get around more. I have no hobbies, but like to play pool occasionally.

"My literary tastes are pretty conventional. I admire Joyce and have been much influenced by him. Henry James has helped me more than any other writer, as far as any understanding of my own craft is concerned—though I do not accept his general view of life, and many of his novels bore me. Stendhal seems to me the best novelist, and among current books I admire Malraux's *Man's Fate* more than any other. Edmund Wilson seems to me to be the best American critic.

"My aversions, both in literature and in my daily contacts, are equally conventional—arrogance, cruelty, indifference. The only thing I really despise is smugness. If I had to choose a single phrase to express the main reason why I want to write, I think I would take that sentence from Malraux, where one of his characters says that he works in order to give working people a sense of their own dignity."

* * *

Mr. Cantwell has been an associate editor of *Time* since 1938. His two novels so far published both belong to the "proletarian" school. He also writes short stories and appeared in both the third and fourth *American Caravan.*

PRINCIPAL WORKS: Laugh and Lie Down, 1933; Land of Plenty, 1934.

ABOUT: New Republic November 8, 29, 1939; Wilson Library Bulletin January 1936.

ČAPEK, KAREL (1890-December 24, 1938), Czech novelist, dramatist, and essayist, was born at Malé Svatonice, Bohemia, the son of a physician. His early bent for science blossomed later in the convincing backgrounds of his scientific fantasies. He was educated at the University of Prague, with courses later in Berlin and Paris, and gradually turned his interest from biology to philosophy. He became very early a close friend of Thomas Masaryk, the great first president of the ill-fated Czechoslovakian republic, and under his influence (Masaryk was a professor of philosophy) considered himself a disciple of  the American pragmatist, William James. Though Čapek's first published work was a translation of French poetry, he was attracted primarily to American and English ways of thought. His novels, indeed are strongly influenced by the early work of H. G. Wells.

When the Versailles Treaty created the new state of Czechoslovakia, Čapek threw himself heart and soul into the struggle to build up a truly democratic nation. "His personal mission," Willi Schlamm remarks, "was to educate the Czech people to the living foundations of democracy." With Beneš he labored to find a basis of reconciliation with the Sudeten Germans. He almost literally died of the death of his country; after the Munich Conference he seemed to lose the will to live, and succumbed quickly to pneumonia. Up to that crisis he had lived the life of three busy men at least: in the morning he worked on his novels and plays and gardened—he was a passionate gardener; in the afternoon he held an editorial position on a Prague newspaper, the *Lidove Noviny*, which was the mouthpiece of the Masaryk and Benes government; and in the evening, especially on his celebrated Friday evenings "at home," he held open house for the liberal intellectual world of Prague. At the same time he was the actuating spirit of the modern theater in Czechoslovakia. He was for a long time art director of the National Art Theater, then built his own Vinohradsky Art Theater, where he produced plays by the great Europeans, as well as by young Czech dramatists of promise. His first plays and stories were written in collaboration with his brother Josef, who shared his home, neither brother being married.

A dark, slender man with a hesitating manner and speech, Čapek seemed younger than his years, and his extreme modesty and the way in which he lost himself in his enthusiasms added to the illusion of youth. Until his dreams and his heart broke together, his mind was set always on the future rather than on the past of his work. In a sense, he pronounced his own obituary: "A short life is better for mankind, for a long life would deprive man of his optimism."

In this country, Čapek is best known as the author of *R.U.R.*, that drama on "the mechanization of the proletariat" which anticipated Aldous Huxley's novel, *Brave New World*, and which gave to English as well as to other languages the word "robot." He liked to play with the idea of scientific discovery—a universal explosive in *Krakatit*, atom-splitting in *The Absolute at Large*; or with the inhuman turned human—insects in *The World We Live In*, salamanders in *War with the Newts*. But his plays are implicit sermons, disguised by the dramatic adroitness of the born playwright. To many critics, however, Čapek's most important work is not his stories, novels, or dramas, or his brilliant travel-pictures and analyses of nations, but the essays in which in the guise of reporting the thoughts of Masaryk he laid bare his own idealistic credo. "Whenever Čapek thought himself to be writing for posterity," says Schlamm, "he was merely a great talent; when he wrote for . . . his Czech contemporaries, he succeeded in achieving greatness."

His name is pronounced chop'-ek.

PRINCIPAL WORKS AVAILABLE IN ENGLISH: *Plays*—The Makropolous Secret (in England: The Makropolous Affair) 1922; R.U.R., 1923; The World We Live In (in England, The Life of the Insects) 1923; Adam the Creator (with Josef Capek) 1929; And so Ad Infinitum (with Josef Capek) 1934; The Power and the Glory (in England, The White Scourge) 1938. *Fiction*—Krakatit, 1925; The Absolute at Large (in England, The Manufacture of the Absolute) 1927; Money and Other Stories, 1929; War With the Newts, 1937. *Essays*—Letters From England, 1925; Letters From Italy, 1926; How a Play Is Produced, 1928; Letters From Spain, 1931; Letters From Holland, 1933; President Masaryk Tells His Story, 1934; Intimate Things, 1935; Masaryk on Thought and Life, 1938; The First Rescue Party, 1939; I Had a Dog and a Cat, 1940.

ABOUT: Drake, W. A. Contemporary European Writers; Nation January 14, 1939; Newsweek January 2, 1939; Saturday Review of Literature January 7, 1939; Slavonic Review April 1939; Time January 2, 1939.

CARCO, FRANCIS (July 31, 1886-), French poet and novelist, was originally named Francis Carcopino-Tussoli, and is of partly Italian descent. He was born in Noumea, New Caledonia, in the South Pacific, where his father was State Domains Inspector. When he was fourteen the family returned to France, to Villefranche-de-Rouerge, where the father was a government official as controller of mortgages. He was educated in the *lycée* there, but was a poor student, most of his attention being given to outside reading. His earliest literary interests were in Poe, Verlaine, Rimbaud, Baudelaire—a bent which prepared him excellently for his later absorption in the artistic Bohemia of Paris. Somehow he secured his degree and became a tutor at the *lycée* in Agen, though a rather unusual one, who spent most of his time writing verse and left his pupils to their own devices. He had some poems accepted, and at the end of

three months he drew up stakes and migrated to Toulouse. This was in 1906. For a short time during this year he edited a literary magazine in Nice. He became widely known as a singer, and contemplated a career singing in cabarets— which he fulfilled thirty years later when he appeared at the Noctambules in Paris.

For a few months he was on the stage, then joined the army, becoming a corporal in Grenoble, where Jules Romains was one of his colleagues. At the end of his military service he founded the magazine *Pan*, in 1909 he published his first volume of poems, and in 1910 he became secretary of the magazine *Le Feu*. He was ready for Paris at last. A friend secured him a sinecure in the Water Supply Division of the Department of Public Works. His real life was spent in Montmartre. His career as a Bohemian had begun. In orthodox fashion he published another precious volume of verse. But he was absorbing into every pore the life and spirit of the underworld—the true underworld of Villon, as distinguished from the artists' Bohemia. It was 1914 before his first novel was published, and meanwhile he experienced every vicissitude. Sometimes, to keep alive, he had to steal milk and rolls from doorsteps, even while he was working (at a starvation wage) as art critic of *L'Homme Libre*. His companions ranged from gutter denizens to men now famous— Pablo Picasso, Modigliani, Utrillo, Max Jacob, Pierre MacOrlan.

His enjoyment of the success of his first novel, *Jésus-la-Caille*, was ended by the First World War. He became a corporal in a field bakery, then joined an aviation school and was a pilot for the remainder of the war. At its end, he returned to Paris, and in novel after novel became recognized as the authentic chronicler of the underworld. On the side he wrote poetry, plays, travel books, art criticism, and literary biography and criticism. In 1922 he received the Grand

Prix of the French Academy for *L'Homme Traqué (The Hounded Man)*, and in 1937 he was received into the Académie Goncourt. Though it was no longer necessary for him to steal milk to live, he remained an *habitué* of the Bohemia which he celebrated in his novels, and whose own story he wrote in 1928.

He looks the Bohemian he is, with his thick, dark hair, pale skin, small but sharp eyes, and beautiful, expressive hands. Charlotte Haldane, admiring his "simplicity and gracefulness of style," called him "sympathetic and nearly first rate." His sentimentality is "tempered by humor," his language is crisp and dynamic. He has been, as one critic remarked, the explorer of the underworld who has put into his novels the obscure creatures scorned by others. But before that he was a poet of fantasy, and in the best of his work both aspects of his talent are inextricably mingled.

Even the occupation of Paris by the Nazis in 1940 failed to separate Carco from his beloved Paris, or to put an end to his running feud with the other members of the Goncourt Academy.

WORKS AVAILABLE IN ENGLISH: The Noose of Sin (in America: The Hounded Man) 1924: The Romance of François Villon, 1927; From Montmartre to the Latin Quarter (in America: The Last Bohemia) 1928; Perversity, 1928.

ABOUT: Peyre, J. Francis Carco (in French); Annales Politiques et Littéraires February 1, 1930, October 25, 1937, December 10, 1937; Bookman (London) January 1933; Journal des Débats August 27, 1926; Revue des Deux Mondes May 1, 1920, February 1, 1936; Revue Politique et Littéraire March 20, 1926.

CARLETON, WILL. See "AMERICAN AUTHORS: 1600-1900"

CARMAN, BLISS (April 15, 1861-June 8 1929), Canadian poet, was born William Bliss Carman in Fredericton, New Brunswick, of a family descended from American Loyalists who had fled to Canada during the Revolution. He was educated at Fredericton Academy and then did graduate work at the University of Edinburgh, during 1882 and 1883. He returned to read

law with his father, a barrister, but finding that not to his liking, he taught school and studied civil engineering. In none of these

pursuits did he discover his own place in life, for from childhood his devotion had been to poetry and particularly to the poetry of nature. In 1885 he cut loose from his surroundings and went to Harvard. There he met Richard Hovey, and the two young men resolved to devote themselves to poetry as a career. They were a striking pair— Hovey bearded and romantic looking, Carman a young giant, with classically beautiful features and a mass of blond hair, who dressed eccentrically as a matter of principle. They were close friends and collaborators until Hovey died in 1900.

In New York, where the two went, poetry as a career meant speedy starvation. Bohemianly poor, Carman managed to keep going by editorial work, on the *Independent* and *Current History* in New York and on the *Atlantic Monthly* and the *Chap Book* in Boston. Later on he wrote a literary column for numerous newspapers and for some time was a popular lecturer. His last undertaking was editorial, the preparation of the *Oxford Book of American Verse*.

Primarily, however, he was the single-minded acolyte of poetry. He had two distinct veins—one, evidenced chiefly in the volumes written with Hovey, was a flair for light romantic verse, very *fin de siècle* today but immensely successful in its own time. The other and more genuine talent he possessed was elegiac, balladic, and nature-celebrating. He was a true lyrist, fresh and spontaneous even in the rigid verse-forms to which he was bound by the tradition of his era. In his nature-poems he aspired to touch the fringe of Wordsworth's mantle; in his ballads he was stimulated by the achievement of his avowed master, Browning. Fame and a settled income injured him; he began to repeat himself, and his work lost its color and its pagan feeling for nature, though technically it was vastly improved.

Like many very large men, Carman was shy and reticent, self-depreciating, and taciturn. Yet he was friendly by nature, and much loved. Celebrity never turned his head, even when the Canadian Parliament bestowed its poet laureate's medal on him in 1928. He was acclaimed as the bard of Canada, and is indeed to date its most considerable poet. He died, not in his native but in his adopted country, at New Canaan, Conn., and was buried there in spite of efforts to have his ashes placed in Canadian earth. He never married.

There is little profundity in Carman's poetry, which even at its best is a bit too fluently cheerful for modern taste; but he himself claimed so little for it beyond a single-minded apostleship that it is supererogatory to judge him by too lofty standards. He wrote his creed once and for all in "Daisies," when he said:

> And all of their singing was, "Earth,
> it is well!"
> And all of their dancing was, "Life, thou
> art good!"

Padraic Colum's obituary in the *Commonweal* praised Carman's "sweet nature," the "gayety and color of his mind," the "frugal dignity" of his life, and the long devotion to his art.

PRINCIPAL WORKS: *Poetry*—Low Tide on Grand Pré, 1893; Songs From Vagabondia (with R. Hovey) 1894; Behind the Arras, 1895; A Seamark, 1895; More Songs From Vagabondia (with R. Hovey) 1896; Ballads of Lost Haven, 1897; By the Aurelian Wall, 1898; A Winter Holiday, 1899; Last Songs From Vagabondia (with R. Hovey) 1901; Ballads and Lyrics, 1902; Pipes of Pan No. I, 1902; Pipes of Pan No. II, 1903; Pipes of Pan No. III, 1904; Pipes of Pan No. IV, 1904; Sappho, 1905; Echoes From Vagabondia, 1912; Daughters of the Dawn (with M. P. King) 1913; Earth Deities (with M. P. King) 1914; April Airs, 1914; Later Poems, 1922; Far Horizons, 1925; Wild Garden, 1929; Sanctuary, 1929. *Essays*—The Kinship of Nature, 1904; The Friendship of Art, 1904; The Making of a Personality, 1908.

ABOUT: Cappon, J. Bliss Carman and the Literary Influences and Currents of His Time; Hawthorne, J. Bliss Carman; Rittenhouse, J. B. The Younger American Poets; Atlantic Monthly May 1906; Canadian Bookman September 1929, March 1932, August 1933; Commonweal December 25, 1929; Overland Monthly July 1929.

CARMER, CARL LAMSON (October 16, 1893-), American essayist and poet, writes: "I was born in Cortland, N.Y. My father, Willis Griswold Carmer, then principal of the Dansville High School, and my mother, who was Mary Lamson of Geneseo, had been visiting on my grandfather's farm at Dryden up to very shortly before my birth, but a good team  of horses got them both into Cortland in time for me to be born in the hospital there.

"My first five years were spent in Dansville. Then my father became superintendent of schools at Albion, N.Y., and took the family, to which my sister had been added, to live there. My school days were spent in Albion. I graduated from the Albion High School in June, 1910, and in the following fall I went to Clinton, where I entered Hamilton College, of which my father is an alumnus. I graduated from Hamilton in the class of 1914.

"After a year of work in English Literature at the Harvard Graduate School I received the degree of M.A. and began teaching college freshmen at Syracuse University to write correctly. After two semesters of that I obtained a better position at the University of Rochester. I had taught in Rochester one year before I was obliged to become a soldier. I drilled recruits for a while at Camp Dix, N.J., became a sergeant in the Division Judge Advocate's office, where I studied army law, and was sent to Officers' Training Camp, from which I graduated as a Second Lieutenant of Field Artillery. At the end of the war I was a First Lieutenant, instructor in the School of Fire at Fort Sills, Okla.

"I went back to teaching peace-time subjects at Hamilton College, then returned to the University of Rochester as assistant professor. I became an associate professor at the University of Alabama two years later and a few years after that achieved a full professorship.

"After six years of teaching in Alabama I went to New Orleans, where I became a columnist on the *Item-Tribune* and wrote a book of verses (privately printed) entitled *French Town.* I lost the job on the paper and went to New York, where I became assistant editor of *Vanity Fair.* At this time I married Elizabeth Black, artist, daughter of Col. Bryan Black of New Orleans. A year later I became associate editor of *Theatre Arts Monthly.* After four years of going to the theatre and writing about the theatre, during which I wrote a book of poems, *Deep South,* published by Farrar & Rinehart, I resigned my editorship to write a prose study of Southern life. This book, *Stars Fell on Alabama,* was a Literary Guild Selection. Two years later I had completed *Listen for a Lonesome Drum,* a similar study of up-state New York. Soon thereafter I began telling American folk-tales over Station WABC of the Columbia Broadcasting Co. These tales were made into my fifth book, *The Hurricane's Children,* which was illustrated with black and white drawings by my wife. For three years I worked on a book about a river, *The Hudson,* one of the series, *Rivers of America,* edited by the late Constance Lindsay Skinner.

"I am a member of the council of the Authors' Guild, of the board of directors of the American Civil Liberties Union, of P.E.N., and The Players. I am particularly fond of tennis, dancing, folk-songs. I have been living in New York City for five years."

* * *

Of Carl Carmer's delightful studies of American folklore, *Time* remarked that "he maintains an aloof compassion, avoiding sentimentality as well as . . . mockery." He has dug out for himself a new and rich claim in the goldfields of American literature and life.

PRINCIPAL WORKS: College English Composition (with E. R. Shoemaker) 1927; French Town, 1927; Deep South, 1930; Stars Fell on Alabama, 1934; Listen to a Lonesome Drum, 1936; The Hudson, 1939; Genesee Fever (novel) 1941.

ABOUT: New York Times Book Review January 11, 1942; Saturday Review of Literature December 11, 1937, July 1, 1939, September 7, 1940, December 6, 1941; Scholastic April 3, 1937; Time June 29, 1936; Wilson Library Bulletin February 1937.

CAROSSA, HANS (December 15, 1878-), German novelist and poet, was born at Tolz, Bavaria, a small watering-place, the son of Karl Carossa and Marie (Voggenreiter) Carossa. The family originally came from Verona, Italy, settled in southern Germany and intermarried with the natives, who were Catholics. Hans Carossa attended the gymnasium at Land-

shut before spending several years in study at the Universities of Munich, Wurzburg, and Leipzig, which then had a famous medical faculty. Receiving his medical degree from Leipzig in 1903, he practiced in Passau, where he married the daughter of a local merchant in 1906. Study of Goethe and Gottfried Keller resulted in poetry of his own; Carossa's first volume of *Gedichte* appearing in 1910. Stemming from the South German Romantic tradition, the poems search the dark corners of consciousness and display a rather fatalistic attitude. In 1913 a novel, *Doktor Bürgers Ende,* was published. On the outbreak of the First World War next year Carossa moved to Munich. In 1916 he was called to the colors as doctor of the 19th Bavarian Reserve Infantry Regiment on the Roumanian front whence came his *Roumanian Diary,* which Frank Swinnerton has called "a fine book, clear-sighted, measured and beautiful." After the Armistice, Carossa continued practice in Munich as a specialist in tuberculosis. Since the consolidation of the Third Reich

Carossa has published only one book, *Geheimnisse des reifen Lebens* (1936). More popular with his own generation than with the Nazi youth, Carossa feels that the new movement is essentially what the youth of Germany needs, while exercising his privilege of age to issue mild warnings and criticisms. He occasionally sighs for the good old days, as a true Bavarian somewhat grieved at the disappearance of pre-war German federalism. Clair Baier writes of Carossa: "Long before the National-Socialists achieved supreme power in Germany, Carossa had been recognized as a truly German writer—'ein volkischer' or 'volksverbundener Dichter,' as one who showed no leanings toward Marxism and Liberalism, nor towards any of the 'decadent' schools of literary thought." He prefers to stress human and personal elements rather than national and political ones; and "appeals not to 'Deutschtum' but to common humanity in his readers." A mild, Germanic, clean-shaven man, Carossa was praised by Arnold Bennett for his unusually broad culture, and once received a graceful tribute from such fellow-writers as Rilke, Stefan Zweig, and Hugo von Hofmannsthal in *Buch des Dankes für Hans Carossa.*

WORKS AVAILABLE IN ENGLISH TRANSLATION: A Roumanian Diary, 1929; A Childhood, 1930; Boyhood and Youth, 1931; Doctor Gion, 1933.

ABOUT: Buch des Dankes für Hans Carossa; Carossa, H. Verwandlungen einer Jugend; Eloesser, A. Modern German Literature; Haueis, A. Hans Carossa: Personlichkeit und Werk; Bookman December 1930; Contemporary Review February 1941; German Life and Letters April 1938, January 1939; London Mercury June 1938; Saturday Review of Literature September 5, 1931; Spectator January 5, 1931.

CARPENTER, EDWARD. See "BRITISH AUTHORS OF THE 19TH CENTURY"

CARR, JOHN DICKSON ("Carter Dickson," "Carr Dickson," pseuds.) (1905-), American-English writer of detective fiction,

was born at Uniontown, Pa., the son of Wooda Nicholas Carr, later U.S. Congressman (1913-15) and currently U.S. Postmaster of Uniontown, and Julia Carr. According to the *Daily News Standard* of that community for August 31, 1939, John Dickson Carr was then paying a visit to his old home town, accompanied by Mrs. Carr,

originally of Bristol, England; their young daughter Julia has been left with her grandmother in Bristol. Mr. Carr had written the majority of his thirty-odd books in the decade he had spent in England, where he was honored by initiation into the Detection Club in 1936. Dorothy Sayers and Anthony Berkeley were his sponsors; and G. K. Chesterton was in the chair for the occasion.

Continuing to judge from the available data, in the manner of Mr. Carr's sleuths—the fat and brusque "H.M.," Dr. Fell, and Bencolin, the Parisian police inspector—one feels fairly safe in stating that the novelist was born twenty-five years before his thriller, *It Walks By Night*, attracted favorable attention in 1930. At the age of eight he was hauled off to Washington, where his father "thundered in Congress" while his young son stood on a table in the members' anteroom and recited Hamlet's soliloquy to Tom Heflin, Pat Harrison, and Claude Kitchin. He sat on "Uncle Joe" Cannon's knee, and learned crap-shooting from the newsboys on the corner. Young Carr's earliest heroes were Sherlock Holmes, d'Artagnan, and the Wizard of Oz. At fourteen he was writing about sports and murder trials for a newspaper. Preparatory school, the Hill School, followed—mentioned with pride by the author because it was the only institution of learning from which, he says, he was not fired. The next step along the way for him was Haverford College. Intended for the study of law, Carr preferred newspaper work; mathematics was another stumbling-block in his academic career, besides such escapades as staging fake murders with a dummy to bring in the police. He later went abroad to study and write, and has made his home in England for many years. He and his family and their possessions were completely bombed-out no less than three times in the 1940-41 blitz, but stayed indomitably on.

J. B. Priestley has said that Carr has "a sense of the macabre that lifts him high above the average run of detective story writers"; another reviewer calls his novels full-bodied, with plenty of connective tissue and that three-dimensional quality lacking in so many detective yarns. His especially-written broadcasts for the British Broadcasting Corporation have proved an emphatic success. The one unforgiveable sin in detective story writing, he believes, is "being dull"—a fault which no reader has discovered in his own stories, characterized equally by ingenuity and liveliness, and in the opinion of connoisseurs among the best available in the *genre* today.

PRINCIPAL WORKS: *As John Dickson Carr*—It Walks By Night, 1930; The Lost Gallows, 1931; Castle Skull, 1931; The Corpse in the Waxworks, 1932; Poison in Jest, 1932; The Mad Hatter Mystery, 1933; Hag's Nook, 1933; The Blind Barber, 1934; The Eight of Swords, 1934; Death-Watch, 1935; The Three Coffins, 1935; The Arabian Nights Murder, 1936; The Murder of Sir Edmund Godfrey, 1937; The Four False Weapons, 1937; The Crooked Hinge, 1938; To Wake the Dead, 1938; The Problem of the Green Capsule, 1939; The Problem of the Wire Case, 1939; The Man Who Could Not Shudder, 1940; The Case of the Constant Suicides, 1941; Death Turns the Tables, 1942. *As "Carr Dickson"*.—The Bowstring Murders, 1933; The Plague Court Murders, 1934; The White Priory Murders, 1934; The Red Widow Murders, 1935. *As "Carter Dickson"*—The Unicorn Murders, 1935; The Punch and Judy Murders, 1937; The Peacock Feather, 1937; The Judas Window, 1938; Death in Five Boxes, 1938; The Reader Is Warned, 1939; And So To Murder, 1940; Nine and Death Makes Ten, 1940; The Department of Queer Complaints (short stories) 1940; Seeing Is Believing, 1941; The Gilded Man, 1942.

ABOUT: Haycraft, H. Murder for Pleasure: The Life and Times of the Detective Story.

*CARRELL, ALEXIS (June 28, 1873-   ), French-American physiologist, was born in Sainte-Foy-lès-Lyon, France, the son of Alexis and Anne (Ricard) Carrel. He received his L.B. at the University of Lyons in 1890, Sc.B. University of Dijon, 1891, M.D. University of Lyon 1900. Since then his honorary degrees have been numerous, including doctorates from Columbia, Brown, Princeton, Belfast, California, and elsewhere. In 1937 Dartmouth made him an honorary Phi Beta Kappa. He was a Nobel Prize winner in 1912 in medicine and physiology, is a commander of the Legion of Honor, and has Belgian, Swedish, and Spanish decorations. He is a fellow of the American College of Surgeons, the American Surgical Association, the American Philosophical Society, and the New York Academy of Medicine, and an honorary fellow of the Royal Society of Medicine. He received the Nordhoff-Jury Cancer Prize in 1931, and the Newman Foundation Award of the University of Illinois in 1937.

This distinguished career began with an internship in the Lyon Hospital, following which Dr. Carrel was for two years prosector at the University of Lyon. Becoming discouraged with his scientific prospects, he came to Canada with the idea of engaging in cattle raising! Fortunately he was deflected from this idea by an appointment to the Hull Physiological Laboratory in Chicago, where he met the celebrated Simon Flexner, who at once saw the possibilities of this young worker and secured his services for the Rockefeller Institute for Medical Research. After six years on the staff, he became a member of the Institute in 1912, and was retired as emeritus in 1939.

In 1913 he married the Marquise de la Marie, a widow who as Anne de la Motte had been his laboratory assistant in Lyon, and who continued to work for him. The Nobel Prize came to him for his work in transplantation of organs and blood vessels and his researches in keeping isolated living matter alive. (The piece of chicken heart which he has kept alive for more than twenty years is known all over the world.)

With the outbreak of the First World War he became a major in the medical department of the French army, and remained in France until 1919, except for a furlough to the United States in 1917 to establish a hospital at the Rockefeller Institute. He and his wife conducted a laboratory hospital at Compiègne, where he developed his system of preventing wound infection, including the universally employed Carrel-Dakin solution for wounds. As soon as the Second World War started, in spite of his age he at once offered his services again to France, and from September 1939 served on a special war mission for the French Ministry of Public Health. He is now associated with the Vichy régime.

During all his years in America, Dr. Carrel spent every summer at his home on the island of St. Gildas, off the coast of Britanny. Charles Lindbergh, after becoming vitally interested in Carrel's work, undertook laboratory research under Carrel's direction and bought a neighboring island where he lived for some time. Dr. Carrel's most striking characteristic is his amazing vitality; as Arthur Train, Jr., remarked, "audacity is the key to his character." He is unusual in appearance—short, bald (he usually wears a skull cap, either black or white), and behind pince nez are concealed near-sighted eyes, one of which is brown, the other blue. He is, in spite of his scientific preeminence, essentially a mystic, and is a devout and practicing Roman Catholic. Throughout his only non-technical book, *Man the Unknown*, this semi-mystical, semi-philosophical note sounds, together with a sort of spiritual monism which believes passionately in the unity of all life. The poet in him contends, in this book, with the scientist. Though he speaks with a marked accent, he writes equally well in English or in French; *Man the Unknown,* however, appeared first in his native tongue.

PRINCIPAL WORKS: Manifested Life of Tissues Outside of the Organism (with M. T. Burrows) 1911; The Treatment of Infected Wounds (with G. Dehelly) 1919; Man the Unknown, 1935; The Culture of Organs (with C. A. Lindbergh) 1938.

ABOUT: Law, F. H. Modern Great Americans; Catholic World December 1936; Current Biography 1940; Hibbert Journal October 1938; Illustration December 23, 1939; Literary Digest December 27, 1919; Reader's Digest March 1941; Revue Scientifique March 1937; Saturday Evening Post July 23, 1938; Scientific American May 1936; Time June 13, 1938, April 24, 1939.

CARROLL, Mrs. GLADYS (HASTY)
(June 26, 1904-), American novelist, writes: "Birthplace, Rochester, N.H.—

Pinchot

though this seems less important, in view both of my personal devotions and my literary material, than the fact that my home from earliest memory has been in South Berwick, Maine. My parents (Warren V. and Emma Dow Hasty), my brother, and I lived with my paternal grandfather, on his farm, until his death, when the farm and the lumber business in which he and my father had been engaged became my father's. Shortly after, I went away to college, though not far away—to Bates College, in Lewiston. I had scarcely spent a night outside the State of Maine when I was married at my Commencement in 1925 to Herbert A. Carroll, of Greenfield, Mass. His work in various departments of education carried us to Fall River, Mass., for three years, to New York for two, and to Minneapolis, Minn., for five.

"My first two books were juveniles, *Cockatoo,* published in 1929, and *Land Spell,* 1930. The next three were novels, all written while we lived in Minnesota—*As the Earth Turns,* 1933, *A Few Foolish Ones,* 1935, *Neighbor to the Sky,* 1937. Our son, Warren Hasty Carroll, was born in Minneapolis in 1932.

"We are now living permanently in a house which we built in South Berwick, across the lane from my grandfather's place, where my father and mother still live. Here for a week each summer, at the foot of the Hasty field, our neighbors present a folkplay based on *As the Earth Turns,* the proceeds

of the undertaking maintaining a church, community social center, and library in the rural neighborhood of Emery's Bridge, bringing in electricity, and providing a reserve fund in case of individual or group emergency.

"Life is and always has been more interesting and precious to me than literature; I read and write only out of eagerness for further clarification of what I see and hear and feel."

* * *

Mrs. Carroll has further exemplified her philosophy in an article in the *Saturday Review of Literature* (November 9, 1935), where she says that her work is devoted to the thesis that New England is not a "ghost region," living only in the glory of its literary and cultural past, but that it is still a living and growing community, full of material for the writer with the seeing eye. That this is so, she has exemplified in her own novels, which carry on the traditions of Sarah Orne Jewett and Mary E. Wilkins Freeman, and complement the Maine seacoast novels of Mary Ellen Chase and Rachel Field.

PRINCIPAL WORKS: Cockatoo, 1929; Land Spell, 1930; As the Earth Turns, 1933; A Few Foolish Ones, 1935; Neighbor of the Sky, 1937; Head of the Line, 1942.

ABOUT: Independent Woman January 1936, Saturday Review of Literature May 6, 1933; April 27, 1935; Wilson Library Bulletin January 1934.

CARROLL, PAUL VINCENT (July 10, 1900-), Irish dramatist, writes: "I was born at a small seaside resort called Blackrock, near Dundalk in the County of Louth, Ireland. My late father, Michael Carroll, was the local schoolmaster on weekdays and on Saturday he was employed by auctioneers to portion out amongst local farmers two, three, and five acre lots in

farms that came under the hammer. My mother has the picturesque name of Kitty and her family, the Sandses, came over to Ireland as planters from Scotland about the middle of the eighteenth century. I was educated by my father until I was thirteen, and he laid into me so hard at lessons that I was delighted when he sent me to the comparative security of St. Mary's College, Dundalk, where I played ducks and drakes with the immensities of literature until I went off to

Dublin in 1916 to St. Patrick's Training College, with a view to graduating as a teacher. In this way I was pitched right into the Irish armed revolution against England, and I got caught up breathlessly in the seething literary and dramatic activity that was finally to roll Ireland in battle-smoke from 1916 to 1921. I learned at the Abbey Theatre the rudiments of play-making and that unquenchable love of the drama that is the chief impetus of my life.

"Refusing to teach, as my father had done, under an unbearable clerical yoke, in Ireland, I sailed out of Dublin on a cattle boat and landed in Glasgow, where I began my active teaching career, and where I spent the happiest days of my life. Here I began to re-educate myself. I rediscovered the Grecians and Shakespeare. Then I stumbled on the Romanticists, and I quoted Byron, Shelley, and Keats in every pub in Glasgow, till one night I blundered into the Augustan period of literature and Swift so shocked and fascinated me that to this day his influence is one of the most potent factors in my writing, and is stronger in me than that of any other great writer except perhaps Thomas Hardy whom I consider the last link of British literature with the Grecians. Yeats, my first love in poetry, remains with me today more strongly than ever, and is challenged only by George W. Russell, ("A.E."), that most holy and saintly of all pagans.

"In drama I first came under the baleful influence of Tolstoy, so that my first play, The Watched Pot, was so diabolical and gloomy that it caused laughter instead of fear. Then, fortunately for my work, Ibsen took a sure and disciplined hand in my development, and with the addition of Synge, whose work taught me colour and rhythm, I began to visualize more sanely the strengths and weaknesses of human character.

"I wrote Things That Are Caesar's, which was an immediate success in Dublin and won the Abbey Theatre Award for that year. But it was only in 1937, when the American theatre endorsed the Abbey Theatre's opinion of Shadow and Substance, that I began to take my place as a professional dramatist. In 1939, owing to the tightening of clerical control in Ireland and other political ramifications the Abbey Theatre refused The White Steed, but America gave it generous treatment. Kindred and The Old Foolishness are my two latest works.

"In 1923, in Glasgow, I married Helena Reilly, a gown designer, and there are three daughters of the marriage. Since coming to maturity, I have had no political opinions. I like a system of government that leaves me alone to do what I want to do, so long as I conform to the ordinary natural laws. I do, however, believe that the needs and the happiness of humanity would be best administered to by a governmental combination of the best people with the best writers. It is not, of course, a new idea, neither is it original. I stole it from Swift. In religion, I cling by conviction to Catholicism, but God save me from its administrators! Thank Heaven I have always managed to separate the one from the other.

"My ambitions are chiefly theatrical—they are the return of the beauty of the spoken word to the drama, and the raising of the emotions back to the level of Shakespearian glamour. I adore children and am happiest when amongst them. I like horses and loathe dogs. I live in Scotland, seven miles out of Glasgow, in a little villa called Torquil which I bought in 1938 with American dollars, from a very lovable young lady who was dying and knew it. She is dead now, but the flowers which she planted all over the garden and lawn are still there, and are carefully tended in memory of her."

* * *

Carroll is a tiny man with a leprechaun air, the brogue heavy on his tongue, and he himself bald and already wrinkled, but the wrinkles are of laughter. He received the Drama Critics' Circle award for the best foreign play in 1938, for Shadow and Substance. George Jean Nathan said his work was "stippled alternately with tenderness and dynamite." He himself says: "I write as Ibsen did. I take the life of a small village and enlarge it to encompass all human life."

PRINCIPAL WORKS: Shadow and Substance, 1937; The White Steed, and Coggerers, 1939.

ABOUT: New Republic May 4, 1938; Newsweek January 23, 1939; Wilson Library Bulletin February 1940.

CARRYL, CHARLES EDWARD. See "AMERICAN AUTHORS: 1600-1900"

*CARSWELL, Mrs. CATHERINE (MACFARLANE) (March 27, 1879-), Scottish biographer, was born in Glasgow, the daughter of George Gray Macfarlane, an East India merchant. She was educated at Park School and the University of Glasgow, and then spent two years studying music in Frankfurt, Germany. In 1903 she was married to Herbet P. M. Jackson, and they had a child who died. They were divorced in 1908. In

* Died February 18, 1946.

1907 she became dramatic critic of the Glasgow *Herald*. The turning point in her career as a writer began with a meeting with D. H. Lawrence in 1914. They grew to be close friends, he criticized and encouraged her work, and after his death she became one of his many biographers. In 1915 she was married to Donald Carswell, also a writer and an administrative officer in the Home Office. (He was killed in a "blackout" accident in January 1940.) They had one son. In the same year as her marriage, Mrs. Carswell lost her position on the *Herald*, for which she had been doing books as well as plays, because of a favorable review of  Lawrence's *The Rainbow*, which had been censored. The Carswells moved from London to Bournemouth (she had been doing her reviewing at long distance) soon after this; Mr. Carswell had been called to the bar, and then had become an officer in the army. These were hard years; she had not yet published a book, she was ill, and they were very poor.

Better times began after the war. Mrs. Carswell's first book was a realistic novel, published in 1920 when she was forty-one. Though she is known now primarily as a biographer, both this and her second novel won some success. She contemplated writing a novel in collaboration with Lawrence, she did some literary criticism, and she began research for her first biography, a life of Burns. This received praise as accurate, complete, and fair. Her next biography, however, the life of Lawrence (who had died in 1930) which was written, from her intimate knowledge, as a counter-blast to J. Middleton Murry's first biography of the novelist, raised a storm. Murry succeeded in having it suppressed, called it a libel, and wrote another book to refute it. It nevertheless remains what Shane Leslie called it, "the most illuminating book about Lawrence," not excluding his widow's. Mrs. Carswell's later books have been less controversial, and have gained her an increasing reputation as a scholarly and sympathetic biographer.

The Carswells lived for some years in Toppersfield, Essex. Mrs. Carswell works slowly, with a passion for exact documentation, and her health is too frail to permit her much social life even in time of peace. She is tall, slender, and fair, with deep-set, brooding eyes and delicately aquiline features. She gives as her disparate "recreations" "doing things" and "sensual contemplation." Before the present war she traveled a good deal on the continent, often making long walking-tours, with her husband and in later years with her son.

PRINCIPAL WORKS: Open the Door (novel) 1920; The Camomile, 1922; The Life of Robert Burns, 1930; The Savage Pilgrimage: A Narrative of D. H. Lawrence, 1932; The Fays of the Abbey Theatre (with W. G. Fay) 1935; The Scots Week-End (with D. Carswell) 1936; The Tranquil Heart: Portrait of Giovanni Boccaccio, 1937.

ABOUT: Carswell, C. The Savage Pilgrimage; Murry, J. M. Reminiscences of D. H. Lawrence; Fortnightly September 1934.

CARTER, JOHN FRANKLIN (April 27, 1897-), American political journalist and writer of detective fiction, who uses the pseudonyms "Jay Franklin" and "Diplomat," was born in Fall River, Mass., one of the seven children of the Rev. John Franklin Carter, an Episcopal clergyman, and Alice Schermerhorn (Henry) Carter. In 1900 the family moved to Wil-  liamstown, Mass, where Dr. Carter, who had been "trained in the hard school of Bishop Lawrence," became rector of St. John's Church. The parish contained a large number of textile workers and college students.

Young Carter's boyhood and youth up to the time of his graduation from Yale in 1920 (his preparatory school was St. Mark's) is described in his informal autobiography, *The Rectory Family*. "Possibly the haphazard method of old-time liberal education was not a bad preparation for the years of economic upheaval which were to sweep over us," he concluded, though "it was hard to leave such a sanctuary for the $30-a-week jobs and the hall bedrooms of city boarding houses, and the bitter struggle for riches and existence in the 1920's." He was at Yale with Stephen Vincent Benét, Thornton Wilder, Archibald MacLeish, and Thomas Coward, who became his publisher. Carter was employed in the American embassies at Rome and Constantinople in 1918-19; was private secretary to the American ambassador at Rome in 1920-21; represented the Williamstown Institute of Politics in 1922; and for the next six years represented newspapers in Rome: the London *Daily Chronicle* in 1922-23 and the

New York *Times* from 1923 to 1928. He was an economic specialist in the State Department at Washington from 1928 to 1932; Washington correspondent of *Liberty* from 1932 to 1934, also writing for *Vanity Fair*; was one of the organizers and first editors of the news-magazine *Time*; and spent 1934 to 1936 in the office of the Under-Secretary of Agriculture, when he began to write (as "Jay Franklin") his syndicated pro-New Deal newspaper column, "We, the People," a brilliant, well-informed, if often obstinately partisan, column which ranges over literature as well as politics and economics. Some Republican papers declared they bought it solely to keep tabs on the doings of the Roosevelt administration. In 1938-39 Carter was radio commentator for the National Broadcasting Company.

At Yale Carter was member of Alpha Delta Phi and Wolf's Head, and he also belongs to the National Press Club in Washington. He is a Democrat, and is a member of the Christian Church. In 1927 he married Sheila Sutherland; they have a daughter, Sonia Franklin Carter, and live in Washington.

A serious infection in childhood left Carter "with bad eyes and a leaky heart," and he learned to write "in self-defence against a world which is, among children at least, thoroughly contemptuous of weaklings."

As the pseudonymous "Diplomat," Carter wrote between 1930 and 1935 a series of unusual and amusing detective stories, featuring the adventures of Dennis Tyler, career diplomat and amateur sleuth, and slyly satirizing the world of diplomacy and politics in Washington and abroad.

PRINCIPAL WORKS: Man Is War, 1926; Conquest: America's Painless Imperialism, 1928; What This Country Needs, 1931; What We Are About To Receive, 1932; The New Dealers (with others) 1934; American Messiahs (with others) 1935; Our Lords and Masters, 1935; The Rectory Family, 1937; La Guardia, 1937; The Future is Ours, 1939; "1940," 1940; Remaking America, 1942. As "Diplomat"—Murder in the Embassy, 1930; Murder in the State Department, 1930; Scandal in the Chancery, 1931; The Corpse on the White House Lawn, 1932; Death in the Senate, 1933; The Brain Trust Murder, 1935.

ABOUT: Carter, J. F. The Rectory Family; Howe, Q. The News and How To Understand It; Time April 7, 1941.

CARUS, PAUL (July 18, 1852-February 11, 1919), German-American philosopher, was born in Ilsenburg, Germany, son of the Superintendent General of the Church of Prussia. He was educated at gymnasia in Posen and Stettin, and at the Universi-

ties of Greifswald, Strassburg, and Tübingen, where he received his Ph.D. in 1876. He then became a teacher in a military school in Dresden, but was forced to resign because of his liberal political views. He went to England, and from there to the United States, about 1883. He settled in Chicago, where in 1887, a zinc manufacturer named Hegeler established a weekly (later a monthly) called the *Open Court*, and made Carus its editor. Until his death Carus was editor of this magazine, of the quarterly *Monist*, and

E. W. Reiss

of the Open Court Publishing Co. In 1888 he married Mary Hegeler, his benefactor's daughter.

Besides his own writing, Carus translated and edited Kant; he was also the author of several dramatic poems. One of these, *De Rerum Natura*, was translated from the German by C. A. Lane in 1895. Most of Carus' work, however, was written in English.

Carus was a pure monist who felt that all nature was one, that psychology was a branch of physiology, and that philosophy could be made an objective science. In spite of his immense erudition and his cogent thinking, he had little influence on American philosophic thought: he was too religious for the Rationalists, and the classical philosophers resented him because he was not one of their own group of university spokesmen.

PRINCIPAL WORKS: Fundamental Problems, 1889; The Gospel of Buddha, 1895; Buddhism and Its Christian Critics, 1897; Kant and Spencer: A Study of the Fallacies of Agnosticism, 1899; Whence and Whither, 1900; The Soul of Man, 1900; The Surd of Metaphysics, 1903; Friedrich Schiller, 1905; Amitabha: A Story of Buddhist Theology, 1906; Our Children, 1906; Chinese Thought, 1907; Foundations of Mathematics, 1908; God: An Enquiry and a Solution, 1908; The Pleroma, 1909; Philosophy As a Science, 1909; Truth on Trial, 1911; The Canon of Reason and Virtue, 1913; Nietzsche and Other Exponents of Individualism, 1914; Goethe: With Special Consideration of His Philosophy, 1915; The Venus of Milo, 1916.

ABOUT: Dial May 3, 1919; Open Court September 1919.

CASSERES. See DE CASSERES

CASTLE, EGERTON (March 12, 1858-September 16, 1920), English novelist, was the eldest son of M.A. Castle of Park Lane, London. His grandfather, Egerton Smith

Castle, was a well-known philanthropist and man of letters who established the Liverpool *Mercury;* Egerton Castle was later chief proprietor of the paper. His father preferred Paris and Vienna to England, and was an intimate friend of Verdi, Donizetti, Rossini, Liszt, George Sand, and Browning. Egerton Castle accompanied his father on walking tours through

the German and Austrian forests and provincial France, and along the Mediterranean. He attended the Lycée Condorset at Paris till 1873, then studied at the Universities of Paris and Glasgow; King's College, London; and Trinity College, Cambridge, where he concentrated on the Natural Science Tripos.

Admitted to the Inner Temple, Castle soon abandoned the law to enter the Royal Military College at Sandhurst; was commissioned lieutenant with the 2nd West India Regiment; served the colors three years; and later was captain in the Royal Engineer Militia (Portsmouth Division, Submarine Miners), having passed through all the courses in submarine mining at Chatham and Gosport. He was a member of English fencing teams which met France and Belgium in international competitions. From 1885 to 1894 Castle was a member of the staff of the *Saturday Review.* His first short story, "A Paragraph in the Globe," was written while he was on his Rome honeymoon with Mrs. Castle, who was Agnes Sweetman of Lamberton Park, Queen's County, Ireland; they had a daughter. Their series of pleasantly romantic novels, once very popular, were signed "By Agnes and Egerton Castle." *The Pride of Jennico; The Bath Comedy,* dealing with Beau Nash and his times, and *The Secret Orchard,* dramatized for Mr. and Mrs. Kendal in 1901, were all best-sellers.

In America, David Belasco produced *Sweet Kitty Bellairs,* a dramatization of *The Bath Comedy.* Castle also wrote a play, *Desperate Remedies,* for Richard Mansfield. He was a member of the Athenaeum, Garrick, Fencing, and Authors clubs in London. The Castles' home was at Hindhead, Surrey, near the homes of Conan Doyle and Grant Allen. He died at sixty-one, and Mrs. Castle died two years later, in 1922.

PRINCIPAL WORKS: The Light of Scarthey, 1895; Young April, 1899. *With A. Castle*—The Pride of Jennico, 1898; The Bath Comedy, 1900; The Secret Orchard, 1901; The Star Dreamer, 1903; The Incomparable Bellairs, 1904; French Nan, 1905; If Youth But Knew, 1906; My Merry Rockhurst, 1907; Flower o' the Orange and Other Stories, 1908; The Ways of Miss Barbara, 1914; A Little House in War Time, 1915; The Black Office, and Other Chapters of Romance, 1917; Wolf Lure, 1917; Pamela Pounce, 1921.

ABOUT: Castle, A. & E. A Little House in War Time; Bookman March 1908.

"CASTLEMON, HARRY." See "AMERICAN AUTHORS: 1600-1900"

*CATHER, WILLA SIBERT (December 7, 1873-), American novelist, was born near Winchester, Va., in the fourth generation of an Anglo-Irish family. Her father was Charles F. Cather, her mother Mary Virginia (Boak) Cather. When she was eight years old her father emigrated to a ranch in Nebraska, then still semi-pioneer country.

N. Muray

To this day Willa Cather seems much more of a Westerner than a Southerner, in spite of her Virginia birth and ancestry. A stocky little girl with reddish brown hair and bright blue eyes (a description which, with her youthful appearance, more or less fits her even now), she grew up a tomboy, at home in the saddle, mingling with the children of other ranchers, most of them foreign-born or second generation Americans, and learning at first hand the lives of the people about whom she was to write in later years. There were no schools near her, and she was taught at home. Both her grandmothers were members of the household, and they schooled her in the English classics and in Latin. It is significant that the first literary influence to affect her strongly was that of Virgil.

The family moved to the little town of Red Cloud, Neb., and there Miss Cather went to high school. She worked her way through the University of Nebraska by doing newspaper correspondence, and after her graduation in 1895 this experience stood her in good stead. She was passionately fond of music, and determined to live in a city where she could find concerts as well as intellectual companionship. Her selection was Pittsburgh, where she became telegraph editor and dramatic critic of the *Daily Leader.*

But newspaper work did not attract her, and in 1901 she turned to teaching, as head of the English department in the Allegheny High School. She was beginning to write verse which was finding its way into magazines. Two years later she published a volume of poetry, and in 1905 a collection of short stories which received favorable comment and led next year to her going to New York, to *McClure's Magazine*. She was managing editor of the magazine from 1906 to 1912, though according to Ida Tarbell she was not much in sympathy with its "muckraking" and crusading methods.

During this time, on vacations and short leaves of absence, she traveled a good deal, in Europe and America, She even tried to live permanently in France, but she was so homesick for the prairie country that she could not endure it. Later she transferred her affection to the desert country of the Southwest, which she has described in such loving detail in *Death Comes to the Archbishop*.

From the time she left *McClure's*, Miss Cather has lived in New York as a free lance writer, the success of her books from *O Pioneers!* on having made it unnecessary for her to take an editorial position. She still travels a good deal, and in fact was in Europe when the Second World War began. She has never married, but lives quietly in an apartment filled with reminders of her travels. Perhaps her chief characteristic in her personal life is her loyalty to the friends of her childhood and youth. She still loves music, and many famous singers have been among her close associates. Though she shuns publicity, five universities have given her honorary degrees, and in 1933 she received the *Prix Femina Americaine*.

Miss Cather first became widely known with *O Pioneers!* in 1913. Her novels may be divided into three groups: those dealing with the West, and particularly with foreign-born farmers and their descendants (*O Pioneers!* the first part of *The Song of the Lark, My Antonia, A Lost Lady*); those short stories and novelettes (such as the stories in *Youth and the Bright Medusa*) which show the influence of Henry James and Edith Wharton, and deal mostly with artists and sophisticated Easterners; and those, merging almost into legend, which evidence **her interest in Roman Catholicism** (*Death Comes to the Archbishop, Shadows on the Rock*).

Even before this phase, however, Miss Cather's work displayed an aloofness, a lack of immediacy, unusual in modern American writing. As the late T. K. Whipple remarked, she is "the exemplar of the pure artist." Passion, humor, and the chaotic life of her own time pass her by; her loose, plotless books give a feeling of timelessness. She herself said she reached her objective when she stopped trying to *write* and began to *remember*. Her two attempts to treat of contemporary events, *One of Ours* and *The Professor's House*, are both comparative failures, even though the former was a Pulitzer Prize winner in 1922.

Her chief defect as a writer is the lack of "a tragic sense," an excessive emotional caution and reserve which result in diminished vitality in her later as compared with her earlier novels. But this is overweighed by a nobility and distinction which have made her a classic while she still lives. As Clifton Fadiman said, her viewpoint is "Virgilian in its grace, its aversion to confusion and violence, its piety, its ancestor-worship, its moral idealism, its gentle stoicism, its feeling for the past, and its sense, touching rather than tragic, of the tears which lie in mortal things." And to the expression of his outlook on life she has brought a style (to quote Howard Mumford Jones) "grave, flexible, a little austere, wonderfully transparent, everywhere economical." She has written comparatively little in recent years, but she has already given to the world a handful of novels which will continue to be read for some time. "She comes closest in American literature of this period," says Henry Seidel Canby, "to the classic ideal of balance, insight, restraint."

PRINCIPAL WORKS: April Twilights (poems) 1903; The Troll Garden, 1905; Alexander's Bridge, 1912; O Pioneers! 1913; The Song of the Lark, 1915; My Antonia, 1918; Youth and the Bright Medusa (short stories) 1920; One of Ours, 1922; A Lost Lady, 1923; The Professor's House, 1925; My Mortal Enemy, 1926; Death Comes to the Archbishop, 1927; Shadows on the Rock, 1931; Obscure Destinies (short stories) 1932; Lucy Gayheart, 1935; Not Under Forty (essays) 1936; Saphira and the Slave Girl, 1940.

ABOUT: Boynton, P. H. Some Contemporary Americans; Rapin, R. Willa Cather; Sergeant, E. S. Fire Under the Andes; Whipple, T. K. Spokesmen; America January 11, 1936; Bookman March 1932; Commonweal November 23, 1927, February 25, 1931; February 7, 1941; Nation December 7, 1932; New Republic June 17, 1925, February 10, 1937; New York Herald Tribune "Books" December 15, 1940; Saturday Review of Literature August 6, 1938; Time December 9, 1940.

"CAUDWELL, CHRISTOPHER." See SPRIGG, C. ST. J.

CAZAMIAN, LOUIS FRANÇOIS (April 2, 1877-), French critic of English literature, writes: "Born at Saint-Denis, Île de la Réunion;

father from the South of France, a teacher at the *Lycée*, mother's family had come to the island at various times from the South of France. Left the island when five, followed father through his career as headmaster in several French cities. Last years of secondary studies in Paris. A pupil at the *École Normale Supérieure*, 1896-1900; about eighteen months spent in England during those four years. Degree in English, 1900; a fellow of the Thiers Foundation, Paris, 1901-1903; degree of Doctor of Letters, 1903; lecturer at the universities of Lyons, Bordeaux, Paris (1908); professor of modern English literature and civilization at the Sorbonne, 1925. Married, 1903; wife died in 1904 giving birth to daughter; married again, 1908, two daughters. During the World War served chiefly in the Intelligence Department of the War and Foreign Offices, Paris. Lectured at various British and Belgian universities and at the University of Toronto. Invited for a period of teaching by several American colleges: the University of California, 1924 and 1929; Rice Institute, Houston, 1925; Columbia University, 1928-29; Wellesley College, 1933-34; addressed many others. A member of the *Mission du Haut Enseignement* [mission of higher instruction] in the United States, November 1918-January 1919; of the *Mission Cavelier de la Salle* in Louisiana and Texas, 1937. Honorary doctor of Oxford University, St. Andrew's (Scotland), Durham (England). For twelve years co-editor of the *Revue Anglo-Américaine*. Officer of the Legion of Honor. Live in Paris, with a country home at Saint-Haon le Châtel, Loire."

* * *

Several of Professor Cazamian's books were originally written in English, of which he is a master; others have been translated from the French. He is working at present on Part II of *The Development of English Humor*. Among his French works still untranslated are books on Kingsley, on Great Britain and the First World War, and on the English social novel and English romantic poetry.

PRINCIPAL WORKS: Modern England (translated) 1911; Carlyle (translated) 1914; Three Studies in Criticism, 1924; A History of English Literature (with É. Legouis) 1927; The Aims and Methods of Higher Literary Studies, 1929; Criticism in the Making, 1929; The Development of English Humor, Part I, 1930; Humor in *Hamlet*, 1937; Essais en Deux Langues [Essays in Two Languages] 1938.

ABOUT: Cazamian, L. F. Essais en Deux Langues (bibliography).

CECIL, Lord EDWARD CHRISTIAN DAVID (April 9, 1902-), English biographer, usually known as Lord David Cecil, is the younger son of the Fourth Marquess of Salisbury (James E. H. Gascoyne-Cecil), who was formerly Lord Privy Seal. His mother was Lady Cicely Alice Gore, daughter of the Fifth Earl of Arran. He was educated at Wadham College,

Oxford, where he was a Fellow. In 1932 he was married to Rachel MacCarthy, daughter of the critic and editor, Desmond MacCarthy, and they have one son. They have a London house, but their usual residence is at Fordinbridge, Hampshire. Lord David is very young in appearance, dark, slim, and poetic looking. Though he actually writes very little verse, he has always been deeply interested in poetry, and is a leading authority on Cowper. In 1940, also, he edited the *Oxford Book of Christian Verse*. He is also well informed on painting, and has been a trustee of the National Portrait Gallery since 1937.

Besides his biographies, he edited the *Anthology of Modern Biography* in 1936, and a selection of Cowper's verse and prose in 1933. He is in the tradition of English authors of noble birth; as a member of one of the oldest and most aristocratic of British families, he has had access to private papers of great value to an historical biographer. However, his chief interest has been, not in the greatest days of the Cecils (the Tudor era), but in the eighteenth and nineteenth centuries, and all of his biographical works have dealt with figures of this period. Arnold Whitridge called him "astute and lively," and said: "He does not write at the top of his voice, but he is never obvious and he is never dull." He is an extremely conscientious biographer, who puts no imagined speeches in his subjects' mouths, and is willing to sacrifice drama to authenticated fact.

Since he has apparently never written the life of anyone with whom he was not personally sympathetic, there is a warmth in his books missing from those of the biting and iconoclastic "new" biographers. Most of his work has dealt with literary personages—though not all of it: his life of Lord Melbourne in the days when he was young William Lamb and married to the appealing and appalling Caroline, is probably the best book yet written on its subject—and he has some standing as a literary critic. His biographical and critical articles appear frequently in the English reviews. His best books to date are undoubtedly the life of Melbourne and *The Stricken Deer* (not the shorter life of Cowper, which is an English Association pamphlet). He has much of Cowper's own sensitivity to beauty and of his intense religious feeling, though without the morbidity which marked the poet's religiosity.

PRINCIPAL WORKS: Life of Cowper (in America: The Stricken Deer: The Life of Cowper) 1929; William Cowper, 1932; Sir Walter Scott, 1933; Essays in Revaluation (in America: Early Victorian Novelists) 1934; Jane Austin, 1935; Leisure of an Egyptian Official, 1938; The Young Melbourne, 1939; The Oxford Book of Christian Verse (ed.) 1940; Men of the R.A.F. (with W. Rothenstein) 1942.

ABOUT: Fortnightly Review March 1940; Saturday Review of Literature May 18, 1935.

"CELINE, LOUIS FERDINAND." See DESTOUCHES, L. F.

CENDRARS, BLAISE (September 1, 1887-   ), French novelist and poet, writes: "I was born in Paris, of a Swiss father and a Scottish mother. From my earliest childhood I traveled, in Egypt, Switzerland, Italy, Germany, England. At fifteen I left my family to go to live in China, and left school. I did business and traveled widely in China, Mongolia, Siberia, Persia, the Caucasus, Russia. In 1907 I returned to Paris, where I secured my bachelor's degree and enrolled in the School of Medicine of the University. But, seized again by the demon of travel, I returned to Russia, and from there to Canada and the United States.

"It was in New York that I wrote my first poem, hence my gratitude to and tenderness for New York. In 1911 I returned to Paris from San Francisco, going by Panama to visit the canal, then in construction. The war surprised me in Paris, where I was on the way to making a name for myself as a poet. I lost my right arm in 1915, on September 29th, in Champagne.

"Meanwhile I had married. I am the father of two sons, one of whom is now in a bank and the other an aviator.

"After the war, I was an editor in Paris, a motion picture director in London and Rome, I have been in business and in industry, produced films, written scenarios, written a ballet for the Swedish Ballets of Rolf de Maré, been a journalistic, an art critic, and I published my first novel, *Sutter's Gold* [*L'Or*] in 1924, just as I was leaving for Brazil. Since then I have never stopped traveling and writing books. I have lived in Brazil, Argentina, Chile, Paraguay, I have traveled throughout Africa; I live in Paris, I have a house in Biarritz, another in the Isle-de-France, I fly often, I love autoing, I have returned many times to the United States, I have visited Hollywood—and in September 1939 [written before the outbreak of war—ED.] I am leaving to tour the world in a sailboat.

"Meanwhile I was divorced. I am not yet a grandfather.

"I do not like politics. I love to loaf, as the list of my works indicates. [M. Cendrars has published some 25 volumes, hence this remark is ironic.] I speak many languages, I have made several translations [from the English, German, and Portuguese], and my books have been translated into fifteen or twenty different languages. Life is my only wealth and I spend it, for I am a spendthrift."

* * *

M. Cendrars has a personality as colorful as his life, and he has put both in his books. *Sutter's Gold*, his best known work in English, was much criticized for inaccuracy by people who forgot it was a novel, not a history. In a sense it, like Cendrars' other novels, is self-revelatory and hence autobiographical, for, as he says, "one can relate no other life than one's own." John Dos Passos called him "an intellectual vagabond, . . . a kind of medicine man trying to evoke the things that are our cruel and avenging gods" (the machinery of modern life, with which he is at war even as he celebrates it).

In 1942 Cendrars was reported to be living in the "Free" Zone, in the South of France.

WORKS AVAILABLE IN ENGLISH: Sutter's Gold, 1926; African Saga, 1927; Little Black Stories for Little White Children, 1929; Panama: or The Adventures of My Seven Uncles, 1931.

ABOUT: Lepage, A. Blaise Cendrars (in French); Putnam, S. The European Caravan; Vox, M. Diagnostic; Saturday Review of Literature October 16, 1926.

CESTRE, CHARLES (May 9, 1871-), French university professor and writer, was born at Tonnerre, Burgundy, and was educated at the Sor

bonne, Paris. He also spent two years as a graduate student at Harvard University (1896-98), receiving his M.A. in 1897, and was an instructor there. Other posts at French universities included a period as Maître de Conférences at the University of Lyons; a professorship at the University of Bordeaux; and his most recent position as Professor of American Literature and Civilization at the University of Paris. Professor Cestre has been exchange professor at Harvard, Bryn Mawr, and the Universities of California, Georgia, Illinois, Michigan, and Wisconsin.

Les États Unis (1928) a big picture-book published by Larousse, with 593 illustrations, and with text by Cestre, and *Initiation à la Vie aux États-Unis*, which he wrote in 1931 in collaboration with Comtesse M. de Bryas, have interpreted America to Frenchmen; in 1931 Professor Cestre assisted in the compilation of the American Library Association list, *French Books for American Libraries*.

Other books by Cestre on American life include *L'Usine et L'Habitation Ouvrière aux États-Unis* (1920) and *Production Industrielle et Justice Sociale aux-États-Unis*, published the same year. In 1925 Professor Cestre gave some public lectures at Bryn Mawr, collected in the volume *An Introduction to Edwin Arlington Robinson* (1929). His first book was *La Révolution Française et Les Poètes Anglais* (1789-1809), published in 1906, and in 1912 he wrote *Bernard Shaw et Son Œuvre*. *John Thelwall: A Pioneer of Democracy and Social Reform in England*, a monograph published in 1906, included in the appendix three hitherto unpublished letters by William Godwin, the originals of which were in Cestre's possession. He has translated the American novelist Robert Herrick's *The World's Decision* as *La Decision Mondiale* (1917).

In 1937 Cestre began editing *Études Anglaises*, a new bi-monthly published in Paris, where he makes his home in the rue de Regard, in the sixth arrondissement. During the First World War he published *L'Angleterre et La Guerre* (1915). Cestre's most recent contribution to Franco-American solidarity was an interesting study of Nathaniel Hawthorne issued in 1934. He holds the degrees of D.Litt. and LL.D.

PRINCIPAL WORK: (originally written in English): John Thelwall: A Pioneer of Democracy and Social Reform in England, 1906; French, English, and European Democracy: 1215-1915, 1918; The Ideals of France, 1922; An Introduction to Edwin Arlington Robinson, 1929; Hawthorne, 1934.

ABOUT: International Who's Who.

CHAMBERLAIN, JOHN RENSSELAER (October 28, 1903-), American critic, was born in New Haven, Conn., the son of Robert Rensselaer Chamberlain and Emily (Davis) Chamberlain. He was educated at Yale (Ph.B. 1925), where he was on the staff of the *Lit*, ran a column in the *Daily News*, and was chairman of the *Record*. On leaving college he

became an advertising copy writer for a year, then got a job on the New York *Times,* at first as a reporter in Washington. In 1928 he returned to New York as assistant editor of the *Times Book Review*, in which position he remained until 1933, building up a reputation as one of the most competent of the younger critics. A year as associate editor of the *Saturday Review of Literature* followed, and then he went back to the *Times*, this time as writer of a daily book column. For three years he reviewed a book a day, writing directly on the typewriter, often just ahead of the deadline. It is no wonder that he says he had no time during this period to do any reading for his own pleasure.

In 1936 he became an editor of *Fortune*; and at the same time did book reviews for *Scribner's Magazine*, until 1938, when he changed to *Harper's*, where he succeeded Harry Hansen. He has lectured at the Columbia School of Journalism, the New School for Social Research, and the Columbia Summer School. In 1942 he became editor of Freedom House. In between times he has managed to write four books, contribute to the anthology, *The Critique of Humanism* (1930), and write frequent articles for the magazines. He also contrives to find leisure to play at least one set of tennis every day in season.

In 1926 he married Margaret Sterling, and they live in Cheshire, Conn. Clifton Fadiman has described him with his "shy, deprecative smile . . . and tentative manner of speaking, both tending to obscure the fact that his mind has sharpness and unbluff-ability." His memory is phenomenal, his mind "naturally orderly," and he has a real passion for books. He says he is "a free-lance radical who refuses to be bound." Van Wyck Brooks and Edmund Wilson are his favorites among contemporary American critics, Archibald MacLeish among contemporary poets; but for his own choice he reads by preference the eighteenth century English writers, chiefly Gibbon and Sterne.

Chamberlain is remarkably young-looking, with wavy dark hair and a still boyish face. Fadiman called him "still profoundly educatable," a rare characteristic for a critic but one that is obvious in his writing. He himself deprecates his work as a reviewer, saying that it leads to "mental fragmentation" and that the exigencies of journalism make it impossible to do any real critical appraising. This, however, is actually true only of the daily reviewing he did for three years; in his magazine departments his work has been solid and thoughtful. His style has been described as "easy, but not trivial, allusive but not pedantic." His books for the most part have reflected his social and political opinions rather than his literary views.

PRINCIPAL WORKS: Farewell to Reform, 1932; Challenge to the New Deal, 1934; After the Genteel Tradition, 1937; Books That Changed Our Minds (ed.) 1939; The American Stakes, 1940.

ABOUT: Publishers' Weekly January 18, 1936; Saturday Review of Literature March 7, 1936; Time April 1, 1940.

CHAMBERLIN, WILLIAM HENRY

(February 17, 1897-), American political writer, was born in Brooklyn, N.Y., the son  of Ernest V. Chamberlin and May E. (McClintock) Chamberlin. He was reared in Philadelphia and educated at the Penn Charter School and Haverford College (B.A. 1917). For a year after leaving college he was assistant magazine editor of the Philadelphia Press. In 1919 he became assistant to the late Heywood Broun, then

book editor of the New York Tribune, and remained there for three years. He was at this time an enthusiastic radical, and in 1922, much to his delight, he was made correspondent of the Christian Science Monitor in Russia. Later he became correspondent also of the Manchester Guardian. At this time James E. Abbe described his work as being "for the reading public which demands facts, and is not particular if they do not happen to be entertainingly strung together."

From being an extreme sympathizer with the Soviet régime, Chamberlin during his twelve years in the U.S.S.R. became one of its bitterest enemies. Nearly every one of his books has been an unqualified attack on the Soviet system and on Communism and collectivism in general. In 1935 the Monitor transferred him to the Far East, where he remained until 1939, when he was again transferred to France. He returned to the United States after the Nazi occupation of France.

In 1920 Mr. Chamberlin married Sonya Trosten, and they have one daughter. He is stocky, inclined to plumpness, with light brown hair, gray eyes, and a still youthful face. Broun called him "an incurably romantic Utopian," and much of his hatred of the Soviets seems indeed to be a violent reaction arising from disillusionment, and growing from emotional expectations which were rudely destroyed by reality. His writing, which Abbe once called dully factual, has in his books been polemic and excited, and even those who share his viewpoint have sometimes felt that he was swung too strenuously to the opposite extreme from that of his early beliefs.

He remains, however, a very competent reporter, careful in his documentation where his feelings are not involved, and cautious in his pronouncements. This is particularly evident in his book on Japan, which, brought up to date after later developments, is a valuable source and reference work. He also contributes frequently to the serious reviews on foreign political topics. He is a member of the Academy of Political and Social Science and of Phi Beta Kappa, the scholars' fraternity. His early interest in literature did not survive his career as a foreign correspondent, and for many years he has done no writing except as a commentator on and critic of political and economic conditions.

PRINCIPAL WORKS: Soviet Russia, 1930; The Soviet Planned Economic Order, 1931; Russia's Iron Age, 1934; The Russian Revolution: 1917-21, 1935; Collectivism—A False Utopia, 1937; Japan Over Asia, 1937 (revised 1939); Japan in China,

1940; Confessions of an Individualist, 1940; The World's Iron Age, 1941.

ABOUT: Chamberlin, W. H. Confessions of an Individualist; Christian Science Monitor Magazine September 30, 1939; Nation October 16, 1935, January 1, 1936; New Outlook December 1933.

CHAMBERS, CHARLES HADDON
(April 22, 1860-March 27, 1921), Australian playwright, journalist, and stockrider, was

born at Stanmore, Sydney, New South Wales, the son of John Ritchie Chambers, a former Ulster man who had joined the N.S.W. Civil Service, and Frances (Kellett) Chambers of Waterford, Ireland. He was educated privately and at the Merrickville and Fort Street public schools in Sydney; and at the age of fifteen entered the (N.S.W.) Civil Service. Two years later he gave up this indoor clerical post to become a stockrider in the Bush.

In addition to his fondness for a decidedly active life, including sports, he had a real fancy for literary experimentation. At the age of twenty-two he went to London to make a serious try at journalism and story-telling. He soon discovered that the drama was his best medium, and after two rather unimpressive attempts he wrote, while he was still well under thirty, a semi-melodramatic comedy called *Captain Swift*. Beerbohm Tree produced it at the Haymarket Theatre in the fall of 1888, and it was many times revived. In 1890 *The Idler* was staged in New York, and in the following year at the St. James in London. Chambers' best comedy was *The Tyranny of Tears,* which Charles Wyndham, then in his last season as a producer, brought through to a rousing finish. It was a "triumph of the commonplace" in four acts.

During the World War Chambers was employed in British propaganda work, and made several journeys to the United States. He died of a stroke in London, at the age of sixty-one, following his return from a trip to France.

He wrote half a dozen other plays in addition to several collaborations with B. C. Stephenson and Comyns Carr. But it is his early plays (and especially "so shrewdly and finely comic a study as *The Tyranny of Tears*") that have earned him a place among the playwrights who enlivened the theatre at the turn of the century.

PRINCIPAL WORKS (dates of publication): Captain Swift, 1902; The Idler, 1902; Tyranny of Tears, 1902; The Saving Grace, 1919; Passers-by, 1920.

ABOUT: Chambers, C. H. The Tyranny of Tears (see Introduction); Australian Biographical Dictionary; Times (London) March 29, 1921.

*CHAMBERS, Sir EDMUND KERCHEVER (March 16, 1866-), British essayist, critic, and educator, was born in Berkshire, the eldest son of the Rev. William Chambers, once fellow and tutor of Worcester College, Oxford, and Anna Heathcote Arnold. He was sent to Marlborough, and went up to Corpus Christi College, Oxford, the very week in which Matthew Arnold paid the University his last visit. In 1892 he entered the Education Department, and there became eventually the Second Secretary of the Board. In 1893 he was married to Nora Bowman, whose father, John Davison Bowman, was associated with the Exchequer and Audit Office. Two years later he edited a book of *English Pastorals* and followed this with *Donne's Poems* and *Vaughan's Poems.* Shortly before the appearance of his *Red Letter Shakespeare* (1904-08) came his two-volume book on the medieval stage. In 1932 he selected the material for the *Oxford Book of Sixteenth Century Verse,* basing his choice on the "absolute poetry" (rather than the historical-interest) content. He admits, however, that he showed a "decent tenderness" to beginners and made concessions to "the glamour of a famous name" in order to include a few pieces by Henry the Eighth and Queen Elizabeth. He was made Companion of the Bath in 1912, and knighted (K. B. E.) in 1925.

All of Chambers' research has been done by methods which he himself has been obliged to work out. Oxford, he says, was his "most kindly nurse" but provided him with no blueprints for building a reputation as one of the ablest of Shakespearean authorities. Unlike J. M. Robertson, whose energetic skepticism is as destructive as it is constructive, Chambers' approach is decidedly conservative. "I come to accept Shakespeare," he has said, "not to praise him." He admits that he belongs to those "many impenitent Victorians who still find in that bygone verse the cool refreshment which it breathed upon its first readers."

PRINCIPAL WORKS: The Medieval Stage, 1903; The Elizabethan Stage, 1923; Shakespeare: A Survey, 1925; Arthur of Britain, 1927; William Shakespeare, 1930; Sir Henry Lee, 1936; Samuel Taylor Coleridge, 1938. *Edited*—English Pastorals, 1895; Donne's Poems, 1896; Vaughan's Poems, 1896;

Red Letter Shakespeare, 1904-08; Aurelian Towns-hend's Poems, 1911; The Oxford Book of Six-teenth Century Verse, 1932.

ABOUT: Chambers, E. K. The Medieval Stage (see Preface); Kelly's Handbook, 1936; Modern Language Review January 1926; Nineteenth Century February 1927.

CHAMBERS, ROBERT WILLIAM
(May 26, 1865-December 16, 1933), Ameri-can novelist and short-story writer, was born

in Brooklyn, N.Y. the son of William Chambers and Caro-line (Broughton) Chambers. He stud-ied painting at the Art Students' League in New York, where Charles Dana Gibson was a member of his class, and in 1886 proceeded to Paris for further training at the École des Beaux Arts and the Académie Julien. The Salon ac-cepted his paintings when Chambers was only twenty-four. Returning to New York in 1893, he did illustrating for Life, Truth, and Vogue. His first book, In the Quarter, a melodramatic story of the student life he had known in Paris, might yield a libretto for another La Bohême. The King in Yel-low, a collection of short stories, attained a kind of sinister celebrity; the reissue in 1938 showed it somewhat dated although one tale, "The Demoiselle D'Ys," has a haunting, poetic eeriness. The Maker of Moons was an imaginative horror story. Chambers soon dropped this style to write four romances centering around the Franco-Prussian War: Lorraine, Ashes of Empire (in which a group of dashing young Americans assist the Empress Eugénie to escape, hat and all, from Paris), The Red Republic, and The Maids of Paradise. These exhibited his ability to handle crowds, invent exciting incident, and exercise his painter's dexterity in painting vivid landscapes.

Continuing his historical-novel phase, Chambers wrote a series about Revolution-ary New York State, Sir William Johnson, Walter Butler, and Indian conspiracies, which still exercise their spell over romantic youth. These were Cardigan, The Maid at Arms, The Hidden Children, and The Little Red Foot. Next came the society problem-novels, concerned largely with love and the obstacles to marriage. The Fighting Chance and The Danger Mark considered the dan-gers of alcoholic tastes in, respectively, a man and girl, while The Younger Set and

The Firing Line took up the question of divorce. In spite of the vogue of the Cham-bers heroine at the time, she was markedly less convincing than his men. His dramatic instinct found vent in The Witch of Ellan-gowan, a vehicle for Ada Rehan, and Iole, a musical comedy based on a novel which was supposed to lampoon Elbert Hubbard of the Roycrofters. The real model was Aristide Bruant, a Parisian diseur (for Bruant see Toulouse-Lautrec, by Gerstle Mack). Mr. Keen, of The Tracer of Lost Persons, is a sentimental detective.

In his first twenty years as a popular writer Chambers produced forty-five vol-umes, "veering in accordance with the breeze of popular demand." The period of 1915-1919 had its quota of war novels. In 1924 he returned to historical fiction, with the same easy fluency but to small critical ac-claim, although magazines continued to pay high prices for his serials. Chambers was able to gratify his tastes for Chinese and Japanese antiques, old china and furniture, armor, and the restoration of his early nine-teenth-century home in the Adirondack foot-hills, called Broadalbin. At a New York office, whose address was unknown even to his family, he wrote from ten to six. Fishing and hunting were his relaxations. The novelist was a well set-up man, with square shoulders and chin and a gray mous-tache. His manner was cordial and genial. The National Institute of Arts and Letters numbered Chambers among its members. On July 12, 1898, he married Elsa Vaughn Moller. A son, Robert Husted Chambers, attained some success as a writer.

PRINCIPAL WORKS: In the Quarter, 1893; The King in Yellow, 1893; The Red Republic, 1894; The Maker of Moons, 1895; Lorraine, 1896; The Mystery of Choice, 1897; Ashes of Empire, 1897; Outsiders, 1899; Cardigan, 1901; The Maid-at-Arms, 1902; The Maids of Paradise, 1903; Iole, 1905; The Fighting Chance, 1906; The Tracer of Lost Persons, 1906; The Tree of Heaven, 1907; The Firing Line, 1908; The Danger Mark, 1909; Special Messenger, 1909; Ailsa Paige, 1910; The Common Law, 1913; The Hidden Children, 1914; The Dark Star, 1915; The Restless Sex, 1917; The Crimson Tide, 1919; The Little Red Foot, 1921; Eris, 1923; The Man They Hanged, 1925; Sun Hawk, 1928; Rogue's Moon, 1928; The Happy Parrot, 1929; The Rake and the Hussy, 1930; Painted Minx, 1930; War Paint and Rouge, 1931; The Whistling Cat, 1932; Whatever Love Is, 1933; Secret Service Operator, 1934; Young Man's Girl, 1934; Love and the Lieutenant, 1935; The Gold Chase, 1935; Beating Wings, 1936; The Fifth Horseman, 1937; Marie Halkett, 1937; Smoke of Battle, 1938.

ABOUT: Baldwin, C. C. The Men Who Make Our Novels; Chambers, R. W. The King in Yellow (see Foreword by R. Hughes to 1938 ed.); Cooper, F. T. Some American Story Tellers; Honee, C.

A Sherlock Holmes Birthday; Overton, G. Authors of the Day; Cosmopolitan April 1911; Forum May 1918; New Republic November 30, 1918; New York Times December 17, 1933.

CHAMSON, ANDRÉ (June 6, 1900-), French novelist and essayist, writes: "André Chamson was born at Nîmes, in the south

of France. He is descended from a family of peasant origin from the mountains of Cevennes. It was in this rough country, which Stevenson has described in *Travels With a Donkey,* that André Chamson passed his childhood. Memories of the wars which the Camisards waged for freedom of conscience, a severe Protestant training, and mountain climbing with the little peasants were his first education.

"A student at the primary school in Vigan, then at the *lycée* at Ales, and finally at the *lycée* at Montpellier, where he secured his degree, Chamson then went to Paris to take a course in history at the Sorbonne. He entered the École des Chartes and on graduation presented a thesis on the historical geography of his native region.

"When hardly out of the university, Chamson published his first book, *Roux the Bandit,* in 1926. Since that date, he has brought out a new volume almost every year. His work is above all the work of a novelist. His first novels—*Roux the Bandit, The Road, The Crime of the Just, Histoires de Tabusse*—were consecrated to the life of the mountaineers of the Cevennes. With *Héritages,* his work plunged into a more complex world. *Barren Harvest* was consecrated to the relations of France and Germany after the victory of Hitler. With *La Galère,* it is the French political life of these latest years and, particularly, the riotous demonstration of February 6, 1939, which serves as the author's theme.

"Besides his work as novelist, Chamson has pursued the work of an essayist, attracted by the philosophy of history and by contemporary politics: *L'Homme Contre l'Histoire, La Révolution de Dix-Neuf, Tyrol, Rien qu'un Témoignage,* written on the return from a trip to Madrid in 1937, during the civil war.

"Chamson has been closely associated with French political life. As chief assistant in the cabinet of Daladier during the upheaval of February 6, he fought, by pen and word

of mouth, against the attempts which were made to install a Fascist régime in France. For three years he edited the weekly *Vendredi* with Jean Guéhenno and Andrée Viollis. His position is that of an advanced democrat.

"Parallel to his literary work and his political activities, Chamson has pursued the scientific career for which he was prepared at the École des Chartes. He has been assistant curator of the National Museum at the Palace of Versailles, on which he published a book in 1937.

"Chamson is married, the father of a little daughter, Frédérique. He loves mountain-climbing and skiing. He has remained faithful to his native land, whose dialect he speaks, and to which he returns to spend his holidays. He would like above all to be able to devote his life more and more to novel-writing."

* * *

André Chamson's simple and austere works have been associated by many critics with his native region of the Cevennes. Ernest Boyd says: "Readers in this country will note in Chamson's novels a quality which is not usual in French literature, although it would not be out of place in some of the Wessex stories of Thomas Hardy.... Chamson is a Cevenole Protestant, with all the rugged austerity, the fundamental respect for human rights, which that breed of Huguenots acquired throughout years of struggle against political oppression and against a countryside as stern and harsh as Calvinism itself." André Rousseaux, the distinguished French critic, after elaborating on the characteristics of the Cevennes region, states that Chamson is at his best in his regional novels, "not only because he depicts with bold strokes the landscape which since childhood has become one with his sensibility, but because that unique, particularly strong character which typifies this country—revolt and heresy—leaves its accent on his literary work." Chamson is the novelist of that revolt and heresy which permeate the history of the Cevennes.

Chamson's present whereabouts, since the writing of the autobiographical sketch above, is unknown to the editors of this volume, but it is unlikely that the Nazis, or the men of Vichy, can be favorably disposed toward one who persistently dared to challenge the reactionary Nationalists, as in these words spoken at a Writers' Congress in Paris in the summer of 1935:

"I want my voice to carry over to the ranks of our enemy because I am French since France herself was formed: I am their enemy because I spring from a long line which has spoken first the old romance tongue before the French tongue, because I am bound to this land by its cemeteries and its furrows . . . because I tried to sing, first of any, this long line of peasants who only knew how to speak in a low voice, following the rhythms and visions of my country."

When last heard of, Chamson was acting as a liaison officer with the French army at the front.

WORKS AVAILABLE IN ENGLISH: The Road, 1929; Roux the Bandit, 1929; The Crime of the Just, 1930; The Mountain Tavern, 1933; Barren Harvest, 1935.

ABOUT: Chamson, A. The Road (see Foreword by E. Boyd); Lefèvre, F. Une Heure Avec; Lehmann, J. New Writing in Europe; Rousseaux, A. Âmes at Visages du Vingtième Siècle; Annales Politiques et Littéraires December 1, 1927, May 15, 1932, December 2, 1932, February 17, 1933, May 25, 1939; Bookman June 1930; L'Europe Nouvelle January 19, 1935; Revue des Deux Mondes February 15, 1935.

CHANNING, EDWARD (June 15, 1856-January 7, 1931), American historian, winner of the Pulitzer Prize, was born in Dorchester, Mass., one of  the five children of William Ellery Channing "the younger," friend of Hawthorne and Emerson, who, according to Thoreau, was "all genius and no talent," and Ellen Kilshaw (Fuller) Channing, a sister of Margaret Fuller. His mother died when 'the boy was three; he seldom saw his father, who was an inveterate wanderer; and he was sent to live with his grandfather, who changed his first-given name of Henry to Edward Perkins Channing. Channing dropped his middle name after leaving college.

Young Channing attended Eayres School, Boston, and graduated from Harvard College in 1878 with a B.A. degree. His grandfather intended him for the law, but when Edward received a mark of 100 on a theme from Henry Adams, "the greatest teacher I ever encountered," he decided to teach history.

"Two years after graduation I received my Doctorate in History from Harvard University," he once wrote the Secretary of his Harvard class, "and at once sailed for Europe. . . . After nine months I sailed for

home, having gained a new outlook on the world. For a couple of years I cooled my heels at the outer doors of university presidents, but finally broke into the Harvard circle, owing to the ill-health of one of the teachers of American history." Albert Bushnell Hart had been given preference because he had a German Ph.D., but Channing eventually gained the McLean Professorship of Ancient and Modern History, which he held until retirement. He was elected at twenty-eight to the Massachusetts Historical Society for his first book, *Town and County Government in the English Colonies of North America* (1884). "In 1896 I took my family to England for nine months and wrote a high-school text book, entitled *A Students' History of the United States,* which took me four months to write and . . . made it possible for me to devote a large portion of [a] quarter of a century to the production of *A History of the United States.*" This *magnum opus,* beginning with 1000 A.D. and concluding with the Civil War, was dictated, the composition of the previous one-volume history having left Channing with a bad case of writer's cramp.

The *History* is more a valuable compilation from original sources than a work of art. Its final volume on the Civil War, was awarded the 1926 Pulitzer Prize. As Samuel Eliot Morison has said, Channing had no knack of vivid narrative or description, and dictation resulted in a rather formless and slipshod style.

Channing married Alice Thacher of West Newton, Mass., in 1886, and they had two daughters. A solitary and astigmatic childhood left him with a shy, gruff, and abrupt exterior, but he was much devoted to his friends even though a terror to undergraduates, whom he later grew to like. "Apart from travel, his only recreation appeared to be in boats, and he was an excellent sailor, threading the mazes and the shoals of Cape Cod without touching keel or centerboard," according to A. Lawrence Lowell. He died in his seventy-fifth year of a cerebral hemorrhage.

PRINCIPAL WORKS: Town and County Government in the English Colonies of North America, 1884; The Narragansett Planters, 1886; The United States of America: 1765-1865, 1895; A Students' History of the United States, 1897; A History of the United States, 1905-25; The Jeffersonian System, 1906.

ABOUT: American Academy of Arts and Letters Publications 1932; Kraus, M. A History of American History; Current History March 1931; Massachusetts Historical Society Proceedings May 1931; Mississippi Valley Historical Review 1931.

*CHAPMAN, FRANK MICHLER (June 12, 1864-), American ornithologist, was born in Englewood, N.J., the son of a Union soldier, Lebbeus

Chapman, and Mary A. (Parkhurst) Chapman. His boyhood was spent in Englewood, where he put in much time aloft in his father's fruit trees, attended Englewood Academy, and became a clerk in the city collection department of the American Exchange National Bank in New York City across the Hudson. When a prize was offered for the best paper tracing migratory movements of birds in various sections of the country, young Chapman rose even earlier in New Jersey. His lunch hours were spent on the corner of Fourteenth Street recording forty different species of native birds on the headgear of women shoppers. After resigning from the bank in 1886 for volunteer work on the top floor of the American Museum of Natural History, he was made associate curator of Ornithology and Mammalogy in 1888, becoming Curator of Ornithology in 1908, a position he still holds. "Out of a life-long devotion to birds he has created on the corner of 81st Street and Central Park West in New York City what has been called the ornithological center of the universe," wrote a colleague recently in *Natural History*, the museum's periodical. Dr. Chapman's *Handbook of the Birds of Eastern North America* is a familiar and prized possession of many home libraries as well as public institutions.

Presenting him with the Roosevelt Medal for Distinguished Service in 1928, Hermann Hagedorn called his "a name beloved wherever in America, in school or home, the birds are permitted to come down from the treetops to be the companions of men." He is a writer and lecturer "of persuasive charm," and has led zoölogical explorations in temperate and tropical America since 1887; was elected president of the Linnaean Society of New York in 1897; and was vice-president of the Explorers' Club from 1910 to 1918. Beginners in bird-study, professional ornithologists, artists, authors, and explorers alike turn to Chapman for aid. His belief is that "if our studies of birds have no bearing on the progress and welfare of mankind they are futile." While he has not elected to work in *belles-lettres*, he is "susceptible

to a certain living quality in the facts." Dr. Chapman married Fannie Bates Embury in 1898; their one son bears his father's name. He is a baldish, gray-haired, clear-eyed gentleman with a neatly-trimmed moustache.

PRINCIPAL WORKS: Handbook of Birds of Eastern North America, 1895; Bird-Life: A Guide to the Study of Our Common Birds, 1897; Bird Studies With a Camera, 1900; A Color Key to North American Birds, 1903; The Economic Value of Birds to the State, 1903; The Warblers of North America, 1907; Camps and Cruises of an Ornithologist, 1908; The Travels of Birds, 1916; The Distribution of Bird-Life in Colombia, 1917; Our Winter Birds, 1918; What Bird Is That? 1920; My Tropical Air Castle, 1929; Autobiography of a Bird Lover, 1933.

ABOUT: Chapman, F. M. Autobiography of a Bird Lover; Kunitz, S. J. & Haycraft H. (eds.) The Junior Book of Authors; Tracy, H. C. American Naturists; Natural History January 1940.

CHAPMAN, JOHN JAY (March 2, 1862-November 4, 1933), American man of letters, was born in New York City, the son of

Henry Grafton Chapman and Eleanor (Jay) Chapman. His father was president of the New York Stock Exchange, but lost money during the panic of the 1870's. Young Chapman tutored at Harvard to help pay his expenses; graduated in

1884; traveled abroad after graduation, visiting an aunt in Russia; and was admitted to the bar in 1888, practicing for ten years. Chapman married Minna Timmins, the half-Italian niece of the Brimmer family of Boston, under melodramatic circumstances. After beating up a man who, he believed, had trifled with Miss Timmins' affections, Chapman went to his dreary furnished room, thrust his left hand deep into a glowing coal fire, then walked to the Massachusetts General Hospital to have it amputated. The marriage to Miss Timmins took place in the summer of 1889. One of their sons was drowned in an Austrian river in August 1903; the other, Victor, the first American aviator to die in the First World War, came into posthumous fame when Chapman edited his letters.

Chapman practiced and hated law, and was passionately, if not always consistently, interested in politics in the last years of the nineteenth century. He was a member of the City Reform Club, founded by Theodore Roosevelt, from 1882; and was president of the Good Government Club, an anti-Tammany organization whose members were known as Goo-Goos. From March 1897 to 1901 he published *The Political Nursery,* which attacked Seth Low, the reformist mayor of New York; Theodore Roosevelt, who had thrown over Chapman's Independents for Boss Platt and the Republican nomination for governor of New York; and which assailed the policy of the United States in Cuba and the Philippine Islands, as well as denouncing the British in South Africa.

Chapman broke down in the middle of a speech in a small Pennsylvania town, spent a year in bed, and for nearly three years was under the delusion that he could not walk without crutches. For thirty years he led the life of a well-to-do squire at Barrytown-on-the-Hudson: his second wife, Elizabeth Chanler, married in 1898, was of a wealthy family. Much of his time was spent badgering Harvard authorities and magazine editors. In August 1914 Chapman went personally to Balfour, Haldane, and Sir Edward Grey, who received him courteously, asking them to announce the Allied aims to be non-aggressive. He rose at the Cosmopolitan Club, New York, in 1920 to denounce the speaker, Siegfried Sassoon, as showing fear and self-pity, and in 1925 became so violently anti-Catholic and anti-Semitic that he was sent abroad to avoid another breakdown. Death came at seventy-one, after an operation.

Edmund Wilson calls Chapman the best writer on literature of his generation, who "made the Babbitts and the Mores and the Brownells look like provincial schoolmasters." His *Emerson* of 1898 is like an extension of Emerson, a recreation of the philosopher for a new generation. Chapman's style is "an instrument of perfect felicity, economy, limpidity, precision and point," and he was the best letter-writer of his time. (He called President Eliot of Harvard "the very highest type of a most limited and inspiring pork-chopism.") Chapman's verse is "only effective when it approximates the qualities of his prose." Fond of writing plays about kings (his dramas were almost purely literary), he had something of a kingly presence himself, with a Jove-like beard and a brooding expression.

PRINCIPAL WORKS: Emerson and Other Essays, 1898; Causes and Consequences, 1898; Learning and Other Essays, 1911; William Lloyd Garrison, 1913; Greek Genius, 1915; A Glance Toward Shakespeare, 1922; Notes on Religion, 1922; Letters and Religion, 1924; Dante, 1927. *Poems:* Homeric Scenes,

1914. *Plays:* The Maid's Forgiveness, 1908; A Sausage From Bologna, 1909; Benedict Arnold: A Play for a Greek Theatre, 1909.

ABOUT: Chapman, J. J. Memories and Milestones; Howe, M. A. D. W. John Jay Chapman and His Letters; Sherman, S. P. Shaping Men and Women; Wilson E. The Triple Thinkers; Atlantic Monthly May 1934; New York Times November 5, 1933; Publishers' Weekly November 25, 1933.

CHAPMAN, JOHN STANTON HIGHAM. See CHAPMAN, M.

CHAPMAN, MARISTAN, is the pen-name of a husband and wife, John Stanton Higham Chapman (May 21, 1891-), and Mary Hamilton (Ilsley) Chapman (September 10, 1895-), under which they have written in collaboration novels, stories for young people, and a biography.

Mr. Chapman was born in London, the son of Joseph John and Alice Mary (Williams) Chapman, and from 1910 to the World War was an aeronautical engineer. In the war he served with the British Air Service and then was transferred to the United States Signal Corps. In London he met and married Miss Ilsley, and went with her to America in 1917, becoming naturalized in 1926. His career as a writer dates from 1928. The Chapmans lived for some time in Sewanee, Tenn., and Jacksonville, Fla., but live now in Pacific Palisades, near Los Angeles, Calif.

Mrs. Chapman was born in Chattanooga, Tenn., the daughter of the Rev. John Henry Ilsley and Mary (Hamilton) Ilsley. Her childhood was spent in her father's mountain parishes, and she grew up with an intimate knowledge of the lives of the Appalachian mountaineers. She was educated at schools in Chattanooga and at the Kemper Hall Convent School, Kenosha, Wis. At the beginning of the war she went to Europe, studied at a secretarial school, and became secretary first to a member of Parliament and then in the British aircraft service. For several years after her marriage she and her husband roamed through the South in a housecar, and from these experiences grew their joint books. She had written secretly for years, but with no thought of publication.

So close is the collaboration between the Chapmans that it was a long time after their first novels appeared before the public knew that "Maristan Chapman" was not a single individual. Their books for adults are marked by deep sympathy for the mountain people of whom they treat; their children's books, which are mostly mystery-adventure stories, have been called "competent and thrilling." (May Lamberton Becker finds the "Glen Hazard" stories the best of their kind in recent years.)

The Chapmans are retiring and dislike the limelight. Mrs. Chapman has written of their work: "I have been haunted always by the Southern highlanders' need of a recorder. Driven to frenzy by outland interpretation, we at last took up the work of their defence. We try to get soundness and sureness into the simple stories of the mountain people as they are. . . . Our object is to show a class of people too long looked upon only *as* a class, to be live and knowing individuals; to make their eyes the eyes through which the outlander may see their world, and, thus seeing, experience an understanding kinship with them, and at the same time feel a sense of adventure for himself, in seeing an unexplored corner of life."

The only excursion of the Chapmans outside the field of fiction has been their detailed and interesting study of the life of the Duc de Morny, a statesman of the Second Empire in France.

PRINCIPAL WORKS: Happy Mountain, 1928; Homeplace, 1929; Imperial Brother: The Life of the Duc de Morny, 1931; The Weather Tree, 1932; Wild Cat Ridge, 1932; Timber Trail, 1933; Glen Hazard, 1933; Eagle Cliff, 1934; The Marsh Island Mystery, 1936; Rogues on Red Hill, 1937; The Girls of Glen Hazard, 1937; The Mystery of the Broken Key, 1938; The Clue of the Faded Dress, 1938; The Flood in Glen Hazard, 1939; Glen Hazard Cowboys, 1940; The Mill Creek Mystery, 1940; The Gulf Coast Treasure, 1941; The Mountain Mystery, 1941.

ABOUT: American Home July 1929.

CHARDONNE, JACQUES (1884-),
French novelist whose real name is Jacques Boutelleau, but who has always written un-

der and is generally known by his *nom de plume*, was born and reared at Barbezieux, Charente, and was graduated from its college. He is a lifelong friend of the novelist Henri Fauconnier, and when the two boys were only fourteen they established a "literary journal" which survived only one number, leaving debts to the printer which they satisfied by establishing a theatre and giving one performance! As a young man he moved to Paris and lived there throughout his active career. Subsequently he moved to La Frette (Seine et Oise), which is in the occupied area of France.

Only two of Chardonne's novels have been translated into English. The first of these, *Epithalamium*, won the Northcliffe Prize in 1922 for the best French novel of the year, and tied with René Maran's *Batouala* for the Goncourt Prize. The chief influences on his work have been those of his friend André Gide, and through Gide, of Montaigne; indeed his chief fault as a novelist is that he is too philosophical, and digresses frequently from his story to reflect on its moral. He himself says: "I write novels to express . . . a debate, a moral drama, a spiritual search." He is an admirable psychologist, with a deep interest in the inner lives of his characters rather than in their outer actions.

His style is quiet and impressionistic. Justin O'Brien remarked of him that "he hits the mark with every sentence, while subtly pretending to leave great gaps for the reader to fill in. . . . His restraint is admirably calculated." Someone has said that Chardonne is a writer to re-read rather than to read.

Although Chardonne has for many years been a recognized author with a considerable following, he took no part in public life and was not prominent in literary or social circles until the German occupation of France in 1940 when he became one of the leaders of the pro-Fascist group of French intellectuals, along with Drieu la Rochelle and Alfred Fabre-Luce. He is now alienated from most of his former friends, including Gide. "The spirit of France," he writes, "is in safe keeping."

WORKS AVAILABLE IN ENGLISH: Epithalamium, 1923; Eva: or, The Interrupted Diary, 1931.

ABOUT: Annales Politiques et Littéraires May 1, 1930, April 25, 1936, December 10, 1937.

*CHARNWOOD, GODFREY RATHBONE BENSON, 1st Baron (November 6, 1864-), English biographer and novelist,

is the fourth son of William Benson, J.P., of Langtons, Alresford, Hampshire, and Elizabeth, daughter of Thomas Smith of Colebrooke Park, Tonbridge, Kent. He was raised to the peerage in 1911. Lord Charnwood is best known to Americans

for his remarkable biographical study of Abraham Lincoln and an outstanding book on Theodore Roosevelt. He also enlists the attention of students of the detective novel for his sole contribution thereto, written as Godfrey Benson: the "modern" and readable *Tracks in the Snow*, first published in 1906; reissued in 1927 under the name of Charnwood.

Lord Charnwood's education began at Winchester, whence he proceeded to Balliol College, Oxford, the stronghold of Benjamin Jowett. He won a first class in Lit. Hum. (classics) in 1887 and remained awhile at Balliol as tutor. His political career was inaugurated by election to Parliament from the Liberal Woodstock Division, Oxford, in 1892. Lord Charnwood (then Godfrey Benson, M.P.) served in Parliament till 1895. He was mayor of Lichfield from 1909 to 1911; Deputy Lieutenant, Justice of the Peace and Chairman of Quarter Sessions, Staffordshire, and Alderman of Lichfield City. In 1897 he married Dorothea Mary Thorpe (author, as Lady Charnwood, of *Call Back Yesterday*, 1937); they have a son, born in 1901, and two daughters, and live in London.

The *American Historical Review* said of *Abraham Lincoln,* "Lord Charnwood has given us the most complete interpretation of Lincoln as yet produced, and he has presented it in such artistic form that it may well become classic." Another critic noted that the author's interest seemed to be chiefly attracted towards the military administration of the Civil War and the workings of conscription. *According to St. John,* a study of the Fourth Gospel, was characterized by a *New Republic* reviewer as "meandering urbanity enwrapped in reverence." Lord Charnwood has also written prefatory memoirs to works of Herbert Murray Burge and John Burnet.

PRINCIPAL WORKS: Tracks in the Snow (as G. R. Benson) 1906 (reissued 1927); Abraham Lincoln, 1916; According to St. John, 1926; **Theodore Roosevelt, 1928.**

CHARTERIS, LESLIE (May 12, 1907-), English crime-and-adventure story writer reports: "I was born in Singapore,

and learned Chinese and Malay from native servants before I could speak English. My parents dragged me three times around the world before I was twelve and then they decided it was time I went to school. This was a mistake, because by that time I had acquired a much

better education than any school had to offer. My mother's collection of my first manuscripts goes back no farther than a story written when I was seven. At ten I was writing and editing a one-man magazine to which my relatives had to subscribe under discreet blackmail. At eleven I first got into print with a poem. It was quite good, too. School was not conducive to literary efforts. I usually seemed to find myself running the school magazines and getting them suppressed on account of the heretical touches which I put into them. I also earned quite a steady amount of spending money with learned articles about music, a subject on which I am remarkably uninformed. At seventeen I sold my first fiction story. It is worth noting that my teachers of English had no great opinion of my aptitude for this subject.

"At eighteen, against my better judgment, I allowed myself to be sent to Cambridge University. At this time a life of crime appealed to me much more strongly. Since I considered myself much too clever to go in for any small-time stuff, I set out to acquire the best possible education in criminal technique by reading every book on criminology that I could lay my hands on. I also read vast quantities of crime fiction. This reading revived my own youthful enthusiasm for writing. It seemed pretty easy. Just to find out how easy it was I wrote a full-length crime novel. A publisher bought it and demanded more. Since then I have had no time to burgle any banks.

"At the end of my first year at Cambridge I announced to my parents that I was going to be a writer. My father, a very conventional gentleman who believed all writers were rogues and vagabonds, told me that if I wanted to be a writer I could do it at my own expense. There followed a gay and sometimes ghastly period during which I wrote consistently books and stories which were usually sold but at very slowly increasing prices. In those days I did more things to scrape a living than I can easily remember. I went back to Malaya and worked on rubber plantations, a tin mine, and a wood distillation plant. I prospected for gold in the jungle and tried pearl fishing. I was a seaman on a freighter and I covered the English countryside with a sideshow in a traveling fair. I was a bartender in a country inn and I played professional bridge in a London club.

"Fortunes changed gradually. I began to earn a reasonable living. I got married and had a daughter. I took a pilot's license. I went to Spain and became a devoted fan of bull-fighting. In 1932 I came to America as a very small literary personality and began to build an American market. I went to Hollywood the following year and did my first picture. I returned to England, bought a large country estate, and went on writing. I got divorced. I returned to New York on a commission to write some magazine stories, and married an American girl. The movies took up my character the 'Saint,' and I became relatively affluent. Just recently I have started to take a more active interest in the picture production of the 'Saint' stories. I have settled into an unadventurous groove of winters in Southern California and traveling in the summers, lately with a trailer of my own design in which I have made two leisurely crossings of the United States. Probably this is all quite temporary, and in the end I shall be a bum again."

* * *

An application for U.S. citizenship in 1941 disclosed Leslie Charteris' "real" name as Leslie Charles Bowyer Lin, and revealed that his father was a Chinese surgeon, his mother an Englishwoman.

The "Saint," Simon Templar, is a latter-day Raffles or Arsène Lupin whose "fierce and fantastic" adventures have become exceedingly popular, both in print and on the screen. Mr. Charteris says it takes him "two years of thinking and two days of high-speed dictating" to write a story. His first wife was Pauline Schishkin, from whom he was divorced in 1937; his second was Barbara Meyer, whom he married in 1938. His invariable monocle and his small moustache are distinctive features of his appearance; he says he likes sunbathing, flying, shooting, and "knocking kill-joys," and that "my favorite writer is myself."

PRINCIPAL WORKS: Meet the Tiger, 1928; The Bandit, 1929; Enter the Saint, 1930; Knight Templar (in America: The Avenging Saint) 1930; Alias the Saint, 1931; Featuring the Saint, 1931; Daredevil, 1931; She Was a Lady (in America: Angels of Doom) 1931; The Holy Terror (in America: The Saint Vs. Scotland Yard) 1932; Getaway, 1932; Once More the Saint (in America: The Saint and Mr. Teal) 1933; The Brighter Buccaneer, 1933; The Misfortunes of Mr. Teal, 1934; Boodle (short stories) (in America: The Saint Intervenes) 1934; The Saint Goes On, 1934; The Saint in New York, 1935; The Saint Overboard, 1936; The Ace of Knaves, 1937; Thieves' Picnic, 1937; Follow the Saint, 1938; Prelude for War, 1938; The Happy Highwayman, 1939; The First Saint Omnibus, 1939; The Last Hero, 1939; The Saint in Miami, 1940; The Saint Goes West, 1942.

ABOUT: American Magazine November 1935; Life May 19, 1941; Time October 27, 1941.

CHASE, MARY ELLEN (February 24, 1887-), American novelist, was born in Blue Hill, Maine, on the east coast, a region she has made peculiarly her own. Her father was Judge Edward Everett Chase, her mother Edith (Lord), Chase, and she was one of eight children. She was educated at Blue Hill Academy and the University of Maine (B.S. 1909). She

earned her way through college by writing juvenile stories, her first published work being a football story in the *American Boy*, for which she received $17!

Miss Chase taught history in several western boarding schools till 1918, then went to the University of Minnesota as instructor in English, rising by 1926 to an associate professorship. At the same time she secured her M.A. at Minnesota in 1918, her Ph.D. in 1922. In 1926 she was called to Smith College, where she is now professor of English literature. She teaches for three days a week and devotes the rest of her time to writing and outside lecturing, and to her hobbies of bird study and gardening. Most of her vacations she spends in England, usually exploring the southern counties. She is unmarried.

She has honorary doctorates from the University of Maine, Bowdoin College, and Colby College, and in 1931 received the *Pictorial Review* prize of $2500 for a short story called "Salesmanship." She writes a great deal for the magazines: stories, essays, and critical reviews; she has published several textbooks, essays, and books for young people. But her novels for adults, of which *Mary Peters* is perhaps the best known, constitute her chief claim to renown. Her native country, the life and people of which are her principal theme, is north of the farming land pictured by Gladys Hasty Carroll; her people are boat-builders, seamen, and fishermen. In a sense she is the successor, as a regional novelist, of Sarah Orne Jewett, who was in her youth her friend and guide. The loving care with which she depicts a by-gone way of living does not debar her from a strict realism, and her novels have historical as well as literary interest.

Miss Chase has done notable work also in interpreting England and the English to Americans, in a manner that is both sympathetic and factual. Her lectures on English literature, and the enthusiasm with which she inspires her pupils to read and to own for themselves the classics of our common tongue, are a further service in the cause of mutual understanding between the two English-speaking nations.

PRINCIPAL WORKS: His Birthday (juvenile) 1915; The Girl from the Bighorn Country (juvenile) 1916; Virginia of Elk Creek Valley (juvenile) 1917; The Art of Narration (with F. K. Del Plaine) 1926; Thomas Hardy From Serial to Novel, 1927; Uplands, 1927; The Writing of Informal Essays (with M. E. Macgregor) 1928; The Golden Asse and Other Essays, 1929; Constructive Theme Writing, 1929; The Silver Shell (juvenile) 1930; A Goodly Heritage (autobiography) 1932; Mary Peters, 1934; Silas Crockett, 1935; This England (in England, England Now) 1936; It's All About Me (juvenile) 1937; Mary Christmas, 1937; Dawn in Lyonesse, 1938; The Goodly Fellowship, 1939; Windswept, 1941.

ABOUT: Chase, M. E. A Goodly Heritage; Publishers' Weekly August 4, 1934; Reader's Digest February 1941; Scholastic April 17, 1937; Wilson Library Bulletin February 1934; Yale Review September 1940.

CHASE, STUART (March 8, 1888-), American economist, writes: "I was born during a blizzard, in Somerworth, N. H., where my father, Harvey Stuart Chase, was working as an engineer installing the town water supply. All my ancestors on both sides, so far as I know, have lived in New England for generations since coming from England in the 1600's.

E. Schaal

"I was a rather normal boy, small for my age, a greedy reader, and devoted to sports. We spent our summers in the White Mountains, where I did a great deal of camping, climbing, and trail building.

"I was graduated from he Newton, Mass., High School in 1906, and entered the Massachusetts Institute of Technology. My father meanwhile had switched from engineering to accounting, and I was to be trained to enter the latter profession. He sent me to Tech to learn how to work. Then I went to Harvard for the comparative relaxation of courses in economics, banking, and accounting. I received my degree *cum laude* from Harvard in 1910, but having entered late I never came to know my classmates very well. John Reed I knew slightly, but I did not know Walter Lippmann, T. S. Eliot, Heywood Broun, and others who have since become prominent.

"I entered my father's accounting firm in Boston, passed my C.P.A. examinations, played in amateur theatricals, and read more than ever. One day in the library of the Boston Harvard Club I picked up Henry George's *Progress and Poverty*. That was the beginning of my interest in social problems. Presently I joined the Boston Fabian Club. A little later (1914) I was married to Margaret Hatfield, who had played opposite to me in some of our theatricals in West Newton.

"When the country entered the war, I tried to register as a conscientious objector. The official in charge of registration said coldly that I might spare myself the trouble; with a wife and young son I was ineligible for the draft anyhow. [Later a daughter also was born.] I went to Washington to take a job with the Federal Trade Commission, and was dispatched to Chicago to investigate the meat packing industry. Some of the findings of our report displeased the Chicago packers. As soon as Harding was elected in the fall of 1920, all of us who were prominent in this investigation were fired from government service. This provided an interesting sidelight on the connection between Big Business and politics.

"I came to New York, and joined the staff of an organization called the Technical Alliance, whose major figure was Thorstein Veblen. The Technical Alliance was the nucleus for a later and more famous organization called Technocracy. I had nothing to do with the latter, however, except to write a pamphlet about it. From the Technical Alliance I went on to the Labor Bureau, incorporated in New York, a research organization which provided technical service for labor unions and cooperatives, on a nonprofit basis.

"In 1925 I wrote my first serious book, *The Tragedy of Waste*. Before that I had written occasional articles. The book was well received, and I began to think of myself as a regular writer. About this time I became a contributing editor of the *Nation*. In 1927 I went to Russia as an economic adviser to a trade union delegation and on returning helped to edit a volume entitled *Soviet Russia in the Second Decade*.

"In the same year *Your Money's Worth* was published, which I had written in collaboration with F. J. Schlink. Presently Mr. Schlink and I organized the first testing bureau for consumers, called Consumers' Research. It is still flourishing, with some 60,000 members.

"In 1930 I was separated from my first wife in a friendly divorce, and married Marian Tyler, whom I had met when we were both on the staff of the *Nation*. She and I now live quietly in the country, where with her help I do most of my writing. Once a year I tour the country lecturing, mostly to teachers' organizations and college students.

"On lecture trips and holidays I have covered a good part of North America. Living on this continent, I am constantly studying it, and sometimes I think that it may become the chief source of civilization in the years before us.

"At home, I write or study about six hours a day and spend several hours out of doors, chopping wood, tending my tennis court, swimming, skiing, skating, walking. It is a free, irregular, but industrious life, and suits my tastes very well.

"Although at first glance the list of my books seems varied, a single theme runs through them all, namely the impact of the machine on human beings. Thus *Mexico* was a comparison between the machine age and the handicraft age. *Rich Land, Poor Land,* besides expressing an interest in nature which goes back to my boyhood in New Hampshire, describes the ravages of land and resources brought about primarily by the misuse of machine techniques. *The Tyranny of Words* suggests ways and means for applying science to language and communication. Perhaps the broadest conclusions I have reached about the impact of technology are contained in *The Economy of Abundance.* That book was written in 1933, but the pattern which it sketched still seems to hold." *The Road We Are Traveling* is the first of a proposed series of six.

PRINCIPAL WORKS: A Honeymoon Experiment, 1916; The Tragedy of Waste, 1925; Your Money's Worth (with F. J. Schlink) 1927; Men and Machines, 1929; Prosperity—Fact or Myth, 1930; The Nemesis of American Business and Other Essays, 1931; Mexico—A Study of Two Americas (with M. Tyler) 1931; A New Deal, 1932; The Economy of Abundance, 1934; Government in Business, 1935; Rich Land, Poor Land, 1936; The Tyranny of Words, 1938; The New Western Front (with M. Tyler) 1939; Idle Money, Idle Men, 1940; A Primer of Economics, 1941; The Road We Are Traveling, 1942.

ABOUT: I Believe (symposium); Carpenter, C. E. Dollars and Sense; Neilson, F. Control From the Top; Catholic World February 1937; Christian Century March 9, 1938; Saturday Review of Literature March 24, 1934, January 22, 1938, August 24, 1940; Time June 19, 1939.

CHENEY, SHELDON (June 29, 1886-   ), American writer on art and the theatre, writes: "Sheldon Cheney was born into an atmosphere of literay ambition and ac-

tivity. His father, Warren Cheney, was editor of the *Overland Monthly* and published a book of verse and three novels.

The family home in Berkeley, Calif., was often visited by Jack London, Mary Austin, and Lincoln Steffens. Sheldon Cheney studied intermittently at art schools, along with a routine 'letters' course at the University of California (B.A. 1908), thus fixing his two major professional interests: the arts and books.

"It was as a designer and engraver of bookplates that he first achieved recognition. While in college he founded and edited a quarterly magazine, which achieved international circulation, for designers and collectors of bookplates. Finding, however, that the world of design could get on very well without him, he turned to the field which was to claim his professional attention for twenty years: the theatre.

"He plunged into the then 'new movement' in the theatre and has been known ever since as an uncompromising modernist and perhaps impossible idealist in that field. In 1916 he founded the pioneering periodical review, *Theatre Arts Magazine,* now *Theatre Arts Monthly,* and edited it for three years, in Detroit and then in New York. His service in the theatre ended in five years' endeavor on Broadway, chiefly with the Actors' Theatre and Augustin Duncan, and in the writing of a now standard history, *The Theatre: 3000 Years of Drama, Acting, and Stagecraft.*

"In the early 1920's, a revived interest in craftswork resulted in his setting up a hand press, at his then home at Scarborough-on-Hudson, N.Y. But the Sleepy Hollow Press printed only two pamphlets. He then wrote *A Primer of Modern Art* (most often reprinted of his books, repeatedly revised and now in its tenth edition).

"From 1926 to 1931 he and his family lived in various parts of Europe, three more books about the arts resulting. He then returned to California and tried to found the 'School for Open-Mindedness' in Berkeley, a project that promptly succumbed under pressure of economic conditions. It took the Great Depression to wipe out his tangible property and his way of making a living, a disaster accompanied by the death of his first wife.

"Idealists, however, have to be fairly indestructible, and he came back with his most uncompromising and controversial book, *Expressionism in Art*. He now lives at Upper Stepney, Conn., and recently lecture tours have taken precedence of writing. He has been made honorary fellow in the fine arts at Union College, and has worked side by side with the students at the annual Mohawk Drama Festival. His books intrinsically are less important than the ideas he has spread, and the art movements in which he has been an often obscure but directive figure. His fights have been against academism in all fields of art, and against what is generally considered 'practical' organized education—but which omits what he considers the most practical elements in preparation for living, creative vision and spiritual experience."

* * *

Sheldon Cheney was originally named Sheldon Warren Cheney, and his books are so listed by the Library of Congress; but he has asked the editors of this volume to omit the middle name, which he never uses. In 1910 he married Maud Maurice Turner, and they had two sons and a daughter. She died early in 1934 and at the end of the year he married Martha Candler, who collaborated with him in his book, *Art and the Machine*. In appearance he resembles the conventional pedagogues he decries—thin and stooped, with graying hair and blue eyes behind pince nez.

Sheldon Cheney's enthusiasm for modern art has exerted a healthy influence on contemporary taste. For over twenty-five years he has waged his fight in defense of the "living, creative vision."

PRINCIPAL WORKS: The New Movement in the Theatre, 1914; The Open-Air Theatre, 1918; Modern Art and the Theatre, 1921; A Primer of Modern Art, 1923; The Art Theatre, 1925; Stage Decoration, 1927; The Theatre: 3000 Years of Drama, Acting, and Stagecraft, 1929; The New World Architecture, 1931; Expressionism in Art, 1934; Art and the Machine (with M. C. Cheney) 1936; A World History of Art, 1937; The Story of Modern Art, 1941.

ABOUT: Bookman January and December 1930; Theatre Arts February 1941.

CHESNUTT, CHARLES WADDELL

(June 20, 1858-November 15, 1932), called "the first American Negro novelist," was born in Cleveland, Ohio, and at sixteen began to teach in the public schools of North Carolina, where his family had moved. At twenty-three he was principal of the State Normal School in Fayettesville. In 1883 Chestnutt did some newspaper work

in New York City, going soon after to Cleveland as a court stenographer. He was admitted to the bar in 1887. In North Carolina Chesnutt had studied the traditions and superstitions of the Negro people, and in August of 1887 the *Atlantic Monthly* presented his first short story, "The Goophered Grapevine," the beginning of a series collected in *The Conjure Woman*, which may loosely be described as a novel. Uncle Julius, the narrator of these tales, compares favorably with Joel Chandler Harris' Uncle Remus in shrewdness, kindliness, and eye for the main chance; if anything, he is more clearly individualized than Uncle Remus, in the opinion of Benjamin Brawley. Chesnutt's dialect is not always above question, Brawley continues, "but, all told, *The Conjure Woman* showed that there had at last appeared among the Negro people a man who was able to write fiction with a firm sense of art." The *Overland Monthly* published another story in the series. The Houghton Mifflin trade edition of the book was preceded by a limited edition subscribed for by members of the Rowfant Club and the Cleveland bar. Several other editions appeared, climaxed in 1929 by a new edition with a "very flattering foreword" by Joel Elias Spingarn.

No American colored writer had previously secured critical recognition except Paul Laurence Dunbar, the poet, and the Colonial poet, Phillis Wheatley. William Dean Howells wrote in the *Atlantic* for May 1900: "The stories of *The Conjure Woman* have a wild, indigenous poetry, the creation of a sincere and original imagination, which is imparted with a tender humorousness and a very artistic reticence."

In 1928 Chesnutt was awarded the Spingarn gold medal, valued at $100, for his "pioneer work as a literary artist depicting the life and struggle of Americans of Negro descent." Brawley calls his later novels forced and unreal; too full of propaganda to be ultimately satisfying. Chesnutt was a court reporter, except in 1900-01, till his death, and educated four children, two at Smith, one at Harvard, and one at Western Reserve.

PRINCIPAL WORKS: *Fiction*—The Conjure Woman, 1899; The Wife of His Youth and Other Stories of the Color Line, 1899; The House Behind the Cedars, 1901; The Colonel's Dream, 1905.

Miscellaneous—Frederick Douglass (Beacon Biographies of Eminent Authors) 1899; The Marrow of Tradition, 1901.

ABOUT: Adler, E. (ed.). Breaking Into Print; Brawley, B. The Negro Genius; Brown, S. The Negro in American Fiction, 1937.

CHESTER, GEORGE RANDOLPH

(1869-February 26, 1924), American novelist and short-story writer, inventor of Get-Rich-Quick Wallingford, was born in Ohio. At an early age he left home to exist by odd jobs in a planing mill, as plumber, paper-hanger, bill-clerk, cook, waiter, and pen and ink artist—a mode of life which enabled him to invent with conviction the jovial company-promoter, Wallingford, and his satellite Blackie Daw, who sailed as closely as possible to windward of the law. Get-Rich-Quick Wallingford has entered the folk-lore of American fictional characters, and the allusion is immediately comprehensible to any reader whose memory extends to the administration of the first Roosevelt. George M. Cohan made a play from the stories, and there is even a dramatization in French: Abel Tarride's *Faire Fortune*. Chester worked on the Detroit *News* and the Cincinnati *Inquirer* (as Sunday editor) until he became a successful syndicate and magazine writer. After divorcing his first wife, Elizabeth Bethermel, he married Lillian De Rimo of Cincinnati, and collaborated with her on several novels, one of which, *Cordelia Blossom* (1914), was dramatized with some success. After the First World War he made $25,000 a year as writer and moving-picture director (*The Son of Wallingford* was one picture), and contributed the *Izzy Iskovitch* stories every three weeks to the *Saturday Evening Post*, at $2,000 apiece. Chester was slim, round-faced and blue-eyed. He died of a heart attack in New York at fifty-seven and was buried in Spring Grove Cemetery, Cincinnati.

PRINCIPAL WORKS: Get-Rich-Quick Wallingford, 1908; The Cash Intrigue, 1909; The Making of Bobby Burnit, 1909; The Art of Short Story Writing, 1910; Young Wallingford, 1910; The Early Bird, 1910; Wallingford and Blackie Daw, 1913; Wallingford in His Prime, 1913. *With Lillian Chester*—The Ball of Fire, 1914; Cordelia Blossom, 1914; Pay, 1915.

ABOUT: Cosmopolitan; May 1911; New York Times, February 27, 1924.

CHESTERTON, GILBERT KEITH

(May 29, 1874-June 14, 1936), English essayist, novelist, polemicist, and man-of-letters, was born at Campden Hill, London, the elder son of Edward Chesterton, a retired realtor, whose wife had Scottish and French-Swiss blood in her veins. In 1887 he went to St. Paul's, a public school (in the English sense) for day-boys, where he

won no distinction in Classics, was looked upon as rather sleepy, but was recognized by the staff to have certain aptitudes and excellences unusual in the conventional English upper middle-class boy. He foreshadowed a long journalistic career by helping to produce a school magazine. In 1892 he left St. Paul's and began to study at the Slade, the art school of University College, London. He made no very startling progress in the graphic arts, though he became a light comic draughtsman of some merit and later illustrated a number of books by himself and his friends E. C. Bentley and Hilaire Belloc. He did not stay long at the Slade, soon moving over to W. P. Ker's English literature course at the same college. There he met (Sir) Ernest Hodder Williams, soon to become governing director of the publishing firm, Hodder & Stoughton, who in due course started him on his literary career by allowing him to review books in that firm's monthly journal, the *Bookman*. He took no degree, but for some years lived a home life propitious for the development of talent, in a family devoted to art and letters and visited by many prominent young men. Before he was twenty-one he was well launched as a reviewer and journalist.

His friend, Archibald Marshall, literary editor of the *Daily News,* gave him work. Association with this Liberal daily brought him into touch with its owner, George Cadbury, and with such other prominent Liberals as Lord Morley, George Wyndham, A. G. Gardiner, and C. F. G. Masterman. But his greatest and most enduring friendship was with Hilaire Belloc, whose views on religion, politics, and history chimed so well with his own that the two men were often lumped together facetiously as "The Chesterbelloc." Chesterton's journalistic contacts included also the *Speaker* and the *Illustrated London News,* for which latter he wrote a regular weekly essay from 1905 to 1930, missing only two numbers in the quarter-century. A review defending R. L. Stevenson against belittlement won him the interest and friendship of Sir Sidney Colvin.

Chesterton was, however, by no means content to be merely a journalist, and soon began to pour out a series of books displaying astonishing energy, remarkable versatility, and authentic literary feeling. The bibliography enumerates the chief titles: here no more can be attempted than a grouping under main heads. The largest group by far consisted of essays, many, but not all, collected from periodicals. *All Things Considered, Tremendous Trifles, The Uses of Diversity,* and *Avowals and Denials* are some of these. Another big section comprised fiction, mainly of a philosophic-fantastic nature, the most accomplished and famous novels being *The Napoleon of Notting Hill* and *The Man Who Was Thursday.* A sub-section related the adventures in crime investigation of a quiet little Roman Catholic priest, Father Brown. (They are better fantasy than detection; but of Father Brown's appeal there can be no doubt: he has become one of the best loved characters in contemporary fiction, and his creation brought new literary stature to the detective story.) Then there were many volumes of poems, gay and rollicking for the most part, beginning with *Greybeards at Play* and eventually brought together in a collected edition in 1927. *Orthodoxy* (1906) was the first of a group of vigorously polemical books expounding Chesterton's views on religion, politics, and sociology. History, literary criticism, and art criticism also engaged the interest of this astonishing man. He contributed a study of Browning to the authoritative "English Men of Letters" series; wrote books on Dickens, Stevenson, Blake, Cobbett, and Chaucer; produced *A Short History of England;* and wrote innumerable introductions to literary classics. Chesterton went to Ireland in 1919, to America in 1922, and to Rome in 1930, bringing back from each place a book; and a visit to Palestine brought forth a volume somewhat misleadingly called *The New Jerusalem.*

Through all this imposing and colorful tapestry certain main threads can be traced. Dominant among them is the religious view of the world. Chesterton was not received into the Roman Catholic Church until 1922, but so profoundly Romanist was his apprehension of metaphysics and morals that many of his readers, hearing of the formal act of submission, were surprised to learn that he had not been a Catholic for twenty years. He once said: "I am one of those people who believe that you've got to be dominated by your moral slant. I'm no art-for-art's-sake man. I am quite incapable of talking or writing about Dutch gardens or the game of chess, but if I did, I have no doubt that what I would say or write about them would be colored by my view of the cosmos." He sought to show that Catholicism, far from being obscurantist and out-of-date, was the world's true refuge from its troubles. In politics he rejected socialism for a theory he called Distributism, which advocated the widest possible ownership of property, and he ran a paper called *G.K.'s Weekly* as its official organ. He detested teetotalism, vegetarianism, and mechanization, and, though he professed not to be an anti-Semite, was unsympathetic with the Jews. With Belloc and his own brother, Cecil, he founded the *New Witness* early in the century to attack political corruption. He had a gay and brilliant style, shot with paradox which was often strained to extremes.

Chesterton was a man of enormous physical bulk, and this, with his unkempt hair and moustache, made him a joy to caricaturists. He often debated in public, and was a splendid after-dinner speaker. In his later years he ran a successful weekly literary *causerie* for the British Broadcasting Corporation. He lectured in 1930 at the University of Notre Dame, South Bend, Indiana, which made him LL.D. He married Frances Blogg, in 1901, and after living in London for a short time, bought a half-timbered house, "Top Meadow," at Beaconsfield, in the delightful Chiltern Hills but within easy reach of the capital. There he died at sixty-two.

A high-spirited, combative, opinionated man, he impressed on everything that he wrote a strong, whimsical, humorous personality which marked him out as a genuine man-of-letters. Deep scholarship he did not claim; and he was fundamentally out of touch with the spirit of an age which counted Shaw, Wells, Hardy, and Arnold Bennett among its major prophets. Yet for all his passionate and unashamed championship of dogma, for all his flashy rapier-play of verbal paradox, his most bitter opponents, infuriated though they may have been by what they deemed a false and tortuous philosophy, freely granted him credit for his wit, his broad humanity, his personal kindliness, love of liberty, and gift of prose.

PRINCIPAL WORKS: *Essays, Travel, and Miscellaneous*—The Defendant, 1901; Twelve Types, 1902; All Things Considered, 1908; The Ball and the Cross, 1909; Tremendous Trifles, 1909; Alarms and Discursions, 1910; A Miscellany of Men, 1912; Simplicity and Tolstoy, 1912; Utopia of the Usurers, 1917; Irish Impressions, 1919; The New Jerusalem, 1920; The Uses of Diversity, 1920; What I Saw in America, 1922; Fancies Versus Fads, 1923; Generally Speaking, 1928; The Thing, 1929; Come To Think of It, 1930; All Is Grist, 1931; Sidelights on New London and Newer York, 1932; "All I Survey," 1933; Avowals and Denials, 1934; As I Was Saying, 1936.

Novels and Tales—The Napoleon of Notting Hill, 1904; The Club of Queer Trades, 1905; The Man Who Was Thursday, 1908; The Innocence of Father Brown, 1911; Manalive, 1912; The Flying Inn, 1914; The Wisdom of Father Brown, 1914; The Man Who Knew Too Much and Other Stories, 1922; The Return of Don Quixote, 1922; Tales of the Long Bow, 1925; The Incredibility of Father Brown, 1926; The Secret of Father Brown, 1927; The Poet and the Lunatics, 1929; Four Faultless Felons, 1930; The Paradoxes of Mr. Pond, 1936.

Verse—Greybeards at Play, 1900; The Wild Knight and Other Poems, 1900; The Ballad of the White Horse, 1911; Poems, 1915; Wine, Water, and Song, 1915; The Ballad of St. Barbara and Other Verses, 1922; The Queen of Seven Swords, 1926.

Polemical Works—Heretics, 1905; Orthodoxy, 1909; What's Wrong With the World, 1910; The Superstition of Divorce, 1920; Eugenics and Other Evils, 1922; St. Francis of Assisi, 1923; The Everlasting Man, 1925; The Catholic Church and Convention, 1926; The Resurrection of Rome, 1930; St. Thomas Aquinas, 1933; The Outline of Sanity, 1936.

Criticism and History—Robert Louis Stevenson, 1902; Robert Browning, 1903; G. F. Watts, 1904; The Characteristics of Robert Louis Stevenson, 1906; Charles Dickens, 1906; William Blake, 1910; George Bernard Shaw, 1910; Appreciations and Criticisms of the Works of Charles Dickens, 1911; The Victorian Age in Literature, 1913; A Short History of England, 1917; William Cobbett, 1925; Chaucer, 1932.

ABOUT: Arns, C. Gilbert Keith Chesterton: Umriss Seiner Künstlerpersönlichkeit; Arocena, R. El Sembrado de Chesterton; Braybrooke, P. Gilbert Keith Chesterton; Bullett, G. The Innocence of G. K. Chesterton; Cammaerts, E. The Laughing Prophet; Chesterton, C. G. K. Chesterton: A Criticism; Haycraft, H. Murder for Pleasure: The Life and Times of the Detective Story; Hoffmann, G. Gilbert Keith Chesterton als Propagandist; Las Vergnas, R. Portraits Anglais; O'Connor, J. Father Brown on Chesterton; Scott, D. Men of Letters; Slosson, E. E. Six Major Prophets; Titterton, W. R. G. K. Chesterton: A Portrait; West, Julius. G. K. Chesterton: A Critical Study.

CHILDERS, ERSKINE (June 25, 1870-November 24, 1922), Anglo-Irish writer and politician, was born in London, the second son of Robert Caesar Childers, a noted Pali scholar, and Anna Mary Henrietta (Barton) Childers, of Glendalough House, County Wicklow, Ireland, which was his only home until he was married. He was named Robert Erskine Childers. The boy's preparatory school was Haileybury; he went from there to Trinity College, Cambridge University, taking the Law Tripos and a B.A. degree in 1893. Soon after

leaving Cambridge, Childers spent his holidays either alone or with a friend or two, navigating some tiny yacht in the English Channel, the North Sea, or the shoals of the German, Danish, or Baltic coasts. From 1895 to 1910 he was a clerk in the House of Commons. He was one of the first to join the City Imperial Volunteer battery of the Honourable Artillery Company in 1899, for service in the Boer War. *In the Ranks of the C.I.V.* (1900) was his first book, followed by *The H.A.C.*  *in South Africa* (1903), written in collaboration.

In the same year appeared his best-known book, a romantic and curiously prophetic novel *The Riddle of the Sands*. In it, an English civil servant and his friend, cruising in the Baltic in a small yacht, the *Dulcibella*, find themselves the discoverers of a carefully planned invasion of England by Germany, in sea-going lighters under escort of the Imperial Navy. The earliest American edition of the romance appeared in 1915, in the early months of the First World War; and the second, largely at the insistence of Christopher Morley, was published in November 1940, when the *Luftwaffe* was hammering London from overhead, and rumors of an invasion of Britain by sea were again rife. (Just why the publisher's "blurb" for the 1940 edition called one of the two principal and indubitably English characters an American was a mystery no casual reader could decipher.) A low-priced Pocket Book Edition appeared at the same time. The novel was republished in England in 1914, when Childers was doing reconnaissance work on the seaplane carrier H.M.S. *Engadine*. He took part in the Cuxhaven Raid in November 1914, and for the rest of the war was intelligence officer and training officer in the Royal Naval Air Service. He was promoted to lieutenant-commander and major in the service, and received a D.S.C. However, he had become "finally and immutably a convert to Home Rule" in Ireland some years before, and after demobilization in March 1919 devoted the rest of his life to securing Irish independence. Even as early as July 1914, after the passage of Asquith's Home Rule bill, Childers and his wife, who was Mary Alden Osgood of Boston, Mass., were carrying cargoes of arms in their yacht "Asgard" from the Continent into Howth harbour. In December 1919 he settled in Dublin to write propaganda for the cause, and in May 1921 was elected to the self-constituted Dail Eireann from County Wicklow. On establishment of the Irish Free State Government Childers joined the Republican army, serving with mobile columns in the south. On November 10, 1922, Free State soldiers surrounded Glendalough House. Childers was arrested and court-martialed in Dublin a week later, by a court whose authority he refused to acknowledge, and on November 24 he was shot by a firing squad at Beggar's Bush barracks, after shaking hands with each of the firing party. He was fifty-two. His wife and two sons survived.

Childers as a writer possessed exceptional lucidity and charm; his qualities as a man won respect even from his most determined opponents.

PRINCIPAL WORKS: In the Ranks of the C.I.V., 1900; The H.A.C. in South Africa (with others) 1903; The Riddle of the Sands, 1903; "The Times" History of the War in South Africa (Vol. 5) 1907; War and the Arme Blanche, 1910; German Influence on British Cavalry, 1911; Home Rule, 1911.

ABOUT: Childers, E. The Riddle of the Sands (see Preface to 1940 ed. by R. T. Bond); Williams, B. Erskine Childers; Living Age March 3, 1923; Nineteenth Century and After January 1923; Saturday Review of Literature August 10, 1940.

*CHILTON, ELEANOR CARROLL

(September 11, 1898-   ), American novelist and poet, writes: "I was born in Charleston, W.Va., the daughter of William Edwin Chilton and Mary Louise (Tarr) Chilton. I was educated at private schools there, at the Masters School at Dobbs Ferry, N.Y., at Dana Hall, and at Smith College, from which I graduated with the class of 1922. I spent the next year and a half in Oxford and London, studying mediaeval literature, and after returning to America wrote and published a novel. I lived in New York City for a year or more, reading manuscripts for two publishers, and then returned to England, where I remained until 1934. During those years I wrote stories and plays and two novels. Herbert Agar *qv* and I were married in 1933, in England, and we are now

living in Louisville, Ky., where he edits the *Courier-Journal."*

* * *

Eleanor Carroll Chilton's father was a United States senator; her husband is a well-known author in his own right, as well as a collaborator with his wife. They have no children. She is a member of the Colonial Dames of America. She started writing while in college, her first work being in verse; she is something of a Smith legend, her poems and articles having been published frequently while she was still a student. She is slender, rather fair, with a delicate, sensitive face. Elinor Wylie was among the earliest admirers of her work, which has a quality of fastidiousness and sensibility that marks her, though chiefly a novelist, as primarily a poet.

PRINCIPAL WORKS: *Novels—* Shadows Waiting, 1926; The Burning Fountain, 1929; Follow the Furies, 1935. *Miscellaneous—*Fire and Sleet and Candlelight (poems, with W. Fisher and H. Agar) 1928; The Garment of Praise (essays, with H. Agar) 1929.

ABOUT: Time December 9, 1940; Wilson Library Bulletin May 1929.

CHOLMONDELEY, MARY (June 8, 1859-July 15, 1925), English novelist, was born at Hodnet, Shropshire, the third child and eldest daughter of the Rev. Richard Hugh Cholmondeley, who was eventually made Rector of Hodnet, and Emily Beaumont Cholmondeley. All her life, from the time she was a child, she suffered from ill health. Her invalid sister, Hester, author of a quantity of miscellaneous verse, died at the age of twenty-two. She herself had a quiet, studious and repressed early life, saddened by an unhappy love affair. Emerson's writings consoled and influenced her.

Before her father's retirement in 1896 and their removal to London, she had published three novels, none of which made much of an impression. But in 1899 she decided to make a satirical raid on what her biographer called "our back-bone"—the English middle class. *Red Pottage* penetrated its shams, make-shifts, and pretentious complacency, with particular reference to the clergy. Its verisimilitude and candor resulted in a minor literary scandal—though its author might more justly have been attacked for having written a novel which,

* Died February 8, 1949.

although it was relatively successful in building up its characters, was at times tediously moralistic and based on a quite implausible intrigue. *Red Pottage* made Mary Cholmondeley a "celebrity."

During the next ten years she published four more novels (none of which stirred as much interest as *Red Pottage*) and also a book of retrospective glances called *Under One Roof: A Family Record*. In 1921, she suffered a severe illness. From this time on she lived quietly in London, dying in Kensington at the age of sixty-eight.

It is said that she belonged and never ceased to belong to "her stock, her county, her England. . . . Pretty she wasn't, but there was a charm of intelligence in her irregular face, distinction in her appearance," a physical description that might have been applied as well to her niece, the novelist Stella Benson. [qv]

That she "spun her moralities too fine" was her chief defect as a novelist. Without doubt it was the outspokenness of *Red Pottage* and the ensuing reverberations that constitute Mary Cholmondeley's primary claim to remembrance.

PRINCIPAL WORKS: The Danvers Jewels, 1887; Sir Charles Danvers, 1889; Diana Tempest, 1893; A Devotee, 1897; Red Pottage, 1899; Moth and Rust, 1902; Prisoners, 1906; The Lowest Rung, 1908; Notwithstanding, 1913; Under One Roof, 1918; The Romance of His Life, 1921.

ABOUT: Lubbock, P. Mary Cholmondeley: A Sketch From Memory; London Times July 17, 1925.

*CHRISTIANSEN, SIGURD WESLEY

(November 17, 1891-), Norwegian novelist, writes (in English): "At eighteen I got a job in the post office at Drammen, Norway, where I was born—a position which I still maintain. My first book was published in 1915. It was the novel *Seireren (The Conqueror)*, which treats the problem of the redress of the criminal through atonement. Some years later came the two connected novels, *Vårt Eget Liv (Our Own Life)* (1918) and *Ved Golgata (At Golgotha)* (1920). The main theme in the first volume is egotism; in the second, sacrifice. Both volumes have later been worked into one volume and published (1939) under the second title. My next important work, the trilogy *Riket (The Kingdom)* appeared during the years 1925-30. It is a story about

the question of guilt, about the yearning of man for a personal and saving faith in life and in religion, and about his struggle to reach such a faith which will carry him not only through life but also through death. In 1931 came the novel *To Levende og en Död (Two Living and One Dead)*, about false hero worship and the right to value life higher than money and outward honor. This novel was awarded first prize in a Scandinavian literary contest. Two years later followed the novel *Agner i Stormen (Chaff Before the Wind)*, a portrait of a woman and a book about the rights of the weaker in relation to those of the strong. In 1935 came *Drömmen og Livet (Dream and Life)*, which was continued by *Det Ensomme Hjerte (The Lonely Heart)* in 1938. These novels portray the growth of a young boy, his encounter with life, and his vocation to the holy martyrdom and the enchantment of the art of poetry.

"Three of my plays have been staged at the National Theatre in Oslo. *En Reise i Natten (A Journey in the Night)* has also been played on several of the main stages of Sweden and Finland and was broadcast in Oslo, Stockholm, Copenhagen, and Paris."

* * *

Sigurd Christiansen's reticence about himself means only that he has little personal life outside his writing. He is unmarried, still lives [at last report from occupied Norway] in the same small town which has always been his home, and is in his office every day. He is a serious-minded man whose preoccupation is largely with spiritual problems. As Rolv Thesen remarked, he possesses "penetrating psychology and fine insight," although his deep concern with the inner being of his characters makes his novels "somewhat heavy and monotonous."

WORKS AVAILABLE IN ENGLISH: Two Living and One Dead, 1932; Chaff Before the Wind, 1934.

ABOUT: Elster, K. Illustrert Norsk Litteraturhistorie; American Scandinavian Review January 1932.

CHRISTIE, Mrs. AGATHA (MILLER)

(1891-), English detective story writer, writes: "I was born [Agatha Mary Clarissa Miller] in Torquay in the county of Devon, one of the most beautiful of all the counties of England. My father, Frederick Alvah Miller of New York, died when I was a child and I was brought up by my mother. She encouraged me from a very early age to write poetry and stories and helped me in my selection of books to read. My mother was an intelligent woman with a very original mind. She had the gift of awakening enthusiasm on a subject, and my education in her hands (I had no governess and did not go to school) became a thrilling game. I was very much the youngest of the family and so was much alone, and being imaginative I created playmates who to me were very much alive (more alive to me than the children who occasionally came in to play with me). Though I had invented stories in my own mind from an early age it never occurred to me to put them on paper. It was my mother who first commanded me

to write a story. I had a cold and could not go out, so I was told, 'You'd better write a story.' It was quite easy to think of one but not quite so easy to write it all down. It became more easy as time went on but all my stories at that time were very sad and very sentimental.

"At sixteen I was sent to school in Paris and studied singing. It was a great blow to me when I realized that my voice was not strong enough for opera.

"My mother took me to Cairo for a winter and there with great laboriousness I wrote a novel. Mr. Eden Phillpotts, our neighbor and friend in Torquay, was very kind to me over my efforts and his encouragement helped me to go on trying. From time to time I had a short story published—a great excitement and pleasure.

"In 1912 I became engaged to be married and in 1914, a few months after the outbreak of war, I was married. My husband was in France, so I entered a V.A.D. hospital in Torquay and had little time for writing. Towards the end of the war I had more leisure, as I was working in the hospital dispensary, and there I planned a detective story. I had read a good many detective novels, as I found they were excellent to take one's mind off one's worries. After discussing one with my sister she said it was almost impossible to find a *good* detective story, where you didn't know who had committed the crime. I said I thought I could write one. She was doubtful about it. Thus spurred on, I wrote *The Mysterious Affair at Styles.* It was written very slowly, by fits and snatches, but when I had a fortnight's leave from hospital I went out to stay on Dartmoor by myself and got it fin-

ished. It was sent to a publisher—and duly returned. This happened several times. When I sent it to the Bodley Head and nothing further happened I forgot all about it. It was a great surprise to me about a year later to get a letter requesting me to come for an interview. I was much excited and signed a contract then and there. I didn't make much money out of it but it stimulated me to further efforts. I had never thought of writing as a regular source of income or of myself as a writer by profession. By the time I had written six books I really felt I was a writer.

"In 1928 I obtained a decree of divorce against my husband, Col. Archibald Christie, C.M.G., D.S.O., and for the next few years I traveled while my daughter, Rosalind, was at school, only coming back to England for the school holidays.

"Traveling has always been one of my chief pleasures. In 1930 I visited Ur, where I met Max Mallowan, who was assisting Sir Leonard Woolley with the archaeological excavations there. In September 1930 I married him, and now I spend several months of every year in Syria or Iraq with my husband. I love the desert, and when I am not writing I help with the photography for the expedition. I enjoy writing when I am in the desert. There are no distractions such as telephones, theatres, operas, houses, and gardens.

"A hobby of mine is to buy houses, decorate and alter them, live in them for a short time, and then sell them. It is an expensive hobby but great fun.

"My chief dislikes are crowds, loud noises, wireless, cinemas, and gramophones. I dislike the taste of alcohol and do not enjoy smoking.

"I like sun, sea, flowers, traveling (except by sea when I am always ill), trying strange food, cooking, swimming, playing tennis, playing the piano, going to theatres, concerts, reading, and doing embroidery."

* * *

Agatha Christie is one of the few writers of detective fiction whose books consistently make best-seller lists, and one of the few whose novels have been serialized in popular magazines on both sides of the Atlantic. Possibly she is the most successful financially of the authors writing in the form today. It has been said that the little Belgian who is the central figure of her stories— Hercule Poirot, with his waxed mustaches, passion for neatness, conceited faith in the infallibility of his "little grey cells," and murderous attacks on the English language—

comes closest of all the sleuths of modern times to being a "household word," as Sherlock Holmes was in an earlier day. Still the best known among Mrs. Christie's books is *The Murder of Roger Ackroyd* (1926), her brilliant *tour de force* with a trick ending. Though the legitimacy of the device she used is still the subject of hot debate, the book itself is one of the few undoubted classics of the modern detective story, and marks what seems to be the farthest possible extension of the "least-likely-person" theme favored by so many writers in the *genre*. (In a later, Poirot-less novel, *And Then There Were None,* Mrs. Christie comes close to surpassing her own feat.) Among her few faults, in fact, is her too great reliance on this theme in one form or another; also, Poirot's detectival methods must be called closer to the intuitive than to the realistic and scientific. Nevertheless, despite the straining of probability in some of her books, Mrs. Christie clearly belongs among the half-dozen most accomplished and consistently entertaining writers in her chosen field today.

PRINCIPAL WORKS: The Mysterious Affair at Styles, 1920; The Secret Adversary, 1922; The Murder on the Links, 1923; Poirot Investigates, 1924; The Man in the Brown Suit, 1924; The Secret of Chimneys, 1925; The Murder of Roger Ackroyd, 1926; The Big Four, 1927; The Mystery of the Blue Train, 1928; The Seven Dials Mystery, 1929; The Mysterious Mr. Quin, 1930; Murder at the Vicarage, 1930; Murder at Hazelmoor (English title: The Sittaford Mystery) 1931; Peril at End House, 1932; The Tuesday Club Murders (English title: The Thirteen Problems) 1933; Thirteen at Dinner (English title: Lord Edgeware Dies) 1933; Murder in the Calais Coach, 1934; Murder in Three Acts, 1934; Death in the Air, 1935; Boomerang Clue, 1935; The ABC Murders, 1936; Cards on the Table, 1937; Dead Man's Mirror, 1937; Death on the Nile, 1937; Poirot Loses a Client, 1937; Appointment with Death, 1938; The Regatta Mystery, 1939; Murder for Christmas, 1939; And Then There Were None (English title: Ten Little Niggers) 1940; The Sad Cypress, 1940; The Patriotic Murders, 1941; N or M?, 1941; Evil Under the Sun, 1941; The Body in the Library, 1942.

ABOUT: Haycraft, H. Murder for Pleasure: The Life and Times of the Detective Story; Thomson, H. D. Masters of Mystery; Delineator February 1937; Saturday Review of Literature January 7, 1939.

CHURCH, RICHARD (March 26, 1893-), English poet, novelist, and literary critic, was born in London, the second son of Thomas John Church and Lavinia Annie (Orton) Church. He was educated at Dulwich and Hamlet School, and entered the civil service at sixteen. Church began writing at eighteen, and in 1917 published his first book of poems, *Flood*

of Life. He has also contributed reviews regularly to the *Spectator*. Other activities include an advisory editorship with J. M. Dent & Sons, publishers; directing the Oxford Festival of Spoken Poetry; and acting as examiner for voice production and verse speaking at the University of London. Church was first married to Caroline Padgett; his second wife was Catherina Anna Schwimmer. He has a son and three daughters. He retired from the civil service at forty, in 1933. His London clubs are the Athenaeum and Savile, and his country home is The Oast House, Curtisden Green, Goodhurst, Kent.

Up to 1930 Church had confined himself to writing poetry, except for a study of Mary Shelley in 1928. *High Summer* (1931), his second novel, is written, according to Peter Quennell, with a sensitiveness in the choice of words which reminds us of the author's training as a poet. It concerns Nora Holgate, a strong purposeful woman who leaves the unreal world of her mother and the incompleteness of her own marriage to enter the business world, and there wins success and the love of a strong man. One critic called the dialogue "sometimes unbelievably stiff, tawdry, and banal." *The Porch* (1937) won the Femina Vie-Heureuse Prize for the most distinctive novel of the year. Louis Untermeyer, including Church in his frequently revised anthology, *Modern British Poetry*, writes: "*Philip* reveals the work of an artist extremely sensitive to the implications behind the physical fact: a poet who, like a lesser Robert Frost, combines the power of sight with insight. *Mood Without Measure* is, as the title indicates, a transcript of emotion in free or cadenced verse instead of meter. *Theme With [sic] Variations*, though a smaller volume, has larger implications. Never a popular poet, scarcely an enjoyable one in a general sense, Church frequently succeeds in sounding, in a subterranean music, currents deeper than surface agitations."

PRINCIPAL WORKS: *Poetry*—Flood of Life, 1917; Hurricane, 1919; Philip, 1923; Portrait of the Abbot, 1926; The Dream, 1927; Theme and Variations, 1928; Mood Without Measure, 1928; The Glance Backward, 1930; News From the Mountain, 1932; Twelve Noon, 1936. *Prose*—Mary Shelley, 1928; Oliver's Daughter, 1930;

High Summer, 1931; The Prodigal Father, 1933; Apple of Concord, 1935; The Porch, 1937; The Stronghold, 1939; Calling For a Spade, 1939; The Room Within, 1940.

ABOUT: International Who's Who; Untermeyer, L. Modern British Poetry.

*CHURCHILL, WINSTON (November 10, 1871-), American novelist, was born in St. Louis, the son of Edward Spauld-

ing Churchill and Emma Bell (Blaine) Churchill. He was graduated from the United States Naval Academy at Annapolis in 1894, but never served in the Navy. Having private means, he was able to devote himself entirely to writing, and

Haesler

after the enormous success of his second novel, *Richard Carvel,* he was made independently wealthy. Two years later, *The Crisis* established him as one of the most popular American novelists. In 1924, by a vote of 1,753 readers of the *Literary Digest International Book Review,* he was named fourth in a list of the ten "greatest" writers appearing after 1900. This was a tribute to the continued popularity of his work, for his final novel had appeared in 1917.

Early in life Mr. Churchill moved to New Hampshire, which has been his home ever since, though so far west in the state that his postoffice address is in Vermont. He has been active in state politics, serving in the legislature from 1903 to 1905, and running for governor on the Progressive ticket in 1913. In 1895 he married Mabel H. Hall; they have no children.

By ceasing to write virtually in the middle of his career, Mr. Churchill has made himself into a subject for historical criticism while still alive; in fact, many readers may be surprised to learn that he is still living. He has always been retiring, keeping his private life out of the limelight. In 1917 he emerged to visit England and France and to tour the British war front, the result being his first work of non-fiction, *A Traveller in War-Time.* He lives quietly in the country, interested in his garden and always accompanied on his walks by a dog or two, usually a setter. He is a slender, smooth-shaven man of medium height, with smooth gray hair once dark, who in spite of his loose country clothes somewhat resembles an actor of the old school.

Almost his only idiosyncrasy as a writer was to see to it that there was almost always a "C" somewhere in the title of his novels. Those novels, as William Allen White remarked, "sold in carload lots." (*Richard Carvel* alone sold over a million copies.) Most of them are now gathering dust on library shelves; they were distinctly of their own era. White called him "the first of the literary reformers." He concerned himself both with American history and with current social problems, ranging from religion to divorce. He was best known, however, as one of the school of historical romancers so popular at the beginning of the century.

Carl Van Doren has summed up Mr. Churchill's strength and weakness as a novelist, and his place in American literature, by saying that he "came when romance was in that ascendant mood . . . which attended the war with Spain. . . . In Mr. Churchill the national imagination found a romancer full of consolation to any who might fear or suspect that the country's history did not quite match its destiny. . . . He habitually moved along the main lines of American feeling. . . . Morally he has been strenuous and eager; intellectually he has been naïve and belated. . . . He has always been the romancer first and the critic afterwards, . . . a sort of unconscious politician among novelists." Nevertheless, he concluded, Mr. Churchill is "a sincere, scrupulous, and upright man who has served the truth and his art according to his lights." Certainly he was conscientious, working hard on the factual background of his novels and careful in the details of research. He was a disciple of Theodore Roosevelt and, like him, earnest, aggressive, and an admirer of the heroic and the extroverted.

The American Winston Churchill is not related to and should not be confused with Winston Leonard Spencer Churchill, the English politician and author.

PRINCIPAL WORKS: The Celebrity, 1898; Richard Carvel, 1899; The Crisis, 1901; The Crossing, 1904; Coniston, 1906; Mr. Crewe's Career, 1908; A Modern Chronicle, 1910; The Inside of the Cup, 1913; A Far Country, 1915; The Dwelling Place of Light, 1917; A Traveller in War-Time, 1917; Dr. Jonathan (play) 1919; The Crisis (play) 1927; The Uncharted Way: The Psychology of the Gospel Doctrine, 1940.

ABOUT: Nation April 27, 1921; New Yorker June 1, 1940. Publishers' Weekly January 17, 1931.

CHURCHILL, WINSTON LEONARD SPENCER (November 30, 1874-), English statesman, soldier, historian, and biographer, was the third son of the late Lord

* Died March 12, 1947.

Randolph Churchill, the grandson of the seventh Duke of Marlborough, and the direct descendant of the victor of Ramillies and Malplaquet.  His mother was an American, the former Jennie Jerome of New York. He was educated at Harrow School and the Royal Military College, Sandhurst, whence he passed into the army, serving in several colonial campaigns. During the South African War he acted as war correspondent for the London *Morning Post,* was captured by the Boers, and escaped under exciting conditions.

Churchill was returned to Parliament as a Conservative in 1900. He joined the Liberals in 1904, participated in their electoral triumph in 1906, and in the same year was made Under-Secretary for the Colonies. Promoted to the Presidency of the Board of Trade in 1908, he was beaten in the consequent by-election at Northwest Manchester, but fought and won Dundee, for which division he continued to sit until 1922. In 1910-11 he held the high office of Home Secretary; and in the latter year he went to the Admiralty as First Lord, and is recognized as the ablest holder of that position in modern times. It was in great measure due to his foresight that the British Fleet was ready at its stations in August 1914.

The abortive expeditions to Antwerp and Gallipoli, though well-conceived strategically, both ended in tragic failure, and did great harm to Churchill's reputation and career. In 1915 he was reduced to minor office as Chancellor of the Duchy of Lancaster, and shortly afterwards resigned and went to France as an officer. He had several narrow escapes from death. In 1917 he returned to politics as Minister of Munitions, and from 1919 to 1921 he was Minister for War and Air. In 1921 he went to the Colonial Office once more. At the election of 1922 he was beaten at Dundee. He had made himself still more unpopular by a third abortive military expedition—to help the White Russians on the Murman Coast; and was rejected by two more constituencies at by-elections in 1923 and 1924; but at the General Election of 1924 he was at last restored to Parliament by the Epping Division (near London), for which he has sat uninterruptedly ever since. Stanley Baldwin (now

Earl Baldwin) made him Chancellor of the Exchequer, and he served as such until a Labor Government came in in 1929. He had no further office until the outbreak of the war against Hitler, which brought him back to the Admiralty. On the resignation of Neville Chamberlain after the Norwegian debacle early in May 1940, Winston Churchill at sixty-five became Britain's Prime Minister—thirty-five years after the first biography of him had been published!

This almost telegraphic account of a great public figure should be supplemented by other reading. What must concern *this* book mainly is Churchill's activity as a printed author, which has always been considerable. Beginning with *The Story of the Malakand Field Force,* in 1898, he has produced many works of history and biography, the most notable of which have been his *The World Crisis, Marlborough,* and *Lord Randolph Churchill.* His personal familiarity with momentous happenings, his fine expository power in matters of strategy and tactics, his welding of source material into an artistic whole, his sense of color and adventure, his polished and felicitous style, make him one of Britain's most skilled writers in his own field.

Yet it may well be that Winston Churchill's lasting reputation in letters, as well as politics, will finally rest on his magnificent, moving war-time orations after his rise to the premiership in his country's darkest hour. That these are "literature" in the most ancient and epic sense of the word, few who have heard or read them will deny. As Lewis Gannett has said, his phrases "seem destined to go ringing down the years, in the mouths of schoolboys who repeat the historic words of history. They do not ape emotion; they express it"; while *Time* has predicted that his "throbbing passages" will live as long as Shakespeare's. Or, as Rosemary and Stephen Benét phrased it, "Through Churchill all England spoke."

Churchill the man is a vivid, dogged, and tenacious character, who has always been a fighter and has always profoundly believed in himself, while remaining able (on occasion) to laugh at himself as heartily as at others. He is master of the pungent phrase, of forensic fisticuffs; but, perhaps more important than that, he never fails to see events and personalities in a large way. In times of peace he lives at Westerham, Kent, where he likes to play at bricklaying. But his real hobby is fine art, and he is a better painter than many who consider themselves professionals. On the personal side he is noted for his cherubic face, his perpetual big cigar, his invariable bow-tie, and his extraordinary variety of hats.

PRINCIPAL WORKS: *Historical and Descriptive*— The Story of the Malakand Field Force, 1898; The River War (2 vols.) 1899; Hamilton's March, 1900; London to Ladysmith via Pretoria, 1900; Mr. Brodrick's Army, 1903; My African Journey, 1908; The World Crisis (6 vols.) 1923-31 (abbreviated and revised, 1931). *Biographical*—Lord Randolph Churchill (2 vols.) 1906; Marlborough: His Life and Times (4 vols.) 1933-38; Great Contemporaries, 1937. *Political*—For Free Trade (speeches) 1906; Liberalism and the Social Problem (speeches) 1909; The People's Rights (speeches) 1910; India: Speeches and an Introduction, 1931; Thoughts and Adventures, 1932; Arms and the Covenant (speeches) 1938; While England Slept, 1938. *Miscellaneous*—Savrola, 1900; My Early Life (also published as A Roving Commission) 1930; Step by Step: 1936-1939, 1939; Blood, Sweat, and Tears (English title: Into Battle) 1941.

ABOUT: Arthur, G. Concerning Winston Spencer Churchill; Broad, C. L. Winston Churchill; George, R. E. S. Winston Churchill; Guedalla, P. Mr. Winston Churchill: A Portrait; Keynes, J. M. The Economic Consequences of Mr. Winston Churchill; Kraus, R. Winston Churchill; Manning, P. & Bronner, M. Mr. England: The Story of Winston Churchill, the Fighting Briton; Martin, H. Battle: The Life Story of Winston Churchill; Moir, P. I Was Winston Churchill's Secretary; Roberts, C. E. B. Winston Churchill; Roberts, C. E. B. A Man Arose; Sencourt, R. Winston Churchill; Scott, A. McC. Winston Churchill in Peace and War; Current Biography March 1942.

*CLARK, BARRETT HARPER (August 26, 1890-), American dramatic critic and editor, writes:

"Born in Toronto, Canada,

Newspictures

of American-born father and Canadian mother. Moved to Chicago 1893. Attended University of Chicago for three years, and (1909-10) University of Paris for one year. Joined Mrs. Fiske's acting company as actor and assistant stage manager, and played season of 1912-13 with her in New York and on the road. In Europe 1913-14, in France, England, and Germany, studying the theatre, contributing articles to American and English magazines, and securing first-hand material which was used in *Contemporary French Dramatists.* Beginning 1913, translated (with introductory material) several French plays which were published in the United States, and edited for the use of amateur actors fifty-five titles in the *World's Best Plays* series. Edited and/ or translated many plays since. In connection with his work of popularization of foreign drama (1913 to 1920), contributed

articles, lectured, and taught dramatic classes at Chatauqua, but from about 1920 interest centered largely on contemporary American drama. Occasional teaching was carried on in the School of Journalism at Columbia University and at Bryn Mawr College. As editorial adviser for Samuel French (until 1936) was instrumental in making known the work of several young native playwrights, writing prefaces to the published work (among others) of Paul Green, Lynn Riggs, Samson Raphaelson, Virgil Geddes, E. P. Conkle, Albert Bein, and Martin Flavin. Between 1924-30 wrote regular drama reviews of the New York theatre for the *Drama* magazine. Latest editorial work was collecting of the manuscripts of 100 famous, and hitherto unpublished, plays in twenty volumes, *America's Lost Plays,* to be published by Princeton University Press.

"Always active in efforts to curb or abolish censorship: at present vice-chairman of National Council on Freedom from Censorship; organized, with Sidney Howard and E. H. Bierstadt, a Protest Committee and published the book *Jurgen and the Censor.* Author of two anti-censorship pamphlets, *Oedipus and Pollyanna* and *The Blush of Shame.* Has been more or less regular contributor to American, English, and Continental dramatic magazines, and was at one time or another regularly attached to the staffs of *Drama,* New York *Sun, Arts Gazette* (London), and Gorky's *Besseda.* Was Dramatic Director (under War Department) at Camp Humphreys, Va., in 1918; Associate Director (1918-21) of Foreign Language Information Service, Washington and New York; spent two years (1922-23) in France and Germany writing on the theatre; play reader for the Theatre Guild (1929-30); on Board of Directors and adviser for the Provincetown Playhouse and Group Theatre; and has since 1936 been Executive Director of Dramatists' Play Service, New York. Author of pamphlets on Maxwell Anderson and Paul Green."

* * *

In 1916 Mr. Clark married Cecile Matilda Smith; they have two daughters and a son. His home is in Briarcliff Manor, N.Y. He is a serious-looking, bespectacled man with stiff dark hair and lined face which expresses both forthrightness and kindliness. His particular interest at present is in encouragement of the "non-professional" theatre.

PRINCIPAL WORKS: The Continental Drama of Today, 1914; The British and American Drama of Today, 1915; Contemporary French Dramatists, 1915; European Theories of the Drama, 1916; How

* Died August 5, 1953.

to Produce Amateur Plays, 1917; A Study of the Modern Drama, 1925; Eugene O'Neill: The Man and His Plays, 1926; Professor Clark: A Memoir, 1928; Speak the Speech, 1930; An Hour With American Drama, 1930; Eugene O'Neill Bibliography (with R. Sanborn) 1931.

ABOUT: Time July 17, 1939.

*CLAUDEL, PAUL (August 6, 1868-   ), French poet, playwright, and diplomat, was born at Villeneuve-sur-Fère-en-Tardenois, a

little village of some three hundred inhabitants in Aisne. His father, Louis-Prosper Claudel, dealt in mortgages and bank transactions; his mother, Louise (Cerveaux) Claudel, derived from a family of Catholic farmers and priests. Paul studied with private tutors and later attended provincial schools. When thirteen, his family moved to Paris where his sister Camille was studying sculpture under Rodin, and he was sent to the Lycée Louis-le-Grand and then to law school and the École des Sciences Politiques. In the summer of 1886 he underwent a profound psychological experience on discovering the poetry of Rimbaud: "I remember, I shall remember always . . . when I bought that little copy of the *Vogue* which contained the *Illuminations.* . . . I emerged at last from that hideous world of Taine, of Renan, and of the other Molochs of the nineteenth century, from that prison, from that frightful mechanism entirely governed by perfect and inflexible laws, which to make it worse, were knowable and teachable. . . . I had a revelation of the supernatural." This mystical adumbration was followed a few months later by his conversion to Catholicism while listening to the Magnificat during Christmas mass, at Notre-Dame: "In one moment my heart was touched and I believed. God exists, He is here. . . . He is just as personal a being as I."

In 1890 Claudel passed the examinations required for the French diplomatic service and after two years in the Commercial Department in Paris was appointed consulate assistant in New York (1893) and later consul pro tem. in Boston (1894). From 1894 to 1909 he served as vice-consul and finally as consul at Shanghai, Fuchow, Hankow, Peking and Tientsin. In 1906 during one of his trips to France he married Mlle. R e i n e Sainte-Marie-Perrin, the daughter of a Lyons architect, and took her

back to China where their first child was born.

Claudel's career as a writer had begun, anonymously, before he left his native country—the first sketch of his drama *Tête-d'Or* having been published in 1890 and *The City* in 1893; but it was not until 1900 that he published a book under his own name, *The East I Know.* His first collection of plays entitled *L'Arbre,* containing new versions of *Tête-d'Or, Le Répos du Septième Jour* and *La Jeune Fille Violane,* was published in 1901. However none of his plays was produced until much later.

In 1909 Claudel was transferred to Prague as consul, in 1911 to Frankfort, in 1914 to Hamburg. During the war he spent a year and a half as financial attaché at Rome and then left for Brazil in the capacity of Minister Plenipotentiary. His secretary, the composer Darius Milhaud, set many of his poems to music, and later composed the score for his *Book of Christopher Columbus,* produced in 1929 at the Berlin Opera House.

Claudel was French Ambassador to Japan (1921-25), to the United States (1926-33), and to Belgium (1933-35). At the outbreak of war in 1939 he was drafted to an important post in the Ministry of Propaganda.

Claudel is a great mystic poet, and his plays are but dramatic poems. Critics as different as the Abbé Dimnet, Duhamel, Turquet-Milnes, and Cattaui have called him the greatest living French poet; his plays, permeated with Æschylean grandeur, reveal his indebtedness to the Greek tragedian whose *Agamemnon, Choephori,* and *Eumenides* he translated. Claudel considers *Tête-d'Or, Partage de Midi,* and *The Satin Slipper* his best dramas, but *The Tidings Brought to Mary* and *The Book of Christopher Columbus* are also profoundly moving.

Claudel has five children and as many grandchildren. He has been described as "a contemplative Napoleon" and even today he looks like a gentler Bonaparte, like "a builder of churches," with a broad forehead, an alert expression—a mystic poet who is also exact, precise, amazingly practical! He speaks slowly, repeats his words carefully as if he were masticating them, sampling their taste. He devotes less than an hour a day to his poetry-writing, actual composition occurring during his strolls. His hobby is—sketching; his aversion—the smell of vanilla. Of his literary influences he has confessed: "Others, and especially Shakespeare, Æschylus, Dante, and Dostoievsky

* Died February 23, 1955.

were my masters and showed me the secrets of my art. But Rimbaud alone had an influence which I shall call seminal and paternal."

In 1941, Claudel, aged seventy-three, was reported in good health and dwelling in his château near Lyons, in Unoccupied France. He was said to be resigned to the "New Order" and a supporter of Vichy's policy of "collaboration" with Germany. His son and grandchildren had come to the United States.

WORKS AVAILABLE IN ENGLISH TRANSLATION: *Essays*—The East I Know, 1914; Letters to a Doubter, 1927; Ways and Crossways, 1933. *Plays* —The Tidings Brought to Mary, 1916; The Hostage, 1917; Tête-d'Or, 1919; The City, 1920; Proteus, 1921; The Book of Christopher Columbus, 1930; The Satin Slipper, 1931. *Poetry*—Three Poems of the War, 1919.

ABOUT: Bregy, K. Poets and Pilgrims; Chaigne, L. Le Chemin de P. Claudel; Duhamel, G. P. Claudel; Lalou, R. Contemporary French Literature; Madaule, J. Le Drame de P. Claudel; Rosenfeld, P. Men Seen; Turquet-Milnes, G. Some Modern French Writers; Bookman (London) January 1932; Dublin Review April 1932; Fortnightly Review September 1, 1924; Outlook March 16, 1927.

CLEGHORN, SARAH NORCLIFFE

(February 4, 1876-), American poet, was born in Norfolk, Va., and spent her early

C. Naar

childhood in Wisconsin and Minneapolis, but both her parents, John Dalton Cleghorn and Sarah Chestnut (Hawley) Cleghorn, were Vermonters, and on her mother's death, in 1885, she and her brother (the only ones to survive of six children) were sent to Manchester, Vt., to be reared by their mother's sisters. She was educated at Burr and Burton Seminary, in Manchester, with one year as a special student at Radcliffe College (1895-96). Her first published work was not verse, but stories, the very first being in Elbert Hubbard's *Philistine*, in 1897. With a small private income, for many years she did no outside work, spending her summers in Vermont, her winters in the South, with frequent trips to New York. Some of her early work was written in collaboration with her close friend, Dorothy Canfield Fisher.

There is a hiatus of twenty years between Miss Cleghorn's first published volumes and her next book, her autobiography. This was caused partly by the fact that her socialism and pacifism made editors and publishers reluctant to use her later writing, and partly by the fact that in middle age she became a teacher, first in Brookwood School, founded by William and Helen Fincke at Katonah, N.Y., and then, after Brookwood had become a labor college, at the Finckes' later school, Manumit. Both of these were so-called "progressive" schools, using the Montessori and Dalton project methods. In 1929, on a year's leave of absence from Manumit, she acted as a substitute Associate Professor of English at Vassar College. A few year later, pernicious anemia, which forced her to return to meat-eating after years of vegetarianism, obliged her to resign as a teacher, and she now lives the year round in Arlington, Vt. She has never married.

Sarah Cleghorn is in many ways typical of the New Englanders of an earlier generation than her own. She was never pretty, being short, stocky, snub-nosed, and blonde almost to albinism, but her face is alight with intelligence. Personally unassuming, rather shy, absent-minded, and retiring, she has been acutely conscious of her social responsibilities, and has allied herself wth many causes—anti-vivisection, peace, socialism, woman suffrage, anti-lynching, opposition to child labor, prison reform. Far too timid ever to be a public speaker, she yet had the courage to remain an uncompromising pacifist during and after America's participation in the First World War. Her poems she divides into what she calls "sunbonnets" (portraits of New England country life in a past age), poems expressive of a rather personal variety of mysticism, and "burning poems" with social content. Her early work one critic called "pensive, touching, and pastoral"; in the later poems he noted her "genuine and impassioned thought and a heart burning with love of her fellowcreatures," united with "skill of versification and haunting phrase." Probably the one thing of hers which will survive longest is a quatrain that she sent hesitantly in 1919 to Franklin P. Adams' "Conning Tower," where it was reprinted on its twentieth anniversary:

> The golf links lie so near the mill
> That almost every day
> The laboring children can look out
> And see the men at play.

PRINCIPAL WORKS: The Turnpike Lady (novel) 1907; The Spinster (novel) 1916; Fellow Captains (essays, with D. C. Fisher) 1916; Portraits and Protests (poems) 1917; Threescore, 1936; Nothing Ever Happens, and How it Does (with D. C. Fisher) 1940.

ABOUT: Cleghorn, S. N. Threescore; Atlantic Monthly December 1925; Christian Science Monitor Monthly April 18, 1936.

CLEMENS, SAMUEL LANGHORNE.
See "AMERICAN AUTHORS: 1600-1900"

*CLENDENING, LOGAN (May 25, 1884-), American physician and writer,
was born in Kansas City, Mo., the son of

Edwin McKaig Clendening and Lide (Logan) Clendening. He attended the University of Michigan from 1903 to 1905 for what is known in the United States as his "pre-medic" course, and received his Doctor of Medicine degree from the University of Kansas in 1907. Two years later he began practice in Kansas City, and from 1910 to 1917 was instructor in internal medicine at the Medical Department of the University of Kansas, which remains his office address. Dr. Clendening married Dorothy Hixon of La Crosse, Wis., in 1914.

During the First World War Dr. Clendening was a major in the Medical Corps and chief of medical service at the Base Hospital, Fort Sam Houston, from 1917 to 1919. He returned next year to the University of Kansas as associate professor of medicine, and has been Professor of Clinical Medicine there since 1928. In the year 1922-23 he was president of St. Luke's Hospital staff. Dr. Clendening figures frequently in the anecdotes and memorabilia of Alexander Woollcott, who spent his formative years in Kansas City. He has also been photographed behind bars (in 1939) as a sequel to an attempt to smash a noisy air-compression drill operated by a WPA street gang a hundred yards from his Kansas City home, where he was trying to concentrate on writing a newspaper column in addition to attending to his practice, university instruction, and miscellaneous literary work.

His most popular book, *The Human Body*, published in 1927, appeared a decade later in a new edition, completely rewritten and printed from new plates. The function of this book, he has stated, is not to give specific advice but to explain how the body works, so that the patient will have a more intelli-

gent, and perhaps a more confident, understanding of what the doctor is doing for him.

Dr. Clendening, a Dickens enthusiast, is an especial authority on *The Pickwick Papers,* which he put in his knapsack when he went to war. He has made a number of English journeys over Dickens territory, beginning in 1911. The doctor is a member of several learned societies, and a freethinker in his religious beliefs.

PRINCIPAL WORKS: Modern Methods of Treatment, 1924; The Human Body, 1927; The Care and Feeding of Adults, 1931; Behind the Doctor, 1933; The Balanced Diet, 1936; A Handbook to Pickwick Papers, 1936; Common Sense Health Chats, 1939.

ABOUT: Clendening, L. A Handbook to Pickwick Papers; Newsweek February 20, 1939.

CLEUGH, Mrs. SOPHIA (1887?-),
was born in Regent's Park, London, the daughter of a moderately wealthy English Liberal, named Sad-

ler. Before she was two the family moved to Paris, which, for three years meant little more to small Sophia than goat-carriages, Punch and Judy shows, and the mastery of a few very useful French words. Soon after their return to England (Surrey), Matthew Arnold became the child's first-claimed "lion."

She began school in London at ten, and for four years learned English literature from Professor Churton Collins. At sixteen she went to Dresden to study violin and piano and then came back to England for a year at the Royal College of Music. But these ambitions faded early. And in the midst of Suffrage activities she wrote not only a play, which was produced at a London matinee, but a fairy tale for which the old *London Magazine* paid her three guineas. Within the next four years she wrote— and saw produced—about a half-dozen comedies.

In London (1911) she met the Canadian-American actress, Margaret Anglin; sailed for the United States in July of that year; and after almost selling a Scotch play to Broadway, decided to remain in New York. She got a small part in *Bunty Pulls the Strings;* and soon afterwards was married to Dennis Cleugh, English playwright and actor, who died in 1928. Both she and her husband were with Nat Goodwin's *Never Say Die* in a transcontinental tour which lasted fourteen months. At the Yale Pageant, in 1916, she was "mistress of the robes" and responsible for the making of about 8,000 costumes.

Then came the war. Her husband went to the French front in the King's Royal Rifles and she herself did volunteer work for the State Audit and Food Ministry. She was "demobbed" in 1920.

In July of the year following she returned to New York, did a little movie publicity, and then settled down to the writing of her first novel, *Matilda: Governess of the English* (1924). In the next ten years she wrote about a dozen more, and among the later ones were: *Song Bird,* the romance of a Spanish opera-singer; *Enchanting Clementina,* written on the Isle of Wight during the winter of 1929-30; *The Angel Who Couldn't Sing,* an episodic novel built on *Cavalcade* lines; and *Wind Which Moved a Ship,* published in 1936. Some of her works have been signed "Ursula Keene." Her name is pronounced *clew.*

In this country she has resided intermittently at Andover, Mass. For over a year (1935-36) she conducted, for Station WHN, New York, a weekly quarter-hour Bookshop of the Air—reviews and interviews. Since that time she has written movie scripts for Universal Pictures. At the outbreak of the Second World War she returned to England to work with the Air Ministry in North Wales.

Mrs. Cleugh is neither a stylist nor a perfectionist in the matter of novel structure. But she writes easily and pleasantly; and her books convey some of the sunnier aspects of an era between two wars.

PRINCIPAL WORKS: Matilda: Governess of the English, 1924; Ernestine Sophie, 1925; Jeanne Margot, 1927; A Common Cheat, 1928; Spring, 1929; Song Bird, 1930; Daisy Boy, 1931; Enchanting Clementina, 1931; Young Jonathan, 1932; Loyal Lady (American title: Anne Marguerite) 1932; The Hazards of Belinda, 1933; Lindy Lou, 1934; The Angel Who Couldn't Sing, 1935; The Wind Which Moved a Ship, 1936.

ABOUT: Cleugh, D. Wanderer's End (see Foreword); American Notes and Queries September 1941; Bookman (London) May 1930; Bloomington, (Ill.) Sunday Pantagraph August 23, 1936; New York Times November 3, 1928; New York World-Telegram June 4, 1936; Staten Island Advance November 7, 1934.

CLIFFORD, Mrs. LUCY (LANE) (?-April 21, 1929), English novelist, letter-writer, and dramatist, was born in Barbados, British West Indies, the daughter of John Lane, who came of a family well

known in those parts. In 1875 Lucy Lane was married to William Kingdon Clifford, who, at the age of thirty was considered a remarkable young intellectual. (William James referred to him as the "delicious *enfant terrible*"; and W. H. Mallock caricatured him as one "Mr. Saunders" in his *New Republic.*)

To the Clifford home in St. John's Wood came many of the literary and scientific "giants" of the day, including Leslie Stephen, Huxley, and Tyndall. Lucy Clifford herself was one of the few women who were privileged to do homage to George Eliot at the famous "Sunday afternoons" at the Priory.

For Mr. Clifford's health they went to the Mediterranean in April 1878. He was better on their return, then suffered a relapse, and was taken to Madeira, where he died in March of the following year. Fortunately George Eliot was able to aid Mrs. Clifford, left with two daughters and inadequate means, to secure a small Civil List pension. Shortly afterwards the editors of the *Standard* began to solicit a few of her pieces and she was for many years a contributor.

Her first novel, *Mrs. Keith's Crime,* in which parents are tried for ending the misery of a hopelessly ill and suffering child, appeared anonymously in 1885. Not until the book had gone into several editions was she identified as the author. Lord Morley thought it "revolting"; Thomas Hardy admired it; and Browning called it "splendid" and wished that he himself had written it. Eight years later came *Aunt Anne,* the study of a dual personality, exemplified in inherent "good-breeding" and a complete lack of scruples. She wrote an extravaganza called *A Wild Proxy;* a relentless and somewhat artful study of female strategems in *Love Letters of a Worldly Woman;* and a book of children's tales (*Anyhow Stories*) which had sufficient merit to have been attributed, by some critics, to Lewis Carroll. In the early 1900's she wrote a number of plays (*The Likeness of the Night, The Searchlight, A Woman Alone,* etc.), some of which appeared first in magazines.

Kipling, it is said, had much faith in her literary judgment; James Russell Lowell wrote her a series of remarkable letters; and

Henry James remembered her in his will. Her *Mrs. Keith's Crime* enjoyed a sweeping though brief popularity: it is not, however, so much for the art of writing itself but for her associations with those who practiced this art that she is remembered.

PRINCIPAL WORKS: Anyhow Stories, 1882; Mrs. Keith's Crime, 1885; Love Letters of a Worldly Woman, 1891; A Woman Alone, 1891; Aunt Anne, 1893; A Wild Proxy, 1894; The Likeness of the Night, 1901; Woodside Farm, 1902; The Modern Way, 1906; Sir George's Objection, 1910.

ABOUT: Haldane, E. S. George Eliot and Her Times; London Times April 22, 1929.

CLOETE, STUART (July 23, 1897-), South African novelist, writes: "Stuart Cloete was born in Paris, but comes of

a well known South African family which first came to South Africa in 1652. His ancestor Jacob Cloeten was the first man to obtain a grant of land there. The earliest trace of the family is a 13th Century tomb in Saxony. Later they moved to Spain where their name became Cloetta, and then moved with the Spanish forces to the Low Countries.

"Educated as a child in Paris, Stuart Cloete went at the age of twelve to school in England, where he remained until the outbreak of war. He has the almost unique distinction of having failed the entrance examination for Sandhurst, the English Royal Military Academy. He was, however, gazetted second lieutenant in 1914 at the age of seventeen. At nineteen he commanded a company in the Ypres salient and was later wounded in the lung on the Somme. Two years later he rejoined the British Expeditionary Force, and at St. Leger was wounded in four places so severely that after being on half pay for five years he was finally put on the retired list. Unfitted for anything but open air life, he decided to go to South Africa, which, though he had never seen it, was the home of his people. After growing cotton for a land company and being manager of a 16,000-acre cattle ranch, he bought his own dairy farm.

"At this time he became interested in writing and showed some of his work to Sarah Gertrude Millin and E. Arnot Robertson, who encouraged him to go on. He sold his cattle and returned to England. Working all day and living on the remains of his capital, he could find no outlet for his work. Actually his sales were: first year, nothing; second year, eight guineas; third year, thirty-six guineas for six stories. Then he wrote a novel which was refused by four publishers and finally accepted by Heinemann. This he withdrew, as he did not like it, and began *The Turning Wheels,* which was accepted with contracts signed both in England and in America when only 50,000 words were completed. It was a Book-of-the-Month Club selection and a choice of the English Book Society—the first time any first novel had been so doubly chosen. It has since been translated into ten languages. *The Turning Wheels* begins a series of novels which will cover a South African family from 1812 to 1930. Each book will be complete in itself, but each will contain characters that appeared in the previous one."

* * *

Mr. Cloete is a tall, moustached man who looks "half ex-Coldstream Guards officer and half Dutch ex-farmer." He is unmarried. At the outbreak of the Second World War, he volunteered for army service but was refused because of his wounds in the 1914-18 struggle. He then came to the United States. His name is pronounced *clew-tee.*

PRINCIPAL WORKS: The Turning Wheels, 1937; Watch for the Dawn, 1939; Yesterday Is Dead, 1940; Young Men and Old, 1941; The Hill of Doves, 1941.

ABOUT: New York Times Book Review November 17, 1940; Saturday Review of Literature November 6, 1937, June 1, 1940; Time November 8, 1937; Wilson Library Bulletin November 1937.

"CLOSE, UPTON." See HALL, J. W.

CLUTTON-BROCK, ARTHUR (March 23, 1868-January 8, 1924), English journalist, critic, and essayist, was born in Weybridge, the third son of John Alan Clutton-Brock, a prominent banker, and Mary Alice (Hill) Clutton-Brock. In 1882 he entered Eton on a scholarship, winning here an English verse prize for an ode in the manner of Shelley, on "England and Her Colonies."

W. Rothenstein

At New College, Oxford, he took third classes in classical honors moderations and Literae Humaniores. After a short time in a stockbroker's office, Clutton-

Brock was called to the bar by the Inner Temple in 1895, and practiced some years. Evelyn Vernon-Harcourt became his wife in 1903, and next year Clutton-Brock began his writing career as literary editor of the *Speaker* (later the *Nation*) and frequent contributor to the new *Literary Supplement* of the London *Times.* In 1908 he was art critic on the *Times,* after serving in a similar capacity on the *Tribune* and *Morning Post.* Two books on the cathedrals of northern France and the cathedral church of York preceded his well-known studies of Shelley, published in 1909 and revised fourteen years later, and of William Morris. Accepting Morris' aesthetic approach to socialism, Clutton-Brock joined the Fabian Society in 1909. His view of Shelley was sufficiently unorthodox to "antagonize the worshipful." Religion did not interest Clutton-Brock until the First World War, when he published two volumes of *Thoughts on the War.* By 1919 he had reached the conclusion that he had attained religious optimism too easily; he believed, however, and preached in his articles in the *Times Literary Supplement,* that religion should be taken in a spirit of love, laughter, and beauty. He was inclined to take flight from the world of existence into a Platonistic sphere of absolute values, and freely acknowledged his debt to Benedetto Croce. Although a fearless critic, he was inclined on occasion to be didactic, and was frequently too impulsive, too rapid, and too versatile. In the words of T. L. Hammond, "To the day of his death [at fifty-eight, after an intermittent illness of three years] he was a boy in the spontaneous candour of his enthusiasms and the unspoilt freshness of his feeling for life." His last conscious act was to point out to his doctor the beauty of an iris.

PRINCIPAL WORKS: The Cathedral Church of York, 1899; Shelley: The Man and the Poet, 1909; William Morris: His Work and Influence, 1914; Thoughts on the War, 1914-1915; The Ultimate Belief, 1916; Studies in Christianity, 1918; Essays on Art, 1918; Essays on Books, 1920; More Essays on Books, 1921; The Necessity of Art, 1924.

ABOUT: Lynd R. Books and Authors; Murray, D. L. Scenes and Silhouettes; Walkley, A. B. More Prejudice.

COATES, ROBERT MYRON (April 6, 1897-), American novelist, writes: "I was born in New Haven, Conn. My father, Frederick Coates, was an expert tool-maker, a type of mechanic that in those days could get jobs anywhere, and since he liked to travel, from the time I was six years old we were pretty constantly on the move—to Cripple Creek, Colo., where he had a try at gold-mining; to Salt Lake City, Portland, Ore., Seattle, Springfield, Mass., New York City, Rochester, N.Y., Cincinnati. By that time he was a machine designer and I was in college at Yale. I graduated, B.A., 1916, having first spent six or eight months in the Naval Aviation at Bay Shore, during the War. I worked for a while, writing features for a newspaper syndicate and pamphlets for the United States Rubber Company; but my heart was not in it, and in 1921 I went abroad—to Paris, to Italy, back to Paris  again, and finally to settle in the town of Giverny, in the Eure.

"I came back to this country in 1926, having out-stayed most of the expatriates I'd gone over with (perhaps because I'd settled in the country in France, instead of in Paris), and for the next year or so (in the course of which I married Elsa Kirpal, a sculptor) I existed pretty precariously in New York writing book reviews, Sunday feature stories for the *Times* and the *Tribune,* etc. Then, chiefly through the intervention of my friend James Thurber, I got a job on the *New Yorker.* I've been associated with that magazine in one capacity or another pretty much ever since—as one of the 'Talk of the Town' editors, then as book critic, and now as art critic, and also as a contributor. Having built a house at Gaylordsville, Conn., I moved there in 1931, and have lived there ever since. We have a son.

"My interest in art dates from the early 1920's, when I used to hang around the Art Students' League. My first published writing was a couple of poems in the *New Republic,* in 1919. I soon turned to prose, and while abroad I contributed to *Gargoyle* (Paris), *Broom* (Rome), and others of the so-called 'little' magazines. Short stories of mine have appeared in the O. Henry Prize Stories of 1937 and in O'Brien's Best Stories of 1939."

* * *

Mr. Coates is over six feet tall, with a shock of red hair and gentle blue eyes. According to Mr. Thurber, he "enjoys reading dictionaries, histories of Ireland, Flaubert, trade journals, and the printing on cans of preserved vegetables; he haunts five-and-ten-cent stores and factories; and spends whole afternoons throwing an ice-pick at a bull's-eye on a barn door." It was he who introduced Ernest Hemingway to Gertrude Stein. His novel, *The Eater of Darkness,* has been called "the first Dada novel in English." His sociological work, *The Outlaw Years,* took three years of research, and is a valuable piece of Americana.

PRINCIPAL WORKS: The Eater of Darkness, 1926; The Outlaw Years: The History of the Land Pirates of the Natchez Trace, 1930; Yesterday's Burdens (novel) 1933.

COATSWORTH, ELIZABETH JANE

(May 31, 1893-), American writer for children, novelist, and poet, writes: "Buffalo, N.Y., when I was born was still a large town where everyone knew everyone else. For eight months of the year I had little time for play, for I went to a school that was modeled on the English system, with long hours and severe discipline. But in the summer we moved to 'the Beach,' overlooking the Canadian shore of Lake Erie. In these two places I grew to girlhood, but since ours was a traveling family, we were not always at home. When I was less than a year old we went to California; when I was five I was looking down on clouds from the high Alps, and galloping on donkeys across Egyptian deserts; when I was twelve we spent two years in Southern California and I had my first glimpses of Mexico and Aztec ruins.

"I was fond of books in those days—more fond than I am now—but my memories of Vassar are more of explorations through that lovely Hudson countryside than of my courses. I took my B.A. in 1915, and an M.A. at Columbia in 1916, and then came a never-to-be forgotten year of adventure in the Orient. There followed years of books and travel. I had always written poetry and began now to publish it more and more. Then one day I wrote *The Cat and the Captain.* Since then writing books for children has become a pleasant habit, and I have written many, including a Japanese tale of *The Cat Who Went to Heaven* which won the Newbery Medal for 1930.

"In 1929 I married Henry Beston,[qv] the writer. We have two daughters, and divide our time between an old house in Hingham, just south of Boston, and a farm that lies on a promontory jutting out into Damariscotta Lake in Maine. There any fine day near noon you might see two tall dark-haired people, with two little curly-haired girls and a black bull terrier, strolling toward the trees that fringe the lake, their morning writing done, and picnic baskets in their hands."

* * *

Miss Coatsworth has also studied at the University of California. Her work has three distinct periods: the first when she traveled extensively and became known, while still in her twenties, as an authority on the Orient; the second when she was known primarily as a poet of talent and promise, whose free verse Dorothy Emerson called "fragile as a paper umbrella, delicately sorrowful as the drone of an insect"; and the third, when she became a very popular writer for children. She seems at this writing to be entering still a fourth period, having written one adult novel and being engaged on a second. She also still writes poetry, though no longer the imagistic verse of her early days, and is said to have appeared more frequently in magazines than any other contemporary American poet.

PRINCIPAL WORKS: *Poetry*—Fox Footsprings, 1923; Atlas and Beyond, 1925; Compass Rose, 1929. *Juveniles*—The Cat and the Captain, 1927; Toutou in Bondage, 1929; The Sun's Diary, 1929; The Boy and the Parrot, 1930; The Cat Who Went to Heaven, 1930; Knock at the Door, 1931; Cricket and the Emperor's Son, 1932; Away Goes Sally, 1934; The Golden Horseshoe, 1935; Sword of the Wilderness, 1936; Alice-All-By-Herself, 1937; Dancing Tom, 1938; Five Bushel Farm, 1939. The Fair American, 1940; The Trunk, 1941; Houseboat Summer, 1942; Runaway Home (with Mabel O'Donnell) 1942. *Novel*—Here I Stay, 1938.

ABOUT: Kunitz, S. J. & Haycraft, H. (eds.). The Junior Book of Authors; Scholastic April 24, 1937.

*COBB, HUMPHREY (1899-), American novelist, was born in Florence, Italy, in Casa Guidi, the famous house which was the

home of Robert and Elizabeth Barrett Browning. His parents, Bostonians, had lived in Italy for some years. In 1912, when he was thirteen, the family returned to the United States in order to give him an American education. But in September

Pinchot

1916, when he was only seventeen, he enlisted in the Canadian Army. He was sent to France the next year, and served through the

First World War, being wounded and twice gassed. After the war he stayed in Europe, living in various parts of England and in Paris. Then, before returning to America, he went around Africa as sailor on a freighter. Meanwhile he was learning to write novels by the process of writing them and then destroying them. His first and second books met this fate.

Back in New York, he became an advertising copywriter. Finding that it was impossible to write after office hours, he threw up his job and settled down in earnest. The result was *Paths of Glory,* which was a sensation in 1935, and later was a successful play in a dramatization by the late Sidney Howard. Incidentally, the novel had no title when it was finished, and was named by means of a prize contest. Mr. Cobb now lives in Pasadena, Calif. He has been married, but is now divorced. He is short, very blond, almost bald, extremely shy and reticent. Only his hatred of war and his liberal social views can force him to the agony of speaking in public.

Paths of Glory, with its excellent title from Gray's *"Elegy,"* is an unsparing exposure of the cruel injustices possible under war psychology. Christopher Morley has called it "more than a book—it is an arrow in the conscience of the world." It tells the story of an incident (based on fact) in which a martinet general, to cover up his own inefficiency, has three men picked by lot from a French regiment and shot for "cowardice" because they were unable to take a hill held by the German forces. It is a painful, powerful work, which has become a minor classic among the post-war novels of the school of Remarque's *All Quiet on the Western Front* and Arnold Zweig's *The Case of Sergeant Grischa* (to the latter of which it bears a certain analogy).

Since publication of his first novel, Mr. Cobb has continued to write, but has published no other books; another novel, *None But the Brave,* ran as a serial in *Collier's Weekly* in 1938.

PRINCIPAL WORK: Paths of Glory, 1935.

ABOUT: New York Times September 22, 1940; Scholastic November 9, 1935.

*COBB, IRVIN SHREWSBURY (June 23, 1876-   ), American humorist and novelist, writes: "My grandfathers both were born on Kentucky soil—one in 1804, the other in 1808. My ancestors were among the earliest settlers in the state, one group coming from Virginia before the state was created, the other emigrating from Vermont in the seventh year of the young commonwealth. I am a direct descendent of Thomas Chittenden, the first governor of Vermont, and of Colonel Linah Mims, who was acting governor of Virginia for a short while in 1812.

"My father, Joshua Clark Cobb, who had been a rich man's son, was for most of his life a poor man. So I never got as far as the second grade in high school at Paducah, Ky., where I was born and reared. At fourteen I was trying to learn shorthand; at fifteen I was driving an ice-wagon, collecting on a newspaper route, delivering circulars, and selling a few crude drawings to allegedly comic papers, being minded to become a cartoonist. At sixteen I was a cub reporter on the local daily. At nineteen I was for a short while its managing editor— the youngest managing editor of a daily paper in the United States, so it was said. I have followed the writing game in one fashion or another ever since—with time out for lecture work, war correspondence, travel, hunting and fishing, collecting Indian relics, and for trying (of recent years) to act in the movies. But I didn't write my first short story until I was in my 37th year—an age when many short story writers either have written themselves out, or else have graduated—or descended, as the case may be and frequently is—into the novel-writing class.

"I was born a Democrat and fetched up as one and still am one, but by no means a subscriber to all the political doctrines and government policies of the New Deal. My literary preferences are comfortable enough, I'd say. I do not care—have never cared— for many of the so-called classics, nor for the fiction of the ultra-modernistic school. I do not believe that it is necessary to be blatantly pornographic and deliberately nasty in order to be realistic and graphic in expression of thought or description of human beings and human events. In religion—as I publicly stated a good many years ago and was soundly scolded by numerous preachers for doing so—I am an Innocent Bystander. My favorite authors and public figures are mostly dead. Among the survivors, at this writing, are Booth Tarkington, Kenneth Roberts, former Governor Al Smith, U.S. Senator Carter Glass, James

* Died March 10, 1944.

Stevens, Prof. Washington Carver, colored, of Tuskegee Institute, Rabbi Cohen of Galveston Texas, Helen Hayes the actress, John Charles Thomas the singer, W. C. Fields the comedian, and Gracie Allen the nut. I give thanks daily that, in the main, my tastes always have been rather vulgar and my preferences for simple people and commonplace things.

"In 1900 I married Miss Laura Spencer Baker of Savannah, Ga. In 1904 we moved to New York. We tried it thirty-four years and we didn't like the place. So we came to Santa Monica, where just lately we celebrated our 40th wedding anniversary. Either we have grown to like Southern California or have just become numb—the jury is still out. We have one daughter, Elizabeth Cobb Rogers, also a writer, and two grandchildren, one of whom, we fear, may grow up to be a writer likewise.

"I have had sixty-odd books published. The exact number doesn't matter, because some of them never sold and some of them should never have been published in the first place. In addition, I have ground out millions of words—essays, special articles, supposedly humorous skits, stray bits of fiction, copy for columns and departments—which were printed in magazines, syndicate outputs, or individual newspapers. I have likewise written numerous playlets which were produced, more or less successfully, in vaudeville; and I wrote myself or collaborated in writing several plays, all of which failed.

"I am now [1940] engaged in writing a series of personal reminiscences: not an autobiography, exactly, but first cousin to one. It started out to be a single volume. From present indications the material may make two volumes, weighing about three pounds apiece. In odd intervals I likewise write moving picture scripts and occasionally play a part in a moving picture. I waited until I was along toward sixty to try the acting game; still I like it. I have never had any trouble controlling my fan mail."

PRINCIPAL WORKS: Back Home, 1912; Cobb's Anatomy, 1912; Cobb's Bill of Fare, 1913; Roughing It De Luxe, 1914; Europe Revised, 1914; Old Judge Priest, 1915; Fiddle, D. D., 1916; Speaking of Operations—, 1916; Local Color, 1916; Those Times and These, 1917; The Glory of the Coming, 1918; The Thunders of Silence, 1918; The Life of the Party, 1919; Oh, Well, You Know How Women Are! 1919; The Abandoned Farmers, 1920; A Plea for Old Cap Collier, 1921; One Third Off, 1921; Sundry Accounts, 1922; Myself to Date, 1923; A Laugh a Day, 1923; Goin' on Fourteen, 1924; Here Comes the Bride, 1925; More Laughs for More Days, 1925; Prose and Cons, 1926; Some United States, 1927; Ladies and Gentlemen, 1927; All Aboard, 1928; This Man's World, 1929; Red Likker, 1929; Both Sides of the Street, 1930; Incredible Truth, 1931; Down Yonder, 1932; Murder Day by Day, 1933; Faith, Hope, and Charity, 1934; Judge Priest Turns Detective, 1937; Azam: The Story of an Arabian Colt, 1937; Exit Laughing, 1941; Glory, Glory, Hallelujah! 1941.

ABOUT: Bennett, A. Your United States; Cobb, I. S. Exit Laughing; Myself to Date; Mencken, H. L. Prejudices, First Series; Neuman, F. G. Irvin S. Cobb: His Life and Letters; Williams, B. C. Our Short Story Writers; American Magazine December 1922; Bookman July 1929; Forum October 1917; Golden Book January 1934; New York Times Book Review November 2, 1941.

COCTEAU, JEAN (July 5, 1891-), French poet, novelist, playwright, and critic, was born in Maisons-Laffitte, on the Seine, some ten miles from Paris, of a family of Parisian lawyers. In 1909, when he was scarcely seventeen, his volume of poems *La Lampe d'Aladin* appeared, followed soon after by *Le Prince Frivole* and *La Danse de Sophocle* which, because of  their orthodoxy and classic restraint, found the reputable Editions du Mercure de France for a publisher. "When I was seventeen," Cocteau declared, "I was charged with the electricity of poetry but bewildered by praise of a doubtful value, and the reading of bad books, I was incapable of forging a transmitting process and spent all my time turning over and over on the same spot, like a sick person trying to fall asleep. I dragged myself about, absurdly puffed up with pride; I was sick of myself and would have been glad to die. It was the Comtesse de Noailles who imparted to me her love of life. . . . Gradually I fell into the sleep of a somnambulist. This became my normal state, and no doubt I shall continue to sleep until the end. Then I set out in search of myself. The first person I met was Gide. How I envied him his Protestant childhood! . . . Our friendship gave me strength."

Cocteau regretted and disowned his early works, his "waking books," and preferred to date his literary debut from the publication of his prose fantasy *Le Potomak*, when he "began to dream." Cocteau was engaged in the composition of *Le Potomak* at the outbreak of war in 1914 and interrupted it to go to the front where he flew with the aviator Roland Garros. The war had a tremendous impact on the young poet as can be seen from the revised edition of *Le Potomak* published in 1919, shortly before his poems *Le Cap de Bonne-Espérance,* which marked his departure toward the imaginative and the baroque even in its typography, and where, in the poem "L'Invitation à la Mort" he describes his first flight with Garros.

During the last twenty years Cocteau has tried all existing literary *genres* plus a few more which he invented, and experimented with nearly every new trend in not only the five traditional arts but the cinema, the ballet, the circus, and jazz as well, for according to him, "art must satisfy the nine muses." Cocteau has been intimately connected with modernist leaders in various spheres, including Picasso, Stravinsky, Diaghilev, frequently collaborating with them. He has been actor, director, scenario writer, novelist, critic.

As a poet the volumes *Poésie 1916-1923* (1925) and *Opéra 1925-1927* (1927) show him an astonishing experimentalist in technique, often amusing, always eccentric, and an inveterate practitioner of his theory of poetry: that "a great literary masterpiece is but a dictionary in disorder." Cocteau made his début as a novelist in 1923 with *Thomas the Impostor,* and then perfected his fictional expressionism with *The Grand Ecart* (1923) and *Enfants Terribles* (1929), which definitely placed him among the most exciting story tellers in contemporary letters.

However it is in the "amusement field" that Cocteau has displayed most effectively his manifold interests and original talent: his collaboration with Picasso, Satie, Diaghilev, Bakst and the "Six" group resulted in such entertaining ballets as *Parade* (1917, music by Satie), *Le Bœuf sur le Toit* (1920, jazz), *Les Mariés de la Tour Eiffel* (1924, music by the "Six"), and *Le Pauvre Matelot* (1927, music by Honegger) ; his adaptation of *Romeo and Juliet* performed on June 2, 1924, at the Théâtre de la Cigale was followed by his refreshing *Orphée* (1926), and the opera-oratorios *Œdipus King* (1927, music by Stravinsky) and *Antigone* (1927, music by Honegger). More recently Cocteau has tried the theatre single-handedly: on February 17, 1930, the Comédie Française performed his one-act monologue *La Voix Humaine,* and on April 10, 1934, the Comédie des Champs Elysées produced *The Infernal Machine,* magnificent *tours de force* which enlarged his group of admirers considerably and enhanced his reputation. He also wrote the scenario *The Blood of the Poet,* and with this strange film which he directed himself

and which fully evidenced his imaginative gifts, his name traveled far beyond the confines of esoteric circles. Finally his satiric drama *Les Parents Terribles* became the Paris theatrical hit of 1939.

Cocteau has touched many extremes of human experience. His rogueries, tomfooleries, and brilliant fireworks mirror the chaos and restlessness of his generation, and although he has tried many means of escape—the Catholic Church, opium, solitude—he has remained the incorrigible *enfant terrible* of contemporary literature, even after his fiftieth birthday.

All photographs of Cocteau are inadequate to picture his personal appearance. Margaret Anderson writes: "His face is so delicate, so constantly in transition, that only the cinema could register its nuances. His hands are even more expressive than his face. They would be merely grotesque—too long, too veined—except that he uses them like words."

Professor Stansbury says that Cocteau's works "must be accepted and enjoyed as a series of glittering and rapidly moving scenes developed by means of clever juggling. . . . His books have charm, even in those passages, unfortunately all too frequent, which seem devoid of meaning. His ability to impart a light touch to everything, he defines as 'a clean vivacity.' The great poet Rainer Maria Rilke exclaimed: "Tell Jean Cocteau that I adore him, the only person for whom the Myth opens its gates, and from which he returns bronzed as from the seaside."

Since the German occupation of France in 1940, Cocteau has disappointed his admirers by veering somewhat helplessly into the Fascist orbit.

WORKS AVAILABLE IN ENGLISH TRANSLATION: *Novels*—Thomas the Imposter, 1925; The Grand Ecart, 1925; Enfants Terribles, 1925. *Plays*—Orphée, 1933; The Infernal Machine, 1936. *Essays*—A Call to Order, 1927; Opium: The Diary of an Addict, 1932; Round the World Again in Thirty Days, 1937.

ABOUT: Lalou, R. Contemporary French Literature; Lefèvre F. Une Heure Avec; Stansbury, M. H. French Novelists of Today; Books June 1 1930; Grande Revue April 1933; Humanité October 6, 1926; Mercure de France April 1, 1930; New Republic August 20, 1930; New York Times June 22, 1930; Oxford Outlook March 1931.

*COFFIN, ROBERT PETER TRISTRAM (March 18, 1892-), American poet, writes: "I am a New Englander by birth, by bringing up, by spirit—while I was living abroad and in New York—and now again, by residence. [Editorial Note: Mr Coffin was born in Brunswick, Maine the son of James William Coffin and Alice Mary (Coombs) Coffin.] My family has roots 300 years deep in the New England soil and sea. The Coffins were once the whalers extraordinary that Edmund Burke speaks of, princes of Nantucket, in Quaker gray.

"I grew up on a Maine saltwater farm, and I began being a poet there among lighthouses and barns and boats, tides and fogs and apples and hired men, on that best kind of farm. I went to a rural red-brick schoolhouse, which, by the way, I have just bought and intend to preserve as a monument to my boyhood and the boyhood of America.

Pinchot

I have put my boyhood into *Lost Paradise,* a prose book that bids fair to become a classic of Maine boyhood and boyhood everywhere. And I have put my father, who was a pioneer in bringing Casco Bay islands into civilization, into such another prose classic, *Portrait of an American.*

"I graduated at Bowdoin, *summa cum laude,* 1915; at Princeton, M.A., 1916; and at Oxford University, B.Litt., 1921, where I was Rhodes Scholar from Maine, just before and after my two years' vacation from civilization in the World War. I taught English at Wells College, Aurora, N.Y., for thirteen years, 1921-34, and I am now back home at Bowdoin as Pierce Professor of English, living in a house a stone's throw from the house where I was born. I have lectured frequently at other colleges: at Columbia, on contemporary poetry, 1937 and 1938; I gave the Turnbull Memorial Poetry Lectures on Frost and Robinson, "New Poetry of New England" at Johns Hopkins University in 1938; and these lectures have been published by the Hopkins Press. I hold honorary Litt.D.'s from Bowdoin, 1930, and University of Maine, 1937. I have been Phi Beta Kappa Poet at Harvard, Hamilton, Virginia, Colby, Tufts, and Boston University. I have been made an Honorary Life Member of the National Arts Club. I am a member of the Author's Club and P.E.N. I was National Honor Poet in 1935, won the Golden Rose of the New England Poetry Society in 1936, and I won the Pulitzer Prize for Poetry in 1936 with my volume *Strange Holiness.*

"For the rest, I am a Republican by politics, a Congregationalist, a member of the Phi Beta Kappa and the Zeta Psi Fraternity.

"Besides writing and teaching poetry, I keep in training as a poet by living through the summers on my two farms, a saltwater one with a sea-captain's mansion, on the coast, and a freshwater one, on Merrymeeting Bay—also an old home of sea-captain farmers, on the banks of that river, the Kennebec, whose history I wrote for the first volume in the *Rivers of America* series. I have four fine-looking children to keep me young. [Editorial Note: Mr. Coffin married Ruth Neal Phillip in 1918.] My relaxations are writing, story telling, gardening, and fishing—both saltwater and fresh. Being an amateur artist, I often draw the jacket designs for my own books, and illustrate them likewise. I have written 20 books in all. I think I have about the widest range of any living author anywhere, all the way from biography, *Laud* and *The Dukes of Buckingham,* through history, *Kennebec,* to lectures and essays, *An Attic Room* and *Book of Crowns and Cottages,* and novels of the Maine Coast, *John Dawn* and *Red Sky in the Morning,* and, of course, my nine volumes of poetry. In poetry, too, my range is wide, from ballad to blank verse lyric. This range is apparent in my *Collected Poems,* published in 1939 with a preface that sums up many of my ideas about poetry and its place in modern life.

"I do most of my creative writing late at night, when the children and neighbors are quiet, when a man can put his best foot forward and say the best things he can about life, which I believe poetry ought to say. I think some of the embittered and despondent modern poets ought to be obliged to write after midnight. I feel that they would find it hard to be cynical and pessimistic at, say three o'clock in the morning. Among my definitions of poetry are these: Poetry is the art of making people feel well about life; poetry is saying the best one can about life; poetry is the art of putting different kinds of good things together: men and plows, boys and whistles, hounds and deer, sorrow and sympathy, life and death.

"One of my three professions now is taking my poems, and my ideas about poetry as a public function, directly to the American people with my own voice. My lecture-readings take me all over our country. I have read before some 500 colleges and schools and clubs in the past few years. I have built up an interest in my poems unique in the contemporary scene. As my interests and themes have been wide, so has the response to my work been. Most of my recent books have sold widely. *Ballads of Square-Toed Americans* and *An Attic Room* have been reprinted; *Lost Paradise* has been reprinted five times; *Strange Holiness* has been reprinted six times; *Saltwater Farm,* my collection of Maine poems, three times; and *Kennebec,* five.

"In addition to my books, I have contributed continuously to magazines, both prose and verse, for the past 15 years. I am at present Book and Poetry Editor for *Yankee.*"

PRINCIPAL WORKS: *Poetry*—Christchurch, 1924; Dew and Bronze, 1927; Golden Falcon, 1929; The Yoke of Thunder, 1932; Ballads of Square-Toed Americans, 1933; Strange Holiness, 1935; Saltwater Farm, 1937; Maine Ballads, 1938; Collected Poems, 1939; There Will Be Bread and Love, 1942. *Prose*—Book of Crowns and Cottages, 1925; A Book of Seventeenth Century Prose, 1929; An Attic Room, 1929; Laud: Storm Center of Stuart England, 1930; The Dukes of Buckingham, 1931; Portrait of an American, 1931; Lost Paradise, 1934; Red Sky in the Morning, 1935; John Dawn, 1936; Kennebec: Cradle of Americans, 1937; New Poetry of New England: Frost and Robinson, 1938; Captain Abby and Captain John, 1939; Thomas-Thomas-Ancil-Thomas, 1941; Christmas in Maine, 1941.

ABOUT: Coffin, R. P. T. Lost Paradise; English Journal September 1936; Literary Digest June 1, 1935; Poetry February and November 1938; Saturday Review of Literature September 22, 1933, April 20, 1935, May 9, 1936, May 27, 1937; Scholastic March 3, 1934, October 3, 1936, October 30, 1937; Time October 9, 1939.

*COHEN, MORRIS RAPHAEL (July 25, 1880-), American philosopher, was born in Minsk, Russia, the son of Abraham M.

Cohen and Bessie (Farfel) Cohen, and was brought to the United States at the age of twelve. He was educated at the College of the City of New York (B.S. 1900) and Harvard University (Ph.D. 1906). From 1899 to 1903 he taught history at the Educational Alliance, New York, and in 1900 and 1901 at the Davidson Collegiate Institute as well. In 1901 and 1902 he was a teacher in the New York public schools. His long association with his alma mater, the College of the City of New York, began in 1902, when for two years he taught mathematics there; in 1904 he left to attend Harvard, but returned in 1906. Until 1912 he continued to teach mathematics; then he became professor of philosophy, and remained in that post until 1938, when he retired. He is now professor emeritus, at an unusually early age.

However, though he said then that he wanted to give up teaching and devote himself entirely to writing, that his health was frail and he felt that nearly forty years in classrooms was enough, he was immediately made professor of philosophy at the University of Chicago and still holds that position. Though he spends some time in Chicago, his permanent residence remains New York. Many times other colleges and universities tried to persuade him to go to them, but he refused to leave C.C.N.Y., where he said the students stimulated him. They in their turn regarded him with respect and some awe, as their "modern Socrates with an acid tongue." During these years he lectured on philosophy in many colleges, including Harvard, Yale, Columbia, Johns Hopkins, Stanford, and St. John's, as well as at the New School of Social Research, with which he is still connected. Though he never studied law, legal philosophy has been his specialty, and Felix Frankfurter (who was his roommate in Harvard) once said that every judge and lawyer in the United States had been influenced by Morris Cohen.

Dr. Cohen was married in 1906 to Mary Ryshpan, and they have two sons and a daughter. He was president of the American Philosophical Association in 1929, on the council of the American Association of University Professors from 1918 to 1921, is a Fellow of the American Association for the Advancement of Science, and organized the Conference on Legal and Social Philosophy in 1913 and the Conference on Jewish Relations, of which he has been president since 1933. A "big-domed, gray-haired" man, his chief recreation is the study of mathematics and physics.

Harold J. Laski has called him "the most penetrating and creative United States philosopher since William James"; Sidney Hook says he is the embodiment of "the spirit of intelligent dissent" and holds "the foremost place in the realm of creative American thought today." Henry Hazlitt finds him "remarkably free from provincialism of place or time . . . deeply traditional . . . he is a rationalist in the sense that he is convinced that philosophers . . . must rely on the validity of logical reasoning . . . but he does not identify knowledge with its rational element. Nature is more than reason." Brilliant and scholarly, he has "too critical a

* Died January 28, 1947.

mind to line up with any party or cult." His style, said Hazlitt, is "not lacking in a fine terseness of its own. . . . He often permits himself a dry irony, and he has a remarkable gift for pithy aphorism." He was the editor of the *Modern Legal Philosophy Series* and of a series of *Jewish Social Studies,* and contributed to the *Cambridge History of American Literature* and *Contemporary American Philosophy.*

PRINCIPAL WORKS: Reason and Nature, 1931; Law and the Social Order, 1933; An Introduction to Logic and Scientific Method, 1934.

ABOUT: Journal of Philosophy January 7, 1932; Monist July 1934; Nation April 15 and August 5, 1931; New Republic July 23, 1930; Open Court February 1932; Philosophical Review November 1932; Time December 27, 1937.

COHEN, OCTAVUS ROY (June 26, 1891-), American novelist, short-story writer, and writer of detective fiction, was

born of Jewish parents in Charleston, S.C., the son of Octavus Cohen and Rebecca (Ottolengui) Cohen. At seventeen he graduated from the Porter Military Academy at Charleston; acquired a degree of B.S. from Clemson College three years later, in 1911; and in 1927 received an honorary Litt.D. from Birmingham-Southern College for his services to Southern literature. These consisted of a long and profitable series of humorous tales about highly original Negroes, from the triumphant Florian Slappey to Epic Peters, the philosophical Pullman porter. For a time an issue of the *Saturday Evening Post* without a Cohen serial or short story was hardly thinkable.

For a year Cohen worked as a civil engineer with the Tennessee Coal, Iron & Railroad Co.; after graduation from Clemson he was a newspaperman, working in the editorial departments of the Birmingham (Ala.) *Ledger,* the Charleston (S.C.) *News and Courier,* the Bayonne (N.J.) *Times,* and the Newark (N.J.) *Morning Star.* Admitted to the South Carolina bar in 1913, he practiced two years. In October 1914 Mr. Cohen married Inez Lopez of Bessemer, Ala., and next year began to write in earnest. The Cohens have a son, Octavus Roy, and live on West Fifty-seventh Street in New York City. Dabbling in the theatre, Cohen, with George Boardhurst, made something of a

success of *The Crimson Alibi* (1919), following this with three plays, *The Scourge, Come Seven,* and *Shadows* in 1920, and *Every Saturday Night* in 1921. He is a lieutenant in the U.S. Naval Reserve Force and a member of the Authors' League of America.

Although Octavus Roy Cohen is known chiefly as a humorist and popular entertainer, some readers prefer him as a detective-story writer. The late Willard Huntington Wright ("S.S. Van Dine") put the seal of approval on "the fat, commonplace, unlovely and semi-illiterate, but withal sympathetic and entertaining Jim Hanvey, who knows all the crooks in Christendom and is their friend."

PRINCIPAL WORKS: The Other Woman (with J. A. Giesy), 1917; The Crimson Alibi, 1919; Polished Ebony, 1919; Gray Dusk, 1920; Come Seven, 1920; Six Seconds of Darkness, 1921; Highly Colored, 1921; Midnight, 1922; Assorted Chocolates, 1922; Jim Hanvey: Detective, 1923; Dark Days and Black Knights, 1923; Sunclouds, 1924; Bigger and Blacker, 1925; The Iron Chalice, 1925; Black and Blue, 1926; The Outer Gate, 1927; Detours, 1927; Florian Slappey Goes Abroad, 1928; Spring Tide, 1928; The Valley of Olympus, 1929; Epic Peters: Pullman Porter, 1930; The Backstage Mystery, 1930; Lilies of the Alley, 1931; Carbon Copies, 1933; Scarlet Woman, 1934; Transient Lady, 1934; Scrambled Yeggs, 1934; Back to Nature, 1935; With Benefit of Clergy, 1935; Child of Evil, 1936; I Love You Again, 1937; East of Broadway, 1938; Florian Slappey, 1938; Strange Honeymoon, 1939; Kid Tinsel, 1941; Lady in Armor, 1941.

COLBY, FRANK MOORE (February 10, 1865-March 3, 1925), American editor and essayist, was born at Washington, D.C., of New England

stock. His parents were Stoddard Benham Colby and Ellen Cornelia (Hunt) Colby. Colby's own children, Stoddard and Harriet, are well known in present-day New York literary and publishing circles. Colby graduated from Columbia University in 1888 and received a master's degree in political science the next year. He was a Seligman Fellow there in 1889-90, lectured in history at Columbia, and was instructor at Barnard College 1892-95, with a year out as acting professor of history at Amherst College, 1890-91. A period at New York University as professor of economics followed. Colby had always eked out his salary by writing, and he left teaching in 1900 to become an editorial writer on the New York *Commercial Advertiser* for two years. His lifelong connection with the *New International Encyclopedia* (when he joined it, the *International Encyclopedia*) began in 1898, when he edited its yearbook, as he continued to do until death. Daniel Colt Gilman and Harry Thurston Peck were his associates in 1900-03, and in 1913-15 he joined Talcott Williams in supervising publication of the second edition of the *New International Encyclopedia,* which owes many of its superiorities to Colby's suggestions. He was literary critic of *Harper's Weekly* for three months, and a contributor to or staff member of the *Bookman,* the *New Republic, Vanity Fair,* the *North American Review,* and *Harper's Magazine.* Colby's dryly witty essays, written in the intervals of his heavy editorial duties, attracted a devoted if comparatively small following, augmented after his death by Clarence Day's editing of *The Colby Essays.* (Colby said, for instance, that "Hamilton Wright Mabie conducted young women into the suburbs of literature and left them there.") Burton Rascoe describes him as a man six feet in height, broad-shouldered, ruddy, with curly sandy hair, a sandy moustache, and a handsome aggressive appearance which belied his native reserve and shyness. Colby had "an unusual and true sense of humor, different from the sense of fun which characterizes so much American humor." He married Harriet Wood Fowler of Amherst in 1896.

PRINCIPAL WORKS: Outlines of General History, 1899 (4th edition 1921); Imaginary Obligations, 1904; Constrained Attitudes, 1910; The Margin of Hesitation, 1921; The Colby Essays (ed. by Clarence Day, Jr.,) 1926.

ABOUT: Colby, F. M. The Colby Essays (see Preface by P. Littell); Rascoe, B. Before I Forget; International Year Book, 1925; New York Times March 4, 1929; Saturday Review of Literature March 21, 1925; May 30, 1936, December 2, 1939.

COLE, GEORGE DOUGLAS HOWARD

(September 25, 1889-   ), English economist and writer of detective stories, who collaborates in both fields with his wife, Margaret Isabel (Postgate) Cole, writes: "G. D. H. Cole was educated at St. Paul's School, London (scholar), Balliol College, Oxford (Domus and Jenkyns Exhibitioner), and Magdalen College, Oxford (Fellow) 1912-19. He was Deputy Professor of Philosophy at Armstrong College, University of Durham, 1913-14; head of tu-

torial classes department, London University, 1919-25; and since 1925 has been a Fellow of University College, Oxford, and reader in economics at Oxford. He has taken an active part from boyhood in the Socialist movement, and was president, shortly after his student days, of the Oxford University Socialist Society and the University Socialist Federation. He is now president of the Oxford University Labour Club and chairman of the Association of University Labour Parties. He has been associated since 1912 with the Workers' Educational Association, of which he was for a number of years vice-president, and for a year acting president. He joined the Independent Labour Party and the Fabian Society at eighteen, and is now chairman of the Fabian Society, in which he has been actively associated with the work of research on economic and social problems. He was connected with the Guild Socialist movement, helped found the National Guilds League in 1915, and  has written extensively on Guild Socialism.

During 1914-18 he was head of the research department of the Amalgamated Society of Engineers and adviser to the trade unions on war-time economic problems. He became in 1918, at the end of the war, the director of the British Labour Party's research work, and was also for a number of years honorary secretary of the Labour Research Department. He was a founder and for some years president of the Association of Tutors in Adult Education, and is now British member of the Board of the International Institute of Social History, in charge of its British Section and library at Oxford. He took to writing detective stories during an illness, as he had been told not to work and found the prospect intolerable. He is vice-chairman of the Diabetic Association of Great Britain. He has been on the staff of the *New Statesman* since 1918. He was married in 1918 to Margaret Isabel Postgate; they have two daughters and a son."

* * *

The Coles are the most celebrated "writing couple" in England except Beatrice and Sidney Webb. All their detective stories are written in collaboration, but both of them have written individually as well as in collaboration on economic topics. Both are frequent contributors to magazines and news-papers, and have edited as well as written many books. Mrs. Cole is the daughter of Prof. J. P. Postgate of Cambridge, and sister of R. W. Postgate, also a distinguished econ-omist. She was educated at Roedean School and at Girton College, Cambridge. From 1914 to 1916 she was classical mistress at St. Paul's Girls' School, and from 1916 to 1925 assistant secretary of the Labour Re-search Department. Thereafter she was lec-turer for Tutorial Classes in London Uni-versity for a number of years. She is now honorary secretary of the Fabian Society. She was an active member of the National Guilds League, and has written a number of pamphlets for the League, for the Labour Research Department, and for other bodies. Mr. and Mrs. Cole live in London, though Mr. Cole spends much time in Oxford.

As writers on economics, the Coles, whom Harold Laski called "an educational move-ment in themselves," have an unusual ability to collect and digest great masses of dry ma-terial and make them intelligible to the lay reader. In their lighter vein as mystery writers they have a tendency sometimes to "write down" to their readers, and do not always observe the sacred canonical rules of crime-story writing; nevertheless, their de-tective stories are always literate and intel-ligent, if often slow by American standards.

Yusuke Tsurumi, a Japanese journalist visiting London, described G. D. H. Cole as "tall, emaciated, pale, and awfully busy." The last phrase, at least, must apply to both the husband and wife in this gifted couple.

PRINCIPAL WORKS: *Economics, by G. D. H. Cole alone and in collaboration*—The World of Labour, 1913; Labour in War-Time, 1915; Trade Unionism on the Railways, 1915; An Introduction to Trade Unionism, 1917; Self-Government in In-dustry, 1917; The Payment of Wages, 1917; Labour in the Commonwealth, 1918; Social Theory, 1920; Chaos and Order in Industry, 1920; Guild Social-ism Re-Stated, 1921; The Future of Local Govern-ment, 1921; Trade Unionism and Munitions, 1923; Workshop Organization, 1923; Labor in the Coal-Mining Industry, 1923; Out of Work, 1923; Rents, Rings, and Houses (with M. I. Cole) 1923; Or-ganized Labor, 1924; The Life of William Cobbett, 1924; The Life of Robert Owen, 1925; A Short History of the British Working-Class Movement (3 vols.) 1925-27; The Economic System, 1927; The Next Ten Years in British Social and Eco-nomic Policy, 1929; Politics and Literature, 1929; Gold, Credit, and Employment, 1930; British Trade and Industry, Past and Future, 1932; Economic Tracts for the Times, 1932; The Intelligent Man's Guide Through World Chaos, 1932; The Intelli-gent Man's Review of Europe Today (with M. I. Cole) 1933; Studies in World Economics, 1934; Some Relations Between Political and Economic Theory, 1934; What Marx Really Meant, 1934; A Guide to Modern Politics (with M. I. Cole) 1934; The Simple Case for Socialism, 1935; Prac-tical Economics, 1937; The People's Front, 1937; The Condition of Britain (with M. I. Cole) 1937; Persons and Periods, 1938; Socialism in Evolution, 1938; The Common People (with R. W. Postgate) 1938; The Machinery of Socialist Planning, 1938; Dare We Look Ahead (with others) 1938; A Plan for Democratic Britain, 1939; British Trade Union-ism Today, 1939. *Economics and Sociology, by M. I. Cole*—Local Government for Beginners, 1927; Marriage, 1938; Women of Today, 1938. *Poems, by G. D. H. Cole*—Poems, 1910; New Beginnings, 1914; The Crooked World, 1933. *Poems by M. I. Cole*—Margaret Postgate's Poems, 1918. *Detective Stories, by G. D. H. & M. I. Cole*—The Brooklyn Murders, 1923; The Death of a Millionaire, 1925; The Blatchington Tangle, 1926; The Murder at Crome House, 1927; The Man From the River, 1928; Superintendent Wilson's Holiday (short stories) 1928; Poison in the Garden Suburb, 1929; Burglars in Bucks (in America: The Berkshire Mystery) 1930; The Corpse in the Constable's Garden (in America: The Corpse in Canonicals) 1930; The Great Southern Mystery (in America: The Walking Corpse) 1931; Dead Man's Watch, 1931; Death of a Star, 1932; The Affair at Aliquid, 1933; End of an Ancient Mariner, 1933; A Lesson in Crime (short stories) 1933; Death in the Quarry, 1934; The Big Business Murder, 1935; Dr. Tancred Begins, 1935; Scandal at School, 1935; Last Will and Testament, 1936; The Brothers Sackville, 1936; Disgrace to the College, 1937; The Missing Aunt, 1937; Mrs. Warrender's Pro-fession, 1938; Off With Her Head! 1938; Double Blackmail, 1939; Greek Tragedy, 1939; Murder in the Munition Works, 1940; Wilson and Some Others, 1940; The Counterpoint Murder, 1941; Knife in the Dark, 1942.

ABOUT: Haycraft, H. Murder for Pleasure: The Life and Times of the Detective Story; Min-sky, D. The Intelligentsia of Great Britain; Book-man; January 1933; Fortnightly Review August 1929; Living Age April 1, 1922, March 21, 1925; Nation December 23, 1939.

COLE, Mrs. MARGARET ISABEL (POSTGATE). See COLE, G. D. H.

COLERIDGE, MARY ELIZABETH. See "BRITISH AUTHORS OF THE 19TH CENTURY"

*COLETTE, GABRIELLE CLAUDINE

(January 28, 1873-), French novelist who signs her books "Colette," was born in the Burgundian village of Saint-Saveur-en-Pui-saye (Yonne). Her father, Jules-Joseph Colette, a retired army captain, was the local tax-collector, a rather picturesque character who loved his bottle and his pol-itics, wrote pamphlets on military matters  and harangued the bewildered **peasants in** the name of "natural history, physics and elementary chemistry." Her mother, Sidonie Colette, was a lovable woman, extremely fond of her pets and books—at mass she frequently read her Corneille hidden inside her prayerbook. By the time Gabrielle was eight she had already discarded her Perrault, preferring writers for grown-ups: Labiche, Daudet, and even Merimée, whom she could not understand. At the local school she became the star pupil, especially because of her fluency in composition, to her as easy "as frying eggs." In 1890 financial reverses forced the family to move to the neighboring town of Chatillon-Coligny where Mme. Colette's son by a former marriage was a doctor. Homesick Gabrielle found her way around and unexcitedly married a friend of the family, Gauthier-Villars, better known as "Willy," a music critic and breezy confectioner of popular light novels. Willy was thirty-four; Colette, twenty and too wild to be of much help in his social climbing: her sharp tongue and bad manners were no asset. Instead she helped him in a "literary" way—by telling him some of her pranks and experiences. These, properly spiced by Willy, resulted in *Claudine at School* (1900), the tremendous success of which led on to a Willy-Colette collaboration which lasted for several years and brought to avid "light" readers the Claudine Series: *Young Lady of Paris* (1901), *Claudine en Ménage* (1902), *The Innocent Wife* (1903).

After divorcing Willy in 1906 (she could not bear the "depressing house" at 28 rue Jacob, nor Willy's Wagnerism, "refinements," and publicity stunts), Colette realized her life dream and went on the stage (music hall)—without detriment to her "solo" writing, however: she published at least a novel a year, of which *The Vagrant* (1910) stands out as one of her finest achievements. In that year she married the writer and statesman Henri de Jouvenel, with whom she lived until 1924. During the First World War, she was a nurse and converted her husband's estate near Saint-Malo into a hospital. For her services she was made Chevalier of the Legion d'Honneur.

Colette's life is not to be told in terms of her ever-growing series of novels. She has at various times been dramatic critic, fashion columnist, book reviewer, feature writer, woman's page editor of *Le Matin*, *Figaro*, *La Vie Heureuse*, *Femina*, *Vogue*, *La Vie Parisienne*, *Gringoire*.

Considered France's leading woman writer, Colette has often been mentioned for the Goncourt Prize. She is a member of the Belgian Academy. Her most important

novels: *The Vagrant*, *The Gentle Libertine*, *Chéri*, *The Last of Chéri*, *The Other One*, are, like most of her works, predominantly autobiographical in nature and show her characteristic power of observation, her intensity of feeling, her warm, personal style. Ehrhard says that her gift for recording sensations "invests her style with a strong flavor" and results in "the most perfect naturalist expressionism of the early decades of the century." The acute critic André Billy has written of Colette: "What the photographs do not show are the feline movement of the pupils, the warm tint of the complexion, the soft and seemingly round voice, its so curious, so nostalgic higher tone, broken suddenly by a burst of laughter or of anger; it is also that impression of muscular strength, of physical solidity and density, which emanates from her whole person and which makes one believe that along with literary genius, another genius of flesh and blood, a privilege of nearly animal invulnerability, abides in her."

Like her mother, Colette loves books, children, flowers and animals, especially cats. "She is," says Prof. Mornet, "the historian and poet of the instincts."

WORKS AVAILABLE IN ENGLISH TRANSLATION. The Vagrant, 1912; Barks and Purrs, 1913; Cats Dogs, and I, 1924; Chéri, 1929; Claudine at School (with "Willy") 1930; Mitsou, 1930; The Gentle Libertine, 1931; The Other One (British title Fanny and Jane) 1931; Young Lady of Paris (British title: Claudine in Paris) (with "Willy") 1931; A Lesson in Love, 1932; Recaptured, 1932 The Ripening (British title: The Ripening Corn) 1932; The Last of Chéri, 1932; Morning Glory 1932; The Pure and the Impure, 1933; The Innocent Wife, 1934; The Indulgent Husband, 1935 Duo, 1935; Cat, 1936; Mother of Claudine, 1937.

ABOUT: Bertaut, J. Le Roman Feminin de George Sand à Colette; Billy A. Intimités Littéraires; Chauvière, C. Colette; Ehrhard, J. E. L. Roman Français depuis Marcel Proust; Fillon, A. George Sand à Colette; Billy, A. Intimités Littéature; Larnac, J. Colette; Mornet, D. Histoire de la Littérature et de la Pensée Françaises Contemporaines; Sachs, M. The Decade of Illusion Voigt, W. Colette.

COLLIER, JOHN (May 3, 1901-), English novelist, was born in London, the son of John George Collier. His uncle, Vincent Collier, was also a novelist, once well known, and his great-grandfather was physician to William IV, the predecessor of Queen Victoria. Mr. Collier was educated privately and never attended a university. At nineteen he started writing verse, and his first poems were published when he was twenty. Four of his poems received *This Quarter's* prize for English poetry in 1922. He was twenty-nine, however, before his first book appeared, and then it was not verse, but a satirical and fantastic novel, *His Monkey Wife.* Several books by him have been privately printed in expensive limited editions. In some cases this was made necessary by the English censorship laws, since his marked talent for satire takes a Joycean turn, and often includes words usually considered unprintable. In addition to novels and short stories and one book of poems, he has published an informal history of Great Britain after the First World War (written in collaboration with Ian Lang), which is frankly modeled on the American Frederick Lewis Allen's *Only Yesterday.* He also edited the works of the seventeenth

century biographer John Aubrey, whose wit, frankness of speech, and irony made him a particularly sympathetic subject. Perhaps the most interesting of Mr. Collier's novels is *Full Circle,* a fantasy of England in 1995—an England destroyed by war, its civilization wrecked, its people reduced to primitive savagery.

For several years Mr. Collier was poetry editor of *Time and Tide.* At this period he lived on a farm in Hampshire, and described himself as "indistinguishable in appearance and pursuits from any other country bumpkin." Since, however, he also said that he did "as nearly nothing as possible, except reading and looking at pictures," the description does not seem to have been very apt. Actually he is a rather urban and sophisticated-looking young man, with keen eyes and an impish smile. He has visited the United States, and in Hollywood met his wife, Shirley Lee Palmer, whom he married in 1936. They have no children. They formerly lived at Wilcote Manor, Oxfordshire, where until the outbreak of the Second World War Mr. Collier spent most of his time gardening and shooting; but in 1942 they were living in Virginia, U. S. A. His other favorite recreation is sailing. He publishes an occasional poem, and more frequently publishes short stories in English and American magazines.

American readers should not confuse Mr. Collier with the late John Collier, the celebrated English painter, or with the American John Collier (1884-), the Commissioner of Indian Affairs, who has written a number of books about the American Indians.

PRINCIPAL WORKS: His Monkey Wife: or, Married to a Chimp, 1930; Gemini (poems) 1931; Epistle to a Friend, 1931; No Traveler Returns (short stories) 1931; Green Thoughts (short stories) 1932; Just the Other Day (with I. Lang) 1932; Tom's A-Cold (in America: Full Circle) 1933; Defy the Foul Fiend: or, The Misadventures of a Heart, 1934; The Devil and All (short stories) 1934; Variations on a Theme (short stories) 1935; Presenting Moonshine, 1941.

ABOUT: Collier, J. Green Thoughts (see Foreword by O. Sitwell).

COLLINS, DALE (April 7, 1897-), Australian novelist and travel-writer, was born in Sydney, an ailing child who spent months each year in bed. Near him lived the future Mrs. Collins, whom he was to meet in Monte Carlo a quarter-century later. He never countenanced the idea of any other career than writing. At eleven young Dale Collins contributed a story,

"A Kangaroo Hunt," to an English comic paper, *Puck.* His father, an Irish doctor and ship's surgeon, had died when Dale was two, leaving Mrs. Collins, whose family had supplied several generations of English clergymen in "the old country," to rear a family of five children.

At fourteen Dale Collins was on the staff of a suburban paper near Melbourne, showing such aptitude as office-boy, proof-reader, and leader-writer, as well as "Evangeline" of the woman's page, that he soon became dramatic critic and chief special writer on the Melbourne *Herald,* and contributed to the Sydney *Bulletin* and other Australian papers. When the Chicago millionaire, A. Y. Gowen, came to port in his motor-yacht, making the first motor-boat voyage around the world, Collins joined up on twenty-four hours' notice and quitted Australia to write up the voyage (*Sea-Tracks of the Speejacks*) for Lord Northcliffe's London *Daily Mail.*

An Irish palm-reader told Collins he should cease wasting time on small things. He wrote *Ordeal,* a harsh, straightforward tale of the sea; published in 1924, it was dramatized by the author and produced in London the following year. In the early 1930's Mr. and Mrs. Collins shipped as steward and stewardess at a shilling a month on a freighter for a two years' cruise, in the course of which they visited America twice and went three times round the world. The novelist has a pleasant, open face, with dark eyes and hair, a wide mouth, and wears horn-rimmed glasses. Several of his novels have been filmed. His first wife died in 1933, and he is now married again and has two daughters.

PRINCIPAL WORKS: Sea-Tracks of the Speejacks Around the World, 1923; Ordeal, 1924; The Haven, 1925; The Sentimentalists, 1927; Vanity Under the Sun, 1928; Idolaters, 1929; Rich and Strange, 1931; Lost, 1933; The Mutiny of Madame Yes, 1934; Race the Sun, 1936.

ABOUT: Miller, E. M. Australian Literature From Its Beginnings to 1935; Wilson Library Bulletin March 1931.

COLLINS, JOHN CHURTON. See "BRITISH AUTHORS OF THE 19TH CENTURY"

COLUM, Mrs. MARY GUNNING (MAGUIRE) (188?-), Irish-American literary critic, is the daughter of Charles Maguire

and Maria (Gunning) Maguire. She is a graduate of the National University of Ireland, and also attended Dominican College, Dublin, and the Pensionnat Sacré Coeur, Vaals, Holland. In 1912 she married the poet Padraic Colum,[qv] and they came to the United States in 1914. Twenty years later Mrs. Colum began her "Life and Literature" department in the *Forum*, continuing until that periodical's expiration in 1940. In 1933 William Rose Benét, commenting on her announced appointment, said: "Everyone of sapience knows that Mrs. Colum is the best woman critic in America. There is no one in her class. She occupies the same place in this country that Rebecca West does in England. To her many friends among writers and editors she is known as "Molly," and the only thing they ever hold against her is that she will continue to get her copy in in her own good time, come Hell or High Water." He also mentioned Mrs. Colum's recent "severe illness and long convalescence abroad." She has contributed to the *Dial, Scribner's, New Republic, Saturday Review, New Statesman and Nation, Yale Review*, and other periodicals. In 1930 she was granted a Guggenheim Fellowship in Literary Criticism, and in 1934 Georgetown University, a Catholic institution in Washington, D.C., awarded her the John Ryder

Randall gold medal. She is currently reviewing poetry for the New York *Times Book Review*.

From These Roots (1937), her one book, deals "with the sweep of literary ideas and literary philosophies as these were manifested in various literatures and by various writers." Modern literature, she declares, begins with Lessing, in whose mind "we have in germ very many of the most modern developments of literary forms."

PRINCIPAL WORKS: From These Roots, 1937.

ABOUT: Boyd, M. Life Makes Advances; Tietjens, E. World at My Shoulder; Saturday Review of Literature October 28, 1933; November 13, 1937, March 16, 1940.

COLUM, PADRAIC (December 8, 1881-), Irish-American poet and miscellaneous author, writes: "When I am asked for an autobiograph-

Pinchot

ical sketch I am filled with dismay. There is hardly anything to be said about my life. I was born nearly in the middle of Ireland. My father happened to be the master of a workhouse; consequently I was born where waifs, strays, tramps congregated. While I was still a child I left the town I was born in and went to live in the next county. There, in my grandmother's house, I heard stories before I could read them, and songs and scraps of poetry before I had to learn any at school. Then I went to live near Dublin. Dunleary, the town I grew up in, has been beautifully described by L. A. G. Strong in *The Sea Wall*. In my twenties I was living in Dublin. The Celtic Revival was a very vital movement then. An Irish Theatre was being promoted by William Butler Yeats; all sorts of talent were looked for in the generation which was coming on. It was a good time to come of age in.

"I was brought into all the activity that was going on; my first poems were published by Arthur Griffith; I entered the group in which were Yeats, Lady Gregory, A.E., and J. M. Synge, and had a play produced when I was twenty; my second play, *The Land*, was the first success that the Irish Theatre had. Later, with James Stephens and Thomas MacDonagh, one of the leaders of the revolution of 1916, I founded the *Irish Review*.

"In 1914 I came to America for the first time. It was there that I began to write stories for children, growing out of translation of a long folk-story from the Irish. In 1923, on the invitation of the Hawaiian legislature, I went to the Islands to make a survey of their traditional stories and reshape them so as to bring the imaginative past of the Polynesian people to the newer groups in the Islands. In 1930 I went to France."

* * *

In recent years Mr. Colum has lived in Connecticut. In 1912 he married Mary Gunning Maguire, who as Mary Colum*qv* is a well known literary critic. The late Llewelyn Powys called Padraic Colum "a faëry cardinal, . . . an authentic poet." L. A. G. Strong said that he "has brought to mature manhood a curious innocence of vision, a power of seeing familiar things as if he had only just come across them." It is this characteristic that has given his versions of folk-stories their freshness and simplicity. He is a noted reader of his own works, and his sensitive, brooding, Celtic face reflects his natural lyric quality, his sympathetic temperament, his gift for fantasy and friendship.

PRINCIPAL WORKS: Wild Earth (poems) 1907; My Irish Year, 1912; A Boy in Eirinn, 1913; Three Plays, 1916; The King of Ireland's Son (juvenile) 1916; Mogu: The Wanderer (play) 1917; The Adventures of Odysseus (juvenile) 1918; The Tale of Troy (juvenile) 1918; The Boy Who Knew What the Bird Said (juvenile) 1918; The Girl Who Sat By the Ashes (juvenile) 1919; The Children of Odin (juvenile) 1920; The Boy Apprenticed to an Enchanter (juvenile) 1920; The Golden Fleece (juvenile) 1921; The Children Who Followed the Piper (juvenile) 1922; Dramatic Legends (poems) 1922; Castle Conquer, 1923; The Island of the Mighty, 1924; At the Gateways of the Day, 1924; The Voyagers, 1925; The Forge in the Forest, 1925; The Bright Islands, 1925; The Road Round Ireland, 1926; Creatures (poems) 1927; The Fountain of Youth, 1927; Balloon (play) 1929; Orpheus—Stories From the Mythologies of the World, 1929; Old Pastures (poems) 1930; Cross Roads in Ireland, 1930; Three Men, 1931; Poems, 1932; A Half Day's Ride (essays) 1932; The Big Tree of Bunlahy (short stories) 1933; The White Sparrow, 1933; The Legend of Saint Columba, 1935; The Story of Lowry Maen (poem) 1937; Flower Pieces (poems) 1939; Where the Winds Never Blew and the Cocks Never Crew (juvenile) 1940.

ABOUT: Kunitz, S. J. & Haycraft, H. (eds.). The Junior Book of Authors; Catholic World July 1928; Commonweal June 7, 1935; Dial February 1928; Poetry July 1931; Saturday Review of Literature April 16, 1932.

COLVIN, Sir SIDNEY (June 18, 1845-May 11, 1927), British critic of art and literature, was the third son of Barzett David Colvin, an East India merchant, and Mary Steuart (Bayley) Colvin. He was born into easy circumstances on a big estate near Woodridge, East Suffolk, and was there educated by private tutors, since his mother had "a horror of schools for her sons." In boyhood he loved fishing and field sports and showed bookish tendencies, taking early to Scott and Spenser, as well as to the ordinary writers for boys like Marryat, Mayne Reid, and Fenimore Cooper. Ruskin was a family friend, and his powerful personality made a strong impression.

In 1863 Colvin went to Trinity College, Cambridge. He found himself in no way inferior to youths who had had a normal schooling, and was placed third in the first class of the Classical Tripos in 1867. He sought the acquaintance of Burne-Jones while still an undergraduate, later knew Rossetti, Watts, and other artists, and orientated his studies in the direction of art criticism. He was made a Fellow of Trinity in 1868, but journalism rather than academic work was his preferred occupation at first. Settling in London, he wrote about books and pictures. His chief employment was that of art critic on the *Pall Mall Gazette*. A series of papers in P. G. Hamerton's *Portfolio* appeared under the title of *Children in Italian and English Design,* to make his first book, in 1873. Valuable social contacts were formed by his membership in the New (later Savile) Club, and by attendance on Sundays at the *salons* of G. F. Watts at Little Holland House and of George Eliot and G. H. Lewes at The Priory, St. John's Wood.

The year 1873 was a memorable one for Colvin. First, he made the acquaintance of Frances, wife of the Rev. A. H. Sitwell, a lady of taste and culture, who became his firm friend and, in 1903, having been widowed, his wife. Secondly, at her house he met the young Robert Louis Stevenson, whose delightful nature and evident genius made strong appeal to Colvin. The critic gave most valuable aid to the novelist, by introduction to clubs and editors, and the two men were in close and affectionate touch with one another until Stevenson's death in 1893. The third big event of 1873 was Colvin's nomination as Slade Professor of Fine Art at Cambridge. Three years later he received the additional appointment of Director of the Fitzwilliam Museum, Cambridge. In 1884 he was called thence to be Keeper of the Department of Prints and Drawings at the British Museum, resigning his Slade chair a year later.

Colvin's tenure of the Keepership (which lasted until his retirement under age-limit regulations in 1912) was marked by extensive improvements in the display of the collection, the issue of excellent booklet guides (some written in collaboration with Arthur M. Hind), and the purchase of various important groups of prints and drawings. Colvin lived in an official residence within the Museum precincts, where he often entertained eminent literary and artistic figures. Browning, Meredith, Gladstone, and in later years Conrad, were among his acquaintances—the Pole, indeed, an intimate friend, succeeding Stevenson in Colvin's highest regard.

Never a narrow specialist on art, he maintained a lively practical interest in pure literature, some fruits of which were his studies of *Landor* (1881) and *Keats* (1887) in the "English Men of Letters" series, his *Selections from Landor* (1882), his edition of Stevenson's *Vailima Letters* (1895) and general letters (1889) and his Edinburgh Edition of Stevenson (1894-97). Notable works on art were *Early Engravings and Engravers in England* (1905) and the *Catalogue of Early Italian Engravings* (1910), both written with Mr. Hind. His best-considered and most authoritative work was *John Keats: His Life and Poetry* (1917). *Memories and Notes of Persons and Places* followed in 1921. In 1927 Colvin died, at the age of eighty-one. He left no children.

A man of deep and wide culture, Colvin was an able and percipient critic. "In person," wrote Campbell Dodgson, "he was tall and thin, in manner animated and nervous, sometimes irritable, but charming in demeanor to those whom he liked. He walked with a slight limp after an accident in which his leg was broken."

PRINCIPAL WORKS: *Writings on Fine Art—* Children in Italian and English Design, 1872; Occasional Writings on Fine Art, 1873; A Florentine Picture Chronicle, 1898; A Descriptive Catalogue of the Pictures in the Fitzwilliam Museum, 1902; Early Engraving and Engravers in England, 1545-1695 (with A. M. Hind) 1905; Catalogue of Early Italian Engravings (with A. M. Hind) 1910. *Literary Criticism and Biography—*Landor (Eng-

lish Men of Letters Series) 1881; Keats (English Men of Letters Series) 1887; John Keats: His Life and Poetry, His Friends, Critics and After-Fame, 1917. *Memoirs—*Memories and Notes of Persons and Places: 1852-1912, 1921. *Works Edited—*Selections From the Writings of Walter Savage Landor, 1882; Letters of John Keats, 1891; The Works of Robert Louis Stevenson (Edinburgh Edition) 1894-97; The Vailima Letters of R. L. Stevenson, 1895; The Letters of Robert Louis Stevenson to His Family and Friends, 1899 (further letters, 1911).

ABOUT: Dictionary of National Biography Supplement: 1922-30; Lucas, E. V. The Colvins and Their Friends; The Times (London) May 12, 1927.

COMFORT, WILL LEVINGTON (January 17, 1878-November 2, 1932), American novelist, journalist, and short-story writer, was born in Kalamazoo, Mich., the son of Silas H. Comfort and Jane (Levington) Comfort. His father was a soldier in the Civil War, one of the youngest cavalrymen in Michigan, who spent his pension on drink. John Levington, Will Comfort's maternal grandfather, was an Irish peasant boy, a British soldier and a Wesleyan Methodist preacher in America. The boy's earliest conscious memories were of a house on Lincoln Avenue, Detroit, where his mother kept the family together by teaching. Will could read before five, began to write at six, and sold a story for $10 while working as an elevator boy. A shooting affray in which a woman was concerned made it necessary for Comfort to leave a post on the Detroit *Journal*. An even rougher newspaper experience in Cincinnat preceded his enlistment in the Spanish-American War. At Tampa, Fla., with a cavalry troop, Comfort contracted a severe case of typhoid and malaria. He was war correspondent in the Philippines for the Detroit *Journal* newspaper syndicate, and in 1904 went to Japan and Russia in a similar capacity for the Pittsburgh *Dispatch* Newspaper Syndicate. After his return from the Philippines, Comfort sold seventeen stories about an imaginary American soldier, Dulin, for forty dollars apiece. They were syndicated, but S. S. McClure refused to publish them as a book. *Routledge Rides Alone*, his best-known novel, emerged from the Russo-Japanese war experience. Comfort was drunk for fifty days after completing the novel, ending in a sanatorium

for a cure. A graphic depiction of the horrors of war, the novel was recommended by Edwin Markham for a Nobel prize and was circulated by peace societies as anti-war propaganda. Comfort supported his family by writing steadily for magazines of large national circulation. The Comforts had a son and two daughters. Mrs. Comfort, the "Penelope" of Comfort's unusually frank autobiography, *Midstream,* was Adith Duffie-Mulholland of Detroit. The *Nation* said the book showed two obsessions: the necessity to write and the determination to philosophize. Comfort died in Los Angeles at forty-four. H. L. Mencken once remarked, "He has done, indeed, some capital melodramas. What Comfort preaches is a sort of mellowed mariolatry, a humorless exaltation of woman. Arm in arm with all this exaltation of woman, of course, goes a great suspicion of mere woman."

PRINCIPAL WORKS: Routledge Rides Alone, 1910; Fate Knocks at the Door, 1912; Down Among Men, 1913; Midstream (autobiography) 1914; Red Fleece, 1915; Lot & Company, 1915; Child and Country, 1916; The Hive, 1918; The Shielding Wing, 1918; Son of Power, 1920; This Man's World, 1921; The Public Square, 1923; Somewhere South in Sonora, 1925; Samadhi, 1927; Apache, 1931.

ABOUT: Comfort, W. L. Midstream; Mencken, H. L. Prejudices; First Series.

CONAN DOYLE. See DOYLE.

CONKLING, Mrs. GRACE WALCOTT (HAZARD) (1878-   ), American poet, was born in New York City, her maiden name being Hazard. She was educated at Smith College (B.L. 1899), and also studied at the Harvard Summer School. She then went to Europe and until 1904 studied music and languages at the University of Heidelberg and in Paris. She is an accomplished organist, and returned to America expecting to make this her profession. However, she had already had experience as a teacher, having been a tutor for two years at South Woodstock, Conn., and having taught English, Latin, and Greek in a New York private school for a year more. In 1905 she married Roscoe Platt Conkling, and they have two daughters, the younger of whom, Hilda Conkling, born in 1910, was a elebrated child prodigy who began to "talk poems" at the age of four and who published a volume at nine.

Mrs. Conkling early in her married life began to lecture on contemporary poetry, and in 1914 she joined the English faculty of Smith College. She is still there, having been associate professor for some years.

She lives in Northampton, Mass. She no longer writes much verse, however, and has published no volume since 1929. In the mid-1920's she became affiliated with the Imagist group which centered in America around Amy Lowell, and much of her work after that time was written in free verse. Miss Lowell valued her poetry highly, and said that it was "a perfectly original utterance, based upon a highly individual response to life, . . . with carefully chiseled technique, . . . and a lively sense of the value of words and the tones and cadences of speech." Other critics, less committed to the "new" poetry, felt that Mrs. Conkling had lost the lyric quality and the feeling of her earlier work. She is a minor poet, and no longer an active one, but some of her nature poems still retain their fluent visual freshness.

PRINCIPAL WORKS: Afternoons of April, 1915; Wilderness Songs, 1920; Imagination and Children's Reading (prose) 1922; Ship's Log and Other Poems, 1924; Flying Fish—A Book of Songs and Sonnets, 1926; Witch and Other Poems, 1929.

ABOUT: Saturday Review of Literature January 24, February 21, 1925; Woman Citizen March 1927.

CONKLING, HILDA. See CONKLING, G. W. H.

"CONNELL, NORREYS." See O'RIORDAN, C. O'C.

*CONNELL, RICHARD EDWARD (October 17, 1893-   ), American novelist and story-writer, reports: "My first writing was

done for the daily newspaper my father edited in Poughkeepsie, N.Y. I covered baseball games. I was ten years old and got ten cents a game. I have been a professional writer ever since.

"I was born in Dutchess County, just over the hill from the Roosevelts. There I grew up, went to school, and worked on the Poughkeepsie *News-Press* in the evenings and in the summers. When I was sixteen I was city editor at $16 a week. Then I went to Georgetown College for a year and also served as secretary to my father, who had been elected to Congress. He died in 1912. I entered Harvard and was graduated in 1915. In college I was an editor of the *Daily Crimson* and the *Lampoon*.

"I went to New York and worked on the city staff of the New York *American,* and then became an advertising copy writer for a big agency. When we went into World War I, I enlisted in the 27th New York Division, and trained at Camp Wadsworth, Spartansburg, S.C., where I was editor of the camp weekly paper, the *Gas Attack.* I served a year with the A.E.F. in France as a private. After the war I went back to work in New York as an advertising writer. In 1919 I became a free-lance fiction writer and have been one ever since, writing chiefly short stories, a few novels, and some motion picture stories and screen plays. Also in 1919, I was married to Louise Herrick Fox, writer and editor.

"We went to Paris in 1920 and lived there and in London, returning, every year or so, for long stays in New York and Westport, Conn. I came to California on a visit in 1925, and have lived here since then. My permanent address (at the moment) is Beverly Hills, Calif. My wife is Hollywood editor of the magazine, *You,* and I work on fiction at home, or, now and then, at a motion picture studio. We do some gardening, and when we can, some deep-sea fishing, especially for sail-fish in Mexican waters.

"Some of the motion pictures I have helped to make are *Meet John Doe, Brother Orchid, Nice Girl, Hired Wife,* and *Milky Way.* I have had about three hundred stories published in American and English magazines."

PRINCIPAL WORKS: The Sin of Monsieur Pettipon (short stories) 1922; Apes and Angels (short stories) 1924; Variety (short stories) 1925; Mad Lover, 1927; Murder at Sea, 1929; Ironies (short stories) 1930; Playboy, 1935; What Ho! 1937.

CONNELLY, MARCUS COOK (December 13, 1890-   ), American playwright who signs his works as Marc Connelly, was born

in McKeesport, Pa., the son of Patrick J. Connelly and Mabel Fowler (Cook) Connelly. He was educated at Trinity Hall School, Washington, Pa. In 1910 he became a reporter for the Pittsburgh *Sun,* went from there to the *Dispatch,* and then wrote a humorous column for the *Gazette Times.* In 1915 he went to New York to see a musical show in which some

of his lyrics were to be sung. The show failed promptly, but Mr. Connelly stayed on, fascinated by the theatre. He made his way by free-lance journalism, the writing of humorous verse, and occasional sketches or lyrics for musical comedies. A few years later he met George Kaufman, in collaboration with whom many of his best plays were to be written. Their first play, *Dulcy,* was a great success, and they seldom had a failure afterward. It was 1926 before Mr. Connelly produced a play except in collaboration. In 1929, however, he achieved his widest celebrity with the production of *Green Pastures,* adapted from Roark Bradford's *Ol' Man Adam and His Chillun.* It received the Pulitzer Prize of the year, and later became a widely popular film. Mr. Connelly himself directed the play.

Mr. Connelly has always been interested in other aspects of stagecraft than writing, and he acted as the director of *Berkeley Square* in 1929. Though he has never published any books except the reading versions of his plays, he still writes a good deal of verse and has had many stories in magazines. One of these, "Coroner's Inquest," won the O. Henry short-short story prize in 1930. Even his stories usually have a theatrical background. He was one of the founders of the *New Yorker,* and occasionally contributes to it. He is director and treasurer of the Dramatists' Guild of the Authors' League of America, and has been active in working for establishment of an international copyright for plays. Testifying before the Patent Office, he told how, when *Dulcy* was played in Holland, all the compensation he received was a copy of the program on which his name was misspelled!

Medium-sized, totally bald, and with keen blue eyes behind spectacles, Mr. Connelly is unspoiled by fame, and is noted for his modesty and his considerateness for others. He was married in 1930 to Madeline Hurlock, and lives in New York, though before the present war he made frequent and extended trips to Europe. He is a former president of the Authors' League, and was elected to the National Institute of Arts and Letters in 1935.

Primarily Marc Connelly is a writer of high comedy, which depends for its appeal on characterization rather than on plot. No one who saw *The Green Pastures* needs to be told that he is also capable of tenderness and pathos. In addition to his plays which have been published in book form, he has been author or co-author of two musical comedies, written with Mr. Kaufman—

Helen of Troy, N.Y., and *Be Yourself*—and of a number of plays, including *The Deep Tangled Wildwood* (with Kaufman), *The Wild Man of Borneo* (with H. J. Mankiewicz), *The Farmer Takes a Wife* (with F. B. Elser), and *Everywhere I Roam* (with A. Sundgaard).

PRINCIPAL WORKS: (dates of publication): Dulcy (with G. S. Kaufman) 1921; The Copperhead (with G. S. Kaufman) 1922; To the Ladies (with G. S. Kaufman) 1923; Beggar on Horseback (with G. S. Kaufman) 1923; Merton of the Movies (with G. S. Kaufman) 1925; The Wisdom Tooth, 1927; The Green Pastures, 1930; Little David (one-act) 1937; The Traveler (one-act) 1939.

ABOUT: Case, F. Do Not Disturb; Scholastic February 13, 1937; Theatre Arts April 1940.

"CONNINGTON, J. J." See STEWART, A. W.

CONNOLLY, JAMES BRENDAN (1868-), American writer of sea stories, was born in South Boston, Mass., the son  of John and Ann (O'Donnell) Connolly. When he was still a boy he loved to frequent the harbor when sailors were on leave. Before he entered Harvard in 1895, he spent three years as a clerk, inspector, and surveyor with a corps of U. S. engineers at Savannah, Ga. At college he excelled in athletics and wanted to compete in the first modern Olympic Games, to be held at Athens in April 1896. When the college authorities refused him a leave of absence, he walked out, never to see the "Yard" again until he lectured, many years later, before the Harvard Union—on literature. By setting the "triple jump" record at the very opening of the Games he became the first modern Olympic champion. (At the Paris Exposition, 1900, he placed second in the running "triple jump"; and as a spectator only—because of an accident *en route*—he attended the Athens meet of 1906.) In 1898 he was with the 9th Massachusetts Infantry and was at the siege of Santiago. In 1904 he married Elizabeth Frances Hurley, of South Boston; they have one daughter, Brenda. He served in the Navy during 1907-8, and in 1912 ran for Congress on the Progressive ticket.

Two months before the American navy ships and army transports landed in Vera Cruz, in the "punitive expedition" of April 1914, Connolly signed up with *Collier's* to report on the navy in Mexican waters, and by special permission got aboard the new battleship "New York." The boat unfortunately reached Mexico a day late for the liveliest part of the battle, but Connolly got his "story." In 1917, becoming European naval correspondent for *Collier's*, he won permission to cruise with an American destroyer, the "Nicolson," which set out from Queenstown to pick up a convoy in the Bay of Biscay, where it fought off some terrific torpedo fire. It is from this kind of adventure and from a lifelong love for all that concerns a sea-going fisherman that his books evolve. In *Port of Gloucester* he returned to the material of his first book, *Out of Gloucester*, and, with a few small exceptions, the salt air has blown through all that came between.

PRINCIPAL WORKS: Out of Gloucester, 1902; The Seiners, 1904; Crested Seas, 1907; An Olympic Victor, 1908; Wide Courses, 1911; The Trawler, 1914; Head Winds, 1916; The U-Boat Hunters, 1918; Hiker Joy, 1920; Steel Decks, 1925; Book of the Gloucester Fishermen, 1927; Navy Men, 1939; American Fishermen, 1940; Port of Gloucester, 1940; Canton Captain, 1942.

ABOUT: Connolly, J. B. Navy Men; Connolly, J. B. U-Boat Hunters; Kieran, J. The Story of the Olympic Games; Saturday Review of Literature September 16, 1933.

"CONNOR, RALPH." See GORDON, C. W.

CONRAD, JOSEPH (December 3, 1857-August 3, 1924), English novelist, was born Jósef Teodor Konrad Korzeniowski, the son of Apollo Nałęcz Korzeniowski and Ewelina (Bobrowski) Korzeniowski, near Kiev, in what was then Russian Poland. Probably no stranger life-story exists than that of this man who, a native of an inland country, spent all his  youth at sea, and who, utterly ignorant of English at twenty, became not only a great novelist in that tongue, but also a supreme English stylist. Yet, though he was a British subject from 1886, he spoke always with a marked accent, and from his carriage, his gestures, his blurred voice, even his gaze, there looked out a spirit inherently Slavic with a touch of the Oriental.

Conrad's father was a poet and a revolutionist, the son of a cavalry officer who had written one very dull tragedy. The maternal uncle, Tadeysz Bobrowski, who became the boy's guardian after he was orphaned, was always warning him against "the Korzeniowski strain"—extravagant, idealistic, full of pose and exaggeration, predestined to ruin. Yet the mother too was an ardent patriot, and when her husband was arrested in 1861 as leader of a Polish revolutionary group, she followed him willingly into exile, with her small son, to Vologda, in northeast Russia. But the privations she met killed her in four years, and three years later her husband too was so broken in health that the Czarist government relented and allowed him to go back with his child to Cracow. There, after a year, he also died.

The boy, reared by his practical-minded uncle, grew up with a dual soul. He was a devout Roman Catholic, a small patriot who could read the forbidden Polish tongue before he was five, a lover of fairy tales who yet was haunted by "the awful sense of the inevitable" and who never really recovered from the shock of his father's death. On the other hand he was an avid devourer of adventure stories—chiefly those of Frederick Marryat—a passionate lover of geography, who earned the derision of his playmates by pointing to the blank "unknown" space on a map of Africa and announcing, "When I grow up, I shall go *there.*" (He did; it was to the Congo, which nearly killed him, with fever and near-drowning, in 1890.) He read Dickens in translation, and England became to him the land of romance. At fifteen he was sent with a tutor to tour the continent, and he began a two-year struggle for permission to go to sea. Reluctantly, in 1873, he was allowed to ship on a French vessel from Marseilles. For four years he served in the French mercantile marine, at one time running contraband for Don Carlos.

Joseph Conrad (his name as a novelist which later he made legally his own) came very near to being a French instead of an English writer. All his life French, not English, was his instinctive secondary language. But the sight of an English ship in the harbor at Marseilles deflected his destiny. He went to Lowestoft, qualified as a seaman, learned English laboriously from a newspaper, and gradually worked upward until in 1880 he passed his examination as master. Until 1894 he served as first or second in command of merchant ships, mostly bound to and from the Orient. Until 1889 he had written nothing.

It was in that year that he began *Almayer's Folly,* his first novel. Always a painfully slow writer, the book was interrupted by voyages, by his African mishaps, by illness and convalescence. The great books of his first period—*The Nigger of the Narcissus, Lord Jim, Youth, Nostromo*—excited the discriminating few, but had small sales. He had resigned from the sea to write; in 1896, against her family's opposition to the foreigner, he had married Jessie George; soon there were two sons to support as well. Ill and discouraged, he forced himself to apply for reinstatement to the service. Fortunately for literature he was refused. Friends finally secured a small Civil List pension for him, which he gave up when his writing began to bring him in a living. He was no business man; he was harassed by debt, and it was not until his last years, in his last home in his beloved Kent, that he was entirely free from monetary worry. But in friends he was always rich. Henry James delighted in the company of this most disparate nature to his; Stephen Crane's last sad months were lightened by the friendship of the older man; Ford Madox Huefer, who became Ford Madox Ford, collaborated with him; his only visit to the United States, in 1923, was solely to visit his American publisher and close friend, F. N. Doubleday, whom he called "Effendi." Nervous, abrupt, with unreasoning likes and dislikes, introverted and depressed, tortured by the aftermath of fever and in later years by gout, Conrad nevertheless was beloved by the few who penetrated the mask of irascibility and gloom. Writing was always agony to him, surrounded by clouds of despair and continued only by herculean effort. His last work shows the weariness and strain. It was not until *Chance,* in 1913, that he became generally popular at all; and he has never been "popular," in the invidious sense.

The one thing Conrad is not is a mere adventure story writer, a "sea story" creator like Cooper or Marryat. For the most part the ocean and the strange lands that border it are his milieu, but his novels are no more "sea stories" than *Moby Dick* is a sea story. There is indeed an affinity between Joseph Conrad the Pole and Herman Melville the American. Like Melville's, Conrad's novels are a long confession: they are egocentric, written around a protagonist who is not the nebulous "I" ostensibly telling the tale. Ruth M. Stauffer correctly called him a "romantic realist." The *New Republic,* in an obituary editorial, amplifies the phrase: "He added to romance (which Robert Louis Stevenson called the poetry of circumstance) the realism of human experience, and made realism significant as the poetry of character."

Conrad deals, in his greatest books—the last of which were *Chance* and *Victory*—most often with what Gamaliel Bradford termed "damaged souls." Almayer himself, Lord Jim, Nostromo—all of them have an almost Byronic flaw somewhere. *"N'y touchez pas, il est brisé."* They are himself. He carried with him always a "guilt complex"—his was the cleaved spirit, he was the foreigner who had deserted his own country, the alien speaking his inmost heart in another's tongue. Hidden and perhaps hardly conscious, that theme warred with his aspiration for "a world governed by sanity and method." He was, to use a Jungian term, an intuitive type; he identified himself with his characters to an unusual extent. That is the probable explanation of the comparative weakness of all his women: unlike that other intuitive, George Meredith, he could identify himself only with the men who were partial aspects of his own nature.

Conrad was fond of a Polish proverb which praises the man who "is conquered, but never submits." It was his own keynote. Fidelity, solidarity, "the community of mankind," were his passion—the obverse of the hidden guilt he bore. Even H. L. Mencken, who proclaims him as a pure realist, who rightly points to his constant effort "to make you hear, to make you feel, above all to make you *see*," acknowledges also that Conrad is "forever setting himself problems and forever coming to conclusions that leave them unsolved." Typically his hero, like Lord Jim, "passes away under a cloud, inscrutable at heart."

To this vision of himself and his world he was permanently true—if we except the product of his last failing years, such as *The Rover* and the unfinished *Suspense*, and perhaps also *The Secret Agent* and *Under Western Eyes,* where he was dealing for once with a background not his own. If this be romance, then Conrad was a romantic. Certainly his creation, in every detail, of the life of a mythical South American country in *Nostromo* is a triumph of romance, achieved by the technique of realism. In unconscious revulsion from the pose and bombast of those "romantic noblemen," the Korzeniowski, yet with their blood in every fiber of his being, he achieved a fusion of the two schools, the romantic and the realistic. Above all authors he hated Dostoievsky. And Dostoievsky is more than a Russian who detested the Poles; he is a mystical genius, the quintessence of the brooding yet exhibitionistic Slav. Partly what Conrad hated was the Dostoievsky within himself.

The revered old author of the last years in prosperous, sleepy Kent, the novelist whose name was spoken with those of Hardy and Meredith; the not-quite-English figure whose walk and direct gaze and broad shoulders betrayed his years on the quarter-deck—though characteristically he never took exercise and seldom left his house: these were not all that suddenly fell asleep forever in 1924. This son of Polish aristocrats and revolutionaries left to the English language a heritage richer than any other has given it who was not born to the nuances of its words. The very fact that a great mind was expressing itself in an alien tongue gave to his work, at its best, a rare beauty. With all its imperfections, *Almayer's Folly* brought into English literature a fresh vigor that is like the salt of the sea, as the powerful rhythm of his phrases is the sea's own rhythm. When such a power is brought to bear on a "passionate contemplation and depiction of reality," Conrad's achievement at his best, the result is the production of that rare thing which may justifiably be named a work of genius.

PRINCIPAL WORKS: *Novels*—Almayer's Folly, 1895; An Outcast of the Islands, 1896; The Nigger of the Narcissus, 1897; Lord Jim, 1900; The Inheritors (with F. M. Ford) 1901; Romance (with F. M. Ford) 1903; Nostromo, 1904; The Secret Agent, 1907; Under Western Eyes, 1911; Chance, 1913; Victory, 1915; The Shadow-Line, 1917; The Arrow of Gold, 1919; The Rescue, 1920; The Rover, 1923; The Nature of a Crime (with F. M. Ford) 1924; Suspense, 1925. *Short Stories* —Tales of Unrest, 1898; Youth, 1902; Typhoon, 1903; A Set of Six, 1908; 'Twixt Land and Sea, 1912; Within the Tides, 1915; Tales of Hearsay, 1925. *Miscellaneous*—The Mirror of the Sea, 1906; A Personal Record (in England, Some Reminiscences) 1912; Notes on Life and Letters, 1921; Last Essays, 1926; Letters to Marguerite Poradowska, 1940.

ABOUT: Adams, E. L. Joseph Conrad: The Man; Bancroft, W. W. Joseph Conrad: His Philosophy of Life; Conrad, J. G. Joseph Conrad and His Circle, Joseph Conrad As I Knew Him; Conrad, J. A Personal Record; Crankshaw, E. Joseph Conrad; Cross, W. L. Four Contemporary Novelists; Cunninghame Graham, R. B. Inveni Portam: Joseph Conrad; Curle, R. Joseph Conrad, The Last Twelve Years of Joseph Conrad; Ford, F. M. Joseph Conrad, Thus to Revisit; Garnett, E. Letters From Joseph Conrad; Jean-Aubry, G. Joseph Conrad; Mason, J. E. Joseph Conrad; Megroz, R. L. Joseph Conrad's Mind and Methods, A Talk With Joseph Conrad; Mencken, H. L. A Book of Prefaces; Morf, G. The Polish Heritage of Joseph Conrad; O'Flaherty, L. Joseph Conrad; Safroni-Middleton, A. Tropic Shadows;

Stauffer, R. M. Joseph Conrad; Stawell, F. C. Conrad; Sutherland, J. G. At Sea With Joseph Conrad; Symons, A. Notes on Joseph Conrad; Walpole, H. Joseph Conrad; Bookman February, June 1923, June 1926, August 1928, March 1932; Catholic World September 1924; Century Magazine February, March 1928; Current Opinion September, November 1924; Edinburgh Review January 1925; Fortnightly May 1921, September 1924; Literary Digest August 23, September 13, 27, 1924; Literary Review August 9, 16, 30, 1924; Nation August 20, 1924, June 30, 1926; New Republic May 16, 1923, August 20, 1924; Outlook May 23, 1923; Scribner's Magazine May 1925; Saturday Review of Literature September 6, 1924, October 18, 1924, November 7, 1925, January 14, 1928, August 19, 1933; Yale Review January 1925, April 1928.

CONSTANTIN-W E Y E R, MAURICE

(April 24, 1881-   ), French novelist, writes: "I was born at Bourbonne, France. Spent part of my life in

Canada and U.S.A. Came back in 1914 for the war. Served first in the infantry as sergeant. Was awarded military medal, November 16, 1914, for gallantry. Promoted officer. Severely wounded on May 10, 1917. Awarded Legion of Honor. Served in the French tank service for the rest of the war.

"Turned to writing after the war. Published successively nineteen novels, and biographies of Champlain and Shakespeare. Goncourt Prize, 1928, for *Un Homme Se Penche sur Son Passé* (*A Man Scans His Past*). The Theatre de l'Atelier produced in 1930 *Le Stratagème des Roués*, adapted by me from Farquhar's *The Beaux' Stratagem*, while the French National Theatre of l'Odéon produced in 1939 *Le Grand Will*, a dramatic biography of William Shakespeare, written in partnership by me and Clara Longworth Chambrun (wife of General de Chambrun and sister to the late Nicholas Longworth).

"As a rule, most of my books have tried to enhance the value of action, courage, and energy. A great number of them have been devoted to the picture of western Canada. *Cavalier de la Salle* is a romantic story of the discovery of the West, while *Champlain* is a biography devoted to the great French pioneer of Canada.

"I am writing at present for the moving pictures. I am also devoting part of my time to writing a book of criticism on Shakespeare's plays. I have contributed to nearly all the leading French newspapers and magazines. From 1924 to 1931, I was editor of French political newspapers. But I have given up politics entirely.

"I was promoted officer in the national order of the Legion of Honor in 1932. I am living in Vichy for the greater part of the year. But I have traveled extensively, more especially through Northern Europe and in Spitzbergen. I have been very keen on mountaineering. But, of late, I have too much suffered from the wounds I received during the last war to do any more climbing."

* * *

M. Constantin-Weyer's father was an army officer. He was educated at the Sorbonne (science faculty), and at twenty published a small volume of poems, *Images,* of which not even he has a copy today. In 1901 his mother lost her fortune and he emigrated to Canada (from childhood he had spoken English, as well as German and Provençal), where he was farmer, cowboy, woodcutter, trapper, fur trader, and sometimes newspaper reporter. In 1912 he established a horse and cattle ranch in Manitoba. He has been called "the French Jack London." Justin O'Brien said that *Vers l'Ouest* (*Towards the West*) "caused a sensation in Paris; he revived the Jack London manner and stamped it with the mark of a national product. He became a best seller overnight and ceased to be discussed in literary circles." Nevertheless, it was six years later that he won the coveted *Prix Goncourt.*

WORKS AVAILABLE IN ENGLISH: A Man Scans His Past, 1929; The Half-Breed, 1931; Towards the West, 1931; The French Adventurer: The Life and Exploits of La Salle, 1931; Forest Wild, 1932.

ABOUT: Annales Politiques et Littéraires December 15, 1928, January 6, 1933, April 21, 1933; Bookman May 1931; Revue des Deux Mondes July 15, 1939.

COOK, GEORGE CRAM (October 7, 1873-January 14, 1924), American novelist, poet, and playwright, was born in Davenport, Iowa, the son of Edward Everett Cook, a railroad lawyer, and Ellen Katherine (Dodge) Cook. Cook's great-grandfather, Ira Cook, had come to Iowa from Whiteston, N.Y., in 1836, three years after land was opened to settlement. Davenport had a Cook Memorial Library, a Cook Home, and a Cook Memorial Church. George Cram Cook attended Griswold College, a military preparatory school; the University of Iowa from 1889 to 1892; and went East

to take his B.A. degree in 1893 from Harvard. In 1894 he received another B.A. from Heidelberg, and still another in 1895 from the University of Geneva. As an Iowa sophomore he had read Emerson, Plotinus, Swedenborg, and Plato, and indulged in much youthful day-dreaming. From 1895 to 1899 he taught English literature at the University of Iowa, and from 1902 to 1903 at Leland Stanford University. In 1902 he married Sara Herndon Swain of Chicago, and later went into chicken-raising and truck-farming, considerably to his wife's distaste. They were separated three years later, and in January 1908 Cook married Mollie A. Price of Chicago, who bore him a son, Harl, and daughter, Nilla, who later attained some success as a dancer and more notoriety as a follower of Gandhi, and who published her autobiography in 1939. Cook

had seventeen-year-old Floyd Dell as a hired hand on his farm; later he was associated with Dell on the Chicago *Evening Post* as literary editor. He figures in Dell's novel *Moon-Calf* as Tom Alden. *The Chasm*, Cook's own Socialist novel, appeared in 1911. His first, *Roderick Taliaferro* (1903), was an historical novel.

In April 1913 Cook was married to Susan Glaspell *qv* of Davenport by the Mayor of Weehawken, N.J., and they took the Fall River boat to Provincetown, Mass., where they organized the Provincetown Players in an old fish-house which Mrs. Wilbur Daniel Steele had taken for a studio, at the end of Mary Heaton Vorse's wharf. Here Cook played Yank in the first production of Eugene O'Neill's *Bound East For Cardiff*, with an actual fog outside and actual tide washing up under the floor timbers to lend extra realism. In 1915 Cook established the Playwrights' Theatre in New York City, to produce native American rather than European plays. Five hundred dollars of his capital of $513 was used to build a plaster dome for special lighting effects in the small theatre on Macdougal Street. The commercial success of O'Neill's *The Emperor Jones* in 1920 caused Cook to lose interest in the project, and in 1921 he sailed for Greece with his wife and family. Here he fraternized with poets, scholars, and peasants; wore the peasant costume; built a wall of Cyclopean rock; and grew a patriarchal beard. When

he died at sixty, of a septic condition caught from a puppy suffering with glanders, shepherds left their flocks to give him a funeral. His grave at Delphi is marked by a stone given by the Greek government from the ruins of the sacred Temple. "Jig" Cook was, says his wife and fellow-playwright, Susan Glaspell, a "great lover and a lusty enthusiastic drinker. He was too generous for his own good as artist. Just as, though at one time the mystic, and again the passionate evolutionist, in it all was the poet richly aware of life, so, socially, through it all he was the democrat." His poems seem "accidental and negligent." In his New York days Cook was a handsome man with a shock of blue-white hair coming down to a widow's peak, very black eyebrows, hazel eyes, and orange-colored flesh.

PRINCIPAL WORKS: Roderick Taliaferro: A Story of Maximillian's Empire, 1903; The Chasm: A Novel, 1911; The Spring: A Play, 1921; Greek Coins: Poems, 1925. *Plays*—Suppressed Desires (with S. Glaspell) 1920; Tickless Time (with S. Glaspell) 1920.

ABOUT. Cook, G. C. Greek Coins (see Memorabilia by Floyd Dell, Edna Kenton and Susan Glaspell); Cook, N. C. My Road to India; Glaspell, S. The Road to the Temple.

COOKE, CROFT-. See CROFT- COOKE

COOLBRITH, INA DONNA. See "AMERICAN AUTHORS: 1600-1900"

COOPER, COURTNEY RYLEY (October 31, 1886-September 29, 1940), American novelist and miscellaneous writer, was born in Kansas City,

Mo., the son of Baltimore Thomas Cooper and Catherine (Grenolds) Cooper. He attended the public schools of Kansas City, running away at sixteen to become a clown in a little circus, the Cook and Barret show. The circus remained the ruling passion of his life, and he worked himself up from performer and sign-painter to press agent for Colonel William F. Cody ("Buffalo Bill"), and head press agent and, for a time, general manager of the old Sells-Floto Circus in 1914-1915. Newspaper work preceded press agentry; Cooper was special writer on the Kansas City *Star* from 1910 to 1912, and worked on the New York *World* in 1912, the Chicago *Tribune* in 1913, and the Denver *Post* the same year. In 1918 he enlisted as a private in the United States Marines, later receiving a commission as second lieutenant and an assignment in France to collate historical matter concerning the marines, and to edit letters written home from the battlefield. *The Eagle's Eye: A True Story of the Imperial Government's Spies and Intrigues in America,* written with W. J. Flynn in 1918, was the first of Cooper's sensational factual books, culminating in his later books about crime, *Here's to Crime* (1937) and *Designs in Scarlet* (1939), which had the endorsement of the Federal Bureau of Investigation, but discussed so many forms of depravity in such explicit vernacular terms that they could hardly have been issued by a reputable publisher in the days when Cooper first began writing. His active magazine-writing career started in 1912, and he wrote many articles on special assignment for the *Saturday Evening Post.*

Courtney Ryley Cooper wrote more than 750 stories besides his books; tales of the jungle, and life in mining and road-construction camps and trading posts of the Canadian Northwest. The circus retained its perennial fascination, however, and in April 1940 Roland Butler, chief press agent for Ringling Brothers Barnum & Bailey Circus, announced that he had signed Cooper as press agent and feature writer for the show at a salary of a cent a year. On his estate at Sebring, Fla., Cooper had a rose garden growing in the shape of a circus ring, with a Roman chariot, a relic of some circus, as a centerpiece. Sebring was near the winter quarters of the circus. He also directed several motion pictures on crime subjects and wrote several scenarios, including those for *Weary River* and *Wild Cargo,* and wrote several radio serials, *The Gibson Family* and *Circus Days* among them. On September 20, 1940, Cooper and Mrs. Genevieve R. Furey Cooper, whom he had married in December 1916, returned from Florida. Nine days later he was found hanging from a steam pipe in the closet of his room on the twenty-third floor of the Hotel Park Central. Mrs. Cooper attributed his suicide to snubs from the F.B.I., which she said disregarded Cooper's reports on fifth column activities in Mexico, where he had spent several months. The Bureau denied that it even knew that Cooper had returned from Mexico, and a New York columnist (Walter Winchell) later asserted that Cooper had been incurably ill with cancer. He was in his fifty-fourth year. He was slight, energetic, with gray hair and a cleft chin.

PRINCIPAL WORKS: The Eagle's Eye (with W. J. Flynn) 1918; Memories of Buffalo Bill, (with L. F. Cody) 1920; The Cross-Cut (novel) 1921; The White Desert (novel) 1922; The Last Frontier (novel) 1923; Under the Big Top, 1923; Lions 'n' Tigers 'n' Everything, 1924; High Country: The Rockies Yesterday and To-Day, 1926; Oklahoma, 1926; Annie Oakley: Woman at Arms, 1927; Colorado, 1928; Challenge of the Bush, 1929; Go North, Young Man! 1929; Avalanche, 1929; Caged (novel) 1930; Ghost Country (novel) 1930; Mystery of Four Abreast (novel) 1930; Trigger Finger (novel) 1930; Circus Day, 1931; Old Mom (novel) 1934; Poor Man's Gold (novel) 1935; Ten Thousand Public Enemies, 1935; Here's to Crime 1937; Designs in Scarlet, 1939.

ABOUT: New York Times September 30, 1940; Saturday Evening Post August 26, 1939.

COOPER, EDITH EMMA. See "BRITISH AUTHORS OF THE 19TH CENTURY"

COPPARD, ALFRED EDGAR (January 4, 1878-), English story writer who writes as A. E. Coppard, was born at Folkstone, Kent, the son of a tailor and a housemaid; "Save these," he says, "I have no notable ancestry." He was educated at Lewes Road Board School, Brighton, until the age of nine, then for two years he was shop boy to a trousers-maker in  Whitechapel, London. He returned to Brighton and became an office boy, meanwhile reading poetry avidly, and continuing his self-education by constant study. He found leisure also to develop into a first-class athlete, and at one time was a professional sprinter. He followed all sorts of occupations, but finally became a clerk and accountant, and in 1907 went to Oxford as accountant to an engineering firm.

It was in Oxford that he first met other people interested in books and writing, and that his own ambition to write was fired. He began writing short stories, in his characteristic poetic and fanciful vein, but met with small success in finding publishers for them. Nevertheless, in 1919, he decided to give up his clerical job and devote all his time to writing. Two years of extreme poverty but of great productiveness followed, which eventuated in *Adam and Eve and Pinch Me,* the first book put out by the Golden Cockerel Press, a communal society of craftsmen

First editions of this and others of Mr. Coppard's books have brought high prices, but he has not benefited by them; his work has always appealed to a small if enthusiastic group, and he has sometimes been obliged to return to clerical work for a time in order to support his family. He married, as his second wife, Winifred May deKok, of the Orange Free State, and has a son and a daughter. He lives now in the country, at Dunmow, Essex.

Folk tales Mr. Coppard considers the best models for a story writer. He dislikes pretension either in writing or in life, and admires the simple and straightforward. He has listed as his favorite prose writers, besides the unknown authors of folktales, "Darwin, Sterne, Dickens, Henry James, Hardy, Shaw, Chekhov, and James Joyce. Favorite poets: Shakespeare, Chaucer, Milton, Wordsworth, Burns, Browning, Hardy, Herrick, Vaughan. Literary dislikes: Swift, Thackeray, the Lawrences (both—D.H. and T.E.), Dryden, and Kipling. Favorite public figures: Cromwell, Lincoln, Kruger." He says that "all the tales concerned with a character called Johnny Flynn are to some extent autobiographical."

Mr. Coppard is primarily a poet—he has written and published much verse, both in conventional and irregular forms—and his prose stories have a definitely poetic quality. They are unique in style, and quite impossible to describe; they read sometimes like a cross between "Saki" and Lord Dunsany. Ford Madox Ford has said of him: "He is almost the first English prose writer to get into English prose the peculiar quality of English lyric poetry. I do not mean that he is metrical; I mean that hitherto no English prose writer has had the fancy, the turn of imagination, the wisdom, the as it were piety, and the beauty of the great seventeenth-century lyricists like Donne or Herbert—or even Herrick. And that peculiar quality is the best thing that England has to show."

PRINCIPAL WORKS: *Prose*—Adam and Eve and Pinch Me, 1921; Clorinda Walks in Heaven, 1922; The Black Dog, 1923; Fishmonger's Fiddle, 1925; The Field of Mustard, 1926; Silver Circus, 1928; Count Stefan, 1928; The Gollan, 1929; Pink Furniture (juvenile) 1930; Nixey's Harlequin, 1931; Rummy, 1932; Dunky Fitlow, 1933; Polly Oliver, 1935; Ninepenny Flute, 1937; You Never Know, Do you? 1939; Tapster's Tapestry, 1939. *Poetry*—Hips and Haws, 1922; Pelegea, 1926; Yokohama Garland, 1926; Collected Poems, 1928.

ABOUT: Bookman (London) April 1933.

CORBETT, ELIZABETH FRANCES

(September 30, 1887-   ), American novelist, was born in Aurora, Ill., the daughter of Richard W. Corbett and Isabelle Jean (Adkins) Corbett. Her father was an official of the National Soldiers' Home near Milwaukee, and she lived there for twenty-five years—probably the only author ever brought up in a similar institution.

Underwood

She received her B.A. at the University of Wisconsin in 1910, being elected to Phi Beta Kappa. She is unmarried. Her first three novels were published while she still lived in Wisconsin, but in 1927 she moved to New York, where she makes her home with her mother, her father having died.

Miss Corbett is one of the many self-critical writers who have had the courage to destroy a first novel when it was finished. The discipline she imposed upon herself has been rewarded; without being "significant" her work is deft, professional, and above the average of popular fiction. Her best-known character has been Mrs. Meigs, a delightfully human old lady whose youth (when "she was Carrie Eaton") was presented after she had become familiar to readers in her charming later years. Others of her novels have dealt with the past of a small Illinois city, undoubtedly stemming from childhood memories of Aurora. She has also written a series of stories for girls centering in a family called the Grapers. The zest for living, the wit, and the warm sympathy evident in all Miss Corbett's novels are not merely literary evocations, but are expressions of her own personality. Charles Hanson Towne remarked: "She has watched, and listened, and comprehended, and reported her findings in smooth and mellow prose." The very uneventfulness and retirement of her private life have fitted her ideally as an observer and reporter of the lives of others.

PRINCIPAL WORKS: Cecily and the Wide World, 1916; The Vanished Helga, 1918; Puritan and Pagan, 1920; Walt: The Good Gray Poet Speaks for Himself, 1928; If It Takes All Summer, 1930; The Young Mrs. Meigs, 1931; The Graper Girls, 1931; After Five O'Clock, 1932; The Graper Girls Go to College, 1932; A Nice Long Evening, 1933; The House Across the River, 1934; Growing Up With the Grapers, 1934; Mr. Underhill's Progress, 1934; The Constant Sex, 1935; Mrs. Meigs and Mr. Cunningham, 1936; The Langworthy Family, 1937; Light of Other Days, 1938; She Was Carrie Eaton, 1938; The Far Down, 1939; Charley Manning, 1939; The Queen's Holiday, 1940; Mr. and Mrs. Meigs, 1940; Out at the Soldiers' Home, 1941; Faye's Folly, 1941; The Kimball Collection, 1942.

CORELLI, MARIE (1855-April 21, 1924), English novelist, was born in London. In later years she claimed to have been born in

1864, and to have been the adopted daughter of the Scottish song writer, Charles Mackay. As a matter of fact, all disinterested biographers now agree that she was Mackay's daughter by a widow, Ellen (Kirtland) Mills, who later became his second wife; and, as his first wife did not die until 1859, her illegitimacy as well as her vanity impelled her to advance her birth date nine years. She was originally known as Mary (or Minnie) Mackay, and adopted her pseudonym not as a writer, but as a musician. She was a brilliant pianist, and was preparing for a concert career when a "psychical experience" turned her suddenly into a writer in 1885. Then she invented "a Scottish mother and an Italian father," and many of her closest friends never knew her correct name.

She was educated by governesses and a short term in a convent school, and after abandoning music issued her first book, *A Romance of Two Worlds,* in 1886, preceded only by one story published in *Temple Bar.* This novel was one of seven—ending with *The Life Everlasting,* in 1911—which dealt with "spirit power and universal love." Her first substantial success, however, came with *Thelma,* her great popularity with *Barabbas,* and her unique appeal to "royalty and servant girls" with *The Sorrows of Satan,* which was the climax of her career and broke all previous sales records.

Miss Corelli's youth was spent in Surrey, near George Meredith, who encouraged her as a musician but not as a novelist. Her mother died in 1876 and six years later her father moved to London. In 1901 she bought a house in Stratford-on-Avon reputed to have belonged to Shakespeare's daughter, and this was her home thenceforth. She never married, but lived alone with her constant companion, Bertha Vyver, who later wrote an admiring book of memoirs about her. Her ill-timed fervor and desire to play Lady Bountiful involved her in constant quarrels with her neighbors, culminating in

an arrest for hoarding during the World War—though she was generosity itself, and her patriotism was unimpugnable. (Michael Sadleir calls her wartime attitude "a collaboration between Niobe and Britannia"!)

Still pouring out books, though her popularity decreased with the years, the pretty little blonde woman imperceptibly faded into an old lady still convinced of her perfect rightness, vast learning, and supreme genius. She died of heart disease, just after the completion of her twenty-eighth novel, in her seventieth year.

Hypersenitive to criticism, Miss Corelli refused in later days to allow her books to be sent to the reviewers. She was insanely vain, a passionate self-dramatizer, and like her own readers from Queen Victoria down, she mistook mystical pretense for knowledge, florid rhetoric for stylistic triumph, and a mild talent for genius which it was blasphemy to attack. Yet on the other side of her nature she was warm hearted, deeply religious in her own individual manner, impulsively generous both with money and with praise, and she did have a flair for "gorgeous scene painting" and extravagantly romantic characterization that put the breath of life into her wildest and poorest stories.

PRINCIPAL WORKS: A Romance of Two Worlds 1886; Vendetta, 1886; Thelma, 1887; Ardath, 1889 Wormwood, 1890; The Soul of Lilith, 1892; Barabbas, 1893; The Silver Domino, 1893 (anon.); The Sorrows of Satan, 1895; The Murder of Delicia 1896; Cameos, 1896; Ziska, 1896; The Mighty Atom, 1896; Boy, 1900; The Master Christian 1900; Jane, 1900; Temporal Power, 1902; God' Good Man, 1904; Free Opinions, 1905; The Treasure of Heaven, 1906; Holy Orders, 1908; The Life Everlasting, 1911; The Innocent, 1914; The Young Diana, 1918; My Little Bit (non-fiction) 1919; The Love of Long Ago, 1920; The Secret Power, 1921; Love and the Philosopher, 1923; The Open Confession, 1925; Poems, 1925.

ABOUT: Bell, R. S. W. & Coates, T. F. G Marie Corelli: The Writer and the Woman Bullock, G. Marie Corelli: The Life and Death of a Best-Seller; Carr, K. Miss Marie Corelli Corelli, M. Open Confession; Vyver, B. Memoir of Marie Corelli; Literary Guide (London) Augus 1940; Saturday Review of Literature August 24 1940.

*COREY, LEWIS (October 13, 1894-) American economist, has, unlike most economic theorists, always been a free lance and has never taught in a college or university. In 1930 he was on the staff of the Institute of Economics, in Washington, and in 1936 he was assistant editor of the *Encyclopedia of the Social Sciences* He has for many years been a frequent contributor to the *Nation* (in which his second book appeared first as a series of

* Died September 16, 1953.

articles), and has also written for the *New Republic,* the *Annalist,* and the *New Freeman.* He has always been a left theoretician,  a convinced Marxist, but belongs to no existing party, and favors a "reconsideration" of Marxism in view of the increasing "proletarianization" of the "new" white-collar middle class. John Chamberlain, discussing Mr. Corey's work, predicted that as a result of his writings, "an American equivalent of the British Labor Party may be in the offing," whose principles would stem from Mr. Corey's critiques of the capitalist system. He favors a modification of Socialist theories to fit the psychology and industrial development of the United States. A sharp-featured man with light brown hair and thick eyebrows over keen eyes, he lives in New York City.

PRINCIPAL WORKS: The House of Morgan: A Social Biography of the Masters of Money, 1930; The Decline of American Capitalism, 1934; The Crisis of the Middle Class, 1935; The Unfinished Task, 1942.

COREY, PAUL (July 8, 1903-), American novelist, was born on a farm in Shelby County, Iowa, the son of Edwin Olney Corey and Margaret Morgan (Brown) Corey,  and the youngest in a family of five boys and two girls. His paternal grandfather was a Mexican War veteran and an adventurer in the gold rush of '49 who did not, however, find gold. Giles Corey, the most famous male victim of the colonial witchcraft craze, who was pressed to death, and who figured in Longfellow's *New England Tragedy,* was another ancestor. When young Paul was not yet two his father died, and the struggles of his mother to keep her family together on the farm were similar to those of the Mantz family in the trilogy of farm life he was later to write, beginning with *Three Miles Square* (1939). When she moved to Atlantic, Iowa, in 1918, Paul went to high school there. In 1921 he entered the University of Iowa, where he worked his way, chiefly as geology librarian; worked the summer of 1923 in a California

redwood lumber mill; and graduated in 1925, the year of his mother's death. Corey left for Chicago to work first in Kroch's bookstore, then on the *Economist,* a trade paper.

He had by now written a novel and several short stories, and brought them to New York City, continuing to write at night, and holding jobs variously with the Retail Credit Company, the Brooklyn Directory of the New York Telephone Company, and the *Encyclopaedia Britannica.* In 1928 he married Ruth Lechlitner, poet, and poetry critic for the New York *Herald Tribune "Books."* Before she came to New York from Michigan, they had met at the University of Iowa while she was working on the *Midland,* a national literary magazine edited by John T. Frederick. They went to Europe on a honeymoon, using their combined savings, and traveled and wrote in France, Spain, and England. On their return to New York they took office jobs again, but gave them up in the spring of 1931 to live on a few acres of land in the highlands of the Hudson near Cold Spring, N.Y. Corey built first a cottage of stone with his own hands; sold it in a few years at a profit; and built a bigger stone house on his hilltop. Having terraced a rocky hillside into level beds, as they had seen the French farmers do, they raised their own vegetables, and also did well with chickens. "On less than $1,000 a year cash income they live in absolute independence," according to William Seabrook in the *Reader's Digest.* A daughter was born to the Coreys in 1941.

Paul Corey is very blond, with hair that is beginning, he says, a forehead "pincer-movement," blue-eyed, and hard-muscled from having mixed, according to his estimate, "a hundred thousand pounds of sand and cement," to say nothing of handling "a thousand tons of stone" at his house-building. He likes good food, railway engines, and cats; his special dislike is the one billboard visible on the Post Road across the fields from the Corey front yard. The manuscript of his first novel has been presented to the University of Iowa library. Lewis Mumford called this novel, *Three Miles Square* (1939), "one of the best novels of agricultural America that anyone has produced in our generation"; while Louis Bromfield pronounced *The Road Returns* (1940), the second volume in the trilogy, "one of the most honest books I have ever read"; and Grant Wood, the Iowa artist, discovered in Corey's work "realism of the best sort."

PRINCIPAL WORKS: Three Miles Square, 1939; The Road Returns, 1940; County Seat, 1941.

*CORTISSOZ, ROYAL (1869-), American art critic and journalist, was born in Brooklyn, N. Y., and at a fairly early age

went to work for McKim, Mead & White, a famous firm of architects. (Cortissoz always regarded Charles Follen McKim, designer of numerous American landmarks, as a highly sensitive artist who happened to be dealing in marble instead of oils.) He remained there six years. In 1891 he joined the staff of the New York *Herald Tribune* and served at first in the double capacity of literary editor and art critic, until the art section, of which he still remains in charge, consumed all his time.

In 1897 he was married to Ellen Mackay Hutchinson, editor and poet, who was responsible for shaping the *Tribune's* Sunday Supplement. Her *Songs and Lyrics* had appeared in 1881, and with Edmund Clarence Stedman she edited an 11-volume *Library of American Literature* . . . (1889-90). She died August 13, 1933.

One of Cortissoz' earliest books was a study of August Saint-Gaudens, followed four years later by a life of John La Farge (1911). Between his *Art and Common Sense,* supporting his belief that "beauty is all," and *Nine Holes of Golf,* a light hearted contention that this same pursuit of beauty was as "legitimate on the links as among works of painting and sculpture," came a biography of Whitelaw Reid. He wrote three more books on craftmanship and art personages and edited a number of biographical and critical volumes.

In his fifty years of professional journalism he has enjoyed some remarkable friendships, as extensive among musical and literary groups as among art-lovers and artists —Richard Aldrich, Henry Krehbiel, William Winter, Ogden Reid, James Gibbons Huneker, Katharine Prescott Wormeley, and Franklin P. Adams. He has made several pilgrimages to the shrines of European art. He is small, white-haired, and bearded; Louis Betts has done a portrait of him for the Century Club, of which Cortissoz has served as president. He is also a member of the American Academy of Arts and

Letters and was awarded the Chevalier Order of Leopold. Wesleyan conferred on him an honorary L.H.D. degree in 1927.

Cortissoz has witnessed what is probably one of the most violent aesthetic upheavals in the history of art, and yet has retained all the while his classic old-masters concept of beauty: ". . . Through all the mutations of schools and traditions, for many centuries, art has recognized the validity of certain fundamental laws. I believe in the art that is faithful to those laws. . . ." He is an avowed conservative, a "Diogenes along the art galleries of 57th Street." And by tribute from the Salmagundi Club: "To him, a straight line has ever [been] and eternally will be the shortest distance between two points." His name is pronounced *cor-tees'uz.*

PRINCIPAL WORKS: August St. Gaudens, 1907; John La Farge, 1911; Art and Common Sense, 1913; Life of Whitelaw Reid, 1921; Nine Holes of Golf, 1922; American Artists, 1923; Personalities in Art, 1925; *Edited*—Don Quixote; The Autobiography of Benvenuto Cellini; Whitelaw Reid's American and English Studies.

ABOUT: Adams, F. P. Diary of Our Own Samuel Pepys; Cortissoz, R. John La Farge; Cortissoz, R. Art and Common Sense; Letters of James Gibbons Huneker; Art Digest April 1, 1937, December 15, 1939; Forum December 1935; New York Herald Tribune August 14, 1933; Time March 10, 1930.

"CORVO, BARON." See ROLFE, F.

CORY, CHARLES BARNEY. See "AMERICAN AUTHORS: 1600-1900"

COUCH. See QUILLER-COUCH.

COUPERUS, LOUIS MARIE ANNE (June 10, 1863-July 16, 1923), Dutch novelist, was born at the Hague, the son of Jan Ricus Couperus and Geertruida Johanna (Reynst) Couperus. When he was ten, his father received a government appointment in Java, and he lived and went to school there (in the Willem III Gymnasium) until he was fifteen, when his

father died and he and his mother returned to Holland. He attended the University at The Hague, but was not a particularly good student; his interest in history, particularly, was not so much scholarly as literary. He became a teacher, and first appeared in print as a poet, with two little

* Died October 17, 1948.

volumes which he himself said were "a mixture of Baudelaire and Rossetti, boiled in syrup."

His first novel, *Elina Veere,* was published in 1889, and he was hailed by the newly risen school of Dutch realism as one of their own. It enabled him to cease teaching and not only to devote all his time to writing but also to indulge his passion for travel. His early experiences in the Dutch East Indies colored all his work; he returned there often and constantly harked back to Javan scenes as background. In 1891 he married Elizabeth Bland. A few years later his mother died and thereafter he and his wife lived in Italy until the outbreak of the First World War. In 1921 he went back to the Dutch East Indies, via Japan, for two years, as a correspondent for the *Haagsche Post,* stopping over in London to visit his friend Sir Edmund Gosse and to be honored by a dinner at the House of Commons.

"I am a Latin of the Latins," he said of himself. "My heart is so tropic." This was true not only physically (he could not stand the cold of Holland), but also in a literary way, for his Puritanical countrymen objected to what they called "morbidity" and "sex obsession" in his books. Nevertheless, when he returned to Holland in 1923, his sixtieth birthday was the occasion of a national celebration. He was awarded the Order of the Netherlands Lion (he had received the Order of Orange Nassau in 1896), and was presented with a country home. Indirectly the gift caused his death. A slight scratch or insect bite received there the next month resulted in blood poisoning and killed him at sixty.

Arnold Mulder called Couperus "unquestionably a major novelist of the world, hidden away in the Dutch language." He wrote more than thirty novels, but although three of them were translated early into English, he did not begin to be widely known in England and America, or known by his best books, until a few years before his death. His able and enthusiastic translator, Alexander Teixeira de Mattos, unfortunately himself died a few months earlier than Couperus. At the time of Couperus' sudden death he was being mentioned prominently for the 1924 Nobel Prize in Literature.

Like Thomas Hardy, Couperus was strongly impressed by the idea of inevitability, of fate operating inexorably through heredity. His best work centered itself about what he called "small souls," people of no importance to themselves or anyone else, but still human. In the "books of the small souls"—*Small Souls, The Later Life, The Twilight of the Souls,* and *Dr. Adriaan* —no individual characters stand out: it is the group and its interactions which interest him. Money and the sense of family cohesion are the motivating themes. To a certain extent this is true also of what is perhaps his best novel— *Old People and the Things That Pass,* the story of the effect of an old and forgotten crime on people, not yet born when it was committed. His historical novels are superficial and dreary, and unworthy of him at his best. His style, according to Dutch critics, is colorful and poetic, and he has sometimes been called a "sensitist."

Gosse, who knew him well, described him as "trim and well groomed, with tufts of gray whiskers on each side of the pale oval of his face, to which black-rimmed glasses gave a certain owl-like aspect." His name is pronounced *coo-pare'us.*

WORKS AVAILABLE IN ENGLISH: *Novels*—Elina Veere, 1889; Footsteps of Fate, 1891; Psyche, 1898; Small Souls, 1914; Later Life, 1915; Twilight of the Souls, 1917; Dr. Adriaan, 1918; Old People and the Things That Pass, 1918; Ecstasy, 1919; The Inevitable (in England: The Law Inevitable) 1920; The Tour: A Story of Ancient Egypt, 1920; The Hidden Force, 1921; Majesty, 1921; The Comedians: A Story of Ancient Rome, 1926; Arrogance: The Conquests of Xerxes, 1930; Eighteen Tales, 1930. *Travel*—Eastward, 1924; Nippon, 1926.

ABOUT: Coenen, F. Louis Couperus (in Dutch); Gosse, E. W. Silhouettes; Deutsche Rundschau July 1924; London Mercury September 1923; Outlook November 28, 1923; Review of Reviews October 1923.

COURNOS, JOHN (March 6, 1881-   ), Russian-American novelist, writes: "I was born in Kieff, and until the age of ten I had yet to hear a word of English. Except for my immediate family, I spent those early years in solitude in the Russian woods. The medical tradition was strong in my family. For many generations it had counted many doctors, and my parents

Oggiano

made up their minds to make me one. (This may account for my tendency to diagnose the ills of society!) This was not to be. My parents lost their money, and with a large family they left for America. I was ten when I came to Philadelphia, and after my idyllic existence in the woods my new life in an industrial city was hard and in some ways incomprehensible. I went to school and in my spare hours I sold newspapers. My first English, which I learned in the streets, was expressive, and I dare say efficient if not exactly elegant. After two years, owing to the fact that I froze a foot one night while selling papers in a blizzard, we moved out of town, and I began my new life as a bobbin boy in a woolen mill. I received $2.50 a week, working ten hours a day, and was eventually promoted to a man's job at an increase of fifty cents a week. I was then about fourteen years old.

"I returned to town and became an office boy on a daily newspaper, and was eventually promoted to an editorial position. This I held for some time, gathering all the while all kinds of experience. My first interest in literature was contracted by an acquaintance with art students, and my first writing consisted chiefly of art criticism. All this time I was the main support of a large family. That I should ever have become an author seems like sheer accident. I feel as if I had been subconsciously driven into literature by some blind will.

"At the age of thirty-one I got 'fed up' with everything. I was in a rut and I felt that if something didn't happen I should end by cutting my throat. Instead I chucked a perfectly good life-job and went to Europe without any introductions or prospects. For years I had been thinking of writing a novel, and at thirty-five I suddenly realized that if I did not get down to work then and there I should regard all my experience as wasted. When I began working on The Mask I had but one book in mind. I found, however, that with work the idea broadened and developed, and that I should never be able to complete it in the single volume I had planned. At the conclusion of 100,000 words, I had to end my book abruptly—a fact which did not escape the critics. I then thought I could finish the narrative in The Wall, but the same thing occurred, and I was forced to continue the story in Babel. The New Candide was my first venture into the purely imaginative field. In the three volumes which preceded it, I unburdened myself of the experiences which drove me to write in the first instance.

"I have no doubt that anybody looking for anything but money would be regarded nowadays by all 'sane' people as something of a fool. Well, I have a fondness for such divine fools, since it is they alone who relieve us of the tedium of our drab existence. Indeed, in that sense, I hope I am something

of a fool myself, and in support of my folly, let me quote still another fool, William Blake: 'If a fool persist in his folly, he shall become wise.' "

* * *

Mr. Cournos was a member of the commission sent to Russia by the British Foreign Office in 1917-18, and later he was on the staff of the Ministry of Information. In 1920 he was a member of a commission investigating conditions in the famine areas of Central Europe. In 1924, in London, he married Helen (Kestner) Satterthwaite, herself a novelist under the name of "Sybil Norton." He has a stepson and a stepdaughter. Until 1931 they lived in England and on the Continent; then they returned to America, to New Haven, Conn. They now live in New York. Mr. Cournos has translated much from the Russian and edited several short story anthologies. His novels include one mystery, Grandmother Martin Is Murdered. He is dark and thin, and has aquiline features.

PRINCIPAL WORKS: The Mask, 1919; The Wall, 1921; Babel, 1922; The New Candide, 1924; Sport of the Gods (play) 1925; Miranda Masters, 1926; O'Flaherty the Great, 1927; A Modern Plutarch (biography) 1928; In Exile (verse) 1928; Wandering Women, 1930; Grandmother Martin Is Murdered, 1930; The Devil Is an English Gentleman, 1932; Autobiography, 1935; Public Affairs; An Open Letter to Jews and Christians (in England: Hear, O Israel) 1938; A Boy Named John, 1941; A Book of Prophecy (ed.) 1942.

ABOUT: Baldwin, C. C. Men Who Make Our Novels; Cournos, J. Autobiography; Cumberland, G. Written in Friendship; Literary Digest International Book Review August 1924; New York Evening Post Literary Review August 2, 1924; T. P.'s and Cassell's Weekly December 13, 1924.

COURTHOPE, WILLIAM JOHN (July 17, 1842-April 10, 1917), English literary critic and historian, was born at South Malling near Lewes, the eldest son of William Courthope, of an ancient Sussex family, who was rector of the parish. Mrs. Courthope was a sister of John Charles Ryle, first bishop of Liverpool. The elder Courthope died in 1849, and the three children were brought up by an uncle who lived at Wiligh near Wadhurst. In 1861 Courthope matriculated at Corpus Christi College, Oxford, coming there from the preparatory schools of Blackheath and Harrow. In 1862 he was an exhibitioner at New College. John Addington Symonds the younger introduced him to John Conington, Corpus professor of Latin, who was Courthope's intimate friend until Conington's death in 1869. In 1868 Courthope won the Chancellor's prize with an English essay on "The

Genius of Shakespeare." *Ludibria Lunae,*
a satire on woman's rights, appeared in
1869, when he left the bar to enter the Education Office as an examiner.   In 1887
Courthope was civil service commissioner,
rising to senior commissioner in 1892, continuing till 1907.   His six-volume *History
of English Poetry,* published from 1895 to
1909, gave him a reputation as a sound,
conservative, and patriotic critic, duly elic-
iting a Litt.D. from Durham in 1895, the
year he was elected to the professorship of
poetry at Oxford for five years.   Courthope
also edited, with a biography, the last five
volumes of the standard edition of Pope in
ten volumes which had been begun by Whit-
well Elwin.   This occupied him from 1871
to 1889.   In 1870 he married Mary Scott,
daughter of the inspector of hospitals at
Bombay, and they had four sons and two
daughters.   Courthope's strength gradually
failing, he spent his last years at Sussex
near Whiligh.   He died at seventy-four.

In poetical theory, Stuart Sherman said
in 1917, Courthope was a profoundly confirmed classicist.   In his reaction against
the excesses of romantic theory and practice
he advocated the revival of the heroic couplet and of ethical and satirical forms of
verse.   His leading idea was "the gradual
and majestic growth of the British Empire
out of the institutions of the Middle Ages,"
and his estimate of individual authors was
likely to be determined by the extent to
which they reflected English public life and
national spirit and character.   Courthope's
virtue—he was not an exceptionally original
thinker—"consists in the philosophical composition of materials amassed by his predecessors."   His own poetry has pastoral
charm.

PRINCIPAL WORKS: Ludibria Lunae, 1869; The
Paradise of Birds, 1870; Addison (English Men
of Letters) 1882; The Liberal Movement in English Literature, 1885; Life in Poetry: Law in
Taste, 1901; A History of English Poetry, 1895-
1909; The Country Town and Other Poems, 1920.

ABOUT: Courthope, W. J. The Country Town
and Other Poems (see Memoir by A. O. Prick-
ard); Nation May 31, 1917.

COWARD, NOEL PIERCE (December
16, 1899-   ), English dramatist, was born
at Teddington, on the Thames, the son of
Arthur Coward, who came of an "enormous, active, and fiercely musical family" and who always wore a blue corn-
flower in his buttonhole, and Violet
(Veitch) Coward, daughter of a captain
in the Navy.   His father was associated
first with a music publisher and then with

a piano manufacturer, and only under considerable strain did the Cowards retain the
accoutrements of a modest respectability.
Noel was sent first to a day school in Surrey, then to the Chapel Royal school in
Clapham; but after
coming under the dra-
matic   tutelage   of
Italia Conti, his pre-
occupation with the
three R's was only
spasmodic.   He made
his first stage appear-
ance in a company
headed   by   Charles
Hawtrey, whose ini-
tial verdict on young

Coward's histrionics was—"Never let me see
that boy again."

In January 1918 he was examined for
active service in the war and declared unfit because of earlier tubercular symptoms.
Shortly afterwards, however, he was assigned to a labor corps composed largely
of elderly physical defectives, and only with
strenuous wire-pulling did he effect a transfer to the Artists' Rifles at Gidea Park, not
far from London.   Here, returning one day
from a drill, he tripped and fell; and the
rest of his army life was divided between
hospital sentences and the execution of "light
duties" at Gidea Park.   He was finally discharged in August with a six-months' pension of 7s. 6d.

Coward's first play, *The Last Trick,* a
melodrama with a revenge *motif,* brought
him $2,000.   But it apparently did not lend
itself to the producer's contemplated re-
vamping; it never emerged.   *The Rat Trap,*
which he himself called his first serious
attempt at psychological conflict, was produced when he was eighteen.   He began to
feel himself "set" as a writer, and a passing
"lurid" phase ensued, during which "tarts,
pimps, sinister courtesans, and cynical adult-
erers whirled across [his] pages."

The *Vortex,* produced in 1923, was his
first great success.   *Hay Fever,* his own
favorite among his plays, was typical
of the sophisticated comedies and farces that
belonged to this period.   He turned shortly
to revues and operettas, doing the writing
and the producing; and he admitted, in 1933,
that *Bitter Sweet,* with its "particular mood
of semi-nostalgic sentiment," had given him
more complete satisfaction than anything else
he had ever written.

Some of the social satire which riddled
Private Lives and *Design for Living* went

319

into several of the nine short plays combined under the title *Tonight at 8:30*. *Cavalcade*, which opened in London in the fall of 1931, was not conceived as a patriotic appeal, Coward insists, but "primarily as the story of thirty years in the life of a family." And he regrets the fact that the critics missed the irony of the war scenes. *Cavalcade* was even more successful on the screen than on the stage.

A. G. MacDonell remarked that Coward is "prepared to act, sing, dance, compose music, write lyrics, stage-manage, produce, and turn out one comedy per fortnight, separately, in pairs, or all at once." Not all his plays have been successes, and he does not do all these things equally well, but he is a first-class actor, his music is something more than acceptable, and he shows marked ability as a stage manager and producer. His acting in the American film made from his own play, *The Scoundrel*, received the critic's plaudits. He has even found time to write three novels, all "terrible," says he. One, it appears, was published.

A young man who long before he was thirty was considered the foremost dramatist of his generation in England might be forgiven if he basked a bit in the sunshine of fame; but Noel Coward is as retiring as he is celebrated. He has said in his impudent autobiography *Present Indicative*: "My sense of my own importance to the world is relatively small. On the other hand, my sense of my importance to myself is tremendous." He has never married. He is supposed to be "the wealthiest playwright in the world" but he is still a tireless worker. He is tall and slender, with sensitive actor's hands, sleek brown hair, and blue eyes. In his forties he still seems inexhaustably young, perhaps because he was already "old at twenty," arrested timelessly in the superficial generation which he has satirized so cruelly, yet typifies himself.

PRINCIPAL WORKS: *Plays* (dates of publication)—The Rat Trap, 1924; The Young Idea, 1924; Fallen Angels, 1925; Hay Fever, 1925; The Vortex, 1925; Easy Virtue, 1926; The Queen Was in the Parlour, 1926; The Marquise, 1927; Home Chat, Sirocco, "This Was a Man," 1928; Bitter Sweet and Other Plays, 1929; Private Lives, 1930; Cavalcade, 1931; Post-Mortem, 1931; Design for Living, 1933; Conversation Piece, 1934; Point Valaine, 1935; To-Night at 8:30 (We Were Dancing; The Astonished Heart; "Red Peppers"; Hands Across the Sea; Fumed Oak; Shadow Play; Ways and Means; Still Life; Family Album) 1936; Curtain Calls, 1940; Blithe Spirit, 1941. *Miscellaneous*—Collected Songs and Lyrics, 1931; Spangled Unicorn, 1933; Present Indicative, 1937; To Step Aside, 1939.

ABOUT: Coward, N. Present Indicative; Arts and Decoration September 1927; Canadian Forum July 1933; Collier's February 10, 1940; Fortnightly Review December 1933; Living Age January 1932; New Republic April 21, 1937; New Yorker July 8, 1940; Queen's Quarterly February 1935; Saturday Review of Literature February 25, 1933, April 8, 1933, March 28, 1937, April 17, 1937; South Atlantic Quarterly July 1938 Theatre Magazine March 1931; Time August 19, 1940.

COWLEY, MALCOLM (August 24, 1898-), American critic and editor, writes: "I was born in Belsano, Pa., a village on the western slope of the Alleghenies. My father, William Cowley, until he retired in the summer of 1939, was a homeopathic physician in Pittsburgh. My mother, Josephine (Hutmacher) Cowley, belonged to a German family established in Quincy, Ill.

Newspictures

Belsano was their summer home, but I always felt that I belonged there rather than in Pittsburgh. It's hard to be loyal to Pittsburgh.

"I was educated in the Peabody High School, Pittsburgh, where I had the time of my life. I went to Harvard in 1915 and stayed till the spring of 1917, when I went to France to serve in the American Ambulance Service. Actually, I was assistant driver of a munition truck for six months. Came home; went to Harvard again for the spring term of 1918; went to the artillery officers' training school at Camp Taylor, just a week before the armistice. Got out of the army, starved for eight months in Greenwich Village (and that's no figure of speech); got married to Marguerite Frances Baird; went back to Harvard for the 1919 fall term and was graduated that winter after a little less than three years in college.

"New York again, this time making money enough to feed wife and self. Worked for a year on *Sweet's Architectural Catalogue*. Had the very good luck in 1921 to get an American Field Service Fellowship that paid my way to the University of Montpellier, ten miles from the Mediterranean but damned cold in the wintertime. Scholarship renewed for 1922-23; this time I lived in Giverny, about fifty miles from Paris. Met all the Dada crowd (later the Surrealist crowd). Helped to get out two of the expatriated magazines, *Secession* and *Broom*.

"Came home in the summer of 1923, and have stayed here ever since, except for a short visit to France and Spain in the summer of 1937. First I went back to work for *Sweet's Catalogue* (eighteen months). Then I free-lanced for a little more than five years, doing mostly book reviews and translations from the French; I think I was a dandy translator. Then, just a month before Black Thursday, I got a job on the *New Republic*. It was something like going into a monastery—at least I have been so busy ever since that I feel a little cut off from the world, like a man in a hospital who doesn't know anything except what he reads in the papers.

"I was divorced from my first wife in 1932, and married Muriel Maurer. We have one child, a boy who makes enough noise for six. We live in a remodeled barn in Sherman, Conn., with an FHA mortgage. My avocations are, for spring, trout-fishing; for summer, gardening; for autumn, hunting; for winter, fill it in for yourself. The torture of my life is writing."

* * *

Mr. Cowley is a handsome, youngish man with thick dark hair, a small moustache, and direct blue eyes. He is now book editor of the *New Republic* and contributes a leading review nearly every week. For a short time in 1942 Cowley was with the wartime Office of Facts and Figures in Washington, but resigned after being attacked by the Dies Committee for his "leftist" record.

PRINCIPAL WORKS: Blue Juniata (poems) 1929; Exile's Return: A Narrative of Ideas, 1934; After the Genteel Tradition (editor and co-author) 1937; Books That Changed Our Minds (editor and co-author) 1939; Dry Season (poems), 1941.

ABOUT: Bookman October 1930; Saturday Review of Literature January 16, 1934.

COX, ANTHONY BERKELEY ("Anthony Berkeley," "Francis Iles?," pseuds.)

(1893-), English author of detective and psychological crime fiction, writes from London concerning his career: "I began by writing sketches for *Punch,* a (so-called) humorous periodical peculiar to this country, but found that detective stories paid better. When I find something that pays better than detective stories, I shall write that. . . . Roger Sheringham

["Anthony Berkeley's" best known detective character] is an offensive person, founded on an offensive person I once knew, because in my original innocence I thought it would be amusing to have an offensive detective. Since he has been taken in all seriousness, I have had to tone his offensiveness down and pretend he never was."

Mr. Cox is much too modest on both scores. For all his claim to merely pecuniary motives, few detective stories produced on either side of the water today are written with such care or literary skill as those that come from the pen of "Anthony Berkeley"; and Roger Sheringham, the human, often fallible, central figure of such memorable adventures in sleuthing as *The Poisoned Chocolates Case,* has been called by H. Douglas Thomson "a less serious edition of [E. C. Bentley's] Philip Trent"—no slight tribute in itself.

"Anthony Berkeley's" stories—beginning with *The Layton Court Mystery,* published anonymously in England in 1925 when the author was thirty-two—brought to the detective novel an urbane and naturalistic quality that was a welcome and needed relief. Their author was also one of the first writers in the field consciously to recognize the necessity of expanding the detective form in new directions, to prevent self-strangulation. As far back as 1930 he was writing in the preface to *The Second Shot*: "I am personally convinced that the days of the old crime-puzzle pure and simple, relying entirely upon plot and without any added attractions of character, style, or even humour, are in the hands of the auditor; and that the detective story is in the process of developing into the novel with a detective or crime interest, holding its readers less by mathematical than by psychological ties. The puzzle element will no doubt remain, but it will become a puzzle of character rather than a puzzle of time, place, motive, and opportunity."

All the "Berkeley" books are excellent illustrations of this credo. As "Francis Iles" (presumptively) the author has gone even farther. Although Mr. Cox freely confesses his identity as "Berkeley," he has consistently refused either to confirm or deny personally the "Iles" *nom de plume*; London publishing and literary circles, however, admit no doubt of the fact. Reversing conventional detective formulae, the "Iles" novels—penetrating psychological studies of murder and horror seen "from the inside out"—started a prolific new school of fiction and have had a far-reaching influence on crime writing generally. Though the idea itself was not particularly new, in "Iles'" skilful hands it left the experimental stage behind and became a definite literary form. The first of the highly praised "Iles" novels was *Malice Aforethought,* published in 1931; *Before the Fact* followed a year later. After a seven-year silence, "Iles" resumed writing in 1939 with *As for the Woman,* announced as the first of three projected novels "about murder as a natural outgrowth of character." Alfred Hitchcock gave *Before the Fact* a notable film production in 1941 under the title *Suspicion.*

In addition to the "Berkeley" and "Iles" books, several works of humorous nature have appeared in England over the author's "legal" name of A. B. Cox, but they are little known in the United States.

In peacetime Mr. Cox lives with his wife in a fine old house in the St. John's Wood district of London and maintains a professional address just off the Strand, where he is one of two directors of A. B. Cox, Ltd. The nature of this corporation is not revealed by any of the London directories. Many readers believe that the author's remarkable knowledge of obscure English legal procedure displayed in *Trial and Error* —one of the most brilliant of the many "Berkeley" *tours de force*—indicates a sometime training for the bar. Other of the works hint at first-hand acquaintance with journalistic, diplomatic, and political backgrounds. Not least among his numerous distinctions, Mr. Cox is one of the few living English writers who comprehends the mysteries of the American language. He is a witty and delightful correspondent, and is described by Malcolm Johnson, of his American publishers, as "an amateur criminologist of considerable standing [he was the founder and first Honorary Secretary of the Detection Club] and one of London's best hosts."

In the field of the modern sophisticated novel of crime and detection, Mr. Cox— under either of his names—must stand very close to the top.

PRINCIPAL WORKS: As *A. B. Cox*—Brenda Entertains, 1925; Jugged Journalism, 1925; The Family Witch, 1925; The Professor on Paws, 1926; Mr. Priestley's Problem, 1927. As *"Anthony Berkeley"*—The Layton Court Mystery, 1925; The Mystery at Lover's Cave, 1927; The Amateur Crime, 1928; The Silk Stocking Murders, 1928; The Poisoned Chocolates Case, 1929; The Picadilly Murder, 1930; The Wychford Poison Case, 1930; The Second Shot, 1930; Top Storey Murder, 1931; Murder in the Basement, 1932; Jumping Jenny, 1933; Mr. Pidgeon's Island, 1934; Trial and Error, 1937; A Puzzle in Poison (English title: Not To Be Taken) 1938; Death in the House, 1939. As *"Francis Iles"*—Malice Aforethought, 1931; Before the Fact, 1932; As for the Woman, 1939.

ABOUT: Haycraft, H. Murder for Pleasure: The Life and Times of the Detective Story; Thomson, H. D. Masters of Mystery; Wilson Library Bulletin December 1939.

COX, PALMER. See "AMERICAN AUTHORS: 1600-1900"

*COYLE, KATHLEEN, Irish novelist, writes: "Born and brought up in the Northwest of Ireland; Irish father and American mother. Tragic, Brontë sort of childhood. From the beginning, I imagine, life never wanted me. I was poisoned when only a few weeks old by a nurse who left me for dead in the cradle while she decamped with trunks full of valuables, and only the timely although unexpected arrival

of my grandmother from New York on that particular morning saved me. A few years later, another nursemaid allowed me to indulge in an accident which has marked all my life. I never went to school or college and have consequently missed all that might be good or bad in these institutions. Educated on the surface by French governesses, at the core by what I inherited from my parents and free access to my father's excellent library, where I read everything from *Virgin Births* to Descartes and Dean Swift and Mrs. Henry Wood. Also, an imaginative child, I was steeped in that particular Celtic atmosphere in which dreams are made over into realities.

"I wrote my first story surreptitiously when I was nine and hid it in a secret place from which it promptly disappeared—swept into flames or the dustbin by a zealous nursemaid, probably. It had almost the same effect upon me to lose it as to lose my head. I was convinced for some time afterwards that no other idea would ever occur to me. Writing, I discovered some years later, was my only outlet and means of expression. I was good for nothing else. Of my novels only one, *A Flock of Birds,* is of any value. The others are, and were meant to be, means of earning a livelihood. *The French Husband* was written in eleven days.

"I have no hobbies, only devotions: my son and daughter, my friends, and my good work—when I am able to write what I like writing."

* * *

* 1886-March 25, 1952.

Miss Coyle is so reticent about the details of her private life that it is impossible to discover even her married name or the date of her birth. She lived in Paris for many years, but is now living in New York. She has a melancholy, sensitive face with great brooding brown eyes. Rebecca West speaks of "the courage with which she has pursued her ends in spite of pitiful ill health, and the joy she can distill from little things in the midst of the most discouraging circumstances." *A Flock of Birds,* her own choice among her novels, is a story of the Irish revolution. Her best known book has been *Liv,* whose heroine is a Scandinavian girl in Paris. To one critic her work suggests that of Virginia Woolf. Eudora Ramsay Richardson said: "Her poetic sensibility . . . struggles through word vehicles inadequate for full expression. . . . [Yet] she seems to have within her the power to develop into a distinguished writer."

PRINCIPAL WORKS: Picadilly, 1923; The Widow's House, 1924; Youth in the Saddle (in America: Shule Agra) 1927; It Is Better To Tell, 1927; Liv, 1929; A Flock of Birds, 1930; There Is a Door, 1931; The French Husband, 1932; The Skeleton, 1933; Morning Comes Early, 1934; Undue Fulfillment, 1934; Immortal Ease, 1936; Brittany Summer, 1940; Who Dwell With Wonder, 1940; Josephine, 1942; To Hold Against Famine, 1942.

ABOUT: Coyle, K. Liv (see Introduction by Rebecca West); Bookman May 1929.

COZZENS, JAMES GOULD (August 19, 1903-), American novelist, writes: "I was born in Chicago, but this was something of  an accident, and I never saw Chicago to my conscious knowledge until 1938. My mother was Bertha Wood, a Nova Scotian of a Connecticut Tory family. My father was Henry W. Cozzens of Newport, R.I., where his people had lived since the be-

E. Schaal

ginning of the eighteenth century. His grandfather was mayor of Newport, and during the Civil War governor of Rhode Island.

"I grew up on Staten Island, N.Y., where I went to the Staten Island Academy until I was old enough to be sent away to school. I graduated from Kent in 1922 and then entered Harvard. During my sophomore year (1923-24) my first book was published. This went to my head, and I took a year's leave of absence to write a second book. It was published in 1925, but instead of going back to college I went to Cuba, where I spent a year teaching the children of the American engineers at a sugar mill in Santa Clara Province. In the summer of 1926 I went to Europe and remained there a year.

"In 1927 I was married to Bernice Baumgarten of the firm of Brandt and Brandt, the literary agents. Since 1933 I have lived on a farm in Hunterdon Co., N.J., with the exception of a year (1938) when I served as an associate editor on *Fortune.*

"My first novel was written when I was nineteen, and that, and the next, and the next, were about what you would expect. I have the advantage of being older now. My social preference is to be left alone, and people have always seemed willing, even eager, to gratify my inclination. I am more or less illiberal, and strongly antipathetic to all political and artistic movements. I was brought up an Episcopalian, and where I live the landed gentry are Republican. I do not understand music, I am little interested in art, and the theatre seems tiresome to me. My literary preferences are for writers who take the trouble to write well. This necessarily excludes most of my contemporaries and I think I would do well to skip the presumptuous business of listing the three or four who strike me as good. I like Shakespeare and Swift and Steele and Gibbon and Jane Austen and Hazlitt."

* * *

Mr. Cozzens approaching forty still looks very young—not much older than the dark, handsome boy who "made" the *Atlantic Monthly* when he was only sixteen. He says that in his present circumstances he "occasionally writes something, but devotes practically all his time to farming." His first book to attract wide attention was the short novel, *S.S. San Pedro,* based on the "Vestris" disaster, and a remarkable *tour de force* for a man who had actually never been to sea except as a passenger. "I try," he remarked to the late Ruth Hale, "to recreate the thing I have felt or retell the thing I have seen. The ordered process is beyond me." He has been particularly praised for the firmness of his drawing of character, and the richness of his word-coloring.

PRINCIPAL WORKS: Confusion, 1924; Michael Scarlett, 1925; Cockpit, 1928; The Son of Perdition, 1929; S. S. San Pedro, 1931; The Last Adam, 1933; Castaway, 1934; Men and Brethren, 1936; Ask Me Tomorrow, 1940; The Just and the Unjust, 1942.

ABOUT: New York Times Book Review June 23, 1940; Saturday Review of Literature June 29, 1940; Scholastic January 11, 1936.

"CRADDOCK, CHARLES EGBERT."
See "AMERICAN AUTHORS: 1600-1900"

CRAIG, GORDON (January 16, 1872-), English actor, scenic designer and writer on the theatre, is the son of Ellen Terry, the

famous actress, and Edward Godwin, an architect and occasional designer for the theatre. With his sister, Edith Craig, later his mother's constant companion and also a successful worker in the theatre, Gordon Craig lived in Harpenden, Hertfordshire, as a small boy. Lady Gordon and Henry Irving were his godparents. At six he was a super with his mother and Irving in *Olivia*; played a gardener's boy in Chicago at thirteen, in *Eugene Aram*; and in 1889 became a member of Irving's famous Lyceum company at £5 a week, playing Arthur St. Valery in *The Dead Heart*. In vacation months Craig played Romeo, Petruchio, Macbeth, and Hamlet at other theatres.

He left the stage in 1897. Lee Simonson, the American scenic designer—notably for Theatre Guild productions—in a candid chapter of his book, *The Stage Is Set,* entitled "Day-Dreams: The Case of Gordon Craig," calls Craig's later career in its totality a compensation for youthful defeat, his failure to make more of an impression in Irving's company. Christopher St. John, in the enlarged edition of Ellen Terry's memoirs, remarks that Gordon Craig has presented himself to the world and to some extent conquered it in the capacity of a thwarted genius. "He is now known mainly as a theatrical antiquary who writes very charmingly about his hobby." In his three years of activity on his own in the theatre, Craig did grandiose and mystical sets for Purcell's *Dido and Aeneas, The Masque of Love,* Handel's *Acis and Galatea,* Laurence Housman's nativity play *Bethlehem* (in the hall of the Imperial Institute), *Sword and Song,* Ibsen's *Vikings,* and *Much Ado About Nothing.* Not even Ellen Terry's presence could save the Ibsen production.

In 1903 Craig left England for Italy, where he founded the School for the Art of the Theatre at the Arena Goldoni, Florence. Isadora Duncan gained him a commission to design Ibsen's *Rosmersholm* for Duse, who discarded the set after one performance, and in 1910 he did the sets for the Moscow Art Theatre's Production of *Hamlet*. Craig married a "small, energetic Italian woman"; his son, Edward Anthony Craig, born in 1904, is an artist, designer and producer for the cinema and theatre who produced *Macbeth* at the Old Vic in 1932. A daughter was named Nelly. Many of Craig's essays first appeared in his periodical, *The Mask*, published in Florence since 1908 and *The Marionette,* founded in 1918. He is a member of the English Wood-Engraving Society, starting off as a young man with a woodcut of Walt Whitman.

Since the outbreak of the Second World War, Craig has presumably returned to his native country. His mailing address is now at Newport, Monmouth, England.

PRINCIPAL WORKS: The Art of the Theatre, 1905; On the Art of the Theatre, 1911; Towards a New Theatre, 1913; The Theatre Advancing, 1921; Scene, 1923; Woodcuts and Some Words, 1924; Books and Theatres, 1925; Henry Irving, 1930; Fourteen Notes, 1931; Ellen Terry and Her Secret Self, 1931.

ABOUT: Housman, L. The Unexpected Years; Simonson, L. The Stage Is Set; Terry, E. The Story of My Life.

CRAIGIE, Mrs. PEARL MARY TERESA (RICHARDS). See "BRITISH AUTHORS OF THE 19TH CENTURY"

CRANE, HART (July 21, 1899-April 27, 1932), American poet, was originally named Harold Hart Crane. He was born in Garrettsville, Ohio, the son of Clarence Arthur Crane and Grace (Hart) Crane. The family moved first to Dayton and then to Cleveland in his early childhood; in the latter city the father became owner of a large candy manufacturing company. His parents

W. Evans

were divorced soon after, and his broken allegiance was the first of the factors which resulted in his personal disintegration.

From the age of thirteen Crane wrote verse of more than usual promise. At seventeen he spent a year with his mother on her father's plantation in the Isle of Pines, Cuba, an experience which gave him the first of his two intricately interwoven themes, the sea. The other, the city, came in Paris and New York the year following.

At the entrance of the United States into the World War, Crane abandoned the idea of college and returned to Cleveland, where he worked as a laborer in munition plants and shipyards. His father then took him into his business, determined to shake the "poetic nonsense" out of him. Several times, maddened by attempts to make him a salesman or shipping clerk, he escaped to New York where he wrote advertising copy; but this was little better, and his ambivalent tie to his father drew him back. The final break came in 1920. Crane, who had already known the Middle West, Cuba, and France, was now ready to have his work synthesized and come to fruition in New York.

Before his first book had been published, he was rescued from the advertising business by the philanthropy of the banker Otto Kahn, who enabled him to devote all his time to writing *The Bridge,* a mystical interpretation of the past, present, and future of America. Soon after its appearance he won the Helen Haire Levinson prize from *Poetry: A Magazine of Verse,* and was one of the Guggenheim Fellowship winners in 1931. He went to Mexico, with the idea of steeping himself in its atmosphere in preparation for another long poem which should do for Latin America what *The Bridge* did for Anglo-Saxon America.

It was by this time too late for Hart Crane to save himself. His heredity, his era, his personal history were all ruinous to him. Alcoholism had grown on him until his sober periods were few; he was besides an overt and aggressive homosexual. In his cups he was quarrelsome, he made violent scenes, he was completely without discipline or social control. His friends gave up in despair, even those who felt most keenly that a great poet was throwing himself headlong to destruction. Returning to New York by ship, the Mexican poem not even started, his achievement all behind him and nothing but blackness ahead, Crane threw himself overboard. In his own words,

> Sleep, death, desire,
> Close[d] round one instant
> in a floating flower.

Yet it was far more than a wasted life that dropped into those waters. If Crane is difficult to comprehend as a poet, it is because (to quote his own declaration) he was "more interested in the so-called illogical impingements of the connotations of words on the consciousness (and their combinations and interplay in metaphor on this basis) than . . . in the preservation of their logically rigid significations at the cost of limiting [the] subject matter and perceptions involved in the poem." Allen Tate says in his introduction to *White Buildings* that Crane has "a fresh vision of the world, so intensely personalized in a new creative language that only the strictest and most unprepossessed effort of attention can take it in." Waldo Frank observes: "The poetry of Hart Crane is a deliberate continuance of the great tradition in terms of our industrialized world." Against this, the accusation by Max Eastman that Crane made a cult of unintelligibility seems factitious and trivial. He was, in fact, a myth-maker in the grand manner, a mystic with enormous sensitivity to his environment. If James Joyce in his special field be worth the labor of decipherment, so too was Hart Crane in his. The packed images of his poems, particularly of *The Bridge,* which stems so strangely from Poe and Whitman, require the closest attention, but they also reward it. His work at its best is, as an obituary in the *Nation* remarked, "very great and pure poetic energy." When, in a lucid moment, he realized that he had "exhausted his will power in the process of composition," that what he had done he could never do again, he who had wished to live always at high emotional pitch chose annihilation.

PRINCIPAL WORKS: White Buildings, 1926; The Bridge, 1930; Collected Poems, 1933.

ABOUT: Eastman, M. The Literary Mind; Horton, P. Hart Crane: The Life of an American Poet; Zinsser, H. As I Remember Him; Atlantic Monthly August 1940; Nation May 11, 1932, May 3, 1933; New Republic April 23, 1930, May 11, 1932; February 15, 1933, April 14, 1941; Poetry: A Magazine of Verse June 1930, June 1932, July 1932, April 1933.

CRANE, STEPHEN. See "AMERICAN AUTHORS: 1600-1900"

CRAPSEY, ADELAIDE (September 9, 1878-October 8, 1914), American poet, originator of the "cinquain," was born in Brooklyn, N.Y., the second daughter of the Rev. Algernon Sidney Crapsey (whose heterodox preaching eventuated in charges of heresy, trial in an ecclesiastical court, and finally deposition from the Episcopal Church) and Adelaide Trowbridge Crapsey, an equally unorthodox mother who gave her nine children extreme intellectual independ-

ence. Before Adelaide was a year old the Crapseys moved to Rochester, N.Y.

She was a student at Kemper Hall, Kenosha, Wis., from 1893 to 1897; and for the school publication she wrote an appreciative review of Charles Reade's *Peg Woffington* and an essay on Charlotte M. Yonge. She also wrote short stories and translated Daudet's *The Pope Is Dead*.

In 1901 she was graduated from Vassar College, and two years later after a long and enforced vacation because of illness she returned to Kemper Hall to teach history and literature. In 1905 she studied archeology in Rome and during the two years following she taught English literature at Miss Low's School, Stamford, Conn.

Her physical condition grew considerably worse, despite a voyage to Holland (1907) with her father, who was a delegate to The Hague Peace Conference. In 1911 she was appointed instructor in poetics at Smith College; ill health compelled her to resign in 1913.

For more than a year before she died of tuberculosis at Saranac Lake, N.Y., in the autumn of 1914, she herself had known that she would never recover. Except for the scattered poems written before 1911, her most significant writing was done during the last grim but not cheerless months of her life. A thin volume of this *Verse* was published a year after her death; seven poems were added when it was reissued in 1922; and twenty additional poems appeared in the 1934 edition. Her *Analysis of English Metrics* (1918), an exhaustive technical thesis on accent, remained only two-thirds completed. Of the "cinquain," a five-line unrhyming stanza containing respectively two, four, six, eight, and two syllables, supposedly suggested by the Japanese "hokku" or "tanka," she was the originator: and in this lay her particular literary merit. Its effect is gossamer, yet highly compressed, and the poetic idea is reduced to its most economical terms.

Like her verse, she herself was "fair and fragile, in action swift, in repose still."

PRINCIPAL WORKS: Verse, 1915 (also 1922 and 1934); Analysis of English Metrics, 1918.

ABOUT: Crapsey, A. Verse (see Foreword and Preface to 1934 edition); Hartley, M. Adventures in the Arts; Jones L. First Impressions; Osborn, M. E. Adelaide Crapsey.

CRAVEN, THOMAS (January 6, 1889-), American writer on art, was born in Salina, Kan., the son of Richard Price Craven and Virginia (Bates) Craven. He was educated at the University of Kansas and Kansas Wesleyan University, receiving his B.A. from the latter institution in 1908. After a short time as a reporter and as a railroad night clerk, he went to Paris, where, as he says, "I embarked seriously into the business of transforming myself into a Frenchman." He wrote poetry and studied art, but as a painter he has never been much more than a good amateur. However, he returned to New York and to Greenwich Village, where he roomed with Thomas Benton and played the artist-Bohemian. Once in a while, in order to live, he had to go away for a few months or a year to teach Greek and Latin in schools located anywhere from the West Coast to Puerto Rico, where he was an instructor in the university in San Juan in 1913. During the First World War he served as a second class seaman in the United States Navy.  Following the war he gradually found himself and his place as an art critic. Today he is well known as writer, lecturer, and editor in this field. Besides his own books, he has edited books of prints; *A Treasury of Art Masterpieces* and *A Treasury of American Prints* both appeared under his editorship in 1939.

In 1923 he married Aileen St. John-Brenon, an English writer, and they have one son. They live in Great Neck, Long Island, N.Y. An acquaintance described him as "living in a comfortable house full of good paintings, with a red-headed wife and son," where he "serves the best fried chicken north of the Potomac." He looks the Middle Westerner he is, with his shrewd, lined face, long nose, and straight lank hair.

Thomas Craven probably has more enemies among artists than any other living man. He is the Mencken of the art world—irreverent, iconoclastic, and positive. Occasionally this attitude degenerates into what has been called "exhibitionistic slapstick and critical buffoonery." His pet detestation is the School of Paris and any manifestation of its influence on American painters; he is the publicist and laureate of American regional painting particularly of the Midwest group led by Grant Wood. "His philosophy of art," Ralph M. Pearson remarked, "is he-man and red-blooded. His general creed is that . . . only art dealing with the human drama of the day . . . has any meaning to contemporary man, that all problems of structure or design should be a means and not an end." Most painters regard Craven as a journalist in art rather than as a critic, but it cannot be denied that he is a lively and provocative writer in a difficult field and that his articles and books have stirred up interest even among those who know and care nothing about painting.

PRINCIPAL WORKS: Men of Art, 1931; Modern Art, 1934. *Editor*—A Treasury of American Prints, 1939; A Treasury of Art Masterpieces, 1939; Thomas Hart Benton: A Descriptive Catalogue, 1939.

ABOUT: Forum January 1936; New York Times December 14, 1939; Saturday Review of Literature September 30, 1939.

CRAWFORD, FRANCIS MARION.
See "AMERICAN AUTHORS: 1600-1900"

CRAWFORD, JOHN WALLACE. See "AMERICAN AUTHORS: 1600-1900"

CRICHTON, KYLE SAMUEL ("Robert Forsythe") (November 6, 1896-   ), American journalist, was born in Peale, Pa., the

son of William Crichton and Margaret (Nelson) Crichton. He received a B.A. degree from Lehigh University, where he was a member of the Phi Delta Theta fraternity, in 1917, and after graduation was manager of the Albuquerque (N.M.) Civic Council and associate editor of *Scribner's Magazine.* He married Mary Collins Collier of Santa Fé, N.M., in July 1921, and they have a daughter, Vivienne, and three sons, Andrew, Robert and William. Kyle Crichton's first book, *Law and Order, Ltd.,* the life of Elfego Baca, an officer of the law who had his own methods of overawing Western bad men, was published in Santa Fé, N.M., in 1928, with the imprint of the New Mexico Publishing Corporation.

Crichton has also been a coal miner, runner of a turret lathe in a machine shop, and an open-hearth puddler in the Allegheny steel mills of Pennsylvania, so that he has first-hand knowledge of the problems of labor. As "Robert Forsythe" he wrote pungent articles about personages in the public eye for the Communist *Daily Worker* and the *New Masses* in the palmy days of the "popular front." These hewed straight to the party line, and he received no money for writing them, according to Burton Rascoe. As associate editor of *Collier's Weekly,* Crichton, under his own name, writes illustrated interviews with screen, stage, radio and pugilistic celebrities for the periodical, making him a dual literary personality, one who does not allow his right hand to know what his Left is doing. Physically he is a giant, described as possessing "that bent-over, hard-ducking crouch common to many men who derive their idea of the general spread of human imbecility by the number of times they have been asked: 'How's the weather up there?'"

"These little essays on current American asininities are by and for someone who has been until quite recently taken in by them," commented the *Nation* on *Redder Than the Rose,* written as "Forsythe." "One has the feeling that Mr. Forsythe chastises such personages as Mae West, H. L. Mencken, Alexander Woollcott, and J. P. Morgan with such jubilant ardor because he recognizes their influence. Communism gives not only a point but a kind of salubrious glow to the best pieces."

PRINCIPAL WORKS: Redder Than the Rose, 1935; Reading From Left to Right, 1938.

ABOUT: Newsweek June 27, 1938.

*CROCE, BENEDETTO (February 25, 1866-   ), Italian philosopher, historian, and literary critic, was born in the village of Pescasseroli (Abruzzi), of middle-class Catholic parents. His father was a businessman, and the son of "a staunch old-fashioned magistrate, devoted to the Bourbons." Benedetto's interest in literature and history dates back to his

early childhood: "At the age of six or seven years I knew no greater delight than that of going with my mother into a bookshop." Signora Croce also took him to the old churches of Naples and these "first aroused in me an interest in the past." When a little over nine, he entered a Catholic school patronized by aristocrats of the Bourbon party, where he ran away with all the prizes. Gradually he developed a "contempt for the cant of Liberalism and a hatred of pompous phrases and all rhetorical ostentation." While at the *liceo,* in 1882, his first sketches appeared in a literary journal: critical essays somewhat satirical in tone. His earliest reading experiences were Pellico's *My Prisons,* "whose pages I sometimes, in an ecstasy of joy, kissed for very gratitude," and, later, the works of De Sanctis and Carducci, whom he preferred for his "violent and combative attitudes."

In the 1883 earthquake of Casanicciola, Benedetto lost his parents and his only sister, and he himself was buried beneath the ruins for some time, and seriously injured. On recovering he went to live in Rome with his father's cousin, Silvio Spaventa. Stunned by the tragedy and ill adjusted to his new *milieu* swarming with deputies, politicians, and journalists, he considered these "the darkest and most bitter years" of his life and even contemplated suicide. Although registered in the law school he never attended classes, "never sat for the examination," spending his days instead in the Casanatense library. During his second year in Rome he attended Antonio Labriola's lectures on moral philosophy, which impressed him deeply and sowed the seeds for his *Philosophy of Practice.* Still he did not recognize as yet his philosophical calling. His *Juvenilia 1883-1887* reveal him as a dilettante only superficially interested in ideas.

On his return to Naples (1886), he leisurely pursued his antiquarian research and even his travels in Germany, Spain, France, and England evidenced his scholastic emphasis. This passion lasted for over six years and resulted in sundry essays on the Neapolitan Revolution of 1799, the Neapolitan theatre from the Renaissance to the end of the eighteenth century, and in the publication, at his own expense, of a "Library of Neapolitan Literature," and a magazine, *Napoli Nobilissima,* dealing with topographical and historical questions.

After reading Vico's *New Science,* in which art and history are connected philosophically, Croce in February or March 1893 sketched his *History Subsumed Under the General Concept of Art.* This was praised by several critics, and, encouraged in his fruitful departure, he wrote in a fortnight (1894) a short polemical treatise on the methods of literary criticism, which caused a stir in his "little world." In April 1895 Labriola sent him the first of his essays on the materialistic conception of history (the one dealing with *The Communist Manifesto*): "I read it and re-read it; and again I felt my whole mind burst into flame. . . . I broke off—I might almost say, gave up—my researches upon Spain in Italian life, and threw myself for several months, with inexpressible fervor, into the study of economy, of which till then I knew nothing." His political passion did not last, however; Croce failed to understand either economics or Marxism: witness his befuddled essays on *Historical Materialism and Marxian Economics* (1895-1900). Shortly afterwards he became closely associated with the idealist Giovanni Gentile, today the outstanding ideologist of Fascism. In January 1903 appeared the first number of *La Critica* under their joint editorship, with Gentile in charge of the philosophy section and Croce of the literary section. Croce planned his editorial work so efficiently that his studies suffered no interruption. In 1905 he discovered Hegel: "When I plunged into the reading of Hegel, I seemed to be plunging into myself." From his exhaustive analysis of Hegelian thought, he drew *What Is Living and What Is Dead of the Philosophy of Hegel* (1906).

Croce's philosophical interests were not confined to specialized, speculative fields; he also wished to see a broader circulation of ideas. In 1906 he persuaded Laterza, the Bari publisher, to issue a series of "Classics of Modern Philosophy," edited with Gentile, as well as a series edited by himself devoted to the Southern Italian writers of the Risorgimento and the early years of the Unity. Croce's broad outlook widened even more in the course of the years—in 1907 he wrote on the philosophy of law and economics, in 1908 on the philosophy of the practical, in 1909 on logic, in 1910 on aesthetic theory, in 1911 on Vico (1668-1744), "the philosopher most closely akin to myself," in 1912 on the theory and history of historiography. This constant shifting from literature to history to philosophy has characterized his work during the past quarter century also.

In 1910 Croce entered the arena of politics: he was elected Senator from Sonnino, and later, served as Minister of Education (June 1920-July 1921) during Giolitti's government. Since the Fascist coup, Croce who is averse to Fascism, has devoted his time to philosophical endeavors. In 1920 he was awarded a gold medal by Columbia University and later he received honorary degrees from Oxford and Freiburg and stood as the strongest candidate for the Nobel Prize in 1934, which, for political reasons, was awarded to Pirandello instead.

Croce's *opera omnia* comprise over twenty volumes, the most remarkable of which are the four volumes of his *Philosophy of the Spirit (Aesthetics, Logic, Philosophy of the*

Practical, and *Theory and History of Historiography),* in the field of philosophy; *Ariosto, Shakespeare, and Corneille,* and *European Literature in the Nineteenth Century,* in the field of literary criticism; and *Italy From 1871 to 1915,* in the field of history. It can be justly claimed, with Crémieux, that Croce "transformed the spiritual physiognomy of Italy" by attacking "the methods and doctrines current in the '90s," by laying bare the weaknesses of "eruditism" and "philogism," and by introducing fresh viewpoints in all his fields of research.

WORKS AVAILABLE IN ENGLISH TRANSLATION: The Philosophy of Giambattista Vico, 1913; Philosophy of the Practical, 1913; Historical Materialism and the Economics of Karl Marx, 1914; The Breviary of Aesthetic, 1915 (enlarged and published later as The Essence of Aesthetic, 1921); What Is Living and What Is Dead of the Philosophy of Hegel, 1915; Logic as the Science of Pure Concept, 1917; Ariosto, Shakespeare, and Corneille, 1920; History: Its Theory and Practice, 1921; Aesthetic as Science of Expression and General Linguistic, 1922; The Poetry of Dante, 1922; Goethe, 1923; The Conduct of Life, 1924; European Literature in the Nineteenth Century, 1924; Benedetto Croce: An Autobiography, 1927; A History of Italy from 1871 to 1915, 1929; Anti-Historical Movement, 1930; Theory and History of Historiography, 1933; History of Europe in the Nineteenth Century, 1933; The Defence of Poetry, 1933; History as the Story of Liberty, 1939.

ABOUT: Carr, H. W. The Philosophy of B. Croce; Castellano, G. B. Croce; Crespi, A. Contemporary Thought of Italy; Croce, B. Benedetto Croce: An Autobiography; Dodds, A. E. The Romantic Theory of Poetry; Flora, F. Croce; Manacorda, G. B. Croce; Pardo, F. La Filosofia di B. Croce; Piccoli, R. B. Croce: An Introduction to His Philosophy; Prezzolini, G. B. Croce.

CROCKETT, SAMUEL RUTHERFORD (September 24, 1860-April 21, 1914), Scottish romantic novelist and clergy-

man, was born at Little Duchrae in the parish of Balmaghie, Kirkcudbrightshire. Between the ages of four and six Samuel attended Laurieston Free Church school, followed by nine gay and adventurous years at an academy known as Cowper's School at Castle Douglas. With a £20 scholarship he entered Edinburgh University at the age of sixteen; finished the arts course in 1879; and then went as a tutor to Germany, Switzerland, and North Italy, absorb-

ing, at this time, much of the romanticism that later crept into his stories.

Meanwhile he had been associated for half a year with a London newspaper; and he maintained these journalistic connections after plunging into theological study at New College, Edinburgh. He was ordained in 1886 in the ministry of the Free Church at Penicuik, Midlothian. In the year following he married Ruth Mary Milner, by whom he had two sons and two daughters.

A series of sketches written for the *Christian Leader* were published in book form in 1893 as *The Stickit Minister,* which, in contrast to the author's dire premonitions, was agreeably received. With this and a volume of poems (*Dulce Cor,* 1886) to his credit, he set about novel writing and in 1894 published two romances, *The Raiders* and *The Lilac Sunbonnet;* both were so rousingly received that he retired from the ministry and devoted full time to writing. In less than twenty years he published more than forty titles, largely novels.

Stevenson, to whom Crockett dedicated *The Stickit Minister,* considered him among the few top-notch letter writers of his day; and in *Songs of Travel* he addressed a set of verses, with flattering borrowings from Crockett's own dedication, to his parochial friend. But Crockett's literary reputation, even during his own lifetime, fell into rapid decline. Perhaps the only durable pieces among his writings were his chronicles of Galloway, his "little fatherland," with its meadows and heath, craggy coast, and lonely lochs. It was after steeping himself in some of these tales of Scotland that Stevenson was forced to admit that his head was "filled with the blessed, beastly place all the time!"

PRINCIPAL WORKS: Dulce Cor, 1886; The Stickit Minister, 1893; The Raiders, 1894; The Lilac Sunbonnet, 1894; The Men of the Moss Hags, 1895; Kit Kennedy, 1899; The Loves of Miss Anne, 1904; White Plumes of Navarre, 1909.

ABOUT: Colvin, S. (ed.). Letters of Robert Louis Stevenson; Harper, M. M. Rambles in Galloway; Glasgow Herald April 22, 1914; Scotsman April 22, 1914; Times (London) April 22, 1914.

CROFT-COOKE, RUPERT (1903-), English novelist and poet, was born in London and educated at Tonbridge School. At seventeen he was a teacher. He went to Paris that year as a private tutor, then spent two years in Buenos Aires, where besides teaching English he edited a magazine called *La Estrella.* In 1925 he returned to London and began to make his way as a free-lance journalist and writer.

In the next four years his poems and stories appeared in "sixty-three periodicals ranging from the *London Mercury* to the *Woman's Weekly.*" He also opened, in 1928, a bookshop, in Rochester, Kent, dealing in first editions. At the same time he turned to broadcasting, giving a series of radio talks on psychology. In 1930 he went abroad again, spending a year in Germany, writing, and later lecturing (in English) in Switzerland and Spain. He is now back in London, and engaged in writing and war work. He is unmarried. He describes himself as "a representative middle-class Englishman," but he certainly has an unusual amount of enterprise and self-confidence.

Mr. Croft-Cooke began his serious literary work as a poet; as early as 1928 he had poems published in *Poetry* (Chicago). His first four books to be published were in verse; they are all out of print now and he feels he has progressed beyond them and prefers not to have even their titles published. He has written three books of nonfiction besides another volume of poems, and had a play produced in 1929, but the bulk of his work has been in fiction. Though he has published better than a novel a year since 1930, his work is far better known in England than in America, where he was almost unheard of until the appearance, in 1938, of *The Man in Europe Street,* a survey of the then existing political and social situation. He also writes frequent articles (usually on sociological subjects) for English periodicals, and he translated the poems of the Spanish author Becquer in 1926. Still young, he is likely to become better known in the future, for his novels have wit and sound technique, and their defects, over-assurance and complacence, are the faults of youth.

PRINCIPAL WORKS: *Novels*—Troubadour, 1930; Give Him the Earth, 1930; Night Out, 1932; Cosmopolis, 1932; Release the Lions, 1933; Picaro, 1934; Shoulder the Sky, 1934; Blind Gunner, 1935; Crusade, 1936; Kingdom Come, 1937; Rule, Britannia, 1938; Same Way Home, 1939. *Miscellaneous* —How Psychology Can Help, 1928; Some Poems, 1929; God in Ruins, 1936; The Man in Europe Street, 1938.

ABOUT: World Today December 1931.

CROFTS, FREEMAN WILLS (June, 1879-   ), Anglo-Irish author of detective

stories, writes: "I was born in Dublin. My father was a doctor in the British Army, and died while on foreign service. My mother was married a second time, to Archdeacon Harding of the Church of Ireland. I was brought up and lived most of my life in what is now Northern Ireland. Educated at Belfast in the Methodist and Campbell Colleges, I became at the age of seventeen a civil engineering pupil of

my uncle, the late Berkeley D. Wise, Chief Engineer of the Belfast & Northern Counties Railway. In 1899 I was appointed Junior Assistant on the construction of the Londonderry and Strabane Extension of the Donegal Railway. From there I became District Engineer at Coleraine upon the Belfast and Northern Counties Railway. Ten years later I was transferred to Belfast as Chief Assistant Engineer of the same railway.

"In 1912 my greatest good fortune befell me in my marriage with Mary Bellas Canning, daughter of the manager of a local bank. We have no children.

"In 1919 I had a long illness, with a slow recovery, and to while away the time I got a pencil and exercise book and began to amuse myself writing a story. It proved a splendid pastime and I did a lot of it before getting about again. Then I put it away, never dreaming that it would see the light of day, but a little later I re-read it, thought that something might be made of it, and began to alter and revise. Eventually it was done and I sent it to a firm of London agents. They succeeded in placing it, and to my immense delight it was published. Now, twenty years later, it (*The Cask*) has sold well over 100,000, and is still selling. Needless to say, I immediately began a second book, *The Ponson Case,* which was also accepted, and since then I have continued to write, now having almost completed my twenty-fourth book. My books have been translated into French, German, Italian, Portuguese, Dutch, Danish, Swedish, Finnish, and Czech. I have also done a number of short stories.

"Up until 1929 I continued both writing and doing engineering work, but then my health gave way and I had to give up one or the other. I decided against railway work, and my wife and I moved to near London, where we still live. Early in 1939

I was elected a Fellow of the Royal Society of Arts."

* * *

Mr. Crofts is an amateur musician, with experience both as organist and conductor. His other recreations are gardening and carpentering. The detective in most of his stories is Inspector French of Scotland Yard. His books are strictly "plot" detective tales, the product of a mind trained in mathematics and engineering. This quality has led John Strachey to complain of "his bleak attention to the mechanics of the detective story, his ostentatious refusal to have anything to do with literary frivols." Nevertheless, *The Cask* is deservedly regarded one of the major classics of the genre, and all the Crofts novels are of special interest to those who enjoy the unraveling of a mystery without psychological characterization or extraneous romance. As Charles W. Purdy has said, Mr. Crofts is "amazingly fair to his readers," scrupulously "planting" his clues and letting the audience start even with the detective in solving the problem involved.

PRINCIPAL WORKS: The Cask, 1920; The Ponson Case, 1921; The Pit Prop Syndicate, 1922; The Groote Park Murder, 1923; Inspector French's Greatest Case, 1925; Inspector French and the Cheyne Mystery, 1926; Inspector French and the Starvel Tragedy, 1927; The Sea Mystery, 1928; The Box Office Murders (in America: The Purple Sickle Murders) 1929; Sir John Magill's Last Journey, 1930; Mystery in the Channel, 1931; Sudden Death, 1932; Death on the Way (in America: Double Death) 1932; The Hog's Back Mystery (in America: The Strange Case of Dr. Earle) 1933; The 12.30 From Croydon (in America: Wilful and Premeditated) 1934; Mystery at Southampton Water (in America: Crime on the Solent) 1934; Crime at Guildford (in America: The Crime at Norne's) 1935; The Loss of the Jane Vosper, 1936; Man Overboard, 1936; Found Floating, 1937; The End of Andrew Harrison (in America: The Futile Alibi) 1938; Antidote to Venom, 1938; Fatal Venture (in America: Tragedy in the Hollow) 1939; Golden Ashes, 1940; Circumstantial Evidence, 1941; A Losing Game, 1941.

ABOUT: Haycraft, H. Murder for Pleasure: The Life and Times of the Detective Story; Thomson, H. D. Masters of Mystery; Saturday Review of Literature January 7, 1939.

CROLY, HERBERT DAVID (January 23, 1869-May 16, 1930), American political writer and magazine editor, was born in New York City, the son of the journalist David Goodman Croly and of Jennie (Cunningham) Croly ("Jennie June," often called the first American newspaper woman). His parents were born abroad; the elder Croly was author of *Glimpses of the Future;* and since both were followers

of Comte, the boy was the first child in the United States to be christened in the Positivist faith, "the dryest, least inspiring or seductive of all the de-supernaturalized faiths." Many of Herbert Croly's later writings represent an attempt, it has been said, to explain to his own rational intelligence a feeling he experienced of growth in spiritual power. He attended the College of the City of New York in 1884-85 and  Harvard College in 1886-87 and 1895-99. In 1900 he became editor of the *Architectural Record,* but devoted himself exclusively to writing after 1906. Three years later came the book on which Croly's reputation chiefly rests, *The Promise of American Life.* It sold only 7,500 copies, but influenced both Theodore Roosevelt and Woodrow Wilson, whose New Nationalism owed much to Croly. Robert Morss Lovett calls it an "extremely clear and interestingly illustrated presentation of a central theme, the necessary association of the American national idea with American democracy." Although Croly wrote as a Hamiltonian, he believed the real failures of the American system to originate in the denial of democratic control.

In October 1914 Croly, with Walter Weyl, Francis Hackett, Philip Littell and Walter Lippmann (who has called Croly the first important political philosopher to appear in America in the twentieth century) began publication of the famous liberal weekly the *New Republic,* called the *Republic* until a Boston publication of that name, partisan towards "Honey Jim" Fitzgerald, protested. It was subsidized by Willard and Dorothy Straight, and supported Wilson up to the Versailles Treaty. Called a journal of opinion, its object was less to reform or entertain its readers than to start little insurrections in the realm of their convictions, in Croly's own words.

Croly was shy and reticent, with a sallow face, green eyes, and a slender, erect figure. Nevertheless he favored gay waistcoats and his own cigars, had a strong taste for gambling, poker and bridge, and sought the company of lively and entertaining people. After a stroke of paralysis in October 1928 he was an invalid until death at Santa Barbara, Calif., a year and a half later, at sixty-one. Croly's articles were painfully written, and his style lacked charm and ease. Nevertheless he was a seminal influence in American journalism and liberal thought.

PRINCIPAL WORKS: The Promise of American Life, 1909; Marcus Alonzo Hanna: His Life and Work, 1912; Progressive Democracy, 1914; Willard Straight, 1924.

ABOUT: Chamberlain, J. The American Stakes; Nation May 28, 1930; New Republic May 28, July 16, 1930; November 8, 1939; New York Times May 18, 1930; Survey June 15, 1930; Time November 13, 1939.

CRONIN, ARCHIBALD JOSEPH (July 19, 1896-   ), Scottish novelist and physician, sends this sketch written by his wife, also a physician: "Archibald Joseph Cronin was born at Cardross, Dumbartonshire, the only child of Jessie (Montgomerie) Cronin and Patrick Cronin. He was educated at Dumbarton Academy, and in 1914 began to study medicine at Glasgow University. His studies were interrupted by war service in the navy [as a surgeon sub-lieutenant]. In 1919 he was graduated M.B., Ch.B., with honors; then he embarked as ship's surgeon on a liner bound for India. There followed various hospital appointments —first at Bellahouston Ministry of Pensions Hospital and finally as Medical Superintendent of the Lightburn Isolation Hospital, Glasgow. In 1921 he married Agnes Mary Gibson, M.B., Ch.B., and commenced practice in South Wales. Whilst working there he took two higher medical degrees. In 1924 he was appointed Medical Inspector of Mines. In 1925 he was awarded his M.D. by the University of Glasgow, with honors. Subsequently he started practice in the West End of London, where he amassed a large and lucrative practice.

"But in 1930 his health broke down, and whilst convalescing in the West Highlands of Scotland he wrote Hatter's Castle, which was published in 1931 and translated into five languages. It was an instantaneous success, and Dr. Cronin then determined to devote himself to literature, an ambition which for years he had cherished in secret. In fact, all his life he had been intensely interested in the world of letters. At the age of thirteen he had won a gold medal in a nation-wide competition for the best historical essay of the year. But besides his

M.D. thesis, A History of Aneurism, his only publication before Hatter's Castle was his report on his survey of the medical regulations in British collieries.

"Dr. Cronin is very keen on all outdoor sports, being particularly fond of trout fishing and golf. In his earlier days he was an enthusiastic footballer. He has a definite interest in the theatre. His taste in literature is catholic, but perhaps his favorite authors are Stevenson, Scott, and Conrad on the romantic side, Balzac, Maupassant, and Flaubert on the realistic. In respect of modern novels, he has little sympathy with the 'stream of consciousness' school, and does not admire the thousand imitators of James Joyce. Of modern writers, he admires Arnold Bennett, Sinclair Lewis, and Somerset Maugham.

"Dr. Cronin resides in an old part of Kensington, London, and also has a country residence in Sussex where he does most of his writing. He has two sons. In literature he has found the sphere of work where he is completely happy. His ambition is simply to write so that not only may his name be known now, but that it may continue to be known."

* * *

Dr. Cronin has a D.P.H. degree from London University and is a member of the Royal College of Physicians. He is a tall, sandy-haired, young-looking man, whom one critic has called "England's new Dickens"— though J. B. Priestley might dispute the title. His medical play, Jupiter Laughs, was produced unsuccessfully in New York in 1940. He has never quite duplicated the freshness and power of his first novel. His work has, however, continued to be immensely popular. Dr. Cronin and his family are now in the United States. He is apparently associated with the British Ministry of Information and has been to Canada to study hospitalization for soldiers.

PRINCIPAL WORKS: Hatter's Castle, 1931; Three Loves, 1932; Grand Canary, 1933; The Stars Look Down, 1935; The Citadel, 1937; Jupiter Laughs, 1940; The Keys of the Kingdom, 1941.

ABOUT: Bookman (London) March 1933; Reader's Digest September 1939.

*CROSS, WILBUR LUCIUS (April 10, 1862-   ), American scholar, biographer, critic, and four-term governor of Connecticut, writes: "Wilbur Lucius Cross was born in Mansfield, Conn., the son of Samuel and Harriet M. (Gurley) Cross. He is in direct descent from William Cross, who fought in the Pequot War, and in collateral descent from Governor Bradford of the Plymouth

* Died October 5, 1948.

Colony. He spent his childhood and early youth in his native town; during vacations he acted as clerk in the village store. After graduating as valedictorian from the Natchaug High School in Willimantic, Conn., he entered Yale College, graduating in 1885 *magna cum laude*. He began his career as a teacher at the age of eighteen, the winter before going to college, in the district school at Gurleyville, in Mansfield. Immediately after graduation from Yale, he was appointed principal of the Staples High School at Westport, Conn. At the end of the school year, he returned to Yale for study in English and philosophy in the Graduate School, receiving his Ph.D. degree in 1889. In September 1889 he was appointed Master of English in Shady Side Academy, Pittsburgh, a position which he resigned in 1894 to accept an English instructorship in the Sheffield Scientific School of Yale University. In 1902 he became full professor, in 1916 Dean of the Yale Graduate School, and six years later the first University Professor of English on the Sterling Foundation. He served as Provost of Yale University from 1922 to 1924. He was made Dean and Professor Emeritus in 1930.

K. Hart

"During this period he edited a number of English classics and wrote several books. In 1911 he established the *Yale Review,* a magazine of international scope, covering art, literature, and public affairs. He is still on the advisory board of this magazine, for which he has written many articles on contemporary fiction.

"In November 1930, four months after he retired from Yale, he was elected Governor of Connecticut on a Democratic platform in a State normally Republican. As a result of three subsequent elections, he held this office for eight years (1931-39).

"Ex-Governor Cross holds honorary degrees (either Litt.D. or LL.D.) from Yale, Harvard, Columbia, California, South Carolina, Michigan, Rochester, Union, Brown, Trinity (Conn.), and Wesleyan. For the part he took in a plan for the interchange of students between Yale and French universities he was decorated by the French government as Chevalier of the Legion of Honor. He is Chancellor of the American Academy of Arts and Letters."

* * *

In 1889 Professor Cross married Helen B. Avery, now deceased. They had three sons and a daughter, of whom two sons are still living. Known familiarly to Yale students as "Uncle Toby" (from *Tristram Shandy*), he is the greatest living authority on Sterne, and an authority on Fielding as well. As governor he introduced many liberal measures, and as Provost and Dean he was a noted executive. His annual Thanksgiving proclamations written when he was governor are classic among American state papers and have been widely reprinted. Silas Bent has said that "he symbolizes a progressive and continuing participation of intellectual men in the American political arena."

PRINCIPAL WORKS: Development of the English Novel, 1899; Life and Times of Laurence Sterne, 1909; History of Henry Fielding, 1918; An Outline of Biography, 1924; The Modern English Novel, 1929; Four Contemporary Novelists, 1930.

ABOUT: American Magazine June 1933; Collier's Weekly November 21, 1931, November 19, 1938; New York Times Magazine April 4, 1937; Saturday Review of Literature October 8, 1938.

CROTHERS, RACHEL (1878-), American dramatist, was born in Bloomington, Ill., the daughter of Dr. Eli Kirk Crothers and Dr. Marie Louise (de Pew) Crothers, who was also a physician and the first outstanding woman doctor in that district. She was graduated from the Illinois State Normal School in 1892. From earliest childhood s h e h a d written "plays" f o r her paper dolls and at the age of twelve she actually wrote and produced a five-act melodrama. Where this gift for the drama came from no one knew, as the theatre was a "remote and somewhat wicked thing" to the Crothers family. Soon after graduation she went to New York and entered the Wheatcroft School of Acting, where after several months as a pupil she became coach and instructor. It was here that she wrote her first one-act plays, coaching the pupils in them and directing and producing them at the annual public matinees. She has ever since directed and supervised the production of her own plays. Her first professional play, *Nora*, was produced in 1906 by Carlotta Nielson. It was a failure and she was left to pay the heavy bills. Her first success was *The Three of Us,* produced by John

333

Golden. Since then she has had a long list of successful plays, until today she is rated by many as the most competent woman dramatist in America. In 1939 she received the Chi Omega National Achievement Award, presented at the White House in 'he presence of President and Mrs. Roosevelt. Up to date she has written and directed nearly thirty plays, many of which have been published in book form. Though she is no propagandist, she has often written on topical subjects, particularly on moral problems affecting women. Her plays, however, also include pure farces like *Expressing Willie,* or touching *genre* pictures like *Old Lady 31.*

An unfortunate venture in 1926 in producing a play by another dramatist put her $45,000 in debt. She refused to go into bankruptcy, and gradually paid off the entire obligation, though she was obliged to mortgage her home in Redding, Conn. and rent it to others. She is back in it now, though she spends her winters mostly in New York. During this period she was forced to take a salaried job as a play reader. Except for this hard period, her entire adult life has been devoted to play writing. She works all morning in bed, in a room purposely kept bare and austere, so that nothing may disturb her. First she writes a rough draft and puts it away to "mellow." Then before she approaches a producer with it she invites some friends to lunch and reads it to them to see if they like it. If they don't, she works on it some more. "I must feel the reactions of an audience," she says.

She is an energetic, executive sort of person, with a round face and grey curly hair. She is smart and "feminine" in her dress and is very fond of jewelry. Aside from her work her chief interest is in her Redding home, a reconditioned farmhouse with terraced gardens. When asked what she likes, she answers, "Everyday life." She is unmarried.

She is an exponent of "sanity in art," and her own work is solidly and conscientiously constructed. Joseph Wood Krutch said of her: "She does have a way of writing which frequently suggests a dramatization of one of the works of Mrs. [Emily] Post. But she is also almost the only remaining composer of what used to be called 'a well made play.' . . . Her neat, careful, measured exposition, while neither profound nor especially subtle, is continuously if gently interesting as well as frequently witty."

PRINCIPAL WORKS: (dates of production): Nora, 1903; The Point of View, 1904; Criss Cross, 1904; Rector, 1905; The Three of Us, 1906; The

Coming of Mrs. Patrick, 1907; Myself, Bettina, 1908; Kiddies, 1909; A Man's World, 1909; He and She, 1911; The Herfords, 1912; Ourselves, 1913; The Heart of Paddy Whack, 1914; Old Lady 31, 1916; Mother Carey's Chickens (with Kate Douglas Wiggin) 1917; Once Upon a Time, 1918; A Little Journey, 1918; 39 East, 1919; Nice People, 1921; Everybody, 1921; Mary the Third, 1923; Expressing Willie, 1924; A Lady's Virtue, 1925; Venus, 1927; Let Us Be Gay, 1929; As Husbands Go, 1931; When Ladies Meet, 1932; Caught Wet, 1932; Susan and God, 1937.

ABOUT: Hackett, F. Horizons; Mantle, B. American Playwrights of Today; Literary Digest August 15, 1936; Nation October 23, 1937; Pictorial Review June 1931; Theatre Arts Magazine March 1931, December 1932; Woman's Home Companion August 1931; Woman's Journal May 1931.

CROTHERS, SAMUEL MC CHORD (June 7, 1857-November 9, 1927), American clergyman and essayist, was born of Scotch-Irish parents, the Hon. John M. Crothers and Nancy (Foster) Crothers, in Oswego, Ill. At sixteen he took a B.A. degree at Wittenberg College, Ohio, and next year, in 1874, a similar degree from Princeton, then the College of New Jersey.  After three years at the Union Theological Seminary in New York City, Crothers was ordained a Presbyterian minister and left for Nevada, where he became "a kind of bishop of the Northwest," starting new centers of liberal faith at Duluth and St. Cloud, Minn., and as far as Helena, Mont. In 1882 he switched to the Unitarian ministry, going to Brattleboro, Vt. (1882-1886), St. Paul, Minn., and becoming minister of the old First Parish of Cambridge, Mass., from 1894 till his death at seventy, thirty-three years later. The same year that Crothers became a Unitarian, he married Louisa M. Bronson of Santa Barbara, Calif. *The Gentle Reader* (1903) made him well known as a new American writer of essays. Hamilton Wright Mabie called them "a happy blending of keen insight and of wit which is neither caustic nor destructive." Essays and sermons were sometimes interchangeable; Crothers's "The Cruelty of Good People" is an excellent sermon. The vagaries of English life and manners caused him much quiet amusement. Arthur Colton once remarked that Crothers was not so witty as Holmes, but witty like Holmes.

Liberty and the freedom of the human soul were favorite topics with Crothers, who protested against tying the church to any particular schemes when John Haynes Holmes proposed to commit the Unitarian Church to a definite program of reform. In some ways he was the most unworldly of men, frankly uninterested in the technical details of conducting a parish. His pulpit manner, quiet, unobtrusive and hesitating —he delivered his sermons without manuscript—was retained in his weekday life. Crothers was an essayist of the familiar type, finding humor in the perception of the incongruous.

PRINCIPAL WORKS: Members of One Body, 1894; The Gentle Reader, 1903; The Pardoner's Wallet, 1905; The Endless Life, 1905; By the Christmas Fire, 1908; Oliver Wendell Holmes and His Fellow Boarders, 1909; Among Friends, 1910; Humanly Speaking, 1912; Three Lords of Destiny, 1913; The Dame School of Experience, 1919; How to Know Emerson, 1920; The Cheerful Giver, 1923.

ABOUT: Newton, J. F. Some Living Masters of the Pulpit; Schelling, F. E. Appraisements and Asperities; Critic March 1906; Nation November 30, 1927; New York Times November 10, 13, 1927; Outlook November 23, 1912; Survey December 15, 1927, January 15, 1928.

*CROW, CARL (1883-), American journalist and writer on the Orient, was born in Highland, Mo., the son of a country

school teacher. From the age of sixteen, when his father died, he supported himself by newspaper work, first as a printer and then as owner of a weekly paper. While a student at the University of Missouri he was the local editor of the Columbia *Missourian* and also Columbia correspondent of the Chicago *Tribune,* St. Louis *Post Dispatch,* and Kansas City *Star.* After doing newspaper work in Texas, he joined the staff of *Hampton's Magazine* in New York in 1909. In 1911 he went to Shanghai as city editor of the *China Press,* and in 1913 to Tokyo as business manager of the *Japan Advertiser.* He returned about 1915 to Missouri and ran a small fruit farm. After America entered the First World War, in 1917, he was asked to return to China as head of the Far Eastern Division of the Committee of Public Information. He stayed on in China after the war as editor of the *Shanghai Post.* In 1931 he resigned his position and started in business for himself as an advertising agent, editing on the side two small magazines about travel

in China. He had published a few minor books on the Orient, but there was a long hiatus in his writing until 1937, when his *Four Hundred Million Customers,* dealing with Occidental business relations in China, became a best seller. His life of Confucius has been called "candid, sympathetic, and engaging"; he is himself a follower of the Confucian philosophy. He was an early advocate of aid to China in the Sino-Japanese conflict, and of a more aggressive attitude by the United States toward Japan. His writing is marked by "wit and facility," though it has been criticized as insufficiently fundamental in its approach. He now lives in Westchester County, just outside New York City.

PRINCIPAL WORKS: America and the Philippines, 1914; Japan and America: A Contrast, 1916; The Travelers' Handbook For China, 1921; Four Hundred Million Customers, 1937; I Speak For the Chinese, 1937; Master Kung: A Story of Confucius, 1937; He Opened the Door of Japan: Townsend Harris, 1937; The Chinese Are Like That (in England: My Friends the Chinese) 1939; Foreign Devils in the Flowery Kingdom, 1940; America in Stamps, 1940; Meet the South Americans, 1940; Japan's Dream of World Empire, 1942.

ABOUT: Saturday Review of Literature December 18, 1937; Scholastic February 26, 1938; Survey Graphic August 1940.

CROY, HOMER (March 11, 1883-), American novelist, writes: "I was born on a farm near Marysville, Mo. I still own

the farm . . . would you like to buy a good farm? I worked at farm labor all my early years; on the side, I wrote. My father nearly fell dead when I showed him a check for $8 from *Puck.* I rode a horse six miles to high school and back  Davart

again that night. No such thing as the city's collecting kids and taking them to school, then. I don't believe we'd have submitted to it. Finally I got off to the University of Missouri, and no greener son of the soil ever stared at the hoary old columns. Paid most of my expenses writing and doing newspaper correspondence. Edited the school papers and magazines and annual. I thought the annual was mighty good. I looked at it, by chance, a few days ago; snapped it shut and hid it under a pile of papers. But I didn't graduate; got flunked in English.

"I was the first student in the first school of journalism: at ol' Missouri University, long before Columbia School of Journalism arrived in the maternity ward. Never could get a job, to amount to anything, after I got out of the school of journalism. Too much prejudice against such schools. Drifted to New York looking for a job, ran one to earth under Theodore Dreiser, who was editor of three women's magazines. I wrote a lot of magazine stories and articles; now and then a good one, but for the most part they were about what you think. After while I wrote a novel and, after a terrific struggle, got it published. They paid in postage stamps.

"I kept on writing them, from time to time, but most of them were not any good. In fact, as I pause and look back, only two of them had any claim to merit—*West of the Water Tower* and *They Had To See Paris*. The latter became Will Rogers' first talking picture and was made into a stage play by my wife and served as a musical comedy for Chic Sale. I'm finishing up a new novel now . . . of course that's going to be a winner."

* * *

Mr. Croy married Mae Belle Savell in 1915; they have one daughter. He is "tall and gangling, with a pate as slick as a china doorknob," "a mild-mannered gentleman from Missouri who wears a Windsor tie and has a twinkle in his calm eye." Though he is primarily a humorist, *West of the Water Tower*, which was published anonymously, is a serious realistic novel, which one critic said had "something of the spirit of Hardy and Dreiser"; but, he added, Croy's outlook "is more hopeful. . . . He sees life without illusion and yet accepts and approves it." He was the first person to go around the world taking motion pictures; he lectures, writes radio scripts, and is famous for the interesting letters he writes his friends (on the backs of letters from other people to him), with such return addresses as "Piano Tuner Technicians' Association" or "Manhattan Home for Wandering Girls," and ending with such signatures as "Yours till China loves Japan, Two-gun Croy, the Law North of 125th Street." His hobby is collecting unusual stationery. As O. O. McIntyre remarked, "No one has more fun out of the business of writing than Homer Croy."

PRINCIPAL WORKS: Boone Stop, 1918; How Motion Pictures Are Made, 1918; West of the Water Tower, 1923; They Had To See Paris, 1926; Fancy Lady, 1927; Caught, 1928; Coney Island, 1929; Headed for Hollywood, 1932; Sixteen Hands, 1938; Mr. Meek Marches On, 1941; Family Honeymoon, 1942.

ABOUT: American Magazine September 1926; Bookman September 1923; Current Opinion September 1923.

CROZIER, JOHN BEATTIE (April 23, 1849-January 8, 1921), Anglo-Canadian philosopher, historian, and political economist, was born in Galt, Ontario, Canada (a village named for John Galt, author of *Annals of the Parish* and *The Ayrshire Legatees*). His ancestors came from Liddesdale in the Scotch border country. Crozier attended the village grammar school, and in 1872 graduated with honors in medicine from the University of Toronto, which gave him an honorary LL.D. in 1899. In 1873 he went to London "to study problems of the world and human life"; Carlyle granted him an interview and cannily reminded him that "medicine is a noble calling." Crozier obtained a degree from St. Thomas's hospital. A grateful *angina pectoris* patient bequeathed him a thousand pounds, which enabled him to marry, raise two daughters, and to write. It was twenty years before magazine editors would print his articles, although he was ready with opinions on Socialism, nationalism, Spencer, Comte, free trade, Cardinal Newman, and Lord Randolph Churchill. *Civilization and Progress* lay dormant for three years, but sold better in a cheaper and rejuvenated edition, with Mrs. Lynn Linton's approval to give it impetus. Fearing his eyesight was threatened, Crozier published an autobiography in 1898. His *The Wheel of Wealth*, according to some critics, was written as a handbook for Protectionists, and W. H. Mallock questioned Crozier's claim that he had substituted a dynamic, or Copernican, system for a static treatment of economic science. Crozier had "picturesqueness of diction and catholicity of appreciation," and could write with asperity on occasion, as when he attacked the tiresome reiteration of the sociologist Benjamin Kidd. He died in London.

PRINCIPAL WORKS: The Religion of the Future, 1880; Civilization and Progress, 1885; History of Intellectual Development on the Lines of Modern Evolution, 1897; The Wheel of Wealth, 1906; Sociology Applied to Practical Politics, 1911; Last Words on Great Issues, 1917.

ABOUT: Crozier, J. B. My Inner Life; Gould, F. J. Chats With Pioneers of Modern Thought; Dalhousie Review January 1922; Fortnightly Review July 1, 1907.

*CULLEN, COUNTEE (May 30, 1903-), American Negro poet, was born in New York City, the son of the Rev. Frederick Asbury Cullen, who founded the Salem

Methodist Episcopal Church, and Carolyn Belle (Mitchell) Cullen. He attended DeWitt Clinton, one of New York City's large secondary schools, and at fourteen wrote a free-verse poem, "To a Swimmer," which was reprinted in the *Modern School Magazine* in 1918. "I Have a Rendezvous With Life," another poem written at DeWitt Clinton, won first prize in a contest conducted by the Federation of Women's Clubs. The *Bookman,* in its issue of November 1923, was the first magazine in general circulation to publish Cullen's verse ("To a Brown Boy"); he also contributed to the *Crisis,* the official magazine of the National Association for the Advancement of Colored People.

Graduating from high school in 1922, Cullen received a B.A. degree from New York University in 1925, followed next year by a master's degree in English literature from Harvard. In April 1928 he married Yolande Du Bois; they were divorced the following year. For two years Cullen was assistant editor of *Opportunity: Journal of Negro Life* (1926-28); studied abroad for a year on a Guggenheim fellowship, writing a poem on lynching in Paris; and returned to teach awhile. At regular intervals Cullen published volumes of verse. The *Medea* of Euripides, translated for Rose McClendon, star of *In Abraham's Bosom,* is written in direct and strong prose except for the choruses, which were set to music by Virgil Thomson for the stage version. Cullen's only novel, *One Way to Heaven,* is a picture of Harlem life not unlike his friend Carl Van Vechten's *Nigger Heaven.*

Countee Cullen began writing as an emotional lyrical poet much under the influence of Keats and Tennyson, and showing his partiality towards Millay, Housman, and E. A. Robinson as well. He has said, "Most things I write I do for the sheer love of the music in them. Somehow I find my poetry of itself treating of the Negro, of his joys and his sorrows—mostly of the latter—and of the heights and depths of emotion I feel as a Negro." A New York *Times* reviewer remarks that some of his verse shows Cullen to be "just a little too much the product of our American colleges." A Methodist like his father, Cullen is a member of Phi Beta Kappa, Alpha

Delta Phi, the Civic Club, and lives on upper Seventh Avenue in New York City.

PRINCIPAL WORKS: Color, 1925; Copper Sun, 1927; Caroling Dusk: An Anthology of Verse by Negro Poets (ed.) 1927; The Ballad of the Brown Girl, 1928; The Black Christ and Other Poems, 1929; One Way to Heaven (novel) 1931; The Medea and Some Other Poems, 1935; The Lost Zoo, 1940; My Lives and How I Lost Them, 1942.

ABOUT: Brawley, B. The Negro Genius; Bookman (London) October 1931.

*CULLUM, RIDGWELL (August 13, 1867-), British novelist, frontiersman, and adventurer, was born in London and lived in England until he was seventeen. In that year he began two decades of sometimes fantastic wanderings. He first joined the earlier gold rush in the Transvaal and is said to have had something to do with mapping out the town of

Mafeking, in the African protectorate of Bechuanaland. A few years later he returned to this region to work in the fabulous diamond mines of Kimberley, Cape of Good Hope province. Here he fell in with an organized band of freebooters who, for the protection of British settlers, were preparing to oppose the reputedly troublesome Boer farmers.

Fur-hunting and trading in the Far Northwest lured him on to the Yukon, where at one time he narrowly escaped starving to death. From there he eventually worked south, crossed the Canadian border and settled down to large-scale cattle-ranching in the state of Montana. He found time, moreover, to take part in some of the later Indian (Sioux) uprisings on the Pine Ridge and Rosebud reservations.

Some accounts credit Cullum with making another journey into Africa before retiring permanently to England in 1904. In any event, the huge success of his first literary sallies encouraged him so much that almost immediately he decided to turn professional novelist. He had already published *The Devil's Keg* (1903), a river-ranch story, and a Canadian yarn called *The Hound From the North.*

Cullum was working in almost virgin ground when he chose Canada for his backgrounds. His knowledge of the country was deepened by his experiences as cow-puncher and prospector; there was certainly no lack of subject matter. He wrote, during that pre-war decade, with a cumulative vigor. Despite Zane Grey's ascendant popularity in England, Cullum, in the years immediately following the Armistice, was more than holding his ground—titles to his credit for the year 1922 numbered fourteen (including republications). He continued writing through the 'twenties and early 'thirties; and in 1938, when he was seventy-one, he appeared again on a publisher's list.

Cullum was married in 1898 to Agnes Winifred Matz; they have no children.

The Zola-esque "rush of elemental passion" that one reviewer ascribed to him was, it would seem, something of an overstatement. Cullum is neither a creator of ageless personalities, nor a stickler for literary niceties. But within his own frame of reference—technicolored fast-moving tales with plot mechanisms that are practically fool-proof—he has romanticized portions of history that might otherwise have wanted for an audience.

PRINCIPAL WORKS: The Devil's Keg, 1903; The Hound From the North, 1904; The Brooding Wild, 1905; The Night Riders, 1906; The Sheriff of Dyke Hole, 1909; The Watchers of the Plains, 1909; The Law of the Gun, 1919; The Heart of Unaga, 1920; The Man in the Twilight, 1922; The Luck of the Kid, 1923; The Child of the North, 1926; Bull Moose, 1931; The Vampire of N'Gobi, 1936; One Who Kills, 1938.

ABOUT: Bookman (Lond.) October 1914 and April 1921.

CUMMINGS, BRUCE FREDERICK
(September 7, 1889-October 22, 1919), English diarist and essayist who wrote under

the pseudonym of "W. N. P. Barbellion" (the initials standing, in sad bravado, for Wilhelm Nero Pilate), was born in Barnstaple, Devon, the son of John Cummings, a journalist, and Maria Elizabeth (Richard) Cummings. He was the sixth and youngest child of the family.

From childhood he showed a bent for natural science, and from the age of thirteen he kept the journal which is the basis of his best known work. At sixteen he was a newspaper reporter, but at the same time he began writing articles for scientific magazines, and in 1910 he obtained a small post in the Plymouth Marine Laboratory. In 1911, in open competition, this self-taught biologist secured a position in the Natural History Museum at South Kensington, Lon-

don, writing technical contributions also to the Proceedings of the Zoological Society, the Journal of Botany, and Science Progress. In 1915 he married Eleanor Benger, and they had one daughter.

But by this time his doom was upon him. His father had died paralyzed, and it is possible that his trouble was hereditary. He was a sufferer from disseminated sclerosis, a fatal disease of the brain and spinal cord, long and agonizing in its course. His wife had been informed of his illness before their marriage, but he himself did not know its nature until he took the army examination during the World War. He was obliged to resign his position in 1917, and two years later he died at Gerrard's Cross, Buckinghamshire.

His Journal of a Disappointed Man, published in the last year of his life, consists of extracts from his diaries from 1903 to 1917, though rather strangely it is usually catalogued by libraries as fiction. What had disappointed Cummings was life, the life-in-death that he had to endure and that made his last years a hell for him and for his devoted and beloved wife. The book is a challenge and a rebuke; he himself wrote, in his Last Diary, "The world has always gagged and suppressed me. Now I turn and hit it in the belly."

But it must not be assumed that this journal, one of the great autobiographies of all time, is whining or complaining. He said: "I am the scientific investigator of myself," and the London Times truly remarked that "he studies himself as he might study any man, or animal; and, as he writes, science and art become in him one." There is humor as well as tragedy in his pages. This "self portrait in the nude," as he called it, is the revelation of a courageous, sensitive, ambitious but objective-minded man whom fate thwarted cruelly. Gradually his "bias changed from intellectual to ethical," but always his mind remained self-critical and his observation keen. Had he lived, he would undoubtedly have grown from a technical writer on science to a creative author, for his style is vivid and shows great natural talent. His other books consist of further extracts from the diaries and some essays which were too long to be included in the journal. Both were published posthumously. Few men who have done so little, and under such untoward circumstances, have accomplished so much.

PRINCIPAL WORKS: The Journal of a Disappointed Man, 1919; Enjoying Life, and Other Literary Remains, 1919; A Last Diary, 1920.

ABOUT: A Book of Great Autobiographies; Barbellion, W. N. P. The Journal of a Disappointed Man, A Last Diary (see Preface by A. J. Cummings); Current Opinion July 1919.

CUMMINGS, EDWARD ESTLIN (October 14, 1894-), or, as he prefers it, "e.e. cummings," American poet, was born

in Cambridge, Mass., the son of Edward and Rebecca Haswell (Clarke) Cummings. He was educated at Harvard, where his father (later a well known Congregationalist minister and lecturer) had been an assistant professor of English. Mr. Cummings received his B.A. in 1915, his M.A. in 1916. Before America entered the First World War, he went to France as an ambulance driver; later he became a private in the American Army, but was stationed at Camp Devens, Mass., and not sent abroad again. It was during his French experience that he was imprisoned for some minor military offense and thus gained the material for his prose work, The Enormous Room, one of the best of the "direct observation" war books by an American—and incidentally his only volume to achieve a measure of popularity.

After the war he went to New York for two years, then (as did nearly every young writer of the period) to Paris, where for several years he studied art. He has much talent as a painter, has exhibited several times with the Society of Independent Artists, and still paints occasionally, though most of his time and energy is given to writing. He returned to New York in 1924, already well known for his prose book and his first volume of poems, won the Dial prize the following year, and remained in America until 1930, when he went back to Paris for several years more. He is now living and working in New York, with a studio in Greenwich Village. In 1928 he married Ann Barton, but they are now divorced. His only play, him, a "phantasmagoria" in twenty-one scenes, was produced by the Provincetown Players in 1928. He is tall and blond, with a face which seems sullen in repose, but lights up when his reserve is occasionally broken by bursts of enthusiastic and brilliant conversation.

Cummings was in the vanguard of the ultra-moderns, experimental, radical, and eccentric both in technique and in typography. Essentially his poetry is highly personal, a private message frankly offered from himself to the few who can receive it. Allen Tate complained that "he replaces the old poetic conventions with equally limited conventions of his own." Unless one has read his work, it is indescribable. As one critic remarked, he has tried "to make words bespeak his all but ineffable theme: the all-importance . . . of being nobody." S. I. Hayakawa, in an illuminating discussion, pointed out that Cummings is by nature shy and exceedingly sensitive: that he has the clear perception and the "breath-takingly clean vision" of a child (he has been very successful in writing for children); that if life had left him alone he would have been able to retain that clarity. But he was "dumped out into the uninnocent and unlyrical world"; his lyricism "ran completely to cover and he turned on the nightmare worlds of reality. . . . His descent into Hell is a trip from which he has not yet come up," and he "gathers together fragments of his inferno, and weaves them into patterns of surprisingly lyric grace." His endeavor is to represent direct experience by the very form of his work as well as by its meaning; it is a sort of super-verbalism that drives some readers to frenzy and others to disgust, but conceals in its depths, if one have sufficient patience and tolerance, much brilliant irony and much poignant beauty.

PRINCIPAL WORKS: The Enormous Room, 1922; Tulips and Chimneys, 1923; XLI Poems, 1925; &, 1925; Is 5, 1926; him, 1927; [no title] 1927; CIOPW (drawings and paintings) 1931; ViVa, 1931; Eimi, 1933; No Thanks, 1935; Tom, 1935; 1/20, 1936; Collected Poems, 1938; Fifty Poems, 1941.

ABOUT: Arts & Decoration March 1925; Canadian Forum July 1930; Hound and Horn, July 1931; New England Quarterly July 12, 1939; New Republic December 2 and 30, 1925; Poetry December 1926, March 1932, August 1938; Saturday Review of Literature April 15, 1933; Southern Review #1 1938.

*CUNLIFFE, JOHN WILLIAM (January 20, 1865-), Anglo-American literary critic, editor, and educator, writes: "My father and grandfather were owners of a daily newspaper at Bolton, Lancashire, and I grew up, so to speak, in the office, my first recollection being that of christening a new steam engine when I was somewhere between three and five years of age. I was educated at the local grammar school, founded in the early seventeenth century. The subjects of instruction were inscribed upon a marble tablet of about that date and were divided into sacred and pro-

fane. The sacred subjects were the Bible and the Church Catechism, but the profane subjects consisting of Greek and Latin classics, were of course much more important. At sixteen I entered my father's office as a reporter. After three or four years of training I went to the Owens College, now the

University of Manchester, where I stayed for some years. I had already taken my B.A. at the University of London in 1884, and in 1886 I took my M.A. in Classics, in 1888 anther M.A. in English and French, and in 1892 the Doctorate in Literature. My first book was *The Influence of Seneca on Elizabethan Tragedy.*

"After taking my doctor's degree, I went back into regular newspaper work, first on my father's paper, of which I became editor, then on the editorial staff of the Montreal, Canada, *Gazette.* In 1899 I was appointed lecturer at McGill University, Montreal, and became associate professor there. In 1906 I was called as a lecturer to Colmubia University. From Columbia I went to the University of Wisconsin to be professor of English and chairman of the department. I stayed at Wisconsin about six years and was then recalled to Columbia as professor of English and associate director of the School of Journalism, which had just been established there under the will of Joseph Pulitzer. On the retirement of Prof. Talcott Williams, the director, I was appointed his successor, and retired as Director Emeritus in Residence in 1931.

"I spent some years at Madison in editing the complete works of the Elizabethan poet, George Gascoigne, which were published in England by the Cambridge University Press. I contributed also to the *Cambridge History of English Literature.* Since 1912 my editorial and critical work has been mainly in the modern field. *Century Readings in English Literature* I began in 1910 in conjunction with two of my younger colleagues at Wisconsin, Prof. J. F. A. Pyre and Prof. Karl Young, now at Yale; the fifth edition is now ready for publication. I revised in conjunction with Prof. A. H. Thorndike the edition of *Warner's Library* in thirty volumes issued in 1917, and was chairman of the Editorial Board of the *Columbia University*

Course in Literature, which was issued in eighteen volumes in 1928 and 1929."

* * *

Dr. Cunliffe was married in 1897 to Jane Erskine, of Montreal. He lives now in New York City, near Columbia.

PRINCIPAL WORKS: The Influence of Seneca on Elizabethan Tragedy, 1893; A Canadian Soldier, 1917; English Literature During the Last Half Century, 1919; French Literature During the Last Half Century (with P. de Bacourt) 1923; Modern English Playwrights, 1927; Pictured Story of English Literature, 1933; English Literature in the Twentieth Century, 1933; Leaders of the Victorian Revolution, 1934; England in Picture, Song, and Story, 1936.

CUNNINGHAME GRAHAM, ROBERT BONTINE (May 24, 1852-March 20, 1936), British travel and story writer and

historian, was born Robert Bontine, in London, the eldest son of William Cunninghame Grahame Bontine and Anne Elizabeth Elphinstone (Fleeming) Bontine. His grandmother was Spanish; he spoke that language before he knew English.

He left Harrow at sixteen to live with relatives in the Argentine on a large cattle ranch. It was then that he reassumed the original form of the family name, the Cunninghame Grahams being a very old Scots family. For fifteen years he steeped himself in the life of South America—Argentina, Brazil, Uruguay, Paraguay. In 1879 he married a Chilean, Gabriela de la Balmondière, who was a mystical poet, but he himself wrote not at all. With his wife he journeyed north, teaching fencing as "Professor Bontini" in Mexico City, punching cows in Texas. His father died in 1884 and he went home to find the ancestral estate at Gartmore burdened with £100,000 of debt, which it took him ten years to pay off. In the end he had to sell it and move to a smaller holding at Ardlack. From 1886 to 1892 he was a Labor Member of Parliament, spending two months in jail in 1887 in consequence of the "Trafalgar Square riots," when he led workers against the police. He organized the Scottish Labor Party with Keir Hardie, and he made of himself the gadfly of Parliament. He lost his seat for North Lanarkshire and several times later contested other seats in vain. He never abandoned his political interests, helping to organize the Scottish Nationalist Party at the age of seventy-six.

In 1897 he heard of a forbidden city in Morocco and, disguised as a Turkish physician, set out for it. Instead of reaching it, he was taken prisoner by the Caid of Kintafi. The result was a first-rate travel book.

For by this time Cunninghame Graham was an author, his first article having appeared when he was thirty-eight and his first book when he was forty-three. He became the close friend and associate of W. H. Hudson, Joseph Conrad, and Bernard Shaw. (Though he quarreled with Shaw later, he furnished the inspiration first for *Captain Brassbound's Conversion* and perhaps for *Arms and the Man*.) His wife died in 1906 and he tried to forget his lasting grief in constant writing, recreating the past of South America and drawing swift pictures of men and their lives. During the First World War he returned to South America to buy horses for the British army. He died in Buenos Aires at nearly eighty-four of pneumonia, having gone there to see a Spanish edition of Hudson through the press.

Cunninghame Graham was one of the great British aberrants. He was of the company of Charles Doughty, Richard Burton, and E. J. Trelawny. It was his Spanish blood that made "Don Roberto" look like a picture by Velasquez; but it was the Celt in him that made him a rover, an adventurer, a grand eccentric. Hudson called him " the most singular of English writers," Conrad called him "a grand seigneur born out of his time." Edward Garnett remarked acutely that though he "paints men and their manners and environment to the life," he is "less of a story-teller than a critical observer and commentator"; and he complains that Cunninghame Graham's style is a little too natural." He himself, with his unshakable verve and wry humor, said he wrote "as a man who has not only seen but lived with ghosts. . . . Thank Heaven I write . . . to please no single being. . . . I write of things without a scrap of interest to right-minded men."

In consequence, "right-minded men" have neglected him; but few writers less deserve neglect.

PRINCIPAL WORKS: *Biography and History—* Notes on the District of Menteith, 1895; A Vanished Arcadia, 1901; Hernando de Soto, 1903; Bernal Díaz del Castillo, 1915; A Brazilian Mystic, 1920; Cartagena and the Banks of the Sinú, 1921; The Conquest of New Granada, 1922; The Dream of the Magi, 1923; The Conquest of the River Plate, 1924; Doughty Deeds, 1925; Pedro de Valdivia, 1926; José Antonio Páez, 1929; Portrait of a Dictator, 1933. *Stories and Sketches—*Father

Archangel of Scotland (with Gabriela Cunninghame Graham) 1898; Aurora la Cugiñi, 1898; The Ipane, 1899; Thirteen Stories, 1900; Success, 1902; Progress, 1905; His People, 1906; Faith, 1909; Hope, 1910; Charity, 1912; A Hatchment, 1913; Scottish Stories, 1914; Brought Forward, 1916; Redeemed, 1927; Bibi, 1929; Writ in Sand, 1932; Rodeo, 1936. *Miscellaneous—*Mogreb-el-Acksa: Journey in Morocco, 1898; The Horses of the Conquest, 1930.

ABOUT: Ford, F. M. Thus to Revisit; Harris, F. Contemporary Portraits; Tschiffely, A. Don Roberto; West, H. F. Cunninghame Graham; Fortnightly February 1933, May 1936; Saturday Review of Literature September 28, 1929, March 28, 1936, April 25, 1936; Time November 23, 1936.

*CUPPY, WILLIAM JACOB (August 23, 1884-), American humorist who signs his work Will Cuppy, writes: "I was born in Auburn, Ind., of pioneer stock. I was one of those sickly children. The fact is that I have never felt very well, though people will not believe it, probably because I am always from five to ten pounds overweight. My happiest childhood memories

Delar

are of the summers passed on the Cuppy farm near South Whitley, Ind., where I acquired my first knowledge of the birds and the flowers and all the other aspects of animate nature which I have treated none too kindly in some of my writings. It was there, too, that I went through a threshing machine by mistake. When not down with measles or some unidentified ailment, I attended the Auburn public schools. To my lasting regret, I was considered bright enough to skip the eighth grade, where I seem to have missed all the main facts of English grammar, punctuation, and that sort of thing. I have tried, by writing as simply as possible and attempting no rhetorical flights whatever, to conceal this weakness in certain branches of my art.

"I entered the University of Chicago in 1902 and was graduated Ph.B. in 1907. The extra year was the result of my outside activities as a reporter for several Chicago newspapers. I hardly expect anyone to believe that I then hung around the campus for another seven years, taking courses in practically everything, with or without bothering to go to examinations. I wanted rather desperately to learn something definite about life, and I thought that was the way to go about it. Besides, I thought it would be a good joke on all concerned for a roistering reporter to become a Ph.D. For three mortal years I read the Elizabethan prose writers and at one time had completed my doctor's thesis. But I am constitutionally unfitted to cope with Old High Middle Gothic and other linguistic riddles which others find so easy. So one day in 1914 I cut my thesis in half, settled for an M.A. degree, and took a train for New York. Someone must have told me that I could find out about life in the East.

"As for my books, there seem to be terrifying—and even to me, perfectly inexplicable—lapses of time between them. This may be because I am always doing something else, newspaper and magazine work or just hermiting in Long Island. For some years I have contributed a column of reviews called 'Mystery and Adventure' to the New York *Herald Tribune 'Books.'* Not long ago I tried lecturing. I cannot lecture.

"I do my writing at night when things are quieter. I can't write an article right off on the typewriter. I have to depend entirely upon the things I have thought of before and jotted down on 3 x 5 cards.

"I do not travel. I am not much of an extrovert, and I'm not much interested in extroverted objects. I do not care for the 'ideas' of novelists. Novels are wonderful, of course, but I prefer the newspapers. I hate authors who cannot see jokes. I am billed as a humorist, but of course I am a tragedian at heart."

* * *

Mr. Cuppy is unmarried, and likes to think of himself as a sort of suburban hermit. His leisurely and quiet humorous style is quite inimitable. His first two books of humor are still in print at this writing, after having gone through numerous printings. For many years he was at work on a new opus known to his friends as *The Decline and Fall of Everything.* It finally appeared in 1941 under the title *How To Become Extinct.*

PRINCIPAL WORKS: Maroon Tales, 1910; How To Be a Hermit, 1929; How To Tell Your Friends From the Apes, 1931; How To Become Extinct, 1941.

ABOUT: Rascoe, B. A Bookman's Daybook; Publishers' Weekly September 30, 1939.

CURRIE, Lady MARY MONTGOMERY (LAMB). See "BRITISH AUTHORS OF THE 19TH CENTURY"

CURTIN, JEREMIAH. See "AMERICAN AUTHORS: 1600-1900"

CURWOOD, JAMES OLIVER (June 12, 1878-August 13, 1927), American popular novelist, was born and died at Owosso,

Mich. His parents were James Moran Curwood and Abigail (Griffin) Curwood. The elder Curwood was related to Captain Marryat, the English novelist, and his wife was reputed to be a remote decendant of an Indian princess. Young James' early environment was a farm close by Lake Erie at Vermilion, Ohio, where he lived from five till thirteen. He had his first gun when eight years old. Expelled from school, he toured the South on a bicycle, peddled medicines, and trapped wild animals. Academic education comprised two years, 1898-1900, at the University of Michigan. From 1900 to 1907 Curwood was a reporter and later editor of the Detroit *News-Tribune*.

At nine he had improvised 200,000 words on a novel of a hundred chapters, but *The Courage of Captain Plum*, his first novel, appeared in 1908 when he was thirty. He was employed for two years by the Canadian government as a writer, lived among Eskimos, and traveled thousands of miles on snowshoes, by canoe and pack train through the Hudson Bay country, always thereafter known to Curwood as "God's Country." His period of greatest prosperity came when the Cosmopolitan Book Corporation took him up and obtained advance orders of over a hundred thousand for *The Valley of Silent Men.*

Curwood wrote twenty-six books in nineteen years, turning out many of them in twelve hours a day of work in a little room he had occupied as a boy in his father's house. He also built a castle on the banks of a river—a writer's workshop of stone; and had a beautiful lodge in the woods of northern Michigan made of logs which he had selected from particularly choice timber. Ray Long, the *Cosmopolitan* editor, described him as a vastly peculiar man; a personality that invited misunderstanding. Intrepid enough to face a trapped grizzly bear, he ran from garter snakes and kept his guests awake at night with screams in his sleep if snakes had been discussed the previous evening. In the last ten years of his life Curwood did no shooting or hunting (although he threatened to shoot bootleggers at sight), and did not go to war in 1917-18, although officially designated war correspondent. He expected to live to a hundred, but died of blood-poisoning before reaching half that age. He left a second wife, Ethel Greenwood Curwood.

Writing of a posthumous novel, *Green Timber,* completed by Dorothea A. Bryant, a New York *Times* reviewer comments: "Mr. Curwood's many admirers will be charmed with it, and the cynics will note again its well worn plot, its group of saintly and uninteresting characters, and the Curwoodian conclusion of eternal happiness to all good people and death and damnation to all the bad 'uns. Mr. Curwood had many of the elements of a good story teller. His books were very popular in France, and in *Green Timber* the exuberant viltality of the man floods his mediocre literary material with a modicum of warmth and grace." Curwood's Indian-like profile suggests that his mother may indeed have had Indian blood.

PRINCIPAL WORKS: The Courage of Captain Plum, 1908; The Danger Trail, 1910; The Honor of the Big Shows, 1911; Flower of the North, 1912; Kazan, 1914; God's Country and the Woman, 1915; The Grizzly King, 1916; Baree, Son of Kazan, 1917; Nomads of the North, 1919; River's End, 1919; The Alaskan, 1923; A Gentleman of Courage, 1924.

ABOUT: Baldwin, C. C. The Men Who Make Our Novels; American Mercury May 1924; Bookman February 1921, November 1927; New York Times January 15, 1923; February 5, 1925; August 15, 1927.

CURZON OF KEDLESTON, GEORGE NATHANIEL CURZON, 1st Marquis

(January 11, 1859-March 20, 1925), states-

man, historian, and traveler, was born at Kedleston Hall, Derbyshire, the eldest of eleven children of the Rev. Alfred Nathaniel Holden Curzon, 4th Baron Scarsdale, and Blanche (Senhouse) Curzon. His governess and private schoolmaster were the formative influences of his childhood. Two year after the death of his mother in 1877 he was afflicted with the first symptoms of curvature of the spine, an ailment from which he never recovered.

In October 1878 he went up to Balliol College, Oxford, won numerous academic awards, and allied himself politically with "Tory democracy seasoned by a strong flavour of imperialism." He left Oxford in 1882, and went to Greece and Egypt, where he wrote what became his Lothian prize essay. In 1883 he was elected a fellow of All Souls College and won the Arnold essay prize. After a journey to Tunis in 1885 he became private secretary to the new prime minister, Lord Salisbury, and in June 1886 he was elected to the House of Commons. He was drifting away from Tory democracy. As a speaker he lacked nothing; yet he was completely unable to sway opinion.

From his travels of 1887-90 and 1893-94 he prepared numerous *Times* articles, reviews, and four books: the extensive *Persia and the Persian Question,* in collaboration with Sir A. Houtum-Schindler, which is still valuable although slightly "watered down" (for Curzon had meanwhile been made under-secretary at the India Office); a volume on Russia; another on the Far East; and *Tales of Travel.*

Shortly after his marriage in Washington, April 1895, to Mary Victoria Leiter, daughter of a Chicago millionaire, Curzon was appointed under-secretary for foreign affairs (the Foreign Office's representative in Commons). At the age of thirty-nine he succeeded Lord Elgin as viceroy of India. The question of the jurisdiction of Indian military heads caused a steadily increasing bitterness during the seven years that followed. Curzon achieved substantial currency reforms, however, and carried on excellent research in Indian art and archeology.

A year after his resignation from the viceroyalty, his wife died, leaving him with three small daughters. In 1907 he was elected chancellor of Oxford University and became active in university reform. Before his second marriage, in 1917, to Grace (Hinds) Duggan, he entered Lloyd George's inner War Cabinet. And in October 1919 he was appointed foreign secretary—but his control was actually only secondary. That the prime ministry was tendered him and, in effect, withdrawn in the same stroke, was an inconceivable blow to him. But he returned to the Foreign Office with energy and magnanimity. He died in London following an operation, at the age of sixty-six, and was buried in Kedleston. As a political figure Lord Curzon achieved "successes rather than success." But regardless of his ultimate diplomatic stature he undeniably broadened Western knowledge of Asiatic art and literature.

PRINCIPAL WORKS: Russia in Central Asia, 1889; Persia and the Persian Question, 1892; Problems of the Far East, 1894; Frontiers, 1907; War Poems and Other Translations, 1915; Tales of Travel, 1923; British Government in India, 1925; Leaves From a Viceroy's Notebook, 1926.

ABOUT: Churchill, W. Great Contemporaries; Nicolson, H. Curzon: The Last Phase: 1919-1925; Political Science Quarterly September 1940; Times (London) March 21, 1925.

CUTLIFFE HYNE. See HYNE

DAGLISH, ERIC FITCH (August 29, 1892-   ), English nature writer and illustrator, writes: "I was born in London, which may seem to have been a heavy handicap for a child destined to find the greatest joy in after life in probing into the intimate secrets of the countryside. I was only five when I first became interested in nature, through a 'grotto' at the end of our garden. Birds, beasts, reptiles, butterflies, and flowers were throughout my school days my chief interests. I began to collect specimens and always had a miniature zoo, housed partly in glass cases in a conservatory, partly in wired pens, in an aviary, and on carefully prepared plots of ground about the garden. So time passed and when I went to a university, I naturally settled down to the serious study of natural science.

"From London I went to Bonn, where I was in 1914 when my world of peaceful studies and happy interests was shattered by the coming of the Great War. Largely owing to the kindly interest and active assistance of a chivalrous American gentleman, whom I had never seen before or have had the pleasure of meeting since, I was able to escape from Germany to Holland and thence to England. Here I joined the army and in due course served in Flanders and France.

"After the war I got back to work and wrote several books for grown-ups. It was not until 1929 that I wrote books for children, at which time I had children of my own. Finding it impossible to obtain the sort of pictures I wanted to illustrate my text, I conceived the idea of cutting my own designs on wood, engraving box-wood blocks which could be machined by the printer for the letter-press. I was a naturalist and author long before I was an engraver."

* * *

Mr. Daglish was married in 1918 to Alice Leslie Mary Archer. They have twin sons and a daughter. He was graduated from Hertford County College and studied at the Universities of London and Bonn (Ph.D.). He was a captain in the war and from 1918 to 1922 was the officer in charge of education at Woolwich Garrison. From 1923 to 1925 he was science correspondent of the London *Evening Standard*. His wood engravings are in many prominent art galleries. His hobby is the breeding of pedigreed animals and plants. He has illustrated many books besides those he himself has written.

PRINCIPAL WORKS: Our Butterflies and Moths and How To Know Them, 1923; Our Wildflowers and How To Know Them, 1923; Marvels of Plant Life, 1924; The Book of Garden Animals, 1928; Animals in Black and White (6 vols.) 1928; The Life Story of Birds, 1930; The Life Story of Beasts, 1931; How To See Birds, 1932; How To See Plants, 1932; How To See Beasts, 1933; The Dog Owner's Guide, 1933; How To See Insects, 1934; How To See Pond Life, 1934; Name This Bird, 1934; Birds' Nests and Eggs, 1935; The Gardener's Companion (with others) 1936; The Junior Bird Watcher, 1936; Book of the Dachshund, 1937.

ABOUT: Kunitz, S. J. & Haycraft, H. (eds.). The Junior Book of Authors; Wilson Library Bulletin May 1932.

*DALY, THOMAS AUGUSTINE (May 28, 1871-   ), American poet and journalist who describes himself as "writer and talker," writes: "T. A. Daly was born in Philadelphia, the son of John Anthony and Anne Victoria (Duckett) Daly. Educated at Villanova College and Fordham University to close of sophomore year, June 1889. Degrees: honorary M.A., Fordham, 1901; Litt.D., Fordham, 1910; LL.D., Notre Dame University, 1917, and Boston College, 1921. First clerk, then reporter and special writer, Philadelphia *Record,* 1889 to 1898. General manager *Catholic Standard & Times,* 1898 to 1915. Columnist, Philadelphia *Evening Ledger,* 1915 to 1918. Editorial writer and columnist, Philadelphia *Record,* 1918 to 1929. Columnist, Philadelphia *Evening Bulletin,* 1929 to date. Began as lecturer and after-dinner speaker in 1905 and rambled all over this country, Canada, and a few scattered spots in England. Pioneer in the writing of Italian dialect verse (beginning 1904), giving many recitals of same. First volume of verse *Canzoni,* published 1906, ran to about 50,000. Then followed seven more books of verse and two of prose.

"Charter member American Press Humorists (president 1906-07), was one of the founders of the Poor Richard Club (advertising) of Philadelphia, 1906; and for many years a member of the Authors' Club and Players' Club. During college days was

* Died October 4, 1948.

second-string pitcher and outfielder, Villanova, and shortstop Fordham Varsity, and quarterback of football team until incapacitated by injury.

"Married Nannie Barrett in 1896. Five sons and three daughters (one daughter deceased). Live in Germantown, Philadelphia."

* * *

"Daly the Troubadour," as "F. P. A." called him, is a medium-sized man with deep-set eyes behind spectacles. Formerly heavily moustached, he is now clean-shaven. Like most professional humorists, he is very solemn in appearance. He was a pioneer columnist (1891); later his close friend Christopher Morley also became columnist on a Philadelphia paper, and they were inseparable until Morley moved to New York. Morley said of him: "He has found good music in very simple hearts, and flowers growing round the heavy wheelbarrows of journalism." He himself remarked: "I have had more pleasure in the writing of many of those simple songs than the reading of them could possibly give to the public." Louis Untermeyer summed up Daly's place in literature very well by saying: "Less popular than [J. W.] Riley or [Paul Laurence] Dunbar, Daly is more skilful and versatile than either; his range and quality are comparable to [Eugene] Field's."

PRINCIPAL WORKS: Canzoni, 1906; Carmina, 1909; Madrigali, 1912; Little Polly's Pomes, 1913; Songs of Wedlock, 1916; McAroni Ballads, 1919; Herself and the Houseful (prose) 1924; The House of Dooner (prose, with C. Morley) 1928; McAroni Medleys, 1932; Selected Poems, 1936.

ABOUT: Daly, T. A. Selected Poems (see Introductory Letter by Christopher Morley); American Magazine June 1920; Cathholic World February 1941; Month January 1913, January 1918; Rosary Magazine July 1913; Scholastic February 20, 1937.

DAMON, SAMUEL FOSTER (February 22, 1893-), American poet, literary biographer, and university professor, was  born in Newton, Mass., the son of Joseph Neal Damon and Sarah Wolf (Pastorius) Damon. He attended Newton High School, received a B.A. degree *cum laude* from Harvard in 1914, and obtained his master's degree in 1927. After graduation Mr. Damon toured Europe with his older sister, returning from the war zone

without any particular inconvenience, and became bayonet instructor in the Harvard R.O.T.C. from May to August in 1917. From July to September 1918 he taught French to soldiers barracked in Boston Harbor; from October to May of the following year he polished gadgets in an airplane factory in New York. Damon enacted a ghost in Eugene O'Neill's one-acter, *Where the Cross Is Made,* at the Provincetown Theatre in New York and contributed an imitation Japanese nō-drama, *Kiri nō Meijiyama,* to the *Dial* of February 1920, fooling one expert into assigning it to a date in the sixteenth century. In April, with a musical setting by F. Flaxington Harker, it was performed at Westhampton College, Richmond, Va.

In 1920-21 Mr. Damon was abroad again as a traveling fellow on an American-Scandinavian Foundation fellowship, returning to become an assistant in English at Harvard until 1927. Two of his "English A" lectures, telescoped and rewritten, appear as "A Lot He Knew" in George Weller's novel of modern Harvard, *Not to Eat, Not for Love.* An essay on the history of free verse written some years previously for a prize contest had not won a prize, but attracted the attention of Amy Lowell, whose expert criticism proved of exceptional value to "a floundering poet."

On April 4, 1925, Mr. Damon was speaker at a dinner tendered Miss Lowell; this was the last time she appeared in public before her death the following month. In 1927 Mr. Damon became assistant professor of English at Brown University, Providence, R.I., and associate professor in 1930. In his sabbatical year, 1933-34, he wrote a bulky, frank, and authoritative life of Amy Lowell, bound uniformly with her *magnum opus, John Keats.* Mr. Damon's *William Blake: His Philosophy and Symbols* (1924) was well reviewed and rapidly became scarce; a second-hand copy has brought $40.

On April 29, 1927, he spoke at a memorial meeting for Abbie Farwell Brown, whom he succeeded as president of the New England Poetry Society. The next February Mr. Damon married Louise Wheelwright of Boston, whose father, Edmund March Wheelwright, was the last civic architect of Boston, the architect of the Lampoon Building and the Larz Anderson Bridge. In 1930 he published a biography of Poe's eccentric predecessor, Thomas Holley Chivers. Two years later the New England Poetry Society awarded Foster Damon its Golden Rose. He was Phi Beta Kappa poet at Tufts May

23, 1934; on March 28, 1927, he had been odist at the Boston Beethoven Centenary Festival.

In 1936 Mr. Damon became a full professor at Brown. Since 1929 he has been curator of the Harris Collection of American Poetry and Plays, the largest collection of its kind in existence. Virgil Thomson made use of it in writing the score for Pare Lorentz's documentary film, "The River"; Mr. Damon himself has composed an orchestral suite, "Crazy Theatre Music," broadcast by the WPA orchestra from the Providence station WJAR January 22, 1938. Mr. Damon is fair, with a calm face and a heavy, well-trimmed moustache. His lyrics have been described as conventional in form and subject matter, with individual rhyme patterns and rather full emotional content. They also display rich humor, a sense of satire, and an ability to handle the longer lyric form. He has contributed regularly to the late *Bookman, Century,* and *Dial,* and the present *Atlantic* and *Harper's.*

PRINCIPAL WORKS: Eight Harvard Poets (ed.) 1917; Eight More Harvard Poets (ed.) 1923; William Blake: His Philosophy and Symbols, 1924; A New Page in Blake's Milton, 1925; Astrolabe (verse) 1927; Tilted Moons (verse) 1929; Thomas Holley Chivers, 1930; The Day After Christmas, 1930; Amy Lowell: A Chronicle, 1935; Series of American Songs (ed.) 1936.

ABOUT: Harvard College, Class of 1914, Twenty-Fifth Anniversary Report.

DANE, CLEMENCE. English novelist and dramatist, was born (Winifred Ashton) and reared in Southern England, and at-

tended several p r i-v a t e schools before going to Geneva, at sixteen, as a teacher of French. After a year she returned to England, studied art for three years at the Slade School, in London, and for another year in Dresden, then gave up a promising career as a portrait painter to teach school in Ireland. She was still very young, in her early twenties, when she abandoned teaching again to go on the stage. She remained an actress for four or five years, then, with the First World War, plunged into war work with so much energy and enthusiasm that her health collapsed. It was while she was recovering from this breakdown that, to occupy her mind, she began her first novel. Her *nom de guerre*—it is more than a pseudonym—

she took from the famous and beautiful church of St. Clements Dane, in London (virtually destroyed in 1940 by a Nazi bomb).

This first novel, *Regiment of Women,* a devastating study of the teachers in a girls' school (the title is taken from John Knox's invective against Mary, Queen of Scots), was an immediate success. Her experience as a teacher had been put to good use. She was next to make use of her stage experience. Her third novel, *Legend,* was so dramatic in form that it was suggested that she make it into a play. She did so, calling the dramatic version *A Bill of Divorcement.* It was remarkably successful, both in London and New York, and proved to be the stepping-stone to fame of the American actress Katharine Cornell. Miss Dane thereafter alternated between plays and novels; she has besides written a book of essays and a critical study of Sir Hugh Walpole. With Helen Simpson[qv] she has also written a series of superior detective novels, centering around "Sir John," who has joined the ranks of the better known fictional sleuths. Among her plays is a dramatization of Max Beerbohm's novel, *The Happy Hypocrite.* Her wide acquaintance with literature frequently appears in her work—for example, she adapted Edmond Rostand's *L'Aiglon* to the English stage (with Richard Addinsell), she wrote one play about Shakespeare, another (*Come of Age*) about Thomas Chatterton and a third (*Wild Decembers*) about the Brontës; and her *Herod and Marianne* is based on a German play by Friedrich Hebbel. One of the most interesting of her novels is *Broome Stages,* which in the guise of the story of an English theatrical family actually renders into fiction the history of the Plantagenet kings.

Miss Dane lives for part of the time in a little flat which overlooks Covent Garden Market in London, and for part of the time in the heart of Devonshire, where she owns an old house. In times of peace she enjoys collecting friends there for house parties, though she says she has never been able to arrange what she would consider the ideal gathering—the guests to consist of Shakespeare, Solomon, Baron Münchhausen, and the Recording Angel! She has visited America several times, and has stayed for some time in Hollywood. She is unmarried. In appearance she is tall, slender, blonde, and aesthetic-looking, with a delicately aquiline profile and a long swanlike neck. With the outbreak of the Second World

War she became once more immersed in war work. In 1941 she was elected president of the Society of Women Journalists.

As a novelist, Clemence Dane is always on the edge of being first-rate. Her best work, like *Regiment of Women* and *Broome Stages,* is very good indeed; but she is not self-critical and she ventures into fields (such as the allegory of *The Arrogant History of White Ben*) where her gift for characterization and deep imaginative sympathy is drowned under a thesis and her voice becomes strident. She must, however, be reckoned among the first half dozen of women writing in English today.

PRINCIPAL WORKS: *Novels*—Regiment of Women, 1917; First the Blade, 1918; Legend, 1919; Wandering Stars, 1924; The Babyons, 1928; Enter Sir John (with H. Simpson) 1928; Gooseberry Fool (with H. Simpson; in America: Printer's Devil) 1929; Author Unknown (with H. Simpson) 1930; Broome Stages, 1931; Re-Enter Sir John (with H. Simpson) 1932; Recapture: A Clemence Dane Omnibus, 1932; Fate Cries Out (short stories) 1935; The Moon Is Feminine, 1938; The Arrogant History of White Ben, 1939. *Plays*—A Bill of Divorcement, 1921; Will Shakespeare, 1921; The Way Things Happen, 1923; Naboth's Vineyard, 1925; Granite, 1926; Mariners, 1926; Adam's Opera, 1928; Wild Decembers, 1933; Come of Age (with R. Addinsell) 1934; Moonlight Is Silver, 1934; Shivering Shocks, 1935; Herod and Mariamne, 1938; Cousin Muriel, 1940. *Miscellaneous* The Woman's Side, 1927; Tradition and Hugh Walpole, 1929.

ABOUT: Bookman (London) August 1924; Literary Digest August 11, 1934; Living Age February 1941; Revue Politique et Littéraire November 21, 1925; Theatre Arts Monthly June 1934.

DANIELS, JONATHAN (April 26, 1902-), American journalist and editor, was born Jonathan Worth Daniels in Raleigh, N.C., the son of Josephus Daniels, editor, former Secretary of the Navy, and United States Ambassador to Mexico, and Addie Worth (Bagley) Daniels. He was educated at the University of North Carolina (B.A. 1921, M.A.

Globe

1922) and at the Columbia University Law School. He did not, however, practise law, but returned to Raleigh as a reporter on his father's paper, the *News and Observer.* He was the paper's Washington correspondent from 1925 to 1928, became associate editor in 1932, and since 1933 has been its editor-in-chief, though his father still retains the formal title. He left the paper twice, in 1930 and again in 1931-32, each time to work on the editorial staff of *Fortune.* In 1930 he also had a Guggenheim Fellowship, and during this period wrote his only novel, an allegorical fantasy.

In 1923 Mr. Daniels married Elizabeth Bridgers, who died in 1929, leaving one daughter; in 1932 he married Lucy Billing Cathcart, and they have three daughters. He still lives in Raleigh, but he and Mrs. Daniels are both fond of travel, and have covered the entire country by automobile. Two of his longest trips were not mere pleasure tours, but were the means by which he gathered the material for his two published surveys of American life, people, and *mores.* A friendly, sociable man with a pleasant, homely face and a winning smile, Mr. Daniels has mingled with every sort of American, from bank presidents to W.P.A. workers, has found it easy to get along with the most varying points of view, and has been able to set down some of the clearest estimates of what Americans are thinking and feeling that have been reported in our time. He finds time, besides his editorial duties and the research for and writing of his books, to write a good deal for the serious reviews; in consequence he has not much leisure for hobbies or recreation, but leads a quiet home life, with gardening and reading to take up his few spare hours. In 1942 he was appointed assistant director of the Office of Civilian Defense.

Without being a distinguished or profound writer, Mr. Daniels commands a pleasing style; as one critic said, "he is gifted with a distinctly non-Northern journalistic ease." His approach is thoughtful, he is well grounded in social and economic theory, and he is careful and accurate in his presentation. He has set down soberly (or sometimes with wry humor) exactly what he has seen, whether local "boosters" objected or not. The result is a valuable guide for other students of the American scene, a source-work for future historians, and the revelation of a civilized and engaging personality.

PRINCIPAL WORKS: Clash of Angels (novel) 1930; A Southerner Discovers the South, 1938; A Southerner Discovers New England, 1940. Tarheels: A Portrait of North Carolina, 1941.

ABOUT: Christian Science Monitor June 15, August 3, 1940; Current Biography 1942; Newsweek August 11, 1934; Time May 13, 1940; Wilson Library Bulletin October 1938.

DANNAY, FREDERIC. See QUEEN, E.

D'ANNUNZIO. See ANNUNZIO

DARGAN, Mrs. OLIVE (TILFORD) ("Fielding Burke"), American poet and novelist, was born in Grayson County, Kentucky, the daughter

of Elisha Francis Tilford and Rebecca (Day) Tilford. She attended the University of N a s h v i l l e (T e n n.) and Radcliffe College, Cambridge, Mass. Olive Tilford taught school in Arkansas, M i s-s o u r i, Texas, and Canada until her marriage to Pegram Dargan of South Carolina. Since then she has lived in New York, Boston, the Carolinas, and abroad, winning critical recognition and various prizes for her poetry: the $500 prize from the Southern Society of New York for the best book by a Southern writer in 1916, and the Belmont-Ward Fugitive prize in 1924. *The Cyclic Rim* (1916) is a cycle of fifty-three poems, written as a memorial to one drowned at sea. Marguerite Wilkinson called her poems conservative in type but with warmth and quaintness of manner. Some of her best work has been in the ballad and in lyrics. Her numerous closet dramas have delicate and fine feeling, but vary in dramatic workmanship, inclining to the didactic and undramatic. Leonard Bacon has called *Lute and Furrow* the record of rather bathetic struggles with insoluble questions, but its ideas "are dictated by a generosity and sweetness not so common that we can afford to take them for granted."

Mrs. Dargan's emotion and her humanitarian sympathies had a rather unexpected flowering in two proletarian novels published under the pseudonym "Fielding Burke" —*Call Home the Heart* (1932) and its sequel *A Stone Came Rolling.* "Kindhearted and nobly intentioned," they reminded Herschel Brickell of some of the intellectual efforts of pre-revolutionary Russians. *Call Home the Heart* is the epic story of Ishma Waycaster, a girl in the North Carolina mountains, who leaves her charming but feckless husband to go with her lover to a mill town, where labor conditions are like those in Gastonia. Elmer Davis calls it for half of its considerable length one of the finest of American novels, until "you suddenly find yourself absorbing a communist sermon that lasts for eight solid pages [and] you feel as if the second

act of *Tristan* has been embellished by a Salvation Army band." In the sequel, Ishma and her husband try to bring about a peaceful social revolution in Dunmow, a Carolina mill town. Bernard Smith has said that the novel shows a sympathy rare in proletarian writers, but suffers somewhat from its excess of emotion.

Mrs. Dargan, a charter member of the Poetry Society of America, is an honorary member of the Radcliffe Club in New York. The University of North Carolina gave her an honorary Litt.D. in 1924. She lives at West Asheville, N.C.

PRINCIPAL WORKS: Semiramis and Other Plays (Carlotta, The Poet) 1904; Lords and Lovers and Other Dramas (The Shepherd, The Siege) 1906: The Mortal Gods and Other Dramas (A Son of Hermes, Kidmir) 1912; Path Flower and Other Poems, 1914; The Cyclic Rim, 1916; Flutter of the Gold Leaf (with Dr. F. Peterson), 1922; Lute and Furrow, 1922; Highland Annals, 1925; Call Home the Heart (as "Fielding Burke") 1932; A Stone Came Rolling (as "Fielding Burke") 1935; From My Highest Hill, 1942.

ABOUT: Wilkinson, M. New Voices.

DARÍO, RUBÉN (January 18, 1867-February 6, 1916), Nicaraguan poet, was really named Felix Rubén Garcia y Sarmiento. His father was Manuel Garcia, his mother Rosa Sarmiento. The parents separated before his birth, and he was reared b y h i s m a t e r n a l grandmother. His birthplace was the village of Metapa, in Léon He published poems before he was thir-

teen, and was a journalist a year later, serving on papers in Santiago, Valparaiso, and Buenos Aires. In 1890 he returned to Nicaragua and married Rafaela Contrera, herself a writer. Disagreement with the political authorities forced him to flee to Guatamala soon after, but he was reconciled with his government and in 1892 was sent to Spain to represent Nicaragua at the Columbus anniversary. He returned home to find that his wife had died in his absence, at the birth of their son. He fell into despair and alcoholism, from which he was rescued by Francisca Sánchez, whom he married later and by whom he also had a son. For many years thereafter he was seldom in his native land, holding various diplomatic, consular, and journalistic posts in Paris and Madrid as well as in Mexico, Argentina, and Colombia. He was in New

York in 1915 in the interests of Pan-American literary relations, but was ill from his arrival. His illness developed into pneumonia, and he reached Nicaragua only in time to die.

Darío, either as a personality or as a writer, was never popular; he was aristocratic and reserved by nature, a born inhabitant of the ivory tower, and was always a bit too precious and "culto" for the general reader. In spite of the jingoistic flavor of some of his later poems, he was really less a South American than a European; in Spain and above all in France he sensed his spiritual home. The influences on his work were all from abroad—first Hugo, then Catulle Mendès, then Gautier, then Poe and Whitman: in other words, the Parnassians, the symbolists, the cosmopolitans. As the American Academy of Arts and Letters put it in a welcoming address in 1915, he "discovered the spirit of the Old World and interpreted it for the New."

But he did more: he effected a real revolution in Spanish poetry, bringing it into touch with the modernist movement in the poetry of other tongues. Technically he was superb. Melodic, and unhampered by tradition, he invented meters of his own—a fifteen-syllable verse, a "free sonnet." His masterwork is the *Cantos de Vida y Esperanza* (*Poems of Life and Hope*) in 1905, which contains his two greatest poems—"Sonato a Cervantes" and "Conción de Otoño en Primavera" ("Song of Autumn in Spring"). His prose sketches, as James Fitzmaurice-Kelly remarks, are "exotic and gallicized." He reached his peak of poetry before he was forty, and his later work showed increasing signs of fatigue and of distraction by other interests. He was at once an innovator and a lover of classicism, but of a classicism defined and in part invented by himself. He is the outstanding figure of modern South American literature, and it is not to the credit of the United States that his name is almost unknown here.

WORKS AVAILABLE IN ENGLISH: Eleven Poems, 1916; Prosas Profanas and Other Poems, 1922.

ABOUT: Darío, R. Vida de Rubén Darío; Escrita por el Mismo; Goldberg, I. Spanish-American Literature; Lugones, L. Rubén Darío; Soto-Hall, M. Revelaciones Intimas de Rubén Darío; Bulletin of the Pan American Union February 1916; Dial June 14, 1917; Literary Digest April 17, 1915; New York Times February 8, 1916.

DARROW, CLARENCE SEWARD (April 18, 1857-March 13, 1938), American criminal lawyer, socio-legal writer, and humanitarian, was born in Kinsman, Ohio, the oldest son of Amirus Darrow, who (unable to hold his faith in any one religious sect long enough to be ordained) had become keeper of a furniture store, and Emily E. (Eddy) Darrow, an energetic and intellectual woman who maintained a kind of Puritanic reserve toward her seven children.

Browsing in his father's humbly accumulated library was considerably more fruitful intellectually than the sum of Darrow's years at the district school or the academy. At the end of his year at Allegheny College in Meadville, Pa., came the panic of 1873; he went to work in a factory; in a store; taught three winters in a country school; and at the age of nineteen had his first year of law at the University of Michigan.  He got his second in an attorney's office, and was admitted to the Ohio bar at the age of twenty-one. At about this time he was married to Jessie Ohl, by whom he had one son, Paul; they were divorced in 1897. He later married Ruby Hammerstrom, who survived him.

He first "flung [his] shingle to the breeze" in the village of Andover (Ohio); went from there to Ashtabula, where he prospered modestly; and in 1888 moved on to Chicago. Meanwhile John P. Altgeld's *Our Penal Code and Its Victims* had provided him with some working premises for the support of his stand on criminal law: poverty is the cause of crime, and man, a helpless organism, is to be condemned for "getting out of step with the crowd, not for doing evil"; and to Darrow capital punishment was "organized, legalized murder."

Among Darrow's famous cases were: the winning of an acquittal for Eugene V. Debs following the American Railway Union strike; another acquittal for "Big Bill" Haywood and two other Western Federation of Miners officials; his plea of mitigating circumstances of insanity, which led to a sentence of life imprisonment instead of death for the child-murderers, Loeb and Leopold; and his crowning triumph over William Jennings Bryan in the Tennessee evolution controversy (in this, the "Scopes case," he lost the jury verdict, but succeeded notably in his real objective—to ridicule similar discriminatory legislation out of existence in other states).

Darrow's briefs, forceful, humane, and clear, were by no means his only writings. In 1899 he edited a collection of essays called *A Persian Pearl;* five years later appeared a somewhat imaginative account of his childhood (*Farmington*); several sociological tracts, including *Resist Not Evil* and *Eye for an Eye,* preceded what was his best known book of this kind, *Crime: Its Cause and Treatment;* and a few years afterwards came *Infidels and Heretics,* "An Agnostic's Anthology," edited in collaboration with Wallace Rice. *The Story of My Life*—"a plain unvarnished account of how things really have happened, as nearly as I can possibly hold to the truth"—sharpened the contours in an old rebel's portrait. "With my last breath I shall probably try to draw another, but, intellectually, I am satisfied that life is a serious burden, which no thinking, humane person would wantonly inflict on some one else." He was an admitted pessimist and agnostic who denied immortality not only on the grounds of lack of evidence but because, he said, physical death and the persistence of memory were logically incompatible. Man, with an acknowledged "will to live," he contended, had little need of any other ethical or spiritual code than a fundamental kindliness, to which all forms of pride, hate, and violence were unknown.

Darrow was of a large build, with well-matched physical and intellectual strengths. It is said that he "dressed with the certainty that clothes do not make the man." For his brilliance as a criminal lawyer he cannot easily be forgotten, and the brave simplicity of his writings has only strengthened the impression.

PRINCIPAL WORKS: A Persian Pearl (ed.) 1899; Resist Not Evil, 1903; Farmington, 1904; Eye for an Eye, 1904; Crime: Its Cause and Its Treatment, 1922; Infidels and Heretics (joint-ed.) 1929; The Story of My Life, 1932.

ABOUT: Darrow, C. Farmington, The Story of My Life; Stone, I. Clarence Darrow for The Defense; Nation March 19, 1938; New Republic March 23, 1938; New York Times March 14, 1938.

DAVIDSON, DONALD (August 18, 1893-), American poet and essayist, writes: "I was born [Donald Grady Davidson] at Campbellsville, Tenn., in the pleasant rural region near Pulaski, the county seat of Giles County. I am the son of William Bluford Davidson and Elma (Wells) Davidson. My people on both sides are of pioneer Tennessee stock. My father was a teacher, and the pattern of my boyhood

memories is built around the rural towns of Middle Tennessee where he taught in the public schools. When I was twelve years old I entered Branham and Hughes School at Spring Hill, Tenn. I finished there in 1909 and entered Vanderbilt University, but I left Vanderbilt at the end of my freshman year and taught school for four years before I returned in 1914. I sat then in the English classes taught by Edwin Mims, John Crowe Ransom, and Walter Clyde Curry; and though I have always been somewhat bookish, that was probably the real beginning of my systematic devotion to literature. My B.A. (a "war degree") came by special dispensation while I was at army camp in 1917, for because of my irregular attendance I had not quite finished my college work, even though I had attended George Peabody College for two summers in an attempt to make up for lost time. I served in the army, at home and in France, for a little over two years—first as Second, then as First Lieutenant.

"I was married in 1918, while I was at Camp Sevier, to Theresa Sherrer; we have one daughter. After discharge from the army I taught for one year at Kentucky Wesleyan College, and then, in 1920, came to Vanderbilt as instructor in English. At Vanderbilt I taught and studied for my M.A. while my wife studied for her degree in law (LL.B.); and we received our degrees at the same Commencement in 1922. I have remained a member of the Vanderbilt department of English, and am now professor.

"My writing began in earnest with the activities that marked the founding of the *Fugitive* by the group of Nashville poets known as the 'Fugitive Group.' I participated with Allen Tate, Ransom, Robert Penn Warren, and others in these activities. From 1924 to 1930 (while teaching and writing poetry) I was literary editor of the Nashville *Tennesseean.* The book page which I edited was also published for a while in the Memphis *Commercial Appeal* and the Knoxville *Journal;* but the enterprise, which had grown to ambitious critical proportions, collapsed with the failure of Caldwell & Co., which dragged down the publisher-sponsor, Colonel Luke Lea.

"In 1930 I was one of the twelve Southerners who published *I'll Take My Stand.* I have contributed to this and to other volumes dealing with Southern problems and have continued to write essays and reviews and poetry. The center of my interests for many years has been in the South as a region and in agrarianism, whether Southern or non-Southern.

"In addition to my regular teaching at Vanderbilt I have been a member of the faculty of the Bread Loaf School of English, in Vermont, for all the summers since 1931."

* * *

Robert Penn Warren has said that Mr. Davidson attempts "to orientate his poetry in terms of his own social tradition. . . . He is engaged in an adventure of self-definition." Louis Untermeyer remarked that his work has been "praised for its 'mysticism' but its outstanding characteristic is its fiery localism."

PRINCIPAL WORKS: *Poetry*—An Outland Piper, 1924; The Tall Men, 1927; Lee in the Mountains, 1938. *Prose*—The Attack on Leviathan, 1938.

ABOUT: Untermeyer, L. Modern American Poetry; Bookman May 1931; Poetry May 1932, May 1939; Time December 26, 1938.

DAVIDSON, JOHN. See "BRITISH AUTHORS OF THE 19TH CENTURY"

DAVIES, WILLIAM HENRY (April 20, 1871-September 26, 1940), Welsh poet, novelist, and author of one of the best autobiographies of modern times, was the son of a publican, and lived his early days at the Church House tavern, Newport, Monmouthshire. All his writing, however, was done in English. Seldom has literary history witnessed so remarkable a career, for until he was over thirty Davies was a hobo and peddler from choice; and yet his later years were entirely devoted to the quiet and innocent pursuits of a man of letters. An unruly strain manifested itself while he was still at his primary school, in youthful thieving exploits carried out with other boys of the same kidney. His education was of the shortest and most rudimentary, and though he duly "served his time" in the picture-frame making trade he had a constitutional dislike for regular work, and made no attempt to set up in business. His grandmother had left him a minute private income of two shillings per week; and when he was twenty-four he succeeded in persuading his trustees to advance him the fare to America.

Arriving in New York with ten dollars in pocket, he soon fell in with a notorious professional beggar called "Brum," who taught him the whole technique of begging, casual labor, and train-jumping. For some six years he covered enormous areas of America, occasionally working for farmers, courting incarceration in jail (for warmth) in the winters, and making eight or nine voyages between Baltimore and Liverpool, England, in the cattle boats. One of these trips had landed him at Newport in 1901. While there he read romantic accounts of the Klondike, and set off in that direction to find gold. At Renfrew, Ontario, he fell while trying to board a moving train, and was so badly injured that his right leg had to be amputated at the knee.

He had saved up his allowance while tramping, and so had 120 pounds to come. He spent half of this in Newport, and then went to London, set on writing as a career. He lived in common lodging-houses, wrote in public libraries, and in 1905, having raised a few pounds by peddling, printed a first book of verse, *The Soul's Destroyer*. He sent copies to various possible purchasers, one of whom, Bernard Shaw, perceived great merit in the work and gave Davies introductions which procured him very favorable publicity. One critic, Edward Thomas, lent the poet a cottage at Sevenoaks, and there he wrote his *Autobiography of a Super-Tramp* (1907), which, by virtue of its plain frankness and wonderful descriptions of professional tramping, made him known to large numbers of the general public.

The days of disreputable indigence were now over. Davies settled in London for a time, mixing with lions like Conrad, Gosse, Hudson, Epstein, and Augustus John. But like Burns in similar circumstances he remained unspoiled. Eventually he moved out into the country village of Oxted, Surrey, and later to Nailsworth, Gloucestershire. He continued writing vigorously until a year or two of his death—poems, novels, more autobiography. In 1911 he was granted a Civil List pension which secured him a bare minimum subsistence irrespective of literary earnings. In 1926 the University of Wales honored him with a Litt.D. degree. He died at sixty-nine after a long illness. Of his marriage little is known.

Davies' untutored muse has produced gently persuasive lyrics inspired by birds, animals, flowers and country life in general. By virtue of these and the splendid, rough, simple, direct prose of his autobiography, he occupies a modestly secure place in the English world of letters.

PRINCIPAL WORKS: *Poems*—The Soul's Destroyer, 1907; New Poems, 1907; Nature Poems, 1908; Farewell to Poesy, 1910; Songs of Joy, 1911; Foliage, 1913; The Bird of Paradise, 1914; Child Lovers, 1916; A Poet's Pilgrimage, 1918; Raptures, 1918; The Song of Life, 1920; The Hour of Magic, 1922; Secrets, 1924; A Poet's Alphabet, 1925; The Song of Love, 1926; A Poet's Calendar, 1927; Forty-Nine Poems, 1928; Moss and Feather, 1928; Ambition, 1929; In Winter, 1931; Poems: 1930-31, 1932; The Lovers' Song-Book, 1933; Love Poems, 1935; The Birth of Song, 1936; The Loneliest Mountain, 1939; Poems, 1940. *Fiction*—A Weak Woman, 1911; The Adventures of Johnny Walker, Tramp, 1926; Dancing Mad, 1927. *Autobiographical and Miscellaneous*—The Autobiography of a Super-Tramp, 1908; Beggars, 1909; The True Traveller, 1912; Nature, 1913; Later Days, 1925; My Birds, 1933; My Garden, 1933. *Opera*—True Travellers; A Tramp's Opera in Three Acts, 1923.

ABOUT: Adcock, A. St. J. Gods of Modern Grub Street; Davies, W. H. The Autobiography of a Super-Tramp, Beggars, The True Traveller, Later Days; Hind, C. L. Authors and I; Kernahan, C. Five More Famous Living Poets; Lucas, F. L. Authors: Dead and Living; Massingham, H. J. Letters to X; Maynard T. Our Best Poets: English and American; Moult, T. W. H. Davies; Sitwell, E. Aspects of Modern Poetry; Catholic World September 1939; Fortnightly Review January 1940. John O'London's Weekly October 11, 1940; New York Herald Tribune September 27, 1940.

DAVIS, CLYDE BRION (May 22, 1894-), American novelist, writes: "Clyde Brion Davis was born in Unadilla, Otoe County, Neb., the son of Charles N. Davis and Isabel (Brion) Davis. Attended public schools in Chillicothe, Mo., and Kansas City. Attended Kansas City Art Institute. Worked as printing pressman, commercial artist, traveling salesman,  private detective. Enlisted in regular army at outbreak of World War, served in France. Worked on *Pontanezen Duckboard*, a soldier publication, in Brest after Armistice. Worked on the Denver *Post*, the Albuquerque, N.M. *Morning Journal*, the Denver *Times*, the Denver *Rocky Mountain News*, the San Francisco *Examiner*, the Seattle *Post-Intelligencer*, the Buffalo *Times*, as reporter, copy reader, telegraph editor, sports editor, Sunday editor, news editor. Married Martha Wirt of Denver in 1926. One son. Hobbies: hypochondria and weed-culture."

* * *

This very brief autobiographical sketch displays excellently Mr. Davis's compound of sober factualism and wry humor. It may be added that in addition to the various occupations he lists, he has also been a steamfitter's helper, chimney sweep, furnace repair man, and electrician. After years of roving, he has settled down now in Hamburg, N.Y.

Mr. Davis is five feet eleven inches tall, weighs 185 pounds, and has an interesting asymmetrical face, with a high forehead under thick wavy dark hair, and an aggressive moustache. Lately he has taken to wearing glasses. His expression is compounded of pugnacity, amiability, sharpness, and dreaminess—just as his books are. In his history, personality, and descent he is peculiarly American, and his novels could have come from no other country. Typically, he places Mark Twain in the forefront of his favorite authors, followed by Anatole France, Flaubert, Voltaire, Lardner, Hemingway, Willa Cather, and Robert Louis Stevenson. His writing shows a bit of the influence of all of these except the last two.

Strangely, the hero of his first novel, *The Anointed*, was not a soldier but a sailor—but a sailor fantastically unlike others. His *"The Great American Novel—,"* in the title of which it is important to retain the quotation marks, is the epic of all the lower-bracket newspaper men in America. *Nebraska Coast* is partly family autobiography, and one of the best of the "Westward migration" stories. Still in early middle age, Mr. Davis bears careful watching; he is one of the most unexpected and unpredictable of current writers.

PRINCIPAL WORKS: The Anointed, 1937; "The Great American Novel—" 1938; Northend Wildcats (juvenile) 1939; Nebraska Coast, 1939; The Arkansas River (Rivers of America Series) 1940; Sullivan, 1940; Follow The Leader, 1942.

ABOUT: Book-of-the-Month Club News May 1938; Scholastic October 16, 1939, September 23, 1940; Time August 2, 1937; Wilson Library Bulletin October 1937.

DAVIS, ELMER HOLMES (January 13, 1890-), American essayist, novelist, and publicist, was born in Aurora, Ind., the son of Elam Holmes Davis and Louise (Severin) Davis. He was educated at Franklin College (B.A. 1910, M.A. 1911), and was a Rhodes Scholar to Queen's College, Oxford (B.A. 1912). In 1909 he taught for a year at the Franklin, Ind., high school. In 1913 and 1914 he was on the staff of *Adventure*, going from there to the New York *Times*, where he remained for ten years. In 1917 he married Florence MacMillan;

they have a son and a daughter. In 1924 he left newspaper work for free-lance writing. At the end of 1939 he was summoned hastily and unexpectedly to "pinch-hit" for H. V. Kaltenborn on the radio as war news analyst for the Columbia Broadcasting System. In spite of the fact that he has never fully recov-

ered from "mike fright," he became in a few months one of the leading broadcasters of the country. His calmness, thoroughness, and pithy simplicity won him millions of discriminating listeners who had tired of the alternate hysteria and unction of radio's more widely publicized "personality boys."

Elmer Davis has really led a triple life: he is a successful writer of stories for the "slick" magazines and of novels, some light, some serious; he is now a prominent publicist; and he is a genuine scholar. He is at present on the editorial board of the *Saturday Review of Literature*, his essays have long been a feature of *Harper's Magazine*, and he is perhaps the only competent Latin scholar who has ever been a popular story writer for the *Saturday Evening Post* and *Collier's*.

He lives with his family in Mystic, Conn., where his prize possessions are his typewriter and "a comfortable chair that looks like hell." He is thick set and square shouldered, with white hair and thick black eyebrows over deep-set dark eyes. He says that Horace and Catullus (in the original) are his favorite poets, Wagner's Ring operas his favorite music, the Bible his favorite book (he wrote a novel about David, Goliath, and Joab), and beefsteak his favorite food. His newspaper career began at fourteen, when he was printer's devil, at a dollar a week, on the Aurora, Ind., *Bulletin*.

His least distinguished writing is in his short stories, which tend to become "formula stories"; his most distinguished is in his scholarly, penetrating, yet witty essays. The Columbia Broadcasting System has perhaps found the most fitting judgment on him: his associates there call him "Master of Understatement."

On June 13, 1942, Elmer Davis was named by President Roosevelt as director of a new Office of War Information, with authority over dissemination of practically all official news and propaganda.

PRINCIPAL WORKS: History of the New York Times, 1921; Times Have Changed (novel) 1923; I'll Show You the Town (novel) 1924; Friends of Mr. Sweeney (novel) 1925; Strange Woman (novel) 1927; Show Window (essays) 1927; Giant Killer (novel) 1928; Morals for Moderns (short stories) 1930; White Pants Willie (novel) 1932; Love Among the Ruins (short stories) 1935; Not To Mention the War (essays) 1940.

ABOUT: Current Biography 1940; Harper's November 1939; Nation May 4, 1940; New York Times June 14, 1942; New York Times Magazine June 21, 1942; Saturday Review of Literature July 15, 1939, March 2, 1940; Time January 22, 1940.

DAVIS, HAROLD LENOIR (October 18, 1896-), American poet and novelist, winner of the Harper and Pulitzer prizes, writes: "Born near Yonoalla in southwestern Oregon. Family originally from east Tennessee, with quarterings principally Welsh. He attended country schools; at nine went to work in a country printing office, learned typesetting through being detailed to set up local poetical ef-

fusions, mostly of an obituary and elegiac character. Also acquired a distaste for poetry that lasted well into early manhood. Moved around, lumbering through public schools, working at various lively-sounding but stultifying occupations (typesetter, cowboy, sheep-herder, packer, deputy sheriff, surveyor), and picking up foreign languages from various immigrant elements that were new to the country then. Still retain a working knowledge of French, German, and Spanish; at one time I also knew the high spots of Gaelic, Greek, Paiute, and the Tilkuni dialect of Sahaptin Indian, also the Chinook trade jargon, all of which I have now completely forgotten. In the army during the World War (rose to the rank of corporal by hard work and strict attention to duty), tried reading for relief from boredom, resorted to foreign-language works because they cost less than English ones, got interested in the short poems of Detlev von Liliencron and tried imitating them. The imitations didn't resemble the originals as much as they might have, but they did pretty well; Harriet Monroe printed some of them in *Poetry* for 1919 and they were awarded the Levinson Prize.

"Wrote poetry after working hours for the ensuing ten years; tried prose at the suggestion and with the unfailing encouragement of H. L. Mencken, and wrote stories and sketches for the *American Mercury* until his resignation as editor. Took to writing short stories for *Collier's Weekly*, received Guggenheim Fellowship to Mexico in 1932, stayed there to do a novel, 1934-35, awarded Harper Novel Prize, 1935, Pulitzer Novel Prize, 1936. Translated a collection of Kechwa Indian songs from Southern Peru, 1938. Working on a novel, live in Northern California on a ranch. Favor a law imposing hanging as a punishment for fanaticism in any form, but have little hope of getting one passed at the present time."

* * *

H. L. Davis is the son of James Alexander Davis and Ruth (Bridges) Davis. In 1928 he married Marion Lay, also a writer. Among his many occupations has been singing folksongs over a Northwestern radio network. He now owns a cattle ranch near Napa, Calif. He is lantern-jawed, with a prominent nose, a small moustache, and rather long hair. Of his first published book, *The Nation* remarked that "its virtues are those of a folktale; its value is anthropological." Malcolm Cowley called it "earth-stained, colt-wild, uproarious." He has been called "a literary pioneer on the Oregon trail," with "a good-humored but thorough contempt for heroics."

PRINCIPAL WORKS: Honey in the Horn, 1935; Proud Riders, 1942.

ABOUT: Publishers' Weekly August 3, 1935; Saturday Evening Post May 6, 1939; Saturday Review of Literature May 9, 1936; Time August 26, 1935; Wilson Library Bulletin October 1935.

DAVIS, OWEN (January 29, 1874-), American playwright, was born in Bangor, Maine, one of the eight children of Warren and Abbie (Gould) Davis. At nine he wrote his first melodrama, *Diamond Cut Diamond: or, The Rival Detectives*. At the end of the first act only one character was left alive, and he committed suicide in a later act. Owen Davis was descended on his mother's side from clipper-ship captains; to this adventurous element in his blood he attributes the fact that he has never done any practical humdrum work, but has remained perfectly content to "make faces at life" and earn his living "by drawing pictures on the wall." His father, a member of the Society of American Iron Manufacturers, moved when Owen was fifteen to the Cumberland Mountains in southern Kentucky.

White

Owen Davis was a student at the University of Tennessee in 1888 and 1889; in 1890 he went to Harvard to stay three years, distinguishing himself chiefly as a hundred-yard sprinter. He assisted the Society of Arts, which presented plays by Howells and Stockton at the Hollis Theatre in Boston with a company headed by Maurice Barrymore. A. M. Palmer put him in a company headed by Mme. Janauschek, where he drew $12 a week and played five parts. Mme. Janauschek gave him an autographed photograph and the advice, "Young man—neffer again be an actor."

Accepting this advice, Davis coached the football team of a New York preparatory school at $50 a month. Seeing a successful melodrama of the period, *The Great Train Robbery*, he studied it intensively and evolved a rather mechanical but effective pattern which served him in the writing of more than one hundred and fifty melodramas of his own, dividing them into Western, New York comedy drama, and "the sexy type." These plays were the contemporary equivalent of the later motion picture; Davis wrote with visual effects in mind rather than any thought of doing realistic dialogue.

Through the Breakers, presented by Gus Hill, ran five years in the United States, England, and Australia. *Under Two Flags*, dramatized in an emergency from "Ouida's" novel, brought a profit of $10,250 in four weeks when played by Davis' summer stock company in Rochester. The most famous of his melodramas, *Nellie; The Beautiful Cloak Model*, with its harried heroine, has assumed an almost legendary place in the history of the American theatre.

In April 1902 Owen Davis married Elizabeth Breyer of Chicago, who had been with E. H. Sothern's dramatic company; to please her he wrote *Icebound*, a New England tragedy which won the Pulitzer drama prize in 1923, and an equally serious play, *The Detour*. Notable plays on which Mr. Davis has worked as adapter include *The World We Live In* (from *The Insect Comedy*, by Josef and Karel Capek); Scott Fitzgerald's drama of a bootlegger, *The Great Gatsby*; and Edith Wharton's *Ethan Frome*.

"A play really is a character driven by an emotion along a definite line to a definite end," states Mr. Davis; and, "the characters of Act I multiplied by the emotions of Act 2 equal Act 3." To fill out the last act of his immensely successful farce, *The Nervous Wreck* (made into Eddie Cantor's musical comedy *Whoopee*), he took a psychoanalytic-laboratory scene from *The Haunted House*, which with freshly written material served

Wallace Eddinger profitably enough for a season. With Lee Simonson, Winthrop Ames, and others, Mr. Davis was a founder of the Cambridge School of the Drama, and he has been active in the affairs of the Society of American Dramatists and the Authors' League of America. *Icebound* made him a member of the National Institute of Arts and Letters. He is short, dark and clean-shaven. Donald Davis and Owen Davis, Jr., his sons, have been workers in the theatre as dramatists, actors, and directors since boyhood.

PRINCIPAL WORKS: (including adaptations and collaborations) At Yale: A Comedy Drama of College Life in Three Acts, 1906; Cupid at Vassar, 1907; Icebound, 1923; The Detour, 1923; The Nervous Wreck, 1923; Lazybones, 1924; Easy Come, Easy Go, 1925; Beware of Widows, 1925; The Haunted House, 1926; At 9:45, 1928; I'd Like To Do It Again (autobiography) 1931; The Ninth Guest, 1932; Ethan Frome, 1936; Mr. and Mrs. North, 1941.

ABOUT: Davis, O. I'd Like To Do It Again.

DAVIS, Mrs. REBECCA (HARDING). See "AMERICAN AUTHORS: 1600-1900"

DAVIS, RICHARD HARDING (April 18, 1864-April 11, 1916), American romancer and journalist, was born in Philadelphia,

P. MacDonald

the son of L. Clarke Davis, a newspaper editor, and Rebecca (Harding) Davis, a novelist who wrote with a grim realism at the literary antipodes from the style of her son. He was educated at Lehigh University and Johns Hopkins, and in 1886 began his journalistic career on the Philadelphia *Record*. After working for two other Philadelphia papers, he went to the New York *Sun* in 1889, under Arthur Brisbane. Brisbane undoubtedly influenced his viewpoint if not his style, which was always vigorous and pure. He was a good newspaper man of the sensational, personally adventurous type then popular.

In 1890 Davis became managing editor of *Harper's Weekly*, and made long journeys in its behalf to the West, the Mediterranean, and Central America. He never ceased to be primarily a reporter, and he "covered" every war of his time—the Greco-Turkish, the Boer, the Spanish-American, and the World War. His story of the German invasion of Belgium, done

for the Wheeler Syndicate, was considered a model of front-line war correspondence, though it was as heavily sentimental and highly colored as were his stories from Cuba during the Spanish-American War in 1898.

But very early he began to supplement his newspaper stories by fiction, and his "Gallegher," which appeared in *Scribner's* in 1890, made him famous overnight. "Gallegher" was a newspaper story; Davis also created at this time the almost equally celebrated "Van Bibber," who was a young man about town.

He was married twice, in 1899 to Cecil Clark, who divorced him in 1910, and in 1912 to Elizabeth G. McEvoy, better known as the musical comedy star, Bessie McCoy. For two decades he combined the careers of journalist, novelist, playwright (he wrote twenty-five plays), and gay social figure. Though he earned $100,000 a year, he left his widow almost penniless when he died suddenly from heart disease at his Mt. Kisco, N.Y., home. Money all but flowed through his fingers, largely because he lived in a bright day-dream. He was Charles D. Gibson's model for the upstanding, handsome young men who squired the famous "Gibson girl"; he was everybody's favorite (except for those who called him prudish and arrogant) and the butt of a hundred affectionately malicious stories of his fastidiousness and innocent swank. As Arthur B. Maurice said, he lived always in his dream-world "with himself in the principal rôle," and then capitalized it in his stories.

The *Nation*, less amiably, points to his "clean-cut engineers and soldiers of fortune who asserted the superiority of the Anglo-Saxon blood among the lower breeds." Yet superficial and over-facile as his work was, and quite without social consciousness, it was always vivid, picturesque, and readable, and he wrote in a condensed, suggestive style that is the mark of the very best in journalism. Journalism in essence all his writing really was. He was truly a bit of a prig, a bit of a *poseur*, and his work betrayed both failings. Nevertheless, in William Rose Benét's words, "Dick Davis was just about the best story he ever wrote!"

Davis fitted his own time perfectly. He never pretended to be more than an entertainer (though he would have liked to insert a moral pill below the sugar-coating), and because he is deservedly forgotten now (except for a few adventure yarns that will always be juvenile favorites) it does not follow that he did not earn the enormous popularity that was his during his lifetime.

PRINCIPAL WORKS: *Fiction*—Stories for Boys, 1891; Gallegher and Other Stories, 1891; Van Bibber and Others, 1892; The Exiles, 1894; The Princess Aline, 1895; Cinderella and Other Stories, 1896; Soldiers of Fortune, 1897; The King's Jackal, 1898; The Lion and the Unicorn, 1899; Episodes in Van Bibber's Life, 1899; In the Fog, 1901; Captain Macklin, 1902; Ranson's Folly, 1902; The Bar Sinister, 1903; The Scarlet Car, 1907; Vera the Medium, 1908; The White Mice, 1909; Once Upon a Time, 1910; The Man Who Could Not Lose, 1911; The Red Cross Girl, 1912; The Lost Road, 1913; The Boy Scout, 1914; The Deserter, 1917. *Plays*—The Dictator, 1904; Miss Civilization, 1905; The Zone Police, 1914; Peace Manoeuvres, 1914. *Travel and Correspondence*—The West From a Car Window, 1892; The Rulers of the Mediterranean, 1893; Our English Cousins, 1894; About Paris, 1895; Three Gringos in Venezuela and Central America, 1896; Cuba in War Time, 1897; The Cuban and Porto Rican Campaigns, 1898; With Both Armies in South Africa, 1900; The Congo and Coasts of Africa, 1907; Notes of a War Correspondent, 1910; With the Allies, 1914; Somewhere in France, 1915; With the French in France and Salonika, 1916; Adventures and Letters, 1917.

ABOUT: Davis, R. H. Adventures and Letters (ed. by C. B. Davis); Downey, F. D. Richard Harding Davis: His Day; Miner, L. S. Mightier Than the Sword; Quimby, H. C. Richard Harding Davis: A Bibliography; Williams, B. C. Our Short Story Writers; Bookman April 1906, June 1916, August 1916; Nation April 20, 1916; Outlook April 19, 1916; Saturday Review of Literature September 23, 1933, February 3, 1940; Scribner's Magazine July 1916, November 1926.

DAVIS, WILLIAM STEARNS (April 30, 1877-February 15, 1930), American historical novelist and college professor, was

born in the old presidential mansion of Amherst College, Amherst, Mass., the son of William Vail Wilson Davis, a descendant of Captain Davis, the first man to fall at Concord in 1775, and Rebecca Frances (Stearns) Davis, daughter of William Augustus Stearns, whose twenty-two year presidency of Amherst had come to an end with his death in June 1876. His childhood was a particularly happy one, and much of it was spent in the family library, ferreting out old atlases which he virtually memorized. He was not physically strong, but he was an ardent fisherman and fond of roaming through the New England mountains. At the age of ten he was stricken with a baffling illness; during the eight years that followed he not only read voraciously in the tales and records of the ancients but prepared himself for college entrance and wrote about five historical romances.

His first book, *A Friend of Caesar*, was published before he finished Harvard in 1900 (M.A. in 1901, Ph.D. in 1905). Not long after the close of a year of European travel and study he became, successively, lecturer at Radcliffe College (1904-05), instructor at Beloit (Wis.) College, associate professor of medieval and modern European history at Oberlin, and from 1909 to 1927 professor of history at the University of Minnesota.

During these years he was turning out good historical novels and romances with considerable regularity. They were wrought out of his so-called "dream-worlds"—Greek, Roman, and feudal societies, the Church, memorable battles, etc. He confessed that when he finished one it seemed, for several weeks, "as if the bottom had dropped out of existence." Among the later of these were *Life on a Medieval Barony*, laid in a thirteenth-century medieval seignory in Northern France; and *The Beauty of the Purple*, a tale drawn from Christian Constantinople in the eighth century. Moreover he prepared several volumes of relatively undiluted history: his timely *Roots of the War* (1918) which rapidly became one of the most widely read of the first origins-of-the-War speculations was followed by a history of France and a study of Southern Europe and the Levant from 330 A.D. to 1922.

For his last years he returned to New England with his wife, Alice Williams (Redfield) Davis, whom he had married in 1911, made his home in Exeter, N.H., and spent his summers in "Clam Rock Cottage." He died in his sixty-third year, following an operation.

Davis wrote nothing extremely brilliant or original, but he should be credited with having welded fact and fiction without loss of either narrative intensity or historical plausibility.

PRINCIPAL WORKS: A Friend of Caesar, 1900; A Victor of Salamis, 1908; The Influence of Wealth in Imperial Rome, 1910; The Friar of Wittenberg, 1912; A Day in Old Athens, 1914; The Roots of the War, 1918; Life on a Medieval Barony, 1923; The Beauty of the Purple, 1924; Belshazzar, 1925; The Whirlwind, 1929.

ABOUT: American Historical Review April 1930; Publishers' Weekly March 8, 1930; Wilson Library Bulletin January 1930.

DAWSON, CONINGSBY WILLIAM

(February 26, 1883-), Anglo-American novelist, was born in High Wycombe, England, the eldest of the three sons of Dr. William James Dawson, a clergyman, literary critic, and historian. Coningsby Dawson received his B.A. with second-class honors in modern history from Merton College, Oxford, in 1905. That year he came with his family to the United States, with the intention of entering the ministry; he did study a year at the Union Theological Seminary in New York. From 1905 to 1910 he traveled extensively in the Hudson Bay country and the Canadian Northwest, and wrote from seven to ten hours a day at his family's home in Taunton, Mass., with dogged determination. Four years of obscure drudgery were rewarded with "a brief burst of fame," as he referred to it in his war letters, when Coningsby Dawson's *The Garden Without Walls*, a somewhat sultry and poetically written romance, was a best-seller in the autumn of 1913. Holt was the publisher, though Dawson was literary adviser of the George H. Doran Company from 1910 to 1913. At the outbreak of the First World War he joined the Canadian Expeditionary Forces as a lieutenant of field artillery, obtaining his training at the Royal Military College, Kingston, Ont., and serving with the First Canadian Division until 1917, then with the Fourth until the end of the war. While on active service he wrote several war books and visited the A.E.F. in 1918. While convalescing from wounds in the same year, he lectured in the United States under the British Mission, returned to the Occupied Territories in 1919, and that year also lectured in every state of the Union on the Anglo-American friendship and social results of the war. Dawson undertook a special mission through Central and Eastern Europe in the interests of American relief for starving children in 1920-21. A Fellow of the Royal Geographical Society, he lists his recreations as traveling, horses, and art-collecting. In 1918 he married Helen Campbell Wright of Newark, N.J., where they make their home, with a son, on Mount Prospect Avenue. The novelist is a handsome man, with aquiline features and curling hair. Most of his novels are serialized before publication, and, while profitable, have hardly fulfilled the promise held forth by *The Garden Without Walls*.

PRINCIPAL WORKS: The Worker and Other Poems, 1906; The House of the Weeping Woman, 1908; The Great English Essayists, 1909; The Great English Letter Writers, 1909; Last Chance River, 1910; The Road to Avalon, 1912; The Garden Without Walls, 1913; The Raft, 1914; Slaves of Freedom, 1916; Khaki Courage (American title: Carry On), 1917; Out To Win, 1918; The Glory of the Trenches, 1918; Living Bayonets, 1919; The Test of Scarlet, 1919; The Little House, 1920; It Might Have Happened to You, 1921; The Kingdom Round the Corner, 1921; The Vanishing Point, 1922; Christmas Outside of Eden, 1922; The Coast of Folly, 1924; Old Youth, 1925; When Is Always? 1927; Pilgrims of the Impossible, 1928; The Unknown Soldier, 1929; When Father Christmas Was Late, 1929; The Test of Scarlet, 1930; Fugitives From Passion, 1930; The Auctioning of Mary Angel, 1930; A Path to Paradise, 1932; The Moon Through Glass, 1934; Inspiration Valley, 1936; Tell Us of the Night, 1941.

ABOUT: Dawson, C. W. Khaki Courage (see preface by W. J. Dawson); Doran, G. H. Chronicles of Barabbas.

DAY, CLARENCE SHEPARD

(1874-December 28, 1935), American essayist who wrote always as Clarence Day, Jr., was born in New York,

the son of Clarence Shepard Day, a stock broker and governor of the Stock Exchange, and Lavinia (Stockwell) Day. It seems almost superfluous to introduce his parents, since they are known to so many readers as "Father" and "Mother." He was educated at St. Paul's School and Yale, and did his first writing as class secretary, when instead of the usual eulogies he produced a candid and objective alumni record. He became a partner with his father, but left Wall Street to join the navy in the Spanish-American War. From this experience dated his arthritis, which from middle age made him a complete cripple, unable to leave his bed or move more than a finger. In his apartment overlooking Central Park he conducted a glove business, still dabbled occasionally in stockbroking, and wrote his books. Before he was too crippled to be active, he had conducted a book department in the *Metropolitan Magazine* and had been on the staff of the *New Republic*. Gradually his inherited fortune disappeared, and it was not until the success of his later books that he regained any considerable part of it.

Day came naturally by writing; though his immediate paternal heritage was financial, his grandfather, Benjamin H. Day, was the founder of the New York *Sun,* and his uncle was the inventor of the Ben Day process for color printing used by newspapers. In 1928 he married Katherine Briggs Dodge, and they had one daughter. He died, not of arthritis, but of bronchial pneumonia.

The nature and work of this almost lifelong invalid, with his bald head fringed with red hair and "the terrible gaze of his big frog eyes" behind their spectacles, are almost impossible to characterize accurately. He was something more than a humorist or a mere ironist, and he would have hooted at the appellation of philosopher. Someone has remarked that he was a replica of his immortal father, choleric, warm-hearted, impetuous, except that he added objectivity and self-realization to the older man's make-up. He was anything but the typical invalid. He was a sympathetic, cordial, affectionate friend, but given also to peremptory commands and bursts of noisy indignation. He was at once tender-hearted and clear-headed, without self-pity and with interests as wide as the sky. In all his books there is implicit a wise and merciful understanding of the pettiness of humanity. His bedroom was a confessional, an audience chamber, a study; he kept his own strange hours, working all night, breakfasting when others dined. He was immensely curious about everything, hospitable to every idea; but, as Philip Littell said, his gullibility was "near to zero."

To most readers he is the author of *God and My Father, Life With Father,* and *Life With Mother,* those unforgettable studies of authentic American types, written with ruthless frankness and ironic tenderness. To a few, he is above all the author of *This Simian World,* in which with passionate scrupulousness he depicts the apelike nature of man, and speculates on what the world would be like had some other kind of animal evolved into the dominant breed.

No mention of Day's books would be just if it omitted the untrained, haunting drawings with which he illustrated them— sketches which are a sort of priceless blend of Art Young with James Thurber. There is more than mere fantasy or mockery in any of the *Scenes From the Mesozoic* or in such pictures as "one of their poets" or "the first thinker" from *This Simian World.* No one has ever appeared in print who was just like Clarence Day; he was *sui generis,*

and the day his crippled hand dropped its pencil something unique and precious went out of the world.

PRINCIPAL WORKS: This Simian World, 1920; The Crow's Nest, 1921 (revised, with additions, as After All, 1936); Thoughts Without Words, 1928; God and My Father, 1932; Life With Father, 1935; Life With Mother, 1936; Scenes From the Mesozoic and Other Drawings (verse) 1935.

ABOUT: New Republic September 11, 1935; Newsweek January 4, 1936; Saturday Review of Literature August 24, 1935, January 4, 1936, February 1, 1936, November 18, 1939; Time January 6, 1936; Wilson Library Bulletin November 1935.

DAY, HOLMAN FRANCIS (November 6, 1865-February 19, 1935), American novelist and writer of verse, was born in Vassalboro, Maine, on the Kennebec River, the son of Captain John R. Day and Mary (Carter) Day. After his graduation from Colby College in 1887, with the degree of B.A., he went to Bangor to serve as managing editor of the publications  of the Union Publishing Co. from 1889 to 1890. After a period as editor and proprietor of the Dexter (Maine) *Gazette,* Day wrote special articles for the Lewiston (Maine) *Journal* and was Maine representative of the Boston *Herald.*

Up in Maine; Stories of Yankee Life Told in Verse (1900), was Day's first book. "No mellow lyre that on which I play: I plunk a strident lute without a glove," the foreword confessed, and this book and its successors, *Pine Tree Ballads* and *Kin o' Ktaadn* were written in not unpleasing doggerel verse. *Kin o' Ktaadn* expressed an attachment to this Maine mountain peak as fervent as Thoreau's in *The Maine Woods,* although rather differently expressed. Either as a tribute to his poetical prowess or because of his journalistic influence, Day was made a major and military secretary on the staff of Governor John F. Hill of Maine, serving from 1901 to 1904.

Squire Phin (1905) was the first of Day's several successful novels about Maine rural types which combined farce, melodrama and broad humor. Dramatized as *The Circus Man,* it was produced in Chicago. *King Spruce, The Ramrodders,* and *The Red Lane* unfolded an epic of far-flung logging and timber-cutting operations, and rank as the most important of Holman Day's novels. A decade later he worked this vein again with *The Rider of the King Log* and *Joan of Arc of the North Woods*. As a writer who dealt with manners and customs "down in Maine" he reigned practically alone, except for the gentler stories of Kate Douglas Wiggin, until a more sophisticated age ushered in R. P. Tristram Coffin, Mary Ellen Chase, and Rachel Field. His play, *Along Came Ruth,* was produced in New York in 1914.

Day's later years were spent in Monterey, Calif., where he wrote numerous scenarios. He died in his seventieth year. Colby College gave him an honorary Litt.D. in 1907.

PRINCIPAL WORKS: Up in Maine, 1900; Pine Tree Ballads, 1902; Kin o' Ktaadn, 1904; Squire Phin, 1905; The Rainy Day Railroad War, 1906; Mayor of the Woods, 1910; King Spruce, 1910; The Ramrodders, 1910; The Skipper and the Skipped, 1911; The Red Lane, 1912; Along Came Ruth (play) 1914; The Landloper, 1915; Blow the Man Down, 1916; Where Your Treasure Is, 1917; Kavanagh's Clare, 1917; The Rider of the King Log, 1919; When Egypt Went Broke, 1920; All Wool Morrison, 1921; Joan of Arc of the North Woods, 1922; The Loving Are the Daring, 1923; Leadbetter's Luck, 1923; Clothes Make the Pirate, 1925; John Lang, 1926; When the Fight Begins, 1926; Starwagons, 1928; Ships of Joy, 1932.

ABOUT: Dunnack, H. E. The Maine Book; New York Times February 21, 1935; Publishers' Weekly March 2, 1935.

DAY LEWIS, CECIL

DAY LEWIS, CECIL (April 27, 1904-), British poet and detective story writer (as "Nicholas Blake"), was born in Ballin-togher, Ireland, the only child of the Rev. F. C. Day-Lewis. His mother, born Kathleen Blake Squires, was a collateral descendant of Oliver Goldsmith, and wrote some poetry (unpublished) herself. She died when her son was four years old; the family had by this time moved to England. The precocious boy wrote verse seriously from the age of six. He attended Sherborne School, where he held a scholarship, and Wadham College, Oxford, where he was an exhibitioner. In 1928 he married the daughter of the headmaster at Sherbourne, Constance Mary King; they have two sons.

Day Lewis was co-editor of *Oxford Poetry* in 1927, but was not financially able to devote all his time to poetry, as he wished, and instead became a teacher until 1935, first at Summer Fields, Oxford; then at Larchfield, Helensburgh, and finally at Cheltenham College. Since then he has given all his time to writing, editing, and political activity. He is usually considered a Communist, though, as Theodore Maynard remarked, his Communism is "hardly more definite than the Shelleyan aspiration, 'The world's great age begins anew.'" However, he has edited the work of Ralph Fox and other avowedly Communist writers. Maynard confidently expects Day Lewis, with his friends W. H. Auden and Stephen Spender, to end their lives in the Roman Catholic Church, but there is as yet no indication that his prophecy will be fulfilled.

After several years in Gloucestershire, Day Lewis moved to his present home in Devonshire. There, "a poet with a gun," he shoots rabbits and watches birds. His other recreations are sailing and singing. He is a tall man with a face already lined, who, Tangye Leon said, "looks strong, almost tough—a young farmer or an aeroplane mechanic." In contrast, his voice is soft, with a lingering Irish intonation.

His freedom from other occupation than writing he owes not so much to his poetry or his critical essays as to the detective stories he has written under the pseudonym of "Nicholas Blake." These were originally undertaken merely as means of making money—in the first place, to pay for repairing a leaking roof!—but he recognizes them now as also "releasing a spring of cruelty" which he thinks is in all human beings, and which, were he a country gentleman, would find expression in hunting. These detective novels, however motivated, are among the very best of their kind; John Strachey noted that "he writes even better when he is, presumably, pot-boiling as Nicholas Blake than when he is 'giving himself to literature' as Day Lewis."

It is as a poet, as the spokesman of the most interesting contemporary English poetic group, however, that Day Lewis is to be judged seriously. He, Auden, and Spender have all been close friends as well as fellow-craftsmen. Of Day Lewis, Malcolm Cowley said: "Politically, philosophically, every way but poetically, he is the best of his group, but he rarely touches Spender's warmth of human emotion or Auden's sharpness of perception." The literary "ancestors" of this school are T. S. Eliot, Wilfrid Owen, and above all Gerard Manley Hopkins; also, as Mary Colum pointed out, there is a strong derivation from Yeats. The three at one time employed "almost a private language," in which favorite words (such as "pylon" or "kestrel") have fixed symbolic meanings. Day Lewis, Cowley remarked, "can be as metaphysical and pedantic as T. S. Eliot. . . . His interests have broadened from the self to the family and at last to society in general. He is a sharp critic, a clear, reasonable, undogmatic expounder."

Another critic, however, noted "a lack of imaginative intensity, occasional undergraduate exuberance, rather obvious derivation." Day Lewis consciously thinks of himself as a poet of revolution—revolution both political and poetic; he has said to himself, "the certainty of new life must be your starting point." It is his belief that only poetry and the fairy tale (or parable) will survive.

PRINCIPAL WORKS: *As C. Day Lewis*—Country Comets, 1928; Transitional Poem, 1929; From Feathers to Iron, 1931; The Magnetic Mountain, 1933; Dick Willoughby (juvenile fiction)1933; A Hope for Poetry (prose) 1934; A Time to Dance and Other Poems, 1935; Collected Poems, 1935; Revolution in Writing (prose) 1935; Noah and the Waters, 1936; The Friendly Tree (novel) 1936; The Starting Point, 1937; Overtures to Death and Other Poems, 1938; Anatomy of Oxford (ed., with C. Fenby) 1938. *As "Nicholas Blake"*—A Question of Proof, 1935; Thou Shell of Death (in America: Shell of Death) 1936; There's Trouble Brewing, 1937; The Beast Must Die, 1938; The Smiler With the Knife, 1939; The Summer Camp Mystery (in England: Malice in Wonderland) 1940; The Corpse in the Snowman (in England: The Case of the Abominable Snowman) 1941.

ABOUT: Haycraft, H. Murder for Pleasure: The Life and Times of the Detective Story; Commonweal August 3, 1935; Current Biography 1940; New Republic February 27, 1935; Poetry December 1935; Saturday Review of Literature March 9, 1935, April 13, 1935, January 7, 1939; Time July 25, 1938; Wilson Library Bulletin April 1938.

DE AYALA. See PEREZ DE AYALA

*DE CASSERES, BENJAMIN (1873-), American essayist, writes: "I am a born writer. Writing has always been my 'escape.' If I am tired mentally and physically I can always rejuvenate myself by going to work—writing. When I was ten years of age I was seriously reprimanded in school for writing surreptitiously *Wrecked on the Island of Dry Tortugas* under my desk instead of studying the school-book on top of my desk. I entered newspaper work at sixteen, becoming the office boy of Charles Emory Smith,

editor-in-chief of the Philadelphia *Press,* at $4 a week. I was soon writing editorials and doing dramatic reviews, being the youngest editorial writer, very likely, in the world, on a first-class newspaper. I never 'learned to write.' Everything I do is 'inspirational'— that is, I have never 'thought out' anything either in my philosophical books or in my newspaper and magazine work. There is a perfect coordination between my conscious and un-  conscious minds. I have a theme—and presto! with a pencil in hand I begin to write.

"I never think logically. I believe logic to be one of the lowest forms of mental activity and imagination the highest, although imagination has an invisible logic of its own. I think in images, flashes, and epigrams. Creators should spurn Reason as an eagle would spurn a ladder.

"I have written about a dozen books that I believe will live long after I'm dead. In doing my private work I have written without any regard for the public or anyone's opinion. My best work is spontaneously me. My favorite among my own books is *Fantasie Impromptu: The Adventures of an Intellectual Faun.*

"The men and books who have influenced me most in my mental, spiritual, and philosophical evolution have been Buddha, Schopenhauer, Ecclesiastes, Nietzsche, La Rochefoucauld, Emerson, Thoreau, Whitman, Amiel, Victor Hugo, Spinoza, *Don Quixote,* Shelley, Heine, Montaigne, Goethe, Dostoievsky, Thomas Hardy, James Huneker, Shakespeare, Omar Khayyam, and Jules de Gaultier. My style is natural to me—never copied. In music (of which I am passionately fond, considering it another dimension) I revere all the masters— particularly Bach, Beethoven, Chopin, and Johann Strauss. I consider *Tristan and Isolde* the greatest music-drama and love story of all time. I know Gilbert and Sullivan almost by heart, believing *The Mikado* and *Patience* to be, masterworks. Rembrandt, Goya, and Renoir are my favorite artists of the brush and Rodin in marbles. I revel in Lewis Carroll and O. Henry. I love good plays and am a picture addict. I enjoy a game of baseball, Scotch and water, and every aspect of nature. Know nothing of sports or stocks.

* Died December 6, 1945.

"My core passion is *liberty.* I am a militant, radical individualist. I hate Communism, Fascism, Socialism, and any system that suppresses the individual and enlarges the powers of the state. I think the United States the best—because the freest—country in the world. Our great man was Thomas Jefferson. Abraham Lincoln appeals powerfully to the imagination. I think of Washington as one of the finest types of revolutionists who ever lived. I admire French culture profoundly.

"What do I know? Only this: 'I am an island of consciousness surrounded entirely by mirages.'"

* * *

Mr. De Casseres was born in Philadelphia, of Sephardic (Spanish) Jewish stock long resident in America; he is a collateral descendant of Spinoza. In 1919 he married Bio Terrill. His home now is in New York. He has had a strange career—never popular, but greatly admired by a few, greatly scorned by others, much better known in France (where he was introduced by Remy de Gourmont) than in America or England. C. de Fornaro called him "a Titan in an inkstand"; George Sterling, "the play-boy of the cosmos" and "supremely our greatest epigrammist."; S. P. Rudens, "a fourth dimensional mind."

In recent years De Casseres has been a columnist for the Hearst papers.

PRINCIPAL WORKS: The Shadow-Eater (poems) 1915; Chameleon—Being the Book of My Selves, 1922; Mirrors of New York, 1925; James Gibbons Huneker, 1925; Forty Immortals, 1925; Anathema! (prose poem) 1928; The Superman in America, 1929; Mencken and Shaw, 1930; The Love Letters of a Living Poet, 1931; Spinoza, 1932; From Olympus to Independence Hall, 1935; The Muse of Lies, 1936; The De Casseres Books (24 volumes issued monthly, including Fantasie Impromptu) 1936-37. Don Marquis, 1938; St. Dantalus, 1938; Sir Galahad, 1938.

ABOUT: Honce, C. A Sherlock Holmes Birthday; Arts and Decoration January 1925; Mercure de France August 15, 1930; Overland Monthly June 1926; Reflex December 1927; Saturday Review of Literature March 16, 1940.

*DEEPING, WARWICK (1877-), English novelist, who was born George Warwick Deeping, writes: "I am the son of a country doctor, educated at the Merchant Taylors' School and by private tutor. I was bored and idle at school, and so escaped some of the repressions and futilities of a merely academic education. I spent four years at Cambridge University, studying science and medicine. I

passed to a London hospital and qualified as a doctor, and practiced as a country doctor for a year.

"I had no urge to write as a youngster. I began to write poetry at twenty, and much of it was very bad poetry. I became infected with medievalism of the romantic school, and produced a series of historical novels with sufficient success to enable me to abandon medicine.

"Married to Maude Phyllis Merrill, we young things had our struggles and our worries, but we managed to find life a great adventure. For a while we lived on a farm in Sussex, and then built ourselves a small house. I became an enthusiastic gardener and designer of gardens.

"I served for four years during the World War in the Royal Army Medical Corps on the Gallipoli Peninsula, in Egypt, France, and Belgium.

"The war, as a great human experience, launched me on deeper seas. Inevitably *Sorrell & Son* was a product of the war. One realized that a nice culture was less important than courage and character. One set out to see life and its realities, its pathos and heroism, and I have managed to find it more splendid than sordid. A negative cynicism seems to me to be a form of cowardice.

"Generally, my characters have been suggested by real people. I saw the originals of Sorrell and Old Pybus and Christopher Hazzard.

"If I have had some success and a good deal of happiness, I can charge much of it to my parents and especially to my wife, who has been the sort of comrade a man dreams of and so rarely finds.

"I like the open air, and traveling, and flowers and trees, and the people who do the work of the world without remembering to be self-consciously clever. I begin work at seven in the morning and go to bed at half past nine. To enjoy the perfume of life one has to cultivate a certain simplicity.

"I agree with my old gardener of seventy-six, who is full of grim humor and of gaiety, and who says: 'I've lived hard and simple.'"

* * *

Though deprecating the sentimentality of many of Mr. Deeping's books, Elmer Davis remarked of *Sorrell & Son,* Mr. Deeping's most successful and widely read novel to date: "The world teems and overflows with art authors; Mr. Deeping is something rarer and perhaps more significant, the producer of a book to which several hundred thousand people came back in grateful relief after sampling the products of the art authors."

PRINCIPAL WORKS: Uther and Igraine, 1903; The Strong Hand, 1912; The White Gate, 1914; Bridge of Desire (in England, Unrest) 1916; Martin Valliant, 1917; Valour, 1918; The Awakening (in England, Second Youth) 1919; The Prophetic Marriage, 1920; The House of Adventure, 1921; The Captive Wife (in England, Orchards) 1922; Apples of Gold, 1923; The Secret Sanctuary, 1923; Three Rooms, 1924; Suvla John, 1924; Sorrell & Son, 1925; Doomsday, 1927; Old Pybus, 1928; Kitty, 1928; Roper's Row, 1929; Exiles, 1930; Stories of Love, Courage, and Compassion, 1930; The Road, 1931; Ten Commandments, 1931; The Challenge of Love, 1932; Old Wine and New, 1932; Smith, 1932; The Eyes of Love, 1933; Two Black Sheep, 1933; The Man on the White Horse, 1934; Seven Men Came Back, 1934; The Golden Cord (in England, Sackcloth Into Silk) 1935; No Hero—This, 1936; Blind Man's Year, 1937; The Woman at the Door, 1937; The House of Spies, 1938; The Malice of Men, 1938; Bluewater, 1939; Folly Island, 1939; The Man Who Went Back, 1940; The Dark House, 1941; Corn in Egypt, 1942.

ABOUT: Saturday Review of Literature February 12, 1927; Wilson Library Bulletin April 1929.

DE FORD, MIRIAM ALLEN (August 21, 1888-   ), American biographer and miscellaneous writer, writes: "I was born in  Philadelphia, the daughter of two physicians [Moïse and Frances (Allen) de Ford]. After graduation from the Girls' High School of that city, I worked for a year as a feature writer on the now defunct Philadelphia *North American*, and then spent a year at Wellesley College. The rest of my college education was gained in the evenings and at week-ends, at Temple University (A.B. 1911) and the University of Pennsylvania; during the day I worked at copy-writing for theatre programs, and went back to the Sunday department of the *North American* for two more years. I received a graduate scholarship at the University of Pennsylvania, and did a year's work there in English and Latin, 1911-12. I then moved to Boston, where until 1915 I worked on various house organs and on *Associated Advertising*, and was official reporter of the Ford Hall Open Forum. In 1915 I went to San Diego, married Armi-

stead Collier, and for two years lived in San Diego and Los Angeles, as a public stenographer and as assistant on another house organ. In 1917 I became editor of still another house organ, this time in Baltimore. The next year I was made a claim adjuster for a large insurance company, and until 1923 served in this capacity in Baltimore, Chicago, and San Francisco. Since then I have been a free lance writer exclusively—I have been having work published since I was twelve.

"In 1920 I was divorced, and in 1921 married Maynard Shipley, writer and lecturer on natural science and president of the Science League of America. Our home for most of the time until his death in 1934 was in Sausalito, near San Francisco. The year after his death I spent in Honolulu, in the East, and in Berkeley; since then I have lived in a downtown hotel in San Francisco.

"Since 1921 I have been San Francisco staff correspondent of the Federated Press, and am active in the Newspaper Guild. Besides my published books noted below, I have written 15 'Little Blue Books' (mostly Latin translations and biographies); contributed to *British Authors of the 19th Century*, *American Authors: 1600-1900*, and the present volume; had stories in two O. Henry anthologies, 1930 and 1934; and have published prose and verse in numerous magazines and in some 35 poetry anthologies. I belong to the Order of Bookfellows and to the Rationalist Press Association of Great Britain, of which I am honorary local secretary.

"In my youth my poetic trinity was Shelley, Poe, and Heine; of late years A.E. Housman and Emily Dickinson have had most to say to me. The two novels I cherish most are *Wuthering Heights* and *Kristin Lavransdatter*. I was born a feminist, and have been a freethinker since I was thirteen. The greatest personal influence in my life was that of Maynard Shipley—the profoundest mind, the most lovable nature, and the noblest spirit I have ever known.

"What with meeting a deadline on a book, doing two research jobs and my newspaper correspondence for 200 labor papers, and trying to work [1942] in a bit of civilian defense assistance in this menaced city which I love, I haven't much leisure; but I am a devoted listener to symphony music and the better radio quiz programs, I am a devout fan for Mrs. Kingsley's 'Doublecrostics,' and I vary the three or four serious books I get through in a week (insomnia is a blessing to the busy!) by allowing myself a weekend ration of one 'whodunit'—psychological variety preferred. I am short and don't weigh much, flatter myself I don't look my age, certainly don't feel it, and am afraid I don't always act it!"

PRINCIPAL WORKS: Love Children: A Book of Illustrious Illegitimates, 1931; Children of Sun (poems) 1939; Who Was When? A Dictionary of Contemporaries, 1940; They Were San Franciscans (biography) 1941; Shaken With the Wind (novel) 1942.

DE GOURMONT. See GOURMONT

DE JONG, DAVID CORNEL (June 9, 1905-   ), Dutch-American novelist, writes: "I was born in Blija, a small village in the

northernmost province of the Netherlands, Friesland, on the Coast of the North Sea. At the age of thirteen my parents brought me with my brothers to the U.S.A., coming straight to Grand Rapids, Mich., where they are still living. I attended grammar school in Grand Rapids, learning English, of which I didn't know a word upon arrival. Because the family fortunes (such as they were) proved to be altogether inadequate to withstand expenses of migration and re-establishment in a new and strange country, I went to work when I was fifteen, after a few months in a business school. Got a job in a bank, pretending I was seventeen, and so from fifteen to eighteen I did all sorts of clerical work, besides manual labor. At eighteen I realized I was sadly in need of 'an education.' So I started high school (a religious local prep school), worked my way through, mainly in drug stores, soda-jerking, clerking, etc., and summers at such odd jobs as bricklaying, house-painting, grave-digging in local cemeteries. Finished the high school work in three years, and then entered Calvin College, in Grand Rapids. From it got my B.A. degree, working my way through, in the fashion mentioned above.

"All in all I attended six colleges, for longer or shorter periods. In my senior year started writing poetry, and was published in *Poetry* and several smaller magazines, and won a few prizes. In 1929-30 I taught high school in Edmore, Mich. Wrote my first short stories at the time, which were printed in *Hound and Horn*, *American Caravan*, etc. On a fellowship from Duke University, I went there to get

my M.A. degree, and while there had several poems and short stories published in *Scribner's, Virginia Quarterly*, etc. After my M.A. degree I accepted a fellowship to Brown University. Studied there one year toward my Ph.D. degree in English, but in the meantime my first novel had been accepted, so quit after one year at Brown. I remained in Providence [R.I.] adopting it as my home town. Apart from a few sporadic jobs, I managed to keep myself alive on writing and translating from the Dutch—precariously, often—one whole year on about $200. Also continued writing short stories.

"In 1938 lived several months in New York City, and received at that time a Houghton, Mifflin Fellowship award for my projected novel *Old Haven*, based largely on Dutch life as I knew it from my childhood. It was published and has been translated into six languages. In 1939 I returned to Holland for the first time since my childhood, and stayed there a few weeks. Then came back to Providence, and am still here, writing, and getting a novel published; still writing short fiction and poetry.

"I weigh about 188 pounds, height just about six feet, currently unmarried. I guess that's just about the story."

* * *

Mr. De Jong is a pronounced reddish blond, with a small moustache. His novels are long, solid, and rich. Howard Mumford Jones spoke of his "sympathy, latent humor, and catholicity of interest which recall the great days of the Russian novels," and considered that his work was "touched with genius."

PRINCIPAL WORKS: Belly Fulla Straw, 1934; Old Haven, 1938; Light Sons and Dark, 1940; The Day of the Trumpet, 1941.

ABOUT: Publishers' Weekly June 12, 1937; Saturday Review of Literature September 24, 1938; Time September 26, 1938; Travel November 1939.

DE JOUVENEL. See COLETTE

DE KRUIF, PAUL (March 2, 1890-   ), American writer on science, was born in Zeeland, Mich., the son of Hendrik and Hendrika J. (Kremer) De Kruif. This part of Michigan is entirely settled by the descendants of Hollanders, and De Kruif belongs to this stock. He was educated at the University of Michigan (B.S. 1912, Ph.D. 1916). The same year he became assistant professor of bacteriology at the university; previously he had worked in the bacteriological laboratory.

During the First World War he was in France as Captain in the Sanitary Corps of the United States Army. From 1920 to 1922

he was associate in Pathology at the Rockefeller Institute. He lost his position because of some of the thinly-veiled portraits in his first book, *Our Medicine Men.* In this same eventful year he married Rhea Barbarin, who has collaborated with him in some of his works.

For the next two years he worked with Sinclair Lewis, providing the background of science and medicine used in Lewis' *Arrowsmith.* The book was written in Central America and Europe, and in his spare moments De Kruif worked in European libraries and collected material later used in *Microbe Hunters.* He had always wanted to write, but first-hand experience of what is needed to write successful novels determined him to stick to the reporting of fact. *Microbe Hunters* was serialized before book publication in the *Country Gentleman,* and in 1925 De Kruif began his still continuing connection with the Curtis Publishing Co., one or another of whose magazines, usually the *Country Gentleman,* has since been his chief magazine outlet. When some medical men objected to his articles on medicine (though he has worked closely with the greatest contemporary medical scientists), Philip S. Rose, the magazine's editor, retorted: "No, he isn't an M.D. and we don't let him peddle pills or write prescriptions for our subscribers. He is a reporter."

About 1935 De Kruif, who had been a reporter and nothing more, became a crusader, aroused by the prevalence of preventable disease merely because of the sufferers' economic inability to pay for cure. Since then the aim of all his work has been to further the spread of preventive medicine, and since 1934 he has been secretary of the President's Birthday Ball Commission for Infantile Paralysis Research.

A big, exuberant, outdoors type of man, with a clipped dark moustache and loose woodsman's clothes, De Kruif lives all year round in his isolated house, "Wake Robin," near Holland, Mich. He swims daily in Lake Michigan, chops wood, drives furiously, and relaxes in the evening with his everpresent pipe, a friendly bottle, and long hours of talk before his fireplace. He leaves

home only to fly to New York or Philadelphia for editorial or committee conferences. To the editors of this volume he writes "My belief is that—taking the long view— the human animal is perfectible, by democratic, not by 'Communazi' means. My activities are concentrated on bringing it about that the time-gap between scientific discovery and its use for the progress of the human animal shall be shortened as much as possible, by democratic means." Personally, he says his ambition is "to grow old very slowly and stay young very long by life in the sun and the moon."

De Kruif's work is always scientifically sound, and always interesting. His full blooded enthusiasm, which results sometime in over-simplification and in a too sprightly style, annoys more staid scientific minds. But he has certainly done more to popularize science, especially medical science, and to bring home to the public its vital importance to daily living, than any other man of his time. His name is pronounced *krife.*

PRINCIPAL WORKS: Our Medicine Men, 1922; Microbe Hunters, 1926; Hunger Fighters, 1928; Seven Iron Men, 1929; Men Against Death, 1932; Yellow Jack (play, with Sidney Howard) 1934; Why Keep Them Alive? (with Rhea B. De Kruif) 1936; The Fight for Life, 1938; Health Is Wealth, 1940.

ABOUT: Hibbs, B. Two Men on a Job; Current Biography 1942; Literary Digest March 28, 1936; Newsweek August 26, 1940; Scholastic October 5, 1935.

DE LACRETELLE. See LACRETELLE.

"DELAFIELD, E. M." (1890-) is the pseudonym of the English novelist and short-story writer, Mrs. Edmée Elizabeth Monica (De La Pasture) Dashwood. Her father was Count Henry De La Pasture of Llandogo, Monmouthshire; her mother, now Lady Clifford, wrote numerous novels under the name of Mrs. Henry De La Pasture. The De La Pastures, of a noble family, came to England

after the French Revolution. Elizabeth De La Pasture had, in her youth, several governesses whose various traits were combined to form the voluble and flighty Mademoiselle of the "Provincial Lady's" diaries. She served as a V.A.D. in Exeter during the First World War from 1914 to 1917, receiving an appointment subsequently under the Ministry

* Died December 2, 1943.

f National Services in the South-Western Region at Bristol. Here she remained until the end of the war, publishing her first novel in 1917. *The War-Workers,* the second, drew upon the experience indicated in the title. In 1919 Elizabeth De La Pasture became the wife of Major Arthur Paul Dashwood, O.B.E., late of the Royal Engineers and the second surviving son of Sir George Dashwood, sixth baronet. The Dashwoods have a son and daughter; the Robin and Vicky of the *Diaries* are "mild likenesses," according to their mother, of them as they were around 1930.

Eighteen books had appeared under "E. M. Delafield's" name, some of them wrought with considerable care and thought, when Lady Rhondda asked her in 1931 to do a serial of some kind for her weekly, *Time and Tide. The Diary of a Provincial Lady* was the result. The popularity of the Lady (with her phlegmatic British husband, her temperamental staff of servants, and such other incidental characters as the affluent and obnoxious Lady B., Our Vicar's Wife, and Old Mrs. Blenkinsop) was immediate and lasting, and somewhat astonished her creator, who scribbled the various installments with no particular effort. Mrs. Dashwood admits to the possession of a photographic and phonographic memory, dating from her childhood, which can, at will, repeat conversations she has overheard in the past with uncanny accuracy. This accounts for much of the verisimilitude of the Diaries, as well as of the colloquies recorded in *As Others Hear Us,* first contributed to *Punch.* She has written three plays, *To See Ourselves* (1930), *The Glass Wall* (1933), and *The Mulberry Bush* (1935). *To See Ourselves,* a dramatization of *The Way Things Are,* whose well-meaning but somewhat baffled heroine, with her husband and children, foreshadowed the Provincial Lady, did well on the London stage and had a mildly successful run in New York.

In 1933 "E. M. Delafield" came to America for a lecture tour, the results appearing serially in *Punch* with illustrations by Arthur Watts, who illustrated the first two diaries, as *The Provincial Lady in America.* The Lady also went to Russia and endeavored to do her bit in the Second World War. From time to time Mrs. Dashwood has shaken her loose long enough to write brilliant novels of manners, from the 'nineties to the present. She lists her recreations as reading other people's books and criminology. Mrs. Dashwood is a Justice of the Peace in Devon, has contributed atmospheric reconstructions of famous criminal cases to *Time and Tide,* and based on an early novel, *Messalina of the Suburbs,* on the celebrated Thompson-Bywaters case. "E. M. Delafield" is a witty, extremely *soignée* person, with a gift for laughter.

PRINCIPAL WORKS: Zella Sees Herself, 1917; The War-Workers, 1918; The Pelicans, 1918; Consequences, 1919; Tension, 1920; The Heel of Achilles, 1921; Humbug, 1921; The Optimist, 1922; A Reversion to Type, 1923; Messalina of the Suburbs, 1924; Mrs. Harter, 1924; The Chip and the Block, 1925; Jill, 1926; The Entertainment, 1927; The Way Things Are, 1928; What is Love? 1928; Women Are Like That, 1929; Turn Back the Leaves, 1930; The Diary of a Provincial Lady, 1931; Challenge to Clarissa, 1931; Thank Heaven Fasting (American title: A Good Man's Love) 1931; The Provincial Lady Goes Further (American title: The Provincial Lady in London) 1932; General Impressions, 1933; Gay Life, 1933; The Provincial Lady in America, 1934; The Provincial Lady Omnibus, 1935; Faster! Faster! 1936; Straw Without Bricks (American title: I Visit the Soviet) 1937; As Others Hear Us, 1937; The Brontës, 1938; Three Marriages, 1939; Love Has no Resurrection, 1939; The Provincial Lady in War Time, 1940; No One Now Will Know, 1941.

ABOUT: Roberts, D. K. Titles to Fame; Christian Science Monitor May 11, 1940.

DE LA MARE, WALTER JOHN (April 25, 1873-   ), English poet and novelist, was born in the Kentish village of Charlton, the son of James Edward Delamare, a church warden of Huguenot descent, and Lucy Sophia (Browning) Delamare, whose father was a naval surgeon at Woolwich Dockyard and the author of two excellent books on convict-ship reform. It has been  fairly well established that de la Mare is related on his mother's side to Robert Browning, by the second marriage of Browning's grandfather.

Young de la Mare was sent to St. Paul's School, and there, at the age of sixteen founded *The Choristers' Journal,* a school magazine. He edited—and probably wrote most of—nine issues, sprinkling in them cautiously veiled advertisements, conceived in the interests of his own stamp album. (This same propensity for collecting has apparently never left him, for the late G. K. Chesterton in his autobiography mentions de la Mare's hobby of searching after "minute objects of the nature of ornaments but hardly to be seen with the naked eye.")

When his formal education ended in the spring of 1890 (he has, however, honorary degrees from St. Andrew's and Bristol Universities), he went directly into the city office of the Anglo-American (Standard) Oil Company, as a bookkeeper. Already he had begun to think of himself as primarily a poet: he kept his hair long and wavy, in the mode of the Latin Quarter Bohemian, and wore a velvet coat. Somewhat ironically the company recognized this strange peacock in its midst by allowing him to edit and write a house organ. It survived only two issues.

His earliest writing was distinctly of the compensatory order; living in the dullest of worlds, he took refuge in fantasy to keep his spirit alive. "Kismet," a short story appearing in *The Sketch* in 1895, represented his first break into public print. Two years later the *Cornhill Magazine* printed "The Moon's Miracle." During these years—and through the publication of his first book, *Songs of Childhood* (1902)—de la Mare used the anagram-pseudonym "Walter Ramal." In 1908 the Asquith Government recognized de la Mare's literary accomplishments: presumably on Sir Henry Newbolt's recommendations, he was given a small grant and put on a Civil List pension of 100 pounds a year. With supplementary free-lance work, largely book reviewing for which he appears to have had little liking, he managed to enjoy a minimum of security. After a second novel and a collection of poems he was veritably set free as an author. He retired to the country and practically ceased to have any career aside from his books. With his wife and four children, two sons and two daughters, he lives at Hill House, Taplow, Buckinghamshire, in times of peace.

His most important novel was *Memoirs of a Midget,* which won the James Tait Black Memorial Prize in 1922. Perhaps only de la Mare could have made real and touching this glimpse into the mind and heart of a woman just like all other human beings except that nature had produced her in miniature.

Like Maeterlinck, de la Mare is a master of the shadowed borderline between the real and the unreal. He has taken this consciously for his own territory, for he says that "our one hope is to get away from realism, in the accepted sense. An imaginative experience is not only as real as but far realer than an unimaginative one." Recently he published a highly illuminating but rather

haphazard study (*Early One Morning*) of "childhood by way of recollection—early memories gleaned from many witnesses ... chiefly from those who were best able to put them into words."

Of his poetry, R. P. Blackmur said that it belongs "in the archaic, . . . haunting realm of the consciousness, where every flight of fancy is final, disarming, and on the verge of the profound." The specific technique by which his effects are brought about has been analyzed by Dorothy Emerson, who pointed out that "his hard beats are usually regular and mark the pattern of the rhythm; the soft beats are sweetly irregular, falling as sparsely or as numerously as the poet's musical ear desires."

G. K. Chesterton once said that "he who is simply the imaginative man can only be found in the images he makes and not in the portraits of him that other people make." Possibly something of de la Mare, then, might be drawn from his own recent delvings (*Behold, This Dreamer!*) into the "reverie, night, sleep, dream . . ." of literature. He has a "dark Roman profile rather like a bronze eagle" and a strange capacity for causing a sort of indefinable legend to grow up around him. J. B. Priestley says that he "remains to criticism an elusive figure, whose outline and gestures are not easily fixed in the memory—a shadowy Pied Piper." His name rhymes with *dare.*

PRINCIPAL WORKS: *Poetry*—Songs of Childhood, 1902; Poems, 1906; The Return, 1910; The Listeners and Other Poems, 1912; A Child's Day 1912; Peacock Pie, 1913; Motley and Other Poems 1918; Flora, 1919; Collected Poems 1901-1918, 1920 The Veil and Other Poems, 1921; Down-adown-Derry, 1922; Come Hither (anthology) 1923; Ding Dong Bell, 1924; Stuff and Nonsense, 1927; Poems for Children, 1930; The Fleeting and Other Poems 1933; A Forward Child, 1934; Early One Morning 1935; Collected Poems 1919-1934, 1935; The Wind Blows Over, 1936; This Year, Next Year, 1937 Memory and Other Poems, 1938; Behold, This Dreamer! (anthology) 1939; Collected Poems, 1941 *Prose*—Henry Brocken, 1904; The Three Mulla-Mulgars, 1910; Crossings (play) 1921; Memoirs of a Midget, 1921; The Riddle and Other Stories 1923; Broomsticks and Other Tales, 1925; The Connoisseur and Other Stories, 1926; Told Again 1927; Stories From the Bible, 1929; Desert Islands 1930; On the Edge, 1930; The Eighteen-Eighties, 1931; Lewis Carroll, 1932; The Lord Fish and Other Stories, 1933; Animal Stories, 1940; Pleasures and Speculations, 1940; Bells and Grass, 1942; Mr. Bumps and His Monkey, 1942.

ABOUT: Chesterton, G. K. Autobiography; Mégroz, R. L. Walter de la Mare; Priestley, J. B. Figures in Modern Literature; Reid, F. Walter de la Mare: A Critical Study; Fortnightly Review March 1940; Poetry September 1936; Scholastic October 26, 1935.

DELAND, Mrs. MARGARET WADE (CAMPBELL) (February 28, 1857-), American novelist and story writer, was

born in Allegheny, Pa., her maiden name being Campbell. Her parents died when she was a child, and she was reared by an aunt and uncle and educated in private schools. The home of her childhood and youth, Manchester, a suburb of Allegheny, is the "Old Chester" of so many of her stories and novels. She wrote from early girlhood, in verse before she turned to prose, and her first poem was published in *Harper's Magazine*. In 1880 she married Lorin F. Deland, and all her books have appeared under her married name. She has no children. Since her marriage she has lived in winter in Cambridge, Mass., and in summer in Kennebunkport, Maine. A lifelong nature-lover, Mrs. Deland lives as much as possible out of doors, and even though at well past eighty she can no longer indulge her passion for gardening very actively, she still knows the flowers and trees intimately.

She has always been a slow and careful worker, writing and rewriting and producing many drafts. She is even given to extensive revision after a story is in type, a practice heavily frowned upon by printers. She is a perfectionist in style, to whom clarity and an easy flow are vitally important, and she scrutinizes every word with that ideal in mind.

She has some talent for art as well, having studied for a while at the Cooper Union, in New York; before her marriage she taught drawing to private pupils. She is a member of the National Institute of Arts and Letters.

Mrs. Deland's first novel was quite unlike all her subsequent ones; it was a thesis novel, dealing with problems of religious faith and doubt in the manner of Mrs. Humphry Ward's *Robert Elsmere*, which appeared earlier the same year. Though neither novel was inspired by the other, it is a curious coincidence that Mrs. Deland named her preacher-hero Ward.

To later readers she became known as a tender and placid chronicler of old days in "Old Chester" among the parishioners of the gentle "Dr. Lavendar." She was never a regional writer; "Old Chester"

might as well have been in New England as in Western Pennsylvania. More than once she tried to return to her early vein of realism, but a large public, mostly feminine, kept demanding more of the nostalgic tales of a village all sweetness and light, seen through the rosy haze of a child's memories and dreams. "Old Chester" belonged in a different world from Gopher Prairie and Winesburg, Ohio; and when they usurped the American small-town scene, it started to fade from view. It is hardly likely that much of Mrs. Deland's work will long survive her, but through a long lifetime she has given innocent pleasure to many. If anything of hers be left to the readers of a harsher age, it may well be her more realistic and less popular novels, *John Ward, Preacher, The Awakening of Helena Richie*, and *The Iron Woman*.

PRINCIPAL WORKS: The Old Garden (poems) 1886; John Ward, Preacher, 1888; A Summer Day, 1889; Philip and His Wife, 1890; Sidney: The Story of a Child, 1892; The Wisdom of Fools, 1894; Mr. Tommy Dove and Other Stories, 1897; Old Chester Tales, 1899; Dr. Lavendar's People, 1903; The Common Way, 1904; The Awakening of Helena Richie, 1906; An Encore, 1907; The Iron Woman, 1911; The Voice, 1912; Partners, 1913; The Hands of Esau, 1914; Around Old Chester, 1915; The Rising Tide, 1916; The Vehement Flame, 1922; New Friends in Old Chester, 1924; The Kays, 1926; Captain Archer's Daughter, 1932; Old Chester Days, 1935; If This Be I (As I Suppose It Be) (autobiography) 1935; Golden Yesterdays, 1941.

ABOUT: Deland, M. If This Be I (As I Suppose It Be); Publishers' Weekly November 21, 1931; Woman's Home Companion June-September 1941.

DE LA PASTURE. See DELAFIELD

DE LA ROCHE, MAZO (1885-), Canadian novelist, was born in Toronto, the daughter of William Richmond de la Roche and Alberta (Lundy) de la Roche, but spent her childhood on her father's fruit farm in Ontario. She hated the city and loved the country, where, a sensitive, shy, and often lonely child, she grew up among horses, dogs, and other pets. She

was educated at home, and was utterly unfitted for city life when her father died and they had to leave the farm and go to Toronto to live. She, her mother, and a cousin who became her adopted sister existed only for the summers, when they went to a cottage on a lake deep in the Ontario woods. There she began to write, first plays, and then novels. The winters she made bearable by taking courses in English at the University of Toronto. In 1918 her mother died, and she and her cousin had to give up their beloved cottage. Miss de la Roche kept house while her cousin held a small civil service job; they lived by the strictest economy, and she kept on writing. She spent hours daily crouched over an old drawing-board (relic of a short-lived attempt to become an illustrator), with a grim determination to succeed as a novelist. Two novels and a volume of short stories were published, but they brought little in either money or glory, though her plays won two prizes in a competition conducted in 1925 by the Daughters of the British Empire.

Then in 1927 all this was suddenly and dramatically changed. Miss de la Roche at one stroke became rich and famous. Her *Jalna*, on which she had been working intermittently for many years, won the *Atlantic Monthly's* $10,000 prize. By 1941 seven other books in the *Jalna* series had appeared, and the end may not be yet. For the information of readers, the proper chronological sequence of the *Jalna* books issued to date (not the order in which they have been published) is as follows: *Young Renny, Whiteoak Heritage, Jalna, Whiteoaks of Jalna, Finch's Fortune, The Master of Jalna, Whiteoak Harvest, Wakefield's Course.* The author also dramatized the books as *Whiteoaks*, and Ethel Barrymore appeared in it in 1936 as the centenarian grandmother.

In 1930 Miss de la Roche moved permanently to England, where she bought a house in Windsor, Berkshire. Canada, and especially the Canadian countryside, are too deeply embedded in her memory, however, for most of her work to have any other background. In 1938 she received the Lorne Pierce Medal of the Royal Society of Canada. Nervous and timid in the ordinary practical affairs of life, she has unquenchable confidence and persistence in her work. She is tall and thin, with coppery hair, brown eyes, and a prominent nose. She is an ardent dog-lover who is seldom seen without her Scottie. She has never married.

It is difficult to analyze the immense popularity of the *Jalna* books, which have overshadowed all her other work. Partly it is due to the fascination of a family chronicle, of the detailed depiction of a richly characterized and populous group. Not a great deal happens to the Whiteoaks, but they are

strongly individualized, they are real people and their history is the history of their time. They may be compared with the *Matriarch* novels of G. B. Stern, or almost with *Gone With the Wind*. They are not great or even major novels, but they have body and texture and life; they are full-blooded, and we read them with the same absorbed interest we give to the life-stories of people we know. Her name is pronounced *roshe*.

PRINCIPAL WORKS: Explorers of the Dawn, 1922; Possession, 1923; Delight (short stories) 1926; Jalna, 1927; Long Life and Other Plays 1929; Whiteoaks of Jalna, 1929; Portrait of a Dog, 1930; Finch's Fortune, 1931; Lark Ascending 1932; The Master of Jalna, 1933; Beside a Norman Tower, 1934; Young Renny (Jalna—1906), 1935 Whiteoak Harvest, 1936; Whiteoaks (play) 1936; The Very House, 1937; Growth of a Man, 1938 The Sacred Bullock and Other Stories, 1939 Whiteoak Heritage, 1940; Wakefield's Course, 1941

ABOUT: North, S. The Writings of Mazo de la Roche; Canadian Bookman October 1938; Canadian Forum July 1932; Canadian Monthly May 1927; Scholastic May 13, 1940.

DE LA SERNA. See GÓMEZ DE LA SERNA

DELEDDA, GRAZIA (September 27 1872-August 16, 1936), Italian novelist, was born in the village of Nuoro, Sardinia

which was the scene of practically all her writing. Her father was Giovanni Antonio Deledda, her mother Francesca (Cambosu) Deledda. She had very little formal education, but except for private lessons in French educated herself by reading. She began writing at fifteen, her first article appearing in a fashion magazine published in Rome. She then began contributing to literary and political magazines in Sardinia. She had never left her native island, and knew nothing of life outside it. Finally, in fear and trembling she wrote a story about the only life she knew, and it was accepted by *La Tribuna* in Rome. From that time she realized her vocation; before she was twenty-one she had published the first three of a long series of novels dealing with the primitive world of the Sardinian shepherds, peasants, and mountaineers.

In 1897 she married a civil officer of the ministry of war named Madesani, and for the first time left Sardinia. Her married life was all spent in Rome, even after her husband's retirement in 1927, and it was here that she died. Although she continued to write regularly and prolifically—and in fact all her best work was still before her—she made her home and a growing family her chief interest, and modestly disclaimed any pride except that by her efforts her children were enabled to secure a better education than they could have been afforded by a civil servant's salary. Almost against her own will she became nationally and even internationally famous, until in 1926 her career culminated in the award of the Nobel Prize for Literature and her election to the Italian Academy. Yet she herself remained unknown to the world outside, and no one meeting this shy, timid little woman with luminous brown eyes and a sensitive face framed in a shock of white hair would have dreamed that she was one of the few women writers ever to receive the highest award in the field of literature. Before Grazia Deledda the only woman to have been awarded the Nobel Prize for Literature was Selma Lagerlöf.

Grazia Deledda's work for the most part remains untranslated into English, and she is therefore less well known in England and America than throughout the Continent. She has, as Lacy Collison-Morlay says, 'done more to make her native Sardinia . . . known to the outer world than any previous writer." She is at one in spirit with the primitive workers and peasants of rural Sardinia, and she describes them in rich and glowing colors and with keen psychological insight. Though three of her score or more of novels have been given English translation, the only one to gain any wide recognition is *The Mother*, a powerful and tragic tale. She was also the author of three plays, one in collaboration, which were produced with success in Rome. Her last novel, published after her death, was *La Chiesa della Solitudine (The Church of the Solitude)*—a title which seems aptly to serve as the valedictory of one of the most retiring and personally reticent authors of her time.

WORKS AVAILABLE IN ENGLISH: After the Divorce, 1905; Ashes, 1910?; The Mother (in England, The Woman and the Priest) 1923.

ABOUT: Collison-Morlay, L. Contemporary Italian Literature; Kennard, J. S. Italian Romance Writers; Publishers' Weekly August 22, 1936; New York Times August 17, 1936.

DELL, FLOYD (June 28, 1887-), American novelist, playwright, and miscellaneous writer, was born in Barry, Ill., the son of Anthony and Kate (Crone) Dell. His family was on the edge of poverty, and he had to leave high school at sixteen to find a job. He worked as a factory hand and at other manual occupations until 1905, when he became a reporter on a Davenport, Iowa, paper. From there he went to Chicago, where he became one of the group of Middle Western authors who constituted the then ascendant "Chicago School," and which included among others Carl Sandburg, Ben Hecht, Francis Hackett, and Charles MacArthur. He worked on various Chicago papers until 1909, when he became assistant literary editor of the *Evening Post,* succeeding Hackett as editor in 1911, when he was less than twenty-four. He built the Friday *Litary Review* of the paper up into one of the best known newspaper literary supplements in the country, then, in

Pinchot

1914, left for New York, the goal of most young Middle Western writers of his time.

A Socialist since boyhood, he gravitated naturally to the old *Masses,* of which he was associate editor from 1914 to 1917; he was one of the defendants when the *Masses* editors were charged with violation of the Espionage Act. When the magazine was succeeded by the *Liberator,* he went with it and was on its staff from 1918 to 1924. The plays which he wrote at this period were produced by the Liberal Club, ancestor of the Provincetown Players and the Theatre Guild. He was one of the best known figures in Greenwich Village, though he was never a playboy or much of a Bohemian, being shy and reserved by nature.

With the rise of Communism and the various Socialist schisms, Mr. Dell, though he retained and still retains his liberal sympathies, ceased to be identified with the radical groups. His first novel, the autobiographical *Moon-Calf,* had been a success, and he signalized his change in viewpoint by deserting the Village for Croton-on-the-Hudson, where he still lives. A first marriage had ended in divorce, and in 1919 he married Berta-Marie Gage; they have two sons. Mr. Dell became increasingly interested, first in psycho-analysis, then in child-training, and has written many articles on both subjects. He seems to have given up novel writing altogether, as well as the writing of plays. *Cloudy With Showers,* a play written with Thomas Mitchell, was produced in 1931; and he had already collaborated with Mr. Mitchell in dramatizing his (Dell's) novel, *An Unmarried Father,* as *Little Accident*—a play which had a successful run in 1928 and added a euphemistic phrase to contemporary English.

In 1935 Mr. Dell became associated with the W.P.A., doing editorial work, and since 1938 he has been chief of the special reports section of its Enforcement Division. With Paul Jordan Smith he edited Burton's *Anatomy of Melancholy* in 1927. His autobiography, published in 1933, goes only to the age of thirty-five, and is a sort of non-fictional commentary on *Moon-Calf,* which remains his best work. It reveals him as essentially a romantic idealist, sentimental and sensitive. He is tall and slender, with a mobile, expressive, face.

PRINCIPAL WORKS: *Novels*—Moon-Calf, 1920; The Briary-Bush, 1921; Janet March, 1923; This Mad Ideal, 1925; Runaway, 1925; An Old Man's Folly, 1926; An Unmarried Father, 1927; Souvenir, 1929; Love Without Money, 1931; Diana Stair, 1932; The Golden Spike, 1934. *Miscellaneous*—Women as World-Builders, 1913; The Angel Intrudes (one-act plays) 1918; Were You Ever a Child? 1919; Sweet-and-Twenty (one-act plays) 1921; King Arthur's Socks and Other Village Plays, 1922; Looking at Life, 1924; Intellectual Vagabondage—An Apology for the Intelligentsia, 1926; Love in Greenwich Village (stories and verse) 1926; The Outline of Marriage, 1926-27; Upton Sinclair—A Study in Social Protest, 1927; Love in the Machine Age, 1930; Homecoming (autobiography) 1933.

ABOUT: Dell, F. Homecoming; Sinclair, U. American Outpost; Young, A. On My Way; Saturday Review of Literature September 30, 1933.

DELMAR, Mrs. VIÑA (CROTER) (January 29, 1905-), American novelist and short-story writer, is the daughter of  Charles and Jean (Guran) Croter. Both were theatrical people, and the future novelist spent her infancy seeing America. At three weeks, she was in San Francisco, sleeping in the top tray of her mother's trunk. When Viña was eight her mother left the stage and settled in the Flatbush section of Brooklyn. Her formal education began in the public schools. Mrs. Croter died when Viña was thirteen, and her father moved to the Bronx, another borough of New York City. There was no more schooling for Viña, who began work-

ing on the stage at sixteen, scoring more notable successes as an usher than actress. Also at sixteen, she married Eugene Delmar on May 10, 1921; a son was born and named Gray. Her experience had also included work as a typist, switchboard operator, and assistant manager of a moving picture theatre in Harlem. She had written stories since she was nine, but the first was published in 1922. Six years later the Literary Guild made Mrs. Delmar's *Bad Girl* one of its 1928 selections. This honest and straightforward tale of the relations, married life, and childbirth experiences of a young typist and a mechanic spoke in the authentic accents of the *milieu* it described. It was dramatized in 1930. Mrs. Delmar has a flair for disconcertingly frank titles; *Loose Ladies,* eleven portraits of girls in American cities, and *Kept Woman,* both published in 1929, at the crest of the Prohibition wave and stock-market boom, occasionally came into collision with the censors. Most of Mrs. Delmar's married life was spent in Inwood, the middle-class residential district of upper Manhattan, which she mirrored with such faithfulness in *Bad Girl;* she now lives in the rather more "select" suburb of Scarsdale. She is a frequent contributor to magazines of large circulation, and several of her tales have been filmed, but at the time of this writing she has produced no books for several years.

PRINCIPAL WORKS: Bad Girl, 1928; Loose Ladies, 1929; Kept Woman, 1929; Women Live Too Long, 1932; The Marriage Racket, 1933.

DEL VALLE INCLAN. See VALLE INCLAN

DE MADARIAGA. See MADARIAGA

DE MONTHERLANT. See MONTHERLANT

DE MORGAN, WILLIAM FREND (November 16, 1839-January 15, 1917) English novelist, was born in London, the son of the famous mathematician Augustus De Morgan and Sophia (Frend) De Morgan. He was educated at University College, and studied art at the Royal Academy school, where he met Burne-Jones, D. G. Rossetti, and William  Morris, who with their families remained throughout his life his closest friends. His father had perceived his literary talent, but De Morgan ignored it and "for forty years never read a book" while devoting himself to the making of artistic pottery. He rediscovered the process of making colored lustres, and his potteries, first in Chelsea, then in Wimbledon and Fulham, were artistically a great success, though he was no businessman and never made more than a bare living. In 1887 he married Evelyn Pickering, a gifted artist; their childless marriage was exceedingly happy though she was eighteen years his junior.

From 1890 the De Morgans were obliged to spend all their winters in Florence, as he showed symptoms of tuberculosis of the spine. Finally, in 1905, he retired—and immediately fell ill. He had been amusing himself for a while by doing some writing in the style of Dickens, whom he worshiped, but had thrown it aside; his only publication to that date had been some technical booklets on pottery. At his wife's insistence he started the story again, and the result was *Joseph Vance,* a first novel at sixty-seven, and an immediate and enormous success. In the eight years or so left to him, De Morgan wrote five more novels besides two unfinished ones which his wife completed after his death. None of them duplicated the great success of *Joseph Vance,* but all were first rate examples of a *genre* which he revived—the leisurely Victorian novel, with the author always prominent in its pages.

De Morgan was as pleased as a child with his sudden and late fame. He was a charming man, sympathetic, generous, sweet-tempered, with a bubbling humor that masked congenital melancholy. He was unorthodox but devout, with an abiding faith in what he called "immortalism." Tall and very thin, with straggling beard and a high-pitched voice, he yet had the genial personality usually associated with a more portly build. He himself said that there was "much of himself" in "Charles Heath" in *Alice-for-Short,* and in the uncompleted *Old Man's Youth.*

With the World War he threw himself whole-heartedly into submarine and aircraft defense; he was a born inventor, and put his talent now at the service of his country, letting his writing go. Ironically, he caught trench fever (or virulent influenza) from a soldier on leave who had called as an admirer of his novels, and died of it. His devoted wife lived just long enough to design his headstone and to finish his two incomplete novels.

"No young man could have written his books," says Arthur Page Grubb. Their "whimsical detachment and placid tolerance" belong to the reflective years. They were discursive, with long lapses from the complicated plots, full of minute detail, often sentimental, but altogether delightful. There is no denying De Morgan was too prolix, though since his time we have learned not to balk at 300,000-word novels. He is always compared to Dickens, whom he thought beyond his reach; but there is much truth in Flora Warren Seymour's remark that "Dickens caricatures, De Morgan characterizes." Certainly his emergence as a novelist at an age when most men's work is over is one of the strangest phenomena in the history of literature. Some of the pleasantest novels in print would have been lost to us had De Morgan died at sixty-five.

PRINCIPAL WORKS: Joseph Vance, 1906; Alice-for-short, 1907; Somehow Good, 1908; It Never Can Happen Again, 1909; An Affair of Dishonour, 1910; A Likely Story, 1911; When Ghost Meets Ghost, 1914; The Old Madhouse (completed by E. P. De Morgan) 1919; The Old Man's Youth (completed by E. P. De Morgan) 1921.

ABOUT: Hale, W. T. William De Morgan and the Great Early Victorians; Scott, W. T. Chesterton and Other Essays; Seymour, F. W. William De Morgan, a Post-Victorian Realist; Stirling, A. M. W. William De Morgan and His Wife; Bookman March 1917; Independent January 29, 1917; Living Age March 3, 1917, May 12, 1917, July 7, 1917; Nation January 25, 1917; North American Review March 1917; Outlook January 24, 1917.

*DENNETT, TYLER (June 13, 1883-), American educator and writer, winner of the Pulitzer Prize for biography, was born in Spencer, Wis., the son of the Rev. William Eugene Dennett and Roxie (Tyler) Dennett. He attended Bates College at Lewiston, Maine, for a year in 1900-01, and received his B.A. degree from Williams College in Massachusetts in 1904, going  to Baltimore for his Ph.D. degree at Johns Hopkins. Dennett was associate editor of the *World Outlook,* a Methodist magazine, from 1914 to 1916, and then till 1918 was director of publicity for the Methodist Centenary, for which large sums of money were expended. The next year he was connected with the Interchurch World Movement (1919-20). He now lists his church affiliation as Congregationalist; his politics as Republican. Dennett married Maybelle Raymond of Washington, D.C., in March 1911, and they have four children: George Raymond, Tyler Eugene, Audrey, and Laurence Dennett.

Dennett was lecturer in American history at Johns Hopkins in 1923-24, and at Columbia in 1927-28, taking time from his post as chief of the Division of Publications, and editor at the U.S. Department of State (1924-29). He was historical adviser to the Department from 1929 to 1931, when he went to Princeton as professor of international relations to remain till 1934. *John Hay: From Poetry to Politics,* written in 1933 for Dodd, Mead's American Political Leaders Series, won the Pulitzer Prize for biography in 1934. An entertaining selection from Hay's letters and diaries, when he was Lincoln's private secretary, was edited with an introduction by Dr. Dennett and published in 1939, also in the American Political Leaders Series. *John Hay* won its author eight honorary doctor's degrees, from Wesleyan, Harvard, Amherst, Columbia, Beloit, Lafayette, Clark, Princeton, and his own *alma mater,* Williams, in 1934. He was president of the latter institution from then till 1937. In 1938-39 he was Carnegie visitor to Australia and New Zealand. Dennett's first three books stemmed from his church and missionary affiliations, and his two extensive tours through Japan, China, the Philippines, Malaysia, and India. He now lives at Hague, N.Y., and his clubs are the Century (New York) and Cosmos (Washington).

PRINCIPAL WORKS: The Democratic Movement in Asia, 1918; A Better World, 1920; Americans in Eastern Asia: A Critical Study of the Policy of the United States with Reference to China, Japan, and Korea in the 19th Century, 1923; Roosevelt and the Russo-Japanese War, 1924; John Hay: From Poetry to Politics, 1933; Editor —Lincoln and the Civil War in the Diaries and Letters of John Hay, 1939.

ABOUT: Dennett, T. The Democratic Movement in Asia.

DENNIS, GEOFFREY POMEROY

(January 20, 1892-), English novelist and essayist, was born in Barnstaple, Devonshire, the son of Austen and Annie (Handford) Dennis. His mother died at his birth. Though he comes of an old and "good" family, it was greatly impoverished, and after a board schooling in North of England schools (his father had moved to Walsall, Staffordshire), he was articled to a real estate agent and auctioneer at fifteen. After three years he secured a scholarship to Oxford, and studied at Exeter College from 1910 to 1914, when he received his

M.A. with first class honors in the School of Modern History. At the university he was co-founder of the Oxford Poetry Series, and treasurer and librarian of the Oxford Union. He returned to Walsall as an elementary school master, but in 1915 joined the army, and served as a captain until 1920, first in France and then in Cologne.

In 1919 he passed third in all England in a civil service examination, and from 1920 to 1937 was associated with the League of Nations in Geneva, eventually becoming chief editor and chief of document services. In 1938 he went to Rome as advisor to the International Institute of Agriculture. When Italy entered the Second World War in 1940 he returned to England.

In 1926 Mr. Dennis married Doris Ethel Hall, who died the following year. In 1928 he married Imogen C. R. Angeli, granddaughter of William Michael Rossetti and great-niece of Dante Gabriel and Christina Rossetti. They have a son and a daughter.

Until *The End of the World,* a powerful fantasy, won the Hawthornden Prize in 1930, Mr. Dennis's novels had had a strange career—hailed by the critics, neglected by the public, and generally assumed to be autobiographical, though the first (and the best) of them, *Mary Lee,* was a study of the religious development of a little girl a hundred years ago! His novels are all highly subjective, even when they deal with "stars and floods and space and time." They contrast markedly with the concerns of his objective career. As Clifton Fadiman remarked, "his major *intellectual* interests are politics and history, but his major interests are spiritual." Aptly enough, it has been said that he looks like "a combined business man and poet," with tortoise-shell spectacles and long, straight blond hair. Fundamentally he is a profound pessimist, with something of the stoical philosophy of A. E. Housman. He himself says that his chief, and really his only, subject is "the divided good-evil nature of the human soul." Louis Golding called him "one of the most important and most unknown authors of our time."

His one excursion into a non-fiction book caused a scandal. It was *Coronation Commentary,* written at the time of the accession of George VI. Since Mr. Dennis had known the then Prince of Wales (the Duke of

Windsor) at Oxford, and was known to have intimate knowledge of the whole royal family, the English Book Society announced his book as its choice of the month without, apparently, reading it. When it appeared it was found to be violently condemnatory of Edward VIII (the Duke of Windsor), and the duke threatened to sue for libel if it were not immediately withdrawn, which it was. Later in the year it was published, with an apologetic foreword, in America.

PRINCIPAL WORKS: Mary Lee, 1922; Harvest in Poland, 1925; Declaration of Love, 1927; The End of the World, 1930; The Devil and XYZ (co-author, under pseudonym of "Barum Browne") 1931; Sale by Auction (in America: The Red Room) 1932; Bloody Mary's, 1934; Coronation Commentary (non-fiction) 1937.

ABOUT: Collins, J. Taking the Literary Pulse; Bookman (London) July 1931, May 1934; Time May 3, 1937.

DERLETH, AUGUST WILLIAM (February 24, 1909-   ), American poet, novelist, and biographer, writes: "Born in Sauk City,

Wis.; parents William Julius and Rose Louise (Volk) Derleth; educated in local parochial and public high school, B.A. University of Wisconsin 1930. Began writing at thirteen, publishing at fifteen, have been publishing consistently since, often more than a hundred long and short titles yearly. Write poetry, essays, reviews, serious novels, short stories, novelettes, mystery novels, plays, biography, criticism. O'Brien Roll of Honor for short story, 1933. Guggenheim Fellow, 1938. At present director of the local Board of Education, special lecturer in American Regional Literature at the University of Wisconsin, head of the local Rangers' Club (a nature organization for young people), contributing editor of Outdoors Magazine. Work in progress includes The Wisconsin (Rivers of America Series); a book-length study of regionalism in America, together with a text, an anthology of regional literature; a biography of Winsor McCay; a history and anecdotal survey of the comics in America; a regional study of the Middle Border country; and various novels. Writing methods—I write very swiftly, from 750,000 to a million words yearly, very little of it pulp material. It is possible that I am perhaps the most versatile and voluminous writer in quality writing fields today, though I should be the last to make a point of this. Responsible educators have called me a one-man fiction-factory, for what that is worth. But I do not write in order to justify any name or title; I write because I must, because I have plots and material to keep me writing for more years than I can possibly live, and I want to put it all down as quickly as I can; or as much of it as I can put down, at any rate. I have actually written over thirty books, including some scheduled for publication two years from now. Some are coming pseudonymously ('Tally Mason,' 'Eldon Heath,' pseudonyms). The initial W. in my writing was used only in my early books; is used still in my work for Weird Tales Magazine, the first market to buy my work.

"My most ambitious work is the Sac Prairie Saga, a projected life-story of Sac Prairie, Wis., from the early 1800's to 1950 or thereabouts, planned to include upwards of fifty books of all kinds, each book to be a perfect unit in itself, and yet each contributing in background to the history of Sac Prairie and of the Mid West generally. It is perhaps the most ambitious project ever undertaken in the history of literature, and has only two contenders in magnitude—Balzac's Human Comedy to which it is often ill compared, and Proust's Remembrance of Things Past. Thirteen volumes of this saga are already published.

"My hobbies are fencing, swimming, hiking, chess, stamp-collecting, and collecting comic strips."

* * *

This dizzying fount of energy is "a burly-chested blond," a "champion letter-writer to the press," the "watchdog of village politics," on which he writes and distributes broadsides. He sponsored the Sauk City community theatre and organized its Parent-Teachers' Association (though he is unmarried!). He reads a book a day, four hundred magazines a year, but says he has no time to read newspapers. In spite of his incredible prolificity, his work, including his poetry, is not superficial, and he is considered a leading authority on regionalism in American literature. His "Judge Peck" mysteries are among the best of their kind. He edited Poetry Out of Wisconsin with R. E. F. Larsson in 1940. With disarming candor, he says, "I enjoy life, and nobody takes me seriously, thank God!"

PRINCIPAL WORKS: Poetry—Hawk on the Wind, 1938; Man Track Here, 1939; Here on a Darkling Plain, 1940; Wind in the Elms, 1941; Rind of Earth, 1942. Novels—Place of Hawks (short stories) 1935; Still Is the Summer Night, 1937; Wind Over Wisconsin, 1938; Any Day Now,

1938; Restless Is the River, 1939; Country Growth (short stories) 1940; Bright Journey, 1940; Village Year, 1941; Sweet Genevieve, 1942. *Mystery Stories*—Murder Stalks the Wakely Family, 1934; The Man on All Fours, 1934; Three Who Died, 1935; Sign of Fear, 1935; Consider Your Verdict, 1937; Sentence Deferred, 1939; The Narracong Riddle, 1940; The Seven Who Waited, 1941. *Miscellaneous*—Still Small Voice: The Biography of Zona Gale, 1940; Atmosphere of Houses, 1940; Village Year: A Sac Prairie Journal, 1941; Evening in Spring, 1941.

ABOUT: Hobbies November 1940; Scholastic November 25, 1940; Time October 30, 1939.

*DE SÉLINCOURT, ERNEST (September 24, 1870-   ), English literary critic and university professor, was born in Streatham, the third son of Charles Alexandre De Sélincourt and Theodora Bruce (Bendall) De Sélincourt. The De Sélincourt family is well known in England for its literary members, native and acquired, such as Anne Douglas Sedgwick.[qv] Ernest De Sélincourt was educated at Dulwich College and University College, Oxford University, where he was lecturer in English Language and Literature from 1906 to 1909, and was made an Honorary Fellow in 1930. He was Professor of English Language and Literature at the University of Birmingham for twenty-seven years, 1908 to 1935, acting as vice-principal in the latter four years. Appointed Professor of Poetry at Oxford in 1928 for five years, his inaugural lecture delivered before the University of Oxford March 1, 1929, was entitled simply "On Poetry." The lectures were gathered together in a volume published in 1934. Professor De Sélincourt has also been in demand as an examiner in Honours Schools over all the academic map of England: Oxford in 1904-06, Wales 1904-07, London 1911-14, Durham 1917-18, Edinburgh 1918-21, Bristol 1923-25, and Leeds 1934-36. Made President of the English Association, in his presidential address he discussed "The Early Wordsworth," the field of his especial interest. This was in 1936, midway in his editing the *Letters of William and Dorothy Wordsworth,* from the early letters from 1787-1805, published in 1935, to the third volume, covering the later years, which came out in 1939. Professor De Sélincourt's home is appropriately in the Lake Region, at Ladywood, Grasmere. His club is the Athenaeum. In 1896 he married Ethel, third daughter of William Tuer Shawcross of Rochdale, by whom he had two sons and two daughters. She died in 1931. In 1934 Professor De Sélincourt was Clark Lecturer at Trinity College, Cambridge University. His honorary degrees include a D.Litt. (Oxford), M.A. (Birming-ham) and LL.D. (Edinburgh). As an authority on Wordsworth, he is a member of an international triumvirate, including the American George MacLean Harper and the French Émile Legouis.

PRINCIPAL WORKS: English Poets and the National Ideal, 1915; The Study of Poetry, 1918; Dorothy Wordsworth: A Biography, 1933; Oxford Lectures on Poetry, 1934. *Editor*—Hyperion A Facsimile of Keats's Autograph Ms., 1905; Poems of John Keats, 1905; Wordsworth's Guide to the Lakes, 1906; The Minor Poems of Spenser 1910, 1912; The Letters of William and Dorothy Wordsworth, 1935-1939; George and Sarah Green A Narrative by Dorothy Wordsworth, 1936; The Journals of Dorothy Wordsworth, 1942.

DE SERNA, ESPINA. See ESPINA

DESTOUCHES, LOUIS FERDINAND (1894-   ), French novelist who signs his works "Louis Ferdinand Celine," was born in Paris, of Breton peasant stock, his father being an elementary school teacher, his mother a seamstress. It is usually considered that his novels, *Journey to the End of Night* and *Death on the Installment Plan,* are autobiographical; they

E. Schaal

are, but not strictly so. However, the events of M. Destouches' life have followed rather closely those of his *soi disant* "hero, Bardamu, at least geographically. After an elementary education, he was working in a ribbon factory when the First World War broke out. He served throughout, was decorated for bravery, and was wounded in the head and shell-shocked. After the war he went to Africa as a petty official of a business concern; while there he began the study of medicine, which he continued on his return, to take his degree at the University of Rennes. Then he sailed to the United States as ship's doctor, and after a while in New York became a staff surgeon at the Ford plant in Michigan. The next year he became associated with the Rockefeller Foundation which sent him to Africa again, this time on a medical mission. From 1921 to 1924 he was connected with the League of Nations, in Geneva, in a political capacity. At the same time he did postgraduate work at the University of Paris, and received another degree in 1924, with a thesis on Ignaz Semmelweiss. In 1926 he became associated with the State Clinic at Clichy, and remained there for ten years, working among the

* Died May 22, 1943.

poorest of the poor and the inhabitants of the underworld, at about $60 a month, though he had built up a small fortune from his royalties.

For he was at the same time writing novels which, though they horrified their readers, were translated into all European languages and sold enormously. His first book, the *Journey to the End of Night,* was rewritten twelve times by longhand before he was satisfied with it. *Death on the Installment Plan* is its sequel. In 1935 he made a visit to Russia, and came back much embittered against the Soviets, though up to that time the Communists had considered him, if not one of them, at least highly sympathetic. He completed this break by writing a violently anti-Semitic book in 1938. When its implications were pointed out to him, he denied any affiliation with Fascism any more than with Communism, and said he had merely tried to "out-rave" the constant ringing in his ears which is his legacy from the war. Since the conquest of France, he has remained in Paris, where his continuing anti-Semitic diatribes have won him the favor of the Nazis. He was last in New York in 1938. He is unmarried.

Both Destouches (or "Celine") and his work are almost indescribable. Outwardly he is a big, heavy-set man with a good-umored, stubborn peasant face. Inwardly he is a seething mass of hatred, profound pessimism, energy, and what must be considered plain insanity. His world is a world of obscenity, cowardice, perversion, murder, treachery, and filth. There are no decent or honest people in it, and there is no hope. Yet in meeting him, as John Marks noted, one finds unbounded vitality, wit, and a passion for conversation, tempered by extreme caution and a touch of penuriousness. He is no moralist in his books; he is not angry, he is only tired, disgusted, despairing, and coldly obscene.

Yet some of the things Leon Trotsky wrote about him in 1935 still hold—his "colossal stock of observations as physician and artist, his sovereign indifference toward academism, his extraordinary instinct for intuitions of life and language." His style, said Trotsky, is "subordinated to his receptivity of the objective world. In his seemingly careless, ungrammatical, passionately condensed language [for the most part the argot of criminals], there lives, beats, and vibrates the genuine wealth of French culture. . . . He has newly threshed the dictionary of French literature."

WORKS AVAILABLE IN ENGLISH: Journey to the End of Night, 1934; Mea Culpa and The Life and Work of Semmelweiss (in one volume) 1937; Death on the Installment Plan, 1938.

ABOUT: Annales Politiques et Littéraires December 9, 1932; Atlantic Monthly October 1935; Bookman (London) October 1934; Living Age December 1935; Time May 30, 1938.

DE UNAMUNO. See UNAMUNO

DEUTSCH, BABETTE (September 22, 1895-), American poet, writes: "Babette Deutsch, daughter of Melanie Fisher and Michael Deutsch, was born in New York City. After graduating from the Ethical Culture School she attended Barnard College, Columbia University. It was her good fortune to study under such stimulating teachers as Franz Boas, Charles A.

Bachrach

Beard, James Shotwell, and the late James Harvey Robinson, and to have contact during those critical years with so salient a personality as Randolph Bourne. While still an undergraduate, Miss Deutsch began contributing to the more serious periodicals of the day, poems of hers appearing in the *North American Review* and the *New Republic*. She received her B.A. in 1917 and thereafter was for a short time connected with the *Political Science Quarterly*. An invitation from Marion Reedy, editor of *Reedy's Mirror* (St. Louis), to contribute critical articles to his one-man journal of opinion resulted in several essays, among them one on Thorstein Veblen. Not long afterward Veblen asked Miss Deutsch to act as his secretary while he was teaching at the New School for Social Research.

"In 1921 Miss Deutsch married Avrahm Yarmolinsky,*qv* Chief of the Slavonic Division of the New York Public Library. They have two sons. Shortly after the birth of their first child, Miss Deutsch went abroad with her husband, visiting Berlin, Riga, Moscow, Leningrad, Warsaw, Florence, Paris, and London. Upon her return to the States she devoted herself to writing, with occasional excursions into the lecturing field. She gave courses on poetry for two seasons at the New School for Social Research, has spoken before a number of university audiences, and has also conducted private classes. Her poem, 'Thoughts at the Year's End,' which appears in her book, *Fire for the*

Night, won the *Nation* Poetry Prize in 1929. She was Phi Beta Kappa poet at Columbia in 1929. In 1933 she was presented with a gold pin by the New York State Federation of Women's Clubs, an honor that might have given her pause, had it not been accorded to poets with whom she is glad to be associated in the public mind.

"The only clubs of which she has been a member are the late lamented Civic Club and P.E.N., the international organization of poets, essayists, and novelists. While not connected with any party, Miss Deutsch belongs to the left wing in politics, and has been active in the Committee for Cultural Freedom, headed by John Dewey, and in liberal movements generally. She dissociated herself from the League of American Writers when she recognized the sectarian character of that organization.

"Miss Deutsch has contributed poetry and criticism to a number of periodicals here and abroad, and her work has been widely anthologized in American and more especially British collections of verse."

* * *

Miss Deutsch has translated a great deal from the Russian and German, particularly in collaboration with her husband. She is slender, dark, and looks the serious student she is—philosophy is her guiding interest. As a reviewer in the *Bookman* remarked, she has "a fine and swift intelligence coupled with extreme subtlety of emotion. . . . Her thought is always at least as important as her feeling." Jessica Nelson North, pointing out that her gravest fault was "the jumbling of too many images into a stanza," said: "She does her best work in a loosely constructed free verse, interspersed with regular rhymed poems where intensity is needed." It is of interest to note that Mark Gideon, in her novel *A Brittle Heaven,* is a portrait of Randolph Bourne.[qv]

PRINCIPAL WORKS: *Poetry*—Banners, 1919; Honey Out of the Rock, 1925; Fire for the Night, 1930; Epistle to Prometheus, 1931; One Part Love, 1939. *Criticism*—Potable Gold: An Essay on Poetry and This Age, 1929; This Modern Poetry, 1935. *Novels*—A Brittle Heaven, 1926; In Such a Night, 1927; Mask of Silenus, 1933. *Miscellaneous* —Walt Whitman, 1941; It's a Secret (juvenile) 1941.

ABOUT: American Scholar January 1941; Poetry June 1931, March 1940; Scholastic November 24, 1934.

DEVAL, JACQUES (June 27, 1893-), French playwright and novelist, was born in Paris, the son of a theatrical producer who died in 1938. Young Jacques Deval was sent to school in England; the knowledge of English acquired there has stood him in such good stead that his last play was written in English, and he can hold his own in Hollywood story conferences. His father did not intend that young Deval should follow a stage career. The son's first play, *Une Faible Femme,* was produced by a theatrical competitor. *Sabre de Bois,* his first novel, was also received favorably by the critics, Victor Méric calling it the finest book of the First World War Jacques Deval rapidly became one of the most prolific and successful of French playwrights, also writing theatrical criticism for the *Revue des Deux Monde* and articles (*chroniques*) for *Gringoire.*

In New York for the production of *Her Cardboard Lover,* a comedy adapte by P. G. Wodehouse in 1926 for the use of Jeanne Eagels, supported by Leslie Howard Deval told a *Herald Tribune* reporter that in Paris he was famous as the one dramatis who had never given an interview or said single quotable thing—to a journalist. Late he allowed it to be known that he was usuall in bed at 9, up at 5, and wrote until 1 when he went for walks, paid social call and read.

Tovarich (1935), Deval's most successfu comedy, which played in 232 cities, is ded cated "à la Memoire d'Anne-Marie Deva Ma Femme." The present Mme. Deval is young French actress, Else Argall, who ap peared for the first time in the film *Club c Femmes,* directed by her husband in 193 from his own script. *Mademoiselle* (1932 was adapted by the American actress Grac George for the use of herself and her ste daughter, Alice Brady. In 1934 Jacqu Deval was in Hollywood, writing two orig nal scripts for Universal.

His most ambitious play, *Pière Pour L Vivants,* which traced sixty years of th life of a middle-class Frenchman and too two years to write, was a quick failur *Tovarich* ("Comrade"), a comedy based one of the oldest romantic and dramat comic situations—members of the nobili forced into service—was produced in stead, in a mood of pique, and rolled up eig hundred performances in Paris alone. the end of the season of its production t play had been shown in translated versio in practically every country in Europ Adapted into English by Robert E. She wood, it ran a year in London, opened in New York in October 1936, and ran through the season. It has been filmed, with Claudette Colbert and Charles Boyer. Deval also once made a *pièce policier* of Agatha Christie's *The Murder of Roger Ackroyd*, Hercule Poirot becoming a Florentine.

Sabre de Bois made a rather belated appearance in English in 1930 as *Wooden Swords*, one reviewer remarking that "somehow it seems like turning back the clock to revive the almost purely humorous war story." The hero, a near-sighted Frenchman in the supply service, fights the enemy with a mop. *That Girl* is the melodramatic chronicle of Chérie, a French girl of the streets lured to Panama, who dies the death of a spy.

M. Deval, who has a Gallic face, smooth black hair, pince-nez and a small moustache, was reported in October 1937 to have taken out his first citizenship papers in the United States.

WORKS AVAILABLE IN ENGLISH TRANSLATION: Wooden Swords, 1930; That Girl, 1932; Tovarich, 1937.

ABOUT: New York Times October 30, 1932.

*DE VOTO, BERNARD AUGUSTINE

(January 11, 1897-), American novelist, and critic, was born in Ogden, Utah, the

son of Florian Bernard De Voto, of Italian descent, and Rhoda (Dye) De Voto, daughter of a pioneer Mormon family. He spent two years at the University of Utah, then transferred to Harvard. War service as a lieutenant of infantry (though he did not go overseas) followed, and he was graduated from Harvard in 1920 as of the class of 1918. In 1923 he married Helen Avis MacVicar; they have one son.

From 1922 to 1927 De Voto was instructor and assistant professor of English at Northwestern University. He then moved to Cambridge, Mass. (where he now lives), and after two years of study and writing began teaching again, this time at Harvard, though most of the time on a part-time basis. In 1936 he went to New York as editor of the *Saturday Review of Literature*, in succession to Henry Seidel Canby. After two years he resigned and returned to Cam-

bridge, but he continues his writing of the "Easy Chair" department in *Harper's Magazine*, which he has conducted since 1935.

Of his own literary interests Bernard De Voto writes to the editors of this volume: "I am more interested in American literature than in any other. I regard *Huckleberry Finn* as the greatest novel written by an American and *Walden* as the greatest work outside of fiction, and I read both very frequently indeed. But I like their exact antitheses almost as well, and have read *Moby Dick* and *Leaves of Grass* almost as often. Similarly with contemporary literature: I think Frost the greatest living poet, but I admire MacLeish almost as much. I have a profound admiration for Hemingway's skill without much liking his books. I like Lewis and Dos Passos, James Farrell and Steinbeck—and so on. I tend to admire skill, mastery of form, more than I should, and so am much distressed by writing like Thomas Wolfe's. In fiction I tend to like psychological treatments more than anything else, and especially psychological subtleties. I like good historical fiction, especially James Boyd's.

"I am profoundly interested in American history, especially frontier history, and more especially the history of the western frontier. I have read and studied it for many years and may claim some authority in the field. I am probably the principal authority on the history of Mormonism, and that involves an intimate knowledge of many other aspects of frontier life. I am also inexhaustibly interested in the history of other crank religions and economic experiments— Shakers, Millerites, Owenites, Brook Farm, Oneida, etc. Probably I shall write books, some time, about both fields.

"For something over a year now I have been working on the unpublished Mark Twain papers. A good many of them will eventually be published under my editorship, and I shall probably revise my book about Mark Twain and write another one. I am also working on a book which I can describe only as a panorama of American expansion during the 1840s. I have been fitfully working on a novel also, but I can hazard no guess or prophecy about its future."

As a disciple of the Italian sociologist Pareto, De Voto has been a storm-center of contemporary American criticism. In his book on Mark Twain he has especially opposed the view of Van Wyck Brooks that

Twain was a genius frustrated by his environment. He is regarded by radicals as a reactionary, and by conservatives as a wild left-winger. As Wilson Follett put it, he has been "a gadfly to all manner of intellectual softies." Edmund Wilson, who conducted a long controversy with him on his economic attitude, nevertheless conceded that "he has maintained among the literary phenomena of his own time a toughness of mind that is uncommon." Despite this mental toughness, he has, to quote *Time*, "enthusiasms just as intense as his animosities."

In 1942 it was revealed that DeVoto is also "John August," writer of thrillers and popular magazine fiction.

PRINCIPAL WORKS: *Novels*—The Crooked Mile, 1924; The Chariot of Fire, 1926; The House of Sun-Goes-Down, 1928; We Accept With Pleasure, 1934. *History and Criticism*—The Writer's Handbook (with W. F. Bryan and A. H. Nethercot) 1927; Mark Twain's America, 1932; Forays and Rebuttals, 1936; Minority Report, 1940; Mark Twain in Eruption (ed.) 1940; Essays on Mark Twain, 1942. As *"John August"*—Troubled Star, 1939; Rain Before Seven, 1940; Advance Agent, 1942.

ABOUT: Mattingly, G. Bernard De Voto: A Preliminary Appraisal; Nation January 23, 1937; New Republic February 3, 1937; Saturday Review of Literature June 16, 1934, May 30, 1936; Time August 26, 1940.

*DEWEY, JOHN (October 20, 1859-   ), American philosopher, was born in Burlington, Vt., the son of Archibald S. Dewey and Lucina A. (Rich)

Dewey. He was educated at the University of V e r m o n t (B.A. 1 8 7 9) a n d Johns Hopkins University (Ph.D. 1884), and has received honorary degrees f r o m the University of Wisconsin, P e k i n g National University, and the University of Paris. He began his teaching career as an instructor in philosophy at the University of Michigan, in 1884. When he left, in 1888, he was assistant professor, and for the next year he was professor of philosophy at the University of Minnesota. He then returned to Michigan as professor, remaining there this time until 1894, when he became professor and head of the philosophy department at the University of Chicago. In 1902 he became director of its School of Education as well. In 1904 he went to Columbia, and remained in active teaching duty there until long past the usual retirement age. In fact, he is still a living force in philosophy and education.

In 1886 he married Alice Chipman, who was his student at the University of Michigan. She died in 1927, and since then Professor Dewey has lived with one of his daughters, in New York in the winter, in Nova Scotia in the summer. He had three sons and three daughters; two sons died, and the Deweys later adopted an Italian boy. Honors have been heaped upon him; he is a past president of the American Psychological Association and of the American Philosophical Society, a member of the National Academy of Arts and Sciences, and a corresponding member of the French Institute. He was the first president of the American Association of University Professors, of which he was one of the founders. Both his seventieth and his eightieth birthdays were widely celebrated in the academic world, though on the second occasion he modestly left town to avoid "a second canonization."

John Dewey has earned distinction in three different fields. In philosophy, he is the chief living exponent of Pragmatism the system established by William James which has been called "the philosophy of the common man." In education, he is the father of the Progressive School movement In the fight for civil and academic freedom he has been in the vanguard for many years In 1929 he became chairman of the League for Independent Political Action; he ha participated in the rough-and-tumble o political campaigns; and was one of the committee which went to Mexico in 1937 to investigate the charges against the late Leon Trotsky. He has been anything but the usual retiring professor. Yet he has all the proverbial professorial absent-mindednes (he sometimes arrives a day early or a day late for appointments), and he is personally shy, gentle, and sweet-tempered. Tall and thin, he bore in middle age a marked resemblance to Robert Louis Stevenson His black eyes behind academic spectacles his sad, drooping moustache, his carelessly combed grey hair, once black, and his disheveled attire have become trademark of "the dean of American philosophers. His voice is a monotonous drawl; his students loved him, but he sometimes put them to sleep. In some ways he seems still to be the small-town son of a Yankee store keeper. He loves the country, though he has never had much flair for farming. His amusements are the reading of detective stories and the solving of acrostics.

* Died June 1, 1952.

Dr. Will Durant has perhaps best summed up Dewey's philosophical system when he says: "The starting-point of his system of thought is biological: he sees man as an organism in an environment, remaking as well as made. Things are to be understood through their origins and their functions, without the intrusion of supernatural considerations. . . . Every idea, to have meaning, must be a way of dealing specifically with actual stimuli and situations. . . . Thought should aim not merely to 'understand' the world, but to control and refashion it. . . . Faith in education as the soundest instrumentality of social, political, and moral reconstruction is justified by the malleability of the instincts and the illimitableness of human growth."

The influence of John Dewey's thought upon American education and philosophy has been incalculable. But it has not been due to any forceful clarity in his writing; it must be confessed that, purely as a writer, he is obscure and sometimes downright bad. His philosophy may be simple and straightforward, but his language is not; it is involved, complicated, and full of "big words." Reading him is a task, as he himself has recognized. Numerous elucidations and glossaries of his work have been written in an attempt to make them more easily understandable to the ordinary cultured reader. As a lecturer, he is not much more lucid, though he has taught now for more than half a century and has lectured in Tokyo and Edinburgh (where he gave the Gifford Lectures in 1929). But it is worth the effort needed to follow his reasoning; and, strange to say, his *Freedom and Culture,* written at eighty, reveals a clearness and crispness which his earlier work markedly lacked. He is still full of vitality. His thinking has integrity and scrupulousness; it is naturalistic, and it is essentially American. In mind and spirit, John Dewey is one of the beacon-lights of American civilization.

PRINCIPAL WORKS: Psychology, 1886; Leibnitz, 1888; Critical Theory of Ethics, 1894; Study of Ethics, 1894; School and Society, 1899; Studies in Logical Theory, 1903; How We Think, 1909; Influence of Darwin on Philosophy and Other Essays, 1910; German Philosophy and Politics, 1915; Democracy and Education, 1916; Reconstruction in Philosophy, 1920; Human Nature and Conduct, 1922; Experience and Nature, 1925; The Public and Its Problems, 1927; The Quest for Certainty, 1929; Art as Experience, 1934; A Common Faith, 1934; Liberalism and Social Action, 1935; Logic: The Theory of Inquiry, 1938; Ethics (with J. H. Tufts) 1938; Freedom and Culture, 1939; Education Today, 1940; The Bertrand Russell Case (ed., with others) 1941.

ABOUT: Essays in Honor of John Dewey on His Seventieth Birthday; Feldman, W. T. The Philosophy of John Dewey; Hook, S. John Dewey, An Intellectual Portrait; The Philosopher of the Common Man: Essays in Honor of John Dewey on His Eightieth Birthday; Schlipp, P. A. (ed.). The Philosophy of John Dewey; Thomas, W. A Bibliography of John Dewey; Thomas, W. A Democratic Philosophy; American Review October 1937; Christian Century November 14, 1934; Current History March 1935; English Review June 1936; International Journal of Ethics October 1935; Philosophical Review September 1938, March 1940; Saturday Review of Literature November 11, 1939; School and Society October 14 and November 11, 1939, January 13, 1940; Sewanee Review January 1940; Southern Review #2 1936, #4 1940; Survey November 1939.

DICKINSON, GOLDSWORTHY LOWES (August 6, 1862-August 3, 1932), English essayist who wrote as G. Lowes Dickinson, was born in London, the son of Lowes Cato Dickinson, an artist, and Margaret Ellen (Williams) Dickinson. While he was an infant the family moved to Hanwell, then a country village though now a London suburb. After a  miserable experience first in private boarding school and then at the Charterhouse, he went up to King's College, Cambridge, from which he was graduated, with a first in classics and the Chancellor's Medal, in 1884. Rather at loose ends, he tried university extension lecturing, decided he was a failure, and began to study medicine. He secured his M.B. degree but never practised, since in 1887 he was made a fellow of King's. With extensions and renewals, he retained his fellowship to his death, forty-five years later. From 1893 to 1896 he was librarian of the college, a sinecure which enabled him to spend most of his time in writing, and from 1896 to 1920 he was lecturer in political science.

Dickinson never married, but spent his whole life as a typical don—so far as his exterior circumstances were concerned. As his friend, the novelist E. M. Forster wrote, "It is difficult to think of a life where so little happened outwardly." He visited Greece in 1900, and made the first of several lecture tours to the United States in 1901, going as far as the University of California. In Yosemite he had a quasi-mystical experience which determined the whole trend of his real life-work—the furthering of the cause of international peace. On this same journey he also saw for the first time India, Japan, and China. To China he was devoted all his life; in his old age he used to wear a Chinese cap to keep draughts from his bald head, and it was to him a symbol of his nearness spiritually to the pacifistic Chinese.

Dickinson's earliest allegiance was to Plato; he started life as a poet and an idealist, and it took years before he could feel himself emotionally at one with present-day humanity. Nevertheless it was to humanity that he dedicated his life. The First World War did not change his convictions; he remained a pacifist, was president of the Union for Democratic Control (which advocated a "peace without victory"), and for a while shared the censorship, persecution, and unpopularity which fell to Ramsay MacDonald and Bertrand Russell. Unlike MacDonald, he never changed his views. He was one of the earliest proponents of the League of Nations, and nearly all his books were dedicated to furthering the cause of international peace. E. Wingfield-Stratford called him "the last Victorian," and certainly he was one of the last of the old noble brood of nineteenth century liberals. He was "an unofficial statesman," as well as "a noble-spirited scholar," and in a Utopia he would have received the public recognition which in actuality he never had.

In appearance he was the lean, spectacled scholar, stooped and with bad skin, but with a sudden smile "which for the moment," said Forster, "made him indescribably beautiful." He dressed dowdily, and was noted for his illegible handwriting (he wrote "good" on a pupil's theme and she asked him indignantly why he had called her a fool!) and for his execrable typewriting. His friendships, especially with younger men, were the one pleasure of his declining years. But failure never discouraged him; to the end he was cheerful, witty, and possessed of "structural charm." He continued to write with youthful verve, often in the Socratic dialogue form he used in his teaching, in that style which was so modulated and persuasive that it was called hypnotic. He died after an operation, three days short of his seventieth birthday.

PRINCIPAL WORKS: From King to King: The Tragedy of the Puritan Revolution, 1891; Revolution and Reaction in Modern France, 1892; The Development of Parliament During the Nineteenth Century, 1895; The Greek View of Life, 1896; The Meaning of Good, 1901; Letters From a Chinese Official (anonymous; in England: Letters from John Chinaman) 1903; Religion: A Criticism and a Forecast, 1905; Justice and Liberty, 1908;

Religion and Immortality, 1911; Appearances: Notes of Travel: East and West, 1914; The European Anarchy, 1916; The Choice Before Us, 1917; The Magic Flute: A Fantasia, 1920; War: Its Nature, Cause, and Cure, 1923; The International Anarchy: 1904-1914, 1926; Goethe and Faust (with F. M. Stawell) 1928; After Two Thousand Years: A Dialogue Between Plato and a Modern Young Man, 1930.

ABOUT: Chesterton, G. K. Heretics; Forster, E. M. Goldsworthy Lowes Dickinson; Fry, R. Goldsworthy Lowes Dickinson; Living Age October 1932, June 1934; London Mercury September 1932; Manchester Guardian August 4, 1932; Nation August 17, 1932; New Statesman and Nation August 13, 1932; Saturday Review of Literature June 9, 1934; Sociological Review October 1932; Spectator August 13, 1932.

DICKINSON, THOMAS HERBERT (November 9, 1877-), American editor and writer on the theatre, reports: "A child of the Civil War, I was born twelve years after its close. In 1865 my maternal grandfather, a maker of cotton machinery in Bedford, England, emigrated to America, going to Charlotte County, Va. My father's family had come to Virginia in 1680. Around 1800 they had taken over a plantation in Charlotte County, near Roanoke. After I was born my father and mother remained in Virginia only until I was four years old. An Ohio boyhood (Richwood, Urbana, Columbus), an Ohio education (Ohio State University), an Ohio marriage (Estelle Reeves, 1900), started me on a course alternating between the formalities of school and the informalities of outdoor life. Running away from college, I joined the Regular Army during the Spanish-American War. Drawn back to the study, I took my M.A. at Columbia, 1900 (Ph.D. Wisconsin, 1906). Then, after a year with the Columbus Dispatch, I proceeded to professorships of English in Texas (Baylor), Ohio State, and Wisconsin.

"The slogan of the first decade of the century in Wisconsin was the return of the government to the people. In my little pond beside the big lake of La Follette the elder Van Hise, Turner, Ely, McCarthy, I began to raise a wind about returning the theatre to the people. In those days there were no Eugene O'Neills, Maxwell Andersons, Robert E. Sherwoods; neither were there a hundred thousand little summer theatres. Most of the writing I did then and for many years after was in an effort to follow through my own speculations about the theatre which would flourish in an ever self-perfecting democracy. The idea had its allurements. That it was over-simplified became clear when the World War and it aftermath demonstrated that democracy is not self-unfolding; it grows only by perpetually combating enemies without and within. Something of the nature and force of these enemies I had an opportunity to observe during the years 1918 to 1922, which I spent with the American Relief Administration in Europe (including some months in Soviet Russia), and during the year 1933 which I spent in Nazi Germany. It happens that the chief lesson that I learned from these experiences was one which I could take to myself as writer: namely, that the particular struggle in which the world is now engaged is one which lays a heavy discipline upon the pen of the writers. Such writing as I have done during recent years has been chiefly directed to the preservation of such records as in a changing world might otherwise be lost or overlooked."

* * *

Professor Dickinson organized the Wisconsin Dramatic Society, from 1913 to 1915 edited the *Play Book*, and edited *Chief Contemporary Dramatists* and *Continental Plays*. He directed the Summer Theatre Institute in Schenectady, N.Y., in 1935, and at Lake George, N.Y., in 1936. He was active in the presidential campaign of Alfred E. Smith in 1928, and the same year was organizer and chairman of the Educational Survey of the Virgin Islands. He lives with his wife on a farm near Wilton, Conn.

PRINCIPAL WORKS: The Case of American Drama, 1915; The Contemporary Drama of England, 1917; The Insurgent Theatre, 1917; Russia in the Red Shadow, 1922; The United States and the League, 1923; The New Old-World, 1923; Playwrights of the New American Theatre, 1925; An Outline of Contemporary Drama, 1927; The Portrait of a Man as Governor, 1928; The Making of American Literature, 1932; The Theatre in a Changing Europe (with others) 1937.

ABOUT: MacGowan, K. Footlights Across America.

"DICKSON, CARTER (or CARR)." See CARR, J. D.

DI DONATO, PIETRO (1911-), American novelist, was born in West Hoboken, N.J., the son of Italian immigrants. His father was a brick-layer. In fact, anyone who has read his only novel so far published knows his simple life-story; for the book is autobiographical in almost every detail. As in the novel, his father was killed in the collapse of a building when he was twelve; his mother died a few years later, leaving him the oldest of a family of eight. He left grammar school to take up his father's trowel and as a young, growing boy he did a man's work at heavy labor. In spite of everything, he managed to attend some night classes and to read voluminously, particularly the Russian novelists. In 1937 *Esquire* printed his first work, a story called "Christ in Concrete." Later this story became the first chapter of his novel, of the same title; it described the hero's father's death, and is one of the big scenes in the book. (Others are the killing of a family friend, and a Gargantuan wedding feast.) At the time, the magazine announced that Mr. Di Donato would expand this story into a book; but he still had his brothers and sisters to support (he still has), and it was not until 1938 that he was able to take a year off to write the

novel. Then he went back to brick-laying, working on the construction of the New York World's Fair. He expects to keep on at his trade at least until all his brothers and sisters are through school. But there is no doubt that he will also keep on writing; he has a real feeling for language.

He is a dark, handsome young man, not tall, but strongly built. He is unmarried, and lives now in New York. His novel has been called by critics passionate, humorous, pathetic, lyrical, bawdy, and crude. His weakness is a certain love of rhetoric for its own sake. But his style is interesting, being based on the spoken language of Italians to whom English is only a second tongue. One critic called his prose "flexible and full of echoes of Italy," and said that the book was "violent in style, incidents, and emotional compression." If he can obtain the leisure to write, Pietro Di Donato still has a great deal to say.

PRINCIPAL WORK: Christ in Concrete, 1939.

ABOUT: Publishers' Weekly January 28, 1939; Time April 10, 1939.

DILLON, GEORGE (November 12, 1906-), American poet, Pulitzer prize winner, writes: "I was born in Jacksonville, Fla. That was my father's home; however, the climate was unsuitable for both my parents, and when I was five years old we moved to Covington, Ky., where my mother's family lived. Thereafter we moved about frequently. I went to school in several places in Kentucky, in Cincinnati, Ohio, and in Webster Groves, Mo. Being an only child and often finding myself in a strange place, I read a good deal for amusement, and this led to an interest in writing. In 1923, after finishing high school, I came to Chicago, where my father had established himself in business some time before. I already felt a strong attraction for the place from reading the books of Dreiser, Ben Hecht, and others. For several months I worked for my father's company helping to make layouts for electrical installations (some of the work being in the stockyards), and in that way got to see some of the more

dynamic aspects of the city's life. I longed to express this new and exciting world in poetry, but realized that I should never be able to do so. My natural predilection was for such poets as Yeats, Housman, Millay, and Frost; and it was the lyrical, subjective type of verse that I attempted to write.

"In the same year, 1923, I entered the University of Chicago, where my interest in verse-writing was further stimulated by contact with the Poetry Club—with two of its graduate members, particularly: Maurice Lesemann and Gladys Campbell. We inaugurated a series of poets' readings, which somehow, against all regulations, we succeeded in putting on in the main University auditorium, charging admission. These were unbelievably successful and ran for several years. Audiences came from all over the city. With the proceeds, after paying the poets' fees, we published a literary magazine, *The Forge.*

"At the University I came under the influence of two remarkable teachers, Edith Foster Flint and Robert Morss Lovett; I also enjoyed the friendship of Robert O. Ballou, at that time literary editor of the *Daily News,* who generously encouraged my efforts at writing poetry. Some of my poems were accepted by magazines. Harriet Monroe invited me to be associate editor of *Poetry,* and during my last two years as an undergraduate I worked part time at the magazine office. My first book of poems, *Boy in the Wind,* was published in 1927.

"After graduation I wrote advertising copy for three years, extolling men's ready-to-wear, motor oil, airplanes—until 1930, when the agency I worked for disbanded. Then I finished another book of poems, *The*

Flowering Stone, published in 1931, and applied for a Guggenheim Fellowship, which enabled me to go abroad the year following. At that time I also received a Pulitzer prize for my second book of poems; so that I was able to travel to most of the European countries, Greece, and North Africa. However, I spent the greater part of two years in Paris alone, attending the University and trying to get a grasp of the language. In 1934 I came back to this country and spent several months with my parents in Richmond, Va., continuing certain studies I had begun abroad—history, economics, Latin poetry. I also finished a number of translations from Baudelaire. 1935 and 1936 I spent free-lancing in New York. I decided to publish some of the Baudelaire translations, encouraged by Edna St. Vincent Millay, who consented to write a preface. While doing so she became greatly interested in Baudelaire and made a number of translations of her own, which she kindly offered to publish in the same volume. This was issued in 1936 as *Flowers of Evil.*

"In 1937 Morton Zabel, who had been editing *Poetry* since Harriet Monroe's death in the previous year, was forced to resign because of his teaching duties, and I was invited to take up the editorship. So far I have been engrossed in learning the job, and I have not done any writing since coming here except an adaptation of Jean Giraudoux's play, *No War in Troy.*"

PRINCIPAL WORKS: Boy in the Wind, 1927; The Flowering Stone, 1931; Flowers of Evil (translations, with E. St. V. Millay) 1936.

ABOUT: Kreymborg, A. Our Singing Strength; Untermeyer, L. Modern American Poetry; Nation February 10, 1932; Poetry March 1932, September 1935; Saturday Review of Literature September 26, 1931.

*DIMNET, ERNEST (July 9, 1866-),

French priest and essayist, best known as Abbé Dimnet, writes: "I was born at Trélon, in northern France. Trélon is a pretty little town in the Fagne, as the western reaches of the Forest of Argonne are called. My early associations were all of woodland or of books, for my people cared for books, and I had free access to the old-fashioned but rich and extremely interesting library of the Trélon

Pinchot

* Died December 8, 1954.

château owned by Comte de Mérode. This nobleman and his wife knew all the best writers of the day, and their conversations gave me a sort of familiarity with literary people. Before I was ten years old I knew, or felt, that I should be a writer myself. I have narrated the story of those early years in *My Old World*.

"Bookish also and old-fashioned was the Cathedral School at Cambria where I was educated. This school presented the extraordinary peculiarity that the students were distinctly superior to their teachers, but had no priggish suspicion that they were: intelligent study was the spirit and the tradition of the school, and this atmosphere reacted on both boys and masters, so that the latter expected and secured more than they could give. I was good at French and Latin composition and developed a knowledge of English which my uncle, who was a priest, had early given me. As the years glided by I took the usual classical degrees, but I specialized in English, went to England as often as I could, and finally competed successfully for *agrégation* in English, a stiff trial which opened for me the doors of establishments of higher education. I taught at the Catholic University of Lille till 1902, and between that date and 1923 at the famous Collège Stanislas, in Paris. After 1923 I found that my literary work and my lecture tours required all my time and resigned from the Collège Stanislas, but I did not leave Paris, where I still reside.

"My first books were written in French, as was natural, but dealt principally with English literature—philosophers or religious apologists in *La Pensée Catholique en Angleterre*, poetry and fiction in *Les Soeurs Brontë* (later admirably translated by Louise Morgan Sill). But I was soon asked to contribute articles in English to the British reviews, and during twenty years I was the Paris correspondent of the *Pilot* and of the well known London *Saturday Review*. This led to the composition of ten books in English as well as to frequent invitations to write for American periodicals. I had not been acquainted with a single American before Col. George Harvey asked me in 1904 to send quarterly letters to the *North American Review*, which he owned at that time. But after a first trip to the United States, in 1908, and especially after the president of Harvard invited me to give a course of Lowell lectures in 1919, America became my field and showed such interest in my books as well as in my lectures that my life seemed to pass from spring into summer. The success of my *The Art of Thinking* in 1928 marked the heyday of this period, and has given me multiform chances to know and appreciate America, as I have tried to show in my latest book, *My New World* (1937). My lecture tours in the United States in the autumn of every year enable me to maintain many happy contacts as well as to feel the pulse of a nation which I have often said would be legally my own if civilization had advanced to the point where a man could be a citizen of the country of his choice as well as of that of his natural allegiance."

* * *

Abbé Dimnet is Canon of Cambrai Cathedral. After the First World War he came to America and raised $100,000 for the restoration of Lille University. Since then, as Lowell lecturer and as lecturer at the Williamstown Institute of Politics, he has become "something of a Franco-American institution." Theodore Purdy, Jr., said of him that he "combines a remarkable faculty for expressing himself in English with the superlative capacity for logical expression so often found in the higher branches of the French educational system."

PRINCIPAL WORKS IN ENGLISH: Paul Bourget, 1913; France Herself Again, 1914; French Grammar Made Clear, 1922; From a Paris Balcony, 1924; France and Her Problems, 1924; The Brontë Sisters, 1927; The Art of Thinking, 1928; What We Live By, 1932; My Old World, 1935; My New World, 1937.

ABOUT: Dimnet, E. My Old World, My New World; Rotarian July 1939, June 1940; Saturday Review of Literature October 19, 1929, March 23, 1935, December 11, 1937; Time December 30, 1937.

"DINE, S. S. VAN." See WRIGHT, W. H.

"DINESEN, ISAK." See BLIXEN, K. D.

"DIPLOMAT." See CARTER, J. F.

DITMARS, RAYMOND LEE (June 20, 1876-May 12, 1942), American naturalist, wrote to the editors of this volume shortly before his death: "I was born in Newark, N.J., and graduated from the Barnard Military School in 1891. Soon after, I obtained a position in the American Museum of Natural History, where by work related to mounting and labeling insect specimens. I remained there for five years, then sought more active work as a reporter for the New York *Times*. While on that paper I was sent to the Bronx to interview Dr. William T. Hornaday, the director of the newly formed Zoological Park. Finding that I was intensely interested in animals, he declared that I should be at the Park, not with a newspaper. I made the change, and have been there ever since, first as curator of reptiles, then in charge of the department of mammals, and since Dr. Hornaday's death as director. In 1903 I was married to Clara Elizabeth Hurd, and we have two daughters.

"Aside from my work at the Park, my principal interest is in writing books and making motion pictures of different kinds of animals. Both record experiences in exploring tropical countries. In recognition of scientific work, I have been made a fellow of the New York Academy of Sciences, a fellow of the New York Zoological Society, a life member of the American Museum of Natural History, a corresponding member of the Zoological Society of London, and in 1930 I was awarded the honorary degree of Litt.D. by Lincoln Memorial University."

* * *

Dr. Ditmars' father was a Confederate veteran who had been on Lee's staff—whence came the son's middle name. He was a slender man, with military bearing, bald, with a clipped gray moustache, aquiline features, and penetrating gray-blue eyes. One of his achievements was perfection of a serum which is an antidote to the bites of all poisonous North American snakes. His hobby was meteorology; he built a weather station in his home, and for years went to the West Indies annually in the hope of observing a hurricane. He probably knew more about reptiles than any man alive, and he wrote factual but lively books both about them and about other animals. As one critic remarked, "he has seldom foisted on his public an uninteresting word."

Dr. Ditmars died at sixty-five, after terminating (January 1942), because of illness, his forty-two years of active service at the New York Zoological Park. He remained honorary curator until his death.

PRINCIPAL WORKS: The Reptile Book, 1907; Reptiles of the World, 1909; Snakes of the World, 1931; Strange Animals I Have Known, 1931; Thrills of a Naturalist's Quest, 1932; Forest of Adventure, 1933; Confessions of a Scientist, 1934; The Book of Zoögraphy, 1934; The Book of Prehistoric Animals, 1935; The Book of Living Reptiles, 1936; The Making of a Scientist, 1937; The Book of Insect Oddities, 1938; The Fight to Live, 1938; A Field Book of North American Snakes, 1939.

ABOUT: Ditmars, R. L. The Making of a Scientist; American Magazine August 1932; New York Times May 13, 1942; Saturday Review of Literature December 17, 1932; Time September 20, 1937.

*DITZEN, RUDOLPH ("Hans Fallada") (July 21, 1893-   ), German novelist, writes: "I was born Wilhelm Friedrich Rudolph Ditzen, in Greifswald, Pomerania. My father was a jurist. The first eighteen years of my life were spent in Berlin and Leipzig, but I never became a real city dweller. It was perhaps from my Frisian and Hanoverian ancestors that I got my

impulse towards the country, flowing water, animals, and the life of the soil. As far as I can recollect, I was pretty much of a good-for-nothing, always sick, given to tears, a pronounced solitary, and happy only in the company of animals. Very early in life I found an escape in the fantasy world of books. At fourteen I had completely gone through my father's library, including the carefully hidden sets of Zola and Boccaccio.

"It is no wonder that I never graduated, but instead, one fine day, found myself in the country as an agricultural student on an estate in Thuringia. For six weeks I worked with a dung fork, in order to show that I was really serious about my love for the land. I spent the next six weeks as a stable boy. I became a notable cow- and horse-midwife.

"Then I became unfaithful to the soil again. Back into the city I went; I became a clerk, a bookkeeper, an estate agent, a dealer in provisions, a potato grower. This lasted for several years.

"In the meantime, between 1920 and 1922, I wrote my first novels. The first enjoyed a very slight success, but it was written entirely in the expressionistic style, and is no longer readable. The next, *Anton und Gerda,* was a failure for my publisher—and yet I still believe it is my most creative book.

"Then followed six years of wandering, silence, inability to write, a surrender of the very thought of writing. Crippled years, sick years, years of beggary and patient waiting, and also, though I did not know it, years of apprenticeship. Then, slowly, a new beginning. I married Anna Issel,

* Died February 6, 1947.

settled down in a little town in Holstein, and solicited classified advertising for a provincial paper. Finally I was allowed to do a little writing. I lived from hand to mouth, and found great joy in living thus quietly with my wife and my child. . . . I found myself again in Berlin. Slowly, with what time I could spare from my office work, I wrote *Bauern, Bonzen und Bomben.*"

* * *

Here, on the threshold of his real career, Herr Ditzen ends his autobiography. The book he wrote after his long silence was a *succès d'éstime*, but little more; he could not yet live by writing alone; and when he wrote *Little Man, What Now?* he was himself a "little man," unemployed and distracted by worry. The immense success of the book dazed him. From its profits he achieved his dream—he bought a farm in Pomerania.

He has never again achieved the universal appeal of the first book which made him known outside of Germany. He has since written two other realistic novels, but for the most part his output has consisted, disappointingly, of rather weak fantasy and sentimentality. Perhaps it is the only thing he can do under current conditions; for he is almost the only author of reputation to remain in Nazi Germany and accommodate himself to the Nazi régime. He said long ago: "I want to write books and live in the country": and to live quietly in the country in Germany under Hitler one must write the kind of books Ditzen has written. He was still at his farm in Carlwitz in January 1940.

Ditzen is blond, slight, and bespectacled. H. A. Wyk spoke of his "wide tranquil face, his luminous gray-green eyes." But under the tranquillity still rests a distrust of good fortune. He is himself still essentially one of the "little men," the "unimportant people," with their simplicity and courage. It was this fact which gave to *Little Man, What Now?* what Christopher Morley called "its quickening sympathy, its softening effect upon our hard crust of daily unconcern," and made it, in spite of its frequent sentimentality, a warm and moving book—almost the last of its kind to appear before sympathy went out of style in Germany.

WORKS AVAILABLE IN ENGLISH: Little Man, What Now? 1933; The World Outside, 1934; Once We Had a Child, 1935; An Old Heart Goes A-Journeying, 1936; Sparrow Farm, 1937; Wolf Among Wolves, 1938.

ABOUT: Living Age June 1933; Neue Rundschau December 1934, December 1938.

*DIVER, Mrs. MAUD (MARSHALL),
English novelist, writes: "I was born [Katherine Helen Maud Marshall] at Murree, a hill station in the Himalayas; my father, Col. C. H. T. M a r s h a l l, having served all his life in India as a soldier-civilian: that is to say, a soldier who enters civilian service, a s they no longer do n o w. From him and from his distin-guished aunt, Honoria Lawrence, wife of Sir Henry Lawrence—I inherited my love for that great country and an affectionate understanding of its people. Many tributes have been paid to me on that head from Indians themselves. In due time my sister and I were sent to England for education; and at sixteen I came back to India, with a sense of returning to things dimly familiar and delightful: the smells of the bazaar, the camels and elephants, the real splendors and tinsel splendors, so sharply contrasted in India, and the delight of riding again. But, for me, the supreme revelation of India was the Himalayas. Born among them, a child of the Hills, I have ever remained so in spirit, as many of my books bear witness.

"A lifelong friend came out with me to India—Mrs. Fleming, sister of Rudyard Kipling. We were quickly drawn together by our love of poets and poetry, our early desire to write, in some way, ourselves. Her genius for criticism helped me much in my early work.

"In India I married a subaltern in the Royal Warwickshire Regiment, now Lt.-Col. T. Diver; and soon after, we went home to England with his regiment. It was only then that I began writing short stories and articles, in the intervals of teaching my only son. Not until 1906 did I write *Captain Desmond V.C.*, which was published in the following year. It was an immediate success and has been translated into several languages. From that time onward, I lived for the work that I had always longed to do. I warm up to a new theme slowly; but once the characters have come to life and taken possession of me, I *live* in them, working practically all day and every day, most often out of doors in my balcony, or sitting on the heather near my present home in Dorset.

"The Indian novels did not at once catch on in America. The first book that gave me a wider public there was *The Strong Hours,* dealing with English characters tested in the Great War. After that, my two chief American successes were Indian novels, *A Wild Bird* and *Ships of Youth.* But the book that has added most to my reputation is the life of my great aunt, Honoria Lawrence.

"One curious faculty that I discovered in myself has helped to enrich the scope and variety of my work. Though I know India well, there are many places described in my books that my actual eyes have never seen. I have read or heard about them. I have visualized them in my mind; and in every case I have received proof abounding that my vivid presentment of those places was true in detail and in spirit. Whether this is a usual or unusual faculty I have no means of judging. I mention it only as bearing on the wide range of scenic setting in my books."

* * *

Mrs. Diver, blonde in youth, is now a dignified white-haired lady with keen blue eyes. She does not use a typewriter, but writes with a pencil, on her knee—out of doors, whatever the weather. The *Bookman* remarked: "With the aid of her vitality, her sympathetic interest in human beings, and her close acquaintance with India, Maud Diver has woven into her many novels a rich and engrossing picture of Anglo-Indian life."

PRINCIPAL WORKS: Captain Desmond V.C., 1907; The Great Amulet, 1908; Candles in the Wind, 1909; The Englishwoman in India (non-fiction) 1909; Lilamani, 1911; The Hero of Herat, 1912; The Judgment of the Sword, 1913; Desmond's Daughter, 1916; Unconquered, 1917; Strange Roads, 1918; The Strong Hours, 1919; Far to Seek, 1921; Lonely Furrow, 1923; Siege Perilous and Other Stories, 1924; Coombe St. Mary's, 1925; But Yesterday, 1927; A Wild Bird, 1929; Ships of Youth, 1931; The Singer Passes, 1934; Kabul to Kandahar (non-fiction) 1935; Honoria Lawrence (non-fiction) 1936; The Dream Prevails, 1938; Phoenix, 1939; Sylvia Lyndon, 1940.

ABOUT: Bookman December 1931.

DIXELIUS-BRETTNER, HILDUR

(1879-), Swedish novelist whose translated works are signed Hildur Dixelius, writes (in English); "I am a child of the North, born in Neder-Kalix in North Sweden. My father was a clergyman; the ancestors of my mother have played a great rôle in the religious life of Sweden. My chief work, the novel trilogy *Prästdottern* (*The Minister's Daughter*), *Prästdotterns Son* (*The Son*), and *Sonsonern* (*The Grandson*), takes its material mostly from the

life of my ancestors. The novels are founded on solid studies in public and family archives. Several of my books, novels as well as collections of shorter sketches, treat of motives taken from the North of Sweden, its landscape and its inhabitants. My later production has been largely influenced by contemporaneous psychology (psycho-analysis). I should like to mention my novel, *I Bojor* (*Enchained*), which had been pointed out by the critics as the most characteristic psycho-analytical novel in Swedish literature. But I must also add that I am by no means an orthodox adherent of the school of Sigmund Freud; I  am, rather, attracted by the profound analysis of the soul-life by C. G. Jung.

"To speak of my external life, I was married in 1923 to the German philosopher Ernst von Aster, at that time professor at the University of Giessen. In 1933 my husband was dismissed for political reasons, and we took up our domicile in Sweden. I bought there in the country a little cottage which was a hundred years old, very characteristic of the style of this time and of the country of Ångermanland, and which I restored and endowed with modern comforts.

"In 1936 my husband was called to the University of Istanbul. These years in Istanbul have been very rich and interesting for me. I have learned to love the Eastern world and especially the Turkish people. I think my literary production will also be influenced by my stay in Turkey."

* * *

Besides her novels and her many short stories, Hildur Dixelius has written several plays. Her social drama, *Mördarin (The Murderer)* was produced in Stockholm in 1928. As might be expected from her interest in psycho-analysis, her books show much depth of insight and her primary emphasis is on the psychological development of her characters. Her work has been translated into German, French, Norwegian, Finnish, and Dutch, as well as into English. In Sweden her most popular novel has been *Far och Son (Father and Son)*, which went into three editions, 1916, 1917, and 1918. Her latest work is a collection of novelettes, *Skohandlare Sandin och hans Barn (The Shoe-Seller Sandin and His Children)*, published in 1936 and not yet translated into English.

WORKS AVAILABLE IN ENGLISH: The Minister's Daughter, 1926; The Son, 1928; The Grandson, 1928 (as "Sara Alelia," 1936).

ABOUT: Dixelius, H. The Minister's Daughter (see Foreword by E. Garnett).

DIXON, RICHARD WATSON. See "BRITISH AUTHORS OF THE 19TH CENTURY"

*DIXON, THOMAS (January 11, 1864-), American novelist and clergyman, was born of Revolutionary stock on a farm in Shelby, Cleveland County, N.C. His parents were the Rev. Thomas Dixon, a Baptist minister, and Amanda Elizabeth (McAfee) Dixon. His first story, written in his teens and published in a college periodical, had to do with the Ku Klux Klan. Dixon received his M.A. degree from Wake Forest College in 1883. At twenty, when he was living in New York, he paid $300 to a theatrical manager to play the Duke of Richmond in a road company of *Richard III.* At Herkimer, N.Y., the manager disappeared with most of the proceeds of the tour.

Dixon returned to the South, spending 1883-84 at Johns Hopkins University studying history and politics. Obtaining an LL.B. from the Greensboro (N.C.) Law School in 1886, he was admitted that year to the bar in all courts—North Carolina, U.S. District, and the Supreme Court. In 1885-86 Dixon was member of the North Carolina legislature; his maiden speech was reported by Walter Hines Page, then of the Raleigh *Chronicle.* Dixon married Harriet Bussey of Columbus, Ga., in March 1886, and they had two sons and a daughter. The present Mrs. Dixon, whom he married in March 1939, was Madelyn Donovan of Raleigh, N.C.

Resigning from the legislature to enter the Baptist ministry in October 1886, Dixon became pastor at Raleigh the next year, and served in Boston, Mass., in 1888-89. The next ten years were spent in New York City, part of them spent wrestling with the problem of providing decent living quarters for three growing children. During this period Dixon was a popular lyceum lecturer. In 1902 his first novel dealing with the race question in America, *The Leopard's*

Spots, was published, followed the next year by *The One Woman: A Story of Modern Utopia,* which was a best seller. It dealt with a crusading clergyman of slightly philandering tendencies who becomes involved in a murder trial, and it was dedicated to his mother, "To Whose Scotch Love of Romantic Literature I Owe the Heritage of Eternal Youth." *The Clansman* (1905) sold even better; exhibiting genuine if still somewhat crude narrative gifts, it was told from a virulently Southern point of view and painted the Ku Klux Klan as a band of dedicated knights extirpating an intolerable menace. The inflammatory episode of Marion Lenoir, who leaps with her mother from a cliff after being assaulted by a Negro, was said to be based on an actual case in Dixon's own home town. It formed one of the most poignant episodes in D. W. Griffith's epochal silent film, *The Birth of a Nation* (1914), based on the Dixon novel.

In 1911 Dixon toured in the leading *rôle* of his own play, *The Sins of the Father.* Successive novels were also written in a rather high-pitched vein. *The Flaming Sword,* published in Atlanta in 1939, visualized the destruction of American democracy by the red menace, primarily through Communistic corruption of the black race. From 1889 to 1903 Dixon was a clerk of the U.S. District Court, Eastern District of North Carolina. A Democrat, but a strong opponent of the New Deal, he makes his home in Raleigh.

PRINCIPAL WORKS: The Leopard's Spots, 1902; The One Woman, 1903; The Clansman, 1905; The Life Worth Living, 1905; The Traitor, 1907; Comrades, 1909; The Root of Evil, 1911; The Sins of the Father, 1912; The Southerner, 1913; The Victim, 1914; The Foolish Virgin, 1915; The Birth of a Nation (photoplay) 1915; The Fall of a Nation, 1916; The Way of a Man, 1918; A Man of the People, 1920; The Man in Gray, 1921; The Black Hood, 1924; The Love Complex, 1925; The Sun Virgin, 1929; Companions, 1931; The Inside Story of the Harding Tragedy (with H. M. Daugherty) 1932; A Dreamer in Portugal, 1934; The Flaming Sword, 1939.

ABOUT: Baldwin, C. C. The Men Who Make Our Novels; Bookman February 1905.

DOBELL, BERTRAM (January 9, 1842-December 14, 1914), English poet and bibliophile, was born in Battle, Sussex, the son of Edward Dobell, a tailor, and Elizabeth (Eldridge) Dobell. Early in his childhood the family moved to London, where the father became paralyzed. The boy had to leave school and become an errand boy and a grocer's clerk; but even then, such was his love of literature, he collected old books from the penny stands in the bookstalls. In 1869 he married Eleanor Wymer, and with a capital of ten pounds opened a stationery shop. This gradually grew into

a large and celebrated second-hand book store, which his sons carried on after his death. It was moved to Charing Cross Road, its present location, in 1887.

In 1874 Dobell, a Rationalist and a reader of Bradlaugh's *National Reformer,* found in its pages the poems of James Thomson ("B.V"). Immensely impressed, he succeeded in meeting the poet, and became that unhappy man's most loyal and devoted friend, bringing about the publication of two volumes of his poems and writing his biography after Thomson's death in 1882. Like Thomson, he was devoted to Shelley, and published facsimiles of some of his poems, as well as his letters to Elizabeth Hitchener. His most noted achievement, however, was the discovery of a forgotten seventeenth century poet, Thomas Traherne. Later he brought forth another, William Strode. His annual catalogues were filled with literary gossip and criticism, and became sought-after items. About his own poems he was very modest, but they were deeply felt and had much nobility, especially his sonnets, which reveal his kindly, sensitive, highly ethical nature.

Temperamentally Dobell had much in common with that other scholar-bibliomaniac, Charles Lamb, about whom he wrote. He shared Lamb's gregariousness, good nature, sleepless intellectual curiosity, and modesty. The World War in a way caused his death; he had long been ill and he became obsessed by the news of death and disaster so that he seemed to lose the will to live, dying just before his seventy-third birthday, at Hampstead. Three sons and two daughters survived him.

Traherne, a fine poet though not so great as Dobell was inclined to think him, had left nothing but an anonymous volume of poems. Scholars who had studied the poems were inclined to ascribe them to Henry Vaughan. It was Dobell whose scholarship led to the identification of the real author, and he followed this by research into Traherne's life and by the critical edition of the poems themselves.

Dobell's other bibliographical triumph was the *Catalogue of Books Printed for Private Circulation* (1906), a tremendous task. Though the catalogue is not complete, it is still the best (and indeed the only) existent list of books in English published by or for their authors. All of Dobell's own works were so printed, either by himself or by private presses in England and America.

PRINCIPAL WORKS: *Prose*—Sidelights on Charles Lamb, 1903; The Laureate of Pessimism, 1910. *Poetry*—Rosemary and Pansies, 1903; Cleon in the Palace of Truth, 1904; A Century of Sonnets, 1910; The Dreamer of the Castle of Indolence, 1915; Sonnets and Lyrics of the War, 1915; A Lover's Moods, 1923.

ABOUT: Bradbury, S. Bertram Dobell; Nation December 21, 1914, February 11, 1915.

*DOBIE, CHARLES CALDWELL (March 15, 1881-), American novelist historian and short story writer, was born in San Francisco,

still lives there, and has been more closely identified with the city than any author of recent times. He had only a grammar school education; his father's death obliged him to go to work at fourteen, first as an office boy in a fire and marine insurance company. He remained in the insurance business until 1915, by which time he was earning enough by his writing to live on the proceeds. For from boyhood he had kept assiduously at work, trying his hand at stories outside of office hours. It was a long time before he met with any encouragement whatever; his first story was published, free, in the *Argonaut*, a San Francisco weekly, when he was nearly thirty; and it was several years more before he made his first sales—to H. L. Mencken, then editor of *Smart Set*. After that his rise was rapid, though it was 1920 before he published a book. He has written many plays, some produced by the Bohemian Club at its Grove in Sonoma County, Calif.

Mr. Dobie has never married. He is in a way a throw-back to the San Francisco of the early 1900's, a dignified but convivial bachelor, an essentially romantic story-teller who thinks of himself as a realist in style, but whose realism strongly resembles that of, say, Frank Norris, and is strictly bounded by the interests of a more stable and limited era. He is in a sense (without any invidious implication) a professional San Franciscan; his native city, in which he has always lived, with which he endured earthquake and fire, is his first love. He has celebrated it in half

* Died January 11, 1943.

a dozen reminiscent books of history and fiction, deftly written, smooth and competent, but all nostalgic for a past which was his youth. As Carey McWilliams has said, he has become the chief "conservative interpreter of San Francisco." The city he knows and adores antedates the bridges and all they involve; it is the city of ferries, cable-cars, and flower-stands, viewed through the eyes of a prosperous middle-class gentleman bred in the old tradition.

PRINCIPAL WORKS: The Blood-Red Dawn, 1920; Broken to the Plow, 1921; Less Than Kin, 1926; The Arrested Moment (short stories) 1927; San Francisco: A Pageant, 1933; Portrait of a Courtesan, 1934; San Francisco Tales, 1935; San Francisco's Chinatown, 1936; San Francisco Adventures (short stories) 1937; The Crystal Ball (short stories) 1937.

ABOUT: Dobie, C. C. Less Than Kin (see Preface by G. Atherton); San Francisco Tales (see Preface by K. F. Gerould).

DÖBLIN, ALFRED (August 10, 1878-), German novelist, playwright, poet, and essayist was born in Stettin, a Pomer-

anian seaport on the Baltic, where he spent the first ten years of his life and attended elementary school. In 1888, his parents, Max Döblin and Sophie Freudenheim, moved to Berlin. Alfred attended Volksschule, a Gymnasium, and the medical schools at Berlin and Freiburg universities. In 1905 he obtained his M.D. degree and left for Regensburg as newspaper correspondent. From the earliest Döblin had been interested in writing, trying his hand at epic poetry, drama, philosophy and criticism. By 1900 he had completed a full-length novel, Die Jagenden Rosse, in 1902 two novelettes—none of them ever published— and in 1903 Der Schwarze Vorhang, which was published in 1919. His first work to appear in print were his short stories occasionally published in the journal Der Sturm (1904-11), the period during which he wrote the one-act Lydia und Mäxchen (1905) and a few essays on philosophy: Gespräche mit Kalypso über die Musik (1906), on aesthetics, and the ontological Das Ich über der Natur (1907), which, in expanded form, was published twenty-one years later.

Returning to Berlin in 1911, Döblin settled down, as a specialist in nervous disorders, in the working-class district of Alexanderplatz. In 1912 he married Miss Erna Reiss and a

son, Peter, was born the same year. Three others followed: Wolfgang, 1915; Klaus, 1917; and Stefan, 1926.

In 1913 Döblin collected under the title Die Ermordung einer Butterblume a dozen of his Der Sturm stories. However, it was not until 1915, when nearing his fortieth birthday, that he attained recognition with his long Chinese novel, Die Drei Sprünge des Wang-lun. During the pre-Expressionist period a tendency toward the exotic already was apparent. Through his mixture of Taoist philosophy and his "profuse display of dragons, lotuses, and Oriental magic," to use A. Eloesser's words, Döblin struck a fashionable chord which won him numerous admirers. However, the First World War soon took people's minds away from literature, and shortly thereafter Döblin joined the army as physician and remained at the front for the next three years, participating in the Verdun campaign. While at the front two of his novels appeared: Wadzeks Kampf und die Dampfturbine (1918) in which he came to grips with machinery, and his early Der Schwarze Vorhang (1919). At the time Döblin was finishing his ambitious novel Wallenstein (1920), in which, against the background of the Thirty Years War, he posed the philosophical problem of Die Drei Sprünge—exemplifying the "wanting-to-do" in the figure of Wallenstein and the "not-wanting-to-do" in that of Emperor Ferdinand.

Back from the War, Döblin turned again to journalism, writing under the pseudonym "Linke-Poot" numerous political satires which were collected in 1921 under the title Der Deutsche Maskenball. After an interlude devoted to play writing, Lusitania (1920) and the four-act Die Nonnen von Kamenaden (1923), Döblin led his satiric vein, illumined by certain utopian elements, to a long fantasy à la H. G. Wells, Berge, Meere, und Giganten (1924), describing the age of the superman (A.D. 2700-3000) in which machinery becomes supreme and brings havoc to man. On his return from a journey to Poland—Reise in Polen (1925)—, his work already well recognized in official circles, he was elected to the Prussian Academy (1926). As soon as he completed the epic poem, Manas (1927), which exhibited a Hindu conception of life, Döblin set to his major work, Alexanderplatz (1929). In this work Döblin the scientist, versed in a professional way in morbid psychology and psychoanalysis, met Döblin, the Expressionist poet, experimenter in literary technique, and Döblin, the old tenant of Alexanderplatz, who knew its secrets and recondite ways. And yet, strictly speaking, Döblin's novel is not a faithful picture of the life of Berlin's *lumpenproletariat* but rather a cinematographic, highly melodramatic version of it, in which life passes rapidly and glamorously amidst sudden death and ghastly crimes. The critics conditioned by *Ulysses'* lurid atmosphere saw then in *Alexanderplatz* "a great masterpiece"; today, in perspective, it is perhaps but an interesting experiment, somewhat *outré*. Thanks to its many translations into French, Spanish, English, Italian, and Dutch, however, it made Döblin's name known the world over.

In 1931 his three-act play *Die Ehe* was extremely successful and the following year his work of fiction, *Giganten,* consolidated his reputation, but with the rising tide of Nazi anti-Semitism, he left the Prussian Academy and Germany, and heard in exile about the burning of his books. Then until Holland fell, his works were published in Amsterdam, including his essays on the Jewish question; his novels, *Babylonische Wanderung* (1934), *Pardon Wird Nicht Gegeben* (1935), available in English as *Men Without Mercy,* and the sequel novel *Das Land ohne Tod* comprising *Die Fahrt ins Land ohne Tod* (1937) and *Die Blaue Tiger* (1938), which dramatizes Indian civilization and the role of Bartolomé de las Casas.

After living for some time with his family in Palestine, Döblin came to the United States and is currently in Hollywood.

WORKS AVAILABLE IN ENGLISH TRANSLATION: Alexanderplatz, 1931; Men Without Mercy, 1937; The Living Thoughts of Confucius (ed.) 1940.

ABOUT: Beach, J. W. Twentieth Century Novel; Bertaux, F. A Panorama of German Literature; Bithell, J. Modern German Literature; Döblin, A. Loerke, O. Alfred Döblin im Buch, zu Haus, auf der Strasse; Eloesser, A. Modern German Literature; Kayser, R. Dichterköpfe; Mann, E. & K. Escape to Life; Mahrholz, W. Deutsche Literatur der Gegenwart; Samuel, R. & Thomas, R. H. Expressionism in German Life, Literature, and the Theatre; Drama April 1391; Neue Rundschau August 1928; Neue Schweizer Rundschau August 1928.

DOBSON, HENRY AUSTIN. See "BRITISH AUTHORS OF THE 19TH CENTURY"

DOLE, NATHAN HASKELL (August 31, 1852-May 9, 1935), American man of letters, was born in Chelsea, Mass., the son of the Rev. Nathan Dole (Bowdoin 1836, Bangor Theological Seminary 1841), descended from one of the early settlers of Newburyport, Bay Colony. His mother was Caroline (Fletcher) Dole,

whose grandfather, William Spaulding, was wounded at the Battle of Bunker Hill. The Rev. Mr. Dole was editor of publications of the Missionary House, Boston. After Phillips Andover Academy, Nathan Dole went to Harvard, graduating in 1874. The next year he taught at De Veaux College, Suspension Bridge, N.Y.; was instructor in Greek and English literature at Worcester High School in 1875-76; and for two years was preceptor at Derby Academy, Hingham, Mass.

In 1880 he came to New York City for a brief period of newspaper work, writing for the Boston *Commonwealth* and the San Francisco *Chronicle.* Next he went to Philadelphia as literary, art, and music critic of the Philadelphia *Press* remaining from 1881 to 1887, when he became literary adviser to Crowell & Co., publishers, for four years. Five months were spent as secretary of the department of publicity for D. Appleton & Co. Dole married Helen James Bennett, also a writer and translator, in 1882, and they had three sons and a daughter. They lived at Jamaica Plain, Mass., spending the summers at "The Moorings," Ogunquit, Maine, and in 1929 moved to Riverdale-on-Hudson, N.Y., to an apartment overlooking the Ethical Culture School. Dole was an active member of the Poetry Society of America, seldom missing a meeting.

Charles Eliot Norton of Harvard benevolently praised the "simplicity, sincerity and grace of rhythm" of some early poems of Dole's. He wrote the Phi Beta Kappa poem for the meeting of the Tufts College chapter in 1904, and was made an honorary member. As an ardent admirer of *The Rubáiyát,* he wrote a romance, *Omar the Tent-Maker* (1899) and was president of the Omar Khayyám Society of America. He edited libraries of famous literature and oratory with Caroline Ticknor; a *Young Folks' Library* with Thomas Bailey Aldrich and others; was responsible for the tenth edition of Bartlett's *Familiar Quotations;* and performed similar useful tasks of literary hackwork. Dole's translations of Tolstoy were for a time the only English versions available; Tolstoy did not particularly care for them, and gave his *imprimatur* to those done by the Englishman Aylmer Maude.[qv] After Dole's death at Yonkers, N.Y., of heart-disease in his eighty-third year, survived by his wife and all four children, the lexicographer Frank Vizetelly wrote to the New York *Times* defending Dole's Tolstoy translations against the animadversions of various English critics. Dole also translated works by Valdès, von Scheffel, Von Koch, Daudet, Verga, and hundreds of songs and lyrical pieces for music from the Russian. His autobiography, which he called his "egotistigraphy" failed to find a publisher. He was a handsome young man, and an old gentleman of engaging appearance.

PRINCIPAL WORKS: Young Folks' History of Russia, 1881; A Score of Famous Composers, 1891; Not Angels Quite, 1893; On the Point (novel) 1895; The Hawthorne Tree (poems) 1895; Life of Francis William Bird, 1897; Joseph Jefferson at Home, 1898; Omar the Tent-Maker: A Romance of Old Persia, 1899; Peace and Progress (poems) 1904; The Building of the Organ (poems) 1906; Six Italian Essays, 1907; Alaska, 1909; The Pilgrims and Other Poems, 1911; Life of Count Tolstoi, 1911; The Spell of Switzerland, 1913; America in Spitsbergen, 1922.

ABOUT: Harvard University, Class of 1874: 25th, 50th, and 60th Anniversary Reports; New York Times May 10, 13, 1935; Poetry July 1935; Publishers' Weekly May 18, 1935.

DONATO. See DI DONATO

DONN-BYRNE. See BYRNE

"DOOLEY, MR." See DUNNE, F. P.

DOOLITTLE, HILDA (September 10, 1886-   ), American poet who writes always as "H.D.," was born in Bethlehem, Pa., the  daughter of Charles L. Doolittle, professor of mathematics and astronomy at Lehigh University, and his second wife, Helen Eugeneia (Wolle) Doolittle. When she was nine the family moved to Philadelphia, where her father became director of the Flower Astronomical Observatory of the University of Pennsylvania. She was educated at the Gordon School, and the Friends' Central School, Philadelphia, and at Bryn Mawr College. She was obliged to leave Bryn Mawr, however, in her sophomore year, because of ill health.

Her first published work consisted of stories for children which appeared in a Presbyterian paper. In 1911 she went to Europe, expecting to stay for the summer. As Iris Barry put it, she "never came back, having been drawn into the Imagist movement by Ezra Pound." Pound sent some of her poems to Harriet Monroe, editor of *Poetry*, who published them in 1913. Soon she became known as one of the leaders of the Imagist poets, a school which tried to convey direct impressions to the reader through the choice of words. In 1938 she won the Helen Haire Levinson Prize offered annually by *Poetry*.

In 1913 Miss Doolittle married Richard Aldington, then also an Imagist poet, but now well known as a novelist. With him she began the translations of Greek poets which she has since carried on alone. When he joined the British army during the World War she took over his editorship of the magazine, the *Egoist*. They were divorced several years after the war.

Her only visit to America since 1911 was in 1920, when she stayed a few months in California. On her return to Europe she settled in a small town near Lake Geneva, which is still her home.

"H.D." looks like a poet, with deep-set gray eyes and delicately aquiline features. Iris Barry, who met her in 1932, speaks of her looking "haunted."

Dorothy Emerson remarked of her work that "we read with our ears, . . . for in her work is the sound of voices." R. P. Blackmur spoke of her "clarity of sound, swift rhythm, economy of words, and a direct appeal to the visual imagination." Harriet Monroe said that she and the other Imagists "shook the Victorian tradition and discarded its excesses."

PRINCIPAL WORKS: Sea Garden, 1916; Hymen, 1921; Heliodora and Other Poems, 1924; Collected Poems, 1925; Palimpsest (novel) 1926; Hippolytus Temporizes (tragedy in verse) 1927; Hedylus (novel) 1928; Red Roses From Bronze, 1932; Ion of Euripides (translation) 1937; Collected Poems, 1940.

ABOUT: Poetry November 1932, December 1937, November 1938; Saturday Review of Literature March 16, 1940; Scholastic January 26, 1935; Wilson Library Bulletin February 1931.

DOREN. See VAN DOREN

DOS PASSOS, JOHN RODERIGO (January 14, 1896-   ), American novelist, writes: "I was born in Chicago, somewhere on Lakeshore Drive, I think, in 1896, was carted around a good deal as a child, to Mexico, to Belgium, lived in England a little, in Washington, D.C., and on a farm in Westmoreland County in tidewater Virginia. My father was a New York lawyer, son of a Portuguese immigrant; my mother's people came from Maryland and Virginia. After graduating from Harvard I went to Spain with the idea of studying in an architectural school; when the United States went into the European War, I got myself into a couple of ambulance services and finally into the United States Medical  Corps as a private. After the peace I worked as a newspaper correspondent and free lance in Spain, Mexico, New York, the near East. The fact that I've managed to scrape up a living by writing has cut me off from

E. Schaal

several other trades and professions I should have liked to follow."

* * *

John Dos Passos is the son of John R. Dos Passos, a "self-made literate," who had entered the Civil War as a drummer boy only to be invalided out at the age of fourteen, and Lucy Addison (Sprigg) Dos Passos. From the reading of Frederick Marryat's novels he acquired a love of the sea, and for a while had his heart set on Annapolis. He prepared at the Choate School, and entered Harvard at a time when E. E. Cummings, Gilbert Seldes, and other young aesthetes were writing for the *Dial*. He was graduated *cum laude* in 1916.

One Man's Initiation—1917, his first book, a somewhat pallid novel, emerged directly from his experiences as an ambulance driver for the French. It was published (1920) in England during a period of severe reaction to inflated patriotism. His much more mature war novel *Three Soldiers*, came two years later. Like William Faulkner's *Soldier's Pay* and Laurence Stalling's *Plumes*, it was one of the earliest of the novels to debunk the so-called glory of the World War, a school which culminated in Remarque's *All Quiet on the Western Front*.

With *Manhattan Transfer*, a novel and a tremendous portrait of ponderous and amorphous New York, Dos Passos hit his stride. It belongs to the same *genre* as his highly significant trilogy, *U. S. A.* (combining *The 42nd Parallel, Nineteen Nineteen,* and *The Big Money*), using Society as the hero in a kind of contemporary history written with a passionate accuracy of detail. The

"movie" technique of his plays—*The Garbage Man, Airways, Inc.,* and others —make them sound better than they read. He has also written several highly unconventional travel books and some verse.

He still has the shyness and enthusiasm of extreme youth. Yet his books leave a somewhat more defeatist than militantly affirmative impression. For some time he has, against his will, been a focus of dissension in radical groups, because he does not adhere in orthodox manner to any one faction but simply veers far to the left. "I'm merely an old-fashioned believer," he says. His novel, *Adventures of a Young Man*, is his answer to the attacks made upon him on this ground. He has always had a sound interest in the underdog and an active indignation over injustices of any kind. During a Sacco-Vanzetti demonstration in August 1927 he was arrested in a picket line and incarcerated in the same cell with the Communist Michael Gold.

Beyond Dos Passos' thick spectacles there are the eyes of a rather dreamy, scholarly man who would rather be left alone to study and write than to be forced by his conscience to stand in picket lines and be thrown into jail for his opinions. When he is not wandering off into some strange region of the earth he lives quietly on Cape Cod, writing in the mornings and swimming and sailing in the afternoons. In his leisure hours he has turned to drawing and painting with more than merely competent results; the illustrations to *Oriental Express* are examples of his work. His wife, Katy, writes for the periodical press over the signature Katherine Smith.

The late T. K. Whipple spoke of Dos Passos' "extraordinary vividness of detail, especially of sensory detail," and of his "keenness of . . . observation of human behavior or of American speech." Mason Wade said that his novels "constitute an unequaled portrait of twentieth century America, . . . peculiarly native and yet fully aware of the universality of our plight."

Dos Passos in early middle age is by no means a fixed and predictable writer. In some ways he has not entirely fulfilled the high promise of his earlier work. But he is still growing. And no critic would be very much surprised by his sudden production of a masterpiece in a completely different Dos Passos mood.

PRINCIPAL WORKS: One Man's Initiation, 1917; Three Soldiers, 1921; Rosinante to the Road Again (essays) 1922; A Pushcart at the Curb (verse) 1922; Streets of Night, 1923; Manhattan Transfer, 1925; Orient Express (travel) 1927; Facing the

Chair, 1927; Manuel Maples Arce Metropolis, 1929; The 42nd Parallel, 1930; Panama, 1931; Nineteen Nineteen, 1932; In All Countries (travel) 1934; Three Plays (The Garbage Man, Airways, Inc., Fortune Heights) 1934; The Big Money, 1936; U.S.A. (The 42nd Parallel, 1919, The Big Money) 1937; Journeys Between Wars (travel) 1938; Adventures of a Young Man, 1939; Living Thoughts From Tom Paine (ed.) 1940; The Ground We Stand On, 1941.

ABOUT: Geismar, M. Writers in Crisis; American Mercury August 1939; Nation February 19, 1938; New York Herald Tribune "Books" September 21, 1941; New York Times Book Review November 23, 1941; North American Review December 1937; Saturday Review of Literature August 8, 1936, June 3, 1939.

DOUGHTY, CHARLES MONTAGU. See "BRITISH AUTHORS OF THE 19TH CENTURY"

"DOUGLAS, GEORGE." See "BRITISH AUTHORS OF THE 19TH CENTURY"

*DOUGLAS, LLOYD CASSEL (August 27, 1877-), American novelist, was born in Columbia City, Ind., the son of the Rev.

Alexander Jackson Douglas (later a physician) and Sarah Jane (Cassel) Douglas. He was educated at Wittenberg College, Springfield, Ohio (B.A. 1900, M.A. 1903), then went to Hamma Divinity School (B.D. 1903). He was ordained as a Lutheran minister, and became pastor of Zion Church, North Manchester, Ind. In 1904 he was married to Bessie Io Porch; they have two daughters.

The next year he moved to the First Church, Lancaster, Ohio, and in 1908 to the Lutheran Memorial Church, Washington, D.C. While there he was chaplain of the First Infantry, District of Columbia. From 1911 to 1915 he was director of religious work at the University of Illinois, then became minister of the First Congregational Church in Ann Arbor, Mich., where he stayed till 1921. From 1921 to 1926 he was at the First Church in Akron, Ohio, from 1926 to 1929 at the First Church in Los Angeles, from 1929 to 1933 at St. James United Church, Montreal. He then retired from the ministry and now devotes all his time to writing.

Mr. Douglas' first books were entirely of a religious or inspirational nature. He was in the midst of a series of lectures on "per-

sonality expansion" when, at over fifty, he suddenly wrote his first novel, *Magnificent Obsession*. No one was more surprised than he at its immense success, or at that of his next novel, *Forgive Us Our Trespasses*. He said modestly: "Most reviewers are agreed that the author has done a clumsy piece of work, and wonder that the thing is read. . . . They are a pair of old-fashioned novels in which the characters are tiresomely decent and everything turns out happily in the end."

Since then Mr. Douglas has added several more novels to the list. All are of the same nature, and all are enormously popular, both as books and, in most cases, as screen plays later on.

To the editors of this volume he writes: "If my novels are entertaining I am glad, but they are not written so much for the purpose of entertainment as of inspiration. There are many people who realize their great need of ethical and spiritual counsel, but are unwilling to look for it in a serious homily or didactic essay. It has been my belief that many such persons can be successfully approached by a novel, offering in a form palatable to them the inspiration they seek.

"Looking back over the novels of the past half century that have contrived to outlive the decade in which they were published, one is impressed by the very considerable number of stories which have endured because of their moral purpose rather than their literary workmanship.

"There will always be room for the 'purpose novel,' and aspiring young writers will do well to consider the importance of the school of fiction that is more concerned with healing bruised spirits than winning the applause of critics."

PRINCIPAL WORKS: Wanted—A Congregation, 1920; The Minister's Everyday Life, 1924; These Sayings of Mine, 1926; Those Disturbing Miracles, 1927; Magnificent Obsession, 1929; Forgive Us Our Trespasses, 1932; Precious Jeopardy, 1933; Green Light, 1935; White Banners, 1936; Home for Christmas, 1937; Disputed Passage, 1939; Invitation to Live, 1940.

ABOUT: Cosmopolitan Magazine November 1938; Newsweek January 16, 1939; Rotarian December 1940; Time January 16, 1939; Wilson Library Bulletin December 1932.

*DOUGLAS, NORMAN (December 8, 1868-), British novelist, scientist and miscellaneous writer, comes of a very old family long established in a castle at Tilquhillie, on Deeside, Scotland. There he was born (George Norman Douglas) and there brought up until 1881, when his formal education began at Uppingham

School. Like many another boy of original and imaginative cast of mind he took very unkindly to the English "public school" routine, so in the autumn of 1883 he was removed from Uppingham and sent to the Gymnasium at Karlsruhe, Germany. There he did well at languages and science, acquiring German, Russian, and French, and precociously contributing to the *Zoologist* in 1886. In 1889 he left Karlsruhe, and in March 1893 passed into the Foreign Office by examination.

Douglas' name remained in the Foreign Office List until 1901, but in point of fact his diplomatic career lasted only some three-and-a-half years. After a year in Whitehall he was sent to St. Petersburg in March 1894. In September of the same year he was granted an allowance for knowledge of Russian; in March 1895 he obtained promotion to the grade of third secretary; and in May 1896 he passed an examination in public law. Six months later he left Russia and never returned to diplomacy. He had already seen Italy in vacations, and now bought a villa at Naples. Towards the end of the century he made a journey to India and Ceylon.

Thus far Douglas had manifested interest successively in music, science and literature. Between 1889 and 1895 he had published several treatises on zoology. In 1901 he broke into fiction, with *Unprofessional Tales,* which, he says, "were published, thank God, under a pseudonym ['Normyx'] and eight copies were sold." He settled on the island of Capri, and devoted himself for some years mainly to scientific work and archaeology, though for a while, prior to the First World War, he was in London acting as assistant editor to Austin Harrison on the *English Review.* His first real work of literature, *Siren Land,* was, in his own words, "hawked about for more than a year without success," but at last came out in 1911, through the good offices of Joseph Conrad and Edward Garnett. Douglas drew only forty pounds royalties, and much of the edition of 1,500 copies was eventually pulped.

In 1917, the worst year of the war, appeared Douglas' amazingly witty and learned philosophic novel, *South Wind,* a spirited, highly colored fantasy on an island called Nepenthe, which was a literary idealization of Capri. The book was naturally hailed for the masterpiece it is, and has since run to a score or more of editions; but at the time of publication Douglas was living frugally in Paris, so he sold out the entire copyright for seventy-five pounds and has not benefited by the repeated reprints. He remained in Paris until after the Armistice.

His next work of any length was the strange novel, *They Went* (1921), founded on an ancient Breton legend. Neither this nor its two successors, *Together* (1923) and *Fountain in the Sand* (1923), added greatly to Douglas' reputation; but another taste of his true quality was savored in *Old Calabria* (1928), which, though nominally a descriptive travel book, has much of the warmth and humor of *South Wind.* According to Muriel Draper, he had spent some twelve years on *Siren Land, South Wind,* and *Old Calabria.* "His varied accumulation of knowledge of the past and present," she continued, "of flesh and blood, untainted by anthropomorphism, his satirical impatience with shams and shibboleths, and his steadily maintained scale of values, would be salutary weapons to use against us [Americans] in this, our critical, period. His style and simplicity of language in using these weapons through the medium of the written word would be a grateful addition to the literature of our times." The same observer speaks of Douglas as "a rugged, sensitive figure," notes "the terrifyingly intelligent humorous gleam in his eye," and remarks an "indescribably rich 'know' flowing from him."

Among Douglas' later books two of the most notable have been *Goodbye to Western Culture* (1930), provoked by Katharine Mayo's *Mother India,* and his memoirs, *Looking Back* (1933), which are constructed from recollections attaching to large numbers of visiting cards collected in a bowl over many years.

Everything that is known about Douglas and everything that emerges from his writings points to his having lived fully, his wide travels and deep reading serving to point and sharpen his joy in good wine, sunny Mediterranean coasts, good conversation, and a free, intelligent existence. The diversity of his interests may have militated against his worldly success in these specialist days; but in *South Wind* he produced something unique and beyond price. Offsetting his many enthusiasms he has some cordial detestations, including socialism, puritanism, and all kinds of set forms, including official Christianity.

In 1898 Douglas married Elsa, daughter of Augustus FitzGibbon, of Mount Shannon, County Limerick, Eire; they had two sons.

For several weeks after the Nazi blitzkrieg in 1940, Douglas was reported missing. Eventually, however, he made his way from France to Switzerland and with great difficulty to Lisbon and thence to London.

PRINCIPAL WORKS: Unprofessional Tales, 1901; Siren Land, 1911; South Wind, 1917; They Went, 1921; Together, 1923; Fountain in the Sand, 1923; Experiments, 1925; Old Calabria, 1928; Birds and Beasts of the Greek Anthology, 1929; One Day, 1929; Three of Them, 1930; Goodbye to Western Culture, 1930; London Street Games, 1931; Looking Back, 1933.

ABOUT: Burke, B. Landed Gentry; Douglas, N. Looking Back; Draper, M. Music at Midnight; British Foreign Office Lists: 1894 to 1908; MacGillivray, R. Norman Douglas; Tomlinson, H. M. Norman Douglas.

DOWDEN, EDWARD. See "BRITISH AUTHORS OF THE 19TH CENTURY"

DOWDEY, CLIFFORD (1904-), American novelist, writes: "I was born in Richmond, Va., of parents who, on both sides,

belonged to families who had lived in Virginia since the early seventeenth century. My father's maternal ancestors, the Blunts, derived from Richard Blunt, who is listed in *Force's Tracts* for 1619 as one of the emigrants to Virginia for that year. They were planters in Tidewater Virginia until after the Confederate War for Independence. Branches of the family migrated to North Carolina and Tennessee, where they won some fame; the Carolina branch produced a signer of the Declaration and the other branch produced the first governor of Tennessee. In Virginia, they attained no prominence whatsoever; nor did any of the other families from whom I was descended. They were all moderately successful, educated, and self-respecting, and they paid much more attention to living than to getting. By now, that viewpoint is a family trait and tradition. I mention these people at such length because all my writings to date have been concerned with them; also, much of my material has come from their records and memories. They are a type

passing from our world, and I have attempted to recapture what they had, what caused their passing, and what of their qualities I believe would serve us well today.

"My first novel, *Bugles Blow No More,* treating the four years of the siege of Richmond, 1861-65, showed them suffering their hardest blow. On the basis of this book, I was awarded a Guggenheim Fellowship to help me research on my second novel, *Gamble's Hundred,* which attempted to depict them at the crucial point in Virginia history when the rising tide of the economic aristocrats first threatened to engulf the independent yeomanry. My third novel— [*Sing for a Penny*] depicts their final end through the rebuilding of Richmond into a part of the new industrial America, reaching its peak in the late '90s. That will be my farewell to Virginia's past and the story of my own people.

"I was graduated from John Marshall High School in Richmond; attended Columbia University; worked first as a reporter on the Richmond *News-Leader,* edited by Dr. Douglas Freeman [qv] (the Lee biographer, who has helped me both in my research and in my first attempts to write—then book reviews). I then returned to New York, to work on the editorial staff of the old *Munsey Magazine* and *Argosy.* For the next ten years, 1926 to 1935, I worked as editor on various pulp-paper magazines and, while writing for them also, researched for the novels I then planned.

"Leaving New York and editorial work in the late fall of 1935 with my wife (formerly Helen Zane-Cetti Irwin, who was also an editor), I went to Florida, then for a year in Richmond to live there while I wrote *Bugles.* Feeling homesick for the metropolitan area, we took a remodeled pre-Revolutionary farmhouse in Silvermine, Conn., where a year's residence brought on a severe sinus trouble. To cure that we came to Tucson in 1939, where we live out of town on the edge of the desert. It is very fine living, though sometimes lonely. It is a good place for work, and that helps. However, we shall eventually return east. Though we have traveled extensively from Vermont to Florida and all points between, I loathe traveling and often wish I had never left Henrico County, Virginia.

"I am an omnivorous reader, but in the past few years rarely read books not concerned with the American scene; of these I prefer history and biography, or historical novels of the type of Walter Edmonds and Jim Boyd. We both like to walk and ride horseback, watch football games and prizefights, and though we diligently study magazines of world events and international opinion, I must admit I would prefer watching a closely packed field finish strong at the Maryland Hunt Cup than read anybody's opinion on Russia. I vote the straight Democratic ticket because my father did, and until a better one comes along, I shall continue to do so . . . and, by better, I mean better designed to interpret and operate the basic democratic principles upon which this government was founded."

* * *

Mr. Dowdey is a serious looking, dark haired, bespectacled youngish man. Bernard De Voto said of his first novel: "He gives us the South primarily as a society [as against an 'idea' or a 'genealogy']. . . . Nowhere else have I seen the disruptive powers of war so truly rendered."

PRINCIPAL WORKS: Bugles Blow No More, 1937; Gamble's Hundred, 1939; Sing for a Penny, 1941.

ABOUT: New York Times Book Review July 13, 1941; Saturday Review of Literature December 18, 1937.

DOWNES. See PANTER-DOWNES

DOWSON, ERNEST. See "BRITISH AUTHORS OF THE 19TH CENTURY"

DOYLE, ARTHUR CONAN (May 22, 1859-July 7, 1930), English romancer and writer of detective fiction, the creator of  Sherlock Holmes, was born at Picardy Place, Edinburgh, the son of Charles Doyle, a civil servant in the Government Office of Works, and Mary (Foley) Doyle. Charles Doyle's father, John Doyle, came to London from Dublin in 1815 and made a reputation, as "H.B.," a political caricaturist relying on wit instead of the grotesque distortions of Gilray and Rowlandson. Richard Doyle, another son of John Doyle, drew the familiar cover of *Punch,* still in use. Artistic and impractical, never earning more than about £240 a year, Conan Doyle's father left the upbringing of his family to his wife and daughters. The Doyles, Anglo-Norman in origin and first called D'Oil, were strong Roman Catholics. Conan Doyle spent nine years with the

Jesuits, first at Hodder, a preparatory school, then seven years of Euclid, algebra, and classics at Stonyhurst, the big Roman Catholic public school in Lancashire. (In later years he left the Church.)

A year at another Jesuit school, Feldkirsh, in the Vorarlberg province of Austria, was followed by a five-years' grind as a medical student at Edinburgh University, ending with Doyle's receiving his Bachelor of Medicine degree in August 1881. More important, he had observed Professor Rutherford, with "his Assyrian beard, his prodigious voice, his enormous chest and his singular manner" (reproduced later in the Professor Challenger of *The Lost World, The Poison Belt,* and *The Land of Mist),* and Joseph Bell, surgeon at the Edinburgh Infirmary. Bell was thin, wiry, angular, a skilful surgeon whose strong point was diagnosis of occupation and character as well as of disease. He was metamorphosed into Sherlock Holmes, when Doyle six years later began to build up a scientific detective who solved cases on his own merits and not through the folly of the criminal. (Bell took a keen interest in the stories and made various rather impractical suggestions.)

Two-penny copies of Tacitus, Swift, Pope's *Homer,* and the *Spectator* helped train Doyle's style, and his student practice plus seven months in the Arctic as ship's doctor on a whaler and three on a steamer bound to the West Coast of Africa, gave him material for the later *Stark Munro Letters* and *The Captain of the Polestar.* Much research went into the historical novels: *Micah Clarke,* which dealt with the Monmouth Rebellion and Jeffreys, the famous hanging judge; and *The White Company,* a story of Edward III's archers in England and France, which has gone through more than fifty editions. Doyle preferred to be remembered as a writer by these and *Sir Nigel,* but Sherlock Holmes came to obscure the issue and take things into his own hands.

Gaboriau had attracted Doyle by the neat dovetailing of his plots, and Poe's masterful detective, M. Dupin, had been one of his heroes from boyhood. Determining to reduce "this fascinating but unorganized business to something like an exact science" (and needing money badly to supplement a starving medical practice) Doyle drew on his memories of Joseph Bell and invented a detective, Sherlock Holmes (a combination of the names of a famous cricketer and Dr. Oliver Wendell Holmes), and a commonplace, unostentatious comrade to serve as a foil, join in the exploits, and narrate them—hence Dr. Watson. Ward, Lock & Co. gave Doyle £25 for the copyright of *A Study in Scarlet* after several other firms rejected the novel, and it became "Beeton's Christmas Annual 1887." The second and best (unless it be *The Hound of the Baskervilles*) of the Holmes long stories, *The Sign of Four*, was written to order for the American *Lippincott's Magazine. The Adventures of Sherlock Holmes,* each short story complete in itself—an innovation in serials—soon began to appear in the *Strand Magazine,* written during Doyle's business hours as an oculist waiting for patients who never came. Eventually he abandoned medicine, at which he had never been successful, to devote his full time to writing.

Holmes, the late Grant Overton stated unqualifiedly, is "without question the most famous character in English literature." Vincent Starrett calls him "a symbol as familiar as the Nelson Monument or the Tower of London; a name that has become a permanent part of the English language." A larger literature has grown around him than any other fictional character save Hamlet. Two Sherlock Holmes clubs, with eminent names in their rosters, meet frequently in London and New York (where they call themselves the Baker Street Irregulars) to read pseudo-scholarly papers based on the details of the stories. The late William Gillette's patrician profile, in his dramatization of the stories, Frederick Dorr Steele's illustrations, and various impersonations in the silent and talking films have made the lean, angular sleuth with his pipe and deerstalker cap almost as immediately recognizable around the globe as Charlie Chaplin.

Sir Arthur—he was knighted and appointed Deputy-Lieutenant of Surrey in 1902 as a reward for his defence of the British cause in *The Great Boer War*—managed to combine the man of action with the man of letters, aided by his sturdy British physique. He is the writer *par excellence* for men and boys. Christopher Morley has spoken of his "great encyclopedia of romance which has given the world so much innocent pleasure." To use another word from the Morley lexicon, he was always the "infracaninophile," the champion of the under dog, as shown by his successful defence of Oscar Slater, imprisoned for the supposed murder of Miss Gilchrist, and George Edalji, a half-caste preposterously accused of horse-maiming. At the time of the World War he advocated a Channel Tunnel, life-saving apparatus for sailors,

and partial armor for soldiers, all against the obstinate opposition of the War Office. Kingsley Doyle, his son, died in London of pneumonia after being badly wounded on the Somme. This death completed Sir Arthur's conversion to spiritualism and led to the devotion of his time and fortune to spreading his beliefs to Australia, Europe, and America. No one who heard him lecture could doubt the deadly earnestness of his convictions. He and Lady Doyle arranged a test communication in the event of the passing of either, but no satisfactory evidence of such communication has followed his death, which occurred at Crowborough, Sussex, in his seventy-first year. Doyle was married twice: to Louise Hawkins in 1885 (she died in 1906) and to Jean Leckie in 1907; he had two sons and a daughter.

Too many ecstatic superlatives have been written about Sherlock Holmes; yet it is no exaggeration to say that after more than half a century he remains the best known and best loved detective in literature. But for him there might have been no detective story in the modern sense. Certainly, few characters of fiction have given so much harmless joy to so great a number of readers.

PRINCIPAL WORKS: *Sherlock Holmes Stories* A Study in Scarlet, 1887; The Sign of Four, 1890; The Adventures of Sherlock Holmes, 1892; Memoirs of Sherlock Holmes, 1894; The Hound of the Baskervilles, 1902; The Return of Sherlock Holmes, 1905; The Valley of Fear, 1915; His Last Bow, 1917; The Case-Book of Sherlock Holmes, 1927. *Other Works*—Micah Clarke, 1888; The White Company 1890; The Refugees, 1893; Exploits of Brigadier Gerard, 1896; Rodney Stone, 1896; The Great Boer War, 1900; Round the Red Lamp, 1902; Sir Nigel, 1906; The Lost World, 1912; The Wanderings of a Spiritualist, 1921; Our American Adventure, 1921; Memories and Adventures, 1924; History of Spiritualism, 1926; The Land of Mist, 1926; The Maracot Deep, 1928; The British Campaign in Europe, 1928.

ABOUT: Bell, H. W. Sherlock Holmes and Dr. Watson; Blakeney, T. S. Sherlock Holmes: Fact or Fiction?; Doyle, A. C. Memories and Adventures; Haycraft, H. Murder for Pleasure: The Life and Times of the Detective Story; Lamond, J. A. A. Conan Doyle; Locke, H. Bibliographical Catalogue of the Writings of Sir Arthur Conan Doyle; Roberts, S. C. Dr. Watson; Starrett, V. The Private Life of Sherlock Holmes; Thomson, H. D. Masters of Mystery; Bookman (London) November 1912 (Conan Doyle number); Collier's Weekly August 15, 1908 (Sherlock Holmes number); John o' London's Weekly July 26, 1930 (Conan Doyle memorial number); Literary Digest July 25, 1930; Saturday Review of Literature August 2, 1930; Times Literary Supplement (London) October 27, 1932.

DRABKIN, YAKOV DAVIDOVICH. See ORENBURGSKY

"DRAGONET, EDWARD." See WIL-
LIAMSON, T. R.

*DREISER, THEODORE (August 27,
1871-   ), American novelist, was born in
Terre Haute, Ind., the son of John Paul

Dreiser and Sarah
(Schanab) Dreiser.
The popular song-
writer, Paul Dresser,
who changed the
spelling of his name,
was his brother, and
Theodore wrote the
chorus of Paul's bar-
ber-shop classic, "On
the Banks of the
Wabash." The father
was a religious bigot who saw his family
escape from him into the world at the earliest
possible opportunity. He moved constantly
from town to town, but Theodore Dreiser
spent most of his childhood in Warsaw, Ind.,
where he attended the public schools. Later
a kindly woman enabled him to go for one
year to Indiana University. By that time
he had already lived for two years in Chicago, and after his one college year he spent
another year in that city, working in a real
estate office and as collector for a wholesale
furniture company, and storing up impressions which later appeared in his novels. In
1892 he began newspaper work on the Chicago *Globe*, and subsequently he worked on
the St. Louis *Globe-Democrat* and *Republic*.
In 1894 he went to New York as editor of
Every Week, a music magazine. From 1898
to 1905 he free-lanced, doing special assignments for various magazines, but he then returned to editorial work with *Smith's Magazine*. In 1906 and 1907 he was managing
editor of *Broadway Magazine*, and for the
next four years editor-in-chief of the But-
terick Publications, principal of which was
the *Delineator*. His only later editorial
position was with the *American Spectator*,
1932-34. He has been twice married and
divorced.

Dreiser's first and perhaps his greatest
novel, *Sister Carrie*, was accepted by its publishers in 1900, on the urgent recommendation of Frank Norris, then a publisher's
reader. But it had hardly appeared when
it was withdrawn, and Dreiser started his
long fight against censorship and for the
right of the serious novelist to present life
as he sees it; at first he fought alone, but
in later years he had able assistance from
H. L. Mencken. He met with censorship
again when *The "Genius"* was interdicted,

and later with the publication of *An American Tragedy*—based on the real-life case of
Chester Gillette, who murdered Grace Brown
at Big Moose Lake in the Adirondacks in
1906. Authors like Faulkner, Hemingway,
Caldwell, Farrell, and Steinbeck can write
freely today largely because of the pioneer
battle fought by Dreiser and Mencken.

Dreiser's earlier work, though there was
implicit in it an acceptance of man as part
of the social mass, was primarily concerned
with the growth, degeneration, or problems
of the individual. In middle life he began
to take an active part in social movements,
was arrested during a civil liberties investigation in Harlan Co., Ky.; studied the Soviet
Union at first hand; and turned from fiction
to write *Tragic America*. He has also
written plays (including the powerful *Hand
of the Potter*), essays, some rather nebulous
free verse, and much autobiography of an
unusually frank and unsparing nature.

But it is as a novelist that he is significant,
and as a novelist that he will live. He did
not reach a really wide audience until publication of *An American Tragedy* in 1926,
followed by its dramatization by Patrick
Kearney. But his most important novels are
probably the earliest ones, *Sister Carrie* and
Jennie Gerhardt. In them, and to a lesser
degree in the studies of an unscrupulous capitalist, *The Financier* and *The Titan*, he established a new school of realism in America.

The man himself, big, slow-moving, his
blond shock of hair turned white, with
"strangely blazing steel gray eyes," is like
one of his own characters. His forehead is
powerful, his eyes keen; the lower part of
his face he terms "lumpy." He speaks
slowly, in a soft, well-modulated voice. He
has known rebuffs and criticism; an air of
humility and equally of pride is stamped
on him, producing the same impression as
his books, that of dogged persistency, honesty, and curiosity about life. He is slow
to anger, but has publicly slapped a Nobel
Prize winner in resentment of a charge of
plagiarism. As Charles R. Walker pointed
out, Dreiser has put himself (though often
not as he actually was, but as he might have
been under other circumstances) into his
novels. "The story of Dreiser's own conflict
with society," said Walker, "is the theme of
all his novels," whether they express the day-
dreams of money, sex, and dominance of an
impressionable boy in a poor, harsh, restricted home, or the dangers that beset a
youth cast by society into mean streets and
narrow drudgery while his spirit cries out
for joy and ease and love.

* Died December 28, 1945.

Grandiose metaphors come easily to the pen in commenting on these novels. Whatever Dreiser does he does hugely. He has been criticized for prolixity, but it would seem that he can be himself only when he can write himself out without regard for space or form. (Even in this respect, however, he is less verbose and chaotic than was Thomas Wolfe, for example.) Henry Hazlitt has remarked on his Gibraltar-like quality, and the phrase connotes size as well as solidity.

It is easy to point out faults in his vast undertakings. Dreiser has never been a stylist; in fact, his English is frequently atrocious—ungrammatical, unwieldy, and confused. He is often sentimental, sometimes to the point of banality. As John Chamberlain noted, "the Ouida strain and the *Tom Jones* strain persist as dominants in all the Dreiser books." He is no master of the sharp and chiseled word, no artist if art means symmetry.

But, to quote Clifton Fadiman, "Dreiser's defects, like a warrior's wounds, are eloquent of struggle." He broods, he is slow and clumsy, he strains and does not always find his foothold; but the spirit that broods is a spirit of understanding and compassion. His pessimism reminds one of the hurt pessimism of a Clarence Darrow; his bewilderment, of the idealistic bewilderment of a Sherwood Anderson. Greatest of all his qualities is a patience for unending detail, so that gradually he reconstructs before our eyes a human being called Hurstwood or Eugene or Clyde or Jennie, a person as real as if we had known him all our lives.

Theodore Dreiser can no more be dismissed with polite superficialities because he is still alive than could Whitman or Hardy were they too still living. He has not become a museum-piece. He does not change; his work shows the same curious lacks and failures as his earliest. "Heavy-handed and clumsy," William Rose Benét called him; but, he added, greater even than "the cumulative effect he gains by laborious presentation of the exact truth" are his "deep human sympathy," his "sincerity that has never swerved." It is in the delineation of average men and women, petty, sordid, faulty, that he is supreme; and the reason is that he has not only known these people intimately, lived with them, worked with them, loved and hated them—he is himself such a person, raised by his own bootstraps, by sheer force of character and intellect, from the mud of provincialism, savage pietism, and deadening poverty.

What differentiates him from the millions born in his same environment is a cumbrous, plodding power of thought and feeling that finds expression, painfully and deliberately, in words. He has little talent, but much genius. He is undoubtedly the most significant realistic novelist America has so far produced.

In 1941 the League of American Writers gave Dreiser the first biennial award of the Randolph Bourne Medal as the American writer who had "performed the most distinctive service for culture and peace."

PRINCIPAL WORKS: *Fiction*—Sister Carrie, 1900; Jennie Gerhardt, 1911; The Financier, 1912; The Titan, 1914; The "Genius," 1915; Free and Other Stories, 1918; An American Tragedy, 1925; Chains, 1927. *Miscellaneous*—A Traveler at Forty, 1913; A Hoosier Holiday, 1916; Plays of the Natural and Supernatural, 1916; Twelve Men, 1919; The Hand of the Potter (play) 1919; Hey Rub-a-dub-dub: A Book of Essays and Philosophy, 1920; A Book About Myself, 1922; Moods (verse) 1922 (as Moods, Philosophic and Emotional, Cadenced and Declaimed, 1935); The Color of a Great City, 1923; Dreiser Looks at Russia, 1928; A Gallery of Women, 1929; My City, 1929; Epitaph, 1930; Fine Furniture, 1930; Dawn, 1931; Tragic America, 1932; The Living Thoughts of Thoreau (ed.) 1939; America Is Worth Saving, 1941.

ABOUT: Boynton, P. H. Some Contemporary Americans; Dudley, D. Forgotten Frontiers: Dreiser and the Land of the Free; Ford, F. M. Portraits From Life; Hapgood, H. A Victorian in the Modern World; Mencken, H. L. A Book of Prefaces; Rascoe, B. Theodore Dreiser; American Mercury January 1926; Bookman April 1926, June 1928; Century August 1925; Forum November 1929; Living Age December 1930; Nation June 3, 1931, October 19, 1932; New Republic December 23, 1936; New York Times Book Review March 16, 1941; Nineteenth Century December 1926; Saturday Review of Literature June 6, 1931, October 15, 1932, March 10, 1934; Virginia Quarterly Review January 1941.

DREW. See BICKERSTAFFE-DREW

DRINKWATER, JOHN (June 1, 1882-March 25, 1937), English dramatist, poet, and biographer, was born at Leytonstone, London, the son of Albert Edward Drinkwater, then a schoolmaster but soon to go on the stage. Owing to his father's peripatetic life in touring companies John was sent, at nine, to Oxford, where he lived with his grandfather, an ironmonger, and attended the Oxford High School (now City of Oxford School). He made no great progress with lessons, but

acquired a love for games and a proficiency at them which long persisted. In 1897 he was taken from school and put in the Northern Assurance Company at Nottingham. He spent three poverty-stricken years there, rising from office boy to guarantee clerk for reinsurances, playing football and cricket on Saturdays, and taking part in amateur theatricals. Early in 1901 he was moved to Birmingham at 60 pounds a year. So far his literary knowledge was of the most meager. His vocation had not declared itself, and, speaking of 1901, he later wrote: "I do not think that at that time I had read a play by Shakespeare." He stayed four years in Birmingham, rising to the rank of junior inspector. His active enthusiasm for theatricals continued; a friendship with H. S. Milligan led to wider reading through emulation, and to acquaintance, in the spring of 1904, with Barry Jackson, then a young man of means keenly devoted to the theatre. In 1903 Drinkwater had paid a bookseller to print a volume of *Poems*. This, and *The Death of Leander* (1906), were later to be regretted as youthful indiscretions. At the fringe of the Barry Jackson circle he stood like the Peri at the gates of Paradise. Jackson gave him a part in *Twelfth Night*; little by little the poor clerk began to find his way about the cultural world, when a business promotion to junior agency inspector exiled him to Manchester in January 1905.

Though there were intellectual flowers on the slag-heap of Manchester they were not for such as he. After fifteen unhappy months in the cotton town he succeeded in getting back to Birmingham as life inspector for the Liverpool, London & Globe Co. at 200 pounds a year—in those days quite a livable salary for a single man in the provinces. He renewed his contacts with Jackson, and acted in the very first production staged by his group, the Pilgrim Players, who led the way towards the foundation of the Birmingham Repertory Theatre. Discharged from his employment in the autumn of 1907, he soon found one more (and, as it proved, his last) insurance post as surveyor to the London and Lancashire Fire Assurance Company. He held it for two years, but his mind was ever more closely set on literature and the drama.

Late in 1909 Drinkwater gave up insurance for good. For a while he solicited advertisements for a trade paper, and he was now earning a little money by contributions to periodicals. After a year of this, Jackson employed him at a salary to augment public

interest in the Birmingham Repertory movement. During their years of association Drinkwater played some forty parts and directed over sixty productions. His own first play, a verse drama called *Ser Taldo's Bride,* written with Jackson, was staged by the Pilgrim Players in January 1911. In the same year he was president of the Birmingham Dramatic and Literary Club. He began to meet people of the first rank and in 1912 published a book on *William Morris* which was well received.

Drinkwater's literary career was now going apace. He published several volumes of verse, reviewed for the Birmingham *Post* and the *Nation,* did editorial work for Routledge's "Muses' Library," was introduced to E. V. Lucas, who put a great deal of work in his way, and wrote in *Rhythm* and the *Poetry Review.* In 1912 he met that great friend of art and letters, Mr. (later Sir) Edward Marsh, who made him free of his London apartment and included him in the anthology, *Georgian Poetry,* with Lascelles Abercrombie, Harold Monro, Rupert Brooke, and others.

In February 1913 Jackson opened the Birmingham Repertory Theatre with Drinkwater as general manager. Here in 1918 his episodic play, *Abraham Lincoln,* made him famous. He followed it with others on such themes as *Mary Stuart* (1921), *Oliver Cromwell* (1921), *Robert E. Lee* (1923), and *Robert Burns* (1925). He continued a prolific writer of verse, and brought out a number of sound biographies and much miscellaneous criticism. From most unpromising beginnings Drinkwater achieved far-flung popularity as a lyrical poet; the intellectuals, however, never placed a high value on his work. His historical dramas, coming after the wilful frivolities which necessarily held the stage during the War of 1914-18, helped to contribute to the revival of the solid drama in England.

Drinkwater's hobby was philately. He married Daisy Kennedy, the violinist, in 1924, and had one daughter. He died at Kilburn, London, in his fifty-fifth year.

PRINCIPAL WORKS: *Poetry*—Poems, 1903; The Death of Leander and Other Poems, 1906; Lyrical and Other Poems, 1908; Poems of Men and Hours, 1911; Poems of Love and Earth, 1912; Cromwell and Other Poems, 1913; Swords and Ploughshares, 1915; Olton Pools, 1916; Poems: 1908-1914, 1917; Tides, 1917; Loyalties, 1919; Poems: 1908-1919, 1919; Cotswold Characters, 1921; Seeds of Time, 1921; Preludes: 1921-1922, 1922; From the German, 1924; From an Unknown Isle, 1924; New Poems, 1925; Persephone, 1926; All About Me, 1928; More About Me, 1929; American Vignettes: 1860-1865, 1931; Christmas Poems, 1931; Summer Harvest, 1933. *Plays*—

Cophetua, 1911; An English Medley, 1911; The Pied Piper, 1912; The Only Legend, 1913; Puss in Boots, 1913; Robin Hood the Pedlar, 1914; The Storm, 1915; The God of Quiet, 1916; Pawns, 1917; Abraham Lincoln, 1918; Mary Stuart, 1921; Oliver Cromwell, 1922; Robert E. Lee, 1923; Robert Burns, 1925; Bird in Hand, 1927; John Bull Calling, 1928; Midsummer Eve, 1932; Laying the Devil, 1933; A Man's House, 1934; Garibaldi, 1936. *Biographies*—Lincoln: The World Emancipator, 1920; Claud Lovat Fraser: A Memoir (with A. Rutherston) 1923; The Pilgrim of Eternity—Byron: A Conflict, 1925; Mr. Charles: King of England, 1926; Charles James Fox, 1928; Pepys: His Life and Character, 1930; The Life and Adventures of Carl Laemmle, 1931; Shakespeare, 1933. *Autobiographies*—Inheritance, 1931; Discovery, 1932. *Critical Works*—William Morris: A Critical Study, 1912; Swinburne: An Estimate, 1913; The Lyric, 1916; Prose Papers, 1917; The Poet and Communication, 1923; Victorian Poetry, 1923; Patriotism in Literature, 1924; The Muse in Council, 1925; A Book for Bookmen, 1926; The Gentle Art of Theatre-Going, 1927; Art and the State, 1930; Poetry and Dogma, 1931; English Poetry: An Unfinished History, 1938. *Miscellaneous Writings*—John Hampden's England, 1933; This Troubled World (papers) 1933; The King's Reign (George V) 1935; Robinson of England (novel) 1937.

ABOUT: Adcock, A. St J. Gods of Modern Grub Street; Agate, J. Alarums and Excursions; Drinkwater, J. Inheritance; Drinkwater, J. Discovery; Hamilton, C. M. Seen on the Stage; Mathews, G. W. The Poetry of John Drinkwater; Newbolt, H. J. New Paths on Helicon; Phelps, W. L. The Advance of English Poetry in the Twentieth Century; Roeder, A. W. John Drinkwater als Dramatiker; Squire, J. C. Books in General: Third Series; Mark Twain Quarterly: Drinkwater Memorial Number.

DRUMMOND, WILLIAM HENRY

(April 13, 1854-April 6, 1907), Canadian poet, was Irish by birth, having been born at Currawn, County Leitrim, where his father, George Drummond, an officer in the Royal Irish Constabulary, was stationed. His mother had been Elizabeth Morris Soden. In 1856 the family moved to County Donegal, and in 1865 to Canada, where the father died. The mother was left penniless with four small sons, of whom William was the oldest. For a few years he attended private school in Montreal, then studied telegraphy and became a telegraph operator at fourteen, on the Rivière des Prairies. It was there that he first knew and learned the ways and speech of the French-Canadian *habitants* and *voyageurs* who later became the subjects of his dialect poems.

In 1876, at twenty-two, he resumed his education with money he had saved, going to the English High School in Montreal, McGill University, and Bishop's College, Lennoxville, where he received his M.D.

degree in 1884. For four years he served a country practice in two small towns, thus coming into still closer contact with the French-Canadian farmers; then he returned to Montreal. In 1895 he became professor of medical jurisprudence at Bishop's College, which gave him an honorary D.C.L. degree. He was also an honorary LL.D. from Toronto University. In 1894 he married May Isabel Harvey, of Jamaica; two of their four children survived. In 1905 he and his brothers bought a valuable silver mine in Cobalt, in northern Ontario, and this claimed the greater part of his time. An epidemic of smallpox at the mining camp sent him there hurriedly in the spring of 1907, and there he died suddenly of a cerebral hemorrhage at fifty-three.

Drummond's French-Canadian poems, such as "The Wreck of the 'Julie Plante'," "Little Bateese," and "Johnny Courteau," became popular wherever "recitations" and "elocution" were in vogue. They were better than this would indicate. Though he was sometimes accused of ridiculing the French-Canadians, actually what he did was to re-create their speech, and to make them articulate. He presents them with mingled tenderness and mirth, and if there is humor in his simple verses there are pathos, sympathy, and tenderness too. His non-dialect poems, though less fresh and appealing, reveal a genuine talent. Louis Fréchette, the French poet laureate of Canada, passed on to Drummond the accolade he himself had received from Longfellow—"pathfinder of a new land of song." Drummond also wrote a few prose sketches or stories in dialect which display the same apt characterization and quick ear for the nuances of language which his verse exemplifies.

Drummond was a man of broad interests, an athlete and a lover of sports, a conscientious physician and teacher, and a poet so modest that he never failed to be amazed at the wide popularity of his work. After his death his widow brought out a posthumous volume of verse and prose, and four years later all his poems were collected in one volume. The best known of his French-Canadian dialect verses still circulate, though many of those who are familiar with them never have heard of their author.

PRINCIPAL WORKS: The Habitant and Other French-Canadian Poems, 1897; Phil-o-Rum's Canoe, 1898; Johnny Courteau, 1901; The Voyageur and Other Poems, 1905; The Great Fight: Poems and Sketches, 1908; Poetical Works, 1912.

ABOUT: Drummond, W. H. The Great Fight (see Biographical Sketch by M. H. Drummond); Poetical Works (see Appreciation by Neil Munro);

Macdonald, J. F. William Henry Drummond; Living Age May 25, 1907; Nation April 11, 1907; Outlook April 13, 1907.

DRUTEN. See VAN DRUTEN

DU BOIS, WILLIAM EDWARD BURGHARDT

(February 23, 1868-), American publicist and novelist, writes: "I was

born in Great Barrington, Mass. My father was a descendant of Jacques Du Bois, a French Huguenot, who came to this country in 1874. My mother was the great-granddaughter of Tom Burghardt, who was born in Africa about 1730, enslaved by the Dutch, and brought to the Valley of the Hudson. I was educated in the public schools of Massachusetts and at Fisk University, Tennessee. I entered the junior class of Harvard and received my bachelor's degree in 1890. I was for two years a fellow, receiving my M.A. in 1891 and my Ph.D. in 1895. Meanwhile I spent two years of study in Germany pursuing courses in history and social science. I returned to the United States to teach for two years in Wilberforce University and one year in the University of Pennsylvania, and then became professor of history and economics in Atlanta University, Atlanta, Ga., where for thirteen years I conducted a series of annual studies of social conditions among American Negroes.

"In 1910 I removed to New York and became an official of the new National Association for the Advancement of Colored People, and for twenty-three years I edited and published the *Crisis,* a 'Record of the Darker Races.' I returned to Atlanta University as head of the department of sociology in 1933, where I am still at work. In 1939 I became editor of *Phylon,* 'the Atlanta University Review of Race and Culture,' issued quarterly, beginning in 1940."

* * *

In 1896 Dr. Du Bois married Nina Gomer, of Cedar Rapids, Iowa. They had a son, now dead, and a daughter.

Dr. Du Bois is the recognized leader of the school of American Negro thought which is in favor of contending for complete equality of opportunity, as against the conciliatory policy of Booker T. Washington and Robert R. Moton. During the Versailles Peace Conference he called the first Inter-

national Congress of Colored Peoples, in Paris. Politically he is a liberal; as a writer his approach is forthright but always informed and scholarly. He shows little trace of Negro blood and in Europe, as Stephen Graham remarked, could easily pass for a Frenchman. He has been all his life a relentless and impassioned fighter, often bitter, but always fair and sometimes brilliant.

PRINCIPAL WORKS: Suppression of the African Slave Trade, 1896; The Philadelphia Negro, 1899; The Souls of Black Folk, 1903; John Brown, 1909; Quest of the Silver Fleece (novel) 1911; The Negro, 1915; Darkwater, 1920; The Gift of Black Folk, 1924; The Dark Princess (novel) 1928; Black Reconstruction, 1935; Black Folk: Then and Now, 1939; Dusk of Dawn, 1940.

ABOUT: Allen, D. (ed.). Adventurous Americans; Calverton, V. F. (ed.). Contemporary Negro Literature; Ovington, M. W. Portraits in Color; American Scholar July 1939; Current Biography 1940; Current Opinion July 1920; New York Herald Tribune "Books" September 8, 1940; Newsweek September 9, 1940; Nineteenth Century November 1920; Outlook (London) April 25, 1925; Southern Review #3, 1936; World Tomorrow August 1929.

"DUDLEY, FRANK." See GREENE, W.

DUFFUS, ROBERT LUTHER

(1888-), American journalist and novelist, was born in Waterbury, Vt. His parents were John McGlashan Duffus and Helen (Graves) Duffus. A boyhood in a typical Yankee community is chronicled in his first novel, *Roads Going South,* published when he was thirty-three. Roads leading away from his native state took Mr. Duffus,

however, to California, where he took his B.A. degree from Stanford University in 1910, his master's degree in 1911, and married Leah Louise Deane of Palo Alto, Calif., in February of 1914. They have two daughters, Nairne Louise and Marjorie Rose.

After leaving Stanford Mr. Duffus was a reporter on the San Francisco *Bulletin* till 1913, when he became an editorial writer. In 1918 he removed to the San Francisco *Call* for a year more of editorial writing in the West, crossing the continent then to serve on the New York *Globe* from 1919 to its demise in 1923. Duffus then launched into a successful career as a free-lance writer and roving reporter. His newspaper experience gave him the knack of writing clearly and informatively on any subject he elected, and his articles appeared in magazines of the type of *Harper's* and the *Forum*. A good friend of public libraries, he wrote *Books— Their Place in a Democracy* in 1930, when the depression had not yet unduly curtailed their resources and services, and *Our Starving Libraries: Studies in Ten American Communities During the Depression Years,* a title which does not require clarification or amplification. Another survey, *Democracy Enters College* (1936), was written under the auspices of the Carnegie Foundation for the Advancement of Teaching, with funds allocated for this purpose by the Corporation.

As a change from factual reporting, Mr. Duffus in 1937 took a fictional excursion into fantasy with *Night Between the Rivers.* That year he resumed an editorial chair, on the staff of the New York *Times,* where his articles in the Magazine Section have been well-known features of that department of the Sunday *Times* for years. Mr. Duffus makes his home in Westport, Conn., but is frequently a summer visitor to his native state, where he still feels entirely at home.

PRINCIPAL WORKS: Roads Going South, 1921; The Coast of Eden, 1923; The American Renaissance, 1928; Tomorrow Never Comes, 1929; Mastering the Metropolis, 1930; Books—Their Place in a Democracy, 1930; The Santa Fé Trail, 1930; The Arts in American Life (with F. P. Keppel) 1933; Our Starving Libraries, 1933; Jornada, 1935; The Sky But Not the Heart, 1936; Democracy Enters College, 1936; Night Between the Rivers, 1937; Lillian Wald, 1938; L. Emmett Holt (with L. E. Holt, Jr.) 1940; That Was Alderbury, 1941; Victory on West Hill, 1942.

ABOUT: Better Homes and Gardens June 1931.

DU GARD. See MARTIN DU GARD

DUGUID, JULIAN (May 24, 1902-), English essayist and travel writer, reports: "I was born at Birkenhead, Cheshire. My

education was conventional. Harrow and New College, Oxford, produced a perfect horror of learning which it took me five years to surmount. Since then I have explored the South American forests, watched jaguars being speared from short range, and seen something of the human spirit in its moments of danger and depression. In the last few years my interests have been increasingly religious; not

the dying dogma of the churches, but the actual basis of contact between the ultimate force and ourselves. These have led me into a scientific study of strange or little understood phenomena: hypnosis, which reaches so far down into the unplumbed depths of our processes; mediumship, which discloses at the least a tremendously increased range of telepathy; spiritual healing, which hints at secrets which our grandchildren may begin to comprehend. It is a fascinating and absorbing range, if undertaken without credulity or superstition. It is possible that this region may lead us into a final knowledge of ourselves.

"I am married, have one child, a daughter."

* * *

Mr. Duguid is a good-looking young man, with thick, dark, curly hair and a small moustache. He lives now on a farm near Fareham, Hampshire. After leaving Oxford he worked for six months with Raymond Savage, the literary critic, and then taught in a boys' school. Then, to his delight, he was enabled to join an expedition, sponsored by the Bolivian government, to explore the limitless jungles of that country, and he immediately "chucked schoolmastering" and set out for South America. All his books, including his two novels (one of which, *Father Coldstream,* is historical) have had this jungle as their background. In 1934 he lectured throughout the United States. *Green Hell,* his first book, "a spirited and deftly written record," enjoyed considerable popularity.

PRINCIPAL WORKS: Green Hell, 1931; Tiger-Man: An Odyssey of Freedom, 1932; A Cloak of Monkey Fur (novel) 1936; Father Coldstream (novel) 1938; I Am Persuaded, 1941.

ABOUT: Literary Digest May 16, 1931.

DUHAMEL, GEORGES (June 30, 1884-), French novelist, playwright, poet, and essayist, was born in Paris of poor parents. His mother was a woman of humble Norman stock and his father, the grandson of a peasant, was a clerk in a herbalist's shop when he married. A hard-working man, he rose to the position of pharmacist and junior surgeon, crowning his career

with an M.D. degree at the age of fifty-one. Two years after his graduation, Georges, the seventh of his eight children, registered in

that same school of medicine at the University of Paris and studied under the same professors who taught his father. Georges' early education showed no particular brilliance, partly because it was so nomadic owing to his elders' constant and unavoidable migration in their struggle for existence.

"When I was between ten and twelve," Duhamel declares, "my father made me perform several throat-operations. The surgical instruments impressed me profoundly, and unquestionably it was then that I decided to become a physician." At twelve Georges had begun quietly to write verse, without glamorous aspirations. At fifteen he attended the sixth class of the Lycée Buffon, and soon after entered the Nevers lycée as a boarder. Wanting to make up for his backwardness, his father permitted him to drop out and study at home with private tutors: he carried this out successfully, completing at eighteen both parts of his baccalaureate and bringing to an end his classical studies. He entered immediately the school of medicine and for several years (1902-07) struggled to get through; insufficient funds forced him to spend his summers working in a law office, an experience which the future novelist used later to his advantage.

In the meantime Duhamel went on with his writing and made friends with other young men interested in literature. In the autumn of 1906 his literary group discovered an old house by the shore of the Marne, at Créteil, some eleven kilometers from Paris, and converted it into an artists' colony. They called it the "Abbaye," in memory of Rabelais' utopian Abbey of Thélème. Among its founders were the poets René Arcos and Charles Vildrac (who had married one of Duhamel's sisters), the painter Albert Gleizes, the politician Henri Martin, and Duhamel. After a month and a half of hard labor the dilapidated mansion was made habitable and the literary utopians moved in, cultivated the gardens, tended the orchards, bought a Minerva pedal-press, and, with the help of master-printer Linard, published their books: *Tragédie des Espaces* by Arcos; *La Vie Unanime* by the twenty-one year old Jules Romains, another of the early Abbeyists; *Images et Mirages* by Vildrac; and a collection of poems, *Des Légendes, des Batailles*—Duhamel's first work. The colony lasted until February 1908, fourteen months all told, and published some twenty books, valuable today not only for their rarity and typographical virtues but also because they marked a most invigorating trend in contemporary French letters. The Abbey introduced Duhamel to the literary world, taught him typography (in composing he attained a speed of 1200 letters per hour), and gave him a wife: at a summer party (1907) he met the actress Blanche Albane whom he married two years later.

On receiving his M.D., Duhamel did research work on the biological activity of colloids, which qualified him for a *licence* in science, and he continued working in a laboratory (1909-14). Nor did he stop writing—after the Abbey's demise he reviewed poetry for the *Mercure de France* and published two volumes of verse: *L'Homme en Tête* (1908) and *Selon Ma Loi* (1910). However it was with his plays *The Light* (1911) and *In the Shadow of Statues* (1912) produced at the Odéon, and *Combat* (1913) produced at the Théâtre des Arts, that his name became widely known in France.

At the outbreak of the First World War the thirty-year-old physician-poet-playwright volunteered for service. He was at the front for over fifty months as assistant surgeon-major, performed 2,300 operations and took care of over 4,000 wounded. Amid the havoc and anguish of war he penned at odd moments the stories contained in *The New Book of Martyrs* (1917), published under the pseudonym "Denis Thévenin," and assembled the material for *Civilization* (1918), which won him the Goncourt Prize.

After the war Duhamel emerged as a mature novelist, one of France's greatest, with the sequel-novel *Salavin*, comprising *Confession at Midnight* (1920), *Salavin's Journal* (1930), *The Lyonnais Club* (1929), and *End of Illusion* (1932); and with the *Pasquier Chronicles*, still in progress, comprising *Papa Pasquier* (1933), *Caged Beasts* (1934), *In Sight of the Promised Land* (1934), *St. John's Eve* (1935), and *House in the Desert* (1937), the latter a dramatic evocation of the Abbey. In the *Salavin* series Duhamel analyzes a Parisian wastrel living on the verge of pathology and always at odds with the "civilized" world—an exhaustive study of a negative hero in the best Dostoievsky-Goncharov tradition. The *Pasquier* cycle, a contrasting study, deals not with a poor neurotic but with a whole family and their associates; as a panorama of French life from 1890 to the war period it bears comparison with Jules Romains' *Men of Good Will* and Roger Martin du Gard's *The Thibaults*.

Duhamel's book on the United States, *Scènes de la Vie Future* (translated as

America: The Menace) gives a grotesque picture of this country, but expresses his horror of an unrestrained material civilization. Duhamel is indeed a moralist above all.

As René Lalou said, "Since the war his work has been one vast inquiry concerning two concepts of civilization—the material and the moral. . . . His honesty forced him to admit that permanent interdependence exists between these two domains." Frank C. Hanighen has perhaps best summed up his entire literary output thus far in saying: "He is a poet whose elegiac cadences melt into a sort of measured prose. He is a dramatist whose dialogue is a succession of chants in honor of the sensibility. And his novels and stories are but cantos in a great epic of human frailty and interior torment."

Duhamel is a modest, retiring man with brightly percipient eyes and soft voice, "violin à la sourdine," witty, and totally devoid of affectation. Before the Nazi conquest he kept an apartment on rue Vauquelin and often rusticated with his three sons, on his estate at Valmondois. He was a member of the French Academy (to which he was elected in 1936), and of the Academy of Medicine—crowning honors for his distinguished contributions in his two fields of activity—as well as President of the Alliance Française and director of the *Mercure de France*. In September 1939 on the outbreak of war with Germany, Minister of Propaganda Jean Giraudoux put him in charge of French radio broadcasting.

At last reports he was still in Paris, but apparently not in favor with the Nazis, who had earlier placed some of his work on their "banned" list.

WORKS AVAILABLE IN ENGLISH TRANSLATION: *Essays*—The Heart's Domain, 1919; America the Menace, 1931; In Defence of Letters, 1938; White War of 1938, 1939. *Fiction*—The New Book of Martyrs, 1918; Civilization, 1919; Papa Pasquier, 1934 (also a British translation with the title News From Havre); The Fortunes of the Pasquiers, 1935 (also a British translation with the title Young Pasquier, and In Sight of the Promised Land); Salavin (Confession at Midnight, Salavin's Journal, The Lyonnais Club, End of Illusion) 1936; Pasquier Chronicles (Papa Pasquier, Caged Beasts, In Sight of the Promised Land, St. John's Eve, The House in the Desert) 1937; Days of Delight, 1939. *Plays*—The Light, 1914; In the Shadow of Statues, 1914; Combat, 1915.

ABOUT: Bidal, M. L. Les Ecrivains de l'Abbaye; Chaigne, L. Vies et Oeuvres d'Ecrivains; Drake, W. A. Contemporary European Writers; Ehrenbourg, I. Duhamel, Gide, etc.: Vus par un Ecrivain d'U.R.S.S.; Humbourg, P. G. Duhamel; Ouy, A. G. Duhamel; Rousseaux, A. Ames et

Visages du Vingtième Siècle; Stansbury, M. H. French Novelists of Today: Nouvelles Littéraires January 27, 1934; Nouvelle Revue Française February 1, 1935.

DUMARCHAIS (or DUMARCHEY), PIERRE. See MAC ORLAN, P.

DU MAURIER, DAPHNE (May 13, 1907-), English novelist, was born in London. She is the granddaughter of the artist and novelist George Du Maurier, author of *Trilby* and *Peter Ibbetson*, and the daughter of Gerald Du Maurier, the noted actor, and of Muriel (Beaumont) Du Maurier. She writes: "I was brought up and educated at home, with my two sisters,  and had six months in Paris when I was eighteen. I read extensively in French and English, and started composing poems and writing short stories during adolescence.

"My earliest literary influences were Katherine Mansfield, Mary Webb, and, curiously enough, Guy de Maupassant. Nowadays I care little for contemporary literature, but read for choice Jane Austen, Anthony Trollope, Robert Louis Stevenson, etc.

"My hobbies are anything to do with the country—walking, gardening, bird-watching, sailing. My dislikes are town life, entertainments, parties, and large social gatherings. I have no feeling for any political party, but am convinced that human selfishness is the root of all the trouble in the world, and that no lasting contribution can be made towards universal peace unless every living man and woman stops thinking and working for *personal* success and profit. I am certain it is possible to live to a high standard and be happy and make other people happy, without adopting a censorious and preaching attitude to the rest of humanity. I believe in the principles of Moral Re-Armament, but am definitely not a member of the Oxford Group."

Miss Du Maurier was married in 1932 to Lt. Col. Frederick Arthur Montague Browning, 2nd, D.S.O., of the Grenadier Guards. They have two daughters and a son, with whom they live, in peace times, in their country home in Hampshire. In 1941 Col. Browning was made a general, the youngest of that rank in the Empire forces.

Besides her novels, Miss Du Maurier is the author of two charming books on her own family—*Gerald,* a study of her father, and *The Du Mauriers,* which goes back three generations and is a delightful *genre* picture and has historical as well as literary interest. *Rebecca,* the theme of which is a little reminiscent of *Vera,* by "Elizabeth" (Countess Russell), is her best known work and was one of the most widely read novels of its year. It was made into an extremely successful motion picture.

PRINCIPAL WORKS: The Loving Spirit, 1931; I'll Never Be Young Again, 1932; The Progress of Julius, 1933; Gerald: A Portrait, 1934; Jamaica Inn, 1936; The Du Mauriers, 1937; Rebecca, 1938; Frenchman's Creek, 1942.

ABOUT: Du Maurier, D. Gerald, The Du Mauriers; Saturday Review of Literature April 24, 1937; Wilson Library Bulletin September 1936.

DU MAURIER, GEORGE. See "BRITISH AUTHORS OF THE 19TH CENTURY"

DUNBAR, PAUL LAURENCE. See "AMERICAN AUTHORS: 1600-1900"

DUNKERLEY, WILLIAM ARTHUR. See OXENHAM, J.

DUNNE, FINLEY PETER ("Mr. Dooley") (July 10, 1867-April 24, 1936), American satirist, was born in Chicago, the son of Peter and Ellen (Finley) Dunne.

After an elementary public school education, he became a reporter on the Chicago *Herald,* in 1884, and during the next eight years served successively as reporter, editorial writer, and city editor on five other Chicago papers. In 1896 he became editor of the *Evening Journal.* Four years later he went to New York, to edit the *Morning Telegraph* for William C. Whitney. Whitney and his son, Harry Payne Whitney, practically adopted Dunne; when the older man died in 1904, the son continued to subsidize him, though the paper had changed hands. He was enabled to become part owner of the *American Magazine,* where he edited a department called "In the Interpreter's House." Next he became editor of *Collier's Weekly,* but when that too was sold he retired from editorial work permanently. Altogether the Whitneys gave him more

than a million dollars, and quite unwittingly killed him as a writer. He had always been lazy, spurred to writing only by necessity, and when the necessity passed he practically stopped working, only occasionally issuing a volume made up mostly of reprints of his earlier work.

In 1902 Dunne married Margaret Abbott; they had three sons and a daughter. He retired to Long Island in 1911, and was almost forgotten by the public when, after a long illness, he died at nearly sixty-nine.

Dunne hated to be called "Mr. Dooley," and yet it is only as "Mr. Dooley" that he will live. It is doubtful if he ever realized how rare a thing he had created. Henry Seidel Canby called the "Dooley" sketches (most of which appeared between 1893 and 1905) "marvelous little satires, each perfectly constructed, with a twist at the end as incomparable as the last line of a sonnet." They made of Dunne our greatest humorist after Mark Twain. They were not merely witty; the fun and the Irish dialect were a mask, a "jester's license," behind which Dunne, in a censorious age, could express his hatred of injustice, selfishness, pretentiousness, and stupidity. Dooley is the eternal skeptic, his friend Hennessey the eternal boob. Using dialect, Dunne could say what he pleased about the stuffed shirts of politics and industry.

And these "light-hearted rapier thrusts" are real works of art, though they appeared first in a newspaper column. Franklin P. Adams said that Dunne "revered the art of saying things perfectly; he hated slovenliness of thought and expression." Some of the sketches are "dated" now, but very many of them are not, as was shown when a collection of the best of them was issued in 1938. Someone has suggested that if they could be reprinted, translated into ordinary English, their penetration, and their appropriateness to contemporary questions, would at once be apparent.

Thomas A. Daly called Dunne "a kind of leprechaun." His scintillating wit was matched by his dislike of the limelight; he was a man generous and genial among his friends, especially in that brilliant group of his early Chicago days, but utterly unmade for the blatancy of popular fame. All these characteristics combined with his natural indolence to cut short his career in mid-course. He was a social satirist of insight and power, who fell into silence just when a voice like his was the nation's greatest need.

PRINCIPAL WORKS: Mr. Dooley in Peace and in War, 1898; Mr. Dooley in the Hearts of His Countrymen, 1898; What Dooley Says, 1899; Mr.

Dooley's Philosophy, 1900; Mr. Dooley's Opinions, 1901; Observations by Mr. Dooley, 1902; Dissertations by Mr. Dooley, 1906; Mr. Dooley Says, 1910; New Dooley Book, 1911; Mr. Dooley on Making a Will and Other Necessary Evils, 1919; The "Mr. Dooley" Papers, 1938.

ABOUT: Ellis, E. Mr. Dooley's America: A Life of Finley Peter Dunne; New Republic May 4, 1938; New York Herald Tribune "Books" November 9, 1941; Publishers' Weekly May 2, 1936; Saturday Review of Literature May 9, 1936.

DUNSANY, EDWARD JOHN MORETON DRAX PLUNKETT, 18th Baron

(July 24, 1878-), Irish dramatist and story writer, was born in London, though of an Irish family, son of the 17th Baron Dunsany. He was educated at Cheam School, Eton, and Sandhurst (the British equivalent of West Point). He succeeded his father at the latter's death in 1899. Lord Dunsany served in the Boer War in the Coldstream Guards, and in the First World War in the Royal Iniskilling Fusiliers, as a captain. He was wounded in 1916.

He was a playwright before he turned to fiction, and was one of the "discoveries" of the Abbey Theater, Dublin, which produced his play, *The Glittering Gates* (about two dead burglars who jimmy the gates of heaven), in 1909. The choice of theme indicates the general trend of Lord Dunsany's work; he deals almost exclusely with what he calls "the mysterious kingdoms where geography ends and fairyland begins."

By his own estimate, 97 per cent of his life has been spent, not in writing, but in sport and soldiering. Ernest Boyd called him "a fox-hunting man . . . with literary talent and a sensitive imagination, . . . the juxtaposition of two people in one, a man of imagination and a fashionable sportsman." When his autobiography appeared in 1938, readers, who knew him only as a dweller in that shadowy realm inhabited by such authors as Algernon Blackwood and Walter de la Mare, were astonished to find that he was actually more interested in hunting, cricket, and similar activities than in any form of artistic life. And he looks the part —a big, genial man, six feet four in height, who once remarked; "Our trenches were only six feet deep; I shall never fear publicity again." Only his spectacles detract from the perfect picture of a typical British squire.

In 1904 Lord Dunsany married Lady Beatrice Villiers, daughter of the Earl of Jersey, and they have one son. He has traveled a good deal, including several trips to America, but spends most of his time in London or in Ireland.

Lord Dunsany believes in writing "literature to please oneself. . . . The main thing is not to interrupt a mood. Writing is an easy thing when one is going strong and fast; it becomes a hard thing only when the onward rush is impeded."

Imaginative power is the salient characteristic of his work both in plays and in stories. He has created a mythology of his own and made it credible. *Gods of the Mountain*, with its atmosphere of menace and horror, is representative of his work. He is a prolific as well as a rapid writer, and the list of his published volumes is a lengthy one. His plays have been produced by the Moscow Art Theater as well as in England, Ireland, and America. He was Byron Professor of English Literature at Athens when Greece fell to the Nazi hordes, and nothing was heard of him for months. Early in 1942 he arrived in Dublin but refused to tell where he had been or what had happened to him.

PRINCIPAL WORKS: *Fiction*—The Sword of Welleran, 1908; The Gods of Pegāna, 1911; Time and the Gods, 1913; Fifty-one Tales, 1915; A Dreamer's Tales, 1916; The Last Book of Wonder (in England, Tales of Wonder) 1916; Tales of War, 1918; Tales of Three Hemispheres, 1919; The Chronicle of Rodriguez, 1922; The King of Elfland's Daughter, 1924; The Charwoman's Shadow, 1926; The Evil Kettle, 1926; The Old King's Tale, 1926; The Blessing of Pan, 1927; The Old Folk of the Centuries, 1930; Travel Tales of Mr. Joseph Jorkens, 1931; The Curse of the Wise Woman, 1933; Jorkens Remembers Africa, 1934; Up in the Hills, 1935; Rory and Bran, 1936; My Talks With Dean Spanley, 1936; The Story of Mona Sheehy, 1940. *Plays*—Five Plays (The Gods of the Mountain, The Golden Dream, King Agimēnēs and the Unknown Warrior, The Glittering Gates, The Lost Silk Hat) 1914; A Night at an Inn, 1916; Plays of Gods and Men, 1917; If, 1921; Alexander and Three Small Plays, 1926; Seven Modern Comedies, 1929; Mr. Faithful, 1935; Plays for Earth and Air, 1937. *Miscellaneous*—Unhappy Far-off Things (essays) 1919; Fifty Poems, 1929; The Pronouncements of the Grand Macaroni (If I Were Dictator) 1934; My Ireland, 1937; Patches of Sunlight (autobiography) 1938, Mirage Waters (poems) 1938.

ABOUT: Bierstadt, E. H. Dunsany the Dramatist; Dunsany, E. J. M. D. P. Patches of Sunlight; Forum February 1935; Living Age April 1941; Revue des Deux Mondes August 15, 1933; Saturday Review of Literature September 24, 1938.

DURANT

DURANT, WILLIAM JAMES (November 5, 1885-), American historian and essayist who writes as Will Durant, was born in North Adams, Mass., of a French Canadian family, his father being Joseph Durant and his mother Marie (Allors) Durant. He was educated at St. Peter's College, Jersey City, N.J. (B.A. 1907, M.A. 1908), and then went to work as a reporter on the New York *Evening Journal.* From 1907 to 1911 he taught languages at Seton Hall, Orange, N.J His parents wished him to become a priest, and he obediently entered the seminary at Seton Hall, but he realized that he had lost his religious faith and withdrew in 1911.

He then became for two years the only teacher of the Ferrer School, New York, an experiment, under Anarchist auspices, in libertarian education. After a year's tour of Europe he entered the graduate school of Columbia University, receiving his Ph.D. degree in 1917. He taught philosophy at Columbia for one term. Meanwhile he had become a director of the Labor Temple School, an adult education project, and did not retire from his teaching there until 1927. He had been a lecturer from 1914, and still continues to give lecture courses throughout the country.

In 1913 Dr. Durant married Ida Kaufman. He lives with his wife, one daughter, and an adopted son at Great Neck, N.Y. He is a slight, round-faced man who wears a small moustache and used to wear a goatee. He says: "I don't drink or smoke, and I have only one wife, but I sometimes mourn what I am missing."

The Story of Philosophy, which made Will Durant famous and opened the flood-gates for an entire school of popularized history, had its genesis in a lecture series and first appeared in printed form under the auspices of E. Haldeman-Julius, in Girard, Kansas. When it was taken over by Simon & Schuster and issued as a bound volume it was a phenomenal best seller, and it has been translated into twelve languages. In 1932 Dr. Durant abandoned all other writing to begin a huge project, a history of civilization in eight volumes, of which two have so far appeared. In preparation for this work he made three tours around the world.

Aside from his books of philosophy, history, and sociological problems, Dr. Durant has written one novel, *Transition,* which is actually nearly all autobiography, and of which he says: "There are some pages in it which I am afraid will remain to the end the best that I have written." He has long since left his early connection with the radical movement, and thinks of himself now as an interpreter of the past to the present, and as a historian of "Man Thinking" who is fortunate enough to live definitely and consciously at the end of a well-marked cultural era.

PRINCIPAL WORKS: Philosophy and the Social Problem, 1917; The Story of Philosophy, 1926; Transition (novel) 1927; The Mansions of Philosophy, 1929; The Case for India, 1930; Adventures in Genius, 1931; A Program for America, 1931; On the Meaning of Life, 1932; The Tragedy of Russia, 1933; The Story of Civilization: Part I, 1935, Part II, 1939.

ABOUT: Durant, W. Transition; Bookman September 1927; Catholic World December 1926; Time November 20, 1939.

DURANTY, WALTER (May 25, 1884-), Anglo-American journalist and novelist, was born in Liverpool and educated at Harrow, Bedford, and Emmanuel College, Cambridge, winning classical scholarships at all. He was graduated from Cambridge with first class honors in classics, and for seven years thereafter led a wandering, Bohemian existence in England, America, and France, sometimes tutoring, often hungry, and occasionally selling an adventure story to an American magazine. In 1913 he ended this aimless life by entering the service of the New York *Times* in its Paris bureau. He has been with it ever since, but he has seldom been in the United States itself since his youth, and is still a British subject (though most readers think of him as an American). During the First World War he was attached as a correspondent to the French Army. In 1921 the *Times* sent him as its correspondent to Moscow, with which his name is most closely identified. He was there until 1933, then was transferred to Paris, returned to Moscow, and after the outbreak of the Second World War returned, first to Paris and then to England. In 1924 he lost his left foot in a railway accident during a visit to France, receiving $10,000 damages. He is reticent

about his private life, but his friends say he is a moody man, sometimes sociable and a *bon vivant,* sometimes reserved and uncommunicative. He is unmarried. He is rather under medium height, somewhat bald, and serious-faced; one would never suspect him of the adventurousness, aggressiveness, and persistence under hardship which are really his. In spite of the strict censorship, and of constant attacks from both conservatives and radicals, he managed during many years to send out factual, fair stories from the U.S.S.R., which gained him a solid reputation as one of the soundest of foreign correspondents. James E. Abbe called him "a straight reporter, with a flair for the bizarre."

In 1932 he won the Pulitzer Prize for reporting. He himself says: "I try to express my thoughts simply, without much care for euphony or grammar," but actually he has exceptional clarity and ease of style. His fiction is not up to the standard of his journalistic writing; he has little gift for characterization or dialogue. In 1928 he won the O. Henry Memorial Prize for a story called "The Parrot," but Alexander Woollcott, at least, says that the actual author of this story was not Duranty, but his colleague, H. R. Knickerbocker! To amuse himself, in moments of depression, he composes prose poems imitative of the manner of E.E. Cummings, but these productions, perhaps fortunately, have never seen the light of print. He says his recreations are "going places, seeing things, and talking to people," all excellent hobbies for a journalist, and which perhaps explain why he is in the forefront of his profession. He is a linguist, who speaks fluent Russian in addition to more usual languages, and has thus been able to present the life of a foreign country not merely as an onlooker, but almost as a participant. It is said that he went to Russia strongly biased against the Soviet régime, but became more or less sympathetic with it on closer acquaintance, a reversal of the usual case. In 1933 he accompanied Maxim Litvinoff when he first came to the United States.

PRINCIPAL WORKS: Moscow Trials, 1929; The Curious Lottery and Other Tales of Russian Justice, 1929; Red Economics (with others) 1932; Duranty Reports Russia, 1934; I Write as I Please, 1935; One Life, One Kopeck (novel) 1937; The Gold Train (novel) 1938; The Kremlin and the People, 1941.

ABOUT: Duranty, W. I Write As I Please; Literary Digest January 13, 1934; New Outlook December 1933; Wilson Library Bulletin April 1936.

DUUN, OLAV (November 21, 1876-September 13, 1939), Norwegian novelist, was born in Namdal, on the west coast of Norway, the son of Johannes Antonius Duun and Ellen (Fossum) Duun. He wrote to the compilers of this volume shortly before his death: "My father was a farmer and fisherman, and so was I from my early years." In 1902 he was enabled to go to the state normal school at Tröndelag, and, as he said, "I worked as a folk-school teacher to my fiftieth year."

His first book, a volume of short stories, appeared in 1907. In 1908 he married Georgina Möller, and they had several children, their oldest daughter being an actress. Duun retired from teaching in 1926 to devote himself entirely to writing; though, since he is a rapid worker, his profession had not prevented almost annual publication of books during his twenty years as a teacher. He lived at Holmestrand, near the Oslo fjord, until his death of a stroke at sixty-six.

Duun wrote, not in the literary Dano-Norwegian, or *riksmaal,* but in the *landsmaal* or spoken language of Norway, and most of his books, moreover, were written in the dialect of the fishermen and small farmers who were his subjects. Because of the difficulty of translation, it was not until he was a major figure at home and elsewhere in Europe that he became known at all to English and American readers. His official translator, Arthur G. Chater, said that "his narrative style closely resembles that of the sagas—plain matter-of-fact, lighted up by flashes of fancy."

In 1918 he began the series of novels known as *The People of Juvik,* six volumes in all dealing with four generations of a family of peasant landowners. H. G. Topsöe-Jensen said of this series: "The style is completely objective. . . . Here are no superfluities, no pointers, no explanations; the author lets his work speak for itself."

Of his own viewpoint Duun said: "I was always a democrat, with but a small interest in politics. Of influences, development, etc., there is not much to be said. There probably are too many influences, so that I cannot see them. As for my development, God knows if there really is any such thing to be found in me."

In spite of this modesty, Phillips Dean Carleton has called Duun "perhaps the greatest living spokesman for the peasant mind. He has had a tremendous task to fulfill and has performed it most creditably." He will inevitably be compared with Hamsun, who deals with much the same kind of people; but Hamsun emphasizes their material problems, Duun their mental and spiritual ones.

Duun had the serious face of a hard worker and a hard thinker. He led a retired life of constant literary labor. His only public connection was with the popular defence movement, which led to the organization of the Norwegian volunteer rifle units.

WORKS AVAILABLE IN ENGLISH: Good Conscience, 1928; The People of Juvik: The Trough of the Waves, 1930; The Blind Man, 1931; The Big Wedding, 1932; Odin in Fairyland, 1932; Odin Grows Up, 1934; Storm, 1935.

ABOUT: Jorgenson, T. History of Norwegian Literature; Overland, A. Olav Duun (in Norwegian); Topsöe-Jensen, H. G. Scandinavian Literature; American-Scandinavian Review September 1937.

DYKE. See VAN DYKE

EASTMAN, MAX (January 4, 1883-   ), American essayist and poet, writes: "I was born [Max Forrester Eastman] in the village of Canandaigua, N.Y.  My father was a minister. My mother was also a minister—the first woman to be ordained in the Congregational church in New York. Her eloquence was quite famous.

"I prepared for college in Mercersburg Academy, Pennsylvania, and was graduated from Williams College in 1905. For four years I taught logic and psychology at Columbia University. I studied at the same time, and passed all the requirements for the degree of Ph.D., which I never went up to get.

"In 1913 I published my first and most successful book, *The Enjoyment of Poetry* —a study of the psychology of literature, which is now in its twentieth edition and is used as a textbook in many American schools and colleges. In the same year I published a volume of poems, *Child of the Amazons.* I also founded, together with a group of revolutionary artists and writers in New York, a humorous, literary, and artistic magazine—left-Socialist in political policy—called the *Masses.*

"I was the editor of this magazine, and also its manager, for five years. We opposed the entrance of the United States into the war in 1917, and also opposed the war. The magazine was suppressed by the government, and four of us, including Floyd Dell, the novelist, Art Young, the cartoonist, and John Reed, the well known Communist writer, were arrested and tried for sedition. We were tried twice, the first time defended by the Socialist lawyer, Morris Hillquit, the second time defending ourselves. I addressed the jury for two hours and forty minutes. The jury disagreed at both trials, and the second time with so large a majority in our favor that the indictment was dismissed.

"I had founded in the meantime a new magazine, the *Liberator,* which I continued to edit until 1923, when I went to Russia to learn the language and study the Soviet civilization. I was for a short time a member of the Communist Party, but I allowed my membership to lapse in 1923 because I wanted to devote myself to literature."

* * *

Mr. Eastman's most popular book since *The Enjoyment of Poetry* has been *The Enjoyment of Laughter,* a study of the psychology of humor. In addition to his creative work, he has edited Karl Marx, translated Leon Trotsky, and acted as compiler and narrator of a film called *From Czar to Lenin.* Since resigning from the Communist Party, he has taken part in many bitter controversies with the orthodox Communists, as a result of his violent opposition to Stalin and "Stalinism." Although he still calls himself a socialist, he contends now that "Marxism is unscientific and complete collectivism a failure."

A tall, strikingly handsome man with a mop of snow-white hair, Max Eastman has been married twice: in 1911 to Ida Rauh, by whom he had a son, and from whom he was divorced in 1922; and in 1924 to Eliena Krylenko, of Moscow. His home is at Croton-on-the-Hudson, N.Y., where he is working on his autobiography.

PRINCIPAL WORKS: Child of the Amazons and Other Poems, 1913; The Enjoyment of Poetry, 1913; Journalism versus Art, 1916; Understanding Germany, 1916; Colors of Life (poems) 1918; The Sense of Humor, 1921; Since Lenin Died, 1925; Leon Trotsky, 1925; Marx and Lenin: The Science of Revolution, 1926; Venture (novel) 1927; Kinds of Love (poems) 1931; The Literary Mind, 1931; Artists in Uniform, 1934; Art and the Life of Action, 1934; The Enjoyment of Laughter, 1936; The End of Socialism in Russia, 1937; Marxism: Is It a Science, 1940; Stalin's Russia and the Crisis in Socialism, 1940; A Letter to Americans, 1941; Heroes I Have Known, 1942.

ABOUT: Brooks, Van W. Sketches in Criticism; Hackett, F. Horizons; Hapgood, H. A Victorian in the Modern World; MacLean, M. S. Men and Books; Young, A. Art Young: His Life and Times; Boston Evening Transcript Book Section November 28, 1931; Current Opinion February 1922; New Republic February 10, 1941; Partisan Review May-June 1942; Saturday Review of Literature November 14, 1936.

EATON, WALTER PRICHARD

(August 24, 1878-), American dramatic critic, essayist, and poet, writes: "I was born in the vicinity of Boston.

My father, Warren E. Eaton, was then and for many years thereafter master of the Harvard School, in Charlestown, Mass. When I was eight, we moved to what was then comparative country, some dozen miles north of Boston, and I was brought up in the simple life of an old New England village, Reading, and in the woods and fields surrounding it. To that early environment I can directly attribute most of the things which have brought me happiness in later years, and also what modest share of literary success I have achieved. The necessity of making with my own hands things which I wanted, like an ice-boat or a canoe, the knowledge of farming and gardening again achieved by necessity, love of the woods and familiarity with their secrets, and in the community life of those pre-radio days the joys of self-created entertainment, all contributed something which has been my future reliance.

"I went to Phillips Andover and Harvard (class of 1900), and then became a reporter on a Boston paper. Ever since I ran a printing-press and edited a paper at the age of thirteen, I had intended to be a journalist. In 1902 I went to New York, on the staff of the *Tribune*, and became assistant dramatic critic, again from early influence. Our village dramatic society had given me a lasting passion for the theatre. For two years I was dramatic critic of the *Sun*, and published a volume of my criticisms, *The American Stage of Today*.

"But in 1910, after my marriage to Elise Morris Underhill of New York, my early environment again took the reins. I couldn't stand city life any longer, and we moved to Stockbridge, in the Berkshire Hills of Massachusetts. I have lived in the Berkshires ever since, and the bulk of my writing has been either juvenile stories for Boy Scouts, or stories and essays about country living, about nature, about gardening. I have made my living and found my happiness, in other words, out of the very things which I learned to do and love as a boy. It is quite possible, of course, that my interest in the theatre could have been aroused, even more strongly perhaps, in a city environment, under favorable circumstances. But for the rest I am pretty exclusively a country product.

"In 1933, on the retirement of George Pierce Baker from the Department of Drama at Yale, I was asked to take over his classes in playwriting, the pioneer classes in this subject in America. That work has filled my winters ever since, almost to the exclusion of any writing of my own. Except for two collaborations produced on Broadway many years ago, my own playwriting has been confined to one-act pieces (such as *The Purple Door Knob*), but the doer in art is not always the most helpful teacher. He wants to re-do the student's work his way. At any rate, the teacher of an art, like playwriting, is a vicarious sharer in the creative process, day in and day out, and discovers that he has little energy left for creative processes of his own. If you want to write, don't teach.

"I used to belong to the Socialist Party, and counted myself a radical. European events of recent years have completely changed that attitude. I hope I shall die under the American system to which I was born."

* * *

Mr. Eaton lectures frequently on gardens and on the drama. From 1930 to 1937 he edited the *Yale One-Act Plays*. He was formerly secretary of the National Institute of Arts and Letters, and has been active in the affairs of the Unitarian Church. His summer home now is in Sheffield, Mass. He is a tall, thin, spectacled man, dignified and professorial in appearance, who attributes to his country living relief from hay-fever, which racked him for years in New York, "where no hay was in sight."

PRINCIPAL WORKS: *Dramatic Criticism*—The American Stage of Today, 1908; At the New Theatre and Others, 1910; Plays and Players, 1916; The Actor's Heritage, 1924; The Theatre Guild: The First Ten Years, 1929; The Drama in English, 1930. *Nature Essays*—Barn Doors and Byways, 1913; Green Trails and Upland Pastures, 1917; In Berkshire Fields, 1919; Skyline Camps, 1922; A Bucolic Attitude, 1926; New England Vista, 1930; Everybody's Garden, 1932; On Yankee Hilltops, 1933; Wild Gardens of New England, 1935. *Juvenile Fiction*—The Boy Scouts of Berkshire, 1912; Boy Scouts in the Dismal Swamp, 1913; Boy Scouts in the White Mountains, 1914; Boy Scouts of the Wildcat Patrol, 1915; Peanut: Cub Reporter, 1916; Boy Scouts in Glacier Park, 1918; Boy Scouts at Crater Lake, 1922; Boy Scouts on Katahdin, 1924; Hawkeye's Roommate, 1927; Boy Scouts on the Green Mountain Trail, 1929; Boy Scouts in Death Valley, 1939. *Adult Stories*—The Runaway Place (with Elise Underhill) 1909; The Man Who Found Christmas, 1913; The Idyll of Twin Fires, 1915; The Bird House Man, 1916; On the Edge of the Wilderness, 1920. *Miscellaneous*—Echoes and Realities (poems) 1918; Penguin Persons and Peppermints (essays) 1922; Queen Victoria (play, with David Carb) 1923.

ABOUT: Burgess, G. (ed.). My Maiden Effort; Bookman July 1909; Country Life April 1923.

EBERHART, Mrs. MIGNON (GOOD)

(July 6, 1899-   ), American detective story writer, writes: "I was born in the West, in a small university town called University Place, in Nebraska, where I went to school. My husband, Alanson C. Eberhart, is a civil engineer and, following my marriage, for some years we traveled constantly. I began to write in 1930. Six of my books have been made into moving pictures and the stories have been translated, I believe, into eleven or twelve languages. My second book, called *While the Patient Slept*, was given the $5,000 Scotland Yard Prize. In 1935 the college I attended, Nebraska Wesleyan University, honored me with a D.Litt. degree. Owing to the fact that my husband's profession took him into many different places, my stories have been written in as great a variety of circumstances, on boats, trains, and in hotels. For some years, however, we lived in Chicago, but I wrote murder mystery stories before I went there. Our present home is in New Canaan, Conn."

* * *

Because so many of Mrs. Eberhart's books center around Nurse Sarah Keate, many readers think she herself has been a nurse; that, however, is not the case. University Place, where she was born, is a suburb of Lincoln, Neb. She is the daughter of William Thomas Good and Margaret Hill (Bruffey) Good. She attended college for only three years and was not graduated. She was married in 1923. She is a pretty, dark-haired woman who confesses to having "a timid soul," and was horrified when she came face to face with real murder in

covering a celebrated case for the Hearst papers.

Mrs. Eberhart started writing in the first place because she had to travel so much, and needed something to relieve her boredom after books and games had given out. She chose mystery stories deliberately because a text-book informed her they paid best; at first she wrote short stories and when they ceased to sell regularly she turned to novels. Her work has been called plausible and entertaining, and her books are noted for their eerie atmosphere of impending danger. She says "writing mystery stories is like walking the tight-rope" between too much and too little realism.

PRINCIPAL WORKS: The Patient in Room 18, 1929; While the Patient Slept, 1930; The Mystery of Hunting's End, 1930; Murder by an Aristocrat, 1931; From This Dark Stairway, 1931; The White Cockatoo, 1932; The Dark Garden, 1933; Cases of Susan Dare (short stories) 1934; The House on the Roof, 1935; Fair Warning, 1936; Danger in the Dark, 1936; The Pattern, 1937; Hasty Wedding, 1938; The Glass Slipper, 1938; The Chiffon Scarf, 1939; Hangman's Whip, 1940; Speak No Evil, 1941; With This Ring, 1941; Unidentified Woman, 1942.

ABOUT: Haycraft, H. Murder for Pleasure: The Life and Times of the Detective Story; Delineator August 1935; Publishers' Weekly January 13, 1934.

*EDDINGTON, Sir ARTHUR STANLEY

(December 18, 1882-   ), English astrophysicist, was born in Kendal, Westmoreland, his father being headmaster of Kendal School. He is of old Quaker descent on both sides. He was educated at Owens College (now Manchester University) and at Trinity College, Cambridge, having an M.Sc. degree from the former and an M.A. from the latter. He is also a B.Sc. of the University of London, and has honorary doctorates from the Universities of Bristol, Leeds, Witwatersrand (South Africa), Edinburgh, Durham, Allahabad and Calcutta (India), and Harvard. At Cambridge he was Senior Wrangler (first in the Mathematics Tripos) in 1904, Smith's Prizeman and Fellow of Trinity in 1907. He was chief assistant at the Royal Observatory in Greenwich from 1906 to 1913, and since that time has been Plumerian Professor of Astronomy at Cambridge and Director of the Cambridge Observatory. He received the medal of the Royal Society (of which

* Died November 22, 1944.

he became a Fellow in 1914) in 1928, is a past president of the Royal Astronomical Society and the Physical Society, and is now president of the International Astronomical Union, and a foreign member of practically all Academies of Science, including the American. He has also received the gold medal of the Royal Astronomical Society and the Bruce Medal of the Astronomical Society of the Pacific. He was knighted in 1930 and received the Order of Merit in 1938. He is unmarried.

As an astronomer, his principal fields have been relativity, stellar evolution, and the motions of stars. He is perhaps better known to the lay public for his semi-popular books in which he is more the philosopher and religionist (he is a strong churchman) than the scientist. He has done more, perhaps, than any other one man to make the theory of relativity understandable to the non-scientific world. In his philosophical aspect, he has joined with Robert A. Millikan and Sir James Jeans in injecting into physics and astronomy a mystical note which is considered indefensible by other cosmologists. He is, however, undoubtedly one of the greatest living astrophysicists.

He is a slender, fair man, with a massive forehead, a soft voice, and a charming manner among his few intimates, but he is almost pathologically shy, and avoids every public or social event from which he can possibly escape. He is a teetotaler, has no hobbies, engages in no recreations; he is almost the perfect incarnation of the retiring, shrinking professor of legend. A bit old-fashioned in all his ways, he still wears the hard collars of a generation ago and a grotesquely heavy watch-chain. He has practically no public life, emerging from his observatory or his study only to deliver a necessary lecture or receive some new honor, and he has very few close associates. But he writes with remarkable lucidity, considering the abstruse and esoteric nature of his subject, and with a disarming grace. He has been in the United States several times, the last time in 1934, when he presided over a meeting of the International Astronomical Union at Harvard. Best known of his non-technical books is *The Nature of the Physical World*.

PRINCIPAL WORKS: Stellar Movements and the Structure of the Universe, 1914; Report on the Relativity Theory of Gravitation, 1918; Space, Time, and Gravitation: An Outline of the General Relativity Theory, 1920; The Mathematical Theory of Relativity, 1923; The Internal Constitution of the Stars, 1926; Stars and Atoms, 1927; The Nature of the Physical World, 1928; Science and the Unseen World, 1929; The Expanding Universe, 1933; New Pathways in Science, 1935; Relativity Theory of Protons and Electrons, 1936; The Philosophy of Physical Science, 1939.

ABOUT: Stebbing, L. S. Philosophy and the Scientists; American Scholar #1 1937; Contemporary Review January 1931; Discovery April 1929; Living Age February 1931; Mind July 1938; Nature June 18, 1938; Nineteenth Century March and May 1929, April 1933; Science January 4, 1929.

EDDY, GEORGE SHERWOOD (January 19, 1871-), American publicist who signs his works as Sherwood Eddy, writes: "Sherwood Eddy was born in Leavenworth, Kan. On his father's side he is a descendant of John and Priscilla Alden. He graduated from Yale in the class of 1891 with a Ph.B. degree. Attended Union Theological Seminary, New York City,

1891 93, and Princeton 1894 96. Received honorary M.A. from Yale in 1916 and honorary LL.D. from College of Wooster, same year. For nearly fifty of his seventy years of life, Dr. Eddy has been compelled, in the nature of his work, to travel almost incessantly, both geographically and ideologically. In 1896 he went to India, where he worked among the students for fifteen years. The next fifteen years, as Secretary for Asia for the Y.M.C.A., he worked and lectured year after year among the students of China, Japan, Turkey, the Near East, and even Czarist Russia. For twenty years between the First and Second World Wars, Dr. Eddy took groups of American educators through all the principal countries of Europe."

* * *

In 1898 Dr. Eddy married Maud Arden, an English missionary, and they had a son and a daughter, both now deceased. He resigned his Y.M.C.A. post in 1931. Always socially minded, he was frequently under fire because of his liberal opinions, and after he left the Y.M.C.A. he joined the Socialist Party. His American Seminar, an annual tour and survey of European conditions, has been transferred to this continent since 1938. In 1936 he started a cooperative farm in Mississippi, using the Rust Mechanical Cotton-picker, as a demonstration of a solution of the sharecropper problem. He lives now on Long Island with his wife and his orphaned grandson, whom he is rearing.

Always eager to find a point of reconciliation between religion and economics, he has been a fearless and dynamic writer and speaker, whose salient characteristic is "a transparent and all-possessing honesty." He has been called "a peripatetic crusader, a trouble-hunter extraordinary"; and the Rev. Frederick K. Stamm listed him among the "ten real Christians" he had known, and said he was "an apostle of good will and understanding."

PRINCIPAL WORKS: India Awakening, 1911; The New Era in Asia, 1913; The Students of Asia, 1915; Suffering and the War, 1916; With Our Soldiers in France, 1917; Everybody's World, 1920; Facing the Crisis, 1922; The New World of Labor, 1923; The Abolition of War (with K. Page) 1924; New Challenges to Faith, 1926; Makers of Freedom (with K. Page) 1926; Religion and Social Justice, 1927; Sex and Youth, 1928; The Challenge of Russia, 1931; The Challenge of the East, 1931; The World's Danger Zone: Manchuria, 1932; The Challenge of Europe, 1933; Russia Today: What We Can Learn From It, 1934; A Pilgrimage of Ideas: The Re-education of Sherwood Eddy, 1934; Europe Today, 1937; Creative Pioneers (with K. Page) 1937; Revolutionary Christianity, 1939; I Have Seen God Do It, 1939; The Kingdom of God and the American Dream, 1941; Maker of Men: The Secret of Character Building, 1941.

ABOUT: Eddy, S. A Pilgrimage of Ideas; Christian Century January 16, 1941; Literary Digest August 12, 1933, April 11, 1936; North American Review December 1929; World Tomorrow October 1929, March 1931.

*EDMAN, IRWIN (November 28, 1896-), American philosopher, was born in New York City, in the shadow of Columbia University, and has lived there all his life—indeed, he says that other parts of the city seem still like a strange land to him. His parents were Solomon and Ricka (Sklower) Edman; his father was a manufacturer of shirts and blouses.

Donaldson

He was educated at Columbia (B.A. 1917, Ph.D. 1920), and began to teach philosophy there in 1918. He has been called "a teacher by instinct," though the story goes that when he was a young lecturer he met his former professor, Felix Adler, on the campus; Adler asked him what he was doing, and when the young man told him, Adler replied, "How cute!" Cute or not, he has been a highly unorthodox teacher and philosopher, who writes light verse, mingles with all sorts of people, is an accomplished essayist, and "an easy blend of the academic and the worldly man." He is still at Columbia, having become instructor in 1920, assistant professor in 1925, associate professor in 1931, and full professor of philosophy in 1935. In that year he was also Henry Ward Beecher lecturer at Amherst College, and in 1939 he taught in the summer school of the University of California. He is book editor (in the field of aesthetics) for the *Journal of Philosophy*, and a member of the editorial board of the *American Scholar*. He also writes and reviews frequently for more general magazines, including the *Nation*, *Harper's*, and the *Saturday Review of Literature*. He is unmarried.

A blond with keen dark eyes behind thick glasses, he suffers from chronic indigestion which he does not allow to interfere with his social and sociable life. His great avocation is music, and his particular musical passion is Brahms. He is "a studied and steadied liberal" in the original meaning of that abused term; even his philosophy is democratically American—though he acknowledges that he is also "a sentimental Anglophile," and he has written charmingly of peace-time England. He is the chief American interpreter of Santayana, though technically he is a Pragmatist, a disciple of John Dewey, and hence at second-hand a disciple of William James. (His Pragmatism is tempered, however, by a touch of idealistic Platonism.) Unlike most authentic philosophers, his main interest has been the study, not of abstract theory alone, but of its application to life. Even in his special field of aesthetics he has none of the superciliousness of the usual writers on this subject.

As Albert Guérard remarked, "he does not set himself apart, like a Pharisee of culture." Professor Guérard has compared reading Dr. Edman to "a delightful conversation with a most urbane teacher." In *Philosopher's Holiday*, which is semi-autobiographical in nature, the conversation is rather with a polished man of the world who happens also to be a teacher of philosophy. Dr. Edman has sometimes been accused of inconsistency and of too definite an attempt to bring philosophy to the level of the lay mind, but laymen who have attempted to read other philosophical books will be grateful for the alleged fault. His philosophy has been aptly called "a blend of Plato, Santayana, and Manhattan"—with a dash of Dewey.

In addition to his own books, Dr. Edman has edited Plato (1927) and Santayana (1936), and has contributed to **many**

* Died September 4, 1954.

anthologies, including *American Philosophy Today and Tomorrow* and *Columbia Studies in the History of Ideas.*

PRINCIPAL WORKS: Human Traits and Their Social Significance, 1920; Poems, 1925; Richard Kane Looks at Life, 1926; Adam, The Baby, and The Man From Mars, 1929; The Contemporary and His Soul, 1932; The Mind of Paul, 1935; Four Ways of Philosophy, 1937; Philosopher's Holiday, 1938; Candle in the Dark, 1939; Arts and the Man, 1939; Fountainheads of Freedom: The Growth of the Democratic Idea (with H. W. Schneider) 1941.

ABOUT: Forum April 1931; Saturday Review of Literature September 2, 1939; Time November 14, 1938; Wilson Library Bulletin June 1932, December 1938.

EDMONDS, WALTER DUMAUX (July 15, 1903-), American novelist, writes:

"My life has little to recommend it, I'm afraid, for it has been smooth sailing right along. I was born in Boonville, N.Y., on a farm belonging to my father. My parents were Walter D. Edmonds and Sarah (May) Edmonds, and my brother and sister and I were brought up in Boonville, for the most part, with winters in New York City, where my father practiced patent law. To me, however, the winters were a mere filling of time, and the life on the farm filled practically all my imagination. I was educated in a day school (Cutler School) in New York, then went to St. Paul's in Concord, N.H., and then to the Choate School at Wallingford, Conn. I graduated from Harvard in 1926. My only academic distinction is a Litt.D. from Union College. At Harvard, however, my chief interest became the *Harvard Advocate,* of which I ultimately became president and on which I think I spent more time and effort than on my studies. Work on the magazine and a failure in my first course in chemistry quickly turned me from a career as a chemical engineer, which had been my father's ambition for me. I majored in English and had the good luck to get into Professor Charles Townsend Copeland's course on English composition. His genius needs no description on my part. He taught me the value of work and of constantly trying to say what I might have to say as simply as possible. Dean Swift was the model he held out to me, and a page of Swift still seems to me the most beautiful example of what prose writing should be in all of English literature. While still in Professor Copeland's course, one of my stories written for him was accepted by *Scribner's Magazine,* and from that moment, with his encouragement, I decided to earn my living by writing.

"Luck has always played into my hands (so far). Mr. Sedgwick of the *Atlantic* decided to take a chance on a novel about the Erie Canal before I had begun it. I wrote *Rome Haul* and it did well. My second effort never sold, and I tore up my third, but since then my books have done well. Marc Connelly made a play of *Rome Haul (The Farmer Takes a Wife)* and it appeared also in the movies, as has *Drums Along the Mohawk.*

"In 1930 I married Eleanor Livingston Stetson, and we have a son and two daughters. They are being brought up much as I was, spending the larger part of the year in Boonville, but the winters in Cambridge. The life in our neighborhood, its origins and history, are what have interested me since I started writing in college. I was lucky to be born in New York State, which is almost in miniature a cross-section of the entire United States. All my books and stories have been about New York, and there is plenty more for me to write about and for a whole flock of writers too. It delights me to see the flock springing up with me— Carl Carmer, Roger Burlingame, Harold Thompson, Mrs. Della Lutes, Chard Powers Smith, Josephine Young Case, I think have all turned to the state in my day.

"My writing is not 'significant,' and I belong to no cliques."

* * *

Mr. Edmonds is a good-looking young man with crisp brown hair, a long, alert face, and an invariable pipe. At the end of 1936 he visited Hollywood to act as technical adviser in the filming of his *Drums Along the Mohawk.* Despite his diffidence and his unwillingness to dramatize himself, he is one of the most successful of contemporary novelists. The days of the building of the Erie Canal have become his special field and property. As one critic remarked, "he is interested less in Congresses and heroes than in the people whom most scholars ignore."

Edmonds' first attempt at working for young people, *The Matchlock Gun,* was awarded the Newbery Medal in 1942 as the most distinguished contribution of the previous year to American literature for children.

PRINCIPAL WORKS: Rome Haul, 1929; The Big Barn, 1930; Erie Water, 1933; Mostly Canallers (short stories) 1934; Drums Along the Mohawk, 1936; Chad Hanna, 1940; The Matchlock Gun, 1941; Young Ames, 1942.

ABOUT: Saturday Review of Literature March 27, 1937, December 11, 1937; Writer January 1941.

EDWARDS, Sir OWEN MORGAN (December 25, 1858-May 15, 1920), British educator, journalist, and reviver of Welsh as a literary language, was born at Coedypry, Llanuwchllyn, Merionethshire, the eldest son of Owen Edwards and Elizabeth (Jones) Edwards. He was first taught at home, and was later sent to a Church of England village school, a grammar school, and a theological college (at Bala), where, during his last year he joined the ministry of the Welsh Calvinistic Methodists.

In 1880 he went to the University College of Wales, Aberystwyth, received a B.A. degree, and in the year 1883-84 attended the University of Glasgow. A year later Balliol College, Oxford, elected him Brackenbury scholar in modern history, and there he won the Stanhope (essay) and Lothian prizes. After a year on the Continent he returned to Oxford, and was shortly appointed lecturer in modern history at Corpus Christi and Trinity Colleges (afterwards at Balliol and Pembroke). From 1889 to 1907 he was tutorial fellow of Lincoln College. In 1891 he married Ellen Davies, by whom he had three children; she died in 1919.

Meanwhile Edwards was elected (1899) without opposition to a seat in Parliament. He disliked politics, however, and resigned in the year following. His conception of Welsh nationalism, roughly formulated during his undergraduate years at Oxford, was of a cultural rather than a political or sectarian autonomy. He was a founder and an influential protagonist of the Dafydd ap Gwilym Society, which took its name from a 14th century Celtic nature poet and love lyricist.

In 1890 he was joint editor of a journal called *Cymra Fydd*—and left when it took on a political coloring. In the two years following he launched successively *Cymru* and *Cymru'r Plant*, a juvenile monthly, and edited both until the time of his death. He founded a quarterly and was associated with *Wales*, a magazine in English. *O'r Bala i Geneva* (1889), his first book, a travel volume, set a new precedent for Welsh prose; his most significant English writing was *Wales*, in the "Story of the Nations" series. He greatly popularized Welsh classics by issuing them in cheap reprints.

He was knighted in 1916 "for his service to Welsh literature." For his achievements in the revival of Welsh as a literary language he is without a peer.

PRINCIPAL WORKS AVAILABLE IN ENGLISH TRANSLATION: Wales, 1901 (in "Story of the Nations" series).

ABOUT: Oxford Magazine June 11, 1920; (London) Times May 18, 1920.

"EGERTON, GEORGE." See BRIGHT, M. C. D.

EGGE, PETER (April 1, 1869-), Norwegian novelist, writes (in English): "Peter Egge was born in Trondheim, a city a thousand years old, the capital of Norway during the Middle Ages. His parents were peasants from Innherad who when young came to settle in Trondheim to make a living there. Want of means prevented Egge from carrying on his studies at the  grammar school and passing his matriculation in classics. Instead he first became a clerk in a tradesman's office, then a sailor, a mason's tender, and a journalist. During the whole of this time he wrote books which he burnt. He was twenty-two years old when his first novel was published. His literary work includes both novels and plays. The theme chosen for his books has chiefly been taken from Trondheim and the country around.

"The novels *The Heart* and *Hansine Solstad* have obtained the greatest success. They have been translated into several languages; *Hansine Solstad* is to be had in ten languages, including English. The comedy *Love and Friendship* has been played hundreds of times in Scandinavia, also in several theatres abroad, including America. The drama *Defect* has been produced in Scandinavia, Germany, Switzerland, Austria, and Italy. According to Norwegian library statistics, Peter Egge has the largest number of readers after Knut Hamsun and Sigrid Undset."

* * *

Egge has also published one volume of poems. He was a "discovery" of Knut Hamsun, who arranged for the production of his first novel, *Common People*. Now over seventy, he is bald, with a gray clipped moustache and beard, a distinguished-looking man about whom one would never guess that he was for two years in his youth a seaman. In the same Scandinavian literary contest in which Sigurd Christiansen won first prize he won third. His work is not static, but has constantly improved and matured with time. Eugenia Kielland spoke of "his fine irony combined with not a little mournful resignation," Rolv Thesen of his "human warmth and sympathetic insight." Kristian Elster remarked that he is "exclusively concerned with the inner world of his characters, with their stream of consciousness, the experiences of the heart and mind. . . . His style is massive: it has power and plenitude, but it can smile too. There is a sincerity, an integrity, and a virility about his craftsmanship; and at the same time something infinitely delicate and full of sensitively reticent feeling." *Hansine Solstad* is considered his masterpiece; Romain Rolland called it "a high-spirited and noble work."

(Peter Egge's autobiographical letter above was written just before the Nazi occupation of Norway. Later information is unavailable.).

WORKS AVAILABLE IN ENGLISH: Hansine Solstad: The History of an Honest Woman, 1929.

ABOUT: Egge, P. Hansine Solstad (see Introduction by H. G. Leach); American Scandinavian Review January 1932, September 1937; Bookman (London) April 1932; Journal des Debats July 29, 1927; Revue Politique et Littéraire March 1, 1930.

EGGLESTON, EDWARD. See "AMERICAN AUTHORS: 1600-1900"

EGGLESTON, GEORGE CARY. See "AMERICAN AUTHORS: 1600-1900"

EHRENBOURG, ILYA (January 27, 1891-), Russian novelist, poet, and journalist, was born in Kiev of a wealthy Jewish family and spent his  childhood in Moscow's Chanovniki suburb, "stale with the odor of hot, sour beer," where his parents moved when he was scarcely five. He attended a Moscow Gymnasium and did his homework with a tutor (a professional hypnotist) who succeeded in controlling the wicked child only because he used hypnotism on him. At the age of thirteen Ilya visited Berlin by himself, gobbled up all the cakes at the Café Victoria, and spent his last pennies on paperweights in the shape of lizards: he had to telegraph home for a return ticket. In Moscow the Ehrenbourgs lived at the Hotel Royal Court, and the boy amused himself by ringing for the waiter who invariably would rush up with a steaming samovar.

In December 1905 Ehrenbourg helped the Revolutionaires in the building of barricades in the Presnya district, and soon thereafter was expelled from the First Moscow Gymnasium for organizing a student strike. Just as he was feeling freer for political activities, he was arrested for distributing leaflets in front of a factory. Subsequently he did organizational work in the Moskvarezk district while trying to master Marx's *Capital*. In 1908 he was imprisoned: "I spent eight months in many jails: in Bassman Prison I was thrashed, regained consciousness lying on the ground; vomited blood; went on a hunger strike for six days—it was tough, but I held on bravely and felt myself a hero. In the Butirki jail, I was scared to death by the rats." Released on bail, and with a "travel permit," Ilya was forced to roam all over Russia.

After 1909 Ehrenbourg traveled widely over Europe, constantly hounded, often hungry for five or six days at a stretch. In Paris his hang-out was the Café Rotonde. The Catholic writers Bloy, Jammes, Claudel, influenced him and he seriously planned joining a Benedictine order.

At the outbreak of the First World War Ehrenbourg offered his services to France. However, he was considered "unfit for service" and had to earn a living as stevedore—loading heavy cases of explosives at the Ivry railway station. Even during these dark days Ehrenbourg had won recognition in Russia for his poems and articles. One day the Paris chief of police summoned him: "Your articles are extremely unjust. We are going to give you a chance: go to the front—after seeing a few things there, you'll write differently!" This was partly true: on his return to Paris he had rid himself of most of his mysticism. On hearing of the Russian Revolution he rushed to his country. At last he reached Kiev and began teaching literature to the workers, supervising children's games, organizing theatre groups. The White Guards were busy too: they staged pogroms every night and Ehrenbourg escaped to Kharkov, then to Koktebel, a desolate place in Crimea, where he "organized an asylum for peasant children. The local priest went from door to door warning neighbors: 'He is driving them into Jewry, he's making devils out of them!' When the children brought milk and bread, things went on fine, when they didn't, I made soup out of pepperhusks. In the end I could not stand it any longer; I was wasting away, rotting," and he escaped in a barge leaving Crimea with a consignment of salt. After two weeks in Tiflis, he obtained a permit for Moscow, but on his way the Cheka grabbed him and it took him two weeks to prove that he was not a Wrangel agent. In Moscow, he found shelter in the Home of Proletarian Writers. It was frightfully cold: "I wrapped myself in an enormous red flag, shivered and pined for the jail of the Cheka with its steam heating." Although he was active helping with the Children's Theatre and reading Pushkin and Mayakovsky to the students of the Higher Chemical School, he could not adjust himself to the conditions of the Civil War.

He went to France, but the authorities advised him to leave immediately, and that is how Ehrenbourg came to write his first serious prose work, *The Extraordinary Adventures of Julio Jurenito* (1921) in Belgium. *Julio Jurenito* deals with the adventures of a Mexican dreamer and his wanderings about Europe with seven disciples. It was in the vanguard tradition of Valéry Larbaud and Pierre MacOrlan, but because of its sharp satiric vein, it attained, according to the critics, "Gargantuan proportions." Its immediate success encouraged Ehrenbourg and he wrote novel after novel: *Nikolay Kurbov* (1923), *The Love of Jeanne Ney* (1924), *The Racketeer* (1925), *The Summer of 1925* (1926), *A Street in Moscow* (1927), as well as numerous volumes of short stories. Although *The Love of Jeanne Ney* (which was made into a successful film) and *A Street in Moscow* dealt with Soviet Russia, the emphasis was on melodramatic aspects of the Revolution. The positive aspects of Soviet life he did not depict until his *Out of Chaos* (1934), unquestionably his best novel. But before the appearance of this mature work, Ehrenbourg had applied his talent to a new *genre*, reportage. With skeptical eye he observed the automobile industry, in *10 H.P.* (1930), and the motion picture business in *Factory of Dreams* (1931); he also reported the trouble in Austria (1934), the Swedish strike, Holland's Five-Year Plan, the Stavisky Affair, and the Civil War in Spain.

Ehrenbourg is a nervous, impressionistic writer of undeniable gifts. A keen observer of contemporary life, in his pamphleteering and satiric gusto he is representative of the raciest contemporary writing. Professor Struve has said: "Ehrenbourg knows how to handle his plot, how to make it thrilling and attractive, he has wit, his satire is often caustic and pointed, he knows how to make shallow thoughts look deep and significant, but the psychology of his characters is usually crude and made to fit in with preconceived abstract schemes." On the whole Struve's criticism accurately summarizes the early Ehrenbourg, but since *Out of Chaos* and the more recent *Without a Pause for Breath* (1937), the imputation of crude psychology is less tenable. Ehrenbourg's personal appearance and habits are as strange as his works. Tall, gawky, with big black eyes and disheveled hair, he usually wears an enormous sombrero and a huge overcoat that makes walking almost impossible. In 1941 he was retained, along with Mikhail Sholokov, by Overseas News Service as a correspondent to report the Russo-German war. His thrilling dispatches from the front, familiar to American newspaper readers, have made him a national hero in the Soviet Union.

WORKS AVAILABLE IN ENGLISH TRANSLATION: The Love of Jeanne Ney, 1929; The Extraordinary Adventures of Julio Jurenito and His Disciples, 1930; A Street in Moscow, 1930; Out of Chaos, 1934; A Soviet Writer Looks at Vienna, 1934.

ABOUT: Mirsky, D. S. Contemporary Russian Literature; Pozner, V. Panorama de la Littérature Russe Contemporaine; Struve, G. Soviet Russian Literature; Nation June 13, 1934; New Republic June 27, 1934; New York Herald Tribune "Books" January 26, 1930, June 22, 1930; New York Times April 17, 1932, June 3, 1934; Outlook July 23, 1930; Saturday Review of Literature January 25, 1930, May 26, 1934.

EHRLICH, LEONARD (1905-   ), American novelist, was born in New York City of a Jewish family and educated at the College of the City of New York (B.A. 1928). From 1930 to 1932 he was an instructor in English at the same college. Thereafter he made his way as a free-lance writer, whose book reviews appeared in the New York newspapers  and in the *Saturday Review of Literature*. In 1933 he was awarded a Guggenheim fellowship, and spent the next year studying in England. At that time, a year after the appearance of his only novel, he said he was contemplating a series of historical novels, but wanted first to finish one to be called *The Free and the Lonely,* which would have a contemporary New York background and apparently was to be autobiographical. Neither this nor any other book by him has, however, as yet appeared.

He is dark and slender, with a sensitive face and thick black hair. He is unmarried, and still lives in New York. He writes very slowly; *God's Angry Man* took four years to finish, and, counting revision and publishing, which he does as he writes, he produced only about two hundred words a day. Once he is satisfied with his work, he does not touch it again, and his first laborious draft is also his last.

The idea of *God's Angry Man,* a fictionalized biography of John Brown of Osawatomie, first came to Mr. Ehrlich from reading the chapter on Brown in Gamaliel Bradford's *Damaged Souls.* Because its excellent parts do not fuse into a consistent whole, Geoffrey Stone called it a partial but creditable failure; at the same time, he said it was "detailed and solid," showing evidence of careful research, a "conscientious report" written with "deep sympathy but lacking the divine fury."

Mr. Ehrlich's chief interest outside history and literature is in music, though he was a junior in college before he heard his first symphony concert. He has since become something of an authority on Brahms and Bach, and has published critical articles on both.

PRINCIPAL WORKS: God's Angry Man, 1932.

ABOUT: Bookman December 1932; Wilson Library Bulletin June 1933.

EIKER, MATHILDE (January 5, 1893-), American novelist, writes: "Mathilde Eiker was born in Washington, D.C.,

the oldest child and only daughter of John Tripner Eiker and Mattie (Eldridge) Eiker. Her father was chief clerk of the Rivers and Harbor Division of the office of Chief of Engineers of the War Department. Her home consequently was in Washington, and she has always lived there. With her three brothers she grew up in a suburb of the city which was then on the verge of farmland and woods and open country, hence enjoying advantages both of rural community and city. She was graduated from Central High School in Washington, and was awarded a scholarship to

George Washington University, from which she was graduated in 1914 with a B.A. degree. Throughout her high school and college courses she was interested in writing. After her graduation from college she published a few short stories under an assumed name. She has never been deeply interested in the short story as a literary form, however, and she soon shifted her attention to plays. She now seriously determined upon a writing career, and in this decision she received the encouragement and assistance of her father. Because of the uncertainties of stage production, she did not confine herself to the field of drama. She began her first novel, which was immediately accepted and published. Since that time she has written only novels. Her interest in the theatre has not vanished, however, and she hopes to include this form of writing again in her work.

"The theatre has always been one of her favorite forms of recreation. The others? Music, bridge, and walking through the beautiful large parks which surround the residential section of the capital."

* * *

Miss Eiker has said: "Unlike many persons who urge for the young writer constant practice in his craft, I believe that the formation of a sure taste and the development of habits of scrutiny are the first and most valuable assets." They have been valuable in her own case, making hers, to quote Elmer Davis, "one of the most inexorably unsentimental minds in modern letters," gifted with "faultless and minute observation, clear-eyed perception, and pervasive irony."

She is unmarried, and still lives at home. For two years, from 1924 to 1926, she was a public school teacher, but resigned "because the inadequacies of the educational system irritated her." She is tall, very slender, with bushy dark hair, a withdrawn, melancholy face, and an unexplained slightly German accent—though her ancestors for many generations have been Americans. She is active in the affairs of the Episcopal Church.

PRINCIPAL WORKS: Mrs. Mason's Daughters, 1925; Over the Boat-Side, 1927; The Lady of Stainless Raiment, 1928; Stranger Fidelities, 1929; My Own Far Towers, 1930; The Senator's Lady, 1932; Brief Seduction of Eva (in England: Flowers by Request) 1932; Heirs of Mrs. Willingdon, 1934; Key Next Door, 1937.

ABOUT: McCall's Magazine January 1928; New York Herald Tribune "Books" March 13, 1932; Saturday Review of Literature November 1, 1930.

ELIOT, CHARLES WILLIAM. See "AMERICAN AUTHORS: 1600-1900"

ELIOT, GEORGE FIELDING (June 22, 1894-), American writer on military affairs, writes: "George Fielding Eliot was

Louelle

born in Brooklyn, N.Y. When he was eight years old, his father accepted a very attractive business offer in Australia, to which he moved with his family. Young Eliot was educated in Melbourne (with the exception of two years during which his parents sent him back to school in the United States). Later he attended Trinity College, at the University of Melbourne, and was graduated there in 1914. Then came the World War. When Australia entered the conflict, Eliot joined up as a second lieutenant (much to his father's disgust), serving with the Australian Imperial Force from 1914 to 1918. As the war progressed, Eliot was promoted to lieutenant, then captain, and finally Acting Major of Infantry. He saw action first during the Dardanelles Campaign, later served in Egypt, and thence went to the Western Front. When the Armistice was signed he was not in France, but aboard a troop-ship bound back to Australia to bring out another load of recruits.

"In 1919 Eliot gave way to his urge to return to his native land. He set sail for Canada, but upon arrival there found that the Royal Canadian Mounted Police were enlisting recruits to their ranks. Eliot enlisted, and served a two-year tour of duty. In 1921 he came to the United States and settled in Kansas City, Mo. After a few years' work as an accountant, he began writing fiction stories about the Great War. Meanwhile, after serving briefly with the Missouri National Guard as a Second Lieutenant of Engineers, he was commissioned in the Military Intelligence Reserve of the United States Army, serving as captain and later as major from 1922 to 1930. During this period he was called to active duty at Fort Leavenworth, Kans., and to the Military Intelligence Division of the War Department at Washington.

"From 1928 to 1936 Eliot devoted himself to the writing of fiction, at the same time delving deep into the study of military history and military research, which later

came to bear fruit. In 1923 he married Sara Hodges, of North Carolina.

"From 1936 to the present time he has given all his time to lecturing and writing on military subjects and related international affairs. He has contributed such articles to many magazines, as well as to newspapers and service journals. Currently he is military and naval correspondent for the New York *Herald Tribune* and for *Life,* military commentator for the Columbia Broadcasting System, and lecturer on national defense."

* * *

Major Eliot is a big, smooth-shaven man, stoop-shouldered in spite of his military training. As a lecturer he is forthright, fluent, and exceedingly well informed. Of his books one critic has said that "he discusses war without sword-rattling, remains genuinely patriotic without a hint of chauvinism."

PRINCIPAL WORKS: Eagles of Death (novel) 1930; If War Comes (with R. E. Dupuy) 1937; The Ramparts We Watch: A Study of the Problems of American Defense, 1938; Bombs Bursting in Air: The Influence of Air Power on International Relations, 1939; Defense of the Americas, 1941; Then Conquer We Must, 1942.

ABOUT: Life May 13, 1940; National Education Association Journal February 1941. Time November 28, 1938.

ELIOT, THOMAS STEARNS (September 26, 1888-), American poet and essayist, was born in St. Louis, Mo., of a distinguished Boston family (President Charles W. Eliot of Harvard was another member) deeply rooted in the New England tradition and in the church. The cordwainer Andrew Eliot (1627-1704), an honest, God-fearing man from East Coker

(Somerset), settled in Boston in middle life. Often chosen Selectman, he became Town Clerk, and sat in condemnation of Salem witches together with one of the Hawthornes. Producing solid merchants and ministers, the Eliots acquired considerable weight in the mundane and divine affairs of Boston. The Rev. Andrew Eliot, D.D. (1718-78), staunch enemy of Episcopalianism, was elected President of Harvard but refused to leave his Congregational pulpit. The Rev. William Greenleaf Eliot, D.D. (1811-87), grandfather of T. S., a graduate of Harvard Divinity School (1834), moved to St. Louis, where he established the first Unitarian

Church and later Washington University which, but for his objection, would have been called Eliot University. Henry Ware Eliot (1841-1919), his second son, named after a famous New England Unitarian leader, married the daughter of a "commission merchant and trader" of Boston, a descendant of Isaac Stearns, one of the original settlers (with John Winthrop) of the Bay Colony in 1630. Charlotte (Stearns) Eliot (1843-1930) was "a woman of keen intellectual interests," witness her biography of William Greenleaf Eliot and her dramatic poem *Savonarola*, piously "introduced" by her seventh and youngest child Thomas.

"Tom" Eliot spent the first eighteen years of his life in St. Louis. On completing his studies at Smith Academy (of Washington University) and spending a year at Milton, he entered Harvard in 1906. Hard-working, brilliant, he finished his undergraduate work in three years and took his M.A. in his fourth. Although extremely reticent, sensitive and reserved, Eliot outshone the luminaries of the Class of 1910—John Reed, Heywood Broun, Hamilton Fish, Jr., Walter Lippmann, Stuart Chase—and was admitted to both literary clubs, the Stylus and the Signet. His interests were "violently eclectic, never popular." He contributed poems to the *Harvard Advocate* during 1907-10 and edited that magazine in 1909-10, but he shied away from Baker's spectacular drama course and from the fashionable readings at "Copey's" rooms. The lectures of Babbitt and Santayana were among his memorable experiences of this time. According to his *Advocate* associates, Eliot "was English in everything but accent and citizenship"—and these he acquired in later years. "His remarks were quiet, witty, precise, but not precious. He smoked a pipe, liked to be alone, carefully avoided slang, and dressed with the studied carelessness of a dandy." As Class Odist, Eliot penned an *Ode* now buried in the *Advocate* for June 24, 1910.

After a year at the Sorbonne, Eliot returned to Harvard and worked for his Ph.D. in philosophy, spicing his logic and metaphysics with some Sanskrit and Pali (1911-14). His dissertation on F. H. Bradley and Meinong's *Gegenstandstheorie* was accepted, he says, "because it was unreadable"—and he never took his degree. Receiving a traveling scholarship, he visited Germany the summer before the outbreak of the war, and that winter read philosophy at Merton College, Oxford.

In the spring of 1915 Eliot married Miss Vivienne Haigh-Wood of London and he earned his living by teaching "French, Latin, lower mathematics, drawing, swimming, geography, history, and baseball" at the Highgate School, London, and later by working at Lloyds Bank, Ltd., where "documentary bills, acceptances, and foreign exchange" took the place of "portraits of ladies." But neither the demands of Highgate nor the prosaic language of Lloyds undid him.

From 1917 to 1919 he was assistant editor of the *Egoist,* having been rejected by the U. S. Navy in 1918 because of poor health. Hitherto confined to the "little" magazines and a couple of slim volumes—*Prufrock and Other Observations* (1917) and *Ezra Pound, His Metric and Poetry*—Eliot now sent to press *Poems* (1919), *Ara Vos Prec* (1920), *Three Critical Essays* (1920), *The Sacred Wood* (1922), *Andrew Marvell* (1922), and *The Waste Land* (1922), which won him the $2000 Dial Award and brought his name to the forefront of contemporary literature. The 434 lines of *The Waste Land* summed up the disillusionment and disgust of the post-war generation, presenting in articulate though often complex form the barrenness of a standardized civilization. The more conservative critics, Mégroz for instance, called it "the greatest hoax of the century," and others, like H. N. Tomlinson in *Gallion's Reach,* objected to some of its features though admitting its "surprising" elements: "What does poetry want with footnotes about psycho-analysis and Negro mythology. . .?" *The Waste Land* has remained, since its first publication in the October 1922 *Criterion* and November 1922 *Dial,* a foundation stone and one of the most influential works not only of contemporary American and English but of world literature: it was translated into half a dozen languages and three versions especially attained wide circulation—the French by the poet Jean de Menasce, the German by the critic Ernst-Robert Curtius, and the Spanish by Angel Flores. *The Waste Land* may be considered a summation also of literary techniques. As early as 1908 Eliot had discovered Laforgue, Corbière, and Baudelaire from Symons' *The Symbolist Movement in Literature,* and their methods he appropriated and combined with his other admirations: Dante and Dryden, Ezra Pound, the Elizabethans and the Metaphysicians, especially Webster, Shakespeare, Middleton, Chapman, and Donne. The result was a poetry of juxtaposition and contrast, extremely modern and sophisticated but also suggestive of older aesthetic norms, of ancient essences and distilled compounds.

In 1922 Eliot established his own magazine *The Criterion,* which during its seventeen years of existence exerted a far-reaching influence in literary and philosophical circles for its serious critical approach and impeccable style. Although at one time it attained wide circulation, it was never self-supporting and Eliot has worked all along as literary editor for Faber & Faber. He became a British subject in 1927. Seeking a way out of "the waste land," Eliot had apparently found it by 1928 when in his famous introduction to *For Lancelot Andrewes* he confessed to being "an Anglo-Catholic in religion, a classicist in literature, and a royalist in politics." His later poetry, as well as his dramatic works, mirrors his conversion to Anglo-Catholicism.

Eliot returned to America for the first time in eighteen years as Charles Eliot Norton Professor of Poetry at Harvard (1932-33). Cordially received by his Alma Mater, he gave "reticent teas," at which expectant young intelligentsia would watch "the silent poet eat cake." "I tend to fall asleep in club arm chairs," declared the supercilious alumnus who has become more British than Henry James, "but I believe my brain works as well as ever, whatever that is, after I have had my tea."

Although Eliot evinced remarkable gifts in *Wanna Go Home, Baby?* (1927), *Sweeney Agonistes,* an Aristophanic melodrama (1932), and *The Rock* (1934), "a pageant play" written "on behalf of the Forty-five Churches fund of the diocese of London," it was not until 1935 that he emerged as an outstanding playwright with *Murder in the Cathedral,* originally intended for a festival of the friends of Canterbury Cathedral. Less successful but equally persuasive in the handling of dramatic situations was his verse play *Family Reunion* (1939).

Eliot's religious-monarchist views find their ripest expression in *The Idea of a Christian Society* (1940), in which he claims that "the only hopeful course" for the world today is in a "truly" Christian society. Eliot champions a National Church, officially recognized by the state, to serve as final authority on dogma, faith and morale—for "a positive culture must have a positive set of values." Such is "the eternal source of truth" and the ultimate return of Thomas Stearns Eliot to the fold of the Rev. Andrew Eliot, D.D., and the Rev. William Greenleaf Eliot, D.D., of Boston.

Eliot has been described as "an Arrow Collar man." He is darkly handsome, sensitive, extremely subtle, always ironical.

He wears his handkerchief in his cuff, drinks burgundy and sherry, plays chess (not so well), and is afraid of cows and high places. He prefers to mingle with the nobility, with church dignitaries and genteel spirits—the Woolfs, for example, or the Sitwells. More than eight years ago D. S. Mirsky said that Eliot had "reached his dead-end with 'The Hollow Men'—all his work since then has been mere flight and evasion." Little did he guess that during the feverish 1940's T. S. Eliot would be preaching the gospel of a "truly" Christian society to a desperate world.

PRINCIPAL WORKS: *Essays*—Sacred Wood, 1920; Andrew Marvell, 1922; For Lancelot Andrewes, 1928; Dante, 1929; Tradition and Experiment in Present-Day Literature, 1929; Thoughts After Lambeth, 1931; Selected Essays, 1917-1932, 1932; John Dryden, 1932; The Use of Poetry and the Use of Criticism, 1933; After Strange Gods, 1933; Elizabethan Essays, 1934; Essays Ancient and Modern, 1936; The Idea of a Christian Society, 1940. *Plays*—Sweeney Agonistes, 1932; The Rock, 1934; Murder in the Cathedral, 1935; Family Reunion, 1939. *Poetry*—Prufrock and Other Observations, 1917; Poems, 1919; The Waste Land, 1922; Poems, 1909-1925, 1925; Ash Wednesday, 1930; Collected Poems: 1909-1935, 1936; East Coker, 1940; Burnt Norton, 1941; The Dry Salvages, 1941.

ABOUT: Gallup, D. C. A Catalogue of English and American First Editions of Writings by Thomas Stearns Eliot; Gordon, G. S. Poetry and the Moderns; Grudin, L. Mr. Eliot Among the Nightingales; Jameson, R. D. Poetry and Plain Sense; Leavis, F. R. New Bearings in English Poetry; Lewis, W. Blasting and Bombardiering; Matthiesen, F. O. The Achievement of T. S. Eliot; McGreevy, T. Thomas Stearns Eliot; Oras, A Critical Ideas of T. S. Eliot; Partridge, A. C. T. S. Eliot; Powell, D. Descent from Parnassus; Williamson, H. R. The Poetry of T. S. Eliot; American Review September 1936; American Scholar January 1940; Commonweal October 16, 1932, February 18, 1938; Nation December 13, 1933, April 17, 1935; New Republic October 26, 1932, May 20, 1936; Poetry December 1934, April 1937, August 1939; Saturday Review of Literature September 19, 1936, January 25, 1941; Time January 2, 1939.

"ELIZABETH." See RUSSELL, M. A. B. R.

ELLIS, HAVELOCK (February 2, 1859-July 8, 1939), scientist of sex, whom H. L. Mencken called the most civilized Englishman of his time, was born Henry Havelock Ellis at Croydon, Surrey. His father, Edward Ellis, was a sea-captain, and on both sides he came of Suffolk families long connected with the sea, and before that including many clergymen. When he was only six he went with his father on a voyage to Australia and South America. He was educated at private schools and at home, his chief early interest being music. At sixteen he was sent to Australia again, since his health was poor, and he stayed in New South Wales from 1875 to 1879 as a country school teacher, part of the time quite alone in a remote part of the country. His only novel, *Kanga Creek,* was an idealized memory of that experience. Solitude and study de-

termined his life course. He was strongly attracted to social philosophy, but felt he must have a fundamental scientific background. He therefore returned to England and studied medicine in St. Thomas' Hospital, London. It was at that period that he met Olive Schreiner, whose friendship had an immense influence on his later life and work.

He practiced medicine only desultorily and for a few years; he had already made connections in the publishing world, and he became a member of the staff of the *Westminster Review* and from 1887 to 1889 was editor of the *Mermaid Series of Old Dramatists.* Gradually—he was always very slow in development—his interests became localized in psychology, and especially in the psychology of sex. The great series of *Studies in the Psychology of Sex* was begun in 1891, and was brought out volume by volume. The publisher was prosecuted for obscenity, and Ellis arranged thenceforth to have his books on the subject published in the United States. They are largely outdated now, and had their defects then, but Havelock Ellis probably did more than any other single individual to bring about a change in the general viewpoint on sex and its scientific elucidation in print.

In 1891 he married Edith M. O. Lees, who died in 1916. The story of their strange and tortured marriage is told in his subjective autobiography, completed just before his death. It revealed that the man who stood as a symbol of sane sexual approach was completely unhappy in his own sexual life. It is a painful and illuminating story, told with entire candor. Toward himself as toward everything else, Ellis' attitude was thoroughly scientific, though in the former case it was also a bit tinged by the natural egotism of an old and famous man. His life outwardly was uneventful, made up of study, hard work, occasional trips to the Continent, and in his last year retirement to Hintlesham,

Ipswich, where he died at eighty in the summer of 1939.

Less than a month before his death, Havelock Ellis sent the editors of this volume the previously unpublished photograph which is reproduced in these pages. Taken in May 1939, in the author's garden summer house at Ipswich, it is in all probability his last portrait. In a courteous accompanying note he wrote apologetically of the "feeble state" of his health, and said, "My work in the world is over." But his mind remained active until the very last, and, frail as his body had always been, he looked like an old sailor—deeply tanned, white-bearded, with deep-set, penetrating blue eyes. He was the last of the great Victorians, and his crusade the last of those they conducted; in a sense he was the Darwin of sex. As *John o'London's Weekly* remarked, "While Ellis' mind was shot with poetry, its business was clear thinking." Primarily, as Joseph Wood Krutch said of him, he was an educator and a scholar. His pioneer work in sexual education tended to obscure in the public mind the fact that he was also a first-class critic. From 1889 to 1914 he edited the volumes of the *Contemporary Science Series* and did it well. In his last years he even conducted a semiphilosophic column for the Hearst papers(!) and made a book out of the questions asked him. He had the old-time appetite (though without humor or gusto) for varied knowledge and the power to synthesize it. "Balance, tact, perceptiveness, candor, emotional warmth"—these, said Lewis Mumford, were Havelock Ellis' outstanding characteristics as a writer. To them may be added a sound and sober knowledge of biology— though in psychology he long ago fell behind the times, as in his shying away from Freud. He had outlived obloquy and, to a large extent, usefulness; but in his time he was a great pathfinder, and if we have out-paced him it is largely because he cleared the way.

PRINCIPAL WORKS: The New Spirit, 1890; The Criminal, 1890; Man and Woman, 1894; Affirmations, 1897; Studies in the Psychology of Sex, 1897-1928, revised edition 1936 (Sexual Inversion, 1897; Evolution of Modesty, 1899; Sexual Selection in Man, 1905; Erotic Symbolism, 1906; Sex in Relation to Society, 1910; Eonism and Other Supplementary Studies, 1928); The Nineteenth Century, 1900; A Study of British Genius, 1904; The Soul of Spain, 1908; The World of Dreams, 1911; The Task of Social Hygiene, 1912; Impressions and Comments, First Series 1914, Second Series 1921, Third Series 1924; Essays in War Time, 1917; The Philosophy of Conflict and Other Essays, 1919; Kanga Creek (novel) 1922; Little Essays of Love and Virtue, 1922; The Dance of Life, 1923; Sonnets with Folk Songs from the Spanish, 1925; The Art of Life, 1929; The Fountain of Life, 1930; More Essays of Love and

Virtue, 1931; Views and Reviews, 1932; George Chapman, 1934; My Confessional, 1934; From Rousseau to Proust, 1936; Questions of Our Day, 1936; My Life, 1939.

ABOUT: Goldberg, I. Havelock Ellis: A Biographical and Critical Survey; Peterson, H. Havelock Ellis: Philosopher of Love; Harper's Magazine October 1939; Literary Guide (London) September 1939; Nation March 25, 1936, July 22, 1939; New Republic April 15, 1936; Publishers' Weekly July 15, 1939; Saturday Review of Literature July 22, 1939, November 4, 1939; Science February 24, 1939; Yale Review September 1939.

ELLSBERG, EDWARD (November 21, 1891-), American naval officer and sea writer, writes: "I was born in New Haven, Conn. When I was  a year old my family removed to Denver, where I grew up. Owing perhaps to a nearly total lack of water on the surrounding prairies, I early took a deep (vicarious) interest in ships and the absent sea. While a freshman at the University of Colorado, destined for a later course in law, I received an appointment to the United States Naval Academy at Annapolis, and entered there in 1910, graduating as honor man in the class of 1914. I was commissioned as Ensign and assigned to the 'U.S.S. Texas' as assistant navigator, with later details as junior torpedo officer, turret officer, and finally division officer for the broadside torpedo defense batteries. In 1916, I received a detail to the Construction Corps of the Navy, was sent back to Annapolis for postgraduate work, and was then transferred to Massachusetts Institute of Technology for a two-year postgraduate course in naval architecture. Upon our entrance into the World War in April 1917, this course was abruptly terminated and I was ordered to the New York Navy Yard and assigned to the reconditioning and refitting of seized German liners as troop transports, and later to the fitting out and operation of mine sweepers. In 1918 (promoted to Lieutenant) I was detailed to the construction of the battleship 'Tennessee,' and on her launching in 1919 was ordered back to M.I.T. In 1920 I receive my M.S. degree and was ordered to the Boston Navy Yard as Planning Superintendent. In 1924, promoted to Lieutenant-Commander, I was loaned to the Shipping Board for a detail

on 'S.S. Leviathan' to redesign and correct deficiencies in her forced draft and ventilation systems. In 1925, upon the sinking of the submarine 'S-51,' I was detailed as Salvage Officer for recovering her from the bottom of the ocean. On the successful raising of the smashed submarine and the bodies of her trapped crew, nine months later, I was awarded the Navy's Distinguished Service Medal.

"In 1926 I resigned from the Navy to become chief engineer of an oil company, a post I held for nine years. In 1927, when the submarine 'S-4' was rammed and sunk, I was called back into the naval service for rescue and the initial salvage work. As a result I was recommissioned in the Naval Reserve and shortly thereafter by Special Act of Congress was promoted to the rank of Commander. I also received the degree of D.E. from the University of Colorado. My first book was published in 1929, and since then eight others have followed. Pigboats was produced as a moving picture under the title Hell Below. In 1935 I resigned from the oil company to become a consulting engineer in private practice. I have done a considerable amount of traveling in Europe, and have lectured extensively on questions involving neutrality, our national situation, and my submarine experiences. I was married in 1918 to Lucy Knowlton Buck; we have one daughter. My home since I left the Navy has been Westfield, N.J., where for some years I have been a member of the Board of Education."

* * *

Commander Ellsberg, a heavy-set, smooth-shaven man, is of Jewish descent. He is considered a leading expert on submarine salvaging and has been responsible for numerous inventions. The Bookman said of him that "he sticks to his last and builds an interesting plot around his extensive knowledge of diving operations." His first story appeared in the Youth's Companion in 1916 and he twice received medals at Annapolis for essays on naval subjects.

PRINCIPAL WORKS: On the Bottom, 1929; Thirty Fathoms Deep, 1930; Pigboats (in England Submerged) 1931; S-54 (short stories) 1932; Ocean Gold, 1935; Spanish Ingots, 1936; Hell on Ice, 1938; Men Under the Sea, 1939; Treasure Below, 1940; Captain Paul, 1941; "I Have Just Begun to Fight," 1942; War at Sea, 1942.

ABOUT: Kunitz, S. J. & Haycraft, H. (eds.) The Junior Book of Authors; Bookman August 1930; New York Times Book Review June 1, 1941; Publishers' Weekly March 29, 1941.

ELTON, OLIVER (1861-   ), English
cholar, Emeritus Professor of English Literature in the University of Liverpool, is
he son of a clergyman, the Rev. C.A. Elton,
B.D. He was educated at Marlborough and
at Corpus Christi College, Oxford, where
he was a Scholar and was graduated in 1884
with a first-class in *literae humaniores*. He
counted among his Oxford friends (Sir)
Michael Sadler, now Master of University
College, Oxford, and D. S. MacColl, later
to be Keeper of the Wallace Collection in
London. He married Letitia, sister of the
last-named, in 1888.

For some six years after graduation Elton
was employed in university extension lecturing, resident tutorships, the taking of
private pupils in Oxford, and the teaching
of Latin at an army coaching establishment; but concurrently he was enlarging his
knowledge of English literature and contributing signed reviews to the *Academy*.
In 1890 he was appointed lecturer in English Literature at Owens College, Manchester (now the University of Manchester), and in 1900 attained professorial
rank in the King Alfred Chair of English
Literature at University College, Liverpool.
He followed two very distinguished men—
Andrew Cecil Bradley and Walter Raleigh;
and before many years had gone by it became evident that the prestige of the Chair
was secure in his hands. He had already
produced a critical volume on *The Augustan
Ages,* an edition of Milton, and a translation of the Mythical Books of Saxo Grammaticus' *Historia Danica* (which dealt with
the Hamlet legend); and he was soon to
add studies of *Michael Drayton* and *Frederick York Powell,* a series of *Modern
Studies* that revealed ripe judgment and an
intimate knowledge of several literatures,
and in 1912 *A Survey of English Literature:
1780-1830,* which last was a major critical
work dealing in great detail with the period
and displaying a most subtle and judicious
sense of literary values. To these two volumes were added two more in 1920, carrying the study forward to 1880, while in 1928
Elton covered the earlier period from 1730
to 1780.

In the purely academic sphere he was
associated with several professors who, like
himself, have since attained international
repute, in an informal committee which
called itself the "New Testament Group,"
this title having no theological bearings, but
indicating a forward-looking policy for the
young university (which had become au-
tonomous in 1903). To the scholarship and

broad humanity of these men the University
of Liverpool largely owed its quick rise
to high status among British educational
institutions. Elton's own lectures always
had a fine sense of proportion and were
especially valuable in guiding undergraduates to appropriate source material; for he
has never believed in spoon-feeding, but has
always given his honors students ample time
for library work. He arranged the English
courses at Liverpool on broad lines, and
insisted on the periodical production of essays, which were always seriously considered
and discussed by him in his room. He was
quick to detect and eradicate any traces of
cant, specious generalization, or careless
writing, and he required his honorsmen to
supplement their purely literary studies
by courses in languages, history, and philosophy.

Elton was a member of the University
Senate, and for a period of interregnum
acted as Vice-Chancellor. He lectured by
invitation at several other universities, including the Panjab University in 1917-18
and University College, London, in 1922-23.
Retiring from Liverpool under age-limit
early in 1926, he went oversea to Harvard,
where he acted as visiting professor and
delivered the Lowell Lectures. In 1927-28
he was visiting professor at Bedford College
for Women, University of London; in 1929-
30 he was lecturer in rhetoric at Gresham
College; and in 1930-31 he made a second
visit to Harvard. He is a Fellow of the
British Academy; he was President of the
English Association in 1932; and he holds
honorary doctorates from the Universities
of Durham, Manchester, Oxford, Liverpool,
and Reading.

In latter years Professor and Mrs. Elton
have lived in the Woodstock Road, Oxford.
Elton was elected an Honorary Fellow of
Corpus in 1930, so that he remains in close
touch with an academic community. Though
past eighty, he pursues an active career as
a writer and external examiner. Already
long familiar with the Classical tongues and
the better-known European languages, he
has lately taken up Slavonic studies and
has produced elegant translations from Russian and Polish poets. He is a tall man, of
fine presence and great dignity, with a high
forehead and well-shaped head, as shown
in the portrait by Augustus John (a former
Liverpool colleague). He is clean-shaven
except for a small imperial. Those who
know him have an immense respect for his
high scholarship and a real regard for his

---

* Died June 4, 1945.

sterling personal qualities of courtesy, generosity and readiness to support those worthy of help. He has two sons, one of whom is a don at Oxford.

PRINCIPAL WORKS: The Augustan Ages, 1899; Frederick York Powell, 1906; Survey of English Literature, 1912 (additional vols. 1920, 1928); C. E. Montagu: A Memoir, 1929; Chekhov, 1929; Robert Bridges and the Testament of Beauty, 1932; The English Muse, 1933; Lascelles Abercrombie...: A Memoir, 1939; Essays and Addresses, 1939.

ABOUT: Blunden, E. C. Votive Tablets; Elton, O: Essays and Addresses, Frederick York Powell, C. E. Montagu.

ERENBURG. See EHRENBOURG

ERNLE, ROWLAND EDMUND PROTHERO, 1st Baron (September 6, 1851-July 2, 1937), English editor and

miscellaneous writer, was born at Clifton-on-Teme, the third son of the Rev. Canon Prothero, Rector of Whippingham. He attended Marlborough; then Balliol College, Oxford (M. A.), receiving a second class in Classical Moderations. In 1875 he took a first class in Modern History at Oxford, and he was a Fellow at All Souls College from that year until 1891. He contested the Biggleswade Division, Bedford, in 1910 as a Conservative candidate (he was land agent to the Duke of Bedford for twenty years) and was a member of Parliament for the University of Oxford from 1914 to 1919, when he resigned and was raised to the peerage as the first Baron Ernle. The five years between 1894 and 1899 were the time of Ernle's greatest literary activity; he not only was editor of the Quarterly Review but edited the Life and Correspondence of Dean Stanley, the Letters of Edward Gibbon, the Letters and Journals of Lord Byron, and, at the Queen's request, Sir R. Holmes' Life of Queen Victoria. From 1913 to 1922 he served on several royal commissions. He was also vice president of the Land Agents' Society and vice president of the Royal Literary Fund. The Psalms in Human Life, a piece of reverent historical potboiling, went through more than twenty editions. Ernle's The Light Reading of Our Ancestors (1927) is a really valuable addition to the history of the English novel, suggested to him by the study made by Sir Walter Raleigh.

Failing eyesight made the collaboration of Lady Ernle and a daughter by his first wife necessary. Lady Ernle, the former Barbara Hamley, died in 1930. His first wife, who died in 1899, was Mary Beatrice Bailward.

PRINCIPAL WORKS: Pioneers and Progress of English Farming, 1887; The Psalms in Human Life, 1903 (21st edition 1928); The Pleasant Land of France, 1908; English Farming: Past and Present, 1912; The Land and Its People, 1925; The Light Reading of Our Ancestors: Chapters in the Growth of the English Novel, 1927; Whippingham to Westminster (reminiscences) 1938. Editor: The Life and Correspondence of Arthur Penrhyn Stanley, 1893; Letters and Verses of Dean Stanley, 1895; Letters of Edward Gibbon, 1896; Letters and Journals of Lord Byron, 1898-1901 (third reprint 1922-1924).

ABOUT: Ernle, R. E. P. Whippingham to Westminster; New York Times July 3, 1937.

*ERSKINE, JOHN (October 5, 1879-) American novelist, poet, and essayist, was born in New York City, the son of James Morrison Erskine and Eliza Jane (Hollingsworth) Erskine. He was educated at Columbia (B.A. 1900, M.A. 1901, Ph.D. 1903), and has honorary doctorates from nine colleges and universities. These degrees are in letters, education, and music,

for Dr. Erskine is a concert pianist of high rank.

He has had an unusual career. It started unremarkably enough, first at Amherst where he was instructor and then associate professor of English from 1903 to 1909, and then at Columbia, where he was adjunct professor of English from 1909 to 1916, professor from 1916 to 1937, and is now professor emeritus. But in 1925 the brilliant teacher who was a campus celebrity but little known otherwise except among other specialists in his own field, suddenly blossomed out as one of the best known satirical novelists in English. Soon after, he appeared as soloist with the New York Philharmonic. He continued to coruscate in these three disparate provinces, living evidence that, for some people at least, life begins not at, but after, forty.

This "huge mast of a man with a bright rudder of a nose, a humorous diagonal mouth, a sabre wit, and the manners of a Sidney," as Henry Morton Robinson called him, "the most colorful person on the campus," with "the rolling gait of a sea captain," to quote Porter Reeves, is known to thousands of readers as the novelist who has brought the legendary tales of Helen of Troy, Lancelot and Galahad, Adam and Lilith, into sparkling contemporary life— readers who never heard of Professor Erskine, the authorized editor of Lafcadio Hearn and an authority on the history of English poetry. Still other thousands know only John Erskine, the president and director of the Juilliard Musical Foundation and the director of the Metropolitan Opera Association. Another public remembers him as the colonel who was chairman of the Army Educational Commission, during the First World War, and who established the A.E.F. University at Beaune, France, or as the advocate of preparedness today. And yet another public respects the co-editor of the *Cambridge History of American Literature* and the *Outline of Literature*, the ex-president of the Poetry Society of America, the former secretary of the Council of Learned Societies, the member of the National Institute of Arts and Letters and the American Academy of Arts and Sciences, the officer of the French Legion of Honor, the recipient of the Distinguished Service Medal. (His other decoration is the David Bispham Opera Medal.)

To live as many lives as these, and to be distinguished in them all, implies development of a "technique of time-saving." *The Private Life of Helen of Troy*, for example, was written between January and June, and between 11 P.M. and 1 A.M., after a full day at the university. He never wastes a minute. He had originally intended to be a pianist, having started to study music at the age of five. He abandoned it for twenty-six years, then returned to it because of a "ferocious urge," and in a few years trained himself to concert capacity. "His erudition," said Mr. Robinson, "is enormous, but he rides it easily. . . . He is a great furnace of energy, but his outward demeanor is leisurely and calm." He even makes time for occasional transcontinental lecture tours.

Dr. Erskine was married in 1910 to Pauline Ives; they have two children. Their home is in New York, where he manages in the interstices of his other activities to serve as a vestryman and a school trustee. For two years he was also a member of the Municipal Art Commission. He denies earnestly that he is merely a witty satirist; he says that he has the same thing to say in his novels, poems, and essays, and that in all of them he is expressing his social ideas. His recent books have been less entertaining and popular than his earlier novels.

PRINCIPAL WORKS: *Poetry*—Actaeon and Other Poems, 1906; Collected Poems, 1922; Sonata and Other Poems, 1925. *Novels*—The Private Life of Helen of Troy, 1925; Galahad, 1926; Adam and Eve, 1927; Penelope's Man, 1928; Cinderella's Daughter, 1930; Jack and the Beanstalk, 1931; Tristan and Isolde, 1932; Helen Retires, 1934; Solomon, My Son! 1935; Mrs. Doratt, 1941. *Miscellaneous*— The Elizabethan Lyric, 1903; Leading American Novelists, 1909; Written English (with H. Erskine) 1910; A Pageant in Honor of Roger Bacon, 1914; The Moral Obligation To Be Intelligent, 1915; The Shadowed Hour, 1917; Democracy and Ideals, 1920; The Kinds of Poetry, 1920; The Literary Discipline, 1923; The Enchanted Garden, 1925; Prohibition and Christianity, 1927; The Delight of Great Books, 1928; Sincerity, 1929; Uncle Sam, 1930; Unfinished Business, 1931; Bachelor of Arts, 1934; Forget If You Can, 1935; The Influence of Women—and Its Cure, 1936; Young Love, 1936; The Brief Hour of François Villon, 1937; The Start of the Road, 1938; Give Me Liberty, 1940; Casanova's Women, 1941; The Philharmonic-Symphony Society of New York (ed.) 1942.

ABOUT: American Magazine May 1930; Bookman August 1927, April 1930; Collier's Weekly September 3, 1927, January 4, 1930; Delineator September 1926; Golden Book March 1934; Musician April 1934; Saturday Review of Literature November 9, 1940; Sewanee Review April 1927; Time October 14, 1940.

ERTZ, SUSAN (1894?-), Anglo-American novelist, was born in England of American parents, both New Yorkers. At a very early age she was brought to America, but returned to England at the age of seven and remained there until she was twelve. From twelve to eighteen she lived in the Sierra Nevada mountains, in California. She writes: "In the company of  two brothers and a sister, I sat at the feet of an English governess who had a liking for adventure. Our studies were pursued in a small cabin, at desks made of rough-hewn pine. The mountain winters were so severe that we went down to the milder climate of San Francisco until the snows were melted. I was in that city at the time of the disaster of 1906. But those long, happy summers in the pine forests of the Sierras are unforgettable."

After "a taste of New York life," Miss Ertz returned to England in May 1914, "to the enjoyment of a few perfect months before the World War." She did war work in London, and was "a spectator of every kind of heroism except the actual heroism of the battlefields." During the war she was in New York for six months, returning to England to do canteen work for American soldiers from late in 1917 until after the Armistice.

Her first novel, *Madame Claire,* appeared in 1922. Its success was not instantaneous, but it grew steadily to popularity. Domestic problems have been the theme of most of her novels: *Nina* treats of a woman's hopeless infatuation for a faithless husband, *After Noon* is a study of a middle-aged man; *The Story of Julian* a portrait of adolescence; and *Now We Set Out* the story of the first years of a marriage. In *Now East, Now West,* she treats of the differences between the American and the English mentality, and *The Proselyte* is a carefully documented and moving account of the great Mormon trek across the plains and mountains to Utah. *No Hearts To Break* is an authoritative account, in fictional form, of the marriage of Jerome Bonaparte and Elizabeth Patterson.

In 1932 Miss Ertz married Major J. Ronald McCrinkle, O.B.E., M.C. She lives in London, visiting America occasionally and in 1937 lecturing there from coast to coast. She spends her holidays in travel or at an old Sussex farmhouse called Pooks Farm. She is greatly interested in painting, and before beginning her literary career studied art with a view to making it her profession.

PRINCIPAL WORKS: Madame Claire, 1922; Nina, 1924; After Noon, 1926; Now East, Now West, 1927; The Wind of Complication (short stories) 1927; The Galaxy, 1929; The Story of Julian, 1931; The Proselyte, 1933; Now We Set Out, 1934; Woman Alive, 1935; No Hearts To Break, 1937; Black, White, and Caroline, 1938; Big Frogs and Little Frogs (short stories) 1939; One Fight More, 1939.

ERVINE, ST. JOHN GREER (December 28, 1883-), Irish playwright, critic, and novelist, was born in Belfast, the son

Pinchot

of William Ervine. He is not a university graduate, but he has an honorary LL.D. from St. Andrews, and is a Fellow of the Royal Society of Literature. He was married in 1911 to Leonora Mary Davis; they have no children. His first one-act play was published in 1907, and in 1910 his first full-length play, *Mixed Marriage,* appeared. He had meanwhile moved to Dublin, and become associate with the Abbey Theatre; in 1915 he became its manager. His best known plays. *Jane Clegg* and *John Ferguson,* were both written before the First World War, the former produced by the Gaiety Theatre Manchester, the latter by the Abbey Theatre

With the war, Mr. Ervine enlisted as trooper in the Household Battalion. In 191 he went to France as a lieutenant in the Royal Dublin Fusiliers. In May 1918 h was severely wounded, and lost a leg i consequence. After the war he did no return to Ireland, but settled in London an continued to write plays, interspersed wit an occasional novel. In 1929 he was em ployed for a year as guest dramatic criti for the New York *World,* and stirred up critical storm, partly by his forthright inde pendence and plain speaking about Amer ican plays of the period, but partly becaus he substituted for his own suave critic style an imitation of "Broadwayese" tha to other critics seemed vulgar and cor temptuous. Nevertheless, he was personall popular and on leaving said that he wa grateful for the kindness he had receive in this country. Like the late David Be lasco, he wears a clerical collar, and indee resembles a clergyman in appearance.

From 1933 to 1936 he was professor o dramatic literature for the Royal Societ of Literature. He is a member of the Iris Academy. Besides his London house, h has a house at Honey Ditches, Seato Devonshire. In later years his work ha broadened to include not only plays (o which he wrote none for eight years) an novels (of which his last was in 1931), bu also biographies and essays on ethical an political subjects. In 1936 he made an ex tended trip to Palestine, described later i a book. He has been active in public lif though always unofficially, and has bee particularly concerned with the raising o theatrical standards. Although in his play especially in the earlier and better know ones, he is a pronounced realist—in fac one of the pioneers of the homespun rea ism of the drama of the Irish Renaissance— he has a strongly ethical bent, and the dra matic impact of his plays and novels i sometimes weakened by his tendency t moralize or to use his characters as vehicle of a social or religious thesis. His is no one of the great names of the group asso ciated with the Abbey Theatre, like thos of Yeats and Synge, but he is a soun craftsman and a competent playwright wh once in a while has exceeded adequacy an roduced a minor dramatic classic such as *John Ferguson* or *Jane Clegg*.

PRINCIPAL WORKS: *Plays*—The Magnanimous Lover, 1907; Mixed Marriage, 1910; Jane Clegg, 1911; John Ferguson, 1914; The Ship, 1922; Mary, Mary Quite Contrary, 1923; The Lady of Belmont, 1924; Anthony and Anna, 1925; The First Mrs. Fraser, 1928 (as a novel, 1931); The Wonderful Visit (with H. G. Wells) 1928; Four One-Act Plays (The Magnanimous Lover, Progress, Ole George Comes to Tea, She Was No Lady) 1928; People of Our Class, 1936; Boyd's Shop, 1936; Robert's Wife, 1938; The Christies, 1939; Boyd's Daughter, 1940. *Novels*—Mrs. Martin's Man, 1914; Alice and a Family, 1915; Changing Winds, 1917; The Foolish Lovers, 1920; The Wayward Man, 1927; The Mountain and Other Stories, 1928. *Miscellaneous*—Some Impressions of My Elders, 1922; The Organized Theatre: A Plea in Civics, 1924; Parnell, 1925; Sir Edward Carson and the Ulster Movement, 1927; How to Write a Play, 1928; The Future of the Press, 1932; The Theatre in My Time, 1933; If I Were Dictator, 1934; God's Soldier: General William Booth, 1934; A Journey to Jerusalem, 1936; The Christian and the New Morality, 1940.

ABOUT: Bookman (London) February 1924; Outlook April 19, 1929; Sewanee Review April 1925.

ESPINA, CONCHA (April 15, 1880-), Spanish novelist, writes: "I was born in Santander, Castille, April 15, 1880. [Other sources give her birth-year as 1877; she herself, on one occasion, gave 1855!] My ancestors were noblemen with a distinguished position in the society of Santander. My first years were happy, with the polished education which then

was given to a girl of my class, with no university studies until later. My character was melancholy and gentle. I published my first work, as a poet, in a very interesting periodical which was published in Santander; I was then twelve years old. Some of the verses gained the greatest honor which a Spaniard could desire in those days: they earned the attention, the praise, and the championship of the famous scholar Marcelino Ménéndez y Pelaya, a man of universal renown and also from Santander. Stimulated by such good fortune I wrote my first prose. It was one of those literary works of which one can say that they have no classification: neither stories, poems, nor essays, it partook of the nature of all three. Both before and after its publication, Ménéndez Pelayo again praised it and urged me to develop as a novelist. In 1910 my

first novel appeared, *La Niña de Luzmela* (*Luzmela's Daughter*), which has been translated into various languages. Since then I have published twenty-nine books, almost all novels, a few short stories or essays.

"My works have been crowned by the Royal Spanish Academy of Letters with prizes, all of them granted for the first time to the books of a woman. I have also received several decorations for my works, including one from Peru, one from Argentina, and the medal of the Academy of Arts and Letters of New York. I am the Spanish representative of the Mark Twain Society and of other Spanish-American societies. My statue was erected by readers from all over the world.

"Above all these honors, undoubtedly undeserved, I have the pure satisfaction which it gives me that my books are equally popular with the cultured public and with simple people. America has given me much of this kind of satisfaction. I have many American girls who were named for my heroines, and many places in the New World bear the names of towns in my literary geography.

"I have tried in my literary work to raise spiritual values above passion, self-interest, and ambition. Next I have sought, in the rich idiom of Castille, the old words of great beauty, which have augmented my vocabulary without making it appear archaic. For this reason some of my books have been studied by the Royal Spanish Academy in the preparation of its dictionary.

"My first youth was spent in Santander; in 1903 I moved to South America. On my return to Spain I settled in Madrid. I am married and have four sons.

"For my religious ideals and my social class, I have been persecuted in every way by the Communists, brought before one of the most frightful Chekas, and finally kept under home arrest until the Day of Liberation. My books and my house were completely destroyed by the Reds. I do not speak, therefore, of my political and social convictions. . . .

"It has frequently been said that one of my favorite works in literature is the marvelous Book of Job; I repeat it.

"I have traveled all over the world and have lived in the United States for long periods. At present I live, as I have done for many years, in Madrid, and my balconies open on the old royal park of the Retiro. Now I have the incomparable happiness of seeing that Spain is reborn, lofty and free, as in the greatest times of its history. In its shadow I live, carrying on my literary work without rest."

* * *

The writer was once unhappily married to a man by the name of de la Serna. Most literary people have respected her wish to be known by her own name of Espina, but some libraries have added the marital "de la Serna," or, even more inaccurately, "de Serna." One of her sons remained in Chile where he is known as a writer.

Annie Russell Marble spoke of the novelist's "vigor and dramatic skill." Of her best known work, *La Esfinge Maragata* (*Mariflor*), the late James Fitzmaurice-Kelly said that it was "a regional tale with realistic elements, whose charm she has not quite succeeded in recapturing in later novels."

WORKS AVAILABLE IN ENGLISH: Mariflor, 1924; The Red Beacon, 1924; Woman and the Sea, 1934.

ABOUT: Espina, C. Woman and the Sea (see Introduction by E. Boyd); Fria Lagoni, M. Concha Espina y sus Criticos; Smith, C. W. Concha Espina and Her Women Characters.

ETSU. See SUGIMOTO

*EVANS, CARADOC (1883-), Welsh novelist and short story writer, writes: "I come from Wales, a country the principal

exports of which are preachers, politicians, and pugilists. My part is Cardiganshire. I come of peasant stock, although my father succeeded in becoming an auctioneer and estate agent. But he died at the age of thirty, leaving a widow and five small children. I was the youngest but one. We went to the board school. The education was free. Next to the preacher the schoolmaster was the worst tyrant in the place. He also was religious. He taught me a little penmanship and a little English reading, but I never had the ghost of an idea what I was reading.

"Mother wanted to place her children in genteel trades. The professions were out of the question. At the age of fourteen, like my elder brother and sister, I was apprenticed to a draper at Carmarthen. It was at this draper's shop that I first tasted fresh meat. My stumbling-block was the English language. I used to make customers laugh by my misuse of words.

"By and by I got another job in Cardiff that job was slavery. We slept eight in a room, and we were badly fed. I came to London, and was sacked from one job after another for my incompetence. I thought that I would like to be a journalist. I attended evening classes at the Working Men's College. But I could not make any progress in English. With all I decided to become a journalist. One day I was discharged from my twelfth job in London, and I vowed not to return to shop work. One morning I put on my frock coat and silk hat, which was the draper's uniform, and walked into the office of a small weekly publication The editor-proprietor engaged me; four weeks later he tried to borrow ten pounds When I said I didn't have it, he replied 'Good God, if I hadn't thought you a rich fellow, I wouldn't have engaged you.' I never received any salary from him, but I had saved about thirty pounds and I lived on that sum. I stayed until the paper broke.

"I wanted to write stories, but I did not know what to write about. Then one night I opened the Bible and said to myself, 'This is the way to learn English.' I said further 'Why not try to write a Welsh story in Biblical English?' I have been trying to do so ever since.

"After *My People* was published people began to talk about me. My uncle, whose memory I hate, noised it about that it was he who had me educated; but the village schoolmaster said: 'If Caradoc can write a book, the village idiot can write a new Bible.' "

* * *

In later years Mr. Evans did editorial work on *Everybody's Weekly, Harmsworth's History of the World,* and *The World's Great Books,* and was acting editor of *T. P.'s Weekly* and *Cassell's Weekly.* He is married to the Countess Barcynska, an Englishwoman whose maiden name was Jervis, and who under the pseudonym of "Oliver Sandys" is a popular novelist. He himself shuns society and leads a very quiet life. Thomas Burke one of his few intimates, describes him as "a lean figure, dark of hair and visage, and heavily lined. He has the smouldering gloom of his race that flashes now and then into nervous heat. Never yet has he been known to keep an appointment. He talks in cascades words tumbling over each other, precisely opposite to the caustic manner of his work He likes plain company, pipes, old taverns and beer." His wife runs a repertory theatre

* Died January 11, 1945.

nd he says his recreation is "scene-shifting and back-stage odd jobs."

He has just one theme in all his writing: detestation of his native land and its people, especially of their miserliness, dishonesty, and religiosity. Naomi Royde-Smith called him "the greatest satirist of his own people since Swift," but he has none of Swift's tortured underlying love of his compatriots. He is sardonic, cruel, and powerful; one of his lectures on the Welsh started a riot, and Lloyd George denounced him as a "renegade," but nothing can keep him from telling the truth as he sees it.

PRINCIPAL WORKS: My People: Stories of the Peasantry of West Wales, 1915; Capel Sion (short stories) 1916; My Neighbors: Stories of the London Welsh, 1919; Taffy (play) 1925; Nothing To Pay, 1930; This Way to Heaven, 1933; Wasps, 1934.

ABOUT: Saturday Review April 1, 1933.

EVARTS, HAL GEORGE (August 24, 1887-October 18, 1934), American writer of Western fiction, was born in Topeka, Kans.,

the son of George Alfred Evarts and Emma Evarts. After attending high school in Topeka for two years he went surveying in Indian Territory, and found that outdoor life appealed to him. Young Evarts lived in Wyoming and other parts of the West as rancher, trapper, licensed guide, and raiser of fur-bearing animals in captivity, and made himself an acknowledged authority on hunting and trapping. In middle life he was outdoor editor of the Saturday Evening Post for several years, contributing many articles on hunting. During the First World War he spent some months as member of the Officers Training Corps, Camp Pike, receiving his commission as second lieutenant shortly before the armistice. In 1911 he married Sylvia Abraham of Kansas City, Mo., who survived him with a son, Hal, Jr., who was a student at Stanford University at the time of his father's death at fifty-seven. Evarts had suffered several heart attacks before he went on a South American cruise in an effort to recover his health. He died aboard the steamship "Malolo" as the vessel neared Rio de Janeiro, Brazil. Evarts was a Republican, a Mason, and a member of the Adventurers and Explorers Clubs. He lived with his family in Los Angeles, Calif., in his later years.

"Mr. Evarts apparently thinks the facts are thrilling enough to stand by themselves without literary artifice or art," commented the New York Times on his fifth "Western," The Settling of the Sage (1922). Nevertheless, he always had a stirring tale to unfold, whatever its technical faults. Like James Oliver Curwood's, his thrillers found favor in France. Tumbleweeds, a novel about the opening-up of the Cherokee Strip—the title referred to riders of the cattle ranges, whose roving and restless nature earned them the sobriquet—was translated as Herbes Volantes: Roman du Far-West, in the "Bibliothèque du Dimanche Illustré." The Boston Transcript called it "one of the 'Western' stories, but in a new environment." Spanish Acres was praised by the Saturday Review of Literature as being "highly meritorious." Evarts, with his bald head and clean-shaven face, looked more like the usual conception of an American business man than a writer of robust outdoor stories.

PRINCIPAL WORKS: The Cross Pull, 1920; The Bald Face, 1921; Passing of the Old West, 1921; The Yellow Horde, 1921; The Settling of the Sage, 1922; Fur Sign, 1922; Tumbleweeds, 1923; Spanish Acres, 1925; The Painted Stallion, 1926; The Moccasin Telegraph, 1927; Fur Brigade, 1928; Tomahawk Rights, 1929; The Shaggy Legion, 1930; Shortgrass, 1932; Wolf Dog, 1935.

ABOUT: New York Times October 19, 1934.

"EVOE." See KNOX, E. G. V.

FABRICIUS, JOHAN WIGMORE (August 24, 1899-), Dutch novelist, was born in Bandoeng, Dutch East Indies, where his father was a government official. He was educated at a secondary school in Batavia, and the family then returned to Holland, where he attended another secondary school in Leyden. His first interest was in art, and he studied for some time in the Art School in Amsterdam. But during the First World War, though he was still in his teens, he was sent by an Amsterdam paper as its war correspondent in the Austrian-Italian front, and with this experience his career as an artist ended and his work as a journalist and writer began. In 1922 he made an extended trip to South and North America, including the United States, again as a newspaper correspondent. Since that time he has devoted himself entirely to novel-writing. He is unmarried. In 1938 he was living in The Hague. Since the Nazi conquest of Holland, no information concerning him has been received, but it is presumed that he is still in the Netherlands, though what he is writing or if he is able to write at all is not known. His work has never had any political implications, so it is probable that no harm has befallen him.

Besides his novels for adults, he has written a seventeenth century historical story for boys, *Java Ho!,* which one critic described as "one of the best sea stories ever written, and one of the most entertaining." Except for this book, he has used the East Indian background of his boyhood very little, most of his novels being laid either in Holland or in Italy, where he has lived and written during extended periods. The latest of his books to be translated has as its scene Austria before, during, and immediately after the First World War. He is so much a citizen of Europe, rather than merely of Holland, that some of the English translations of his books have been made not from Dutch, but from German.

Fabricius' prevailing mood is light hearted; he has a strong vein of humor and a keen eye for idiosyncrasy. His historical work, however, is firmly grounded, though romantic in temper, and he has a marked gift for characterization. He is not in the front rank even of contemporary Dutch authors, but is (or was in times of peace) extremely popular in his homeland. The first of his novels to attract wide attention in English-speaking countries was *The Son of Marietta. Lions Starve in Naples,* which preceded it, was too slight to do much to extend his reputation; but *A Castle in Carinthia,* published in 1940, bids fair to make him better known in the United States and England than any of his previously translated works has done.

Besides his novels, he has published poems and articles in Dutch, which have not been translated.

Works Available in English: The Love of Mario Ferraro (in England: Vain Love) 1931; Java Ho! (juvenile) 1931; The Girl in the Blue Hat, 1932; Lions Starve in Naples, 1935; The Son of Marietta, 1936; A Castle in Carinthia, 1940.

FADIMAN, CLIFTON (May 15, 1904-   ), American literary critic, was born in New York City, the son of Isidore Michael Fadiman and Grace Elizabeth Fadiman. After receiving his B.A. degree from Columbia University in 1925, he taught English at the Ethical Culture High School in New York for two years, marrying Pauline Elizabeth Rush of that city in August of 1927. The Fadimans have a son, Jonathan Rush Fadiman, and live in Manhattan.

Mr. Fadiman was a contributor to magazine and newspapers at twenty. From 1925 t 1933 he was a lecturer for the People's Inst tute, serving as secretary of the lecture sta in the last two years. He was also assistan editor of Simon & Schuster, the publisher former friends at Columbia, from 1927 t 1929, becoming editor then and continuin till 1935. In 1933 he was made book edit of the *New Yorker,* where his brilliant book reviews have been notable features ever since. Douglas Bush complained in the *Bookman* of November 1932 that Fadiman "combines the functions of Ko-Ko and Pooh-Bah; he is the Lord High Executioner among reviewers and he wa born sneering." Time has somewhat soft ened Mr. Fadiman's asperities, and he i always engagingly ready to reverse som previous dictum or opinion when summin up at the end of a literary season.

R. L. Jackson

Clifton Fadiman's comparatively small an sophisticated audiences, reached through hi career as a lecturer and as a reviewer for th *Nation* and the *New Yorker,* became im mensely expanded through the medium o the radio, beginning in the fall of 1938. As sisted by a permanent board of experts, wit and specialists in general information such a Franklin P. Adams ("F.P.A.," the colum nist), John Kieran, sports-writer for the Ne York *Times,* and Oscar Levant, pianist, com poser, and author of *A Smattering of Ignor ance,* Mr. Fadiman conducts his half-hou program, "Information Please," with a run ning fire of quips and comments. In 1940 h received on behalf of his colleagues an sponsors the first plaque ever awarded b the *Saturday Review of Literature* for "Dis tinguished Service to American Literature. Awarding the plaque to Mr. Fadiman, Henr Seidel Canby commented, "The questions an answers which radiate from this room ever week have sent thousands to useful referenc volumes; they have brought to life goo books unopened; the wit and erudition i this hour have electrified the minds of thou sands listening in. An intellectual curiosit aroused and active is the beginning of litera ture."

Mr. Fadiman is big, blond, bespectacle personable; his style of vocal delivery wa perfected on the lecture platform and i pleasant, well modulated, and casual. He has as yet published no original books, though he contributed a section to the symposium, *America As Americans See It,* in 1932; edited *I Believe,* a collection of credos written by living celebrities, in 1939; published, with a long critical introduction in his characteristic off-hand style, a best-selling prose anthology entitled *Reading I've Liked,* (1941); and in 1942 wrote the introduction to a new edition of Tolstoy's *War and Peace.*

Mr. Fadiman also finds time, somehow, to serve as one of the four editors of the Readers Club, which re-issues monthly a book that was neglected on first publication.

ABOUT: Bookman November 1932; Current Biography May 1941; Saturday Evening Post January 11, 1941; Saturday Review of Literature April 6, 1940.

*FAIRBANK, Mrs. JANET (AYER), American novelist, was born in Chicago, apparently some time after 1875, the daughter of Benjamin Ayer and Janet (Hopkins) Ayer. A sister, Margaret Ayer Barnes*qv* is also a well-known novelist, and the two once collaborated in writing the concluding chapters of a novel left unfinished by a lifelong friend, Henry Kitchell Webster. Margaret Ayer Barnes dedicated her novel *Westward Passage* "To J. A. F. Who Blazed the Trail." Janet Ayer attended the University of Chicago, marrying Kellogg Fairbank of that city in May 1900. There are three children, Janet, Kellogg, and Benjamin Ayer.

Janet Ayer Fairbank has been described as one of the busiest and most influential women in Chicago, combining amazing energy with shrewd intelligence. She was active in the cause of woman suffrage, and chairman of the western division of the woman's finance committee of the Progressive Party prior to the outbreak of the First World War. In 1919 she was a member of the executive committee of the Democratic National Committee. During the war she had helped put over various Liberty Loan campaigns, and was active on the Council for National Defense. Thirteen years elapsed between the publication of her first novel, *At Home* (1910) and the next, *The Cortlandts of Washington Square* (1923).

Since then she has devoted more time to writing, though continuing such civic activities as acting as chairman of the board of managers of the Chicago Lying-In Hospital. From 1924 to 1928 she was a member of the executive committee of the Woman's Division of the Illinois Democratic National Committee. Besides belonging to six clubs in Chicago, she is a member of the Cosmopolitan Club in New York. The Fairbank family lives on North State Street, Chicago.

The Smiths, Mrs. Fairbank's novel of 1925, was runner-up for the Pulitzer novel prize in the year the prize was refused, with some contumely, by Sinclair Lewis. *The Bright Land,* a 1932 best-seller, covered the Jackson administration, the Civil War, and Reconstruction. Mrs. Fairbank gave an interviewer, Dorothea Lawrence Mann, an impression of vitality and energy, of controlled and conscious power. She "has her reserves, but it is her warm friendliness, vibrant humor, quick understanding which dominate the scene."

PRINCIPAL WORKS: At Home, 1910; The Cortlandts of Washington Square, 1923; The Smiths, 1925; Idle Hands (short stories) 1927; The Lion's Den, 1930; The Bright Land, 1932; Rich Man— Poor Man, 1936.

ABOUT: Wilson Library Bulletin December 1933.

"FAIRLESS, MICHAEL." See BARBER, M. F.

"FALLADA, HANS." See DITZEN, R.

"FANE, VIOLET." See "BRITISH AUTHORS OF THE 19TH CENTURY."

FANTE, JOHN, (April 8, 1911-), American novelist, writes: "Full name: John Thomas Fante. The time: April 8. 1911. The place: Denver, Colo. Mother's maiden name: Mary Capolungo. Father's full name: Nicholas Peter Fante. Father born in Abruzzi, Italy. Mother born in Chicago, Ill.

W. Gall

"I went to Catholic school, Boulder, Colo. Then to Jesuit High School named Regis, in Denver. Then to University of Colorado. Hated school, all the time. Quit Colorado University. Came to California, 1930. Then worked as cannery flunky, hotel clerk, stevedore, grocery clerk. Bad job at all. Started school again: Long Beach Junior College. Was kicked out for general laxity and hell-raising. Started writing. Quick results: *American Mercury, Atlantic Monthly, Story, Woman's Home Companion.* Wrote first novel, 1934. Bad, unpublished. Wrote it again, 1938: good, very good. Called *Wait Until Spring, Bandini.* Wrote another novel, 1939. Called *Ask the Dust.* Good, but not as good as first. Now writing *Mater Dolorosa* (tentative title) for my biggest effort. Have worked in motion pictures considerably, writing stories too stupid to mention.

"Married Joyce Smart, 1937. California girl. Writes poetry, great poetry. At this writing father and mother still alive, also two brothers and a sister: everybody's happy, if a bit tight-lipped."

* * *

Mr. Fante's first two novels were almost entirely autobiographical, and give a better idea of his history and background than anything that could be written about him by another. He comes of Italian working people, and it is particularly with the second-generation Italians in America that he is concerned.

Fante's books have been called super-realistic and bawdy, and they are both; they are also full of vitality and sympathetic humor. They could have been written only by a young man. His second novel, with its relative triviality and conventionality, was a disappointment to admirers of the full-bodied flavor of the first; but once he gets his past out of his system, he has talent and energy enough to produce some really striking work. Personally, he is short, dark, and excitable, and rather shy. He lives in Roseville, Calif. His name is pronounced *fan'tee.*

PRINCIPAL WORKS: Wait Until Spring, Bandini, 1938; Ask the Dust, 1939; Dago Red (short stories) 1940.

ABOUT: San Francisco Chronicle March 9, 1941; Time October 7, 1940.

FARGE. See LA FARGE

FARJEON, ELEANOR (1881-   ), English writer for children, writes: "I was born in London, and was the third child of B. L. Farjeon, the novelist, and Margaret (Jefferson) Farjeon, the eldest daughter of Joseph Jefferson, the American actor. I never went to school, and

such nursery governesses as came to the house were told not to bother me. But my parents knew everybody in the Bohemian literary and dramatic world, and we grew up in an atmosphere rich with imaginative suggestion. From the age of four I was taken to the theatre and opera freely, and as soon as I could read I was immersed in my father's enormous and very varied library. At seven I was writing my own works on the typewriter.

"I made my public bow (in pigtails) at sixteen, as librettist of an opera called *Floretta,* music by my brother Harry, and produced by the Royal Academy of Music. This was followed by two operettas, based imitations of W. S. Gilbert, who, instead of bearing rancor, sent me kind letters about them. My father died in 1903 and my grandfather sent for all of us to come over to America. We went back to England in a year, and I continued to write at home, slowly discovering what I most wanted to write, and how. I never really 'found' myself until during the war. My first successes were with two series of *Nursery Rhymes of London Town,* which I set later to simple tunes, that are now sung in most of the junior schools in England. Then to avoid the effect of the London air-raids on my mother, I took a tiny laborer's cottage in Sussex. Here *Martin Pippin in the Apple Orchard* was written, and when it had been published I felt that I had found my feet.

"After the war I settled in a cottage with a tiny walled Queen Anne garden in the old part of Hampstead. I wrote innumerable things—fantastic fiction, poems, music, children's tales and games, and one novel. Then I took to writing plays, some of which have been produced."

* * *

Miss Farjeon has never married. She is living at present in Sussex again. Now gray-haired (her hair was once dark), she is still bright-eyed and rosy-cheeked. "Joy," one critic said of her, "is the keynote of all her stories, her poems, and her music."

PRINCIPAL WORKS: Martin Pippin in the Apple Orchard, 1922; Soul of Kol Nikon, 1923; Mighty Men, 1925; Italian Peep Show and Other Tales, 1926; Joan's Door, 1927; Come Christmas, 1928; Collection of Poems, 1929; Faithful Jenny Dove and Other Tales, 1929; The King's Daughter

Cries For the Moon, 1929; Westwoods, 1930; Young Gerard, 1930; Ladybrook, 1931; Fair of St. James, 1932; Katy Kruse at the Seaside, 1932; Ameliaranne and the Magic Ring, 1933; Ameliaranne's Prize Packet, 1933; Over the Garden Wall (poems) 1933; Ameliaranne's Washing-Day, 1934; Jim at the Corner and Other Stories, 1934; A Nursery in the '90s (in America: Portrait of a Family) 1935; Jim and the Pirates, 1936; Two Bouquets (with H. Farjeon) 1936; Wonders of Herodotus, 1937; Martin Pippin in the Daisy Field, 1938; One Foot in Fairyland, 1938; Granny Gray (juvenile play) 1939; Jack Yeats (in Dublin Poets and Artists) 1939; A Sussex Alphabet, 1939; Miss Granby's Secret March, 1941.

ABOUT: Farjeon, E. Portrait of a Family; Kunitz, S. J. & Haycraft, H. (eds.). The Junior Book of Authors.

*FARJEON, JOSEPH JEFFERSON

(1883-), English mystery story writer, was born in London, the son of the novelist Benjamin Farjeon. His maternal grandfather, after whom he was named, was the American actor Joseph Jefferson. He is the brother of Eleanor *qv* and Herbert Farjeon, the novelist and playwright respectively, and he has himself written two plays: *No. 17*, produced as a play in 1924 and later made into a novel, and *Enchantment*, produced in 1930. He is married, and lives in London.

Within his special field he is unusually versatile; as one commentator remarked, he never tells two tales alike: "variety is always his aim." He was one of the first detective story writers to mingle romance with crime. Moreover, he can really write; William Lyon Phelps said he gave distinction to his detective novels by his "excellent literary style." Desmond MacCarthy called him "thrilling but funny," and he is noted personally, as well as in a literary way, for his keen humor and flashing wit. He is capable, however, of the "grandly sinister," of the appalling and terrifying. His mastery of a background of horror is particularly fine. Dorothy Sayers, who certainly should be an infallible judge of mystery stories, says Farjeon is "quite unsurpassed for creepy skill." Although many of his books have been published in America, he is not nearly so well known in this country as in England, or as he deserves to be among connoisseurs of the "whodunit." His only non-fiction book is an entertaining historical study of smugglers and smuggling.

PRINCIPAL WORKS: The Master Criminal, 1924; Uninvited Guests, 1925; No. 17, 1926; The House of Disappearance, 1927; The Crook's Shadow, 1927; At the Green Dragon, 1927; Underground (in America: Mystery Underground) 1928; Shadows by the Sea, 1928; The "Z" Murders (in America: A Person Called Z) 1929; The 5:18 Mystery, 1929; Appointed Date, 1930; Following Footsteps, 1930; Mystery on the Moor, 1931; The House Opposite, 1931; The Murderer's Trail, 1931; Phantom Fingers, 1931; Ben Sees It Through, 1932; Trunk Call, 1932; Sometimes Life's Funny, 1933; Old Man Mystery, 1933; The House on the Marsh, 1933; Sinister Inn, 1934; Fancy Dress Ball (in America: Death in Fancy Dress) 1934; Confusing Friendship, 1934; His Lady Secretary, 1934; Mystery of Dead Men's Heath, 1934; Windmill Mystery, 1934; Holiday Express, 1935; Little God Ben, 1935; Mountain Mystery, 1935; Adventure of Edward, 1935; Golden Singer, 1935; Detective Ben, 1936; Dangerous Beauty, 1936; Thirteen Guests, 1936; Yellow Devil, 1937; Holiday at Half Mast, 1937; The Compleat Smuggler (non-fiction) 1938; End of an Author, 1938; Mystery in White, 1938; Dark Lady, 1938; Seven Dead, 1939; Exit John Horton (in America: Friday the Thirteenth) 1939; Aunt Sunday Sees It Through (in America: Aunt Sunday Takes Command) 1940; Death in the Inkwell, 1942.

ABOUT: Farjeon, E. Portrait of a Family.

*FARNOL, JEFFERY (February 10, 1878-), English novelist, was born John Jeffery Farnol in Warwickshire, the son of Henry J. and Katherine Farnol. His interest in books was aroused at an early age, largely by listening in surreptitiously while his father read novels aloud to his mother after the children's bedtime. He determined to become a novelist himself.

But his family was unable to send him to a university (he had been taught privately, at home), and when he insisted he wanted to write, they decided to "put that nonsense out of his head" by apprenticing him to the owner of a brass foundry in Birmingham. He was soon sent home with a note from the foreman, reading: "No good for work, always writing."

He had some talent for drawing, so was sent next to the Westminster School of Art. But it was soon apparent that he would never make an illustrator. In the end he took a job in his father's business, and on the side wrote stories, a few of which he sold. His spare time he spent in cycling around Kent, Surrey, and Sussex. In 1900, at twenty-two, he married an American girl, Blanche V. W. Hawley, daughter of a New York artist. Two years later, with no money whatever, he set sail for New York, where his wife lived with her parents while he dwelt in a slum room, painted scenery at the Astor Theatre, and wrote feverishly at night by the aid of strong tea. It was thus, homesick for England, that he wrote his first novel, *The Broad Highway*. No

---

* Died June 6, 1955.

American publisher would look at it, and he was ready to burn it when his wife sent it to his mother, who found an English publisher for it. It was so successful that in 1910 the Farnols were able to return to England. They settled in Kent, where they had a daughter, and then moved to Sussex. In 1938 they were divorced, and the same year Mr. Farnol married Phyllis Clarke. He lives now in Eastbourne, Sussex.

Mr. Farnol has never entirely given up drawing, and himself illustrated his two books for children. His other hobby is prizefighting, of which he has written a vivid historical survey. In appearance he suggests the business man his parents tried to make him, rather than the author he became: he is round faced, spectacled, and dresses very conservatively. But though there is nothing at all of the Bohemian about him, he is a romanticist *par excellence.* His novels are purely "escape literature" of the sword-and-cloak school, and are not intended to be anything else. Those with most likelihood of survival are the two earliest, *The Broad Highway* and *The Amateur Gentleman,* which established him in popularity and created a public which has welcomed and rewarded the spate of books which has flowed from his pen since. A fluent and prolific writer, with an easy if undistinguished style, he still produces a volume or more a year, and is now at work on a new novel even in the midst of war.

PRINCIPAL WORKS: The Broad Highway, 1910; The Chronicles of the Imp (in America: My Lady Caprice) 1911; The Money Moon, 1912; The Amateur Gentleman, 1913; The Honourable Mr. Tawnish, 1914 (as a play, 1924); Beltane the Smith, 1915; The Definite Object, 1917; Some War Impressions (in America: Great Britain at War) 1918; The Geste of Duke Jocelyn, 1919; Black Bartelmy's Treasure, 1920; Martin Conisby's Vengeance, 1921; Peregrine's Progress, 1922; Sir John Dering, 1923; The Loring Mystery, 1925; High Adventure, 1926; The Quest of Youth, 1927; Epics of the Fancy (in America: Famous Prize Fights) 1928; Gyfford of Weare, 1928; The Shadow and Other Stories, 1929; Another Day, 1929; Over the Hills, 1930; The Jade of Destiny, 1931; Voices From the Dust (short stories) 1932; Charmian Lady Vibart, 1932; The Way Beyond, 1933; Winds of Fortune (in America: Winds of Chance; short stories) 1934; John o' the Green, 1935; A Pageant of Victory, 1936; The Crooked Furrow, 1937; Book for Jane (juvenile) 1937; The Lonely Road, 1938; The Happy Harvest, 1939; New Book for Jane (juvenile) 1939; A Matter of Business and Other Stories, 1940; Adam Penfeather, 1941.

FARRELL, JAMES THOMAS (February 27, 1904-   ), American novelist, writes: "I was born in Chicago and attended parochial schools on the South Side of Chi-

cago. In June 1923 I was graduated from St. Cyril High School in Chicago, an institution conducted by the Carmelite Fathers. I was a student of De Paul University (evenings) for six months, and of the University of Chicago for almost three years. I have held the following jobs: wrapping shoes in a chain shoe store in Chicago; clerk in an express office; gasoline filling station attendant; clerk for a chain cigar company on upper Broadway in New York City; advertising salesman for Donnelly's 'Red Book,' selling in Queens, L.I.; work-

ing in an undertaking parlor in Chicago; and campus reporter for the Chicago *Herald Examiner.*

"Various of my works have been published in England, France, Sweden, and South America. In 1937, *A World I Never Made* was the subject of a censorship trial in New York, but the charges against the novel were dismissed by Magistrate Henry Curran in a written decision. In 1937 also, I won a $2,500 Book-of-the-Month Club prize for *Studs Lonigan.* I was awarded a Guggenheim Fellowship for creative writing in 1936.

"My fiction is written in the naturalistic or realistic tradition. What I have already written is part of a plan of books on which I have been engaged for over ten years. When and if this plan is completed, it will consist of twenty-five or more works, including novels, novelettes, short stories, sketches, and plays. These works are to be loosely integrated through the associations of the characters depicted, and the scenes and the environments recreated. The purpose of these works is, stated generally, to recreate a sense of American life as I have seen it, as I have imagined it, and as I have reflected upon and evaluated it. I am concerned in my fiction with the patterns of American destinies, and with presenting the manner in which they unfold in our times. My approach to my material can be suggested by a motto of Spinoza which I have quoted on more than one occasion: 'Not to weep or laugh, but to understand.'

"All too frequently critics and reviewers have attempted to explain books of mine by attributing to me motivations which did not consciously play any rôle in the writing of these books. If there is any hatred in my books, for example, it is not directed against eople but against conditions which brutalize human beings and produce spiritual and material poverty."

* * *

James T. Farrell, short, serious-faced, owlish, with thick spectacles and rumpled dark hair, lives in New York, near Columbia University, with his wife and small son. In the living room of their apartment he writes indefatigably from eight each morning till late in the afternoon.

Farrell is a stickler for accuracy of details in his books, and writes and rewrites before he is satisfied. He has said: "It took me a long time to write so slowly that you would think it was written quickly." Though frank and photographic in his reporting of folk speech and manners, there is nothing pornographic in his intent. ("Emetic" is an adjective frequently applied to his works.) His chief defect is the prodigality of expression which draws his novels out to undue length and sometimes results in monotony of effect.

Mr. Farrell adds to his autobiographical sketch: "Among my favorite authors, I might list Dostoievsky, Turgeniev, Tolstoy, Gogol, Chekhov, Stendhal, Balzac, Flaubert, Marcel Proust, James Joyce, Dickens. Just about my only hobby is baseball. I like to follow baseball from year to year, to see games, and to keep track of records such as batting and pitching averages."

He is radical in his political and economic convictions, though violently at outs with the "orthodox" Communists.

PRINCIPAL WORKS: Studs Lonigan, 1932-35 (Young Lonigan, 1932; The Young Manhood of Studs Lonigan, 1934; Judgment Day, 1935); Gas House McGinty, 1933; Calico Shoes and Other Stories, 1937; No Star Is Lost, 1938; Fellow Countrymen (short stories, published in England) 1938; Tommy Gallagher's Crusade, 1939; Counting the Waves and Other Stories, 1940; Father and Son, 1940; Ellen Rogers, 1941; $1,000 a Week, 1942.

ABOUT: Canadian Forum April 1939; Library Journal April 15, 1937; New Republic November 3, 1936, October 28, 1940; New York Times Book Review May 17, 1942; Publishers' Weekly January 9, January 30, February 6, 1937; Saturday Review Literature March 28, 1940; Time September 19, 1938; Wilson Library Bulletin March 1935.

FARSON, NEGLEY (May 14, 1890-   ), American journalist and novelist, was born in Plainfield, N.J., the son of Enoch Farson and Grace (Negley) Farson. He was named James Scott Negley for his grandfather, a Civil War veteran, one of the four generals who plotted and rode with Sherman from Atlanta to the sea. Young Farson attended Phillips Andover Academy in Massachusetts, whence he was expelled for helping duck a master. Before advancing upon the University of Pennsylvania to take a B.S. degree in civil engineering, he sailed his boat, the "Nimrod," on the Delaware River, with a friend, and became interscholastic shot-put champion. Farson began work as engineer in 1914 with a Manchester, England, firm whose ambition was to make the best chains in the world. Later in the

Pinchot

year he went to Petrograd to sell army and navy supplies to the Russian government for another firm; from 1915 to 1917 he did business for his own company, Landby & Farson. Petrograd in the first year of the war offered "the perfect life of dissipation."

Enlisting in the British Royal Flying Corps, Farson attained the rank of lieutenant and saw service in Egypt. Two subsequent years were spent in British Columbia for the recuperation of a wounded leg. Farson had married Eve Stoker in September 1920; they have a son, Daniel Negley. They spent the year 1923-24 in Chicago, where he was sales manager of the Mack International Motor Truck Co. Tiring of the strain and confinement of office life, Farson obtained an appointment as foreign correspondent for the Chicago *Daily News,* and went abroad in 1924 to stay for eleven years. Soon after reaching Europe he purchased a 26-foot Norfolk Broads centre-board yawl, the "Flame."

Sailing Across Europe (1926) is the record of this cruise, and Farson's first book. His work took him into India, Egypt, and throughout Europe. *Black Bread and Red Coffins* was the result of his tour of duty in Russia. From 1931 to 1935 Farson was stationed in London, where he is a member of the London Association of American Newspaper Correspondents, serving as president in 1933-34, and also a member of the Savage Club. His permanent address in both the American and British *Who's Who* is given as London. In December 1935 Farson added *The Way of a Transgressor* to the growing list of reminiscences of American war correspondents; it was one of the liveliest and most candid of them all. Farson's Aunt Edith once wrote his flight commander that Negley was "such a wild, reckless boy" and needed especial attention; there was nothing in this record to prove her wrong. Its sequel, *Transgressor in the Tropics,* appeared in 1937. Farson is also the author of a number of readable, if pot-boiling, novels. Hospitals bulk large in his reminiscences, since his physical mishaps have been many.

PRINCIPAL WORKS: Sailing Across Europe, 1926; Daphne's in Love, 1927; There's No End To It, 1929; Black Bread and Red Coffins (English title: Seeing Red: Today in Russia) 1930; The Way of a Transgressor, 1935; Transgressor in the Tropics, 1937; Story of a Lake, 1938; Fugitive Love, 1939; Behind God's Back, 1941; Bomber's Moon, 1941.

ABOUT: Farson, N. The Way of a Transgressor; Transgressor in the Tropics, Behind God's Back.

FAUCONNIER, HENRI, French writer of travel books, writes (in English): "I have always held that, in art or literature,

what matters is not the man who works, but the man's work. The greatest writers are only great as writers and appear, in ordinary life, just as petty and foolish as anyone else. Perhaps more so. For no man can be universal, especially a specialist. "Now I am called upon to give an account of myself, not as a writer but as a man, which means confessing my many follies. A cruel task if you consider that, having written but little, I must have acted a good deal.

"To begin with, after studying for the law like a good boy, I suddenly absconded and found myself landed in a far-away foreign country with the idea of making a fortune out of nothing—which was absurd. Then, having made it, I decided that rubber, which had enriched me, could not but go on inflating forever—until it burst most sadly in my hands. When war came, I warred away with as much spirit as one can put into such a dismal occupation—because I hoped there would never be another war after that. And now, though it becomes quite clear that humanity is mad—especially the white part of it to which I belong—here am I, in this tottering old world, still waiting for miracles.

"Still waiting for miracles . . . why not? Have I not seen a country which was practically nothing but virgin jungle absorb in a space of twenty years twenty centuries of civilization, with its roads and railroads and vast cities brimming with modern life? And is not another part of the world, looked upon as civilized, receding just as fast into barbarism? What can be said to be possible or impossible, wise or unwise? Utopia, sooner or later, must come true. Humanity must arise some day to another ideal than that of being led like cattle, and fooled and slaughtered.

"We shall not live to see the change. That is why we must take refuge in fiction. I tell myself many beautiful tales which I mean to write—but I often desist because, in the writing, their beauty fades."

* * *

This sketch, it need hardly be added, was sent by M. Fauconnier (from Barbezieux, Charentes, France) before the French defeat by Hitler. Until the present war his permanent address was Radès, Tunisia. Barbezieux was his birthplace, and he studied law at Bordeaux, fifty miles South. His father died when he was twenty and he had to help bring up a large family of brothers and sisters. He went to Singapore in 1905 as assistant to a British rubber planter, and soon became a planter in his own right. After the First World War, in which he served throughout, he returned to Malaya until the collapse of the rubber boom, when he settled in Tunisia to write. Malaisie received the Goncourt Prize for 1930. Basil Davenport called it "an exquisite book." M. Fauconnier, a dark, slim man with a small moustache, is unmarried. He is a member of the Royal Society of Literature, in London.

WORKS AVAILABLE IN ENGLISH: Malaisie (England: The Soul of Malaya) 1931.

ABOUT: Lalou, R. Histoire de la Littérature Contemporaine; Saturday Review of Literature December 12, 1931; Spectator November 21, 193[

FAULKNER, WILLIAM (September 25, 1897-), American novelist, who sometimes spells his name Falkner, was born in

New Albany, Miss. Statements that he was born in Ripley, Miss., in October, 1897, are incorrect; both villages, however, are near Oxford, seat of the University of Mississippi, which has been his home since childhood. His father was Murry

C. Faulkner, owner of a livery stable but also treasurer of the university; his mother Maud (Butler) Faulkner. On both sides the family belonged to the wealthy and powerful Southerners ruined by the Civil War and

reduced to genteel poverty. William was the oldest of four brothers, one of whom became a well-known aviator before he was killed in 1935. After the fifth grade he attended school only desultorily, though he took some high school work and also some special courses at the University of Mississippi. For the most part, in his late teens, he merely hung around Oxford, read a great deal, wrote bad verse imitative of Swinburne and Omar Khayyám, and tried to find himself. The First World War woke him from this lethargy. Flying caught his imagination, but he refused to enlist with the "Yankees," so went to Toronto and joined the Canadian Air Force, becoming a lieutenant in the R.A.F. Biographers who say he got no nearer France than Toronto are mistaken. He was sent to France as an observer, had two planes shot down under him, was wounded in the second shooting, and did not return to Oxford until after the Armistice.

He re-entered the university, and attended it off and on from 1919 to 1921, though he was never graduated. As a veteran, he was able to waive the requirement of high school graduation before becoming a regularly enrolled student. In between times he worked as a house painter, painting the roofs of several university buildings. He served later as university postmaster, until he was dismissed for inattention to duty. Then, at loose ends again, he drifted to New Orleans, where he became a friend of Sherwood Anderson, through whom he came to the notice of the *Double Dealer,* one of the pioneers of "little" literary magazines. Faulkner's first published work was a poem in this magazine, in 1922. He wrote *Soldiers' Pay* in New Orleans, and Anderson recommended it to a publisher on condition that he would not have to read the manuscript first! It was accepted, and Faulkner started work on *Mosquitoes,* the background of which was the New Orleans Bohemia. Before either of them appeared, however, he had suddenly left on a freighter for Europe, where he spent most of 1925. He had previously spent a few unhappy months in New York as a clerk in a book-store, an utter misfit in both the city and the occupation.

Back in Oxford again, he worked as a carpenter, farmed, fished, and hunted, saw his first two novels through the press, received critical acclaim but not much money, and wrote *The Sound and the Fury.* Not surprisingly, since it is the first of the Faulkner novels written in his cryptic stream-of-consciousness style, at first no publisher would look at it. The long first section consists of the sense-impressions of an idiot; there are two characters in it, man and woman, with the same name; and it is difficult to understand until after one has finished it. Discouraged but not daunted, he went to work on *Sartoris,* the first of his many novels centering loosely around the Sartoris (for which read Faulkner) family and the town of Jefferson (Oxford), Miss. The principal character, Colonel Sartoris, was a mingling of his grandfather and his great-grandfather and namesake, a pioneer railroad builder who was also author of a sentimental novel of the South, once popular, called *The White Rose of Memphis. Sartoris* was published in 1929, the same year that its author married Mrs. Estelle (Oldham) Franklin, a widow with two children. They now have a child of their own.

Unable to live by his writing, Faulkner took a job as night superintendent of a power plant. There, writing on an upturned wheelbarrow in the small hours of the morning, he revised *The Sound and the Fury,* and at the same time deliberately set about writing a pure horror story, aimed at the collection of royalties, which he called *Sanctuary.* After the establishment of his reputation by *The Sound and the Fury* and *As I Lay Dying,* he rewrote *Sanctuary* also, so that now it is part of the Jefferson cycle. It was the first of his novels to become popular. From that time on he has not had to worry about money; he was able to modernize his century-old house, to buy a private plane, to finance his brother's barnstorming career, and to travel where he pleased. Hollywood bought *Sanctuary* and turned it into a movie, and Faulkner was asked to assist in its filming. Since then he has spent much time in Hollywood, though on his own terms. (On one occasion he asked permission to do his writing "at home"; the studio consented, but when they tried to telephone him in Santa Monica one day, they discovered that he had meant "at home" in Mississippi, to which he had returned!)

He lives in Oxford for most of the time now, though he also has a thirty-five-acre farm in the hills. His mornings are given to writing, his afternoons to hunting, fishing, and conviviality. He takes his farming seriously, and even does his own brewing. Except among his intimates, he is silent and unsocial, and has even been called "insolent"; the fact is that his manner is the result of acute sensitiveness. In 1939 he won the first prize in the annual O. Henry Memorial Award. He writes his books by hand—a fine, unreadable hand—on the right-hand side of legal-sized sheets of paper, reserving the left-hand side for corrections. He is slow and hesitant in his speech, much more eager to talk about farming or hunting than about literature, and completely uncritical of his own work. For example, he once told a college class that he had "never given the subject of form a single thought," whereas Conrad Aiken said that form was his constant preoccupation. His own comment on fiction-writing is: "If a story is in you, it has got to come out."

Faulkner's world is a nightmare realm, "darkly reflected through distorting lenses," as Anthony Buttitta put it. Inordinately imaginative, bitter, undisciplined, brilliant, and difficult, he is, as one critic remarked, "extraordinarily powerful but extremely uneven." Burton Rascoe gave him credit for sardonic humor and a comic sense, but it is the humor of the grotesque. He is the chronicler of decay, of viciousness, of perversion, of cruelty. Earle Birney said there were two Faulkners—"a stylized and morbid mystic. attempting a sequence of novels on the scale of an epic," and "a sharp and brilliant narrator of short stories." Granville Hicks called his characters "twisted shapes in the chaotic wreckage of a mad world," and said that he was in the tradition, not of the high tragedy of John Webster and Robinson Jeffers, but of the "technical ingenuity" and horror of Poe and Ambrose Bierce: "it is too easy for him to produce shudders for him to bother to try to create tragedy." And all this is presented in what Aiken called "a strangely fluid and slippery and heavily mannered prose." In all his major novels, Faulkner has to be *re-read* to be comprehended, and in some cases only an acquaintance with all the novels makes for complete understanding of his intricate cross-narrative.

It is curious that this master of a complicated prose is in his verse flat and derivative, hardly more than what Bernard DeVoto called him—"a gifted amateur." But he cannot be dismissed so cavalierly as a novelist, even by those who dislike his grimness, his morbidity, and his wallowing in horror. He is in a way a minor Balzac of a sub-human world, no more obsessed with abnormality than was Dostoievsky, though completely lacking in the spiritual implications which are Dostoievsky's signature.

In appearance Faulkner is rather short, slender, with very black hair and moustache now beginning to gray, and "sharp-eyed as a gambler." He is never likely to conform to any rules, either as a person or as a writer;

he cannot be tamed into a drawing-room lion; he remains what he began—a child o the Deep South, a product of social disinte gration and decay, who is also an authenti and powerful story-teller.

PRINCIPAL WORKS: The Marble Faun (poems 1924; Soldiers' Pay, 1926; Mosquitoes, 1927; Sar toris, 1929; The Sound and the Fury, 1929; As I Lay Dying, 1930; Sanctuary, 1931; These Thirtee (short stories) 1931; Idyll in the Desert, 1931 Light in August, 1932; A Green Bough (poems 1933; Pylon, 1933; Absalom, Absalom! 1936; Un vanquished, 1938; Wild Palms, 1939; The Hamle 1940; Go Down Moses and Other Stories, 194.

ABOUT: Geismar, M. Winters in Crisis; Atlan tic Monthly November 1939; Bookman Septembe and December 1931; Canadian Forum June 1938 Nuova Antologia January 16, 1938; Poetry Octobe 1933; Saturday Review of Literature May 21, 1938 Sewanee Review July 1932; Time January 23, 193

FAURE, ÉLIE (April 4, 1873-October 3] 1937), French art critic and historian, wa born at Ste. Foy, Gironde, the son of Pierr Faure, a peasant grower of wine grapes. At fifteen he was sent to Paris, to the Lycée Henri IV. With his brother, he studied medicine at the University, and received his degree in 1899. Though he practised his profession, and was a sur-

D. Rivera

geon for many years, his primary interes was always in art—as an amateur, not as painter himself. From childhood picture had entranced him, and he estimated th worth of his life at any period by th number of paintings he was able to se All through his student days he haunted th Louvre as a relief from the dissecting roon He was married, to Suzanne Gilard, befoi he was twenty-one, and one of their tw sons died in infancy. He described th period as "Boredom. Sickness. Death. Su fering. A precocious education in respons bility and unhappiness. I saw hardly an painting." The famous Dreyfus case wa indirectly the cause of his salvation. A ardent *Dreyfusard*, through his championshi of the accused officer, Faure met Zola an Anatole France, and through their influenc he was appointed art critic of *L'Auror* the paper which had become Dreyfus' chic organ of defense.

Through these connections he met th artists he had admired, and he began his re career with the publication of a brochur on Velasquez in 1904. In 1905 he helpe to found the Université Populaire, a scho of adult education: it was as an outgrowth of his lectures there that his greatest work, his *History of Art,* appeared. He continued to study while he taught and wrote, and gradually he evolved his synthesis of art and life, which is his chief contribution to the history and criticism of painting. Art he considered a social expression, and he treated of it primarily in its relation to civilization as a whole.

He served through the First World War as a surgeon, returning to his art work at its conclusion. Always a liberal in his sympathies, a close friend of the martyred socialist leader Jean Jaurès, gradually his theme expanded until he became more an aesthetic philosopher than an art critic in the narrow sense. However, he continued to issue brochures on individual artists, including Corot, Cézanne, Derain, and Matisse, and he wrote introductions for numerous collections of prints, one outstanding example being his essay on Goya. He knew Diego Rivera well, and the Mexican artist painted his picture in army uniform—a black-bearded, baldish man who looks almost comically the "typical" Frenchman. He died in Paris at sixty-four.

Montaigne, Shakespeare, Pascal, Cervantes he thought the type of the truly civilized man. He recognized, however, that it is emotion, not intellect, which rules mankind. "I have come to look upon the universe itself as an aesthetic phenomenon," he said, "and God as an artist creating and retouching it incessantly, in a kind of unconscious rapture and lyricism." As his circumstances became easier, he began to collect paintings himself, and had some fine originals, especially of the Impressionist and Post-Impressionist school. Travel was his greatest joy, and in 1931 he spent a year on a world tour, in the course of which he visited the United States.

WORKS AVAILABLE IN ENGLISH: History of Art, 1921-30 (Ancient Art, 1921; Mediaeval Art, 1922; Renaissance Art, 1923; Modern Art, 1924; Spirit of the Forms, 1930); Art of Cineplastics, 1923; Napoleon, 1924; Dance Over Fire and Water, 1926; The Italian Renaissance, 1929; The Spirit of Japan, 1930.

ABOUT: Ellis, H. The Philosophy of Conflict; American Historical Review January 1938; Dial February 1922, August 1925, October 1926; Mercure de France December 1, 1937, April 1, 1938; Revue de Littérature Comparée April 1938.

FAUSET, JESSIE REDMON (1884?-),

American Negro novelist, was born in Philadelphia, Pa., and attended the public schools, where she was the only colored child in her class. She graduated from Cornell University in 1905, took her master's degree at the University of Pennsylvania, and studied French at the Alliance Francaise and at the Sorbonne.

She taught in Washington, D.C. until she tired of the growing racial discrimination shown there; did editorial work on the *Crisis* in New York, which she has called "free and friendly, a very good town indeed to live in"; and taught French at the De Witt Clinton High School.

Jessie Fauset wrote several poems which were included in *Caroling Dust,* an anthology of Negro verse edited by Countee Cullen, but she desired to write fiction. "Out of the figures weaving themselves into the tapestry of our national life," she once said, "I see sometimes the colored man as the last stronghold of those early American virtues which once we fought so hard to preserve integrity, pride, indomitableness, and a sort of gay hardihood. Drama is the colored man's portion every day, with its immediate response and adjustment to all the stimuli induced by all the slings and arrows which the meaningless ferocity of life lets fly at him. He parries them so well and with what shrewd philosophy; what superb address, and what rueful humor! A pity to let the archives of Americana build up without a record of the deeds and thoughts of these people, so brave and grave and gay! So I have tried to set them down." Zona Gale wrote a preface to Miss Fauset's third novel, *The Chinaberry Tree.* An explanatory note seemed necessary, for, as Marion L. Starkey remarked in an interview with Miss Fauset, "When along comes a novel writer like Jessie Fauset who writes neither of the backwoods nor of Harlem dives, but of Negroes of background and ambition, white readers become disconcerted." Some of her themes were racial discrimination, and the question of Negroes' "passing" in white society when they happened to be fair-skinned.

Miss Fauset also taught at Tuskegee, to learn the Deep South, and has lectured on Negro writers. With her husband, Herbert Harris, who served in the First World War, she has lived in a cooperative apartment house on upper Seventh Avenue in New York's Negro quarter, Harlem. A brother, Arthur, has been a principal of a Philadelphia school, and studied for a doctor's degree in anthropology.

PRINCIPAL WORKS: There Is Confusion, 1924; Plum Bun, 1929; The Chinaberry Tree, 1931; Comedy, American Style, 1933.

ABOUT: Brawley, B. The Negro Genius; Boston Transcript October 29, 1933.

FAUSSET, HUGH I'ANSON (June 1895-), English critic, poet, and literary biographer, was born in Killington, Westmorland, the second son  of the Rev. T. E. Fausset. His grandfather, Canon A. R. Fausset of York, was a classical scholar and one of the foremost Biblical commentators of his time. Ten days after Hugh Fausset's birth, his mother died of an embolism following puerperal fever. The result on her husband was to drive him to the verge of insanity. Hugh Fausset's home life was Samuel Butler's *The Way of All Flesh* translated into reality; the house became "the terrifying vortex of nerve-storms," with his father not only maintaining incessant vigilance over the two boys at home, but watching them afield with a telescope and beating them with sadistic violence if they seemed to attempt to thwart his wishes.

Drilled by his father in English, Greek and French syntax at six, at ten Hugh was day boy in a preparatory school. Sedbergh was his public school. At Cambridge Hugh Fausset was a student at Corpus Christi College, where he won the Chancellor's Medal for English verse and cultivated the outward seeming of an orthodox poet, with long hair, a straggling moustache and flowing black tie (his father refused to be seen in public with him). A knee dislocated when playing football, and general debility following two operations for an abscessed appendix kept him out of the First World War. Fausset joined the Choir of King's College Chapel as Choral Scholar, singing daily for two years.

In 1918 Fausset married Marjory Rolfe and supported his family, augmented by a son and two daughters, by reviewing three and four hundred books a year for the *Times Literary Supplement,* the Manchester *Guardian,* the Yorkshire *Post,* the *Listener,* and the *Aryan Path.* He edited Donne and Cowper for Everyman's Library and wrote penetrating studies of these poets as well as of Coleridge, Tennyson, Keats, and Tolstoy. Schooldays in the Lake Country made him an early convert to Wordsworth. Disillusioned with D. H. Lawrence,

he turned to Jacob Boehme and other mystics. An experience of "supernatural peace" in Westminster Cathedral led Fausset beyond Christianity to study and approve the philosophies of the East, particularly the Vedantas. The Faussets now live at Widdington, Newport, Essex. A pronounced romantic in his first poems, Fausset now writes a contemplative, disillusioned, flexible prose. "It is good that the hard world of fact, of tangible demands and difficult circumstances, should have made it impossible for me to indulge the easy, romantic dream, or effect a pleasant compromise," he concludes in the autobiographical *A Modern Prelude.*

PRINCIPAL WORKS: The Lady Alcuin and Other New Poems, 1918; The Spirit of Love: A Sonnet Sequence, 1921; Keats: A Study in Development, 1922; Tennyson: A Modern Portrait, 1923; Studies in Idealism, 1923; John Donne: A Study in Discord, 1924; Samuel Taylor Coleridge, 1926; Tolstoy: The Inner Drama, 1928; The Proving of Psyche, 1929; The Modern Dilemma, 1930; The Lost Leader: A Study of Wordsworth, 1933; A Modern Prelude (autobiography) 1933; Poet of Democracy: Walt Whitman, 1942.

ABOUT: Fausset, H. I. A Modern Prelude.

"FAUST, FREDERICK." See BRAND, MAX

FAŸ, BERNARD (April 3, 1893-), French historian, educator, and lecturer, was born Marie Louis Bernard Faÿ in Paris, the son of Henri Faÿ and Cécile Rivière Faÿ. When he was only seven, an uncle who was sailing for the United States, glibly promised him that some day he should go to Harvard. Not until about twenty years later, however, when Bernard Faÿ was awarded a Victor Emmanuel  Bachrach Chapman Memorial Fellowship, did this become an actuality. Meanwhile he had not only graduated from the Sorbonne but had served in the French Army as a captain from 1914 to 1919; been "re-endeared" to the New World by a young American volunteer (from Harvard) whom he had met behind the lines; and decorated for bravery in Belgium and at Verdun.

Following the war and at the end of two years at Harvard and in New York, he returned to France and was made a professor of French Literature at the University of Clermont-Ferrand, belonging to that old town in Auvergne where Peter the Hermit preached the first crusade. He held that post for about ten years. During this period, however, he was away from France for months at a time; and his approach to French letters (in his literary panorama *Since Victor Hugo,* 1927) had, therefore, an extremely healthy objectivity. In 1929 came his *Franklin,* enhanced by an abundance of unpublished correspondence and generally conceded to be the best study of the subject that had yet appeared. He collaborated with Avery Claflin on *The American Experiment,* an attempt, in part, to quiet a kind of hateful fear of America, which, Faÿ contended, was gaining ground in Europe.

In February 1932, while Faÿ himself was in the United States, the Collège de France created a Chair of American Civilization and called him to fill it. He was the youngest ever to be appointed to that faculty.

The Two Franklins (the lesser-known, Benjamin Franklin Bache, Faÿ regarded as the most outspoken "the most reckless, the most generous, and the most neglected" of Revolutionary figures) and *Roosevelt and His America,* largely devoted to the thesis that Americans thrive on crises, were issued in 1933.

In October 1935 Faÿ made his twenty-second visit to the United States. As president of the French Committee of the Academy for the Rights of Nations, he spoke, in March 1937, to that organization's Berlin branch. During these months, moreover, he wrote a number of articles for the Sunday magazine section of the New York *Times:* speculations on the nearness of Europe's explosion and a paradoxical suggestion that Germany might win as long as she is weak and lose as soon as she becomes really strong.

It was announced in August 1940 that Faÿ has been appointed general director of the French National Library, succeeding Julian Cain, who left France just before the surrender. He is reported by Edgar Ansel Mowrer, to be "on good terms with the German authorities."

PRINCIPAL WORKS: Since Victor Hugo, 1927; Franklin: The Apostle of Modern Times, 1929; The American Experiment (with A. Claflin) 1929; George Washington: Republican Aristocrat, 1931; The Two Franklins: Fathers of American Democracy, 1933; Roosevelt and His America, 1933; Revolution and Freemasonry, 1935.

ABOUT: Faÿ, B. Roosevelt and His America; Harper's December 1932; Harvard Graduates Magazine June 1920; Illustration February 20, 1932; New York Times March 12, 1937 and August 9, 1940.

FAY, SIDNEY BRADSHAW (April 13, 1876-), American historian, writes: "Sidney B. Fay was born in Washington, D.C., the son of Professor Edward Allen Fay, for fifty years a teacher of the deaf and vice-president of Gallaudet College. Educated at Sidwell's Friends' School and the Washington High School; at Harvard University (B.A. 1896, Ph.D. 1900); and at the

Bachrach

Universities of Paris and Berlin; honorary L.H.D. from Smith College, 1929. As teacher of European History was Austin Teaching Fellow at Harvard, 1900-02, professor of history at Dartmouth, 1902-14, at Smith, 1914-29, and at Harvard and Radcliffe since 1929. Also lecturer in Modern European History at Amherst and Columbia during several semesters between 1917 and 1928. Conducted a round table at the Williamstown Institute of Politics in 1924.

"Member of the Editorial Board of the *American Historical Review* (1924-30), of the *Smith College Studies* (1915-29), and of the *Journal of Modern History* (since 1937). Member of the Massachusetts and American Historical Societies, American Society of International Law, American Political Science Association, American Academy of Arts and Sciences, of French and German historical societies, and of the Finnish Academy of Sciences. Contributor of articles and book reviews to numerous historical and literary periodicals. Principal interest in recent years, modern German history, and the causes of the World War of 1914 and of the Second World War of 1939. Principal recreations, tennis, and travel in Europe. Married, 1904, Sarah Proctor; three daughters."

* * *

Professor Fay lives in Cambridge, Mass., in the winter and in Nantucket in the summer. He is clean-shaven, with a high forehead, a long upper lip, and drooping eyelids behind rimless glasses. He was the first American scholar to attack the theory of Germany's sole guilt in the First World War, and has been described as a "benign revisionist." Harry Elmer Barnes has praised his "scholarly competence as a diplomatic historian" and his "mastery and marshaling of the evidence."

PRINCIPAL WORKS: A History Syllabus for Secondary Schools, 1904; The Records of the Town of Hanover, N.H. 1761-1818, 1905; A Syllabus of European History (with H. D. Foster) 1912; The Hohenzollern Household in the Sixteenth Century, 1916; The Origins of the World War, 1929; Guide to Historical Literature, 1931; The Rise of Brandenburg-Prussia to 1786, 1937.

ABOUT: Current History December 1928; Living Age December 1928.

FEARING, KENNETH (1902-   ), American poet, writes: "I was born [Kenneth Flexner Fearing] in Oak Park, Ill. My

father, Harry L. Fearing, is an attorney practicing in Chicago. My mother's name was Olive Flexner. I was brought up and educated in the public schools of Oak Park, and graduated from the University of Wisconsin in 1924. In Chicago, I did newspaper work as a reporter, have been salesman, mill-hand, clerk, etc. Since 1924 I have lived almost continuously in New York City, and most of that time has been spent as a free-lance writer. Much of that work was purely commercial, done under pseudonyms. As for influences: many, not the least of them in music and cartooning; and in poetry, I would say that they range from Villon to Keats. But generally speaking, that is for practical purposes, I should say I was in the Whitman tradition, not because I have an exaggerated liking for his actual performance, but because I regard Whitman as the first writer to create a technique indigenous to the whole of this country's outlook. Literary and social preferences: I will suffer fools, though not gladly, but I can't endure stuffed shirts. Political convictions: a mystery to me. I voted for LaFollette in 1924, for William Z. Foster in 1932, and passed on most of the other dates. My favorite authors are those, and there are very few, who can write exciting books. As pre-requisite to suit my taste an author must be clear, not repeat himself too much, not pretend to know more about life than the rest of us fools, and not lie too much, or if so, plausibly. I am married, have one son, live in New York City, and am at work on prose and poetry."

* * *

In 1936 Mr. Fearing received a Guggenheim Fellowship, which was renewed in 1939. He is serious, thin-faced, spectacled, and shy, far less aggressive than his dynamic poems would indicate.

His poems may be called a subway mosaic of currently topical phrases arranged so as to present a corrosive, wierdly lighted picture of contemporary American life. As William Rose Benét remarked, "A good deal of his work reads like nightmares induced by New York newspapers and modern civilization, . . . not cheering to read, but it haunts one." His approach is from the Left and his motivating force is healthy anger. Horace Gregory said that he had "converted the bromides of tabloid journalism . . . into a brilliant art."

Without any question Kenneth Fearing is one of the significant phenomena of twentieth century American poetry. Written in the living idiom, his verse speaks for the uneasy, unhappy troglodytes of the metropolitan world.

The novels to which Fearing has lately been devoting himself, have not yet achieved the distinction and force of his verse.

PRINCIPAL WORKS: Angel Arms, 1929; Poems, 1935; Dead Reckoning, 1938; The Hospital (novel) 1939; Collected Poems, 1940; The Dagger in The Mind (mystery story) 1941; Clark Gifford's Body (novel) 1942.

ABOUT: Poetry February 1937, April 1939, July 1939, September 1940; January 1941; Saturday Review of Literature June 15, 1935; Time September 4, 1939; February 17, 1941.

FENOLLOSA, ERNEST FRANCISCO. See "AMERICAN AUTHORS: 1600-1900"

FERBER, EDNA (August 15, 1887-   ), American novelist, was born in Kalamazoo, Mich., the daughter of Jacob Charles Ferber, a storekeeper, and Julia (Neuman) Ferber. Both her parents were Jewish, her father born in Hungary, her mother in Milwaukee. In her childhood they moved to Appleton, Wis., where she lived through her girlhood. Her father became

N. Muray

blind, and she was obliged to give up her ambition to study for the stage, and to take a job as reporter on the Appleton *Daily Crescent,* at $3 a week. Previously she had never thought of writing. Her work attracted the attention of the editor of the Milwaukee *Journal,* who sent for her;

she continued her newspaper work there and on the Chicago *Tribune.* Meanwhile she had published a short story in *Everybody's Magazine* and written a novel which she did not like and threw it away. Her mother rescued it and sent it to a publisher, and in 1911 it came out as her first book, *Dawn O'Hara.* Her first big success was as the author of a series of stories, later collected in several books, about a woman traveling "salesman" named Emma McChesney. She was graduated into the best seller class with *So Big,* in 1924, followed by two other very popular novels, *Show Boat* (made into a musical play, a movie, and a radio program) and *Cimarron,* a story of the opening up of Oklahoma, also a big hit as a motion picture. She has also been most successful as a playwright, in collaboration with George S. Kaufman, their best known plays being *Dinner at Eight, The Royal Family, Stage Door,* and *The Land Is Bright.* All these, except the last (1941), have also been filmed. Miss Ferber lives now in New York with her mother. She has never been married.

Edna Ferber is a tremendously vital person, who works hard and plays hard. She does her work directly on the typewriter (as do most authors with newspaper training), and devotes all her mornings to writing, though she never seems to need seclusion or to be annoyed by interruptions. When she is working on a book she sometimes spends a few whirlwind days in the locale, interviewing its residents and gathering impressions; on other occasions she relies entirely on memory or even reading, without ever having seen the place. She is short, with a large head covered with thick, crinkly dark hair, a paper-white skin, and vivid dark eyes. Her speaking voice is low and husky, with a dramatic quality. She is forthright, direct, energetic, and warm-hearted, typically of the Middle West in her outlook.

Though she knows her books have been for the most part escapist stories, written in an escapist era, she yet feels that they contain a social message which readers have failed to catch. She says she has never written a book with which she was completely satisfied. Grant Overton, who pointed out the zest and gusto which make her books such easy reading (and also sometimes mar them by evidence of haste and superficiality), nevertheless considered her "the keenest social critic among our fiction writers." William Allen White said she is "the legitimate daughter of the Dickens dynasty," and added: "the historian will find no better

picture of America in the first three decades of this century than Edna Ferber has drawn." Other critics have been far less enthusiastic, and when *Saratoga Trunk* was published in 1941, more than one reviewer noted that it was written ready-made for the movies, "lacking nothing but the Technicolor."

PRINCIPAL WORKS: Dawn O'Hara, 1911; Buttered Side Down, 1912; Roast Beef Medium, 1913; Personality Plus, 1914; Emma McChesney & Co., 1915; Fanny Herself, 1917; Cheerful—By Request, 1918; Half Portions; 1919; The Girls, 1921; Gigolo, 1922; So Big, 1924; Show Boat, 1926; Mother Knows Best, 1927; Cimarron, 1929; American Beauty, 1931; They Brought Their Women, 1933; Come and Get It, 1935; Nobody's In Town, 1938; Stage Door (with G. S. Kaufman), 1938; A Peculiar Treasure (autobiography) 1939; Saratoga Trunk, 1941; No Room at the Inn, 1941; The Land Is Bright (with G. S. Kaufman) 1941.

ABOUT: Ferber, E. A Peculiar Treasure; Bookman June 1925, October 1926; Life September 23, 1940; New York Times Magazine September 1, 1940; Saturday Review of Literature June 16, 1935, February 4, 1939; Time February 6, 1939; World's Work June 1930.

FERGUSSON, HARVEY (January 28, 1890-), American novelist, writes: "Albuquerque, N.M., at the turn of the century, when I was ten years old, still had somewhat the character of a frontier town. Gambling was wide-open and cow-punchers and sheep men crowded the saloons on Saturday nights. The surrounding country still was wild and it was the first

White

thing that caught my interest. I had a horse and gun by the time I was eleven and spent nearly all my spare time hunting and riding, mostly alone. I was bored by school and read very few books before I was twenty, but I liked to draw pictures. One year I went to school in Washington, D.C., where my father was a delegate to Congress from the territory of New Mexico, and one year I went to the New Mexico Military Institute in Roswell, where I was drilled so thoroughly that I still know the manual of arms and still jump when I hear reveille in the morning. At Roswell I acquired a greatly improved carriage and a lasting aversion to military discipline. At the age of eighteen I went to Washington and Lee University, in Virginia, for the somewhat irrelevant reason that my father had gone there in 1870 when General Lee was president. I there acquired a B.A. degree and a profound distaste for academic instruction. Emerging at the age of twenty-one, I went into the United States Forestry Service, chiefly because I had a great longing to get back into the mountains. If left to myself I might have remained there a long time, but my father, who was in Washington again, sent for me and put me in a law school. Two weeks of legal study convinced me that I would never be a lawyer. I sold my textbooks for sixteen dollars and got a job on the old Washington *Herald* at nothing a week. When my sixteen dollars was gone, they gave me a salary of eight dollars a week.

"I have been writing for a living ever since. I have been successively a reporter, a Washington correspondent, editor of a syndicate, a corporation publicity man in New York, and a scenario writer in Hollywood; but most of my time and energy for twenty years have been devoted to the writing of books. I have published ten of them, including eight novels, a history, and a book which is classified in libraries as philosophy. For ten years I lived in Washington, for eight years I commuted between New York and New Mexico, and for the past seven years I have lived in Hollywood."

* * *

In 1927 Mr. Ferguson married Rebecca McCann, who died the same year. His first novel, *The Blood of the Conquerors,* opened up a new vein in American fiction—the realistic interpretation of New Mexican history and contemporary life; and he has returned to it often, especially in *Wolf Song* and *In Those Days.* His aim, he has said, is to "abolish journalism from novel writing, . . . [to] keep description only in so far as it is description from the point of view of a character, and as it affects the person."

His sister, Erna Ferguson, has written several interesting books about South America.

PRINCIPAL WORKS: The Blood of the Conquerors, 1921; Capitol Hill, 1923; Women and Wives, 1924; Hot Saturday, 1926; Wolf Song, 1927; In Those Day, 1929; Footloose McGarnigal, 1930; Rio Grande (history) 1933; Modern Man: His Belief and Behavior, 1936; The Life of Riley, 1937.

ABOUT: Baldwin, C. C. The Men Who Make Our Novels; Mencken, H. L. Prejudices (Fourth Series).

*FERRERO, GUGLIELMO (July 31, 1871-   ), Italian historian of Jewish descent, was born in Portici, near Naples. Although he has been for many years a university professor of history, he is not a university graduate, his doctorates of letters and

laws being honorary. Few historians, however, have gone more thoroughly into their chosen fields than has Ferrero, though his achievements are based largely on private study. He entered journalism when very young, as a member of the staff of *Secolo,* Milan, a Republican, but not Socialist, paper. He has traveled extensively both in Europe and America, his last lecture tour in the United States being in 1931. He is married to Gina Lombroso, daughter of the eminent criminologist, Cesare Lombroso, and herself (rather strangely) an antifeminist writer; they have a son and a daughter. Signor Ferrero has lectured on Roman History at the Collège de France,  in Paris, as well as at colleges in North and South America.

Radical Republican in politics, he sided strongly with the Allies in the First World War, and his influence helped to bring Italy into the war on the Allied side. From the beginning of the Fascist régime he was strongly and outspokenly opposed to it. For a while he was allowed to live in peace in his home in Florence, but it soon became evident that he would no longer be able to raise his voice while he remained in Italy. He moved with his family to Switzerland, and since 1930 has been Professor of European Military History at the Institut Universel des Hautes Études Internationales and Professor of Modern History at Geneva University. All his books were condemned and destroyed in Italy in 1935. He is a small man, with aquiline features, a cavalry moustache, and an imperial, partly bald, with keen eyes behind large tortoise-shell spectacles. He is an officer of the Legion of Honor.

Because of his lack of academic background, and also because at one time he was taken up and exploited by certain newspaper interests in the United States, orthodox historians often speak contemptuously of Ferrero and condemn him as sensational. It is true that his statements have often seemed exaggerated and even hysterical, and the close analogy which he believes to exist between the fall of the Roman Empire and the condition of Europe and America in the recent past and present is not wholly tenable. Nevertheless, events are giving evidence daily that his "sensationalism" has often been prophetic. As early as 1933 he said

* Died August 4 (?), 1942.

that "the next war will destroy civilization," and some of his prophetic warnings antedate those of Oswald Spengler.

Ferrero is a novelist as well as historian and journalist, though his novels are mostly fictionalized history and sociology. His massive history of Rome he has never finished; he says he has all the material on hand, but lacks the incentive to go on with what must be a gloomy narrative. Hugh Ross Williamson, though recognizing him as primarily an iconoclast, marked his "profound knowledge, penetrating insight, and definite contemporary relevance." G. Hubert-Rodier called him "our greatest consultant physician on those political diseases from which our social body suffers periodically; indeed, he is perhaps the greatest diagnostician Europe has produced since de Tocqueville."

WORKS AVAILABLE IN ENGLISH: The Female Offender (with C. Lombroso) 1895; Militarism, 1902; The Greatness and Decline of Rome (5 vol.) 1907-09; Characters and Events of Roman History from Caesar to Nero, 1909; The Women of the Caesars, 1911; Between the Old World and the New: A Moral and Philosophical Contrast, 1914; Ancient Rome and Modern America, 1914; Who Wanted the European War? 1915; Europe's Fateful Hour, 1918; A Short History of Rome (with C. Barbagallo) 1918-19; Problems of Peace, From the Holy Alliance to the League of Nations, 1919; The Ruin of the Ancient Civilization and the Triumph of Christianity: With Some Consideration of Conditions in the Europe of To-day, 1921; The Soul of Woman; Four Years of Fascism, 1924; Words to the Deaf: An Historian Contemplates His Age, 1926; The Third Rome (novel) 1927; The Seven Vices (novel) 1929; The Unity of the World, 1930; Peace and War, 1933; The Life of Caesar (revision of Vols. 1 and 2 of The Greatness and Decline of Rome) 1933; The Gamble: Bonaparte in Italy, 1796-97, 1939; The Reconstruction of Europe: Talleyrand and the Congress of Vienna, 1941.

ABOUT: Annales Politiques et Littéraires February 10, 1935; Living Age April 10, May 22, 1926, May 1, 1930, September 1939; Revue Politique et Littéraire March 1, 1930.

FEUCHTWANGER, LION (July 7, 1884-), German novelist, writes: "I was born in Munich, the son of a wealthy Jewish

industrialist. I studied German philology and the history of literature at the Universities of Munich and Berlin between 1 9 0 3 and 1907. I learned ancient and modern languages. In 1918 I was made a Ph.D., my thesis being a study of Heinrich Heine's *Rabbi von Bacherach*. In

the same year I founded a literary newspaper, *Der Spiegel* (*The Mirror*), which spoke for contemporary literature in so far as it embraced revolutionary artistic tendencies.

"From 1908 to 1911 I worked regularly on the literary critical paper, *Die Schaubühne* (*The Stage*), and interested myself in a literary society, Phoebus, which worked for the modern movement in German literature. I traveled much, most of all in Italy. Continuing my literary-scientific studies, I wrote an aesthetic novel, *Der Tönerne Gott* (*God of Thunder*).

"In 1912 I was married to Marthe Löffler, and left Germany. I traveled in Italy and French North Africa. In 1914 I was caught by the war in Tunis and taken prisoner. I succeeded in escaping, and returned to Germany. I was taken as a soldier, but soon discharged. During the war I wrote the plays *Vasantasena* and *Warren Hastings* which, at first forbidden, later had great success. I wrote the anti-war plays, *Die Kriegsgefangenen* (*Prisoners of War*) and *Peace* (after Aristophanes), which were both suppressed. I produced at the Munich Folk Theater, among other plays, Gorky's *Lower Depths*. Then I wrote drama, *1918* (*Thomas Wendt*), which described the end of the war and the betrayal of the German Revolution, and whose first performance at Münster led to 'disturbance of the public peace' and political suppression.

"In 1921 I finished the novel *Jud Süss* (*Power*), but could find no publisher. The next year I wrote *Die Hässliche Herzogin* (*The Ugly Duchess*). In 1925 I moved to Berlin. *Jud Süss* finally appeared and had a great success in Germany, and also in France and Spain, where I traveled in 1926. *Erfolg* (*Success*) appeared in 1930, and was sharply attacked. I began the *Josephus* trilogy the next year. In 1932 and 1933 I traveled in America.

"In 1933 my house in Berlin and my fortune was confiscated, and I went into exile. I moved to France, where I wrote the novel, *The Oppermanns*. In 1936 and 1937 I was in Moscow, where I began the novel, *Exile*."

* * *

After the collapse of France, Feuchtwanger was reported to have fallen into Nazi hands and, by some accounts, to have been beheaded, by others, interned in a concentration camp. Actually he and his wife escaped across Spain and Portugal with the aid of American friends (he was, indeed, under sentence of death by the Germans) and eventually reached the United States late in 1940, and makes his home here today. He is a short, thin man with a face not handsome, but intelligent and expressive. Among his other works, not mentioned by him, is *Pep,* a book of satirical poems about America which he wrote under the pseudonym (a literal translation of his name) of "J. L. Wetcheek." At that time (1929) he had never seen the United States, but his hits at American foibles were very keen.

Outside of pre-Nazi Germany, where he was perhaps best known as a playwright, his historical novels are considered his most important work. Such books as *Power, The Ugly Duchess, Josephus, The Jew of Rome,* and *The Pretender* have what *Time* called "vivid immediacy," bringing the past to life brilliantly. Louis Untermeyer called him "a master of imaginative construction," and Horace Gregory has spoken of his "rare gifts of historical observation and understanding of individual character." Thanks to his careful mastery of detail, the same characteristics obtain in his novels of contemporary life, like *Success* and *The Oppermanns.*

The Devil in France (1941) described his concentration camp experiences in France and his eventual escape in female disguise.

WORKS AVAILABLE IN ENGLISH: Power, 1926; The Ugly Duchess, 1928; Two Anglo-Saxon Plays (The Oil Islands, Warren Hastings) 1928; Pep: J. L. Wetcheek's American Song Book, 1929; Success, 1930; Josephus, 1932; The Oppermanns, 1934; Three Plays, 1934; The Jew of Rome, 1935; Marianne in India, 1936; Moscow 1937, 1937; The Pretender, 1937; The Devil in France, 1941; Josephus and the Emperor, 1942.

ABOUT: New Statesman and Nation September 11 and 18, 1937; New York Times Magazine January 19, 1941; Review Politique et Littéraire April 15, 1933; Time May 24, 1937, November 11, 1940.

*FÉVAL, PAUL, fils (1860-   ), French novelist, poet, and seaman, was born in Paris, the son of the elder Paul Féval, *feuilletonist,* rival of Victorien Sardou, and patron of Émile Gaboriau. Before he was thirty the younger Féval had not only become something of a searover, but had also written three books; and before the appearance of *Fils d'Artagnan,* a character-borrowing from the elder Dumas, published in the year of the outbreak of the First World War, he experimented in play writing (*Chantepie*) and

produced a substantial crop of novels and epic poetry.

With the coming of the war he became a member of the Board of Governors of the Ligue Maritime Française; and for propaganda purposes he traveled with the French fleet and took photographs of battleships in action. After the Armistice he maintained at least indirect relations with the Ligue, and for its illustrated review, devoted to the strengthening of France's Colonial good-will, he retold some of the nation's famous sea battles, both old and recent. A year later the same journal published fourteen of his sailors' songs, music for which had been written by various hands. In 1922 he wrote an assortment of tales originating in the folk-ways of various French colonies; some of these had reached him first-hand in the course of his own wanderings.

In 1928 he continued his transformation of the two famous fictional stand-bys, D'Artagnan and Cyrano, in *Years Between* a collaboration with M. Lassez. Again in 1930 and 1931 he carried these same characters through *Comrades at Arms* and *Salute to Cyrano,* neither of which can stand comparison with Dumas. Accepted on their own merits, however, they are good, swift-moving tales.

Féval is vice-president of La Societé des Gens de Lettres, a founder of the Society of French Novelists, and has also written scenarios for several French moving pictures. Very few of his books have been translated, and it is therefore difficult to "place" him for an English-speaking public. His father, of course, had set precedents in literary prestige and personal legendry which would have been very hard to maintain. As a young man Féval, now over eighty, appears to have lived a normal, busy life and to have regarded his own writing not as the careful execution of a prodigious task but as an experiment in literary variety.

PRINCIPAL WORKS AVAILABLE IN ENGLISH TRANSLATION: Years Between (with M. Lassez) 1928-29; Comrades at Arms, 1930; Salute to Cyrano, 1931; Heir of Buckingham (with M. Lassez) 1932.

*FICKE, ARTHUR DAVISON (November 10, 1883-   ), American poet, writes: "I was born at Davenport, Iowa, a small city in the Mississippi Valley. My father, Charles August Ficke, an eminent lawyer, had been brought to this country from Germany when an infant; my mother, Frances (Davison) Ficke, was of New England stock. My father was an inveterate traveler, and in my youth I was taken on numerous trips all over the world. I studied at Harvard under such eminent men as Santayana, Kuno Francke, William James; one of my classmates was Franklin D. Roosevelt. From my earliest youth I was more interested in the writing of poetry than in anything else; but I yielded to my father's wishes and became a lawyer. However, I found time during the first ten years

in his office to write eight books of poems and two treatises on Japanese art. When the First World War came along, I volunteered; and after long service in the American Army in France eventually became a lieutenant-colonel,

Bachrach

though probably there is no one alive who is less of a real soldier than I am.

"After my army service I never went back to the law, but became solely a writer. I am married to the painter, Gladys Brown, and live half the time in New York City and half the time in the beautiful Berkshire Hills at Hillsdale, N.Y. I am [currently] working on a long poem, *Beggar's Wallet: 1940,* in which I try to express something of the confusions that beset us all in this troubled hour. I have no political preferences, for all present American parties seem to me equally betrayers of the hopes of man, and no party has yet emerged that gives true expression to that honest sharing of opportunity which alone can save us.

"As to what I am like personally—that is a hard question to answer: all I can say is that I have infinite intellectual curiosity, and that I am passionately devoted to a large variety of such friends as are beyond the deserts of any man. I do not believe that civilization is coming to an end, nor do I despair of our some day creating a decent world, in spite of all present appearances to the contrary. But it will take a long time, and the devout labors of many men yet unborn.

"I forgot to mention the thing which, alas, is probably known to many people who have never read my serious poetry—a preposterous volume called *Spectra,* in which, in 1914, my oldest friend, Witter Bynner[iv] and I perpetrated a harmless hoax, under the names of 'Emanuel Morgan' and 'Anne Knish,' and pretended to found a new 'school' of poetry that was designed to satirize certain affectations in the fashionable poetry of that moment. Many critics swallowed the bait and gave high praise to the utter nonsense we had concocted. I fear I shall never live down my reputation as a clever person— whereas the truth is that I am a very serious and confused person."

* * *

Though Conrad Aiken complained that Mr. Ficke's free verse was "shapeless and ungoverned," he conceded that he had "done some charming things"; and C. A. Millspaugh characterized his serious poetry as being governed by "passion and rumination." His best-known volume is *Sonnets of a Portrait Painter* (new and revised edition 1922). Mrs. Ficke, whom he married in 1923, is his second wife; in 1907 he married Evelyn Bethune Blunt and they had a son; the marriage was later dissolved. In 1906 and 1907 he taught English at the State University of Iowa.

PRINCIPAL WORKS: From the Isles, 1907; The Happy Princess, 1907; The Earth Passion, 1908; The Breaking of Bonds, 1910; Twelve Japanese Painters (prose) 1913; Mr. Faust, 1913; Sonnets of a Portrait Painter, 1914; The Man on the Hilltop, 1915; Chats on Japanese Prints (prose) 1915; An April Elegy, 1917; Spectra (with W. Bynner) 1917; Out of the Silence, 1924; Selected Poems, 1926; Mountain Against Mountain, 1929; The Secret and Other Poems, 1936; Mrs. Morton of Mexico (novel) 1939; The Blue Jade Sceptre, 1941; Tumultuous Shore and Other Poems, 1942.

ABOUT: Starrett, V. Books Alive; Poetry August 2, 1937; Publishers' Weekly August 19, 1933; Scholastic May 19, 1934.

"FIELD, MICHAEL." See "BRITISH AUTHORS OF THE 19TH CENTURY"

FIELD, RACHEL LYMAN (September 19, 1894-March 15, 1942), American novelist and writer for children, was born in New York City, the daughter of Dr. Matthew D. Field and Lucy (Atwater) Field. Dr. Field was the nephew of three exceptionally distinguished uncles: Cyrus Field, who laid the first Atlantic cable; David Dudley Field, international lawyer; and Justice Stephen J. Field of the United States Supreme Court. Rachel

Pinchot

Field's early childhood was spent in western Massachusetts, at Stockbridge, the ancestral home of the Field family, and at Springfield. From the time she was fifteen the family went each summer to one of the picturesque Cranberry Isles, off the coast of Maine. All of these localities were later turned into rich backgrounds for her books.

"It is humiliating to confess," Rachel Field wrote to the compilers of this volume not long before her untimely death at forty-seven, "that I wasn't one of those children who are remembered by their old school teachers as particularly promising. I was more than ten years old before I could read. I was notably lazy and behind others of my own age in everything except drawing pictures, acting in plays, and committing pieces of poetry to memory." Poetry, in fact, was her greatest love, and at an early age she was contributing verse to her school paper and the *St. Nicholas* League. From high school in Springfield, where twenty dollars for a prize essay constituted her first literary earnings, she went to Radcliffe College.

In Professor George P. Baker's celebrated "English 47" workshop at Harvard-Radcliffe (where her classmates included Thomas Wolfe and many others since famous) Rachel Field scored her first success with a one-act play, *Three Pills in a Bottle,* which has been played by groups all over the country on the average of once a week ever since. After Radcliffe she went to New York and supported herself for six years by writing synopses for a motion picture company and by similar editorial piece-work. In her spare time she continued to write verse and short plays ". . . and, yes, the usual thing—a novel. It went the rounds and was turned down as it should have been. But some of the editors wrote me letters about it and they all said the first part, dealing with the heroine's childhood, was the best."

This criticism launched her on her first career, as a writer for children. The going was slow at first, but before many years she had to her credit a full shelf of children's books: verse, stories, and sometimes illustrations. Few authors in the field have been more consistently successful. Her books have been highly praised by librarians and specialists in children's literature, and taken to their hearts by the child readers themselves. Most of them are still in print, many years after they were written. She herself credited her success to *not* "writing down" to her youthful audience.

Gradually her interest in the American historical scene began to creep more and more into her writing, and this resulted, in 1929, in the appealing story of *Hitty* ("the only true juvenile classic written in America since the World War"). Illustrated by Dorothy Lathrop, who with Miss Field found the real Hitty (a quaint hundred-year-old doll) in a New York antique shop, the book became something of a publishing sensation. It was awarded the Newbery Medal—the first time the award had gone to a woman writer—as the most distinguished work of children's literature for the year, and attracted almost as many adult as younger readers. Its sale set a modern record for literature of its type.

Hitty marked another turning point in Rachel Field's career. In 1930 she published *Points East,* narratives of New England in verse, her first book written exclusively for adults. *God's Pocket,* a semi-fictional biography based on an old journal, followed in 1934. The next year saw her first full-length adult novel, *Time Out of Mind,* a warmly romantic story of the Maine coast in the twilight of the age of sail. Highly praised by critics and public alike, it became an outstanding success of the season.

In 1935 also, Miss Field married Arthur Pederson, literary agent; they had one daughter, Hannah. An interlude in Hollywood was the basis of their joint-novel, *To See Ourselves,* a compassionate tale of the "little people" who make up the wistful outer fringe of the moving picture capital. In 1938 Miss Field achieved her greatest popular success with *All This, and Heaven Too,* a fictionized life of her great-aunt, who before she became the wife of the Rev. Henry M. Field had been the famous "Mademoiselle D." of Paris, a central figure in the dramatic and still-debated de Praslin murder case. The book was a national best-seller for months and was made into a highly successful moving picture.

Rachel Field was described by those who knew her as friendly, gracious, unassuming, informed and informative, open minded in discussion but determined once she reached a conclusion. A delightful conversationalist, she possessed also "the gift of silence." Of medium height, she had curly auburn hair, blue eyes, a generous mouth, a low-pitched voice, and an infectious laugh. She enjoyed housework and "growing things" and was an enthusiastic cook.

The wealth and acclaim of her last years failed to change her tastes, and she lived quietly and modestly with her husband and infant daughter in Beverly Hills, Calif. Failing to rally after an operation complicated by pneumonia, she died following an illness of ten days, in her forty-eighth year. She was survived by her mother, a nonagenarian. Burial was in the ancestral plot at Stockbridge, Mass. Her last novel, *And Now Tomorrow*, the story of a New England mill town, was appearing serially in a national magazine at the time of her death and was issued posthumously in book form.

In a tribute in the *Saturday Review of Literature* after Rachel Field's death, Laura Benét called her "a tonic and a stay to those who loved her." Thousands of readers who did not know her personally valued her books for the same qualities.

PRINCIPAL WORKS: *Children's Fiction and Verse*—The Pointed People, 1924; Taxis and Toadstools, 1926; Eliza and the Elves, 1926; The Magic Pawnshop, 1927; Little Dog Toby, 1928; Hitty: Her First Hundred Years, 1929; Calico Bush, 1931; Hepatica Hawks, 1932; Just Across the Street, 1933; Susanna B. and William C., 1934. *Plays*—Six Plays, 1924; The Cross-Stitch Heart and Other One-Act Plays, 1927. *Poetry*—Points East, 1930; Branches Green, 1934; Fear Is the Thorn, 1936; At Christmas Time, 1941. *Adult Fiction and Biography*—God's Pocket, 1934; Time Out of Mind, 1935; To See Ourselves (with Arthur Pederson) 1937; All This, and Heaven Too, 1938; And Now Tomorrow, 1942.

ABOUT: Kunitz, S. J. & Haycraft, H. (eds.). The Junior Book of Authors; Horn Book 1928; Library Journal April 1, 1942; New York Times March 16, 1942; Publishers' Weekly June 28, 1930, March 21, 1942; Saturday Review of Literature March 28, 1942.

FIELD, SARA BARD (1882-), American poet, writes: "Born in Cincinnati a short time before one of the worst Ohio River floods, I remember hearing my father tell of escapes in packing boxes from second-story windows. When I was about three years of age my family moved to Detroit, elm-shaded and serene, in its pre-automobile days. There I received my education through high school. At eighteen, I married a minister many years my senior.

A. Arkatov

He had just accepted a call to a Eurasian Baptist Church in Rangoon, Burma. We went there in 1900, and my son was born there in 1901. I saw 'Christian' English exploitation of a brave, free, simple, and essentially spiritual people. I saw the famine sufferers from India whose distress, I knew, had drawn pennies from the ragged pockets of bootblacks and washerwomen in America, and watched quantities of rice, wheat, and tea being exported from the land by the wealthy landlords. I saw 'pagans' whose morality shamed many Christians. These things wakened my mind and soul. I grew up.

"Forced by ill health to return to America, we spent some months in New Haven, where I was privileged to audit the courses of the late Professor Lounsbury of Yale. It was he who first told me I was a poet.

"We went to a poor parish in Cleveland at the time when that city's mayor, Tom Johnson, and a brilliant company of his disciples were teaching municipal ownership and the necessity for social control of all public utilities and monopolies. I listened and learned. I met Clarence Darrow and learned more. My sister, Mary Field Parton, then head of a social settlement in Chicago, visited me with books and liberal conversation. I, and afterwards my husband, became Socialists. The wealthy and orthodox trustees of our church thereupon asked for our resignation, and we went to a small parish in Portland, Ore., with our son and a daughter born in Cleveland.

"In Portland, introduced by Darrow, I met Charles Erskine Scott Wood. My history thereafter is largely in this association. As organizer of the College Equal Suffrage League in the year of Oregon's suffrage victory, I traveled over the whole state, speaking in all small and larger towns. I also helped in the Nevada campaign when that State won suffrage. Later, under the brilliant leadership of Alice Paul, I traveled over the whole country speaking in the interests of national suffrage.

"My intensive literary career began in 1927, with the publication of *The Pale Woman*. This was followed by *Barabbas*, a long dramatic narrative, partially historical, on which I worked for many years. I have now in preparation another book of poetry and one of prose.

"In the foothills of the Santa Cruz Mountains, in California, my husband and I live literally under our own vine and figtree, whose juice and fruit we love to share. On these forty acres of rocky land we try to preserve a small world of Peace and Love and Justice despite the wide boundaries of War and Hate and Inhumanity that lie beyond and around us."

* * *

Mrs. Wood's maiden name was Field; her first husband's name was Ehrgott. Though she is frail and has had long sieges of serious illness, she is still a handsome and distinguished-looking woman. At present she is "eyes and often hands and feet" for her poet-husband[qv] who is ninety at this writing [1942] and whose sight has become very bad. Her own poems William Rose Benét called "coruscatingly imaginative" and "poignantly human"; Sara Bard Field herself he called "one of the finest spirits of our time." Of *Barabbas* Max Eastman said that it contains "many passages as fine as any poetry of its kind in America."

PRINCIPAL WORKS: The Pale Woman, 1927; Barabbas, 1932; Darkling Plain, 1936.

ABOUT: Saturday Review of Literature December 19, 1936.

FIELDING, A. E. is a name which has appeared on the title-page of English detective and mystery fiction since 1924. Until recently it was believed by most authorities on such matters, including the Library of Congress, that this signature represented an Englishman by the name of Archibald E. Fielding who was born in 1900. However, the editors of TWENTIETH CENTURY AUTHORS are assured by the American publishers of the Fielding books, H. C. Kinsey Co., of New York, that the author behind the initials is really a middle-aged Englishwoman by the name of Dorothy Feilding (*sic*), whose peace-time address is Sheffield Terrace, Kensington, London, and who enjoys gardening. No other factual or personal details are available. Neither "Mr." Fielding nor "Miss" Fielding figures in any of the usual books of biographical or literary reference. For many years the Fielding novels were signed with the first initial only. In 1927 the author adopted for American (but not for English) publication the two initials.

The first Fielding novel was *The Eames-Erskine Case* (1924), which was also received successfully in America a year later. When Inspector Pointer of Scotland Yard, the central Fielding character, solved the mystery of *The Footsteps That Stopped* (1926), the London *Times* commented that "Mr. Fielding has added to his reputation, but his narrative requires careful reading." *The Net Around Joan Ingilby* (1928) usually considered the best of the Fielding stories, was devious and unexpected in winding the coils around a young woman who proved to be a murderess. Additional Fielding novels have followed at a steady flow of one or two each year and have found general favor with readers on both sides of the Atlantic, although they are somewhat uneven in quality. Isaac Anderson once complained in the New York *Times* of Fielding's "muddled manner of writing"; but the Chicago *Tribune* pronounced "him" a writer of distinction "who ennobles his chosen field."

PRINCIPAL WORKS: The Eames-Erskine Case, 1924; Deep Currents, 1925; The Charteris Mystery, 1925; The Footsteps That Stopped, 1926; The Clifford Affairs, 1927; The Net Around Joan Ingilby, 1928; The Cluny Problem, 1928; The Mysterious Partner, 1929; Murder at the Nook, 1929; The Craig Poisoning Mystery, 1930; The Wedding-Chest Mystery, 1930; The Upfold Farm Mystery, 1931; Death of John Tait, 1932; The Westwood Mystery, 1932; The Tall House Mystery, 1933; The Cautley Conundrum (U.S. title: The Cautley Mystery) 1934; Tragedy at Beechcroft, 1935; The Case of the Two Pearl Necklaces, 1936; Mystery at the Rectory, 1936; The Case of the Missing Diary, 1937; The Paper Chase (U.S. title: The Paper Chase Mystery) 1937; Black Cats Are Lucky, 1937; Scarecrow, 1937; Murder in Suffolk, 1938.

FIELDS, Mrs. ANNIE (ADAMS). See "AMERICAN AUTHORS: 1600-1900"

FINEMAN, IRVING (April 9, 1893-   ) American novelist, writes: "I was born in New York City of middle-class Jewish parents [Joseph and Rebecca Rachel (Blanc) Fineman], and early decided I was going to be an engineer. I had no difficulty in achieving that ambition. I got my degree in civil engineering from both the Massachusetts Institute of Technology and Harvard in 1917 (having interrupted my training to take various engineering jobs on steel and concrete structures in the United States and Canada) and had been awarded a fellowship for graduate work in technological research when the United States entered the war, and I was given a commission as engineer officer in the Navy. I continued in the service until 1922, and then returned to civil engineering—design and construction of bridges, subways, etc.—and also taught for several years, theoretical and applied mechanics, in the engineering college of the University of Illinois. It was there, in 1928, that I took it into my head to write a novel —quite secretly, of course, since our American cult of specialization makes it dangerous for a man in technology to exhibit any serious interest in the arts, although for my own part I have never felt that the functions of the scientist and artist are unrelated.

"This first novel, *This Pure Young Man*, was submitted to the Longmans, Green contest in 1930, and won the prize—$7,500. I was thus auspiciously launched upon a new career (although I had been contented enough in the other), and proceeded to write a second novel. In 1932 I had a short but not unpleasant experience writing in Hollywood, which was followed by my appointment to the faculty of literature of the newly founded Bennington College in Vermont. When my third novel was published and received unanimous critical acclaim, it encouraged me in the belief that with these three books I had served my apprenticeship in this new craft and might turn to the treatment of materials for which my background particularly prepared me but which I had heretofore reserved—in the field of science. I spent some four years on the next book, *Doctor Addams*, a long novel with a highly technical background dealing with a biophysicist in our time.

"I was a voracious reader from childhood but never, before I engaged in writing, had thought of literature objectively—as something to be studied—and the few literature courses I had in my schooling certainly had little influence on my writing. It was only when I undertook to teach the subject that with my students I made a thoroughgoing and conscious study of literature and the techniques of writing; but by then I had written two books. So long and wide has been my reading of the classic literatures that it would be impossible now for me to say which books (excepting the Bible) or authors among them have influenced me. But among moderns I may easily point to Thomas Mann (whom I consider the greatest writer of our time), James Joyce, Joseph Conrad, and Virginia Woolf as writers from whom I have, at one point or another, learned a great deal.

"I have now resigned from teaching to devote myself to writing the novels I have projected. I was married in 1935 to Helene Hughes, and we live with our two sons in an old farmhouse in the Green Mountains. In 1939 we went to California and I wrote for Warner Brothers. I look to the development of the motion picture as a narrative medium with all the range of style and content which our fiction now has. Between books I lecture, but I cannot imagine why people want to see or listen to a writer who must, it seems to me, put the best of himself into his writing.

"In politics I am not an orthodox party man, though I generally vote Democratic.

I am a lover of true democracy, which I believe will survive only if it progresses toward democratic socialism. I dislike intensely the shoddy aspects of crowded, high-pressure big-city life. I hope for a highly civilized rural community of life, when we have learned not only to develop but to distribute our actual and potential blessings —both natural and technological."

PRINCIPAL WORKS: This Pure Young Man, 1930; Lovers Must Learn, 1932; Hear, Ye Sons, 1933; Doctor Addams, 1938; Jacob 1941.

ABOUT: Wilson Library Bulletin December 1940.

FINGER, CHARLES JOSEPH (December 25, 1869-January 7, 1941), Anglo-American writer on travel and adventure, wrote to the compilers of this volume shortly before his death: "Charles J. Finger, born in Sussex, England, became an American citizen in 1896. He is now living near Fayetteville, Ark. His education was somewhat of a haphazard affair. His activities in the world  of affairs were equally haphazard, for, after following the sea in his youth, he landed in Patagonia, where, for five years, ending in 1896, he roved from Chile down to the southernmost part of Tierra del Fuego, sometimes trapping and hunting, at times prospecting for gold in the Andes, at other times associating with the Indians.

"It was an experience that he was to turn to account later in his books. But the arts he had learned in that South American experience left him unfitted for life in the United States, though singularly enough his talent for and knowledge of music were turned to account when, by an odd set of circumstances, he became director of the San Angelo (Texas) Conservatory of Music, 1898-1900, during which time he also interested himself in economics and was a frequent contributor to the *Public* (Chicago), a Single Tax periodical subsidized by Joseph Fels.

"Striking out into a new mode of life, he took up railroad work, beginning in Alamogordo, N.M., as a boilermaker's helper. He advanced rapidly through devious channels, and, in Ohio, became an auditor, and finally general manager of the Ohio Southeastern System, then receiver of several railroads. His literary efforts were confined to articles in *Railway Age*.

"Meanwhile his short stories in Mencken's *Smart Set*, in the *Century*, and other magazines had attracted the attention of William Marion Reedy, who invited him to the editorial chair of the *Mirror* (St. Louis). On the death of Reedy, Mr. Finger bought land in Arkansas and settled down to authorship and sheep raising, with frequent trips to satisfy his yearning for travel. His *Tales From Silver Lands* was awarded the Newbery medal (for juvenile books) in 1925, and his *Courageous Companions*, an historical romance, won the $2000 Longmans Juvenile Fiction prize in 1929.

"In all, he has had thirty-two books published. He has, forthcoming, a companion volume to *Tales From Silver Lands*, an historical romance dealing with the War of 1812, and a novel dealing with the fur traders of 1812-14. In addition, he is the author of 34 brochures in the Haldeman-Julius 'Little Blue Book' series. For twelve years, 1920-32, he owned and edited a one-man journal, *All's Well*, which was intended to keep up the *Reedy's Mirror* tradition, and in the last three years of that journal's existence he was in partnership with Jacob Omansky, manager of the New York *Post*. In 1933 Mr. Finger became managing editor for the Bellows-Reeve Company of Chicago, and now edits a monthly journal for that firm.

"His political views are advanced. He is sociable but not social-minded, so belongs to no organization. In view of his literary achievements Knox College gave him a Litt.D. degree and the University of Arkansas an LL.D. He is on the editorial board of *Story Parade* and is a frequent contributor to magazines and reviews. Married to Nellie B. Ferguson in 1902, he has five children three sons and two daughters; his daughter Helen is a gifted artist. He dislikes social artificialities. His hobbies are sailing and riding and pool-playing."

* * *

Mr. Finger was born at Willesden, the son of Charles H. Finger and Julia (Connolly) Finger. He was educated at King's College, London, and studied music at Frankfort, Germany; he was an authority on Wagner, Chopin, and Grieg. He was a heavy-set, handsome man with a high forehead framed by wavy white hair. He died after a heart attack at his home at Fayetteville, Ark., at seventy. Though much of his work was written for young people, older people with young hearts enjoy it as well. Margaret Wallace called him "an adventurous spirit . . . capable of reflection and analysis."

PRINCIPAL WORKS: Choice of the Crowd (novel) 1921; In Lawless Lands, 1923; Highwaymen, 1923; Tales From Silver Lands (juvenile) 1924; Bushrangers, 1924; Spreading Stain (novel) 1927; David Livingstone: Explorer and Prophet, 1927; Frontier Ballads, 1927; Heroes from Hakluyt (ed., juvenile) 1927; Ozark Fantasia, 1927; Tales Worth Telling (juvenile) 1927; Romantic Rascals, 1927; Courageous Companions (juvenile fiction) 1929; Man for A' That, 1929; Seven Horizons, 1930; Adventures Under Sapphire Skies, 1931; Paul Bunyan Geography, 1931; Foot Loose in the West, 1931; Magic Tower, 1933; After the Great Companions, 1934; A Dog at His Heels (juvenile) 1935; The Distant Prize, 1935; Valiant Vagabonds, 1936; Our Navy (juvenile) 1936; Guns Thundered at Tripoli, 1937; Give a Man a Horse (juvenile) 1937; Bobbie and Jock and the Mailman (juvenile) 1938; Golden Tales From Faraway, 1940.

ABOUT: Child, H. El Jimmy; Faraday, J. G. Twelve Years of Children's Books; Finger, C. J. Seven Horizons; Fletcher, J. G. Life Is My Song; Gannett, L. Sweet Land; Hudson, W. H. A Hind in Richmond Park; Lucas, E. V. Post Bag Diversions; Powys, J. C. Autobiography; West, H. F. Life of Cunningham Grahame; Bookman June 1930; Saturday Review of Literature July 12, 1941; Southern Folklore Quarterly June 1937.

FINNEY, CHARLES GRANDISON (December 1, 1905-), American novelist, writes: "I was born in Sedalia, Mo. My parents were Norton J. Finney, whose father was president of the M.K.T. Railroad, and Florence (Bell) Finney, daughter of the city counsellor of St. Louis. For education, I went to the public schools of Sedalia. The only honor I attained there

Pereira

was the presidency of the debating club in my senior high school year. After that I attended the University of Missouri for a year and a half. On leaving the university, I enlisted in the army and was assigned to the 15th Infantry, at that time stationed in Tientsin, China. I served the full three years of the enlistment (1927-30), rising to the rank of Private First Class and achieving the rating of Sharpshooter with both the Springfield rifle and the Browning semi-automatic. I was discharged with 'excellent character' and recommended for re-enlistment. I came to Tucson, Ariz., where I have since lived. I secured a job as proofreader on the *Arizona Daily Star*, which I still hold. In 1934 I finished my first novel, which I had begun in my last year in China. *The Circus of Dr. Lao* was awarded the American Bookseller's Association prize for 'the most original novel' of the year, that year being the first the Association had awarded prizes. The critical reception accorded my second novel was largely hostile, but the third has received an excellent press and, I believe, will far outsell the former two books. I was married in 1939 to Marie Doyle. My hobbies are pistol-shooting and snake-catching. I have no present work in progress."

* * *

Mr. Finney is the great-grandson and namesake of a celebrated Congregationalist minister, the founder of Oberlin College. His spectacles and his thin, serious face make him much more literary than martial in appearance. *The Circus of Dr. Lao,* his first and still his best-known novel, was, he has said, the result partly of dreams, partly of observation in China, and presents the impact of Oriental culture and necromancy on a small Southwestern town. It is a fantastic, ribald piece of work; F. H. Britten spoke of it as a series of "obstreperous imaginative orgies" with a background of "sardonic gayety under fire." His latest novel, *Past the End of the Pavement,* is in a very different vein, dealing with an imaginative family of boys and their zoological collections, but it displays the same *outré* humor. It was a candidate for the same award his first novel received in 1935, but came out second to Dalton Trumbo's *Johnny Got His Gun.*

Mr. Finney writes only after his hours as a proofreader, and cannot therefore be very prolific. He chose Tucson as his home after his army term because his brother was living there, but now is permanently attached to it and to the near-by desert—where there are plenty of snakes to catch. He is one of the few contemporary American novelists who have never lived in New York.

PRINCIPAL WORKS: The Circus of Dr. Lao, 1935; The Unholy City, 1937; Past the End of the Pavement, 1939.

ABOUT: Wilson Library Bulletin June 1936.

FIRBANK, ARTHUR ANNESLEY RONALD (1886-May 21, 1926), English

novelist, essayist, and dramatist, better known as Ronald Firbank was born in London, second son of Sir Thomas Firbank, M.P., a contractor, and his wife, Jane Harriette (Garret). The founder of the family wealth (which was considerable) had been his grandfather, who began as an illiterate laborer in the north. Ronald was pampered by his mother and attended no school until he was 14. He was then sent to Uppingham, but was withdrawn after

two terms and put under a private tutor at Buxton. In 1904 he went to Tours to improve his French, and read Gautier, Baudelaire, Mallarmé, Flaubert, Maeterlinck, and Henri de Régnier. The following year he issued a small book containing the stories, *Odette d'Antrevernes* and *A Study in Temperament,* spent some time in Madrid, and, towards the end of the year, was entered at Scoone's, a private

A. John

college in London, where his mother prepared the way by putting in a new bed and a special armchair.

In the autumn of 1906 Firbank went up to Trinity Hall, Cambridge. He was already an extremely "precious" character, with *fin de siècle* tastes in literature, sinuous gestures, a high-pitched voice, a penchant for decorative rings, and a detestation of what he called "the mob." Rupert Brooke was his exact college contemporary, and the two had some contact during the poet's tentative period. Firbank gave lavish parties in his exotically decorated rooms, developed a great pride in his own good looks, and flirted with Catholicism, to which he became a definite convert in 1908. In June 1909 he left Cambridge without a degree, and after dallying with the idea of seeking a post in the Vatican, settled in London as a sort of literary and artistic man-about-town, drinking a lot of champagne and exciting considerable mockery by his affectations. He is described as "undulating" along Piccadilly; Edward Marsh met him at the Russian Ballet, "a strange figure pirouetting about the corridor and making little faces to itself"; while Lord Berners, to avoid the embarrassment of a public conversation one day, shouted: "You are my favorite author," and hurried off. C. W. Beaumont, bookseller and student of ballet, describes him thus:—

"He was tall and slender in figure; his physique was almost feminine in its delicacy; he had the wasp waist affected by Victorian exquisites. His hair was dark and sleek and brushed flat to the head; his eyes were blue or bluish-grey; his features were oval in shape, the eyebrows thin and arched, the nose long, the chin weak; his complexion was fresh, with a rosy blush on the cheekbones. . . . His hands were white and very well kept, the nails long and polished, and what was unusual in a man is that they were stained a deep carmine."

For all his superficial silliness, which made him intolerable to many, Firbank had, in the words of Sir Sydney Cockerell, "fine discernments in art and literature," and won the appreciation of friends like Evan Morgan, Albert Rutherston, and Augustus John. He was painted by John, Charles Shannon, Wyndham Lewis, and Alvara Guevara.

Always delicate in health, Firbank spent much time abroad in mild climates. He was in Egypt during the winter of 1911 and often went to Bordighera and Rome. When the war broke out it does not seem to have occurred to him that he might have any obligations (though in any case his health would have debarred him from any strenuous form of service). He buried himself in Oxford, seeing nobody, and wrote four books, *Vainglory, Inclinations, Caprice,* and *Valmouth.* In 1919 he took rooms in Jermyn Street, London, and tried with small success to revive his old existence in a changed world. His play, *The Princess Zoubaroff,* was published in 1920 but never produced. In the summer of 1921 he was at Versailles, where he wrote *The Flower Beneath the Foot.* The next year a visit to Haiti gave him the material for *Prancing Nigger.* Bordighera, Rome, London, and then Rome again, were his next living places, and at Rome he died, in his fortieth year.

Firbank's best-known novel is *Prancing Nigger,* which presents the Negro in an original light and has been highly praised by Carl Van Vechten. His works are too short to fall within the ordinary definition of the novel, and are more concerned with character than with action. Their eccentric personages are cleverly limned, and among a small but eclectic body of readers Firbank enjoys a considerable reputation. He detested women, and so never married.

PRINCIPAL WORKS: Odette d'Antrevernes, and A Study in Temperament, 1905; Vainglory, 1915; Odette: A Fairy Tale for Weary People, 1916; Inclinations, 1916; Caprice, 1917; Valmouth: A Romantic Novel, 1918; The Princess Zoubaroff: A Comedy, 1920; Santal, 1921; The Flower Beneath the Foot, 1923; Prancing Nigger (first issued in England as Sorrow in Sunlight) 1924; Concerning the Eccentricities of Cardinal Pirelli, 1926; The Works of Ronald Firbank (5 vols.) 1929.

ABOUT: Firbank, R. Prancing Nigger (see Introduction to American ed. by C. Van Vechten); Firbank, R. Works (see Biographical Memoir by O. Sitwell and Introduction by A. Waley); Fletcher, I. K. Ronald Firbank; Muir, P. H. A Bibliography of the First Editions of Books by Ronald Firbank; Life and Letters, March 1929; Times (London) Literary Supplement January 15, 1931.

FIRKINS, OSCAR W. (1864-March 7, 1932), American literary and dramatic critic and university professor, was born in Minneapolis, the son of Otis W. and Mary O. (Ten Eyck) Firkins. The family was a mixture of Anglo-Saxon, French, and Dutch. Firkins' great-grandfather, Coanrad Ten Eyck, a Dutch Reformed clergyman in New York State, was tried for heresy in 1819.  His paternal grandmother was a Langlois from New England; the family came to America at the time of the Revolution.

The boy could read at five, and required special glasses at thirteen. Bad eyesight, a shy, introverted nature, and an uncertain nervous constitution made his life one of disappointment and frustration, enlivened for his friends and students by flashes of ironic humor and a sardonic appreciation of the life outside his own small orbit.

He received his B.A. degree from the University of Minnesota in 1884 and an M.A. in 1898. A brief and wretched experience as timekeeper in his father's lumber yard and an attempt to teach at a boys' school in Moorhead, Minn., was fortunately succeeded by an instructorship and later professorship in the university's English department.

Eventually, at his own request, he was made Professor of Comparative Literature, thus making him independent of departmental interference. The National Institute of Arts and Letters made Firkins a member on the strength of his literary essays in various periodicals before his acute, subtle, and mannered studies of Jane Austen and William Dean Howells had found publishers.

In 1919 Harold Fuller and Fabian Franklin of the *Weekly Review* imported Firkins to New York to write dramatic criticism for two years for a small but appreciative audience, including William Archer, the English critic, who insisted on meeting him. Firkins' New York letters to his mother and a sister, the late Ina Ten Eyck Firkins, a well-known librarian and bibliographer, make curious and amusing reading. (They were usually signed with his full name.) *La Bohême,* for instance, gave him a slight chill, because "an opera in a garret seems as misplaced as a bird of paradise in a hencoop." Pavlova stirred this inquiry: "What emotion is there in a horizontal leg?" Firkins' later trips to New York to see plays invariably were followed by thronged university lectures about his impressions of them. He spoke before the New York Library Club and several other organizations, if he did not deem the occasion and subject beneath him. Firkins' body, after death at sixty-eight, was cremated at Lakewood Chapel, Minneapolis.

PRINCIPAL WORKS: Ralph Waldo Emerson, 1915; Jane Austen, 1920; William Dean Howells: A Study, 1924; Two Passengers for Chelsea and Other Plays, 1928; The Bride of Quietness and Other Plays, 1932; The Revealing Moment and Other Plays, 1932; Collected Essays, 1934; Power and Elusiveness in Shelley, 1937.

ABOUT: Chase, M. E. A Goodly Fellowship; Firkins, O. W. Memoirs and Letters (see Memoirs by Ina Ten Eyck Firkins, Richard Burton, and Netta W. Wilson); Morley, C. Streamlines; American Review June 1933; New York Times March 8, 1932; Saturday Review of Literature June 30, July 21, 1934.

FISHER, Mrs. DOROTHEA FRANCES (CANFIELD) (February 17, 1879-), American novelist who writes both

E. Schaal

as Dorothy Canfield and Dorothy Canfield Fisher, was born in Lawrence, Kan., the daughter of James Hulme Canfield, a prominent educator, and Flavia (Camp) Canfield, an artist. She had a year's schooling in Paris at the age of ten, since which time she has spoken French as fluently as English. Later (after having received a Ph.B. from Ohio State University in 1899, while her father was its president), she studied at the Sorbonne, and she received her Ph.D. in French from Columbia in 1905. She was preparing to be a professor of languages. Instead, in 1907, she married James Redwood Fisher. They have a son and a daughter.

Mrs. Fisher has always been interested in education, even though she never became a teacher. From 1902 to 1905 she was secretary of the Horace Mann School in New York. In 1912, in Italy, she became interested particularly in the educational work of Dr. Maria Montessori, and she has written several books bearing on it. Another of her chief concerns during this part of her life was her war work. The Fishers went to France for three years during the first World War, and while Mr. Fisher was in

the ambulance service, Mrs. Fisher worked with blinded soldiers and later established a Convalescent Home for refugee French children from the invaded areas. The family returned to the United States in 1919, but in 1923 they spent another year abroad. Since then, though she still travels a good deal, most of her time has been spent in a remodeled Canfield farm (the Canfields were Vermont pioneers), near Arlington, Vt. There she and her husband farm and live simply, as friends and neighbors of the rural New Englanders who, with university teachers and her beloved French, have shared the spotlight in Mrs. Fisher's novels. For a year she served on the Vermont Board of Education.

Mrs. Fisher has thus to an unusual extent combined a life of scholarship, art, and domesticity. She has translated several books, the best known being Papini's widely read *Life of Christ*; she has a long list of published works; and she is above all a wife, mother, grandmother, and homemaker. At first glance one would take her for the brisk, executive, motherly farm woman that she essentially is, with her square jaw, deft hands, and her soft waves of blonde hair now turned gray. It is only when one notes her high, wide forehead and her deep-set, keen blue eyes that one sees also the thinker and the novelist. For, though her novels have been very popular, she is not a "popular" novelist in the invidious sense. She has studied the Middle Western, and later the New England, milieu intensively and shrewdly, and her psychological touch is acute and sure.

Mrs. Fisher's first widely read novel, *The Squirrel Cage*, appeared in 1912. Since then her work has shown increasing maturity and depth. *The Deepening Stream*, a finely conceived story, is perhaps her highest achievement so far. She writes of the life she has known—of people on college faculties, French peasants, women in small towns, New England villagers. Her background and experience have combined to make one of her salient characteristics as a writer a deep-seated Americanism entirely free from parochialism. As Elizabeth Wyckoff said, she is "full of motherly understanding and tolerance of human beings, . . . fluent, deeply emotional, . . . an old-fashioned born novelist with a good working style, flexible and ready to hand." And William Lyon Phelps, though he feels that her "conscientious realism" has spun out some of her books to undue length, thinks as highly of her work. "All her novels," he said, "are autobiographical, being written exclusively out of her own experience and observation."

PRINCIPAL WORKS: *Fiction*—Gunhild, 1907; The Squirrel Cage, 1912; Hillsboro People (short stories) 1915; The Bent Twig, 1915; The Real Motive, 1916; Understood Betsy (juvenile) 1916; Home Fires in France (short stories) 1918; Day of Glory (short stories) 1919; The Brimming Cup, 1921; Rough-Hewn, 1922; Raw Material, 1923; The Home-Maker, 1924; Made-to-Order Stories, 1925; Her Son's Wife, 1926; The Deepening Stream, 1930; Basque People (short stories) 1931; Bonfire, 1933; Fables for Parents (short stories) 1936; Seasoned Timber, 1939. *Miscellaneous*—Corneille and Racine in English, 1904; English Rhetoric and Composition (with G. R. Carpenter) 1906; What Shall We Do Now? (juvenile) 1907; The Montessori Mother, 1912; Montessori Manual, 1913; Mothers and Children, 1914; Self-Reliance, 1916; Fellow-Captains (with S. N. Cleghorn) 1916; Why Stop Learning? 1927; Our Young Folks, 1941.

ABOUT: Cleghorn, S. N. Threescore; Kirkland, W. & F. Girls Who Became Writers; Bookman September 1931; Reader's Digest December 1940; Saturday Review of Literature October 11, 1930; Scholastic May 13, 1939.

FISHER, HERBERT ALBERT LAURENS (March 21, 1865-April 17, 1940), English historian, college president, sometime President of the Board of Education, was the eldest son of Herbert W. Fisher, Vice-Warden of the Stannaries (tin and smelting districts) of Cornwall and Devon. Educated at Winchester, he passed thence by scholarship to New College, Oxford. He read Classics and took a double first; but history was his real interest, and he followed it up in advanced studies at the École des Chartes and the University of Göttingen. In 1888 he was elected a Fellow of New College and began his tutorial career. His lectures were not specially eloquent. His most influential work as a teacher was done (as often happens under the Oxford system) by private historical talks in his rooms, wherein his splendid grasp of his subject was evident to undergraduates fortunate enough to participate. As a writer he first made his mark with *Studies in Napoleonic Statesmanship* (1903) which he followed by *Bonapartism* and by a popular but scholarly account of *Napoleon* in the Home University Library (of which series he was one of four joint editors). To the big *Political History of England: 1485-1558,* he contributed a volume on the Early Tudors.

In 1912 Fisher was nominated Vice-Chancellor of the University of Sheffield.

After twenty-four years in the calm beauty of Oxford the transition to this grim Midland steel city must have been brusque; but Fisher had practical educational ideals which here found an outlet in linking town and university more closely, in fostering the expansion of the Workers' Educational Association, and in advocating trade schools. With the onset of the war, Fisher worked hard to put the scientific departments fully at the service of the State. In 1916 Lloyd George was beginning to give evidence of his prescience by choosing for high office men of expert ability who had thus far taken no part in political life. Fisher was one he singled out; and after being returned to Parliament for the Hallamshire division of Sheffield, this eminent educationist was very fitly appointed President of the Board of Education. He proved to be an idealistic and highly efficient Minister, looking forward to a more broadly based educational system for the whole country and a higher status for the teacher. His Education Act of 1918 was shorn of some of its most useful provisions (notably a wide extension of compulsory day continuation classes) by post-war economy demands, but it introduced some far-reaching reforms. Fisher stayed on as Minister until the Lloyd George Coalition was broken up in 1922, and was mainly responsible for the Burnham Award, which gave all teachers a regular rising salary-scale, and for the settlement of a reasonable superannuation scheme for them. He was a delegate to the first League of Nations Assembly in 1920-22. He remained in Parliament as National Liberal Member for the English Universities until 1926; but in 1925 he was chosen Warden of New College and a year later took up residence in Oxford once more.

Years of public life had not disabled Fisher for the presidency of a learned community. His wide knowledge had been supplemented by participation in the actual shaping of history; he was genuinely solicitous for the welfare of undergraduates; and on the social side he was gracefully aided by his wife, the eldest daughter of Sir Courtenay Ilbert. He was a handsome man, of fine presence, possessed of wide liberal views, humanity, and fairness of mind, which came out as well in his personal dealings as in his writings. The most celebrated of these, *The History of Europe,* was a product of his later Oxford years. It was history in the great tradition, and had an immense vogue everywhere except in Germany and Italy, where it was banned.

From 1912 to 1915 Fisher had served on the Royal Commission on the Public Services in India, paying a visit there during the period. Over a space of years he worked with Sir Michael Sadler on the Oxford Preservation Trust, and he did distinguished service on many public bodies, including the British Academy (of which he was a Fellow), the British Museum, the Rhodes Trust, the London Library, the National Trust for Places of Historic Interest or Natural Beauty, the Governing Body of Winchester College and the B.B.C. In 1930 he delivered the Tercentenary Oration of the State of Massachusetts, and in 1933 he was a member of the British Delegation to French Canada. In April 1940 he was serving on the London Tribunal when he was knocked down by a lorry in Millbank, on Thames-side, dying of his injuries a week later.

PRINCIPAL WORKS: *Historical*—The Medieval Empire, 1898; Studies in Napoleonic Statesmanship: Germany, 1903; Bonapartism, 1908; The Republican Tradition in Europe, 1911; Napoleon, 1913; Studies in History and Politics, 1920; A History of Europe (3 vols.) 1936 (rev enlarged ed., 1938); Pages From the Past, 1939. *Biographies*—Frederick William Maitland: A Biographical Sketch, 1910; Viscount Bryce of Dechmont, 1927; Paul Vinogradoff: A Memoir, 1927. *Miscellaneous*—Educational Reform, 1918; Orthodoxy (Essex Hall Lecture) 1922; The Common Weal, 1924; Our New Religion (on Christian Science) 1929; An Unfinished Autobiography, 1941.

ABOUT: Cohen, M. R. Law and the Social Order; Fisher, H. A. L. An Unfinished Autobiography; Raymond, E. T. Uncensored Celebrities; Riddell, G. A. R., 1st Baron. More Things That Matter. The Times (London) April 19, 20, 1940.

FISHER, VARDIS (March 31, 1895-   ), American novelist, writes: "I was born on a wild windy night that ushered in All Fools' Day a few minutes later; in a one-room cottonwood shack on a bleak Mormon outpost in Idaho; with a caul which for my mother augured that I'd be a bishop at least and perhaps an apostle. Nursed on a cow, allowed to yell night and day, and despised by relatives for whom I was the most sickly runt in a pioneer clan, I headed straight into the most introverted childhood that ever had nightmares on an American frontier. To the age of ten or eleven, when I first entered school, my memories are chiefly of howling wolves, screaming cougars, venison, deer skins for bedding, and neigh-

borless loneliness. My father, Joseph, and mother, Temperance Thornton, stemmed from Mormon converts who went west with Joseph Smith. I have one brother, Dr. V. E. Fisher, a psychologist, and an atheist like myself; and a sister, Irene, who is pious enough for a whole tribe.

"I took a B.A. from the University of Utah; an M.A. and Ph.D. (*magna cum laude*) from the University of Chicago. I have taught in those and in other universities. My doctoral thesis was on the literary reputation of George Meredith. No linguist, I had a deuce of a time learning Old English and German. I was corporal in the first war to save democracy but never got shot at.

"My career began, I suppose, early in high school; for before I was half way through a wild-eyed and sentimental adolescence, I wrote what I called a novel, as well as a ton of horrible verse. Inasmuch as by that time I had an incurable feeling of inferiority, I decided to be a writer. I read so much before the age of thirty that I nearly went blind, and that great and noble scholar, John Matthews Manly, pointed out to me that I was a book drunkard. Doubtless many authors have influenced me for good and ill. I think of Keats, Meredith, France, Cabell. My only literary preference is for *intelligent* books.

"And that goes for persons. I belong to no political party, no societies or clubs. My political convictions are summarized in the last chapters of *No Villain Need Be*. My favorite public figures are men of integrity like George Norris. My chief dislikes include evasions in their multitude of forms; increasing taxes that assume the dubious privilege of being governed to be worth all the tribute it costs; college graduates who, unable to find a job, set up as literary critics; dictatorships and any suppression anywhere of freedom of thought and voice; the sentimental chivalry of a nation that encourages parasitic women; radio advertising; and my own books as soon as they are finished. I like intelligence; persons who do not think with their emotions; and persons who discipline their egoistic demands with a rebuking sense of irony."

* * *

In 1918 Mr. Fisher married Leona McMurtrey; they had two sons, and after her death he married, in 1928, Margaret Trusler, a philologist; in 1940, Laurel Holmes. In 1935 he was director of the Federal Writers' Projects in Idaho, and since unemployed writers are scarce in that sparsely populated state, he wrote almost single-handed the *Idaho Guide* and the *Idaho Encyclopaedia*. He first became widely known through his autobiographical tetralogy, with titles taken from Meredith's *Modern Love;* Fisher's hero bore the transparent name of "Vridar Hunter." This exceedingly introverted and frank series, at first rejected by every eastern publisher and published by the Caxton Printers in Idaho, was later taken over by a large New York firm. With *Children of God,* the long novel on the history of Mormonism which won the Harper Novel Prize in 1939, Fisher suddenly revealed himself in a completely new light—as an objective writer of historical fiction. As Burton Rascoe said: "Hitherto Fisher's fame has been limited to a handful of admirers [who considered him] . . . a more profound delver than Proust into the abysses of the subconscious, an introverted writer with a sensitivity so abnormal as to be the exquisite refinement of genius. . . . His metamorphosis is astonishing. . . . He has told a grand story in a grand manner."

PRINCIPAL WORKS: Sonnets to an Imaginary Madonna, 1927; Toilers of the Hills, 1928; Dark Bridwell, 1931; In Tragic Life, 1932; Passions Spin the Plot, 1933; We Are Betrayed, 1935; The Neurotic Nightingale (essays) 1935; No Villain Need Be, 1936; April—A Fable of Love, 1937; Odyssey of a Hero, 1937; Forgive Us Our Virtues, 1938; Children of God, 1939. The City of Illusion, 1941.

ABOUT: Newsweek August 28, 1939; Southern Review Summer 1937; Written August 1940.

FITCH, CLYDE. See "AMERICAN AUTHORS: 1600-1900"

FITTS, DUDLEY (1903-), American poet, was born in Boston, and was educated in the public schools of that city and at Harvard, where he received his B.A. degree in 1925. While there he was editor of the *Harvard Advocate,* in which his first work was published. He writes: "I owe my literary education to my association, as an undergraduate, with John Wheelwright, Foster Damon, Grant Code, and Richard Blackmur." He has been closely connected with *Hound and Horn* during the whole of its lifetime, and his first serious work was published in that magazine, in *Poetry,* and in *transition.* Since then, he says, "I have contributed verse and criticism to numberless magazines here and abroad, from the *Atlantic Monthly* and the *Criterion* down (or up)." He has worked both at the Yaddo and at the MacDowell colonies for writers. Since 1927 he has been instructor in English at the Choate School, Walling-

ford, Conn., and he is now connected with *New Directions,* Norfolk, Conn. In 1932 he went to Spain and there began a translation into Spanish of Archibald MacLeish's *Conquistador.* "The Fascist insurrection of 1936," he writes, "put an end to this project." Since 1936 he has been engaged with Robert Fitzgerald in translations from the Greek and Latin. He says: "My chief literary preoccupation now is with the Greek and Roman classics. Fitzgerald and I are interested in the radio as a medium for the resuscitation of Greek drama, and we intend to keep on experimenting along the line opened up for us by the very successful broadcasts of our translation of the *Alcestis* of Euripides by the British Broadcasting Company in 1937 and the National Broadcasting Company in 1939, and of the *Antigone* of Sophocles by the latter in 1939."

William Rose Benét said of his poetry, which he classed with the school of "erudite implications," that it is "highly intellectual, wayward, and quite difficult." He added: "He has a subtle mind, a sensitivity to beauty, an esoteric sense of humor, and a most elliptical manner." He himself, with a sense of humor not at all esoteric, notes that his poetry is distasteful to two critics who have nothing else in common, in that he has received "a bitter aside by Mr. Allen Tate, who dislikes my work, and another bitter aside by Mr. Granville Hicks, who dislikes my work (and how!)."

PRINCIPAL WORKS: Two Poems, 1932; Ten Introductions (with G. Taggard) 1935; The Alcestis of Euripides (with R. Fitzgerald) 1936; Poems 1929-1936, 1937; One Hundred Poems from the Palatine Anthology, 1938; The Antigone of Sophocles (with R. Fitzgerald) 1939; More Poems From the Palatine Anthology, 1941; Latin American Poetry (ed.) 1942.

ABOUT: Poetry November 1937; Saturday Review of Literature July 3, 1937.

FITZGERALD, FRANCIS SCOTT KEY (September 24, 1896-December 21, 1940), American novelist, was born in St. Paul, Minn., the son of Edward and Mary (McQuillan) Fitzgerald, on both sides of Irish descent. The family was prosperous, and he was educated first at St. Paul Academy and then at the Newman School, in New Jersey, to which he was  sent very young in his parents' hope of making him attend to his studies instead of "wasting his time scribbling." He went on "scribbling," however, both there and at Princeton, which he left in 1917, after four years, as author of a Triangle Club operetta, but as a non-graduate. He left to join the army, and served as an infantry lieutenant and aide-de-camp to Gen. J. A. Ryan until 1919.

After he was demobilized he went to New York, where it is said that seven newspapers in turn refused to give him a trial as a reporter, and where for three months he wrote street car advertising slogans for an advertisement agency. Then he sold a short story or two to the *Smart Set,* under the editorship of H. L. Mencken and George Jean Nathan, and, elated, returned to St. Paul to work on a novel. He was not yet twenty-four. During leisure hours in his army service he had been working on a novel never finished and never published, but he wasted none of it, for he filched all the best passages for the new book on which he now started work. In fact, when his first novel appeared, one wit called it "the collected works of F. Scott Fitzgerald," since it contained the best portions of everything he had written hitherto.

The book was *This Side of Paradise* (1920), which was accepted by special delivery and at once established the young author as a conspicuous figure in the current literary world. This was not because of any remarkable merit in either the story or its writing, but because it was the perfect expression of the world of the post-war American adolescent—the "jazz age." Fitzgerald received the subsequent celebrity and money undazzled but delighted; he had always had faith in himself, always had been "determined to be a genius." In the same year, he married Zelda Sayre, also a writer; they had one daughter. He went on writing—short stories, another novel, a play. The play was a failure and involved him in debts which he had to work hard to liquidate. After his first success he lived mostly on Long Island and abroad, chiefly on the Riviera and in Rome.

A pale blond with very fair hair and light blue eyes, F. Scott Fitzgerald, after a precocious beginning (which he exaggerated occasionally to make it still more remarkable), kept on being young. Youth and contemporaneity were his strength and in the end his weakness. He was the voice of his generation, the generation of "flaming youth"—disillusioned, flippant, hard-boiled—and he spoke its exact language. The trouble was that the generation grew up and was succeeded by a very different one, to which Fitzgerald never made a quite successful adjustment. In the world of his last years he was lost, though only in early middle age. Describing himself as "a cracked plate," he spent his final three years, almost in retirement, in Hollywood.

In his adult years Fitzgerald, unlike his imitators, never made a virtue of cynicism. He took himself and his work seriously; he tried desperately to fulfill the magnificent promise of his youth. Of his finest novel, *The Great Gatsby* (1925), which celebrates the spectacular rise and fall of a bootlegger-dreamer of the post-war decade, he remarked later:

"Now that this book is being reissued, the author would like to say that never before did one try to keep his artistic conscience as pure as during the ten months put into doing it. Reading it over one can see how it could have been improved—yet without feeling guilty of any discrepancy from the truth, as far as I saw it. . . . I think it is an honest book, that is to say, that one used none of one's virtuosity to get an effect, and, to boast again, one soft-pedalled the emotional side to avoid the tears leaking from the socket of the left eye, or the large false face peering around the corner of a character's head."

His letter of advice to young writers concludes with a characteristically poignant warning: "But remember, also, young man: you are not the first person who has ever been alone and alone."

At the end, before his heart gave way in Hollywood at forty-four, he worked on an unfinished novel of filmland, *The Last Tycoon,* which was published posthumously (together with *The Great Gatsby* and *Selected Short Stories*). Edmund Wilson, in his foreword to the volume, called it Fitzgerald's most mature work.

John Peale Bishop worked out, very interestingly, two strains in Fitzgerald's undoubted talent—the Irish, with its inverted romanticism, its moody sentimentalism, its innate prudery; and the Middle Western, with its awe at wealth, power, and urbanity: "The rich are not as we." To quote Mr. Bishop, the author was fascinated by "the expensive charm and sensational display of the post-war decade, but he began counting the cost long before the bills came in"—and when, figuratively, the bills came in he had no coin good for their payment. He had extraordinary imagination, utterly undisciplined and "without intellectual control"· he had immense verve, but was incapable

461

of genuine abstract thought. No one ever so got under the skin of that particular generation (because he was himself part of it, and its most articulate spokesman) ; and, as Mr. Bishop remarked, his work had "every fault, except failure to live."

PRINCIPAL WORKS: This Side of Paradise, 1920; Flappers and Philosophers (short stories) 1920; The Beautiful and Damned, 1921; Tales of the Jazz Age, 1922; The Vegetable (play) 1923; The Great Gatsby, 1925; All the Sad Young Men (short stories) 1926; Tender Is the Night, 1934; Taps at Reveille (short stories) 1935; The Last Tycoon, 1941.

ABOUT: American September 1922; Bookman England: Heads or Tails) 1939; Marrons Glacés, March, May 1922; New Republic February 17, 1941; March 3, 1941; Saturday Evening Post September 18, 1920; Saturday Review of Literature June 12, 1937, January 4, 1941; Scholastic October 12, 1935; Virginia Quarterly Review January 1937.

FITZMAURICE-KELLY, JAMES (June 20, 1858-November 30, 1923), English authority on Spanish literature, was born in Glasgow, the eldest son of Colonel Thomas Kelly of the 40th Foot, formerly of the Egyptian Police, and Catherine (Fitzmaurice). His mother dying abroad, the boy, who was deeply attached to her, added her name to his patronymic. In 1885 Fitzmaurice-Kelly was in Spain acting as tutor to Don Ventura Misa in Jerez de la Frontera. Returning to London next year, he reviewed books for the *Spectator, Athenaeum,* and *Pall Mall Gazette,* and was one of William Ernest Henley's young men. Archer Huntington, in New York (where his Hispanic Museum, with its fine library, stands) and Raymond Foulché-Delbosc were other close friends. Fitzmaurice-Kelly's authoritative work on Cervantes, his life and times, began with a *Life* in 1892 followed by the definitive *Memoirs* twenty years later, in 1913. He edited the *Complete Works* of Cervantes (1901) and, with John Ormsby, *Don Quixote* (1899-1900). A wider public knows him by the *Oxford Book of Spanish Verse* (1913) and the *History of Spanish Literature,* first published in 1898, which was also translated into Spanish and French.

He contributed thirty-nine articles on Spanish literature and authors to the notable eleventh edition of the *Encyclopaedia Britannica,* showing the advance made in Spanish studies since George Ticknor, and displaying notable gifts for analysis and synthesis, and was made Knight Commander of the Order of Alfonso XII. He was Norman MacColl lecturer at Cambridge in 1907, and Gilmour Professor of Spanish Language and

Literature at the University of Liverpool from 1909 to 1916, when he occupied the Cervantes chair of Spanish Language and Literature at King's College, London. Fitzmaurice-Kelly was self-taught in his Spanish studies. Reading Pascal deterred him from entering the priesthood, and his zest for life made the decision a wise one. He married Julia Sanders, herself a Spanish scholar, in 1918; they had no children. He died at Sydenham at sixty-six.

PRINCIPAL WORKS: Life of Miguel de Cervantes Saavedra, 1892; A History of Spanish Literature, 1898; Lope de Vega and Spanish Drama, 1902; Cervantes in England, 1905; Chapters on Spanish Literature, 1908; Miguel de Cervantes Saavedra: A Memoir, 1913; Bibliographie de l'Histoire de la Littérature Espagnole, 1913; Complete Work of Cervantes, 1901; The Oxford Book of Spanish Verse, 1913.

ABOUT: (London) Times December 1, 1923; Manchester Guardian December 5, 1923; Revue Hispanique 1924.

FLANDRAU, CHARLES MACOMB (December 9, 1871-March 28, 1938), American novelist, short-story writer and essayist, was born at St. Paul, Minn., a son of Charles Eugene Flandrau, who wrote a history of Minnesota, and Rebecca Blair (McClure) Flandrau. Grace C. (Hodgson) Flandrau, the writer, is his sister-in-law. Charles Flandrau graduated from  Harvard College in 1895. The Cambridge scene, observed with Western irreverence and a sharp, rather feminine humor, soon elicited two books, *Harvard Episodes* and *The Diary of a Freshman. Harvard Episodes,* published by the young firm of Copeland and Day, depicted the college rounders, *poseurs,* and butterflies of the period, as Paul Rosenfeld has said, and also showed "the sentimental idealization of socially privileged and prominent classmen." The stories provoked enough public attention and protest to interest George Horace Lorimer, editor of the *Saturday Evening Post,* who commissioned the cheerfully amusing *Diary of a Freshman* and its sequel, *Sophomores Abroad,* the latter not published in book form till thirty years later. Flandrau's *Prejudices* (1911), first contributed to the *Bellman,* are essays done with "charm, skill and easy tolerant humor," as were the *Loquacities* published twenty years later. In 1908 his *Viva Mexico,* written from material gathered while he was living on a coffee plantation, attracted much favorable attention. An account of Mexico under the reign of Diaz, it has been called one of the best travel books ever written. Flandrau, whose ancestry was French, also passed much time in a villa near Bizy, Normandy, the section from which the family emigrated. The village, he said, caused the pages of *Madame Bovary* "to seem like a work of contemporary fiction—the book of the month." From 1915 to 1920 he was music and dramatic critic of the St. Paul *Pioneer Press and Dispatch*. Flandrau died in St. Paul at sixty-six, after a year's illness. He had an alert, humorous face, fair hair, and wore eye-glasses. Some of his special admirers included Owen Wister, who praised his charm of style and literary acumen in discursive writing; Alexander Woollcott; and Edmund Pearson, who persuaded Rutger Jewett of Appleton-Century to publish *Sophomores Abroad* in 1935.

PRINCIPAL WORKS: Harvard Episodes, 1897; The Diary of a Freshman, 1901; Viva Mexico, 1908; Prejudices, 1911; Loquacities, 1931; Sophomores Abroad, 1935.

ABOUT: Woollcott, A. Enchanted Aisles. New York Times March 31, 1938; Publishers' Weekly April 9, 1938; Saturday Review of Literature June 12, July 3, 1937; April 9, 1938.

FLAVIN, MARTIN (November 2, 1883-), American dramatist, writes: "I was born in San Francisco. My father,  Martin J. Flavin, was a merchant, born in New York but of Irish extraction. My mother, Louise Archer, was the daughter of California pioneers whose ancestral roots were in Virginia and South Carolina. My father died in my childhood

Keystone

and my mother remarried. I grew up in Chicago, attended the public schools there and, for a short time, the university, where my principal activities centered about the comic opera and dramatic clubs. On leaving college I tried my hand at writing short stories for the magazines, supplementing the irregular rewards with a night job on a newspaper. I met with some success and established a market for a certain type of story, but the medium did not satisfy me and, after a year or two, I decided to go into a family manufacturing business in the Middle West, and continued in this occu-

pation for twenty years—always with the reservation that some time I would return to creative writing. Twelve years elapsed and I was in the middle thirties before I began again to write, this time for the theatre—in such leisure as my duties as a business executive allowed me. For several years I managed to combine both occupations. I was forty years old before I had a play produced on Broadway, and not until three years later did I definitely turn my back on an active business career and burn my bridges behind me.

"I have been married twice: in 1914 to Daphne Virginia Springer, from whom I was divorced three years later. By this marriage I have a daughter. In 1919 I married Sarah Keese Arnold, and in 1921 we began the creation of a home on a rocky point in the Pacific Ocean, a few miles south of Carmel, Calif. This place, 'Spindrift,' has been for eighteen years, and still is, my home. Most of my plays have been written there, my two sons have grown up there; and there, in 1937, my wife lost her life by a fall into the sea.

"My writing life has been devoted to the theatre. Except for the stories which I wrote as a youth and a book which I have recently completed, I have known no other medium. I have worked for motion pictures at different times, but the synthetic method of production is not adapted to me. For one quarter, not long ago, I taught a class in playwriting at Stanford University. It was an interesting experience but it is not my *métier*. I have always worked alone and am without experience of collaboration. I am, I suppose, both politically and spiritually, an individualist."

* * *

Mr. Flavin looks a little like a less obese and less extreme Irvin Cobb, with a hint of his Irish ancestry in his features. He says he was "stage struck from birth." One of his best known plays, *The Criminal Code*, was the result of the emotional effect on the playwright of a visit to San Quentin Prison. Besides his published plays, his acted dramas include *The Road to the City, Dancing Days*, and *The Road to Damascus*. The other one-acters included in a volume with *Brains* are *Casualties, The Blind Man, An Emergency Case, A Question of Principle*, and *Caleb Stone's Death Watch*. After the death of the second Mrs. Flavin, the author was married a third time, in 1940, to Mrs. Connie Bell. Since writing the autobiographical note above, Mr. Flavin appears to have become more interested in novel-writing than heretofore.

PRINCIPAL WORKS: (Date of Publication): Children of the Moon, 1924; Lady of the Rose, 1925; Brains and Other One-Act Plays, 1926; Service for Two, 1927; The Criminal Code, 1929; Spindrift, 1930; Broken Dishes, 1930; Cross Roads (Grist to the Mill) 1930; Amaco, 1933; Achilles Had a Heel and Tapestry in Gray, 1936; Around the Corner, 1937; Mr. Littlejohn, 1940; Corporal Cat, 1941.

ABOUT: Wilson Library Bulletin January 1931.

FLECKER, JAMES ELROY (November 5, 1884-January 3, 1915), English poet and dramatist, was born at Lewisham, Lon-

don, elder son of the Rev. W. H. Flecker, D.D., and his wife, Sarah (Ducat). His baptismal names were Herman Elroy, and he changed the first to James while at Oxford. In 1886 Dr. Flecker became headmaster of Dean Close School, Cheltenham, and most of Roy's youth was spent there. He learned to read from shop signs, and was a highly strung, clever, and quarrelsome child. As early as thirteen he began to write verse. His father brought him up on strict Evangelical lines, but was a real friend and companion to him. At the age of sixteen he was sent to Uppingham, whence, after only five terms, he passed to Trinity College, Oxford, with a classical scholarship and a school-leaving scholarship. He was there from 1902 to 1906.

At Oxford Flecker won no academic honors, taking only a third in both "Mods." and "Greats." But this was because he was interested in many other things than the classical curriculum—in French poetry, for example. He became an agnostic, made many friends, and wrote much verse, which was so good as to lead Professor Sir Walter Raleigh to prophesy a great future for him.

The home civil service, journalism, or schoolmastering, were considered possible careers. Roy (as he was always called) taught at a private school in Hampstead for a few weeks at the end of 1906. Early in 1907 he made an abortive attempt to live by writing, at Oxford. He then set to work seriously on modern languages, with a view to the examination for a student-interpretership in the consular service. He already knew much French and German. He now added Italian, Spanish, and mod-

ern Greek, and passed the examination early in 1908. The next step in his training was a two-year course in modern languages at Caius College, Cambridge. He disliked the academic atmosphere of Cambridge, but found consolation in outdoor pursuits like walking and punting (of which he was very fond), in hard work, and floods of talk. Francis Birrell, a great friend of those days, wrote that "he was not a complicated character, but fundamentally simple and boyish, with some of the vanities of boys"; while Rupert Brooke described a visit from him at Grantchester, "poling a canoe up the river at night. There were lanterns in the bow and stern and Flecker, dressed in flannels, a tall, swarthy and rather sinister figure, erect in the canoe, wore a garland of red flowers on his head."

An engagement of marriage, contracted in 1909, was soon broken by mutual consent. Flecker was posted to Constantinople in June 1910; but after only a few weeks he was found to have tuberculosis, and returned to England for a three-months' stay at a sanatorium in the Cotswolds. By this time he had already published two books of verse, The Bridge of Fire and Thirty-six Poems, and was at work on the play, Don Juan, and on a school text, The Scholar's Italian Book. From the sanatorium he went to Paris, then via London, back to Constantinople and thence to Beirut. On a period of leave in Athens in May of this year he married a Greek lady, Helle Skiadaressi. He acted as vice-consul in Beirut until March 1913, delighting in the scenery but longing for home. In May 1913 his health broke completely, and under urgent medical advice he went to Leysin, Switzerland. The rest of his short life was spent in Swiss sanatoria, at Leysin, Montana, Locarno and Davos, at which last place he died at only thirty. Re-converted to Christianity in his latter days, he received communion on his death-bed.

Flecker's verse was distinguished by gorgeous color and by a search after perfection of form that was more French than English. Indeed the French "Parnassian" poets, especially Heredia, were his avowed masters. The play, Hassan, was his chief contribution to literature, and when produced in 1923-24, with ballets by Fokine and music by Delius, it had the highest success. Flecker's knowledge of the East was profound, and based both on personal experience and wide reading. He was an accomplished linguist and translator, a keen bibliophile, and by temperament a convinced optimist.

PRINCIPAL WORKS: *Poetry*—The Bridge of Fire, 1908; The Last Generation, 1908; Thirty-Six Poems, 1910; Forty-Two Poems, 1911; The Golden Journey to Samarkand, 1913; The Old Ships, 1915; The Burial in England, 1915; God Save the King, 1915; Collected Poems, 1916; Selected Poems, 1918. *Plays*—Hassan, 1922; Don Juan, 1925. *Miscellaneous Prose*—The Grecians: A Dialogue on Education, 1910; The Scholar's Italian Book, 1911; The King of Alsander, 1913; Collected Prose, 1920; Some Letters From Abroad (with Reminiscences by Helle Flecker and an Introduction by J. C. Squire) 1930.

ABOUT: Cunliffe, J. W. Modern English Playwrights; Dukes, A. The Youngest Drama; Flecker, J. E. Collected Poems (see Introduction by Sir John Squire); Flecker, J. E. Some Letters From Abroad; Goldring, D. Reputations; Hodgson, G. Life of James Elroy Flecker; Lucas, F. L. Authors: Dead and Living; Lynd, R. Old and New Masters; Massingham, H. J. Letters to X; Morgan, A. E. Tendencies of Modern English Drama; Phelps, W. L. The Advance of English Poetry in the Twentieth Century; Shanks, E. Second Essays on Literature; Swinnerton, F. The Georgian Literary Scene; Waugh, A. Tradition and Change. Bookman August 1916; Bookman (London) January 1931; Living Age February 1917; Fortnightly Review February 1924.

FLEMING, PETER (May 31, 1907-),

English travel writer and novelist, was born in London, the son of Major Valentine Fleming, D.S.O., a Member of Parliament, and Evelyn Beatrice (Ste. Croix) Fleming. He was educated at Eton (where he edited the school paper) and at Christ Church College, Oxford, where he edited the weekly *Isis* and was graduated with First Class Honors in English Literature, in 1929. He went into journalism after leaving the university, was on the staff of the London *Evening Standard,* was connected with the British Broadcasting Corporation, and for some time conducted a department in the *Spectator.* Much of his journalistic writing has been done under the pseudonym of "Moth."

Travel, however, is his real passion. He has traveled for long periods in Mexico, Brazil, Russia, China, Japan, and Manchuria, most of his journeys in West and Central Asia being made as special correspondent for the London *Times.* He accompanied the famous woman explorer, Ella Maillart, in a journey through Tartary in 1935. Nearly all his books have been vivid

accounts of these trips, many of which were nearer to exploration than to mere travel. In 1940 he published a fantastic novel positing an accidental visit by Hitler to England.

Mr. Fleming is a reserve lieutenant in the Grenadier Guards, called to active duty in the Second World War. (He was erroneously reported killed in Norway in the spring of 1940.) He was married to Celia Johnson in 1936, and they have one son. His favorite recreations in time of peace are shooting, stalking, and squash. His permanent home is in London. He is a good-looking young man, with smooth hair and regular features—a typical well-bred young Englishman in appearance, though he has had plenty of experience in "roughing it" in wild countries. He is a prolific short story writer.

As a writer, his virtues are vividness, humor, and enthusiasm; his chief defect a trifle too much self-confidence and self-esteem. But his books are among the best of contemporary accounts of travel, written with the narrative verve of fiction but thoroughly reliable as to fact. He is still connected officially with the *Times,* and when circumstances permit he will doubtless go on other far journeys under its auspices, and write engaging books about them on his return. His stories are above the average in competency, though his one novel, *Flying Visit* (1940), had only a fair press, most reviewers pronouncing it psychologically false. It enjoyed a small revival, however, in the year after publication when Rudolf Hess' flying visit to Britain made Fleming's wartime fantasy seem far less implausible than before. His travel books have one unusual distinction, in that they continue constantly to improve.

PRINCIPAL WORKS: Brazilian Adventure, 1933; Variety, 1933; One's Company, 1934; News From Tartary, 1936; Flying Visit (novel) 1940; A Story To Tell and Other Tales (short stories) 1942.

ABOUT: Spectator March 17, 24, 31, 1939.

"FLEMING, WALDO." See WILLIAMSON, T. R.

*FLETCHER, JOHN GOULD (January

3, 1886-), American poet, winner of the Pulitzer Prize, writes: "I was born at Little Rock, Ark., the only son of a Confederate soldier, John Gould Fletcher, aged fifty-five, and of Adolphine (Krause) Fletcher, of German and Danish descent, and twenty-four years his junior. My boyhood was that of almost any young Southern boy of the time, except for the fact that, my parents being well-to-do, I was given good teachers and the use of a large library. At the age of about seven, I started studying Latin and German under private tutors, and I did not go to school till I was ten—having already shown a marked fondness for reading poetry. At sixteen, I left for the North, and after one year at Phillips Andover entered Harvard.

At college, I was a misfit. The new England atmosphere was unfamiliar, and I made few friends. I began to read widely and extensively, and to scribble verses. The first I recall writing were in the summer of 1905, during the course of a

Pinchot

Western trip that had taken me and my older sister as far as the Yosemite Valley.

"In 1906 my father suddenly died, leaving me, temporarily, financially independent, but still unaware of what I could make of myself. My idea was to go abroad, and start my writing career in Europe. College, in my case, had already proven itself largely a failure; and beyond the career of a poet, I could see nothing. The next year I quit Harvard, when within four months of my graduation. After a vain attempt to turn to archaeology, in the course of a trip to Southwestern Colorado and Northern New Mexico, I returned to Boston, unable to make up my mind to return to college. In the upshot, I left America the next year, 1908, for Italy. The next year found me in London, where I decided to settle; and I remained there, with numerous visits to the Continent, till 1914. Then the World War drove me back.

"When I returned, I had already written and published five books of poetry at my own expense. These I thought not very good at the time, and I think so still. But I had already begun work on two others which represented me more completely. I had joined the Imagists, and had a good friend in America in Amy Lowell. I stayed in America till 1916. Then, in the midst of the war, I went abroad again and married Florence Emily Arbuthnot, of London. Finally, after five tentative attempts to return to America, I came back for good and all in 1933. My first marriage and my old life had ended together.

"Since then, my travels have been made in the confines of the American continent. In 1936 I married Charlie May Simon. We have traveled together from New Hampshire to Oaxaca in Mexico, and from the Atlantic to the Pacific. The only permanent home I have lived in for as much as a year has been in Arkansas.

"In 1939 I was awarded the Pulitzer Prize on the basis of my *Selected Poems,* representing twenty-five years' continuous work on poetry. In 1936 I had been commissioned to write *The Epic of Arkansas* in honor of the centenary of my State, by the leading newspaper of Little Rock. These two achievements, along with representation in almost every anthology, are what I have to show for having devoted myself to poetry since I was twenty. Apart from poetry, my chief interests are painting and music. Some day I would like to show the parallel lines of development on which painting and poetry travel. At present I am writing a novel. I have long since lost the feeling that I will die young. I now expect to live twenty more years and to die at the same age as my father."

* * *

Albert Kreymborg has described Mr. Fletcher: "Earnest and impassioned, thoroughly self-aware and quite aware of the world to which his being responds, . . . [but] humor, or the ability of weighing oneself in the balance, is absent." R. P. Blackmur says that Fletcher has "talent, sincerity, and verve," but that his work is "rhetorical, loose, and unsyntactical. . . The poems are not objects, but media, . . . versions, not discoveries." Conrad Aiken's characterization is probably the fairest: "The sort of poet who reaches his greatest brilliance when allowed to develop rapidly successive musical variations on a theme capable of prolonged treatment."

PRINCIPAL WORKS: *Poetry*—The Dominant City, 1913; Fire and Wine, 1913; Fool's Gold, 1913; The Book of Nature, 1913; Visions of the Evening, 1913; Irradiations—Sand and Spray, 1915 (these two as Preludes and Symphonies, 1922); Goblins and Pagodas, 1916; Japanese Prints, 1918; The Tree of Life, 1918; Parables, 1925; Branches of Adam, 1926; The Black Rock, 1928; XXIV Elegies, 1935; The Epic of Arkansas, 1936; Selected Poems, 1938; South Star, 1941. *Prose*—Paul Gauguin, 1921; Some American Poets, 1921; John Smith—Also Pocahontas, 1928; The Two Frontiers: A Study in National Psychology, 1930; Life Is My Song (autobiography) 1937.

ABOUT: Aiken, C. Skepticisms; Fletcher, J. G. Life Is My Song; Hughes, G. Imagism and the Imagists; Kreymborg, A. Troubadour; Lowell, A. Poetry and Poets; Monroe, H. Poets and Their Art; A Poet's Life; Untermeyer, L. American

Poetry Since 1900, From Another World; Nation August 29, 1928; New Republic November 17, 1937; Poetry January 1926, May 1932, March 1936, September 1938; August 1939; Saturday Review of Literature August 27, 1938, May 6, 1939; Sewanee Review July 1938; Southern Review #4, 1936.

FLETCHER, JOSEPH SMITH (February 7, 1863-January 31, 1935), English antiquarian and writer of mystery and de-

tective fiction, was born in Halifax, the son of a Nonconformist minister whom he candidly called a most bigoted protestant. Orphaned at eight months, he was taken in by his grandmother, who lived at Darrington, Yorkshire, on the Great North Road. He was cured of lameness by an old country wife's specific and at eighteen went to London to try his hand at journalism. After an apprenticeship in sub-editorial work at a guinea a week, he turned free-lance writer. From 1890 to 1900 he contributed sketches of rustic life to the *Leeds Mercury* under the pseudonym, "Son of the Soil." *When Charles the First Was King*, published in 1892, was one of the last of the old-fashioned three-decker novels and attracted favorable attention. Fletcher wrote poetry, theology, biography, topographical history, historical fiction and romance, pastoral-comedy, pastoral-tragedy, and short stories, as well as the detective and mystery novels for which he is best known. His "Leet Livvy" has been called the finest poem ever written in the Yorkshire dialect form. He also turned out an authoritative history of Yorkshire and several related archaeological and antiquarian works, and wrote the lives of Lord Roberts and Cardinal Newman. He was a direct, forceful narrator who rarely permitted interest to stagnate. His complete output ran to more than one hundred volumes.

Fletcher's antiquarian researches gave him rich background material when he began to write detective fiction, which he did for some years without any special recognition. Then, in 1918, President Woodrow Wilson discovered and enjoyed an English edition of *The Middle Temple Murder* (still, with *The Charing Cross Mystery*, Fletcher's best known work). With the weight of presidential approval behind them, Alfred A. Knopf, published in the United States a steady stream of Fletcher's detective stories from then until his death. His output was exceeded only by Edgar Wallace's. The books were translated into fifteen European languages and into Chinese. There were far too many of them, and they were of unequal value, but they played an important part in creating the modern vogue for detective stories—with a bias in favor of the British product. Their once great popularity, however, has waned rapidly since their author's death. Fletcher's detectives were not memorable, they were not supermen or super-sleuths, but muddled through to their solutions in approved British style. None of them, save possibly Roger Camberwell, is remembered by name today. Fletcher "impresses by wealth of invention and skilful manipulation of plot-material rather than by human portraiture." His settings, too, are often the best part of his books. Some readers find his spasmodic style, filled with dashes and exclamation points, rather trying. He often roughed out his plots while on walking trips, and the stories frequently give the impression of being spontaneous improvisations. Fletcher gave a great deal of pleasure in his time, but he has been superseded by fresher and better writers in his chosen field.

PRINCIPAL WORKS: *Detective Stories*—Adventures of Archer Dawe, 1909; The King Versus Wargrave, 1915; The Rayner-Slade Amalgamation 1917; The Amaranth Club, 1918; Paul Campenhaye: Specialist in Criminology (short stories) 1918; The Middle Temple Murder, 1918; The Talleyrand Maxim, 1919; Dead Men's Money, 1920; The Paradise Mystery, 1920; Scarhaven Keep, 1920; The Borough Treasurer, 1921; The Chestermarke Instinct, 1921; The Lost Mr. Linthwaite, 1921; The Orange-Yellow Diamond, 1921; The Root of All Evil, 1921; The Markenmore Mystery, 1922; The Middle of Things, 1922; Ravensdene Court, 1922; The Charing Cross Mystery, 1923; The Copper Box, 1923; Rippling Ruby, 1923; The Secret of the Barbican (short stories) 1925; The Great Brighton Mystery, 1925; The Kang-he Vase, 1926; The Cartwright Gardens Murder, 1926; Marchester Royal, 1926; The Missing Chancellor, 1927; The House in Tuesday Market, 1929; The Yorkshire Moorland Murder, 1930; Murder at Wrides Park: Being Entry Number One in the Case-Book of Ronald Camberwell, 1931; Murder in Four Degrees, 1931; Murder in the Squire's Pew, 1932; And Sudden Death, 1936; The Mill House Murder: Being the Last of the Adventures of Ronald Camberwell (finished by "Torquemada") 1937. *Other Fiction*—When Charles the First Was King, 1894; At the Blue Bell Inn, 1898; Anthony Everton, 1903; Daniel Quayne: A Morality, 1907; I'd Venture All for Thee! 1913. *Miscellaneous*—Ballads of Revolt, 1897; A Picturesque History of Yorkshire (3 vols.) 1899-1901; All About Yorkshire, 1908; The Cistercians in Yorkshire, 1919; Leeds, 1919; Collected Verse (1881-1931) 1931.

ABOUT: Haycraft, H. Murder for Pleasure: The Life and Times of the Detective Story; Bookman (London) February 25, 1912; New York Times, February 1, 1935.

FLEXNER, ABRAHAM (November 13, 1866-), American educator and author, was born in Louisville, Ky., the sixth of

nine children, seven of whom were boys. His father, Morris Flexner, a successful merchant, was a Bohemian by birth and had made his New World start as a peddler. His mother, Esther (Abraham) Flexner, a native of the Rhineland village of Roden, had witnessed Louis Napoleon's *coup d'état* in Paris and in her late teens had come to America—nine weeks at sea—in a sailboat.

The panic of 1873 worked its hardships on the Flexners but in no way discouraged them intellectually. Young Abraham got a job in the public library and began to show much promise. He entered Johns Hopkins in 1884; and by hard work and concentration earned a bachelor's degree in two years. He was still nineteen when he settled down to four pleasant but unadventurous years of high-school teaching. This experience, however, thoroughly convinced him that the public school system tended to "catch" a child where he is weak instead of where he is potentially strong and can be made stronger. Moreover, he had done considerable tutoring on the side, and in the fall of 1890 he founded the very successful "Mr. Flexner's School."

In 1898 he was married to Anne Laziere Crawford, the playwright, who first attracted attention with her stage versions of *Miranda of the Balcony* (for Mrs. Fiske) and *Mrs. Wiggs of the Cabbage Patch.* They have two daughters.

He pursued graduate work at Harvard (M.A., 1906); and studied at Berlin and at Heidelberg. There, more and more enamoured of the German university and more and more critical of ours, he wrote his first book, *The American College,* published in 1908.

On his return from Europe he began, for the Carnegie Foundation for the Advancement of Teaching a two-year tour of the medical schools of United States and Canada. The fruits of his efforts fell like a bombshell in the form of a modest *Bulletin Number Four,* issued in 1910. The simple and sound essentials for adequate medical education, it appeared, were wanting. And a fearless and completely salutary reform followed.

In 1913 he joined the staff of the General Education Board to which Rockefeller, largely through Flexner's own efforts, gave almost fifty million for the improvement of medical education in America. By 1928, the year of Flexner's "retirement," the academic level, in the American medical field, had risen stupendously. Meanwhile he had published an account of prostitution in Europe and several books on various phases of education. *Universities—American, English, German* appeared in 1930. He has written innumerable articles for both newspapers and magazines.

He held Rhodes (1927-28) memorial and Taylorian (1928) lectureships at Oxford; and since 1930 has been director of the Institute for Advanced Study at Princeton. "Throughout my life," he says, "I have pursued the will o' the wisp excellence. " and he seconds Jules Cambon's cry against mediocrity in all its forms. He is, primarily, an educator and reformer; but his clear-thinking analyses and his own tremendous success story belong to both the literature and history of medical science.

PRINCIPAL WORKS: The American College, 1908; Medical Education in the United States and Canada, 1910; Prostitution in Europe, 1913; A Modern School, 1916; A Modern College, 1923; Medical Education: A Comparative Study, 1925; Universities—American, English, German, 1930.

ABOUT: Flexner, A. I Remember; Harper's October 1939 and August 1940; New York Times Magazine January 5, 1941; School and Society June 26, 1937 and October 21, 1939; Time October 7, 1940.

FLINT, FRANK STEWART (December 19, 1885-), British poet, translator, and civil servant, was born in London, the

son of a commercial traveler who could provide no more than a "fleabitten" existence for his family. Young Flint went to common school and by special examination was allowed to leave before his fourteenth birthday. He took any job that

came his way, and worked part of the time in a warehouse. In his late teens he began to buy cheap books from the street stalls, and here on one momentous day he fell heir to a volume of Keats which almost immediately swept him into an entirely new world.

At the age of nineteen he entered the Civil Service as a typist; at the same time he was enrolled at a workingman's night school, digging into Latin and French. He had two children by his first wife, whom he married in 1909; and not long after her death in 1920 he married a second time.

His first published volume, *In the Net of the Stars* (1909), devoted largely to love lyrics, was considered youthful (he was only twenty-four), romantic, and dangerously derivative. But it bore a few hints of an emergent poetic personality. His stylistic departures, indeed, fell short of his prefatory claim: "I have . . . not rimed where there was no need to . . . I have followed my ear and my heart, which may be false. I hope not." But the free verse movement in England was yet unborn; these were, therefore, fairly bold words.

In March of that same year he and a small group of serious young iconoclasts— all of whom shared a decided "dissatisfaction with English poetry as it was being written"—began a series of Thursday evening sessions at a restaurant in Soho. They proposed to break down the boundaries of conventional versification and to substitute cadence for meter, and became the original Imagists. They were, indeed, much indebted to Amy Lowell, who, after several sojourns in England, carried their credo to America (it was she who popularized Flint's phrase "unrimed cadence").

Meanwhile Flint had written a number of essays on the new French poetry, which, more than almost anything else, awakened interest in this subject in England; and Ezra Pound's *Des Imagistes* contained five of Flint's now more mature poems. His *Cadences* (1915) was a far cry from the "nightingale" and "magic casement" of nineteenth century verse. With *Otherworld*, issued in the same year, he became a poet of real stature.

During the First World War he served the Army eleven months in England. After his discharge in 1919 he was taken into the Ministry of Labor, where, with several promotions, he became chief of the Overseas Section, Statistics Division. His literary work from the early twenties on seems to have been confined almost entirely to translations—*Memoirs of Madame de Pompadour, Gandhi the Holy Man, Rasputin,* and numerous others. He has succeeded in teaching himself ten languages and was, at one time at least, England's foremost linguist. As a poet, however, he would seem to have burned out. John Gould Fletcher says that Flint is ever conscious of his Cockney forebears and that this growing sense of inferiority has made him a "tragically ineffectual figure."

Flint stopped writing at a time when he appeared to be really finding himself. Yet in those few years he had become part of a movement which, though extremist and short-lived, has undoubtedly had a salutary effect on modern English poetry. Most of his work is signed F. S. Flint.

PRINCIPAL WORKS: In the Net of the Stars, 1909; Cadences, 1915; Otherworld, 1915.

ABOUT: Fletcher, J. G. Life is My Song; Hughes, G. Imagism and the Imagists; Letters of D. H. Lawrence; Egoist May 1, 1915; English Review January 1921.

FLYNN, JOHN THOMAS (October 25, 1882-), American journalist, biographer, and writer on financial topics, was born in Bladensburgh, Md., the son of John and Margaret (O'Donnell) Flynn, and was educated in the parochial schools of New York City. He attended Georgetown University, Washington, D.C., and married Alice Bell of Michigan in April 1910.  They have a son, Thomas; the elder son, John, is deceased. Mr. Flynn was a reporter on and later city editor of the New Haven (Conn.) *Register* from 1916 to 1918; city editor of the New York *Globe* in 1920; and managing editor of that newspaper until its purchase and extinction by Frank Munsey in 1923. A successful freelance writer for some years, Mr. Flynn began to write a column for the *New Republic* in 1931. *Investment Trusts Gone Wrong,* his first book (1930), was collected from the files of the weekly. It is "a volume so uncomfortable that it provoked an investigation of investment trusts by the attorney-general of New York," states *Harper's Magazine,* to which Mr. Flynn has contributed numerous articles. He is "one of the best-known of living pathologists of capital," according to the same source. "Mr. Flynn, a vigorous advocate of the idea that telling the truth is not a bad practice, has been an extremely busy man since 1929. No one has done more than he to demonstrate that the crash was anything but an Act of God."

In 1933-34 he was adviser to the U.S. Senate Committee on Banking and Currency in its investigation of the Stock Exchange, and in 1934-35 economic adviser to the U.S. Senate committee investigating munitions. Appointed a member of the Board of Higher Education of New York City by Mayor LaGuardia in July 1935, he was head of the board in 1937. Mr. Flynn has lectured on contemporary economics at the New School of Social Research, New York, in 1935 and 1936. A past president of the New York Press Club, he is also a member of the Authors' League of America and the Players Club. His home is at Bayside, Long Island. *God's Gold*, a searching biography of John D. Rockefeller, Sr., and *Country Squire in the White House,* a campaign-year diatribe against President Roosevelt, have made his name familiar to a less specialized public.

With the approach of the Second World War to the Americas, Flynn became an ardent isolationist leader and was active with Charles A. Lindbergh and the American First Committee. Lewis Gannett called him "a combative Irishman with an equal dislike for money changers and for Franklin D. Roosevelt." Political differences led to a termination, in 1940, of his long association with the *New Republic,* for which he had been conducting a column called "Other People's Money."

PRINCIPAL WORKS: Investment Trusts Gone Wrong, 1930; Graft in Business, 1931; God's Gold, 1932; Security Speculation: Its Economic Effects, 1934; Country Squire in The White House, 1940; Men of Wealth, 1941.

ABOUT: Review of Reviews October 1934; New Republic December 9, 1940, February 3, 1941.

"FLYNT, JOSIAH." See WILLARD, J. F.

FOERSTER, NORMAN (April 14, 1887-), American critic and educator, was born in Pittsburgh, the son of Adolph Martin Foerster and Henrietta M. (Reineman) Foerster. He was educated at Harvard (B.A. 1910) and the University of Wisconsin (M.A. 1912.), and received an honorary Litt.D. from the University of the South in 1931. In 1920 and 1921 he studied in England, and in 1927 and 1928 in France and Germany. From 1911 to 1914 he was instructor in English in the University of Wisconsin. He then went to the University of North Carolina as associate professor of English, became pro-

fessor in 1919, and remained there until 1930, when he went to the University of Iowa as director of the School of Letters and professor of English. He has been there since that date. His home is in Iowa City, where he lives with his wife, Dorothy Haskell, whom he married in 1911, and their two sons. He is a member of the executive council of the Modern Lan-

guage Association, and belongs also to the Modern Language Association of America and the Modern Humanities Research Association.

During the public prominence of the "humanist" group represented by Irving Babbitt and Paul Elmer More, Professor Foerster was usually accepted as one of that coterie of critics, and he is still in accord with its classical and conservative preconceptions. He has written and edited text-books in English as well as works of literary criticism, and others with a philosophical and sociological approach. In addition to his own books, he was editor of *Essays for College Men* (with F. A. Manchester and Karl Young), 1913-15; *Chief American Prose Writers,* 1916; *American Ideals* (with W. W. Pierson, Jr.) 1917; *English Poetry of the Nineteenth Century* (with G. R. Elliott) 1923; *American Poetry and Prose,* 1925; *Reinterpretation of American Literature,* 1928; *Humanism and America,* 1930; and *American Critical Essays,* 1930.

PRINCIPAL WORKS: Outlines and Summaries, 1915; Nature in American Literature, 1923; American Criticism, 1928; The American Scholar, 1929; Sentences and Thinking (with J. M. Steadman, Jr.) 1929 (as Writing and Thinking, 1931); Towards Standards, 1931; The American State University: Its Relation to Democracy, 1937; The Future of the Liberal College, 1938.

ABOUT: New England Quarterly January 1931; Sewanee Review October 1939; Southern Review Spring 1938.

FOGAZZARO, ANTONIO (March 25, 1842-March 7, 1911), who has been called "the most important Italian novelist since [Alessandro] Manzoni" (1785-1873, the author of *I Promessi Sposi*), was born near Vicenza, the son of Mariano and Teresa (Barrera) Fogazzaro. His early youth was spent in exile, since his parents had to leave home to escape the oppressive and inquisitorial government of the Austrians. Antonio studied the classics under a wise tutor, Professor Zanella, then took up law at the Universities of Padua and Turin. He practiced law at Turin, where his father was living in voluntary exile, and from November 1865, in Milan.

In religious polemics, young Fogazzaro was a disciple of Rosmini, whose *Five Wounds of the Holy Church*, translated by Canon Liddon of England and presented to Pius IX, in 1848, was prohibited by the Congregation of the Index, but cleared in 1854. Fogazzaro was himself to encounter the censorship of Holy Church, when he published *Il Santo* in 1905. The founda-

tion of his literary work, however, was poetry, not fiction or polemics. *Miranda* and *Valsolda* (1874 and 1876), the first a story in verse, the second a collection of lyrics, preceded *Malombra* (1881), his first novel, which was a study in psychopathology.

In 1895 he began his famous trilogy of novels dealing with the politics and religion of northern Italy before the Risorgimento (the War of Liberation, beginning before the middle of the nineteenth century and completed by 1870). It is a family chronicle, beginning with Franco Maironi, who finds in Catholicism the strength to meet sorrow which crushes his more intellectual wife. His son, Piero, survives a disastrous married life, and is spurred on to religious rejuvenation of the Church. In *Il Santo*, Piero Maironi is driven by conscience to expiate by a life of penance a sin which he intended but did not complete. When he takes refuge in a monastery, his exalted mysticism is regarded as heresy, and he is driven out. He becomes a mouthpiece of proposed reform in the Church which he expounds to the Pope himself, telling him the Church is assailed by four evil spirits—lying, domination, avarice, and immobility. *Il Santo* ran as a serial in the *Revue des Deux Mondes,* and appeared in Germany in *Hochland*. The censors of the Index called it heretical, the good work and righteous conduct of Maironi (who became the lay brother Benedetto) counting less with them than his failure to subscribe to orthodox formulas. The novel was accepted as "the platform, even gospel" of Italian Christian Democrats. Fogazzaro protested mildly at the Church's action; his *Leila,* concerning a woman who changes to re-

ligion from atheism under the influence of love, was regarded in some quarters as a recantation.

Dying after an operation just before his sixty-ninth birthday, Fogazzaro received extreme unction from a friar. With his striking face and figure, thick gray hair and melodious voice, Fogazzaro showed few signs of age. He married Margherita Valmarana in July 1866; they had three sons.

PRINCIPAL WORKS AVAILABLE IN ENGLISH TRANSLATION: The Patriot, 1907; The Sinner, 1907; The Saint, 1907; The Woman, 1907; The Politician, 1908; Leila, 1910.

ABOUT: Gallarati-Scotti, T. The Life of Antonio Fogazzaro; Kennard, J. S. A Literary History of the Italian People, Italian Romance Writers; Thayer, W. R. Italica; Catholic World, May 1911, July 1911; Contemporary Review May 1911; Dial March 16, 1911; Edinburgh Review October 1911; North American Review April 1911; Yale Review October 1911.

FÖLDES, JOLÁN (1903-   ), Hungarian, novelist, writes, in English: "I was born in a village of the Hungarian plain called Kenderes. At the time it was a village like any other in the country, without electric light, gas, water, or a railway station. Later it was to receive all these blessings, being the family seat of Admiral Horthy, Regent of Hungary. My father

was the chemist, one of the five 'gentlemen' of the village, the other four being the doctor, the town clerk, and the two divines: the Catholic priest and the Protestant vicar. The rest of the inhabitants were peasants, working in the fields from dawn to midnight for about twopence a day, walking barefoot on weekdays to save their boots for Sunday.

"I had the Hungarian equivalent of a college education. As I showed a certain gift for languages, especially Latin and Greek, I went on to the university, firmly resolved to become a classical philologist. Very soon I was attracted by modern languages, English and French, and went to the Sorbonne, in Paris, to study them. Being curious, and apparently an unstable character, I soon threw them over for sociology and psychology.

"My first attempts at writing were little essays on sociological problems published, to my great astonishment, by quite serious papers. To earn my bread I did a number of things: worked in a Paris factory; in offices as typist, secretary, and such; at schools, teaching languages; for publishers as reader and translator. I cannot say how I began writing novels—I never meant to. My first novel, *Prelude to Love*, won a literary prize. Other novels followed. I often long for the meditative quiet of philology.

"It might have been political-mindedness that kept me from it. I am intolerant and a fighter; my own little obsession is human dignity, which, so it seems to me, has sunk lower in our days than ever before. For my own domestic use I divide people—and writers—into two groups: those who feel insulted in their own person by any affront to the human rights and dignity of others, and those who don't. The latter, whether enjoying the humiliation of others or accepting it with equanimity, are a kind of animal altogether different from mine; I want to kill them.

"This, I expect, is a full confession as well of preferences and likes and dislikes, as of political convictions. Of course, I am violently anti-Nazi and anti-Fascist.

"For the last few years I have been living in England, a country I love. I hope to see America some time. I just had a letter from a refugee friend of mine who used to be a successful doctor. Now he is a cleaner in a hairdresser's shop in New York, working twelve hours a day. He writes: 'I have never been so happy and free in all my life.' So that's why. I have been married twice, second marriage is still in vigor."

* * *

"Jolán" is the Hungarian for "Yolanda," by which name Miss Földes now prefers to be known, since she is now permanently a Londoner. Her married name is not available. Mistakenly addressed as if she were a man, she writes: "Do you mind my being a woman? I do, sometimes!" However English her soul, she is in appearance typically Hungarian, with dark curly hair, a generous mouth, and bright dark eyes. She began writing at sixteen. At one period of her career she was secretary of the Hungarian Embassy in Egypt. Her second novel, *The Street of the Fishing Cat*, won the All-Nations Novel Prize in 1936. Her work has been characterized as "clever, smooth, and thoroughly international."

WORKS AVAILABLE IN ENGLISH: The Street of the Fishing Cat, 1937; I'm Getting Married, 1937; Prelude to Love, 1938; Egyptian Interlude (in England: Heads or Tails) 1939; Marrons Glacés, 1940; Rudi Finds a Way, 1941.

ABOUT: Publishers' Weekly October 24, 1936.

FORBES, ESTHER (1894?-), American historical novelist and short story writer, was born in Westborough, Mass., the daughter of William Trowbridge Forbes and Harriet (Merrifield) Forbes. Her mother is the author of *Gravestones of Early New England and the Men Who Made Them*. Young Esther Forbes spent much of her childhood poring over ancient copies of *Godey's Lady's Book*, and

E. Schaal

various tomes on witchcraft which she found in her father's typically New England attic. She graduated from the Bradford (Mass.) Academy in 1912, and from 1916 to 1918, inclusive, was a student at the University of Wisconsin. Returning to Massachusetts, she became a member of the editorial staff of the old publishing house of Houghton Mifflin in Boston, remaining from 1920 until her marriage to Albert Learned Hoskins, Jr., of Devon, Pa., in 1926. They were divorced in 1933. Miss Forbes regards her "discovery" of Rafael Sabatini as her most noteworthy achievement during her stay with Houghton Mifflin.

O Genteel Lady! her first historical novel published in 1926, was at once a consequence of and a reaction from her early perusal of *Godey's*. In it, a woman stages her own private revolt against prevailing Victorian standards of behavior. One of Miss Forbes' ancestresses died in a Cambridge jail under accusation of witchcraft; another was troubled by visions of the devil and by black imps biting her feet. *A Mirror for Witches* (1928), her next romance, was at first conceived as an ultra-modern psychological novel, but "as soon as I got the idea of using the style of the great diarists of the period, Cotton Mather and kindly Judge Sewall, I felt my feet were on firm ground and I knew what I was doing." The title page read, in part: *A Mirror for Witches in Which Is Reflected the Life, Machinations, and Death of Famous Doll Bilby Who, With a More Than Feminine Perversity, Preferred a Demon to a Mortal Lover.* Seven years elapsed before the publication of *Miss Marvel* (1935) and two more before the appearance of Miss Forbes' most ambitious effort, the historical romance *Paradise*, a long novel of colonial Massachusetts culminating in King Philip's War

"Enough this side of the antiquarian to be historical rather than pedantic, her massing of detail is entirely trustworthy," commented Frances Winwar. It viewed Puritanism with mocking humor, but preserved a proper spirit of detachment. Next year's romance, *The General's Lady,* was a lighter effort, but as definitely a product of intensive research, laid in the last years of the American Revolution. The *New Yorker* called it "a pretty period piece but not quite the real thing," and Stephen Vincent Benét conceded that it was "no *Paradise.*" Her biography of Paul Revere, a Book-of-the-Month Club selection in 1942, was praised by John Chamberlain as "a book which goes straight to the heart of life in old Boston without sacrificing an iota of universal quality"

Miss Forbes, who has a pleasant, good-humored face crowned by unruly hair, and who is fond of dogs, makes her home in Worcester, Mass. "Break-Neck Hill," one of her short stories, was included in the *O. Henry Memorial Award Stories of 1920.*

PRINCIPAL WORKS: O Genteel Lady! 1926; A Mirror for Witches, 1928; Miss Marvel, 1935; Paradise, 1937; The General's Lady, 1938; Paul Revere and the World He Lived In, 1942.

ABOUT: Scholastic October 26, 1935.

FORBES, Mrs. ROSITA (TORR)
(1893-), English travel writer, was born at Swinderley, Lincolnshire, the daughter of  Herbert J. Torr. Her name originally was Joan Rosita Torr. She writes under the name of her first husband, Col. Ronald Forbes, whom she divorced later. Her present husband is Col. Arthur T. McGrath of the British War Office. Her father and grandfather were both members of Parliament, and she has a brother and a first cousin in the diplomatic service. She has been a really phenomenal traveler; literally the only countries on earth she has never visited have been Tibet and New Zealand, and she has touched on both of them "unofficially." Among her many journeys are one trip around the world, to thirty countries, in thirteen months; an expedition to Kufara, Libya, in 1920, the first by a European since 1879; and expeditions to Abyssinia, Syria (where she was in the secret service), Asir and Yemen; an unsuccessful attempt to make a pilgrimage to Mecca disguised as an Arab (she speaks

Arabic fluently), a journey to the Atlas Mountains to write the life of Raisuli, and extensive travels in the Balkans, Central Asia, South America, India, Africa, and Cochin China. In 1934 she flew her own plane 14,000 miles around Central and South America. In 1924, in the United States, she gave eighty-eight lectures in ninety-one days; early in 1940 she gave sixty-four lectures and nine broadcasts in Canada for the National Council of Education. She is now in the Bahamas, where she is building a house, but it is not likely that she will stay "put" in it very long. This amazing career began in 1915, when she drove an ambulance for the French Societé de Secours aux Blessés Militaires until invalided out of the service with two medals for valor. She has many other decorations and medals, and is a Fellow of the Royal Geographical Society and an honorary member of Geographical Societies in France, Italy, and Belgium.

Yet this intrepid traveler, who often lives among the people as one of them, is a rather frail-looking, very "feminine" person, slender, with large, expressive eyes and masses of fluffy dark hair framing a delicate, mobile face. She has interviewed the great of all the earth, met them in their informal hours "off the record," and together with a clear-headed grasp of international politics she unites a gift for racy, exciting writing. Her novels are not nearly so interesting as her straightforward yet romantic stories of real people and events.

In the latest word from "the Rosita Forbes front," she writes: "I am now building a house on Eleuthera, sixty-four miles from Nassau—so far an almost uninhabited island, where I've bought four hundred acres of bush. I'm going to live there after the war." On her own incredible adventures she comments: "I am now prepared to believe a great deal that in more ignorant years I would have discarded without a second thought."

PRINCIPAL WORKS: Unconducted Wanderers, 1919; The Sultan of the Mountains: The Life Story of Raisuli, 1924; A Fool's Hell (novel) 1924; From Red Sea to Blue Nile, 1925; If the Gods Laugh (novel) 1925; Sirocco, 1927; Adventure, 1928; King's Mate (novel) 1928; One Flesh (novel) 1930; Conflict: Angora to Afghanistan, 1931; Ordinary People, 1931; The Secret of the Sahara! Kufara, 1931; Eight Republics in Search of a Future, 1933; Women Called Wild, 1935; Forbitten Road: Kabul to Samarkand, 1937; These Are Real People, 1937; India of the Princes, 1939; A Unicorn in the Bahamas, 1940.

ABOUT: Sykes, Sir P. Explorers All, The History of Exploration; Country Life September 1935; Independent Woman July 1936; Wilson Library Bulletin February 1939.

FORD, FORD MADOX (originally Ford Madox Hueffer) (1873-June 26, 1939), English novelist and miscellaneous writer, was  born in Merton, England, a son of Dr. Francis Hueffer, a German, at one time musical editor of the *Times.* His English grandfather was Ford Madox Brown, the painter, and his aunt married William Rossetti, brother of Dante Gabriel Rossetti. Brown was one of the founders of the pre-Raphaelite movement in art, which Ford professed to loathe, although he was very fond of Christina Rossetti. Dr. Hueffer had started, with "distinguished ill success," according to his son, a journal in Paris in support of Wagner; another in Rome in support of Schopenhauer, and two in London, the *New Quarterly* to spread the fame of the latter, and *The Musical World,* in Wagner's behalf.

The Brown Owl, a fairy tale written when Ford was seventeen and published two years later, was his first printed work. At twenty-two he had four books to his credit. Germany and France as well as England contributed to his education, especially France. German poetry, particularly Heine, appealed to him, but he thought out his novels in French before writing them in English, and had a deep love for French culture. *Poems for Pictures* appeared in 1897, and next year Joseph Conrad suggested that Ford act as his collaborator. William Ernest Henley, the critic, had recommended him, saying that Ford was the finest stylist then writing in English. *The Inheritors* (1901), *Romance* (1903), parts of *Nostromo,* and *The Nature of a Crime* were the result. The volumes were signed under Ford's original name of Hueffer.

Hueffer changed his name to Ford in 1919 for reasons probably connected with his complicated marital affairs. In 1909 he left his wife, Mrs. Elsie Hueffer, whom he had married in 1894. There were two daughters, born in 1897 and 1900. Ordered in 1910 to pay his wife 3 pounds a week, he refused to do so, and was committed to Brixton Gaol for ten days, where he made post-bags, ate prison bread, and was given a girls' story by Mrs. L. T. Meade for intellectual diversion. Subsequently, in 1925, Ford figured in another court action when Mr. Justice Branson made perpetual an injunction re-straining Miss Violet Hunt, the writer and his former secretary, from describing herself as his wife or suggesting that the first Mrs. Hueffer was not his wife. Miss Hunt's lawyer said in her defence that "Mr. Hueffer, who has now adopted another name and lives in another country, had represented that he was a German, and had obtained a divorce in Germany."

The *English Review* was launched in 1908 for the express purpose of publishing a poem by Thomas Hardy, "The Sunday Morning Tragedy," which had been rejected by every magazine in England. Conrad, William James, W. H. Hudson, and Galsworthy were other contributors, as well as T. S. Eliot, Robert Frost, Norman Douglas, Wyndham Lewis, and H. M. Tomlinson. It published H. G. Wells' *Tono-Bungay* and the only articles Anatole France and William Howard Taft (while President) ever wrote for an English review. After the First World War, Ford founded the *transatlantic review* in Paris, to which James Joyce and Ernest Hemingway contributed.

Notable historical novels written by Ford prior to the war included two on Catherine Howard, wife of Henry VIII (*The Fifth Queen* and *The Fifth Queen Crowned*) and *The 'Half Moon',* about Henry Hudson. *The Good Soldier,* written in 1914, Ford intended to be his last novel. He went to war as a lieutenant in a Welsh regiment, was severely gassed, and returned to write his most celebrated series of novels, the saga of Christopher Tietjens, which dealt with England and the war. These comprised *Some Do Not, No More Parades, A Man Could Stand Up,* published consecutively 1924 to 1926, and a concluding volume, *The Last Post,* 1928. Tietjens' prototype was Arthur Pearson Marwood, Ford's partner, or backer, in the founding of the *English Review.* The view taken of war was not in the least romantic, but one of detachment and disenchantment.

Ford wrote more than sixty books in all, including several volumes of highly interesting but not always factually reliable works of autobiography. Feeling that England would not be normal again until the post-war generation had grown up, he preferred to live in Provence and the United States. His last years were spent at Olivet College in Michigan, in an "attempt to restore to the youth of this state a lost art—that of reading." He was a celebrated gourmet and connoisseur of food and wines, and was over six feet in height, with a fair skin, yellow hair, a gray moustache and pale blue eyes. As a result of his gassing in the war he spoke with a pronounced wheeze. He was a Roman Catholic. Ford's death occurred at a Deauville clinic, not long after he had left Olivet for a vacation.

PRINCIPAL WORKS: *Novels*—The Fifth Queen: And How She Came to Court, 1906; The 'Half Moon': A Romance of the Old World and the New, 1909; The Fifth Queen Crowned, 1910; Mr. Apollo, 1910; The Portrait, 1910; Ladies Whose Bright Eyes, 1911; The Panel, 1912; Mr. Fleight, 1913; Ring for Nancy, 1913; The Young Lovell, 1913; The Good Soldier, 1915; Privy Seal: His Last Venture, 1917; Some Do Not, 1924; No More Parades, 1925; A Man Could Stand Up, 1926; The Last Post, 1928; When the Wicked Man, 1931. *Critical and Historical Works*—Ford Madox Brown: A Record of His Life and Work, 1896; The Cinque Ports, 1900; Rossetti: A Critical Essay, 1902; Hans Holbein: The Younger, 1905; The Soul of London, 1905; The Pre-Raphaelite Brotherhood, 1907; The Spirit of the People: An Analysis of the English Mind, 1907; Henry James: A Critical Study, 1913; Between St. Dennis and St. George, 1915; When Blood Is Their Argument, 1915; Joseph Conrad: A Personal Remembrance, 1924; A Mirror to France, 1926; New York Is Not America, 1927; The English Novel: From the Earliest Days to the Death of Joseph Conrad, 1929; Provence: From Minstrels to the Machine, 1935; The Great Trade Route, 1937; The March of Literature, 1938. *Autobiography*—Memories and Impressions, 1911; Thus To Revisit, 1921; It Was the Nightingale, 1933; Mightier Than the Sword: Memories and Criticisms, 1938.

ABOUT: Aldington, R. Life for Life's Sake; Hunt, V. I Have This To Say; New York Times June 27, 1939; Newsweek July 3, 1939; 19th Century August 1939; Saturday Review of Literature July 1, 8, 1939.

"FORD, LESLIE." See BROWN, Z. J.

FORD, PAUL LEICESTER. See "AMERICAN AUTHORS: 1600-1900"

FORD, WORTHINGTON CHAUNCEY

(February 16, 1858-March 7, 1941), American bibliographer, historian, and statistician,

was born in Brooklyn, N.Y., "into an historical Paradise," according to James Truslow Adams, writing in the *Saturday Review of Literature* after Ford's death, at sea, at the age of eighty-three. His father, Gordon Lester Ford, had been successful in several lines of business, was a founder of the Brooklyn Library, Art Association, and Academy of Music, and had accumulated and used the most valuable private library of Americana in the United States, comprising 50,000 volumes and 100,000 manuscripts and a vast amount of other material. His sons, including Paul Leicester Ford, the novelist and historian, gave the collection to the New York Public Library after their father's death. Their mother was Emily Ellsworth (Fowler) Ford, and Noah Webster was one of their ancestors.

Worthington Ford was educated at the Brooklyn Polytechnic Institute and at Columbia University, receiving an honorary M.A. degree from Harvard in 1907, an honorary Litt.D. from Brown in 1919, and an honorary LL.D. from the University of Michigan in 1920. He was chief of the Bureau of Statistics of the Department of State in Washington from 1885 to 1889; went to the Treasury Department in a similar capacity from 1893 to 1898; and in October of the following year married Bettina Fillmore Quinn of Washington. Their children were Crimora Chauncey Ford and Emily Ellsworth Ford.

Ford was connected with the Boston Public Library from 1897 to 1902, lecturing on statistics at the University of Chicago in 1909; and was chief of the Division of Manuscripts at the Library of Congress from 1902 to 1909, also becoming editor of the Massachusetts Historical Society in 1902 and continuing until 1929. He was lecturer on historical manuscripts at Harvard from 1910 to 1929 and on history at the University of Michigan, 1921-26. In 1929 Ford became director of the European mission of the Library of Congress designed to select manuscripts in all chief archives abroad to be copied for deposit in the Library of Congress. "This task, which called for complete mastery of his field and a fine discrimination, was completed fortunately just before the outbreak of war and the destruction or dispersion of great masses of documents never to be recovered," according to J. T. Adams, who calls Ford "a remarkable combination of a very great scholar, of a man of the world, of a Humanist to whom nothing human was alien, and above all of a great gentleman." He was fond of music and the theatre, good food and rare vintages. When the Germans occupied Ford's country place near Paris, he left with a suitcase for the Pyrenees, and later was evacuated with other Americans from Marseilles on the liner "Excalibur." He died on shipboard before reaching New York.

PRINCIPAL WORKS: American Citizen's Manual, 1882-83; The Standard Silver Dollar, 1884; George Washington, 1889. *Editor*—The Writings of George Washington, 1889-93; The Spurious Letters Attributed to Washington, 1889: Washington As an

Employer and Importer of Labor, 1889; Winnowings in American History (with P. L. Ford) 1890-91; Letters to William Lea, 1891; Wills of George Washington and His Immediate Ancestors, 1891; Correspondence and Journals of Samuel Blachley Webb, 1893-94; British Officers Serving in America: 1754-1774, 1894; ... 1774-1783, 1897; Defence of Philadelphia in 1777, 1897; Journals of the Continental Congress, 1904-37 (first 15 volumes); Some Social Notes Addressed to Samuel Blachley Webb: 1776-1791, 1911; Writings of John Quincy Adams, 1913-17; Thomas Jefferson Correspondence, 1916; The Boston Book Market: 1679-1700, 1917; The Isle of Pines, 1668: An Essay in Bibliography, 1920; Some Papers of Aaron Burr, 1920; A Cycle of Adams Letters: 1861-1865, 1920; Broadsides, Ballads, &c, Printed in Massachusetts: 1639-1800; 1922; War Letters . . . of John Chipman Gray and John Codman Ropes, 1927; Letters of Henry Adams, 1930-38.

ABOUT: Library Journal April 1, 1941; New York Times March 8, 1941; Saturday Review of Literature April 19, 1941.

FORESTER, CECIL SCOTT (August 27, 1899-), English novelist 'and miscellaneous writer, was born in Cairo, Egypt,  the son of George Forester and Sarah (Troughton) Forester. He saw Corsica, Spain, and France before spending his boyhood in a busy London suburb, with all its "bustle and jollity of life." From 1910 to 1917 Young Forester was in the Lower School of Dulwich College, then attended the college itself. For a time he studied medicine at Guy's Hospital, but a number of reasons, "laziness and indiscipline" among them, impelled him, like Somerset Maugham and A. J. Cronin, to forsake medicine for a career as a writer. Some verse contributed in 1917 to Nash's and the *English Review* has never been collected.

With *Payment Deferred,* a painfully gripping study of the disintegration of the mind of a murderer, Mr. Forester made an auspicious entry into the writing of prose-fiction. Dramatized, the book also firmly established the reputation of Charles Laughton, who repeated the impersonation in New York on the stage and, soon after, in the talking pictures. In 1926, the year of the publication of *Payment Deferred,* Mr. Forester married Katherine Belcher (they have two sons) and went voyaging on the "Annie Marble," a punt-built dinghy fifteen feet long and five feet wide at its widest point, which was named after a character in the thriller. They explored the backwaters of Germany, France, and England. The first log of the journey, published in 1929, was followed next year by *The Annie Marble in Germany. The Gun* (1933), which was a novel of the Peninsular War, anticipated Mr. Forester's later triumphant career as an historical novelist. *The General* (1936), a dispassionate study of the mentality and behavior of some of the higher command in the First World War had an inexplicably—for the author—large sale in Germany until he discovered that it was regarded by the Nazis as a sublime deification of the militaristic spirit.

Mr. Forester, who chooses to regard himself as a newspaperman who writes novels rather than a novelist who occassionally takes foreign assignments for the *Times,* was a correspondent in Spain in 1936-37 and covered Prague during the Nazi occupation of Czechoslovakia. In 1937 *The Happy Return,* soon followed by *Flying Colours* and *A Ship of the Line,* inaugurated the appearance of Captain Horatio Hornblower in the gallery of British romantic heroes of fiction. Combining the prowess of a Marryat character with the psychological complexity of a Conrad sea captain, Hornblower won his creator the James Tait Black Memorial prize for Literature. The Book Society of England and the Book-of-the-Month Club in the United States (which named the trilogy *Captain Horatio Hornblower*) sent the work in its entirety to their subscribers. The New York *Times* praised the book's "fine forthright prose and careful antiquarianism." William McFee commented that Mr. Forester "writes as if nobody had ever written a tale before." One of his critics thought some of Hornblower's mannerisms and obsessions too insistently pointed up. The novelist wrote a play, *Nurse Cavell,* with C. E. Bechhofer Roberts, in 1934, and has spent some time in Hollywood, a place which he violently dislikes. Most recently he has been living in Berkeley, Calif.

Physically Mr. Forester is slightly built; weighs about 135 pounds; and has a pleasant, low-pitched voice that "could be easily drowned out by one small bellow from Captain Horatio Hornblower," according to Anne Ford. Retiring by nature, he makes no pose of undue seclusiveness and willingly goes through the expected interviews and public appearances. He claims to be the fastest eater in the British Isles.

PRINCIPAL WORKS: Payment Deferred, 1926; Love Lies Dreaming, 1927; The Wonderful Week, 1927; Victor Emmanuel II and the Union of Italy, 1927; Louis XIV, King of France and Navarre,

1928; The Shadow of the Hawk, 1928; Brown on Resolution, 1929; The Voyage of the Annie Marble, 1929; The Annie Marble in Germany, 1930; Two-and-Twenty, 1931; Death to the French, 1932; The Gun, 1933; The Peacemaker, 1934; The African Queen, 1935; The General, 1936; Marionettes at Home, 1936; The Happy Return (American title: Beat to Quarters) 1937; Flying Colours, 1938; A Ship of the Line, 1939; Captain Hornblower, R. N., 1939; To the Indies, 1940; The Captain From Connecticut, 1941.

ABOUT: Book of the Month Club News April 1939; New York Herald Tribune "Books" March 2, 1941; New York Times Book Review February 23, 1941. Wilson Library Bulletin February 1940.

FORMAN, HENRY BUXTON. See "BRITISH AUTHORS OF THE 19TH CENTURY"

FORSTER, EDWARD MORGAN
(1879-   ), English novelist, with admixture of Welsh blood, is the son of Edward Morgan Llewellyn Forster and Alice Clara Forster. He went as a day boy to Tonbridge School, and afterward to King's College, Cambridge, where he thoroughly appreciated the intellectual atmosphere and won the friendship of one of his preceptors, G. Lowes Dickinson, author of *A Modern Symposium,* whose *Life* he was to write in 1934.

He had roughed out a novel at twenty, but it was never completed. After his graduation he began to write short stories, some of which appeared in the *Independent Review* and elsewhere. Before long he took up his domicile in Italy, writing there the two novels, *Where Angels Fear to Tread* (1905) and *A Room With a View* (1908), and producing a school edition of the *Æneid* (1906). The novels just named had an Italian background; but *The Longest Journey* (1907) dealt with Tonbridge and Cambridge. Forster returned to England in 1907, delivered some lectures at the Working Men's College, and finished off *A Room With a View,* which he oddly describes as having been "liked by the young, and business men." *Howard's End* (1910) was his most mature work thus far.

In 1911 Forster was engaged in literary journalism, wrote a play, *The Heart of Bosnia,* which never saw the stage, and went with Dickinson to India, where he accumulated material for what was to be his subtlest novel. During the First European War he was in Alexandria, doing civilian war work. While there he contributed to the *Egyptian Mail* a number of studies which in 1923 came out as *Pharos and Pharillon* and wrote *Alexandria: A History and Guide* (1922).

On the conclusion of peace Forster returned to London and did a great deal of reviewing for the *New Statesman, Spectator,* and several daily papers, acting for a short time as literary editor of the Labor *Daily Herald.* He went to India again in 1921, cast a new eye over his old notes, and in 1924 brought out *A Passage to India,* which is usually considered his *magnum opus.* It is a very brilliant and delicate study of the difficulties experienced by a cultivated Indian and a Britisher of similar caliber in making ordinary human social contact; and it won the Femina Vie Heureuse and James Tait Black Memorial prizes in 1925.

In 1927 Forster was invited by King's College, Cambridge, to deliver the annual Clark Lectures. He chose as his theme *Aspects of the Novel* (the book appeared the same year), which is a well-reasoned analytical study of this art form, lightened by considerable humor. It cuts across many of the accepted notions about the novel; and perhaps the most remarkable thing about it, as the production of a practicing novelist, is the comparatively humble status it accords to fiction in an age when fiction heavily preponderates over other classes of literature. In 1928 he published *The Eternal Moment,* a collection of short stories which he says "represent together with those in *The Celestial Omnibus* volume all that I am likely to accomplish in a particular line. Fantasy can be caught in the open here by any who care to catch her."

Another production of the 1920's, *Abinger Harvest* (1926), deserves at least a passing word. It consists of reprints of reviews and articles out of various journals, and shows Forster's worth as a critic of agile mind and nice appreciation. Its title comes from the pleasant Surrey village in which the author lives.

Forster is anything but a prolific author. He is not harassed by the need to produce, and he sometimes takes years in maturing a literary project. One critic wrote of him: "So erratically and spasmodically has he worked that one cannot think of his genius as in course of development; it comes and goes, apparently as it wills." He is the complete man of letters, not only in his devotion to literature but in his care for the rights of authors as such. He has from time to time contributed to the *Author* on subjects of professional moment; and during the last ten years or so, in common with most liberal-minded men, he has viewed with increasing concern the inroads of totalitarian censorship and book-burning on freedom of expression. There is a high degree of freedom in England (not in Eire, which has a formidable list of banned books); but even in England there has been stupid police action over works of the highest merit like *Lady Chatterley's Lover* and *Ulysses*; and Forster has expressed his feelings on this matter in articles and in his preface to Alec Craig's *The Banned Books of England* (1937).

Forster's power of characterization, subtlety in plot, wit, irony, and 'resilient style are likely to give permanence to more than one of his works. He is an honorary Fellow of King's College, Cambridge; he was made an honorary LL.D. of Aberdeen in 1931; and in 1937 he received the Benson Medal of the Royal Society of Literature.

PRINCIPAL WORKS: Where Angels Fear to Tread, 1905; The Longest Journey, 1907; A Room With a View, 1908; Howard's End, 1910; The Celestian Omnibus, 1923; Pharos and Pharillon, 1923; A Passage to India, 1924; Goldsworthy Lowes Dickinson, 1934; Abinger Harvest, 1936; What I Believe, 1939; England's Pleasant Land, 1940.

ABOUT: Hoare, D. M. Some Studies in the Modern Novel; Macauley, R. The Writings of E. M. Forster; Swinnerton, F. A. The Georgian Scene; Verschoyle, D. (ed.). English Novelists; White, I. H. (ed.) Essays in Value; American Review May 1937; Kenyon Review Spring 1942; Living Age May 1937, September 1935; London Mercury September 1938; Nation October 22, 1938; Saturday Review of Literature August 27, 1938.

"FORSYTHE, ROBERT." See CRICHTON, K.

FORT, CHARLES HOY (August 9, 1874-May 3, 1932), American critic of science, was born in Albany, New York, and was

largely self-educated. As a boy he was an amateur naturalist, then became a reporter, and wrote short stories which were published in the *Broadway Magazine* when Theodore Dreiser was its editor. In 1896 he married Anna Filan, who survived him by five years; they had no children. It was about 1908 that he began the incredible work of research which resulted in his four published books—the last issued after his death. Gradually he evolved a series of very

bizarre theories on scientific phenomena; but what people forget, who (like Edmund Pearson) classify him as a "literary freak and curiosity," is that all these theories were firmly grounded in established, documented, and apparently reliable facts and occurrences. He toiled for years in the British Museum, literally blinded himself, and for several years was unable to work at all until his sight was recovered. During his last years he lived in the Bronx, New York, a large but shy, reticent, gray-haired man with spectacles and a walrus moustache, surrounded by hundreds of boxes of notes and clippings, still working long hours in the library to collect more data. His recreation from these labors was principally a game he invented and called super-checkers. He died at fifty-seven of enlargement of the heart.

It is impossible to describe in brief compass the nature or contents of Fort's books. Both he and his disciples have been called credulous and gullible, and undoubtedly Fort was insufficiently grounded in science, particularly in astronomy, to justify many of his generalizations: but the work he did may some day prove an invaluable source for later investigators. (William Seabrook, in *Witchcraft*, echoes many of Fort's statements in *Wild Talents*.) He himself called it "a kind of non-fictional fiction. . . . Maybe I am a pioneer in a new writing that instead of old-fashioned heroes and villains will have floods and bugs and stars and earthquakes for its characters and motifs." His style was as strange as his subjects, peculiarly his own --a sort of court reporter's jargon (he was an expert shorthand reporter) that yet managed to convey his constant excitement. He was no solemn fanatic; he had great humor, was as caustic as he was daring. The Fortean Society, founded by Tiffany Thayer (he is still secretary) in 1931, included such men as Booth Tarkington, Theodore Dreiser, Ben Hecht, Alexander Woollcott, and John Cowper Powys (none of them, it may be noted, a scientist). "One of the most original and courageous thinkers in the world today," J. David Stern called him.

"Portents, the horrors and mysteries of Nature, disappearances, strange forms of demise—these were Fort's sustenance," said Idwal Jones. "He compiled books in an apocalyptic prose, and in a cold excitement recited wonders that would have frozen the blood of Sir John Mandeville." "He is rash; he ventures where angels fear to tread; often his daring overtops his knowledge," wrote Maynard Shipley in the New

York *Times Book Review.* "But his data—if not his conclusions—are thoroughly grounded and well documented, and he is perhaps the enzyme orthodox science most needs. . . . He is the *enfant terrible* of science, bringing the family skeleton to the dinner table when distinguished guests are present. . . . Reading Fort is a ride on a comet. . . . Discount everyone of his hypotheses, and the solid body of his data remains—a lifework in itself."

PRINCIPAL WORKS: The Book of the Damned, 1919; New Lands, 1923; Lo! 1931; Wild Talents, 1932; The Books of Charles Fort (omnibus collection) 1941.

ABOUT: Fort, C. The Books of Charles Fort (see Introduction by T. Thayer); Smith, H. A. Low Man on a Totem Pole; Fortean Society Magazine September 1937 et seq.; Time February 23, 1931.

FOSDICK, CHARLES AUSTIN. See "AMERICAN AUTHORS: 1600-1900"

FOSS, SAM WALTER. See "AMERICAN AUTHORS: 1600-1900"

FOURNIER, ALAIN (sometimes written Alain-Fournier) (October 3, 1886-September 22, 1914), French novelist, was born

Henri Alban Fournier at Chapelle-d'Angillon, north of Bourges in the Department of the Cher, on the border of Sologne. A country of marshes, ponds and decayed châteaux between the rivers Cher and Loire, this region reappeared in Alain Fournier's later fiction. Childhood and youth were spent in the tiny village of Epineuil, where his parents were teachers. At thirteen Henri went into training at Brest for a post as naval officer, disliked it, and at seventeen entered the Lycée Lakanal, a secondary school, to prepare for the École Normale Supérieure. (He failed its entrance examinations in 1907). At the Lycée he found a friend, Jacques Rivière, later editor of the *Nouvelle Revue Française*, who married Fournier's sister; Mme. Isabella Rivière later collected and edited the correspondence between her brother and husband. Fournier spent July to September of 1905 in England as French correspondent for a London merchant. He lived at Chiswick, and familiarized himself with the work of the pre-Raphaelites, whose realistic detail and dreamlike vision had their influence on *Le Grand*

Meaulnes, his best-known work, based on his boyhood experiences at school and to some extent on the life of John Keats. The central figure, Augustin Meaulnes, is a young visionary, bent on an adolescent search for the ideal, whom his schoolfellows call Le Grand Meaulnes. Published in 1912, it attracted comparatively little attention except from some discriminating critics. An English translation, *The Wanderer* appeared in 1928, with an introduction by Havelock Ellis. Fournier's posthumous *Miracles* (1924) contains a fragment of an unfinished novel, *Colombe Blanchet,* which was to be a story of Parisian life.

Fournier took his required military training in 1907-09. He was killed early in the First World War during a scouting expedition in the Bois Saint-Remy, on the river Meuse, less than two weeks before his twenty-eighth birthday. His body was never found. Ellis describes him as slender, with a dark serious countenance, a slight moustache, and "the face of an imperious young prince."

PRINCIPAL TRANSLATED WORKS: The Wanderer, 1928.

ABOUT: Chaix, J. De Renan à Jacques Rivière; Wall, E. von der. Alain-Fournier: Sein Wesen und sein Werke; Bookman October 1928; études: Revue Catholique l'Intérêt Général February 5, 1938; Revue Hebdomadaire July 3, 1920.

FOWLER, FRANCIS GEORGE. See FOWLER, H. W.

FOWLER, GENE (1890-   ), American novelist and biographer, was born in Denver. His name was originally Eugene Devlan, and

he was the son of Charles F. Devlan and Dora G. Devlan. His father died when the boy was an infant, and his mother later married Frank Fowler, who adopted his stepson and gave him his name. When he was thirteen his mother also died.

Long before that time, when he was only ten, the boy had left school and gone to work for a taxidermist. The net result of that early experience was that he has for most of his life been a vegetarian! He escaped from this job to become a printer's devil, and from that minute his career was settled. He would be a reporter and a writer. He studied at home in his spare hours, and worked his way through one year at the

University of Colorado; and as soon as he was old enough he began work as a reporter on a Denver newspaper. After several years on both the major papers of his native city, he went to New York, in 1924, as sports editor of the *Daily Mirror*. The next year he was managing editor of the *American,* then promotion manager of King Features (a syndicate), and in 1928 managing editor of the *Morning Telegraph,* primarily a sports sheet. He lost this position because of his large ideas for the paper's prestige, paying enormous sums to attract well-known writers to its pages.

Hollywood called him; at first he went for short stays, then lived there for several years, writing films for all eight of the largest picture companies. He is now living in New York again, with his wife, formerly Agnes Hubbard, whom he married in 1916. They have three children. In between books and pictures he has done any number of odd jobs, from representing the late Queen Marie of Rumania when she visited the United States to managing prizefighters and wrestlers. Gene Fowler is a newspaper legend in both Denver and New York; his prankish exploits and his witticisms have become a myth in the *Front Page* tradition. He calls himself "an American peasant," but if he has a peasant's earthy shrewdness he has none of his taciturnity or stolidity. He is the friendliest man on earth; he himself says that "anyone who gives him a pat on the back earns his immediate and unquestioning devotion." He has a weakness for animal pets of the most varied sort—perhaps in belated apology for his years in taxidermy. Patriarch of these pets is a remarkable parrot.

Mr. Fowler has never lost his grip on the semi-pioneer Colorado in which he was reared. Most of his novels reconstruct the Denver of his youth and of the generation before it; they are the outgrowth of hours and years spent in talking to old-timers with long memories, and of other hours and years spent as a first-rate newspaper reporter, usually on the City Hall beat. His biographies are equally racy and equally of the soil. He is interested in human beings, whom he regards with tolerance and without illusions. He is no stylist, and seldom aspires beyond good journalese, but he has a primary virtue: he is always readable.

PRINCIPAL WORKS: Trumpet in the Dust, 1930; Shoe the Wild Mare, 1931; The Great McGoo (play, with B. Hecht) 1931; The Great Mouthpiece (biography) 1931; Timberline (biography) 1933; Father Goose, 1934; The Mighty Barnum (with

B. Meredyth) 1935; Salute to Yesterday (non-fiction) 1937; Illusion in Java, 1939.

ABOUT: Smith, H. A. Low Man on a Totem Pole; New York Times September 15, 1940; Newsweek October 18, 1937; Wilson Library Bulletin December 1937.

FOWLER, HENRY WATSON (1858-December 26, 1933), English philologist, best known for his works in collaboration with his younger and shorter-lived brother Francis George Fowler (1870-1918), was one of seven sons of Robert Fowler of Christ's College, Cambridge, and Caroline (Watson) Fowler. He attended Rugby and won minor and major exhibitions at Balliol  College, Oxford, where he went on a scholarship in 1877. He stood only second both in Moderations and Litterae Humaniores, however, and failed in his qualifying Divinity examination for a degree, but took his B.A. and M.A. together in 1886. After a temporary mastership at Fettes, an outstanding school in Scotland, he went in 1882 to Sedbergh School in the extreme northwest corner of Yorkshire. The headmaster, H. G. Hart, had been reared at Harrow in the Arnold tradition. Fowler was regarded with some awe by his boys, among whom he was privately known as "Joey Stinker," from his pervading aroma of tobacco, but was admired as a first-rate swimmer, skater, and climber. One former student recalled his reading Conan Doyle's *The White Company* aloud, "in a beautiful voice."

Fowler refused to prepare his students for confirmation, and this, together with a disagreement with Hart over the mastership of a house, which he apparently believed should have been offered to him, determined him to leave Sedbergh in 1899. He settled in Chelsea on £120 a year inherited from his father, to which he added £30 a year from journalistic work. For exercise he bathed in the Serpentine in all weathers and drilled in the Inns of Court Volunteers ("The Devil's Own"), where he shared a tent with the author "F. Anstey." At the end of 1903 he joined his brother Francis (who had meantime taken an M.A. at Cambridge, after preparing at St. Paul's) in a cottage on the Isle of Guernsey, and their brief but fruitful collaboration began. At fifty H. W. Fowler married Jessie Marian Willis, who ran a nursing home. F. G.

Fowler married later, but the name of his wife is not available. (The *Dictionary of National Biography* has ignored the Fowlers, and *they* ignored *Who's Who.*) In spite of their ages, both brothers enlisted for service in France in the First World War; there Francis contracted the tuberculosis which ended his life in 1918, at only forty-eight.

Besides the guide to correct speech called *The King's English,* their best known collaboration, the Fowlers made a translation of Lucian together, as well as compiling the *Concise Oxford Dictionary,* a condensation of the larger work, and outlining the *Dictionary of Modern English Usage,* which, however, Francis Fowler did not live to finish. (His name, appearing below his brother's on the title-page, caused one myopic reviewer to remark that "the lady was sometimes more brilliant than her husband.") George Dangerfield called *The King's English* "an accurate chart of style with all the shoals and reefs carefully marked and liberally sprinkled with wrecks. . . . It is more than a guide to correct English—it is a work of art." After a third of a century it is still standard authority wherever English is studied and taught.

Almost to the day of his death at seventy-five, H. W. Fowler continued his work for the Clarendon Press, doing his own housework as well as looking after his wife in her last stages of cancer. A hale old man with high color and a carefully kept beard, he died finally of influenza and bronchial pneumonia at Hinton St. George, in Somerset. A third brother, recorded only as A. J. Fowler, assisted H. W. Fowler in his later works and lived to 1938.

PRINCIPAL WORKS: *With Francis George Fowler*—The Works of Lucian, 1904-1915; The King's English, 1906; The Concise Oxford Dictionary, 1911; A Dictionary of Modern English Usage, 1926. *By Henry Watson Fowler*—Some Comparative Values, 1929; If Wishes Were Horses, 1929; Rhymes for Darby and Joan, 1931.

ABOUT: Society for Pure English: Tract xliii; Bookman June 1932; New York Times Book Review February 25, 1940; Saturday Review of Literature January 6, 1934.

FOX, JOHN, JR. (1862-July 8, 1919), American novelist, was born in Paris, Ky. the eldest son of John William Fox, of Virginia descent, and his second wife. His exact birth-date is unknown, for he always refused to tell his age. His older half-brother was his first teacher. After two years at Transylvania University (where he knew and was influenced by James Lane Allen, who was then living in Lexington), he transferred to Harvard, and was graduated in 1883 as the youngest of his class. For brief periods he was next a reporter on the New York *Sun,* a law student at Columbia, and a reporter on the *Times.* Illness then forced him to return for a year of idleness. Finally, in 1887, he went into the mining business at Big Stone Gap, Virginia. He returned to journalism twice—first during the Spanish-American War, when after a short time as a Rough Rider he became correspondent for *Harper's Weekly,* and later during the Russo-Japanese War, when he was correspondent for *Scribner's Magazine.* In 1908 he married the

musical comedy star, Fritzi Scheff, but they were divorced within a few years.

Fox attracted close friends as disparate as Thomas Nelson Page and Theodore Roosevelt. There was something childlike about his personality, and about what Page called his "quaint physiognomy and spare, sinewy figure." He was afflicted with almost pathological indecision in practical matters, in which he was chronically vague and unpunctual. But these defects and others were outweighed by his "absolute naturalness and absence of pose" and a charm and courtesy which endeared him to his intimates. He died at only fifty-seven, from pneumonia contracted on a fishing trip in the mountains, after a long visit in Europe.

Fox's stories, which after a slow start became almost automatic best sellers, were a direct outgrowth of his mining experiences, which brought him into touch with the then little known mountaineers of Kentucky, Tennessee, and West Virginia. *The Little Shepherd of Kingdom Come* and *The Trail of the Lonesome Pine* (which sold about a million and a quarter copies) made his name a household word throughout America. He really knew the mountaineers, had closely observed their life and customs and caught their dialect well. But devotion to "the old romantic formulas," a heavy pall of conventionalism, and a cloying "sweetness" mar his work. As the *Nation* remarked: "He knew how to tell a story with contagious speed." But he shared with most of the Southern writers of that period an "admixture of sentimentalism which . . . will do more than anything else to deprive his novels of a long life." Page, who suffered from the same disability and therefore discounted it in his friend, praised his love of beauty (his descriptions of landscape are indeed done with loving fidelity, though a bit too ornately), and his "richness of sentiment." In a field where he was a more objective critic, that of style, Page said truly that Fox had a gifted and easy command of language: "he had never written a page that did not sing." Within severe limitations, his novels and stories must be included in any survey of regional literature in the United States.

PRINCIPAL WORKS: *Novels*—The Kentuckians, 1899; Crittenden, 1900; The Little Shepherd of Kingdom Come, 1903; A Knight of the Cumberland, 1906; The Trail of the Lonesome Pine, 1908; The Heart of the Hills, 1913; Erskine Dale: Pioneer, 1920. *Short Stories*—A Mountain Europa, 1894; A Cumberland Vendetta, 1895; Hell Fer Sartain, 1897; Blue Grass and Rhododendron, 1901; Christmas Eve on Lonesome, 1904; In Happy Valley, 1917. *Non-Fiction*—Following the Sun Flag, 1905.

ABOUT: Literary Digest October 17, 1925; Nation July 19, 1919; Scribner's Magazine December 1919.

FOX, RALPH WINSTON (1900-January 3, 1937), Anglo-Canadian novelist and political writer, was born in Halifax, N.S.,

 the son of comfortable middle-class parents. His home environment would have conditioned the average person for a conventional approach to life and letters. But by the time young Fox had finished Oxford he had become incensed over the social apathy of the intelligentsia, and in 1920 he undertook a journey into the most hard-hit famine area of the Soviet Union. His own observations on the recovery phase and the period of first expansion of private enterprise—1922 and the early part of 1923 —went eventually into his *People of the Steppes* (1925), in which he set down "people, good and bad of all parties. . . ." This however, was not his very first plunge into print: a "romantic comedy for all Socialist children," which he called *Captain Youth*, had been issued in pamphlet form three years earlier.

In 1928 came his novel, *Storming Heaven*, a modern picaresque with a sufficiency of love and politics. It was laid largely in Siberia, opening at the Japanese evacuation of Vladivostok just before it was incorporated into what is now the U.S.S.R. Five years later he published a life of Lenin, a

study of British Colonial imperialism, and a Marxian analysis of the Irish question. His two-volume study of the *Class Struggle in Britain* appeared in 1934. By 1935 his literary and political energies had visibly strengthened each other: and in that year he went to Paris to attend a world congress of writers. The hall in which the sessions took place, Fox afterwards wrote, was thickly surrounded by police, detectives, and armed *gardes mobiles*—"lest the subversive influence of Aldous Huxley . . . Heinrich Mann [etc.] should set Paris on fire with revolt."

In fairly rapid succession came a volume on Communism, a book on Genghis Khan, and some political conclusions under the title *Frances Faces the Future*.

He went to Portugal, in 1936, to get some idea of the extent of Italy's armament aid to Franco; and wrote a full account of the dangerous expedition in a pamphlet called *Portugal Now*. *The Novel and the People*, published posthumously, represents the integration of his literary judgment and political faith. In it he examined the state of the English novel, analyzed the "crisis of ideas which had destroyed the foundation on which the novel seemed once to rest so securely," and established the relationship between the novel and humanity's struggle for a new, democratic, and hateless set of social values. "They Hanged Frank Whittam," a dream narrative from an unfinished piece, part of which was published under the title "A Wasted Life," and "Conversation With a Lama," are, in themselves, sufficient evidence of Ralph Fox's *finesse* as a writer of imaginative fiction. And it was into this *genre* that he wanted eventually to direct more and more of his literary energy.

Late in 1936 he joined the Loyalist cause in Spain, and spent the first days of December in the "funny little town" of Albacete— waiting, restless, but cheerful. On January 3, 1937, while Fox was acting in the capacity of assistant political commissioner to a brigade of the International Legion stationed near Lopera, in Andalusia, it looked as if a shift in the position of the Loyalist machine gunners would cover the Fascist right flank. Fox bent low and set off on a fast run to organize the maneuver. Bombing and gunning became intense, and before long the whole front had changed; trapped in the cross-fire, Fox was killed in action.

For a while his reputation as an active political worker appeared to be eclipsing his reputation as a writer. To Mike Gold who commented on this fact, Fox said, on one occasion, "Damm it, everyone thinks it of me! I must write a string of novels to break down this silly notion." He died too young to fulfill this intention.

PRINCIPAL WORKS: Captain Youth, 1922; People of the Steppes, 1925; Storming Heaven, 1926; Lenin: A Biography, 1933; Colonial Policy of British Imperialism, 1933; Marx and Engels and the Irish Question, 1933; The Class Struggle in Britain, 1934 (2 vols.); Communism, 1935; Genghis Khan, 1936; France Faces the Future, 1936; Portugal Now, 1937; The Novel and the People, 1937; Ralph Fox: A Writer in Arms (ed. by O. Lehmann, T. A. Jackson, & C. Day Lewis) 1937.

ABOUT: Fox, R. Ralph Fox: A Writer in Arms, The Novel and the People, People of the Steppes, Portugal Now, Storming Heaven; Lehmann, J. New Writing in England; Rust, W. Britons in Spain; Labour Monthly February 1937; New Masses April 13, 1937; New Statesman and Nation December 29, 1934.

"F. P. A." See ADAMS, F. P.

"FRA ELBERTUS." See HUBBARD, E.

FRANCE, ANATOLE (April 16, 1844-Ocotber 12, 1924), French novelist and critic, was born at the Quai Malaquais,  Paris, only son of François Noël Thibault, bookseller and bibliophile, and was baptized Jacques Anatole François. The name by which he is universally known is thus only a partial pseudonym. One of his grandfathers had fought at Waterloo; and he himself was brought up in a Royalist and Catholic atmosphere, which he was to dispel in due course as a result of his reading and thinking.

He went to the Collège Stanislas, a high-class Jesuit school, where he was excellently grounded in the Graeco-Roman classics. The spirit and savor of these works remained ever with him, but so far as general reading and inquiry were concerned he learned less in school than he did from his father's library, the bookstalls on the quais, and the group discussions of artists, critics and bibliographers which took place in the evenings at home. In later life he often made literary use of his childhood days, the best of the books concerning them being Pierre Nozière and Le Livre de Mon Ami. In adolescence there was formed his character-

istic attitude towards Catholicism and its priests—a standpoint comprehending keen interest in theological paraphernalia and deep mistrust of priestly ethics and metaphysics. His higher education was concerned with poetry and philosophy, and he took a historical course at the École des Chartes.

In 1867 France published in La Gazette Rimée two poems which helped to cause the suppression of that magazine on political grounds. In the following year his first book, a study of Alfred de Vigny, brought him into touch with the Parnassian group and their leader, Leconte de Lisle. He obtained a post in the Senate library, published two volumes of verse, quarrelled with Leconte de Lisle (which lost him his post), and in 1877 began for the publisher, Lemerre, a series of ten introductions to French classics. He had, be it added, seen military service in 1870 at the Siege of Paris.

France's first considerable work of literature (also a publishing success) was the novel, Le Crime de Sylvestre Bonnard, which gained a prize from the Académie Française in 1881. Its tender, kindly charm won it many friends then and since, but in the years of his fame its author described it as "insipid and tedious."

He married, about this time, one Mlle. Guérin, by whom he had one daughter. In 1883 he began a friendship which vitally affected his life for twenty-seven years, with Mme. Arman de Caillavet, who goaded his naturally indolent nature to work, took care of his small material needs and petty details, and surrounded him, in a manner thoroughly French, with all the apparatus of the literary lion. His genius now rapidly matured, manifesting itself in Thaïs, a novel of antiquity (1890); L'Étui de Nacre (1892), a collection containing his most memorable short story, "The Procurator of Judaea"; La Rôtisserie de la Reine Pédauque (1893), in which the character of the Abbé Jérôme Coignard first appeared; Le Lys Rouge (1895), a love story; and the skeptical Le Jardin d'Épicure (1895). Election to the Académie confirmed his status in 1897.

Meanwhile journalism occupied a good deal of his time. Between 1886 and 1891 he was literary critic of Le Temps, producing a mass of highly subjective criticism which appeared in book form as La Vie Littéraire. He was no admirer of Zola's style and temper, but nevertheless supported him in the Dreyfus affair in 1898. More journalism followed, from 1897 to 1901, when he wrote in L'Écho de Paris a series of satirical episodes at the expense of "the priest, the soldier and the financier," which were collected in four volumes as *La Vie Contemporaine.*

For many years France's custom was to travel extensively in France and Italy with Mme. de Caillavet during the summer and to spend the winter at his Paris house, the Villa Saïd, on the Bois de Boulogne. His routine there has been piquantly described by his secretary and "Boswell," J. J. Brousson, who came to him as a raw young man to check and methodize his references for a life of Joan of Arc. On getting up in the morning France would put on trousers with huge feet attached to them (like those worn by Balzac), and a flannel dressing-gown, and would choose a skull-cap from a huge collection he harbored. Seated in his library he would ring for his housekeeper, who then dragged in a mass of envelopes, sheets of paper and notebooks, done up in a sheet secured with safety-pins. This was the "manuscript" of *Joan of Arc,* which Brousson had to sort out. After some twenty years of intermittent work the book appeared in two volumes in 1908. It took an entirely secularist and realist view of the Maid, as against the orthodox romantic and Catholic view.

The decade just before the war was rich in works of genius. In 1904 appeared the short sketch called *L'Affaire Crainquebille,* which dealt with great delicacy and pity with an old hawker's conflict with the law; *L'Ile des Pingouins* (1908), a burlesque allegory of French history, full of keen irony and out-of-the-way erudition, was perhaps his master-work; and *La Révolte des Anges* (1914) ran it very close as a political satire. The death of Madame de Caillavet, in 1910, had plunged France into the deepest nervous depression, which left him unable to work for months; and a minor annoyance was a lawsuit by Lemerre, consequent on the author's failure to write a promised history of France. A compromise was reached, and in 1913 there appeared *Le Génie Latin,* a collection of biographical sketches written thirty years before.

In September 1914 he removed to an estate called La Bechellerie, near Tours, which remained his home thenceforward. He was anything but a wholehearted supporter of the war, though he wrote a book called *Sur La Voie Glorieuse,* the profits of which were devoted to the aid of the wounded. In the spring of 1918 he attended a performance of his poetic drama, *Les Noces Corinthiennes* at the Comédie Française

while an air raid on Paris was taking place. The peace terms pleased him as little as they did most advanced thinkers.

During the spring of 1919 France undertook a lecture tour in South America. In the following year he made his second marriage (the first having long since ended in divorce) to Emma Laprévotte, and became guardian to his grandson, Lucien Psichari, whose father had fallen in the war. In 1921 he received the Nobel Prize for literature; in 1922 all his works were put on the Papal Index. He died at Tours on October 13, 1924, after an illness which had lasted the whole summer. He was buried in Paris on October 18 with full military honors but without religious service. The President of the Republic attended the ceremony, as did the Premier, the entire cabinet, the ambassadorial corps and the Académie. The gigantic crowd was estimated to be the biggest since the Victory Parade of 1919. Funeral orations were delivered by M. Albert, Minister of Education, and by MM. Gabriel Hanotaux, Léon Jouhaux, and Léon Blum. A collection of France's unfinished papers was published in America by Michel Corday in 1926, and his Collected Works appeared in 1930. The English and American *éditions de luxe* were illustrated with rich fantasy and singular appositeness by Frank C. Papé.

In an introduction to the English edition of *La Rôtisserie* (1922) Wiliam J. Locke writes: "He hovers over the world like a disembodied spirit, wise with the learning of all times and with the knowledge of all hearts that have beaten, yet not so serene and unfleshly as not to have preserved a certain trickiness, a capacity for puckish laughter which echoes through his pages and haunts the ear when the covers of the book are closed." A profoundly skeptical thinker, the color of his mind was yet heavily suffused with the Catholicism of his early years. He had an extraordinarily deep and minute acquaintance with the Scholastic method of ratiocination, and used it constantly, but with satirical intent, the *locus classicus* being the discussion in Heaven, in *L'Ile des Pingouins,* on the theological dilemma caused by the baptism of the penguins. He was as much soaked in Catholic lore as was that other lapsed Catholic, James Joyce, and welcomed someone's description of himself as a mocking monk. He constantly projected his own personality into his characters, and Pierre Nozière, Monsieur Bergeret, Sylvestre Bonnard, and Jérôme Coignard all represent aspects of his nature. Irony and a passion tor reform, tempered by delightful humor and supported by astonishing erudition, are his chief characteristics. Of his style Jules Lemaître wrote: "It has traces of Racine, Voltaire, Flaubert, Renan, and it is always Anatole France."

France was a connoisseur of food and furniture. He liked to be free of all financial dealings and domestic detail, leaving these to his womenfolk. He was slender in build, with pointed beard and moustaches, shaggy eyebrows, beautiful hands, and faun-like ears.

PRINCIPAL WORKS AVAILABLE IN ENGLISH TRANSLATION: Monsieur Bergeret, 1902; The Crime of Sylvestre Bonnard, 1906; Mother of Pearl, 1908; The Red Lily, 1908; The Garden of Epicurus, 1908; Thaïs, 1909; The Life of Joan of Arc, 1909; The Well of St. Clare, 1909; The White Stone, 1909; Penguin Island, 1909; Balthasar, 1909; Works (25 vols.) 1909; Merrie Tales of Jacques Tournebroche, 1909; The Wickerwork Woman, 1910; The Elm Tree and the Mall, 1910; Honey Bee, 1911; On Life and Letters, 1911, 1914, 1922, 1924; Jocasta and the Famished Cat, 1912; The Aspirations of Jean Servien, 1912; The Opinions of Jerome Coignard, 1912; At the Sign of the Reine Pedauque, 1912; My Friend's Book, 1913; The Gods Are Athirst, 1913; Girls and Boys, 1913; The Revolt of the Angels, 1914; Crainquebille, Putois, Riquet, and Other Profitable Tales, 1915; The Man Who Married a Dumb Wife, 1915; Pierre Nozière, 1916; The Amethyst Ring, 1916; The Human Tragedy, 1917; The Bride of Corinth and Other Poems and Plays, 1920; Little Pierre, 1920; The Seven Wives of Bluebeard, 1920; Marguerite, 1921; The Mummer's Tale, 1921; Clio, 1922; Count Morin, Deputy, 1922; The Bloom of Life, 1923; Latin Genius, 1924; Representative Stories of Anatole France, 1924; Little Sea Dogs and Other Tales of Childhood, 1925; Riquet (selected and adapted from France's novels) 1925; Pierre (selected chapters from the four autobiographical novels) 1926; Under the Rose (unfinished works) 1926; Unrisen Dawn (speeches and addresses) 1928; Rabelais, 1929; Works (41 vols.) 1930.

ABOUT: Brousson, J. J. Anatole France Abroad, Anatole France Himself; Cerf, B. Anatole France; Eastman, M. Heroes I Have Known; George, W. L. Anatole France; Gsell, P. The Opinions of Anatole France; Le Goff, M. Anatole France at Home; May, J. L. Anatole France; Pouquet, J. M. Last Salon: Anatole France and His Muse; Segur, N. Conversations With Anatole France, The Opinions of Anatole France; Shanks, L. P. Anatole France; Shishmanova, I. V. Philosophical Novels of Anatole France; Starrett, V. Bookman's Holiday; Stewart, H. L. Anatole France: The Parisian.

FRANCK, HARRY ALVERSON (June 29, 1881-), American travel author, writes:

"It is a pleasure, not to say honor, to appear in TWENTIETH CENTURY AUTHORS, though some of my readers now and then imply that I am a century earlier than that. I am up to my ears in trying to get material for a book on South America

(my twenty-ninth, so help the poor public). [Mr. Franck writes from Chile.] Taking up from 1930, I spent a year, with two lecture seasons, in the British Isles, and wrote them up not entirely to the pleasure of their inhabitants; a year with my wife and five children on the Continent with Aix en Provençe, France, as headquarters; traveled that year by my very own second-hand Citroen car through most of

Pinchot

Europe; a touch of North Africa on the way home, end of 1931.

No place like home (even if you have none of your own) during the depression; but by October 1933 I was on my way again —most of Europe as far as Malta—I've been in every country in Europe except San Marino, which is so small I have never been able to find it. Back home (Philadelphia and finally New Hope, Pa., where we bought a farm with a 1774 stone farmhouse, and have had a *pied à terre* as well as a head in the clouds ever since) to June 1934, then off to Russia for the summer; wrote that off my chest by New Year's Eve and off to Mexico with wife to follow the Cortez trail; to Hawaii with most of the family winter of 1935-36; an air trip around the Caribbean in 1937; to Alaska with oldest son summer of 1938; since when I have been able to stay put and plant potatoes until October 1940, when with wife and youngest son set out to do South America.

"Just to emphasize that it is some job to be a vagabond writer and raise a family too, I met my wife, Rachel Whitehill Latta, in France during the war; our oldest son was born on a British freighter in the Caribbean, within three miles of the coast of Colombia, so he is American, English, and Colombian by birth; one daughter was born in China; our youngest son in England."

* * *

Harry A. Franck was born in Munger, Mich., and worked his way through the University of Michigan (B.A. 1903), starting his vagabond career—on a cattle-boat to England—at the end of his freshman year. Later he did graduate work at Harvard. At first he combined teaching with vagabondage, but from 1911 abandoned teaching. During the First World War he was a lieutenant in the American army in France and Italy. He has covered some ninety countries intensively and he still retains his vigor for adventure and his zest for recording it. He is known (at least to his publishers) as "the prince of vagabonds."

PRINCIPAL WORKS: A Vagabond Journey Around the World, 1910; Four Months Afoot in Spain, 1911; Zone Policeman 88, 1913; Tramping Through Mexico, Guatemala, and Honduras, 1916; Vagabonding Down the Andes, 1917; Vagabonding Through Changing Germany, 1919; Roaming Through the West Indies, 1920; Working North From Patagonia, 1921; Wandering in Northern China, 1923; Glimpses of Japan and Formosa, 1924; Roving Through Southern China, 1925; East of Siam, 1926; The Fringe of the Moslem World, 1928; I Discover Greece, 1929; A Scandinavian Summer, 1930; Marco Polo, Junior, 1930; Foot-Loose in the British Isles, 1933; A Vagabond in Sovietland, 1935; Trailing Cortez Through Mexico, 1935; Roaming in Hawaii, 1937; Sky Roaming Above Two Continents, 1938; The Lure of Alaska, 1939; Pan-American Highway, 1941; Rediscovering South America, 1942.

ABOUT: Century Company. The Prince of Vagabonds: The Story of Harry A. Franck; Franck, R. L. I Married a Vagabond.

*FRANK, BRUNO (June 13, 1887-   ), German novelist, writes: "I was born at Stuttgart, south Germany. The ancestors of

my father, however, lived in the Rhineland for centuries, always in the same small town near the Dutch border. Many of them were physicians; my grandfather and father were bankers. In our family that spirit of liberal democratic views prevailed which was so characteristic of the majority of German Jewry.

"I first attended the preparatory college (Gymnasium) at Stuttgart, after that one of the modern colleges (Landschule) in Thuringia. Among my teachers there were one of Germany's foremost pedagogues, Paul Geheeb, and Theodor Lessing, the philosopher, whom the Nazis murdered in old age.

"As was the custom in Germany I changed universities several times. I studied law, philosophy, and history at the Universities of Tuebingen, Munich, Leipzig, and Strassburg. I received my Doctor's degree in philosophy and literature at the University of Tuebingen.

"Then restless years of travel began for me, for the most part under restricted conditions, since my parents looked upon my mode of living and my plans for the future with apprehension, for which I cannot censure them. I entered upon my literary work at an early age. My first book, a

collection of poems, appeared when I was barely eighteen. The book met with success; today these early literary efforts appear to me epigonous and weak. The same may be said of my first stories and novels. In later years, I have never been able to read anything through of my early work.

"After that I lived mainly in Munich, at that time the most beautiful and the gayest city of Germany, in close contact with the authors residing there, among whom Frank Wedekind and Rainer Maria Rilke excelled. Two of the younger authors, Wilhelm Speyer and Lion Feuchtwanger, were among my closest friends. During that time the acquaintance with Thomas Mann was of great significance to me. When I first met him, he was a young man of a little over thirty, but his wonderful novel *Buddenbrooks* had already brought him fame. The friendship that began at that time has lasted during a lifetime. My enthusiasm for the work of this extraordinary writer has steadily increased for more than a quarter of a century.

"I was twenty-seven years old when the World War broke out. I saw service on the Western Front and then in Russia. I returned from the front in a bad state of health and spent several years in complete solitude in the country, in southern Bavaria.

"I thought I would never marry. And I was a man of thirty-six when I met a girl, not yet sixteen, Elisabeth Pallenberg-Massary, who broke down this resolution at once. Her mother was the actress Fritzi Massary, at whose shrine the German public worshipped for thirty years, her stepfather was Max Pallenberg, the great comedian, later on killed in an airplane accident. My marriage has become the great unclouded happiness of my life.

"We settled in Munich permanently, and now that part of my literary productivity began at which I can look in retrospect without discomfort. Since I am by nature little ambitious and just as little inclined to amass a fortune, I undoubtedly needed someone who was passionately interested in my work, someone for whose comforts I wanted very much to care.

"Between 1924 and 1928 I published three novels and a large number of short stories. Simultaneously I wrote much for the stage. I was quite successful with my ten or twelve plays; some statistician has figured out that my plays were performed more than 12,000 times all over the world. Yet I believe that my work as a novelist is of better quality than as a playwright. I have also

* Died June 20, 1945.

adapted about fifty plays, written in foreign languages, for the German stage, among them plays by Noel Coward, Sacha Guitry, Marcel Pagnol, and many others.

"At the beginning of 1933 Adolf Hitler assumed power in Germany. The day after the ill-famed Reichstag fire we left Germany. We knew then that for a long time to come no author would have the possibility of a free and decent existence, particularly if he were a Jew. Like so many others we lost our home, our position, and our possessions. My wife left it all behind without one word of complaint. In the years that followed she has had but one thought: to help all those whose plight is worse than our own.

"Thereafter we changed our domicile several times; we lived in Switzerland, in the southern part of France, in London. We spent two summers near Salzburg, the most marvelous countryside in Europe, enjoying the wonders of music and drama presented there at the once renowned festivals. We knew full well that this meant a second leave-taking, since Austria's rape by Hitler was manifestly imminent.

"In 1937 I received an offer to come to Hollywood. In the fall of that year we moved to the United States. Since then I have been connected with several of the large studios. I intend, however, to interrupt this activity and to return, for a time at least, to my literary domain. Since my departure from Germany, two novels of mine have appeared and a collection of my shorter stories which has not yet been published in English.

"As to my political convictions, they are definitely and bluntly opposed to every nationalism and 'dynamism.' By tradition and instinct I am a democrat. Radicalism is not in my line, but I am convinced that only very thorough social reforms will bring about economic and political world recovery.

"My principal interests are centered around history and literature. The authors whom I read again and again are Thucydides, Tacitus, Gibbon, Macaulay, Michelet, Taine, Ranke, and Burckhardt. In dramatic literature my highest admiration goes (after Shakespeare) to Aristophanes, Molière, Kleist, and Nestroy; in lyric poetry to Goethe, Hölderlein, Verlaine, and Baudelaire, Shelley and Keats; in novels to Cervantes, Flaubert, Swift and Thackeray, Tolstoy and Turgeniev. Of contemporary authors Thomas Mann and W. Somerset Maugham seem to me the most admirable. Were I to make a decision as to painters, I should name Holbein, Vermeer, Goya, and the French Impressionists; in plastic art Donatello; in music Beethoven is to me the very idea of all that is greatness, Rossini the epitome of all that is grace. Historical figures whom I admire particularly are Henry IV of France, William of Orange, William Pitt (Earl of Chatham), Thomas Jefferson, and Abraham Lincoln.

"My recreations are reading, music, quiet enjoyment of beautiful scenery, conversations with friends. I am not a collector. Sport has never interested me. I love the feeling of independence, travel, all animals, dogs in particular. From the very bottom of my heart I loathe boring people and every kind of noise."

* * *

Bruno Frank's historical novels are so accurate as to detail that they are sometimes classed as history. In 1937 the Theatre Guild produced his *Storm Over Patsy* (elsewhere titled *Storm in a Teacup*) and *Young Madame Conti*. Clifton Fadiman called him "one of the most gifted of that band of German writers and artists who have faith in Europe as a psychological entity," while a reviewer in the *Bookman* particularly praised his "sensitive insight."

WORKS AVAILABLE IN ENGLISH: The Days of the King, 1927; Trenck, 1928; Twelve Thousand (play) 1928; The Persians Are Coming, 1929; A Man Called Cervantes, 1934; Closed Frontiers (in America, Lost Heritage) 1937; Storm in a Teacup, 1938; Young Madame Conti, 1938.

FRANK, LEONHARD (September 4, 1882-), German novelist, short story writer, and playwright, was born in the ancient episcopal see of Würzburg in Lower Franconia (Bavaria), the son of a carpenter. Leonhard attended the local *volksschule,* but due to the poverty and uncertainties which visited the homes of German workers, was soon  forced to start helping his family. At thirteen he was apprentice in a bicycle factory, and later house painter, attendant in a hospital-laboratory, and chauffeur to a country doctor. Having succeeded in saving a meager sum, he moved to Munich to study art. However his artistic sensibility found readier expression in literature and in 1914 he made a brilliant *début* with *The Robber Band.* In this first novel Frank depicted

with sympathy and humor a band of Würzburg schoolboys who, with heads full of
Wild West stories, formed a secret society
and played at robbers and Indians but in
the course of time became exactly like
the mediocre lower-middleclass elders with
whom they had come in conflict. In his
next novel, *The Cause of the Crime,* Frank
deepened his psychological research by showing how a half-starved young poet came
back from Berlin and strangled his old
schoolmaster who had treated him severely
twenty-one years before. Frank showed the
poet's inner-life, "all its alternations of
misery, apathy, self-contempt, and irrelevant
trifles, both before the crime and all through
his fully detailed trial, to the moment when
the axe fell." While the First World War
raged over Europe Frank wrote, between
1916-17, his anti-war novel, *Der Mensch ist
Gut* (1918), which circulated widely in Germany and, as some critics claim, seriously
weakened German morale on the home front.

In his next work, *A Middle-Class Man*
(1924) (re-titled, in the American edition,
Clamoring Self), Frank portrayed an idealistic youth trained to conscious inferiority
by the contemptuous attitude of parents and
teachers. He longs to help others, becomes
a Socialist, and leaves home to live with a
comrade in freedom and free love, but
eventually capitulates to respectability and
achieves remarkable success as a banker.
The haunting knowledge of self-betrayal
drives him finally into madness and he goes
off on a wild journey about Europe endeavoring to find the man he should have been.

With his novelette *Carl and Anna* (1926),
immediate cause of his election to the German Academy of Letters, Frank attained his
greatest and most universal success. The
simple plot is stated in clear, vigorous language: Richard and Carl are prisoners in
the Russian steppe; Richard talks so much
about his wife, Anna, that Carl falls in love
with her, contrives to escape and seeking
her out, tells her he is her husband. Puzzled
but not deceived, Anna yields to love. When
Richard returns, Carl and Anna leave him to
his misery and set out to find a new home.
With but the slightest technical modifica-
tions, Frank was able to convert his novelette
into an extremely actable play, a great hit in
several German cities and later in Paris in
J.-R. Bloch's version and in New York
where it had its première in October 1929
at the Guild Theatre. The story was filmed
in Germany in 1928.

Encouraged by this success Frank dramatized in 1929 *The Cause of the Crime* and

wrote the three-act comedy *Hufnägel* (1930).
In the field of the novel he followed *Carl
and Anna* with *The Singers* (1927) in which
he picked up the characters of *The Robber
Band* and presented them again in Würzburg, "middle-aged men now, impoverished
by the war, and with the spirit of adventure
knocked out of them." In *Brother and
Sister* (1929) two children—the boy eight,
the girl three—separated by their parents'
divorce, meet seventeen years later, fall in
love and marry. Frank analyzes with great
precision their psychological upheaval on
discovering their blood relationship. *Three
of the Three Million* (1932), the last novel
Frank wrote in his native country, deals
with a trio of unemployed men in Germany
in the first engulfing wave of the great
depression, their adventures in South America and their return in 1931 to their home
town. According to a distinguished critic,
"it is a compact story, without frills and
decorations and deriving from its anonymity
a touch of the universal which is never
strained or self-conscious." At various times
—in 1925, 1926, 1929—Frank collected in
book form his masterly short stories: *Im
Letzten Wagen, An der Landstrasse, Die
Schicksalbrücke, Absturz,* most of which
have been translated into English and collected under the title *In the Last Coach and
Other Stories.*

After the advent of the Nazis Frank had to
leave Germany, and lived in Paris, England,
and Switzerland. His most recent works
are the novel, *Die Traumgefährten* (1936),
and the three-act comedy, *Der Aussenseiter*
(1937). In 1940, with the help of American
writers, he was able to escape to the United
States from that Europe whose torment and
horror he has depicted so masterfully. In
spite of his wide travels, he is reported not
to know any language but German.

Of Frank's work the critic Alfred Polgar
said: "Leonhard Frank's creative writing is
a perception of the deeper relationships of
events within the human domain. A hark-
ening to the voices which in the chaos of
voices of the inner life are the dominant
ones. In his books the world is discovery,
not invention; the latter, rich and full of
meaning, serves only as a means of presenting the former. His characters bring forth
fate as the tree brings forth leaves and
flowers; they are set forth so true to life
that it seems as though their creator has
added nothing to his own but only hearkened
to organic growth. . . . His prose is built
compactly, the narrative chooses the shortest
line, scorns embellishments. Melancholy

ives Frank's books their dark foundation; umor plays many-colored lights over it. 'rank's work helps to lengthen the lever-rm that is to lift the burden of oppressive njustice and misery from the breast of mankind."

AVAILABLE IN ENGLISH TRANSLATION: The ause of the Crime, 1928; The Robber Band,)28; Carl and Anna, 1929; Karl and Anna drama) 1929; Brother and Sister, 1930; Clamor-g Self (British title: A Middle-Class Man) 1930; arl and Anna and Breath, 1930; The Singers,)33; In the Last Coach and Other Stories, 1934; hree of the Three Million, 1936; Carl and Anna nd The Cause of the Crime, 1936; Carl and Anna nd In the Last Coach, 1938.

ABOUT: Bertaux, F. A Panorama of German iterature; Bithell, J. Modern German Literature; loesser, A. Modern German Literature; Frank, . Absturz; Hewett-Thayer, H. W. The Modern erman Novel; Mahrholz, W. Deutsche Literatur er Gegenwart; Samuel, R. & Hinton Thomas, R. xpressionism in German Life, Literature, and the heatre; Nation October 30, 1929; New Republic ctober 23, 1929; Review of Reviews December 29.

RANK, WALDO DAVID (August 25, 889-   ), American novelist and essayist, rites: "Previous articles published on me give the impression that I am a polygraph, with no unity in my w o r k, a n d disastrously u n d e r-estimate the most important facet of my writing: my imagina-t i v e books—fiction. The truth is that all my work has a strict polyphonic unity: and s two principal phases, the novels and the ultural portraits'—such as Virgin Spain nd America Hispana and Rediscovery of merica—are as closely allied as movements f a symphony. Both forms are essentially esthetic; and this aspect of my work, the ormal, is the most important and naturally, herefore, the least understood in the United tates, where formal literary values are lmost entirely ignored, except in the minor orms, such as lyric verse. The strongest ppreciations of my work as a formal artist's ave come from Russia, France, and South merica.

"But since the symphonic unity of my work becoming articulate in that work itself— aving reached, I think, its fullest maturity two recent novels, The Death and Birth f David Markand and The Bridegroom ometh—an articulation which I hope to be le to proceed with in subsequent novels,

independent, but allied like panels of a great mural, I need not expatiate upon it here.

"The trouble is that the central command-ment of my aesthetic vision of life compels me frequently into the fields of action. And so my recent actions in Spain, my close alliance with the progressive movements of Latin America. (Ex-President Cardenas of Mexico is a dear friend, and I profoundly love as well as respect him), etc., are also facets of the action I undertake in my books. For my sense of literature is that of an action. To me a good book is an act; or, if you prefer, an acting and an enacting indi-vidual. That is why, in the long run, a book's formal quality is what counts most— makes it most effective. Where mine comes in, in such a hierarchy, it is too early to say."

* * *

Mr. Frank was born in Long Branch, N.J., the son of Julius J. Frank and Helene (Rosenberg) Frank. He was educated at Yale (B.A. and M.A. 1911), and has an honorary Litt.D. from the National Univer-sity of San Marcos, Lima, Peru. In 1917 he married Margaret Naumburg, by whom he had a son; they were divorced later, and in 1927 he married Alma Magoon, by whom he has two daughters. After some months on a Wyoming ranch, between 1911 and 1913 he worked on the New York Evening Post and Times. He was a founder and edi-tor of the Seven Arts, 1916-17, and has been American correspondent of Europe and the Nouvelle Revue Française. He has lived in Europe and Mexico and toured South America. He has written several "modern-istic" plays, best known of which is New Year's Eve (1929). He is a slender, dark man, handsome in an intense and nervous manner. A hard and steady worker, outside his scheduled hours for writing he is genial and sociable. His recreations are playing the 'cello' when he is in New York, and sailing and swimming when he is at his country home on Cape Cod. He keeps regular office hours in his work, turning out about 2,000 words a day.

Time remarked that "for some twenty years he has been adjuring, adverting, ad-vising his countrymen," and he himself says: "Every critical work that I have written has been inspired by my love of my country, and . . . by my faith in the high destiny of my country." He has done much to establish a firm friendship between the Latin Amer-ican nations and the United States.

"He alone among us," said Gorham B. Munson, "tries to write the prophetic novel." Others have commented on his "testamental quality of speech, permeated with a new mysticism," and on what William Troy called his "lyrical prose." Some critics, on the other hand, find his writing murky and over-wrought.

PRINCIPAL WORKS: *Fiction*—The Unwelcome Man, 1917; The Dark Mother, 1920; City Block, 1922; Rahab, 1922; Holiday, 1923; Chalk Face, 1924; The Death and Birth of David Markand, 1934; The Bridegroom Cometh, 1938, Summer Never Ends, 1941. *Essays*—The Art of the Vieux Colombier, 1918; Our America (in England, The New America) 1919; Salvos, 1924; Virgin Spain, 1926; Time Exposures (by "Search-Light") 1926; The Rediscovery of America, 1929; America Hispana, 1931; Dawn in Russia, 1932; In the American Jungle, 1937; Chart for Rough Water, 1940; Virgin Spain (revised) 1942.

ABOUT: Benardete, M. J. (ed.). Waldo Frank in America Hispana; Munson, G. B. Waldo Frank; A Study; Mercure de France April 15, 1930; New York Times Book Review April 15, 1942; Saturday Review of Literature June 15, 1940; Sewanee Review October 1932; South Atlantic Quarterly January 1936.

*FRANKAU, GILBERT (April 21, 1884-), English novelist and short-story writer, is the eldest son of the late Arthur

Frankau and J u l i a F r a n k a u, who, as "Frank Danby," was the author of *Pigs in Clover* and other successful novels. The boy was "brought up Church of England," and was not made acquainted with h i s Jewish ancestry until he was sixteen. After leaving Eton in 1904 Gilbert Frankau went into the wholesale cigar business with his father, marrying Dorothea Drummond Black next year. Two daughters were born, one of them the novelist and short-story writer Pamela Frankau.[qv] This marriage was dissolved. *The Love Story of Aliette Brunton* (1922), which derived from this experience, was, like the later *Holy Deadlock* of A. P. Herbert, a plea for more liberal divorce laws. In 1912 Frankau left for a two-year trip around the world, to open new markets for the family tobacco business.

In the First World War he received a commission with the 9th East Surrey Regiment in October 1914, transferring to the R.F.A. in March 1915. Appointed adjutant to his brigade, Frankau went overseas and fought at Loos, Ypres, and on the Somme. Promoted Staff Captain for special (propaganda) duty in Italy, October 1916, he was invalided from the service with shell-shock and granted the rank of captain, February

1918. *The Guns* (1916), a volume of wa poems, and the best-selling *Royal Regimen* a novel published nearly a quarter-cen tury later, utilized his war experience Frankau's first experiments in writing in cluded novelettes in verse, and Byroni poems in the vein of *Don Juan*. His *Poetic Works* were collected in 1923. In 1922 h married Aimée de Burgh, and lived an wrote on a lavish scale in London and o the Riviera. This marriage was also dis solved, and in 1932 Susan Lorna Harr became Frankau's third wife.

Patrick Braybrooke, who finds a meld dramatic streak in the Frankau fiction, nc unlike "Frank Danby's," calls him "a admirable novelist for ordinary people." I the foreword to Frankau's knowing, allu ive autobiography, *Self-Portrait,* the nove ist states, "This is the story—in so far a it can be told without giving pain, causin undue offence, or landing my worthy pub lishers in the Law Courts—of my own li up to the age of fifty-five." Frankau quote a candid friend as having said of him tha he cared for only two things on earth— women and "copy."

PRINCIPAL WORKS: One of Us, 1912; Tid'ap 1914; The Guns, 1916; The City of Fear, 191 The Woman of the Horizon, 1917; The Judgemei of Valhalla, 1918; One of Them, 1918; Seeds (Enchantment, 1921; The Love Story of Aliet Brunton, 1922; Men, Maids, and Mustard: A Co lection of Tales, 1923; Gerald Cranston's Lad 1924; Life—and Erica, 1925; Masterson, and M Sentimental Journey, 1926; Twelve Tales, 192 So Much Good, 1928; Dance, Little Gentlemar 1929; Martin Make Believe, 1930; Concernir Peter Jackson and Others, 1931; Christoph Strong, 1932; Wine, Women, and Waiters, 193 The Lonely Man, 1932; Everywoman, 1933; Secr Services, 1934; Three Englishmen, 1935; Farewe Romance, 1936; Experiments in Crime, 1937; Mo of Us, 1937; Dangerous Years, 1937; That Fier Light, 1938; Royal Regiment, 1938; Self-Portrai A Novel of His Own Life, 1940; Air Ministry- Room 28, 1942.

ABOUT: Braybrooke, P. Novelists, We Are Se en; Frankau, G. Self-Portrait; Frankau, P. I Fir Four People.

FRANKAU, PAMELA (1908-), Eng

lish novelist and short-story writer, is th younger of the two daughters of the noveli Gilbert Frankau[qv] and Dorothea Drum mond (Black) Frankau, the first of h three wives. The girl lived at Windsor wit her mother and sister Ursula. She went school at Stapleton, where she won swimming prize and first scholastic honor (by last-minute cramming) and was a ardent Girl Guide. Mrs. Frankau's seriou illness made it imperative for her to ear money, and Pamela Frankau began her li erary career in London at eighteen with th

Amalgamated Press, at 37s. 6d. a week. Her closest friend there was Pat Wallace, Edgar Wallace's daughter. *Marriage of Harlequin* 1927), her first novel, originally titled *Hamlet and Harlequin*, was written in a third-class carriage of her business train, on paper stolen from Fleetway House, with a scarlet fountain-pen given her by her novelist father, with whom Pamela Frankau was generally on friendly terms. Promoted to a sub-editorship on the *Woman's Journal* at five pounds a week, she continued to write, and developed an excellent market for her vivacious short stories and newspaper articles. This halcyon state of affairs did not last. In February

1931 Miss Frankau was living in a London boarding house with her sister and grandmother, and was glad to have the security of a salaried post with an advertising agency (apparently the same one with which Dorothy Sayers was once connected) as copy writer, at 600 pounds a year.

Miss Frankau has had five American publishers. She took advantage of an illness to write her autobiography in a nursing home. Published in 1935, *I Find Four People* (referring to the successive phases of her career) is a frank and diverting account of her business experiences and affairs of the heart, with some sensible reflections on the practical details of a writer's career. A successful publisher must, she states, be an astute tradesman, "a seeker not after souls but library subscriptions." She is a little regretful that she did not continue from school to a university, instead of "conniving at the popular stupidities of a woman's magazine." She usually writes three thousand words a day, always in longhand. In parody of a popular song, Miss Frankau once breaks forth: "I'll be writing rot, always. Rot that's rather hot, always. Written for the dense, It does not make sense. . . ." Her fiction, however, has sprightly and distinctive qualities, especially *The Devil We Know*, a study of a young Jewish scenario writer's struggles with a sense of inferiority, and *A Democrat Dies* (American title: *Appointment With Death*), a combined mystery and political satire. Miss Frankau once described herself as "a little overweight, with severely short black hair and a pale round face."

PRINCIPAL WORKS: Marriage of Harlequin, 1927; Three, 1929; She and I, 1930; Letters From a Modern Daughter to Her Mother, 1931; Born at Sea, 1932; Women Are So Serious, 1932; I Was the Man, 1932; Foolish Apprentices (American title: Walk Into My Parlour) 1933; Tassell-Gentle (American title: Fly Now, Falcon) 1934; Fifty-Fifty and Other Stories, 1936; Jezebel (Biblical Biographies Series) 1937; The Devil We Know, 1939; A Democrat Dies (American title: Appointment With Death) 1940.

ABOUT: Frankau, P. I Find Four People.

FRANKEN, ROSE (Rose Franken Meloney) (1898-), American playwright, novelist, and director was born in Texas.

At an early age, Miss Franken, as she is known professionally, was brought to New York. At seventeen, on the day that she was to have entered college, she married Dr. Sigmund Walter Anthony Franken. Three sons were born of this marriage. Dr. Franken died in 1933. In 1937 Rose Franken married her present husband, William Brown Meloney, well known author, playwright and producer. In addition to the many novels and plays which she has written and published in her own name, Miss Franken and Mr. Meloney have collaborated in the writing of numerous magazine serials and motion picture screen plays.

Miss Franken has become one of the outstanding playwright directors of the contemporary stage, with a string of hits behind her name. Her short stories appear in the foremost magazines where she is recognized as the highest paid and one of the most successful of the modern short story writers. Her novels, like her plays, range from the incisive and penetrating portrayals of human drama and emotion such as *Pattern, Of Great Riches, Another Language, Outrageous Fortune,* to the warm and universal portraits of modern marriage such as *Claudia* and her lighter plays. Her work commands an equal audience in England and she enjoys the reputation of being the most translated American writer, her works currently appearing in twenty countries. *Claudia,* one of her most successful plays, was tested in the short story form and in the novel before she chose it as a theme for a play; its subsequent life would seem to have exhausted the possible literary fields, for it has twice appeared as a motion picture. A radio serial made from the play was also highly successful and profitable. (*Claudia* was dramatized from her novels dealing with this heroine.)

Mrs. Franken is candidly feminine in her viewpoint. In her opinion, "In a love story it is always the woman's relation to the man that is the more interesting, that makes the story." In her joint novels with her husband, he creates the plots, she writes the dialogue. She is very facile; she never rewrites; her first draft is invariably her last. A certain superficiality of style is inevitable with such a method, but her verve and naturalness of expression carry her through, and there is fresh life in all her work. She is not "significant" either as novelist or as playwright, but as both she is alive, penetrating, and always entertaining.

PRINCIPAL WORKS: *Novels*—Pattern, 1925; Twice Born, 1935; Of Great Riches (in England: Gold Pennies) 1937; Claudia, 1939; Claudia and David, 1940; The Book of Claudia, 1941. *As "Margaret Grant"*—Call Back Love, 1938. *As "Franken Meloney"*—Strange Victory, 1939; When Doctors Disagree, 1940; American Bred, 1941. *Plays*—Another Language, 1932; Mr. Dooley, Jr. (juvenile, with J. Lewin) 1932; Claudia, 1941.

ABOUT: New York Times Magazine May 4, 1941.

"FRANKLIN, JAY." See C A R T E R, J. F.

FRAZER, Sir JAMES GEORGE (January 1, 1854-May 7, 1941), Scottish anthropologist, was born in Glasgow, the son of a Presbyterian minister.

He was educated at Larchfield Academy, Helensburgh, at Glasgow University, and at Trinity College, Cambridge, which he entered on a scholarship. Throughout most of his long life (after 1879) he was a Fellow of Trinity. He also read law in the Middle Temple, was admitted to the bar in 1879 and was made an Honorary Bencher of the Middle Temple in 1931. He was knighted in 1914 and received the Order of Merit in 1925. He was made a Fellow of the Royal Society in 1920, was an honorary Fellow of the Royal Society of Edinburgh and an associate member of the French Institute, and a Commander of the Legion of Honor. He had honorary doctorates from Oxford, Cambridge, Glasgow, St. Andrews, Durham, Manchester, Paris, Strasbourg, and Athens, and was a Fellow of the British Academy. In 193 he was made an Honorary Freeman of th City of Glasgow. In 1896 he married Mrs Lily Grove, an author in her own right they had no children.

Sir James won world-wide fame as a anthropologist, but he was also a classica scholar, who edited and translated Apollo dorus, Pausanias, Ovid, and Sallust; and critic of English literature, particularly o the eighteenth century, who edited Cowpe and Addison. Edmond Jaloux describe him, during a visit to Paris in 1935, as "sti agile and quick," with a short white bearc eyes of a brilliant sapphire blue behind hi glasses, a sociable, convivial nature for a his more than eighty years, and a "restless encyclopedic mind." In his honor the Fraze Lectures are given in rotation at Glasgo and Cambridge, by authorities in anthro pology, and ten years of them have also bee published in book form.

The Golden Bough, Sir James' greates work, the first volume of which appeare in 1890, is one of the great seminal book of our era. Of it Samuel C. Chew said "Anthropologists of the future must re-sif and rearrange his vast stores of material, . . [but] even if every one of his theories is a length swept away by the rising tide o knowledge, I find it impossible to believe tha in any future state of literary cultur thoughtful people will allow this grea achievement of learning and imagination an literary art to accumulate dust on th shelves." Its central thesis is that in the ex planation of "the remarkable rule which reg ulated the succession to the priesthood o Diana at Aricia" lies a universal religious sys tem depending on the ritual killing of a kin by his successor. From this central fact ha been built up an account of the evolution o religion paralleled only by that of Sigmun Freud—to whose theories, incidentally, Si James was always ardently opposed. I is impossible, however, for any future stu dent of the subject to dispense with eithe of these fundamental contributions to socia anthropology, which, disparate as they ma seem to be at first glance, nevertheless ma be reconciled by later-comers building upo the work of these mighty pioneers.

A retiring scholar for all his amiable so ciability, Sir James Frazer's was a name t conjure with among his colleagues, but rela tively unfamiliar to the lay public, in spit of the one-volume edition of *The Golde Bough* brought out in 1922. But he was on of the truly great and original moder thinkers, and his conclusions are presented ot in dry discussions, but in a "subtle, firm, nd musical" prose. As the New York *Herald Tribune* said editorially at the time f his death: "The impact of his extraordinary labor seems certain to be felt for ecades to come."

Sir James succumbed to the infirmities of ge at Cambridge in his eighty-seventh year. Lady Frazer, also in her eighties, died ess than twelve hours later.

PRINCIPAL WORKS: Totemism, 1887; The Golden Bough (16 vols.) 1890-1915 (1-vol. edition, 922); Pausanias and Other Greek Studies, 1900; Lectures on the Early History of the Kingship, 905; Adonis, Attis, Osiris: Studies in the History f Oriental Religion, 1906; Questions on the Customs, Beliefs, and Languages of Savages, 1907; The Scope of Social Anthropology, 1908; Psyche's Task, 1909; Totemism and Exogamy, 1910; The Dying God, 1911; The Magic Art and the Evolution of Kings, 1911; Taboo and the Perils of the Soul, 1911; Spirits of the Corn and of the Wild, 912; The Scapegoat, 1913; Balder the Beautiful, 913; The Belief in Immortality and the Worship f the Dead (3 vols.) 1913-24; Folk-Lore in the Old Testament, 1918 (abridged 1923); Jacob and he Mandrakes, 1918; The Magical Origin of Kings, 1920; Sir Roger de Coverley and Other Literary Pieces, 1920; Sur Ernest Renan (in French) 1923; The Worship of Nature, 1926; The Gorgon's Head and Other Literary Pieces, 1927; Man, God, and Immortality; Thoughts on Human Progress, 1927; The Growth of Plato's Ideal Theory, 1930; Myths of the Origin of Fire, 1930; Garnered Sheaves, 1931; Lecture on Condorcet, 933; The Fear of the Dead in Primitive Religion 3 vols.) 1933-36; Creation and Evolution in Primitive Cosmogonies and Other Pieces, 1935; Aftermath: Supplement to The Golden Bough, 1936; Totemica: A Supplement to Totemism and Exogamy, 1937; Greece and Rome, 1937; Anthologia Anthropologica (ed., 4 vols.) 1938-39.

ABOUT: Besterman, T. Bibliography of James George Frazer; Dawson, W. R. (ed.). Frazer Lectures 1922-32; Downie, R. A. James George Frazer; Heape, W. Sex Antagonism; Living Age April 1934; New Republic February 28, 1923; North American Review December 1923; Virginia Quarterly Review July 1936.

FREEMAN, AUSTIN. See FREEMAN, R. A.

FREEMAN, DOUGLAS SOUTHALL May 16, 1886-), American historian, Pulitzer Prize winner, was born at Lynchburg, Va., the son of Walker Burford Freeman, later Commander-in-Chief of the Confederate Veterans, and Bettie (Allen) Freeman. The family moved to Richmond in 1892, where Douglas Freeman attended McGuire's University School and Richmond College (B.A. 1904). He entered Johns Hopkins as a fellow in history, and received his Ph.D. in 1908. That year he issued his first book, a *Calendar of Confederate Papers.* The following spring he was engaged by the Richmond *Times-Dispatch* to write a

series of editorial articles on the reform of the tax-system of Virginia. Out of this connection came appointment as secretary of the Virginia Tax Commission (1910-12), and from 1913 a position as editorial writer on the jointly owned Richmond newspapers, the *Times-Dispatch* and the *News-Leader.* Upon the sale of the former in 1914, he remained with the *News-Leader,* of which he became editor in 1915, a position he still holds. The outbreak of the First World War found him editing, in leisure time, the confidential dispatches of General Robert E. Lee to President Jefferson Davis, a notable collection of unpublished papers that belonged to W. J. De Renne of Savannah, Ga. Through this work he became familiar with military terminology, and it was through his editorials on military operations that he first became known outside his own constituency.

In 1914 Mr. Freeman undertook to write, on publisher's order, a short biography of Lee, but he soon found that such a book would be a mere repetition of what had already been published, whereas the amount of new, unused material would justify a full-length biography. To this he devoted most of his spare time after 1915, and finally published the work in 1934. It received that year's Pulitzer Prize in biography.

He bought an interest in the *News-Leader* in 1923, and, from the very nature of his vocation, found himself responsible, in time, for a variety of enterprises. In 1934 he was visiting Professor of Journalism at Columbia University, and since 1935 he has been lecturing one day a week there on editorial method and editorial technique. He is rector of the board of the University of Richmond, president of the Poe Foundation, president of the Southern Historical Society, president of the Confederate Memorial Institute, and president of the Society of American Historians. He is also a trustee and member of the Rockefeller Foundation and General Education Board. Much of his time is given to lectures and public speeches, though he seldom goes on long lecture tours.

Such an enormous amount of work can be accomplished only by strict regulation of his time. He is in his newspaper office every day at 5:40 A.M. After a daily radio

---

* Died June 13, 1953.

broadcast, his afternoon is given to writing, and he is in bed by 8:45 P.M. In his house he has a study with a chapel or shrine near it which he uses for meditation. Even conversation with his wife and family, or listening to symphonic music on the radio, has to have its scheduled hour. He was married in 1914 to Inez Virginia Goddin, and has two daughters and a son. A lean man with thinning gray hair and spectacles, he looks more like a college professor than like a newspaper editor. He has twelve honorary degrees. In 1933 he received the Parchment of Distinction of the New York Southern Society.

His editorials on the present war are all written in terms of analogy with the Civil War. *Life* called him "probably the sanest and soundest observer of the European war in the United States today." His monumental life of Lee, in four volumes, is probably the definitive biography of the Confederate leader.

PRINCIPAL WORKS: Calendar of Confederate Papers (ed.) 1908; Reports on Virginia Taxation, 1912; Lee's Dispatches (ed.) 1914; Virginia—A Gentle Dominion, 1924; The Last Parade, 1932; R. E. Lee (4 vols.) 1934; The South to Posterity, 1939.

ABOUT: Life May 13, June 3, 1940; Saturday Review of Literature May 11, 1935; Time April 1, 1940; Wilson Library Bulletin June 1935.

FREEMAN, HAROLD WEBBER

(1899-), English novelist, was born in Essex and educated at the City of London

School. He served in the British army for the last year of the First World War, then spent four years at Christ Church, Oxford University. Two years as a farm laborer followed, part of the time with a short-lived poultry concern, then as helper to farmers in the district which forms the background of *Joseph and His Brethren* (1928) which was made a choice of the Book-of-the-Month Club in the United States. The novel, first conceived as a short story of 800 words and so published in January 1926, was expanded in five months of 1927-28 in Florence, Italy. Mr. Freeman had left the land in 1924 to do odd jobs, educational work, and so on, going abroad at intervals. *Down in the Valley* is another agrarian novel of style and distinction. Its author does not claim any further knowledge

of farming than that of a rough general farmhand—his associates in Suffolk would not have called him either a first-class cow man or horseman; and in biographical dictionaries Mr. Freeman lists himself merely as "writer," with no elaborative details. He still lives in the country in Suffolk, but admits to his publishers that "he travels when possible." Some of these travels evidently took the novelist to Spain, which figures prominently in *Andrew to the Lions*, in which Suffolk is only a corner of the map and which has unusual gayety and irony of tone.

As a regional novelist, H. W. Freeman has been compared with Sheila Kaye-Smith who also writes of farming life in East Anglia. *Fathers of Their People* and its sequel, *Pond Hall's Progress*, display the same deep attachment to the soil and country life that appeared in *Joseph and His Brethren*, and are told in the same style of almost Biblical simplicity. A *Bookman* reviewer once commented that Freeman's main purpose seems to be showing the world a form of life of which he approves, letting consideration of expression and clear portrayal, development and inter-relation of character go by the board. The novelist is a handsome man, with a firm mouth, prominent chin, and thick, waving hair.

PRINCIPAL WORKS: Joseph and His Brethren, 1928; Down in the Valley, 1930; Fathers of Their People, 1932; Pond Hall's Progress, 1933; Hester and Her Family, 1936; Andrew to the Lions, 1938; His Own Place, 1941.

ABOUT: Wilson Library Bulletin February 1929.

FREEMAN, JOHN

(January 29, 1880- September 23, 1929), English poet, critic and novelist, was born at Dalston, Middlesex, the elder son of John Freeman, a commercial traveller of country origin, and Catherine (Botham) Freeman, grand-

daughter of a captain in the regiment of the Guards. A scarlet-fever attack in his fourth year left him with heart trouble which was a constant threat to him all his life. He was entered in an academy in Hackney, but left school at the age of twelve to become a junior clerk in the head office of the Liverpool Victoria Friendly Society (industrial and national health insurance), of which he eventually (1927) was made secretary and director, supervising 000 employees and capital amounting to £20,000,000.

At a very early age he taught himself Greek and applied himself to a wide reading in English literature. His unpretentious attempts at writing, at the age of eighteen, marked the beginning of a literary life which was abetted by friendships with Roger Ingpen and Walter de la Mare and which remained always completely distinct from his commercial activities. In 1902 he married Gertrude Farren, by whom he had two daughters.

Freeman's first literary recognition came in 1916 with the appearance of *Stone Trees,* a book that completely eclipsed his earlier *Twenty Poems* and *Fifty Poems.* Seven more volumes of verse followed, including his *Collected Poems* (1928) and his posthumous *Last Poems,* issued in 1930. *Poems New and Old,* awarded the Hawthornden Prize in 1920, introduced Freeman to American readers. His *Portrait of George Moore* and later *Herman Melville* established him as a sensitive and perceptive critic.

He was a slight man, with large eyes, somewhat long but well-kept hair, an expressive mouth, and a receding chin. Those who knew him best said that for the graceful humor of his conversation he had no peer; his letters, thirty-odd of which were edited in 1936 by Gertrude Freeman and Sir John Squire, are intelligently discursive. He died in Anerley at the age of forty-nine.

One of his contemporaries said, in a strictly complimentary sense, "If ever a poet sang simply to please himself and because he could not help singing, that poet was John Freeman." But because his verse was "melodious, slow-flowing, and mellifluous," its audience was somewhat restricted. There was a poet's strength of rhythm in his prose, which, he contended, should be written rather for the ear than for the eye. "I have," he himself once said, "a lover-like palate for phrases."

PRINCIPAL WORKS: Twenty Poems, 1909; Fifty Poems, 1911; Presage of Victory, 1916; The Moderns, 1916; Poems New and Old, 1920; Music, 1921; Portrait of George Moore, 1922; English Portraits, 1924; Herman Melville, 1926; Solomon and Balkis, 1926; Last Poems, 1930; John Freeman's Letters, 1936.

ABOUT: Freeman, J. Last Poems (See Introduction); Freeman, J. John Freeman's Letters (See Introduction); London Mercury February 1930; Insurance Mail October 5, 1929

FREEMAN, JOSEPH (October 7, 1897-   ), American poet, editor, and critic, writes: "I was born in the Ukraine, came

A. Albee

to the United States in 1904, grew up in Brooklyn's slums. I began drawing at five, writing at twelve; my first poems and stories were published when I was about fifteen. At seventeen I became a Socialist and a public speaker. Graduating from Columbia University in 1919 (Phi Beta Kappa), I became (after a year with Harper & Bros.) a professional newspaperman, was Chicago *Tribune* correspondent in Paris in 1920, and the following year in London. At this time I wrote and published a great deal of poetry. Returning to the U.S.A. in 1921, I joined the editorial staff of the *Liberator.* Three years later the magazine folded up, and during 1924 I was publicity director for the American Civil Liberties Union. The following year I joined the staff of the TASS News Agency and worked there, on and off, until 1931. I continued writing poetry and started to publish Marxist literary criticism; but, as an enthusiast for the classless Socialist society, could not escape economics. My first book, written, in collaboration with Scott Nearing, was a pioneer study of American foreign relations from a left viewpoint. It was translated in Germany, Spain, Mexico, and Russia.

"In 1926 I cooperated with a group of writers and artists in founding the *New Masses,* then a monthly of literature, art, and politics. Later that year I went to the Soviet Union, and in the spring of 1927 I stayed for several months in Germany. Back in the U.S.A., I spent my days at the news agency, my nights writing Marxist literary criticism, teaching journalism and literature to workers' classes, and lecturing in and around New York. In 1929 I went as newspaper correspondent to Mexico City, since then my favorite town. On my return to New York, I wrote *Voices of October* in collaboration with Joshua Kunitz and Louis Lozowick. This was the first full length study of Soviet art, literature, and films published by Americans. The next year I worked in Hollywood with the Russian novelist Boris Pilnyak. We did a script called *Soviet* for M.G.M. under the supervision of Irving Thalberg. But it was a touchy subject; the picture was never produced.

"For the next five years I was active in the development of the left literary movement. On and off, I edited the *New Masses*. In 1933 I published the first anti-Nazi pamphlet in this country, and helped found the first anti-Nazi organizations. In 1934 a publisher asked me to collect a volume of poems with a preface. The more I labored on that preface, the more I thought of my experiences in general, so I had to go off to the country to write a narrative about our times in autobiographical form. *An American Testament* was chosen by the Writers' Congress as the best autobiography of the year. It did fairly well in this country, but was a best seller in England. Distance does lend enchantment.

"The following two years I edited the *New Masses*, published a number of literary essays, lectured extensively on literature and politics, and made a second visit to Mexico (this time as delegate of the League of American Writers to the Mexican literary congress). On this visit I obtained the first extensive interview with President Cardenas given to an American journalist. At present I am in the country editing my poems and essays into books, and working on an historical study from which I hope to learn something about the real nature of democracy. I have completed a movie script about the work of Sigmund Freud, and published some short stories. I am married to Charmion von Wiegand, painter and art critic, and we have our home at Accord, N.Y., among the foothills of the Catskills. Our neighbors are all farmers; twenty miles away is the art colony of Woodstock.

"I like to read Plato, Dante, Shelley, Marx, Proust, Dostoievsky, Balzac, Lenin, Tolstoy, Freud, Hart Crane, Hemingway, Joyce, and Gertrude Stein; to hear the music of Bach, Mozart, Borodin, César Franck, and Benny Goodman; to see paintings by Ingres, Cezanne, Picasso, and Walter Quirt; to watch the acting of John Barrymore, Greta Garbo, Charles Laughton, Mickey Mouse, and Charlie Chaplin."

* * *

Mr. Freeman's prose is often polemic, but his poetry is for the most part purely lyrical. Malcolm Cowley called him "a citizen of two worlds, the bohemian and the revolutionary, [whose] essential position has always been that of a translator and intermediary."

PRINCIPAL WORKS: Dollar Diplomacy: A Study in American Imperialism (with S. Nearing) 1925; Voices of October: Art and Literature in Soviet Russia (with J. Kunitz & L. Lozowick) 1930; The

Soviet Worker: An Account of the Economi Social, and Cultural Status of Labor in th U.S.S.R., 1932; An American Testament: A Na rative of Rebels and Romantics, 1938.

ABOUT: Dell, F. Homecoming; Farrell, J. Notes on American Literature; Fischer, L. Me and Politics; Freeman, J. An American Test ment; Nation October 24, 1936; New Republ October 28, 1936; Saturday Review of Literatur October 31, 1936.

FREEMAN, Mrs. MARY ELEANO (WILKINS) (October 31, 1852-March 1, 1930), American novelist and story write was born in Ran-dolph, Mass., the daughter of Warren E. Wilkins, an archi-tect and storekeeper, and Eleanor (Loth-rop) Wilkins. Both parents were of old New England stock. In later years she claimed to have been born in 1862, but  was really ten years older. From childhoo she was too frail to attend school or lea the life of a normal child, and when fo one year, 1870, she went to Mount Holyok Seminary (now Mount Holyoke College she was obliged to leave because of he poor health: yet she lived to be seventy seven. Her last formal education was few months in a boarding school at Wes Brattleboro, Vt., in 1873, her family havin moved to that town.

Her first published work was vers mostly for children. Her sister, mother, an father were all dead by 1883, and she re turned to Randolph and lived with a gir hood friend. She had an aunt as well a herself to support, and her first stories fo adults were written in the hope of makin more by them than the juvenile magazine could pay. She also acted as secretary t Oliver Wendell Holmes (Sr.), and throug him became acquainted with the famou Massachusetts writers of the day. With th publication of *A New England Nun*, in 1891 she began to achieve recognition in her ow right. In 1902 she married Dr. Charle Manning Freeman, and for the remainde of her life her home was with him i Metuchen, N.J., where she died.

Small, with luxuriant brown hair an deep blue eyes, Mrs. Freeman looked wha she was for most of her life—a spinster o good family from a small New Englan town. She had the simplicity, frankness and dry humor of her type. She had, how ever, much more, including a keen and orig inal talent. Owing to the haphazard method of self-education she underwent, her reading was wide but uneven, and (perhaps fortunately) she missed knowing most of the authors who might have influenced her work. Her novels are poorly constructed and quite inferior to her short stories, which are unique of their kind. As John Macy said, "her genius was original, not of a school. . . . She had no tears except the tears of things. . . . Her material was close at hand, plain and simple; she had the genius to see it and render it objectively." Her field is the New England village, and there is no bitterness, no satire, in her depiction of its frustrated lives. "The gentle woman merely records a grimness for which she is not responsible."

For a decade before her death Mrs. Freeman wrote little, though before her marriage she had been a prolific writer. (She is credited with 238 short stories in all, besides twelve novels, a play, and two volumes of verse.) By the time of her death she was largely forgotten, though in 1925 she was awarded the Howells Medal for fiction by the American Academy of Arts and Letters and the next year was elected a member of the National Institute of Arts and Letters. She was the last of the great *genre* writers in New England—she and Sarah Orne Jewett, whom she had not read. In style she was, at her best, noteworthy: her phrasing, as Macy remarked, is "economical and unadorned but easy, flexible, muscular."

PRINCIPAL WORKS: *Short Stories*—The Adventures of Ann (juvenile) 1886; A Humble Romance, 1887; A New England Nun, 1891; The Pot of Gold, 1892; Young Lucretia, 1892; Comfort Pease and Her Gold Ring, 1895; The People of Our Neighborhood, 1898; Silence, 1898; The Jamesons, 1899; The Love of Parson Lord, 1900; Understudies, 1901; Six Trees, 1903; The Wind in the Rose Bush, 1903; The Givers, 1904; The Fair Lavinia, 1907; The Winning Lady, 1909; The Green Door, 1910; The Yates Pride, 1912; The Copy-Cat, 1914; Edgewater People, 1918. *Novels*—Jane Field, 1893; Pembroke, 1894; Madelon, 1896; Jerome: A Poor Man, 1897; The Heart's Highway, 1900; The Portion of Labor, 1901; The Debtor, 1905; "Doc" Gordon, 1906; By the Light of the Soul, 1906; The Shoulders of Atlas, 1908; The Butterfly House, 1912; An Alabaster Box (with F. M. Kingsley) 1917. *Miscellaneous*—Decorative Plaques (verse) 1883; Giles Corey; Yeoman (play) 1893; Once Upon a Time and Other Child Verses, 1897.

ABOUT: Brooks, V. W. New England Indian Summer; Overton, G. Our Women Novelists; Pattee, F. L. Side-Lights on American Literature; Atlantic Monthly June 1899; Bookman August 1931; Publishers' Weekly March 22, 1930.

*FREEMAN, RICHARD AUSTIN

(1862-), English scientific detective story writer, creator of Dr. Thorndyke, who signs

his work R. Austin Freeman, was born in London, the youngest son of Richard Freeman. He was a surgeon by profession, having received his medical training at the Middlesex Hospital Medical College. In 1886 he became a Member of the Royal College of Surgeons and a Licentiate of the Society of Apothecaries, and immediately was appointed house physician of the Middlesex Hospital. The next year he went to the Gold Coast, in Africa, as Assistant Colonial Surgeon, and in the same year he married Annie Elizabeth Edwards. They had two sons.

In 1889 Freeman joined a medical expedition to Ashanti and Bontuku, an experience which led to a travel book nine years later. He was then appointed Anglo-German Boundary Commissioner, but the African climate affected his health and he was invalided out, a victim of blackwater fever. Back in England, he served temporarily as surgeon at his old hospital, and then became acting assistant medical officer at Holloway Prison, meanwhile engaging in private practice. (His specialty was the ear, nose, and throat.) For a short time also he was acting assistant medical officer for the Port of London.

His health, however, continued to be unsatisfactory, and he was forced practically to abandon his profession. He turned to writing as a whole-time occupation in 1904, having published nothing previously but his book of African travels in 1898. His only later medical service (except for a small country practice) was during the World War, when he was commander of ambulance service as a member of the Royal Army Medical Corps. He was placed on the retired list in 1922, and since then has lived at his home in Gravesend, Kent, remaining there, in the heart of "Hell's Corner," throughout the 1940-41 blitzkrieg, working methodically each day in his personally constructed bomb-shelter in his garden. During recent years he has engaged in handicrafts as a hobby, being an expert in bookbinding and wax and clay modeling as well as a good amateur painter. A shy, modest man, he lives quietly: "I have no desire for personal publicity," he informed the editors of this book.

Though Freeman wrote one other non-fiction book—*Social Decay and Regeneration,* a biologico-sociological study—and one novel (his first) without crime elements, it is as a scientific detective story writer that he is primarily known. Both his medical training and experience and his acquaintance with prison routine have stood him in good stead. Dr. John Thorndyke, protagonist of all his detective stories, whom Christopher Morley has called "the most carefully established crime savant since Sherlock Holmes," is a thorough scientist, based, like Doyle's character, on a former instructor of the author; in Freeman's case a professor of medical jurisprudence. "Thorndyke's material," his author writes, "is real, authentic material, and is recognized as such by the lawyers and men of science who are among my most constant readers." Freeman maintains a laboratory in which he carefully works out every experiment described in his fiction, and the interest in a Thorndyke story is not in discovery of the criminal so much as in the *means* used to discover and convict him. For this reason, his following is perhaps greatest among the more intellectual enthusiasts for this type of fiction. To these, the Thorndyke stories are not only intensely interesting but often valuable as well. As Freeman himself has remarked: "In each book, a particular problem in medical jurisprudence is worked out, and although the cases are fictitious, the facts are real facts and in many cases contribute new matter to the science." In several instances the methods evolved and described in the stories have been put into actual, later use by the police.

Among contemporary practitioners of the detective story, Freeman is the undoubted international *doyen* of the scientific division.

PRINCIPAL WORKS: *Non-Fiction*—Travels and Life in Ashanti and Jaman, 1898; Social Decay and Regeneration, 1921. *Fiction*—The Golden Pool, 1905; The Red Thumb Mark, 1907; John Thorndyke's Cases, 1909; The Eye of Osiris, 1911; The Mystery of 31 New Inn, 1912; The Singing Bone, 1912; Unwilling Adventurer, 1913; The Uttermost Farthing, 1913; A Silent Witness, 1914; The Exploits of Danby Croker, 1916; The Great Portrait Mystery, 1918; Helen Vardon's Confession, 1922; The Cat's Eye, 1923; The Mystery of Angelina Freed, 1923; The Shadow of the Wolf, 1923; Dr. Thorndyke's Case Book, 1923; The Blue Scarab, 1924; The Puzzle Lock, 1925; The D'Arblay Mystery, 1926; A Certain Dr. Thorndyke, 1927; The Surprising Experience of Mr. Shuttlebury Cobb, 1927; The Magic Casket, 1927; Flighty Phyllis, 1928; As a Thief in the Night, 1928; Famous Cases of Dr. Thorndyke, 1929; Mr. Pottermack's Oversight, 1930; Pontifex, Son and Thorndyke, 1931; The Thorndyke Omnibus, 1931; Dr. Thorndyke's Discovery, 1932; When Rogues Fall Out, 1932; The Great Platinum Robbery, 1933; Dr. Thorndike Intervenes, 1933; For the Defense: Dr. Thorndyke, 1934; The Penrose Mystery, 1936; Death at the Inn, 1937. The Stoneware Monkey, 1939; Mr. Polton Explains, 1941; The Unconscious Witness, 1942.

ABOUT: Haycraft, H. Murder for Pleasure: The Life and Times of the Detective Story; Thompson, H. D. Masters of Mystery; Ward, A. C. Aspects of the Modern Short Story.

FRENCH, ALICE. See "AMERICAN AUTHORS: 1600-1900"

*FRENSSEN, GUSTAV (October 19, 1863-   ), German novelist and playwright, was born in Barlt, a little village in which his family had dwelt for five hundred years, on the western coast of Schleswig-Holstein. Friedrich Hebbel, Theodor Storm, and Klaus Groth spent their youth in the same district of Ditmarschen. His father, a joiner, managed with difficulty to send him to a nearby Latin school, wishing him to become a minister of the Lutheran church. After training at the universities of Tübingen and Berlin, and passing his state examinations at Kiel, Frenssen at twenty-seven became pastor at Hemme, thirty miles from Barlt. In that year he married the youngest daughter of Lehrers Walter in Meldorf. The young minister before long was famous all over Germany as a preacher and writer of sermons.

N. Yontoff

In 1896, when Frenssen was thirty-three, *The Sand Countess,* his first novel appeared, followed in 1898 by *The Three Comrades.* The next year he published the first of his three volumes of *Village Sermons* (1899-1902). With the almost unprecedented success of *Jörn Uhl* (1901), which had an immediate sale of 216,000 copies (by 1937 it had sold 428,000 copies), Frenssen in order to write resigned his pastorate, but not his ministry in the broad sense of the word. Moving to a beautiful wooded bluff in Blankenese, overlooking the busy harbor traffic of Hamburg, he devoted himself to describing the simple peasantry of his native region, descendants of the ancient Frisians and Saxons. During the First World War he returned to the thatched cottage of his parents in Barlt, where he

* Died 1945.

has lived ever since. His second and, according to some critics, his last great novel, was *Holyland* (1906), for which he received an honorary doctorate from the University of Heidelberg.

Frenssen is called "the novelist of Schleswig-Holstein," whose color and atmosphere he has portrayed with imagination and fidelity. His hard-working toilers of the barren soil are as monumental as Millet figures. "Frenssen has a natural talent of a peculiarly epic quality. . . . What he lacks is judgment or what may be called taste—not a very popular word in Germany—an artistic discrimination and conscience, which he and his admirers repudiated as forming part of the pretentious claims of Berlin and its literary world," says Arthur Eloesser. Frenssen's novels form a part of the *Heimatkunst* or regional movement in German literature of the early twentieth century, marking a reaction from both naturalism and decadent neo-Romanticism. While Frenssen has often been criticized for his platitudinous, didactic tendencies and his diffuse, careless style, his warmth, energy, and optimism give his books a charm which won him tremendous popularity in Germany, where they are still a household commodity.

PRINCIPAL WORKS AVAILABLE IN ENGLISH TRANSLATION: Jörn Uhl, 1905; Holyland, 1906; The Three Comrades, 1907; Peter Moor's Journey to South-West Africa: A Narrative of the German Campaign, 1908; Klaus Hinrich Baas: The Story of a Self-Made Man, 1911; Village Sermons of a Novelist, 1924; The Anvil (British title: Otto Babendiek) 1930; The Pastor of Poggsee, 1931.

ABOUT: Alberts, W. Gustav Frenssen; Eloesser, A. Modern German Literature; Florer, W. W. German Liberty Authors; Francke, K. (ed.). The German Classics; Hauser, O. Gustav Frenssen; Johnsen, W. Gustav Frenssen; Numsen, N. Gustav Frenssen.

FREUCHEN, PETER (1886-), Danish

autobiographer and travel writer, writes (in English): "I am just a writer from

a small country, and this will mark people all the time. I used to be an Arctic explorer and managed a station in the northernmost house in the world for many years. Also I traveled and explored new countries as long as such were to be found. Unfortunately, I froze my left leg off, and that turned me into a writer. And as I had started, I could never stop again.

"To write I had quite some experience, having stayed with Eskimos for years and shared their life, as we were cut out from civilization during the last war. Next, I was terribly sorry not to be able to use what knowledge I had collected about traveling and hunting in the Arctic, so I put it in writing. And as I had seen much of the ways human beings act, I made up my mind to do novels to make readers swallow it. Nothing is worse than diaries to the public. But if you are careful never to give them what you don't know about, and never try to fake them, they will trust you and learn from your books just as well.

"I wrote some novels and they caught on. Fourteen languages have been used for translations of my books, which gave me a thrill more than money. I also had the pleasure of going to Hollywood and seeing a novel of mine turn into a picture [*Eskimo*, 1932]. That taught me much, and I will stay a lover of the movies as a way of getting in touch with people. I also tried a play—also dealing with Eskimos—and it had quite a success in Denmark, Norway, Finland, and Germany. Then turned up Mr. Hitler, and down went my play in Germany. So did all my books in his countries.

"I expect to have about ten books to write yet. I planned to do all the Eskimo spirit as a token of the world's people put in a nutshell (that means the immense Arctic coast). I wrote about the Eskimos' contacting the Mounted Police in Canada. I wrote about them trying to live alone away from civilization. In my novel *Ivalu* (which I value most) I related my own experience with my beloved little Eskimo wife, Navarana. At the time being I work on a huge novel about the first Danes coming to Greenland. And then I will tell about how civilization did good for Eskimos, as it did for all primitive people. This will be my next book. Just wait. I also wrote books about traveling and exploring. I used to be a surveyor, but my time was when the dog sledge was the instrument to get along. Two autobiographical books, *Arctic Adventure* and *It's All Adventure*, made me great pleasure. Later on I traveled in Siberia and did a book about this; it is a good book all right, but editors are scared that I am too much in favor of the Soviet Government, the Bolsheviks are sore that I criticized too much. I just told what I saw as I saw it.

"My life as an explorer was connected with my late friend Knud Rasmussen, a most distinguished Danish explorer, with whom I was partner and friend from 1910 until his death in 1933. I wrote a book about him too.

"After I quit staying constantly in Greenland—my wife Navarana passed away on an expedition in 1921— I settled down in Denmark and bought me a little island, Enhoje, from where I wrote my books and from where I traveled to North and South. I spend much time lecturing. I like to lecture, and lectured all over Denmark and the whole of Scandinavia, Germany (during the republic), England, and the United States. I visited South America once, flying round to see the difference from the Arctic, where I had lived for so many years. Wonderful, and I did a book about the voyage, but just in Danish and Portuguese (for Brazil).

"And now I think I have no more to tell. Times here in Denmark are hard, but I have my wife, Magdalene, and my daughter, Pipaluk [half-Eskimo; her brother could not endure European life and had to be sent back to Greenland], who found the most understanding mother in Magdalene and is educated in Denmark. What will come next nobody knows at the time being. But I will keep on writing and try to give my readers my true opinion on things and people. I really believe that even if I have been far away from the center of the world, I might have picked something to show how wonderful the world is—even in our days. In fact I got a touch of something very few writers sense: the desire for company and the demand to talk and tell and listen. That is what I write about."

* * *

Although a member of many learned societies, endowed with many honors, Peter Freuchen remains the huge six-foot-six, red-bearded giant who left a medical school at twenty to go to the Arctic—absent-minded, implusive, childlike, a warm-hearted, simple bear of a man. It is not generally known that he is of Jewish descent, though he seems an incarnation of the ancient Vikings. A long-time Social Democrat, he was for many years a contributor to *Politiken*, the famous Copenhagen newspaper, and for some time also edited a Danish magazine financed by the family of his present wife, heiress to a great fortune made from oleomargarine. His "unconscious eloquence," as much as his strange life, has made him one of the most attractive and likable of present-day travel writers. His letter above was written before the Nazi occupation of Denmark. No later information has been received from or about him.

AVAILABLE IN ENGLISH: Eskimo, 1931; Sea Tyrant (novel) 1932; Ivalu (novel) 1935; Arctic Adventures, 1935; It's All Adventure, 1938.

ABOUT: Freuchen, P. Arctic Adventures, It's All Adventure; Literary Digest April 4, 1936; Newsweek April 4, 1936; Time July 4, 1938.

FREUD, SIGMUND (May 16, 1856-September 23, 1939), Austrian psychologist and founder of psychoanalysis, was born at Freiburg, Moravia, but was taken to Vienna at four and grew up there. His father was a merchant; the Freud family were middle-class Jews. That was no barrier to his educational advancement in the nineteenth century, and he received his  M.D. from the University of Vienna in 1881. However, though he had studied medicine his interests lay outside practice, in the field of general science; botany and chemistry both claimed his attention more than did his medical studies. From 1876 to 1882 he worked in the Physiological Institute under Brücke, and on his obtaining his degree he was appointed demonstrator there. He also became an assistant physician at the great Vienna hospital, the *Allgemeine Krankenhaus,* and his experiences there first led him to study neuropathology. He enrolled in the Institute for Cerebral Anatomy, and in 1885 he went to Paris, to study at the university and also at the Salpetrière under the famous Charcot. By this time he was groping his way toward the system of treatment and philosophy with which his name will always be associated. His colleague, Dr. Breuer, had interested him the year before in the treatment of hysteria by hypnosis. He returned to Vienna, to become lecturer on neuropathology at the university, in 1886. As his psychological theories developed, they met with great resistance from the orthodox authorities; nevertheless he was appointed "professor extraordinary" of neurology at the university in 1902. (In 1920 he became full professor, and so remained until the Anschluss in 1938.)

His first book to develop the systematized theory of psychoanalysis was the *Traümdeutung (Interpretation of Dreams),* in 1900. About 1902 his work began to attract attention outside of Vienna, and in 1909 he was invited by G. Stanley Hall to visit and lecture at Clark University, which conferred an honorary LL.D. on him. He had long ago broken with Breuer, who continued to use hypnotism as a means of ascertaining the underlying causes of hysteria and its allied complexes. Psychoanalysis did not spring full-fledged from Freud's mind, like Minerva from Jove's forehead, but was gradually evolved, altered, and amended through the years. By the time (approximately the end of the World War) when it had become internationally known, it was a very different thing from the first simplified and tentative elucidations of the early 1900's. It had developed an unfortunately formidable vocabulary, and had already given birth to "heresies" like those of Jung and Adler.

It had also become a world movement, with disciples in every country, an enormous literature, and International Congresses, beginning in 1908. Though Vienna was still the recognized home of the movement, Freud himself had long ceased to make personal analyses, and confined himself to writing, to editing and directing four psychoanalytical journals (including the *International Journal of Psychoanalysis*), and to his teaching post in the university.

It is impossible in brief compass to give a satisfactory account of psychoanalytical theory. Briefly, it posits the existence in us of a subconscious mind, which retains memories, impressions, and experiences forgotten by the conscious mind. These appear in dreams, slips of the tongue, and similar "purposeless activities," and they cause in us the "psychic knots" which are known as complexes, and which express themselves in sexual and social inadequacies and disturbances, neuroses, and even psychoses. Freud also takes for granted two antagonistic impulses, existent from birth—the self-centered and destructive, and the outward-going and constructive, which he called sexual. Had he used the word "social," which is just as descriptive, he would have avoided reams of controversy and abuse. The interrelation of these impulses leads to what is called "ambivalence"—co-existing love and hatred of the same object. Among the commonest of complexes is the Oedipus complex in men and the Electra complex in women—unconscious attachment to the parent of the opposite sex, with accompanying unconscious hatred and jealousy of the parent of the same sex. The therapeutic method of psychoanalysis consists in leading the patient gradually to externalize and make conscious his hidden and "forgotten" complexes, transferring to the analyst the emotions he felt originally for, perhaps, his father or mother. The task of the analyst is then to "break the transference" and restore the patient to a conscious realization of the meaning of his neuroses and their consequent dissolvement. The million objections and questions which may be aroused by this very superficial and inadequate exposition will find their answers in the published works of Freud and his disciples, chief of whom in England and America at present are Ernest Jones of London, A. A. Brill of New York, and Karl F. Menninger of Topeka.

In any event, by 1930, when he celebrated his seventieth birthday, Sigmund Freud was a figure of world fame, by many coupled with Alfred Einstein, another German Jew, as the two greatest men of their time. Even his enemies (and they have been many) never questioned the epoch-making nature of his theory. Psychoanalysis had by that time grown to be much more than a way of curing neurotics. It had had immense repercussions on anthropology, art, the study of religion, and literature. It had affected schools of thought, political and religious theories, and artistic movements. It was behind "stream-of-consciousness novels," the revolutionary writing of James Joyce and Gertrude Stein, surrealist paintings, atonal music. It has even been held that there are Freudian elements in Nazi philosophy— surely a strange irony if true. At seventy, Freud was awarded the Goethe Prize in Frankfurt, and given the freedom of the city of Vienna. He had lived in the same house in Vienna for half a century; it housed also his laboratory, his publishing business, and the international offices of the psychoanalytical society. He had been married in 1886; his wife, Martha, and their three sons and three daughters were still with him. He himself had come very near death from cancer of the jaw; his lower jaw had to be excised and his gray beard hid the artificial replacement. He was an old man who, if still attacked venomously on half a dozen fronts, yet was reverenced and honored by the learned associations of the world.

In 1938, when the Nazis conducted their "bloodless invasion" of Austria and the Austrian Republic ceased to exist, Freud was so ill that his family did not tell him the truth of events. It took all the persuasions of his "Aryan" disciples to keep the Nazis from arresting him and throwing him from his sick-bed into a concentration camp. His books were burned, his collections seized and destroyed. His publishing house was confiscated and all his property lost. Palestine offered him a refuge but it was too far away for a man who had been Viennese of the Viennese, and who had shed, a lifetime ago, any affiliation with the Jewish or any other religion. He applied for a visa to Holland but it was refused. His passport was seized and not returned for weeks. Finally, by herculean effort of his associates, he was given permission to go to England. He reached there in June, 1938, and at once made application for British citizenship. "How peaceful it is!" he murmured. "I hope they will let me stay." For three months he had not left his house in Vienna, dreading the insults thrown at every Jew.

His wife, daughter, and nephew, and two old servants accompanied him; his son, an architect, had preceded him to London. He had rescued the manuscript of the book on which he had been working—his last book, *Moses and Monotheism*. In London he was received with honor. Since he was too ill to leave his home except in a wheelchair, by an almost unprecedented action the charter-book of the Royal Society was brought to him to sign. He was happy for the year still before him, as happy as a man can be who has lost nearly everything. Then came another operation, from which the eighty-three-year-old man did not recover. By his wish, he was cremated quietly without a public funeral.

It is hardly possible to evaluate Freud as a writer, since books were to him merely a means of exposition of his theories. His style was not simple, though it was far less involved than that of some of his followers, whose jargon makes their work almost unreadable. Even his more "popular" works, like *Totem and Taboo, The Future of an Illusion,* and *Moses and Monotheism,* take for granted a preliminary acquaintance with their premises. He was primarily a scientist, not a literary stylist. Perhaps his chief contribution to literature is not in anything he himself wrote, but in the influence of all his writings and teachings on the writing of authors who were young or unborn when he gave to the world his theory of psychoanalysis.

WORKS AVAILABLE IN ENGLISH: The Interpretation of Dreams, 1913; The Psychopathology of Everyday Life, 1914; On Dreams, 1914; Wit and Its Relation to the Unconscious, 1916; Delusion and Dream, 1917; Totem and Taboo, 1918; Dream Psychology, 1920; A General Introduction to Psychoanalysis, 1920; Beyond the Pleasure Principle, 1922; Group Psychology and the Analysis of the Ego, 1922; Collected Papers, 1924-25;

The Ego and the Id, 1927; The Problems of Lay Analyses, 1927; The Future of an Illusion, 1928; Civilization and Its Discontents, 1930; New Introductory Lectures on Psychoanalysis, 1933; Autobiography (in England: An Autobiographical Study) 1935; Inhibitions, Symptoms, and Anxiety, 1936; The Problem of Anxiety, 1936; The Basic Writings of Sigmund Freud (ed. by A. A. Brill) 1938; General Selection From the Works of Sigmund Freud (ed. by J. Rickman) 1938; Moses and Monotheism, 1939.

ABOUT: Belgion, M. Our Present Philosophy of Life; Eastman, M. Heroes I Have Known; Freud, S. Autobiography; Jastrow, J. The House That Freud Built; Low, B. Psychoanalysis; McDougall, W. Psychoanalysis and Social Psychology; Mann, T. Freud, Goethe, Wagner; Osbert, R. Freud and Marx; Reik, T. From Thirty Years With Freud; Wittels, F. Freud and His Time, Sigmund Freud; Zweig, S. Mental Healers; American Journal of Psychology October 1933; Annales Politiques et Littéraires March 23, 1936, October 10, 1939; Christian Century May 20, 1936; Fortnightly Review October 1938; Mercure de France April 1, May 1, July 15, 1938; Nation May 20, 1936; Nature July 9, 1938; New Statesman and Nation September 30, 1939; Psychological Review September 1933; Saturday Review of Literature July 25, 1936; September 3, 1938; Science September 30, 1939; Spectator September 29, 1939; Virginia Quarterly Review October 1934.

"FROME, DAVID." See BROWN, Z. J.

FROST, ROBERT (March 26, 1875*-), American poet, was born in San Francisco, the son of a New England father, William Prescott Frost, and a Scottish mother, Margaret (Moodie) Frost. That his father was a Southern sympathizer, however, is indicated by the son's given name, Robert Lee. He was active in San Francisco politics, but he died when the boy  was ten, and the mother (a teacher) moved back with him to New England, to Lawrence, Mass. It was in high school there that he learned—appropriately—from Virgil that he was a poet. He tried a year at Dartmouth, but it was too academic for his taste, so he went to work as a bobbin-boy in a Lawrence mill. At twenty he married Eleanor Miriam White, who remained his critic and his basic inspiration until her death in 1938. They had four daughters, of whom one has died.

In 1897 Frost tried college again—this time Harvard—and stuck it out for two years. He never received a regular degree, but has honorary ones from sixteen colleges, including the two at which he was a stu-

* Correction: Year of birth, 1874.

dent. He tried his hand at many trades— as a country school teacher, a cobbler, a small town editor (on the weekly Lawrence *Sentinel*), and finally a farmer. He retired to almost absolute isolation on a farm near Derry, N.H., and stayed there for eleven years. His only published work was a few poems in the *Independent*. The farm failed, and he was at loose ends again. His wife made "the only romantic remark of her life" —"Let's go to England and live under thatch." They sailed in 1912, and settled in a cottage in Beaconsfield.

There Frost's real career began. He met other poets—Rupert Brooke, Lascelles Abercrombie, Wilfrid Gibson, Edward Thomas— and he secured publication of his first book, *A Boy's Will*. *North of Boston* followed it the next year. The stone rejected by the American builder proved to be the foundation of the temple. He returned to the United States in 1915 to find himself famous.

Since then his life has been a succession of honors. He was "poet in residence" at Amherst and the University of Michigan, and he is now Emerson Professor of Poetry at Harvard. In between times he made futile attempts to escape from academic responsibilities on farms in New Hampshire and Vermont. He still has a farm at South Shaftsbury, Vt., though for most of the year he has to live in Boston. He lectures every summer at the Breadloaf School at Middlebury College, a school he helped to found in 1920. He received the Pulitzer Prize for poetry three times, in 1924, 1931, and 1937; the Loines Prize in 1931, the Mark Twain Medal in 1937, the gold medal of the American Academy of Arts and Letters in 1938, and the Poetry Society of America medal in 1941.

And he has remained essentially just what he was when he farmed in New Hampshire or tramped the Carolinas looking for work. Louis Untermeyer has described him: the face "carved out of native granite," the "pale blue but quizzical eyes, the quickly bantering smile and the sensual bee-stung underlip, . . . a stubborn scholar's face masking the irrepressible poet's." He still slouches in his chair, drawls his words in his "creaking, cranky voice," possesses "the mannerisms of a Yankee hired man." Elizabeth Shepley Sergeant added to the picture: "eyes colored like juniper, hair shaded like gray bark, eyebrows of a rogue, lips of a caustic wit."

Frost has been compared with Wordsworth, but he is far less bloodless. There is no doubt that he is, as Gorham B. Munson put it, "the purest classical poet of America today," or that he is in the great tradition. Half Scottish, and born in California, he is nevertheless the authentic voice of New England, the last blossom of its flowering: his is, to quote Carl Van Doren, "the sound of a Yankee voice." His characteristic forms are "conversation pieces, aphoristic verses, autobiographical riddles, blank-verse "novels," interspersed with pure lyrics. He himself says that to him "the thing that art does for life is to clip it, to strip it to form": a poem, to him "begins in delight and ends in wisdom," C. Henry Warren called his verse "as direct and unmoral as the song of a bird." The only dissenting word in the long chronicle of adulation is Isidor Schneider's; even he granted that Frost is a great poet, but he considered him "singularly out of touch with his time, . . . weakest in ideas." Frost does not pretend to be a philosopher, except by implication; and what philosophy he has is a mingling of traditional New England individualism and Stoic renunciation. But his work "partakes of the dignity and serenity of the hills among which much of his life has been passed." It is "a book of people, not merely a translation of backgrounds," "teasing and twisting new values out of old commonplaces."

Frost does not force himself to write, preferring to wait until he can write at his best. "It takes me two days to unscrew and two to screw up again," he says. He does not believe in fancy esthetics. "A poem," he explains, "begins with a lump in the throat; a homesickness or a lovesickness. It is a reaching-out toward expression; an effort to find fulfilment. A complete poem is one where an emotion has found its thought and the thought has found the words."

PRINCIPAL WORKS: A Boy's Will, 1913; North of Boston, 1914; Mountain Interval, 1916; New Hampshire, 1923; West-Running Brook, 1928; A Way Out (play) 1929; The Lovely Shall Be Choosers, 1929; Collected Poems, 1930 and 1939; The Lone Striker, 1933; A Further Range, 1936; From Snow to Snow, 1936; The Witness Tree, 1942.

ABOUT: Boynton, P. H. Some Contemporary Americans; Brooks, Van W. New England: Indian Summer; Coffin, R. P. T. New Poetry of New England: Frost and Robinson; Lowell, A. Tendencies in Modern American Poetry; Munson, G. B. Robert Frost; Squire, J. C. Contemporary American Authors; Thornton, R. (ed.). Recognition of Robert Frost: Twenty-Fifth Anniversary; Untermeyer, L. From Another World; Van Doren, C. & M. American and British Literature Since 1890; American Literature November 1937; American Review March 1924; American Scholar March 1936; Bookman December 1926, July 1930; Bookman (London) January 1931; Commonweal January 13, 1932; English Journal October 1927; Fortnightly Review February 1931, May 1940; London Mercury December 1925; Nation January 28, 1931; New England Quarterly June 1937; New Republic September 30, 1925; Poet Lore December 1929; Poetry December 1924, July 1939; Saturday Review of Literature March 28, 1925, January 17, 1931, December 28, 1935, February 15, 1936, April 10, 1937, January 1, 1938; Sewanee Review July 1940; Time May 15, 1939; Virginia Quarterly Review July 1925; Yale Review March 1934.

FRY, ROGER ELLIOT (1866-September 9, 1934), English art critic and painter, informed the compilers of this work shortly

before his death: "Roger Fry, the son of the late Sir Edward Fry, Lord Justice of Appeal, was born in London. After taking an honors degree in natural science at King's College, Cambridge, he decided to devote himself to art, and studied in the London studio of Francis Bate for some years, before going to Paris. During the 'nineties of last century he was a member of the New English Art Club. This was the home of Impressionism in England. Impressionism was still regarded at that time as a dangerous foreign innovation. To some extent he reacted against Impressionist practice and increasingly sought for direction in the works of the older masters, particularly of the Italian school.

"In 1899 he published his first book. This was on Giovanni Bellini (now out of print) and this, having earned him a certain reputation as an authority on the subject, led, in the early years of the present century, to his being appointed curator of paintings of the Metropolitan Museum of Art in New York. The president of the board of trustees was the late J. Pierpont Morgan. As frequently happens in museums, a difference of opinion arose between the trustees and the curator regarding the policy of the museum, which, after a few years, led to the termination of his connection, and his return to Europe.

"About this time [1905] he produced an annotated and critical edition of Sir Joshua Reynolds' *Discourses*. He became much interested in the *Burlington Magazine*—an interest which has been continued up to the present date.

"In 1911 he organized the first exhibition of Twentieth Century French art. Up to that time the works of Cézanne, Van Gogh, and Gauguin, not to mention Matisse and Picasso, were practically unknown to the English public. For the purpose of exhibition he gave to this group the name of "Post-Impressionists." The fact that he had hitherto been regarded mainly as an authority on early Italian art, and now came forward to defend what seemed extravagantly revolutionary, was something of a shock to the British public, but increasing familiarity with the work of these masters has made his attitude appear less paradoxical.

"He has written several books of essays on aesthetic questions, notably *Vision and Design* and *Transformations*. He has also written short studies on *Flemish Art* and *Characteristics of French Art* besides monographs on Cézanne and Henri Matisse. His only excursion into more general literature consists of a book of his impressions of Spain, called *A Sampler of Castille*.

"In the current year [1933] he has been appointed Slade Professor of Fine Arts at Cambridge University."

* * *

As a painter Roger Fry was hampered rather than helped by his great learning. He lacked feeling, and attained to no more than a cold correctness. As a critic he was a pioneer in the attempt to appraise painting as a self-contained activity, and readily drew on his knowledge of the past to reinforce arguments on the art of today. A logical and forceful lecturer, he accomplished the remarkable feat of filling the large Queen's Hall, London, for two successive nights, to hear his discourses on British art. He went back to first principles, and may be said to have done more than any other man in the re-orientation of British taste. D. S. MacColl wrote of his "intent gaze" and his "shock of hair above a well-shaped forehead." E. M. Forster wrote that he was "charming, polite, courageous and gay in his private life; he was generous and energetic; he was always helping people, especially the young and obscure . . . he believed in reason . . . rejected authority, mistrusted intuition."

He married Helen Combe in 1896 and had one son and one daughter. He was still the incumbent of the State Chair when he died at the age of sixty-eight, as the result of injuries received in a fall.

PRINCIPAL WORKS: Giovanni Bellini, 1899; Edition of Reynolds' Discourses, 1905; Vision and

Design, 1920; A Sampler of Castile, 1923; Transformations, 1926; Cézanne: A Study of his Development, 1927; The Arts of Painting and Sculpture, 1932; Reflections on British Painting, 1934; Last Lectures, 1939.

ABOUT: Forster, E. M. Abinger Harvest; Hannay, H. Roger Fry and Other Essays; Laver, J. Portraits in Oil and Vinegar; Woolf, V. Roger Fry: A Biography; Burlington Magazine, October and November, 1934; Saturday Review of Literature October 12, December 7, 1940; The Times (London) September 10, 11 & 12, 1934.

FUESS, CLAUDE MOORE (January 12, 1885-), American biographer and educator, was born in Waterville, N.Y., the

Nation-Wide

son of Louis Philip Fuess and Helen Augusta (Moore) Fuess, and graduated from the local high school at sixteen. In 1905 he received his B.A. degree from Amherst College, the *alma mater* of Calvin Coolidge, a biography of whom Fuess published thirty-five years later. Fuess received his master's degree from Columbia in 1906, and two years later went to Andover, Mass., to become instructor in English and editor of the *Phillips Bulletin* of the long-established boys' school, Phillips Andover Academy. He remained here a quarter-century (1908-33) in those capacities and as Elizabeth Milbank Anderson Foundation professor of English (from 1928). Since 1933 Fuess has been headmaster of the academy.

In 1912 Fuess fulfilled the requirements for a Ph.D. at Columbia and published his thesis, *Byron as a Satirist in Verse.* In 1917 he published a history of Phillips Andover as *An Old New England School,* and followed it up two years later with histories of the academy and of the town of Andover in the First World War. He took an active part himself, notably as civilian chief of the Personnel Division, Camp Joseph E. Johnston, Jacksonville, Fla., from April to September 1918, and major in the Quartermasters' Corps till December. Previously he had served as New England secretary of the American Red Cross fund drive in 1917, and member of the Legal Advisory Board of Selective Service.

After the alarums and excursions of war, Fuess returned to Andover to write, edit, and compile an astonishing array of books, from productions of local pride such as *All For Andover, The Andover Way,* and *Men of Andover,* to anthologies of verse (*Selec-*

tions From the Victorian Poets and *A Little Book of Familiar Verse*), and long, painstakingly documented biographies such as the *Life of Caleb Cushing,* of Newburyport, Mass.; *Daniel Webster,* his *magnum opus; Carl Schurz;* and a shorter, more popularized account of *Rufus Choate. Calvin Coolidge: Man From Vermont* (1940), written as it is from the New England point of view, is understandably a friendlier account of the Yankee president than the more objective conception of the man found in the biography by the Kansan, William Allen White. His fellow-historians, such as Henry Steele Commager and Allan Nevins, have been appreciative in reviewing books by Dr. Fuess.

Claude Fuess is a Republican, a Presbyterian, was president of the New England Association of Teachers of English of 1927-28 and national president of Alpha Delta Phi from 1937 to 1939; has contributed to the *Dictionary of American Biography,* and is a member of numerous social clubs and learned societies. Amherst, Columbia, Dartmouth, Yale, and Princeton have honored him with the degree of Litt.D., and Williams varied the list with an L.H.D. He married Elizabeth Cushing Goodhue of Andover in June 1911, and twenty-four years later their son, John Cushing Fuess, graduated from Harvard. The family divides its time between Andover and Dublin, N.H.

PRINCIPAL WORKS: Byron as a Satirist in Verse, 1912; An Old New England School, 1917; Phillips Academy, Andover, in the Great War, 1919; The Town of Andover, Mass., in the World War, 1921; The Life of Caleb Cushing, 1923; All for Andover, 1925; The American Legion in Massachusetts, 1925; The Andover Way, 1926; Peter Had Courage, 1927; Rufus Choate, 1927; Men of Andover, 1928; Daniel Webster, 1930; Carl Schurz, 1932; Amherst: Story of a New England College, 1935; Creed of a Schoolmaster, 1939; Calvin Coolidge: The Man From Vermont, 1940. Editor—Narrative Poems, 1908; Milton's Minor Poems, 1913; English Essays, 1914; Selected English Letters, 1914; Selected Short Stories, 1914; A High School Spelling Book, 1915; A Little Book of Familiar Verse, 1922; Selections From the Victorian Poets, 1922; Good Writing, 1923; Amherst Memorial Volume, 1926; Practical Précis Writing, 1929; History of Essex County, Mass., 1935.

ABOUT: Fuess, C. M. Creed of a Schoolmaster.

FULLER, HENRY BLAKE (January 9, 1857-July 28, 1929), American novelist, critic, and satirist, was born in Chicago, the son of George Wood Fuller, a bank cashier whose father was a cousin of the Transcendentalist intellectual Margaret Fuller, and Josephine (Sanford) Fuller. After his graduation from the Chicago

High School and an interlude of bank work, came the first of his European pilgrimages, undertaken, presumably, for the study of music and architecture. Fuller, however, pursued neither art seriously. He could play the 'cello and organ and improvised freely on the piano.

Under the pseudonym "Stanton Page" he wrote his first book, *The Chevalier of Pensieri-Vani,* a crisply witty novel laid in Italy; it became a "sensation of the 'nineties" and ran to at least five editions. *The Chatelaine of La Trinité,* a sequel (in manner only), was less highly praised; and the third, *The Last Refuge,* was veritably ignored. Fuller's critics are considerably divided on his ability to maintain his original "high." But Carl Van Vechten calls *The Chatelaine* "quite as charming and distinguished" as *The Chevalier,* and trusts. that "the future will do more justice to" *The Last Refuge.* Of the two Chicago novels that interrupted this Continental "series," *Cliff-Dwellers* was less successful than *With the Procession.*

Meanwhile Fuller had privately printed *The New Flag,* a volume of belligerently satiric verses directed at President McKinley and numerous other political figures. His later *Lines Long and Short,* profiles in free verse, was hardly more than an experiment.

In 1901 and 1902 the book review section of the Chicago *Evening Post* was, in part, his achievement; and in 1912 and 1913 the editorial page of the Chicago *Record-Herald* bore the Fuller mark. His valued services to Harriet Monroe's *Poetry: A Magazine of Verse,* from its founding in 1912 until the time of his death, included reviewing, proof-reading, and dummy-pasting. He was a member of the Little Room, a group of Chicago's artistic *élite,* among whom were several of *Poetry's* guardian angels.

After a long hiatus in the writing of books, Fuller completed, during the last six months of his life, a volume of reflective philosophy and travel called *Gardens of This World;* and a semi-successful attempt to satirize the motion picture industry's overuse of the "modern generation" theme, published posthumously as *Not on the Screen.*

Despite Fuller's early familiarity with Europe, he was only moderately cosmopolitan. He never left the Midwest, after his return in 1896, save for a brief trip abroad in 1924. Yet Carl Van Vechten sees a strong parallel between Fuller and Henry James. "His *genre,*" he remarks, "is the miniature. In the words of one of his characters it may justifiably be said of him that he combines 'the fortunate moment and the felicitous hand.'"

PRINCIPAL WORKS: The Chevalier of Pensieri-Vani, 1890; The Chatelaine of La Trinité, 1892; The Cliff-Dwellers, 1893; With the Procession, 1895; From the Other Side: Stories of Transatlantic Travel, 1898; The New Flag, 1899; The Last Refuge: A Sicilian Romance, 1900; Lines Long and Short, 1917; Gardens of This World, 1929; Not on the Screen, 1930.

ABOUT: Garland, H. Roadside Meetings; Griffin, C. M. Henry Blake Fuller; Monroe, H. A Poet's Life; Morgan, A. Tributes to Henry B. from Friends; Van Vechten, C. Excavations; New Republic August 21, 1929; New York Times July 29 and August 1, 1929.

FÜLÖP-MÜLLER, RENÉ (March 17, 1891-), Rumanian biographer and political writer, writes: "I was born in the city of Caransebes, which at that time belonged to Hungary [now to Rumania]. I spent my youth at this place, which is situated at a point where four countries meet: Rumania, Serbia, Hungary, and the Turkish island of Ada Kaleh in the

Danube. My father was a pharmacist and wanted me to study pharmacy. But at the age of fourteen I ran away from home, for I planned to write a big work, called *Thaumaturgy.* Traveling through the Balkans, I led the life of a vagabond. When I arrived at Vienna I was deprived of all means and had to pass my nights in the open on the benches of the *Ringstrasse.* I experienced great poverty, and wrote my first article to make a living. In the Viennese coffee-houses I came into contact with literary people, and later on in Paris I became part of the literary circle of the *Closerie des Lilas.*

"After having finished my high school education I studied at the Universities of Kolozsvar, Vienna, Lausanne, and Paris, taking courses in medicine, psychiatry, pharmacy, chemistry, and philosophy. In Switzerland I became a student of the renowned Professor August Forel at Ivorne, and in Paris the world-famous Professor Babinsky taught me psychiatry at the Salpetrière.

"At the outbreak of the First World War I was in Vienna, where I joined the sanitary staff of the army. I served in an auxiliary first aid position at the Russian front in Galicia, and was later on entrusted with directing an adventurous transport of cholera patients to Hungary.

"Keenly interested in the intellectual-political development of the post-war period, I attended the Conference of Geneva, where the economic reconstruction of Europe was planned, and later on I took an active part in the first Peace Congress. Here I met the leading spiritual creators of a Europe between world wars. As journalist and travel editor I spent two years in Russia, and went to Asia, Africa, and the United States. I also experienced the quaint life of holy Mount Athos, the monks' republic near Greece.

"The results of all these experiences, voyages, and studies is a number of books, translated into many languages, articles, and plays. My latest book, *Triumph Over Pain,* is the first volume of a triology which deals with the problems of pain, insanity, and death. The two other volumes, *Power of Insanity* and *Struggle Against Death,* are in preparation. Also in preparation is an autobiography, entitled *Adam, Where Art Thou?* With this book I shall try to give a synthesis of personal and super-personal, by showing the fate of a man who lives his life at the time of intellectual and political change from the individualistic to the de-individualized twentieth century."

* * *

Fülöp-Müller is on his father's side of Huguenot descent; his mother was a Macedonian. After his early experience at Vienna, his parents rescued him from a hospital where he had been sent after his health collapsed, and took him home. His precious manuscript on thaumaturgy he lost in a tramway. He has a degree in pharmaceutical chemistry, has edited the posthumous works of Tolstoy and Dostoievsky, and has written a book on the Russian theatre with Dr. Josef Gregor, curator of the Vienna National Library Theatre Collection. He is married to the Hungarian soprano, Fanny Bendiner (1916). They have no children. Soon after the outbreak of the Second World War he came to America and went to Hollywood.

WORKS AVAILABLE IN ENGLISH: The Mind and Face of Bolshevism, 1927; Lenin and Gandhi, 1928; Rasputin: The Holy Devil, 1928; The Russian Theatre (with J. Gregor) 1930; Power and Secret of the Jesuits, 1930; The Unknown Tolstoy, 1930; The Ochrana, 1930; The Imagination Machine, 1931; Gandhi the Holy Man, 1931; Leo XIII, 1935; Leaders, Dreamers, and Rebels, 1935; The Motion Picture in America, 1938; Triumph Over Pain, 1938.

ABOUT: Vance, W. René Fölüp-Müller's Search For Reality: A Biographical Study.

FURNIVALL, FREDERICK JAMES. See "BRITISH AUTHORS OF THE 19TH CENTURY"

FUTRELLE, JACQUES (April 9, 1875-April 15, 1912), American journalist and writer of detective fiction, creator of "The Thinking Machine," was born in Pike County, Ga., the son of Wiley H. H. Futrelle and Linnie (Bevill) Futrelle. He was educated at public and private schools and was a theatrical manager while he was still in his twenties. In 1895 he married L. May Peel, also a writer. For several  years he was a member of the editorial department of the Boston *American,* in which many of his tales first appeared, proceeding from newspaper work (like Earl Derr Biggers, who also started in Boston, a few years later) to the successful writing of detective stories. "The Thinking Machine," Futrelle's amusingly eccentric contribution to the ranks of American fictional detectives, made his first appearance in the closing chapters of an adventure novel, *The Chase of the Golden Plate* (1906). The sleuth's full name was Augustus S. F. X. Van Deusen and he was cast as a professor in an unnamed American university. Short stories featuring the character appeared in the popular magazines and were collected in two volumes. *The Thinking Machine* (1907) was reissued in 1918 as *The Problem of Cell 13,* the title of the first and best known story, which has appeared in many anthologies.

Before his heroic and tragic death in the "Titanic" catastrophe in 1912, Futrelle also wrote a number of tales in light romantic vein. They are forgotten today, but his detective stories have survived remarkably well. In a contest conducted in 1937 by the publishers of an anthology of detective stories chosen specially for boys, the young readers voted the thirty-year old "Problem of Cell 13" their favorite tale. And more than a quarter of a century after the author's death, the stories were re-serialized in England by the Beaverbrook newspapers [information from Mrs. Futrelle, who survived her husband].

Futrelle was a far abler writer than his better known contemporary in detective fiction, Arthur B. Reeve,[qv] the "Craig Kennedy" man. Had he lived beyond his thirty-seventh year, he would almost certainly have become a major figure in the development of the American detective story. As it was, he brought to the form a lightness of touch in advance of his time, and even by modern standards his plots are still ingenious and his narratives readable.

PRINCIPAL WORKS: The Chase of the Golden Plate, 1906; The Thinking Machine, 1907 (reissued as The Problem of Cell 13, 1918); The Thinking Machine on the Case, 1908; The Simple Case of Susan, 1908 (elaborated by May Futrelle into Lieutenant What's-His-Name, 1915); Elusive Isabel, 1909; The Diamond Master, 1909; The High Hand, 1911; My Lady's Garter, 1912.

ABOUT: Haycraft, H. Murder for Pleasure: The Life and Times of the Detective Story; New York Times April 19, 1912.

FYLEMAN, ROSE (1877-), English poet and writer for children, writes: "I was born in Nottingham, of Jewish descent.

I wrote stories and verses when I was quite a little girl, and even had one printed in a local paper, a much less usual thing then than now. I went to college [University College, Nottingham], intending to be a teacher, and did teach for a year or two. Then it was found out that I had a voice, so I went abroad and studied singing in Germany and Paris and London. I sang in public, gave lessons, taught in my sister's school, and still wrote verses; so I had a busy life. And then one day a friend suggested to me that I might write for Punch. The idea seemed ridiculous, but I thought I might as well try, and they accepted my verses. Of course I was very much elated. Since then I have gone on writing verses and stories. Before long I gave up my other work and only wrote and sometimes lectured. It has been great fun.

"I am very fond of traveling and have been to nearly all European countries and have enjoyed it all immensely. I've been twice to the States. And I hope you won't think I'm just flattering when I say that I have never seen anything more impressive than the first sight of New York from the steamer. Another thing that very much impressed me was the efficiency of your children's libraries wherever I went. I should like to say what an appreciative public I have found in the States and how much I value it. I've been to Canada too and I had a glorious time on each trip to the American continent."

* * *

Miss Fyleman is unmarried. "R. F.," as she is known to her friends, is credited with "seeing her own particular brand of fairies everywhere." In London she lives in a quaint old house which she passed for years, always hoping some day to own it. She was for years a regular contributor to Punch, and has translated a great deal from French, German, and Italian. She has a diploma from the Royal College of Music, and her musical knowledge has meant a great deal in the lilt and rhythm of her verses. She wrote the Christmas Play for the famous theatre, "the Old Vic," in 1926, and in 1933 had a children's opera, written with Thomas Dunhill, produced in Guildford. She writes at odd times, wherever she happens to be, and her writing is an expression of her buoyant, whimsical nature.

PRINCIPAL WORKS: Fairies and Chimneys, 1918; The Fairy Green, 1919; The Fairy Flute, 1921; The Rainbow Cat, 1922; A Small Cruse, 1922; Forty Good Night Tales, 1923; Eight Little Plays for Children, 1924; Fairies and Friends, 1925; Letty, 1926; Forty Good Morning Tales, 1926; A Princess Comes to Our Town, 1927; Seven Little Plays for Children and Some Old-Fashioned Girls, 1928; Gay Go Up, 1929; Twenty Tea Time Tales, 1929; The Katy Kruse Play Book, 1930; Fifty New Nursery Rhymes, 1931; The Adventures of Captain Marwhopple, 1931; Heyding-a-ding, 1931; The Easter Hare, 1932; Rose Fyleman Birthday Book, 1932; The Princess Dances, 1933; Jeremy Quince, 1933; Nine Small Plays, 1934; Bears, 1934; Widdy-Widdy-Wurky, 1934; Six Short Plays, 1935; Monkeys, 1936; Billy Monkey, 1936; Six Longer Plays for Children, 1936; The Magic Pencil (eight plays) 1938; Book of Saints, 1939; Red Riding Hood (operetta, with W. Grand) 1939; Fairies and Chimneys (poems) 1940; Runabout Rhymes, 1941.

ABOUT: Kunitz, S. J. & Haycraft, H. (eds.) The Junior Book of Authors; Bookman (London) October 1929; Horn Book January 1940; Saturday Review of Literature November 16, 1929.

*GÁG, WANDA (March 11, 1893-), American artist and writer for children, reports: "I was born in this country but, because of my background, I often feel that I spent my early years in Europe. My father and my mother's parents came from Bohemia. My birthplace, New Ulm, Minn., was settled by Middle Europeans and I grew up in an atmosphere of Old World customs

* Died June 27, 1946.

and legends. In our home creative expression was taken for granted: my father, the son of a wood-carver, decorated houses and churches on weekdays; on Sundays he painted pictures in his attic studio. We children (seven of us) all drew, and most of us wrote stories and poems besides.

"Our father died when I was barely fifteen years old. My mother was ill, there  was very little money left, and life was difficult for many years. I was the oldest and I earned what I could by painting place cards and by writing and illustrating stories for the Minneapolis *Journal* junior page. After graduating from high school I taught country school. Then we lost our mother.

Pinchot

"By means of scholarships and help from friends in St. Paul and Minneapolis I studied art there and in New York City. I stayed in New York and, after the usual disappointments, I managed to eke out a bare living by painting lamp shades and doing commercial work. During this period I used to visit some friends who had two children. They often begged me for stories and I would tell them whatever popped into my head. *Millions of Cats, The Funny Thing,* and *Snippy and Snappy* came into being this way. Later I wrote them down, illustrated them, and took them around to publishers, but no interest was shown in them.

"I was not interested in a commercial future. I took my savings, rented a cheap house in the country, and, in a frenzy of freedom, drew and painted practically everything I saw. When I returned to New York in the fall the Weyhe Galleries bought some of these drawings and gave me a one-man show. Soon my work found its way into museums and private collections. This, in turn, created an interest in my juveniles and, one by one, my three neglected stories, later others, were made into books and published.

"I now live for the greater part of the year in the country. My hobbies are gardening and predicting the weather. I love to go barefooted, I don't like high heels, and I wear hat and gloves only when they are needed to protect me from the elements.

"I work hard and long at both the text and illustrations in my books. I rewrite my stories many times, my aim being to get something which is simple but not dull, colorful but not florid, and explicit but not long-winded. I think children's stories should be suitable for reading out loud and, with this in view, I recite mine to myself when out walking, to test them for rhythm, sound values, and clarity."

* * *

"Miss Gág is black-haired and has been called "pretty in a truculent sort of way." She is unmarried. In her autobiographical sketch she has omitted the heroic story of how, single-handed, as a young girl she educated her five sisters and her brother before she felt free to do her own work, but it is told in her *Growing Pains* (1940). As Helen Ferris said: "She is real. She will not fool with life, or be put off with easy prizes."

PRINCIPAL WORKS: (with illustrations): Millions of Cats, 1928; The Funny Thing, 1929; Snippy and Snappy, 1931; The ABC Bunny, 1933; Gone Is Gone, 1935; Tales From Grimm (translated) 1936; Snow White and the Seven Dwarves (translated) 1938; Growing Pains, 1940; Nothing at All, 1941.

ABOUT: Gág, W. Growing Pains; Kirkland, W. & F. Girls Who Became Artists; Kunitz, S. J. & Haycraft, H. (eds.). The Junior Book of Authors; Century Magazine August 1928; Creative Art December 1927, November 1931; Horn Book November-December 1935; Prints March 1931; Saturday Review of Literature October 5, 1940; Woman's Journal January 1929.

GALDOS. See PEREZ GALDOS

GALE, ZONA (August 26, 1874-December 27, 1938), American novelist, short story writer, dramatist, and poet, was born in Portage, Wis., once a pioneer fur trading center, of "Yankee stock," the daughter of Charles Franklin Gale and Eliza (Beers) Gale. She was graduated from the University of Wisconsin in 1895 (M.A. 1899), and in 1929 received an honorary Litt.D. from her alma mater.

She had written from early childhood (her first "book" was printed and bound by herself at the age of seven), and it was natural that she should turn to newspaper work. She was employed by various Milwaukee papers from 1899 to 1901, when she went to New York and became a reporter on the *World*. She wrote indefatigably meanwhile, mostly short stories, but it was not until 1904 that her first story was published, prophetically by *Success*. The same year she went back to Portage, which she was to make famous as "Friendship Village," and there she lived for the remainder of her years, though she died in a Chicago hospital, of pneumonia. The girl who had jotted down bits of poems and stories while she waited for interviews had the habit of industry; she worked ceaselessly, and neither fame nor prosperity slackened her labor. In 1928, at fifty-four, she married William L. Breese, a Portage manufacturer whom she had known since childhood. She had previously adopted two little girls. She was always socially minded, and served as chairman of the Wisconsin Free Library Commission (her very last published article was on "Why Libraries Need Friends," in the *Library Journal*), as a regent of the University of Wisconsin, and as a campaigner for the Progressive Party in the 1936 state elections.

"Fragile, flower-like, and feminine" seemed fitting words to describe Zona Gale in her youth. Her face expressed wistfulness and idealism, but it expressed determination, too. A loyalty to her native *milieu* which yet avoided provincialism was one of her outstanding characteristics. When she received the Pulitzer prize for her dramatization of *Miss Lulu Bett* in 1920, it was amid universal approval. In her later work there was a falling off of power which disappointed her admirers; she seemed to have written herself out in the vein which was peculiarly hers; a curious, over-anxious strain of mysticism appeared in her writing.

But there can be no question of the fineness and strength of her best work, of novels like *Miss Lulu Bett* and *Birth*. The *Nation*, in an obituary notice, summed up very well her place in American literature when it called her "a fellow-realist with Sinclair Lewis and Theodore Dreiser." It noted that *Miss Lulu Bett* was "exactly contemporaneous with *Main Street*, and called it "hardly less influential in establishing a new tone in fiction dealing with provincial America." Miss Gale began her career as a regional writer, a local colorist whose work was somewhat tinged with sentimentality, though even then it showed her command of sharp observation and fidelity to reality. With Miss Lulu Bett, unregarded "doormat" in her married sister's home, sentimentality gave way to true realism; and in the dramatization of the novel there appeared one of the very first American plays to eschew convention and herald the dawn of a mature American drama.

PRINCIPAL WORKS: *Novels*—Romance Island, 1906; Heart's Kindred, 1915; A Daughter of Tomorrow, 1917; Birth, 1918; Miss Lulu Bett, 1920;

Faint Perfume, 1923; Preface to a Life, 1926; Borgia, 1929; Papa La Fleur, 1933; Light Woman, 1937. *Short Stories*—The Loves of Pelleas and Etarre, 1907; Friendship Village, 1908; Friendship Village Love Stories, 1909; Mothers to Men, 1911; Christmas, 1912; Neighborhood Stories, 1914; Peace in Friendship Village, 1919; Yellow Gentians and Blue, 1927; Bridal Pond, 1930; Old Fashioned Tales, 1933. *Plays*—Miss Lulu Bett, 1920; Mr. Pitt (dramatization of Birth) 1924; Evening Clothes, 1932. *Miscellaneous*—When I Was a Little Girl, 1913; The Secret Way (poems) 1921; Portage, Wisconsin, and Other Essays, 1928; Frank Miller of Mission Inn, 1938. Magna, 1939.

ABOUT: Derleth, A. Still Small Voice; Gale, Z. When I Was a Little Girl; Nation January 7, 1939; Newsweek January 9, 1939; Saturday Review of Literature January 7, 1939; Wisconsin Magazine of History March 1939.

GALLIENNE. See LE GALLIENNE

GALSWORTHY, JOHN (August 14, 1867-January 31, 1933), English novelist, dramatist, poet, and man of letters, was born at Kingston, Surrey, the son of John Galsworthy, attorney, and Blanche Bailey (Bartleet) Galsworthy. The family was of old Devonshire stock and in easy circumstances, so that the boy spent his childhood in comfort, not to say luxury.

After going to a preparatory school at Bournemouth he was sent, in 1881, to Harrow, one of the two most famous public schools of England and the kindly nurse of many statesmen and men of letters. He played in the first football eleven and became its captain, but showed no special literary bent either at school or at New College, Oxford, to which he went on. At college he was described as "lazy, dressy, sporting," and took a keen interest in racing. He graduated with honors in law and was called to the Bar in 1890. He continued reading law till 1894, but, being under no compulsion to earn a living, he made small attempt to practice, and soon went on a series of long journeys, to Russia, Egypt, Fiji, America, Canada, Australia, and the Cape. Journeying by sailing ship from Adelaide to South Africa, he made friends with a Polish officer who showed him a half-written novel, with which Galsworthy encouraged him to proceed. The officer's name was Joseph Conrad, the book was *Almayer's Folly,* and the meeting was the beginning of an affectionate friendship which lasted until Conrad's death.

In 1891 Galsworthy's cousin, Arthur, married Ada Cooper, daughter of a Norwich doctor. Charming, intelligent and beautiful, she was much loved by all the family, but the marriage proved disastrous. As time went on she and John became drawn together. In 1904 they went away to Dartmoor, were duly served with divorce papers, and married on September 23, 1905, the day after the decree *nisi* had been made absolute.

Galsworthy had read deeply in Dickens, Turgenev, Maupassant, Anatole France, and Tolstoy just after graduation, but it was some years before he himself seriously attempted to write, with Ada's encouragement. He learnt by doing, and once said: "I was writing fiction for five years before I could master even its primary technique." His first four volumes, all issued under the pseudonym of John Sinjohn, appeared between 1897 and 1901. These were *From the Four Winds, Jocelyn, Villa Rubein,* and *A Man of Devon.* All were immature, as indeed was *The Island Pharisees,* which came out under his own name on 1904; but in this last could be seen the outlines of his distinctive view of life. Patrician by birth, instincts, and education, he was yet very keenly sensible of the tragedy of poverty and full of pity towards victims of cruelty and injustice. He detected in his own compeers a crass complacency and indifference to the plight of the wage-earner; and *The Island Pharisees* was the first of a long series of books and plays which showed the wealthier Edwardian middle class in all its insensitive commercialism.

The first word of what became known as the "Forsyte Saga" was written on Campden Hill, London, in May, 1903, and the last at Hampstead, London, on August 15, 1920. But to speak of the Saga is to anticipate. Its first component part, *The Man of Property* (a separate novel in itself) was published in 1906, introducing the public to Galsworthy's most rounded character, Soames Forsyte, embodiment of all the pre-war conceptions of the propertied classes, to his disturbing and fascinating wife, Irene, to James ("nobody ever tells me anything"), to Old Jolyon, kindest and most equable of the Forsytes, to June, protector of "lame ducks," and many others who have become almost as firmly established in the consciousness of British readers as the personages of Dickens. With this book Galsworthy emerged from his long novitiate to become a writer of power and influence.

In the same year, 1906, he first appeared as a dramatic author, with *The Silver Box,* which was put on at the Court Theatre.

Henry Arthur Jones, Pinero, and Bernard Shaw had brought the drama of social problems into popularity, and Galsworthy followed on. *The Silver Box* drew a bitter contrast between justice administered to the rich and the poor; *Strife* (1909) brought current industrial troubles out of the realm of statistics into that of hard fact; *Justice* (1910) painted so terrible a picture of prison life that it was the proximate cause of various reforms. Other plays produced prior to the war were *The Eldest Son, The Pigeon, The Fugitive,* and *The Mob.* None was a work of a high order. Of the rest of Galsworthy's dramatic output the pieces called *The Skin Game* (1920) and *Loyalties* (1922) are generally considered the best. The plays are interpenetrated with a burning sense of social injustice, which shines the more brightly because of the transparency of the medium. In the novels, with their much greater resiliency of technique, moral judgments are far less overt and more subtle, so that certain of them (to their author's amusement) have actually been taken by naïve readers as documents supporting the aristocratic view of life.

During the winter of 1912-13 Galsworthy was fighting actively for the introduction of humane slaughtering. He was passionately fond of animals, especially dogs, which abounded in his various houses and figured with some prominence in the novels. He loved horses too, and rode every day when in the country, but, with his humanitarian convictions, he did not follow hounds. Music was another of his enthusiasms.

He continued writing through the war period, and in 1918, twelve years after his first Forsyte book, he returned to that family with an exquisitely delicate short sketch of the old age and death of Old Jolyon, called "Indian Summer of a Forsyte" (in *Five Tales*). *In Chancery* (1920) and *To Let* (1921) completed the Saga proper, though the fortunes of the younger Forsytes (and some surviving elders) were later pursued in *The White Monkey* (1924), *The Silver Spoon* (1926), and *Swan Song* (1928), which were in this last year issued together in an omnibus volume as *A Modern Comedy.* Noteworthy novels outside this great series were *The Dark Flower* (1913), a frank study of passion, *The Freelands* (1915), an expression of belief in the land as "the very backbone and blood of our race," and *Saint's Progress* (1919), which showed a clergyman confronted by a grave moral situation.

Just after the war Galsworthy refused a knighthood, but in 1929 he accepted the Order of Merit, the most exclusive and genuine of British honors. In 1932 the Nobel Prize for literature was awarded to him. He was honorary fellow of New College, Oxford, and held honorary doctorates from Oxford, Cambridge, and five other universities. Never a great committee man, he yet took a keen interest in the work of the P.E.N. Club. He visited the United States on various occasions. The play, *Escape,* was written in California in 1926. Galsworthy came over again in the fall of 1930 and spent that winter in Arizona. He possessed various country houses at different times (after one of which, at Manaton, on Dartmoor, the collected edition of his works was called). From 1919 onwards his London home was Grove Lodge, at the highest point of Hampstead. There he died, of pernicious anaemia. By his own direction his ashes were scattered to the winds.

Galsworthy's personal character was in the last degree upright, kindly, and modest. Frank Harris described him as being "about medium height, spare of habit and vigorous, his head long, well-shaped; his features fairly regular, a straight nose, high forehead; he is almost completely bald and wears glasses. . . . Seen close to, his face becomes more interesting; the serious blue eyes can laugh; the lips are large and well-cut, promising a good deal of feeling, but the characteristic expression of the face is seriousness and sincerity."

He often worked in an armchair with a pad on his knee, writing rapidly and in a bold hand, and later making many corrections; but he could and did write almost anywhere. He would only begin composition when inspiration pressed. It was not his habit to construct elaborate outlines for plays or novels, and he allowed himself to be carried along by the development of his characters as the work progressed. His prose was lucid, evocative, often plain almost to the point of being colloquial. He was a master of the ordinary scene—a peaceful garden on a June day, a dog greeting its master, a business man eating his lunch or walking along a city street. His incisive sense of character, his grasp of the social milieu of which he wrote, and his humanitarian sympathies would seem, despite the dimunition of his reputation since his death, to assure him a respected place in the history of modern English literature.

PRINCIPAL WORKS: *Fiction*—From the Four Winds, 1897; Jocelyn, 1898; Villa Rubein, 1900; A Man of Devon, 1901; The Island Pharisees, 1904; The Man of Property, 1906; The Country House, 1907; Fraternity, 1909; A Motley, 1910; The Patrician, 1911; The Dark Flower, 1913; The Little Man, 1915; The Freelands, 1915; Beyond, 1917; Five Tales, 1918; The Burning Spear, 1919; Saint's Progress, 1919; Tatterdemalion, 1920; In Chancery, 1920; Awakening, 1920; To Let, 1921; The Forsyte Saga, 1922; Captures, 1923; The White Monkey, 1924; Caravan, 1925; The Silver Spoon, 1926; Two Forsyte Interludes, 1927; Swan Song, 1928; A Modern Comedy (The White Monkey, The Silver Spoon, and Swan Song) 1928; Four Forsyte Stories, 1929; On Forsyte 'Change, 1930; Maid in Waiting, 1931; Flowering Wilderness, 1932; Over the River, 1933; End of the Chapter (Maid in Waiting, Flowering Wilderness and Over the River) 1935; Forsytes, Pendyces, and Others, 1935. *Plays*—Plays: The Silver Box, Joy, Strife, 1909; Justice, 1910, The Little Dream, 1911; The Eldest Son, 1912; The Pigeon, 1912; The Fugitive, 1913; The Mob, 1914; A Bit o' Love, 1915; The Foundations, 1920; The Skin Game, 1920; Six Short Plays, 1921; Loyalties, 1922; A Family Man, 1922; Windows, 1922; The Forest, 1924; Old English, 1924; The Show, 1925; Escape, 1926; Exiled, 1929; The Roof, 1929; The Winter Garden: Four Dramatic Pieces, 1935. *Essays*—A Commentary, 1908; The Inn of Tranquillity, 1912; A Sheaf, 1916; Another Sheaf, 1919; Addresses in America, 1919; Castles in Spain, 1927; The Creation of Character in Literature (Romanes Lecture) 1931; Glimpses and Reflections, 1937. *Letters*—Letters From John Galsworthy, 1900-32 (ed. by Edward Garnett) 1934. *Poems*—Moods, Songs, and Doggerels, 1912; The Bells of Peace, 1921; Verses, New and Old, 1926; Collected Poems, 1934. *Collected Works*—Manaton Edition (21 vols.) 1923-24.

ABOUT: Archer, W. The Old Drama and the New; Chevrillon, A. Three Studies in English Literature; Coats, R. H. John Galsworthy as a Dramatic Artist; Croman, N. John Galsworthy: A Study in Continuity and Contrast; Cross, W. L. Four Contemporary Novelists; Delattre, F. Le Roman Social de John Galsworthy; Ervine, St. J. Some Impressions of My Elders; Galsworthy, A. Over the Hills and Far Away; Harris, F. Contemporary Portraits; Kaye-Smith, S. John Galsworthy; Marrot, H. V. A Bibliography of the Works of John Galsworthy; Marrot, H. V. The Life and Letters of John Galsworthy; Ould, H. L. John Galsworthy; Phelps, W. L. The Advance of the English Novel; Reynolds, M. E. Memories of John Galsworthy, by His Sister; Rohmer, C. Buddenbrooks und The Forsyte Saga; Schalit, L. John Galsworthy; Trumbacher, W. H. R. Gerhardt Hauptmann and John Galsworthy: A Parallel; Atlantic Monthly December 1916; Fortnightly Review May 1909, March 1922; North American Review February 1922; Yale Review October 1924.

GALTON, Sir FRANCIS. See "BRITISH AUTHORS OF THE 19TH CENTURY"

GANNETT, LEWIS (October 3, 1891-), American critic, writes: "Lewis Gannett, literary critic of the New York *Herald Tribune* since 1930, became a literary critic more or less by accident, and still regards his work rather as a form of reporting than as an exercise in aesthetics. He was born in Rochester, N.Y., the son of a New England Unitarian minister and a Pennsylvania Quaker mother. After graduating from the East High School in Rochester, he went to Harvard, intending to become a biologist, but decided instead to be a philosopher. This indecision, so frequently manifested in his life, adds to the range covered in his daily newspaper column, 'Books and Things,' but detracts somewhat from its depth and consistency. Mr. Gannett studied economics at German universities in the year before the World War, and returning to

Pinchot

Harvard, took his M.A. in that subject, then decided that academic economics was a 'phony' science, and determined to learn about life as a newspaper reporter. He harassed Herbert Bayard Swope into taking him onto the staff of the New York *World,* where he served as reporter and war rewrite man.

"The war [1914-18] found Mr. Gannett a bellicose pacifist. He went to France in the summer of 1917 with a Quaker relief unit; and, after the Armistice, became the *Survey's* correspondent at the Peace Conference. Returning to America in 1919, he joined the staff of the *Nation* where he crusaded for ten energetic years of combative 'liberalism.' He returned to Europe for the *Nation* in 1921, and spent the winter of 1925-26 in China. In 1928 he took a long leap to the staff of the *Herald Tribune,* expecting to become a national reporter and discovering himself as a book columnist.

"He translated, in 1915, Dr. A. H. Fried's *The Restoration of Europe,* and, in 1930, Dr. Hjalmar Schacht's *The End of Reparations.* In 1934 he wrote *Sweet Land,* a record of the first of those transcontinental automobile trips which periodically interrupt his literary columning. In 1940 he edited Walter Nelles' *A Liberal in Wartime: The Education of Albert De Silver.* He has written in various magazines on race prejudices, patterns of imperialism, wild gardens, the history of American beards, road signs and tourist cabins, covered bridges and American food, and of his dream of settling down some day at Cream Hill in Connecticut, and writing. In 1917 he married Mary Ross, and in 1931 he married Ruth Chrisman. He has a son and a daughter born of his first marriage."

* * *

In person, Lewis Gannett is gregarious, bespectacled, pleasant-mannered, almost diffident. As a writer, he is clear and incisive. After well over a decade of daily book-reviewing, his criticisms remain fresh, considered (despite his disclaimer), and comprehensive.

PRINCIPAL WORKS: Young China, 1926; Sweet Land, 1934.

GARCÍA LORCA, FEDERICO (June 5, 1899-August 1936), Spanish poet and playwright, was born in Fuente Vaqueros, a small town only seven kilometers from Granada. His parents, both Andalusians, are still living. His father, an enterprising farmer, owns a farm, Callejones de García, in the fertile vega surrounding Granada, and a comfortable mansion in the heart

of the city, directly across the casino. His mother, Doña Vicenta, whom he idolized, is a gifted pianist and from the earliest imparted to him the rudiments of music which later he perfected with a local teacher and his godfather, Manuel de Falla, later to become the celebrated composer.

Despite his predilection for farm life with its folklore and music, and the carefree days romping with his brother Paco and his two sisters and staging in the evening his first plays, Federico followed regular classes: first at an elementary school in Almería and later in Granada, at the school of the Sacred Heart, at the Institute and finally at the University where he took up law as well as the regular course in the Faculty of Philosophy and Literature. With one of his favorite teachers, Martín Domínguez Berrueta, the art professor, and several of his fellow-students, he journeyed through Castile in 1917, and this unforgettable experience inspired him to write *Impresiones y Viajes* (1918), his first book, a lyrical interpretation in prose of the austere, melancholy Castile by a sensitive romantic youth from the South. In 1919 another of his favorite teachers, Fernando de los Ríos, persuaded his parents to let him go to Madrid, where he remained for the next fifteen years with but brief sojourns in the provinces. Giving up his university studies, he soon devoted himself entirely to his literary endeavors. He organized theatrical performances, read his poems in public, wandered in Castile collecting and transcribing old folksongs. To this period belongs *El Maleficio de la Mariposa*, a Maeterlinckian pastiche which caused a great scandal when produced at the Eslava of Madrid in 1920, and *Libro de Poemas* (1921), a compilation of poems based on folklore material. In 1922, backed by such recognized older men as Zuloaga and de Falla, he organized the first "Cante Jondo" festival at the Alhambra at which Spain's most famous "deep song" singers and guitarists participated. This festival may be considered one of the climaxes in the poet's career, and although his *El Poema del Cante Jondo*, written at this time, was not published until ten years later, it is evident that the "deep song" form permeated his poems of 1921-24 (*Canciones*, published in Málaga in 1927) and his consummate ballads of 1924-27 (*Romancero Gitano*, published in Madrid in 1928).

But before the far-reaching triumph of this latter volume, which attained seven editions during his lifetime, García Lorca had shown talent in two other fields: his drawings had been exhibited in Barcelona (1927) and his three-act play, *Mariana Pineda*, had been successfully produced at Madrid's Teatro Fontalva. His drawings revealed a child-like simplicity somewhat Cocteau-ish and that Gongoristic trend which later his chum Salvador Dalí made famous in Paris.

In 1929-30 García Lorca lived in John Jay Hall, Columbia University, and his poems appeared for the first time in English in the magazine *Alhambra*. The poet's favorite hideout was Harlem. He loved Negro spirituals, finding in them a primitive quality not unlike that of the "deep song," and inspired by them he wrote his splendid *Oda al Rey de Harlem*, published recently in a posthumous collection, *The Poet in New York*.

In 1930, after a vacation in Cuba and Mexico, García Lorca returned to Spain shortly after the proclamation of the Spanish republic. At the Second Ordinary Congress of the Federal Union of Hispanic Students held in Madrid in November 1931 it was decided to build a big wooden shed or "barraca" at some central point in Madrid with the idea of performing important plays for the masses and thus raising their taste. With the help of Fernando de los Ríos, then Minister of Education, "La Barraca" became a car of Thespis and during 1932 toured many Spanish towns, performing on the public squares.

García Lorca's first theatrical success of 1927, *Mariana Pineda*, followed by the "violent farce" in two acts, *La Zapatera Prodigi-* *osa* (1930) and the *Títeres de Cachiporra* (1931) had prepared the young poet-playwright for *Amor de Don Perlimplín con Belisa en su Jardín* (1933) and especially for the strong rural tragedy which climaxed his career when it was produced in Madrid in 1933, and which two years later was presented to a baffled New York audience at the Lyceum Theatre under the title *Bitter Oleander*.

In 1933-34 García Lorca toured Argentina and Uruguay, delivering lectures, reading his poems and presenting his shorter pieces in puppet shows before groups of friends and admirers. On his return to Spain he finished his tragi-comedy *Yerma*. A year later he saw his last play, *Doña Rosita la Soltera*, a piece which combined some of the violence of his rural tragedies and some of the broad humor of his farces.

At the outbreak of the Civil War, García Lorca was staying at Callejones de García, his country home. One day, toward the end of July, while visiting his friend Rosales Vallecillo, a merchant, he was arrested by Franquist soldiers. After a few days in jail he was invited to go with them to see his brother-in-law, Manuel Fernández Montesinos, the Socialist ex-Mayor of Granada whom they had murdered and dragged through the streets. When they reached the cemetery they told Federico to get out of the car. Suddenly they struck him with the butt of their rifles and as he lay in his blood they riddled his body with bullets. His books were burned in Granada's Plaza del Carmen and today are banned from Franco's Spain.

Thus Spain was deprived of one of her most authentic poets, the tall, broad lad of the dark, round face all covered with moles, of the black hair smooth and shining, with the body of the Granadan peasant and the hoarse voice so sweetly Andalusian, who played the piano and sang with savage sadness the old delicious, uncouth songs of Castile, Galicia, and Andalusia.

PRINCIPAL WORKS AVAILABLE IN ENGLISH: Bitter Oleander, 1935 (as Blood Wedding, 1939); Lament for the Death of a Bullfighter and Other Poems, 1937; Poems, 1939; The Poet in New York and Other Poems, 1940; From Lorca's Theatre: Five Plays, 1941; Selected Poems 1941.

ABOUT: Gomez de Baquero, E. Los Poetas; García Lorca, F. (See Prefaces and Introductions to various works); González Carvalho, V. Obra y Muerte de Federico García Lorca; Río, A. del. El Poeta Frederico García Lorca; Souviron, J. M. La Nueva Poesía Española; Trend, J. B. Alfonso the Sage; Valbuena Prat, A. La Poesía Española Contemporánea; Cursos y Conferencias November 1939; Left Review May 1938; Nation September 18, 1937; New Yorker June 1, 1940; Poetry December 1937, September 1940; Revista de las Indias March

1937; Revista Iberoamericana November 1939; Revista Socialista September 1939; SECH December 1936; Sustancia September 1938; Universidad de Panamá August 1937.

GARD. See MARTIN DU GARD

GARDNER, ERLE STANLEY (July 17, 1889-), American detective story writer, writes: "I was born in Malden, Mass., but

Whitesell

as my father was a mining man my early boyhood was largely spent in mining camps. At seventeen I was in the Klondike. My education was unorthodox, gravitating between amateur four-round exhibition fights at Oroville, Calif., to studying law in the office of the deputy district attorney. Was admitted to the California bar at twenty-one, started practicing law in Ventura County, Calif., and remained actively engaged for some twenty-two years, specializing mostly in trial work, preferably before juries. For three years I was president of the Consolidated Sales Company, a sales organization which specialized in taking over the entire output of factories and furnishing merchandizing facilities. Started writing in 1921, selling two or three scattered stories, then did nothing with writing until 1924, when I decided to develop it as a sideline. By 1928, I was established as a quantity producer in the pulp field and averaged better than a million words a year, in addition to carrying on a rather extensive law practice.

"I have always been fascinated by the Chinese people, and because I had numerous Chinese clients, started studying the language and psychology. In 1931, I went to China, and lived for some time in various parts of the country. In 1934 began devoting my attention almost exclusively to writing and travel. Have lived in Honolulu, the South Seas, Mexico, and various parts of the United States and Alaska. Lived for two years in house trailers, having three trailers in which I maintained field offices, with secretaries, chauffeurs, etc.

"Have done a great deal of hunting with bow and arrow, both for large and small game. At present spend most of my time in travel, spending winters either in the desert, Mexico, or the French Quarter of New Orleans, summers in the mountains, the fall in hunting trips with bow and arrow,

and the rest of the time on a 200-acre ranch in California. With the use of dictating machines, I maintain a fairly large and steady output of mystery fiction. Chief desire is for bigger and better adventures, undertaking search for the unusual, meeting new people, studying human motivation and psychology."

* * *

In 1912 Mr. Gardner married Natalie Talbot, and they have a daughter. He is a heavy-set but light-stepping man with a powerful, nervous grip, with light brown hair worn in a pompadour, who looks like a sheriff in a movie "horse opera." He loves the outdoors, likes to follow the sun, seldom smokes or drinks, and is known to his friends as made up of energy and determination, with a frank bit of superstition thrown in. His approach to his work is purely commercial, not literary—it is a "product" which he turns out; but his books are nevertheless among the top-notchers in the "time-killer" division of the mystery field. Most of them, with titles starting with *The Case of the . . .*, center about Perry Mason, a lawyer who rather resembles Erle Stanley Gardner. The *D.A.* series concerns Douglas Selby, a country district attorney. A third series has as its sleuth Terry Clane. Mr. Gardner is also believed to write under at least two pen-names. His total annual wordage (he sometimes keeps as many as five secretaries busy transcribing his dictation) is said to be the largest of any writer since Edgar Wallace, and his combined annual book sales the greatest of any author now active in the mystery field.

As might be imagined, characterization (apart from the hero) and background are of secondary importance in the Gardner stories, though adequate to the day. But the plots are baffling and the style is always swift-paced and exciting. His handling of legal points has brought high praise from members of the profession. His books appeal chiefly to masculine readers and those who take the detective story as an anodyne.

PRINCIPAL WORKS: The Case of the Velvet Claws, 1932; The Case of the Sulky Girl, 1933; The Case of the Lucky Legs, 1933; The Case of the Howling Dog, 1934; The Case of the Curious Bride, 1935; The Case of the Counterfeit Eye, 1935; The Case of the Caretaker's Cat, 1935; The Case of the Sleepwalker's Niece, 1936; The Case of the Stuttering Bishop, 1936; The Case of the Dangerous Dowager, 1937; The Case of the Lame Canary, 1937; The D.A. Calls It Murder, 1937; Murder Up My Sleeve, 1937; The Case of the Substitute Face, 1938; The Case of the Shoplifter's Shoe, 1938; The D.A. Holds a Candle, 1938; The Case of the Perjured Parrot, 1939; The Case of the Rolling Bones, 1939; The D.A. Draws a Circle, 1939; The Case of the Baited Hook, 1940; The D.A. Goes to Trial, 1940; The Case of the Silent Partner, 1940; The Case of the Turning Tide, 1941; The Case of the Empty Tin, 1941; The D.A. Cooks a Goose, 1942; The Case of the Drowning Duck, 1942.

ABOUT: Haycraft, H. Murder for Pleasure: The Life and Times of the Detective Story; Saturday Review of Literature July 16, 1938.

GARLAND, HAMLIN (September 14, 1860-March 4, 1940), American novelist and essayist, wrote to the editors of the present volume a few months  before his death at seventy-nine: "T h e home in which I was born was a pioneer l o g-cabin near the village of West Salem i n Wisconsin. M y father, R i c h a r d Hayes Garland, was a transplanted New Englander, a native of Oxford County, Maine. My mother, Isabelle Charlotte (McClintock) Garland, was of Scotch-Irish derivation. From the Garlands I get my literary endowment, such as it is, and from the McClintocks my love of music and my Celtic temperament. In 1869 my people moved to Iowa and I spent twelve years on a 'Middle Border' farm. After graduating from the Cedar Valley Seminary in Osage, Iowa, in 1881, I helped my father establish a new home in Ordway, S.D. In 1883 I 'held down' a claim in MacPherson County, N.D. In 1884 I sold this and on the proceeds, $200, went to Boston to prepare myself for teaching American literature.

"I made my home in Boston for nine years. In 1887 I wrote *Main-Travelled Roads,* a volume of short stories, following it with my first novel, *A Spoil of Office,* in 1891. In 1893 I bought an old home in my native village of West Salem and brought my invalid mother back to the valley where she had spent her girlhood. I made Chicago my literary headquarters, however.

"In 1895 I began a life of Ulysses S. Grant and in 1899 I married Zulime Taft, a sister of Lorado Taft, the sculptor, and established a home in Chicago. A daughter was born to us in West Salem in 1904 and another in Chicago in 1907. In 1915 we moved to New York City, and in 1917 *A Son of the Middle Border* was published. In 1922 its sequel, *A Daughter of the Middle Border,* won the Pulitzer Prize for that year. These two books led to my election as one of the directors of the American Academy of Arts and Letters.

"In 1930 I built a home in Laughlin Park, Los Angeles, Calif. [it was here that he died, after a cerebral hemorrhage], where my wife and I now live in comparative leisure and undeniable comfort. Our daughters are near at hand and we have two grandchildren. The University of Wisconsin, Northwestern University, Beloit College, and the University of Southern California have honored me with the degree of Litt.D., and the Theodore Roosevelt Memorial Society awarded me its gold medal."

* * *

Active mentally and physically to the last, Hamlin Garland continued to work and write virtually to the day he died. He left an almost-finished book describing his ten years in Southern California, which he had instructed his family to publish only after his death. At his bedside when he died were his wife and two daughters. He was a tall, lean man, with thick white hair and moustache and strongly aquiline features. For forty years he was an eager investigator of psychic phenomena, and he wrote several books on the subject, but professed himself to be still agnostic regarding personal survival after death. Of his own work he said modestly: "I have no illusions concerning my achievements . . . I realize all my shortcomings and some of my mistakes, but . . . with all their faults, I am content to have my books serve as witness of my good intent."

Wallace Stegner, in reviewing Iowa's literary history, said: "As a man of the gifted Midwestern group that gathered in Chicago and as a forerunner of the many writers who now profess cultural regionalism as a literary creed, Garland is of the first importance." Granville Hicks, though his economic bias made him impatient of Garland's latter-day conservatism, as opposed to his radical youth, nevertheless had high praise for his early Middle Western novels: "He wrote some of the finest fiction we have— direct, comprehensive, moving, and savagely honest." *A Son of the Middle Border* is Hamlin Garland's enduring monument—and perhaps the finest regional work American literature has produced. By a curious coincidence, Garland's death occurred within three days of that of Edwin Markham— often called the dean of American poets as Garland was of novelists; and though Markham died in New York, both were buried in Los Angeles, within a week.

PRINCIPAL WORKS: Main-Travelled Roads, 1890; A Spoil of Office, 1891; Crumbling Idols, 1894; Rose of Dutcher's Coolly, 1895; Life of Ulysses S. Grant, 1898; The Trail of the Gold-

Seekers, 1899; The Captain of the Gray Horse Troop, 1901; Hesper, 1902; The Shadow World, 1908; A Son of the Middle Border, 1917; A Daughter of the Middle Border, 1922; The Book of the American Indian, 1923; Trail-Makers of the Middle Border, 1926; Roadside Meetings, 1930; Companions on the Trail, 1931; My Friendly Contemporaries, 1932; Afternoon Neighbors, 1934; Forty Years of Psychic Research, 1936; The Mystery of the Buried Crosses, 1939.

ABOUT: Federal Writers' Project (American Guide Series). Hamlin Garland Memorial; Garland, H. Roadside Meetings, Companions on the Trail; Nation October 21, 1931; New York Herald Tribune March 5, 1940; New York Times March 5, 1940; Saturday Review of Literature July 30, 1938, February 3, 1940, March 16, 1940; Scholastic March 26, 1938; Step Ladder April 1940.

GARNETT, DAVID (1892-), English novelist, and formerly publisher, comes of a literary family. His grandfather, Dr.

Richard Garnett, was a well-known writer w h o superintended the Reading Room at the British Museum. His father, the late E d w a r d Garnett,*qv* was the best-esteemed publisher's reader in L o n d o n, and his mother, Constance, has won renown for her translations of Dostoievsky and other Russian authors. David was privately educated as a boy, passing in due course to the Royal College of Science, where he studied botany (and incidentally discovered a new species of mushroom). His first book was an adaptation and abridgment of V. A. Dasent's *The Kitchen Garden and Its Management*. During the War of 1914-18 he was, in common with some others who later made themselves known in the literary world, a conscientious objector to military service; but he worked with the Friends' War Victims Relief.

During the war period Garnett met another bookish young man, Francis Birrell, and in 1919, disregarding Edward Garnett's solemn warning to have nothing to do with the book trade or authorship, the two started a book shop in Gerrard Street, Soho (the Italian quarter abutting on London's West End). Both men wrote books besides selling them; and Garnett's *Lady Into Fox* (1922) was so original in conception and treatment that it was everywhere talked about and read and in 1923 won the Hawthorden Prize and the James Tait Black Memorial Prize. Garnett followed it up in

1924 with *A Man in the Zoo,* in which a young man, after a lovers' quarrel, offers himself to the Zoological Society of London as a specimen of *homo sapiens.*

Garnett has written a number of pleasant novels since then, but has never caught the public imagination so well as in these first two. He is also known as a well-informed and judicial critic, having run a weekly page on "Books in General" in the *New Statesman* for many years.

In 1923 Garnett became a publisher, acting as literary adviser to that eminent typographer, Francis Meynell, on the Nonesuch Press. For some ten years this firm published some of the best-produced works in England, and had a salutary influence on the practice of the ordinary journeyman publisher. For typography and layout the credit goes to Meynell; but Garnett showed fine discrimination in his selection of texts, both old and modern, and helped to make more than one reputation. The American slump of 1929 dealt a crippling blow to the fine book market, and the British financial panic of 1931 finished it off. Garnett severed his connection with the Press in 1932, and soon Meynell went to advertising.

Garnett's writings are notable for their humor, sympathy, imagination, and for a chaste, simple, forthright style that has nothing in common with the starkness of the Hemingway school but harks back to the pre-Johnsonian epoch. He has a keen eye and ear for country sights and sounds, lives in the country, at St. Ives, Huntingdonshire, and is fond of fishing. Some ten years ago he taught himself to fly, and described his first efforts in *A Rabbit in the Air* (1932). He is a tall, fair man, of excessive diffidence, but by no means frosty or remote. He married Rachel Alice, daughter of the architect W. C. Marshall, who illustrated several of his books with woodcuts. She died in 1940.

Garnett's *War in the Air* (1941) is a study of the British air war from the outbreak of hostilities to May 1941, during which period he was a flight lieutenant R.A.F.V.R. and a staff officer in the Intelligence at the Air Ministry in London.

PRINCIPAL WORKS: Dope-Darling (by "Leda Burke"), 1919; Lady Into Fox, 1922; A Man in the Zoo, 1924; The Sailor's Return, 1925; Go She Must! 1927; The Old Dovecote and other stories, 1928; No Love, 1929; The Grasshoppers Come, 1931; A Rabbit in the Air, 1932. A Terrible Day, 1932; Pocahontas: or, The Nonpareil of Virginia, 1933; Beany-Eye, 1935; War in the Air, 1941.

ABOUT: Gould, G. The English Novel of Today; MacCarthy, D. Criticism; Swinnerton, F. A. The Georgian Literary Scene. Bookman (London) October, 1931.

GARNETT, EDWARD (1868-February 21, 1937), English critic, essayist, and dramatist, was born in London, the son of the  celebrated Dr. Richard Garnett, man of letters who succeeded his own father as Keeper of Printed Books in the British Museum. His mother was Olivia (Singleton) Garnett, an Irishwoman. He was educated privately, his most valuable schooling being the family atmosphere of culture and scholarship. Indeed, Garnett's whole life was passed in the midst of books, their reading and making, and he had almost no personal existence apart from them. He did, however, have a great gift for friendship. Among the writers who became his close friends, whom he advised, encouraged, and helped to publicize, were Joseph Conrad, John Galsworthy, and D. H. Lawrence. He acted professionally also as a literary adviser, being attached at different periods to the English publishing firms of Fisher, Unwin, Heinemann, and Jonathan Cape.

Garnett married Constance Black, who as Constance Garnett became famous in her own right for her translations into English from the Russian. Her translations of Tolstoy, Turgeniev, and others of the great Russian novelists did a signal service to both literatures. Of their two sons, one, David,[qv] also has become a novelist of merit.

Edward Garnett, besides his original writing, edited Charles M. Doughty's famous *Arabia Deserta* and compiled an anthology of selections from the writings of W. H. Hudson. He also edited volumes of letters from Conrad and Galsworthy, after their deaths—the former volume containing letters written to him from 1900 to 1932, the latter from 1895 to 1924. These, with their notes by Garnett, are among the most valuable biographical sources for both authors.

Essentially, Garnett was a bookish man. Even his social satires, though they have pungency, smell of the lamp. His "poems in prose," *An Imaged World,* are modeled on those of Oscar Wilde. His plays are essentially undramatic, and are meant to be read rather than to be acted. His talent was derivative, and he was overshadowed during most of his life by the greater renown of his father and his wife, and during the end of it by the growing recognition of his son.

Nevertheless, he was something more than a mere reflex of a literary environment. Galsworthy, no mean critic himself, called Garnett "one of the greatest of English critics." He was a slow worker, thorough in his research to the point of exhaustion of the material, and in consequence he is represented by few volumes. He was not a precocious writer, and in addition many of his critical essays are still uncollected from the magazines in which they appeared.

A kindly, genial man, Garnett was retiring and modest to a fault; he pushed his friends forward but never himself, and was quite content to be known as the son, husband, and father of writers far more familiar to the general public than was he himself. His critical writing is sound and acute, and it will survive with the authors whom it evaluated.

PRINCIPAL WORKS: An Imaged World, 1894; Hogarth, 1911; Turgeniev, 1917; Papa's War and Other Satires, 1919; Friday Nights (essays) 1922; The Trial of Jeanne d'Arc and Other Plays, 1931.

ABOUT: New York Tribune October 29, 1922; Publishers' Weekly March 20, 1937.

GARNETT, RICHARD. See "BRITISH AUTHORS OF THE 19TH CENTURY"

*GARRETT, GARET (February 19, 1878-), American publicist, was born at Pana, Ill., and educated in the public schools. He was originally named Edward Peter Garrett, but has adopted his present name personally as well as for writing. He was a financial writer on the New York *Sun* from 1903 to 1905, on the *Times* in 1906 and 1907, on the *Wall Street Journal* in 1907 and 1908, and on the *Evening Post* from 1909 to 1912. He was editor of the *Times Annalist* from 1912 to 1914, and assistant editor of the *Tribune* from 1916 to 1918, since which time he has been a free-lance writer on political and economic topics, most of his work appearing in the *Saturday Evening Post.* He is unmarried, and lives in Tuckahoe, N.J.

He is the author of several novels, mostly with political backgrounds, but is far better known for his articles. *Ouroboros,* an economic forecast, was characterized by E. M. Nicholson as "lively and penetrating." He is a thoroughly competent, professional writer, strongly conservative in his viewpoint, and violently opposed to the New Deal and to liberalism in general. He has a gift for satire and his work is genuinely witty when the wit is not drowned by irritation. He is a specialist in financial

* Died November 6, 1954.

questions, especially in problems of taxation, and frequently succeeds in making even this dry subject readable and interesting to the layman.

PRINCIPAL WORKS: Where the Money Grows, 1911; The Blue Wound (novel) 1920; The Driver (novel) 1921; The Cinder Buggy (novel) 1922; Satan's Bushel (novel) 1923; Ouroboros, 1925; Harangue, 1927; The American Omen, 1929; The Bubble That Broke the World, 1932.

GASSET. See ORTEGA Y GASSET

GEDDES, Sir PATRICK (1854-April 16, 1932), British biologist and educator, was born in Perth, Scotland, the son of a captain in the Royal

Highlanders. He spent a year in the National Bank of Perth and attended University College, London, the University of Edinburgh, and the Sorbonne in Paris. Geddes was Huxley's assistant as demonstrator of physiology at University College, and taught zoology at the University of Aberdeen and botany at the University of Edinburgh. He was lecturer on natural history at the Edinburgh School of Medicine; in 1883 became professor of botany at University College, Dundee (St. Andrews University); and in 1919 professor of sociology and civics at the University of Bombay, India. At the time of his death Geddes was director of Scots College, Montpellier University, France. At Dundee he had taken up only a third of his teaching salary so that he might give attention to some of the multifarious projects that interested him. Lewis Mumford, an ardent disciple, remarked that, "One might get the impression that Professor Geddes is a vigorous institution, not a man." *Nature* called him "a figure apart in modern science." Besides being "one of the fathers of modern geography, and of much in modern psychology and biology," Geddes was a pioneer in city planning; directed the printing establishment of Geddes & Colleagues, which was chiefly interested in publishing works of Asiatic literature; and designed the Hebrew University building in Jerusalem. He was knighted in 1932. During his wanderings a home was maintained for his wife and three children on the top of Castle Hill in old Edinburgh. Mrs. Geddes died of fever in 1917, and a son, Alasdair, "ace of balloons," was killed in the First World War.

Besides his academic work, Geddes worked at marine zoological stations, made an expedition to Mexico to dig fossils, and toured India with his "Cities and Town Planning Exhibition." The first exhibit was sunk in the Indian Ocean by the German raider "Emden," but a new one was assembled by friends in England and sent to him. Amelia Defries describes Geddes as an agile, thin man, swift in movement and sudden in action, with shaggy eyebrows and beard. He died at seventy-eight.

PRINCIPAL WORKS: The Evolution of Sex (Outlines of General Biology, with Sir J. Arthur Thomson) 1889; Chapters in Modern Botany, 1893; A Study in City Development, 1904; Cities in Evolution, 1913; The Coming Polity (with V. V. Branford) 1917; Ideas at War (with Gilbert Slater) 1917; Our Social Inheritance (with V. V. Branford) 1919; The Life and Work of Sir Jagadis C. Bose, 1920.

ABOUT: Defries, A. D. Pioneers of Science; Gardiner, A. G. Pillars of Society; Zangwill, I. Without Prejudice; Nation May 4, 1932; New Republic April 27, 1932; October 30, 1929.

GEDDES, VIRGIL (May 14, 1897-), American playwright and poet, writes: "Born on a farm in Dixon County, Nebraska. Educated in country grade schools and small town high school. Served in the United States Navy during World War I. Worked at various jobs, from 1920 to 1930, in Boston, Chicago, and Paris. Was financial editor of the Chicago *Tribune,* Eu-

ropean edition, from 1924 to 1928. Wrote first play in 1926, *The Frog,* which was produced by the Boston Stage Society in 1927. First play produced in New York was *The Earth Between,* produced by the Provincetown Players in 1929, in which Bette Davis made her first appearance on the New York professional stage. In 1932 I founded and directed the Brookfield Players, of Brookfield, Conn. (where I live), one of the first of the summer try-out theatres. From 1935 to 1937 I was managing producer of Unit 1-A of the New York City branch of the Federal Theatre, which produced *Chalk Dust, Battle Hymn, Hymn to the Rising Sun,* and other plays.

"I have been active in the theatre as dramatist, producer, and critic for about fifteen years. I have had no formal training for any part of this profession. I took to writing plays because it seemed to me the most direct means of getting down in black and white the feelings and thoughts of the kind of people I was interested in. Through my plays I have endeavored to present phases of American life not heretofore seen on the stage. This has necessitated my using methods unestablished by traditional playwriting. I am, therefore, I suppose, an unorthodox playwright.

"Through my numerous pamphlets and articles in theatrical journals I have endeavored to educate that public (and those critics) interested in the theatre as to the true nature of dramatic material and art, as I see it. Many of my plays have caused considerable controversy, notably *The Earth Between, In the Tradition, Native Ground.* Nevertheless, I have had numerous productions of my work, in New York and throughout the United States, even on the radio. I have also written considerable poetry and since 1920 have published many poems in magazine and book form."

* * *

Mr. Geddes is unmarried. When the Theatre Guild bought an option on *Native Ground* and then refused to produce it, he conducted a one-man picket of its theatre. In 1938 he was connected with the Washington office of the Federal Theatre, and remained with it until the project was killed.

Of *Native Ground,* whose theme of incest violated one of the great traditional taboos, Horace Gregory said: "There is no one writing for the American stage today . . . who equals Virgil Geddes' command of diction. . . . Here are no experiments in verbal technic but the mature development of a genuine style. . . . The potentialities of Mr. Geddes' work are very great, indeed, and with each publication of a new play it seems to show a steady gain in power and direction." Whitney Bolton said that "his devotion to the theatre, his experience in it, his calm literate mind, all enforce a respectful hearing for him." As a minority report on his "Freudian and cosmological overtones," Grenville Vernon (in the *Commonweal*) called his plays "so starkly underwritten that they are little more than scenarios, . . . repetitious, discursive," and said that in his opinion Mr. Geddes was "neither a poet nor a dramatist." Barrett Clark said of him: "He is not much inclined to talk, and when he does it is with a slow, suppressed, and passionate restraint."

PRINCIPAL WORKS: *Plays:* The Frog, 1928; The Earth Between and Behind the Night, 1930; Native Ground, The Plowshare's Gleam, As the Crow Flies, 1932; The Stable and the Grove, 1933; Pocahontas and the Elders, 1933; Four Comedies From the Life of George Emery Blum (In the Tradition, I Have Seen Myself Before, The Drink in the Body, By the Soul You May Bury) 1934. *Criticism*—Beyond Tragedy, 1930; The American Theatre: What Can Be Done? 1933; Towards Revolution in the Theatre, 1933; The Theatre of Dreadful Night, 1934; The Melodramadness of Eugene O'Neill, 1934; Left Turn For American Drama, 1934. *Poetry*—40 Poems 1926; Poems: 41-70, 1926; Decisions Before Battle, 1939.

ABOUT: Block, A. The Changing World in Theatre and Plays; Clark, B. H. An Hour of American Drama; Flanagan, H. Arena; Geddes, V. The Earth Between . . . (see Preface by B. H. Clark); Commonweal April 9, 1937; French's Bulletin April 1930.

GEDYE, GEORGE ERIC ROWE (May 27, 1890-), English journalist, writes: "The day when my English literature master a t Queen's College, T a u n t o n, said: "Gedye, y o u a r e d o o m e d to one of three callings—writing, the stage, or the church," was the highlight of my school-d a y s. By environment destined for a business career which I not only detested  but knew myself entirely unfitted for, I was not discouraged when my parents' first enquiries in journalistic circles met with the advice: 'Do all you can to start your boy in any other career.' For several years I persisted in accumulating a varied collection of rejection slips for short stories, articles, and even a poem or two, with an occasional glorious appearance in print, the while my family patiently endeavored to acclimatize me successively in a bank and an insurance office. In August 1914 I joined the London University Officers' Training Corps, was gazetted to a commission in the Gloucestershire Regiment, went to France in November 1915, served in the front line until blown up and shell-shocked in 1916, served as instructor to an officer cadet battalion in England, returned to France as captain in the Intelligence Corps, and was finally attached to the Intelligence Section of 2nd Army Headquarters. Attached to the cavalry as German interpreter in the advance to the Rhine, I served on the staff of the

Military Governor of Cologne, and later on the International Allied Rhineland High Commission until 1922, when I resigned to take up journalism at last.

"I picked up a space rate job for the London *Times,* and six months later with the French occupation of the Ruhr I became special correspondent of the *Times* and held the post until 1926. After six months on the desk in London I went in 1925 to Vienna as correspondent for Central Europe and the Balkans. Fired by the *Times* because I insisted on showing up the Franc Forgery scandal, which involved many leading Hungarian political personalities, I took up a parallel post with the *Daily Express.* Two years later I resigned to take up the same job with the *Daily Telegraph* and to become 'second man' in the New York *Times* Vienna Bureau. Two years later I became correspondent for Central and Southeastern Europe for the New York *Times,* and miraculously managed not to be expelled from Vienna during the four years of clerico-Fascist dictatorship. I covered the last hours of free Austria, the Nazi invasion, and the horrors of the first persecution of the Jews, Socialists, and Communists in Vienna. I was given two orders of expulsion by the Gestapo. I then asked for permission to cover Czechoslovakia's six months' agony which ended with the Nazi invasion of March 1939. Eventually the British Legation got me a safe conduct to leave. After a brief visit to the United States I was appointed Moscow correspondent.

"Besides my books, I translated George London's *Red Russia* from the French in 1928. Between whiles I have contributed many articles to publications grave and gay, chiefly the former, especially those of liberal and anti-Fascist color."

* * *

G. E. R. Gedye was born in Clevedon, Somerset, and educated at Clarence School (Weston-super-Mare), Queen's College (Taunton), and London University. He was married to Elisabeth Bremer, of Cologne, in 1928; they have no children. Among his recreations, with swimming, skiing, and sun-basking, he lists "irritating the conventional." His books have frequently achieved that end, but their headlong style and immediacy have made them best sellers in England and exceedingly popular in this country. In the summer of 1940, frustrated by rigid censorship, he left Moscow for Istanbul. His name is pronounced *ged'ee.*

PRINCIPAL WORKS: A Wayfarer in Austria, 1928; The Revolver Republic, 1930; Heirs to the Habsburgs, 1932; Betrayal in Central Europe (in England: Fallen Bastions) 1939.

ABOUT: Gedye, G. E. R. Heirs to the Habsburgs (see Foreword by G. P. Hooch); Howe, Q. The News and How to Understand It; Time September 3, 1940; Wilson Library Bulletin October 1939.

GEIJERSTAM, GÖSTA af (1888-   ), Swedish novelist and artist, is one of four sons of Gustaf af Geijerstam. He was reared in Sweden, and educated to be a painter, studying at Munich, Berlin, and Paris. His work belongs to no particular school, his favorite subjects comprising sweeping landscapes in water-color, generally black and white and blue. Geijerstam came to Norway in 1906; he had been a sickly child and it was thought that the air in Norway would benefit him. He returned there every summer thereafter, and lived in a hut in Gudbrandsdalen, where he painted and lived as the people there lived. Exhibitions of his oil and water-color paintings have been held in both Oslo and Bergen.

Memories of Geijerstam's first summer in the old mountain pasture land are reproduced in a charming "open-air" book, *Ormpojken Roald och Jag,* illustrated with his own sketches. During the first World War, Geijerstam, whose mother was Finnish, went to Germany to enlist in the Finnish battalion which the Germans were training for a organized attempt to help Finland break away from Russia. The book which he wrote about the Finnish battalion (*Finska Bataljonen*), one of his first, is the only one in which he has found his subject outside rural Norway. Geijerstam's novels in general deal with aliens, isolated beings, "outsiders" in this world, people who are unable to adapt themselves, writes Sigrid Undset in a biographical sketch. "All Geijerstam's books deal with a problem which is not one of the least fundamental in our age when most values are being re-assessed—the question of what a human life is worth. What right has a human being to live and be himself, if he is predestined by his entire nature to be an outsider, a recluse? And are there other and less conventional human values than the usefulness of a human being to society?"

Lewis Gannett applies his favorite adjective, "sunlit," to Geijerstam's *Northern Summer,* which the New York *Times* called "a charming and almost idyllic story, written with unaffected simplicity and good humor." *Storevik,* the sequel, continues the story of a Norwegian family growing up in their island refuge in a Norwegian fjord. *Iva,* on the contrary, is restrained and sombre. Joran Birkeland, Geijerstam's translator, in her account of a visit to his home in Gudbrandsdalen before the 1940 German invasion of Norway, described the writer as having deep gray eyes, straight graying hair, and a deep-lined, thin, dark face. She reported that he spends his summers in a low gray-brown house, surrounded by wild gladioli and rowan trees, with his wife, Astri, and several children.

WORKS AVAILABLE IN ENGLISH TRANSLATION: Northern Summer, 1937; Storevik, 1938; Iva, 1939; Northern Winter, 1940.

ABOUT: Undset, S. Gösta of Geijerstam.

GEISEL, THEODOR SEUSS (March 4, 1904-), American humorist and artist, who writes and draws under the pseudonym  of "Dr. Seuss," was born in Springfield, Mass., the s o n o f Theodor R. Geisel, Superintendent of Parks in that city, and Henrietta (S e u s s) Geisel. After graduation from the Central High School he w e n t to Dartmouth College, w h e r e h e edited *Jack-o'-Lantern* and took advantage of the institution's famous winter sports, notably skiing. After graduation in 1925 young Geisel wrote a column for the Springfield *Union,* then set out for Lincoln College, Oxford University. Finding a course in the punctuation of Shakespeare dull, he drew pictures during lectures, discovering a real ability in cartooning. In a period of travel and study on the continent, chiefly in France and Italy, he wrote a long novel in longhand, which remains unpublished. On his return to the United States Geisel began to draw in earnest, coining his pen-name (in a double sense) from his mother's maiden name and a long-coveted Ph.D. which he never got around to earning. Fantastic representations of bears, lions, flying cows, "hippocrasses and blinkets" were less successful than depictions of turtles. *Judge* bought three turtles for seventy-five

dollars, on the strength of which Dr. Seuss married Helen Palmer, a classmate at Oxford, in November 1927. More tangible means of support came from the Flit Company, which had spotted a *Judge* cartoon, dealing sympathetically with a mediaeval knight who, after spending the whole day spraying every cranny of his castle with that insecticide, was thanklessly awakened from sound sleep by a dragon. The success of Dr. Seuss' subsequent campaign encouraged humor in advertising.

Ten years later Dr. Seuss essayed the writing and illustrating of books for children, with encouraging results. Anne Carroll Moore said of *And To Think That I Saw It on Mulberry Street* that it had the dynamic quality of the comic strip without its vulgarity. Two other juveniles followed, alternated by an adult hilarity, *The Seven Lady Godivas,* written not only to correct the ageless belief that there was only one, but to escape the monotony of writing about nothing but "men folks and children, dragons or fish." Mr. Geisel has also painted a number of murals for private homes; modeled several of his weird creations in plaster; and traveled in over thirty countries in Europe, the Near East, and South America. His work combines bland American foolishness with the humorous exaggeration of German comic artists and the insane ingenuity of the British Heath Robinson. Dr. Seuss has capable, sensitive hands; a pleasant, strong, dark face; and wears modern rimless spectacles. In 1941 he blossomed as a political cartoonist for the newspaper *PM,* directing most of his satirical fantasy against the Isolationist Ostrich. His pseudonym is pronounced *sooss.*

PRINCIPAL WORKS: And to Think That I Saw It on Mulberry Street, 1937; The 500 Hats of Bartholomew Cubbins, 1938; The King's Stilts, 1939; The Seven Lady Godivas, 1939; Horton Hatches the Egg, 1940.

ABOUT: Wilson Library Bulletin November 1939.

GELLHORN, MARTHA ELLIS (1908-), American novelist and journalist, was born in St. Louis, of a well-to-do Middle Western family. She traveled in Europe, where she met her first husband, Marquis Bertrand de Juvenel, a French journalist; published her first novel, *What Mad Pursuit* (1934) at twenty-six, while she was still the Marquise; and worked on a newspaper in Albany, N.Y. "Crude as it is," remarked the New York *Times* about *What Mad Pursuit,* "there is something fresh and appealing about this book." It deals with three neurotic young women from

n exclusive Eastern woman's college who
ave an invariable knack of getting into
rouble. Miss Gellhorn was introduced to
Harry L. Hopkins when the latter was in
harge of the Federal Emergency Relief
Administration, and got from him an assignment to survey living conditions of people

on relief in indus-
trial areas. After
turning in her report,
Miss Gellhorn re-
wrote four sections of
it as short stories that
formed a novel on a
central theme and
which she entitled
*The Trouble I've
Seen*. It was an im-
pressive if depressing

Blackstone

human document for which H. G. Wells
wrote an introduction.

In Spain during the civil war, where she
had gone on a magazine assignment, Miss
Gellhorn met Ernest Hemingway[qv] behind
the lines of the Loyalist army, and is supposed to have been the original of the girl
in his play, *The Fifth Column.* Hemingway
dedicated *For Whom the Bell Tolls* to her,
and on November 21, 1940, after his second
wife had obtained a Florida divorce, married
her at Cheyenne, Wyoming.

Early in 1941 Miss Gellhorn, with
Hemingway, went to the Orient as special
correspondent for *Collier's Weekly,* the new
odyssey taking her along the Burma Road.
She had previously been in Czechoslovakia
and Finland for *Collier's,* covering news
events after the Munich pact and during
the war waged on Finland by Russia.

A Stricken Field (1940), a novel narrated by one Mary Douglas, a journalist,
deals with refugees in Czechoslovakia after
the latter was absorbed by Germany. Edith
Walton of the New York *Times* stated that
it "wavers on the borderline of fiction and
non-fiction." It is "a compelling book and
a moving one, but as a novel it is weak."
She concluded that Miss Gellhorn was an
admirable reporter; that verdict seems to be
unanimous. Of *The Heart of Another*
(1941), a book of short stories, the New
York *Times* said: "The noise of guns
rumbles in these tales that take readers
to Cuba and Finland, Paris, Madrid, and
Corsica." The author is slim and blonde.

PRINCIPAL WORKS: What Mad Pursuit, 1934;
The Trouble I've Seen, 1936; A Stricken Field,
1940; The Heart of Another, 1941.

ABOUT: Cowles, V. Looking for Trouble;
Life January 6, 1941; New York Times November
22, 23, 1940.

GEORGE, STEFAN ANTON (July 12,
1868-December 4, 1933), German poet,
was born in Büdesheim, of a middle-class
Catholic family orig-
inally from Lorraine;
in his veins ran
French, Walloon, and
Celtic blood as well as
German. When he
was five the family
moved to Bingen,
where he was reared.
He was for a time a
student at the Gym-
nasium in Darmstadt,

and after 1888 studied art and philosophy at
the Universities of Berlin, Munich and Paris;
from the beginning, however, his family
realized that he was destined for no ordinary
profession, and left him free to wander
through Europe and study as he pleased.
He traveled in England, Switzerland, France,
Belgium and Italy, became proficient in all
the Latin tongues, and in Paris became a
close associate of the Symbolists—Mallarmé,
Viélé-Griffin, and their group. The other
great influence on his work was that of the
English Pre-Raphaelite school. He translated
D'Annunzio, Verlaine, Rimbaud, Mallarmé,
Regnier, Rossetti, Shakespeare's *Sonnets,*
and Dante's *Divine Comedy* into German; but
his own poetry for years was published and
circulated only privately. In 1892 he founded
a magazine, *Blätter für die Kunst* [*Pages
on Art*], but this too was circulated only
among his own small and rigid group of
disciples, chief of whom was Hugo von
Hofmannsthal. He thus came to public attention already the leader of a "strict and
exclusive" school of poetry.

George throughout his life refused to concern himself with mundane affairs or to have
any personal association except with a very
small and selected group. He had hardly
any intimates—though ironically, considering
his last days, his closest friend was a Jew.
He made no secret of his homosexual tendencies, and never married. It may be said
that he had no private life, and very little
of a public one. Gradually, however, he
became recognized as the spokesman in Germany of a neo-romanticism which grew into
a new classicism; he was, to quote Arthur
Eloesser, "the renovator and enricher of German intellectual life" for many years. In
1927 he received the Goethe Prize, of 10,000
marks. His views were openly Nietzschean;

he was "against the mass man," "for the heroic man." It is not surprising, therefore, that the Nazis, finding Germany almost denuded of writers of any rank, enthusiastically adopted George, proclaiming him as the prophet of their régime. Goebbels offered him membership in the Prussian Academy of Arts and Sciences. He did not answer; he never answered letters. He was inordinately shy and haughty, a withdrawn aristocrat of the spirit. But by way of reply he left Germany at once (accompanied by his Jewish friend) and went first to Italy and then to Switzerland, where he lived with a sister. It was in Lugano that he died. Once he was dead, the Nazi officials took him over bodily; they gave their greatest literary prize his name, and he is now officially *the* Nazi poet. But on his deathbed he asked to be buried in Switzerland until Germany was free. And Goebbels sent a wreath "from the German "Reich" to be laid on his Swiss grave!

There is much in George's work which might justify the Nazi assumption. He made Nietzsche's Superman a present reality, he lived in an ivory tower where he practised formal art for art's sake and that alone. He was independent of time: as Eloesser put it, he "practised the noble abstinence of standing aside from the life of his own age . . . and entering into no communication with it save through his work. . . . His poetry is at once an antique temple and a mediaeval cathedral." He considered poetry to be "static": a poem is a surmounting of passions and privations; it does not communicate. It is an expression of "the cosmic ego." What Morton Dauwen Zabel called his "calm ascetic nobility" gradually became, with the events of the First World War and its aftermath, unmistakably nationalistic. His is, said Zabel, "an art dispassionate and intolerant, yet of a pure and ordered idealism," producing "some of the finest formal poetry in modern literature." His work, the German critic W. Scheller remarked, is "severe and noble," he is "the guardian of the temple." His aloof spirit could not realize what meaning lesser men might take from his words.

He looked the poet, with dark wavy hair and a broad brow with remarkable eyebrow bulges. His handwriting was like print; his books were published in a special antique type. His work was almost entirely in lyric poetry, though the evolution of a new formal drama was one of his interests. Very little of it has been translated into English; it is difficult and utterly remote from our spirit or the times. But Paul Rosenfeld

said of George's poetry: "It is immediately perceptible to all the senses, exquisitely resonant and pictorial, often of a brocade-like or satiny splendor. . . . Rilke alone among contemporary German poets equaled him in point of artistic stature and intellectual scope. . . . Hard, gem-like, his sapiently modulated poems approach the classic idea of the finite, self-contained, serenely immobile object."

In addition to his poems included in the translated edition listed below, ten appeared in issues Nos. 3 and 4 of the magazine *Poet Lore* for 1939.

WORKS AVALABLE IN ENGLISH: George Hofmannsthal, Rilke (ed. by M. Sommerfield) 1938.

ABOUT: Düberg, F. Stefan George (in German); Eloesser, A. Modern German Literature Klage, L. Stefan George (in German); Mann K. & E. Escape to Life; Scheller, W. Stefan George (in German); Contemporary Review June 1935; Deutsche Rundschau July 1928, January 1934 July 1939; Europe Nouvelle March 24, 1934 Journal des Débats December 8, 1933, January 12 1934; Mercure de France July 1, 1928, January and February 15, 1934, October 15, 1938; Neue Rundschau October 1932, January 1934; New Republic October 28, 1940; Nuova Antologia March 16, 1926, January 16, 1934; Poetry March 1934 Preussische Jahrbuch July 1928, November 1934 Publications of the Modern Language Association June 1936; Queen's Quarterly November 1937 Revue Politique et Littéraire January 6, 1934 Saturday Review of Literature July 18, 1931 Westermanns Monatshefte July 1928.

GEORGE, WALTER LIONEL (March 20, 1882-January 30, 1926), English novelist, who wrote as W. L. George, was born in Paris and reared there until the age of twenty-three. Until he was twenty he could not speak English at all, and his entire outlook was that of the French lower middle class. Moreover, although his parents were British subjects, his

mother was a Jewess. Temperamentally, he was singularly ill equipped to essay a career as an English writer.

Before he turned to writing, he had studied chemistry, engineering, and law, and had served in the French army. When in 1905 he finally went to England, it was to work in a business office. He turned next to journalism, and was a special correspondent for various London papers on the Continent until 1911, when the immediate success of his first novel, *A Bed of Roses*, enabled him to devote his entire time thereafter to creative work. During the World War he served in the Ministry of Munitions. In 1920 he made an extended lecture tour in the United States.

George was married three times: in 1908 to Helen Porter, who died in 1914; in 1916 to Helen Agnes Madden, by whom he had two sons, and who died in Houston, Texas, in 1920; and in 1921 to Kathleen Geipel, a novelist, who survived him.

He died at forty-three, horribly, of creeping paralysis, which started in his right hand and gradually made him completely helpless. He faced the end with indomitable courage, dictating his last work to his wife and a secretary who alone could understand his almost unintelligible speech. He was a dark, handsome, burly man, who all his life spoke English with a French accent.

In some ways George as a personality reminds one of Arnold Bennett, who also never realized that in the eyes of many of his acquaintances he was considered "a bit of a cad." The French logic and the French thrift which were part of his earliest training both betrayed him; he never understood how he outraged people, or how *outré* some of his actions appeared to conventional Englishmen and Americans. When he wrote *The Triumph of Gallio* he intended it to be largely a self-portrait in disillusionment and stoicism, and was amazed to find it hailed as a good study of a bounder! He had, as someone has remarked, wit but no humor, conscience but no taste. The misunderstanding he met embittered him, and he over-compensated by arrogance which further alienated those who knew him.

Yet he was a sincere and genuine liberal, a forward-looking man who embraced pacifism, republicanism, labor organization, and feminism among his earnest beliefs. Because *A Bed of Roses* was a book about a prostitute, his public insisted on his specializing in the problems of women, and resented his attempts to write of other things. Indeed, this and *The Second Blooming* are among his best books, though he was annoyed when his serious attempts to portray sociological and psychological problems were reviewed only in terms of the sexual elements involved. He was the most generous of authors, with no professional jealousy; a great believer in the devotion of writers to their own time and place, he constantly encouraged young novelists who seemed to him to be truly modern in their outlook.

As Sheila Kaye-Smith remarked, the outstanding characteristic of George's work is its extraordinary vitality. "It may not live forever," she said, "but at least it lives now." His early promise was not all fulfilled, but it came near enough to fulfilment to make one feel that it just missed being first class.

PRINCIPAL WORKS: *Novels*—A Bed of Roses, 1911; The City of Light, 1912; Israel Kalisch, 1913; The Little Beloved (in England, The Making of an Englishman) 1914; The Second Blooming, 1914; The Strangers' Wedding, 1916; Blind Alley, 1919; Caliban, 1920; The Confession of Ursula Trent, 1921; The Stiff Lip, 1922; One of the Guilty, 1923; The Triumph of Gallio, 1923; Gifts of Sheba, 1926; Children of the Morning, 1926; The Ordeal of Monica Mary, 1927. *Short Stories*—Olga Nazimov, 1915; Selected Short Stories, 1927. *Non-Fiction*—Engines of Social Progress, 1907; France in the Twentieth Century, 1908; Labour and Housing at Port Sunlight, 1909; Woman and Tomorrow, 1913; Dramatic Actualities, 1914; Anatole France, 1915; The Intelligence of Woman, 1917; A Novelist on Novels, 1918; Eddies of the Day, 1919; Hail, Columbia! 1921; A London Mosaic, 1921; The Story of Woman, 1925.

ABOUT: Harris, F. Contemporary Portraits: Third Series; Hind, C. L. More Authors and I; Swinnerton, F. A London Bookman; Bookman November 1920; Fortnightly Review April 1, 1926; Saturday Review of Literature March 13, 1926.

GERHARDI, WILLIAM ALEXANDER

(November 21, 1895-), English novelist, was born in St. Petersburg (now Leningrad), but he was the son of English parents, Charles Gerhardi, a cotton-spinning manufacturer of remote Belgian descent, and Clara (Wadsworth) Gerhardi. He was educated at the St. Annen Schule and the Reformierte Schule  in St. Petersburg and at Worcester College, Oxford. His career as a "polyglot" began in childhood, when he could already speak fluent English, Russian, French, and German. When the First World War started he enlisted as a trooper in the Fifth Reserve Cavalry of the British Army, soon becoming a cadet and ending as a captain and as military attaché to the British Embassy in Petrograd (Leningrad). From 1918 to 1920 he was with the British Military Mission to Siberia. He thus observed both the Russian Revolution and the Civil War and Allied Intervention at first hand, and these stirring scenes form the background of his first two novels. He has been decorated with the Order of the British Empire, the Czecho-Slovakian Croix de Guerre, and the Russian Order of St. Stanislav.

Mr. Gerhardi began writing at fourteen—with "a monstrous novel on Tolstoyan lines—in Russian." (He published a novel in 1934 called *Resurrection*—but it was not Tolstoyan, and not in Russian!) Chekhov, whose biography he wrote, is his literary idol, but in English his model is H. G. Wells. What he likes about them both is their vividness, which to him is "everything." He wrote his first book on a card index; but now he dictates his books into a dictaphone, designing his novels "like a carpet or a tapestry," and "enriching the design" as he goes along. He has a strong vein of satire, underlying a gift for realism and acute characterization. It may be said of him that he is one of the few genuinely European writers, whose nationality is almost unguessable from his work; one critic remarked that his short stories read like excellent translations from some foreign language.

Slender, blond, nervous, with deep-set eyes and a sensuous mouth, Gerhardi looks younger than his age. He is unmarried, and has for some years lived in London. His breadth of experience, his proficiency with languages, and his international viewpoint make him invaluable to the government in times like the present, and he has, of course, been a British subject from birth. Among his closest friends were the late Lord Northcliffe and his brother, the late Lord Rothermere; he rides, dances, plays tennis, and in times of peace leads a very active social life. He has lived in most countries of the civilized world and has twice circumnavigated the globe. He is a true cosmopolitan, in his temperament as well as in his work. He is objective and a lover of reason who hates every sort of mysticism. But perhaps his salient characteristic is the cool amusement with which he regards and depicts, by preference, neurotic, emotional, and idiosyncratic persons and peoples.

PRINCIPAL WORKS: Futility, 1922; Anton Chekhov (biography) 1925; The Polyglots, 1925; A Bad End, 1926; The Vanity Bag, 1927; Donna Quixote (play) 1927; Perfectly Scandalous (play) 1927; Pretty Creatures (short stories) 1927; Jazz and Jasper (in America: Eva's Apples) 1928; Pending Heaven, 1930; Memoirs of a Polyglot (autobiography) 1931; The Memoirs of Satan (with B. Lunn) 1932; The Casanova Fable (with H. Kingsmill) 1934; Resurrection, 1934; Of Mortal Love, 1936; Meet Yourself As You Really Are (non-fiction, with Prince L. Loewenstein) 1936; My Wife's the Least of It, 1938; The Romanovs: Evocation of the Past As a Mirror for the Present, 1939.

ABOUT: Gerhardi, W. Memoirs of a Polyglot; Bookman November 1927.

*GEROULD. Mrs. KATHARINE (FULLERTON) (February 6, 1879-   ), American novelist, essayist, and short-story writer, was born in Brockton, Mass., the daughter of Bradford Morton Fullerton (D.D.) and Julia M. (Ball) Fullerton. Educated at Radcliffe College, she received her B.A. degree in 1900 and a master's degree next year, when she went to Bryn Mawr College as Reader in English. A year's leave of absence in 1908-9 was spent in England and France. She "sat in quiet *tête-à-tête* with Henry James in the garden of Lamb House"; in her childhood years Katharine Fullerton had heard the deep notes of George Meredith's voice. She left Bryn Mawr in June 1910 to marry Gordon Hall Gerould, professor of English at Princeton since 1916. The Geroulds have a son Christopher, and a daughter, Sylvia. For other personal details, one may quote Mrs. Gerould herself: "The color of my eyes is no secret to my acquaintance, and is something I have long ceased to consider of any importance, even to myself. But when strange women in Oklahoma demand to be told it, I feel that I am being morally burglarized. I feel even more as an innocent woman must feel if accident causes her to be searched by a police matron." The quotation is from an essay in her second book of essays, *Ringside Seats*. Of the first, *Modes and Morals*, the Springfield *Republican* remarked, "A little superior, a little supercilious Mrs. Gerould doubtless is, and not a little paradoxical." Lawrence Gilman paid the same book the following backhanded compliment: "One salutes Mrs. Gerould of the short stories as a fictional artist of subtle power and distinguished skill. One views her secondary personality, the social philosopher, the student of manners and morals, as an example of the perturbing truth that a mind which creates with brilliancy and force may be feeble and unrewarding in ratiocination."

Mrs. Gerould's writing career began in 1900, when she won a prize for the best story in the *Century's* competition for college graduates. One of her stories in *Vain Oblations* concerns a New England woman who ends up as a more or less willing member of a particularly savage African tribe. Herself a tenth-generation New Englander, Mrs. Gerould "emerged from that bleakness into the more tepid air of the Middle Atlantic States. For the first time I saw men and women frankly preoccupied not only with life and liberty, but with the pursuit of happiness." Her name is pronounced *jer'uld*.

PRINCIPAL WORKS: Vain Oblations, 1914; The Great Tradition, 1915; Hawaii: Scenes and Impressions, 1916; A Change of Air, 1917; Modes and Morals (essays) 1919; Lost Valley, 1922; Valiant Dust, 1922; Conquistador, 1923; The Aristocratic West, 1925; The Light That Never Was, 1931; Ringside Seats (essays) 1937.

ABOUT: Sherman, S. P. The Genius of America.

'GIBBON, LEWIS GRASSIC." See MITCHELL, J. L.

GIBBONS, FLOYD PHILLIPS (July 16, 1886-September 24, 1939), American journalist, was born in Washington, D.C.,  the son of Edward Thomas Gibbons and Emma Theresa (Phillips) Gibbons. He attended Gonzaga College and the Georgetown (D.C.) University, and at twenty-one was a reporter on the Minneapolis *Daily News*. After working on the Milwaukee *Free Press* and the Minneapolis *Tribune* he landed a job on the staff of the Chicago *Tribune* in 1912, one which he badly needed. Burton Rascoe recalls his arrival at the paper, when he obtained an advance to get a bath and shave, and a skin-tight suit of large gray checks. Gibbons was war correspondent with Villa in the Mexican Revolution in 1915, reporting his raid on Columbus, N.M., in March 1916, and accompanied Pershing on his punitive expedition into Mexico as a correspondent accredited by the War Department. His series of articles on poorly-equipped state troops was quoted extensively during the campaign for universal military training in the United States. He accompanied General Funston on his last inspection of American militia and regulars on the border and in Mexico.

In 1917 Gibbons was a passenger on the S.S. "Laconia," torpedoed and sunk on February 25 two hundred miles off the Irish coast. He was on his way to London as a *Tribune* correspondent, and after his rescue cabled 4,000 words on the disaster to his paper. As war correspondent in France in 1918, Gibbons had his left eye shot out at the battle of Château-Thierry. For this, and for services as foreign director of the *Tribune* and editor of the European edition published in Paris, Gibbons was awarded the French and Italian Croix de Guerre with palm. He was likewise made an officer of the Legion of Honor in 1923. That same year Colonel Robert McCormick, owner of the *Tribune,* sent Gibbons to Algiers and Timbuctoo to investigate the sheiks there and find if they were anything like the romantic cavaliers of E. M. Hull's current novel, *The Sheik.* He traveled in airplanes over the greater part of Europe, North Africa, Asia Minor, and the Gobi desert, experiences "which made the famous message to Garcia sound like a ride on a Fifth Avenue bus," according to Rascoe, who said Gibbons possessed "a virility that [was] simple, honest, direct, homely and ingenuous."

In the late 1920's Gibbons was a popular radio commentator, sponsored by the now defunct *Literary Digest* as "The Headline Hunter," broadcasting his experiences and opinions at a maximum speed of 245 words a minute. As a journalist he also covered revolutions in Germany and Russia, the Spanish war against Riff tribes in Morocco, the Sino-Japanese war, and the civil war in Spain. Gibbons died at fifty-three of a heart ailment at his farm at Saylorsburg, Pa., near Stroudsburg. A requiem mass was sung for him at Dahlgren Chapel, Georgetown University, and he was buried in Mount Olivet Cemetery in Washington. He was survived by two brothers and two sisters. Gibbons' books were written in a rapid, sensational, journalistic style. He had full lips, a "rugged ringside face," stood six feet and weighed 190 pounds, and usually wore a gray suit, a soft hat, and a linen patch over his lost eye (the other was blue). He is recalled principally as a legend—even in his lifetime—of American journalism.

PRINCIPAL WORKS: How the Laconia Sank, 1917; Militia Mobilization on the Border, 1917; And They Thought We Wouldn't Fight, 1918; The Red Knight of Germany, 1927; The Red Napoleon, 1929.

ABOUT: Gilbert, D. Floyd Gibbons: Knight of the Air; New York Times September 25, 26, 28, 1939; Newsweek October 2, 1939; Publishers' Weekly October 14, 1939; Time October 2, 1939.

GIBBONS, STELLA (January 5, 1902-), English novelist and poet, writes: "My father was a doctor in a poor district in North London. I was the eldest of three children. Our home life was not happy, and certainly this fact made me rely on my own imagination for entertainment and what is now called 'escape.' Before I could read I used to entertain my two little brothers and other children with fantastic romances. Story-telling and the

creation of imaginary people and situations was thus one of my earliest habits. I loved reading, too. We had an old bookcase carved from black oak and decorated with figures of Adam and Eve and bunches of apples, and herein I discovered Lord Beaconsfield's gorgeous Jewish romance, *Alroy*, and Thomas Moore's Oriental poem, *Lallah Rookh*. The glowing Eastern landscapes and brilliant figures charmed me, I am sure, because they were so different from the squalid, dull streets in which I walked every day.

"My father had eccentric ideas about our education, and I was not sent to school but was educated at home by a series of governesses until I was thirteen. I became precocious and spoilt, and when at thirteen I went to the North London Collegiate School for Girls (founded by the famous pioneer in women's education, Frances Mary Buss), I was naturally not happy at this excellent school. But I made two lifelong friends there; and I used to write school stories and sketches which had a long waiting-list of girls eager to read them. At nineteen I went to University College, London, where I stayed for two years and took the journalism course—at that time the only one of its kind in London.

"My first job was a decoder of cables with the British United Press at three pounds a week. Here I learned to write professionally; to interest the reader, reject irrelevancies, and present facts simply and (I hope) vividly. I spent ten years or so in Fleet Street at various jobs—dramatic criticism, special reporting, fashion writing, literary criticism. I also wrote short stories and poetry.

"In 1933 I married Allan Bourne Webb, the actor and singer (not to be confused with Alan Webb, the actor). We have one daughter.

"I love writing. I use a pen and scribbling blocks from Woolworth's, and keep notebooks to jot down plots and characters and ideas. I go out very little to parties, but take every opportunity of broadening my experience by going to the places ordinary people go to—church, hospitals, the cinema, school prize-givings, social service committee meetings, etc. I find ample material here for stories, without looking for exotic settings.

"I believe in a good God and the Christian faith, and detest politics."

* * *

Miss Gibbons' burlesque of rural novels *Cold Comfort Farm*, won the *Femina Vie Heureuse* Prize in 1933. She has a story in *Modern English Short Stories*, and the one she considers her best, "Sisters," is in *Penguin Parade No. 3*. Her poems are in many anthologies. She lives with her husband and daughter in London.

PRINCIPAL WORKS: *Poetry*—The Mountain Beast and Other Poems, 1930; The Priestess and Other Poems, 1934; The Lowland Venus and Other Poems, 1938. *Fiction*—Cold Comfort Farm, 1932; Bassett, 1934; Enbury Heath, 1935; The Untidy Gnome, 1935; Miss Linsey and Pa, 1936; Roaring Tower (short stories) 1937; Nightingale Wood, 1938; My American, 1939; Christmas at Cold Comfort Farm, 1940.

ABOUT: Publishers' Weekly May 19, 1934.

GIBBS, ARTHUR HAMILTON (March 9, 1888-), Anglo-American novelist who writes as A. Hamilton Gibbs, was born in

London, the son of Henry James Gibbs and Helen (Hamilton) Gibbs, and the younger brother of Cosmo Hamilton [qv] (who dropped his last name) and of Sir Philip Gibbs.[qv] He was educated at the College de St. Malo, in France,

where he acquired fluent colloquial French, and at St. John's College, Oxford. Between the two colleges, he worked for a firm of gold assayers and refiners. At Oxford he and his brother Cosmo founded the *Tuesday Review*, which he edited; but he also rowed on the college crew and was noted as an amateur boxer.

Long before this he was already a published author, for at fourteen he wrote a weekly London letter for a Cambridge University magazine, and at fifteen began to have short stories published. When he left the university he became his brother Cosmo's secretary, and in 1912 he came to America as an actor in his brother's play, *The Blindness of Virtue*. At the beginning of the First World War he returned to England and enlisted as a trooper in the 21st Lancers. He was soon commissioned as an officer and transferred to the Royal Field Artillery, with which he served in France, Egypt and

Serbia. He was demobilized in 1919 with the rank of major. He received the Military Cross.

The same year he married Jeannette Philips, of Boston, a practicing attorney, and since 1920 he has lived permanently in the United States, his home now being in Middleboro, Mass. "I like the bigness of the United States," he says. "It has breathing spaces." Mrs. Gibbs has turned from the law to authorship, and has published several novels. Though it is necessary for Major and Mrs. Gibbs to spend much time in Boston or New York, they both prefer the country, and live there as much as possible. Tall, rangy, very dark, Major Gibbs "looks like a Mohawk Indian," and is an eager and skilled athlete—boxer, swimmer, tennis player, and "par" golfer. His hobby is the collection of old brass. He dislikes making speeches or attending social teas, and he says his two-fold ambition is, first, to win an amateur golf championship, and second, to write a book that satisfies *him*.

Four of Major Gibbs' books have been best sellers—*Soundings, Labels, Harness,* and *Chances.* He wrote *Gunfodder* in the intervals of military service at the front, and brought the completed manuscript back with him in his knapsack. In spite of his love of athletics and the outdoors (he says he is "a collector of sunshine"), his novels are not adventure stories, but narratives based on contemporary social and ethical problems. He has not the suavity and urbanity of his brother Cosmo, nor the scholarliness of his brother Philip, but his writing has a solidity that makes him not the least considerable member of the "writing Gibbses." Though his work is "popular" and neither esoteric nor profound, it is not cheap, and his books are unfailingly interesting and sincerely felt. Like so many others, his war experiences made him hate war, and he has fought the militaristic spirit ever since.

PRINCIPAL WORKS: The Complete Oxford Man, 1910; Cheadle and Son, 1911; The Hour of Conflict, 1913; The Persistent Lovers, 1914; Gunfodder (non-fiction) 1919; Soundings, 1925; Labels, 1926; Harness, 1928; Chances, 1930; Undertow, 1932; Rivers Glide On, 1934; Bluebottles (verse) 1935; The Need We Have, 1936; The Young Prince, 1937; A Half Inch of Candle, 1939.

ABOUT: Bookman August 1929.

GIBBS, Sir PHILIP HAMILTON (May 1, 1877-) English journalist and novelist, is the son of the late Henry Gibbs, a departmental chief at the Board of Education, and his wife, Helen Hamilton. He was privately educated, and was encouraged to write by his elder brother, who uses the name Cosmo Hamilton [qv] for literary work. Another brother, A. Hamilton Gibbs,[qv] is also a writer of reputation. At nineteen Philip was appointed educational editor to the publishing house of Cassell & Co.; in 1901 he left for Bolton, where he served for a year as managing editor to Tillotson's Literary Syndicate; after which he was taken on by the late Lord Northcliffe to run "Page 4" of the *Daily Mail* in association with Filson Young. This lasted only a few months, as did his next engagement with the *Daily Express.* A period of two years as literary editor of the *Tribune,* a radical daily started by Franklin Thomasson, a Bolton business man, ended in the failure of the paper (by no means through lack of merit), and caused Gibbs to go off to the South coast town of Littlehampton and write *The Street of Adventure,* a poignant novel of the joys and hazards of journalism in Fleet Street. A libel action, started by a journalist who deemed himself to have been defamed as one of the characters, was settled out of court, but Gibbs suffered a loss on the book at its first issue.

He worked for some time as a free-lance, writing a life of Buckingham and *Men and Women of the French Revolution,* and then became special correspondent to the *Daily Chronicle,* reporting such sensational events as the Sidney Street battle with anarchists and the cross-Atlantic chase after Crippen, the murderer. His biggest "scoop" was his alleged exposure of the late Dr. Frederick Cook, the Polar claimant, on which he staked his reputation in the face of bitter opposition. In 1911 he went to Portugal to report on the prisons after the revolution which ejected Manoel; in 1912 he covered the Balkan war for the *Graphic;* and in 1914 he reported on public opinion in Germany for the *Chronicle* and dealt with the Ulster troubles in Ireland.

Immediately on the outbreak of the First World War in 1914 Gibbs went to France for the *Chronicle.* After working under heavy restrictions for months, he became one of the five accredited correspondents with the Allied forces and produced some of the best war correspondence that has ever been written. All five correspondents were made

Knights of the Order of the British Empire in 1920.

Realities of War (1920) and the novel, *The Middle of the Road* (1923) told of the horrors and dreariness of long conflict and the impatience of youth with pre-war values. Gibbs travelled widely just after the war, lecturing in the United States in 1919, 1920, and 1921, interviewing the Pope (an astounding journalistic feat), and investigating conditions in Russia during the famine of 1921. About this time he resigned from the *Daily Chronicle* through disagreement with its Irish policy. He edited the *Review of Reviews* in 1920-21.

For the last twenty years Gibbs has been a prolific novelist and commentator on the European scene. His work is marked by a keen idealism, an impatience with shams, and a sense of the high adventure of life. The last war profoundly affected his nature and made him a fervent apostle of peace. He served on the Royal Commission on Armaments in 1935.

Lightly built and of middle height, Gibbs is a quiet-mannered man, very unlike the typical news-gatherer, and yet, apart from his purely literary reputation, he is known as one of the most expert journalists of the age. He is a member of the French Legion of Honour, and is a Roman Catholic. In 1898 he married Agnes, daughter of the Rev. W. J. Rowland; she died in 1939. Their son, Anthony, carries on the literary tradition of the family.

PRINCIPAL WORKS: The Street of Adventure, 1900; Beauty and Nick, 1914; The Soul of the War, 1915; Battles of the Somme, 1916; Now It Can Be Told, 1920; Adventures in Journalism, 1923; Young Anarchy 1926; Darkened Windows, 1928; Since Then, 1930; The Winding Lane, 1931; European Journey, 1934; England Speaks, 1935; Ordeal in England, 1937; Across the Frontiers, 1938; This Nettle, Danger, 1939; Broken Pledges, 1939; Sons of the Others, 1941, The Amazing Summer, 1941; The Long Alert, 1942.

ABOUT: Falk, B. Five Years Dead; Gibbs, P. Adventures in Journalism; Hamilton, C. People Worth Talking About; Hind, C. L. More Authors and I; Marble, A. R. A Study of the Modern Novel; Overton, G. M. Cargoes for Crusoes; Catholic World September 1938; Rotarian April 1937; Saturday Review of Literature December 4, 1937; Time November 6, 1939.

GIBRAN, KAHLIL (1883-April 10, 1931), Syrian-American mystical writer and artist, was a native of Bechari, Lebanon. The Lebanites, Claude Bragdon explains, are as different from other Syrians as the Scotch highlander is different from the lowlander, being a Nordic, not a Semitic, stock. Gibran's people were affluent and cultured, his mother's family the most musical in the countryside. The boy displayed precocity in drawing, building, modeling, and writing; at eight he was greatly impressed by Michelangelo and Leonardo. At twelve Gibran was in the United States, returning to enter a Syrian college at fourteen and a half. In Paris he studied drawing at the École des Beaux Arts. His earlier literary work comprised prose poems in Arabic. His plays were known to the entire Arabic world, from China to Spain, and gave rise to a new word Gibranism. They displayed "mystical vision, metrical beauty, a simple and fresh approach to the so-called problems of life." Before he was twenty Gibran adopted English exclusively as his medium of expression. *The Prophet* discussed man's relation to fellowman; *The Garden of the Prophet,* man and nature; and *The Death of the Prophet,* man and God. Their aim was to discover some workable way of feeling, thinking, and living which would lead man to mastery of his life. As an artist, Gibran's portraits and ideal heads are "frequent-

ly magnificent and possess a strikingly Leonardesque quality." (See his *Twenty Drawings,* 1919).

Gibran's well-known *Jesus, the Son of Man* is an attempt to show Christ through the consciousness of his immediate contemporaries, enemies and friends alike. At the time of his death at forty-eight in St. Vincent's Hospital, New York City, Gibran had been working on a book of parables, issued posthumously. Claude Bragdon describes him as being "compact, strong, swarthy," with a sensitive face; austere, but with nothing of the ascetic about him, modest and unpretentious.

PRINCIPAL WORKS: The Forerunner: His Parables and Poems, 1920; The Prophet, 1923; Sand and Foam: A Book of Aphorisms, 1926; Jesus the Son of Man, 1928; The Earth Gods, 1931; The Garden of the Prophet, 1933.

ABOUT: Bragdon, C. F. Merely Players, More Lives Than One; Christian Century September 30, 1911; Publishers' Weekly April 25, 1931.

GIBSON, WILFRID WILSON (October 2, 1878-   ), English poet, was born in Hexham, near Newcastle, in the extreme North of England. He was educated privately and spent some time in travel as a boy. He started writing poetry in earliest youth, and except for his war service has devoted his whole life to it ever since. He never attended a university or practised any profession. From the time his first poem was published in the *Spectator* in 1897 he has

poured out books of verse almost without interruption, though his production has slackened in recent years. Since 1910 he has been primarily "the poet of the industrial poor." His earlier work was "musical but undistinguished verse"; his reputation today rests entirely on the work of the past thirty years.

He moved to London in 1912, and married. But the country was always his first choice (he lives now in a Northwestern London suburb), and the next year he moved to the Malvern Hills. Four times he tried to enlist in the First World War, but was rejected each time because of poor sight; he is very near-sighted. In 1917 he made a long lecture tour in the United States, spending three months in Chicago. On his return he was finally accepted for service, and served as a private until he was demobilized in 1919. His home for some years thereafter was in Hertfordshire, until his final return to the outskirts of London. With Lascelles Abercrombie, Rupert Brooke, and John Drinkwater, he was a founder of the short-lived "Georgian" magazine of poetry, *New Numbers;* and he was a joint-beneficiary with Abercrombie and Walter de la Mare of Brooke's will.

John Freeman remarked of Gibson that he is "without imitators and almost without rivals in his poetic mode. He is one of the most prolific of writers and one of the most realistic.... He takes his subjects from common life.... His lyrics are all point—acute, clear, often piercing, unsuperfluous in expression." He is not a poet of nature, and yet his observation of nature is close and acute. What interests him is human beings, and since the human beings who most interest him are the obscure and lowly, the general effect of his work is grim and depressing. With further reading, however, the depression vanishes; his viewpoint is essentially healthy, austere, and with an underlying stoicism which in the end is bracing. Though he calls his poems lyrics, he is not a lyricist; his work seldom sings. His charactertistic mode is the short dramatic piece written like a play. (Strangely enough, his only formal play was diffuse and rather

weak.) Like his friend Siegfried Sassoon, he has written some powerful verse exposing the horrors of war, though like all other Englishmen he is now once more deeply engaged in another conflict.

Gibson's weakness is his constant effort to raise ordinary matter into poetry by heightening its dramatic effect; the effort sometimes becomes a visible strain. He is too much given to artificial "surprise endings" in the manner of an O. Henry story, and sometimes instead of being dramatic he becomes melodramatic. But in his best work he can in a few lines reconstruct a whole man or even a whole class. The worst that can be said of him is that he has written too much, too easily. The best that can be said is that, emotional and unintellectual as his writing is, he is the self-chosen voice of the inarticulate. He is the most English of writers; no one could ever mistake him for anything else. And the England in whose tongue he speaks is the England of those who have been silent because they did not know how to speak. At his best he raises their voices to the plane of genuine poetry.

PRINCIPAL WORKS: Urlyn the Harper, 1902; The Queen's Vigil, 1902; The Golden Helm, 1903; The Nets of Love, 1905; Stonefolds, 1907; Daily Bread, 1910; Fires, 1912; Thoroughfares, 1914; Borderlands, 1914; Battle, 1915; Friends, 1916; Livelihood, 1917; Poems, 1917; Whin (in America: Hill Tracks) 1918; Home, 1920; Neighbours, 1920; Krindlesyke and Other [Verse] Plays, 1922; Kestrel Edge and Other [Verse] Plays, 1924; I Heard a Sailor, 1925; Collected Poems, 1926; 63 Poems: A Selection, 1926; The Golden Room and Other Poems, 1928; Between Fairs: A Comedy (play) 1928; Hazards, 1930; Islands, 1932; Highland Dawn, 1932; Fuel, 1934; Coming and Going, 1938; The Alert, 1942.

ABOUT: Bookman (London) December 1928; Living Age April 15, 1927; Saturday Review of Literature January 17, 1931, April 15, 1933, January 12, 1935; Scholastic March 11, 1940; South Atlantic Quarterly January 1927.

*GIDE, ANDRÉ PAUL GUILLAUME
(November 22, 1869-), French novelist and essayist, was born in Paris into a very strict, religious family. His father, Professor Paul Gide of the Faculty of Law, was born in Uzès (Languedoc) and derived from an old Huguenot stock of Cévennes peasants. His mother, Juliette Rondeaux, born at Le Havre, came from

a wealthy Protestant family, tempered by a Catholic strain, of jurists from Normandy.

According to Gide: Nothing could be more different than the influences of these two families, or than these two provinces of France [harsh Languedoc and lush green Normandy], whose contradictory influences unite in me. Often I have persuaded myself that I had been compelled to produce a work of art simply because it was the only way to bring about an agreement between these two divergent elements which otherwise would have fought constantly with each other or at least have pursued a dialogue within me." Professor Gide, whom his colleagues nicknamed *vir probus* because of his absolute probity and honesty, died when André was only eleven and the boy's upbringing was left entirely to three women "who were dominated by the fear of thinking or acting otherwise than with perfect rectitude." To the consternation of these ladies, André at six years of age trampled over his playfellows' sand castles and mud pies, bit the bare shoulders of young girls, and obstinately misbehaved. Mme. Gide was forced to keep changing her son's environment: now it was La Rocque or Cuverville, the Vosges Mountains or the Riviera or Montpellier where they sojourned at "Uncle Charles's," the famous economist Gide. André's schooling, therefore, was erratic and from the earliest was left almost entirely to tutors who interested the boy more for the stories of their private lives than for their knowledge—with one exception, M. de Lanux, a true musician, who introduced André to Bach and Schumann. Later Gide confessed that music had been of paramount importance in his work, that Chopin taught him more, technically, than any literary master.

Despite his irregular schooling, Gide obtained his baccalaureate in 1890 from the École Alsacienne, where his two chief influences were the Greek poets and his classmate Pierre Louÿs, later known for his pagan *Aphrodite*. On finishing school, André rented a little châlet near Annecy and there shut himself up, with a piano. In his seclusion a struggle ensued between the strict religious outlook which his background and especially his mother had left upon him, and the urgent appetites of the flesh; this struggle, vastly exaggerated in his imagination and couched in the vague ethereal form of Symbolism, resulted in his first book, *Cahiers d'André Walter,* printed at his own expense in 1890. The young writer soon won entrance to Stéphane Mallarmé's literary Tuesday evenings; with other school friends he founded esoteric little magazines. Gide was one of the typical eccentrics of literary France in the 'nineties: a thin, tall, pale young man with a black beard, brown cloak, black felt hat, and in his hand his life-long companion, the Holy Bible.

In 1893 the young painter Paul Albert Laurens obtained a traveling scholarship and Gide accompanied him to North Africa. After crossing Tunisia, they finally settled in Biskra, a little oasis at the edge of the Sahara desert. Gide believed himself tuberculous (like his father) and feared an early death. However at Biskra he found himself wonderfully recovered, and wild with joy he commenced to lead an almost animal existence, shaving his beard, discarding his garments, and playing in the nude with the native children. His newly-won happiness found lyrical echo in his *Nourritures Terrestres,* an invitation to the life of the senses. But his doctors sent him for a "cure" to the Jura Mountains; on his return to Paris he wrote *Paludes,* expressing his disappointment with "civilized" society. Unable to stand Paris any longer, he sailed again for Algiers. At Blidah he met Oscar Wilde and Lord Alfred Douglas. Finally Gide bought some land in Biskra, and decided to remain there forever, but suddenly, in 1895, he was summoned to his dying mother's bedside, in La Rocque. Gide had been bitterly estranged from his mother; but at her death he "felt all his being sink into an abyss of love, distress, and freedom." Gide inherited a large fortune, including a Louis XIII chateau in La Rocque-Baignard.

Shortly thereafter, in October 1895, Gide married his cousin, to whom he had been attached since his twelfth year, and returned with her to Algeria. In that year he finished *Nourritures Terrestres,* not published till 1897. The conflict between the meaning of his marriage (spirit, celestial purity, vow to protect the austere Emmanuèle), and the content of his book grew unbearable. On learning of Gide's vices Emmanuèle recoiled to her Cuverville estate and "took refuge in God." Gide, on the contrary, gave himself over completely to his instincts. At the beginning of the century Gide was far from solving his great dilemma: he loved life with pagan enthusiasm while at the same time he aspired after holiness. This frame of mind is reflected in *The Immoralist* (1902), a book which was overlooked by his vanguard colleagues, not so much because of its frank laudation of carnal audacities as because it was a realistic "novel," at a time when esoteric circles wanted only "symbols." Partly because of this, partly because of his excessively frank confessionalism, Gide re mained silent for the next six years (1902-08) except for brief critical articles. During this period he traveled extensively, rushing madly through Germany, Italy, Turkey, Austria, Spain, Greece....

In February 1909 the first number of the *Nouvelle Revue Française* made its appearance. Although his name was not included among the editors (he always evaded official titles), Gide was the moving spirit of what became the most influential literary magazine in the French language. With his activities in this journal, Gide's role as discoverer and promoter of fine literature assumed paramount importance: he discovered and encouraged Schlumberger, Alain Fournier, Cocteau, Jean-Richard Bloch, Roger Martin du Gard (Nobel Prize winner for 1937), Jules Romains, Jean Giraudoux. In 1909 also appeared *Strait Is the Gate*, Gide's first novel to have any real sale. All these factors encouraged Gallimard, the publisher, to invest some of his capital in the *Nouvelle Revue Française* and to print the work of its contributors—the beginning of the most enterprising and progressive publishing house in France. With the advent of the war, just as Gide had scored his greatest popular success with *The Vatican Swindle* (1914), the *Nouvelle Revue Française* had temporarily to cease publication: most of the contributors left for the front and Gide for a Franco-Belgian center to help refugees. For eighteen months Gide devoted himself to this work and the experience brought him once more to the threshold of mystical exaltation: he wrote then his dialogue with Jesus, *Numquid et Tu*.

When the war ended André Gide had reached the age of fifty. But he was still young in spirit and participated in the tempestuous literary and artistic *isms* of post-war Europe. His Lafcadio, the amoralistic hero of *The Vatican Swindle*, became the symbolic figure of the new era. As his influence on the younger generation increased, enemies appeared on all sides. In 1924, when the Catholic nationalist Henri Massis accused Gide of corrupting public morals by means of his subtly mendacious art, Gide answered with a popular edition of *Corydon*, a defense of homosexuality which he had nervously circulated privately. In that same year his autobiography *If It Die* was printed, but this was withheld from circulation till 1926.

The repercussion of these two books was almost annihilating; his enemies ostracized him, claiming that Gide had overstepped the bounds of decency. Left alone, Gide replied

to the shocked literary world by selling the books of most of his "friends," disposing of his estates, and taking a boat bound for French Equatorial Africa with the young Marc Allégret. In his absence his masterpiece, *The Counterfeiters* (1926), was published, one of the great novels of contemporary literature. For a whole year Gide explored the Congo and Chad; what began as an innocent chase after rare butterflies ended in a mighty exposé of the ruthless exploitation of the African colonies by the French concessionary companies. *Travels in the Congo* appeared in 1927, its sequel in 1928, but from his return to France in 1927 Gide waged a gallant fight against the French government and the magnates responsible for the abuses depicted in his book. His struggles met with only a slight success but they convinced him that the basic cause of it all was the social system as a whole. Gide gradually turned to Marxism and in 1932 openly accepted the program of communism. However, a ferocious individualist like Gide could not assimilate Marxism entirely; on his visit to the Soviet Union in 1935-36 he became disillusioned with collectivist society, too. During the Spanish Civil War, Gide helped the Loyalists by selling his books and manuscripts and sending them the proceeds. In 1941 he was reported living "true to himself" in Cannes; he is an unappeasable anti-Fascist.

André Gide's tortuous career mirrors, perhaps melodramatically, the crisis of modern man. He impersonates the inquisitive spirit of our age, its zig-zags, its counterpoints of bliss and anguish, its maelstrom, and also its deepest concern for sincerity even if it leads to outrageous confession. *The Vatican Swindle, The Counterfeiters*, and his revealing autobiography *If It Die* have assured him of a high place in contemporary world literature—but clever and profound as are his translations of his inner struggles, they do not excel his contributions as friend, adviser, and influence—for more than a man Gide has been, above all, a force.

WORKS AVAILABLE IN ENGLISH TRANSLATION: *Fiction*—Prometheus Illbound, 1919; Strait is the Gate, 1924; The Vatican Swindle, 1925 (later published as Lafcadio's Adventures); The Counterfeiters, 1927; The Prodigal Son, 1928; The School for Wives, 1929; The Immoralist, 1930; Two Symphonies (Isabelle, The Pastoral Symphony) 1931. *Travel and Criticism*—Oscar Wilde, 1905; Dostoievsky, 1925; Essay on Montaigne, 1929; Travels in the Congo (To the Congo, Back From Chad), 1929; Return From the U.S.S.R., 1937; Afterthoughts, 1937; The Living Thoughts of Montaigne (ed.) 1939. *Autobiography*—If It Die, 1935.

ABOUT: Curtius, E. R. Die Literarischen Wegbereiter des Neuen Frankreich; Du Bos, C. Le Dialogue avec André Gide; Fernandez, R. André Gide; Gabory, G. André Gide; Grosse, E. Portraits and Sketches; Hytier, J. André Gide; Jones, P. M. French Introspectives. Lalou, R. André Gide; Martin-Chauffier, L. André Gide, Mille, P. The French Novel; Pfleger, K. Wrestlers With Christ; Pierre-Quint, L. A. Gide: His Life and His Work; Stansbury, M. H. French Novelists of Today; Bookman October 1927; Europe January 15, 1937; New York Herald Tribune "Books" April 13, 1930; Suisse Romande April 1, 1939; Yale Review December 1931.

GILBERT, Sir WILLIAM SCHWENK.
See "BRITISH AUTHORS OF THE 19TH CENTURY"

GILDER, RICHARD WATSON. See "AMERICAN AUTHORS: 1600-1900"

GILMAN, LAWRENCE (July 5, 1878-September 9, 1939), American music critic, journalist, and writer on musical subjects,

Pinchot

was born in Flushing, Queens Borough, New York, the son of Arthur C. and Bessie (Lawrence) Gilman. After attending the public schools of New York he went to the Classical School, Hartford, Conn. Gilman also studied painting with William M. Chase, and illustration at the Art Students' League in New York. Entirely self-taught in musical theory, composition, orchestration, organ, and piano, Gilman's love for music dated from his teens, when he amassed nickels and dimes until he had enough to buy a conductor's score of Wagner's *Tristan und Isolde*. From this time, also, dated his lifelong passion for Wagner's music and for such outstanding exponents of his operas as the de Reszke brothers and Kirsten Flagstad. From 1896 to 1898 Gilman was on the staff of the New York *Herald;* from 1901 to 1913 music critic and assistant editor of *Harper's Weekly*, its assistant editor from 1903 to 1911, and managing editor from then until 1913. When he transferred to the editorial staff of *Harper's Monthly*. Eight years as dramatic and literary critic on the *North American Review*, edited by George Harvey, followed. In 1923, after the death of Henry Edward Krehbiel, music critic of the New York *Tribune,* Gilman became musical editor and critic of that newspaper (later the *Herald Tribune*) until

his death from heart disease in his White Mountain cottage at Peckett's, Sugar Hill, N.H. A daughter, Elizabeth (Mrs. Malcolm E. Anderson, editor of young people's books) and his wife, Mrs. Elizabeth Wright (Walter) Gilman, survived.

Mr. Gilman, a modest and reserved, but genial and generous man, was called "the poet and seer" of his profession. A colleague once remarked that Gilman was "the only critic in town; the rest of us are just reviewers." George Stevens, editor of the *Saturday Review of Literature,* said that he wrote with a purple typewriter ribbon, referring to the literal ecstasy which Gilman reserved for the special objects of his affection, like Wagner, Toscanini, and Chaliapin. He drew upon an apparently inexhaustible store of quotations from mystics; no two reviews ended with the same ascent into the empyrean. Gilman's program notes for the New York Philharmonic Society and the Philadelphia Orchestra, as well as his quiet, dry voice in Sunday radio broadcasts of the Philharmonic made him known to an immense public. His newspaper justly remarked that "his peculiar, inimitable gift was that of the noble eulogist."

PRINCIPAL WORKS: Phases of Modern Music, 1904; Edward MacDowell (Living Masters of Music Series), The Music of Tomorrow, 1906; A Guide to Strauss's "Salomé," A Guide to Debussy's "Pelléas and Melisande," Stories of Symphonic Music, 1908; Nature in Music, 1914; Music and the Cultivated Man, 1929; Wagner's Operas, 1937; Toscanini and Great Music, 1939.

ABOUT: Etude November 1939; New York Times September 10, 1939; Time September 18, 1939.

*GILPATRIC, GUY (January 21, 1896-),
American novelist and short-story writer, was born in New York City, the son of

John Guy Gilpatric and May (Smith) Gilpatric. He attended Columbia Grammar School and in 1912, at sixteen, established a passenger altitude record (4665 feet) at Dominguez, Calif., three months after receiving his pilot's license. From August 1917 to December 1918 Gilpatric was a first lieutenant and captain in the U.S. Air Service, with the American Expeditionary Force in France. He returned to enter the advertising business in 1918, marrying Louise Lesser of Manville, R.I., in 1920. In the fall of 1930 Gilpatric resigned the vice-presidency of a well-known advertising agency and went to the Riviera to live and write in the Villa L'Yeuse, Parc Saramartel, Antibes, France. Here he spent about six hours a day at actual writing, indulging in fencing, in which he is an expert, and pistol-shooting for diversion. Gilpatric is at home in both stratosphere and bathysphere; from 1912 to 1917 he was an aerial instructor and test pilot for various firms in the United States and Canada; and in 1938 he published *The Compleat Goggler* ("Being the First and Only Exhaustive Treatise on the Art of Goggle Fishing, That Most Noble and Excellent Sport Perfected and Popularized by Guy Gilpatric in the Mediterranean Sea Though Long Practiced Elsewhere By Other Benighted Savages. . . Together With Descriptions of Many Marvels Witnessed Upon the Bottom of the Sea and Fully Exposing the Author's Cunning Methods of Swimming, Diving, and Spearing Fish and Octopi"). The outbreak of the Second World War brought Mr. Gilpatric back to his native country and California, to come into closer contact with a large and enthusiastic reading public who follow the exploits of Muster Colin Glencannon, chief engineer of the "S.S. Inchcliffe Castle," in the pages of the *Saturday Evening Post*. Most of Gilpatric's books are collections of these stories. The New York *Times Book Review* admits that the stories "are full of raucous hawhaws," while one enthusiastic reader wrote to the author that Glencannon was "undoubtedly the biggest, drunkenest, 'fightenest' blackguard in either steam or sail, on any ocean." Others note his similarity to Kipling's adventurer, Mulvaney.

PRINCIPAL WORKS: Scotch and Water, 1931; Half Seas Over, 1932; French Summer, 1933; Brownstone Front, 1934; Mr. Glencannon, 1935; Three Sheets in the Wind, 1936; The Compleat Goggler, 1938; The Gentleman in the Walrus Moustache, 1939; Glencannon Afloat, 1941.

GILSON, ÉTIENNE HENRY (1884-),
French historian and philosopher, was educated at the Sorbonne (Ph.D.), and also has honorary D.Litt. and LL.D. degrees. From 1913 to 1919 he was a professor at the University of Lille, then for two years was at Strasbourg University. From 1921 to 1932 he was professor of mediaeval philosophy at the Sorbonne. Since 1929 he has been director of the Institute of Mediaeval Studies at Toronto, Canada, and since 1932 a professor at the Collège de France, dividing his year between the two posts until the Second World War. He has lectured frequently in Great Britain and the United States; he first lectured at Harvard in 1926, was a half-time professor there from 1927 to 1929, and was one of the invited lecturers at the tercentenary celebration in 1936. The following year he lectured at the University of Virginia. He lectures and writes in English as well as in French. A kindly man who lightens his dry subject with much humor, he was described by William W. Gunn as of "sturdy build, erect carriage, dark hair, sanguine complexion." He is a corresponding member of the British Academy and the Royal Academy of the Netherlands, and until the present war lived, when he was in France, in Paris, with a country home at Vermenton, Department of Yonne. The Nazi conquest is believed to have caught him "somewhere in occupied France."

M. Gilson is one of the greatest living mediaevalists. A devout Roman Catholic, he is a disciple of St. Thomas Aquinas, and with him advocates "philosophical unity as a safeguard against chaos." Generally liberal in his outlook, he believes that faith and reason are interrelated and inseparable, and that "there is a spiritual order of realities whose absolute right it is to judge even the state and eventually to free us of its oppression."

WORKS AVAILABLE IN ENGLISH: The Spirit of Mediaeval Philosophy, 1936; The Philosophy of St. Thomas Aquinas, 1937; The Unity of Philosophical Experience, 1937; The Philosophy of St. Bonaventure, 1938; Reason and Revelation in the Middle Ages, 1938; Christianity and Philosophy, 1939; The Mystical Theology of St. Bernard, 1940; God and Philosophy, 1941.

ABOUT: Commonweal May 1, 1929, November 20, 1936; Dublin Review October 1933; Mercure de France October 15, 1931; Mind January 1933; Nation September 12, 1936; Revue Philosophique November 1935, January 1936.

GIONO, JEAN (March 30, 1895-),
French novelist, was born in Manosque, a small town in the Basses Alpes, southeastern France. His grandfather was a Carbonaro officer who participated, with Émile Zola's father, in ruthlessly crushing the revolts of the Clerical Peasants in Calabria, after which he conspired against the authorities and escaped a death sentence by hiding in Montezenello, and then flee-

ing to Algeria. Giono's father, an itinerant cobbler who "mended shoes in a wooden stall which still stands near the Marseilles post-office," was fifty-two when his only son was born, three years after his marriage to Pauline Pourcin, a thirty-eight-year-old Parisian laundress, the daughter of a Provençal father and a Picard mother. "He was very handsome with his great white beard, but she was still more beautiful.

Schreiber

Jean entered the local school at the age of six but dropped out in 1911 during his first year at the *collège*: "My father was old and worn out; I was sixteen, he, sixty-seven. In order to help him I began to look for work. I would have preferred some sort of manual labor, to be a joiner or a blacksmith, but above all a shoemaker. Instead, I had to enter a bank as messenger boy. Later on I was promoted to clerk." When away from the prosaic world of the Comptoir National d'Escompte, Jean read the Bible and Homer's *Odyssey* (he had little money for new writers) and wrote poetry.

At the outbreak of the First World War Jean left for the front immediately and remained as second-class soldier until 1918. He fought at Verdun. Shortly after his demobilization and his return to the Comptoir National, his father died (April 1920), aged seventy-seven, and he married Eliza, the daughter of the hairdresser across the street. "She was the first person to have confidence in me, for I had already begun to write, although I did not show my work to anyone. I used to write in the evening after work and in the morning before work."

In October 1921 Giono's poem "Sous le Pied Chaud du Soleil" appeared in the Marseilles journal *La Criée* and three years later the Editions des Cahiers Livres of Saint-Paul de Vence published, in an edition limited to three hundred copies, his first volume, *Accompagnés de la Flute*. Besides Eliza, the poet Lucien Jacques and painter Maxime Girieud encouraged him and through their intercession Giono found his place in vanguard literature when in August 1928 the *Nouvelle Revue Française* published his short story "Champs." Soon thereafter (February 1929) Bernard Grasset published his novels *Hill of Destiny* and *Lovers Are Never Losers* which were imme-

diate successes (the latter won the Prix Brentano for 1931).

In the United States Giono is best known for his novels *The Song of the World* and *Harvest* which were originally published in 1934 and 1930, respectively. *Harvest* (*Régain*) was adapted to the movies in France, and when the film was shown in the United States, despite the truculent intervention of the censor, it was awarded the 1939 prize for the best foreign motion picture of the year. Giono's play *Lanceurs de Graines* (1936), produced in Paris and, in translation, in London, Frankfurt, Prague, Vienna and Oslo, reveals him as a gifted playwright.

Since 1930 Giono has lived in his own house, a little bungalow he calls "Paraïs," on the slope of Mont d'Or overlooking the valley of the Durance, in his native Manosque, with his old mother, almost blind, his wife and his two daughters: Aline, born in 1926, and Sylvie, born in 1934. Near Manosque a colony of his disciples has been organized.

Giono's novels of the soil are characterized by their profound understanding and love of the peasantry as well as their rustic, vigorous style which, as André Maurois remarked, "in its simple grandeur is very nearly epic." Was not Giono's main literary influence the *Odyssey?* His appreciative audience widened and since 1930 he has produced one fine novel after another, at least one a year, often more. To his pagan, nature-loving outlook he has added a new theme: hatred for war, expressed in his admirable *Le Grand Troupeau* (1931). This preoccupation led him to action: in 1934 he joined the "Association des Écrivains et des Artistes Révolutionaires" and waged a fierce struggle against war and Fascism. More recently, however, he reverted to a Tolstoyan position, praising the solitude of the country and pacifism, regarding the toilers of the soil as a race rather than a class. "Peasant civilization possesses as a gift human qualities which philosophical civilizations spend centuries first defining, then desiring, and finally losing." However his crusade is not against the familiar ogre, the machine age: "I am not an enemy of machines. I am the enemy of modern ways of using machines. I do not wish to destroy airplanes, phonographs, cinemas and radios. I say only that there is something beyond that and better: it is man. I say furthermore that all the countries, all the territories, all the mysticisms are not worth the life of a man. Furthermore I take a firm and unshakeable position against wars of all sorts." In October 1939 he was imprisoned by French authorities for inciting the peasants to oppose the war, but after the German victory was reported back in his native Manosque, where he has promoted a venture to produce motion pictures.

This affable, broad-shouldered nature apostle, with his deep blue eyes and winning smile, preaches social abstention: "No political régime has been able to give man in a thousand years one thousandth part of the happiness brought by a night's sleep."

WORKS AVAILABLE IN ENGLISH TRANSLATION: Hill of Destiny, 1929; Lovers Are Never Losers, 1931; The Song of the World, 1937; Harvest, 1939.

ABOUT: Ciossek, H. H. Jean Giono; Ehrhard, J. E. Le Roman Français Depuis Marcel Proust; Michelfelder, C. Jean Giono et les Religions de la Terre; Rousseaux, A. La Littérature du Vingtième Siécle; Etudes February 5 and 20, 1937; Neue Rundschau April 1935; Nouvelles Littéraires December 20, 1930; Scrutiny December 1934; Times (London) Literary Supplement December 3, 1938.

GIOVANNITTI, ARTURO (January 7, 1884-), Italian-American poet, was born in Ripabottoni in Southern Italy, and edu-

cated at the *lycée* in Campobasso. Coming hopefully to the United States in 1900 at seventeen, he was speedily disillusioned with the American dream. After working for a time in Pennsylvania coal mines Giovanitti attended theological school, but was repelled by the "formalism of prescribed thinking." He joined the Socialist party, believing it had a constructive program besides constituting a powerful protest against the inequalities of society, and for a time edited an Italian radical paper, *Il Proletario.* Becoming involved in the textile mill strike at Lawrence, Mass., he was "railroaded" to jail for several months. A consequent poem, "The Walker," as a personal document of a man in prison is unrivaled even by *The Ballad of Reading Gaol,* in the opinion of Louis Untermeyer, who continues, "I do not think that the growth of Socialism has produced, with the exception of *The Communist Manifesto,* a more noble or inspired piece of literature." Giovannitti's "stark and barbaric hymns of labor" are in unrhymed verse, but show scant traces of any other Whitmanian influence. His other poems in strict meters are apt to be merely conventionally effective and stud-

ded with the *clichés* of poetic expression. He was an impatient advocate of American intervention in the First World War against Germany, long before his comrades were finally persuaded of its advisability by the terms of the Brest-Litovsk treaty. Helen Keller contributed an indignant and lyrical preface to Giovannitti's book of poems, *Arrows in the Gale,* writing, "He finds voice for his message in the sighs, the dumb loves and hopes, the agonies and thwartings of men who are bowed and broken by the monster hands of machines." In October 1917 Giovannitti contributed to the *New Masses* "When the Cock Crows," a poem inspired by the brutal lynching of Frank Little, a labor leader. In recent years he has been inactive as a poet.

PRINCIPAL WORKS: Arrows in the Gale, 1914.

ABOUT: Giovannitti, A. Arrows in the Gale (see Introduction by H. Keller); Kreymborg, A. Our Singing Strength. Untermeyer, L. The New Era in American Poetry.

*GIRAUDOUX, JEAN (October 29, 1882-), French novelist, playwright, and diplomat, was born in Bellac, a small town

in Limousin, of a lower middle-class family. His father, a civil engineer in the public service, was in charge of the numerous bridges of the region. Jean grew up in the typically tranquil milieu of a provincial town, remarkable neither for its natural nor its historical beauty, yet to him "unquestionably the most charming spot in the world," but the damp climate aggravated his father's rheumatism and he had to move with his family to Cérilly, a town in Allier, smaller than Bellac, where he served as tax-collector. After a brief schooling at Bellac and Pellevoisin, Jean entered the *lycée* at Châteauroux, which he classified as "the ugliest town in France." Here he studied not only the French classics but the Greek and Latin. "I could almost say," he confessed recently, "that the first language I wrote in a literary way was Latin."

On graduating "with the highest distinction," Jean was awarded a scholarship for the Lycée Lakanal in Paris where he followed the classical course and at its completion left to serve his military period in Lyon and Clermont-Ferrand. Finally, in 1903 he entered the École Normale Supérieure planning to become a professor. But the scholarly-looking blond young man with the incipient moustache and well-dressed hair and the occasional monocle was not of the bookish type: he loved sports and often achieved creditable performances on the running track. After changing from French literature to philology, he came out with a diploma in "higher German studies," only to give up once and for all the idea of an academic career. Neither did he think of literature as a career even though one of his stories, "Le Dernier Rêve d'Edmond About," had appeared in the *Marseille-Éturiant* in 1904. For five years (1905-10) Jean explored the world, often on foot, generally penniless. He visited Germany, Holland, Norway, Austria, Italy, the Balkans, the United States, Canada, Mexico; he tutored the German prince, Saxe-Meiningen, taught French at Harvard, served as private secretary to the owner-editor of *Le Matin* and later became short-story editor, which explains how it came to pass that the conventional readers of *Le Matin* were treated for a while to the strange stories of Guillaume Apollinaire and Charles-Louis Philippe.

In 1910, partly through influential connections, Giraudoux, aged twenty-eight, was appointed *élève* vice-consul in the French Ministry of Foreign Affairs, and his travels began again, more leisurely and comfortably, of course; important missions took him to northern Russia and the Orient. His writing, too, continued: the admirable story "La Pharmacienne" had appeared in 1907 in the *Revue des Temps Présents,* and while the publisher Grasset (whom he had accidentally met in a café) was reading the five stories of *Les Provinciales,* Giraudoux finished the three in *L'École des Indifférentes* which were printed immediately—one (Gide's discovery) in the *Nouvelle Revue Française,* another in the *Mercure de France,* and the third in the *Grande Revue.* Grasset published *Les Provinciales* in 1911 and sold thirty copies in four years, netting Giraudoux twenty francs in royalties. His first attempt at a novel, *Simon le Pathétique,* was appearing in *L'Opinion* at the outbreak of the First World War and had to be discontinued. Its disappointed author joined the infantry, fought with distinction on the Marne, in Alsace, at the Dardanelles, was three times cited for bravery and decorated with the cross of the Légion d'Honneur. While recuperating in Portugal from a shrapnel wound, he wrote *Campaigns and Intervals* (1918), one of the few genuinely literary reports of the war. After the armistice, Giraudoux accompanied Marshal Joffre and

Bergson in their good-will tour to America, and on his return resumed his duties in the Ministry of Foreign Affairs, eventually qualifying for the consular service. Because he was married and a father, he preferred to remain in Paris. His novel *Simon le Pathétique,* entirely overhauled and published in 1918, and his variations on a Greek Theme, *Elpénor* (1919), and *Adorable Clio* (1920) had made his name famous in esoteric circles as a writer of original fantasy and mature poetic gifts, but in 1922 with *My Friend From Limousin* he scored a tremendous success, winning half of the Prix Balzac (the other half went to Baumann's *Job le Prédestiné*), and widening his public to include international readers.

The personal antagonism and political feud between his chief, Berthelot and Poincaré resulted in Giraudoux's "exile" to the French embassy in Berlin (1924). But Poincaré was soon overthrown, and Giraudoux returned to his Ministry and was placed in charge of its Press Bureau; to avenge Poincaré's "punishment" he wrote *Bella* (1926), one of his finest if most virulent novels.

In 1928, with Jouvet's advice and "collaboration," Giraudoux converted *My Friend From Limousin* into the play *Siegfried,* and discovered, at the age of forty-six, that the theatre was his most adequate vehicle of expression. *Siegfried's* tremendous success was followed by another hit, *Amphitryon 38* (1929), and from then on, the theatre has received Giraudoux's major attention. Besides his adaptation of Margaret Kennedy's *The Constant Nymph,* as *Tessa* (1934), he wrote *Judith* (1932), *Intermezzo* (1933), *La Guerre de Troie* (1935), *Electre* (1937) and one of the 1939 theatre hits, *Ondine,* a fantasy based on La Motte Fouqué's romantic classic *Undine.*

The versatile Giraudoux, "France's most distinguished playwright," Minister Plenipotentiary, General Inspector of Diplomatic and Consular Posts, was head of France's wartime propaganda and iron censorship in 1939-40. After the Nazi conquest he went to Vichy as director of propaganda.

Giraudoux has been compared to Anatole France, Renan, Bernard Shaw, Voltaire. In his extremely personal art are mixed some of the virtues of these masters—he is a poet, an ironist, a subtle thinker, a consummate stylist, in short, a strange summation of all the eclectic currents and refinement in European culture, and also a bit of a dandy, a lover of sports, of books and politics, reserved and elegant—pale lips, prominent forehead, well-dressed hair, deep blue eyes, tortoise-rimmed spectacles. Jouvet has called him "a true magician of the theatre," claiming that "if the language of Racine is still spoken in France two hundred years from now, the works of Jean Giraudoux will still be performed."

WORKS AVAILABLE IN ENGLISH TRANSLATION: Campaigns and Intervals, 1918; Suzanne and the Pacific, 1923; My Friend From Limousin, 1923; Bella, 1926; Siegfried, 1930; Amphitryon 38, 1938; Paris Impromptu, 1938; Racine, 1938.

ABOUT: Bourdet, M. J. Giraudoux; Brasillach, P. Portraits; Drake, W. A. Contemporary European Writers; Humbourg, P. J. Giraudoux; Lemaitre, G. Four French Novelists; Rousseaux, A. Le Paradis Perdu; Stansbury, M. H. French Novelists of Today; Living Age October 1939; Nouvelle Revue Française July 1, 1933; Plaisir de France, February 1936; Revue de Paris November 15, 1934; Theatre Arts Monthly February 1938.

GISSING, GEORGE. See "BRITISH AUTHORS OF THE 19TH CENTURY"

GLADKOV, FEDOR VASILIEVICH (1883-), Russian novelist and dramatist, was born in Chernavka, a province of

Saratov, in the district of Petrovsk, the son of poor peasants. At nine he learned to read and write from an educated Old Believer, the sect to which his parents belonged. His grandmother, who had been a serf, and visiting preachers taught young Fedor apocryphal legends. Music he knew only through ancient religious hymns, psalms, and litanies. His mother and grandmother, "both expert in the art of story telling and tears" strongly influenced the boy's childhood. When Fedor was nine the family left the village to live among the fisher folk of the Volga and peasants of the Caucasus. In 1895 they settled at Krasnodar, where his father was employed in a steam-mill, and his mother went out to work by the day. Young Gladkov began to read Russian classics: Lermontov, Dostoievsky, and Tolstoy "intoxicated" him, while Pushkin and Gogol left him cold. He passed entrance examinations to high school brilliantly, but was too poor to enter. Successive apprenticeships to a druggist, a lithographic shop, and a printing plant proved failures. At seventeen Gladkov began to write for local papers, from his knowledge of the ways of workers and vagabonds, and did some tutoring. Chronic undernourishment—his meals were usually the scraps from the cafés of the Old Bazaar —sent him to hospital for two months. When his father was sentenced to Siberia for six months for uttering counterfeit money, Gladkov followed him there to act as schoolmaster in a little lost hamlet among the Chaldons, and to buy him a farm on the elder Gladkov's release in 1905. Fedor left for Moscow with the intention of studying at the university, but instead attended a Normal School in Tiflis. Initiated into revolutionary activity, he went to Kuban to work among Social-Democratic groups, fell afoul of the police, and was sentenced to three years' exile on the banks of the Lena. Returning to Kuban as a Communist, he fought throughout the civil war. Gorky showed his literary work consideration and sympathy, and Korolenko also proved kind.

Gladkov's *Cement* was "the first novel to rise out of the turbulence of the Revolution." It is an important but by no means great novel, wrote Joshua Kunitz in the *Nation*; the materials were magnificent but their profound possibilities were superficially exploited, according to V. F. Calverton. It shows Soviet life "as represented in the relationship of the masses to the economic policies of the nation."

WORKS AVAILABLE IN ENGLISH TRANSLATION: Cement, 1929.

ABOUT: Gladkov, F. V. Cement (see autobiographical note); Ost-Europa March 1931.

GLAESER, ERNST (1902-), German novelist, is a product of the First World War. His education was interrupted and his emotional growth hampered by the unnatural conditions in which his boyhood was passed. The war did not establish a moratorium on puberty, as he once remarked sardonically to an interviewer after his novel *Jahrgang 1902* (1928),

which sold 70,000 copies in Germany, was published in English as *Class of 1902,* with some episodes of adolescent eroticism expunged. The title referred to the military class in which Glaeser was placed automatically by the year of his birth. Imprisoned for a time in a French prison at Mainz, Glaeser was obliged to repeat the last year in his *lycée* at Darmstadt. After graduation from this preparatory school, he attended the Universities of Freiburg, Munich,

Frankfort, and Berlin. He began his writing career with expressionistic plays, *Souls Overboard,* and *Uberwindung der Madonna,* a play in the manner of Wedekind which cost him a trial for heresy. After acquittal, Glaeser edited the literary section of the Frankfurter *Zeitung* and directed the newspaper's radio station.

When he was twenty-six, Glaeser published *Jahrgang 1902,* a story which must be added to *Sergeant Grischa* and *All Quiet On the Western Front* when we are assembling the most significant work which the war produced, according to William Soskin. "It does not deal directly with the materials of warfare except in so far as the tragedy of murdered minds and souls and diseased temperaments in the noncombatant social body are material of war." Glaeser himself remarked that he was "more troubled by the awakening of my senses than by a victory in Mesopotamia." He proceeded to get rid of his obsessions by the method of Goethe —freedom through expression. "Cynicism and irony are our defensive weapons," he told an interviewer in 1929, who described him as a tall, pale young man with a gaunt expression. "I am going to tell stories that it requires courage to tell, stories which certain men would pay me well to keep silent. I only want to write useful books. I don't give a snap for beauty."

The Last Civilian (1935), his next novel, had as epigraph a quotation from Heinrich Heine: "If ever liberty disappeared from the face of the earth—which God forbid—a German dreamer would rediscover it in his dreams." This ironically prefaced a novel which traced the development and increasing power of National Socialism in Germany. Ben Ray Redman called it "rich in substance, tight of texture, charged with emotion, and perfectly constructed."

After Hitler's coming to power, Glaeser had voluntarily left Germany and lived successively in Prague, Zurich, Paris (where *The Last Civilian* was published), and again in Zurich. Another production of this period was the novelette, *The Indestructible,* published in Amsterdam and never translated into English. In Zurich he shocked his fellow-exiles by writing a newspaper article dissociating himself from them and condoning Hitler's policies. Shortly afterward, he received a contract from a Berlin publisher and returned to Germany, where at last report he was still living.

WORKS AVAILABLE IN ENGLISH TRANSLATION: Class of 1902, 1929; The Last Civilian, 1935.

ABOUT: Les Annales Politiques et Littéraire November 10, 25, 1937.

*GLASGOW, ELLEN ANDERSON GHOLSON (April 22, 1874-   ), American novelist, was born and still lives in Richmond Va. She is the daughter of Francis Thomas Glasgow and Anne Jane (Gholson) Glasgow, and is unmarried. Because of delicate health as a child, she had only a little training in private schools, and for the most part educated herself by read-ing in her father's extensive library. From the beginning she was surrounded by a classical culture, and she learned the alphabet not out of a primer but out of Scott. Since that time she has received honorary degrees from the University of North Carolina, the University of Richmond, Duke University, and the College of William and Mary, and is an honorary member of Phi Beta Kappa.

She started to write very young, though her first novel, *Sharp Realities,* written at eighteen, she herself destroyed. Her first work, mostly verse, appeared anonymously, and her own family (like Jane Austen's) did not know she was doing any serious writing until she was revealed as the author of *The Descendant*—which was so "masculine" in style that one critic ascribed it to Harold Frederic.

Although she has traveled much abroad, and for a short time lived in New York, for many years she has lived and worked quietly in a century-old grey stone house in the heart of Richmond, a house covered with ivy and wisteria, its garden concealed by box and magnolia and by a high iron fence. Miss Glasgow has strongly the feeling of "belonging" to a place. "We live," she has said, "where we are born." James Branch Cabell called her "a grande dame of a rare and almost extinct type." She is in the true sense of the phrase a great lady, urbane, and sophisticated. "As fearlessly unconventional as she is in thought," said the late Sara Haardt, "she is precisely and as uncompromisingly conventional in manner." Emily Clark, trying to describe her, spoke of her "autumn leaf coloring," and the description is apt; her hair is a dark bronze, her eyes brown, and she loves the colors of the autumn leaves and the autumn sky. She is slightly deaf, though not observably so. She leads an active life, her interests and affiliations ranging from the Colonial Dames to the Richmond S.P.C.A., of which

* Died November 21, 1945.

she is president, and from the American Academy of Arts and Letters to the Modern Language Association. She plays, besides, a fair game of golf. In 1940 she was awarded the Howells Medal for Fiction by the American Academy of Arts and Letters, in 1941 she received the annual *Saturday Review of Literature* plaque for outstanding service to American letters, and in 1942, for *In This Our Life*, she received the Pulitzer Prize for novels.

From her early youth Ellen Glasgow was a realist and a feminist. "By temperament," she has said of herself, "I was on the side of the disinherited, . . . [though] my sense of humor was an adequate defense against the more destructive winds of doctrine. I prefer the spirit of fortitude to the sense of futility."

An "ironic idealist," J. S. Wilson called her, while to Henry Seidel Canby she is an "ironic tragedian." She is both. Stark Young noted how "as a young girl she determined to write of the South not sentimentally, not as a conquered province, but as part of the larger world." He spoke of her literary manner, marked by "affability that consists of a certain reserve," her "caustic insight and social satire," with "an undercurrent of intensity and courage." Her pictures of Southern life, in both the upper and the lower social strata, and particularly her pictures of Southern women and their relations to Southern men, are devastating, and all the more so because they are softened by humor and affection. "The realism which engages this author," said Emily Clark, "is the penetration of shams, a perpetual rebellion against hypocrisy." In her earlier novels, such as *The Voice of the People*, there was more overt revolt and less implied exposure, but in every one of her books there is "her own sort of realism, which she has never interpreted as drabness." "Her handling of her characters is that of a thoroughbred," Miss Clark concluded. Ellen Glasgow may be hailed as one of the true and enduring leaders of the literary renaissance of the South.

PRINCIPAL WORKS: The Descendant, 1897; Phases of an Inferior Planet, 1898; The Voice of the People, 1900; The Freeman and Other Poems, 1902; The Battle-Ground, 1902; The Deliverance, 1904; The Wheel of Life, 1906; The Ancient Law, 1908; The Romance of a Plain Man, 1909; The Miller of Old Church, 1911; Virginia, 1913; Life and Gabriella, 1916; The Builders, 1919; One Man in His Time, 1922; The Shadowy Third, 1923; Barren Ground, 1925; The Romantic Comedians, 1926; They Stooped to Folly, 1929; The Sheltered Life, 1932; Vein of Iron, 1935; Collected Works, 1933 and 1938; In This Our Life, 1941.

ABOUT: Hatcher, H. Creating the Modern American Novel; Quinn, A. H. American Fiction; Sherman, S. P. Critical Woodcuts; Bookman April 1929; Nation April 12, 1933; New Republic June 7, 1933; New York Herald Tribune "Books" July 24, 1938, November 17, 1940; New York Times Book Review December 18, 1938; Saturday Review of Literature November 23, 1929, August 31, 1935, September 10, 1938, March 29, April 5, 1941; Virginia Quarterly Review January 1939.

*GLASPELL, SUSAN (July 1, 1882-   ), American novelist and dramatist, winner of the Pulitzer Prize for drama, writes: "My

early life was spent in the Middle West and for the last twenty-five years my home has been in New England. My mother, Alice Keating, was of Irish parentage; the ancestry of my father, Elmer S. Glaspell, is early American of English descent. We were a middle-class, not very well-to-do family. My education was in the public schools of Davenport and later at Drake University, Des Moines. I cannot remember the time I did not want to write, and creative efforts began while still in grammar school. In college I was sending out stories to the magazines. Most of them came back but a few of them stayed. I also helped myself through college by some work for the Des Moines newspapers, and the day after my graduation I joined the staff of the *News* there. I was assigned to the State House and covered the Legislature when in session. There I was always running into things I saw as short stories, and after less than two years of newspaper reporting I boldly gave up my job and went home to Davenport to give all my time to my own writing. I say boldly, because I had to earn my living. These short stories were published in *Harper's,* the *American,* and other magazines—though I wrote a number that weren't published at all, and that was perhaps just as well. After a few years I wanted to do a novel, and again, with some trepidation, I called a halt on the short stories to write *The Glory of the Conquered.*

"In 1913 I married George Cram Cook,*qv* a writer, also of Iowa. We knew other writers who were living at Provincetown on Cape Cod, and after a summer there we bought a house. This has been my home ever since.

"I wrote several other novels, and when, in 1915, my husband organized the Provincetown Players, I became interested in writing for the theatre. My first ventures were one-act plays—*Trifles,* which was suggested to me by a newspaper experience in Iowa, and, in collaboration with my husband, *Suppressed Desires.* Both have been given ever since by little theatres all over the country. After writing other short dramas I began to do the full length play. *Bernice, Inheritors,* and *The Verge* were of that period.

"My husband had always had a strong feeling about the culture of ancient Greece, and in 1922 we went to that country and lived for two years at Delphi on Mount Parnassus. Mr. Cook died there, and after my return to America I wrote *The Road to the Temple,* the story of his life which also included a good deal of my own. Since then I have written four novels. I also wrote other plays, and *Alison's House* was awarded the Pulitzer Prize in 1931.

"I have been a good deal in France and England. Many of my winters are spent in New York. But most of my novels and plays have their roots in the Middle West, doubtless because that is where my formative years were spent. And though I have for years lived in other places, I have never lost the feeling that that is my part of the country."

* * *

George Cram Cook died in 1923. In 1925 Mrs. Cook married Norman Häghejm Matson, also a writer; this marriage has been dissolved. With Mary Heaton Vorse, she is one of the last remaining figures of the early days of Provincetown as an art colony and as the "mother" of the American Little Theatre. After a long silence, she published in 1939 *The Morning Is Near Us,* a novel characterized by keen psychological insight. Ludwig Lewisohn said of her work that it is "morbidly frugal in expression, but candidly naked in substance."

PRINCIPAL WORKS: *Novels*—The Glory of the Conquered, 1909; The Visioning, 1911; Lifted Masks, 1912; Fidelity, 1915; Brook Evans, 1928; Fugitive's Return, 1929; Ambrose Holt and Family, 1931; The Morning Is Near Us, 1939. *Plays*—Trifles, 1917; Suppressed Desires (with G. C. Cook) 1917; Bernice and Other Plays, 1920; Inheritors, 1921; The Verge, 1922; The Comic Artist (with N. Matson) 1927; Alison's House, 1930. *Miscellaneous*—The Road to the Temple, 1926.

ABOUT: Glaspell, S. The Road to the Temple; Bookman July 1925; Drama June 1931; Life July 15, 1940; Nation November 3, 1920, April 4, 1923.

GLASS, MONTAGUE MARSDEN (July 23, 1877-February 3, 1934), Jewish-American humorist, playwright, and short-story writer, was born in Manchester, England, the son of James D. Glass, who until the late 'eighties was a wealthy napkin manufacturer, and Amelia (Marsden) Glass. He was brought to America in 1890 and spent his late boyhood on New York's East

NBC

Side. He attended the College of the City of New York and New York University. With contributions to the university *Item* and with a short story in the *Metropolitan Magazine* he broke into print. He joined the law office of David & Kaufmann, but abandoned all practice in 1909.

Magazine editors refused his story about the petty kings of the garment industry ("Potash and Perlmutter") in the fear that it might offend some of their advertisers. A trade journal in Detroit gambled on it; and immediately asked for another in the same vein. (Glass, however, had to threaten suit before he got his forty dollars for the two of them.) His first collection of tales, *Potash and Perlmutter,* appeared in 1910, followed a year later by *Abe and Mawruss.* Both books were converted into great stage successes, Charles Klein collaborating on the first adaptation and R. C. Megrue on the second. Short stories comprised the bulk of his prose for the next decade, but in *Worrying Won't Win* (1918) he introduced a little good-natured opinion on the Czar, war finances, and other matters. In 1907 he had married Caroline Patterson, by whom he had a son who died at the age of three, and a daughter who survived him. He went to Europe in 1919 to cover the Peace Conference; and again in 1931 to send back despatches on the Spanish revolution. Over the signature "Theophilus Cossart" he published (privately) a farce called *The Prodigious Experiment Brought to Perfection in Boston at Father Burke's Academy . . . ,* with a "biographical sketch" of Father Burke. It proceeded on the assumption that

> . . . few would be contaminated
> By vice if early vaccinated.

Broadway's last glimpse of the Potash and Perlmutter manner came in 1932 with *Keeping Expenses Down,* a Montague Glass-Dan Jarrett collaboration that retained the old cloak-and-suit favorites under new names.

Glass died, following an embolism, at Westport, Conn., in his fifty-seventh year. German, French, and Italian he spoke with ease—but not Yiddish. He wore a shell-rimmed pince-nez, smoked powerful cigars, and was a connoisseur of wines. He exchanged quips with Franklin P. Adams, played piano duets with John Erskine, and was an accompanist for Hendrik Willem Van Loon's fiddling. Glass will be remembered largely for his creation of a stage "type" and for his many associations with the literary, theatrical, and musical figures of his day.

PRINCIPAL WORKS: *Stories, etc.*—Potash and Perlmutter, 1910; Abe and Mawruss, 1911; Elkan Lubliner—American, 1912; Competitive Nephew, 1915; Worrying Won't Win, 1918. *Plays*—Potash and Perlmutter (with Charles Klein) 1913; Abe and Mawruss (with R. C. Megrue) 1915; Present Company Excepted, 1921; Lucky Numbers, 1927; You Can't Learn Them Nothing, 1929.

ABOUT: Adams, F. P. The Diary of Our Own Samuel Pepys; New York Herald Tribune February 5, 1934; introductory notes in the works.

GLENN, ISA (1888-), American novelist, was born in Atlanta, Ga., the daughter of John T. Glenn and Helen A. (Garrard) Glenn. Her father was mayor of Atlanta, and she is a cousin of the actress, Cora Urquhart Potter. Her earliest talent was for art, and after private schooling in Atlanta and New York, she was sent, very young, to Paris, where she studied

Harris & Ewing

painting for a year in the studio of another of her cousins, James McNeil Whistler. Then he told her bluntly that she would never make an artist and that she would better turn to "scribbling." She did not, however, though she left Paris soon after, take his advice immediately. Instead she returned to Atlanta, and in 1903 was married to Brigadier General J. S. Bayard Schindler. They had one son, who is now a novelist. General Schindler died in 1921. During their life together he was stationed at many posts—in the Philippines, all over the Orient, in South America, and in the South Sea Islands. The experiences and background of those years formed the material for Mrs. Schindler's first novels.

In 1925, when he was living in New York, she studied motion picture producing at Columbia, and since this did not take up all her time, she also entered a short-story writing class. Though she says, "I don't think you can teach writing," this nevertheless was the final impetus which made her a writer. She began publishing stories in the magazines, and soon afterwards finished her first novel, *Heat,* a study of the effect of the tropics on natives of the temperate zones. Her next novel had much the same theme, with special reference to children and young people; her third was a devastating record of factitious "Southern charm." Indeed, as Ford Madox Ford remarked, all her earlier novels were "expressions of dislike"; she evidently had a great deal of repressed indignation and disgust to work off before her maturer work began with *A Short History of Julia.* Her novels and stories since then have been increasingly what Ford called this book, "beautiful and touching," though she has not lost the "sense of the ridiculous" which T. S. Matthews thought her most salient characteristic: he called her work "not pretty, but true." John Farrar hailed her in 1927 as already of the caliber of Willa Cather and May Sinclair, but she has not confirmed this estimate. The author whom she most resembles, though lighter in touch and less profound and inclusive, is Ellen Glasgow.

Isa Glenn is a tiny, red-haired woman, who lives in a New York apartment full of Whistler items. Her chief interests aside from her work are the National Arts Club and the Society of Colonial Dames. She is a painstaking and methodical writer, who says it takes "six months in my head, two months on the typewriter" to complete a novel. She writes a long synopsis first, tracing out every detail of chronology and interrelationship of characters, and meanwhile she dwells constantly on the persons of her book until she knows them intimately. The rest, she says, is "almost like copying."

PRINCIPAL WORKS: Heat, 1926; Little Pitchers, 1927; Southern Charm, 1928; Transport, 1929; A Short History of Julia, 1930; East of Eden, 1932; Mr. Darlington's Dangerous Age, 1933; The Little Candle's Beam, 1935; According to Mac Tavish, 1938.

ABOUT: Bookman April 1927.

*GLYN, Mrs. ELINOR (SUTHERLAND) (1864-), British novelist and short-story writer, was born in Jersey, the Channel Islands, the younger daughter of Douglas Sutherland of Toronto, Ont., and Elinor (Saunders) Sutherland. Her maternal grandfather, Colonel Thomas Saunders, was born in Paris at the end of the French Revolution in 1795, and was related to the Admiral Saunders who helped to take Quebec. He married an Irish girl, and they settled in Canada on a tract of land near Guelph, Ont. Douglas Sutherland was a civil engineer, played the violin and spoke several languages. He took his wife to New York before the Civil War, then went to Brazil to build a railroad. Their

first child, Lucy ("Lucile"), later Lady Duff Gordon, was born in London, and sixteen months later Elinor was born in Jersey, where her mother was spending the winter with a half-French aunt. She was taken to the Guelph estate, Summer Hill, when she was ten months old; Sutherland had died of typhoid fever.

Elinor's mother married David Kennedy, a selfish, domineering man who reminded his step-daughter of Elizabeth Barrett's father, and they lived in Ireland, in Yorkshire, and in Jersey in the 1870's, at Richelieu, a house at Bagot, St. Saviour. Elinor had the range of a large library here, and read Greek and French classics, Pepys, Byron, Kingsley's *Heroes,* Strickland's *Queens of England,* St. Simon, Sterne, Voltaire, *Don Quixote* in French, and Lady Blessington's novels. La Rochefouchauld's *Maxims* and Chesterfield's *Letters to His Son* became Bibles to her: "the whimsical, cynical views in these old books began to mould me in a new way."

In Paris with a friend of her mother's, old Mlle. Duret, Elinor saw Sarah Bernhardt in *Theodora,* which made a deep impression on her, and acquired a passion for tiger skins dating from a visit to the Jardin des Plantes with a young man. Her stepfather died; Lucy had to have an expensive divorce; and Mrs. Kennedy used the remains of her fortune to set up Lucile Ltd., which became a well-known dressmaking establishment. In April 1892 Elinor Sutherland married Clayton Glyn, J.P., of Durrington House and Sheering, Harlow, Essex. They lived on a lavish scale, entertaining and being entertained in large country houses; Mrs. Glyn's exotic beauty and red hair, regarded as a misfortune when she was a girl, began to be appreciated. *The Visits of Elizabeth* (1900), her first book, reflects this period, and was serialized in the *World.*

The famous, or at least notorious, novel *Three Weeks* (1907) was compounded of a period of romantic starvation which Mrs. Glyn had spent in Venice with her husband,

who failed to appreciate the city; the assassination of Queen Draga of Servia in 1906; and a meeting with a young Englishman in a castle near Glamis. Mrs. Glyn points out in her disarming autobiography, *Romantic Adventure,* that the novel is really highly moral in tone; Paul pays willingly with his life for a single passionate romance, and the book, translated into all European languages, was treated seriously as tragedy. Glyn had a financial failure soon after (he died in 1915) and his wife began to write novels in deadly earnest to pay off his debts. Faulty and ungrammatical as they were, says Mrs. Glyn, they have nevertheless given a good deal of happiness to a large number of people, and were faithful portrayals of the manners and customs of their periods. A popular edition of her books issued in 1917 sold over a million copies. "On looking back at my life I see that the dominant interest, in fact the fundamental impulse behind every action, has been the desire for *romance.* I have sought it continuously, and have . . . tried to hand on my faith to others by means of my books and my films."

Mrs. Glyn spent 1922 to 1927 in Hollywood, and made the word "It" synonymous with sex-appeal. In New York, she lived at the Ritz Tower, and wrote daily articles and magazine stories. She lost £40,000 in the making of films in England, and her later years have not been so prosperous. She lives, in peacetime, on Hertford Street in London, and is a member of the Bath Club.

PRINCIPAL WORKS: The Visits of Elizabeth, 1900; The Reflections of Ambrosine, 1902; The Damsel and the Sage, 1903; The Vicissitudes of Evangeline, 1905; Beyond the Rocks, 1906; Three Weeks, 1907; The Sayings of Grandmamma, 1908; Elizabeth Visits America, 1909; His Hour, 1910; The Reason Why, 1911; Halcyone, 1912; The Contrast and Other Stories, 1913; The Sequence, 1913; Letters to Caroline, 1914; Three Things, 1915; The Career of Katherine Bush, 1917; Destruction, 1919; Points of View, 1920; The Philosophy of Love, 1921; Man and Maid, 1922; The Great Moment, 1923; Six Days, 1924; Letters From Spain, 1925; This Passion Called Love, 1926; Love's Blindness, 1926; It, 1927; The Flirt and the Flapper, 1930; Love's Hour, 1932; Sooner or Later, 1933; Did She? 1934; Romantic Adventure: The Autobiography of Elinor Glyn, 1936; The Third Eye, 1940.

ABOUT: Bennett, A. Books and Persons; Douglas, N. Experiments; Glyn, E. S. Romantic Adventure.

GODDEN, RUMER (1909*-), Anglo-Indian novelist, writes: "Rumer Godden was born in Sussex, England, but lived as a child in a small town on the banks of India's greatest river. She was very happy playing out of doors or writing poems and

* Correction: Date of birth, December 10, 1907.

stories on her mother's notepaper. When she was sent back to England she found life in a cold South Coast town dull and colorless, could never settle down at school, and was glad to go back to India as a young girl. After training in London she started a children's dancing school in Calcutta. This school became large and successful and after some years she was glad to sell it and to spend all her time at her real work, which is writing. Now she has lived half her life in England and half in India and is always a little homesick for one country or the other. In private life she is Mrs. Laurence S. Foster and lives in Calcutta with her husband and two little girls. Here she works hard, runs a small day school after her own ideas for her daughters, is not at all interested in

games or in a social life, but has a beautiful garden, a great many books and a piano, and breeds white Pekinese. In England she has a stone cottage in a lonely part of Cornwall, where, high on the moors and in sight of the sea, she

K. Vaughan

finds it easiest to write her books.

"Rumer Godden has written ever since she can remember, but her first book to be published was finished just before the birth of her first child. She enjoyed writing this book more than any other; it is about a Chinese man and a Pekinese dog and is the result of a lifelong interest in Chinese literature and life. She dramatized *Black Narcissus,* which, with *Gypsy, Gypsy* has been translated into Norwegian, Dutch, Danish, Polish, and Italian—the contract for the Italian translation being signed two days before Italy came into the war. When the war began she was in Europe completing her latest book. After the fall of France she took her children to India. There, after training as an Auxiliary Nurse, in case the war should reach India, she means to go on writing."

* * *

Of Rumer Godden's work Gladys Graham said: "The tale is told, the spell is woven, and to ask for more is to ask for a different book." Another commentator remarked that she had "three saving graces: an acute sense of psychological tension and overtone, a coolly notable skill at prose, a peculiar ability in atmosphere." Of *Gipsy, Gipsy* this same critic said that it "might have been written by

Emily Brontë if she and her prose had pernicious anemia but were not otherwise seriously indisposed."

PRINCIPAL WORKS: Chinese Puzzle, 1936; The Lady and the Unicorn, 1938; Black Narcissus, 1939; Gypsy, Gypsy, 1940; Breakfast With the Nikolides, 1942.

ABOUT: Time July 17, 1939, August 12, 1940.

GOETEL, FERDYNAND (1890-   ), Polish novelist and short-story writer, was born at Krakow. His great-grandfather, the first Goetel to settle in Poland, married a German woman. The family, of Swedish stock, had settled in Germany in the eighteenth century. Goetel's father was a railroad conductor who died when Ferdynand was a boy. His mother sup-

ported herself and her children by dressmaking, and managed to give the boy a good education. After finishing high school at Krakow young Goetel went to Vienna to study architecture at the Polytechnic there. After four years in Vienna he went to Warsaw to work as a journalist. In Warsaw when the First World War began, he was interned by the Russian government as an Austrian subject. After five months in prison Goetel was taken to Tashkent in Asiatic Russia, where, still a prisoner, he worked draining swamps and building bridges, progressing from common laborer to overseer and directing engineer. While a prisoner at Tashkent, Goetel married a Polish girl, Panna Madalinska, whose great-grandfather was a general in the Polish army who had been exiled with his family to the Caucasus for his part in the 1830 uprising. Shortly after his marriage Goetel was forced into the Red army, but escaped over the Persian frontier with his wife and daughter when the Bolshevists attacked Warsaw. After a period of wandering through Persia, Afghanistan, and India, he returned to Poland by way of Egypt and England with no money, no property, and no position. He had, however, an enviable store of memories and experiences which were soon turned to profitable account. Writing of the weird people he had seen, adventurers and refugees, of people and institutions upset by the Revolution and floundering in the new order, Goetel's books captured the imagination of his readers and won him, in 1929, a literary prize from the

Polish government. *From Day to Day,* translated from the Polish by Winifred Cooper and with an appreciative foreword by John Galsworthy, was a selection of the Literary Guild of New York in 1931. G. K. Chesterton contributed a preface to *Messenger of the Snow,* published in England in 1931. Goetel has also written short stories, travel books on India and China, a six-act play with prologue and epilogue, and edited *Przeglad Sportowy,* besides other Polish journals. The editors of this volume are uninformed as to his present whereabouts.

WORKS AVAILABLE IN ENGLISH TRANSLATION: From Day to Day, 1931; Messenger of the Snow, 1931.

ABOUT: Wings: The Literary Guild Magazine, May 1931.

GOETZ, GEORGE. See CALVERTON, V. F.

GOGARTY, OLIVER ST. JOHN (August 17, 1878-   ), Irish poet, novelist, and essayist, was born in Dublin, where he still makes his permanent home, and educated at Stonyhurst and at Trinity College, Dublin. He is a surgeon, a noted throat specialist still in active p r a c t i c e, and is a Fellow of the Royal College of Surgeons of Ireland. He was a Senator of the Irish Free State from 1922 to 1936. An open enemy of the Sinn Feiners and of de Valera, during the "troubles" in 1921 he was kidnapped and shot at, his country house was burned down, and he was obliged to take refuge, with his family (he was married in 1906 and has two sons and a daughter), in England. He returned a year later, and though still opposed to the present government of Eire, he takes no active part in politics now and the feeling against him has died down. He has a pilot's license and is keenly interested in aviation. His other hobby is archery, which he practises at his country home in Renvyle, County Galway. He used to engage in motorcycle racing in his younger years.

Dr. Gogarty is perhaps chiefly famous as the original of "Buck Mulligan" in the *Ulysses* of his fellow-student James Joyce. He never liked Joyce, however, objecting to the future author's habit of taking notes on every conversation. He has known intimately nearly all the great figures of the Irish Literary Renaissance. Best of all he knew William Butler Yeats, of whom he might be said to be a disciple, though an irreverent one. He was also an intimate of George Moore, whose garden his house overlooks. George Russell ("A.E.") called him "the wildest wit in Ireland," and his sayings have become legendary in Dublin. Francis Hackett said he was "at once sensitive and savage, poet and ghoul, hero and knave"; he is utterly unpredictable, a man of moods and violent contrasts. No one who knows him is indifferent to him; he is either ardently loved or ardently hated. Even his enemies, however, grant his coruscating wit—what Hackett called his "rapid and dazzling utterance and tumbled speech."

All these characteristics appear in his prose work, especially in his memoirs, *As I Was Going Down Sackville Street,* and his autobiographical novel of his student days, *Tumbling in the Hay.* Here he is indiscreet, puckish, mischievously outspoken, though his writing tends to be careless and occasionally obscure.

Horace Reynolds, an inveterate admirer of Gogarty's work, called his lyrics "as cool and fresh as a fountain, and delicate as a beautiful change of light." He is a big man, with a face usually melancholy in expression, even in the midst of a side-splitting remark. He is many-sided in temperament as well as in interests; it is a totally different Gogarty who performs an operation, writes a poem, flies a plane, and bursts out with a brilliant epigram or a bit of withering invective. Added to everything else, he is a devout Catholic. Perhaps only Ireland could produce so vari-colored a personality. If his prose had no other merit, it would survive as a gold-mine of information on Irish culture of his day. His verse, which is little known in America, lays claim to survival in its own right; it is not "important," but it is delicate, gay, and sometimes bold.

Gogarty is at present living in the United States.

PRINCIPAL WORKS: An Offering of Swans and Other Poems, 1924; Hyperthuliana, 1930; Wild Apples, 1930; Selected Poems, 1933; As I Was Going Down Sackville Street, 1937; I Follow St. Patrick, 1938; Others to Adorn (poems) 1938; Tumbling in the Hay (novel) 1939; Elbow Room (poems) 1939; Going Native, 1940; Mad Grandeur, 1941.

ABOUT: Gogarty, O. St. J. Others to Adorn (see Preface by W. B. Yeats, Forewords by G. Russell and H. Reynolds); Gogarty, O. St. J. As I Was Going Down Sackville Street; Newsweek June 19, 1939; Saturday Review of Literature December 23, 1933, April 6, 1940, January 25, 1941; This Week January 26, 1941; Time April 5, 1937; Wilson Library Bulletin June 1937.

GOLD, MICHAEL (April 12, 1894-), American novelist, playwright, and journalist, was born Irving Granich in New York,

the son of poor Jewish immigrants from Rumania. His father was a peddler and a suspender-maker, and and he was brought up on the East Side, going to work at thirteen. For four years he was night porter, clerk, and driver for an express company;
then he worked as a carpenter's helper, a section gang laborer, a shipping clerk, a factory hand, and an office boy. About 1915 he went to Boston, where he lived for several years; it was at this time that he began to write. He also became a radical there; after a short time in the I.W.W., he became a Socialist and was copy reader on the New York *Call* when it was a Socialist daily. It was about this time also that he adopted Michael Gold as his name. After the Russian Revolution, when the Communists split off from the Socialists, he joined them and has been active in Communist journalism since that time. He was assistant editor on the *Masses*, was one of the founders of the *Liberator* and was its editor from 1920 to 1922. In 1933 he and Hugo Gellert founded the *New Masses*, with which he is still connected. He has lived and worked all over the United States, largely as a reporter and copy-reader on newspapers, and spent two years in Mexico which proved a fertile experience; much of his writing stems from his Mexican experiences, and his life there confirmed him in his political views. He is married, and lives now in New York. For many years he has been a contributor to the *Daily Worker*, official Communist newspaper.

Michael Gold is dark, with a mass of black hair, now turning gray, and the tanned, broad face of a countryman, though most of his life has been spent in cities. Good-humored and indolent by nature, circumstances have turned him into a hard worker and a hard, vindictive fighter. His very real talent has been submerged for years by his propaganda activities; as long ago as 1932 Upton Sinclair lamented his letting fiction go by the board. His only novel is

a powerful study of the Jews of New York's ghetto; he has a gift for vivid characterization. His play on John Brown, *Battle Hymn,* is strongly and finely conceived. The only book he has published out of character is the juvenile work, *Charlie Chaplin's Parade,* illustrated by Soglow, which is full of sophisticated "wise cracks." His potentialities as a writer were by no means negligible, but they have long been overshadowed by his career of political journalism.

PRINCIPAL WORKS: John Brown, 1923; A Damned Agitator (short stories; published in Moscow) 1924; La Fiesta (play) 1925; Moncy (play) 1929; 120 Million, 1929; Jews Without Money (novel) 1930; Charlie Chaplin's Parade (juvenile) 1930; Proletarian Literature in the United States (co-editor) 1935; Battle Hymn (play, with M. Blankfort) 1936; Change World! 1937; Hollow Men, 1941.

ABOUT: American Mercury September and November 1929; Menorah Journal January 1930.

GOLDBERG, ISAAC (November 1, 1887- July 14, 1938), American biographer, philologist, and miscellaneous writer, was born in Boston, the son of Simon Mordecai Goldberg and Ida (Silverman) Goldberg. While he was only a small child he acquired a fascination for words. It sprang from what he

has called his "plurilingual heritage"—the English which he
himself was taught, the "solemnity, majesty, masculinity" of the Hebrew of his father's prayers, and the soft, sympathetic Yiddish that his mother spoke. From grammar school he was sent to the English High School in Boston, and here, under the excellent tutelage of William B. Snow, then a teacher of French, he became reassured that language was more than "parsing, prosody, and paradigm." He devoured, with "passionate indigestion," Max Müller's two-volume *Lectures on the Science of Language* as well as two books on the history of linguistics.

He was graduated from Harvard in 1910, and received his M.A. and Ph.D. degrees in the two years following. The intellectual energies and philosophies of Denis Mathias Ford, Edward Sheldon, Charles Hall Grandgent, and George Santayana left their mark on Goldberg during these years.

His first book, however, had very little relation to the Romance Philology that had been the subject of his postgraduate research: *Sir William G. Gilbert: A Study in Modern Satire and the Gilbert-Sullivan Operas* (1913). In September of the year following he married Elsie Frieda Horvick. During the World War, he wrote, for the Boston *Transcript,* a series of informative articles on European activity and opinion, basing them on his own translations from the foreign press. From 1923 to 1932 he was literary editor of the *American Freeman;* and in 1930 began two years as music critic of the *American Mercury.* In the fall of 1933 he founded *Panorama,* a monthly news magazine, editing it until its demise in January 1935. He was, at the same time (1933-34), special lecturer at Harvard on Hispano-American literature.

His *Studies in Spanish American Literature,* representing some scholarly spadework in a much-neglected field, was issued in 1920. Before the appearance of *The Drama of Transition,* two years later, he had completed the translation of many Yiddish and Italian plays. Then came his studies of H. L. Mencken and Havelock Ellis. In the 'thirties he produced *George Gershwin—A Study in American Music;* a psychological biography of Lola Montez; a life of the American Jewish pioneer, Major Mordecai Noah; several monographs on criticism, aesthetics, and sex; a book of short tales; and some popular philosophy.

Goldberg said that the source of his "radicalism" was his "great impatience with humanity." His "widely receptive curiosity" (which overstepped religious orthodoxies, social convention, and economic safety) led him to divert his energies into too many channels. Except for his pioneer pieces on Spanish-American literature, no single enterprise seems likely to exert any lasting influence.

PRINCIPAL WORKS: Sir William G. Gilbert: A Study in Modern Satire and the Gilbert Sullivan Operas, 1913; Studies in Spanish-American Literature, 1920; The Drama of Transition, 1922; The Fine Art of Living, 1929; Tin Pan Alley: A Chronicle of the American Music Racket; 1930; George Gershwin: A Study in American Music, 1931; Madame Sex, 1932; The German Jew: His Share in Modern Culture (with Dr. A. Myerson) 1933; Major Noah: American Jewish Pioneer, 1937; The Wonder of Words, 1938.

ABOUT: Harvard Class of 1910: Twenty-Fifth Anniversary Report, 1935; New York Herald Tribune "Books" July 15, 1938; Panorama (scattered issues); introductions to his works.

GOLDING, LOUIS (November, 1895-   ), English novelist, writes: "Louis Golding was born in Manchester, England, of Jewish

parents. Manchester is the 'Doomington' of his best-known novels (*Magnolia Street* and *Mr. Emmanuel*). His father was a ritual orator, whom his son described as the most exquisite he had ever heard. The background of his mother's people and their origins are described in the Russian section of *Five Silver Daughters.* He was educated at Council Schools (synthesized in *The Pursuer*), at the Manchester Grammar School (an ancient foundation described in his first novel, *Forward From Babylon*), and at Queen's College, Oxford. But he considers himself to have acquired the more serious part of his education during that series of world-wide wanderings which have made him one of  the most experienced literary travelers of our time.

"His first work was a novel, entitled *The Advanchers of Three on Bludy Island,* written at the age of six. In his disappointment at its failure to find a publisher, and under the aegis of Tennyson and Poe, he became a poet, and *Sorrow of War,* a volume of poems, became his first published work. He had written about thirty books before *Magnolia Street* established him, with its wide acclamation and its translation into over a score of languages. He himself, however, considers *The Miracle Boy* and *Five Silver Daughters* to be his best work. His writings include novels and short stories, poetry, belles lettres, travel books, criticism, and poetic drama. He has written for the stage, broadcasting, and the cinema. He has lectured in America and played ping-pong in four continents.

"Politically, he is strongly inclined to the left, though the [Soviet] attack on Finland was a severe jolt on the side of the jaw. He is an ardent champion of the Jewish people, whose problems he has expounded in a volume which has been read all over the world. He is unmarried and an *aficionado* of the linked arts of ballet and boxing. In his house in St. John's Wood, in London, which he has composed as lovingly as any of his novels, he has assembled a collection of cherubs which are at once remembrances of his work and of his travels."

* * *

Elsewhere, Mr. Golding gives his recreations as "wandering, reading, talking, and listening." His poems still appear in magazines, though he has had no recent volumes. He modestly omits to mention that he interrupted his university course to enlist in the war and serve in Macedonia. At Oxford he was editor of the *Queen's College Miscellany* and one of the editors of the Oxford books of verse, and his first two volumes were published while he was still a student. Brought up in poverty, he earned all his schooling after the age of twelve by means of scholarships. He has traveled much in the Mediterranean area, "enduring forced and sometimes deliberate discomfort, tramping and writing," but says he has suffered much more discomfort in Pullman sleepers across the American continent! He is a heavy-set, good-looking man, clean-shaven, with wavy dark hair.

PRINCIPAL WORKS: *Novels*—Forward From Babylon, 1920; Seacoast of Bohemia, 1923; Day of Atonement, 1925; Store of Ladies, 1927; The Miracle Boy, 1927; Luigi of Catanzaro, 1927; Give Up Your Lovers, 1930; Magnolia Street, 1931; The Doomington Wanderer, 1934; Five Silver Daughters, 1934; The Camberwell Beauty, 1935; The Pursuer, 1936; The Dance Goes On, 1937; Mr. Emmanuel, 1939. *Non-Fiction*—Sorrow of War (poems) 1919; Shepherd Singing Ragtime (poems) 1921; Prophet and Fool (poems) 1923; Sunward: Being Adventures in Italy, 1924; Sicilian Noon, 1925; These Ancient Lands, 1928; Adventures in Living Dangerously, 1930; James Joyce, 1933; A Letter to Adolph Hitler, 1933; In the Steps of Moses the Lawgiver, 1937; In the Steps of Moses the Conqueror, 1938; The Jewish Problem, 1938; Hitler Through the Ages, 1939; The World I Knew, 1940.

ABOUT: Golding, L. The World I Knew; Bookman (London) June 1928; Saturday Review of Literature July 22, 1939.

GOLDRING, DOUGLAS (January 7, 1887-), English novelist, critic, and travel writer, writes: "Douglas Goldring was born at Greenwich. Both grandfathers were lawyers; father was an architect. Educated at Felsted School. Matriculated at Oxford University, 1906; joined the editorial staff of *Country Life* a year later; in 1908 became associated with Ford Madox Ford (then Hueffer) as sub-editor of the newly-founded *English Review*. In 1910 founded and edited the *Tramp,* an illustrated literary magazine which became famous for its verse. (Among the contributors were James Elroy Flecker, P. Wyndham Lewis, John Drink-

water, Edward Thomas, Rose Macaulay, Arnold Bennett, Ford Madox Hueffer, Violet Hunt, W. H. Davies, Francis Brett Young.) In 1912 became literary editor to a publisher, and was responsible for the publication of *The Golden Journey to Samarkand* and *The King of Alsander,* by his friend James Elroy Flecker. From 1917 to 1920, he worked for the promotion of a better understanding between England and Ireland.

"In 1917 he married Beatrix Duncan, of Dublin, by whom he has two sons. This marriage was subsequently dissolved. In 1919 he visited Germany on behalf of the Fight the Famine Council; joined the London '1917 Club,' and came under the influence of his friend the late E. D. Morel. In 1925 he was appointed English reader at the University College of Commerce, Gothenburg, Sweden, relinquishing this appointment on his marriage to Malin Nordström in 1927. In November 1927 he visited New York and Boston. On returning to Europe, he settled in the South of France, in Nice, and remained there till 1930, when he transferred to London. He is now living in a country cottage in Hampshire. His principal interests, apart from modern art and literature, are civil liberties (he has served on the executive committee of the National Council for Civil Liberties), foreign travel, rural England, and Georgian architecture. In 1937 he founded the Georgian Group, a branch of the Society for the Protection of Ancient Buildings."

* * *

Mr. Goldring, a tall, blond man, is far better known in England than in America, though many of his books have been published here. He was known for years as a book reviewer who believed that "savage, rasping criticism" was "needed for the rebirth of poetry and fiction in England." As a novelist, his creed is that "a real book should send the reader back to life refreshed and stimulated."

PRINCIPAL WORKS: *Fiction*—The Permanent Uncle, 1912; The Fortune, 1917; Nobody Knows, 1923; The Cuckoo, 1926; The Facade, 1927; Margot's Progress, 1929. *Non-Fiction*—Ways of Escape, 1912; Dream Cities, 1913; The Loire, 1913; Dublin: Explorations and Reflections, 1918; A Stranger in Ireland, 1919; The Fight for Freedom (play) 1920; Reputations: Essays in Criticism, 1920; Streets: A Book of London Verses, 1921; James Elroy Flecker, 1923; Northern Lights and Southern Shores, 1926; The French Riviera and the Valley of the Rhone, 1928; People and Places, 1929; Sardinia; The Island of the Nuraghi, 1930; Impacts, 1931; The Coast of Illusion, 1932; Pacifists in Peace and War, 1932; Liberty and Licensing, 1932; To Portugal, 1934; Royal London, 1935;

Odd Man Out (autobiography) 1935; Pot Luck in England, 1936; A Tour in Northumbria, 1938; Facing the Odds (autobiography) 1939.

ABOUT: Goldring, D. Odd Man Out, Facing the Odds; Bookman June 1928; Current Opinion September 1920.

"GOLDSMITH, PETER." See PRIEST-LEY, J. B.

*GOLLOMB, JOSEPH (November 15, 1881-), Russian-American novelist and writer on criminology and politics, writes:

"I was born in St. Petersburg (Leningrad), and I remember it pretty clearly, though I left Russia when I was ten. My father, an engraver, fell out of humor with the Czar and decided that America was the place for him and his. So we came to New York and settled down on the lower East Side, in the world's hugest tenement slum. I attended public schools, the City College of New York, and Columbia University. Then I taught in some of the public schools I attended as a pupil; and later in the DeWitt Clinton High School, the 'Lincoln High' of my books for boys. After school teaching I fulfilled a boyish vow to become a reporter, to travel in Europe and elsewhere, to write some novels, and to go on writing plays. I have the plays still to do."

* * *

Mr. Gollomb received his B.A. from the College of the City of New York in 1902, and his M.A. from Columbia in 1908. He taught from 1902 to 1912, then for two years was a reporter for the Evening World, Evening Mail, and Evening Post. In 1914 he married Zoë Beckley, also a journalist. After three years as dramatic critic of the Evening Mail, the Call, and the Nation, he served on the staffs of scenario departments of several motion picture companies. His interest in criminology began when he was a member of the "Grand Street gang," which produced painters, actors, professors, business men, lawyers, engineers, and writers —and also several notorious gangsters. He has been called the only American journalist ever to get past certain doors in Scotland Yard, the Paris Sureté, and several other undercover agencies. Immediately after the First World War he was a correspondent in Europe for the New York Evening Post.

Of late years he has turned his attention in books and articles largely to the history of labor. He is dark and powerfully built. He lives now in New York.

PRINCIPAL WORKS: Songs for Courage (with Z. Beckley) 1917; That Year at Lincoln High, 1918; Working Through Lincoln High, 1921; The Girl in the Fog, 1923; Tuning in at Lincoln High, 1925; The Portrait Invisible, 1928; Master Man Hunters, 1928; The Subtle Trail, 1929; Crimes of the Year, 1931; Unquiet, 1935; Armies of Spies, 1939; What's Democracy to You? 1940; Captains of Labor, 1940.

ABOUT: Kunitz, S. J. & Haycraft, H. (eds.). The Junior Book of Authors.

GOLSSENAU. See VIETH VON GOLSSENAU

GOMBERG. See LIDIN

GÓMEZ DE LA SERNA, RAMÓN (July 5, 1891*-), Spanish humorist, short story writer, playwright, and novelist, universally known as "Ramón,"
was born in Madrid of a middle-class family. A captious and rebellious child, he often absented himself from school to play handball or discuss Tierra y Libertad, the Anarchist newspaper, with his friends or to edit his

hectograph paper with its solemn editorials on the "disaster of 1898." After a two-year sojourn in Frechilla, a small town in Castilla la Vieja, Ramón returned to Madrid at the dawn of the century and in 1904 celebrated his thirteenth birthday by publishing his first book, significantly entitled Entrando en Fuego (Entering the Fray) which means literally "coming under fire"—and, as a humorous critic remarked, "getting burned." Ramón has never left the literary fire: his life has reflected most of the literary struggles of contemporary Spain and he has always been in the heart of the fire.

After completing his studies at the Institute, he entered the Madrid University law school and graduated in 1908; he claims that he took up law in order "to have his picture taken in cap and gown." By this time Ramón had published his second book, Morbideces (1907), and the intellectual élite had honored him with a banquet: thus literary recognition came to him when scarcely sixteen. And so he decided to see the world: with a meager one hundred and fifty pesetas he journeyed to Paris and then

* Died May 23, 1950.   * Correction: Year of birth, 1888.

toured through Italy, Portugal, and Switzerland, with a short stop at London. In 1908 he met the novelist Carmen de Burgos, his most helpful and stimulating friend.

To follow Ramón's work for the last thirty years is an extremely arduous task: in 1909 he sent five works to press, a feat he repeated in 1917 and again in 1923. More than one hundred volumes of fiction, drama, and criticism now stand to his credit.

Ramón has been, above all, a literary rebel; he has anticipated or participated in most of the post-war vanguard literary movements. In 1910, a decade before the blossoming of Futurism, he was launching a "futurist" manifesto, "My Seven Words": "Oh, si llega la imposibilidad de deshacer"— which in more than seven words means "Alas, if the day should come when it would be impossible to destroy!" Waldo Frank claimed that if "Proust made a portrait of a society in deliquescence, of its break-up into the essences, atoms, maggots of dissolution, Ramón also weaves the filmy shell of a dissolving world, although in him the dissolution is not social, but subjective." This breaking-up is Ramón's major theme: he has devoted volume after volume to the fragmentary, to descriptions of junk-shops and all the oddities, curios, and bric-a-brac that the world has produced. His muse is the same that inspired Goya to do his *Coprichos*. Playful Ramón, lover of absurdities and good fun, has tried all forms of naughtiness—he has lectured on "The Complex Beauty of the Circus" from a trapeze, on "Elephants" from the back of an elephant at the Paris Cirque d' Hiver, he has discoursed eloquently "On Street Lamps," perched on a streetlamp in the city of Gijón. These performances are consistent with the literary genre he has "discovered," the *greguería,* a sort of aphorism or metaphorical maxim thus defined by Christopher Morley: "merry, bitter, and casual trivia of inward observation; sometimes sentimental, sometimes pure iodine. . . . They are worthy to stand beside Chekhov's Notebook; they are more condensed than Pearsall Smith's little sweetbreads." This permeates all of Ramón's works which consist of such exciting fantasies as *La Viuda Blanco y Negro* (1917)— considered by the *Paris-Journal* as one of the five greatest novels of our generation(!) —*El Doctor Inverosímil* (1921), *El Incongruente* (1922), *Movieland* (1922), *El Torero Caracho* (1926), *El Dueño del Atomo* (1928), two penetrative studies, *Goya* (1928) and *Azorín* (1930), and a few plays, the most entertaining of which is perhaps the surrealist *Medios Seres* (1929). Besides his prolific output and his contributions to numerous journals all over the world, Ramón is a most active lecturer and often takes long tours in Latin America. During the Civil War he sympathized with Republican Spain and now lives in Buenos Aires, a voluntary "exile." Ramón makes friends easily. He is a short, plump, witty bachelor, with chubby face and sideburns, inquisitive eyes and contagious smile.

WORKS AVAILABLE IN ENGLISH TRANSLATION: Movieland, 1930. Stories and *greguerías* in the following magazines: *Alhambra* June 1929 and January 1930; *Broom* May 1922; *Bookman* June 1928; *Criterion* January 1923; *Fortnightly Review* January 1929; *Living Age* November 1, 1927; also in Eaton, R. (ed.). The Best Continental Short Stories of 1927; Gorkin, J. G. (ed.). Great Spanish Short Stories; Putnam, S. (ed.). The European Caravan.

ABOUT: Boyd, E. Studies From Ten Literatures; Cansinos-Assens, R. La Nueva Literatura; Cassou, J. Panorama de la Littérature Espagnole; Frank, W. Virgin Spain; Lefèvre, F. Une Heure Avec; Bookman June 1928; Broom May 1922; Fortnightly Review January 1929; New York Herald Tribune Magazine October 12, 1930; Revue Européenne March 1, 1924; Revue Hebdomadaire January 20, 1923; Vie des Peuples June 10, 1922.

GORDON, CAROLINE (October 6, 1895-   ), American novelist, writes: "I was born on Merry Mont Farm, in Todd County, Ky. My mother was a Kentuckian, Nancy Meriwether. My father, James Morris Gordon, was born in Louisa County, Va., and came to Kentucky in the 1880's as a tutor in the Meriwether connection. My people on both sides have been tobacco planters since the weed was first cultivated by white men. My father conducted a classical school for boys in Clarksville, Tenn., and it was in this school and from him that I received my early education. In 1924 I was married to Allen Tate,[qv] the poet and critic. We have one daughter. We live —when we are at home—on a farm on the Cumberland River, near Clarksville, Tenn. The region around Clarksville, which includes a part of Kentucky, is the scene of my first four novels. My fifth is of the pioneer period, with scenes laid in North Carolina and in the Old Watauga section of Tennessee. I was a Guggenheim Fellow

in 1932 and in 1934 I won the second O. Henry prize."

* * *

Caroline Gordon is a slender woman with big dark eyes under thick brows and straight dark hair worn in a coronet braid. Her home in the Cumberland Valley is a more than hundred-year-old house in which Lafayette stayed during his triumphal last tour of America. She is an ardent gardener and prides herself on her cooking and housekeeping. When she and her husband are at home she loves to organize and act in charades. From 1920 to 1924 she was a reporter on the Chattanooga *News.* Her short stories have not been collected in a volume, but many of them have appeared in the annual O'Brien collection; the 1930 volume was dedicated to her by Mr. O'Brien. Ford Madox Ford, who was enthusiastic over her work (which he hailed as "a classical phenomenon"), spoke of its "great composure and tranquillity, . . . an achievement at once of erudition and of sombre and smouldering passion." Her Civil War novel, *None Shall Look Back,* had the misfortune to be published soon after *Gone With the Wind,* which kept it from having the wide circulation it deserved; it is a study particularly of the Confederate general, Nathan Bedford Forrest. *Penhally,* her first and best known novel, is a story of three generations on a Kentucky plantation.

PRINCIPAL WORKS: Penhally, 1931; Aleck Maury, 1934; None Shall Look Back, 1937; The Garden of Adonis, 1937; Green Centuries, 1941.

ABOUT: Bookman December 1931; Southern Review Summer 1937; Wilson Library Bulletin September 1937.

GORDON, CHARLES WILLIAM

("Ralph Connor") (September 13, 1860-October 31, 1937), Canadian novelist, was

P. MacDonald

born in Glengarry, Ontario. His father was the Rev. Daniel Gordon, a Scottish Highlander and a Presbyterian minister; his mother, born Mary Robertson, was also of Scottish descent and was a graduate of Mt. Holyoke (Mass.) Seminary (now Mt. Holyoke College). In 1870 the family moved from the primitive settlement where the father had served as minister to a more settled area, Zorra, Ontario—but it was Glengarry and its wild scenery that lingered in his son's memory.

He and his devoted brother together worked their way through the University of Toronto, and then after a year of teaching classics he put himself through Knox College, a divinity school. Two years at the University of Edinburgh followed, from 1883 to 1885. He then became a missionary to the miners and lumbermen of the Canadian Rockies. In 1893 he was sent to England for a year in the interest of the Canadian Western Missions. During the World War he served as chaplain of the 43d Cameron Highlanders. From 1894 to shortly before his death, he was minister of St. Stephen's Church (Presbyterian), in Winnipeg. In 1920 he was made chairman of the Council of Industry for Manitoba, and he was an idefatigable campaigner for the League of Nations. In 1921 he was moderator of the General Presbyterian Assembly in Canada.

Gordon became an author by accident. At the request of a friend who was editor of the *Westminster Magazine,* he wrote a story which was really a glorified tract, but which aroused so much interest that it gradually grew into his first novel, *Black Rock.* His pseudonym was also an accident; the editor wired him for one, and he responded, "Use Cannor" (taken from a letter-head reading "Brit. Can. Nor. West Mission"). The telegrapher changed it to "Connor," and the editor added the "Ralph" for euphony. So immensely popular was his first book that though he never gave up the ministry, he continued to write novel after novel, practically one a year, and in time he answered equally to either name and came to feel as if he were two men in one.

In 1898 Gordon married Helen King, daughter of a fellow-clergyman and much his junior. The marriage was markedly happy. Their first child was a son; followed by six daughters.

Though in appearance Gordon was a rather severe, scholarly preacher, actually he remained the boy who had rejoiced in the rough life of the wilderness. He was a champion canoer; his summer home—really a camp in the wilds—was his chief joy; he loved the strenuous Scottish game of curling, and he said his best recreation was "driving, always." He was for years a member of a college glee club, and had a good tenor voice. In both religion and politics he was a liberal, and even marched with the militant suffragists in London before the war.

The Canadian west, Scottish Highlanders,
nd the ministry were the three main threads
f his life and interest, and they all come out
a his books. The combination of exciting
dventure and moral purity won for them
ousands of readers who had never before
ndulged in novels—indeed, many of them
aunchly affirmed they were not fiction, for
minister "couldna tell lies." In all his
ovels (in many of which a minister is the
ero), strict morality, temperance, purity,
nd piety are stressed; and yet he was a
orn story-teller, and the scenery and life
f the Canadian Rockies were in his very
ood. His novels are not literature, but
ey are good reading if one can discount
eir smugness, and though they were written
or adults they make excellent juveniles still.

PRINCIPAL WORKS: *Novels*—Black Rock, 1898;
he Sky Pilot, 1899; Beyond the Marshes, 1899;
he Man From Glengarry, 1901; Glengarry School
ays, 1902; The Doctor, 1906; The Foreigner,
09; Corporal Cameron of the Northwest Moun-
d Police, 1912; The Patrol of the Sundance
rail, 1913; The Major, 1917; The Sky Pilot in
o Man's Land, 1919; To Him That Hath, 1921;
ne Gaspards of Pine Croft, 1923; Treading the
inepress, 1925; The Friendly Four, 1927; The
unner, 1929; The Rock and the River, 1931;
he Arm of Gold, 1932; The Girl From Glen-
rry, 1933; Torches Through the Bush, 1934;
ne Rebel Loyalist, 1935. *Non-Fiction*—The Life
James Roberton, 1908; Postscript to Adventure,
38.

ABOUT: Connor, R. Postscript to Adventure;
anadian Bookman April 1930.

GORDON, NEIL." See MACDONELL,
A. G.

GORKY, MAXIM (March 14, 1868-June
4, 1936), Russian novelist, playwright, and
ort story writer, was born Alexei Maximo-

vich Pyeshkoff in
Nizhni Novgorod
(now Gorky) on the
Volga River, the son
of an upholsterer.
Until he was ten he
lived with his mater-
nal grandfather, a
dyer and one-time
Volga boatman, who
taught him to read.
His grandmother, an
curable romantic with an endless fund of
ories and love for human beings, was
rhaps the greatest influence of his life.
lexei had two years of schooling in 1876-
7; at the same time he picked junk in the
ty dumps in order to earn his keep. When
s mother died of tuberculosis in 1878, the
y was put to work in a bootshop, and later

in a draftsman's office. In the spring of
1880 he fled down to the river, and got a
job as dishwasher on a Volga steamer, working under Smury, the cook, who is credited
by Gorky with having first turned his mind
toward literature. At the end of the summer
Alexei found himself back at the draftsman's as boy of all work—scrubbing floors,
washing diapers in icy springwater, and
fighting for the privileges of reading books.
Only revolutionists and terrorists read books,
he was told; when they measured his candle,
he read by moonlight.

In 1884 Alexei left Nizhni Novgorod for
Kazan, hoping to enter the university there.
Little did he guess how dangerous it was
considered in Holy Russia to educate children of the lower classes. Ineligible for the
Tsar's university, he resumed his informal
education later described under the title *My
Universities*. He became acquainted with a
Narodnik group, worked as stevedore,
gardener-janitor, choir boy (being hired in
preference to Chaliapin), and finally in an
underground bakery memorably described in
Twenty-six Men and a Girl. At the age of
eighteen, disenchanted with the Narodniks,
whose faith in the peasantry he could not
share, he shot himself through a lung. The
next three years were spent wandering all
over South and Southeastern Russia working at odd jobs and studying "the lower
depths." In 1890 he returned to Nizhni to
volunteer for service, only to be jailed for
rooming with political suspects. Released,
he became interested in the nascent Marx-
ians, brought a poem to Korolenko, who
criticized it severely, and resumed his
wanderings—down the Volga, across the
Ukraine to Bessarabia, Odessa, the Crimea,
then along the Black Sea to Tiflis, where in
1892 his first story, "Makar Chudra," was
published in a local newspaper over the
signature Maxim Gorky—"Maxim the
Bitter"—the name by which he was thereafter known to the end of his life.

Stories and sketches in various newspapers
soon won him an invitation to contribute to
the influential monthly *Russkoye Bogatstvo*
(*Russian Wealth*), edited by Korolenko and
Mikhalovsky. "Chelkash," written in two
days, established his reputation. Nevertheless he was compelled to take a job on the
Samarskaya Gazeta writing "bad *feuilletons*
under the good pen name of Jehudiil
Chlamyda." In Samara, Gorky wrote about
twenty stories drawn from his wealth of
experiences, and his first two novels, *Foma
Gordyéeff* and *Three of Them*, were based
on Samaran observations. In 1896 Gorky

married Katerina Pavlovna Volzhina, proof-reader on the *Gazeta,* who bore him his only son, Maxim. Shortly thereafter Gorky's column became "too bitter" in its exposé of local corruption and economic exploitation, and he lost his job. Back in his native city, he wrote "Rambling Notes" for the radical daily *Nizhegovodsky Listok* and continued writing stories, all mercilessly mutilated by the censor. Gorky's rebellious note was nonetheless apparent to censor-wise Russians, and Marxists and other revolutionists were quick to hail him. In March 1898, after being rejected by numerous commercial publishers, Gorky's *Sketches and Stories* was published by two idealistic radicals.

The result was unprecedented in Russian literature. Gorky became the most famous writer in Russia. His picture was everywhere, on postal cards, cigarette boxes, in every newspaper. Moscow literary circles led the vogue for Gorky's costume, a blouse and high boots; society ladies raved about those "charming riffraff"; tramps stopped people in the street and demanded vodka in the name of Maxim Gorky, patron of hoboes and rebels. Chekhov tried to entice him to Moscow with tickets for *Uncle Vanya,* urged him to use fewer adjectives, simpler language; he introduced him to Tolstoy, who accused the young writer of "inventing" characters.

Gorky's considerable literary income was devoted almost entirely to the revolutionary movement in which he became a leading figure. The Tsarist police kept meticulous files of his activities down to 1917, but because of his tremendous popularity they treated him warily. In 1901 he was arrested for the third time charged with tendentious activities, just after his poem "The Stormy Petrel" had caused the suspension of the Marxian review *Zhizn (Life)*; but he was soon released, after intercession by Tolstoy. Deported from his native town, Gorky was met by wild demonstrations; his train was stopped by crowds and had to be re-routed around Moscow; train whistles and steam could not drown out his admirers. Gorky's election to the Academy in 1902 was promptly rescinded, whereupon Chekhov and Korolenko resigned and Gorky's reputation was further enhanced.

Smug Citizens, written after endless importunings by Chekhov and a two-weeks' siege by the Moscow Art Theatre, was permitted only after a special performance for government officials; even then it was censored and banned to all but subscribers;

policemen in evening dress took up th tickets. *The Lower Depths,* studiously cer sored, was allowed only because of th government's certainty that it would fai but the play was an international sensatior

Gorky suggested and led the deputation t Prime Minister Witte and other officials o the eve of Red Sunday, 1905, asking that th workmen be permitted to petition the Tsa For his part in the procession and his revc lutionary declaration describing that ever he was again imprisoned, but the goverr ment was besieged with protests from a over the world, and he was released. E took part in the October manifestations : Moscow, organized a Bolshevik newspape in St. Petersburg, *Novaya Zhizn (Ne Life),* the first number of which was co fiscated. After the December barricades I fled the country to raise funds abroad fc the revolution. His arrival in the Unite States in April 1906 was as triumphant : his journey through Finland and Scand navia: Mark Twain, William Dean Howell Arthur Brisbane, Jane Addams, H. G. Well Edwin Markham, and Charles Beard partic pating in the reception. The Russia Embassy in Washington, having failed have Gorky barred as an anarchist, ar nounced that Andreyeva, the actress wh accompanied the writer as Mrs. Gorky, wz not legally his wife. After Gorky sent telegram of greeting to the imprisoned labc leaders Haywood and Moyer, the pre played up the story sensationally, publishir pictures supplied by the embassy of Gorky wife in Russia from whom he had separate years before. Immediately Gorky's par was ejected from the hotel and put out the street in the middle of the night. Pres dent Theodore Roosevelt cancelled a recer tion scheduled at the White House. New papers changed their attitude from adulatic to alarmed concern over "the purity of ou inns." Gorky's resentment is expressed his collection of American stories.

His American campaign a fiasco, Gorky the fall of 1906 settled in Capri, Italy, whei he remained until 1914, when he was grante permission to return to Russia. In Cap Gorky organized a school to train Russia workmen in Bolshevik propaganda. He ha sided with Lenin's Bolshevik faction at th London conference of 1907, but his politic vagueness gave Lenin much trouble. *Tl Confession* (1908) conveyed the religiou mood of those philosophical and politic opponents whom Lenin fought for mar years.

During the war Gorky edited the monthly *Letopis* (*Annals*) until the advent of the Kerensky regime, when he headed the revived daily *Novaya Zhizn*. After the Revolution he devoted himself to saving Russian culture and aiding distressed writers and intellectuals. Lenin never refused Gorky's requests. In 1919 Gorky was made head of the World Literature Series issued by the State Publishing House. At Lenin's insistence he went abroad for his health (1921), returning in 1928 for thunderous celebrations of his sixtieth birthday. He was awarded the Order of Lenin; his birthplace and Moscow's main street were named after him, as well as a literary museum.

Gorky died at sixty-eight, the victim, it is alleged, of a poison plot by internal enemies of the Soviet régime, although he had been in poor health most of his life. At his funeral Molotov declared: "Since Lenin, the death of Gorky is the heaviest loss for our country and for humanity."

Gorky was a man whom fate could not crush. He was intoxicated with life—even his one attempt to leave it was a gesture of sheer desperation. Tall, slender, youthful in motions and figure and in his deep bass voice, he remained to the end an enthusiast. He was a naturalistic realist, but there was in him a strong poetic vein. As a writer he has obvious faults, nearly all traceable to the conditions of his early years. He is noisy, sentimental, turgid, confused; sometimes he wanders vaguely away into a sort of Slavic drunkenness of mere words. But that is only the underside of the garment. Implicit in all his writing, and insuring for the best of it a relative immortality at least, are the pity, the hatred of the hateful, the understanding and aspiration which "flow out of the fable to fix the truth of a way of life." More than a litterateur, Gorky was an institute—"I was all my life busy," he confessed. At the time of his death he was finishing the huge sequel-novel *The Life of Klim Samgin*, four volumes of which had appeared in English translation—a vast panorama of Russian history from the assassination of Alexander II (1889) to the death of Lenin.

WORKS AVAILABLE IN ENGLISH TRANSLATION: *Autobiography*—My Childhood, 1915; In the World, 1917; My University Days, 1923 (later published as Reminiscences of My Youth); Fragments From My Diary, 1924. *Novels*—Foma Gordyéeff, 1901 (later published as The Man Who Was Afraid); Three Men, 1902 (later published as Three of Them); Mother, 1907 (later published as Comrades); The Spy: The Story of a Superfluous Man, 1908; A Confession, 1910; Decadence, 1927; Bystander, 1930; The Magnet, 1931; Other Fires, 1933; The Spectre, 1938. *Plays*—In The Depths, 1903 (later published as A Night's Lodging, The Lower Depths, Submerged, At The Bottom, Down and Out); Summer-Folk, 1905; The Smug Citizen, 1906; The Children of the Sun, 1906; The Judge, 1924; The Last Plays of Maxim Gorki (Yegor Bulichoff, Dostigaeff, The Others) 1937. *Short Stories*—Orloff and His Wife, 1901; Twenty Six and One and Other Stories, 1902 (later published as Twenty Six Men and a Girl, and Other Stories); Tales From Gorki, 1902; The Outcasts and Other Stories, 1902; Creatures that Once Were Men, 1905; Tales From Maxime Gorky, 1910; Tales of Two Countries, 1914; Chelkash and Other Stories, 1915; The Individualists, 1916; Stories of the Steppe, 1918; Through Russia, 1921; The Story of a Novel and Other Stories, 1925; A Book of Short Stories, 1939. *Writings on Literature, Politics, etc.*—Reminiscences of Leo Nicolayevitch Tolstoi, 1920; Reminiscences of Anton Chekhov, 1921; Reminiscences of Leonid Andreyev, 1928; Days With Lenin, 1932; To American Intellectuals, 1932; On Guard for the Soviet Union, 1933.

ABOUT: Dillon, E. J. Maxim Gorki: His Life and writings; Dukes, A. Modern Dramatists; Fox, R. The Novel and the People; Gruzdev, I. A. Das Leben Maxim Gorkis; Kaun, A. Maxim Gorky and His Russia; Olgin, M. J. Maxim Gorky: Writer and Revolutionist; Ostwald, H. O. A. Maxim Gorki; Perski, S. Contemporary Russian Novelists; Usthal, A. Maxim Gorki; Europe August 15, 1936; International Literature January 1933, July 1936, August 1936, October 1936, April 1937, June 1937, August 1937, October-November 1937, December 1937, March 1938; Internationale Literatur June, July 1937, November 1938; Literature of the Peoples of the USSR (VOKS Illustrated Almanac 1934); Monde Slave September 1936; Nation April 1918; Revue de France August 1936; Slavonic Review January 1939; Virginia Quarterly October 1929.

*GORMAN, HERBERT SHERMAN (January 1, 1893-   ), American biographer, novelist, and essayist, writes: "Born: Springfield, Mass. Father, Thomas Gorman, born in Ireland, fought in the Civil War. Mother, Mary (Longway) Gorman, of French and English stock. Education: public schools and high school, Springfield. But most of it came from the public  library; I used to read about fifteen hours a day for months on end. Jobs: was assistant to a cobbler, pasted up newspapers in a newspaper mailing room, worked in a rubber-stamp factory where I nearly lost a finger, spent a year in a bank as the worst bank-clerk ever born, labored for a lumber company. Spent about a year and a half (*circa* 1912) trying to be an actor. Was frightfully stagestruck. Played in stock, in vaudeville, and with Robert Mantell. About 1914 started reviewing books for Springfield *Republican*. Had written oceans of poetry, some of it placed in small newspapers and fly-by-night magazines. About 1915 became reporter for Springfield *Union,* later assistant literary editor, then motion picture editor. In 1918 was called to New York to work for the Liberty Loan Publicity Bureau. Subsequently worked on the New York *Sun, Evening Post, Times,* and *Herald Tribune,* to 1928. Was an extension lecturer at New York University from 1926 to 1929.

"Travels: after end of war went to Europe every chance I could get. Returns home became farther and farther between. Lived for a number of years in France. I hope to return to Paris as soon as this war is finished. Lived also for a year or more in London. Spent some time in Mexico, also Switzerland, Scotland, Ireland.

"Married Jean Wright, 1921; marriage dissolved 1932. She is now Mrs. Carl Van Doren. In 1932 married Claire O. (Schneider) Crawford; one daughter.

"Was book reviewer for *Century Magazine* for a year. Was close friends with Edwin Arlington Robinson, Vachel Lindsay, Elinor Wylie, Ford Madox Ford, James Joyce, and still am with Padraic Colum. Am anti-Communist and anti-Nazi. Lean rather to the Right. As bad as it is, it isn't as bad as the Left. No religious affiliation, but lean toward Roman Catholicism. Do not believe in the equality of people but do believe in justice for all. Desire the utmost freedom—every man and woman in the world to be able to say anything he or she desires to say at any time and in any place, but *not* by persuasion or conspiracy to limit the freedom of others. No political affiliations. When I vote (which I never have done) I'll vote for whom I please. Love (outside literature) music (*not* swing); painting (very pro-Picasso, Modigliani, Vlaminckhl, and Utrillo); sculpture, football (to watch), boxing, and dancing. Passion for hot spicy foods, curries, Chinese dishes. Two secret passions: to be a chef, and to meet Myrna Loy."

PRINCIPAL WORKS: The Fool of Love (novel) 1920; The Barcarolle of James Smith (verse) 1922; The Procession of Masks, 1923; The Peterborough Anthology (with Jean Wright Gorman) 1923; James Joyce—His First Forty Years, 1924; Gold by Gold, 1925; The Two Virginities, 1926; A Victorian American—Henry Wadsworth Longfellow, 1926; Notations for a Chimaera, 1926; Hawthorne—A Study in Solitude, 1927; The Place Called Dagon (novel) 1927; The Incredible Marquis, 1929; Scottish Queen, 1932; Jonathan Bishop (novel) 1933; Suzy (novel) 1934; The Mountain

and the Plain (novel) 1936; James Joyce: Biography, 1940; Brave General, 1942.

ABOUT: Bookman December 1932; Bookm (London) October 1927; Current Biography 194

GOSSE, Sir EDMUND WILLIAM (Se tember 21, 1849-May 16, 1928), Engli critic, essayist, and biographer, was born London, the son of Philip H. Gosse, who somehow managed to be both a zoologist and a religious bigot, and Emily (Bowes) Gosse. Both parents were Plymouth Brethren, and their home was a gloomy place. His mother, besides, was forty-three years

old at his birth, and even more narrow i tellectually than his father. She died wh the frail boy was seven, and his rearing w in his father's hands. Half a century late in *Father and Son* (crowned by the Fren Academy), he revealed behind the tempora veil of anonymity the oppressive years his youth.

Strangely (or perhaps not strangely from such an environment came one of t most urbane, deeply cultured, and sensiti of English critics. His education was enti ly private; he never knew the give-and-ta of a school. In consequence he was alwa fundamentally shy, though the shyness w masked in self-assertion.

In 1867, through Charles Kingsley, was appointed assistant librarian of t British Museum, with Coventry Patmore an associate. In 1875 he became translator the Board of Trade, where Austin Dobs was his colleague. Gradually he became t friend of every living English author note—Swinburne, Hardy, Kipling, Sha Henry James, Max Beerbohm, and ma others. From 1884 to 1890 he was a lectur in English Literature at Trinity Colleg Cambridge (as a successor to Sir Les Stephen), though he himself had no degr In 1904 he left the Board of Trade a for ten years was librarian to the House Lords. In 1875 he had married Nellie Ep sister-in-law of the painter, Sir Lawren Alma-Tadema. They had a son and tv daughters. He was knighted in 1925 (Co mander of the Order of the Bath 1907). I was also a Commander of the French Legi of Honor and had three Scandinavi decorations.

Gosse's family had American connectio and he was always close to the Unit ates, which he first visited in 1884 as a lecturer. Another hereditary interest—the family was of Scandinavian descent—led to his championship of Ibsen and other Scandinavian writers. He was keenly interested also in French literature, and introduced many of the modern French authors to the English public. He was aware of his tendency toward conservatism, and endeavored (not always successfully) to guard against it; but in spite of his innate prejudices he was always as fair in intention as he was frank and outspoken in practice.

Although Gosse wrote verse, plays, a novel, and innumerable essays, it was as a critic that he most nearly approached greatness. His one claim to immortality as a creative writer is *Father and Son,* a human document of the first rank. A high-strung, small man with very fair skin and hair and light eyes, who spoke in a quick, slurring voice, he was happiest basking in the adulation of a circle of famous men and women who all deferred to him. Yet he had many enemies also, largely derived from his habit (as he once wrote to Philip Guedalla) of always meaning "exactly the whole of what I write." Toward the end he grew very weary; in one of his last letters, he wrote to Stark Young of the world "which I am soon to leave behind with some regretful curiosity, but with some baffled satisfaction." He died following an operation, four months after he had served as pallbearer at Hardy's funeral.

PRINCIPAL WORKS: *Prose*—King Erik (play) 1876; The Unknown Lover (play) 1878; Studies in the Literature of Northern Europe, 1879; Gray, 1882; Seventeenth Century Studies, 1883; From Shakespeare to Pope, 1885; Raleigh, 1886; Life of William Congreve, 1888; A History of Eighteenth Century Literature, 1889; Robert Browning: Personalia, 1890; The Life of Philip Henry Gosse, 1890; Gossip in a Library, 1891; The Secret of Narcisse: A Romance, 1892; Questions at Issue, 1893; The Jacobean Poets, 1894; Critical Kit-Kats, 1896; Henry Fielding, 1898; The Life and Letters of John Donne, 1899; English Literature: An Illustrated Record (with Richard Garnett) 1903; Jeremy Taylor, 1904; French Profiles, 1905; Coventry Patmore, 1905; Sir Thomas Browne, 1905; Ibsen, 1907; Father and Son, 1907; Swinburne: Personal Recollections, 1909; The Life of Swinburne, 1912; Portraits and Sketches, 1912; The Future of English Poetry, 1913; Two Pioneers of Romanticism, 1915; The Novels of Benjamin Disraeli, 1918; Some Diversions of a Man of Letters, 1919; Malherbe and the Classical Reaction in the Seventeenth Century, 1920; Books on the Table, 1921; Aspects and Impressions, 1922; The Continuity of Literature, 1922; More Books on the Table, 1923; Personal Relations Between Literature and Medicine, 1924; Silhouettes, 1925; Leaves and Fruit, 1927. *Poetry*—Madrigals, Songs, and Sonnets, 1870; On Viol and Flute, 1873; New Poems, 1879; Firdausi in Exile and Other Poems, 1885; In Russet and Silver, 1894; Collected Poems, 1911

ABOUT: Bellows, W. Edmund Gosse: Some Memories; Braybrooke, P. Considerations on Edmund Gosse; Charteris, E. Life and Letters of Sir Edmund Gosse; Freeman, J. English Portraits and Essays; Pater, W. Essays From The Guardian; Bookman July 1931; Bookman (London) July 1926; Harper's Magazine May 1939; London Mercury June, July, October 1928; New Republic June 6, 1928.

GOUDGE, ELIZABETH (1900-   ), English novelist, writes: "I was born at Wells, in Somersetshire, a cathedral town which I have described as 'Torminster' in *A City of Bells.* My father was vice-principal of the Theological College. When I was three years old he became the principal. Though I was an only child I was never lonely. My invalid mother was, and is,  the most wonderful story-teller in the world. With a family of boy neighbors I wrote a magazine which came out each month and lasted until the labor of writing out my stories palled on me. One of these little boys and I did lessons together with a governess. When this family left Wells I was lonely for the first time; I trailed round the garden weeping bitterly—I was always a watery child—and wished I was dead. My greatest excitement in childhood was being taken every other summer to visit my grandparents in the Channel Islands, where my mother's family, Norman-French in origin, had lived for generations. In my first novel, *Island Magic,* I tried to draw a picture of Guernsey and of the family as I imagined they might have been when my mother and her sisters and brother were young. When I was eleven years old my father was made a canon of Ely Cathedral, in Cambridgeshire, and we moved to yet another small and beautiful cathedral city. There I had lessons with a new governess, too kind to be a good teacher. When I was fourteen my parents suddenly discovered to their horror that their only child knew nothing at all except the dates of the kings of England and the multiplication table. I was promptly sent to boarding-school on the South Coast and was there through the years of the war. At school I was a dunce at everything except English composition and the court curtsey.

"When I returned home I said grandly that I would be a writer. I set blithely to work on children's stories. I did actually achieve a little published volume of fairy stories, which did not sell. Throughout this whole period of strenuous literary labor I earned exactly fifteen shillings. So I decided that literature was no good, and left home for the Art School of Reading University. I stayed there for two years; then I again returned home, and announced with a confidence that now staggers me that I was capable of teaching design and applied art. The ladies of Ely believed me and actually had the generosity to pay me.

"When I was twenty-three my father was made Regius Professor of Divinity at Oxford University, and we moved to Christ Church College. In time Oxford life lost its terrors and the stimulation of it woke up in me the old longing to write. I still went on with my teaching, but I got up early and wrote before breakfast. I chose to start with plays. I was thirty-two before any success came my way: a Sunday night performance in London of a play about the Brontës. I was so encouraged that I gathered my plays together into a book and sent it the round of several publishers. One kind publisher told me: 'Your work shows promise. Why not try to write a novel?' Fired with fresh enthusiasm I sat down and wrote, with a speed and ease which will never be mine again. On the third try with the novel I was lucky. Since then I have written novels and short stories. But plays, just because they are so difficult and I never have any success with them, are still my first love."

* * *

Miss Goudge has never married. Her father died in 1939, and she now lives with her mother in a cottage in South Devon. "Romantic beauty," "lyrical prose," "irrepressible gayety," "a curious charm," are some of the phrases which have been used by critics to describe her work. She is blonde, with an oval face and large, deep-set eyes under a broad forehead. Her name is pronounced *Goozh*.

PRINCIPAL WORKS: Island Magic, 1934; The Middle Window, 1935; A City of Bells, 1936; A Pedlar's Pack (short stories) 1937; Towers in the Mist, 1938; The Sister of the Angels (short stories) 1939; Three Plays (The Brontës of Haworth. Suomi, Fanny Burney) 1939: The Bird in the Tree, 1940; The Smoky House, 1940; Golden Skylark, 1941; Well of the Star, 1941; The Castle on the Hill, 1942.

ABOUT: Christian Science Monitor Magazine June 8, 1940; Current Biography 1940; Scholastic March 4, 1939.

GOURMONT, RÉMY DE (April 4, 1858- September 28, 1915), French poet, novelist, and critic, was born at Bazoches-en-Houlme, Orne (Normandy), the son of Auguste and Marie (de Montfort) de Gourmont. On his father's side he was descended from a famous family of printers and engravers, on his mother's he was related to the 16th century poet Malherbe. He was educated at the University of Caen, and in 1883 went to Paris, where he secured a minor post at the *Bibliothèque Nationale.* Three years later he read Stéphane Mallarmé and first became aware of the Symbolist movement in poetry which has had so great an influence on modern verse and which he himself defined as the necessity to "say things not said before and say them in a way not formulated before." He also met J. K. Huysmans, and through him became one of the founder and a co-editor of the *Mercure de France*

An article in this magazine in 1891 offended the "official patriots" and was construed as pro-German, and Gourmont was discharged. An unfortunate love affair and a disfiguring facial affection combined with his dismissal to throw him into a life of seclusion. He became and for many years remained almost a hermit, with brief incursions into the outer world. As Huneker put it, he lived "in an ivory tower, but on the ground floor." He never married, but was prey to a series of infatuations none of which seemed to have any conclusion except to furnish him with literary material. Though in youth he was considered handsome, in later years he was by no means prepossessing—fat and bald, with no moustache but with a heavy beard, and dressed more like a monk than like a 20th century Frenchman. According to Richard Aldington, Gourmont was afflicted with chronic *lupus,* which caused his horror of society.

The World War awoke his latent patriotism and he became, belatedly, violently anti-German. He was, indeed, writing an impassioned attack on the bombing of the Rheims Cathedral when he was stricken by a cerebral hemorrhage and died soon after. His much younger brother, also an author, was devoted to him and was with him when he died.

Rémy de Gourmont had an encyclopedic mind. Not only was he poet, critic, dramatist, and novelist, but he was also a grammarian, an authority on aesthetics, a philologist, and even a biologist. He contributed to or was on the staff of reviews in France, Germany, Austria, and North and South America—though he disliked Americans until he fell in love with one. Havelock Ellis called him "the finest of living critics," and Amy Lowell spoke of his mastery of technique, his enormous influence on European terature, and celebrated him as "the great teacher of certain effects, the instructor in verbal shades." Ludwig Lewisohn perhaps summed him up best as "a great man of letters, if a poet of but secondary rank."

Yet his best poems—"Litanies de la Rose," "Fleurs de Jadis," "Le Dit des Arbres"— achieve calculated effects. They are beautiful not from feeling, of which they have none, but in the nuances of their sound— for Gourmont's poetry is best read aloud. Louis Dumur said well that "one must be lettered, fully to appreciate de Gourmont"— all his work was what he called one of his novels, a *roman de la vie cérébrale*. Except in his literary criticism, where he was forthright and authoritative, there is something "precious" about most of his writing, something that belongs to the end of the 19th century rather than to the 20th. It was not for nothing that many of his earlier books were privately published in very small editions, in tiny format, with special paper and type; Amy Lowell wittily remarked that he was "a bibliographical dandy."

Yet this is the same man whose series of *Promenades Littéraires* and *Promenades Philosophiques* have been compared to the *Causeries de Lundi* of Sainte-Beuve; whose books on style, aesthetics, and pure literature were classics as soon as they were published; who, in the *Physique d'Amour*, wrote a completely Rationalist and scientific biology and philosophy of sex; and who introduced to the general French reading public the then almost unknown names of Nietzsche, Villiers de l'Isle Adam, Huysmans and Mallarmé. His novels do indeed dwell in "a delicate dream world"; his poems are so purely personal that they approach fantasy and vagueness; but above all he was a great scholar and a great critic, and his influence remains inextricably woven in the fabric of contemporary literature.

PRINCIPAL WORKS AVAILABLE IN ENGLISH: *Novels*—A Night in the Luxembourg, 1912; The Virgin Heart, 1921; A Very Woman, 1922; The Horses of Diomedes, 1923; Mr. Antipholos, 1925; The Dream of a Woman, 1927; Colors, 1929; Letters to the Amazon, 1931. *Essays and Criticism*—Philosophic Nights in Paris, 1920; The Book of Masks, 1921; Decadence and Other Essays on the Culture of Ideals, 1921; The Physiology of Love, 1932. *Poems*—Selections From the Works of Rémy de Gourmont, 1928.

ABOUT: Aldington, R. Rémy de Gourmont, Life for Life's Sake; Gosse, E. W. Aspects and Impressions; Huneker, J. G. Unicorns; Lewisohn, L. The Poets of Modern France; Lowell, A. Six French Poets; Powys, J. C. Suspended Judgments; Querlon, P. de. Rémy de Gourmont; Vorluni, G. Rémy de Gourmont; Current Opinion

November 1915; Dial November 25, 1915; Fortnightly Review October 1927; Nation October 10, 1928.

GRAEFE. See MEIER-GRAEFE

GRAF, OSKAR MARIA (July 22, 1894-), German novelist, writes: "Oskar Maria Graf was born in the little Bavarian resort town of Berg am Starnberger See. His father was a baker, his mother came of peasant stock, both of them Catholics. Like his five older brothers he started life by learning the baking business from the ground up, doing an enormous amount of surreptitious reading while delivering rolls on his morning rounds. At the age of sixteen he ran away to Munich, determined to become a writer. He worked at many jobs, as a baker, miller, elevator boy, reader, postal clerk, and delivering circulars. At the same time he was writing stories and books and being initiated into the world-famed Munich Bohemia, which he still considers his 'university.' He considers Tolstoy to be his outstanding teacher, so far as ethics and writing are concerned.

"In 1913 Graf hiked through South Switzerland and Italy as a hobo. The outbreak of the war found him back in Berlin, at loose ends. From 1914 to 1917 he served at the Russian front. Obedient to his creed, 'thou shalt not kill,' he refused to carry out the orders of his superiors and had to suffer the consequences. In 1918 he saw the Munich Revolution, under the leadership of Kurt Eisner, at close quarters. There he experienced the growth of National Socialism, which he fought openly from the beginning. In 1933, when Hitler seized power, Graf voluntarily went into exile in Austria. Recognized by the Nazis as a 'Nordic' and an 'Aryan,' the regime tried to win him over and recommended his books as true 'blood-and-soil' literature. But Graf refused to swallow the bait and replied by publishing, on the day when the books of the most representative German authors were burnt in Germany, a demand that his books be burnt also, asking, 'What have I done to earn this disgrace?' Thereupon Graf's books were banned and burnt in the Third Reich, and he became one of the first to be deprived of his citizenship.

"In 1934 Graf emigrated to Czechoslovakia, where he remained until 1938. Since then he has been in New York, where he is president of the German-American Writers' Association."

* * *

Graf's novels are all about the Bavarian peasants from whom he springs, and he looks like one of them, big, round-faced, and florid. *Prisoners All* is an autobiographical volume. *Life of My Mother* tells the story of his mother, "whose Catholic stability and sense of relativism form the pivot of his writings." P. Beaumont Wadsworth called him "the Bavarian Gorky, . . . a born storyteller, with a complete absence of propaganda, . . . in the great German tradition of peasant authors."

WORKS AVAILABLE IN ENGLISH: Prisoners All, 1928; The Stationmaster, 1932; The Wolf, 1933; Life of My Mother, 1940.

ABOUT: Graf, O. M. Prisoners All; Bookman June 1932; New Republic April 26, 1939; Time November 18, 1940; Wilson Library Bulletin December 1940.

GRAHAM, CUNNINGHAME. See CUNNINGHAME GRAHAM

GRAHAM, DOROTHY (December 13, 1893-   ), American novelist, writes: "Born in Westchester County, N.Y., in a large

house overlooking the waters of Long Island Sound, I was educated in private schools where an appreciation of Renaissance art was considered essential—and economics never mentioned. Then came Europe, at an impressionable age, experi-

D. Carpenter

encing the pleasant pre-war days which left an influence never to be eradicated. Then intensive study of French, Italian, and German, alternating with jaunts to remote places. School at Lausanne in Switzerland; contacts with many nationalities. Subsequently school in Florence, reading Dante's *Divine Comedy* every morning and having tea with the descendants of the personages whom Dante had consigned to the Inferno. Always interested in writing, my work began to appear in magazines about 1922. In 1924 I married James W. Bennett, who had been in the consular service in China and Australia and who resigned his commission to write about the Orient. My first book, *Through the Moon Door,* was an account

of our life in Peking, and I published fou[r] novels with backgrounds in Europe or Chin[a]. The most significant was *The China Ve[n]ture,* which accurately predicted the prese[nt] Japanese aggression. The United State[s] Navy bought five hundred copies so that th[e] officers and men of the fleet might unde[r] stand conditions in the Far East. Later, thre[e] years were spent in collecting material fo[r] *Chinese Gardens,* an aesthetic history o[f] China and a study of Chinese philosoph[y] I have also lived in Hawaii, Italy, and Franc[e] made several visits to Malaya, Ceylon, S[u] matra, India, Japan, Egypt, seen somethin[g] of Central and South America—always re[-] turning to New York, for three generation[s] of ancestors have made me a confirmed Ne[w] Yorker.

"The record is of travel and writing. A[t] the moment I am doing a novel of Hawa[ii] in the 1890's, Victorianism superimposed o[n] the tropics—the last days of Lilioukalan[i] and the annexation of the Islands by th[e] United States. After that I shall write o[f] America—in its present interesting evolu[-] tion."

* * *

Mrs. Bennett is the daughter of Leo an[d] Emma (Weltech) Graham. She is a Fello[w] of the American Geographical Society an[d] a member of the International Society o[f] Woman Geographers. When she is no[t] traveling, she lives in New York City an[d] in Riverside, Calif., Mr. Bennett's firs[t] home. They have no children. Edmun[d] Kennedy spoke of the "delicate satire" o[f] Dorothy Graham's novels, and of her intens[e] love of beauty. Her best known book i[s] *Candles in the Sun,* a story of internationa[l] society in Italy.

PRINCIPAL WORKS: Through the Moon Doo[r] (non-fiction) 1926; Lotus of the Dusk, 1927 Brush Strokes on the Fan of a Courtesan (vers[e] with J. W. Bennett) 1927; The French Wife, 1928 The China Venture, 1929; Candles in the Su[n] 1930; Chinese Gardens (non-fiction) 1938.

ABOUT: Wilson Library Bulletin February 1931

GRAHAM, STEPHEN (1884-   ), Eng[-] lish writer and authority on Russian litera[-] ture and history, is the son of P. Anderso[n] Graham. At twenty-five, in 1909, he mar[-] ried Rosa Savory. Attracted by th[e] Russian spirit as shown in the litera[-] ture of the country, he gave up life i[n] London and cast in his lot with Russia[n] peasants and students, living wit[h] them in Little Russia and Moscow. Graha[m] tramped in the Caucasus and the Crimea the Ural Mountains, in the far north o[f] Russia, and accompanied Russian peasant[s] pilgrims to Jerusalem. He also "followed up the tide of emigration from Europe to America," going steerage with a party across the Atlantic and tramping to the farms of the West. In 1914 he was in Central Asia; the next year in Egypt, Bulgaria, and Roumania; and in 1916 he traveled to Northern Norway and Murmansk. A year's experience in the First World War, as private in the British Scots Guards, resulted in a book which is an unvarnished account of the brutalizing influence of war on superior officers and army chaplains, and which led to an inquiry in Parliament.

In 1919 Graham walked across Georgia (in Europe) and tramped the American Far West with Vachel Lindsay, the poet, in 1921. He toured Mexico in 1922-23 with the novelist Wilfred Ewart, who was accidentally killed in his hotel New Year's Eve by a spent bullet which came through the window. He edited Ewart's *Life and Last Words* the next year, when he also explored the Soviet frontier from Lake Ladoga to the Black Sea. In 1925 he was in Dalmatia and the Balkans; in the Carpathians in 1926; in New York in 1928; Bosnia in 1929-30; Macedonia in 1935; and Swaziland and the Transvaal in 1936. That year Graham received the Order of St. Sava, Yugoslavia. Books of competent journalism appeared with the same clockwork regularity as his travels. Isidor Schneider has called him "an excellent example of the traveler who rolls over the globe in his own impenetrable little microcosm." In the twenties Graham was the accepted interpreter of the greatness of the Russian soul to English readers, through his translations, introductions and editions. *The Lay Confessor,* his one novel, is a naïve, dreamy, all-accepting narrative, with sudden transitions and a sincerely Russian flavor, according to the *Spectator.* He returned to London in recent years to live on Frith Street in Soho.

PRINCIPAL WORKS: A Vagabond in the Caucasus, 1910; Undiscovered Russia, 1911; A Tramp's Sketches, 1912; With the Russian Pilgrims to Jerusalem, 1913; With Poor Immigrants to America, 1914; Russia and the World, 1915; The Way of Martha and the Way of Mary, 1915; Through Russian Central Asia, 1916; Russia in 1916, 1917; Priest of the Ideal, 1917; Quest of the Face, 1918; A Private in the Guards, 1919; Children of Slaves (American title: The Soul of John Brown) 1920; The Challenge of the Dead, 1921; Tramping With

a Poet in the Rockies, 1923; Under-London, 1923; In Quest of El Dorado, 1924; Life and Last Words of Wilfrid Ewart, 1924; Russia in Division, 1925; London Nights, 1925; The Gentle Art of Tramping, 1927; New York Nights, 1928; The Lay Confessor, 1928; The Tramp's Anthology (ed.) 1928; Life of Peter the Great, 1929; The Death of Yesterday, 1930; St. Vitus' Day, 1930; A Modern Vanity Fair, 1931; Great Russian Short Stories (ed.) 1931; Stalin, an Impartial Study, 1931; Life of Ivan the Terrible, 1932; One of the Ten Thousand, 1933; Twice Round the London Clock, 1933; Boris Gudunof, 1934; Lost Battle, 1934; Balkan Monastery, 1935; Characteristics, 1936; African Tragedy, 1937; Alexander of Yugoslavia, 1938; The Moving Tent, 1939; Stalin, 1939; From War to War, 1940.

ABOUT: Masters, E. L. Vachel Lindsay.

GRAHAME, KENNETH (March 3, 1859-July 6, 1932), British story writer, was born in Edinburgh, the son of J. C. Grahame, a barrister. Both his parents died when he was very young, and he was reared by relatives in Berkshire, England. After leaving St. Edward's School, Oxford, he found himself financially unable to go to college, and so secured a position in the Bank of England. There he rose rapidly, becoming acting secretary in 1893 and secretary in 1898. Like the American E. C. Stedman, he combined banking with literature. He became one of "Henley's young men," when that celebrated writer was editing the *National Observer,* and later was one of the contributors to the *Yellow Book,* that epitome of the end-of-the-century period in English literature.

Grahame, like the "Sunday painters," was a "Sunday writer." Writing was always secondary to his work and his personal life, and he was merely a quiet looker-on at Henley's gatherings of eager young men to whom it was all in all. In 1899 he married Elspeth Thompson, a Scotswoman. Their one son, Alastair, better known as "Mouse," for whom *The Wind in the Willows* was written, died in an accident at twenty. Grahame never recovered from the sorrow. (There is a touching parallel between Grahame's career and that of the American stockbroker-author Charles E. Carryl, whose timeless fantasy *Davy and the Goblin* was also written for the delight of a son who also died prematurely.)

After a full day at the bank Grahame did not hurry home to his desk. Instead, he served in the London Scottish Regiment, or forgot his shyness in social work among slum dwellers at Toynbee Hall. Then in 1907 his health broke down and he was obliged to retire from the bank. He went back to Berkshire and settled at Blewbury. He never wrote again, though he did edit the *Cambridge Book of Poetry for Young People.* His London friends never saw him, but "he knew the name of every horse, cow, and pig in the neighborhood." As Clayton Hamilton noted, he was "not at home beneath a roof"—under the open sky he became friendly and at ease. When Hamilton asked him why he, whom the American considered "the last great master of English prose," had ceased writing, he replied that he was "not a professional writer," that it was not worth while to slave at a desk for some half dozen appreciative readers when there was all outdoors to live in. He had a sort of direct feeling for nature that is rare among intellectuals. After his son's death he moved to Pangbourne, on the Thames, and there father and son lie buried side by side.

Maxfield Parrish had illustrated Grahame's books, and the author was curious to know if the artist "looked like himself." Grahame, too, looked like himself—as one would expect him to look from his books. He was a big, handsome man, with prematurely white hair but a fresh youthful face, with the clear skin of an extreme blond.

Except for an early volume of essays, and a posthumous collection, all Grahame's published work was three books—ostensibly books for children. Actually, as the *Nation* remarked, "the books are not really for children to read, but for adults who remember." They belong in more than one sense to a Golden Age, to a world that is gone—the world before the war of 1914. They contain "treasure once precious and still cherished . . . to protect [it] from an unfriendly world." He himself said he wrote for children because they were "the only really living people." What he was interested in, in other words, primarily was life itself.

Grahame is always compared with Lewis Carroll, but their resemblance is really slight. The later writer "thought his way much deeper into the mind of childhood" than did the earlier. There is not an ounce of rebellion in Alice; she is the good little girl whose parents are always right. Grahame's children, on the other hand, live quite consciously in a world of their own opposed to that of the grownups—the "Olympians," and

half their energy is employed in circumventing and evading these loving enemies. Moreover, Lewis Carroll never began to write the lovely prose that distinguishes Kenneth Grahame's fancies.

Grahame's children talk sometimes like Borrow's gypsies, because Grahame, like Borrow, was a nature poet in prose. In *The Wind in the Willows* (dramatized by A. A. Milne as *Toad of Toad's Hall*), the animals are real animals in the midst of fantasy, and the whimsicality never becomes mawkish. *The Golden Age* and *Dream Days* are books that belong on the shelf, not with *Alice in Wonderland* (supreme as that is in its own mood), but between Charles Lamb and Richard Jefferies.

PRINCIPAL WORKS: Pagan Papers, 1893; The Golden Age, 1895; Dream Days, 1898; The Wind in the Willows, 1908; The Kenneth Grahame Book, 1933.

ABOUT: Chalmers, P. R. Kenneth Grahame; Hind, C. L. Authors and I; Bookman January 1933; Bookman (London) December 1932; Literary Digest August 6, 1932; Nation July 20, 1932; Saturday Review of Literature September 17, 1932.

GRANBERRY, EDWIN (April 18, 1897-), American novelist and university professor, was born in Meridian, Miss., the son of James Asath Granberry and Elizabeth Jane (Phillips) Granberry. Five years in the Indian Territory left him vivid impressions of prairie fires, roaming bands of Indians and prairie wolves. When he was ten the family moved to Florida  where he attended the state university from 1916 to 1918, serving abroad as private in the Marine Corps in the First World War and obtaining his bachelor's degree from Columbia University in 1920. Granberry's original training had been for the career of a concert pianist, but he turned to teaching. After two years as assistant professor of Romance languages at Miami University, Oxford, Ohio, he attended the drama course at Harvard, working in the English 47 Workshop of Professor George Pierce Baker from 1922 to 1924, when he married Mabel Leflar; they have three sons. He was Latin and French master at Stevens School, Hoboken, N.J., from 1925 to 1930, and was appointed associate professor of creative literature at Rollins College, Winter Park, Fla., in 1933. He had received the

O. Henry Memorial Prize for the best short short-story published in an American magazine in 1931-32, for a tale entitled "A Trip to Czardis." Three novels before this award had attracted favorable attention for their "virile imaginative style." Tales of primitive passions in frontier settings, they derived largely from the wild forests, plains and seacoasts of Florida. The *Nation* said of *Strangers and Lovers*, his second novel, that Granberry had an "uncanny sense of natural atmosphere and dexterity in the use of dialect. . . . The evident sincerity with which he writes has caused him to be overpraised, however." Granberry has translated Jacques Lacretelle's *L'Amour Nuptial* as *A Man's Life*, and a novel of André Chamson's as *Mountain Tavern*. He has also contributed articles and short stories to numerous magazines, among them an article on "The Private Life of Margaret Mitchell" to *Collier's* for March 13, 1937. His recreation is deep sea fishing in the keys south of the Florida peninsula. Besides the university address in Winter Park, he lists Orange, N.J., as a residence.

PRINCIPAL WORKS: The Ancient Hunger, 1927; Strangers and Lovers, 1928; The Erl King, 1930.

*GRAND, SARAH (pseudonym of Mrs. Frances Elizabeth [Clark] McFall) (1862-   ), was born in Ireland of English

parents. Edward John Bellenden Clark, a lieutenant in the Royal Navy, and Margaret Bell Sherwood Clark, daughter of George Henry Sherwood, lord of the manor of Rysome Garth, Yorkshire, were her parents. At sixteen she married Brigade-Surgeon Lieutenant-Colonel McFall, who died in 1898. They had one son. Mrs. McFall traveled for five years in the East, China, and Japan; wrote two books, *Singularly Deluded* and *A Domestic Experiment*, and at twenty-six wrote *Ideala*, her first success, which was published in 1888. Five years later "Sarah Grand" made a name for herself with a long romantic novel, *The Heavenly Twins,* which became a best-seller in 1893 along with E. F. Benson's *Dodo.* The Hamilton House twins, Angelica and Theodore (called Diavolo when his true nature asserted itself); The Tenor, and other figments of Mrs. McFall's imagination were imbedded in a complicated plot

narrated in a lush, highly colored style. Like her contemporary Mrs. Humphry Ward, whom otherwise she did not resemble, Sarah Grand was at her most effective when weaving discussion of current problems into her narratives of the doings of good and bad factions of the higher circles of British "society." The land question comes up for exhaustive discussion in *Adnam's Orchard* and its sequel, *The Winged Victory.* The London *Times* called the latter novel a preposterous story preposterously related; the *Saturday Review* remarked that the novel was frankly impossible, viewed from the standpoint of art, but that one must pay a tribute to a personality which contrives to be entertaining "in spite of pleonastic excesses and creative failure." "Sarah Grand," who has interested herself in the woman's movement since the publication of *Ideala* in 1888, has also had first-hand acquaintance with the levels of society of which she wrote; she was Mayoress of Bath, England, where she makes her home at Sion Hill Place, in 1923, and in successive years from 1925 to 1929. Her recreations are sociology, music, and country life.

PRINCIPAL WORKS: Ideala, 1888; The Heavenly Twins, 1893; Our Manifold Nature, 1894; The Beth Book, 1897; The Modern Man and Maid, 1898; Babs the Impossible, 1900; Emotional Moments, 1908; Adnam's Orchard, 1912; The Winged Victory, 1916; Variety, 1922.

GRANT, ROBERT (January 24, 1852-May 19, 1940), American novelist and jurist, was born in Boston, the son of Patrick and Charlotte Bordman (Rice) Grant. He was educated at Harvard, receiving his B.A. degree in 1873, Ph.D. 1876, LL.B. 1879, and an honorary Litt.D. in 1922. He is also a Litt.D. of Columbia. In 1883 he married Amy Gordon Galt,

E. C. Tarbell

daughter of Sir Alexander Tilloch Galt, of Montreal, and they had four sons. She died in 1936. He was chairman of the Water Commission Board of Boston from 1889 to 1893, and Judge of the Probate Court and Court of Insolvency of Suffolk County, Mass., from 1893 to 1923—when, at seventy-one, he resigned because of age. (He lived seventeen years longer, alert and active to the last.) He was graduate president of Phi Beta Kappa in Harvard from 1923 to

* Died May 12, 1943.

1925, and an Overseer of Harvard from 1895 to 1921. He was a member of Governor Fuller's Advisory Committee which in 1927 sealed the death-sentence of Sacco and Vanzetti. He was a Fellow of the American Academy of Arts and Sciences and a member of the American Academy of Arts and Letters and of the Massachusetts Historical Society.

In the early 1920's, Judge Grant created a popular *furore* by his advocacy of more liberal divorce laws. After a series of light romances and adventure stories, his novels became more realistic, and were once widely read, though they are neglected by a later generation. *Unleavened Bread* is the best known of his books. Judge Grant published nothing after his autobiography in 1934. In February 1940, just three months before his death in his eighty-ninth year, he addressed a lively note to the editors of this volume, while *en route* to Hawaii. He died in Boston shortly after his return. The New York *Times* called him "a Boston patrician, who moved in that social circle populated by the Lowells, Cabots, and Lodges."

PRINCIPAL WORKS: The Little Tin Gods on Wheels, 1879; The Confessions of a Frivolous Girl, 1880; The Lambs, 1882; Yankee Doodle, 1883; An Average Man, 1883; The Oldest School in America, 1885; The Knave of Hearts, 1885; A Romantic Young Lady, 1886; The Carletons, 1886; Face to Face, 1886; Jack Hall, 1887; Jack in the Bush, 1888; Mrs. Harold Stagg, 1889; The Reflections of a Married Man, 1892; The Opinions of a Philosopher, 1893; The Bachelor's Christmas and Other Stories, 1895; The Art of Living, 1895; Search-Light Letters, 1899; Unleavened Bread, 1900; The Undercurrent, 1904; The Orchid, 1905; The Law-Breakers, 1906; The Chippendales, 1909; The Convictions of a Grandfather, 1912; The High Priestess, 1915; Their Spirit, 1916; Law and the Family, 1919; The Bishop's Granddaughter, 1925; Occasional Verses, 1926; The Dark Horse, 1931; Four Score—An Autobiography, 1934.

ABOUT: Grant, R. Four Score—An Autobiography; Boston Evening Transcript October 17, 1931; New York Times May 20, 1940.

*GRANVILLE-BARKER, HARLEY GRANVILLE (1877-), English dramatist and writer on drama, was born in London, the son of Albert James Barker and Mary Elisabeth Bozzi-Granville, his mother being partly of Italian descent. His education was in private schools, but ended at thirteen, when after coaching from his mother he entered the combined dramatic school and stock company then at Margate. At fourteen he appeared on the London stage, under (Sir) Charles Hawtrey. His first play, written when he was

sixteen, had an amateur production. His first play to see the professional stage, *The Weather Hen* (1899), was written in collaboration with Herbert Thomas. After appearing with Ben Greet and other stars in a repertoire of plays by Shakespeare and Marlowe, he became associated, in 1900, with the Stage Society, as actor and producer. His first play to attract wide attention, *The Marrying of Ann Leet,* was performed by the Society in 1901. In 1905, with J. E. Vedrenne, he became manager of the Court Theatre. Under his management, the theatre brought out plays, principally by Shaw and Ibsen, which could not then find a place on the conventional commercial stage. Granville-Barker himself acted the chief male rôle in most of Shaw's early plays. The scenery and lighting of the theatre were done by Gordon Craig, Ellen Terry's son. Granville-Barker was thus one of the first apostles of the "new drama" in England, and his association with those of its exponents now living still continues.

In 1907 he married Lillah McCarthy, an actress in his company. They were divorced later, and in 1918 he married Helen Manchester Gates, an American poet and novelist, who has collaborated with him in many translations and adaptations of foreign (particularly Spanish) plays. He ceased acting in 1910, but continued as a producer until 1914. He has honorary degrees from Oxford, Edinburgh, and Reading, is a Fellow of the Royal Society of Literature, and until the outbreak of the Second World War he lived in Paris as Director of the British Institute of the University of Paris. He has written no plays in the past ten years, but has devoted himself to translation and to speeches and books on the theory and technique of drama. Among the many dramatists whose work he has paraphrased or adapted for English use are Schnitzler, Brieux, Martínez Sierra, Joaquín and Serafín Álvarez Quintero, and Jules Romains.

Granville-Barker has a round face, with the mobile features of the actor, and thinning dark hair over a high forehead. Someone has said that he looks like a cross between a bishop and a butler! His interests are intellectual, and social in the broader sense of that word. Personally he is a re-

* Died August 31, 1946.

ring man, who shuns publicity and has
been too busy, since his earliest boyhood,
for much recreation. Thomas H. Dickinson
said of his plays that they "are like reminis-
ences of passionate things after emotion
as cooled, for they are aloof and cyni-
al. . . . He is like Shaw in liking discussion,
a feeling that ideas are among the most
important things in the world." He has
dealt frequently with themes once consid-
red "daring," one of his plays, *Waste*,
being banned by the British censor; but his
treatment is so dispassionate that the most
sensational subjects become at his hands in-
llectual arguments.

PRINCIPAL WORKS: *Plays*—Prunella (with Lau-
nce Housman) 1906; Three Plays (The Marry-
g of Ann Leete, The Voysey Inheritance, Waste)
'09; The Madras House, 1910; Souls on Fifth,
'16; Three Short Plays (Rococo, Vote by Ballot,
arewell to the Theatre) 1917; The Secret Life,
'23; His Majesty, 1928. *Miscellaneous*—A Na-
onal Theatre (with William Archer) 1907; The
ed Cross in France, 1916; The Harlequinade:
n Excursion (with D. C. Calthrop) 1918; The
xemplary Theatre, 1922; Prefaces to Shakespeare,
'23.-37; On Dramatic Method, 1931; The Study of
rama, 1934; A Companion to the Shakespeare
udies (ed., with G. B. Harrison) 1934; On
oetry in Drama, 1937.

ABOUT: Dickinson, T. H. The Contemporary
rama in England; Dukes, A. Modern Drama-
sts; Henderson, A. European Dramatists.

RATTAN, CLINTON HARTLEY (Oc-
ber 19, 1902-   ), American biographer
and critic who signs his works C. Hartley

Grattan, writes: "I
was born in Wake-
field, Mass., of Cana-
dian parents. My
family name is a cor-
ruption of a French-
Swiss name once
spelled Gratteau or
Gratto; I have no
connection with the
famous family of
Irish patriots.

llied

"Although a graduate of the commercial
ourse of New Bedford High School
1920), I obtained my B.A. from Clark
ollege in 1923, specializing in the history
thought and culture under Harry Elmer
arnes. The decided shift in interests came
my third year of high school when, under
e influence of an unusual English teacher,
was introduced to Maxim Gorky, Thomas
ardy, and similar figures. Also from this
ne I date my devotion to liberal social
ews. These interests were confirmed and
larged at Clark, at that time still power-

fully influenced by the ideals of its intellectual founder, G. Stanley Hall.

"After college, I taught English for two
years at Urbana Junior College in Ohio.
When H. L. Mencken started the *American
Mercury* in 1924, Harry Elmer Barnes suggested to him that I might do an acceptable
article. I offered an essay on James Russell
Lowell which was my first published piece
outside of high school and college papers.
In 1926 I came to New York, where I have
ever since been a free-lance writer, contributing chiefly to the 'quality' magazines.
I have never been employed by a newspaper
and but briefly by a magazine. To date
(1940) I have contributed to twenty-two
different magazines and twelve different
newspapers, to some of them many times.
I have written in the fields of literature,
politics, sociology, and economics, with the
result that I do not fit readily into any
established descriptive category. My books
have been similarly diverse in content.
While I am not ashamed of any, I value
most highly *Why We Fought* and *The
Three Jameses*. If I could disown any, it
would be my first, *Bitter Bierce*, which I
now regard as inadequate, though far from
worthless.

"I have made two trips in Australia, the
first for nine months in 1927 and the second
from 1936 to 1938. The latter was made
possible by a grant from the Carnegie Corporation for travel, study, and the collection
of materials for a social history of the Commonwealth. Nothing Australian fails to interest me. My collection of Australian
books is thought by Australian librarians to
be the largest in private hands in the United
States. Another continuing interest of
which I have thus far made no use in writing is modern art, especially American.

"In 1926 I married a New York actress,
Beatrice Kay, from whom I was divorced
in 1934. In 1939 I married Marjorie Sinclair Campbell, of Philadelphia, who sat in
one of my classes at Urbana.

"It has not been my fate to suffer the
burdens of popularity, nor have I ever
courted that fate. I have hewn to my self-
chosen line and the chips have fallen in
strange places."

* * *

Mr. Grattan gave two series of lectures
at the University of Melbourne, as well as
numerous single lectures, while in Australia
in 1937 and 1938. In 1934 and 1935 he
was editor of the Research Section of the
Federal Emergency Relief Administration
in Washington. Besides his own books, he

has contributed to numerous symposia and has edited Burton Rascoe's *A Bookman's Daybook*, Timothy Flint's *Recollections of the Last Ten Years; 1815-1825*, and *The Critique of Humanism* (1930). He is considered the leading American authority on Australian life and literature, and his *Introducing Australia* (1942), coming at a time when Australian and American interests were united in a joint war effort, proved more popular than most of his previous books.

Early in 1942 Grattan served briefly on the Board of Economic Warfare, but he resigned after opposition legislators charged him with being both a Communist and a Fascist! Neither of the obviously contradictory charges was justified, and he was probably the unfortunate victim of political cross-fire.

Grattan's name is accented on the first syllable.

PRINCIPAL WORKS: Bitter Bierce: A Mystery of American Literature, 1929; The Peerless Leader: William Jennings Bryan (with Paxton Hibben) 1929; Australian Literature, 1929; Why We Fought, 1929; The Three Jameses: A Family of Minds, 1932; Preface to Chaos: War in the Making, 1936; The Deadly Parallel, 1939; Introducing Australia, 1942.

GRAVES, ROBERT (July 26, 1895-   ), English poet and novelist, was born Robert von Ranke Graves in London, the son of Alfred Percival Graves (poet, collector of folk-songs, inspector of schools, and son of the Protestant Bishop of Limerick) and of Amalie (von Ranke) Graves, daughter of the professor of medicine at the University of Munich,

W. Hutchinson

and A. P. Graves's second wife. By each marriage the father had five children, so that Robert Graves grew up as one of an unusually large family. There was a large library at home, which provided much of the boy's education, for he was sent to six preparatory schools in all before he entered the Charterhouse in 1914. Boxing and mountain climbing (in Germany and Wales) were much more to his taste at the time than were his studies. Nevertheless he won an exhibition to St. John's College, Oxford. But instead of entering the university, he enlisted in the Royal Welch Fusiliers, where he was an officer in the same regiment with Siegfried Sassoon. Under this stimulating acquaintance he began to write poetry in earnest, and by 1917 had published three volumes, while still on active service. He was wounded and sent to Oxford to convalesce, and there in 1918 he married Nancy Nicholson.

Discharged at the end of the war, he and his wife went to Harlech, Wales, where his mother had built a house. There the first of their four children was born. They were very poor, for his published poems brought him hardly any money. Yet Graves decided to complete his education. They moved to a suburb of Oxford, and for a while ran a shop, without much success while the young husband attended St. John's. While there he edited *Oxford Poetry 192*[ ] with Alan Porter and Richard Hughes. [It] was 1926 before he received his degree. [At] this time he was continuing to issue books of poetry. Meanwhile his wife's health had broken down, and in 1926, partly to find a better climate for her, he became professor of English at the University of Cairo. They returned to England from Egypt in 192[ ] and two years later they separated permanently.

Graves went to Majorca, where with Laura Riding[qv] he conducted the Seizin Press until the Spanish Civil War forced them to leave the island. Many of his books were published by this press, and he and Miss Riding also wrote several critical books in collaboration. He had poured forth his agony of mind—no less acute for being clothed in abstract terms—in a series of critical essays. Now he evolved a theory of poetry as "non-literary," "pure," and "integral," as a "spiritual cathartic" first to the poet and then to his reader. In the words of Geoffrey Grigson, this is "romanticism boiled dry. . ." The poetic logic destroys the sense logic. Nelson Algren compared him to Skelton in his wit and satire, but added: "his fierce preoccupation with trivia and his sometimes forced facetiousness [are] a form of suicide. . . .'A decent mystery' his progress remains. . . . His verse of 1939 is richer and more original even than his verse of 19[ ] but seems to have less importance to the outer world. . . .The leaven of sadness in his early work is replaced more and more by terror"—by what Grigson called his "certainty of despair of life."

It is not only as a poet, however, that Robert Graves has become noted. With *I, Claudius,* he became at one stroke a novelist to be reckoned with, winner of both the Hawthornden and the James Tait Black prizes for 1934. This novel and its sequel *Claudius the God,* are magnificent reconstructions of Roman life. His later novels

ount Belisarius, won the Femina-Vie Heu-
:use prize for 1939—perhaps the last time
will ever be awarded. He has besides
ritten a stirring and candid autobiography;
number of volumes of essays, including a
aluable volume on his friend T. E. Law-
:nce; and (following an American visit)
vo interesting novels dealing with a British
oldier in the American Revolution.

With Laura Riding he edited a semi-an-
ual called *Epilogue: A Critical Summary*
nd translated the autobiography of Georg
chwarz under the title, *Almost Forgotten
ermany.* He has close affiliations with the
xtreme modernists among American (as
ell as among English) poets, and wrote
ie introductions to John Crowe Ransom's
race After Meat (1924) and E. E. Cum-
ings' prose volume, *The Enormous Room*
1928). He is dark and heavy-set, with
stubborn, brooding face which shows his
ish blood far more than his German.
Quietly independent and masculine," T. S.
atthews called him; while Edwin Muir
oted his "candid and unconventional intelli-
:nce."

PRINCIPAL WORKS: *Poetry*—Over the Brazier,
16; Goliath and David, 1916; Fairies and Fusi-
rs, 1917; The Treasure Box 1919; Country Sen-
nent, 1920; The Pier Glass, 1921; Whipperginny,
23; The Feather Bed, 1923; Mock Beggar Hall,
24; Welchman's Hose, 1925; Poems (Augustan
ooks of Modern Poetry) 1925; The Marmosite's
iscellany (as "John Doyle") 1925; John Kemp's
ager: A Ballad Opera, 1925; Poems: 1914-1926,
27; Poems, 1929; Ten Poems More, 1930; Poems:
26-1930, 1931; Poems: 1930-1933, 1933; Collected
oems, 1938; No More Ghosts, 1940. *Novels*—
y Head! My Head! Being the History of
isha, 1925; No Decency Left (with L. Riding)
32; I, Claudius, 1934; Claudius the God and
s Wife Messalina, 1934; Antigua, Penny, Puce
1 America: The Antigua Stamp) 1936; Count
:lisarius, 1938; Sergeant Lamb's America, 1940.
iscellaneous—The English Ballad, 1921; On Eng-
h Poetry, 1922; The Meaning of Dreams, 1924;
etic Unreason, 1925; Contemporary Techniques
Poetry, 1925; Another Future of Poetry, 1926;
wrence and the Arabs, 1927; John Skelton, 1927;
ipenetrability: or, The Proper Habit of English
27; Lars Porsena: or, The Future of Swearing,
27; A Survey of Modernist Poetry (with L.
ding) 1927; A Pamphlet Against Anthologies
ding) 1928; Mrs. Fisher: or, The
ture of Humour, 1928; The Shout, 1929; Good-
e to All That (autobiography) 1929; But It
ll Goes On (autobiography) 1930; The Real
vid Copperfield, 1933; T. E. Lawrence to His
ographers (with B. H. Liddell Hart) 1939;
e Long Week End (with A. Hodge) 1941;
oceed, Sergeant Lamb, 1941.
ABOUT: Graves, R. Goodbye to All That, But
Still Goes On; Bookman (London) March
1; Catholic World February 1941; Nation (Lon-
i) August 14, 1926; New Republic February
1930; Poetry December 1939; Publishers'
eekly April 19, 1930; Time May 15, 1939, No-
nber 4, 1940.

GRAY, JAMES (June 1899-), American
critic and novelist, was born in Minneapolis, the son of a newspaperman, so that
his destiny was de-
termined practically
in the cradle. When
the boy was thirteen
the family moved to
Washington. After
the death of his
father, Mrs. Gray re-
turned to Minnesota
with her son. James
Gray attended the
University of Minne-

Pinchot

sota, graduating in 1920, and began newspaper work next year. He has thus completed nearly twenty years with the St. Paul
Pioneer Press & Dispatch, for which he has
written editorials, dramatic criticism, and a
daily column chiefly devoted to books. He
has also reviewed books in the field of his
specialty, Middlewestern life, for book reviewing mediums on the Atlantic seaboard.
His first book, *The Penciled Frown* (1925),
was followed by two regional and psychological novels which received favorable attention. *Shoulder the Sky* (1935), a study
of the struggle of a young doctor and his
wife in a small town of the Middle West
to overcome psychological and emotional
barriers between themselves, was called by
Burton Rascoe "one of the most intelligent
and agreeable works of fiction we have had
in this generation." The *Nation,* however,
objected that the dialogue in the book was
not human conversation but stylized smart
talk. His subsequent novels have been praised
for the "beautifully composed prose" and
critized for the use of "the rapier . . . where
a blunt instrument would be more effective."
His study of the Illinois River is an outstanding contribution to the Rivers of America series. The novelist is married, and has
a daughter and two sons.

PRINCIPAL WORKS: The Penciled Frown, 1925;
Shoulder the Sky, 1935; Wake and Remember,
1936; Wings of Great Desire, 1938; The Illinois
1940; Vagabond Path, 1941.

"GRAYSON, DAVID." See B A K E R,
R. S.

GREEN, ANNA KATHARINE (November 11, 1846-April 11, 1935), American
writer of detective fiction, who has been
variously called the "mother" and "godmother" of detective stories, was born in
Brooklyn, N.Y., the daughter of James
Wilson Green, a well known defense law-

yer, and Katharine Ann (Whitney) Green. She received a B.A. degree from the Ripley Female College, Poultney, Vt. Her genteel ambition was to write poetry, and she did so to the extent of *The Defense of the Bride and Other Poems,* and *Risifi's Daughter,* a drama in verse. E. C. Stedman approved her verses; Emerson wrote her cordially. As a curious preparation for a poetic career, she wrote a detective story, *The Leavenworth Case* (1878), and overnight found herself the author of a best-seller and the inventor of a detective, Ebenezer Gryce, who beat Sherlock Holmes to the post by nearly a decade. (Gryce appeared in a few later stories; but to say, as *Newsweek* did, that his adventures filled twenty-six subsequent volumes is inaccurate reporting.)

The novel was dramatized—her husband, Charles Rohlfs, whom she married November 1884, playing in it —and achieved the distinction of a special re-issue in 1934 prefaced by "S. S. Van Dine," the creator of Philo Vance.

Mrs. Rohlfs had a respectable knowledge of criminal law and kept her detective work (nearly all her remaining writing was in this *genre*) within the bounds of probabilities. The American detective, she postulated, cannot be a free-lance in the land of mystery, and must act in conformity with established law. The murderer, she thought, should be the first to announce the crime. Her own favorite among her books was *The Hand and the Ring.* (Connoisseurs prefer *The Filigree Ball, Lost Man's Lane,* and *The House of the Whispering Pines.*) The essentials of a good mystery story, she said, are first of all an interesting plot with a new twist, a queer turn that has never been attempted. The story should rise in steps from one unfolding to another, reaching a climax that must be a pleasant surprise, never a disappointment.

Mrs. Rohlfs was a mild-mannered person who enjoyed life, in Buffalo, N.Y., with her husband and family (a daughter and two sons), and was described in her eighty-third year as "gentle, courteous, gracious—even shy." She lived to be nearly ninety.

No one will pretend that Anna Katharine Green's novels were distinguished literature. Yet by virtue of precedence and sustained popularity she holds an honored place in the development of the American detective story. Her style was stilted and old-fashioned, her characterizations forced and artificial; but her plots were models of careful construction that can hold their own against modern competition. She is, perhaps, best read at the impressionable age.

PRINCIPAL WORKS: The Leavenworth Case, 1878; A Strange Disappearance, 1880; The Defense of the Bride and Other Poems, 1882; Hand and Ring, 1883; Marked "Personal," 1893; The Doctor, His Wife, and the Clock, 1895; That Affair Next Door, 1897; Lost Man's Lane, 1898; Agatha Webb, 1899; The Circular Study, 1900; The Filigree Ball, 1903; The House in the Mist, 1905; The Millionaire Baby, 1905; The Amethyst Box, 1905; The Woman in the Alcove, 1906; The Chief Legatee, 1906; The Mayor's Wife, 1907; The House of the Whispering Pines, 1910; Initials Only, 1911; Masterpieces of Mystery, 1913 (reissued in 1919 as Room Number Three and Other Detective Stories); The Mystery of the Hasty Arrow, 1917; The Step on the Stair, 1923.

ABOUT: Haycraft, H. Murder for Pleasure: The Life and Times of the Detective Story; New York Times April 12, 1935; Newsweek April 2, 1935; Publishers' Weekly April 20, 1935, April 27, 1935; Reading and Collecting January 1938.

GREEN, ANNE (November 11, 1899-) American novelist, was born in Savannah, Ga., the daughter of Edward Moon Green and Mary (Hartridge) Green. She is by ten months the elder sister of Julian Green, the novelist,[qv] who was born in Paris after their parents had gone abroad. Anne Green was educated at the Lycée Molière, Paris, and was a war nurse be-

fore she was eighteen, spending four years in military hospitals during the First World War. Her mother had died at the beginning of the war. She toured Europe and sailed for America, where her Southern relatives proved as pleasantly agreeable as had been anticipated. After Anne Green had written some fashion and technical articles for a newspaper group, her cousin John Macrae, president of the publishing firm of E. P. Dutton, suggested that she try her hand at novel-writing. *The Selbys* (1930), her first novel, was as autobiographical as first novels are likely to be, the author explaining to a *Bookman* interviewer: "In my mother there was real fecklessness and inconsequence which were just a coating to a kind and generous nature. Everything she is described as doing in my book, and all her amusing remarks, are transcriptions of

fact. . . . I wish I could explode the myth
so many readers seem to hold that the
author 'made up' this character, giving me
credit for more imagination than I possess.
The Selbys, both of them, were drawn from
life." The statement hardly holds true of
the succeeding novels, most of which are
whimsical and fantastic in character and incident, as pronounced a contrast to the
somber plots of her brother Julian's fiction
as could well be imagined. Both Greens
are bi-lingual, but Anne writes in English,
whereas Julian plots and writes his novels
in French. Vivacious, bright-eyed, and
soignée, she shared an apartment with her
brother on the Avenue de President Wilson
in Paris up to the time of the Second
World War. Both reside in the United
States now.

PRINCIPAL WORKS: The Selbys, 1930; Reader,
Married Him, 1931; A Marriage of Convenience,
1933; Fools Rush In, 1934; That Fellow Percival,
1935; Winchester House, 1936; 16 Rue Cortam-
bert, 1937; Paris, 1938; The Silent Duchess, 1939;
The Delamer Curse, 1940; The Lady in the Mask,
1942.

ABOUT: Bookman August 1932.

GREEN, JULIAN (September 6, 1900-),
French novelist, was born in Paris less
than a year after his American parents had

settled in that city.
His father, an agent
for an American bus-
iness concern, hailed
from Virginia and
his mother from
Georgia, but more re-
motely the blood of
Irish, Scotch and
English ancestors
mingled in his veins.
Although he was ed-
ucated in a French lycée, Julian's mother
forced him to speak and read English at
home. "I learned English in my childhood
and have spoken it continually ever since,
but even so I cannot write it as well as I
should. It is like a uniform that is too
tight." And this despite the fact that at the
age of nineteen he came to America and
spent two years at the University of Virginia. After the death of his mother at the
beginning of the First World War, the sensitive, lonely child who had already shown
his inclination for the Latin classics and
French and English literature, interrupted
his studies and enlisted in the army. In
1917 he drove an ambulance on the French
and Italian fronts and the following year
joined the French artillery.

At the University of Virginia, "where
he had been sent to brush up his native
language and acquire an easy degree," Green
did not follow the regular curriculum but
took only English and American literature
and in his spare time tutored French and
wrote short stories. His only published
piece written originally in English, "The
Apprentice Psychiatrist," appeared at this
time in the university literary magazine.

On his return to Paris the earnest young
man tried to discover his vocation. Uncertain of his fiction writing, he took courses
in painting at La Grande Chaumière, studied
music at home and wrote stories and essays.
Forced by a publisher's contract to complete
a novel within six months, Green applied
himself to the writing of *Mont-Cinère*
(*Avarice House*), his first novel, which was
published in 1926, winning him immediate
recognition. The "avarice house" of the
story was a real house belonging to his aunt
in Virginia. His second novel, *Adrienne
Mesurat* (*The Closed Garden*) (1927) won
the Femina-Bookman Prize and was
crowned by the French Academy and when
translated into English was selected by the
Book-of-the-Month Club. His third novel,
Leviathan (*The Dark Journey*) (1929) was
chosen by the French Book-of-the-Month
Club and was later awarded the $10,000
Harper Prize Novel Contest for 1929-30.
Thus his reputation was soundly established
as an important novelist in two countries:
France and the United States. It is most
remarkable, indeed, how this American boy
who became a Frenchman led his lugubrious
muse and channeled his Gidean concerns
into producing a thoroughly French art expressed in impeccable French Herbert Gorman says: "Though not French in blood,
he is, in all essentials, a Frenchman. And
yet there is often enough obvious in his
work (and very fine work it is) a subtle
objectiveness before the French scene that
could hardly be attained by a born Frenchman."

While living with his sister Anne,[qv] also
a novelist, in the same apartment where his
father and mother died in Passy, not far
from the Trocadero, Green wrote his
memoirs, *Personal Record,* in which in a
rather reticent manner he reveals, with pristine honesty, his distinctive personality. In
his *Record* he shows his love for death and
the night, his dissatisfaction with our turbulent epoch, but he has no axe to grind,
nothing glamorous to confess. He talks
intelligently about painting, about André
Gide who influenced him so profoundly, and

a few figures of the day—Dali, Malraux, Cocteau, Gertrude Stein—pass fleetingly through his pages. But his paramount considerations are mystical, a constant search for peace and for God, which led him to study Hebrew in order to read the Bible in the original. Bernard Fay's early prophecy, "Julian Green is going to be one of the greatest living French writers; his novels in less than a year have made of him the foremost novelist of the younger generation," was not far from the mark: Green has won for himself one of the loftiest places in contemporary French fiction.

Green generally dresses in dark clothes, he is clean-cut of face, repressed, and, until the fall of France forced his return to Virginia, wrote only in French. Edmond Jaloux describes him thus: "a slender young man with the bearing, the grace and reserve of a young girl—and a young girl of former days. His regular features are delicately modeled, and lighted by handsome eyes. He has an extreme modesty and a high integrity to his art."

AVAILABLE IN ENGLISH TRANSLATION: Avarice House, 1927; The Closed Garden, 1928; The Dark Journey, 1929; The Pilgrim on the Earth, 1929; Christine, and Other Stories, 1930; The Strange River, 1932; The Dreamer, 1934; Midnight, 1936; Personal Record, 1939; Then Shall the Dust Return, 1941.

ABOUT: Ehrhard, J. E. Le Roman Français Depuis Marcel Proust; Green, J. Closed Garden (see introduction by A. Maurois), Personal Record; Lauresne, H. Deux Romanciers de la Solitude: George Eliot et Julian Green; Lefèvre, F. Une Heure Avec. . .; Rousseaux, H. Littérature du Vingtième Siècle; Stansbury, M. H. French Novelists Today; Bookman August 1932; Harper's Magazine September 1941; Hochland Jahrgang 30, 1939; New York Times December 3, 1939; Publications of the Modern Language Association June 1939; Time November 13, 1939, July 29, 1940.

GREEN, PAUL (March 17, 1894-), American playwright and novelist, writes: "Paul [Eliot] Green was born on a farm near the town of Lillington in eastern North Carolina, the son of William Archibald Green and Betty Lorine (Byrd) Green. His people were English and Highland Scotch who had settled along the banks of the Cape Fear River in the early 18th century. There they cleared their fields, built churches, dug canals, cut roads, built their water mills, and civilized the

wilderness the while they worshiped their God in English and Gaelic. The life that Paul Green grew up to know was much the same as that of his ancestors. On his father's farm he and his brothers worked the cotton and corn and cut timber shoulder to shoulder with the Negro laborers. Here his imagination fed on the beauty and loneliness of the wide fields and sky, the ever-changing life of the wooded swamps and hills, and the pathos and humor of the Negroes and fervid poorer whites.

"In many a poetic notebook of his early days he tried to set down something of what he felt about it all, but contrived nothing better than a cartload or two of doggerel. Finally he saved enough money to attend the state university at Chapel Hill, where he won a prize for a one-act play which was produced in the Forest Theatre there. He was a witness at his own play, the first he had ever seen. At the end of his freshman year he enlisted in the army and served for two years, the majority of the time being spent with the American Expeditionary Force in Belgium and northern France. In 1919 he returned to college and began writing other plays for Professor Frederick H. Koch and his newly-established Carolina Playmakers. After graduation he continued his study of philosophy at Chapel Hill and then at Cornell University. In 1922 he married Elizabeth Atkinson Lay, a member of the Playmaker Group and a poet. They have one son and three daughters.

"His first volume of one-act plays, completed at Cornell, was published and received such favorable comment that he was encouraged to go on writing plays. However with few interruptions he has continued his teaching at his alma mater, where he formerly taught philosophy and is now Professor of Dramatic Art. In 1927 he had his first New York productions, two in one season— In Abraham's Bosom and The Field God. For the former he was awarded the Pulitzer Prize for the best American play of the year. In 1928 he received a Guggenheim Fellowship for study abroad. With his wife and children he spent a year in Germany and England studying the theatre. While abroad he wrote Potter's Field, a symphonic drama of the Negro people, later produced in New York under the title, Roll, Sweet Chariot. On his return he completed The House of Connelly for the newly established Group Theatre. This was the first production of that organization.

"Green has always been interested in experimenting with new forms. All of his plays, even his one-acters, make use of music and ballad and song, and he feels that in the present liberated American theatre there is a great chance for the dramatist to let his imagination loose. Because of the continued industrial pattern of the movies, his experience in Hollywood in 1935 was not the happiest. He wrote several successful scripts, however, singly and in collaboration, mostly for Will Rogers and George Arliss, but soon returned to his teaching at the University of North Carolina and to writing plays. In 1936 he wrote *Johnny Johnson* for the Group Theatre, with music by Kurt Weill (his first play with any but a North Carolina background), and in 1927 found a chance to try out without hindrance his theories of music, song, dance, and pantomime in the drama. In a huge amphitheatre on Roanoke Island, N.C., Green's play which he chose to call a symphonic drama (the use of all theatre elements sounding together)—*The Lost Colony*—was produced by a company of 150 persons, made up of local actors, Federal Theatre actors, members of the Carolina Playmakers, and a chorus of Westminster Choir College singers. It was a success from the first and is being repeated for two months each summer for the thousands who come from all parts of the nation to see it. In such large outdoor communal productions as this Green sees a challenge and opportunity for American drama, and he is working on a second project for a vast musical drama to be presented high in the mountains of western North Carolina with the store of folklore, music, ballad, song, and dance as the raw material for the piece.

"His literary preferences are Aeschylus, Shakespeare, Tolstoy and Thomas Hardy. In religion he feels that the sacred books of the Hindus and Chinese incorporate more wisdom than any others. His favorite composer is Beethoven. He thinks that some day there will be a great awakening of music in America as well as of drama, and that what is being done now is pioneer work for the appearance of the great artists to be. He believes that the inspiration of true art comes from the people and not from the pull of any of its mediums or attendant fads from above."

* * *

Mr. Green's profile, with his long head and aquiline features, is classically Roman. But he has his lighter aspects—he is, for example, a fine tennis player and a good baseball pitcher with either hand, besides being a champion cotton picker. Julian R. Meade spoke of his "natural and unassuming manner, his friendly wit, boyish smile, soft and indolent voice, and decidedly Southern speech." He works very fast and has completed some of his plays in a few days. His aim, which he is gradually accomplishing, is to produce "a story, to be gradually written down, of my home folk, black and white."

PRINCIPAL WORKS: *Plays*—The No 'Count Boy, 1924; Fixin's (with Erma Green) 1924; The Lord's Will and Other Carolina Plays, 1925; In Abraham's Bosom, 1926; The Field God, 1927; Last of the Lowries, 1927; In the Valley and Other Carolina Plays, 1928; Tread the Green Grass, 1928; Potter's Field, 1929 (as Roll, Sweet Chariot, 1934); The House of Connelly and Other Plays, 1931; Shroud My Body Down, 1935; Hymn to the Rising Sun, 1936; Johnny Johnson, 1936; The Lost Colony, 1937; Alma Mater, 1938; The Enchanted Maze, 1939; Out of the South: The Life of a People in Dramatic Form (collected plays) 1939; Highland Call: A Symphonic Drama of American History, 1941. *Fiction*—Wide Fields (short stories) 1928; The Laughing Pioneer, 1932; This Body the Earth, 1935. *Miscellaneous*—Trifles of Thought (verse) 1917; Contemporary American Literature (with E. L. Green) 1925; The Lost Colony Song Book, 1937; America in Action (with others) 1941.

ABOUT: American Magazine April 1936; Bookman January 1932; Commonweal May 21, 1937; Life April 7, 1941; Theater Arts Monthly December 1932.

GREENE, Mrs. ANNE (BOSWORTH)

(1878-   ) Anglo-American writer of travel books, books on country life, and children's stories, was born in Chippenham, Wiltshire, England, the daughter of Homer Lyman Bosworth and Delia Evelyn (Rood) Bosworth. Her typical English childhood, with its well-regulated pattern of nursemaids, governesses and riding lessons, is described in  a charming essay in her *Lambs in March*. Business plans made it necessary for Mr. Bosworth to remove his family to America in 1885. Here Anne Bosworth studied painting with Eric Pape in Boston, and married Dr. Harrie William Greene of Springfield in 1900. She exhibited regularly at Provincetown, Mass., and made a trip to the Yellowstone to do watercolor sketches commissioned by magazines. When Provincetown became too crowded, after Dr. Greene's death, Mrs. Greene bought a century-old farmhouse on a hillside farm in South Woodstock, Vt., and moved there with her small daughter Lorna to write and to raise Shetland ponies. A sketch in the *Century Magazine* describing the personality and antics of the rabbit cat on the farm attracted favorable attention, and led to two books about life on an isolated Vermont farm, written with genuine distinction, unusual descriptive power, and engaging humor. In both *The Lone Winter* and *Dipper Hill,* in the book of essays, *Lambs in March,* and in two European travel-books, *Lighthearted Journey* and *Sunshine and Dust,* the central and recurring figure was her daughter Lorna, who studied at London University and gave promise of a brilliant career. Not far past twenty, Lorna Greene died in a hospital at Hanover, N.H., one summer, after she had been pinned under her overturned automobile. A posthumous book in free verse forms, *Morning Moods,* was edited by her mother. Mrs. Greene, who has for several years acted as vice-president of the League of Vermont Writers, is a woman of distinguished appearance, with a nimbus of white hair, and a manner which combines kindliness with a certain remoteness.

PRINCIPAL WORKS: The Lone Winter, 1923; Greylight, 1924; Dipper Hill, 1925; Lambs in March, 1928; Lighthearted Journey, 1930; Sunshine and Dust, 1936; Punch, the Cruising Dog, 1940.

ABOUT: Burlington (Vt.) Free Press September 5, 1936.

GREENE, GRAHAM (October 2, 1904-), English novelist, was born at Berkhampstead, Hertfordshire, where his

father, Charles Henry Greene, was headmaster of the Berkhampstead School. His parents were cousins, his mother having been Marion Raymond Greene before her marriage. Mr. Greene is a distant connection of Robert Louis Stevenson; one of his brothers is a well-known foreign correspondent, another a noted surgeon and mountain-climber. He was educated at Berkhampstead School and at Balliol College, Oxford, and then was sub-editor of the London *Times* from 1926 to 1930. In 1927 he married Vivien Dayrell-Browning, and they have a son and a daughter. He has traveled a good deal in America and lived for some time in Mexico, which has been a scene of more than one of his books.

From 1935 to 1939 he was film critic of the *Spectator.* In 1934 he edited a series of memoirs called *The Old School.* He lives in London.

So much for the unexciting outer life of this remarkable young novelist. His inner life is considerably more important. A convert to the Roman Catholic Church, his religion has colored everything he has written. His preoccupation is psychology, particularly abnormal psychology, and he is a passionate analyst of every shade of religious feeling. Harry Sylvester, in the *Commonweal,* called him the first major English novelist who was a Catholic; and though some allowance may be made for natural predilection in his favor, it is undoubtedly true that (omitting perhaps some Irish names) no novelist has written in English who has so combined great talent and the Catholic point of view. To find analogies for Graham Greene, one would have to go to French literature. He has, of course, made as many enemies as friends by this characteristic; his non-fiction book on Mexico, particularly, has impressed most non-Catholic readers as prejudiced, reactionary and wrong-headed. Even some of his co religionists in America have been antagonized by his essentially European attitude toward the Church.

On the other hand, his fiction has been subtilized and deepened because of the implications behind all his work. Even in his so-called "entertainments"—semi-mystery gangster novels—the interest is not in events but in persons, and not in the outward actions of the persons but in their minds and feelings. Phyllis Bentley remarked that he "seems able to investigate sinister psychologies without sentimentalizing them; his prose has tension, but is never overwritten. His weakness lies, not in stress or stridency but in too great facility and in the over-use of coincidence. Nevertheless, his novels on the whole deserve the encomium bestowed on them by William Rose Benét, who called them "novels of action dealing with peculiarities of psychology," and added: "No man writing today is more a master of suspense . . . He is one of the finest craftsmen of story-telling in our time." The filming of *This Gun for Hire* in 1942 probably presaged a growing popularity for Greene's work in the future.

PRINCIPAL WORKS: The Man Within, 1929; The Name of Action, 1930; Rumour at Nightfall 1932; Stamboul Train (in America: Orient Express) 1932; It's a Battlefield, 1934; The Bear Fell Free, 1935; England Made Me (non-fiction) 1935; The Basement Room (short stories) 1936; Journey Without Maps (non-fiction) 1936; A Gun

For Sale (in America: This Gun For Hire) 1936; Brighton Rock, 1938; The Lawless Roads: A Mexican Journey (in America: Another Mexico) 1939; The Confidential Agent, 1939; The Power and the Glory (U.S. title: The Labyrinthine Ways) 1940.

ABOUT: Commonweal October 25, 1940; Saturday Review of Literature January 28, 1939, March 30, 1940.

GREENE, WARD (December 23, 1892-   ), American novelist, was born in Asheville, N.C., the son of Allison Lawson

Greene and Susan Cary (Rosenburg) Greene, but lived in Atlanta, Ga., from infancy until he was twenty-nine. He is descended from one of General Nathanael Greene's brothers who wandered to Georgia from Rhode Island during the Revolu-

E. Schaal

tion. His mother was a Buffalo, N.Y., girl, with Connecticut Storrs and German von Rosenburgs in her ancestry. Ward Greene was educated in the public schools of Atlanta, and while at grammar school studied afternoons at the Atlantic Art School. In 1912-13 he was a student at the University of the South, Sewanee, Tenn., and in the latter year went to work on the Atlanta Journal as assistant sports editor, working a twelve-hour day for $7.50 a week.

"For ten years I was on the Atlanta Journal under Major John S. Cohen and John Paschall, two of the best newspaper men I have ever known. I went through the mill from police to 'star' reporter. We had some good stories in that time. Hearst had bought the opposition paper and we had to hump. The Grace shooting. The Leo Frank case. The unsolved disappearance of the Nelms sisters. Well, finally we had the war and the Journal sent me to France as its correspondent with Georgia troops. I trailed around in 1918-19 from St. Nazaire to Coblenz, hitting as many scattered outfits as I could—82nd Division, Rainbow Division, 17th Engineers, and so on. Once before, like every newspaper man, I had had the New York bug. In 1917 I came to New York with a job on the Tribune, worked two months, hated the town, and left it flat on Christmas eve. Atlanta was good enough for me. But two years after the war, suddenly it wasn't. I wrote to a friend with a newspaper syndicate, came up on short notice to a rewrite job under Jack Lait, and stuck it out." Then Greene "got an idea for

a short story that didn't seem to fit any of the formulae. It was simply this: A woman can be a success as well as a man, but if you told the truth about it, a lot of go-getters of both sexes got there by fair means or foul. I wrote the story as a novel, Cora Potts, and the first publisher took it on the strength of 40,000 words."

Ride the Nightmare (1930), published the year after Cora Potts, describes a man spurred by an urge to be different from other men; Weep No More (1932) concerns a hard-drinking Southern "smart set"; Death in the Deep South (1936), which made a successful talking picture, is based on the Leo Frank case; Route 28 (1940) weaves a design of frustration along the highway between New York and the New Jersey countryside. As "Frank Dudley" Greene wrote a fictionized exposé of a secret society called the "Red Raiders."

Since 1921 Greene has been executive editor of King Features Syndicate. He is a member of Sigma Alpha Epsilon and the Players Club, and married Hallie Bowden of Atlanta in April 1918. A novelist of the hard boiled school, Greene is also a "fair tennis player, can play any hymn on the piano, and would rather write than be President."

PRINCIPAL WORKS: Cora Potts, 1929; Ride the Nightmare, 1930; Weep No More, 1932; Death in the Deep South, 1936; Route 28, 1940; King Cobra (as "Frank Dudley") 1940.

ABOUT: Wilson Library Bulletin April 1932.

GREENWOOD, WALTER (December 17, 1903-   ), English novelist and playwright, was born in Salford, Lancashire. He came of a very poor family; his father, Tom Greenwood, was a music-loving hairdresser who died of alcoholism when the boy was nine; his mother, Elizabeth M. Greenwood, supported him by working as a waitress. He had no edu-

cation except in council school and by his own reading, and after working in odd hours as a milkman's helper, he left school at twelve to become a pawnbroker's clerk. He has tried his hand at all the dead-end occupations opened to unskilled workers—as office boy, stable boy (in a racing stable and in the private stable of a millionaire cotton manufacturer), repairman in a packinghouse, sign-writer, chauffeur, warehouseman, and salesman. The only time he made more than thirty-five shillings a week was when he worked for a few months in an automobile factory. Several times he was unemployed and had to go on the dole.

Then, in 1933, he wrote a novel about his life and the life of others like him. It was *Love on the Dole,* which he made into a play the next year with Roland Gow. The book became a subject for questions in Parliament; it led to investigations and reforms. Also, it "made" its author. He was famous, and he had enough money to live henceforth by writing. In 1936 he visited the United States, where his play was having a successful run. An added sentimental interest fell flat; it was expected that he would now marry the thinly disguised heroine of the novel, his faithful sweetheart during his years of destitution. Instead, she sued him for breach of promise, and he was obliged to settle out of court. In 1937, he married, instead, Pearl Osgood. The affair was the more embarrassing to him because he had by this time been elected a member of the City Council of Salford. It was perhaps for this reason that he and his wife moved soon after to London, where they now live.

Mr. Greenwood lists his favorite recreations as "riding, rowing, sleeping, arguing, and propagating Socialism." He has continued to write in the strain of *Love on the Dole,* though none of his subsequent books has met with the same great success. His novels are all primarily social documents, drab and photographic, detailing the miseries of the very poor, the injustices of the means test, the horrors of unemployment.

In contrast to James Hanley, another "proletarian novelist" whose work is painfully vivid, there is little characterization in Walter Greenwood's work. Its actuating motive is indignation, but the indignation is based on a dull despair. What difference the war and the social changes actuated by it will make in his writing remains to be seen. So far, his books are almost pure propaganda, and sentimentalized propaganda at that. But they are forceful and straightforward, and few writers have had his first-hand experience of the things of which he treats. He is himself a proletarian, and has never forgotten that fact; with increasing maturity he may discover the spark needed to bring his veracious case-studies to life.

PRINCIPAL WORKS: Love on the Dole, 1933 (as play, with R. Gow, 1934); The Time Is Ripe, 1934; His Worship the Mayor, 1934; My Son's My Son (play) 1935; Give Us This Day (play) 1936; The Practised Hand (one-act play) 1936; Standing Room Only 1936; The Cleft Stick (short stories) 1937; The Secret Kingdom, 1938; Only Mugs Work (as novel and play) 1938; How the Other Half Lives (non-fiction) 1939.

ABOUT: Wilson Library Bulletin October 1936.

GREGORY, HORACE (April 10, 1898-   ), American poet, writes: "I was born in Milwaukee, Wis. On my mother's side I am of German stock, a mixture of Prussian and Bavarian blood, the family emigrating to Southwestern Wisconsin in the early 1840's. On my father's side the blood is a mixture of Roman Catholic and Protestant Irish, and English. My grandmother's father was Henry Goadby, who worked with Darwin, Huxley, Owen, and Tyndall and in the early 1860's accepted the chair of sciences in the then newly-founded University of Michigan. My grandfather was Dr. John Gregory, one-time astronomer and mathematician at Trinity College, Dublin, and first city surveyor of Milwaukee. My grandmother was among the first translators of Turgeniev from current French translations into English. My uncle edited the *Evening Wisconsin* for twenty years.

L. Jacobi

"My first job was with my father, Henry Bolton Gregory, president of a firm dealing in baker's supplies and machinery. I was educated in a private school, the German-English Academy, and, during the summers, in the Milwaukee School of Fine Arts. At the University of Wisconsin (1919-23) my chief interests lay in Lucretius and Catullus. I began to write poetry under the strictest of classical influences, Pope and Landor.

"With this background I came to New York in 1923 and contributed formal verse to *Vanity Fair,* the *Nation,* and *Books,* but I soon found the facile 'charm' of these verses lacking in everything I wanted to say. I began a new phase by writing *Chelsea Rooming House,* merely the beginning of my effort to combine the idiom of contemporary life with my early (and entirely literary) influences. Following this, I wrote my translation of Catullus, which, in spite of the many faults it may have, restores, I think, something of the vitality and freshness that Catullus must have had for *his* contemporaries.

"In 1925 I married Marya Zaturenska, whose second book of poems, *Cold Morning Sky,* received the Pulitzer Award for poetry in 1938. We have a son and a daughter, and live in New York. Since 1934, on my return from a stay in England, I have been a member of the English faculty at Sarah Lawrence College, Bronxville, N.Y., where I conduct a poetry hour once a week, and in alternate years lecture on Classical Literature in Translation and Seventeenth Century Literature. In addition to this my yearly college schedule includes a writing course under the title of Observation and Writing.

"At present I am at work on a book of essays and a new book of poems. No matter what others may think of my work I should like to have said of me what was said of Baudelaire, a far greater poet than I: 'He belonged to no school. . . . He copied no one, but he used everyone that suited him, making what he had taken his own and something new.'"

* * *

Thin, spectacled, and serious-looking, Horace Gregory is nevertheless anything but a dry-as-dust professor of literature. In his work he continues consciously to identify himself "with the tradition in American poetry that springs from Emerson." With Eleanor Clark, he edited *New Letters in America* (1937), and he is one of the foremost champions of experimental writing among the younger generation of poets.

PRINCIPAL WORKS: Chelsea Rooming House, 1930; No Retreat, 1933; Pilgrim of the Apocalypse (biography of D. H. Lawrence) 1933; Chorus for Survival, 1935; Poems: 1930-1940, 1941.

ABOUT: Poetry April 1931, July 1935, June 1941; Publishers' Weekly August 14, 1937; Saturday Review of Literature March 4, 1933.

GREGORY, ISABELLA AUGUSTA (PERSSE), Lady (March 5, 1852-May 22, 1932), Irish dramatist, was born at Rox-

borough, County Galway, the youngest daughter of Dudley Persse, a wealthy landowner. She was privately educated, and nothing was farther from her apparent destiny than authorship when, in 1881, she married Sir William Gregory, of Coole, near Dublin, a member of Parliament and former governor of Ceylon. They had one son, an artist who was killed in the World War, but not before leaving children to whom Lady Gregory was devoted. Her husband died in 1892, and it was this in-

directly that led to her interest in writing, for she edited his autobiography, and from it began to turn to an interest in Irish folklore and history. Sir William, though a Protestant like his wife, was a strong Nationalist, and Lady Gregory remained all her long life an intense partisan of Irish independence.

A chance meeting with Yeats in 1898 determined her future. She became so deeply a part of the Celtic literary renaissance, and particularly of the renaissance of the Irish theatre, that she became known as "the godmother of the Abbey Theatre," and George Bernard Shaw called her its "charwoman." There was no task she did not perform for it, from writing "brief comedies to close the performances" to traveling with the company when it took its repertory abroad. She was with the Abbey Players in the United States in 1911 and 1912, during the series of riots over Synge's *Playboy of the Western World* in Philadelphia, New York, and elsewhere, and she returned to America many times thereafter, the last time in 1921.

Lady Gregory translated from the Gaelic of Douglas Hyde (later President of the Irish Free State) and others; she translated Molière from the French into the beautiful idiom of western Ireland which she and Synge and Yeats made familiar to every reader and theatre-goer; she acted as stage manager and business manager of the Abbey. In the town nearest her home at Coole, she was ostracized and boycotted in the early stormy days, but she was never daunted; calm and serene, she carried on to the time when those who had shunned her delighted to honor her.

Her own plays, though overshadowed by the greater genius of some of her associates, have a simplicity and a tender irony that have given them enduring life. *The Workhouse Ward* and *The Rising of the Moon,* the two best known, are beautiful examples of the fusion of poetry and irony, of a laughter that is very close to tears. It was as a focus of influence, however, that her chief service was given. Mario Rossi, an Italian admirer, in a posthumous tribute to her said: "Wherever you have passed, the poets . . . have come around you. . . . You have been their good sister. . . . You have created what did not exist, a common soul for the Catholics and Protestants, for poets and artists, for diverse and hostile spirits." The *London Mercury* said of her death, at eighty: "The gaiety of nations has been diminished."

PRINCIPAL WORKS: *Plays*—Cuchulain of Muirthemne, 1902; Gods and Fighting Men, 1904; Seven Short Plays, 1909; The Kiltartan Molière,

1910; The Image, 1910; Irish Folk History Plays, 1912; New Comedies, 1913; The Golden Apple, 1916; The Dragon, 1920; The Story Brought by Brigit, 1924; Last Plays, 1928. *Miscellaneous*— The Kiltartan History Book, 1909; Our Irish Theater, 1913; The Kiltartan Poetry Book, 1919; Visions and Beliefs in the West of Ireland, 1920; Hugh Lane's Life and Achievement, 1921.

ABOUT: Blunt, W. My Diaries; Boyd, E. A. The Contemporary Drama of Ireland, Ireland's Literary Renaissance; Moore, G. Hail and Farewell; Robinson, L. (ed.), The Irish Theatre; Rossi, M. M. Pilgrimage in the West; Weygandt, C. Irish Plays and Playwrights; Yeats, W. B. Cutting of an Agate; Literary Digest June 11, 1932; London Mercury June 1932; Nation June 8, 1932; Saturday Review of Literature June 11, 1932; Theatre Arts Monthly July 1932; Yale Review April 1925.

*GREGORY, JACKSON (March 12, 1882-   ), American novelist, writer of Western and detective stories, was born in Salinas, Calif., the son of Durell Stokes Gregory and Amelia (Hartnell) Gregory. In 1906 he received the degree of B.L. from the University of California, then, like so many young American college graduates, went directly into teaching. After serving as principal of several California high schools he shifted to newspaper reporting in several of the larger cities of the United States and Canada. With growing family responsibilities—he had married Lotus McGlashan of Truckee, Calif., in December 1910, and they had two sons, Jackson and Roderick—Gregory published his first novel in the year of the First World War; wrote five more Westerns before the war was over; and by 1940 had produced nearly forty books. As Will Cuppy once remarked, Jackson Gregory always slings a readable Western. They are not quite in the class of Eugene Manlove Rhodes, Frank Spearman, and Honoré Willsie Morrow, but stand a cut above B. M. Bower and Zane Grey. *Lords of the Coast* is a more ambitious historical novel. Paul Savoy, his contribution to the ranks of fictional detectives, is well known to not-too-critical readers. The London *Times* found the manner of narrating the three successive cases of Paul Savoy tortuous and hampered by interminable speculations, while the mystery expert of the *Saturday Review of Literature* remarked that the "Ellery-Queenlike artificiality of dialogue and characterization obscure certain good points of the mystery." Mr. Gregory, who is a Democrat and a Catholic, is a member of the Author's League of America and makes his home in Auburn and Altadena, both in California.

PRINCIPAL WORKS: Under Handicap, 1914; The Outlaw, 1916; The Short Cut, 1916; Wolf Breed,

1917; The Joyous Trouble Maker, 1918; Six Feet Four, 1918; Judith of Blue Lake Ranch, 1919; The Bells of San Juan, 1919; Ladyfingers, 1920; Man to Man, 1920; Desert Valley, 1921; The Everlasting Whisper, 1922; Timber-Wolf, 1923; The Maid of the Mountain, 1925; The Desert Thoroughbred, 1926; Captain Cavalier, 1927; Redwood and Gold, 1928; Sentinel of the Desert, 1929; Mystery at Spanish Hacienda, 1929; The Trail to Paradise, 1930; The Silver Star, 1931; The House of the Opal, 1932; Splendid Outlaw, 1932; A Case for Mr. Paul Savoy, 1933; The Shadow on the Mesa, 1933; Ru, The Conqueror, 1933; Red Rivals, 1933; Riders Across the Border, 1933; High Courage, 1934; The Emerald Murder Trap, 1935; Lords of the Coast, 1935; Into the Sunset, 1936; Mountain Men, 1936; Under Handicap, 1936; Sudden Bill Dorn, 1937; Powder Smoke on Wandering River, 1938; Far Call, 1940; Ace in the Hole, 1941; Red Law, 1941; Border Line, 1942; Two in the Wilderness, 1942.

GRENFELL, JULIAN (1888-May 26, 1915), English poet of the First World War, was the eldest son of Lord Desborough.

He attended Summer Fields school, entered Eton at thirteen, and from 1906 to 1910 was at Balliol College, Oxford University. At Eton, Grenfell was master of the Eton Beagles, edited the Eton *Chronicle,* and stood near the top of the Sixth Form. His brother Billy, who seemed like his twin and was killed two months after Julian Grenfell's own death in the First World War, wrote to a friend at Oxford: "You knew all the mysticism and idealism, and that strange streak of melancholy which underlay Julian's war-whooping, sun-bathing, fearless exterior." He entered the army first of all university candidates. With his regiment, the Royal Dragoons, he went in for buck-stalking and polo. In the winter of 1911 he transferred to South Africa, and grew to love the veldt with its "terrific greatness and greenness and dullness and bleakness." He put his horse Kangaroc six feet five inches over a wall with bricks on top, a record for South Africa. In September 1914 Grenfell went with his regiment to Salisbury Plain, and on October 5 was sent to France. "Here we are, in the burning centre of it all, and I would not be anywhere else for a million pounds and the queen of Sheba," he wrote. He was mentioned twice in dispatches, and was awarded the D.S.O. ribbon. In May Grenfell sent home his poem, "Into Battle," which has appeared in most anthologies of war poems, and was called by Viola Meynell "stalwart, great and pure poetry." He was

* Died June 12, 1943.

not destined to write more; on the evening of May 12, 1915, he was struck by a shell-splinter on a hill near the Ypres-Menin Road. Poisoned by the wound, he died at Boulogne Hospital two weeks later. His sister had come from Wimereux to nurse him, and his brother was also present.

PRINCIPAL WORK: Into Battle, 1915.

ABOUT: Dublin Review January-April 1917; English Review January-June 1918.

GRENFELL, Sir WILFRED THOM-ASON (February 28, 1865-October 9, 1940), Anglo-Canadian philanthropist, sur-geon, and author, was born at M o s t y n House, Parkgate, near Chester, England, the second of the four sons of A l g e r n o n Sydney Grenfell and J a n e Georgiana (Hutchinson) Gren-fell. His father was owner and headmas-ter of the boys' school where he was born. Wilfred Grenfell at-tended Marlborough College—college, in England, being a word often applied to large university preparatory schools—and Oxford University, where he took a medical degree and played rugby with the university team. He obtained his training as physician at London Hospital under Sir Frederick Treves (later personal physician to Edward VII) who with Dwight Moody, the American evangelist, inspired Grenfell with a desire to visit the northeastern American coast. In 1889 he entered the medical service of the Royal National Mission to Fishermen, cruised with the fishermen in the North Sea, and established houses and mission vessels for them. In 1892 Dr. Grenfell sailed to Newfoundland in the *Albert,* a ninety-nine-ton ketch, with a crew of ten. The vessel was fitted out with a small hospital amid-ships, and in three months treated 900 patients there. The following winter the Governor and Council of Newfoundland in-vited him to take up regular work along the Labrador coast, then, as now, a part of the colony of Newfoundland. Jacques Cartier once described it as the land God gave to Cain: "Not a cartload of earth on the whole of it."

Dr. Grenfell made his name almost syn-onymous with the country through his medical missions there and the numerous books he wrote about life in that barren land.

His picturesques tales of rugged adventure, risk, and hardship had a natural and inevita-ble appeal to young men and boys; several of the biographies of Dr. Grenfell were written especially for boys. Norman Dun-can's *Dr. Luke of the Labrador* is supposed to be based on Sir Wilfred's personality and career (he was knighted in 1927 by George V, twenty years after Edward VII had dec-orated him a C.M.G.). Lady Grenfell, who was Anne MacClanahan of Lake Forest, Ill., gave him practical assistance in the hospitals and missions from their marriage in 1909 until her death in 1938.

By 1937, the forty-fifth anniversary of the first voyage, the International Grenfell Association had six hospitals, seven nursing stations, four hospital ships, and many other facilities. Hundreds of students from Amer-ican and English colleges assisted Grenfell as volunteer workers. Scotch students gave him an ovation when he was installed rector of St. Andrew's University in Scotland, and made an LL.D. in 1929. Many other uni-versities gave him honorary degrees. As major in the Harvard Surgical Unit in the First World War, he used already tested methods in his treatment of trench feet. Sir Wilfred, who had a pleasant, weather-beaten Scotch face, with silver-gray hair and mous-tache, died of a heart-attack at seventy-five at his home, Kinloch House, Charlotte, Vt. His ashes were sent to St. Anthony, New-foundland, where Lady Grenfell was buried.

PRINCIPAL WORKS: Vikings of Today, 1896; Harvest of the Sea, 1906; Off the Rocks, 1906; A Man's Faith, 1908; Labrador, 1909; Adrift on an Ice-Pan, 1909; Down to the Sea, 1910; What Life Means to Me, 1910; A Man's Helpers, 1910; What Will You Do With Jesus Christ? 1911; What the Church Means to Me, 1911; Down North on the Labrador, 1911; The Adventure of Life, 1912; On Immortality, 1912; What Can Jesus Christ Do With Me? 1912; The Attractive Way, 1913; The Prize of Life, 1914; Tales of the Lab-rador, 1916; Labrador Days, 1919; A Labrador Doctor (autobiography) 1923; Northern Neigh-bors, 1923; Yourself and Your Body, 1925; Labra-dor Looks at the Orient, 1928; Forty Years for Labrador (autobiography) 1932; The Romance of Labrador, 1934; A Labrador Logbook, 1939; Your-self and Your Body, 1941.

ABOUT: Duncan, N. Dr. Grenfell's Parish; Grenfell, W. T. A Labrador Doctor, Forty Years for Labrador; Hall, A. G. Dr. Wilfred Grenfell; Hayes, E. H. Forty Years on the Labrador; Lee, C. With Dr. Grenfell in Labrador; Mathews, B. J. Wilfred Grenfell the Master Mariner; Waldo, F. L. Grenfell: Knight-Errant of the North; Mis-sionary Review April 1936; New York Times Oc-tober 10, 1940; Time October 21, 1940.

GREY, Sir EDWARD. See GREY OF FALLODON, E. G.

GREY, ZANE (January 31, 1872-October 23, 1939), American popular novelist, was born in Zanesville, Ohio, the son of Lewis

Grey, an Ohio backwoodsman, farmer, hunter, preacher, and doctor, and of Alice Josephine (Zane) Grey, a descendant of Col. Ebenezer Zane, a Quaker exiled from Denmark, who shipped to America with William Penn in 1682. Although several other institutions competed for his services as a ball-player, Grey attended the University of Pennsylvania. He struggled conscientiously from 1898 to 1904 to establish a dental practice in New York, but acute boredom and an itch to write made him give up the profession for a hallroom in the shadow of the Elevated Railroad, with a tomcat for company. No publisher would take the result in 1904, an historical novel, *Betty Zane,* so Grey published it himself. His brother, a professional ball-player, provided a cottage on the Delaware River, near Lackawaxen, Pa., where he assembled a superb collection of rejection slips.

In 1908 Grey took a fruitful trip to the West with Colonel C. J. ("Buffalo") Jones. Ripley Hitchcock, literary editor of Harper & Brothers, turned down the resultant book, *The Last of the Plainsmen,* with the usual promptitude. Two years later Harper's accepted *The Heritage of the Desert.* The next novel, *Riders of the Purple Sage,* written on the same formula of Western romance, and issued after long hesitation by Harper's in 1912 rolled up a sale of a million copies, with a later 800,000 in reprints. Twenty-five Zane Grey novels in twenty years sold seventeen million copies, reaching at least three times as many readers. He wrote fifty-four in all, many of which were filmed. A lavish income assured, Grey indulged himself in big-game fishing off Australia and New Zealand. He died of a sudden heart attack in Altadena, Calif., a suburb of Pasadena, at sixty-seven; the body was cremated. Grey had rugged features and profuse gray hair. Mrs. Grey (Lina Elise Roth), two sons, and a daughter survived, as well as three unpublished novels.

"It is difficult to imagine any writer having less merit in either style or substance than Grey and still maintaining an audience at all," Burton Rascoe said, but added that "he brought about the vicarious wish-fulfillment of millions of sedentary workers in the offic warrens of cities and industrial towns." I should be added that Grey's Southwester: backgrounds have color and authenticity.

PRINCIPAL WORKS: Betty Zane, 1904; The Spi it of the Border, 1905; The Last of the Plainsme 1908; The Heritage of the Desert, 1910; Riders o the Purple Sage, 1912; Desert Gold, 1913; Th Border Legion, 1916; The U. P. Trail, 1918; Tale of Fishes, 1919; The Man of the Forest, 1920 The Mysterious Rider, 1921; To the Last Mar 1922; The Call of the Canyon, 1924; The Thur dering Herd, 1925; Tales of Fishing, 1925; Virgi Seas, 1925; Tales of Swordfish and Tuna, 1927 Code of the West, 1934; Western Union, 1939 Twin Sombreros, 1941; Majesty's Rancho, 1942

ABOUT: New York Times October 24, 1939 Publishers' Weekly October 28, 1939; Saturday Re view of Literature November 11, 1939.

GREY OF FALLODON, E D W A R I GREY, 1st Viscount (April 25, 1862-Sep tember 7, 1933), English statesman and na ture-lover, was born in London, the eldest of seven children of Colonel George Henry Grey and Harriet Jane (Pearson) Grey. He always felt that his brothers and sisters had the advantage of him that they were not only reared but born in Fallodon,

the family seat in Northumberland. Colone Grey, a handsome, unintellectual man, diee in Edward's twelfth year and the boy wa thereafter brought up by his grandfather Sir George Grey, Bart., a onetime Libera cabinet member and a man of intellect and perception. When he died in 1882 th twenty-year-old youth inherited his title and became Sir Edward. After preparing a Winchester, Grey went to Balliol College Oxford, and was "sent down" in January 1884 for "incorrigible idleness." He returnee in June to take a Third in Jurisprudence which with a previous Second in Classica Moderations entitled him to a B.A. degree which he neglected to take. Grey's firs Oxford degree was his honorary D.C.L. ir 1907, and he was elected Chancellor of the University in 1928. At the end of 1885 he married Dorothy Widdrington, a reservec but intense woman, also devoted to country life.

Grey took up politics from a sense of duty: Gladstone once remarked "I never knew in a man such aptitude for political life and such disinclination for it." From 1885 to 1916 he was in the House of Commons as Liberal member for Berwick-on-

weed. Becoming Secretary of State for
Foreign Affairs in Sir Henry Campbell-
Bannerman's cabinet, he had eleven consecutive years at the head of the Foreign Office,
beginning in December 1905. Two months
later Lady Grey, who had been ill, was
thrown from a dog-cart and died without
recovering consciousness. Grey's biographer,
George Macaulay Trevelyan, says that Grey's
face, "in youth beaked and bright-eyed like
hawk's, became like that of the king of
birds. Men spoke of his 'sad eagle eyes.'"

On Monday, August 3, 1914, Grey as
Foreign Secretary made the historic speech
in the House of Commons giving Great
Britain's reasons for entering the First World
War. That evening he stood in the windows
of his room in the Foreign Office overlooking St. James's Park, and said to a friend:
"The lamps are going out all over Europe;
we shall not see them lit again in our lifetime." Grey's own eyesight was badly affected when he retired to Fallodon in 1916,
when Lloyd George became Premier. He
was raised to the peerage that year. The
second Lady Grey (Pamela Tennant, whom
he married in 1922 and who died in 1928)
persuaded him to write the charming papers
which—even more than his important memoirs—enable him to be included in a dictionary of authors. Fallodon had a beautiful
bird-sanctuary and Grey had a genius, says
G. M. Trevelyan, akin to that of his friend
W. H. Hudson, for the observation of bird
life in a manner which fused poetry with science. "The author of The Charm of Birds,
Fallodon Papers, and Fly Fishing, is in the
category with Izaak Walton, White of Selborne, Richard Jefferies and Hudson." He
died at seventy-one and his ashes were placed
beside those of Dorothy Grey under Fallodon
trees.

PRINCIPAL WORKS: Fly Fishing, 1899; Twenty-
Five Years; 1892-1916 (memoirs) 1925; Fallodon
Papers, 1926; The Charm of Birds, 1927.

ABOUT: Grey of Fallodon, E. Twenty-Five
Years; Trevelyan, G. M. Grey of Fallodon; New
York Times September 7, 1933; Nineteenth Century May 1934; Publishers' Weekly September 16,
1933.

GRIERSON, FRANCIS (September 18,
1848-May 29, 1927), American essayist, mystic, and musician, was born Benjamin Henry
Jesse Francis Shepard in Birkenhead, Cheshire, England, the son of Joseph Shepard
(among whose ancestors was Thomas
Shepard, New England divine and contemporary of John Harvard) and Emily
(Grierson) Shepard, descended from the
ninth century Clan MacGregor. He was

brought to the United States before he was
a year old, and spent his boyhood on an
Illinois prairie. His family moved first to
Alton, where the
youth heard the last
of the memorable
Lincoln-Douglas de-
bates, and then to St.
Louis where at the
age of thirteen he was
a page to General
Frémont, enjoying the
coveted acquaintance
of both Grant and
Sherman.

With only two years of formal musical
training Shepard exhibited an extraordinary talent at the piano. At barely twenty-one
he set out for Paris—with scarcely enough
money to buy his passage—and almost overnight became a sensation. At the close of a
fabulous tour and several return visits to
America he settled in London to develop
another art, that of writing. And lest his
literary efforts be regarded as the mere
diversions of a musician he changed his name
to Francis Grierson, by which he was known
for the rest of his life.

In the early 'eighties the Chicago Times
had published a series of his essays; and
La Révolte Idéaliste, a collection of essays
and aphorisms, had been extravagantly
praised for the purity of its French and the
poetry of its thought. But not until he was
fifty did he publish his first book in English,
Modern Mysticism and Other Essays. Two
years later came The Celtic Temperament
and Other Essays, afterwards adopted as a
textbook by Japanese universities. For
seven years he wrote intensively on The
Valley of Shadows: Recollections of the
Lincoln Country; it had a prophetic freedom and a delicacy of reminiscence which
he never later equaled. Along with H. G.
Wells, George Bernard Shaw, and Hilaire
Belloc he was writing, in 1910, for the New
Age. But of that formidable group only
Grierson foresaw the approach of a world
upheaval. By 1913 it had become so real
to him that he returned to America; devoted
two of his six years in the East to lecturing;
published two books (Illusions and Realities
of the War and Abraham Lincoln: The Practical Mystic); and retired to Los Angeles.
In 1921 he issued a pamphlet of spiritualistic
Psycho-Phone Messages (the term "psycho-
phone" was his own invention); he had a
serious interest in psychic phenomena, although the extent of his own ability as any
kind of medium appears somewhat unde-

fined. His last days passed in extreme poverty. He died while seated at a piano during an evening recital. He was unmarried.

Grierson put little trust in reason or in science. Intuition and emotion were the sources of his artistic energy; aesthetically he was a mystic. His writing is sometimes wandering and labored, but it contains flashes of weirdly lyric charm.

PRINCIPAL WORKS: La Révolte Idéaliste, 1889; Modern Mysticism and Other Essays, 1899; The Celtic Temperament and Other Essays, 1901; The Valley of Shadows: Recollections of the Lincoln Country, 1858-63, 1909; Portraits, 1910; La Vie and Les Hommes, 1911; The Humour of the Underman, 1911; The Invincible Alliance, 1913; Illusions and Realities of the War, 1918; Abraham Lincoln: The Practical Mystic, 1918; Psycho-Phone Messages, 1921.

ABOUT: Tonner, W. The Genius of Francis Grierson; Trend March 1914; autobiographical passages in the works.

GRIERSON, Sir HERBERT JOHN CLIFFORD (1866-), British scholar, critic, and historian, is the second son of

Andrew J. Grierson, Deputy-Lieutenant of Queendale, Shetland Isles. He was educated at King's College, Aberdeen, Scotland, and at Christ Church, Oxford University. Grierson became professor at Aberdeen at twenty-eight, in 1894, there he stayed until 1915, when he received an appointment as professor of Rhetoric and English at the University of Edinburgh, where he taught until his retirement twenty years later in 1935. He was knighted in 1936. Homage was paid to him in 1938 with a volume of *Seventeenth Century Studies Presented to Sir Herbert Grierson,* published by the Clarendon Press at Oxford and containing twenty-three essays in the fields of Sir Herbert's interests. The book included a dedicatory poem, written in Dutch, and an essay on "The Love Poetry of John Donne." Sir Herbert had edited the *Poems* of Donne in 1912 and published a study of *Metaphysical Poets: Donne to Butler,* in 1921.

Sir Herbert's first wife was Mary Letitia Ogston, daughter of Sir Alexander Ogston, K.C.V.O. Their eldest daughter, Bruce Dickins, M.A., professor of the English Language at Leeds University since 1931, has edited *Yorkshire Celtic Studies* since 1938 and is the author of *The Conflict of*

Wit and Will, among others. The present Lady Grierson, whom he married in 1938 was Margaret Storrs, M.A., Ph.D., daughter of Lucius Seymour Storrs, president of the Los Angeles Railway. Sir Herbert has lectured in America, at Toronto University and Johns Hopkins. Since 1936 he has been Lord Rector of Edinburgh University, and holds numerous honorary degrees from universities in Scotland, England, and Ireland. He has ascetic, strongly marked features with a large nose and wide mouth. The London *Times* has spoken of his "massive learning, breadth of view, clear insight, and kindling power of sympathy [which] made him an inspiring teacher."

PRINCIPAL WORKS: The First Half of the Seventeenth Century (Periods of European Literature) 1906; Metaphysical Poets: Donne to Butler, 1921; Blake's Illustrations to Gray's Poems 1922; The Background of English Literature and Other Collected Essays, 1925; The Poems of John Milton, 1925; Lyrical Poetry From Blake to Hardy, 1928; Cross-Currents in the Literature of the Seventeenth Century, 1929; Carlyle and Hitler, 1933; Milton and Wordsworth: Poets and Prophets, 1937; Sir Walter Scott, Bart, 1938; Essays and Addresses, 1940; Thomas Carlyle, 1941 *Editor*—The Poems of John Donne, 1912; Letters of Sir Walter Scott, 1937; Songs and Lyrics of Sir Walter Scott. *Compiler*—Oxford Book of Seventeenth Century Verse (with G. Bullock) 1934.

ABOUT: Seventeenth Century Studies Presented to Herbert Grierson.

GRIEVE, CHRISTOPHER MURRAY

("Hugh McDiarmid") (August 11, 1892-) Scottish poet and essayist, was born in Langholm, Dumfriesshire, and educated at Langholm Academy and the University of Edinburgh. His family were prosperous landowners, and he has always had an independent income and been able to devote his time to writing and to public activities. Chief of these latter has been the cause of Scottish Nationalism; he was a founder of the Scottish Nationalistic Party, which advocates independence for Scotland, and he says his "recreation" is "Anglophobia." In spite of this, he lives in London most of the time, though he also owns a house in Whelsay, in the Shetland Islands. He was at one time Justice of the Peace in Forfarshire (Angus). He has been married twice: first to Margaret Skinner, by whom he had a son and a daughter, then to Valda Trevlyn, by whom he has a son. He is editor of the *Voice of Scotland,* a quarterly, which is the organ of the Scottish Nationalist Party, and he was the founder of the Scottish section of the P.E.N. Club. In addition to his books of poetry and prose, and his articles on literature and politics in many magazines, he has translated Alexander MacDonald's *The Birlinn of Clanranald* from the Gaelic, and a novel by Ramón María de Tenreiro, *The Handmaid of the Lord,* from the Spanish; and he was the editor of *Living Scottish Poets* and *The Golden Treasury of Scottish Poetry.*

His personality has become something of a legend; he is perhaps the most prominent living Scots Nationalist, and in this rôle his stature as a poet has been somewhat obscured. This "wiry, ruddy-haired little man in shabby tweeds," as Horace Gregory called him, is actually a great satirist and, on occasion, a great lyrist as well; to Edwin Muir his poetry is "pure inspiration; nothing could be better of its kind, and the kind is rare"; to A. C. Frost he is "a strong, masculine, clear-thinking poet." The chief difficulty in becoming acquainted with his work is the language in which much (though by no means all) of it is written—a vocabulary combining ancient and modern Scottish dialect, plus contemporary spoken English: "the naked speech of the Glasgow and London Streets." It requires constant consultation of a glossary, but it is worth the effort; Grieve (or "McDiarmid," for he writes always under his pseudonym) has freshness, vigor, flexibility, and at his best a Swiftian quality of satire. Mr. Frost, who called him "Scotland's vortex-maker," and "the chief insubordinate in a subdominant country," summed up his poetry as consisting of "the actual-grotesque grasped by a particularly shrewd fantasy, . . . switching about from the sardonic to the speculative."

In spite of his strong nationalism, he is socially and politically far to the left, though not technically a Communist. A few years ago at least, he was of the opinion that the Soviet Union was a beacon-light for Scotland to follow. His prose, except for his idyllic travel books, is likely to be argumentative and rhetorical—the besetting weaknesses also of his poetry, which sometimes falls into what Mr. Muir calls "false genius." But he remains a true original, and one of the most interesting men writing today.

PRINCIPAL WORKS: *Poetry*—Sangschaw, 1925; Penny Wheep, 1926; A Drunk Man Looks at the Thistle, 1926; To Circumjack Cenrastus, 1930; First Hymn to Lenin, 1932; Scots Unbound, 1932; Cornish Heroic Song For Valda Trevlyn, 1933; Selected Poems, 1934; Second Hymn to Lenin, 1935. *Prose*—Annals of the Five Senses, 1922; Contemporary Scottish Studies, 1924; The Present Condition of Scottish Arts and Affairs, 1926; Albyn: or, Scotland and the Future, 1927; Scottish Scenes: or, The Intelligent Man's Guide to Albyn (with J. L. Mitchell) 1934; At the Sign of the Thistle, 1934; What Lenin Has Meant to Scotland, 1935; Scottish Eccentrics, 1936; The Islands of Scotland: Hebrides, Orkneys, and Shetlands, 1939. *Edited*—The Golden Treasury of Scottish Poetry, 1941.

ABOUT: Grieve, C. M. First Hymn to Lenin (see Introduction by G. Russell); Bookman (London) September 1934; Canadian Forum February 1936; Englische Studien #3 1933; New Republic May 26, 1937; Poetry February 1937; Sewanee Review January 1940.

GRIFFIN, VIÉLÉ-. See VIÉLÉ

GRISWOLD, FRANCIS (1902-), American novelist, is a native of Albany, N.Y., but lives by preference in the Carolina low country. His first novel, *Tides of Malvern* (1930), unrolled a chronicle of Charleston and the lowlands, from the first incursion of white men from Jamaica down to the world of the 1930's. Burton Rascoe said of this novel: "Make  note of Griswold's name, because it is a name that will be blazoned on the literary scene in a few years and there is a certain satisfaction in getting the jump on things."

This first novel went into six printings. "The *Tides of Malvern* is but a prelude to a decade of writing on the Carolina low country," according to its author. "Little justice, it seems to me, has been done to this section of the South . . . full of beauty and pain, full of profound implications for the heart of man." *A Sea Island Lady,* the next novel in the series, was seven years in the writing; time passed in exploring old houses, ransacking attics, talking with Oldest Inhabitants, and jotting endless notes from old books and faded newspapers. The original draft of the novel was longer than *Gone With the Wind,* and Griswold spent a year in revision. Most of the actual composition was done in Augusta, at his summer shack on a remote peak of the North Carolina mountains, and latterly at Santa Barbara, Calif. "Preoccupied with the passage of time as the one fixed factor in the lives of his characters, he was willing to risk time's obscuring of his own vogue in order to do justice to the literary home of his adoption—'my world in small'—as he called the Carolina lowlands," according to his publishers.

A Sea Island Lady in its final form extended to 964 pages, and covered a time-period of the years between the Civil War and the 1920's. "In his first four-hundred-odd pages Mr. Griswold has told an admirable and moving story," according to Stephen Vincent Benét. Its predecessor, *Tides of Malvern,* drew negative reviews from the New York *Times* and *Nation,* but the late Guy Holt called it "a sound romantic novel, competent and poised and at moments reaching a high level." Elmer Davis commented that "the whole is more effective and more impressive than some of its parts. Covering six generations in three hundred pages requires a good deal of compression."

PRINCIPAL WORKS: Tides of Malvern, 1930; A Sea Island Lady, 1939.

GRUENING, ERNEST HENRY (February 6, 1887-), American journalist and publicist, was born in New York and edu-cated at Hotchkiss School and Harvard University (B.A. 1907, M.D. 1912). He never practiced medicine, but became a reporter and special writer for the Boston *American* (1911-13), assistant editor of the Boston *Herald* (1913-14), managing editor of the Boston *Traveler* (1914-16), and editor of the Boston *Journal* (1916-17). After assisting in organizing the Bureau of Imports of the War Trade Board in Washington, he was managing editor of the New York *Tribune* in 1918. He then enlisted in the Field Artillery, being stationed at Camp Zachary Taylor, in Louisville, to the end of the First World War. In 1919 and 1920 he was president of a printing company and also general manager of *La Prensa,* the only Spanish daily in the United States. (He speaks Spanish, French, and German fluently.)

He joined the staff of the *Nation* as managing editor in 1920, and was with it for three years. Later he was editor in 1933 and 1934. He was national director of publicity in the elder Robert La Follette's presidential campaign in 1924. In 1927 he founded the Portland, Maine, *Evening News,* and was its editor until 1932, and for two years more contributing editor. These were stormy years, as he conducted a single-handed fight against the power trust in Maine. From February to April, 1934, he was editor of the New York *Evening Post.*

Dr. Gruening had always been keenly interested in problems of colonial policy and

had been a member of the Cuba Commission of the Foreign Policy Association. In 1934 he was appointed director of the Division of Territories and Island Possessions of the United States Department of Agriculture, with jurisdiction over Alaska, Hawaii, Puerto Rico, the Virgin Islands, and all South Sea and Equatorial Islands. This post he held until the end of 1939, when he became governor of Alaska, his present office. He was Federal Emergency Relief Administrator for Puerto Rico, and administrator of Puerto Rico Reconstruction.

In 1932 he went to Mexico for *Collier's Weekly.* He was appointed general advisor to the United States delegation to the Montevideo Pan-American Conference in 1933. He is a member of the Council on Foreign Relations of the American Academy of Political and Social Science, and a director of the Foreign Policy Association. In 1914 he married Dorothy Elizabeth Smith; they had three sons, one of whom is deceased. In 1925 he edited a symposium, *These United States,* which attracted much attention. He has lectured at the New School for Social Research and contributed to the *Dictionary of American Biography,* the *Encyclopaedia Britannica,* the *Encyclopedia of Social Science,* and the *American Year Book.* He also writes frequently for the serious reviews.

PRINCIPAL WORKS: Mexico and Its Heritage, 1928; The Public Pays, 1931.

ABOUT: Bookman May 1925; Literary Digest October 21, 1933; Nation August 20, 1934; New Republic March 20, 1929, February 28, 1934; Publishers' Weekly February 24, 1934; Time July 17, 1939.

*GUEDALLA, PHILIP (March 12, 1889-), English historian and essayist, was the first-born son of David Guedalla and Louise (Soman) Guedalla. He went to Rugby School, where he edited *The Meteor,* and to Balliol College, Oxford University. Here he ran the gamut from president of the Oxford Union Society, the famous debating organization, in 1911, to actor in the O.U.D.S. (Oxford University Dramatic Society). Young Guedalla was also an Exhibitioner at Oxford, taking first class honors in Moderations in 1910 and another first class in modern history in 1912. After receiving an M.A. degree in

* Died December 16, 1944.

1913 he became a barrister in the Inner Temple, retiring from practice ten years later to devote his entire time to writing. At Oxford he had published a volume of poetry and another of parodies, and a sober, scholarly dissertation, *The Partition of Europe 1715-1815*. The glittering, coruscating Guedalla style was to be evolved a little later. During the First World War Guedalla served as legal adviser of the Contracts Department of the War Office and Ministry of Munitions. In 1917 he organized and acted as secretary to the Flax Control Board, leaving this post in 1920. Developing Parliamentary ambitions, Guedalla unsuccessfully contested North Hackney in 1922, North-East Derbyshire in 1923 and 1924, Rusholme in 1929, and Withington in 1931. He has been a honorary director of the Ibero-American Institute of Great Britain, and member of the Cinematograph Film Council Board of Trade. In 1919 Mr. Guedalla was married to Nellie Maude Reitlinger.

"A liberal, a sceptic, a Zionist, and the fine quintessence of Balliol," a writer "whose mental frontiers are closed against the *cliché*," Philip Guedalla shared with Lytton Strachey the glory of revivifying the writing of history and historical biography. While some of the earlier books merit the *Nation and Athenaeum's* accusation of "brilliance without balance and color without proportion," Guedalla's later work has gained in sobriety and verisimilitude, while relying less on such easy triumphs as calling a German-Turk alliance "Deutschland über Allah," referring to "the scrap of Papen," and remarking that "any stigma is good enough to beat a dogma." Early in his career as a writer his work received favorable attention in the United States, to which he devoted a book on the American Revolution fully as sympathetic as George Macaulay Trevelyan's. (It was entitled *Independence Day* in England; *Fathers of the Revolution* in America.) *Wellington* (1931), known in England as *The Duke*, was a selection that year of the (American) Literary Guild. *The Hundred Years* (1936), a book covering the century from the accession of Victoria in 1837 to the ascension to the throne of Edward VIII in 1936, was unrolled in thirty episodes, which included several phases of American history. "The past should, for the historian, be his present," Guedalla has written. "He must never write from the angle of today, but almost always from the angle of contemporaries with the events that he describes. . . . When his reader is set dreaming of the past, the historian has done his work, only provided that the dream be true. For then *temps perdu* has become *temps retrouvé*, and the quest is ended." As for his subjects, "to resurrect, to set them moving, catch the tone of their voices, tilt of their heads, and posture of the once living men" is the task of the historian. Mr. Guedalla, who is dark, handsome, and urbane, lists his addresses as Hyde Park Street, London, and The Laundry, Easton Park, Dunmow, Essex. His clubs are the Athenaeum, Garrick, and Beefsteak.

PRINCIPAL WORKS: Ignes Fatui: A Book of Parodies, 1911; Metri Gratia: Verse and Prose, 1911; The Partition of Europe 1715-1815, 1914; Supers and Supermen, 1920; The Industrial Future, 1921; The Second Empire, 1922; Masters and Men, 1923; A Gallery, 1924; A Council of Industry, 1925; Napoleon and Palestine (Davis Lecture) 1925; Independence Day (American title: Fathers of the Revolution) 1926; Palmerston, 1926; Conquistador, 1927; Gladstone and Palmerston, 1928; Bonnet and Shawl, 1928; The Missing Muse, 1929; The Duke, 1931; Argentine Tango, 1932; The Queen and Mr. Gladstone, 1933; The Hundred Days, 1934; The Hundred Years, 1936; Idylls of the Queen, 1937; Rag-Time and Tango, 1938; The Hundredth Year, 1939; Mr. Churchill, 1941.

ABOUT: Adcock, A. St. J. The Glory That Was Grub Street; London Mercury July 1926.

GUÉRARD, ALBERT LÉON (November 3, 1880-   ), Franco-American historian and critic, writes: "I was born in Paris, and lived for twenty years within a quarter-mile of the Pont Royal and the Louvre; I may claim the quays of the Seine as my first teachers. The second decisive influence in my education was the Dreyfus case. The third, just as I was growing into con-  scious manhood, was a protracted sojourn in London, with no program of study except to absorb English life; the second year was spent at Toynbee Hall [a famous settlement house], a bit of Oxford and Cambridge in the slums and ghetto of Whitechapel. I came to America in 1906. My academic experience [as college teacher of French] was singularly fortunate: Williams, aloof and quaint; Stanford, which in those days seemed infinitely remote—still partly in ruins after the earthquake, still with an aura of pioneering adventure under the genial and generous leadership of David Starr Jordan; Rice, in Houston, city of friendliness; Los Angeles [at the Los Angeles branch of the University of California] for a few months; then Stanford again in 1925, this time until night falls.

"My father was a free-thinking Catholic —not an unusual combination in the land of Montaigne and Voltaire. My mother belonged to the pitiful remnant of the Gallican Church, reduced to a single chapel in the poverty-stricken Croulebarde Quarter. My wife's family were of Scottish Covenanter stock. From these conflicting experiences, I have retained an odd blend of ideals: a deep love for long-rooted things, mellow books, old cities, ancient creeds; and also the sense that they were but toys or garments for the eternal and ever new thoughts of living man. The Dreyfus case taught me that the noblest tradition, when exclusive and infallible in its own conceit, could become a power of evil. England at the time of the Boer War strengthened me in my rebellion against tribal idols. Thus I have been an obstinate 'Liberal,' against all the 'eternal verities' that seek to crush man's spirit: in politics, not unpartisan, but antipartisan; in religion, not unsectarian, but anti-sectarian. In international affairs, I believe with William Lloyd Garrison that 'my country is the world, my countrymen are all mankind.' Napoleonism is my sole enemy; and by Napoleonism I mean the prestige and power of sheer force, whether represented by Louis XIV, William Pitt, Bismarck, or Hitler. Such is my way of being '100 per cent American': America to me is not a territory and not a code, but a way of life. It is, in words that David Starr Jordan taught me, the land where hate dies away.

"These conflicting ideals I have endeavored to express in my various studies in French civilization, and, since 1925, in the wider field of General and Comparative Literature. Of such a spirit, respectful of every nation and culture, but eager for friendly cooperation, an international language would be the best symbol and the most efficient instrument. I have endeavored to keep myself free; but liberty without purpose is futile. If I am a follower of Montaigne, Voltaire, and Renan, I am also a disciple of Pascal and Alfred de Vigny. I started my career, three decades ago, with *French Prophets of Yesterday,* an anxious survey of religious thought; I am preparing to close it with my religious testament, *A Bottle in the Sea.*"

* * *

Professor Guérard is at present professor of General Literature at Stanford University. He is a Chevalier of the Legion of Honor. During the World War he was in the intelligence and liaison services of the United States. In 1907 he was married to Wilhelmina Macartney; they have a son and daughter, and had another son who died. The beauty and vigor of his English style may be adduced from this autobiographical sketch, which he says is "A 'posed' portrait, no doubt; what I think I am, and what I try to be. My wife, my children, my students, and my dog have in their minds a totally different picture."

PRINCIPAL WORKS: French Prophets of Yesterday, 1913; French Civilization in the Nineteenth Century, 1914; Five Masters of French Romance, 1916; French Civilization From Its Origins to the Close of the Middle Ages, 1920; International Languages, 1921; The Napoleonic Legend, 1923; Honoré de Balzac, 1924; Beyond Hatred, 1925; Life and Death of an Ideal: France in the Classic Age, 1925; L'Avenir de Paris [The Future of Paris] 1929; Literature and Society, 1935; Art for Art's Sake, 1936; Preface to World Literature, 1940; The France of Tomorrow, 1942.

GUILLOUX, LOUIS (1899-), French novelist, was born in Brittany, the son of Albert-Gaston Guilloux, a well known sculptor. He was educated in Rouen, but h a s lived in small Breton towns during most of h i s life. Not much is known about his personal history, not even whether or not he is married. But from early youth he h a s been a liberal leaning far to the left,

and his first novel, *La Maison du Peuple* (*The People's House,* 1927) traced the birth and growth of political ideas among the workers in a small Breton town. He is dark, with a thin, melancholy face, and the high, bulging forehead of a thinker. At the beginning of the Second World War he was very active in the *Secours Populaires* (the relief association which was engaged in caring for the refugees in France from Spain after the civil war there), and he was the association's regional secretary. At that time he was writing a book on his experiences in the refugee camps, besides being engaged on another novel. Portions of this book appeared in English translation in the *New Republic* and also in English magazines. Since his home is in the occupied portion of France there is the gravest cause for fear for his present welfare, in view of his liberal interests; nothing has been heard from or of him since the Nazi conquest.

M. Guilloux has thus far published five novels: *La Maison du Peuple, La Nymphe au Coeur Fidele* (*The Nymph With the Faithful Heart*, 1928), *Dossier Confidentiel* (*Confidential Report*, 1930), *Angelina* (1934), and *Le Sang Noir* (*Black Blood*, 1935). Of these, only *Le Sang Noir* has been translated into English, under the title of *Bitter Victory*. It is, to use the words of Harold Strauss, a powerful "study of moral cowardice in a person of fine intelligence." M. Guilloux has, said Mr. Strauss, "the grand style of the nineteenth century"; in contrast to the condensation characteristic of the contemporary novel, his books are "almost formless." His style, however, is sober and concise, and his work is equally marked by intelligence and by compassion. He himself says that he has been greatly influenced by the American William Faulkner, but traces may be found also in his writing of the influence of Balzac, Dostoievsky, and Flaubert.

André Malraux said of him that his work evinces "the eternal grudge against reality of a poet whom the very nature of his talent compels to express himself not through lyricism but through this same reality." In his books is "the constantly recurring encounter of the grotesque and the tragic— saved from the artistic dangers that always beset such an encounter by the author's own feeling for what is right." His characters "give the impression of being seen in a kind of phosphorescent light, which they themselves emanate," and *Le Sang Noir* especially, with its minute study of the meannesses and festering sores of a provincial town, has "the atmosphere of parrots in a cemetery."

WORK AVAILABLE IN ENGLISH: Bitter Victory, 1936 (in England, 1940).
ABOUT: Living Age March 1936.

GUINEY, LOUISE IMOGEN (January 7, 1861-November 2, 1920), American poet and essayist, was born in Roxbury, Mass., a suburb of Boston, the daughter of Patrick Guiney and Jane Margaret (Doyle) Guiney. Her father, a native of Tipperary, was wounded in the battle of the Wilderness in the American Civil War, and breveted a brigadier general. He died suddenly when his daughter was sixteen, leaving her with a sense of irreparable loss; his sword and spurs always hung over her

desk. Six years of Louise's childhood were spent among the nuns of the Convent of the Sacred Heart at Elmhurst, R.I., founded by Frenchwomen who emigrated to New England in 1818. Here she repudiated "the Black Arts of mathematics and sewing." As Sir Edmund Gosse said, "Her generous and romantic nature, which dwelt habitually in the past, and was only at ease  in the atmosphere of a chivalrous and antique dreamland, was starved at the outset."

For a time she did newspaper work for a livelihood; after the appearance of her second book of verse, *A Roadside Harp*, containing some of her best and most characteristic poems (admired by Stevenson, for one), O. W. Holmes, E. C. Stedman, R. W. Gilder, and T. B. Aldrich helped her obtain the position of postmistress at Auburndale, Mass., whither she moved her mother and St. Bernard dog. Boycotted by the Protestant community, who refused to buy stamps of a Catholic, Miss Guiney received orders from admirers from all over the United States when the facts became known. After a dreary interlude in the cataloging division of the Boston Public Library, in 1895 she realized her ambition to go to England to study at the Bodleian Library at Oxford, make foot-tours through the Cotswolds, and publish the results of her researches and walking trips. "I came to England not for excitement, not for vogue, but for the velvety feel of the Past under foot, like moss of the forest floor to a barefooted child," she said. In later years her health began to fail (she preferred to spend what money she had on books rather than food), and she died at sixty-eight in her little house at Chipping Campden, Gloucestershire, leaving unfinished an anthology of Recusant Poets—men of the sixteenth and seventeenth century who refused to attend the Established Church—from the time of Surrey to that of Pope.

Louise Guiney lies buried in Wolvercote Cemetery, near Oxford, at the foot of a Celtic cross. Handicapped by deafness and weak eyes, she had chestnut hair, a high color, and indisputable charm. Alice Brown called her "the champion of lost causes, the restorer of names dropped out of rubricated calendars." She revived forgotten worthies of the age of Charles I and poured gaiety and passion into her verse. Katherine Tynan wrote, "she carries her learning delicately. Her poetry has the high note of resolve and courage." Her name is pronounced *guy'nee.*

PRINCIPAL WORKS: Songs at the Start, 1884; Goose Quill Papers, 1885; The White Sail and Other Poems, 1887; Three Heroines of English Romance (with H.P. Spofford & A. Brown) 1894; A Little English Gallery, 1894; The Martyr's Idyl and Shorter Poems, 1899; Monsieur Henri: A Footnote to French History, 1892; A Little English Gallery, 1894; Patrins: A Collection of Essays, 1897; Hurrell Froude, 1904; Happy Ending, 1909 (revised 1927).

ABOUT: Brégy, K. M. C. Poets and Pilgrims; Brown, A. Louise Imogen Guiney; Chislett, W. Moderns and Near Moderns; Gosse, E. W. Silhouettes; Morley, C. Modern Essays: First Series; Rittenhouse, J. B. Younger American Poets; Tenison, E. M. Louise Imogen Guiney; Catholic World August 1925, August 1928.

*GUITERMAN, ARTHUR (November 20, 1871-), American poet and light versifier, writes: "Arthur Guiterman was born in

Vienna, Austria, and because of the anxiety of his mother, a native of Ohio, that there should be no future doubt of his citizenship, his name was registered at the American consulate within twenty-four hours. The family returned to New York when he was in his third year. He was educated mainly in the New York public schools and in the College of the City of New York, from which he was graduated in 1891. During his college years he was active in lacrosse, tennis, and rowing, was on the track team in the Intercollegiate Games as the best sprinter of his year, was captain of the bicycle club, class secretary and poet, and one of the stars of the dramatic club. He received the Ward Medal for highest rating in English composition, was elected to Phi Beta Kappa, and in 1936 received from the Associated Alumni the Townsend Harris Medal for distinguished achievement in postgraduate activities. In 1940 he received the degree of D.Litt. at Rollins College.

"After several years of work as reporter and editor, he became a free-lance writer, devoting himself almost entirely to verse. For many years he was the chief contributor of verse to *Life,* in which he originated the widely imitated 'Rhymed Reviews.' His family name being frequently mispronounced, one of his editorial friends tried

to enlighten inquirers on that point with the couplet:

There ain't no better, fitter man
Than Mister Arthur Guiterman.

"In collaboration with Lawrence Langner, Mr. Guiterman prepared an adaptation of Moliere's *L'École des Maris,* in English rhymed verse, which, as *The School for Husbands,* was successfully produced by the Theatre Guild in 1933. He also wrote the libretto and lyrics for the opera, *A Man Without a Country,* with a score by Walter Damrosch, produced by the Metropolitan Opera Company in 1937 and 1938. He has served as president of the Authors' League Fellowship and of the Poetry Society of America.

Mr. Guiterman was married in 1909 to Vida Lindo. They now spend the autumn and spring in New York, the worst part of the winter in Florida, and the summer in what they now consider their real home, in Arlington, Vt."

* * *

Mr. Guiterman is still an athlete, a mountain climber, skater, and crack tennis player, in spite of his glasses and his scholarly appearance. Joyce Kilmer called him "the most American of poets." Edmund Pearson said, he is "our best writer of light verse and a serious poet with deep and sincere feeling."

PRINCIPAL WORKS: Betel Nuts, 1907; Guest Book, 1908; Rubiayat, 1909; Orestes (with André Tridon) 1909; The Laughing Muse, 1915; The Mirthful Lyre, 1918; Ballads of Old New York, 1920; Chips of Jade, 1920; A Ballad Makers' Pack, 1921; The Light Guitar, 1923; A Poet's Proverbs, 1924; I Sing the Pioneer, 1926; Wildwood Fables, 1927; Song and Laughter, 1929; Death and General Putnam and 101 Other Poems, 1935; Gaily the Troubadour, 1936; Lyric Laughter, 1939; Ballads of Old New York, 1939.

ABOUT: Literary Digest August 24, 1934; Poetry July 1937; Saturday Evening Post August 18, 1928; Saturday Review of Literature August 24, 1935, January 2, 1937; Time January 1, 1940.

GUITRY, SACHA (February 21, 1885-), French actor and playwright, was born in St. Petersburg, Russia, the son of Lucien Guitry, also a well-known actor, who was fulfilling a nine-year contract in the Imperial Theatres of Russia. He was christened Alexandre Pierre Georges Guitry. Mme. Guitry, who had been a Mlle. de Pont-Jest, divorced his father some years later, assumed custody of Sacha and his elder brother, and herself went on the stage as Mme. de Pontry. At five Sacha Guitry played Pierrot, Jr., in a pantomime at St. Petersburg. He attended a succession of schools, a dozen in all, and "finished his

education without having ever begun it."
The theatre was in his blood. *Le Page*, a
one-act play in verse, was performed in

1902. In 1904 Sacha
Guitry played with
his father in a drama
by Maurice Donnay;
was dismissed for put-
ting in a late appear-
ance, minus an essen-
tial wig, and did not
see his father again
for thirteen years.

He wrote sketches
for *Gil Blas* and *La
Clef*, and a successful play, *Nono*, produced
in 1905, followed by a dozen others, which
with the exception of *Le Mufle* did not do
so well. *Deburau* was produced in Paris in
1918, with Lucien Guitry playing the famous
pantomimist. Staged by David Belasco in
New York, with Lionel Atwill in the title-
rôle, in 1920, the play ran several months
and was succeeded by Guitry's *The Grand
Duke*, also with Atwill. In 1927 Guitry himself and his young wife, Yvonne Printemps,
played in New York in *Mozart* and *L'Illu-
sioniste*. (Sarah Bernhardt was a witness of
the Guitry-Printemps wedding, as she had
attended the marriage of his parents thirty-
seven years before.) *Pasteur* was well received in Paris in 1919, but failed to arouse
interest in the United States.

It has been said that Guitry staged a "one-
man revolt against the lugubrious and disillusioned French theatre." On the screen he
has been equally triumphant, among his successes being *Roman d'un Tricheur, Champs
Elyseés, Pearls of the Crown*, and *Nine
Bachelors*. His competence extends beyond
the realms of actor and author: he is a first-
class director and producer as well. Irrepressible, clever, talented, a perennial provider of
sensations to the domestic press, alternately
enfant terrible and blasé boulevardier, he
stands in many minds as the very "quintessence of Gallicism."

Guitry has a mobile actor's mask, a clean
shaven face with a large nose, oval chin, and,
in his own words, "a look of slightly arrested
development." He has been married four
times, most recently to Geneviève de Serre-
ville, in 1939.

In 1941 Guitry was in occupied Paris,
whence contradictory reports have emanated
concerning his relations with the Nazis.

WORKS AVAILABLE IN ENGLISH TRANSLATION:
Deburau, 1921; Pasteur (in Dickinson, T. H. *Chief
Contemporary Dramatists: Second Series*); If
Memory Serves (autobiography) 1935; Remem-
bering the Champs Elysées, 1940.

ABOUT: Benjamin, R. Sacha Guitry: Roi du
Théâtre; Guitry, S. If Memory Serves; Leeds,
S. B. These Rule France; Whitridge, A. Critical
Ventures in Modern French Literature; New York
Times February 1, 1942; Revue de Paris July 15,
1939.

GULBRANNSEN, TRYGVE (1894-),
Norwegian novelist, was born in a town, but
his parents were farmer folk who did not
come to the town un-
til they were about
thirty, so that they
always remembered
and talked of their
farming origin—
hence their son's in-
timate knowledge of
the country. The
boy's grandfather had
been a wealthy man,
with landed property,

but lost every cent when Gulbranssen was
only six years old. The boy took a job as
errand boy, and left school at thirteen, the
legal age. He continued, however, to attend
night classes in art, as a star pupil, until he
was twenty. A boys' athletic club that he
started at this time was the inception of the
successful organization of such clubs in Norway. He is an artist of considerable ability,
contributing to *Oslo Illustrerte*, among other
periodicals.

Gulbranssen was manager of a tobacco
factory at twenty-three and successfully
started his own business with another young
man when he was twenty-six. From the
time he was twenty he wrote steadily, but
made no serious effort to publish anything,
except a story in a newspaper, until *Beyond
Sing the Woods* appeared in 1936. Gulbranssen can write only after midnight, a
habit dating from the time when he lived
in cramped quarters with his parents and
four brothers and sisters, and could write
in peace only after the rest had gone to bed.
He wrote steadily until three or later, getting
up in time to reach his office at nine. When
Gulbranssen married and started a home of
his own, the habit continued. It is only at the
stroke of midnight that his ideas begin to
flow. He writes in pencil, refusing to have a
typewriter or any other machine in his study.
Surrounded by machines in the office, he
prefers to be rid of them when at home.

The novelist is an impressive figure, with
a broad brow, a mass of brown hair that
grows on his head like a Viking's helmet,
eyes with a look of overstrain from reading,
a well-shaped nose, and sensitive mouth.
His Norwegian fellow-authors are inclined
to resent the phenomenon of a business man

and an amateur becoming a best seller, and with novels of a romantic trend at that. He has taught himself English and German. S. R. Mitchneck has said of Gulbranssen, "While he lacks the sculptural quality attained by Jens Peter Jacobsen, the Danish Flaubert and the cynosure of Scandinavian writers, Gulbranssen possesses an unsurpassed picturesqueness of style." Lewis Gannett writes that his chronicles of an aristocratic Norwegian family living on their huge hill estates "possess something of the earthy richness of Knut Hamsun's early books, some of the magic of old Norway that inspired Sigrid Undset."

So far as is known Gulbranssen is still in Norway.

WORKS AVAILABLE IN ENGLISH TRANSLATION: Beyond Sing the Woods, 1936; The Wind From the Mountains, 1937.

GUMMERE, FRANCIS BARTON

(March 6, 1855-May 30, 1919), American university professor and authority on poetic origins, was born in Burlington, N.J., the son of Samuel James Gummere and Elizabeth Hooton (Barton) Gummere. He attended Haverford College, of which his father was president (his grandfather was superintendent of Haverford School), receiving a B.A. degree in 1872; spent a year as clerk in an iron foundry, read law another year in a Philadelphia office, and obtained a second B.A. at Harvard in 1875, the same year that Haverford granted him a master's degree. At Harvard, Gummere came under the tutelage of Francis James Child, the great American authority on English and Scottish popular ballads. Gummere began teaching at the Friends' School, Providence, R.I., spending his long vacations in Europe, where he attended the universities of Leipzig, Berlin, Strasbourg, and Freiburg, and obtained his Ph.D. in 1881. After a year's instructorship at Harvard and a period as headmaster of the Swain Free School, New Bedford, Mass., he became professor of English and German at Haverford in 1887, receiving an appointment as professor of English literature in 1909. Gummere remained at Haverford over thirty years, refusing posts at Harvard and the University of Chicago, but lecturing at Northwestern, Johns Hopkins, and the University of California.

Gummere's theory of the origin in group dancing of English and Scottish ballads, drawing analogies to communal dancing in the Faroe Islands, owed something to Hamann, Herder, and Grimm, and was worked out in thorough if not entirely convincing

detail in his *The Popular Ballad,* supplemented by the earlier collection of *Old English Ballads* with its notes and long critical preface. He also contributed the chapter on ballads to the *Cambridge History of English Literature.* In 1907 Gummere suffered a nervous breakdown and lost the use of his right eye; the next year he overtaxed his heart while walking in Virginia, but lived eleven more years, to the age of seventy-four. He married Amelia Smith Mott in September 1882. Gummere's courses at Haverford comprised Shakespeare, Milton, Goethe, popular ballads, and Chaucer. Christopher Morley, whose *The Trojan Horse* stems from the Chaucer course, wrote of Gummere: "To listen to him was a purifying of wit, an enriching of memory, an enabling of judgment, an enlarging of imagination." Gummere was "a man of the rarest and most delicate breeding," one who "moved among all human contacts with unerring grace." His name is pronounced *gum'er-ee.*

PRINCIPAL WORKS: Handbook of Poetics, 1885; Germanic Origins, 1892; Old English Ballads, 1894; The Beginnings of Poetry, 1901; The Popular Ballad, 1907; The Oldest English Epic, 1909; Democracy and Poetry, 1911.

ABOUT: Harvard College Class of 1875: Fiftieth Anniversary Report; Morley, C. Essays; Modern Philology September 1919; Nation July 26, 1919; Philadelphia Press May 31, 1919.

GUNN, NEIL MILLER (November 8, 1891-), Scottish novelist, writes: "Neil M. Gunn was born in Caithness, the most northerly county of Scotland, and his earliest memories center round his father's fishing boats and the tall cliffs, with inland straths and moors for background. There was the village school, but his real education was absorbed as a matter  of joy from his environment, its long hours of independence and freedom, its fishing and hunting, its legends and traditions. At the age of thirteen he went down to Galloway, in the South of Scotland, where he was privately educated for a couple of years. But at the end of that time he grew restless, and, seeing an advertisement for boys in the Civil Service, set off for the given address, passed the examination, and was sent to London, where he found himself facing life on fifteen shillings a week. In two years he saw enough life in that great city to last him for a long time, so he went to Edinburgh for

a change. But after two years there, he decided to go in for a higher post in the Civil Service, which would at once give him more money and take him back to the Highlands. So he studied and passed the examination and got back to the Highlands.

"For that northland would not keep out of his head. And now his job took him for some years all over the Highlands, until he knew the inlets and fishing lochs of the Hebrides as intimately as the cliffs of Caithness. Hunting and fishing, all the local sports and pastimes, were his; and he started writing as an extra pastime—short stories, poetry, essays. His second novel, *Morning Tide,* won a Scottish award, was a choice of the English Book Society, and was successfully translated. His sixth novel, *Highland River,* was awarded the James Tait Black Memorial Prize as the best British novel of 1937. But before that he had thrown up his Civil Service post, bought a boat, and gone to sea with his wife, cruising down the West coast of Scotland.

"This Northern land is in his blood and therefore in his books. Its culture is a very old one and particularly fascinates him because at an early age it managed to hold a fine balance between individual freedom and the duty the individual owes to society. He is an authority on the modern movement called Scottish Nationalism, having taken part in its economic, political, and literary ventures. He is an authority also on Scotch whiskey, and has written a book on the subject. For there is indeed little of his native land that he does not know at first hand."

* * *

Mr. Gunn married Jessie D. Frew in 1921. He is typically Scotch in appearance, tall and rawboned, with aquiline features and dark curly hair. His greatest pleasure still is in sea-boats and fishing, and he loves to "go back to his native village and re-explore the old haunts." Robert Mallory said of him: "His style is distinguished by brilliance and color. He creates images."

PRINCIPAL WORKS: Grey Coast, 1926; Hidden Doors (short stories) 1929; Morning Tide, 1931; The Lost Glen, 1932; Sun Circle, 1933; Butchers Broom, 1934; Whiskey and Scotland (non-fiction) 1935; Highland River, 1937; Off in a Boat (non-fiction) 1938; Wild Geese Overhead, 1939; Second Sight, 1940; The Silver Darlings, 1941.

ABOUT: Bookman April 1931; New York Times Book Review November 9, 1941.

GUNNARSSON, GUNNAR (May 18, 1889-), Icelandic novelist, was born in Valbjófsstaður, in Fljótsdal, Norður Múlasýsla, Iceland, the son of Gunnar H.

and Katrin (Dorarinsdóttir) Gunnarsson, both of old farming families. When he was eight his parents moved to another farm at Ljóttstaðir, Vopnafjörður. Until he was eighteen he went to country schools and helped on the farm, then he went to Denmark to Askov Folk High School, where he studied from 1907 to 1909. At this time he had already published two small collections of poems in Icelandic, which he himself says were "of no importance."

His first Danish publication was also poetry, a volume issued in 1911. He began to attract attention as a writer with his four-volume "Borg" series, covering three generations of an Icelandic farm family such as the one from which he himself sprang. The only one of these so far to be translated into English is *Guest the One-Eyed.* Another series of related novels is *The Church on the Hill,* of which the first two volumes, *Ships in the Sky* and *Night and the Dream,* have appeared in English. These are partly autobiographical, the former being a sensitive portrayal of the fresh, direct mind of a child. Gunnarsson is also celebrated in Denmark (all his later books are in Danish) as an historical novelist, chiefly of the discovery and early days of Iceland: *The Sworn Brothers,* almost an adventure story, belonging to this category. His only other novel so far to appear in English is *Seven Days' Darkness,* a powerful study of the disintegration of a mind through the deliberate malice of a villain.

In 1912 Gunnarsson married Franzisca Jörgensen, and they have two sons. Until 1939 he lived in Denmark; then he bought an old farm near his birthplace, Skriðuklaustur, which is now his home. He has traveled a great deal—eight times to Iceland (via Scotland) from Denmark between 1913 and 1938, frequently to Sweden, Norway, Germany, Switzerland, and Austria, and also to Italy, Portugal, Spain, North Africa, England, Finland, and Russia. He is an honorary professor of the University of Iceland, in Reykjavík, and has an honorary Ph.D. from Heidelberg. He is also a Commander of the Icelandic Falcon and a Knight of Dannebrog, a Danish order.

Gunnarsson is blond, smooth-shaven, wears glasses, has a high scholarly forehead and an habitually rather cynical expression. Indeed, as W. W. Worster says, he sees "life as a tragedy, humanity as the helpless prey of gods that kill us for their sport, or blindly." Some of the authors whom he names as his favorites—Shakespeare, Dickens, Maupassant, Dostoievsky, Hamsun, Lagerlöf, Goethe, "and the unknown writers of the Icelandic sagas"—are those who might be expected to influence a writer of his prevailingly gloomy tone. His other chief weakness, undue repetition, may be traced to the long-winded sagas, originally chanted for illiterate hearers and hence constantly repeating themselves to impress the auditors' memory. On the other hand, Gunnarsson is capable of quiet humor and has a loving concern for the slightest details of natural description; and Julius Clausen says of his historical novels, which he calls "a sort of literary ancestor-worship," that Gunnarsson "has both the epic repose of the saga and its circumstantiality."

PRINCIPAL WORKS AVAILABLE IN ENGLISH. The Sworn Brothers, 1921; Seven Days' Darkness, 1930; Guest the One-Eyed, 1930; Ships in the Sky; Compiled from Uggi Greipsson's Notes, 1938; Night and the Dream, 1938; The Good Shepherd, 1940.

ABOUT: American-Scandinavian Review March 1934; Edinburgh Review October 1923.

GUNTHER, JOHN (August 30, 1901-   ), American newspaper correspondent, writes: "I have devoted myself for twenty years to

writing of some sort or other. My bent has been toward journalism from the beginning. I was a Chicago boy, educated in the public schools there, and I remember writing pieces about the Russian Revolution and so on even when I was in high school. At college (the University of Chicago) I was the literary editor of the campus paper, the *Daily Maroon*. I had several articles published in national magazines like *Smart Set* and the *Bookman* while I was still an undergraduate. I went to Europe for the Chicago *Daily News* in 1924 and worked for the *News* there for twelve years. I had exceptionally good luck in that for a long time I was used as a kind of 'swing man,' taking charge of various bureaus while the senior correspondents were away, and then covering various special news stories in between.

Thus I was at one time or another in charge of *Daily News* offices in London, Berlin, Vienna, Moscow, Rome, and Paris, and I also visited Poland, Spain, the Balkans, and Scandinavia. I have worked in every European country except Portugal. I saw at first hand the whole extraordinary panorama of Europe from 1924 to 1936. I was lucky enough to have a ringside seat for almost the entire spectacle.

"In 1936 I wrote *Inside Europe*, which drew on these experiences. This book has had a striking success all over the world. I was fortunate in that it appeared at just the right time, when the three totalitarian dictators took the stage and people began to be vitally interested in them. *Inside Europe* has been repeatedly revised and republished; the newest edition appeared in February, 1940. It has been translated into fourteen languages, I believe, and its total distribution must be something over 500,000 copies.

"As a serious political journalist I decided even before *Inside Europe* became so widely known to extend my work with an analagous survey of Asia, and so I spent most of 1937 and 1938 traveling in Asia and then writing about it. I am hoping to do a third book of the same general nature about the United States. My basic idea is to attempt to draw a kind of political map or chart of the contemporary American world."

* * *

Since writing the autobiographical sketch above, Mr. Gunther has produced *Inside Latin America*, the result of a short but intensive visit to our Southern neighbors.

Mr. Gunther married Frances Fineman in 1927; they have one son. James E. Abbe called him "a two hundred-pound connoisseur of good food and good liquor, who enjoys European life, with other things secondary to that." That was in 1933, and Mr. Gunther's views have broadened; his work, which began with journalistic travel books, has become much more serious since then.

PRINCIPAL WORKS: The Red Pavilion, 1927; Eden for One, 1927; The Golden Fleece, 1929; The Bright Nemesis, 1932; Inside Europe, 1936; Inside Asia, 1939; Inside Latin America, 1941.

ABOUT: Current History July 1939, January 1940; New York Herald Tribune "Books" April 29, 1942; New York Times Book Review October 26, 1941; Newsweek June 12, 1939; Time June 12, 1939; Wilson Library Bulletin June 1937.

G U S E V (or GUSSIEV). See OREN-BURGSKY

GUTHRIE, THOMAS ANSTEY ("F. Anstey") (August 8, 1856-March 10, 1934), English humorist, fantasist, and playwright,

was born in London, the son of a tailor of the same name. His mother, Augusta Amherst (Austen) Anstey, was an accomplished pianist and copyist. Thomas, the eldest son—he had two brothers and a sister—enjoyed the pleasant childhood of a well-to-do Victorian family and was destined by his father to become a barrister. With that intention he entered Trinity Hall, Cambridge University.

In the spring of 1877 a friend, Walter Frith, started an undergraduate weekly, *The Cambridge Tatler.* Guthrie, combining his eccentric headmaster at school and the magic transformations and exchanges of bodies in W. S. Gilbert's *Bab Ballads,* contributed a serial entitled "Turned Tables." (He signed the work "T. Anstey," and a printer's error made the "T" an "F." Thus originated the pseudonym he used throughout his life—though he never made any secret of the identity behind the signature.) In 1881 he was called to the Bar by the Benchers of his Inn, the Middle Temple. Frith, meanwhile, had given James Payn, reader for the famous publishing firm of Smith & Elder, the manuscript of Guthrie's *Vice Versa,* rewritten from the earlier serial. Heralded by a cordial review by Andrew Lang in the *Saturday Review,* whose verdict in those days carried enormous weight, this story of an elderly, pompous English business man who exchanged bodies with his schoolboy son under the influence of a magic stone, at once became a runaway best-seller, the publishing event of 1882. (Reading it gave Anthony Trollope his fatal paralytic stroke!)

F. C. Burnand invited Guthrie to contribute to *Punch,* and he joined the staff in 1887, to remain off and on until 1930. John Tenniel, George du Maurier, and Charles Keene, among others, were his associates. Henry James, Kipling, Bram Stoker, and the Frederick Lehmanns became his friends. His *Voces Populi,* a series of overheard conversations, proved a popular *Punch* feature before it appeared in book form. *The Man From Blankley's,* also first printed there, made a successful play in England and a farcical talking picture for John

Barrymore in America. *The Brass Bottle,* inspired by Rossetti's *Rose Mary* and Lane's translation of the *Arabian Nights,* was a notable *Strand Magazine* serial in 1899. Its dramatization had 244 performances in England (1909) but ran only a fortnight at the Lyceum Theatre in New York the next year. Except for the pirated editions of *Vice Versa,* "F. Anstey's" work never sold well in America.

Guthrie's most successful and engaging books all had a basis of fantasy. *The Brass Bottle* described the benevolent but ill-advised efforts of a Djinn to enrich the young architect who released him from his bottle; *The Tinted Venus* dealt with an enraged walking statue of Venus; *A Fallen Idol,* with a malevolent image; and *In Brief Authority,* with a bourgeois English family suddenly transferred to the Grimm Brothers' Märchenland. These wild extravagances, says Doris Langley Moore, biographer of E. Nesbit, whose tales of magic somewhat resembled Guthrie's, "are rendered at once plausible and delightfully humorous by being given a realistic setting and a dramatis personae of perfectly normal individuals." The serious novels he attempted, like the three-decker *The Pariah,* were unsuccessful; but the stories of magic (six of them are reprinted in the omnibus *Humour and Fantasy,* 1931) still have their stout adherents. *The Pocket Ibsen* (1895) is also first-rate criticism in the form of parody.

His royalties wisely invested, Guthrie lived a peaceful and happy life, beloved by dogs and children. He never married. Sir J. C. Squire, editor of the late *London Mercury,* testified to the sweetness and serenity of his character. He was of medium stature, and precisely dressed, complete with top-hat and umbrella. He died of pneumonia at seventy-seven, and his ashes were placed in the grave of his friend and brother-in-law, George Millar, in Blatchington churchyard. An autobiography, *A Long Retrospect,* written 1929-1933, was published posthumously in 1936.

PRINCIPAL WORKS: *Novels and Stories*—Vice Versâ: or, A Lesson to Fathers, 1882; The Giant's Robe, 1884; The Black Poodle and Other Tales, 1884; The Tinted Venus, 1885; A Fallen Idol, 1886; The Pariah, 1889; Voces Populi: First Series, 1890, Second Series, 1892; Tourmalin's Time Cheques, 1891; The Talking Horse and Other Tales, 1892; Mr. Punch's Pocket Ibsen, 1893; The Man From Blankley's and Other Sketches, 1893; Love Among the Lions, 1898; The Brass Bottle, 1900; A Bayard From Bengal, 1902; Only Toys, 1903; Salted Almonds, 1906; Percy and Others, 1915; In Brief Authority, 1915; The Last Load, 1925. *Autobiography*—A Long Retrospect, 1936. *Plays*—The Man From Blankley's, 1901; The

Brass Bottle, 1911; Vice Versa, 1911; The Would-Be Gentleman (adaptation from Molière) 1926; The Imaginary Invalid, 1929; Four Molière Comedies (The Miser, A Doctor Perforce, The Learned Ladies, The Misanthrope) 1931; Three Molière Plays (Tartufe, Scapin the Trickster, The School For Wives) 1933.

ABOUT: Guthrie, T. A. A Long Retrospect; Lucas, E. V. Reading, Writing, and Remembering; Turner, M. J. Bibliography of the Works of F. Anstey; London Mercury April 1934.

*GWYNN, STEPHEN LUCIUS (February 13, 1864-), Irish poet, critic, and biographer, writes: "I was born in county Dublin,

son of the Rev. John Gwynn, distinguished as a Biblical Scholar. I was the eldest of eight brothers, mostly conspicuous in various ways. I went to Oxford, took a classical degree (first class), and for ten years was a teacher, but began to contribute prose and verse to periodicals. In 1896 I came to London to live by writing essays, criticism, novels, and some verse—especially on Irish subjects. In 1904 I went to live in Ireland with my family (wife and six children), and in 1906 was elected a Member of Parliament for the city of Galway, as one of Redmond's [Nationalist] party. From then until 1918 my work was chiefly in politics. In 1914 I enlisted and after three months' service as a private was given a commission in the Connaught Rangers. In December 1915 I went to France with the 16th Irish Division, as captain in command of a company. In 1917 I was invalided home after trench fever, and subsequently received the Legion of Honor. After Redmond's death in 1918, when Dillon succeeded to the party leadership, I found myself at odds with his policy and broke with the party. After the war my constituency ceased to exist and I returned to the status of a free lance journalist. Up to 1925 I acted as Irish correspondent of the London Observer, and had to write much that was unpopular about both the actions of the 'Black and Tan' police and the methods used by Irish guerila war. After the formation of the Free State, I backed Mr. Cosgrave's party as strongly as I could, and my house on the outskirts of Dublin was blown up by the 'Irregulars' who supported Mr. de Valera.

"In 1923 I went back to London to re-establish my interrupted literary career. I continued to write a great deal on Irish subjects—history, travel books, fishing sketches, etc.—but other things interested me. Every year I went to France and wrote about that country. Much biography also—largely eighteenth century; and I prepared the Memoirs of Sir Cecil Spring-Rice, and wrote a life of the explorer, Mary Kingsley, which was given a prize as the best biography of the year in which it appeared. I have a weakness for my books on France and also for my Collected Poems and some of my essays, more especially Fond Opinions. In my French excursions I wrote so much about French wines that I was honored with the rank of Officier de l'Instruction Publique. The National University of Ireland recently gave me an honorary D.Litt. degree. I am also a member of the Irish Academy of Letters."

* * *

Mrs. Gwynn is the author's cousin as well as his wife. One of his sons is publisher and editor of the Dublin Review. Since 1932 Stephen Gwynn has been president of the Irish Literary Society. He contributes a regular department to the Fortnightly Review. His home is in Dublin.

PRINCIPAL WORKS: An Eighteenth Century Portrait Painter (Northcote) 1898; The Repentance of a Private Secretary, 1898; Tennyson, 1899; Highways and Byways in Donegal and Antrim, 1899; The Decay of Sensibility, 1900; The Old Knowledge, 1901; The Queen's Chronicler (poetry) 1901; Today and Tomorrow in Ireland, 1902; John Maxwell's Marriage (novel) 1903; Fishing Holidays, 1903; The Masters of English Literature, 1904; Thomas Moore, 1904; The Fair Hills of Ireland, 1906; The Glade in the Forest (novel) 1907; A Holiday in Connemara, 1909; Robert Emmet: An Historical Romance, 1909; The Famous Cities of Ireland, 1916; For Second Reading (essays) 1918; John Redmond's Last Years, 1919; Irish Books and Irish People, 1919; The Irish Situation, 1921; Garden Wisdom, 1921; Collected Poems, 1923; The History of Ireland, 1923; Ireland: A Survey of Historical Forces, 1924; Duffer's Luck (essays) 1924; Experiences of a Literary Man (autobiography) 1926; In Praise of France, 1927; Ireland, 1927; Saints and Scholars, 1929; The Life of Sir Walter Scott, 1930; Burgundy, 1930; The Life of Horace Walpole, 1932; Mary Kingsley, 1932; Life and Friendships of Dean Swift, 1933; Claude Monet and His Garden, 1934; Mungo Park, 1934; Ireland in Ten Days, 1935; Life of Oliver Goldsmith, 1935; Irish Literature and Drama, 1936; The Happy Fisherman, 1936; From River to River, 1937; Fond Opinions, 1938; Dublin Old and New, 1938; Henry Grattan and His Times, 1939; Robert Louis Stevenson, 1939; Scattering Branches (ed.) 1940; Salute to Valour (verse) 1941.

ABOUT: Gwynn, S. Experiences of a Literary Man.

* Died June 11, 1950.

HABBERTON, JOHN. See "AMERI-
CAN AUTHORS: 1600-1900"

HACKER, LOUIS MORTON (March 17,
1899-), American historian, writes: "I
was born in New York City, the son of
immigrant p a r e n t s
both of whom had
been born in Austria
and who had come to
this country in their
teens. T h e y were
b o t h needle-t r a d e
w o r k e r s and were
quickly sucked into
the sweat-shop indus-
tries of New York.
When I was about
ten my father became a small storekeeper
and continued so until the enterprise folded
up years later. I was therefore brought up
in a lower middle class environment in a
populous city, with the limitations of such
a boyhood. I went to the New York public
schools, played on the city streets, and did
not see the country until I was thirteen.
In fact, I never ventured far from the
parental roof until I was twenty, when I
went to Illinois for a short stay.

"I went to the Brooklyn Boys' High
School and attended Columbia from 1916
to 1918, serving a few months in the
S.A.T.C. At college, I was stimulated most
by Charles A. Beard and Benjamin B.
Kendrick, and I became interested in the
writing of American history. In fact, I followed Beard to the Bureau of Municipal
Research for a year from 1918. Return
to college was out of the question, so I
worked at a variety of jobs, meanwhile continuing my studies sporadically at night.

"In 1921 I married Lillian Lewis, and
thanks to her encouragement and assistance
(for by that time my wife was teaching in
the public schools) I was able to go back to
college. In 1922 I was extraordinarily
fortunate: I won a nation-wide competition
conducted by the Knights of Columbus with
an essay entitled 'The Genesis of the Inter-
state Commerce Act.' The $500 I received
helped me pay off some heavy debts and
continue my schooling. I received my B.A.
from Columbia in 1922 and my M.A. there
also in 1923.

"My first real job followed my graduation; for Frank Moore Colby, who was
editor of the *New International Encyclopaedia*, hired me as an assistant. Colby
was a great and understanding man; he gave
me his friendship and also my head. I

learned to write on that job; for, as an
average daily chore, I turned out 1,500
words on everything and anything—history,
politics, public administration, geography
and the like. This went on for almost two
years.

"After that I got lost somehow. I was
unemployed for a long time and then was
compelled to take an office job which paid
me well enough but drove me deeper and
deeper into a blind alley. Fortunately, I was
able to keep my hand in at writing, for
every year I turned out 50,000 words for
the *New International Year Book* on a
curious miscellany of subjects. My first
child, a son, was born in August 1929 (later
we had a daughter) ; at the end of the year
I quit my job. Harry Elmer Barnes and
B. B. Kendrick had got me to write a history
of the United States since the Civil War,
and without a contract or funds I started
out. Fortunately, a fine friend helped me
a little; my wife did odd jobs; a good part
of the time we simply did without. In 1930,
when the larder was entirely bare, Henry
L. Mencken took three articles from me
(naturally I was entirely unknown to him)
for the *American Mercury*, and Suzanne
LaFollette, who had revived the *Freeman*
as the *New Freeman*, took three more. In
less than eighteen months—such are the
urgencies and confidences of youth—I wrote
(doing the research at the same time) a
manuscript of more than 400,000 words.
B. B. Kendrick helped me whip it into shape
and in 1932 it was published as *The United
States Since 1865*, under the joint authorship of Kendrick and myself. The book
reflects my background and training—Beard
is writ large all over it—and I have incorporated into it a sympathy for the common
man (from whom I myself sprang and who
has built America).

"The other writings now followed fast,
for I was able to keep going as a free-lance
with occasional odd jobs. In 1935 I got
my first regular job in almost six years when
I began to teach at Columbia. I have continued to teach there, as well as at the
University of Wisconsin and Ohio State University. At the present time I am committed
to the writing of three new books, two of
which are already in progress.

"I have written several millions of words,
been paid for almost all of them, and yet I
have come to the conclusion that the hardest
job in the world is the complete earning of
a livelihood from the pen.

"My orientation is plain: emotionally, I
am committed to the American way of life—

for I am more and more impressed by the truly democratic spirit, the friendliness, the hardheaded, pragmatic qualities of the typical American. But I feel that our civilization is in process of transformation; it is becoming more and more collectivized, with the authority of the central state increasingly powerful. This is the leading question of our time: how to permit collectivization to continue and at the same time hold in check the growth of a state bureaucracy. In America, I feel that it can and will be done: so that the long-term outlook, as I see it, is not dark.

"Intellectually, my greatest debts are to the men of the Enlightenment and those people who brought that spirit into American culture—Jefferson, Emerson, Dewey, Veblen, Parrington, Beard. In my special field—historical writing—I seek to follow in the tradition of the great historical sociologists—Marx, Sombart, Weber, Perienne, Sée. I write economic history, never losing sight, however, of the close links between politics and economic development. To that extent, history is a philosophic discipline."

PRINCIPAL WORKS: The United States Since 1865 (with B. B. Kendrick) 1932; The Farmer Is Doomed, 1933; A Short History of the New Deal, 1934; The United States: A Graphic History, 1937; American Problems of Today, 1938; The Triumph of American Capitalism, 1940.

ABOUT: Civic Leader December 7, 1936.

HACKETT, FRANCIS (January 21, 1883-   ), Irish-American critic, biographer, and novelist, was born in Kilkenny, one

of the numerous children of John Byrne Hackett, M.D., and Bridget (Doheny) Hackett. Hackett was "not born a liberal," he states in the autobiographical *I Chose Denmark* (1940). "I [was] born a myopic, astigmatic, fatty, apprehensive bundle of human expectancy." One brother became an army doctor and another a Jesuit priest. Francis Hackett was educated at Clongowes Wood College, Kildare, and came to the United States at eighteen. In 1902 he made a connection with a law firm in New York City as office-boy at $3.50 a week, and from 1906 to 1909 was an editorial writer on the Chicago *Evening Post*. For the next two years he edited the weekly literary review of the paper, in "a spirited, liberal vein," according to a colleague, Harry

Hansen. Another, Burton Rascoe, writes: "The literary page of the Chicago *Evening Post* was already an intellectual institution when I arrived in Chicago. It had been created by Francis Hackett, an immigrant from Ireland, whose prose had such freshness and power and his information had been so wide and his untutored learning so great that he was called to New York as literary critic for the *New Republic* when that magazine was established in 1912."

While in Chicago Hackett also taught classes at Jane Addams' Hull House. Once he gave up a $40-a-week job to write a compendium called *Beauty and Health*, living in an unheated house on Superior Street in a dollar-a-week room. Hackett remained with the *New Republic* from 1914 to 1922. In 1918 he married Signe Toksvig, who had come down from Cornell to work on *Vogue*, and had been sent to Frank Crowninshield to see Herbert Croly of the *New Republic* about a position, which she was given. Two years after their marriage the Hacketts paid their first visit to Denmark, her native land. The year of his marriage Hackett published two books, one a study of his native isle, and *Horizons*, a collection of book reviews. "When I left Chicago I thought, indeed, that I had done with book reviewing," Hackett wrote by way of preface. "I had slipped into the trade without any apprenticeship, drawn by love of it; I left it because it seemed like writing in water. But one's past is the parent of one's future: I returned to it in 1914. . . . I do not propose to defer to the current American superstition that pedantry is the equivalent of ideas." *The Invisible Censor* (1920) was another volume of critical essays, *That Nice Young Couple* (1924), a triangle novel, received rather mixed notices.

In 1929 the Book-of-the-Month Club in New York sent its subscribers Hackett's *Henry the Eighth: A Personal History*, on which he had been working for years. "Henry shall be finished if the gasoline holds out," he promised his publishers once from the South of France. The actual writing of the book was done in his little house by the sea in Ireland. Robert Morss Lovett called it "a work of scholarship alive with imagination and gorgeously apparelled in style." Leonard Woolf complained, apropos of this same style, that Hackett occasionally "forces the pace madly and maddeningly, and tries to write much better than he or anyone else can." *Queen Anne Boleyn* (1938), the book's companion-piece, is cast in the form of fiction, although taking but few liberties with the biographical and historical facts concerning Henry's queen and Elizabeth's hapless mother.

When Hackett's novel *The Green Lion* (1936) and his wife's *Eve's Doctor* were prohibited by government censors in Ireland, they left the island on the anniversary of Parnell's death and went to live in Hellerup, a section of Copenhagen. Hackett found so much to admire in Denmark that he wrote his book about it, finishing it at Martha's Vineyard, Mass., in the summer of 1940; he had come to the United States the previous December to see about the production of a play about Anne Boleyn, and the Nazi invasion of Denmark prevented his return. He was later reported living in the Virgin Islands. Hackett left the Catholic church long ago. "My bias was to be outside all regimentations and standardizations, all totalities, all absolutes." Physically he is rugged, with thick curling hair.

PRINCIPAL WORKS: Ireland: A Study in Nationalism, 1918; Horizons, 1918; The Invisible Censor, 1920; The Story of the Irish Nation, 1922; That Nice Young Couple (novel) 1924; Henry the Eighth, 1929; Francis the First, 1934; The Green Lion (novel) 1936; Queen Anne Boleyn (novel) 1938; I Chose Denmark, 1940; What "Mein Kampf" Means to America, 1941.

ABOUT: Dell, F. Homecoming; Hackett, F. I Chose Denmark; Hansen, H. Midwest Portraits; Rascoe, B. Before I Forget.

"HADDON, CHRISTOPHER." See "BEEDING, F."

HAGEDORN, HERMANN

(July 18, 1882-), American poet, novelist, and biographer, was born in New York City, the son of Hermann and Anna (Schwedler) Hagedorn, was educated at the Hill School, Pottstown, Pa., and received a degree of B.A. from Harvard in 1907. The next year was spent traveling in Switzerland with a classmate, Wilder Goodwin, author of some novels, and attending the winter session of the University of Berlin. He returned to marry Dorothy Oakley of Englewood, N.J., in June 1908—they have a son and two daughters—and attend Columbia for a year. After instructing in English (1909-11) at Harvard, where he was assistant to Barrett Wendell and gave a course in composition of his own, Hagedorn moved his family to California for a while, bought a farm in Connecticut, and wrote two novels which he dismisses as "formless and jejune." The First World War made him somewhat guiltily conscious of his Germanic blood.

With Porter Emerson Browne, Julian Street, and Charles Hanson Towne, he founded The Vigilantes, which was designed to train boys for citizenship, but served recruiting purposes in the war. He was later ashamed of "silly chants and little hymns of hate." Meantime Hagedorn had became well known as an occasional poet. Poems read at Harvard from 1907 to 1937 are collected in *This Darkness and This Light* (1938). Meeting Theodore Roosevelt during the war, he became deeply attached to his personality, and after the death of Roosevelt was chiefly instrumental in organizing the Roosevelt Memorial Association, of which he was secretary and executive director. Later Hagedorn spent three years at the Library of Congress in preparation for writing a two-volume biography of Leonard Wood, Roosevelt's crony and *protégé*. As director and vice-president of the Edward MacDowell Association he studied Edwin Arlington Robinson at close range at the Peterborough, N.H., colony, and wrote a eulogistic biography of the poet. His own poetry is melodious and conventional. In recent years Hagedorn has been active in the Oxford Group, and is now organizer and director in the National Rededication Movement. A dark, slim, handsome man, Hagedorn has found life "complex, disturbing, somewhat exhausting, a bit harrowing, romantic and beautiful beyond belief."

PRINCIPAL WORKS: The Woman of Corinth, 1908; Poems and Ballads, 1912; Faces in the Dawn (novel) 1914; Makers of Madness (play) 1914; The Great Maze and The Heart of Youth, 1916; You Are the Hope of the World, 1917; Barbara Picks a Husband (novel) 1918; The Boys' Life of Theodore Roosevelt, 1918; Roosevelt in the Bad Lands, 1921; Ladders Through the Blue (poems) 1925; Dreams of Zach Peters, 1925; The Rough Riders (novel) 1927; The Book of Courage, 1929; Leonard Wood: A Biography, 1931; The Magnate: A Biography of William Boyce Thompson, 1935; Brookings; A Biography, 1936; Edwin Arlington Robinson, 1938; This Darkness and This Light: Harvard Poems (1907-1937) 1938; Combat at Midnight, 1940; The Bugle That Woke America, 1940. *Editor*—Fifes and Drums, 1917; The Americanism of Theodore Roosevelt, 1923; Memorial Edition of the Writings of Theodore Roosevelt, 1923-1925.

ABOUT: Baldwin, C. C. The Men Who Make Our Novels; Harvard College, Class of 1907: Twenty-Fifth Anniversary Report.

HAGGARD, Sir HENRY RIDER

(June 22, 1856-May 14, 1925), English romancer, was born at Bradenham, Norfolk, the son of William Meybohm Rider Haggard and Ella (Doveton) Haggard. He was educated at the Ipswich Grammar School, with frequent journeys to the Continent

during his childhood and youth. At nineteen he went to South Africa as secretary to the governor of Natal. Two years later, in 1877, when the Transvaal was annexed by Great Britain, he was on the staff of the special commissioner, and was made Master of the High Court at Pretoria. In 1879 he resigned to take up ostrich farming. In 1880 he returned to England to be married to Mariana Margitson, then returned to his ostrich farm with his wife.

In 1881 the Transvaal was re-ceded to the Dutch, and Haggard came back to England and read for the bar. In 1884 he became a barrister in London, but was never very active in his profession. He had begun writing with a privately published novel in 1882, and with *King Solomon's Mines,* in 1885, he met with such success that he was assured of financial independence and abandoned the law altogether.

Politics interested him, for he was a strong Imperialist and was regarded as an authority on the empire and colonialism, but he was unsuccessful in a candidacy for Parliament, and the only elective office he ever held was that of chairman of the bench of magistrates at Ditchingham, Norfolk, where he lived. What meant most to him, and what earned for him numerous official honors, was not his novels (which he wrote hurriedly, he claimed, merely, as a source of income) but agriculture and the condition of the farmer and rural worker. It was for his writings in this field (which he considered his real claim to celebrity) that he was knighted in 1912 and was made Knight Commander of the Order of the British Empire in 1919. Labor colonies, colonial emigration, and kindred topics were his special field. Walter Tittle, who drew his picture in 1922, described him as "very tall, angular, huge of frame," and said he looked "like a capable farmer."

Yet his novels were more to him, in spite of his avowals, than pot-boilers. He would not otherwise have named his three daughters after three of his heroines. He might be prouder that a mountain and a glacier in Canada were called after him, but the unabating spontaneity and enthusiasm with which he poured out fiction at the rate of a book every year or oftener indicate that another side of his nature was deeply satisfied by the fashioning of these romantic tales of adventure and mystery. When he died at sixty-eight, in London, he had published more than forty novels, and several more were issued posthumously.

These novels of Rider Haggard, "mildly derided by literary critics, deplored sometimes by parents and teachers and librarians," nevertheless are among the best yarns of their sort. They belong in the same category, in a sense, as the works of Jules Verne and Dumas *père*—works of fiction written for adults but for the most part devoured by adolescents. Their heroines are all beautiful, their heroes brave and strong, and something happens every minute. There is not a dull page in them, any more than there is the slightest cerebration. They are pure novels of action. But the African ones particularly are based on first-hand observation, and they have served to make strange parts of the world less strange to three generations of avid readers. No one who has read them is likely to forget *She* ("She who must be obeyed"), or *King Solomon's Mines,* or *Montezuma's Daughter.* Perhaps no one was ever especially improved by reading a Haggard novel, but neither was anyone ever injured by it, or (what is more important) ever bored. *She* especially has become a classic of its kind, and has passed into the vocabulary of many who have never even read the book.

PRINCIPAL WORKS: *Novels*—Cetywayo and His White Neighbors, 1882; Dawn, 1884; The Witch's Head, 1885; King Solomon's Mines, 1885; She, 1887; Allan Quatermain, 1887; Maiwa's Revenge, 1888; Allan's Wife, 1889; Beatrice, 1890; Eric Brighteyes, 1891; Nada the Lily, 1892; Montezuma's Daughter, 1894; The People of the Mist, 1894; Heart of the World, 1896; Swallow: A Story of the Great Trek, 1899; Black Heart and White Heart, 1900; Lysbeth: A Tale of the Dutch, 1901; Pearl Maiden, 1903; Stella Fregelius, 1903; Ayesha: The Return of She, 1905; Fair Margaret, 1907; The Ghost Kings, 1908; The Yellow God, 1909; Queen Sheba's Ring, 1910; Red Eve, 1911; Child of Storm, 1912; The Wanderer's Necklace, 1914; Allan and the Holy Flower, 1915; The Ivory Child, 1916; Moon of Israel, 1918; When the World Shook, 1919; The Ancient Allan, 1920; She and Allan, 1921; The Virgin of the Sun, 1922; Queen of the Dawn, 1925; Treasure of the Lake, 1926; Marion Isle (in England, Mary of Marion Isle), 1929; Belshazzar, 1930. *Miscellaneous*—A History of the Transvaal, 1899; A Farmer's Year, 1899; A Winter Pilgrimage, 1901; Rural England, 1902; A Gardener's Year, 1905; The Poor and the Land, 1905; Regeneration, 1910; Rural Denmark and Its Lessons, 1911; The Days of My Life, 1926.

ABOUT: Haggard, R. The Days of My Life; Mansfield, K. Novels and Novelists; Bookman (London) November 1926; Century May 1923;

Edinburgh Review October 1926; English Review January 1920; Living Age March 6, 1920; London Mercury November 1924; Outlook May 27, 1925.

HALDANE, JOHN BURDON SANDERSON (November 5, 1892-), English biologist who signs his works as J. B. S.

Haldane, writes: "I was born at Oxford. My father was Professor John Scott Haldane, the physiologist. [His uncle was Viscount Haldane, the statesman and philosopher; his sister, Naomi Mitchison, the novelist.] I was educated at Eton and New College, Oxford. I learned much of my science by apprenticeship, assisting my father from the age of eight onwards, and my university degree is for classics, not science. I was in a British infantry battalion from 1914 to 1919, and was twice wounded. I began scientific research in 1910, and became a Fellow of New College, Oxford, in 1919. I was at Cambridge from 1922 to 1932 as Reader in Biochemistry, and have been professor first of physiology, then of biometry, in London University since 1933. I was visiting professor in the University of California in 1932. In the same year I was elected a Fellow of the Royal Society of London.

"My scientific work has been varied. In the field of human physiology I am best known for my work on the effects of taking large amounts of ammonium chloride and ether salts. This has had some application in treating lead and radium poisoning. In the field of genetics I was the first to discover linkage in mammals, to map a human chromosome, and (with Penrose) to measure the mutation rate of a human gene. I have also made some minor discoveries in mathematics.

"Whilst I may have been a credit to my universities, I have been a trial in other ways. I was dismissed from Cambridge University in 1926 in connection with a divorce case, but regained my post on appeal to a higher tribunal, which found that the university authorities had decided to dismiss me without hearing my case. At present [1940] I have refused to evacuate University College, London, and, with two assistants, am its sole academic occupant. I am carrying on research there under difficulties.

"Besides strictly scientific books I have written a number of popular works, including a book of children's stories. I consider that a scientist, if he can do so, should help to render science intelligible to ordinary people, and have done my best to popularize it.

"Till 1933 I tried to keep out of politics, but the support given by the British Government to Hitler and Mussolini forced me to enter the political field. In 1936 I spent three months in Republican Spain, first as an adviser on gas protection, and then as an observer of air raid precautions. I was at the front line during fighting, and in several air raids behind the line. Since then I have tried, with complete lack of success, to induce the British Government to adopt air raid protection measures which had proved their efficacy in Spain.

"Mr. Chamberlain's policy, and recent developments in physics and biology, combined to convince me of the truth of the Marxist philosophy. Though I am a member of no political party, I have of late years supported the Communist Party on a number of issues. At present I am engaged on research in genetics, on research intended to save the lives of members of the British armed forces, and on writing and public speaking designed to prevent the spreading of the present war, and if possible to bring about peace. I am a fairly competent public speaker.

"I have been married to Charlotte Franken, a writer, for fourteen years; measure six feet one-inch, weigh 245 pounds; and enjoy swimming and mountain walking. I am bald and blue-eyed, with a clipped moustache; a moderate drinker and a heavy smoker. I can read eleven languages and make public speeches in three, but am unmusical."

* * *

Professor Haldane is a "burly, tweedy, shaggy man," who says he is dogmatic but is actually a delightfully witty talker, forthright and informal. His remarkably large head caused Sir Arthur Keith, the celebrated anthropologist, to induce Haldane to will it to him if he should predecease Keith. Haldane is noted for his willingness to serve as "his own chief guinea pig" in all sorts of hazardous scientific experiments. In addition to the academic distinctions he lists, he was president of the Genetical Society from 1932 to 1936, and is a Chevalier of the Legion of Honor. In the spring of 1942 he was reported from London to have applied for formal membership in the Communist party.

PRINCIPAL WORKS: Daedalus: or, Science and the Future, 1924; Callinicus: A Defense of Chemical Warfare, 1925; The Last Judgment, 1927; Animal Biology (with J. S. Huxley) 1927; Possible Worlds and Other Essays, 1927; Science and Ethics, 1928; Enzymes, 1930; The Inequality of Man and Other Essays, 1932; Science and Human Life, 1933; The Causes of Evolution, 1933; Fact and Faith, 1934; Science and the Supernatural (with A. Lunn) 1935; Scientific Progress (with others) 1936; My Friend Mr. Leakey (juvenile) 1937; The Marxist Philosophy and the Sciences, 1938; A.R.P. [Air Raid Protection] 1938; Science and You, 1939; Science in Peace and War, 1940; New Paths in Genetics, 1941.

ABOUT: Dublin Review July 1928; Nation July 23, 1930; News Week January 22, 1940; Time March 13, 1939; Wilson Library Bulletin May 1929.

HALL, GEORGE BIRBECK NORMAN.
See "BRITISH AUTHORS OF THE 19TH CENTURY"

HALL, GRANVILLE STANLEY (February 1, 1844-April 24, 1924), American psychologist and university president, was

born on his grandfather's farm in Ashfield, Mass., the son of Granville Bascom Hall, a descendant of Elder William Brewster, and Abigail (Beals) Hall, a descendant of John Alden. Experiences in a country school made young Hall cognizant of the depths of corruption possible in adolescent human nature, and of the strains and stresses of the period of adolescence, which he called one "of great temporary plasticity." He graduated from Williams College in 1867 with Phi Beta Kappa ranking; studied psychology in Germany; and received the degree of B.D. in 1871 from Union Theological Seminary in New York City. After experience as a pastor in Cowdesport, Pa., and as tutor in the family of Jesse Seligman, the banker, Hall spent four years as professor of psychology at Antioch College, Ohio, from 1872 to 1876. In 1878 Hall received his Ph.D. from Harvard, where he studied psychology, then a budding science, with William James. On a second trip to Germany, Hall married Cornelia Fisher in Berlin, in 1879, and kept house in Leipzig next door to Gustav Fechner, the founder of modern psychology, studying also with the experimental psychologist Wilhelm Wundt and with Karl Friedrich Ludwig, the physiologist.

Back in the United States, the Halls lived in Somerville, Mass., and he lectured a Harvard for five dollars a course. John Hopkins called him in 1881 as professor o psychology. Jonas Clark, a retired merchan of Worcester, Mass., decided in 1888 to per petuate his name with a university. Hall whom A. E. Hamilton has called the fathe of Clark University and the chief agen after Eliot and Gilman in revolutionizin higher education, was given free rein here and from 1892 to 1900, when Clark died, a salary of $28,000 a year. Clark's will pro vided for an undergraduate college, bu made no provision for Hall, whose inde pendent attitude and unconventionality al ways made him numerous enemies. He re signed in 1920. Lorine Pruette, one of Hall' students and now a well-known practicin psychologist, called him the Playboy o Western Scholarship, "a fierce old dictator.'

He founded and edited the *American Jour nal of Psychology* in 1887, edited the *Journa of Race Development* after 1910, and th *Journal of Applied Psychology* after 1917 The two-volume *Adolescence* of 1904 is hi best-known work. Hall "never evolved mor than the barest rudiments of a system o psychology," but was called the pioneer an prophet of a young and growing science, it most influential and enthusiastic propagand ist. A "thin, fine old figure of indisputabl presence," G. Stanley Hall succumbed a eighty to heart-failure after a two-day sieg with pneumonia, and was survived by a son Dr. Robert G. Hall, an Oregon children' specialist. (The first Mrs. Hall died in 1890 nine years later Hall married Florence E Smith of Newton, Mass.) In his writin and practice Hall had well served "handi capped, adult-ridden youth." His "genera psychonomic law" held that the child an the race are the key each to the other.

PRINCIPAL WORKS: Aspects of German Culture, 1881; The Contents of Children's Minds on Entering School, 1894; Adolescence, 1904; Youth: Its Education and Regimen, 1906; Educational Problems, 1911; Jesus the Christ in the Light of Psychology, 1917; Morale, 1920; Recreations of a Psychologist, 1920; Senescence, 1922; Life and Confessions of a Psychologist, 1923.

ABOUT: Clark, G. S. Life and Confessions o a Psychologist; Pruette, L. G. Stanley Hall: A Biography of a Mind, 1926; Wilson, L. N. G Stanley Hall; American Mercury July 1924 National Academy of Sciences of the U.S.A. Biographical Memoirs 1929; New York Time April 25, 29, 1924; Psychological Review Marc 1925.

"HALL, HOLWORTHY." See POR-
TER, H. E.

*HALL, JAMES NORMAN (April 22,
1887-   ), American man of letters, writes:
'James Norman Hall was born at Colfax,
Iowa. He attended the

public schools of his
home town and en-
tered Grinnell Col-
lege, graduating with
the class of 1910.
From 1910 to 1914 he
was engaged in social
work, in Boston, as
agent for the Society
for the Prevention of
Cruelty to Children.
In August 1914 he joined Lord Kitchener's
Volunteer Army, the First Hundred Thous-
and, enlisting as a private in the 9th Battalion Royal Fusiliers. He served with this
unit as a machine gunner, in France, during
the spring, summer, and early winter of
1915-16, and took part in the Battle of Loos.
Having obtained his release from the British
Army, he re-enlisted October 1916, in the
Aviation Division of the French Foreign
Legion, as a member of the Lafayette Flying Corps, and after his period of training
went to the front as a member of the Escadrille Lafayette (Spad 124). When, later,
the Escadrille Lafayette was incorporated
into the American Air Service, as Pursuit
Squadron 193, he was commissioned as captain and transferred to the 94th Pursuit
Squadron, U.S.A.S. He was shot down behind the German lines in May 1918 and
remained a prisoner in Germany during the
last six months of the war.

"After his release from the army in March
1919, he spent some months in the United
States, and in January 1920 set out for the
island of Tahiti, in French Oceania, where
he has since lived, engaged in literary work
of various kinds. He is married and has
two children, a son and a daughter. Sometimes he writes to provide his family's bread
and butter and sometimes for his own pleasure.

"He belongs to an Anarchist party with
an enrollment of one member."

* * *

Mr. Hall, tall, lean, and saturnine in appearance, but described as a paragon of
amiability and affability, is half of the writing team of Nordhoff and Hall, though he
has also written books without collaboration.
He and Charles Nordhoff,[qv] who had been
with him in the Lafayette Escadrille, went

to Tahiti together. In 1923, for a complete
change of climate, he went to Iceland to
spend the autumn and winter. After that he
lived continuously in Tahiti for many years,
though at the present writing he makes his
home at Sausalito, Calif. which he loves and
refuses to leave again.

In 1925 Mr. Hall was married to Sarah
Winchester, half-Tahitian daughter of a
British sea captain. He is an ardent mountain climber, and once a year traveled around
Tahiti on a bicycle. He says that formerly
he was "an amateur on the ocarina," the
so-called "musical sweet potato" (shown in
the accompanying portrait). He loves music,
and has a large collection of classical records,
but abhors jazz and swing. After the great
success of their books, especially *Mutiny on
the Bounty*, both Nordhoff and Hall were
pestered by tourists, and since Hall is unable
to be severe except in writing (where he is
"a master of subtle invective"), he was
forced to hide out whenever a ship was in
port. He says: "It seems indecent for a man
to be as content with life as I am.... I have
irrevocably lost ... social- and political-mindedness."

Nordhoff and Hall in their collaborations
work very closely together. Often a single
paragraph will be made up of sentences by
both hands. They say the hardest part of
their joint books to make satisfactory is the
beginning. In his own capacity, Mr. Hall is a
skillful writer of light verse and, to quote
James McConnaughey, "one of the most
delightful of living essayists."

PRINCIPAL WORKS: *With Charles Nordhoff—*
The Lafayette Flying Corps, 1920; Faery Lands
of the South Seas, 1921; Falcons of France, 1929;
Mutiny on the Bounty (in England: Mutiny!)
1932; Men Against the Sea, 1933; Pitcairn's Island, 1934; The Hurricane, 1936; The Dark River,
1938; No More Gas, 1940; Botany Bay, 1941; Men
Without Country, 1942. *Individual Works—*Kitchener's Mob, 1916; High Adventure, 1918; On the
Stream of Travel, 1926; Mid-Pacific, 1928; Flying
With Chaucer, 1930; Mother Goose Land (juvenile) 1930; The Tale of a Shipwreck, 1935; The
Friends, 1939; Dr. Dogbody's Leg, 1940.

ABOUT: Atlantic Monthly April 1926, Septem-
ber 1932; Bookman May 1932; Literary Digest
February 22, 1936; New York Times Book Re-
view August 18, 1940; Saturday Evening Post
April 23, 1938; Saturday Review of Literature
September 9, 1933, September 28, 1940.

HALL, JOSEF WASHINGTON ("Up-
ton Close"), (February 27, 1894-   ), American traveler, historian, and lecturer, was
born in Kelso, Wash., the son of Joseph and
Lina (Ganty) Hall. He was graduated
from George Washington University, in
1915. In the year following he became
investigating officer for the United States

Government in Shantung, a post which he held for three years. Out of this very unquiet period came his first book, *In the Land of the Laughing Buddha* (1925), wherein he observed that "a white barbarian may be *in* the Chinese world but he never becomes *of* it. He may be an onlooker, an adviser, or a highly flattered lackey, but he never becomes more than the utensil of the more cunning and sophisticated Chinese mind." He contended that the Republic was, to the Chinese themselves, never more than a "sham," which by their wit they have "elevated . . . into a farce at least. . . ."

On one occasion he had sent *sub rosa*, a number of Japanese invasion stories to a friend, John B. Powell, editor of the *China Weekly Review* in Shanghai. To let Powell know where he was he put the words "Up Close" at the end of the dispatch; these evolved easily into "Upton Close"; and the name never left him.

Subsequently, he was made chief of foreign affairs under Wu Pei-fu. In the path of a dangerous epidemic he contracted a fever, but was fortunate enough to get satisfactory care in an "ancient and cockroachy hospital tucked away in the grounds of the German legation." He took part, somewhat later, in several National Geographic Society explorations.

In 1926 Hall collaborated with Dr. Herbert Henry Gowen on an *Outline History of China*; a year later he produced another study of Far East revolt and a novel. In 1929 he published a collection of well-informed "unadorned sketches" (*Eminent Asians*), written from a variety of sources ranging from the obscurest of languages to the simplest of table-talk. He had, he said, seen the "reading of a Chinese lyric do more to remove the blindness that threatens to destroy our world than an entire course of sermons against race prejudice." His other books include *The Challenge Behind the Face of Japan* (1934) and a novel, *Son of Mine* (1936).

"Upton Close" was married in 1915 to Nettie Lipkaman, of Denver, Colo.; they have four children. For almost twenty years he has been a public lecturer. One need no longer be apologetic, he says, about "a business with three million customers." The radio, he says, makes people want to

talk back; but they have to attend a forum to do it. Nothing, therefore, he believes, has given lecturing a greater impetus than radio. He is heard regularly on the air as N.B.C. news reporter from the Pacific coast.

PRINCIPAL WORKS: In the Land of the Laughing Buddha, 1924; Outline History of China (with H. H. Gowen) 1925; The Revolt of Asia, 1927; Moonlady, 1927; Eminent Asians, 1929; Challenge Behind the Face of Japan, 1934; Son of Mine, 1936.

ABOUT: Hall, J. W. In the Land of the Laughing Buddha; Hall, J. W. Behind the Face of Japan; American Mercury January, November 1940, April 1941; Living Age June and August 1940; Saturday Review of Literature January 13, 1940.

HALL, LELAND (July 20, 1883-), American musician and miscellaneous writer, was born in Malden, Mass., the son of Osborn Boylston Hall and Lydia Abbott (Lord) Hall. He attended Hopkinson's School in Boston, and then continued in logical succession to Harvard, where he received the degree of B.A. in 1905. Hall's master's degree was obtained at

the University of Wisconsin in 1912, at the end of two years as teacher of music and history. From 1913 to 1917 he lectured at Columbia, and from 1920 to 1922 at Harvard and Radcliffe. From 1914 to 1917 he had edited *The Art of Music,* leaving in 1918 for a period with the American Red Cross in France. Hall's left eye is defective; with his right eye he "saw a little between Montfaucon and Varennes, but it wasn't pretty." Since 1930 he has been professor of music at Smith College, Northampton, Mass. "The Lord made me a musician, and in spite of all my efforts at reconstruction, I still remain one." *Listeners' Music* (1937) is a book which discusses rhythm, tempo, melody and harmony for the amateur musician, employing a minimum of technical terms.

Salah and His American, the book on which Leland Hall's reputation as a writer chiefly rests, first appeared serially in *Asia,* and is a thoughtful, charmingly written study of a Negro, a former slave, who was his personal servant at Marrakesh in Morocco, where Hall had gone to study Arabic. After seeing to it that Salah was taught an occupation, he indulged in some speculation as to the relative desirability of the state of slavery and the privilege of competing for a livelihood in the modern world. Professor Hall has traveled in Cornwall, France, Morocco, and the French Sudan. The United States has given him two shocks, "the betrayal of Woodrow Wilson by his countrymen and the execution of Sacco and Vanzetti." He is bald, bespectacled, and somewhat professorial in appearance.

PRINCIPAL WORKS: Sinister House, 1919; Timbuctoo, 1927; Salah and His American, 1934; They Seldom Speak, 1936; Listeners' Music, 1937.

ABOUT: Harvard College, Class of 1905; Twenty-Fifth Anniversary Report.

*HALL, RADCLYFFE (188?-), English novelist and poet, was born in Bournemouth, Hampshire, the daughter of Radclyffe Radclyffe-Hall, and was christened Marguerite Radclyffe Hall. She was educated at King's College, London, and in Germany, and began her literary career by writing verses, collected into four volumes of poetry. Many of them were set to music, notably The Blind Ploughman, set by Coningsby Clarke, and several others by Coleridge-Taylor, Liza Lehmann, Amy Woodeforde-Finden, Mrs. George Batten, etc. In 1924 Radclyffe Hall published two novels, The Forge and The Unlit Lamp. The latter was the first of her works of fiction to treat of inverted love, and was three years in the writing. William Heinemann, her publisher, had read some of her short stories and suggested that she could easily write novels.

Adam's Breed (1926), the story of a sensitive Italian restaurant-keeper, was awarded the Femina-Vie Heureuse prize and the James Tait Black Memorial Book Prize for that year, and in 1930 also received the gold medal of the Eichelbergher Humane Award. In 1928, against the advice of some of her friends, Radclyffe Hall published The Well of Loneliness, a long and intensely earnest novel whose theme was the attachment between a young girl and an older woman. It soon ran afoul of British censorship. A London magistrate, Sir Chartres Biron, ruled that although the book was dignified and restrained in manner, it presented an appeal for the recognition by "decent people" that sexual inversion exists and is not the fault of the person who suffers from it; therefore he judged the book an obscene libel and ordered all copies of it destroyed. John S. Sumner of the American Society for the Suppression of Vice promptly followed suit, but met with another of his frequent reverses when an American court handed down a decision disagreeing with the English ruling that the theme of homosexuality is per se indiscussable and indecent. A Victory Edition of the novel was published in celebration of the ruling.

Radclyffe Hall, pleased with her victory, did not press her advantage by writing more controversial thesis-novels. Writing is only one of her numerous interests, which include riding, traveling, attending first nights, collecting antique oak, and breeding dogs, many of which have appeared on show benches in America. She is a Fellow of the Zoological Society, and has been for some time member of the Council of the Society for Psychical Research, in which she has shown great interest. Radclyffe Hall has never found any difficulty in writing under any circumstances, even on the top of a trunk in a noisy hotel bedroom. Her books have been written in such rooms in Florence, northern Italy, Normandy, and Paris. When the writing fever is in the ascendant, Miss Hall continues for ten or twelve hours at a stretch, while meals and appointments go by the board. Her home before the Nazi bombardment was The Forecastle, The Hucksteps, Rye, Sussex. Radclyffe Hall's novels have distinction, if little humor, and are decorated with set-pieces of nature description. Miss Hall is dark, distinguished in appearance, and wears severely-tailored clothes.

PRINCIPAL WORKS: 'Twixt Earth and Stars: Poems, 1906; Poems of the Past and Present, 1910; Songs of Three Counties and Other Poems, 1913; The Forgotten Island (poems) 1915; The Forge (novel) 1924; The Unlit Lamp, 1924; A Saturday Life, 1925; Adam's Breed, 1926; The Well of Loneliness, 1928; The Master of the House, 1932; Miss Ogilvy Finds Herself (short stories) 1934; The Sixth Beatitude, 1936.

HALLGREN, MAURITZ ALFRED (June 18, 1899-), American journalist and essayist, was born in Chicago, of Scandinavian descent on both sides, and was educated at the University of Chicago (non-graduate). After a few months as reporter on the Chicago Daily News, he became, in 1920, telegraph editor of the South Bend, Ind., Tribune, and remained there until 1922. He was then, briefly, assistant news editor of the Cincinnati Times-Star, and went from there to become a member of the staff of the Associated Press at Chicago for three years.

From 1926 to 1928 he was Washington correspondent of both the International News Service and the United Press, attached to the State Department.

For the next two years he was the Berlin correspondent of the United Press. From 1930 to 1934 he was an associate editor of the *Nation.* From 1934 to 1938 he did editorial work on the Baltimore *S u n,* since which time he has been free-lancing. During the First World War he served in France with the United States Marine Corps.

In 1921 he married Elizabeth Stone; they have a son and daughter. Their home is on a farm near Glenwood, Md.

A serious-looking, spectacled man with a mass of dark hair over a high forehead, Mr. Hallgren actually is amiable and witty in his private associations, but desperately in earnest as a writer. Though he is rather far to the left in his political and economic views, he has no hard-and-fast affiliations. His hobby is philately. James Truslow Adams called him "an able journalist," and he is precisely that; he is, besides, a man who is upset by things he sees that he thinks wrong, and who voices his opinion of them in a direct and forthright manner. His chief defect as a writer is that he does not go to the roots of his subject, but contents himself with surface effects, so that the final verdict on his work so far must be that of Mr. Adams: "worthwhile though not outstanding."

PRINCIPAL WORKS: Seeds of Revolt, 1933; The Gay Reformer, 1935; The Tragic Fallacy, 1937; All About Stamps, 1940; Landscape of Freedom, 1941.

HALLIBURTON, RICHARD (January 9, 1900-March 23/24, 1939), American writer of romantic travel books, wrote to the compilers of this volume before his death:

"Born in Brownsville, west Tennessee. [Parents: Wesley and Nell (Nance) Halliburton.] Moved to Memphis in infancy, and though rarely there have called that 'home' ever since. Went to Memphis University School till fifteen—interested even then in literature and the arts. In 1915 was sent to Lawrenceville Preparatory School at Lawrenceville, N.J. Finished there in class of 1917. War having been declared that April, I made valiant efforts to get into it. Got only as far as Princeton summer military camp. Entered Princeton in fall of 1917, taking mostly military courses. More student encampments the following summer. Then, weary of army life, I switched to Princeton Naval Unit. The war ended before I got to sea. So, the following summer vacation, overcome with restlessness, I skipped off to New Orleans, signed on a freighter, sailed up and down the Atlantic, vagabonded about Europe, and missed my junior year completely from Princeton. The dean, hearing of my adventures, let me carry on with my class. I did nothing distinguished at Princeton, except to be very solitary, and to tramp the New Jersey hills restlessly, hungry for the liberated and colorful life lived the year before.

"Promptly after graduation (B.A. class of 1921) with a room mate I went back to sea, and sailed and tramped for two years here and there around the world. My adventures were sufficiently unusual to suggest a book. I wrote one, called it *The Royal Road to Romance.* Nine publishers turned it down. The tenth took it only because he had heard me tell the stories professionally at the Princeton Club. This was not until 1925, when I was twenty-five.

"Before the book was launched I went to Greece, to follow the travels of Ulysses, climb Mount Olympus, explore the Marathon race course, and swim the Hellespont. *The Glorious Adventure,* my story of Greece, appeared in 1927.

"Never having had any special instruction in writing, and having read no more than my Princeton classes required, I was surprised when both books, appearing close together, went into twenty editions. But it was not until they were published in a couple of dozen foreign languages that I felt convinced they must be unusual books.

"Encouraged, I struck out for Latin America, visited Yucatan, Mexico, swam the Panama Canal from ocean to ocean, and spent the summer on Devil's Island. These stories ran in the *Ladies' Home Journal.* The book was called *New Worlds to Conquer.*

"The wanderlust still possessed me. A year later, 1930, I bought an airplane and took off with a pilot companion to fly from Hollywood to Timbuctoo. Arriving there we flew next to Persia, Mount Everest, Borneo, and the Philippines, spending eighteen months, and seeking everything that might amuse us. The record of these air adventures appeared in 1932 under the title *The Flying Carpet*.

"New York, at brief and irregular intervals, has been my address since Princeton. My great ambition in life is to keep myself free enough from possessions and responsibilities to be able to obey the moment's impulse. I like swimming and history and beer. I've spoken at most of the colleges and private schools in the country and greatly enjoyed these contacts. I've played the leading rôle in one moving picture—but this was rather painful both to the audience and to myself."

* * *

To collect material for his books, two thousand lectures, and *Ladies' Home Journal* serials, Halliburton engaged in countless manufactured adventures. In 1937 he decided to sail a seventy-five-foot Chinese junk, the *Sea Dragon*, from Hongkong to the San Francisco World's Fair. After two years' preparation the junk, equipped with an auxiliary engine and a radio, left Hongkong March 4, 1939, and was last heard from March 24, when the liner *President Coolidge*, 1,200 miles west of Midway Island, in seas forty feet high, received a radio message from Captain John Wenlock Welch that the junk's lee rail was under water. The craft, never heard from since, probably sank in the typhoon that night. In October 1939 a Memphis jury declared Halliburton legally dead on March 23 or 24, the uncertainty arising from the fact that he was near the international date line.

Halliburton's books sold more than a million copies, not—as the New York *Herald Tribune* observed, because he was a great writer or a great adventurer, but because his formula was sound. "Even in death his formula for popularity did not fail him"; his books still sell. He was deceptively delicate in appearance, slim, with auburn hair.

PRINCIPAL WORKS: The Royal Road to Romance, 1925; The Glorious Adventure, 1927; New Worlds To Conquer, 1929; The Flying Carpet, 1932; Seven League Boots, 1935; The Book of Marvels: The Occident, 1937; Second Book of Marvels: The Orient, 1938; Richard Halliburton: His Story of His Life's Adventures as Told in Letters . . ., 1940.

ABOUT: American Magazine October 1926; Publishers' Weekly August 12, 1939; Time June 19, 1939; World Review March 5, 12, 1928.

HALPER, ALBERT (August 3, 1904-   ), American novelist, writes: "I was born in Chicago, and grew up on that city's great West Side. I  went to grammar school, high school, then went to work, drifting from job to job like other youths of America, who, destined neither for the professions nor for specialized posts in the industrial world, burn out their strength in jobs that lead nowhere. I was an order-picker in a mail-order house, machine operator in a factory making looseleaf binders, salesman for a beauty parlor supplies firm, jewelry clerk, advance agent for a tobacco company, shipping clerk and plate stamper in an electrotype foundry for over three years, and postal sorter on the night shift of the Chicago central postoffice. I always wanted to become a writer, but I could never work myself out of the rut of the dull, monotonous West Side streets and my dreary bread-and-butter labor.

"Instead, in my spare time I tried to become a song writer, and, with the help of a small-time orchestra leader, several of my numbers were played in hard-boiled roadhouses just beyond the city limits of Chicago. I enrolled in evening courses in accounting at Northwestern University, but dropped out. Went to evening law school a while, also dropped out.

"Finally, I figured that what I needed was some sort of personal crisis so that I could find out where I was heading for. (This statement, on the face of it, sounds like heavy thunder in light opera, but at that time it was serious business to me.) So I got a job on the night shift at the postoffice, sorting mail and slinging heavy, dusty mailsacks, seven nights a week. I worked there for fourteen months. The dead flow of days and weeks finally straightened me out, and on the day I was notified that I was about to be promoted to a regular clerkship with increased wages, I resigned right away and left town the next morning, to burn my bridges, to get away from the gray West Side and my family, and to try, once and for all, to become a writer.

"From then on (the autumn of 1928), I have made Manhattan more or less my headquarters and have been writing steadily. I had a hard time getting started, but I suppose my experiences in unheated tenements, with 'thrifty' meals, etc., were no different from other writers' difficulties. *Union Square*, published as my first novel, was my fourth full-length piece of work.

"Because of the subject matter of my novels and short stories, I have been labeled by various critics of the Left and of the Right as a 'proletarian' writer. Frankly, I dislike labels. We writers of America live in a capitalistic society; some of us describe the hopes, faiths, and despairs of people who earn their daily bread in factories, stores, and offices; others of us describe the hopes and despairs of the middle class; still others of us describe the mores and the decay of the upper classes, and their hopes for the continuance of the *status quo*. Why not do away with labels and merely call ourselves commentators, or historians, of present-day society as we see it? That is less pretentious, it seems to me, and more truthful.

"In 1934 I was awarded a Guggenheim Fellowship and spent a year in Europe, chiefly in London. I have few hobbies: walking, ice-skating, swimming, a little tennis, and looking for good 50c-60c *prix fixe* restaurants in Manhattan."

* * *

Mr. Halper's parents were immigrants from Lithuania, who came to Chicago in the early 1890's, where his father opened a small store that sold everything from groceries to clothes. They moved frequently, but always in the same general neighborhood. Since Halper's books are drawn directly from his own experience, the critic was correct who said that "he knows what he's talking about." He is a dark, short, stocky young man, now growing bald, and wears a small moustache. His manner of speech has been described as "simple, direct, and suddenly graphic." In addition to his novels, he has written many short stories; in fact, his first appearance in print was with a story in the *Dial*, in 1929. Carl Van Doren said of him that he is "rich in raw materials and skillful in dramatization."

PRINCIPAL WORKS: Union Square, 1933; On the Shore (short stories) 1934; The Foundry, 1934; The Chute, 1937; Sons of the Fathers, 1940.

ABOUT: Literary Digest September 1, 1934; Saturday Review of Literature November 6, 1937; Scholastic April 6, 1935, February 18, 1939; Wilson Library Bulletin April 1935.

*HAMILTON, CLAYTON (November 14, 1881-), American dramatist and drama critic writes: "Clayton Hamilton was born in Brooklyn, N.Y., the only child of George Alexander and Susie Amelia (Corey) Hamilton. He was educated at the Polytechnic Institute (B.A. 1900). Awarded a competitive University Scholarship, he proceeded to Columbia, where he took his M.A. in 1901. Though only nineteen years of age, he was immediately appointed to teach in the department of English, serving as first assistant to Prof. Brander Matthews. Through twenty years he continued to lecture at Columbia, mainly on the modern drama. Meanwhile he had given other courses in the general field of literature, at a dozen of the fore-

Blackstone

most private institutions in New York, headed by the Brooklyn Institute of Arts and Sciences.

"Quite early in his teens he had begun to contribute short stories, poems, sketches, reviews, and essays to various magazines. For two years he served as associate editor and dramatic critic of the *Forum*, for eight years as dramatic editor of the *Bookman*, for two years in a similar capacity with *Everybody's Magazine*, for eight years with *Vogue*, and for one year with *Vanity Fair*. Starting in 1910, he began to issue a series of many books concerned primarily with the art of the drama and the technic of the theatre. In addition to the preparation of his own books, he has served as a sort of midwife for the issuance of many others.

"Clayton Hamilton's career in the theatre began also at an early age. His first play, *A Night at an Inn*, was acted on Broadway when he was twenty-one years old; he was twenty-four when Henry Miller produced *The Love That Blinds* (written in collaboration with Grace Isabel Colbron). The same year, 1906, he was appointed literary adviser to Richard Mansfield, and he continued in this capacity until the death of this great actor in 1907. A few years later, he collaborated with A. L. Thomas in the composition of several plays—*The Big Idea, Thirty Days,* and *The Better Understanding.* For two years from 1920 to 1922, he served as story editor for the old Goldwyn Corporation in Hollywood. After a trip to the South Seas, he returned to New York.

"In recent years he has been concerned in one way or another, with the production of plays for the living theatre. Meanwhile he has embarked upon two or three trans-

* Died September 17, 1946.

continental lecture tours which have taken him to every state of the Union except Florida and to more than half the provinces of Canada. In his comparatively idle moments, he has always been a traveler, an adventurer, and an explorer. He has visited nearly every region of the habitable world. At home he has been for several years an amateur yachtsman. This devotion of his later life ties up logically with the period in his early twenties when he served as purser, ship's doctor, and third officer of a tramp steamer in the British Mercantile Marine. In 1912, he was elected to the National Institute of Arts and Letters, and has served both as vice-president and as secretary. He has been a member of the Players, in New York, since 1903, and has served three times as secretary of the club."

* * *

Mr. Hamilton is stout, with thick, wavy white hair, once blond, and clean-cut features. In 1913 he married Gladys Coates; they have two sons. The *Literary Digest* called him "a top-flight dramatist, lecturer, and pulse-holder to 10,000 eager, breathless, neophytic young playwrights." B. Virginia Lee remarked that "he has a faculty of getting to the bottom of things."

Mr. Hamilton is listed by the Library of Congress as Clayton Meeker Hamilton, but he writes to the editors of this volume: "Please suppress entirely the middle name of 'Meeker,' which I deliberately deleted from my professional name before I reached the age of twenty-one. The parents of Woodrow Wilson called him 'Tom' and the parents of Rudyard Kipling called him 'Joe,': but every adult author should be entitled to choose the trademark by which he chooses to be known." [The point raised by Mr. Hamilton is the occasion of frequent friction between authors and librarians. Most modern librarians will agree with Mr. Hamilton's contention, but will point out that the name-form to which he objects would not be used in library cataloguing, had not he himself at some time reported it in that guise. The way for an author to assure that only the name-form he prefers will be used in library cataloguing is never to use or report any other form, even parenthetically in *Who's Who* and the like. Or, if a form objectionable to the author has already come into library use, a letter to the Library of Congress will in most cases obtain a correction in the future.]

PRINCIPAL WORKS: Materials and Methods of Fiction, 1908; The Theory of the Theatre, 1910; Studies in Stagecraft, 1914; On the Trail of Stevenson, 1915; Problems of the Playwright, 1917; The Big Idea (play) 1917; A Manual of the Art of Fiction, 1918; Seen on the Stage, 1920; Thirty Days, 1923; The Better Understanding (play) 1924; Conversations on Contemporary Drama, 1924; Wanderings, 1925; Friend Indeed (play) 1926; So You're Writing a Play! 1935; The Theory of the Theatre, 1939.

ABOUT: Literary Digest October 12, 1935; Overland and Out West February 1925.

*HAMILTON, COSMO (187?-), English novelist, dramatist, and short-story writer, is the second son of Henry James Gibbs and Helen (Hamilton) Gibbs. He assumed the name Cosmo Hamilton by deed poll. He is a brother of Sir Philip Gibbs and Arthur Hamilton Gibbs.*qv*

J. M. Flagg

His father, who was a civil servant, a departmental chief of the Board of Education and a colleague of Matthew Arnold, had "a' large family, a delicate wife, and an unresilient salary." Cosmo Hamilton began to write at an undetermined age. His first book, *Which Is Absurd,* was reviewed by Jerome K. Jerome in two words, "Quite so." After writing articles for the *Pall Mall Gazette* and a daily London letter for a syndicate, Hamilton edited the *Sovereign,* and became editor of the more important *World,* remaining until it was bought by Northcliffe and a more amenable editor installed. The theatre now beckoned, and Hamilton wrote *The Catch of the Season,* a musical comedy starring Seymour Hicks; *The Belle of Mayfair,* in which Edna May made a final appearance and was succeeded by Billie Burke; and a long succession of other plays, notably *Scandal, The Blindness of Virtue, Mr. Pickwick, Arsène Lupin,* a dramatization of the crook-stories by Maurice Leblanc, and *Mrs. Skeffington.* Most of Hamilton's drawing-room comedies, spiced with mildly daring situations, were produced by Charles Frohman, who went down with the torpedoed liner *Lusitania.* During the First World War Hamilton was gazetted a sublieutenant in the Royal Naval Air Service, and in 1938 he held the post of Head Warden and recruiting officer in the Air Raid Precautions service. During the 'twenties a familiar figure in the New York theatre, Hamilton also lectured throughout the country.

* Died October 14, 1942 at the home of his brother, Sir Philip Gibbs, at Shanley Green, Surrey, England.

His first wife was Beryl Faber, who died in 1912; his second, the divorced wife of Guy Bolton, the playwright. The Hamiltons have a son and daughter, and make their home at Mills Croft, Wonersh, Surrey. George Doran described him as handsome, suave, ingratiating, with jet black hair slicked back from his forehead, revealing the face of a modern St. John. "Earnest, zealous, compassionate, and attracting, he became the evangelist of sex contentment." His fiction has been described as amiable, light-hearted, sophisticated, with modern backgrounds.

PRINCIPAL WORKS: Through a Keyhole, 1899; Impertinent Dialogues, 1901; The Duke's Son, 1905; Adam's Clay, 1907; Brummell, 1907; The Blindness of Virtue, 1908; The Infinite Capacity, 1910; The Outpost of Eternity, 1912; The Door That Has No Key, 1913; A Plea For the Younger Generation, 1915; The Miracle of Love, 1915; His Friend and His Wife, 1920; The Rustle of Silk, 1922; The Laughing Mask, 1924; Unwritten History (autobiography) 1924; Caste, 1925; The Three Passions, 1928; The Little Gold Ring, 1929; The Pleasure House, 1930; Happiness, 1931; People Worth Talking About, 1934; The Splendour of Torches, 1934; Adam and Evelyn, 1936; The Armour of Light, 1937; Discord and Harmony, 1938; Everyman for His Wife, 1938; Thy Lamp o' Memory, 1939.

ABOUT: Doran, G. H. Chronicles of Barabbas; Hamilton. S. Unwritten History; Overton, G. Cargoes for Crusoes.

HAMILTON, EDITH (1869*-), American educator and writer on Greek and Latin literature, is the daughter of Montgomery

 Hamilton and Gertrude (Pond) Hamilton. A sister, Dr. Alice Hamilton, is the only woman to have served on the faculty of the Harvard Medical School. Edith Hamilton attended Miss Porter's School in Farmington, Conn., and re-

ceived B.A. and M.A. degrees in Greek and Latin courses from Bryn Mawr College in 1894. She was a Fellow in Latin at Bryn Mawr the next year, and went to Germany on a Mary E. Garrett European fellowship to study at the Universities of Leipzig and Munich in 1895-96. She had the distinction of being the first woman ever to be admitted at the University of Munich. A chance remark in a lecture by Professor Williamowitz-Mollendörff fired her with the ambition to write a book some day which would communicate to others the genuine pleasure

she had experienced in her contacts with the Greek and Roman ways of life, as reflected in their respective literatures. She had read Latin "ever since my father, who knew nothing about methods for softening the rigors of study, started me at the age of seven on Six Weeks' Preparation for Caesar. I have read it, except during the brief intermission of college, for my own pleasure merely, exactly as I would read French or German. . . . What the Romans did has always interested me much less than what they were, and what the historians have said they were is beyond all comparison less interesting to me than what they themselves said." On her return from Germany, Miss Hamilton was persuaded to organize the Bryn Mawr School at Baltimore, Md., where she was headmistress for twenty years, beginning in 1896. On her retirement she found time to begin her long-projected book. The first chapters of The Greek Way (1930) were published in Theatre Arts Monthly, to whose editors, Mrs. Edith Isaacs, John Mason Brown, and Rosamond Gilder, Miss Hamilton makes her acknowledgements in the preface to her book.

"They have endured much in the making of this book; listened tirelessly to my vehement and wearing enthusiasms; made me rewrite all my favorite passages; never spared me the faithful wounds of friends; cheered me in the terrible moments that come to those who take up what a great Frenchwoman has called le sale métier d'écrivain; in short, shown themselves the staunch and patient supporters without whom I believe no one would have courage to write a book."

The Greek Way at first had a modest sale, but later went into several printings. The Roman Way (1932) emphasized the similarities between life in ancient Rome and in modern America, and leaned less on secondary sources than The Greek Way which was rather heavily indebted to W. Macneile Dixon's Tragedy and R. W. Livingston's The Greek Genius and Its Meaning to Us. The Prophets of Israel (1936), called by Kirsopp Lake "accurate without being pedantic," represented a departure into new fields for Miss Hamilton, but retained the characteristics of its predecessors. It expresses, said the Christian Century, "in a crisp and vigorous style, not a few sound insights into the values of Hebrew prophecy. [The essays] reflect much more her vigorous reaction to her own world than her understanding of the world about which she writes." The chapter on the prophet Isaiah was particularly pungent in expression. Alfred Kazin remarked that Miss Hamilton "makes one feel the intensity that once shook a narrow earth." Miss Hamilton has also reviewed books in the field of her specialty. She is unmarried, and lives on the East Side in New York City.

PRINCIPAL WORKS: The Greek Way, 1930; The Roman Way, 1932; The Prophets of Israel, 1936.

ABOUT: Bryn Mawr College: Register of Alumnae and Former Students; Hamilton, E. The Roman Way (see Preface).

HAMILTON, Mrs. MARY AGNES (ADAMSON) (1883-), Scottish novelist and political writer, was born in Man-

C. Harris

chester but reared in Glasgow, where her father, Robert Adamson, was professor of logic at the university. She was educated at Newnham College, Cambridge, and after a year in Germany and a year as assistant lecturer in history at the University of Cardiff came to London, where she assisted Sir Philip Gibbs in editing the *Review of Reviews*. In 1905 she married C. J. Hamilton, secretary of the Royal Economic Society; they have no children. In 1924 she ran for Parliament as a Labor Party candidate but was defeated. In 1929 she was elected from Blackburn and served for two years, until the Labor Party's national defeat. She was a member of the British delegation to the League of Nations Assembly in 1929 and 1930, and on the Royal Commission on Civil Service from 1929 to 1931. From 1933 to 1937 she was a governor of the British Broadcasting Corporation. Before becoming a Member of Parliament she was parliamentary private secretary to the Postmaster General. Since 1937 she has been an alderman of the London County Council. At present she is on the staff of the Ministry of Information. She recently completed a brief history of women in the trade union movement, but a novel which she was writing when the war broke out has been suspended "for the duration."

Mrs. Hamilton's life of J. Ramsay MacDonald, published under the pseudonym of "Iconoclast" in 1925, first brought her to wide public attention. In 1929 she com-

bined this book with her *Man of Tomorrow* as a definitive biography of MacDonald published under her own name. She has been an unusually versatile writer, among her books being works (some for young people) on ancient history, labor and political essays and biographies, and novels, two of which are mystery stories. She is a tall, animated woman with a brisk walk, emphatic gestures, and a hearty laugh. She was graduated from Newnham with honors in classics and history, and until after her marriage, when labor politics became her first interest, the history of Greece and Rome was her special field. Among her hobbies she lists sketching and listening to music. Besides her own works, she has translated books by Max Nordau and Gustav Frenssen. She has visited the United States several times.

PRINCIPAL WORKS: *Novels*—Less Than the Dust, 1912; Yes, 1914; Dead Yesterdays, 1916; Slings and Arrows, 1918; Full Circle, 1920; Follow My Leader, 1922; The Last Fortnight, 1924; Special Providence (in America: Three Against Fate) 1930; Murder in the House of Commons, 1931; Life Sentence (in America: Sentenced to Life) 1935. *Non-Fiction*—The Story of Abraham Lincoln, 1906; Junior History of Rome, 1910; Greek Legends, 1912; Outlines of Greek and Roman History, 1913; Outlines of Roman History, 1915; Ancient Rome, 1922; The Man of Tomorrow, 1923; England's Labor Rulers, 1924; James Ramsay MacDonald, 1925; Outline of Ancient History (with A. W. F. Blunt) 1925; Margaret Bondfield, 1926; Mary Macarthur, 1926; Greece, 1926; Thomas Carlyle, 1926; Folly's Handbook, 1927; J. Ramsay MacDonald, 1929; Rome, 1932; In America Today, 1932; John Stuart Mill, 1933; Sidney and Beatrice Webb, 1933; Boat Train (essays) 1934; Newnham, 1936; Arthur Henderson, 1938; The Labor Party, 1939; Women at Work, 1941.

ABOUT: Harper's Magazine April 1932; Independent Woman February 1938; Wilson Library Bulletin May 1930; Woman's Journal February 1930.

HAMMETT, DASHIELL (May 27, 1894-), American founder of the "hardboiled" school of detective fiction, was born Samuel Dashiell

Hammett on the Eastern Shore of Maryland, the son of Richard Thomas Hammett and Annie Bond (Dashiell) Hammett. The name "Dashiell" (accent on the second syllable) is of French origin and was originally

"de Chiel"; Hammett says the chief characteristic of his de Chiel ancestors was that they fought in every war and never won. After the Baltimore Polytechnic Institute, which he left at thirteen, Hammett turned his hand to all sorts of occupations. He has worked as a newsboy, freight clerk, railroad laborer, messenger boy, stevedore, and as advertising manager for a San Francisco jeweler. Eight years of his life were spent as a Pinkerton detective, the experience that gave him ground for his later novels; among the celebrated cases with which he was connected were those of Nicky Arnstein and "Fatty" Arbuckle, and he won his first promotion by catching a man who had stolen a ferris wheel. During the First World War he served as a sergeant with the Motor Ambulance Corps, and in consequence of his war experiences contracted tuberculosis (from which he later recovered). After first trying a leave of absence, he was obliged to give up work as a detective and turned perforce to writing for a living. Previous to 1922 he had published nothing except some verse. The war injured his health, but it made him a writer, and it also gave him a wife, for in 1920 he married his hospital nurse, Josephine Annas Dolan, of Anaconda, Mont. They have two daughters.

Hammett's first detective story (he had for some years been reviewing detective fiction for the New York *Evening Post*) was *Red Harvest* (1929), a loosely constructed blood-and-thunder novel with more gangsterism than detection, even of his particular definition, in it. *The Dain Curse* marked an improvement in his method, and he reached his zenith with *The Maltese Falcon*. Generally considered his greatest achievement, this novel holds an unusual distinction in being the only contemporary detective story to be "immortalized" by inclusion in the Modern Library. *The Glass Key* was regarded by critics as a worthy successor (and is Hammett's favorite among his own works); but *The Thin Man*, written with an apparent eye toward mass sales, marked a softening and falling off in the author's powers, in the opinion of *aficionados*. This, however, did not prevent the story, with William Powell and Myrna Loy in the leading rôles, from becoming a sensational Hollywood success—a better film, in the opinion of many, than it was a book. A series of cinematic sequels with the same actors have contributed to the author's increasing financial independence.

Hammett has written but little for publication in recent years, spending most of his time on Hollywood payrolls. He is a nightworker, who starts in the small hours and works until daylight; sometimes, at a crucial

moment, he works on a book or picture thirty-six hours at a stretch. A slender six-footer with a crest of prematurely gray hair and a small moustache, he might serve as the physical model for one of his own detectives. But he does not greatly admire his detective stories. What he wants to do is write plays and "straight" novels. He admires Ernest Hemingway, William Faulkner, and Ben Hecht, all writers as grim and swift-paced in their fields as he is in his. In poetry his great admiration is for Robinson Jeffers.

Perhaps no other writer of detective fiction in the present generation has so changed and influenced the form as Hammett. An entirely new school of writing has grown up following the pattern he set. Few readers today will follow the *Bookman's* exaggeration, "It is doubtful if even Ernest Hemingway has written more effective dialogue"; but there is no doubt of Hammett's real talent in this direction, as in his realistic portrayal of character. His detectives are all private agents, drawn from real life: brutal, grasping, lecherous "heels," but each with his own hard and distinct code. The action is machine-gun-paced and the events so violent that they sometimes threaten credibility. But for all their external speed and violence, Hammett's novels are among the best examples extant of the blending of detection and the psychological study of character. His name will long remain a mile-post in detective literature.

Politically Hammett belongs to the Left, and he has been active for many years in defense of civil liberties. He is president of the League of American Writers.

PRINCIPAL WORKS: Red Harvest, 1929; The Dain Curse, 1929; The Maltese Falcon, 1930; The Glass Key, 1931; Creeps by Night (ed.) 1931; The Thin Man, 1932.

ABOUT: Haycraft, H. Murder for Pleasure: The Life and Times of the Detective Story; Bookman June 1932; Literary Digest December 9, 1933; New York World-Telegram June 22, 1931, April 13, 1942.

HAMMOND, PERCY (March 7, 1873-April 25, 1936), American journalist and dramatic critic, was born in Cadiz, Ohio, the son of Alexander Hammond and Charlotte (Hunter) Hammond, and was christened Percy Hunter Hammond; the "Percy" rankled all his life. Both his father and grandfather fought in the Civil War; Alexander Hammond enlisted as a drummer boy at seventeen, fought at Kenesaw Mountain, and marched to the sea with Sherman. Printer's ink was also in his blood; in the north of Ireland an ancestral Hunter owned one of the first printing presses in the country. Percy Hammond

began at twelve as a printer's devil on the Cadiz *Republican* (now past its 125th year) and saw his first show at thirteen, in a tent at the Cadiz county fair. (It was *Little Nugget,* with Joseph Cawthorne, playing the leading comedy rôle.) In an

M. Goldberg

Anti-Saloon League parade, Percy carried a banner reading "Tremble, King Alcohol, for I shall grow up."

At fifteen he ran away to Pittsburgh, where he sold papers to buy gallery seats in the theatre, and continued on to Washington. Here he fainted in the front hall of the mansion occupied by Senator John Sherman of Ohio; the senator saw to it that he had crackers and milk, a printer's union card, and a job in the Government Printing Office which he held four years. Back in Ohio, Percy worked two years on the Chillicothe *News-Advertiser,* his uncle's paper, then obtained an $8-a-week job with the City Press, a news-gathering association. In May 1896 he married Florence Carnahan of Cadiz; he completely lost interest in life after her death in 1935.

From 1898 to 1908 Hammond was reporter, editorial writer, and dramatic critic for the Chicago *Evening Post,* and was also press agent for the Grand Opera House, owned by the Hamlin family; hence his sobriquet, probably first given him by his long-time friend "F.P.A." of "The Pied Piper of Hamlin's." Hammond became dramatic critic of the Chicago *Tribune* in 1908, and as Paris correspondent saw something of the First World War and a good deal of the Peace Conference. In 1921 W. O. McGeehan, sports writer of the New York *Herald Tribune,* but then by some odd chance its city editor, went to Chicago and returned in triumph with Hammond as the paper's new dramatic critic. Hammond was frankly terrified of the New York theatre, and did not strike his stride until the end of his first year, when he decided he had been too lenient, "got out the old horsewhip and joined in the game" of badgering actors and producers. The elaborate irony of his style, which John Mason Brown called "as highly polished as marquetry" and John Anderson described as mixed subtly of perfume and carbolic acid, seldom allowed him to express a definite enthusiasm for any play or player, and he was "a wonderful hater." "With an intricate and subtle mind he managed, somehow, to have a simple heart," said another colleague, Richard Lockridge, while George Jean Nathan declared that with his Chestertonian bulk, Gilbert Stuart countenance, and venerable white locks, he *looked* like a dramatic critic. Hammond had a crimson face and blue eyes. In his later years his constant companion was his only son, John, who wrote an indignant letter to the newspapers refuting some of the statements in *Before I Forget,* by Burton Rascoe, who found Hammond singularly unlovable in his Chicago days. Hammond died at nearly sixty-three, of pneumonia, in the Rockefeller Institute Hospital in New York City.

PRINCIPAL WORKS: But—Is It Art, 1927; This Atom in the Audience, 1940.

ABOUT: Hammond, P. This Atom in the Audience, 1940. Percy Hammond: A Symposium in Tribute; Rascoe, B. Before I Forget; New York Herald Tribune May 7, 1941; New York Times April 26, 1936; Time April 28, 1941.

*HAMSUN, KNUT (August 4, 1859-), Norwegian novelist and Nobel Prize winner, was born at Lom, Norway, in the northern Gudbransdal Valley,

the son of Peder Pederson and Tora Olsdatter. Following the ancient Norwegian peasant custom, his name properly would be Knut Pedersen; Hamsun was the name of his ancestral farm, and hence legally his. On both sides he belongs to the robust "peasant aristocracy," small landholders who are deeply rooted in the soil and fiercely conservative. In his own sketch for the English *Who's Who* he says proudly that he had "no education," and that is almost literally true. From the age of four he lived with an uncle in the remote and isolated Lofoten Islands, and then was apprenticed to a cobbler. As a boy of nineteen he published a long poem and a novel, and on their proceeds he left the shoemaker's last and began twelve years of wandering, with the idea of earning his way through the university in Christiania (Oslo). He was a coal-trimmer, a longshoreman, a private tutor, a clerk in a store and the postoffice, a court messenger; and then he entered the university only to discover that he could not possibly study and at the same time make enough to live on. So he went by steerage to the United States, and there he continued his nomadic life, working his way westward to the Dakotas. There he decided to prepare himself for the Unitarian ministry, but instead, after being a farmhand and a dairyman, and then incongruously lecturing on French literature in Minneapolis, he wound up as a street car conductor in Chicago. The legend is that he read Euripides on the back platform instead of letting passengers on and off, and in consequence was discharged. He returned to Norway, still found no means of livelihood, tried America once more as a lecturer in the Northwest, and ended up, in the late 1880's, as a fisherman off the Grand Banks of Newfoundland.

He was now nearly thirty years old, and had so far accomplished practically nothing. But he had accumulated, by bitter experience, a vast fund of first-hand information on how the poor exist, and nature had already endowed him with keen sympathies and with a mystical rapport with nature. He was ready to express himself. In 1888, in a Danish magazine, he published a fragmentary novel which he called *Sult* (*Hunger*). It created a sensation. From that time on he was a noted writer. Since 1889, he says, he has been "mostly writing, the last thirty years also farming." He lives at Noerholmen, near Grimstad, a fishing village where Ibsen spent his youth. In a white two-story house, "at the end of a quiet bight of the sea," he lives and works, with his wife, who was Marie Andersen and who is something of a linguist, and with his two sons and three daughters.

"No living writer," said the *Living Age*," "has a soul that bruises more easily." Hamsun's aversion to publicity, especially as he grows older, is almost pathological. On his seventieth birthday the Norwegian Society of Authors wished to present him with a loving cup, and newsmen came from all over Europe to interview him. He simply ran away, and stayed in hiding for three days. As for the loving cup, he wrote the society to scratch his name off it and give it to someone else! He writes sometimes in an untidy, dusty little block-house in his garden which no one is allowed to set in order but himself; but just as frequently he goes to some near-by fishing village and works on his books in a country inn. His only hobby is typical—it is solitaire.

During the First World War Hamsun made no secret of his sympathy with the Ger-

man side, and he has since been accused with reason of being openly and aggressively pro-Nazi. (The German invasion of Norway in 1940 received his public "blessing" almost as soon as the Nazi troops had reached Oslo.) But he is past eighty years old now, and what little strength he has left he wishes to give to his work. Asked by his publishers what he most admired, he answered that he esteemed fairness and justice as the highest human qualities, and his continuing hold on life, true to his tenacious peasant ancestry, was evidenced in his spontaneous reply to a further question as to his chief aversion—"never should I die, if I had not to do it!"

In earlier life Hamsun looked not so much the peasant as the country school-teacher which he has also been, with bristly hair brushed back from a high forehead, thin, ascetic face, a formidable moustache, and nose glasses. Now the moustache is clipped and without the glasses he resembles more a tall, wiry old farmer. He is unmistakably Scandinavian in appearance.

Hamsun's work is largely autobiographical —that is, it deals usually either with his own painful youth and young manhood or with observation of the people among whom he was born and grew up. His milieu is often the same as Johan Bojer's, but whereas Bojer is concerned primarily with the material and social situation of his characters, it is their psychology, particularly their subconscious psychology, which most interests Hamsun. In 1920 he received the Nobel Prize for literature; his books have been translated into some twenty-five languages. He is one of the major figures of European literature, but his fame is as it were in spite of himself, for he remains innately introverted and unassuming. "We penetrate straight into the core of Knut Hamsun's works," said Walter A. Berendsohn, "if we bear in mind his close relationship with nature, emphasized by his deep religion." His aim in writing is "to grant the individual soul its due," and the influences on him are as disparate as Rousseau and Strindberg. Though he has treated of daring themes, he himself is rather conservative in most of his social views. His style, however, is modern, vivid and apt, with a remarkable gift for verisimilitude in portraiture. He is a shy man, most at home with children, kindly and sensitive, with the keen wit of the observant and taciturn. His lack of formal education has made him wary and a bit touchy, and this accounts for much of the myth of his almost aggressive shrinking from public notice. "Isn't culture," he has asked, "really the education of the heart?"

PRINCIPAL WORKS AVAILABLE IN ENGLISH: Shallow Soil, 1914; Growth of the Soil, 1920; Pan, 1920; Hunger, 1921; Dreamers (in England, Mothwise) 1921; Mysteries, 1927; The Women at the Pump, 1928; Chapter the Last, 1929; Vagabonds, 1930; August, 1931; The Road Leads On, 1934; The Ring Is Closed, 1937; Look Back on Happiness, 1940.

ABOUT: Gustafson, A. Six Scandinavian Novelists; Larsen, H. A. Knut Hamsun; Contemporary Review July 1938; Living Age September 15, 1929, February 1934; New York Herald Tribune "Books" April 7, 1940; Wilson Library Bulletin March 1929, December 1936.

HANLEY, JAMES (1901-), Irish novelist, was born in Dublin, the son of Edward H. Hanley and Bridget (Roche) Hanley,

of a poor working-class family on both sides. He left a board school at thirteen to become a stoker and sailor, and followed the sea from 1914 to 1924. Back on shore, he worked as butcher, railwayman, cook, clerk, and postman before he finally broke into journalism. In 1930 he published his first book; but his first success did not come until the following year, with Boy. Since that time, and especially since The Furys, in 1934, he has been able to live by writing alone. He is unmarried, and lives in London. From boyhood he has had a passion for music, and taught himself to play the piano; though his hands were too stiff from years of manual labor to enable him ever to become a really competent pianist, music is still his chief recreation. His only exercise is walking. He looks like a poet rather than a novelist, with wild blond hair and strange, far-seeing light eyes— sailor's eyes.

And it is of the sea he writes; the sea and the worker on land are his two themes. He says: "The more insignificant a person is in this whirlpool of industrialized and civilized society, the more important he is for me." His novels do for the sailor in fiction what Eugene O'Neill's early plays did for him in drama; it is not surprising that he dislikes Conrad, who saw the ship from the officer's deck. The influence of Balzac and Turgenev is patent in his work.

Mr. Hanley has a peculiar gift for evoking pity and terror; his books are full of horror, and for the most part make painful reading. His work seems to strike the critics in very disparate ways; whereas a writer in the London Mercury said that he possessed "a detachment so chill it sometimes seems close to scorn," Edwin Muir found in him "imaginative sympathy, the ability to enter into any situation without prejudice and without bitterness, an undeviating humanity." He has sometimes seemed overwhelmed himself by the misery he depicts, and to lose himself in a welter of hysteria. But this defect of his novels on Irish workers never appears in his stories of seamen, where, to quote Mr. Muir again, he remains "reasonable in a mad setting."

In his earlier work there was plenty of evidence that he was an uneducated man, untrained in writing, who yet had something of which to unburden his heart, and the native talent with which to express it. His style was formal, bookish, and strained. But he has learned his craft since that time, until now his narrative flows easily and bears the stamp of its own maker. Nevertheless, his best work remains Boy and The Furys; in these he was not so good a writer as he is now, but he was possessed of an urgency, an immediacy, which in his later books he has inevitably lost.

The Furys, The Secret Journey, and Our Time Is Gone compose a trilogy of lower-class Dublin life; an infernal picture of lives twisted and spoiled; a long, unsparing accumulation of misery, desperation, and despair.

PRINCIPAL WORKS: Drift, 1930; A Passion Before Death, 1930; Boy, 1931; The Last Voyage, 1931; Ebb and Flood, 1931; Men in Darkness (short stories) 1931; Aria and Finale (short stories) 1932; Captain Bottell, 1933; The Furys, 1934; The Maelstrom, 1935; Stoker Bush, 1935; The Wall, 1936; The Secret Journey, 1936; Half-an-Eye (short stories) 1937; Broken Water (autobiography) 1937; Grey Children: A Sociological Study, 1937; Soldiers Wind (essays) 1938; People Are Curious (short stories) 1938; Hollow Sea, 1938; Between the Tides (essays) 1939; Our Time Is Gone, 1940; The Ocean, 1941.

ABOUT: Hanley, J. Broken Water; London Mercury July 1937; Time July 22, 1935.

*HANNAY, JAMES OWEN ("George A. Birmingham") (July 16, 1865-), Anglo-Irish novelist and clergyman, was born in Belfast, the son of the Rev. Robert Hannay, Vicar of Belfast. He was educated at Temple Grove, Sheen, in Ireland; Haileybury School, in England; and at Trinity College Dublin (B.A. 1887, M.A. 1895). He was ordained deacon in 1888 and priest in 1889, and served as a curate in County Wicklow and a rector in County Mayo. In 1901 and 1902 he was a lecturer at Dublin University He remained as rector in Mayo until 1912, when he was appointed canon of St. Patrick's Cathedral in Dublin. From 1905 to 1915 he was a member of the General Synod of the Church of Ireland. He continued at St. Patrick's until 1921, except that in 1916 he was a temporary army chaplain. From 1922 to 1924 he was chaplain of the British Legation at Budapest, was rector of Wells from 1924 to 1934, and then became rector of Holy Trinity Church, in Kensington, London, which is still his post.

In 1926 he was university preacher at Durham University, in 1927 at Oxford. His wife, who was Ada Wynne, daughter of the Bishop of Killaloe, died in 1933, leaving two sons and two daughters. He made a lecture tour in the United States in 1913, and again in 1915—he is a popular lecturer as well as a clergyman and a novelist.

His first book, done under his own name, was ecclesiastical in nature. He began writing stories about 1890, but published no novels until fifteen years later. All his fiction is written under his pseudonym, "George A. Birmingham." He learned Gaelic in County Mayo, and edited a volume of Irish short stories in 1932. His first novel, a *roman à clef*, brought him more notoriety than money; but from the publication of *Spanish Gold* in 1908, he was established as a novelist. Though his salient characteristic to most readers is his racy humor, he himself says his novels are "dull, hard work," and he can see nothing amusing about them. He has written plays, books of essays, and travel works, but primarily he is known as a novelist of Irish life. His play, *General John Regan,* caused a riot when it was produced in his own town of Westport, County Mayo, in 1913; the populace considered it derogatory and attacked the actors, seriously injuring one of them.

Mr. Hannay is tall, still robust in appearance despite his seventy-odd years, with gray curly hair and twinkling blue eyes behind spectacles. His hobby is yachting, and he is a member of the Royal Irish Yacht Club. Among his rather unexpected productions is a light opera, *The Mermaid,* written with S. H. Nicholson in 1927. He has cheerfully survived the days when his anonymity was first pierced and he was burnt in effigy,

"mildly boycotted," and booed by compatriots who detected, or thought they detected, in his work an attitude of "Protestant patronage." He has been a most prolific writer, and a vastly popular one, though he himself would be the last to claim for his work any great literary value. The only ones of his books he sets store by are those dealing with church history.

PRINCIPAL WORKS: The Spirit and Origin of Christian Monasticism, 1903; The Wisdom of the Desert, 1904; The Seething Pot, 1905; Hyacinth, 1906; Benedict Kavanaugh, 1907; The Northern Iron, 1907; The Bad Times, 1908; Spanish Gold, 1908; The Search Party, 1909; Lalage's Lovers, 1911; The Lighter Side of Irish Life, 1911; Eleanor's Enterprise (play) 1911; The Major's Niece, 1911; The Simpkins Plot, 1911; The Inviolable Sanctuary, 1912; The Red Hand of Ulster, 1912; Doctor Whitty, 1913; General John Regan (novel and play) 1913; Irishmen All, 1913; The Lost Tribes, 1914; From Connaught to Chicago (in America: From Dublin to Chicago) 1914; Minnie's Bishop and Other Stories, 1915; Gossamer, 1915; The Island Mystery, 1918; A Padre in France, 1918; Up the Revels, 1919; Our Casualty and Other Stories, 1919; An Irishman Looks at His World, 1919; Good Conduct, 1920; Insheeny, 1920; Lady Bountiful, 1921; The Lost Layer, 1921; The Great-Grandmother, 1922; A Public Scandal and Other Stories, 1922; Send for Dr. O'Grady (play) 1923; Found Money, 1923; King Tommy, 1923; The Grand Duchess, 1924; Bindon Parva, 1925; The Gun-Runners, 1925; A Wayfarer in Hungary, 1925; Goodly Pearls, 1926; The Smugglers' Cave, 1926; Spillikins (essays) 1926; The Lady of the Abbey, 1926; Can You Answer This? 1927; Children, Can You Answer This? 1927; Now You Tell One: Stories of Irish Wit and Humour, 1927; Ships and Sealing-Wax (essays) 1927; The Runaways, 1928; The Major's Candlesticks, 1929; Murder Most Foul: A Gallery of Famous Criminals, 1929; Wild Justice, 1930; The Hymn-Tune Mystery, 1930; Fed Up, 1931; The Silver-Gilt Standard, 1932; Elizabeth and the Archdeacon, 1932; Angel's Adventure, 1933; Two Fools, 1934; Millicent's Corner, 1935; Mrs. Miller's Aunt, 1936; Isaiah (non-fiction) 1937; Magilligan Strand, 1938; The Birmingham Bus and Other Stories, 1938; Appeasement (non-fiction) 1939; God's Iron: A Life of the Prophet Jeremiah, 1939; The Search for Susie, 1941.

ABOUT: National Review September 1940.

HANSEN, HARRY (December 26, 1884-), American critic, writes: "Harry Hansen was born in Davenport, Iowa, and began writing for the local newspapers while in high school. The day after his graduation he became telegraph editor of the Davenport *Republican,* and in the next two years held the posts of city editor and editor and reported national conventions and started a book column. Octave Thanet, George Cram Cook, Floyd Dell, Susan Glaspell, and Arthur Davison Ficke were writing in Davenport at that time. While attending the University of Chicago,

Hansen used his summer vacations to work for the Davenport *Times*. At the university he majored in English literature, his instructors including Robert Herrick, Robert Morss Lovett, and Richard Green Moulton. Graduating in 1909, he became alumni secretary, editor of the *University Magazine,* and promotion copy-writer for the University of Chicago Press. He then became a reporter for the Chicago *Daily News*, which sent him as correspondent to Berlin to succeed Raymond Gram Swing, who was being transferred to Paris. Just before the declaration of war Hansen was ordered to Belgium. He covered the retreat of the Belgians, joined the Germans in Brussels, and marched with the German army into France. With Irvin Cobb, John T. McCutcheon, James O'Donnell Bennett, and Roger Lewis, he signed a statement saying they had witnessed no atrocities on their march of a hundred miles, a document that created a sensation on both sides. After various vicissitudes he covered Flan-

ders and the Siege of Antwerp, Austria, and Italy, and made a special journey to the Scandinavian countries, taking over the foreign desk in the Chicago office when the United States entered the war. In 1919 he attended the Peace Conference in Paris and on his return to Chicago became literary editor of the *Daily News*.

"At that time Chicago was the center of intense literary activity and books and poems were being written there by Carl Sandburg, Sherwood Anderson, Ben Hecht, Edgar Lee Masters, Harriet Monroe, Maxwell Bodenheim, Keith Preston, Burton Rascoe, and dozens of others. In 1926 Hansen succeeded Laurence Stallings as 'The First Reader,' in the New York *World*. This column of book reviews was published three times a week; Hansen made it a daily column and until the *World* was sold it published a page about books practically every day. This daily feature was followed by all other New York newspapers. In 1931 when Scripps-Howard bought the *World* and merged it with the *Telegram,* the 'First Reader' column became a daily feature of the *World-Telegram.* From 1933 to 1940 inclusive Hansen edited the O. Henry Prize Stories, an annual anthology of short stories chosen from American magazines. From 1923 to 1939 Hansen wrote book comment

for *Harper's Magazine*. He also wrote numerous introductions and special chapters for other books, lectured at Columbia University on reviewing and biography, had a radio program on books in Chicago from 1924 on, and similar programs over the Columbia Broadcasting System and the National Broadcasting Company in New York City. He has lectured nationally and his book comment is syndicated in magazines and newspapers. He translated Jakob Wassermann's *Faber* in 1925.

"He married Ruth McLernon in 1914 and has two daughters, and frequently sails with them in their sloop on Long Island Sound. He lives in Mount Vernon, N.Y."

* * *

Mr. Hansen was described by R. W. Davis as "a literary Viking," with "a dreamy eye but a firm mouth." He says of himself: "The artist should write about life as he pleases and choose his materials where he finds them." He says he is wedded to the West because he understands it and he has faith in the ultimate emergence of its artists."

PRINCIPAL WORKS: The Adventures of the Fourteen Points, 1919; Midwest Portraits, 1923; Carl Sandburg: The Man and His Poetry, 1924; Your Life Lies Before You (novel) 1935.

ABOUT: Bookman July and October 1930; Nation June 4, 1924; Publishers' Weekly January 21, 1933, May 4, 1940.

HANSEN, MARCUS LEE (December 8, 1892-May 11, 1938), American sociologist and winner of the Pulitzer Prize in history in 1941 (posthumous award), was born in Neenah, Wis., and was educated at Central College (Iowa). He graduated from the University of Iowa in 1906, receiving his M.A. degree next year. He then entered the Harvard Graduate School, but

left when the United States entered the First World War to serve in the army at Camp Taylor, Ky. He received his Ph.D. degree (or "academic work-card," as Elmer Davis calls it) in 1924 from Harvard.

That year Congress passed the immigration law which became effective in 1929, and virtually ended the great era of American immigration. Hansen spent nearly four years in Europe on stipends from the Social Science Research Council and the American

Council of Learned Societies, gathering materials in the British Isles, Germany, France, Switzerland, the Netherlands and the Scandinavian countries for his studies in immigration.

Dr. Hansen's first study, "German Schemes of Colonization Before 1860," was published in *Smith College Studies in History,* October 1923-January 1924. In 1928 Hansen returned to become associate professor of history at the University of Illinois, being given a full professorship in 1930. He died at Redlands, Calif., eight years later, in his forty-sixth year. *The Atlantic Migration, 1607-1860: A History of the Continuing Settlement of the United States,* published in 1940 by the Harvard University Press with a foreword by Arthur M. Schlesinger of Harvard's history department, was posthumously awarded the Pulitzer Prize for history. *The Immigrant in American History,* also edited and prefaced by Professor Schlesinger, contained nine essays developing Hansen's larger views on the historical rôle of the immigrant in American life.

Dr. Hansen was a clean-shaven, rugged-featured man. He "will be remembered for his painstaking scholarship and his sincere interest in students, and his ability to transform the so-called dry bones of history into living realities," according to the *American Historical Review.* H. P. Fairchild stated of his prize-winning study that "the material is handled so sympathetically that the high scholarship of the work does not preclude a powerful human appeal."

In 1935 Dr. Hansen had given eight public lectures at the University of London on nineteenth-century immigration in relation to American history. The *London Times* reviewer who wrote that he "was prone to introduce elaborate and excessively profound theories of historical causation" may have heard some of these lectures.

PRINCIPAL WORKS: Old Fort Snelling: 1819-1858, 1918; Welfare Campaigns in Iowa, 1920; Welfare Work in Iowa, 1921; The Atlantic Migration, 1607-1860: A History of the Continuing Settlement of the United States, 1940; The Immigrant in American History, 1940; The Mingling of the Canadian and American Peoples, 1940.

ABOUT: Hansen, M. L. The Atlantic Migration (see Foreword by A. M. Schlesinger); American Historical Review July 1938; New York Times May 12, 1938.

*HAPGOOD, HUTCHINS (May 21, 1869-), American novelist and essayist, writes: "I was born of New England and New York parents, in Chicago, and was lost for a time with my nurse in the great fire of 1871. I went to the University

of Michigan and to Harvard (B.A. and M.A.); studied for a year and a half at German universities; taught for a year at Harvard and the University of Chicago. I joined the staff of the New York *Commercial Advertiser* in 1897, when Lincoln Steffens was city editor. I married Neith Boyce in 1899. From this marriage there were two sons (one deceased) and two daughters. My travels began in 1893, and involved a trip round the world in 1895 and a brief sojourn in Japan. After my marriage I traveled with my wife, living in Italy in 1903; and later with my family, living in Italy and France. I have worked on the staff not only of the *Commercial Advertiser,* but also of the New York *Evening Post,* the New York *Telegraph,* the Chicago *Evening Post,* and the New York *Globe,* where I did my most important

Bouchard

signed and unsigned newspaper work. I also wrote for magazines and delivered lectures.

"I consider the general character of my work an interpretation of the developing labor, sociological, philosophical, and aesthetic movements of the country. The readers of my autobiography will see how closely I have been connected with almost all the 'movements' of the last forty years. My attitude of mind has consistently been what is called progressive. Sometimes I have been known as a radical, but I think those who best understand me feel that mine was a consistent effort to interpret the developing movements of all kinds."

* * *

Hutchins Hapgood has been a fructifying influence in American thought of the past half century. As Robert Morss Lovett has remarked, "For many years in America and parts of Europe it has been an open sesame to say 'Friend of Hutchins Hapgood.' . . . Everything he writes reflects the period in which he has lived." His autobiography, "a picture of the modern world strained through the Victorian culture," takes its place beside that of Lincoln Steffens. Mr. Hapgood lives now in the summer in Winchester, N.H., and in the winter in Key West, Fla. There is a twenty-year hiatus in his publications, and he was long over-shadowed by his better-known brother Norman, but there is much in the interpretation of American life which is understandable to the younger

* Died November 18, 1944.

generation only through reading a very few men and women, of whom he is one.

PRINCIPAL WORKS: Paul Jones, 1901; The Spirit of the Ghetto, 1902; The Autobiography of a Thief, 1903; The Spirit of Labor, 1907; An Anarchist Woman, 1909; Types From City Streets, 1910; Enemies (play, with N. Boyce) 1916; The Story of a Lover, 1919; A Victorian in the Modern World (autobiography) 1939.

ABOUT: Chamberlain, J. Farewell to Reform; Dodge, M. Movers and Shakers; Filler, L. Crusaders for American Liberalism; Hapgood, H. A Victorian in the Modern World; Kreymborg, A. Troubadour; Symes, L. & Clement, T. Rebel America; New Republic October 18, 1939; Time September 25, 1939.

HAPGOOD, NORMAN (March 28, 1868-April 29, 1937), editor, journalist, and reformer, was born in Chicago, the oldest  son of Charles Hutchins Hapgood, a socially-minded manufacturer who came of a long line of Puritan stock, and Fanny Louise (Powers) Hapgood. (Hutchins Hapgood,*qv* also an author and journalist, was a slightly younger

Harris & Ewing

brother.) He was a "bright boy . . . who was expected to do great things." Shortly after entering Harvard he became a much admired young intellectual. He was graduated in 1890 and three years later received a degree from the law school. At the end of a year's practice in Chicago he turned to journalism, and because his parents were relatively secure financially he could afford to take a $5-a-week reporting job on the Chicago *Evening Post.* He had, also, a few months with the Milwaukee *Sentinel,* and then set out for New York, where he did space-reporting for the *Evening Post.* With Lincoln Steffens, then a crack police-reporter, he was added to the staff of the reconstructed *Commercial Advertiser* (later the *Globe*). After an active turn at dramatic criticism he sailed for Europe, and while abroad was offered the editorship of *Collier's Weekly.* His drives against shoddy parliamentary procedure in Congress and against the sale of harmful foods and drugs, and his exposure of land-grab scandals made him a national figure.

Following a number of quarrels with Robert Collier he went over to *Harper's Weekly* in 1912, lending strong editorial support to the Wilson administration. In 1918, in the columns of *Leslie's Weekly,* he

suggested eventual recognition of Russia. That same year President Wilson, in an indirect move for the solution of the Russian problem, appointed Hapgood minister to Denmark. But the discord of United States' official opinion about Russia measurably crippled Hapgood's mission. At the beginning of Al Smith's first term as Governor of New York, Hapgood became his adviser, and with Henry Moscowitz wrote a campaign biography of Smith called *Up From the City Streets* (1927). Hapgood had already published a volume of collective biography; lives of Washington, Lincoln, and Webster; a book on the theatre in America; and two pieces of social history. In 1930 came his autobiography, *The Changing Years.* Hapgood's first wife, Emilie Bigelow, divorced him in Paris in 1915; and in December of the year following he married Elizabeth K. Reynolds. He died of an operation in New York, after a brief illness.

Hapgood enjoyed a long friendship with Mark Twain, who, when he was an old man, once confessed to him that through all the really constructive years of his life he had been fundamentally unhappy. "Norman lived," said his brother Hutchins, "in a way, in the externals of life, active, unsentimental, unreflective, clever, able, extroverted and ambitious." His editorial prestige, during the first quarter of this century was considerable, and it was inevitable that he should influence the social thought of that period.

PRINCIPAL WORKS: Literary Statesmen, 1897; Daniel Webster, 1899; Abraham Lincoln, 1899; George Washington, 1901; The Stage in America, 1901; Industry and Progress, 1911; The Advancing Hour, 1920; Up From the City Streets (with Henry Moscowitz) 1927; Why Janet Should Read Shakespeare, 1929; The Changing Years, 1930.

ABOUT: Hapgood, H. Victorian in the Modern World; Hapgood, N. The Changing Years; New York Times April 30, 1937.

HARDING, Mrs. BERTITA (LEONARZ) (November 1, 1907-   ), American biographer, was born Bertita Carla Camille Leonarz, in Nuremberg, Germany, and inherited from her mother the Magyar title of Countess Karolyi. Her ancestry was Rhenish and Hungarian, and her education was cosmopolitan in the extreme. When she was an infant her parents  took her to Mexico, on a diplomatic mission for Emperor Franz Joseph of Austria; she went later to the Convent de Sacré Coeur, in France, then to a Philadelphia boarding-school; she has attended the University of Wisconsin, and is a graduate in music of the National Conservatory of Mexico. She is a violinist and singer, educated for the concert stage, and has refused several operatic offers because she prefers to write and lecture. In 1926 she married Jack Ellison de Harding, of Manchester, England. They came to the United States the same year, she was naturalized in 1927, and her home now, when she is not on a lecture tour, is in Indianapolis, though she also has a regular address in Monterey, Mexico.

From childhood her imagination was captured by the tragic story of the Hapsburg dynasty, and fed by stories told her by her maternal grandmother and by former ladies-in-waiting to the ill-starred Empress Carlotta, She has been called "a person whose manifest destiny was to become the biographer of the Hapsburgs," but she does not confine her royal biographies to the Hapsburgs alone.

Mrs. Harding sings Spanish and Hungarian folk songs, lectures on the lives of past and present European royal figures, and is a frequent contributor to the *New Yorker*. Her books have been translated into French, Hungarian, and Spanish.

She is a fair-haired, pretty young woman, who likes to dress in the old national costume of Hungary, but who is much more Viennese than Magyar in appearance. She, like her books, is "brimming with exuberance and *joie de vivre*." Although her biographies are carefully documented, they read like novels. "She is a born story-teller, writing in swift-moving, frank, breezy style," commented Blair Niles. "Refreshingly, she was no case to prove, but is animated solely by her own interest in the tale she has to tell." Another reviewer summed up her books by saying that they are marked by "reader interest, writing craftsmanship, and vigorous characterization."

PRINCIPAL WORKS: Phantom Crown, 1934; Royal Purple, 1935; Golden Fleece, 1937; Farewell 'Toinette, 1938; Imperial Twilight, 1939; Hungarian Rhapsody, 1940; Amazon Throne, 1941.

ABOUT: Newsweek February 20, 1937.

HARDY, ARTHUR SHERBURNE

(August 13, 1847-March 13, 1930), American novelist, poet, and diplomat, was born at Andover, Mass., the son of Alpheus and Susan W. (Holmes) Hardy. His father was a well-to-do merchant and trustee

of Amherst College, where his son spent the year 1864-65, after attending the Boston Latin School, Phillips Andover Academy, and spending some of his formative years at a school in Neuchâtel, Switzerland. Arthur Hardy's charming if minor literary talent had a natural affinity for the clarity, grace, and precision of the best French writing. He graduated from the United States Military Academy at West Point in 1869; a year's soldiering with the Third Artillery Regiment on the Dry Tortugas proved more than sufficient, and he resigned to become professor of civil engineering at Iowa College, now Grinnell, from 1871 to 1873. After studying scientific bridge-building and road-constructing in Paris, Hardy taught at Chandler Scientific School, connected with Dartmouth, and at the College itself, until

June 1893, when he succeeded William Dean Howells as editor of the *Cosmopolitan Magazine*.

His novel, *But Yet a Woman*, had attracted attention in 1883 (*Francesca da Rimini*, a long poem published in 1878, was his first purely literary work), and in 1888 the *Atlantic Monthly* serialized *Passe Rose*, the romance of a dancing girl at the court of Charlemagne, probably the most enduring of Hardy's books. In 1897 he entered the diplomatic service, holding posts at Persia, Greece (minister, 1899-1901), and Switzerland, concluding with three years as minister to Spain (1903-05) until recalled in a moment of pique by Theodore Roosevelt, who mistakenly believed that Hardy had refused to undertake a post as Under Secretary of State. Hardy retired to Woodstock, Conn., where his wife's family lived (he had married Grace Aspinwall Bowen in 1898), dying there in his eighty-third year. He also had a son by a previous marriage, who lived with him in Persia. At seventy-six Hardy published a rambling autobiography. Books of his later years included *Aurélie*, a child's story; *Diane and Her Friends*, a collection of short stories; and *Peter*, legends about dogs.

PRINCIPAL WORKS: Francesca da Rimini, 1878; Elements of Quaternions, 1881; But Yet a Woman, 1883; Wind of Destiny, 1886; Passe Rose, 1889; Elements of Calculus, 1890; Songs for Two, 1900; His Daughter First, 1903; Aurélie, 1912; Diane and Her Friends, 1914; Helen, 1916; Peter, 1920; Things Remembered, 1923.

ABOUT: Hardy, A. S. Things Remembered; Book Buyer September 1890; New York Times March 14, 1930.

HARDY, THOMAS. See "BRITISH AUTHORS OF THE 19TH CENTURY"

HARE, AUGUSTUS JOHN CUTHBERT. See "BRITISH AUTHORS OF THE 9TH CENTURY"

HARKER, Mrs. LIZZIE ALLEN (WATSON) (1863-April 14, 1933), English novelist and playwright, was born in  Gloucester, the daughter of William Watson, according to the London *Times.* The New York *Times* obituary states that she was born in Edinburgh. She was educated at Cheltenham Ladies' College, and married James Allen Harker, a professor of the Royal Agricultural College at Cirencester, where she died at seventy. The Harkers had two sons. She began her literary career by writing short stories in the *Outlook* and other magazines, and published her first novel in 1902. *Miss Esperance and Mr. Wycherley,* published in both England and the United States in 1908, was her first real success; it deals with two engaging children brought up by an old maid and her bachelor brother in Scotland, and had a sequel, *Mr. Wycherley's Wards.* Kate Douglas Wiggin contributed a preface to *Concerning Paul and Fiammetta,* published two years previously. "Perhaps Mrs. Harker's most pleasing characteristic was her insight into the ways of children and old people, and she presents many delightful pictures of them in her book," according to the London *Times,* which was referring to *The Ffolliots of Redmarley* (1913). The *Springfield Republican* called it "not a striking tale but . . . a very charming and agreeable one"—epithets which might be applied to all her novels and the short stories gathered into *Children of the Dear Cotswolds* (1920).

Marigold: An Arcadian Comedy, written by Mrs. Harker in collaboration with F. R. Pryor, ran eighteen months at the Kingsway Theatre in London, from April 1927, and was revived there in August 1930 prior to its being taken to Canada and the United States for a run. Pryor also collaborated with her on *His Proper Pride,* which was performed by John Drinkwater's Birmingham repertory company. Other successful novels of Mrs. Harker's were *The Bridge Across,* dealing with a middle-aged couple; and *The Really Romantic Age* (1922), concerning a baby orphan, the son of an Anzac and a munition girl of the First World War.

PRINCIPAL WORKS: Concerning Paul and Fiammetta, 1906; His First Leave, 1907; Miss Esperance and Mr. Wycherley, 1908; A Romance of the Nursery, 1909; Master and Maid, 1910; Mr. Wycherley's Wards, 1912; The Ffolliots of Redmarley, 1913; Jan and Her Job, 1917; Allegra, 1919; Children of the Dear Cotswolds (short stories) 1920; The Bridge Across, 1921; The Really Romantic Age, 1922; The Vagaries of Tod and Peter, and Other Stories, 1923; The Broken Bow, 1924; Hilda Ware, 1926; Black Jack House, 1929.

ABOUT: London Times April 15, 1933; New York Times April 15, 1933.

HARLAND, HENRY. See "AMERICAN AUTHORS: 1600-1900"

"HARLAND, MARION." See "AMERICAN AUTHORS: 1600-1900."

*HARPER, GEORGE MCLEAN (December 31, 1863-), American biographer and scholar, writes: "I was born at Shippensburg, Pa., of Scotch ancestry, my parents being William Wylie Harper and Nancy (McLean) Harper. I prepared for college at the Cumberland Valley State Normal School and graduated at Princeton in 1884, greatly indebted for literary  training to Professor S. R. Winans. After six months as reporter and copy reader on the New York *Tribune* I spent nearly two and a half years in Europe, England, and Scotland, studying literature and history. From 1887 to 1889 I was a member of the editorial staff of *Scribner's Magazine.* Called to Princeton as instructor in French in 1889, made assistant professor in 1891 and professor of Romance languages in 1894, I took every opportunity to revisit France and Italy. In 1895 I married Belle Dunton Westcott. We have a daughter and a son (professor of classics in Williams College), and four grandchildren. In 1900 I was transferred to the department of English, and in 1926 appointed to the Woodrow Wilson Chair of Literature, founded by Edward Bok.

---

* Died July 14, 1947.

"In 1915 I was a delegate of the American Commission for Relief in Belgium, and was in charge of operations at Ghent for supplying food in East Flanders. In 1917 my son and I served as orderlies in the American Ambulance Hospital at Neuilly, France.

"Having reached the age limit, I retired from my professorship in 1932, but was retained by the university for two years longer, as special lecturer. I taught once in the summer session of Cornell University. I contributed to the *Enciclopedia Italiana* the English basis of its article on 'Literature in the United States.' I have edited works by Hugo and Balzac, Woodrow Wilson's addresses, and two volumes of Wordsworth, and have contributed to many magazines. If any one of my essays is important it is 'A Declaration of Dependence,' published in the *Quarterly Review* for October 1938. I am a director of the C.R.B. Educational Foundation, and Officer of the Crown of Belgium, and a member of the National Institute of Arts and Letters.

"I am in favor of the New Deal, though not of its agricultural policy nor of maintaining a large navy. I am an advocate of federal union of the democratic peoples of the world. In 1939 the Princeton University Press published in my honor a volume of studies entitled *Wordsworth and Coleridge*, edited by Earl Leslie Griggs."

PRINCIPAL WORKS: The Legend of the Holy Grail, 1893; Masters of French Literature, 1901; Charles Augustin Sainte-Beuve, 1909; William Wordsworth: His Life, Works, and Influence (2 vols.) 1916 (one volume edition 1929); John Morley and Other Essays, 1920; Wordsworth's French Daughter, 1921; Dreams and Memories, 1922; Spirit of Delight, 1928; Literary Appreciations, 1937.

ABOUT: Griggs, E. L. (ed.). Wordsworth and Coleridge.

HARRADEN, BEATRICE (January 24, 1864-May 5, 1936), English novelist, was the youngest daughter of Samuel and Rosalie Harraden. She was educated in Dresden, at Cheltenham College, at Queen's College, and at Bedford College, London. At a time when a university-bred woman was something of a novelty, she received a B.A. degree from London University, with honors in classics and mathematics, in 1883. *Things Will Take a Turn*, a story for children, was her first published book.

Miss Harraden's short stories also appeared in *Blackwood's Magazine,* but William Blackwood rejected her greatest success, *Ships That Pass in the Night* (the title, of course is from Longfellow's *Evangeline*), on the ground that it was too short and probably would not sell! Lawrence & Bullen bought the novel outright, and published it with some misgivings. It was an immediate success, and has sold more than a million copies. The novel is comparatively brief, and ends abruptly with the heroine's death from a street accident, not from the tuberculosis which finds her, at the beginning of the story, one of the 250 guests of the Kurhaus at Petershof, a winter resort for consumptive patients. The setting, theme and varied types of people presented gave the novel its popular appeal. (Thomas Mann did not disdain to use these same elements in *The Magic Mountain*.) Miss Harraden's next book was *In Varying Moods*, collected short stories written in Sussex, Cannes, and Mentone: she frequently traveled on the Continent.

In spite of extreme shyness, Beatrice Harraden at fifty was in the thick of the suffrage movement, a leader of the Women's Social and Political Union, selling papers at street corners, marching in parades, and speaking at meetings. She also set herself down as actively interested in the promotion of international comity, and visited the United States in 1894-95. Her photographs show a woman with an intense, spiritual face wearing pince-nez, with thick hair and a firm mouth. She died at Barton-on-Sea at seventy-two.

PRINCIPAL WORKS: Things Will Take a Turn, 1891; Ships That Pass in the Night, 1893; In Varying Moods, 1894; Hilda Strafford, 1897; The Fowler, 1899; Katharine Frensham, 1903; Interplay, 1908; Out of the Wreck I Rise, 1912; The Guiding Thread, 1916; Where Your Treasure Is, 1918; Spring Shall Plant, 1920; Thirteen All Told, 1921; Youth Calling, 1924; Rachel, 1926; Search Will Find It Out, 1928.

ABOUT: New York Times May 6, 1936.

HARRIMAN, JOHN (1904-), American novelist and short-story writer, reports "I was born in Purchase, N.Y., the son of Oliver Harriman, the banker. I attended St. Mark's School, Southboro, Mass. I left school at fifteen, convalescing from a pulmonary disorder, and traveled in Europe and Northern Africa for two years with a tutor: France, Italy, Greece, and a winter in Egypt and Algiers. I did not go to college. Instead, at seventeen, I went into a banking firm in Tennessee, traveling for them in Mississippi and Arkansas. Then went back to Europe, this time as secretary to a representative of one of the big New York banking firms. My employer's firm was interested in Central European loans, and we traveled extensively in Germany and Austria. The project of connecting the Rhine and the Danube by a canal was under consideration by the Weimar Republic at that time. My employer was interested in secur-

ing the financing. With him I met and came to know fairly well the leaders in business and politics in the Germany of that day. We lived in Munich, and traveled back and forth between Berlin and Vienna, which was at that time in the final stages of inflation, and where the suffering was frightful to see.

"I returned to New York in 1924, and spent five years on the staff of the *Evening World*: the usual reporter's jobs, police headquarters, West Side court, Federal Courts, and finally general reporting. The last two years I specialized in aviation and in trial work: the second Hall-Mills trial, Ruth Snyder and Judd Gray, René Fonck's attempted flight to Paris for the Orteig Prize which Lindbergh won the following year. I had one year's leave of absence which I spent in Paris and London, and I wrote some fiction for magazines which I am more than willing to forget.

"Just before the newspaper was sold, I left it and went into Wall Street. I worked for a Boston firm of investment counsels, specializing in analysis of the copper and steel stocks, visiting the mines and mills in the Middle West. I left Wall Street to go to Boston, where my first novel was written, returning upon its publication to New York. My second novel takes a family whose background is Wall Street through a cycle of financial depression. I am married and have a daughter."

* * *

John Harriman's first novel, *Winter Term*, a caustic study of a rich boys' private school, aroused much controversy on its appearance. William Rose Benét praised it as an accurate and frightening story of a gentleman's "so-called education." He is currently working, at his home in Bucks County, Pa., on a trilogy devoted to the public utilities industry.

PRINCIPAL WORKS: Winter Term, 1940; The Career of Philip Hazen, 1941.

HARRIS, FRANK (February 14, 1856-August 26, 1931), British-American man of letters, claimed that he was born in Galway, Ireland. Because his personal accounts are so untrustworthy, his family origin remains obscure. It is certain that at fifteen he was awarded a scholarship to Cambridge University, but because of his youth it was taken from him and instead he was

given ten pounds and told to wait a year. Instead, he used the money to come by steerage to the United States, where he worked as bootblack, ditch digger, and in similar occupations until he became a hotel clerk in Chicago. From Chicago he went to Texas, where he seems to have been a cowboy—though how much of his story of his Texas experiences is true, no one knows. He did go to the University of Kansas, worked his way through college and law school, became naturalized, and was admitted to the bar in Kansas in 1875. Then he returned to Europe and seems to have studied briefly at various continental universities. He drifted back to England at some time in the 1890's and became editor of the *Evening News*. Later he edited the *Fortnightly*, then the *Saturday Review* (which had an immense influence, and "discovered" Shaw and Wells), *Vanity Fair* (in connection with which he served a brief prison sentence for libel), and the *Candid Friend*. His biography of Oscar Wilde was too frank for any English publisher to touch, so he came back to America and printed and sold it himself. Then he bought and edited *Pearson's Magazine* until his "pro-German" views caused its suspension. He left New York in 1922, and the remainder of his life was spent on the Riviera. His period of power and celebrity had been in the "mauve decade"; his embittered last years were increasingly poverty-stricken, and in the end he was writing gossip for a "chitchat magazine" published for British visitors to Nice and Cannes. Much of the obloquy of his last years was due to the scandal aroused by his *My Life and Loves*, printed in Germany because no English or American publisher would run the risk of printing it. He was married twice (at least), but had no children—or no acknowledged children. He died at Nice: the biography of Bernard Shaw on which he was engaged was sufficiently finished for it to be published a few months later—though some doubt has been expressed as to how much of it was really his own work.

Harris was a strange creature, bombastic, violent, prejudiced, and seemingly offensive on principle. (Wilde said he was "invited to all the great houses in London—*once*.") Shaw called him a ruffian and a monster, Francis Hackett said he was a foul-mouthed crook, Joseph Wood Krutch called him an exhibitionistic satyr. He was utterly devoid of humor, envious, malicious. In appearance he resembled a cheap gambler, with his brigandish moustache, beady eyes, and flashy clothes. Yet he was also, as Heywood Broun remarked, "an inspired literary scout," and Norman Douglas, who disliked him, yet spoke of his "heartfelt and outspoken reverence for all that is admirable in art or literature." He had an immense appetite for life, a turbulent vitality, what the *Bookman* aptly described as "a theatrical nature, a mixture of poetry and fireworks." A few of his stories—"Montes, the Matador" most of all—are masterpieces; his biographical studies (in actuality also largely fictional) nevertheless are the work of a man of uneven but indubitable talent. Norman Douglas has said the final word on him: "Owing to a fatal flaw in his alloy he lost all that his rare combination of gifts should have gained for him."

PRINCIPAL WORKS: *Fiction*—Elder Conklin, 1894; Montes, the Matador, 1900; The Bomb, 1908; Unpath'd Waters, 1913; Great Days, 1914; The Veils of Isis, 1915; Love in Youth, 1916; A Mad Love, 1920. *Plays*—Mr. and Mrs. Daventry, 1900; Shakespeare and His Love, 1910; Joan la Romée, 1926. *Biography and Criticism*—The Man Shakespeare, 1909; The Women of Shakespeare, 1911; Contemporary Portraits (Four Series) 1915-23; Oscar Wilde, 1916; Latest Contemporary Portraits, 1927; Life of Bernard Shaw, 1931. *Autobiography*—My Life and Loves (3 vols.) 1923-27; My Reminiscences As a Cowboy, 1930.

ABOUT: Harris, F. My Life and Loves, My Reminiscences As a Cowboy; Lunn, H. K. Frank Harris; Sherard, R. H. Bernard Shaw, Frank Harris, and Oscar Wilde; American Mercury February 1932; Bookman November 1931, August 1932, February 1933; Catholic World December 1932; Literary Digest September 19, 1931; Nation September 9, 1931, December 23, 1931, May 4, 1932.

HARRIS, JOEL CHANDLER. See "AMERICAN AUTHORS: 1600-1900"

HARRISON, FREDERIC. See "BRITISH AUTHORS OF THE 19TH CENTURY"

HARRISON, HENRY SYDNOR (February 12, 1880—July 14, 1930), American novelist, was born in Sewanee, Tenn., where his father, Dr. Caskie Harrison, was professor of Greek and Latin at the University of the South. His mother, Margaret Coleman (Sydnor) Harrison, came from Halifax County, Va. In 1885 Dr. Harrison established a private school of his own, the Brooklyn (N.Y.) Latin School, and his family joined him in 1885. Henry Sydnor Harrison graduated in 1900 from Columbia University, where he edited the *Morningside* and *Spectator,* and played in productions of the Columbia Dramatic Society, notably in the old Daly farce, *A Night Off,* as Professor Babbit. Dr. Harrison died in 1902, and the family moved to Richmond, Va. Henry went into journalism, but "found it was nothing but newspaper work." In 1910 he retreated to Charleston, W.Va., and wrote a novel in six months. Completed in August 1910 and published May 6, 1911, as *Queed,* the romance of an absent-minded and public-spirited young newspaper man, the novel caught the public fancy. *Queed* and its successor *V.V.'s Eyes,* which advocated reforms in tobacco factories, sold 400,000 copies, and Harrison found his short stories, hitherto rejected with the exception of a dozen or so, in demand by editors. (He could not forbear to twit them with the fact in an article in the *Atlantic Monthly,* in April 1914.) *V.V.'s Eyes* was, in its way, as uncomplimentary to Southern womanhood as Lillian Hellman's play, *The Little Foxes.*

H. L. Mencken, in one of his early swashbuckling moods, rather unfairly dubbed Harrison a "merchant of mush," and called *Queed* William J. Locke diluted with vast drafts from *Laddie* and *Pollyanna.* In *Angela's Business,* Harrison dealt with a woman who was intent on getting married; and *Saint Teresa,* which William Lyon Phelps called "a rather wild story," culminates in a knock-down-and-drag-out fight between Teresa de Silver, who refuses to turn her steel mill into a munitions factory, and her efficiency manager.

When I Come Back (1919) was designed as a tribute to Harrison's brother, who fell in the Argonne in the First World War, and was based to some extent on his letters from France. In 1929 Harrison contributed a series of articles to the Richmond *News Leader*. He died in a hospital at Atlantic City, N.J., at fifty, four days after an operation. Harrison never married. His royalties enabled him to travel abroad and put up at good American hotels. A *Bookman* interviewer described him as being of medium height, and slender, with light hair and blue eyes.

PRINCIPAL WORKS: Captivating Mary Carstairs (as "Henry Second"), 1910; Queed, 1911; V.V.'s Eyes, 1913; Angela's Business, 1915; When I Come Back, 1919; Saint Teresa, 1922; Andrew Bride of Paris, 1925.

ABOUT: Baldwin, C. C. The Men Who Make Our Novels; Mencken, H. L. Prejudices: First Series; Atlantic Monthly April 1914; Bookman September 1913; June 1914; New York Times July 15, 1930; Publishers' Weekly July 19, 1930.

HARRISON, Mrs. MARY ST. LEGER (KINGSLEY) ("Lucas Malet") (1852-October 27, 1931), youngest daughter of

the author Charles Kingsley, was born at her father's rectory in Eversley. She was a student at the Slade school for a while, and then enjoyed some rather extensive travel on the Continent, in America, and in the East. Her marriage to the Rev. William Harrison was unhappy, and they eventually separated. Five years after his death in 1897, she was received into the Roman Catholic Church, and her religion became more preoccupying.

She had already produced one novel when, in 1885, she published *Colonel Enderby's Wife*, a book that marked her as a writer of considerable promise. Six years later with *Wages of Sin* and still later with *Sir Richard Calmady* she braved some rather daring and unpleasant subject matter and the consequent resentment of Victorian critics. But her sense of comedy and her structural soundness were sufficiently evident. Some time after her acceptance of Catholicism, she found herself obliged, for the sake of her own conscience, to revise certain portions of her earlier writings.

Her father's literary remains, both published and unpublished, came nominally into her possession in 1892. Not until twenty-two years later, however, did she have complete access to them. She "developed the characters, disentangled the plot, and completed the story" of 150 foolscap pages of handwritten manuscript which Charles Kingsley had, presumably, written just before *The Water Babies*. In it (*The Tutor's Story*, published with some success) she said she wanted most of all to preserve that "pathetic charm of 'a day that is dead' "—but for the literary, social, and political methods of that day she held no brief whatsoever.

She was tall and strangely handsome and was much admired in intellectual circles. With about a dozen titles to her credit, she extended a family literary tradition of distinction.

PRINCIPLE WORKS: Colonel Enderby's Wife, 1885; Little Peter, 1887; The Wages of Sin, 1891; The Gateless Barrier, 1900; Sir Richard Calmady, 1901; The Far Horizon, 1906; The Golden Galleon, 1910; Deadham Hard, 1920; The Survivors, 1923; The Dogs of Want, 1924.

ABOUT: Kingsley, C. The Tutor's Story (see Prefatory Note); Thorp, M. F. Charles Kingsley: 1819-1875; London Times October 29, 1931.

*HART, ALBERT BUSHNELL (July 1, 1854-), American historian and university professor, was born in Clarksville, Pa.,

the son of Albert Gaillard Hart and Mary Crosby (Hornell) Hart. "I have traced the Hart clan back to Stephen Hart of Ipswich, England, father of Steven Hart the emigrant, who came to Boston in 1632, lived in Cambridge, and helped to found Connecticut," Hart once wrote the secretary of his Harvard class, 1880: "On my mother's side I have run back five generations to the first Hornell, and have visited his birthplace at Hor, Sweden."

Hart attended the West High School, Cleveland, Ohio, and after his graduation from Harvard, where he was a classmate of Theodore Roosevelt, spent a year in the graduate department of the University of Berlin and with Professor von Hoist at Freiburg (Baden), receiving his Ph.D. degree in August 1883. Returning to Harvard as instructor in politics and history, Hart was made a full professor in January 1897. In 1903-04 Hart spent his second sabbatical year making a foot journey among the southern valleys of the Alps, "and then with my family spent four months in the Southern states, and a like period in California. This experience has given rise to a renewed interest in the race problem of the South, resulting in numerous addresses and articles. In 1902 I undertook the editing of a cooperative history of the United States in 28 volumes"—the well-known American Nation Series.

"I count myself fortunate in having, rather by chance indirection than by deliberate intent, steered into a profession where the opportunities were great," wrote Hart to his class secretary in 1930. "By the inspiration of several of my professors—notably Emerton, Torrey, Dunbar, Nat Shaler, and more than anybody else, [Charles Eliot] Norton—I was led to enter the field of history. Henry Adams and Cabot Lodge lectured while we were there, but I knew them not. Then came the good-will and confidence and support in perilous difficulties of Charles William Eliot, the greatest man (except a member of our Class) whose friendship I have ever had. The developments of the subject in which I take most pride and pleasure are the opening up of source material, the combination of groups of scholars on historical tasks too great for any one mind, and a share in introducing stimulating methods for undergraduate lecture courses and for the historical training of advanced students. For all the weary hours spent over bibliographies and source books and textbooks, at the end of over fifty years I have the satisfaction of believing that I was one of a group of young men who made history and government vital subjects for college and graduate school."

President Coolidge appointed Hart one of the nineteen members of the Commission for the celebration of the 200th anniversary celebration of the birth of Washington, and he visited more than 250 localities in England connected with Washington.

Dr. Hart, also the holder of four honorary degrees, became professor-emeritus in 1926. Mrs. Hart (Mary Hurd Putnam, whom he married in 1889) died some years ago. His home in Cambridge, Mass., is on Plympton Street, and he has an office in the Widener Library. He has written and edited about a hundred volumes.

PRINCIPAL WORKS: Introduction to the Study of Federal Government, 1891; The Formation of the Union, 1892; Studies in American Education, 1895; Guide to the Study of American History (with E. Channing) 1897; Salmon Portland Chase, 1899; The Foundations of American Foreign Policy, 1901; Source-Book of American History, 1903; Handbook of the History, Diplomacy and Government of the United States, 1903; The Romance of the Civil War, 1903; Slavery and Abolition: 1831-1841, 1906; National Ideals His-

torically Traced, 1907; Manual of American History, Diplomacy and Government, 1908; The Southern South, 1910; Essentials in American History, 1911; The Obvious Orient, 1911; The War in Europe: Its Causes and Results, 1914; The Monroe Doctrine: An Interpretation, 1915; Handbook of the War (with A. C. Lovejoy) 1917; America at War, 1917; We and Our History, 1923; Wall Maps of American Government, 1927. Editor—American History Leaflets (with E. Channing) 1892-1910; American History Told by Contemporaries, 1901-29; The American Nation Series, 1903-18; American Yearbook, 1911-20, 1926-32; American Patriots and Statesmen from Washington to Lincoln, 1916; Commonwealth History of Massachusetts, 1927-29; The Roosevelt Encyclopedia, 1927- ; George Washington Pamphlets, 1932.

ABOUT: Harvard University, Class of 1880: Twenty-Fifth and Fiftieth Anniversary Reports.

*HART, Mrs. FRANCES NEWBOLD (NOYES) (August 10, 1890-), American novelist and writer of detective fiction under the name of Frances Noyes Hart, was born a  Silver Springs, Md., the daughter of Frank Brett Noyes, editor and proprietor of the Washington Star and president of the Associated Press, and Janet Thurston (Newbold) Noyes. She was educated at private schools and in Italy; also attending the Sorbonne and Collège de France in Paris and taking extension courses at Columbia University. Experiences in 1918-1919 as a Y.M.C.A. canteen worker in France were the basis of a popular book about the American troops in France during the World War, My A.E.F. (Her first book was Mark, a "society novel," published in 1913.) For six months in 1917-1918 she was a translator with the Naval Intelligence Bureau. Miss Noyes married Edward Henry Hart of New York City, in 1921. They live with their two daughters in Washington, D.C. Mrs. Hart is a member of the Authors' League of America, the Colony Club, and the National Woman's Country Club.

In Mrs. Hart's best-selling novel, The Bellamy Trial, a notable tour de force among detective stories, "the customer," said Will Cuppy, "gets full journalistic accounts of eight days in court, complete with speeches, testimony and excitement in the press seats, the whole offered in a sprightly and entertaining manner." Some trial lawyers declared that the lib-

* Died October 25, 1943.

erties taken with the rules of evidence in the book would have made it necessary to declare a mistrial in real life; others praised its fidelity to legal procedure. *Hide in the Dark,* another popular favorite, is said to have started the game of "Murder." *The Crooked Lane,* a novel of Washington society, introduced scientific detection of the Viennese school, although the plot, according to Ralph Partridge, was not helped by the "luscious padding" of the background and characters.

PRINCIPAL WORKS: Mark, 1913; My A.E.F., 1920; Contact, 1923; The Bellamy Trial, 1927; Hide in the Dark, 1929; Pigs in Clover, 1931; The Crooked Lane, 1934.

ABOUT: Haycraft, H. Murder for Pleasure: The Life and Times of the Detective Story; Saturday Evening Post January 28, 1928.

HART, LIDDELL. See LIDDELL HART, B. H.

HART, MOSS (October 24, 1904-), American playwright, was born in New York City, the son of Barnett Hart and Lillian (Solomon)

Vandamm

Hart. He was educated in the public schools of New York; lived in the "close drabness of an 107th Street tenement," and wrote his first play at twelve, acting it before an admiring audience of relatives at the Bronx Y.M.H.A. For a time Hart was with the Thalian Players, which won the Belasco cup in a Little Theatre competition one year. He became a floorwalker for a cloak-and-suit concern, and wrote and directed the employees' annual show. Once he appeared with the late Charles Gilpin in Eugene O'Neill's *The Emperor Jones.* Hart directed little theatre groups in Brooklyn and Newark during the winters, and spent several strenuous summers as social director in summer camps, rising from $30 to $200 a week. "It wasn't work merely; it was slavery which took the form of really macabre play," Edna Ferber wrote once. The clerks, shop-girls, and stenographers "paid $35 a week, everything included. And everything included Moss Hart." During one really horrible summer, when it rained fifteen consecutive days, Hart had to call on all his inventive powers to keep his charges amused. He worked at Camp Utopia, Pa., and the Crescent Country Club, Vt.

When Hart began to write plays, the first, *The Hold-Up Man,* produced appropriately in Chicago, was a failure. *Once in a Lifetime* (1930), when expertly doctored by George S. Kaufman,[qv] collaborator in most of his succeeding works, became a hit. It was an uproarious satire on life in Hollywood, which Hart had not yet visited; later he repaired the omission. Kaufman stated that 75 per cent of the play was Hart's, and the 60 per cent he received from the royalties made Moss Hart affluent at twenty-six. A long list of Kaufman-Hart plays has followed, representing collaboration in all degrees; in some cases the original work is almost entirely Hart's with technical polishing by Kaufman, in others the partners have worked together from the start. *Face the Music* (1932) was a musical comedy satirizing the free and easy New York City municipal government, and featured Mary Boland. *As Thousands Cheer* (1933) was a successful Music Box revue starring Beatrice Lillie, Ethel Waters, and the late Marilyn Miller; the music was written by Irving Berlin. *Merrily We Roll Along* (1934), the most serious of the collaborations, considered by many critics the team's finest work, was played in reverse and laid bare the spiritual degradation of a successful New York dramatist. *You Can't Take It With You* (1936), a comedy of a "screwball" family, brought the joint-authors the Pulitzer Prize for drama in 1937 and made a hugely successful motion picture.

In 1938 Hart's income was estimated at $175,000, and he is said to have spent $100,000 on a farm in New Hope, Pa., and a house on 57th Street off Sutton Place in New York City. *The American Way* (1939), a patriotic spectacle, was at first conceived by Hart as *Wind Up an Era* before Noel Coward's *Cavalcade* was produced on much the same lines in England. *The Man Who Came to Dinner* (1939), which ran well over a year on Broadway and in numerous companies, was tailored for Alexander Woollcott's talents. One of the few "uncollaborative" products of Moss Hart's versatile talent is the psychoanalytic musical comedy written for Gertrude Lawrence, *Lady in the Dark* (1941), with music by Kurt Weill. Hart is unmarried. He visited Europe in 1932; went around the world with Cole Porter, the composer, in 1934.

PRINCIPAL WORKS: (mostly in collaboration with G. S. Kaufman): The Hold-up Man, 1925; Once in a Lifetime, 1930; Face the Music, 1932; As Thousands Cheer, 1933; Merrily We Roll Along, 1934; The Great Waltz, 1934; Jubilee, 1935; You Can't Take It With You, 1936; I'd Rather Be Right, 1937; The Fabulous Invalid, 1938; The American Way, 1939; The Man Who Came to Dinner, 1939; George Washington Slept Here, 1940; Lady in the Dark, 1941.

ABOUT: Parker, J. Who's Who in the Theatre; Look April 9, 1940; New York World-Telegram June 4, 1938.

HARTE, BRET. See "AMERICAN AUTHORS: 1600-1900"

HAŠEK, JAROSLAV (April 30, 1883-1923), Czech novelist and short-story writer, was born in Prague, the son of a teacher of mathematics in the Bohemian capital, Josef Hašek, and Katerina Hašek. He was named Jaroslav Matej Frantisek Hašek, and was a cheerful youth, fond of hoaxes and practical jokes. The dictates of necessity forced him into a clerkship in a bank. Hašek was determined to be a writer, however, and had published sixteen volumes of short stories before the First World War broke out and he was called to the colors by the Austrian army.

When assigned to a sanitary corps, Hašek indulged in the same sort of light-hearted sabotage as is perpetrated by his famous soldier-creation, Schweik. He was taken prisoner on the Eastern front, and spent several years in Russian camps. Later he enrolled in the Czechoslovakian army; was an assistant editor on a Czech newspaper; and joined the Bolshevists to hold some important offices in the Communist party. When, finally, Hašek returned to his liberated country, he did not live to enjoy the success he had never expected to attain. He began to write The Good Soldier: Schweik, "the gargantuan book which was to inflame a nation to resistance and sweep all Europe with the virility of its satire," which was titled Osudy Dobrého Vojáka Švejka za Světové Války. According to his original plan, Schweik was to be completed in six volumes. Hašek died at forty, however, with only four volumes written.

"That good old soldier, Schweik, this quiet, unassuming, shabbily dressed man: the heroic dauntless man who was the talk of all citizens in the kingdom of Bohemia when they were under Austrian rule" (so described by the author, tongue in cheek) appealed to the rank and file of Hašek's fellow-countrymen, but did not interest the intelligentsia of Czechoslovakia until they began to hear rumors that a character had appeared in their literature who was being compared to Cervantes' Sancho Panza. In a few months translations were on sale in Vienna, Berlin, Moscow, and Paris. The French regarded Le Brave Soldat Chveïk not so much as a work of national character as a manifestation of an absolute pacifism. Some Czech critics feared that the book would be received as fact and so mislead strangers into thinking that Schweik was truly representative of the Czech character.

In 1928 a dramatization was produced by Erwin Piscator at his Nollendorfplatz Theatre in Berlin. Piscator, now on the staff of the New School for Social Research in New York City, told an interviewer in 1940 that his own nightmare experiences in the war suggested the treadmill he used in staging Schweik, in which he also employed film as a substitute for a chorus. Hašek, "the incoherent Bohemian and drunkard of genius," is depicted by the illustrator of Schweik as a powerfully built man with a round face covered by a stubble of beard, fuzzy hair growing low on his forehead, a hairy chest, and a pipe and a stein of beer as adjuncts to his pen. He was a Catholic, having joined the church in 1910. The English translation, made by Paul Selver and illustrated by Joseph Lada, appeared seven years after his death.

WORK AVAILABLE IN ENGLISH TRANSLATION: The Good Soldier: Schweik, 1930.

ABOUT: Jelinek. Histoire de Littérature Tchèque de 1890 à Nos Jours; Menger. Jaroslav Hašek Doma; Rivista di Letterature Slave April 1928.

HATCH, ERIC (October 31, 1901-), American novelist and story writer, was born Eric Stow Hatch in New York City and educated at St. Paul's School, Concord. He was not graduated, however, and did not go to college; instead, at seventeen, he entered his father's investment banking business and remained in it for ten years. His business career was interrupted only by the First World War, during which he served for two years in the New York National Guard. In 1922 he married Sylvia Whiton-Stuart, and they had a daughter; after a divorce, he married, in 1929, Gertrude Thomas. Even while he was in Wall Street he started to write sto-

ries, and by 1928 he was sufficiently successful to be able to leave business and devote himself entirely to writing. Before long he was summoned to Hollywood, and for the past half dozen years he has spent about half his time as a screen writer. He lives in Beverly Hills, Calif. He continues, however, to pour out short stories for the popular magazines and an occasional novel.

The work of Eric Hatch is light and entertaining, never profound and probably not "literature," but always deft, competent, and professional. He has a great fund of humor and a gift for apt characterization and for a half-affectionate, half-satirical depiction of the idiosyncrasies of his fellow-humans. His chief recreation is yachting, and he is an experienced sailor. He still spends part of every year in New York, but seems to be permanently a part of the Southern California group of motion picture staff writers. Perhaps his best-known picture was *My Man Godfrey*, originally a story, and rewritten for the screen. It comes nearer than anything else Mr. Hatch has written to having "social implications," but he belongs distinctly to the school of authors whose aim is not instruction or reform, but pure entertainment.

PRINCIPAL WORKS: A Couple of Quick Ones, 1928; Domestic Animal, 1929; Romance Prescribed, 1930; Lovers' Loot, 1931; Five Days, 1933; Road Show, 1934; Fly by Night, 1935; My Man Godfrey, 1935; Good Old Jack, 1936; The Captain Needs a Mate, 1937; June Remembers, 1938; Unexpected Uncle, 1941.

HATCHER, HARLAN HENTHORNE

(September 9, 1898-), American critic and novelist, writes: "I was born by the great bend in the Ohio River that sweeps around the southernmost tip of Ohio. Shortly after McKinley was shot, we moved over to Kentucky, where my father taught school. I left the academy of the Morehead Normal School in my senior year to join the army in the S.A.T.C. at Miami University. I was mustered out, taught history the rest of the year, and entered the Ohio State University in 1919 (B.A. 1922, M.A. 1923, Ph.D. 1928). Except for an interlude as a graduate student at the University of Chicago, a year in Europe, and various minor leaves of ab-

sence, I have lived and worked at Ohio State ever since. I became a professor of English in 1932. It is a good but not a quiet life; there is nothing 'cloistered' about a modern state university with 15,000 students! In fact I periodically escape from the rush of the university into the peace and contemplative quiet of New York.

"My first novel was largely written in London. I temporarily parted company with Ariosto and the Medici, rented a chair above the Serpentine, and wrote about life on the Kentucky side of the Ohio River. It was apparently most widely read by sheltered souls who found it shocking

"My next novel was about the Big Sandy country of Kentucky. The State of Kentucky issued a special number of the *Kentucky Progress Magazine* on the Big Sandy Valley, reprinted parts of the book, and illustrated it with photographs of the region. A personal book on my native state, *The Buckeye Country*, pleased Ohioans and they made it a best-seller.

"At Ohio State University I specialize in the novel and the modern drama, giving half my time to large undergraduate lecture courses and half to directing the work of graduate students. I write during the morning hours and during the quarter vacation from teaching. I plan my writings in Columbus, draft them at Concord, Mass., where, with my wife, Frank Wilson Colfax, I usually live a few weeks of each year, and complete them at a sunny window on the tenth floor of a New York hotel. I have lectured far and wide all over the Republic. I wrote a weekly book column for the Columbus *Citizen*, and serve as editorial advisor to *College English*. For two years I directed the Federal Writers' Project in Ohio, and edited the *Ohio Guide* and other publications. I was once upon a time Junior Assistant County Sanitary Engineer of Franklin County; I made a drainage map of the area around Columbus. For recreation I play golf and tennis, and travel much about Ohio and Walden Pond."

PRINCIPAL WORKS: The Versification of Robert Browning, 1928; Tunnel Hill (novel) 1931; Patterns of Wolfpen (novel) 1934; Creating the Modern American Novel, 1935; Central Standard Time (novel) 1937; The Buckeye Country: A Pageant of Ohio, 1940; Modern Dramas; Continental, British, American (ed. with introductory essays) 1941.

ABOUT: Scribner's Magazine November 1937.

*HAUPTMANN, GERHART JOHANN ROBERT

(November 15, 1862-), German dramatist and novelist, Nobel Prize winner, was born in Ober-Salzbrunn, Silesia, the son of Robert Hauptmann, an innkeeper (whose own father had been one of the poor Silesian weavers celebrated in the grandson's most widely known play), and of Marie (Strahler) Hauptmann. The boy was sent to school in Breslau, where he did not at all distinguish himself. Then his father lost his hotel and his savings, and Gerhart was taken from school and sent to stay with an uncle, a devout Moravian who was also musically inclined, so that Hauptmann in his most impressionable years came under the influence both of religion and of art. It was not music, however, but sculpture, which first seemed to be his chief gift. He returned to Breslau in 1880 to attend the Royal College of Art, his father's and uncle's intention of making a farmer of him having

Times Studios

proved doomed to failure. Again he was an ungovernable pupil, who was rusticated for several months. He did not leave the college, however, until 1882, and then to join his brother (later a noted scientist and a minor poet) at the University of Jena, where Haeckel and Eucken were among his teachers.

In 1883, still considering himself a sculptor, Hauptmann set out for Italy, and for some time practiced his art in Rome. There also he was stricken with typhoid fever, and a German girl, Marie Thienemann, nursed him back to health. In 1884 they were married, his two brothers later marrying her two sisters. The Hauptmanns had three sons; but the marriage was unhappy and was later dissolved. Hauptman married his present wife (Margarete Marschalk) in 1905, they have one son.

For a short time, in Berlin, he went on the stage, but he was never a success as an actor. He had by now published his first volume, a Byronesque poem called *Promithedenlos*, all copies of which he later withdrew from publication. Another volume of poems and his first unimportant novel appeared in 1887. It was at this time that he met Arno Holz, the father of literary naturalism in Germany, and became in some sense his disciple. His first play, *Vor Sonnenaufgang (Before Dawn)*, produced by the Free Stage Society in Berlin, in 1889, was purely naturalistic, and produced a storm of protest. It was not, in fact, till

the end of his first and second literary periods—the realistic and the socialistic—that Hauptmann ceased to be a storm-center, condemned and attacked by the authorities and the orthodox critics, and began the slow ascent to the almost canonized position of his last years.

His first really important work was the famous play, *The Weavers,* dealing with the first stirrings of labor among the exploited weavers of the 1840's. As late as *The Rats,* written in 1911, some of Hauptmann's plays continued to be naturalistic in tone and treatment; but the mystical, symbolic phase was inaugurated with *Hannele,* in 1894, and *The Sunken Bell,* in 1897. These, with perhaps *Rose Bernd, The Beaver Coat,* and *Lonely Lives,* are the best known of Hauptmann's plays to the English-reading public, but he has produced and published thirty-eight in all, two in 1939 when he was seventy-six years old.

Though he began writing as a poet, Hauptmann has only two volumes of lyrics in print. As a novelist he has been much more prolific, though few of his novels have been translated into English. Two of these, *The Fool in Christ: Emanuel Quint,* and *The Heretic of Soana,* belong to his mystical period. He was never so strong a realist in fiction as in the drama, and none of his naturalistic novels has appeared in English.

As the years went on, honors fell thick on the aging author. A Hauptmann-cult sprang up, not discouraged by himself. His palatial house in Agnetendorf, in the mountains of western Germany, where he still lives, became a shrine. He was compared to Goethe, and like Goethe he had his disciples who took down his most casual conversation to preserve it for posterity. Oxford and Columbia universities gave him honorary degrees, as well as Leipzig and Prague. In 1912 he won the Nobel Prize for literature. Once the Kaiser removed the royal insignia from his theatre box because a Hauptmann play was to be produced there; but there was hardly any honor or medal of the German Republic that he did not receive. He was a close friend of President Ebert, and in the days before the Nazis came to power they constantly attacked and derided him. Nevertheless, he is the only German author of distinction who has not left Nazi Germany voluntarily or been exiled. As an anonymous German writer in the English *Spectator* put it: "That the old gentleman on the threshold of old age and of the Third Reich no longer found the strength to eat with tears the bread of strangers, no one can find offense who knows his Stoicism and his credulity."

Doubtless he no longer can live in the resplendent state of his sixth decade—the baronial hall, the exquisite dress, the lordly banquets described by Rothenstein. But he still finds it possible to live in peace and in as much comfort as possible. Looking like a cross between the aged Goethe and a benign old priest, with his fluffy white hair and his tall, still erect form, he tramps about his estate in all kinds of weather, receives with dignity those who still travel to see him, and keeps on writing. He has written his own quasi-apology for what in a younger man would be judged more harshly:

> Weak, you may say, were his weapons,
> Still were his courage and his good
> will great!

It is by the work of his early years that, when the record is closed, Gerhart Hauptmann will be permanently judged and acclaimed. He was never, whatever his sympathy with the poor, a radical; as the *Nation* remarked: "he never stepped beyond the confines of an individualist bourgeois attitude. . . . He lives in an airtight chamber apart from world events. . . . He was a young man whose ardor flared up for a span and then burned out into innocuous fantasy." And August Closs confirmed this judgment by saying that Hauptmann's "gospel" is "the redemption of sinful man by the uniting force of love." He himself remains the indifferent Olympian: "I write because I can do nothing else. Whether it is good or bad is the affair of the critics, who do not interest me at all." He has indeed "put his Pegasus through many paces." But a great German writer who found it impossible to live in Germany today has nevertheless paid only recently a tribute to the golden residue of Hauptmann's work that will be left when time has burnt off all the slag: Thomas Mann said of him, "He did not speak in his own guise, but let life itself talk."

PRINCIPAL WORKS AVAILABLE IN ENGLISH: *Plays*—Lonely Lives, 1898; The Coming of Peace, 1900; The Sunken Bell, 1900; Hannele, 1908; Dramatic Works (9 vols., ed. by Ludwig Lewisohn) 1912-29. *Novels*—Atlantis, 1912; Parsival (juvenile) 1915; Phantom, 1922; The Heretic of Soana, 1923; The Island of the Great Mother, 1925; The Fool in Christ: Emanuel Quint, 1926.

ABOUT: Hale, E. E. Dramatists of Today; Heller, O. Studies in Modern German Literature; Holl, K. Gerhart Hauptmann; His Life and Work; von Hulsen, H. Gerhart Hauptmann; Huneker, J. G. Iconoclasts; von Klenze, C. From Goethe to Hauptmann; Rothenstein, W. Men and Memories; Voigt, F. A. Hauptmann-Studien; Commonweal February 15, 1933; Contemporary Review December 1932; Current History November 1932; Journal des Débats September 16, 1932, November 25, 1932; Living Age July 1929, March 1933; Nation March 3, 1932; Spectator November 10, 1933, November 26, 1937.

HAUSER, HEINRICH (1901-), German novelist, was born of Danish parents in Berlin. At seventeen he quit school to join the navy as a midshipman, but saw little of the First World War, the German revolution supervening. At nineteen he was searching for mines in the North Sea. Deciding to study medicine, he attended a series of universities, until  compelled to leave to make a living in coal mines and steel mills. Returning once again to the sea, Hauser journeyed to Australia, India, to Mediterranean ports of call, and South America. Articles describing his experiences were accepted by newspapers. Receiving an order for articles on Mexico, he shipped there and sold six articles for ten dollars. Marriage gave Hauser temporary respite from wandering, and he settled down for a while in a little village on the German coast. After another trip to South America he took an editorial job on the *Frankfurter Zeitung*, varied the monotony of this by becoming publicity manager for a German circus, and wrote the novel which was translated into English as *Bitter Waters*. The book had a preface by Liam O'Flaherty, whom Hauser had met in Ireland in 1928. As a return courtesy, Hauser translated O'Flaherty's *The Informer* into German, and made a motion picture with him. Hauser took his moving-picture camera into the mining and steel industries of the Ruhr and by slow stages, in 1931, down the Mississippi, stopping off in New York to let his publishers have a look at him and in Chicago to take some background shots. Experiences in the West Indies as an apprentice deep-sea diver and a trip to Chile on the four-masted sailing ship "Pamir" preceded the American visit.

His publishers saw a handsome, well-knit, robust man with crisp brown hair, speaking excellent English. Antipathetic to the Hitler régime, Hauser now makes his home in the United States. Thomas Mann, praising *Bitter Waters*, which won the Gerhart Hauptmann Prize in Germany, spoke of Hauser's "original and natural talent, great stock of living experience, and marked faculty for form." Harry Hansen, reviewing *Thunder Above the Sea,* spoke of Hauser's rare ability in sketching wayward, forlorn, suffering and scarcely articulate women. "His chief difficulty seems to be in bringing his introspective musings in line with his story-telling."

WORKS AVAILABLE IN ENGLISH TRANSLATION: Bitter Waters, 1929; Thunder Above the Sea, 1931; Fair Winds and Foul: Ship, Crew, Sea, Horizon, 1932; Once Your Enemy, 1937; Last Port of Call, 1938; Battle Against Time: a Survey of the Germany of 1939 From the Inside (English title: Hitler Versus Germany) 1939; The Folding Father (juvenile) 1942; Time Was: Death of a Junker (autobiography) 1942.

ABOUT: Hauser, H. Time Was; Wilson Library Bulletin, May 1932.

HAWES, CHARLES BOARDMAN

(January 24, 1889-July 15, 1923), American writer of sea tales, was born at Clifton Springs, N.Y., the

son of Charles Taylor Hawes and Martha (Boardman) Hawes. He spent a decidedly out-of-doors boyhood in Bangor, Maine. In his preparation for college he found that he must either stay "up" in Latin or stay out of football, and therefore applied himself seriously to his Horace. He entered Bowdoin in 1907, edited a campus magazine, won a number of literary awards, was class poet during his junior and senior years and was graduated in 1911. He was awarded the Henry Wadsworth Longfellow graduate fellowship for Harvard. His summers had been spent on surveying parties in the Maine woods and in his first year out of college he worked as a linesman. Then he began a year's teaching at Harrisburg Academy, Pennsylvania. In 1916 he married Dorothea Cable, daughter of George Washington Cable. They had two sons.

Not long after he had joined the editorial staff of the *Youth's Companion* he began a long and exhaustive series of researches on sea life, collecting stories from the sailors at the wharves, spending long hours in the Peabody Marine Museum and Essex Institute, and even making voyages in search of some much-coveted log, chart, land map, or book about the sea. In 1919 *The Mutineers* was serialized in the newly launched boys' magazine, *The Open Road,* of which Hawes was soon to become associate editor, and

appeared in book form the following year. *The Dark Frigate,* his best known work, won the Newbery Award as the most distinguished "juvenile" of 1923, the year of its author's untimely death at thirty-four. *Gloucester: By Land and Sea* and *Whaling,* a detailed history of the industry extending from the very earliest records down to the period of its decline, were published posthumously; the latter was completed by his wife.

Hawes was an accomplished fencer and was fond of chess and its Japanese counterpart, *shogi.* As he wrote he constantly revised and re-revised, in his effort to strike the smoothest prose rhythm and the best formula for combining sea-faring imaginativeness and historical authenticity. His sudden and early death brought an end to several ambitious literary objectives which would doubtless have enhanced an already enviable achievement.

PRINCIPAL WORKS: The Mutineers, 1920; The Great Quest, 1921; The Dark Frigate, 1923; Gloucester; By Land and Sea, 1923; Whaling, 1924.

ABOUT: Ernst, C. H. Charles Boardman Hawes: An Appreciation; Kunitz, S. J. & Haycraft, H. (eds.). The Junior Book of Authors; Boston Evening Transcript July 17, 1923; Publishers' Weekly August 18 and 25, 1923.

HAWKINS, Sir ANTHONY HOPE

("Anthony Hope") (February 9, 1863-July 8, 1933), English novelist, was born in London, the son of the Rev. Edward C. Hawkins, headmaster of St. John's Foundation School for the Sons of Poor Clergy. He was educated at Marlborough School and Balliol College, Oxford, receiving his M.A. with honors in 1885. He then read

for the bar, and was admitted from the Middle Temple in 1887. Clients were slow in arriving, and he filled his enforced leisure by writing novels, the first of which was published at his own expense. He dabbled in politics also, and ran for Parliament as a Liberal, but was badly defeated.

Success as a barrister and as a novelist arrived together, and he immediately chose the latter. In the same year, 1894, he achieved celebrity and prosperity with two very disparate books—*The Dolly Dialogues,* which George Meredith admired, but which now are very dull humor, and *The Prisoner of Zenda.* With this adventurous romance of

mythical kingdom (first of the *genre* later
exploited by Richard Harding Davis, George
Barr McCutcheon with his "Graustark" series, and others), he had found his *métier.*
He followed it thenceforth, in a long series
alternated with other novels of a light "society" tone. All his books were written
under his first and middle names as a pseudonym; he regretted this later, but had
adopted the pseudonym when he still expected to remain in the law.

Hawkins visited the United States on a
lecture tour in 1897, and frequently thereafter. In 1903 he married an American,
Elizabeth Somerville Sheldon, of Vermont
and New York. They had two sons and a
daughter.

He was knighted in 1918, and soon after
bought a house at Tadworth, Surrey, which
was his home until he died, after a long
illness, at seventy. He loved to play the
country squire, and was most hospitable,
though his working hours were sacred, and
he sat at his desk regularly for seven hours
a day, six days a week. A bald, ruddy,
long-headed man of medium size, he was
handsome in youth and, says his classmate
and biographer, Sir Charles Mallet, "far
more serious at eighteen than at thirty-
eight." In later years, his natural seriousness induced him to try his hand at "problem
novels," but they were not his *forte.* The
field that he had made his own and in which
he was supreme was the "sword and cloak"
school of fiction, which stemmed directly
from the novels of the elder Dumas. In
the happy days before the World War, when
one had to go to the realms of fancy to
supply tales of war and intrigue, "Anthony
Hope's" romances provided a literature of
escape. Their popularity is no longer so
great, though the motion pictures have made
them familiar to a younger generation.
Hawkins was a lover of the theatre, and
had an aptitude for the dramatic. Both
Rupert of Hentzau and *The Prisoner of
Zenda* had long runs as plays, and have not
yet entirely left the stage. He wrote several
other plays as well, the most successful being
Simon Dale, Pilkerton's Peerage, and *The
Adventure of Lady Ursula.*

Cyril Clemens, who visited Hawkins in
1930, noted that he was "a bigger man than
his books showed him" to be. And Mallet,
who knew him well, said he had "the scholar's sense of style, the philosopher's ironic
observation, and wit both fine and rare, . . .
gifts . . . a little wasted on the subjects
chosen." Those dashing stories, instinct with
verve, are the best of their kind in English—
even though the kind has no pretension to
enduring life.

PRINCIPAL WORKS: A Man of Mark, 1889;
Father Stafford, 1890; Mr. Witt's Widow, 1892;
The Dolly Dialogues, 1894; The Prisoner of
Zenda, 1894; The God in the Car, 1894; Rupert
of Hentzau, 1898; Quisante, 1900; Tristram of
Blent, 1901; The Intrusions of Peggy, 1902; The
Indiscretion of the Duchess, 1904; Double Har-
ness, 1904; A Servant of the Public, 1905; Sophy
of Kravonia, 1906; Tales of Two People, 1907;
The Great Miss Driver, 1908; Second String,
1910; Mrs. Maxon Protests, 1911; A Young Man's
Year, 1915; Captain Dieppe, 1918; Beaumaroy
Home From the Wars, 1919; Lucinda, 1920;
Little Tiger, 1925; Memories and Notes, 1927.

ABOUT: Adcock, A. St. J. Gods of Modern
Grub Street; Hope, A. Memories and Notes;
Mallet, C. E. Anthony Hope and His Books;
Contemporary Review August 1933; Overland
Monthly December 1930.

HAWTHORNE, JULIAN (June 22,
1846-July 21, 1934), American novelist, was
born in Boston, the only son of the novelist
Nathaniel Hawthorne
and his wife Sophia
(Peabody) Haw-
thorne. The family
removed to Liver-
pool, England, where
Nathaniel Hawthorne
was consul, when
Julian was seven, and
the elder writer's
English Notebooks
record many "long
walks with J—." After seven years abroad
the boy returned to enter the Lowell Scientific School at Harvard in 1863, taking
post-graduate work at a polytechnic school
in Dresden. *Putnam's Magazine* for August
1869 published two sonnets sent from Germany. Julian returned to America in 1870
and became a hydrographic engineer in the
New York Dock Department. Another
seven years, beginning in 1874, were spent
in London on the staff of the *Spectator.*
Julian Hawthorne's position as the son of
America's most famous novelist, his own
work always judged with that fact in mind,
made him capricious and irritable, anxious
to shock his critics. His novels, usually
sensational, outspoken, and fantastic, represented a transition between the Gothic romanticism of the earlier American novelists
and the scientific naturalism of the period
into which he lived on, dying at the advanced age of eighty-eight. Admitting he
wrote for money, Hawthorne turned out
three and four books a year. *A Fool of
Nature,* a novel written in Jamaica in nineteen days, under the pseudonym "Judith
Hollinshed," won the $10,000 prize offered

by the New York *Herald,* which then sent him as a special correspondent to India to investigate famine and plague. After 1900 Hawthorne wrote no more fiction, becoming an indefatigable writer of popular histories, short stories, and syndicated articles. Late in the eighties he had developed a new variant of the detective story, using the real experiences of the famous New York policeman Inspector Byrnes in *The Great Bank Robbery, An American Penman,* etc. Two books on his famous father were in the modern informal tradition of biography.

On March 26, 1913, firmly protesting his innocence, Hawthorne entered Atlanta Penitentiary for a year, convicted with Dr. William James Morton, son of the discoverer of ether, for misusing the mails in sending through them a misleading prospectus about mining properties in northern Ontario. Hawthorne took a lively interest in prison life, editing *Good Words,* the prison paper, and condemning conditions in the penitentiary in *The Subterranean Brotherhood,* written after his release. In later life he edited the book page of the Pasadena (Calif.) *Star News* for seventeen years. A posthumous book of memoirs was edited by his widow, Edith (Garrigues) Hawthorne. A daughter, Hildegarde Hawthorne, became a well known author of children's books.

PRINCIPAL WORKS: *Fiction*—Bressant, 1873; Idolatry; 1874; Garth, 1877; Archibald Malmaison, 1879; Sebastian Strome, 1880; Noble Blood, 1884; John Parmlee's Curse, 1886; A Fool of Nature, '899; One of Those Coincidences and Other Stories, 1899. *Miscellaneous*—Saxon Studies, 1876; Nathaniel Hawthorne and His Wife, 1885; Confessions and Criticisms, 1886; American Literature, 1891; A History of the United States, 1899; Hawthorne and His Circle, 1903; The Subterranean Brotherhood, 1914; Memoirs, 1938.

ABOUT: Hawthorne, J. Memoirs; Honce, C. A Julian Hawthorne Collection, Mark Twain's Associated Press Speech; Bookman April 1931; New York Times July 15, 1934; Saturday Review of Literature July 21, 1934.

"HAY, IAN." See BEITH, J. H.

"H.D." See DOOLITTLE, H.

HEADLAM, WALTER GEORGE (February 15, 1866-June 20, 1908), English classical scholar and poet, was born at Hyde Park, the second son of Edward and Mary (Sowerby) Headlam. He was a direct descendant of Richard Bentley, the famous Master of Trinity College, Cambridge University, the great classical critic. Walter absorbed classics and cricket at Elstree, a pioneer preparatory school; took prizes at Harrow; and in 1885-

87 won seven Browne medals at King's College, Cambridge, as well as a first class (third division) in the first part of th Classical Tripos.

Elected a fellow of King's in 1890, Headlam spent the rest of his life there on a meager stipend, "teaching and studying in the grand manner." He read through the entire extant *corpus* of Greek literature and did some uncannily thorough restoration and editing of the complete text of the *Mime* of Herodas, "the least poetic of Greek authors." Headlam's *Book of Greek Verse,* in 1907, with a prefatory essay on the art of translation, showed taste and poetic feeling It included his revised translations of poems by Meleager. Headlam had a mercurial temperament ("a rich and boyish humanity," E. F. Benson says) and a hypochondriac preoccupation with death. He died suddenly at forty-two in a London hotel and was buried at Wycliffe, Yorkshire. He had been editing the Fragments of Sophocles. Much uncollected material by him appeared in the *Classical Review.*

PRINCIPAL WORKS: Fifty Poems of Mealager 1890; The Mimes of Herodas, 1891; The Book of Greek Verse, 1907. Letters and Poems, 1910.

ABOUT: Benson, E. F. As We Were; Headlam W. G. Letters and Poems; Academy October 8 1910; Cambridge Review October 15, December 3 1908.

HEARD, GERALD (October 6, 1889-), English essayist who was born Henry Fitz-Gerald Heard, writes: "Gerald Heard's family was Anglo Irish. Unlike his brothers he was born in London. Education followed in the Wessex of Thomas Hardy's novels, at a school where Alfred the Great had been taught, but not many people had learned much since. Academic education finished at Cambridge which then was becoming—with the interest in atom-splitting and psychical research—the home of new-found causes. History was, however, his own 'Honours Course,' and the wish to write took historical themes. Education, however, was not finished and so authorship had to wait. A back-view into

imperial politics was first given by a couple of years' attendance on a British Attorney General. That was during the last big war. It was hardly over before the scene shifted to Ireland, where, assisting Horace Plunkett, the founder of Co-operation in that country, a close-up was obtained of nationalist politics at fever-heat. That scene closed with Plunkett's house being blown up while Heard was alone in residence—a climax rather like a badly staged movie. Such a send-off returned him to England, where at last writing could begin. After some essays on political history, his first book, attempting to work out historically the connection between architecture and costume, was published in 1925. A far heavier essay was slowly maturing and three years later this attempt to suggest that history is due to a change in man's consciousness appeared with the title *Ascent of Humanity.* The British Academy gave this the Henrietta Hertz award, instructing the author to try again. That led to *The Social Substance of Religion.* Meanwhile there had been a year editing a monthly effort which, backed by a number of writers and scientists, was to advocate Scientific Humanism. It called itself the *Realist,* but as it had no money backing, its title was as ill-chosen as its history was brief.

"In a few months a more lasting and even more broadly scientific an opening was offered as popular science commentator for the British Broadcasting Corporation. This kept Heard busy most of five years, but meanwhile the interest in history went on. The present, though, was getting too insistent for long back-looks. So in the middle of the last decade Heard began to take part in direct attacks on public opinion. The veteran Ethical Society of Britain offered a pulpit. The hospitality of Dr. Maude Royden's pulpit was next accepted. The war-pressure mounting, Heard joined, with Aldous Huxley, Dick Sheppard's last effort. There began a year or so of meetings trying to rouse public opinion and point out the kind of price—in liquidated imperialism—which would have to be paid if war was averted. Even progressives felt that was going too far. It was clear, Britain would refuse to wake up till too late. There was work to which American friends were calling, and it was all too clear that only in America was there left any freedom for men to choose their course and to avoid blind collisions. Realizing that here alone has democracy a chance and thought an opportunity of influencing action, Heard

entered America in 1937. Since then he has continued to try to draw the attention of those who still have time to the basic trends and choices which at present lie before free men."

* * *

Mr. Heard, who is unmarried, lives now in Hollywood, Calif. His father, H. J. Heard, was a Prebendary of the Church of England. His highly controversial books are conceded, even by enemies of his beliefs, to be brilliantly and provocatively written. As H. F. Heard he contributed two notable *tours de force* to the mystery field with *A Taste for Honey* (1941) and *Reply Paid* (1942).

PRINCIPAL WORKS: Narcissus: An Anatomy of Clothes, 1924; The Ascent of Humanity, 1929; Social Substance of Religion, 1931; This Surprising World, 1932; The Emergence of Man, 1932; These Hurrying Years, 1934; Science in the Making, 1935; The Source of Civilization, 1935; Exploring the Stratosphere, 1936; The Third Morality, 1937; Pain, Sex, and Time, 1939; The Creed of Christ, 1940; The Code of Christ, 1941; A Dialogue in the Desert, 1942. *As H. F. Heard*—A Taste for Honey, 1941; Reply Paid, 1942.

ABOUT: Mind April 1930; Saturday Review of Literature October 2, 1937.

HEARD, H. F. See HEARD, G.

HEARN, LAFCADIO. See "AMERICAN AUTHORS: 1600-1900"

HECHT, BEN (February 28, 1893-), American novelist and dramatist, was born in New York, the son of Joseph and Sara (Swernofsky) Hecht, immigrants from Southern Russia. In his childhood his family moved to Chicago and then to Racine, Wis., where he attended high school. He was a child prodigy on the violin, and gave a concert in Chicago at the age

A. Petersen

of ten. His maternal uncle had been "strong man" of a circus, and Hecht spent his summer vacations touring Wisconsin as acrobat with a small circus. At sixteen he ran away to Chicago, and after some experience as owner and manager of an "art theatre," he got a job on the Chicago *Journal.* Four years later, in 1914, he transferred to the Chicago *News,* where he remained until 1923. This was the era of the Chicago "literary renaissance," and he was an integral part of it, publishing stories in the

Little Review and the *Smart Set.* In 1918 his paper sent him to Berlin as its correspondent for a year; then he returned to Chicago, where he founded a daily short column (the stories later being collected as *1001 Afternoons in Chicago*). In 1923 he started his own newspaper, the Chicago *Literary Times,* and edited it for two years. His first novels were published during this period. He also began his career as a playwright, though it was not until 1930, in *The Front Page,* written with Charles MacArthur, that he became widely known in this field.

Hecht and MacArthur, after collaborating on plays and motion pictures, in 1934 formed their own producing company in New York, the best known of their motion pictures being *The Scoundrel.* Hecht also wrote, with MacArthur, the motion picture version of *Wuthering Heights.* In 1940-41 he conducted a department called "1001 Afternoons in Manhattan" in the newspaper *PM;* these writings were soon collected in a similarly titled volume. His play *Lily of the Valley,* set in a morgue, closed after eight performances early in 1942. Hecht's reply to the critical roasting of his earnest production was an angry sonnet sent to the New York newspapers and published by some of them.

He has been twice married: in 1915 to Marie Armstrong, by whom he had a daughter; and after his divorce in 1925 to Rose Caylor. He lives in Nyack, N.Y. In his leisure he studies botany, sails a small gaff-rigged boat, and plays baseball. Henry F. Pringle described him as "short and stubby, with sharp blue-gray eyes and stringy black hair. . . . He looks tough. He is."

Time has described his novels as "gaudy, swashbuckling, ranting books." He has also a strong vein of "a sort of ouija-board mysticism," as evidenced in *A Book of Miracles.* Frederick Dupee remarked that he has "more gross talent than net accomplishment," and his work is very uneven. It is always, however, full of vitality and a roaring gusto. He seems always capable of doing much better work than he has thus far done, and if he can ever take his time and write a book at his leisure, he should be able to harness his really great talent and produce a work fully worthy of the initial promise of his youthful years in Chicago, when he was haled, on the publication of *Erik Dorn,* as one of the real hopes of contemporary American literature.

PRINCIPAL WORKS: *Fiction*—Erik Dorn, 1921; Gargoyles, 1922; Fantazius Mallare, 1922; 1001 Afternoons in Chicago (short sketches) 1923; The Florentine Dagger, 1923; Humpty Dumpty, 1924; The Kingdom of Evil, 1924; Count Bruga, 1926; A Jew in Love, 1930; Broken Necks (short stories) 1931; The Champion From Far Away (short stories) 1933; Actor's Blood, 1937; A Book of Miracles (novelettes) 1939; 1001 Afternoons in New York (short sketches) 1941. *Published Plays*—The Wonder Hat (one-act plays, with K. S. Goodman) 1912; The Egotist, 1923; The Front Page (with C. MacArthur) 1928; The Great Magoo (with G. Fowler) 1932; Twentieth Century (with C. MacArthur) 1933; To Quito and Back, 1937; Fun To Be Free: Patriotic Pageant (with C. MacArthur) 1941.

ABOUT: Bookman October 1929; Collier's Weekly October 20, 1934; Scholastic March 30, 1935; Time February 17, 1936, June 19, 1939.

*HEDIN, SVEN ANDERS (February 19, 1865-   ), Swedish geographer, traveler, and writer, was born in Stockholm, the son of Ludwig Hedin, Chief Architect of Stockholm, and Anna Berlin Hedin. He was just fifteen when Baron Erik Nordenskjöld, conquerer of the Northwest passage steamed into Stockholm harbor in triumph. Young Sven's career, in his own opinion, was irrevocably decided. He consumed books on the Arctic, made innumerable maps, and during Northern winters rolled about in the snow and slept by open windows in order to harden himself.

But when he was twenty he was offered a post as tutor to a child who was being sent to Baku, on the Caspian Sea. He crossed the Baltic and the Gulf of Finland and from St. Petersburg made the journey, by train and troika, to the Peninsula of Apsheron. On the south of it was Baku and on the east, the "Black Town," seat of the oil king's refineries. After seven months in this strange "forest of derricks" he set out for Teheran with a young Tartar, Baki Khanoff, who had taught him the Tartar and Persian languages. He not only had his first glimpse of Nasr-ed-Din, the Shah of Persia, but on a blue-blooded horse made an adventurous ride across to Kermanshah. *A Journey Through Persia and Mesopotamia* afterward covered this period.

Then came a return to Sweden and a little formal study—at the Universities of Upsala and Berlin. Meanwhile he sold a self-illustrated story of the Persian journey for six hundred dollars. Not long afterward he was sent as an ambassador to the

* Died November 26, 1952.

Shah; and in September he began a journey into China. It was not until many years later (1933) that he helped the Chinese government stake out two auto highways running between China proper and the province of Sinkiang. He made another journey to China in 1935, forty-five years after his first one, and expressed a conviction that Japan will never conquer China. No white man knows more about Central Asia than he.

Politically, Hedin appears to be pro-Nazi, despite his pro-Chinese bias in the Orient. In August 1936 he willingly dashed off, for a Nazi publisher, an introduction to a series of pamphlets (*Whither Europe*). The Swedish Government condemned these booklets as "a foul and vicious attack on a particularly friendly nation" (Czechoslovakia), and questioned Hedin's gesture. He admitted that he had not read the manuscripts to which his prefatory note was attached. In October 1939 he was sent to Berlin to sound German sentiment for mediation of the war. And in February 1940 Hitler awarded him a Grand Cross of Distinguished Service of the German Eagle. Hedin made another journey to Berlin—this time *incognito*—to accept the honor.

Someone has said that Hedin is "his own best publicity agent." According to one tale, a dispatch from Peiping, five days before the publication of his *A Conquest of Tibet,* stated that Hedin had been captured and was being held on the Western border. On the very day before the book came out, however, a wire from Hedin himself arrived—with utterly no mention of any kidnaping. His saga of adventure in the region of Lop-nor appeared in England in 1937 and in the U.S. in 1940 (as *The Wandering Lake*). Hedin also put the finishing touches on a study of *Chiang Kai-shek*; and wrote a letter urging that the United States use its position as a great power to "compel a peace that would lead the way to a sensible reconstruction of Europe and a just and right division of the productive areas of the world."

PRINCIPAL WORKS AVAILABLE IN ENGLISH TRANSLATION: Journey Through Persia and Mesopotamia, 1887; Adventures in Tibet, 1904; Overland to India (2 vols.) 1910; With the German Armies in the West, 1915; Mount Everest, 1922; From Peking to Moscow, 1924; My Life As an Explorer, 1925; Across the Gobi Desert, 1932; Jehol, City of Emperors, 1933; Riddles of The Gobi Desert, 1933; The Silk Road, 1936; The Wandering Lake, 1937; Chiang Kai-shek, 1940.

ABOUT: Hedin, S. A. My Life As an Explorer; Forum April 1940; Living Age March 1934; Newsweek July 21, 1934, November 7, 1936, December 12, 1938; New York Times February 19, 1940, March 5 and 7, 1940.

HEIDENSTAM, VERNER VON (July 6, 1859-May 20, 1940), Swedish poet and novelist, winner of the Nobel Prize, was born on the estate of his father, Nils Gustaf von Heidenstam, at Olshammer, Orebro, Sweden. The family was of ancient noble lineage; many Heidenstams had served in the Swedish diplomatic and military service. He was a child of precarious  health who was much given to reading poetry and heroic tales, and soon became familiar with the work of Bellman, Tegnér, Vitalis, and Topelius, as well as tales of the common people. Ill-health forced him to leave school in Stockholm, and in 1876 young von Heidenstam went abroad to recuperate in Italy, France, Germany, Switzerland, and the Orient, for eight years. In 1879-80 he was in Rome, and next year studied art under Gérôme at the École des Beaux-Arts in Paris. His marriage to Emilia Uggla, a Swiss, was the cause of his estrangement from his family from 1880 until 1887, when he was summoned to his father's deathbed. The summer of 1882 was spent in Norway; the next year they rented an ancient castle in Switzerland, where they led a hermit-like life of study and seclusion.

His first collection of poems, *Pilgrimage: the Wanderyears,* published in 1888, drew on his Oriental experiences and described Italian and Swiss landscapes. With Oscar Levertin, a Jewish poet of mystical and aesthetic bent, von Heidenstam collaborated in 1890 in writing *Pepita's Wedding,* which urged a return to idealism and the search for inner truth, as opposed to the fashionable literalism represented by his friend August Strindberg. *Endymion* (1889), a novel of travel reminiscences and Oriental experiences, showed von Heidenstam to be an "imaginative realist." It represented an Orient doomed to death by the civilization of the Western world. In 1893 his wife died; three years later he married Olga Wiberg, but soon divorced her. In 1899 he was elected to the Gotenburg Academy of Science and Letters. In 1900 he bought a country estate, Naddö ur Vadstena, and married his third wife, Greta Sjöberg, almost twenty years his junior. Their closest friends were Scandinavian and German scholars. His second novel, *Hans Alienus,* whose Faust-like hero continues a painful search for the meaning of life, maintained the ancient Greek conception that the joy of living was the ideal aim. Turning to his native country for fresh themes, von Heidenstam produced *St. George the Dragon-Killer, The Pilgrimage of St. Bridget,* and the prose poems *Sweden and Her Leaders* and *Swedish Tales. Charles XII and His Warriors,* a national epic, had monumental simplicity and classic beauty of style, and is considered his most important work. With the publication of *Nya Dikter* (1915) von Heidenstam won the reputation of being one of the greatest of contemporary Swedish lyrists, and the award of the Nobel Prize for literature in 1916 came as no surprise.

In 1912 he had been elected one of the eighteen immortals of the Swedish Academy. The University of Stockholm made him an honorary Ph.D. in 1909. *Nya Dikter* was his last work, except for *The Swedes and Their Chieftains,* a popular reader for young students. Von Heidenstam died in Stockholm at nearly eighty. He was a national idealist who scorned alike the pessimism of the naturalists and the poverty of fantasy of the realists.

WORKS AVAILABLE IN ENGLISH TRANSLATION: A King and His Campaigners, 1902; The Soothsayer, 1919; Selected Poems, 1919; The Birth of God, 1920; The Charles Men, 1920; The Tree of the Folkungs, 1925; The Swedes and Their Chieftains, 1925.

ABOUT: Gustafson, A. Six Scandinavian Novelists; Heidenstam, V. von. Sweden's Laureate, Selected Poems by Verner von Heidenstam (see Preface); Landquist, J. Verner von Heidenstam; Marble, A N. Nobel Prize Winners in Literature; Bookman February 1917; Nation November 30, 1916; New York Times May 21, 1940; Poetry April 1917; Review of Reviews January 1917.

Pinchot

HELLMAN, LILLIAN (June 20, 1905-), American dramatist, writes: "I was born in New Orleans. My mother's name had been Julia Newhouse until she married my father, whose name is Max B. Hellman. They were both Southerners: my mother came from Alabama, my father from New Orleans. I moved to New York when I was five years old, returned to New Orleans for long visits each year, went to public schools in both places. I went to New York University, did not graduate. Immediately upon leaving college I worked for Horace Liveright, the publisher. I have been writing since I was a child. I wrote many short stories, had few accepted—understandably. In 1931, I wrote an unproduced play [*Dear Queen*] with Louis Kronenberger. In 1934 I wrote *The Children's Hour,* in 1936 *Days To Come,* in 1939 *The Little Foxes,* in 1940 *Watch on the Rhine.* I have adapted plays for pictures: *The Dark Angel, These Three* [screen version of *The Children's Hour*], *Dead End.*

"Politically, I am a liberal: I choose to think that means that I believe more in the rights of the working man than I believe in any other rights. I like to read Henry James, Dreiser, Dostoievsky, Mark Twain, melodrama, poetry. I was married to Arthur Kober; we were divorced in 1932. I live at Hardscrabble Farm, Pleasantville, N.Y."

* * *

Miss Hellman is of medium height, slim, with light reddish-blonde hair but dark eyebrows and eyes. She left New York University at the end of her third year, but later went to Columbia for one semester, when she studied chiefly Dante. She was at one time promotion and subscription manager for a stock company in Rochester, N.Y., and was for several years a play reader: Vicki Baum's *Grand Hotel* was one of her "discoveries." In 1936-37 she made a long trip to Europe, spending much time in Soviet Russia and in Spain, where she was under bombardment by the Franco forces.

The Children's Hour, a powerful play hinting at sexual abnormality, created a furor and ran for 691 performances. Its screen version was much milder. When the play opened on Broadway, Miss Hellman's bank account was down to $55. Since then, aside from *Days To Come,* which ran only a week, she has won for herself the appellation, "Number One Woman Playwright," with *The Little Foxes,* a vivid study of avarice against a Southern background, and *Watch on the Rhine,* the American stage's first successful anti-Nazi play, which received (1941) the annual award of the New York Drama Critics Circle.

"I am a writer," she has said. "I am also a Jew. I want to be quite sure that I can continue to be a writer and that if I want to say that greed is bad or persecution is worse, I can do so without being branded by the malice of people who make a living by that malice."

PRINCIPAL WORKS: The Children's Hour, 1934; Days To Come, 1936; The Little Foxes, 1939; Watch on The Rhine, 1941; Four Plays, 1942.

ABOUT: Current Biography 1941; Literary Digest May 4 and September 14, 1935; New York Times Magazine May 4, 1941; New Yorker November 8, 1941; Wilson Library Bulletin May 1939.

HEMINGWAY, ERNEST (July 21, 1898*-), American novelist, was born Ernest Miller Hemingway in Oak Park, Ill.,  near Chicago, the son of Clarence Edmonds Hemingway, M.D., and Grace (Hall) Hemingway. His father was not only a physician who often took the boy with him on his country visits (experiences recorded in *In Our Time*), but also an ardent sportsman, who gave his son a fishing-rod at two and a gun at ten. The boy was educated in the Oak Park public schools, and later did some desultory studying in France. His earlier work was written under his full name; he dropped his middle name about 1930. His father wanted him to study medicine; his mother, musical in tastes, tried in vain to make a 'cellist of him. He ran away from home at fifteen, but returned, and was graduated from high school in 1917. He got a job soon after as a reporter on the Kansas City *Star*, but in a few months left for Italy to serve as an ambulance driver in the First World War, soon transferring to the Italian infantry. This is the background of *Farewell to Arms*, though actually he was not present at the retreat from Caporetto. He was severely wounded, and still wears a platinum knee-cap and bears numerous scars of shrapnel. He was invalided home, and in 1919 was married to Hadley Richardson, a boyhood sweetheart. They had a son, but were divorced in 1926. In 1920 the Toronto *Star* sent Hemingway to cover disturbances in the Near East, and about 1921 he settled in Paris. At this time he had written nothing except for his newspaper stories.

In Paris, Hemingway met two persons, with both of whom he is now at "outs," but who had a profound effect on his career—Ezra Pound and Gertrude Stein. His first books were published in Paris, and it was there that he formed part of the world of expatriates who became the people of his first successful novel, *The Sun Also Rises*. (A burlesque of Sherwood Anderson, *The Torrents of Spring*, had appeared earlier in the same year.) Like Byron, with whom he has very much in common, Hemingway awoke to find himself famous; automatically he became the voice of "the lost generation." In 1927 he returned to the United States, and in the same year married Pauline Pfeiffer, mother of his two younger sons. They were divorced in 1940, and soon afterwards he married the writer, Martha Gellhorn.[qv] In 1930 he bought the house in Key West, Fla., which is now his home (and the scene of *To Have and Have Not*). In 1936, at the beginning of the Spanish Civil War, he went to Spain and wrote the commentary for the film, *The Spanish Earth*. The next year he returned to Spain as a correspondent for the North American Newspaper Alliance, and there he absorbed the background of his play, *The Fifth Column*, and of his novel *For Whom the Bell Tolls*; it was in Spain also that he became an *aficionado* of bullfighting. Add a journey to Africa (*The Green Hills of Africa* and one of his best short stories, "The Snows of Kilimanjaro"), and it will be seen how closely Hemingway has tied together his personal experience and the subject-matter of his writing.

A big, dark, "square-featured" man, Hemingway has become a sort of legend in his own lifetime. He has fostered the myth by mystery; he is exceedingly reserved and reticent, and tries hard to keep his private and public lives separate, without much success. He is still an ardent fisherman, proud of having had a fish named after him, and a contributor of rare specimens to museums. At one time he called himself a Catholic, though he was no more an orthodox Catholic than, in later years, he was a Communist or even a "fellow-traveler"; he has an amazing faculty for taking on the atmosphere of the group which at that moment is engaging his passionate interest. He is, quite unashamedly, exceedingly superstitious, and he is rather self-consciously convivial; he gives as his hobbies ski-ing, fishing, shooting, and drinking. All this, of course, points to an overstressed masculinity which has always been one of his hallmarks; according to Max Eastman, with whom later on he staged an embarrassing public feud, he has "genuine masculinity and cool courage, [but is at heart] gentle and sensitive, and rather puritanical." Eastman considered Hemingway's obscenity and his celebration of cold-blooded toughness "a lot of internal bluster." Clifton Fadiman acutely remarked that "he is the hero who distrusts heroism; he is the prophet of those who are without faith."

At the very base of all his work is the death-cult. Wyndham Lewis noted that "the 'I' in Hemingway's stories is the man that things are done to": and the final and always impending thing that is done to him is death.

He has, as the Freudians would say, over-rationalized a profound revulsion. Bull-fighting, big game hunting, war, gangsterism —all of these are variations on the same theme: man is a doomed creature, whose only virtue and only hope is to face the inevitable stoically. Sometimes, in his lesser works, he has descended into what Sinclair Lewis called "puerile slaughter and senile weariness," but when his subject has been great enough for him to lose himself in it, as in *A Farewell to Arms,* and most of all in *For Whom the Bell Tolls,* he has approached true greatness. To quote Edmund Wilson, "if he has sometimes, under the menace of the general panic, seemed on the point of going to pieces as an artist, he has always pulled himself together the next moment."

He is a master of the short story; to name only two well-anthologized specimens, "The Killers" and "The Undefeated" are triumphant narrations. In his stories even more than in his novels there appears the famous "Hemingway dialogue"—inimitable though, alas, too often imitated—short, clipped, and bare, the very essence of speech. As John Peale Bishop said, he has "made Midwestern speech into a prose living and alert, capable of saying at all times exactly what he wanted it to say." When it is added that, in the words of Edmund Wilson, "with his barometric accuracy he has seized the real moral feeling of the moment," even though "his vision of life is one of perpetual annihilation," it can be understood that Ernest Hemingway is among the few genuinely important fiction writers of his generation.

PRINCIPAL WORKS: Three Stories and Ten Poems, 1923; In Our Time, 1924; The Torrents of Spring, 1926; The Sun Also Rises, 1926; Men Without Women (short stories) 1927; A Farewell to Arms, 1929; Present-Day American Stories (with others) 1929; Death in the Afternoon (non-fiction) 1932; Winner Take Nothing (short stories) 1933; Green Hills of Africa (non-fiction) 1935; To Have and Have Not, 1937; The Fifth Column [play] and the First Forty-Nine [stories] 1938; For Whom the Bell Tolls, 1940.

ABOUT: Stein, G. The Autobiography of Alice B. Toklas; Atlantic Monthly July 1939; Canadian Forum December 1937; Colophon July 1935; Current History November 7, 1940; Harper's Magazine December 1940; Nation January 18, 1933; New Republic June 7, 28, 1933, November 11, 1936, January 20, 1941; New York Times August 11, 1940; Saturday Review of Literature November 6, 13, 20, December 4, 1937; Sewanee Review July 1940; Southern Review #4 1938; Time October 18, 1937; Virginia Quarterly Review January 1937.

HÉMON, LOUIS (October 12, 1880-July 8, 1913), French novelist, was born in Brest, the son of Felix Hémon, inspector-general of the University of Brest. Instead of entering the diplomatic career for which he was educated at the École Coloniale, he wrote sports articles and short fiction for Parisian newspapers, and won a small literary prize in 1906.

Soon he moved to London, where he was married and wrote six short stories and two novels of London life. Left a widower in 1911, he migrated to Canada, recording the trip in a fragmentary journal.

At the village of Péribonka, near St. John's Lake, in the northern section of Quebec province, Hémon worked for six months, beginning in June 1912, as an eight-dollar-a-month laborer on the farm of a French-Canadian named Samuel Bédard. On the adjoining farm lived Eva Bouchard, sister of Madame Bédard. Hémon made her the heroine of *Maria Chapdelaine,* the novel that brought him posthumous fame; the heroine's parents were modeled after Samuel Bédard and his wife.

After posting the manuscript to the editor of *Le Temps* in Paris, he set off westward on foot along the tracks of the Canadian Pacific Railroad, with a few pennies in his pocket, in search of further literary material. He was killed by a train at a curve near Chapleau in Ontario and was buried in the village cemetery.

The astounding success of *Maria Chapdelaine* in 1920 led to a search of the author's papers and manuscripts and publication of his four other books.

A white marble slab was placed over Hémon's grave at Chapleau, a commemorative stone was erected at Péribonka, and two Canadian lakes were renamed Lake Hémon and Lake Chapdelaine in his honor. The farm of Samuel Bédard became a popular tourist shrine, and Eva Bouchard built a little cottage nearby in which to receive the strangers who made pilgrimages to her.

Hémon was remembered as a shy and self-contained person, frail in health, who "fled from the world and loved solitude and meditation." He was a master of Oriental languages. He has a place, in the words of Edouard Rod, as "the historian of the people without a history, whether they lived beside the Thames or the Péribonka."

WORKS AVAILABLE IN ENGLISH TRANSLATION: *Novels*—Maria Chapdelaine, 1921; Blind Man's Buff, 1925; Monsieur Ripois and Nemesis, 1925. *Short Stories*—My Lady Fair, 1923. *Travel*—The Journal of Louis Hémon, 1924.

ABOUT: Boyd, E. Studies From Ten Literatures; Catholic World May 1927; Living Age April 1929; Canadian Magazine January 1935.

HENDERSON, ARCHIBALD (June 17, 1877-), American mathematician, historian, biographer, and critic, writes: "Archibald Henderson was born in Salisbury, N.C., the son of John Steele Henderson and Elizabeth Brownrigg (C a i n) Henderson, and grew up at beautiful 'Blythewood,' where he was an avid reader in a library composed of three libraries com-

bined in one and already famous a hundred years ago. He experienced two 'awakenings ' in childhood and youth: the reading as a child of *Huckleberry Finn,* and as a lad being deeply moved by the social implications of *Les Miserables.* He attended the Episcopal Church School in Salisbury, showing unusual aptitude for mathematics. He was graduated with high honors from the University of North Carolina in 1898, won a gold medal for mathematical proficiency, and on graduation was appointed to an instructorship in mathematics. He became in turn assistant professor, associate professor, professor, and finally head of the department, which position he still holds. He took his M.A. degree from the University of North Carolina in 1899 and his Ph.D. in 1902. He took a second Ph.D. at the University of Chicago in 1915. He has studied at Cambridge University, the University of Berlin (under Einstein), and the Sorbonne. He has an international reputation as a relativist and for his work on cubic surfaces.

"His literary interests began in undergraduate days, with two essays in the *North Carolina University Magazine.* From 1903 to 1906 he published many literary essays under the name of 'Erskine Steele.' In 1903, while a fellow and tutor in mathematics at the University of Chicago, he attended a performance of Bernard Shaw's *You Never Can Tell,* and then and there, subconsciously, if not consciously, resolved to become

Shaw's biographer. After some correspondence with Shaw, he began writing the dramatist's life on a large scale, at Shaw's instance. He was aided unstintedly by Shaw, who corresponded with him voluminously and whom he visited in 1907, 1910, and 1911. The biography was completed after six years of hard work.

"Professor Henderson was married in 1903 to Minna Curtis Bynum, who is a translator and writer under the name of 'Barbara Henderson.' They have three daughters and two sons."

* * *

Archibald Henderson's studies of Shaw, over a period of nearly forty years, make him the world's leading authority on "G.B.S." His second biography (1932) is the most complete and fully documented of any published in recent years, and is said to be the most elaborate biography of a dramatist ever published. He is also well known as an historian of the early United States. He has done much editorial work, particularly in the field of dramatic history and criticism.

PRINCIPAL WORKS: Interpreters of Life and the Modern Spirit, 1911; George Bernard Shaw, His Life and Work, 1911; The Twenty-Seven Lines Upon the Cubic Surface, 1911; Mark Twain, 1911; European Dramatists, 1913; O. Henry: A Memorial Essay, 1914; The Changing Drama, 1914; The Revolution in North Carolina in 1775, 1916; Isaac Shelby, 1917; The Star of Empire, 1919; Conquest of the Old Southwest, 1920; The Teaching of Geometry, 1920; Washington's Southern Tour, 1791, 1923; Relativity: A Romance of Science, 1923; The History of St. Luke's Parish, 1924; Table Talk of G.B.S., 1925; Is Bernard Shaw a Dramatist? 1929; The Transylvania Company and the Founding of Henderson, Ky., 1929; Contemporary Immortals, 1930; Washington the Traveler, 1931; Dr. Thomas Walker, 1931; Bernard Shaw: Playboy and Prophet, 1932; The Significance of the Transylvania Company in American History, 1936; The Church of the Atonement and the Chapel of the Cross, 1938; Old Homes and Gardens of North Carolina, 1939; North Carolina (5 vols.) 1941.

ABOUT: Brock, H. I. Archibald Henderson; Johnson, G. W. & MacKaye, P. Archibald Henderson; Smith, C. A. Archibald Henderson; Starr, E. L. Makers of America; Bookman (London) May 1911; Carolina Magazine December 1922; North Carolina Review April 1911; Sewanee Review October 1918.

HENDERSON, WILLIAM JAMES (December 4, 1855-June 5, 1937), American music critic and writer, was born in Newark, N.J., the son of William Henderson and Ettie Henderson. In 1876 he received a B.A. degree from Princeton, his master's degree ten years later, and an honorary Litt.D. in 1922, when he was generally recognized as America's finest music critic, even though contemporary with Richard Aldrich and Lawrence Gilman. Henderson always considered himself primarily a reporter with

a specialty, music. He worked on the New York *Times* as staff reporter from 1883 to 1902, and published, in 1895, a standard work on *Elements of Navigation*. (He regarded the rigging of operatic ships in *L'Africana, Tristan,* and *Fliegender Höllander* with a super-critical eye.)

The Metropolitan Opera House opened in New York the year he became a *Times* reporter; in 1902 he went to the New York *Sun* as music critic, to remain until a nervous breakdown in 1936. Early the following summer Henderson put a rifle-bullet through his head in his Forty-Fourth street apartment, probably feeling, at eighty-one, that he had fulfilled his musical mission in life. Lawrence Gilman called him a mellow ironist; his successor on the *Sun*, Oscar Thompson, wrote of his fresh, clean-cut penetrating style, which proceeded from idea to idea with magisterial certainty. Henderson was never stampeded by the popular furore over certain singers, notably Marion Talley; his books on singers and on the art of singing are particularly authoritative. Withal he was a kindly, neighborly, pleasant-faced soul, genial though firm with his staff of assistants.

PRINCIPAL WORKS: The Story of Music, 1889; Preludes and Studies, 1891; Elements of Navigation, 1895; Afloat With the Flag, 1898; What Is Good Music? 1898; How Music Developed, 1898; The Orchestra and Orchestral Music, 1899; Richard Wagner, 1901; Modern Musical Drift, 1904; Pipes and Timbrels (poems) 1905; The Art of the Singer, 1906; Some Forerunners of Italian Opera, 1911; The Soul of a Tenor: A Romance, 1912; Early History of Singing, 1921; The Art of Singing, 1938.

ABOUT: Musical Quarterly October 1937; New York Times June 6, 1937.

*HENDRICK, BURTON JESSE (December 8, 1870-), American biographer, historian, journalist, three-time winner of the Pulitzer Prize, was born in New Haven, Conn., the son of Charles B. Hendrick, an inventor, and Mary Elizabeth (Johnston) Hendrick. He prepared at Hillhouse High School (New Haven) for Yale, where he acquired a decided fondness for the Grub Street crowd and became editor of the *Yale Courant* and the

Yale Literary Magazine, more intimately referred to as "The Lady in Brown." With a B.A. degree (1895) he returned for graduate work in English under Henry Augustin Beers. Meanwhile he wrote occasional pieces for the New York *Post* and served as New Haven correspondent for the New York *Sun.* In December 1896 he was married to Bertha Jane Ives; they have two children, Ives and Hobart Johnston. Hendrick received a master's degree in 1897, became editor of the New Haven *Morning News,* where he remained until its decease. Then came seven years with the New York *Post,* the last two of which he

Disraeli

devoted largely to the writing of editorials.

In 1905 he was "caught in the fearful orbit of Sam McClure," when *McClure's,* with an admitted tendency "to view with alarm," was, in many respects, America's No. 1 magazine. For it Hendrick wrote political and social articles. In 1913 he left, and plunged into an entirely different environment at *World's Work.* Here it was not customary to hold a mirror to corruption, but rather to "point with pride." These fourteen years, against his earlier muckraking, were certainly less colorful. For his "accuracy, honest thinking, and good humor" (it is said that he never let his anger upset his judgment) he won an enviable reputation.

Not until the 'twenties did he begin to devote full time to the writing of books. The Chronicles of America series had, to be sure, published his *Age of Big Business* in 1919; but it was his joint capture, with Admiral William Snowden Sims (*Victory at Sea,* 1920) of the Pulitzer Prize in history that began a succession of literary honors. For his own *Life and Letters of Walter Hines Page* (1922) he received his second Pulitzer Prize (biography); and his third in 1928, for *The Training of an American,* which covered Page's earlier years. His *Bulwark of the Republic,* a biography of the Constitution, was a Book-of-the-Month Club choice in 1937. In 1939 came a study of the South's failure in the Civil War, *Statesmen of a Lost Cause.*

Journalism's effect on Hendrick—if any—has been only salutary. The Fourth Estate spared him from the writing of either drab or stuffy history: and his own scholarliness, on the other hand, has kept him a "first-rate journalist who knows his subjects to the very roots."

PRINCIPAL WORKS: The Age of Big Business, 1919; Victory at Sea (with W. S. Sims.) 1920; The Life and Letters of Walter H. Page, 1922; The Jews in America, 1923; The Training of an American, 1928; The Life of Andrew Carnegie, 1932; The Lees of Virginia 1935; Bulwark of the Republic, 1937; Statesmen of the Lost Cause, 1939.

ABOUT: Hendrick, B. J. Statesmen of the Lost Cause (see Prologue); Atlantic Monthly October 1935; Book-of-the-Month Club News May 1937; Newsweek January 15, 1937; Time June 7, 1937.

HENLEY, WILLIAM ERNEST. See "BRITISH AUTHORS OF THE 19TH CENTURY"

HENRY, O. (September 11, 1862-June 5, 1910), American short-story writer, was born William Sydney Porter at Greensboro, N.C., the son of  Algernon Sidney Porter and Mary Jane Virginia (Swaim) Porter. His father was a physician, but more interested in perpetual motion. The mother died when her son was only three. He left school, conducted by an aunt, at fifteen, and worked for five years in his uncle's drug store. In 1882 he went to Texas for reasons of health, spending two years on a ranch owned by friends from Greensboro. Here Porter picked up a little French and German and a good bit of Spanish, an accomplishment he was to find useful later. Leaving for Austin, he spent ten years as clerk and bookkeeper, draftsman in a state land office, and bank teller. A romantic elopement with his first wife, Athol Estes, took place July 5, 1887. Some first sketches appeared in the Detroit *Free Press.* In 1894 he bought Brann's *Iconoclast* for $250, rechristening the paper *The Rolling Stone* when the erstwhile owner asked to have the name restored to him. Giving up the paper a year later, Porter tried a year in Houston, Texas, where the *Daily Post* printed his "Tales of the Town" and "Some Postscripts." These were collected and edited in 1939.

Suddenly Porter was summoned to Austin to stand trial for the embezzlement of funds from the First National Bank, where he had been teller. It is probable that Porter was only technically guilty, since the methods of management there were amazingly lax. On the way back for trial, however, he caught a train going in an opposite direction and made his way to New Orleans, where he unloaded bananas. Honduras was the next stop, where he "knocked around with the refugees and the consuls." Al Jennings, famous outlaw, and his brother Henry were two of the refugees. Porter traveled with them from Honduras to South America to Mexico, using the $30,000 which had been the proceeds of a Jennings robbery. News of his wife's serious illness brought Porter back to Austin in 1897. In March of the next year he was sentenced to the Federal ward of the Ohio State Penitentiary for five years, lessened to three years and three months by his exemplary behavior. His durance was not wholly vile, since he was allowed to practice his old profession of pharmacy, sleep in the prison hospital, and occasionally to roam the streets at night. Al Jennings was another inmate of the prison. Another pal, Jimmy Connors, gave him the plot for "A Retrieved Reformation," which later became *Alias Jimmy Valentine,* a highly successful play (for its adapter), a popular song, and a motion picture. Porter wrote several stories in prison under various pen names. The exact derivation of "O. Henry" is somewhat of a mystery; it possibly refers to Orrin Henry, a prison guard.

Leaving prison in July 1901, Porter went to Pittsburgh, thence to his beloved Bagdad-on-the-Hudson, New York City, at the invitation of Gilman Hall, an editor of *Ainslee's Magazine.* He haunted streets, parks, and restaurants, talking to all sorts and conditions of people. In 1904 he wrote sixty-five stories, fifty the next year, usually putting off the actual writing until goaded by editors, from whom he had received advances. Porter's life centered about Madison Square and Irving Place two blocks below Gramercy Park. An average daily consumption of two quarts of whiskey failed to paralyze his creative faculty: in his lifetime he turned out 600 pieces of original fiction. A venture in the theatre (*Lo,* written in 1909 in collaboration with Franklin P. Adams,[qv] the columnist) was not a success. Porter had few intimate friends apart from his editors and his second wife, Sara Lindsay Coleman, whom he married November 27, 1907. A daughter, Margaret, married Oscar Cesare, the cartoonist. From time to time he went to Asheville, but returned to New York to die of tuberculosis at forty-eight. He was stricken at the

Caledonia Hotel June 3, and his death occurred two days later at the Polyclinic Hospital, East 35th street. "Pull up the shades," O. Henry asked the nurse, adding, in a paraphrase of the words of a popular song of the day, "I don't want to go home in the dark." His funeral at the Little Church Around the Corner, it so happened, was scheduled at the same hour as a wedding.

O. Henry's popularity reached its apogee after his death, when his collected works had an immense sale. He was essentially a raconteur who, in the words of Carl Van Doren, "saw human life as a tissue of episodes rather than as any broad general process." His vision was ironic but not embittered. The characters he devised were familiar and simple to his readers; the stories were "written in plain vernacular, diversified by adventurous slang." The slang, naturally, is sometimes unintelligible when read today, and the local allusions have lost their point. His stories have a sameness in theme and structure, relying on a few formulae, such as the essential inertia of human nature. The "sharp unlooked-for twist at the end of the stories" is almost the O. Henry trademark. In 1918 the Society of Arts and Sciences founded the O. Henry Memorial award for the best American short story published each year, and Greensboro commemorated its son with the O. Henry Hotel. His once immense vogue has, however, waned in an era when even the popular magazines show a trend away from the formularized, machine-made plot. He still remains, nevertheless, the acknowledged master of the *genre* he so largely created, and the fact remains that a few of his stories have survived the generation of their writing.

WORKS: Cabbages and Kings, 1905; The Four Million, 1906; Waifs and Strays, 1906; Hearts of the West, 1907; The Trimmed Lamp and Other Stories, 1907; The Gentle Grafter, 1908; The Voice of the City, 1908; Options, 1909; Roads of Destiny, 1909; Strictly Business, 1910; Whirligigs, 1910; Sixes and Sevens, 1911; Rolling Stones, 1913; Collected Works (12 volumes), 1913.

ABOUT: Clarkson, P. S. A Bibliography of William Sydney Porter; Davis, R. H., & Maurice, A. B. The Caliph of Bagdad; Harrell, M. S. (ed.). O. Henry Encore (see Biographical Introduction); Henry, O. Collected Works; O. Henry Papers; Jennings, A. Beating Back: Through the Shadows With O. Henry; Mais, S. P. B. From Shakespeare to O. Henry; Maurice, A. B. O. Henry; Sinclair, U. Bill Porter: A Drama of O. Henry in Prison; Smith, C. A. O. Henry Biography; Wilson, L. C. Hard To Forget; Bookman June 1925, August 1931; Golden Book April 1930; Literary Digest March 10, 1928; New York Times Book Review

January 5, 1941; Review of Reviews August 1928; Saturday Review of Literature June 27, 1931.

HENTY, GEORGE ALFRED. See "BRITISH AUTHORS OF THE 19TH CENTURY"

HERBERT, ALAN PATRICK (September 24, 1890-), English novelist and essayist who signs his work A. P. Herbert, or "A.P.H.," was born in London, his father being P. H. Herbert of the India Office, his mother Beatrice (Selwyn) Herbert. He was educated at Winchester and New College, Oxford, being an Exhibitioner in both, and graduating  with a First Class in Jurisprudence in 1914. He served for three years of the First World War with the Royal Naval Division, in Gallipoli, on the Peninsula, and in France, until he was wounded and invalided out. He was admitted to the bar from the Inner Temple in 1918, and though he has never practised law he has made good use of his professional knowledge in his writings. He was married in 1914 to Gwendolen Quilter, and has a son and three daughters. For two years he was private secretary to Sir Leslie Scott, K.C., a Member of Parliament. Since 1910 he had been a regular contributor to *Punch,* under the initials "A.P.H.," and in 1924 he joined its staff, on which he still is. In 1925 he represented *Punch* at the Third Imperial Press Conference, in Melbourne.

He lives in Hammersmith, overlooking the Thames, the freedom of which for non-commercial craft has been one of his ardent "causes." (He wrote *The Water Gipsies,* in fact, during the eighteen months he cruised in a remarkable "ark" of his own devising up and down the river, to prove his point—after numerous letters to the *Times* had failed to secure action.) Since 1935 he has been a Member of Parliament, as an Independent, representing Oxford; his chief triumph in this capacity has been his bringing about the passage of the Matrimonial Causes Bill, in 1937, thus modifying the obsolete English divorce laws. An aggressive champion of his beliefs, he lists among his other "ogres" prohibition and bad English. In 1940, with brilliance and eloquence, he led the successful fight in Parliament against the imposition of a war-time tax of 12 per cent on the sale of books.

Mr. Herbert is one of the greatest after-dinner speakers alive, bubbling over with wit. He has made a lecture tour in the United States which proved this assertion. He is a devotee of skittles, a game something like ninepins, and is president of the Black Lion Skittles Club. He also likes to sail, play tennis, and perform on the piano. Florid and heavy-set, he looks a bit like a sporting man-about-town, but back of his *bonhommie* and his humor there is a serious and logical mind. There is always a pill under the sugar-coating. Some of his light satirical essays may be a bit too British for American comprehension, but his novels are delightful. He is also the author of a number of comic operas, some written with Sir Nigel Playfair; best known of these are *Riverside Nights, Helen, Tantivy Towers,* and *Derby Day.*

In his more serious work, Mr. Herbert reveals himself as a writer of power and sensitivity. Though he calls himself "a crusted Tory," he actually has a passion for justice, and not the slightest compunction against going counter to current prejudices in fighting for it. He is a modern Don Quixote whose windmills are all real.

PRINCIPAL WORKS: Secret Battle (novel) 1920; Light Articles Only, 1921; A Man About Town, 1923; Tinker, Tailor (juvenile verse) 1923; Double Demon and Other One-Act Plays, 1924; Old Flame (novel) 1925; Laughing Ann (verse) 1926; She-Shanties (verse) 1927; Plain Jane (verse) 1927; Topsy, M. P., 1929; Misleading Cases in Common Law, 1929; More Misleading Cases, 1930; Wisdom for the Wise (verse) 1930; The Water Gipsies (novel) 1930; A Book of Ballads, 1931; No Boats on the River, 1932; Still More Misleading Cases, 1933; Holy Deadlock, 1934; Mild and Bitter, 1936; Uncommon Law, 1936; What a Word! 1936; The Ayes Have It, 1937; Sip! Swallow! 1937; General Cargo, 1939; Siren Song (verse) 1940; Let Us Be Glum (verse) 1941.

ABOUT: New York Times Magazine September 15, 1940; Rotarian July 1940; Time April 6, 1936.

HERBST, JOSEPHINE (March 5, 1897-), American novelist, writes: "I was born in Sioux City, Iowa, of parents who

had come to I o w a from the East in the late 1880's with great expectations. B o t h m y parents w e r e f r o m Pennsylvania f a m i l i e s who had come to this country from Germany a n d Switzerland b e f o r e 1700. I was brought up on my mother's

C. Fenn

nostalgia for the East; and her admiration for those members of her family who had ventured, often to their downfall, dramatized for me my entire conception of American life. As a family, we were omnivorous readers; my first gift of a book was Bunyan's *Pilgrim's Progress.* The family for generations had kept diaries and letters, and the first inkling I had of the complexity and significance of people in relation to each other and the world came from these documents. Living seemed constantly fertilized and damned by the tragic burden one generation passed to the next.

"I was never satisfied with my home town, and the beautiful Iowa land never came alive for me until years in Europe had taught me to see it. College life, too, was never satisfying, and I went to four different colleges (Morningside College, the University of Iowa, the University of Washington, and finally the University of California) before graduating in 1918. While still in college, I began to earn my way, typing, teaching, and working in a print shop. By 1920 I was in New York. By 1922 I had worked in a department store, had been a case-worker for a charity organization, a publicity writer for a fly-by-night concern, and an editorial reader for H. L. Mencken, and was on my way to Europe. Thereafter, for three years, I lived in Germany, Italy, and France.

"During these years the content and purpose of my work began to shape themselves. My first story to be published appeared in the *Smart Set* in 1923, when Mencken and Nathan were its editors. Although I knew many of the so-called 'lost generation' in Paris, I have always considered myself to be in a constant state of new discovery. After my marriage to John Herrmann (one of the *transition* group) in 1925, we went to live on an old farm in Connecticut. I now live in an old stone house in Erwinna, Pa., about fifteen miles from the Old Blue Church at Emaus where many of my people were buried for a hundred years. I have also lived in Mexico, visited the Soviet Union in 1930, returned to Germany to report the effect of Hitler's régime for the New York *Post* and the *Nation* in 1935, was in Cuba during the general strike of 1935, in my own state, Iowa, for the farm strike of 1932, in Flint, Mich., during the automobile strike of 1937, and in that same year I was in Madrid during its bombardment. In 1939 I went to South America. I received a Guggenheim Award in the field of the novel in 1936.

"My third novel, *Pity Is Not Enough,* was the first of a trilogy (followed by *The Executioner Waits* and *Rope of Gold*) to cover not only the decay of capitalistic society but also the upthrust of a new group society. To write historical stuff not in the romantic method or as history but as living, breathing language and life is my job."

* * *

In June 1942 Miss Herbst became the protagonist of a *cause célèbre* when she was discharged without warning from the German desk of the Donovan Committee in Washington (office of the Coordinator of Information), to which she had volunteered her services. The only possible explanation seems to have been her long and proud record of militant anti-Fascism.

PRINCIPAL WORKS: Nothing Is Sacred, 1928; Money for Love, 1929; Pity Is Not Enough, 1933; The Executioner Waits, 1934; Rope of Gold, 1939; Satan's Sergeants, 1941.

ABOUT: New Republic June 15, 1942; Saturday Review of Literature March 4, 1939.

HERFORD, CHARLES HAROLD

(1853-April 25, 1931), English scholar and critic, was the eldest son of a Manchester merchant. At an early age he was given some rudimentary training as an architect but the only later vestige of this was a decided fondness for sketching. At Owens College he began an academic life which at Trinity, Cambridge, earned for him the eighth place in the Classical Tripos of 1879. For two of his essays he was a winner of both the Members' Prize and, jointly, the Harkness award. In 1887 he was elected to the Chair of English in the College of Aberystwyth, but in 1901 he returned to Manchester and held, until his retirement in 1921, the first independent Chair of English Literature. Herford's wife died in the summer of 1930. Herford himself died at his home in Oxford the following spring, survived by an only daughter.

His indifference to matters of routine made him a not too successful teacher and lecturer in the technical sense, but indirectly his influence on his students was considerable. He was also an examiner for the Civil Service Commissions and for the universities of Oxford, Cambridge, and London. He edited Spenser's *Shepherd's Calendar,* a ten-volume Shakespeare, and, with Percy Simpson, an exhaustive Ben Jonson: He wrote a book on Browning in the "English Writers" series and four additional biographies; and he made some excellent pioneer translations that helped to introduce Ibsen to the English reading public. In

newspapers and periodicals he protested social injustices and political tyrannies. After the War of 1914 he became zealously interested in bringing English readers into touch again with German writers, and aided in founding the English Goethe Society. His literary achievements were motivated, in part, by his great faith in the efficacy of things of the mind to lay the foundations of perpetual peace.

PRINCIPAL WORKS: Studies in the Literary Relations Between England and Germany in the 16th Century, 1886; Memoirs of W. H. Herford, 1911; Treatment of Love and Marriage and Other Essays, 1921; The Post-War Mind of Germany and Other European Essays, 1927.

ABOUT: Abercrombie, L. Herford and International Literature; Bulletin of the John Rylands Library July 1931; Spectator May 2, 1931.

HERFORD, OLIVER

(December 1863-July 5, 1935), Anglo-American poet, illustrator, and wit, was born in Sheffield, England, the son of a Unitarian clergyman, the Rev. Dr. Brooke Herford and Hannah (Hankinson) Herford. The elder Herford, an author of religious books, moved his family to the United States when Oliver was six,  and held pastorates in Boston and Chicago. Oliver was educated at Lancaster College in England and at Antioch College, Ohio. After studying art at the Slade School in London and at Julien's in Paris, he began his long and brilliant career as versifier and artist on *Life, Harper's Weekly,* and other magazines. Between 1893 and 1931 he wrote and illustrated about fifty books of artistic nonsense. "No one is more successful than he," wrote Carolyn Wells, "in personifying animals or inanimate things. . . . His realm is Fancy and his scope the material universe. His success is due to his innate comprehension and mastery of the principle of *reductio ad absurdum.*" William Dean Howells called him the Charles Lamb of his day.

Herford's oral humor was remembered as often as his verse. In his heyday he was called "the most quoted man in America." Many of his famous quips were first delivered at the Players Club, his favorite haunt. He wore a monocle in the English fashion and clung to the high stiff collar. He died in the New York apartment where he lived for more than thirty years, near Gramercy Park, and was buried at Wayland

Mass., the home of his sister Beatrice Herford (Mrs. Sidney W. Hayward) whose book of *Monologues* (1908) he illustrated. His wife, Margaret Regan, herself a poet and playwright, came from London in 1903 with the actress Cissie Loftus. They met at the home of E. H. Sothern and were married in 1904. She died in 1935, in her early fifties, after a long illness.

An accurate bibliography of Herford's books would be difficult to compile, for they appeared under various imprints and frequent dates, and many are no longer to be found except in private collections. He himself did not know how many he had written and remembered only a few of their titles.

PRINCIPAL WORKS: Pen and Inklings, 1893; Artful Anticks, 1894; The Bashful Earthquake and Other Fables and Verses, 1898; An Alphabet of Celebrities, 1899; A Child's Primer of Natural History, 1899; Overheard in a Garden, 1900; More Animals, 1901; The Cynic's Calendar (with Ethel Watts Mumford and Addison Mizner) 1902-17; Rubaiyat of a Persian Kitten, 1904; Two in a Zoo (with Curtis Dunham) 1904; The Fairy Godmother-in-Law, 1905; A Little Book of Bores, 1906; The Astonishing Tale of a Pen and Ink Puppet, 1907; The Peter Pan Alphabet, 1907; The Smoker's Year Book, 1908; Cupid's Almanac and Guide to Hearticulture (with J. Cecil Clay) 1908; The Simple Jography, 1908; Cupid's Fair Weather Book, 1909; Cupid's Encyclopedia, 1910; Happy Days (with J. Cecil Clay) 1911; The Kitten's Garden of Verses, 1911; The Mythological Zoo, 1912; The Bishop's Purse (with Cleveland Moffett) 1913; The Jingle-Jungle Book, 1913; Confessions of a Caricaturist, 1917; The Laughing Willow, 1918; This Giddy Globe, 1919; The Herford Aesop, 1921; Neither Here Nor There, 1922; Poems from "Life" (ed.) 1923; Excuse It Please, 1929; Sea Legs, 1931; The Deb's Dictionary, 1931. *Plays*—The Devil (adapted from Ferenc Molnar) 1908; The Florist Shop; The Love Cure; Con & Co.; What'll You Have? (with Karl Schmidt) 1925.

ABOUT: Masson, T. L. Our American Humorists; Overton, G. M. When Winter Comes to Main Street; Atlantic Monthly January 1936; New York Times July 6, 1935; Newsweek July 13, 1935; Publishers' Weekly July 13, 1935; Saturday Review of Literature July 13, 1935; Scholastic April 15, 1940; Time July 15, 1935.

*HERGESHEIMER, JOSEPH (February 5, 1880-), American novelist, writes: Joseph Hergesheimer was born in Philadelphia of Protestant German and Scots antecedents. For a while he studied at an orthodox Quaker school in Germantown, and at sixteen left there for the Pennsylvania Academy of Fine Arts. This was not a success; he began to write and published his first novel, *The Lay Anthony,* in 1914. Since then he has written uninterruptedly—novels, history, biography, stories, and critical papers. He composes slowly or rapidly after elaborate preparation

and research with an increasing need for corrections. Consequently his life is dull and without incident; he has no spectacular tastes or ability, no picturesque habits; his opinions are positive in a negative sense:

opposed to liberal visions and conservative materialism, skeptical about democratic benefits and certain about the disabilities of absolute government; with no affection for an abstract humanity or universal good in the Platonic sense but rather on the side of nominalism; deeply engaged by the history of belief, he has no faith whatever.

"On a more terrestrial plane he lives in a very old stone house, in Pennsylvania, empty of ornament, with severely whitewashed walls and walnut furniture; once filled by a constant stream of people, the Dower House is now mostly a tranquil place of books. Mr. Hergesheimer likes simple food elaborately served, and discovered, after living nearly sixty years, an inherent distaste for potent drinks. He likes learned men and polite women, and would prefer to see few if any poets, in either prose or verse, painters, sculptors, singers, and no *dilettanti* of the arts at all. He cannot read Scott, Dickens, Thackeray, Mark Twain, or *Alice in Wonderland.* He thinks that, today, at best letters is a respectable and pleasant trade. Opera and jazz equally discourage him, and a single bar, a line, of Gilbert and Sullivan are beyond his endurance.

"By association a Democrat, he finds two parties under every system of government— one in power and the other out of power. A conservative, in this philosophy, is an individual with a bank account; and a radical, one innocent of temporal rewards and satisfactions. The difference becomes extraneous. He avoids, with admirable physical result, every form of exercise, conventional pastimes including the theatre and games; the competitive spirit, especially between horses, strongly depresses him. Actually it was the dullness of pleasure that drove him to the pleasures of dullness— constant reading and limited artifices of the pen. He has had no children and, more than willing to forego both the biological justification and joys of parenthood, he believes that in this particular he has benefited humanity. He has seen no equality in people and opportunities, nothing to indicate the possibility of creating or maintaining it.

"In his books women are frequently lovely because he thinks that loveliness, a pleasant actuality, is indispensable to the purpose of fables. There are, clearly, different kinds of beauty, but all immeasurably superior to a commonplace merit. At the same time he has labored to provide comparable men—primarily masculine individuals of simple courage, satisfactory austerity and engaging envelope: men and women who lend existence, and fables, a momentary and flickering reassurance. The truth is that his own main supports, rather than higher splendors, have been imagination, a resolute vanity, and cigars. Ignorance, not his vices, has continuously defeated him. He would like to write the narrative of an English nunnery laid in the reign of Edward the Confessor and an autobiography that took no account of names and personages; it would omit them entirely and neglect the inseparable burdens of women and love; a work only concerned with the hidden principle of literary endeavor, the world as a panorama, and theological speculation. Nothing more unpromising could well be imagined."

* * *

Mr. Hergesheimer is the son of Joseph and Helen Janet (MacKellar) Hergesheimer. He was married to Dorothy Hemphill in 1907. Sara Haardt described him as "powerfully built, eyes gray-blue [concealed behind large spectacles], dark-skinned, voice quick, assertive, unequivocal." She spoke also of his "incalculable, almost appalling energy and unassailable dignity," and his "sensitive rather than inquiring mind." "His times," she remarked, "are antagonistic to his spirit." Clifton Fadiman, in a brilliantly devasting article, called him "the Sargent of the modern American novel" and "the jongleur of a—regrettably—modern feudalism."

PRINCIPAL WORKS: The Lay Anthony, 1914; Mountain Blood, 1915; The Three Black Pennys, 1917; Gold and Iron, 1918; Java Head, 1919; The Happy End, 1919; Linda Condon, 1919; San Cristobal de la Habana (non-fiction) 1920; Cytherea, 1922; The Bright Shawl, 1922; The Presbyterian Child (autobiography) 1923; Balisand, 1924; From an Old House (non-fiction) 1925; Tampico (non-fiction) 1926; Quiet Cities (short stories) 1928; Swords and Roses, 1929; The Party Dress, 1930; The Limestone Tree, 1931; Sheridan (non-fiction) 1931; Berlin (non-fiction) 1932; Tropical Winter (short stories) 1933; The Foolscap Rose, 1934.

ABOUT: Hergesheimer, J. The Presbyterian Child; Bookman June 1929; Canadian Forum April 1931; Nation February 15, 1933, March 15, 1933; New York Times December 22, 1940.

HERNE, JAMES A. See "AMERICAN AUTHORS: 1600-1900"

HERRICK, ROBERT (April 26, 1868– December 24, 1938), American novelist wrote before his death to the compilers o this volume: "I was born in Cambridge, Mass. My father, William Augustus Herrick, a lawyer, was descended from an unbroken line of New England farmers dating from 1636. My mother was Harriet Emery, whose father and uncles  were Congregational ministers in Massachusetts. I went to the Cambridge Latin School then to Harvard, where I received the B.A degree (the only one I have) in 1890. M sophomore year was spent in travel to th West Indies, Mexico, California, and Alaska I began to have my stories published, firs in the Harvard Advocate and then in th Harvard Monthly. I was an editor of th Monthly for several years, and editor-in chief for half a year, sharing this honor wit Norman Hapgood. It was in the effort t establish the Harvard system of teaching undergraduates to write that I gave man years of my life.

"After graduation I was an instructor i English at the Massachusetts Institute o Technology from 1890 to 1893, and the instructor, assistant professor, and professo of English at the University of Chicag until 1923, when I resigned. Much of tha time I had been on part-time service, th rest of my time being spent in travel an authorship. From 1913 I have had a hom in York Village, Maine. During the [First World War I was in Europe, writing signe articles for the Chicago Tribune and othe periodicals.

"Thus I have been both teacher and write for most of my mature life, and the cente of my activity during those years was Chi cago, the characteristic American metropolis but my ties to my birthplace of New Eng land have been maintained, and I have als lived for considerable periods in Europe, th West Indies, and Mexico, and have visite almost every State of the Union, notabl Arizona, California, and Florida. In 193 I was appointed secretary to the governo of the Virgin Islands.

"I hope that my novels are in some wa a contribution to the understanding of cor temporary American life, about which for the most part they are concerned. I do not believe in 'propaganda' writing, or so-called 'problem fiction,' though most of my fiction has been concerned with problems of one kind or another. But I have endeavored to deal with these problems less in an argumentative or controversial manner than as crises in human lives. Although by education, training, and conviction I belong to the realistic school of novelists, nevertheless I recognize the futility of critical labels, and realize that in my fiction there are romantic and idealistic elements that do not conform to strict realism. Life presents itself to me as a dream, often sordid, sometimes tragic, rarely insignificant. It has been my constant effort as an artist to render its significances, which in the bustle of actual living are so often ignored or blurred."

* * *

It was as a direct result of overwork in his duties in the Virgin Islands that Mr. Herrick suffered a heart attack and died (at Charlotte Amalie) at seventy. He was a handsome man, with regular features and thick white hair. In 1894 he married Harriet Emery, his mother's namesake but no relation. Alfred Kazin called him "a pioneer realist"; Henry Seidel Canby, "a writer of careful prose, of novels that were always good even when not widely publicized, . . . a realist when realism was still unfashionable and a satirist when Americans did not like satire"; Newton Arvin, "the most humane, the most capacious, and the most truly critical mind at work in American fiction since Howells and [Frank] Norris."

PRINCIPAL WORKS: *Fiction*—The Man Who Wins (short stories) 1895; Literary Love Letters and Other Stories, 1896; The Gospel of Freedom, 1898; Love's Dilemmas (short stories) 1898; The Web of Life, 1900; The Real World, 1901; Their Child (short stories) 1903; The Common Lot, 1904; The Memoirs of an American Citizen, 1905; The Master of the Inn, 1908; Together, 1908; A Life for a Life, 1910; The Healer, 1911; One Woman's Life, 1913; His Great Adventure, 1913; Clark's Field, 1914; The Conscript Mother (short stories) 1916; Homely Lilla, 1923; Waste, 1924; Wanderings (short stories) 1925; Chimes, 1926; The End of Desire, 1932; Sometime, 1933. *Miscellaneous*—Composition and Rhetoric (with L. T. Damon) 1899; The World Decision, 1916; Little Black Dog, 1931.

ABOUT: Baldwin, C. C. The Men Who Make Our Novels; Cooper, F. T. Some American Story Tellers; Hansen, H. Midwest Portraits; Van Doren, C. Contemporary American Novelists; Bookman November 1913; Dial August 16, 1910; Nation October 7, 1925; New Republic June 17, 1931, March 6, 1935, January 18, 1939; Saturday Review of Literature January 7, 1939, July 8, 1939.

HERZOG, ÉMILE. See MAUROIS, A.

HESSE, HERMANN (July 2, 1877-), German novelist, writes: "I was born in Calw, in the Black Forest, of a pious Protestant family; my ancestors and relatives were preachers, physicians, missionaries, and the origin of the family from different nations brought it about that I was not susceptible to nationalistic sentiments. I have twice changed my nationality, and  am today a Swiss citizen; without considering the Swiss people a nation of half-gods, I am from my heart an admirer and adherent of our political state. My youth and schooldays were divided between Germany and Switzerland; since 1912 I have lived continuously in Switzerland. I was as a boy called to the ministry. I broke away from this career very early, was for a number of years a bookseller and dealer in antiques, and have published many books since 1899. Since the success of my first novel (*Peter Camenzind*, 1904), I have lived without any profession but literature.

"In my youth I traveled much; my favorite country was Italy. In 1911 I was in India, thus following the tradition of my father and grandfather, both of whom were missionaries there, and my grandfather also an outstanding authority on India. The study of the ancient Hindus and the ancient Chinese has had as great an influence on me as the Christianity, tinged with piety, of my parents' home. My political faith is that of a democrat, my world-outlook that of an individualist. What has all my life long occupied, attracted, and actually formed me, was not social problems, but the problems of the individual; and the tendency of the new history to subordinate the personality to the pleasure of the conventional mass, is something I hate to the death.

"My books, which include many purely lyrical in nature, are written without any ruling purpose; they have, however, in the course of the years, brought me a reading public mostly of young men who have been drawn to me both personally and as a writer and to whom I have become a counselor. The difficulties which in the world today confront the individual and his building of a harmonious personality, are felt, as I daily discover, to be very great by many, especially young people within the authoritative churches and states, and a part of this youth, at least within the limits of the German language, seems to see in me the poet with whom it has most kinship.

"Most of my books have been translated into the Scandinavian and Slavic languages, several into Japanese, a few into English and French. My hobbies are gardening and watercolor painting. My residence since 1919 has been the town of Montagnola, near Lugano, Switzerland. For eight years I have been working on a poem of a Utopian nature."

* * *

In 1904 Herr Hesse was married to Maria Bernoulli, of Basel; they have one son. Hesse was educated in a classical school and also in a theological seminary, and for a short time in his early youth was a mechanic. He is a poet and an essayist as well as a novelist. John Bronson has spoken of his "sensitive, colorful, and harmonious prose," and another critic called him "one of the most cultured and sensitive of contemporary German writers. . . . His language is majestic and biting and at times transcendental." He is very little known in America and England, and it is unfortunate that so few of his books have been translated into English.

WORKS AVAILABLE IN ENGLISH: Steppenwolf, 1929; Death and the Lover, 1932.

ABOUT: Bookman January 1933; Deutsche Rundschau July 1927; Mercure de France January 1, 1926; Neue Rundschau January 1934, July 1937; Nuova Antologia March 1, 1928.

HEWLETT, MAURICE HENRY (January 22, 1861-June 16, 1923), English novelist, poet, and essayist, was born in Adding-

ton, Kent, the eldest son of Henry Gay Hewlett, an amateur critic and poet. He was a bookish, dreamy boy, who steeped himself in romance and poetry and n e v e r took a university degree, though he attended the London International College. For twelve years he studied law in a desultory fashion, finally being called to the bar in 1891. He never practiced. His first visit to Italy, made in his youth, was the beginning of a lifelong "love affair"; he returned often, though briefly, and some of his finest work is a reflection of his adoration of medieval Italy. In 1888 he married Hilda Beatrice Herbert, a vicar's daughter who rather surprisingly became an aviatrix and

during the First World War built planes for the British government.

Hewlett lectured on medieval art at the South Kensington University, wrote critical papers for literary reviews, was an authority on heraldry, and for two years, from 1898 to 1900, was Keeper of the Land Revenue Records and Enrollments for the Record Office. He and his wife settled at Broad-Chalke, near Salisbury, where for nearly twenty years their home was the rectory of the village church, dating from 1350. All this was grist for his literary mill, which, however varied its product, revolved always around reconstruction of the past, and especially of the medieval past. He himself, however, lived in the present: in his later years he was preoccupied with the condition of the rural poor and the workers, and moved from the rectory to a stone workman's cottage in an endeavor to share the circumstances of the laborers for whom he felt so deeply. His wife's war activities had earned her a fortune, but she gave it all away. She and their daughter were in close sympathy with his views.

He was a changeable, moody man—a Bohemian and a dreamer in the country, a crisp, decisive man of business in the city, which he hated. His long, sensitive face, with its high bald forehead and deep-set, dark blue eyes, his upturned moustache and goatee, proclaimed him one of the intellectual aberrants who give flavor to the stodginess of Anglo-Saxon character. He belonged to no group or faction, for he lived almost entirely in the realm of theory and of erudition. His mind, like his writing, was both romantic and archaic.

Hewlett's writing is so varied that half a dozen unrelated judgments may be rendered on it. His historical novels have a richness of detail and a power of evocation of personality that place them among the classics; it is unfair to say, as did the *Outlook* in an obituary notice, that he wrote them "to satisfy his own passion for the quaintness of ancient things." *Richard Yea-and-Nay* and *The Queen's Quair* belong in a high and permanent category of fiction. His Italian essays and stories—*Earthwork Out of Tuscany, Little Novels of Italy*, and the rest —do more than testify to his passion for the land: they re-create its past. His novels of eighteenth century and contemporary life, from *Open Country* to *Rest Harrow*, with *Mainwaring* as an epilogue, move on a rather lower plane, seem less happily in the peculiar vein of his genius. His later Icelandic folktales and legends have perhaps little more than historical interest. His poetry, the main preoccupation of his last years, is occasionally fine and moving—most of all *The Song of the Plow*. His style, lush and decorative and sometimes a bit precious, is out of fashion; but the literary mode will change again, and when it does it will rediscover Hewlett. He himself thought of his novels as historical reincarnation, fictionized as little as possible. *The Forest Lovers, Richard Yea-and-Nay, The Queen's Quair,* and *Little Novels of Italy* have the best chance to endure. His writing had strength and beauty, and for their sake his rank romanticisms and his archaisms may alike be overlooked. Like Lord Acton, he believed that "books are made from books," and his lasting work is the fruit of learning rather than of life. But he was in love with his subjects, and so he brought to the dry bones of the Middle Ages a rich and curious robe that clothed them in evocative magic for our modern sight.

PRINCIPAL WORKS: *Novels*—The Forest Lovers, 1898; Richard Yea-and-Nay, 1900; The Queen's Quair, 1904; The Fool Errant, 1905; The Stooping Lady, 1907; Half-Way House, 1908; Open Country, 1909; Rest Harrow, 1910; Brazenhead the Great, 1911; The Song of Renny, 1911; Mrs. Lancelot, 1912; Gendish, 1913; A Lover's Tale, 1915; The Little Iliad, 1915; Frey and His Wife, 1916; Love and Lucy, 1916; Thorgils, 1917; Gudrid the Fair, 1918; Light Heart, 1920; Outlaw, 1920; Mainwaring, 1920. *Short Stories*—Little Novels of Italy, 1899; The New Canterbury Tales, 1901; Fond Adventures, 1905; Lore of Proserpine, 1913; *Essays*—Earthwork Out of Tuscany, 1895; The Road in Tuscany, 1904; In a Green Shade, 1920; Wiltshire Essays, 1921; Extemporary Essays, 1922; Last Essays, 1924. *Poetry*—The Masque of Dead Florentines, 1895; Songs and Meditations, 1897; Pan and the Young Shepherd (poetic play) 1898; Artemision: Idylls and Songs, 1909; Helen Redeemed and Other Poems, 1913; Gai Saber: Tales and Songs, 1916; The Song of the Plow, 1916; The Village Wife's Lament, 1918; Flowers in the Grass, 1920. *Miscellaneous*—Letters to Sanchia Upon Things as They Are, 1910; Letters, 1926.

ABOUT: Bronner, M. Maurice Hewlett; Freeman, J. English Portraits and Essays; Haworth, P. English Hymns and Ballads and Other Studies in Popular Literature; Hewlett, M. Letters; Priestley, J. B. Figures in Modern Literature; Squire, J. C. Sunday Mornings; Stonehill, C. A. & H. W. Bibliographies of Modern Authors: Series 2; Sutherland, B. Maurice Hewlett; Historian and Romancer; Century June 1923; Edinburgh Review January 1924; Fortnightly Review July 1925, October 1938; Outlook June 27, 1923, August 15, 1923; Saturday Review of Literature December 31, 1927.

"HEXT, HARRINGTON." See PHILLPOTTS, E.

HEYER, GEORGETTE (August 1902-), English writer of historical novels and detective fiction, was educated at "numerous high-class seminaries," but did not go to college or pass matriculation or any other kind of examination. She did attend history lectures given by the late Professor Forbes at Westminister College. Miss Heyer's first novel was written when she was seventeen, and published in 1921, two years later.

In 1925, aged twenty-three, Miss Heyer married G. R. Rougier, and accompanied him to East Africa, where she remained until 1928. Their son was born in 1932. Miss Heyer also spent a year in Yugoslavia, going there at the end of 1928. She is an omnivorous reader; her special preferences among fiction writers include Jane Austen, whose works she would choose if restricted to one novelist for desert island reading, and Thackeray, Meredith, Maupassant, H. C. Bailey, Stephen Leacock, W. W. Jacobs, and Kipling.

Miss Heyer's historical romances have sweep, excitement, and color, rather like the Baroness Orczy's. As to her detective stories the Boston *Transcript* stated that she had the delightful talent of blending humor and mystery, and Isaac Anderson, the New York *Times'* mystery-story expert, remarked approvingly that "there are not so many shudders in Georgette Heyer's murder mysteries as there are in those of some other writers, but there is a lot more fun." But "Nicholas Blake" (Cecil Day Lewis) commented of one of her stories that the detection was perfunctory, to say the least, and the *Saturday Review of Literature* noted a "double fracture of mystery story ethics" in the same tale. *Merely Murder* (1935) was her first book to achieve wide popularity with American readers.

PRINCIPAL WORKS: The Black Moth: A Romance of the 18th Century, 1921; The Great Roxhythe, 1922; Instead of the Thorn, 1923; Simon the Coldheart, 1925; These Old Shades, 1926; Helen, 1928; The Masqueraders, 1928; Pastel, 1929; Beauvallet, 1929; The Conqueror, 1931; Footsteps in the Dark, 1932; Devil's Cub, 1932; Why Shoot a Butler? 1933; The Convenient Marriage, 1934; The Unfinished Clue, 1934; Death in the Stocks (U. S. title: Merely Murder) 1935; The Regency Buck, 1935; Behold, Here's Poison, 1936; The Talisman Ring, 1936; They Found Him Dead, 1937; An Infamous Army, 1937; A Blunt Instrument, 1938; Royal Escape, 1938; No Wind of Blame, 1939; The Spanish Bride, 1940; Beau Wyndham, 1941; Envious Casca, 1941; Faro's Daughter, 1941.

HEYWARD, DU BOSE (August 31, 1885-June 16, 1940), American novelist and dramatist, was born in Charleston, S.C., the  son of E d w i n W. Heyward and J a n e (Du Bose) Heyward, and the oldest son of the oldest son in direct line from Judge Thomas Heyward, a signer of the Declaration of Independence. He therefore belonged to the innermost circle of South Carolina aristocracy. However, the family was impoverished by the Civil War, and his father's death, when the boy was two, further reduced its fortunes, so that at nine he was selling newspapers and at fourteen had left the public school and was a clerk in a hardware store. At seventeen an attack of infantile paralysis made him an invalid for three years. Then he became a warehouse clerk and later an insurance salesman, succeeding in this occupation but overworking until after ten years he had a bad breakdown.

His first writing was poetry, much of it in collaboration with his friend Hervey Allen. Emily Clark remarked that he "regarded his poetry as a training school for prose." He and Allen were among the founders of the Poetry Society of South Carolina, which had a strong influence on the rebirth of literature in the South, and later they arranged a congress of Southern writers at Richmond, of which Heyward was chairman. In 1923 he married Dorothy Hartzell Kuhns, whom he had met at the MacDowell Colony at Peterborough, N.H., and who later collaborated with him on the dramatization of *Porgy* and *Mamba's Daughters*. She persuaded him to give up his insurance business, and without either job or money they went to the Great Smokies, where Heyward wrote his first novel, *Porgy*. It was an immense success, as a serial, as a novel, and later on as a play and an opera (*Porgy and Bess*, with music by George Gershwin). From that date he was established as a novelist and playwright, his subject nearly always being the primitive Gullah Negroes of South Carolina and the Sea Islands, though *Peter Ashley* is an historical novel, *Angel* deals with the mountaineers, and *Star Spangled Virgin* is laid in the Virgin Islands.

The Heywards with their only daughter lived in Charleston in a house overlooking the White Point Gardens, and in summer in Hendersonville, N.C. They also kept their house on Folly Island as a quiet place to work free from social interruptions. For many years Heyward accustomed himself to do a year's writing in four months, spending eight months in earning a living. He wrote slowly, and considered his output small. He died at Tryon, N.C., near his Hendersonville home, of a heart attack following a period of illness, at fifty-four.

Mr. and Mrs. Heyward were thought by their friends to resemble each other to a remarkable degree. Both were tall and thin, with large brown eyes and an appearance of fragility. Heyward's most characteristic expression, said Emily Clark, was "his tired, luminous smile." She remarked also that he remained "quite hopelessly a Southern gentleman." Since the Southern aristocracy has always had for the Negro a sympathy and understanding alien to the poor whites who have to compete with the Negroes economically, this may in part account for the freshness and immediacy of Heyward's portrayals, in which, as Eudora Ramsay Richardson noted, he "resisted a temptation to sentimentality." Many readers, in fact, mistakenly assumed Heyward to be a Negro, a circumstance which he said made him feel "very proud," for he considered it a tribute to the verisimilitude of his writing. On one occasion, it is told, he arrived at a large university to deliver a lecture and found that he was billed on the program as "not only a member of Harlem's intellectual colony, but a Southern Negro of the old tradition!"

Heyward had honorary degrees from the Universities of North and South Carolina and from the College of Charleston, and was an honorary member of Phi Beta Kappa. He was a member also of the National Institute of Arts and Letters. In addition to his work between covers, *The Brass Ankle*, an unpublished play, was produced in 1931.

PRINCIPAL WORKS: Carolina Chansons (verse, with H. Allen) 1922; Skylines and Horizons (verse) 1924; Porgy, 1925; Angel, 1926; Mamba's Daughters, 1929; The Half Pint Flask, 1929; Jasbo Brown and Selected Poems, 1931; Peter Ashley, 1932; Lost Morning, 1936; Star Spangled Virgin, 1939.

ABOUT: Bookman January 1930; New York Herald Tribune June 17, 1940; Saturday Review of Literature June 29, 1940; Virginia Quarterly Review October 1930.

*HICHENS, ROBERT SMYTHE (November 14, 1864-   ), English novelist, writes: "I was born at Speldhurst, in Kent. My education took place at Tunbridge Wells, at Clifton College, and at the Royal College

* Died July 20, 1950.

of Music, in London. I also spent one year at a London school of journalism, and I studied the piano and organ for a considerable time at Bristol, under the Cathedral organist and conductor. My father (Canon F. H. Hichens of Canterbury) wished to send me to Oxford, but I preferred to study music and was allowed to. On leaving the

school of journalism I started to write. At first I wrote for papers. Then I wrote short stories, which were published in the *Pall Mall Magazine,* etc. A winter in Egypt gave me the idea for a short book, and I wrote *The Green Carnation,* which was published both in England and America, and was successful.

"Soon after, I joined the staff of the London *World* as music critic, succeeding George Bernard Shaw. After holding the post for about three years I resigned, and began to travel and live abroad during a great part of the year, returning to England in the summer months. I devoted myself to the writing of books and short stories, and also did some work for the stage. I have published about fifty books and have written many stories for various magazines.

"I have lived a great deal in North Africa, and in Sicily, Italy, and Switzerland. I have never married. Travel has, I think, influenced my career a good deal. A visit to Northern Africa induced me to write *The Garden of Allah,* of which about 800,000 copies have been sold. This book has been turned into a successful play, and filmed three times. My acquaintance with Egypt led to my writing *Bella Donna,* which has also been adapted with success to the stage and filmed three times. Many of my other books have been filmed.

"I usually write in the mornings, and again between six and eight o'clock in the evenings. I play tennis and golf, and in Egypt I ride a great deal in the desert, which is close to my house there, usually starting out at 6 A.M. I think that my chief pleasures in life have been traveling, reading good literature, listening to fine music, riding on horseback, and games—but not card games, which I never play. I prefer hot climates to cold, and living in the country to living in any town.

"I have paid one visit to America and enjoyed it. The languages I speak besides my own are French and Italian. My Arabic is confined to a few words, although I have been so much in North Africa."

* * *

Although Mr. Hichens is known now only as a novelist (and primarily as the author of the once immensely popular *Garden of Allah*), in his youth he also published many poems, some of which were set to music as concert songs. One, "A Kiss and Goodbye," had the distinction of being on the repertoire of Adelina Patti. In his late seventies he is still hale, tanned and white-moustached, and still hard at work as a writer. His name is pronounced *hitch'enz.*

PRINCIPAL WORKS: *Fiction*—The Coastguard's Secret, 1885; The Green Carnation, 1894; An Imaginative Man, 1895; The Folly of Eustace (short stories) 1896; Flames, 1897; Byeways, 1897; The Londoners, 1898; The Slave, 1899; Tongues of Conscience, 1900; The Prophet of Berkeley Square, 1901; Felix, 1902; The Woman With the Fan, 1904; The Garden of Allah, 1904; The Black Spaniel (short stories) 1905; The Call of the Blood, 1906; Barbary Sheep, 1907; A Spirit in Prison, 1908; Bella Donna, 1909; The Dweller on the Threshold, 1911; The Fruitful Vine, 1911; The Way of Ambition, 1913; In the Wilderness, 1917; Mrs. Marden, 1919; Snake-Bite (short stories) 1919; The Spirit of the Time, 1921; The Last Time (short stories) 1922; December Love, 1923; After the Verdict, 1924; The God Within Him (in America: The Unearthly) 1926; The Bacchante, 1927; Doctor Artz, 1929; The Gates of Paradise (short stories) 1930; The Bracelet, 1930; My Desert Friend, 1931; Mortimer Brice, 1932; The Paradine Case, 1933; The Power to Kill, 1934; The Gardenia, 1934; "Susie's" Career (in America: The Pyramid) 1935; The Afterglow, 1935; The Sixth of October, 1936; Daniel Airlie, 1937; Secret Information, 1938; The Journey Up, 1938; That Which Is Hidden, 1939; The Million, 1940; Married or Unmarried, 1941; A New Way of Life, 1942.

ABOUT: Adcock, A. St. J. The Glory That Was Grub Street; Chevalley, A. The Modern English Novel; Williams, H. Modern English Writers.

HICKS, GRANVILLE (September 9, 1901-), American critic, writes: "Born in Exeter, N.H., the son of Frank Stevens Hicks and Carrie Weston (Horne) Hicks, I attended the public schools of Framingham, Mass., and was graduated from Harvard in 1923; M.A. 1929. After two years at Harvard Theological School, I gave up my somewhat inexplic-

able plan of entering the ministry, and in 1925 began teaching Biblical Literature and English at Smith College. In the same year I was married to Dorothy Dyer, and we have one daughter. From 1924 to 1927 I was literary editor of the *Universalist Leader,* and out of the reading I did in that position came my first book, *Eight Ways of Looking at Christianity.* In 1927 I published an article in the *American Mercury* called 'The Parsons and the War,' which involved me in some controversy and led to the ending of my connection with the *Leader.* In the next year or two I published other articles in the *Mercury,* the *Forum,* and elsewhere, and began reviewing for the *Nation.*

"Up to the time I went to Smith I had been greatly influenced by the liberal sociologists and mildly affected by the impressionistic critics. At Smith I became acquainted with Newton Arvin, and largely because of him came under the influence of Van Wyck Brooks. Although my critical opinions later took definite shape as a result of reading Marx and the Marxists, I have always been under obligations to Brooks.

"In the autumn of 1929, after a year of graduate study at Harvard, I became assistant professor of English at Rensselaer Polytechnic Institute. During the next few years I wrote reviews for many periodicals, and began reading manuscripts for the Macmillan Company, which I have continued to do. My interest in Marx and in the Communist Party came soon after the depression. When the weekly *New Masses* was founded in 1934 I served for a time as literary editor, and I remained a member of the editorial staff for more than five years.

"*The Great Tradition,* a study of American literature since the Civil War, was published in 1933, when Marxism was still news. That year and those that followed were full of controversy, both literary and political, and my dismissal from Rensselaer in the spring of 1935 was no surprise. In 1936-37 I held a Guggenheim Fellowship for a study of recent British literature. Except for one year, 1938-39, when, to the great displeasure of the Boston press, I served as Counsellor in American Civilization at Harvard University, the period since Rensselaer fired me has been spent on a farm we were lucky enough to own in Grafton, N.Y. No farmer, I liked the incidental tasks of life in the country. Aside from such activities, I have divided my time between literature and politics. With Ella Winter I edited the letters of Lincoln Steffens. Although I resigned from the editorial staff of the *New Masses* and from the Communist Party in the fall of 1939, because of disagreement with the party's position on the Soviet-German pact, I continue to believe in Socialism and to work for it as best I can."

* * *

Time called Granville Hicks "a Yankee moralist," and the phrase is apt. Allowing for the changes of time and history, he is of the breed of New England social philosophers of the early and middle nineteenth century. Thin-faced, with spectacles and mussed dark hair, he is unmistakably Yankee in appearance. His writing, though argumentative, is also persuasive, and he is one of the best of the school of leftist literary critics which ultimately stems from V. L. Parrington. His first novel, *Only One Storm,* "a protracted town meeting in disguise," a "mental clearing-house for Mr. Hicks' own thoughts," scored a substantial popular and critical success in 1942.

PRINCIPAL WORKS: Eight Ways of Looking at Christianity, 1926; The Great Tradition, 1933; One of Us (with L. Ward) 1935; John Reed—The Making of a Revolutionary, 1936; I Like America, 1938; Figures of Transition, 1939; The First To Awaken (with R. M. Bennett) 1940; Only One Storm (novel) 1942.

ABOUT: Nation February 14, 1935, June 12 and 26, 1935; New Republic June 2, 1935, October 4, 1939, June 17, 1940; Newsweek June 8, 1935, October 9, 1939; Time April 25, 1938, May 27 1940.

HIGGINSON, THOMAS WENTWORTH. See "AMERICAN AUTHORS: 1600-1900"

HILL, FRANK ERNEST (August 29, 1888-   ), American writer, was born in San José, Calif., the son of Andrew P. Hill and Florence (Watkins) Hill. He received his B.A. degree from Stanford University in 1911, his master's degree three years later, and in 1915 married Elsa Hempl of Stanford. They had two children, Russell and Anabel, and were divorced in 1936. In May 1938 Hill married Ruth Arnold Nickel.

The next year after graduating from Stanford, Hill was assistant in English at the University of Illinois (1912-13), returning to Stanford then to hold an instructorship in English for three years. Coming east, he was connected with the Extension Department of Columbia University in 1916-17. After the First World War, Hill took a post as editorial writer on the New York *Globe and Commercial Advertiser* in 1920, eaving in 1923 when the newspaper was ⹁ought up and destroyed by Frank Munsey. ⹁e spent 1923-25 on the New York *Sun* be⹁oming literary editor in 1925. Six years ⹁1925-31) as editor-in-chief of Longmans, ⹁reen & Co., the publishers, followed. In ⹁927 Hill was co-author with Joseph Aus⹁ander of *The Winged Horse,* which the ⹁uthors called a book for all readers who ⹁re curious about poetry, children and adults ⹁ncluded. A reviewer who knew both men ⹁tated that he could "see the brilliancy of the ⹁ne lighting on the serenity of the other, and ⹁oth glowing"—serenity apparently being the ⹁uality observable in Hill. In the following ⹁ears Hill published *Stone Dust,* the poems ⹁f an American flyer. Percy Hutchison ⹁rote in the New York *Times* that Hill had ⹁an eye for color, an ear for rhythms, and ⹁e combines lyric poise with lyric ecstasy." ⹁n 1930 he rendered Chaucer's *Canterbury Tales* into modern verse. *The Westward Star* (1934) is a novel in verse, and a fairly ⹁uccessful example of that difficult form.

Hill spent 1931 to 1937 writing and lec⹁turing. Since the latter year he has been ⹁ield representative of the American Asso⹁ciation for Adult Education, and has aban⹁doned verse for expository prose. His home ⹁s in Brooklyn, his office in New York. Hill ⹁s a Democrat, a Unitarian, and a member ⹁f the Players Club in New York City.

PRINCIPAL WORKS: The Winged Horse (with J. Auslander) 1927; Stone Dust, 1928; What Is American? 1933; The Westward Star, 1934; The School in the Camps, 1935; Listen and Learn, 1937; Man-Made Culture, 1938; Educating for Health, 1939; Training for the Job, 1940; Radio's Listening Groups, 1941.

*HILL, Mrs. GRACE (LIVINGSTON)

(April 16, 1865-), American novelist, was born in Wellsville, N.Y., the daughter of the Rev. Charles Montgomery Livingston and Marcia (Macdonald) Livingston. There were seven Presbyterian ministers in her immediate family, and even her name, Grace, was given her because of its theological meaning. Her mother wrote stories for religious magazines, and her aunt was the writer of juveniles, Isabella Alden ("Pansy"). She was educated at home under private tutors and at the Cincinnati Art School and Elmira College, where she also studied art. From childhood, however, she had loved to write

* Died February 23, 1947.

stories. Her mother as long as she lived was her helpful critic.

In 1892 she married another Presbyterian minister, the Rev. Thomas Franklin Hill, and they had two daughters. He died in 1899, and her father immediately after. Now she was obliged to write, to support her children. She conducted a weekly syndicated column in religious papers, and she continued to write the novels which she had begun merely as an avocation. Of her early days as a writer she says: "The truth is I never did consciously prepare for my literary career, and, furthermore, I have no method at all. Coming from a family of authors, it never came into my mind that preparation was necessary."

She has been an immensely voluminous writer, still turning out about three books a year. She writes in the midst of interruptions, without disturbance. In middle life she remarried, and is now Mrs. Flavius J. Lutz. She lives in Swarthmore, Pa., in an old stone house, and works in a second-story room "littered with books and magazines." She is active in church work, and speaks frequently before religious groups, traveling to her lecture engagements in a big automobile which is her only luxury. She refuses to charge anything for speaking, and supports a mission Sunday School single-handed. At seventy-five she could pass for sixty, with "quick step, full firm voice, deep laugh, and only slightly grayed hair." In her youth she played tennis and rode horseback, and she has never lived a cloistered life, though religion has been her chief preoccupation.

Mrs. Hill's many novels are all really sugar-coated tracts. At one time she changed publishers in dudgeon because her long-time publisher asked her to soft-pedal her evangelical message. (Her usual method, when she disapproves of anyone, is to write a novel about him!) She has an immense audience, made up mostly of people who do not usually read novels; in all some three million copies of her books have been sold. Some of her later novels were written under the pseudonym of "Marcia MacDonald."

PRINCIPAL WORKS: A Chatauqua Idyl, 1887; A Little Servant, 1890; The Parkerstown Delegate, 1892; Katharine's Yesterday, 1896; In the Way, 1897; Lone Point, 1898; A Daily Rate, 1899; An Unwilling Guest, 1901; The Angel of His Presence, 1902; The Story of a Whim, 1902; According to the Pattern, 1903; Because of Stephen, 1903; The Girl From Montana, 1907; Marcia Schuyler, 1908; Phoebe Dean, 1909; Dawn of the Morning, 1910; The Mystery of Mary, 1911; Aunt Crete's Emancipation, 1911; Lo, Michael, 1913; The Best Man,

1914; The Man of the Desert, 1914; Miranda, 1915; The Obsession of Victoria Gracen, 1915; The Finding of Jasper Holt, 1916; A Voice in the Wilderness, 1916; The Witness, 1917; The Red Signal, 1918; The War Romance of the Salvation Army (non-fiction) 1919; The Search, 1919; Cloudy Jewel, 1920; Exit Betty, 1920; The Tryst, 1921; The City of Fire, 1922; The Big Blue Soldier, 1923; Tomorrow About This Time, 1923; Recreations, 1924; Not Under the Law, 1925; Ariel Custer, 1925; A New Name, 1926; Coming Through the Rye, 1926; Job's Niece, 1927; The White Flower, 1927; The Honor Girl, 1927; Crimson Roses, 1928; Blue Ruin, 1928; Found Treasure, 1928; Duskin, 1929; The Prodigal Girl, 1929; Out of the Storm, 1929; Ladybird, 1930; The Gold Shoe, 1930; The White Lady, 1930; Silver Wings, 1931; The Chance of a Lifetime, 1931; Kerry, 1931; Happiness Hill, 1932; The Challengers, 1932; The Patch of Blue, 1932; The Ransom, 1933; Matched Pearls, 1933; The Beloved Stranger, 1933; Rainbow Cottage, 1934; Amorelle, 1934; The Christmas Bride, 1934; Beauty for Ashes, 1935; White Orchids, 1935; The Strange Proposal, 1935; April Gold, 1936; Mystery Flowers, 1936; The Substitute Guest, 1936; Sunrise, 1937; Daphne Dean, 1937; Brentwood, 1937; Marigold, 1938; Homing, 1938; Maris, 1938; Patricia, 1939; The Seventh Hour, 1939; Stranger Within the Gates, 1939; Head of the House, 1940; Rose Galbraith, 1940; Partners, 1940; By Way of the Silverthorns, 1941; In Tune With Wedding Bells, 1941; Astra, 1941; Girl of the Woods, 1942.

ABOUT: Time July 3, 1939.

HILLYER, ROBERT SILLIMAN (June 3, 1895-   ), American poet, writes: "Robert Hillyer comes of an old Connecticut family founded by John  Hillyer of Windsor in 1633. He was born in Orange, N.J. and educated at Kent School, Harvard (class of 1917), and the University of Copenhagen (1920-21). During the World War he served as ambulance driver with the French Army, saw service at Verdun, and won a citation from the French government (1917). He then transferred to the American Army, in which he served as first lieutenant. After the Armistice he was courier for the Peace Conference—the mistakes of which he clearly saw; but what could he do about it? In 1919 he took up his career of teaching at Harvard, where he is now Boylston Professor of Rhetoric and Oratory, a chair previously held by the late Dean L. B. R. Briggs and Prof. C. T. Copeland. From 1926 to 1928 he was an assistant professor at Trinity College, which, on his departure, gave him an honorary M.A.

J. Durup

"In 1916, when he was an undergraduate, he won the Garrison Prize for poetry. That year, too, marked the publication of his first poem to appear in a national magazine the *New Republic*. He and his friend John Dos Passos joyously spent the check in Boston. In 1934 he was awarded the Pulitzer Prize for his *Collected Verse*. He was president of the New England Poetry Club, 1923-25, and is a member of the National Institute of Arts and Letters and of the American Academy of Arts and Sciences. He has been Phi Beta Kappa poet five times: at Tufts, at Columbia, at the College of William and Mary, and twice at Harvard (the second time for the Tercentenary celebrations). In 1926 he married Dorothy Hancock Tilton, of Haverhill, Mass., a direct descent of Elder Brewster and the great-great grandniece of Gov. John Hancock. They have one son.

"Hillyer's home, 'Venily,' is in Pomfret, Conn., a beautifully wooded acreage with a small lake in its center. There he passes as much time as may be with his family and friends, his music and books, and those moments of contemplation more than ever necessary to a conservative and religious poet in a radical and blasphemous age."

* * *

Hillyer has been praised for his craftmanship, his "faith in spiritual continuance," but has frequently been attacked, mostly by left-wing critics. It is perhaps significant that he considers Robert Bridges the greatest poet of his era. As he indicates, he feels consciously out of tune with his time, and "an air of loss and unconsoled brooding hovers over his work."

PRINCIPAL WORKS: Sonnets and Other Lyrics, 1917; The Five Books of Youth, 1920; Alchemy—A Symphonic Poem, 1920; A Book of Danish Verse (trans., with S. Foster Damon) 1922; The Hills Give Promise, 1923; The Coming Forth by Day, 1923; The Halt in the Garden, 1925; The Happy Episode, 1927; The Seventh Hill, 1928; The Gates of the Compass, 1930; Riverhead (novel) 1932; Collected Verse, 1933; A Letter to Robert Frost and Others, 1937; First Principles of Verse, 1938; In Time of Mistrust, 1939; Pattern of a Day, 1940.

ABOUT: New Republic November 4, 1940; Poetry November 1934, February 1938; Saturday Review of Literature January 6, 1934.

*HILTON, JAMES (September 9, 1900-   ), English novelist, was born in Leigh, Lancashire, and was taken at an early age to London, where his father was a schoolmaster. Young Hilton attended various London schools, then Leys School, Cambridge. In 1921 he received a B.A. degree in history and the English tripos (first class) from Christ's College, Cambridge University. Too young by a few

* Died December 20, 1954.

months for service, he was a member of the Cambridge University R.O.T.C. when the First World War finished. He had done some writing as an undergraduate,  the *Manchester Guardian* accepting an article when he was seventeen, and in the same year he wrote his first novel, *Catherine Herself,* published two years later while Hilton was still in college. He wrote a twice-a-week column for the Dublin *Irish Independent,* and kept it up for several years afterwards.

"I came out of the university at an unfortunate time," Hilton once told an interviewer. "I wanted a job, and so did thousands of other men, in the post-war slump. I did not become overburdened with riches from royalties. Really, the first one of the many [books] I had written which brought me in a good return was *And Now Good-Bye,* which appeared in 1931. My first real stroke of good luck came all unknown to me when in the latter part of 1933 I was approached by the editor of the *British Weekly,* the great nonconformist Protestant publication, who asked me to write a long short story for his special Christmas supplement, to be completed within a fortnight." His mind remaining total blank on the subject, and the deadline for submitting the story approaching, Hilton went out on his bicycle to clear his brain, and returned home to write *Goodbye, Mr. Chips* in four days. The editor of the *British Weekly,* which was owned by a great London book publishing company, suggested that the story deserved an American market. The *Atlantic Monthly,* the first periodical to which Hilton submitted the story, published it in its April 1934 issue. Alexander Woollcott eulogized, in the *New Yorker* and on the air, this pleasing if sentimental tale of an old English schoolmaster looking back over his uneventful life. Published in June 1934, the little book became a best-seller; was reissued next year with pen-and-ink illustrations by a well-known English artist, H. M. Brock; was dramatized in 1938; and the next year appeared in a painstaking film version made in an actual English public school, with Robert Donat playing Mr. Chips and Greer Garson his young wife. The success of the book bore along with it *Lost Horizon,*

an older Hilton novel (1933), winner of the Hawthornden Prize, to the best-seller ranks and to the screen, with the consequence that "Shangri-la," Hilton's mythical country, became a household word. *Lost Horizon* combined adventure with romance and metaphysics, and was told in Hilton's usual smooth and accomplished style. *Knight Without Armour,* a novel of pure adventure, was effectively filmed with Marlene Dietrich. *We Are Not Alone* was popular as novel, play, and film. *Random Harvest,* a novel of amnesia, "is overlaid with [his] not unpleasant but faintly mauve sentimentalism."

Hilton has spent much time lately in the United States, particularly in Hollywood, where he has assisted in the filming of his books. Reporters found him "a smallish, unassuming, fresh-faced Englishman with a very contained manner. His hair was neat, and his speech was neatly turned."

PRINCIPAL WORKS: Catherine Herself, 1920; And Now Goodbye, 1931; Murder at School (by "Glen Trevor"; U. S. title: Was It Murder?) 1931; Contango (U. S. title: Ill Wind) 1932; Rage in Heaven, 1932; Knight Without Armour (U. S. title: Without Armour) 1933; Lost Horizon, 1933; Goodbye, Mr. Chips, 1934; We Are Not Alone, 1937; To You, Mr. Chips, 1938; Random Harvest, 1941.

ABOUT: Stevens, G. Lincoln's Doctor's Dog and Other Famous Best Sellers; Scholastic October 2, 1939; Wilson Library Bulletin December 1935.

HINDUS, MAURICE GERSCHON

(February 27, 1891-), Russian-American writer, was born in Bolshoye Bikova, Russia, one of the eleven children of Jacob and Sarah (Gendeliovitch) Hindus. His father was a hardworking man, a kulak, but hardly the grasping, overfed kulak of Soviet films. After his death Maurice Hindus came to the United States  with his mother, in 1905, and began work in New York City, as an errand boy, setting himself to learn twenty new English words a day and attending night school. He attended lectures in Madison Street given by a benevolent Scotsman, who also made young Hindus a gift of George Eliot's *Adam Bede* to perfect his English. After two years in Stuyvesant High School he applied to Cornell State Agricultural College, which refused him entrance because of lack of credits; Colgate University proved more hospitable. Hindus graduated there with honors in 1915; took his M.S. degree in 1916, and received an honorary Litt.D. in 1931. After a year of graduate study at Harvard in 1917, he launched out as a free lance writer.

In 1922 Hindus spent several months among the Russian Doukhobors in western Canada; Glenn Frank, then editor of the *Century Magazine,* accepted several articles about them and gave Hindus useful advice as well as a commission to return to Russia to investigate collective farms under the Soviet régime. Of the resultant books, *Humanity Uprooted* (1929) and *Red Bread*—which had a foreword by John Dewey—were the most favorably received. *Humanity Uprooted* procured Hindus several lecture engagements, especially in January to March of 1930, when he traveled throughout the United States. His autobiography, *Green Worlds: An Informal Chronicle,* has been called by John Gunther the most useful kind of autobiography because it throws light on the author's other books. Most of it is the record of his experiences as a young man on an upper New York State farm; the contrasts drawn between American farms and Russian collective farms proved illuminating. Of his books in general, the *Nation* has remarked that Hindus has a gift for dramatization and is a master of narrative and description, but is sometimes weak in analysis. The writer, who is unmarried, is a member of Phi Beta Kappa and Delta Sigma Rho, and makes his home, when he is not traveling, in New York City. Recently he has turned to the novel with some success.

PRINCIPAL WORKS: The Russian Peasant and the Revolution, 1920; Broken Earth, 1926; Humanity Uprooted, 1929; Red Bread, 1931; The Great Offensive, 1933; Moscow Skies, 1936; Green Worlds (autobiography) 1938; We Shall Live Again, 1939; Sons and Fathers (novel) 1940; To Sing With the Angels (novel) 1941; Hitler Cannot Conquer Russia, 1941; Russia and Japan, 1942.

ABOUT: Hindus, M. Green Worlds; Wilson Library Bulletin February 1931.

HINKSON, Mrs. KATHERINE. See TYNAN, K.

HOBART, Mrs. ALICE TISDALE (NOURSE) (January 28, 1882-), American novelist, was born in Lockport, N.Y., the daughter of Edward Henry Nourse and Harriet Augusta (Beaman) Nourse. The Nourses were an old New England family, descendants of Rebecca Nourse, one of the victims of the Salem witchcraft mania. When she was two the family moved to Chicago; when she was ten her mother died and her father moved to a farm in Downer's Grove, Ill. At seventeen

an accident to her spine made her a semi invalid for many years. However, she was a student at the University of Chicago from 1904 to 1907, and spent two years in organization work at the Kansas State University. In 1908 she went to China to visit a sister who was a teacher in a missionary school, and stayed there for two years. In 1914 she was married in Tientsin to Earle Tisdale Hobart, an American who was in buisiness in China, and went to live in the frontier villages of Mon-golia and Manchuria as well as in the larger cities.

She began to write, with the original idea of "presenting in a series of novels the interesting and dramatic interplay of Eastern and Western minds brought together in the Orient." With the Chinese Revolution, of which she was a close-up observer, the nature of her work deepened and intensified. In 1927 the Hobarts returned to America, though for the next two years they also spent much time in Europe. The first of her novels to achieve wide popularity was *Oil for the Lamps of China,* in which for the first time the life of white men in China who are business men, no missionaries or government officials, was presented. In *Their Own Country* the same American couple are brought to America to face economic problems there. Both novels, without being strictly autobiographical, owe much to Mrs. Hobart's own experiences.

Since her return to the United States she has lived in New York, in Washington, D.C., in Virginia, and now lives in Martinez, Calif., on San Francisco Bay. Her passion is gardening, and she enjoys recalling the many gardens she has planted in far-sundered portions of the globe. Largely because she is still often in pain, she writes very slowly; she is very careful in the research for her novels, and rewrites them many times until she is satisfied with them. She says she likes "quiet living in the country, the woods better than the seashore." In appearance she is attractive, with soft gray hair and clear-cut, delicate features. She is a member of the P.E.N. and the Society of Women Geographers of America.

PRINCIPAL WORKS: Pioneering Where the World Is Old (non-fiction) 1917; By the City of the Long Sand (non-fiction) 1926; Within the

Walls of Nanking (non-fiction) 1928; River Supreme, 1929; Oil for the Lamps of China, 1933;
Yang and Yin, 1936; Their Own Country, 1940.

ABOUT: Saturday Review of Literature April
20, 1940; Wilson Library Bulletin November 1933.

"HOBBES, JOHN OLIVER." See
"BRITISH AUTHORS OF THE 19TH
CENTURY"

HOCKING, JOSEPH (1860-March 4,
1937), English Wesleyan clergyman and
novelist, was born at St. Stephen's, Corn-

wall, the youngest
son of James Hock-
ing. An elder brother
Silas (1850-1935)
was also a novelist.
Joseph attended Cres-
cent Range College,
Victoria Park, where
he was Prizeman,
and Victoria Univer-
sity, Manchester. At
eighteen he was a
and surveyor, then entered the Nonconformist ministry in 1884. Three years later
Hocking traveled through Egypt, Palestine,
Syria, Turkey, and Greece, gathering material for discourses and background for
some of the fifty-odd novels he produced.

They were chiefly stories of the simple,
old-fashioned type, describing the middle-
class life of the day, and, sometimes, conflicts
between Protestant and Catholic. In the
early nineteen-hundreds Hocking breasted
the then popular wave of historical fiction;
a novel laid in the time of the Great Armada
and published in the United States in 1903
as A Flame of Fire had almost as long a
title-page as Conan Doyle's Micah Clarke.
It purported to be an authentic historical
document edited by Joseph Hocking; the
Nonconformist conscience evidently allowed
this innnocent literary deception, although
it is possible that some of his Cornish
parishioners may have been fooled. Hocking
retired from the ministry at fifty. In 1887
he had married Annie Brown; they had
four daughters and a son who was killed
in active service in 1918. Hocking listed
his recreations as golf, motoring and tennis;
his clubs as the Reform and Whitefriars.

He died at St. Ives, Cornwall. Cornwall
had given him settings and characters for
many of the novels, such as The Birthright:
A Romance of Cornwall and Felicity Treverbyn; his theological training, for The
Trampled Cross, The Eternal Challenge,
and The Jesuit; while the two combine happily in such a title as Ishmael Pengelly.

The Sword of the Lord is a novel of the
time of Luther.

PRINCIPAL WORKS: Jabez, 1891; Zillah, 1892;
Ishmael Pengelly, 1894; All Men Are Liars, 1895;
Fields of Fair Renown, 1896; The Birthright: A
Romance of Cornwall, 1897; The Scarlet Woman,
1899; O'er Moor and Fen, 1901; Follow the
Gleam, 1903; Esau, 1904; A Strong Man's Vow,
1907; The Trampled Cross, 1907; The Soul of
Dominic Wildthorne, 1908; The Sword of the Lord,
1909; The Jesuit, 1911; God and Mammon, 1912;
All for a Scrap of Paper, 1914; The Path of
Glory, 1917; In the Sweat of Thy Brow, 1920;
Prodigal Daughters, 1922; Prodigal Parents, 1923;
Felicity Treverbyn, 1927; The Eternal Challenge,
1929; Out of the Depths, 1930; Caleb's Conquest,
1932; Deep Calleth Deep, 1936.

ABOUT: New York Times March 5, 1937.

*HODGES, Mrs. BARBARA K. (WEB-
BER) ("Elizabeth Cambridge") (October
7, 1893-), English novelist, was born
in Rickmansworth,
Herefordshire, her
maiden name being
Webber, and her
father a physician.
She was educated at
private schools in
Plymouth, Westgate-
on-Sea, and Paris.
She began publishing
short stories at seven-
teen, but stopped

writing at twenty-one, when she married G.
M. Hodges, also a physician and surgeon.
For a short time she worked in the Voluntary Aid Detachment, the women's defense
organization of the First World War. She
has two sons and a daughter, and lives in
Deddington, near Oxford. In times of
peace her avocations are reading and gardening; at present she is again doing volunteer
war work.

Mrs. Hodges began writing again in 1930
—not short stories this time, but novels,
of which she has since published six, all
written under the pseudonym of "Elizabeth
Cambridge." The daughter of one medical
man, and married to another, it is natural
that in several of them (notably The Two
Doctors) there is a medical background.
Although her books have all been published
in America, she has not become nearly so
well known here as in her native land. The
two latest, however, have attracted more attention than any of her previous work. She
is an easy, graceful writer, rather domestic
and parochial in her interests, but possessing
quiet humor and a genuine gift for observation and description.

PRINCIPAL WORKS: Hostages to Fortune, 1933;
The Sycamore Tree, 1934; Susan and Joanna,

1935; The Two Doctors, 1936; Spring Always Comes, 1938; Portrait of Angela (in America: Mrs. Dufresne) 1940.

HODGSON, RALPH (1871-   ), English poet, was born in Yorkshire. A recluse who believes his private life is not the

public's concern, little is known about him. It is known, however, that he lived in the United States for a short time, that he was a draughtsman on a London evening paper, that he was for several years editor of *Fry's*

W. Rothenstein

Magazine, and that he lectured on English literature at Sendai University, Japan, in 1924. He was a co-founder of a private press called the Sign of the Flying Flame, which published, besides other broadsides and chapbooks, booklets of his own poems. He won the Polignac Prize of 100 pounds in 1914 for "The Bull." Among former winners of this prize were Walter de la Mare and John Masefield. He is a lover of dogs, especially of bull-terriers, which he breeds and which he judges in shows; indeed, he is a lover of all animals, domestic and wild, and detests hunting as well as every other kind of killing. He likes billiards and enjoys watching boxing matches, and he is devoted to his pipe and its extra-strong tobacco. He is unmarried, and lives in London. His favorite poets are Shelley and Wordsworth. He does not like his own first published volume. That about sums up all that is known of him personally. Sir William Rothenstein described his appearance: "a powerful head, held rather high; his face irregular and deeply lined, with wide, sensitive nostrils and an ample, rather loose mouth."

Mr. Hodgson simply stopped writing in 1917, and he has published nothing since. This is the more remarkable, since his work was steadily growing in power. Neither his subject-matter nor his style is particularly original, but his poetry has a ballad-like quality that is inimitable; it is "clear, melodic, matter-of-fact, and yet magical." Maud Slessor said that there was "never a less self-conscious writer," and remarked that his spirit of "Franciscan comradeship" with all that exists, from man to inanimate objects, is implicit in everything he writes. His few best-known poems, such as "Eve," "The Bells of Heaven," "Stupidity Street,"

"Time, You Old Gipsy Man," and "The Bull," have appeared innumerable times in anthologies, and are likely to be woven into the permanent fabric of English poetry. He is at once tender and angry, raising his voice for the inarticulate, most of all for hunted, defenseless, birds and animals; and sometimes, as in "Eve," he has a rich pictorial tone that recalls the Pre-Raphaelites, particularly D. G. Rossetti. His is a major place among minor poets, and it is a matter for profound regret that he has apparently decided that he has nothing more to say. E. V. Lucas said very truly that Ralph Hodgson "has written a few of the truest poems of our time."

PRINCIPAL WORKS: The Last Blackbird and Other Lines, 1907; The Bull, 1913; Eve and Other Poems, 1913; The Mystery and Other Poems, 1913; The Song of Honour, 1913; Poems, 1917.

ABOUT: Aiken, C. Skepticisms; Davies, W. H. Later Days; Maynard, T. Our Best Poets; Monroe H. Some Contemporary Poets; Newbolt, H. J. New Paths on Helicon; Phelps, W. L. The Advance of English Poetry in the Twentieth Century; Rothenstein, W. Men and Memories; Squire, J. C. Books in General; Bookman January 1918; Bookman (London) July 1917, April 1931; Dial July 19 and August 30, 1917; English Journal February 1926; Nation September 17, 1914, August 24, 1918; Nineteenth Century July 1920; Saturday Review (London) May 25, 1907; Scholastic March 21, 1936.

*HOFFENSTEIN, SAMUEL (October 8 1890-   ), American poet and humorist, was born in Lithuania, the son of Josiah Mayer Hoffenstein and

Taube Gita (Kahn) Hoffenstein. Coming to the United States and Pennsylvania, Hoffenstein attended the public schools of Wilkes-Barre, and was himself principal of the North Main Street School after graduation from La-

Kessler

fayette College, Easton, Pa. After serving for a time on the city staff of the Wilkes Barre *Times-Leader,* he became a reporter for the New York *Sun* in 1912, a special writer the next year, and dramatic critic in 1914-15, writing a department as "The Playgoer." As press agent for Al Woods the theatrical producer, from 1916 to 1927 Hoffenstein was the creator of various legends about this rough diamond among impresarios. Concurrently, in 1923-25, Hoffenstein contributed a column, "The Dome," to the New York *Tribune.* Hoffenstein's parody of the *Daybook* written by Burton Rascoe, the paper's literary critic, had

* Died October 6, 1947.

amused Rascoe, who invited him to be a regular contributor. When Hoffenstein justified his faith by publishing *Poems in Praise of Practically Nothing,* Rascoe called them "technically perfect, original as far as originality in poetry can go, in the main line of Heinesque tradition, the epitome of lyrical wit." Herbert Gorman noted their "savage irony." The book's successor, *Year In, You're Out,* was more uneven in quality, reminding Harry Hansen of "a vaudeville program with an outstanding headliner and a lot of cheaper acts." In recent years Hoffenstein has been writing for the screen in Hollywood, making his home on Wilshire Boulevard in Beverly Hills. His conversation, it is said, is often of sardonic raillery, barbed with the most astonishing word combinations, spoken "in tones of strained bitterness that make for him a sort of vocal sanctuary against the world." He married Edith M. Morgan in 1927.

PRINCIPAL WORKS: Life Sings a Song, 1916; Poems in Praise of Practically Nothing, 1928; Year In, You're Out, 1930.

ABOUT: Rascoe, B. A Bookman's Daybook.

HOFMANNSTHAL, HUGO HOFMANN, Edler von (February 1, 1874-July 15, 1929), Austrian poet and dramatist who

wrote as Hugo von Hofmannsthal, was in spite of his excessively German name the descendant of a Spanish-Jewish family long settled in Vienna, where he was born. He attended the University of Vienna and received a Ph.D. degree, but while still a student his writing attracted the attention of Hermann Bahr, who made a social lion out of his "discovery." The work which earned this early fame comprised three poetic dramas, the first published under the pseudonym of "Theophil Morren," the next two under that of "Loris." Indeed, Hugo von Hofmannsthal may be said to have originated the neoromantic school in Austria while he was still an undergraduate.

For twenty years he was a close collaborator with Richard Strauss, the composer. It can hardly be said that he wrote the librettos for Strauss' operas; his words and Strauss' music were rather two sides of the same fabric, and *Salome, Elektra, Der Rosenkavalier, Die Aegyptische Helene,*

would be as unthinkable without Hofmmansthal as without their composer. Later he collaborated in much the same manner with Max Reinhardt, in this case providing the dramas while Reinhardt provided the staging. The first of their joint productions was an adaptation of the English morality play, *Everyman,* in 1912, which held the stage at Salzburg until political conditions uprooted all German and Austrian art. It was indeed fortunate for Hofmannsthal that he died before the Nazi invasion of Austria, for to his disciples he seemed to live utterly removed from the world, scarcely noting the passage of a World War, untouched by what happened around him. M. Joubert remarked that he "had no biography in the usual sense, for external events influenced his life but little or not at all."

Because of the operation of this "Hofmannsthal legend," very little personal information about him is available. Yet Hofmannsthal himself, in his posthumous *Buch der Freunde* (1929), expressed his belief in "art for life's sake," and said that to be a complete human being "active life and suffering are necessary." Prof. E. R. Curtius has pointed out that after 1914 Hofmannsthal "ceased to be a romantic aesthete and became a 'conservative-revolutionary,' seeking to set up intellectual authority based on spiritual motives." Curtius called him "a man and artist of broad international sympathies but essentially Austrian in his genius."

Hofmannsthal's life ended tragically. He was married and had three children, and he was especially devoted to his oldest son, Franz, who killed himself on July 14, 1929. The next day while the father was dressing for the funeral he dropped dead of heart failure. His mind had dwelt much on death —far more than it had dwelt on the reality of mundane life. Yet his appearance belied his brooding, sensitive spirit, for he was dark and heavy-set and amiable, what Arnold Bennett, who seldom saw beneath the surface, called "a very jolly fellow."

Actually this "very jolly fellow" was also a brilliant classical scholar, possessor of a mind of rare receptivity, "the eternally young, modest, and joyfully appreciative artistic gourmet." Raymond Henry, the French critic, said he "should have been born in Greece at the time of Pericles. . . . [He was] southern in spirit and in temperament, . . . at the very depth of his nature an aesthete, . . . a brilliant essayist, a magician of words, and a lyric poet more than a dramatist." His poetry is mystical and symbolistic, but too close to the classical tradition to belong in the "modernist" group. It has melody and color, and it is the perfect medium of expression for complicated, half-articulate nuances of the spirit. His sense of dramatic plot was poor; many of his plays are close though modernized adaptations of those of Calderon, Molière, Otway, Sophocles; so susceptible was he to literary influences, from the Greeks to Oscar Wilde and d'Annunzio, that, especially in his prose, it is almost impossible to unravel the threads and find what was ultimately his own. It is for this reason that he had for two decades practically no evolution as an artist, but was at forty-five almost exactly what he had been at twenty. What might have been his further development, on the lines suggested by Curtius, can, of course, never be known now because of his death in his prime. He himself, as his own best critic, described in one couplet his strength and his weakness:

> To dreams I say: stay with me, oh, be real!
> And to reality: be dreams and fade!

PRINCIPAL WORKS AVAILABLE IN ENGLISH: Elektra, 1908; The White Fan, 1909; Ariadne at Naxos, 1912; Everyman, 1912; The Rose Cavalier, 1912; Death and the Fool, 1913; Venice Preserved, 1913; Madonna Dianora (The Lady at the Window) 1916; Prologue for a Marionette Theatre, 1916; Cristina's Homecoming, 1917; Lyrical Poems, 1918; The Death of Titian, 1920; The Adventurer and the Singer, 1920; The Marriage of Sobeide, 1924.

ABOUT: Chandler, F. W. Modern Continental Playwrights; Dukes, A. Modern Dramatists; Eloesser, A. Modern German Literature; von Hofmannsthal, H. Lyrical Poems (see Introduction by C. W. Stork); Strauss, F. (ed.). Correspondence Between Richard Strauss and Hugo von Hofmannsthal; Commonweal July 31, 1929; Contemporary Review November 1929; Literary Digest September 21, 1929; Saturday Review of Literature September 6, 1930.

HOGBEN, LANCELOT THOMAS (December 9, 1895-   ), English scientific and economic writer, writes: "According to my

parents, who did not always divulge to me the truth about matters connected with human reproduction, I was born on December 9, 1895, in Portsmouth, England, where my father engaged in the profession of converting the personnel of His Majesty's Navy to belief in the literal interpretation of the authorized (James I) version of the New and Old Testaments—

especially the latter. By the time I was eleven he had come to the conclusion that prayer was more efficacious than his persuasive powers. So we moved to London. There I attended Tottenham County School, where I learnt very little except what, in spite of the obstacles put in my way by schoolmasters, I was able to teach myself; but I still cherish grateful memories of a schoolmistress who surreptitiously introduced me to Fabian Tracts and Bernard Shaw's plays. In 1912 I got a scholarship to Cambridge, and had my first opportunity of sampling the merits and disabilities of our governing class. Between 1919, when I married Enid Charles, now Britain's leading population statistician, and 1925, I held jobs in the Universities of London and Edinburgh, and then went to McGill as Assistant Professor in Zoology. After making many friends in America, I went to South Africa as Professor and Head of the Department of Zoology in Cape Town. There I remained till 1930, when I became Professor of Social Biology in London University. Since this appointment was located in the London School of Economics, it goes without saying that no scientific man could stay there indefinitely. In 1936 I became Regius Professor of Natural History in the University of Aberdeen. In the same year I was elected a Fellow of the Royal Society.

"The part of my research work which I have enjoyed most has been concerned with the role of the pituitary gland in relation to color change in animals. I have also been awarded the Neill prize and gold medal of the Royal Society of Edinburgh for my contributions to mathematical genetics. In my spare moments I have written several apparently successful books, of which *Science for the Citizen* entertained me most.

"I like Scandinavians, skiing, swimming, and Socialists who realize that it is our business to promote social progress by peaceful methods. I dislike football, economists, eugenists, Fascists, Stalinists, and Scottish conservatives. I think that sex is necessary and that bankers are not."

* * *

The tone of this sketch indicates why Lancelot Hogben was able to attract innumerable readers for books with such titles as *Mathematics for the Million* and *Science for the Citizen*. Leonard Bacon called him "an economist who has taken all knowledge for his province, . . . a scientist who does make the elementary clear." He himself says that his creed is that of "a scientific humanist." His scientific work has also covered experimental physiology and animal breeding research; he has written much for Rationalist publications. *Dangerous Thoughts* is largely sociological and economic in subject. In 1938 he edited *Political Arithmetic,* a symposium on social statistics.

Hogben was lecturing in Norway when the Nazis invaded Scandinavia. The story of his attempts to get back to England, in the course of which he journeyed thousands of miles and visited the United States, as well as many other countries, is told in *Author in Transit* (1940).

He is a scholarly looking, thin-faced man with a mass of wavy dark hair and a mouth which betrays his lurking sense of humor. In his middle forties, he is remarkably young in appearance. He and his brilliant wife (who says her recreation is maternity!) have two sons and two daughters. Their present home is in Aberdeen, Scotland, where he succeeded the famous Sir J. Arthur Thomson in one of the world's most important scientific teaching positions.

PRINCIPAL WORKS: Alfred Russel Wallace, 1918; Introduction to Recent Advances in Comparative Physiology (with F. R. Winton) 1925; Comparative Physiology, 1926; The Comparative Physiology of Internal Secretion, 1927; The Nature of Living Matter, 1930; Principles of Animal Biology, 1930; Genetic Principles in Medicine and Social Science, 1931; Nature and Nurture, 1933; Mathematics for the Million, 1936; Retreat From Reason, 1936; What Is Ahead of Us? (with others) 1937; Science for the Citizen, 1938; Dangerous Thoughts, 1939; Author in Transit, 1940.

ABOUT: Ethics July 1938; Eugenic Review January 1940; Nation November 12, 1938; New York Times August 4, 1940; Nineteenth Century March 1940; Saturday Review of Literature January 14, 1939; School and Society September 10, 1938; Wilson Library Bulletin March 1940.

HOLDEN, RAYMOND PECKHAM

(April 7, 1894-), American poet and novelist, writes: "I was born in New York City, and spent the first seventeen years of my life in a small town bounded by 72d St., Grant's Tomb, Riverside Drive, and Central Park. I never got out of that region except in summer for vacations, at Christmas time when I was allowed to visit 23d St. for shopping, and on Sundays when I visited my grandparents in that other and very different city in 79th St. just east of Fifth Avenue. Perhaps because I had been exposed to books (my father, Edwin Bab-

cock Holden, had a very large library), I began to write at the age of about fifteen; but having nothing to write about except the effect which the sound of words had on my somewhat empty head, I achieved little but a feeling of scorn for people who were not tortured by the vastness of undisciplined emotion. Four years at Princeton did little to advance my intelligence, as anyone who wishes to consult the old files of the *Nassau Literary Magazine* will discover.

"The war, the subsequent collapse of my too easily acquired personal economy, and an early acquaintance with Robert Frost took me off the wrong track, even if those events did not set me on the right one. My first book of poems was better received than it deserved to be, and its reception made me begin to think about myself as a writer rather than a mere fugitive from those who did not understand the soul. An unstable emotional nature, however, kept me from doing any real work for many years. I worked at odd jobs in the publishing business and with magazines, wrote a detective novel and a biography, neither of which, so far as I can tell, were read by anyone. I did not write what I should have been writing because it was hard to do and my thoughts were unfocussed.

"In 1931 I published another mystery novel, but still shied away from real production. I presume that, as almost any kind of meat, no matter how fundamentally bland, acquires some flavor if you hang it long enough, it was only natural that I should eventually begin to ripen. Be that as it may, I produced in 1935 a novel which turned out to be the first of what I hope will be a long series of studies of a group of interrelated people. The second of the series appeared in 1939 and the third will be ready soon. In the meantime I published another mystery novel and two more volumes of poems.

"In 1937 I married Sara Henderson Hay, the poet. I still haven't been able to get away from New York City, where I am on the staff of the Book-of-the-Month Club. My chief pleasures are simple ones, related to human living. I like people, the country, boats, baseball, books, music, food, and drink. Although I still hope to see reason, common sense, and decent consideration for the common man enter into political and economic life, I believe that the problems of government in the modern world are as yet unsolved. I am vitally interested in their solution and I hope that I shall be able to contribute to that end. For the present, I believe that there are fewer bad Democrats than bad Republicans: I believe that, no matter who wins the war, the human race is going to lose it. Nevertheless, if participation in it becomes necessary, I should not be in the least averse to taking my place in it. I don't believe that even war can stop a man from thinking; and thinking, by those who have never taught themselves to follow others, is what the human race most needs."

* * *

Mr. Holden's first wife was Louise Bogan, the poet, whom he married in 1925 and from whom he was divorced in 1937. His mystery novels are written under the pseudonym of "Richard Peckham."

PRINCIPAL WORKS: *Poetry*—Granite and Alabaster, 1922; Natural History, 1938; The Arrow at the Heel, 1940. *Novels*—Murder in Strange Houses, 1929; The Penthouse Murders, 1931; Chance Has a Whip, 1935; Death on the Border, 1937; Believe the Heart, 1939. *Miscellaneous*—Abraham Lincoln: The Politician and the Man, 1929.

ABOUT: Poetry June 1938.

*HOLLIDAY, ROBERT CORTES (July 18, 1880-   ), American editor and essayist, writes: "They say that having been born in

Pinchot

Indiana is something you never get over. You may go far from that rich and singular loam, and have your sides sandpapered in various parts of the world, but the Indiana never gets rubbed out. I was born in the 'original square mile' of Indianapolis. Though Mr. Tarkington did not have me individually in mind, my boyhood has been described by him with remarkable accuracy in his *Penrod* books and in *Seventeen*. It was the boyhood, I guess, of the Wabash Valley of that period. I left high school to go to New York to become an illustrator and painter. While living in a garret on Broome Street had work published by a Scribner publication now forgotten. Eyes failed.

"Turned up next as a 'special' student at the University of Kansas. Returned to New York and became a clerk 'on the floor' in a celebrated bookstore. And now began the kind of thing which an illustrious advertising man has termed 'a lifetime of jobs instead of the job of a lifetime.' Roustabout librarian, professional philanthropist, hotel detective, several times a literary editor, student of 'pubs' in England, reporter, hard-

driven feature writer, voluminous book reviewer, editorial writer, 'essayist,' ghost writer, general editorial handyman with in turn three famous publishing houses (sometimes simply called 'help,' one time 'literary adviser'), publicity man, advertising 'account executive,' instructor in writing, literary agent, pedigreed dog breeder: all these things have I been. I have been 'in' fish, as editor of a trade journal; in mausoleums, as a 'public relations' expert, and, as an historian, in ladies' underwear. At all of this I have been successful and am now a rich man—in experience.

"The unaccountable thing is that for a sizable stretch of years I had become so sunk in Newyorkerie that I was one of those strange beings who believe you can't get your breath off of Manhattan Island. I wrote, part of the time, under the name of 'Murray Hill,' and received letters seriously beginning 'Dear Mr. Hill.'

"And now—I guess it is what Stevenson called 'the romance of destiny'—I have lived for the past decade in a Dutch stone house amid the mountains at the tip-top of New Jersey; a house with one part something over a hundred and fifty years old, another part about two hundred years old. I don't know where I may go from here, but I know where I want to go at the last. The author of *Walking Stick Papers* hopes to be reunited in dust with the pioneer of the gold-headed cane [his paternal grandfather, the Rev. Fernando Cortez Holliday], upon whose family monument are cut these portentous words: "I am the Resurrection and the Life—Holliday.' "

* * *

From 1918 to 1923 Mr. Holliday was closely connected with the *Bookman,* and was its editor in 1919-20. He has been a free-lance writer and teacher of writing since 1926. In 1913 he married Alice Hickman; later they were divorced. He was a close friend of Joyce Kilmer, and became his editor and literary executor. Christopher Morley called Holliday "a burly soul, gazing with shy humor through thick-paned spectacles," and his essays "racy, vigorous, and genuinely flavored." Benjamin de Casseres said he wrote "with all his senses." Less favorable critics have called him slight and derivative. His *The Business of Writing* is one of the most useful technical books for the beginning writer, full of valuable and practical marketing advice.

PRINCIPAL WORKS: Booth Tarkington, 1918; Walking Stick Papers, 1918; Joyce Kilmer: A Memoir, 1918; Peeps at People, 1919; Broome Street Straws, 1919; Men and Books and Cities,

* Died December 1, 1946.

1920; Turns About Town, 1920; In the Neighborhood of Murray Hill, 1922; The Business of Writing, 1923; Literary Lanes and Other Byways, 1925; Our Little Brother Writes a Play, 1928; Unmentionables From Fig-Leaves to Scanties, 1933.

ABOUT: Doran, G. H. Chronicles of Barabbas; McFee, W. Harbours of Memory; Morley, C. Mince Pie; Library Journal March 1, 1934; Publishers' Weekly November 25, 1933; Scholastic May 6, 1940.

HOLLOWAY, EMORY (March 16, 1885-), American biographer and Pulitzer Prize winner, writes: "Most of my writing  has been a by-product of my lifelong occupation as a teacher. In mountain summer schools near Little Rock, Ark., I began teaching when I was eighteen, to earn money to finish college. Since then I have taught in the grades, in a high school, in a small church college, in a state university, in an urban college for girls, in the A.E.F. University at Beaune France, and in Queens College, the youngest of the institutions of high education of the City of New York. After twenty-three years at Adelphi College—a long and happy employment—I joined the small staff which organized Queens, where, for the four years of its existence [1941], I have been the elected chairman of the English department. In that time the student body expanded from 400 to 2,200, and the English staff from seven to twenty-two.

"While doing graduate work at Columbia University I became interested in a then little studied but now widely acclaimed poet. After seven years of research I published, in two volumes, *The Uncollected Poetry and Prose of Walt Whitman*, which students of the poet, who are now very numerous, have used in much later scholarship. I then turned to the editing of Whitman's preserved writings. Professor Bliss Perry was then the only American scholar who had written a life of Whitman that made any pretensions to research into a life which, for all its candor, yet cultivated certain shadows and myths. So I next wrote a narrative biography, using this form in the hope of increasing the number of intelligent readers of a poet who had too long been the property of the sophisticate and the cultist. The book, though intended for the general reader, yet contained a good deal of criticism, for my purpose was not only to

present a complex personality but also to show the social and artistic significance of the great poet, all against a picture of his time. *Whitman* was awarded the Pulitzer Prize in biography for 1927.

"With the exception of a utopia written for girls (and inspired by my own daughter when she was twelve), my writing has been largely limited to Whitman and Whitmaniana, even when I contributed to the *Encyclopaedia Britannica* and the *Cambridge History of American Literature*. Such concentration of effort might seem narrowing to some American (rather than European) scholars, but as a matter of fact I have stuck to the subject because there was so much to be done and because of its ever-widening and perennially contemporary significance. Not only the student but the country as a whole, if democracy is to thrive, has need of Whitman's 'steady faith' in itself. In a way, the circumstances of my ancestry and early life were a good preparation for the understanding of such a writer as Whitman, because they helped me to understand the America which he 'absorbed' in his personality and poetry. My paternal grandfather owned a slave or two, but my mother's father, a Kentuckian descended from Daniel Boone, was for freedom. My own life has been spent almost equally on the two sides of the Mason and Dixon line, and I have been educated and have taught in both sections. My travels have taken me over practically all the states in the Union and I have made acquaintance with life in the mountains, on the farms, in towns and villages, and in the largest of our cities. I have a firm faith in the common sense of the American people and in their devotion to the way of life which they have progressively (if sometimes slowly and with many blunders and injustices) worked out for themselves, and I doubt not their willingness to protect it, once they realize that it is endangered."

* * *

Professor Holloway was born in Marshall, Mo., and was educated at Hendrix College, Conway, Ark. (B.A. 1905) and the University of Texas (M.A. 1912, LL.D. 1935). He also studied at Columbia. From 1906 to 1908 he taught English at the Amity, Ark, high school, and from 1910 to 1911 in Scarritt-Morrisville College, Morrisville, Mo. In 1912 he became instructor in English at the University of Texas; from 1914 to 1937 he was professor of English at Adelphi College, and in 1937 he went to Queens College, Jamaica, N.Y. In 1918 he served as a transport secretary of the Y.M.C.A. in France, and in 1919 taught at Beaune. In 1925 and 1926 he was a lecturer in the Workers' University. He married Ella Brooks Harris in 1915, and they have two sons and a daughter. They live in Brooklyn, with a summer home in Meddybemps, Maine. He was chairman of the Walt Whitman Memorial Committee in 1925, and since 1940 has been editor of *American Literature*.

PRINCIPAL WORKS: Whitman: An Interpretation in Narrative, 1926; Janice in Tomorrow-Land (juvenile) 1936.

HOLME, CONSTANCE, English novelist and short-story writer, was born the youngest of the fourteen children of John Holme, J.P., D.L., of Owlet  Ash, Milnthorpe, Westmorland. Her mother's family had a strain of Spanish blood, perhaps derived from waifs cast up by storm-tossed Armada vessels. The village of Milnthorpe lies on a small estuary in the Morecambe Bay. In 1916 Miss Holme married Frederick Burt Punchard, J.P., F.S.I., resident agent for Lady Henry Bentinck's Underley Estates. Constance Holme's novel, *The Trumpet in the Dust* (1921), which derived its title from Rabindranath Tagore's poem, "The Trumpet," is dedicated "To Lord Henry Bentinck: This Weed From an Uncultivated Garden." Mr. Punchard retired in 1937. His wife speaks of Owlet Ash as a place where she was born, lived, was married, and probably will be buried. It has an "unexciting and probably quite unproven ghost."

Constance Holme's "peculiar gift to the modern novel," according to Doris N. Dalglish, is "the gift of an intellect which has been kept immune from the fretfulness of the ailing society of cities, enriched by the messages of hill and sea, and instructed thereby to appreciate the nobility of man's dependence." She has written of a band of Westmorland gentry and farmers of whom a dozen certainly "come alive." The Oxford University Press has included an unprecedented number of her novels and collections of short stories in its World Classics series; *The Splendid Faring* (1919) won the French literary prize awarded by Femina-Vie-Heureuse; and in February 1938 the *Saturday Review of Literature* launched a "crusade for Constance Holme"

to make her books better known to an American audience sure to appreciate them. Her novels treat of Westmorland types with sure authority. One of her best descriptive devices is the correlation of natural phenomena with mental or spiritual states in her characters; she also uses the supernatural with telling effect. Constance Holme has a blond, typically English type of beauty; has lived at The Gables, Kirkby Lonsdale, and now lists her ancestral home, Owlet Ash, as her residence.

PRINCIPAL WORKS: Crump Folk Going Home, 1913; The Lonely Plough, 1914; The Old Road From Spain, 1916; Beautiful End, 1918; The Splendid Faring, 1919; The Trumpet in the Dust, 1921; The Things Which Belong, 1925; He-Who-Came? 1930; The Wisdom of the Simple and Other Stories, 1937.

ABOUT: Adelphi May 1925; Saturday Review of Literature February 19, 1938; Wilson Library Bulletin May 1938.

HOLTBY, WINIFRED (1898-September 25, 1935), English novelist and essayist, was born in Rudstone, Yorkshire, the daughter of David Holtby. She was a brilliant student at both Queen Margaret's School, Scarborough, and Somerville College, Oxford, though her university career was interrupted by a year of war service in the Signals Unit of the Women's Aux-  iliary Army Corps, when she was hostel-forewoman at a post near Huchenneville. After graduation from Oxford she went to London, in 1921, where she became associated with Lady Rhondda on her magazine, *Time and Tide*, of which eventually (from 1926) Miss Holtby was director. In London she lived with her classmate Vera Brittain, though she was always nostalgic for her native Yorkshire, and gave her home address as Cottingham. Besides her editorial work and her writing, she traveled all over Europe as a lecturer for the League of Nations Union. She never married.

An indefatigable worker, she gave, with her tall slender figure, her golden hair and bright blue eyes, the appearance of fragility; and this impression was not an inaccurate one. Overwork contributed as much as anything else to a fatal heart disease, which increasingly disabled her during the last four years of her short life. Nevertheless, she refused to give way to it, and her novel, *South Riding*, was actually finished less than four weeks before her death, when she was quite aware that she was running a race against time. She died in London, but was buried in her native town of Rudstone.

Few persons have died within recent years in England of whom it could so truly be said that their death was premature and that their best potentialities died with them. For Winifred Holtby was constantly maturing, and each of her books was better than the last. Until her posthumously published novel, her work was little known in the United States, and several of her volumes have never been published in America. She was a clever essayist and a keen critic, but it is as a writer of fiction that she will be remembered. *Mandoa! Mandoa!* is a devastating satire on industrial civilization cast in a primitive African community. But her greatest triumph was in *South Riding,* a Yorkshire novel (its exact locale hidden by the fact that Yorkshire in actuality is divided into only North, West, and East Ridings) based in part on her own mother's experiences as a County Council member. It was made into a motion picture by a British company with considerable artistic and some financial success. In it is implicit the whole social and economic scene, the slightly urbanized rural community which is its setting being merely the microcosm of a nation, and indeed of a civilization shared on both sides of the Atlantic. It is a triumph marred only by the melancholy thought that it was its author's last work. Winifred Holtby had in her the makings of a novelist of the very first rank; like Arnold Bennett's in his Five Town stories, her regionalism was universal. As the *Literary Digest* remarked, *South Riding* is "a magnificent epitaph" for its creator.

PRINCIPAL WORKS: Eutychus: or, The Future of the Pulpit, 1928; Virginia Woolf, A Critical Study, 1932; Mandoa! Mandoa! 1933; Truth Is Not Sober and Other Stories, 1934; Women and a Changing Civilization, 1934; South Riding, 1936; Pavements at Anderby (short stories) 1937; Letters to a Friend, 1937.

ABOUT: Brittain, V. Testament of Friendship; Holtby, W. Letters to a Friend; Holtby, W. South Riding (see Ave atque Vale, by V. Brittain); Christian Century October 30, 1935; Literary Digest April 11, 1936; Publishers' Weekly October 12, 1935; Scholastic January 22, 1938; Wilson Library Bulletin April 1934, November 1935.

*HOOTON, EARNEST ALBERT (November 20, 1887-), American anthropologist, was born in Clemansville, Wis., the son of William Hooton and Margaret Elizabeth (Newton) Hooton. His father was a Methodist minister, of English

* Died May 3, 1954.

birth, who in spite of a small salary saw to it that all his children had a college education. The unusual spelling of Professor Hooton's first name is an evidence of the atmosphere of serious endeavor which surrounded his childhood. In spite of extreme near-sightedness, which made him wear spectacles at six, he was a very bookish child, ready for high school at eleven—he himself says he was "a horrid little squirt." By this time the family lived in Manitowoc, Wis., where the frail little boy went to high school with husky, tobacco-chewing grown men from the lumber camps.

Bachrach

At fifteen he entered Lawrence College, in Appleton, Wis. He majored in Latin, and expected to become a teacher of classical archaeology. He received his Ph.D. in Latin and Greek at the University of Wisconsin in 1911, teaching Latin at the university meanwhile, and then secured a Rhodes Scholarship and went to Oxford. There he discovered how fragmentary was his classical training as compared to that of English students. He became interested in anthropology, and transferred to Exeter College, where the celebrated R. R. Marrett was the apostle of anthropological science. Through Marrett's influence he became an instructor in Harvard in 1913, and has been there ever since. He became a full professor in 1930, and has been curator of the Peabody Museum since 1914.

In 1914 he married Mary Beidler Camp, and they have two sons and a daughter, all of whom, to his chagrin, are more interested in athletics than in scholarship. In spite of his bad sight, he went into training at Plattsburg in 1916, but never entered the war. He lives in Cambridge, where outside his hours of teaching and of writing he likes to have open house for his students and to hold long conversations over his favorite jasmine tea. He is an enthusiastic golfer, and among his other likings are cats and sherry. Lately he has amused himself by turning illustrator of his own books, his fantastic drawings, of which he makes fun but to which he is devoted, having a touch about them of Van Loon, Bemelmans, or even Thurber. He is slender, of medium height, with a thin moustache, a characteristic pipe his constant accompaniment in leisure hours, and a surprised appearance behind his thick spectacles, because of the strain to which he must put his eyes.

Professor Hooton is widely known as the "anthropological Cassandra," with a very poor opinion of the accomplishments and prospects of the human race; yet "beyond his immediate pessimism is a sort of long-sighted optimism." His work is unfailingly entertaining, yet it has a sound substratum of scientific authority. Walter Stockley called him "a brilliant scientist who happens to have a flair for showmanship. . . . He makes more noise in public and gets more newspaper space than any other anthropologist in the world."

As evidence of the validity of the research behind his provocative wit, he is a fellow of the American Association for the Advancement of Science, the American Academy of Arts and Sciences, and the Royal Anthropological Institute, and in 1933 received an honorary Sc.D. degree from Lawrence College.

PRINCIPAL WORKS: Ancient Inhabitants of the Canary Islands, 1925; The Indians of Pecos, 1930; Up from the Ape, 1931; Apes, Men, and Morons, 1937; The American Criminal, 1939; Crime and the Man, 1939; Twilight of Man, 1939; Why Men Behave Like Apes and Vice Versa, 1940.

ABOUT: American Mercury November 1939; Current Biography, 1940; Life August 7, 1939; Saturday Review of Literature October 16, 1937; Time November 8, 1937, December 2, 1940.

"HOPE, ANTHONY." See HAWKINS, A. H.

HOPE, LAURENCE (April 9, 1865-October 4, 1904), English poet, was born Adela Florence Cory at Stoke House, Stoke

Bishop, Gloucestershire, the daughter of Arthur Cory, a colonel in the Indian Army, and Fanny Elizabeth (Griffin) Cory. After attending private school at Richmond, she went out to India to join her parents. In 1889, at twenty-four, "Laurence Hope" married Colonel Malcolm Hassels Nicolson of the Bengal Army, an expert linguist. The couple settled at Madras, and the young wife devoted her leisure time to poetry. Nicolson was made a lieutenant-general in 1899. In 1891-1894 he was aide-de-camp to Queen Victoria, who died in the year that Mrs. Nicolson published The Garden of Kama and Other Love Lyrics From India, Arranged in Verse by Laurence Hope

(1901). It is unlikely that the Queen would have approved this torrid, Swinburnian verse, which illustrated "a lover's aim for destruction of self-consciousness in union with the object of his desires" and insisted on the right of woman to share this ecstasy. Mrs. Nicolson's note of passion, expressed in a medium of Oriental temperament and imagery, seemed like something new in English literature. Her inspiration was attributed, somewhat doubtfully, to "the world of Islam and the Persian poets." In any case, the poems became immensely popular; set to music, "Pale hands I loved beside the Shalimar" and others became the standby of drawing-room sopranos and, later, of radio tenors. The poems were reissued in 1908 as Songs From the Garden of Kama. They were generally reviewed as the work of a man. Two more volumes of verse, one posthumous, followed the first. General Nicolson, who called his wife "Violet," died in 1904 at Mackay's Gardens, a nursing home in Madras. After two months of grief and acute depression, "Laurence Hope" swallowed perchloride of mercury and died at Dunmore House, also in Madras. She was buried with her husband in St. Mary's cemetery.

PRINCIPAL WORKS: The Garden of Kama, 1901; Stars of the Desert, 1903; Indian Love, 1905; Songs From the Garden of Kama, 1908.

ABOUT: Rothfeld, O. Indian Dust; Studies of the Orient. Athenaeum October 29, 1904.

HOPKINS, GERARD MANLEY. See "BRITISH AUTHORS OF THE 19TH CENTURY"

HORGAN, PAUL (August 1, 1903-), American novelist, writes: "I was born in Buffalo, N.Y., the second son of Edward D. and Rose Marie (Rohr) Horgan. My father and mother were first-generation Americans, and from my grandparents I inherit English-Irish and French-German blood. The European ties of family life were still strong enough and evident

enough, when I was a child, to take effect in my character and to be echoed in several of my books. I was educated at a private school in Buffalo until my eleventh year, when my family removed to Albuquerque, N.M., because of my father's health. Thereafter I went to the public schools in Albuquerque, and saw a new world of land. The most interesting thing about the place to me was the nearness of 'the country.' At the end of familiar streets, you could see the mesa, and sand hills, and cliffs made by gravel-haulers; and every time you looked East you could see the mountains.

"Thus in childhood I knew two worlds, as only a child can know them, the impression shaping the clay. This will explain why my books have been about both the East and the West of our country.

"During my high school years I entered New Mexico Military Institute as a cadet. There I had three years of schooling, which ended my 'formal' education. My father died in 1922, and it was decided that our family return to the East. In 1923 the move was made, and instead of staying in Buffalo with the rest, I went to Rochester, N.Y., to study singing. Before long I was working on the production staff of the Eastman Theatre, and during the next three years I had an intensive experience doing everything there was to do with the stage: acting, singing, helping the director, Rouben Mamoulian, making scenery, writing, even dancing. I had always leaned toward the theatre. My first piece of writing was a play for a toy theatre. I had always heard music at home. The Rochester years included much music. I was thrown with many brilliant musicians, foreign and domestic. We were a curious crew serving with an enthusiastic energy alien to an American industrial city.

"In 1926 I left the Eastman Theatre and returned to New Mexico, going as librarian to the New Mexico Military Institute. Once again the West brought me new views, but this time I was not a stranger. I began to write books, and produced five before finding a publisher for the sixth—a novel. This was *The Fault of Angels*, and it was awarded the Harper Prize in 1933. It was a comedy celebrating the atmosphere of those Rochester experiences mentioned above. Since then I have published ten more books, and have written many plays."

* * *

Captain Horgan (his professional title) is still librarian at the New Mexico Military Institute. He is unmarried. He is a dark-haired, good-looking man who is a fine tennis player and coaches the tennis team at the school. He still sings, but was obliged to give up a professional musical career because of his health. At sixteen he was music critic of the Albuquerque *Morning Journal*. He comes honestly by his literary talent, his grandfather, Mathias Rohr,

having been a German poet who left the University of Bonn to emigrate to Buffalo.

Mr. Horgan's first publication was in *Poetry*. A story of his appeared in the O. Henry Memorial volume for 1931. He has some aptitude for drawing also, and illustrated his first book, a history of soldiers of all times written for boys. He is a Catholic.

His best work, except for his prize novel, is in descriptions of the Southwest. In his other novels he is a bit given to what one critic called "fancy writing," but his Western background is keenly and vividly presented.

PRINCIPAL WORKS: Men of Arms, 1931; The Fault of Angels, 1933; From the Royal City, 1934; No Quarter Given, 1935; The Return of the Weed, 1936; Main Line West, 1936; A Lamp on the Plains, 1937; New Mexico's Own Chronicle (with M. G. Fulton) 1937; Far From Cibola, 1938; The Habit of Empire, 1938; Figures in a Landscape, 1940; Firelight, 1942.

ABOUT: Library Journal August 1933, September 1, 1933; Publisher's Weekly May 3, 1941; Time April 29, 1940; Wilson Library Bulletin September 1933.

HORN, ALFRED ALOYSIUS ("Trader" Horn) (1861?-June 26, 1931), English adventurer, was born Alfred Aloysius Smith in Lancashire, of an old Preston family. Two brothers became priests, and one took to farming. Young Smith entered St. Edward's College, Liverpool, September 21, 1872, aged eleven; his "lively behavior" made the authorities request him  to leave in 1878. (All this according to the Liverpool *Post* for July 8, 1927). He went to the West Coast of Africa as a trader for ivory and rubber, for the London firm of Hatton & Cookson. "Trader" Horn was unknown to fame until he turned up, an old man living in a Johannesburg doss-house, at the back door of Ethelreda Lewis,[qv] an English novelist then living in South Africa, to sell her a gridiron and spin some romantic yarns. They seemed like good copy to Mrs. Lewis, who gave him pencil and paper to write them down on quiet Mondays at the doss-house. John Galsworthy, who called on the old man, wrote an appreciative introduction to his book as edited and expanded by Mrs. Lewis, and the Literary Guild in New York City published the volume as its fourth selection.

Four publishing houses had rejected it before Clifton Fadiman, reader for Simon & Schuster, recommended the book to his firm. The "jumble of jungle adventure" received favorable, if occasionally amused, notice from the critics; and in spite of one reviewer who called the book "senile drivel touched up with loving care by a third-rate novelist," it sold 170,000 copies.

"Trader" Horn was imported by his publishers to New York to enjoy the fruits of his success, and proved to be a "vague, mild old man of the type that frequents Bowery saloons." With his long cape and five-gallon hat, he bore some resemblance to the picturesque American poet Joaquin Miller. He died in a hospital at Whitstable, England, after a brief illness, leaving his daughter an estate of $8,520, the remainder of royalties estimated at $100,000. *Trader Horn* was the title of a moving picture based on his adventures, full of wild animals and destined to long litigation because the leading lady contracted a slow fever in Africa during its filming. The book's two sequels did not sell so well as the original volume of adventures.

PRINCIPAL WORKS: Trader Horn, 1927; Harold the Webbed: or, The Young Vykings, 1928; The Waters of Africa, 1929.

ABOUT: New York Times June 26, July 1, August 20, 1931; New Yorker October 7, 1939.

HORN, "TRADER." See HORN, A. A.

HORNADAY, WILLIAM TEMPLE
(December 1, 1854-March 6, 1937), American zoologist, wrote before his death to the compilers of this volume:

"I was born on a backwoods farm in central Indiana. Eighteen months later my family moved to Iowa. But it was in 1873, on the campus of the pioneer Iowa State Agricultural College, that the present historian found his manhood self, and was born into a raw and unharrowed field of practical zoology. My lifetime task took definite form: bringing the most interesting wild creatures of the world to the millions of people who cannot go to them. The means? Travel, collecting, museum-building, and books. The zoological parks were born twenty-five years later.

"This sketch is supposed to concern books and their making—a subject that is one lap nearer to my heart than even the wild animals. The desire of my sober young manhood to talk to 'the millions' about wild animals has (for me) most gloriously been gratified. My favorite of my books is the Imp of the brood, *Wild Animal Interviews, and Wild Opinions of Us.* Perhaps that is because these (fiction?) stories all were syndicated to a total of 1,547,638 readers for nearly a year.

"I was an associate member of a book-loving family. It was Audubon's *Birds of North America,* Samuel's *Birds of New England,* and Tenney's excellent *Manual of Zoology* that revealed to me the existence of the great world of wild creatures, and fired my farm-bred soul with a desire and purpose to see a whole lot of it. My 'fortune' in books, figuratively speaking, was made by *Two Years in the Jungle;* I think my *American Natural History* is my *magnum opus;* my most scholarly and best written book is my *Minds and Manners of Wild Animals.*"

* * *

From 1875 to 1879 Mr. Hornaday visited Cuba, Florida, the West Indies, South America, India, Ceylon, the Malay Peninsula, and Borneo, as a collecting zoologist. From 1882 to 1890 he was chief taxidermist of the United States National Museum. Then for six years he engaged in the real estate business in Buffalo, N.Y. In 1896 he began his real lifework with the New York Zoological Park (the "Bronx Zoo") in New York, of which he was still director when he died at his home in Stamford, Conn., at eighty-four. He had an Sc.D. degree from the University of Pittsburgh (1906), and received gold and silver medals for creating the Montana Bison Range and the Elk River Game Preserve, and instigating the Bayne law to prohibit sale of the nation's game. A great conservationist, he was no mild, white-bearded scientist, but "a tireless fighter who battened on controversy." He was married in 1879 to Josephine Chamberlain, and they had one daughter.

PRINCIPAL WORKS: Two Years in the Jungle, 1885; Free Rum on the Congo, 1887; The Extermination of the American Bison, 1887; Taxidermy and Zoological Collecting, 1892; The Man Who Became a Savage, 1895; Guide to the New York Zoological Park, 1899; The American Natural History, 1904; Camp-Fires in the Canadian Rockies, 1906; Our Vanishing Wild Life, 1913; Minds and Manners of Wild Animals, 1922; Tales From Nature's Wonderlands, 1924; A Wild-Animal Round-Up, 1925; Wild Animal Interviews, 1928; Thirty Years' War for Wild Life, 1931.

ABOUT: Kunitz, S. J. & Haycraft, H. (eds.). The Junior Book of Authors; Commonweal March 19, 1937; Science May 7, 1937.

HORNUNG, ERNEST WILLIAM (1866-March 22, 1921), English novelist, short-story writer, and inventor of Raffles, the  Gentleman Cracksman, was born at Middlesborough, Yorkshire. He was educated at Uppingham. After he left school, ill health compelled him to go to Australia, where he remained from 1884 to 1886, absorbing local color for two successful works of fiction, *A Bride From the Bush* and *Stingaree.* On Hornung's return to England he married Constance Doyle, a sister of A. Conan Doyle, in 1893. Six years later the gentleman crook, Raffles, and his satellite and chronicler, Bunny, made their appearance in *The Amateur Cracksman,* with a dedication: "To A.C.D., This Form of Flattery." Doyle always felt a special affection for his brother-in-law, "Willie" Hornung, and praised in his autobiography Hornung's charm and wit. (It was Hornung who said, "Though he might be more humble, there is no police like Holmes.") This did not prevent Doyle's feeling some justified apprehension over Hornung's glorification of a criminal. Kyrle Bellew, an American matinée idol of the day, also lent his romantic presence to the dramatization of the stories, *Raffles,* produced in New York in 1903.

The Raffles tales, four volumes of them, were told with a fine economy and an admirable choice of words and gave the author wide fame. Hornung, a man of genuine culture, did not particularly pride himself on them, and it must be admitted that a faint suggestion of decadence hovers over the stories. *Stingaree,* the romance of a chivalrous Australian bushwhacker, benefits by its outdoor setting. *Fathers of Men* is one British story of public school life which is neither sensational nor unduly sentimental. Hornung wrote many other novels, mainly forgotten today.

In the First World War, although he was a great sufferer from asthma, Hornung went to France with a Y.M.C.A. library, leaving the field of Arras only after heavy bombardment which put the Germans in possession of the library. His only son was killed at the front. His war poems, *The Young Guard,* were printed in the London *Times* and circulated as leaflets. *Notes of a Camp Follower,* his book of war

reminiscenses, is charming and unaffected. He died at St. Jean-de-Luz, France, where George Gissing lies buried.

Like Raffles, wrote Hugh Caister in the *Outlook,* Hornung was a cricketer, a sentimentalist, and a craftsman. "He had, indeed, talents which in a generation less brilliant than his own might have commanded immediate respect, and which in any generation might, had he bothered, have been made the vehicle of great ideas. But he did not bother. Raffles came to him once, and he wrote a minor classic." Doyle, writing a preface to the posthumous *Old Offenders,* attributes Hornung's effectiveness as a writer to his sudden use of the right adjective and the right phrase.

PRINCIPAL WORKS: The Amateur Cracksman, 1899; Dead Men Tell No Tales, 1899; Raffles: Further Adventures of the Amateur Cracksman, 1901; At Large, 1902; The Shadow of the Rope, 1902; No Hero, 1903; Stingaree, 1905; A Thief in the Night: Further Adventures of A. J. Raffles, 1905; Mr. Justice Raffles, 1909; The Camera Fiend, 1911; The Crime Doctor, 1914; Notes of a Camp-Follower on the Western Front, 1919.

ABOUT: Doyle, A. C. Memories and Adventures; Miller, E. M. Australian Literature From Its Beginnings to 1935; London Mercury May 1921; New York Times April 8, 1921; Outlook (London) May 19, 1923.

HORVÁTH, ODÖN VON (1901-June 1938), Hungarian-German dramatist and novelist, was born in the country then known as Serbia, where his father was a member of the Austro-Hungarian embassy, and educated in Budapest. When still in his twenties Horváth enjoyed popularity as a writer of comedies in Germany; the seriousness of his two anti-Nazi novels pub-  lished in this country after his tragic death has somewhat obscured the fact. Of the amusing and satirical *Italienische Nacht* produced in 1931, Alfred Kerr remarked in the *Berliner Tageblatt* that "one laughs oneself sick." A novel in three parts, *Der Ewige Spiesser,* possessed, according to the *Münchner Post,* "what is so rare in our time: humor." When Odön von Horváth was only twenty-seven, European critics awarded him the Kleist Prize, roughly equivalent to the American Pulitzer Prize for drama. Johann Strauss' enchanting waltz, "Tales From the Vienna Woods," was his inspiration for the gay farce, *Geschichte aus dem Wiener Wald: Volksstück in Drei Teilen,* with its action laid in Vienna and the Wiener Wald, which played in Berlin in 1931. The famous theatrical producer Max Reinhardt was one of Horváth's intimate friends, as were the writers Alfred Neumann, Franz Werfel, and Stefan Zweig, who said after his untimely death at thirty-seven that, "Literature has lost the most gifted writer of the younger generation."

Early in June 1938, Horváth was strolling along the Champs Elysées in Paris, where he was living as a self-imposed exile from the Nazi régime (although his 100 per cent Aryanism had saved him from persecution) when a sudden gust of wind cracked a huge, dying chestnut tree. The trunk crashed down, instantly killing the writer. No one else was hurt. He may well have been wearing his customary expression of cheerful good-humor; the day was a fine one.

Of *The Age of the Fish* (1938), which was written without anger, Lewis Gannett said: "There is beauty and dignity in this gentle, distinguished story." Dorothy Canfield declared: "We have had nothing from Nazi Germany which so conveys the atmosphere of ordinary life under Nazi rule. It is a fiery glassfull of distilled essence of what happens to men, women, boys and girls if they do not singly and individually renounce what they know to be human decency, dignity, and integrity." *A Child of Our Time* (1939) represents Everyman in Nazi Germany; it is the story of a young man, born into a post-war world which had no place for him, who loses the use of his right arm in an undeclared war on a neutral neighboring country. It is, states the *New Yorker*, "told in a bleak, swift prose reminiscent of Franz Kafka's," and is "a sort of allegory, with an average man for a combined hero and villain. He mouths the propaganda which is fed to him, carries out the violent commands, and feels quite empty inside."

WORKS AVAILABLE IN ENGLISH TRANSLATION: The Age of the Fish, 1938; A Child of Our Time, 1939.

ABOUT: Horváth, O. von. A Child of Our Time (see foreword by Franz Werfel and Appreciation by Stefan Zweig in the British edition); Time February 20, 1939.

HOUGH, EMERSON (June 28, 1857-April 30, 1923), American novelist, was born in Newton, Iowa, the son of Joseph Bond Hough and Elizabeth Hough. His father was a Virginia schoolmaster who had moved to Iowa when it was still a virgin wilderness.

Hough taught public school after graduating (as one of a class of three) from the Newton High School, then went to the University of Iowa to study law. This profession, though he secured his degree, was admitted to the bar, and even started practice in Whiteoaks, N.M., was his father's choice rather than his own. While still in college he had started to sell stories to the popular magazines, and his actual life was devoted to what he called "professional out of door journalism"—camping out, roughing it all through the United States and Canada, and writing about his experiences. Then he worked for a while on papers in Des Moines, Iowa, and Sandusky, Ohio, and in Chicago managed the branch office of *Field and Stream*. He was forty-two when his first book was published and he was not able to live wholly by writing until after the success of *The Mississippi Bubble*, in 1902.

In 1897 he married Charlotte A. Cheseborough. His headquarters, so to speak, was in Chicago, but all his life he continued to wander. For years he edited a department, "Out-of-Doors," in the *Saturday Evening Post;* and out of doors remained his most preferred environment. He was an ardent advocate of conservation, and did much for the movement to preserve the national parks. He was president of the Midland Society of Authors in 1917-18, but can hardly be said to have belonged to the so-called "Chicago Renaissance group."

Hough's constant wandering, his incessant need of leaving the cities and renewing contact with nature, though ostensibly in the cause of historical research and the cause of natural conservation, actually came very near to nomadism. He was in a sense a throw-back to the pioneer generations he so admired. As Wallace Stegner has remarked, he "fits no patterns and left no legacies except his keen interest in the western migrations of settlers."

Hough, a burly, heavy-set man who looked like one of his own pioneers, was of the type that Theodore Roosevelt loved—aggressive but genial, provincial, intensely patriotic, and a skilled woodsman. His style had no distinction, though he himself had a very high opinion of his place as a writer. Historical fiction dealing with the building of the West was his special field, and in that he did seek for accuracy of detail and prided himself on seldom being caught in an error. His work had a certain force, but it was conventional and often awkwardly worded. His novels were ideally suited for the motion pictures, which found a gold mine in *The Covered Wagon*. The *Outlook*, in an obituary notice, said that he "described pioneer life as it truly was," and the *Review of Reviews* spoke of his "life-long burning passion for nature, for the hardy virtues of our pioneer forebears." Charles C. Baldwin summed up Hough's career in words that explain both his popularity and the lack of survival-value of his books: "He ran away from life, from his fellows; he hid in the forests; he played at being back in the days of the great explorers. . . . He was . . . a boy with a boy's love for beckoning roads and the hunter's trail." His name is pronounced *huff*.

PRINCIPAL WORKS: The Singing Mouse Stories, 1895; The Story of the Cowboy, 1897; The Girl at the Half-Way House, 1900; The Mississippi Bubble, 1902; The Way of the West, 1903; The Law of the Land, 1905; The King of Gee Whiz, 1906; The Story of the Outlaw, 1906; The Way of a Man, 1907; Fifty-Four Forty or Fight, 1909; The Sowing, 1909; The Young Alaskans (juvenile) 1910; The Purchase Price, 1911; John Rawn: Prominent Citizen, 1912; The Lady and the Pirate, 1913; Young Alaskans on the Trail (juvenile) 1914; Let's Go Afield, 1916; The Magnificent Adventure, 1916; The Man Next Door, 1917; The Broken Gate, 1917; Young Alaskans in the Far North (juvenile) 1918; The Way Out, 1918; The Sagebrusher, 1919; The Web, 1919; The Covered Wagon, 1922; North of Thirty-Six, 1923; Mother of Gold, 1924; The Ship of Souls, 1925; Young Alaskans on the Missouri (juvenile) 1929.

ABOUT: Baldwin, C. C. The Men Who Make Our Novels; Stone, L. A. Emerson Hough: His Place in American Letters; Outlook May 9, 1923; Review of Reviews June 1923; Saturday Evening Post June 7, 1924.

"HOUGHTON, CLAUDE." See OLDFIELD, C. H.

HOUGHTON, WILLIAM STANLEY

(February 22, 1881-December 11, 1913), English dramatist who wrote as Stanley  Houghton, was born at Ashton-on-Mersey, Cheshire, the son of John Hartley Houghton, a cotton merchant in the neighboring city of Manchester. Educated at Bowdon College, the grammar schools of Stockport and Wilmslow, and for a final year at the Manchester Grammar School (where he was

contemporary with Gilbert Cannan), he entered his father's warehouse in 1897 as a salesman of "grey cloth." He worked a regular business-man's day, from 9 to 5, and his occupation brought him into contact with the dour, forthright commercial types he was later to put so successfully on the stage.

As soon as he left school he joined the Manchester Athenaeum, founded the Swan luncheon club for the discussion of the arts, and spent almost the whole of his small leisure in amateur dramatic work, acting over 70 parts between 1901 and 1912. Manchester has been a notable dramatic centre for forty years, and produced the "Lancashire school" of playwrights, of whom Houghton, Allan Monkhouse, and Harold Brighouse are the chief.

From 1900 onwards Houghton began to write for the stage, beginning with farces and one-act plays, many of which were put on by amateurs. It should be emphasized that his own amateur acting was by no means merely a hobby, and that he kept it up in order to learn stagecraft from the inside. He also acted as unpaid dramatic critic to the Manchester *City News* during 1905-06. Between 1907 and 1912 he did a good deal of free-lance dramatic criticism and general literary journalism for the Manchester *Guardian*, meeting through this work men of the calibre of C. E. Montague, Monkhouse, and G. H. Mair.

Houghton's first play to be put on the professional stage was *The Dear Departed*, produced by Miss A. E. F. Horniman at her Manchester repertory theatre, the Gaiety, in November 1908. It was subsequently translated into, and produced in, French, Dutch, and Welsh. *Independent Means* followed in 1909, *The Younger Generation* and *The Master of the House* in 1910, and then several more. With the production (on June 16, 1912) of *Hindle Wakes* by Mr. Lewis Casson at the Aldwych Theatre, London, Houghton sprang into fame and fortune. The company was Miss Horniman's, from Manchester, and the big part of Nathaniel Jeffcote was taken by Herbert Lomas, a superb Lancashire actor. Within a year the play had been acted 2,000 times in London, Manchester, New York, and Chicago.

Houghton was now able to give up the cotton trade. He removed to London, was elected to the Savage (the premier literary club) and to the exclusive Dramatists' Club, and was much fêted, lionized, and run after by editors and fellow-dramatists. He soon found that he was too accessible to all this, and went to Paris to escape it. There he wrote six chapters of a novel, *Life,* and lived happily and busily. But while on holiday in Venice in the summer of 1913 he was attacked by an infection which necessitated two operations and his eventual return to Manchester. Finally meningitis supervened, and he died at the age of thirty-two.

Houghton's plays have something of the Ibsenian realism without that master's far-reaching social sense. They display a section of society *in petto,* the section comprising the Lancashire millowner and millhand, whose rough, unromantic, common-sensical attitude is done to the life. Problems of youth *versus* age, of emancipated ideas trying to break down narrow, money-bred conventions, are his chief themes. *Hindle Wakes,* which deals with a moral lapse by a mill-girl with the owner's son, and her spirited refusal to be married offhand, is beautifully constructed, true in dialogue down to the last word, and just misses real greatness. The title puzzled New York, so it may be usefully stated that Hindle is a fictitious town and the "wakes" are the annual holiday, when the mills close for a week.

Houghton worked quickly, jotting ideas in note-books and then planning the whole play before writing a line. His politics were advanced, but were not obtruded in his work. He was popular, but reserved in company until he "thawed." He played cricket, lawn tennis and hockey (as a left-hander) and a respectable game of bridge.

PRINCIPAL PUBLISHED WORKS: The Dear Departed, 1910; The Younger Generation, 1910; Independent Means, 1911; Fancy Free, 1912; Hindle Wakes, 1912; Five One Act Plays (The Dear Departed, Fancy Free, The Master of the House, Phipps, The Fifth Commandment) 1913; Works (with Biographical Introduction by Harold Brighouse) 1914.

ABOUT: Agate, J. Short View of the English Stage: 1900-1926; Archer, W. The Old Drama and the New; Cumberland, G. Set Down in Malice; Cunliffe, J. W. Modern English Playwrights; Dickinson, T. H. The Contemporary Drama of England; Houghton, W. S. Works (see Biographical Introduction by Harold Brighouse); Morgan, A. E. Tendencies of Modern English Drama; Palmer, J. The Future of the Theatre. English Review January 1914; Living Age February 1914.

HOULT, NORAH (1901*-), Irish novelist, writes: "Born in Dublin of Anglo-Irish parentage. Owing to death of both parents in her early childhood was educated in English schools. After leaving school joined the editorial staff of the Sheffield *Daily Telegraph,* where she remained for two years. Then went to London, having obtained a small post with Pearson's Maga-

zines, Ltd. Later supported herself by clerical work and some free-lance journalism, and book reviewing for the Yorkshire *Evening Post.* In 1928 a book of stories, *Poor Women,* was published and very favorably received. Lived in Dublin from 1931 to 1937, in New York City from 1937 to the outbreak of war, when she returned to London. Work in progress is the story of a colored American girl who suffers from no 'inferiority complex.'

"No political convictions except an intense dislike of Fascism and Communism, any 'ism' that believes in the suppression of individual rights. Favorite authors, Dickens and Dostoievsky; present-day authors: the earlier, more intelligible, Henry James; James Joyce, John Steinbeck, Henry Handel Richardson, Arthur Machen, 'Elizabeth,' William McFee, Frank Swinnerton."

* * *

Miss Hoult is unmarried. She is a strikingly handsome woman, with smooth dark hair, fine dark eyes, and a searching, direct gaze. Two of her novels have not yet been published in the United States. Her first publication, the volume of short stories to which she refers, attracted much attention; it was a sort of forecast of her intensive study of human beings, especially Irish people, in relation to their economic background and problems. She has the observant eye of a naturalist, and though she is openly feminist in her viewpoint, her grasp of masculine character is unusual in a woman writer. One critic called her work "a simple, stark type of realism with great emphasis on details." Howard Mumford Jones remarked also on her "wealth of observed detail, wonderful reporting of talk." He said that her writing was "direct, simple, and to the point," yet "the total effect is poetic." Her style in general is clear, pointed, and fluent, though occasionally pedestrian. Between the lines one may read her hatred of superstition and fanaticism. She is one of the most interesting of the contemporary novelists to come out of Ireland, a school of chroniclers of universal life in the terms of Dublin life, who carry on from the early work of Joyce in *Dubliners* and *Portrait of the Artist as a Young Man.*

PRINCIPAL WORKS: Poor Women (short stories) 1928; Time! Gentlemen, Time! (in America: Clos-

ing Hour) 1930; Apartments To Let 1932; Youth
Can't Be Served, 1933; Nine Years Is a Long
Time, 1935; Holy Ireland, 1936; Coming From
the Fair, 1937; Four Women Grow Up, 1939;
Smilin' on the Vine, 1941.

ABOUT: Bookman March 1930; Saturday Review of Literature May 21, 1938.

HOUSE, JAY ELMER (April 3, 1872-January 5, 1936), American journalist and syndicated columnist, was born in Plymouth,

Ill., the son of Benjamin Franklin House and Sarah Jane (Wier) House. His father was a "bottoms" farmer. In one of his many rambling, confidential columns, full of homespun philosophy and reminiscences of the hardships of his childhood and years as a country printer, editor, and reporter, House wrote that having been reared on bottoms farms, he was never comfortable on high prairies. Aside from a few terms in country schools, he was self-educated. "He could write with the clarity and simplicity which comes rightly out of the West country," said a fellow newspaperman, Don Rose, after House's death. "He was brought up in a tough school and kept his stamina a long time." In 1900 House was "a peppery youngster with an unconfirmed reputation as a smart newspaperman and a good writer" and he went to Atchison, Kan., to run an opposition newspaper to Ed Howe's *Globe.* This did not last long.

In 1901, House began to write a column for Middle Western newspapers, and continued with the Philadelphia *Public Ledger,* the Philadelphia *Inquirer,* and the New York *Evening Post.* Listing the chronology of the column on one occasion, House recorded, "This column is sneered at by the New York intelligentsia, 1920 to 1932, inclusive." House also contributed to the *Saturday Evening Post* and other periodicals. From 1915 to 1919 he was mayor of Topeka, Kan.

House could "spin a yarn and paint a picture" in his column, usually written between 2 and 4 P.M. His opinions, as recorded in frequent dialogues between two ungrammatical interlocutors, Lash and Bill, were conservative. Books are mentioned rarely (he published only one book himself—and that posthumously). He "read Whitman only sketchily and with no appreciation whatsoever." *Jurgen* "meant nothing to us and we found it exceedingly boresome." House was happily married. A sturdy con-

stitution kept him going until nearly sixty-four. Somewhat rustic in appearance, he had a kindly, lined face.

PRINCIPAL WORKS: On Second Thought, 1937.

ABOUT: House, J. E. On Second Thought (see Introduction by Don Rose); New York Times January 6, 1936.

HOUSEHOLD, GEOFFREY (1903-), English novelist and short-story writer, is a graduate of Oxford University, where he received a First Class

in English Literature. Since then he has lived in the four quarters of the earth, first in Bucharest, where he was confidential secretary to the management of the Bank of Rumania, then in Spain, which became his "other country." Household speaks the Spanish language with the fluency of a native. He did his first writing in Spain. One of his earliest stories, "El Quixote del Cine," was published by the *London Mercury* and was included in its anthology, *The Second Mercury Story Book.* Leading English magazines published other Spanish stories, and after this success in writing, Household "rashly decided to earn his living thereby."

Crossing the Atlantic, Household arrived in the United States simultaneously with the depression. Hack work kept him alive in Manhattan for the next two years. "It was not bad fun, but too exhausting. I took the thing seriously." Among other jobs, he wrote the historical playlets which the American School of the Air (Columbia Broadcasting Company) broadcast weekly to the schools, in 1932 and 1933. He was married in 1930 to Elisaveta Kopelanoff in New York City. After 1933 he returned to England, spending two years as an overseas representative in Europe, the Near East, and South America. In the spring of 1935 he had a chance to spend six months in London for the first time in his life, and decided once more to become a professional writer. The *Atlantic Monthly* gave *The Salvation of Pisco Gabar,* a long short story of Spain, the lead position in the June 1936 issue, and in 1939 serialized his novel of adventure, escape, and pursuit, *Rogue Male.* Until just before the Spanish Civil War, Household and his wife lived in Southern Spain in a fishing village across the bay from Malaga, within view of the majestic Sierra Nevadas. They now live in England.

Rogue Male dealt with an Englishman who went hunting for a dictator (presumably in Germany.) Captured, tortured, and given up for dead by his inquisitors (at first), the sportsman-hero escapes to England, finds himself in renewed jeopardy, and goes to cover like a badger in an underground refuge. *The Salvation of Pisco Gabar*, appeared in company with other stories in a collection published in 1939, and ranked high as an authoritative addition to the books of fiction dealing with Spanish life. The *Atlantic* described Household in June 1936 as "an Englishman in his mid-thirties" and later published a woodcut portrait which showed this to be excellent if succinct description.

PRINCIPAL WORKS: The Terror of the Villadonga, (in America: The Spanish Cave) 1936; The Third Hour, 1937; Rogue Male, 1939; The Salvation of Pisco Gabar and Other Stories, 1939.

ABOUT: Atlantic Monthly July 1939; Saturday Review of Literature September 2, 1939.

HOUSMAN, ALFRED EDWARD (March 26, 1859-May 1, 1936), English poet and scholar, was born in Fockbury, Worcestershire; h i s  childhood was spent two miles away, at Bromsgrove. T h u s the author of *A Shropshire Lad* actually never lived in Shropshire, t h o u g h i t s hills were the "western horizon" of his youth. He was the oldest of a family of seven, his younger brother being Laurence Housman,[qv] the well known playwright and essayist.

A. E. Housman was educated at Bromsgrove School, and in 1877 went up to St. John's College, Oxford. Something happened to him in the years between 1877 and 1881—something unknown even to his own family—which changed his entire nature. He had been gay, witty, lively, outgoing; he became rigidly reserved, melancholy, a recluse. He never changed again. The nature of this secret calamity cannot even be guessed at. Certainly he had one heavy disappointment, which his pride exaggerated in his own eyes—he failed in his examination for honors, took a merely pass degree the next year, and never even received the degree formally until he was appointed to University College in 1892. But something more personal also seems to have occurred. A few things are certain: he had then a

capacity for deep and warm friendship, whereas in later years he had no intimates; he never married, and so far as known had no love affairs. The rest, as he would have wished it to be, is silence.

In 1882 he passed a civil service examination and became a higher division clerk in the Patent Office. He held the post for ten years. During all these years he lived in London and was completely alienated from his family. When in 1892 he was made Professor of Latin at University College, London, his pride allowed him at last to make overtures to his brothers and sisters, who were glad enough to be on good terms with him again. In later years his brother Laurence came as near to him as did any human being, and was named as his literary executor.

Housman was at University College until 1911, when he became Professor of Latin at Trinity College, Cambridge. This was the last move in an outwardly uneventful life; he died at Trinity twenty-five years later.

Inwardly his was a curious and involved career. He was an authentic, an exquisite poet—a great minor poet, if one may dare the contradiction—but during his lifetime he published only two slim volumes. In his famous *Name and Nature of Poetry*, in 1933, he explained, so far as such things can be explained, how this was so: poetry to him was a sort of fever, which he had strength to endure only during a few brief periods. He deliberately called his second volume *Last Poems*, and wrote that he did not expect ever to publish poetry again. The posthumous volume edited by his brother was for the most part made up of work written long before; Laurence Housman had explicit orders to destroy anything that was not up to the rigid standard the poet had set himself.

So fearful was he of leaving behind him anything, in prose or verse, which might represent less than his greatest, that he himself destroyed more than he left. His biographer, A. S. F. Gow, remarked that "few can have shown such anxious solicitude in selecting the stones of which his 'monument' was to be composed." Housman himself exclaimed: "What a slow and barren mind I have, . . . what a trouble composition is to me (in prose, I mean: poetry is either easy or impossible)."

Aside from his poems and his essay on poetry, all his work is in editions and translations of the Latin (and a few of the Greek) classics. His greatest accomplishment as a scholar was his definitive edition

(1903-32) of M. Manilius, a rather arid astronomical poet of the Augustan Age. As a critic of other scholars' work, however, Housman was anything but arid. He was the dread of other classicists—ruthless, violent, arrogant. Careless or inept work met with no mercy from him, no matter how honored the name or revered the age of the offender. Yet face to face with a stupid student or an inefficient teacher, he could be kindly compassion itself.

He was a lonely man, austere, fastidious, aloof. There were incongruous elements in his personality—for example, an unexpected chauvinism which warred embarrassingly with the universality of his philosophy: as Conrad Aiken remarked, in his poems "something like the Kipling note was always lurking just around the corner." Under the authoritative scholar hid the poet who was "at his first appearance already a minor classic" and who remained always the poet of bitter youth. "He somehow managed," said Edmund Wilson acutely, "to grow old without in a sense ever having come to maturity."

And disparate as were the subjects of his prose articles and his poems, separated from each other by a continent and two thousand years—from the Shropshire Lad to ancient Rome—still there was no mistaking that the same man wrote them both. "The skill behind the savage prose and the force behind the poetry," said Chauncey B. Tinker, "are the same shattering power."

Housman was a really great scholar—the equal of Richard Bentley, John Sparrow has noted, "for learning, ingenuity, and controversial vigor." But it is as a poet that he most concerns the world. He was an extraordinarily limited poet in range; there were few strings to his lyre, but those strings were nearly all pure gold. Louis Kronenberger was unjust in saying that he was "plainly a perfect poet and just as plainly not a great one." The lyric style of his earlier poems is easy to parody. Indeed, a whole generation of younger poets, successors of those who fed on the *Rubáiyát*, have built up their reputations on imitations of Housman. But what cannot be parodied or imitated are, first, the marvelous singing fall of his greatest lines, and secondly, the atmosphere of stoically borne but inevitable doom. It is not fair to call him merely a defeatist; he is no more a defeatist than was Thomas Hardy, who is nearer to him in spirit than most other men of his time. He is great enough, at his best, to rise over even his own occasional bathos. His verse

forms are all traditional and conventional, his irony is simple and open. In his own narrow field this arrogant and lonely man, this fierce defender of a dead learning, is unique and beautiful.

PRINCIPAL WORKS: A Shropshire Lad, 1896; Last Poems, 1922; The Name and Nature of Poetry, 1933; More Poems, 1936.

ABOUT: Gow, A. S. F. A. E. Housman: A Sketch; Housman, L. A. E. H. (in America, My Brother: A. E. Housman); Richards, G. Housman: 1897-1936; Symons, K. E. *et al.* A. E. Housman: Recollections; Catholic World April 1935; Fortnightly Review June 1936; Harper's Magazine June 1939; Living Age October 1936; Nation December 18, 1937; New Republic November 11, 1936, September 29, 1937; New Yorker June 10, 1933; Poetry June 1936, May 1938; Saturday Review of Literature December 21, 1936, May 9, 1936, September 19, 1936, April 16, 1938; Yale Review September 1935, December 1936.

HOUSMAN, LAURENCE (July 18, 1865-), English dramatist, novelist, and illustrator, writes: "The man who bears my name, and who claims to be me was born the sixth in a family of seven. He was an u g l y child, and remained ugly till his eighteenth year, when h i s looks gradually improved. He w a s also, in those early years, rather a weakling, bad at athletics, not fond of exercise, a continuous but slow reader, lazy at work which did not interest him—and at his school, did little; in solitary leisure a persistent day-dreamer; in company a victim of 'the inferiority complex,' from which he has never got free, and is still, in consequence, defensively pugnacious. His father was a lawyer, an inventor who never gained a penny by invention, who also cooked, gardened, and composed poetry; living persistently above his income. The mother of the family died in the author's fifth year; two years later her place was taken by a valiant stepmother to whom the family owed much. At eighteen Laurence left school and went with a sister to London to train as an art student; and it was not till five or six years later that he returned definitely to authorship, beginning with fairy-tales, legends, and poems, illustrated by himself. His first—almost his only—popular success [before *Victoria Regina*] came by accident. He published anonymously *An Englishwoman's Love Letters*. The public insisted on the letters' being genuine, and attributed them to forty different people

from Queen Victoria downwards. As a result the book did harm rather than good to the author's attempts to be recognized as a serious writer.

"Five years later, he was dragged into playwriting by the insistence of Granville-Barker, at whose encouragement he has continued writing for the uncommercial stage ever since. Between 1912 and 1918 he also published three novels, of which he thinks much more highly than does the general public. Political satire in the form of fiction now definitely attracted him and has continued to do so. But he knows for certain that his best work, and that which is most likely to live after him, is his play cycle of the life of St. Francis.

"He is unmarried, a rabid pacifist and internationalist, and a great admirer of the work of his brother, A. E. Housman,*qv* the poet—who, however, did not return the compliment. He lives with a group of Quaker friends in a village two miles from Glastonbury. His main activity, outside his literary work, is the local production of plays—sometimes his own, but more often other people's. For the University College London Dramatic Society, he wrote, in 1932, a scene representing his own deathbed under the title of *Nunc Dimittis*. In this scene he himself took the part of the dying author with such success that it threatens to become an annual event, until the representation becomes a reality."

* * *

Mr. Housman has been called "England's most censored playwright." Thirty-two of his plays in all have been censored (though in most cases the ban has been lifted later), because they represented either Biblical personages or living members of the royal family. (In America, however, his *Victoria Regina*, with Helen Hayes in the title part, was hugely successful.) He has continued to illustrate the books of others as well as to write his own. Agnes Repplier called him "so brilliantly versatile that there is hardly a field of letters which he has left untried and unadorned. . . . He has done flawlessly the work he assigned himself." Louis Untermeyer has described him as "bearded, dark-browed, staring into eternity like a bashful, even a benevolent, Mephistopheles."

PRINCIPAL WORKS: *Plays*—Bethlehem, 1902; Prunella (with H. Granville-Barker) 1906; The Chinese Lantern, 1908; Lysistrata, 1910; Pains and Penalties, 1911; Lord of the Harvest, 1916; As Good As Gold, 1916; Nazareth, 1916; The Return of Alcestis, 1916; Bird in Hand, 1916; The Wheel, 1919; The Death of Orpheus, 1921; Angels and

Ministers, 1921; Possession, 1921; Little Plays of St. Francis: First Series, 1922; Second Series, 1931; Third Series, 1935; Dethronements, 1922; False Premises, 1922; Followers of St. Francis, 1923; The Comments of Juniper, 1926; Ways and Means, 1927; Cornered Poets, 1929; Palace Plays, 1930; The New Hangman, 1930; The Queen's Progress, 1932; Ye Fearful Saints! 1932; The Queen, God Bless Her! 1933; Four Plays of St. Clare, 1934; Victoria Regina, 1934; The Golden Sovereign, 1937; Palace Scenes: More Plays of Queen Victoria, 1937. *Poems*—Spikenard, 1898; Rue, 1899; Selected Poems, 1909; The Heart of Peace, 1919; The Love Concealed, 1928; Collected Poems, 1937. *Fiction*—A Farm in Fairyland (short stories) 1894; The House of Joy (short stories) 1895; All Fellows (short stories) 1896; The Field of Clover (short stories) 1898; An Englishwoman's Love Letters, 1900; A Modern Antaeus, 1901; Sabrina Warham, 1904; The Blue Moon (short stories) 1905; The Cloak of Friendship (short stories) 1905; John of Jinaglo, 1912; The Royal Runaway, 1914; The Sheepfold, 1918; A Doorway in Fairyland (short stories) 1922; Trimblerigg, 1924; Odd Pairs (short stories) 1925; Uncle Tom Pudd, 1927; Turn Again Tales, 1930; What O'Clock Tales, 1932; What Next? (short stories) 1938. *Miscellaneous*—The New Child's Guide to Knowledge, 1911; St. Francis Poverello, 1918; Ploughshare and Pruning-Hook, 1919; The Life of H. R. H., The Duke of Flamborough (ed.) 1928; War Letters of Fallen Englishmen (edited) 1930; Histories (4 vols., with C. H. K. Marten) 1931-32; The Unexpected Years (autobiography) 1936; A. E. H. (in America: My Brother, A. E. Housman) 1937; What Can We Believe? (with D. Sheppard) 1939.

ABOUT: Balmforth, R. The Problem Play; Blunden, E. C. Votive Tablets; Hind, C. L. Authors and I; Housman, L. The Unexpected Years; Atlantic Monthly January 1940; Saturday Review August 9, 1930; Time July 26, 1937.

HOVEY, RICHARD. See "AMERICAN AUTHORS: 1600-1900"

HOWARD, BRONSON CROCKER. See "AMERICAN AUTHORS: 1600-1900"

HOWARD, SIDNEY COE (June 26, 1891-August 23, 1939), American playwright and short-story writer, was born at Oakland, Calif., one of the four sons of John L. Howard, who started an early steamship line to Alaska, and Helen (Coe) Howard, a professional organist, pianist and accompanist, daughter of a Forty-Niner. Sidney inherited his self-educated father's enthusiasm for music, books, and gardening, and began writing poetry at an early age. At twelve he was taken to Italy, and went abroad again five years later. After graduating from the University

of California at Berkeley in 1915 (and writing several plays there) he studied playwriting with the late George Pierce Baker at the latter's "English 47 Workshop" at Harvard. He served with the American Ambulance corps on the Western Front and in the Balkans in the early part of the First World War, and was later commissioned captain of a bombing squadron in the aviation corps of the U. S. Army.

After the Armistice, Howard became a special investigator and feature writer for the *New Republic* (contributing a series of articles on labor spies) and for *Hearst's International Magazine*. He joined the staff of the humorous weekly *Life* in 1922 and was its literary editor.

Swords, a poetic melodrama of the Italian Renaissance, was Howard's first play, opening at the National Theatre in New York, September 1921. Clare Eames, niece of the famous American opera singer Emma Eames, was the leading lady. She married Howard soon afterwards and starred in several of his plays, notably *Neb McCobb's Daughter,* in which she played a New England spinster of indomitable courage, with excellent effect. She bore him a daughter, Clare Jenness. (They separated in 1928; Howard obtained a divorce in March 1930, charging desertion; and Miss Eames died in a nursing home in London the next November.) *Half Gods,* one of the least successful plays, was a drama of married life, somewhat marred by personal bitterness.

They Knew What They Wanted, produced by the Theatre Guild in 1924 and starring Pauline Lord and Richard Bennett, was a character play about Italian fruit-growers in California which won Howard the year's Pulitzer Prize for drama. Clare Eames' acting next year could not keep *Lucky Sam McCarver* going long, although it deserved a better fate. *The Silver Cord,* a drama of oppressive mother love produced in 1928, was an artistic and financial success. Besides Howard's original plays, he made several adaptations from foreign sources and dramatizations of novels, particularly Sinclair Lewis' *Dodsworth.* He also did a number of screen adaptations for Samuel Goldwyn in Hollywood. *The Late Christopher Bean,* another success starring Pauline Lord, was "suggested" by René Fauchois' *Prenez Garde à la Peinture.* Katharine Cornell, Fay Bainter, Fay Compton, and Ethel Barrymore were among the stage stars who acted in Howard's plays. At the time of his death he was at work

on a dramatization of Carl Van Doren's Pulitzer-prize-winning biography, *Benjamin Franklin,* and had agreed to dramatize an English crime-novel, Graham Greene's *Brighton Rock,* for Gilbert Miller. *Benjamin Franklin* was to have ended the second season of the Playwrights' Company, in which Howard's associates were Robert E. Sherwood, Maxwell Anderson, S. N. Behrman, and Elmer Rice.

Howard met his death in the garage of his farm at Tyringham, Mass., when a tractor which had been left in gear leaped forward and pinned him against the wall, crushing his chest. In conversation with Dorothy Thompson some time before, he had made a casual remark that "the machine has a life of its own." He left his second wife, Mrs. Leopoldine Blaine (Damrosch) Howard, daughter of Walter Damrosch, the orchestra conductor, their three children, and the daughter by Clare Eames.

Sidney Howard resembled an actor as much as a playwright, with dark, handsome features and a nervous manner. The New York *Herald Tribune* spoke of him as being quiet and incisive, with no patience for cant, sham, and affectation. Candor and integrity were combined in him with humor, sensitiveness, and perceptiveness. Howard brought to the American theatre keen intelligence, a sense of character, and expert craftsmanship. Most of his plays were tailored to the abilities of certain actors, although he tried, as Walter Prichard Eaton pointed out, to produce at the same time something of social value.

PRINCIPAL WORKS: *Plays*—Swords, 1921; They Knew What They Wanted, 1924; Lucky Sam McCarver, 1926; Ned McCobb's Daughter, The Silver Cord, 1927; Half Gods, 1929; The Late Christopher Bean, Alien Corn, 1933; Ode to Liberty (dramatization of Michel Duran's *Liberté Provisoire*), Yellow Jack 1934; Paths of Glory, 1935; The Ghost of Yankee Doodle, 1937. *Short Stories*—Three Flights Up. *Sociology*—The Labor Spy.

ABOUT: Mantle, B. Contemporary American Playwrights; New York Times August 24, 1939; Saturday Review of Literature September 2, 1939.

HOWE, EDGAR WATSON (May 3, 1853-October 3, 1937), American editor, essayist, and novelist, was born in Treaty, Ind., the son of Henry Howe, a farmer and preacher, and his second wife, Elizabeth (Irwin) Howe. When he was three the family moved in a covered wagon to Fairview, Mo., the "country town" of his first novel. He had very little schooling, but started work as a farmhand at seven, and as a printer's apprentice at twelve. In later years he received honorary Litt.B. degrees from Rollins and Washburn Colleges, but he never saw the inside of a high school. At nineteen he was publishing the Golden (Colo.) *Globe*. In 1877 he moved to Atchison, Kan., always afterwards identified with his name (though he traveled much and in later years spent his winters in Miami, Fla.) ; and there he

bought a single-sheet newspaper, also called the *Globe*, which he built up into probably the best known small town paper in America. He was its editor and proprietor to 1911, when he turned it over to his sons and established *E. W. Howe's Monthly*, which he owned, edited, and indeed wrote, to his death.

In 1875 Howe married Clara L. Frank. They had two sons, both newspaper men, and a daughter, the novelist Mateel (Howe) Farnham. Mr. and Mrs. Howe were divorced in 1901, and thereafter he lived with a niece who took charge of his home, "Potato Hill." (He was called "the sage of Potato Hill.") He died at eighty-four after a long illness which had resulted in paralysis.

Howe had the virtues and defects of his era, his place of birth, and his upbringing. He became the apostle of "common sense," a gruff, grouchy, cranky man of unswerving honesty and independence. He distrusted all theory, and prided himself on his incapacity for abstract thought. His gospel was that of material success, but it was the success of a small-town Middle Westerner, earned by hard work, strict attention to business, and fair dealing. If that were all he had had to offer, he would have been lost among the millions of those like-minded to him. But he was also a keen critic, a wit of almost the first rank, and a master of the pungent paragraph. The *Nation* called *E. W. Howe's Monthly* "one of the best things of its kind in any age," and Howe himself "the best paragrapher alive." Wilbur L. Schramm remarked that Howe had "built a career which a century before, and under the right conditions, might have made him known as another Benjamin Franklin, but which in his own day made him merely a five-cent Carnegie."

Yet if Howe is to have any enduring fame it is not for his aphorisms or his generally discredited and out of date philosophy; it is because he wrote perhaps the first and

certainly one of the best realistic novels of the Middle Western small town, *The Story of a Country Town*. A generation before *Main Street* and *Winesburg, Ohio*, Howe had set it all down—the smugness, the meanness, the boasting, the cruelty. No publisher would touch it, and he finally had to print the book himself. Yet be it said to the glory of the publishers of the 'eighties that after it made its way to New York and was "discovered" by Mark Twain and William Dean Howells, he was besieged by offers of publication. This powerful, bitter story is still a classic in its field. Howe followed it by other novels, but they were all failures; he had written himself out, in the novel form, with his first attempt.

PRINCIPAL WORKS: *Fiction*—The Story of a Country Town, 1883; A Moonlight Boy, 1886; A Man Story, 1888; The Mystery of the Locks, 1889; An Ante-Mortem Statement, 1891; The Confessions of John Whitlock, 1891; The Anthology of Another Town, 1920. *Essays*—Paris and the Exposition (2 vols.) 1907; Trip to the West Indies, 1910; Lay Sermons, 1911; Travel Letters From New Zealand, Australia, and Africa, 1913; The Blessing of Business, 1918; Ventures in Common Sense, 1919; The Indignations of E. W. Howe, 1925. *Autobiography*—Plain People, 1929.

ABOUT: Howe, E. W. Plain People; Nation October 16, 1937; Saturday Review of Literature February 5, 1938.

HOWE, MARK ANTONY DE WOLFE (August 28, 1864-), American biographer, editor, and Pulitzer Prize winner, who writes as M. A. De Wolfe Howe, was born in Bristol, R.I. and reared in Philadelphia, but for so many years has been so closely identified with Boston that he has been called "the nearest to carrying on the Oliver Wendell Holmes tradition." After receiving his B.A. from Lehigh University in 1886 (the same university gave him an honorary Litt.D. in 1910), he went to Harvard, was graduated B.A. again in 1887, and secured his M.A. in 1888. From 1888 to 1893 and again from 1899 to 1913 he was associate editor of the *Youth's Companion;* from 1893 to 1905 he was associate editor of the *Atlantic Monthly*, and from 1911 to 1929 was vice-president of the Atlantic Monthly Company. He edited the *Harvard Alumni Bulletin* from 1913 to 1919, and the *Harvard Graduates' Magazine* in 1917 and 1918. For twenty-five years he was a trustee of the

Boston Athenaeum, and its director from 1933 to 1937. He was an Overseer of Harvard from 1933 to 1939, and a trustee of the Boston Symphony Orchestra from 1908 to 1933. From 1929 to 1931 he was consultant in biography at the Library of Congress. In 1932 he was visiting scholar at the Huntington Library, San Marino, Calif. He is a Fellow of the American Arts and Sciences. His biography of Barrett Wendell won the Pulitzer Prize in 1925.

In 1899 Mr. Howe married Fanny Huntington Quincy, who died in 1933. They had a daughter and two sons, both of whom are well known in letters—Mark as the editor of the notable Holmes-Pollock correspondence, Quincy as editor, publisher, and author of books on America's foreign relations, and radio commentator.

Mr. Howe has been called "a professional Harvard man," "a genial wit who looks like a diffident banker," and it has been rumored that he is the original of the biographer in John P. Marquand's *The Late George Apley*. He is frank to say that he prefers to write biographies of those he admires, and he has little love for the "new biography" stemming from Lytton Strachey. But, as Clarice Lorenz remarked, he is "in one sense a connecting link between the old and the new, for his biographies contain virtues of both schools. His style is polished, urbane, and succinct. . . . [He has devoted] his life to the work of snatching the great and the near-great out of the bog of oblivion."

PRINCIPAL WORKS: Shadows (poems) 1897; American Bookmen, 1898; Phillips Brooks, 1899; Boston: The Place and the People, 1903; Life and Letters of George Bancroft, 1908; Harmonies (poems) 1909; Boston Common, 1910; Life and Labors of Bishop Hare, 1911; Letters of Charles Eliot Norton (with S. Norton) 1913; The Boston Symphony Orchestra, 1914; The Atlantic Monthly and Its Makers, 1919; George von Lengerke Meyer —His Life and Public Services, 1919; Memoirs of the Harvard Dead in the War Against Germany (5 vols. with others) 1920-24; Memories of a Hostess, 1922; Barrett Wendell and His Letters, 1924; Causes and Their Champions, 1926; Classic Shades, 1928; James Ford Rhodes: American Historian, 1929; Yankee Ballads, 1930; Bristol, R.I.,: A Town Biography, 1930; Representative Twentieth Century Americans, 1930; Portrait of an Independent: Moorfield Storey, 1932; The Children's Judge: Frederick Pickering Cabot, 1932; Songs of September (poems) 1934; John Jay Chapman and His Letters, 1936; Holmes of the Breakfast Table, 1939; A Venture in Remembrance, 1941. *Edited*— The Beacon Biographies (21 vols.) 1899-1910; The Memory of Lincoln, 1899; Home Letters of General Sherman, 1909; Harvard Volunteers in Europe, 1916; Later Years of the Saturday Club, 1927; New Letters of James Russell Lowell, 1932.

ABOUT: Howe, M. A. De W. A Venture in Remembrance; Time April 19, 1939.

HOWELLS, WILLIAM DEAN. See "AMERICAN AUTHORS: 1600-1900"

HUBBARD, ELBERT ("Fra Elbertus") (June 19, 1856-May 7, 1915), American "inspirational" essayist, was born in Bloomington, Ill., the son of Dr. Silas Hubbard and Juliana Frances (Read) Hubbard. After a common school education, he went in 1872 to Chicago, where he engaged in free lance newspaper work. In 1880 he moved to Buffalo as salesman  and advertising writer for a soap factory. The next year he married Bertha C. Crawford, and established his home in a Buffalo suburb, East Aurora, thereafter identified with his name. He retired from business in 1892 and entered Harvard. College life at thirty-six, however, was too difficult, and he soon left and took a tramping tour through Europe which changed and determined his career, for he met and became a disciple of William Morris—not Morris the artist and Socialist, but Morris the writer and craftsman. On his return to America, Hubbard settled in Boston, where he worked in the office of the Arena Publishing Co. His essays and novels began to appear in this company's magazine, the *Arena,* and were later published by it in book form.

In 1895 he returned to East Aurora, and established the Roycroft Shop, named for two seventeenth century English printers. Here he built up an enterprise that made and sold pottery, leather and metal work, *objets d'art* of various kinds, conducted a hotel, and published a pocket-size magazine called the *Philistine,* whose familiar brown craftpaper cover, printed in red, with hand-set type, typified for a while the advance-guard of literary Bohemia at the end of the century. As one looks over the *Philistine* now, it is hard to see why its success was so sensational, and why it was considered so scandalous; but with Hubbard as its publisher and editor, and soon its entire author, even to advertisements, it went from 2500 copies, given away, to a paid circulation of 225,000. He published also a larger magazine, the *Fra,* and his press poured out a constant stream of "Little Journeys" to the houses of famous people and other essays, including the phenomenal *Message to Garcia* in 1899, with its record sale of 40,000,000 copies. There were 500 employees in the Roycroft enterprises, working in a pseudo-communal organization at extremely low wages. From 1900 Hubbard spent his summers in lecturing, and his slight, frail figure, with "artistic" clothes and waving bow tie, became known on platforms from coast to coast.

In 1903 his wife divorced him, and the next year he married Alice Moore. Both Hubbard and his wife were drowned when the "Lusitania" was sunk by the Germans in 1915. So thoroughly was the *Philistine* his personal organ, that it lived only two months after him. The Roycroft Shop, under his son's management, survived for a longer period, but without pretense of being anything but a commercial enterprise.

Accused of being a radical, Hubbard was in reality a reactionary of the reactionaries, and the apostle of Big Business. There is no doubt that at the core of his theatricalism lay a sincere longing to create beauty, an aesthetic impulse rendered grotesque by his incurably "go-getting" personality. Yet, in spite of what Percy H. Boynton called his "breezy and somewhat recklessly informal style," "Fra Elbertus" was a real educative influence. Even his superficial philosophy was better than none. To quote Leigh Mitchell Hodges: "His pencil was a plough that let light and air into brains baked hard by centuries of vicarious thinking."

PRINCIPAL WORKS: *Novels*—One Day: A Tale of the Prairies, 1893; Forbes of Harvard, 1894; No Enemy (But Himself) 1894. *Essays*—Time and Chance, 1899; Life of Ali Baba, 1899; The Man of Sorrows, 1906; So Here Cometh [*sic*] White Hyacinths, 1907; The Roycroft Dictionary, 1915; Memorial Edition, Little Journeys (14 vols.) 1915; Selected Writings (14 vols.) 1923; Elbert Hubbard's Scrap Book, 1923; The Note Book of Elbert Hubbard, 1927.

ABOUT: Balch, D. A. Elbert Hubbard: Genius of Roycroft; Heath, M. H. The Elbert Hubbard I Knew; Lane, A. Elbert Hubbard and His Work; Shay, F. Elbert Hubbard of East Aurora; Current Opinion April 1923; Scribner's Magazine September 1938.

HUBBARD, FRANK McKINNEY ("Kin Hubbard," "Abe Martin") (1868-December 26, 1930), American humorist and journalist, was born at Bellefontaine, Ohio, the son of Thomas Hubbard and Sarah Jane Hubbard. His father was publisher of a weekly newspaper, the *Examiner*, which had been in the family since 1830. After attending the public schools of Bellefontaine young Hubbard set type in his father's printing shop, proceeding to Indianapolis, Ind., in 1891 to work as a cub reporter, cartoonist and staff artist on the Indianapolis

News. His rural philosopher "Abe Martin," retailing the cracker-box philosophy, sayings, and doings of a mythical rural community "direct from the Paw Paw belt of Indiana" was born in 1904, and eventually appeared as a syndicated feature in three hundred newspapers. Hubbard rejected many importunities to appear in person as "Martin," yielding once in 1926 to read an essay on boosting the community to a dinner of Indianapolis business men engaged in some community effort. He firmly turned down all radio offers. A good-looking, pleasant-featured, light-haired Hoosier, he fell dead of heart disease the day after Christmas, 1930, aged sixty-two. He was survived

by Mrs. Josephine (Jackson) Hubbard, a son, Tom, and daughter, Virginia.

Often compared with Artemus Ward and Josh Billings, Hubbard was more modern in his implications than either, and was as adept at conveying home truths in the disguise of dialect as "Mr. Dooley" (Finley Peter Dunne.[qv] A few typical remarks may be quoted from the *Abe Martin Almanacks*: "Miss Fawn Lippincutt went t' see the Dghffihjkzk Rushy ballet, an' says it was th' limit, but well done." "A warnin' is all th' average American needs t' make him take a chance." "Th' hardest thing t' stop is a temporary chairman." "Mrs. Tilford Moots is scarcely able t' do her housework, an' th' doctor says she'll have t' have her 'phone taken out." To accompany his aphorisms, Hubbard sketched scrawny but cheerful animals and natives inhabiting an undetermined backwoods district. His published books were mostly reprintings of his newspaper columns.

PRINCIPAL WORKS: Abe Martin's Almanack, 1907; Abe Martin's Primer, 1914; Abe Martin on the War and Other Things, 1918; Abe Martin's Home Cured Philosophy, 1919; Comments of Abe Martin and His Neighbors, 1923; Abe Martin: Hoss Sense and Nonsense, 1926; Abe Martin's Barbed Wire, 1928; Abe Martin's Town Pump, 1929.

ABOUT: Stillson, B. & Russo, D. R. Abe Martin—Kin Hubbard; New York Times December 27, 1930.

*HUCH, Frau RICARDA OCTAVIA (July 18, 1864-), German novelist, was born in Brunswick (Braunschweig), the daughter of a merchant, and was educated there and at the University of Zurich, where she received a Ph.D. degree in 1892.

* Died November 17, 1947.

Her brother Rudolf and her cousin Friedrich are also writers. Until 1896 she was secretary of the city library of Zurich, then became a teacher, in Bremen. She had already published two volumes of poems and

a novel, and she soon moved to Vienna to devote herself entirely to writing. There, in 1897, she married Dr. Ermanno Ceconi. They had one daughter. They were divorced in 1906 and in 1917 she married her cousin, Richard Huch, a lawyer. They lived first in Munich and then in Berlin, her present home being in Freiburg.

Ricarda Huch's novels may be divided into three categories, chronological as well as thematic: first, the romantic, idealistic, novels, often médiaeval in setting; then the historical novels (really fictionized biography) centering around Garibaldi and the *Risorgimento* in Italy; and third the philosophical novels, sometimes historical but always primarily concerned with the search for spiritual fundamentals. She has also written a number of historical monographs.

Her defects are a complete lack of humor, frequent sentimentality, and unquestioning acceptance of the egoistic family-solidarity which (as Thomas Mann showed in *Buddenbrooks*) has made middle-class nineteenth century life, particularly in the Teutonic countries, smug, dull, and cruel. Her strength is in her characterization and in the brooding atmosphere of impending doom which she can evoke. William A. Drake spoke of her "extraordinary talent for divination and representation, . . . her erudite, conscious mastery of her materials."

Her seventieth birthday, in 1934, was widely noticed throughout Germany. She stands aloof from politics or contemporary problems, living in a world of her own. When she was elected to the Nazi Academy of Writers she firmly declined the honor. In appearance she is frail, with fluffy white hair and her portraits show the clever, disillusioned face of an eighteenth century *salonière*.

WORKS AVAILABLE IN ENGLISH: Defeat, 1928; The Deruga Trial, 1929; Victory, 1929; Eros Invincible, 1931.

ABOUT: Gottlieb, E. Ricarda Huch (in German); Hewitt-Thayer, H. W. The Modern German Novel; Walzel, O. Ricarda Huch (in German); Bookman (London) May 1933; Deutsche Rundschau July 1934; Neue Rundschau August 1934; Nuova Antologia March 1, 1924.

HUDSON, JAY WILLIAM (March 12, 1874-), American philosopher and novelist, was born in Cleveland and educated at Hiram College, Oberlin, the University of California, and Harvard (Ph.D. 1908). He was assistant in philosophy at the University of California from 1904 to 1906, and then went to Harvard, resigning as associate professor of philosophy in 1913, since when he has been professor of philosophy at the University of Missouri. He spent the year of 1930-31 in philosophical research in Europe. He has also taught at summer sessions of the George Peabody College for Teachers. In 1918 he was Commanding Captain of the American Red Cross in France, and he was a member of the National Advisory Board of the World's Court League. He has been chairman of the board of officers of the American Philosophical Association and president of the Western Philosophical Association. He is also a lecturer on philosophical, literary, and sociological subjects. He was married in 1909 to May Bernard Small, who died in 1915, and in 1918 to Germaine Sansot, a Frenchwoman. He writes a great deal of poetry, but has never been willing to have it published. He thinks it natural that a philosopher should also be a novelist, and says: "Literature is indeed my vocation and philosophy only my avocation." He is intimately acquainted with the Gascon country in France, and before the war spent his summers there. His recreations are tennis, billiards, and walking. His novel, *Abbé Pierre's People,* was awarded the Catholic Press Association Prize for 1928. Its predecessor, *Abbé Pierre,* was a best seller. R. D. Townsend said that Dr. Hudson's fiction is characterized by "honest simplicity, . . . restrained humor, and unobtrusive sentiment —not sentimentality."

Blackstone

PRINCIPAL WORKS: *Novels*—Abbé Pierre, 1922; Nowhere Else in the World, 1923; The Eternal Circle, 1925; Abbé Pierre's People, 1928; Morning in Gascony, 1935. *Non-Fiction*—The Treatment of Personality by Locke, Berkeley, and Hume, 1911; America's International Ideals, 1915; The College and the New America, 1920; The Truths We Live By, 1921; Why Democracy, 1936; The Old Faiths Perish, 1939.

ABOUT: Outlook June 7, 1922

*HUDSON, STEPHEN, is the pseudonym of Sydney Schiff, an English novelist who is probably unique in his firm resistance to letting anything whatever be known about his private life. Even his age is unknown, except that he must by now be very old, since he did not start to write until after he was fifty, and his first volume was published in 1916. Up to

M. Beerbohm

that time, he has said, he was regarded by his family as a failure; then he set himself deliberately to learning to write as he would learn any other trade. He is a man of wealth and is an art collector and connoisseur, and he has been a friend in need to many European artists and musicians now celebrated. He was a close personal friend of Marcel Proust, to whom he dedicated *Prince Hempseed,* and one of whose volumes in *À la Recherche du Temps Perdu* he translated. He was also an intimate friend of Katherine Mansfield. He is married, and he lives at Abinger Common, near Dorking, Surrey. That is absolutely all that he allows to be known about himself by the public, except that he says "there is, and will be, as much of my life in my books as it is possible for me to mould into the form of literature." This is not to be taken too literally, however; it is the feeling and background of his novels, not the specific incidents, which he wishes to be understood as autobiographical.

The only published photograph of "Stephen Hudson" shows a pretty little blond boy of four or five. A caricature drawing gives him a bald head, a jutting chin, a long, thin neck, a white moustache, and horn-rimmed spectacles. His dislike for publicity he calls his "paradoxical idiosyncrasy," since "I take the public into my confidence and tell them all about myself in my books while reserving my personal privacy."

Nearly all these books center about one group of persons, Richard Kurt, his brother Tony, his first wife, Elinor Colhouse, and his second wife, Myrtle. Most of them are written in the first person singular, Richard being the "I," but *Tony* is entirely in the second person, and is in the form of a long speech from Tony to his brother Richard. Motivation is "Hudson's" single interest in the delineation of his characters. Edwin Muir said of him: "In his grasp of the motives of action he shows a more complete mastery and a greater sincerity than anyone else. . . . Action is never separated in his novels . . . from its results. . . . He writes about passions and sentiments only when they are motives. . . . His is a condensed, eliminative, almost taciturn art. His work has clarity, but it also has depth." Other critics have echoed this opinion: Frank Rutter spoke of his "undeviating sincerity of thought and emotion, the utmost possible simplicity and clarity of utterance," and Harry Hayden Clark of his "symmetry of structure and a certain beauty born of economy, bareness, lucidity, and precision." As against this, the only dissenting note comes from the criticism that his leading character, Richard Kurt, is essentially spineless, and hence that the novels are "much ado about nothing." Stephen Hudson is far better known in England than in America, though his books have all appeared here. A penetrating estimate of his work and his place in literature, however, appeared in the *Nation* in 1925, written by Edwin Muir. Ironically, Muir, knowing nothing personally of the author, spoke of him as a young and promising novelist—when he must at that time have been about sixty years old!

PRINCIPAL WORKS: War Time Silhouettes (short stories) 1916; Richard Kurt, 1919; Elinor Colhouse, 1921; Prince Hempseed, 1923; Tony, 1924; Myrtle, 1925; Richard, Myrtle, and I, 1926; A True Story (including Prince Hempseed, Elinor Colhouse, Richard Kurt, and part of Myrtle) 1930; Céleste and Other Sketches, 1930; The Other Side, 1937.

ABOUT: Bookman August 1930; Bookman (London) May 1925; Nation December 9, 1925.

HUDSON, WILLIAM HENRY (August 4, 1841-August 18, 1922), English nature writer, was born at Quilnes near Buenos Aires, Argentina, South America, of American-born parents: Daniel Hudson, born at Marblehead, Mass., in 1804, and Katherine (Kimball) Hudson, a native of Maine and of English descent. Hudson's paternal grandfather emigrated to Massachusetts from Exeter, and was a member of a family which came over on the "Mayflower." Daniel Hudson, after being injured in a brewery, went to Argentina and "farmed sheep" until his death in 1868. There were seven children, William being the next-to-youngest of five boys. *Far Away and Long Ago,* which was composed in the author's

seventy-seventh year in a convent hospital at Brighton, under the influence of Aksakov's *Memoirs,* tells with nostalgic charm the story of his life on the pampas up to his fifteenth year. The time was the era of dictatorship under the Argentine tyrant, Rosas. Little law existed among the wild gauchos; murder was a commonplace.

Hudson's health was permanently impaired at fifteen by an attack of rheumatic fever, brought on by a harrowing experience when he drove cattle through a blizzard, and it remained precarious all his life, which, however, extended well past eighty. His mother, who died in 1860, fostered his love of nature, and he roamed the pampas, examining the exotic plant and animal life with a microscopic eye and absorbing material for his ornithologies, especially the *Argentine Ornithology,* (1888-1889) in two volumes, done in collaboration with Dr. P. L. Sclater.

Hudson left the Argentine for England in 1870, but did not become a naturalized English citizen (sponsored by Joseph Conrad) until thirty years later. He had an intense dislike for dated events, connecting them with age and death, and lied about his age without shame. To live for the present hour was Hudson's philosophy, and he refused to recall anything unhappy or unpleasant in his experience. His early years were bitter ones; recognition was slow in coming and he had little practical ability. R. B. Cunninghame Graham called him a bird in London, caged in ill-health and poverty. His curious marriage with Emily Wingreave, a heavy, plodding woman, much his elder in age and with no intellectual perception, at least gave him food and shelter. (When asked once by Sir William Rothenstein how long he had been married, he replied gloomily, "As long as I can remember!") The ill-assorted pair operated boarding houses, in one lean time living for a week on milk and one tin of cocoa. Later Mrs. Hudson inherited a dismal tower on Cornwall Road near Westbourne Park Station. She was devoted to her difficult husband, and could divert his mind by her singing, since she had been a friend of Adelina Patti and had once appeared on the light-opera stage. The loss of her voice late in life was a blow to Hudson, who survived his wife by ten years. During that time he usually lived at Penzance on the Cornwall coast.

Frank Swinnerton recalls Hudson's appearances in the offices of J. M. Dent, his publishers, swathed in a long cylindrical coat surmounted by a hard bowler hat, his bright eyes black as black-currants, his brows thick to bushiness and his nose hooked like some exotic bird's.

Green Mansions, Hudson's best-known book, was published in 1904 and drew attention to his other work. Too emotionally and imaginatively cold to be a complete novelist, Hudson did not realize the full potentialities of his theme in this strange, haunting novel, although Rima, the bird-girl, is a strikingly original creation (at least until the time that she begins to speak, or chirp) and her horrible end lacerates the feelings of sensitive readers. "Like Borrow, whom he does not otherwise resemble," Frank Swinnerton says, "he has a power to encounter strange people and converse with them, so that his books teem with tantalizing episodes." Hudson, if he has no kinship with Gilbert White (of *The Natural History of Selborne*) "has neither the emotionalism of Jefferies nor the vanity of Thoreau." (*The Purple Land,* his other novel, Swinnerton calls broken and spasmodic, the sort of highly unsystematic invention which critics are driven to dub "picaresque.") Rima became a well-beloved figure in English fiction, so much so that Jacob Epstein's impression of her in stone, done in his best archaic and Assyrian style, drew a roar of outrage when the figure was unveiled at the Hyde Park bird sanctuary in London three years after Hudson's death.

John Galsworthy, who wrote the preface to the definitive edition of Hudson's collected works in twenty-four volumes, testified that "of all living authors—now that Tolstoy is gone—I could least dispense with W. H. Hudson." Joseph Conrad thought that "Hudson writes as the grass grows. The good God makes it be there. And that is all there is to it." His books have been studied in schools as models of style. Morley Roberts called him a "half-tamed hawk." Hudson had his mild eccentricities and tolerant but honest prejudices. His uncertain health was the cause of his irritable unreasonableness and abrupt savage laughter. He had distinguished and devoted friends: Conrad first of all, Cunninghame Graham, Morley Roberts, Ford Madox Ford, Edward Thomas, Edward Garnett of the British Museum, George Gissing (another social recalcitrant), Sir William Rothenstein, Sir Edward Grey—who got him a civil pension —and the Ranee of Sarawak. Kind to wounded birds and animals, Hudson was especially bitter against sportsmen. People turned to look at him on the street, with his unusual height, massive head, shaggy hair, close-cropped beard, brown until late in life, prominent features, high cheekbones, giving rise to the rumor that he had Indian blood, and ungainly gait, a "strange and rather crab-like" walk. Hudson's physical strength was unusual, enabling him to bicycle till in his old age, and to tramp and cycle all over southern England. After a protracted siege with heart disease he died in his sleep, and was discovered dead in bed by his house-keeper. Hudson's burial place is Broadwater, on his favorite Sussex downs.

After 1900, writes E. L. Woodward in the *Dictionary of National Biography,* a turn in literary fashion and beginning of revolt against reason helped the popularity of Hudson's romances and his studies of the life and thought of country folk. The background of Hudson's early life, and the setting of his stories were so very different from the environment of most professional literary men that Hudson was able without effort to "add strangeness to beauty" in his work. Lord Grey spoke of his "gift for pure observation—the power of being moved to think and feel, without any desire to interfere." Hudson read Fabre with pleasure, but thought Maeterlinck unreal. He described himself as "a naturalist in the old, original sense of the word, one who is mainly concerned with the 'life and conversation of animals.'" Of *Green Mansions,* he remarked "The story doesn't move—it simmers placidly away." A combination of circumstances gave Hudson a place in English literature which is unlikely to be disputed by any rival in the present day.

PRINCIPAL WORKS: The Purple Land That England Lost, 1885; Argentine Ornithology, 1888-1889; The Naturalist in La Plata, 1892; Fan (under pseudonym of "Henry Harford") 1892; Birds in a Village, 1893; Idle Days in Patagonia, 1893; British Birds, 1895; Birds in London, 1898; Nature in Downland, 1900; Birds and Man, 1901; El Ombu, 1902; Hampshire Days, 1903; Green Mansions, 1904; A Little Boy Lost, 1905; A Crystal Age, 1906; Land's End, 1908; South American Sketches, 1909; Afoot in England, 1909; A Shepherd's Life, 1910; Adventures Among Birds, 1903; Far Away and Long Ago: A story of My Early Life, 1918; Birds in Town and Village, 1919; The Book of a Naturalist, 1919; Dead Man's Plack, 1920; A Traveler in Little Things, 1921; A Hind in Richmond Park, 1922; Collected Works, 1923.

ABOUT: Bennett, A. Books and Persons; Ford, F. M. Thus To Revisit; Garnett, E. Friday Nights; Garnett, E. (ed.). Letters From William Henry Hudson to Edward Garnett; Galsworthy, J. Castles in Spain and Other Screeds; Harper, G. McL. Spirit of Delight; Hewlett, M. Extemporaneous Essays; Massingham, H. J. Untrodden Ways; Roberts, M.

W. H. Hudson: A Portrait; Squire, J. C. Life and Letters; Swinnerton, F. The Georgian Scene; Wilson, G. F. A Bibliography of the Writings of W. H. Hudson. Bookman July 1929; Fortnightly Review February 1926; New York Times Book Review December 7, 1941; Outlook September 13, 1922.

HUDSON, WILLIAM HENRY (May 2, 1862-August 12, 1918), English-American educator and miscellaneous writer, was born in London, the son of Thomas Hudson, Fellow of the Royal Statistical Society, and Mary Ann (Swash) Hudson. He was educated privately, worked as a journalist in London, and was for several years private secretary to Herbert Spencer, the philosopher and sociologist, and librarian of the City Liberal Club, London. In 1890 he married Florence Amy Leslie of London, and that same year transferred activities to the United States, where he was successively assistant librarian of Cornell University, 1891-92; professor of English literature at Leland Stanford University in California, 1892-1901; and professorial lecturer in the University of Chicago, 1902-03. At the time of his death Hudson was staff lecturer in literature to the University Extension Board of the University of London, leaving unfinished a school history, *The United States From the Discovery of the American Continent to the End of the World War,* which he had carried only as far as John Adams. The book, designed as a companion to Hudson's history of France in the "Great Nations" series, was completed by I. S. Guernsey and published in 1922.

Hudson had not a gleam of the distinction of his famous namesake, the great nature writer (1841-1922)*ᵍʷ*, but wrote pleasant literary essays and more than twenty volumes of popularization. His American stay produced an edition of Walt Whitman, as well as the United States history, and a book on the missions of California. A useful handbook on Keats and his poetry in 1911 was succeeded by similar handbooks on Grey and Lowell the next year, Milton in 1912 and Schiller and Wordsworth in 1913. Hudson published one novel, *The Strange Adventures of John Smith* (1902), and edited numerous school texts.

PRINCIPAL WORKS: The Church and the Stage, 1886; Introduction to the Philosophy of Herbert Spencer, 1894; Idle Hours in a Library, 1897; Sir Walter Scott, 1900; The Sphinx and Other Poems, 1901; The Famous Missions of California, 1901; The Meaning and Value of Poetry, 1901; Rousseau and Naturalism in Life and Thought, 1903; The Story of the Renaissance, 1912; A Quiet Corner in a Library, 1915; The Man Napoleon, 1915; A Short History of English Literature in the

Nineteenth Century, 1918; The United States From the Discovery of the American Continent to the End of the World War (with I. S. Guernsey) 1922.

HUEFFER. See FORD, F. M.

*HUGHES, HATCHER (1886?-   ), American dramatist and university professor. was born in Polkville, N.C., the son  of Andrew Jackson Hughes and Martha (Hold) Hughes. He graduated from the University of North Carolina in 1907 with the degree of B.A., obtaining his master's degree in 1909, when he resigned his instructorship in English at the university and went north to Columbia University for two years of graduate study. Here he organized a playwriting course, in 1912; lectured in the English department from 1912 to 1917, when he was a captain in the U.S. Army for two years; and has been an assistant professor of English since 1922. In the early 1920's he spent several vacation months tramping over the Carolina mountains, mingling unobtrusively with the mountain people and studying their *mores* and idiom. Two plays resulted, *Ruint,* and the more successful *Hell-Bent fer Heaven,* which the late H. T. Parker of the Boston *Transcript* called a high-pitched folk play. A study of religious fanaticism, it won the Pulitzer drama prize that year (1923) over George Kelly's homespun American comedy, *The Show-Off,* which was its chief competitor. Professor Hughes' excursions into farce have been less happy. *Honeymooning on High: A Silly Play For Silly People* had a somewhat cool reception in Boston in 1927, and Howard Barnes of the New York *Herald Tribune* classified *The Lord Blesses the Bishop* (1932) as a wordy and stilted farce concerning paternity out of wedlock. *Wake Up, Jonathan!* (1921), a comedy of family life written in collaboration with Elmer Rice, gave Minnie Maddern Fiske a couple of profitable seasons in New York and the hinterlands. Another unsuccessful collaboration was *It's a Grand Life* (1930), written with Alan Williams. Professor Hughes, who is a member of the National Institute of Arts and Letters and the Century Association, and Mrs. Hughes (Janet Ranney Cool, whom he married in May 1930) make their home in the Columbia University neighborhood in New York City.

PRINCIPAL WORKS (Dates of publication): Hell-Bent for Heaven, 1924; Ruint, 1925; Wake Up, Jonathan! (with E. Rice) 1928; The Lord Blesses the Bishop, 1932.

ABOUT: Mantle, B. The Best Plays of 1923-1924.

HUGHES, LANGSTON (February 1, 1902-   ), American poet, writes: "I was born in Joplin, Mo. My mother, Carrie (Langston) Hughes, had been a schoolteacher in a grammar school at Guthrie, Okla., where she met my father, James Nathaniel Hughes, a storekeeper there. Until the age of twelve, I was brought up largely by my grandmother, Mary  Sampson Patterson Leary Langston (in case anybody wants to trace genealogies), who lived to be the last surviving widow of John Brown's Raid, for her first husband, Sheridan Leary, died there.

"After my grandmother's death, I went to live in Lincoln, Ill., with my mother, now Mrs. Homer Clark, for she had long divorced my father, who had gone to live in Mexico when I was still a baby. I went to Central High School in Cleveland, then, at graduation, to Mexico for a year or so with my father. My first poems were written in high school and published in the school magazine.

"From Mexico in 1921 I went to Columbia University for a year. Then I went to work on my own at various jobs in and about New York, ending up as a seaman on transAtlantic trips to Africa and to Holland; then as a cook in a Montmarte night-club for a winter in Paris. Back in America I was a bus boy at the Wardman Park Hotel in Washington, where Vachel Lindsay attracted attention to my work by reading three poems (that I left beside his plate in the dining-room) to his audience at a recital in the Little Theatre of the hotel.

"In 1925 I received the first poetry award in the *Opportunity* literary contest conducted by that journal of Negro life. Through the contest, Carl Van Vechten became interested in my work and asked to see all my poems. These he sent to Alfred A. Knopf, who published them under the title of *The Weary Blues,* my first book. Also through my poetry, from a kind and generous woman who had shown interest in my work, there came a scholarship to complete my education at Lincoln University, in Pennsylvania. I graduated, B.A., from there in 1929. Since then I have been a professional writer earning my living from various kinds of writing, and from lecturing. I have published a novel, short stories, poems, done motion picture work in Moscow and in Hollywood, and written various plays (including *Mulatto*, which ran for almost two years on Broadway and on the road), enough songs to make me a member of ASCAP, and a number of travel articles for various magazines, also two children's books.

"My chief literary influences have been Paul Laurence Dunbar, Carl Sandburg, and Walt Whitman. My favorite public figures include Jimmy Durante, Marlene Dietrich, Mary McLeod Bethune, Mrs. Franklin D. Roosevelt, Marian Anderson, and Henry Armstrong. I live in Harlem, New York City. I am unmarried. I like: *Tristan*, goat's milk, short novels, lyric poems, heat, simple folk, boats, and bullfights; I dislike *Aida*, parsnips, long novels, narrative poems, cold, pretentious folk, busses, and bridge.

"My writing has been largely concerned with the depicting of Negro life in America. I have made a number of translations of the poems of Negro writers in Cuba and Haiti. In 1931-32 I lectured throughout the South in the Negro schools and colleges there, and one of my main interests is the encouragement of literary ability among colored writers. The winter of 1934 I spent in Mexico, where I translated a number of Mexican and Cuban stories. I was the only American Negro newspaper correspondent in Spain, in 1937—for the Baltimore *Afro-American*. I am executive director of the Harlem Suitcase Theatre, the only Negro Workers' Theatre in New York. I received the *Palms* Intercollegiate Poetry Award in 1927, the Harmon Award of Literature in 1931, in 1934 was selected by Dr. Charles A. Beard as one of America's twenty-five 'most interesting' personages with a 'socially conscious' attitude, and in 1935 was granted a Guggenheim Fellowship for creative work."

* * *

Mr. Hughes' poems have been translated into German, French, Spanish, Russian, Yiddish, and Czech, and many of them have been set to music by John Alden Carpenter, William Grant Still, and others. Many, though by no means all, of them are in Negro dialect.

PRINCIPAL WORKS: *Poetry*—The Weary Blues 1926; Fine Clothes to the Jew, 1927; Dear Lovely Death, 1931; The Dream Keeper (juvenile) 1932; Scottsboro Limited (play and poems) 1932; Shakespeare in Harlem, 1942. *Fiction*—Not Without Laughter, 1930; Popo and Fifina (juvenile) 1932 The Ways of White Folks (short stories) 1934 *Non-Fiction*—The Big Sea, 1940.

ABOUT: Hughes, L. The Big Sea; Ovington M. W. Portraits in Color; Saturday Review of Literature November 12, 1932, June 22, September 21, 1940.

HUGHES, RICHARD ARTHUR WARREN (1900-), English novelist and dramatist, is Welsh by birth and descent though born in Weybridge, Surrey. His father was Arthur Hughes, his mother Louisa (Warren) Hughes. He was educated at the Charterhouse and at Oriel College, Oxford. (B.A. 1922). His university life was varied by vacations  in which he diverted himself in rather *outré* ways—by tramping, begging, acting as a pavement artist, and once leading an expedition through Central Europe on some obscure mission which involved political intrigue. All this was merely high youthful spirits, which found better outlet in his first play, written while he was still an undergraduate. This was *The Sisters' Tragedy* which was sponsored for its London production by John Masefield and called by George Bernard Shaw "the finest one-act play ever written." He was still at Oxford also when he published his first book of poems.

He has continued to be interested in the theatre, though after 1928 he turned primarily to fiction as his mode of expression. He was one of the founders of the Portmadoc Players in Wales, and up to 1936 was vice-president of the Welsh National Theatre. He also claims to have written the first radio play in the world.

Early in his career Mr. Hughes' health broke down, and he was obliged to spend the better part of a year in recuperation. Most of it he spent in the United States, three months on a farm in Virginia. In 1932 he married Frances Bazley, and they had a son and two daughters (one daughter deceased). His home now is in Carmarthenshire, Wales.

He was Petty-Constable of Laugharne, Wales, in 1936. His recreations are sailing and, in peacetime, traveling; besides the United States he has traveled in Canada, the West Indies, and the Near East. He is rather a strange-looking man, still young in appearance in spite of early baldness and a pointed red beard. Harry Salpeter called him "frail of body, kind of disposition." Rebecca West spoke of his "Shelleyan innocence and preoccupation with ethereal matters," and told a story of a servant who was afraid to announce him to her mistress because "he looked so much like Our Lord!"

But there is nothing ethereal about his writing, which Rebecca West again called 'a hot draught of mad, primal fantasy and poetry." The novel variously known as *High Wind in Jamaica* and *The Innocent Voyage*, Burton Rascoe truly said, was "unlike any novel ever before written, . . . a classic in English literature, certain of permanence." It reads in part, with its fiendish children and its soft-hearted pirates, as if Jonathan Swift had written *Alice's Adventures in Wonderland. In Hazard,* ostensibly a sea story, is in reality a terrifying allegory of the British Empire at this crisis of its existence. Richard Hughes is a completely unpredictable writer, because he preserves the devastating innocence of the child reflected through a highly sophisticated mature intellect.

PRINCIPAL WORKS: Gipsy Night (poems) 1922; The Sisters' Tragedy and Other Plays, 1924; Confessio Juvenis (poems) 1926; A Moment of Time (short stories) 1926; Plays, 1928; The Innocent Voyage (in England: High Wind in Jamaica) 1929; The Spider's Palace (juvenile short stories) 1931; In Hazard, 1938; Don't Blame Me (short stories) 1940.

ABOUT: Arts and Decoration June 1929; Bookman December 1929; Canadian Forum January 1930; Newsweek October 10, 1938.

* * *

HUGHES, RUPERT (January 31, 1872-), American novelist, dramatist, biographer, and miscellaneous writer, was born

in Lancaster, Mo., of Southern stock. His father, Felix Turner Hughes, was a railroad lawyer, and his mother was Jean Amelia (Summerlin) Hughes. The family moved not long after to Keokuk, Iowa, on the Mississippi River, in whose waters Hughes spent a large part of his boyhood. He attended boarding school at St. Charles, Mo., and in 1892 received a B.A. degree from Adelbert College, now part of Western

Reserve University, Cleveland, Ohio, followed by a master's degree in 1894 and another M.A. from Yale five years later, in 1899. A studious boy, he was nicknamed "History" at school. His first book was a story for boys, first serialized in *St. Nicholas*; a generation now tottering past middle-age has pleasant recollections of the Dozen from Lakerim and their escapades. "On leaving Yale I spent a few months as a reporter on a New York daily paper," Hughes told a reporter when his successful farce, *Excuse Me,* laid in a Pullman car on the Overland Limited, was launched on its New York run in 1911, "and learned a good deal about the city. My first theatrical production was a terrific failure, lasting one night in New York. I was twenty-two at the time." This was *The Bathing Girl,* produced at the Fifth Avenue Theatre. From May 1901 to November 1902 Hughes was in London acting as chief assistant editor of the *Historians' History of the World,* in twenty-five volumes, frequenting both the British Museum there and the Bibliothèque Nationale in Paris. Back in the United States, he consulted libraries in New York, Boston, and Washington (the Library of Congress) and worked four years seeing the set through the press. He was also assistant editor of *Godey's Magazine, Current Literature,* and the *Criterion.*

He served in the New York National Guard as private to captain, 1897-1908, and was a captain in the Mexican border service in 1916. He was commissioned a captain of infantry in January 1918; promoted to major in September; and received an honorable discharge the next January. The following April he was made a major in the Reserve Corps, and became a lieutenant-colonel March 10, 1928. He was decorated with the order of Polonia Restituta, a Polish order, in 1923. This military experience proved of value when Hughes began to write his realistic and well-documented biography of George Washington, for which he will probably be remembered longer than for his sensational and ephemeral novels, with their profusion and confusion of styles. An extemporaneous speech made by Hughes in January 1926 at a private banquet of the Sons of the Revolution in Washington was the primary impetus to his doing a life of Washington stripped of fable and sentiment but preserving his subject's greatness. Research was done both in the Library of Congress and in the Huntington Library in California. Hughes married Agnes Wheeler of Syracuse in 1893; they were divorced in

1903. In 1908 he married Adelaide Mould, known on the stage as Adelaide Manola. She died in 1923, leaving a son and daughter. Next year he married Elizabeth Patterson Dial, an actress. Besides writing *Excuse Me* and other plays, Hughes adapted *Two Women* from the Italian for Mrs. Leslie Carter, and dramatized *Tess of the Storm Country* (1911) and his own *Miss 318.* He has composed songs and written and directed many motion pictures; his present address is Los Angeles, Calif.

PRINCIPAL WORKS: The Lakerim Athletic Club, 1898; American Composers, 1900; Gyges Ring (poems) 1901; The Whirlwind, 1902; Love Affairs of Great Musicians, 1903; Zal, 1905; Miss 318, 1911; The Old Nest, 1912; What Will People Say? 1914; Music Lovers' Cyclopedia, 1914; Empty Pockets, 1915; Clipped Wings, 1916; The Thirteenth Commandment, 1916; In a Little Town, 1917; We Can't Have Everything, 1917; The Unpardonable Sin, 1919; Long Ever Ago (short stories) 1919; The Cup of Fury, 1919; The Fairy Detective (juvenile) 1919; What's the World Coming To? 1920; Beauty, 1921; Momma, 1921; Souls for Sale, 1922; Within These Walls, 1923; The Golden Ladder, 1924; Destiny, 1925; The Old Home Town, 1926; We Live But Once, 1927; The Patent Leather Kid, 1927; The Lovely Ducklings, 1928; Mermaid and Centaur, 1929; Ladies' Man, 1930; No One Man, 1931; Static, 1932; The Uphill Road, 1933; Love Song, 1934; The Man Without a Home, 1935; Stately Timber, 1939; Music Lovers' Encyclopedia, 1939; City of Angels, 1941. *Biography*—George Washington, 1926, 1927, 1930; Attorney for the People: The Story of Thomas E. Dewey, 1940.

ABOUT: Des Moines (Ia.) Register May 28, 1911; New York Dramatic Mirror March 8, 1911.

*HUIDOBRO, VICENTE (January 10, 1893-), Chilean poet and novelist, was born in Santiago of an ancestry three-quarters Spanish and one-quarter French. On both sides he is of aristocratic lineage, but he has been a Socialist from his earliest years. He was educated at the Jesuit College in Santiago and at the Berthelot Lyceum, where he studied law.

He did not practice law, however, but began the study of medicine, first in Chile, then in Paris, where he went at the age of nineteen. Between his seventeenth and his twentieth years he published various books and edited various magazines in Chile. Some of the poems in his first volume, *La Gruta del Silencio (The Grotto of Silence)* caused a literary scandal among the critics; but it was these very poems which were most attacked

that served him as the basis for the "great poetic revolution" he fathered, which he called "Creationism." In Paris, in 1916, he founded with Guillaume Apollinaire and Pierre Reverdy the review *Nord Sud (North South),* which was of great importance in the development of poetry and painting on the extreme modernist schools. In 1917 his first volume of poems in French appeared in Paris, *Horizon Carré (Square Horizon)* From this period (he lived in Paris throughout the First World War) date his best known volumes of poetry, *Ecuatorial (Equatorial)* and *Poemas Articos.* In July 1918, worn out by the privations of war, he went to spend a vacation in Madrid. His visit caused a sensation in literary circles, and a circle of young disciples formed around him. At the end of the war he returned to Chile. There his work continued to be the center of attack and discussion, the most common criticism being that it was unintelligible. He began also at this time to write prose works two of which have been translated into English.

When the Spanish Revolution broke out he went to Spain hoping to find a means of assisting the Loyalists, and lived there for three months, visiting the front and lending his services as a writer to the Loyalist cause. In recent years he has lived again in Paris but returned to Santiago at the beginning of the present war. He is unmarried.

The critic A. Rozade said of him that he was "not only the founder of the Creationist school, but also a truly great poet doubled with a profound student of aesthetics, a poet who has always been considered a revolutionist because he is a builder."

WORKS AVAILABLE IN ENGLISH: Mirror of a Mage, 1931; Portrait of a Paladin, 1932.

ABOUT: Holmes, H. A. Vicente Huidobro and Creationism; Putnam, S. (ed.) European Caravan; Valle, J. del Vicente Huidobro (in Spanish).

HULL, EDITH MAUDE, is an Englishwoman best known for her novel, *The Sheik* which scored a *succès de scandale* in 1921 and was made into a silent motion-picture which exploited the sex-appeal of Rudolph Valentino, with financial results which must have been gratifying to its author. The *Literary Review* called the central idea of the novel "poisonously salacious," and its English heroine, Diana Mayo, indubitably a sister under the skin of Justine, the heroine created by the Marquis de Sade. The New York *Times* remarked that the story, viewed from a sane literary standpoint, was preposterous.

* Died January 2, 1948.

"Scenes of incandescent passion" are also features of Miss Hull's *The Lion Tamer* (1928). *The Sheik* had its inevitable sequel, *Sons of the Sheik* (1925); and *The Shadow of the East* (1921) and *The Desert Healer* (1923) delved in the same vein. *Camping in the Sahara* (1927) is a straightforward travel book which shows the author's genuine knowledge of the *milieu* employed in her shockers. For some reason, the author's personal life is a closely guarded secret. She presumably lives in England today and has appeared on the book lists quite recently, but she is virtually forgotten in her own lifetime.

PRINCIPAL WORKS: The Sheik, 1921; The Shadow of the East, 1921; The Desert Healer, 1923; Sons of the Sheik, 1925; Camping in the Sahara, 1927; The Lion Tamer, 1928; Captive of the Sahara, 1931; The Forest of Terrible Things, 1939; Jungle Captive, 1939.

HULL, HELEN ROSE, American novelist, writes: "My grandfather Hull was for many years editor and publisher of the *Advertiser-Mercury*, in  Constantine, Mich. The smell of printer's ink was part of my summer holidays through the early years of my life, and getting into print seemed a natural and easy accomplishment, especially as Grandfather on my eighth birthday printed as a small booklet one of my first stories. My father and mother, Warren C. Hull and Louise (McGill) Hull, were both teachers. Father was Superintendent of Schools in Albion, Mich., where I was born. The study in our house there had bookshelves which reached to the ceiling, and I still have a scar under my chin, the result of a fall when I climbed up the shelves to reach a book on the top. Books and printing were so much the background of those early years that I do not remember when I did not intend to write.

"I was educated at Michigan State College and the University of Michigan, and in 1912 took a Ph.B. degree at the University of Chicago, where I later did graduate work. I then came East to teach at Wellesley, and have since then had a double career. At present I am associate professor in the English department at Columbia University, where I have three courses in fiction writing. My first short stories began to appear in 1915; my first novel was published in 1922. In 1930 I was awarded a Guggenheim Fellowship for Creative Writing, upon which I spent six months in England, ending in a motor trip in a small Morris-Cowley, which I drove to the left without mishap. I have also traveled in Southern Europe and in the Near East, and through the Southern part of the United States.

"Summers I spend in Maine, in an old house on Blue Hill Bay. In the mornings I write, with a small wire-hair terrier guarding the door of my work-shop (once a poultry house). In the afternoons—well, there are gardens to work in; or deck tennis, or a new game called Socci; or bicycling; or sailing; or going off in the motor boat to explore islands; or walking through the woods with the dogs, keeping a wary eye for porcupines and skunks; or driving. I like to dig clams and then to steam them in seaweed on a beach fire. I like to dig potatoes I have helped hill. Although I enjoy life in New York, because I like the theatre and music and dinner parties, I usually spend part of the week in the country (in Westchester) even during the winter.

"I still read, but think I am something of an ostrich as far as preferences in books are concerned. I like detective stories, current magazines, modern poetry (perhaps Robert Frost and Gerard Hopkins are my favorite poets), contemporary novels, philosophy, psychology, criticism."

* * *

Miss Hull is unmarried. She wrote for ten years before receiving any encouragement, and says she papered one whole wall of her house with rejection slips. She works furiously when she has a novel in hand, destroying and revising until she is satisfied; then takes a rest until "the strange urge to write another book" rises within her. Roberts Tapley said of her: "Shrewd, pointed, immediate, Miss Hull's novels spring from direct observation." Olga Owens remarked: "She is a realist in the best sense. . . . Yet because she possesses a fine creative fire, this detailed realism is raised to the plane of art."

PRINCIPAL WORKS: Quest, 1922; Labyrinth, 1923; The Surry Family, 1925; Islanders, 1927; The Asking Price, 1930; Heat Lightning, 1932; Hardy Perennial, 1933; Morning Shows the Day, 1934; Uncommon People (short stories) 1936; Candle Indoors, 1936; Frost Flower, 1939; Experiment (novelettes) 1940; Through the House Door, 1940.

ABOUT: Bookman May 1932; Saturday Evening Post June 1, 1935.

"HULL, RICHARD." See SAMPSON, R. H.

HULME, THOMAS ERNEST (September 16, 1883-September 28, 1917), English philosopher, was born at Endon, North Staffordshire. He was educated at Newcastle-under-Lyme High School and at St. John's College, Cambridge, from which he was "sent down" (expelled) in 1904 in consequence of a student prank. He went to London, where he studied without being registered in a university, and two years later he went to Canada for three months. In 1907, he was in Brussels, where he taught English and studied French and German.

By this time his chief interest was in philosophy, and, back in London again, he became the focus of a group of philosophers, writers, and artists. He founded the Poets' Club in 1908, and the beginnings of the Imagist school of poetry among its members made him known as "the father of Imagism." Ezra Pound and "H.D." were among this group. In 1911 Hulme attended the Philosophical Congress in Bologna and remained in Italy for three months.

The next year he was readmitted to Cambridge, by the good offices of the French philosopher, Henri Bergson, who predicted a great philosophical career for him. But the university was impossible to him after eight years of absence, and he soon left and went to Berlin, where for nine months he studied German philosophy and psychology. His first book, a translation of Bergson's *Introduction to Metaphysics,* appeared this same year. This, a translation of Georges Sorel's *Reflections on Violence,* and a few short poems appended by Pound to *Ripostes* were the only work by Hulme, except for articles in the *New Age* and a few other magazines, to be published during his short lifetime. In 1913 he delivered some lectures in London on Bergson which he intended to make into a book.

Hulme, like so many others of high talent and great promise, was a casualty of the World War. He enlisted at the beginning and was sent to France in 1915. He was wounded, invalided home, returned, and two years later was killed near Nieuport, Belgium, at thirty-four. His published articles during the war were for the most part an intellectual defense of militarism. At his death he left a mass of unarranged, fragmentary notes and manuscripts. These his friend Herbert Read with much labor pieced together and was able finally to bring out in two volumes of essays on humanism, modern art, aestheticism, and similar themes.

Hulme's aesthetic theories were based solidly on his philosophy, which was nearer to the "humanism" of Irving Babbitt and Paul Elmer More in America than to the teaching of any other school. To Hulme, as to Babbitt and More, neither romantic subjectivism nor progress had any real validity. As Montgomery Belgion said, Hulme "wanted to revive an awareness of the importance of dogma." To him, "ethical values were absolute and objective." He considered man incapable of perfectionism, and discipline in art as in life an unassailable necessity.

Hulme was slow in developing, and what his work might have been had he lived for the usual span of years cannot now be ascertained. Certainly he had a fruitful talent, and he was full of plans for future work. "His passion for the truth was uncontrolled," remarked Jacob Epstein, the sculptor. "His whole life was a preparation for the task of interpretation which he set himself." Unfortunately, this unfinished period of preparation was all the life he had, and so all that can be said of him now is that his mind turned naturally to abstract thought, that he would undoubtedly have done work of value in the theory of art, and that he had unusual potentialities which were never fulfilled.

His name is pronounced *hume.*

PRINCIPAL WORKS: Speculations, 1924; Notes on Language and Style, 1929.

ABOUT: Hughes, G. Imagism and the Imagists; Hulme, T. E. Speculations (see Foreword by J. Epstein and Introduction by H. Read); Notes on Language and Style (see Introduction by H. Read); Lewis, W. Blasting and Bombardiering; Roberts, M. & E. Hulme; Saturday Review of Literature October 1, 1927; Sewanee Review July 1930.

HUME, CYRIL (March 16, 1900-) American novelist, was born in New Rochelle, N.Y., the son of Thomas J. and Harriet (Kean) Hume. He was sent to the Canterbury School at New Milford, Conn., and very shortly after his graduation he began four months' service in the United States Army (219th Engineers). He entered Yale with the Class of 1922, but did not remain to take a degree.

When his first book, *Wife of the Centaur* appeared in 1923 one critic credited him with Meredith's gift of "hurling truth and realism in a cloud of petals." But along with other extravagant claims were also charges of over-exuberance and an insufficient sense of humor. The movies, however, seized upon the sensational aspects of the book, and with the subsequent profits Hume went abroad and took a Florentine villa, "complete to an underground passage and a hant." Here he wrote considerable poetry as well as prose, and returned with a novel called *Cruel Fellowship*. As a psychological portrait of a modern ne'er-do-well the critics admired it; but to some of the details by which the effect was achieved they strenuously objected.

The *Golden Dancer* followed shortly—presumably too shortly; it received no special praise. But by the time fourteen of his short stories had been collected into *Street of the Malcontents* (1927), reviewers were in a mood to tolerate Hume's lavishness of words and to acknowledge a certain "beauty of cynicism" that runs through the book. Sexual tragedy was the theme of *A Dish for the Gods* (1929) as it was of *My Sister My Bride,* published three years afterwards. In 1932 he issued a book of poems and short stories, *Myself and the Young Bowman,* not only "pleasant reading" but evidence of Hume's ability to write good English prose.

Cyril Hume's first wife was Charlotte Dickinson, of Grand Rapids, Mich. Three years after this first marriage came his second (1929), to Helen Chandler, the actress. This too was afterwards dissolved, and Miss Chandler became the bride of Bramwell Fletcher, the English actor.

Cyril Hume has published little in recent years; since 1930 he has done screenplay adaptations and collaborations for Hollywood. The early promise of an impressive talent is yet to be fulfilled.

PRINCIPAL WORKS: Wife of the Centaur, 1923; Cruel Fellowship, 1925; The Golden Dancer, 1926; Street of the Malcontents and Other Stories, 1927; A Dish for the Gods, 1929; Myself and the Young Bowman and Other Fantasies, 1932; My Sister My Bride, 1932.

ABOUT: Arts & Decoration August 1925; Bookman August 1924, March 1929; Harper's December 1925, September 1926, May 1928.

HUME, FERGUS (July 8, 1859-July 13, 1932), Anglo-Australian "story-teller" (as he styled himself), was born Ferguson Wright Hume in England, the second son of James Hume of Dunedin, New Zealand. The family soon returned to Dunedin where the elder Hume was for a time joint-proprietor of a mental hospital and where Fergus attended high school, later continuing his education at the University of Otago. Intended for the bar, he "served

articles" in New Zealand and Melbourne. Although he wrote more than 130 books in his long lifetime, his sole claim to remembrance today rests on his first novel, a detective story written while he was still a barrister's clerk and published in Melbourne in 1886 (the date is usually wrongly given as 1887) as *The Mystery of a Hansom Cab.* Virtually unreadable today, it received vastly more attention at the time of its publication than Conan Doyle's epochal *Study in Scarlet,* issued a year later; a full-length parody was based on it; and by the time of Hume's death it had reputedly sold above half a million copies—the greatest commercial success, according to Willard Huntington Wright, in the annals of detective fiction. Curiously enough, only one copy of the Melbourne edition is known to survive (in the Mitchell Library, Melbourne), and there has arisen more than a suspicion of thimble-rigging in the purported printing figures of the various London editions, beginning in 1887. Nevertheless, the  book's popular reception was truly astounding and remains one of the unexplained mysteries of publishing history.

Hume had foolishly sold the copyright of his *magnum opus* outright, for only fifty pounds, and in 1887 or 1888 he set out for England to attempt to capitalize on his reputation. He spent the rest of his life there, residing in Essex—appropriately near a hamlet called Thundersley. (To make the pun even more apposite, for a crime-hack, his address part of the time was Kiln Road.) He wrote and published his prolific mysteries and romances until the late 1920's—without, however, approaching his initial success—and died at seventy-three. He and his one remembered book belong to the realm of literary *curiosa.*

PRINCIPAL WORKS: The Mystery of a Hansom Cab, 1887; The Piccadilly Puzzle, 1889; The Black Carnation, 1892; The Lone Inn, 1894; The Lady From Nowhere, 1900; The Other Person, 1920: The Caravan Mystery, 1926.

ABOUT: Carter, J. (ed.) New Paths in Book-Collecting; Haycraft, H. Murder for Pleasure: The Life and Times of the Detective Story; Honce, C. A. Sherlock Holmes Birthday; Miller, E. M. Australian Literature From Its Beginnings to 1935; Wright, W. H. (ed.). The Great Detective Stories; Illustrated London News October 6, 1888; New York Times July 14, 1932.

*HUMMEL, GEORGE FREDERICK

(September 3, 1882-), American novelist, was born at Southold, Long Island, N.Y.,

Pinchot

the son of Gottlieb Friedrich Hummel and Anna Hummel. Expelled from public school, he was prepared for college by his sister, and made a brilliant scholastic record at Williams, which gave him a B.A. degree in 1902. The next year he obtained a master's degree from Columbia University, where he took other post-graduate work. His tenure of life seeming precarious after a series of operations, Hummel went to the Southwest, where the rough life of the open plains of Texas and Mexico gave him fresh vitality. Besides ranching, he taught in preparatory schools from 1903 to 1909, and was university scholar and alternate fellow at Columbia in 1911, where he completed the residence work for a doctor's degree in German and English literature. From 1912 to 1916 Hummel organized business enterprises, also organizing schools of industrial education from 1916 to 1921 and becoming (on paper at least) a millionaire in Wall Street. He married Lillie Conrad Busch of St. Louis in 1914, and in 1923 published his first novel, *After All,* a sincere treatment of marriage. His regional novels will generally be found to have their roots in Southold, where he still makes his home. *Heritage,* the study of a similar village, was praised by the New York *Times* for being "as completely American as a strawberry festival." Variants from this genre are *Evelyn Grainger,* a minute realistic study of a woman; and *Lazy Isle,* a picture of Capri which is perhaps intentionally reminiscent of Norman Douglas' *South Wind.* Mr. Hummel also produced several plays for Elliott Productions and made an unsuccessful foray into the theatre himself with a play, *The World Waits,* produced in 1933. Cleanshaven, and somewhat Teutonic in appearance, he is a member of Phi Beta Kappa, Phi Gamma Delta, and the Williams Club of New York City.

PRINCIPAL WORKS: After All, 1923; Subsoil, 1924; A Good Man, 1925; Evelyn Grainger, 1927; Lazy Isle, 1927; Summer Lightning, 1928; Heritage, 1935; Tradition, 1936; Adriatic Interlude, 1938.

ABOUT: Wilson Library Bulletin November 1936.

* Died December 19, 1952.

HUMPHRIES, ROLFE (November 20,

1894-), American poet, writes: "I was born in Philadelphia, the oldest of five children of John H. and Florence (Yost) Humphries. Educated at home, and in public school; graduated from the Towanda (Pa.) High School in 1910, and from Amherst College with the B.A. degree in 1914. The family moved to California in 1912,

and my school year 1912-13 was spent at Stanford University. After graduation I had a job in San Francisco in a private school for boys. Taught Latin, and a little of everything else, coached athletics, ran a boys' camp in the summer time, refereed intercollegiate football in the fall. I worked at these activities for eight years, with the exception of the time from October 1917 to December 1918. I was drafted into the army, sent to Camp Lewis in Washington and Camp Gordon and Camp Hancock in Georgia, and discharged with the rank of First Lieutenant of Infantry, having been student and instructor in machine gun school.

"In 1923 I came to New York, and since 1924 have been teacher of Latin in a coeducational country day school just outside New York City. Married in 1925 to Helen Ward Spencer (M.D.), graduate of Radcliffe and the University of California. A son was born in 1931; that same summer we bought a small frame house and eight or ten acres of hillside land in Warren Court, N.J.

"In 1938 I was awarded a Guggenheim Fellowship for creative writing in the field of poetry, and during the year traveled in Mexico and Europe. In the summers of 1938 and 1939 I taught poetry at the Writers' Conference at the University of New Hampshire. A book of poems was published in 1929. Poems and critical articles have appeared in many magazines. In 1921 I compiled *A Little Anthology* of poems. In 1936 I edited, with Prof. M. J. Benardete, the anthology *And Spain Sings,* and translated about a third of the fifty poems in that collection. I also translated Federico Garcia Lorca's posthumous collection, *The Poet in New York.* A second volume of my own verse, *Out of the Jewel,* appeared in 1942.

"Most of my education has been in languages. My father began to teach me some Latin before I could read, and one of my earliest books was a Latin primer. My father was the superintendent of schools in Towanda and taught the high school Latin; my mother taught the English. Yeats lectured at Amherst my freshman year, and read from his works; and Gilbert Murray taught classes in Greek; a logic class directed by Alexander Meiklejohn was important to my senior year. I wrote verses in high school and before; contributed, without conspicuous success, to *St. Nicholas,* wrote for high school and college literary magazines.

"Always liked athletics, especially baseball and football. (My father played professional baseball briefly after his graduation from Cornell; my two brothers and I used to barnstorm Sundays, and get in fights, in small towns in California.) Outdoor life in the summers is good; I used to enjoy hiking in the High Sierras, and fishing of a bungling sort. (My manual dexterity is very limited.) I like horse races, including betting.

"I have, at one time or another, enjoyed reading Shaw, Chesterton, Conrad, Nietzsche, Kipling, Shakespeare, Keats, Milton, Yeats, Housman, Eliot, Auden, Rilke, Catullus, Virgil, Dante, Propertius, Theocritus, Hemingway, Steinbeck—the list would be too long, and needs to be thought about more carefully and systematically than I have time and space for here. There is almost no public figure at the moment whom I can look upon without loathing. My political convictions are not popular."

PRINCIPAL WORKS: Europa and Other Poems and Sonnets, 1929; Out of the Jewel, 1942.

HUNEKER, JAMES GIBBONS (January 31, 1860-February 9, 1921), American art and music critic and miscellaneous writer, was born in

Philadelphia, the son of John H. Huneker, and Mary (Gibbons) Huneker. James Gibbons, the Irish poet and patriot, was the maternal grandfather. The Huneker family, of Hungarian origin, had been in America since 1700. Huneker senior, a well-to-do business man, was an amateur baritone who collected etchings and entertained celebrities in his home. James was sent to Roth's Military Academy in Philadelphia, but disliked the discipline and was taken out at twelve. He was much more interested in theatres and museums. To im-

prove his "abominable" penmanship, he was sent to a writing academy. Of his own accord James outlined a vast program of reading, outlining more than five hundred selected authors in a copy-book, to be covered in a five-year program. A brief apprenticeship at the Baldwin Locomotive Works ended when his clothes caught in a machine and he was nearly killed.

At thirteen James began to study law in various Philadelphia offices. In 1875 he studied the piano with Michael Cross, rising at 6 to practice before going to the law office at 9. On Saturdays he played the organ at a Jewish synagogue, and on Sundays at a Roman Catholic church. A short story, "The Comet," sold for $5 in 1876, appeared ten years later in the *Telephone,* a West Philadelphia journal. Huneker's career as music critic began with his reporting Charles H. Jarvis's "Classical Sunday Soirées" for the *Evening Bulletin,* and contributing paragraphs to Theodore Presser's *Etude,* the well-known musical magazine, when it was started.

At eighteen Huneker attained Paris, in a "music mad" state. He was fortunate in two teachers: George Mathias, a pupil of Chopin, about whom Huneker wrote an authoritative book, and Theodore Ritter, a pupil of Liszt. Piano practice took six to ten hours each day. Returning to Philadelphia, Huneker studied and read "enormously." In 1881 he came to New York City as critic and journalist, studying the piano with Rafael Joseffy and acting as assistant in the National Conservatory for ten years. For fifteen years Huneker was connected with the *Musical Courier,* serving without salary till 1888. From 1891 to 1895 he was music and dramatic critic of the New York *Recorder;* from 1895 to 1897 he worked on the short-lived *Morning Advertiser.* In Huneker's own words, he lived luxuriously and worked like a dog. *Mezzotints in Modern Music* was published in 1899. *Chopin; The Man and His Work,* his most important work, gave him an established reputation. (Huneker also edited much of Chopin's piano music.)

In 1902 began Huneker's fifteen-year connection with the New York *Sun,* as writer on drama, art, music, and literature. Again he went to Europe, visiting theatrical centers and art shrines and writing articles. Five months were spent in Spain writing about Velasquez pictures. He admitted to a "travel mania," loving Holland and Belgium particularly. Bruges was his favored city. In Paris Huneker contributed to the *Paris*

Weekly Critical Review, in London to the *Saturday Review.* He interviewed Pope Pius X in 1905, and visited Calabria for the *Sun,* after the earthquake. Periodically his essays were expanded into books, of which *Iconoclasts: A Book of Dramatists* attained the greatest success. His own favorites were *Melomaniacs, Visionaries,* and *Egoists,* because they were "despised and rejected."

H. L. Mencken said of Huneker, quite justly, that "it would be difficult, indeed, to overestimate the practical value to all the arts in America of his intellectual alertness, his catholic hospitality to ideas, his artistic courage, and above all, his powers of persuasion."

Huneker's "polyphonic mind" embraced Ibsen, Nietzsche, Shaw, Huysmans, Rimbaud, Villiers de l'Isle Adam, Strindberg, Stirner, Richard Strauss, Edward McDowell, and William McFee. Edgar Saltus was a particular pet of his. A genial critic, he never wrote destructively, and was particularly fond of praising Mary Garden in and out of season. *Painted Veils,* a privately printed novel about an unprincipled *prima donna,* was regarded as very daring in its day, but can now be obtained in a popular reprint.

Huneker's "amazing eclecticism," while enabling him to discuss many and diverse practitioners of all the arts, was not conducive to the formulation of any very consistent system of aesthetics. His literary method is somewhat spasmodic and disjointed; sentence following sentence, not always in logical sequence. He was known for his geniality and wit and is credited, somewhat dubiously, with the origin of the frequently paraphrased *bon mot:* "It's pretty— but is it Art?" His conversation was even more stimulating than his writing.

In 1918 Huneker left the *Sun* for the *Times,* where he stayed two years, and was critic for the New York *World* from 1919 till his death. For two years he also traveled to Philadelphia as critic for the *Press.* Saddened by Prohibition (though he himself drank nothing but beer, which he had loved to consume with selected companions at Lüchow's famous restaurant in New York), he seldom left his home in the Flatbush section of Brooklyn. Huneker died of pneumonia after an illness of four days; his body was cremated. At the memorial services held in the New York Town Hall, four friends spoke in eulogy, and a string quartet played. He left a second wife,

Josephine Lasca; his first, Clio Hinton, a sculptor, bore him a son, Eric. His name is pronounced *hun'aker.*

PRINCIPAL WORKS: *Critical*—Mezzotints in Modern Music, 1899; Chopin: The Man and His Music, 1900; Melomaniacs, 1902; Overtones, 1904; Iconoclasts: A Book of Dramatists, 1905; Visionaries, 1905; Egoists: A Book of Supermen, 1909; Promenades of an Impressionist, 1910; Franz Liszt, 1911; The Pathos of Distance, 1913; Ivory, Apes, and Peacocks, 1915; The New Cosmopolis, 1915; Unicorns, 1917; The Philharmonic Society, 1918; Charles Baudelaire, 1919; Bedouins, 1920; Variations, 1921; Essays (ed. by H. L. Mencken) 1929. *Autobiographical*—Old Fogey, 1913; Steeplejack, 1919; Letters, 1922; Intimate Letters, 1925; *Novel*—Painted Veils, 1920 (reissued 1929).

ABOUT: Boynton, P. H. Some Contemporary Americans; De Casseres, B. James Gibbons Huneker; De Mille, G. E. Literary Criticism in America; Hind, C. L. More Authors and I; Holliday, R. C. The Bookman Anthology of Essays; Mencken, H. L. A Book of Prefaces; Prejudices: Third Series; Saturday Review of Literature August 19, 1933; Scribner's Magazine March 1922.

HUNT, VIOLET (1866-), English biographer and novelist, was born in Durham, the daughter of the famous Pre-Raphaelite painter Alfred William Hunt and of Margaret (Raine) Hunt, who was a writer. She grew up in "the Rossetti circle," in intimate companionship with the most famous authors and artists of the time, and was educated at one of  the first high schools for girls, where her schoolmates were the daughters of William Morris and Edward Burne-Jones. Her first poetry was submitted to Christina Rossetti for criticism. But she was intended by her father to be, not a writer, but a painter; she studied art almost before she could handle a brush, and was twenty-eight before she abandoned it altogether.

Then began what she calls her "years of usefulness," when she was a well-known novelist, a still better-known hostess to the artistic and political great, a journalist—she did a weekly column for the *Pall Mall Gazette*—and an active worker for woman suffrage. For a number of years after 1911 she was known as Mrs. Hueffer, having formed an alliance with the late Ford Madox Ford (originally Ford Madox Hueffer), also a child of the Pre-Raphaelite group. However, since Hueffer's wife refused to divorce him, he and Miss Hunt were never legally married, and they were estranged for many years before his death. Iris Barry described her about 1910—"slightly distracted but amusing," "obviously a beauty of the Edwardian era," with "her distraught golden hair," and her conversation "at once good-natured and sharp-tongued, . . . chattering with a sublime disregard for practically everything." At seventy-odd, she still lives in London, in a house with a garden adorned by a large stone statue of Ezra Pound made by Henri Gaudier-Brzeska, the house being run not so much for her comfort as for that of her blue Persian cats.

Her work as a novelist is very nearly forgotten, though it was at once robust and subtle; Godfrey Childe said she "tells her stories clearly and vigorously, and invests them with a valiant significance." Her biography of D. G. Rossetti's wife has been attacked for a certain aristocratic snobbishness apparent in it. But her autobiography and, to a certain extent, this biography as well are priceless source-books; other people have written about the Pre-Raphaelites from the outside, but she has been able to write of them as a younger contemporary, almost as one of them. She has known so many people well whose names are legendary now; she was friendly in later years with Joseph Conrad and Henry James and W. H. Hudson, and she was one of the "discoverers" of D. H. Lawrence. Although she no longer writes much or takes a very active part in the world, she is still occasionally seen in literary circles. As a writer she has considerable talent and a mastery of technique, though her interests have been too scattered and her mind too unfocused to insure permanence for her novels. As a living evocation of a rich past she has been and still is unique.

PRINCIPAL WORKS: The Maiden's Progress, 1894; A Hard Woman, 1895; Unkissed, Unkind! 1897; The Human Interest, 1899; Affairs of the Heart, 1900; The Celebrity at Home, 1894; Sooner or Later, 1904; The Cat, 1905; White Rose of Weary Leaf, 1909; The Wife of Altamont, 1910; Tales of the Uneasy, 1910; The Doll, 1911; The Desirable Alien, 1913; The House of Many Mirrors, 1915; Their Lives, 1916; The Last Ditch, 1918; Their Hearts, 1921; The Tiger Skin, 1924; More Tales of the Uneasy, 1925; The Flurried Years (in America: I Have This To Say) (autobiography) 1926; The Wife of Rossetti, 1932.

ABOUT: Adcock, A. St. J. The Glory That Was Grub Street; Hunt, V. The Flurried Years; Richards, G. Memories of a Misspent Youth; Bookman October 1931; Bookman (London) June 1932.

HURLBUT, JESSE LYMAN (February 15, 1843-August 2, 1930), American clergyman and Biblical commentator, was born in New York City, the son of Samuel Hurlbut and Evelina Hurlbut. He was

educated at Wesleyan College, Conn., receiving his B.A. degree in 1864, his master's degree in 1867, and an honorary S.T.D. (when he was eighty) in 1923. Ordained a Methodist minister in 1865, Hurlbut was pastor in Newark that year, continuing to pastorates in Montclair, Paterson, Plainfield, and Hoboken, in New Jersey, until 1879. From 1872 to 1874 he was on Staten Island, N.Y. From 1879 to 1884 Hurlbut was agent of the Sunday School Union of the Methodist Episcopal Church, receiving the degree of D.D. from Syracuse University in 1883.

A publishing interlude found him secretary of the Sunday School Union and Tract Society from 1888 to 1890, when he began to write more ambitious works than manuals and syllabi. Studies in the Four Gospels (1888), Studies in Old Testament History (1892), and Our Church (1899) were followed by Hurlbut's Story of the Bible in 1901, which sold close to a million-and-a-half copies and insured that at least two generations of American youth would recognize Biblical allusions in their current reading. Hurlbut returned to pastorates in New Jersey, at Morristown, South Orange, and Bloomfield, and was superintendent of the Newark District from March 1909 to his retirement in 1914. He was also well known as a Chautauqua counselor and director. Dr. Hurlbut died in Bloomfield, N.J., at the patriarchal age of eighty-seven.

PRINCIPAL WORKS: Outline Normal Lessons, 1884; Manual of Biblical Geography, 1885; Studies in the Four Gospels, 1888; Studies in Old Testament History, 1892; Revised Normal Lessons, 1895; Our Church, 1899; Hurlbut's Story of the Bible, 1901; Sunday Half Hours With the Great Preachers, 1905; Handy Bible Encyclopedia, 1906; Teacher Training Lessons, 1908; Organizing and Building Up the Sunday School, 1909; Traveling in the Holy Land Through the Stereoscope, 1913; Hurlbut's Story of Jesus, 1915; The Story of the Christian Church, 1918; The Story of Chautauqua, 1921.

ABOUT: New York Times August 4, 6, 1930.

HURST, FANNIE (October 18, 1889-   ), American novelist and short story writer, was born in Hamilton, Ohio, but was taken back a few weeks later to her parents' home in St. Louis, where she spent her childhood and girlhood. She was the

only child of Samuel Hurst, owner of a shoe factory, and Rose (Koppel) Hurst. She was educated at Washington University (St. Louis), receiving her B.A. in 1909. The immense vitality which is still her outstanding characteristic was evidenced early, by her activity in athletics and private dramatics as well as by her precocity and indefatigability as a writer. From her early teens she poured out essays, stories, and

Oggiano

verses and besieged magazines with them, beginning with a verse masque which she innocently sent to the *Saturday Evening Post* at fourteen. While she was still in the university her work began to appear in *Reedy's Mirror,* and she also did a few free-lance assignments for St. Louis newspapers.

A year after her graduation she persuaded her parents to let her go to New York to do graduate work at Columbia. She did work in the English department there, but she also "went into training for fiction" by living in the slums, working in sweat shops and department stores and on the stage, acting as nursemaid and waitress, and going by steerage to Europe. The next year, 1912, she met Robert H. Davis, then editor of *Munsey's,* who has helped so many young writers to celebrity. He said to her: "Fannie Hurst, you are a writer!" That was enough encouragement; she set to work harder than ever, and in 1914 she brought out her first book, a volume of short stories called *Just Around the Corner.* She published four volumes of stories before she appeared as a novelist.

In 1915 Miss Hurst married Jacques S. Danielson, a pianist, though the marriage was not announced until 1920. Then it attracted a great deal of attention, because she and her husband had separate homes as well as separate work. In her own apartment, surrounded by a menagerie of pets (including a monkey), Miss Hurst works six hours steadily every day. She has been active in civic work, has traveled a great deal, including two visits to Russia, lectures frequently, and was president of the Authors' Guild in 1936-37, chairman of the Woman's National Housing Commission in the same year, and secretary of the New York World's Fair Commission. She is a handsome, dark woman of the opulent type,

who loves vivid colors and luxurious clothing. Her interests in reading are mainly in the fields of science, history, and exploration. She sleeps only four or five hours a night, but is always in radiant health and full of energy. Her temperament is naturally sanguine and extroverted; she is a born publicist for causes in which she believes, but about her own work she is modest, saying, "If I write down, it is because I am down. I am low."

Harry Salpeter quite aptly called her "the sob sister of American fiction." Several of her books have been turned into popular motion pictures. "Her chief problem," he said, "has been to make the reader shed the tears from which she has forced herself to refrain." She is the friend of the underdog, especially when the underdog is a woman; it is significant that her own favorite of her books, her "love child" she calls it, is *Lummox,* the story of an inarticulate servant-girl. She is guilty sometimes of stridency and poor taste, but her work is always warm, vital, and sympathetic. As Arthur Bartlett Maurice said, "She began writing in the shadow of Balzac," and she still sees life in terms of a *Comédie Humaine.* She would like to write "a history of woman in four or five volumes," but that in a sense is what all her work has been.

PRINCIPAL WORKS: Just Around the Corner (short stories) 1914; Every Soul Hath Its Song (short stories) 1916; Land of the Free (play) 1917; Gaslight Sonatas (short stories) 1918; Humoresque (short stories) 1919; Stardust, 1921; Back Pay (play) 1921; The Vertical City (short stories) 1922; Lummox, 1923; Appassionata, 1926; Song of Life (short stories) 1927; A President Is Born, 1928; Five and Ten, 1929; Procession (short stories) 1929; Back Street, 1930; Imitation of Life, 1933; Anitra's Dance, 1934; No Food With My Meals (non-fiction) 1935; Great Laughter, 1936; We Are Ten (short stories) 1937; Lonely Parade, 1942.

ABOUT: Bookman May 1929, August 1931; Christian Science Monitor Monthly August 7, 1935; Independent Woman March 1934, January 1938; Literary Digest April 21, 1934; Saturday Review of Literature October 9, 1937.

HURSTON, ZORA NEALE (January 7, 1903-), American novelist, writes: "I was born at Eatonville, Fla. (the first *incorporated* Negro town in America). My father, the Rev. John Hurston, was a Baptist preacher and carpenter. My mother, Lucy Hurston, sewed for the community. They both came from Alabama and had been in Eatonville three years when I was born.

"I went to grammar school in the village and was generally considered a bright pupil, but impudent and a bit stubborn. There were many beatings, both at home and at school, and a great deal of talk at both places about 'breaking my spirit.' One mile away was a white village, mostly inhabited by white people from Wisconsin, Michigan, and upper New York State. They often visited our village school, and they found me and I found them. They gave me books to read and sent me more when they went North in the summer. I played with their children on their estates. I felt no fear of white faces. The Southern whites in the neighborhood were very friendly and kind, and so I failed to realize that I was any

different from them, in spite of the fact that my own village had done its best to impress upon me that white faces were something to fear and be awed by. So I have never been able to achieve race prejudice. I just see people. I see the *man* first, and his race as just another detail of his description.

"I went to high school at Morgan Academy of Morgan College, Baltimore. Started in college at Howard University at Washington, D.C., but transferred to Barnard College in my sophomore year and took my B.A. there in 1928. Dr. Franz Boas got me a fellowship in anthropology to do research in folklore, and I returned to the South immediately upon my graduation. This work went on for four years. By reason of my work, I was invited to join the American Folklore Society, American Ethnological Society, and American Anthropological Society.

"While I was working I began to think of writing. I had done a few things for school publications as an undergraduate. I saw that what was being written by Negro authors was all on the same theme—the race problem, and saturated with our sorrows. By the time I graduated from college, I had sensed the falsity of the picture, because I did not find that sorrow. We talk about the race problem a great deal, but go on living and laughing and striving like everybody else. So I saw that what was being written and declaimed was a pose. A Negro writer or speaker was supposed to say those things. It has such a definite pattern as to become approximately folklore. So I made up my mind to write about my people as they are, and not to use the traditional lay figures.

"I love sunshine the way it is done in Florida. Rain the same way—in great slews or not at all. I am very fond of growing things; I shall end my days as a farmer if I have my way. I like strong displays of nature like thunder-storms, with Old Maker playing the zigzag lightning through his fingers. I feel a kinship with animals and things. I am sorry that snakes are so misunderstood and hated by their kinfolk on two legs. I dislike cold weather and all of its kinfolk: that takes in bare trees and a birdless morning.

"I love courage in every form. I worship strength. I dislike insincerity, and most particularly when it vaunts itself to cover up cowardice. Pessimists and grouches and sycophants I do despise. I like all kinds of pretty-looking tasteless salads.

"In authors I like Anatole France, Maxim Gorky, George Bernard Shaw, Victor Hugo, Mark Twain, Dickens, Robert Nathan, Willa Cather, Irvin S. Cobb, Anne Lindbergh, the Chinese philosophers, and Sinclair Lewis. I read every bit of Irish folk material that I can get hold of. Among public figures I like Lindbergh, Thomas E. Dewey, A. L. Lewis, George W. Carver, the Duke of Windsor; among deceased Americans, Lincoln, Edison, Franklin, Washington, Alexander Hamilton, Robert E. Lee (he fought for an unfortunate cause, but he was a worthy foe), Robert G. Ingersoll, Thomas Paine.

"I want my residence to be Orange County, Fla., but my career keeps me living in my Chevrolet. At present I am drama coach at North Carolina College for Negroes, at Durham, N.C. My work in progress is a novel of upper-class Negro life, two full length plays, and several short stories."

* * *

Miss Hurston is unmarried. She was at one time amanuensis for Fannie Hurst. She received a fellowship from the Rosenwald Foundation in 1935, and Guggenheim Fellowships in 1936 and 1938. Her play, *From Sun to Sun,* was produced at the John Golden Theatre in New York. For three years she was a principal speaker at the Boston Book Fair.

PRINCIPAL WORKS: Jonah's Gourd Vine, 1934; Mules and Men, 1935; Their Eyes Were Watching God, 1937; Tell My Horse, 1938; Moses: Man of the Mountain, 1939.

ABOUT: Saturday Review of Literature June 22, 1940; Wilson Library Bulletin May 1939.

HUTCHINSON, ARTHUR STUART-MENTETH (1880*-), English novelist, writes: "A.S.M. Hutchinson was born in India. His father, General H. D. Hutchinson, C.S.I., was a distinguished soldier of the British Indian Army, becoming later Director of Staff Duties at the War Office. His mother was a member of a noble and ancient Scottish house, the Stuart-Menteths. General Hutchinson was the writer of several military text-books, also of studies of Waterloo and of the Peninsular Campaign; and 'A.S.M.,' as this author is always familiarly known, took up as his professional weapon not his father's sword but his father's pen. Debarred by deficient eyesight from going with his two brothers into the army, he was set for the medical profession, studying medicine at St. Thomas's Hospital, London.

"To be a writer was, however, the career on which he was determined; and after three years as medical student he broke into Fleet Street, to which already he had been contributing articles and stories. To write novels was his design, but success in journalism, culminating in his appointment as editor of the *Daily Graphic,* made breaking out of Fleet Street a more difficult matter than had been breaking in.

"Three novels were written during this period, and then came the Great War of 1914-18 to make the break for him. In that first round of the World War, 'A.S.M.' served in France with the Royal Engineers and with the Third Canadian Tunneling Company, also, during the occupation of Germany after the Armistice, on the Headquarters Staff of the Tenth Corps.

"On being demobilized he settled down as novelist, to achieve sounding success with his first book of this phase, *If Winter Comes.* In spite of this success, Hutchinson brought his wares into the market only at considerable intervals, and himself into the public eye as little as he could possibly help. He is a writer of slow yield and a man of eminently retiring disposition. He married late in life, in 1926, Una Rosamond Bristow-Gapper, granddaughter of General Bristow-Gapper, and he has two sons. Riding and hunting were his chief delights while he was able to enjoy them after the 1914 war. Always before that had been walking and

reading as his outstanding sources of pleasure, and these remain with him as his inexhaustible recreations, shared now in renewed flavor with his two boys.

"On the outbreak of the 1939 war he became first an Air Raid Warden, later a member of the Home Guard of his home town, Eastbourne, where he has lived now for some years, delighting in the Downs and the sea."

* * *

Walter Tittle called Mr. Hutchinson "shy to the verge of timidity," with "extreme modesty, amounting almost to an inferiority complex," yet with "decided personal charm" and "whimsical, self-sacrificing humor." Tall and slender, with an eager, sensitive face, he is the exact opposite of the conventional successful novelist; he shuns all sorts of social gatherings, works hard, and in peacetime lives almost like a recluse. He writes by hand, in a diminutive script, and is so self-distrustful that he revises his work constantly, sometimes to the extent of completely rewriting an almost finished book. It is true that in one sense his novels are second-rate, but they are good second-rate. He is a romantic and a sentimentalist, and makes no pretense of being anything else. Not quite so moralistic as Warwick Deeping, he nevertheless belongs to the same general school. But he has deep sincerity, disarming candor, and a neat touch of humor, besides an agreeable, smoothly running style. He puts his heart into his books, and they have a lasting appeal to a large, responsive public.

PRINCIPAL WORKS: Once Aboard the Lugger —, 1908; The Happy Warrior, 1912; The Clean Heart, 1914; If Winter Comes, 1920; This Freedom, 1922; The Eighth Wonder and Other Stories, 1923; One Increasing Purpose, 1925; The Uncertain Trumpet, 1929; The Book of Simon (non-fiction) 1930; Big Business, 1932; The Soft Spot, 1933; A Year That the Locust . . . (autobiography) 1935; As Once We Were, 1938; He Looked For a City, 1940.

ABOUT: Hutchinson, A. S. M. A Year That the Locust...; Century June 1923; Outlook April 12, 1922; Time January 13, 1941.

HUTCHINSON, RAY CORYTON (January 23, 1907-), English novelist who signs his works as R. C. Hutchinson, writes: "I was brought up in an exceedingly comfortable home in a London suburb, and at thirteen went to school at Monkton Combe (where I spent three miserable homesick years) and then to Oriel College, Oxford. There I joined the cavalry section of the Reserve Officers Training Corps but found that riding was not my

forte. The horses threw me constantly, so I transferred to the air squadron, where I did succeed in bringing a plane down without wrecking it.  I wasted my time at Oxford, the only sensible thing I did was to pay court to Margaret Jones, a graduate (the English equivalent of the American co-ed). We became betrothed immediately after I had passed my Schools (examinations).

"After college I went with a large mustard manufacturing company in Norwich, becoming chief assistant to the manager of the advertising department. But selling things never gave me a thrill, and in 1935 I resigned to devote all my time to writing, as long as the publishers and/or Hitler will allow me. I have written from childhood, and produced a 20,000-word 'novel' while still at school. My short stories, one of which appeared in O'Brien's *Best British Short Stories* for 1928 and a few of which were published in the *English Review,* and my first novels were written after long hours in the office, in my spare time. Few novels have been so excruciatingly naïve as was my first one. *Testament* won the London *Sunday Times* gold medal for fiction and was translated into five languages. Several of my novels have sold badly at home but had a good press in America, and *vice versa.*

"I live now in a converted sixteenth century farmhouse in Hampshire, with my wife and two sons and two daughters. I have [1940] taken a temporary commission in the army for the duration of the war. I have very little of a 'life' to write about. It is all negatives: I was *not* one of fourteen children born to an impoverished knife-grinder, nor did I spend my childhood in the Australian bush. I have never rounded up cattle in Arizona or been a schoolmaster in Dundee or a police court reporter in Cape Town or an elevator man in Pittsburgh. In fact, I have done none of the things that every self-respecting writer has done as a matter of course. I am simply a standard English bourgeois who has written a few books.

"I can justify this shocking state of affairs only by giving the opinion—it is nothing more—that a novelist's job is a whole-time job in itself; that a body who wants to produce novels must teach himself to write as best he can (no one else can teach him) and then get on with it—again, as best he can. Sinclair Lewis (I think) said that there was enough copy for a dozen novels just around the block; no need to go bumming all round the world after it. I think the essence of that observation was sound. I should say that a novelist requires not width but depth of experience, that his concern is with the pattern of life rather than the superficial variations in a multitude. I am talking of the novel in its most important function. It brings other functions within its scope, of course; it informs, and mocks, broadens, clarifies, and amuses; but I think that the great novel, when it comes again, will be devoted primarily to the portrayal of man as man.

"I might add that, as things are at present, I see more chance of that novel's being written in America than in Europe. In Europe one is too hard-pressed by life to interpret it, in these years. This is a day for journalists. The novelists can't keep up with the stream; the breadth and depth and fullness and lovely proportions of the art—as the masters have revealed it—cannot show themselves in this uproar. I thank God there is a great democracy sufficiently far from Europe to get on with the business of democracy.

"I might say, with regard to my own work, that I try within the limits which fiction allows to let it reflect the Christian philosophy, as far as my knowledge of that philosophy allows; because I believe, albeit with a very scanty theological equipment, that no other attitude towards the mystery of pain, which is the great mystery, has any value."

* * *

R. C. Hutchinson is a handsome young man, with regular features, dark hair and clipped moustache, and blue eyes. He himself likes *Shining Scabbard* best of his novels, but the ones best known in America are *The Answering Glory* and *The Unforgotten Prisoner.*

PRINCIPAL WORKS: Thou Hast a Devil, 1930; The Answering Glory, 1932; The Unforgotten Prisoner, 1933; One Light Burning, 1935; Shining Scabbard, 1936; Testament, 1938; Last Train South (play) 1938; The Fire and the Wood, 1940.

ABOUT: Book-of-the-Month Club News December 1936; New York Herald Tribune "Books" September 1, 1940; San Francisco Chronicle June 2, 1940; Saturday Review of Literature January 28, 1939; Wilson Library Bulletin May 1939.

HUXLEY, ALDOUS LEONARD (July 26, 1894   ), English novelist and essayist, writes: "I was born at Godalming, in the county of Surrey.  My father was Leonard Huxley, eldest son of T. H. Huxley, the biologist. My mother was Julia Arnold, daughter of Thomas Arnold, a brother of Matthew Arnold. I was educated at a preparatory school and at Eton, to which I went with a scholarship in 1908. My intention was to become a doctor, and I had just begun to specialize in biology at school, when I contracted keratitis and became in a few months almost completely blind. I learned to read books and music in Braille and to use a typewriter, and continued my education with tutors. At this period, when I was about eighteen, I wrote a complete novel which I was never able to read, as it was written by touch on the typewriter without the help of eyes. By the time I could read again, the manuscript was lost. After two years, one eye had sufficiently recovered to make it possible for me to read with the aid of a magnifying glass, and I proceeded to Oxford. A scientific career was now out of the question, owing to defective vision, and at Oxford I read English literature and philology.

"I took my degree in 1915 and spent the rest of the war doing odd jobs, such as cutting down trees, working in a government office, and teaching. In 1919 I married Maria Nys. (My wife, who is Belgian, had come to England during the war as a refugee, and it was then that I first met her.) About the same time I began to work on the staff of the *Athenaeum,* under the editorship of John Middleton Murry. For the next few years I did a great variety of literary journalism for many periodicals— dramatic criticism, art criticism, musical criticism, book reviews, miscellaneous essays.

"Having accumulated a little money, I removed with my wife and son to Italy, where I spent the greater part of the time between 1923 and 1930. In Italy I was free to devote most of my time to the writing of novels, essays, and short stories. In 1925 and 1926 my wife and I spent the best part of a year traveling in India and the Dutch Indies. On our return we re-established contact with Frieda and D. H. Lawrence, whom we had hardly seen since the war, and from that time until Lawrence's death in 1930 were much together in Italy and France.

"In 1930 I bought a small house in the South of France, which became our home when we were not in London. In 1934 and 1935 we were in Central America and the United States, and three years later returned to America, where a series of lucky accidents brought to my notice the method of eye-training devised by the late Dr. W. H. Bates of New York. Working with experienced teachers of the method, I have already obtained very striking improvement in vision and hope, by patient work, to restore my sight even further.

"At present, I am living in Southern California, where facilities for eye-training by the Bates method are particularly good. While in California I have worked on a treatment of the life of Madame Curie and a screen play of Jane Austen's *Pride and Prejudice.*

"The most important single event in my life was unquestionably the onset of eye trouble. This had the effect of isolating me during my years of adolescence and of forcing me to live very largely on my own inner resources. In recent months the discovery of a method whereby, through properly directed conscious effort, the disability can be remedied has been for me of the highest significance and importance, as demonstrating, in one particular sphere, the possibility of becoming the master of one's circumstances instead of their slave. The problem of freedom, in the psychological rather than the political sense of the word, is in large measure a technical problem. It is not enough to wish to become the master, it is not even enough to work hard at achieving such mastery. Correct knowledge as to the best means of achieving mastery is also essential. In one limited field of human disability, Dr. Bates has provided such knowledge. Similar techniques for controlling unfavorable circumstances in other isolated fields have been independently developed and are available for anyone who cares to learn them. All these techniques, however, are secondary and, so to say, peripheral to a great central technique. This central technique, which teaches the art of obtaining freedom from the fundamental human disability of egotism, has been repeatedly described by the mystics of all ages and countries. It is with the problem of personal, psychological freedom that I now find myself predominantly concerned."

* * *

Aldous Huxley has often been described, with his "legs twice as long as Lytton Strachey's," his bent shoulders, and (previously) his heavy-lensed spectacles. A recent visitor writes of him: "I expected to find him wrinkly-browed and skinny and querulous, like his pictures, but he is filled out pretty well, calm, and happy." His thought and work may be divided into two sharp chronological sections, the change coming somewhere between 1930 and 1935. In his earlier period, he was well described as "Example No. 1 of the skeptical brilliance that burst forth after the First World War." This is the period of *Crome Yellow, Antic Hay,* and *Point Counter Point,* those almost too bright pictures of a society in decadence. They were hard, glaring, objective, brittle. That they represented Aldous Huxley's world as he saw it is witnessed by the obvious portraits (for example, of Murry and Lawrence in *Point Counter Point*).

The disgust implicit in these novels first became explicit in the "Utopian" novel, *Brave New World.* It became open and conscious in his *Eyeless in Gaza.* Indeed, Mr. Huxley's revulsion was so complete that it threw him headlong into the camp of the mystics, where he is likely to remain. The other influence perceptible in his later books is that of Gerald Heard.[qv] From being (to quote Sidney Case) "too anxiously intellectual," he became too confusedly anti-intellectual. As William Soskin said, "he adopts a rather childish manner of revulsion against phenomena, people, and manners which most men, perhaps healthier but probably no less sensitive men, can accept quite humanly. Mr. Huxley's manifestations of learning and wit are impressive. His personality, as it is exhibited in a novel of this nature [*After Many a Summer Dies the Swan*], is not."

David Daiches puts the same criticism in another way, "Huxley, starting with a preconceived romantic view of life, turns to disillusioned satire on finding that life as it is lived by his contemporaries does not justify his view. . . [He comforts himself in the end] with a personal mysticism, a romantic view that will not require to be tested by the facts."

It has been suggested that Huxley is not inherently a novelist, and that he is on the way to abandoning this form. To cite Daiches again, "His real genius is as an essayist. . . . His novels are either a series of character sketches, or a group of essays, or simple fables, or tracts. His essays, however, are always brilliantly executed." *Grey*

Eminence (1941), a penetrating study of Father Joseph, 17th century French mystic and politician, represents the kind of book that Huxley currently seems most interested in writing.

From the brother of Julian Huxley,[qv] the nephew of Mrs. Humphry Ward, the grandnephew of Matthew Arnold, and the grandson of Thomas Henry Huxley and Thomas Arnold, much is expected—even from a man who has spent a great part of his life in fighting incipient blindness. The severity of the criticism Aldous Huxley meets is a gauge of his proved ability. It is because he has shown himself capable of extraordinarily brilliant work that the Oliver Twists of criticism keep asking for more. Where they err is in the demanding more of the fare they once so relished; as is obvious from Huxley's autobiographical sketch above, there is no possibility of that.

PRINCIPAL WORKS: *Fiction*—Limbo, 1920; Crome Yellow, 1921; Mortal Coils, 1922; Antic Hay, 1923; Little Mexican and Other Stories (in America: Young Archimedes and Other Stories) 1924; Those Barren Leaves, 1925; Two or Three Graces, 1926; Point Counter Point, 1928; Brave New World, 1932; Rotunda (selected stories and essays) 1932; Eyeless in Gaza, 1936; After Many a Summer Dies the Swan, 1940. *Poetry*—The Burning Wheel, 1916; Jonah, 1917; The Defeat of Youth, 1918; Leda, 1920; The Cicadas and Other Poems, 1931. *Essays*—On the Margin, 1923; Along the Road, 1925; Jesting Pilate, 1926; Proper Studies, 1927; Do What You Will, 1929; Brief Candles, 1930; Vulgarity in Literature, 1930; Music at Night and Other Essays, 1931; Texts and Pretexts, 1932; The Olive Tree and Other Essays, 1936; Ends and Means, 1937. *Play*—The World of Light, 1931. *Biography*—Grey Eminence, 1941.

ABOUT: Duval, H. R. Aldous Huxley: A Bibliography; Henderson, A. Aldous Huxley; Joad, C. E. M. Return to Philosophy; Muir, P. H. Bibliography of Aldous Huxley; American Review December 1934, February 1937; Bookman November 1924; Catholic World August 1934, October 1936; Contemporary Review April 1939; Englische Studien #1, 1937; Harper's Magazine November 1939; Living Age September 1930, February 1932; London Mercury September 1938; Nation February 10, 1926; New Republic January 19, 1938, November 1, 1939; Queen's Quarterly February 1935; Revue Littéraire Comparative January 1939; Revue Littéraire et Politique August 15, 1936, May 15, 1937, November 1938; Saturday Review of Literature March 19, 1938, January 27, 1940; Sewanee Review July 1935, January 1939; Spectator March 12, 1937; Virginia Quarterly Review Autumn 1937.

HUXLEY, JULIAN SORELL (June 22, 1887-), English writer on science, comes of distinguished ancestry. He is the grandson of Thomas Henry Huxley, the grandnephew of Matthew Arnold, the nephew of Mrs. Humphrey Ward, and the older brother of Aldous Huxley.[qv] His father was Leonard Huxley, who followed the family tradition as an essayist. He was born and lives in London, and was educated at Eton and at Balliol College, Oxford. At

both Eton and Balliol he held scholarships, and he won a first in natural science in 1909. Rather more surprisingly, he also won the Newdigate Prize (poetry) in 1908, though his later verse has been dismissed as "intellectual doggerel."

The year following his graduation from Oxford, Huxley held a scholarship at the Naples Biological Institute. From 1910 to 1912 he was lecturer on zoology at Balliol, then he came to America, to the newly founded Rice Institute at Houston, Tex., and from 1912 to 1916 was first research associate and then assistant professor of zoology there. He served in the First World War as a staff lieutenant at General Headquarters in Italy, and then for six years was Fellow of New College and Senior Demonstrator in Zoology at Oxford. In 1921 he was with the Oxford Expedition to Spitzbergen. From 1927 to 1935 he was professor of zoology at King's College, London, and also Fullerian Professor of Physiology at the Royal Institution from 1926 to 1929. In 1929 he was sent to East Africa as an advisor on native education, his book, *Africa View,* being a fruit of that journey. He is now secretary of the Zoological Society of London, which in effect makes him director of the famous Regent's Park Zoo. He was biology editor of the 14th edition of the *Encyclopaedia Britannica,* was general supervisor of biological films for Great Britain Instructional Limited from 1933 to 1936, now holds the same position for Zoological Film Productions Ltd., was president of the National Union of Scientific Workers from 1926 to 1929, and is now president of the Institute of Animal Behaviour and vice-president of the Eugenics Society. His motion picture, *Private Life of the Gannets,* prepared with R. M. Lochley, was produced in 1934. He has collaborated a great deal with H. G. Wells and his son G. P. Wells, as well as with others. His book with A. C. Haddon, *We Europeans,* an exposure of the "Nordic race theory," won the Anisfield Award in 1936.

Physically, he much resembles his famous grandfather (minus the latter's whiskers), with his dark curly hair, generous mouth, and quizzical expression. Thomas Henry

Huxley said of him when he was a small boy: "I like that chap. I like the way he looks you straight in the face and disobeys you." The same spirit of calm determination is still one of Julian Huxley's leading traits. His interests are almost entirely scientific, though he has a strong social conscience and is rather leftist in his political views. Though he enjoys travel, swimming, and tennis, his chief recreation is bird-watching, about which he has written a book. He was married in 1919 to Marie Juliette Baillot, a French Swiss, and has two sons.

The high literary standard of *The Science of Life* may perhaps be due to H. G. Wells, but Huxley's books written without collaboration are non-technical and evidence command of an easy, flexible style. He has not the purely literary genius of his younger brother, but he is certainly one of the most readable, as well as reliable, of the current popularizers of science.

PRINCIPAL WORKS: The Individual in the Animal Kingdom, 1911; Essays of a Biologist, 1923; The Outlook in Biology, 1924; The Stream of Life, 1926; Essays in Popular Science, 1926; Religion Without Revelation, 1927; Animal Biology (with J. B. S. Haldane) 1927; Ants, 1929; The Science of Life (with G. P. & H. G. Wells) 1929; Bird-Watching and Bird Behaviour, 1930; What Dare I Think? 1931; Africa View, 1931; An Introduction to Science (juvenile, with E. N. da C. Andrade) 1931 (as Simple Science, 1934); The Captive Shrew and Other Poems of a Biologist, 1932; Problems of Relative Growth, 1932; A Scientist Among the Soviets, 1932; If I Were Dictator, 1934; Science Research and Social Needs, 1934; We Europeans (with A. C. Haddon) 1935; More Simple Science (with E. N. da C. Andrade) 1935; T. H. Huxley's Diary of the Voyage of H.M.S. Rattlesnake (ed.) 1935; At the Zoo, 1936; Beginnings of Life, 1938; Living Thoughts of Charles Darwin (with J. Fisher) 1939; The Uniqueness of Man (American title: Man Stands Alone) 1941; Democracy Marches, 1941; Evolution Up-to-Date, 1942.

ABOUT: Saturday Review of Literature November 7, 1936; Wilson Library Bulletin June 1938.

*HYDE, DOUGLAS (1860-), Irish historian, poet, and folklorist. and President of Eire, was born in Frenchpark, County Roscommon (the old Connaught, on the borders of Mayo), the son of the Rev. Arthur Hyde and Elizabeth (Oldfield) Hyde, daughter of an Archdeacon. He was educated at Trinity College, Dublin, where he studied divinity but never took his degree, graduating instead B.A., 1884, with the highest honors. In 1887 he took his

* Died July 12, 1949.

LL.D., but never practiced law. From earliest childhood he was familiar with the Gaelic language, then a very rare phenomenon except among peasants, and said he even dreamed in Gaelic. After a year as interim professor of modern languages at the University of New Brunswick, in Canada, he returned to Ireland and at once began to work actively for restoration of the Irish language and culture. He founded the Gaelic League in 1893, and was its president until he resigned in 1915 because it was becoming identified with Irish nationalism and he wished the movement to remain non-political. In 1906 he toured the United States on behalf of the League (he was banqueted in San Francisco just before the earthquake and fire in April), and returned with 11,000 pounds donated by Americans of Irish descent. In acknowledgement of his efforts he was given the freedom of the cities of Dublin, Cork, and Kilkenny, and later that of Limerick as well. From 1909 to 1932 he was professor of Modern Irish and Dean of the Celtic Faculty at University College, Dublin. He then retired to his home at Ratra, County Roscommon, with his wife, the former Lucy Kurtz, whom he had married in 1891, and their two daughters. (She has since died.) He served two brief terms in the Senate of the Irish Free State, but was entirely without political affiliations or interests when, in 1938, he, though a Protestant, was elected the first president of Eire. He was then seventy-eight, and the term is for seven years. As president he has little direct power, but immense influence, and he holds much the same position of reverence and honor as Masaryk did in Czechoslovakia.

Most of Dr. Hyde's writings are in Gaelic. His first work was done under the pseudonym of "An Craoibhin Aoibhinn" ("delightful little branch"), and he is usually known by that name in Ireland. He was one of the founders of the famous Abbey Theatre in Dublin, and many of his plays have been produced there, notably *The Workhouse Ward,* translated into English by Lady Gregory. He has had many literary and scholarly honors, has been president of the Irish Literary Society, the Irish Texts Society, and the Folklore Institute of Ireland, received the Gregory Medal in 1937, and has honorary doctorates from every Irish university. His translations of the Connaught love songs and religious songs show his marked talent as a poet; in fact, Yeats said he was "a poet sacrificed to a movement."

He is a tall, gaunt man, swarthy, with black hair and walrus moustache now turned white, light eyes, and a massive head. His only avocation is golf. W. M. Crook called him "one of the most lovable of human beings. . . . His mission is spiritual and intellectual." Padraic Colum called him "a scholar and poet who has struggled to preserve the Celtic heritage . . . one of the most unassuming men one could meet anywhere; he has never put himself forward as a writer." Although most of his writing, being in Gaelic, is unavailable for the average American or English reader, many of his verse translations have found their permanent home in anthologies.

WORKS IN ENGLISH: Beside the Fire, 1890; Love Songs of Connaught, 1894; Three Sorrows of Story-Telling, 1895; Story of Early Irish Literature, 1897; A Literary History of Ireland, 1899; Mediaeval Tales From the Irish, 1899; Raferty's Poems, 1904 (enlarged edition 1933); The Bursting of the Bubble and Other Irish Plays, 1905; The Religious Songs of Connaught, 1906; Legends of Saints and Sinners From the Irish, 1915.

ABOUT: Coffey, D. Douglas Hyde: President of Ireland; Canadian Bookman June 1938; Commonweal June 2, 1939; Fortnightly Review June 1938; Nineteenth Century July 1938; Spectator May 7, 1938.

*HYNE, CHARLES JOHN CUTCLIFFE WRIGHT (Cutcliffe Hyne) (May 11, 1865-), English novelist and short-story writer, inventor of Captain Kettle, was born in Bibury, Gloucestershire, the son of the Vicar of Bierley, The Rev. Charles Weight Noble Hyne, and Frances (Wootton) Hyne. The boy went to the  local grammar school at twelve, and worked in the coal pits, turning bases of Davey lamps. At fifteen he had reached a height of six-feet-three. In due course Hyne received a B.A. and M.A. from Clare College, Cambridge University, where he pursued the Natural Science Tripos courses, and hunted, rowed, boxed, and sailed on Scottish lochs in the vacations. "Neither gaiters nor gown" (the Church or schoolmastering) appealing much to his tastes, young Hyne began the hard, grinding apprenticeship necessary to writing. He intended his style to be free of padding, obsolete words, obscure phrases, and personal mannerisms. Charles Dickens, Jr., editor of *All the Year Round,* gave him a guinea and encouraging praise for a story of 12,000 words. Pot-boilers, boys' books, and advice to readers as a mythical Aunt Ermyntrude kept Hyne going until he hit on the idea of his pugnacious little Welsh sea-captain, with the red torpedo beard and strait-laced ideas. Kettle made his first appearance in a serial written for *Answers,* published by Alfred Harmsworth, later Lord Northcliffe. Named *The Giant Sea Swindle,* it appeared in book form as *Honour of Thieves,* and later as *The Little Red Captain,* in which form it still sells. Cyril Arthur Pearson, then starting a sixpenny magazine (*Pearson's Magazine*) rather on the lines of the *Strand Magazine,* thought it a good idea to compete with the latter in presenting a series of stories with a central figure like Sherlock Holmes. He offered Hyne fifty guineas apiece for six Kettle stories; after which Hyne "never looked back." The ideal illustrator was found in the late Stanley L. Wood. Kettle was as popular in the United States as in England, has appeared in a play, and put his creator in the upper income-tax brackets.

Mr. Hyne has travelled 400,000 miles, in the Shetlands, Lapland, the Arctic, the Spanish Main, the Congo, Mexico (where he was interested in mining), and Brazil. A son died at home of wounds received as an ensign of Guards in the battle of the Somme. As a novelist Hyne prefers to improvise, believing that "clamped-down, prearranged plot is the reason why characterization in current detective stories is either childish or completely absent." He is now engaged in research into the causes of congenital deafness; and lists his recreations as big-game shooting and cave-hunting.

PRINCIPAL WORKS: *Captain Kettle Stories*—Adventures of Captain Kettle, 1898; Further Adventures of Captain Kettle, 1899; The Little Red Captain, 1902; Captain Kettle, K.C.B., 1903; The Marriage of Captain Kettle, 1912; Captain Kettle on the Warpath, 1916; The Reverend Captain Kettle, 1925; President Kettle, 1928; Mr. Kettle, Third Mate, 1931; Captain Kettle, Ambassador, 1932. *Others*—The Lost Continent, The Filibusters, 1900; McTodd, 1903; Trials of Commander McTurk, 1904; Kate Meredith, Financier, 1907; The Escape Agents, 1911; People and Places, 1930; But Britons *Are* Slaves, 1932; Ivory Valley, 1938; Wishing Smith, 1940.

ABOUT: Hyne, C. J. C. W. My Joyful Life.

HYNE, CUTCLIFFE. See HYNE, C. J. C. W.

IBAÑEZ. See BLASCO IBÁÑEZ

"ICONOCLAST." See HAMILTON, M. A. A.

"ILES, FRANCIS." See COX, A. B.

ILF, ILYA ARNOLDOVICH (October 16, 1897-April 14, 1937), Russian humorist was born in Odessa, the son of a bank clerk. In 1913 he was graduated from a technical school and went to work in a draftsman's office. Later he worked in a telephone station, in an aviation plant, and in a factory that manufactured hand-grenades. After that he was a statistician,  and then the editor of a magazine called *Sindektikon,* a humorous journal for which he wrote verses under a feminine pseudonym. He was also a member of the presidium of the Odessa Union of Poets, and its bookkeeper; but after the first trial balance was taken, it became evident that the preponderance of his talent was on the side of literary rather than bookkeeping activity! In 1923 he moved to Moscow, where at last he found his real profession, working on newspapers and magazines of humor. He was married in 1924.

All Ilf's work was done in conjunction with Eugene Petrov *qv* whom he met in Moscow, in the offices of the *Whistle,* daily organ of the railway workers. Ilf was of Jewish descent, Petrov Russian. Much of their writing appeared in the famous Moscow satirical magazine, *Crocodile,* and in the newspaper *Pravda.*

The two together were the most noted humorists of post-revolutionary Russia, not Communists, but sympathetic if keen-eyed "fellow travelers," known to the people as the Soviet Mark Twain. Ilf's farcical extravaganza, with its "rich, unflagging variety of invention," made his work extremely popular, especially as his shafts were directed always toward minor discrepancies or inadequacies of the government, not toward its main purpose. In 1936 he and Petrov visited the United States, publishing later a humorous account of their experiences. He died the following year, at only forty, of tuberculosis.

Ilf was tall, slender, and blond. He was a moody man, self-conscious, introverted, and reflective, with a touch of the dreamer and the poet about him.

WORKS AVAILABLE IN ENGLISH: (all with Eugene Petrov): Diamonds To Sit On, 1930; Little Golden Calf, 1933; Little Golden America, 1937.

ABOUT: Nation September 25, 1935; New Masses July 21, 1942.

*IMBS, BRAVIG (October 8, 1904-), American novelist and poet, writes: "My parents were Norwegian-Americans, my  birthplace, Milwaukee, Wis. My father was a cost accountant and came from a long line of Norwegian mariners. My paternal grandmother, the only Irish person in the family, wrote poems in Gaelic. Unfortunately these were all lost in a fire, but I remember her reciting them to me when my parents visited her. I was brought up in Chicago, attending the public schools there. I was given such a dose of Bible study and hymn-singing in the United Brethren Church in my childhood that I had enough for the rest of my life. My only escape was music and I studied the violin assiduously. I also started writing poems as soon as I could write; my first opus began:

> Swat the fly
> And swat it hard,
> I say, say I.

"When I was in the eighth grade my family was smitten with the common Middle Western disease—a longing for California. We went out to Riverside, but seventeen 'tremors' in five weeks sent us back to Chicago. On graduating from the Carl Schurz High School I decided I wanted to go to Princeton. I had to spend a year at a preparatory school, the Elgin Academy, the most awful year in my life. Then I flunked trigonometry and consequently could not go to Princeton. I went to Dartmouth instead. I had to earn my way there, buttering and stoking and teaching violin to thirteen nerve-wrecking children. At the end of two years I left for Europe on a cattle boat. I landed in Paris with five dollars in my pocket. I got a job at the Chicago *Tribune* within three days. I worked a month before my glaring incompetency was discovered, and with the money I had made I went on a troubadour trip in the Loire Valley, playing my violin in the cafés. When I returned to Paris I got another job teaching in an American school. I learned French that year, got back on the Chicago *Tribune* in the advertising department, and eventually got a post as music critic on the Paris *Times*. Meanwhile I studied composition with George Antheil, attended Gertrude Stein's salon with wor-

shipful regularity, met James Joyce and many others. I wrote my first novel, which was rejected everywhere until Bernard Faÿ, with whom I had been working on American Revolutionary history, recommended it to the editor of the Dial Press. *transition* appeared at this time, too, and I helped proof-read some of the first numbers.

"In 1928 I went on a tour of Germany, Poland, Lithuania, and Latvia. I met Countess Valeska Balbarischky in Riga and married her almost immediately afterwards. We returned to Paris where I joined an advertising agency and remained with it until the war. I devoted my leisure to writing, playing in a string quartette, learning the virginals and harpsichord, and going skiing whenever I could. We have two daughters, one born in Paris, the other in New York, where we have now made our home."

PRINCIPAL WORKS: Eden: Exit This Way (poems) 1927; The Professor's Wife (novel) 1928; Chatterton, 1934; The Cats (novel) 1935; Confessions of Another Young Man, 1937.

ABOUT: Imbs, B. Confessions of Another Young Man.

INCLÁN. See VALLE INCLÁN

*INGE, WILLIAM RALPH (June 6, 1860-), English clergyman and writer, was born in Crayke, Yorkshire, a place far from a railroad and thinly populated. He was the eldest son of the Rev. William Inge, D.D., Provost of Worcester College, Oxford, and Mary (Churton) Inge, daughter of the Venerable Edward Churton, Archdeacon of Cleveland. The future  Dean of St. Paul's attended Eton and King's College, Cambridge University, where he was Bell Scholar and Porson Prizeman in 1880; Porson Scholar in 1881; Craven Scholar and Browne Medallist in 1883; and Hare Prizeman in 1885. He took first class honors in the Classics in 1882 and 1883, and occasionally indulged in cricket. Deafness and persistent hypochondria prevented his enjoying an assistant mastership at Eton particularly, from 1884 to 1888. From 1886 to 1888 he was also a Fellow of King's College, becoming a Fellow and Tutor of Hertford College, Oxford, in 1889, remaining till 1904. Inge was ordained a deacon in 1888. In 1903 he was vicar of the aristocratic parish of All Saints'. Ennismore

Gardens, remaining until 1907 when he returned to academic life as Lady Margaret Professor of Divinity—the oldest foundation at the university—and Fellow of Jesus College, Cambridge. In 1911 Herbert Asquith, then Prime Minister, appointed him Dean of St. Paul's Cathedral, hoping to revive the scholarly prestige of the office, which had been held by Donne, Milman, and Church. Inge accepted, though confessing himself "terribly bored by long musical services," and finding that relations with his colleagues required all his tact.

His sermons soon attracted attention, and the *Daily Mail* was inspired to dub the new incumbent "The Gloomy Dean." Other newspapers and journals came forward to seek his opinions and solicit articles. Dean Inge, who had three sons and a daughter to educate, was glad to execute these commissions, while sometimes complaining bitterly of his treatment at the hands of "the guttersnipes of Fleet Street." He also made a name as a scholarly writer on mystics and as a student of the ancient philosopher and Neo-Platonist, Plotinus. A rationalist, pluralist, and pragmatist, he never hesitated to speak his mind on birth-control, pacifism, and similar controversial topics, with wit and force. After his retirement as dean in 1934, he continued to contribute regularly to the *Evening Standard*. Distinctly cadaverous, with sunken cheeks and thin nose, Dean Inge walks with a limp and speaks in a slow even tone. In 1905 he was married by Archbishop Davidson to Mary Catharine Spooner, daughter of the Archdeacon of Maidstone and grand-daughter of Bishop Harvey Goodwin. The holder of numerous honorary degrees, he was also given a C.V.O. in 1918 and a K.C.V.O. in 1930. His address is Brightwell Manor, Wallingford. His name is pronounced *ing*.

PRINCIPAL WORKS: Society in Rome Under the Caesars, 1886; Christian Mysticism, 1899; Faith and Knowledge, 1904; Selections From the German Mystics, 1904; Studies of English Mystics, 1906; Truth and Falsehood in Religion, 1906; Personal Idealism and Mysticism, 1907; Faith, 1909; Speculum Animi, 1911; The Church and the Age, 1912; Types of Christian Saintliness, 1915; The Philosophy of Plotinus, 1918; Outspoken Essays, 1919; Outspoken Essays: Second Series, 1922; The Idea of Progress (Romanes Lecture) 1920; Personal Religion and the Life of Devotion, 1924; The Platonic Tradition, 1926; England, 1926; Lay Thoughts of a Dean, 1926; The Church in the World, 1927; Assessments and Anticipations, 1929; Christian Ethics and Modern Problems, 1930; Every Man's Bible, 1931; More Lay Thoughts of a Dean, 1931; Things New and Old, 1933; God and the Astronomers, 1933; Vale (autobiography) 1934; The Gate of Life, 1935; Freedom, Love and Truth, 1936; A Rustic Moralist, 1937; Modernism in Literature, 1938; Our Present Discontents, 1938;

A Pacifist in Trouble, 1939; The Fall of the Idols, 1941.

ABOUT: Begbie, H. Painted Windows; Belloc, H. Essays of a Catholic; Chesterton, G. K. A Miscellany of Men; Dark, S. Five Deans; Gardiner, A. G. Many Furrows; Portraits and Portents; Guedalla, P. Masters and Men; Hewlett, M. H. Wiltshire Essays; Inge, W. R. Vale; Kircher, R. Engländer; Mais, S. P. B. Some Modern Authors; Newton, J. F. Some Living Masters of the Pulpit; Rothenstein, W. Twenty-Four Portraits; American Review April-May 1935; Contemporary Review March 1923; Current Opinion, February, April 1920; Dalhousie Review January 1928; Fortnightly Review November 1934; Literary Digest July 15, 1922; November 24, 1923; Living Age July 23, 1921; New Republic May 22, 1929.

"INNES, MICHAEL." See STEWART, J. I. M.

IRWIN, Mrs. INEZ (HAYNES) (March 2, 1873-), American novelist and short-story writer, was born in Rio de Janeiro, Brazil, the daughter of Gideon Haynes and Emma Jane (Hopkins) Haynes. Her ancestors came from New England, and New England "seems to be a good place for ancestors to come from if one intends to write," says May Lamberton  Becker in a prefatory note to Mrs. Irwin's "The Frog in the Well," the first story in Mrs. Becker's anthology, *Under Twenty,* a collection of stories for girls of that age. "From New England men set out in sailing ships to far corners of the world, bringing home Turkey carpets and Nankin china still to be found in dim mansions near the coast; from New England came writers whose works it is part of our American education to read, and men and women who crusaded for great unpopular causes. There is something of all three in Mrs. Irwin's work for the world."

Inez Haynes attended the Girls' High School and Normal School, Boston, and was a special student at Radcliffe College from 1897 to 1900, marrying Rufus Hamilton Gillmore of Boston in 1897. Her second husband, whom she married in 1916, was Will Irwin,[qv] also a writer. *June Jeopardy* (1908) was her first book, followed by *Maida's Little Shop* (1910); Maida's subsequent possessions, always diminutive, were described in other books, up to *Maida's Little Island* (1939) and *Maida's Little Camp* (1940). The author's very popular Phoebe and Ernest stories first appeared in the *American Maga-*

zine. "They were so nearly typical of American high school boys and girls in a suburb or small town where people are well-to-do, that every one who lived in such a place seemed to recognize them among his acquaintance," says Mrs. Becker. "They appeared twice in book-form, *Phoebe and Ernest,* and *Phoebe, Ernest, and Cupid,* and not long after came a similar set of stories about a family of self-reliant young people, *The Ollivant Orphans.* Her novels are for the most part sympathetic studies of family relations."

In 1916-18 Inez Haynes Irwin was correspondent for various magazines in France, England, and Italy. She was a founder, with Maud Wood Park, of the National Collegiate Equal Suffrage League, and has been a member of the National Advisory Council of the National Women's Party. *Angel Island* (1914) was a feminist novel, and in 1921 she published *The Story of the Woman's Party.* She won the O. Henry Memorial Prize for the best short story of 1924, and was president of the Authors' League of America from 1931 to 1933. From 1935 to 1940 Mrs. Irwin was chairman of the Board of Directors of the World Centre for Women's Archives. Her New York clubs are the Cosmopolitan, Heterodoxy, and Query. The Irwins live on West Eleventh Street in New York City, spending their summers at Scituate, Mass. *Murder Masquerade* (1935), published in Great Britain as *Murder in Fancy Dress,* was a well-received account of a polite murder; *A Body Rolled Downstairs* (1938) was not up to the standard of its predecessor.

PRINCIPAL WORKS: June Jeopardy, 1908; Maida's Little Shop, 1910; Phoebe and Ernest, 1910; Janey, 1911; Phoebe, Ernest, and Cupid, 1912; Angel Island, 1914; The Ollivant Orphans, 1915; The Californiacs, 1916; The Lady of Kingdoms, 1917; The Happy Years, 1919; The Native Son, 1919; The Story of the Woman's Party, 1921; Out of the Air, 1921; Maida's Little House, 1921; Gertrude Haviland's Divorce, 1925; Maida's Little School, 1926; Gideon, 1927; Family Circle, 1931; Confessions of a Business Man's Wife, 1931; Youth Must Laugh, 1932; Angels and Amazons, 1933; Strange Harvest, 1934; Murder Masquerade, 1935; The Poison Cross Mystery, 1936; Good Manners for Girls, 1937; A Body Rolled Downstairs, 1938; Maida's Little Island, 1939; Maida's Little Camp, 1940; Many Murders, 1941.

ABOUT: Becker, M. L. (ed.). Under Twenty; Overton, G. M. The Women Who Make Our Novels.

IRWIN, WALLACE ADMAH (March 15, 1876*-), American novelist, writes: "I was born in Oneida, N.Y., as was my older brother, Will Irwin. My father was David Irwin, of Pennsylvania farming stock.

My mother, Edith Emily Greene, was the daughter of Charles Chauncey Greene, a portrait painter and collateral descendant of Gen. Nathanael Greene. When I was four our parents moved from Canandaigua, N.Y., to Leadville, Colo., to follow the boom in silver. The Irwins got plenty of experience, but very little silver. I attended public school sporadically; my mother conducted my education. We moved to Denver when I was fourteen. An unsympathetic school board, remarking that I knew more Shakespeare than long division, put me in the third grade; however, I graduated from the West Denver High School in 1896. I was an assayer in Cripple Creek for a year before I matriculated at Stanford University. I was more interested in writing than in study, and after three years of devotion to college publications I was expelled for delinquency in scholarship. After a period of starvation in San Francisco the editor of the *Examiner* took me on his staff. In odd moments I dashed off rhymed leaders for local news. A year later I took over the editorship of the *Overland Monthly.* In 1902 I wrote a little book of verse called *Love Sonnets of a Hoodlum,* a classic Petrarchian sonnet cycle in American slang. It was intended as a literary joke, and the young author when rather dazed when  Barrett Wendell of Harvard incorporated it in his lecture before the Sorbonne.

"I came to New York in 1904, and for a year wrote a daily verse for the *Evening Globe.* On the day of the San Francisco earthquake I was admitted to the staff of *Collier's Weekly,* for which I began the *Letters of a Japanese Schoolboy,* under the *nom de plume* of 'Hashimura Togo.' This feature went on for twenty years in various magazines and syndicates. About 1915 I wrote my first serious prose: short stories which appeared in *McClure's.* In 1919 the *Saturday Evening Post* sent me to California to investigate the Japanese question. In 1927 I visited the South Sea Islands with the late Martin Egan. In Fiji I met Dr. S. M. Lambert, leader of the Rockefeller Foundation's health compaign over the entire South Pacific. In 1938 I became Dr. Lambert's literary adviser for his autobiography.

"My first wife, Grace Luce, whom I married in 1901, died in 1914. In 1915 I married Laetitia McDonald, who wrote the play *Lady Alone* and two novels, *Young and Fair* and *Silver Platter*. We have two grown sons. During the [First] World War I served on the Committee on Public Information and later was commissioned Lieutenant Commander U.S.N.R. In 1911 I was elected honorary life editor of the Harvard *Lampoon*. My name, I hope, is still on Lampy's roll."

* * *

It was not until years after the first appearance in print of "Hashimura Togo" that it was certainly known that the author was not really a Japanese. Mr. Irwin, though not so well known as his brother, is one of the deftest of American humorists, and has also written well-conceived and solid realistic novels. It was Gelett Burgess' San Francisco magazine, the *Lark,* which, according to Charles Caldwell Dobie, "launched both the Irwins." Wallace Irwin is a heavy-set man with spectacles and a clipped moustache. He lives now in East Setauket, Long Island, in the summer, and in Southern Pines, N.C., in the winter.

PRINCIPAL WORKS: The Love Sonnets of a Hoodlum, 1902; The Rubaiyat of Omar Khayyam, Jr., 1902; Fairy Tales Up to Now, 1904; Nautical Lays of a Landsman, 1904; At the Sign of the Dollar, 1904; Chinatown Ballads, 1905; Random Rhymes and Odd Numbers, 1906; Letters of a Japanese Schoolboy, 1909; Mr. Togo: Maid of All Work, 1913; Pilgrims Into Folly, 1917; Venus in the East, 1918; The Blooming Angel, 1919; Suffering Husbands, 1920; Seed of the Sun, 1921; Lew Tyler's Wives, 1923; The Golden Bed, 1924; Mated, 1926; Lew Tyler and the Ladies, 1928; The Days of Her Life, 1931; The Julius Caesar Murder Case, 1935; Young Wife, 1936.

ABOUT: Delineator March 1932; Harper's Magazine August 1937; Sunset Magazine April 1921.

*IRWIN, WILLIAM HENRY (September 14, 1873-), American novelist, short-story writer, and journalist who signs his  works as Will Irwin, was born in Oneida, N.Y. He was the son of David S. Irwin and Edith E. (Greene) Irwin. He received his B.A. degree at twenty-five from Stanford University, Calif., in 1899, and next year published a volume of *Stanford Stories,* written in collaboration with C. K. Field. With Gelett Burgess, a fellow San Franciscan, he wrote two books of picaresque adventure with Californian settings, *The Reign of Queen Isyl* (1903) and *The Pica-*

roons (1905), the latter of which was serialized in *Pearson's Magazine.* On graduation from college Irwin became assistant editor of the San Francisco *Wave,* and in 1900 was its editor. In 1901 he went to the San Francisco *Chronicle* as a reporter, serving as a special writer the next year, and editing the Sunday edition from 1902 to 1904, when he removed to New York City to become a reporter on the New York *Sun.* He stayed there until 1906, when he became managing editor of *McClure's Magazine* for a year. In 1907-08 he was a writer for *Collier's Weekly,* and then became a successful and well-paid free-lance journalist. Irwin's first wife, married in 1901, was Harriet Hyde of San Francisco; they had a son, William Hyde Irwin. In 1916 he married Mrs. Inez (Haynes) Gillmore, who also writes, as Inez Haynes Irwin.*qv* They live in New York City.

Will Irwin was war correspondent with the German, Belgian, and British armies for various American publications and the London *Daily Mail,* in 1914-15. At the same time he was a member of the executive committee of the Commission for Relief in Belgium. From 1916 to 1918 he was war correspondent for the *Saturday Evening Post* with the French, Italian, British, and American armies, also serving in 1918 as chief of the foreign department of the Committee on Public Information. He was decorated with the ribbon of the Legion of Honor from France; the King Albert Medal, first class, from Belgium; as well as the Medaille de la Reconnaissance; the commemorative medal of the Olympic Games, from Sweden; and the Order of Gedeminas from Lithuania. Like his wife, Will Irwin has been president of the Authors' League of America; he has also served as president of the Authors' Guild. From 1929 to 1931 he was president of the American Centre of P.E.N. Club. His clubs are the Bohemian (San Francisco), and the Players and Dutch Treat clubs in New York City. A play, *The Thirteenth Chair* (1916), written with Bayard Veiller, had a successful run; *The House That Shadows Built* (1929) is a history of the motion picture. In 1930 he collaborated with the late Sidney Howard on a play, *Lute Song.* Will Irwin is an excellent journalist, and a writer who knows the uses of suspense and mystery.

PRINCIPAL WORKS: Stanford Stories (with C. K. Field) 1900; The Reign of Queen Isyl (with G. Burgess) 1903; The Picaroons (with G. Burgess) 1905; The Hamadryads (verse) 1904; The City That Was, 1907; Old Chinatown, 1908; The Confessions of a Con Man, 1909; Warrior the Untamed, 1909; The House of Mystery, 1910; The

Readjustment, 1910; The Red Button, 1912; Where the Heart Is, 1912; Beating Back (with A. J. Jennings) 1914; Men, Women, and War, 1915; Latin at War, 1916; A Reporter at Armageddon, 1918; The Next War, 1921; Columbine Time, 1921; Christ or Mars, 1923; Youth Rides West, 1925; How Red Is America? 1927; Highlights of Manhattan, 1927; Herbert Hoover: A Reminiscent Biography, 1929; The House That Shadows Built, 1929; Propaganda and the News, 1936; Spy and Counterspy (with E. V. Voska) 1940.

About: Baldwin, C. C. The Men Who Make Our Novels; Masson, T. L. Our American Humorists.

"I. S." See SCHNEIDER, I.

ISHERWOOD, CHRISTOPHER (August 26, 1904-), English novelist, writes:
"I was born at Disley, Cheshire. My family

Disraeli

had lived in the neighboring village of Marple since the sixteenth century, when, as successful farmers, they were able to buy 'The Hall'—an Elizabethan mansion standing in a big waterlogged park. An ancestor of mine, Judge Bradshaw (the full family name is Bradshaw-Isherwood) was president of the court which condemned Charles I to death. My father was an army officer who had fought in the Boer War—a talented musician, amateur actor, and water-color artist. My childhood was spent traveling around with his regiment, which was stationed first near York, then at Aldershot, and later in Ireland. In 1914, I was sent to a boarding school, where I made friends with the future poet, W. H. Auden. In 1915, my father was killed at Ypres. In 1919, I entered Repton School—the background of the motion picture, Goodbye, Mr. Chips. In 1924, I went to Corpus Christi College, Cambridge, with a history scholarship.

"After Cambridge, I worked for a time as secretary to André Mangeot, the French violinist and leader of a string quartette, in which John Barbirolli played the 'cello. I also earned my living as a private tutor. In 1928, I became a medical student—for two semesters only—and published my first novel. In the following year I went to Berlin, to visit Auden, who had been sent there by his parents to learn German. As a result of this visit I decided to settle in Germany. I remained there, on and off, for

the next four years. During this time I supported myself by giving English lessons.

"Hitler's coming into power made me what one of my German friends has described as an 'honorary refugee.' Since that time, I have always remained in fairly close touch with the circles of the Emigration. Between 1933 and 1937, I traveled a great deal, and spent several months in many of the European countries—Greece, Portugal, Spain, France, Belgium, Holland, and Denmark. During this period I wrote two plays in collaboration with Auden; both were performed in London. At the beginning of 1938 Auden and I, financed by our publishers, made a trip to China. While I was away my autobiographical book appeared. It contains portraits of most of my friends—including Auden and Stephen Spender—under fictitious names.

"In the autumn of 1938, after Auden and I had returned from China, our third play was produced—and coldly received by an audience which had just experienced the Appeasement of Munich; for it describes the outbreak of a European war. In January, 1939, we sailed for New York, intending to become permanent residents of the United States. Since that time I have written nothing of importance. I am now employed as a dialogue-writer by Metro-Goldwyn-Mayer."

* * *

Mr. Isherwood is unmarried, and lives in Santa Monica, Calif. He had had previous experience as a script-writer for Gaumont-British. In his book on China written with Auden he wrote all the prose narrative, Auden contributing the poems. Their joint plays are marked by an almost surrealist fantasy, but Mr. Isherwood's own novels are in a different and quite realistic vein.

His works, in the viewpoint of many critics as reported by John Lehmann, offer "the greatest promise for the future of our imaginative literature among all the younger novelists. . . . [He] was one of the first prose artists of his generation to receive the full impact of Europe as the Fascist tidal wave began to roll over it. . . . His prose is easy and flowing, not a word is wasted, and everything is seen in precise and daylight-clear shape."

Principal Works: All the Conspirators (novel) 1928; The Memorial (novel) 1932; The Dog Beneath the Skin: or, Where Is Francis? (play, with W. H. Auden) 1935; Mr. Norris Changes Trains (American title: The Last of Mr. Norris) (novel) 1935; Ascent of F. 6 (play, with W. H. Auden) 1937; On the Frontier (play, with W. H. Auden) 1938; Lions and Shadows (autobiography) 1938;

Journey to a War (with W. H. Auden) 1939; Good-bye to Berlin, 1939.

ABOUT: Isherwood, C. Lions and Shadows; Lehmann, J. New Writing in Europe; Time August 7, 1939.

ISTRATI, PANAÏT (August 11, 1884-April 16, 1935), Rumanian novelist who wrote in French, was born at Braïla, Rumania, the son of a Greek smuggler and a Rumanian washerwoman.  At the age of fourteen he left his parents, urged by an imperious need of wandering, in the course of which, in Rumania, Egypt, and Turkey, he was a grocery and butcher's clerk, a domestic servant, an apprentice mechanic and locksmith, a porter, and a house painter. In 1906 he stowed away in a Rumanian ship and for two years visited, by the most varied forms of transportation, Egypt, Greece, Naples, Port Said, Jaffa, Jerusalem, Beirut, and all the Near East. His journeys were made, without a ticket, on board ships where, when he was discovered, he had to work his way, and, on land, by riding the rails. It was in Egypt and Italy that he learned Italian, Arabic, and German.

In 1913, when for the first time he spent three months in Paris, he did not know a word of French. He returned soon to Rumania, where he made the acquaintance of Christian Rakovsky, later Soviet Ambassador in Paris, but at that time an exile from Russia. Istrati organized with him the first strikes and the first revolutionary uprisings in Rumania. When the First World War broke out, he had just established a small farm to raise pigs, and had just married a Jewess, a militant Socialist. But marriage and agriculture both suited him ill. The pigs died, and at the end of March 1916, deserted by his wife, he went on foot to Switzerland, after having crossed all of Austria in the midst of the war.

He spent four years in Switzerland, where he learned French by reading the classics; the first book he read was Fénelon's Télémaque, with the aid of a French-Rumanian dictionary. But the poverty to which he was reduced soon exhausted him, and after four months of happiness he underwent a distressful crisis. He was, at that period, sometimes a road-mender, sometimes an erector of telegraph poles, and he offered his services from village to village between Zurich, Basle, Berne, and Geneva. It was there that he discovered the Jean-Christophe of Romain Rolland, to whom he wrote a long letter which never reached its destination.

In 1919, he was at Nice with a camera with which he took pictures of the winter tourists on the promenade. In absolute destitution, despairing of ever being able to reach the ear of the French writer whom he most admired, he tried to kill himself by cutting his throat. At the end of six months in the hospital he recovered. He wrote again to Rolland, a letter of fifty pages, to which he received at last a letter which encouraged him to write. It was in 1923 that his first book, Kyra Kyralina, appeared, and he continued meanwhile his trade of wandering photographer on the shores of Brittany and Normandy.

From a Socialist, he had become a Communist, without any very clear idea of what Communism meant. He became an enthusiastic adherent of the doctrine, and was invited, in 1928, to take part in the celebration of the tenth anniversary of the Bolshevik Revolution. He went to Russia in the automobile of Rakovsky, whom he had met again in Paris and who had just been recalled from his ambassadorship. He arrived in Russia in a state of extreme exaltation, hailed the Soviet state as his chosen land, and decided to live there. He obtained permission to travel where he wished, and during the sixteen months he spent in Russia, he covered it from East to West and from North to South. His journeys disillusioned him with the U.S.S.R., and he wrote three anti-Communist books expressing a complete repudiation, not of revolution itself, but of the Russian Revolution. Thereafter he was naturally repudiated by the Communists who had been his strongest supporters; and he even broke with Rolland on this issue.

The hardships of Istrati's life had made him a prey to tuberculosis. 1933 found him at Nice, married again, this time to a much younger woman, a physico-chemist from Bucharest, and again in the utmost poverty; for though he had become a very popular novelist, he had no sense of money and had been inveigled into an outrageously unfair arrangement with his French publisher. His wife was homesick and in 1934 they returned to Rumania. There he was obliged to apply to ex-King Carol, as head of the Royal Foundation which governed all publication in the country, for a pension in return for the copyright and Rumanian translation of his books. He was, of course, accused of selling out to the king, and hence to the anti-Semitic and Fascist forces with which at that time Carol was identified. However, Istrati was by this time a dying man, with no resources except his writing, and with eight persons to support. The arrangement was made, but never fulfilled; Istrati died in destitution, and his wife was left penniless. He described himself at the end as "a man conquered in his belief in human regeneration, and who today no longer believes in anything." But it is as "the indefatigable lover who was the singer of the Mediterranean spring" that he will be remembered. He never felt thoroughly at home in French, and found writing a difficult task; he always had to have a friend read his manuscripts later to correct their grammar. But the end result was a limpid, flowing style, utterly at variance with the author's fiery and essentially melancholy temperament.

WORKS AVAILABLE IN ENGLISH: Kyra Kyraline, 1926 (as Kyra, My Sister, 1930); Uncle Anghel, 1927; The Bandits, 1929; Thistles of the Baragan, 1930; Balkan Tavern, 1931; Bitter Orange Tree, 1931; Russia Unveiled, 1931.

ABOUT: Mercure de France May 1940; Publishers' Weekly May 4, 1935; Romanic Review April 1935; Saturday Review (London) May 4, 1935.

JACKS, LAWRENCE PEARSALL

(1860-), English philosopher, essayist, and editor, was born in Nottingham, and educated in the University School of that city. He next attended the University of London, receiving an M.A. degree in 1886 and entering the ministry next year as assistant to the Rev. Stopford Brooke in Bedford Chapel. The

Underwood

Rev. Mr. Brooke is best known to American college students for his primer of English literature. His assistant married Olive Cecilia Brooke, Stopford Brooke's daughter, in 1889 (they had five sons and a daughter), and edited his father-in-law's letters and wrote his *Life*. After Bedford, Dr. Jacks was subsequently in charge of Renshaw Street Chapel, Liverpool, and the Church of the Messiah, Birmingham. With the foundation of the *Hibbert Journal* in 1902, Dr. Jacks became its editor and has so continued. In 1903 he became professor of philosophy at Manchester College, Oxford, "The Seat of Unitarianism," serving also as Principal of the College from 1915 until his retirement from both posts in 1931. He has received honorary degrees of LL.D., D.D., and D.Litt. from Glasgow, Harvard, Liverpool, McGill, Oxford, and the University of Rochester, (N.Y.). A son, Maurice Leonard Jacks, has been director of the Department of Education, Oxford, since 1938. Dr. Jacks' address is Far Outlook, Shotover Hill, Oxford.

Harold Begbie ("The Gentleman With a Duster") remarks that the face of Dr. Jacks resembles that of the great Unitarian, James Martineau, his head crowned with white hair and his "nobly coloured, ivory face ploughed up and furrowed by mental strife . . . the face of a man who has lived out of doors." He has pale blue eyes, a short thick-set body, heavy shoulders, and deep chest. His movements are slow, "as it were of a peasant."

Dr. Jacks is undoubtedly the best known of living Unitarian clergymen, from his long eminence as editor of the *Hibbert Journal* and his list of nearly thirty published works. He believes that the universe is a living, not a dead, lifeless mechanism, and that human beings are fellow-workers in its creative evolution. The *Nation* once remarked, "There is a vigor in his sturdy heresies which testifies to the strength of his orthodoxy." A talk he once gave in Liverpool Cathedral, at the invitation of the Dean and with the approval of the latter's Bishop, resulted in an outburst of *odium theologicum* early in 1934, when higher ecclesiastical authorities of the Church of England registered disapproval of a Unitarian (who by implication questioned the divinity of Christ) being allowed to occupy the pulpit. A favorite vehicle of Dr. Jacks' ideas is his imaginary industrial city, Smokeover, through the mouths of whose fictitious inhabitants he makes his criticisms of life.

PRINCIPAL WORKS: Mad Shepherds and Other Human Studies, 1910; The Alchemy of Thought, 1910; Among the Idolmakers, 1911; All Men Are Ghosts, 1913; From the Human End, 1916; Philosophers in Trouble, 1916; The Country Air, 1917; Life and Letters of Stopford Brooke, 1917; From Authority to Freedom: The Spiritual Pilgrimage of Charles Hargrove, 1920; Religious Perplexities, 1922; The Legends of Smokeover, 1922; A Living Universe, 1923; Realities and Shams, 1923; The Challenge of Life, 1924; Responsibility and Culture, 1925; The Faith of a Worker, 1926; The Heroes of Smokeover, 1926; Constructive Citizenship, 1927; My Neighbour the Universe, 1928; The Inner Sentinel, 1930; The Education of the Whole Man, 1931; Education Through Recreation, 1932; My American Friends, 1933; Elemental Religion, 1934; The Revolt Against Mechanism, 1934; Co-operation or Coercion, 1938; The Stolen Sword, 1938; The Last Legend of Smokeover, 1939; Construction Now, 1940.

ABOUT: Begbie, H. Painted Windows; Overton, G. M. When Winter Comes to Main Street.

*JACKSON, HOLBROOK (December 31, 1874-), English essayist, literary historian, and editor, writes: "Holbrook Jackson was  born in Liverpool and was self-educated. He began earning his living at the age of fifteen, and hoped ultimately to make enough money to subsidize himself as a writer, in which ambition he never succeeded, though he did contrive to become a writer. He published his first articles when he was sixteen. He tried his hand at verse, and in 1903 published an anthology of verse for children entitled *Everychild*. He abandoned business for journalism in 1907, and became joint editor of the *New Age* with the late A. W. Orage. He practiced in Fleet Street as a free lance from 1908 to 1910. His *Bernard Shaw* was the first book on the playwright-philosopher. He turned his pen to almost every branch of the craft and contributed to many of the leading London daily and weekly periodicals. He succeeded T. P. O'Connor as writer of the 'Book of the Week' on the *Sunday Sun*. He joined the staff of *Black and White*, and was successively and sometimes simultaneously literary, art, and musical critic, and even found time to do a little editing by taking over control of the *Idler* for several months whilst its proprietor, Robert Barr, wrote short stories to pay the printing bills.

"His real career as an editor began with his association with T. P. O'Connor in 1910, of whose publications he became managing director, and eventually edited both *T. P.'s Magazine* and *T. P.'s Weekly*. He was a regular contributor to the journals under his control and to other journals. In 1913 *The Eighteen Nineties*, the first complete review of art and letters in England at the close of the nineteenth century, made its appearance.

"At the beginning of 1917 he published the literary pocket journal, *To-Day*, of which he was owner as well as editor. It lived for seven years with no other object than the presentation of the literary tastes of its editor. Among its contributors were Richard Aldington, W. H. Davies, John Drinkwater, Walter de la Mare, T. S. Eliot, Ralph Hodgson, Ezra Pound, William Watson, and Augustine Birrell.

"He has taken a practical interest in the revival of good printing, and has taken part in several typographical ventures, notably

Flying Fame (1913). Under this title, he and his friends Ralph Hodgson and the late Claude Lovat Fraser published the now famous series of chapbooks and broadsides containing original poems and essays by de la Mare, James Stephens, and Hodgson, illustrated by Fraser. Since 1917 he has been editorial director of the National Trade Press, Ltd., and is an acknowledged authority on many business problems, notably the display of merchandise and the determination of fashion colors, on both of which he has done pioneer work. The latter interest led to the formation of the British Colour Council, of which he was chairman in 1933 and 1934.

"Despite his interest in business affairs, he is primarily a bookman, and has formed an interesting small library, rich in seventeenth and eighteenth century works. His recreations are reading, writing, and buying books; traveling; looking at the human comedy; and talking. He was married in 1900 and has one daughter."

* * *

John T. Winterich said of *The Eighteen Nineties* that it was "the finest history of the Beardsley to Wilde to Beerbohm era that has yet seen the day." It is an invaluable sourcebook; and so, for literary anecdotes, is his later *Anatomy of Bibliomania*.

PRINCIPAL WORKS: Edward Fitzgerald and Omar Khayyam, 1899; The Eternal Now (verse) 1900; Bernard Shaw, 1907; William Morris, 1908; Great English Novelists, 1908; Platitudes in the Making, 1911; All Manner of Folk, 1912; Town, 1913; The Eighteen Nineties, 1913; Southward Ho! and Other Essays, 1914; Occasions, 1922; End Papers, 1923; A Brief Survey of Printing (with S. Morison) 1923; Essays of Today and Yesterday, 1928; The Anatomy of Bibliomania, 1930; The Fear of Books, 1932; William Caxton, 1933; Maxims of Books and Reading, 1934; The Printing of Books, 1937.

ABOUT: More, P. E. Decadent Wit; Publishers' Weekly January 1931; Saturday Review of Literature, September 30, 1933.

*JACKSON, JOSEPH HENRY (July 21, 1894-), American literary critic and travel writer, was born in Madison, N.J., the son of Herbert Hallett Jackson and Marion Agnes (Brown) Jackson. He was educated at the Peddie School, Highstown, N.J., and at Lafayette College, where he was a student from 1915 to 1917, but was not graduated. During the First World War he served first as a private in the Ambulance Corps and later as a first lieutenant of infantry and instructor in the Intelligence School. After the war he came to San Francisco, which is still his headquarters. He had previously written advertising copy for a New York agency, but since 1920 has been associated with various magazines and one newspaper. From 1920 to 1923 he was associate editor of *Sunset,* then a general magazine, from 1923 to 1926 its managing editor, and from 1926 to 1928 editor-in-chief. For the next three years he was literary editor of the *Argonaut,* a San Francisco weekly. In 1930 he became literary editor of the San Francisco *Chronicle,* a position he still holds, writing a daily column, "Notes of a Bookman," with a four- to twelve-page Sunday department as well. He has become one of the best-known literary critics and reviewers in the United States, writing reviews frequently for literary magazines, and having been one of the board of judges of the O. Henry Memorial Award in 1935. He has a large local following, and publishers value him because "he sells books." Circulating libraries always stock up in San Francisco after a Jackson review. But he is

best known nationally as a radio broadcaster on books. He started a local book review broadcast over KGO in 1924, and though it has occasionally been interrupted, it is now one of the oldest sustaining programs on the air. At first heard only on a Coast network, it is now released nationally every week by the National Broadcasting Company.

Mr. Jackson was married in 1923 to Charlotte E. Cobden, and they have one daughter. His home is in Berkeley, Calif., across the bay from San Francisco. He has traveled a good deal in Central and South America, and each of his trips has resulted in an informal travel book. He has also been a student of California history, and has written much in a popular yet accurately documented style on this subject as well.

David Bramble called Mr. Jackson "sane, balanced, and highly intelligent. He has a sense of humor that delights in the ridiculous." (His hobby is the collection of what he calls "insaniana"—books of the freakish and *outré* variety, the archetype of which is the work of the egregious "Sweet Singer of Michigan" and similar members of the lunatic fringe of literature.) Most people who have known Mr. Jackson only over the radio are surprised to find him a good-looking, youngish man; he happens to have a rather thin voice which gives the impression of

patriarchal age until one discovers it belongs to a man with a full, fresh-skinned face, light brown hair, and twinkling eyes.

Mr. Jackson's books, both of travel and of history, are in a sense by-products of his main job as a book critic. But they make excellent reading, and if they are neither philosophical nor profound, they present sympathetic and appealing pictures of our Southern neighbors and our Western past.

PRINCIPAL WORKS: Mexican Interlude, 1936; Notes on a Drum, 1937; Tintypes in Gold, 1939; Extra! Extra! 1940; Anybody's Gold: The Story of California's Mining Towns, 1941.

ABOUT: Christian Science Monitor August 12, 1939; Publishers' Weekly November 5, 1932.

JACOB, NAOMI ELLINGTON (July 1, 1889-   ), English novelist, writes: "Naomi Jacob was born in the city of Ripon, in York-

shire, England. Her mother's family were yeomen, who had held the same piece of land for over three hundred years; her father's family came from Spain, having worked their way— taking several hundreds of years to do it—through Holland

to Poland. Her great grandmother and great grandfather were both killed in 'pogroms' in that country, her grandfather escaping as a small child to Germany. Owing to family reverses, Naomi Jacob began work at the age of fifteen, as a teacher in a 'church school' in the North of England, at a salary of twelve pounds a year. On this wage, augmented by some help from her mother— the best mother in the world—she managed to live and pass examinations. Then, when fully qualified, she realized that she disliked the limits put on free education in those days, and left, going on to the vaudeville stage for some years. With the beginning of the Great War, she became an officer in the Women's Legion [working as superintendent of a munition factory]; at the end of the war, she went into a sanatorium, suffering from consumption. Leaving the sanatorium, she went on the legitimate stage, and had considerable success, playing in London with most of the best known actors and actresses of the day. She also appeared in several films. It was about this time that she wrote her first novel, *Jacob Ussher,* which was — and still is — a first-rate seller. Again her health gave way, and in 1930 she was ordered to leave England and see what the milder

711

and sunnier climate of Italy would do for her. In a year she was cured. She continued to write, and produces two books a year. In addition, she returns to England every summer for a long lecture tour, speaking every day and often twice and three times a day for six weeks.

"Politically she calls herself a 'Conservative Socialist.' She is a Catholic by religion. Her amusements are: work, work again, and more work. She lives in Sirmione, on the shores of Lake Garda. She is passionately fond of music, particularly Italian opera; a pacifist; a collector of old furniture. She boasts that at fifty she can still work for twelve hours a day, that she has never allowed a 'fan' letter to go unanswered, and that she answers them all personally. She is a confirmed optimist, and declares that the best song in the world is, 'It's a lovely day tomorrow.' "

* * *

Miss Jacob omits one of her chief hobbies —cooking, on which she has written a book. She is devoted to animals, works for their protection, and "keeps a Pekinese." Though she says she never takes exercise, she does enjoy "a little mild swimming." She is unmarried. Her pre-war lectures were on peace, literature, and the theatre. She has written two one-act plays. With the advent of the Second World War in 1939, shortly after the writing of this autobiographical sketch, Miss Jacobs returned to England from Italy.

PRINCIPAL WORKS: Jacob Ussher, 1926; Power, 1927; The Man Who Found Himself, 1929; Rock and Sand, 1929; That Wild Lie—, 1930; The Beloved Physician, 1930; Roots, 1931; "Seen Unknown . . ." 1931; Props, 1932; Young Emmanuel, 1932; Poor Straws! 1933; Groping, 1933; Me: A Chronicle About Other People (autobiography) 1933; The Plough, 1934; Four Generations, 1934; The Loaded Stick, 1934; "Honour Come Back—" 1935; Me—in the Kitchen (non-fiction) 1935; The Founder of the House, 1935; Timepiece, 1936; Our Marie (biography of Marie Lloyd) 1936; Fade Out, 1937; Barren Metal, 1937; Me—Again (autobiography) 1937; The Lenient God, 1938; No Easy Way, 1938; Straws in Amber, 1938; This Porcelain Clay, 1939; Full Meridian, 1939; They Left the Land, 1940; Sally Scarth, 1940; Cap of Youth, 1941; Under New Management, 1941.

ABOUT: Jacob, N. Me, Me—Again; Saturday Review of Literature January 1, 1938.

JACOBS, JOSEPH. See "BRITISH AUTHORS OF THE 19TH CENTURY"

*JACOBS, WILLIAM WYMARK (September 8, 1863-), English story writer, best known as W. W. Jacobs, writes: "I was born in London and educated at private schools. After passing (with some trouble) a Civil Service examination, I was ap-

pointed to the Savings Bank Department of the General Post Office. I cannot flatter myself that I was a good clerk, nor has anybody else attempted to do so. From the age of twenty I tried my hand at writing, mostly humorous articles. It was a pleasant hobby and the more agreeable because it brought me a little extra pocket-money. In 1896, however, I published my first book, *Many Cargoes*, and three years later resigned my post in the Civil Service to join the great and increasing army of authors.

"My father, William Gage Jacobs, was the manager of South Devon Wharf, Wapping, and it is probably owing to that connection that some tang of the sea *and* the foreshore of the Thames insinuated itself into my work. That did not happen until some years after I had left the house on the wharf at Wapping. I suppose distance lent enchantment to a view that certainly needed it.

"I married five months after leaving the Service, and two sons and three daughters appeared to help persuade me to push a never very industrious pen. My political opinions have always been Conservative and individualistic since I arrived at adult age. Before then I suppose I had the same vague yearnings for Utopia as the adolescents of today. As to likes and dislikes, I have many of both, but expression of them would mean criticism—a thing I avoid."

* * *

This autobiographical sketch illustrates excellently W. W. Jacobs' two most salient characteristics—his dry humor and his self-effacing modesty. He is a taciturn, shy little man who lives very quietly and avoids controversy or publicity. His once blond hair is now white, but his face is still extraordinarily young, and his habitual expression is "wistful, almost sad," though his occasional smile lights it surprisingly. His voice is low, and his manner gentle, and it is only in his watchful blue eyes and his "humorist's tell-tale mouth" that one sees the teller of so many lusty sea-stories. Many of these stories he picked up on walking tours on the sea-coast with Will Owens, his illustrator, where the silent listener turned to good advantage the yarns poured into his sympathetic ears.

Mrs. Jacobs was Agnes Eleanor Williams, a suffragette who was one of the "prison

* Died September 1, 1943.

martyrs" of the pre-war campaign, and a Socialist. The family lives in London in the winter and near Epping Forest, in Essex, in the summer. For nearly fifteen years now Mr. Jacobs has ceased to write, except for an occasional short story; his last published book, in 1931, was an omnibus of previously printed stories.

He is known chiefly as a humorist, a tale-teller in what John Drinkwater called "the Dickens tradition." Though his characters are mostly seafaring men, it has been noted that he seldom follows them beyond the shore, and his main protagonist is the night watchman on the dock, who tells the story as he heard it from the man who sailed away. There is little development in his work, his earliest stories being of just the same *genre* as his latest. The humor is quiet, arousing a chuckle rather than a laugh. But this same man has produced some spine-chilling horror-stories, including that classic in this *genre*, "The Monkey's Paw," without which no anthology of its kind would be complete. He has also written a number of plays, mostly one-act comedies, several of them in collaboration with Louis N. Parker. Best known of his plays are *Establishing Relations, The Warming Pan, A Distant Relative,* and *Dixon's Return.*

PRINCIPAL WORKS: Many Cargoes, 1896; The Skipper's Wooing, 1897; Sea Urchins, 1898; A Master of Craft, 1900; Light Freights, 1901; At Sunwich Port, 1902; The Lady of the Barge (with L. N. Parker) 1902; Odd Craft, 1903; Dialstone Lane, 1904; Captains All, 1905; Short Cruises, 1907; Salthaven, 1908; Sailor's Knots, 1909; Ship's Company, 1911; Night Watches, 1914; The Castaways, 1916; Deep Waters, 1919; Sea Whispers, 1926; Snug Harbor (omnibus) 1931.

ABOUT: Adcock, A. St. J. The Glory That Was Grub Street; Bennett, A. Books and Persons; Hind, C. L. More Authors and I; Priestly, J. B. Figures in Modern Literature; Ward, A. C. Aspects of the Modern Short Story; Bookman (London) October 1926; Century Magazine July 1923; London Mercury November 1923; South Atlantic Quarterly July 1919; Wilson Library Bulletin January 1933.

JAMES, HENRY (1843-1916). See "AMERICAN AUTHORS: 1600-1900"

*JAMES, HENRY (1879-), American writer and trustee, winner of the Pulitzer Prize for biography, was born in Boston, the son of William James, the philosopher and psychologist, and Alice H. (Gibbens) James. In the letters of his famous uncle, Henry, he figures as "Harry," especially when a guest at the novelist's home, Lamb House, at the old Cinque Port of Rye, Sussex. (Later the home of E. F. Benson, the Georgian man-

* Died December 13, 1947.

sion was wrecked by Nazi bombs in the Second World War.)

Henry James received his B.A. degree from Harvard in 1899, and after obtaining an LL.B. at the Law School practiced law in Boston for the next eight years. In 1912 he came to New York as manager of the Rockefeller Institute for Medical Research, serving as member of the War Relief Commission of the Rockefeller Foundation in 1914-16. He married Olivia Cutting of Westbury, Long Island, in 1917; they were divorced in 1930 and in 1938 he married Mrs. Dorothea (Draper) Blagden, widow of Linzee Blagden. Civil and military service took James to Washington; to France with the American Expeditionary Forces; and to Versailles for the Peace Conference, in 1918-19.

Some years later Henry James was requested by the family of Richard Olney, Cleveland's somewhat belligerent Secretary of State, to write a biography of Olney. The result was a competent biography, both from the literary and legalistic points of view, which served as a trial exercise for the prize-winning *Charles W. Eliot,* published in two volumes in 1930. The New York *Times* called the latter "more than the biography of a man, albeit one of the most notable figures of his time. It is the romance of education as education evolved under the guidance of the man who was Harvard's president for forty years." William Dana Orcutt remarked that the work brought out "with amazing clarity each phase of an extraordinarily many-sided character." James' edition of his father's *Letters,* published in 1919, is so detailed as to take rank as a third biography, perhaps the most appealing of the trio.

As a member of the Harvard Board of Overseers (he has been a Fellow of the College since 1936) James visited principally the biological departments. His work in recent years has been as chairman of the board of the Teachers Insurance and Annuity Association. "I hate and dread war, but I'm sure there is a good deal in our kind of civilization for which we must be willing to fight," he wrote the secretary of his Harvard class in 1939. For recreation, he hunts in the wildest regions of Vermont. "Working over trees and shrubs is an outdoor recreation that I can enjoy at every season, and by way of sport I play a little golf and sometimes exercise a bird-dog, although without very important results for the larder." His home is in New York

City, where he is a trustee of the New York Public Library.

PRINCIPAL WORKS: Richard Olney, 1923; Charles W. Eliot, 1930. *Editor*—The Letters of William James, 1930.

ABOUT: Harvard University, Class of 1899: Secretary's Fortieth Anniversary Report.

*JAMES, MARQUIS (August 29, 1891-), American journalist and biographer, twice winner of the Pulitzer Prize, writes: "I

was born in Springfield, Mo. My parents, Houstin James and Rachel Marquis, were descended from colonial Virginia stock, Scotch-Irish on my father's side and French Huguenot on my mother's. Socially they ranged from Tidewater gentry to mountaineers. At the time of my birth my father was practicing law before the rude courts of the Indian and Oklahoma Territories. Before I was three, to be near my father's law practice my mother took me to Oklahoma. Our home was a raw prairie claim near Enid in the Cherokee Strip which had been opened to white settlement six months before. We had a large collection of books for the time and place and most of them dealt with my mother's favorite subject—history. My mother taught me to read when I was about four. The western sagas I heard and my mother's books were my earliest intellectual fare.

"When I was ten we moved to Enid. The country was settling down. I went to school but had considerable difficulty with my classes. Grammar and arithmetic I could not understand, and cannot now. History I liked and read continuously, though often my reading failed to coincide with the day's lessons. The study of literature I liked because I liked the sound of words. I liked the lives of writers because they are a branch of history. Exploring the mysteries of a county seat town, the printing shops interested me most. The processes by which the printed page came into being fascinated me. I hung around and learned the rudiments of the trade. These associations led to my first newspaper 'writings,' most of which were never written at all but composed out of my head at the case and inserted in type in the forms of the weekly Enid *Events*. At fourteen I was a fullfledged reporter for the *Events*. Two years later my father died and my newspaper earnings were needed.

I finished high school and even attended Oklahoma Christian (now Phillips) University for a few months. I left college because I thought I could learn as much in a newspaper office — and certainly have a better time.

"At twenty I took the road as a tramp reporter. In three years I covered fairly well the triangle bounded by Chicago, New Orleans, and New York. On the New Orleans *Item* I met a blonde girl reporter named Bessie Rowland. In 1914 we were married. I decided to settle down in earnest and try my hand at other writing on the side. I got to be assistant city editor of the Chicago *Evening Journal* but I could not land my literary output any higher than the pulps. A year later we were in New York, my wife on a Brooklyn paper and I on the *Tribune*. When we went in the war I declined a newspaper assignment abroad and joined the army; was nineteen months in France, discharged as Captain of Infantry.

"I took up press agentry and ghost writing, in which there was good money, but after three years quit for a subordinate job with a client. The *American Legion Monthly*, which in my capacity as National Director of Publicity of the Legion I had helped to found, was printing historical sketches based on sound research and embodying what aimed to be a literary quality. Having made a job to my liking I took it and began to write such pieces. They interested other editors and I began to get offers elsewhere. For a few months I doubled in brass on the staff of the *New Yorker*, but quit that to begin a biography of Sam Houston, in whom I had been interested since boyhood. It took four years. The book sold 100,000 copies and won the Pulitzer Prize in 1930. This encouraged me to tackle Andrew Jackson, in two volumes, which took seven years, and sold 250,000 copies, and won the Pulitzer Prize in 1938.

"We live in Pleasantville, N.Y. We have a daughter. My library-and-office is over the garage in the back yard. It contains no telephone. My recreations: riding, tennis, draw poker, travel. Major dislike: radio. Politics: a non-partisan New Dealer. Do enough magazine work to keep my hand in and write—not talk—some for radio. Have never been to a literary tea or cocktail party. Favorite American writers: fiction— Mark Twain, Bret Harte, Willa Cather, Sinclair Lewis, James Boyd; non-fiction— Benjamin Franklin, Thomas Jefferson, Francis Parkman, Carl Sandburg.

* Died November 19, 1955.

"When I feel capable of doing a man of thought—all my subjects so far have been men of action, who are simpler to handle—I want to tackle Jefferson and possibly Franklin. Maybe that will be the work of my very ripe years when I have actually settled down for good."

* * *

Mr. James, "a fifth or sixth cousin of Jesse James," is six feet tall, with rumpled gray hair and an alert, intelligent face. Lynn Anderson called his biographies "gorgeous historical documents"; he himself says it his aim "to raise historical writing from its present lowly state to be a branch of letters in the literary sense." His biographies of Garner and DuPont, however, were received much less favorably than his earlier works.

PRINCIPAL WORKS: A History of the American Legion, 1923; The Raven: A Biography of Sam Houston, 1929; Six Foot Six (juvenile biography of Houston, with B. R. James) 1931; Andrew Jackson: The Border Captain, 1933; They Had Their Hour, 1934; The Courageous Heart (juvenile biography of Jackson, with B. R. James) 1935; Andrew Jackson: Portrait of a President, 1937; Mr. Garner of Texas, 1939; Alfred I. du Pont: The Family Rebel, 1941.

ABOUT: New York Times Book Review March 11, 1934; Newsweek October 4, 1937; Publishers' Weekly April 26, 1941; Saturday Review of Literature May 7, 1938.

JAMES, MONTAGUE RHODES (August 1, 1862-June 12, 1936), English antiquarian and writer of ghost stories, was

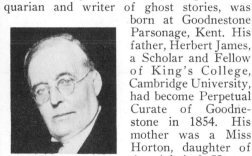

born at Goodnestone Parsonage, Kent. His father, Herbert James, a Scholar and Fellow of King's College, Cambridge University, had become Perpetual Curate of Goodnestone in 1854. His mother was a Miss Horton, daughter of the Admiral Horton who fought in the Napoleonic wars. In 1865 Dr. James was given the living of Great and Little Livermere, Suffolk, by Mrs. Jane Broke of Livermere Hall, and Montague James regarded this Rectory as his home till his father's death in 1909. Montague burst into tears at his first children's party and was comforted when left in the library of his hostess; at seven he begged for a seventeenth-century Dutch Bible to console him during convalescence, and also wrote the lives of nineteen northern saints. In 1873

he attended Temple Grove, entering Eton three years later as King's Scholar, and taking several prizes for Latin prose and verse. He wasted no time on games, although of great physical strength and popular with his school-fellows. In 1882 James entered Cambridge as Eton Scholar of King's, and won further prizes, including the Chancellor's Medal in 1886. Next year he went with Dr. Hogarth to Cyprus to excavate, and might well have become a great classical archaeologist. "But apocryphal literature and medieval manuscripts had already claimed him for their own," as S. G. Lubbock says, James was given a Fellowship at King's in 1887, and 1893 moved into rooms at the top of Wilkins' Buildings, where he stayed twelve years, always accessible to undergraduates and always working steadily on his catalogues of manuscripts, assisted by a prodigious memory. Collections at Trinity, Emmanuel, Pembroke, Corpus Christi, and several other colleges, and those in some private libraries, such as J. P. Morgan's, were included in the scope of his work; the James bibliography takes up thirty pages of S. G. Lubbock's monograph. From 1894 to 1908 Dr. James directed the work of the Fitzwilliam Museum. As Provost of King's College, 1905-18 (Vice Chancellor 1913-15), he was also Senior Fellow of Eton, and he became Provost of Eton in 1918, remaining till his death.

The minutes of the Chitchat Society meeting held at King's October 28, 1893, recorded that "Mr. James read 'Two Ghost Stories.'" Lord Frederic Hamilton, editor of the Pall Mall Gazette, secured "Lost Hearts" and published it with illustrations; "Canon Alberic's Scrapbook" was published by Leo Maxse in the National Review. Every year a small party assembled at King's before Christmas to hear "Monty James'" latest. James admitted that Sheridan Le Fanu was his chief inspiration, especially where walking corpses were concerned, but James surpassed most writers of ghost stories in the eeriness of his atmosphere, the individual and peculiarly creepy quality of his plots, and the vindictiveness and malignancy of his ghosts, who had an uncomfortable habit of operating in broad daylight. Basil Davenport, in an article on the genre, "The Devil Is Not Dead," remarks truly that James wrote a greater number of consistently first-rate ghost stories than any one else. He "remained young and even boyish in all but bodily presence to the very end" (at seventy-four) and was an unparalleled mimic, his favorite stunt being the reproduction of a complete Masters' meeting.

PRINCIPAL WORKS: *Ecclesiastical and Antiquarian*—Psalms of the Pharisees, (with H. E. Ryle) 1891; The Testament of Abraham, 1892; The Gospel According to Peter, 1892; Sculptures of the Lady Chapel at Ely, 1895; Life and Miracles of St. William of Norwich (with Dr. Jessopp) 1896; Verses in the Windows of Canterbury Cathedral, 1902; Ancient Libraries of Canterbury and Dover, 1903; Stained Glass at Ashridge, 1906; Frescoes at Eton, 1907, 1923; Biblical Antiquities of Philo, 1917; Wanderings and Homes of MSS, 1919; The Lost Apocrypha of the New Testament, 1920; The Apocryphal New Testament, 1924; The Book of Tobit, 1929. *Ghost Stories*—Ghost Stories of an Antiquary, 1905; More Ghost Stories of an Antiquary, 1911; A Thin Ghost and Others, 1919; Twelve Medieval Ghost Stories, 1922; The Five Jars, 1922; Collected Ghost Stories, 1931. *Editor*—Madam Crowl's Ghost and Other Tales of Mystery (by J. S. Le Fanu) 1923.

ABOUT: Honce, C. A. Sherlock Holmes' Birthday; James, M. R. Eton and King's: 1875-1925; Lubbock, S. G. A Memoir of Montague Rhodes James; Sayers, D. L. The Omnibus of Crime; Saturday Review of Literature February 15, 1936.

JAMES, NORAH CORDNER (1900-   ),

English novelist, writes: "I was born in London. My father was a consulting mining  civil engineer. He had traveled all over the world and our house generally had some visitor in it from another country. I was a delicate child, and went to many schools in the hope that they would prove beneficial to my health. The last one I attended was the Francis Holland School in Baker Street, London. I left there to study art in the Slade School. The war came and I worked for a while on the land. Later, I got a job at the Ministry of Pensions. It was while I was there that I realized the need for organization of the staff for the betterment of the bad conditions prevailing. When I left the Ministry, I became a trade union organizer and was responsible for 25,000 men and women members of the clerical association for which I worked.

"Later, owing to ill health, I had to take six months' rest. During this time I began to write. When I was better I helped to design book jackets for a firm of commercial artists. My next job was secretary to the poet, Gerald Gould, and political secretary to his wife, Barbara Ayrton Gould. Eventually I went to a publishing firm, where I became advertising and publicity manager. I was there for five years. During my last

year with them, I wrote my first novel, *Sleeveless Errand*. After it had been published in America and eight other countries, I left the publisher and lived on my earnings as a novelist. I supplemented these by representing American publishers over in this country.

"In 1931 I visited America and learned at first hand what a very lovely city New York is. I did a good deal of traveling during the next five years, Germany, France, Italy. And all the time I was writing.

"I have had Labor sympathies ever since I was old enough to think at all, and I loathe injustice of any kind. After Munich, I realized that war was inevitable. Just before it broke out, I returned from France and joined the London Auxiliary Fire Service. But now [March, 1940] I am waiting to go to France as a driver of a mobile canteen van.

"My favorite authors, apart from detective fiction, which I like best, are American writers; I still prefer William Faulkner to any others. The novel I have just finished is a long one, the life of a London charwoman, interwoven with the stories of the people she works for. The book has a London background. I have written over thirty books. I have also done a certain amount of short story writing and journalism."

* * *

Miss James is pretty, with short light hair and very blue eyes. She is unmarried. Behind her London background she is of Irish ancestry. She still paints and does sculpture as a recreation, and she is a good swimmer.

Sleeveless Errand was probably the most suppressed novel ever published in England; every store containing copies was raided, and a guard stood for a week-end at the window of one store containing one copy, until the owner could be found to remove it. Nobody has ever given an adequate explanation of why it was thus censored and, in the later English edition, expurgated—the theory is that the objection was to one word in the book. Nearly all of Miss James' novels are tragic in theme; one critic remarked that "she loves suffering too dearly." but added that "she writes well enough to redeem the tritest story." She is a prolific writer, with a witty style.

PRINCIPAL WORKS: Sleeveless Errand, 1929; Hail! All Hail! 1929; Shatter the Dream, 1930; To the Valiant, 1930; Wanton Way, 1931; Hospital (in America: Nurse Adriadne) 1932; Tinkle the Cat, 1932; Jake the Dog, 1933; Jealousy, 1933; Mrs. Puffy, 1934; Strap-Hangers (in America:

Sacrifice) 1934; Cottage Angles, 1935; The Lion Beat the Unicorn, 1935; Return, 1935; By a Side Wind, 1936; Return Cheaper, 1936; Sea View, 1936; Two Divided by One, 1936; Women Are Born To Listen, 1937; The House by the Tree, 1938; As High As the Sky, 1938; Mighty City, 1939; Stars Are Fire, 1939; I Lived in a Democracy (autobiography) 1939; Gentlewoman, 1940; The Long Journey, 1941.

ABOUT: James, N. C. I Lived in a Democracy; Bookman October 1929.

*JAMES, WILL (June 6, 1892-   ), American Western writer and illustrator, writes: "I was born close to the sod of the Judith Basin country in Montana. My dad was a Texan, my mother a Southern Californian, both Scotch Irish, with a little Spanish on my mother's side. My dad had come North to start in the cow business when I was born. I stopped the outfit, headed from Texas to Canada, in Montana. I was a year old when my mother died, and four when my dad was killed while handling cattle. I was then adopted by a French Canadian trapper and prospector named Jean Beaupré. A kinder and wiser man I've never known. He had very little education as to books but was past master at all outdoors. That way he was my only teacher. I done my first book learning from old magazines and saddlery catalogues we'd find in different scattered cow camps. During late summers Bopy, as I called the old trapper, got to take me far to the North to his trapping territories, sometimes as far as the Peace River country. I done a lot of studying by the fireplace of the dugouts up there, also drawing, which I took to from the time I picked up a piece of charcoal from a branding fire.

Apeda

"Many years later when I started in the art game, by accident with a horse that bucked too hard, fell on me, and laid me up, I was given two art scholarships which I didn't use enough to say I did. It was the same with my writing and such, I could never seem to memorize long phrases, dates, or names. Like also with drawing, I can't copy, not even my own work, and I've never drawn or painted from life. I never went into a school-house, only for a shindig a couple of times. With Bopy's French, which was mixed with Indian, and his look on life and knowledge of nature he teached me more than, I think, I could of learned from any school. With speaking his mixed

French for the ten years I was with him, then mixing in afterwards with Spanish, Mexican, and Indian, sort of turned my talk and writing in a way very different than most others.

"Bopy left me late one spring, when I was going on fourteen, and from all evidence he was drowned while getting a bucket of water at the edge of a swirling river. Being that horses was my failing ever since I can remember and I'd got to riding quite a bit for different outfits while Bopy would fool around at prospecting during summers, I went right on to that after Bopy had gone, and rode with many of the biggest cow and horse outfits from Canada down to Mexico. I'd got battered up quite a bit while riding all kinds of horses while I worked, and it finally took one horse to sudden bring the turning point in my life, from riding to writing. But drawing was my first try with no thought of writing, for I figured a good education would sure be necessary for that. Looking back now I think I was lucky, for after only a couple of months of struggling, all ignorant of the publishing game, I sold my first drawing to *Sunset* for $25. I sold that outfit many more after that, enough to keep alive on and finally to get to New York, where I done some magazine illustrating, painted covers and such, and sold some idea drawings to *Life*. I went back West in 1921.

"It was in 1923, I was not making ends meet, my saddle was still in hock. A friend got after me to try my hand at writing with my drawing. I laughed at him but he was serious, and finally I made him a bet of five dollars that any writing of mine would be returned faster than I could send it. The result was my first article, 'Bucking Horses and Bucking Horse Riders,' in *Scribner's*. The next four following was accepted straight hand running, and then I figured I sure enough was a writer. But the blow came with the sixth one and took the feathers off my hat, it was returned.

"But I still am lucky, I think, for I now have only two short stories left on hand, and I'm letting them ferment till the right time comes. Since I started in the writing game in 1924 I've had nineteen books published, also had two in the movies and now plan on having more.

"I was married once, to a very fine girl, but being brought up as I was, so free, ignorant of conventional ways, I figured it best for us both that I be the Lone Cowboy again. That's the title of my book of my life story. My residence is in Montana.

I still as always have my horses, which are my pet likes. As to my pet dislikes, that's crowds. But I like to mingle with a few good friends. At a rodeo I hit for the chutes. The work I'm on now is short stories for the magazines, something I haven't done for some years."

* * *

Will James, whose "autobiography" is given here as written, is the typical cowboy in appearance—long, rangy, with a tanned, aquiline face. He owns a 12,000-acre ranch near Billings, Mont. He illustrates all his own books—*Smoky* won the Newbery Medal in 1934, and has been filmed, as has *Lone Cowboy*. His wife was Alice Conradt, whom he married in 1920. Doris Montague said of him: "He can't spell worth a cent and he doesn't know much about grammar. But he has a lot he wants to say and he gets it out in the easiest, simplest way he can."

PRINCIPAL WORKS: Cowboys, North and South, 1924; The Drifting Cowboy, 1925; Smoky, 1926; The Cow Country, 1927; Sand, 1929; Lone Cowboy, 1930; Sun-Up (short stories) 1931; Big-Enough, 1931; All in the Day's Riding (short stories) 1932; The Three Mustangeers, 1933; Uncle Bill, 1934; In the Saddle With Uncle Bill, 1935; Home Ranch, 1935; Scorpion: A Good Bad Horse, 1936; Cowboy in the Making, 1937; Look-See, 1938; Dark Horse, 1939; Horses I've Known, 1940; The American Cowboy, 1942.

ABOUT: James, W. Lone Cowboy; Kunitz, S. J. & Haycraft, H. (eds.). The Junior Book of Authors; American Magazine May 1931; Journal National Education Association October 1927.

JAMES, WILLIAM. See "AMERICAN AUTHORS: 1600-1900"

JAMESON, STORM (1897-), English novelist, was born Margaret Storm Jameson in Whitby, Yorkshire, the daughter of William S. Jameson. As  might be gathered from her novels, she comes of a family of shipbuilders. On the Yorkshire moors she romped with her brothers: one of them, Lt. Harold Jameson, a Flying Corps pilot, was shot down in France in January 1917. Storm was frequently thrashed by her mother for reading before breakfast, but this same mother took her, at fifteen, twenty miles to the Municipal School at Scarborough, to obtain one of the three open scholarships offered in the North Riding of Yorkshire. At Leeds University Miss James took a First Class in the Honours English school and won a research scholarship at University College, London, where, with her thesis *Modern Drama in Europe* (published 1920), she received an M.A. degree. She has worked as copywriter for a publicity company, for a publisher, as a dramatic critic, and as editor of a weekly magazine. She visited the United States for the first time in 1930. She is married to Guy Patterson Chapman, and has one son. She still lives in Whitby, though she usually spends several months of the year in London, where she is president of the British section of the P.E.N. Club. An attractive blonde who looks younger than she is, Storm Jameson is a typical Yorkshirewoman, stubborn, rather secretive and reticent, with a hot temper, bulldog persistence, and immense vitality. She rides, drives, and bicycles, likes to dance, is a good cook, collects models and pictures of ships, and reads everything she can get relating to shipbuilding. Three of her books, *The Lovely Ship, The Voyage Home,* and *A Richer Dust,* form a trilogy of a shipbuilding family (probably her own) and its Victorian matriarch; some of her later novels have carried on the story of Mary Hervey's descendants. She is an outspoken liberal, whose horrifying *In the Second Year* was the English analogue of Sinclair Lewis' *It Can't Happen Here.*

Strange to say, this intense and rather aggressive personality melts to self-deprecation when it comes to her profession. She is surprised when her writings are praised, regards her own books with a jaundiced eye, and never feels that she has accomplished what she set out to do. As one critic remarked, "Her strong fighting spirit with regard to life is counteracted to some extent by her misgivings toward literature." She has even proposed that reviewers as a class be abolished because of the discouragement they bring to authors! Of herself she writes: "I have every talent of the good business man, shrewdness, persistence, a taste for strategy—except a talent for enjoying business. . . . The domestic routine of a house and a settled life worries me to death; I can't endure it. . . . I shall always be content that my mother was a Congregationalist and that what religion I got in my youth was colored by that stiff, self-regarding faith. It would be no use for me to deny to myself my noncomformist upbringing. Its narrow ideas of right and wrong, its distrust of enjoyment, are in my bones. . . . If I could begin my life again, but with half of the experience I have had of it, I would not live by writing. I am not what you call a born writer, and I should have been much happier as an engineer."

Yet Storm Jameson is one of the strongest as well as one of the most interesting of contemporary English novelists. It is true that, as John Chamberlain said, she "has the trick of skipping her big scenes"; she is given to understatement, to keeping all melodrama, and too often all drama, off-stage. But she can build real personalities, can bring her characters to solid life, and can construct a three-dimensional world. She is particularly happy in her evocation of the Victorian era. Her trilogy is no *Forsyte Saga,* but her Herveys and Russells are almost as real, background and all, as the Forsytes. That she is a woman is unmistakable in all her books; her feminism is so profound that she takes it for granted, and she is merciless to the kind of female of whom Clare Boothe writes; but, unlike many woman novelists, she can create credible masculine characters as well, who are both male and human. Toward struggling strength, she has deep and warm sympathy; for weakness, she has no pity at all.

Perhaps Storm Jameson's attitude toward life can be summed up in two sentences: She edited with enthusiasm a symposium called *Challenge to Death.* And she gave her autobiography the title, *No Time Like the Present.* She is as English as Yorkshire pudding, and as direct, clean-cut, and seabreasting as one of her own beloved ships.

In the Second World War, Storm Jameson's son, like his uncle before him, fought in the Royal Air Force.

PRINCIPAL WORKS: The Pot Boils, 1919; Happy Highways (non-fiction) 1920; Modern Drama in Europe, 1920; The Clash, 1922; The Pitiful Wife, 1923; Three Kingdoms, 1926; The Lovely Ship, 1927; Farewell to Youth, 1928; The Voyage Home, 1930; The Decline of Merry England (non-fiction) 1930; A Richer Dust, 1931; That Was Yesterday, 1932; The Triumph of Time, 1932; No Time Like The Present (autobiography) 1933; Women Against Men (novelettes) 1933-1937; Company Parade, 1934; Love in Winter, 1935; None Turn Back, 1936; In the Second Year, 1936; The Moon Is Making, 1937; Here Comes a Candle, 1938; Farewell Night, Welcome Day, 1939; Civil Journey (essays) 1939; Europe To Let: The Memoirs of an Obscure Man, 1940; Cousin Honoré, 1941; The Fort, 1941; The End of This War, 1941.

ABOUT: Atlantic Monthly February 1941; Bookman February 1933; Bookman (London) June 1926; Revue Politique et Littéraire November 21, 1925; Saturday Review of Literature January 29, 1938.

JAMMES, FRANCIS (December 2, 1868-November 1, 1938), French poet and novelist, was born at Tourney, Hautes-Pyrénées.

His father, a notary, had been born in Guadaloupe, French West Indies. The father became Keeper of Records at Bordeaux, and the son attended the university there, (he had previously studied at the Collège de Pau), but was a poor scholar. On the death of his father, Francis Jammes abandoned his half-hearted pursuit of the law, and with his mother set-

tled in her ancestral village of Orthez, Basses-Pyrénées. He lived there in seclusion for most of his life, moving a few years before his death to Hasparren, in the same province, where he died a month before his seventieth birthday. For a short time he worked in Orthez as a notary's clerk. He was married in 1906, and had seven children, one of whom became a nun. Although he had been reared as a Catholic he had been a very indifferent one, a nature-lover and almost a pantheist, until the poet Paul Claudel (later French ambassador to the United States) "converted" him in 1905. Thereafter he was primarily a Catholic poet; as Mary Duclaux put it, he was "a faun who turned Franciscan." Though in consequence he was hailed eagerly and highly lauded as "reconciling Nature and Grace" by critics among his co-religionists, actually the influence on his work was bad; his poetry became increasingly insipid, and he himself little more than a "pious shadow."

But his earlier poetry, though he had no scientific knowledge, was so informed by a passion for nature that, to quote W. A. Drake, he became, "so to speak, the Thoreau of France." Drake said that Jammes loved nature and animals "better than any poet since the Greeks had loved them. They have rewarded him . . . by making him a poet." His nature poems possessed a profound spontaneity and simplicity, and "an extraordinary faculty of objective and ironical, yet sympathetic, observation." In his prose fiction, he has written mostly about humble, provincial people, and has been particularly successful in depicting sensitive, spiritual young girls. Mme. Duclaux described him with his "ruddy, jocund, rustic face, a crown of grizzling curls, behind which Nature had provided the tonsure"; in his last years he became a gray-bearded patriarch. Only one volume of Jammes' work, *Romance of the Rabbit,* 1920, has been published in English, though many of his poems have appeared in English translation in magazines, mostly in *Poet Lore*: see particularly seven poems in that magazine, No. 2, 1940.

ABOUT: Braun, T. Des Poètes Simples: Francis Jammes; Bersancourt, A. de. Francis Jammes, Poète Chrétien; Drake, W. A. Contemporary European Writers; Duclaux, M. Twentieth Century French Writers; James F. Mémoires; Lowell, A. Six French Poets; Catholic World May 1926; Europe Nouvelle November 12, 1938; Mercure de France December 15, 1938; Poet Lore #4 1938; Publications Modern Language Association June 1932; Revue des Deux Mondes November 15, 1937, December 1, 1938; Saturday Review of Literature September 30, 1933.

JARRETT, Mrs. CORA (HARDY) (February 21, 1877-   ), American novelist, short-story writer, and writer of detective fiction, was born in Norfolk, Va., the daughter of Frederick and Charlotte Frances (Graves) Hardy, and educated at Pollock-Stephens Institute, Birmingham, Ala., from 1890 to 1894. After a succeeding year at Miss Baldwin's School, Bryn Mawr, Pa., she attended Bryn Mawr College itself, and received a B.A. degree in 1899. Abroad the next year, Miss Hardy studied at the Sorbonne, the Collège de France, and at Oxford University. From 1903 to 1904 she taught English and Greek at Ward-Belmont Seminary, Nashville, Tenn., following with three years as teacher of English at St. Timothy's School, Catonsville, Md. In 1906 her marriage to Edwin Seton Jarrett, a civil engineer, of New York City, took place. The Jarretts have two sons, Edwin Seton Jarrett and William Armistead Jarrett, and a daughter, Olivia Heather Jarrett, and make their home at Wild Goose Farm, Shepherdstown, W.Va. Mrs. Jarrett is a member of the Cosmopolitan Club in New York City, the Present Day Club in Princeton, N.J., and the Woman's Club of her place of residence.

Nearly twenty years elapsed between Mrs. Jarrett's first book, *The Cross Goes Westward,* published in 1910, and her next, *Peccadilloes* (1929). *Night Over Fitch's Pond,* the third, gained respectful and rather startled attention from critics as an unusual mystery story with psychological overtones. M. C. Dawson wrote in the New York *Herald Tribune "Books"*: "Every now and then a writer of discrimination hits on the fact that a mystery story growing out of the psychology of the characters is a thing capable of infinitely richer development than any ordinary thrillers." The *Nation* remarked that the author had not lived among college professors and their wives for nothing. Mrs. Jarrett's *Pattern in Black or Red,*

was published under the pseudonym of "Faraday Keene," but few critics were fooled by that. Her stories are much in demand by magazines. William Soskin has said that her chief fondness is for psychological overtones, the aberrations and violences caused by restraint in a polite social pattern. *The Ginkgo Tree* is a notable example of this preoccupation.

PRINCIPAL WORKS: The Cross Goes Westward, 1910; Peccadilloes, 1929; Night Over Fitch's Pond, 1933; Pattern in Black and Red (as "Faraday Keene") 1934; The Ginkgo Tree, 1935; Strange Houses, 1936; I Asked No Other Thing (short stories) 1937; The Silver String, 1937.

*JASTROW, JOSEPH (January 30, 1863-   ), American psychologist, was born in Warsaw, Poland; his father, Marcus (or Morris) Jastrow, was a rabbi. His mother was Bertha (Wolfsohn) Jastrow. He was brought to America at an early age, and educated at the University of Pennsylvania (B. A. 1882, M.A. 1885) and at Johns Hopkins University (Fellow

Keystone

in Psychology 1885-86, Ph.D. 1886). In 1928 he received an honorary 'LL.D. from the University of Würtemberg. He was professor of psychology at the University of Wisconsin for almost exactly forty years, from 1888 to 1927, and is now professor emeritus. He was president of the American Psychology Association in 1900, and was in charge of the psychology section of the Chicago World's Fair in 1893. From 1928 to 1932 he conducted a daily syndicated article in newspapers under the title, "Keeping Mentally Fit," and from 1935 to 1938 he broadcast weekly talks on psychology through the National Broadcasting Company, on a national hook-up.

Dr. Jastrow was married in 1888 to Rachel Szold, who died in 1926. They had no children of their own, but adopted a son. He lives now in New York, and is officially retired, though he is still a frequent contributor of articles to scientific and general periodicals. In 1910 he lectured at Columbia, and from 1927 to 1933 at the New School for Social Research.

For many years Dr. Jastrow has been the psychological gadfly, with his sting ready for any theory he considers absurd. He has been the outspoken enemy on the one hand of Freud and psychoanalysis, and on the

* Died January 9, 1944.

other of spiritualism and supernaturalism, including the "supersensory" experiments at Duke University. Though not devoid of prejudices himself, he has been a doughty foe of prejudice, and has been quick to point out emotional elements in public thought. He has a real gift for popularizing complex subjects, without descending to a merely journalistic level. On the whole he has exercised a healthful influence, puncturing with force and sometimes with wit the excesses arising from undue enthusiasm. He has found no psychological school to possess a panacea for our defects in thinking, and has in general been more engaged in pointing out defects and errors than in building up any opposition system of his own. His style, without being distinguished, is strong and lucid.

Besides his own books, he edited and contributed to *The Story of Human Error,* in 1936. He was also a contributor to *Epitomes of Three Sciences,* in 1890. He is rather heavy-set and stocky, bald, with a full face, a small moustache, and eyeglasses. His older brother was the late Morris Jastrow, Jr. (1861-1921), the distinguished Orientalist and professor at the University of Pennsylvania.

PRINCIPAL WORKS: Time Relations of Mental Phenomena, 1890; Fact and Fable in Psychology, 1900; The Subconscious, 1906; The Qualities of Men, 1910; Character and Temperament, 1915; The Psychology of Conviction, 1918; Keeping Mentally Fit, 1928; Piloting Your Life, 1903; Effective Thinking, 1931; The House That Freud Built, 1932; Wish and Wisdom, 1934; Sanity First, 1935; The Betrayal of Intelligence, 1938.

*JEANS, Sir JAMES HOPWOOD (September 11, 1877-), English astronomer and mathematical physicist, was born in London,  the son of W. T. Jeans. He was educated at the Merchant Taylors' School and at Trinity College, Cambridge, where he was Second Wrangler (second highest in mathematics) in 1898, Smith's Prizeman in 1900, and a Fellow in 1901. He has had honorary doctorates since from Oxford, Manchester, Benares, Aberdeen, Johns Hopkins, St. Andrew's, Dublin, and Calcutta. He was created a knight in 1928 and received the Order of Merit in 1939. He was a lecturer in mathematics at Cambridge until 1904, and then went to Princeton as professor of applied mathematics, staying in America from 1905 to 1909. In 1907 he married an American, Charlotte Tiffany Mitchell, who died in 1934, leaving a daughter. In 1935 he married Susi Hock, an Austrian, and they have a son.

From Princeton he returned to Cambridge, where he was Stokes Lecturer in Applied Mathematics from 1910 to 1912. From 1919 to 1929 he was secretary of the Royal Society. In 1922 he was Halley Lecturer at Oxford, and from 1924 to 1929 professor of astronomy for the Royal Institution; in 1934 he resumed this post, which he still holds. Since 1923 he has also been a research associate of Mount Wilson Observatory in California. His honors have been innumerable: he is a Fellow of the Royal Society, was president of the Royal Astronomical Society from 1925 to 1927 and of the British Association for the Advancement of Science in 1934, was president of the Indian Science Congress Association at its Jubilee Congress in 1938, and has received the Royal Medal of the Royal Society (1919), the gold medal of the Royal Astronomical Society (1922), the Franklin Medal of the Franklin Institute, Philadelphia (1931), the Mukerjee Medal of the Indian Association for the Cultivation of Science (1937), and the Calcutta Medal of the Royal Asiatic Society of Bengal (1938). He is also a member of the Advisory Council to the Privy Council Committee for Science and Industry. He lives in Dorking, Surrey.

In physics Sir James has developed the kinetic theory of gases and worked on various aspects of radiation, particularly the interrelation of radiation and free electrons. In astronomy, his special field has been cosmogony, with particular reference to mathematical analysis of its problems. He has developed theories of the effect of gravitational motion on the motion of stars, of the nature and formation of binary stars, spiral nebulae, giant and dwarf stars, and gaseous stars, and on the source of stellar energy. With Professor Harold Jeffreys of Cambridge, he is the author of a theory of the origin of our solar system which, though still debated, has been widely accepted by other cosmogonists.

It will thus be seen that Jeans is one of the great scientists of all time, and one of the greatest living today. He has also, especially in his non-technical books, such as *The Mysterious Universe* and *The Stars in Their Courses,* undertaken to be a philosopher as well. In the spirit of the saying that "man made God in his own image," Sir James' God is "the great mathematician." To him nothing real exists except mathematics; mathematical formulae are the only objective reality. Like other distinguished physicists, such as Sir A. S. Eddington and Dr. Robert A. Millikan, he has exalted Heisinger's "indeterminacy principle" into a philosophical concept, and has evolved from the study of electrons a theory of supernaturalism. More materialistic thinkers have attacked him as "a modern Pythagoras," because of this bent.

Apart from this tendency, Sir James is not only a profound scientist, but also, in the words of Ivor Thomas, "a master of the arresting phrase," with "a rich imagination working through a flexible pen." As H. L. Mencken said, he has "a really extraordinary gift for making the most difficult of scientific concepts understandable." It is not strange that his popular works have actually become best-sellers.

PRINCIPAL WORKS: A Dynamical Theory of Gases, 1904; Theoretical Mechanics, 1906; The Mathematical Theory of Electricity and Magnetism, 1908; Radiation and the Quantum-Theory, 1914; Problems of Cosmogony and Stellar Dynamics, 1919; Atomicity and Quanta, 1926; Astronomy and Cosmogony, 1928; Eos, or the Wider Aspects of Cosmogony, 1928; The Universe Around Us, 1929; The Mysterious Universe, 1930; The Stars in Their Courses, 1931; The New Background of Science, 1933; Through Space and Time, 1934; Science and Music, 1937; An Introduction to the Kinetic Theory of Gases, 1940.

ABOUT: Stebbing, L. S. Philosophy and the Physicists; American Mercury February 1931; American Scholar #1 1937; Contemporary Review January 1931; Hibbert Journal April 1931; Nature December 8 and 29, October 13, 1934, January 7, 1939; Nineteenth Century October 1934; Philosophical Magazine February 1935; Science August 21, 1931, April 19, 1935; Scientific American May 1932.

JEFFERS, ROBINSON (January 10, 1887-   ), American poet, was born in Pittsburgh, Pa., the son of Dr. William Hamilton

Jeffers and Annie Robinson (Tuttle) Jeffers. He was educated by tutors and at private schools in Switzerland and Germany, at the University of Pittsburgh, and at Occidental College, Los Angeles, where he received his B.A. in 1905. He then

E. Weston

did graduate work in English and three years' medical work at the University of Southern California, and studied "desultorily" at the University of Zürich. He has besides done a year's work in forestry at the University of Washington. All this was

a futile effort to find an occupation of interest to him; as a matter of fact it was only poetry that concerned him deeply, and in those years he had no money to contemplate a purely literary life. He was an athlete in college—a mile runner and a champion swimmer—and he has retained his athletic ability. In later years he received honorary doctorates from Occidental and the University of Southern California, and he is an honorary Phi Beta Kappa. In 1937 he received the Book Club award for distinguished work.

In 1913 Jeffers married Una Call Kuster. They have twin sons. In 1914, when he was about to set out for England in the hope of finding it easier to live by writing there, an uncle died and left him a legacy sufficient to enable him to lead the life he desired. It was then that he went to Carmel, Calif., and on Point Sur, the scene of so many of his poems, built with his own hands the stone house and its accompanying stone tower in which he works, where for thirty-five years he has led almost a hermit existence.

Not entirely so, however: he has traveled often in the West, and in 1929 and 1937 made extended trips to the British Isles; the myths of his inaccessibility are largely myths alone. He has good friends but they are few, and he does not want new ones; least of all does he want the easy publicity and sociability which come from dealing with strangers. He is a slow worker, and he prefers for the most part to be alone with his work and his family, leaving Mrs. Jeffers as his "buffer" with the outside world. In his own words, his amusements are "stonemasonry, tree-planting, swimming, pipe-smoking, drives and walks in the Coast Range, reverent admiration of hawks, herons and pelicans; discarded amusements, long-distance running, wrestling, alcoholism, canoeing; idiosyncrasies, almost perfect inability to write a letter or kill an animal, love of monotony and wet weather." Six feet tall, powerfully built, bronzed by the sun, with searching blue-gray eyes, he looks like an Indian, and has aptly been called "tomahawk-faced."

It is from the world in which he lives, and which in his philosophy is a place of stern, lonely beauty marred by the infestation of doomed and perverted animals called human beings, that he has drawn the long measures of his cadenced poetry, which is nearer to the Greeks than to Whitman, and at its best has the rhythm of the sea. As Delmore Schwartz said, the background of Jeffers' poems is "the world-picture of nineteenth century science, the World War, and Jeffers' portion of the Pacific Coast." Frajam Taylor noted the constant antithesis of his two chief symbols—the hawk, the wild undirected spirit of man, and the stone, the rooted and immemorial earth. To Jeffers, civilization is toppling to its doom, man himself may be a dying race, and the world will be all the better for it. It is a viewpoint which makes for bare, unrelieved tragedy; and though at its heights it produces supreme poetry, it hesitates always on the very verge of hysteria and absurdity. "Civilization is a transient sickness." "Humanity is needless." That is a creed for a hawk, not for a man.

"His attitude," said Hildegarde Flanner in a penetrating study, "is supremely negative, his protest has been set down in tragic and distorted sexual images. . . . All his themes are of vehemence, intensely and frequently frustrated passion, perversion, bitter introspection, . . . symbols . . . of civilization turning in upon itself, . . . a kind of willing insanity. . . . His powers of realism and tempo are miraculous, [but they are] used on people whose pathology is so absolute that their problems can be only the problems of the mad."

Jeffers is a unique phenomenon in American and indeed in world literature. Sometimes he is grandiose rather than grand, sometimes his unremitting monotony of doom grows wearying, but of his fierce and original genius there can be no doubt.

PRINCIPAL WORKS: Flagons and Apples, 1912; Californians, 1916; Roan Stallion, Tamar and Other Poems, 1925; The Women at Point Sur, 1927; Cawdor and Other Poems, 1928; Dear Judas and Other Poems, 1929; Descent to the Dead, 1931; Thurso's Landing and Other Poems, 1932; Give Your Heart to the Hawks, 1933; Solstice, 1935; Such Counsels You Gave to Me, 1937; Selected Poetry, 1939; Two Consolations 1940; Be Angry at the Sun, 1941.

ABOUT: Adamic, L. Robinson Jeffers: A Portrait; Alberts, S. Bibliography of Robinson Jeffers; Bennet, M. Robinson Jeffers and the Sea; Gilbert, R. Shine, Perishing Republic: Robinson Jeffers and the Tragic Sense in Modern Poetry; Greenan, E. Of Una Jeffers; Powell, De L. C. Robinson Jeffers: The Man and His Work; Sterling, G. Robinson Jeffers: The Man and the Artist; Van Wyck, W. Robinson Jeffers; Canadian Forum January 1939; New Republic January 27, 1937; Poetry March 1934, February 1937, January 1938, October 1939, December 1941; Saturday Review of Literature September 5, 1931, March 9, 1935, December 2, 1935, October 23, 1937.

---

*JENSEN, JOHANNES VILHELM (January 20, 1873-), Danish novelist, was born in Farsö, North Jutland, of peasant stock, though his father was a veterinarian. He went to school in Viborg, and then

* Died November 25, 1950.

began the study of medicine at the University of Copenhagen. He did not complete the course, however, but left college to write and travel. He has been and still is an intensive traveler. He came to America first in 1897 and has been here many times since; two of his early novels were laid in Chicago. His first novel was published in 1896, but he did not attain any wide celebrity until the publication of *Himmerland Stories* in 1898, a volume based on his memories of his childhood home in Jutland. Although he had long been a noted figure in Scandinavian literature, he was not widely known in other countries until the appearance of his six-volume epic of the emergence and history of the Cimbrians, the Teutonic race, probably originating in Jutland, which gradually overran Europe. This work, called in English *The Long Journey*, covers the period from the Ice Age to the time of Columbus, whom Jensen claimed as a Cimbrian. ("Himmerland" is supposed to be derived from "Cimberland," and Cumberland in England may have the same derivation.)

In Denmark previous to the publication of this epic (beginning in 1908), Jensen had been known principally as the leader of the younger generation of novelists and the arch-enemy of the nineteenth-century school led by Georg Brandes. He is not only a novelist, but is also a poet and dramatist (he translated *Hamlet* into Danish), an essayist and philosopher, and a journalist who for many years has contributed regularly to *Politiken*. Though he did not finish his medical studies, he retained from them a life-long interest in science, and he was one of the leading exponents of Darwinism in the Scandinavian countries. In religion he is an outspoken Free Thinker. He lectures a great deal, and in the course of his talks has introduced to Denmark many American authors, from Walt Whitman to Ernest Hemingway. He has done yeoman work on behalf of the preservation of the relics of Denmark's history, and also for the provision of adequate housing for Danish university students. He is a keen sportsman and hunter, an amateur sculptor, a good smith, mason, and woodcarver—he has even made violins. He is married, with three sons, two of whom are physicians. With his family [before the Nazi occupation] he lived in Copenhagen, with a summer home in Zealand, on the seashore, which he and his sons built themselves. Personally he is a very retiring, modest man who shuns publicity. He was blond before he turned gray, but though he has the Nordic fairness he has not the Nordic height, being short in stature. With his lined, smooth-shaven face, his horn-rimmed glasses, and his nervous speech, to his fellow-countrymen he seems to be "American" in appearance.

Jensen has been for many years the foremost fighter in Denmark for a realistic, naturalistic literature, as contrasted with the "Europeanism" of Brandes. He has often written in too much haste and under too much pressure, and his knowledge of science is sometimes too superficial for the use he makes of it, but at his best—in his lyric poems (which unfortunately have not been translated into English) and in his great epic "myth"—he is undoubtedly, as Walter Berendsohn put it, "one of the best brains and most fertile writers in Scandinavia." Knut Hamsun called him "a visionary by means of all his five senses," and Berendsohn said of him: "He breaks the old shape of the myth . . . by giving it new content. . . . He is full of the sense of reality. . . . His imagination never flags." His language is fresh and plastic, his style is masterly, and his poetry, which is often in the old ballad forms, has been called "firm yet visionary."

WORKS AVAILABLE IN ENGLISH: The Long Journey (Fire and Ice, The Cimbrians, Christopher Columbus) 1923-24; The Fall of the King, 1933.

ABOUT: Gelsted O. Johannes V. Jensen (in Danish); Rosenfeld, P. Men Seen; Topsöe-Jensen, H. C. Scandinavian Literature; American-Scandinavian Review October 1929; Bookman October 1923; Contemporary Review July 1938.

JEROME, JEROME KLAPKA (May 2, 1859-June 14, 1927), English humorist and playwright, was born at Bradford street,

Walsall, Staffordshire, the son of Jerome Clapp Jerome and Marguerite (Jones) Jerome. The boy's middle name was not derived from that of his father, an impecunious Nonconformist preacher, but from George Klapka, a Hungarian general in exile, a frequent guest of the Jeromes. The family moved to the Poplar district of London near Limehouse where the elder Jerome worked as an ironmonger. The

boy's chief reading matter was Foxe's Book of Martyrs, but after the passage of W. E. Forster's Education Bill he entered the Philological School, where he stayed until fourteen. His mother died the next year, and Jerome became a clerk at £26 a year for the London & Northwestern Railway Company at Euston, living in one cheap lodging house after another and reading in the British Museum. Working as a super whetted his theatrical appetite, and he toured the provinces for three years, becoming thoroughly acquainted with the Hero, Heroine, Comic Man, Peasantry, and so on, amusingly described in Stageland (1886). Jerome also tried his hand as a shorthand reporter, parliamentary agent, and assistant schoolmaster. His well-known Idle Thoughts of an Idle Fellow, sold to Home Chimes at fourteen guineas apiece, gave him confidence to enter journalism, and he began to conduct a "Gossip's Corner" in the magazine. In 1888 he married Georgina Henrietta Stanley. Four years later Jerome became joint editor of the Idler, with Robert Barr, and in 1893 launched his own paper, To-Day, with Stevenson's Ebb-Tide as a star serial attraction. A damage suit, in which his opponent was awarded one farthing but Jerome incurred costs of £9,000, made it necessary to sell both papers.

Now he began to write plays in earnest. Charles Hawtrey produced Barbara; Bernard Partridge played in New Lamps for Old; and various one-act plays and curtain-raisers were accepted. Jerome's collaborators included Haddon Chambers, Eden Phillpotts, and Justin McCarthy. He recommended Mary Ansell as an actress to J. M. Barrie, who married her. Miss Hobbs was an especially good money-maker, but was eclipsed by The Passing of the Third Floor Back, which the late Johnston Forbes-Robertson and his wife, Gertrude Elliott, introduced to the London public September 1, 1908, and which played for seven successful years in Great Britain and America. The characters were Bloomsbury boarding-house lodgers respectively labelled Cheat, Slut, Painted Lady, Hussy, and so on; they were converted by a "Stranger" who was the better self or real self of each. Sybil Thorndike remarked dryly of this modern morality play that "the play seems to me to go further in the direction of actual preaching than is, in my opinion, truly representative of the theatre."

Jerome's immensely successful book of humor, Three Men in a Boat, was written in his thirtieth year, shortly after his marriage. A million (pirated) copies were sold in America. This and his autobiographical novel, *Paul Kelver,* were highly regarded in Russia, and *Three Men* was used as a school text in Germany. Dickens and Mark Twain were evident influences in his work. During the First World War he volunteered his services to France as an ambulance driver, and was sent as a propaganda agent to Washington. *My Life and Times,* his autobiography, appeared in 1926.

Jerome was a handsome man, with black eyes, silver-white hair and a well-knit, robust frame. He was occasionally mistaken for Lord Oxford and Asquith. His later years were spent on a country estate, Monk's Corner, in Marlow, Buckinghamshire. While traveling in England he was stricken with a cerebral hemorrhage and removed to Northampton Hospital, where he died. His burial place is Ewelm, Oxfordshire, in the chancel of the same church where Chaucer's son is interred.

PRINCIPAL WORKS: On the Stage and Off, 1885; Idle Thoughts of an Idle Fellow, 1889; Three Men in a Boat, 1889; New Lamps for Old, 1889; Novel Notes, 1893; John Ingerfield, 1894; The Second Thoughts of an Idle Fellow, 1898; Miss Hobbs, 1900; Paul Kelver, 1902; The Passing of the Third Floor Back, 1907; They and I, 1909; The Great Gamble, 1914; Malvina of Brittany, 1917; Anthony John, 1923; My Life and Times, 1926.

ABOUT: Adcock, A. St. J. The Glory That Was Grub Street; Chevalley, A. The Modern English Novel; Kernahan, C. Celebrities; Moss, A. Jerome K. Jerome; Bookman (London) September 1926; Golden Book August 1933; London Mercury July 1927; Outlook June 29, 1927; Saturday Review of Literature June 25, 1927.

JESSE, FRINIWYD TENNYSON, Eng-
lish novelist, dramatist, and criminologist, writes: "I am (like most people!) the child

of a clergyman—the Rev. Eustace Tennyson d'Eyncourt Jesse. I am a great-niece of Alfred Lord Tennyson. I have earned my own living since I was twenty. I started as a journalist 'on space' for the *Times* and the *Daily Mail,* and also did book reviewing for the *Times Literary Supplement* and the *English Review.* [In 1914 she came to New York and worked briefly on the *Metropolitan Magazine.*] I was a war correspondent in the last war, but not accredited to any newspaper, as in those days it was not considered decent to send a young girl to the front. Naturally I went, though in much less safety than had I had

any credentials. I also worked during the last war for the Ministry of Information, which was not so laughable as it is now; also for the National Relief Commission, of which the head was Herbert Hoover, later your president, but who of course was far too great and far-away for me ever to meet him, as I was the smallest cog in that great wheel. I also was *Visiteuse des Hôpitaux de la Croix Rouge Française* [visitor for the French Red Cross] in small French frontline hospitals.

"I am married to one of England's best-known playwrights, H. M. Harwood. He is a doctor and a business man as well as a playwright. Since we were married in 1918 we have lived almost all over the world, and we know and love America well, hence our letters to our friends there which are now [1941] being published in book form. Our chief hobby in the days when we could afford such a thing was sailing; it is many years since we have been able to indulge in that. I started life as an art student and have found even my slight knowledge of drawing and painting invaluable to me in writing, as it does enable one to see. I am very fond of flying, and my chief passion is murder."

* * *

This last statement of course is to be taken as having purely literary significance! One of Miss Jesse's chief contributions to criminological theory is the suggestion that just as there are "born murderers," there are also born "murderees"—people who seem destined to be murdered. In collaboration with her husband, she wrote and produced the plays, *The Mask, Billeted, The Pelican,* and *How To Be Healthy Though Married,* and is the sole author of *Quarantine* and *Anyhouse.* In addition to her novels (some of which have a murder background) and her *Murder and Its Motives,* she has edited a number of cases for the Notable British Trials Series. The Harwoods' wartime letters from the "London Front" were written to S. N. Behrman, Alexander Woollcott, and other American friends. The Harwoods live in St. John's Wood, London; they have no children.

PRINCIPAL WORKS: *Novels*—The Milky Way, 1913; Beggars on Horseback, 1915; Secret Bread, 1917; The White Riband, 1921; Tom Fool, 1926; Moonraker, 1927; The Lacquer Lady, 1929; Solange Stories, 1931; A Pin To See the Peep-Show, 1934; Act of God, 1936. *Non-Fiction*—The Sword of Deborah: First Hand Impressions of the British Women's Army in France, 1919; The Happy Bride (poems) 1920; Murder and Its Motives, 1924; Many Latitudes, 1928; Sabi Pas: or I Don't Know, 1935; London Front (with H. M. Harwood) 1940; While London Burns (with H. M. Harwood) 1942.

ABOUT: Jesse, J. The London Front, While London Burns; John O' London's Weekly January 6, 1939; World Today July 1924.

*JEWELL, EDWARD ALDEN (March 10, 1888-), American art critic and novelist, writes: "Pisces froze. I helped bring

in the blizzard of 1888. I was born at Grand Rapids, Mich. Ancestral strains (mingling in deep-rooted American stock): English on the side of my father, Frank Jewell, and Dutch on that of my mother, whose maiden name was Jennie 'Agnes Ousterhout. Early life spent in Michigan. Educated in public and private schools; but not until entering Friends' School, in Washington, D.C., at the age of seventeen, did I feel that 'education' was worth the pain of it. Up to the age of about twenty-two interest centered, passionately, in the theatre. From the age of eight on, managed, wrote plays for, and acted in, my own theatre. It was in the attic and was called the Imperial. As playwright, gradually gave way to Shakespeare. This long passion for the stage ended in a brief professional career (with Louis James, then with Donald Robertson).

"Around 1910, a radical change. Realized at that time it was creative, not interpretive, work that I wanted. Turned to the writing of epic poetry (!) and novels. In lieu of college, for which no use was had, lived and studied abroad (1910-11). Returning home, became a cub (later drama critic) on the Grand Rapids *Herald*, a paper then owned by my uncle, Senator William Alden Smith, and edited by Arthur Vandenberg.

"Married Manette Lansing Carpenter in 1914. A year in Washington as one of Senator Smith's secretaries. Then we moved to New York, with our infant daughter (an only child). Bessie Breuer, at that time Sunday editor of the old *Tribune*, gave me my first New York job. In 1916 edited the *World Court Magazine*. Served, 1916-17, as an associate editor of *Everybody's*. Returned to the *Tribune* as Sunday editor (Garet Garrett was then the executive editor) and remained until the close of 1919. Interlude: just, as it developed, at the tail-end of the World War, got a commission (second lieutenant) in the Chemical Warfare Service; trained for a few weeks at Camp Humphreys in Virginia and at Camp

Kendrick in New Jersey; expected to be sent overseas; then the Armistice, and I was back at the *Tribune*.

"Meanwhile, for years, had been pegging away at fiction, writing at 4 A.M. and on the top of busses. At the close of 1919 we went to Bermuda, where, over a period of months, two manuscripts, long in progress, were completed, and a third novel was got well under way. The three novels were published in rapid succession. An *impasse* reached in writing the fourth novel is still operative. Finally abandoning fiction, I returned to magazine work (a few months with *Success*) and to journalism, spending some time abroad—first as a free lance, then (in Ireland) as foreign correspondent for the *Christian Science Monitor*. Early in 1925, joined the Sunday department of the New York *Times*, and in 1927 became associate art critic, continuing as such until the death, in 1936, of the senior critic, Elizabeth Luther Cary. Since then have been art critic and editor.

"I do some lecturing and have written two books on art. I have no hobbies, and my sole recreation is taking trips on freighters."

PRINCIPAL WORKS: The Charmed Circle, 1921; The White Kami, 1922; The Moth Decides, 1922; Americans (art criticism) 1930; Have We an American Art? 1939.

ABOUT: Forum November and December 1935.

JEWETT, SARAH ORNE. See "AMERICAN AUTHORS: 1600-1900"

*JOAD, CYRIL EDWIN MITCHINSON (August 12, 1891-), English philosopher who writes as C. E. M. Joad, was born in London, the son of Edwin and Mary (Smith) Joad. He was educated at Blundell's School, Tiverton, and at Balliol College, Oxford, where he was John Locke Scholar in Moral Philosophy in 1914. He became a pacifist and a Social-

ist in Oxford, and was a conscientious objector during the First World War. He was also at this time a feminist, but since then (perhaps because of an unsuccessful marriage) has expressed himself freely on the "inferior mind" and "nuisance value" of women. He was an early disciple of Wells and Shaw, and has remained unchanged in the changing years since. He has also been all his adult life a Rationalist of the nine-

* Died October 11, 1947. * Died April 9, 1953.

teenth century variety; he has been a life-long student of psychic phenomena, but his judgment on their credibility is adverse, and he is unalterably opposed to what he calls "the cult of unreason," in which he includes psycho-analysis, Behaviorism, and Marxism (his Socialism being of the un-Marxian school).

He was for sixteen years in the Civil Service, first in the Board of Trade, then in the Ministry of Labor. He retired in 1930 to become head of the department of philosophy and psychology in Birbeck College, University of London. This university gave him a D.Litt. degree in 1936. He lives in Hampstead, "in an ugly but comfortable house overlooking the Heath." His recreations are tennis, chess, and bridge; his mornings he gives to work, the rest of the day to social life. He is a passionate champion of the freeing of caged or performing animals, and has written bitterly on the spoiling of the English countryside, scene of his many walking tours. He is fond of good cooking and good eating, loves music (but nothing later than Beethoven), and says he would rather do any other kind of work than write. He wears a full beard and dresses deliberately in a slovenly manner more suggestive of a tramp than of a college professor. It was he who in 1938 shocked the academicians by proposing a moratorium on science, which he blamed for the industrialization and standardization of society. In other words, he has been well called "the Mencken of England," though he and Mencken would be at sword's points on most issues.

He himself says: "I admire reason and the free movement of the mind. I like art that is measured and formal, and I think of the good life as an affair of playing games and rambling over mountains as a relief from the rigors of intellectual effort, . . . the backbone of one's life." Literary style he considers "a nuisance," and he says: "Writing is the most arduous form of occupation I know"—in which condemnation he includes the physical labor of writing as well as the mental toil.

Leonard Bacon, who is in hearty disagreement with Joad's views, called his "a mind of the second order with a flair for exhibitionism," but even he acknowledged that Joad was "skillful at the legerdemain of dialectics." Another kindlier critic called him "by turns persuasive, glib, caustic, and profound." However he may antagonize others by his forthrightness as well as by a certain hide-bound quality of mind, much of his writing is based on solid work and

straight thinking, and where it is not marred by "professorial archness and cockney philistinism" (to quote Bacon again), it is stimulating and provocative. In addition to his books on philosophy and similar subjects, he is the author of several early novels, which he is content to have forgotten.

PRINCIPAL WORKS: Essays in Common Sense Philosophy, 1919; Common Sense Ethics, 1921; Common Sense Theology, 1922; Introduction to Modern Political Theory, 1924; Thrasymachus: or, The Future of Morals, 1924 (revised, as The Future of Morals, 1936); Samuel Butler, 1924; Introduction to Modern Philosophy, 1924; Mind and Matter, 1925; The Babbitt Warren, 1927; Diogenes: or, The Future of Leisure, 1928; The Mind and Its Workings, 1928; The Future of Life, A Theory of Vitalism, 1928; The Meaning of Life, 1929; Matter, Life and Value, 1929; The Present and Future of Religion, 1930; The Story of Civilization (juvenile) 1931; The Horrors of the Countryside, 1931; Great Philosophies of the World, 1931; Philosophical Aspects of Modern Science, 1932; Under the Fifth Rib: A Belligerent Autobiography, 1933 (as The Book of Joad, 1937); Counter-Attack From the East, 1933; Is Christianity True? (with A. Lunn) 1933; Guide to Modern Thought, 1933; A Charter for Ramblers, 1934; Liberty Today, 1935; Return to Philosophy, 1935; The Story of Indian Civilization, 1936; The Dictator Resigns, 1936; Guide to Philosophy, 1936; Guide to the Philosophy of Morals and Politics, 1938; Why War? 1939; A Philosophy for Our Times, 1940; Journey Through the War Mind, 1940; What Is at Stake, and Why Not Say So? 1940.

ABOUT: Joad, C. E. M. Under the Fifth Rib; Saturday Review of Literature June 3, 1933; Time August 22, 1938.

*JOHNS, ORRICK (June 2, 1887-), American poet, writes: "I was born in St. Louis, Mo., educated at its public schools, the University of Missouri, and Washington University. During vacations, I was a reporter and man-of-all-trades— among them Deputy City Marshal. My first swell job was as assistant to William Marion Reedy, editor of *Reedy's Mirror*  and one of the last really great 'personal journalists.' I reviewed plays, books, music, and fine arts! Helped to found the Players' Club of St. Louis, with which were associated such future stars as Morris Carnovsky, Henry Hull, and Sidney Blackmer, and became president of it for a term. Winner *Lyric Year* national poetry prize, 1912, with 'Second Avenue.' In New York I was an early member of the Liberal Club, meeting over Polly's restaurant in Macdougal Street, saw the first productions of the Provincetown Players, and was a fellow of the first

American 'Left Bank' in Greenwich Village. Was one of the early contributors to *Poetry,* and an associate of Alfred Kreymborg, the poet and editor of *Others.* Went into advertising copy writing for many years, but continued to publish verse and prose in magazines. In 1923 Margaret Anglin produced my comedy, *A Charming Conscience,* of which she was the most charming feature. Went to Italy in 1926 for a short vacation and stayed three and a half years. Lived in Capri, Naples, Florence, Venice, Sicily—and was probably the only American to be operated on for appendicitis on the slopes of Mt. Etna. Migrated to Carmel, Calif., in 1929, and married Caroline Blackman. Our daughter was born there. In San Francisco, associated with liberal and left-wing groups, organizing fruit and vegetable workers— ranch-running in an old Ford; also labor defense, the movement to free Tom Mooney and other labor leaders. Continued this work in Missouri and New York City, became an associate editor of the *New Masses,* and co-organizer of first American Writers' Congress and the League of American Writers. Was appointed Director of Federal Writers' Project, WPA, in New York City, served 1935-36.

"I have seen nothing but wars in my time: labor wars, national and international wars, slave insurrections, civil wars, cultural wars, and literary wars. Sad, but necessary to great change. I was exempted from military service by physical disability, but have had a modest share in two civil victories: the revolution in American arts and literature, their release from the anaemia of my boyhood days; and the awakening of labor and social consciousness in America. I have voted for Bryan, Wilson, Debs, Norman Thomas, William Z. Foster, and Franklin Roosevelt for president. The last-named is the best we have had for seventy years, not for achievement but for transfusing government arteries with human blood. I am about what I was years before the big dollar dive: a radical Missouri Democrat and a Roman Catholic.

"Hobby: wood carving and carpentry. Present occupations: writing a book short enough to take a long time, and trying to keep a few Connecticut acres free from snowdrifts in winter, weeds, sassafras, rocks in summer, and the sheriff all the time. After my first wife's death, married, in 1937, Doria Berton."

* * *

Mr. Johns was one of the pioneers of the "new poetry" in America. He is best known,

however, as the author of *Time of Our Lives,* largely a biography of his father, an old-time newspaper man.

PRINCIPAL WORKS: *Poetry*—Asphalt, 1919; Black Branches, 1920; Wild Plum, 1926. *Miscellaneous*—Blindfold (novel) 1923; Time of Our Lives, the Story of My Father and Myself, 1937.

ABOUT: Johns, O. Time of Our Lives; Untermeyer, L. American Poetry Since 1900.

JOHNSON, JAMES WELDON (June 17, 1871-June 26, 1938), American Negro poet and essayist, had a truly amazing career. Born in Jacksonville, Fla., the son of James and Helen Louise (Dillette) Johnson, he received his B.A. and M.A. degrees at Atlanta University, in 1894 and 1904 respectively, and also studied for three years at Columbia. He started as teacher  in and principal of a Negro school in Jacksonville which he built up to high school grade, and at the same time studied law. In 1897 he was admitted to the Florida bar, as the first Negro attorney since the Civil War. In 1901 he went to New York where he and his brother, J. Rosamund Johnson, together with Bob Cole, collaborated in the writing of popular songs and light opera with great success. On one song they cleared $13,000, which they took to France and promptly spent in several light-hearted months. Johnson then was appointed United States Consul, first in Venezuela, then in Nicaragua, and was as successful a diplomat as he had been a song writer.

In 1910 he married Grace Nail, and two years later his first book, the fictional *Autobiography of an Ex-Colored Man,* appeared anonymously (its authorship was not acknowledged until 1927). He edited a book of American Negro poetry and two of Negro spirituals; he wrote the English libretto for the opera *Goyescas,* which was produced at the Metropolitan in 1915; he was long secretary of the National Association for the Advancement of Colored People, and he received the Spingarn Medal in 1925. Finally, without ceasing to write, he returned to teaching. In 1930 he became professor of creative literature at Fisk University, and from 1934 was also visiting professor of literature at New York University.

This remarkably useful career was cut short in its prime when, near his summer home at Dark Harbor, Maine, a railroad train struck his automobile. Johnson was killed instantly, his wife seriously injured.

The anonymous novel which first made his fame is probably the best piece of writing Johnson did. He was a vigorous and shrewd polemic writer in defense of his race, but as a poet he clung too closely to conventional forms; as Harold Rosenberg put it, he was "a Negro poet only in the sense that he applied his academic art to the situation of the American Negro." Occasionally, however, as in the free verse sermons entitled *God's Trombones,* he transcended the academic tradition and gave utterance to simple, powerful and truly poetic lines.

It was in personality that Johnson came nearest to greatness. Oswald Garrison Villard, who called him, in no invidious sense, "a fine gentleman," commented that in a long friendship he had found Johnson "never discouraged or without hope of a better world, with a judgment sane, calm, and detached."

PRINCIPAL WORKS: The Autobiography of an Ex-Colored Man, 1912; Fifty Years and Other Poems, 1917; Self-Determining Haiti, 1920; God's Trombones, 1927; Black Manhattan, 1930; St. Peter Relates an Incident of the Resurrection Day (verse) 1930; Negro Americans, What Now? 1934; Along This Way, 1934; Selected Poems, 1936.

ABOUT: Johnson, J. W. Along This Way; Christian Century July 13, 1938; Etude October 1938; Nation July 2 and 9, 1938; Poetry October 1936; Saturday Review of Literature July 9, 1938; School and Society September 3, 1938.

JOHNSON, JOSEPHINE WINSLOW
(June 20, 1910-   ), American novelist and poet, writes: "My parents were Benjamin

and Ethel (Franklin) Johnson, of Irish, Scotch, and English ancestry. I was born in Kirkwood, Mo., and attended private and public schools there. We moved to the country in 1922 on a hundred-acre farm. I have always loved the country and nature more than anything else. I went to Washington University, St. Louis, and specialized in English courses. I also took art training there. I started publishing short stories and poetry in magazines at this time. I painted murals in two children's schools in St. Louis and exhibited water color paintings. I traveled in the West, South, East, and in Europe. I did not graduate but left college and started writing and painting. I wrote *Now in November* [which won the

Pulitzer Prize for fiction in 1934], taught at the Bread Loaf Writers' Conference in Middlebury, Vt., became interested in social work, wrote newspaper articles for the St. Louis *Post-Dispatch* and *Star-Times* on sharecroppers and local strike and relief conditions. I was president of the Consumers' Co-operative organization in 1938, and am actively interested in co-operatives and in social and political reform. I believe in abolishing the 'profit system' and desire a true democracy—economically as well as politically.

"I am very much interested in books, particularly poetry, in cooking, walking, the making of puppets, in all forms of art, in animals (pigs, hedgehogs, hawks, bats, sheep, and all the others too). I have no discrimination in literary tastes. I love beautiful writing. I hate to speak in public. I am on the board of the St. Louis Urban League, a member of an organization to aid sharecroppers, a member of the American Civil Liberties Union, the Fellowship of Reconciliation, the Authors' Guild, the Co-operative Consumers of St. Louis, and various other organizations. I was married in 1939 to Thurlow Smoot, regional attorney for the National Labor Relations Board. I am living at present in St. Louis and Webster Groves, Mo."

* * *

In addition to the Pulitzer Prize, in the same year Miss Johnson was represented in the O. Henry Memorial Volume, with her first published short story, called variously "Dark" and "Genacht," which has often been reprinted. At that time Ellery Sedgwick spoke of her "unmistakable gift of style," which is the most obvious aspect of her writing. Louis Untermeyer praised the "unpretentious but unmistakable power" of her "quiet and beautiful prose." It has depth and music, though it is sometimes lacking in clarity. She is still young, and it remains to be seen whether she will develop beyond her present rather rigidly limited *genre.* Her poetry is at once lyric and intellectual, and rather cold. She herself looks like a poet, with blown dark hair and a long, delicately aquiline face which somewhat recalls the aristocratic beauty of Elinor Wylie. "I hate standardization, ugliness, narrowness of life," she says. "I wish that everyone could see the significance and beauty of ordinary things."

Miss Johnson should not be confused with Josephine Johnson of Norfolk, Va., one of the *Lyric* group, who has published only poetry and has never appeared as a prose-writer.

PRINCIPAL WORKS: Now in November, 1934; Winter Orchard and Other Stories, 1935; Jordanstown 1937; Year's End (poems) 1937; Paulina (juvenile) 1939.

ABOUT: Saturday Review of Literature May 11, 1935; Scholastic January 8, 1938; Wilson Library Bulletin June 1935.

JOHNSON, LIONEL PIGOT. See "BRITISH AUTHORS OF THE 19TH CENTURY"

*JOHNSON, OWEN MC MAHON (August 27, 1878-   ), American novelist and short-story writer, was born in New York

City, the son of Robert Underwood Johnson, poet and magazine editor,^{qv} and Katherine (Mc-Mahon) Johnson. Literature was in the air; young Owen received $1 for a story printed in *St. Nicholas* when he was six, and at twelve he got out a paper with the assistance of a young son of the poet and editor Richard Watson Gilder. At Lawrenceville School in New Jersey he founded and edited the first *Lawrenceville Literary Magazine,* and a dozen years later put the school permanently on the map of school-story fiction with *The Eternal Boy* (1909) and successive stories— some of them illustrated by Frederic Dorr Steele—of the exploits of the Tennessee Shad, Doc Macnooder, the Prodigious Hickey, Hungry Smeed, the Gutter-Pup, Skippy Bedelle, and other imperishable adolescents who would greatly have mystified Mr. Chips. At Yale, Owen Johnson was chairman of the *Yale Literary Magazine* for the Class of 1900 (he received his B.A. degree in 1901), and a decade later scandalized some Yale men by the best-selling novel, *Stover at Yale,* which attacked the solemn mumbo-jumbo of senior societies and the intellectual incuriosity of the average undergraduate in no uncertain terms.

Soon after receiving his degree from Yale Owen Johnson published a novel of the Civil War, *Arrows of the Almighty,* and married the first of five wives, Mary Galt Stockly of Lakewood, N.J., who died in 1910. His second wife was Esther Cobb of San Francisco, and her successors were Cecile Denis de la Garde of Chignens, France, who died less than a year after their marriage in 1917; Catherine Sayre Burton of New York, whom he married in January 1921 and who died

March 2, 1923; and Gertrude Boyce, widow of John A. Leboutillier, who married the novelist in January 1926. After their house at Stockbridge, Mass. burned in 1929, the Johnsons came to New York City to live. Several of the Johnson novels discuss marriage problems. His other preparations for a career of writing were a period as police court reporter, after graduation, and a stay in France during the First World War. He was made Chevalier of the Legion d'Honneur in 1919, and is also a Member of the National Institute of Arts and Letters. Johnson's rather sensational, dated fiction has not worn so well as his stories of (not necessarily for) boys.

PRINCIPAL WORKS: Arrows of the Almighty, 1901; In the Name of Liberty, 1905; Max Fargus, 1906; The Comet (play) 1908; The Eternal Boy, 1909; The Humming Bird, 1910; The Varmint, 1910; The Tennessee Shad, 1911; Stover at Yale, 1911; A Comedy for Wives (play) 1911; The Sixty-First Second, 1912; Murder in Any Degree, 1913; The Salamander, 1913; Making Money, 1914; The Woman Gives, 1915; The Spirit of France, 1915; Virtuous Wives, 1917; The Wasted Generation, 1921; Skippy Bedelle, 1923; Blue Blood, 1923; Children of Divorce, 1927; Sacrifice, 1929; The Coming of the Amazons, 1931.

ABOUT: Farrar, J. (ed.). The Literary Spotlight; Bookman October 1913, June 1914, December 1921; Time August 17, 1936.

JOHNSON, ROBERT UNDERWOOD (January 12, 1853-October 14, 1937), American editor, diplomat, and poet, was born in Washington, D.C., the

son of Nimrod H. Johnson and Catherine C. (Underwood) Johnson. He received the degree of B.S. from Earlham College, Indiana, in 1871 (and an honorary Ph.D. in 1889), and at twenty went on the staff of the *Century*

Magazine, then a conservative, highly regarded periodical with exalted standards, most carefully edited by Richard Watson Gilder. Johnson was associate editor from 1881 to 1909, and editor-in-chief from November 1909 (succeeding Gilder) until May 31, 1913. (A respectfully amused impression of the magazine's office and editor appears in *The First Person Singular,* an early novel by William Rose Benét, who joined the staff soon after leaving Yale.) Johnson also worked with the Century Company, the book-publishing affiliate, having charge with Clarence Clough Buel of editing the "Century War Series," subsequently ex-

* Died January 27, 1952.

tending it to *Battles and Leaders of the Civil War*. In 1887-88 he succeeded in inducing Grant to write his memoirs, half of which appeared in the series. (The Century Company lost the full book-rights, by a narrow margin, to Mark Twain and his publishing concern.) Johnson's services to international copyright were long and valiant, and of more permanent value to literature, probably, than his fluent, conventional verse.

With John Muir, Johnson set on foot the movement resulting in the creation of the Yosemite National Park, and was also chiefly responsible for the marble Hall of Fame, an adjunct of New York University, in New York City. He was director of the Hall from 1919 and part-arbiter of the inclusions therein, as well as secretary of its living counterpart, the American Academy of Arts and Letters. Johnson originated the "American Poets' Ambulances in Italy," which presented 112 ambulances to the Italian army in four months of 1917. He was ambassador to that country from February 1920 to July 1921. Another of Johnson's gifts to American literature was his son, Owen McMahon Johnson,*qv* author of the Lawrenceville stories, *Stover at Yale*, and many popular novels. The elder Johnson was a bearded, kindly, rather consciously literary presence.

PRINCIPAL WORKS: The Winter Hour and Other Poems, 1891; Songs of Liberty and Other Poems, 1897; Poems (collected) 1902; (enlarged, 1908); Poems of War and Peace, 1916, Italian Rhapsody and Other Poems of Italy, 1917; Collected Poems, 1919; Poems of the Longer Flight, 1928; The Pact of Honor and Other Poems, 1929; Poems of the Lighter Touch, 1930; Poems of Fifty Years (definitive edition) 1931; Aftermath, 1933; Heroes, Children, and Fun, 1934; Your Hall of Fame (prose) 1935.

ABOUT: Johnson, R. U. Remembered Yesterdays (autobiography); New York Times October 15, 1937; Newsweek October 25, 1937; Publishers' Weekly October 23, 1937; Wilson Library Bulletin November 1937.

JOHNSTON, Mrs. ANNIE (FELLOWS) (May 15, 1863-October 5, 1931), American author of stories for children, was born in

Evansville, Ind., the daughter of Albion and Mary (Erskine) Fellows. Her father, a Methodist minister, died when she was two years old and her mother took the three daughters to the country near Evansville, where they grew up with ten cousins. Annie attended district school, read the entire

Sunday School library, and wrote stories and poems in imitation of those she found in *Godey's Lady's Book, St. Nicholas,* and the *Youth's Companion.* After studying for a year at the University of Iowa, she spent the next few years teaching in the public school at Evansville, working in an office, and traveling in New England and Europe. At twenty-five she married her cousin William L. Johnston, a widower with three children. Encouraged by him, she contributed occasional stories to the *Youth's Companion.* When her husband died after three years, leaving her the three children to support, she set to writing in earnest.

On a visit to Pewee Valley, near Louisville, Ky., she was charmed by the atmosphere of leisure and aristocratic living, and by the character of a spirited little girl who had the temper of her grandfather, an old Confederate colonel. On her return to Evansville she wrote *The Little Colonel,* the first of a series of twelve popular volumes centering about this little heroine. Three years after its publication she went to live permanently in Pewee Valley. In search of health for her step-son, she made a temporary home for him successively in Arizona, California, and Texas, from 1901 to 1910, when he died. The Southwest furnished settings for several of her books.

Thousands of children were entertained and inspired by Mrs. Johnston's characters, who had integrity and lived in a world where good intentions prevail and simple virtues are glorified. "By drawing upon her own idealized childhood and the scenes and people she loved," wrote a critic, "she created a glamor about her characters which charmed youthful readers." She did this without any superior gifts of imagination, observation, or psychological acuteness.

PRINCIPAL WORKS: Big Brother, 1893; The Little Colonel, 1895; Joel—A Boy of Galilee, 1895; Ole Mammy's Torment, 1897; Songs Ysame (poems, with her sister Mrs. Albion Fellows Bacon) 1897; Two Little Knights of Kentucky, 1899; The Little Colonel's House Party, 1900; The Little Colonel's Holidays, 1901; The Little Colonel's Hero, 1902; Little Colonel at Boarding School, 1903; Little Colonel in Arizona, 1904; Little Colonel's Christmas Vacation, 1905; The Little Colonel's Knight Comes Riding, 1907; Mary Ware, 1908; Legend of the Bleeding Heart, 1908; The Jester's Sword, 1909; Little Colonel Good Times Book, 1909; Mary Ware in Texas, 1910; Travellers Five, 1911; Mary Ware's Promised Land, 1912; Miss Santa Claus of the Pullman, 1913; Georgina of the Rainbows, 1916; Georgina's Service Stars, 1918; Story of the Red Cross, 1918; The Road of the Loving Heart, 1922; The Land of the Little Colonel, 1929.

ABOUT: Johnston, A. F. The Land of the Little Colonel; Kunitz, S. J. & Haycraft, H. (eds.).

The Junior Book of Authors; Publishers' Weekly October 10, 24, 1931; St. Nicholas December 1913; Saturday Review of Literature November 15, 1930.

JOHNSTON, Sir HARRY HAMILTON (June 12, 1858-July 31, 1927), English explorer, novelist, and miscellaneous writer,

was born at Newington Terrace, Kensington Park, South London, the third son of John Brookes Johnston and eldest child of Esther Laetitia (Hamilton) Johnston, of Scotch descent. His father's first wife had died two years before, of puerperal fever. The precocious child, who traced descent from several painters through the Hamilton line, admired peacocks and proceeded to draw pictures of them. At fourteen he amused zoo officials by painting the biggest and most ferocious subjects there. At eleven, during a visit to Rochester, he caught a fleeting glimpse of Charles Dickens taking notes in the Cathedral porch, presumably for *Edwin Drood*. Johnston, who knew Dickens' novels by heart, amused himself as a man by writing continuations of some of them. At eighteen he toured Spain, painted a Provençal picture that was accepted by the Royal Academy, and soon after learned the Latin languages and Arabic by touring in the Mediterranean countries and through Tunis. His formal education included periods at Stockwell Grammar School; King's College, London; and four years (1876-80) at the Royal Academy of Arts.

Harry Johnston "not only wrote the history of Africa, but often made it." He explored Portuguese West Africa and the River Congo in 1882-83; commanded a scientific expedition of the Royal Scientific Society to Mt. Kilimanjaro, in 1884; was vice-consul in the Cameroons in 1885; and consul for the province of Mozambique in 1888. Next year he led an expedition to Lakes Nyasa and Tanganyika, and founded the British Central Africa Protectorate. In 1897 Johnston was Consul-General of the Regency of Tunis for two years. He was in the Uganda Protectorate in 1901 when the Joseph Chamberlain clique forced his resignation. That year he established the identity of the okapi, a zebra-like beast of the Congo forest which he had been looking for ever since some remarks of Philip Gosse, Sir

Edmund Gosse's father, about an African unicorn had interested him. For the rest of his life Sir Harry Johnston (K.C.B. 1896; K.C.M.G. 1901) wrote the history of Africa—of whose territory he had added 400,000 square miles to the Empire—and, at the instigation of H. G. Wells, his amusing and outspoken pseudo-novels, continuations of Dickens' *Dombey and Son* and *Our Mutual Friend* and of Bernard Shaw's *Mrs. Warren's Profession*. Lady Johnston was the Hon Winifred Irby, O.B.E., daughter of the fifth Lord Boston. A little, plump man, with a feminine voice, Sir Harry was not notable for tact. "Elizabeth" (Lady Russell) was a close friend. He died in his seventieth year at the home of a sister in the north of England, and was buried in the churchyard of the village, Poling, Arundel, where he lived at St. John's Priory.

PRINCIPAL WORKS: The River Congo, 1884; Kilimanjaro, 1885; History of a Slave, 1889; Life of Livingstone, 1891; British Central Africa, 1897; A History of the Colonization of Africa by Alien Races, 1899-1913; The Uganda Protectorate, 1902; British Mammals, 1903; Liberia, 1906; A History of the British Empire in Africa, 1910; The Negro in the New World, 1910; The Opening-Up of Africa, 1911; Views and Reviews, 1912; Phonetic Spelling, 1913; Pioneers in West Africa, Canada, India, Australasia, Tropical America and South Africa (3 vols.) 1911-1913; The Truth About War, 1916; The Gay-Dombeys, 1919; Comparative Study of Bantu and Semi-Bantu Languages, 1919-1922; Mrs. Warren's Daughter, 1920; The Backward Peoples, 1920; The Man Who Did the Right Thing, 1921; The Veneerings, 1922; Little Life-Stories, 1923; The Story of My Life, 1923; Relations, 1925.

ABOUT: Johnston, A. The Life and Letters of Sir Harry Johnston; Johnston, H. H. The Story of My Life; Swinnerton, F. Swinnerton: An Autobiography; New York Times August 1, 1927.

JOHNSTON, MARY (November 21, 1870-May 9, 1936), American novelist, was born in Buchanan, Va., the daughter of John William and Elizabeth (Alexander) Johnston, both of early Virginia families, her father being a lawyer and a major in the Confederate Army. She was educated at home, and grew up in her father's library, which was particularly rich

in books of history. Her girlhood was spent in Birmingham, Ala., but on her father's death she moved to Richmond, and lived there until in her later years she built a house in Warm Springs, Va., where she died. She never married.

Her life was uneventful: a youth spent in ministering to her motherless brothers and sisters, much ill health, journeys to New York and abroad, and from her earliest years the scribbling of stories, which she sent out once and then burned on their first rejection. Her first novel, in 1898, created no stir; but two years later, with *To Have and To Hold,* she became a phenomenal best seller. *Audrey,* in 1902, was also successful, but thereafter, though she had established a *genre* and continued to exemplify it, she produced no such sensationally popular novels as the two just named. Historical fiction, particularly of the South, continued to be her dominant theme, though in *Silver Cross,* in 1921, she ventured into the realm of mysticism. Her books were thoroughly documented, and she spent much time in careful research. A shy, retiring little woman, with dark hair and a firmly set jaw, Miss Johnston remained what she had been born—a Southern lady of the old dispensation.

It was in her books, which the *Commonweal* called not so much historical novels as "romantic novels about history," that she lived vicariously a career of adventure and danger. They were rosy-hued, swashbuckling novels, skimming the surface of thought and reveling in action. The *Saturday Review of Literature* called them "part tinsel, part silk, part old-fashioned stage illusion," and William Allen White remarked that she "made historical novels out of the wax portraits of the early aristocrats of the Atlantic Coast." Nevertheless, her facts were sound, her story-making instinct true, and with the possible execption of *Silver Cross* she did not know how to be uninteresting. Probably no better story of capture by and escape from the Indians has been written than *The Great Valley.* A whole generation formed its picture of early days in Virginia from *To Have and To Hold.* And the *Commonweal* paid her the final compliment when it said of this book and *Audrey* that, in their "rich concentration of evocative detail and magically compelling historic atmosphere," they were, however minor, "in the authentic tradition of the great Sir Walter."

PRINCIPAL WORKS: Prisoners of Hope, 1898; To Have and To Hold, 1900; Audrey, 1902; Sir Mortimer, 1904; The Goddess of Reason, 1907; Lewis Rand, 1908; The Long Roll, 1911; Cease Firing, 1912; Hagar, 1913; The Witch, 1914; The Fortunes of Garin, 1915; The Wanderers, 1917; Pioneers of the Old South (non-fiction) 1918; Foes, 1918; Michael Forth, 1919; Sweet Rocket, 1920; Silver Cross, 1921; 1492, 1922; Croatan, 1923; The Slave Ship, 1924; The Great Valley,

1926; The Exile, 1927; Hunting Shirt, 1931; Miss Delicia Allen, 1932; Drury Randall, 1934.

ABOUT: Commonweal May 22, 1936; Saturday Review of Literature May 23, 1936.

JOHNSTON, MYRTLE (March 7, 1909-), Irish novelist, writes: "I was born, the eldest of three sisters, in Dublin. Our branch of the Johnston family had come from Annandale, Scotland, to Ireland during the persecution of the Covenanters in the seventeenth century, one of them building Magheramena Castle on the shores of Lough Erne in the  beautiful, but wild and desolate, County Fermanagh. We were the last of his descendants to inhabit the Castle. My father, Captain James Johnston, was Master of the Horse, and later private secretary to Lord Aberdeen during his second term as Lord Lieutenant of Ireland. My mother, the daughter of an Irish District Inspector of Police, and one of ten sisters celebrated in Irish society as 'the ten lovely Miss Waterses,' was, like my father, an ardent Nationalist. 'Ireland' and 'Home Rule' are words I remember early attending to in grown-up conversation at the Private Secretary's Lodge.

"I was six when my father was killed at the Dardanelles in 1915. Left without the means to keep on Magheramena, my mother sold it and for the next five years, the most formative for me as an author, we lived in Dublin. Before I could read I had determined that I would write stories. It became my abiding purpose. At ten, I received my first rejection from a magazine, the London *Windsor.* I continued writing stories, poems, plays—most historical or fantastic—often submitting my work to magazines, but never being in the least cast down by rejection, which I almost welcomed as an inevitable part of the business of becoming an author. My family was in no sense literary—although an ancestor was Maria Edgeworth, so celebrated in her day and so forgotten in ours—and we knew no writers, so that I pursued my ambition happily, without criticism, influence, or advice.

"Not long before my twelfth birthday, the Irish 'Troubles' of 1920-21—that betrayal of Nationalist dreams—decided my mother to follow the example of nearly all our friends and leave Ireland for England, where we have since lived quietly in Bournemouth, Dorset. I did not go to boarding school or university. In Ireland we had had governesses, and in Bournemouth we attended a small P.N.E.U. day school which I left at seventeen.

"At fifteen, I sent my first full-length novel to a publisher. It was turned down, and so was my second, although with very kindly encouragement from the London firm which accepted my third novel, *Hanging Johnny*—my first published work—when I was eighteen. Three other novels and a volume of short stories followed. I was deflected, in those years, from the straight path to a measure of financial and literary success, which my first book had seemed to indicate, by a desire to experiment with form and subject which I fear has not left me yet. Having begun early to publish, I regard much of my work as the cast-off clothes of a growing child, bearing little relation, perhaps, to any ultimate achievement of mine.

"My second sister Marjorie was, also at eighteen, the author of a commentary on certain episodes of Napoleonic history entitled *Domination*."

PRINCIPAL WORKS: Hanging Johnny, 1927; Relentless, 1930; The Maiden, 1935; Laleen and Other Stories, 1938; The Rising, 1939; Amiel, 1941.

JONES, HENRY ARTHUR. See "BRITISH AUTHORS OF THE 19TH CENTURY"

JONG. See DE JONG

JORDAN, Mrs. HELEN ROSALINE (ASHTON). See ASHTON, H.

JOSEPHSON, MATTHEW (February 15, 1899-), American critic and biographer, was born in Brooklyn, N.Y., the son

B. Abbott

of Julius and Sarah (Kasendorf) Josephson. He received his B.A. at Columbia University in 1920, and soon after became one of the group of American literary "expatriates" in Paris. He was an intimate of the original group of Surréalist authors and painters, was associate editor of *Broom*, 1922-24, and was contributing editor of *transition*, 1928-29. He then returned to New York, where he tried to revive and continue *Broom*, but without success. In 1929 he was book editor of the Macaulay Co. He was then persuaded to try his hand as a financier, in connection with a Wall Street brokerage firm, but though he made money the strain brought him near a nervous breakdown, and he abruptly deserted finance for literature, to which he has remained faithful ever since. In 1920 he married Hannah Geffen, and they have two sons.

His first prose book was an authoritative and well-documented biography of Zola. In 1930, when he was at work on his second biography, of Rousseau—in fact, the night before he was to sail for Europe to complete his research in France—his house was burned to the ground and he himself was injured in trying to rescue his manuscript. The book was completed on the farm in Gaylordsville, Conn., which is his present home.

With the publication of *The Robber Barons,* in 1934, Mr. Josephson changed his focus of interest from literary to economic history. This book was written while he was the holder of a Guggenheim Fellowship. His sympathies are leftist, but this book and his later *Politicos* are, to quote John Chamberlain, "a measured, sober, and subtle work of synthesis and reinterpretation." He is not a muckraker, but an historian.

He is a thin, dark, intense-looking man, with a moustache and deep-set, thoughtful eyes. He says of himself: "I am comparatively young and, as I feel, 'in the midst of life.'" His most important work, he feels, is still before him. Long ago he expressed "the dilemma of the American artist," who must either risk submersion in the tide of industrialism or exile himself from his homeland. Nevertheless he has made his choice, and (long before the war made it physically impossible for him to continue to live in Europe) his choice lay with America. "I must live here," he says, "to see the battle fought out and to see the nature of the transformation that will take place here; to see whether mechanism will enjoy the ultimate triumph over ideas."

PRINCIPAL WORKS: Galimathias (poems) 1923; Zola and His Time, 1928; Portrait of the Artist as American, 1930; Jean-Jacques Rousseau, 1932; The Robber Barons, 1934; The Politicos, 1938; The President Makers, 1940.

ABOUT: Boston Evening Transcript April 1, 1933.

JOUVENEL. See COLETTE

JOYCE, JAMES (February 2, 1882-January 13, 1941), Irish novelist, was born James Augustine Aloysius Joyce in Rathgar,

B. Abbott

a suburb of Dublin, in the seething political era when Parnell was the hope of Ireland. His father, John Stanislaus Joyce, is described as an Irish Micawber, a jolly, bibulous, pugnacious good fellow notorious in Dublin for his reckless extravagance, his biting wit, and his monocle. Having lost his youthful patrimony in a distillery that made its whisky in an old convent, he became secretary to the National Liberal Club and later Collector of Rates of the City of Dublin. John Stanislaus liked to boast of his "devil of a good tenor voice," but he had few books in his library, regarding the sedentary occupation of reading as fitting enough for Jesuit fathers but otherwise a sign of declining manhood. The only mark of his three years at Queen's College, Cork, he would say, was his name carved on a desk. He was inordinately proud of his eldest son James, favorite of his "sixteen or seventeen children." His wife Mary Jane, a brilliant pianist, was a proud, handsome, sensitive woman whose life was dominated by two masters: John Stanislaus and the Roman Catholic Church.

As a small, sensitive lad of six, James Joyce was sent to the best Jesuit school in Ireland, historic Clongowes Wood College, Clane, where he spent three unforgettable years. At nine, hearing his father's friends discussing Parnell, the boy wrote a virulent attack against Tim Healy which his father had published as a small pamphlet, all copies of which have been lost.

In 1891, doubtless for financial reasons, James was withdrawn from Clongowes Wood and for two years he remained at home in Dublin until his father secured a free tuition for him at Belvedere College, Dublin, a similar Jesuit institution. Here he remained from his eleventh to his fifteenth year, excelling in essay writing. One, entitled "My Favourite Hero," was on Ulysses. With the prizes won for these essays, the youth took his family to the theatre and to fine dinners in popular restaurants. They admired these early essays more than his later works. Joyce was an

excellent scholar, an omnivorous reader, captain of the school in his last year. He wrote poetry, translated from the Latin, studied four languages. At Belvedere he considered joining the Jesuit Order, but despite the wishes of his mother, who became more pious with age, he decided against it. From 1898 to 1902 Joyce attended University College (also Jesuit). He studied Aristotle and Aquinas, Latin, Italian, French, and even Norwegian in order to read Ibsen. Gaelic he would not touch.

In April 1900 the venerable *Fortnightly Review* printed an essay entitled "Ibsen's New Drama," a criticism of *When We Dead Awaken,* which Joyce had read in the original immediately upon publication. In 1901 when the proposed National Theatre for Ireland was being launched, Joyce denounced it as a surrender to the mob, a betrayal of the artist who should know no national boundaries. Unable to get this essay regularly published, he had it printed as a two-penny pamphlet, *The Day of the Rabblement.*

Shortly after taking his bachelor's degree in October 1902 Joyce left Dublin for Paris. "I will not serve that in which I no longer believe," he wrote later in *A Portrait of the Artist as a Young Man,* "whether it calls itself my home, my fatherland or my church." He had two letters of introduction, one from the Lord Mayor of Dublin, a pound or so, and some poems. He attended one class at the Collège de Médecine but dropped out on learning that fees had to be paid in cash in advance. Soon he was practically starving. He wrote some plotless sketches called "Epiphanies," later introduced into the *Portrait.* In his favorite café he almost got into a duel with a German poet who worshipped the Aryan race— a prejudice inimical to Joyce. In April 1903 he was summoned home to his dying mother's bedside, and for four months he watched her die. In 1904 he left home and lived in cheap rooms, carrying his own bedposts around with him. An entire section of *Ulysses* is based on his experiences as a teacher at Clifton School, Dalkey, in the spring of 1904, at which time he lived for a short while in the Martello Tower at Sandycove, one of fifteen battlements built in 1804 when invasion of Britain was threatened.

On June 10, 1904, Joyce met Nora Joseph Barnacle, a witty, auburn-haired girl, nonliterary but charming, who had come to Dublin from Galway to earn her living. By October they were married and on their way to Zurich, where an employment agency promised him a job in the Berlitz School. [In 1931 the Joyces were re-married in London, "for testamentary reasons."] The agency proved to be a swindle but Joyce did get a job in the Berlitz School in Trieste (then Austria) at 80 pounds a year.

Joyce's history for the next quarter of a century is the history of one long struggle for publication, a struggle probably unmatched in the annals of literature.

Chamber Music, a slight volume of lyrics written during his last year in Dublin, was rejected by four London publishers, one of whom failed to return the manuscript, before it was finally published by Elkin Mathews in 1907. Although press notices were favorable, and at least five composers made settings of the songs, *Chamber Music* brought Joyce not a penny in royalties.

Dubliners, a group of short stories begun in 1904, was completed the following year, but such was the squeamishness of the Edwardian era that the work was not published until 1914. Two publishers broke contracts rather than risk sponsoring the book. Thinking to publish the book himself Joyce came to Dublin in 1912 to buy the sheets, but the printer refused to sell, destroyed them, and broke up the type. Joyce left Ireland never to return, despite personal invitations from Yeats and proffered membership in the Irish Academy of Letters.

A Portrait of the Artist as a Young Man, a strictly autobiographical novel depicting Joyce's Jesuitical schooling and his gropings toward a working aesthetic, was tentatively entitled "Stephen Hero." Joyce conceived it as a huge book running to more than three hundred thousand words, but he decided instead to write a sequel called *Ulysses.* The *Portrait* is dated "Dublin, 1904. Trieste, 1914." During these ten years, isolated and unrecognized, he had "the delicate task of living and of supporting two [later three: Giorgio was born 1905; Lucia 1907] other trusting souls on a salary of 80 pounds a year for teaching the English language . . . as quickly as possible with no delays for elegance." This he called his "interrupted life," and he regarded his writing as his only hope.

In 1914 Ezra Pound, leader of a new "revolutionary" movement of vanguard writers including Wyndham Lewis, Richard Aldington, and T. S. Eliot, who wished to "blast" out the stuffy Edwardian epoch, asked Joyce's permission to include a poem from *Chamber Music* in his first *Imagist Anthology.* To Pound, Joyce sent his manuscript of the *Portrait,* and serial publication was immediately arranged in the vanguard English magazine, *Egoist.* The Egoist Press attempted to publish this novel in book form, but no printer in the British Isles would "for one moment entertain any idea of printing such a production," as one of them said; ultimately the Egoist Press had to import sheets from America, where Ben W. Huebsch published the book in 1916.

Ulysses was conceived in 1906 as a story for *Dubliners,* but Joyce did not begin writing this most elaborate of novels until 1914, in Trieste, just after completing his three-act play *Exiles* (published 1918 in America and England). During the First World War, in which Joyce took little interest and no sides, he managed to leave Trieste and settled in Zurich. Here, tormented by poverty and increasing eye troubles, he struggled to complete *Ulysses.* Hearing of his difficulties, Ezra Pound induced Yeats, George Moore, and Edmund Gosse to intercede with Prime Minister Asquith for aid, with the result that the Privy Purse sent Joyce 100 pounds. Joyce refused to serve in the British Army, but he did lend his services to the English Players, a semi-propagandistic acting company formed in Zurich during the war. In 1919 Joyce returned to the now-Italian Trieste; the following year Pound persuaded him to go to Paris, where in 1921 *Ulysses* was finally ended with the word "Yes."

In England the *Egoist* had serialized those parts of the novel which the printer would consent to set up; in America the *Little Review* published twenty-three installments in 1918-20, three of which (January and June 1919, January 1920) caused the magazine to be confiscated by the U.S. Post Office for alleged obscenity. The editors, the Misses Heap and Anderson, were fingerprinted and fined $100. Thereupon Mr. Huebsch declined to publish the book unless Joyce would make it "conform to the law." Publication in England was out of the question.

In Paris, however, Miss Sylvia Beach decided to publish *Ulysses* under the imprint Shakespeare & Co., the name of her vanguard bookshop. The vast novel was completely reset six times, Joyce practically rewriting every proofsheet sent him by the "scrupulous and understanding" French printers, whose task was simplified by the fact that they did not realize what strange English they were putting together. On Joyce's fortieth birthday he received the first printed copy of *Ulysses*, a heavy book bound in the blue and white of the Greek flag. The thousand numbered copies of this edition were exhausted within a month.

First reactions varied from A.E.'s "greatest fiction of the twentieth century" to Alfred Noyes' "It is simply the foulest book that has ever found its way into print." The *Dublin Review* declared: "A great Jesuit-trained talent has gone over malignantly and mockingly to the powers of evil."

Of the second printing of 2,000 copies (printed from the same plates but by John Rodker, Paris, for the Egoist Press, London), 500 were burned in New York by the U.S. Post Office. The English customs authorities at Folkestone confiscated 499 copies of the third edition of 500 copies.

Wherever *Ulysses* was banned, it was smuggled in. In the United States bowdlerized, pirated, and forged editions appeared which Joyce could not protest because he held no copyright. It was not until 1933 that Americans were legally permitted to read the book, when U.S. District Judge John M. Woolsey ruled, in a now famous decision, that "whilst in many places . . . *Ulysses* . . . is somewhat emetic, nowhere does it tend to be an aphrodisiac." This decision was upheld by the Federal Circuit Court of Appeals, with a lone dissent by Judge Martin J. Manton (later removed and jailed for corruption in office). The Random House edition of 1934 was the first legally printed in any English-speaking country. Thirty-five thousand copies were sold immediately.

Ulysses describes a single day in Dublin, June 16, 1904. The characters and events parallel in an ingenious and sometimes imperceptible manner the *Odyssey* of Homer, almost every detail of which can be found disguised in *Ulysses*. Each episode is written in a style appropriate to the subject matter, moreover each episode features an organ of the human body, a science or art, a symbol, and a color. "Keys" and "guides" have been written interpreting *Ulysses*, the best of which, by Stuart Gilbert, is almost as long as the novel itself.

As *Ulysses* deals with the day and the conscious mind, *Finnegans Wake* (1939), which occupied Joyce for seventeen years, deals with the night and the subconscious; it is the first attempt to articulate the wordless world of sleep. Written in a dream language compounded of dozens of languages, including Eskimo, it contains not a single sentence to guide the reader in interpreting it, not a single direct statement of what it is about. "Whether Joyce is eventually convicted of assaulting the King's English with intent to kill, or whether he has really added a cubit to her stature, she will never be quite the same again," said *Time*; while Harry Levin, in his essay "On First Looking into *Finnegans Wake*," concluded: "Among the acknowledged masters of English—and there can be no further delay in acknowledging that Joyce is among the greatest—there is no one with so much to express and so little to say. . . . The detachment which can look upon the conflicts of civilization with so many competing vocables is wonderful and terrifying."

Joyce spent his latter years in Paris with his wife, his son Giorgio, and Giorgio's son Stephen, who called his adoring grandfather "Nono." Joyce's daughter Lucia, afflicted with a nervous disorder, was in a sanatorium; on her Joyce spent much of the income left him by Harriet Weaver, an admirer of his work.

In June 1940, when the French army fell back from Paris before the onrushing Germans, the Joyces were forced out of Vichy, where they were visiting. They took refuge in nearby St. Gérand-le-Puy and applied for a visa to Switzerland, but the Swiss government demanded a $7000 bond (reduced eventually to $3500, contributed by friends). The Joyces arrived practically penniless in Zurich, dependent on money raised for them in the United States. Worry over the poor reception of *Finnegans Wake*, their financial plight, and the fate of Lucia, whom they could not rescue from occupied France, finally induced Joyce's collapse. The end came after an operation for a malignant duodenal ulcer, followed by two blood transfusions.

For years he had been nearly blind, having undergone ten major eye operations, all without anaesthetics. His later writing was done in a big hand on large sheets of paper. A family man, he called himself a "born monogamist." He spoke Italian as smoothly as English, flawless French, fluent German, knew some twelve other tongues including Lapp, and numerous dialects as well. He smoked cigarettes or thin cigars and drank only white wines, but never during the day. He loved to dance—flinging himself about with wild abandon, as if he had no bones—and to sing. Tall, slender, and very erect though loose of carriage, he was quiet, self-contained, and courteous, almost courtly. He dressed with conservative elegance, be-ringed hands being his only exoticism aside from his inevitable walking-stick. Sometimes he wore a black patch over his left eye beneath the almost spherical lens of his glasses. Greeks, he believed, brought him good luck; nuns, bad luck. He feared thunder, dogs, and riotous waters.

In many respects the death of Joyce marked the end of an era. His writings, in the words of *Time,* "had been the most massive, inclusive, eloquent statement of Europe's intellectual and moral chaos, a chaos now audible and visible in the falling walls of Europe's cities. And Joyce had died in the midst of this downfall—perhaps because of it. There was something about his death that suggested the great Bishop of Hippo, St. Augustine, dying at the close of the Roman world to the echo of Vandal swords against the city gates."

WORKS: Chamber Music, 1907; Dubliners, 1914; A Portrait of the Artist as a Young Man, 1916; Exiles, 1918; Ulysses, 1922; Pomes Penyeach, 1927; Collected Poems, 1937 (containing Chamber Music, Pomes Penyeach, and Ecce Puer); Finnegans Wake, 1939 (some excerpts from this work were published as "Work in Progress," in *transition,* 1927-1930, and as Haveth Childers Everywhere, 1931; Anna Livia Plurabelle, 1932; Two Tales of Shem and Shaun, 1932; The Mime of Mick, Nick and the Maggies, 1934).

ABOUT: Baake, J. Das Priesenscherzbuch *Ulysses*; Beach, J. W. The Twentieth Century Novel; Beckett, S. On Exagmination . . . of Work in Progress; Broch, H. James Joyce und die Gegenwart; Budgen, F. James Joyce and the Making of *Ulysses*; Curtius, E. R. James Joyce und Sein *Ulysses*; Daiches, D. The Novel and the Modern World; Duff, C. James Joyce and the Plain Reader; Gilbert, S. James Joyce's *Ulysses*; Golding, L. James Joyce; Gorman, H. James Joyce; Hanley, M. L. Word Index to James Joyce's *Ulysses*; Hentze, R. Die Proteische Wandlung im *Ulysses* von James Joyce; Kulemeyer, J. Studien zur Psychologie in Neuen Englischen Roman; Levin, H. James Joyce; Miller-Budnitskaya, R. James Joyce's *Ulysses,* (in *Dialectics*: No.5); Muir, E. Transition; Muller, H. J. Modern Fiction; Obradovic, A. Die Behandlung der Räumlichkeit im Späteren Werk des James Joyce; Schwartz, J. Bibliography of Joyce's Works; Smith, P. J. A Key to the *Ulysses* of James Joyce; Strong, L. A. G. "James Joyce" (in D. Verschoyle, ed. *The English Novelists*); Waldock, A. J. James Joyce and Others; Waldock, A. J. Some Recent Developments in English Literature; West, A. Crisis and Criticism; Wilson, E. Axel's Castle; Boston Transcript May 20, 1939; Colophon Spring 1936; Nation February 14, 1934, May 6, 1939; New Republic June 28, 1939; January 20, 1941; New York Herald Tribune "Books" January 21, 1934, May 21, 1939; New York Times October 10, 1937, May 7, 1939, January 13, 1941; New Yorker May 6, 1939; Poetry March 1941; Saturday Review of Literature January 27, 1934, May 6, 1939, January 25, 1941; Time January 29, 1934, May 8, 1939, February 10, 1941; Times (London) Literary Supplement May 6, 1939; Yale Review Spring 1938.

JUNG, CARL GUSTAV (July 26, 1875-), Swiss psychologist, was born at Kasswyl, Thurgovie, Switzerland. His family were citizens of Basel. His father was a liberal clergyman, a philologist with an interest in the Orient; his maternal grandfather had been a professor of medicine, a political refugee from Germany. Jung intended at first to be an ar-

chaeologist, but after entering the University of Basle transferred to the medical faculty, receiving his first medical degree in 1900, his M.D. in 1902. Later he studied in Paris under Pierre Janet, his chosen field from the beginning being psychiatry. He was physician to the Psychiatric Clinic of the University of Zurich from 1900 to 1909, lectured on psychiatry at the University from 1905 to 1913, and has been professor of psychology at the Federal Polytechnical University, Zurich, since 1932. In 1903 he married, his wife being "also a member of a conservative Swiss family, a woman of unusual character and distinction." He has four daughters and one son, and eleven grandchildren.

He was early attracted to the researches of Sigmund Freud, although they did not meet until 1906, at which time he says he already had doubts as to the universal validity of Freud's theory of psychoanalysis, particularly as to its sexual aspects. Nevertheless, he was considered Freud's chief disciple and associate. Both of them came to America in 1909 to lecture at Clark University, at the invitation of G. Stanley Hall. Jung was by this time in private practice in Zurich. It was not until 1913 that he finally broke with Freud and advanced his own "heretical" psychoanalytic theory. Since he had been founder and president of the International Psychoanalytic Society, and editor of Freud's and Bleuler's *Annual for Psychological and Psychopathological Research,* his abandonment of the Freudian movement caused a sensation in scientific circles.

During the First World War, Jung was Medical Commander of the British interned in Switzerland. In 1919 he went to North Africa, the first of several African journeys, notably to Kenya, to conduct researches in primitive psychology. He has also made six trips in all to the United States, traveling in the Southwest, lecturing at Fordham University in 1912, and speaking at the Harvard Tercentenary Celebration in 1936, and at Yale the following year. In 1938 he spoke at Calcutta University, India, and received an honorary D.Sc. degree from Oxford. In 1933 he was president of the International Medical Society of Psychotherapy. At present he is doing historical and comparative research in the psychology of symbolism.

Jung is tall, large-boned rather than stout, with white hair and a face that has been called "unpaintable, since its planes are always changing." He lives quietly in an old-fashioned house in Zurich, and drives his own red automobile about the city.

His books are hard reading, since he makes no concessions to popularity, but they are closely reasoned. In contradistinction to Freud, he plays down the influence of sex on the unconscious and emphasizes the role of myth; dream analysis is very important in his system. He is subjective, synthetic, and constructive, his object being the re-creation of the individual. Science he considers "a tool, not a god." "Everything that befalls us is necessary." It is to Jung that we owe the current conception of introverted and extroverted personalities. Elizabeth Shepley Sergeant says of him that "in the forefront of every page is a dynamic, thinking, modern man, . . . and in the background a wise, redeeming figure, a very ancient and intuitive man." She calls him "one of the earth people," the "wise men": "one leaves his presence feeling enriched and appeased." His name is pronounced *yoong.*

PRINCIPAL WORKS: Psychology of Dementia Praecox, 1906; The Theory of Psychoanalysis, 1912; Psychology of the Unconscious, 1916; Collected Papers on Analytical Psychology, 1917; Psychological Types, 1923; Contributions to Analytical Psychology, 1928; Two Essays on Analytical Psychology, 1928; The Secret of the Golden Flower (with R. Wilhelm) 1930; Modern Man in Search of a Soul, 1933; Psychology and Religion, 1938; The Integration of the Personality, 1939.

ABOUT: Corrie, J. ABC of Jung's Psychology; Hoop, J. H. van der. Character and the Unconscious; Jacobi, J. Psychology of C. J. Jung; Harper's Magazine May 1931; Journal of Abnormal Psychology January 1924, January 1930; Monist January 1924; Time March 7, 1938.

JUSSERAND, JEAN ADRIEN ANTOINE JULES (February 18, 1855-July 18, 1932), French diplomat and literary historian, first winner of the Pulitzer Prize for history, was born in Lyons of prosperous middle-class parents. The family seat, where their springs and summers were passed, was Saint-Haon-le-Châtel, in the district of the Loire. At ten Jules entered the Collège des Chartreux at Lyons, run by secular priests with a liberal turn of mind, where he studied ancient and modern languages and had plenty of physical exercise. In Paris, he pursued legal studies, receiving a university degree of *licencié en droit,* while Lyons gave him two bachelor's degrees in science and letters. His theses in both the latter were on English topics. In 1875 young Jusserand was in England, perfecting his knowledge of the language, and returned to Paris to take first place in the competitive examination to enter the consular service. His first important critical study was published when he was twenty-three (*Le Théâtre en Angleterre Depuis la Conquête jusqu'aux Prédecesseurs Immédiates de Shakespeare,* 1878). The first volume of Jusserand's *A Literary History of the English People* was crowned by the French Academy and awarded the Bordin prize. Taine, author of the famous *Histoire de la Littérature An-*

glaise, corresponded with Jusserand, who regarded his own work as a supplement to Taine's, designed to show that in England society and literature resembled and complemented each other. Critics generally agree that he successfully did so, and, especially, made a definite contribution to the history of English fiction.

Jusserand's early diplomatic career embraced a period as Councillor to the Embassy at London (1887-90) and Minister to Denmark (1898-1902). On February 7, 1903, he presented his credentials in Washington as American Ambassador, replacing Jules Cambon. He remained till the end of the Coolidge administration, and there was general regret when he was recalled at the end of 1924. Theodore Roosevelt, whom he persuaded to read the *Chanson de Roland* in preference to the *Nibelungenlied,* regarded Jusserand as a superior kind of playmate, taking him frequently on strenuous walks through Rock Creek Park and making him a member of his tennis cabinet. Jusserand was the only non-American ever to head the American Historical Society, and in 1917 he received the Pulitzer Prize in history for his *With Americans of Past and Present Days.* Sixteen American universities gave him honorary LL.D.'s, William Lyon Phelps speaking at Yale of his "union of honest, scrupulous, original research with critical insight, human sympathy, and grace of style."

Jusserand made a radio broadcast to the United States in 1932, the year of his death at seventy-seven. He was survived by Mme. Elise (Richards) Jusserand, who was born in France of American (Bostonian) parents. She attended the memorial services when a terraced exedra in Rock Creek Park was dedicated to Jusserand's memory, with President Franklin D. Roosevelt as speaker. Jusserand was a medium-sized, typically Gallic individual, with carefully trimmed beard and moustaches.

PRINCIPAL WORKS AVAILABLE IN ENGLISH TRANSLATION: English Wayfaring Life in the Middle Ages, 1889; The English Novel in the Time of Shakespeare, 1890; A French Ambassador at the Court of Charles II, 1892; A Literary History of the English People, 1906-1913; With Americans of Past and Present Days, 1916; The School for Ambassadors and Other Essays, 1924.

ABOUT: Jusserand, J. J. What Me Befell: The Reminiscences of J. J. Jusserand; Jusserand Memorial Committee. Jean Jules Jusserand; Lauzanne, S. Great Men and Great Days; Orcutt, W. D. Celebrities Off Parade; New York Times July 19, 1932.

* * *

KAFKA, FRANZ (July 3, 1883-June 3, 1924), Austrian novelist and short story writer, was born in Prague of a wealthy

family of Czech Jews. Franz idolized his father, Hermann Kafka, a self-made man who after persistent struggles had established a solid wholesale business in fancy goods. Franz's mother, Julie, was an exceptionally intelligent woman, an indispensable and indefatigable partner to her husband.

Franz's two elder brothers died in their childhood and, as the oldest child, he was left very much to himself, separated from his three younger sisters by more than six years. The boy's upbringing was entrusted to a French girl who prepared him for elementary school and tutored him in many subjects, not excluding love-making. On finishing the Volksschule Franz attended the Gymnasium in the Alstadter Ring, a strict German institution of extremely high scholastic standards. Subsequently he enrolled in the law school, although his main concern was already for literature. He joined the liberal "Lese-und Redehalle der Deutschen Studenten" and waged his first literary battles, attacking the then fashionable artifici-

alities of Oscar Wilde and Wedekind and endorsing the solid values of Thomas Mann's *Tonio Kröger* and Flaubert's *Sentimental Education.*

In 1906 Kafka entered a story in a contest sponsored by the Viennese periodical *Zeit.* This was the beginning of his career as a writer. In June of that year he received his doctorate in jurisprudence from the German university Karls-Ferdinand at Prague. For lack of anything better he took a small job with an Italian insurance company. In 1908 he obtained a much coveted semi-governmental job, with good pay and short hours, in a workers' accident insurance institute.

After office hours Kafka studied the Czech language and, although not active in politics, attended Czech discussions and mass meetings. He suffered from splitting headaches and frayed nerves; finally in despair he became a vegetarian, and he even took seriously the nonsense of the anthrosophists, being tremendously impressed when Dr. Rudolph Steiner told him he had clairvoyant powers. He gradually drifted towards the Cabbala and became convinced that he had a mission (a mandate, as he used to call it) in life. This mystic strain became more and more pronounced as he came under various intellectual influences, such as his friendship with the Zionist Max Brod, with Franz Werfel, etc., and his study of Kierkegaard and Pascal. Paradoxically enough, Kafka also loved sports. He always looked forward to his Easter and summer vacations and spent many a weekend swimming and boating in nearby resorts and strolling in the woods with his friends.

It was not until 1912 that Kafka emerged as a writer fully conscious of his powers. At Brod's instance, Kafka finally put together some of his "observations," which, despite the huge type used, made only a 99-page brochure, Kafka's first book, *Observations (Betrachtung)*, 1913. Between the end of September and the end of November, Kafka, having now contracted the habit of literary work, finished *The Judgment (Das Urteil)*, published in Brod's yearbook *Arkadia*, and the first chapter, entitled *The Stoker (Der Heizer)*, of his projected novel *Amerika. The Stoker* was published in 1913, when Kafka was already working "with incredible ecstasy," often without stopping to eat or sleep, on his *Metamorphosis (Verwandlung)*. *The Judgment* was dedicated to Fraulein F. B. whom he had met in August 1912 and who for the next five years inspired him to his loftiest creativeness and also, more often, drove him to the most abject depths of despondency. The outcome of the disastrous love affair was that Fraulein F. B. married some one else and had two children, while Kafka, despite his outdoor exercises, his gardening, and his sojourns at various resorts, became more seriously ill.

When the First World War broke out, Kafka was exempt from military service because of his government position, and once when he insisted on going to the front his health failed him altogether. In October 1915 the Fontane Prize was awarded to Kafka for *The Stoker,* and during the winter 1916-17 he worked steadily on *The Trial* while his health steadily declined. He was strongly advised to go to a sanatorium, but consented only to join his youngest sister who had taken over the management of a small estate in Zurau. From this charming spot he derived the slight nature setting of *The Castle.*

Kafka remained in Zurau until summer 1918 when he returned to his office in Prague. The war made itself felt with increasing ruthlessness (poor food, coal shortage, etc.) and bore down heavily upon the sick poet trying to earn his living and write his books with his last drop of energy. In order to stave off death he moved around desperately from one sanatorium to another. In the summer of 1923 he met Dora Dymant, a young Polish Jewess, still in her teens, in whom the forty-year old writer found the last and most satisfactory love of his tormented life. Soon Dora and Kafka settled in Prague, where he wrote his most cheerful story, *A Little Woman (Eine Kleine Frau).* Between Christmas and New Year Kafka lay ill with a continuous high fever; when he recovered, the couple moved to Zehlendorf. On March 17, 1924, Max Brod took Kafka to his parents, where he remained with Dora till April 10, when, in an open car and with rain pouring down upon them, they transferred him to the Wiener Wald Sanatorium for consumptives. With no private rooms available, Kafka had to lie next to a dying man. Not even Werfel's intercession helped to make things more comfortable for Kafka, and he had to be taken to the Kierling Sanatorium in Klosterneuburg, where he died. He was buried in the Jewish cemetery in Prag-Straschnitz.

During his short literary career of about ten years Franz Kafka published only a few stories. He destroyed as many, and before his death told his friend Brod to burn all his manuscripts. Fortunately, Brod did not carry out his orders and today Kafka's works are available in six volumes, which have exerted a tremendous influence in contemporary world literature. Kafka's writings are predominantly autobiographical and deal with the misunderstanding between man and his environment. They dramatize symbolically the ideas of Kierkegaard and Pascal concerning the implacable fatality of life. The problems involved are moral and spiritual: how to find one's true place and vocation and how to act in accordance with the will of heavenly powers.

Kafka's influence on modern writing has been openly acknowledged by such young writers as Christopher Isherwood and Rex Warner; among older writers Thomas Mann, Alfred Döblin, Jakob Wassermann, Conrad Aiken, Waldo Frank, and Denis Saurat have expressed themselves in most glowing terms on discovering Kafka's work. Saurat called Kafka "the greatest German writer since Nietzsche, the only writer of our time that can stand beside Proust." Waldo Frank claimed that "when the history of the novel of the past hundred years is finally written, Kafka will be accepted as the equal of Dostoievsky and as his immediate successor," and Kafka's incomparable translator, the English critic Edwin Muir, said that "there is no other writer of his age—and it was the age of Rilke and Proust —whose work carries so continuously the mark of greatness. Kafka has that complete integrity that makes all the artistic means he uses so infallibly right, so absolutely suited to his purpose and what he has to say."

WORKS AVAILABLE IN ENGLISH TRANSLATION: The Castle, 1930; The Great Wall of China, 1933; The Metamorphosis, 1937; The Trial, 1937; Amerika, 1938; A Franz Kafka Miscellany, 1940.

ABOUT: A Franz Kafka Miscellany; Brod, M. Franz Kafka; Eloesser, A. Modern German Literature; Kafka, F. The Castle (see Preface to 1941 ed. by T. Mann); Naumann, H. Die deutsche Dichtung der Gegenwart; Schoeps, H. J. Gestalten an der Zeitenwende; Soergel, A. Dichtung und Dichter der Zeit; Bookman November 1930; Colosseum April-June 1939; German Life and Letters October 1937, July 1938; Life and Letters June 1934; Die Literarische Welt June 4, 1926, June 29, 1928, July 15, 1927, August 30, 1929, September 6 and 13, 1939; Literary World August 1934; Nation October 15, 1930; Neue Schweizer Rundschau April 1930, July and August 1931; New Freeman December 10, 1930; New York Herald Tribune "Books" September 21, 1930; Nouvelle Revue Française April 1933; Scribner's December 1930; Scrutiny June 1938.

KAGAWA, TOYOHIKO (July 10, 1888-), Japanese social worker and novelist, was born in Kobe, one of the four illegitimate children of a secretary to the Privy Council (advisers to the Emperor) and a geisha, or dancing girl. On the death of his father, when the boy was four, young Kagawa was sent with his older sister to his ancestral village home, where he was brought up by his foster-grandmother and his father's wife. He attended the Boy's Middle School at Tokushima, a large city on the island of Shikoku. At sixteen he met the missionary Dr. Harry W. Myers, and resolved to become a Christian minister. Kagawa studied at the Presbyterian College, Tokyo; began his professional training at Kobe Theological Seminary; and went to live in Shinkawa, the worst slum of Kobe, where ten thousand people were huddled into houses six feet square. Kagawa filled his room with outcasts; sleeping for four years with the hand of a haunted murderer clutching his; becoming half-blind when he contracted trachoma from another inmate; and on one occasion wearing a red kimono contributed by a courtesan of the district when he had given his trousers away. In May 1914 he married a girl called Spring, a bookbinder and a student of his; left her to carry on his work, and departed to the United States, returning after three years at Princeton (1914-17) with the degree of Doctor of Theology. His autobiographical novel, *Across the Death Line,* was published serially in the monthly *Kaizo (Reconstruction)* and sold 250,000 copies in book form. Of

his fifty books and thirty pamphlets, over a million copies have been sold. Kagawa has earned more than $100,000 in royalties, reserving $40 a month for his family of wife and three children, and spending the rest to maintain a dispensary, a visiting nurse, night schools, and cheap dormitories and eating houses.

A believer in communism of the early Christian or Tolstoyan brand rather than Marxism, Kagawa has been sometimes in collision with the government and on other occasions has enlisted its support. In 1921 he inaugurated the first labor union in Japan, and he has been head of the Osaka Spinners' Union and adviser and reorganiser of the All-Japan Peasant Union. In 1926 he persuaded the government to appropriate a million dollars to wipe out slums in six large cities; after the slump of 1930-31 he was adviser to Tokyo's Social Welfare Bureau, refusing a salary of $9,000 a

year. In 1940 he was imprisoned briefly for his pacifistic opposition to the war with China.

Sturdy and stocky, Kagawa has a sensitive mouth and expressive eyes. As literature, his *Meditations* rank higher than his novels. He lectured in the United States in 1931 and 1935-36.

Several months after the outbreak of war between the United States and Japan in December 1941, a Tokyo short-wave broadcast used Kagawa as a "peace feeler" by quoting him to the effect that all Japan was praying for "an end of war."

WORKS AVAILABLE IN ENGLISH TRANSLATION: Across the Death Line (U.S. title: Before the Dawn) 1924; A Shooter at the Sun, 1925; Love: The Law of Life, 1929; The Religion of Jesus, 1931; New Life Through God, 1931; A Grain of Wheat, 1933; Christ and Japan, 1934; Jesus Through Japanese Eyes, 1934; Meditations on the Cross, 1935; Songs From the Slums: Poems, 1935; Brotherhood Economics, 1936; The Thorn in the Flesh, 1936; The Land of Milk and Honey, 1937; Meditations on the Holy Spirit, 1939; The Challenge of Redemptive Love, 1940; Behold the Man, 1941; The Two Kingdoms, 1941.

ABOUT: Axling, W. Kagawa; Baumann, M. Kagawa: An Apostle of Japan; Hunter, A. A. Three Trumpets Sound; Reid, T. W. Kagawa: Mystic and Man of Action; Current Biography 1941; Homiletic Review December 1923.

*KAISER, GEORG (November 25, 1878-), German dramatist, was born Friedrich Karl Georg Kaiser in Magdeburg, the son of Friedrich Kaiser, a wealthy merchant, and Antonie (Anton) Kaiser. He was educated in the Gymnasium in his native town, but at eighteen left school and entered business. When he was twenty-one he was sent to Argentina, and spent three years as an official of a big German electric company in Buenos Aires. The climate disagreed with him, and after an attack of tropical fever he returned to Europe. He was not able to live in Germany, however, and he went to Spain and Italy, at the same time beginning to write. His first play, *Rektor Kleist,* appeared when he was twenty-four, in 1902. In 1908 he was married to Margarethe Habenicht, and they have two sons and a daughter.

He seems to have taken no part in the First World War (probably because of the condition of his health), but settled in Weimar, with summers at the seashore, and con-

* Died June 6, 1945.

tinued to write. Later he lived in the country, near Berlin, and in the small town of Grünheide. A curious episode in his life occurred in 1920, when this distinguished dramatist spent a term in jail in Munich for stealing furniture from a sublet villa! He stated that he had done this deliberately because he could not live without the comforts and luxuries to which he had always been accustomed, and his and his family's large fortune had been swept away by the inflation. He became a Fellow of the German Academy in 1930. No information regarding him has come out of Germany since the present war began, and where he is now is not known. He never took any part in politics, but the fact that one of his plays, *A Day in October,* was produced in London in 1939 indicates that he is not a Nazi or a Nazi sympathizer. He is a bald, once blond man with a small moustache, and a lined, sad face rather reminiscent of that of Strindberg, one of his masters in the drama.

Herr Kaiser is considered, with the late Ernst Toller, as the outstanding German exponent of Expressionism. Victor Wittner called him "probably the greatest dramatist of our time writing in the German language," and "a poet with vision, [but] never lyric, always dramatic." W. A. Drake said that "the invisible protagonist of all Kaiser's plays is energy—raw, splintering energy.... He is exclusively a dramatist of ideas." He himself says his plays are not *Schauspiele* (entertainments) but *Denkspiele* (plays to make one think). Arthur Eloesser called him "the best pyrotechnician of the German theatre" and "the most versatile of all German dramatists." Like all the Expressionists, his plays are written in a clipped "telegram style." He has been called cold, mathematical, a mere play-architect, yet the keynote of his work is compassion and resentment of wrong, though he has little knowledge or vision of social problems. His best and most characteristic plays are the loosely-connected trilogy, *The Coral, Gas I,* and *Gas II.* These are half social study, half fantasy. He has also written satirical historical dramas and comedies; in almost every case, however, the real hero of his play is the large group or the mass, who act on and are acted on by individuals. In him may be seen many seemingly disparate influences—Strindberg and Wedekind, Bernard Shaw, Schopenhauer, Nietzsche, Dostoievsky, Plato, Hölderlin. W. A. Drake summed up Kaiser's position by saying:

"In his plays are indistinguishably mingled the impulses of a pure craftsman with those of an obstreperous pamphleteer. . . . He knows almost more than is decent of the meanness of his fellow-creatures, but loves them all with an impetuous commiseration that transcends finite judgment."

WORKS AVAILABLE IN ENGLISH: From Morn to Midnight, 1920; Gas, 1924; Fire in the Opera House, 1927; The Phantom Lover, 1928; The Coral, 1929; Vera (also another edition as Villa in Sicily) 1939.

ABOUT: Diebold, B. Anarchie in Drama; Drake, W. A. Contemporary European Writers; Eloesser, A. Modern German Literature; Fuchter, M. J. Social Dialetic in Georg Kaiser's Dramatic Works; Steinbauer, H. Das Deutsche Drama; Canadian Forum May 1931; Theatre Arts Monthly October 1931.

KALLAS, Mrs. AINO JULIA MARIA (KROHN) (August 2, 1878-   ), Finnish-Estonian novelist, writes (in English): "I was born in Wiipur-ki (Viborg), Suomi (Finland). My father was Julius Leopold Friedrich Krohn, Professor of Finnish Literature at the University of Helsinki (Helsingfors), my mother Maria Wilhelmina (Lindroos) Krohn. I was married in 1900 to Dr. Oskar Philipp Kallas, the Estonian scientist, who was first Estonian Minister to Helsinki and later for twelve years minister at the Court of St. James, in London, and at The Hague. We have two sons and two daughters. I have published short stories, novels, essays, and plays, some of which have been translated into English, French, Dutch, Swedish, German, Italian, Danish, and Hungarian. I have made lecture tours in Finland, Estonia, Holland, Great Britain, Canada, and the United States. I have several times received the Prize for Literature in Finland, and also received the Lyceum Club Literary Prize in London. My husband retired from the diplomatic field in 1934, and we live now in Talinn, Estonia."

* * *

This was written before the Soviet conquest of Estonia, so that Mme. Kallas' present welfare and whereabouts are unknown. Until the present crisis at least, she had lived quietly for some years in Talinn. Although she writes in Finnish, her native language, her subjects are frequently Estonian, and drawn from the customs and folklore of her adopted land. Three of her books have been translated into English, one

743

a novel based on an Estonian tradition and containing elements of the supernatural; the other two, collections of realistic short stories and novelettes. Her fiction is tragic and emotional in tone, but never sordid; her general mood is that of exaltation. John Galsworthy, the late English novelist, who was a great admirer of her work, called her "one of the strongest and most individual of living writers." It is unfortunate that a writer of her stature has been compelled to make her appeal to public attention in a difficult tongue unknown to the great mass of readers in Europe and America, and one which there are few competent to translate. It is probably because of this that nothing of hers has appeared in English for ten years or more. *The White Ship* particularly was well received in England (where all her English translations have been published first) and in America, and since she is the author of a long list of novels and stories in Finnish, it is to be hoped that in less troubled times we may be given other specimens of her powerful and interesting talent.

WORKS AVAILABLE IN ENGLISH: The White Ship: Estonian Tales (short stories) 1924; Eros the Slayer: Two Estonian Tales (novelettes) 1927; The Wolf's Bride, 1930.

ABOUT: Kallas, A. The White Ship (see Preface by J. Galsworthy); Saturday Review of Literature July 16, 1932.

KANG, YOUNGHILL (1903-), Korean-American author, writes: "As a child I wrote mostly in classical Chinese characters.

O. Garber

The direct result of contact with Western thought and Western knowledge was to turn my attention to science. When I went to college in America, I meant to study in some definite field of science, as being most valuable to myself and most serviceable to society. I found myself very unhappy and I did not feel at home in the laboratory. The only subject that gave me relief and delight was literature and poetry, read and re-read and unconsciously memorized in the solitary room. Writing was forced upon me, since I could not find my peace anywhere else. For three years (1924-27) I wrote in the Korean language or else in Japanese. But since 1928 I have been trying to write in English. I made a definite decision to seek a job related somewhat to the spiritual realm of my choice (I had no money at all at this time and I was very hungry indeed), and this I have ever since been able to secure. My connection with the *Encyclopaedia Britannica,* under W. B. Pitkin, the managing editor, was very encouraging and broadened my knowledge through the writing and editing of articles on world art and literature. In the same way my teaching at New York University department of English has helped to familiarize me with the great English and American poets, and prepared me for creative writing.

"*The Grass Roof* treated my own life in the Orient, and *East Goes West* (more mature in style and technique) treated my life and that of other Orientals in America. Its original title was *Death of an Exile. The Grass Roof* (translated into several languages, including French and German) may be said to have been written in the mood of the Everlasting Nay of Carlyle; *East Goes West* may be compared to the mood of the Everlasting Yea.

"Now I have been teaching for the last ten years. I do not mind teaching. I am sincere in saying that it is congenial to me to teach literature—but I found so little time to do writing, which is my chief work. That is why I gave up the greater part of my teaching. The only time I did nothing else but writing was when I had a Guggenheim Fellowship in Europe for two years (1933-35)."

* * *

Mr. Kang came to New York from Korea when he was eighteen. He is married to Frances Keely, also a writer. One of his chief concerns at present is an effort to secure his citizenship papers in the United States by means of a special bill in Congress. He was born in the Korean village of Song-Dune-Chi, was seven years old when Japan annexed Korea, and received his first education in Confucian and then in Christian mission schools in his native land. He was one of the last immigrants to reach America before Oriental immigration was prohibited. He has never returned to Korea, his family being dead or scattered. He is now connected with the Metropolitan Museum of Art in New York. Thomas Wolfe said of him: "Kang is a born writer, everywhere he is free and vigorous; he has an original and poetic mind, and he loves life."

PRINCIPAL WORKS: Translations of Oriental Poetry, 1929; The Grass Roof, 1931; The Happy Grove, 1933; East Goes West (novel) 1937.

ABOUT: Kang, Y. The Grass Roof; New Republic December 8, 1937; New Yorker September 18, 1937; Saturday Review of Literature April 4, 1931; Scribner's Magazine November 1931.

KANTOR, MACKINLAY (February 4, 1904-   ), American novelist, writes: "My mother's parents, of Scotch, English, Irish, and Pennsylvania German blood, were pioneers of Hamilton County, Iowa. My mother, Effie Mac-Kinley, married John Martin Kantor, a young Jew who was born in Sweden. They were divorced a few years later. I was born in my grandparents' home in Webster City, Iowa, and spent most of my childhood and youth there. In 1917 my father re-entered our lives temporarily, and the result was a year in Chicago during war-time—a puzzling and chaotic year for an Iowa boy to grow up in. When I was seventeen we were living in Des Moines—living in poverty and on some kind of hopes, I suppose, for I had just decided that the only thing I wanted to do was to write. That same year came an offer to my mother that she edit a daily newspaper in Webster City, and she and I spent the next four years doing just that. The paper didn't belong to us, but we thought it did. I served an apprenticeship valuable to any writer: the daily necessity of writing, words, words, words — handling them and managing them by the thousands, trying to learn how to put them together. High school was only a valueless incident along the way. I did win a Des Moines *Register* short story contest; the prize was awarded when I was just eighteen, and I thought that my future was assured. It was exactly five and a half years later that I received any money from another story.

"In the meantime I had been writing a lot of verse (much of it bad, but still like some of the ballads), and after wandering through newspaper columns and fly-by-night poetry magazines and the back pages of women's magazines with these wares, I found myself twenty-one years old, with no great skill at verse, and a newly completed and perfectly frightful novel. Our newspaper failed, and I went to Chicago in the spring of 1925. There I worked at one job after another, and wrote endless dirges and ballads for B. H. L.'s "Line-o-Type" column in the Chicago *Tribune*. The following year I met Irene Layne, a young commercial artist, and we were promptly married. I got back into newspaper work on the Cedar Rapids *Re-*

publican, but when it was sold suddenly in 1927 I lost the last regular job I ever held.

"My second-written and first-published novel, *Diversey,* I wrote during 1927 at Webster City, while my wife and I were existing in a kind of summer hibernation in my grandparents' old house, and living on four dollars a week. It was not until *Long Remember,* 1934, that I achieved any particular financial or widespread critical success.

"There is one form of criticism which I resent instantly, and that is being taken to task for not sticking to one subject. I write about what interests me most at the time; sometimes the subject is historical, sometimes contemporaneous, and it has even verged on the fantastic [in *The Noise of Their Wings*]. My principal ambition is to become so successful as a novelist that I shall not need to write popular magazine fiction in order to win a generous income, and can thus devote all my time to my novels. In this savage and upset world, I believe firmly that a comfortable income is the greatest sustaining factor which an individual may have, and I marvel not at the frequent manifestations of bitterness in this country, but at the fact that there are not more of them. It seems to me that the world is cruel indeed when two-thirds of the families of the world's richest nation have incomes amounting to less than $1500 per year.

"I am a member of no church or political party or fraternal group. I am not a Democrat, but am an enthusiastic admirer of Franklin D. Roosevelt. In 1937 I built a house in Florida, but no longer live there. My wife and I spend most of our time in and around New York, where our son and daughter attend school."

* * *

Mr. Kantor is a good-looking young man, long-headed, with thick blond hair. In his youth he made several hobo journeys through the Middle West, reflected in his third novel. His hobbies are many: he is an expert fifer, an honorary member of the National Association of Civil War Musicians, he collects butterflies, is an authority on mushrooms, plays golf, and likes "exploring caves and battlefields." He explored battlefields to good purpose in *Long Remember,* one of the finest of Civil War novels. His mind works best at night, and he has been known to telephone his friends at 2 A.M. for advice and criticism. His versatility has made him a realistic novelist of contemporary lower-class life, an historical novelist, and a writer of moving if rather sentimental novelettes.

PRINCIPAL WORKS: Diversey, 1928; El Goes South, 1930; The Jaybird, 1932; Long Remember, 1934; Turkey in the Straw, 1935; The Voice of Bugle Ann, 1935; Arouse and Beware, 1936; The Romance of Rosy Ridge, 1937; The Noise of Their Wings, 1938; Valedictory, 1939; Cuba Libre, 1940.

ABOUT: American Magazine August 1935; Scholastic December 8, 1934; Wilson Library Bulletin October 1932.

KAPEK. See CAPEK

KARLFELDT, ERIK AXEL (July 20, 1864-April 8, 1931), Swedish poet, winner of the Nobel Prize, was born in Folkärna,

Dalecarlia, the part of Sweden which has been the background of much of Selma Lagerlöf's work. His father was Erik Ersson Karlfeldt, a lawyer; his mother, whose second marriage this was, had been Anna Jansdotter. On both sides he came of peasant stock and of a long line of small farmholders; his father had been self-educated and practised among his peasant neighbors, and the boy was brought up beside the rivers and in the forests of his Northern homeland. He was educated at Vesterås and at the University of Upsala; in his first year in college his father lost his money and his ancestral home, and soon died because of shock and grief; the boy, however, continued his studies in poverty and was graduated as a licentiate in 1902. For a time he was a teacher, first in Djursholm, then in the Vermland Folk High School at Molkom. In 1903 he became librarian of the Academy of Agriculture at Stockholm, and remained in this post until 1912. He had been made a member of the Swedish Academy in 1904, and since 1907 had been a member of its Nobel Prize Committee; in 1912 he was made its permanent secretary, and still held that post at his sudden death in Stockholm. It was he who made the official address of welcome to Sinclair Lewis when he received the Nobel Prize for Literature in 1930. (This speech is one of Karlfeldt's two works available in English translation.) In 1906 he had also become a member of the Academy of Social Sciences and Literature of Goteberg.

He married late in life, his wife being nearly twenty years his junior; they had two daughters. Although he had small leisure for writing, he published in the midst of his heavy duties five volumes of poems, in 1895, 1898, 1906, 1918, and 1927. His work became widely known from the first, and in 1912 he was offered the Nobel Prize, but refused it on the ground that it had already been awarded to other Swedish authors and that his poetry was unknown outside of Sweden. He was the only person who has ever refused it. After his death, it was awarded to him posthumously, in 1931. He was a rather fleshy, blond man, looking younger than his years, and with more of the executive than of the poet in his appearance; he has been described as possessing "a resolute face and firm-set figure," and the same commentator said that his salient characteristics were "courage, consistency, directness, and a lonely but deeply sincere and affectionate spirit."

It is indeed strange that this man, truly a major poet, was for his whole lifetime not even a name outside his native country, where his work was known to everybody. Only one volume of his poems has been published in English (and that seven years after his death, by the University of Minnesota Press), though many of the individual poems have been translated, chiefly by Charles Wharton Stork, and have appeared in magazines, principally in *Poetry* and *Poet Lore*. He was purely a lyrist, whose twin sources of inspiration were nature and the peasants of his homeland; Stork called him "a tribal spokesman, . . . in substance strongly national, even local. . . . In form, however, he has the definite and sharply-chiseled technique of classic tradition." All his work was in regular meter and in rhyme "He does not moralize, he presents." His early poems were simple, but "his most characteristic work is highly decorative, with a certain quaintness of design." Yngve Hedvall said one must be Swedish to get the full flavor of Karlfeldt, of "the interweaving of words and rhymes that in its bold splendor has something of peasant baroque." "At first a serene singer of his homeland," said a German critic, "later he became the mournful poet of the demonic elements of Nature."

WORKS AVAILABLE IN ENGLISH: Why Sinclair Lewis Got the Nobel Prize, 1931; Arcadia Borealis, 1938.

ABOUT: Fogelqvist, T. Erik Axel Karlfeldt (in Swedish); Mangard, C. En Bok om Karlfeldt; American-Scandianavian Review January 1925, June 1928, June and October 1931; Bookman January 1932; Poetry June 1932, August 1940; Saturday Review of Literature October 24, 1931.

KATAEV, VALENTIN PETROVICH
(1897-   ), Russian novelist and playwright,
and older brother of Eugene Petrov,^{qv}

was born in Odessa,
the son of a school-
master. On both sides
he was of "bourgeois"
stock; his grand-
fathers were respec-
tively a priest and a
general. While he was
still at school the First
World War began and
he enlisted in the ar-
tillery in 1915. He
served throughout the war and was wounded
twice. After the Bolshevik Revolution he
fought in the Ukraine, on the Red side;
however, he was not always an orthodox
Communist, and at one time spent eight
months in jail as a prisoner of the Cheka.
In 1922 he went to Moscow to live, and the
following year was married. He worked as
a journalist, wrote movies and librettos for
comic operas, and did comic verse and nursery rhymes to earn a living. At the same
time he was hard at work on his first major
novel, *The Embezzlers*. Before its appearance he had published two adventure novels
which were mere pot boilers.

Kataev had indeed been writing from early
childhood, for he began composing verses
at the age of nine, and actually had some
published at twelve. He has since then
published two other novels (translated into
English), two volumes of short stories, and
several plays, of which the most popular is
the farcical *Squaring the Circle*, performed
some six thousand times in Europe and
America, a thousand times in Russia alone.

Valentin Kataev is the licensed humorist
of the Soviets. Doubtless because it is so
thoroughly evident that his boisterous fun
covers a deep conviction, and that his satire
is directed only against superficial aspects of
the Soviet régime, he has been immensely
popular and remains unsuppressed. Joseph
Wood Krutch said that his art is "a two-
edged weapon, and the skill with which he
wields it is revealed in the fact that he
manages somehow not to cut himself on
either edge." He provides a safety-valve
for discontent and a means of working off
irritation through hearty laughter. As a
novelist he derives obviously from the Gogol
of *Dead Souls,* but he is far more earthy
and less sentimental than was his great predecessor among Russian humorists. He has
been called "the Noel Coward of Russia,"
but actually there is little resemblance, except

in the rough-and-tumble of his farces, for
he has none of the brittle sophistication of
the English playwright. At the same time
he is no mere *farceur;* Sir Hugh Walpole
said of *The Embezzlers* that "it can be read
by anyone as a lark, by anyone also as a
sociological study, and then read again as a
piece of literature." In style, his novels
belong to the contemporary "stream of consciousness' school, diffuse, fluid, and loosely
devised.

Few persons look more exactly what one
should expect than does Kataev; with his
pointed ears, the two peaks of his dark hair
on his forehead, his long nose and his wide
smile, he resembles uncannily a classic
faun. And like a faun, he has been called
a bumptious buffoon, who conceals within
his broad comedy a joyous desire to slap
down pretentiousness, hypocrisy, and silliness, no matter in what exalted quarters
they may raise their heads.

WORKS AVAILABLE IN ENGLISH: The Embezzlers, 1929; Time, Forward! 1933 (in England:
Forward, Oh Time! 1934); Squaring the Circle
(play) 1936; Peace Is Where the Tempests Blow
(in England: Lovely White Sail: or, Peace Is
Where the Tempests Blow) 1937; Semyon Kotko,
1941.

ABOUT: Kataev, V. The Embezzlers (see Introduction by Stephen Graham).

KATZ, H. W. (December 31, 1906-   ),
German novelist, writes (in English): "H.W.
Katz, although of Eastern European [Gali-
cian] background, was
reared in Germany
and, in the years be-
fore the Nazi coup,
was the youngest edi-
tor of the important.
German weekly, *Die
Welt am Montag*
(*The World on Mon-
day*). In 1933 he fled
Berlin. He passed a
good part of his exile

Wolff

in France, where he worked as a glass-blower
and a dish-washer, learned to tailor leather
jackets, translated commercial letters, gave
German lessons, and distributed circulars.
His first novel, *The Fishmans,* was written
late at night, for at other hours Katz was
working at odd jobs or looking for them. It
won in 1938 the Heinrich Heine Prize,
awarded by a group of famous refugee writers (Feuchtwanger, Bruno Frank, Mann,
etc.); 220 manuscripts from all over the
world were sent to the jury anonymously.
The book was translated into many languages,
and its success permitted him to concentrate
on the series of projected novels in which

747

he intends to portray the fantastic and catastrophic world through which he and his people have lived since the turn of the century. *No. 21 Castle Street* is the second of this series.

"When the war broke out in 1939, Katz joined the French forces as a volunteer and was awarded the Croix de Guerre with citation; he had become a naturalized French citizen. On April 15, 1941, Katz arrived in New York with a special visa granted by the Department of State."

* * *

Mr. Katz is married and has one daughter. His wife and child were left in Paris while he retreated with the French army almost to Spain. "By a miracle," he ran into them in a village near Bordeaux. At present they are living in Brooklyn. Lion Feuchtwanger said that he "sees things poetically. With all its tribulations, life for him is a colorful fairy story." Norman L. Rollins called his work "utterly honest. . . . There is little art here, no artifice." And N. L. Rothman remarked that though he "works on a small scale, modestly," he is yet "a contemporary voice crying havoc." His novels, which suffer from being poorly organized, have been described by Harold Strauss as a "curious pastiche of history-as-seen-from-below. . . . He writes with a kind of clear-eyed, friendly objectivity that contrasts with the morbid introspection common to most novels about Central European Jews."

WORKS AVAILABLE IN ENGLISH: The Fishmans, 1938; No. 21 Castle Street, 1940.

ABOUT: Saturday Review of Literature July 23, 1938, November 16, 1940.

KAUFMAN, GEORGE SIMON (November 16, 1889-), American playwright and journalist, was born in Pittsburgh, Pa., the

White

son of Joseph S. Kaufman and Nettie (Schamberg) Myers Kaufman. After graduating from the public high school, young Kaufman studied law for a few months, but gave it up as being too difficult. He was successively chainman and transitman on a surveying corps; window clerk in the Allegheny County tax office; stenographer; and traveling salesman for the Columbia Ribbon Co. *The Butter and Egg Man* (1925), his only published play written without a collaborator, which mingles the usual kind of business with show business, perhaps owes something to the latter experience. In 1908 Kaufman became a voluntary contributor of prose and verse to the column then edited by Franklin P. Adams ("F.P.A.") in the New York *Evening Mail.* Adams helped him to obtain a post as columnist on the Washington *Times,* owned by Frank Munsey, who failed to appreciate the humor of his new staff-member. After this year (1912-13) in Washington, Kaufman returned to New York to succeed Adams as columnist on the *Mail,* in 1914-15, when Adams went to the *Tribune.* Kaufman next worked on the dramatic staffs of the New York *Times* and *Tribune,* bringing the Sunday theatrical page up to its present standard of liveliness, variety, and readability, instead of giving it the perfunctory treatment previously accorded to this section of the respective newspapers.

When Henry R. Stern of the Joseph W. Stern Music Co. formed an organization for the encouragement of young playwrights, Kaufman submitted *Going Up,* a farce which was never produced, but which attracted the attention of John Peter Toohey, associated with George C. Tyler, the theatrical producer. Toohey (now Kaufman's press agent) introduced Kaufman to Tyler, who commissioned him to write, with Marc Connelly, a play around the character Dulcy, an amiable nitwit and dispenser of platitudes who had figured for some time in Adams' column. The title-rôle gave the actress Lynn Fontanne an excellent opportunity to show her skill as a comedienne.

To the Ladies and *Merton of the Movies,* also written in collaboration with Connelly, were produced in 1922 and were solid successes. *Merton* was based on the novel by Harry Leon Wilson. Kaufman has written about forty plays in collaboration with Irving Pichel, Larry Evans, Marc Connelly, Edna Ferber (*Minick, The Royal Family,* a comedy about a stage family not unlike the Barrymores, and *The Land Is Bright*), Katherine Dayton, Alexander Woollcott (*The Channel Road,* from a story of Maupassant's, *Boule de Suif,* and *The Dark Tower,* a mystery play), Ring Lardner (*June Moon,* a satire on writers of popular songs), Morrie Ryskind (*Of Thee I Sing,* with a score by George Gershwin, which won the Pulitzer drama prize in 1931, and its sequel, *Let 'Em Eat Cake*), and Moss Hart (*Merrily We Roll Along, You Can't Take It With You,* the Pulitzer prize play of 1936; *The Man Who Came to Dinner*—reputedly satirizing Alexander Woollcott; and *George Washing-*

ton Slept Here). He wrote *The Cocoanuts* and *Animal Crackers,* musical comedies, for the Marx Brothers; *Strike Up the Band,* with Gershwin music; collaborated with Howard Dietz on *The Band Wagon,* a musical revue of 1931; and helped write the patriotic spectacle, *The American Way* (1939). Kaufman has been called the most successful master of stage technique in the contemporary theatre, and an outstanding satirist (although he once defined satire as "what closes Saturday night").

Kaufman married Beatrice Bakrow in March 1917; they have an adopted daughter, Anne. Kaufman, a tall saturnine individual with a swarthy complexion, oversized glasses, and hair cut in a pompadour, exercises close supervision over his acting companies, and once played the part of Laurence Vail, a disgruntled playwright stranded in a Hollywood studio, in his *Once in a Lifetime. Merrily We Roll Along,* a play told "backwards," and one of Kaufman's few serious works, is regarded by many critics as his finest effort, though it did not have the vast popular success of some of his comedies. He has staged *The Front Page* and most of his own plays. He has a palatial country estate at Holicong (near New Hope), Pa.

PRINCIPAL WORKS: Dulcy, (with M. Connelly) 1921; To the Ladies (with M. Connelly) 1922; Merton of the Movies (with M. Connelly) 1922; Beggar on Horseback (with M. Connelly) 1924; The Butter and Egg Man, 1925; The Royal Family (with E. Ferber) 1927; The Channel Road (with A. Woollcott) 1929; Once in a Lifetime (with M. Hart) 1930; Of Thee I Sing (with M. Ryskind) 1931; Dinner at Eight (with E. Ferber) 1932; The Dark Tower (with A. Woollcott) 1933; Let 'Em Eat Cake (with M. Ryskind) 1934; Merrily We Roll Along (with M. Hart) 1934; First Lady (with K. Dayton) 1935; Stage Door (with E. Ferber) 1936; You Can't Take It With You (with M. Hart) 1936; I'd Rather Be Right (with M. and L. Hart) 1937; The Fabulous Invalid (with M. Hart) 1938; The American Way (with M. Hart) 1939; The Man Who Came to Dinner (with M. Hart) 1939; George Washington Slept Here (with M. Hart) 1940; The Land Is Bright (with E. Ferber) 1941.

ABOUT: Adams, F. P. The Diary of Our Own Samuel Pepys; Brown, J. M. Two on the Aisle; Ferber, E. A Peculiar Treasure; Krutch, J. W. American Drama Since 1918; Nathan, G. J. Passing Judgments; Mersand, J. Traditions in American Literature; Current Biography August 1941; Scribner's Magazine May 1933.

*KAYE-SMITH, SHEILA (1888†-),

English novelist, was born at St. Leonards-on-Sea, near Hastings, the daughter of Edward Kaye-Smith, M.R.C.S., L.R.C.P., a prominent physician and surgeon. She was educated privately and published her first novel at twenty, having written from childhood. In 1924 she married T. Penrose Fry, then Anglican rector at St. Leonards-on-Sea, later at Norland and in London. In 1929 he and his wife were both converted to the Roman Catholic Church, and he resigned his ordination. They have no children. When they moved to London, Mrs. Fry bought an ancient oast-house in Sussex so as to have a foothold always in her beloved home county, and after his retirement they returned permanently to Sussex to live. Their home now is in Northam, where in 1940 she was reported playing hostess to three mothers and four children evacuated from London because of the war. At Northam the Frys actually farm their land, so that besides being a prolific and hard-working writer, Mrs. Fry also has the duties

Pinchot

of a land-owner and a farmer's wife. She is slight, very slender, with serious gray eyes under heavy eyebrows.

Sussex belongs to Sheila Kaye-Smith just as thoroughly as Wessex belonged to Thomas Hardy. In the words of Andrew Malone, she has made of it "a special preserve which she has cultivated with great skill and assiduity." Mary Stack called her Sussex novels, so many of which center around the Alard family in its past and present generations, "a Galsworthian saga presented against a Hardyesque background." Love of land is the dominating theme in her novels, and next in prominence is a deep religious strain. Love, in her work, is nearly always tragic, but there is a profound vitality, a passionate life-urge, in all her characters. Though her outlook has been called masculine, she has been most successful in her creation of living, breathing women, from Joanna Godden to Susan Spray.

She speaks frequently in public, having developed by sheer will-power from a poor and hesitant lecturer to an unusually assured and smooth one. Besides her novels and short stories, and her autobiography (which is almost entirely on the spiritual plane), she has written plays and much poetry. As a verse-writer, however, she is rather a competent versifier and balladist than a poet.

Sheila Kaye-Smith's fiction is objective, richly inventive, and written with a loving adherence to the very forms of rustic speech. But too many of her books are too much like one another, she repeats herself far too frequently, and the end-effect is monotony. Mary Stack has summed her up justly if severely in saying: "In spite of brilliance in characterization, she is not a novelist of character, any more than she is a novelist of local color. She is, rather, a novelist with a deep understanding of life and love, with a rich feeling for the land. . . . She has the power of presenting all this in prose that is often beautiful and sometimes masterly. And yet . . . she has all gifts in abundance but greatness is excepted."

PRINCIPAL WORKS: The Tramping Methodist, 1908; Starbrace, 1909; Spell-Land, 1910; Isle of Thorns, 1913; Three Against the World, 1914; Willow's Forge and Other Poems, 1914; Sussex Gorse, 1916; The Challenge to Sirius, 1917; Little England, 1918; Tamarisk Town, 1919; Green Apple Harvest, 1920; Joanna Godden, 1921; The End of the House of Alard, 1923; Saints in Sussex (poems) 1923; The George and the Crown, 1925; Joanna Godden Married and Other Stories, 1926; Iron and Smoke, 1928; The Village Doctor, 1929; Mrs. Adis, and The Mock-Beggar (plays, with J. Hampden) 1929; Shepherds in Sackcloth, 1930; Mirror of the Months (essays) 1931; The History of Susan Spray: The Female Preacher (in America: Susan Spray) 1931; Summer Holiday, 1932; The Children's Summer, 1932; The Ploughman's Progress, 1932; Superstition Corner, 1934; Gallybird, 1934; Selina Is Older (in America: Selina) 1935; Rose Deeprose, 1936; Three Ways Home (autobiography) 1937 The Valiant Woman, 1938; Faithful Stranger and Other Stories, 1938; Ember Lane: A Winter's Tale, 1940; The Secret Son (in England: The Hidden Son) 1942.

ABOUT: Kaye-Smith, S. Three Ways Home; Commonweal January 18, 1935; Contemporary Review January 1925; Fortnightly Review August 1926; Nineteenth Century June 1925; Saturday Review (London) May 3, 1930; Yale Review October 1925.

KEABLE, ROBERT (March 6, 1887-December 23, 1927), English novelist, was born in Bedfordshire, the son of the Rev. Robert

Henry Keable, an evangelical minister. He was educated at Whitgift School and at Magdalene College, Oxford, where he was an exhibitioner and was graduated with First Class honors in the History Tripos. Then, having become an Anglican, he was ordained in 1911, and after a year as a curate went to Africa as a missionary. In 1914 he became rector at Leribe, Basutoland. In 1917 and 1918 he was chaplain with the South African forces in France. The experiences he underwent at this time, and his conflicts with the church authorities, caused him to revolt violently against the church

and everything it stood for. He resigned his ordination, and in poverty began to write a novel which would express his righteous anger. This act, seemingly suicidal to his career, was actually the making of it. He had previously published poems, essays, and religious studies which had attracted no attention whatever. His novel, Simon Called Peter, was a sensation. (There were not lacking critics to say that it was sensational as well.) It became a best-seller on both sides of the Atlantic, was filmed, and made its author at once rich and famous. Like two earlier novels dealing with a clergyman's disillusionment and loss of faith, Mrs. Humphry Ward's Robert Elsmere and Margaret Deland's John Ward, Preacher, it aroused the greatest excitement in the reading public—and like them both, it has been thoroughly forgotten.

Keable never exactly repeated his success, though Peradventure, which was partly autobiographical, was written with the same urgency of feeling. For the most part he tended to repeat himself, and in the end became "a rather monotonous rebel against convention and prudery." In the two or three years between writing Simon Called Peter and reaping the financial rewards of a best-selling novel, he was obliged to take to teaching, at Dulwich and Dunstable, a profession he detested. As soon as he was able to do so, and warned by his physician of failing health, he went to live in Tahiti. It was too late, however, for recovery of his health. Writing against time, he made himself more ill; and he died in Tahiti, of Bright's disease, when he was only forty. He was never married.

The great influence on his youth was that of Monsignor Hugh Benson, of the famous Benson family of writers, who almost made him a Roman Catholic. (He ended as an aggressive Freethinker.) It has been remarked that at times his style resembles a serious parody of Benson's. On one side of his nature, he was weighed down by a sense of social responsibility and by spiritual unrest; on the other, he was a buoyant, boyish man, generous and eager, remembered by his friends for "his bright whimsical sideglance, his quick, uneven gait," life-hungry, sensitive, imaginative, sympathetic. In a sense he never matured either as a writer or as a man; cut short in full tide, he never developed, as a longer life would have enabled him to do, his real powers. Nevertheless, he left enough to evidence him as a writer of simplicity and sincerity, with imaginative gifts and a faculty for close observation, whose work was injured, but also created, by the fact that no matter what the changes in his religious viewpoint he remained always a preacher.

PRINCIPAL WORKS: A City of the Dawn, 1915; Standing By; War Time Reflections in France and Flanders, 1919; Pilgrim Places, 1920; Simon Called Peter, 1921; Mother of All Living: A Novel of Africa, 1922; Peradventure: or, The Silence of God, 1923; Recompence (sequel to Simon Called Peter) 1925; Numerous Treasure, 1925; Tahiti: Isle of Dreams, 1926; Recognition, 1926; Lighten Our Darkness (in America: Ann Decides) 1927; The Madness of Monty (in America: Though This Be Madness) 1929; The Great Galilean, 1929.

ABOUT: Bookman (London) February 1928; London Mercury February 1928.

"KEENE, FARADAY." See JARRETT, C. H.

KELLAND, CLARENCE BUDING-TON (July 11, 1881-), American novelist and short-story writer, was born in

Portland, Mich., the son of Thomas Kelland and Margaret (Budington) Kelland. He was educated in the private schools of Detroit; received his LL.B. degree from the Detroit College of Law in 1902, and five years later married Betty Carolina Smith of Ludington, Mich. From 1903 to 1907 Kelland was a reporter and political editor of the Sunday edition of the Detroit *News.* Now one of the most prolific and successful purveyors of popular fiction, he got his start as a writer of juvenile stories. He edited the *American Boy* from 1907 to 1915, and is still a contributing editor. In the last three years of his editorship he lectured at the University of Michigan on juvenile literature and on writing as a profession. *Mark Tidd* (1913), his first book, launched its plump young hero on a career which included experiences, in several sequels, as business man, editor, manufacturer, and in the backwoods. In 1918 Kelland was director of overseas publicity for the Y.M.C.A. and its war-work for the American Expeditionary Force in France. Scattergood Baines, a fat, resourceful Yankee promoter, was another creation of Kelland's who became familiar to the multi-million readers of the *Saturday Evening Post* and the *American Magazine. Cosmopolitan* paid him $75,000 for the serial rights to *Star Rising* (1938). *Mr. Deeds Goes To Town* (1936), one of the most popular moving pictures ever made, and

starring Gary Cooper, was based on one of Kelland's short stories. He is a member of the Players, Century, Coffee House, and North Hempstead (N.Y.) Country Clubs; is a Mason; and has been for several years president of the Dutch Treat Club, for whose annual shows, presented in New York for members and their friends, Kelland has more than once written skits and sketches. The Kellands' permanent residence is near Phoenix, Arizona, where they own the Scattergood Date Gardens. Kelland is also part-owner of Rancho Santa Marita, a 50,000-acre cattle ranch in Yavapai County, Arizona.

Kelland's more sophisticated magazine fiction is humorous, well plotted, and usually well written, but his most popular figure is still Scattergood Baines. In this wide acceptance Mr. Kelland finds a moral. "Scattergood Baines came into being in 1915 while I was in Vermont inefficiently helping my brother-in-law to manufacture clothes-pins. There was no human original, but rather he expressed my notion of what a true Vermonter was like. The first three stories of his exploits appeared in the *Saturday Evening Post.* Then John Siddall of the *American Magazine,* took him over, and he has continued to inhabit the *American's* pages through the reign of the present editor, Sumner Blossom. In the *American* he has appeared in at least a hundred short stories and in one novel, so you will see that he has been a very good friend to his inventor. Probably he has been the most persistent example of longevity in the history of American fiction. . . . To my surprise and to my pleasure I have had news of his existence in nearly every state of the Union. . . . It may be that in the Scattergood stories there is little literary merit visible to the critical eye, but nevertheless I am content with them and even a little proud to have been the conduit through which they flowed. To satisfy the demanding eye of those who read alone to discover literary excellence is a fine thing; to satisfy the homely, decent emotions and to give pleasure to millions is also a splendid thing. To combine the two is a miracle. If I were compelled to choose between the two, being impotent to work miracles, I believe I would with deliberation choose the latter."

Early in 1942 Mr. Kelland was appointed executive and publicity director of the Republican National Committee. He had long been an opponent of President Roosevelt's "New Deal" policies.

PRINCIPAL WORKS: Mark Tidd, 1913; Mark Tidd in the Backwoods, 1914; Pieces of Silver, 1914; The American Boy's Workshop, 1914; Mark

Tidd in Business, 1915; Into His Own, 1915; The Hidden Spring, 1915; Mark Tidd's Citadel, 1916; Sudden Jim, 1916; The Source, 1917; Mark Tidd, Editor, 1917; Mark Tidd, Manufacturer, 1918; The Little Moment of Happiness, 1919; Conflict, 1920; Scattergood Baines, 1921; Contraband, 1922; The Steadfast Heart, 1923; Miracle, 1924; Rhoda Fair, 1925; Dance Magic, 1926; Dynasty, 1929; Hard Money, 1930; Gold, 1931; Speak Easily, 1932; The Great Crooner, 1933; Cat's-paw, 1934; Dreamland, 1935; Roxana, 1936; Mr. Deeds Goes to Town, 1936; Jealous House, 1937; Spotlight, 1937; Star Rising, 1938; Arizona, 1939; Skin Deep, 1939; Scattergood Baines Returns, 1940; The Valley of the Rising Sun, 1940; Scattergood Baines Pulls the Strings, 1941; Silver Spoon, 1941.

ABOUT: Kelland, C. B. Scattergood Baines Returns (see Preface); New York Herald Tribune January 5, 1942; New York Times Book Review April 27, 1941.

KELLER, ALBERT GALLOWAY

(April 10, 1874-), American sociologist, was born in Springfield, Ohio, the son of

Jeremiah Keller and Laura Stephenson (Smith) Keller. He received his B.A. at Yale in 1896 and his Ph.D. in 1899. In 1898 he married Clara Louise Gussmann; they have two daughters and a son.

Dr. Keller became connected with the social science department of Yale in 1900, when he entered as instructor. In 1907 he was appointed professor of the science of society, succeeding and carrying on the work of the eminent William Graham Sumner. For a brief time at the end of the First World War he was a captain on the General Staff of the United States Army. Besides his own works, he has been the authorized editor of Sumner's essays, and also edited J. Scott Keltie's History of Africa. On January 16, 1942, Dr. Keller met his last class at Yale before taking a leave of absence until his normal retirement, at 68, in June. He had been fifty years at Yale as student and teacher. On his retirement he became secretary of the Graham Sumner Club, formed in 1914 by a group of Dr. Keller's students.

Dr. Keller was known as a "hard" teacher who took no nonsense from his pupils. With his heavy dark eyebrows and dark eyes contrasting with white hair and moustache, he looks the rigid disciplinarian he is. His economic views may be justly described as reactionary; he is even farther to the right than his colleague and master Sumner was, and thrift and private enterprise are his

economic idols. He is by no means, however, a stodgy writer, for a great deal of biting wit is hidden in his tirades against liberal social philosophy. John Chamberlain, who was his pupil, called him "gruff, ursine, sardonic in his humor, and conservative as a clam in his economics." He is an authority on the technical aspects of his subject, and his book on ethnography has been translated into Spanish and published in Mexico. His Societal Evolution has been translated into Japanese. He was one of the contributors to the anthology, Evolution of Man, 1922 (published as Evolution of the Earth and Man, 1929).

PRINCIPAL WORKS: Homeric Society, 1902; Queries in Ethnography, 1903; Colonization, 1908; Physical and Commercial Geography (with H. E. Gregory & A. L. Bishop) 1910; Commercial and Industrial Geography (with A. L. Bishop) 1912; Societal Evolution, 1915; Industry and Trade (with A. L. Bishop) 1918; Through War to Peace, 1918; Starting-Points in Social Science, 1923; Science of Society (4 vols., with W. G. Sumner) 1927; Man's Rough Road, 1932; Reminiscences of William Graham Sumner, 1933; Brass Tacks, 1938.

ABOUT: New York Herald Tribune January 16, 1942; Saturday Review of Literature July 9, 1938.

KELLY, Mrs. ELEANOR (MERCEIN)

(August 30, 1880-), American novelist and short-story writer, was born in Milwaukee,

Wis., the daughter of Thomas Royce Mercein, descendant of an émigré Royalist family of Southern France, and Lucy (Schley) Mercein, who belonged to a long-established Maryland family. She spent her childhood in the Middle West,

and lived in a rather noble, dark, old house that overlooked Lake Michigan. In 1898 she was graduated as valedictorian from the Georgetown Convent of the Visitation, in Washington, D. C. Three years later she married Robert Morrow Kelly, Jr., son of a prominent journalist in Louisville, Ky. Here they made their home and converted an antebellum hillside barn into a studio house. Mr. Kelly died in 1926.

Her first book, Toya the Unlike, was indifferently received; Kildares of the Storm, however, noticeably widened her reading public. Then came three novels native to Kentucky. Beginning with Basquerie (1927), she wrote a trilogy laid in the Pyrenees sector of Spain, her most successful setting for novels. Spanish Holiday is a book of semi-travel tales of a country that seemed to Mrs. Kelly to be "gentle, fiercely chivalrous, complex and yet as simple as the eternal verities...." Others of her books have as back-drops Moorish Africa and Syria and the ancient port of Ragusa and Corfu.

Since the late 'twenties she has done much traveling, always collecting new grist for her seemingly inexhaustible supply of travel sketches and tales in the *Saturday Evening Post, the Ladies' Home Journal,* and *Collier's.* She is primarily a story-teller, of the old "local color" school.

PRINCIPAL WORKS: Toya the Unlike, 1913; Kildares of the Storm, 1916; Why Joan? 1918; The Mansion House, 1923; Basquerie, 1927; Book of Bette, 1929; Spanish Holiday, 1930; Nacio: His Affairs, 1931; Arabesque, 1933; Sounding Harbors, 1935; Mixed Company, 1936.

ABOUT: Overton, G. The Women Who Make Our Novels; Louisville (Ky.) Courier-Journal November 3, 1940; Saturday Evening Post October 31, 1936; Forewords to the works.

KELLY, GEORGE EDWARD (1887-),
American playwright, was born in Philadelphia, one of ten children of John Henry Kelly and Mary (Costello) Kelly. Walter Kelly (d. 1939) vaudeville's "Virginia Judge," who afterwards invaded the legitimate stage, was his brother. Young George was educated privately in the Quaker City;

N. Muray

avoided college altogether; took some special work in mathematics, and in 1911, presumably smitten by his brother's stage ascendency, tried his own hand at acting. For about five years he was on the road, playing juvenile rôles; and then plunged into vaudeville, when Nazimova and Madame Bernhardt were headliners in the field. Kelly traveled the Keith and Orpheum circuits, using largely his own sketches. "The Woman Proposes," "Finders Keepers," and "Poor Aubrey" (afterwards enlarged for *The Show-Off*) were some of the favorites.

His first full-length play, *The Torchbearers,* a piece that poked fun at the Little Theatre movement, was produced in 1922; Fox Films, about fifteen years later, bought it for $17,500. In 1924 *The Show-Off,* a plotless study of a winsome braggart, made Kelly the most talked-of playwright on Broadway and was recommended for the Pulitzer Prize—but the awarding committee's vote went to Hatcher Hughes' *Hell-Bent fer Heaven.* Next year, however, *Craig's Wife* made him a Pulitzer winner;

it was a technically excellent characterization of a "pitiless nag" who sacrifices the happiness of those around her for material security. Neither *Daisy Mayme,* in 1926 nor *Behold the Bridegroom* (1927), which from a literary point of view was conceded to be "far above the level," was very well received. In October 1929 Rowland Stebbins produced *Maggie the Magnificent,* with a cast that included Joan Blondell and James Cagney, but it was too "distressingly truthful" to win the hearts of playgoers; *Philip Goes Forth* (1931) fared no better. For several years Kelly remained "enormously uninterested" in the theatre, but he spoke up again in 1936 with *Reflected Glory,* directing it himself. But the play, presumably, did more for Tallulah Bankhead's reputation as an actress than for Kelly's name as a playwright, and, except for the unadulterated comedy of a few superb short scenes, made one critic "wish that the theatre would stop trying to behave itself."

Kelly is tall, lithe, and noticeably Gaelic, with a quick flash of his eye, a nervous intensity of gesture, and a quiver about his mouth that easily breaks into a smile. He is unmarried and has spent most of his time, during the last few years, in Hollywood— "coasting," says Burns Mantle. "I don't care," Kelly has often said, "to what devastation my work is subjected, but I do dislike any publicity concerning myself." He has, however, admitted that winter is the tragedy of his life: "In fact that is my one genuine distinction—that I have hated cold weather more than any other human being."

PRINCIPAL WORKS: The Torchbearers, 1922; The Show-Off, 1924; Craig's Wife, 1925; Daisy Mayme, 1926; Behold the Bridegroom, 1927; Maggie the Magnificent, 1929; Philip Goes Forth, 1931; Reflected Glory, 1936.

ABOUT: Flexner, E. American Playwrights 1918-1938; Mantle, B. Contemporary American Playwrights; Morehouse, W. Forty-Five Minutes Past Eight; Nation October 3, 1938; New Republic October 7, 1936; Scholastic March 6, 1935; Theatre Guild Magazine July 1930.

KELLY, JAMES FITZMAURICE-. See
FITZMAURICE-KELLY

*KENNEDY, CHARLES RANN (February 14, 1871-), Anglo-American playwright
and actor, was born in Derby, England, the son of Edmund Hall Kennedy and Annie Leng (Fawcett) Kennedy. His grandfather, also named Charles Rann Kennedy, was a well known Greek scholar. Originally intended for holy orders, young Kennedy instead worked as an office boy and clerk from thirteen to sixteen; as

lecturer and writer to twenty-six, when he married Edith Wynne Matthison of Birmingham, Warwickshire, in July 1898; and thenceforth was an actor, press-agent, writer of short stories, articles and poems, and a theatrical business manager to 1905, when he devoted his time mainly to dramatic writing. With Miss Matthison, who appeared in several of his plays and is widely known for her portrayal of Everyman in the old English morality play of that name, Kennedy  headed for several years the dramatic department of Bennett Junior College in Millbrook, N.Y. They have now retired, and live in Los Angeles, Calif. Kennedy is a member of the Players Club in New York City, and a thirty-third degree Mason. He became a naturalized American citizen in 1917.

Kennedy made his first appearance on the stage at Her Majesty's Theatre, London, April 28, 1897, as a starving citizen in *The Seats of the Mighty*. After touring as Lord Drelincourt in *Jim the Penman*, he became treasurer at the Metropole Theatre, Camberwell, for two years, then business manager and actor with Ben Greet, playing Shakespearean parts and the Doctor in *Everyman*. His first appearance in New York was made at Mendelssohn Hall, 1903, as the Doctor and the Messenger in *Everyman*. In 1913 he played in Chicago as John Heron in his own *The Necessary Evil*. In January 1918 he appeared at the Cort Theatre in *Everyman*, and that same month produced his own play, *The Army With Banners*, at the Vieux Colombier Theatre. The British Censor refused to license his Biblical play, *The Chastening*, and Kennedy took it to St. Paul's Church in June 1924, also showing it at the Mary Ward Settlement, playing the Carpenter himself. *The Servant in the House* (1908), Kennedy's first and best-known drama, showed a Christ-like figure solving the problems of a modern household. *The Passing of the Third-Floor Back*, by Jerome K. Jerome, deals with a similar theme, and the two are often confused. *The Idol-Breaker* (1914) was also a symbolic, if a more secular play; in the figure of The Man of Letters it poked some fun at Acton Davies, then dramatic critic of the New York *Evening Sun*. *The Terrible Meek* (1911), which has been read and acted in thousands

of churches, seemed to H. T. Parker of the Boston *Transcript* to be "written oftenest in big, swelling, cadenced abstract words. The ideas that underlie all these words are the abstractions beloved of Mr. Kennedy's visionary spirit." All his plays are distinguished by sonority and earnestness, but, with the exception of *The Servant in the House*, have not been very well fitted to the requirements of the commercial theatre. As an actor, Kennedy also toured the United States in *The Chastening, The Admiral, Old Nobody*, and *The Salutation*. He retired from the American stage in 1924, but in July 1926 played Dante Alighieri in *The Salutation* at the St. Pancras People's Theatre. At Millbrook he staged and usually appeared in the annual Greek play. An imposing-looking man of a rather old-fashioned theatrical type, Charles Rann Kennedy reminded Joyce Kilmer, who interviewed him once, of Chesterton's *Manalive*. He once jocularly proved, by approved cryptogrammic methods, that Shakespeare's plays were written by C. Rann Kennedy! Most of his own plays have been assembled in omnibus volumes.

PRINCIPAL WORKS: The Servant in the House, 1908; The Winterfeast, 1908; The Terrible Meek, 1911; The Necessary Evil, 1913; The Idol-Breaker, 1914; The Rib of the Man, 1916; The Army With Banners, 1917; The Fool From the Hills, 1919; The Chastening, 1922; The Admiral, 1923; The Salutation, 1925; Old Nobody, 1927; Crumbs, 1931; Flaming Ministers, 1932; Face of God, 1935; Beggar's Gift, 1935.

ABOUT: Chesterton, G. K. A Miscellany of Men; Kilmer, J. Literature in the Making; Atlantic Monthly January 1909; Independent July 30, 1908, April 4, 1912.

KENNEDY, MARGARET (1896-), English novelist, was born in London, the daughter of Charles Moore Kennedy, a barrister. Her later childhood was spent in Kent and in Cornwall. She was educated at Cheltenham School and at Somerville College, Oxford, taking a degree in history. She had been writing since early childhood—in fact before she could read  or write, she had composed a "play" which was performed frequently by her small cousins and playmates; and before she entered college she had written (and destroyed) five novels and three plays. Her first published work, however, was a textbook on modern European history, one of a series, written on assignment. It took her two years to do, but she is grateful for the experience, since it provided an excellent training-course in handling words and arranging material. Her first real success was with her second published novel, *The Constant Nymph,* a delightful if a trifle sentimental novel which was a best-seller and which, when dramatized the year after its publication by the author and Basil Deane, was also a success as a play. (And still later as a film.)

In 1925 Miss Kennedy married David Davies, a barrister who had formerly been secretary to Lord Asquith and Oxford, and who is now Judge of the County Courts and a King's Counsellor. They have a son and two daughters. Their home in London is on the top of a hill, in Campden Hill Square. In peacetime she did all her writing pacing up and down in her drawingroom study, usually reciting her work aloud as it came to her—a reversion, perhaps, to the very early days of her life when she refused to learn to write because it was so much easier to dictate! Her avocation is music; she is an accomplished pianist and has a fine singing voice. Besides her novels, she has done a great deal of writing for the movies, and calls herself a "film fan." She is tall, fair, and slender, "typically English" in appearance. She has a passion for mountain-climbing, with the Welsh mountains her favorites.

In an interview with Edith Olivier, she said: "I hardly ever read a modern book which is not well written; their weakness seems to me that they are often *too* bookish." No one can allege this of Margaret Kennedy's own novels. Asked if she drew her vivid characterizations from life, she said: "I never make a real portrait. I borrow people's *appearances* from all over the place. Then someone *suggests* a kind of character to me, but by the time I've finished working on it, it's unlike anyone I've ever known." The freshness and spontaneity of her work are unfailing, her humor bubbles, and despite a weakness for her heroines which sometimes degenerates from tenderness to sentimentality, her novels are so full of her own love of life that they captivate the reader as well. She is never solemn (though sometimes pathetic) or profound, but she is nearly always engaging.

PRINCIPAL WORKS: A Century of Revolution, 1922; The Ladies of Lyondon, 1923; The Constant Nymph, 1924; A Long Week-End, 1927; Red Sky at Morning, 1927; Come With Me (play, with B. Deane) 1928; The Fool of the Family (sequel to The Constant Nymph) 1930; Return I Dare Not, 1931; A Long Time Ago, 1932; Escape Me Never! (play) 1934; Together and Apart, 1936;

Autumn (play, with G. Ratoff) 1937; The Midas Touch, 1938; Where Stands a Wingèd Sentry, 1941; The Mechanized Muse, 1942.

ABOUT: Arts and Decoration May 1925; Bookman (London) October 1925; Life February 10, 1941.

KENT, ROCKWELL (1882-   ), American artist and travel writer, was born in Tarrytown Heights, N.Y., the son of Rockwell and Sarah (Holgate) Kent. He was educated at Columbia, where he studied architecture, and then studied art under William M. Chase, Robert Henri, and other famous painters. His first exhibition was held at the National Academy of Design in 1905. In 1909 he married Kath-

B. Martinson

leen Whiting, and they had two sons and three daughters. In 1926 he married Frances Lee, by whom he has one son. They were divorced in 1940. He was famous as an illustrator, cartoonist (under the pseudonym of Hogarth, Jr.), and painter long before he took to writing. His books are a by-product of his adventures and travels, and are all semi-autobiographical in character, though *Salamina* is supposedly a novel. All except *Voyaging,* which has its background in Terra del Fuego, deal with Alaska. When he is not on one of his one-man expeditions to the North, he lives in Ausable Forks, N.Y. He is a "character," an individualistic, controversial, contradictory man, who insists on his own independence but patriarchally governs his family, a born wanderer who is yet an avid home-builder, a gray-eyed, sinewy man who in spite of his bald head seems much younger than he is. He says of himself: "I dislike criticism and critics. I have only one life and I'm going to live it as nearly as possible as I want to live it. I think of all the arts as by-products of life. Life has always been, and God help me, always will be, so exciting that I'll want to talk about it. I rate even my being an artist and a writer by being heart and soul a revolutionist. I think that the ideals of youth are fine, clear, and unencumbered; and that the real art of living consists in keeping alive the conscience and the sense of values that we had when we were young. If I amount to anything today it is because to some extent I have done that." In many a political and economic fight Kent has demonstrated his loyalty to the cause of the underprivileged.

Louis Untermeyer called Kent's books "completely unaffected, richly delineated, wholly revealing, . . . extended letters to the reader, . . . fresh and provocative, immediate in their compulsion." In addition to his own books, he has illustrated many books by others, including Voltaire's *Candide*, Melville's *Moby Dick*, and Chaucer's *Canterbury Tales*. He once had himself incorporated to facilitate sale of his work, and is reputed to be the world's first incorporated artist.

PRINCIPAL WORKS: Wilderness, 1920; Voyaging, 1924; N by E, 1930; Rockwellkentiana, 1933; Salamina, 1935; This Is My Own, 1940; A Northern Christmas, 1941.

ABOUT: Armitage, M. Rockwell Kent; Kent, R. Rockwellkentiana; Untermeyer, L. From Another World; American Magazine March 1925; Arts & Decoration March 1920; Collier's June 5, 1920; Colophon June 1936; Demcourier September 1937; Forum February 1932; International Studio June 1919; July 1924; New Republic May 4, 1927; Outlook July 9, 1930; Saturday Review of Literature January 3, 1931; Scribner's September 1937; Time September 20, 1937.

KER, WILLIAM PATON (August 30, 1855-July 17, 1923), Scottish educator and authority on medieval literature, was born

in Glasgow, the eldest son of William Ker, merchant, and Caroline Agnes (Paton) Ker. After attending Glasgow Academy and Glasgow University he proceeded in 1874 to Balliol College, Oxford, where Benjamin Jowett was Master. In 1876 Ker took a First Class in Classical Moderations, followed in 1878 by a Second Class in *Literae Humaniores*. Winning a Taylorian scholarship in 1878, he was elected to a fellowship at All Souls College, Oxford, in November 1879, and clung to this connection for forty-four years. In 1878, also, he was appointed assistant to William Young Sellar as Professor of Humanity at the University of Edinburgh and in 1883 was made professor of English literature and history at the new University College of South Wales, Cardiff— "hard, pioneering work." In 1889 Ker succeeded Henry Morley in the Quain Chair of English language and literature at University College, London, and when the university was reorganized in 1900 was appointed chairman of the modern languages board. A conservative in politics and everyday life,

Ker hated officialdom and slackness. During the First World War he organized the department of Scandinavian studies at London University, was made first director, and resigned all posts in 1922. His heart was at Oxford which elected him to the Chair of Poetry in 1920. There, as R.W. Chambers has said, he was "at once a wit, a sage and an institution." On his week-ends he took the young Fellows for walks in the country, or sat with them in the Common Room. Ker never married. He loved "children, animals, climbing, rowing, dancing, good wine and good fellowship." He fell dead of heart failure while climbing in the Alps (at sixty-seven!) and was buried in the old churchyard in Macugnaga, Italy.

Ker's best-known work, *Epic and Romance*, appeared when he was forty-two. He was considered an authority on the history of poetic forms, the relation of form and substance, and medieval literature in general.

PRINCIPAL WORKS: Epic and Romance, 1897; The Dark Ages, 1904; Essays on Medieval Literature, 1905; The Art of Poetry: Seven Lectures, 1920-1922, 1923; English Literature: Medieval, 1924; Form and Style in Poetry (ed. by R. W. Chambers) 1928. *Editor*—The Essays of John Dryden, 1900; Froissart's Chronicles (trans. by Lord Berners) 1901-1903.

ABOUT: McCunn, J. & F. Recollections of W. P. Ker by Two Friends; Alpine Journal November 1923; London Times July 20, 21, 23, 25, 1923; Revue Anglo-Américaine February 1926.

KERR, SOPHIE (August 23, 1880-), American novelist and short story writer, was born in Denton, on the Eastern Shore of Maryland, her maiden name being Kerr. She was educated at Hood College, Frederick, Md. (B.A. 1898), and at the University of Vermont (M.A. 1901). In 1904 she married John D. Underwood, and during her married life lived in New England.

Buschke

However, she was divorced in 1908 and has not remarried. For a few years she wrote under her married name, but some time ago resumed her maiden one. In her youth she did some newspaper work: was woman's editor successively of the Pittsburgh *Chronicle-Telegraph* and *Gazette Times*, and later was for several years managing editor of the *Woman's Home Companion*. She has traveled widely, but now spends most of her time in a New York apartment, the real owner of which, she says, is a cat. She is a delightful hostess, and Ann Hark called her "a culinary expert and a connoisseur of food." Besides her stories, she wrote a play, *Big-Hearted Herbert,* with A.S. Richardson, which was produced in 1934, and which one critic called "good clean fun, laid on with a steam-shovel." Her *forte* is stories and serials in the women's magazines, and she has been a popular and prolific writer for them for many years. Her novels belong in the same category—done with a sure professional touch, but lightly skimming the surface of life. Gerald Hewes Carson remarked of her: "She might tell us much about human nature as it peers out from beneath its humdrum shell of business. But she is ambitious only to amuse. One must grant that she can do that to perfection."

PRINCIPAL WORKS: Love at Large, 1916; The Blue Envelope, 1917; The Golden Block, 1918; The See-Saw, 1919; Painted Meadows, 1920; One Thing Is Certain, 1922; Confetti, 1927; Mareea-Maria, 1929; Tigers Is Only Cats, 1929; In for a Penny, 1931; Girl Into Woman, 1932; Stay Out of My Life, 1933; Miss J. Looks On, 1935; There's Only One, 1936; Fine To Look At, 1937; Adventure With Women, 1938; Curtain Going Up, 1940; Michael's Girl, 1942.

ABOUT: Ladies' Home Journal May 1928; Reader's Digest August 1940.

KESTEN, HERMANN (January 28, 1900-), German novelist and playwright, was born in Nuremberg. He writes: "I am  a Jew. My father's father was a farmer; my mother's father a merchant. My father was an agent in the import and export of eggs. His office was in our apartment and it seemed to me that his whole business was to send and receive cables, from Cairo to London, from Shanghai to Trieste. At least twenty messenger boys came daily to our place with cables and telegrams, and they became my friends. As a little child I got accustomed to answering telephone calls from faraway cities. My father was my best teacher, friend, model, and ideal. He was a man of leisure and dignity, a lover of books and coffeehouses, children and men, an admirer of Voltaire and Lessing, Swift and Heine, the Bible and Tolstoy. He was a Spinozist and a fanatic on the question of children's education and in matters of honor. He died as a soldier in the First World War and is buried in Lubin, Poland. I studied at the Humanistisches Gymnasium in Nuremberg, and at universi-

ties at Erlangen and Frankfurt-on-the-Main, specializing in history and literature. I wrote a dissertation on Heinrich Mann."

From the age of five, Kesten was a voracious reader: "I began with the Bible and Schiller, with Swift and Heine (I hated children's books) and have not yet finished reading." His first story, "Vergebliche Flucht," appeared in the *Frankfurter Zeitung* in 1926 and was later included with another novelette which gave title to *Die Liebes-Ehe* (1929). He became widely known in 1928 when his first novel, originally serialized in the *Frankfurter Zeitung* in 1927, won the Kleist Prize—this was *Joseph Breaks Free,* a vivid depiction of the struggles of a child to break away from his family. In his second novel, *Ein Ausschweifender Mensch* (1929), the struggle widens into that of a man trying to free himself from the bonds that link him to his fatherland.

But Kesten's mordant humor was not circumscribed to fiction: his comedy *Maud Liebt Beide* was staged in Kassel in 1928; *Admet,* based on the Alcestis-theme, in Oberhausen in 1929; and *Die Heilige Familie* in 1930 at Berlin's Schiffbauerdamm theatre. He wrote, besides, *Babel* (1930) and *Einer Sagt die Wahrheit* (1931) and in 1931 he collaborated with Ernst Toller in *Wunder in Amerika* which was performed at Mannheim and translated into English as *Mary Baker Eddy* (1935).

Before Hitler, his vitriolic novels, *Happy Man* (1931) and *Der Scharlatan* (1932), in which he attacked the hypocrisy and false ideology of Nazism, won Kesten the hatred of the Hitlerites. On Hitler's seizure of power he was forced to flee from Germany; he was at that time literary editor of the vanguard Berlin publishing house, Gustav Kiepenhauer. In exile in Amsterdam he founded the first great anti-Nazi publishing house, Allert de Lange, of which he was literary editor from its inception in 1933 until the invasion of the Lowlands in 1940 compelled yet another flight. He became an American resident in 1940.

During his Netherlands exile Kesten, on completing the sardonic novel *Der Gerechte* (1934), turned to a vein, historical recreation, which has enhanced his reputation: he has written two monumental historical romances: *Spanish Fire* (1936), dealing with Ferdinand and Isabella, and *I, the King* (1937), based on the life and times of Philip the Second of Spain. Of *I, the King* Hendrik Willem Van Loon wrote: "It is supposed to be the story of Philip of Spain, but it is much more than that. It seems like the final word upon the hideous and age-old problem of man's tyranny over man. In writing this book, Hermann Kesten has done well by the country of his adoption. In addition, he has richly deserved the gratitude of those in every part of the world who still believe that the personal freedom and the integrity of the individual are the beginning and end of happiness for a truly civilized people." Spain's contemporary tragedy also affected Kesten profoundly and his concern resulted in the vivid and intense novel, *The Children of Guernica* (1939).

Besides his fecund literary creation which has found its way into all civilized languages, Kesten has compiled several anthologies— French and German short stories, Heine's verse and prose; has translated into German, with his sister Gina, works by Julian Green, Jules Romains, and Jean Giraudoux; has found time to travel extensively in Europe and Africa and has lived in Amsterdam, Brussels, Paris, Nice, London, and New York, where he is at present writing.

WORKS AVAILABLE IN TRANSLATION: Joseph Breaks Free, 1930; Happy Man, 1935; Mary Baker Eddy (in collaboration with E. Toller) 1935; Spanish Fire, 1937; I, the King, 1939; The Children of Guernica, 1939.

ABOUT: Boston Transcript July 30, 1938; Commonweal August 12, 1938; National July 23, 1938; New Republic November 16, 1938; New York Herald Tribune "Books" July 10, 1938, November 3, 1940; New York Times July 10, 1938, November 10, 1940; New Yorker July 9, 1938; Saturday Review of Literature July 23, 1938, November 16, 1940; Times (London) Literary Supplement December 3, 1938.

KESTER, VAUGHAN (September 12, 1869-July 4, 1911), American novelist and short-story writer, was born in New Bruns-

wick, N.J., the son of Franklin Cooley Kester and Harriett (Watkins) Kester. The greater part of his boyhood was passed at Mount Vernon, Ohio, at the home of his grandmother. Here he contracted a severe cold which left him with permanent hoarseness and difficulty of speech, and eventually led to his death in his forty-second year after a series of throat operations. In Ohio young Kester attended various private schools conducted by women teachers; spent a term at public school at Cleveland, where his mother conducted a School of Design for Women for seven years; and with his brother studied under

a tutor from Adelbert College. He also spent some time on his uncle's ranch on the River Platte, near Denver. When he was nineteen Mrs. Kester resigned from her school, and the family went to Florida to live in a camp. Here Kester, tall, broad-shouldered, with pipe in mouth and dressed in his favorite "filthies," as he termed his oldest clothes, mixed and talked with poor whites, himself the soul of simplicity, according to his brother Paul. Later they had a log cabin as a permanent camp on the banks of the Potomac, twenty miles from Washington. Once Kester looked up Dan Emmett, composer of *Dixie*, finding the old man chopping wood for a living, at eighty, near Mount Vernon, Ohio. Kester wrote various newspaper articles about the erstwhile famous minstrel, *Kate Field's Washington* printing the first article, and gave the money to Emmett.

When Kester was living at what he termed "The Little White House" on Riverside Drive in New York City, he collaborated with Paul Wilstach and Paul Kester in writing *The Cousin of the King*, a play. *The Looker-on*, another drama, was later played by Walker Whiteside. For a time he served on the editorial staff of the *Cosmopolitan*, at Irvington-on-Hudson, N.Y., also working on its syndicate. After reading manuscripts for Harper & Bros. for a few months, Kester had his first novel, *The Manager of the B. & A*, published by the firm in 1901, at the recommendation of his mother's cousin, William Dean Howells. Three years earlier he had married Jessie Jennings. Kester also contributed short stories to *Munsey's Magazine*, the *Century*, the *Bellman*, and the *American Magazine*. *The Prodigal Judge*, his most important novel, appeared in 1911, the year of his death. Kester lived long enough to know that it had made a definite impression on the critics—some of whom were slightly scandalized by its melodramatics and by the roguery of Uncle Bob Yancy, the judge— as well as being eagerly read by a novel-reading public then unaccustomed to such stimulating fare. It is a genuine contribution to the shelves of American regional fiction, as well as a faithful picture of the manners, customs, and dialects of North Carolina and Tennessee of the 1830's. Kester's one romantic novel, *John o' Jamestown*, dealing with Captain John Smith, came out in the year of the tercentenary of the settlement of Virginia. *The Fortunes of the Landrays* (1905) appeared while Kester and his brother were in the north of England. He died at Gunston Hall, Fairfax County, Va.

PRINCIPAL WORKS: The Manager of the B &
A, 1901; The Fortunes of the Landrays, 1905;
John o' Jamestown, 1907; The Prodigal Judge,
1911; The Just and the Unjust, 1912; The Hand
of the Mighty and Other Stories, 1913.

ABOUT: Kester, V. The Hand of the Mighty
(see "Sketch of the Author" by P. Kester); Bookman May 1911; Review of Reviews June 1911.

KEYES, Mrs. FRANCES PARKINSON (WHEELER) (July 21, 1885-), American novelist and essayist, writes:

Bachrach

"My background and traditions were decidedly variegated. My mother was a fashionable New Yorker transplanted to a Vermont village, the home of her paternal ancestors; my father was a scholarly Bostonian transplanted to hospitable Virginia, where he became a professor of ancient languages. Before I was seven weeks old I had traveled seven hundred miles, and except for an interval of fourteen years when I was first married, and when I lived summer and winter on a New Hampshire farm, I have traveled more or less constantly ever since. My alleged education, which was brief and intermittent, was received partly in Boston, partly in Geneva, and partly in Berlin, not to mention a long period in the country with a German governess. Nominally, I now live in New Hampshire in the summer and in Washington in the winter. Actually, I have spent four summers during the last ten years in Europe, one in California, and one divided among Cuba, Haiti, Panama, Hawaii, and Japan; and winter-time has found me at such divergent points as Teheran, Singapore, and Lima. Moreover, I have kept house quite as contentedly in the capital of Chile as in the capital of New Hampshire and the capital of the United States.

"My natural proclivity for wandering, which my mother encouraged and developed all through my youth, has been intensified during the last decade because my profession has taken me to the far corners of the earth. I have been writing ever since I was four years old, though the products of my pen were tucked away in bureau drawers, secluded from the eyes of a derisive family, until a happy accident, which occurred during the World War, encouraged me to send them out to try their fate with editors. At first I found most of these rather indifferent, not to say stony-hearted; but gradually I have discovered that many are, after all, kindly, cooperative, and receptive to ideas that have any saving graces. My first novel was published in 1919. My first article written from Washington, in 1920, was the forerunner of the Letters From a Senator's Wife, dealing with events and personages of national and international importance, which have continued ever since. I have written a large number of articles on miscellaneous subjects, some short stories, and a little verse. I have also done a good deal of public speaking in connection with my writing. I have had long periods of invalidism and semi-invalidism, but I have always continued to recover, and expect to attain a ripe old age. I am fond of housekeeping, and until I abandoned a needle for a typewriter, did a great deal of fine sewing. My favorite diversions include reading, motoring, contract bridge, and the theatre, though I am almost never bored under any conditions or in any surroundings. I love the ocean, and regard flying as an ideal mode of transportation. I enjoy people even more than I do places, and I am convinced that the Spanish explorer of old was right when he maintained that it is the search for treasure no less than treasure itself which makes life worth while."

* * *

Mrs. Keyes was born at the University of Virginia, where her father, John Henry Wheeler, was professor of Greek. She has honorary Litt.B. degrees from George Washington University and Bates College. In 1904 she married Henry Wilder Keyes, who was Republican governor of New Hampshire from 1917 to 1919, and United States senator from 1919 to 1937. He died in 1938. They have three sons. She has been for many years a regular contributor to Good Housekeeping and has traveled much for it. From 1937 to 1939 she edited the D.A.R. Magazine, though she has since left the D.A.R. because of disagreement with its policy. She has remodeled an old house in Alexandria, Va., where she keeps her collections of national costumes, fans, and peasant dolls from all over the world. She has graying brown hair and bright brown eyes, and has never lost the New England accent she acquired in her long years in New Hampshire. Her style has been called "gaily professional"; she is a kind of liaison officer between the women of America and professional and social Washington. She has also written two religious biographies.

PRINCIPAL WORKS: The Old Gray Home-stead (novel) 1919; The Career of David Noble (novel) 1921; Letters From a Senator's Wife, 1924; Queen Anne's Lace (novel) 1930; Silver Seas and Golden Cities, 1931; Lady Blanche Farm, 1931; Senator Marlowe's Daughter (novel) 1933; The Safe Bridge, 1934; The Happy Wanderer, 1935; Honor Bright, 1936; Written in Heaven, 1937; Capital Kaleidoscope, 1937; Parts Unknown, 1938; The Great Tradition, 1939; Along a Little Way, 1940; The Sublime Shepherdess, 1940; Fielding's Folly, 1940; Grace of Guadalupe, 1941; All That Glitters, 1941.

ABOUT: Keyes, F. P. Along a Little Way; Good Housekeeping May 1929; Time June 21, 1937.

*KEYNES, JOHN MAYNARD (June 5, 1883-), English economist, was born in Cambridge, where his father, John Neville

Keynes, was regis-trary of the uni-versity; his mother was Florence Ada (B r o w n) Keynes, daughter of a well-known dissenting minister. He was ed-ucated at Eton and at King's College, Cam-bridge, where he was president of the Cam-bridge Union Society, and was graduated as Twelfth Wrangler in 1905. From 1906 to 1908 he was in the India Office. Soon after, he became connected with the Treas-ury, in which he served during the First World War; the year before the war he was a member of the Royal Commission on Indian Finance and Currency. At the Paris Peace Conference he was principal repre-sentative of the Treasury and for six months served as deputy for the Chancellor of the Exchequer on the Supreme Executive Coun-cil. Since 1912 he has edited the *Economic Journal,* and he was also formerly chair-man of the editorial board of the *Nation* (London). From 1929 to 1931 he was a member of the government's Committee on Finance and Industry. He was made a Companion of the Bath in 1917, and is a Fellow of the British Academy. He is a Fellow and the Bursar of King's College, and divides his residence between Cambridge and London. In 1925 he married Lydia Lopokova, the dancer. He is interested as an avocation in the theatre, and is chairman of the Cambridge Arts Theatre.

His friend A. G. Gardiner has described Mr. Keynes as slight and sallow, with thin face, vivacious eyes, dark eyebrows, and a longish nose which gave him the schoolboy soubriquet of "Snout." His is "an incandes-cent spirit . . . a mind always cool but always at the gallop." He speaks rapidly and volubly. He is no pedant, and carries his erudition lightly; he knows art, litera-ture, and philosophy well, and it is said that only three living men can understand his *Treatise on Probability!* He has no ear for music, hates early rising, and plays solitaire to cool his heated brain. He has "no superstitions, no faith, no tact, no patience, his sympathies are cold." H. N. Brailsford called him "the most daring of English economists," but though he is the great enemy of capitalistic *laissez-faire,* he is not a Socialist of any school, but calls himself a Liberal. His influence on English and foreign economic opinion has been con-siderable. A. L. Rowse has commented on his "pathetic desire for a creed with inability to believe in one."

Mr. Keynes's economic specialty is finance; it was disagreement with his plan of paying the war reparations that led to his resigna-tion from the Treasury and the subsequent publication of his best-known book, *The Economic Consequences of the Peace.* His latest important proposal is for financing the present war by means of a forced loan on industry, to be repaid after the war is over. Abstruse and deadly dull as much of his chosen subject is, he is one of the few economists who almost invariably writes, not only lucidly, but wittily as well.

In 1941 the financial world was startled by the appointment of Keynes as a director of the arch-conservative Bank of England, whose fiscal policies he had often criticized.

In 1942 he was created a Baron by King George VI. His name is pronounced *kanes.*

PRINCIPAL WORKS: Indian Currency and Fi-nance, 1913; The Economic Consequences of the Peace, 1919; A Treatise on Probability, 1921; A Revision of the Treaty, 1922; A Tract on Monetary Reform, 1923; A Short View of Russia, 1925; The End of Laissez-Faire, 1926; Laissez-Faire and Communism, 1926; A Treatise on Money (2 vols.) 1930; Essays in Persuasion, 1931; Essays in Biog-raphy, 1933; The General Theory of Employment, Interest, and Money, 1936; How To Pay for the War, 1940.

ABOUT: Greidanus, T. Development of Keynes's Economic Theories; Hopkins, L. E. Political Fi-nance; Marget, A. W. Theory of Prices; Saulnier, R. J. Contemporary Studies of Some Recent The-ories of Money, Prices, and Production; American Economic Review June 1937; Canadian Forum December 1939; Current Biography 1941; Inter-national Labour Review June 1940; Journal of Political Economy October 1936, October 1939; Living Age March 13, 1926; New Republic May 13 and July 29, 1940; New Statesman and Nation September 28, 1940; Nineteenth Century September 1932, September 1936; Philosophical Review May 1930; Quarterly Journal of Economics February and August 1938; Spectator March 24, 1933, November 24, 1939, March 1, 1940; Time November, 27, 1939.

* Died April 21, 1946.

*KEYSERLING, HERMANN ALEX-ANDER, Graf von (July 20, 1880-   ), Russo-German philosopher, writes: "I was

born in the year 1880, on July 8, Russian style (July 20, Gregorian calendar) on the feudal estate of Könno, in what was then Russian Livonia [now in Estonia]—a scion of a family interested in intellectual and spiritual matters for the last seven generations. My grandfather, Alexander Keyserling, was the founder of Russian geology. My father was Count Leo Keyserling, a typical Russian *grand seigneur,* my mother Baroness Jane Pilar von Pilchau, of the baronial family Ungern-Sternberg of Grossenhof.

"I spent my youth as a child of nature on my ancestral estate, educated by private tutors until, on my father's death in 1894, I entered the highest class of the Russian Gymnasium at Pernau. I then spent a year at the University of Geneva and a year and a half at the University of Dorpat. After receiving an almost fatal injury in a student duel I left Dorpat for Heidelberg, where, following my grandfather's example, I studied geology. It was then that I read Houston Stewart Chamberlain's *Foundations of the Nineteenth Century.* The impression produced on me was tremendous. It was really in order to become acquainted with Chamberlain that I went to complete my studies in Vienna, where I took my Ph.D. degree in 1902. I then traveled and studied independently in Paris, London, and Berlin, and in 1904 wrote my first philosophical work, which determined my vocation. In 1908 I took over the ancestral estate and settled in Rayküll as a farmer and forester.

"In October, 1911, I embarked on the world-journey that led to *The Travel Diary of a Philosopher,* the book that made me famous. When the World War broke out I was correcting the second proofs of the first volume. Publication was indefinitely postponed. At the close of the war my entire fortune was swept away. I settled in Darmstadt, Germany, and in 1919 I married Bismarck's granddaughter, Gräfin Goedala von Bismarck-Schoenhausen. We have two sons. On November 23, 1920, I founded the School of Wisdom at Darmstadt. This 'school' never was a school proper; it meant a center of inspiration as opposed to information and education. From 1920 to 1927 it was a focus of general and world-wide interest. Many latter-day leaders who think little of my world-philosophy are without any doubt my disciples as far as the understanding of mass psychology and the primacy of vital (as opposed to abstract) problems goes. From 1927 to 1932 I did most of my work in other countries, traveling and lecturing, and my books written during those years, *America Set Free* and *South American Meditations,* were applications of my life-philosophy to Continental as opposed to generally human problems.

"I do not mean to write more books before having reached a new and higher stage of spiritual unfoldment. Since 1936, I have led the life of a solitary, to whom, it is true, more and more people come for the sake of heart-to-heart talks. I feel it to be more and more the real duty of spiritual man at this age of the great 'Revolt of the Earth-Forces' to act in silence—very much as the early Christians acted during the first centuries after Christ. My life is growing more and more impersonal and selfless. All that matters is my spiritual life."

* * *

As George E. G. Catlin said, "The essence of Keyserling's philosophy is one of artistic egoism 'triumphing over destiny.'" He himself has said: "The meaning of my life is to dispense living impulses. By 'wisdom' I mean simply 'self-expression.'" Although he is a scholar and a remarkable linguist (he writes in English and French as well as he does in German), Keyserling has little use for intellect or learning, but is the exponent of an intuitional "popular mysticism." On his American tour in 1929 he amazed his hosts by his insistence on the details of personal luxuries, and his deliberate inattention to the facts regarding a country on which he was writing a book aroused the irritation of critics and fellow-philosophers. Irwin Edman called his philosophy "a weird amalgam of random insights and idiocies," but for a time it was exceedingly popular. His most valuable book is probably *Europe,* since he has real knowledge of the psychological undercurrents of that distressed continent. In appearance Keyserling is half the aristocrat, half the mystic, as he is in actuality—with a long head and high forehead, a straggling beard, light, flashing eyes, and an authoritative manner. He is a fascinating talker, with whom conversation is a fine art, and his arresting personality conceals the obscurantism of his philosophic system.

* Died April 26, 1946.

PRINCIPAL WORKS AVAILABLE IN ENGLISH: Creative Understanding, 1922; The Travel Diary of a Philosopher, 1925; The Book of Marriage, 1926; The World in the Making, 1926; The Recovery of Truth, 1927; Europe, 1928; America Set Free, 1929; South American Meditations on Hell and Heaven in the Soul of Man, 1932; Problems of Personal Life, 1934; The Art of Life, 1936; Immortality, 1937; From Suffering to Fulfillment, 1938.

ABOUT: Durant, W. Adventures in Genius; Keyserling, H. Das Buch vom Persönlichen Leben; Parks, M. G. Introduction to Keyserling; l'Europe Nouvelle June 24, 1933; La Grande Revue January 1939; Journal des Débats May 17, 1929, March 13, 1931; Living Age August 1, 1930, November 1930; Neue Rundschau May 1931; New English Weekly July 28, 1938; New Republic July 31, 1929; Nuova Antologia November 1, 1932; Outlook July 23, 1930; Revue Politique et Littéraire July 21, 1928; Saturday Review of Literature October 26, 1929; Visva-Bharati Quarterly January 1938.

KIDD, BENJAMIN (September 9, 1858-October 2, 1916), English sociologist, was the eldest son of Benjamin Kidd, formerly of the Royal Irish Constabulary.

At nineteen he was holding a post with the Inland Revenue department, Somerset House. Kidd was an obscure civil-service clerk until the publication of *Social Evolution* in 1894 gave him fame. He resigned, traveled to the United States and Canada in 1898, and to South Africa in 1902, the year when his *Principles of Western Civilization* was published. These works, while not regarded seriously in academic circles, reached the wide popular audience at which they were aimed; were hailed by theologians, and were translated into several languages. Written in a pretentious, rhetorical style, which "had no antiseptic to keep the books from slow decay," Kidd's works drove home their central theses by self-confident and emphatic reiteration. *Social Evolution* seeks to establish that religion is the central feature of human history, the chief agency for promoting philanthropy and the political enfranchisement of the masses (Kidd, however, was a deadly foe of Socialism). Women readers liked his contention that woman is naturally anti-pagan, that is, unselfish, and devoted to the interests of the race, which he said, is in accordance with the spirit of Christianity. "It is a strange and even melancholy thought," Harold Laski has said, "that so glittering a mass of sophistries should have been received with respect and gratitude by reasonable and even distinguished men."

Kidd's later years were secluded. In 1903 he left London for Tonbridge, and later moved to Ditchling, Sussex. In 1908 he gave the annual Herbert Spencer lecture at Oxford, and in 1911 contributed the article on sociology to the *Encyclopaedia Britannica. The Science of Power,* a successful posthumous work, published by his son Frederick in 1918, dated from 1910. Kidd completed it in 1914, but the First World War made a revision necessary. He died of heart disease at Croydon. His wife was Maud Emma Isabel Perry. They had three sons.

PRINCIPAL WORKS: Social Evolution, 1894; The Control of the Tropics, 1898; Principles of Western Civilization, 1902; The Science of Power, 1918.

ABOUT: London Times October 3, 1916; Nation October 12, 1916; New Republic December 30, 1916.

KILMER, JOYCE (December 6, 1886-July 30, 1918), American poet and essayist, was born Alfred Joyce Kilmer in New Brunswick, N.J., the son of Frederick Barnett Kilmer, a professional chemist, and Annie (Kilburn) Kilmer. His mother was a writer of sorts, the author of *Whimsical Whimsies,* among others. Joyce Kilmer, who became a Catholic in later

years, after his infant daughter Rose contracted infantile paralysis, liked to call himself "half-Irish," but his ancestry was German-English-Scotch. He attended Rutgers College from 1901 to 1906, and received an A.B. degree from Columbia in 1908. Immediately on graduation he married Aline Murray, stepdaughter of Henry Mills Alden, editor of *Harper's Monthly.* Mrs. Kilmer was a well-known poet until her death in 1941. Kilmer taught Latin for a year at the Morristown (N.J.) High School; worked on the *Standard Dictionary* from 1909 to 1912; was literary editor of the *Churchman,* an organ of the Episcopal Church, of which he was then a member; and in 1913 landed a more lucrative job with the Sunday Magazine and Book Review sections of the New York *Times.* Possessed of exuberant vitality, and with a good deal of the actor in his make-up, Kilmer enjoyed turning out reams of excellent copy and pontificating to women's clubs on the writing of poetry. His first book, *Summer of Love,* in 1911, showed the influence of Yeats and other Celtic poets. *Trees and Other Poems* appeared in 1914, the phenomenally popular title-poem having first appeared in *Poetry* in August 1913.

Kilmer embraced Catholicism with fervor, patterned his later work on Coventry Patmore, and aimed to combine "piety with mirth." Traces of Crashaw, Vaughan, Herbert, Housman, and E. A. Robinson appear in his verse, which has been called "a broken bundle of mirrors."

The sinking of the "Lusitania" turned Kilmer's sympathies towards the Allies (he wrote "The White Ships and the Red," a poem about the disaster, on order for the *Times*). Enlisting as a private in the Seventh Regiment of the New York National Guard, —he was later transferred to the 165th Regiment of the Rainbow Division—Kilmer was an earnest and sincere soldier in France until he received a bullet through his brain while scouting for a machine-gun nest. He was buried beside the Ourcq, a French stream not far from Seringes, and was awarded a posthumous Croix de Guerre. Mrs. Kilmer and four children survived. He was remembered in the Second World War when Camp Kilmer, an embarkation station in New Jersey, was dedicated (1942) in his honor.

Joyce Kilmer was said to be a bit pompous in manner, physically on the plump side, with reddish-brown hair and intelligently glowing eyes.

PRINCIPAL WORKS: Summer of Love, 1911; Trees and Other Poems, 1914; The Circus and Other Essays, 1916; Literature in the Making (interviews) 1917; Main Street and Other Poems, 1917.

ABOUT: Brégy, K. M. C. Poets and Pilgrims; Daly, J. J. A Cheerful Ascetic and Other Essays; Kilmer, A. Memories of My Son, Sergeant Joyce Kilmer; Kilmer, J. Joyce Kilmer (see Memoir by Robert Cortes Holliday); Morley, C. Pipefuls; America August 31, 1918; Bookman October 1918; Catholic World July 1939; New York Times August 18, 22, 25, 1918.

KING, BASIL (February 26, 1859-June 22, 1928), American novelist, short-story writer, and spiritualist, was born William Benjamin Basil King at Charlottetown, Prince Edward Island, Canada, the son of William King and Mary Anne Lucretia King, and was named for his father, his mother's father, and an uncle. He attended St. Peter's School in Charlottetown, and King's College, Windsor, entering the Episcopalian ministry and going to St. Luke's Procathedral, Halifax, as rector in 1881. In 1892 King was called to Christ Church, Cambridge, Mass. *Griselda,* his first novel, was published at forty-one, followed by four others of no particular note until *The Inner Shrine* aroused speculation by its anonymous appearance in *Harper's Magazine.* It was a striking novel, declared the *Dial,* though highly artificial and even tricky; and dealt with the later life of a French-Irish girl whose American husband was killed in a duel with a Frenchman who slandered her. King explained later that *Harper's,* which had had serials by Hardy, Gilbert Parker, and Margaret Deland, thought a novel by a newcomer would have a more favorable reception if published without his name. Suffering from ill-health and already failing eyesight, King was glad to accept these terms and to retire to Europe for a rest of two years. He took the precaution of learning to use a typewriter before his sight completely failed. *The Wild Olive, The Street Called Straight,* and *The Way Home* were all published as "By the Author of *The Inner Shrine,"* in spite of the fact that a man in Peekskill, N.Y., took upon himself to confess on his deathbed that he was the real author of the novel. Aligning himself with Sir Arthur Conan Doyle and Sir Oliver Lodge, King announced his belief in spiritualism and the guidance of a spirit personality in his work. A famous man who had recently died helped him finish two stories, King declared. They often dealt with transition from life to death with, however, retention of consciousness, and appeared in *Cosmopolitan, Red Book, McCall's,* the *Saturday Evening Post,* and *Pictorial Review.* King's work was characterized by "a certain finished commonplaceness" and a strong didactic strain. He died at sixty-nine after an illness of four years, leaving a daughter and his widow, Esther Manton (Foote) King of New Hampshire.

PRINCIPAL WORKS: Griselda, 1900; In The Garden of Charity, 1903; The Steps of Honor, 1904; The Giant's Strength, 1907; The Inner Shrine, 1909; The Wild Olive, 1910; The Street Called Straight, 1912; The Way Home, 1913; The Letter of the Contract, 1914; The Side of the Angels, 1916; The Lifted Veil, 1919; The Abolishing of Death, 1919; The Conquest of Fear, 1921; The Dust Flower, 1922, The Discovery of God, 1923; The Happy Isles, 1923; Faith and Success, 1925; The Spreading Dawn: Stories of the Great Transition, 1927; Adventures in Religion, 1929; Satan As Lightning, 1929.

ABOUT: Baldwin, C. C. The Men Who Make Our Novels; New York Times June 23, 1928.

KINGSLEY, SIDNEY (October 18, 1906-), American playwright, was born Sidney Kieschner.

He attended Townsend Harris Hall, one of New York City's large secondary schools, and here wrote some one-act plays on social problems. Winning a state scholarship, he went to Cornell University, where he was a member of the university dramatic club, writing more one-act plays, and acting with Franchot Tone in *The Glittering Gate* and an ambitious revival of Sheridan's *The Critic*. In 1928 Kingsley received a prize for *Wonder-Dark Epilogue*, selected as the year's best one-act play by a student playwright. After four months in the Tremont Stock Company in New York's Borough of the Bronx, where he was paid $12 a week, he played a part in the Broadway production of *Subway Express*. Several years of play-reading and scenario-writing for Columbia Pictures followed.

Kingsley's first play to be produced professionally was *Men in White*, originally titled *Crisis*. The Group Theatre presented it at the Broadhurst Theatre in the autumn of 1933, and it received the Pulitzer Prize as the best play of the year. In 1934 it was produced at the Lyric Theatre in London, and has also been staged in several continental centers, Budapest among them. In preparation for writing this hospital play, Kingsley had quietly investigated the Lebanon, Montefiore, Bellevue, and Beth Israel hospitals in New York City, and was allowed by a friend to masquerade as an amateur interne and take notes on a multitude of clinical details. Brooks Atkinson of the New York *Times* called it "warm with life and high in aspiration, and it has a contagious respect for the theme it discusses." Arthur Pollock termed Kingsley "a matchless copier, and a copier with a social consciousness. He has a message." The play was sold to Metro-Goldwyn-Mayer for $47,000, and made a successful film.

Dead End, a spectacular play with striking settings by Norman Bel Geddes, that almost "stole the show," presented the bitter contrast between the adjoining luxurious apartment houses and run-down slums of New York's upper East Side, and the effect of these on their respective inhabitants. John Mason Brown wrote that Kingsley had "sharp ears for the speech of gangsters, policemen, street waifs, poor mothers and prostitutes," but that the language of his smart set was decidedly less convincing. The play's convincing juvenile actors, however, had not been imported from the East Side, as most audiences believed, but were products of various New York dramatic schools. As "The Dead End Kids" they helped make an effective film of the play and stayed on in Hollywood to work in other pictures.

In *Ten Million Ghosts,* a war play, the new technique of stagecraft which Kingsley employed failed to carry the play beyond eleven performances, in October 1936. He had received $165,000 for the picture rights to *Dead End*, and could afford to experiment. *The World We Make* (1939), dramatized for Labor Stage from Millen Brand's novel, *The Outward Room*, had a creditable run. In July of the same year Kingsley married Madge Evans, an actress, at York Village, Maine; she had been playing in a summer theatre at Ogunquit. The still-youthful playwright has a clean-shaven face and strong features.

Kingsley was called into service as a private in the U. S. Army in 1941. He was reported to be working at camp, when off duty, on a play about Thomas Jefferson.

PRINCIPAL WORKS: Men in White, 1933; Dead End, 1936; The World We Make, 1939.

ABOUT: Brown, J. M. Two on the Aisle; Theatre Arts Monthly July 1938.

"KINGSMILL, HUGH." See LUNN, H. K.

KIPLING, RUDYARD (December 30, 1865-January 18, 1936), English imperialist, poet, and writer of short stories and novels, was born at Bombay, India, the only son of John Lockwood Kipling, pottery designer and connoisseur of Indian art. His mother was Alice (Macdonald) Kipling, daughter of a Wesleyan minister and sister of Lady Burne-Jones, Lady

Poynter, and Mrs. Alfred Baldwin—whose son Stanley, Rudyard's cousin, became Prime Minister of England and afterwards Lord Baldwin. The Kiplings had one younger child, a daughter Beatrice. The boy's infancy was spent largely in the care of native *ayahs,* so that he learned Hindustani concurrently with English and absorbed much of the spirit of India during his most impressionable years. At the age of six he was sent home to the charge of an elderly relative at Southsea. A delicate child, he was not wisely used by his guardian. It was not until 1878, when he was twelve, that he went to school, being then entered at the United Services College, Westward Ho!, North Devon, a public school taking chiefly Anglo-Indians. He did not excel either at studies or at athletics, though he was a fine swimmer; but here he took his very first steps in letters, editing the college magazine for a stretch and placing some verse with a local paper. The exuberant book, *Stalky and Co.*, gives a picture of his schooldays.

In 1883, rejecting the parental offer of a University course, Kipling returned to India. His father had exchanged the headship of the Bombay School of Art for the post of Director of the Lahore Museum, and by his influence Rudyard was appointed to the staff of the Lahore *Civil and Military Gazette*. He soon learned the craft of journalism, living a strenuous and harried life. But his abounding energy and high ambition were by no means satisfied by routine, and he began to write short stories for his paper—stories containing the now celebrated characters, the "soldiers three": Ortheris, Mulvaney, and Learoyd, which later formed the substance of *Plain Tales From the Hills* (1888). His editor of those days has recorded that he was far from impressive in appearance, but was a brilliant conversationalist and a man of sterling character. He was indefatigable, not only in his work but in his exploration of Indian life and customs.

From 1887 to 1889 Kipling worked on the Allahabad *Pioneer*, gaining further valuable journalistic experience and vigorously carrying on that private work by which he hoped to become known in London. He had already issued, at Lahore, in 1886, a collection of verses which had appeared in the *Gazette*, as *Departmental Ditties*. This volume is now a rare collector's item, ranking high among Kipling's first editions, many of which have brought fantastic prices at auction. He brought out *Soldiers Three, Under the Deodars*, and several other pictures of Anglo-Indian civil and military life while at Allahabad. In 1889 the *Pioneer* sent him to England by way of Japan, San Francisco, and New York, the literary results being *Letters of Marque* and *From Sea to Sea*.

Once in London, Kipling settled in Villiers Street, near the Thames and the great newspaper quarter of Fleet Street, and set out to conquer the Capital. A eulogistic article in the London *Times* did much to help. That same year he met Caroline Starr Balestier, sister of the American writer, Charles Wolcott Balestier, and in 1892 married her. (He had published *The Light That Failed* and had taken a voyage to South Africa in 1891.) The year 1892 also saw the issue of *Barrack-Room Ballads*, perhaps Kipling's best-known book. The couple went over immediately to Brattleboro, Vt., where Mrs. Kipling had a property, and lived there for some four years, during which two daughters were born to them. Kipling wrote busily. His *Many Inventions* (1893), introducing the character of Mowgli, is considered by some judges to show him at his apogee. The *Jungle Books* (1894-95), another work which attained international celebrity, *The Seven Seas* (1896), and *Captains Courageous* (1897) were other products of the American period.

Returning to England in 1896 after a quarrel with his brother-in-law, Beatty Balestier, Kipling settled at Torquay. A cruise with the Channel Fleet produced a brilliant piece of reportage, *A Fleet in Being*. A visit to New York early in 1898 was disastrous, Kipling's elder daughter dying and he himself narrowly escaping death from double pneumonia. In 1900 Kipling went to South Africa to see the Boer War at first-hand, acting as associate editor to *The Friend*, of Bloemfontein, for which he wrote "King Log and King Stork" and other pieces of worth. "The Absent-Minded Beggar" also appeared here. *Kim* (1901) was his first really successful long novel, presenting a remarkably colorful, expert, and dramatic picture of Indian social life, character, custom, and religion.

After the Boer War, Kipling made his home first at the seaside village of Rottingdean, near Brighton, and later at a house called "Batemans," at the village of Burwash, also in the county of Sussex. He had a great love and appreciation for the rolling green downland of this region and its notoriously "difficult" inhabitants, who have earned from less friendly observers the adjective "silly." He was by this time rich and famous. The *Barrack-Room Ballads* were known to all. "Gunga Din," with its celebrated opening and closing lines, "The Widow at Windsor" (*i.e.*, Queen Victoria), the facile heroics of "If," and the doubtful modesty of "Recessional" were familiar to every literate household, as were phrases like "the white man's burden" and the whole paraphernalia of Kiplingesque imperialism. In the uneasy period prior to the War of 1914-18 Kipling tended more and more to identify himself with highly controversial political issues, like conscription and woman's suffrage, the former of which he supported and the latter opposed. He came to be considered the incarnation of the more truculent type of British imperialism, so much so that in 1907 he was cartooned taking out his "girl," Britannia, for a day on Hempstead Heath (a lovely wild tract of land in northwest London, part of which is metamorphosed into a sort of Coney Island on three national Bank Holidays). Yet for all the bitter controversy his political attitude aroused, there were hardly two opinions as to his superb literary craftsmanship. Foreign approval was marked the same year (1907) by the award of the Nobel Prize for Literature.

Two plays, *The Harbour Watch* (1913) and *The Return of Imray* (1914), were staged in London, but both missed fire. Then came the First World War. As might have been expected, Kipling became furiously active as a propagandist by speech and writing. Two books, *The New Army in Training* and *France at War*, were devoted to the cause; and also *The Irish Guards in the Great War*, which he edited (1923). In this regiment his only son had fallen in action. Kipling was one of the first public men to be "co-opted" to the Imperial War Graves Commission, and was responsible for the obituary phrase used for war dead: "Their Name Liveth Forevermore." His later books included *Debits and Credits* (1926), *Thy Servant a Dog* (1930), and *Limits and Renewals* (1932). He died rather suddenly in London at just past seventy, leaving one daughter, Elsie.

In addition to his Nobel award Kipling was the recipient of many high honors. The highest of all, the Order of Merit, he refused, but in 1926 he was given the Gold Medal of the Royal Society of Literature, which only Scott, Meredith, and Hardy had received before him. As early as 1897 he had been elected to the Athenaeum under Rule II (a special provision for the co-option of distinguished men). He held honorary degrees from the Universities of Oxford, Cambridge, Edinburgh, Durham, McGill, Athens, Paris, and Strasbourg, valuing his two French doctorates most of all. He was Lord Rector of the University of St. Andrews from 1922 to 1925, and in

1933 was elected a foreign associate member of the French Académie des Sciences et Politiques. The French translations of his works, by André Chevrillon, had a surprising vogue, considering how typically English an author he was.

If, indeed, there can be said to exist a "typical Englishman" (and when we juxtapose Blake, Johnson, Keats, Tennyson, and Hardy it may be doubted), then Kipling represented his apotheosis. He stood for all those qualities of bravery, doggedness, self-sufficiency, complacency even, which have often antagonized those whom he was pleased to call "lesser breeds without the law." But in his own right, and apart from politics, Kipling has powerful claims to eminence as a man of letters. No one, scarcely, has given such a twist of humor or horror to a short story. No one has produced anything quite like the playful whimsicality of the *Just So Stories*, or so complete a picture of Indian life as *Kim*, or such perfect expressions of the British soldier's language and viewpoint as the *Barrack-Room Ballads*. At his worst he could be cheap, flashy, and sentimental; but at his best he was a finished and perfect artist. He was a master of language (drawing freely on the Bible at whiles) and wrote very delightfully of children and animals. He was one of the most parodied authors of modern times, the jingle of his meters lending itself easily to such treatment.

Kipling was slight in build, not very tall, bald in later years, and possessed of a rather fierce semi-military moustache. Shortsighted from infancy, he always wore spectacles, and looked anything but the combatant character he was.

PRINCIPAL WORKS: *Poems*—Departmental Ditties, 1886; Barrack-Room Ballads, 1892; Seven Seas, 1896; Five Nations, 1903; Collected Verse, 1907; Songs From Books, 1912; The Years Between, 1919; Verse (inclusive edition, 3 vols.) 1919; Verse (inclusive edition, with various additions since 1919) 1933; Songs of the Sea, 1927; Poems, 1886-1929 (3 vols.) 1929. *Novels and Short Stories*—Plain Tales From the Hills, 1888; Soldiers Three, 1888; The Story of the Gadsbys, 1888; In Black and White, 1888; Under the Deodars, 1888; The Phantom Rickshaw and Other Tales, 1888; Wee Willie Winkie and Other Child Stories, 1888; The Light That Failed, 1890; Mine Own People, 1891; Naulakha (with Wolcott Balestier) 1892; Many Inventions, 1893; The Jungle Book, 1894; Second Jungle Book, 1895; Captains Courageous, 1897; The Day's Work, 1898; Stalky and Co., 1899; Kim, 1901; Just So Stories, 1902; Traffics and Discoveries, 1904; Puck of Pook's Hill, 1906; Actions and Reactions, 1909; Rewards and Fairies, 1910; Diversity of Creatures, 1917; Select Stories, 1921; Land and Sea Tales, 1923; "They" and Brushwood Boy, 1925; Debits and Credits, 1926; Thy Servant a Dog, 1930

Limits and Renewals, 1932. *Travel and Description*—Letters of Marque, 1891; American Notes, 1891; From Sea to Sea, 1899; Sea and Sussex, 1926. *Naval and Military*—A Fleet in Being, 1898; The New Army in Training, 1915; France at War, 1915; Sea Warfare (reprinted newspaper pieces) 1916; Graves of the Fallen, 1919; The Irish Guards, 1923.

ABOUT: Brion, M. Rudyard Kipling; Chandler, L. H. A Summary of the Works of Rudyard Kipling; Charles, C. Rudyard Kipling; Cooper, A. P. Rudyard Kipling; Dunsterville, L. C. Stalky's Reminiscences; Falls, C. Rudyard Kipling: A Critical Study; Hopkins, R. T. Rudyard Kipling; Le Gallienne, R. Rudyard Kipling: A Criticism (with bibliography by John Lane); Munson, A. I. Kipling's India; MacMunn, Sir G. Rudyard Kipling: Craftsman; Palmer, J. W. Rudyard Kipling; Wilson, E. The Wound and the Bow; Young, W. A. Kipling Dictionary.

KITTREDGE, GEORGE LYMAN (February 28, 1860-July 23, 1941), American philologist, university professor, and Shake-

Bachrach

spearean authority, was born in Boston, the son of Edward Lyman Kittredge and Deborah (Lewis) Kittredge. His mother's ancestors settled in Barnstable, Mass., in 1639, and Kittredge was descended from those who knew the vigorous, exacting discipline of the sea." He carried this stern authority into his own classrooms, beginning with his Latin classes at Phillips Exeter Academy in 1884. He had graduated from Harvard College in 1882, first scholar in his class, coming there from Roxbury Latin School.

From 1888 to 1890 Kittredge was instructor in English at Harvard, assistant professor from 1890 to 1894, and professor from 1894 to his retirement in 1936. To generations of students he was "Kitty." His last lecture as an active member of the Harvard faculty was delivered Friday, May 1, 1936, in his course, English 22; formerly English 2. Kittredge gave this course with Professor Francis J. Child in the later years of Child's life, and since Child's death in 1896 had conducted it alone. Six Shakespeare plays were studied each year, line for line and word for word. For his last lecture as Gurney Professor of English Literature, conducted in the usual masterful, impatient, and brilliantly discursive style, students and faculty packed the room to the doors and crowded at the windows and in an entry. Professor Kittredge retired to his Hilliard Street home in Cambridge to

edit his long-promised edition of Shakespeare in several volumes. He had married Frances Gordon of Exeter, N.H., in 1886; they had a son (Harvard, 1912) and two daughters.

In 1892 Kittredge instituted the study of Middle English romance at Harvard. His *Chaucer and His Poetry* has done, it is said, more than any other single work to make clear the greatness of Chaucer to the modern reader. He edited the final volume of Professor Child's monumental edition of *English and Scottish Popular Ballads,* and, with Mrs. Helen Child Sargent, made a one-volume recension. Kittredge also prepared several editions of Latin poets with James B. Greenough, and edited various literary series. He received honorary degrees from Harvard, Chicago, Johns Hopkins, McGill, Brown, Yale, Oxford, and Union College, where he was made honorary chancellor for 1936. Dixon Ryan Fox, Union's president, called Kittredge "a scourge to stupidity and pretense, but an inspiring friend to earnest competence; versed in the history of witchcraft, and thought by some to practise the black arts in divining students unprepared; exploring with piercing thoroughness the foundations of the English language and with unique authority expounding the accomplishment of its greatest master." "War to the death," according to Stuart P. Sherman, was the cry in his Shakespeare course, "on gushing Mrs. Jamesons, moralizing clergymen, and fantastic Teutonic metaphysicians." Professor Kittredge, with "luminous white hair and beard a frame around a face the eyes of which are difficult for most people to meet, and with a swift-moving figure familiarly attired in pale gray" was a memorable figure in Cambridge, where he sometimes stopped traffic in Harvard Square with uplifted cane or snatched off the hats of students tardy in recognizing him. His pungent, biting wit made him a legend in his own lifetime, and anecdotes about him were innumerable. One of his few recreations was singing ribald songs.

"He feared general ideas and destroyed them," Sherman, one of his most brilliant students, said in 1913, reviewing *Anniversary Papers by Colleagues and Pupils of George Lyman Kittredge.*" His ardor was towards the establishment of readings, the ascertainment of dates, the understanding of separate literary phenomena."

Professor Kittredge died at eighty-one at his summer home at Barnstable, Mass.

PRINCIPAL WORKS: The Language of Chaucer's Troilus, 1894; The Mother Tongue (with S. L. Arnold) 1900; Words and Their Ways in English

Speech (with J. B. Greenough) 1901; The Old Farmer and His Almanack, 1905; English Witchcraft and James I, 1912; Chaucer and His Poetry, 1915; A Study of Gawain and the Green Knight, 1916; Shakespeare, 1916; Dr. Robert Child; The Remonstrant, 1919; Sir Thomas Malory, 1925; Witchcraft in Old and New New England, 1929; Virgil and Other Latin Poets (with J. B. Greenough and T. Jenkins) 1930.

ABOUT: Anniversary Papers by Colleagues and Pupils of George Lyman Kittredge; Harvard University, Class of 1882: Secretary's Seventh Report; Sherman, S. P. Shaping Men and Women; Harvard Alumni Bulletin November 6, 1936; Nation September 8, 1913; New York Herald Tribune July 24, 1941; New York Times April 19, 1936, July 24, 1941; Time August 4, 1941.

*KNIBBS, HARRY (or HENRY) HERBERT (October 24, 1874-), Canadian verse- and story-writer, writes:

"Born at Niagara Falls, Ont. Went at fourteen to Woodstock College, Woodstock, Ont. When fifteen went to Ridley College, St. Catherines, Ont. Spent three years there. Migrated to Buffalo, N.Y., and because of American parentage and because of coming of age in the United States, automatically I became an American citizen.

"Worked as a wholesale coal salesman, traveling in Ontario and Michigan. Took a job as clerk in the Lehigh Valley Railroad office. Hoboed in the Middle West for two years. Returned to Buffalo and married Ida J. Pfeiffer (1899). Went to work as stenographer in Division Freight Office of B.R. & P. Railway. Was summoned to general office in Rochester, N.Y., became private secretary to the traffic manager. Built a home in Rochester. At the age of thirty-four, rented it, and went to Harvard College to specialize in English. Spent three years in Harvard. A class exercise in post-graduate work was published; it was a novel. Spent the summers in Maine. Migrated to California in 1910. Made an eleven-months camping trip over, around, and through California. Returned to Los Angeles and wrote a Western novel. It was accepted.

"Since then have traveled extensively in California, New Mexico, and Arizona. And I have written something like twelve novels of the West. Incidentally, wrote and published five books of verse. Wrote for the *Popular Magazine* for about twenty years. Wrote for other pulpwood magazines and

the *Saturday Evening Post.* Still writing for the magazines. I live in La Jolla, Calif. And that is the news up to this moment."

* * *

Mr. Knibbs's *forte* in verse is verse narrative, of an unpretentious, popular nature. He has also done some writing for the movies. His Western stories are strongly individualized as to characterization; he is primarily a "man's writer."

PRINCIPAL WORKS: First Poems, 1908; Lost Farm Camp, 1912; Stephen March's Way, 1913; Overland Red, 1914; Songs of the Outlands, 1914; Sundown Slim, 1915; Riders of the Stars, 1916; Tang of Life, 1917; Ridin' Kid From Powder River, 1919; Songs of the Trail, 1920; Partners of Chance, 1921; Saddle Songs, 1922; Wild Horses, 1924; Temescal, 1925; Sungazers, 1926; Sunny Mateel, 1927; Songs of the Lost Frontier, 1930; Gentlemen, Hush! (with T. Lummis) 1933; The Tonto Kid, 1936.

*KNIGHT, ERIC (April 10, 1897-), Anglo-American novelist; sends this biographical sketch written by his wife:

"Born [Eric Mobray Knight] in Menston, Yorkshire, the third son of Quaker parents. His father (a diamond merchant) died in South Africa two years later. Soon after, his mother went to St. Petersburg (Leningrad) as governess to Princess Xenia's children. She left Russia in 1905 and came to America. One at a time the sons were sent for to join their mother; they had been living with relatives in Yorkshire. It was not until 1912 that he came to America. By that time he had already worked in a steel mill, a cotton mill, a worsted mill, a sawmill, a glass-blowing factory, starting half-time at twelve and full-time at thirteen. On this side he worked as a copy boy on the Philadelphia *Press.* Within a short time the copy boy in his spare hours was writing feature articles for the syndicate bureau. Then he started on his schooling again, and went quickly and briefly through a number of educational institutions, including the Cambridge (Mass.) Latin School. Being interested in art, he went to the Boston Museum of Fine Arts School, then to the National Academy of Design in New York, the Art Students' League, and the Beaux Arts Institute.

"The First World War had started, and he left art and went to Toronto and enlisted as a private in the 'Princess Pat's' (Princess

* Died May 7, 1945.

* Died January 15, 1943.

Patricia's Canadian Light Infantry). Both his brothers were killed on the same day in France, in the American Army, in 1918. When Eric Knight returned to America after the war, he found that his art career was a trifle blocked by the fact that he was almost totally color-blind. For a while he tried cartooning, then went back to his first love, newspaper work. He worked on several Connecticut papers, the *Bronx Home News* in New York, and the Philadelphia *Sun* and *Public Ledger,* with an interlude in the United States Army and trips to Central America and Europe.

"He had married for the second time in 1932 and gone to live on a farm in Valley Forge, Pa., but he did not leave his post as dramatic critic on the *Ledger* until 1934, when he went to do film writing in Hollywood. On the Coast, E. E. Cummings read some of his stories and suggested that he send something to *Story,* which published his first story (except for a short-short in *Liberty*) in 1935. In 1936 a story was reprinted in the O. Henry Memorial Collection of prize stories. He had already published one novel. In California, he worked a small alfalfa ranch and wrote another novel. In 1937 the Knights escaped from Hollywood and came East. But in 1938 he was back in Yorkshire and ·he visited the Distressed Areas. He wrote an article about it, but could not say it all, so he wrote more in a novel, *The Happy Land.* Of his recent novel, *This Above All,* he says: 'It seems as if everything I've written points and pours and directs itself into this one.'

"He has lectured at the Writers' Conference in Boulder, Colo., and at the State University of Iowa. He lives in a very rickety farmhouse in Pennsylvania and raises pigs, chickens, ducks, geese, potatoes, etc. His favorite pastimes in season (and when not doing the farm chores) are jumping horses, figure ice-skating, making furniture, wood-carving, and building stone walls."

* * *

Mr. Knight's marked originality of thought and theme, his skilful handling of Yorkshire idiom, and his easy command of a style alternating between deep and indignant earnestness and a kind of "burlesque subtlety," combine to make him one of the most interesting of contemporary novelists. Although a British subject, he is a major in the United States Army, working in the Special Services Division since April 1942. With his ruddy English complexion he looks younger than his years. He had three children by his first marriage.

His present wife, Jere Knight, also a writer, is "as American as buckwheat cakes and Philadelphia scrapple."

PRINCIPAL WORKS: Invitation to Life, 1934; Song on Your Bugles, 1936; The Flying Yorkshireman (with other novellas, ed. by W. Burnett) 1936; You Play the Black and the Red Comes Up (as "Richard Hallas") 1938; The Happy Land (in England: Now Pray We For Our Country) 1940; Lassie Come-Home (juvenile) 1940; This Above All, 1941; Sam Small Flies Again (short stories) 1942.

ABOUT: Current Biography 1942; New York Times Book Review April 5, 1942; Saturday Evening Post January 18, 1938; Wilson Library Bulletin March 1941; Writer June 1940.

KNIGHT, GEORGE WILSON (September 19, 1897-), English-Canadian literary critic, was born in Sutton, Surrey, the son of George and Caroline Louisa (Jackson) Knight. He was educated at Dulwich College, London, and at St. Edmund Hall, Oxford, receiving his B.A. in 1925 and his M.A. in 1931. During the First World War he was a motor  cycle dispatch rider, serving in Mesopotamia, Persia, and India. He began his professional career as a teacher not of literature but of mathematics. From 1920 to 1925 he taught at Seaford House, Littlehampton, St. Peter's, Seaford, and Hawtrey's, Westgate-on-Sea; from 1925 to 1931 he taught at Dean Close School, Cheltenham. In 1931 he was appointed Chancellors' Professor of English at Trinity College, Toronto University, and Toronto has become his permanent home. His principal interest is in Shakespearian criticism, and since 1932 he has produced Shakespeare's plays at the Hart House Theatre in Toronto.

Professor Knight writes infrequently for the magazines, usually for those published in Canada. His books are philosophical and critical in nature. The *Bookman* remarked that his was "a new form of Shakespeare interpretation which . . . emphasizes the 'temporal' and 'spatial' elements and the poetic symbolism."

He is unmarried, and between his teaching duties, his literary work, and his year-long preparation for his annual dramatic productions has little time for social life or outside interests. He is a member of the Anglican Church.

PRINCIPAL WORKS: Myth and Miracle, 1929; The Wheel of Fire, 1930; The Imperial Theme, 1931; The Shakespearian Tempest, 1932; The

Christian Renaissance, 1933; Principles of Shakespearian Production, 1936; Atlantic Crossings, 1936; The Burning Oracle, 1939; This Sceptred Isle, 1940.

ABOUT: Bookman November 1930.

KNITTEL, JOHN (March 24, 1891-   ), Swiss novelist, linguist, and archaeologist, was born John Herman Emanuel Knittel

in Dharwar, India, the son of the Very Reverend Herman Knittel and Anna (Schultz - Bodmer) Knittel, both of whom returned to Switzerland when the child was six years old. He was educated at Basel and Zurich; and took special studies in philosophy. After his mother's death a few years later, he went off to London; got a humdrum job in a bank; and then left it to join an American film export house.

Robert Hichens, the novelist, sympathized with Knittel's literary aspirations and aided him in the publication of his first book, *Aaron West.* He became temporarily absorbed in theatrical management, in the very early 'twenties, and brought record audiences to the Apollo (London) for solid tragedy bills. At this same theatre his own play, *The Torch,* which, said one critic, might have been real tragedy had it not at the end thinned out into "sheer bathos," survived twenty-seven performances.

He wrote steadily for a while, and finished a love tale called *Into the Abyss.* Wanderlust took him into Egypt, where almost without effort, he turned out his third novel, *Nile Gold* (1929), a modern legend. Two years later came *Midnight People,* laid in the French Morocco.

Knittel went back to Europe; rested a while in Switzerland; and then set out again for Africa, bought an oasis, and began to raise date palms and sheep. In the four years following he wrote: *Cyprus Wine From My Cellar,* a travel book; two novels (*Via Mala and Dr. Ibrahim*), both of which were structurally and stylistically imperfect but praised for their psychological perceptions; and *The Asp and Other Stories.*

Between *The Commandant,* the tale of a Russian officer in the French foreign legion who is accompanied to a mountainous region of Morocco by two English women, and *Power for Sale,* a somewhat long-winded romance of a young engineer-idealist who

established a power plant in the Swiss Alps and attempted to run it according to his own set of values, came a play, *Protektorat* (Knittel writes in both German and English).

Knittel is of a sturdy youthful build and has gay piercing eyes. He was married in 1915 to Frances Rose White-Bridger, an English girl; they have a son and two daughters. He has three times been National Golf Champion of Switzerland, and at last report was still making his home in that country.

Most of Knittel's critics appear to be of the opinion that in his great variety of subject matter he does indulge in a certain amount of sensationalism, along with his obvious insight and perception of character.

PRINCIPAL WORKS: Aaron West, 1921; Into the Abyss, 1928; Nile Gold, 1929; Cyprus Wine From My Cellar, 1933; Dr. Ibrahim, 1935; Via Mala, 1935; The Asp and Other Stories, 1936; Power for Sale, 1939.

ABOUT: Books Abroad 1933 and 1936; Dramatic Index 1922; Wilson Library Bulletin February 1935.

KNOX, EDMUND GEORGE VALPY (July 27, 1881-   ), English humorist, parodist, and poet, editor of *Punch* and contributor to that periodical under the pseudonym "Evoe," is the eldest of the six sons of the Rt. Rev. E. A. Knox, D.D., and Ellen Penelope (French) Knox, daughter of Dr. Valpy French, Bishop of Lahore. Father Ronald Knox, the well-

known writer and Roman convert[qv] is his youngest brother. E. V. Knox was educated at Rugby and at Corpus Christi College, Oxford University. In 1912 he married Christina Frances Hicks, youngest daughter of the Bishop of Lincoln, and they had a son and daughter. For practically the whole course of the First World War he served in the Lincolnshire Regiment, receiving a wound at Passchendaele. *The Brazen Lyre,* E. V. Knox's first book of humorous verse, was published in 1911. In 1921 he joined the staff of *Punch* and issued a book of parodies illustrated by George Morrow, *"Parodies Regained."* Both books could have passed as the work of Owen Seaman, editor of *Punch,* whom Knox succeeded as editor in 1932. The first Mrs. Knox died in 1935. Two years later Mr. Knox married Mary Eleanor Jersey Shepard, daughter of Ernest

Howard Shepard, the *Punch* artist who illustrated A. A. Milne's *When We Were Very Young.*

At frequent intervals Knox has collected into books his poems, parodies, skits, and reflections on human foibles, very much in the *Punch* tradition of mild (to the American taste) humor. Many of "Evoe's" observations are undoubtedly instructive to readers overseas, who may, for instance, have wondered just what the budgerigars may be which figure so frequently in fiction as members of British households. "Observations on the Behaviour of the Budgerigar" will inform them that the objects in question are love-birds from South Africa. Knox's recreations are golf and fishing, and his clubs the Athenaeum, Savile, Garrick, and United University.

PRINCIPAL WORKS: The Brazen Lyre, 1911; A Little Loot, 1919; "Parodies Regained," 1921; These Liberties, 1923; Fiction As She Is Wrote, 1923; An Hour From Victoria and Other Excursions, 1924; Fancy Now, 1924; Quaint Specimens, 1925; This Other Eden, 1931; Here's Misery! 1931; Slight Irritations, 1931; Folly Calling, 1932.

KNOX, RONALD ARBUTHNOTT
(February 17, 1888-   ), English priest, satirist, essayist, and detective story writer,

was born in England, the fourth son of the Rt. Rev. Edmund Arbuthnott Knox, Anglican Bishop of Manchester. His father (1847-1937) wrote *Reminiscences of an Octogenarian* (1935) and a study of the *Tractarian Movement* (1933). One of his brothers is Edmund George Valpy Knox[qv] ("Evoe" of *Punch*). "Ronnie," as he is still popularly known at Oxford, began his literary career at the age of ten by writing Latin and Greek epigrams. He stood high in scholarship at Eton and at Balliol College, Oxford, where he was president of the Union and won the Hertford and Ireland scholarships. After taking a first in Greats he was for two years a fellow and lecturer at Trinity College, Oxford, then took holy orders, and was Anglican chaplain of the college for five years. Converted to Roman Catholicism in 1917, he was ordained priest in 1919 and in 1925 became Catholic chaplain at Oxford. He was made domestic prelate to the Pope in 1936. In the summer of 1939 he retired from Oxford to prepare a new translation of the Vulgate (Latin) scriptures.

Father Knox is known as one of the most influential Catholic apologists in England; he is called remarkable for his urbanity, his exuberance, his light-heartedness, and his ability as a satirist to "turn a serious controversy into a glorious joke without injuring the force of his argument." In the words of J. G. E. Hopkins, "He has wit to give point and bite to his satire and he has an impish humor which flickers over all his work, illuminating it with a fantastic and charming light." He is a voluminous magazine contributor, and most of his books are collections of essays previously published in that form, or of his brilliant sermons.

Best known of his original books is *Barchester Pilgrimage,* a parody on Trollope's manner and style, which continues the adventures of the characters in the Barsetshire novels, bringing the action down to 1934.

Among his numerous activities, Monsignor Knox is a prominent member of the English Detection Club—although his own detective novels, rather too erudite and involved for the general taste, have been accused of violating the rules established by that body. His inquiry into the Sherlock Holmes canon in *Essays in Satire,* the most popular of his collections of essays, has become a classic of Sherlockiana.

PRINCIPAL WORKS: Some Loose Stones, 1913; Reunion All Round, 1914; A Spiritual Aeneid, 1918; Patrick Shaw-Stewart (ed.) 1920; Memories of the Future, 1923; The Miracles of King Henry VI (tr.) 1923; Sanctions: A Frivolity, 1924; The Viaduct Murder, 1925; Other Eyes Than Ours, 1926; The Three Taps, 1927; The Belief of Catholics, 1927; An Open Air Pulpit, 1928; The Footsteps at the Lock, 1928; The Mystery of the Kingdom (sermons) 1928; Essays in Satire, 1928; On Getting There, 1929; The Best Detective Stories of the Year, 1928-1929 (ed., with H. F. Harrington) 1929-1930; Caliban in Grub Street, 1930; Difficulties (with Arnold Lunn) 1932; Broadcast Minds, 1932; The Body in the Silo, 1933; Still Dead, 1934; Heaven and Charing Cross (sermons) 1935; Barchester Pilgrimage, 1935; The Holy Bible: An Abridgement and Rearrangement (ed.) 1936; Double Cross Purposes (American title: Settled Out of Court) 1937; Let Dons Delight, 1939; Captive Flames, 1940; Nazi and Nazarene, 1940.

ABOUT: Alexander, C. Catholic Literary Revival; Begbie, H. Painted Windows; Drinkwater, J. This Troubled World; Lunn, A. H. M. Roman Converts; Singer, E. A. Fool's Advice; Catholic World October 1937; Dublin Review July 1918; Living Age November 1932; Time March 27, 1939.

KOBER, ARTHUR
(1900-   ), American humorist and dramatist, was born in Brody, Austria-Hungary, later Poland. At two he came to the United States with both his

parents. He attended the public schools in Harlem and spent a year and a half at the High School of Commerce. Leaving school at fourteen, Kober served as stock-clerk at Gimbel's department store, stenographer for the Maxwell Automobile Co., and bell-boy on a ship going to San Francisco via the Panama Canal. Becoming assistant to Claude Greneker, press representative for the Shuberts, theatrical producers, he wrote publicity for their musical revue *Artists and Models* and for *Is Zat So?,* a successful farce about prize-fighting. Kober was also press agent for Marc Connelly's Negro morality play, *The Green Pastures,* and the late George Gershwin's musical, *Strike Up the Band.* He also publicized Maurice Schwartz and Ruth Draper, the celebrated *diseuse;* produced *Me,* by Henry Myers, which ran four weeks; and made an unsuccessful attempt to bring the Moscow State Theatre to this country, with backing by the late Otto Kahn.

Besides conducting columns for the *Morning Telegraph, Theatre Magazine,* and the Paris *Comet,* Kober spent eight years with the Fox and Metro-Goldwyn-Mayer motion picture companies in Hollywood, writing screen plays for Carole Lombard, Kay Frances, Joan Blondell, Ginger Rogers, and other stars. For a time he was married to Lillian Hellman, who later wrote *The Children's Hour* and *The Little Foxes;* the marriage ended in a divorce. With an uncannily accurate ear for the conversations conducted by the inhabitants, old and young, of the Jewish sections of New York City's Borough of the Bronx, Mr. Kober has a warm regard for his young clerks and stenographers, as shown by his play, *Having Wonderful Time,* which won the Roi Cooper Megrue prize as the best comedy of 1937. The play was a dramatization of sketches which appeared in the *New Yorker,* unfolding the romances which spring up in a summer camp in the Catskill Mountains in vacation time (the playwright had once been the social director of such a camp); it was made into a successful talking picture. The adventures of the Gross family, chronicled in the *New Yorker,* were collected in book form as *Thunder Over the Bronx. Pardon Me for Pointing* comprises forty-four sketches which "probe deep into the minds of producers, directors, Park Avenuveau riche, movie agents, Hollywood stars, and plain little people." *Time* remarked of *Dear Bella* (1941) that "all the stories achieve the distinction of being not only funny, but sympathetic"; but some other reviewers thought that his *métier*

was nearing exhaustion. Mr. Kober is of medium height, and dark.

In 1941 Kober married Margaret Frohnknecht of New York, sister of Mrs. Erich Leinsdorf, wife of the Wagnerian conductor at the Metropolitan Opera.

PRINCIPAL WORKS: Thunder Over the Bronx, 1935; Having Wonderful Time, 1937; Pardon Me for Pointing, 1939; My Dear Bella, 1941.

ABOUT: New York Journal-American August 19, 1937.

KOMROFF, MANUEL (September 7, 1890-), American novelist, was born in New York, the son of Samuel and Belle (Borkes) Komroff. He went to Yale, where he studied engineering, but left in 1912 without a degree. He had also studied music and painting, both of which he put to good account—the first by writing musical scores for motion pictures,  L. Nelson and the second by acting as art critic for the New York *Call.* He was at that time a Socialist, and when the first Russian Revolution occurred he went to Petrograd (now Leningrad) and soon found himself editor-in-chief of the *Russian Daily News* (published in English)—the rest of the staff having hastily left the country at the coming into power of the Bolsheviks. Komroff, who was far from a Communist, soon followed them, making his way to Japan via Siberia. Then he went to Shanghai, where he worked on the *China Press* for several months before finally returning to America.

In 1918 he married Elinor M. Barnard, an English artist, from whom he was divorced in 1937. For his first few years back in New York he had a hard time earning a living. For a long time he reviewed movies (twenty or so a week) for *Wid's,* now the *Film Daily,* wrote three editorials a day for the *Daily Garment News,* and in his so-called spare hours worked away at stories. In 1924 he joined the staff of Boni & Liveright, who published his first book, a volume of short stories called *The Grace of Lambs.* He also edited a number of volumes of the Modern Library, then published by this firm. One of these books was Marco Polo's *Travels,* and becoming interested in the great explorer he spent some months of 1926 in Rome, doing research for another book on Marco Polo, which, however, was never written. Instead, his first novel, *Jug-*

gler's Kiss, came out in 1927, and was followed two years later by *Coronet.* This two-volume historical novel was a pronounced success; it is estimated that it has had at least a million readers. It enabled him to leave his editorial job and devote himself exclusively to creative work.

With but few exceptions, Mr. Komroff's novels are historical, his favorite period being the seventeenth and eighteenth centuries in central Europe. However, *Two Thieves* goes a great deal farther back, being the story of the two crucified on either side of Jesus. For this, as for his other historical stories, he did an unusual amount of research, his usual method being to read everything published on the era he can find and to fill many notebooks with details before he begins writing. This attention to detail may account for the principal fault found with his work, that its transitions are too abrupt, and that it is crowded with so much material that important episodes are scamped in order to include less significant ones. He struck a new vein in *The March of the Hundred,* a sort of allegory (perhaps stemming from Xenophon) of a band of soldiers of an unknown country lost and marching they know not where; in the end the reader perceives that it is a picture of modern Europe. His short stories appear regularly in the better magazines.

Mr. Komroff is red-haired, with a straggling red moustache, a long head, and near-sighted dreamy eyes. Combined with his Russian-sounding name, his appearance causes many people to think that he must be a foreigner, instead of that even rarer object, a native New Yorker. No one, however, thinks this after having met him and listened to his purposely slangy and colloquial speech. His handwriting is practically illegible, in strange contrast to his chiseled sentences. His style is polished, some of his descriptions—notably that of the Battle of Waterloo in his novel of that name—being minor classics in their *genre.*

PRINCIPAL WORKS: The Grace of Lambs (short stories) 1925; Juggler's Kiss, 1927; The Voice of Fire, 1927; Coronet, 1929; The Fool and Death, 1930; Two Thieves, 1931; A New York Tempest, 1932; I, the Tiger, 1933; Waterloo, 1936; The March of the Hundred, 1939; The Magic Bow, 1941; In the Years of Our Lord, 1942.

ABOUT: Literary Digest August 1, 1936; Reader's Digest April 1941; Scholastic February 15, 1936.

KRAPP, GEORGE PHILIP (September 1, 1872-April 21, 1934), American philologist and university professor, was born at Cincinnati, Ohio, the son of Martin Krapp and Louisa (Adams) Krapp, and took his bachelor's degree at Wittenberg College in 1894, his master's degree three years later. Krapp came East in 1897 to become an instructor in English at the Horace Mann School in New York City, and remained with Columbia University for ten years. Appointed an adjunct professor of English in Columbia College in 1907, he went in 1908 to hold a similar chair at the University of Cincinnati, remaining until 1910, when he returned to Columbia as professor of English. He had obtained his Ph.D. at Johns Hopkins University in 1899. His first published works concerned English grammar and the growth and present use of modern English, but with the publication of *Pronunciation of Standard English in America* (1919) he entered the field of philology, which he made preëminently his own. The first edition of H. L. Mencken's *The American Language* had appeared in 1918, but Krapp's comprehensive two-volume *The English Language in America* (1925) was called the first history, if not the first study, of the American language. The second volume is almost entirely devoted to pronunciation. "Certainly it is not possible to detach American writing with ease from the whole body of literature written in the English language or to say that by the possession of this or that precise quality it has established itself," he contended.

Mencken said of Krapp's *Pronunciation of Standard English in America* that "no one can henceforth write about American pronunciation without leaning heavily upon Professor Krapp's work." His was the scholarship "of enormous field work and spadework," as the New York *Times* said editorially after Krapp's sudden death at sixty-one of a cerebral hemorrhage at his home on Riverside Drive in New York City. He also had a remarkable collection of phonograph records preserving variations of American pronunciation. Three volumes of a monumental collection of Anglo-Saxon poetry had been published at the time of Professor Krapp's death. He was survived by Elizabeth (von Saltza) Krapp, whom he had married in 1911, a daughter, and two sons. *Tales of True Knights* and *The Kitchen Porch* were books written primarily for his children.

PRINCIPAL WORKS: Andreas and the Fates of the Apostles, 1906; The Elements of English Grammar, 1908; Modern English—Its Growth and Present Use, 1909; In Oldest England, 1912; The Rise of English Literary Prose, 1915; Pronunciation of Standard English in America, 1919; Tales of True Knights, 1921; First Lessons in Speech Improvement, 1922; The Kitchen Porch, 1923; The English Language in America, 1925; Comprehensive Guide to Good English, 1927; The Knowledge of English, 1927; Anglo-Saxon Reader, 1929; (ed.) The Junius Manuscript, 1931.

ABOUT: New York Times April 22, 25, 29, 1934; Publishers' Weekly May 12, 1934.

*KRASSNOFF, PETER NIKOLAE-VICH (1869-), Russian monarchist, novelist, and short-story writer, was born in

the southeast of Russia, the son of Nikolai Ivanovich Krassnoff. He was sent to both elementary and secondary military academies; and was afterwards commissioned to the Imperial Regiment, with which he served until 1909 when he was appointed head of a training school for Cossack officers.

Meanwhile, 1897-98, he had made a pilgrimage to Abyssinia as head of the Russian Imperial Mission (recorded in a book on the Cossacks in Africa); in 1902 he was made official military correspondent of the Russian *Invalid;* and the Russo-Japanese hostilities took him, in 1904, to the Orient. He was advanced to the rank of Colonel in 1910 (he had already received several coveted military decorations), and in 1911 he became commander of the First Siberian Cossack Regiment.

Krassnoff was an officer of the old school and no admirer, in the fall of 1917, of Alexander Kerensky, the recently deposed head of the Provisional Government. But, on the other hand, he was anxious to strike a blow against the Bolsheviki who had already taken over considerable power. As Commander of the Third Cavalry Corps he succeeded in penetrating Gatchina on the 9th of November and Tsarske Selo on the 10th; and he was approaching Petrograd with hardly more than a scattered brigade and eight weak squadrons. Red strength there, at that moment, was almost negligible. But Krassnoff, woefully lacking in infantry reinforcements, soon found his own demoralized Cossacks in retreat.

Krassnoff was arrested on the 15th and brought to Smolny under guard. The treatment of political prisoners was still a fairly casual matter and he was reputedly released on the promise that he would never fight the

* Died in 1947.

Soviet régime. He went immediately south into the Don Region; on May 11 (1918) was elected Ataman of the Don; and by the following winter had raised an anti-Soviet army which, including its reservists, numbered about 50,000 men. He received arms from Germany, and even went so far as to make numerous flattering appeals to the Kaiser (despite his earlier denunciation of the Bolsheviki as Wilhelm's agents). For a while he more than held his own against the Reds, but with the eventual defeat of Germany in 1918 his position fell abruptly.

Following a number of bitter military disputes he resigned, and went to live in Batum, where he wrote the first portion of a long saga, *From Double Eagle to Red Flag,* too emotional to be historically convincing, too vivid to be dull. Among his earlier writings were an account of his Abyssinian adventures, tales emerging from the Russo-Japanese War, and various articles for semi-military periodicals. Since the time of his withdrawal from army life he has written about a dozen books—novels, short stories, fictionalized reminiscences—which might be said to contribute something to a study of the Russian people but which, from a literary point of view, have small chance of survival.

PRINCIPAL WORKS AVAILABLE IN ENGLISH TRANSLATION: From Double Eagle to Red Flag, 1926; The Unforgiven, 1928; Amazon of the Desert, 1929; The White Coat, 1929; Kostia the Cossack, 1930; Yermak the Conqueror, 1930; Napoleon and the Cossacks, 1931; Largo, 1932.

ABOUT: Chamberlin, W. H. The Russian Revolution; Trotzky, L. History of the Russian Revolution.

KREY, Mrs. LAURA LETTIE (SMITH) (December 18, 1890-), American novelist, writes: "I was born in

Galveston, Texas, and grew up on a plantation in Texas on the Brazos River. My mother died when I was a few months old. I was a child growing up pretty largely in the world of men, who taught me the working of politics and the prac-

G. Garrett

tical management of a plantation, and told me many amazing stories about the past—how Texas was won in the first place and then, in the '70s, rewon. I did some writing during those years, a good deal of it, I remember. Then I was sent to Staunton, Va., to Mary Baldwin Seminary. I returned to Texas to the university, where I fell happily under the tutelage of Stark Young, who led all of us who could keep panting pace with him through all kinds of reading. In college I served on all the various college publications, acquiring some practical experience in editing and a Phi Beta Kappa key. There were, however, to be many years after I graduated in 1912 before I was again to have the time and the strength together to do much writing. I was married in 1913 to August Charles Krey, professor of mediaeval history at the University of Minnesota, and we had a son and daughter. My husband had more confidence in me than I had in myself; a writer himself, he urged me to take the attic for a study, and I began to write steadily, hours on a stretch—at last trying to write a novel. For a long time I had wanted to write about actual cotton planters —not those in the movies or in uplift novels. My story had lain on my mind for ten years, and for two, the first chapter had been, off and on, set down on paper, but it never suited me. It does not now. The book could never be so beautiful and perfect as I had dreamed it might be.

"My second novel deals with Spanish Texas and the Republic of Texas."

* * *

Mrs. Krey's baptismal name was Laura Letitia Smith. Her first published work, articles in women's magazines, appeared under the pseudonym of "Mary Everett." . . . And Tell of Time, which has been called "a kind of apology for Texas aristocracy and for the plantation set-up," is ultimately to be the first of three related novels, which Mrs. Krey says are technically not to be a trilogy.

PRINCIPAL WORKS: . . .And Tell of Time, 1938; On the Long Tide, 1940.

ABOUT: Wilson Library Bulletin October 1939.

KREYMBORG, ALFRED (December 10, 1883-), American playwright, poet, and critic, writes: "Alfred Kreymborg was born in New York City. His father, Hermann Charles Kreymborg, was born in Germany, and his mother, Louise (Nasher) Kreymborg, in New York of German parentage. Most of the facts of his youth and early manhood are revealed in his autobiography, Troubadour. Kreymborg, whose parents were poor, had no academic education beyond public schools and the two years he spent at Morris High, then in its infancy. His earliest aesthetic influ-

ences came out of music and the theatre, and his literary progress was slow. At twenty-one, after the death of his parents, he began a patient career in a traditional garret on West 14th Street, where, after ten hard years, he succeeded in publishing practically nothing. Once he found his own style, in free verse, his development was rapid and was stimulated by the arrival of other poetic and dramatic pioneers of the pre-war era. Many of these pioneers found their first hearing in Kreymborg's early editorial ventures, the Glebe

R. L. Jackson

and Others and Broom, and his interest in his fellow American authors has never died down.

"Of his unpublished work there are four full-length plays in tragedy, comedy, or tragi-comedy. There is also a volume of nine one-act plays under the general title of Ballad of Youth and a volume of poems under the tentative title of Poet and Prose. Work in progress includes plans for a second Troubadour, an animal book in verse, Music on the Mandalute (the instrument with which Kreymborg has often toured America), and the Collected Poems and Collected Plays.

"The poet has been twice married: once for exactly one year to Gertrude Lord, and then for the rest of his life, since 1918, to Dorothy Bloom. His literary and social preferences are fairly catholic as a rule and contain too many names for a strict catalogue. The same may be said for his favorite authors and public figures. His political convictions embrace any leader or average person who never loses sight of the social under-dog and who does his utmost toward making democracy a really living process for everyone concerned. In other words, Kreymborg is an ardent humanist. His likes and dislikes are likewise too numerous to mention and vary with the temperamental seasons. They may be found in the body of his work. He has lectured in many places here and abroad and taught for two years at Briarcliff Junior College. He has published about forty books with about twenty different publishers."

* * *

Kreymborg learned chess from his father as a small child, and for eight years supported himself as a professional chess-player. It is still his chief recreation. He has been a great fructifier of other people's writing and has lent a helping hand to more than one beginning writer. Alfred Kreymborg believes everyone should "know and make poetry." He himself has won a verse play prize from *Poetry,* and the Sergel Prize of the University of Chicago (in 1936) for his play, *Commencement.* He is described as "a quiet, small man, fond of good talk." A critic has noted that "he points out the spiritual weaknesses of mankind in affectionate indulgence or harsh irony. Man is both the hero and the villain of the piece." From 1927 to 1936 he was co-editor, with Van Wyck Brooks, Lewis Mumford, and Paul Rosenfeld, of the *American Caravan,* an influential anthology of experimental writing which introduced many new authors.

PRINCIPAL WORKS: *Poetry*—Mushrooms, 1916; Blood of Things, 1920; Less Lonely, 1923; Scarlet and Mellow, 1926; Funnybone Alley, 1927; The Lost Sail, 1928; Manhattan Men, 1929; Lyric America (ed.) 1930; The Little World, 1914 and After, 1932. *Plays*—Plays for Merry Andrews, 1920; Puppet Plays, 1923; Rocking Chairs and Other Comedies, 1925; Lima Beans, 1925; There's a Moon Tonight, 1926; How Do You Do, Sir, and Other Short Plays, 1934; The Four Apes and Other Fables of Our Day, 1939. *Miscellaneous*—Love and Life and Other Studies, 1910; Apostrophes, 1912; Erna Vitek (novel) 1914; Troubadour; An Autobiography, 1925; Our Singing Strength (in England, Outline of American Poetry) 1929; I Am No Hero (novel) 1933; Poetic Drama: An Anthology of Plays in Verse (ed.) 1941.

ABOUT: Aiken, C. Skepticisms; Beach, J. W. The Outlook for American Prose; Johns, O. Time of Our Lives; Kreymborg, A. Troubadour; Monroe, H. Poets and Their Art; Rosenfeld, P. Men Seen; Newsweek March 31, 1934; Scholastic April 2, 1938, October 30, 1939.

KRUIF. See DE KRUIF

KRUTCH, JOSEPH WOOD (November 25, 1893-   ), American dramatic critic and essayist, was born in Nashville, Tenn.,

the son of Edward Waldemore Krutch and Adelaide (Wood) Krutch. He was educated at the University of Tennessee (B.-A. 1915) and at Columbia (M.A. 1916, Ph.D. 1923). He originally intended to be an engineer, but his attention was diverted to literary analysis and criticism. In 1917 and 1918 he was instructor in English at Columbia, and during the following year was

a traveling fellow of the university. From 1920 to 1923 he was associate professor of English at the Brooklyn Polytechnic Institute. The next year he was a special lecturer on English at Vassar College, with the rank of professor; from 1925 to 1931 associate professor in the School of Journalism at Columbia; from 1932 to 1935 lecturer at the New School for Social Research; and since 1937 he has been professor of English at Columbia.

Dr. Krutch has been associated with the *Nation* since 1924: for eight years as dramatic critic and associate editor, for the next five years as a member of the editorial board, and since 1937 as dramatic critic again. He lived in Europe on a Guggenheim Fellowship in 1930 and 1931. During the First World War he was a member of the Psychological Corps of the United States Army. He is a member of the National Institute of Arts and Letters. In 1923 he married Marcelle Leguia, of Hendaye, France; they live in downtown New York, with a summer home at Redding, Conn. He is a blond, slender man, tall, dignified, and reserved, with a small moustache.

Besides his own books, he has edited the plays of Congreve and of Eugene O'Neill, and is the editor of the many-volumed English translation of Marcel Proust's *Remembrance of Things Past.* He has contributed to three major anthologies: *Our Changing Morals,* 1925; *Living Philosophies,* 1931; and *America Now,* 1938. He was one of the founders of the Literary Guild.

Without being a member of the so-called Southern Agrarian group, Dr. Krutch shares much of their conservative viewpoint. Though he is less gloomy now than in years past, and from the beginning has accepted his dark conclusions with stoicism and an almost cheerful pragmatism, he remains the prime pessimist among American critics. "Gallant despair" has been his watchword, an attitude sometimes indicted by other critics as not being altogether free from affectation. A decade ago Ralph Barton Perry remarked on his "pious acceptance of the creed of Spengler and Keyserling." He sees little hope for literature, the nation, Western civilization, or humanity as a whole. He is also a thorough convert to psychoanalysis; in fact, one objector called his biography of Poe "a Freudian melodrama." He has been accused of being "drab and tedious," of being washed in "the tepid waters of melancholy."

On the other hand, he has not lacked admirers. Robert Morss Lovett praised his "clear thinking and interesting presentation," and many of his unhappy prophecies have come all too true in the present unfortunate crisis of world affairs. In one field he has few rivals, and that is in dramatic criticism. He has none of the verve and impudent wit of a George Jean Nathan, but he is sound and just. In the words of Edith J. R. Isaacs, he is "one of the most thoughtful and literary of American dramatic critics." His name is pronounced *krootch.*

PRINCIPAL WORKS: Comedy and Conscience After the Restoration, 1924; Edgar Allan Poe—A Study in Genius, 1926; The Modern Temper, 1929; Five Masters, 1930; Experience and Art, 1932; Was Europe a Success? 1934; The American Drama Since 1918, 1939.

ABOUT: Harris, M. The Case for Tragedy; Bookman January 1930, February 1932; Ethics July 1938; Saturday Review of Literature June 1, 1929; Sewanee Review January 1936; Southern Atlantic Quarterly July 1938.

KÜLLER. See AMMERS-KÜLLER

KUPRIN, ALEXANDER IVANOVICH
(August 1870-October 25, 1938), Russian novelist and short-story writer, born in Na-

rovchat, a village in the province of Penza, came from fairly well-to-do parents; his mother was descended from the old aristocratic Tatar family of the Kolonchaks, and his father was a petty government official, with a pronounced artistic temperament—he played the violin and dabbled in oils. Before his sixth birthday Alexander was sent to a rather austere boarding school for boys and later to the Second Cadet School in Moscow, experiences which proved rather painful to judge by such stories as "The Fugitives" (in *The Star of Solomon*) and "At the Cross Roads." The Cadet School led young Kuprin to the Alexander Military Academy for Infantry (Moscow) where after two years of rigorous training he qualified for lieutenant and in 1890 joined the 46th Infantry Regiment.

While at the Military Academy, Kuprin had begun to write stories—one of them had been published in a satirical journal as early as 1889—and now in the army more than ever he found solace from annihilating boredom in literary exercises which his Commander did not approve in the least, and which frequently brought him solitary confinement in a dark dungeon. In 1897, after four years of persecution, Kuprin rebelled, quitting the service but remaining at Kiev with exactly thirteen kopeks in his pocket. This was the beginning of his long vagabondage. However, he was confident of his literary future and regarded his adventures as necessary steps in search of material. At various times he worked as longshoreman, dentist's apprentice, surveyor, printer, chorister, circus performer, tobacco salesman, and office boy for a machinery concern; he hunted in the Polessye forests and for two years caught sturgeon and mackerel with the fishermen of Balaklava in Crimea. At the turn of the century he settled in Petersburg: he joined the staff of *God's World* (*Mir Bozhyi*) and of *Knowledge* (*Znanie*), the publishing house founded by Maxim Gorky. Work abounded, but not money.

In 1905 Kuprin registered his first great success: his novel *The Duel* made an instant hit, partly because it was an excellent novel but to a larger extent because of its timeliness. The reading public saw in *The Duel* a burning indictment of Russian military bureaucracy, an explanation of Russia's catastrophic defeat in the Russo-Japanese war. The truth of the matter is that Kuprin had conceived his novel long before the war, during the time when he was in the infantry regiment. Kuprin's exposé crossed the frontiers: within a short time *The Duel* was available in Polish, German, French, and Italian translations. Although Kuprin added to his picture of army life in "Captain Rybnikov" (in *A Slav Soul and Other Stories*), his public did not receive it so warmly and unanimously as *The Duel.* Three years later, however, Part I of *Yama: The Pit* once more caught his readers' attention. *Yama* was primarily a *succès de scandale,* and although Mirsky called it "a journalistically realistic, crude, and sentimental novel," undoubtedly it contains a penetrative analysis of the lot of the prostitutes in Czarist Russia. Although Parts II and III of *Yama* did not appear until 1914-15, by 1912 the author was recognized as one of the major figures in Russian letters.

At the outbreak of the First World War Kuprin joined the army. At the time of the Russian Revolution he was stationed at Gotchina and expressed his dislike for the Soviet régime. He joined the White Army and fought with General Yudenitch who with the support of the British Admiralty launched a sudden attack on Petrograd, which was repulsed by the rallying of the workers of Petrograd. Kuprin escaped with his family to Helsingfors and obtained a position on the staff of *New Russian Life* (*Novaya Russkaya Zhizn*). For seventeen years, 1920-37, he lived in exile in Paris and Ville-d'Avray, where he continued to write, not too successfully, about his life experiences. In 1937 he returned to the Soviet Union and died in Leningrad the following year, at the age of sixty-eight.

Kuprin was a satirical realist, often unbearably sentimental but always thoroughly aware of the contradictions of his fatherland. Stephen Graham said in 1916: "After Chekhov the most popular tale-writer in Russia is Kuprin, the author of fourteen volumes of effusive, touching, and humorous stories. . . . Perhaps the greatest of living Russian novelists is Kuprin—exalted, hysterical, sentimental, Rabelaisian Kuprin!"

WORKS AVAILABLE IN ENGLISH TRANSLATION: Olessia, 1909; The Duel, 1916 (abridged version under title In Honour's Name, 1907); The River of Life and Other Stories, 1916; A Slav Soul and Other Stories, 1916; The Bracelet of Garnets and Other Stories, 1917; Sasha, 1920; Yama: The Pit, 1922; Sulamith, 1923; Gambrinus and Other Stories, 1925.

ABOUT: Grigorkov, Y. A. Aleksandr Ivanovich Kuprin; Mirsky, D. S. Contemporary Russian Literature; Olgin, M. J. Guide to Russian Literature; Persky, S. Contemporary Russian Novelists; Phelps, W. L. Essays on Russian Novelists; Grande Revue February 1932; Mercure de France, September 15, 1938.

KYNE, PETER BERNARD (October 12, 1880-), writer of popular American novels, was born in San Francisco, Calif.,

the son of John and Mary (Cresham) Kyne. He attended the public schools and business college and at the age of sixteen left his family and found a job in a "general store," working fifteen hours a day for $20 a month. But he loved to sell things, and instinctively felt that he had failed if a man refused to buy overalls two inches too long merely because the store hadn't the right size in stock. At the end of nine months, however, he decided to join the Army. That year in uniform left him with far more literary grist than military zest; he did, nevertheless, see service in the Philippine Rebellion.

Then came seven eye-opening years in a lumber and shipping office, where, during the bloody San Francisco waterfront strike of 1903 he got his first real impressions of "scab" hiring and the wretchedness of living-quarters on the Pacific Coast lumber schooners. With Andrew Furuseth, a colorful labor leader, he worked tirelessly for the eventual passage of the La Follette Seamen's Bill, a law which was later nullified, however, by government "interpretation."

He left the shipping office and bought a workingmen's haberdashery on the Embarcadero, the waterfront street of San Francisco; and a little later turned lumber broker "sadly undercapitalized, but long on industry and courage." A curiosity which prompted him to ask questions at very opportune moments was the secret, he contends, of his ability to sell.

Kyne has invested, without success, considerable sums in gold mines. Once he invented a combination hot-water bottle and ice-pack with a "center of gravity," but when the idea failed to make his fortune, he bought a farm and raised Holstein-Friesian cows and Duroc-Jersey hogs.

In 1910 he was married to Helen Catherine Johnston, and about this same time he made the leap from business to letters— "the world lost a good salesman when I became a writer." He had already published several books before he went to France (War of 1914) as Captain of the 144th Field Artillery; among them was *Cappy Ricks*, which with its extensions and variations virtually froze Kyne's reputation as a writer of popular fiction. In the post-war decade he wrote almost a dozen books in addition to *They Also Serve*, slightly fantastic "memoirs" of ranch adventures in California and soldier days abroad. The 'thirties brought fewer tales than had the 'twenties, but in his sixties Kyne is still writing steadily.

There is nothing finished, profound, or durable about Kyne's writing, but his stories are well-paced and charged with sentimental values. For a quarter of a century they have found a large and constant reading public.

PRINCIPAL WORKS: Three Godfathers, 1913; Cappy Ricks, 1916; The Valley of the Giants, 1918; Kindred of the Dust, 1920; The Pride of Palomar, 1921; Never the Twain Shall Meet, 1923; The Understanding Heart, 1926; They Also Serve, 1927; Comrades of the Storm, 1933; Cappy Ricks Comes Back, 1934; Dude Woman, 1940.

ABOUT: American Magazine June 1933; Reader's Digest December 1939; New York Times February 3, 1939.

LACRETELLE, JACQUES DE (July 14, 1888-   ), French novelist, was born at Cormatin, in a Burgundy castle which his  grandfather, himself a poet, playwright, and "extreme left" Deputy, had bought in the nineteenth century in order to be close to the poet Lamartine. Until the age of ten Jacques traveled widely, especially in the Orient; his father was in the diplomatic service. On his return to Paris he attended the Lycée Janson-de-Sailly where the distinguished stylist André Bellessort taught him composition. Then he entered Cambridge University and enlarged his list of favorite authors (Anatole France, Dostoievsky, Flaubert, Stendhal, Gide) with English novelists, especially the Brontës and Hardy. Jacques was not sure of his vocation till his friend Jacques de Zogheb persuaded him to become a writer. During short sojourns at Moret and Provins, and while traveling in San Salvador (1914), he wrote his first novel, La Vie Inquiète de Jean Hermelin which was published in 1920. In that same year he met Anatole France and, shortly after, Marcel Proust, and his contact with these masters encouraged him further in his literary pursuits.

In 1922 Lacretelle attained full recognition with *Silbermann,* a work he had written with utmost care in the Jewish quarters of Tunis and in his retreats at Maisons-Laffitte and Montfort-l'Amaury, and which won him the Prix Femina. *Silbermann* narrates, simply and touchingly, the persecution of a Jewish fellow-student by Catholic boys in a Paris lycée. During his vacations in Compiègne and Beauvais, Lacretelle completed *Marie Bonifas* (1925), a portrait of a provincial woman in the realistic tradition of Balzac and Flaubert, but peppered with Freudian effects. For the next few years he wrote only short stories for magazines and the theatre column for the *Nouvelle Revue Française*—often he escaped to the solitude of Ermenonville and Chantilly. In 1926 he traveled extensively in Greece, Italy, and Spain. Soon thereafter he returned to his novel-writing and in 1929 strengthened his reputation with *A Man's Life,* a profound psychological novel which has been compared to Gide's *The Immoralist* and which won him the Grand Prix of the French Academy.

Lacretelle then devoted himself to his most ambitious plan, the sequel-novel *Les Hauts-Ponts,* of which several volumes, beginning in 1932, have been published in France, without as yet any translation into English.

Les Hauts-Ponts is the detailed history of a family in the atmosphere of a period and a province (Vendée), during the course of half a century. Of it Jeannert says, "Since *Remembrance of Things Past,* this is truly the most solid work which can be imagined, that in which the characters are the most clearly drawn, and the tone most constant, in the sense that artists give to this word."

On April 6, 1933, Lacretelle married Mlle. Yolande de Naurois, a descendant of Turgot and Racine, and with her translated Emily Brontë's *Wuthering Heights* (1937). They have two children, Anne and Amaury, and live in Paris. In September 1939 they visited New York as the guests of the French Institute, and Monsieur Lacretelle lectured on contemporary literature at the World's Fair. No information as to his present whereabouts is available.

Lacretelle is tall, over six feet, and broad-shouldered; his profile is rugged and he speaks English with a distinctly Cambridge accent; his voice is grave and metallic. He suffers from deafness, loves solitude, and has been described as "reticent, a trifle sententious, minutely observing his own thoughts as he speaks, doubtful of himself, discreet and frank at the same time."

Works Available in English Translation: Silbermann, 1923; Marie Bonifas, 1927; A Man's Life, 1931; "Delos" (in John Myers O'Hara's *Hellas the Immortal*) 1932.

About: Bethléem, L. Romans à Lire et à Proscrire; Billy, A. Intimités Littéraires; Chaigne, L. Vies et Oeuvres d'Écrivains; Dumas, F. R. These Moderns; Ehrhard, J. E. Le Roman Française Depuis Marcel Proust; Lefèvre, F. Une Heure Avec; Rousseaux, A. Ames et Visages du XXe. Siècle; Sachs, M. The Decade of Illusion; Annales Politiques et Littéraires June 15, 1929, February 15, 1930; Nouvelles Littéraires April 18, 1925; Revue des Deux Mondes August 1, 1925; La Vie Nouvelle June 1929.

LACY, ERNEST. See "AMERICAN AUTHORS: 1600-1900"

"LADY OF QUALITY." See BAGNOLD, E.

*LA FARGE, CHRISTOPHER (December 10, 1897-   ), American poet and novelist, was born in New York City, a son of Christopher Grant La Farge and Florence Bayard (Lockwood) La Farge, and was given his father's full name. The senior La Farge was an architect and lecturer on architecture, and his father was John La Farge, the well-known painter and worker in stained glass. Oliver La Farge,*qv* the American novelist, is a younger brother of Christopher La Farge.

Christopher La Farge, says Paul Hyde Bonner, was not born with a gold spoon in his mouth, "but within easy reach of plenty of old family silver." His home was "one in which culture and field sports were considered more important than the amassing of utility bonds." The boy's world was one of woods, meadows, salt marshes, streams, books, and paintings. Even before he entered the First Form at Groton, young La Farge could ride well, shoot moderately, and cast a wet fly with enough skill to catch a trout. From St. Bernard's School he went to Harvard, where he helped edit both the *Advocate* and the *Monthly,* and wrote plays

for the Hasty Pudding Club. When the First World War interrupted his studies, "there followed an interlude of contra-espionage" — says Bonner — "which might easily have tempted a less erudite artist to follow in the footsteps of E. Phillips Oppenheim." He was commissioned a second lieutenant.

On his return from the war La Farge spent the years 1919-21 in the Harvard School of Architecture, receiving his B.A. degree in 1920. After obtaining a B.Arch. degree from the University of Pennsylvania in 1923, he went to work in his father's office. Then came the depression. "If the T-square could no longer be used, his typewriter could. Without a sigh, he packed his wife, children, and his trunks and headed straight for the Weald of Kent," where they lived in a cottage among the oast houses. Here La Farge wrote his first narrative poem, *Hoxie Sells His Acres.* Mrs. La Farge was Louisa Ruth Hoar of Washington, D.C. They were married in 1923, and have two sons.

Hoxie was a "restrained *tour-de-force,* summing up old Rhode Island memories." On his return to the United States soon after, La Farge wrote *Each to the Other: A Novel in Verse,* which was made a choice of the Book-of-the-Month Club for April 1939. "It uses every device of verse," said Stephen Vincent Benét, "but it has the weight and texture of a novel." Each epi-

sode of this story of a happy marriage was preceded by a sonnet. Clifton Fadiman commented that "the beautiful passages should have been collected as a short book of lyrics, and Mr. La Farge's talent for characterization should have been utilized in a conventional piece of prose fiction." La Farge's first venture into the novel form was *The Wilsons* (1941), a slight but readable study of American snobbism, chapters of which had appeared in the *New Yorker.*

The poet, like his brother, is long, lean and dark. He likes fishing and shooting woodcock.

PRINCIPAL WORKS: Hoxsie Sells His Acres, 1934; Each to the Other: A Novel in Verse, 1939; Poems and Portraits, 1940; The Wilsons: A Story of a family (novel) 1941.

ABOUT: Harvard University, Class of 1920: Twentieth Annual Report; Book-of-the-Month Club News March 1939.

LA FARGE, OLIVER (December 19, 1901-), American novelist, was born Oliver Hazard Perry La Farge in New York, the son of Christopher Grant La Farge, noted architect, and Florence Bayard (Lockwood) La Farge. He comes of a distinguished family, being descended both from Benjamin Franklin and Commodore Oliver Hazard Perry (his name-

D. Ulmann

sake). He is a grandson of the famous painter and artist in stained glass, John La Farge and a brother of Christopher La Farge.*qv*

Oliver La Farge was educated at St. Bernard's School, Groton, and Harvard (B.A. 1924, Hemenway Fellow 1924-26, M.A. 1929); he also has an honorary M.A. from Brown University (1932). At Harvard he was president of the *Advocate,* editor of the *Lampoon,* and class poet. Although born in New York, he spent most of his boyhood in Rhode Island, is a fine sailor, and is as devoted to the sea as he is to the desert. His interest in and sympathy with the American Indians dates almost from his infancy, when he dubbed himself "Indian Man," the name he was always known by as a child. In college this interest became specialized into anthropological, ethnological, and archaeological research; to this day there are anthropologists who hope devoutly that he will fail as an author and come back to their field. He made three archaeological expeditions to Arizona for

Harvard, two ethnological expeditions to Mexico and Guatemala for Tulane University, and one to Guatemala for Columbia; and he was assistant in ethnology at Tulane from 1926 to 1928 and research associate in anthropology at Columbia from 1931 to 1933. He has been president of the American Association on Indian Affairs since 1937, and was president of its predecessor, the National Association on Indian Affairs, for four years previous. From 1930 to 1932 he was director of the Eastern Association in Indian Affairs, and in 1931 directed the Intertribal Exhibitions of Indian Arts. Deeply tanned, with black hair, long arms, and the gait of an Indian, he is often taken by Indians for one of themselves, only from another tribe. The Navajos have been his special interest, though he is also official adviser to the Hopis, and has been a member of the advisory board of the Laboratory of Anthropology at Santa Fé, N.M., since 1935.

He was married in 1929 to Wanden E. Mathews, and they had a daughter. In 1937 they were divorced, and in 1940 Mr. La Farge married Consuelo Odil Baca, a literary agent, whose father was lieutenant governor of New Mexico and whose mother was its secretary of state. In 1941 he was awarded a Guggenheim Fellowship.

Most of Mr. La Farge's novels and stories center about the Indians, especially the Navajos. His first story was published in the O'Brien Anthology for 1927, and another won the O. Henry Memorial Prize in 1930. His first novel, *Laughing Boy*, won the Pulitzer Prize for Fiction in 1929. Better than perhaps any other articulate white man, he has understood the Indians and been able to act as their spokesman; his Indians are real men and women, with human thoughts and emotions and speech. Both in fiction and non-fiction he has exposed and protested against the whites' bad faith with the Indians on the one hand, and the attempts to "Americanize" them away from their native culture on the other. One critic summed up Oliver La Farge's mission as a writer by saying that he brought to his work "accurate observation, sensitive understanding of the complex Indian psychology, and respect for their cultural dignity." In the few stories he has written about other peoples, he has shown that besides these characteristics he possesses a natural gift for easy and vivid narrative.

PRINCIPAL WORKS: Tribes and Temples (with F. Blom) 1927; Laughing Boy, 1929; Sparks Fly Upward, 1931; The Year Bearer's People, 1931; Long Pennant, 1933; All the Young Men (short stories) 1935; The Enemy Gods, 1937; As Long As the Grass Shall Grow (non-fiction) 1940; The Changing Indian (ed.) 1942; The Copper Pot, 1942.

ABOUT: Bookman September 1930; Literary Digest May 31, 1930; Saturday Review of Literature October 16, 1937; Scholastic March 17, 1941; Time October 25, 1937.

LAGERLÖF, SELMA OTTILIANA LOVISA

(November 20, 1858-March 16, 1940), Swedish novelist, the first woman to win the Nobel Prize for Literature, was born in Värmland, Southern Sweden, the older daughter of Lieutenant Erik Lagerlöf and Louise (or Lovisa) (Wallroth) Lagerlöf. When she was three years old she suffered what apparently was an at-

tack of infantile paralysis, and was always lame as a result, though much of her childhood was spent in sanatoria or in warm climates in the hopes of regaining her health.

Her life outwardly was uneventful. During her early childhood, her grandmother was a constant source of stories, many of which appeared later in the granddaughter's books. Being a delicate child, she was not sent to school, but was taught at home. Her parents were both persons of culture, her father descended from a long line of army officers, her mother from clergymen. Her first literary interest was in the drama, thanks to a winter in Stockholm when she was introduced to the theatre, but her first published work was verse, which appeared in the local papers, but for a volume of which she could find no publisher. Later she thought so little of it that she made no attempt to collect it in book form.

The great attachment of her life was to the ancestral home, Mårbacka. Her father died when she was in her early twenties, and in the financial troubles that followed, the family lost this dearly loved estate. As in one of her own stories, Miss Lagerlöf bought it back with her Nobel Prize money, remodeled it, lived there for many years, and eventually died there.

By the time of her father's death she was preparing to be a country school teacher. At twenty-two she had gone to Stockholm, studied at the Teachers' Seminary, and was assigned to a school in Landskrona, in Northern Sweden (Dalecarlia). This is the region about which she wrote so much and so sympathetically; Värmland and Dalecarlia became her two sources and backgrounds, and she seldom strayed far from them except to follow their peasants when they too left the homestead.

In spite of her occasionally published verses, it seemed likely by the time Selma Lagerlöf was thirty that she was doomed to a lifetime of teaching and obscurity. It would have been hard for her to believe that in a few years more she would be the most popular author Scandinavia has ever had except Hans Christian Andersen. The book which accomplished this miracle was *Gösta Berling,* into which she poured all the overflow of Värmland legends with which her mind had been full since childhood. Its style was not prepossessing, for she had found her first great literary influence in Thomas Carlyle, and nothing could have been less appropriate as a model for fiction. The effect of *Heroes and Hero Worship* on *Gösta Berling* is only too apparent. Nevertheless the richly romantic mood of the book, its evocation of a hitherto unmined past, made it immensely popular. With the first five chapters she won a prize from the magazine *Idun,* the first real recognition she had ever had. The book has been translated into many languages, and is still widely read.

The following year, 1895, she was given a traveling fellowship, and left teaching permanently. She went to Italy, to the enriching of her literary background. Later, in spite of her lameness, she traveled all over Europe and even to Palestine. With the earnings from her books, she bought a small house in Falun, in which she lived with her mother and aunt. She never married, and except for a very youthful and platonic attachment appears to have had no love affairs.

In 1904 she received the gold medal of the Swedish Academy, and ten years later was elected its first woman member. In this capacity she was on the board which annually decides the recipients of the Nobel Prizes. In 1909 she herself had been the first woman so honored. Two years earlier she had been given an honorary Ph.D. degree by the famous Upsala University, at its Linnaeus Jubilee.

As the years passed, Miss Lagerlöf lived more and more in retirement, though her fiftieth birthday was celebrated nationally and her seventieth internationally. In the winter she lived in Falun, in the summer in the reconstructed Marbacka, where she really farmed the 140 acres and was an old-time lady of the manor for the fifty-three peasants employed on the place. The grain she raised was made into a breakfast food, bearing the farm's name, which was sold widely in Stockholm. In 1911 she addressed an international woman suffrage convention; she had always been a feminist, and was a pacifist as well. Her last months were made miserable by the spread of the war to Scandinavia and the threat to Sweden. She died of peritonitis, after a long illness and twenty-four hours of unconsciousness. Perhaps one of the last things she ever wrote was a note (in English) to the editors of this volume, regretting that because of her illness she was unable to prepare an autobiographical sketch.

Selma Lagerlöf was never pretty, but in old age, with her very white skin and bright steel-gray eyes, she had real distinction. Her soft, beautifully modulated voice was one of her chief attractions. On politics and religion she never expressed herself except indirectly, but it seems apparent that she had an amiable weakness for the supernatural, and shared in the world of fantasy which so often appears in her novels.

For critics of a later generation, her philosophy often seemed too simple, her outlook too limited; they complained of the lack of social content in her work, and said that "where she stops questioning, we begin." But that simplicity, as Walter Berendsohn remarked, is perfected: "the miraculous in our life on earth is her true theme. . . . She is a teller of homely legends and stories to which old and young children all over the world love to listen." Actually for children, she wrote two books, at the request of the Swedish school authorities; in translation, *The Wonderful Adventures of Nils* and his *Further Adventures* have been used as supplementary reading in American schools. To quote Hanna Larsen, "she conveys her facts through a golden haze of fiction." Or, as Agnes C. Hansen put it, hers is "a romantic and paradoxical interpretation of the familiar."

After she grew away from the early influence on her style of Carlyle, her work, passing through a rather exclamatory and over-emphasized period, settled into her true *genre*—a deep calm, a naïve simplicity like Andersen's, which makes her later books read as if they were tales told quietly in a summer twilight.

Works Available in English: The Story of Gösta Berling, 1898 (as Gösta Berling's Saga, 1918); Invisible Links (short stories) 1899; The Miracles of Anti-Christ, 1899; From a Swedish Homestead (short stories) 1901; Herr Arne's Hoard, 1904; The Wonderful Adventures of

Nils (juvenile) 1907; Christ Legends, 1908; The Girl From the Marsh Croft, 1910; The Further Adventures of Nils (juvenile) 1911; Lilliecrona's Home, 1914; Short Stories, 1915; Jerusalem, 1915; The Emperor of Portugallia, 1916; The Holy City, Jerusalem II, 1918; The Outcast, 1922; Mårbacka: The Story of a Manor, 1924; The Treasure, 1925; Charlotte Löwensköld, 1927; The General's Ring, 1928 (the last two, with Anna Svärd, as The Ring of the Löwenskölds, 1931); Memories of My Childhood, 1930; The Queens of Kungahälla, 1930; Harvest, 1935; The Diary of Selma Lagerlöf, 1936.

ABOUT: A Book of Great Autobiographies; Berendsohn, W. Selma Lagerlöf; Her Life and Work; Gustafson, A. Six Scandinavian Novelists; Jepson, M. Selma Lagerlöf (in Swedish); Kirkland, W. M. Girls Who Became Famous; Kristensen, M. Selma Lagerlöf (in Swedish); Lagerlöf, S. Mårbacka, Memories of My Childhood, The Diary of Selma Lagerlöf; Larsen, H. A. Selma Lagerlöf; Leverson, O. I. Selma Lagerlöf (in Swedish); Maule, H. E. Selma Lagerlöf; American Scandinavian Review December 1928, December 1938; Bookman (London) October 1927; Contemporary Review July 1938; Deutsche Rundschau November 1928; Family July 1937; Living Age October 6, 1923, December 1932; Publishers' Weekly March 23, 1940; Revue Politique et Littéraire November 3, 1934; School and Society March 23, 1940; World Today December 1928.

LAING, ALEXANDER KINNAN (August 7, 1903-   ), American poet and novelist, writes: "I was born at Great Neck,

L.I., N.Y., but my parents were New Yorkers. When I was six we moved to Pelham Manor, where I attended high school. My somewhat self-centered father insisted upon maintaining a farm in the middle of a suburb, and my memories are somewhat speckled with pictures of 'Squire Laing's cow' impeding the progress of the trolley that inspired Fontaine Fox to create his 'Toonerville.' While in high school I set up a mail-order enterprise dealing in the gadgets from which radios could be constructed. When I went to Dartmouth College my somewhat dreamy lieutenant in the business allowed it to fail. This helped to turn my interest from the scientific to the aesthetic, and I began to write a great deal of verse, though at college I became inordinately opulent by writing popularized technical pieces for newspaper radio supplements.

"I left Dartmouth in 1925 without taking my degree, spent a couple of weeks in Wall Street, began to publish verse, and then became technical editor of *Radio News*. After

a few months I took to the road and presently became a seaman. Back on dry land I edited the *Power Specialist,* but quit in 1928 and went to sea again, with a spell 'on the beach' in the Pacific Northwest. My first book was issued that year. In 1929 I wrote advertising copy, but took time off to put my first novel into shape. In 1930 I joined the faculty of Dartmouth College as tutorial adviser in English, a connection which with changes of title has continued since, except for a year of two commencing in 1934, when I took advantage of a Guggenheim fellowship for a jaunt around the world, with major pauses to study in London, Singapore, and Honolulu. In 1933 I had taken my B.A. at Dartmouth as of the Class of 1925.

"My first marriage, to Isabel Lattimore Frost in 1930, had ended with a divorce. In 1936 I married Dilys Bennett; we have a son. Since 1937 I have been assistant librarian at Dartmouth. I live on a Vermont hillside, across the river from Hanover [N.H.], a couple of miles from the library tower. My current avocations are carpentry, gardening, and skiing, depending on the season."

*   *

For the sake of verisimilitude, Mr. Laing has listed himself as "editor" of his macabre and fantastic novel, *The Cadaver of Gideon Wyck.* He has actually edited *The Haunted Omnibus* (1938) and *The Life and Adventures of John Nicol, Mariner* (1936). Both in prose and verse he is a sedulous stylist, with theories for utilizing the full resources of the English language. His wife, Dilys Bennett Laing, is a poet, author of *Another England* (1941).

PRINCIPAL WORKS: Fool's Errand, 1928; End of Roaming, 1930; Wine and Physic, A Poem and Six Essays on the Fate of Our Language, 1934; The Sea Witch, 1934; The Cadaver of Gideon Wyck (with T. Painter) 1934; The Motives of Nicholas Holtz (with T. Painter; in England: The Glass Centipede) 1936; Dr. Scarlett, 1937; Sailing In (juvenile) 1937; The Methods of Dr. Scarlett, 1938.

LALOU, RENÉ (September 3, 1889-   ), French essayist and critic, was born in Boulogne-sur-mer, and spent all his childhood in the North of France. He studied at a school in Calais; finished off with two years (1906-08) at the Lycée Henri-IV; and was subsequently accredited for entrance at École Normale Supérieure. During the four years following he was a student at the University of Lille, making frequent excursions to England—London, Oxford, and Dover.

From 1909 to 1910 he was assistant master at the Manchester Grammar School; two years later he accepted a post at the Lycée d'Oran; and in 1914 he had fulfilled all the requirements for a University professorship. Then came the First World War. Lalou went first to Algeria with the French infantry; and from 1916 to 1919 he was attached to the État-Major-General de la Marine, as an officer-interpreter. He afterwards taught in the Naval School at Brest; and then filled a succession of *lycée* appointments, the last of which was at the Henry-IV in Paris.

Meanwhile (1913-20) he had written four novels (none in English translation): *Les Deux Ordres,* a pre-war saga which analyzes the conflict of two generations; *L'Investiture* the story of discordant love; *Tristan Launey: Romancier,* a philosophic drama of life and death; and *Le Chef,* a tragedy embodying the endless struggle between a strong vigorous intelligence and commonplace minds. Lalou submitted them in manuscript to Georges Crès, who read them carefully, held them some time, and eventually (1923) published *Le Chef.* In a long conference Crès proposed that Lalou undertake the writing of a much-needed history of contemporary French literature.

To more than fifteen years of methodical study Lalou added two further years of uninterrupted labor. *La Littérature Française Contemporaine* appeared in 1922 and is the only important book of Lalou's that has been translated into English. (A revised and augmented edition was issued in French in 1941.) Because he wore no "school tie" whatsoever, Lalou could risk considerable frankness on literary faddists and opportunists; and his own historical discrimination gave the book ample authenticity. Its only enemies, in fact, seem to have been those authors who felt themselves and their thoughts too summarily dealt with.

Défense de l'Homme (Intelligence et Sensualité) was issued in 1926 and shortly afterward came *Une Alchimie Lyrique, Panorama de la Littérature Anglaise Contemporaine,* and *Le Clavecin Non Tempéré.* He wrote monographs on André Gide, Paul Valéry, and Roger Martin du Gard, whose work he had admired as early as 1913 and with whom he himself enjoyed a slight acquaintance. In addition to translations of Shakespeare, Poe, and Meredith, Lalou has written prefaces to French translations of books by Virginia Woolf, D. H. Lawrence, and Charles Morgan; and many critical articles for academic and literary reviews.

He and Mme. Lalou (née Dubonnet) have a home in Paris on the rue de Seine. Lalou is an officer of the Légion d'Honneur, has been recognized by the French Academy, and holds an honorary degree in agriculture and a membership in various Parisian outing clubs. As a literary craftsman he avoids categorizing, labeling, and blue-print writing: "Life is deeper than dogmatism. I have tried to follow life faithfully, looking at it closely until some order appeared rather than accepting any order imposed upon it from without."

Lalou's critical work, in translation, has served to introduce and interpret to the English-speaking world the leading modern writers of France, in the same way that he has presented to his own countrymen the best contemporary writers in English.

PRINCIPAL WORK AVAILABLE IN ENGLISH TRANSLATION: Contemporary French Literature, 1924.

ABOUT: Mercure de France December 1, 1930.

LA MARE. See DE LA MARE

LAMB, HAROLD (September 1, 1892-), American story writer and historian, writes: "I was born in Alpine, N.J., with damaged eyes, ears, and speech, and grew up so. For some twenty years it was an ordeal to meet people, and I am still uncomfortable in cities or crowds, although by now the damages of childhood have nearly righted themselves. 'To build up,'  I was sent from the gymnasium to the open country; but all my free time was spent in my grandfather's library, to my huge satisfaction and to the detriment of my eyes. School was torment, and college—Columbia —was worse. The hours that really counted were spent in the library at Columbia. There I dug into something gorgeous and new, chronicles of people in Asia. I wrote all the time; set up my stories in the attic in school and printed them on a hand-press and then carried on with the Columbia literary magazine. I was flunked unconditionally in general history and was only tolerated in John Erskine's and Carl Van Doren's classes. Brander Matthews awarded me the Bunner medal in American literature, and this saved me from dismissal, since I had devoted the hours outside the library to the soccer and tennis teams.

"In 1914 my father broke down and I found a job as make-up man on a motor trade weekly, then tried to do financial statistics for the New York *Times* and write stories at the same time. The stories were gleaned from the Oriental digging, and *Adventure* printed them. An understanding editor, Arthur Sullivant Hoffman, allowed me to write anything I wanted.

"I wandered more than a bit, turned up in Plattsburg, 1916, and in the 107th Infantry, as a private, but did not see any fighting. [He also received his B.A. from Columbia in 1916.] In 1917 I married Ruth Barbour, and I have wondered since then why men write books about unhappy marriages. We have a son and a daughter. We went out to the Pacific Coast soon after our marriage. Two years of that time were spent at Fort Bragg, in the forest along the Northern California coast. I live now in Piedmont, in Southern California.

"I have had to gather together my own collection to work with—the mediaeval travelers, Persian and Russian chronicles, histories of elder China. I spend months in going through the scenes of a book in imagination until all details are clear. Then I try to put it all down in words. I shirk revising, which is an ordeal. When study oppresses I go straight to the Northern lumber camps or the decks of a schooner. My relaxations are chess, tennis, and gardening. I am six feet one inch in height, weigh 160 pounds, and have prematurely gray hair."

* * *

Mr. Lamb won the medal of the Persian government for scientific research in 1932, and the silver medal of the Commonwealth Club, San Francisco, in 1933. He was a Guggenheim Fellow in 1929. He has written several motion pictures, including *The Plainsmen*. He reads Arabic and Chinese, and Mr. Hoffman, his "discoverer," called him "always the scholar first, the good fictionist second," praising also his imagination and enthusiasm, and his "dogged fighting spirit."

PRINCIPAL WORKS: Genghis Khan, 1927; Tameralen, 1928; The Crusades—Iron Men and the Saints, 1930; The Crusades—The Flame of Islam, 1931; Nur Mahal, 1932; Kirdy (juvenile) 1933; Omar Khayyam, 1934; The March of the Barbarians, 1940.

ABOUT: Kunitz, S. J. & Haycraft, H. (eds.). The Junior Book of Authors; Bookman March 1930.

LAMONT, CORLISS (March 28, 1902-), American essayist, writes: "Born at Englewood, N.J., in the year 1902, I think there can be no doubt that physically and to a large extent spiritually I am a child of the twentieth century. I received my formal education at Exeter and Harvard, going on to post-graduate work at Oxford and Columbia. At Columbia I served for four years as instructor in philosophy and wrote my first book in the form of a Ph.D. thesis on the subject of immortality.

"Later I expanded this study into what has been my major piece of work in the field of philosophy, *The Illusion of Immortality*. In this book I undertook, quite in the spirit of the age, to give in modern and scientific terms the complete case against the idea of personal survival after death and to present an affirmative philosophy of life based on the this-earthly enjoyment of human existence. Then, in order to make the job complete, I edited an anthology of poetry, *Man Answers Death* (1936), centering around this same philosophy of Humanism. It is, I believe, the only anthology of poetry which fully presents the more realistic side of what the poets of the race have had to say about death.

"Turning to the question of *how* the two billion inhabitants of this planet can attain the Humanist goals of peace, freedom, and happiness, I reached the conclusion that a planned and democratic Socialist order is the only possible means of establishing a stable and abundant world civilization in which the Good Life of the individual can flourish in the Good Society of all. I worked through this conclusion in some detail, from the viewpoint of an independent radical, in *You Might Like Socialism: A Way of Life for Modern Man*. As the title indicates, Socialism not only offers lasting solutions for our fundamental social and economic problems, but also gives men and women a total and inclusive way of life around which they can integrate themselves in a psychological and spiritual sense. Though these are distressing times everywhere, I remain basically optimistic about the future of mankind for the simple reason that I see real hope for the not distant emergence of a genuine Socialist system throughout Europe and large portions of Asia.

785

"For a decade and more I have maintained a general though critical sympathy for the Soviet Union, where the first Socialist society in history has become a functioning reality. In several pamphlets and many articles that I have written about the Soviet Republic I have been able to embody direct observations made in visiting the U.S.S.R. in 1932 and again in 1938. In the latter year I witnessed the tremendous economic and cultural progress that had been achieved since my first trip. I do not believe, however, in any mechanical imitation of Soviet Russia, since Socialism must necessarily differ from country to country, adjusting itself to the cultural patterns and specific economic conditions of whatever nation is involved.

"As Plato says, the philosopher is 'the spectator of all time and all existence'; he is a specialist only in the sense of viewing the whole of life and in trying to make a rounded synthesis of its various aspects. Philosophy as thus interpreted is peculiarly suited to my temperament, since I relish by nature a many-sided life and feel interested literally in everything. My chief personal problem is to find time for all the things I want to do both in the field of creative writing and of pure enjoyment in the exciting worlds of literature and art, drama and music, travel and sport, social intercourse, and family relations. I try to keep abreast of all these worlds, though the presence of four children in the house sometimes threatens to disrupt the process."

* * *

As the son of Thomas W. Lamont, a partner of J. P. Morgan, Mr. Lamont has attracted some public attention because of his radicalism. He was married in 1928 to Margaret Hayes Irish, also a writer, and they have two daughters and two sons. He is chairman of the board of directors of the *People's Press,* member of the editorial council of *Soviet Russia Today,* and a contributing editor of *Science and Society.* He was one of the representatives of the American Civil Liberties Union who was arrested in Jersey City in a test of Mayor Hague's anti-free speech law (later declared unconstitutional by the U.S. Supreme Court). He taught philosophy at Columbia from 1928 to 1932, since when he has devoted all his time to writing.

A suit for libel brought by Mr. Lamont against the Bobbs-Merrill Co., publishers of *The Red Decade* by Eugene Lyons,[qv] was settled out of court in 1942 to Mr. Lamont's satisfaction.

PRINCIPAL WORKS: Issues of Immortality, 1932; Russia Day by Day (with M. Lamont) 1933; The Illusion of Immortality, 1935; You Might Like Socialism, 1939.

ABOUT: Literary Digest July 14, 1934.

LAMPMAN, ARCHIBALD. See "BRITISH AUTHORS OF THE 19TH CENTURY"

LANCASTER, BRUCE (August 22, 1896-), American novelist, was born in Worcester, Mass., the son of Walter Moody Lancaster and Sarah Jenkins (Hill) Lancaster. He attended Sanford School at Redding Ridge, Conn., in 1913-14. His military service began in 1916, when he served with Battery A, 1st Massachusetts Field Artillery, on the Mexican border; and he  spent twenty months with the American Expeditionary Force in France, serving in Battery A, 101st Field Artillery, 26th Division, of the U.S. Army. He is a second lieutenant in the Officers' Reserve Corps. Bruce Lancaster obtained his B.A. degree from Harvard University in 1918, and is usually listed in class reports by the secretary of the class, Franklin E. Parker, Jr. as a "Lost Member." From 1919 to 1927 he was engaged in administrative and sales work, then served six years in the Foreign Service of the U.S. Department of State.

As vice-consul, Lancaster lived at Kobe, Japan, from 1928 to August 1930, when he went to Nagoya for two months, returning to Kobe to stay until June 1932, when he again spent two months in Nagoya. His last year in the consular service was spent at Kobe. He married Jessie Bancroft Payne in December 1931; they now live on Linnaean Street, Cambridge, Mass. Lancaster was assistant secretary to the board of governors of the Society of New York Hospitals from 1933 to 1937, when he began to write novels. After *The Wide Sleeve of Kwannon,* a 17th-century romance of the Dutch East India Company, he wrote *Guns of Burgoyne* (1939), a realistic and exciting novel of this ill-fated British expedition during the Revolutionary War, dealing with the same campaign as did Kenneth Roberts' *Rabble in Arms. The Bride of a Thousand Cedars* (1939), written with a Harvard classmate, the writer and publisher Lowell Brentano, has for its locale Bermuda during the

American Civil War. *Bright to the Wanderer* (1942) is a novel of the Upper Canadian rebellion of 1837, "frankly intended to entertain."

Bruce Lancaster is a member of the Society of Japanese Studies of New York and the American P.E.N. His clubs are the Harvard and Downtown Harvard clubs in New York City, and formerly, the Kobe and Concordia in Kobe. He is a Republican and an Episcopalian.

PRINCIPAL WORKS: The Wide Sleeve of Kwannon, 1938; Guns of Burgoyne, 1939; The Bride of a Thousand Cedars (with L. Brentano) 1939; For Us the Living, 1940; Bright to the Wanderer, 1942.

ABOUT: New York Times Book Review December 1, 1940.

LANDAU. See ALDANOV

LANE, Mrs. ROSE (WILDER) (December 5, 1887-   ), American novelist and miscellaneous writer, was born in a "claim

shanty" near De Smet, Dakota Territory (now S.D.), the daughter of pioneering parents, Almanzo James Wilder and Laura Elizabeth (Ingalls) Wilder. They were unable to get by on the homestead, and so while she was still a small child they pulled up stakes and migrated to the Ozark Mountains, where she was reared. This is the country which has been the background of many of her novels and stories. Later they moved again to Crowley, La., where she was graduated from high school. She then went to San Francisco, where she did newspaper work, and where in 1909 she married Gillette Lane, from whom she was divorced in 1918. Besides being a reporter and feature writer, Mrs. Lane has worked as an office clerk, a telegrapher, and at selling farmland. In 1920 she made her first trip to Albania, living there for some time in almost medieval surroundings in the mountains, the first "foreign woman" many of the inhabitants had ever seen. Later she made another trip there, and from her experiences grew not only a book, *The Peaks of Shala*, and numerous stories and articles, but also a translation of *The Dancer of Shamakha* (1923).

Among Mrs. Lane's published works, she includes the once-famous best-seller, *White Shadows in the South Seas*. Her claim is that she "ghost-wrote" this book for the late Frederick O'Brien.[qv] He always alleged that she merely acted as his secretary, and that the book was entirely his. Inasmuch as O'Brien died in 1932, the controversy will probably always remain unsettled.

Mrs. Lane now lives most of the time in New York. Her interest has become more and more concentrated on the history and customs of the Ozark Mountains where she lived as a child, and many people in Missouri and Arkansas think of her as their official spokesman. She is a stocky woman, gray-haired, with a determined expression beneath which lurks a keen sense of humor. She is direct and outspoken, and a good mixer with all kinds of people.

Although she is not a prolific novelist, she is constantly at work on short stories and articles for the popular magazines. Besides her fiction, she has written "official" biographies of Henry Ford and Herbert Hoover. As a novelist, she may be described as competent and sympathetic, with a good journalistic style and not much depth. Perhaps her best as well as her most unusual writing has been about Albania, where she really did have a unique experience, not without its personal dangers, and one she knew how to tell about vividly and impressively.

PRINCIPAL WORKS: Henry Ford's Own Story, 1917; Diverging Roads, 1919; The Making of Herbert Hoover, 1920; The Peaks of Shala (non-fiction) 1923; He Was a Man, 1925; Hill-Billy, 1926; Cindy, 1928; Let the Hurricane Roar, 1933; Old Home Town, 1935; Give Me Liberty, 1936; Free Land, 1938.

ABOUT: Good Housekeeping February 1931; Scholastic February 11, 1939.

LANG, ANDREW. See "BRITISH AUTHORS OF THE 19TH CENTURY"

LANGDON-DAVIES, JOHN (1897-   ), British anthropologist and sociologist, was born in Zululand, South Africa, where his

father, the Rev. Guy Langdon-Davies, ran a frontier school. The elder Langdon-Davies, who died when the boy was three, was a remarkable man; from an orthodox clergyman he had become a Huxleyan, a Voltairean, and a Tolstoyan pacifist. On  his death the mother, reluctant to take her son back to smug suburban life in England, opened a toy store and worked as a milliner in Natal, while the boy ran wild and largely took care of himself. But when he was seven she was obliged to give up, and they sailed for England; her son has never seen Africa since. He was placed in Tonbridge School, where the persecutions of the other boys made his school days a hell on earth, and gave him a lasting inferiority complex. Nevertheless he struggled through to a scholarship to St. John's College, Oxford, and he became a recognized anthropologist and a Fellow of the Royal Anthropological Institute. He was a teacher for a number of years, both of children and of adults, and is a popular lecturer both in England and in America, where he has made several lecture tours, the first in 1926. He was married first to Constance Scott, by whom he had two sons, and, after a divorce, to Elizabeth Barr, by whom he has a daughter. His home now is in London; he has written several recent short books bearing on the war crisis.

Far to the left in his views, though not officially a Communist, he took part on the side of the Loyalists in the Spanish Civil War from its beginning in 1936. Another of his interests is in physics and especially in radio, on the technical side of which he has become something of an expert. Indeed, Mr. Langdon-Davies' pitfall is his unusual versatility, which exposes him to the danger of easy superficiality. He is a vivid and engaging writer, and this very fact, together with his radical tendencies, has made the orthodox scientists and economists alike suspicious of him. He is a born popularizer, with a gift for making abstract subjects clear and simple. But he is no smooth-speaking optimist: in his words, we live today "in a savage epoch, when almost nothing seems self-evident"; and he has foretold a universal triumph of Fascism, and eventually a regimented humanity biologically altered as are the regimented social insects! It is this dark outlook which has probably kept him from feeling full enthusiasm for any social panacea, though all his sympathies are with the exploited and oppressed.

In appearance, Mr. Langdon-Davies might come straight from the editorial board of the *Yellow Book,* with his curly hair, high forehead, small features, and a certain indefinable *fin-de-siècle* air about him. But in mind (though the influence of his early years in Africa and of his unhappy boyhood are still both strong within him), he is ultra modern. It may be expected that as world conditions change, his vision will change with them. If he can concentrate all his energies on one worth-while field of inquiry, better books may be expected of him yet than he has hitherto produced—for all his work so far,

even the popular *Man and His Universe,* has been just on the edge of achievement.

PRINCIPAL WORKS: The New Age of Faith, 1925; A Short History of Women, 1927; The Future of Nakedness (in America: Lady Godiva: The Future of Nakedness) 1929; Dancing Catalans, 1929; Militarism in Education, 1930; Man and His Universe, 1930; Science and Common Sense (in America: Man Comes of Age) 1931; Inside the Atom, 1933; How Wireless Came, 1935; Radio; The Story of the Capture and Use of Radio Waves, 1935; A Short History of the Future, 1936; Behind the Spanish Barricades, 1937; Air Raid: The Technique of Silent Approach, High Explosive, Panic, 1938; Parachutes Over Britain, 1940; The Fifth Column, 1940; Nerves Versus Nazis, 1940; Invasion in the Snow, 1941; Home Guard Warfare, 1941; Home Guard Fieldcraft Manual, 1942; Home Guard Training Manual (ed.) 1942.

ABOUT: Harper's Magazine October 1926, May 1930.

LANGNER, LAWRENCE (May 30, 1890-), Anglo-American playwright, was born in Swansea, South Wales, the son of Braham Langner and Cecile Langner. He attended grammar schools in Swansea and in Margate, England, then became a pupil of Wallace Cranston Fairweather, a chartered patent agent in London. Langner passed the examinations of the

M. Stein

British Chartered Institute of Patent Agents at twenty, and came to the United States next year, in 1911. He established his own firm as a patent lawyer in New York in 1913, and next year organized the Washington Square Players, which produced one-act plays at the Bandbox and Comedy theatres. In 1916 Langner married Estelle Roege; they had a daughter, Phyllis Adair Langner, and were later divorced. Langner was one of the chief founders of the Theatre Guild, which supplanted the Washington Square Players but retained members of their personnel, such as Helen Westley and Lee Simonson, who also became directors of the Guild. After producing plays for some years at the Garrick Theatre, the Guild built its own handsome playhouse on West 52nd Street.

During the First World War, Langner served as consultant to the Ordnance Department on munitions inventions and was a member of the Advisory Council to the American Committee for preparation of patent sections of the Treaty of Versailles. (He had become a naturalized American citizen in 1917.) He is now a member of the firm of Langner, Card & Langner, international patent solicitors, with offices in New York, Chicago, and Washington; he is also a member of the firm of Stevens, Langner, Parry & Rollinson of London, chartered patent agents.

Langner's avocation has always been the theatre. He wrote several one-act plays for the Washington Square Players, including *Another Way Out, Family Exit, These Modern Women, Matinata* and *Pie,* which the Provincetown Players produced. As a Theatre Guild director he conducted the negotiations with George Bernard Shaw for the production of *St. Joan* and *Back to Methuselah.* He has adapted several plays, including *School for Husbands,* from the French of Molière, with Arthur Guiterman, and Strauss's *Der Fledermaus,* with Robert Simon. Two plays founded on early American sexual *mores* and written in collaboration with his second wife, Armina Marshall (they were married in 1924 and have a son, Philip) were comedies which combined archness with suggestiveness. *The Pursuit of Happiness* (1934) considered the Colonial custom of bundling, and *Suzanna and the Elders* (1940) the Oneida experiment in communal living. The Langners, who live on West Eleventh street in the winter, own and operate a summer theatre, the Westport (Conn.) Country Playhouse.

PRINCIPAL WORKS: *Plays*—Moses, 1924; Henry Behave, 1927; The Pursuit of Happiness (with A. Marshall) 1934; Suzanna and the Elders (with A. Marshall) 1940. *Others*—Outline of Foreign Trade Mark Practice (with H. Langner) 1923.

ABOUT: Eaton, W. P. The Theatre Guild: The First Ten Years; New York Herald Tribune April 27, 1941.

LARBAUD, VALÉRY (August 29, 1881-   ), French critic, novelist, short story writer, translator, and poet, was born in the

cosmopolitan city of Vichy, where his father founded the still profitable Établissement Larbaud, a bathing resort. A delicate only child, he loved books and solitude. His library of more than twelve thousand volumes— all bound in appropriate national colors—was started at an early age, as were his huge assortment of maps, charts and flags and his international collection of tin soldiers.

At Sainte Barbe des Champs in Fontenay-aux-Roses, "an old school, more cosmopolitan

than a world's fair," Valéry excelled in Greek and French literature, geology and philology; his Spanish and Spanish-American classmates inspired his life-long predilection for things Spanish. Valéry attended the *lycées* Henri-IV, Bainville, and Louis le Grand, and obtained his *licencié ès lettres* from the Sorbonne, meanwhile travelling extensively all over Europe. Having already made translations from Whitman and won acclaim for his superb rendering of *The Ancient Mariner* (1901), Larbaud decided to translate foreign writers and introduce them to French literature. To this end he learned half a dozen languages, and assimilated the literature of twice as many countries. Larbaud was the first Frenchman to study or translate Samuel Butler, Chesterton, Conrad, Landor, Hardy, Stevenson, Joyce, Ramón Gómez de la Serna, and many others into French; no less valuable was his service in introducing to the English-reading public Rimbaud, Claudel, Péguy, and Giraudoux. The Mexican Azuela, the Italian Svevo, the Argentine Güiraldes have been subjects of his encomiastic essays, as well as Huxley, Coventry Patmore, Francis Thompson, and Edith Sitwell. Larbaud recognizes no national boundaries.

Foreign lands as well as foreign books attract him, and his travels range as wide as his literary tastes. His suave, sophisticated reports of his journeys in every corner of Europe and northern Africa started the vogue for travelogues years before the globe-trotting expeditions of Claudel, Morand, et al.

Larbaud's books, few and far between, are usually interconnected and form a sort of continuous veiled autobiography. *A. O. Barnabooth, Le Pauvre Chemisier: Les Poésies,* prose poems written between 1900 and 1907, appeared in a limited edition in 1908, the review copies bearing the title *Poèmes d'un Riche Amateur. Fermina Marquez,* his first novel, begun in 1906, was published 1909. Unconventional in form, this was coolly received, but with the publication, after ten years in the writing, of *A. O. Barnabooth: His Diary* (1913), Larbaud was recognized as a major novelist of his generation. This depicts the restless cosmopolitan spirit of a young millionaire poet in search of exotic adventures, and has been called the *Adolphe* of our time. *Enfantines,* sensitive stories of childhood, was begun in 1908, published 1918. Larbaud was a pioneer and master in the portrayal of adolescence. *Amants, Heureux Amants* (1924) consists of three stories two of which are entirely interior monologues in the Joycean manner.

Larbaud was introduced to Joyce, then still unknown, by Sylvia Beach in 1919. Upon reading the portions of *Ulysses* which she gave him (expecting to find them an excellent sleep-inducer), Larbaud recognized Joyce immediately as one of the greatest writers of the century. It was largely due to Larbaud's efforts, says Herbert Gorman, that Joyce became widely known among French writers and critics. Larbaud edited the French translations of *Ulysses*. In 1920 he gave Joyce the use of his quarters in Paris.

"Vast culture, distinction of tone and serenity of spirit combine to make Larbaud a writer of unusual charm," writes Milton H. Stansbury. "He can infuse dreamy glamour through a book like *Enfantines,* distill the subtle aroma of poetry through every page of *Amants, Heureux Amants,* or with grace and vivacity portray the vacillating Barnabooth. He has not been a prolific writer, and except for his continued activity in translating and promulgating foreign authors, his literary career seems prematurely ended."

Up to the time of the fall of France in 1940, Larbaud wrote articles on the more sophisticated French writers for papers such as the *New Weekly* of London and *La Nación* of Buenos Aires; these, it is said did not have to be translated. On his desk in Paris, to symbolize his eclecticism, stood a figure of Buddha next to one of Minerva wearing the Phrygian cap of the Republic. Possessed of a remarkable memory, Larbaud can recite entire poems not only in French but in their English or Italian versions. One of his superstitions is that all his books must be published on the fourth of July. He will not allow them to be publicized in any way. Physically, Larbaud is rather short and stocky, with swarthy complexion and large dark eyes that smile serenely and good-naturedly.

AVAILABLE IN ENGLISH TRANSLATION: A. O. Barnabooth: His Diary, 1924.

ABOUT: Contreras, F. Valéry Larbaud; Crémieux, B. XXme Siècle; de Voisins, G. Valéry Larbaud; Jaloux, E. L'Esprit des Livres; Lalou, R. Contemporary French Literature; Lefèvre, F. Une Heure Avec; Lièvre, P. Esquisses Critiques; Rousseaux, A. Littérature du Vingtième Siècle; Stansbury, M. H. The French Novel Today; Grande Revue August 1924; Nouvelle Revue Française February 1, 1924; La Revue de Paris December 15, 1932; Symposium July 1932.

LARDNER, RING (March 6, 1885-September 25, 1933), American short-story writer and journalist, was born Ringgold Wilmer Lardner, the son of Henry Lardner and Lena Bogardus Phillips Lardner. He was graduated from high school in his native Niles, Michigan, wanted to go to the University of Michigan "and take football and dentistry," but soon found himself enrolled at Armour Institute, Chicago, for the study of mechanical engineering. At the end of the first semester he "passed in rhetoric and out of Armour." He got a job as local freight agent, but lost it when he misdirected a consignment of cream cheese. For six dollars a week he was bookkeeper and handy-man in a gas office, and then one day, succeeded in "stealing" an opening (which his brother had been unable to accept) on the South Bend (Ind.) *Times.* He covered police stations, courts, ball games and movies, and in his second year (1907) went over to the staff of the Chicago *Inter Ocean.* Almost immediately the *Examiner* singled him out as a man of particular ability hired him, and sent him South with the White Sox. In 1910 and 1911 he was editor of *Sporting News,* a baseball weekly in St. Louis. He did some sports stories for the Boston *American,* and became a copyreader for the Chicago *American.* But when it was discovered that he printed an account of the death of one Tom Shevlin instead of Tom Shevlin's father, young Lardner found himself involuntarily transferring his interests to the Chicago *Herald Examiner.* In 1913 he began to conduct a column in the *Tribune,* "In the Wake of the News," which survived until he became associated with the Bell syndicate in 1919.

Meanwhile Lardner had sent, in 1914 some of the adventures of Jack Keefe, a White Sox pitcher, and his wife Florrie conceived in a series of analphabetic epistles to the *Saturday Evening Post.* They caught hold immediately and their audience was country-wide; in book form they became the *You Know Me, Al* series; and in their wake sprang up a new debunking school of sport criticism to displace the traditional simon pure eulogies. Everything he wrote during the five years that followed was regarded as thoroughgoing humor, but in 1924, with the appearance of a collection called *How*

To Write Short Stories ("Some Like Them Cold," "Golden Honeymoon," "My Roomy," et al.) and in 1926 with *The Love Nest*, it became obvious that Lardner was fundamentally not a laugh-for-laugh's sake humorist but a satirist obsessed with a black melancholy. His repugnance for boors, morons, and swine, either explicit or implicit, had a Swiftian cynicism, and yet there was always that thin top layer of wild nonsense to make "people who do not read books" laugh at the "funny man."

In 1927 he published his mad autobiography called *The Story of a Wonder Man*. With George M. Cohan he collaborated on *Elmer the Great*, a piece about a ball-player, and with George S. Kaufman, on *June Moon*, both of which had good runs on Broadway. Lardner's close friend F. Scott Fitzgerald said that he had "stopped finding any fun in his work ten years before he died." His last actual output was a series of reviews of radio broadcasting for the *New Yorker*, under the date-line, "No Visitors, N. Y." and "Out for Lunch, N. Y." One source of resentment was that he had gotten his foothold as a sports specialist, and he heartily disliked being unable to rid himself entirely of that identification. He died of heart disease at forty-eight at his home in East Hampton, L.I., after four years of poor health.

Lardner was tall, broad, big-boned, and lean, with brooding eyes and a rather heavy and inert voice; but he was unmistakably handsome. He married Ellis Abbott in 1911 and by her had four sons. (James Lardner fought with the Lincoln Batallion in the Spanish Civil War and was lost during the Ebro offensive.) He was a quiet man, says Franklin P. Adams, "who might sit in a room for three hours without saying a word." Adams credits him, moreover, with a tremendous strength both as an observer and as a "sympathetic hater of the human four-flusher." He wrote about Americans in the language of Americans, and he left a firmer, richer soil for later colloquial writers to dig in. He has two sets of readers: those who only laugh, and those who, like the late William Bolitho, are shaken with horror and despair and regard him as "the greatest and sincerest pessimist America has produced."

PRINCIPAL WORKS: Bib Ballads, 1915; You Know Me, Al, 1916; Gullible's Travels, 1917; Treat 'Em Rough, 1918; The Real Dope, 1918; The Big Town, 1921; How To Write Short Stories, 1924; What of It? 1925; The Love Nest and Other Stories, 1926; The Story of a Wonder Man, 1927; Round Up (reprint) 1929; June Moon (play, with G. S. Kaufman) 1930; Lose With a Smile,

1933; First and Last (non-fiction) 1934; Ring Lardner's Best Stories (reprint) 1938.

ABOUT: Adams, F. P. Diary of Our Own Samuel Pepys; Geismar, M. Writers in Crisis; Masson, T. L. Our American Humorists; Commonweal October 10, 1933; Living Age December 1933; Nation March 22, 1933, October 11, 1933; New Republic May 22, 1929, October 11, 1933.

LA ROCHE. See DE LA ROCHE

LARSEN, JOHANNES ANKER. See ANKER LARSEN

LA SERNA. See GÓMEZ DE LA SERNA

*LASKI, HAROLD JOSEPH (June 30, 1893-), English political scientist, was born in Manchester, the second son of Nathan Laski. Brought up in an orthodox Jewish household, he attended Manchester Grammar School and New College, Oxford, where he was an Honorary Exhibitioner, won the Beit Prize in 1913, and was graduated with first-class honors in the  School of Modern History in 1914. For the next two years he was a lecturer on history at McGill University, in Canada, and then for four years held the same post at Harvard. During his last year there, 1919-20, he was also Harvard Lecturer at Yale, and in 1917 he was Henry Ward Beecher Lecturer at Amherst. He left Harvard in 1920 after a disagreement with the authorities over the Boston police strike, and returned to London.

There he formed an academic connection, existing to this date, with the London School of Economics. He also became a lecturer on political science at the University of London, and since 1926 has been its professor of that subject. He has also lectured at Magdalene College, Cambridge (1922-25), Yale (1931-1933), Moscow (1934), and Trinity College, Dublin (1936).

Professor Laski was vice-chairman of the British Institute of Adult Education from 1921 to 1930, a member of the Fabian Society Executive from 1922 to 1936, a member of the Lord Chancellor's Committee on Delegated Legislation in 1929, of the Departmental Committee on Local Government in 1931, and on Legal Education in 1932, has been a member of the Industrial Court since 1926, and is now a member of the

Council of the Institute of Public Administration, of the editorial board of the *Political Quarterly,* and of the executive committee of the Labor Party. He received an honorary LL.D. degree from the University of Athens in 1937.

He is married to Frida Kerry and they have one daughter. His present home is in London. A dark, round-faced man with spectacles and a large moustache, his only recreation and hobby is book-collecting. In spite of his interest in politics, he prefers to work on committees rather than to hold public office, and turned down the offer of a certain election as a Labor Member of Parliament.

A convinced Marxian, Professor Laski has of course long been under fire from conservatives both in England and in America. He is not, however, and never has been a Communist. Probably no Englishman since Lord Bryce has known American politics, history, and law as thoroughly as he does. He has written a great deal about America, and may be considered more of an authority on our government than are most Americans. In addition to his books, he is a prolific writer of articles for the serious reviews both here and in England, and he has edited the works of Edmund Burke and John Stuart Mill.

Patience and brilliance, in equal proportions, are the hallmarks of his writing. One critic called him "one of the most progressive and fearless thinkers of the day. A whole school of political science has arisen around him." Arnaud Dandieu, praising his "ardor and fighting spirit," remarked: "The problem of authority is the one around which all Laski's work revolves. . . . He is an individualist first and foremost. . . . His economic science is supplemented to a rare and perhaps unique degree by his historical and psychological abilities." Laski's current writing is largely concerned with the political aspects of the Second World War and, looking ahead, with the problems of post-war reconstruction.

PRINCIPAL WORKS: Studies in the Problem of Sovereignty, 1917; Authority in the Modern State, 1919; Political Thought in England From Locke to Bentham, 1920; The Foundations of Sovereignty and Other Essays, 1921; A Grammar of Politics, 1925; Communism, 1927; The Dangers of Obedience and Other Essays, 1930; Liberty in the Modern State, 1930; An Introduction to Politics, 1931; Studies in Law and Politics, 1932; The Crisis and the Constitution, 1932; Democracy in Crisis, 1933; The State in Theory and Practice, 1935; The Rise of European Liberalism, 1936; Parliamentary Government in England: A Commentary, 1938; The Danger of Being a Gentleman and Other Essays, 1940; The American

Presidency: An Interpretation, 1940; Where Do We Go From Here? 1940; Strategy of Freedom, 1941.

ABOUT: American Political Science Review May 1924; American Review October 1936; Book-of-the-Month Club News July 1940; Century Magazine November 1928; Christian Century June 12, 1935; Living Age November 1930; New Statesman and Nation July 21 and 28, August 11, 1934; Nineteenth Century March 1940; Wilson Library Bulletin November 1935, January 1941.

"LATHAM, O'NEILL." See O'NEILL, R. C.

LATZKO, ADOLPH ANDREAS (September 1, 1876-   ), Hungarian novelist, writes: "Andreas Latzko, born in Budapest; at the end of his studies and his military service, at the age of twenty-two, started his career of writing in the Hungarian language as a journalist, on the editorial staff of the same paper which Ferenc Molnár joined at the same time. His  first play, *Ten Years,* was performed in the Budapest National Theater in 1898; a second, *Sisters,* was played in the Hungarian National Theatre. Latzko's first play in German was performed in the Little Theatre in Berlin in 1901. His first novel appeared in 1909, *Der Roman des Herrn Cordé* [*The Novel of Mr. Cordé*]. He then wrote travel-letters from a journey in 1913 and 1914 to North Africa, Egypt up to the second cataract of the Nile, the Canary Islands, Portugal and Spain, Ceylon, all of British India, Burma, Singapore, and the whole island of Java. There a severe attack of malaria interrupted his travels, and Latzko returned to Europe, landing in the last ship to arrive before the outbreak of the war. After being shell-shocked as an artillery reserve officer on the Tyrolean front, he went on military furlough in 1917 to Switzerland, at Davos, where he wrote his volume of stories, *Menschen im Krieg* [*Men in War*]. This book was suppressed and confiscated in all belligerent countries including America, yet was translated into twenty-two languages. A novel of the war, *Friedensgericht* [*Judgment of Peace;* translated as *Men in War*] appeared just before the close of the war, and was translated into eleven languages.

"Born on the eastern border of Europe Latzko is ending his life on the extreme western border as a citizen of Holland. This journey corresponds exactly to his direction from his first written line to his last important battle (in the field of *belles lettres*)— from urging better living conditions for the poor, and the extension of democracy in the world, to belief in complete spiritual and political liberty and the freeing of mankind from all the misery of an insecure life."

* * *

Not only was Latzko's *Menschen im Krieg* suppressed, but he himself was demoted to the ranks and condemned to death. He saved his life by staying in Switzerland. (It should be noted that the forbidden book of short stories, written under the title *Menschen im Krieg*, was *not* the novel published as *Men in War* in 1918). Latzko comes of a family of bankers, and was the first to break away from the family profession. He is married and has one child. He wrote to the editors of this volume in April 1940 from Amsterdam, where he had lived for some years. His whereabouts and fate, since the Nazi occupation of Holland, are unknown.

WORKS AVAILABLE IN ENGLISH: Men in War (in England: Men in Battle) (short stories) 1918; Men in War (Judgment of Peace) (novel) 1919; Seven Days, 1931; Lafayette: A Life (in England; Lafayette: A Soldier of Liberty) 1936.

ABOUT: Bookman October 1931; Time February 10, 1936.

LAVER, JAMES (March 14, 1899-) English novelist, poet, playwright, and art critic, writes: "I was born in Liverpool.

On the paternal side my forebears were captains of coasting vessels trading between Liverpool and Bristol. My great-grandmother was Welsh and my grandmother from the North of Ireland. My mother died when I was barely four years old; my father married again a few years later. We were Methodists, and the atmosphere of our home was one of Puritan piety, although there was nothing harsh or intolerant in my father's religion. There were a good many books in the house, and reading was encouraged. Ungrammatical speech was always corrected and the use of slang discouraged, and this is one of the great debts I owe my father, as well as that familiarity with the splendid sonority of the Bible which has never left me.

"I went, in spite of our being Methodists, to a 'Church School.' It was intended at first that I should enter the family printing and stationery business, but at the age of twelve I won a scholarship to the Liverpool Institute. My literary bent soon declared itself—indeed, I had already written stories and verses at the elementary school— and was encouraged by the master in charge of history and literature. A Liverpool shipowner, a great benefactor of the school, believed in my immature talents, and provided the money to keep me at New College, Oxford, for three years. But immediately after matriculation, in 1917, I was gazetted second lieutenant in the King's Own (Royal Lancaster) regiment. I joined the Expeditionary Force in France two days before the signing of the Armistice, but was kept in France for nearly a year before being demobilized. I then returned to Oxford.

"Most of my friends were surprised, and a few were horrified, when I received the Newdigate Prize in 1921 for a poem on Cervantes. This was so well received by the press that I rushed into print with a volume of poems, which sold about thirty copies. After taking my degree I stayed at Oxford for another year. In 1922 I was appointed assistant keeper of the print room at the Victoria and Albert Museum. I wrote art criticism and thought of myself as a poet. My enthusiasms were, and have continued to be, eighteenth century and French. In writing I cultivated a precise, dry, humorous style. I was a little mad on the theatre, and translated several plays from the French and German. I also produced plays for amateur societies, and in 1928 married the actress Veronica Turleigh (Bridget Veronica Turley). We now have a son and a daughter, and live in Chelsea.

"Nearly all my writing is done in the evening after dinner. In 1937 I became keeper of my department, and until the outbreak of war, I spent my working day at the Museum, examining and cataloguing prints. I also became interested in biography, and research on this led to a considerable amount of lecturing. About 1926 I became interested in the Working Men's College, founded by Frederick D. Maurice and Thomas Hughes, author of *Tom Brown's School-days*. At first I taught English literature, and then was appointed art director, a post held in the past by Ruskin, Burne-Jones, and Rossetti.

"In spite of these serious occupations, however, and the production of the philosophic poem *Macrocosmos*, my natural attitude to life remained humorous and satirical, and my 'naughtier' works have been the only ones to reach a wide public. *Nymph Errant,* which was banned in Eire, was successfully produced as a play in 1933. In 1938 my play, *The Heart Was Not Burned,* was produced in London. I edited the standard edition of the poems of Charles Churchill, and in 1940 completed an edition of the poems of Baudelaire for the Limited Editions Club of New York. I do not, however, allow my more imaginative writings to be swamped by works of scholarship, and I hope to continue in play, novel, or poem in the vein of humorous fancy and social satire first explored in *Nymph Errant* and *A Stitch in Time.*"

* * *

In appearance, James Laver the art critic, with his tortoise-shell spectacles and intellectual forehead, effectually blankets James Laver the writer of frivolous and cynical books, and doubtless many persons know him in one capacity who never suspect the other.

PRINCIPAL WORKS: *Verse*—Cervantes, 1921; His Last Sebastian, 1922; The Young Man Dances, 1925; A Stitch in Time, 1928; Love's Progress, 1929; Macrocosmos, 1929; New Poems, 1933; Ladies' Mistakes, 1933; Background for Venus, 1934; Panic Among Puritans, 1936. *Fiction*—Nymph Errant, 1932; The Winter Wedding, 1934; The Laburnum Tree (short stories) 1935; Tommy Apple, 1935; Tommy Apple and Peggy Pear, 1936. *Miscellaneous*—Portraits in Oil and Vinegar, 1925; Design in the Theatre (with G. Sheringham) 1927: A History of British and American Etching, 1929; Nineteenth Century Costume, 1929; Etchings of Arthur Briscoe, 1930; Whistler, 1930 (revised edition 1938); Eighteenth Century Costume, 1931; Wesley, 1932; "Vulgar Society": The Romantic Career of James Tissot, 1936; French Painting of the Nineteenth Century, 1937; Taste and Fashion From the French Revolution Until Today, 1937; Adventures in Monochrome: An Anthology of Graphic Art, 1941; Nostradamus, 1942.

ABOUT: New Statesman and Nation November 26, 1938; Saturday Review of Literature February 19, 1934.

"LAWLESS, ANTHONY." See MAC-DONALD, P.

LAWRENCE, DAVID HERBERT (September 11, 1885-March 2, 1930), English novelist, poet, essayist, and playwright, was born at the colliery village of Eastwood, Nottinghamshire, son of John Arthur Lawrence, coal miner, who had married Lydia Beardsall, a teacher, a woman several stages above him in manners and cultivation. The boy was one of five children, brought up in an atmosphere of poverty, brutality, and drink. An early attack of pneumonia sowed the seeds of tuberculosis. Lawrence was a frail and studious child who was encouraged to develop his mind by his mother, to whom he was passionately devoted. At thirteen he entered Nottingham High School with a scholarship. Leaving at sixteen, he was a clerk for a short time and then went to the British School at Eastwood as pupil teacher. Ambitious to become a certified teacher, he entered the training department of University College, Nottingham, at the age of eighteen, and after a two-year course won his certificate and was appointed to Davidson Road elementary school at Croydon, near London.

Meanwhile he had begun to write verse, encouraged by an Eastwood girl who figures as "Miriam" in *Sons and Lovers*. His friendship with her (not liaison) continued some ten years, and it was she who gave him a start by copying five of his poems and sending them to the *English Review*. Ford Madox Hueffer (later Ford), who was then editing this magazine, published several, invited Lawrence to call, and handed over his novel, *The White Peacock,* to the publisher's reader, Edward Garnett, who recommended it for publication. The book came out in January 1911, but Lawrence's pride was submerged by deep gloom over the death of his mother, which had occurred a month earlier.

Though the novel brought in only fifty pounds Lawrence now decided to live by literature, quitting his school with an excellent reputation. In April 1912 he called on Professor Ernest Weekley, of Nottingham, to inquire as to the possibilities of a lectureship in a German university, and instantly fell in love with Weekley's wife, a lady of thirty-one with three children. Mrs. Weekley was born Frieda von Richthofen, daughter of Baron von Richthofen, military governor of Metz. Before long it was evident that she reciprocated Lawrence's feelings, and in a few weeks the two threw in their lot together and set out for Metz. Not unnaturally the Baron was uncongenial; so for a time Lawrence stayed at Waldbröl, in the Rhineland, while Frieda remained with her people. They then reunited and stayed for a space at Isartal, Bavaria, perforce living very frugally. In August they went to Austria, and thence on foot over the Brenner Pass to Gargnano, on Lake Garda, where they remained until April 1913. They had only a very little money accruing from a second novel, *The Trespasser.* Housekeeping on next to nothing was a new experience for Frieda, and of the two Lawrence was the practical hand at cooking and cleaning. Another visit to Germany followed, then a short time in England, and from September 1913 to June 1914 they lived at Lerici, Italy. During 1913 had appeared Lawrence's first book of poems, *Love Poems and Others* and a novel, *Sons and Lovers,* which showed mature powers.

In July 1914 Professor Weekley's decree *nisi* against Frieda was made absolute and she at once married Lawrence. By this time he had some little reputation and a literary acquaintance which included John Middleton Murry and his wife Katherine Mansfield, Cynthia and Herbert Asquith, (Sir) Edward Marsh, and Sir Walter Raleigh. The war brought special problems, practical and psychological. Lawrence's pulmonary weakness debarred him from military service (though he was several times called up for medical examination), but Frieda's nationality was in itself a cause of trouble, especially as her cousin, Baron Manfred von Richthofen, became the most famous and intrepid of the German airmen. Lawrence and his wife lived in or near London for a month or two, then in a Buckinghamshire cottage, and then, early in 1915, on the Meynell estate at Greatham. After returning to London towards the end of 1915 the Lawrences took a cottage in 1916 in the hamlet of Zennor, a few miles south of St. Ives, Cornwall, remaining in this wild spot some eighteen months. The Murrys were with them for a time, relationships varying between cordiality and strain. The Lawrences were most indiscreet, being careless with their lights though living on the coast, and singing German songs in their cottage at night. They became the objects of deep suspicion on the part of the authorities, and in October 1917 were ordered by the police to leave Zennor and not to reside in any prohibited area.

During these first three years of conflict Lawrence had done a good deal of work, in spite of grave unsettlement and deep disgust with the war. At the end of 1914 he published a book of short stories called (not by him) *The Prussian Officer;* in 1915 came the first of many brushes with the pruriency of the police, his novel, *The Rainbow,* being condemned as obscene and the entire edition destroyed; in 1916 appeared a travel book, *Twilight in Italy,* and a volume of verse, *Amores;* and in 1917 another, dealing with his life with Frieda, called *Look! We Have Come Through.*

After leaving Zennor, Lawrence wrote little for some months. The war dragged on, police surveillance continued, and since some of the author's best and most poetical work had gone into *The Rainbow* its fate was an abiding source of bitterness. Lack of its expected royalties, too, caused long-continuing money worries. The two stayed in London for a brief period at the end of 1917, after which they lived in country cottages, first at Hermitage, Newbury, Berkshire, and later at Middleton-by-Wirksworth, Derbyshire. With the peace, at the end of 1919, Lawrence went abroad, thereafter returning only for brief periods. From Florence he went to the Abruzzi, thence to Capri, and thence to Taormina, Sicily, where he remained until 1922. *The Lost Girl* (1920) was one attempt to give the public what he believed it wanted. *Women in Love,* which had been written five years before but rejected by the London publishers, was issued late in the same year by private subscription in New York. It may now, perhaps, be considered the most rounded expression of Lawrence's conception of life and love. *Movements in European History* (1921) was a commissioned task, done for money. *Sea and Sardinia* (1921), on the other hand, was a quick, joyous, unconventional record of a journey made. *Psychoanalysis and the Unconscious* (1921) and *Fantasia of the Unconscious* (1922) were attempts to systematize the philosophy implicit in the novels and poems.

The next journey, begun early in 1922, took the Lawrences to the Antipodes by way of Ceylon. At Thirroul, in Australia, was written *Kangaroo,* a book full of the dreariness of colonial provinciality. But Australia was only a stopping place on the way to Taos, New Mexico, whither Lawrence had been recommended by Mabel Dodge Luhan, who persuaded him by letter that there he would find health and the conditions for the establishment of an intellectual community (of which he had long dreamed). He arrived there in the autumn, by way of New Zealand, Tahiti, and San Francisco. After three months he moved to Del Monte ranch, seventeen miles higher up in the Rockies, but wintered in old Mexico for warmth. The autumn of 1923 saw a visit to England, Frieda preceding "Lorenzo" (as he was always called) by two months. They returned to Del Monte ranch (now presented to them by Mrs. Luhan) in the spring of 1924. The next winter was again spent in Mexico. Late in 1925, after revising *The Plumed Serpent* and suffering a severe illness, Lawrence left America and went to live at Spotorno, Italy. At this place occurred one of those marital crises which illustrate very well the relations between him and his wife. He gave her the stimulus of living with a genius; she gave him peace and love; but at intervals they fought like tigers, not stopping at the throwing of crockery. They differed, be it remembered, in race, social class, and temperament, and Frieda's natural hankering for her children (she had none by Lawrence) often aroused jealousy and resentment in him. Here at Spotorno she rashly invited a daughter to stay. Lawrence riposted by inviting his sister, Ada. Before long the whole establishment went up in metaphorical smoke, and it took weeks to quench the flames.

For two years from the spring of 1926 he lived at Scandicci, near Florence (with visits to England and to Austria for a cure), and there wrote *Lady Chatterley's Lover*, making no less than three versions. This is an account of the sexual relations of a high-born lady with a gamekeeper. These are recorded with the utmost physical detail, with the use of all the forbidden words. So the book, which was privately set up in Florence, was prohibited both in England and the United States, and remains tabu, though thousands of copies must have been smuggled through. Trouble with copyrights resulted in the appearance of many pirated editions, chiefly in America.

During the Florentine period Lawrence's health had gone from bad to worse and he had several times been near death. Two more years remained to him. He lived successively at Chexbres and Kesselwatte, in Switzerland, and at Le Lavandou and Bandol, visited Mallorca and revisited Florence. He had been painting since 1925, and in 1928 held an exhibition in London. It was raided by the police on grounds of immorality; and in 1929 the manuscript of his poems, *Pansies*, was confiscated on the same count. He spent the winter of 1929-30 at Bandol and in February went to a sanatorium at Vence, where he died at forty-four of tuberculosis.

The vivid, challenging genius of Lawrence and his preoccupation with sexual themes quickly made him the subject of a very considerable literature, much of it highly controversial. Middleton Murry's *Son of Woman* (1931) elaborated with subtlety the theory that Lawrence's extreme devotion to his mother amounted to a "mother-fixation" and prevented him from attaining fulfilment in love with a wife. Frieda Lawrence very naturally took the strongest exception to the publication of this book while she was alive, and her own volume, *"Not I, But the Wind"*, should be read as a corrective. Catherine Carswell, Ada Lawrence, Richard Aldington, Mrs. Luhan, Dorothy Brett and many others who knew him contributed to the flow of reminiscence and criticism.

Lawrence's whole powers were devoted to the pursuit of a fuller, freer, more intense life than is permitted by our industrial civilization and our social system. Despite his insistence on the physical aspects of sex he was far from being an immoralist; and indeed is described by many who knew him well as a puritan. He lived with the utmost frugality, did not smoke, and drank little. To restore a natural balance in living (destroyed by sexual squeamishness, mean motives and mechanical monotony) was the underlying purpose of one who was worlds away from being "the idle singer of an empty day."

He was a quick worker but often re-wrote two or three times, writing out of doors when he could. He disliked discussion of his work, and lost interest in a book as soon as it was printed. Frieda records that the only newspapers she ever saw him read were the *Corriere della Sera* and the Sydney *Bulletin*. In person Lawrence was tall, slight and frail, with gray eyes and a red beard.

PRINCIPAL WORKS: *Novels*—The White Peacock, 1911; The Trespasser, 1912; Sons and Lovers, 1913; The Rainbow, 1915; The Lost Girl, 1920; Women in Love, 1920; Aaron's Rod, 1922; Kangaroo, 1923; The Boy in the Bush (with M. L. Skinner), 1924; St. Mawr, 1925; The Plumed Serpent, 1926; Lady Chatterley's Lover, 1928; The Virgin and the Gipsy, 1930; The Escaped Cock, 1929 (republished in 1931 as The Man Who Died). *Poems*—Love Poems and Others, 1913; Amores, 1916; Look! We Have Come Through, 1917; New Poems, 1918; Tortoises, 1921; Birds, Beasts, and Flowers, 1923; Collected Poems, 1928; Pansies, 1929; Nettles, 1930; Last Poems, 1933. *Short Stories*—The Prussian Officer, 1914; England, My England, 1922; The Ladybird (American title: The Captain's Doll), 1923; Glad Ghosts, 1926; The Woman Who Rode Away, 1928; The Lovely Lady, 1933; Love Among the Haystacks and Other Stories, 1933; Christ in the Tyrol, 1933. *Plays*—The Widowing of Mrs. Holroyd, 1914; Touch and Go, 1920; David, 1926; Plays, 1933. *Travel Books*—Twilight in Italy, 1916; Sea and Sardinia, 1921; Mornings in Mexico, 1927; Etruscan Places, 1932. *Miscellaneous*—Psychoanalysis of the Unconscious, 1921; Movements in European History, 1921; Fantasia of the Unconscious, 1922; Studies in Classic American Literature, 1923; Pornography and Obscenity, 1930;

Apocalypse, 1931; Letters of D. H. Lawrence (ed. by Aldous Huxley) 1932.

ABOUT: Aldington, R. D. H. Lawrence; Brett, D. Lawrence and Brett; Carswell, C. Savage Pilgrimage; Carter, F. Lawrence and the Body Mystical; Corke, H. Lawrence and Apocalypse; Fabes, G. H. D. H. Lawrence: His First Editions; Lawrence, A. The Young Lorenzo; Lawrence, A. & Gelder, G. S. The Early Life of D. H. Lawrence; Lawrence, F. "Not I, But the Wind"; Luhan, M. D. Lorenzo in Taos; MacDonald, E. D. Bibliography of the Writings of D. H. Lawrence; Moore, O. Further Reflections on the Death of a Porcupine; Murry, J. M. Reminiscences of D. H. Lawrence; Murry, J. M. Son of Woman; Nin, A. D. H. Lawrence; Potter, S. D. H. Lawrence; Seligmann, H. J. D. H. Lawrence; Tindall, W. Y. D. H. Lawrence and Susan His Cow; West, R. D. H. Lawrence.

LAWRENCE, JOSEPHINE (1897?-   ),

American novelist, was born and still lives in Newark, N.J. Her father was Dr. Elijah

H. Phyfe

Wiley Lawrence, her mother Mary Elizabeth (Barker) Lawrence. She was graduated from the Newark High school and took special courses in English at New York University. Immediately after leaving school in 1915 she joined the staff of the Newark *Sunday Call* and is still on it, as editor of the household service departments and the children's page. She is unmarried.

Miss Lawrence's first writing was as a juvenile author; she brought out thirty-three books for children, many of them anonymously, before she wrote a novel for adults. She also wrote a radio series for children, "The Man in the Moon." She was the first writer to have two successive books selected by the Book-of-the-Month Club, these being *Years Are So Long* and *If I Have Four Apples.*

Describing herself as "an old-fashioned conservative," Miss Lawrence is very averse to personal publicity, and even her publishers have been unable to get many of the details wanted by press-agents. She is what *Time* called her, "a conscientious, self-effacing newspaper woman." She is small and slender, with dark hair, bright eyes, and a pleasant voice. Her only interest outside her job and her books is in the New Jersey Women's Press Club; she is also a member of the Authors' League and the Authors'

Guild. She is a Democrat and a Presbyterian.

Miss Lawrence's novels are all, in a sense, propagandistic; that is to say, they are all sugar-coated pills, or, to vary the metaphor, streamlined "moral tales." Each poses a problem—dependent old age, family budgets, unemployment, the servant question, the egoism of "self-sacrifice"—and then tells an illustrative story. Sometimes the sugar-coating wears a bit thin, and there are dull stretches; but at her best (as in *Years Are So Long*, which also made a successful motion picture) she is really moving. Her view of humanity, and especially of women, is an astringent one. As Frances Woodward said of her work: "She is not comforting. But she does not sneer." She makes no attempt to solve the problems she posits, but lays them in the reader's lap with a hinted "What are *you* going to do about it?"

All her stories are laid in Newark, which hitherto unnoticed territory she has taken for her own; and all her people are men and women of the middle class, in business or the lesser professions. The common sense and reticence which are her chief personal characteristics appear in her novels as well, but she has a quiet humor too, and occasional passages of tenderness and pity. She has reconstructed with loving care the world of the inhibited people who write letters to the woman's editor of a Sunday newspaper, and she has done it well. In a sense, her novels are a sort of expansion of her newspaper work, and her love for long expository titles increases the journalistic effect. Sinclair Lewis said of her: "This world of hers is America, superlatively, . . . [with] its touching, gently tragic people. . . . She snarls with gaiety, she smites with tenderness. . . . She has a truly unusual power of seeing and remembering the details of daily living."

PRINCIPAL WORKS: *Juveniles*—Brother and Sister Books (6 vols.) 1921-27; Rosemary, 1922; Elizabeth Ann Books (8 vols.) 1923-29; Rainbow Hill, 1924, The Berry Patch, 1925; Linda Lane Books (6 vols.) 1925-29; Next Door Neighbors, 1926; Rosemary and the Princess, 1927; Two Little Fellow Books (5 vols.) 1927-29; Glenna, 1929; Christine, 1930. *Novels*—Head of the Family, 1932; Years Are So Long, 1934; If I have Four Apples, 1935; The Sound of Running Feet, 1937; Bow Down to Wood and Stone, 1938; A Good Home with Nice People, 1939; But You Are Young, 1940; No Stone Unturned, 1941.

ABOUT: Newsweek March 7, 1938; New York Times Book Review January 12, 1941; Saturday Review of Literature January 9, 1937; Time December 30, 1935; Wilson Library Bulletin March 1936.

LAWRENCE, THOMAS EDWARD

(August 16, 1888-May 19, 1935), English traveler, archaeologist, and soldier,  was born at Tremadoc, Carnarvonshire, North Wales, second of five sons of Thomas Lawrence, whose family, though English, had been long settled in Ireland. His infancy was divided between Scotland, the Isle of Man, Brittany, the Channel Islands, and Hampshire. From September 1896 to July 1907 he was at Oxford High School (now City of Oxford School), not a "public school" but an ordinary secondary school. He described his schooling as "an irrelevant and time-wasting nuisance, which I hated and condemned"; yet his mother records that he was at this time apparently happy enough, that he was an orderly and punctual boy, and that he passed first in English in the Oxford Local Examination, taken by thousands of boys all over the United Kingdom. He showed an early interest in archaeology, spending much of his leisure in taking rubbings from monumental brasses, hunting out fragments of Roman pottery, and traveling over a wide area in France with the principal aim of examining castles and cathedrals. A foretaste of his extraordinary bravery and stoicism under hardship is provided by an anecdote which tells how, having broken an ankle at school, he pedaled home on a bicycle with the one sound foot.

In the autumn of 1907 he went up to Jesus College, Oxford, with an exhibition. He attracted the notice of the archaeologist, Dr. D. G. Hogarth, whose friendship became a paramount shaping influence in his life. In 1910 he took a first in modern history and was then elected a senior demy of Magdalen. A vacation journey to Syria in undergraduate years was followed, on graduation, by a period of Jebail, in Syria, working at Arabic, during the winter of 1910-11, a five-months digging at Carchemish with Hogarth and R. Campbell Thompson, and an expedition through Northern Mesopotamia in the summer of 1911, doing any kind of odd job to pay his way. From the spring of 1912 to that of 1914 he was working in Egypt under Sir W. M. Flinders Petrie and at Carchemish under Sir Leonard Woolley. In the early part of 1914 he was occupied on a survey of Sinai. These years laid the foundation of his intimate knowledge of the geography, ethnology, history, folk-lore, and languages of the Near East, which enabled him to live among the Arabs during the First World War as one of themselves, and enormously assisted him in his colossal enterprise against the Turkish rulers.

From December 1914 to October 1916 Lawrence was attached to the British Intelligence Department in Egypt as a staff captain. He was a difficult colleague for soldiers whose minds ran along conventional lines; and when he at length applied for leave to go to the Hejaz with Sir Ronald Storrs there were many who were glad to be rid of him. The Arab chiefs, beginning with the Sherif of Mecca, were in revolt against the Turks. Lawrence now devoted all his indomitable energy and the powers of his subtle brain to coordinating the activities of widely scattered tribes, ill-equipped, differing enormously in ways of life, and having long traditions of internecine warfare. In Feisal he found a leader with enough fire, personal prestige, and tact, and thenceforward, taking on Arab costume, he worked and thought unremittingly to encompass the downfall of the Turk. For the full appreciation of the complicated operations and long camel marches of 1917-18 the reader must turn to *Seven Pillars of Wisdom*. In essence Lawrence's strategy consisted in destroying as much Turkish *matériel* (trains, and so forth) as possible by surprise attacks or secret mining, conserving the Arab forces with few casualties. He took Wejh, then the port of Akaba, and brought the Arabs into collaboration with the British in the invasion of Syria. A masterly and resounding victory at Deraa opened the way to Damascus, which was taken in October 1918, the Arabs arriving there ahead of the British.

From January to October 1919 Lawrence was with the Arab delegation to the Peace Conference, and while in Paris he began to write his account of the revolt, irrelevantly called *Seven Pillars of Wisdom*. In October he was elected to a Fellowship at All Souls College, Oxford, and continued writing, but round about Christmas lost the whole manuscript, except the introduction and drafts of books 9 and 10, at Reading Station. Like Carlyle in similar circumstances, he began again, this time without the help of his notes, which he had destroyed as each section of the first draft was finished. The second text was completed in London in less than three months and ran to some 400,000 words. The author considered it "substantially complete and accurate" but "hopelessly bad as a text," so from it he constructed Text III, working during 1921-22 in London, Jeddah, Amman, and London again. He then burnt Text II and had eight copies only of Text III (some 330,000 words) set up by the *Oxford Times*. Five of these were read by fellow-officers who had served in the Hejaz. Still another revision was then made, and in December 1926 a limited edition, reduced to some 280,000 words, was issued to subscribers at thirty guineas a copy. An abridgement called *Revolt in the Desert* (130,000 words) was issued for general circulation in Great Britain and America in 1927; and in 1935, after Lawrence's death, the *Seven Pillars* itself was made available to the public. A splendid series of illustrations, chiefly by Eric H. Kennington, adorned the book.

Meanwhile Lawrence, scorning all the wealth and power that could have been his for the asking, lived in comparative obscurity. He had accepted the C.B. and the D.S.O. and ended the war as a colonel, but refused both a knighthood and the Victoria Cross. He consented to help the War Office as political adviser on Middle Eastern affairs in 1921-22. But he was hurt because of what he conceived to be the unfair treatment meted out to the Arabs after the war; he detested publicity; he seemed utterly without ambition to play a further big part in world affairs. So at the end of 1922 he enlisted in the Royal Air Force as a simple aircraftman, under the name of Ross. Discovery of his identity led to his discharge, so he joined the Royal Tank Corps as Private Shaw. In 1925 he returned to the Air Force (still as Shaw—a name he adopted by deed poll in 1927), served in England and India, and did valuable work on flying boats, despite his humble rank. He was discharged in March 1935 and went to live at a country cottage at Moreton, Dorsetshire, promising himself a restful period with his books and gramaphone. But on May 13 he sustained terrible injuries when thrown off his motorcycle in avoiding a collision, and died at Bovington Camp military hospital on May 19.

The King headed the list of distinguished men paying tribute to Lawrence's memory. Memorials were erected in St. Paul's Cathedral and in his old school, eloquent addresses being given at the first unveiling by Lord Halifax and at the second by Winston Churchill.

In 1932 Lawrence produced a colloquial prose translation of the *Odyssey*. His place in letters, however, will depend on *Seven Pillars of Wisdom*, and in spite of its inordinate length and plethoric detail this is likely to survive as one of the great books of our age, comparable, as Mr. Churchill said, with *Robinson Crusoe* or *Gulliver's Travels*. His was perhaps the strangest, most adventurous life of modern times. His enigmatic personality was fully revealed to none, and the impact of it on many minds is described in a symposium called *T. E. Lawrence: By his Friends*. Very short in stature and slight in build, he had blue eyes of almost mesmeric power, and it was impossible to talk to him without sensing his greatness. He had an impish and puckish humor. He seemed without human weaknesses. He neither smoked nor drank, and was indifferent to women. Soldier, diplomat, scholar, linguist, archaeologist, mechanic, and man of letters, he impressed all he touched with the mark of genius. King George V, writing to A. W. Lawrence, said simply: "Your brother's name will live in history." There can be no doubt that it will.

PRINCIPAL WORKS: Carchemish: Report on the Excavations at Djerabis (with C. L. Woolley) 1914; The Wilderness of Zin (with C. L. Woolley) 1915; Seven Pillars of Wisdom: A Triumph, 1926; Revolt in the Desert, 1927; The Odyssey of Homer (translation) 1932; Letters From T. E. Shaw to Bruce Rogers, 1933; Crusader Castles (2 vols.) 1936; More Letters From T. E. Shaw to Bruce Rogers, 1936; The Letters of T. E. Lawrence (ed. by David Garnett) 1938.

ABOUT: Duval, E. W. T. E. Lawrence: A Bibliography; Edmonds, C. T. E. Lawrence; Graves, R. Lawrence and the Arabs; Lawrence, A. W. (ed.) T. E. Lawrence: By his Friends; Lawrence, T. E. Seven Pillars of Wisdom, and Revolt in the Desert; Liddell Hart, B. H. Colonel Lawrence: The Man Behind the Legend; Richards, V. Portrait of T. E. Lawrence; Robinson, E. Lawrence: The Story of his Life; Sanders, F. W. T. Lawrence of Arabia; Thomas, L. J. With Lawrence in Arabia.

LAWSON, JOHN HOWARD (September 25, 1895-), American playwright, writes: "I was born in New York City, and attended Cutler School in New York and Williams College. I graduated in 1914, and my first job was as a cable editor in the New York office of Reuter's, Ltd. I worked there for somewhat more than a year, and resigned under the mistaken impression that a quick success as a playwright was awaiting me. This curious delusion was the result of receiving a small payment for an option on a play, from the partnership of George M. Cohan and Sam H. Harris. The partners gave me helpful advice; Mr. Sam Forrest worked with me in an effort to whip the embryonic play into shape. But it wouldn't whip! I sold a number of options, and had two disastrous out-of-town try-outs in 1916 and 1917. I went abroad in 1917, serving in the volunteer ambulance service with the French Army, later being transferred to the Italian front. I returned to Europe for two years after the war, living chiefly in Paris, and came back to the United States with *Roger Bloomer,* produced by the Actors' Theatre in 1923, and described by the late Percy Hammond as 'Nightmare in 48th Street.'

Harris & Ewing

"*Processional,* presented by the Theatre Guild in 1925, was the center of a spirited critical controversy. It is my opinion that both the applause and the censure were unwarranted, and that the play was more important as an indication of an approach to the theatre than for its rather specious originality. *Nirvana* followed *Processional* in 1926. In 1927, the New Playwrights' Theatre began its short and rather hectic career. I was one of the directors of the enterprise, and the initial production was my political farce, *Loudspeaker.* In the following year, the New Playwrights produced another play of mine, *The International.*

"In the 1930's I divided my time between Hollywood and Broadway. I learned a great deal in both fields; indeed, I feel that the past twenty years have been a sort of apprenticeship, and that I am just beginning to undertake serious dramatic work. The Group Theatre produced *Success Story* in 1932. I had two plays in 1934: *Gentlewoman* and *The Pure in Heart. Marching Song* was staged by the Theatre Union in 1937. Among my recent motion pictures are *Blockade, Algiers,* and *They Shall Have Music* (the last-named being in collaboration with Irmgarde Von Cube). A new play, *Parlor Magic,* has been under way for two years. I am also planning a Social History of American Literature, with special reference to various popular forms of expression—newspapers, magazines, dramatic and vaudeville entertainment, etc. The research on this work has led to its almost fourth-dimensional extension. I don't know how many volumes or years may be involved.

"My father was Simeon L. Lawson, my mother Belle (Hart) Lawson. I have been married twice: first to Kathryn Drain, 1919; one son. We were divorced. In 1925, I married Susan Edmond, and we have a son and a daughter. I am a member of the Council of the Authors' League of America, a former president of the Screen Writers' Guild, and a member of the League of American Writers."

* * *

Mr. Lawson is of Jewish descent, the family name originally being Levy. He lives now with his family in North Hollywood, Calif., and he also owns a beautiful early Long Island house at Mastic, N.Y. His plays are well to the left both in viewpoint and in style, many of the earlier ones being "expressionistic" in mode. George Jean Nathan once called him "in many respects a typical specimen of the little theatre young American playwright," an estimate that fails to say enough for the intelligence, dynamism, and exciting effectiveness of his writing. His later work shows power and simplicity.

PRINCIPAL WORKS: *Published Plays*—Roger Bloomer, 1923; Processional, 1925; Loudspeaker, 1927; The International, 1928; Success Story, 1932; With a Reckless Preface (The Pure of Heart, Gentlewoman), 1934; Marching Song, 1937. *Miscellaneous*—The Theory and Technique of Playwriting, 1936.

ABOUT: Lawson, J. H. Roger Bloomer (see Introduction by John Dos Passos); Loudspeaker (see Introduction by Joseph Wood Krutch); American Mercury May 1926; Catholic World May 1934; Theatre Arts Monthly June 1934.

*LEA, FANNY HEASLIP (October 30, 1884-), American novelist and short story writer, was born in New Orleans and educated at Newcomb College, Tulane University (B.A. 1904). In 1911 she married Hamilton Pope Agee, and they had a daughter. During most of her married life she lived in Honolulu, but she was divorced in 1926 and returned to the mainland. At present she lives in New York. She says of herself: "I was born wanting to write . . . and loving books more than anything else in the world. . . . It is an incredible piece of luck, being paid to do a thing which one would fight to do anyhow." She has been writing ever since she was seven—verse, plays, and stories. Her first published work was in verse. She says she "aspires to the light touch," to ro-

* **Died January 13, 1955.**

mance, to emotion deftly concealed behind a surface sophistication; and this modest ambition she has fulfilled in a competent, professional manner. Most of her work appears in the large women's magazines, and she belongs to that group of novelists who are read almost entirely by middle-aged, middle-class women. Although she once impressed people as "a fluffy blonde," there is nothing fluffy about her mind; she is keenly intelligent, knows her exact limitations as a writer, and never exceeds them. In her particular field she is unerring, with ability as well as charm. On the surface she seems to be the kind of person she writes about—light-hearted, responsive, and none-too-intellectual: underneath she is a hard-working professional writer who loves the outdoors and spends much of her leisure roughing it, and who in spite of an ebullient manner reads serious books and earned the membership she holds in Phi Beta Kappa.

PRINCIPAL WORKS: Quicksands, 1911; The Jaconetta Stories, 1912; Sicily Ann, 1914; Chloe Malone, 1916; With This Ring, 1925; The Dream-Maker Man, 1925; With or Without, 1926; Wild Goose Chase, 1929; Lolly (play) 1930; Happy Landings, 1930; Goodbye Summer, 1931; Half Angel, 1932; Summer People, 1933; Dorée, 1934; Anchor Man, 1935; The Four Marys, 1936; Once to Every Man, 1937; Not for Just an Hour, 1938; There Are Brothers, 1940; Nobody's Girl, 1940.

ABOUT: Saturday Evening Post May 29, 1926.

*LEACOCK, STEPHEN BUTLER (December 30, 1869-), Canadian humorist and scientist of economics and politics

was born at Swanmoor, Hampshire, England, the son of W. P. Leacock and Agnes (Butler) Leacock. "I am not aware that there was any conjunction of the planets at the time, but I should think it extremely likely. My parents emigrated to Canada in 1876, and my father took up a farm near Lake Simcoe, in Ontario. This was during the hard times of Canadian farming, and my father was just able by great diligence to pay the hired man, and, in years of plenty, to raise enough grain to have seed for the next year's crop without buying any. By this process my brothers and I were inevitably driven off the land, and have become professors, business men, and engineers, instead of being able to grow up as farm laborers. I was educated at Upper Canada College, Toronto,

of which I was head boy in 1887. From there I went to the University of Toronto, where I graduated in 1891. At the University I spent my entire time in the acquisition of languages, living, dead, and half-dead, and knew nothing of the outside world. I spent my time from 1891 to 1899 on the staff of Upper Canada College, an experience which has left me with a profound sympathy for the many gifted and brilliant men who are compelled to spend their lives in the most dreary, most thankless, and the worst-paid profession in the world. In 1899 I gave up school teaching in disgust, borrowed enough money to live upon for a few months, and went to the University of Chicago to study economics and political science. I was soon appointed to a fellowship in political economy, and by means of this, and some temporary employment by McGill University, I survived until I took the degree of doctor of philosophy in 1903. From this time I have belonged to the staff of McGill University, first as a lecturer in political science, and later as the head of the Department of Economics and Political Science. Many of my friends are under the impression that I write humorous nothings in idle moments when the wearied brain is unable to perform the serious labors of the economist. My own experience is exactly the other way. The writing of solid, instructive stuff, fortified by facts and figures, is easy enough. But to write something out of one's own mind, worth reading for its own sake, is an arduous contrivance, only to be achieved in fortunate moments, few and far between. Personally I would rather have written *Alice in Wonderland* than the whole *Encyclopaedia Britannica*."

* * *

The sketches in *Literary Lapses* were written between 1891 and 1899, when the author was in his early twenties, and were published in *Saturday Night, Life, Truth, Puck,* and the Detroit *Free Press.* "Later on I gathered these sketches together and sent them to the publishers of my *Elements of Political Economy.* They thought I had gone mad. I therefore printed the sketches on my own account and we sold them through a news company. We sold 3,000 copies in two months. In this modest form the book fell into the hands of my good friend—as he has since become—Mr. John Lane. He read the sketches on a steamer while returning from Montreal to London, and cabled me an offer to publish the book in regular form."

Professor Leacock married Beatrix Hamilton of Toronto at the Little Church Around the Corner in New York City in August 1900; their son was born fifteen years later in the same month, and was named Stephen Lushington Leacock. Mrs. Leacock died in 1925. Stephen Leacock the elder might without exaggeration be called the most popular humorist in America since Mark Twain. Parts of the *Nonsense Novels* have gone into the currency of familiar and immediately recognized quotations. Professor Leacock, who retired from teaching in 1936, is the holder of honorary degrees of Litt.D., LL.D., and D.C.L. He is a member of the University Club in Montreal; has a summer home in Orillia; and lists his recreations as fishing, camping, and gardening. He has a fine, grave face; a head well thatched with hair; a deep, vibrating voice; and he walks with a stride.

PRINCIPAL WORKS: Elements of Political Science, 1906; Baldwin and La Fontaine (Makers of Canada Series) 1907; Literary Lapses, 1910; Nonsense Novels, 1911; Sunshine Sketches of a Little Town, 1912; Behind the Beyond, 1913; Arcadian Adventures With the Idle Rich, 1914; Moonbeams From the Larger Lunacy, 1915; Essays and Literary Studies, 1916; Further Foolishness, 1916; Frenzied Fiction, 1917; The Hohenzollerns in America, 1919; The Unsolved Riddle of Social Justice, 1920; Winsome Winnie, 1920; My Discovery of England, 1922; Over the Footlights, 1923; College Days, 1923; The Garden of Folly, 1924; Winnowed Wisdom, 1926; Short Circuits, 1928; The Iron Man and the Tin Woman, 1929; Economic Prosperity in the British Empire, 1930; Back to Prosperity, 1931; Afternoons in Utopia, 1932; Mark Twain, 1932; Charles Dickens: His Life and Work, 1933; Lincoln Frees the Slaves, 1934; Humour: Its Theory and Technique, 1935; Greatest Pages of Charles Dickens, 1935; Greatest Pages of American Humour, 1936; Hellements of Hickonomics in Hiccoughs of Verse, 1936; Funny Pieces, 1936; My Discovery of the West, 1937; Humour and Humanity, 1937; Here Are My Lectures and Stories, 1937; Model Memoirs and Other Sketches From Simple to Serious, 1939; Too Much College, 1939; The British Empire: Its Structure, Its Unity, Its Strength, 1940; My Remarkable Uncle and Other Sketches, 1942; How To Write, 1942.

ABOUT: Adcock, A. S. J. The Glory That Was Grub Street; Allen, C. K. Oh, Mr. Leacock; Becker, M. L. Golden Tales of Canada; Braybrooke, P. Peeps at the Mighty; Hind, C. L. More Authors and I; Locke, G. H. Builders of the Canadian Commonwealth; McArthur, P. Stephen Leacock; McGill University Library School: Class of 1935. A Bibliography of Stephen Leacock; Masson, T. L. Our American Humorists; Canadian Magazine May 1922; Living Age December 30, 1916, November 5, 1921; New York Herald Tribune Magazine December 10, 1933; Ontario Library Review February 1928; Reader's Digest March 1940.

LEAF, MUNRO (December 4, 1905-   ), American writer for children (of all ages), reports: "I was born just outside of Baltimore, at Hamilton, Md. My mother and father were both born in Maryland. So I moved to Washington, D.C., before I was two months old. I went to school in Washington and then there I was right back where I started, in Maryland at the state university.

Pinchot

In 1927 I got my varsity letter in lacrosse and a B.A. degree. Then I went to Harvard to the graduate school and took a Master of Arts degree in English literature. The following year I went back to Harvard. This time I had a wife, Margaret Pope—a very nice wife, I might add, and I liked her so well that I still have the same one. We have a son, Andrew Munro Leaf, born in 1939.

"I did some special research work at Harvard on the early novel and coached football at the Roxbury Latin School until Harvard gave me an assistantship in English and sent me to England the following summer to buy books for the Widener Library. Then I took a job in the fall of 1929 to teach and coach at Belmont Hill School. I stayed there two years, then went to Montgomery School in Wynnewood, Pa., to spend one more year in teaching and coaching.

"By then I had begun to suspect that what I had always hazily been wanting was crystallized in book publishing. We came to New York in 1932 and I read manuscripts for the Bobbs, Merrill Co. until 1933, when I went to the Frederick A. Stokes Co., where I am still. In 1934 I wrote a book for children called *Grammar Can Be Fun*, in which I tried to take some of the dullness out of the really painful business of correcting children's slips of the tongue. I drew some scratchy pencil indications of what an artist was supposed to draw in the book and finally wound up by doing them myself. So then I was a full-fledged author and illustrator all in one lump.

"In 1936 I wrote a book that I thought was for children but now I don't know. It was the story of a little bull who would not fight. Robert Lawson (who can really draw) illustrated that."

*   *   *

The rest is history. *Ferdinand,* reproduced in everything from movies to soap, is now a fixed part of the American scene. The story was written in forty minutes on a rainy Sunday afternoon. Mr. Leaf is currently "streamlining the classics" in the *American Magazine* and doing "Watchbirds" for the *Ladies' Home Journal.* He is short and dark, with a wide humorous mouth, and he says his mission in life is "to ridicule the stuffed shirt." A second son was born to the Leafs in 1941.

PRINCIPAL WORKS: Grammar Can Be Fun, 1934; Robert Francis Weatherbee, 1935; Manners Can Be Fun, 1936; Ferdinand, 1936; Noodle, 1937; Wee Gillis, 1938; Safety Can Be Fun, 1938; Listen, Little Girl, Before You Come to New York, 1938; The Watchbirds, 1939; Fair Play, 1939; More Watchbirds, 1940 (ed.) Aesop's Fables, 1940; John Henry Davis, 1940; Fly Away, Watchbird, 1941; The Fun Book, 1941; Simpson and Sampson, 1941; A War-Time Handbook for Young Americans, 1942.

ABOUT: American Magazine December 1939; Publishers' Weekly October 23, 1937, August 26, 1939; Wilson Library Bulletin May 1937.

LEAF, WALTER (November 28, 1852-March 8, 1927), English banker and translator, was born in Upper Norwood, the

eldest son of Charles John Leaf and Isabella Ellen (Tyas) Leaf. John Tyas, her father, was a fine classical scholar who for twenty years was on the staff of the London *Times.* Leaf's father was a partner in a firm of dealers in silks and ribbons. After being tutored at home, Leaf won an entrance scholarship at Winchester, but instead went to Harrow as a home boarder, his parents going along too. Here he was at a disadvantage so far as sports and games were concerned; he was short-sighted and no effort was made to fit him with glasses. Made head boy of a house, The Park, by his tutor, Frederick William (later Dean) Farrar, he nevertheless managed to maintain discipline. In October 1870 Leaf entered Trinity College, Cambridge University, on a classical scholarship; was a member of the "Apostles"; amused himself in vacations with mountaineering and figure-skating; won the Craven scholarship in 1874 and was made a Fellow of Trinity in 1875. Some of his family dying, Leaf re-entered the "rag business" and by an abrupt transition made himself a power in the City. His firm became a limited liability company, and

Leaf was elected chairman in 1888-1892, also becoming chairman of the London and Westminster Bank in 1918 and, in 1919, of the Institute of Bankers. Asquith admired his speeches on financial subjects. In 1924 he was president of the International Chamber of Commerce; in 1926, he visited Germany to advise on economic reconciliation. Leaf's health failing—he was a small man, lacking a physical vigor—he took a sea voyage to South Africa and returned to die at Torquay. In 1894 he had married Charlotte Mary, daughter of John Addington Symonds; they had a son and two daughters.

Leaf's fame as a translator rests chiefly on his translation of the *Iliad,* with Andrew Lang and Ernest James Myers, into archaic and poetical prose. It has been called the best edition in English, perhaps in any language. Gilbert Murray said that everything he wrote was interesting, alive and business-like; but that his books of Homeric criticism did not allow sufficiently for myth, fiction, and mere conventional ornament in Homeric poetry. His work on *Banking* is standard in its field.

PRINCIPAL WORKS: Troy: A Study in Homeric Geography, 1912; Homer and History, 1915; Strabo on the Troad, 1923; Banking, 1926. *Translations*—The Iliad of Homer (with Andrew Lang and Ernest James Myers) 1882 (second edition enlarged and improved, 1900-1902).

ABOUT: Leaf, C. M. Walter Leaf (with fragment of autobiography.

LEBLANC, MAURICE (1864-November 6, 1941), French fiction writer and playwright, best known as the creator of Arsène Lupin, was born in Rouen, the son of Émile Leblanc, of partly Italian descent. He was frequently identified as the brother-in-law of Maurice Maeterlinck,*qv* the noted Franco-Belgian dramatist; but his sister, the actress Georgette

Leblanc, was never married to Maeterlinck, though she was his companion for many years. In early youth Leblanc became a hack-journalist and wrote fiction for some years without important success. One day, probably about 1906, he was asked by the editor of a new journal, *Je Sais Tout,* for a short story of crime to fill a particular space. Without an idea in his head, said Leblanc, and with no knowledge of criminals, he took up his pen, and his impudent hero Arsène

Lupin sprang into being. From this almost accidental beginning came one of the most successful careers in contemporary French letters, culminating in the ribbon of the Legion of Honor for the author. Until the Nazi occupation, at least, Leblanc lived in retirement in rural France, near Paris. (He did *not* die in 1926, as Willard Huntington Wright erroneously stated in *The World's Great Detective Stories.*) He was described as a quiet, friendly man of middle height, with a large cheerful face, bright, kindly eyes, and a large moustache over a humorous mouth. Much of his writing was done in the open air. He enjoyed chess and had a taste for the works of Poe and Balzac.

Arsène Lupin, Leblanc's best known creation, underwent a curious transition in the course of his career. In all the earlier books (the first was *Arsène Lupin: Gentleman-Cambrioleur,* published in 1907), he was the dashing gentleman-burglar of the original title; then, as more and more readers insisted that he should turn his brilliant talents to the *pursuit* of crime, a new epoch set in, and he devoted himself to correcting the blunders of the official police; in the final volumes, he works almost openly as a detective with his old enemies of the law. An early parody in the worst Gallic vein, introducing Lupin and Sherlock Holmes in unequal conflict, deserves mention as a literary curiosity; but as a work of fiction it is best forgotten. Lupin's position as a modern picaresque hero is undoubted, and has recently been reinforced by the moving pictures, following earlier stage successes. He is also a detective of more than average ability—Willard Huntington Wright praised *Les Huit Coups de l'Horloge* (The Eight Strokes of the Clock) as including "some of the best and most characteristic examples of modern detective stories." "To the skill of Sherlock Holmes and the resourcefulness of Raffles," wrote Charles Henry Meltzer, Arsène Lupin "adds the refinement of a casuist, the epigrammatic nimbleness of a La Rochefoucauld, and the gallantry of a Du Guesclin."

Leblanc died shortly before his seventy-seventh birthday at the home of a son in Perpignan, only two weeks after the death of his sister Georgette. Accounts from Vichy in Unoccupied France said that his final illness was brought about by exposure while traveling on an unheated train to visit his son who was ill. Obituary accounts stated that part of his education had taken place in Manchester, England, and Berlin, Germany, and that he had worked in his

youth in his father's shipbuilding establishment and had later studied law before publishing his first novel, *A Woman,* in 1887.

Maurice Leblanc may not have been the equal of his compatriots Gaboriau and Gaston Leroux[qv] in the realm of ratiocination, but he was an infinitely better storyteller than either of them.

PRINCIPAL WORKS AVAILABLE IN TRANSLATION: The Exploits of Arsène Lupin, 1907; Arsène Lupin versus Holmlock Shears, 1909; The Hollow Needle, 1910; "813," 1910; The Crystal Stopper, 1913; The Confessions of Arsène Lupin, 1913; The Return of Arsène Lupin, 1917; The Eight Strokes of the Clock, 1922; Memoirs of Arsène Lupin, 1925; Arsène Lupin: Super-Sleuth, 1927; Arsène Lupin Intervenes, 1929.

ABOUT: Haycraft, H. Murder for Pleasure: The Life and Times of the Detective Story; Thomson, H. D. Masters of Mystery; Wright, W. H. (ed.). The Great Detective Stories; Cosmopolitan Magazine May 1913; New York Times November 8, 1941.

LEDWIDGE, FRANCIS (June 19, 1891- July 31, 1917), Irish poet, was born at Slane, County Meath, the eighth child of Patrick Ledwidge, an evicted tenant-farmer, afterwards a farm laborer, and Annie (Lynch) Ledwidge. After leaving the Slane national school at twelve, the boy worked in the fields and as a domestic servant. At fourteen he was apprenticed to a Dublin grocer, but in a homesick mood tramped thirty miles back to his mother's cottage. He became a ganger on the roads, later overseer of roads in the Slane area, after being dismissed from work as a copper-miner for fomenting a strike. Some first verses were printed in the Drogheda *Independent*; these and others Ledwidge collected in an old copybook and sent to Lord Dunsany, who responded enthusiastically with advice and introductions to the literary world. Ledwidge served as secretary of the County Meath farm laborers' union, on the Navan district council, and as insurance commissioner for the county. Although a strong Nationalist, at the outbreak of the First World War he joined Dunsany's 5th Battalion Royal Inniskilling Fusiliers, soon earning his stripe as lance-corporal. In August 1915 he was present at the Suvla Bay landing at Gallipoli, and was with the first detachment sent from Gallipoli to Salonika in October. He fought through the Vardar retreat in December.

After a spell in a hospital in Egypt he was sent to France, and was killed in action in Belgium.

Called the Burns and the John Clare of the Irish (and once advertised as "The Scavenger Poet" by his publisher), Ledwidge's genius was not distinctively Irish. His themes were those common to most nature poets—May-blossoms, roses, and birds. (Dunsany called him the poet of the blackbird.) His joy in nature was purely sensuous, its "sorrow at root the pagan grief that all things pass." Ledwidge made remarkable strides in a short span of years: John Drinkwater spoke of his "break from hesitant and alloyed grace into sure and bright authority." The poet was well-built, tall, with an eager gentle face, arresting eyes, dark soft hair, and a shy, reserved manner.

PRINCIPAL WORKS: Songs of the Field, 1915; Songs of Peace, 1916; Last Songs, 1918; Complete Poems (with prefaces by Lord Dunsany) 1919.

ABOUT: Drinkwater, J. The Muse in Council; Tynan, K. The Years of the Shadow; Bellman November 10, 1917; Catholic World November 1917; Century January 1918; English Review February 1918; Living Age September 17, 1918, July 31, 1920; Nation October 19, 1918; New Statesman August 11, 1917; South Atlantic Quarterly July 1922.

LEE, MANFRED. See QUEEN, E.

LEE, Sir SIDNEY (December 5, 1859-March 3, 1926), British biographer and Shakespearean scholar, was born in London,

son of Lazarus Lee, merchant, of Jewish descent, and Jessie (Davis) Lee. His true forenames were Solomon Lazarus, but he abandoned them for Sidney in 1890. Educated at the City of London School, under the celebrated Dr. E. A. Abbott, he won an exhibition to Oxford and matriculated from Balliol in 1878. His academic record was no more than mediocre, for he took only a third in Classical Moderations and a second in Modern History. But his promise as a researcher in Tudor annals was early recognized by that doyen of Elizabethan scholars, Dr. F. J. Furnivall, who remarked sterling qualities in two undergraduate papers on Shakespeare published in the Gentlemen's Magazine, and on the strength of them gave Lee the task of editing Huon of Bordeaux for the Early English Text Society. Furnivall it was, too, who put Lee in the way of doing the great work of his life. In 1882 the publisher, George Smith, began to plan the Dictionary of National Biography, with (Sir) Leslie Stephen as editor. A good sub-editor was needed, and Lee (abandoning a proffered lectureship at Groningen) was appointed at Furnivall's instance, beginning work in March 1883 at £300 a year.

This colossal editorial task, planned to cover fifty volumes but actually filling sixty-three, proved eminently congenial to Lee's taste and admirably suited to his capacities. He had the industry of a mole, an orderly methodical mind, a fine sense of proportion and a hawk-like eye for errors. Stephen was a bad and unwilling proof-reader, so Lee undertook all that part of the work, and was responsible also for keeping contributors up to time—a duty he fulfilled so well that the volumes appeared regularly every quarter. He wrote 870 articles himself, covering a very wide range. He deputized most ably for Stephen during the latter's two illnesses of 1888 and 1889, became joint editor in 1890 and sole editor in May 1891. He gathered an excellent staff around him and worked them hard, but preserved the most cordial relations with all. Frequent staff dinners helped to foster esprit de corps, and at one of these, in July 1897, Canon Alfred Ainger produced the celebrated mot on the austere style of D.N.B., saying that the editor's motto was "No flowers, by request." The last volume appeared in October 1900 and the First Supplement in three volumes a year later. Thenceforward Lee was no longer fully employed on D.N.B., though he edited the Index and Epitome in 1903, a volume of Errata in 1904 and a Second Supplement in 1912.

Lee's Queen Victoria, written for the First Supplement, came out in expanded form as a book in 1902. His Shakespeare had been similarly treated in 1898, and this finally appeared, doubled in length, as the Life of Shakespeare in 1915. Lee was Clark Lecturer at Cambridge (England) in 1901-02, visited America in 1903, later publishing the lectures given there as Great Englishmen of the Sixteenth Century, edited numerous Shakespeare facsimile reprints, and brought out a twenty-volume Shakespeare for the University Press (Harvard) of Cambridge, Mass., in 1907-1910. In 1910 this was published in England also. From 1913 to 1924 he was Professor of English at East London College. A first volume of a Life of King Edward VII came out in 1925, but Lee's health was rapidly breaking up, and he died at sixty-six, without completing the second volume.

Lee was described by Stephen as always calm, confident, and conscientious, while George Saintsbury said of him: "He is about the only man, I think, of the whole lot of us (including myself) from whom I have never heard an unkind speech about a fellow craftsman." He was the pattern of an editor, judicial, accurate, scholarly, choosing contributors with care and managing them with firmness and tact. He was a prime authority on Shakespeare. His knighthood, conferred in 1911, was only one of many honors, which included Fellowship of the British Academy, honorary degrees from Oxford, Manchester and Glasgow, membership of a Royal Commission on Public Records and trusteeship of the National Portrait Gallery. He was a foreign member of the American Academy of Arts and Sciences and a corresponding member of the Massachusetts Historical Society. He did not marry.

PRINCIPAL WORKS: Stratford-on-Avon From the Earliest Times to the Death of Shakespeare, 1885; A Life of William Shakespeare, 1898 (rewritten and very greatly enlarged, 1915); Memoir of George Smith, 1902; Queen Victoria: A Biography, 1902; The Alleged Vandalism at Stratford-on-Avon, 1903: Great Englishmen of the Sixteenth Century, 1904; Shakespeare and the Modern Stage, 1906; The French Renaissance in England, 1910; Principles of Biography, 1911; Shakespeare and the Italian Renaissance, 1915; The Perspective of Biography, 1918; Life of King Edward VII (finished by F. S. Markham), 1925-27; Elizabethan and Other Essays, 1929.

ABOUT: Cromer, E. B. Political and Literary Essays; Dictionary of National Biography Supplements; 1912-21 and 1922-30; Firth, C. H. Sir Sidney Lee: 1859-1926; Greenwood, G. G. Lee, Shakespeare, and a Tertium Quid; Orcutt, W. D. Celebrities off Parade; Parsons, J. D. Ben Jonson and Sidney Lee; Parsons, J. D. Sir Sidney Lee and Absolute Proof About the Poet Shakespeare; Parsons, J. D. Sir Sidney Lee Challenged; Smith, F. E. [Earl of Birkenhead]. Law, Life, and Letters; Stephen, L. Some Early Impressions; Stephen, L. Studies of a Biographer; Times (London) March 4 and 6, 1926; Bulletin of the Institute of Historical Research June 1926; Proceedings of the British Academy 1929.

"LEE, VERNON." See PAGET, V.

*LE GALLIENNE, RICHARD (January 20, 1866-   ), English poet and essayist, was born in Liverpool, the son of John and Jane Le Gallienne. His father was of French descent. He was educated at Liverpool College, and was then apprenticed to a firm of chartered accountants, who wrote his father that "his head was so filled with literature . . . that he was demoralizing the

whole office." After seven years he secured a pleasanter position as secretary to Wilson Barrett, the actor-manager, the high light of which was a meeting with Swinburne. His first encouragement as a writer came from the elder Oliver Wendell Holmes, to whom he sent his first poems. In 1891, through the publisher John Lane, he became literary critic of the London *Star,* succeeding Clement K. Shorter and having as colleagues George Bernard Shaw and A. B. Walkley. He next became a reader for John Lane.

In 1898 he moved to America and lived in New York for many years. After a few years' residence in Woodstock, N.Y., and in Rowayton, Conn., he left the United States again and settled on the Riviera, at Mentone. His daughter, Eva Le Gallienne, the noted actress, was born in London.

Le Gallienne has been married three times: in 1891 to Mildred Lee, who died in 1894; in 1897 to Julie Norregaard, a writer and actress of Scandinavian descent (Eva Le Gallienne's mother), from whom he was divorced; and in 1911 to Irma Hinton Perry.

He is a strikingly handsome man, who cultivated his "poetic" appearance. Holbrook Jackson called him "a sort of *fin de siècle* Leigh Hunt"; and he belongs peculiarly to the era of the *Yellow Book* and the rise of Oscar Wilde. His verse is highly derivative, rather pretty than beautiful; his prose mannered and sentimental. In recent years he has lived largely in the past, writing with sad nostalgia of the golden days he helped to adorn, and with the death of which his own place in the sun passed away.

Le Gallienne has written far too much for the good of his reputation, and he never recovered from the weakening influence of the writers, from Wilde to Dowson, who were the London literary lions of his youth. His work is full of precious mannerisms and makes dull reading nowadays. It is a voice from another world, and a world which wearies the readers of today. But he had a fresh if not a deep-rooted talent, and he did have the inestimable advantage of knowing intimately everybody who mattered in a small circle historically interesting to the student of literature. In the end all that survives of his work may be the reminiscent books—*The Quest of the Golden Girl, The*

* Died September 15, 1947.

Romantic Nineties, and *From a Paris Garret.*

PRINCIPAL WORKS: *Verse*—My Ladies' Sonnets, 1887; English Poems, 1892; Robert Louis Stevenson and Other Poems, 1895; Omar Repentant, 1908; New Poems, 1910; October Vagabonds, 1910; The Lonely Dancer and Other Poems, 1913; The Silk Hat Soldier and Other Poems, 1915; The Junk-Man and Other Poems, 1921; A Jongleur Strayed, 1922; The Magic Seas, 1930. *Prose*—Volumes in Folio, 1888; George Meredith, 1890; The Book-Bills of Narcissus, 1891; The Religion of a Literary Man, 1893; Prose Fancies (two series) 1894, 1896; Retrospective Reviews, 1896; The Quest of the Golden Girl, 1896; If I Were God, 1897; The Romance of Zion Chapel, 1898; Walt Whitman, 1898; Young Lives, 1899; The Sleeping Beauty, 1900; The Beautiful Lie of Rome, 1900; Rudyard Kipling: A Criticism, 1900; The Life Romantic, 1900; An Old Country House, 1902; Mr. Sun and Mrs. Moon, 1902; Old Love Stories Retold, 1904; Painted Shadows, 1904; How To Get the Best Out of Books, 1904; Romances of Old France, 1905; Little Dinners With the Sphinx, 1907; Love Letters of the King, 1908; Orestes, 1910; Attitudes and Avowals, 1910; Loves of the Poets, 1911; Maker of Rainbows, 1912; Highway to Happiness, 1912; Vanishing Roads and Other Essays, 1915; Pieces of Eight, 1918; Woodstock, 1923; The Romantic Nineties, 1926; The Philosophy of Limited Editions, 1929; There Was a Ship, 1930; From a Paris Garret, 1936; From a Paris Scrapbook, 1938.

ABOUT: Archer, W. Poets of the Younger Generation; Burdette, O. The Beardsley Period; Jackson, H. The Eighteen Nineties; LeGallienne, E. At Thirty-three; Rothenstein, W. Men and Memories; Bookman (London) April 1914; Catholic World February 1928, April 1932.

LÉGER, ALEXIS ST. LÉGER (May 31, 1887-   ), French poet who uses the pseudonym "St.-J. Perse," was born on Saint-

Léger les Feuilles, a small family-owned coral island off Guadeloupe. An old bishop was his instructor; his nurse was a Hindu, in secret a priestess of Shiva. His early memories have to do with sea and storms, tropical lushness, exotic plantation life. At eleven he was brought to France, where he began his education in letters, medicine, and law, prior to joining the diplomatic service in 1914. Three years later he went to China as Secretary of the Diplomatic Corps; his friends were Chinese philosophers; his favorite refuge was a temple that he rented in the hills. During his furloughs he traveled in the Gobi Desert and explored the islands of the South Seas between Fiji and the New Hebrides.

In 1922, at the personal request of that apostle of peace, Aristide Briand, Léger came to Washington for the Disarmament Conference, serving as expert on the Far East. Returning to France with Briand, he devoted himself for the next decade as the latter's intimate collaborator and friend, his "right arm." On Briand's death in 1932, Léger became Permanent Secretary for Foreign Affairs. At night he worked on his poems, but none of his associates, not even Briand, had any knowledge of them. In this period he refused ambassadorships to Brussels, Rome, and Washington.

"Of Léger's record as a statesman," writes Archibald MacLeish, poet and Librarian of Congress, "history will have much to say.... None knew better than Léger the complexion of French politics or the natures of the French politicians. . . . Léger, opposed always to appeasement, opposed also the appeasers. . . . When France capitulated, Léger embarked upon a British ship, still laden with food intended for the French army. But the Nazis remembered him. Immediately upon occupying Paris they looted his apartment in the Avenue Camoëns. His unpublished poems, of which there were about five volumes in manuscript, are now ashes.... Léger arrived in Canada on June 14th, [1940] the anniversary of the burning of the Bastille, a day of significance to France, to him and to us."

Léger now lives in the United States. He has been appointed a Fellow of the Library of Congress, consultant in French poetry.

MacLeish remarks that Léger's publications "have the quality of inadvertence. His first poem *Images à Crusoé* (1909) and the collection known as the *Éloges* (1910) [with the signature Saint Léger Léger] were published without his consent, in the first volume of the *Nouvelle Revue Française*. *Poème* was published in November 1922 on the insistence of Valéry Larbaud in a small magazine called *Intentions*. Similar circumstances surround the *Amitié du Prince*. It was published in facsimile done by Jacomet for Ronald Davis and appeared in 1924. The publication of *Anabase* (1924) also was entirely fortuitous."

Léger's world-wide reputation as a poet rests almost exclusively on *Anabase*, a long poem, which was translated into English by T. S. Eliot in 1930, and into German, Italian, Rumanian, and Russian.

"*Anabase* is already well known, not only in France, but in other countries of Europe," wrote Eliot. "One of the best Introductions to the poem is that of the late Hugo von

Hofmannsthal, which forms the preface to the German translation. There is another by Valéry Larbaud, which forms the preface to the Russian translation. And there was an informative note by Lucien Fabre in the *Nouvelles Littéraires.*" The poem has no particular reference to Xenophon or the journey of the Ten Thousand. It is "a series of images of migration, of conquest of vast spaces in Asiatic wastes, of destruction and foundation of cities and civilizations of any races or epochs of the Ancient East. . . . Any obscurity of the poem, on first reading, is due to the suppression of 'links in the chain,' of explanatory and connecting matter, and not to incoherence or to the love of cryptogram. The justification of such abbreviation of method is that the sequence of images coincides and concentrates into one intense impression of barbaric civilization. Its sequence, its logic of imagery, are those of poetry and not of prose. I believe that this is a piece of writing of the same importance as the later work of James Joyce, as valuable as *Anna Livia Plurabelle.* And this is a high estimate indeed."

In March 1942 *Poetry: A Magazine of Verse*, printed, in the original French, Léger's powerfully symbolic *Exil*, written on Long Beach Island and dedicated to Archibald MacLeish. It was the first long poem in a foreign language ever to appear in *Poetry.*

Léger's literary "ancestors" are Tacitus, Persius, Racine. The poet, he asserts, must rely upon the subconscious, but the subconscious mastered by reason. He remains indomitably, passionately French: "About France there is nothing to say: It is myself and all of myself."

WORKS AVAILABLE IN ENGLISH TRANSLATION: Anabasis, 1930.

ABOUT: Léger, A. Anabasis: A Poem by St.-J. Perse (see Introduction by T. S. Eliot); Poetry March 1942 (see A Note on Alexis Saint Léger Léger by Archibald MacLeish); Sewanee Review January-March 1936.

LEGOUIS, ÉMILE HYACINTHE (October 31, 1861-October 16, 1937), French literary critic and educator, was born in Honfleur, Normandy, a small harbor town at the mouth of the Seine. His father was a mercer; his mother died when the boy was three. Staying at home until he was seventeen, young Legouis attended the local college or preparatory school, then spent two years at the Lycée Louis le Grand, where he was taught English by Professor Alexandre Beljame, later lecturer at the Sorbonne. A year at the University of Caen gave Legouis the degree of *licencié-ès-lettres*, equivalent to an M.A. degree, and at twenty he taught English at the college of Avranches for a year, perfecting his knowledge of the language in 1881-82 by six months apiece in London and Leamington. Studying again with Beljame at the Sorbonne in 1883-85, Legouis was made *agrégé*, or fellow, in English, and at twenty-four joined the Faculté des Lettres of Lyons as *maître de conférences d'anglais. Le Général Michel Beaupuy* (1891), a study of the officer referred to in the ninth book of Wordsworth's *Prelude*, was Legouis' first book, itself a prelude to a lifelong interest in the English poet. In 1894 Legouis lectured on English at the Sorbonne, which gave him a doctor's degree and a full professorship for *La Jeunesse de William Wordsworth* (1896), which was crowned by the Academy and superseded all former studies. Wordsworth's relations with Annette Vallon, "the voluble impulsive sentimental woman who develops under the stress of adverse circumstances into a devoted mother and a heroic devotee of the Royalist cause," are considered at length in *William Wordsworth and Annette Vallon* (1922). In 1912-13 Legouis was exchange professor of English at Harvard, lecturing also at Princeton, and in 1922 at Johns Hopkins.

His *History of English Literature*, written with Louis Cazamian,[qv] a colleague at the University of Paris, is called by George McLean Harper, the American authority on Wordsworth, a better history than Taine's or Saintsbury's. Harper also states that "no other foreigner has ever, by the variety, fullness, soundness, and intimacy of his work, shown such competence in this sort and done so great service, his books being useful not only to French readers but to ourselves." Legouis retired in 1932 to spend his declining years with two sons, a daughter, and ten grandchildren, Mme. Legouis having died in 1929. A handsome old man with white moustache and beard, he died just before his seventy-sixth birthday.

WORKS AVAILABLE IN ENGLISH TRANSLATION: The Early Life of William Wordsworth: 1770-1798, 1897; Geoffrey Chaucer, 1913; William Wordsworth and Annette Vallon, 1922; Wordsworth in a New Light, 1923; A History of English Literature, 1926; A Short History of English Literature, 1934.

ABOUT: English Studies December 1937; Études Anglaises July-September 1938; Quarterly Review January 1938.

LEHMANN, JOHN (1907-), English poet and essayist, writes:

"John Lehmann was born at Bourne End in the Thames Valley. His father was R. C. Lehmann,^{qv} well-known journalist and oarsman, and his mother comes from Massachusetts and is a sister of the late H. P. Davis (the 'Father of Broadcasting'). He has three sisters, one of them Rosamond Lehmann^{qv} the novelist, and another Beatrix Lehmann the actress. He was educated at Eton (King's Scholar) and Trinity College, Cambridge. He has published two books of poetry, a novel, a travel book about the Caucasus, and a study of Austrian and Danubian problems. He is founder and editor of the book-periodical *New Writing*, the first number of which was published in 1936. He lived in Vienna for some years previous to the Anschluss, was a member of the Anglo-American Press Association, and contributed articles to the *New Statesman*, the *Geographical Magazine* (London), *Travel*, etc. A short study of English literary trends was published in New York in 1939, leading to a similar work, though considerably wider in scope, for the Penguin (Pelican) Books. In 1938 he became partner and managing director in the Hogarth Press, the London publishing firm founded by Leonard and Virginia Woolf. He is single, and lives in London."

PRINCIPAL WORKS: A Garden Revisited (poems) 1931; The Noise of History (poems) 1931; Prometheus and the Bolsheviks, 1937; Evil Was Abroad (novel) 1938; Down River, 1939; New Writing in England, 1939; New Writing in Europe, 1940.

LEHMANN, ROSAMOND (1903-),

English novelist, was born in London, the daughter of Rudolph Chambers Lehmann,^{qv} for many years on the staff of *Punch,* and of Alice Marie (Davis) Lehmann, a cousin of the American playwright, Owen Davis. John Lehmann,^{qv} the poet, is her brother, and Beatrix Lehmann, the actress, is her sister. She was educated at Newnham College, Cambridge, the scene of her first very successful novel, *Dusty Answer*. She has been married twice, first to Leslie Runciman and then to her present husband, the Hon. Wogan Philipps, eldest son of Lord Milford, and a well known painter. They have a son and a daughter, and live at Ipsden, Oxford.

She wrote from earliest childhood, her first writing being verse; in fact her first published work was a poem in *Cornhill* when she was sixteen. She still writes verse, which she prefers to prose, but only for her own pleasure, since she does not consider it good enough for publication. Many critics, however, have noticed the poetic strain in her novels. Her chief recreation is reading, but she says that no author has particularly influenced her, though her greatest admiration is for Walter de la Mare. She is an unusually pretty woman, with regular features and beautifully shaped eyes under delicate eyebrows. One interviewer called her "the youngest and prettiest of British novelists."

The most salient feature of Rosamond Lehmann's novels is her persistent backward glance. From the beginning, she has been possessed of a nostalgia for youth, a feeling that maturity is dull and drab and that everything worth while in life comes in its earlier years. The delicacy of her touch may be indicated by the fact that a year before the furore over Radclyffe Hall's *The Well of Loneliness,* Miss Lehmann was able to present the same theme in *Dusty Answer* without offense and almost without notice. She was never a "promising" novelist, her very first work being a full-fledged achievement; Oliver Warner said truly that "her future is full of the most exciting possibilities. . . . She has proved the sureness of her selection and the range of her potentialities." But George Dangerfield, though a great admirer of her "delicate and lyrical prose," sounded the warning that "her progress has been from the universal to the local, from the wide arena to the narrow." He expressed the hope that she would "set her imagination free," and so "take a major place in modern British fiction."

In spite of this one weakness, there is universal praise for the beauty and depth of her work at its best. A reviewer in the New York *Times Book Review* summed her up very well when he noted as her leading characteristics "technical brilliancy, impeccable style, sensitivity, and deep, almost intuitive, knowledge of the thought-processes of women." For her work is unmistakably that of a woman; her men are likely to be either cads or weaklings or both, but her women are exquisitely delineated; she "sees through persistently feminine eyes."

PRINCIPAL WORKS: Dusty Answer, 1927; A Note in Music, 1930; Invitation to the Waltz,

1932; The Weather in the Streets, 1936; No. More Music, 1939.

ABOUT: Bookman February 1933; Bookman (London) December 1934; Newsweek May 23, 1936.

LEHMANN, RUDOLPH CHAMBERS

(January 3, 1856-January 22, 1929), English humorist and sportsman, was born near

Sheffield, the eldest son of Frederick and Nina (Chambers) Lehmann. Liza Lehmann, the well-known composer, was his cousin, and he was a nephew of Rudolph Lehmann, the painter. In due course of time his daughter, Rosamond,[qv] grew up and wrote the best-selling novel *Dusty Answer.* His only son, John,[qv] born in 1907, has written notable poetry and travel books and is editor of the *New Writing* series. Another daughter, Beatrix, is a well known English actress.

Lehmann was educated at Highgate School and Trinity College, Cambridge University, where he was president of the Union, edited the *Granta,* and was captain of the first Trinity Boat Club, "the best oar who never got a Blue." In the 1890's and early 1900's he coached victorious crews for both Oxford and Cambridge, as well as at Leander, Dublin, Berlin, and as far afield as Harvard (which gave him a master's degree). He became a barrister of the Inner Temple in 1880, and in 1887 was co-author of Dale and Lehmann's *Digest of Overruled Cases.* He contested Cheltenham as a liberal candidate in 1885, Central Hull in 1886, and Cambridge Town in 1892, and was Member of Parliament for the Harborough Division of Leicester, 1906-1911. Lehmann's connection with *Punch* extended from 1890 to 1919, his chief contribution being "neat and kindly verses about sports and manners, the country, rowing, and rocketing pheasants." As another Liberal, A. A. Milne found his presence at the *Punch* round table a great solace, the editor, Owen Seaman, being a hidebound conservative.

Lehmann's other activities included a year as editor of the *Daily News,* in 1901. He died of pneumonia, after a long and painful illness, at Bourne End, his home. Mrs. Lehmann (Alice Marie Davis) was an American. They had a son and three daughters. The *Spectator* spoke of him as "a man of dis-

tinction and charm and one of the best of friends."

PRINCIPAL WORKS: Harry Fludyer at Cambridge, 1890; In Cambridge Courts, 1891; The Billsbury Election, 1892; Mr. Punch's Prize Novels, 1893; Rowing (Ishmian Library) 1897; Anni Fugaces, 1901; Adventures of Picklock Holes, 1901; Crumbs of Pity, 1903; The Sun-Child, 1904; The Complete Oarsman, 1908; Light and Shade, 1909; Charles Dickens as Editor, 1912; Sportsmen and Others, 1912; A Spark Divine, 1912.

ABOUT: The H [Harvard] Book of Athletics; Lehmann, R. Memories of Half a Century; Marshall, A. Out and About; Milne, A. A. Autobiography. London Mercury February 1929; Spectator January 26, 1929.

LEIGHTON, CLARE VERONICA HOPE

(1900-   ), English illustrator and writer, is the daughter of the late Robert

Leighton, boys' story writer, and Marie Conner Leighton, writer of melodramas; they collaborated at the turn of the century in writing *Michael Dred: Detective,* which has some historical interest as the earliest story to make the de-

Disraeli

tective the murderer. Clare Leighton was educated at first by inadequate governesses, she says, then at the Brighton School of Art and later at the Slade School of Art. At the Central School of Arts and Crafts, Southampton Row, Miss Leighton learned the art of wood-engraving of which she is today one of the foremost practitioners. Since she began her work as a wood-engraver, she has won the first prize and medal at the International Exhibition of Engravings at the Chicago Art Institute; has represented Great Britain in wood-engraving at the International Exhibition in Venice in 1934; and has had works purchased for permanent collections by the British Museum, the National Galleries of Stockholm and Canada, and galleries in New York and other cities. She has also illustrated a number of books, including Emily Brontë's *Wuthering Heights,* Thornton Wilder's *The Bridge of San Luis Rey,* H. M. Tomlinson's *The Sea and the Jungle,* and Thomas Hardy's *The Return of the Native* and *Under the Greenwood Tree,* the latter being completed toward the end of 1940, when she was reported in the deep South of the United States, gathering material for another book of her own, to accompany her *The Farmer's Year, Four Hedges,* and *Country Matters.*

Clare Leighton has written and illustrated various books for children, and a technical book on wood cuts and engraving; she is a member of the Society of Wood Engravers and a Fellow of the Royal Society of Painters, Etchers, and Engravers. She was a close friend of the novelist Winifred Holtby.

In November 1935 Miss Leighton came to the United States to spend some weeks, with the intention of going as far west as St. Paul and painting Negro types in Florida. She also gave a few lectures on engraving and exhibited some of her work. *Four Hedges,* her book of that year, tells of the happenings in her garden in the Chiltern Hills month by month throughout the year, and is illustrated with engravings of the flowers, the birds, the snails and tortoises, and the human denizens of the garden. Like her other books, it was written with grace, humor and elevation of spirit. "The best of this work, as of any other good work in the great tradition of English wood-cutting, is its nobility," Hilaire Belloc wrote of her work in 1925. "It rings true; not only to what it represents, but to the kind of life we have to lead during our little passage through the daylight. It does good. . . . I find that the things I know, the realities of a moment, have been fixed. I find that the hand which drew or cut the line was sure." Miss Leighton was so saturated with her subject-matter that she did the scenes of Hardy's *Under the Greenwood Tree* from memory, while detained in the United States by the Second World War.

PRINCIPAL WORKS: How To Do Wood Engraving and Woodcuts, 1932; The Musical Box, 1932; The Farmer's Year, 1933; The Wood That Came Back, 1934; Four Hedges, 1935; Wood Engraving of the 1930's, 1936; Country Matters, 1937; Sometime—Never, 1939.

ABOUT: Brittain, V. Testament of Friendship: The Story of Winifred Holtby; London Mercury August 1925.

LEMAîTRE, JULES (August 27, 1853-August 5, 1914), French critic and playwright, was born François Élie Jules Lemaître at Vennecy, in Loiret, the son of a teacher in a religious institute. After attending religious schools in Orléans and Paris and the École Normale, he became instructor of rhetoric at the Havre lycée in 1875, remaining there four years. During the next few years Lemaître taught at Algiers (1880-82), Besançon (1882), and Grenoble (1883), but without ever relegating his literary interests to second place: he contributed essays on Flaubert, Leconte

de Lisle, and other French writers to various journals and in 1880 published his first book, a volume of verse entitled *Les Médaillons.*

In 1881 Lemaître had married Pauline des Chalais, a quiet, religious girl. He took her to cafés and insisted on making her a sophisticated woman of the world. She learned quickly—and deceived him. They separated but soon he "pardoned" her and they went to Grenoble where she died in 1883.

After the tragic interlude, Lemaître gave up definitely his teaching career, went to Paris, and contributed regularly to the *Revue Bleue* those "silhouettes" on contemporary writers which later appeared in the seven-volume *Les Contemporaines* (1885-99). In 1885 he became dramatic critic for the *Débats* and two years later for the conservative *Revue des Deux Mondes.* Lemaître made his debut as a playwright with *Revoltée* (1889), an Ibsenian retelling of his marital conflict. Although it was an utter fiasco, he was not discouraged and the following year produced *Le Député Leveau,* a political satire, which fared much better. However much greater success awaited his dramatization of his own novel, *Les Rois* (1893), a psychological study based on a newspaper account of the disappearance of an Austrian prince. His dramatic career reached its apogee in 1895 with the production of *The Pardon.* This play and the influence of his mistress—the Countess de Loynes, originally a demi-mondaine, whose salon had become the rendezvous of literary and political men—won Lemaître election to the French Academy in January 1896.

Lemaître's uninterrupted critical work gradually overshadowed his creative achievements and today he is better known for his criticism than for his plays or fiction. In addition to his series *Les Contemporains* and his collected dramatic criticism, the ten-volume *Theatrical Impressions* (1888-98), he wrote memorable studies of his favorite classics: Rousseau (1907), Racine (1908), Fénelon (1910) and Chateaubriand (1912). Lemaître's critical approach was not based on any esthetic system; he was rather an impressionist deeply imbued with the skepticism of his master, Renan. Gamaliel Bradford called him the French Charles Lamb. To Lemaître criticism was "the art of enjoying books" and what he understood by "criticizing" was simply chatting informally about books, indulging in anecdote and gossip, trusting nothing but his first impressions. As Lalou said, Lemaître merely cultivated his "garden of delicate taste. . . . His wisdom remained that of a cultivated bourgeois who does not abandon his prejudices, but in his best moments he added to them the mocking delicacy of a peasant from the valley of the Loire." Lemaître's viewpoint was inextricably bound to his conservative outlook: he lauded public morality, classicism, and patriotism. For years he was president of the Ligue de la Patrie Française and a member of the Action Française. Royalist and anti-Semitic, he was one of Dreyfus' bitterest enemies. He died at Tavers in 1914 at the age of sixty, two days after Germany declared war on France.

WORKS AVAILABLE IN ENGLISH TRANSLATION: *Criticism*—Jean Jacques Rousseau, 1907; Literary Impressions, 1921; Theatrical Impressions, 1924; Selections, 1930. *Fiction*—On the Margin of Old Books, 1929. *Plays*—Protection, 1890; White Love, 1892; The Eldest Miss Peterman, 1899; Forgiveness, 1913 [same as The Pardon, 1914]; Poor Little Thing, 1915.

ABOUT: Babbitt, I. The Masters of Modern French Criticism; Baring, M. Punch and Judy; Chandler, F. W. Modern Continental Playwrights; Clark, B. H. Contemporary French Dramatists; Henry, S. French Essays and Profiles; Lalou, R. Contemporary French Literature; Morice, H. Jules Lemaître; Squire, J. C. Books Reviewed; Walkley, A. B. Pastiche and Prejudice; Bookman September 1907; Fortnightly Review March 1905.

LENGYEL, EMIL (April 26, 1895-   ), Hungarian-American writer on international affairs, writes: "I was born in Budapest. My

father was a merchant. He died when I was two years old. My school days were dull. One of my teachers told me that I lacked linguistic talent. Just to spite him, I have been writing for publication in English, French, and German, in addition to my native Hungarian. After my graduation from the secondary classical school I matriculated in the Law Faculty of the Royal Hungarian University of Budapest. The war was on, and I was drafted for service in 1915. I was sent to the Eastern Front as an ensign. The Russians started their big offensive in June 1916. I was among those whom they took prisoner. They took us to a prison camp in Siberia, Irbit. I spent

Bachrach

twenty months there. I suffered a nervous breakdown, and my hair turned white at twenty-one. Luckily I also got malaria, a neutral Red Cross commission was passing through, and they sent me to Norway for hospitalization. After a fortnight there, in February 1918 I was sent back to Budapest. I was bedridden till the end of the war. While in the hospital I was studying furiously, and quickly passed my examinations and was graduated as Doctor of Laws. I wanted to become a lawyer. Instead, I became a journalist. For some time, I also was an interpreter—a kind of liaison officer between the French and the Hungarians. In the summer of 1920 I went to Prague, then to Vienna. There I got a job as a correspondent of Hungarian newspapers. By 1921 I was co-editor of the *Ungarische Rundschau*, a German language newspaper syndicate. I induced some of my editors to let me cover the Washington Disarmament Conference. I have been in America ever since. In 1927 I became an American citizen.

"I started in America as a messenger boy. I first started to write for American newspapers six months after my arrival. For years after 1925 I wrote regularly for the New York *Times*. Besides my books, I have written a scenario, *The World in Revolt,* shown in New York in 1934, and have translated many books from the French, German, and Hungarian. For the last eight years I have also been a lecturer, and have been pretty much all over America. In 1935 I got a teaching job at the Brooklyn Polytechnic Institute. Three years later I became a lecturer on education in the School of Education of New York University. I was married in 1938 to Livia Delej, and we have one son."

* * *

As a journalist Mr. Lengyel was known as "the terror of celebrities," because he tracked them down until they talked to him. His *Cattle Car Express* won the Strassburger Peace Prize in 1931. Christopher Stull remarked that he "has a faculty for writing books on timely subjects." Not invariably profound, they are always entertaining and packed with information.

PRINCIPAL WORKS: Cattle Car Express (in England: Beyond the Eastern Front) 1931; Hitler, 1932; The Cauldron Boils, 1932; The New Deal in Europe, 1934; Millions of Dictators 1936; The Danube, 1939; Turkey, 1941; Dakar 1941.

ABOUT: Wilson Library Bulletin December 1939.

*LENORMAND, HENRI-RENÉ (May 3, 1882-   ), French dramatist, writes: "My entire childhood was passed under the influence of music, and I believe that a critical mind could discover the source of my dramatic production in the musical work of my father, the composer René Lenormand: his admirable exotic melodies, that spirit of things far from this earth that breathed through him. A sedentary Parisian, there, in those Asiatic, Polynesian, or African inspirations, is the origin and the explanation of my *Simoun, À l'Ombre du Mal, Asie.* I have traveled, it is true. With my wife, the dramatic artist Marie Kalff, a Hollander by birth and who passed her early childhood in Java, I have journeyed through Oceania, the Sahara, the Arctic lands, the Near East. But these travels were the realization of my father's dream, the accomplishment, at twenty years' distance, of a musical task undertaken by my father, at his piano, behind the partition of the room where I lived.

"I have always dreamed of a dramatic art which would be neither exclusively of my time, nor exclusively of my country: a theatre which would comprehend all human anguish and which would try to soothe it in the light of eternity. I hate the theatre of the 'boulevard,' its arbitrary divisions, its bourgeois intrigues, its aridity, and its spirit. But I have tried to live in an eternal 'becoming.' I have avoided abstraction, system, 'general ideas.' I have tried to put the greatest possible amount of truth in my works. And if, in the background of all my exotic plays, one finds a feeling of revolt against 'colonial realities,' of hope for the liberation of the oppressed races, one will not find either sermons or illusions. I detest both 'thesis plays' and sentimentality.

"At bottom I feel, by my education and my literary preferences, a more intimate relation to the Elizabethan dramatists than to those of my own country. (I earned my degree in English at the Sorbonne.) It is perhaps for this reason that *man,* the psychological animal, the exclusive subject of the French tragedians, cannot, it seems to me, be separated from the natural forces which condition him. Around man I have tried to make real the nature which overwhelms

* Died February 17, 1951.

or exalts him, the mysteries which surround him.

"This great ambition which I brought to my plays has, naturally, made my life difficult. Long suppressed, derided, attacked, my plays have only recently been recognized in France. *Le Simoun* took twenty years to appear in the repertoire of the Comédie Française. It is true that very early in my career precious encouragements came from abroad. Max Reinhardt in Vienna, the Theatre Guild in New York, produced *Les Ratés* [*The Failures*] soon after its creation. And several of my dramas have been generously welcomed in South America, in Greece, at Prague, Madrid, Warsaw, in fact in nearly every land on earth.

"I am far from considering my task finished. I have four plays ready and I plan to write many others. I lack neither strength nor courage. But dramatic authors address a public which is no longer a very good theatre public. The masses, made intellectually indolent by the motion pictures, obsessed by the fear of war, morally disturbed by the transmutation of standards by which we are surrounded, overcome by the last twenty years of world history, of amazing happenings, of melodramatic events and horrible tragedies, are more and more rebellious against the magic of the balanced art of the theatre. At least we know nothing in France of the monster born under the totalitarian régimes, by the will of the governments and the weakness of the writers: the 'directed theatre.' If our art is imperiled in its material prosperity, it is not menaced in its essence. The theatre, in France, is free." [Written before the fall of France. No subsequent word has been received from or about M. Lenormand.—ED.]

* * *

Lenormand, with the eyes and forehead of a dreamer, looks like the man who might well write this thoughtful analysis of himself and his art. He explores, said Ashley Dukes, "the dramatic field that lies on or beyond the borderland of verbal expression. . . . His preoccupation is with the darker forces of the human mind." His plays, broken into many short scenes, call for revolutionary stage settings. Though he says he has never read Freud, he has been called "a psycho-analytical craftsman." Edmond Sée, who called Lenormand "the great dramatist of the unconscious and the subconscious," remarked that his work as a whole "forms the pathetic demonstration of some great human law, social or philosophical." As he says, he has had a hard row to hoe, and though even in France he had from the beginning a small group of admirers, he was practically unknown for a long time. Besides his plays, he has written a few stories and a volume of prose poems.

WORKS AVAILABLE IN ENGLISH: The Failures, and Time Is a Dream, 1923; Three Plays (The Coward, Man and His Phantoms, The Dream Doctor) 1928; In Theatre Street (in Famous Plays of 1937) 1937.

ABOUT: Monner Sans, J. M. El Teatro de Lenormand; Palmer, J. Studies in Contemporary Theatre; Rops, D. Sur la Théâtre de H.-R. Lenormand; Literary Digest July 27, 1936; Revue Politique et Littéraire April 21, 1928.

*LEONARD, WILLIAM ELLERY (January 25, 1876-), American poet, essayist, and teacher, was born in Plainfield, N.J., the son of the Rev. William James Leonard and Martha (Whitcomb) Leonard, who named the boy William Ellery Channing Leonard after the famous New England divine; he dropped the "Channing" in later years. He was educated at Boston University (B.A. 1898; later fellow in philology), Harvard (M.A. 1899), the Universities of Göttingen and Bonn, and Columbia (fellow 1902 and 1903, Ph.D. 1904). He was instructor in Latin at Boston University in 1898; principal of the Plainville, Mass., High School, 1899; instructor in German at the Lynn, Mass., High School, 1904; and editor of Lippincott's English Dictionary for two years thereafter. He then went to the University of Wisconsin, first as instructor in English; he rose gradually in rank until in 1926 he became full professor, which he still is. In 1916, when he was still able to travel to some extent, he was visiting professor of English at New York University.

Professor Leonard's fully acknowledged and recorded neurosis is one of the most important facts of his life; it is a salient part of his career that since 1911 he has been unable to go very far from home, and since 1922 has been a prisoner within four or five blocks. When he was a very small child he was badly frightened by a locomotive, which he identified with God. This psychic trauma was suppressed, but determined his life. In 1909 he married Charlotte Freeman, who killed herself two years later. Added to the grief and shock of this was the vile slander that he had forced her to take poison.

The agony he underwent whitened his hair and fixed his compulsion neurosis. In 1914 he married Charlotte Charlton, who divorced him in 1934. The following year he married one of his pupils, Grace Gordon, more than thirty years his junior; she too was unable to endure the peculiar conditions made necessary by his affliction, and they were later amicably divorced. In April 1940 he remarried his second wife, Charlotte Charlton, making his fourth marriage.

In spite of this "fear of spacial distance from a centre of safety," Leonard is no invalid. In his hale sixties, he swims and skates on the lake fortunately near his home, plays a good game of tennis, and is still a lean, sinewy, unstooped six feet. He may be "the country's best-known phobiac" but his mind is still "fun-loving and razor-keen." The same intellect which cannot curb his emotional dread "holds the learning of thirty centuries and a mastery of a dozen ancient and modern languages." He is a staunch liberal, stood valiantly against participation in the First World War, and has not hesitated to take a firm stand for civil liberties in several unpopular cases. Ernest L. Meyer has described him, with his loose "outdoor" clothes and his flowing purple tie, "gaunt-cheeked, Indian-featured though not tawny, with dark brown intent eyes behind glasses and arched by black eyebrows."

He is a great scholar, who has made definitive translations of Empedocles, Lucretius, Beowulf, the Babylonian legend of Gilgamesh, and has published works on the scansion of Middle English and the meter of The Cid. But primarily he is a poet. His poetry, though traditional in form, is either intensely personal or outspokenly social in feeling. To the former category belong such poems as Two Lives (the story of his first marriage), to the latter, such as The Lynching Bee. To quote Ernest Meyer again, "he enriches the present with the vitality of the past; . . . he has made of his scholarship not pedantry but power." His autobiography, The Locomotive God, though painful to read, is so valuable in its minute self-analysis that it is in use as a psychological textbook in several colleges.

PRINCIPAL WORK: Poetry—Sonnets and Poems, 1906; The Vaunt of Man and Other Poems, 1912; Poems: 1914-16, 1916; The Lynching Bee and Other Poems, 1920; Two Lives, 1925; A Son of Earth, 1928; This Midland City, 1930. Prose—Byron and Byronism in America, 1905; The Poet of Galilee, 1909; Glory of the Morning (play) 1912; Æsop and Hyssop, 1913; Socrates, 1915; Red Bird (play) 1923; Tutankhamen and After, 1924; The Locomotive God, 1927. Lucretius: The Man, the Poet, and the Times, 1942.

* Died May 2, 1944.

ABOUT: Leonard, W. E. The Locomotive God; American Mercury July 1934; Newsweek July 6, 1935.

LEONOV, LEONID MAKSIMOVICH

(June 1, 1899-   ), Russian novelist, writes: "I was born in Moscow on June 1, 1899 (May 19 by the old calendar), by origin a peasant from Kaluga, Gubernia. My father, who was an obscure journalist, was from 1905 to 1910 banished to the north of Russia for political activity, and incarcerated in a fortress for two years. I studied at the Moscow Third Gymnasium, from which I graduated as a journalist on the staff of the Red Army newspaper. I took part in the Civil War. I wrote much verse from the days of my youth. It was no loss to world literature, however, when I burned it all in 1920. In 1923 I married the daughter of N. V. Sabashnikov, the Russian publisher.

"My favorite authors are Balzac and Dostoievsky. The novels I have written are *Badgers* (1924), which was also published in France, Poland, Germany, Spain, and other countries; *The Thief* (1927), also published in Germany, England, Czechoslovakia, etc.; *Sot* (1929), also published in Germany, France, England, Sweden, Spain, etc.; *Skutarevsky* (1931), also published in England, America, Czechoslovakia, and Poland; and *The Road to the Ocean* (1936). I have two volumes of short stories to my credit, as well as a volume of plays, several of which have been staged. The Moscow Art Theatre has produced *The Gardens of Polovchansk*; the Maly Theatre, *The Wolf* and *Skutarevsky*; the Vakhtangov Theatre, *The Badgers*.

"My works have been published in the USSR in editions totaling more than a million copies. My hobbies are gardening, rearing cactuses, and motoring. My future work will show whether it will pay the American publisher to interest himself in a fuller biography of me."

* * *

Despite the modesty of this last statement, Maxim Gorky considered Leonov "one of the chief representatives of the contemporary group of Soviet writers who continue the work of classical Russian literature. . . . His talent is increasing with extraordinary rapidity. . . . Each new book has a more convincing ring than the last. . . . He uses words as a painter uses colors."

Leonov has lived both in central Russia and as far north as Archangel, where his father was exiled, and has traveled in Germany, France, and Italy. His peacetime home is Moscow. A dark, clean-shaven young man, he looks even younger than he is. Though he was denied a university education because of his bourgeois family, he is strongly pro-Soviet, and his later novels celebrate the industrialization and feats of construction of the U.S.S.R. The color and sonority of Leonov's style are of course lost in translation, but not the originality of his thought and his mastery of technique.

Leonov wrote the preceding autobiographical sketch before the German invasion of Russia in 1941. A dispatch in 1942 noted that Leonov had lost one eye in the fighting before Leningrad. Leonov was one of the six script writers to contribute to the making of the great Soviet war film, "This Is the Enemy."

WORKS AVAILABLE IN ENGLISH: The Thief, 1931; Soviet River (in England, Sot) 1932; Skutarevsky, 1933.

ABOUT: Mirsky, Contemporary Russian Literature; Living Age April 1932; New York Herald Tribune "Books" March 6 and 13, 1932; Slavonic Review July 1933, April 1937.

LERNER, MAX

(December 20, 1902-   ), American authority on sociology and politics, writes: "I was born near Minsk, in Russia.

Harris & Ewing

My father has fluctuated between shopkeeping and petty trade on one hand and teaching on the other. I was brought to the United States in 1907, at the age of four. After wandering about a good deal, my family settled in New Haven when I was about ten, where I had most of my schooling. A scholarship enabled me to get to Yale, and there I did most of my work in English literature. Toward the end of my college term (I got my B.A. in 1923) I got interested in economics and social theory, and after a year's try at law school, spent three years in graduate work at the Robert Brookings School of Economics and Government at Washington. I was deeply influenced there by Walter Hamilton. After getting my Ph.D. at Brookings in 1927, I spent five or six years helping Alvin Johnson and Edwin Seligman in editing the *Encyclopedia of the Social Sciences*. During these years I was mainly struggling to find my proper form for writing, and was soaking myself in the whole past literature of the social sciences. Since 1931 I have devoted myself mainly to teaching, writing, and journalism. My first book, *It Is Later Than You Think*, tries to give a perspective of the problems of contemporary politics and contemporary minds. My second book, *Ideas Are Weapons*, enabled me to bring together a large variety of essays in fields ranging from literature to law and politics. I spent three years (1936-39) as editor of the *Nation*, and still maintain my interest in journalism.

"My political convictions are on the left, although I belong to no party. I feel that my energies must lie with the movement toward a democratic socialism. My favorite author is Thorstein Veblen, and my favorite public figure is the late Justice Holmes. In 1928 I was married to Anita Marburg, have three daughters, and live at Williams College, where I am a professor of political science. I am at present at work on two long-range projects: a history of the cult of power and anti-humanist trends in Europe since Machiavelli, and a book on the American Supreme Court."

* * *

Mr. Lerner received an M.A. degree at Washington University, St. Louis, before he went to Brookings. He taught at Sarah Lawrence College, Bronxville, N.Y., from 1932 to 1936, and was chairman of the faculty of the Wellesley Summer Institute from 1933 to 1935. For a year thereafter he lectured on government at Harvard. He was director of the consumers' division of the National Emergency Council in 1934.

PRINCIPAL WORKS: It is Later Than You Think, 1938; Ideas Are Weapons, 1939; Ideas for the Ice Age: Studies in a Revolutionary Era, 1941.

ABOUT: New Republic December 20, 1939; Southern Review #4, 1939.

LEROUX, GASTON (1868-April 16, 1927), French writer of mystery and detective stories, had an adventurous life which

he translated into his sensational fiction. According to his own account he was a lawyer, legal chronicler, stage critic, writer on hygiene, dramatist, newspaper correspondent, globe-trotter, and novelist, and tramped up and down the world, his daring spirit carrying him into faraway corners and into and out of a dozen scrapes. His travels took him into Sweden, Prussia, from Finland to Nijni Novgorod and south to the Caspian Sea, and through Italy, Egypt and Morocco. Disguised as an Arab, he risked his life twenty times—he said—at Larache and Fez while in Morocco. *L'Illustration* called him "the eternal reporter," a journalist first and last who was able to make copy out of the most unpromising materials and situations. Leroux, for instance, once attempted to interview Joseph Chamberlain during the gloomy days of the South-African war. He made his way into Chamberlain's study at Birmingham, and took his seat opposite the statesman's desk. Dismissed in short order by a secretary, he turned out a three-column article, "How I Failed To See Chamberlain," which was regarded as a little masterpiece of good humor and wit. His career as a writer of popular fiction began in the early 1900's.

Although *The Phantom of the Opera* had a notable success in the silent moving pictures with Lon Chaney in the starring rôle, and although such sensational mysteries as *The Secret of the Night* and the Cheri-Bibi books were popular in their time both at home and abroad, Leroux's lasting reputation rests on the half-dozen *aventures extraordinaires* of Joseph Rouletabille, reporter-sleuth, which have been called by Willard Huntington Wright "among the finest examples of detective stories we possess." The first and by far the best known of the Rouletabille novels was *Le Mystère de la Chambre Jaune* (*The Mystery of the Yellow Room*), published in France in 1907 and translated a year later, which, it has been said, has seldom been surpassed in the *genre* for plot manipulation and ratiocination. Whether or not Leroux was the originator of the popular gambit of the crime committed in a sealed room is debatable; but, as one writer has declared, the idea has never been used "so logically, so brilliantly, or so simply as in the chubby hands of Rouletabille." Too, the author's revelation of the official detective on the case as the culprit has been termed "a classic *tour de force* on the 'least-likely-person' theme." The only one of the succeeding novels to approach the popularity of the initial volume was its direct sequel, *Le Parfum de la Dame en Noir* (1908), translated in 1909 as *The Perfume of the Lady in Black*.

But for all their ratiocinative excellence, Leroux's Rouletabille novels belong today among those books everybody "knows," but which comparatively few have actually read. Typical of the French detective story since the beginning, they followed the tradition begun by Gaboriau—meticulous logic combined with yellow-back sensationalism. Surpassing as is the detection, the second quality makes them difficult going for modern readers past the impressionable age.

PRINCIPAL WORKS AVAILABLE IN ENGLISH TRANSLATION: The Mystery of the Yellow Room, 1908; The Perfume of the Lady in Black, 1909; The Phantom of the Opera, 1911; The Man With the Black Feather, 1912; The Secret of the Night, 1914; Bride of the Sun, 1915; Cheri-Bibi, 1916; The Dancing Girl, 1925; The Man of a Hundred Faces, 1930.

ABOUT: Haycraft, H. Murder for Pleasure: The Life and Times of the Detective Story; New York Times April 17, 1927.

LESLIE, Mrs. DORIS (OPPENHEIM)

English novelist, writes: "I did not intend to be a writer. I showed no particular literary talent as a child, but I seem to have exhibited a definite gift for drawing, which induced my father to remove me from school in Brussels and send me to a school of art in London. I became stage-struck at fifteen. I did not want to be an artist. I wanted to be an actress. My father sternly repudiated the idea. But unknown to him I had secured a scholarship in the dramatic section of the Guildhall School of Music, and its principal, the late Sir Landon Ronald, eventually persuaded my father to allow me to go on the stage. My first appearance was at the 'Old Vic,' where I played Viola in *Twelfth Night*. I married in my teens the late John Leslie, who was also a member of the 'Old Vic' company. When shortly afterwards my husband died, my ambition to be an actress died too, and I went off to study art in Florence. I studied life more. I kept a daily diary of impressions, and when I came back to England I decided that art, after all, was not to be my goal.

"So I wrote a book about Florence. I showed it to a real author, the first I had met in my life, and he sent it to a publisher, who to my utter astonishment accepted it. I had now become a writer, without having any idea how to write—or what to write. I was bound by contract to deliver three more books and somehow or other I wrote them. They were all incredibly bad. I think I can safely say that my literary career began from the moment I discovered and could acknowledge how very bad those early efforts were.

"My first big success was *Full Flavour*. I wrote it for my mother, but she did not,

to my sorrow, live to see it published. It became a world best seller and has been dramatized and translated into five languages.

"I am now married to Dr. W. Fergusson Hannay, a well known London physician.

"It may be interesting to know that I cannot type. All my books are written in longhand and every chapter is rewritten about six times, so that I have written eight million words by hand! That is probably a record."

* * *

Because she cannot type or dictate, and because of the danger of accident to her right hand while horseback riding (her favorite recreation), Doris Leslie has had the hand insured for a considerable sum. She lived for a long time in Devon, and does not like cities or their noise, but is now living in London. Her literary favorites are Emily Brontë, Galsworthy, and Aldous Huxley. Her maiden name was Oppenheim, and she is of Jewish descent, black-eyed and with black hair worn in a Dutch bob. Her second husband was R. Vincent Cookes. Frances Woodward said she "writes fluently," but classed her as "one of the dozens of competent English novelists who appear to have been permanently deafened by the Ypres guns, and unaware that there are now new thunders over England." Circumstances since then have doubtless changed this situation.

PRINCIPAL WORKS: The Starling, 1927; Fools in Mortar, 1928; The Echoing Green, 1929, Terminus, 1930; Puppets Parade, 1932; Full Flavour, 1934; Fair Company, 1936; Concord in Jeopardy, 1938; Another Cynthia, 1939; Royal William, 1941; House in the Dust, 1942.

ABOUT: Saturday Review of Literature July 2, 1938.

"LESLIE, HENRIETTA." See SCHÜTZE, G. H. R.

LESLIE, SHANE (September 29, 1885-), Irish biographer and critic, writes: "Shane Leslie was born [John Randolph Shane Leslie] in London, on a site now commemoratively covered by Selfridge's Stores, where his remaindered works may be purchased cheap. Parents: Sir John Leslie, an Irish baronet, and Leonie Jerome of Madison Square, New York. Background: old Irish home in Ulster on the borders of Monaghan where sport and Conservative politics were dominant. Education: Eton College followed by a year in Paris in the Latin Quarter and three years

at Cambridge, at King's College. At the university he became interested in the Oxford High Church Movement, the Irish Literary Renaissance, and Christian Socialism.

"He took a degree in 1907 and went that winter to Russia where he became a friend of Tolstoy and adopted his social opinions. In the following year he became a Roman Catholic and took to a tramp's life. While wandering and lecturing in America he married Marjorie Ide, the daughter of the Governor General of the Philippines and Ambassador to Spain. He has since lived between London and Glaslough, Ireland, and added two sons and a daughter to the world's over-population.

"The authors whom he has studied closest are Æschylus, Milton, Tolstoy, Huysmans, Leon Bloy, Baron Corvo, Stendhal, and Thomas Aquinas, on all of whom he has written appreciations. His recreations are forestry (trained as an axeman), long-distance walking (invented 'hiking' while an undergraduate at Cambridge), and proof-reading. Interested in bird sanctuaries and considers Audubon as a patron saint. Collects old Irish books and relics and digs for Celtic antiquities. Wears the Irish saffron kilt and studies Old Irish in his leisure.

"Most of his books are out of print. At present he is chiefly known and dreaded as a reviewer on the London *Daily Telegraph* and *Sunday Times.* He still believes it necessary to read through a book before writing its review.

"He claims to have had an unsuccessful life though a happy one. He has stood twice for Parliament as an Irish Nationalist and been defeated each time. He has often been blackballed but never blackmailed. He believes it is better to interest or amuse people than to make them rich or prosperous. He is proud of being a relation of Mr. Churchill and Mr. Parnell and of the Red Indians through his American grandmother."

* * *

Shane Leslie is bald, long-headed, and more Irish than "Red Indian" in appearance. He is an associate of the Irish Academy, and has an honorary LL.D. from Notre Dame University. His books, like his temperament, display a commixture of erudition, conservatism, humor, and truculence. He has written novels, history, and verse, but is best known as a biographer. His most widely read book has been *The Skull of Swift.* His novel, *The Cantab,* was withdrawn because of protests from Cambridge University, and *The End of a Chapter* was withdrawn in consequence of a libel suit by the late Sir Thomas Lipton. His two main interests in life are indicated by his statement that his two "American friends whom he admires immensely" are Cardinal O'Connell and Dr. A. S. W. Rosenbach, the book collector.

PRINCIPAL WORKS: *Novels*—The Oppidan, 1922; Doomsland, 1923; Masquerades, 1924; The Cantab, 1926; The Anglo-Catholic, 1929. *Verse*—Verses in Peace and War, 1916; Poems, 1928; The Epic of Jutland, 1930; Poems and Ballads, 1933. *Biography*—Cardinal Manning, 1921; Sir Mark Sykes, 1923; Gordon Bailey, 1924; George IV, 1926; The Skull of Swift, 1928; J. E. C. Bodley, 1930; Studies in Sublime Failure, 1932; The Script of Jonathan Swift and Other Essays, 1935; Men Were Different, 1937; Sir Evelyn Ruggles-Brise, 1938; Life of Mrs. Fitzherbert, 1939. *Miscellaneous*—The End of a Chapter, 1916; A Ghost in the Isle of Wight, 1929; St. Patrick's Purgatory, 1932; The Oxford Movement, 1933; The Passing Chapter, 1934; The American Wonderland, 1936; The Film of Memory (autobiography) 1938.

ABOUT: Leslie, S. The Film of Memory; Monro, H. Some Contemporary Poets.

LEVIN, MEYER (October 8, 1905-), American novelist, writes: "I was born in Chicago and raised on the West Side, which changed from a Ghetto to a Little Italy during my childhood. My father was a tailor, and owned a house. We couldn't move out of the district until long after it became famous as the Bloody Nineteenth ward of gangsterdom. I visited our

street recently and found a Federal Housing Project extending over the site of my childhood home. I started to write in grammar school, setting up my stories in the print shop. In high school and college—University of Chicago—I followed the usual pattern of contributing to and editing school papers. During my second year at college I went to work part time as a picture-chaser for the Chicago *Daily News.* In due time I became a reporter, a feature writer, and eventually a columnist. My column was called 'A Young Man's Fancy,' and got no mail, so I suppose nobody read it.

"In 1925 I went abroad and fooled around with painting for a while, in Paris. Fernand Leger told me I might become a painter in ten years and that seemed too long, so I stuck to writing—which turned out to take longer. For five more years I was in and out of newspaper work; during that time I wrote *Reporter,* which was published in 1929 and withdrawn shortly after publication, due to a threat of suit from a newspaperwoman who thought she had been pictured in the book. Though their lawyers said she had no case, the publishers did not want to go to the expense of defending the suit, and prevailed on me to agree to withdrawal. By that time I was in the post-publication phase of thinking it a weak book, so I agreed.

"I went to Palestine and lived in a new settlers' farm community there, and wrote a book called *Yehuda;* meanwhile my second novel appeared. Back in the United States, during the early depression years, I was an actor for a while, and also produced marionette plays at the New School for Social Research. I had been active in experimental marionette theatres for many years, doing such plays as O'Neill's *The Hairy Ape* and Georg Kaiser's *From Morn to Midnight.* I heard of a new magazine called *Esquire,* about to be published. Got a job on the staff, doing a marionette-caricature feature with verse and writing motion picture reviews. The verse-caricatures took up too much time, so I gave up the marionette business, with a final mercenary fling doing a Buster Brown Show at the Chicago World's Fair. As reader for *Esquire,* I inaugurated the personally-written rejection note, which became an awful headache when the scripts started coming in at the rate of 1500 a week. For about five years I kept up with this and movie reviewing, and in the meantime wrote *The Old Bunch;* about three hundred pages of this were cut to get it down to publishable length.

"I married Mabel Schamp Foy; we have one son. We went to Spain during the war, where she did laboratory work in a hospital. On returning from Spain, I dropped my editorial work with *Esquire* in order to write *Citizens.* The first draft of this novel was done in Gary, Ind.; I put the manuscript into a suitcase and drove back to Chicago, parking the car while I reviewed a movie. The car was broken into, and the suitcase and a typewriter stolen. I went to Hollywood to rewrite the book. Stayed on in Hollywood but never got a job in the movies."

* * *

Mr. Levin also served for a time as editor of *Ken.* His novel *Citizens* is a fictionized version of the killing of ten steel mill strikers at Chicago on Memorial Day, 1937. Ernest Hemingway called it "a fine and exciting American novel." Clifton Fadiman observed that "its meaningful and arresting content compels the reader to overlook the author's obvious shortcomings as an artist."

PRINCIPAL WORKS: Reporter, 1929; Frankie and Johnnie: A Love Story, 1930; Yehuda (nonfiction) 1931; The Golden Mountain (folk tales) 1932; The New Bridge, 1933; The Old Bunch, 1937; Citizens, 1940.

ABOUT: Current Biography 1940; Scholastic April 23, 1938.

LEVY, HYMAN (March 7, 1889-), British scientist, philosopher, and essayist, was born in Edinburgh, and there attended George Heriot's School. As a youngster he had a decidedly inventive curiosity and amused himself with experiments in steam energies—filled an egg shell with boiling water, etc. In 1911 he was graduated from Edinburgh University with First Class Honors in mathematics and physics and then pursued further studies at Oxford and Göttingen. All the while he was acquiring a considerable love of argument, and would sometimes even impose upon the good nature of the green grocer or the charwoman in order to strengthen in his own mind some still tenuous hypothesis.

In 1916 he became a member of the aerodynamics research staff of the National Physical Laboratory. At the end of four years' service there he accepted an assistant professorship (mathematics) at the Royal College of Science. In 1923 he was made a professor of mathematics at the Imperial College of Science and Technology, and still retains this post. Between 1924 and 1930 he was chairman of the Science Advisory Committee of the Labour Party. He was married in 1918 to Marion A. Fraser; they have two sons and a daughter.

Levy has always contended that science must become the means of creating — not destroying—an "abounding civilization." The theme is implicit in almost everything he has written, from his earlier books that included *The Universe of Science* down to his more recent *Modern Science* and *A Philosophy for a Modern Man.* Related to this basic assumption are sociological and ethical interpretations that are inseparable from his left-wing political beliefs. War, moreover, has neither muddled his thinking nor shaken his courage. He is wholeheartedly anti-Fascist but believes that an armed resistance is meaningless unless it is strengthened by an extension of peoples' rights and liberties, working-class organization, and socialized industry. His books and articles have a more-than-average effectiveness: he not only has considerable to say but his manner of saying it has neither the technical arrogance of a scientific tract nor the saccharine simplicity of an overly popularized piece of writing.

PRINCIPAL WORKS: The Universe of Science, 1932; Science in an Irrational Society, 1934; The Web of Thought and Action, 1934; Thinking, 1935; Elements of the Theory of Probability, 1936; A Philosophy for a Modern Man, 1938; Modern Science, 1939; Science—Curse or Blessing? 1940.

ABOUT: Adams, M. (ed). Science in the Changing World; Huxley, J. Science and Social Needs; Levy, H. A Philosophy for a Modern Man; Macmurray, J. (ed.). Some Makers of the Modern Spirit; New Statesman and Nation July 27, 1940 and August 17, 1940.

LEWIS, DAY. See DAY LEWIS

LEWIS, DOMINIC BEVAN WYNDHAM (1894-   ), British essayist, humorist, and biographer, who signs himself D. B.

Wyndham Lewis, was born in Wales, the descendant of an old and distinguished Welsh family, his father being a clergyman. (He should not be confused with the novelist and painter Wyndham Lewis,^{qv} to whom he is unrelated.) He was intended for the law, but the First World War broke out while he was still a student at Oxford, and he enlisted as a private in the infantry. He served at the front in France, was shellshocked twice, then was sent to Macedonia, where he became seriously ill with malaria. He was invalided out as a second lieutenant in 1918, from Malta, and was just about to return to France when the war ended. He himself says of his entry into literature: "In 1919 I thought of journalism for some reason, and joined the staff of the London *Daily Express* as a columnist, conducting the 'By the Way' column under the pseudonym of 'Beach Comber.' After four years of this I left the *Express,* and since then have written a weekly article of an alleged light nature for the London *Daily Mail.*"

Mr. Lewis is far too modest concerning his achievements; Jan Gordon rightly called him "one of Britain's most brilliant humorists." He is also something of a French scholar, having lived in Paris for many years before the present war, and having done much translation from the French (notably Barbey d'Aurevilly's *Anatomy of Dandyism,* in 1928). He has not only a keen wit of his own, but also an unerring eye for the ludicrous elsewhere, as witness the delightful anthology of bad verse, *The Stuffed Owl,* which he edited in 1930 with Charles Lee.

But he is besides all this a sound—and fascinating—historian, who has written serious works on Louis XI of France, Charles V of the Holy Roman Empire, and François Villon. He has the face of a thinker, with a high broad brow and brooding eyes. Like many professional humorists, he is rather melancholy by nature. He is unmarried.

Mr. Lewis' reputation outside England has been injured by a trivial and regrettable accident—the unfortunate similarity of his name to that of the novelist and painter Wyndham Lewis, a much more assertive personality, and no relation whatever. No two writers could be more unlike. D. B. Wyndham Lewis' position in England is roughly analogous to that of Christopher Morley or of the late Heywood Broun in America—he is warm, gossipy, and whimsical, with scintillating wit half-concealing unusual literary erudition. None of these characteristics can be attributed to the older man of this name except the literary erudition. D. B. Wyndham Lewis describes himself temperamentally (again most unfairly) as "impulsive, lazy, easily imposed upon (except by the Grave and Good), distinctly Celt, full of strong loves and hates, and generally unpleasant."

PRINCIPAL WORKS: A London Farrago, 1922; At the Green Goose, 1923; At the Sign of the Blue Moon, 1924; At the Blue Moon Again, 1925; François Villon: A Documented Study, 1928; King Spider, 1929; On Straw and Other Conceits, 1929; (ed. with Charles Lee) The Stuffed Owl, 1930; Welcome to All This, 1931; Emperor of the West (in America: Charles of Europe) 1931; The Nonsensibus, 1936; (ed.) I Couldn't Help Laughing! An Anthology of War-Time Humour, 1941.

*LEWIS, Mrs. ETHELREDA (189?-   ), South African novelist, is best known as the editor of the reminiscences of "Trader" Horn,^{qv} although she has published works of her own. Her name does not appear in *Who's Who,* the *International Who's Who,* or the *South African Who's Who.* Some references in her works indicate that she was born in England. She came to London in the autumn of 1923 with an introduction to Winifred Holtby, the York-

shire novelist, from Jean McWilliams of Johannesburg, Mrs. Lewis' home, in order to find a publisher for her first novel, *The Harp,* which appeared in the United States in 1925, and was followed by *Flying Emerald* the next year. Both were regarded as competent pieces of story-telling, with authentic African backgrounds and an excellent understanding of human motives and actions. "Winifred and I had tea with her at her Earl's Court boarding house and talked publishers for hours," writes Vera Brittain in *Testament of Friendship.* "Her intense, serious mind (which nevertheless conveyed so successfully the salty, ribald humour of Aloysius Horn) was then, as always, deeply preoccupied with the welfare of the African natives, and her tales of their exploitation stirred Winifred's dominant passion for justice into a longing to go to their aid." When Winifred Holtby was in South Africa in the spring of 1926, Mrs. Lewis organized a small band of white experts to talk over racial problems at a series of meetings in the Workers' Hall, in Johannesburg. She had met "Trader" Horn in 1925, when he came to the back door of her home to sell her a gridiron. "When Alfred Horn first swam into my ken I was about to settle down to a morning's work on the stoop.... With notebook and pencil I approached the doorstep full of the possibilities of Chapter Fourteen" of her novel then in hand. A few minutes' conversation with the old man convinced Mrs. Lewis that she had found a literary treasure-trove. The first volume of *Trader Horn,* edited and rewritten from the patriarch's pencil-scrawled manuscript and amplified from his conversation, was published in June 1927, with an introduction by John Galsworthy, who was in South Africa at the time, and called on both Horn and Mrs. Lewis. It was made a choice of the Literary Guild in New York, and had large bookstore sales also. Mrs. Lewis gathered material for a second and third volume between October 1925 and March 1927. "As for the conversations, he had no idea my constant note-taking was to be part of the book. He knew I was a journalist, always doing vague things with pencil and note-books, and ready to catch any phrases that might fall from the poor man's table."

PRINCIPAL WORKS: The Harp, 1925; Flying Emerald, 1926; The Life and Works of Alfred Aloysius Horn, an Old Visitor. . . .Taken Down and Edited by Ethelreda Lewis (ed.) 1927-32.

ABOUT: Brittain, V. Testament of Friendship: The Story of Winifred Holtby.

*LEWIS, SINCLAIR (February 7, 1885-), American novelist, the first American to win the Nobel Prize for literature, was born in Sauk Center, Minn., which in spite of his denials is generally considered to be the original of Gopher Prairie in *Main Street,* just as Zenith in *Babbitt* is mostly Minneapolis. His father, Dr. Emmet J. Lewis, was a country doctor who

H. Stein

gave his son much of the background for Dr. Kennicott in *Main Street* and some of that for *Arrowsmith* (though Paul DeKruif supplied most of the technical details for that book). His mother, a Canadian but the daughter of a physician who fought in the Union Army during the Civil War, was Emma Kermott. The Lewises were orginally Welsh, but lived in Connecticut and New York State for several generations before immigrating to Minnesota.

"Red" Lewis, a gangling, pink-skinned, freckled, red-haired boy, went from the Sauk Center High School to Yale, where he was graduated in 1908. In 1936 he received an honorary Litt.D. from his alma mater. In college he began to write, and was an editor of the literary magazine. He also became a Socialist, and interrupted his college career to become a janitor of Upton Sinclair's colony, Helicon Hall, until it burnt down. Like most mid-Western boys with literary ambitions, Lewis drifted to New York and tried his luck at free-lancing without marked success. For a while he was assistant editor of *Transatlantic Tales,* then went to Panama to try in vain to get a job on the canal, then under construction. He returned to Yale and finished his course, then began two years of wandering. He worked on a paper in Waterloo, Iowa, returned to New York as a worker for a charity organization, sold a story to *Red Book* and on the proceeds went to California. There he lived in Carmel as part-time secretary to Alice MacGowan and Grace MacGowan Cook, lived with William Rose Benét, his classmate at Yale, ghostwrote for Jack London, and was fired from both the Associated Press and the *Bulletin* (then edited by Fremont Older) in San Francisco as an incompetent reporter. Next came Washington, as assistant editor of the *Volta Review,* a magazine for teachers of the deaf. New York again, and a job as manuscript reader for Frederick A. Stokes; next assistant editor of *Adventure,* then editor of the Publishers' Newspaper Syndicate, and finally editor for the George H. Doran Co. This, his last office position (though he is now book editor of *Newsweek*) he held until 1916, when as the author of two published novels and half a dozen stories in the *Saturday Evening Post,* he felt it was safe to become once more a free-lance writer.

In 1914 Lewis had married Grace Hegger, and they had a son, Wells, named for H. G. Wells. They were divorced in 1925, and later she wrote a thinly-veiled *roman â clef* about their marriage. In 1928 he married Dorothy Thompson,*qv* the celebrated columnist. On their divorce in 1942 Miss Thompson was given custody of their child, Michael.

Until 1920, Sinclair Lewis was just a run-of-the-mill story teller, his novels and stories alike quite in conformity with the current standards of bourgeois entertainment. Then he broke loose, and decided to write a novel for his own pleasure, saying just what he thought, whether it sold or not. The novel was *Main Street.* It has sold some 500,000 copies, has been translated into nearly every European language, has given a new phrase to our dictionaries, and made Lewis a world-figure. It also involved him in a storm of controversy which worried him not at all. He has followed it since by other tendentious and provocative books—*Babbitt, Elmer Gantry,* even *Arrowsmith* and *Ann Vickers.* Each one meant a howl of rage from the groups—Rotarians, evangelists, medical foundations, social workers—who felt themselves attacked. When *Elmer Gantry* was published, a minister in Virginia invited Lewis to come down and be lynched, and one in New Hampshire tried to have him jailed.

Lewis is a most uneven writer. In between his important novels he has kept turning out a series of trivial and superficial books which do nothing to help his reputation and only bewilder his disciples. He seems genuinely uncritical of his own work. The fact is that in spite of his love for a thesis and its exposition, he is not at heart a reformer; he is only presenting a picture of American life as he sees it, and appears to be naively surprised when it outrages the people it portrays. The latest of his books of any social (or literary) value was *It Can't Happen Here,* a savage forecast of an imminent American Fascism which in dramatized form was played by the Federal Theatre Project in cities all over the country. His following novel, *The Prodigal Parents,* disgusted his admirers, who felt betrayed by this bald apology to Babbitt, in the form of an externalization of all Babbitt's views of the younger generation. But that does not worry Lewis, either. He still looks out on the world with the innocent stare of an observant baby, and may at any time upset all the critics by producing another book which will become the Bible of the liberals. It is true, however, that with the years he has become increasingly conservative, as well as increasingly bitter. His humor is all satire now, and frequently it is only sarcasm.

Lewis has the habit of working intensively for months on a book, then loafing for a year or so until he is ready to start the next one. He is an indefatigable researcher, at least so far as his books with social content are concerned. He calls in the assistance of experts in the field (the Rev. L. M. Birkhead of Kansas City for *Elmer Gantry,* De Kruif for *Arrowsmith*), he travels in search of material, and he piles up an imposing array of notes and clippings, before he begins the actual writing. When he is not working hard, he is playing hard. His house in Vermont, where for several years he has lived, is then full of people. When he is a work he lives like a hermit. Recently he has tried his hand (not too successfully) as an actor. He has many fast friends but his truculence has earned him as many enemies as have his novels. Louis Untermeyer has called him "a native blend of boldness and enthusiasm, of skepticism and affirmation." Fundamentally he is still the non-conforming son of a small Middle Western town.

In 1926, when he was awarded the Pulitzer Prize for *Arrowsmith,* he refused it, saying he did not believe in prizes, and though many other authors more worthy than he to receive this one. In 1930, however, he accepted the Nobel Prize, and went to Stockholm to receive it formally. This, he said, was more of a world event than a mere provincial prize-giving. But in his speech of acceptance he named the Americans he considered more eligible to receive it than himself, including Dreiser, Cabell, Willa Cather, and Upton Sinclair.

The critics have never known just how to judge Sinclair Lewis, for the very reason given by one of them, Robert Cantwell, that he is "too prolific, one of the most plunging and erratic writers in our literary history." The late T. K. Whipple said he "studied American society like a Red Indian stalking through the land of his enemies," and the simile is very apt. He is really not so much a constructive or creative novelist as what

J. Donald Adams called him—"the greatest photographer in fiction that we have produced." He has a remarkable gift for slogans, for mimicry of speech, for surface accuracy of delineation. Whether he goes far beneath these is a question. "He is better at caricature than at character," Henry Seidel Canby said. He is often a moralist, sometimes a sentimental moralist; his passion for complete reproduction frequently makes for very dull pages. But he has undoubtedly made a large section of the United States self-conscious; Babbitt can never be quite so openly Babbitty now as he was before, a Dodsworth, an Arrowsmith, a Carol Kennicott, even a Gantry, must now realize themselves as their own type. He has enriched the vocabulary of "the American language" as have few authors. And, as E. M. Forster remarked, "he has lodged a piece of a Continent in the world's imagination." When an Englishman thinks of our Middle West, it is Sinclair Lewis' Middle West, Zenith and Gopher Prairie, that for good or evil he has in mind. "A restless, determined, tall flame," is Carl Van Doren's succinct characterization of Lewis.

PRINCIPAL WORKS: Our Mr. Wrenn, 1914; The Trail of the Hawk, 1915; The Job, 1917; The Innocents, 1917; Free Air, 1919; Main Street, 1920; Babbitt, 1922; Arrowsmith, 1925; Mantrap, 1926; Elmer Gantry, 1927; The Man Who knew Coolidge, 1928; Dodsworth, 1929; Ann Vickers, 1933; Work of Art, 1934; It Can't Happen Here, 1935; Jayhawker and Dodsworth (plays, with Sidney Howard) 1935; The Prodigal Parents, 1938; Bethel Merriday, 1940.

ABOUT: Bechofer-Roberts, C. E. The Literary Renaissance in America; Boyd, E. A. Portraits; Lippmann, W. Men of Destiny; Van Doren, C. Sinclair Lewis (with Bibliography by Harvey Taylor); Whipple, T. K. Spokemen; American Mercury August 1930; Arts and Decoration May 1925; Bookman April 1925, March 1929, July 1931; Bookman (London) January 1924, January 1931; Catholic World May and December 1930; Century July 1925; Current History January 1931; Journal des Débats November 14, 1930; Living Age May 23, 1925; Nation May 19, 1926; New Republic October 11, 1922, October 21, 1936; New York Times Book Review June 30, 1940; North American Review June 1938; Outlook July 6, 1927, November 19, 1930; Revue Politique et Littéraire January 17, 1931; Saturday Evening Post December 26, 1931; Saturday Review of Literature January 28, 1933, January 20, 1934, April 14, 1934, June 12, 1937, February 4, 1939; Time July 12, 1939, November 18, 1940.

LEWIS, WYNDHAM (1886-), English novelist, essayist, and artist (not to be confused with the humorous essayist D. B. Wyndham Lewis,[qv] to whom he is unrelated), was actually born (Percy Wyndham Lewis) in Maine, but of English parents, and was taken to England while still an

infant. He was educated at Rugby and at the Slade School of Art in London. During the First World War he was a bombardier (non-commissioned) in the Royal Artillery, and later a battery officer. He was long editor of the *Blast*, the magazine in which many now well-known writers, including its co-founder Ezra Pound, appeared; and he was the leader of the Vorticist movement, one of the ultra-modern artistic movements of the era of Dadaism, Cubism, and Surrealism. He first became widely known as a novelist, next as  a critic and philosopher, next as a political pamphleteer.

All this time he has continued to paint; his work is hung in many museums, including the Victoria and Albert. It was the rejection of his portrait of Augustus John which caused that distinguished painter to resign from the Royal Academy in 1932. He has traveled all over Europe, and made one long journey to Morocco in 1931. Following the death of the *Blast,* he edited for a while two other "little" magazines, *Tyro* and the *Enemy.* To describe his career in his own words: "I am a novelist, painter, sculptor, philosopher, draughtsman, critic, politician, journalist, essayist, pamphleteer, all rolled into one, like one of those portmanteau-men of the Italian Renaissance. . . . I have been a soldier, a yachtsman, a baby, a hospital patient, a traveler, a total abstainer, a lecturer, an alcoholic, an editor, and a lot more."

In between these various phases of his existence, he has gone for years at a time into total retirement and obscurity, each time to reappear in some new phase. Storm Jameson, differentiating him from the humorous essayist D. B. Wyndham Lewis, called him "the angry one," and that describes him very well. G. W. Stonier accused him of "deadly humorlessness, invective for its own sake," and of "periodical bombing raids on the public." His later works especially conform to no definable category; they are part novel, part essay, part prose poem, but all satire. D. G. Bridson, who called his actual poetry mere flat "pamphleteering in verse," nevertheless said that at his best he "can lash with his rope-end harder as a satirist than any other living writer."

He is bitterly opposed to the social degeneration theory of Spengler and Keyserling, but his philosophical and political opinions are so uniquely his own that they can hardly be elucidated except by reading him. Stonier remarked that he "cannot write badly when he writes at full power," and certainly *Tarr* was a remarkable novel and *Time and Western Man* a thought-provoking discussion.

He is unmarried. Since the outbreak of the Second World War he has been living obscurely in the United States. In appearance he is almost as unusual as in his writing: his self-portraits show a sleek and solemn philosopher, whereas his photographs betray the vitriolic (though pipe-smoking) satirist and bitter fighter, whose formidability is accented by over-sized shell-rimmed spectacles.

PRINCIPAL WORKS: Tarr (novel) 1918; The Art of Being Ruled, 1925; The Lion and the Fox: A Study of the Rôle of Hero in the Plays of Shakespeare, 1926; Time and Western Man, 1927; The Childermass, 1928; Wild Body (short stories) 1928; Paleface: The Philosophy of the Melting-Pot, 1929; Apes of God (novel) 1930; The Diabolical Principle, 1930; The Dithyrambic Spectator, 1931; Hitler, 1931; The Doom of Youth, 1932; Filibusters in Barbary, 1932; Snooty Baronet, 1932; One-Way Song (verse) 1933; Men Without Art, 1934; Left Wings Over Europe: or, How To Make a War About Nothing, 1936; Blasting and Bombardiering (autobiography) 1937; The Revenge for Love (novel) 1937; Count Your Dead: They Are Alive, 1937; The Mysterious Mr. Bull, 1938; Wyndham Lewis: The Artist From "Blast" to Burlington House (autobiography) 1939; The Jews—Are They Human? 1939; The Hitler Cult, 1939; America, I Presume, 1940; The Vulgar Streak, 1941.

ABOUT: Lewis, W. Blasting and Bombardiering, Wyndham Lewis: The Artist From "Blast" to Burlington House; American Review October-November 1935; Canadian Forum June 1936; New Statesman and Nation August 13, 1932; Poetry December 1934; Sociological Review July 1928.

*LEWISOHN, LUDWIG (May 30, 1882-   ), American novelist and critic, was born in Berlin, the son of Jacques Lewisohn

and Minna (Eloesser) Lewisohn (who were first cousins), but was brought to America at the age of seven. He was reared in Charleston, S.C., and says, "at the age of fifteen I was an American, a Southerner, and a Christian." (He had joined the Methodist Church.) He was educated at the College of Charleston (B.A. and M.A. 1901, Litt.D. 1914) and at Columbia (M.A. 1903). After a year with a publishing

company (1904-05), he became a free-lance writer for five years, then in 1910 was appointed an instructor in German at the University of Wisconsin. The next year he became professor of German Language and Literature at Ohio State University, meanwhile building up a reputation as a literary critic and as a translator from French and German. His opposition to the First World War, together with his German birth, finally made this position so uncomfortable that he resigned, and in 1919 became dramatic critic of the *Nation.* From 1920 to 1924 he was its associate editor. Then he went to Paris, where he lived for a number of years. It was there that he first began to interest himself in the Jewish problem and in Zionism, and to think of himself as a Jew. In 1925 he made his first trip to Palestine. He is now honorary secretary of the Zionist Organization of America. In Paris also was written *The Case of Mr. Crump,* which was suppressed in America. His present home is in New York.

A brief word must be said as to Mr. Lewisohn's complicated matrimonial history. In 1906 he was married to Mrs. Mary Arnold (Crocker) Childs, an Englishwoman who is now a dramatist and poet under the pseudonym of "Bosworth Crocker." (Lewisohn's view of the marriage may be obtained from *Up Stream* and from *The Case of Mr. Crump.*) They were divorced about 1925. After a sixteen-year alliance with Thelma Spear, a singer, by whom he had a son, he married Edna Manley, a young journalist. The sordid embarrassments which followed in the courts have been amply recorded by the newspapers and need not be discussed here.

It is rather difficult to evaluate Mr. Lewisohn's personality without making him seem ridiculous, which he is not. He is an abnormally sensitive man, a born romantic, who accepted guilelessly and whole-heartedly all the "promises" of Americanism, and then found himself faced by prejudice and intolerance, which were not lightened by his markedly Jewish appearance. The result was the formation of a real persecution complex, until Benjamin De Casseres could call him "the Great Ostracized" and "The Wandering Jewish Niobe of the ages." There is no doubt that his work has deteriorated as a result. It is not true, as De Casseres puts it, that "there is a sickly plaint in all he writes," but there is a sickly plaint, a whining note of self-defense and self-justification, in far too much of his later work. Only occasionally now does a flash of his old brilliance come through. He is capable of what the late Ernest Sutherland Bates called "creative malice." He has become almost a fanatic and he has made a public show of himself more than once (though in some of these exhibitions he has been the victim rather than the instigator).

But these things must not be allowed to obscure the fact that, despite the limitations of his taste, for the first quarter of the twentieth century he was one of the bright lights of American literature; that his dramatic and literary criticism was as brilliant as it was serviceable; that his translations of Hauptmann and Sudermann "set a new standard"; and that his judgment so far as technique is concerned was once "more nearly infallible than that of any other contemporary writer."

PRINCIPAL WORKS: *Novels*—The Broken Snare, 1908; Don Juan, 1923; The Case of Mr. Crump, 1926; Roman Summer, 1927; The Island Within, 1928; Stephen Escott, 1930; The Last Days of Shylock, 1931; The Golden Vase, 1933; This People, 1933; An Altar in the Fields, 1934; Trumpet of Jubilee, 1937; Forever Wilt Thou Love, 1939. *Criticism*—The Modern Drama, 1915; The Spirit of Modern German Literature, 1916; The Poets of Modern France, 1918; The Drama and the State, 1922; The Creative Life, 1924; Expression in America, 1932 (as the State of American Literature, 1939). *Miscellaneous*—Up Stream (autobiography) 1922; Israel, 1925; Cities and Men, 1927; Mid-Channel: An American Chronicle (autobiography) 1929; Adam (play) 1929; The Permanent Horizon, 1934; The Answer: The Jew and the World, 1939; Haven (with E. M. Lewisohn) 1940; The Renegade, 1942.

ABOUT: Lewisohn, L. Up Stream, Mid-Channel; Lewisohn, L. & E. M. Haven; American Mercury April 1934; American Review December 1933; Bookman July 1931; Canadian Bookman September 1930; Canadian Forum February 1931.

LIDDELL HART, BASIL HENRY

(October 31, 1895-), English military historian, was born in London and educated at St. Paul's School and at Corpus Christi College, Cambridge. While he was still in the university the First World War broke out, and he served through its entirety as a captain of infantry, being severely wounded. He was put on half pay in 1924 and retired in 1927. He gained attention immediately as a military expert, and in 1920, when he was only twenty-five, he was called to write the official post-war manual on infantry training and appointed by the War Office to edit *Small Arms Training.*

Even before that, in 1917, he had evolved the Battle Drill System and other tactical methods which are now official in the British Army; he modernized infantry drill and introduced the theory of indirect approach in strategy. He became military editor of the *Encyclopaedia Britannica,* and from 1925 to 1935 was military correspondent of the London *Daily Telegraph.* He then became military correspondent and adviser on defense for the *Times,* and continued on the staff of this paper until 1939, when he had a nervous breakdown and was obliged to go to the West of England to recover his health. Leslie Hore-Belisha, the former War Minister, was considered to be Captain Liddell Hart's disciple, and they were closely associated in 1937 and 1938; sixty-two of the organizational reforms suggested by Liddell Hart had been achieved by 1939, to the undoubted benefit of the service if to the disgruntlement of the army hierarchy. As the outstanding exponent, in broader military theory, of defense as opposed to attack, his popular prestige naturally declined after the fall of France 1940. He claimed, however—and more impartial observers were inclined to grant him a hearing—that bureaucracy and dissension (or worse) in the French army had prevented any fair test of his "defense principle."

Captain Liddell Hart was Lees-Knowles Lecturer on military history at Trinity College, Cambridge, in 1932-33. In 1934 he held a Leverhulme Research Fellowship. At the International Studies Conference in 1935 his critiques were circulated by the General Staffs; he was one of the British Delegation. He was co-opted a member of the County of London Territorial Association, is an advisory member of the Executive Committee of the League of Nations Union, and is on the Council of the Society for Army Historical Research. In the literary field, he is an active member of the Association of Writers for Intellectual Liberty, and was a vice-president of the P.E.N. Club.

He was married in 1918 to Jessie Stone, and they have one son. Their home is in London. He is a remarkable linguist, who speaks fluently and has made translations from French, German, Italian, Russian, Arabic, "and sixteen other languages." A moustached, long-nosed, long-jawed man, growing bald, with observant eyes behind pince-nez, Captain Liddell Hart was at one time acclaimed as "the architect of Britain's defense." He writes frequent articles for English and American reviews on military history and tactics, and his military biographies, particularly those of Scipio Africanus and of his close friend, the late T. E. Lawrence, are models of their *genre*. His recreation is tennis, which he plays with almost professional skill.

PRINCIPAL WORKS: New Methods of Infantry Training, 1919; Science of Infantry Tactics, 1921; Paris: or The Future of War, 1925; A Greater Than Napoleon: Scipio Africanus, 1926; Lawn Tennis Masters Unveiled, 1926; Great Captains Unveiled, 1927; The Remaking of Modern Armies, 1927; Reputations: Ten Years After, 1928; The Decisive Wars of History: A Study in Strategy, 1929; Sherman: Soldier, Realist, American, 1929; The Real War, 1930 (as A History of the World War 1914-1918, 1935); Foch: The Man of Orleans, 1931; The British Way in Warfare, 1932 (as When Britain Goes to War, 1935); The Future of Infantry, 1933; The Ghost of Napoleon, 1933; Colonel Lawrence: The Man Behind the Legend, 1934; T. E. Lawrence: In Arabia and After, 1934; The War in Outline, 1914-1918, 1936; Europe in Arms, 1937; Through the Fog of War, 1938; T. E. Lawrence to His Biographers (with R. Graves) 1939; The Defense of Britain, 1939; Dynamic Defense, 1940; The Current of War, 1941.

ABOUT: Time March 18, 1940; Wilson Library Bulletin November 1939.

LIDIN, VLADIMIR (1894-), Russian

novelist and short story writer whose name was originally Vladimir Germanovich Gomberg, was born and still lives in Moscow. His work before the Soviet Revolution was mostly in the short story form, and his novels read like expanded short stories; he is still, in form, a disciple of Chekhov and Maupassant, although in spirit he is completely a child of the new era in Russia. He was for many years on the staff of *Izvestia*, the official daily newspaper of the Soviet Government, and still writes articles for it. He has been called "one of the most readable of Soviet reporters." "His milieu," said Gleb Struve, "is that of the Soviet employees, of the old and the new bourgeoisie, the so-called 'Nepmen,' and the new rich of the period of the New Economic Policy, and his subject is as often as not the seamy side of Soviet life." He is nevertheless in good favor with the government, and is a member of the Union of Soviet Writers. He has traveled to some extent outside of Russia, and as recently as 1935 made an extended visit to France, from which he wrote travel articles for *Izvestia*.

As is the case with many Soviet writers, Lidin lays little emphasis on his private life, and little is known of it. Only one of his novels has been translated into English, and though it was published in both England and America, it attracted little attention. Two of his stories have appeared in English: "Glaciers" in *Short Stories Out of Soviet Russia* (edited by John Cournos, 1929), and "Harps" in *Bonfire: Stories Out of Soviet Russia* (edited by S. Knovalov, 1935).

WORK AVAILABLE IN ENGLISH: The Apostate (in America: The Price of Life) 1931.

ABOUT: Struve, G. Soviet Russian Literature.

LIEPMANN, HEINZ (1905-), German-American novelist, writes: "I was born

twice: the first time in Hamburg. My father and grandfather had been seamen. When the World War broke out, my father volunteered, and was killed in action in 1917. Ten months later my mother died of malnutrition. In 1933, the German government had me thrown into a concentration camp  and took my German citizenship away, because I was—as a Jew—not worthy to belong to the German people. As furthermore had committed the crime of believing in liberalism and practical democracy, and the greater crime of not changing these convictions when the Nazis came into power, I was treated in a rather unfriendly manner in the Witmoor concentration camp. After I had succeeded in escaping from the camp, in the spring of 1934, I spent altogether fourteen months in French and English hospitals, and to today I carry one deformed kidney and twelve scars, as memories of my first Fatherland.

"After having spent several winters in the United States, lecturing, I entered New York as an immigrant and since then have lived there. October 12, 1937, is my second birthday, because I believe that a man's real Fatherland is not the country in which he was accidentally born, but the Fatherland of his convictions. I regard myself, though I am not yet a citizen, as a member of this great, humane corporation, the United States.

"After both my parents died, I became a seaman. I returned to Europe in 1922, and walked all over the continent, working here and there. At last I remained in Frankfurt, where I watched the beginnings of the German inflation. Working during the day, I learned bookkeeping and banking at night. After a few clerical jobs, I became a member of a bank. In 1923, at the height of the German inflation, when a loaf of bread cost a billion marks, and you could buy an apartment house for five dollars, I earned big money. After the inflation was over, I first finished my school education, and then began to study at the university in Frankfurt. When I saw that my money wouldn't last long enough for me to finish my medical schooling, I changed to psychology and philosophy. In 1926, I got my Ph.D. degree.

"Around that time, I began to write for the *Frankfurter Zeitung,* the greatest liberal newspaper in Germany. I became assistant theatre critic. When I was offered an engagement at the excellent city theatre of Frankfurt, I accepted. At the end of 1928, I received a call to the Hamburger Kammerspiele, one of the very best theatres, as director and assistant producer. In Hamburg I wrote my first novel, *Nights of an Old Child,* a realistic and lyrical kind of autobiography. My second novel, *Wanderers in the Mist,* received the American Harper Prize for the best German novel.

"Then came Hitler. I joined the secret opposition movement against the Nazis. In hospital in Paris I wrote *Murder Made in Germany,* the first authentic report about Hitler's Germany. This book was published in twelve countries, and became a best seller. The German government tried to suppress the book; the embassies in Holland, England, Poland, Norway, and the United States demanded its confiscation and my arrest for having "insulted the head of a friendly nation." In Holland I was sentenced to one month's imprisonment. After I had spent a pleasant month in the prison of Amsterdam, I went to the next trial, in London. I was discharged, but on appeal by the German Embassy the new sentence was confiscation of the book and £1000 fine, to be paid by the publishers, or six months' imprisonment. I preferred imprisonment. I spent five months (one month off for good behavior) in Wormwood Scrubs, and there wrote the first part of my new book, *Fires Underground.* In 1936 the Nobel Committee commissioned a dozen famous chemists from many countries to collect material for a 'philosophical history,' of chemistry and chemical warfare. They selected me to write the book made from their researches.

"Since 1937, in New York, I have been writing only in English. I have published stories and articles in American magazines and now I plan to start a new novel. I have also lectured frequently."

* * *

Dr. Liepmann escaped from Wittmoor by swimming the Elbe. After two and a half hours he was rescued by a Belgian steamship. He is dark, thin, and earnest looking, and is unmarried.

PRINCIPAL WORKS: Wanderers in the Mist, 1930; Peace Broke Out, 1932; Murder—Made in Germany, 1934; Fires Underground, 1936; Nights of an Old Child (in England: Escape to Life) 1937; Poison in the Air (in England: Death From the Skies) 1937.

ABOUT: American Magazine January 1939; Scholastic February 12, 1940.

LIN, YU-T'ANG (1895-), Chinese-American essayist, writes: "I was born in Amoy, Fukien Province, China. As a third-generation Christian, I was sent to Christian schools, learning English and Western subjects. After marriage, my wife and I went abroad to learn together, and I studied at Harvard, Jena, and Leipzig Universities. I took my B.A. from St. John's,

Shanghai, my M.A. from Harvard, and my Ph.D. from Leipzig. Returning to China, I became in 1923 professor of English philology at Peking National University, and a radical. I aided the radical students, watched massacres, was blacklisted and had to hide, and joined the new revolutionary government in Wuhan as secretary in the Ministry of Foreign Affairs. Finally, when I got tired of that and saw through the farce of revolution, I graduated into an author, partly by inclination, partly by necessity.

"I am the founder and editor of the following: *Analects Fortnightly* (*Lunyü*) a magazine devoted to humor and satire, founded 1932; *This Human World* (*Jenchienshih*), literary fortnightly devoted to essays and criticism, founded 1934; *The Cosmic Wind* (*Yüchoufeng*), containing general articles on literature and contemporary events, founded 1935. I have been on the editorial staff of the *China Critic,* English weekly of Chinese opinion, since 1927, and of *T'ien Hsia Monthly,* English monthly, since 1936.

"I love contradictions. Though I am now a pagan, I think I am about as moral a man as anybody. I am devoted to literature, but have always considered it a mistake that I did not enroll in a scientific school at the start of college. I love China, and I criticize her more frankly and honestly, I believe, than any other Chinese. I admire the West intensely, but am contemptuous of the West's educational psychologists. I have always liked a revolution, but never the revolutionists.

"My wants are few. I want particularly a good library, some good cigars, and a woman who understands and who leaves me free to do my work. My likes are diverse. I like whimsical writers with a fine fancy, but equally I like realistic common sense. I am interested in literature, pretty peasant girls, geology, atoms, music, electrons, electric shavers, and every kind of scientific gadget. I model clay and drip colored wax from candles onto glass to make landscapes and portraits. I enjoy walking in the rain; swim about three yards; blow soap bubbles with my three daughters. I love debates on theology and adore all mountains.

"I love Heine and Stephen Leacock and Heywood Broun; Mickey Mouse and Ronald Colman; Lionel Barrymore and Katherine Hepburn. I hate Kant and economics.

"I don't mind sitting with either ambassadors or common people, but I can't stand ceremonious restraint and have no desire to impress people. I hate a tuxedo because it makes me look like a Chinese waiter. Nor can I endure standing still. I walk up three flights rather than wait for an elevator. My only sport is walking about the streets and lying on the ground in New York's Central Park, when the police don't see me. I am fast at washing dishes, always breaking a few. My prose is composed of nicotine, as I smoke every waking hour, and I can tell on what page the nicotine is thickest. I get dizzy on a glass of beer, but have a sentiment for wine.

"I have never written a line that pleased the authorities, nor have I said anything that would please everybody, or tried to. Some in high places in China criticized *My Country and My People,* saying it was unpatriotic to write so frankly. On the contrary, to hide truth would be to dishonor my country.

"I have never rescued any girls in the city or heathen in the country. I have never been conscious of sin. I am not afraid of old age or death. The ideal man is not a perfect man, but just a likable, reasonable human being, and that is what I am trying my best to be."

* * *

This autobiographical sketch will give an idea of Dr. Lin's delightful style and his easy command of idiomatic English, while for a still closer intimate view of him one should read the naïve and charming book by his three young daughters, called *Our Family.* His own *My Country and My People* and *The Importance of Living* were both best-sellers in the United States, and

Dr. Lin on several nation-wide tours has expounded the philosophy of the latter book. After having tried London and the Continent, the Lins settled in New York. Dr. Lin is a slender, bespectacled man who looks the amiable scholar he is.

PRINCIPAL WORKS IN ENGLISH: Letters of a Chinese Amazon, 1927; Readings in Modern Journalistic Prose, 1928; The Little Critic, 1935; My Country and My People, 1935; Confucius Saw Nancy (a drama) and Essays About Nothing, 1936; A Nun of Taishan and Other Translations, 1936; A History of the Press and Public Opinion in China, 1937; The Importance of Living, 1937; The Wisdom of Confucius, 1938; Moment in Peking (novel) 1939; With Love and Irony, 1940; A Leaf in the Storm, 1941.

ABOUT: Lin, A., A., C.M. Our Family; New York Times Book Review May 4, 1941; Newsweek December 6, 1937; Scholastic March 19, 1938; Wilson Library Bulletin January 1937.

*LINCOLN, JOSEPH CROSBY (February 13, 1870-), American novelist and humorist, was born in Brewster, Mass., on Cape Cod, the son of Joseph Lincoln and Emily (Crosby) Lincoln. His father was a seaman, as his father and grandfather had been before him. "For a mile in each direction from the plain little house of the Lincolns every house contained a  Cap'n." When the boy was a year old, his father died of a fever in Charleston, S.C., and his mother took him up to Boston. In summers, however, the boy got back to the Cape, with its sand dunes and cranberry bogs, and "rode the old stage coach from Harwick to Chatham; he knew the lightkeepers, the fishermen, the life savers, and the cracker-box oracles in the village stores." He went to school at Brewster and Chelsea. College was out of the question, so the Lincolns went to Brooklyn, N.Y., where he entered a broker's office. He hated the work, and has "always felt that they were fully as glad to get rid of me as I was to leave them." Young Lincoln took drawing lessons from Henry ("Hy") Sandham and went to Boston to open an office for commercial art work. He sometimes wrote a verse or joke which was accepted when the drawing it accompanied was refused. Verses published in the *Bulletin* of the League of American Wheelmen, of which he became associate editor in 1896, reached a public of 125,000. In 1897 Lincoln married Florence E. Sargent of Chelsea, Mass.; their son, Joseph Free-

* Died March 10, 1944.

man Lincoln, was later to collaborate with his father on writing two novels.

In 1899 the elder Lincoln moved to New York to write, and in 1902 Albert Brandt of Trenton, N.J., published *Cape Cod Ballads,* his first book, in a yellow-backed volume with illustrations by E. W. Kemble. The *Saturday Evening Post* accepted a Cape Cod short story, and Lincoln wrote more stories and began a novel, written during laborious week-ends. In 1904 came *Cap'n Eri,* the story of three old sea captains who despaired of their joint efforts at housekeeping and advertised for a wife. Its immediate and lasting success assured Lincoln that he had found his vocation. He was enabled to build a Colonial house in Hackensack, N.J., near his friend Sewell Ford, and a summer home at Chatham, Cape Cod. His present address is Villa Nova, Pa. In 1912 the Lincolns lived for a while in England, traveled on the Continent, and visited Switzerland. He has also traversed the United States, delivering his lecture on "Cape Cod Folks" or giving readings from his own books, which follow the same unerring formula and gratify a very large public.

"It would be very hard for me to write a long story which should end dismally," Mr. Lincoln has confessed. "It is only too true that stories in real life frequently end that way, but I don't like my yarns to do so. So it is fair to presume that in whatever books I may hereafter write, the hero and the heroine will be united, virtue rewarded and vice punished, as has happened in those for which I am already responsible." The late Hamlin Garland once wrote of Lincoln: "He looks like . . . an old skipper, hearty, unassuming and kindly. The task which he has set himself is one which calls for a keen sense of character, democracy of sentiment and fancy which never—or very seldom—loses its hold on the solid ground of experience. His plots are sometimes negligible, but his characters, even when they seem a bit repetitious, are a joy. His prosperity is well earned." Lincoln is a member of the Players Club in New York, and the Franklin Inn and Arts clubs in Philadelphia. He writes from 9 A.M. to noon, with a stubby pencil, on large sheets of yellow paper. One of his novels, *Shavings,* was successfully dramatized. *All Alongshore* (1931) is an omnibus volume.

PRINCIPAL WORKS: Cape Cod Ballads, 1902; Cap'n Eri, 1904; Partners of the Tide, 1905; Mr. Pratt, 1906; Cy Whittaker's Place, 1908; Our Village, 1909; The Depot Master, 1910; Cap'n Warren's Wards, 1911; The Woman Haters, 1911; The Rise of Roscoe Paine, 1912; The Postmaster, 1912; Mr. Pratt's Patients, 1913; Kent Knowles,

"Quahaug," 1914; Thankful's Inheritance, 1915; Mary 'Gusta, 1916; Extricating Obadiah, 1917; Shavings, 1918; The Portygee, 1919; Galusha the Magnificent, 1921; Fair Harbor, 1922; Doctor Nye, 1923; Rugged Water, 1924; Queer Judson, 1925; The Aristocratic Miss Brewster, 1927; Silas Bradford's Boy, 1928; Blair's Attic (with J. F. Lincoln) 1929; Blowing Clear, 1930; All Alongshore, 1931; Head Tide, 1932; Back Numbers, 1933; Storm Signals, 1935; Cape Cod Yesterdays, 1935; Great-Aunt Lavinia, 1936; Storm Girl, 1937; A. Hall & Co., 1938; Christmas Days, 1938; Ownley Inn (with J. F. Lincoln) 1939; Out of the Fog, 1940; The New Hope (with J. F. Lincoln) 1941.

ABOUT: Baldwin, C. C. The Men Who Make Our Novels; Overton, G. M. American Nights Entertainment, Authors of the Day; American Magazine July 1919; Forum February 1919; Life July 15, 1940; Publishers' Weekly April 17, 1920; Time August 14, 1939.

LINDBERGH, Mrs. ANNE SPENCER (MORROW) (1906-), American poet and essayist, was born in Englewood, N.J., the daughter of Dwight Whitney Morrow, late United States Ambassador to Mexico, and Elizabeth Reeve (Cutler) Morrow. She was educated at Miss Chapin's School and at Smith College (B.A. 1927, honorary M.A. 1935). She also received

P. Cordes

honorary LL.D. degrees from Amherst College and the University of Rochester in 1939. In 1934 she received the Hubbard Medal of the National Geographical Society. Soon after her marriage she took up flying and received a pilot's license; she is also a licensed radio operator, and has acted in that capacity in the several long air trips she has taken with her husband. Two of her three books have been records of and reflections on these journeys.

All the world knows that Miss Morrow was married to Charles Lindbergh in 1929, that they have had three sons and two daughters, and that their oldest son was kidnapped and murdered. Following that tragedy they went to live first in England, then on an island off the coast of France, then in the Channel Islands, returning to America only after the outbreak of the Second World War. Few such shy, diffident, sensitive persons have been obliged so to live their private lives in public as has been the case with Mrs. Lindbergh. It is to her credit that she remains just what she was in her college days—simple, direct, and unassuming, bearing tragedy with dignity and fame with genuine modesty. She is a person to whom one warms at sight, and much of the criticism of her husband for his political statements has been qualified by the reservation that Mrs. Lindbergh still commands general admiration—even though in *The Wave of the Future* she provided a quasi-mystic, philosophic base for his isolationist (some say totalitarian) views.

From earliest girlhood she wrote poetry, at first merely charming light verse but later lyric poems of some distinction. Indeed, there is a poetic vein in all her prose; no one but a poet could have written her books. She shrank always from the social life considered suitable to the daughter of wealthy and prominent parents; at college she won honors and prizes for her writing. Her poems appear occasionally in the magazines, but they have not yet been collected in a volume. Without being exactly pretty, she is attractive, with dark hair, a face still round and girlish in spite of all she has endured, and great dark eyes which look straight at one. The late Amelia Earhart said of her: "She is small of stature and has a charming dignity when surrounded by people."

North to the Orient, her first book, was evidence of her possession of the first of the characteristics attributed to her as a writer by Amy Loveman—"the seeing eye." With *Listen, The Wind,* through which the wind seems actually to blow, she proved her possession of the second characteristic—"the singing heart." In her brief, sharply criticized essay, *The Wave of the Future* (1940), which many liberal writers condemned as a document of "appeasement" and a defeatist acquiescence to the Fascist menace—"a wave of the past"—Mrs. Lindbergh tried to explain her sense of the inevitability of history in a simple (perhaps too simple) poetic metaphor. Even her severest critics, however, concede her personal integrity and sincerity.

PRINCIPAL WORKS: North to the Orient, 1935; Listen, The Wind, 1938; The Wave of the Future, 1940.

ABOUT: Life January 20, 1941; Literary Digest March 9, 1929, January 11, 1936; Time October 14, 1940.

LINDSAY, JACK (1900-), Australian novelist and classical scholar, writes: "I was born in Melbourne. My father is Norman Lindsay,^{qv} the artist. My teens were spent in Brisbane, Queensland, where (wholly on scholarships) I was educated at the Boys' Grammar School and the University, taking a first class honors in Latin and Greek. After some largely misdirected efforts to start a literary movement in Sydney (to find the next stage after the used-up bush-school), I came to England in 1926. For some four years I was associated with the fine-press movement in London, doing mainly translations from Greek and Latin, verse and prose. With the break that occurred at the end of the 1920's, I had to find some new application of whatever faculties I owned; and after a difficult period hammered out a method for historical novels. From 1933 to the present my work has been on those lines, though I have now turned more towards direct historical analysis.

"My early work was largely in verse, abortive efforts to write poetic drama without getting the point of contemporary contact. With the novel I began to find a medium for coming to grips with all my intellectual interests. Starting with a certain philosophic discipline created by apprenticeship to Plato and Nietzsche, I began making strenuous efforts to stabilize a world-view based subjectively on Freud and objectively on Frazer's *Golden Bough.* My classical bias took me to the period of the Caesarian revolution for my material. Hence my first four novels. I found that the work of getting the political aspects into focus with the world-view derived from Freud and Frazer led me into more generalized questions of the nature of development, on the one side into pantheist philosophy such as Spinoza's, and on the other into science, especially the work of Darwin. I thus arrived, on my own, at a Dialectical Materialistic philosophy before I had read a word by any of the writers of that school.

"All these efforts to reformulate continually more comprehensive theses of development I kept on trying to put into my novels —one on ancient Egypt, another on Bruno, and a triad on the main points of struggle in England. *Brief Light* was a return to the Roman scene [it is a fictionalized biography of Catullus]; and in another novel I have dealt with the Carthage of Hannibal.

"One side-line (1937-39) has been mass-declamation poems which enable me to claim the position of the only English poet with a mass-audience, as they have been performed before many tens of thousands; for instance, before huge crowds in Trafalgar Square, though taking some half an hour to declaim. Beginning in 1930 without any political position, I was thus quickly led by my historical analyses to an active anti-Fascist position and to a realization of the bases of cultural vitality in the liberating movements of mass-life. Recently, however, my main interest has been history in general, especially with reference to the problems of cultural development. In *A Short History of Culture,* I essayed a broad view; but raised far too many new issues for the space. I am therefore working on separate aspects of the theme, treating them with extreme detail and documentation."

* * *

Mr. Lindsay is still living in London. He is unmarried. He is an enormously prolific writer, issuing several volumes a year; besides these he has edited several anthologies (including, with Edgell Rickwood, *A Handbook of Freedom*) and has published translations of numerous Greek and Roman authors, among them Theocritus, Catullus, Propertius, Petronius, Ausonius, and the Mediaeval Latin poets. His only recreation, he says, is sun-bathing, opportunities for which in London are hardly frequent. Many of his translations are illustrated by his father, one of the best known contemporary British artists.

PRINCIPAL WORKS: *Poetry and Verse Drama*— Marino Faliero, 1927; Fauns and Ladies, 1928; Passionate Neatherd, 1929; Hereward, 1930; Helen Comes of Age, 1931; Dionysos, 1932. *Novels*— Cressida's First Lover, 1932; Rome For Sale, 1934; Caesar Is Dead, 1935; Last Days With Cleopatra, 1935; Despoiling Venus, 1935; Storm at Sea, 1935; Runaway, 1935; The Wanderings of Wenamen, 1936; Come Home at Last (short stories) 1936; Rebels of the Goldfields, 1936; Shadow and Flame, 1937; Adam of a New World, 1937; Sue Verney, 1937; 1649, 1938; Lost Birthright, 1939; Brief Light, 1939; Stormy Violence, 1941; Hannibal Takes a Hand, 1941; Light in Italy, 1941. *Miscellaneous*—William Blake: Creative Will and the Poetic Image, 1929; The Romans, 1935; Marc Antony: His World and His Contemporaries, 1936; John Bunyan: Maker of Myths, 1937; The Anatomy of Spirit, 1937; A Short History of Culture, 1939.

LINDSAY, NORMAN (February 23, 1879-   ), Australian artist and novelist, was born Alfred William Norman Lindsay in  Creswick, Victoria, the son of a physician. However, he, his brother Lionel, and his sister, all turned to art at an early age. The sister married the famous cartoonist W. H. Dyson; in fact, Dyson is doubly related to Lindsay, since Lionel Lindsay married Jean Dyson. Norman Lindsay, after an elementary schooling, at sixteen joined the staff of a Melbourne paper, drawing illustrations. Since 1901 he has been the chief cartoonist of the Sydney *Bulletin,* and is undoubtedly the best-known black-and-white artist in Australia. He has worked in many mediums—oil, water-color (which he prefers), etching, lithography, wood-engraving, and modeling in cement. In black-and-white he has illustrated many books, chiefly "the bawdier classics"— Petronius, Boccaccio, Casanova, and the like. His *Pen Drawings* have been collected in several volumes, and he is represented in many galleries in the Antipodes and in England, including the Exhibit of Australian Art in London. He is married, and the father of three sons, all of whom, Jack,[qv] Philip, and Raymond, have become novelists, since the Lindsay family seems to move in professional cycles from one generation to the next. His home is in Springwood, N.S.W. His hobby is the making of ship-models, many of them genuine works of art, such as his model of Captain Cook's "Endeavor," which is now in the Melbourne Art Gallery.

As a writer, Norman Lindsay first became known outside his native land by *Red Heap,* censored in Australia but popular in America under the title of *Every Mother's Son.* This was not, however, by any means his first book or even his first novel. Writing is to him purely an avocation, a further outlet for his bubbling spirits. It is an absorbing avocation, nevertheless, which has consumed a good deal of his time and energy, as witness his co-sponsorship of the Endeavor Press, and of the family magazine, *Vision,* which he and his sons founded in 1924. (By "family magazine" is meant merely that it was the joint enterprise of the Lindsay family, not at all that its contents were suited to what our grandparents called "family reading!") In literature as in art, indeed (with the exception of his powerful political cartoons), Norman Lindsay is, to quote C. Hartley Grattan, "a sort of healthy, roistering Aubrey Beardsley."

Much of this insistence in his work and that of his sons on "drinking and wenching" is pure reaction from the drab and Puritanical conventionality of Australian life. It has actually injured Norman Lindsay as a novelist, since it smacks more than a little of an outmoded era even earlier than the "jazz age"—the era of the *Yellow Book* and *fin de siècle* in England. As *The Cautious Amorist* and *Age of Consent* show, Lindsay is "an expert plot-builder" and a master of cool irony. His rowdyism is three-quarters rebellion, and only obscures his authentic merits as a writer. But it may be expected that every Lindsay novel will be "frank and funny." Since he is a true humorist, the frankness is actually equalled by the fun.

Rex Hunter has described Norman Lindsay: "He has the Australian gauntness without the Australian height; moves like quicksilver; possesses the enormous energy of the true creator. His thin, pale face is lit by keen blue eyes, punctuated by a beaked nose like an exclamation mark, fringed by gray hair cut straight across the forehead." He and his sons are the "horrible examples" of all the blue-noses (known as "wowsers") in Australia. In a less provincial environment he would be seen in a juster light, as a brilliant artist and cartoonist, and an exceedingly clever and uninhibited novelist.

PRINCIPAL WORKS: A Curate in Bohemia, 1913; The Magic Pudding, 1919; Creative Effort: Essays on Life and Art, 1920; Red Heap (in America: Every Mother's Son), 1931; Mr. Gresham and Olympus, 1932; Saturdee, 1933; Pam in the Parlour, 1934; The Cautious Amorist, 1934; Age of Consent, 1938.

LINDSAY, THOMAS MARTIN (October 18, 1843-December 6, 1914), Scottish historian, was born at Lesmahagow, Lanarkshire, the eldest son  of Alexander Lindsay, a minister of the Relief Church, and Susan Irvine (Martin) Lindsay. He was educated at the universities of Glasgow and Edinburgh. At Edinburgh Lindsay was awarded the Ferguson scholarship and Shaw fellowship, both open to graduates of any Scottish university, and made a brilliant record in philosophy. He became assistant to Professor Alexander Campbell Fraser, and studied for the ministry of the Free Church of Scotland. Leaving New College, Edinburgh, in 1869, Lindsay became assistant to the minister of St. George's Free Church. The Church's General Assembly elected him to the chair of church history in its theological college at Glasgow, and in 1902 he became its principal. Lindsay's zeal for social work, especially for foreign missions, matched his ability as an inspiring teacher of history; he visited the mission fields in Syria and spent a year in India. Brief textbooks on the gospels of St. Mark, St. Luke, and the Acts of the Apostles; a long article on Christianity for the ninth edition of the *Encyclopaedia Britan-*

nica (1875-88), and a chapter on Luther for the second volume of the *Cambridge Modern History* were preliminary exercises for his largest and most important work, *A History of the Reformation in Europe,* in 1906-07. Descriptive of "a great religious movement amid its social environment," it broke fresh ground with its investigations into family religious life in Germany in the decades immediately preceding the Reformation. Lindsay's collections of caricatures and illustrations of costume testified to his belief in the value and significance of records of domestic and social life. He had "learning, candor and full-blooded humanity," shown for instance in his defense of William Robertson Smith in the courts of the Free Church against a heresy prosecution (1877-81); his interest and active participation in the crofter agitations in the West Highlands associated with the early career of Joseph Chamberlain; and the enthusiasm he shared with his wife, Anna Dunlop Lindsay, for the education of women. They had three sons and two daughters. Lindsay has been called the most important Scottish contributor to European history since William Robertson.

PRINCIPAL WORKS: Luther and the German Reformation, 1900; The Church and the Ministry in the Early Centuries, 1903; A History of the Reformation in Europe, 1906-1907.

ABOUT: Ross, J. The Fourth Generation. Glasgow Herald December 8, 1914.

LINDSAY, VACHEL (November 10, 1879-December 5, 1931), American poet, was born Nicholas Vachel Lindsay in Springfield, Ill., a town which he was to regard afterwards with a sort of mystical adoration, largely because of its association with Lincoln. He attended Hiram College for three years, but left to go to Chicago to study at the Art Institute. He had never  thought of himself as a poet at that time, and in fact never completely lost interest in drawing. Some of his books he illustrated himself.

Harris & Ewing

Lindsay attended the Art Institute for three years, at night, working in a department store during the daytime. In 1904 he went to New York and studied at the New York Art School. But he was utterly unable to sell any of his drawings or even to find any other kind of work, so in 1905 he set out on a vagabond tour through the west, reciting his own poems in return for food and lodging and distributing a leaflet which he called *Rhymes To Be Traded for Bread*. This was by no means the last tramping trip he took, and in one sense he continued them all his life, for recitation (or rather chanting) of his poems remained, in spite of his many published volumes, his main source of livelihood. During nearly all the winters between 1905 and 1910, when he could not tramp through the country districts of the West and South, he lectured for the Y.M.C.A. (in New York and Springfield) or for the Illinois Anti-Saloon League. In his habits and cultural viewpoint he remained what he had been born—a small town Middle Western American.

As the years went on, Lindsay grew increasingly weary of this incessant wandering, the constant repetition of utterances already made. As early as 1922 he complained that when he spoke on some such subject as the principles of versification the audience always demanded that he "cease his trifling" and give them "The Congo" or "General William Booth Enters Into Heaven." In 1925 he married Elizabeth Conner, whom he had first met when he lectured at Mills College, in Oakland, Calif., where she was a student and where after his death she taught English. Soon there were a son and a daughter to support as well, and Lindsay kept on in the same deadening treadmill. Whether he had any better and greater work in him which he could not find time to do is a nice question, though he himself certainly believed so. After the first three books he showed a steady deterioration of power; how much of this was due to the life he was forced to lead, to poverty, ill health, and worry, and how much to the fact that he had written himself out, can of course never be known now.

For a while the Lindsays lived in Spokane, Wash., Mrs. Lindsay's home; then they returned to Springfield, to the house in which Lindsay had been born. It was there that he died at fifty-two. Edgar Lee Master's biography is unreliable, but it does give a hint of the gloom and despair of the poet's last years. There seems little doubt that to some extent his mind was affected; he lost himself in a maze of symbolism and hieroglyphics. The official cause of his sudden death was coronary thrombosis (he was besides a sufferer from diabetes); Masters says he took poison.

The fact seems to be that the immense gusto of his earlier years finally wore itself out. He had the impulse of a troubadour or a minnesinger to sing directly to the people, but he lacked sustained vitality. Also, the narrowness of his childhood environment cramped and limited his power. Lindsay was never an intellectual; as Ernest Sutherland Bates said, he was "essentially intuitive, and almost devoid of critical ability. . . . His manner grew steadily more pompous, hieratic. . . . He had already become a legend rather than a living reality long before his death."

He conceived of himself primarily as a teacher, an evangelist. His was to be the voice of the true, the genuine America. Hazelton Spencer said that his "optimism was exactly the same brand as Emerson's or Whitman's," but he had much less to communicate than they. It is true, however, as Spencer added, that "no man ever had a loftier vision of his country or tried harder to help his fellow-citizens realize it."

His poems were meant to be chanted, as he did chant them. Their first appearance in *Poetry* heralded a new *genre* in American verse, a note which no one else has ever caught exactly and which he himself as last ceased to do more than echo. Benjamin De Casseres dubbed him "the jazz Blake, St. Francis of Assisi playing the saxophone at the Firemen's Ball," and though the intention was unfriendly the characterization is apt. He was raucous, noisy, exuberant, but so was the America he knew and represented. He thought it was the national spirit in its eternal aspect; actually it was the tone of an era, and the era is dead.

But that does not mean that all of Vachel Lindsay's poetry is dead as well. If they had no more than historical significance, his Negro, Indian, Salvation Army, and Western themes would still find interested readers. They have more than that. There is in them the unmistakable voice of a real talent, a much frailer talent than Lindsay and his first admirers thought he had, a talent largely frustrated by the limitations of his mind, but still authentic and in some measure unique. The "Gospel of Beauty" seems quaintly outdated today, and it is hard to think of a poet who could with complete conviction speak on behalf of the Anti-Saloon League. Perhaps he was the last spokesman of a time and place that had been largely inarticulate, and that now belong only in the archives. Time has moved so swiftly of late years that the present treads on the heels of the past. Lindsay has been dead for little more than a decade, but in many ways he seems farther away than do Emerson or Thoreau. He was a tired, sick, unhappy man who, whatever the actuating means, was glad to die. He was not a great poet nor will he have any appreciable influence on American poetry of the future. But while the drums still beat in the Congo and still pound at the gate of heaven for General William Booth to enter in, Vachel Lindsay will not be entirely forgotten. In his few best poems, the pulse still throbs.

PRINCIPAL WORKS: *Poetry*—General William Booth Enters Into Heaven and Other Poems, 1913; The Congo and Other Poems, 1914; The Chinese Nightingale and Other Poems, 1917; The Golden Whales of California and Other Rhymes, 1920; The Daniel Jazz, 1920; Going-to-the-Sun, 1923; Collected Poems, 1924; Going-to-the-Stars, 1926; The Candle in the Cabin, 1926; Johnny Appleseed, 1928; Every Soul Is a Circus, 1929; Selected Poems, 1931. *Prose*—The Tramp's Excuse, 1909; Adventures While Preaching the Gospel of Beauty, 1914; The Art of the Moving Picture, 1915; A Handy Guide for Beggars, 1916; The Golden Book of Springfield, 1920; The Litany of Washington Street, 1929; Letters to A. Joseph Armstrong, 1940.

ABOUT: Davison, A. Some Modern Poets; Graham, S. Tramping With a Poet in the Rockies; Kreymborg, A. Our Singing Strength; Lewisohn, L. Expression in America; Lindsay, V. Adventures While Preaching the Gospel of Beauty; Masters, E. L. Vachel Lindsay: A Poet in America; Morley, C. Ex Libris Carissimis; Trombley, A. E. Vachel Lindsay, Adventurer; Van Doren, C. Many Minds; American Mercury December 1926, April 1932, July 1933; Bookman October 1926, March 1932, April 1932; Commonweal December 23, 1931; Magazine of Art August 1938; Nation December 16, 1931; Poetry January 1927, January 1932; Saturday Review of Literature December 19, 1931, January 9, 1932, August 10, 1935, August 10, 1940; Spectator January 23, 1932.

LINKLATER, ERIC (1899-), Scottish novelist, was born in Dounby, Orkney Islands (which is still his home), the son of Robert Linklater. He  was educated at the Aberdeen Grammar School (from which he ran away, at twelve, to join the army, but to which he was ignominiously returned) and at the University of Aberdeen (M.A. 1925). He served throughout the First World War as a private in the Black Watch, was severely wounded in 1918, and as invalided home.

For a while at the university he studied medicine, but changed his mind as to his profession midway in his course, and majored in English instead. Immediately after receiving his degree he went to India, where he was assistant editor of the *Times of India,* in Bombay. From there he went to Iran (Persia), returning to England in 1927 as assistant to the professor of English literature at Aberdeen University. After a year he won a Commonwealth Fellowship for travel in the United States. He spent two years, from 1928 to 1930, in this country and covered it assiduously, instead of merely touring the Eastern seaboard as so many transatlantic visitors do.

He had already gained some reputation as a poet, but his first novel, Scottish in background, was written and published during his stay in America. He has never returned to teaching, but has been a successful freelance writer ever since that time, alternating between novels and biographies. In 1933 he married Marjorie MacIntyre, and they have two sons. He is stocky, almost bald, with a fringe of sandy hair, and wears a clipped moustache and gla..es, giving him the appearance of being older than his actual years. His gusto and high spirits, however, are those of youth rather than of middle age. Even his biographical work is lively, though sound; his novels are sometimes more "smart" than clever. But his enthusiasm is infectious, and if he sometimes seems to put down whatever comes next into his head, good or bad, at other times he carries the reader along in a whirlwind of carefree ebullience. On the other hand, when he is deeply concerned with his subject, as in *Men of Ness,* he is capable of a stark, bare style which is highly effective.

Until the Second World War, Eric Linklater varied the monotony of his island life (first in Finstown, then in his native Dounby) by occasional travel, at which times he gave instructions that no mail was to be forwarded to him, since he was intending to bury himself in the life of another country, with an eye to future writing. One of these trips was to China, in 1936, which resulted in a further recital of the adventures of his picaresque hero "Juan," who first appeared as the author's *alter ego* in America. When Mr. Linklater restrains a tendency to pretentious style, which sometimes runs away with him and occasionally (as in *Magnus Merriman*) makes him almost unintelligible, he is one of the most gifted of the less profound contemporary novelists.

Linklater belongs to the Scottish Nationalist Movement and has stood, unsuccessfully, for Parliament. During the Second World

War, as a major, he is actively concerned with the defense of the Orkneys.

PRINCIPAL WORKS: *Novels*—White Man's Saga, 1929; Poet's Pub, 1929; Juan in America, 1931; The Men of Ness: The Saga of Thorleif Coalbiter's Sons, 1932; The Crusader's Key, 1933; Magnus Merriman, 1934; God Likes Them Plain, 1935; Ripeness Is All, 1935; Juan in China, 1937; The Sailor's Holiday, 1937; The Impregnable Women, 1938; Judas, 1939. *Miscellaneous*—A Dragon Laughed and Other Poems, 1930; Ben Jonson and King James, 1931; The Devil's in the News, 1934; The Revolution, 1934; Robert the Bruce, 1934; The Lion and the Unicorn: or What England Has Meant to Scotland, 1935; The Man on My Back (autobiography) 1941; The Northern Garrisons, 1941; Cornerstones: A Dialogue Between Confucius, Lincoln, Lenin and a British Pilot, 1941.

ABOUT: Linklater, E. The Man on My Back; Canadian Forum December 1931.

LIPPMANN, WALTER (September 23, 1889-   ), American editor and publicist, was born in New York, the son of Jacob and

R. L. Jackson

Daisy (Baum) Lippmann. He was in the class of 1910 at Harvard, but took his degree in 1909, acting in what would have been his senior year as assistant to George Santayana, the philosopher, and taking graduate courses in philosophy. He then became an investigator for Lincoln Steffens on *Everybody's Magazine,* but when Steffens left the magazine, Lippmann also resigned and for a while made his way by free-lance journalism and reviewing. Through Graham Wallis, the English sociologist, he had become a Socialist, and in 1912 he went to Schenectady, N.Y., as private secretary to George R. Lunn, elected that city's first Socialist mayor. After a few months he left this position to go to Maine to help on an English translation of Freud; while there he began writing a book which became his first volume, *A Preface to Politics,* and which had the curious honor of being praised by Freud and becoming the Bible of the future Progressive Party under Theodore Roosevelt.

When the *New Republic* was founded in 1914, Lippmann became an associate editor, and so remained until 1919, though in 1917 he took leave of absence to become assistant to Newton D. Baker, then Secretary of War, and to help prepare the Versailles Peace Conference, which he attended. From the *New Republic* he went to the old New York *World,* and by 1924 was its chief editorial writer, by 1929 its editor. When the *World*

died in 1931, Lippmann made explicit a complete reversal of viewpoint which had been implicit, though unnoticed, in his books for some time. He went to the *Herald Tribune* as a special writer and still holds that post. From a liberal with distinctly leftist tendencies he had become a pronounced right-winger, and in 1936 he shocked his former associates by openly announcing himself as a Republican. As Max Lerner said: "The compass of his thinking has swung round under the pressure of events. . . . *The Good Society* [1937] is his renunciation of the earlier Lippmann and his consolidation of the latter-day Lippmann." And John Flynn commented: "As Mr. Lippmann marched from left to right, from camp to camp, he neglected to change the flag he carried. . . . Now he has formally hauled down the old flag he once bore so high."

Walter Lippmann is now the oracle of the conservative intellectuals, a senator of Phi Beta Kappa, a member of the Board of Overseers at Harvard, of the National Institute of Arts and Letters, and of the American Academy of Arts and Letters. He has houses in New York, on Long Island, and in Florida, and is fond of riding, fishing, and refereeing polo games, though he does not himself play polo. There is no reason to suppose that there was any ulterior reason for his political about-face except the natural effect of increasing prosperity on a fundamentally conservative nature. Mabel Dodge Luhan has remarked that he "might lose his glow in a fight, but he will never lose an eye." He is not a fighter; he is a scholar in politics, much as Henry Cabot Lodge was in another time. He has been consistent in his later views; he left the American Newspaper Guild when it affiliated with the C.I.O., and he proposed as a solution for the Jewish problem in Europe that refugee Jews all be colonized in Africa.

The *American Magazine* called him "the great elucidator" and "the man with the searchlight mind," and it is as a philosophic critic of the political, economic, and ethical scene that he has built his reputation. In 1931 he won a $2,000 prize from the *Yale Review* for an article on the American press, and his newspaper articles, like his books, have a markedly scholarly tinge. But his writing is never stodgy; on the contrary it is unfailingly brilliant.

Mr. Lippmann looks younger than his years, with his hair still dark, his eyes still keen and searching, and his face unlined. In 1917 he was married to Faye Albertson;

they were divorced at the end of 1937 and in 1938 he married Helen Byrne Armstrong. He has no children. He has received honorary LL.D. degrees from twelve American colleges and universities, and Litt.D. from Columbia and Dartmouth.

PRINCIPAL WORKS: A Preface to Politics, 1913; Drift and Mastery, 1914; The Stakes of Diplomacy, 1915; The Political Scene, 1919; Liberty and the News, 1920; Public Opinion, 1922; The Phantom Public, 1925; Men of Destiny, 1927; American Inquisitors, 1928; A Preface to Morals, 1929; The United States in World Affairs (with W. O. Scroggs) 1931, 1932, 1933; Interpretations, 1932 and 1933-35; The Method of Freedom, 1934; The New Imperative, 1935; The Good Society, 1937; The Supreme Court: Independent or Controlled? 1937; Some Notes on War and Peace, 1940.

ABOUT: Christian Century September 23, 1936; Commonweal March 13, 1936, August 4, 1939; Nation November 27, 1937; New Republic September 23, 1936; Saturday Review of Literature January 7, 1933; Time September 27, 1937, November 13, 1939.

"LLEWELLYN, RICHARD." See LLEWELLYN LLOYD, R. D. V.

LLEWELLYN LLOYD, RICHARD DAVID VIVIAN ("Richard Llewellyn")

(1907?-   ), Welsh novelist and playwright w h o understandably signs a shortened form of his compound name to his works, w a s b o r n a t St. David's, in Pembrokeshire, Wales. "My school years were spent in St. David's, Cardiff, and London," he writes. "At sixteen I was sent to Italy to learn hotel management, starting in the kitchen. In Venice I studied painting and sculpture in my spare time, and worked with an Italian film unit, learning the rudiments of the cinema. I should describe the years up to nineteen as turbulent. Realizing a need for discipline, I joined the ranks of H. M. Regular Army and served both at home and abroad [for five years]. Returning in 1931, jobless, I turned to the cinema, and entered the studios as extra player in order to study the methods of men then in charge of production. In an interval I became a reporter on a penny film paper, and it was during this period that I started writing for pleasure."

Returning to the cinema, Llewellyn Lloyd became assistant director, scenarist, production manager, and, finally, director. Then a slump in the industry turned him to playwriting, and his *Poison Pen,* a psychological mystery play, was successfully produced in London.

How Green Was My Valley was begun in St. David's, from a draft written while he was serving with the army in India, and was rewritten in Cardiff, and again "in St. James's Park, London, during a period of unemployment." After another period of work in Wales—at St. David's, and Cardiff, and Llangollen—he returned to London to sign an agreement with Michael Joseph, the London publisher, to whom he had been introduced by a friend. In the summer of 1939 Llewellyn turned over the manuscript of the completed novel, and it was published in Great Britain in October of the same year. It sold 50,000 copies in four months, and went far past the hundred thousand mark in the United States when published early in 1940. There is not a character or an incident in this lyrical story of the vicissitudes of a mining family in South Wales from the late 1870's to the beginning of the present century which does not have some basis in fact. Every scene and character, however, is a composite creation.

"Mr. Llewellyn has used the novelist's license to rearrange Nature," says the editor of *John o'London's Weekly.* "His Valley is not one valley but a dozen. There are fifty Gwilyn Morgans and Reverend Mr. Gruffydds. The conflict between God and Mammon still goes on, exactly as he describes it, in any one of a hundred communities. . . . It still astonishes me that a man who has led the life Mr. Llewellyn has led, who has roughed it as he has roughed it, should have come out of the blue as a finished literary artist, with every resource of tenderness, pity, humor, and realism at his fingers' ends. I expected to meet a dreamer, and I met a man who as Chief Transport Officer for E.N.S.A. [Entertainments National Services Association] is directing the movements of nearly 500 concert parties which are going about entertaining the troops in England and France." (This was written early in 1940; a few weeks later the author rejoined the army, with the rank of Captain in the Welsh Guards.)

"Richard Llewellyn Lloyd is a man of medium height, with small hands and feet, and with eyes and hair as black and shining as a lump of Welsh coal. The bridge of his roman nose is a little out of line. The reason for this is that at one stage of his extraordinary career he was a boxer. It cannot have been easy to hold his own with such small—even delicate—hands, but one has only to feel his firm grip, to observe his steady eye, his alert step, and the jaunty tilt of his head to realize that he is well able to look after himself."

Clifton Fadiman called *How Green Was My Valley* "very Welsh in its defects no less than in its qualities," and another critic comments that the novel seems to fall off in vigor towards the end. But the book's myriad readers seem to agree with the *Atlantic Monthly* that it is "a story as noble as it is simple and strong. It is a beautiful story, too, told in words which have Welsh music in them." Filmed in 1941, *How Green Was My Valley* was judged the best American motion picture of the year by the industry's "Academy."

PRINCIPAL WORKS: Poison Pen: A Play in Three Acts, 1938; How Green Was My Valley (novel) 1939.

ABOUT: Christian Science Monitor Magazine February 24, 1940; Current Biography 1940; John o' London's Weekly March 15, 1940.

LLOYD, RICHARD LLEWELLYN.
See LLEWELLYN LLOYD, R. D. V.

LOAN. See VAN LOAN

*LOCKE, ALAIN LE ROY (September 13, 1886-), American Negro essayist, writes: "I was born in Philadelphia, only  son of Pliny I. and Mary (Hawkins) Locke, native Philadelphians and school teachers; and thus into smug gentility. A professional career was mandatory, all the more so because of the frantic respectability of the free, educated Negro tradition, their main bulwark against proscription and prejudice. First, it was to be medicine, which early ill health toned down to the family calling. After the public schools, the Central High School (1902), and the Philadelphia School of Pedagogy (1904), I entered Harvard College, from which I was graduated with honors in philosophy and English in 1907. There I was exposed to the Golden Age of liberalism and, deeply influenced by Barrett Wendell, Copeland, Briggs, and Baker, shed the Tory restraints for urbanity and humanism, and under the spell of Royce, James, Palmer, and Santayana, gave up Puritan provincialism for critical-mindedness and cosmopolitanism. On a

J. L. Allen

Rhodes Scholarship from Pennsylvania, the next three years were spent expanding these viewpoints at Oxford, followed by a year of further specialization in philosophy at the University of Berlin. Returning home in 1911, I spent six months traveling in the South—my first close-range view of the race problem—and there acquired my lifelong avocational interest of encouraging and interpreting the artistic and cultural expression of Negro life, for I became deeply convinced of its efficacy as an internal instrument of group inspiration and morale and as an external weapon of recognition and prestige.

"So, while teaching philosophy at Howard University from 1912 to the present, I have devoted most of my literary effort and time to this avocational interest of Negro culture, with occasional excursions into the sociological side of the race question. My connection with the literary and art movement, styled in 1925 the 'New Negro' Renaissance, was thus a logical outcome of this artistic creed and viewpoint."

* * *

Dr. Locke received his Ph.D. at Harvard in 1918. He is a member of Phi Beta Kappa, the American Philosophical Association, the International Institute of African Languages and Cultures, and the League of American Writers, and a corresponding member of the Académie des Sciences Coloniales, Paris. He is unmarried, lives in Washington, D.C., and is an Episcopalian. Besides his books, he has edited volumes of Negro poems and plays, and writes frequently for the literary and sociological magazines.

PRINCIPAL WORKS: Race Contacts and Inter-Racial Relations, 1916; The Problem of Classification in Theory of Value, 1918; The New Negro, 1925; The Negro in America, 1933; Negro Art: Past and Present, 1936; The Negro and His Music, 1937; (ed.) The Negro in Art, 1940; (ed.) When Peoples Meet: A Study in Race and Culture Contacts (with B. J. Stern) 1942.

LOCKE, WILLIAM JOHN (March 20, 1863-May 15, 1930), English novelist, was born in Demerara, British Guiana, the elder son of a Barbados banker, John Locke, and his wife, Sarah Elizabeth. Locke senior removed to Trinidad in 1864, and William, after being sent home to England at the age of three and remaining there until he was twelve, completed his schooling at Queen's Royal College, Trinidad. From there he won an exhibition to St. John's College, Cambridge, which he entered in 1881, graduating three years later with honors in

* Died June 9, 1954.

the mathematical tripos. Locke's exact movements for the next five years are hard to trace in detail, but he seems to have spent some considerable time in France improving his knowledge of Gallic life and culture, both of which held out very great appeal to him. In 1889-90 we find him schoolmastering at

the Oxford Military College, Temple Cowley, his subject being not mathematics but senior French. From there he passed for a brief period to Clifton College, Bristol, where he fell seriously ill and contracted tuberculosis. In 1891 he went to Trinity College, Glenalmond, where he taught modern languages until 1897.

Locke had already begun to write, having brought out his first novel, *At the Gate of Samaria,* in 1895; but even after the publication of three more in the two following years, he felt he could not rely on his pen for a livelihood. Yet in 1897 he was able to abandon teaching (which was slavery to him) for a far more congenial occupation, being selected from a large number of candidates as Secretary to the Royal Institute of British Architects, who were seeking a cultivated layman rather than an architect. He was highly interested in architecture, and held this post very happily for ten years until in 1907, having made a great deal of money by his ninth and tenth novels, he resigned. These two books were *The Morals of Marcus Ordeyne* (1905), which he dramatized the next year and which was later filmed, and *The Beloved Vagabond* (1906), the quintessence of Lockean gay romanticism, which made his name known to great bodies of readers in Great Britain and America.

Now free of all routine, Locke produced books rapidly year after year and had much stage success as well, being responsible for five plays staged in London between 1907 and 1912. *The Joyous Adventures of Aristide Pujol* (1912) was one of the gayest and best of his works, containing, among other things, the delightful episode of a young Frenchman teaching his language in a girls' school and instructing his charges very thoroughly in Parisian slang.

During the War of 1914-18 Locke turned his country home at Hemel Hempstead, Hertfordshire, into a rankers' hospital at his own cost. He was very active, too, on behalf of Belgian refugees, his services in this cause

being rewarded by the conferment of the Belgian Ordre de la Couronne. He went to Cannes in 1921 for reasons of health. He was taken seriously ill in the winter of 1929 and died in Paris at sixty-seven after an operation.

Not among the serious, "psychological" novelists, Locke had no "mission" save to entertain, and this he did supremely well in his best works, evincing a light-hearted gaiety and wit, a good power of story telling, and a real charm which was the reflection of his personality. For all friends and observers concur in reporting on the sympathy, modesty, generosity, and winning quality of his nature. His favorite fictional type was the vagabond who is the despair of dull and pompous people.

In appearance Locke was sharp-featured, with a high forehead, and wore pince-nez. He married Aimée Hamilton Meath in 1911. She survived him, and there was an adopted daughter, Sheila.

PRINCIPAL WORKS: *Novels*—At the Gate of Samaria, 1895; A Study in Shadows, 1896; The Demagogue and Lady Phayre, 1896; Derelicts, 1897; Idols, 1899; The White Dove, 1899; The Usurper, 1901; Where Love Is, 1903; The Morals of Marcus Ordeyne, 1905; The Beloved Vagabond, 1906; Septimus, 1909; Simon the Jester, 1910; A Christmas Mystery, 1910; The Glory of Clementina Wing, 1911; The Joyous Adventures of Aristide Pujol, 1912; Stella Maris, 1913; The Fortunate Youth, 1914; Jaffery, 1915; The Wonderful Year, 1916; The Red Planet, 1917; The Rough Road, 1918; Far Away Stories, 1919; The House of Baltazar, 1920; The Mountebank, 1921; Moordius and Co., 1923; The Coming of Amos, 1924; The Golden Adventure of Mr. Paradyne, 1924; The Great Pandolfo, 1925; The Old Bridge: A Florentine Tale, 1926; The Kingdom of Theophilus, 1927; Perella, 1928; Ancestor Jorico, 1929; The Town of Tombarel, 1930. *Plays*—Mr. Cynic, 1899; The Lost Legion, 1900; The Morals of Marcus, 1906; The Palace of Puck, 1907; Butterflies, 1908; The Beloved Vagabond, 1908; A Blank Cheque, 1908; The Man From the Sea, 1910; An Adventure of Aristide Pujol, 1912; The Mountebank (with Ernest Denny) 1923; The Light on the Mountain, 1926.

ABOUT: Adcock, A. St. J. Gods of Modern Grub Street; Cooper, F. T. Some English Story Tellers; Dictionary of National Biography Supplement: 1922-30, 1937; Hind, C. L. Authors and I; Marble, A. R. A Study of the Modern Novel; Phelps, W. L. The Advance of the English Novel; Williams, H. Modern English Writers; Bookman (London) January 1907; Times (London) May 17, 19, 20 and 21, 1930.

LOCKHART, ROBERT HAMILTON BRUCE (September 2, 1886-), Scottish journalist, was born in Anstruther, Fifeshire, the son of Robert Bruce Lockhart and Florence Stuart (Macgregor) Lockhart. In his infancy the family moved to Beith. Most of his early life was spent

in the Highlands. He was educated at Fettes College, Edinburgh, and at the Universities of Paris and Berlin. In 1907 he went to British Malaya to assist an uncle on his rubber plantation. Malaria obliged him to return to Europe in 1910. In 1911, after a competitive examination, he was appointed British vice-consul in Moscow, and from 1914 to 1917 was acting consul general. The next year he headed a special British mission to the U.S.S.R. At the time of Dora

Kaplan's attempt on Lenin's life, Lockhart was arrested as an accomplice—largely thanks to his lack of discretion in expressing his opinions. He was condemned to death, and held prisoner in the Kremlin, but was finally exchanged for Maxim Litvinoff, whom the British had arrested in reprisal.

From 1919 to 1922 he was commercial secretary of the British Legation at Prague. Being heavily in debt, he then resigned from the consular service and in an endeavor to recoup his fortunes engaged in banking enterprises in Central Europe and the Balkans from 1923 to 1928. He became disgusted with the financial life, and in 1929, though reluctant to tie himself down, he joined the staff of the London *Evening Standard,* and remained with this paper until 1937. His books meanwhile (most of them autobiographical) had begun to appear, and the first, *British Agent,* proved an immense success, both as a book and later as a motion picture. Accordingly in 1937 he retired from journalism to devote himself entirely to free-lance writing. On the outbreak of the present war, he rejoined the Foreign Office, and as these lines are written is employed in the Political Intelligence Department.

Mr. Lockhart began his career as a writer about 1912, with short stories written and published under a pseudonym. His first book, however, was not published until 1932. Hailed as "the man who chose the golden mean," he has been surrounded by stirring historical events but their impact on him has been entirely personal. He has been called "a compound of Scottish romanticism, sentimentality, and vanity." He himself acknowledges that his temperament and viewpoint are essentially Scottish. He says that, "having passed most of my life in cities (I have been in every capital in Europe), I

hate big towns. My chief recreation is trout and salmon fishing, and my sole ambition is to own a cottage in my native Scotland." In 1913 he married Jean Haslewood, an Australian; they had one son, but were divorced in 1938. He is a heavy-set man with dark wavy hair and blunt features.

Edmund Wilson, though severely critical of Lockhart, yet granted him high literary skill, and added that "his books are something more than a valuable and highly entertaining record of the official strata of modern Europe; they are a genuine contribution to the history of the human spirit in the late phases of imperialist activity."

PRINCIPAL WORKS: British Agents, 1932; Retreat From Glory, 1934; Return to Malaya, 1936; My Scottish Youth, 1937; Guns or Butter, 1938.

ABOUT: Lockhart, R.H.B. British Agent, Retreat From Glory, Return to Malaya, My Scottish Youth; New Republic November 28, 1934; Wilson Library Bulletin April 1939.

LOCKRIDGE, Mrs. FRANCES LOUISE (DAVIS). See LOCKRIDGE, RICHARD

LOCKRIDGE, RICHARD (September 25, 1898-), American drama critic and novelist, was born in St. Joseph, Mo., and was educated at the Kansas City Junior College and the University of Missouri (non-graduate). His studies were interrupted by a year in the United States Navy, in 1918. In 1921 and 1922 he was a reporter on the Kansas City *Kansan;*

D. Rolph

then, after a few months on the Kansas City *Star,* he went to New York, and for six years was a reporter on the *Sun.* He is still on the *Sun,* but since 1928 he has been its drama critic. He has also maintained a sort of loose editorial connection with the *New Yorker* magazine from time to time.

In 1922 Richard Lockridge married Frances Louise Davis, who is his collaborator in the charming and delightful mystery stories centering around his characters, Mr. and Mrs. North, who first appeared (with only one literary parent) as a series of stories in the *New Yorker.* (The accompanying photograph shows both Lockridges.) So successful was this combination of murder and domesticity that the Norths were made into a play by Owen

Davis, which appeared on the New York stage in 1941 and was later sold to Hollywood.

Mr. Lockridge is a versatile author. He writes extensively—and lectures as well—on the theatre; he is a master of the *New Yorker* type of sketch; and besides the stories and novels about the Norths, he has written a definitive and exhaustive biography of the tragedian, Edwin Booth. He has grace and wit, and though he is hardly likely to confine himself henceforth to mystery stories, he and his wife can be counted among the select few who appeal both to the general reader and to the more intellectual enthusiasts of that *genre*. As a drama critic his judgment is reliable and his style entertaining. But his *forte* is as a writer of the loosely-woven sketch which is the contemporary equivalent of the familiar essay, and of the half-plotless short story which is really a study of character and a depiction of personality. If there be such a thing, he may be called a typical *New Yorker* contributor.

Mr. and Mrs. Lockridge live in downtown New York, on the edge of Greenwich Village—as do the Norths—and have a country residence on a lake not far from the city—as also do the Norths. Richard Lockridge's newspaper post and his outside writing leave him little leisure for other interests, but he plays a good game of tennis—as does Gerald North.

PRINCIPAL WORKS: Darling of Misfortune: Edwin Booth, 1932; Mr. and Mrs. North, 1936; The Norths Meet Murder (with F. Lockridge) 1940; Murder Out of Turn (with F. Lockridge) 1941. A Pinch of Poison (with F. Lockridge) 1941; Death on the Aisle (with F. Lockridge) 1942.

ABOUT: New York Post April 9, 1941.

LODGE, HENRY CABOT. See "AMERICAN AUTHORS: 1600-1900"

LODGE, Sir OLIVER JOSEPH (June 12, 1851-August 22, 1940), English scientist and writer on psychic phenomena, was born

in Penkhull, Staffordshire, the son of Oliver Lodge, a manufacturing potter of Irish descent, and Grace (Heath) Lodge. He was educated in the Newport Grammar School, Shropshire, and at fourteen left school to assist his father in his business. He was already interested

in physics far more than in pottery, and in 1873, after passing the examinations with the highest honors, he went to London as a demonstrator and instructor in physics, and at the same time a student, at University College. He took his Sc.D. degree in 1877. In 1881 he was made professor of physics at University College, Liverpool, and remained there until 1901, when he became principal of the University of Birmingham. He resigned this position in 1919.

He had meanwhile become one of the foremost physicists of the world, his special field being in electro-magnetism and pioneer work in wireless telegraphy. Among his innumerable honors may be mentioned the Rumford and Albert Medals of the Royal Society and the Faraday medal of the Institute of Electrical Engineers. He was Romanes Lecturer at Oxford in 1903, president of the Physical Society of London in 1899 and 1900, and president of the British Association for the Advancement of Science in 1913 and 1914.

His interest in psychic phenomena dated from 1889, though it was increased by the death of his favorite son Raymond in the First World War. He was president of the Society for Psychical Research from 1901 to 1904 and again in 1932. He was knighted in 1902. Lady Lodge, the former Mary F. A. Marshall, who had some reputation as a painter, died in 1929. They had been married in 1877, and had six sons and six daughters.

Modern broadcasting would be largely impossible without use of the basic Lodge patent for selective tuning by use of self-induction. His researches on radiation and on the existence of an ether of space are also basic in modern physics. He was best known to the general public, however, as a writer, lecturer, and broadcaster on psychic phenomena. He accepted survival as proved, but was not officially a Spiritualist, remaining a member of the Church of England.

Intellectually active to the last, Sir Oliver lived near Salisbury, three miles from Stonehenge. He died at eighty-nine. He was a large man (six feet three inches, weighing over 200 pounds) with a white beard. Walter Tittle called him "a great oak-tree of a man, with head like the dome of St. Paul's, and a fine heavy voice with a rich Staffordshire burr." Sir Arthur Keith said: "His presence is commanding and imposing, his carriage easy and dignified, his expression both friendly and sagacious. Time has mellowed his features; the fact that his most cherished ideas have been rejected with contumely by many of his scientific contemporaries has left his temper unsoured." He was the last of the great scientists who in a sense were contemporaries of Tyndall, Huxley, Darwin, Wallace, and Crookes; and the last of the psychic researchers who were colleagues of Frederick W. H. Myers and William James. J. H. Poynting well called him "a great experimenter and a brilliant expounder of his own work and of the work of others."

PRINCIPAL WORKS: Elementary Mechanics, 1879; Modern Views of Electricity, 1889; Lightning Conductors and Lightning Guards, 1892; Pioneers of Science, 1892; The Work of Hertz and Some of His Successors, 1894; Modern Views on Matter, 1903; Easy Mathematics, 1905; Life and Matter, 1905; Electrons, 1907; The Substance of Faith, 1907; Man and the Universe, 1908; The Ether of Space, 1909; The Survival of Man, 1909; Parent and Child, 1910; Reason and Belief, 1911; Modern Problems, 1912; Continuity, 1914; The War and After, 1915; Raymond: or, Life and Death, 1916; Christopher: A Study in Human Personality, 1918; Relativity, 1921; Making of Man, 1924; Atoms and Rays, 1924; Ether and Reality, 1925; Electrical Precipitation, 1925; Talks About Wireless, 1925; Evolution and Creation, 1926; Modern Scientific Ideas, 1927; Science and Human Progress, 1927; Why I Believe in Personal Immortality, 1928; Energy, 1929; Phantom Walls, 1929; Conviction of Survival, 1930; The Reality of a Spiritual World, 1930; Beyond Physics, 1930; Demonstrated Survival, 1930; Advancing Science, 1931; Past Years: An Autobiography, 1931; My Philosophy, 1933.

ABOUT: Lodge, O. Past Years; Poynting, J. H. Sir Oliver Lodge; Bookman (London) February 1927; Century Magazine June 1923; Fortnightly Review September 1934; Hibbert Journal July 1917; Homiletic Review July 1932; London Quarterly Review July 1925; New York Times August 23, 1940; Outline (London) November 10, 1927; Pall Mall Magazine January 1904; Publishers' Weekly September 21, 1935; School and Society January 31, 1920; Scientific American December 26, 1903; Strand Magazine September 1928.

*LOFTING, HUGH (January 14, 1886-),

English-American writer for children, creator of Dr. Dolittle, writes:  "It was during the Great War [1914-18], and the children at home wanted letters from me—and they wanted them with illustrations. There seemed very little of interest to write to youngsters from the front, and it was all censored. One thing, however, that kept forcing itself on my attention was the very considerable part the animals were playing in the war. That was the beginning of the idea [of the Dr. Dolittle stories]— an eccentric country physician with a bent for natural history and a great love of pets, who finally decides to give up his human practice for the therapy of the animal kingdom. This was a new plot for my narrative letter for the children. It delighted them, and at my wife's suggestion I decided to put the letters in book form.

"I make no claim to be an authority on writing or illustrating for children. The fact that I have been successful merely means that I can write and illustrate in my own way. There has always been a tendency to classify children almost as a distinct species. For years it was a constant source of shock to me to find my writings amongst 'Juveniles.' It does not bother me any more now, but I still feel there should be a category of 'Seniles' to offset the epithet."

* * *

Mr. Lofting was born in Maidenhead, Berkshire, and is as much Irish as he is English. When he was eight he was sent to a Jesuit boarding school in Derbyshire. He came to America and attended the Massachusetts Institute of Technology in 1904 and 1905, returning to England to complete his education at the London Polytechnic in 1906 and 1907. After a short period as an architect, he worked as a civil engineer in Canada, Africa, and the West Indies. In 1912 he settled in New York, and married Flora Small, an American. She died in 1917, leaving a daughter and a son. In 1918 he married Katherine Harrower, who died the same year. In 1935 he married Josephine Fricker, and he lives now with her and their son in Madison, Conn. He served with the British Army in Flanders and France in 1917 and 1918, and was seriously wounded and invalided out. He was awarded the Newbery Medal, "the Pulitzer Prize of children's literature," in 1922.

PRINCIPAL WORKS: The Story of Dr. Dolittle, 1920; The Voyages of Dr. Dolittle, 1922; The Story of Mrs. Tubbs, 1923; Dr. Dolittle's Post Office, 1923; Dr. Dolittle's Circus, 1924; Porridge Poetry, 1924; Dr. Dolittle's Zoo, 1925; Dr. Dolittle's Caravan, 1926; Dr. Dolittle's Garden, 1927; Dr. Dolittle in the Moon, 1928; Noisy Nora, 1929; The Twilight of Magic, 1930; Gub Gub's Book, 1932; Dr. Dolittle's Return, 1933; Tommy, Tilly, and Mrs. Tubbs, 1937.

ABOUT: Kunitz, S. J. & Haycraft, H. (eds.). The Junior Book of Authors.

---

* Died September 26, 1947.

LOFTS, NORAH (1904-), English novelist, writes: "I was born in Norfolk, on a farm. All my people have been farmers for uncounted years, and I still regard growing food as the most important work anyone can do. Lots of other people are beginning, rather belatedly, to share this view. I had, for nine years, the inestimable advantage of a country upbringing and the tutelage of a father who was a great reader, a wit, and a raconteur. His untimely death in 1913 altered life altogether. We moved into Bury St. Edmund's, a small though very old market town in Suffolk, and it was decided that I should train as a teacher, since teaching offered, as few things did at that time, comparative economic independence for women. A complete inability to do sums resulted in a failure to matriculate and condemned me to the lower reaches of the profession, which I pursued, sometimes very unhappily, for some twelve years.

"All my life I have written stories. I used to print them very carefully in large letters and sew the sheets into cardboard covers, endow them with very highfalutin titles, and present them to my long-suffering family for birthdays and Christmas. In 1931 I began to have more ambitious ideas about publishing, and began a round of touting my wares which bade fair to discourage me for ever. The manuscripts— and frequently myself—were cast with scorn out of almost every publishing house in London. It was four years before the current manuscript, *I Met a Gypsy,* now much tattered, and the author, now almost desperate, fell into the keeping of receptive publishers in London and New York. After a year and the publication of a second book, I somewhat dubiously relinquished my teaching post.

"I am married. I live in a seventeenth century house with a growing collection of old furniture. I have a passion for dogs and regret that space enables me to keep only two, a Scottish terrier and a dachshund. If civilization survives this war, I hope one day to lash out and own a place with a kitchen garden and a paddock, and be able to buy up any tired old horse I see and allow it to end its days in peace and plenty under the shade of my trees. That is really my dearest wish, because the woes of horses are a matter of deep concern to me. If we revert to barbarism, I hope to be allowed to carry my mat from place to place and tell stories for copper coins: quite an appealing idea, because if one were nimble one could always be one day's jump ahead

of the critics. At present I am very busy, with bits of war work added to the usual round of writing. I fear my autobiography is quite the dullest ever known, and most unlikely to interest anyone."

* * *

Mrs. Loft's (not dull) autobiography is incomplete; she fails, for example, to vouchsafe her maiden name (which appears to have been Robinson) or the name of her husband. She is dark-haired and dark-eyed, with a serious, direct gaze. Her cottage in historic Bury St. Edmunds is actually built on the wall of the ancient Benedictine Library. Her concern for ill-treated horses is so genuine that at one time she offered to give 10 per cent of the royalties of her books for their rescue and care. Her first book, *I Met a Gypsy,* received the American Booksellers' Association's award for the most undeservedly neglected book of 1935. Her belief is that "style should be clear and neutral," like window-glass, and that marked mannerisms obscure the reader's view and should be regarded as a defect.

PRINCIPAL WORKS: I Met a Gypsy (short stories) 1935; Here Was a Man: A Romantic History of Sir Walter Raleigh, 1936; White Hell of Pity, 1937; Out of This Nettle (in America: Colin Lowrie) 1938; Requiem for Idols, 1938; Blossom Like the Rose, 1939; Hester Roon, 1940; The Road to Revelation, 1941.

ABOUT: Wilson Library Bulletin March 1939.

*LOHRKE, EUGENE WILLIAM (April 8, 1897-), American novelist and essayist, writes: "I was born in East Orange, N.J. My father was from Memel, East Prussia; my mother was born in New York. I attended the Newark Academy and later went to Williams College. When America joined the Allies in the First World War, I trained with the college R.O.T.C. and  later at Camp Devon, Mass. I was sent overseas in April 1918 with a 'casual' detachment destined to be further trained and commissioned at the Saumur Artillery School in France. Here I received a commission as second lieutenant, and served with the First Division during the Argonne Offensive, and later with the Army of Occupation, with headquarters at Coblenz, Germany.

"After the war I became a reporter, first on the *Evening Sun* of New York. I worked

* Died May 17, 1953.

as City Hall reporter for this paper and the *Evening Post* between intervals of traveling, living abroad, trying to write fiction, and knocking about the world in Europe and America generally [including a summer working in the Canadian wheat harvest]. My first short story, a thoroughly bad imitation of Joseph Conrad's *Heart of Darkness*, was bought by *Munsey's Magazine*. Another product of this phase of imitation, *Overshadowed*, was expanded into a thoroughly bad novel and published in 1929. After another trip to Europe in 1930, I returned and edited *Armageddon: The World War in Literature*. In 1930 I married Arline Cone, and after six months of living in England, we returned and followed the crowd by buying an old farm in Sharon, Conn. *Deep Evening*, my first successful novel from a literary standpoint, appeared at this time. While living in Connecticut I wrote two other novels.

"In July 1936 we returned to England and took up residence in a very ancient farmhouse near the coast in Sussex. Here both my wife and I had our attention drawn to the political conditions in England and the Continent. Profoundly moved by the events at the time of Munich, we returned to New York and wrote together *Night Over England*, which was published partly in *Harper's Magazine* before appearing in book form. We returned to England in March 1939 to explore the background further and write *The Long Watch in England*, a condensation of which also appeared in *Harper's*. I am planning other works, in the same personal narrative style, on the European backgrounds that led to war."

* * *

Mr. and Mrs. Lohrke are at present living in New York. Mrs. Lohrke was born in Brooklyn and educated at Packer Collegiate Institute. She was in the educational department of Harcourt, Brace and Company, and has written many reviews and articles for magazines. Mr. Lohrke has translated Romain Rolland's *Les Leonides* (1929), and revised Johannes Lang's *Crime and Destiny* (1930) for its American edition. His prose is called "suave and musical" by the New York *Times*. The two books on England, though pessimistic and disheartening, make impressive reading.

PRINCIPAL WORKS: Overshadowed, 1929; Armageddon: The World War in Literature (ed.) 1930; Deep Evening, 1931; The First Bus Out, 1935; The Long Exile, 1936; Night Over England (with A. Lohrke) 1939; The Long Watch in England (with A. Lohrke) 1940; Night Raid, 1941.

ABOUT: Harper's Magazine 1939.

LONDON, JACK (January 12, 1876- November 22, 1916), American novelist and short-story writer, was born in San Francisco, Calif., the illegitimate son of W.H. Chaney, an itinerant Irish astrologer whom his son never saw, and Flora Wellman, the black sheep of a pioneer Wisconsin family of Welsh stock. She left Massillon, Ohio, at twenty-five and met Chaney at the home of Mayor Yesler of Seattle. Chaney, born in Maine of Irish stock, was a linguist, and student of history and the Bible. In general his writing, attack, attitudes and turnings of phrase are said to resemble those of his famous son. The secret of London's paternity was so carefully guarded that Carl Van Doren, writing five years after his death in *The American Novel*, stated that he was the son of a frontier scout and trapper (which is probably a fabrication of Jack's). London, however, was fully aware of his origin, which probably conditioned the uneasy bravado with which he faced life, his occasional longing for conventional respectability—as shown by his wooing of Mabel Applegarth—and his desperate efforts to become a landowner and householder on the grand scale.

Eight months after Jack's birth as John Chaney, Flora married John London of Pennsylvania, and the pair led a precarious existence running a grocery store, taking boarders, and conducting a chicken ranch. London had no childhood, he said later, and the pinch of poverty was chronic. But he soon discovered the world of books. At ten he was borrowing books of adventure, travel, sea voyages and discoveries from the Oakland Public Library, guided by the librarian, Ina Coolbrith, poet laureate of California, who also lent him *Madame Bovary* and *Anna Karenina* from her private collection. Odd jobs on paper routes, ice-wagons, bowling alleys, in canneries and jute mills—at ten cents an hour for a ten-hour day—gave him an intimate sympathy with working-class life and a permanent distaste for its drudgery. At fifteen he went on the road as a tramp, earning the sobriquet of "Sailor Kid" by riding the blinds over the Sierra Nevadas. (At eighteen he joined Kelly's branch of Coxey's Army of the Commonwealth and started beating his way east on freights. Niagara police gave him thirty days' hard labor as a vagrant,

which he served at the Erie County Penitentiary unloading canal boats.) Jack, at sixteen, was an oyster-pirate and longshoreman
in and near the bay of San Francisco, the
owner of the "Razzle Dazzle," which he acquired for $300 (the purchase price included
Mamie, queen of the oyster pirates), and a
seaman before the mast on the "Sophie
Sutherland," an 80-ton sealing vessel which
reached the coasts of Japan and Siberia. The
heavy drinking bouts recorded in *John
Barleycorn* took place at this time.

London became an enthusiastic believer in
Socialism on reading the Communist Manifesto. Deciding to live "by his brain rather
than his brawn," he entered the freshman
class of Oakland High School at nineteen.
At the Henry Clay Debating Society, the one
rallying point for the city's intellectuals, he
met Edward and Mabel Applegarth, members of a cultivated English family. Jailed
for an attack on capitalism at City Hall
Park, he was labeled "The Boy Socialist" by
the Oakland papers. By cramming nineteen
hours a day he managed to enter the University of California, but left before the
year was up to support his mother and
foster-father by working in a laundry. When
gold was discovered in the Klondike in 1896
Jack caught the universal fever. He packed
8,000 pounds (including the *Origin of
Species*, Spencer's *Philosophy of Style*,
Marx's *Das Kapital*, and *Paradise Lost*)
over the Chilkoot Pass, and returned home
without having mined an ounce of gold, but
with experience which he transmuted into
The Call of the Wild, a genuine contribution
to American literature. (It sold just under
a million and a half copies.)

John London had died in his absence, and
Jack returned to day labor until acceptance
of stories by the *Overland Monthly* and
Black Cat encouraged him to turn down a
postoffice job and devote his time to writing.
His omnivorous reading continued; Kipling
and Stevenson were his literary gods, and
Darwin, Spencer, Karl Marx, and Friedrich
Nietzsche his "literary godparents." In particular he adopted Nietzsche's doctrine of
the superman, the man on horseback who
could conquer all obstacles and rule the slave
mass. This might seem to match oddly with
his Socialistic convictions, but inconsistencies
never bothered London. His beliefs were a
mixture of Socialism, Haeckel's monism,
Spencer's materialistic determination, and
Darwin's evolution.

Late in 1899 the *Atlantic Monthly* bought
a long story, "An Odyssey of the North,"
for $120, and Houghton Mifflin, then its
book-publishing affiliate, offered him a contract for a volume of short stories (*The Son
of the Wolf*). Next year he married Bessie
Maddern, a cousin of the actress Minnie
Maddern Fiske; three years later he was to
leave her and his daughters to marry Charmian Kittredge, who appealed to his lush
streak of romanticism. It was part of London's pose to be a Great Lover.

S. S. McClure subsidized London for a
time, at $125 a month. Macmillan's, through
its editor, George P. Brett, increased this to
$150, and when he became a best-selling
author usually acceded to his insatiable demands for advance royalties. (London made
over a million dollars on his fifty books, and
spent it all). An astute advertising campaign,
aided by an excellent press, put *The Call of
the Wild* in the best-selling lists of 1903.
The *Century Magazine* published *The Sea
Wolf*, London's chief glorification of the
Blond Beast, and paid him $4,000. In 1904,
he reported the Russo-Japanese War for the
Hearst papers. (An assignment in 1902 to
cover the aftermath of the Boer War left
him stranded in London, where he gathered
material in the poverty-stricken East End
for *People of the Abyss*). In 1905 he ran
for mayor of Oakland on the Socialist ticket,
receiving 981 votes, and went on a lecture
tour of the country. Sailing the "Snark," the
ketch which cost him $30,000 to build, to
Hawaii, he wrote *Martin Eden*, his fine autobiographical novel. The Applegarths and
George Sterling also figure in it (Sterling
as the poet Brissenden). In 1907 came *The
Iron Heel*, with an introduction by Anatole
France; this is a remarkable anticipation of
fascism, describing a revolution in 1932, and
has been called in some quarters his most
interesting and important book. London's
baronial (and badly abused) hospitality at
his Beauty Ranch in California forced him
to write incessantly to meet his bills and the
cost of building the fantastic castle, The
Wolf House, destroyed by fire before its
completion. By 1913 he was called the highest-paid, best-known, and most popular writer in the world, with books translated into
eleven languages. He left Macmillan for
Century in 1912, but quarreled with them
over *John Barleycorn* and returned. Overwork, financial difficulties and heavy drinking caused his literary output to deteriorate.
Although the cause of London's death was
given out as uremic poisoning, a pad on his
night-table, with a calculation of the lethal
dose of morphine sleeping tablets, and two
empty vials on the floor indicated that, like

his autobiographical hero Martin Eden, he had taken refuge in suicide.

London had a muscular build, light curling brown hair, blue eyes, a soft voice and a boyish charm. He saw human history in terms of the evolutionary dogma, says Carl Van Doren, "a glorious, continuous epic of which his stories were episodes. He set them in localities where the struggle could be most obvious: in the wilds of Alaska, on remote Pacific Islands, on ships at sea out of hearing of the police, in industrial communities during strikes, in the underworlds of various cities, on the routes of vagabondage."

PRINCIPAL WORKS: The Son of the Wolf, 1900; The God of His Fathers, 1901; Children of the Frost, 1902; The Call of the Wild, 1903; The Kempton-Wace Letters, 1903; The People of the Abyss, 1903; The Sea Wolf, 1904; The War of the Classes, 1905; The Game, 1905; White Fang, 1905; Before Adam, 1906; The Iron Heel, 1907; The Road, 1907; Martin Eden, 1909; Burning Daylight, 1910; Revolution, 1910; The Cruise of the Snark, 1911; Smoke Bellew, 1912; John Barleycorn, 1913; The Night Born, 1913; The Valley of the Moon, 1913; The Star Rover, 1914.

ABOUT: Johnson, M. E. Through the South Seas With Jack London; London, C. K. The Book of Jack London; London, J [oan]. Jack London and His Times; Noel, J. Footloose in Arcadia; Stone, C. I. Sailor on Horseback; Van Doren, C. The American Novel; Bookman, February 1929; Literary Review January 26, 1924; Living Age January 13, 1917; Overland Monthly May 1917, October 1920; Saturday Review of Literature September 24, 1938.

*LONG. Mrs. **GABRIELLE MARGARET VERE (CAMPBELL)** (October 29, 1886-), English historical novel-

ist and short story writer, whose work appears (among other disguises) under the pseudonyms of "Marjorie Bowen" and "George Preedy," † is the second daughter of Vere Douglas Campbell and Josephine Elisabeth Ellis (Bowen) Campbell, daughter of the Rev. Charles Bowen, a Moravian clergyman. She was born on Hayling Island, in a cottage, between the days of All Saints and All Souls, and "inherited a double misfortune, the unhappiness of my parents and their poverty."

A reserved, sensitive child, who deeply disliked the bohemian life led by her emotionally unstable mother; was haunted by nocturnal fears; and taught herself to read and

paint, the girl philosophically disregarded the fact that she seldom had enough to eat and made the most of the materials at hand. She studied art at the Slade School in London and spent a year in Paris, absorbing French history and local color. Her first novel, published at sixteen, was a success, although she had waived royalties and received only sixty pounds by grace of her publisher. More favorable terms were arranged for succeeding books, and "Marjorie Bowen" began a steady grind of writing to support her extravagant mother and sister. Her singularly frank autobiography describes the writer as "a woman who earned her living by writing fiction—with occasional essays in that kind of history deplored by historians. . . . I knew my little gifts to be genuine. I was a born story-teller. I had an inexhaustible fund of invention, a fluent and easy style, a certain gift for color and drama, and such a passionate interest in certain periods of history that I was bound, in reproducing them, to give them a certain life." Marjorie Bowen's novels with Dutch and Italian backgrounds were particularly successful. General Crack, written under the pseudonym of "George Preedy," made an effective film.

The novelist's first marriage, in 1912, to Don Zeffrino Emilio Costanzo, a Sicilian, was in general a tragic and unhappy experience, ending with his death after a long illness in 1916. An infant daughter died of meningitis in England, while a son survived. By her second marriage, to Arthur L. Long of Richmond, Surrey, in 1917, she had two sons. Tall, with straight golden-brown hair, she lists her recreations as painting, needlework and reading, and her address as Markham Square, London. In her own words, "I have stood by the Vyverburg and gazed down the valley of the Boyne. I have seen Maximilian's tomb at Innsbruck and Goujon's statue of Diane de Poitiers. I can still hear, in Herbert's lovely phrase, 'music at midnight,' that I interpret as the courage to find beauty in dark places."

PRINCIPAL WORKS: As "Marjorie Bowen"—The Viper of Milan, 1906; The Glen o' Weeping, 1907; The Sword Decides, 1908; Black Magic, 1909; I Will Maintain, 1910; Defender of the Faith, 1911; God and the King, 1911; God's Playthings, 1912; The Rake's Progress, 1912; A Knight of Spain, 1913; The Governor of England, 1913; The Two Carnations, 1913; Prince and Heretic, 1914; The Carnival of Florence, 1915; Mr. Washington, 1915; Because of These Things, 1915; Shadows of Yesterday: Stories From an Old Catalogue, 1916; "William, By the Grace of God—" 1916; The Third Estate, 1917; Curious Happenings; Short Stories, 1918; The Burning Glass, 1918; Crimes of Old London, 1919; Mr. Misfortunate, 1919;

---

* Died December 23, 1952.
† Also "Joseph Shearing."

The Cheats, 1920; The Haunted Vintage, 1921; Affairs of Men, 1922; The Love Thief, 1922; The Jest, 1922; The Presence and the Power, 1924; Five People, 1925; Seeing Life and Other Stories, 1925; The Seven Deadly Sins, 1926; Boundless Water, 1926; Dark Ann and Other Stories, 1927; "Five Winds": A Romance, 1927; The Countess Fanny, 1928; The Golden Roof, 1928; Dickon: An Historical Romance, 1929; The Third Mary Stuart, 1929; Exits and Farewells! 1930; The English Paragon, 1930; Old Patch's Medley, 1930; Brave Employments, 1931; Dark Rosaleen, 1932; The Last Bouquet: Some Twilight Tales, 1932; The Gorgeous Lovers and Other Tales, 1929; Mary Queen of Scots: Daughter of Debate, 1934; The Triumphant Beast, 1934; The Scandal of Sophie Dawes, 1935; Patriotic Lady: A Study of Emma, Lady Hamilton, 1935; Trumpets at Rome, 1936; Peter Porcupine: A Study of William Cobbett, 1936; Crowns and Sceptres: The Romance and Pageantry of Coronations, 1937; William Hogarth: The Cockney's Mirror, 1937; Giant in Chains: Prelude to Revolution, 1938; Wrestling Jacob: A Study of the Life of John Wesley, 1938; Ethics in Modern Art, 1939; Mr. Tyler's Saints, 1939; Exchange Royal, 1940; Today Is Mine, 1941. As "George Preedy"—General Crack, 1928; Captain Banner, 1930; Bagatelle and Some Other Diversions, 1930; The Pavilion of Honour, 1932; Violante, 1932; The Autobiography of Cornelis Blake, 1934; Laurell'd Captains, 1935; This Shining Woman: Mary Wollstonecraft Godwin, 1937; Painted Angel, 1938; The Dove in the Mulberry Tree, 1939; The Fair Young Widow, 1939; Child of Chequer'd Fortune: The Life of Maurice de Saxe, 1939; Primula, 1940; The Life of John Knox, 1940; The Life of Rear-Admiral John Paul Jones, 1940; Findernes' Flowers, 1941; Black Man, White Maiden, 1942. As "John Winch"—The Mountain of Gold, 1928; The Hunting of Hilary, 1929; When the Tide Runs Out, 1930; Idlers' Gate, 1932. As "Robert Paye"—The Devil's Jig, 1930; Julia Rozengrave, 1933. As "Margaret Campbell"—The Debate Continues (autobiography) 1939.

ABOUT: Campbell, M. The Debate Continues (autobiography).

LONG, HANIEL (March 9, 1888-), American poet and publisher, writes: "My father and mother went over to Burma

from Allegheny College (my father was a missionary), and I was born in Rangoon, about which I can remember very few things (though most charming). When we came back to the States it was still the horse and buggy age. There were some telephones about, and I remember an early version of moving pictures. In 1910 I was driving a car on a cross-country newspaper assignment. The radio began in Pittsburgh. Highways began to improve, and wonderful bridges appeared. Pretty soon people began flying to New York in airplanes. This was

all excellent, but industrial strikes and the First World War showed that science and engineering had another face, too, not so pleasant.

"That brings us to the psychological age, which we are now entering, painfully. It began to dawn on bright people that what was wrong with the outside world merely reflected what was wrong with us inside. We used science and engineering as our feelings prompted us to use them, and it is not easy to learn how to fight, love, and acquire, in ways advantageous to society.

"Hence, everywhere I've lived in the United States—airy New York, Pittsburgh warm under its pall, Duluth on its hill, Minneapolis around its lakes (I found my wife [Alice Lavinia Knoblauch] there in 1913), sun-drenched Santa Fé, the bright people (the kind ones) have been talking about the values of feeling, and studying human relationships. It's the first faint beginning of a world of balance and sanity. In a triumphant age of applied science, all you can do is to come down to earth and the truths that never change, and think of people not as parts but as wholes, and in creaturely kindness.

"At Harvard I won a medal for an essay on George Meredith. I have since written a book on Walt Whitman. If I could, I'd write books also on Montaigne, William Blake, and William James. But I hope that influences from all these men are to be felt in what poems and prose I have been able to get down on paper. I'm glad I was born in the horse and buggy age. I prize especially my friends of the same vintage, and we can talk it all over and understand one another perfectly."

* * *

Mr. Long received his B.A. from Harvard in 1910, but did part of his work *in absentia,* as during his senior year he was a reporter on the New York *Globe* and *Commercial Advertiser.* From 1910 to 1929 he taught English at the Carnegie Institute of Technology, Pittsburgh. In 1929 he moved to Santa Fé, N.M., where he still lives. In 1933 he organized a non-profit, cooperative publishing business called Writers' Editions, of which he has been director since 1935. In 1937 and 1938 he edited the literary page of the *New Mexico Sentinel.* He and Mrs. Long have one son. His own first name is pronounced *Han-eye-el,* with accent on the second syllable.

PRINCIPAL WORKS: Poems, 1920; Notes For a New Mythology, 1926; Atlantides, 1933; Pittsburgh Memoranda, 1935; Interlinear to Cabeza de

Vaca, 1936; Walt Whitman and the Springs of Courage, 1938; Malinche (Doña Marina) 1939; Piñon Country, 1941.

About: Poetry January 1935; Survey Graphic July 1935.

*LONSDALE, FREDERICK (February 5, 1881-), British dramatist, was born Lionel Frederick Leonard in St. Helier,

Jersey, the Channel Islands, which also gave Lillie Langtry and Seymour Hicks to the British theatre. His first lucrative work was as a bell-boy on a transatlantic steamer, and he has also been an able-bodied seaman, and a private in the South Lancashire Regiment. In 1908, when he was twenty-seven and was writing for the theatre as Frederick Lonsdale, he had no less than three plays produced, *The Early Worm, The King of Cadonia,* and *The Best People. The Balkan Princess,* written with Frank Curzon, was a success of 1910, but was eclipsed by *The Maid of the Mountains* (1916) which was a favorite with British troops who went to see it repeatedly during their London leaves, and which piled up almost as many performances as the contemporary *Chu Chin Chow.* In 1919 Lonsdale adapted Booth Tarkington's romantic novel *Monsieur Beaucaire* for the stage. *Aren't We All?* was the first of his "smooth and sprightly comedies" to achieve American success; it was presented by the late Charles Dillingham in 1923 at his Globe Theatre in New York, with Cyril Maude as star and the then obscure Leslie Howard in the cast. *Spring Cleaning,* in the same season, though preceding Noel Coward's *Vortex,* was much in the same *genre,* with its satirical observation of a high-living "upper class." *The Last of Mrs. Cheyney* (1925), one of Lonsdale's most entertaining comedies, was also a crook-play with amusing complications. It made a successful moving picture. Its star was Ina Claire, who also played in *Once Is Enough* (1938), written in Lonsdale's familiar style, which by then seemed rather dated in a world which was more concerned with revolutions and impending war than with the tribulations of the English aristocracy, as set forth in drawing-room comedies which stemmed directly from Oscar Wilde and Arthur Wing Pinero. *Time* called the play "full of fish-wife manners but ducal breeding."

In the '20s, at the height of Lonsdale's career, Hesketh Pearson in one of his "Intimate Impressions," contributed to *Theatre World,* confided that "everybody calls him 'Freddie,' which is perhaps the most significant thing about him. There is a boyishness, a naughty boyishness, in his whole manner and attitude toward life that necessitates the abbreviation of his Christian name." Lonsdale once changed his mind between Southampton and Cherbourg about coming to America, debarked at the latter port, and returned to his country home in Kent. He is a member of the Garrick, Green Room, Savage, and Beefsteak clubs in London, and the Stage Golfing Society, Buckinghamshire; his favorite recreations are golf, tennis, and motoring.

Michel Mok, the New York *Post's* interviewer, found Lonsdale in February 1938 "looking like a weather-beaten Punch dressed by the best Bond Street tailor," and with smooth, well-brushed iron-gray hair. "A comedy is a tragedy averted," Lonsdale told him. "I try to tell my story in terms of humorous action and dialogue. The tragedy impends and then I avert it." He rises at 8, and writes with pencil on foolscap paper till 1 P.M., taking about two months to write a play. He has written or collaborated in writing several moving-picture scenarios, notably *The Private Life of Don Juan.* Mrs. Lonsdale was Leslie Brooke Hoggan.

Principal Works: *Plays*—The Early Worm, 1908; The King of Cadonia, 1908; The Best People, 1908; The Balkan Princes (with F. Curzon) 1910; Betty (with G. Unger) 1915; Waiting at the Church, 1916; The Maid of the Mountains, 1916; Aren't We All? 1923; Spring Cleaning, 1923; Madame Pompadour (with H. Graham) 1923; The Fake, 1924; The Street Singer, 1924; The Last of Mrs. Cheyney, 1925; On Approval, 1927; The High Road, 1927; Lady Mary (with W. J. H. Turner) 1928; Canaries Sometimes Sing, 1929; Never Come Back, 1932; The Foreigners, 1932; Once Is Enough, 1938.

About: New York Post February 4, 1938; Newsweek December 18, 1939; Time February 28, 1938.

LOON. See VAN LOON

LOOS, ANITA (April 26, 1893-), American novelist and dramatist, was born in Sisson, Calif., the daughter of Richard Beers Loos, a humorist and theatrical producer, and Minnie Ella (Smith) Loos. Anita appeared with her father's stock company at five, and at a slightly more advanced age played Little Lord Fauntleroy and the heroine of *The Prince Chap,*

* Died April 4, 1954.

at her various ages, as the play advanced, of six, twelve, and fifteen.

Anita Loos attended high school at San Diego, Calif., where her parents moved when she was thirteen. Between stock productions, her father had run motion pictures, which Anita watched from the wrong side of the screen. Before causing a flurry of excitement by running away from home and marrying an orchestra leader, she wrote her first scenarios, sending one to the Biograph Co., whose address she had noted on the top of a film can. David Wark Griffith

paid her $15 apiece for several, notably *The New York Hat,* in which Mary Pickford and Lionel Barrymore played. Griffith was considerably taken aback when he first met Miss Loos, under her mother's wing, and saw in this child, wearing pigtails and sailor suit, the writer who had been responsible for some of his roughest comedies.

Anita Loos had won a prize at twelve for a school essay, setting forth her ambition to be a ship's architect, and she won prizes from the New York *Evening Telegram* with such monotonous regularity that the newspaper finally put her on salary and set her to writing a humorous column. In 1919 she married John Emerson, who had come from New York with Douglas Fairbanks, and the two concocted for Fairbanks *His Picture in the Papers,* the screen's first satire, which won favorable notices from the *Fòrum* and the *Atlantic Monthly.* Miss Loos wrote scenarios for Fairbanks for three years—she had written for Griffith for five years—and also collaborated with Emerson in supplying Constance Talmadge with stories. For a time they had their own film unit, the John Emerson-Anita Loos Productions. They are now connected with the Metro-Goldwyn-Mayer Studios at Culver City, Calif., and live on Ocean Front, Santa Monica.

Gentlemen Prefer Blondes (1925) was Anita Loos' first book of fiction, and was written as a serial for *Harper's Bazaar* at a time when her husband was desperately ill. This hilarious chronicle of a thoroughly hard-boiled and conscienceless little gold-digger operating under a disguise of bland innocence represented, according to Miss Loos, her concentrated knowledge of Hollywood and other places. It sold 400,000 copies, and earned its author in all more than $600,000. With June Walker, a brunette actress wearing a blonde wig in order to play Lorelei Lee, a dramatization of the book was produced at the Times Square Theatre, New York, in 1926. Next year Miss Loos toured Europe; met Mussolini and H. G. Wells, who told her not to write another purely humorous book. *But Gentlemen Marry Brunettes* (1928) was a fairly amusing sequel. Among recent talking pictures, the best-known Loos-Emerson scenarios are those for *Red Headed Woman, San Francisco,* and *The Women.* Miss Loos is petite, has a wind-blown black bob and big black eyes, and speaks rapidly in a tremulous voice.

PRINCIPAL WORKS: Breaking Into the Movies (with J. Emerson) 1921; Gentlemen Prefer Blondes, 1925; But Gentlemen Marry Brunettes, 1928.

ABOUT: Lawrence M. School of Femininity; Shaw, C. G. The Low-Down; New York Times December 6, 1931, July 5, 1936; New Yorker November 6, 1926

LORCA. See GARCÍA LORCA

LOTHROP, Mrs. HARRIETT MULFORD (STONE). See "AMERICAN AUTHORS: 1600-1900"

"LOTI, PIERRE" (pen-name of Julien Viaud) (January 14, 1850-June 10, 1923), French novelist, was born in Rochefort of an old middle-class family of Huguenot stock. For generations his ancestors on both sides were intrepid navigators, many of whom had gone down with their ships. Julien's early life in a lugubrious home regulated by an austere mother, a sis-

ter twenty years his senior, and some fussy old aunts was extremely unhappy. His education consisted of compulsory Bible readings and odious private tutors in Greek, Latin, and English; later he attended the Rochefort Lycée (now called Lycée Pierre Loti), where he evidenced little talent and which he abhorred. His parents intended Julien for the ministry but upon the death of their older son in 1865—a surgeon in the navy who died at sea—they were forced for financial reasons to permit the younger Viaud to become a sailor. After a short course at the Paris Lycée Henri IV, Julien entered the naval academy at Brest in 1865, and two years later embarked as junior midshipman on the "Jean Bart" for a training cruise around the world. The ship touched at all five continents but was suddenly recalled to Brest at the outbreak of the Franco-Prussian War. On July 31, 1870, first-class midshipman Viaud set sail for the Baltic on the corvette "Decrès."

For twelve years Julien Viaud, rebaptized "Pierre Loti" by the Tahitians in 1872 (*loti* means "rose" in their language), sailed the seven seas and absorbed the qualities of every land, all of which he translated into numerous exotic novels that have made the name of Loti famous. From his first book (1879) to his last (1921) Loti never tired of describing the countries he had seen: Constantinople appears in *Aziyade* and *The Disenchanted*, Brittany and its surrounding seas in *My Brother Yves*, Tahiti in *The Marriage of Loti*, Senegal in *The Romance of a Spahi*, Japan in *Madame Chrysanthème*, the Basque country in *Ramuntcho*, and the Northern seas in *An Iceland Fisherman*, probably his best-known masterpiece.

"Pierre Loti" scored his first literary success in 1880 with his second novel, *The Marriage of Loti*. Both the public at large and the discriminating critics hailed it as a *chef-d'œuvre*; the arbiter of taste Jules Lemaître declared: "I have never been so deeply moved by a book!" Thus "Loti" did not have to struggle to get to Parnassus: Daudet befriended him and introduced him to the Goncourt circle, and in 1892, defeating Émile Zola as candidate for the French Academy, he sat among the immortals. His swift victory must not be attributed to such tangential influences as salons, women, or clericals—rather it was due to his gift for supplying the public's demands, a note of exoticism wrapped in a perfumed, vaguely melancholy style. The period of French colonial imperialism had begun, and soft music was the order of the day.

"Loti's" services to his country during the world war, embodied in his hysterical anti-German pamphlets *The Trail of the Barbarians, War,* etc., won him the Grand Cross of the Legion of Honor in 1922. In his old age he found solace in his grandchild, his cats, and his "palace" which boasted a Gothic hall, a Renaissance hall, a mosque, and a vast Chinese hall in red and gold adjoining a pagoda. He died in 1923 at the age of seventy-three and was buried with national honors at the Pierre d'Oléron cemetery.

" 'Loti' is romantic in his acute sensibility, his recurrent pessimism and ennui, his absorption in nature, and his absorption of nature into himself," say Nitze and Dargan. "Extremely, even naïvely self-centered, he is yet capable of pity for the suffering, especially for the 'toilers of the sea.' His style, with all its simplicity, has the undulating and suggestive power of music. . . . Emotional rather than thoughtful, not elaborate in characterization or plot, his idylls move us through his capacity for sincerely realizing alien landscapes and alien souls."

WORKS AVAILABLE IN ENGLISH TRANSLATION: *Fiction*—My Brother Yves, 1887 (also as A Tale of Brittany); An Iceland Fisherman, 1887; From Lands of Exile, 1888; Madame Chrysanthème, 1889 (also as Japan); Rarahu, or; The Marriage of Loti, 1890; The Romance of a Spahi, 1890 (also as The Sahara); A Child's Romance, 1891 (also as The Story of a Child); A Phantom From the East, 1892 (also as Constantinople); The Book of Pity and of Death, 1892; Ramuntcho, 1897 (also as A Tale of the Pyrenees); Disenchanted, 1906; Stories From Pierre Loti, 1933. *Travel, etc.*—Into Morocco, 1889; Last Days of Pekin, 1902; Madame Prune, 1905; India, 1906; Egypt, 1909; Carmen Sylva and Sketches of Orient, 1912; Siam, 1913; Turkey in Agony, 1913; On Life's By-Ways, 1914; James, H. Essays in London and Elsewhere; Jerusalem, 1915; The Trial of the Barbarians, 1917; War, 1917; Notes of My Youth, 1924.

ABOUT: Assolant, G. P. Loti; Barry, W. F. Heralds of Revolt; D'Auvergne, E. B. P. Loti, The Romance of a Great Writer; Flottes, P. Le Drame Intérieur de P. Loti; Gosse, E. Franch Profiles; Guérard A. L. Five Masters of French Romance; James, H. Essays in London and Elsewhere; Lefêvre, R. La Vie Inquiète de P. Loti; Lemaître, J. Literary Impressions; Mariel, J. P. Loti; Serban, N. P. Loti; Sherman, S. P. Critical Woodcuts; Stephen, W. French Novelists of Today; Contemporary Review July 1930; Mercure de Flandre August-September 1930.

LOUNSBURY, THOMAS RAYNESFORD. See "AMERICAN AUTHORS: 1600-1900"

LOUŸS, PIERRE (December 10, 1870-June 4, 1925), French poet and novelist, was born in Paris during the Franco-Prussian war; the Goncourt Brothers' *Journal* remarks on the *tristesse de ce jour*—Louÿs' birthday. One of his parents was related to Victor Hugo, and Louÿs was a grandnephew of the Duc d'Abrantes through his great-grandmother, Louise Junot,  sister of the hero of Austerlitz. The boy was instructed in *rhetorique* at L'École Alsacienne, for which he had small affection, and in *philosophie* at the Lycée de Sailly, where he received baccalaureate degrees in science and letters. He also studied intermittently at the Sorbonne. At nineteen he met Leconte de Lisle, and became a close friend of other Parnassian poets as well, particularly José-Maria de Heredia, whose younger daughter Louise he married in 1899. In 1890 Louÿs began to issue *La Conque*, each copy containing an unpublished poem by an illustrious name, among the contributors being Swinburne, Mallarmé, Verlaine, and Judith Gautier. In 1893-94 *Astarte*, his own first volume, appeared. According to one story, Louÿs inherited 300,000 francs on attaining his majority, and spent it all in three years when a doctor mistakenly told him he had only that length of time to live. In December 1894 the first of the *Chansons de Bilitis* appeared, poems celebrating in a style of classical precision the pleasures of Sapphic love, and purportedly written by a Greek poetess. Bilitis had no more real corporeal existence than Prosper Mérimée's Clara Gazul, but the inevitable dupe bobbed up to claim that he knew the original Greek text.

Aphrodite, subtitled *Amours Antiques,* was equally voluptuous in tone, but dealt this time with an Alexandrian courtesan, Chrysis, who requires her lover, the sculptor Demetrios, to commit a theft, a murder, and a sacrilege to gain her favors. He performs the deeds, then spurns her; she drinks hemlock, and Demetrios makes a perfect statue over her corpse. Censorship played a large part in the history of *Aphrodite*; the book was refused by several publishers before appearing as a *feuilleton* in the *Mercure de France* (August 1895); Senator Bérenger denounced it in the name of public morality, and François Coppée called it a masterpiece (whereupon it sold over 150,000 copies and set up Louÿs in life once more); and a diluted but extravagant stage spectacle based on the romance, produced at the Century Theatre in New York, created much advance excitement. Louÿs lived in a secluded villa on the rue de Boulainvilliers in Passy, sleeping all day and working all night, sustained by a daily quota of eighty cigarettes. Resembling a Van Dyck painting with his pale face, brown hair and moustache, serene, ironical eyes, and regular features, Louÿs sometimes appeared in his father-in-law's salon; other friends included Mallarmé, Regnier, Claude Farrère, Valéry, and Claude Debussy. The outbreak of the First World War seriously disturbed him; letting his beard grow, he became even more of a recluse. Three years after the death of Louÿs

at fifty-five, *Psyche*, another classical romance, was published, with a conclusion and notes by Farrère. Louÿs was a classical scholar of the first rank, a man of encyclopedic knowledge. His poems had the brilliant color and light and pictorial qualities of the Parnassians and the Symbolist poets. He also claimed to be a strict moralist, his purpose being to show the ravages caused by passion.

Works Available In English Translation: The Songs of Bilitis, 1904; Aphrodite, 1925; Psyche, 1928; Satyrs and Women, 1930; The Woman and Puppet, 1930; The Collected Tales of Pierre Louÿs, 1930; The Collected Works of Pierre Louÿs (Liveright's Black and Gold Library ed. contains: Aphrodite, Woman and Puppet, The Songs of Bilitis, The Adventures of King Pausole, The Twilight of the Nymphs, Sanguines, Psyche) 1932.

About: Gaubert, E. Pierre Louÿs, Louÿs, P. The Woman and the Puppet (see Introduction by Arthur Symons); Mercure de Flandre March, April 1928.

LOVELACE, Mrs. MAUD (HART) and DELOS WHEELER (April 25, 1892- and December 2, 1894-), novelists, write (over Mrs. Lovelace's signature): "We are both from Minnesota. Delos came *via* Brainerd and the Northern pine forests, I came *via* Mankato and the Minnesota River Valley, to Minneapolis, where in 1917 we met and married.

Pinchot

Both of us had attended the University of Minnesota, and Delos was in the army, having enlisted when America entered the Great War. He served for twenty-seven months, went to France with a machine-gun battalion. After being demobilized he went to newspapering with the Minneapolis *Tribune* and both of us went to writing. At first we collaborated on short stories, but presently I left him to do these alone and turned to novels. In 1933, by mutual inclination we took to writing together again and did two novels in collaboration. In 1931 our daughter and only child was born. After she grew old enough to listen to stories I found myself most interested in inventing stories which would interest her. These centered chiefly around my own childhood and grew into a book.

"Having watched other collaborators getting into each other's hair and on each other's nerves, we have reached the conclusion that happy collaborations, like happy marriages, are made in heaven. When we do a book together, we simply share the work. Some instinct tells us which chapters belong to Delos, which belong to me, and which must be tussled with together. Some parts of the work, such as any necessary research, fall naturally to me, and other parts, such as whipping up a plot, fall naturally to him. Collaborations aside, he has a finger in all my literary pies and I in his.

"We live in a white, blue-shuttered house in Garden City, L. I., near New York, where Delos is a member of the editorial staff of the New York Sun. In exchange for the lakes and prairies and pine woods of Minnesota, we have received the Atlantic. We all like swimming and Delos likes tennis. We motor a lot because I like to and play bridge a lot because he likes to. Our daughter and her father are studying the piano —running neck to neck. The piano is one of the centers of our home; the fireplace is another, and the terrace a third. We are incorrigible eaters-out-of-doors. We all like the theatre, and Sunday mornings, and books, and journeys long or short, but especially long."

* * *

Mrs. Lovelace's novels written by herself are all historical. She does careful research for them, and works regularly five hours a day. A reviewer of one of her books hailed "the usual Lovelace vivacity." As a young man Mr. Lovelace worked on newspapers in Fargo, N. D., and Minneapolis; he has studied at Cambridge University, England, and Columbia.

PRINCIPAL WORKS: By Maud Hart Lovelace— The Black Angels, 1926; Early Candlelight, 1929; Petticoat Court, 1930; The Charming Sally, 1932; Betsy-Tacy (juvenile) 1940; Betsy, Tacy and Tib (juvenile) 1941. By Delos Wheeler Lovelace— Rockne of Notre Dame, 1931. In Collaboration— One Stayed at Welcome, 1934; Gentlemen From England, 1937; The Golden Wedge (juvenile) 1942.

ABOUT: Wilson Library Bulletin November 1930.

LOVELACE, DELOS WHEELER. See LOVELACE, M. H. & D. W.

*LOVETT, ROBERT MORSS (December 25, 1870-   ), American literary critic and university professor, was born in Boston on Christmas Day, the son of Augustus S. Lovett and Elizabeth (Russell) Lovett. He graduated from Harvard College with the degree of B.A. in 1892, remaining in the English Department that year as assistant in English and becoming instructor in 1893. Removing to Illinois that year, Lovett was first instructor in rhetoric, then

assistant professor of English from 1896 to 1904, at the University of Chicago. He was associate professor until 1909, then full professor until retirement in 1936. On the administrative side, he was dean of junior colleges from 1903 to 1920.

With his colleague and close friend William Vaughn Moody, the poet and dramatist, Lovett was co-author of A History of English Literature, known to many college students as "Moody and Lovett." He also wrote two forgotten novels, Rachel Gresham (1904) and A Winged Victory (1907). In 1919 he edited the Dial, still published in Chicago and still on the conservative side; became a member of the editorial board of the New Republic in 1921; and has advocated numerous liberal causes, being the president of the League for Industrial Democracy, president of the Sacco-Vanzetti National League, member of the executive committee of the  Acme American Civil Liberties Union, and member of the League for Independent Political Action.

President Roosevelt appointed Lovett governmental secretary of the Virgin Islands in 1939; his address is Charlotte Amalie, St. Thomas. His only son, Robert Morss Lovett, Jr., was killed at Belleau Wood, France, in the First World War. Mrs. Lovett was Ida Mott-Smith of Boston. They were married in 1895, and have two daughters and three grandchildren. A member of the National Institute of Arts and Letters, Lovett is also a member of the University and Cliff Dwellers clubs in Chicago and the Harvard and Coffee House clubs in New York. He writes a clear and distinguished prose, and is well known as an authority on English fiction. One of his best-known studies is the monograph on Edith Wharton, to whose friend and mentor, Henry James, Lovett bears some physical resemblance. For diversion he "particularly enjoys" chess.

PRINCIPAL WORKS: A History of English Literature (with W. V. Moody) 1902; Rachel Gresham (novel) 1904; A First View of English Literature (with W. V. Moody) 1905; A Winged Victory (novel) 1907; Edith Wharton, 1925; Preface to Fiction, 1930; History of the Novel in England (with H. S. Hughes) 1932. Compiler— British Poetry and Prose (with R. K. Root & R. Lieder) 1928; The College Reader (with H. M. Jones) 1936. Editor—Selected Poems of William

Vaughn Moody, 1930; Eminent British Poets of the Nineteenth Century.

ABOUT: Harvard College, Class of 1892: Twenty-Fifth and Fortieth Anniversary Reports; Time November 13, 1939.

LOWELL, AMY (February 9, 1874- May 12, 1925), American poet and critic, was born in Brookline, Mass., the daughter of  Augustus Lowell and Katherine Bigelow (Lawrence) Lowell. She was a Brahmin of the Brahmins, born to wealth, high culture, and intellectual interests. One of her brothers was Abbott Lawrence Lowell, president of Harvard; another was Percival Lowell, the astronomer. She was a collateral descendant of James Russell Lowell, and her grandfather founded the cotton manufacturing town of Lowell, Mass.

These matters are important in any estimate of Amy Lowell, because they influenced her profoundly. She was educated in private schools and began early the trips abroad which enriched her mind though they often resulted in severe nervous strain. Before she was thirty her parents had died, and she bought the family estate, "Sevenels," in Brookline, which was her home—almost her shell—for the rest of her life. A glandular imbalance caused her to become immensely stout, and precluded any probability of marriage or romantic attachments. Her life was necessarily to be one of intellectual attainment. But in spite of her bulk, her black cigars, and her oaths, there was nothing masculine about her; she was given to rather grotesquely feminine garments for formal wear, and behind the autocracy of her manner there hid a rather pathetic and very feminine softness.

It was not until 1902 that she "discovered" that poetry was her "natural mode of expression." Before that she had interested herself mainly in civic affairs—she was always a pronounced conservative, a die-hard Republican with iron views on the place of the working-class—though she had entertained vague plans of some time becoming a writer. She did not burst into poetry. She set herself to learn the trade like any other, studied hard, and was thirty-six before she published a volume of poems.

In 1913, in England, she met Ezra Pound, "the father of Imagism." Pound's theories interested her profoundly, and with her customary decisiveness she proceeded to take the movement over bodily. She did not succeed, since Pound was a tough adversary, but he remained in Europe and she returned to America, and in her own mind at least the Imagist school was thenceforth her property. It was in this phase that her most characteristic poems were written, in free verse fine in technique and displaying what John Livingston Lowes called "her almost unrivaled command of the vocabulary of sensuous impressions." For some years before her death, however, she ceased to think of herself as an exponent of Imagism, and she wrote many poems in more traditional forms. The best known of her poems to the casual reader is the dramatic "Patterns"; her own favorite was "Lilacs."

Since she was in her own way a reigning monarch, Amy Lowell had no particular concern with the reputation of eccentricity which made her a sort of monstrous legend. Everyone knew that she slept in the daytime and worked at night; that she slept on sixteen pillows and that everywhere she went all mirrors must be covered and a dozen pitchers of ice water must be at hand; that visitors to "Sevenels" not important enough to be sent for in the big maroon car must run the gamut of seven untrained sheep dogs, for protection against whose endearments guests, after dinner, were provided with towels to place over their evening clothes. (When the dogs became a nuisance, however, with characteristic nonchalance she had them all killed.) She had always had a passion for the stage—Eleanora Duse was her idol, and her faithful and patient companion, Ada Russell, had been an actress —and it is probable that she dramatized herself consciously.

But she was no *poseur*. She was a scholar, not a dilettante; she had a critical faculty both powerful and discriminating, and a strong and subtle command of expression. She was not, as she had hoped and meant to be, a poet of the first or even the second rank. As Louis Untermeyer said, "she had genius for everything except the thing she wanted most: permanence as a poet." Undoubtedly her great biography of her lifelong idol Keats will outlive any of her poems. The book was coolly received in England, and when she died soon after (of a cerebral hemorrhage), silly commentators said that, like Keats himself, she had been "slain by an article." It was as untrue of her as of him. It was not criticism which killed her, but Keats: the terrible labor of bringing the book to birth was too much for her always precariously balanced health.

Amy Lowell was an autocrat to editors, but it was often on behalf of others. She was a good friend and a good fighting enemy. She took her political and economic views from her family, but nothing else: in everything pertaining to herself as an individual she was a forthright rebel. By her own orders, for example, there was no religious service at her funeral. She made her own judgments in religion as she did in literary criticism, or in the writing of her "unrhymed cadence" (a phrase she preferred to "free verse") or "polyphonic prose." John Livingston Lowes called her "a vivid and powerful personality which dominated handicaps. . . . In her paradoxes lay the richness of her character—her mind was endlessly acquisitive. . . . She had an extraordinary catholicity of interests and a passion for adventures in technique."

"Her genius," said Robert Morss Lovett, "was militant, . . . her poetry alive, because she lived in it. . . . She lived and gave life." And Elizabeth Shepley Sergeant, who said "she lived dramatically and opulently, always for spectators," remarked that her death was "like the fall of a dynasty."

Her chief pitfall, in fact, was the very profuseness of her talent, pruned as it might be by an exigent technique. In her anonymous *Critical Fable,* which she finally acknowledged after accusing half a dozen others of being its author, she notes that very fault in herself. Knowing it, she yet could not curb it. In consequence her influence as a poet outweighed her direct contribution. As a critic, however, she spoke with her own voice. Her most important critical work, the biography of Keats, has taken its place among the great biographies in the field of English poetry.

PRINCIPAL WORKS: *Poetry*—A Dome of Many-Coloured Glass, 1912; Sword Blades and Poppy Seeds, 1914; Men, Women, and Ghosts, 1916; Pictures of the Floating World, 1919; Fir-Flower Tablets (with Florence Ayscough; translations from the Chinese) 1921; Legends, 1921; A Critical Fable, 1922; What's O'Clock, 1925; East Wind, 1926; Ballads for Sale, 1927; Selected Poems, 1928. *Prose*—Six French Poets, 1915; Tendencies in Modern American Poetry, 1917; Can Grande's Castle, 1918; John Keats, 1925; Poetry and Poets, 1930.

ABOUT: Aiken, C. Skepticisms; Boynton, P. H. Some Contemporary Poets; Brooks, V. W. New England Indian Summer; Bryher, W. Amy Lowell: A Critical Appreciation; Cestre, C. The Poetry of Amy Lowell; Damon, S. F. Amy Lowell: A Chronicle; Hunt, R. & Snow, R. H. Amy Lowell: Sketches Biographical and Critical; Monroe, H. Poets and Their Art; Sergeant, E. S. Fire Under the Andes; Untermeyer, L. American Poetry Since 1900; Wood, C. Amy Lowell; Arts and Decoration September 1925; Bookman June 1925, July 1925, March 1926; Catholic World June 1925; Dial November 2, 1918; Forum July 1925; Harper's Magazine August 1939; Nation May 27, 1925; New Republic May 25, 1925, November 18, 1925; North American Review March 1925; Saturday Review of Literature May 30, 1925, October 3, 1925, December 5, 1927, November 16, 1935; Scribner's Magazine September 1927.

LOWENTHAL, MARVIN (October 6, 1890-), American essayist, writes: "I am a native of Bradford, Pa., a boom oil-town and one of America's last frontiers. My parents, who were both born in Syracuse, N. Y., had lived through wild times in Titusville and the upper Allegheny. I first read Plato in the deep woods with the hoot-hoot of a 'barker' from a far-away  derrick ringing in my ears. Even today the smell of leaking gas is nostalgic perfume.

"At the age of fourteen I was technically an author. Channing Pollock published a short story of mine in *Stage,* and thereafter sent me numerous rejection slips with excellent but unheeded advice. A year later I took a job as a bobbin-boy in a local silk mill for ten and a quarter hours a day at $2.50 a week; and in six years I was assistant superintendent. During this time I became a graduate of our Carnegie Public Library—having thumbed or read every book in its stacks.

"Thanks to the encouragement of William Ellery Leonard, who had been induced to read some of my scribbling, I went to Madison, Wis., in order to make myself into a writer. Somehow, in the course of three years (1912-15), I found myself entered into the university and a graduate with honors. I was a columnist on the college paper and a Phi Beta Kappa. I earned my room and board by serving gaily at one and the same time as publicity man and dramatic critic for the Madison vaudeville and legitimate theatres. Prize-winning essays furnished me with clothes, beer, and pleasant vacations. Passes to the Orpheum won me the friendship of a co-ed whom I was eventually to marry. In 1915 a scholarship in philosophy gave me a year at Harvard and a master's degree. By that time I had enough of academic atmosphere, and through the persuasion of Louis D. Brandeis I moved to San Francisco, where for three years I furthered the Zionist movement up and down the Pacific Coast. In 1918 the U. S. Army rejected me as too light in weight for a hero, and Sylvia Mardfin accepted me as a husband.

"After the Treaty of Versailles was signed, I lived in New York as an editor of the *Menorah Journal* and contributor to the *Dial,* the *Freeman,* and the *Nation.* In 1922 I set out for Europe, and remained abroad for most of the time until 1933. I occupied an 'observation post' at the League of Nations, served as a secretary to the World Conference for International Peace Through Religion, traveled in all European countries except the Scandinavian, visited the Near East and North Africa, contributed to American periodicals and press, went up with the stock market and down with the crash to the serious life of an author and lecturer.

"My *Autobiography of Michel de Montaigne* is composed and translated from his writings and family documents, together with an interpretative preface. I translated, with preface, *The Memoirs of Glueckel of Hamelin* (1932), the narrative of a seventeenth century merchant's wife in Hamburg. My recent book, *New York: The City Washington Knew,* written in collaboration with Frank Monaghan, is a portrait of New York City and its life for the one year, 1789, when Washington was inaugurated as President and the first session of Congress met on Wall Street. It is a return to my earliest and deepest interest—the American past as it shaped our life today. I hope soon to be able to go back, in another book, to one of the springs of that past in the headwaters of the Allegheny."

PRINCIPAL WORKS: A World Passed By, 1933; The Autobiography of Michel de Montaigne, 1935; The Jews of Germany: A Story of Sixteen Centuries, 1936; New York: The City Washington Knew (with F. Monaghan) 1940; Henrietta Szold: Life and Letters (ed.) 1942.

*LOWES, JOHN LIVINGSTON (December 20, 1867-), American scholar and critic, was born in Decatur, Ind., the son of Abram Bower Lowes and Mary Bella (Elliott) Lowes. He was educated at Washington and Jefferson College, in Pennsylvania (B.A. 1888, M.A. 1891), at the Universities of Leipzig and Berlin, and at Harvard (Ph.D. 1905). He has received honorary doctorates from Washington and Jefferson, McGill, University of Maine, Brown, Tufts, Yale, Harvard, and Oxford. He was married in 1897 to Mary Cornett, and has one son. During his years of graduate

study at Washington and Jefferson he also taught mathematics. The remainder of his academic career has been in the department of English: at Hanover College, Indiana, 1895-1902; Swarthmore College to 1909; Washington University (St. Louis) to 1918 (serving also as dean of the college in 1913 and 1914). In 1918 he went to Harvard as professor of English; in 1930 he became Francis Lee Higginson Professor of English Literature, and in 1940 he was retired with the title of Professor Emeritus. He was also dean of the Graduate School of Arts and Sciences in 1924 and 1925. In 1930 he spent a year in Oxford as the first George Eastman Visiting Professor, and Fellow of Balliol College. He has lectured in universities all over the United States, including Texas, California, and Northwestern, and at the University of Wales. He is a Senior Fellow of the Society of Fellows, a corresponding fellow of the British Academy, a fellow of the National Institute of Arts and Sciences, the American Academy of Arts and Sciences, the Mediaeval Academy of America, and the

D. Ulmann

American Association for the Advancement of Science, and a member of many learned societies.

These honors are all well earned. Professor Lowes is undoubtedly one of the greatest of living scholars in his field. Sir John C Squire called his *Convention and Revolt in Modern Poetry,* his first volume, "the best book about poetry which has been written in our generation." His *Road to Xanadu,* a study of the subconscious sources of Coleridge's *Kubla Khan,* in spite of its extreme erudition and the subtlety of its style, became almost a popular sensation; as Theodore Baird remarked, "it transformed source-hunting into something new," a sort of sublimated detective process. He has been a great and inspiring teacher, "a teacher" (to quote the *Outlook*) "who knows that the end of life is not learning but that the end of learning is life." His own highly allusive style, someone has suggested, may some day serve as the starting point for some later critic's delving in turn into the sources of his work, as he delved into Coleridge's.

A small, slight, but wiry man, whose black hair turned gray very late in life, he is still

* Died August 15, 1945.

full of energy and enthusiasm. His resonant bass voice comes as a surprise from so small a person. He is an inveterate smoker, and has more than once set fire to himself in class by absent-mindedly stuffing his lighted pipe into his pocket. Aside from this, however, he is no "absent-minded professor," but has a precise, quick mind of razor-blade sharpness. With George Lyman Kittredge, he edited the synonyms in the *New International Dictionary*. He is a wit as well as a scholar, and he is genuinely interested in young people, as human beings as well as in their capacity as students. His retirement from active teaching merely means that he will now have more time to devote to his work as a literary critic and editor.

PRINCIPAL WORKS: Convention and Revolt in Poetry, 1919; The Road to Xanadu, 1927; Of Reading Books and Other Essays, 1930; The Art of Geoffrey Chaucer, 1931; Geoffrey Chaucer and the Development of His Genius, 1934; Essays in Appreciation, 1936.

ABOUT: Bookman July 1930; London Mercury September 1927; Modern Language Association Publications June 1928; Nation May 18, 1927; New Republic October 5, 1927; Outlook September 10, 1919.

*LOWNDES, Mrs. MARIE ADELAIDE (BELLOC) (1868-), English mystery story writer and playwright, writes: "Through

my French father, Louis Belloc, I am descended from the last colonel of the famous Berwick Brigade, raised in Scotland and Ireland to fight for the Stuarts. My English mother was great-granddaughter to Joseph Priestley, the Unitarian minister and chemist who discovered oxygen. I am the sister of Hilaire Belloc.[qv] I was born a Catholic, and hold firmly to the tenets of that faith.

"I had practically no education at all, save two years in a beautiful and well managed convent school. I lived half the year in France and half in England, which in a way was an education in itself, for it gave me the immense privilege of an intimate knowledge of the literature of two nations—or indeed I may say three nations, for *Rollo* was most certainly my first sweetheart, and the *Little Women* were my first girl friends. Seventeen of my French relations fought in the First World War, and my heart is all French.

"I began writing at the age of sixteen, being at the time deeply interested in history.

Many years went by before I wrote my first novel, though I had always intended to write stories, and very early developed a plot mind. I have no literary preferences. Everything I think good, old or new, whether in poetry, imaginative literature, or *belles lettres*, appeals to me. I do not care for games. Writing, reading, and knowing people are my greatest pleasures. I am proud of having discovered for myself many obscure authors who afterwards became famous. These include Theodore Dreiser, Arnold Bennett, Willa Cather, Walter de la Mare, and Sinclair Lewis.

"I am married to Frederic Sawrey Lowndes, a member of the staff of the London *Times*. I have a son and two daughters.

"I think I may say I work every day of the year, writing in bed in the early morning. I rewrite more, I think, than any author living. Thus a five-thousand-word story often means for my secretary the typing of fifty thousand words."

* * *

It was with *The Lodger* (1913; a fictionized representation of the Jack-the-Ripper murders) that Marie Belloc Lowndes became established as a writer of mystery stories, her previous work having been historical or fictional studies of character. The late Edmund Pearson called this book "the best book about murder written by any living author." A great many of her crime stories are similarly imaginative studies of actual murder cases. She resents being thought of merely as a crime story writer, and says that what really interests her is character and sex. "What has always seemed to me of paramount interest . . . is contained not in the word 'Who?' but in the word 'Why?'"

Besides her brother, Mrs. Lowndes has other celebrated relatives. Her French grandmother was the translator of *Uncle Tom's Cabin* in France. Her mother, who was Bessie Raynor Parkes, was a pioneer English feminist and editor of one of the first women's magazines in England. Mrs. Lowndes herself is small, plump, friendly, with "pale gray-blue eyes with a jolly twinkle, and an ingratiating smile," and with "considerable natural vivacity curbed by even more considerable graciousness and self-possession."

In peacetime Mrs. Lowndes is a frequent visitor to the United States. A recent letter to American friends reports the bombing and burning of her London house in an air raid.

PRINCIPAL WORKS: *Novels*—The Philosophy of a Marquise, 1899; The Heart of Penelope, 1904;

---

* Died November 14, 1947.

Barbara Rebell, 1905; The Pulse of Life, 1907; The Uttermost Farthing, 1908; Studies in Wives, 1909; No Man Pursueth, 1910; Jane Oglander, 1911; The Chink in the Armor, 1912; Mary Pachell, 1912; Studies in Love and in Terror, 1913; The Lodger, 1913; The End of Her Honeymoon, 1914; Good Old Anna, 1915; The Red Cross Barge, 1916; Lilla: A Part of Her Life, 1916; Love and Hatred, 1917; The Lonely House, 1920; From the Vasty Deep, 1920; What Timmy Did, 1921; The Terriford Mystery, 1924; Some Men and Women (short stories) 1925; Bread of Deceit, 1925; What Really Happened, 1926; Thou Shalt Not Kill, 1927; The Story of Ivy, 1928; Cressida, 1928; One of Those Ways, 1929; Duchess (in America; The Duchess Intervenes) 1929; Letty Lynton, 1930; Vanderlyn's Adventure, 1931; Jenny Newstead, 1932; Another Man's Wife, 1934; The Chianti Flask, 1935; Who Rides on a Tiger, 1936; The House by the Sea, 1937; The Marriage-Broker, 1937; Motive, 1938; And Call It Accident, 1939; Reckless Angel, 1939; The Christine Diamond, 1940. *Plays*—With All John's Love, 1932; The Second Key, 1935; Her Last Adventure, 1936; Empress Eugenie, 1938; The Injured Lover, 1939; Christine Diamond, 1940; Before the Storm, 1941. *Miscellaneous*—Life and Letters of Charlotte Elizabeth, Princess Palatine, 1889; Pages From the Journal and Correspondence of Edmond and Jules de Goncourt (ed.) 1894; Lizzie Borden: A Study in Conjecture, 1939; I, Too, Have Lived in Arcadia (autobiography) 1942.

ABOUT: Lowndes, M. A. B. I, Too, Have Lived in Arcadia; Bookman (London) March 1929; London Mercury February 1932; Overland September 1930; Publishers' Weekly January 14, 1933.

LUBBOCK, PERCY (June 4, 1879-   ), English essayist, historian, and novelist, is the son of Frederic Lubbock and Catherine

(Gurney) Lubbock. He had a traditionally happy upper-class childhood. At Eton, where he wrote a whole book of rhyme, life was equally cloudless. From there he went to King's College, Cambridge.

On the recommendation of Howard Sturgis, a close literary friend, he was appointed, in 1906, Pepysian Librarian at Magdalene College, a post which he held about two years, and which gave him access to a wealth of sources for his study (1909) of that ever-popular diarist. In December 1907 he went to Italy with Arthur Christopher Benson, and spent a month in Rome and Florence. At about this time he formed close friendships with several literary celebrities, among them Henry James.

In 1921 Lubbock dissected a number of great novels—the works of Tolstoy, Flaubert, Henry James, and others—and reduced his findings to *The Craft of Fiction*. In

the two years following came, successively, *Earlham,* a tender recollection of his grandparents' home in Norfolk where Lubbock had spent most of his childhood; and *Roman Pictures,* a book of unerring profiles and casually refreshing observations. In 1925 he published a novel, *The Region Cloud,* a somewhat static study in mental relationships; and in the year following he edited the diary of Arthur Christopher Benson, his much admired housemaster and friend at Eton. Still later he wrote the affectionate, faithful, and discreet *Shades of Eton.*

Lubbock is tall, pale, and languid, and has a heavy shock of once black hair. A. C. Benson said that human relationships were for him a "series of deep thrills—exultations and agonies—"and that generous unsuspecting affability, on the other hand, appeared to be for him a kind of "emotional harlotry." He was married, in 1926, to Lady Sybil Desart, who had been previously married to William Bayard Cutting and to Geoffrey Scott.

Italy, Lubbock's home for the decade preceding the Second World War, failed to rekindle his literary energies. "It seems in the nature of things," wrote one of his critics more than ten years ago, "that Lubbock cannot write a great deal more. He has little to do with the fleeting and mediocre, with the hasty and the frivolous."

PRINCIPAL WORKS: Samuel Pepys, 1909; The Craft of Fiction, 1921; George Calderon: A Sketch From Memory, 1921; Earlham, 1922; Roman Pictures, 1923; The Region Cloud, 1925; Diary of Arthur Christopher Benson (ed.) 1926; Mary Cholmondeley: A sketch From Memory, 1928; Shades of Eton, 1929.

ABOUT: Lubbock, P. The Diary of Arthur Christopher Benson; Lubbock, S. M. C. A Page From the Past; Bookman (London) August 1929.

LUCAS, EDWARD VERRALL (1868-June 26, 1938), British essayist, anthologist, novelist, and writer of light verse, was born at Eltham, Kent, not far from London, the son of Alfred and Jane Lucas. The family were Quakers, and themselves quite ordinary people, though their line included in its ambit Lord Lister, A. W. Verrall, the Cambridge classicist, and

Roger Fry, the artist and critic. E. V. was brought up at Brighton, attending eleven schools in all, and at sixteen was apprenticed to a bookseller in that seaside town. From

1889 to the beginning of 1892 he worked as a reporter on the Sussex *Daily News,* and then, thanks to the generosity of an uncle, spent eighteen months at University College, London, where his most useful work was done in the literature class of W. P. Ker. He had an introduction to Richard Whiteing, the novelist, at whose house he began to meet literary people of mark.

In April 1893 he joined the *Globe,* a London evening paper, and, having very easy hours, spent a great deal of time on private work in the British Museum. He formed a useful friendship with C. L. Graves, frequented the bookshops, and in his first professional year, 1893, was asked by the Society of Friends to compile a memoir of Lamb's Quaker friend, Bernard Barton. This was the beginning of his extensive researches on Lamb, which later led to a request from the publishers, Methuen & Co., to prepare a new edition of the essayist's work and a new biography. In 1896 he helped for a brief period on the reconstituted *Academy.* His real start arose out of the publication of an essay on poetry for children in the *Fortnightly,* which caught the eye of the publisher, Grant Richards, who got Lucas to compile *A Book of Verses for Children* (1897) and made him one of his readers. He became an inveterate anthologist, and one of his most successful gleanings, *The Open Road,* was also one of his earliest, coming out in 1899. *Punch* began to give him hospitality about the end of the century. In the autumn of 1903 he was invited to sit at its famous Table. Meanwhile in 1900 he had been commissioned by Methuen to work on Lamb, and he gradually became more and more closely connected with that house, first as reader, and eventually, on Sir Algernon Methuen's death in 1924, as chairman.

Lucas was a most prolific and versatile writer. Apart from his work on Lamb, which is authoritative, he produced about a dozen novels (of which the only one generally read is *Over Bemerton's*), more than thirty collections of essays, sundry works on travel, topography, and art, a series of comic skits with C. L. Graves, two books of reminiscences, and a play. The travel books began in 1905 with *A Wanderer in Holland,* and the most popular of them was *A Wanderer in London.* Lucas never had any success with the stage, but did some useful "lyric" writing during the war of 1914-1918 for light shows like *Business as Usual.* His comical anti-German skits, (done with C. L. Graves and illustrated by George Morrow) had really little malice

in them and were good fun. In 1919 he traveled round the world, giving his impressions in *Roving East and Roving West.*

Lucas' chief claim to remembrance will probably be his work on Lamb and his familiar essays, which are utterly charming and take their place in the best tradition. He had the widest social and literary contacts, belonged to many clubs, loved champagne and good living, rejoiced in his success without being spoiled by it, and was a hard worker all his life. Cricket was one of his enthusiasms, and he would have liked to excel at riding but always remained a little nervous of horses. Dark, heavily built, with prominent nose and ruddy complexion, he looked what he was—a man of the world. From 1896 to 1908 he lived in Kent and thereafter in Sussex, with a London house as well. James Agate, who knew him intimately, once wrote: "I have an idea that the serenity of the writer was a mask hiding the torments of a man knowing as much about hell as any of Maupassant's characters, or even Maupassant himself."

Lucas died at seventy. He had married in 1897 Elizabeth, daughter of James T. Griffin of Rochester, N.Y., whose wife was a Scotswoman. Of the marriage there was born one daughter, Audrey, who wrote a posthumous memoir of her father.

PRINCIPAL WORKS: *Essays*—Fireside and Sunshine, 1906; Character and Comedy, 1907; Good Company, 1909; One Day and Another, 1909; Old Lamps for New, 1911; Loiterer's Harvest, 1913; Cloud and Silver, 1916; Baghdad, With Diversions, 1917; 'Twixt Eagle and Dove, 1918; Mixed Vintages, 1919; The Phantom Journal and Other Essays and Diversions, 1919; Adventures and Enthusiasms, 1920; Urbanities, 1921; Giving and Receiving, 1922; You Know What People Are, 1922; Luck of the Year, 1923; Encounters and Diversions, 1924; Events and Embroideries, 1926; A Fronded Isle and Other Essays, 1927; A Rover I Would Be, 1928; Turning Things Over, 1929; Traveller's Luck, 1930; Visibility Good, 1931; At the Sign of the Dove, 1932; Lemon Verbena and Other Essays, 1932; Saunterer's Rewards, 1933; Pleasure Trove, 1935; Only the Other Day, 1936; All of a Piece, 1937; Adventures and Misgivings, 1938. *Travel & Topography*—Highways and Byways in Sussex, 1904; A Wanderer in Holland, 1906; A Wanderer in London, 1906; A Wanderer in Paris, 1909; A Wanderer in Florence, 1912; A Wanderer in Venice, 1914; London Revisited, 1916; Roving East and Roving West, 1921; Introducing London, 1925; Zigzags in France, 1925; A Wanderer in Rome, 1926; Introducing Paris, 1928; French Leaves, 1931; English Leaves, 1933; London Afresh, 1936. *Art Criticism*—The British School, 1913; Edwin Austin Abbey, 1921; Vermeer of Delft, 1922; Little Books on Great Masters, (8 vols.) 1924-26; A Wanderer Among Pictures, 1924; John Constable the Painter, 1924; Vermeer the Magical, 1929. *Biography & Reminiscences*—Bernard Barton and his Friends, 1893; Charles Lamb and the Lloyds (ed.) 1898;

The Life of Charles Lamb, 1905; A Swan and Her Friends [Anna Seward] 1907; David Williams, 1920; The Colvins aand Their Friends, 1928; Reading, Writing, and Remembering, 1932; The Old Contemporaries, 1935. *Novels*—Listener's Lure, 1906; Over Bemerton's, 1908; Mr. Ingleside, 1910; London Lavender, 1912; Landmarks, 1914; The Vermilion Box, 1916; Verena in the Midst, 1920; Rose and Rose, 1921; Geneva's Money, 1922; Advisory Ben, 1923; Windfall's Eve, 1929; Down the Sky: An Entertainment, 1930; The Barker's Clock, 1931. *Poetry*—Sparks From a Flint, 1891; Songs of the Bat, 1892; All the World Over, 1898; The Book of Shops, 1899; Four and Twenty Toilers, 1900; Visit to London, 1902; Mr. Punch's County Songs, 1928; The Pekinese National Anthem, 1930; No-Nose at the Show, 1931.

ABOUT: Adcock, A. St. J. The Glory That Was Grub Street; Bennett, A. Books and Persons; Gosse, E. W. More Books on the Table; Lucas, A. E. V. Lucas: A Portrait; Lucas, E. V. Reading, Writing and Remembering; Overton, G. M. Cargoes for Crusoes; Swinnerton, F. The Georgian Literary Scene; Cornhill Magazine July 1938; Times (London) June 27 1938.

*LUDWIG, EMIL (January 25, 1881-   ), German biographer, was born in Breslau. His father was Hermann Cohn, an eminent ophthalmologist and professor at Breslau University, who gave him the name of Ludwig at birth to offset the difficulties attending possession of an obviously Jewish name. He himself, however, though at one time he was formally a Christian (he is now a Rationalist), has never denied his Jewish ancestry. He was educated at Breslau and Heidelberg Universities, and from the latter received the degree of Jur. Dr., his main interest as a young lawyer being social welfare. He did not practice long, nor was his subsequent commercial career of much importance. From the age of twenty-five he has been a writer and nothing else. His first writing, however, was entirely in dramatic form, much of it in verse. He was a disciple then of Hoffmannsthal and d'Annunzio, with the nostalgia for classicism of the former and the lush romanticism of the latter. Up to the age of thirty he had never written anything but plays and poems.

In 1912 he visited Africa, and there met Elga Wolff, whom he married a few years later. They have two sons. In 1914, shortly before the outbreak of war, he went to London as correspondent for a German paper. This was his first experience in journalism, and he learned it from the ground up: "I learned more than I achieved," he remarked later. With the war, he returned to Germany, and for four years acted as a correspondent in the countries allied to the Central Powers. Though not a Socialist, he was heartily in favor of the Weimar Republic. The murder of Rathenau, in 1922, stirred him to the depths. In the same year, he had his own brush with the reactionaries. His play on the career of Bismarck was suppressed in Berlin; he sued the suppressors and won its right to appear, and it played for a thousand performances.

Since his middle twenties Ludwig has had a home at Ascona, in the Italian section of Switzerland, on Lake Maggiore. After the Nazis came into power in Germany, this voluntary expatriation of course became compulsory. From Switzerland he set out on his incessant journeys in search of material for his biographies. The first work, however, which arose from his journalistic years (years during which he learned a realistic interest in human beings and an acquaintance with the cross-currents of politics) was not biography, but fiction—two novels, in 1918 and 1919, which ten years later were translated into English as one, under the title of *Diana*.

He was meanwhile gradually evolving his biographical style, which has Plutarch and Carlyle as its models. Plutarch is his ideal, but his "masters in thought," Harry Salpeter noted, are a disparate pair—Goethe and Nietzsche. It was a life of Goethe in which he first appeared as a biographer, and which first made him a part of the new school of biography the chief English exponent of which was Lytton Strachey. Ludwig, however, lacks Strachey's acid wit, though he shares his primary interest in the personality of the subject.

Many of his books have aroused heated criticism, perhaps most of all, in Germany, the biography of Kaiser Wilhelm II, and in all countries his "biography" of Jesus, *The Son of Man*. He has been called meretricious, superficial, a "retrospective journalist," and in some of his work he is every one of these. His style is sometimes flamboyant to an annoying degree, and he is apt to be carried away by his enthusiasms and his prejudices alike. But against this must be placed what George A. Johnston called his "transparent compactness, . . . his precise literary simplicity," and his vividness, sympathy, and power of humanizing the sometimes arid great. Stefan Zweig said truly that "he has revivified biography," especially in German, where before him it was notably dull and stodgy.

* Died September 17, 1948.

Ludwig continues to travel much, and made one long lecture tour in the United States, followed by another visit which led to his book on President Franklin D. Roosevelt. He has a sensitive face, with hair still dark and "deep scrutinizing eyes." He is excitable by nature, and apt to lose his temper with interviewers though he himself is a consummate conductor of interviews. He is an indefatigable worker, and even in late middle age has plans ahead for innumerable books. At the present writing he is making his home in California.

WORKS AVAILABLE IN ENGLISH: Genius and Character, 1927; Napoleon, 1927; William Hohenzollern, 1927; Bismarck, 1927; The Bismarck Trilogy (plays) 1927; Goethe, 1928; The Son of Man, 1928; Diana (novel) 1929; On Mediterranean Shores, 1929; Art and Destiny, 1929; Lincoln, 1929; July 14, 1929; Three Titans, 1930; Schliemann of Troy, 1931; Gifts of Life: A Retrospect (autobiography) 1931; Talks With Mussolini, 1932; Nine Etched From Life (in England: Leaders of Europe) 1934; Talks With Masaryk (in England: Masaryk Speaks) 1934; Hindenburg, 1935; Defender of Democracy: Masaryk of Czecho-Slovakia, 1936; The Nile, 1936; The Nile in Egypt, 1937; Cleopatra: The Story of a Queen, 1937; Roosevelt: A Study in Fortune and Power, 1938; Three Portraits: Hitler, Mussolini, Stalin, 1940; The Germans, 1941; Bolivar, 1942; The Mediterranean, 1942.

ABOUT: Ludwig, E. Gifts of Life; Atlantic Monthly March 1929; Bookman November 1928; Living Age May 15, 1930, April 1931; Outlook February 20, 1928; Saturday Review of Literature March 14, 1931; Yale Review July 1928.

LUHAN, Mrs. MABEL (GANSON) DODGE

(February 26, 1879-), American autobiographer, was born in Buffalo, N.Y., the daughter of Charles F. Ganson and Sara McKay (Cook) Ganson. The family was wealthy and of high social standing, but her parents' marriage was unhappy and she passed a disturbed childhood, most of it spent in private boarding schools in Buffalo, New York City, and Chevy Chase, Md. In 1900 she married another wealthy Buffalonian, Carl Evans, and they had one son, John Ganson Evans, who is now himself a writer. Two years after their marriage her husband was killed in a hunting accident, and the young widow set out for Europe with her baby. On the ship she met Edwin Dodge, an architect from Boston, and soon afterwards they were married. They made their home in Florence, which was the scene of the first of her many salons; this was the "aesthetic phase" of her career. The marriage was a troubled one, and was dissolved ten years later, when Mrs. Dodge returned to the United States to put her son in school. She settled in New York and started another salon, the habitués of which this time were not only artists but also liberals and radicals of all persuasions. After a heated love affair with John Reed, Mrs. Dodge married as her third husband the artist Maurice Sterne. They too were divorced, in New Mexico, where she had gone with him to the new art colony growing up in Taos. In 1923 she married her fourth and present husband, Tony Luhan, a full-blooded Pueblo Indian.

Mrs. Luhan has told her own life-story much more vividly and in infinitely greater detail than it can be recounted elsewhere. She describes herself as "a patron of art and artists and poets, congregating those famous as artists, writers, and musicians in her home salon." Malcolm Cowley has remarked that "she collects people in exactly the same spirit as she collected china dogs for her mantelpiece. . . . She is a species of head-hunter." Actually, however, she has frequently become deeply involved emotionally with some of her "collections," notably D. H. Lawrence, about her relations with whom half a dozen books have been written. As a writer she has concerned herself (except for some early newspaper *feuilletons* in her New York period) almost exclusively with "solemnly indiscreet records" of her own life, which has brought her into touch with most of the well known Americans of her time. Much of her still-continuing autobiography is not to be published until twenty-five years after her death. She lives now in Taos, indomitably combining the social conventions of a wealthy society woman with the free life and the spiritual depths she has discovered in the Pueblo Indians. She is short and inclined to plumpness, with glossy hair still brown and "shiny observant brown eyes." (They *are* brown, though Dorothy Brett called them gray.) She is an indubitable "personality," a phenomenon possible only in her own country and her own era. She has described what *Time* called "a dissatisfied, determined, uneasy career" with (to quote Elizabeth Shepley Sergeant) "a frankness rarely met with among the worldly minded." Her books are a rich source for future historians and biographers, though naturally they are written from the viewpoint of her own nature and her own attitude toward those of whom she writes.

PRINCIPAL WORKS: Lorenzo in Taos, 1932; Intimate Memories: Background 1933; Winter in Taos, 1935; European Experiences, 1935; Movers and Shakers, 1936; Edge of Taos Desert, 1937.

ABOUT: Brett, D. Lawrence and Brett; Hapgood, H. A. Victorian in the Modern World; New Republic November 25, 1936; Saturday Review of Literature November 26, 1938; Time November 23, 1936, January 22, 1940.

LUMPKIN, GRACE, American novelist writes: "The Lumpkins came from England and settled in Virginia in the middle of the seventeenth century.

About 1780 two brothers, one of whom was my direct ancestor, migrated to Georgia. My Virginia ancestors fought in the Revolution, and four of my great-uncles were killed in the Civil War. After I was born my family moved to the country near Columbia, S.C. I graduated from high school and had an added year of school in Georgia. After that I taught school near the place where we lived in the country and organized an adult night school for farmers and their wives. Later I had a position with the Government as Home Demonstration Agent, and learned more about the economic and other problems of farmers and their wives. During most of the summers I lived out in the mountains of North Carolina and at different times stayed with people who worked in cotton mills. During my school days I published stories in the school magazines. I liked to write and wanted to write, but at that time I seemed to be concerned with only two things, the hard details of making a living, and the easier and more pleasant experience of going out at night and enjoying myself with dancing and other pleasures. I worked for two years as industrial secretary for the Y.W.C.A., and though I think this organization does good work in its field, my industrial work only convinced me that the workers could better their lives only by means of unions.

"When I was twenty-five years old I decided that I must begin to write if I was ever to do so. I saved a little money and came to New York for some evening courses in writing at Columbia University. My money was stolen from me the third day I was in New York. Fortunately I found a job almost at once in an office and so was able to attend the classes that I had planned to take. I stayed in my first job for three

years and then, thinking it would give me more time for writing, I became a chambermaid. But with fifty beds to make and rooms and bathrooms to clean I found there was not much time or energy left for writing. So I returned to work in offices, with some extra time in between jobs spent in writing on borrowed money.

"Along with other things I did at this time, I went down to City Hall and was married. Our best man did not show up for three hours. Since for sentimental reasons we wanted him to be present when we were married, we waited for him and I had all the sensations of a bride who is kept waiting at the church.

"By the spring of 1931 half of my novel, *To Make My Bread,* was completed. I was then working in an office and a friend persuaded me to take what I had done to the Macaulay Publishing Co. Four days later I signed a contract which gave me an advance, so that I was able to drop the office work and finish the novel. Later Albert Bein dramatized it and the play opened at the Broadhurst Theatre on November 6, 1935. It was transferred to the Civic Repertory Theatre and ran until April 1936.

"I have written a number of short stories, which have been published in the *Virginia Quarterly Review,* the *North American Review,* and elsewhere; my first story appeared in the *New Masses.* At present I am finishing my fourth novel."

* * *

Miss Lumpkin still lives in New York. She is round-faced, with long blond hair worn in a coronet braid around her head. Her first novel seemed to "type" her as a "proletarian novelist," but with her third, a study of small town Southern life, it became apparent that she had more than one string to her literary bow, and she is now considered one of the most promising of the younger members of the "new" Southern school.

PRINCIPAL WORKS: To Make My Bread, 1932; A Sign for Cain, 1936; The Wedding, 1939.

ABOUT: Bookman November 1932.

*LUNN, HUGH KINGSMILL (1889-), English biographer, literary critic, and anthologist, who signs his works with the partial pseudonym of Hugh Kingsmill, writes: "I was born in London. My father, Sir Henry Simpson Lunn, had recently returned from India, where he had been a Wesleyan medical missionary. During my early years he was engaged in establishing the travel business which bore his name,

* Died May 15, 1949.

and much of my childhood was passed in Switzerland. My education was of the ordinary kind favored by the prosperous classes in England. After Harrow I went to Oxford, but did not take a degree there. For a short time I was associated with Frank Harris, the biographer of Shaw [also Shakespeare and Wilde] and autobiographer of himself. On the outbreak of the last war I joined the Royal Naval Division, and spent the last two years of the conflict as a prisoner of war in Germany. For some years after the war I worked in my father's travel business, chiefly in Switzerland. Leaving it in 1927, I devoted myself entirely to writing until May, 1940, when the shortage of schoolmasters owing to the present war led to my becoming a schoolmaster [at the Merchant Taylors School, Sandy Lodge, Middlesex]. I have been married twice.

"As a biographer, I recognize that an outline of a man's life tells the reader very little about him, unless he has led an active life. My own life has been active only, as it were, in spite of myself. In an age of private and public earthquakes I have frequently had to move farther and faster than suited my temperament. This has doubtless been good for me and my work, but I should be glad if my last years could be passed in the tranquillity suitable to my nature, and in adding to the number of my novels—for in spite of the great interest which biography has for me, I do not think it possible to go as deep in biography as in fiction.

"The books of mine which I prefer are, in the following order, *The Fall* (a novel), *The Dawn's Delay* (short stories), *The Return of William Shakespeare, Samuel Johnson, D. H. Lawrence, Frank Harris,* and a volume of parodies, *The Table of Truth;* and a collaboration with Hesketh Pearson, *Skye High,* an account of a journey through the Highlands in the wake of Johnson and Boswell."

* * *

Mr. Lunn is the younger brother of Arnold Lunn, the Catholic apologist. His only novel was published under his full name. In 1922 he co-operated with "Frederick De Valda" in a short-lived scheme to find homes in France and other Continental countries for retired English officers and other persons of limited means.

PRINCIPAL WORKS: The Fall (in America: The Will To Love) 1919; The Dawn's Delay (short stories) 1924; Matthew Arnold, 1928; After Puritanism: 1850-1900, 1929. The Return of William Shakespeare, 1929; Frank Harris, 1932; The Table of Truth, 1933; Samuel Johnson, 1933; The Sentimental Journey: A Life of Charles Dickens, 1934; The Casanova Fable: A Satirical Revalua-

tion (with W. Gerhardi) 1934; Brave Old World: A Mirror for the Times (with E. Muggeridge) 1936; Made on Earth: A Panorama of Marriage, 1937; Skye High (with H. Pearson) 1937; 1938: A Preview of Next Year's News (with E. Muggeridge) 1937; The English Genius: A Survey of the English Genius and Character, 1938; D. H. Lawrence, 1938; Johnson Without Boswell: a Contemporary Portrait of Samuel Johnson, 1940. *Anthologies (edited)*—An Anthology of Invective and Abuse, 1929; More Invective, 1930; The Worst of Love, 1931; What They Said at the Time, 1935; Parents and Children, 1936; Courage, 1939.

ABOUT: Lunn, A. Come What May; Wilson Library Bulletin April 1941.

"LUSKA, SIDNEY." See "AMERICAN AUTHORS: 1600-1900."

LYND, Mrs. HELEN (MERRELL). See LYND, R. S.

*LYND, ROBERT (April 20, 1879-), Irish essayist, was born in Belfast, the son of the Rev. R. J. Lynd, D.D. and Sarah (Rentoul) Lynd. (He should not be confused with the American sociologist, Robert Staughton Lynd,[qv] the  author of *Middleton,* to whom he is in no way related.) He was educated at the Royal Academical Institution and at Queen's College, Belfast (B.A. 1899). Soon after his graduation he went to London, where he now lives, and entered journalism. He was successful from the beginning, and early in his career specialized in literary criticism and in a kind of light essay-writing which made him one of the earliest and most popular of the newspaper columnists. He is now, and has been for many years, literary editor of the London *News Chronicle.* At the same time, he is a regular staff editorial writer for the *New Statesman and Nation,* his work in that weekly being under the pseudonym of "Y.Y." (What these initials mean, Mr. Lynd has never told.) In 1909 he married Sylvia Dryhurst, who under the name of Sylvia Lynd has become well known as a poet and has also published novels. They have two daughters.

Mr. Lynd is a man of medium height, with a thin humorous face and one whimsically raised eyebrow. He has no time for hobbies or avocations, for he is an almost terribly prolific essayist, who writes in no other form but writes (and publishes) literally dozens of short essays every month.

Many of these, but far from all, have been collected into volumes. They range in subject from literature to politics, from country life to history, but most of them are quite indefinable, since they are the random reflections of a man with a well-stocked mind and a facile fancy. He is by no means so well known in America as in England, largely because his type of light essay, still existent in Great Britain, has almost ceased to be written or read on this side of the Atlantic. He writes too much to be always at his best, but his best is very good indeed—light but not superficial, shrewd, quietly humorous, and as polished as if he wrote one essay a month instead of several a day.

Besides his essays, Mr. Lynd has written four books on Ireland and its people, and two or three of actual literary criticism and history. Ernest Boyd called him "a distinguished essayist," possessing "masculine humor and fancy." In 1932 he edited an anthology called, rather surprisingly, *Love Through the Ages*. Technically, he is known in England as a "middle-writer," which means a writer of short editorials and journalistic essays not of sufficient current importance in subject to be counted as "leaders." He is undoubtedly the best "middle-writer" now functioning in Great Britain, and if an omnibus collection could be made of the very best of the essays in his many volumes, American readers would readily understand why his reputation is so great in England.

PRINCIPAL WORKS: Irish and English: Portraits and Impressions, 1908; Home Life in Ireland, 1909; Rambles in Ireland, 1912; The Book of This and That, 1915; If the Germans Conquered England and Other Essays, 1917; Ireland a Nation, 1919; Old and New Masters, 1919; The Art of Letters, 1920; The Passion of Labour, 1920; The Pleasures of Ignorance, 1921; Books and Authors, 1922; Solomon in All His Glory, 1922; The Sporting Life and Other Trifles, 1922; The Blue Lion and Other Essays, 1923; The Peal of Bells, 1924; The Money-Box, 1925; The Little Angel, 1926; The Orange Tree, 1926; The Goldfish, 1927; Dr. Johnson and Company, 1928; The Green Man, 1928; It's a Fine World, 1930; Rain, Rain, Go to Spain, 1931; The Cockleshell, 1933; Both Sides of the Road, 1934; I Tremble to Think, 1936; In Defense of Pink, 1937; Searchlights and Nightingales, 1939; Modern Poetry (ed.) 1939; Life's Little Oddities, 1941.

LYND, ROBERT STAUGHTON (September 26, 1892-), American sociologist, was born in New Albany, Ind., the son of Staughton Browning Lynd and Cornelia (Day) Lynd. (He is in no way related to and should not be confused with Robert Lynd,[qv] the British essayist.) He was educated at Princeton (B.A. 1914), Union

Theological Seminary (B.D. 1923), and Columbia (Ph.D. 1931). Diverted from his original intention of becoming a clergyman, he next entered, not his final chosen field of sociology, but the publishing world, being editor of the *Publishers' Weekly* from 1914 to 1918, in which year he served as a private in the United States Field Artillery. He then worked as manager of advertising and publicity for the book department of Charles Scribner's Sons, in 1919, and the following year was assistant on the staff of B. W. Huebsch and of the *Freeman*. In 1921 he married Helen Merrell, who has collaborated with him

Steiner-Morris

on his two major books. They have a son and a daughter, and live in New York.

From 1923 to 1926 Dr. Lynd was director of the Small City Study of the Institute for Social and Religious Research. The ultimate result of this work was the publication of *Middletown* (commonly supposed to be Muncie, Ind.), the first attempt to study a modern city of the Occidental world in exactly the same objective spirit and with the same technical methods as had been employed theretofore only in anthropological and social studies of savage communities or prehistoric peoples. Before writing this book with his wife, however, Dr. Lynd spent another year as assistant director of the division of educational research of the Commonwealth Fund. From 1927 to 1931 he was first assistant to the chairman and then permanent secretary of the Social Science Research Council. Since 1931 he has been professor of sociology at Columbia University. In 1937 appeared the "sequel" to *Middletown,* a re-evaluation of the town in the light of the changes brought about by the depression. Dr. Lynd has also written, without collaboration, a rather pessimistic survey of our educational and cultural status, and he is a frequent contributor to sociological and general periodicals. He has been a trustee of the Twentieth Century Fund since 1938, and is a Fellow of the American Association for the Advancement of Science.

The two books on "Middletown" were not only pioneer work, which has given rise to at least one similar English book and to a whole new school of sociological research, but they are also as fascinating reading for those with a love of objective detail and a real interest in the meaning of America and Americanism as can well be imagined. "To study ourselves as through the eye of an outsider is the basic difficulty," remarked Clark Wissler of the American Museum of Natural History; and this difficulty the Lynds were the first to surmount. R. L. Duffus called the two books "the most valuable record we shall ever have of an American community of that period," a "magnificent piece of work which should interest all thoughtful readers," and a work "recognized instantly as a classic."

PRINCIPAL WORKS: Middletown: A Study in Contemporary American Culture (with H. M. Lynd) 1929; Middletown in Transition (with H. M. Lynd) 1937; Knowledge For What? 1939.

LYONS, EUGENE (July 1, 1898-), American journalist and editor, was born in Uzlian, Russia, the son of Nathan Lyons and Minnie (Privin)  Lyons. His family came to the United States when he was nine, and settled in the lower East Side, New York, where "coarseness, vermin, want . . . became routine common-places" and where they felt themselves "aliens and intruders in a nation of Americans."

Young Lyons thought himself a Socialist, he says, almost as soon as he thought at all: he attended a "Socialist Sunday School"; graduated in time to the Young People's Socialist League, and (almost always) carried a volume of Dostoievsky under his arm. From high school he went to the College of the City of New York and then to Columbia, working in the evening to meet his expenses. During the First World War he was "herded" into the Students' Army Training Corps, and shortly after the Armistice he began writing workers' stories for the New York (Socialist) *Call.* Although he worked subsequently on the staff of the Erie (Pa.) *Dispatch* and Wall Street's *Financial America*, his loyalties and most valued contacts remained with the radical labor movement.

In the fall of 1920, convinced that the "impending Italian revolution needed its John Reed out of America," he sailed for Naples, with credentials from the Federated Press and from the *Liberator.* Before long, however, he was taken into custody and then given twenty-four hours to get out of the country. Almost immediately on his return to the States he set out for Boston,

where in a chilly little office he helped to whip up world protest (1921-22) against the conviction of Sacco and Vanzetti. His own extensive account of this case was translated into German, Italian, Russian, and Yiddish; and in 1933 it was fuel for the Nazis' burning of the books. He was married in 1921 to Yetta Siegel; they have a daughter Eugenia Rose.

After a year with *Soviet Russia Pictorial* and four with Tass (then Rosta) the official Soviet news agency, the United Press, in an exchange of facilities with Tass, made him its Moscow correspondent. He succeeded in obtaining the coveted first interview with Stalin after his rise to power.

On a temporary return to the United States in March 1931 he had, already, a few qualms about the new Russia; and back there once again, he began to feel a real disillusionment. Soviet authorities had frowned on several of Lyons' earlier reactions and stories, but his scoop (November 1933) on the bagging of Japanese bombers by Russian aircraft guns wrote his ticket home. He left Moscow on January 31, 1934; got some good glimpses of European dictatorships—largely for *Collier's*; and came home. He joined the publicity firm of Ames and Norr in 1935 and left in January 1939 to become editor of the *American Mercury.*

Lyons edited *Six Soviet Plays* (1936) and *We Cover the World* (1937) tales of wandering correspondents, among which was his own account of the first press interview with Riza Pahlevi, the self-made Shah of Persia. His bitter-titled *Assignment in Utopia* (anticipated in part by *Moscow Carrousel*, 1935) left nothing unsaid on disillusionment with Russian Socialism, until, indeed, his vitriolic study of *Stalin: Czar of All the Russias* (1940). *The Red Decade* (1941) is a detailed invective against American leftist intellectuals which led at least one of the victims to bring suit against Lyons and his publisher. [See sketch of Corliss Lamont.]

PRINCIPAL WORKS: The Life and Death of Sacco and Vanzetti, 1927; Moscow Carrousel, 1935; Six Soviet Plays (ed.) 1936; Assignment in Utopia, 1937; We Cover the World (ed.) 1937; Stalin: Czar of All the Russias, 1940; The Red Decade: The Stalinist Penetration of America, 1941.

ABOUT: Lyons, E. Assignment in Utopia; New York Herald Tribune "Books" January 17, 1939; Saturday Review of Literature October 9, 1937.

LYTTON STRACHEY. See STRACHEY

"MAARTENS, MAARTEN." See SCHWARTZ, J. M.

MABBOTT, THOMAS OLLIVE (July 6, 1898-), American scholar and leading authority on Edgar Allan Poe, writes: "I  was born in New York City, and went to Collegiate School in New York, then entered Columbia and stayed there until I took my Ph.D. in 1923, by editing Poe's unfinished play, *Politian,* not previously published in full. In 1922 I worked for a while as assistant in the New York Historical Society, then was assistant in charge of masters' essays at Columbia; became assistant professor of English at Northwestern University in 1925, went to Brown, 1928-29, then came to Hunter College, where I still am associate professor of English. I've been elected most popular instructor at Northwestern and Hunter. In summer sessions I've taught at Chicago and Duke. In 1928 I married Maureen Cobb, and have one daughter.

"My work has been in several fields, characterized by only one common factor, with enough complexity to make them interesting. In my teaching I emphasize the human significance; in my writings abstract truth in history and letters. I began early to plan a complete edition of Poe's works, with notes, and have in preparation or published a good deal of material by and about him, including, besides his play his *Doings of Gotham,* the *Letters of Eveleth to Poe,* and the play, *Merlin,* by L. A. Wilmer, about Poe, as well as facsimiles of *Al Aaraaf* and *Tamerlane* (this last with very elaborate comment). Incidentally I have collected some short stories by Walt Whitman, *The Half-Breed,* and with Rollo Silver published Whitman's *A Child's Reminiscences.*

"In 1936 I became president of the Edgar Allan Poe Society of New York. I've written a good many articles for the learned journals on literary history, probably over a hundred in London *Notes & Queries,* many in *American Literature,* etc. I was asked to edit such writings of Milton as were not edited by other contributors to the *Columbia Milton,* and with J. Milton French took charge of most of two of the large volumes. This was my chief interest from 1930 to 1938.

"In 1927 I became associated with W. L. Schreiber, then preparing the *Handbuch der Holz- und Metalischnitte des XVten Jahrhunderts* (*Handbook of Wood- and Steel-Cuts of the Fifteenth Century*), and was his assistant in listing separate fifteenth century woodcuts in America. Later I wrote four volumes of the Heitz Series, publications with reproductions of these unique prints. I also wrote on the most puzzling type of fifteenth century printing, the Pasteprints, my monograph of which, published by the Metropolitan Museum, is my own favorite work. My hobby is coin collecting, and my training for work in other fields is always influenced by numismatic method; I spent much time during three summers studying in the Department of Coins and Medals at the British Museum. My discoveries in this field are minor, but I am a veteran reviewer of numismatic books for the *Numismatist.* My other hobbies are reading weird fiction, helping students, and my dog, Muttsy."

PRINCIPAL WORKS: Poe's Brother (with H. Allen) 1926; Pasteprints and Sealprints, 1932. *Edited*—Poe's Politian, 1923; Life and Works of Edward Coote Pinkney (with F. L. Pleadwell) 1926; Walt Whitman's Half-Breed and Other Stories, 1927; Selected Poems of Poe, 1928; Poe's Doings of Gotham (with J. E. Spannuth) 1929; Whitman's A Child's Reminiscences (with R. G. Silver) 1930; Complete Poetical Works of William Wilberforce Lord, 1938; Poe's Raven, 1942.

ABOUT: America's Young Men.

MABIE, HAMILTON WRIGHT (December 13, 1845-December 31, 1916), American editor and literary critic, was born in Cold Spring, N.Y., a village on the east bank of the Hudson opposite Cornwall, the son of Levi Jeremiah Mabie and Sarah (Colwell) Mabie. On his mother's side he was of Scotch-English stock, and on his father's French Huguenot; the  American founder of the family was Sergeant Gaspard Mabille, who settled in New Amsterdam in the middle of the seventeenth century. When the boy was about five the family moved to Buffalo, where Hamilton attended the public schools and his father engaged in the wholesale lumber business. They moved in 1858 to Brooklyn, where the elder Mabie went into the wholesale boot and shoe business, and in 1864 to Tarrytown, N.Y. Hamilton Mabie was ready for college at sixteen, but was advised to read law with a Brooklyn attorney; he probably read more fiction and poetry in the office than law. August 1863 found him back at Williams for the entrance examinations.

In college Mabie read five and six hours a day; helped edit the *Williams Quarterly;* and in his senior year was president of the Adelphic Union, which once imported Emerson to speak to its members. Mabie's particular cronies in Williams were Francis Lynde Stetson and G. Stanley Hall. In 1869 he received a Bachelor of Laws degree from the Columbia Law School and was admitted to the New York bar. Legal work rubbed decidedly against the grain, but Mabie stuck to it for eight years, when he was invited in 1879 by Lyman Abbott to help edit the *Christian Union,* which in July 1893 took the name of the *Outlook.* Mabie married Jeannette Trivett in October 1876. After living for ten years in Greenwich, Conn., they moved to the home of their later years at Summit, N.J., in 1888. For sixteen years Mabie was a member of the vestry of the Calvary (Episcopal) Church there, and took great interest in the Kent Place School for Girls, which he hoped to make a national school equivalent to the Phillips Andover Academy for boys.

Mabie's first book, *Norse Stories Retold From the Eddas,* was published by Roberts Bros. of Boston, in 1882. He edited *Fairy Tales Every Child Should Know* in 1905, and followed it with similar volumes covering folk tales, stories, legends, myths, hero tales, and stories of famous heroines. In 1909 he edited the "After School Library" in twelve volumes. Much of Mabie's work was designed for the *jeune fille;* in the well-known phrase of Frank Moore Colby, he conducted young women into the suburbs of literature and left them there. A high moral tone pervaded his work, which was written in a graceful and fluent style; the distinguishing characteristic of his taste was that it was "correct," rather than good. *The Life of the Spirit* (1899) was one of his most popular books, and the *William Shakespeare* of the next year was well regarded. In 1902 he became a contributing editor of the *Ladies' Home Journal.* Mabie lectured in Japan for six months in 1912 and 1913, speaking on "American Ideals, Character, and Life" under the auspices of the Carnegie Endowment for International Peace. He was first secretary of the National Institute of Arts and Letters, founded in 1898; and in 1908 was elected to the American Academy of Arts and Letters, founded four years before.

In 1915 Mabie suffered a heart attack at the University Club in Philadelphia, and died at seventy-one of cardiac asthma and pneumonia. He was described by an *Outlook* associate as a short, solid-looking, well-dressed man with an invariably cheerful manner.

PRINCIPAL WORKS: Norse Stories Retold From the Eddas, 1882; My Study Fire, 1890; Under the Trees and Elsewhere, 1891; Short Studies in Literature, 1891; Essays in Literary Interpretation, 1892; Short Studies in Literature: Second Series, 1894; Essays on Nature and Culture, 1894; Essays on Work and Culture, 1896; In the Forest of Arden, 1898; The Life of the Spirit, 1899; Our Country in Peace and in War, 1899; William Shakespeare, 1900; A Child of Nature, 1901; Parables of Life, 1902; Works and Days, 1902; In Arcady, 1903; Backgrounds of Literature, 1903; The Great Word, 1905; Christmas Today, 1908; Introductions to Notable Poems, 1909; The Writers of Knickerbocker New York, 1912; American Ideals, Character, and Life, 1913; Japan Today and Tomorrow, 1914; Fruits of the Spirit, 1917; Essays in Lent, 1919.

ABOUT: Morse, E. W. The Life and Letters of Hamilton W. Mabie; Pearson, E. L. Books in Black or Red; New York Times January 1, 4, 14, 20, 1917; Outlook January 10, 1917; Williams Alumni Review January, April 1917.

MACAULAY, ROSE, English novelist, was born in Cambridge, the daughter of G. C. Macaulay, lecturer in English literature at Cambridge University, but was reared in Italy, where she acquired her lifelong love of swimming, sailing, and the sea. She attended both school and college at Oxford, and was still in her teens and a student when (1911) her first novel  was published. She lives in London, with a country home in Beaconsfield, though between the First and Second World Wars she spent much of her time in France and Italy; and she has never married. One critic applied to her her own description of one of her characters in *Staying With Relations*— "ironic, amused, passionless, detached, elegantly celibate . . . a traveled European, a bland mocker, a rather mincing young gentlewoman." She has been called "a feminist, a big-hearted spinster, a gentle cynic, an indulgent recorder of human weakness and folly"; Odell Shepard said she had "abundant wit and deficient warmth. . . . There is something of the feminine dandy in her . . . but more of the maiden aunt." She lives alone and is very reticent about her private life. She calls herself "inefficient," and finds it difficult to discover time enough for her work. Love she thinks "the greatest adventure in people's lives, but not the only one."

Her favorite writers, not unsurprisingly, are Anatole France and Virginia Woolf; her aversions are Thomas Hardy and Henry James. In other words, what she admires is deftness and the light touch; what she dislikes is seriousness and lack of clarity. These preferences are an index to her own writing; she is extremely clever, and she is apt to sacrifice emotion to cleverness, so that she can seem superficial or even heartless. Yet to her, "ignorance, vulgarity, and cruelty are the three black jungle horrors." Doris N. Dalglish, who noted that Miss Macaulay's recurrent theme was "the tragic futility and chaos of the post-war world, which she reproduces with an interest which is partly disgust," called her "a mirror of contemporary opinion and strife," but added that her wit was sometimes "far too easily satisfied with itself."

Her wide recognition came with the satirical novel, *Potterism,* a sort of British analogy to and predecessor of Sinclair Lewis' *Babbitt.* Since then, even when she avows a serious purpose, her books have been unfailingly judged as satire. In the end she has become the victim of her own reputation —as witness her novel *And No Man's Wit,* in which she manages to be caustic and merry in the midst of the tragedy of the Spanish Civil War. In *I Would Be Private,* again, she fell into the pitfall of pure superficial topicalism. Yet her best work—*Potterism, Told by an Idiot, Staying With Relations*—has a personal flavor that is inimitable, and whatever else she is, she is always entertaining. Her inner self has perhaps never come out in her fiction, but only in her poems and in her study of religion in English literature. She is dark, thin, intense-looking.

Most of Rose Macaulay's possessions, including her valued library, were destroyed during the Blitz raids on England.

PRINCIPAL WORKS: *Novels*—The Valley Captives, 1911; What Not, 1919; Potterism, 1920; Dangerous Ages, 1921; Mystery at Geneva, 1922; Told by an Idiot, 1923; Orphan Island, 1924; Crewe Train, 1926; Keeping Up Appearances, 1928; Staying With Relations, 1930; The Shadow Flies, 1932; Going Abroad, 1934; I Would Be Private, 1937; And No Man's Wit, 1940. *Miscellaneous*—The Two Blind Countries (poems) 1914; Three Days (poetry) 1919; A Casual Commentary, 1926; Poems, 1927; Some Religious Elements in English Literature, 1931; They Were Defeated, 1932; The Minor Pleasures of Life, 1934; (as: Personal Pleasures, 1936); John Milton, 1934; The Writings of E. M. Forster, 1938; (ed. with D. George) All in a Maze: a Peace Anthology, 1940.

ABOUT: Braybrooke, P. Some Goddesses of the Pen; Hastings, W. T. (ed.). Extemporary Essays; Johnson, B. Some Contemporary Novelists; Schelling, F. E. Appraisements and Asperities; Sherman, S. P. Critical Woodcuts; Anglia (Halle, Germany) June 1928; Book Window Spring, 1931; Bookman May 1927; Contemporary Review January 1925; Nation December 16, 1931.

*MAC CARTHY, DESMOND (1878-   ), English journalist and critic, is the son of Charles Desmond MacCarthy and Louise (de la Chevallerie) MacCarthy. He was educated at Eton and Trinity College, Cambridge, and spent a term at Leipzig University in an attempt to perfect his German. On one occasion young MacCarthy met Frank Wedekind, the German dramatist, in a beer-hall where the latter was speaking; another literary acquaintance of his youth was Samuel Butler, author of *The Way of All Flesh* and *Erewhon.* In 1906 MacCarthy married Mary Warre-Cornish; they have two sons, and a daughter who married Lord David Cecil. MacCarthy's first experience as an editor was with a periodical called the *New Quarterly.* He edited the *Eye Witness,* whose proprietor was later charged with bigamy and embezzlement. The paper became the *New Witness* and "continued to employ me till it lost the Marconi libel case, after which it became a shakier support."

In 1913 Clifford Sharp invited MacCarthy to write for the *New Statesman,* where the atmosphere was sometimes "a trifle wintry, and Jack Squire, Robert Lynd and I used occasionally to give each other little warm shower-baths of praise and support." MacCarthy's genuine admiration for Sharp is attested in a long dedicatory essay prefixed to one of the volumes of the uniform, collected edition of his (MacCarthy's) work. He became literary editor of the weekly in 1920, later dramatic critic, one who could not "be relied upon to support any particular line of dramatic effort through thick and thin." During the First World War, MacCarthy was a member of a section of the Red Cross attached to the French Army in 1914-15. His later editorial experiences included the editorship of *Life and Letters.* MacCarthy has also contributed weekly articles to the London Sunday *Times;* broadcast literary talks for the British Broadcasting Corporation; and delivered the Leslie Stephen lecture at Cambridge University in 1937. He is generally regarded as one of the soundest and most consistently entertaining of British journalists.

PRINCIPAL WORKS: The Court Theatre: 1904-1907, 1907; Remnants, 1918; Portraits, 1931; Criticism, 1932; Letters of the Earl of Oxford and

* Died June 8, 1952.

Asquith (ed.) 1933; Experience, 1935; Leslie Stephen, 1937; Drama (collected essays) 1940.

ABOUT: MacCarthy, D. Criticism; Marsh, E. A Number of People.

MC CARTHY, JUSTIN. See "BRITISH AUTHORS OF THE 19TH CENTURY"

MC CARTHY, JUSTIN HUNTLY (1860-March 21, 1936), English novelist and historian, was the eldest son of Justin McCarthy, one-time

leader of the Irish Nationalist party in the House of Commons and author of *History of Our Own Times* and of novels in collaboration with Mrs. Campbell Praed.*qv* His mother was Charlotte (Aliman) McCarthy. Justin Huntly McCarthy was educated at University College School and University College, London, began to write at twenty-one, and was himself a Member of Parliament from 1884 to 1892. Two years later he began his career as romanticist by marrying in Edinburgh Marie Cecilia ("Cissie") Loftus, a star of the music halls and once leading woman for Sir Henry Irving. The marriage was dissolved in 1899 in America. McCarthy's name became still more firmly identified with the theatre by the play *If I Were King,* dramatized from his best-selling novel about François Villon which appeared at the beginning of the twentieth century. It gave E. H. Sothern one of his best romantic rôles and a struggling young artist, John Barrymore, a commission to execute a poster. In the middle 1920's the play became the basis of a successful music-drama, *The Vagabond King,* in which Dennis King had his first singing rôle.

Justin Huntly McCarthy, in his own words, engaged in "much journalism and much traveling"—in Europe, Egypt, the Holy Land, and the United States; wrote popular history in the vein of and in collaboration with his distinguished father, and was a prolific writer of romantic historical novels, none of which attained the status or popularity of *If I Were King,* and which could generally be described in the terms the *Nation* applied to one of their number, "an animated and effectively costumed story, ripe for a fall from the bookshelf to the footlights." Plays of his composition included *The Candidate, The White Carnation, The*

O'Flynn, Caesar Borgia, Charlemagne, and (with R. C. Carton) the prosperous *Nurse Benson.* His second wife was Louillie Killick of Budapest. In his prime McCarthy was a singularly handsome Irishman. He died at seventy-five in London, after a long illness.

PRINCIPAL WORKS: *Novels*—If I Were King, 1901; Marjorie, 1903; The Proud Prince, 1903; The Lady of Loyalty House, 1904; The Dryad, 1905; Flower of France, 1906; Seraphica, 1907; The Duke's Motto, 1908; The Georgeous Borgia, 1908; The God of Love, 1909; The O'Flynn, 1910; The King Over the Water, 1911; A Health Unto His Majesty, 1912; Calling the Tune, 1913; Fool of April, 1913; Pretty Maids All in a Row (American title: The Glorious Rascal) 1915; In Spacious Times, 1916; Henry Elizabeth, 1920; The Golden Shoe, 1921. *History*—The French Revolution, 1890-1897; A Short History of the United States, 1898; History of the Four Georges and of William IV (with J. McCarthy) 1901.

ABOUT: Neale's Monthly November 1913; New York Times March 22, 1936.

*MC CORMICK, Mrs. ANNE (O'HARE), American journalist, winner of the Pulitzer Prize, was born in Yorkshire, England, but

was brought to the United States in infancy and reared in Dayton, Ohio. Her maiden name was O'Hare, and she is married to Francis J. McCormick. In 1921, when she began to do free-lance work for the New York *Times,* she was about thirty-five, already married, and her only experience in journalism had been as associate editor of the *Catholic Universe Bulletin.* Her main interest was in art and architecture, and she was a trustee of the Dayton Art Museum (she still is). Her work at once attracted attention by its "accuracy and brilliancy," and she very soon became a regular member of the *Times* staff. The paper sent her abroad, first to Italy (where she was one of the first to foresee the coming importance of Mussolini, and where the fact that she herself is a Catholic gained her an inside connection with the Vatican), then to Germany and to Russia. She has interviewed practically every important international figure of the past two decades, and wrote her only book on what she saw in Russia. In 1936 she became the first woman ever to be appointed to the small editorial council which really governs the *Times,* and she remains the only woman in an important position on that paper, her signed column of

* 1882(?)-May 29, 1954.   **867**

comment on foreign affairs appearing on the editorial page. In 1937 she was the first woman to receive a Pulitzer Prize in journalism. In 1939 Smith College gave her an honorary LL.D. degree, and she was given the Achievement Award of the American Woman's Association, for (to quote Fannie Hurst) "a cumulative achievement in the field of interpretive journalism over a period of years." Carrie Chapman Catt named Mrs. McCormick as one of "America's ten greatest women." Yet this short, retiring, rather shy woman, her once reddish hair now gray, is painfully modest about her accomplishments, saying that the honors given her are merely accidental, because her work has thrown her among stirring events. Be that as it may, she is regarded by most of her colleagues as an unusually keen analyst of world affairs, with a reputation for accuracy. Her general viewpoint is that of a liberal democrat who is very far indeed from being a radical, but in her one book, on so controversial a subject, she has obviously made every effort to be impartial.

PRINCIPAL WORKS: The Hammer and the Scythe (in England: Communist Russia) 1928.

ABOUT: Current History July 1939; Independent Woman July 1939; New York Times Magazine March 24, 1940; Newsweek June 20, 1936.

MC CRAE, JOHN (November 30, 1872-January 28, 1918), Canadian physician and poet, author of "In Flanders Fields," was

born in Guelph, Ontario, of Scottish Covenanter stock, the son of David McCrae and Janet (Simpson) McCrae. After attending the Guelph Collegiate Institute he received a degree in biology from the University of Toronto in 1894, illness preventing his taking a medical degree until 1898. He was a medical officer in the Boer War. For a time McCrae was instructor in pathology at the University of Vermont, returning soon to Montreal to practice. He was reading proof on his *Text-Book of Pathology,* written with a Dr. Adami, in 1914, when the First World War broke out. Before long Dr. McCrae was in France as medical officer with the First Brigade Artillery. During the second battle of Ypres, in April 1915, his dressing-station was established at the foot of a bank of the Yser Canal; men who were shot rolled down the bank into the station. McCrae had written some creditable poetry during the Boer War and for *McGill University Magazine,* but he is remembered only for the fifteen-line poem which *Punch* printed December 8, 1915 ("In Flanders Fields"). The poem was reprinted, for use as an incentive to recruiting in the United States, and was found smeared with blood in the pockets of soldiers. About two years later McCrae died of double pneumonia and massive cerebral infection at No. 14 General Hospital, Wimereux, Boulogne. He was tall, well-knit, cheerful, and boyish, especially in the civilian clothes which he always had cut on the same pattern as in his medical-student days.

PRINCIPAL WORKS: A Text-Book of Pathology, 1914; In Flanders Fields, 1919.

ABOUT: McCrae, J. In Flanders Fields (see Memoir by A. Macphail in 1919 ed. and Introduction by Bishop W. T. Manning in 1921 ed.); Canadian Bookman August 1926; McGill University Magazine April 1918; South Atlantic Quarterly January 1920.

MC CULLERS, Mrs. CARSON (SMITH) (February 1917-), American novelist and short-story writer, was born in Columbus, Georgia,

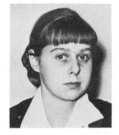

the daughter of Lamar and Marguerite (Waters) Smith. "I have been writing since I was sixteen years old," she has said. "After finishing high school very early I loafed for almost two years before getting off to New York to school again. I began to write at about this time. For several years before then my main interest had been in music and my ambition was to be a concert pianist. My first effort at writing was a play. At that phase my idol was Eugene O'Neill and this first masterpiece was thick with incest, lunacy, and murder. The first scene was laid in a graveyard and the last over a catafalque. I tried to produce it in the family sitting room, but only my mother and my eleven-year-old sister would cooperate. My father, who was startled and rather dubiously proud, bought me a typewriter. After that I dashed off a few more plays, a novel, and some rather queer poetry that nobody could make out, including the author. When I was seventeen I went to New York with the idea of going to classes at Columbia and at the Institute at Juilliard [the Juilliard Foundation]. But on the second day I lost all my tuition money on a subway. I was hired and fired for various part-time jobs and went to school at night. But the city and the snow (I had never seen snow before) so overwhelmed me that I did no studying at all. In the spring I spent a great deal of time hanging around the piers and making fine schemes for voyages. The year after that *Story* bought two of my short stories and I settled down to work in earnest. For two years my husband and I lived in North Carolina. I like to go out for long walks in the woods around here. Also I enjoy playing the piano and listening to phonograph records. . . . All the characters in my book would perhaps be called entirely fictional. I have never in my life been acquainted with a deaf mute, and I would be hard put to tell you just how the book happened to be written. It seems to me that writing, or any art, is not dependent on an act of will but is created spontaneously from some objective source the author can only shape, control and form."

* * *

The novel in question, *The Heart Is a Lonely Hunter* (1940) was intended to present an ironic parable of Fascism. Its central figure is a deaf-mute who loses the only companion to whom he can talk in sign-language, and is compelled to listen to the life-histories of an intellectual Negro doctor, a half-crazy, drunken radical, and a small girl. "Without any lushness, with a hard maturity, Carson McCullers presents poor people in a town in the deep South, the sort Dostoievsky might have written about—but quite differently," Lorine Pruette has said. Lewis Gannett called it "a strange and uneven book, at times almost miraculous in its concise intensity, at times baffling in its meandering immaturity." The Negro author of *Native Son*, Richard Wright, found the most impressive aspect of the novel "the astonishing humanity that enables a white writer, for the first time in Southern fiction, to handle Negro character with as much ease and justice as those of her own race."

Reflections in a Golden Eye (1941) is a brief, intense novel, by most reviewers labeled "neurotic," about the domestic tragedy of an Army officer in a Southern camp.

Mrs. McCullers was awarded a fellowship at the Bread Loaf Writers' Conference, Middlebury, Vt., in the summer of 1940. Her husband is Reeves McCullers, whom she married in 1937. She is living once more in New York. In 1942, at work on a new novel, she was granted a Guggenheim Foundation award.

PRINCIPAL WORKS: The Heart Is a Lonely Hunter, 1940; Reflections in a Golden Eye, 1941.
ABOUT: Current Biography 1940; Time February 17, 1941.

MC CUTCHEON, GEORGE BARR (July 26, 1866-October 23, 1928), American novelist, was born on a farm near Lafayette, Ind., the son of John Barr McCutcheon and Clara (Glick) Mc-Cutcheon. He thus belonged to the so-called "Hoosier School" of writers and was a close friend of George Ade and Booth Tarkington. His brother John became the cartoonist.

The McCutcheons moved in 1876 to Lafayette, where the father became a banker and politician, ending up as sheriff and county treasurer. From early childhood George wrote stories, somewhat in the vein of the then popular dime novels; then he tried plays; but he was nineteen before the *Waverly Magazine* finally accepted a story, which even then was not published for two years more.

He was educated at Purdue University, running away after a year to join a touring theatrical company, but returning disillusioned to college, after being stranded and obliged to walk home. By 1889 he had sold just two stories, for the sum of $25 for both. Despairing of becoming a professional writer, he joined the Lafayette *Journal* as a reporter. By 1893 he was city editor of the Lafayette *Courier*. But he disliked newspaper work, and soon after the success of his second novel resigned. The paper insisted that he work half time, which he did until he moved to Chicago in 1905.

His first, and most popular, novel, *Graustark*, he sold to the publisher for $500. It made half a million for the publisher, and as much more, later, as a play; but the publisher voluntarily paid royalties on reprint editions. This romantic tale of an imaginary Balkan kingdom became a best seller; people tried to buy tickets for Graustark, or pretended they knew characters in the novel. Actually McCutcheon had never been to Europe, had never read Anthony Hope's *Prisoner of Zenda* (nearest to the vein of his book), and said his only inspiration was the *Arabian Nights*.

Another novel which became a long-running play as well, *Brewster's Millions,* was published under a pseudonym on a bet that it would outsell *The Sherrods,* published at the same time under his own name. McCutcheon won the bet. His own favorite of his novels was not *The Sherrods,* as has been said, but *Mary Midthorne,* a realistic story of Indiana. Yet he himself said: "Why read for realism when one can read for thrills?"

In 1904 McCutcheon married Marie (Van Antwerp) Fay, a widow, whose son by her first marriage he adopted. He was president of the Authors' League, 1924-26, and was a collector of first editions, Corots, and Brangwyn etchings. He died suddenly of a heart attack at a luncheon of the Dutch Treat Club in New York, after having suffered from a cardiac disease for a year and a half. McCutcheon in his latter years, was bald, with aquiline features and keen, deep-set eyes.

McCutcheon's novels in all sold over five million copies, to say nothing of the long runs of his plays. He himself lamented the lack of romance in modern life, and was pleased that his most popular books in some measure supplied it, though he attempted over and over again to take the public fancy with more realistic work. To the end of his days, however, he was known as the author of *Graustark, Castle Craneycrow,* and *Beverly of Graustark*—and as an authority on the Balkans, which he never saw.

PRINCIPAL WORKS: Graustark, 1901; Castle Craneycrow, 1902; Brewster's Millions, 1903; The Sherrods, 1903; Beverly of Graustark, 1904; The Day of the Dog, 1904; Nedra, 1905; Jane Cable, 1906; The Flyers, 1907; The Husbands of Edith, 1908; Truxton King, 1909; The Butterfly Man, 1910; Mary Midthorne, 1911; The Hollow of Her Hand, 1912; A Fool and His Money, 1913; Black Is White, 1914; The Prince of Graustark, 1914; Mr. Bingle, 1915; From the House Tops, 1916; Green Fancy, 1917; The City of Masks, 1918; Sherry, 1919; Anderson Crow: Detective, 1920; Quill's Window, 1921; Yollopp, 1922; Oliver October, 1923; East of the Setting Sun, 1924; Romeo in Moon Village, 1925; Kindling and Ashes, 1926; The Inn of the Hawk and Raven, 1927; Blades, 1928; The Merivales, 1929.

ABOUT: Baldwin, C. C. The Men Who Make Our Novels; Bookman May 1925, January 1929; Collier's Magazine April 11, 1925; Literary Digest November 17, 1928.

"MC DIARMID, HUGH." See GRIEVE, C. M.

MAC DONAGH, THOMAS (1878-May 3, 1916), Irish poet and patriot, was born at Cloughjordan, a town in County Tipperary. His parents were both teachers in primary schools. He was trained by a religious order and was a religious novice in early youth, then taught in a college in Kilkenny and afterwards in Fermory. Perfecting

himself in Gaelic, MacDonagh traveled to the Aran Islands and spent some time in the Irish-speaking districts in Munster. Padraic Pearse[qv] had established a bi-lingual secondary school for boys in Rathmines, a suburb of Dublin, called Sgoil Eanna or St. Enda's; MacDonagh joined the staff and became fast friends with Pearse. The school was one of the two lay Catholic schools in Ireland. MacDonagh's five volumes of poems published between 1902 and 1913 show many characteristics of the poetry of the Celtic Renaissance, in their lyrical freshness, quaint humor, and fondness for the ballad form. They also show, as A. Raybould says, an intensely speculative mind; MacDonagh was "in subtle philosophizing another Crashaw, however surcharged with passion."

After a reading session in Paris, MacDonagh obtained his M.A. degree in the National University, Dublin, which made him assistant professor of English literature after the submission of his thesis, "Thomas Campion and the Art of English Poetry." MacDonagh knew poetry well in English, French, Latin, and Irish; he was particularly drawn to Catullus, Dante, and Racine. With his wife, small son, and infant daughter he lived at Grange House Lodge, Rathfarnham. When the Irish Volunteers were organized in the winter of 1913 he was placed on the "Executive" with command of a corps. After the uprising in the spring of 1916, MacDonagh, Pearse, and others were shot by a British firing squad in Dublin Castle on Holy Cross Day. MacDonagh was thirty-eight. An officer who witnessed the executions said, "They all died well, but MacDonagh like a prince." Padraic Colum wrote that he had a short figure, a scholar's brow and dominating nose. "He looked a man of the Gironde—a party he often spoke of."

PRINCIPAL WORKS: Through the Ivory Gate, 1902; April and May, 1903; The Golden Toy, 1906; Songs of Myself, 1910; Lyrical Poems, 1913; Poetical Works, 1917.

ABOUT: Colum, P. & O'Brien, E. J. Poems of the Irish Revolutionary Brotherhood; MacDonagh, T. Poetical Works (see Introduction by James Stephens); Irish Monthly September 1919; New York Times May 4, 7, 1916.

MAC DONALD, GEORGE. See "BRITISH AUTHORS OF THE 19TH CENTURY"

MAC DONALD, PHILIP (189?-), English novelist and writer of detective fiction, is as reticent about the details of his personal life as some others

in his mysterious clan, such as "Ernest Bramah" and "John Rhode," though unlike them his best known books appear over his own name. He is known to be the grandson of George MacDonald, the Scottish novelist, author of the children's classics *At the Back of the North Wind* and *The Princess and the Goblin.* According to his publishers, Philip MacDonald has been a gentleman sportsman, breaking in horses imported for Army service from the Argentine; served in a cavalry regiment in Mesopotamia in the First World War; and published his first novel about a boxer, before he turned to the more profitable business of setting up straw men of crime. He had never made any special study of criminology nor had any connection with Scotland Yard when he became a gentleman-ranker in the regiment of crime-story writers.

MacDonald's first detective novel *The Rasp* (1924), introducing his sleuth, Colonel Anthony Gethryn, was an immediate success and has become a small classic of the *genre.* It has been followed by a dozen others which are almost invariably choices of the Crime Clubs in both England and the United States. *Escape,* a non-Gethryn thriller, is held in particularly high regard by devotees of "the blood." In quite another vein, *Patrol* is a distinguished story of a desert patrol of English soldiers in Mesopotamia, which has been filmed with marked success. Horses have always remained MacDonald's greatest hobby; he has done a good deal of fancy riding and jumping at horse shows, and has always admitted to the ambition to ride in the Grand National, England's most famous and dangerous steeplechase. H. C. Harwood calls him, as a detective-story writer, "gay, forcible, and a fair player." Norman Klein appraises his writing as decently loaded with exclamation points, and the books in general as extremely workmanlike and cleverly plotted. MacDonald is something of a fanatic on the point of giving his readers a fair chance, concealing no clues or essential details: *Persons Unknown* was written expressly to illustrate this thesis: "a due and proper unfolding to

the reader of the tale and of the relevant pieces, however small, of the puzzle. . . . The ideal detective story is a sort of competition between author and reader."

Philip MacDonald has also written under the pseudonyms of "Oliver Fleming," "Anthony Lawless," and "Martin Porlock."

At the present writing MacDonald is in Hollywood as a scenarist, where he has produced some notable scripts, among them the screen-play of Daphne du Maurier's *Rebecca,* as filmed by Alfred Hitchcock.

PRINCIPAL WORKS: Gentleman Bill: A Boxing Story, 1922; The Rasp, 1924; Patrol, 1928; The White Crow, 1928; Likeness of Exe, 1929; The Link, 1930; The Noose, 1930; Persons Unknown: An Exercise in Detection, 1930; Rynox, 1930; The Choice, 1931; Moonfisher, 1931; The Wraith, 1931; Murder Gone Mad, 1931; The Crime Conductor, 1932; Escape, 1932; Rope to Spare, 1932; Death on My Left, 1933; Menace, 1933; Mystery of the Dead Police, 1933; R. I. P., 1933; The Nursemaid Who Disappeared (U. S. title: Warrant For X.) 1938. *As "Oliver Fleming"*—The Spandau Quid, 1923. *As "Anthony Lawless"*—The Harbour, 1931. *As "Martin Porlock"*—Mystery at Friar's Pardon, 1931; Mystery in Kensington Gore, 1932; Moonfisher, 1932; X v. Rex, 1933.

ABOUT: Haycraft, H. Murder for Pleasure: The Life and Times of the Detective Story; Thomson, H. D. Masters of Mystery; Bookman (London) June 1929.

MACDONELL, ARCHIBALD GORDON (November 3, 1895-January 16, 1941), Scottish novelist, satirist, and writer of detective fiction, was born at Aberdeen, the son of William Robert Macdonell, LL.D., and Alice Elizabeth (White) Macdonell; the name is accented on the final syllable. He was educated at Winchester, and in the First World War

was a lieutenant in the Royal Field Artillery of the 51st Highland Division (Territorial Forces), from 1916 to 1918. From 1922 to 1927 Macdonell was a member of the headquarters staff of the League of Nations Union. In 1923 and 1924 he contested Lincoln as a Liberal candidate for Parliament. For some of his writings he employed the pseudonym "John Cameron," and as "Neil Gordon" he wrote nearly a dozen detective stories, some of them choices of the Crime Club in both England and the United States. In *The Shakespeare Murders* (1933) his detective, Peter Kerrigan, solves a mystery which involves a cipher concocted from

Hamlet, although he is no Shakespeare student himself. In 1933, also, Macdonell published his riotously amusing study of British manners and customs, *England, Their England.* "The Scot does not laugh hastily," wrote Christopher Morley in his Foreword to the American edition. "I imagine Mr. Macdonell watching the oddities of England, calmly self-contained, for (say) fifteen mature years. Then he could bear it no longer. Something snapped. He uttered a long and echoing guffaw. But in the actual relief of this explosion he realized also that while laughing he had learned to love." Macdonell was secretary of the Sherlock Holmes Society of London, and attended the state dinner of the American organization, the Baker Street Irregulars, on December 7, 1934, in New York City. Observers saw a tall, athletic, energetic young Scot with a close-cropped moustache. His book of American reminiscences, *A Visit to America* (1935), was circumspectly written. *Lords and Masters* (1936) and *The Autobiography of a Cad* (1939) were other volumes of satire, somewhat overweighted by suppressed indignation. *Napoleon and His Marshals* (1934) is an interesting historical study which shows Macdonell's grasp of strategy. He contributed *My Scotland* to the My Country Series in 1937, and in 1939 wrote a play, *What Next, Baby,* and published a volume of short stories, *The Spanish Pistol.* His recreations were golf, cricket, and tennis. He was killed in an air raid at Oxford two months after his forty-fifth birthday.

PRINCIPAL WORKS: England, Their England, 1933; Napoleon and His Marshals, 1934; How Like an Angel, 1934; A Visit to America, 1935; Lords and Masters, 1936; My Scotland, 1937, Autobiography of a Cad, 1939; The Spanish Pistol and Other Stories, 1939; The Crew of the Anaconda, 1940. *As "Neil Gordon"*—The New Gun Runners, 1928; The Professor's Poison, 1928; The Silent Murders, 1929; Seven Stabs, 1930; The Big Ben Alibi, 1930; The Factory on the Cliff, 1930; A Body Found Stabbed, 1932; Murder in Earl's Court, 1933; The Shakespeare Murders, 1933.

ABOUT: Macdonell, A. G. England, Their England (see Foreword by Morley); New York Times January 18, 1941; Wilson Library Bulletin April 1941.

MC FALL, Mrs. FRANCES ELIZABETH. See GRAND, S.

MACFALL, HALDANE (July 24, 1860-July 25, 1928)

British novelist and art historian, was christened Chambers Haldane Cooke Macfall. He was the eldest son of Lieut.-Col. D. Chambers Macfall and Mabel (Plumridge) Macfall, the daughter of an admiral. After attending Norwich

Grammar School and Sandhurst, the military school, Macfall was gazetted to a West India Regiment in 1885, served in Jamaica, where he took notes for his famous picaresque novel, *The Wooings of Jezebel Pettyfer* (1897). Macfall served also in West Africa, retiring as lieutenant in 1892. In the First World War he was made Captain of the Essex Regiment in January 1915 and was major (second in command) of the Sherwood Foresters. Beginning with his *Whistler* of 1905, Macfall published several erudite and fascinating books on the history and criticism of art, culminating in the eight-volume *History of Painting* published in 1910. Besides writing monographs on the work of Boucher, Fragonard, and Vigée Le Brun, Macfall was himself a painter, exhibiting at the Royal Academy, the International, etc. He was awarded a Civil List pension for distinction in literature, in 1914. At sixty-six he published *The Three Students,* a closely-packed historical novel of eleventh - century  Persia which critics compared to Flaubert's *Salammbô.* Omar Khayyám is one of its chief protagonists.

Macfall's novel, *The Masterfolk* (1905), dedicated to George Meredith, is a novel of Bohemian life in literary London and artist Paris of the 1890's. Frequently Dickensian in tone, and full of romantic sentiment, it is nevertheless a biting satire on English decadents, in which the most obvious caricature was a personage named Quilliam O'Flaherty Macloughlin Myre (Oscar Wilde). His best-known novel, *The Wooings of Jezebel Pettyfer,* has been called by Vincent Starrett a "West Indian blend of *Pickwick, The Three Musketeers,* and the Spanish romances of roguery." Jezebel is a Barbadian Negress, "reckless, unmoral and delightful," whose first recorded lover is John Sennacherib Dyle, barrack boy, butler, soldier, deserter, and fugitive. The book has "uncensored and uproarious humor, fine humanity and tolerance, tumult and gusto of style." It is the last of a great line of picaresque romances. Meredith told Macfall the novel was the finest of his generation, but "ought never to have been written." Macfall, who died the day after his sixty-eighth birthday, seems to have been a man of rich and fascinating personality, although a terror to the *poseurs* and *claquers* of the

London art world. He could address himself to any level of the reading public, as is shown by the popularity of his war books, written for the man in the street. He listed his recreations as the playhouse, designing covers and decorations for books, and the study of life and people.

PRINCIPAL WORKS: The Wooings of Jezebel Pettyfer, 1897; The Masterfolk, 1903; Whistler, 1905; Irving, 1906; Ibsen, 1906; Old English Furniture, 1908; Beautiful Children, 1909; The French Pastellists of the Eighteenth Century, 1909; History of Painting, 1910; The Splendid Wayfaring, 1913; The Nut in War, 1914; Battle, 1914; Germany at Bay, 1917; Beware the German's Peace, 1918; The Book of Lovat, 1923; The Three Students, 1926; The Life of Beardsley, 1927; Songs of the Immortals, 1927; Persuasions to Joy, 1927.

ABOUT: Starrett, V. Buried Caesars; American Magazine of Art September 1930.

MC FEE, WILLIAM (June 15, 1881-),

Anglo-American novelist and essayist, writes: "Being born in 1881, I was brought

Gorska-Hill

up in a Victorian household. My father, John Henry Mc-Fee, a master in sail, had recently retired from the sea and settled in London, which was the center of the maritime world, as a professional ship's-husband, or, as they now call

themselves, marine superintendent. My father had been part owner of a shipyard at Countney Bay, near St. John's, N.B., and there married my mother, Hilda Wallace, daughter of William Wallace, a farmer on the Petitcodiac River. For three years she sailed, as captain's wife, in the ship 'Erin's Isle.' My father died in 1891. I was the eldest of three young children whose Canadian mother had some difficulty in adjusting her colonial ideas to suburban life in London. I must have been sent to all the schools in the district before I finally found refuge from home life and suburban suppression in the East Anglian School at Bury St. Edmunds, Suffolk, now known nationally as Culford School.

"In my seventeenth year I was articled as a premium apprentice to Richard Moreland & Sons, mechanical engineers of Old Street, in the City. This cost £300. It lasted three years, and I learned something about engines. I studied at night. The American method, of going to college to learn what any man of energy can acquire

at night, strikes me as namby-pamby, and an unfortunate prolongation of adolescence.

"At the end of the three years, in spite of the £300, as I had no influence, I was fired. I had several months of unemployment. I was then adopted by a successful consulting engineer as his assistant in the London office of a large Yorkshire firm manufacturing laundry machinery. I say 'adopted' because Thomas George Newton was very much in loco parentis to me for over four years. He had a large family of sons and daughters of his own, but he must have liked me, for he treated me very handsomely and taught me a lot of selling and designing. Once or twice he fired me, but decided to give me another chance. Then one day, I ran away. I simply bolted. One of my father's brothers was a Marine Superintendent in London. I persuaded him to give me a job on a tramp. He was gloomy. He did not believe I would stick it. I got on a train and went to Newcastle-on-Tyne and went to sea. I stuck it. I stuck it for the years 1906-1911, when I quit as chief engineer of 'S.S. Fernfield' and came to live in the United States. I was thirty years old.

"My former employer, Mr. Newton, must have been surprised to get a letter from Newcastle announcing my flight. I called on him some six months later. He was very much amused. I had refunded my week's wages, which I had forfeited by not giving notice, and he made me take it back. God rest his soul. He was a man who had a big hand in making something of me.

"I wrote several books in America. I completed Casuals of the Sea, which I had been writing at sea for some time. My first book, Letters From an Ocean Tramp, came out with Cassell in 1908. I was in Kobe, Japan, at the time. When we reached Boston, with a cargo of sugar from Java, Christmas 1908, my book was on sale ($1.50 net). I did not buy a copy; $1.50 was a lot of money in those days, and I knew I would get six free copies at home.

"Barring the war, I have been in America since 1912. If America can stand it, I can. I am still an associate member of the Institute of Mechanical Engineers in London, my sole remaining link with my former profession. I was honored by Yale with an M.A. degree a few years ago, which I try to live up to. I have lived in Westport, Conn., since I quit the sea in 1922. My former employers, the United Fruit Co., gave me 'leave of absence,' but I fear I turn up nowadays only as a passenger."

* * *

William McFee served through the World War as sub-lieutenant in the British Navy. In 1920 he married Pauline Khondoff, from whom he was divorced in 1932. The same year he married Beatrice Allender. He was born at sea, homeward bound from India, and most of his novels and stories have concerned the sea. In his home he likes to amuse himself by making ship models to scale. He conducts a weekly column on shipping for the New York *Sun.* A big, blond man, with bright blue eyes, he is a lover of outdoor life, of animals and children. He is often compared with Conrad, but they have nothing in common except their maritime profession; McFee is neither so romantic nor so interested in psychology as was the great Polish novelist. He is primarily a teller of tales, his recurrent character being Chief Engineer Spenlove, "his garrulous, ironic, goateed *alter ego.*"

PRINCIPAL WORKS: Letters From an Ocean Tramp (non-fiction) 1908; Aliens, 1914; Casuals of the Sea, 1916; A Port Said Miscellany, 1918; Captain Macedoine's Daughter, 1920; A Six-Hour Shift, 1920; Harbours of Memory (essays) 1921; An Engineer's Notebook, 1921; The Gates of the Caribbean, 1922; Studies in Patriotism, 1922; Command, 1922; Race: A Prelude (non-fiction) 1924; Swallowing the Anchor, 1925; Sunlight in New Granada (non-fiction) 1925; Life of Sir Martin Frobisher, 1928; Pilgrims of Adversity, 1928; Sailors of Fortune, 1929; North of Suez, 1930; The Harbourmaster, 1932; No Castle in Spain, 1933; More Harbours of Memory (essays) 1934; The Beachcomber, 1935; The Derelicts, 1938; The Watch Below, 1940; Spenlove in Arcady, 1941.

ABOUT: A Book of Great Autobiography (symposium); Adamic, L. From Many Lands; Babb, J. T. Bibliography of William McFee; Maule, H. E. William McFee; Saturday Review of Literature October 3, 1931; Time November 21, 1938; Yale Review June 1939.

MAC GRATH, HAROLD (September 4, 1871-October 30, 1932), American popular novelist, was born in Syracuse, N.Y., the

son of Thomas H. MacGrath and Lilian Jane MacGrath, was educated there, and in 1890 went to work on the Syracuse *Herald* as a reporter under E. H. O'Hara, its publisher, who later set him to conducting a humorous column. *Arms and the Woman,* MacGrath's first novel, appeared in 1899. *The Grey Cloak* (1903)

capitalized the current vogue for historical novels. *The Man on the Box,* a best-seller of the year, was published in 1904 and was promptly dramatized. Henry E. Dixey gave 123 performances in New York of this light-hearted farce of the horse-drawn cab era, about a young Washington "society man," who masqueraded as his inamorata's coachman. The play was a stock-company favorite and was filmed; MacGrath's best-known contributions to moving pictures, however, were the early "silent" serials "The Perils of Pauline" and "The Million Dollar Mystery," one of the greatest money-makers of pioneer cinema history. After a short time with the Albany *Knickerbocker Press,* MacGrath conducted a column for the Chicago *Evening Mail,* when George Ade and Eugene Field were on rival newspapers across the street. His income, at its peak, was $30,000 a year, and he bought a villa at Lake Como and took his wife around the world. MacGrath kept regular office hours, wrote in longhand, and did not take too seriously either himself or his career as a romancer and story-teller. He frankly termed his novels "fairy-tales for grownups" and turned them out by the score, writing 7,000 words a day or more in his prime. He died in Syracuse at sixty-one after an illness of several months. His "books reflect his own enjoyment and mirror his own optimistic philosophy, imbibing no taint of forced enthusiasm," remarked the editor of the *Reader* when *The Man on the Box* was on the crest of its popularity.

PRINCIPAL WORKS: Arms and the Woman, 1899; The Grey Cloak, 1903; The Man on the Box, 1904; The Princess Elopes, 1905; Enchantment, 1905; Half a Rogue, 1906; The Lure of the Mask, 1908; The Goose Girl, 1909; The Carpet From Bagdad, 1911; Drums of Jeopardy, 1920; The Cellini Plaque, 1925.

ABOUT: New York Times October 31, 1932; The Reader July 1903.

*MACHEN, ARTHUR (1863-   ), Welsh novelist and essayist, was born in Caerleon, England, the only child of a clergy-

man. He was a dreamy, introspective child, early under the spell of that haunted region one of the last stands of the ancient Britons. He grew up a solitary and a mystic, his literary idols De Quincey and Scott. The private schools he attended made little impression upon him.

* Died December 15, 1947.

Anyone less fitted than this boy, who lived as much in the past as in the present, to make his own way in London can not well be imagined. Yet at eighteen he found himself in Paddington, a clerk in a publishing house who wrote poetry to ease his misery. He had already published a long poem, *Eleusinia* (1881), of which he says that "fortunately" he possesses the only copy extant. For the saving grace of this young dreamer was his quiet humor, without which much of his life would have seemed to him insupportable. His whole London career in its early years was wretched; when he could endure office work no longer he became a badly paid teacher; then even this failed him and he tried vainly to make his way as a free-lance writer until all his money was gone and he returned home.

There he supported himself by translations from the French. *The Anatomy of Tobacco*, which he had written in London, was published under a pseudonym. He found himself called "a second-rate imitator of Stevenson." Considering that writing has always been torture to him, it is a wonder that he persisted. But he did persist, and his major work began with the first of his "long picaresque romance of the soul," *The Hill of Dreams*, published ten years after he wrote it—and after a publisher who had rejected it announced the appearance of a book on exactly the same theme (which, however, never came out).

In 1902, with five books already to his credit, Mr. Machen suddenly became an actor, at thirty-nine. For several years he toured with the Benson Shakespearian Repertoire Company. He has retained to this day many of the mannerisms and much of the appearance of the old-time Shakespearian actor, including the deep sonorous voice which must first have caused him to think of the stage as a career. He married, in middle age, one of the actresses of the Benson Company, and they have two sons.

At fifty he began still a third career, as a journalist, and for nearly a decade was a regular contributor to the *Evening News*. Then he deserted London for Old Amersham, Buckinghamshire, where he lives now, his chief recreation being shooting or, as he puts it, "dog and duck." In the course of his life he had inherited a small fortune, but spent it all on travel. His books have never earned him a real livelihood. They have been the treasures of a few. The only thing he ever wrote which gained widespread popularity was the wholly fictional account of the "angels of Mons," which thousands of soldiers believed in devoutly during the World War.

Arthur Machen's literary career is over; his only recent book is a compilation from the past. In his early sixties he deliberately killed himself as an author, since writing had always been painful and he had won by it neither fame nor economic security. He writes: "I was born in 1863; in other words, I am now rather old and tired." John Gunther has described him as he was fifteen years ago, and as he still is—with his thick white hair "in a horizontal bob," his "clouded blue eyes," his "waxen hands." Oliver Warner called him "the last of the literary dictators, the best talker, and greatest 'character' left in letters."

His work is literary caviar, wry in the mouths of most people but a passion with those susceptible to its ghostly powers. His evocation of the depths of evil is masterly. More than any other writer he can materialize the shuddering forces of another world—perhaps because he himself has lived all his life across its border. While he still lives he has become a legend, and so long as stories of the supernatural are read, Arthur Machen's will be among them.

His name is pronounced *mach'en*.

PRINCIPAL WORKS: *Fiction*—The Chronicle of Clemendy, 1888; The Great God Pan, and The Inmost Light, 1894; The Three Imposters, 1895; Hieroglyphics, 1902; The House of Souls, 1906; The Hill of Dreams, 1907; The Great Return, 1915; The Bowmen, and Other Legends of the War, 1915; The Terror, 1917; The Shining Pyramid (short stories) 1924; The Children of the Pool, 1936. *Miscellaneous*—The Anatomy of Tobacco (as "Leolinus Siluriensis") 1884; Far Off Things, 1922; Things Near and Far, 1923; Strange Roads, 1923; The London Adventure, 1924; Dog and Duck, 1924; Notes and Queries, 1926; Dreads and Drolls, 1926.

ABOUT: Machen, A. Far Off Things, Things Near and Far, The London Adventure; Bookman July 1925; Bookman (London) March 1932; Mercure de France January 1, 1938; Revue Politique et Littéraire September 3, 1927; Sewanee Review July 1924.

MC HUGH, VINCENT (December 23, 1904-), American novelist writes: "I was born in Providence, R.I., of Irish- and Scotch-American stock. My father is a printer and amateur painter. My mother, Mary Young, was assistant superintendent of evening schools in Providence. She died when I was eleven years old. I was brought up as a Roman Catholic, sent to parochial schools and Providence College. At the end of my freshman year, I was forced out of the latter institution for reasons not unlike Shelley's in similar circumstances. I had been very reluctant to bring up my non-religious views. My family had a house at West Barrington on Narragansett Bay. There and in Providence I played baseball, football, hockey,

learned swimming, gardening, and sailing—in a three dollar skiff. From my thirteenth year I worked at odd jobs—soda jerker, bottler, newspaper bundler, etc. but my four years as a public library messenger probably decided my tastes.

Pinchot

I can think of no better place for a writer to learn his trade.

"At seventeen I did book reviews for the New Orleans *Double Dealer,* and began my first novel at twenty. I went to New York in 1928, and did book reviews, verse, articles, and fiction for newspapers and magazines. I also worked for a time as associate editor of the New York *Evening Post Literary Review* [which eventually became the *Saturday Review of Literature*]. In 1933 I returned to West Barrington and lived there till 1936. Then for two years I was editor-in-chief of the Federal Writers' Project in New York City. I helped to edit *American Stuff,* and planned and directed work on *New York Panorama* and the *New York City Guide* up to their final stages. I contributed the essays 'Metropolis and Her Children' and 'The Urban Pattern' to *New York Panorama.* I am now writing the short non-fiction book reviews for the *New Yorker* and teaching a seminar in the technique of the novel at New York University. I have in preparation a book of verse, a short novel about New York, and two sequels to *Caleb Catlum's America.* In collaboration with Valentine Davies, I am also working on a musical comedy in which Caleb Catlum is the chief figure.

"I have been married continuously for eleven years, have no children, and live in Lindenhurst, L.I. My taste in politics runs to democratic pluralism. I admire John Dewey, Jules Romains, Arthur Singleton, and Edward Ellington. My avocations are sharpie sailing and hot music. Besides the books mentioned, my work has also appeared in *American Stuff, Best Short Stories of 1935,* and *A Quarto of Modern Literature.*"

* * *

Mr. McHugh's best known novel, *Caleb Catlum's America,* is practically indescrib-

able; Caleb Catlum is an imagined folk-figure, roistering, full-blooded, and, to quote his author, "a kind of devil in the American cheese."

PRINCIPAL WORKS: Touch Me Not, 1930; Sing Before Breakfast, 1933; Caleb Catlum's America 1936.

ABOUT: Wilson Library Bulletin November 1936.

MC ILWAIN, CHARLES HOWARD

(March 15, 1871-), American historian and Pulitzer Prize winner, was born in Saltsburg, Pa., and was educated at the College of New Jersey (now Princeton University) (B.A. 1894, M.A. 1898) and Harvard (M.A. 1903, Ph.D. 1911). He also has honorary doctorates from Harvard, Williams, and the College of Wooster. He was admitted to the Pennsylvania bar in 1897, but after a year turned to teaching, being teacher of Latin and history at Kiskimenetas School from 1898 to 1901. From 1903 to 1905 he was professor of history at Miami University, Oxford, Ohio; from 1905 to 1910 preceptor at Princeton; in 1910 and 1911 Thomas Brackett Reed Professor of History and Political Science at Bowdoin College. In 1911 he went to Harvard, first as assistant professor of history, then as professor of history and government; since 1926 he has been Eaton Professor of the Science of Government. He is a trustee of Princeton, a Fellow of the American Academy of Arts and Sciences and the Mediaeval Academy of America, a corresponding member of the Royal Historical Society, and past president (1935) of the American Academy of Arts and Sciences and the Mediaeval Academy of America, a corresponding member of the Royal Historical Society, and past president (1935) of the American Historical Association. In 1899 he married Mary B. Irwin, who died in 1906, leaving a son and daughter; in 1916 he married Kathleen Thompson, and they had a daughter and two sons (one deceased). They live in Belmont, Mass.

In 1924 Professor McIlwain received the Pulitzer Prize in history for *The American Revolution,* described as "a constitutional interpretation."

PRINCIPAL WORKS: The High Court of Parliament and Its Supremacy, 1910; The American Revolution, 1923; The Growth of Political Thought in the West, From the Greeks to the End of the Middle Ages, 1932; Constitutionalism and the Changing World, 1939; Constitutionalism, Ancient and Modern, 1940.

MAC INTYRE, CARLYLE FERREN

(July 16, 1890-), American poet, was born "on a train somewhere in the Middle

West," and reared in Southern California. His father was a furniture maker, Scotch by birth; his mother, who was partly of German descent, was cultured and scholarly-minded, and had a great influence on his literary development. He was graduated from the University of Southern California in 1917, and received his Ph.D. in 1922 at Marburg University for a thesis (in German) on the use of color in Rossetti's poems. He became a teacher of English at Occidental College, where he was something of a campus celebrity, thanks to his invariable black sombrero (somebody stole it once and he threatened to flunk every student unless it was returned) and his old auto in which he rushed around town. In 1928 he became a member of the faculty of the University of California at the Los Angeles branch. This was his "romantic" or "bohemian" phase, when he lived in a cabin in the foothills of the Sierras, with a vineyard and a private winery, and wrote reams of verse, but circulated it only in typed copies for his friends. A flood wiped out his cabin, his library, and all his manuscripts, leaving only these typed copies. This ended what he now calls his period of "romantic slush." He became both more serious and more social-minded, and his later poetry, by which he is best known, is distinctly in the social manner. In 1938 he received a Guggenheim Fellowship, which financed part of his translation of Goethe's Faust. He has also translated Rainer Maria Rilke. He lives now in Berkeley, Calif., where he teaches at the university. He was married in 1929 to Marian Hammond.

Still colorful, he says that though he considers the contemporary literary "batter" to be "not without yeast," and is pleased to be included in it, he cares "more for what a man writes than for what he is." However, of himself he adds: "Ironically enough, with General Francis Marion on my father's side, and Commodore Preble on my mother's, I merely taught mathematics in the army in the war. The combined breeds in my thin blood-stream include Scotch, Irish, Welsh, and German. I have done oyster-fishing in the Gulf. I have hoboed over six thousand miles in the United States, and I have ridden camels in the Sahara. I was a judge on the Shelley Memorial

Award (1939-40). I am married, have a son, am out of debt, and I do not care for Ezra Pound."

* * *

Lawrence Clark Powell called Mr. MacIntyre "a hopped-up, super-charged, twentieth century Byron," but he is more than this; he is a poet of considerable power and unusual brilliance. In addition to his own books he has been co-editor of two textbooks in English literature, Elements of Discourse in English Literature (1934) and English Prose of the Romantic Period (1938). He is tall and thin, and characteristically says of his appearance that since the photograph accompanying this biography was taken, which "looks as well as I can expect," he has lost "one tooth and nine hairs" to which he adds, unnecessarily: "I am not vain."

PRINCIPAL WORKS: The Brimming Cup, 1930; Poems, 1936; Cafés and Cathedrals, 1939; Fifty Selected Poems by Rainer Maria Rilke (translation) 1940; Faust (translation) 1941; The Black Bull, 1942.

ABOUT: Poetry August 1937, June 1940; Saturday Review of Literature July 3, 10, 1937, June 24, 1939, July 6, 1940; Southern Review Summer 1937; Wilson Library Bulletin March 1939.

*MC INTYRE, JOHN THOMAS (November 26, 1871-), American novelist, short story writer, and dramatist, was born in Philadelphia, the son of Patrick and Sarah (Walker) McIntyre. He was educated in the public schools, and began to write for Sunday papers. At that time the "Sun" story, the sort of thing done so well in Charles Dana's New York

Sun, was popular in those newspapers which liked to think of themselves as being well written. Thomas Wharton, Sunday editor of the Philadelphia Times, and a cousin of Owen Wister, was the first to accept McIntyre's stories of this type. They had to do with people and events about the cheaper end of town. Talcott Williams, later of the Columbia School of Journalism, then editor of the Philadelphia Press, advised McIntyre to continue to write stories of common life. One of his several tales of the kind was published in the Chicago Chap Book, and his first published book, The Ragged Edge (1902) was an exercise in the same genre. McIntyre was also the author of several successful stage melo-

* Died May 21, 1951.

dramas. Arnold Daly played in "a tight, real ugly little play called *The Wedding Journey*" which proved too strong meat for the audiences of the period. In 1919 George C. Tyler produced McIntyre's fantasy, *A Young Man's Fancy*, concerning a young fellow who became infatuated with a wax model in a shop window. Two period novels, *Blowing Weather* (1923) and *Shot Towers* (1926), were favorably received and still sell. *Slag*, published by Scribner's in 1927, was a grim tale about gangsters which again proved to be rather in advance of its time. In 1932 McIntyre published an historical novel, *Drums in the Dawn*, and in 1936 came into his own with *Steps Going Down*, which won the $4,000 prize as the United States winner in the All-Nations Prize Novel Competition, sponsored by the Literary Guild, Farrar & Rinehart, Warner Brothers, and eleven foreign publishers. William Soskin, one of the judges, reported that the author "contrived to represent a new, hard, deflated American mood with superb realism. His book comes to us, sirens screaming, at 80 miles an hour—and that is a truly modern spirit." Carl Van Doren wrote, "There is hardly a page without an act, thought, or speech which is as natural as experience." As a person, state Mr. McIntyre's publishers, "he is tall, vigorous, hearty and humorful. He tells stories as very few people can." He has published several mystery and adventure stories pseudonymously, as well as over his own name.

PRINCIPAL WORKS: The Ragged Edge, 1902; Blowing Weather, 1923; A Young Man's Fancy, 1925; Shot Towers, 1926; Slag, 1927; Stained Sails, 1928; Drums in the Dawn, 1932; Steps Going Down, 1936; Ferment, 1937; Signing Off, 1938.

ABOUT: Boston Evening Transcript December 24, 1932. Wings: The Literary Guild Magazine 1936.

MC INTYRE, OSCAR ODD (February 18, 1884-February 13, 1938), American journalist and columnist, was born in Platts-

burg, Mo., of Scottish blood, the son of Henry Bell McIntyre, a hotel-keeper and a heavy, inarticulate man of whom his son was inclined to be shy, and Frances, or Fanny (Young) McIntyre, who died when O. O. McIntyre was three. The boy had been named for an uncle

named Odd (pronounced Udd). He was taken to his grandmother in Gallipolis, Ohio for rearing and education. The boys of the town were prompt to gang up on the new arrival, with his kilts and his shrinking manners, and implanted in McIntyre a lifelong inferiority complex which he was always the first to admit. McIntyre was also a hypochondriac, in constant fear of death but avoiding any reference to it or to ill-health. He was a Christian Scientist for the last twenty years of his life. In 1902 he was a reporter of local items for the Gallipolis *Journal*, a four-page daily, at $2 a week, and next year went to Cincinnati to spend nine months taking a four-months' course at a business college. Here he learned to typewrite. In his later years Scotch thrift and various phobias compelled him to type his daily column single-spaced on one sheet, making no carbon copies and writing corrections in red ink. He preferred to rewrite the column if it was lost in transit.

In 1904-05 McIntyre was a feature writer on the East Liverpool (O.) *Tribune*, and in 1906 a political writer and later managing editor of the Dayton *Herald*. In 1907 he was back in Cincinnati as telegraph editor, city editor, and assistant magazine editor of the *Post*, staying until 1911, when he went east to New York City to work for a few months as associate editor of *Hampton's Magazine*, edited by Ray Long, cousin of McIntyre's wife, who was Maybelle Hope Small of Gallipolis. (They were married in February 1908.) *Hampton's* was in the hands of the sheriff in a few weeks, and McIntyre found uncongenial work as a copyreader on the *Evening Mail*. He was discharged in eight months for incompetence.

The McIntyres took a room in a small hotel on West Seventy-Second Street, and he began to send out a New York newsletter on hotel stationery, offered to various newspapers for whatever they thought the feature worth to them. A complimentary reference to the new manager of the Hotel Majestic on Central Park West obtained him a post as resident press-agent with an almost unlimited expense account. (He was also press-agent for Florenz Ziegfield, producer of the Follies.) McIntyre went to the Hotel Majestic in December 1915, and moved out in a white rage in December 1920 to the Ritz-Carlton Hotel, which had no objection to dogs, which had been banned from the other hotel. In May 1922 the McNaught Syndicate took over McIntyre's column, "New York Day By Day," paying him $400 a week. When McIntyre died in his Park Avenue apartment five days short of his fifty-fourth birthday (probably of pernicious anemia) he was averaging $3,000 a week. For twenty years he had also contributed a monthly article to *Cosmopolitan,* edited for a long period by his friend Ray Long. "I write from a country town angle of a city's glamour and the metropolis has never lost its thrill for me," McIntyre said more than once. His reports of a thrilling and semi-mythical metropolis reached an estimated public of over a hundred million readers, whose uncritical adoration passed lightly over his uncertain spelling and dubious French. His prose was occasionally embellished by purple patches, and his custom of using buried quotations elicited a lengthly protest from Christopher Morley, who traced vestiges of his own work all through McIntyre's *The Big Town.*

He was just short of six feet, usually weighed 142 pounds, had a long, sensitive face (he called himself horse-faced), thick unruly white hair, and dark brown eyes. McIntyre's funeral was held from Gatewood, a house he had never used, in Gallipolis.

PRINCIPAL WORKS: White·Light Nights, 1924; Twenty-Five Selected Stories, 1929; Another Odd Book: Twenty-Five Short Stories, Second Series, 1932; The Big Town: New York Day by Day, 1935.

ABOUT: Driscoll, C. B. The Life of O. O. McIntyre; McIntyre, O. O. Twenty-Five Short Stories (see "Odd McIntyre's Own Story"); Starrett, V. Books Alive; Christian Century March 2, 1938; New York Times February 15, 16, 18, 1938; Newsweek February 21, 1938; Publishers' Weekly February 26, 1938; Rotarian July 1940; Saturday Evening Post November 20, 1937; Wilson Library Bulletin March 1938.

MACKAIL, DENIS (June 3, 1892-), English novelist, was born in London, the only son of the great Latinist and some-

time Professor of Poetry at Oxford, J. W. Mackail.*qv* His mother was Margaret Burne-Jones, only daughter of the Pre-Raphaelite painter Sir Edward Burne-Jones, and through her he was related to Kipling and to Stanley Baldwin. Angela Thirkell *qv* is his sister. Mackail was educated at St. Paul's School and at Balliol College, Oxford, but because of ill health he left the university without a degree and made a trip to Africa instead. This was in 1912, and soon after his return to England he became a stage designer, an outgrowth of an early hobby of a miniature theatre. He designed the sets for James Barrie's *The Adored One,* and for Shaw's *Pygmalion* (the play, not the motion picture), during the run of which he spent six months in the United States. During the First World War, being barred by frail health from active service, he worked in the War Office and the Board of Trade, and for a while in the print room of the British Museum. He then tried his hand, first in business, then as a publisher's reader, but in neither was he a success, and, unemployed at twenty-seven, he became an author. The novel he wrote in five weeks (he says it now takes him a year to finish one as long) proved popular, and he has continued to follow it with annual books which a critic has said are "a cross between Lamb and Milne, with a dash of Wodehouse." He had meanwhile acquired a family, having in 1917 married Diana Granet, daughter of a railway magnate; they have two daughters. *Greenery Street,* which is largely autobiographical, deals with their courtship and early married days. "I write," he tells the editors of this work, "only about people and places I consider I know well."

Mackail is sharp-featured, clean-shaven, and looks rather like an actor. He lives with his family in Sussex. Of his writing methods he says: "The whole thing is pain and agony, largely out of my control, and I have never yet written anything remotely resembling the vision that has set me off. I write by the clock and by the number of words. It is my ambition to retire with a large fortune made out of literature. At least, I think that is my ambition, but I don't suppose anything would ever really stop me. I am quite unable to read anything that I've ever written once I've corrected the proofs. It is my whimsical wish to be accepted as a highbrow by other highbrows, and of course I never shall be."

Mr. Mackail's novels are much better known in England, where they are very popular, than in America, though several of them have appeared here. They are distinctly light, and their humor is their chief characteristic, but they have much charm. They are unmistakably English in tone, and often contain vivid thumb-nail portraits that stick in the memory. Their outstanding defect is sentimentality, but that may be forgiven in books that have so little pretension. Certainly they are pleasant reading, and that is probably all their author has seriously aspired to—if (which may be doubted) he is ever serious. His name is pronounced *may'k'l.*

PRINCIPAL WORKS: What Next? 1921; Romance to the Rescue, 1921; Bill the Bachelor, 1922; According to Gibson, 1923; The *Majestic* Mystery, 1924; Summertime, 1924; Greenery Street, 1925; The Fortunes of Hugo, 1926; The Flower Show, 1927; Tales From Greenery Street, 1928; Another Part of the Wood, 1929; How Amusing! 1929; The Young Livingstones, 1930; The Square Circle, 1931; David's Day, 1932; Ian and Felicity, 1932; Peninsula Place, 1932; Chelbury Abbey, 1933; Having Fun, 1933; Summer Leaves, 1934; The Wedding, 1935; Back Again, 1936; Jacinth, 1937; Morning, Noon and Night, 1938; London Lovers, 1938; Barrie: The Story of J.M.B., 1941.

ABOUT: Bookman (London) June 1929; Scholastic May 5, 1934; Wilson Library Bulletin February 1933.

*MACKAIL, JOHN WILLIAM (1859-),

English literary historian and university professor, received his education in the universities of Edinburgh and Oxford. He became a member of the staff of the Ministry of Education in 1884, continuing until his sixtieth year in 1919. From 1906 to 1911 Mackail held the chair of Poetry at Oxford University. In 1888 he had married Margaret Burne-Jones, daughter of Sir Edward Burne-Jones, the painter, and they had a son and two daughters; two of the children are well known writers: Denis Mackail and Angela (Mackail) Thirkell.[qqv] He was an intimate friend of the painter, writer, and typographer William Morris, who designed borders and initials for Mackail's *Biblia Innocentium,* a child's history of the Jews, printed by Morris' Kelmscott Press in 1892. At Kelmscott House, Hammersmith, on a November day eight years later, Mackail delivered a memorial address on Morris which was printed by the Doves Press. In 1919, he delivered the Leslie Stephen lecture before the University of Cambridge. Professor Mackail, who translated the *Odyssey* into English verse, was president of the Classical Association in 1922-23. He has also been Professor of Ancient Literature at the Royal Academy of Arts, President of the British Academy, and holds numerous honorary degrees. Mackail's *Studies in Humanism* (1938) —humanism in the ordinary, not the Irving Babbitt and Seward Collins, sense—gathered together papers such as "What is the Good of Greek?" "The Italy of Virgil and Dante," "Allan Ramsay and the Romantic Revival," and essays on Ariosto and John Ruskin. He contributed *Virgil and His Meaning to the World of Today* to the series entitled "Our Debt to Greece and Rome." The aesthetes of the 'nineties rejoiced in his well-chosen *Select Epigrams From the Greek Anthology* (which was re-issued exactly fifty years later) and his authoritative biography of William Morris. Mackail's lectures and studies of poetry are not iconoclastic in their general tenor, and make pleasant reading. He is a member of the Athenaeum, and lives at Pembroke Gardens, London.

PRINCIPAL WORKS: Select Epigrams From the Greek Anthology, 1890; Biblia Innocentium, 1892; Latin Literature, 1895; The Life of William Morris, 1899; The Springs of Helicon: A Study in the Progress of English Poetry From Chaucer to Milton, 1909; Lectures on Greek Poetry, 1910; Lectures on Poetry, 1911; Russia's Gift to the World, 1915; Life and Letters of George Wyndham (with G. Wyndham) 1925; Classical Studies, 1925; Studies of English Poets, 1926; The Approach to Shakespeare, 1930; Studies in Humanism, 1938. *Translator*—The Odyssey in English Verse, 1903-10.

ABOUT: International Who's Who.

*MC KAY, CLAUDE (September 15, 1890-), American poet and novelist, was born in Sunny Ville, Jamaica, West Indies,

the son of Thomas Francis McKay and Ann Elizabeth (Edwards) McKay, poor Negro farm workers. He received no formal schooling whatever, but an older brother gave him some elementary instruction. At about fourteen he went to Kingston, where eventually he became a member of the native constabulary. There he began to write dialect verses, and became a sort of unofficial poet laureate of the colony. At twenty-two he had had two books of poems published, and was the first Negro to receive the medal of the Institute of Arts and Sciences. The award also included a sum of money, and he came to the United States, where he entered Tuskegee Normal and Industrial Institute. After a few months he found himself at odds with the methods and aims of this school, and went to Kansas State College. Two years showed him that neither farming nor teaching agriculture, even to help his countrymen, was his *forte,* and he used the balance of his scholarship fund to go to New York. In 1914, after he had opened a restaurant which failed, he was obliged to earn his living by waiting on table in summer hotels and in dining-cars. He began to write poetry again, his first work appearing in the *Seven Arts* under the name

* Died December 13, 1945.   * Died May 22, 1948.

of "Eli Edwards." It attracted the attention of other writers and critics, especially those of the left wing, and he began again to be known as a poet. In 1918 he managed to go to London, where Frank Harris acclaimed him as a genius, and where he worked as a reporter on Sylvia Pankhurst's radical pacifist paper, the *Workers' Dreadnaught*. Back in New York, he became a protégé of Floyd Dell and Max Eastman and joined them as associate editor of the *Liberator*, from 1919 to 1922.

During his American years Mr. McKay had married, and had been separated from his wife. She appeared in New York in 1922, and he decided to leave for abroad. He was sent to the U.S.S.R. as observer at the fourth congress of the International (he was at this time generally considered to be a Communist), and from there he went to France, where he stayed for some ten years. Without funds, he was forced to work as an artist's model. Deprivation injured his health; he was threatened with tuberculosis, and it was finally made possible for him to go to the warmer climate of the Riviera. There he worked for a time in Rex Ingram's motion picture studio at Nice, and later spent some time in Marseilles and in Morocco. Meanwhile he had turned from poetry to fiction. His first novel, *Home to Harlem*, was a success, and since its publication he has been a free-lance writer, now living in New York.

Claude McKay was one of the foremost figures in the so-called "Negro literary renaissance" of the 1920's. Many of his poems are hot protests against discrimination and injustice—perhaps the most anthologized has been "If We Must Die," ending: "Pressed to the wall, dying, but—fighting back!" His novels are vividly realistic pictures of Negro workers and of the riff-raff, black and white, of European waterfronts. His work is uneven, and his novels are episodic, betraying the fact that his natural medium is not prose but verse; but he has a powerful gift for narrative and characterization.

PRINCIPAL WORKS: *Poems*—Songs of Jamaica, 1911; Constab Ballads, 1912; Spring in New Hampshire, 1920; Harlem Shadows, 1922. *Novels*—Home to Harlem, 1927; Banjo, 1929; Gingertown, 1931; Banana Bottom, 1933. *Miscellaneous*—A Long Way From Home (autobiography) 1937; Harlem: Negro Metropolis, 1940.

ABOUT: McKay, C. A Long Way From Home; American Mercury August 1939; Publishers' Weekly October 30, 1937; Time March 22, 1937.

MACKAYE, PERCY (March 16, 1875-   ), American dramatist and poet, writes: "The life-work of an author is the summa-

tion of those spiritual influences which have wrought it. In my own case, by far the greatest of those influences has been the immeasurable love of one steadfast friend, the sharer and inspirer of all my creative work during more than forty years, my wife, Marion (Morse) Mackaye,  who died in 1939. The remainder of my life is dedicated to revealing to others, if I can, the incomparable charm and grandeur of her gallant spirit. Of earliest influences, the most compelling were those of the gods and demigods of Greek and Norse mythology, with their legends and sagas, as first brought to me, by word of mouth, by my older brother Will, artist, actor, poet. Next, the wonders of great literature, especially of the poets: Chaucer, the old balladists, and all-engulfing Shakespeare; not learned from school-books (for I went little to school, and prepared myself for college) but chiefly from readings aloud with members of our large family, all of whom became well-known authors. I was born into a heritage of the theatre, to which a large part of my life has been devoted.

"After graduation from Harvard, in 1897, my sojourns in Europe and studies at Leipzig resulted in several published volumes. But more creatively influential than such studies have been my first-hand encounters with the variedly wonderful backgrounds of my own country, America, which I have toured from Maine to California, at times on horseback, or on foot, in the wilder mountain regions. From these experiences have sprung many enriching friendships, especially with living poets and artists of my time, at home and abroad.

"Looking back on half a century, my life seems to loom—almost as in fantasy—like some enchanted tree, bearing on its boughs many kinds and forms of strange fruits, some ripened and fallen, some still quickening into flower, all burgeoning from one central trunk, rooted deep in the ages, and fed there by ever-renewing springs. The name which I have given to that central source of creative life is the title of my recent volume—*Poesia Religio* (*The Faith of Poetry*), published in four languages, at Mulhouse, France. The motto of its vignette-design is 'Liberty, Diversity, Fraternity.'"

* * *

Mr. Mackaye was born in New York, the son of the noted actor Steele Mackaye and of Mary Keith (Medbery) Mackaye. Besides his Harvard degree, he has an honorary M.A. from Dartmouth and an honorary Litt.D. from Miami University; he was a student at Leipzig University in 1899. He married Marion Homer Morse (1872-1939), who collaborated with him in many of his books, in 1898, and they had two daughters and a son. The first fellowship in creative literature in the United States was founded for him at Miami in 1900. He taught poetry and folk-backgrounds at Rollins College from 1928 to 1930, and was advisory editor of *Folk-Say*. His keen interest in folk-literature came from a sojourn in the mountains of Kentucky in 1921. He received the first commission from the Federal Government to write and produce a national festival-drama, in 1931. He was visiting professor at Sweet Briar College in 1932, and director of the White Top (Virginia) Mountain folk-festival in 1933. From 1933 to 1936 he and his wife collected folk-material in North Carolina, Florida, and Virginia, though his home at this time was in Windsor, Vt. He went to Europe to live in 1938, setting up a pre-war residence in Dornach, Switzerland.

He is an intense-looking man with spectacles, a small moustache, and abundant brown hair. His influence has been more extensive than his individual celebrity, but his is a famous name among those interested in preservation of our native arts. He is primarily what one critic called him, "the man who has fought for a dream."

PRINCIPAL WORKS: The Canterbury Pilgrims (play) 1903; Fenris the Wolf (play) 1905; Jeanne d'Arc (play) 1906; Sappho and Phaon (play) 1907; The Scarecrow, 1908; Lincoln Centenary Ode, 1909; Poems, 1909; A Garland to Sylvia (play) 1910; Anti-Matrimony (play) 1910; To-Morrow (play) 1911; Yankee Fantasies (one-act plays) 1912; The Civic Theatre, 1912; Uriel and Other Poems, 1912; Sinbad the Sailor (play) 1912; Sanctuary (masque) 1913; St. Louis (masque) 1914; A Thousand Years Ago (play) 1914; The Present Hour (poems) 1914; The Immigrants (play) 1915; The New Citizenship, 1915; A Substitute for War, 1915; Poems and Plays, 1916; Caliban (masque) 1916; American Consecration Hymn, 1917; Community Drama, 1917; The Evergreen Tree (masque) 1917; The Roll Call (masque) 1918; James Russell Lowell Centenary Poem, 1919; Washington (play) 1919; The Will of Song (with Harry Barnhart) 1919; Rip Van Winkle (opera) 1920; The Pilgrim and the Book, 1920; Dogtown Common (poem) 1921; This Fine-Pretty World (play) 1923; The Skippers of Nancy Gloucester (poem) 1924; Kinfolk of Robin Hood (juvenile play) 1924; Untamed America (with M. M. Mackaye) 1924; April Fire (poem) 1925; Tall Tales of the Kentucky Mountains, 1926; Napoleon Crossing the Rockies (play) 1927; Winged Victory (poem) 1927; Epoch—The Life of Steele Mackaye, 1927; The Gobbler of God (poem) 1928; Kentucky Mountain Fantasies, 1928; The Sphinx (play) 1929; Songs of a Day, 1929; Weathergoose-Wool, 1929; William Vaughn Moody—Twenty Years After (poem) 1930; Wakefield (masque) 1932; American Theatre-Poets, 1935; In Another Land (poems, with A. Stetten) 1936; The Far Familiar (poems) 1937; Poog's Pasture, The Mythology of a Child, 1938; Poesia Religio, 1940; My Lady Dear, Arise! . . . Songs and Sonnets in Remembrance of Marion Morse Mackaye, 1940.

ABOUT: Annals of an Era: Percy Mackaye and the Mackaye Family; Dickinson, T. H. The Playwrights of the New American Theatre; Mackaye, P. Epoch—The Life of Steele Mackaye; American Speech April 1931; Everybody's Magazine May 1919; Outlook March 25, 1925; School and Society March 26, 1921.

MC KENNA, STEPHEN (February 27, 1888-   ), English novelist, was born in London, the son of Leopold and Ellen McKenna.

His paternal uncle was Reginald McKenna, noted financier and statesman, and the family was wealthy. Stephen was educated at Westminster, where he held a scholarship, and at Christ Church, Oxford, where he held an exhibition. He received his B.A. in 1909 and his M.A. in 1914. Always of rather frail health, he was unable to serve in the army during the First World War, but was attached from 1915 to 1919 to the War Trade Intelligence Department. In 1917 he was with the Balfour Mission to the United States. He has traveled a great deal, in Europe, Asia, and Africa, as well as in America. Much of his traveling has been in search of a warm climate, for his health is still delicate. He has never married.

He lives now in London, with a country home in Berkshire. Though he is an indefatigable writer, turning out two or three books a year with alarming prolificness, he finds time also for much social life. He himself says his favorite recreation is walking, but to his associates he is known rather as a genial and continual host. The opera is his passion; he attends it nightly during the season and always entertains afterwards at his chambers in Lincoln's Inn, where the mornings are consecrated to writing. He is tall and slender, with light hair and blue eyes and an aquiline profile.

With lifelong entreé into the heart of London's social and political life, McKenna has based all his stories on the sophisticated society he knows best. He writes only of real people, and often of himself; his actual autobiography was only, in a sense, a continuation of the "long confession" of his novels. But that confession, though it may be ironical and even lightly cynical, is never bitter or cruel; he has an affection for his private world, however clearly he sees it.

The limited nature of his background makes him far more widely read at home than abroad, and even in England more than one critic has pointed out the narrowness and superficiality of his treatment. He is a brilliant conversationalist, both orally and in print; in some ways he seems a successor to the epigrammatic style of Oscar Wilde, except that he also has a gift for sheer storytelling that Wilde did not possess. *Sonia*, written during the war, has remained his most popular work. It struck a new note in fiction—a note untouched since Disraeli—in its pictures of the political and social inner circle. The note has now been sounded many times, establishing McKenna as the official historian of his class and time, but also arousing some exasperation at the solemnity with which he treats essentially trivial people and problems. Not his most disgruntled critic has ever denied him, however, the possession of a brilliant style and of a master's hand at narrative.

Stephen McKenna the novelist should not be confused with Stephen MacKenna (1872-1934), the classical scholar and translator of Plotinus and Porphyry.

PRINCIPAL WORKS: The Reluctant Lover, 1912; Sheila Intervenes, 1913; The Sixth Sense, 1915; Sonia, 1917; Ninety-Six Hours' Leave, 1917; Midas and Son, 1919; Sonia Married, 1919; Lady Lilith, 1920; The Education of Eric Lane, 1921; The Secret Victory, 1921; While I Remember (autobiography) 1921; The Confessions of a Well-Meaning Woman, 1922; Tex: A Chapter in the Life of Alexander Teixeira de Mattos, 1922; Soliloquy, 1922; The Commandment of Moses, 1923; Vindication, 1923; By Intervention of Providence, 1923; To-Morrow and To-Morrow, 1924; Tales of Intrigue and Revenge, 1924; An Affair of Honour, 1925; The Oldest God, 1926; Saviours of Society, 1926; The Secretary of State, 1927; Due Reckoning, 1927; The Unburied Dead, 1928, The Shadow of Guy Denver, 1928; The Datchley Inheritance, 1929; Happy Ending, 1929; The Redemption of Morley Darville, 1930; The Cast-Iron Duke, 1930; Dermotts Rampant, 1931; Beyond Hell, 1931; Pandora's Box, 1932; Superstition, 1932; The Way of the Phoenix, 1932; The Magic Quest, 1933; Namesakes, 1933; The Undiscovered Country, 1934; Portrait of His Excellency, 1934; Sole Death, 1935; While of Sound Mind, 1936; Lady Cynthia Clandon's Husband, 1936; Last Confession, 1937; The Home That Jill Broke, 1937; Breasted Amazon, 1938; Life for a Life, 1939.

ABOUT: Adcock, A.St.J. Gods of Modern Grub Street, McKenna, S. While I Remember; Mais, S.P.B. Books and Their Writers; Overton, G. Authors of the Day; Wilson Library Bulletin May 1933.

MC KENNEY, RUTH (November 18, 1911-), American sociological writer and humorist, writes: "I was born in a little

E. Schaal

town in Indiana which it took me nearly twenty years to learn how to spell—Mishawaka. I grew up in Cleveland, Ohio— the first thing I remember about growing up was a book my mother gave me called *Child's History of Evolution*. This made such a sensation in my Sunday School that my sister Eileen and I were evicted, for having pernicious views. My mother, whose maiden name was Flynn, was an Irish Nationalist, and gave me a lifelong bias for freedom and independence. I went to the public schools in Cleveland, where my mother taught until she died, when I was eight years old. I was graduated from Shaw High School in 1928 and I still have dismal memories of a class oration about taking the marines out of Nicaragua. My college education was disjointed and rather spotty—I worked on the Columbus *Dispatch* between attending some classes at Ohio State University. I never got a diploma, but on the other hand, I was a pretty good printer and had a union card. I learned the trade when I was fourteen, and switched over to newspaper reporting when I was seventeen. In between I was an extremely bad waitress, and an enormously unsuccessful book salesman (house to house).

"The Ohio Newspaper Women's Association gave me some prizes the years I worked on the Akron *Beacon-Journal*—in those days I liked to remind myself that I had a man's job and wasn't stuck on the society page. I finished off my stint on newspapers with two years on the New York *Post* (1934-1936), where I was what they called a feature writer. In 1936, after seven years before the mast of various city desks, a friend loaned me $80. With this fortune I was able to pay off the money I had borrowed from my kindly employers on the *Post*. Thus, free at last, I quit.

"Since then, I have written books. Two of them are meant to be humorous, collections of stories which appeared first in the *New Yorker* and other magazines. However, I am not a humorist. I only wrote the funny stories to make a living while composing weightier *opera;* I doubt if I shall ever write anything else funny, for the truth is, I have very little sense of humor, and suffer a good deal while writing what is supposed to be funny. I have published one book which I like, called *Industrial Valley.* This is a true story of what happened to Akron, Ohio, from 1932 to 1936. Nobody in Akron liked the book, but it won a prize at the Writers' Congress as the best non-fiction book of the two years 1938 and 1939. My next book is a novel entitled *Jake Home*— I have it about half done now. When I quit the *Post* I made a resolution to publish four books before the end of 1940, but by then I had only one and a half done that I liked, and the half isn't published yet, so I didn't do so well.

"Besides writing books, I am an editor of the *New Masses* and write a weekly column for it called 'Strictly Personal.' I was married in 1937 to Richard Bransten. My husband is an historian, who uses the pen-name of "Bruce Minton." My sister Eileen was married in 1940 to Nathanael West, the novelist, and *her* brother-in-law is Sidney Perelman. So we are thick with writers in the family, including my nine-year old stepson, who is currently writing a novel."

* * *

Three days before the appearance (in January 1941) of the smash-hit dramatization of *My Sister Eileen,* and shortly after the account above was written, Ruth McKenney was called to Los Angeles by the tragic death of her sister and Mr. West in an automobile accident as they were returning from a hunting trip in Mexico.

PRINCIPAL WORKS: My Sister Eileen, 1939; Industrial Valley, 1939; The McKenneys Carry On, 1940.

ABOUT: McKenney, R. My Sister Eileen, The McKenneys Carry On; Scholastic January 13, 1941.

MACKENZIE, COMPTON (January 17, 1882*-   ), English novelist, writes: "I was born in West Hartlepool. My father, known as Edward Compton, and my grandfather, known as Henry Compton, were both distinguished actors who used the name Compton for stage purposes; my grandfather took the name from his maternal grandmother. My great-grandfather, John Mackenzie, was a writer of historical and theological works. My great-great-aunt, Mary Mackenzie, was a popular novelist of the first quarter of the nineteenth century. I am related on the paternal side to John Addington Symonds, Sir Rowland Hill (of

Penny Post fame), and many other distinguished figures in literature, scholarship, medicine, law, and the theatre. My mother's father was Hezekiah Linthicum Bateman, of an old Baltimore family, who was the first of the American theatrical impresarios to exploit Britain, and who gave Henry Irving his chance at the Lyceum Theatre. My maternal grandmother wrote many successful plays. She was a daughter of the popular English actor, Joseph Capwell, who left the British Navy to spend most of his life in America.

"I was educated in St. Paul's School, London, and Magdalen College, Oxford. I took an Honours Degree in modern history, founded and edited a magazine called the *Oxford Point of View,* in the pages of which many well-known figures of our time made their first appearance in print, and I was business manager of the Oxford University Dramatic Society. I became a student of the Inner Temple, but soon gave up the law for literature. In 1905 I married Faith Stone, who has herself written several successful books.

"I started out as a dramatist, and my first play, *The Gentleman in Grey,* was produced in Edinburgh in 1907. That year I published a volume of poems. In 1911 my first novel, *The Passionate Elopement,* was published with such success that my future career was fixed. My second book, *Carnival,* appeared in 1912. Nearly half a million copies of this book have been sold. It has been dramatized and performed both in America and England; it has been a silent and a talkie film, a radio play, and a radio opera. It was followed by *Sinister Street,* which still sells yearly as many copies at its original price as many new novels.

"In April 1914 I was received into the Catholic Church. During the World War I served in the Royal Marines at Gallipoli. In 1916 I was Military Control Officer in Athens. In 1917 I was Director of the Aegean Intelligence Service, until invalided in September of that year. I received the Legion of Honour from the French, the White Eagle from the Serbians, the Redeemer from the Greeks, and was made an officer of the Order of the British Empire. After the war I left Capri, where I had set-

* Correction: Year of birth, 1883.

tled in 1914, and acquired the two Channel Islands of Herm and Jethou. In 1923 I started a monthly magazine called the *Gramophone,* which I still edit. In 1928 I was one of the founders of the National Party of Scotland—which demanded the restoration of Scottish sovereignty and a Scottish Parliament—and moved from the Channel Islands to Scotland, where I now reside on the island of Barra in the Outer Hebrides. In 1931, standing as a Scottish Nationalist, I was elected Lord Rector of Glasgow University, defeating among others Prof. Gilbert Murray and Sir Oswald Mosley. The following year I was prosecuted by the Crown for a breach of the Official Secrets Act in the third volume of my War Memories. I was fined 100 pounds, and *Greek Memories* was suppressed. In 1939, after the publication of *The Windsor Tapestry* [which was nevertheless hotly attacked for its attitude toward the reigning family], the ban was withdrawn and *Greek Memories* was published [as *Aegean Memories*]. For five years I wrote a weekly article on gramophone records for the *Sunday Pictorial,* and for another five years I was literary critic of the *Daily Mail.*

"My political convictions are most nearly embodied in those of Éamon de Valera and the Portuguese statesman Salazar. I regard the National Government of Great Britain since 1931 with loathing, and consider the abdication of King Edward VIII the greatest political disaster Britain has suffered in my lifetime. My pet abominations in the past are Queen Elizabeth and Oliver Cromwell. My favorite novelists are Stendhal and Jane Austen; my favorite dramatist is Aristophanes; my favorite historians are Tacitus and Herodotus; my favorite poets are Blake, Keats, and Dante. I detest blood sports. My favorite game is Rugby football. I detest golf. I love billiards. I prefer cats to dogs and I am president of the Siamese Cat Club of Great Britain. My favorite composers are Beethoven, Mozart, and Sibelius. I hate Imperialism, believe that Jefferson Davis was right and Abraham Lincoln wrong. I am a believer in Social Credit, and I consider that the use of the word 'democracy' for the political systems of Great Britain and the United States is a libel upon the Greek conception embodied in the word."

* * *

As will be seen from the above, Mr. Mackenzie's is a forthright and individualistic character. Other items concerning him which he does not mention are that Fay Compton,

the well-known actress, is his sister; that he has an honorary LL.D. from the University of Glasgow; that he has had four plays produced in all, including his own dramatization of *Carnival;* that his original name was Edward Montague Compton; that he founded a weekly called *Vox,* whose object was to criticize the radio programs of the British Broadcasting Company; that he is dark, thin-faced, and in some of his pictures bears a curious resemblance to Aubrey Beardsley.

Though he has been immensely popular, critics never know quite how to classify him as a novelist. He has written of the London half-world, of international politics, of expatriates (almost in the style of Norman Douglas), and rather overwhelmingly of his religious views, which are as strong as his political opinions. He has been accused of everything from pornography to theological propaganda, and of "a crude determination to shock" which is eminently unfair to his serious objectives as a writer. John Freeman called him "diligent, observant, and experienced," which faint praise is countered by another critic's notations on his "colored and mellifluous style, picaresque action, humorous character study, and a sympathetic portrayal of religious sensibility."

PRINCIPAL WORKS: *Novels*—The Passionate Elopement, 1911; Carnival, 1912; Sinister Street (in America: Youth's Encounter) 1913-14; Guy and Pauline, 1915; Plashers Mead, 1915; Sylvia Scarlett, 1918; Sylvia and Michael, 1919; Poor Relations, 1919; The Vanity Girl, 1920; Rich Relations, 1921; The Altar Steps, 1922; The Seven Ages of Woman, 1922; The Parson's Progress, 1923; The Heavenly Ladder, 1924; Santa Claus in Summer, 1924; The Old Men of the Sea, 1924; Coral, 1925; Fairy Gold, 1926; Vestal Fire, 1927; Rogues and Vagabonds, 1927; Extraordinary Women, 1928; Extremes Meet, 1928; The Three Couriers, 1929; The Adventures of Two Chairs (juvenile) 1929; The Enchanted Blanket (juvenile) 1930; Told, 1930; April Fools, 1930; Buttercups and Daisies (in America: For Sale) 1931; Our Street, 1931; The Darkening Green, 1934; Figure of Eight, 1936; The Four Winds of Love (The East Wind, 1937; The South Wind, 1937; The West Wind of Love, 1940; West to North, 1940); The Red Tapeworm, 1941. *Non-Fiction*—Poems, 1907; Kensington Rhymes, 1912; Gramophone Nights (with A. Marshall) 1923; Gallipoli Memories, 1929; Athenian Memories, 1931; Greek Memories, 1932; Unconsidered Trifles, 1932; Prince Charlie, de Jure Charles III, 1932; Water on the Brain, 1933; Literature in My Time, 1933; Reaped and Bound, 1933; Marathon and Salamis, 1934; Prince Charlie and His Ladies, 1934; How Does Your Garden Grow? (with others) 1935; Catholicism and Scotland, 1936; The Book of Barra (with J. L. Campbell) 1936; Pericles, 1937; The Windsor Tapestry, 1938; A Musical Chair, 1939; Aegean Memories, 1940.

ABOUT: Mackenzie, C. Reaped and Bound; Mackenzie, F. S. As Much as I Dare, More Than I

Should; Swinnerton, F. The Georgian Scene; Bookman December 1925; Catholic World, September 1922; Living Age March 6, 1920.

"MACLAREN, IAN." See "BRITISH AUTHORS OF THE 19TH CENTURY."

*MC LAUGHLIN, ANDREW CUNNINGHAM (February 14, 1861-), American historian and Pulitzer Prize winner, writes: "Andrew Cunningham McLaughlin was born in Beardstown, Ill. His father was ruined financially by the stopping of commerce on the Mississippi during the Civil War, and in 1865 removed to make a fresh start in Muskegon, Mich. At the age of seventeen Andrew entered the University of Michigan. Graduating in 1882, he returned to Muskegon to teach Latin in the high school and to read law. In 1884 he entered the Michigan Law School, and was awarded the LL.B. the next year. After a few months with a law firm in Chicago he was called back to Ann Arbor to teach Latin at the university, and in 1887 was appointed instructor in history there. His literary contributions to the field of American historical scholarship soon began to appear.

"In 1890 McLaughlin married Lois Thompson Angell, daughter of James B. Angell, president of the University of Michigan. [Three sons—two deceased—and three daughters.] After a year's study in Europe, 1893-94, he returned to Michigan to resume teaching and writing. In 1898 he became one of the editors of the *American Historical Review,* a capacity in which he served till 1914, four years (1901-05) as managing editor. In 1903 he was called to the Carnegie Institution in Washington, D.C., as head of the newly organized Bureau of Historical Research. He returned to Michigan in 1905, and in 1906 accepted the headship of the department of history at the University of Chicago. [Professor Emeritus, 1929.] In 1914 he became president of the American Historical Association.

"After the entry of the United States into the First World War, he lectured in Great Britain upon American political institutions and attitudes. *The Constitutional History of the United States,* the most important work of his pen, was awarded [1936] the Pulitzer Prize for the best historical writing of the year. His latest contribution to American legal historical scholarship was an article written in 1940, entitled 'The Court, The Constitution, and Conkling.' "

PRINCIPAL WORKS: Lewis Cass, 1891; History of Higher Education in Michigan, 1891; Civil Government in Michigan, 1893; The Western Posts and British Debts, 1894; A History of the American Nation, 1899; The Confederation and the Constitution, 1905; The Courts, the Constitution, and Parties, 1912; Cyclopaedia of American Government (ed., with A.B. Hart) 1914; America and Britain, 1918; Steps in the Development of American Democracy, 1920; Foundations of American Constitutionalism, 1932; A Constitutional History of the United States, 1935.

MAC LEISH, ARCHIBALD (May 7, 1892-), American poet, winner of the Pulitzer Prize, Librarian of Congress and Director of the Office of Facts and Figures, was born in Glencoe, Ill., the son of Andrew MacLeish, and Martha (Hillard) MacLeish. He received his preparatory education at the Hotchkiss School, then went to Yale (B.A. 1915) and Harvard (LL.B. 1919).

Washington Press-Photo

In 1932 he received an M.A. degree from Tufts College. He himself says modestly that he attended Harvard Law School "to avoid going to work." Be that as it may, he did not want or like the law as a profession, since he "never could believe in it." While he was still a student he married Ada Hitchcock, a singer; they had three sons (one deceased) and a daughter. The First World War found MacLeish, in spite of his wife and baby, first a member of an ambulance unit and then in the Field Artillery at the front; he was discharged with the rank of captain. His brother, an aviator, was killed in Belgium.

"Again to avoid going to work," he taught for a year at Harvard. He had had a volume of poems published while he was in France, but he was dissatisfied with his writing. For the next three years, 1920 to 1923, he practiced law in Boston, but found he could write less than ever. Finally, in 1923, by this time with two children to support, he decided to throw everything overboard and take a chance on living by poetry alone. He and his family went to France and stayed there (with one five-months journey to Persia) until 1928. "I date the beginning of my life from 1923," he says. He read intensively, mostly French poetry, but also T. S. Eliot and Ezra Pound, the two manifest influences on his earlier work. From 1924, released from the inhibitions which had oppressed him, he published a volume of verse nearly every year.

* Died September 24, 1947.

Back in America he settled on a farm in Farmington, Conn. He made one long trip alone in Mexico, following the route of Cortez, the result being *Conquistador,* which won the Pulitzer Prize for poetry in 1932. For some time he was on the staff of *Fortune.* In 1938 he became curator of the Nieman Collection of Contemporary Journalism at Harvard, and advisor to the Nieman Fellows. In 1939 he was named by President Roosevelt as Librarian of Congress, succeeding Herbert Putnam. At first there was opposition on the part of some professional librarians, not so much against MacLeish himself as against the appointment of a creative writer instead of a technical expert, and in a few cases for less creditable political reasons. But other prominent librarians (including Dr. Putnam) as ardently endorsed the choice, and the opposition died down soon after MacLeish's appointment was confirmed and he entered upon his duties, for it soon became apparent that he would make an excellent librarian and an inspiring leader. What effect the heavy duties now devolving on him will have on his poetic output remains to be seen.

He had meanwhile been developing far beyond the young man who wrote in the idiom of Pound and Eliot, who was one of the voices of the nostalgic "lost generation," and who kept his poetry "inviolate" from the conflicts of his era. Always, as Lewis Galantière remarked as long ago as 1929, "extremely sensitive to his time and its perturbations," he was gradually drawn into the dominant current of post-depression literature, until as Chairman of the 1937 National Congress of American Writers, he could say: "In that war [against Fascism] . . . we, writers who contend for freedom, are ourselves, and whether we so wish or not, engaged." He began experimenting with "socio-economic grafts" on poetry— with the ballet, in *Union Pacific,* with the drama, in *Panic,* with the radio, in *The Fall of the City* and *Air Raid,* with "the art-form of the news-picture magazine" in *Land of the Free.* It was a far call from the intense subjectivity of *The Hamlet of A. MacLeish.*

His mastery of words, what Mason Wade called "his singular ability to get at the roots of language," his command of cadence and rhythm, survived his changes of social viewpoint, but his most recent work seems to have lost its edge and purity of tone and to be dominated by rhetorical compulsions.

One of the significant precursive (American) documents of the Second World War was MacLeish's denunciation, in a public address made June 1940, of "the irresponsibles," meaning specifically the generation of post-First World War writers whose revulsion against war and the values of war, he charged, had "done more to disarm democracy in the face of Fascism than any other single influence." This indictment, though it was hotly contested by many of MacLeish's former political associates of the Left, marked the swift alteration of America's intellectual climate preparatory to our direct involvement in the war against the Axis powers.

With regard to MacLeish's own fluctuations of opinion, Morton Dauwen Zabel commented in a blistering two-part attack in the *Partisan Review* (January-February, March-April 1941): "It is hopeless to try to cope with MacLeish's statements when those of one year are set against those of another; it is often impossible to clarify his contradictions or ambiguities within a single essay." In Zabel's estimation, MacLeish is "a phenomenon of our time and culture": "Poet, scholar, gentleman, and librarian, he has become a major American prophet and Voice of Destiny."

In Washington, as Librarian of Congress, MacLeish rapidly won his way into the "inner cabinet" of President Roosevelt's confidential advisers. He is indubitably one of the most influential figures in our national life. His appointment, in 1941, as Director of the newly created Office of Facts and Figures, placed him in a key post respecting wartime propaganda in America. Although he still retains title as Librarian of Congress, his activities are centered in O.F.F.

In an interesting commentary on his family—his father, a "devout, cold, rigorous man of very beautiful speech," and his mother, his father's third wife, who came of "very passionate people with many mad among them," MacLeish has tried to analyze his own inheritance. Physically he probably inherits from his Scotch father his height, his long-headedness, and his bright, large, dark eyes.

PRINCIPAL WORKS: Tower of Ivory, 1917; The Happy Marriage, 1924; The Pot of Earth, 1925; Nobodaddy (play) 1925; Streets in the Moon, 1926; The Hamlet of A. MacLeish, 1928; New Found Land, 1930; Conquistador, 1932; Frescoes for Mr. Rockefeller's City, 1933; Union Pacific, 1934; Panic, 1935; Public Speech, 1936; The Fall of the City, 1937; Land of the Free, 1938; Air Raid, 1939; America Was Promises, 1940; The Irresponsibles, 1940; The American Cause, 1941; A Time to Speak, 1941; Prophets of Doom, 1941; Next Harvard, 1941.

ABOUT: American Mercury November 1940; American Review May 1934; Atlantic Monthly June 1940; Current Biography, 1940; Library Journal July 1939; Nation April 17, 1929, January 10, 1934, May 18, 1940; New Republic January 17, 1934, May 5, 1941; Newsweek March 24, 1941; North American Review June 1937; Partisans Review January-February, March-April 1941; Poetry August 1930, June 1931, September 1938; Publishers' Weekly July 15, 1933; Saturday Review of Literature July 29, 1933, January 27, 1934, June 16 and 24, July 1, 1939; Time March 17, 1941.

MAC MANUS, SEUMAS (1869-   ), Irish story writer, writes: "I was born in County Donegal, which is Ireland's Northwestern

Witzel

cornerstone. I am one of the mountain people. As a barefoot boy I herded cattle and sheep on the hills, labored on the farms, attended the mountain school where I got the little education that is mine. By the time I was seven, I could tell a hundred

of the old tales, as I had learned them by a hundred firesides. I was passionately fond of books, and during my boyhood devoured every book that was to be found among our hills—altogether as many as fifteen.

"At the age of sixteen I began making poems, while I herded or plied the spade on my father's hillside, chiefly patriotic poems. Within another year I was publishing prose and verse in the little weekly newspaper of our county. At the end of three years the editor gave me my first pay—a check for ten shillings. And I was a proud man. Then he printed for me my first book of poems, with the Irish title *Shuilers*, meaning Vagrants.

"By now I had become the schoolmaster of our mountain school. Now also a penny weekly newspaper in Dublin ordered from me a series of nine stories at ten shillings each. Hearing that American story papers paid higher than $2.50 a story, I wrote the full of a bag of stories, and then, closing my school, sailed for America in the steerage of a big liner. Arrived in New York I asked the names of magazines that would pay well for stories. I sold every one of them, and sailed back to Ireland eight months later with a fortune, with which I bought a fairy hill in Donegal, of which I had always been enamored. I returned to America the next autumn with a new bag of stories, and carried home in the spring three times as big a fortune. My Donegal neighbors, knowing that anyone who wished could shovel up bagfuls of such stories among our hills, could hardly credit the simplicity of the American people!

"American publishers began putting out my folk-tale books, original stories of Irish life, and Irish history. And I, who had never seen a college before I came to America, found a great field lecturing to the big colleges and universities of this country. This I have been doing for many, many winters. But for my summers I always go back to my own Donegal hills, and my own Donegal people, and my own Donegal fairies."

* * *

Mr. MacManus received an LL.D. degree from Notre Dame University in 1917. He has had many plays produced besides his published stories. In 1901 he married Anna Johnston, who as "Ethna Carbery" was a well-known Irish poet. She died the next year, and in 1911 he married Catalina Violante Paez, of Venezuela. They have two daughters. He is a faithful chronicler of the old tales, and his books have charm for young people as well as for adult readers.

PRINCIPAL WORKS: Shuilers (poems) 1893; The Leading Road to Donegal, 1895; 'Twas in Dhroll Donegal, 1897; Humours of Donegal, 1898; Bend of the Road, 1898; Through the Turf Smoke, 1899; In Chimney Corners, 1899; The Bewitched Fiddle, 1900; Donegal Fairy Stories, 1900; Lad of the O'Friels, 1903; The Red Poocher, 1903; The Hard-Hearted Man, 1903; Irish Nights, 1905; Yourself and the Neighbors, 1914; Ireland's Case (non-fiction) 1915; Lo, and Behold Ye, 1919; Top o' the Mornin', 1920; The Story of the Irish Race (non-fiction) 1921; The Donegal Wonder Book, 1926; O Do You Remember, 1926; Bold Blades of Donegal, 1935; The Rocky Road to Dublin (autobiography) 1938; Well of the World's End, 1939; Dark Patrick, 1939.

ABOUT: Kunitz, S. J. & Haycraft, H. (eds.). The Junior Book of Authors; MacManus, S. The Rocky Road to Dublin; Catholic World July 1919, June 1925.

MAC NEICE, LOUIS (September 12, 1907-   ), Irish poet, writes: "Born in Belfast. Both parents Irish, from Connemara. Father (Rt. Rev. John Frederick MacNeice) now Protestant Bishop of Down, Connor, and Dromore; mother Elizabeth Margaret Clesham) MacNeice. Sent to Marlborough School, in England, 1917. Read classics and philosophy at Oxford, 1926-30; Merton College. First in 'Greats.' 1930, married Giovanna Marie Thérèse Ezra, and appointed lecturer in classics at the University of Birmingham. Held this post till 1936, when appointed lecturer in Greek at Bedford College for Women in the University of London. Think the present English system of teaching the classics is bad. One son; marriage dissolved 1936. 1940, special lecturer in English for the spring semester at Cornell University.

"At various periods have done a lot of book-reviewing, etc. Contributed to most of the English periodicals, *e.g.*, the *Spectator*, the *New Statesman & Nation*, the *Morning Post*, *New Writing*, the *London Mercury*, the *Criterion*, the *Times Literary Supplement*.

"Influences: at Oxford, T. S. Eliot, James Joyce, D. H. Lawrence, sundry philosophers (have long ago ceased reading philosophy). Nowadays prefer history, biography, statistics. Rarely read novels. Consider the world's greatest novel is Tolstoy's *War and Peace*. Wrote three novels in my early twenties—all bad.

"Politics: distrust all parties but consider capitalism must go. Visited Barcelona, New Year's 1939, and hold that in the Spanish Civil War the balance of right was certainly on the side of the Republican Government; the situation, however, much more complex than represented in the English press. Am opposed to Partition in Ireland. Would normally vote Labour in England, but think the Labour Party won't get anywhere till they have got rid of their reactionary leaders.

"Have been connected with the English Group Theatre in London, who produced my translation of the *Agamemnon* of Aeschylus (1936) and my bad experimental play, *Out of the Picture*. Am now writing a trilogy of one-act plays, possibly for the Abbey Theatre, Dublin. Think the London West End stage is moribund.

"Forthcoming works include a new book of poems; *The Roman Smile* (literary criticism), a verse translation of the *Hippolytus* of Euripides, and a quasi-autobiographical book. Have also, in addition to my own books, contributed articles to various books of literary criticism. Most of my books have been published in America."

* * *

Louis MacNeice is one of the group of younger British poets which includes W. H. Auden and Stephen Spender; and it is usually considered that they constitute a related trinity. Delmore Schwartz characterized his work as being "adroitly naïve." Unlike Auden and his friend Christopher Isherwood, he did not become a permanent resident of the United States, but returned to England for military service.

Some of his earlier work was written under the pseudonym of "Louis Malone." His chief recreation is tennis. In 1937 he visited Iceland with Auden, a joint book resulting from the journey. Another trip to the Hebrides also inspired a travel book. Although he is of pure Irish stock, he has not lived in Ireland since his boyhood, but has for many years been a Londoner.

PRINCIPAL WORKS: *Poetry*—Blind Fireworks, 1929; Poems, 1935; The Agamemnon of Aeschylus (verse translation) 1936; Out of the Picture (play in verse and prose) 1937; The Earth Compels, 1938; Autumnn Journal, 1939; The Last Ditch, 1940; Poems: 1925-1940, 1940; Plant and Phantom, 1941. *Prose*—Letters from Iceland (with W. H. Auden) 1937; I Crossed the Minch, 1938; Zoo, 1938; Modern Poetry, 1938; The Poetry of W. B. Yeats, 1941.

ABOUT: Christian Science Monitor Magazine June 22, 1940; London Mercury January 1938; Poetry May 1936, March 1938, February 1939, May 1940.

MC NEILE, HERMAN CYRIL ("Sapper") (1888-August 14, 1937), English writer of popular adventure and crime fiction, the creator of Bulldog Drummond, was the son of Captain Malcolm McNeile of the Royal Navy. He attended Cheltenham College and the Royal Military Academy, Woolwich. For a dozen years he served in the Royal Engineers,  entering in 1907, receiving his lieutenant's commission seven years later, and retiring as lieutenant-colonel in 1919. "Sapper," his pseudonym, was derived from this experience, Sappers, (according to the *Oxford Dictionary*) being the unofficial title of the Engineers, whose wartime duties include tunneling under and mining the enemy lines. McNeile began to write short stories during the World War, and after 1920, when athletic-alcoholic Bulldog Drummond made his prosperous début, averaged a volume a year to the time of his death. The first book of the long Drummond series carried the revealing sub-title "The Adventures of a Demobilized Officer Who Found Peace Dull"; which explains both McNeile's own reason for writing the stories and their vast popularity with ex-service men. They were "escape fiction" of a very specialized sort. NcNeile was working with his friend Gerard Fairlie (a fellow-novelist and sportsman who is generally regarded as Drummond's original) on a play, *Bulldog Drummond Again*, at the time of his death at his home at Pulborough, Sussex, at forty-nine, of an illness traceable to his wartime service.

Bulldog Drummond was created on the stage by the late Sir Gerald du Maurier in London and was played to excellent effect in New York by A. E. Matthews. Ronald Colman turned in a brilliant impersonation in one of the first full-length talking pictures, in 1929; and this began a very uneven cinematic series, concocted by a variety of scenarists and played, usually, by second-rate film actors, that continued long after McNeile's death.

Inevitably, as the New York *Times* pointed out, McNeile will be remembered as Drummond's creator, though he wrote good adventure tales featuring several other characters. His formula was by no means new, but "Sapper" "invested his picaresque hero with daring, wit, ingenuity, and ability to turn out on the right side of the law in the long run." Drummond is a prime representative of a long line of crime-*cum*-detection adventurers of the Robin Hood school: a "blood" brother of D'Artagnan, of Raffles, of Arsène Lupin, and of Leslie Charteris' The Saint.

PRINCIPAL WORKS: The Fatal Second, 1916; Men, Women, and Guns, 1916; No Man's Land, 1917; Bulldog Drummond: The Adventures of a Demobilized Officer Who Found Peace Dull, 1920; The Dinner Club, 1923; Bulldog Drummond's Third Round, 1924; The Hidden Witness, 1929; Bulldog Drummond Strikes Back, 1933; Challenge, 1937.

ABOUT: New York Times August 15, 1937.

MAC ORLAN, PIERRE originally Pierre Mac Orlan Dumarchais or Dumarchey) (February 28, 1882-). French novelist, writes: "Pierre  Mac Orlan was born in Péronne (Somme), where his father was an infantry officer. H*e* was a backward pupil of the *lycée* in Orleans. In 1901 he arrived in Paris, where he suffered much distress and want. He tried his hand at any number of odd jobs, from ditch digger to house painter and proofreader. He lived in Belgium, Holland, and Italy. He returned to Paris, and in 1911 good luck seemed to smile at him, as he became humorous columnist for *Le Journal*. The war blighted this slight streak of prosperity. He fought as a private in the infantry from August 2, 1914, to September 1916 when he was wounded at the siege of Pèronne, his native town.

"It was not until 1918 that he became established as a writer. His first works were tales of adventure. Gradually his taste changed, and now he seeks for the social adventure of our times. He is a reporter as well as a novelist, and all his books have reporting for their basis. He has lived in Germany, and has visited the Foreign Legion in Morocco.

"Physically he is thick-set and round-faced. He lives all the year round in the country, at St. Cyr-sur-Marin, in a little farm adapted to his taste. He is married and has no children—but he has two dogs. He lives in some seclusion; another way of saying he hates the social swirl. His literary preferences emphasize the books which portray our times and those reflecting the social lyricism of adversity, of the downtrodden. His liking for English books is very profound. At a very young age he was much moved by Kipling and Stevenson. Among the French writers he loves particularly Barrès and Zola, for reasons without any connection. If he were twenty years younger he would work directly for the moving pictures, for he believes that this could become the highest lyrical expression of the social fantasy of our times. His amusements consist in doing nothing. He smokes his pipe under the apple-trees, and relishes with pleasure whatever spare time his tasks leave him."

* * *

M. Mac Orlan is of Breton, and ultimately of Flemish, descent, with some Scottish ancestry. He was for years in his youth an art student, who now, as Charlotte Haldane said, "paints with his pen." Robert Bourget-Pailleron called his work "mechanism mingled with fantasy," with "a depth of irony which persists always." His story, Miss Haldane remarked, "is the slenderest thread on which to hang impressionistic pictures." The characters seem merely incidental to his theme. He is "a romantic who expresses himself only by means of formal, classical gestures."

There is no news of his activities since the Nazi conquest.

WORKS AVAILABLE IN ENGLISH: On Board the "Morning Star," 1924; One Floor Up, 1932.

ABOUT: Annales Politiques et Littéraires May 1, 1932; Bookman (London) December 1932; Revue des Deux Mondes November 15, 1933; Revue Européenne October 1924; Revue Mondiale September 16, 1926.

MACY, JOHN ALBERT (April 10, 1877-
August 26, 1932), American critic and
biographer was born in Detroit, Mich., the

son of Powell Macy
and Janet Foster
(Patten) Macy. In
his childhood the fam-
ily moved to Malden,
Mass., where he at-
tended school. He was
graduated from Har-
vard in 1899 (M.A.
1900). For a year
thereafter he was in-
structor in English at
Harvard, and also taught at the Perkins Institution for the blind and deaf, and at a
similar school in Worcester, Mass. It was
through these connections that he met Helen
Keller and her teacher, Anne Sullivan. In
1905 he and Miss Sullivan were married,
the ceremony being performed by Edward
Everett Hale. They were divorced later,
though they always remained friends. Mrs.
Macy was eleven years older than her
husband, and her first duty and loyalty
remained to Miss Keller.

Macy had always been radical in his economic views, and in 1911 joined the Socialist
Party. He succeeded Walter Lippmann as
secretary to George R. Lunn, the Socialist
mayor of Schenectady, N.Y., but held the
position only a few months. After a long
trip to Europe, he became literary editor of
the Boston *Herald*. In 1922 and 1923 he was
literary editor of the *Nation*, and in 1926
became literary advisor to William Morrow
& Co., the publishers. He also lectured a
great deal in addition to his editorial work
and his writing, and someone has written
of his "swishing hair and flowing tie" on
the platform—a Bohemian gesture which accorded ill with his professorial countenance
and his horn-rimmed glasses.

He died, indeed, almost on the lecture
platform—of coronary thrombosis, in an attack following immediately after a lecture on
"Revolution and Rebellion in Classical American Literature," at the summer school of the
International Ladies' Garment Workers'
Union. At the time of his death he was a
teacher at the Rand School of Social Science
in New York, and also, rather curiously,
director of a girls' "finishing school" in Richmond, Va. He was fifty-five.

Few more lovable or more beloved men
than "Jack" Macy have ever lived. He
poured himself out in generosity and kindness, and every cause of the underdog found
him prompt to help. Few knew of his en-

couragement of young writers, or of the
modesty with which he regarded his own not
unimportant writing. As the *Nation* remarked after his death, he "saw literature
always to some extent in . . . a social and
economic context," but his best known book,
The Spirit of American Literature, was (to
quote the *Nation* again) "a pioneer volume
in the attack against the genteel tradition."

Gorham B. Munson pointed out the chief
defect in Macy's work when he said, "He
professes the wish, not so much to write
intelligently and beautifully as to write entertainingly. That is, his center of interest is
in the public." But Carl Van Doren added,
with as much truth: "His range is wide, his
information sound, his gusto generous. He
does not go beyond his depth, because he
knows what his depth is."

Besides his own books, Macy edited Helen
Keller's *Story of My Life,* James Branch
Cabell's *Between Dawn and Sunrise,* and a
symposium, *American Writers on Literature.*

PRINCIPAL WORKS: Edgar Allen Poe, 1907; A
Guide to Reading, 1909; The Spirit of American
Literature, 1913; Socialism in America, 1915; Walter James Dodd, 1918; The Critical Game, 1922;
The Story of the World's Literature, 1925; The
Romance of America as Told in Our Literature,
1929; About Women, 1930; Feminism and Femininity, 1930; Do You Know English Literature?
(with B.C. Williams) 1931.

ABOUT: Braddy, N. Anne Sullivan Macy; Bookman January 1926; Freeman January 10, 1923; Nation September 7, 1932; New Republic November
15, 1922; New York Herald Tribune August 27,
1932; New York Times Book Review October 25,
1925; Publishers' Weekly September 3, 1932.

MADARIAGA, SALVADOR DE (July
23, 1886-), Spanish publicist and literary
critic, was born in Corunna, the son of

Colonel Don Jose de
Madariaga and Doña
Ascencion (Rojo) de
Madariaga. He was
educated at the Insti-
tuto del Cardenal Cis-
neros, Madrid, and in
Paris, at the College
Chaptal, the École
Polytechnique, and
the École Nationale
Superieure des Mines.
He received an honorary M.A. from Oxford
University in 1928, and is a Fellow of Exeter
College. He began his career as a mining
engineer, being technical advisor to the Span-
ish Northern Railway from 1911 to 1916.
He then went to London, where for five
years he was a journalist, critic, and pub-
licist. He writes in Spanish, French, and
English.

From the beginning of the League of Nations, Señor de Madariaga was closely associated with its work. He was a member of the press section of its secretariat from 1922 to 1927, and from 1931 to 1936 was the Spanish permanent delegate and chairman of the conciliation committee. An active pacifist, he was long secretary of the World Federation. In 1931 he was Spanish Ambassador to the United States, and from 1932 to 1934 was Spanish Ambassador to France.

In 1928 he became King Alfonso XIII Professor of Spanish Studies at Oxford, and in 1932 he returned to this university, and is still on its faculty. He was one of the earliest Spanish Republicans, but since the civil war has held himself aloof from the politics of his native country. Once an ardent liberal, his disillusioning experiences in the diplomatic and political worlds have made of him a sardonic cynic. Perhaps the last time he made any attempt to activate the ideals of his youth was when as chairman of the conciliation committee of the League of Nations he tried vainly to secure justice for the Ethiopians against Fascist Italy.

Primarily he is a poet, though he has never published a volume of poems. A Spaniard, he is a leading authority on English poetry of the late eighteenth and early nineteenth century Romantic school. His wit has been called "Voltairian," and it has lost none of its brilliancy with his growing cynicism. Briand said he was one of the ten best conversationalists in Europe, and his writing is as coruscating as his speech. As Lewis Gannett remarked, "he has a kind of French clarity of mind." He can no longer be thought of, as he once was, as "a good European," since he has withdrawn farther and farther into an ivory tower of refuge from this disturbing era; but he is still one of the most powerful publicists and most devastating wits of the day. His love of paradox is apparent in nearly everything he writes, even on the dryest of subjects.

Señor de Madariaga is married to a Scotswoman, a classical scholar, the former Constance Archibald. They have two daughters, whom he calls his "Spanish daughter" and his "English daughter," from their different birthplaces and babyhood environments. He is a lean, bespectacled, sharp-nosed man, his former shock of hair now vanished, but still with heavy black eyebrows over keen dark eyes. He is a frequent lecturer, and has made several lecture tours in the United States, in addition to the year he spent as Ambassador.

PRINCIPAL WORKS AVAILABLE IN ENGLISH: Shelley and Calderon and Other Essays on Spanish and English Poetry, 1920; Spanish Folksongs, 1922; The Genius of Spain, 1923; The Sacred Giraffe, 1926; Englishmen, Frenchmen, Spaniards, 1928; Disarmament, 1929; Spain, 1930; Sir Bob, 1930; I Americans, 1930; Don Quixote, 1934; Anarchy or Hierarchy, 1937; Theory and Practice in International Relations, 1938; The World's Design, 1938; Christopher Columbus, 1939; Hernán Cortés: Conqueror of Mexico, 1941.

ABOUT: Annales Politiques et Littéraires February 1, 1932; Bookman November 1924, April 1929, September 1930; Deutsche Rundschau May 1938; Europe Nouvelle June 27, 1936; Hibbert Journal July 1938; Illustration March 25, 1933; New Statesman & Nation October 26, 1935; Revue des Deux Mondes November 1, 1929.

MADELEVA, Sister MARY. See WOLFF, M. E.

*MAETERLINCK, MAURICE, Comte (August 29, 1862-   ), Belgian dramatist, essayist, philosopher, winner of the Nobel Prize for literature, was born Maurice Polydore Marie Bernard Maeterlinck, at Ghent, the son of Polydore Maeterlinck, a man of small independent means. Coming of ancient Flemish stock, he has always prided himself on his origin, and in 1886, when he first began to write, he used to spell his forename "Mooris." For seven years of his boyhood he was under the Jesuits at the local College Sainte-Barbe. The régime was rigorous; and he was glad to move in due course into the more humane atmosphere of the University of Ghent. There a literary propensity became apparent, and it was fostered by acquaintance with the poet, Émile Verhaeren. Maeterlinck's family would have no trifling with poetry, however Maurice was put to the law, and in 1886 became a member of the Ghent bar. He did not practise long as an advocate, and is reported to have lost every case in which he appeared. His heart was not in the matter; he had a shy address most unsuited to his profession, and a harsh, thin voice that did not help. Moreover he was unsettled for legal work by a six-months' visit to Paris in 1887. There he saw the Promised Land. The legal studies which were the reason for the journey were somewhat neglected in favor of foregatherings with Villiers de l'Isle Adam, the Symbolist, and other literary people to whom he was introduced by a school-friend, Grégoire Le Roy. He even managed to get

* Died May 6, 1949.

into print, placing a few poems and an essay called "The Massacre of the Innocents" with a little monthly entitled *La Pléiade*.

Back in Belgium he continued his advocacy for a brief period but soon gave it up for a career in letters. He contributed to *La Jeune Belgique*, brought out a book of gently languorous and melancholy poems called *Serres Chaudes* in 1889, and in the same year became a dramatist with *La Princesse Maleine*. This play produced one of those startling events that are commoner in fiction than in life. It was read by the Parisian critic, Octave Mirbeau (who occupied a position something like that of Edmund Gosse in England) and he found it so excellent that in the *Figaro* of August 24, 1890, he compared it with Shakespeare.

Naturally uplifted by this eulogy (but not spoiled, for he was a modest man) Maeterlinck was encouraged to go on with his work. In 1891 he wrote two more plays, *L'Intruse* and *Les Aveugles*, and made evident his philosophic trend by a translation from the Flemish of the mystical work, *L'Ornement des Noces Spirituelles*, by Ruysbroeck l'Admirable. In his Introduction to this work Maeterlinck showed his own formative reading among authors ancient and modern, including Plato, Plotinus, Jacob Boehme, Coleridge, Novalis, and Emerson. The German writer, Novalis, had an especially strong influence on him, and in 1895 he was to translate that philosopher's *Disciples at Sais*.

Thus far Maeterlinck had, besides his book of verse, written eight plays which, in Edward Thomas' words, revealed "the disquiet of a mind that has given itself wholly to mystery." Best known among them was his *Pelleas and Melisande*, which inspired Claude Debussy's famous opera of the same name. His outward life had been uneventful. He had lived quietly at Oostacker in summer and Ghent in winter, writing, reading, canoeing, and skating. But in this year, 1895, there occurred an event of paramount importance to his development as a man and an author. This was his meeting with the French actress, Georgette Leblanc (whose brother was the popular novelist Maurice Leblanc[qv]). She had had a stormy and unhappy childhood, from which she had escaped by marriage at an early age—only to find that life with her Spanish husband was impossible. After a few months he disappeared, leaving her hopelessly bound in the toils of a Catholic marriage with a person whose whereabouts was unknown.

Georgette was a woman of parts and culture. She read Maeterlinck's works, admired the personality behind them, and at last contrived a meeting. Other encounters followed. Georgette soon perceived instances of the philosopher's complete humanity, as when, refusing to go into a room specially rigged out in a decorative scheme supposedly suited to his temperament, he collapsed comfortably into an old armchair, puffing at his pipe. Before long the two were together, and the peace and inspiration Georgette brought to Maeterlinck are expressed in the greater optimism and objectivity of his next few books.

In 1896 Maeterlinck left his native country for Paris, where he continued to live quietly. After some little time he took a country house at Gruchet-Saint-Simon, where he lived for nearly ten years. Then came the opportunity to acquire a magnificent home. The expulsion of the religious orders from France had left vacant the Norman Abbey of Saint Wandrille, near Rouen. It was available at a most reasonable rent, so the author moved in (regardless of the difficulty of keeping servants in this huge pile). The Abbey was for long his home, and he used it often as the setting for private performances of his own plays and those of Shakespeare. As a seasonal residence he had Quatre Chemins, near Grasse, in the Alpes-Maritimes. This opulent way of life, covering the years immediately prior to the first European War, was made possible by the considerable fortune brought to him by *The Blue Bird*.

Returning to the story of Maeterlinck's literary career, we find in 1896 the first of his delightful books of gravely wise familiar essays, *Le Trésor des Humbles*. It was followed in 1898 by *La Sagesse et la Destinée*, a work showing a broad moralistic attitude typical of his mature thought. To describe it as an ethical or metaphysical treatise would be inexact. It has no set system and presents no hard-and-fast moral rules, but is rather a widely discursive, gently persuasive guide to the leading of a sane spiritual life motivated by love. Both these books were dedicated to Georgette Leblanc. She ran his home, looked after his welfare, and took the leading parts in many of his plays.

With *La Vie des Abeilles* (1901) a new side of Maeterlinck's genius became apparent. Bee-keeping had been one of his hobbies from his youth up. He now supplemented his personal observations by extensive reading, and in this book showed that the so-called mystic could be as exact and scientific as any man. The scientific aspect was supplemented by a philosophic apprehension of the ways of these fascinating and orderly communities. The drama kept its place, too, in the forefront of his interests. *Monna Vanna* (1902) and *Joyzelle* (1903) reinforced his reputation in this field, as did *Le Temple Enseveli* (1902) in the essay. The vague half-lights of his early period were now almost gone, and there was increasing social emphasis.

L'Oiseau Bleu (*The Blue Bird*) had an enormous and widespread success, due less, probably, to its allegorical concomitants than to the light fantasy interpenetrating it, and the decorative, fairylike quality that has put it in the same category of popularity as *Peter Pan*. After more than thirty years, it is still Maeterlinck's best known single work. It had a curious theatrical and bibliographical history. Sent to Stanislavsky at the Moscow Art Theatre, it was put on in 1908 and ran for nearly a year. In December 1909 it was produced at the Haymarket Theatre, London, again totaling more than three hundred performances. The English version was also published that year, before the French (as has often happened with this author), which did not appear until 1910. The New York production followed that October and it was not until March 1911 that the play was at length seen in Paris, at the Théâtre Réjane. It has also been a favorite of the films, both in silent and talking versions, for many years.

The year 1911 also brought Maeterlinck the Nobel Prize for literature. (He had to decline another proferred honor—membership of the Académie Française, for its acceptance would have meant taking out papers as a Frenchman, and this he was unwilling to do. His own king in due course, recognized his eminence by raising him to the rank of count, on the occasion of his seventieth birthday.) About this time he also published a translation of *Macbeth* (the main dialogue in prose, but the witches' pieces in verse) which showed profound comprehension of the spirit and language of that difficult play.

Though Maeterlinck had deserted Belgium he remained a patriotic Belgian, and in 1914, despite his age of fifty-two years, tried hard to join the civil guard of his native country. Balked in this, he essayed the French Foreign Legion, but he was told officially that his pen would be more useful than his sword, and so went off enthusiastically to Italy to lecture in the Allied cause. An attempt to make similar propaganda in Spain was frustrated tactfully by the powers there. *Les Débris de la Guerre* (1916) was a collection of war articles and *The Burgomaster of*

Stilemonde (1918) a play on the German occupation of Belgium.

Soon after the war the long association with Georgette Leblanc was broken for reasons that remain obscure. [Georgette died at Cannes in October 1941.] Maeterlinck married Renée Dahon and made his summer home at the Château de Médan, Seine-et-Oise, with a winter villa called "Les Abeilles," near Nice. Ten years prior to the present writing, he had humorously dismissed himself as a spent force; but his actual practice has belied the then expressed intention to devote himself to eating, sleeping, drinking and living well for what years remained to him. He has, in fact, gone on with his work, despite his advanced age. Philosophy and natural history have remained alternate interests.

Maeterlinck visited the United States in 1920 but his lectures had little success owing to his poor command of spoken English (his *reading* knowledge is deep). In 1924 he went to Greece and the Near East and in 1926 to Algeria and Tunisia.

Maeterlinck has never been a formal philosopher in the sense that Benedetto Croce is such. His mind has not run to systems. His care has been the exploration of the vague, twilit regions that lie just behind the visible world and the inculcation of humane spiritual values in a mechanistic age. In the words of Sir Edmund Gosse, "His spirit is one of grave and disinterested attachment to the highest moral beauty." Most of the vast critical literature his work has evoked is eulogistic, but Giovanni Papini acts as *advocatus diaboli*, describing him as "a solemn man with a black cat in a dark room" and finding fault with his ambiguity, hair-splitting, and fondness for unfinished sentences.

Some years ago Frank Harris described Maeterlinck as "a broad Fleming of about five feet nine in height, inclined to be stout." He has a large, round head and blue-gray eyes. He hates formality and lionizing, and is entirely earthy and democratic in his distractions, which in the full vigor of his age included walking, skating, cycling, motoring, boxing, and beer. There is, it will be seen, nothing of the "pale aesthete" about this man. He loves animals, and was one of the first members of the Ligue Internationale Antivivisectiste. Gérard Harry records the very human trait of cursing *in Flemish* at small annoyances.

Following the Hitler conquest of France in 1940, Maeterlinck, at seventy-eight, and his wife fled to America, where he is still residing at the present time.

Works Available In English Translation: *Plays*—The Princess Maleine, 1892; Pelleas and Melisande, 1892; Alladene and Palomedes, 1898; Aglavaine and Selysette, 1899; The Death of Tintageles, 1899; The Blue Bird, 1909; Betrothal, 1912; The Wrack of the Storm, 1916; The Burgomaster of Stilemonde, 1918. *Essays and Philosophy* —The Treasure of the Humble, 1897; Wisdom and Destiny, 1898; The Buried Temple, 1902; The Double Garden, 1904; The Life of Space, 1922; The Magic of the Stars, 1930; The Hour Glass, 1936. *Natural History*—The Life of the Bee, 1901; The Life of the White Ant, 1926; The Life of the Ant, 1931; Pigeons and Spiders, 1935.

About: Griggs, E. H. Maeterlinck: Poet and Mystic. Harry, G. Vie de Maurice Maeterlinck; Leblanc, G. Maeterlinck and I; Leneveu, G. Maeterlinck and Ibsen; Le Sidaner, L. Maurice Maeterlinck; Marble, A.R. The Nobel Prize Winners; Papini, G. Four and Twenty Minds; Thomas, E. Maurice Maeterlinck; Walkley, A.B. Frames of Mind; American Magazine January 1941; Contemporary Review November 1910, February 1940; Newsweek February 10, 1941; Time July 22, 1940, February 10, 1941.

MAHAN, ALFRED THAYER. See "AMERICAN AUTHORS 1600-1900"

MAIS, STUART PETRE BRODIE (July 4, 1885-), English novelist, essayist, and radio broadcaster who signs his writ-

ings S. P. B. Mais, was born in Matlock, the son of the Rev. Brodie Mais. He was educated at Heath Grammar School, Halifax, Denstone College, and Christ Church, Oxford, graduating with his "blue" as a runner and with honors in mathematics and English literature. He received his B.A. in 1909 and his M.A. in 1913. From 1909 to 1920 he was a gamesmaster and army class tutor at Rossall, Sherbourne, and Tonbridge. From 1918 to 1936 he was literary critic successively of the London *Evening News*, *Daily Express*, and *Daily Graphic*, and from 1926 to 1931 leader writer and book reviewer on the *Daily Telegraph*. He is one of the leading broadcasters and televisors for the British Broadcasting Company, and is also a lecturer on books, travel, and the English countryside. As "the modern Columbus," in 1934, he has given radio talks in the United States as well as in England. During the First World War he was professor of English at the Royal Air Force Cadet College, and has been an examiner and lecturer at the University of London. Many of his broadcasts have later been published as books. He is married and has three children. His home, called "Toad

Hall," is at Shoreham-by-Sea. He gives as his favorite recreations cricket, walking, riding, bicycling, flying, and in fact travel of any sort, by any means, anywhere. A thin-faced blond with scant eyebrows over penetrating dark eyes, his face is thoughtful and melancholy in repose, but actually his salient characteristics as a writer and speaker are spontaneity and humor. He is an exceedingly prolific writer, who acknowledges he has little time for reading, and confesses that among the classics he has never read are works by Goethe, Smollett, Baudelaire, and Darwin's *Origin of Species*. He feels his special mission as a broadcaster is to interest children in English literature, and adults in the beauty of their country and its pressing social needs.

Principal Works: Shakespeare for Schools, 1913; An English Course for Army Candidates, 1915; A Public School in War Time, 1916; April's Lonely Soldier, 1916; Interlude, 1917; Rebellion, 1917; From Shakespeare to O. Henry, 1917; A Schoolmaster's Diary, 1918; An English Course for Schools, 1918; The Education of a Philanderer, 1919; Books and Their Writers, 1919; Uncle Lionel, 1920; Color Blind, 1920; Why We Should Read, 1920; An English Course for Everybody, 1921; Caged Birds, 1922; Quest Sinister, 1922; Oh! To Be in England, 1922; Prunello, 1923; Some Modern Authors, 1923; Perissa, 1924; Eclipse, 1925; Orange Street, 1926; See England First, 1927; Do You Know? 1927; Glorious Devon, 1928; The Cornish Riviera, 1928; First Quarter, 1929; Sussex, 1929; Frolic Lady, 1930; It Isn't Far From London, 1930; England of the Windmills, 1931; Southern Rambles, 1931; This Unknown Island, 1932; The Highlanders of Britain, 1932; Some Books I Like, 1932; These I Have Loved, 1933; S.O.S. Talks on Unemployment, 1933; Week-Ends in England, 1933; A Modern Columbus, 1934; Isles of the Island, 1934; More Books I Like, 1934; Road About England, 1935; England's Pleasance, 1935; The Writing of English. 1935; Walking at Week-Ends, 1935; A Chronicle of English Literature, 1936; England's Character, 1936; All the Days of My Life, 1937; The Three-Colored Pencil, 1937; Let's Get Out Here, 1937; Light Over Lundy, 1938; Old King Coal, 1938; Walking in Somerset, 1938; Britain Calling, 1938; Highways and Byways in the Welsh Marches, 1939; Listen to the Country, 1939; Hills of the South, 1939; Fifty Years of the London County Council, 1939; Raven Among the Rooks, 1939; Fear Lent Us Wings, 1939; Men in Blue Glasses, 1940; There'll Always Be an England, 1940; Diary of a Public Schoolmaster, 1940; Calling Again, 1941; The Black Spiders, 1941; Diary of a Citizen, 1941.

About: Mais, S.P.B. All the Days of My Life.

MAITLAND, FREDERIC WILLIAM. See "BRITISH AUTHORS OF THE 19TH CENTURY"

MAJOR, CHARLES (July 25, 1856-February 13, 1913), American historical novelist, was born at Indianapolis, Ind., and was educated in the public schools of Shelbyville and Indianapolis. His parents were

Stephen and Phoebe (Gaskill) Major. The elder Major was born in Granard, County Longford, Ireland, and came to the United States in 1829. He practiced law in

Shelbyville, whither the family moved when Charles was thirteen. Charles Major read law in his father's office, was admitted to the bar in 1877, and practiced law all his life except for serving in the Indiana legislature as a Democrat. In September of 1877 he married Alice Shaw of Shelbyville.

Of a quiet and retiring disposition, Major found his chief recreation in reading, especially English and French history of the Renaissance period. Publishing *When Knighthood Was in Flower* at forty-two, Major became a figure to be reckoned with in the astonishing renaissance of the historical novel at the turn of the century, in which so many Hoosier writers participated. Like Booth Tarkington, who wrote *Monsieur Beaucaire*, Major preferred European periods to the American scene covered by his fellow-Indianan Maurice Thompson in *Alice of Old Vincennes*, and by the Easterner Winston Churchill in *The Crossing*. Major's historical fiction, however lacking in psychological depth or penetration, had enough surface color, glitter, movement, and excitement to appeal to an extensive reading public, who bought 200,000 copies in two years and flocked to see the dusky beauty of Julia Marlowe in Paul Kester's dramatization of the novel. The love story of Mary Tudor, sister of Henry VIII, and Charles Brandon, Duke of Suffolk, was played against a background of sixteenth-century England. Marion Davies played the rôle in the silent moving pictures in 1922, and Mary Pickford appeared as Dorothy Vernon in the film version of *Dorothy Vernon of Haddon Hall*, Major's second best-seller. Major had his own theories concerning the writing of historical fiction, believing that the novelist should not try to reproduce contemporary speech, and should make a thorough study of original sources and the whole background of the life and people of the period attempted before setting pen to paper. With *The Bears of Blue River* he came nearer his own milieu, but his heart was not in it. The last two novels written before his death at fifty-six were *A Little King,* describing the child-

hood of Louis XIV, and *The Touchstone of Fortune,* which dealt with a certain Baron Clyde in the reign of Charles the Second.

PRINCIPAL WORKS: When Knighthood Was in Flower, 1898; The Bears of Blue River, 1900; Dorothy Vernon of Haddon Hall, 1903; A Forest Hearth, 1903; Yolanda, Maid of Burgundy, 1905; A Gentle Knight of Old Brandenburg, 1909; A Little King, 1910; The Touchstone of Fortune, 1912.

ABOUT: Pattee, F.L. The History of American Literature Since 1870; Book Buyer March 1900; Bookman November 1900; Current Literature May 1900.

"MALET, LUCAS." See HARRISON, M. ST. L. K.

MALINOWSKI, BRONISLAW (April 7, 1884-May 16, 1942), Anglo-Polish anthropologist, was born in what was then Austrian Poland, of a long line of Polish nobility and landed gentry, his father, Lucyan Malinowski, being a professor and scholar of Slavic philology. He was educated at the Polish University of Cracow, from which he received his Ph.D. in 1908 with the highest honors of the Austro-Hungarian Empire— *sub auspiciis Imperatoris.* He also studied at the University of Leipzig before going to London, where he did research at the British Museum and from 1910 was connected with the London School of Economics. In 1914 he was a member of the Robert Mond Expedition to New Guinea and North Melanesia.

This anthropological expedition, however, had scarcely reached its location when the First World War broke out. Malinowski was technically an Austrian (he subsequently became naturalized as a British subject), and therefore an enemy alien. He was interned for the duration of the war, but with rare perspicacity his place of internment was named as the Trobriand Islands—in other words, throughout the war he continued, under merely formal restriction, to do his anthropological research. After the Armistice he went to Australia, and a year later returned to England. There in 1919 he married Elise Rosaline Masson, daughter of Sir David Masson, K.B.E., F.R.S. She died in 1935, leaving three daughters. In 1940 he married Anna Valetta Hayman-Joyce, sister of Brigadier Hayman-Joyce of the British General Staff. Mrs. Malinowski paints under the name of Valetta Swann.

In 1924 Dr. Malinowski became a reader in social anthropology at the University of London, and in 1927 its professor of anthropology. At the invitation of the Laura Spelman Rockefeller Memorial, he visited the

United States and Mexico in 1926, touring the universities and doing anthropological research among the Pueblo Indians. He returned here three more times, in 1933 as Messenger Lecturer at Cornell, in 1936 as a delegate from Great Britain to the Harvard Tercentenary, when he received an honorary D.Sc. degree from Harvard, and in 1938 when he came here to spend his sabbatical leave.

In 1934 Dr. Malinowski did survey work among the Bantu tribes of South and East Africa. In 1936 he lectured at the Institute for Comparative Study of Cultures at Oslo. He was honorary member or correspondent of numerous anthropological and scientific bodies.

As a founder of the so-called functional school of anthropology, he insisted on studying human culture as a pragmatically connected whole and in examining human institutions in the light of their functioning within the framework of that whole. His special province was social anthropology, with particular reference to primitive religion and sexual customs. The scientific organization of his materials in this field marked the advance of cultural anthropology beyond its merely descriptive stage.

When war broke out again in Europe in 1939, Dr. Malinowski was still in this country on sabbatical leave. Advised to remain for the duration, he became visiting professor at Yale University and chairman of the board of exiled members of the Polish Academy of Arts and Sciences. His students found him thin and bright-eyed, with a "mouse-thatched head" and quick, nervous gestures. When he died at his home in New Haven of a heart attack at fifty-eight, the New York *Times* commented editorially:

"This integrator of ten thousand cultural characteristics was no ordinary professor. Parisian cafés, the islands of the South Pacific, the jungle of West Africa, European salons—he was at home in all, both as man of the world and as a scientist. . . . Both in English and American universities students flocked to him, enthralled by his command of his material."

PRINCIPAL WORKS: The Family Among the Australian Aborigines, 1913; Argonauts of the Western Pacific, 1922; Myth in Primitive Society, 1926; Crime and Culture in Savage Society, 1926; The Father in Primitive Psychology, 1927; Culture, the Diffusion Theory (with G.E. Smith & Others) 1927; Sex and Repression in Savage Society, 1927; The Sexual Life of Savages in Northwestern Melanesia, 1929; Coral Gardens and Their Magic, 1935; The Foundations of Faith and Morals, 1936.

ABOUT: American Anthropologist April 1937; Current Biography 1941; Newsweek September 19, 1936; New York Times May 17, 1942.

MALRAUX, ANDRÉ (November 3, 1895*-), French novelist and critic, was born in Paris of well-to-do parents. After completing his classical studies at the Lycée Condorcet he studied Sanskrit, Chinese, and archaeology at the School of Oriental Languages. In 1921 he published his first book, a collection of prose poems entitled *Lunes en Papier*, and married Clara Goldschmidt, the daughter of a German financier of Jewish extraction. Two years later he visited his father, a civil servant in Indo-China. Here, for almost a year, he dug through the ruins of fallen temples and collected Kmer statues. Suddenly abandoning his archaeological research, he joined with the Young Annam League in its fight for Indo-China dominion status. Thereupon the government laid claim to his Kmer statues, and he was allowed to keep them only after appealing to a higher court and proving that the evidence against him dealt not with art but with his connection with the Young Annam League.

Malraux's political interests sharpened as the situation in China intensified. In 1925 he acted as associate Secretary General of the Kuomintang, and played a leading role in the National Liberation Movement. On June 23, 1925, a mob in Canton protesting the shooting of some workers during a strike in Shanghai was fired upon by British police; as a result a general strike was called which paralyzed Hong Kong and Shameen (the Anglo-French concession in Canton), the struggle lasting fifteen months. These events form the background of Malraux's first important novel, *The Conquerors* (1928), which had been preceded by *La Tentation de l'Occident* (1926), a series of imaginary letters between a young Chinese and a Frenchman, revealing the need to find "the course and demands of action" that "will correspond with the dignity and intensity of human desires." This underlying philosophical motif pervades the turbulent world of *The Conquerors* as well as Malraux's subsequent works. Although it was lauded by the most exacting critics, *The Conquerors* sold poorly, but found its way gradually into eleven languages. His next

* Correction: Date of birth, November 3, 1901.   **897**

book, *The Royal Way* (1930), an adventure story set in Indo-China, a passionate variation on a Conrad theme, not only sold poorly but was generally condemned by the critics.

In 1933, however, *Man's Fate* won Malraux the Goncourt Prize and he was hailed as one of France's outstanding writers. In this novel he dramatized another historical event in which he had participated, the Chinese Revolution of 1924. In 1926 Malraux had been made a member of the Committee of Twelve (Chiang Kai-Shek was another member) and during the 1927 Revolution he occupied the post of propaganda commissioner for the key provinces of Kwangsi and Kwantung. All the themes outlined in *The Conquerors* are brought to a full and splendid statement in *Man's Fate*. The story—which records two eventful days in March 1927—is one of human crisis sustained at a level that becomes almost unbearable. Philip Henderson says that "outside Dostoievsky or Maxim Gorky, there is perhaps no other book comparable to this in the sheer naked intensity of its suffering." In *Man's Fate* Malraux succeeded in grasping an objective historic situation and in integrating it, with acute sensitiveness, in the subjective world of his characters. When Chiang Kai-Shek broke with the Third International and the Revolution collapsed with a series of betrayals, executions, and assassinations, Malraux left China. After collecting Graeco-Buddhist art in Persia and Afghanistan, he returned to Paris, edited de luxe editions for Gallimard, helped Mme. Malraux with her translations from the German, and put in order his apartment at the Rue du Bac for the birth of his daughter Florence (1933).

In the early part of 1934 Malraux took aviation lessons with Captain Corniglion Molinier; one day they flew over the Strait of Bab-el-Mandeb into the world's most desolate desert (crossed only once before, in 1932, by an English camel expedition), and on March 9 they reported the discovery of the Queen of Sheba's legendary city, north of Ruba-al-Khali. Although specialists were non-committal, newspapers the world over played up the event melodramatically.

In Malraux's next work, *Days of Wrath* (1935), he focussed his attention on the Hitler terror. This short novel is a tribute to the heroism of the anti-Fascists. He depicts the feelings of a Communist who after being beaten up by the Nazis and imprisoned in a dark cell for nine days is freed when a fellow Communist whose name

he does not know surrenders in his place. *Days of Wrath* scored an international success (it was a Book-of-the-Month selection), but Malraux went on with his treatise on aesthetic theory (*The Psychology of Art*, still in progress), and intensified his practical activities, speaking at mass meetings in defense of Thaelmann, the imprisoned German Communist; protesting at the invasion of Abyssinia; founding with Louis Aragon the International Association of Writers for the Defence of Culture, which held its first congress in the Salle de la Mutualité (Paris), June 21-25, 1935.

When the Franco revolt broke out in Spain on July 18, 1936, Malraux organized an air corps for the Loyalists and, despite his limited flying experience, made sixty-five flights over Fascist territory, was twice injured, but helped in stopping the Rebel advance on Madrid. Besides fighting at the front, Malraux toured France and the United States raising funds for the Loyalists and in his spare time wrote *Man's Hope* (1937), "a big, fast-paced, sprawling, 511-page novel," which seizes with intense dramatic power on the events of the first nine months of the Spanish conflict. Edgell Rickword says: "If imagination means the power to communicate intense experience, then *Man's Hope* is a magnificent imaginative work. Without deviating from the strictest objectivity, Malraux has developed a prose which is more supple than that of his earlier works, which describes, suggests, evokes without self-consciousness, seemingly without effort."

Malraux celebrated his thirty-eighth birthday filming *Man's Hope* in Barcelona, with cameraman Louis Page of *Carnival in Flanders* fame. Back in Paris (1939), now separated from his wife, he returned to his job at Gallimard's, resumed his *Psychology of Art* and his manifold political activities.

A number of conflicting reports concerning Malraux reached America after the downfall of France in 1940. The most accurate information seems to be that after serving in a French tank column, he escaped safely to Unoccupied France.

Malraux has been described as "volatile, restless, sharp-eyed, thin-featured. . . . He talks a great deal, and very rapidly, smokes constantly, is disturbed by a facial tic which stayed with him after illness in China. Gloomily handsome, mildly sardonic, he enjoys the companionship of pretty women." Malraux knows Spanish, English, German, Italian, Russian as well as Chinese and minor Oriental tongues. He is fond of English and American writers (especially D. H. Lawrence, Dashiell Hammett, Hemingway, Faulkner) and introduced to France *Sanctuary* and *Lady Chatterley's Lover.*

WORKS AVAILABLE IN ENGLISH TRANSLATION: The Conquerors, 1929; Man's Fate (British title: Storm in Shanghai), 1934; The Royal Way, 1935; Days of Wrath (British title: Days of Contempt), 1936; Man's Hope (British title: Days of Hope), 1938.

ABOUT: Ehrhard, J.E. Le Roman Français Depuis Marcel Proust; Henderson, P. The Novel Today; Lefevre, F. Une Heure Avec; Stansbury, M.H. French Novelists Today; The Literary World August 1934; Marianne May 24, 1933; New Masses November 15, 1938; New Republic August 9, 1933; New Writing Autumn 1938; New York Post June 25, 1934; New York Times June 25, 1934, November 6, 1938; Saturday Review of Literature January 11, 1941; Time January 13, 1931, November 7, 1938, October 30, 1939.

MALTZ, ALBERT (October 28, 1908-), American dramatist and novelist, writes: "I was born in Brooklyn. My father came

Talbot

to this country as a boy from what is now Lithuania, and followed the usual course of immigrants — that of laborious work from childhood in a desperate attempt to gain security—and then to keep it. He was a grocer's boy, a salesman, later a house painter, and, for some years, a farmer. In middle life he became a successful builder. He went to a comparatively early grave, worn out, carrying with him a love for America and painter's lead-poisoning. My mother came to this country as an infant from Poland. She wanted to be a schoolteacher and spent her adolescent years instead as a seamstress in a sweatshop. There she contracted trachoma, and the girl who wanted to be a schoolteacher lived out the rest of her life unable to read. That too I have remembered.

"I went to the public schools and then to Columbia. While I now look back upon much of my elementary and college work as wasted because of the primitive methods of education upon which it was based, there is no question that without it I would have been a dunce. College, particularly, provided a period of sharp awakening, especially to one of my background. There I spent most time on philosophy—a subject taught with maximum love by the instructors, I believe, and with maximum errors and innocence in pedagogy—but a subject most provocative

in itself. I remember Irwin Edman and Peter Odegarde and Mark Van Doren with gratitude, and others as well. At college, too, I got a hankering to write. John Erskine gave me a first encouraging push. He wouldn't recall it, but it meant a good deal.

"After graduation, in 1930, I went to Yale to study at the Drama School with George Pierce Baker. I was terribly ignorant and learned a great deal there, particularly from two persons: the late Alexander Dean, who, I believe, knew more about theatre in all phases than anyone I have ever known; and George Sklar, a fellow-student then, who collaborated with me on two plays. He spurred me on, above all, to the conclusion upon which all my work is and will be based: that individuals live not in a vacuum but in society, and that a writer cannot write truly of people or characters unless the world in which they live is equally illumined. Together, while at Yale, we wrote *Merry Go Round*, and stepped from school into Broadway in one feverish semester. That play was temporarily censored because it dealt with political corruption and the shoe pinched on the gangrenous foot. The episode provided a second great lesson: that not all dogs are honest.

"I have been writing since. My wife is Margaret Larkin and we have one child."

* * *

Mr. Maltz began as a dramatist, with *Merry Go Round, Peace on Earth,* and *Black Pit,* all strongly "social," the two latter produced by the Theatre Union. His one-act pacifist play, *Private Hicks,* won first prize in the New Theatre League Contest in 1935. He turned next to. short stories. One of these, "Man on a Road," almost was a forecast of the Congressional investigation of silicosis among West Virginia miners. Another, "The Happiest Man on Earth," an almost unbearable study of unemployment, won first prize in the 1938 O. Henry Memorial Volume. "Season for Celebration," a corrosive study of a Bowery flophouse, was included in the anthology, *The Flying Yorkshireman.*

He is dark, with strongly marked features, and still so young that one may prophesy great things of him. He was married in 1937, and lives in New York except when he is writing scenarios in Hollywood. Maltz has taught two sessions of the Rocky Mountain Writers' Conference and has been an instructor of playwriting at New York

University. He is a member of the Council of the Authors' League.

PRINCIPAL WORKS: *Plays* (*dates of publication*)—Peace on Earth (with G. Sklar) 1934; Black Pit, 1935; Private Hicks (in Best Short Plays of the Social Theatre) 1939. *Fiction* — The Way Things Are (short stories) 1938; The Underground Stream, 1940.

ABOUT: Scholastic March 5, 1938; Wilson Library Bulletin September 1939.

MANN, ERIKA (November 9, 1905-), German-American journalist, is the oldest child of Thomas Mann,[qv] the great German writer. She  was born in Munich, and after finishing school went to Berlin to study with Max Reinhardt. She prepared further for the stage in Bremen and Hamburg, where she played one of the leading parts in the

S. Deutch

first play of her brother, Klaus—*Anja und Esther*. This was in 1925, and the same year she was married to Gustaf Gründgens, at that time a prominent left-wing actor, now a Nazi, a personal friend of Hermann Goering, and director of the Berlin State Theatre. They were divorced when their ways separated after the Nazi conquest of Germany. Like her brother, to whom she is very close, Erika Mann lived two or three lives at once in those early years—acting, writing, traveling, and even taking part in a race of Fords around Europe, in which she won first prize for driving six thousand miles in ten days, meanwhile sending in newspaper stories of her progress! She staged her own satirical revue, "Peppermill," which opened in Munich at the beginning of 1933. After Hitler's coup it was taken to other countries, running a total of more than a thousand performances; in 1936 it was put on in New York. She traveled around the world with her brother, wrote with him an account of their trip called *Rundherum* (*Round-about*), and published an adventure story for boys, *Stoffel Flies Over the Seas*.

Then came Hitler. Her parents were in Switzerland at the time he seized power, and it was Erika who, disguised in a peasant dress and dark glasses, rescued the manuscript of *Joseph and His Brethren*, taking it out of Germany in the tool-box of the Ford car she had won as her prize in the driving contest. She can give no more definite date for this than the spring of

1933, because of people concerned in the enterprise who are still in Germany.

In 1935 she was married to the English poet, Wystan Hugh Auden. She came to the United States with her family in 1936, and has lived here since, mostly in New York, though she has made transcontinental lecture tours. Before coming to America she had spent some time in Czechoslovakia, and she went to Spain in 1938. From a girl who thought politics "the business of the politicians," she has become a leader of anti-Fascism, as is evidenced by all her recent books. She writes now in English and expects soon to be an American citizen, like her father and brother. She is handsome, with dark hair and eyes, and in her lighter moments likes to practice Bavarian cooking, swim, and ski.

WORKS AVAILABLE IN ENGLISH: School for Barbarians, 1938; Escape to Life (with K. Mann) 1939; The Other Germany (with K. Mann) 1940; The Lights Go Down, 1940.

ABOUT: Current Biography 1940; Nation October 19, 1940; Time February 26, November 2, 1940; Wilson Library Bulletin June 1939.

*MANN, HEINRICH (March 27, 1871-), German novelist, writes: "I was born in Lübeck. My father was Senator Heinrich Mann. My mother came from Brazil, one of my great-grandfathers was from Geneva. The family built their house in the seventeenth century. I studied in Berlin, traveled in French Switzerland, and lived much in Italy. By my fortieth year I knew  the Italian people well enough to write my novel, *The Little Town*. In the following decade I gave, in three novels, a portrait of German society under the Empire. *Der Untertan* [*The Subject,* translated as *The Patrioteer*] treated of the bourgeoisie, *Die Armen* [*The Poor*] of the proletariat, *Der Kopf* [*The Chief*] of the ruling classes.

"I produced another considerable effect with the play *Madame Legros,* which toward the end of the World War pleased its spectators, because it celebrated all humanity. The film, *Der Blaue Engel* [*The Blue Angel*] was in 1930 dramatized from the novel *Professor Unrat*, which appeared in 1904.

"The Prussian Government called me to Berlin to the Academy of Arts. In 1931 I was elected to the presidency of the Poetry Section. I remained in this office, until the

* Died March 12, 1950.

beginning of the persecution of literature under the Nazi régime made it necessary for me to resign my post and leave the country.

"In exile it was important to assert courage and strength. I have since 1933 composed new books and written for the freeing of Germany. I learned to express myself in French and informed a large public of the facts about a German régime that had reinforced its war against civilization with the extremest outrages, since the time when it banished me myself.

"In exile I have written my largest and most ambitious novels. *Die Jugend des Königs Henri Quatre* [*The Youth of King Henri IV*, translated as *Young Henry of Navarre*] appeared in 1936, *Die Vollendung des Königs Henri Quatre* [*The End of King Henri IV*, translated as *Henry King of France*] in 1938. The hero of both books is one of the greatest figures of European history. The problem treated is human greatness, its questionable value and merit.

"These works of an author who is in his sixty-ninth year, dare not at present be known in his own country. Other lands and languages have received him with honors."

* * *

Heinrich Mann is the older brother of Thomas Mann.[qv] In 1914 he married Marie Kahn, of Prague; they have one daughter. Until the Nazi occupation he lived at Nice, on the Riviera, from where he wrote the preceding account. Subsequently he escaped to America where he now lives. He looks not unlike his famous brother, with the same long head and dark skin, indicative of their partly Portuguese ancestry. In Heinrich Mann the Latin appearance is accentuated by a heavy moustache and a goatee.

Heinrich Mann is an unusually gifted writer, who combines beauty of style and richness of narrative with deep earnestness of feeling. S. Kracauer has said of him: "He is the defender of the mind and the champion of intellectual freedom, with as much accent on intellect as on freedom, . . . a friend of enlightenment, a disciple of wisdom."

WORKS AVAILABLE IN ENGLISH: The Poor, 1917; The Patrioteer, 1918; The Goddess, 1918; The Chief, 1925; In the Land of Cockaigne, 1925; Diana, 1929; The Royal Woman, 1930; Mother Mary, 1930; The Little Town, 1931; The Blue Angel, 1932; The Hill of Lies, 1934; Young Henry of Navarre (in England: The Youth of Henri IV) 1938; Henry King of France (in England: Henri Quatre, King of France) 1939; The Living Thoughts of Nietzsche (ed.) 1939.

ABOUT: Living Age September 1932.

*MANN, KLAUS (November 18, 1906-), German-American novelist, essayist, and playwright, writes: "I was born in Munich, the second child of Thomas Mann[qv] and Frau Katja Mann, *née* Pringsheim. I went to school in Munich, and later became a pupil of a progressive German country school (*Freie Schulgemeinde im Odenwald*, near Heidelberg). I started  my literary career when I was seventeen years old. In 1924 I published short stories and articles in various leading Berlin papers, during the winter of 1924-25 I was active as a theatrical critic for a Berlin morning paper, and in the spring of 1925 I published my first book, a volume of short stories called *Vor dem Leben* (*Before Life*). In the fall of the same year my first novel appeared (*Der Fromme Tanz* [*The Pious Dance*]), and at the same time I came out with my first play, *Anja und Esther*, which was produced in Munich, Hamburg, Berlin, Vienna, and several other cities. It was also translated into Italian and produced in Rome. In the first performance, at Hamburg, my sister Erika and Pamela Wedekind, the daughter of the famous poet Frank Wedekind, played the two leading parts, while Gustaf Gründgens and I appeared as the two leading men. Fraülein Wedekind was then my fiancée.

"I appeared as an actor in another play I wrote—a comedy entitled *Revue zu Vieren* (*Revue With Four Characters*). With this play we toured Germany, and also went to Copenhagen. In 1927-28 I made a tour around the world with my sister. We spent half a year in this country, having a wonderful time in New York, Hollywood, etc. We also delivered lectures on modern German literature to various universities, such as Princeton and Harvard. In collaboration with Erika, I wrote a book describing our exciting journey.

"During the years from 1929 to 1933 I wrote two more novels and produced two more plays—a comedy with an American background, and a stage adaptation of Jean Cocteau's novel, *Les Enfants Terribles*, entitled *Geschwister* (*Brother and Sister*), produced for the first time at Munich, with Erika in the leading role. I published another volume of short stories, a volume of literary and political essays, and a book of

* Died May 21, 1949.

childhood memories, *Kind Dieser Zeit* (*Child of Our Time*).

"The fatal year 1933 meant a turning-point in my life. When Hitler came to power, I realized, without hesitation, that I had to leave the country—although I am no Jew and never belonged to any political party. But I knew from the beginning that I could not bear life under the Nazi dictatorship. I left Germany in March 1933 and have never set foot there since. Even before Hitler's rise to power, however, I used to travel a great deal, and I actually spent more time in Paris and the South of France than in Munich or Berlin. So the exile—cruel as it may be—meant less of a tragedy for me than it did for many of my fellow-refugees; for I always felt myself to be a European rather than a German, and a citizen of the world rather than a European.

"Between 1933 and 1936 I lived in Amsterdam, where I was active as the editor of a literary monthly called *Die Sammlung* (*The Collection*), the sponsors of which were André Gide, Heinrich Mann (my uncle), and Aldous Huxley. I also spent a great deal of time in Zurich (where my father then had his home), in Paris, Nice, Budapest, Salzburg, and Prague. Thanks to the generosity of President Beneš, I became a citizen of Czechoslovakia, after having been deprived of my German citizenship by the Nazis. I moved to America in the autumn of 1936. A year later my parents settled at Princeton, N.J. My headquarters are our Princeton home and a hotel room in New York City. Besides, I travel a great deal, lecturing—usually on topics such as 'After Hitler—What?' or 'A Family Against a Dictatorship.' Sometimes, however, I am even allowed to speak about literature.

"I am at work now on a series of historical portraits, presenting various distinguished persons who visited this country during the last two centuries. During the summer of 1938 I went to Spain, a few months before the final collapse of the Loyalists.

"I stubbornly hope to live long enough to witness a state of international affairs which may be a little less confused and horrifying than the world we have to face at this moment."

* * *

Klaus Mann is editor of *Decision*, a magazine of free culture, which he founded in New York.

WORKS AVAILABLE IN ENGLISH: The Fifth Child, 1927; Alexander (novel) 1930; Journey Into Freedom, 1935; Pathetic Symphony (novel) 1938; Escape to Life (with E. Mann) 1939; The Other Germany (with E. Mann) 1940; The Turning Point (autobiography) 1942.

ABOUT: Mann, K. Kind Dieser Zeit; Bookman June-July 1932; Current Biography 1940; Time February 26, 1940, January 20, 1941.

*MANN, THOMAS (June 6, 1875-   ), German novelist and essayist, winner of the Nobel Prize, was born in the ancient Hanseatic city of Lübeck, of a prosperous influential mercantile family. His great grandfather was a freethinker, a follower of the Rationalists; his grandfather, a political liberal, was Consul to The Netherlands, while his father, Johann Heinrich Mann, was a Senator and twice Mayor of the free city. A most dignified gentleman, he was unconventional enough to read Zola's novels and to marry Julia da Silva-Bruhns, daughter of a German planter at Rio de Janeiro and his Portuguese-Creole wife, who had been taken to Lübeck at the age of seven. "When I ask myself the hereditary origin of my characteristics I am fain to recall Goethe's famous little verse and say that I too have . . . from my mother the sensuous, artistic side," says Mann. She was fiery, temperamental and romantic, in her youth a much-admired beauty, and extraordinarily musical. It has been said that Mann combines the French concern for form with the German concern for substance, the French gift of lucid, logical analysis with the German genius of pure poetry and music.

F. Warschauer

With his older brother Heinrich, his younger brother and two younger sisters (both of whom later committed suicide), Thomas led a sheltered, happy childhood in a big house built by his father near the ancestral dwelling later shown to the curious as "the Buddenbrook house."

Slated to be another merchant, dreamy, indolent Thomas was sent to the Realgymnasium, at the Katherineum, where he had a "stagnating, unsatisfying time." He loathed the stiff Prussian regimen, mocked the manners of its masters, and "early espoused a sort of literary opposition to its spirit, its discipline, and its methods of training." A poor student, he completed his disgrace in the eyes of the authorities by "writing"—poems, a romance, plays, and, under the pseudonym "Paul Thomas," "philosophic and revolutionary leaders" for a periodical called *Spring Storm*—"not a very proper

* Died August 12, 1955.

school paper, I fear"—established, together with some radical-minded fellows, "for art, literature and philosophy." In May 1893 this magazine carried the first work signed Thomas Mann—a poem.

Not long after the pompous funeral of Johann Mann in 1890, his hundred-year-old grain business went into liquidation, having been declining for some time. His great house was sold, as the old family homestead had been sold before it, and Frau Mann soon quit Lübeck for gayer, sunnier Munich, leaving Thomas to finish his schooling. At nineteen he received his certificate and followed his family to Munich, where, "with the word temporary in my heart," he took an unsalaried job in an insurance office, and sat at a sloping desk copying out accounts and writing, surreptitiously, his first tale, a love story called "Fallen," which brought him his first literary success.

After a year of "business activities," Thomas with the aid of his mother's lawyer won his freedom and attended courses in literature, art, history and political economy at the University, after which he joined his brother Heinrich in Rome. They spent the summer in Palestrina, the winter in Rome, which they regarded as "the refuge of our irregularity." Heinrich, who meant to be an artist, sketched, while Thomas devoured Russian and Scandinavian literature, and wrote. While still in Rome his first book was published by the famous Berlin house of Fischer, whose editor had been greatly taken by *Little Herr Friedemann*, and asked for more stories.

In 1898 Mann returned to Munich with the huge but incomplete manuscript of *Buddenbrooks*, on which he continued to work until the turn of the century, despite a pleasant post on the staff of *Simplicissimus* which he held for about a year. His great influences at this time were Schopenhauer, whom he read "day and night, as perhaps one reads only once in his life," and whose mysticism he wove into the close of his novel; and Nietzsche, whom he loved but rejected almost entirely. He scorned the great immoralist's cult of the superman, his glorification of "life" at the expense of the mind. "What to me were his blond beast and his philosophy of force? Almost an embarrassment."

Buddenbrooks was sent to Fischer by registered mail; the post office clerk smiled when Mann wrote "Manuscript" on the wrapper and then insured it for a thousand marks. At this unwieldy production by an obscure young author the publishers balked.

Cut it in half, they urged. But Mann, then serving a brief term in the army, persuaded them to risk it, and *Buddenbrooks* appeared in two expensive volumes at the end of 1900, with a 1901 imprint. At first the book seemed doomed to failure. Critics resented its size, the public its price; but in a year the first edition of 1000 copies was sold out and Fischer decided on a cheap one-volume reprint with William Schultz's Biedermeier cover design. Whereupon the book began to sell, printings overlapped, the twenty-five-year old author was "snatched up in a whirl of success," his picture appeared in the papers; "the world embraced me amid congratulations and shouts of praise." Until it was burned and banned by Hitler, *Buddenbrooks*, considered everywhere a classic, sold over a million copies in Germany alone; it has been translated into almost every modern language.

In February 1905 Mann married Katja Pringsheim, only daughter of a cultured mercantile family of Munich in whose elegant salon he was lionized after his great success. Henceforward, until 1933, Mann's life was calm, joyous, and fruitful. He owned a fine home in Munich, a summer home in Tölz on the Isar, and later a cottage on the dunes of Nidden in Memelland. He lectured in Holland, Switzerland, England, Scandinavia, with holidays in Spain and the Lido. Six children were born to him; the oldest, Erika, became an actress and writer, Klaus, his oldest son, is also a writer.[qqv]

Tonio Kröger, Mann's own favorite work, appeared in 1903 in the volume of tales entitled *Tristan*. Like *Death in Venice* (1913), acclaimed "the finest novelette produced in our generation," these stories are psychological studies of genius. After *Royal Highness* (1909), "an attempt to come to terms, as a writer, with my own happiness," fifteen years elapsed before his next novel. During this war period Mann wrote a series of groping, soul-searching treatises, notably *Reflections of a Non-Political Man* (1918) in which he painfully examined his conscience. Out of this spiritual travail came *The Magic Mountain* (1924). This second major masterpiece had occupied Mann since 1912, when he spent three weeks in a Davos sanatorium with his wife, who had a catarrh of the lung. Envisioning a short, humorous tale of "the fascination of death, the triumph of extreme disorder over a life founded upon order and consecrated to it . . . a droll conflict between macabre adventure and bourgeois sense of duty," Mann began to write his grim epic of a civilization in decay.

Thinking to write about himself, he discovered himself, as usual, depicting the world and his age. *The Magic Mountain* "represents German 'liberalism,' its fluctuation between extremes of nationalism and mysticism, technics and esthetics," says H. Slochower. "In Thomas Mann the German middle class has its most eloquent spokesman in the novel and *The Magic Mountain* is its greatest artistic and intellectual achievement."

Between 1924 and 1933 Mann produced, among other works, two novelettes, *Disorder and Early Sorrow* (1926), an exquisitely tender and sympathetic story of parental love whose childish heroine is Mann's favorite daughter Elizabeth, and *Mario and the Magician* (1930), a symbolic representation of the evils of dictatorship.

In 1926 a Munich artist asked Mann to write an introduction to a portfolio of illustrations depicting the story of Joseph the son of Jacob, of which Goethe once said, "This natural narrative is most charming, only it seems too short, and one feels inclined to put in the detail." Mann looked up the old family Bible; meditating and groping he felt "an indescribable fascination . . . at this idea of leaving the modern bourgeois sphere so far behind and making my narrative pierce deep, deep into the human." Mann studied the Biblical legend, made archaeological excursions, visiting Egypt and Palestine after receipt of the Nobel Prize in 1929. He was nearing the end of what he realized would be only the first volume when the Reichstag went up in flames. Mann, lecturing at the time in Holland, never returned to Germany, but settled in Zurich to finish *Joseph and His Brothers* (1933). His children Erika and Klaus and his brother Heinrich pleaded with him to denounce the Nazis, but the "non-political man" hesitated. Finally Mann could contain himself no longer. An attack upon *emigré* Germans in the *Neue Zuricher Zeitung* brought his first open denunciation of the Nazis as enemies of Christianity, of Occidental morality, and of civilization itself (February 3, 1936); whereupon Mann was deprived of German citizenship. On December 19, 1936, Mann was informed by the Dean of the Philosophy Faculty of the University of Bonn that his honorary doctorate had been rescinded. In reply Mann wrote a scorching denunciation of fascism published all over the non-Fascist world: *An Exchange of Letters* (1937). Mann's works are now banned in the Third Reich as "un-German." He believes with excellent rea-

son, that had he remained in Germany he would not be alive today.

Since coming to the United States in 1938, Mann has given himself unstintingly to the anti-Fascist cause, relinquishing "that dangerous . . . habit of thought which regards . . . life and intellect, art and politics as totally separate worlds." He has lectured to capacity audiences across the country on the subject of his book *The Coming of Democracy* (1938). He considers the United States the classic ground of democracy, the center to which Western culture is shifting for " the duration of the present European dark age." These activities have not deflected him from his work as artist, the conclusion of the fourth part of his monumental Joseph story. Meanwhile he has relaxed from this heavy labor with two slighter narratives. Among the honors he has received here is his appointment as Fellow of the Library of Congress, consultant in German literature.

For several years Mann made his home at Princeton, N.J., where he lectured at the University, but in 1941 he built a permanent home at Santa Monica, Calif. He spends his mornings in creative writing, afternoons on correspondence, dictating to his wife and two secretaries, one German, one English. At five o'clock high tea is served. He is an inveterate concert-goer (his tastes run from Brahms to Stravinsky but his favorite is Wagner); on occasion he consents to a literary evening at which he reads aloud his latest work. Walking is his only exercise, his old gramophone his favorite fun. Like many mystics, he is superstitious about numbers. In *The Magic Mountain,* for example, the number seven recurs again and again as a unifying symbol representing the completion of a cycle. It pleases his mathematical sense that he has three boys and three girls, born in somewhat symmetrical succession; and that most of the important events of his life occurred in mid-decade. He believes he will die at the same age as his mother, in 1945.

WORKS AVAILABLE IN ENGLISH TRANSLATION: *Novels*—Royal Highness, 1916; Buddenbrooks, 1924; The Magic Mountain, 1924; Joseph and His Brothers, 1933; Young Joseph, 1935; Joseph in Egypt, 1938; The Beloved Returns, 1940; The Transposed Heads, 1941. *Short Stories and Novelettes*—Death in Venice (including Tristan and Tonio Kröger) 1925; Children and Fools (nine short stories) including Little Herr, 1928; Early Sorrow, 1930; A Man and His Dog, 1930; Death in Venice (new translation) 1930; Mario and the Magician, 1931; Nocturnes (three stories) 1934; Stories of Three Decades (all of Mann's fiction except the novels) 1936. *Essays and Criticism*—Three Essays, 1929; A Sketch of My Life

1930; Past Masters, and Other Essays (thirteen essays) 1933; An Exchange of Letters, 1937; Freud, Goethe, and Wagner, 1937; The Coming Victory of Democracy, 1938; This Peace, 1938; This War, 1940.

ABOUT: Baer, L. The Concept and Function of Death in the Works of Thomas Mann; Bithell, J. Modern German Literature; Burke, K. Counter-Statement; Cleugh, J. Thomas Mann: A Study; Cather, W. Not Under Forty; Eloesser, A. Modern German Literature; Eloesser, A. Thomas Mann: Sein Leben und Sein Werk; Havenstein, M. Thomas Mann; Helbling, C. Thomas Mann; Jacob, G. Das Werk Thomas Manns; Kapp, M. Thomas Manns novellistische Kunst; Lion, F. Thomas Mann in Seiner Zeit; Mann, T. A Sketch of My Life; Peacock, R. Das Leitmotiv bei Thomas Mann; Slochower, H. Thomas Mann's Joseph Story; Slochower, H. Three Ways of Modern Man; Weigand, H. J. Thomas Mann's Novel "Der Zauberberg"; Books May 5, 1927, December 8, 1929, December 24, 1933, May 5, 1935; Chicago Post February 29, 1924; New Masses March 29, 1938; New Republic October 13, 1937; New York Herald Tribune "Books" June 29, 1941; New York Times May 19, 1940; New Yorker June 6, 1936; Publications of the Modern Language Association of America June 1928 and September 1931.

MANNIN, ETHEL EDITH (October 1900-   ), English novelist and essayist, writes: "I was born in London of working-class parents of Irish descent, Robert Mannin and Ethel (Gray) Mannin. I be-

lieve that the working-classes, who are the great mass of people, are the salt of the earth and the hope of the civilized world— if there be any hope for it, which is to my mind debatable. I was educated at board school (state school). There was no high-falutin nonsense about my 'gift' for writing, which I developed at about the age of seven. I left school at fifteen and got a job in an advertising agency as a stenographer. At seventeen I was editing various house-organs and the old theatrical and sporting paper, the *Pelican*, which (Sir) Charles Higham, my employer, had acquired. I published my first novel in 1922. My third novel, *Sounding Brass*, a satire on the advertising world, was much talked of in Fleet Street, as everyone identified the hero as Higham, and I began to be known from that book. *Confessions* in 1929 was a *succès de scandale*. Soon after this I published my first book on child education and psychology, *Commonsense and the Child*, having come under the influence of that most radical of all educationists, A. S. Neill. I joined the Independ-

ent Labor Party (revolutionary Socialist) in 1932. I am still [1940] a member, but have lately adopted the pacifist position of non-violence, whilst still maintaining the revolutionary Socialist position, having come a few years ago under the influence of the late Bart de Ligt (the author of *The Conquest of Violence*). *South to Samarkand* is the story of my final disillusionment with the U.S.S.R. Of my novels, I like nothing before *Linda Shawn*, and my own preference is for *Venetian Blinds*, a study of working-class and lower-class life as I knew it and lived it (see *Confessions*).

"I like mountains, gardening, and simple people. My passion is for Eire, the land of my ancestors. I like walking, but don't play any games or go in for any sports. I am opposed to capital punishment, orthodox education, and blood sports. I married Reginald Reynolds, the author of the anti-Imperialist book *White Sahibs in India* a few years ago. I have a daughter of nineteen by a former marriage [to John Porteous].

"I have a six-roomed cottage and lovely garden outside of London, and am acquiring a two-roomed cabin in Connemara, in Eire. I admire the works of Somerset Maugham and Aldous Huxley. I like Bach and Purcell. I loathe radio, telephones, cars, red fingernails, American films, synthetic blonde hair, and writing about myself."

* * *

A critic in 1926 described Miss Mannin as "gentle, shy, pretty, and thoroughly charming: one would never suspect her of being serious-minded." But her work he called "sound, cruel, and wise," and spoke of her "caustic wit and her observing eye." It has been objected that sometimes "she allows words to get in her way," and her work is uneven, but it has body and power.

Miss Mannin has been married twice: to J. A. Porteous in 1919 and in 1938 to the author Reginald Reynolds. She was a member of the Independent Labour Party from 1932 to 1942, when she resigned, "preferring anarchism to Marxism," she writes. She is a pacifist.

PRINCIPAL WORKS: *Fiction*—Martha, 1922; Hunger of the Sea, 1924; Sounding Brass, 1925; Pilgrims, 1927; Green Willow, 1928; Crescendo, 1929; Children of the Earth, 1930; Ragged Banners, 1931; Bruised Wings (short stories) 1931; Green Figs (short stories) 1931; Tinsel Eden (short stories) 1931; Love's Winnowing, 1932; Linda Shawn, 1932; Venetian Blinds, 1933; Dryad (short stories) 1933; Men Are Unwise, 1934; The Falconer's Voice (short stories) 1935; Cactus, 1935; The Pure Flame, 1935; Women Also Dream, 1937; Rose and Sylvie, 1938; Darkness My Bride, 1938; Julie: The Story of a Dance Hostess, 1940; Rolling in the Dew, 1940; Red Rose, 1941. *Non-*

Fiction—Confessions and Impressions (autobiography) 1929; Commonsense and the Child, 1931; All Experience, 1932; Forever Wandering, 1935; South to Samarkand, 1936; Women and the Revolution, 1938; Commonsense and the Adolescent, 1938; Privileged Spectator (autobiography) 1939, Christianity—or Chaos? 1940; All Experience, 1941; Commonsense and Morality, 1942.

ABOUT: Mannin, E. Confessions and Impressions, Privileged Spectator; Bookman August 1926.

MANNING, FREDERIC (1887-February 22, 1935), Australian poet and miscellaneous writer, was born in Sydney and attended Sydney Grammar School. He was chiefly self-educated, however, spending much time reading in Italy and England. Throughout his life he suffered from asthma, only his indomitable determination enabling him to serve through the Flanders, Artois, and Picardy campaigns of the First World War. His fine anonymous war book, *Her Privates We* (1930), which took its title from *Hamlet* and headed each chapter with a quotation from Shakespeare, is the history of a platoon and a battalion on the Somme and Ancre front, with typical characters and conversations fundamentally true, if laying less stress on the scatological aspects of war than is to be found in *All Quiet on the Western Front*. "My concern has been mainly with the anonymous ranks, whose opinion, often mere surmise and ill-informed, but real and true, I have tried to represent faithfully," Manning wrote. He carried his concern with anonymity to the title-page, which represented the book to be the work of "Private 19022." The true authorship was not generally known until after his death. Manning lived in Italy after the war, making one visit to Australia and going to London to die at forty-eight.

Arnold Bennett, E. M. Forster, St. John Ervine, and T. E. Lawrence all hailed *Her Privates We* as a great book. *Scenes and Portraits* (1909) is a series of imaginary conversations which has the range of Landor and the delicacy of touch of Anatole France. Manning's London publisher, Peter Davies, wrote after his death: "Constant ill-health, combined with an extreme fastidiousness, curtailed the literary output which might have been expected from so fine and penetrating a mind, and the modesty and aloofness which prevented him from putting his name to the most successful of his books robbed him of the personal fame which would have been his had he cared to claim it."

PRINCIPAL WORKS: The Vigil of Brunhild, 1907; Scenes and Portraits, 1909; Poems, 1910; Eidola, 1917; The Life of Sir William White, 1923; Her Privates We (by "Private 19022") 1930.

ABOUT: Rothenstein, W. Since Fifty; Australian Quarterly June 1935; Saturday Review of Literature May 18, 1935.

MANSFIELD, KATHERINE (October 14, 1888-January 9, 1923), British short story writer and critic, was born Kathleen Mansfield Beauchamp at Wellington, New Zealand. Her father, Harold Beauchamp, was a banker and industrialist, knighted a week before her death, who had married Annie Burnell Dyer. Her early years were spent in the village of Karori,

near Wellington, where she had the ordinary schooling of the local country children. Her literary bent declared itself so early that when she was nine her first story was published in a magazine called *The Lone Hand*. In 1903 she was sent to London and attended Queen's College, in Harley Street, where she edited the college magazine. But during these first London years her interests turned rather to music than to writing. She became an excellent 'cellist, and projected a musical career. In 1906 she returned to New Zealand (very unwillingly, for the wider life of the capital had taken hold of her), but she was so wretched at what she deemed a remote provincial existence that after two years she persuaded her father to let her go to London again, on an allowance of £100 a year.

Such a sum could provide nothing but the minimum necessities. Miss Mansfield, abandoning music for a now plainly evident literary vocation, experienced the usual dreary ill-luck of aspirants and had no acceptances. The year 1909 was a dangerous and unhappy one. She married George Bowden, but left him after only a few days, and for a short time toured as a super in opera. She was soon with child by another man and went to Woerishofen, a quiet, unfashionable Bavarian spa to avoid scandal. Always delicate in health, she became ill and gave birth to a still-born child. Her Bavarian days formed the groundwork of her first stories, *In a German Pension*, which came out in book form in 1911.

They had meanwhile appeared during 1910 and 1911 in a journal called *The New Age*, edited by A. R. Orage. In 1911 she did some reviewing for the *Westminster Gazette*, but she was still anything but a literary success when, in December of that year, there occured an event which was to prove of crucial importance both to her emotional and her literary life. This was her meeting (at the house of W. L. George, the novelist) with the critic, John Middleton Murry.*qv* He was then an Oxford undergraduate, running a magazine called *Rhythm* in company with Michael Sadleir. To its pages, and those of its successor, *The Blue Review,* she contributed stories regularly until the demise of the second paper in July 1913. Murry meanwhile had left Oxford and embarked on a precarious journalistic career in London. He wanted a room at not more than two dollars a week. Katherine rented him one in her apartment; and they would meet in the evenings and talk literature and plans. By April 1912 it became obvious that a far deeper feeling than literary sympathy swayed them. They lived thenceforward as man and wife, though it was not until 1918 that a divorce allowed them to contract a legal alliance.

Ill-health and ill-success pursued Miss Mansfield unappeasably. She was to win wide literary reputation eight years later, but from the beginning of the war or thereabouts her pulmonary weakness became ever greater, and she did much traveling about from place to place to find a climate in which she could live. Early in 1915 she and Murry spent some weeks at Zennor, in Cornwall, in close association with D. H. Lawrence and Frieda von Richthofen. The autumn found her in London, where she was visited for a week by her only brother, Leslie Heron Beauchamp, on his way to fight in France. They spent long hours talking of childhood days, and Miss Mansfield, deeply distressed by the war, now decided to escape backwards in time to this period. A new and terrible grief followed immediately, for Leslie was killed almost as soon as he reached the front. In November 1915 Katherine went to Bandol, in the south of France, and wrote *The Aloe,* which was eventually shortened and published as *Prelude* in 1920, and *Je ne Parle pas Français,* which was privately printed by Murry in 1919.

During 1916 she helped Lawrence and Murry with a small review called *The Signature,* which ran only to three issues. In 1917 she lived in Chelsea. December of that year brought a serious attack of pleurisy, which left her definitely consumptive. In January 1918 she went to Bandol again, only to find it dirty, neglected, changed out of all recognition. Ill and depressed, she dragged up to Paris at the end of March,

arriving just at the moment when the Germans had begun their long-range bombardment of the city. Civilian cross-channel traffic was suspended, official red tape kept her in Paris for three weeks, but at last she arrived back in London, exhausted and in a very grave state of health. She spent the summer at Looe, in Cornwall. This year she and Murry were able to marry, and several of her stories appeared, one published by the Hogarth Press and two others in the *English Review* and *Art and Letters.* Murry became editor of the *Athenaeum* in the spring of 1919. Katherine reviewed for him week by week under the initials, K.M., attracting some attention. *Bliss and Other Stories,* issued in 1920, at last brought her real reputation. She had spent the winter of 1919-20 at Ospedaletti and Mentone, continuing her work in spite of passing much time in bed. She went on until the *Athenaeum* was absorbed by the *Nation* in February 1921.

The physical and spiritual conflicts of these last years are set out in the pathetic but brave *Journal* which was posthumously published. She strove after an "inner calm," which she in fact attained, but failed to realize her wish that she might produce "a full body of work." In January 1922 she went to Paris for special treatment. The following October she entered the Gurdjieff Institute, near Fontainebleau, an establishment which aimed to combine spiritual and physical healing. She died there of a pulmonary hemorrhage at thirty-four and was buried at nearby Avon (France).

Katherine Mansfield's short stories are outside the British tradition, depending for their power (which is very great) less on outward event than on atmosphere subtly bodied forth. They have been compared with those of Chekhov, but there are important differences. She could be satirical; her descriptive and analytical powers were of abounding richness; and throughout her work there is a feeling of vivid awareness of life. She was an exact and careful manipulator of word and phrase; she found it hard to begin work, but once launched she wrote easily and swiftly. In person she was slim, small, with dark bobbed hair and intense dark eyes. Middleton Murry wrote that she "was natural and spontaneous as was no other human being I have ever met. She seemed to adjust herself to life as a flower adjusts itself to the earth and to the sun." She valued the praise of ordinary people above that of the critics. The great force that maintained her during her last years of pain was a consuming desire to give out the truth.

PRINCIPAL WORKS: *Short Story Collections*— In a German Pension, 1911; Je ne Parle pas Français, 1919: Bliss, 1920; Prelude, 1920; The Garden Party, 1922; The Dove's Nest, 1923; Something Childish (American title: The Little Girl) 1924; Selected Stories, 1929; The Aloe, 1930. *Poetry*—Poems, 1923. *Autobiography*— Journal, 1927; Letters, 1928; Scrapbook, 1940 (all ed. by J. M. Murry). *Criticism*—Novels and Novelists, 1930.

ABOUT: Brewster, D. & Burrell, A. Dead Reckonings in Fiction; Carco, F. Souvenirs sur Katherine Mansfield; Cather, W. S. Not Under Forty; Collins, J. The Doctor Looks at Literature; Dictionary of National Biography Supplement: 1922-30. Gould, G. The English Novel of To-day; Lang, W. Sprache und Stil in Katherine Mansfields Kurzgeschichten; Mais, S.P.B. Some Modern Authors; Mantz, R.E. The Critical Bibliography of Katherine Mansfield; Mantz, R.E. & Murry, J. M. The Life of Katherine Mansfield; Maurois, A. Prophets and Poets; Murry, J. M. Reminiscences of D. H. Lawrence; Orage, A. R. Selected Essays and Critical Writings; Squire, J. C. Books Reviewed; Swinnerton, F. A. The Georgian Literary Scene; Wiegelmann, T. Das Weltbild der Katherine Mansfield.

*MANTLE, BURNS (December 1873-   ),

American dramatic critic and theatre annalist, was born in Watertown, N.Y., the

son of Robert Burns Mantle and Susan (Lawrence) Mantle, and was given his father's full name. After attending public school and normal college, Mantle struck out for the Far West. In 1892 he started East again

Oggiano

with the Chicago World's Fair in view, but tarried in Denver. He was dramatic editor of the Denver *Times* from 1898 to 1900, and the Denver *Republican* in 1900-01. The latter year found him in Chicago working on the *Inter-Ocean*, remaining until 1907 and marrying Lydia Holmes Sears of Denver in August 1903. From 1908 to 1911 Mantle was Sunday editor of the Chicago *Tribune*, after a preliminary year as dramatic editor, and "was just as bad a Sunday editor as any of them, too," according to the *Dramatic Mirror*. "Three years later, when he had printed the story of the Hope diamond for the third time, he decided it was again time to move." Mantle then came to New York, where he has remained for thirty years, and is now regarded as the dean and Nestor of dramatic critics. He was dramatic editor of the now defunct *Evening Mail* from 1911 to

1922, and has been dramatic editor and critic of New York's most prosperous tabloid newspaper, the *Daily News,* from 1922 to the present. Since 1911 he has also written dramatic correspondence for the Chicago *Tribune,* from which the *News* stemmed.

His opinions on current dramatic offerings are sound, and are expressed in clear, explicit language suited to the comprehension of his vast multitude of readers. Producers covet the literal "four-star" rating given by Mantle to plays which meet with his entire approval. He also selects the ten plays of each season which in his opinion are the best it has afforded, and incorporates them in his useful series, *Best Plays and Year Book of the Drama in America,* which he inaugurated in 1919. The plots of the selected plays are given in actual dialogue and running summary; all other plays produced in the season are listed with their casts and briefly described. A single volume edited on similar lines closed the gap between 1909 and 1919. In 1935 Mantle published a fat omnibus of plays, *A Treasury of the Theatre.* His two volumes on twentieth-century playwrights are similarly useful, if not particularly profound. Mantle, a pleasant-faced gentleman with prominent eyes, is a member of the Dutch Treat and Pomonok Country Clubs, has served as president of the Critics' Circle, and lives in Forest Hills, a suburb of New York City. The Mantles have a daughter, Margaret Burns Mantle.

PRINCIPAL WORKS: American Playwrights of Today, 1929; Contemporary American Playwrights, 1938. *Editor*—Best Plays and Year Book of the Drama in America, 1919-date; Best Plays of 1909-1919 (with G. P. Sherwood) 1933; A Treasury of the Theatre (with J. Gassner) 1935; Contemporary American Playwrights, 1938.

ABOUT: Who's Who in Queens; Dramatic Mirror October 16, 1912.

MARE. See DE LA MARE

MARITAIN, JACQUES (November 18, 1882-   ), French philosopher and Catholic apologist, was born in Paris and was educated at the Sorbonne,

from which he received a Ph.D. Reared in an atmosphere of liberal Protestantism, he became dissatisfied and sought for a definitive philosophy. His search took him to Henry Bergson, but though Bergsonism

restored his shaken faith in metaphysical

* Died February 9, 1948.

solutions it provided no answer to his need for an Absolute. He says the only good thing he got out of his association with Bergson was his meeting with his future wife. Mme. Raïssa Maritain has collaborated with her husband in several books and has also written several of her own. Both he and his fiancée were converted to the Roman Catholic Church in 1906. For two years thereafter Maritain studied biology at the University of Heidelberg, under Hans Driesch, who is known among scientists as an antimaterialist. The philosophy of St. Thomas Aquinas strongly attracted Maritain, and on his return to France he spent several years in its study. He is today the leading neo-Thomist of the contemporary world and was the foremost spokesman of the "Catholic revival" in France.

In 1913 Maritain became professor of modern history and philosophy at the Institut Catholique, in Paris, founded to offset the "skeptical tendencies" of the Sorbonne. He has also taught at the Collège Stanislas in Paris and the Petit Seminaire in Versailles. His first book, an attack on Bergsonism, was written in 1917 at the request of the bishops in charge of the Institut Catholique. He has since produced almost a score of volumes, including a series under the general heading of *Elements of Philosophy;* and he is besides a voluminous contributor to the philosophical reviews. He is a retiring, reticent man whose life centers around his philosophical and religious theories, and whose only interest outside them is in a quietly happy home life. He is a young-looking, still dark-haired man, with regular features and a keen and sensitive face.

George N. Shuster, a leading American Catholic layman, has called Maritain "the most interesting living revivalist," and Justin O'Brien called him "the most active of modern French exponents of a return to mediaeval ideals." Maritain has not hesitated to call himself an "anti-modernist." To Kenneth Burke he is "a subtle dialectician," whose "most characteristic trait is his tact.... The mere suavity of his work restores our faith in the culture of his religion." He is not easy reading, but this is primarily because of the nature of his subject; his style is graceful, and as lucid as the intricacies of scholastic thought permit.

After the fall of France in 1940, the Maritains came to the American continent, where he is professor at the Institute of Mediaeval Studies at Toronto and visiting professor at Columbia and Princeton.

WORKS AVAILABLE IN ENGLISH: The Life of Prayer (with R. Maritain) 1928; Three Reform-ers: Luther, Descartes, Rousseau, 1928; The Things That Are Not Caesar's, 1930; Art and Scholasticism, 1930; An Introduction to Philosophy, 1930; Primacy of the Mind, 1930; The Angelic Doctor, 1931; Théonas, 1933; Freedom in the Modern World, 1935; Temporal Power and Liberty, 1935; The Degrees of Knowledge, 1937; An Introduction to Logic, 1937; True Humanism, 1938; Anti-Semitism, 1939; Preface to Metaphysics, 1939; Scholasticism and Politics, 1940; Science and Wisdom, 1940; Religion in the Modern World, 1941; Living Thoughts of St. Paul (ed.) 1941; France My Country, 1941; Ransoming the Time, 1941.

ABOUT: Fadiman, C. (ed.). I Believe; Bookman September 1929; Catholic World September 1933; Commonweal March 23, June 1, July 13, December 7, December 28, 1934, October 13, November 24, 1939; Le Correspondant June 25, 1926; International Journal of Ethics January 1931; London Mercury September 1929; New Republic May 21, 1930; Nineteenth Century June 1939; Time October 28, 1940.

MARKHAM, EDWIN (April 23, 1852-March 7, 1940), American poet, wrote to the editors of this volume some time before his death: "I was born in Oregon City, [Ore.], not far from the Pacific Ocean. My father, Samuel Markham, had been captain of an emigrant train from Illinois. My mother, Elizabeth (Winchell) Markham, became one of the early apple-grow

ers of the Northwest. She was also the poet laureate of the new settlement—the earliest woman writer recorded in Oregon. My father, a farmer and hunter, died in Oregon. When I was about five, my mother, taking her younger children, went down to California and settled on a cattle range near the Coast Mountains in the Suisun Valley. Here I grew to be a shepherd and a vaquero, following the flocks and herds. Our public school was open only three months of the year. I was one of its most eager pupils. Here, one fortunate year, there chanced to come to us a teacher who was an ardent lover of poetry. He made me a life-long reader and writer of poetry.

"For about ten years I continued to be a farmhand, devouring all the books available. At fifteen, we left our foothill home and went down to the Santa Clara Valley, where I was graduated from the State Normal School at San Jose. Later I was graduated from a college at Santa Rosa, and now I launched forth as a school teacher, first in Southern California, then later in the Sierras, in the little town where gold was discovered. Here I was made superintendent of schools of the county, and here I came upon a magazine containing Millet's famuos picture of The Man With the Hoe, an event which has meant a great deal in my life.

"From El Dorado County I went down to the San Francisco Bay area, where I was made principal of the Observation School of the University of California. I had begun in the Sierras to write my poem, 'The Man With the Hoe.' I finished the poem at the end of 1899. It caught public attention, was copied across the country, and has since gone around the world and been translated into almost every language.

"That year I left off teaching to devote myself to writing and lecturing. I have traveled all over the United States, visiting every large city, lecturing on poetry and on the social and industrial problem. I am spending my last years on Staten Island, N.Y., where I can breathe the fresh air on my sleeping porch and can keep in close touch with the stars."

* * *

Edwin Markham died of pneumonia at his Staten Island home after a four-day illness, less than two months before his eighty-eighth birthday and only three days after the death in Los Angeles of his contemporary Hamlin Garland—often called the dean of American novelists as Markham was of poets. Following public funeral services in Brooklyn, he was taken to Los Angeles to be buried beside his wife. Up to 1937, when he was eighty-five, the poet continued to be "hale and hearty," as he had described himself in the sketch above. It was in 1937 that he received the $5,000 prize of the Academy of American Poets. In the same year he was declared incompetent by a court, an attack of encephalitis, added to the effects of age, having almost obliterated his memory. The death of his wife in 1938 was another heavy blow. They had been married in 1897, and were an ideally devoted couple. She was Anna Catherine Murphy, also a writer; their son, Virgil Markham, is well known as an author of mystery stories.

Louis Untermeyer described Edwin Markham as "looking like a blurred composite photograph of four Hebrew prophets and all the New England poets"—a very apt description. He was the last left of the authors of the Golden Age of California literature. His eightieth birthday was celebrated by a big meeting in Carnegie Hall in New York, when he recited once again his famous "Man With the Hoe." Another of his poems, "Washington, the National Builder," was written in 1931 for the United States George Washington Bicentennial Committee. His second best known poem is undoubtedly "Lincoln." He belonged to an earlier age, declamatory, hortatory, and moralistic; but, as William Rose Benét pointed out, he had "vigor, great liberality of spirit, and an accomplished knowledge of versification."

PRINCIPAL WORKS: *Poetry*—The Ballad of the Gallows Bird, 1896; The Man With the Hoe and Other Poems, 1899; Lincoln and Other Poems, 1901; The Shoes of Happiness and Other Poems, 1915; Gates of Paradise and Other Poems, 1920; New Poems: Eighty Songs at 80, 1932; The Star of Araby, 1937; Collected Poems, 1940. *Prose*—The Children in Bondage (with B. B. Lindsay and George Creel) 1914; California the Wonderful, 1915. *Edited*—Foundation Stones of Success, 1925; The Book of Poetry, 1927; California in Song and Story, 1930; Poetry of Youth, 1935.

ABOUT: Fitch, G. H. Great Spiritual Writers of America; Hind, C. L. Authors and I; Stidger, W. L. Edwin Markham; American Magazine September 1928; American Mercury December 1926; Christian Century April 7, 1927, May 31, 1933, March 18, 1940; Literary Digest December 22, 1934; Overland Monthly July 1932; Poetry April 1940; Saturday Review of Literature April 23, 1932, March 16, 1940.

MARKS, JEANNETTE AUGUSTUS (August 16, 1875-   ), American poet, playwright, and educator, writes: "Jeannette Marks was born in Chattanooga, Tenn., the daughter of William Dennis Marks and Jeannette Holmes (Colwell) Marks. Her father was Whitney Professor of Dynamics in the University of Pennsylvania and an early friend of Edison. She  received part of her preliminary education in Europe; received the B.A. degree from Wellesley College in 1900 and the M.A. degree in 1903, and did post-graduate work in England at the Bodleian Library and the British Museum. An instructor and associate professor of English literature at Mt. Holyoke College from 1901 to 1910, and lecturer from 1913 to 1921, since 1921 she has been Kennedy Professor of English Literature there. Until 1939 she was chairman of the Department of English Literature and Drama. In 1916 she established at Mt. Holyoke the Play and Poetry Shop Talk, a forum to which American poets and dramatists are invited to read their productions and discuss present-day aspects of their art. Since 1928 she has been director of the Laboratory Theatre, which she founded, the first little theatre built as such in the Connecticut Valley.

"In 1911 she was awarded the Welsh National Theatre prize for two plays, *The Merry Merry Cuckoo* and *Welsh Honeymoon.* Her Welsh plays have been given many hundreds of times throughout this country, in Great Britain, and even in Japan. Her literary interests have been as important in her life as the dramatic. As a result of her Browning research, she has been made a Sponsor of the Pacific Coast Browning Foundation, an Honorary Member of the Browning Society of Los Angeles, a Corresponding Member of the Institute of Jamaica, B.W.I. (which awarded her the Silver Musgrave Medal in 1939 for *The Family of the Barrett*), and a Fellow of the Institute of American Genealogy.

"She is a member of the Society of Friends (Quakers). Her devotion to social justice found expression in seven years of work for Sacco and Vanzetti and in her book, *Thirteen Days,* about this famous trial. It is also represented by the award of the Kossovo Medal by the Royal Red Cross of Jugo-Slavia (1931), and at home by her membership in the National Woman's Party."

* * *

Miss Marks has never married. She lives in South Hadley, Mass., with a summer home at Westport, N.Y., on Lake Champlain. She is a lover of out of doors, fond of riding, mountain-climbing, motor-boating, sailing, and driving, fearless without being foolhardy. She loves dogs and is never without one. Of her work, the late Margaret Wilkinson said that she "is at her best when she writes brief and simple lyrics in conventional meters."

PRINCIPAL WORKS: The Cheerful Cricket, 1907; The English Pastoral Drama, 1908; Through Welsh Doorways, 1909; The End of a Song, 1911; Gallant Little Wales, 1912; Leviathan, 1913; Early English Hero Tales, 1916; Three Welsh Plays, 1917; Courage, 1919; Children in the Wood Stories, 1919; Goeffrey's Window, 1921; Willow Pollen (poems) 1921; The Sun Chaser (play) 1922; Genius and Disaster: Studies in Drugs and Genius, 1925; The Merry Merry Cuckoo and Other Welsh Plays, 1927; Thirteen Days, 1929; The Family of the Barrett, 1929.

MARKS, PERCY (September 9, 1891-   ), American novelist and educator, was born in Covelo, Calif., the son of Henry Marks and Sarah (Lando) Marks. He obtained a B.L. degree from the University of California in 1912, and his master's degree from Harvard University in 1914. Mr. Marks

makes some pungent remarks on the waste and futility involved in getting the average Ph.D. degree, in his book on American colleges and universities, *Which Way Parnassus?* (1926), and he is *not* a Doctor of Philosophy.

After leaving Harvard, Marks was supervisor of education at the State Infirmary, Tewksbury, Mass., for a time, following up this initial experience in teaching with four years as instructor in English at the Massachusetts Institute of Technology. He went from Boston to Hanover, N.H., to teach English at Dartmouth, and finally to Providence, R.I., to hold an instructorship at Brown University. C. C. Baldwin states in his *The Men Who Make Our Novels* (1924) that Marks "was fired from Brown because he could not see eye to eye with the average college trustee." Marks is described in this book as "thin, a little stooped, well-dressed in a casual sort of way, with a whiff of tobacco about him. He is not the sort the ordinary trustee would elect as an instructor."

The Plastic Age (1924), Marks' first and best-selling novel, was, according to Baldwin, turned down by Alfred Harcourt before it found a publisher elsewhere. Baldwin's impression was that the novel was "deliberately scandalous." "It overemphasizes youth's interest in sex, but it is well-written and unafraid." "I have found to my horror," Marks himself has said, "that many people thought I was muckraking in my novel of college life, *The Plastic Age.* In that book I tried to present dramatically both the good and bad in undergraduate life." He believes that even in the colleges with the highest standards not 10 per cent of the undergraduates have first-class minds. "The American college is an extremely sentimental institution, and much of its value lies in its sentimentality."

Writing in *Harper's* for July 1926, Marks was as pessimistic about "The Pestiferous Alumni." "There is no intellectual life in a college club: there is only the musty odor of death. When most seniors graduate they put away for the last time their mortar boards and gowns and their intellectual life with them. Books become a thing of the past."

After leaving the academic world, Marks began to write and publish other novels at regular intervals. They are not designed for the super-sophisticated, as one critic has remarked, but range, sometimes naïvely but usually entertainingly, over various social and emotional problems of modern life. Marks was a second lieutenant of infantry in the First World War. He married Margaret Ellen Gates in December 1927.

PRINCIPAL WORKS: The Plastic Age, 1924; Martha, 1925; Which Way Parnassus? 1926; Lord of Himself, 1927; A Dead Man Dies, 1929; The Unwilling God, 1929; The Craft of Writing, 1932; Better Themes, 1933; A Tree Grown Straight, 1936; And Points Beyond, 1937; What's a Heaven For? 1938; The Days Are Fled, 1939; No Steeper Wall, 1940; Between Two Autumns, 1941; Full Flood, 1942.

ABOUT: Baldwin, C. C. The Men Who Make Our Novels; Harper's July 1926; Scholastic March 2, 1935.

MARQUAND, JOHN PHILLIPS (November 10, 1893-), American novelist, short-story writer, author of detective fic-

Bachrach

tion, and winner of the Pulitzer Prize, was born in Wilmington, Del., the son of Philip Marquand and Margaret (Fuller) Marquand. Margaret Fuller, the famous New England bluestocking, was his great-aunt; most of her famous contemporaries at one time or another visited "Curzon's Mill," the Marquand farm near Newburyport, Mass., in the possession of the family for more than a century. Echoes of this environment and circle are audible in his novel Wickford Point. Marquand lived at Rye, N.Y., until he was fourteen, spending his summers at "the Mill." After graduation from the Newburyport High School he won his B.A. degree from Harvard College, Class of 1915, in three years, and two weeks later was a reporter on the Boston Transcript.

Marquand's novel H. M. Pulham, Esquire (1941) hinges on the difficulty experienced by the central character in writing an interesting "class life" for the twenty-fifth anniversary report of the class secretary. Marquand himself had no such difficulty. In the 1940 Report, copyrighted by the secretary, he wrote in part: "Since that date [1915], I have supported myself without any outside help, but with, as I look back, quite a lot of outside hindrance. After a trip to the Texas border with Battery A,

and the usual hiatus in '17 and '18 of making a bad job trying to be a West Point graduate [he was a first lieutenant in the Fourth Brigade, Field Artillery, A.E.F. and participated in the Marne-Aisne, St. Michiel, and Meuse-Argonne offensives] I found myself on the magazine department of the New York Tribune, where my services could not have been conspicuous, because Mrs. Ogden Reid told me last year that she couldn't remember my being around the place at all. The next position turned out to be a desk in the copy department of the J. Walter Thompson Company, just vacated by Richard Connell on his way to greener pastures. At the end of a year I began to have what might be mildly termed a negative reaction toward the routine of creative selling. During a summer in Massachusetts I wrote a novel of the cloak and sword school. This work was purchased by the Ladies' Home Journal, and once I asked the editor why he ever did it. The Journal, he explained, had just acquired presses for a five-color illustration process, and they wanted to do pictures of men with lace about their throats. I sold the next story I wrote to the Saturday Evening Post, and very nearly all I have written subsequently has appeared there. I have been successful from the start at writing short stories, and lately I have not been bad at a more difficult branch of the craft, the magazine serial. There is a risk in writing for periodicals of large circulations of falling into the rut of sure-fire formula and of developing brittle superficial fluency. . . . Geographically speaking, I have seen a good deal of the world since I left Harvard—most of the United States, including Hawaii and Canada, England, France, Germany, Persia, Malay and Indo-China, Mongolia and Japan. [Some of these backgrounds were used in his Mr. Moto mystery stories, which bear a generic resemblance to the earlier Charlie Chan novels of another Harvard graduate, Earl Derr Biggers.[qv]] But the most remarkable sights I have witnessed are those in which we all have shared in our 25 years at home—years which have kicked us out of a comfortable Victorian era into a war, out of it into the 20's, when we could pour champagne into Ford radiators, and thence into the crash and the New Deal, while we approach another war."

According to a favorite literary legend, when Marquand took The Late George Apley (a purported memoir of a self-satisfied Bostonian) to the lady literary agent who had handled his magazine fiction, she called it humorless fantasy and advised him to put it away and forget it! But after serialization, this first-rate social satire won the Pulitzer Prize 1937 as the best novel of the year. A modified version of its almost identical successor, *H. M. Pulham, Esquire,* appeared in *McCall's* as *Gone Tomorrow.*

J. P. Marquand, says Constance M. Fiske, is of average build and average-colored hair, with "a kindly, harassed face," and dresses with typical Bostonian disregard of current fashion. "His apparent ineffectiveness [in coping with the mechanics of living] disguises a keen appreciation of fundamentals. He can sum up any situation or personal equation with incisiveness, with tenderness, and always with a strong flavor of that disturbingly amusing cynicism that is Yankee humor." It was probably the sardonic side of this humor that led him to remark on one occasion that he had only three friends in the world—and two of them didn't like him! He married Christina Davenport Sedgwick of Stockbridge, Mass., in 1922, and they had a son and a daughter. They were divorced in 1935; two years later Marquand married Adelaide F. Hooker. They have a daughter, born 1940, and divide their time between Kents Island, Newburyport, Mass., and New York City.

According to the *Publishers' Weekly,* Marquand figured as the "murderee" in Timothy Fuller's thinly disguised mystery novel of the Boston literary scene, *Three-Thirds of a Ghost* (1941).

PRINCIPAL WORKS: The Unspeakable Gentleman, 1922; Four of a Kind, 1923; Black Cargo, 1925; Lord Timothy Dexter, 1925; Warning Hill, 1930; Haven's End, 1933; Ming Yellow, 1934; No Hero, 1935; Thank You, Mr. Moto, 1936; The Late George Apley, 1937; Think Fast, Mr. Moto, 1937; Mr. Moto Is So Sorry, 1938; Wickford Point, 1939; H. M. Pulham, Esquire, 1941; Last Laugh, Mr. Moto, 1942.

ABOUT: Harvard University, Class of 1915: Twenty-Fifth Anniversary Report; New York Times April 7, 1940; Book-of-the-Month Club News, March 1941; Life March 24, 1941; New York Herald Tribune "Books" March 16, July 5, 1941; Saturday Review of Literature December 10, 1938; Wilson Library Bulletin September 1938.

MARQUIS, DON (July 29, 1878- December 30, 1937), American novelist, poet, and dramatist, was born Donald Robert Perry Marquis in Walnut, Ill., the son of James Stewart Marquis and Virginia Elizabeth (Whitmore) Marquis. After a high school education, he tried his hand at many occupations — country school teaching,

clerking, hay baling. Then he became a student at the Corcoran School in Washington, D.C., but after a year and a half decided he had not sufficient talent, and took a job in the Census Bureau. He acted also as part time reporter for the Washington *Times.*

Next he went on the stage, with a touring stock company which soon met the fate of most third-class theatrical troupes. He did not really find himself until he secured a job as editorial writer on the Atlanta *Constitution.* Joel Chandler Harris, the editor, and author of the *Uncle Remus* stories, took an interest in the young man, made him assistant editor of *Uncle Remus' Magazine,* and turned him in the direction of creative writing. In 1912 Marquis went to New York, and started the famous "Sun Dial" column in the *Sun.* Many of his best known characters first saw the light in that column and in the later "Lantern" on the *Herald Tribune.*

Christopher Morley, who was Marquis' close friend, said he looked "like a careful blend of Falstaff and Napoleon III." But none knew better than Morley that this prince of humorists, bubbling over with wit and mirth, was at heart an embittered cynic. His last years were tragic; for six years he was "a penniless and hopeless cripple" (*Newsweek*) before he finally died (at Forest Hills, Long Island) of a cerebral hemorrhage.

Marquis was married twice: in 1909 to Reina Melcher, who died in 1923, and in 1926 to Marjorie Vonnegut, who survived him. Before his long illness Marquis was a heavy-set man, with a round face under a high forehead, looking not unlike a prosperous Middle Western farmer.

Benjamin De Casseres called Marquis "Shelley trying to lasso the Golden Calf: a born poet and bitter satirist." He himself noted that he had worked three days on *The Old Soak,* which was a success, and ten years on *The Dark Hours,* a drama of the Crucifixion, which was a flop; and he said: "It would be one on me if I should be remembered longest for creating a cockroach character." Yet it is to be feared that his gloomy prediction will come true; it is archy and mehitabel, Hermione, and the Old Soak who are likeliest to survive of all Don Marquis' creations. He will be remembered, not as the serious author of *Poems and Portraits* or *Out of the Sea,* but as the humorist who wrote *The Almost Perfect State* or *The Old Soak's History of the World.*

Yet even in these apparently lighter works there is caustic and sometimes corrosive satire, markedly in *Chapters for the Orthodox.* It was in his last unfinished novel, posthumously published, *Sons of the Puritans,* that Don Marquis tried at last to write himself out, without satire and in simple earnestness. It is a fine realistic picture, obviously autobiographical, and a devastating exposure of the Puritanical small town. In many ways it remains, incomplete as it is, his best work.

His name is pronounced *mar'kwis.*

PRINCIPAL WORKS: Danny's Own Story, 1912; Dreams and Dust, 1915; Cruise of the Jasper B., 1916; Hermione, 1916; Prefaces, 1919; The Old Soak, 1921; Carter and Other People, 1921; Noah an' Jonah an' Cap'n John Smith (verse) 1921; Poems and Portraits, 1922; The Revolt of the Oyster, 1922; Sonnets to a Red Haired Lady, 1922; The Old Soak's History of the World, 1924; Words and Thoughts (play) 1924; The Dark Hours (play) 1924; Pandora Lifts the Lid (play, with C. Morley) 1924; Out of the Sea (play) 1927; The Almost Perfect State, 1927; archy and mehitabel, 1927; Love Sonnets of a Cave Man and Other Verses, 1928; When the Turtles Sing, 1928; A Variety of People, 1929; Off the Arm (novel) 1930; Chapters for the Orthodox, 1934; The Old Soak's History of the World, 1934; archy does his part, 1935; Sun Dial Time (short stories) 1936; Sons of the Puritans, 1939.

ABOUT: De Casseres, B. Don Marquis; Bookman July 1931; Catholic World April 1930; Commonweal November 23, 1932; Newsweek January 10, 1938; Publishers' Weekly January 8, 1938; Saturday Review of Literature May 15, 1937, June 5, 1937; Scholastic January 22, 1938; Wilson Library Bulletin February 1938.

MARRIOTT, CHARLES (1869-), English novelist and art critic, was born in Bristol. His father was a brewer. Young

Marriott was educated by the Rev. Arthur Tooth, of Woodside, Croydon, and at an art and technical school in South Kensington. For a while he worked at photography; qualified, in 1890, as a dispenser at Apothecaries' Hall; and combined both capacities at the County Asylum, Rainhill, from 1889 to 1901. Relinquishing the pestle for the pen, Marriott became a successful purveyor of popular fiction, alternating these by more subtle psychological romances with an infusion

of art criticism. Some of these were published in the United States, where critics praised the "restraint and delicacy" of his literary manner. In 1924 Charles Marriott became art critic of the London *Times,* after publishing several studies on modern art, notably *Modern Art* (1917), *Modern Movements in Painting* (1920), *Modern English Architecture* (1924), and a study of Augustus John. He also translated Lionello Venturi's *History of Art Criticism* from the Italian, and joined the Comtesse Marie Van Heuvel in a translation of Venturi's *Italian Paintings in America* (1933). Another of Marriott's translations is *Perfection* (1923), from the Portuguese of Eça de Queiroz. He was Sydney Jones Lecturer in Art at Liverpool University in 1938-39.

Charles Marriott was first married to Dora M. M'Loughlin in 1892, and they had a son and two daughters. Mrs. Marriott died in 1917, and two years later he married Bessie Wigan of Portishead. Their peacetime home is in the Chelsea district of London.

PRINCIPAL WORKS: The Column, 1901; Love With Honour, 1902; The House on the Sands, 1903; Genevra, 1904; Mrs. Alemere's Elopement, 1905; The Lapse of Vivien Eady, 1906; Women and the West, 1906; The Remnant, 1907; The Wondrous Wife, 1907; The Kiss of Helen, 1908; A Spanish Holiday, 1908; The Happy Medium, 1908; When a Woman Woos, 1909; The Intruding Angel, 1909; "Now!" 1910; The Romance of the Rhine, 1911; The Dewpond, 1912; The Catfish, 1913; Subsoil, 1913; (U. S. title: What a Man Wants) 1913; The Unpetitioned Heavens, 1914; Davenport, 1915; Modern Art, 1917; Augustus John, 1918; Modern Movements in Painting, 1920; The Grave Impertinence, 1921; An Order To View, 1922; Modern English Architecture, 1924; Key to Modern Painting, 1938.

ABOUT: International Who's Who.

MARSH, NGAIO (April 23, 1899-), New Zealand detective story writer, writes: "I was born at Christchurch, New Zealand, of what the Victorians used to call poor but genteel parentage. My father is a descendant of an ancient English family, the piratical de Mariscos, Lords of Lundy. They were kicked out of Lundy on general grounds of lawlessness and turned up in Kent, where they changed their names to Marsh, and many, perhaps on the rebound from piracy, turned Quaker. My maternal grandfather was an early colonist of New Zealand, his father, a Jamaican

planter, having been ruined by the emancipation of slaves. I was educated in New Zealand at St. Margaret's College and the Canterbury University College School of Art, where I was a student for five years. In those days I hoped to make painting my job but I wrote a bit at the same time, and having completed a terrible romantic drama, had the temerity to show it to Mr. Allan Wilkie, the Shakespearian actor-manager. He rejected the play but offered to take me into his company, so I became a touring actress and stuck to it for two years. In 1928 I went to London, where, in partnership with the Hon. Mrs. Tahu Rhodes, I ran a house-decorating business for four years. The business still prospers, but domestic reasons called me back to New Zealand in 1932. I left at a day's notice and dumped with an agent the typescript of my first novel. I had written it to amuse myself during odd hours and was astonished when I learned it was accepted for publication.

"I stayed in New Zealand for four years, wrote five more detective books, returned to London in 1937, spent six months traveling about Europe, wrote another book, and came back to New Zealand, where I am at present living with my father. I still do a good deal of theatrical work, mostly as producer for repertory. My interests are art, Shakespeariana, books in general. My manias are the theatre and travel. My favorite authors are the Elizabethans, Somerset Maugham, Charles Morgan, George Moore, Aldous Huxley, Dickens, and Stella Benson. I have written many travel articles, short stories, and verse."

* * *

Miss Marsh is unmarried. As for the pronunciation of her first name (the Maori name of a flowering tree), she herself says it has three syllables, and is pronounced as spelled except that the "g" is silent; an acceptable approximation, however, is *ny'-o.* Her books are in the very first rank of their kind, suave, intelligent, and amusing; one reviewer remarked of her that "Dorothy Sayers had better be sure her crown's on straight!"

PRINCIPAL WORKS: A Man Lay Dead, 1934; Enter a Murderer, 1935; Nursing Home Murder (with H. Jellett) 1936; Death in Ecstasy, 1937; Vintage Murder, 1937; Artists in Crime, 1938; Death in a White Tie, 1938; Overture to Death, 1939; Death at the Bar, 1940; Death of a Peer, 1940; Death and the Dancing Footman, 1941; New Zealand (non-fiction) 1942.

ABOUT: Haycraft, H. Murder for Pleasure: The Life and Times of the Detective Story; Wilson Library Bulletin September 1940.

MARSHALL, ARCHIBALD (September 6, 1866-September 29, 1934), English novelist, short-story writer, and humorist, was the eldest son of Arthur Marshall, a London business man, and Louisa (Hammond) Marshall. He was educated at Highgate School, and at Trinity College, Cambridge University, where he obtained a B.A. degree. His father had intended  that Marshall should become a partner in his business, but after eight months in Australia, and a visit to the United States, Marshall decided to study for holy orders in the Church of England. Instead, however, he married Helen May Pollard in 1902, and settled at Beaulieu in the New Forest to write fiction and spend three years planning and making a four-acre garden. *Peter Binney: Undergraduate,* a farcical novel of university life as experienced by an elderly undergraduate, was the first; its successor, *The House of Merrilees,* was unanimously rejected by English publishers. With two associates, Marshall founded the publishing house of Alston Rivers and issued the book himself. In 1907 Lord Northcliffe engaged him as sub-editor of *Books,* the four-page literary supplement to the *Daily Mail,* and he assumed complete charge six months later when the chief editor, Edmund Gosse, was tactfully let out. The Marshalls now moved from Beaulieu to a cottage in the country between Rye and Winchelsea, two of the old Cinque Ports. Henry James proved to be a genial and amusing neighbor. They stayed here from 1908 to 1913, Marshall writing 3,000 words a day on serials for the *Daily Mail,* of which *The Mystery of Redmarsh Farm* proved to be the most popular.

From 1913 to 1917 the family lived in Switzerland. As correspondent for the *Daily Mail,* Marshall traveled to Australia and America again, and reported the aftermath of the Messina earthquake. He was Paris correspondent for the *Daily News* during the First World War, removing then to Cambridge to edit the *Cambridge Review.* *The Squire's Daughter,* his novel of 1909, was the first of the Squire Clinton series, the best-known of Marshall's work in the United States, which drew the inevitable comparison with the chronicle novels of Anthony Trollope. They "described a world we know, and of which we are getting a little tired, but which the Americans do not know," one English critic explained; "an interesting and remote form of civilization with which they would not willingly lose touch." The "naïve snobbishness and right feeling" of the Squire were described with tolerance and humor, and his young twin daughters were two of Marshall's happiest creations. William Lyon Phelps called his books exciting without being sensational, and inspiring but not didactic, when presenting the novelist for Yale's honorary Litt.D. in 1921. The Anthony Dare series, and those books dealing with the Graftons and the Allbrights aroused less interest. Marshall became a regular contributor to *Punch,* the solemn absurdities of his *Simple Stories* being particularly relished. A ruddy, curly-haired, prepossessing man, his chief diversions were golf, shooting, walking, and reading history, Victorian novels, and poetry. He died suddenly at Cambridge, less than a month after his sixty-eighth birthday.

PRINCIPAL WORKS: *Novels*—Peter Binney: Undergraduate, 1899; The House of Merrilees, 1905; Richard Baldock, 1906; Exton Manor, 1907; Many Junes, 1908; The Squire's Daughter, 1909; The Eldest Son, 1911; The Mystery of Redmarsh Farm, 1912; The Honour of the Clintons, 1913; Roding Rectory (U. S. title: The Greatest of These) 1914; Rank and Riches (U. S. title: The Old Order Changeth) 1915; Upsidonia, 1915; Watermeads, 1916; Abington Abbey, 1917; The Graftons, 1918; Sir Harry, 1920; The Hall and the Grange, 1921; Big Peter, 1922; Pippin, 1923; Anthony Dare, 1923; The Education of Anthony Dare, 1924; Anthony Dare's Progress, 1925; The Allbright Family, 1926; Joyn, 1926; That Island, 1927; Simple People, 1928; Miss Wolby at Steen, 1929; Two Families, 1931; The Appletons of Herne, 1931; The Birdikin Family, 1932; The Lady of the Manor, 1932; The Claimants, 1934. *Short Stories*—The Terrors, 1913; The Clintons and Others, 1919; Peggy in Toyland, 1920; Audacious Anne, 1924; Joan and Nancy, 1925; Simple Stories, 1927; Simple Stories From Punch, 1930; Angel Face, 1933. *Autobiography*—Out and About, 1933.

ABOUT: Adcock, A. St. J. The Glory That Was Grub Street; Ford, F. M. Return to Yesterday; Marshall, A. Out and About; Phelps, W. L. Archibald Marshall: A Realistic Novelist; Bookman (London) September 1925; Boston Evening Transcript August 5, 1933; New York Times October 1, 1934.

MARSHALL, BRUCE (June 24, 1899-), English novelist and satirist, is the son of Claude Niven Marshall of Edinburgh. He was christened Claude Cunningham Bruce Marshall, and attended Edinburgh Academy; Trinity College, Glenalmond, till his seventeenth year; and St. Andrews and Edinburgh Universities. Serving in the First World War as second lieutenant in the 3d Royal Irish Fusiliers, Marshall lost a leg in battle and was for a time a prisoner of war. Edinburgh gave him a master's degree in 1924, and made him a Bachelor of Commerce in 1925. Next year Marshall was admitted a member of the Society of Accountants in Edinburgh, the only profession which would enable him to live abroad, or so it seemed to him. Marshall enumerates his recreations as "writing novels if regarded as a chartered accountant, accountancy if regarded as a novelist," and has been fortunate in making both his recreations pay dividends.

Father Malachy's Miracle (1931), one of the best-liked novels of its decade, is an obstreperously humorous but fundamentally reverent recounting of the commotion caused in lay and ecclesiastical circles when a quiet little Irish priest, set down in the dour environs of Edinburgh, succeeded in translating a *palais de dance* from the city to the top of the Bass Rock in the Firth of Forth. Like a similar performance of the Queen of Babylon at the British Museum in E. Nesbit's *The Story of the Amulet,* it was generally regarded as "an impertinent miracle." Brian Doherty adapted the novel into a play which, featuring Al Shean of Gallagher and Shean fame as the daring priest, was a pleasant feature of the 1938 New York theatrical season. The *Catholic World* called the stage version "not only Catholic but very beautifully Christian." Bruce Marshall's subsequent satires have lampooned boys' schools, incompetent bishops, provincial Englishmen, Big Industry, and billboards. Good novels, he states, are written not by using a camera but by piecing together the patterns of life which the novelist finds thrown at his feet. "For life is good literature escaping just as surely as good literature is life held fast." A dark, smiling man, the novelist lives in Edinburgh.

PRINCIPAL WORKS: Stooping Venus, 1926; Father Malachy's Miracle, 1931; Prayer For the Living, 1934; The Uncertain Glory, 1935; Canon to the Right of Them, 1936; Luckypenny, 1937; Delilah Upside Down, 1941.

ABOUT: Wilson Library Bulletin October 1938.

"MARTENS, PAUL." See SOUTH-WOLD, S.

"MARTIN, ABE." See HUBBARD, F. McK.

MARTIN, EDWARD SANDFORD

(January 2, 1856-June 13, 1939), American humorist, essayist, and magazine editor, was

born at Willowbrook on the shore of Lake Owasco, N.Y., the son of E. T. Throop Martin and Cornelia (Williams) Martin. After attending Phillips Andover Academy he graduated in 1877 from Harvard, which gave him an honorary M.A. in 1916. Here he helped found the *Lampoon,* undergraduate humorous publication. In 1879 he was in the State Department at Washington; returned to New York to work awhile on Charles Anderson Dana's *Sun;* studied law and was admitted to the bar at Rochester, N.Y.; and was assistant editor of the Rochester *Union and Advertiser.* With Thomas L. Masson and Andrew Miller, Martin founded the national humorous weekly *Life;* it was said that no one whose name did not begin with "M" or had not graduated from Harvard could hope for a position on the staff of the periodical. He became its first editor, in 1883, and wrote sane, balanced, and reasonably humorous editorials from 1887 to 1933. *Life* reached a circulation peak of 250,000 in 1921; but after a steady decline was sold in October 1936 to the *Time-Fortune* organization for $85,000. It had introduced to the world such men as Charles Dana Gibson, Oliver Herford, and John Kendrick Bangs, and crusaded against vivisection and for fresh-air camps for slum-children. Of *The War Week by Week* (1914) and *The Diary of a Nation* (1917), collections of Martin's editorials, the *Spectator* commented that they had no parallel in British journalism—"unconventional, colloquial, but trenchant, often intensely serious though appearing in what is nominally a comic paper." Martin's work was called by other critics sprightly and interesting, a mingling of wit and wisdom in fluent talk.

From 1920 to 1935 he conducted the department "The Easy Chair" in *Harper's Monthly;* he had written for *Harper's Weekly* from 1898 to 1913. Martin died at eighty-two in the New York Orthopedic Hospital after a three-months' illness, leaving a gross estate of $114,956. Two daughters and a son survived; Mrs. Martin (Julia Whitney of Rochester, whom he married in 1886) had died some years previously. Martin was gray-haired, quiet and retiring in manner.

PRINCIPAL WORKS: Slye Ballads in Harvard China, 1882; A Little Brother of the Rich (verses) 1890; Pirated Poems, 1890; Windfalls of Observation, 1893; Cousin Anthony and I, 1895; Lucid Intervals, 1900; Poems and Verses, 1902; The Luxury of Children, and Other Luxuries, 1904; The Courtship of a Careful Man, 1905; In a New Century, 1908; Reflections of a Beginning Husband, 1913; Unrest of Women, 1913; The War Week by Week, 1914; The Diary of a Nation, 1917; Abroad With Jane, 1918; The Life of Joseph Hodges Choate, 1920; What's Ahead, and Meanwhile, 1927.

ABOUT: Downey, F. Portrait of an Era; Gibbs, W. Bed of Neuroses; Harvard College, Class of 1877; Fiftieth Anniversary Report; New York Times June 14, 17, 1939; Publishers' Weekly July 8, 1939; Time June 26, 1939; Wilson Library Bulletin September 1939.

*MARTIN, EVERETT DEAN (July 5, 1880-   ), American sociologist, was born in Jacksonville, Ill., the son of Buker E. Martin and Mollie (Field)

Martin. He received a B.A. degree from Illinois College, Jacksonville, in 1904 (the same institution gave him an honorary Litt.D. in 1929); was graduated from Mc-Cormick Theological Seminary in 1907; and was ordained as

a Congregational minister. That same year Mr. Martin married Esther W. Kirk of Jacksonville. Three daughters were born: Mary, Margaret, and Elizabeth. Mr. Martin was pastor of the First Church, Lombard, Ill, 1906-08; Peoples Church, Dixon, Ill., 1908-10; and the Unitarian Church of Des Moines, Ia., from 1910 to 1914. He left the ministry in 1914 to write on philosophical subjects; was divorced from his first wife and married to Persis E. Rowell in 1915; and in 1916 began to lecture on social philosophy at the Peoples Institute, New York. Here Mr. Martin was assistant director and secretary from 1917 to 1922, when he became director. His *The Behavior of Crowds* (1920) was one of the first popular studies of mob psychology. As director of the Cooper Union Forum, the largest center for free discussion of politics and educational subjects in America, he has had other opportunities for observing large bodies of people in action. He has been head of the Union's department of social philosophy since 1934. Other lecturing and teaching experience includes a period as lecturer in social psychology at the New School for Social Research in New York City (1922) and instructor in social psychology at Brookwood Workers College, Katonah, N.Y., in 1922-23. From 1919 to 1922 Mr. Martin was chairman of the National Board of Review of Motion Pictures. His second marriage was also terminated by divorce—his son, Everett Eastman Martin, is the child of this marriage—and in 1931 he married Daphne Crane Drake. Mr. Martin has a deserved reputation as a mass educator and popularizer of psychology. *The Meaning of a Liberal Education,* a non-fiction best seller, condemned the utilitarian aim of modern education. His Colver lectures at Brown University, 1931, were collected in *The Conflict of the Individual and the Mass in the Modern World* (1932). He contributed *Psychology and Its Use* to the American Library Association's "Reading With a Purpose" series. The chapter on education in *Whither Mankind* (1928) is his work. A Democrat, Mr. Martin is also a member of four learned societies, the Century Association and P.E.N. Club of New York, and the Authors' Club of London.

PRINCIPAL WORKS: The Behavior of Crowds, 1920; The Mystery of Religion: A Study in Social Psychology, 1924; Psychology: What It Has to Teach You About Yourself and Your World, 1924; Psychology and Its Uses, 1926; The Meaning of a Liberal Education, 1926; Liberty, 1930; The Conflict of the Individual and the Mass in the Modern World, 1932; Civilizing Ourselves: Intellectual Maturity in the Modern World, 1932; Farewell to Revolution, 1935; Some Principles of Political Behavior, 1939; A Philosophical Analysis of the Present World Conflict, 1940.

ABOUT: Harper's Magazine May 1927; Parents' Magazine May 1935.

MARTIN, Mrs. HELEN (REIMENSNYDER) (October 18, 1868-June 29, 1939), American novelist and short-story writer, was born at Lancaster, Pa., the

daughter of the Rev. Cornelius Reimensnyder and Henrietta (Thurman) Reimensnyder. Her father was a Lutheran clergyman. After attending Swarthmore College and taking special courses in English at Radcliffe she married Frederic C. Martin at thirty, in 1899. At thirty-six Mrs. Martin published her first novel of the Pennsylvania Dutch people, *Tillie: A Mennonite Maid* (1904), a field which she shared only with Elsie Singmaster,*qv* and of which she remained the undisputed mistress till her death at seventy in New Canaan, Conn. The first impetus to her investigating the

simple, frugal, and sometimes—for the Mennonite women-folk—narrowly restricted lives of this unusual body of religionists was given by a Philadelphia magazine, which requested a lawyer-friend of Mrs. Martin's acquaintance to write the history of his Pennsylvania-Dutch ancestry. The first colony of Mennonites settled at Germantown, Pa., in 1683, coming from Europe to escape persecution for their religious beliefs. Occasional upheavals in Mennonite communities, which insist on having their own schools, still testify to the persistence and pertinacity of the sect.

Mrs. Martin succeeded in gaining their confidence, and wove her findings into simple romantic plots, in which overbearing Mennonite elders and boorish young suitors frequently got their "comeuppance" from rebellious Mennonite maids, who were sometimes abetted by more liberal-minded arrivals from the outside world. Mrs. Martin's serials were, as a natural consequence, in demand by editors of women's magazines. *Erstwhile Susan,* long an effective vehicle for Minnie Maddern Fiske, the dry little American comedienne, was a dramatic version of one of Mrs. Martin's stories of oppression and revolt, *Barnabetta.* After the Martins had lived for many years in Harrisburg, Mrs. Martin's husband died in 1936, and her own death occurred three years later at the home of a daughter, Mrs. Hans Heinemann. She had written over thirty novels. A son, Dr. Frederic Martin of the University of Maine, also survived.

PRINCIPAL WORKS: Tillie: A Mennonite Maid, 1904; Sabina: A Story of the Amish, 1905; The Betrothal of Elypholate and Other Tales, 1907; The Revolt of Anne Royle, 1908; The Crossways, 1910; When Half-Gods Go, 1911; The Fighting Doctor, 1912; The Parasite, 1913; Barnabetta, 1914; Martha of the Mennonite Country, 1915; Those Fitzenbergers, 1917; Maggie of Virginsburg, 1918; The Schoolmaster of Hessville, 1920; The Marriage of Susan, 1921; The Church on the Avenue, 1923; The Snob, 1924; Ye That Judge, 1926; Sylvia of the Minute, 1927; Wings of Healing, 1929; Yoked With a Lamb and Other Stories, 1930; Porcelain and Clay, 1931; Lucy Anderson, 1932; From Pillar to Post, 1933; The House on the Marsh, 1936; Emily Untamed, 1937; Son and Daughter, 1938; The Ordeal of Minnie Schultz, 1939.

ABOUT: New York Times June 30, 1939; Wilson Library Bulletin September 1939.

MARTIN, VIOLET FLORENCE ("Martin Ross") (June 11, 1865-December 21, 1915), Irish novelist and essayist who wrote always in collaboration with her cousin, Edith Oenone Somerville,*qv* was born at Ross House, County Galway, Ireland. She took her pseudonym from her native place.

She was the youngest daughter of James Martin, Deputy Lieutenant of Ireland, and his second wife, Anna Selina (Fox) Martin. She was educated first by governesses at home, and then at Alexandra College, Dublin. Although her mother and Dr. Somerville's were first cousins, the two girls did not meet until 1886. Dr. Somerville was then primarily an illustrator, and Miss Martin became her model. It was a crucial moment for both of them; Dr. Somerville described it later as "the hinge of my life, the place where my fate, and hers, turned over." Before long they had decided to try their hands at joint authorship, and their long collaboration ended only with Miss Martin's death— did not, indeed, end there, for since then her cousin has continued to publish all her work as by "Somerville and Ross."

Neither cousin ever married, and from their girlhood on they lived together, mostly at Drishane, County Cork, the Somerville home. They traveled a great deal together on the Continent, and spent months at a time in Paris. Their first joint novel was published in 1889, their original pseudonyms being "Martin Ross" and "Geilles Herring." Besides their novels, they published travel books, volumes of essays, and memoirs.

In 1898 Miss Martin was severely injured by being thrown by her horse, and several years of invalidism resulted; it may indeed have contributed to her premature death at fifty. She was singularly fragile in appearance, near-sighted, and it was hard to believe that actually she was almost as ardent a hunter and sportsman as her cousin. She was musical, and had a good singing voice. She was also an ardent suffragist, and was vice-president of the Munster Women's Franchise League. Her cousin, who always called her "Martin," described her as "a rare and sunny spirit," and her bubbling humor was one of her chief characteristics. Their books went slowly, because they were constantly interrupted; in fact, they never had a professional approach to writing, but considered it their avocation, and the life of country gentlewomen their vocation. They never took themselves seriously, but they did take their work seriously; they labored for two years over *The Real Charlotte,* their first serious book and

their masterpiece. Their most popular book, however, was the rollicking *Some Experiences of an Irish R. M.,* which had a success they were never able to duplicate.

A note of the forced and mechanical intrudes itself into their later work, which lacks the spontaneity of the earlier books. Theirs was, however, as C. L. Graves said, "the most brilliantly successful example of creative collaboration in our times." Miss Martin died at Cork twenty-seven years ago, but so long as her cousin continues to write she still lives in Irish literature. Dr. Somerville said of this: "In whatever, during these later years, I have written, I have known her help and have thankfully received her inspiration. She has gone, but our collaboration is not ended."

PRINCIPAL WORKS: (all with E. O. Somerville): *Fiction*—An Irish Cousin, 1889; Naboth's Vineyard, 1891; The Real Charlotte, 1895; The Silver Fox, 1897; Some Experiences of an Irish R. M., 1899; All on the Irish Shore, 1903; Further Experiences of an Irish R. M., 1908; Dan Russel the Fox, 1911; In Mr. Knox's Country, 1915. *Miscellaneous*—Through Connemara in a Governess Cart, 1893; In the Vine Country, 1893; Beggars on Horseback, 1895; Some Irish Yesterdays, 1906; Irish Memories, 1918.

ABOUT: Gwynn, S. L. Irish Books and Irish People; Somerville, E. A. O. & Ross, M. Irish Memories; Williams, O. Some Great English Novels; Edinburgh Review October 1921; Living Age October 4, 1913; Spectator, January 1, 1916.

MARTIN DU GARD, ROGER (1881-   ), French novelist and playwright, winner of the Nobel Prize for literature, was born at Neuilly-sur-Seine, near Paris, of an old Catholic family of lawyers and magistrates from Lorrain and Bourbon. Roger attended two of the finest Paris *lycées,* the Condorcet and the Janson-de-Sailly, and after three years at the École des

F. Margaritis

Chartes he was graduated in 1906 with the degree of archivist-paleographer. He evinced his literary vocation from the earliest—at the age of twenty he held Tolstoy's *War and Peace* as his Bible—but his father curbed it until after the young man had completed his work at the École and married. The methodology of research imbued the future novelist with a deep respect for historical truth, for painstaking documentation, and for scientific scruples. In 1908 he published his first novel, *Devenir,* which he later repudiated as a bad novel, "*un mauvais roman de jeunesse."* The archeologist was a most fastidious critic of his own endeavors: he never finished two long novels written during 1906-10 and mercilessly destroyed whatever he had completed.

From April 1910 until May 1913 he worked on the novel which marks the real beginning of his literary career, *Jean Barois.* His school chum, the publisher Gaston Gallimard, saw the bulky manuscript but did not dare risk his money on it until he heard André Gide's laudatory remarks. *Jean Barois* (1913) suggests in many ways some of the problems which later preoccupied Martin du Gard in *The Thibaults.* It deals with the short-lived triumphs and recurring defeats of youth in its conflict with the stable, inert clerical order of 1890. Through Gide and the *Nouvelle Revue Française* group, Martin du Gard become acquainted with Schlumberger and Copeau and these two interested him in playwriting.

In August 1914 Martin du Gard was mobilized and for the duration of the war he was at the front in charge of a transport division. He saw the war from many fronts and at close range. During the Armistice he was sent to the Rhine region where he left his twenty-one trucks in time to begin work on his ten-volume novel *The Thibaults* which took most of his time from 1920 to 1936 and won him the Nobel Prize for 1937 as well as the recently established Literary Prize of the City of Paris (1937). *The Thibaults* has been universally recognized as a masterpiece of contemporary literature. Although conceived originally as the study of a French family (a broader *Jean Barois*) it grew into a veritable panorama of French life from 1903 to 1914.

By 1922 Martin du Gard had finished and published Parts I and II (*The Grey Notebook* and *The Penitentiary*), and by 1923, Part III (*High Summer*) in two volumes. Then he took a long rest. In 1925 he settled in Bellême (Orme) and lived a secluded life. He wrote leisurely and by 1928 completed *La Gonfle*—"a very facetious farce concerning an old woman with dropsy, a sacristan, a veterinary, and a stomach-pump for animals"—which showed that profound knowledge of French peasant mentality and extraordinary mastery of dialogue which made his other farce, *Le Testament du Père Leleu*, completed in 1920, such a success when produced by Copeau at the Vieux Colombier. In 1928 Martin du Gard finished also two more parts of *The Thibaults*: IV and V (*The Consulting*

Day and *Sorellina*), followed in 1929 by Part VI (*Death of the Father*).

In 1930, just as he had completed *L'Appareillage*, intended to be the concluding volume of *The Thibaults*, Martin du Gard met with a serious automobile accident. On leaving the Mans clinic, three months later, he re-read the manuscript and destroyed it. What the history of literature lost by this action will never be known; all that is known is that this volume linked the death of the father (December 1913) to the summer of 1914. The present conclusion, *Summer 1914* (1936), originally in three volumes, was written by Martin du Gard in the solitude of the Midi during 1933-36.

Martin du Gard's three plays justify his inclusion among France's outstanding dramatists, and his *Vieille France*, "a simple album of village sketches," would alone rank him among the most significant novelists, but *The Thibaults* makes him one of the really great writers. This long novel measures scrupulously the moral forces of our day, shows the old tissue tearing slowly, irrevocably. His artistic feat is unique: he manages to reproduce the complex modern scene within a highly integrated form. His dialogue is of an unusual fluidity and exactitude. He has a gift for depicting scenes of violent action, and his whole book breathes an intense, almost brutal, physical life.

Until the Nazi invasion, Martin du Gard lived with his wife and daughter in Paris at 10 Rue du Dragon, where the young Victor Hugo had an attic room at the outset of his literary career. After the fall of France the Martin du Gards escaped to Unoccupied territory after great suffering and hardship. Martin du Gard is a serious, retiring writer who has never discussed his travels, his books, or his love affairs; he does not like to publish his photograph or his autograph; he refuses to give interviews or speak over the radio.

André Rousseaux, a critic who knows him well, says that the best description of Martin du Gard is to be found, in a somewhat caricaturesque form, in the following description of one of his characters (minus the moustache): "The Fat One was ugly with an ugliness which was ridiculous and yet sympathetic. He was tall, with great shoulders and a large stomach. The most prominent feature of his face were his nostrils. He had an overweening nose protruding from the middle of his comedian's white and fatty face. His hair was brown and combed back. Two thin lines of a meager moustache emphasized the outline of the upper lip, while the lower one hung limp and fleshy. The chin deepened into two fatty furrows. The rather heavy impertinence of the nose and the subtle irony of the eyes gave to his whole physiognomy a mocking expression which offended at first, but which was softened by the general good nature expressed in his features, particularly by the mouth, and by a certain fleeting quality of gentleness in his eyes."

WORKS AVAILABLE IN ENGLISH TRANSLATION: The Thibaults (Parts I-VI) 1939 (an earlier and quite inadequate translation of Parts I-III was published in 1926); Summer 1914, 1940.

ABOUT: Ehrhard, J. E. Le Roman Français depuis Marcel Proust; Gheon, H. Parti Pris; Lalou, R. Roger Martin du Gard; Rice, H. C. Roger Martin du Gard; Figaro July 23, 30, 1932; Living Age January 1938; Mercure de France January 15, 1931, December 1, 1937, April 1, 1938; New Republic November 24, December 29, 1937, January 5, 1938; New Yorker March 1, 1941; Nouvelle Revue Française January 1924 and August 1929; Revue de Paris, August 15, 1937; November 20, 1937; Saturday Review of Literature November 20, 1937, March 25, 1939; Statesman & Nation December 4, 1937; Time November 29, 1937, February 24, 1941.

MARTÍNEZ RUIZ, JOSÉ (June 8, 1873-), Spanish essayist, novelist, and playwright, better known under his *nom de plume* "Azorín," was

born in Monóvar (Alicante). His mother, Luisa Ruiz, derived from a rich family of landlords, and his father, the lawyer Isidro Martínez, mayor of the town, later became Conservative deputy from that district.

José had five sisters and two brothers. On completing his elementary studies at Monóvar and Yecla, José attended the law school in Valencia but soon discovered his dislike for jurisprudence and devoted most of his time to literature: he wrote atheistic articles, book reviews, and dramatic criticisms for the local papers; Baudelaire's *Flowers of Evil* was his great reading experience at the time. Tired of the University of Valencia, he moved to that of Granada, but his legal studies still remained in the background. In 1893 he published his first books: a critical monograph on the eighteenth century playwright Fernández de Moratín, and *Buscapiés,* dealing satirically with eighteenth century Spain. During the next few years he traveled to Salamanca and Valencia, and,

finally, in 1896, settled down in Madrid and joined the staff of the newspaper *El País.*

In the Spanish capital, José, already known as "Azorín," soon found his way to the vanguard literary circles. His major interests then were literary criticism and sociology. According to "Azorín," his first important work is *El Alma Castellana* (1900), which introduced his characteristic theme and style: in it the Spanish landscape with its old towns, ancient buildings, stagnant souls, is evoked in an impressionistic style full of pungent phrases, repetitions, and subtle nuances. "Azorín," sought the really authentic Hispanic sensibility, extolled Larra (who in the nineteenth century satirized Spain's lethargy and self-complacency) as "the master of our generation" and attacked Echegaray whose literary tradition (crowned by the Nobel award for 1904) he considered obsolete.

In 1907 and 1914 "Azorín" was elected Deputy, and in 1917 and 1919 he served as Under-Secretary of Public Instruction. In 1908 he married Julia Guinda Urzanqui. During the war, "Azorín" supported the Allies, but was sent in 1917 to Paris as correspondent of the reactionary pro-German paper *ABC.* His war experiences were recorded in several volumes. With the appearance of *El Chirrión de los Políticos* in 1923, one feels "Azorín's" disappointment with politics: in this "moral fantasy" he exposes the machinations of petty tyrants and dishonest politicians. From then on he devoted himself more exclusively to his literary creation, and on May 28, 1924, was elected, by unanimous vote, to the Spanish Academy. His academic career was very short, for he did not return to his chair after Gabriel Miró was refused entrance.

One of "Azorín's" earliest passions was the theatre; recently he made versions of Gantillon's *Maya* and of Evreinov's *Dr. Fregoli*—another way of saying that despite his love for the classics he has kept in touch with vanguard literature. With the emergence of surrealism, "Azorín" renewed his art. Since 1926 he has written *Old Spain* (1926), *Brandy, Mucho Brandy* (1927), and *El Clamor* (1928, in collaboration with the popular playwright Muñoz Seca), a scathing satire of the journalistic world, for which they were expelled from the Madrid Newspaper Guild. In 1930 "Azorín" broke with the Monarchist paper to which he was one of the leading contributors, and declared openly for the most advanced and boldest Republican ideas. He did not participate in the Spanish Civil War, however, but lived in Paris for its duration, contributing a weekly column to *La Nación* (Buenos Aires). He was reported to have returned to Madrid in 1940, a circumstance suggesting still another change in ideology.

"Azorín's" more recent works stand in sharp contrast to his previous clearness and simplicity: his "etopeya" *Félix Vargas* (1928), like his "pre-novel" *Superrealismo* (1929), his short stories *The Syrens* (1929), and his novel *Pueblo* (1930), contain a certain density difficult to grasp. Because of his felicitous juxtaposition of the old and the new, the sexagenarian Azorín who loves the classics as much as Rilke and Proust, has remained one of the youngest and most discussed writers of contemporary Spain. Cassou has called him "the most perfect realization of European impressionism" and, praising his gift for perceiving and depicting objects, he said "Azorín" has poured the Spanish language into a new mould of brevity and precision." The writer is tall, robust, blonde, with a scar on his face (remnant of a childhood prank); a sensitive, affable gentleman and scholar, he wears monacle and spats and says that he is in love with subways! His *nom de plume* is pronounced *ah-tho-reen'*.

WORKS AVAILABLE IN ENGLISH TRANSLATION: Don Juan, 1924; An Hour of Spain, 1931; The Syrens, 1931.

ABOUT: Alfonso, J. Azorín; Bell, A. F. G. Contemporary Spanish Literature; Boyd, E. Studies From Ten Literatures; Cassou, J. Panorama de la Littérature Espagnole Contemporaine; Gómez de la Serna, R. Azorín; Madariaga, S. The Genius of Spain; Mulertt, W. Azorín; Warren, L. A. Modern Spanish Literature.

*MARTÍNEZ SIERRA, GREGORIO (May 6, 1881-), Spanish dramatist, was born in Madrid, which has been his home  ever since, and educated at its university. Through Jacinto Benavente he became interested in the drama, and immediately after graduation joined the older playwright's semi-professional Spanish Art Theatre. He acted in its performances for ten years, meanwhile working as a journalist and turning out a series of novels, only one of which, *Anna María*, has been translated into English. His own first play was published in 1905. In 1899 he had married María Lejárraga. She was a poet, and they wrote jointly, and published under his

name, two volumes of verse; he had previously first appeared in print as the author of a volume of poems. Since that time he and his wife have collaborated in nearly all the plays published and produced as by Martínez Sierra; sometimes her name appears as co-author, and sometimes not.

For a year, from 1907 to 1908, Martínez Sierra traveled in Central and Northern Europe and in England. He then returned to Madrid, and began an intensive career of playwriting and adaptation and translation of plays by foreign dramatists. His own first great success was with *Canción de Cuña (The Cradle Song)*, in 1911, which later scored an equal success in America. In 1916 he organized his own theatre in Madrid, and through war and revolution has kept it open most of the time since, producing both his own plays and those of others. He has found time also to edit a library of translated *World's Classics,* to edit a magazine, and to found a publishing house. He has adapted and translated some fifty plays, written some thirty volumes of non-dramatic work, and written about forty plays, either alone or in collaboration with his wife. He brought his own company to New York in 1927, and in 1931 spent some time in Hollywood, supervising the filming of his play *Mamá,* and translating, filming, and directing other Spanish plays for presentation in Spanish-speaking countries. Although he has taken no part in politics, his sympathies during the Spanish Civil War were apparently with Franco, for he is a devout Catholic and deeply religious. He seems to have lived undisturbed in life or property during the years of revolution, and he is still at work in Madrid.

Martínez Sierra is now considered one of the leading dramatists of Spain. The main influence on his work has been, not his first mentor Benavente, who is a realist, but the romantic Belgian, Maurice Maeterlinck. Except for a slight tendency to feminism, he espouses no social causes and abhors social tendencies in literature. Joseph Wood Krutch called him "unabashedly romantic," with a charm that is "quaintly exotic." Stark Young said that his work has "a kind of realistic mysticism," and is made up of "poetry, plain fact, and loving irony. . . . It has a simple outline, but within this outline are a fertile content and warm luminosity." Desmond MacCarthy accredited him with "an immediate directness, an instinctive balance between subtlety and reticence." Other critics less kindly disposed to his strongly mystical bent have called his work soft and

* Died October 1, 1947.

formless, and sometimes boring; they grant, however, that he has a capacity for inspiring banal and outworn plots with warm sensibility and poetic warmth.

WORKS AVAILABLE IN ENGLISH: The Cradle Song, 1917; Love Magic, 1917; The Lover, 1917; Theatre of Dreams, 1918; Poor John, 1920; Madame Pepita, 1921; The Mountebank, 1921; Anna Maria (novel) 1921; The Kingdom of God, 1922; The Romantic Young Lady, 1922; The Two Shepherds, 1922; Wife to a Famous Man, 1922; Plays, 1923; Idyll, 1926; The Road to Happiness, 1927; The Forgotten Song, 1928; Holy Night, 1929; A Lily Among Thorns, 1930; Take Two From One, 1931; Spring in Autumn, 1933.

ABOUT: Bell, A. F. G. Contemporary Spanish Literature; Boyd, E. Studies From Ten Literatures; Chandler, F. Modern Continental Playwrights; Warren, L. A. Modern Spanish Literature; Bookman July 1923; Contemporary Review February 1924; Hispania November 1922, February 1923; New Statesman and Nation July 30, 1932.

MARTÍNEZ ZUVIRÍA, GUSTAVO ADOLFO ("Hugo Wast") (1883-), Argentine novelist, writes: "Gustavo Martínez

Zuviría was born in Córdoba, Argentina. He studied at the College of the Immaculate Conception at Santa Fe, and secured a degree of Doctor of Social Science. He has been professor of political economy at the University of Santa Fe,

Pinchot

and represented the province of Santa Fe as a national deputy in Congress from 1916 to 1920. His first two books were published under his true name. All the others have appeared under his pseudonym.

"The first edition of Flor de Durazno (Peach Blossom) (1911) took seven years to exhaust. This same work, which was sold with such difficulty, has now reached its 150,000th copy, has been dramatized and filmed, and has been translated into ten languages. The Royal Spanish Academy gave its Grand Prize to Valle Negro (Black Valley), and incorporated in its dictionary many of the Argentine idioms first incorporated in literary form by 'Hugo Wast.' Among his novels is a trilogy dealing with the history of Argentine independence. For his novel Disierto de Piedra (Stone Desert), he received the National Grand Prize for Literature, $30,000. His works have been translated into French, German, English, Italian, Russian, Portuguese, Dutch, Polish, and Czech. The Argentine Government, at the foundation of the Argentine Academy of Letters, in 1931, named him as one of the members. He is a correspondent of the Royal Spanish Academy and of the Colombian Academy of Letters. He is also a member of the National Committee of Culture, of the National Committee for Intellectual Co-operation, and of the Argentine-Uruguayan Cultural Institute. Pope Pius XI made him a Pontifical Commander of the Order of St. Gregory the Great. He is at present director of the National Library of Buenos Aires.

* * *

"Hugo Wast" is an anagram of Sr. Martínez Zuviría's given name, Gustavo. He adopted the pseudonym soon after his marriage, in 1918, to avoid confusion with his many other interests—his teaching, his law practice, and his large holdings in cattle ranches. He retired from his position as Deputy in order to have more time for his writing, and he has long been the most popular novelist in Argentina, if not in South America. Actually, however, the general public did not discover his identity until he received the National Athenaeum's prize of $10,000 in 1916 for La Casa de los Cuervos (The House of the Ravens.). His work has been called "impressive, somber, and powerful," but critics generally agree that he suffers from the same tendency to melodrama which is noted in the work of Blasco Ibáñez, by whom Sr. Martínez Zuviría has been strongly influenced.

WORKS AVAILABLE IN ENGLISH: Black Valley, 1928; Stone Desert, 1928; Peach Blossom, 1929; The Strength of Lovers, 1930.

ABOUT: Martínez Zuviría, G. A. Las Espigas de Ruth (Ruth's Gleanings); Hispanic-American Historical Review February 1929; Literary Digest May 12, 1928; Pan-American Magazine September 1930.

*MARVIN, FRANCIS SYDNEY (August 6, 1863-). English educator, writes: "I was born in the City of London. My father was a business man and churchwarden in one of the many small parishes of the City, full of life and business during the week and as still as a churchyard on the Sunday. He was one of the latest business men to go out into the nearer countryside for his residence. In his case he went to the North and I spent most of my childhood in Southgate, about a dozen miles from the center of the city. Unhappily I had lost my mother before I was two years old. This was a deprivation of loving and careful influence which I have felt all my life. There was, however, one sister, who has given her life

to the betterment of the natives of Jamaica, where she lives.

"My father, being a 'City man,' was able to obtain for me a 'presentation' to the Merchant Taylors' School, which is linked up by scholarships with St. John's College at Oxford. Being a rather lonely child, I spent all my free time on my lessons, and made sure of a St. John's scholarship some years before it was my turn to take. This came in 1882, when I went to Oxford with a posse of the other top boys in various subjects at school. Before that time, however, I had made the acquaintance of the leaders of Positivism in London—Frederic Harrison, Professor Beesly, and above all Dr. J. H. Bridges, who was the most philosophical and spiritually-minded of the group. I was thus, on entering Oxford, already more mature and systematic in my thought than most of my companions or tutors. I stood religiously somewhere on the road marked out by George Eliot, whom I once saw at a concert in London.

"Having determined early to be a clergyman, when the old beliefs of my father and school faded away, I turned to the nearest bit of social and religious work which I could think of, and became on leaving college an elementary teacher. I spent two years at this work, first in Oxford and then in the East End of London. This work led to an inspectorship of schools in the year 1890 and the thirty-four years which followed form the main part of my life. During them I visited schools and training colleges of all kinds and spent my spare time in reading and lecturing on educational and historical subjects, mainly to teachers' audiences. One of these courses was the basis of my best known book, *The Living Past*, which was supplemented during the Great War by a volume sketching the history of the nineteenth century under the title of *The Century of Hope;* the phrase became proverbial in many mouths, and in the time of trouble which accompanied and followed it has acquired a somewhat pathetic significance. The hope, however, which it embodies still stands firm in the hearts of many who are witnessing the catastrophes of the present time.

"From the year 1915, at the beginning of the Great War, I initiated a series of Unity History Schools, largely with the cooperation of the Society of Friends. These Conferences continued till 1939 and have led to the publication of a number of volumes of collected essays on *The Unity of Western Civilization, Progress and Unity,* etc."

* * *

Mr. Marvin was married in 1904 to Edith Mary Deverell; they have two sons. He resigned as Staff Inspector of the Board of Education in 1924, after having served in Lancashire, Cornwall, Cumberland, and Yorkshire. In 1929 and 1930 he was professor of modern history in the University of Egypt. He lives now in Welwyn Garden City, where his recreations are tennis, swimming, and music. He is a Fellow of the Royal Historical Society.

PRINCIPAL WORKS: The Living Past, 1913; The Century of Hope, 1919; The Making of the Western Mind (with others) 1923; The Adventures of Odysseus (juvenile, with R. J. G. Mayor & F. M. Stawell) 1924; India and the West, 1927; The Modern World, 1929; The Nation at School, 1933; Old and New, 1935; Comte: The Founder of Sociology, 1936; The New Vision of Man, 1938. *Edited*—The Unity of Western Civilization, 1915; Progress and History, 1916; Recent Developments in European Thought, 1920; The Evolution of World Peace, 1921; Western Races and the World, 1922; Science and Civilization, 1923; England and the World, 1925; Art and Civilization (with A. F. Clutton-Brock) 1928; The New World Order, 1932.

ABOUT: Christian Century September 20, 1923; Contemporary Review August 1939.

MARY MADELEVA, Sister. See WOLFF, M. E.

MASEFIELD, JOHN (June 1, 1878-   ), Poet Laureate of England, novelist, playwright, critic, military and nautical historian, is the son of George Edward Masefield, a solicitor of Ledbury, Herefordshire, and his wife, Caroline Parker, a clergyman's daughter. The father died while John was very young, so the boy was brought up by an uncle, William. He went to King's  School, Warwick, for a few years, but as he had ambitions to be an officer in the merchant service he was sent, at the age of thirteen, to the famous training ship, "Conway," which is moored in the River Mersey off Rock Ferry. At fifteen-and-a-half, having done very well at his studies, he was apprenticed aboard a "windjammer," and sailed in her round Cape Horn to Iquique, Chile. There he became seriously ill and returned home by steamer; and when recovered he obtained the post of sixth officer on the

White Star liner, "Adriatic." The ship was in dock at New York, and he went out to join her there, but changed his mind and abandoned the sea as a profession.

Masefield was in or around New York for some three years. His first plan was to take up medicine, working his way through college, but this scheme he also abandoned. For some months he passed from one humble job to another, working in a bakery, a livery stable, and a saloon; until a post in a carpet factory at Yonkers provided him with a poor but regular wage. During his two years there his private preoccupations became more and more literary. He began not only to read the English classics but to write poems and essays of his own; and in 1897 he returned to London with his mind set on a career in letters.

Five years were yet to elapse before his first book appeared. They were years spent in a hard apprenticeship, writing a great deal of miscellaneous matter—poems, short stories, articles, and book reviews. The *Outlook*, the *Academy*, and the *Speaker* all took his contributions; and J. L. Hammond, editor of the last mentioned, in due course made Masefield his literary editor, and moreover recommended him to the powerful *Manchester Guardian.* For some time he divided his week between Manchester and London (in many ways preferring the former city). For the *Guardian* he wrote miscellaneous articles, and originated a "Miscellany" feature which was (and remains, in other hands) an admirable *causerie*, very greatly superior to the fatuous "gossip columns" so beloved of the popular press.

In the fourteen years prior to the outbreak of the First World War Masefield built up a firm reputation as a poet, playwright and novelist. His first collection of poems, *Salt-Water Ballads,* which came out in 1902, contained promise of greater things and included the fine lyric, "Sea Fever," which remains his best-known short poem. Further volumes appeared in 1903 and 1910, while in the *English Review* of October 1911 there was published the long poem, *The Everlasting Mercy,* which brought him fame. It was fierce, rough stuff, dealing with the redemption of a country libertine. It contained disreputable passages of low life and used words which before the First World War were not considered admissible in literature; and in consequence there were critics who refused it the praise it deserved. But its fire and vigor, its knowledge of the harsher side of village life, and the real lyrical beauty of its later passages, won for

it the acceptance of many good judges. *The Widow of Bye Street* (1912 and *Dauber* (1913) were other long poems in similar vein. They were all rapid and racy, full of tragic fervor and brilliant descriptive power, and marred only by frequent carelessness in the matter of rhymes and an occasional brusque descent into bathos.

Meanwhile *The Tragedy of Nan* (1909) and *The Tragedy of Pompey the Great* (1910) had shown that Masefield was also a writer of strong dramatic power. And in fiction he had made a good beginning, though his most successful novels were products of the post-war period. The best of the early fiction was *Multitude and Solitude* (1909), the story of a successful dramatist who grows to despise his success and turns to an active scientific career. Masefield's output included sundry stories for boys, in which his love of action and adventure showed to great advantage.

Like most men of letters with their way still to make, Masefield turned his hand to various editorial tasks. One such was the editing of collections of voyages for Messrs. Dent's highly successful "Everyman's Library." For another admirable series, Messrs. Williams & Norgate's "Home University Library," he wrote in 1911 a book on *Shakespeare,* full of illuminating, if not always orthodox, criticism. His book on *John M. Synge* (whom he had known well in his early London days) came out after the war had started, in 1915.

With the onset of the war, Masefield undertook Red Cross service, first in France and later on a hospital ship at Gallipoli. He was profoundly moved by the tragic and terrible things he saw, and his book on *Gallipoli* (1916) is considered to be one of the finest and most vivid accounts of that appalling adventure. In 1916, and again in 1918, he lectured in America in aid of the Allied cause. His speeches on these occasions were collected in 1918 as *St. George and the Dragon* (in America entitled *The War and the Future).* Two further war products were *The Old Front Line* (1917) and *The Battle of the Somme* (1919).

For all his propensity for the adventurous life, Masefield, like all other sensible men, was glad to turn his back on the sordid squalor of the War. He was now forty years of age, and at the height of his powers and threw himself energetically into the work of composition. The first post-war fruits of his pen were represented by *Reynard the Fox* (1919)—a splendid long poem which displayed his finest narrative powers and characterization, and pictured the hunt not only from the point of view of the hunters but (in breathless and pathetic passages) that of the straining, hunted fox. *Right Royal* (1920) did similar service for horse racing. With *Sard Harker* (1924) Masefield took up the novel again after an interval of many years, producing a story packed with every kind of thrilling hazard. *Odtaa* (1926) was in the same order of fiction, and the series continues unabated to the present time.

So great has been Masefield's literary activity in latter years that only its main tendencies can be here reviewed. Apart from his fiction he has kept up a constant output of poetry, most of it lamentably inferior to his best, and has turned more and more towards the poetic drama as a medium of expression. He takes the keenest interest in the right speaking of verse, and has a small theatre at his house.

He has lived for many years now on Boar's Hill, a quiet, pine-clad region above Oxford, where he can indulge his liking for writing out of doors and where he is in easy touch with scholars and men of letters. The University of Oxford granted him the honorary degree of D.Litt. in 1922 and the University of Aberdeen made him LL.D. the same year. In 1930 he was appointed Poet Laureate in succession to the late Robert Bridges, and in 1935 he received the most coveted honor England can bestow, being admitted to the small and eminent company of the Order of Merit. He has lectured in Turkey and many European countries for the British Council (the chairman of whose Books and Periodicals Committee he is); and in connection with the war now raging (1942) he is making strong efforts to see that the troops are kept well supplied with books.

Masefield (regarded as the writer of his prime) has superb gifts as a storyteller, both in prose and verse. His sense of pity and tragedy is highly developed, and his subject matter comes straight out of the lives of humble people. He loves and understands the country and the sea, and he is probably the most "unliterary" Laureate that England has ever had in the sense that forms and conventions interest him far less than actuality and the warm movement of life itself. His poetic diction is hewn out of the ordinary vocabulary; and he makes up in passion and fire what he lacks in humor and the gentler virtues.

In person, indeed, Masefield is the gentlest and quietest of men, courteous, understanding, and utterly free from affectation of any kind; generous, and sensitive to criticism. In 1903 he married Constance de la Cherois-Crommelin, of Cushendun, County Antrim, Northern Ireland, and had a son and a daughter. The daughter, Judith, has illustrated several of his books. In 1942 the son, Lewis Crommelin Masefield, a former newspaperman, aged thirty-two, was reported "killed in action far from home in recent fighting."

PRINCIPAL WORKS: *Poetry*—Salt-Water Ballads, 1902; Ballads, 1903; Ballads and Poems, 1910; The Everlasting Mercy, 1911; The Story of a Round-House and Other Poems, 1912; The Widow in Bye Street, 1912; The Daffodil Fields, 1913; Dauber, 1913; Philip the King and Other Poems, 1914; Good Friday, 1915; Good Friday and Other Poems, 1916; The Cold Cotswolds, 1917; Lollingdon Downs and Other Poems, 1917; Rosas, 1918; Reynard the Fox, 1919; Animula, 1920; Enslaved and Other Poems, 1920; Right Royal, 1920; King Cole, 1921; The Dream, 1922; King Cole and Other Poems, 1923; Sonnets of Good Cheer to the Lena Ashwell Players, 1926; Midsummer Night and Other Tales in Verse, 1928; South and East, 1929; Minnie Maylow's Story and Other Tales and Scenes, 1931; A Tale of Troy, 1932; Pontus and Other Verse, 1936; The Country Scene, 1937; Tribute to Ballet, 1938; Some Verses to Some Germans, 1939; Gautama the Enlightened, 1941; Natalie Maisie and Pavilastukay, 1942.

Plays—The Tragedy of Nan and Other Plays, 1909; The Tragedy of Pompey the Great, 1910; The Faithful, 1915; The Locked Chest; The Sweeps of Ninety-Eight, 1916; Melloney Hotspur, 1922; A King's Daughter, 1923; The Trial of Jesus, 1923; Tristan and Isolt, 1927; The Coming of Christ, 1928; Easter: A Play for Singers, 1929; End and Beginning, 1933. *Fiction*—A Mainsail Haul (stories) 1905; A Tarpaulin Muster (stories) 1907; Captain Margaret, 1908; Multitude and Solitude, 1909; A Book of Discoveries, 1910; Lost Endeavour, 1910; Martin Hyde, 1910; Jim Davis, 1911; The Street of To-day, 1911; The Taking of Helen, 1923; Sard Harker, 1924; Odtaa, 1926; The Midnight Folk, 1927; The Hawbucks, 1929; The Bird of Dawning, 1933; The Taking of the Gry, 1934; The Box of Delights, 1935; Victorious Troy: or, The "Hurrying Angel," 1935; Eggs and Baker, 1936; The Square Peg: or, The Gun Fella, 1937; Dead Ned: The Autobiography of a Corpse, 1938; Live and Kicking Ned, 1939; Basilissa, 1940; Conquer, 1941. *Critical and Biographical Works*—William Shakespeare, 1911; John M. Synge, 1915; John Ruskin, 1920; A Foundation Day Address, 1921; Shakespeare and Spiritual Life (Romanes Lecture) 1924; With the Living Voice, 1925; Chaucer, 1931; Poetry, 1931; Some Memories of W. B. Yeats, 1940. *Historical and Miscellaneous Works*—Sea Life in Nelson's Time, 1905; On the Spanish Main, 1906; My Faith in Woman Suffrage, 1910; Gallipoli, 1916; The Old Front Line, 1917; The Battle of the Somme, 1919; St. George and the Dragon (American title: The War and The Future) 1918; Recent Prose, 1924; The "Conway": From her Foundation to the Present Day, 1933; The "Wanderer" of Liverpool, 1930; In the Mill (autobiography) 1941; The Nine Days Wonder, 1941.

ABOUT: Biggane, C. John Masefield: A Study; Gosse, E. W. Books on the Table; Hamilton, W. H. John Masefield: A Critical Study; Lynd,

R. Old and New Masters; Mason, J. E. Makers of Literature: No. 4: John Masefield; Newbolt, H. J. New Paths on Helicon; Rickword, E. (ed.) Scrutinies; Rothenstein, W. Twenty-Four Portraits; Simmons, C. H. A Bibliography of John Masefield; Squire, J. C. Tricks of the Trade; Thomas, G. John Masefield; Williams, I. A. John Masefield; New York Times Book Review March 17, 1940; Newsweek September 16, 1940.

*MASON, ALFRED EDWARD WOODLEY (1865-   ), English romantic novelist and playwright, writer of adventure and

detective fiction, was born at Dulwich, London, the youngest son of William Woodley Mason of Everleigh. He was educated at Dulwich and Trinity College, Oxford, where he was an amateur actor and received an A.M. degree. Turning to the professional stage, for which his rather theatrical good looks eminently fitted him, Mason toured the provinces with the Benson Company and the Compton Comedy Company (Compton Mackenzie's family name is Compton, and his sister Fay uses that name), and was a soldier in Bernard Shaw's *Arms and the Man*. His first novel, *A Romance of Wastdale*, written in 1895 after he had left the stage as an actor, was fairly well received by the critics. *The Courtship of Morrice Buckler* of the next year had large sales. After *Clementina* (1901), Mason left historical fiction for novels of contemporary life based on his own experience. *The Four Feathers*, whose pageantry and intense human interest make it a perennial joy to the makers of moving pictures, is a study of a British guardsman who resigned his commission when his regiment was about to start for Egypt, was branded as a coward, ostracized, and spectacularly redeemed. For local color, Mason made an arduous journey into Egypt by camel train. He took a steamer from Suez down the Red Sea, disembarked at Suakin, and pushed off into the eastern Sudan with his half-dozen camels, arriving eventually at Berber and Khartum. Omdurman he found as it was during the life of the Kalifa; the house of stone, the famous prison, still stood.

The Broken Road drew a nine-page letter of praise from Lord Curzon, viceroy of India, for the faithful atmosphere of its Indian scenes. Mason was a member of the House of Commons from Coventry in

1906, making a notable maiden speech from the floor of the House in 1907. He did not stand again in 1910. During the First World War he was abroad as chief Naval Intelligence, with rank of major. Short stories constituted his sole literary output during this period. He explored the western Mediterranean, Jamaica, Ceylon, Mexico and the Caribbean, being an enthusiastic sailor of small boats and a member of the Royal Yacht Squadron (as well as a keen cricketer). Several dramatizations of his novels had successful runs, notably *Morrice Buckler*, done in collaboration with Isabel Bateman, and *Miranda of the Balcony* (produced in New York in 1901). *The Witness for the Defense* (1911) was the most successful. *Fire Over England* made a striking film.

At the Villa Rose, the novel which first introduced Mason's notable detective, M. Hanaud, and fussy little foil, Mr. Ricardo, appeared in 1910 and brought a needed freshness to the detective story of that period. Willard Huntington Wright ("S.S. Van Dine") spoke enthusiastically of Hanaud as almost the Gallic counterpart of Sherlock Holmes. *The House of the Arrow* (regarded by many detective-fiction *aficionados* as almost perfect in its *genre*) together with *No Other Tiger* and *The Prisoner in the Opal*, are "excellent examples of detective fiction, carefully constructed, consistently worked out and pleasingly written. They represent . . . the purest expression of this type of diversion." Mason was an early experimentalist in the use of believable character and psychology in the detective story. He blends convincing mood and color with excellent detection.

PRINCIPAL WORKS: Novels—A Romance of Wastdale, 1895; The Courtship of Morrice Buckler, 1896; The Philanderers, 1897; Lawrence Clavering, 1897; Parson Kelly (with Andrew Lang) 1899; Miranda of the Balcony, 1899; The Watchers, 1899; Clementina, 1901; The Four Feathers, 1902; The Truants, 1904; Running Water, 1907; The Broken Road, 1907; At the Villa Rose, 1910; The Turnstile, 1912; The Witness for the Defence, 1913; The Summons, 1920; The Winding Stair, 1923; The House of the Arrow, 1924; No Other Tiger, 1927; The Prisoner in the Opal; 1929; The Dean's Elbow, 1930; The Three Gentlemen, 1932; The Sapphire, 1933; They Wouldn't be Chessmen, 1935; Fire Over England, 1936; The Drum, 1937; Königsmark, 1938. Short Stories—Ensign Knightly, 1901; The Four Corners of the World, 1917. Biography—Sir George Alexander and the St. James' Theatre, 1935; The Life of Francis Drake, 1942.

ABOUT: Adcock, A. St. J. Gods of Modern Grub Street; Barrie, J. M. The Greenwood Hat; Haycraft, H. Murder for Pleasure: The Life and Times of the Detective Story; Swinnerton, F. The Georgian Scene; Bookman (London) April 1931.

* Died November 22, 1948.

MASON, VAN WYCK (November 11, 1897-), American novelist, writes: "Born Francis Van Wyck Mason] in Boston.

Berkshire School, 1920, Harvard, B.S., 1924. Two and a half years overseas: First Lieutenant Interpreter's Corps, A. E. F.; Sergeant, Troop C, Squadron A, New York; First Lieutenant Field Artillery Reserve, 110th F. A. Played much polo in

Globe

Maryland and Boston. Speaks French and some Spanish and German. Has lived abroad over four years at various times and has traveled extensively in Eastern Europe, Russia, North Africa, Central America, and the West Indies. Spent three years in Bermuda. Married Dorothy Louise Macready, 1927; two sons. Member of Loyal Legion.

"In 1931 he studied with John Gallishaw for some six months, then entered the literary business seriously. From that time built himself into a position as one of the more important writers among the better popular fiction magazines. Nowadays, he contributes articles to such other publications as *The Writer, Town and Country, Country Life,* and various publications dealing with horses. He has written Foreign Legion stories, juveniles, historical romances, war stories, flying stories, and many types of adventure-action stories. He has had published twelve international mysteries with Captain Hugh North as their hero. Two others were written under the pseudonym of 'Geoffrey Coffin.' Besides fourteen detective stories, he has published three historical romances. *Three Harbours* is probably his best-known book, remaining on the best-seller list for almost a year. It achieved a country-wide acclaim and was also published in Sweden, Holland, and England; and, but for the war, would also have appeared in Germany, Denmark, and Hungary. To date, his books have been published in France, England, Italy, Denmark, Czechoslovakia, Spain, Greece, Norway, and Hungary. *Stars on the Sea* is the second of four volumes which will depict the maritime peoples of the American Colonies during the Revolution."

* * *

Mr. Mason's home is in Baltimore. He comes of an old Nantucket family, but as his grandfather was American Consul in Berlin and Paris his first eight years were spent abroad. He had intended to enter the diplomatic service, but on his father's death he started an import business dealing in antique books, maps, rugs, and embroideries. Until 1927 he wrote only in his leisure time. His detective stories belong to "the Oppenheim tradition" of international intrigue; his historical novels are well documented melodramas. In 1942 Major F. Van Wyck Mason was placed in charge of the War Department's Publication Section, the official contact between the U.S. Army and book and magazine publishers.

PRINCIPAL WORKS: *Mystery Stories*—Seeds of Murder, 1930; Yellow Arrow Murders, 1930; Vesper Service Murders, 1931; Shanghai Bund Murders, 1931; Sulu Sea Murders, 1932; Budapest Parade Murders, 1932; Washington Legation Murders, 1934; Seven Seas Murders (as "Geoffrey Coffin," with H. Brawner) 1935; Murder in the Senate (as "Geoffrey Coffin," with H. Brawner) 1935; Spider House, 1936; Forgotten Fleet Mystery (with A. H. Young-O'Brien) 1936; Castle Island Case, 1937; Hong Kong Airbase Murders, 1937; Cairo Garter Murders, 1938; Singapore Exile Murders, 1938; The Bucharest Ballerina Murders, 1940; The Rio Casino Intrigue, 1941. *Historical Novels*—Captain Nemesis, 1936; Three Harbours, 1938; Stars on the Sea, 1940; Hang My Wreath (as "Ward Weaver") 1941.

ABOUT: Country Life October 1939; New York Times Book Review June 9, 1940; Publishers' Weekly November 2, 1940; Wilson Library Bulletin January 1940; Writer March 1941.

MASON, WALT (May 4, 1862- June 22, 1939), American humorist, was born in Columbus, Ont., Canada, the son of John and Lydia Sarah (Campbell) Mason. His father, a wool dyer, was killed when the boy was four, and when he was fifteen his mother died. He came to the United States in 1880, worked as a farm hand in New York state, and drifted to

Kansas, where he worked on the Atchison *Globe* (1885-87), the Lincoln (Neb.) *State-Journal,* and other papers. Mason married Ella Foos of Wooster, Ohio, the year he began to do paragraphs for the Washington *Evening News.* In 1907 he arrived in Emporia, Kans., with an extra shirt, $1.35 in cash, and an old pony and "buggy." Here he was taken in by William Allen White, editor of the Emporia *Gazette,* who was later to call Mason "the Homer of modern America and particularly of Middle-Western America, the America of the country town." George Ade termed him "the high priest of horse sense." His lays were sung in rhymed prose, full of unexpected collocations and ingenious twists. To quote from the obituary in *Time* (and illustrate Mason's style): "Walt Mason's doggerel, couched in slang, hit the syndicates with a bang; rich, respected, worth his salt grew reformed Booze-hoister Walt." Death came at seventy-seven in La Jolla, Calif., after an illness of several weeks. An adopted daughter, Mary, survived. Mason had a rugged humorous face, framed in a shock of gray hair, and weighed up to 240 pounds.

PRINCIPAL WORKS: Uncle Walt, 1910; Walt Mason's Business Prose Poems, 1911; Rippling Rhymes, 1913; Horse Sense, 1915; Terse Verse, 1917; Walt Mason, His Book, 1918.

ABOUT: New York Times June 23, 1939; Newsweek July 3, 1939; Poetry August 1939; Time July 3, 1939; Wilson Library Bulletin September 1939.

MASPERO, Sir GASTON CAMILLE CHARLES (June 23, 1846-June 30, 1916), French archaeologist, was born in Paris; his

parents were of Italian (Lombard) origin. In his second year at the École Normale, Maspero met Auguste Edouard Mariette, the famous Egyptologist, who encouraged the young man after he had successfully translated in eight days an Egyptian inscription on a stela. In 1869 Maspero was *répétiteur* (teacher) of Egyptian language and archaeology in the École des Hautes Études; took part in the battle of Montretout as a member of the *garde mobile* in 1870, and was appointed to the chair of Champollion in 1874 at the Collège de France. In November 1880 Maspero headed an archaeological mission to Egypt which later became the Institut Français de l'Archéologie Orientale. This post he held until June 1886, struggling with natives and cholera, and uncovering the mummies of whole families of Pharaohs at Deir el-Bahri. Professorial duties recalled him to Paris, where from 1895 to 1899 he wrote his *Histoire des Peuples de l'Orient*, an enlargement of a manual published in 1875, which showed the inter-relations between Egyptians, Chaldeans, Syrians, and Medes and Persians that had been obscured by Greek writers, who had been the sole interpreters heretofore of ancient peoples to modern. Maspero believed that an archaeologist must know modern Egypt thoroughly to understand the ancient country, so he traversed the whole terrain and sailed up the Nile. In 1899 he returned to Egypt as director-

general of the department of antiquities. When the government proposed to lift the Assuan dam seven meters, Maspero raised 1,600,000 francs to explore and strengthen monuments threatened with inundation, including forty temples between Philae and Wady Halfa. By 1909 he had published twenty-four volumes of catalogues of collections. The remarkable discoveries made at the temple of Karnak were largely his. In 1887 Oxford University gave him an honorary degree of D.C.L., and in 1909 the British government made him a knight commander of the order of Saints Michael and George, "in reward for services to the Crown in the foreign affairs of the Empire." Maspero had an agreeable, bearded face; an attractive bearing, and soft, clear voice. He collapsed at seventy with a heart attack at a meeting of the Academie des Inscriptions of the Institut de France.

WORKS AVAILABLE IN ENGLISH TRANSLATION: Egyptian Archaeology, 1888; Life in Ancient Egypt and Assyria, 1892; The Dawn of Civilization, 1894; The Struggle of the Nations: Egypt, Syria, and Assyria, 1896; The Passing of the Empires, 1900; History of Egypt, Chaldea, Babylonia, and Assyria, 1901; Egypt: Ancient Sites and Modern Scenes, 1911; Art in Egypt, 1912; Popular Stories of Ancient Egypt, 1915.

ABOUT: Institut de France, Academie des Inscriptions: Compte Rendu 1917; Revue des Deux Mondes August 15, 1916.

*MASSINGHAM, HAROLD JOHN (March 25, 1888-   ), English biographer and writer on natural history, writes: "I am actually writing a kind of autobiography at the moment, but it is rather an account of mental experience rather than a record of events. I was educated at Westminster School and Queen's College, Oxford. A very severe illness pre-

vented my taking my degree in the Honours School of English Literature, and I became a journalist in London, including a post as literary editor of the *Athenaeum*. My health, however, broke down again, and during the war of 1914-18 I was in the country, principally Dorset, pursuing ornithological studies and gradually extending these to include other aspects of natural and animal life. After the war, I joined the staff of the *Nation*, of which my father (H. W. Massingham) was editor; founded the 'Plumage Bill Group' to agitate for a bill to stop the importation of plumage for millinery purposes; and traveled over various parts of England in search of material for my books on the country.

"In 1931 I left London altogether and became a permanent resident in the country (Gloucestershire and the borders of Oxon and Bucks). Up to the present day I have written from thirty to forty books, chiefly about various aspects of country life (landscape, architecture, wild life, husbandry, gardening, topography, geology, and particularly rural craftsmanship). I have also written a book about London, a biography of Shelley's friend Trelawney, an anthology of seventeenth century poetry in the Golden Treasury Series (1919), an edition of Gilbert White, and a long book about the prehistoric origins of English civilization (*Downland Man*). I have written a good deal about our archaeological remains, and I also built a private museum for housing various tools, implements, etc., of bygone husbandry and crafts. In 1938 I fell over a concealed trough in long grass, and the accident resulted in a long and dangerous illness through which I lost my leg. I have not yet recovered from this."

* * *

In 1933 Mr. Massingham married Anne Penelope Webbe; they have no children. In 1925 he edited a selection from the writings of his distinguished father, Henry William Massingham (1860-1924). He has also edited an anthology, *Poems About Birds* (1922), which Sir J. C. Squire in his preface called "delightful and representative."

PRINCIPAL WORKS: St. Francis of Assisi, 1913; Letters to X, 1919; People and Things, 1919; Dogs, Birds, and Others, 1919; Natural History Letters From the Spectator, 1921; Some Birds of the Countryside, 1921; Untrodden Ways, 1923; In Praise of England, 1924; Sanctuaries for Birds, 1924; H. W. M.: A Selection From the Writings of H. W. Massingham (ed.) 1925; Downland Man, 1926; Fee, Fi, Fo, Fum, 1926; Pre-Roman Britain, 1927; The Golden Age: The Story of Human Nature, 1927; The Heritage of Man, 1929; The Friend of Shelley: A Memoir of Edward John Trelawny, 1930; Birds of the Sea Shore, 1931, Wold Without End, 1932; London Scene, 1933; Country, 1934; Through the Wilderness, 1935; English Downland, 1936; The Genius of England, 1937; Cotswold Country, 1937; Shepherd's Country, 1938; Country Relics, 1939; Rural England, 1939; Sweet of the Year, 1939; Chiltern Country, 1941; Fall of the Year, 1941.

*MASTERS, EDGAR LEE (August 23, 1868-   ), American poet, novelist, and biographer, was born in Garnett, Kan., the son of Hardin Wallace Masters, an attorney and politician, and Emma J. (Dexter) Masters. He was reared in Petersburg and Lewistown, Ill., the "Spoon River

country" he afterwards made famous. He was educated at Knox College, then read law in his father's office and was admitted to the bar in 1891. The next year he left home abruptly and went to Chicago. He had already had experience as a reporter on local papers and learned the printer's trade, and he had contributed poems and stories to papers and magazines. He had had only a year of college, but his own reading had made of him at twenty-three an educated man, especially in the fields of history and philosophy. He opened a law office in Chicago, and before long had a large and flourishing practice. It was 1920 before he finally abandoned the law for literature. He married Helen Jenkins in 1898, left her and their three children in 1917, and was later divorced from her. His second wife

Pinchot

was Ellen F. Coyne, whom he married in 1926.

It was William Marion Reedy, editor of *Reedy's Mirror* in St. Louis, who made a real poet out of Masters. A book could be written on Reedy's influence on the young writers of his time and region. To Masters he gave a copy of *Epigrams From the Greek Anthology,* in 1913. Masters had written hundreds of derivative poems, had even published three unnoticed volumes of them. Now his feeling for America, for the Middle West, his love and hate of it, his delving into its history, and his turn for rhythmical expression, suddenly fused, under the magic of the Greek epigrams, into the *Spoon River Anthology.* This collection of apocryphal epitaphs from the graveyard of an Illinois town has been called "one of the most original pieces of imaginative literature" ever written. Fundamentally its idea is not new, but the treatment of it is new. In it Masters made articulate a whole ignored or forgotten part of the American soul, and even a part of the human soul.

And in the twenty-five years since then, Masters has kept on writing, industriously, prolifically, earnestly. He has written much more verse—even gone back to Spoon River; he has written novels and boys' stories and lives of Whitman and Mark Twain (he received the Twain Medal in 1927) and Vachel Lindsay, and a bitter attack on Lincoln, which alienated his old friends Lindsay and Carl Sandburg. He has written dramatic and narrative poems, some based on history,

* Died March 5, 1950.

some on the processes of law. In his autobiography he tells frankly the long dreary story of his many quarrels, his troubled personal affairs, his experiences with ingratitude and neglect and injustice. He is a cynic and a pessimist, but one with a lively sense of humor, a love for nature and for the fullness of life, and even with a quality of reverence, the constant disillusionment of which perhaps creates his open bitterness. He has never duplicated either the immense popular success or the literary achievement of the original *Spoon River Anthology*. Much of his work has been long-winded, dull, and opinionated beyond endurance. He has washed his dirty linen in public and embarrassed his admirers; he seems always surrounded by turmoil and carries a chip on his shoulder. Yet this is the same man whose exquisite sympathy, poetic clairvoyance, restrained irony, and delicate simplicity gave us a book that will be a classic while America is America. John Cowper Powys called him "a poet of enduring depth and originality," Harry Roskolenko said that "he has left sharp nuances throughout the hard past of American life and letters, and as a poet he has contributed along with some few others the sense of history which has been accepted and moulded into a tradition." Constantly disappointed, those who know his potentialities wait with unfailing hope for their second burgeoning.

Physically, Masters looks more the lawyer than the poet. Robert van Gelder described him in 1942: "Mr. Masters walks very slowly and erectly. He wore a blue suit that, it is reasonable to believe, some tailor considers a masterpiece. The suit shows off good shoulders and a trim waist. His face is ruddy with a combative expression, but . . . his tone is mild and his manner, though impersonal, essentially friendly. He is now in his early seventies, and when he comments that he has 'always been vigorous' the statement is easy to believe." He has lived for some years in New York, but is seldom seen at literary gatherings. "I don't want to be tied up with anyone, with any group," he protests. "As a writer, I have no relationships." In seclusion, and regularly at work on some new volume (he has hundreds of unpublished poems), he nurses what Powys called his "solidity of mind, grim pot-house humor, and massive quizzical passivity."

PRINCIPAL WORKS: *Poetry*—A Book of Verses, 1898; Songs and Sonnets (anonymous) 1910 and 1912; Maximilian (blank verse drama) 1902; Spoon River Anthology, 1915; Songs and Satires, 1916; The Great Valley, 1917; Toward the Gulf, 1918; Starved Rock, 1919; Domesday Book, 1920; The Open Sea, 1921; The New Spoon River, 1924; Selected Poems, 1925; Lee: A Dramatic Poem, 1926; Jack Kelso, 1928; The Fate of the Jury, 1929; Gettysburg, Manila, Acoma, 1930; Godbey, 1931; The Serpent in the Wilderness, 1933; Richmond, 1934; Invisible Landscapes, 1935; Poems of People, 1936; The New World, 1937; More People, 1939. *Novels*—Mitch Miller, 1920; Children of the Market Place, 1922; Skeeters Kirby, 1923; The Nuptial Flight, 1923; Mirage, 1924; Kit O'Brien, 1927; The Tide of Time, 1937. *Miscellaneous*—Blood of the Prophets, 1905; Althea (play) 1907; The Trifler (play) 1908; Lichee Nuts, 1930; Lincoln—The Man, 1931; The Tale of Chicago, 1933; Dramatic Duologues, 1934; Vachel Lindsay, 1935; The Golden Fleece of California, 1936; Whitman, 1937; Across Spoon River (autobiography) 1937; Mark Twain, 1938; The Living Thoughts of Emerson (ed.) 1940; The Sangamon, 1942.

ABOUT: Hansen, H. Mid-West Portraits; Jones, L. First Impressions; Lowell, A. Tendencies in Modern American Poetry; Masters, E. L. Across Spoon River; American Mercury December 1926; American Review September 1924; Bookman August 1929; Century Magazine August 1925; Modern Language Notes June 1930; New York Times Book Review February 15, 1942; Poetry May 1931, April 1936, March and July 1937, January 1940; Revue Littéraire Comparée April 1930; Saturday Review of Literature August 26, 1933, September 12, 1936; Sewanee Review July 1933; Time November 16, 1936, November 22, 1937.

*MATHER, FRANK JEWETT (July 6, 1868-), American art critic, was born in Deep River, Conn., the son of Frank Jewett Mather and Caroline Arms (Graves) Mather. He was educated at Williams College (B.A. 1889, L.H.D. 1913), Johns Hopkins University (Ph.D. 1892), the University of Berlin, and the École des Hautes Études, Paris. From 1893 to 1900 he taught English and Romance languages at Williams College. For the next ten years he was successively an editorial writer and art critic on the New York *Evening Post* and assistant editor of the *Nation*. He has also, since 1923, been joint editor of *Art Studies*. From 1910 to 1933 he was professor of art and archaeology at Princeton; he is now emeritus professor. He is a member of the National Institute of Arts and Letters, the American Academy of Arts and Sciences, the American Philosophical Society, and the Dante Society, and a corresponding member of the Hispanic Society of America. In 1905 he married Ellen Suydam Mills; they have a son and a daughter. In 1917 he was an ensign in the United States Navy Reserve Force. He lives now at Washington Crossing, Pa.

Although he lists himself as a Socialist, Dr. Mather was one of the "old guard" of the school of Humanism represented by Irving Babbitt and Paul Elmer More, but decidedly less reactionary than either, and was one of the contributors to the symposium, *Humanism in America*. His special field in art is

* Died November 11, 1953.

classic art, but in his works he leans over backward to be tolerant to all schools and entirely objective; in fact his chief fault is too rigid a discipline over his personal feelings and views. In spite of this, he has sometimes been called "our leading critic of art." Guy Pène du Bois has called him "a rare man able to look at pictures and judge them on their merit."

PRINCIPAL WORKS: Homer Martin: Poet in Landscape, 1912; The Collectors (short stories) 1912; Estimates in Art, 1916 (Series 2, 1931); The Portraits of Dante, 1921; A History of Italian Painting, 1923; Ulysses in Ithaca, 1926; Modern Painting, 1927; Concerning Beauty, 1935; Venetian Painters, 1936; Western European Painting of the Renaissance, 1939.

ABOUT: Bookman March 1930.

MATSON, NORMAN HÄGHEJM

(1893-   ), American novelist and journalist, is of Norwegian stock. "When, speaking the literal truth, I say  that I was born in the shadow of a factory in an industrial town in the Middle West and raised in a tenement in a working-class district of San Francisco, the pictures that flash in the minds of my friends from London — and Moscow (for an example) are likely to have very little to do with the pictures stored in my memory," Matson wrote in "The Shortest Way Out Was to the Left," an autobiographical article, in the American Review for September 1934. The house, as a matter of fact, had eight rooms, and a damson plum grew by the door of the white barn. The tenement was a corner flat with a bay-windowed parlor, and a library where Matson's father used to lie on the couch and chuckle over Pickwick Papers. In a dream recorded in 1930, Matson recalls "the scrub-oak forest in Michigan where I built a shack as a small boy. Again seated on the slope of Twin Peaks I felt the heat and blinked the vast glare of San Francisco in flames." "The trouble with the district [where he was raised], according to a young equalitarian like me, was that there was too much equality there." Young Matson decided to rise above his environment; attended night high school; and wrote poems for the Masses. He achieved a two-room apartment of his own in an Italian slum, with woodcuts on the walls of his living room. After a short time in railroading, Matson turned to journalism, working on a California labor news-

paper; going East to work at the copy desk of the Socialist paper, the Call, in New York; and also holding jobs on the London Daily Herald and L'Humanité, in Paris. "I am not keen for fantasy (but I like my own very much)," according to Matson, whose first novel, Flecker's Magic (1926) was termed by the Boston Transcript "delightful fantasy produced without effort, and without affectation." It concerns Spike Flecker, a Minnesota art student in Paris, who meets a young witch who causes an omnibus to overturn, and grants him his choice of wishes.

Day of Fortune (1928), its successor, was written in Norway; and describing the pleasure and tragedy of childhood and middle-class life in a Scandinavian-American family, was regarded by some reviewers as semi-autobiographical. The New York Times called it a "powerful naturalistic novel." In 1925 Matson married Susan Glaspell,qv the American playwright, and they settled in Truro, Mass. The marriage was later dissolved.

The Log of the Coriolanus (1930) is the record of Matson's 3100-mile voyage from New Bedford to Cape Verde and Praia, Brazil, on an old iron bark. "Never—not in California, New York, here and there in Europe, in youth or during youth's long funeral, have I felt such peace," he wrote one day in his log.

Matson has written short stories for the Saturday Evening Post and Collier's, and his Pop Bigelow stories written for the Woman's Home Companion in 1933-34 were also much enjoyed. His satirical play, The Comic Artist, written with Susan Glaspell, was more than once on the verge of being brought into New York. Doctor Fogg (1929), like Flecker's Magic, was an excursion into fantasy, and was ranked by John Carter ("Jay Franklin") with Wells' When the Sleeper Wakes as a scientific satire.

E. M. Forster quotes approvingly from Flecker's Magic in his Aspects of the Novel, as an example of fantasy in the novel. "Thus again and again—the mark of the true fantasist—does Norman Matson merge the kingdoms of magic and common sense by using words that apply to both, and the mixture he has created comes alive. . . . There are always surprises in the working of a fresh mind, and to the end of time good literature will be made round this notion of a wish." In 1941 Matson completed The Passionate Witch, a novel left unfinished by its author, the American fantasist Thorne Smith.qv Bats in the Belfry (1942) is a sequel to this novel.

PRINCIPAL WORKS: Flecker's Magic, 1926; The Comic Artist: A Play in Three Acts (with S. Glaspell) 1927; Day of Fortune, 1928; Doctor Fogg, 1929; The Log of the Coriolanus, 1930; Bats in the Belfry, 1942.

ABOUT: Forster, E. M. Aspects of the Novel; American Review September 1934; Saturday Evening Post June 1, 1935.

MATTHEWS, BRANDER. See "AMERICAN AUTHORS: 1600-1900"

*MATTHIESSEN, FRANCIS OTTO

(February 19, 1902-   ), American educator and literary critic, writes: "Since my chief interest is in the art  and cultural history of America, I count it particularly fortunate that as a child I had already become acquainted with many regions of our country. Born in Pasadena, Calif., my first years were spent partly there, partly with

Bachrach

my grandfather in central Illinois. After attending Hackley School at Tarrytown, N.Y., and a brief interval in the Royal Air Force at Toronto in 1918, I went through Yale [B.A. 1923], and thereafter as a Rhodes Scholar to New College, Oxford [B.Litt. 1925]. I was attracted to Harvard to do my doctorate [M.A. 1926, Ph.D. 1927], since I wanted to work under Professor John Lowes. My undergraduate concentration had been in English and Greek, and little attention had been called to our own cultural heritage. But stimulated by the early work of Van Wyck Brooks, I became interested in its rediscovery. I wanted to place our master-works in their cultural setting, but beyond that I wanted to discern what constituted the lasting value of these books as works of art.

"I was an instructor at Yale for two years, and since 1929, with the exception of a year in New Mexico and a year in Kittery, Maine, I have been teaching at Harvard, where I am now an associate professor of history and literature. I enjoy teaching as a spur to further knowledge, and I greatly value the stimulus of contact with the students. But I have long felt that the tragic defect in our education was that most of its scholarship was in a vacuum, that our scholars did not even recognize, let alone perform, their social responsibilities. I was, therefore, very glad to become one of the charter members of a local of the Teachers' Union at Harvard in 1935. I believed then

and believe increasingly, in this time of crisis, that the main hope for a healthy democracy lies in the progressive labor movement. The only healthy state for the critic and scholar is to keep breaking down all the barriers of segregation and false privilege that shut him away from the fullest participation in the life of the community."

* * *

Dr. Matthiessen is unmarried, and lives in Eliot House, Cambridge, Mass. He is chairman of the Board of Tutors in history and literature at Harvard. His style has been called "closely written, compact, mature," and Dorothy Van Doren has said: "His tone is distinguished and civilized." His major work to date, *American Renaissance* (1941), was called by the *Saturday Review of Literature* "perhaps the most profound work of literary criticism on historical principles by any living American."

PRINCIPAL WORKS: Sarah Orne Jewett, 1929; Translation: An Elizabethan Art, 1931; The Achievement of T. S. Eliot: An Essay in the Nature of Poetry, 1935; American Renaissance: Art and Expression in the Age of Emerson and Whitman, 1941.

MAUDE, AYLMER (March 28, 1858-August 25, 1938), English writer, best known as the leading translator of Tolstoy, was born at Ipswich, the son of the Rev. F. H. Maude and Lucy (Thorpe) Maude, both Quakers. After preliminary education at Christ's Hospital in London (1868-74) he went to Moscow, at sixteen, to enter the Lyceum for further study. After leaving the Lyceum he remained in the country three years as a private tutor of the English language. Maude returned to London to engage in business for about ten years, then returned to Russia to become head of the Russian Carpet Company in Moscow from 1890 to 1897. Still interested in literature, he found time to pay many visits to the country estate of Count Leo Tolstoi, Yasnaya Polyana, which eventually became a sort of shrine to the novelist's admirers throughout the world. Maude, with his Quaker heritage, had been attracted to Tolstoy's philosophy of absolute non-resistance to violence. He also studied the Doukhobors, a Russian nonconformist sect persecuted for many years by the Czarist government for their refusal to bear arms and their contention that all men are equal, and in 1899 he assisted Tolstoy and committees of British and American Quakers in arranging the migration of 7500 of the sect to Canada, where they settled in Saskatchewan, and still occasionally perplex the local authorities with their beliefs. In 1897 Maude had resigned from the carpet company to devote all his time to writing and translating, and he became a frequent contributor to the *Fortnightly Review,* the *Times Literary Supplement,* and other periodicals. He married Louise Shanks in 1884, and she collaborated with him in much of his literary work. They had four sons. Besides writing several biographies of Tolstoy, he edited a twenty-one volume centenary edition of Tolstoy's works, and ten years later, although then seventy-nine years old, supervised rehearsals of a London production of Tolstoy's play *The Living Corpse.* In 1932 he had been placed on the Civil List to receive a pension of 100 pounds a year. He died at eighty at Ladywell House near Chelmsford.

"Translators are traitors to those they serve," runs an old Italian proverb, which Maude was fond of quoting. His own first experience of translations had been his introduction, as a boy, to an attractively illustrated edition of *Don Quixote,* the text of which proved much less pleasing than its pictures. When he came to translate Tolstoy, he had a thorough knowledge of the Russian language and was not obliged, like some of his predecessors, to work from a sometimes inaccurate French text. In the last twelve years of his life Tolstoy made emphatic and repeated commendation of Maude's translations; he did not approve those made by the American, Nathan Haskell Dole.*qv* Bernard Shaw once remarked that Maude was to Tolstoy what William Archer had been to Ibsen or Ashton Ellis to Richard Wagner.

PRINCIPAL WORKS: Tolstoy and His Problems: Essays, 1901; A Peculiar People: Ten Doukhobors, 1905; Life of Tolstoy: The First Fifty Years, 1908, Later Years, 1910; Tolstoy on Art and Its Critics, 1924; Marie Stopes: Her Work and Play, 1924; Family Views of Tolstoy, 1926; Leo Tolstoy and His Works, 1930.

ABOUT: New York Times August 25, 1938; Publishers' Weekly September 3, 1938; Slavonic Review April 1939; Wilson Library Bulletin October 1938.

MAUGHAM, WILLIAM SOMERSET

(January 25, 1874-), English novelist and dramatist, was born in Paris, where his father, Robert Ormond Maugham, was solicitor to the British Embassy. He spoke French before he spoke English, though he was of pure English descent. He was the youngest of six sons (his brother is now Lord Maugham and Chief Justice of England). His mother died of tuberculosis when he was eight. Two years later the father followed, from cancer, and the or-

phaned child was sent to his paternal uncle, a clergyman in Whitstable, Kent. What he underwent in that cold and rigid environment he has told poignantly in *Of Human Bondage,* his greatest novel, which except for its ending is almost entirely autobiographical. It was not enough that he could scarcely speak his ancestral tongue, but he was undersized and shy, with the seeds of tuberculosis in his lungs and cursed by a marked stammer—the equivalent of Philip Carey's clubfoot. At thirteen he was sent to King's School, Canterbury, and the intention was that he should proceed to Oxford and prepare to enter the church.

But from the beginning he wanted to write, and he finally secured his uncle's permission to go, when he had been graduated, not to Oxford, but to Heidelberg. There he never matriculated, but he attended lectures and for the first time was able to live a carefree life appropriate to his years. He must, however, his uncle said, choose a profession. He chose medicine, and for six years "walked" St. Thomas's Hospital, London, being qualified in 1898 as a Member of the Royal College of Surgeons and a Licentiate of the Royal College of Physicians. But he never practised, except for his year in the Lambeth slums as an interne—an experience which produced his first novel, *Liza of Lambeth.* He had tried his best to please his uncle; he had worked himself in school into incipient tuberculosis, so that he had to be sent to the South of France to convalesce; he had even endured six weeks apprenticed to a chartered accountant; and now he had qualified as a physician. He still wanted to write.

So for ten years, mostly in Paris, he wrote and starved. His luck turned in 1907, with his first successful play, *Lady Frederick.* Since that time he has never had to think about any means of livelihood except his writing. He poured out plays—at first he was far better known as a dramatist than as a novelist or short story writer; later the balance was reversed—and he traveled, the one thing he had wanted to do even more than to write. He has been several times around the world, knows all Europe well, and has spent long periods in the United States, the South Seas (source of *The Letter* and *Rain*—which first appeared as "Miss

Thompson" in *The Trembling of a Leaf*—and much else of his work), and China. His most beloved country is Spain, on which he has written two interpretative books.

The sole approach to medicine in his later life came during the First World War, when he enlisted with a Red Cross Ambulance Unit. Later, however, he was transferred to the Intelligence Department; out of his experience in secret service grew *Ashenden*. In 1915 he married Lady Wellcome, a widow who had been Syrie Barnardo, daughter of Dr. T. J. Barnardo the philanthropist. They had a daughter, but were divorced in 1927, and Maugham has never remarried. His war experiences caused a flare-up of tuberculosis, and he spent some time in a sanitarium in Scotland. Early in the 1930's he settled, permanently as he thought, in Cap Ferret, Alps Maritimes, France, in his famous Villa Mauresque. (The Moors have some private significance to Maugham; an esoteric Moorish symbol is his "mark" which is on everything he owns.) There, though he proclaimed himself an unsocial being, his hospitality was boundless. At the outbreak of the Second World War, he was assigned to special work at the British Ministry of Information in Paris. The Nazi advance overtook him there. After weeks when he was missing and his fate was unknown, he managed to reach England on a crowded collier, leaving behind him his villa, all his belongings, and his unfinished manuscripts. In October 1940 he came to the United States, ostensibly on a visit but in all probability on a government mission.

Richard A. Cordell has described Maugham as he is now: "a short, slender, middle-aged man with thin brown hair combed straight back, a narrow moustache, and a somewhat sallow complexion." Other characteristics are his observant eyes, his frequent gestures, and his mellow voice, which still retains the hesitancy once a stammer. He is a brilliant though cruel *raconteur*, but a good listener as well. He practically never speaks in public, and shuns publicity. All his life he has been, religiously, an agnostic; in social and political views he is rather far to the right, though he believes that his is a lost world and a dying way of life.

It is the hard truth that Somerset Maugham has many devoted admirers, but also an unusual number of enemies. The reasons are obvious. As Mary M. Colum remarked, he has "the habit of depicting living people in his books, with what often has seemed calculated malice." (*Cakes and Ale*, for example, was taken as a libel on both

Thomas Hardy and Sir Hugh Walpole; Elinor Mordaunt wrote *Gin and Bitters* as an angry riposte. And many who knew Gaugin resented *The Moon and Sixpence*.) His "bland contempt for humanity," his "pukka sahib" attitude combined with an actual dislike for the very upper middle class of which he prefers to write, what Malcolm Cowley called his "patronizingly, smugly, and insultingly tolerant" attitude, "the milk of human kindness, half-soured," are not likely to endear him to his victims or their friends. He himself says: "My sympathies are limited. . . . I can never forget myself. . . . I have never felt some of the fundamental emotions of normal men." Mrs. Colum summed him up by saying that he is "too intelligent for the rest of his equipment." Only in *Of Human Bondage* has he ever lowered the mask which by now is firmly fixed to his countenance. Only for that great book may he be named a genius.

And yet when all this is said of Maugham (and when one has omitted the hundred little kindnesses and generosities which actually have marked his private life), how much there is left! Richard Aldington saluted him as "a master of the hard long art of writing," and he is that above all. Cowley praised his "clean prose and solid form," William R. Benét called him not unjustly "the English de Maupassant," Grant Overton noted that "his writing is always visual. . . . He makes every word count, every character, every situation, every scene." His mastery of the dramatic form has redounded to the good of his work as novelist and short story writer. He resents being called a "professional" writer, a "competent" writer; and yet there is no denigration involved in recognizing his superb lucidity, his urbanity, his precision, his acid irony, his brilliant wit. It is his very competency, his professionalism as distinguished from amateurism, which enables him to skim lightly over taboos (as in "The Book Bag"), to win and hold a huge audience without ever flattering or catering to it, to push his cheerful cynicism down his readers' throats and make them like it. He is definite and clear, deft and sure of himself; and if, as Mrs. Colum laments, he lost early "his flare and his wings," at least he has never lost his head. To quote Aldington again: "Maugham's work gives the impression of coming from an accomplished man of the world and not from a man in a library. . . . He refuses to conform to anybody's idea of what he ought to think and feel and do, and has labored with the utmost sincerity to discover what he really does think and feel, what sort of things he really wishes to do. . . . Out of such essential integrity and truth to himself comes the genuine artist."

PRINCIPAL WORKS: *Fiction*—Liza of Lambeth, 1897; The Making of a Saint, 1898; Orientations (short stories) 1899; The Hero, 1901; Mrs. Craddock, 1902; The Merry-Go-Round, 1904; The Bishop's Apron (novelization of Loaves and Fishes) 1906; The Explorer (novelization of play) 1907; The Magician, 1908; Of Human Bondage, 1915; The Moon and Sixpence, 1919; The Trembling of a Leaf (short stories) 1921; On a Chinese Screen (short stories) 1922; The Painted Veil, 1925; The Casuarina Tree (short stories) 1926; Ashenden: or, The British Agent, 1928; Cakes and Ale: or, The Skeleton in the Cupboard, 1930; First Person Singular (short stories) 1931; The Narrow Corner, 1932; Ah King (short stories) 1933; Altogether, 1934; East and West (collected short stories) 1934; Cosmopolitans (short stories) 1936; Theatre, 1937; Christmas Holiday, 1939; The Mixture as Before (short stories) 1940; Up at the Villa, 1941. *Plays (dates of production)*—Man of Honour, 1903; Lady Frederick, 1907; The Explorer, 1908; Jack Straw, 1908; Mrs. Dot, 1908; Penelope, 1909; Smith, 1909; The Tenth Man, 1910; The Trivial Shepherd, 1910; Landed Gentry, 1910; Loaves and Fishes, 1911; Plays (published) 1912; The Land of Promise, 1914; Caroline, 1916; Love in a Cottage, 1918; Caesar's Wife, 1919; Home and Beauty, 1919; The Unknown, 1920; The Circle, 1921; East of Suez, 1922; Our Betters, 1923; The Camel's Back, 1924; The Letter, 1927; The Constant Wife, 1927; The Sacred Flame, 1929; The Breadwinner, 1930; For Services Rendered, 1932; Sheppey, 1933. *Miscellaneous*—The Land of the Blessed Virgin, 1905; The Gentleman in the Parlour, 1930; Don Fernando, 1935; The Summing Up (autobiography) 1938; Books and You, 1940; Strictly Personal, 1941; The Hour Before the Dawn, 1942.

ABOUT: Bason, F. Bibliography of W. Somerset Maugham; Cordell, R. A. W. Somerset Maugham; Dottin, P. Le Théâtre de W. Somerset Maugham; Maugham, W. S. The Summing Up; Ward, R. H. William Somerset Maugham; Bookman November 1926; Canadian Forum May 1936; Century Magazine May 1925; Forum May 1938; Life December 2, 1940; New Republic August 22, 1934, March 30, 1938; New Statesman and Nation June 15, 1940; New York Times Book Review November 24, 1940; New Yorker June 7, 1941; Saturday Review of Literature June 17, August 19, 1939, July 27, 1940; World Today August 1928.

MAURIAC, FRANÇOIS (October 11, 1885-), French poet, playwright and novelist, was born in the rue du Pas-Saint-Georges in Bordeaux, of a middle-class family of landlord-farmers, clothiers and sugar refiners. Fatherless when only twenty months old, François was brought up in the strictest Roman Catholic orthodoxy by his mother, who guided the destiny of her daughter and four sons: Raymond, the oldest, became a lawyer and writer whose novel *Individu* won him the Prix du Prémier Roman for 1934; Jean, a priest; Pierre, professor at the Faculty of Medicine of the

University of Bordeaux; François, one of France's greatest writers.

Until he was twenty François lived in Bordeaux, spending his vacations and holidays at the Saint-Symphorien estate which his father had inherited from a grand-uncle, at his maternal grandmother's Château-Lange, or at his paternal grandfather's Langon by the Bordeaux-Cette railway line. This background of his boyhood, the Gascon Landes, with their pine-woods, vineyards, and melancholy landscape, exerted a strong influence during his formative years and appears as the setting of his novels.

At five the boy was sent to the Jardin d'Enfants, a kindergarten run by the Sisters of the Holy Family in the rue Mirail, and then to the Institution du Grand-Lebrun of the Marionites fathers, in Candéran, some five miles from Bordeaux. The child's routine was rather strenuous: he was up at five-thirty and never returned home till seven in the evening, when at last free he devoted himself to his diary, his poems and his favorite authors. Gradually Lamartine, Musset and Vigny usurped the place of his early favorites: Mme. de Ségur, Jules Verne, and Paul Feval, but never that of Zénaïde Fleuriot—"I think I can say with truth that no book has moved me more deeply than a simple and innocent novel called *Feet of Clay* which I adored when I was fourteen. It was the work of an old and virtuous woman called Zénaïde Fleuriot, and it was full of imagination and sensibility. . . . Yet when a journalist asks me the names of the writers who have influenced me most I quote Balzac and Dostoievsky, but I never dare mention Mlle. Fleuriot." François was a sad child, easily hurt, *"un enfant triste et que tout blessait,"* who loved from the earliest "the liturgy, and the music and—I hardly dare say it—the sacraments. . . . At the age of sixteen I tried desperately to prove to myself the truth of this religion to which I was eternally bound. On my table—as a witness to this adolescent obsession of mine —there lies a battered edition of Pascal's *Pensées.*"

At the Bordeaux *lycée* (whose principal was André Gide's brother-in-law) Mauriac proved himself a brilliant student, winning a first prize in French. Besides Pascal and Racine, "required" authors, he became particularly fond of Verlaine, Rimbaud,

Baudelaire and Francis Jammes. With his *licence* from the Faculty of Letters Mauriac went to Paris in 1906 and was admitted, after a short preparation, to the École de Chartes. He remained only a few months, but became acquainted in his pension at 104 rue Vaugirard with other young men interested in literature, was elected President of the Cercle Montalembert and wrote poems and poetry criticism for *Temps Présent* and *Revue de la Jeunesse*. Finally in 1909 he collected his poems and published them under the title *Les Maints Jointes*. The veteran writer Paul Bourget liked them so well that he recited one of them to Barrès who immediately ordered a copy of the book Mauriac had not dared send him one originally because he idolized Barrès).

From then on Mauriac was sure of his vocation. After another gifted sheaf of verse, *L'Adieu à l'Adolescence* (1911), dedicated to Barrès, he turned to the novel. Following a visit to Francis Jammes at Orthez, and a short retreat with the Dominican monks at Saulchoir, in 1912 he founded with Lafon *Les Cahiers*, a magazine devoted exclusively to Catholic arts and letters. The following year he published his first novel, *L'Enfant Chargé de Chaines*, and married Jeanne Lafont, the daughter of a functionary in the Ministry of Finances. On his return from a trip in Italy, war broke out and he joined the auxiliary service in the capacity of hospital assistant in a sanitary unit. For months he worked in Salonika but had to be repatriated, the victim of malaria—during the upset he lost the manuscript of his biography of Lacordaire.

After the war Mauriac published *La Chair et le Sang* (1920) and *Préséances* (1921); the latter, considered a satiric picture of Bordeaux society caused a great stir. However it was not until February 1922, with *The Kiss of the Leper*, that, aged thirty-seven, he attained renown. The troubled, adolescent gropings of his early work gave way to a mature, skilful series of novels: *Le Fleuve de Feu* (1923), *Genitrix* (1924), *The Desert of Love* (1925), *Thérèse* (1927), *Coups de Couteaux* (1928) and *Destinies* (1928), in which, limiting his observation to Bordeaux and its countryside, he scourged the narrow-minded bigotry, snobbery, and meanness of old provincial Catholic families. The literary worth of these novels was fully recognized by the French Academy when in 1925 it awarded their author the Grand Prix du Roman, but from a religious viewpoint Mauriac's soul, broken up by unceasing strife, was an arena

of contradiction. Grace and peace he did not attain until his conversion, autumn 1928-spring 1929. While *Suspicion* (1930) reflected this period of transition, *The Viper's Tangle* (1932) definitely showed the emergence of the *Catholic* novelist. Now he refused to sponsor guilt (both in *Thérèse* and *Destinies* he had sympathized with the guilty ones), and portrayed the transgressor in all his abject reality, demonstrating the misery of lives deprived of God. A similar conciliatory attitude toward the Church is evident in *Le Mystère Frontenac* (1933) and *La Fin de la Nuit* (1935) in which Thérèse is brought back to suffer for her sins.

By this time the poet, novelist, and critic —he had written penetrative essays on Racine (1928), Molière, Rousseau, and Flaubert (1930), Pascal (1931)—had became a national figure: on March 14, 1932, he was elected President of the Société des Gens de Lettres and on June 1, 1933, to the French Academy to occupy Eugene Brieux's *fauteuil*.

More recently Mauriac has shown his mastery of fiction in *Les Anges Noirs* (1936), *Plongées*, and *Les Chemins de la Mer* (1939), and has explored new fields: biography, with his magnificent *Life of Jesus* (1937); and the drama, with *Asmodée: or, The Intruder* (1938), which has been called "one of the great plays of our time, the first by a living author to be produced by the Comédie Française."

Mauriac is described as a fragile, invalidish man, "a buried heart"—"the musical inflections of [whose] voice recall the South of France. His language is marked by provincial words. The indifference of this man, the somber light in his eyes, the reticences of his compressed, evasive lips, conceal a bitterness which is in keeping with all his work."

After the fall of France in 1940, "Mauriac, whose Catholicism," writes Frank Jones, "is singularly free from the taint of reaction, published a long and eloquent statement of admiration for writers as diverse as Bergson, Maurras, Valéry, Claudel, Proust, Gide, Montherlant, Giono, and Malraux." The concluding passage reads: "On the morrow of a crushing defeat, let us not be taken in by the niggardly, envious or knavish men who presume to exact a synthetic moralism from the writers of France. Let us not become accomplices of the impotent creatures who are convinced, in the great silence after the cyclone, that their turn has come at last. . . . After our disaster as before it, great books will remain great books; and, for all their sublime principles, writers who are nothing will not cease to belong to nothing."

WORKS AVAILABLE IN ENGLISH TRANSLATION: *Drama*—Asmodée: or, The Intruder, 1939. *Essays and Criticism*—Maundy Thursday, 1932; God and Mamnon, 1936; Life of Jesus, 1937; Communism and Christians, 1938; The Living Thoughts of Pascal (ed.) 1940. *Fiction*—Thérèse, 1928; The Desert of Love, 1929; Destinies, 1929; The Family (The Kiss of the Leper and Genitrix) 1930; Suspicion, 1932; The Viper's Tangle, 1933.

ABOUT: Archambault, P. Jeunes Maîtres; Chaigne, L. Vies et Oeuvres d'Ecrivains; Du Bos, C. Mauriac et le Problème du Roman Catholique; Fillon, A. François Mauriac; Mauriac, F. Commencements d'une Vie, God and Mamnon, and Journal; Rousseaux, A. Littérature du Vingtième Siecle; Schwarzenbach, J. Der Dichter Zwiespätligen Lebens F. Mauriac; Stansbury, M. H. French Novelists of Today; Bookman January 1931; Commune March 1939; French Review December 1939; Nouvelle Revue Française February 1939; Revue de Deux Mondes June 15, 1933; Revue de l'Université de Bruxelles May-July 1932; Revue Hebdomadaire, June 26, 1937; Studies December 1933.

MAURIER. See DU MAURIER

MAUROIS, ANDRÉ (1885-), French biographer and novelist, writes: "I was born at Elbeuf, Seine-Inferieure. My parents were both Alsatian in origin, but had left Alsace for Normandy after the war of 1870.

"I was educated first at the little *lycée* at Elbeuf, then at the *lycée* at Rouen, which was the nearest large city. I received there my bachelor's degree in letters and science, then studied for a degree in philosophy at the University of Caen.

"I wanted to write, but I did not know if I should be able to do it. My father was an industrialist and wished me to enter his factory. The man who has had the greatest influence on my life, and who was my professor of philosophy (Alain), advised me to do what my father wanted. 'If you wish to write,' he told me, 'nothing will be more useful to you than to have lived first, to have employed yourself in a trade and to have known responsibility.'

"The great influences of my youth were, first that of this Alain, who was himself a remarkable writer, and next, among books, those of Anatole France, the great French classics, and also the works of Kipling, whose philosophy of action pleased me.

"I remained at the factory from the age of eighteen to twenty-six, then the war of 1914 broke out. As I knew English, I was attached first as interpreter, then as liaison officer, to the British Army. There I continued, as I had done all my life, to write for my own pleasure, describing what I saw without any intention of publishing my notes. These were read by one of my comrades, a French officer like myself, who asked me why I did not give them to a publisher. I answered that I did not know any. He then took it upon himself to take them to Paris, and got them published very quickly. They formed my first book, *Les Silences du Colonel Bramble* [*The Silence of Colonel Bramble*]. This book, partly because of circumstances (it was published in 1918, in the midst of the war) had a great popular and critical success, so that I found myself, from one day to the next, transformed from a factory official and an officer into an author.

"After that, I was naturally only too happy to continue a career which had been since my childhood the object of my desires. Since then I have published in twenty years a great number of books.

"I am married to Simone de Caillavet, herself the daughter of a French writer and playwright. I have three children. I live in winter at Neuilly-s/-Seine, in summer at Perigord (Excideuil). [Written 1939.]

"My literary friends are the writers of my generation: Mauriac, Morland, Giraudoux, Jules Romains, Duhamel. I have much friendship and admiration for Paul Valéry. I was the intimate friend of Marshal Lyautey, whose life I have written.

"I shall soon publish in America an *Art of Life*, which has already appeared in France, and in two or three years a life of Woodrow Wilson."

* * *

André Maurois' original name was Émile Herzog, and he is of Jewish descent; but he has taken the name of Maurois in his personal life as well as in his writing. His first wife was Janine de Szymkiewicz, whom he married in 1912, and who died in 1924 leaving two sons. He has a daughter by his second wife, whom he married in 1926. He is a Knight of the British Empire (1938), a member of the French Academy and of the Legion of Honor, and has honorary degrees from Oxford, Edinburgh, St. Andrews, and Princeton. His manner is alert and vivacious, his speech quick and nervous. He is a sophisticate who writes for people who love the urbane and the witty. As Harold Laski has remarked: "He is always elegant, always well bred. . . . He ministers to those who want the elements of culture without the need to stir the muddy waters of scholarship." His silvery hair, receding from a high forehead, frames (to quote Sisley Huddleston) "heavy-lidded bright eyes in a hatchet-shaped, sensitive face." He has visited the United States several times, and has lectured at Yale and Princeton, as well as at Cambridge University in England. After the fall of France he came to America "for the duration."

It has been said that Maurois writes "novelized biographies and autobiographical novels." The first half of the criticism is undoubtedly true. He has little creative power, but much power of imaginative adaptation. His pitfalls are sentimentality and superficiality, but they are offset by sympathy, delicacy of style, ironic wit, and brilliant description. He is one of the foremost practitioners of the "new" biography whose father was Lytton Strachey.

WORKS AVAILABLE IN ENGLISH: *Fiction*—The Silence of Colonel Bramble, 1919; The Conversation of Dr. O'Grady, 1921; Bernard Quesnay, 1927; The Atmosphere of Love, 1929; The Weigher of Souls, 1931; The Family Circle, 1932; Ricochets (short stories) 1935; The Thought-Reading Machine, 1938; A Time for Silence, 1942. *Biographies and Essays*—Ariel: The Life of Shelley, 1924; Mape: The World of Illusion, 1926; The Life of Disraeli, 1927; Aspects of Biography, 1929; Next Chapter, War Against the Moon, 1929; Byron, 1930; Conversation, 1930; The Country of Thirty-Six Thousand Wishes, 1930; Lyautey, 1931; Tourgeniev, 1931; A Private Universe, 1932; Voltaire, 1932; The Edwardian Era (in England: King Edward and His Times) 1933; Dickens, 1934; Prophets and Poets, 1935; The Miracle of England (in England, A History of England) 1937; Chateaubriand, 1938; Tragedy in France, 1940; Why France Fell, 1941.

ABOUT: Chaigne, L. André Maurois; Lemaître, G. E. André Maurois; Atlantic Monthly March 1929; Living Age January 1931, June 1933; Pictorial Review November 1933; Time November 13, 1939.

MAWSON, CHRISTOPHER ORLANDO SYLVESTER (1870-November 4, 1938), Anglo-American lexicographer,

was born in England, a member of the Yorkshire family which included Sir Douglas Mawson, the famous Antarctic explorer, and Professor Thomas H. Mawson, city planner and remodeler of Athens. He spent years of study and research in Europe and the Orient, and was a member of the Royal Asiatic Society and the Société

Asiatique. After acting as consulting specialist to the late Sir James Murray of the great Oxford English Dictionary, he was engaged by Dr. Benjamin E. Smith, editor of the *Century Dictionary* published by the Century Company of New York, as revising editor of Sanskrit and Anglo-Indian terms. Dr. Mawson (he was both Ph.D. and Litt.D.) next proceeded to Webster's *New International Dictionary* at Springfield, Mass., working also on the *Webster Collegiate Dictionary*. His home was in Wellesley, Mass., and for several years he ran the Mawson Editorial School in Boston. *Professional Book Editing* (1926) is an outgrowth of the correspondence-school work of this establishment. Dr. Mawson's years of travel in all parts of the globe gave weight to his *Geographical Manual and New Atlas* done for Doubleday, Page & Co. in the year of the entry of the United States into the First World War. Work on various revisions of Roget's *Thesaurus* also made his name familiar to literary and editorial workers. His *Dictionary of Foreign Terms* includes eleven thousand entries from fifty-six languages, with translations and explanations.

Dr. Mawson, a tall, well set-up individual with a pronounced English accent, died at sixty-eight while motoring with his wife, Mrs. Katharine (Whiting) Mawson, in Boston. He succeeded in bringing the car to a stop before he succumbed to a heart-attack. His last work, *The Complete Desk Book,* was finished by his collaborator, J. W. Robson.

PRINCIPAL WORKS: Doubleday, Page & Co.'s Geographical Manual and New Atlas, 1917; Style-Book for Writers and Editors, 1926; Professional Book Editing, 1926; The Roget Dictionary of Synonyms and Antonyms, 1931; The Dictionary Companion, 1932; The International Book of Names, 1933; Dictionary of Foreign Terms Found in English and American Writings of Yesterday, 1934; The Complete Desk Book (completed by J. W. Robson) 1939.

ABOUT: Boston Transcript November 5, 1938; New York Times November 5, 1938.

*MAXTONE GRAHAM, Mrs. JOYCE (ANSTRUTHER) ("Jan Struther") (June 6, 1901-), English writer, is the

daughter of the late Hon. Dame Eva Anstruther, D.B.E., who was made a Dame of the British Empire because of her service to the Empire in the First World War, as Director of the Camps Library, which sent millions of books to the troops overseas. (Since her mother wrote books as Eva Anstruther, and since her mother-in-law also wrote, the adoption of a pseudonym seemed advisable when Joyce herself began to contribute to English magazines. She combined her first initial with the family name to create Jan Struther. She was educated in London, and in 1923 married Anthony Maxtone Graham, of an old Perthshire family, "more highland than lowland—to be exact, from the border country," explain Stephen Vincent Benét and Rosemary Benét in a biographical sketch of Jan Struther. Her

father-in-law was the senior partner of Maxtone Graham & Sime, of Edinburgh, London, and Canada. The Maxtone Grahams have two sons and a daughter. The eldest son, James, is a farmer and a Home Guard in England; the two younger children are with their mother in New York City for the duration. Mr. Maxtone Graham, an insurance broker before he joined the Scots Guards, was taken prisoner in Libya in 1942.

Jan Struther's book of sketches of family life, *Mrs. Miniver,* was a summer choice in 1939 of the Book-of-the-Month Club, a best-seller, and a hugely successful movie. "The success is not surprising," wrote the Benéts, "because these essays are beautifully written, with form, with style and a deceptive simplicity. They may look easy to do. So does Mr. Housman's poetry look simple to a beginner. In both cases, every word is in place, like the flowers in a pruned and tended garden. Mrs. Miniver also manages to project the warmth and wisdom of an engaging personality." She first appeared on the court page of the London *Times;* the series was suggested by Peter Fleming of the *Times.* The family of Mrs. Miniver became inextricably confused in the public mind with Jan Struther's family; her husband had to inure himself to being addressed as Clem at his club; and James, Janet, and Robert Maxtone Graham have been assumed to be Toby, Judy, and Vin, which their mother says is decidedly not the case. She prefers to write poetry rather than prose. *The Glass Blower* is "grim and stark and not at all charming." *Try Anything Twice* (1938) is a collection of some fifty pieces, mostly humorous, from *Punch,* the *Spectator,* and other magazines. In appearance Jan Struther is "small, dark-haired and very attractive. Like Elizabeth Bennet she has 'a pair of fine eyes' in an expressive face. She is intelligent, outgiving and pleasant."

PRINCIPAL WORKS: Betsinda Dances and Other Poems, 1931; Sycamore Square and Other Poems, 1932; The Modern Struwwelpeter, 1936; When Grandmother Was Small (verses) 1937; Try Anything Twice (essays and sketches) 1938; Mrs. Miniver, 1939; The Glass Blower, 1940; Women of Britain (ed.) 1941.

ABOUT: Book-of-the-Month Club News July 1940; New York Herald Tribune "Books" October 13, 1940; PM Picture News August 30, 1942; Scholastic January 27, 1941.

MAXWELL, WILLIAM BABINGTON

(1866-August 4, 1938), English novelist who signed his works W. B. Maxwell, was the son of an Irishman, John Maxwell, a successful publisher of magazines, and his wife, a Cornish lady, M. E. Braddon, who in her day enjoyed enormous vogue as the writer of *Lady Audley's Secret* and other popular novels (see *British Authors*

of the Nineteenth Century). Brought up in easy circumstances at Lichfield House, Richmond, Surrey, the boy had a happy childhood, loving his parents and indulged by them, and accustomed to meeting famous people of the social, literary, artistic, and theatrical worlds. Educated at a private school, he left early to take up pictorial art, encouraged by W. P. Frith. He studied at the school run by the animal painter, Frank Calderon, then at Ridley's and finally on his own account at the British Museum; but he merely played at art and gave it up before he was twenty.

For some time he pursued only the lighter occupations of a wealthy young man: theatre-going, traveling, hunting fox and deer from the family's country house, Bank, near Lyndhurst, in the New Forest. On his twenty-first birthday his father made him manager of an annual called *The Mistletoe Bough.* He saw that it badly needed modernizing, but though he improved its literary and illustrative standard his reforms were insufficiently thorough and in a few years the annual died through lack of support from advertisers. There followed more hunting and social life, then a space in which he acted as secretary to his busy and successful mother, and then a few writings of his own. He became a regular contributor of stories and sketches to *The World,* edited by Edmund Yates, a friend of the family. His first two books, *The Countess of Maybury* (1901) and *Fabulous Fancies* (1903), were reprints of these periodical pieces. Neither caused notice, but in 1903, Grant Richards, publisher of the second, took Maxwell out to lunch and virtually dragooned him into starting a long novel. Skeptical of his ability, he yet persevered, and when *The Ragged Messenger* appeared in 1904 it had big sales. In later years it was dramatized and three times filmed.

Thenceforward Maxwell never looked back. *Vivien* (1905) and *The Guarded Flame* (1906) consolidated his success, and he was to produce some forty books. *The Devil's Garden* (1913) was banned by the Library Association and so attained big circulation figures for the wrong reasons. When war broke out in 1914, Maxwell helped raise a battalion in the City of London. The novelist himself was partially lame from a skating accident at the age of eleven, but a Richmond doctor now cured him before the end of the year. He had been gazetted lieutenant in the Royal Fusiliers in September 1914; and being now fit, went to France with his unit in July 1915 as railway transport officer. He was at Loos, the Somme and Passchendaele, and served as aide-de-camp (with rank of captain) to General Sir Reginald Barnes, who, however, insisted on sending him home on health grounds at the end of 1917. He had been mentioned in dispatches and had more than once narrowly escaped death.

His mother had died in 1915. In 1920 Maxwell sold the Richmond house and settled in Kensington, London. He became chairman of the Society of Authors and the National Book Council and member of council of the Royal Society of Literature and the Royal Literary Fund. He visited America as delegate to the International Congress of the Motion Picture Arts.

Maxwell's memoirs, *Times Gathered* (1937), bristle with celebrities, ranging from Wilde to Irving, from Lord Curzon to Charles Reade. Almost literally, he "knew everyone and went everywhere." His novels are pleasant realism, lit up by imagination and sympathy and made solid by fine characterization. He could not work to plan, and was a "bad starter." He became more industrious as time went on, but never lacked for long holidays at home or abroad and all kinds of amusement. He was over six feet in height, had a heavy face and high forehead, and the general aspect of compassion for human weakness, and understanding of human character.

He was very happily married, early in the century, to Sydney Brabazon, youngest daughter of the late Charles William Moore, of the Indian Civil Service, by whom he had one son and one daughter. He died at seventy-two.

PRINCIPAL WORKS: *Novels*—The Countess of Maybury, 1901; The Ragged Messenger, 1904; Vivien, 1905; The Guarded Flame, 1906; Hill Rise, 1908; Seymour Charlton, 1909; The Rest Cure, 1910; Mrs. Thompson, 1911; General Mallock's Shadow, 1912; In Cotton Wool, 1912; The Devil's Garden, 1913; The Mirror and the Lamp, 1918; A Man and His Lesson, 1919; A Remedy Against Sin, 1920; A Little More: A Morality, 1921; Spinster of This Parish, 1922; The Day's Journey, 1923; Elaine at the Gates, 1924; Fernande, 1925; Gabrielle: A Romance, 1926; Life: A Study of Self, 1926; The Case of Bevan Yorke, 1927; We Forget Because We Must, 1928; To What Green Altar? 1930; The Concave Mirror, 1931; Amos the Wanderer, 1932; This Is My Man, 1933; And Mr. Wyke Bond, 1934; People of a House, 1934; Men and Women (Tudor Green, The Emotional Journey, Everslade) 1935-37. *Collections of Short Stories*—Tales of the Thames, 1892; Fabulous Fancies, 1903; Odd Lengths, 1907; The Great Interruption, 1919; Children of the Night, 1925; Jacob's Ladder and Other Stories, 1937. *Autobiography*—Time Gathered, 1937. *Plays*—The Last Man In, 1910; The Naked Truth (with "G. Paston") 1921.

ABOUT: Adcock, A. St. J. Gods of Modern Grub Street; Gould, G. The English Novel of To-Day; "Lacon" (pseud.). Lectures to Living Authors; Maxwell, W. B. Time Gathered; The Times (London) August 5, 1938.

MAYNE, ETHEL COLBURN (187?-April 30, 1941), English novelist, short-story writer, literary historian, and translator, was the daughter of Charles E. B. Mayne, sometime of the Royal Irish Constabulary and the Irish Resident Magistracy, and Charlotte Emily Henrietta (Sweetman) Mayne, daughter of Captain William Sweetman of the 16th Lancers. The girl was  educated at private schools in Ireland, and published her first short story in John Lane's *Yellow Book* in 1895, under the pseudonym of "Frances E. Huntly." Other stories were contributed to *Chapman's Magazine* and to the *Yellow Book* under this name, but Miss Mayne dropped it when her first book of short stories, *The Clearer Vision*, was published in 1898. As an all-round journalist, Miss Mayne reviewed much fiction in the (London) *Nation* and the *Daily News* and wrote many articles in the *Daily Chronicle* and Yorkshire *Post*. She was also favorably known for her studies of Byron. She was a versatile translator, ranging from Marcelle

Tinayre's *Madame de Pompadour* (1925) and Emil Ludwig's *Wilhelm der Zweite* (1926 and *Goethe* (1928), to the *Letters* of Dostoievsky (1914). Others of her translations were R. A. Bermann's *The Forest Ship*, Margarete Böhme's *The Department Store*, the *Selected Poems* of Carl Spitteler, and, in the field of her own specialty, Charles Du Bos' *Byron* (1932).

Miss Mayne lived at St. Margaret's, Middlesex, and found recreation in her translation and original work, in walking, reading, and playing patience. Her short stories, according to Allan Nevins, showed exquisite pains addressed to essentially inconsequential themes. "Miss Mayne's touch upon reality is delicate, reserved, withdrawing," Robert Morss Lovett once wrote. *Enchanters of Men,* studies of two dozen sirens from Diane de Poitiers to Adah Isaacs Menken, is vivacious and readable. *Regency Chapter: Lady Bessborough and Her Friendships* (1939) is linked to Miss Mayne's Byronic studies through Lady Caroline Lamb, Byron's mistress and the daughter of Lady Bessborough. Miss Mayne died at a nursing house in Torquay, Devonshire, presumably in her late sixties.

PRINCIPAL WORKS: The Clearer Vision (short stories) 1898; Jessie Vandeleur (novel) 1902; The Fourth Ship (novel) 1908; Enchanters of Men, 1909; Things That No One Tells (short stories) 1910; The Romance of Monaco, 1910; Byron, 1912; Browning's Heroines, 1913; One of Our Grandmothers (novel) 1916; Come In (short stories) 1917; Blindman (short stories) 1919; Nine of Hearts, 1923; Inner Circle, 1925; The Life and Letters of Anne Isabella, Lady Noël Byron, 1929; Regency Chapter: Lady Bessborough and Her Friendships, 1939.

ABOUT: West, R. Ending in Earnest; New York Herald Tribune May 3, 1941.

MAYO, KATHERINE (1868-October 9, 1940), American journalist and miscellaneous writer, was born in Ridgeway, Pa., the

K. S. Woerner
1896

daughter of James Henry Mayo and Harriet (Ingraham) Mayo. Her ancestry was American for ten generations. She was educated at private schools in Boston and Cambridge, Mass., and lived for some time in Monmouth, N.J., contributing several articles on colonial, Revolutionary, and mid-century topics, chiefly in the setting of that town, to the New York *Evening Post,* under the pseudonym of

"Katherine Prence." About 1900 Miss Mayo accompanied her father, a mining engineer, to Dutch Guiana, South America, where the population was one-third British East-Indian. Returning to the United States, she traveled thousands of miles verifying data for Oswald Garrison Villard's biography of John Brown, and also assisted in the writing of Horace White's *Life of Lyman Trumbull.* Miss Mayo's own first book was the outcome of the murder of a young paymaster on the Bedford Hills, N.Y., estate of her lifelong friend, Miss Moyca Newell, in August 1913. Although Sam Howell had identified his three murderers, the sheriff-constable proved too timorous to apprehend them. *Justice To All,* a study of the Pennsylvania State Police system, influenced the establishment of the New York State Police in the spring of 1917. Theodore Roosevelt had presented a copy to each of the senators and assemblymen of the state legislature. Twenty-five state troopers were to act as pall-bearers at Miss Mayo's funeral twenty-three years later.

During the First World War Miss Mayo went overseas to study the workings abroad of the Y.M.C.A., at the invitation of Association headquarters, wearing their uniform but paying her own expenses. She exonerated the "Y," but was less lenient to the American administration of the Philippine Islands in her *Isles of Fear* (1925). Two years later came *Mother India,* a sensational study of child-marriage in India with which Katherine Mayo's name is chiefly identified. Indignant students burned a copy in Calcutta; Gandhi repudiated "the charge but not the substance"; and several rebuttals were published, notably *A Son of Mother India Answers,* by Dhan Gopal Mukerji. *Volume Two* is Miss Mayo's own documentation for her statements. In 1934 she published a study of American veterans' compensation; in 1938 a historical study of the type with which she began her career, *General Washington's Dilemma;* and at the time of her death was working on a book about the traffic in narcotics. Miss Mayo died at seventy-two after an illness of several months at her own and Miss Newell's home. She was buried at Bedford Hills. She was an Episcopalian; her club was the Cosmopolitan in New York City. Two sisters survived. Miss Mayo's militant journalism was of the lineage of the "muckrakers" of the first decade of the century.

PRINCIPAL WORKS: Justice to All, 1917; The Standard Bearers, 1918; That Damn Y, 1920; Mounted Justice: True Stories of the Pennsylvania State Police, 1922; Isles of Fear: The Truth

About the Philippines, 1925; Mother India, 1927; Slaves of the Gods (short stories) 1929; Volume Two, 1931; Soldiers What Next! 1934; The Face of Mother India, 1935; General Washington's Dilemma, 1938.

ABOUT: Field, H. H. After Mother India; New York Times October 10, 1940; Newsweek October 21, 1940; Wilson Library Bulletin December 1940.

MAYOR, JOHN EYTON BICKER-STAFFE. See "BRITISH AUTHORS OF THE 19TH CENTURY"

MEAD, MARGARET (December 16, 1901-), American anthropologist, was born in Philadelphia, of Quaker descent, the

Blackstone

daughter of Professor Edward Sherwood Mead, of the University of Pennsylvania, and Emily (Fogg) Mead. She was educated at the Doylestown, Pa., High School, New Hope School for Girls, De Pauw University, Barnard College (B.A. 1923) and Columbia University (M.A. in Psychology 1924, Ph.D. in Anthropology, 1929). Her major expeditions, each of which has resulted in a book embodying her findings, have been: to Samoa as a Fellow of the National Research Council in 1925-26, to study the adolescent girl; to the Admiralty Islands as a Fellow of the Social Science Research Council in 1928-29, to study the thought of the pre-school child; study of an American Indian tribe, 1930; to New Guinea, to study the relationship of sex and temperament in the Arapesh, Mundugumor, and Tchambuli tribes, 1931-33; and to Bali and New Guinea in 1936-39, to study the relationships between character formation and culture, under the auspices of the American Museum of Natural History and the Committee for Research in Dementia Praecox of the 33d Order of Masons, Scottish Rite, Northeastern jurisdiction. Since 1926 she has been assistant curator of Ethnology at the American Museum of Natural History. She has been lecturer in psychology at Washington Square College, New York University, and has been visiting lecturer in child study at Vassar College. She is a member of the American Anthropological Society, the American Ethnological Society, and the Polynesian Society. In 1925 she was an associate of the Bishop Museum, Honolulu.

Margaret Mead's father was an economist, her mother a sociologist, and she says she "probably became attached to social science because it had always been around the house." She has been married twice, first to Reo Franklin Fortune, also an anthropologist, and in 1936 to Gregory Bateson, professor of anthropology at St. John's College, Cambridge. They have an infant daughter.

Miss Mead has done the seemingly impossible in writing scholarly and authoritative books on anthropology that yet have been popular best-sellers. Strongly influenced by Franz Boas, she links anthropology with scientific education, and emphasizes cultural conditioning. She calls herself a specialist in primitive education and cultural mechanisms of character formation. On her expeditions she lives with the natives as one of themselves, gaining their complete confidence. The result in printed form is what one critic called "an extraordinary subtle performance." No one would think to look at her that she was one of America's leading anthropologists; she is a tiny person with fly-away light brown hair, a sort of pocket edition of Amelia Earhart in appearance. She has a passion for the theatre, reads "all the good poetry that comes out," and "makes good corn fritters with crocodile eggs."

PRINCIPAL WORKS: Coming of Age in Samoa, 1928; An Inquiry Into the Question of Cultural Stability in Polynesia, 1928; Growing Up in New Guinea, 1930; Changing Culture of an Indian Tribe, 1932; Sex and Temperament in Three Primitive Societies, 1935; Co-operation and Competition Among Primitive Peoples (edited and part author) 1937; Mountain Arapesh, 1938-40.

ABOUT: American Magazine September 1935; Asia August 1940; Literary Digest November 11, 1933; Natural History November 1939; Woman's Journal July 1930.

MEERSCH. See VAN DER MEERSCH

MEIER-GRAEFE, JULIUS (June 10, 1867-July, 1935), German art critic, was born in Resitza, near Berlin, the son of an official. His paternal grandfather was a professor of philology. Meier-Graefe was educated at the Universities of Munich, Berlin, Luttich, and Zurich. He was married in 1895. Although not himself a painter, his chief interest had always been in art, particularly from the historical standpoint. He traveled widely, particularly in Egypt and Greece, and from his journeys came many of his books—some merely discursive travel diaries, like *Pyramid and Temple,* but others of the first importance in

his iconoclastic theories, chief of which was that Egyptian art was superior to that of ancient Greece.

He was the founder of four art magazines —*Pan* in 1894, *Dekorative Kunst* in 1896, *L'Art Décorative* in 1898, and *Germinal* in 1899—and of the Marèes Society in 1917. A clean-shaven man with aquiline features, who had somewhat the appearance of an actor of the old school, he retained his energy and enthusiasm to his old age. At least half his time was spent in traveling, and he was indefatigable. No difficulties or discomfort could keep him from a journey which had art treasures as its goal. At the time of the opening of the tomb of Tutankhamen, he was one of the experts called to evaluate the discoveries, which he appraised as belonging to a decadent period of Egyptian art.

During his latter years he lived, when between journeys, in Berlin or Dresden. After the Nazi *coup d'état,* however, he left Germany, and his last days were spent in Saint Cyrsur Mer, Var, France, where he died at sixty-eight.

Meier-Graefe, besides his almost fifty books of art and travel, wrote one novel, *Der Vater (The Father)*, and a volume of short stories, which, however, were entirely concerned with art and artists. He is best known in England and America for his definitive biography of Vincent van Gogh, followed several years later by a fictionized account of the life of the unhappy Dutch artist. He was one of the first to insist on the importance of van Gogh's work and to familiarize the public with his name. His chief art-interests were in two extremes— ancient art and Impressionism and Post-Impressionism. He wrote also a finely sympathetic biography of Dostoievsky, who was among his greatest admirations; his thesis was that under the wrappings of genius, mysticism, melancholia, and neurosis in Dostoievsky was "that final miracle, the child"—and he said very much the same thing, in essence, of van Gogh.

Until his death Meier-Graefe's articles, in translation, appeared frequently in English and American art magazines, chiefly in *International Studio*. His writing was seldom technical, but was characterized by an easy style, quiet humor, and warm sympathy.

WORKS AVAILABLE IN ENGLISH: Modern Art, 1908; Vincent van Gogh, A Biographical Study, 1922; Degas, 1923; Cezanne, 1927; The Spanish Journey, 1927; Dostoievsky: The Man and His Work, 1928; Pyramid and Temple, 1930; Vincent: A Life of Van Gogh, 1936.

ABOUT: Neue Rundschau August 1935.

*MENCKEN, HENRY LOUIS (September 12, 1880-), American editor and essayist, writes: "I was born in Baltimore, and am the son of parents who were both American-born. My two grandfathers and my maternal grandmother were all born in Germany; my paternal grandmother, by name McClellan, was born in the Protestant North of Ireland, and came to

Pinchot

Baltimore by way of Jamaica in the West Indies. The Menckens originated in Oldenberg and were business men and public officials there for centuries; some of them still survive. My own branch of the family migrated to Saxony in the seventeenth century, and turned to learning. It produced a great many professors during the 150 years following. The Napoleonic wars wrecked it, and my great-grandfather went back to business. In that he was followed by my grandfather (who came to the United States in 1848) and my father, August Mencken. They did well in this country, and left their families decently provided for.

"I went to F. Knapp's Institute, a private school in Baltimore, as a boy, and later to the Baltimore Polytechnic. Why I was sent to the latter I don't know: I have never had any taste for mechanics, though I am much interested in the physical sciences. On my graduation my father took me into his tobacco business, but I didn't like it, and when he died in 1899 I got a job on the Baltimore *Morning Herald*. When the paper suspended publication in 1906 I was its editor. I then moved to the Baltimore *Sun,* and have been on its staff ever since. Newspaper work has always been my chief interest. I began to do a monthly book review for the *Smart Set,* became one of its editors in 1914, and from 1924 to the end of 1933 was editor of the *American Mercury,* but these were only left-hand jobs. I continued to live in Baltimore all the while, and, save for a brief interval, to write for the *Sun.* I do so still.

"My first book was a volume of dreadful juvenile verse, published in 1903. Two years later I did a small volume on George Bernard Shaw—the first about him to be published anywhere. I have written many books since, and edited many others. My best-seller has been *The American Language,* first brought out in 1919. My best book, in my own judgment is *Treatise on the Gods,* first printed in 1930. Many years of hard reading went into it. At the moment [1939] I am completing a volume of reminiscences of my childhood in Baltimore, to be called *Happy Days.* When it is finished I hope to do another small volume to be called *Advice to Young Men,* with a supplemental volume to *The American Language* following. I have plans also for half a dozen other books, but I am nearly sixty, and can't hope to write all of them.

"In religion I am a complete skeptic, as my father and grandfather were before me. But I have no prejudice against theology, and get on with the clergy very amicably. In politics I am a libertarian. That is, I believe thoroughly in the strict limitation of governmental powers. I am thus opposed to all the paternalisms now prevailing, whether Communism, Nazism, Fascism, or the New Deal. I believe in free speech up to the last limits of the unendurable. I am in grave doubt that the so-called democracy of the United States will last much longer. It is a set-up for demagogues, and they have pretty well wrecked it. But the country itself seems to me to be almost bullet-proof, and my guess is that it will come out of the mess very little damaged. In the long run, I believe, the obviously stupid and incompetent will be disfranchised, and some effort will be made to reduce the birth-rate among them. Personally, I am in favor of offering them cash in hand for their consent to be sterilized. That will bring them in by the million, and avoid the danger of giving discretion to public agencies, all of which are muddle-headed and most of which are corrupt.

"I was married in 1930 to Sara Powell Haardt, of Montgomery, Ala. She died on May 31, 1935."

* * *

No one who was not adult and young in the 1910's and early 1920's can understand what a tremendous influence H. L. Mencken had on the more literate and articulate and especially on the literary-minded youth of the United States. He was the man who had pushed Dreiser and Sinclair Lewis to public esteem, the arch-enemy of Puritanism and all its works, the champion of heterodoxy. What many of his disciples tended to ignore was that he was never a political or economic liberal. He was, as Louis Kronenberger has said, "an 'advanced' individualist, not so much rebellious as subversive. . . . He hid a conservative's taste under a firebrand's vocabulary." He belonged

to the boom era; he was its gadfly: but at base he was always just what he is now— primarily a newspaper man and a good one, temperamentally an anarchist, and fundamentally one of the solid middle-class German Baltimoreans, who drink their beer, love music, pay their bills, save their money, and surlily denounce any government that interferes with their private profits and pleasures. What distinguishes him from them is that under it all he is immensely kind, soft-hearted, and even sentimental. Much of his cross-grained invective is self-defense, some of it is mischief—and some of it is real. In essence he is still as Louis Untermeyer described him: "a chubby, moon-faced familiar, a cross between an English Puck and a German Spitzbube. His yellow hair was parted in the middle and neatly plastered down; his eyes were jolly and blue; his snub nose was impudent. He despised humanity . . . and loved persons. . . . Though he still wears the mask of the clown, there emerges the earnest anti-reformer . . . the erudite foe of academicians, . . . the pioneer crusader against crusades. . . . His sportiveness has turned bitter . . . trying to reconcile the irreconcilables."

What distinguishes him also is what Kronenberger called "a superb gift for communication." If the famous Mencken vocabulary seems a little worn now, it was fresh and vivid when he first gave it birth. He still has the vigor, but the pattern has worn thin from repetition. However much the liberal and the young may disagree with him today, it would be well for them to remember that once he was the "censor-baiting, freedom-roaring Mencken of 1920" (to quote Malcolm Cowley), a highly sanative enzyme in the body politic.

PRINCIPAL WORKS: Ventures Into Verse, 1903; George Bernard Shaw—His Plays, 1905; The Philosophy of Friedrich Nietzsche, 1908; Men vs. The Man (with R. R. Lamotte) 1910; The Artist (play) 1912; Europe After 8:15 (with G. J. Nathan and W. H. Wright) 1913; A Book of Burlesques, 1916; A Little Book in C Major, 1916; In Defense of Women, 1917; A Book of Prefaces, 1917; Damn—A Book of Calumny, 1917; The American Language, 1919 and 1936; The American Credo (with G. J. Nathan) 1920; Prejudices (Six Series) 1919-1927; Notes on Democracy, 1926; James Branch Cabell, 1927; Treatise on the Gods, 1930; Making a President, 1932; Treatise on Right and Wrong, 1934; The Sunpapers of Baltimore (with others) 1937; Happy Days: 1880-1892 (autobiography) 1940; Newspaper Days (autobiography) 1941; A New Dictionary of Quotations on Historical Principles (ed.) 1942.

ABOUT: Boyd, E. H. L. Mencken; Goldberg, I. H. L. Mencken; Henderson, F. C. A Bibliography of H. L. Mencken; Lippmann, W. H. L. Mencken; Mencken, H. L. Happy Days, Newspaper Days; O'Sullivan, V. The American Critic; Rascoe, B. &

Others. Fanfare; Untermeyer, L. From Another World; Bookman June 1930; Nation February 4, 1939; New Republic November 21, 1934, October 7, 1936; New York Times Book Review February 11, 1940; North American Review December 1938; Saturday Review of Literature December 11, 1926, January 27, June 29, 1940.

MENNINGER, KARL AUGUSTUS

(July 22, 1893-), American psychiatrist, writes: "I was born in Topeka, Kan., where

I still live and expect always to live. My father came here as a very young man to help in the foundation and development of a small pioneer college. He is still teaching people, including me. My mother also came to pioneer Kansas from the Pennsylvania Dutch country. She has described her life in her book, *Days of My Life*. She taught school while my father went to medical school; he began the practice of medicine in Topeka in 1890.

"I went to school in Topeka through high school and two years of Washburn College. Then I went to the University of Wisconsin for three years and to Harvard Medical School for two more (M.D. 1917, *cum laude*). Following a medical internship I returned to Boston to work with Dr. Ernest Southard, who became one of the great inspirations of my life. I worked under him in the Boston Psychopathic Hospital and taught under him at the Harvard Medical School. From him I gained a conception of the vast scope and potentialities of psychiatry. He died suddenly in February, 1920, and I returned then to Topeka permanently. My father and I laid plans to develop a psychiatric clinic in which we could utilize his two principles of group practice and the developing importance of psychiatry. My brother William graduated from Cornell Medical School and joined us. We built a hospital and to this we added a school for the resident treatment of children with characterological and behavior problems. Young psychiatrists came to us for training, some of whom we ultimately added to our staff.

"In 1916 I married Grace Gaines, and we have two daughters and a son.

"I have tried to reduce to systematic writing the ideals of psychiatric teaching and practice which my brother and father and I and our associates have carried on in our clinic, in three books, *The Human Mind*, a general survey of the field; *Man Against Himself*, which analyzes in detail the destructive tendencies of human beings; and a third book on which I am now at work, analyzing the constructive powers and the technique for developing them.

"Nothing of human concern is really outside of psychiatry; so, in one sense, I have no hobbies: they are all part of my work. My favorite recreation is watching things grow on my tree farm, which I have tried to make into a bird refuge, because birds are as much a part of trees as are leaves and blossoms and fruit. I have an amateur collection of symphonic records and a good many books. Besides these, I like good food and wines—but who doesn't?"

* * *

Dr. Menninger, besides being a witty and companionable man, has an unusual gift for not so much popularizing as factualizing the most abstruse points of psychiatry. He is a firm advocate of psycho-analysis and has been called "more Freudian than Freud." The Menninger Clinic has been of great influence on psychiatric practice in America, and in his books and his many magazine articles he has made its methods and viewpoint widely known among the reading public. He was a lieutenant in the U.S. Naval Reserve from 1918 to 1921, and belongs to and has held office in innumerable learned and technical societies.

In February 1941 Dr. Menninger was divorced from his first wife; in September of the same year he married Jeanetta Lyle, formerly his secretary.

PRINCIPAL WORKS: Why Men Fail (with others) 1918; The Human Mind, 1930 (revised and enlarged, 1937); The Healthy-Minded Child (with others) 1930; Man Against Himself, 1938.

ABOUT: Menninger, F. K. Days of My Life.

MERCER, CECIL WILLIAM (August

7, 1885-), English novelist who writes under the pseudonym "Dornford Yates," is the

eldest son of Cecil John Mercer, solicitor, King's Bench Walk, and Helen (Wall) Mercer. The junior Mercer was educated at Harrow and University College, Oxford University, where he received the degree of M.A. and was presi-

dent of the Dramatic Society in 1906-07. Two years later he was a barrister of the Inner

Temple, but forsook the law for literature. During the First World War he served with the 3rd County of London Yeomanry as second lieutenant, fighting in Egypt in 1915-16 and at Salonika in 1916-17. At Salonika he was signals officer with the 8th Mounted Brigade, rising to a captaincy in 1918. Next year Captain Mercer married Bettine Stokes Edwards of Philadelphia, Pa., divorcing her in 1933. A son was born of this marriage. The second Mrs. Mercer, whom he married in 1934, was Elizabeth Bowie, youngest daughter of David Mather Bowie of Clement's Inn. *The Courts of Idleness* (1920) launched the career of "Dornford Yates" as a writer of light-hearted, irresponsible farce, alternated by rapid-paced tales of dangerous adventure, of which *Storm Music* (1934) is a notable example. They are in the tradition of the adventure stories of Francis Beeding and Roland Pertwee and the Richard Hannay series of John Buchan, and were once characterized by the London *Times* as affording the maximum of entertainment with the minimum of likelihood. The works of "Dornford Yates" are also popular in the United States, where they frequently appear as magazine serials and as publications of the Crime Club. Mr. Mercer's clubs are the Cavalry and the Conservative; his recreations, appropriately, are traveling and motoring. The Second World War curtailed these, and terminated his customary residence in Pau, South France, at his Villa Maryland.

PRINCIPAL WORKS: The Courts of Idleness, 1920, The Brother of Daphne, 1920; Berry and Co., 1921; Anthony Lyveden, 1921; Jonah and Co., 1922; Valerie French, 1923; And Five Were Foolish, 1924; As Other Men Are, 1925; The Stolen March, 1926; Blind Corner, 1927; Perishable Goods, 1928; Maiden Stakes, 1929; Blood Royal, 1930; Fire Below, 1930; Adèle and Co., 1931; Safe Custody, 1932; Storm Music, 1934; She Fell Among Thieves, 1935; And Berry Came Too, 1936; She Painted Her Face, 1937; This Publican (U.S. Title: The Devil in Satin) 1938; Gale Warning, 1939; Shoal Water, 1941.

ABOUT: Bookman (London) August 1928.

MEREDITH, GEORGE. See "BRITISH AUTHORS OF THE 19TH CENTURY"

MEREZHKOVSKY, DMITRY SERGEYEVICH (August 2, 1865-December 10, 1941), Russian novelist and philosopher, was born in St. Petersburg (Leningrad), the son of Serge Ivanovich Merezhkovsky, inspector of buildings for the Imperial Court.

His home life was stern and puritanical; one of his brothers (later a celebrated biologist) was thrown out of the house for expressing sympathy for a woman Nihilist who had been executed, and the eight children hardly dared call their souls their own except when with their gentle mother. The father, however, was proud of his youngest son, and when Dmitry began to write immature verses and pallid essays, he took the fifteen-year-old boy to Dostoievsky to read his

"works" aloud. Dostoievsky's only comment was that "to write, one must suffer."

Merezhkovsky was graduated from the University of St. Petersburg, specializing in philology and saturating himself in the Greek and Roman classics. He was a brilliant student, who covered the whole course in two years. So reactionary was the Imperial government at this period that when the students formed a harmless Molière Club it was suppressed and the lad was barely saved from exile through the influence of his father. There was thus small objection by his family to his spending the year after the university traveling in Crimea and the Caucasus; he was frail in any case, with weak lungs, and needed the warm climate. There he met Zinaida Hippius, then the best known woman poet in Russia, whom he married in 1889. Scarcely had they been married when she became long and gravely ill, and before she had recovered his beloved mother died. Merezhkovsky had begun to obey Dostoievsky's advice. Suffering made him a mystic, and turned his predominant interest toward religion. From 1891 he and his wife spent several years in Greece, Turkey, and the Near East. From this double experience grew the trilogy of philosophical novels dealing with Julian the Apostate, Leonardo da Vinci, and Peter the Great, which appeared under the general title of *Christ and Anti-Christ*. About 1900 his mysticism crystallized into an apocalyptic, neo-Christian (and of course heretical) religion which he called "The New Road," which synthesized the pagan cult of the flesh and the Christian cult of the spirit into one entity. He drew about him a group of disciples, with a magazine as their organ. This Society of Religion and Philosophy was later dissolved by the government.

In the abortive revolution of 1905, Merezhkovsky was closely allied with the revolutionaries, and was obliged to escape to Paris, where he and his wife lived for several years, returning to Russia about 1910. He opposed Russia's participation in the First World War. But when the Bolshevik Revolution of 1917 arrived, it found in him a violent enemy, as might be anticipated from his religious views. To him the Communists were not even human—they were "anti-Christ," "men from Mars." He spent two years in prison in Russia, then in 1920 escaped and found his way to Paris. After the Nazi conquest of France in 1940, Merezhkovsky was reported to be near starvation; he died in Paris at seventy-six.

Merezhkovsky was at one time deeply interested in the theatre, and with Lèon Bakst produced the plays of Euripides in St. Petersburg. Edwin E. Slosson described him as "slight, dark, soft in voice, nervous in manner, vivacious in conversation," bearded, with "large black, tired eyes." In Russia he was best known as a literary critic— a very severe critic, especially of Tolstoy and Gorky—but abroad his reputation rests on his historical and philosophical novels. Edouard de Morsier called these "penetrating and luminous," and said that through them he "belongs to universal literature."

WORKS AVAILABLE IN ENLISH: *Novels*—Julian the Apostate, 1901; Peter and Alexis, 1906; Leonardo da Vinci, 1917 (as The Forerunner, 1931); December the Fourteenth, 1923; Tutankhamen, 1925; Akhnaton: King of Egypt, 1927. *Miscellaneous*—Tolstoy as Man and Artist: With an Essay on Dostoievsky, 1902; Ibsen, 1907; Montaigne, 1907; Pliny the Younger, 1907; Calderon, 1908; Flaubert, 1908; Marcus Aurelius, 1909; Joseph Pilsudski, 1921; Menace of the Mob, 1921; Life of Napoleon, 1929; Napoleon, A Study, 1929; Michelangelo and Other Sketches, 1930; Secret of the West, 1931; Jesus the Unknown, 1934 (as Jesus Manifest, 1935).

ABOUT: Mirsky, D. S. Contemporary Russian Literature; Olgin, M. J. Guide to Russian Literature; Persky, S. Contemporary Russian Novelists; Independent November 15, 1906; Literary Digest February 26, 1921; Mercure de France April 15, 1929; September 15, 1936; Saturday Review of Literature February 21, 1925.

MERRICK, LEONARD (1864-August 7, 1939), English novelist, was born Leonard Miller at Belsize Park, on the outskirts of Hampstead, a son of William Miller, of Jewish stock. He was educated in private schools and at Brighton College, but his father's sudden financial reverses made it impossible to continue on to Heidelberg to complete his education in the law, for which his father had destined him. Forced

to work for a bare subsistence, he went to South Africa when he was eighteen and found work superintending Kaffir laborers in the diamond fields. A job in the local courthouse as a clerk lasted until the judge committed suicide. He worked in a solicitor's office in Kimberley for two years, almost died of camp fever, and eventually returned to London. Always stage-struck, he toured England with a sensational Drury Lane melodrama, using the surname of Merrick, which later became his own by legal process.

Merrick left the stage after two years and turned his hand unprofitably to short-story writing. Borrowing fifty pounds, he went to New York and tried to find work in the theatre. He refused to sell a novel, *Violet Moses,* for $150, and returned to London ill and beaten. Published in London the book was compared with Meredith and George Eliot, but had only a small sale. Mild success greeted *The Man Who Was Good,* completed in 1892.

Grant Richards, who published *Conrad in Quest of His Youth,* supplied the plot of *The Actor-Manager,* and cheerfully dropped a hundred pounds on *One Man's View,* speaks of Merrick as being a "dark, Semitic, sensitive type." A determined effort by a group of fellow-writers, headed by Sir William Robertson Nicoll, led to the unusual procedure of issuing a special collected edition of a writer's work during his lifetime, with prefaces by Nicoll, J. M. Barrie, H. G. Wells, W. J. Locke, Sir Arthur Wing Pinero, William Dean Howells, Maurice Hewlett, and others less known. Merrick had met only three of the twelve contributors. Barrie called *Conrad in Quest of His Youth* "the best sentimental journey written in this country since the publication of the other one; so gay it is, so sad, of such an alluring spirit, so firm a temper." There is no such thing as plot in Merrick's books, Barrie observed; he is a writer of comedies always, though "tragedy lurks at all the corners."

Merrick, said another critic, had a horror of excess; he never attempted minute characterization. He was really at home in only two worlds, the theatre, and literature and journalism. He is in no sense a didactic writer, seeing in life not so much retribution as catastrophe. The spirit of Merrick's literary gift and method, said Pinero, was conciseness and ease. "The somber figure of tragedy tugging at comedy's sleeve cost him thousands of readers."

Merrick married Hope Butler-Wilkins, also a writer, who died in 1917. His own death occurred at a nursing-home in London, following an operation. Besides his novels, he wrote five plays in collaboration.

His daughter, Miss Lesley Merrick, writes to the editors of this volume that her father always felt more at home in Paris, where he lived many years, than in London, though he considered London a much more comfortable place. Having known Paris before the First World War, Merrick could estimate how much that city had lost since then in the way of vivacity and charm. One of his strongest convictions was that hunting, in all its forms, is a barbarous form of amusement. The cruelties that men commit in the name of sport horrified him, and he never hesitated to speak against blood-sports.

PRINCIPAL WORKS: The Man Who Was Good, 1892; This Stage of Fools, 1896; Cynthia, 1897; One Man's View, 1897; The Actor-Manager, 1898; The Worldlings, 1900; Conrad in Quest of His Youth, 1903; The Quaint Companions, 1903; Whispers About Women (short stories) 1906; The House of Lynch, 1907; Lynch's Daughter, 1908; The Man Who Understood Women (short stories) 1908; The Position of Peggy, 1911; When Love Flies Out of the Window, 1914; While Paris Laughed, 1918, A Chair on the Boulevard, 1921; The Little Dog Laughed, 1930.

ABOUT: Merrick, L. Collected Works (see special introductions); Dutton News of Books and Authors October-November 1939; New York Times August 8, 1939; Saturday Review of Literature August 19, 1939.

MERRILL, STUART FITZRANDOLPH (August 1, 1863-December 1, 1915), American-French poet, was born at  Hempstead, L.I., near Whitman's birthplace. He was the son of George Merrill, a New York attorney from New England, whose name originally had been Tibbetts, and of Emma Fitzrandolph (Laing) Merrill, a Virginian. In 1866 the father was appointed counsellor of the American Legation at Paris, and took his wife and three sons with him. A narrow, harsh man, he made his family live in Paris as if they were in a New England village.

Stuart Merrill attended school at Vanves, and then the Lycée Fontanes, where his English teacher was Stéphane Mallarmé, the poet and one of the founders of the Symbolist school. He received his degree in 1884, but immediately afterward his father returned to New York and dragged the son, not yet of age, with him. Against his will he attended the Columbia Law School; but he devoted most of his time to the writing of French poetry instead of to studying American law. In 1887 his first volume, Les Gammes, was published in Paris.

A disciple of William Morris (and later of Tolstoy and Whitman), Merrill early became an active radical. Because he campaigned for Henry George for mayor of New York and supported the defendants in the Haymarket Riot in Chicago, his father disinherited him, and it was only by surreptitious help from his mother that he was able to live. George Merrill finally died in 1888, and the mother at once went with her sons to Europe. During the next four years Merrill returned three times to New York, but on each occasion stayed only a few months. He was in Paris again in 1891, as one of the managers of the New Art Theater, when his second book of French poems, Les Fastes, was published. After 1892 he never saw America again, and he who was noted for his amiability and sweetness of nature never spoke of his native land without hatred—undoubtedly a reflex of his hatred of his father.

For twelve years Merrill lived the typical existence of the Latin Quarter artist of the period. When his mistress, a model named "Bob" to whom he was devoted, married another man, he began a period of dissipation and constant wandering to cure his grief, in the course of which roaming he met in Belgium a young girl named Claire Rion, whom he married in 1908. They settled in Versailles, which was his home thereafter. In 1913 he engaged in a long and bitter controversy with Guillaume Apollinaire on the morals of Walt Whitman, the only American he acknowledged as his master—though William Dean Howells had been and remained his constant friend.

The First World War killed Stuart Merrill as surely as if he had enlisted in the army—which he tried to do without success. An idealist and a pacifist, he was unable to survive the wreck of all his hopes for humanity, and he died suddenly of a heart attack directly brought on by emotion. By his wish, he was buried without religious services. In 1929 a tablet was affixed to his house in Versailles, and a street in Paris has been named for him. For many years the place of his American birth was forgotten, until 1939, almost a quarter-century after his death, when residents of Hempstead, L.I., discovered the fact by accident and, on the anniversary of his birthday, erected a memorial tablet to him.

Merrill's early poems were decorative, beautiful, but without passion. After the crucial year of his desertion by his mistress his work deepened, and his greatest book, *Une Voix dans la Foule,* 1909, is indeed a voice, a voice of pity for all the suffering of man. His poems were all symbolistic and expressionistic, the analogue in words of Debussy in music. Vincent O'Sullivan remarked that he wrote the only French verse which had the romantic dreaminess of the pre-Raphaelite school in English; and Philippe Berthelot called his work "a poetry that leaves after it ineffaceable luminous traces." He wrote only one volume (of prose translations) in English, and his French poems have never been translated except fragmentarily—in fact, like all Symbolist poetry, they are practically untranslatable.

WORK AVAILABLE IN ENGLISH: Pastels in Prose, 1890.

ABOUT: Henry, M. L. Stuart Merrill (in French); Commemoration de Stuart Merrill à Versailles; Dial January 20, 1916; Literary Digest September 14, 1929; Mercure de France October 16, 1909, January 1, 1916, July 15, 1929; New York Herald Tribune August 1, 1939.

MERWIN, SAMUEL (October 6, 1874-October 17, 1936), American popular novelist, was born in a typically American frame house on Orrington

Avenue, Evanston, Ill. His parents were Orlando H. Merwin and Ellen (Bannister) Merwin, and he was a nephew of Frances E. Willard, ardent champion of women's rights. Her nephew later supported woman suffrage and contributed a chapter to the composite suffrage novel, *The Sturdy Oak* (1917), edited by Elizabeth Jordan, but reached the conclusion that the chief result of the vote had been the creation of the "flapper" type.

Merwin lived in other houses in Evanston, went to school there, and attended the local university, Northwestern. With Henry Kitchell Webster,*qv* a boyhood friend, he collaborated in the writing of fiction about American railroad-building: *The Short Line War,* which introduced Jim Fisk and Jay Gould, and the best-selling *Calumet K.* From 1905 to 1909 he was associate editor of *Success Magazine,* succeeding to the editorship in 1909. In 1907 he spent six months in China studying the opium trade as special investigator for *Success. Drugging a Nation* was the resultant book, besides later novels. "Life, as I see it," Merwin told C. C. Baldwin, "is largely what, in fiction, would be classed as melodrama. In writing I must confess to a love of surface color and contrast." As a lover of the theatre he operated a playhouse at Concord, Mass., for fifteen years, obtaining a municipal subsidy; wrote *The Girl Outside* with John King Hodges, produced at the Little Theatre in New York, 1932, with little success; and wrote of the Players in Gramercy Park New York city, as "My Favorite Club." He died there at sixty-two of a stroke of apoplexy during dinner; at his funeral services Walter Hampden, president of the Club read the Dirge from *Cymbeline,* Whitman's "When Lilacs Last in the Dooryard Bloomed," and Kipling's "Envoi" to *The Seven Seas.* The body was cremated. His wife, Edna Earl (Fleshiem) Merwin, whom he married in Evanston in 1901, and a son Samuel Kimball Merwin, survived. The latter has written *Murder in Miniatures,* a detective story, as Sam Merwin, Jr.

Merwin's personal philosophy was evolved from reading John Stuart Mill, Shaw, Ellen Key, and Ibsen. His "society" novels are fairly sensational and superficial, but *Temperamental Henry* and its sequel, *Henry Is Twenty,* the first written about the same time as Tarkington's *Seventeen,* had sound adolescent psychology, and evoked the period of the Illinois town of the 'nineties with skill and charm. Merwin was "round and fat and jolly, Babbitt in the flesh," and wore horn-rimmed glasses.

PRINCIPAL WORKS: The Road to Frontenac 1901; The Whip Hand, 1903; His Little World 1903; The Merry Anne, 1904; The Road Builders 1905; Drugging a Nation, 1908; The Citadel, 1912 The Charmed Life of Miss Austin, 1914; Anthony the Absolute, 1914; The Honey Bee, 1915 The Trufflers, 1916; Temperamental Henry, 1917 Henry Is Twenty, 1918; The Passionate Pilgrim 1919; Hill of Han, 1920; In Red and Gold, 1921 Goldie Green, 1922; Silk, 1923; The Moment of Beauty, 1924; Anabel at Sea, 1927; Lady Can Do 1929. *With Henry Kitchell Webster*—The Short Line War, 1899; Calumet K, 1901; Comrade John 1907.

ABOUT: Baldwin, C. C. The Men Who Make Our Novels; New York Times October 18, 19 20, 1936.

MERZ, CHARLES (February 23, 1893-   ), American editor and essayist, writes: "Charles Merz was born in Sandusky, Ohio. He attend-

N. Y. Times Studio

ed the public schools of that city and left Ohio for the first time in 1911, to enter the class of 1915 at Yale University. Following his graduation he entered magazine work, first on the staffs of *Harper's Weekly* and the *New Republic;* later as a contributor to *Century, Harper's Magazine,* the *Atlantic Monthly,* etc. During the war he served as First Lieutenant with the A.E.F. in France. After the war he traveled as a correspondent in Europe and Asia. In 1924 he became associate editor of the New York *World,* in which position he served until the death of the paper in 1931. In the latter year he joined the staff of the New York *Times.* He was made editor of that paper, succeeding Dr. John H. Finley, in November 1938. The first of his two books is an appreciation of the American scene; the second, a history of the prohibition movement in this country. He is a member of Phi Beta Kappa, the Century Association of New York, and the Board of Governors of the Yale University Press. Colgate University and Wooster College conferred on him in 1939 the degree of LL.D."

* * *

Mr. Merz was married in 1924 to Evelyn Scott (not to be confused with the novelist of the same name). His name is pronounced as if it were spelled "murrs." He is tall, with graying hair, a small black moustache, and thick black eyebrows. He began newspaper work while still in high school in Sandusky, as cub reporter on a local paper, and at the same time edited the school magazine. He is noted for his quick wit, and his earlier book at least is as full of humor as it is of keen observation. The *Bookman* spoke of his "admirable skill in making homely detail or shrewdly culled statistics speak out the general and symbolic meaning he is after," and Fred T. Marsh praised his 'gift for quiet, skillful, ironic analysis of social conditions."

PRINCIPAL WORKS: The Great American Bandwagon, 1928; The Dry Decade, 1931; Days of Decision: Wartime Editorials From the New York Times (ed.) 1941.

ABOUT: Bookman April 1928, May 1929, March 1931; Newsweek November 28, 1938; Time November 28, 1938.

METCALFE, JOHN (1891-   ), English novelist, writes: "I was born at Heacham, Norfolk. My people have been, for the most part, seafaring. My father was at sea until the middle of his life, when he retired to marry my mother. After leaving the merchant marine, he wrote sea-stories for boys. When I was five, my parents went out to Canada, as superin-

tendents of a Dr. Barnardo's Girls' Home. This lasted until I was nine; and when we went back to England, my father and mother carried on similar 'rescue' work for Dr. Barnardo, in the East End of London, in Limehouse, and in Stepney. Later, for a while, they had charge of an orphanage in Scotland. I have not, up to the present, made any direct use of my childhood impressions in Scotland and Canada, but the Limehouse-Stepney period is covered in my novel *Foster-Girl.*

"After my father gave up the profession for which he was best fitted, the fortunes of my parents seem to have fluctuated considerably, but to have 'upped' a shade when I was of prep school age, so that I was able to attend good schools, St. Felix College, at Felixstowe, Suffolk, and Nelson's School in North Walsham, Norfolk. From them I went to the University of London, majoring in philosophy, and graduating in 1913. For a year after this I had a teaching post in Paris.

"I joined the Royal Naval Division in 1914, and was subsequently commissioned in the Royal Naval Volunteer Reserve. By the end of the year I was flying officer (armaments) in the Royal Air Force, and remained on the Reserve until I entered the United States on the quota at the end of 1928. My first job in America was that of 'barge captain' on the East River. This was pleasant (though cold) and quite conducive to writing; but one January night I was run down by a tug; my craft foundered, and I myself escaped narrowly on a fireboat. My books up to this time had been written at odd hours, after midnight and in the early morning, while I was master at Highgate, a 'public school' in London; and I had hoped the leisure enjoyed by a barge captain would provide wonderful opportunities for work. I had another job,

951

actually at sea, after this, but it allowed me no time whatever for literary pursuits.

"Since my marriage in 1928 to Evelyn Scott,[qv] the novelist, I have seen a good deal of America, and have especially enjoyed the Southwest. We have traveled pretty extensively, in France, Spain, Portugal, and North Africa. In 1939 I rejoined the Royal Air Force and am now on active service. Writing, while the war is on, takes second place, but I have another novel on the way."

* * *

Mr. Metcalfe says he had "scribbled" from the age of six. In his early days as a writer he often got up at 4 A.M. to put in three or four hours before his teaching duties began, and wrote again from 7 to 10 in the evening. His novel *Arm's Length* was written on the barge on the East River, and the manuscript was rescued with him after the wreck. It was finished at Yaddo, Saratoga Springs, N.Y. His favorite recreations he gives as cricket, golf, and yachting, and his chief ambition to buy a topsail schooner. His work is characterized by a rather grim, bizarre, and sinister humor, and is markedly individual and *sui generis*. He should not be confused with John Metcalfe, an Australian librarian who writes frequently on his special subject, or with John J. Metcalfe, a writer on India and the British Empire.

PRINCIPAL WORKS: The Smoking Leg (short stories) 1925; Spring Darkness (in America: Mrs. Condover) 1928; Arm's Length, 1930; Judas (short stories) 1931; Foster-Girl (in America: Sally) 1935.

ABOUT: Scribner's Magazine December 1930.

MEW, CHARLOTTE (November 15, 1870-March 24, 1928), English poet, was born in London, the daughter of Frederick

Mew, an architect who died when she was a child, and Anne (Kendall) Mew. There is very little to tell of her outward life, any more than there is of Emily Dickinson's or Emily Brontë's. She was educated privately, she lived for some time in Paris, she loved someone deeply and hopelessly, she endured poverty and illness and despair. Her existence was profoundly entangled with that of her mother, her two sisters, and her brother. They all died, her mother and her dearest sister last of all. In 1922 Thomas Hardy, John

Masefield, and Walter de la Mare procured for her a Civil List pension of 75 pounds a year, so that she need not starve to death. At the end of 1927 she became desperately ill and was taken to a nursing home. She had nothing left to live for. When she had to face another spring, her "defiant reserve" finally snapped. Not yet fifty-eight, she took her own life.

She wrote prose before she wrote poetry; as early as 1894 she was writing stories for the *Yellow Book*. She left a few other uncollected stories and essays. Her poems were wrung out of her, infrequently, when she could no longer contain them. They appeared in all serious journals, and in 1916 the Poetry Bookshop brought out a small volume of them. It won her the friendship of Thomas Hardy, the only joyous thing that ever happened to her. When she lay on what was to be her death-bed, he sent her one of her own poems which he had copied in his own eighty-seven-year-old hand. It was her last message from the world.

"Her reserve," said Harold Monro, "amounted to a kind of secretiveness." And John Freeman echoed him: "Everything is uttered in the manner of telling secrets [which] do not betray her except to those who hold the clue." Her wind-blown gray hair, her startled gray eyes, her thin white face, belonged to a reluctant visitor from another world frightened at what she had undergone in this one. Yet she shared the passions of humanity, only the passion was distilled; she said she had "a scarlet soul," and Louis Untermeyer remarked that "her work, like herself, had a deceptive fragility, a cameo cut in steel." She was rigidly self-critical, her imaginative power curbed and firmly ridden. She just lacks the touch of genius by the narrowness of her range, but within its compass her work is nearly of first rank. "All her poetry is strict religion," said Monro, and Lorna Keeling Collard added that "the secret of her power lies . . . in her sense of spiritual values." Thomas Moult, too, felt the flood pressing against the dam: "Ostensibly always the impersonal observer, yet she imparts to her theme as much intensity as though she were actually expressing her own subjective mood." One line that ends one of her poems is herself *in petto*: "Take it. No give it back!" Technically, her poetry is staccato, broken in meter, fluctuating, unevenly rhymed, but all this is intentional; the form follows the feeling. Like Emily Dickinson, she wanted her manuscript burned; less fortunately for the world, she did not leave the task to others, but performed it herself. Few poets who have left so little have left so much that will endure.

PRINCIPAL WORKS: The Farmer's Bride, 1916, 1921 (in America: Saturday Market, 1921); The Rambling Sailor, 1929.

ABOUT: Monro, H. Some Contemporary Poets; Monroe, H. & Henderson, A. C. The New Poetry; Newbolt, H. J. New Paths on Helicon; Untermeyer, L. Modern British Poetry; Williams-Ellis, A. An Anatomy of Poetry; Bookman (London) July and December 1921, January 1924, May 1928, June 1929; Contemporary Review April 1930; English Journal May 1926; Freeman March 15, 1922; New Statesman April 2, 1921; Poetry June 1922; Spectator March 26, 1921; Yale Review December 1932.

MEYNELL, Mrs. ALICE CHRISTIANA (THOMPSON) (August 17, 1847-November 27, 1922), English poet and essayist,

was born at Barnes, Surrey, near London, though most of her childhood was spent in Italy. Her father, a man of wealth and culture but no profession, was a friend of Dickens; her mother, Christiana Weller, a concert pianist and a not bad painter. Her older sister, Elizabeth (Lady Butler) was a painter of distinction and great reputation (her battle-pictures made her famous in girlhood).

The father was the sisters' only teacher; in their roving life in France and Switzerland and England, but mostly in Italy (where Thomas James Thompson had a grown daughter by his first marriage), he tutored them to such good purpose that few writers of English have had so intimate a knowledge of their native literature as Alice Meynell; Italian and French were also at her full command. Her girlhood was full of love and peace, though tinctured by an adolescent melancholy; its first episode of importance was her conversion to the Roman Catholic Church, which took place when she was twenty. Her mother had preceded her, and her sister and in the end her father followed her.

In 1875 her first volume of poems appeared, Preludes, issued by Tennyson's publisher and sponsored by the praise of Ruskin and Rossetti and George Eliot. All her life the great writers of her time gravitated naturally to her and she to them; Coventry Patmore and George Meredith and of course Francis Thompson were among her intimates. Indirectly his admiration for the poems led to her meeting with the Catholic journalist and literary critic Wilfrid Meynell, slightly her junior in years, whom she married in 1877—the beginning of almost exactly thirty years of a singularly devoted, cooperative, and tender union. Eight children were born to them, four girls and four boys, of whom one died in infancy.

The Meynells were poor, and constant labor in journalism was their only means of livelihood. They toiled together incessantly, amidst the cares of a large family. Alice Meynell contributed one day's offering of the weekly column, "The Wares of Autolycus," in The Pall Mall Gazette, and wrote regularly also at various times for half a dozen periodicals, including Henley's National Observer. She did also much of the hack editorial work of her husband's Weekly Register (a Catholic paper) and Merry England. Her successive volumes of prose essays were largely made up of selections from these magazine articles.

Somehow, with all this toil, and the life-long torture of migraine, she managed also to take a part in social endeavors—to do humanitarian work, and to become an active advocate of woman suffrage, above all, with her husband, to rehabilitate and care for the derelict genius, Francis Thompson. Simple, frugal living and the most open hospitality were the rule at the Meynells—Rothenstein speaks of their uncarpeted floors and their ever-welcoming table. Mrs. Meynell never lost in the narrow confines of domesticity her outward-looking vision on the world; she might almost have been described—did sometimes so describe herself—as a Christian Socialist, and she was most ardently a feminist "in lawful and dignified ways."

Recognition came to her while she was yet young. Her home was a meeting-place for all who were most celebrated in London. When Tennyson died, she was seriously advocated—especially by Patmore—for the laureateship. The one break in her routine of writing and occasional returns to her beloved Italy was eight months spent in America, mostly in California. The adulation she received humanly pleased her, but it could not change her essential simplicity; she was too innately aloof, too reticent, too turned toward a central religious purpose, to be flattered or confused by literary acclaim.

As her children grew up and married, several of them following in the steps of their parents' profession, her life became less restricted and her leisure a little more spacious. The Meynells had moved from their famous house in Palace Court to a flat in the City, and then became the owners of eighty acres, with an old house and cottages for the children and grandchildren, in Sussex. The war brought to her, as it brought to every thinking and feeling being, years of intense preoccupation and pain; a son-in-law died of wounds, her second son enlisted. In the Boer War she had been openly pro-Boer; but in the World War she, with so many others, attached herself to the belief in "a war to end war," a crusade against arrogant militarism.

Though her dark hair never grayed, her slim erect posture never stooped, her health became increasingly frail. Against her strong will she had finally to yield to the weakness of a failing heart. On November 27, 1922, after seven weeks of illness, she died in her sleep, in the dawn.

Alice Meynell is spoken of commonly as a mystic. She was hardly that; she had no turn for philosophy and metaphysics; but she was profoundly and in every atom of her being devoted to the religious impulse. Cool, composed, intellectual (even with "flashes of intellectual arrogance"), austere in spite of a deep-seated keen humor, she had the makings of a saint, of which wifehood and motherhood could not divest her.

Considering her as a writer, Theodore Maynard is perhaps a trifle unjust when he says that "all her essays are touched with the spirit of poetry and all her poetry with the spirit of essays." She herself was unfair to herself in saying she was "a poet of one mood." Her work rarely fails in distinction, unexpectedness of phrase, fine freshness of outlook shining through its surface formality—the freshness brought to old subjects by a sharp and original mind. Katherine Brégy has the last and best word when she speaks of her "classic gold smithery, exquisite and austere."

The family name is pronounced *men'el*.

PRINCIPAL WORKS: *Poetry*—Preludes, 1875; Poems, 1893; Later Poems, 1901; Poems, 1913; A Father of Women, 1917; Last Poems (posthumous) 1923. *Essays*—The Poor Sisters of Nazareth, 1889; The Rhythm of Life, 1893; The Color of Life, 1896; The Children, 1896; London Impressions, 1898; The Spirit of Place, 1899; John Ruskin, 1900; The Children of the Old Masters, 1903; Ceres' Runaway, 1909; Mary: The Mother of Jesus, 1912; Childhood, 1913; Hearts of Controversy, 1917; The Second Person Singular, 1921.

ABOUT: Brégy, K. The Poet's Chantry; Maynard, T. Our Best Poets; Meynell, V. Alice Meynell: A Memoir; Tuell, A. K. Mrs. Meynell and Her Literary Generation; Catholic World March 1923; September 1929, November 1934.

MEYNELL, VIOLA (1886-), English poet, novelist, and short-story writer, was born at Phillimore Place, Kensington, London, sometime prior to 1889, when her parents, Wilfrid Meynell and Alice (Thompson) Meynell,*qv* moved to their new house at Palace Court, London. (Viola Meynell, who married John Dallyn in 1922, now lives there with her husband and son.)  Her father was then editing, as he did for eighteen years, *The Weekly Register*, a Catholic periodical, begun at the request of his friend, Cardinal Manning. He was aided by his wife, the well-known poet and essayist, who also wrote for the *Spectator* and the *Saturday Review*. For relaxation, they edited *Merry England*. "One of the things the childhood of all the young family was chiefly aware of was the indescribable effort and struggle against time on those Thursdays, with both parents silent and desperate with work," writes Viola Meynell in her biography of her mother. Sheila Kaye-Smith speaks of Palace Court as "a household of charming Catholics." The three daughters were passionately devoted to their beautiful and gifted, if occasionally absent-minded, mother.

Some of Viola Meynell's verse appeared in an anthology of 1912, *Eyes of Youth: A Book of Verse*, which had a foreword by G. K. Chesterton. Her poems frequently appeared in the *New Statesman* and the *Observer*, and were collected in *The Frozen Ocean and Other Poems* (1931). She has also edited *The Poet's Walk: A Nature Anthology* (1936). The Dallyns have a country place, Manor Farm, Greatham, Pulborough, Sussex. *Young Mrs. Cruse*, including short stories on rather tenuous themes, chiefly psychological in interest, was published in the United States in 1924. Three years later came *A Girl Adoring*, a novel which probably owes something to Viola Meynell's own family life, and which the *Saturday Review* stated showed emotional power of a high quality. (Edwin Muir complained that the movement of the story was indecisive.) Mrs. Dallyn's memoir of her mother is perhaps her most notable piece of work.

PRINCIPAL WORKS: Lot Barrow, 1913; Modern Lovers, 1914; Columbine, 1915; Narcissus, 1916; The Second Marriage, 1918; Antonia, 1921; Young Mrs. Cruse (short stories) 1924; A Girl Adoring, 1927; Alice Meynell: A Memoir, 1929; The Frozen Ocean and Other Poems, 1931; Follow Thy Fair Sun, 1935; The Poet's Walk: A Nature Anthology, 1936; Kissing the Rod and Other Stories, 1937; Friends of a Lifetime (ed.) 1940.

ABOUT: Johnson, R. B. Some Contemporary Novelists; Kaye-Smith, S. Three Ways Home; Meynell, V. Alice Meynell: A Memoir.

*MICHAËLIS, KARIN (March 20, 1872-), is the partial-pseudonym of the Danish novelist and short-story writer, Kath-

arina Marie (Bech-Brøndum) Michaëlis Strangeland. She was born at Randers, Denmark, the daughter of Jac. Brøndum, who died in 1921. Her mother, *née* Bech, who died in 1932, was memorialized three years later in *Mor* (*Mother*).

After receiving an education in private schools and under tutors, the girl married Sophus Michaëlis, a Danish author. Soon after their separation Mrs. Michaëlis married an American, Charles Emil Strangeland. As Karin Michaëlis she had published several books, from the *Højt Spil* of 1898 and *Barnet* (1901) and *Lillemar* (1901), the two latter translated respectively into fourteen and twenty languages, to her best-known novel, *The Dangerous Age* (*Den Farlige Alder*), first serialized in the *Revue de Paris* in 1911. Over eighty thousand copies were sold in Germany, where the novel and its feminist theme were made the subject of caricatures and cartoons, notably in *Jugend*. Marcel Prévost called it "the most sincere, the most complete, the most humble and the most disquieting feminine confession perhaps ever written."

Subtitled *Letters and Fragments From a Woman's Diary,* it told the story of Elsie Lindtner (who gave her name to the sequel published next year), who felt an inner bleakness at forty-two which led her to separate from her husband. Retiring to the country to think things over, she eventually summons a young man who once aspired to be her lover, but finds that his passion has cooled. Karin Michaëlis concluded that "between the sexes reigns an ineradicable hostility." Some of the feminine

readers of her novel complained that she had betrayed the freemasonry of womanhood. George Middleton, reviewing *The Dangerous Age* in the American *Bookman,* pointed out that "the fictive literature of menopause is small," confined almost entirely to Octave Feuillet's *La Crise* and George Moore's *Sister Theresa.* Photographs of the novelist showed a large-featured, smiling woman. The Boston *Transcript* remarked of her novel of mediaeval Denmark, *The Governor* (1913), that it read like a Norse saga. "Despite the fact that every page contains something to jar sensibility, the reader is held fascinated, as though under a snake-like spell." Karin Michaëlis' children's books, especially the Bibi series, have proved popular. She is the author of more than fifty books.

Karin Michaëlis left her Villa Bergmannshus, at Thurö, before the Nazi invasion, and is currently living in New York with her sister, the Baroness Dahlerup.

WORKS AVAILABLE IN ENGLISH TRANSLATION: The Dangerous Age: Letters and Fragments From a Woman's Diary, 1911; Elsie Lindtner, 1912; The Governor, 1913; Bibi: A Little Danish Girl, 1927; Venture's End, 1927; Bibi Goes Travelling, 1935; Green Island, 1936.

ABOUT: Bookman October 1911; Current Literature August 1911; New York World-Telegram May 14, 1941.

MIDDLETON, GEORGE (October 27, 1880-), American playwright and literary critic, was born in Paterson, N.J., the son of George Middleton and Ida V. (Blakeslee) Middleton. He

received a B.A. degree from Columbia in 1902. Two years were spent in Paris, becoming acquainted with the French theatre, the work of whose dramatists he was later to adapt to the American stage, and absorbing the history, tory and traditions of the city. In 1911 Middleton married Fola La Follette of Madison, Wis., daughter of Senator La Follette and sister of the "Bob and Phil" (U.S. Senator Robert La Follette, and ex-Governor Philip La Follette) to whom Middleton dedicated his *Hiss! Boom!! Blah!!!* of 1933, a play of the boom and depression in fifty scenes, which was never attempted by a Broadway producer. Middleton's first play, written with Paul Kester, *The Cavalier,* was produced by Julia Marlowe in 1902. Margaret Anglin, Robert Edeson, James K.

* Died January 11, 1950.

Hackett, and George M. Cohan played in other dramas and adaptations. Stars in his production of the 'twenties included Nazimova, in *The Unknown Lady*; Marjorie Rambeau, in *The Road Together*; Fay Bainter, in *The Other Rose*, from Edouard Bourdet's *L'Heure du Berger*; and E. H. Sothern, in *Accused*, an adaptation of Eugene Brieux's *L'Avocat*. *Polly With a Past*, written with Guy Bolton and produced by David Belasco in 1917, was one of Middleton's most solid successes, and established Ina Claire as a light comedienne. From 1912 to 1930 Middleton was also literary editor of *La Follette's Weekly*. He was president of the Dramatists' Guild of the Authors' League of America from 1927 to 1929; honorary vice-president of the League in 1930-31; and honorary vice-president of the Confédération Internationale de Société des Auteurs et Compositeurs in 1929. He also spent two years with the silent moving-pictures as associate producer of the Fox Film Corporation, in 1929-31. Besides belonging to the British Authors' Society of London, he had the distinction of running afoul of the British censor, who refused to license his divorce play, *Collusion*, already in rehearsal with Sybil Thorndike. *The Light of the World* (1920), accepted by Firmin Gémier for production at the Odéon in Paris, was the first play by an American to be accepted by a French state theatre. In 1938 Middleton adapted Marcelle Maurette's *Madame Capet*, in ten scenes, to give Eva Le Gallienne an opportunity to appear as Marie Antoinette. Mr. Middleton, a round, cheerful gentleman, wears horn-rimmed spectacles and is a skillful craftsman, if not a dramatist of first importance. He has also written numerous one-act plays.

PRINCIPAL WORKS: Embers, 1911; Tradition, 1913; Nowadays, 1914; Possession, 1915; The Road Together, 1916; Masks, 1920; Hiss! Boom!! Blah!!! 1933; That Man Balzac, 1936; The Dramatists' Guild, 1939.

ABOUT: Mayorga, M. G. Representative One-Act Plays by American Authors.

MIDDLETON, RICHARD BARHAM

(October 28, 1882-December 1, 1911), English poet and story writer, was born at Staines, Middlesex. His middle name was evidence of his descent from Richard Harris Barham, author of the *Ingoldsby Legends*. He was educated at four different "public" schools, including St. Paul's and the Merchant Taylor's School in London. He then did special work at the University of London, and in 1900 secured a higher certificate in mathematics, physics, and English after passing the Oxford and Cambridge examinations. He was not able to attend either university, however, but instead became a clerk for the Royal Assurance Exchange Corporation. Six years of this (1901-07) proved to be the limit of his endurance. He "escaped" by resignation, though he had no other means of livelihood and all his writing up to that time had netted him little more than the five-guinea prize he won for a story in the *New Leader* in 1905. His only recreation up to that time had been the theatre; he

was a passionate theatre-goer, who at one time saw an average of two plays a week.

Shortly before this period Middleton had become one of a group calling themselves the "New Bohemians," who met at the Prince's Head. It was his first chance for acquaintance with literary men, and there he met among others G. K. Chesterton, Hilaire Belloc, and Arthur Machen. Just how he lived is a question—doubtless very much as his adored Ernest Dowson had done, by starving, by the kindness of his friends, by odd jobs and occasional bits of literary luck. The spring of 1911 found him for some reason in Brussels. There, leaving a note in which he told his faithful friend Henry Savage that he was "going adventuring again," he committed suicide by chloroform. He was just twenty-nine. He was buried in Belgium, with the rites of the Church of England, though he had been an avowed atheist.

Collins Brooks rightly called Middleton "a strange relic of the mood of the '90s." He never got past the immature bohemianism of the generation preceding his own, the generation of the *Yellow Book*. Swinburne, Dowson, and Symons were his idols. He lingered briefly like the ghost of a dead past, a "dreamer and a talker," either boisterous with mirth or sunk in the depths of gloom, a nostalgic romanticist who was born some forty years too late. He even looked and dressed like the men he admired; Herman Scheffauer, who lamented his suicide and was soon to follow him, described his "piratical" appearance, with his "slouch hat, cumbrous figure, plump face with its curly black beard."

And yet Middleton was no mere poseur. He was, as Brooks remarked, "a minor master" of his craft, a pure lyrist, a writer of powerful prose. "Words were his trade, words were his fulfilment, and men of letters rather than life shaped him." He liked to sing of "lily maids," but actually women were of small interest to him; nor was he a drunkard like Dowson or like the earlier Swinburne. He was simply a poet born out of his time and unable to accommodate himself to the world in which he found himself. As Robert Shafer said, "He has no message for the world save that of the traveling singer." He had genuine talent for satire, for "a kind of humor peculiar to himself," for the writing of "idylls, grave or gay," for the depiction of the minds of children, for prose in general "remarkable for meaning rather than for form." But it was not until he was dead that anyone recognized his value.

PRINCIPAL WORKS: Poems and Songs, 1912; The Ghost Ship and Other Stories, 1912; The Day Before Yesterday (essays) 1923; The District Visitor (play) 1924; Letters to Henry Savage, 1929; The Pantomime Man, 1932.

ABOUT: Chapman, J. A. Papers on Shelley, Wordsworth, and Others; Savage, H. Richard Middleton: The Man and His Work; Starrett, V. Buried Caesars; Bookman May 1923; Bookman (London) September 1933; Current Literature October 1912; Dial April 16, 1914; English Review July 1912; Fortnightly Review October 2, 1916; Forum June 1913; Harper's Weekly April 5, 1913.

*MILLAY, EDNA ST. VINCENT (February 22, 1892-), American poet, was born in Rockland, Maine, the daughter of  Henry Tolman Millay and Cora L. (Buzzelle) Millay. Kathleen Millay, the writer, is her younger sister. Her first college work was done at Barnard College. She received her B.A. at Vassar College in 1917 and has since had honorary degrees from Tufts College, the University of Wisconsin, and Russell Sage Foundation College. She began writing verse in her childhood, encouraged by her mother, who recognized her unusual talent. She was still a student when her first major published poem, *Renascence* (which appeared in *The Lyric Year* in 1912) aroused general interest by its note of fresh beauty—though it was full of echoes as well; and the year she was graduated from Vassar she published her first volume of poetry. She had already won the Intercollegiate Poetry Society prize. (Incidentally, Miss Millay, like Stephen Vincent Benét and many others, first saw her poems in print in the "club" pages of the juvenile magazine, *St. Nicholas.*)

A period in Greenwich Village in its Golden Age followed, the period when one lived in an attic, wrote anything one could find an editor willing to accept, and when, to quote Miss Millay herself, the young artists and writers of the Village were "very, very poor and very, very merry." In all the later and more mature work of Edna Millay, two persons persistently crop out— the barefoot, red-headed tomboy of Maine, and the sophisticated innocent of Greenwich Village. She became interested in the theatre, joined the Provincetown Players in their early days, and published three plays in verse. Later she wrote the libretto of one of the few American grand operas, *The King's Henchman*, by Deems Taylor.

In 1923 she was awarded the Pulitzer Prize for *The Harp-Weaver*. It was in this volume that she first emerged as a consummate sonneteer. In the same year she married Eugen Jan Boissevain, a Hollander by birth, an importer, and the former husband of the beautiful young feminist, Inez Milholland, who died in the midst of her crusade. Mr. Boissevain abandoned his business to devote himself to fostering and protecting his wife's genius, and has since acted as her secretary, her buffer, and her bodyguard. They moved to a farm in upper New York, in the southern Berkshires, and live there still, though she spends most of her summers in Maine.

In the earlier years of her marriage, Miss Millay frequently visited Europe. Now she tends more and more to isolate herself in the country, where all day she gardens in rough tweeds, and in the evening dresses in formal clothes and dines in state with her husband. She has always loved clothes, and even in her days of direst poverty in New York she managed somehow to look dainty and distinguished. She writes by fits and starts, working hard while she is working, then doing nothing for idle weeks. Her poems are scrawled in cheap notebooks, and sometimes she herself cannot read her own handwriting later on. She is a member of the American Academy of Arts and Letters.

Gradually a social consciousness has grown up within her, and she has begun to write (not invariably, but with increasing frequency) of the world outside herself. In a way she has always had objectivity, for she could stand aside and write of her own emotions as if she were observing a stranger. Starting with her work on the Sacco and Vanzetti defense, but most apparent in the one book—*Conversation at Midnight*—in which she does not appear at all, or appears effectively disguised, she has become definitely a citizen of her own era. She had, as Selden Rodman remarked, "long ago reached the limit of what she could say about herself."

Though Edna Millay is not a "poet's poet," she is certainly the most popular poet (as opposed to versifiers) of her time, the only one who can live well by her writing, whose books are best sellers and collectors' items. She found it unnecessary long ago to write the light satiric prose which she published occasionally under the pseudonym of "Nancy Boyd." She has not even for several years given the public readings of her work with which she used to tour the country. In any poll of literate (not professional) opinion, she would almost certainly be named first among the contemporary poets of America—though she herself would award the palm to Robinson Jeffers.

The hair that was red in childhood has turned to copper, but she still has her "sharply-cornered witch-green eyes," which Llewelyn Powys compared to a leprechaun's. Never beautiful or even pretty, she has the unmistakable stamp on her face of the different, the superior human being. Her fragile appearance, her clear, precise voice, contribute to this impression of a creature straying mistrustfully in an alien world.

Undoubtedly some of the furore aroused by her earlier poems was due to the period of their appearance; in those first volumes Edna Millay was the voice of rebellious "flaming youth," of the young people who were bent on gathering "figs from thistles" and burning their candles at both ends, of the girls who claimed for themselves the free standards of their brothers. Her personality, a bit touched by an aloof arrogance, has made her more than one articulate enemy, and she has been lampooned in one novel at least. But even those who have written of her most scornfully have granted her genuine poetic power, and if nothing else were left of her work there would remain a few poignant lyrics and a few magnificent sonnets of individual stamp. Her style is intensely personal, and some of her youthful work now seems meretricious, but even that had tautness of line and precision of phrase. She is one of the few poets with keen humor, which emerges wryly from the heartbreak-verses and saves her always from mawkishness.

Those who like her as a "satirical realist" do not care for her as a lyricist. But both alike must concede her distinction in the sonnet. With the exception of Elinor Wylie in her last great series, no woman since Elizabeth Barrett Browning, it has been argued, excels her in that form. Hildegarde Flanner spoke of "the sense of freshness and transparent revelation that her early lyrics conveyed," of "the infusion of personal energy and glow into the traditions of lyric poetry, and the deceptively artless ability to set down the naked fact unfortified." Her work is uneven, and every so often one hears it said that her best days are over: then, in a volume which may contain some of her poorest achievement, one comes across two or three poems that seem to stand up and testify to the persistence of her power.

PRINCIPAL WORKS: Renascence and Other Poems, 1917; A Few Figs From Thistles, 1921; Aria da Capo (play) 1921; The Kamp and the Bell (play) 1921; Two Slatterns and a King (play) 1921; Second April, 1921; The Harp-Weaver and Other Poems, 1923; Distressing Dialogues (as "Nancy Boyd") 1924; The King's Henchman (play) 1927; The Buck in the Snow, 1928; Fatal Interview, 1931; Wine From These Grapes, 1934; Flowers of Evil (translation From Baudelaire, with George Dillon) 1936; Conversation at Midnight, 1937; Huntsman, What Quarry? 1939; Make Bright the Arrows, 1940; There Are No Islands Any More, 1940; Collected Sonnets, 1941.

ABOUT: Atkins, E. Edna St. Vincent Millay and Her Times; Brooks, V. W. New England: Indian Summer; Dell, F. Autobiography; Powys, L. The Verdict of Bridlegoose; Yost, K. Bibliography (see Essay by H. L. Cook); Nation November 14, 1934; Neue Rundschau June 1938; New Republic January 27, 1937; Newsweek May 22, 1939; North American Review March 1938; Poetry July 1931, October 1939; Saturday Review of Literature May 20, 1939; South Atlantic Quarterly January 1938; Virginia Quarterly Review Autumn 1927.

MILLER, Mrs. ALICE (DUER) (1874-August 22, 1942), American novelist and poet, was born in New York City, the daughter of G. K. Duer and Elizabeth (Meads) Duer. Graduating from Barnard College, the woman's college of Columbia University, in June 1899, she married Henry Wise Miller of New York in October, and they set sail for Costa  Rica. Mr. Miller had had a tip on the location of the Nicaraguan canal, and had bought a coffee plantation in the path of the coming land boom—which never materialized. Their son, Denning, later to graduate from Harvard, was born "amid the venomous hardships of bungalow life" in the tropics. The Millers returned penniless to New York, where Mr. Miller went into Wall Street as a telephone boy (he later became a successful stock-broker) and his wife taught mathematics, kept house, sold coffee at night to eke out the family income, and wrote fiction. Light in tone, but soundly grounded—critics usually spoke of their charm, distinction, and sincerity—Mrs. Miller's novels and short stories generally appeared first in periodicals of large national circulation, and lent themselves easily to dramatization. *The Charm School* (1919) and *Come Out of the Kitchen* (1916) were transferred almost bodily to the stage; while *Gowns by Roberta* formed the basis of the Kern-Harbach musical comedy *Roberta*.

The Millers lived in Scotland, London, on the French Riviera, and in an apartment on the East River in New York which shared a balcony with Alexander Woollcott's. Mrs. Miller was a charter member of the latter's literary colony on Neshobe Island, Lake Bomoseen, Vt. She also wrote original screen scenarios in Hollywood. In a Hecht-MacArthur picture, "Soak the Rich," made at the Astoria, N.Y., studios, Mrs. Miller played the spoiled daughter of a millionaire, the producers claiming that she was physically the perfect type for such a rôle.

In 1940 .Mrs. Miller had her greatest popular success with, strangely enough, a long narrative poem extolling Britain's resistance in the Second World War. *The White Cliffs* appeared originally in a small printing, after being rejected by several publishers, but gradually caught on and became a runaway best-seller after a reading on the air by Lynn Fontanne. The 200,000th copy was sold in April 1942. Critics seemed to agree that the emotions aroused by *The White Cliffs* had little to do with the quality of the verse.

Alice Duer Miller was fairly tall, rather thin, with black hair (that turned gray), keen, humorous eyes, and a modulated voice with a cultured accent. A loyal alumna of Barnard, she was a trustee of the college and helped write its semi-centennial history. She died in New York at sixty-eight after a illness of eight months.

PRINCIPAL WORKS: The Modern Obstacle, 1903; Calderon's Prisoner, 1904; Less Than Kin, 1909; The Blue Arch, 1910; Are Women People? 1915; Come Out of the Kitchen, 1916; The Charm School, 1919; The Beauty and the Bolshevist, 1920; Manslaughter, 1921; Priceless Pearl, 1924; Are Parents People? (short stories) 1924; The Reluctant Duchess, 1925; Instruments of Dark-

ness and Other Stories, 1926; The Springboard (play) 1927; Forsaking All Others (verse), 1930; Gowns by Roberts, 1933; Come Out of the Pantry (short stories) 1933; Death Sentence, 1934; The Rising Star, 1935; Four Little Heiresses, 1935; Not for Love, 1937; And One Was Beautiful, 1937; Barnard College: The First Fifty Years (with S. Myers) 1939; The White Cliffs (verse) 1940; I Have Loved England, 1941.

ABOUT: Overton, G. M. The Women Who Make Our Novels; Arts and Decoration November 1932; New York World-Telegram January 8, 1938; New Yorker February 19, 1927, August 9, 1941; Scholastic December 17, 1938; New York Times Book Review June 29, 1941.

MILLER, CAROLINE (August 26, 1903-), American novelist and short-story writer, winner of the Pulitzer prize, was born in Waycross, Georgia, a few miles from the place where the Suwanee River rises. She attended the Waycross High School, but did not continue to college, marrying her English instructor instead, in the August following the June of her graduation. The Millers—later divorced—had

Pinchot

three sons, two of whom are twins. For a time they lived in Baxley, where Mr. Miller was superintendent of schools, but later moved back to Waycross, in southern Georgia. *Lamb in His Bosom* (1933) a story of pioneer life in the back country of Georgia in pre-Civil War days, is Mrs. Miller's only novel, and won the Pulitzer prize for the most distinctive novel of its year. It was written in the intervals of her days as housewife and mother.

Much of the material for the book was gathered while Mrs. Miller was buying chickens and eggs ten miles in the backwoods. She writes: "Almost every incident in *Lamb in His Bosom* actually occurred. Some of them I heard from my uncles and aunts, some from my mother. I got most of the local color from hereabouts, but the facts from family history and history of other families. My grandfather built with his hands a little church which still stands fifteen miles from nowhere. . . . All my people are buried there and there's not one house in twenty miles in any direction . . . nothing but the little church and the graves, and the spring and sand and pines and whippoorwills. My mother's grandfather came to this section as a 'New Light' preacher. I could hardly tell where fact left off and fancy

959

began." Mrs. Miller has written short stories in recent years.

Lamb in His Bosom, described by the Boston *Transcript* as an excellent piece of sectional history, had numerous passages of lyrical descriptive prose. Louis Kronenberger commented that the book was notable not as a novel, but as a picture, and said that it seemed to dry up in the last half, becoming "mere jottings in a parish register."

PRINCIPAL WORKS: Lamb in His Bosom, 1933.

ABOUT: Boston Evening Transcript September 8, 1934; Saturday Review of Literature February 29, 1936.

MILLER, HENRY (December 26, 1891-), American novelist, writes: "I was born in New York City of American parents.

C. Van Vechten

My grandfathers came to America to escape military service. All my ancestors are German and come from every part of Germany. The men were mostly seafarers, peasants, poets, and musicians. Until I went to school I spoke nothing but German and the atmosphere in which I was raised, despite the fact that my parents were born in America, was German through and through. From five to ten were the most important years of my life; I lived in the street and acquired the typical American gangster spirit. My parents were relatively poor, hard-working, thrifty, unimitative. (My father never read a book in his life.) I was well cared for and had a very happy, healthy time of it until I had to shift for myself. I defied my parents and those about me almost from the time I was able to talk. I left City College a few months after I entered it, disgusted with the atmosphere of the place and the stupidity of the curriculum. Took a job in the financial district, with a cement company, and quickly regretted it. Two years later my father gave me the money to go to Cornell; I took the money and disappeared with my mistress, a woman old enough to be my mother. I returned home a year or so later and then left for good, to go West. Worked in various parts of the country, mostly the Southwest. Did all sorts of odd jobs, usually as a ranch hand. Was on my way to Juneau, Alaska, to work as a placer miner in the gold fields, when I was taken down with fever. Returned to New York and led a roving, shiftless, vagabond life, working at anything and

everything but never for very long. I lived recklessly and rebelliously up to my thirtieth year, was the leader in everything, and suffered primarily because I was too honest, too sincere, too truthful, too generous.

"Was forced to study the piano at an early age, showed some talent, and later studied it seriously, hoping to become a concert pianist, but didn't. Gave it up entirely, my motto always being 'all or nothing.' Was obliged to enter my father's tailoring establishment, because he was unable to manage his affairs. Learned almost nothing about tailoring; instead, I began to write. Probably the best thing I ever wrote was in my father's shop—a long essay on Nietzsche's *Anti-Christ*.

"When America entered the war [1917] I went to Washington to work as a clerk in the War Department—sorting mail. In my spare time I did a little reporting for one of the Washington papers. Came back to New York again and took over my father's business during his illness. During the war I married and became a father. Though jobs were plentiful at that time, I was always out of work. I held innumerable positions, for a day or less, often.

"The most important encounter of my life was with Emma Goldman in San Diego, Calif. She opened up the whole world of European culture for me and gave a new impetus to my life, as well as direction. I was violently interested in the I.W.W. movement at the time it was in swing. I was never a member of any club, fraternity, or social or political organization. As a youngster I had been led from one church to another. I later followed with great interest the Bahaists, Theosophists, New Thoughters, Seventh Day Adventists, and so on. I was thoroughly eclectic and immune.

"In 1920, after serving as messenger, I became the employment manager of a large public utility corporation in New York City. I held the job almost five years and still consider it the richest period of my life. During a three weeks' vacation, in 1923, I wrote my first book—a study of twelve eccentric messengers. It was a long book and probably a very bad one, but it gave me the itch to write. I quit the job without a word of notice, determined to be a writer. From then on the real misery began. From 1924 to 1928 I wrote a great many stories and articles, none of which was ever accepted. Finally I printed my own things and with the aid of my second wife I sold them from door to door, later in restaurants and night clubs. Eventually I was obliged to beg in the streets.

"Through an unexpected piece of fortune I was able to go to Europe in 1928, where I stayed the whole year, touring a good part of the continent. Remained in New York the year of 1929, again broke and miserable, unable to see a way out. Early in 1930 I raised the money to return to Europe, intending to go direct to Spain, but never getting any farther than Paris, where I stayed for nine years.

"I completed two novels while in America, and I brought with me to Europe a third one, which was unfinished. A publisher in Paris lost my only copy of this book— three years' work gone up the flue. *Tropic of Cancer,* which is announced as my 'first' book, was written about a year after landing in Paris, from place to place on all sorts of paper, often on the backs of old manuscripts. I had little hope, when writing it, of ever seeing it published. It was an act of desperation. The publication of this book by the Obelisk Press, Paris, opened the door of the world to me. I still have no money and still do not know how to earn a living, but I have plenty of friends and well-wishers, and I have lost my fear of starvation, which was becoming an obsession.

"In June, 1939, I left Paris to go to Greece, where I remained until the end of the year—until ordered to return to America by the American Consulate in Athens. As soon as conditions permit I intend to leave America in order to visit Polynesia, the Malay Archipelago, China, India, and Tibet. While in Paris I was the European editor of the *Phoenix,* and on the editorial staff of the literary review, the *Booster* (later *Delta*), Paris, which was published in several languages, and a contributing editor of the French review, *Volontes,* the continuance of which has been interrupted by the war.

"I am a city man through and through; I hate nature, just as I hate the 'classics.' I owe a lot to the dictionary and the encyclopedia. My greatest influences were Dostoievsky, Nietzsche, and Elie Faure. Proust and Spengler were tremendously fecundating. Of American writers the only real influences were Whitman and Emerson. On the whole I dislike the trend of American literature; it is realistic, prosaic, and 'pedagogic,' and is good, in my opinion, only in the realm of the short story. I owe much to the Dadaists and the Surrealists.

"My aim in writing is to establish a greater *reality.* I am at bottom a metaphysical writer, and my use of drama and incident is only a device to posit something more profound. Above all, I am for imagination, fantasy, for a liberty as yet undreamed of. I want to be read by fewer and fewer people; I have no interest in the life of the masses, nor in the intentions of the existing governments of the world. I hope and believe that the whole civilized world will be wiped out in the next hundred years or so. I believe that man can exist, and in an infinitely better, larger way, without 'civilization.'"

* * *

Miller has been called "the heir of D. H. Lawrence in the struggle to re-assert the natural in man." *The Cosmological Eye* was the first of his books which, in view of the unabashed frankness of his treatment and the nature of his material, any American publisher dared to bring out.

PRINCIPAL WORKS: Tropic of Cancer, 1931; Tropic of Capricorn; Black Spring; The Cosmological Eye, 1939; The Wisdom of the Heart, 1941; The Colossus of Maroussi, 1941; (with Fraenkel, M.) Hamlet: a Philosophic Correspondence (2 vols.) 1939-41.

ABOUT: Muir, E. The Present Age From 1914.

MILLER, JOAQUIN. See "AMERICAN AUTHORS: 1600-1900."

MILLER, MAX (February 9, 1901-), American journalist, writes: "I could say that I started writing when eight years old, on a homestead in Montana. I comprised my only reading public. But my stories must have been excellent, inasmuch as I knew my subject well, the stories all being about me. I was sent to school in Everett, Wash., and worked before school wrapping bread in a bakery. The Everett *Tribune* let me write school notes for it, free. When we entered the war I joined the navy. Eighteen months of it—no medals but a lot of water. I was a first class petty officer. When the war was over I finished high school and entered the University of Washington. I edited the university daily during my senior year. I got tired of papers suddenly, but they were the only way I knew to make my living. After the university I was ten years on the San Diego *Sun* before writing *I Cover the Waterfront.* I have grown weary of the title. [The book was later made into a movie.]

"I have built a home on the cliff shoreline of La Jolla, Calif. [a suburb of San Diego]. The winter storms at sea supply me with my driftwood for the rest of the year. The reefs also supply me with my lobsters and my abalone, and I wish that typewriters could float. Then I might find a new one of those some day—washed ashore from the battle-fleet flagship."

* * *

Mr. Miller married Margaret Ripley in 1927. Gordon Pates, who called him "a reporter with a beautifully formed world philosophy," said "he has established a reputation for a quiet, contemplative, conventional style of writing." William S. Thomson spoke of his "freshness of tone and manner . . . simplicity and individuality of approach and style," and John E. Conley called him "intimate, casual, expressive." The late Constance Lindsay Skinner said he was "a reporter par excellence." By way of minority report, other critics have thought him sentimental, often long-winded, and sometimes dull.

PRINCIPAL WORKS: I Cover the Waterfront, 1932; He Went Away for a While, 1933; The Beginning of a Mortal, 1933; The Second House From the Corner, 1934; The Man on the Barge, 1935; The Great Trek, 1935; Fog and Men on Bering Sea, 1936; For the Sake of Shadows, 1936; Mexico Around Me, 1937; A Stranger Come to Port, 1938; Harbor of the Sun, 1939; Reno, 1941; It Must Be the Climate, 1941.

MILLER, RENÉ FÜLÖP. See FÜ-LÖP-MILLER

MILLIN, Mrs. SARAH GERTRUDE (LIEBSON) (1889-), South African novelist, writes: "My first memories are

of Kimberley and the Diamond Fields, where my grandfather was a pioneer but made no money. As my father also made no money there, we moved to the diamond diggings at the Vaal River, where we were the only European family among thousands of natives. There I stayed until, at the age of seven or eight, I went to school in Kimberley, and there I spent my holidays until I married and went to live in Johannesburg. My father gradually acquired trading rights, ferry rights, waterworks, and a farm, here and there along the river. I had six brothers, of whom three remain.

The eldest was killed, after receiving the Military Cross, in France, in March, 1918. My husband (Philip Millin) was a barrister when I married him. He is now a judge of the Supreme Court of South Africa.

"I began writing for publication at the age of sixteen. I began with short stories, articles, and book reviews. Then I wrote novels. Then I wrote a study of South Africa. Then I wrote lives of Cecil John Rhodes and General Smuts. I also wrote a small volumeful of short essays, and made my book, *Mary Glenn,* into a play called *No Longer Mourn,* which was put on at the Gate Theatre in London in 1935.

"*God's Stepchildren* has been my most successful book in America and on the Continent. *Rhodes* has been my most successful book in England. I think my study of South Africa called *The South Africans* is, in actual fact, my best book."

* * *

Winifred Holtby, in 1926, called Sarah Gertrude Millin "a lively, vivacious Jewess, dark, plump, very well waved and shingled —no side, no sentiment." She was born Sarah Liebson, the daughter of Isaiah and Olga Liebson. She was graduated from school at the top of the list of all girl graduates in South Africa, but decided she would rather write than go to college. As Ethelreda Lewis remarked, "she has no dreams"; instead, she has "a clear, relentless, logical sense of the realities of life." She is brisk and unsentimental, a notable housekeeper, a formidable bridge player. But she is not, as she has been called, "heartless." Under her matter-of-factness is deep compassion. Francis Brett Young summed Mrs. Millin up well: "A woman of keen observation, an inquisitive intellect, with a genuine literary gift, . . . a thoughtful and dignified intelligence, . . . a sense of beauty qualified by a certain self-consciousness in its expression, a profound yet somewhat troubled ethical bent, a faith and pity slightly tinged with despair." Though she is the most widely read of living South African writers, her detachment makes her seem always an observer from the outside. Her style Herbert Gorman called "pared, . . . bare and succinct." Clarity and definiteness are her keynotes; "with her," said Ethelreda Lewis again, "thought is born as the written word." But no one could read *God's Stepchildren,* that tragic study of the mixed-blood "Cape colored people," and doubt the warmth and passion that underlie her cool and logical mind.

PRINCIPAL WORKS: *Novels*—The Dark River, 1920; Middle Class, 1921; Adam's Rest, 1922; The Jordans, 1923; God's Stepchildren, 1924; Mary Glenn, 1925; An Artist in the Family, 1927; The Coming of the Lord, 1928; The Fiddler, 1929; The Sons of Mrs. Aab, 1931; Three Men Die, 1934; What Hath a Man? 1938; The Dark Gods (in England: Bucks Without Hair) 1941; The Herr Witch Doctor, 1941. *Non-Fiction*—The South Africans, 1926; (revised and enlarged edition, 1934); Men on a Voyage (essays) 1930; Rhodes: A Life, 1933; General Smuts, 1936; The Night Is Long, 1941.

ABOUT: Annales Politiques et Littéraires September 10, 1936; Bookman October 1925, March 1929.

MILLIS, WALTER (March 16, 1899-), American journalist and publicist, was born in Atlanta, Ga., the son of John Millis and  Mary (Raoul) Millis. He was educated at Yale (B.A. 1920), and at once joined the staff of the Baltimore *News*. In 1923 he went to the New York *Sun* and *Globe* for a year altogether, since which time he has been an editorial and staff writer on the *Herald Tribune*. His college years were interrupted by service as a second lieutenant in the Field Artillery in 1918; he was not, however, sent to France. In 1929 he married Norah Kathleen Thompson, an Englishwoman, and they have a son and a daughter. They live in New York.

A very young-looking man, with regular features and wavy brown hair, Mr. Millis is still a busy working journalist; with his books and his frequent articles in magazines he has small leisure for outside activities or recreation. He has seldom lectured or appeared much in public, and his private life is very much his own. His first book to attract any attention was *The Martial Spirit*, an economic-historical study of the Spanish-American War, written in a spirit of candid realism. When this was followed by *The Road to War*, an equally devastating account of the economic and propaganda influences which preceded our entry into the First World War, it was generally assumed that Mr. Millis was a pacifist and even (in spite of his connection with a conservative newspaper) a radical. His attitude of unjustified optimism toward the then current European situation, in 1937, seemed to confirm that belief. Nothing could have been further from the truth, as his book, *Why Europe Fights*, and his later magazine articles, after the outbreak of the Second World War, demonstrated. He was early in the forefront of those who advocated all possible aid to Great Britain.

The fact seems to be that his interest is primarily journalistic and historical; he wants to know what actually happened, and the conclusions drawn from his findings are of minor importance. He is not, in other words, opposed to all wars or to our participation in them; he simply sees realistically that the war with Spain in 1898, and to a lesser degree our sending of troops abroad in 1917 and 1918, were a mistake in policy. The isolationists have claimed him, but he is not an isolationist and he has openly repudiated them.

It may be added that he writes persuasively and lucidly, and that he has a faculty for making ordinarily dull matter interesting and even at times exciting. His first book was not published until he was thirty, and he is still in earliest middle age.

PRINCIPAL WORKS: Sand Castle, 1929; The Martial Spirit, 1931; Road to War, 1935; Viewed Without Alarm: Europe Today, 1937; Why Europe Fights, 1940; The Faith of an American, 1941.

MILLS, ENOS ABIJAH (1870-September 21, 1922), American naturalist, was born at Fort Scott, Kans., and attended  school at Kansas City until he earned enough money, when fourteen, to go to Colorado; his mother had told him stories about the state which inflamed his imagination. Here he worked as ranch hand, and as tool boy and "hard-rock man" at

Harris & Ewing

Cripple Creek. In his sixteenth year he built his own cabin in Estes Park in the Rockies. Mills managed to attend business college a while in California, where a chance meeting with John Muir,[qv] on a strip of beach near San Francisco in 1889 determined his future as a naturalist. He built the Long's Peak Inn, which he had no trouble filling for the summer season. (No dancing, card-playing, and destruction of wild flowers or game were permitted, and no religious services except in the guests' rooms.) The rest of the year Mills held the unique post of state Snow Observer, climbing isolated peaks to estimate next summer's water-supply, and filled his notebooks with details about mountain sheep, beaver, and grizzly bears which he sold as articles to Eastern editors. Appointed by Theodore Roosevelt as lecturer in the Forest Service (which he fought on occasion for hampering the national park movement) Mills lectured as far east as Boston. He helped create the Glacier National Park, and fought seven years for the creation of the Rocky Mountain National Park. The bill providing for the National Park Service was sponsored by Mills. He tramped the Rocky Mountains from Arizona to Alaska, once crossing the Chilkoot Pass, and usually subsisted on honey and cream, raisins and oranges. In 1918 Mills married Esther A. Burnell, and they had one daughter. He died four years later, at fifty-two. He was slim, alert, with wide eyes, a wide mouth, and hair receding from a high brow. John Burroughs, Mills, and Muir form a triumvirate of American naturalists not likely to be duplicated in these times.

PRINCIPAL WORKS: Wild Life in the Rockies, 1909; The Spell of the Rockies, 1911; In Beaver World, 1913; The Rocky Mountain Wonderland, 1915; The Story of Scotch, 1916; Your National Parks, 1917; The Grizzly, Our Greatest Wild Animal, 1919; Being Good to Bears and Other True Animal Stories, 1919; The Adventures of a Nature Guide, 1920; Waiting in the Wilderness, 1921; Watched by Wild Animals, 1922; Wild Animal Homesteads, 1923; The Rocky Mountain National Park, 1924; Romance of Geology, 1926; Bird Memories of the Rockies, 1931.

ABOUT: Chapman, A. Enos A. Mills; Ward, B. E. (ed.). Essays of Our Day.

MILN, Mrs. LOUISE (JORDAN)
(March 5, 1864-September 22, 1933). American novelist and short-story writer, was

born at Macomb, Ill. Her father was a physician and surgeon in the Civil War, the mayor of the town for three years, and founder of its first bank. Louise was educated by her father and traveled with him. An opportune visit to relatives in San Francisco, where she was shown Chinatown by a Chinese laundryman met at Sunday School, made apparent to the girl where her real interests lay. As a small-part actress she toured America, Europe, Australia, and Asia, where she visited Chinese peasant huts and the homes of higher class Chinese. (She had gone on the stage at eighteen, after some time at Vassar, where she was known as a remarkably bad speller). Her marriage to the English actor, George Crichton Miln, and the birth of four boys and three girls hindered her writing until 1894, when a first book, When We

Were Strolling Players in the East, appeared. That year and the next she covered the China-Japan war in Korea and wrote a series of articles about the personnel of London embassies and the legations of Eastern countries. The Chinese Minister was one of her best friends. Miln died in 1917. All their sons were in the Royal Air Force during the First World War.

A novelization of Mr. Wu, a successful pseudo-Chinese play by H. M. Vernon and Harold Owen, made Mrs. Miln better known to an American public in 1918. Two years later came The Feast of Lanterns, a novel picturing aristocratic Chinese family life and national ideals, love for beauty, nature, justice, and esteem for womankind. The book, which took its title from a principal Chinese holiday, was written in longhand in thirteen weeks.

Mrs. Miln, as compared with Pearl Buck, her nearest literary parallel, is less austere and more superficial. (She said she wrote for amusement, and fitfully). She had a round face, gray hair and plump cheeks; was called a strong Tory in England and an intense royalist in China. Her death occurred at her house near Calais, France.

PRINCIPAL WORKS: Novels—The Invisible Foe (from play by Walter Hackett) 1917; Mr. Wu (from play by H. M. Vernon & Harold Owen) 1918; The Purple Mask, 1918; The Feast of Lanterns, 1920; The Green Goddess (from play by William Archer); Mr. and Mrs. Sên, 1923; In a Shantung Garden, 1924; Ruby and Ivy Sên, 1925; It Happened in Peking, 1926; The Flutes of Shanghai, 1928; By Soochow Waters, 1929; Rice, 1930; The Vintage of Yon-Yee, 1931; A Chinese Triangle (American title: Anne Zu-Zan) 1932; Peng Wee's Harvest, 1933. Non-Fiction—When We Were Strolling Players in the East, 1894; Quaint Korea, 1895; An Actor's Wooing, 1896; Little Folk of Many Lands, 1899; A Woman and Her Talent, 1905; Were Men But Constant, 1918. Short Stories—The Soul of China, 1925; Red Lily and Chinese Jade, 1928.

ABOUT: Century Magazine November 1928; Publishers' Weekly October 7, 1932.

*MILNE, ALAN ALEXANDER (January 18, 1882-   ), English novelist and playwright who writes as A. A. Milne, was born in London, the son of John Vine Milne. He was educated at Westminster School and at Trinity College, Cambridge, where he edited the Granta. He took his degree in 1903 and returned to London to become a journalist. In his own words: "By the end of a year I had spent my money and had earned by writing— twenty pounds. So I moved to two cheap and dirty rooms in a policeman's house in Chelsea and went on writing. The second

* Died January 31, 1956.

year I made about 120 pounds and lived on it. In the third year I was making two hundred pounds, for several papers were now getting used to me, but in February 1906 a surprising thing happened. I was offered the assistant editorship of *Punch*. I accepted and was assistant editor until the end of 1914."

Early in 1915 Milne joined the Royal Warwickshire Regiment. He had been married in 1913 to Dorothy (Daphne) de Sélincourt, who is also a writer. While at training camp he wrote a fairy play in which both he and his wife acted, together with other soldiers and their wives. He had already published three volumes of essays from *Punch* and was becoming known as a humorist. On the Western Front, to which he was sent, he found time to write a play, *Wurzel-Flummery*.

Soon after, he was invalided and on his recovery was made signaling instructor at a camp in England. During this time he wrote three more plays. By the time he was demobilized, he was sufficiently established as a writer to decline to go back to *Punch* and to give all his time to authorship.

It is hardly necessary to remark that Mr. Milne has a son, Christopher Robin. The son is grown now, and also a writer, and he has recounted his fellowship of suffering with Frances Hodgson Burnett's son, who never escaped from being "Little Lord Fauntleroy." Christopher Robin in his childhood inspired a whole series of verses, stories, and plays, including the volumes dealing with "Winnie-the-Pooh." Mr. Milne must by this time feel very much like Frankenstein or like Edgar Bergen—he has produced a monster of whimsicality which threatens to overwhelm his serious work as a dramatist. A thousand people know his juvenile verses who never heard of his comedies, though some of these, like *Mr. Pim Passes By, The Dover Road,* and *The Truth About Blayds,* have been immensely popular. Other readers would be surprised to learn that he has written a first-class detective novel, *The Red House Mystery,* a minor classic of its kind, as well as a highly successful mystery play, *The Perfect Alibi,* and several novels for adults. As a matter of fact, like many humorists, Mr. Milne takes himself and his work very seriously. He would prefer to be known by his powerful and impassioned plea against war, *Peace With Honour.* But he is so inextricably woven into the public mind with the gossamer strands of Christopher Robin and Winnie-the-Pooh that when he came to write his own autobiography he found it necessary to devote the larger part of it to his childhood.

He is not at all the sort of man that one would expect to write children's verses. Tall, tanned, and athletic, with light receding hair and alert blue eyes, he lives much out of doors and is a better than average golfer. But the curse of whimsicality, often of a rather milk-and-water variety, clings to him, and infects even his adult plays. He is apt to be a bit ponderous and dull when he would be lightest; too often he reminds one of Barrie minus Barrie's genius. Nevertheless, in his best plays and in his novels there is apparent a genuinely witty and satirical talent. His name is pronounced *miln*.

PRINCIPAL WORKS: *Plays*—First Plays (Wurzel-Flummery, The Red Feathers, Belinda, The Boy Comes Home, The Lucky One) 1917; Make-Believe, 1918; Mr. Pim Passes By, 1919; The Romantic Age, 1920; Three Plays (The Dover Road, The Truth About Blayds, The Great Broxropp) 1923; Success, 1923; Ariadne, 1925; The Ivory Door, 1927; The Fourth Wall, 1928; Toad of Toad Hall (adaptation) 1930; Four Plays (Michael and Mary, To Meet the Prince [in England, To Have the Honour], The Perfect Alibi, Portrait of a Gentleman in Slippers) 1932; Miss Elizabeth Bennett, 1936; Sarah Simple, 1937. *Novels*—Mr. Pim, 1921; The Red House Mystery, 1921; Two People, 1931; Four Days' Wonder, 1933. *Juveniles*—When We Were Very Young, 1924; Winnie-the-Pooh, 1926; Now We Are Six, 1927; The House at Pooh Corner, 1928; The Christopher Robin Story Book, 1929; The Christopher Robin Reader, 1929; The Christopher Robin Birthday Book, 1931; The Christopher Robin Verses, 1932. *Miscellaneous*—The Day's Play, 1910; The Holiday Round, 1912; Once a Week, 1914; Once on a Time, 1917; Not That It Matters, 1919; If I May, 1920; The Sunny Side, 1922; By Way of Introduction, 1929; Peace With Honour, 1934; Autobiography, 1939; Behind the Lines (verse) 1940; War Aims Unlimited, 1941; War With Honour, 1941.

ABOUT: Milne, A. A. Autobiography; Living Age March 1934; Scholastic November 10, 1934.

MINNIGERODE, MEADE (June 19, 1887-), American biographer and novelist, was born in London and educated at Harrow. His parents, however, were Americans of old Southern families. At nineteen he was brought to the United States and went to Yale, receiving his B.A. degree in 1910. For three years thereafter he was on the staff of a New York publisher, and then for three years with a shipping company. When the United

States entered the First World War, Mr. Minnigerode was sent to France as representative of the United States Shipping

Board; then for another year he served as first lieutenant with the American Red Cross, attached at various times to the American and the French Armies. He received the French Commemorative and Victory Medals. In 1932 he married Mildred Bright Mailliard, and they live in Essex, Conn.

His career as a writer did not begin until after his return from France in 1919, but his success was immediate and he has been a free-lance writer ever since, contributing frequently to magazines. His books have been about equally divided between historico-biographical works and novels: he is perhaps rather better known as a biographer and a writer on social history—as in his popular *The Fabulous Forties*. Most of his novels are historical in nature, and in both forms his special *forte* is vivid character-drawing, so that his style is unmistakable whether he is writing of actual persons and occurrences, or of similar persons and occurrences slightly masked by the requirements of fiction.

PRINCIPAL WORKS: Laughing House, 1920; The Big Year, 1921; Oh, Susanna; Some Personal Letters of Herman Melville and a Bibliography, 1922; The Queen of Sheba, 1923; The Seven Hills, 1923; The Fabulous Forties, 1924; Lives and Times, 1925; Aaron Burr (with S. H. Wendell) 1925; Some American Ladies, 1926; Cordelia Chantrell, 1926; Cockades, 1927; Certain Rich Men, 1927; Presidential Years, 1928; Jefferson, Friend of France, 1928; Some Mariners of France, 1930; The Magnificent Comedy, 1931; The Son of Marie Antoinette, 1934; Marie Antoinette's Henchman, 1936; Black Forest, 1937; The Terror of Peru, 1940.

ABOUT: Saturday of Literature November 6, 1937.

MIRSKY, DMITRY SVYATOPOLK
(formerly Prince) (1890-   ), Russian literary critic and historian, was born in Czarist Russia and was educated at St. Petersburg University. From 1914 to 1918 he served in the Foot Guards, and in the White Army from 1919 to 1920. Removing to England, he lectured on Russian literature at King's College, London University, for the decade 1922-32, at the end of which he surprisingly returned to Russia. Making his home in Moscow, he has been a member of the Union of Soviet Writers and a literary critic and contributor to various Russian papers, publishing, for instance, an essay on T. S. Eliot in *Krasnaia Nov'*, in the March 1933 issue. His admiration for Lenin has apparently made him acceptable to the Soviet régime, despite his birth and inherited title (which he now disavows, as befits a "comrade"). In his *Lenin* (1931) Mirsky wrote: "It has been pointed out to me that, coming as it does from a member of the class that was most effectively eliminated by the great Russian Revolution, and adopting at the same time a pro-revolutionary standpoint, the present book calls for some explanation *pro domo sua*. . . . Whatever the Communists might be worth in their international function, as a Russian party they had preserved the independence of the country from foreign intervention [and] made of Russia a cultural and political force of universal significance. To recognize the unique greatness of Lenin had already become a commonplace among all the younger émigrés of good faith by 1925."

D. S. Mirsky occupies a unique position as interpreter of Russian literature to English readers, and as an exponent of English literature to his countrymen. His *The Intelligentsia of Great Britain* (1935), translated by Alec Brown, makes piquant and amusing reading, especially his remarks on Aldous Huxley and the Bloomsbury set. G. D. H. Cole, he declares, for instance, "has from his academic eminence at Oxford been busy preparing many young people in the art of pot-roasting Marx (or cooking Marx in his own steam in order to de-Marx him)." Mirsky has also translated Gogol's *Diary of a Madman* into English for a limited edition, and, with A. D. Miller, published in 1936 an English-Russian dictionary as part of the *Soviet Encyclopedia*. But his most important works are his objective and definitive histories of Russian literature, written in English. In this field he stands pre-eminent.

He is described as a thickset, bearded man, almost ursine in appearance and manner; a thorough scholar who has few other interests. Though he is regarded as a political apostate by fellow "White" Russians, they respect his sincerity and his achievements as a man-of-letters and historian.

PRINCIPAL WORKS: Contemporary Russian Literature: 1881-1925, 1925; Pushkin (Republic of Letters Series) 1926; A History of Russia, 1927; A History of Russian Literature: From the Earliest Times to the Death of Dostoyevsky, 1927; Lenin, 1931; Russia: A Social History, 1931; The Intelligentsia of Great Britain, 1935.

ABOUT: International Who's Who 1940.

MITCHELL, JAMES LESLIE ("Lewis Grassic Gibbon") (February 13, 1901-February 21, 1935), Scottish novelist, archaeologist and historian, was

born at or near Auchterless in Aberdeenshire. At an early age he was taken by his parents, James and Lilias Mitchell, to Arbuthnott in Kincardineshire, the Mearns country of his stories. There as a boy he attended the local school where he met Miss R. Middleton whom he later married. Mitchell's career began as a journalist (1917-18). After four years in the army (1918-22), he turned to exploration and archaeological research. While still in his twenties his work in archaeology so impressed the editors of the Today and Tomorrow Series that he was commissioned to write *Hanno: or, The Future of Exploration* (1928), his first book. Previously Mitchell had published only a short story, "For Ten's Sake," which after many rejections he had sent to H. G. Wells who encouragingly wrote him that he could "do this sort of thing well," and which finally was published in 1927 in the *Cornhill Magazine*. Its editor, Leonard Huxley, liked from the first Mitchell's stories and published them continually. Later a cycle of twelve were collected in *Calends of Cairo* (1931). These tales of adventure purported to be recounted in Cairo by one Anton Saloney, "dragoman, guide, ex-colonel of horse in the army of Denikin, and one-time professor of English literature in the gymnasium of Kazan." In rapid succession Mitchell sent to press his first two novels: *Stained Radiance* (1930) and *The Thirteenth Disciple* (1931). The impact of these early works made John Lindsey declare in the *Twentieth Century*:

"It seems to me that Leslie Mitchell has justified his inclusion among the very few people—men or women—writing today whose work we cannot spare. The work is individual: perhaps almost annoyingly so. It demands a certain mental adjustment on the part of the reader. But, granted that adjustment, it is important work, indicating a certain line of thought that is too seldom treated of: *a certain freedom from preconceived notions of what is right and wrong.* And the explorer along that line of thought is, I am sure, a writer who will have an influence, and a very definite one, on the thought and literature of the twentieth century."

In 1932 Mitchell published three novels, including *Sunset Song,* Part I of *A Scots Quair,* a magnificent trilogy of Scottish life. L. A. G. Strong considered *Sunset Song* "the biggest book I know which has come out of modern Scotland," and *The Scots Magazine* said: "All our land is there in its sourness, its harshness, in its beauty and its sorrow." *Sunset Song* established "Lewis Grassic Gibbon" as a novelist of first magnitude. Part II of *A Scots Quair, Cloud Howe* (1933), made another Scottish novelist, Neil M. Gunn, confess: "I don't think I have ever been before put under the illusion of the earth itself having a voice."

During 1934 Mitchell collaborated with "Hugh McDiarmid" in the searching *Scottish Scene,* depicting Scotland from all angles and through all forms of literary technique: poems, plays, short stories, essays. To these must be added a novel, *Gay Hunter,* and three volumes in the scientific field: *Earth Conquerors,* which narrates the lives and achievements of great explorers; *Niger: The Life of Mungo Park,* an account of the explorer's terrible hardships in the quest for the river's eastward flow; and *The Conquest of the Maya,* a standard history of the Maya civilization, described in a foreword by the famous archaeologist Sir Gordon Elliot Smith as "a great work which will earn the gratitude of Human History." In this culminating year of Mitchell's short but brilliant career appeared also the last part of his trilogy, *Grey Granite.* Just as *Sunset Song* depicts the pre-war Scottish countryside, and *Cloud Howe* a small Scottish town in the grip of the first post-war depression, *Grey Granite* deals with a Scottish industrial city in the throes of the economic crisis. Mitchell, who called himself "a revolutionary writer," grappled with the problems of social revolution. Whatever his message, he produced in *A Scots Quair* "the greatest Scots novel in Scottish literature," according to James Barke. Historian, aviator, novelist, archaeologist and explorer, Mitchell (whose hobby was deep-sea diving) died at the age of thirty-four, at Welwyn, Garden City. His ashes were interred at Arbuthnott Churchyard.

PRINCIPAL WORKS: Hanno: or, The Future of Exploration, 1928; Stained Radiance, 1930; The Thirteenth Disciple, 1931; The Calends of Cairo (American title: Cairo Dawns) 1931; Three Go Back, 1932; The Lost Trumpet, 1932; Sunset Song, 1932; Persian Dawns, Egyptian Nights, 1933; Image and Superscription, 1933; Spartacus, 1933; Cloud Howe, 1933; Scottish Scene (with "H. MacDiarmid") 1934; Gay Hunter, 1934; Earth

Conquerors (British title: Nine Against the Unknown) 1934; Niger: The Life of Mungo Park, 1934; Grey Granite, 1934; The Conquest of the Maya, 1934.

ABOUT: Christian Science Monitor May 8, 1935; Left Review February 1935, February 1936; New Republic April 12, 1933, February 28, 1934; New Statesman & Nation January 5, 1935; New York Times April 2, 1933, January 27, 1935, April 7, 1935; Saturday Review of Literature February 17, 1934, April 13, 1935; Spectator (London) September 24, 1932, August 4, 1933, December 7, 1934; Times Literary Supplement (London) October 6, 1932, September 7, 1933, April 6, 1934; Yale Review Spring 1934.

*MITCHELL, MARGARET (1900-

American novelist, was born in Atlanta, Ga., the daughter of Eugene Muse Mitchell, a prominent attorney and president of the Atlanta Historical Society, and Maybelle (Stephens) Mitchell. Her mother and her older brother were also deeply interested in local history, and she grew up hearing interminable stories of the War Between

Asasno

the States. She was ten before she learned, with shock, that the Confederacy lost the war! She was graduated from Washington Seminary, Atlanta, and went to Smith College, with the intention of becoming a physician. However, her mother died at the end of a year, and she was obliged to return home, to keep house for her father and brother and to make her début in Atlanta society. In 1922 she tired of a purely social life, and went to work on the Atlanta *Journal,* as a member of the Sunday Magazine staff. Her newspaper work was done under the name of Peggy Mitchell. In 1926 she sprained her ankle badly, it was slow to heal, and she resigned her newspaper job. A year previously she had married John R. Marsh, manager of the advertising department of the Georgia Power Company.

It was during the ten years from 1926 to 1936 that she wrote *Gone With the Wind.* It was written in chaotic fashion, the last part first, and the manuscript piled up without method or completeness. She was in a way unburdening herself of the immense accumulation of minute information on pre-war, war, and post-war days poured into her ears from childhood. When H. S. Latham, Macmillan Company's vice-president, heard of the book and came to Atlanta in 1935 to see it, she insisted that it was not finished. He was so much impressed by it that he arranged for its publication the following spring.

Gone With the Wind is less a novel than a phenomenon. As someone remarked, nobody except Franklin D. Roosevelt has been so much in the public eye since Lindbergh flew the Atlantic as has Margaret Mitchell since 1936. The book sold as many as 50,000 copies in a single day, two million copies by 1939; it has been translated into sixteen languages; in 1940 the technicolor moving picture version with Vivian Leigh and Clark Gable broke all attendance records despite the unexpected disapproval of the Legion of Decency (the novel itself had aroused no moralistic opposition); it has been transcribed in Braille; it received the Pulitzer Prize for fiction in 1937, was selected by the American Booksellers' Association as the outstanding novel of the year, received the first Carl Bohnenberger Memorial Award of the Florida Library Association and the gold medal of the New York Southern Society; and Miss Mitchell's alma mater, Smith College, gave her an honorary M.A. degree in 1939.

The terrific furore which has accompanied all this has effectually kept Margaret Mitchell from writing anything else. She is attempting valiantly to live her normal life, in the same apartment, with the same friends as before, but she conscientiously answers all the tens of thousands of letters written her (with the help of one and sometimes two secretaries), and she autographed books and addressed meetings until her strength gave out. After the world premiere of the movie in Atlanta, she was actually forced to go into hiding. Several impostors have been detected in various parts of the country who have impersonated her. She is still hoping for the excitement to die down, so that she can return to a peaceful existence and show that *Gone With the Wind* is not the only novel she has it in her to write.

She is a tiny woman with blue eyes and dark auburn hair, who has often heard the remark that she could not have written that huge novel because she is "too little." Actually, she is sturdy and a bundle of energy. Like most people with newspaper training, she works directly on the typewriter and is "unable to write" without access to it.

Gone With the Wind, with its 1,037 pages, hardly needs description; it is in essence "an old-fashioned romantic narrative" which appeared at just the right time. It is not a great novel, but it has charm, excitement, and continued interest, it reconstructs vividly a lost time and place, its people are real and alive, and Scarlett O'Hara at least is likely to remain a favorite fiction character for many years. Mrs. Marsh must feel sometimes a little like Frankenstein.

ONLY PUBLISHED WORK: Gone With the Wind, 1936.

ABOUT: Collier's Weekly March 13, 1937; Independent Woman April 1940; Pictorial Review March 1937; Saturday Review of Literature January 8, 1938; Time July 6. 1936; Wilson Library Bulletin September 1936.

MITCHELL, SILAS WEIR. See "AMERICAN AUTHORS: 1600-1900"

MITCHISON, Mrs. NAOMI MARGARET (HALDANE) (November. 1, 1897-), English novelist, writes: "Born  Edinburgh, daughter of physiologist and philosopher John Scott Haldane and Kathleen (Trotter) Haldane. [Her brother is J. B. S. Haldane,*qv* the biologist.] Social origin: land-owning both sides, but brought up at Oxford with professional class outlook; non-religious, high ethical standards, Conservative politics. Well educated as child in boys' school, then by governess. University career interrupted almost before begun by engagement and marriage. Worked as V.A.D. nurse during World War. Husband G. Richard Mitchison, barrister, Labour politican, author *The First Workers' Government.* First child born 1918.

"Early friendship and influence: Aldous Huxley. Hoped to be scientist, but owing to incomplete education and no degree had to write. Husband, first-class historian, lured her into reading history, which found fascinating. Early books written in London, largely while pushing prams [perambulators]. Read immensely in English and French, lived in London, ordinary bourgeois home. Was always rather incompetent housewife. Had four boys and two girls: eldest son died. Became gradually interested in social problems, helped with first birth control clinics in London. Went on writing. Became interested in politics about 1931, when husband stood for Parliament in industrial Division. Got to know working people. Went to Russia 1932. After that constantly becoming involved with political action: counter-revolution in Austria, 1934; sharecroppers in Arkansas, 1935; etc. Always interested in Scottish Nationalism.

"At first favorite high-brow author, gradually began to be disliked by high-brows—perhaps because woman, because interested in ethics rather than direct politics, or because uncomfortably truthful. Dropped historical novels for a time, because of interest in present-day social problems and education. Then re-started because it seems better sometimes to look in a mirror for what one is trying to see. Much influenced by Gerald Heard, but not entirely in agreement.

"Likes collaborating and seldom loses temper: thinks it essential for any modern worker. Also likes writing for children. Apt to engage in newspaper controversy. Answers correspondents.

"Stood for Scottish Universities as Labour Party candidate. Otherwise thinks it more useful to help husband: does not want to get into Parliament, as waste of time. Considers local political and social activities very valuable. Has done a good deal of speaking: usually good, though too emotional. Worked on Popular Front campaign: thinks Cripps and Lansbury best British politicians.

"In end of 1937, husband bought house in West of Scotland; at first did not want to go back to land-owning position, having escaped from it. But gradually became entangled; now living there permanently, glad to have left London. Almost forced into semi-feudal position, now as much part of Carradale as, say, Post Office, and as much used by community, collaborating with them in all ways. Hopes to keep there a corner of democracy, freedom, and civilization during war, and if war ends in revolutionary manner, to stay on as part of Socialist community among friends, perhaps in free Scotland, liberated from English ties but in Federal Union of nations.

"Deeply and practically interested in housing, agriculture, education, herring fishing, evacuation of children from war areas. At present writing poems for Carradale community in collaboration with workers: some set to tunes and sung by workers. Hoping shortly to become local magistrate."

* * *

The clipped style of this sketch gives no idea of Mrs. Mitchison as a novelist. Her historical novels are fascinating, with their homely detail and what Mabel A. Bessey called their "curious fidelity" to historical fact. They deal mostly with ancient Greece and Rome or go still farther back into prehistory. Henry Seidel Canby justly called her "the most interesting historical novelist now writing in English." Humor and decision are in her firm features. She is an efficient but self-effacing enthusiast, who takes far too much time from her writing to do practical work for the causes in which she believes. She deserves a wider public than she has had, especially in America. She was made an officer of the French Academy in 1924.

PRINCIPAL WORKS: The Conquered, 1923; When the Bough Breaks, 1924; Cloud Cuckoo Land, 1925; The Laburnum Branch (poems) 1926; Black Sparta, 1928; Anna Comnena, 1928; Nix-Nought-Nothing, 1928; Barbarian Stories, 1929; The Hostages, 1930; Comments on Birth Control, 1930; The Corn King and the Spring Queen, 1931; The Price of Freedom (play, with L. E. Gielgud) 1931; Boys and Girls and Gods, 1931; The Powers of Light, 1932; The Delicate Fire, 1932; The Home and a Changing Civilization, 1934; Vienna Diary, 1934; Beyond This Limit (with Wyndham Lewis) 1935; The Fourth Pig, 1936; Socrates (with R. H. S. Crossman) 1937; The Moral Basis of Politics, 1938; As It Was in the Beginning (play, with L. E. Gielgud) 1939; Kingdom of Heaven, 1939; The Blood of the Martyrs, 1939; Black Sparta, 1940.

ABOUT: English Review November 1932; Review of Reviews (London) November 1932; Saturday Review of Literature September 19, 1931, September 3, 1933; Scholastic February 10, 1934, December 2, 1940.

MOLESWORTH, Mrs. MARY LOUISA (STEWART). See "BRITISH AUTHORS OF THE 19TH CENTURY."

*MOLNÁR, FERENC (January 12, 1878-), Hungarian dramatist, was born in Budapest, the son of a physician, and was

educated at the Royal College of Science there and in the Law Faculty of Budapest and Geneva Universities. But he never practised law; even in his college days he was writing stories and plays, and after his graduation, instead of an attorney he became a reporter. He was attached to several Budapest papers in turn, and he himself thinks the experience was of value to him in supplying material for his later plays. His last journalistic post was as a war correspondent in 1914-18. He has, however, continued to write short humorous articles (*feuilletons,* as they are known in Europe) for magazines and papers in many countries. He was a regular contributor to the New York magazine, *Vanity Fair,* during its life-time.

Molnár first established his reputation, both at home and abroad, with *The Devil,* in 1907. Two years later he became famous as the author of *Liliom. The Guardsman* and *The Wolf* followed, then *The Swan,* which won him the cross of the French Legion of Honor. His later plays have failed to maintain the high standard of these. George Halasz has suggested that Molnár's "meteoric rise to fame" was primarily due to his "ingenious basic ideas and novel situations"; that when "the well of ideas dried, . . . in order to live up to his reputation he began a frantic search for fantastic and uncommon themes," the result too often being incredibility and triviality. These earlier plays, *Liliom* above all, a classic during its author's lifetime, are characterized by their wit and grace: as Francis Fergusson put it, Molnár could write "light comedy which is really light, really innocent of didacticism, prophecy, and self-pity." Apparently he could not keep it up, and for some years he has been living on his past reputation although he continues to write plays, novels, and stories. Only his articles and sketches are as clever as ever, sophisticated and cynical.

It may be that Molnár's failure to live up to his early promise is a natural consequence of his prominence as a man about town, a noted figure in the gay, mundane society of Budapest. His wife was Lili Darvas, a noted actress and a famous beauty, and all his personal affiliations are with the theatre and with Bohemian circles. In Budapest he did much of his writing in cafés, talking and drinking while he worked, and sitting up all night, sleeping in the daytime. Once his preliminary draft was done, he retired to the hotel suite where he lived, locked himself in with plenty of black coffee, and wrote feverishly until in a few days he emerged with a new play or story. A fugitive from Nazism because of his Jewish origin, he came to America early in 1940; the chief market for his writing here has been Hollywood.

He is a heavy-set man with thick, straight gray hair, once dark. He is noted for his witticisms and is a sought-after companion. *Liliom* and, to a lesser extent, *The Guardsman* and *The Swan,* will continue for a long time to hold their own. *The Guardsman* was very successful as a film. Molnár's special gift, as one critic remarked, is that "he speaks always in an ordinary tone of voice and thus lends to all his work an air of intimacy and familiarity."

WORKS AVAILABLE IN ENGLISH: *Plays*—Liliom, 1921; Fashions for Men and The Swan, 1922; The Guardsman, 1924; Olympia, 1928; Plays, 1929;

* Died April 1, 1952.

The Good Fairy, 1932. *Fiction*—Husbands and Lovers (sketches) 1924; Prisoners, 1925; Eva and The Derelict Boat (novelettes) 1926; Paul Street Boys, 1927.

ABOUT: Arts and Decoration April 1923; Bookman December 1929; Mentor February 1929; Nation May 11, 1921, May 26, 1926; New York Times Magazine January 19, 1941; New Yorker April 15, 1940.

MONCRIEFF. See SCOTT-MON-CRIEFF

MONKHOUSE, ALLAN NOBLE (May 7, 1858-January 10, 1936), English playwright and novelist, was born in Barnard

Castle, Durham, the third son of J. W. S. Monkhouse, and was educated at private schools. In 1893 he married Lucy Dowie, who died the next year; by his second wife, Elizabeth Dorothy Pearson, married in 1902, Monkhouse had two sons and two daughters. (A nephew and namesake, Allan Monkhouse, is a British engineer who figured with other engineers in the Soviet sabotage trial and wrote a book about it.)

The year of his second marriage, Monkhouse became a member of the staff of the *Manchester Guardian*, where he remained thirty years, notably as the paper's dramatic critic. His numerous plays were generally produced, if at all, in the repertory theatres of Manchester, Liverpool, and Birmingham. Guilty of no concessions to popular tastes, as Edward Garnett has said, their situations were "often tragic in their issues, lit by ironical lights, devoid of orthodox comments and sentimental solutions." Monkhouse's "trenchantly intellectual" novels had the same characteristics. *The Conquering Hero* (1923) was one of the first serious plays about the First World War; it is a study of a young intellectual, Chris Rokeby who, egged on by his family and fiancée to enlist, makes a creditable record, and is vociferously welcomed back by the village, knowing secretly that his moments of heroism were counterbalanced by moments of abject cowardice. *The Education of Mr. Surrage*, Monkhouse's wittiest and least sardonic comedy, shows an English provincial so successfully brought up to date by his children and their pseudo-artistic friends that he goes up to London and turns the tables on them. *Mary Broome* is a study of a housemaid, seduced by the son of the

house, who resolutely refuses to make an honest man of him. Of Monkhouse's novels, *My Daughter Helen* and its sequel *Marmaduke* are perhaps the best known; *True Love* is another war study, in which an English newspaperman dies in the trenches, and his German-born wife, whose life has been made miserable by her neighbors, succumbs in childbirth. Monkhouse retired from the *Guardian* in 1932, contributing weekly literary articles, however, until his death at seventy-seven. His home was at Meadow Bank, Disley, Cheshire, where his favorite recreation was "loitering in a garden."

PRINCIPAL WORKS: *Novels*—A Deliverance, 1898; Love in a Life, 1903; Dying Fires, 1912; Men and Ghosts, 1918; True Love, 1919; My Daughter Helen, 1922; Marmaduke, 1924; Alfred the Great, 1927. *Plays*—Mary Broome, 1912; The Education of Mr. Surrage, 1913; Four Tragedies, 1913; War Plays, 1916; The Conquering Hero, 1923; First Blood, 1924; The Grand Cham's Diamond, 1925; O Death, Where Is Thy Sting? 1927; The King of Barvender, 1928; The Rag, 1928; Paul Felice, 1930; Cecilia, 1932. *Essays*—Books and Plays: Essays of To-Day and Yesterday, 1894.

ABOUT: Adelphi May 1924; Fortnightly Review October 1924; Manchester Quarterly July 1914; New York Times January 11, 1936.

MONRO, HAROLD EDWARD (March 14, 1879-March 16, 1932), British poet and critic, was born and reared in Brussels, but was of pure Scottish

descent, the son of Edward William Monro, an engineer. All his life, as F. S. Flint said, "the wild Celt in him was at odds with the thrifty heir of a line of cautious physicians" (on his mother's side). He was bilingual as a child, not leaving Belgium until he was seven. He was then educated at Radley Grammar School and, after a year in France, at Caius College, Cambridge, where he received his degree in 1901. His chief interest —and grief—in the university was horse-racing. In a walking tour in the Hartz Mountains he met his first wife, whom he married in 1903, and by whom he had a son. They were divorced in 1916, and in 1920 he married Alida Klemantaski, who survived him. At Haslemere, where he settled in 1903, he established the Samurai Press. Then he went abroad again, but returned to London in 1911 and the next year established the celebrated *Poetry Review* — the same year that *Poetry* was started in Amer-

ica. As a sort of annex to the magazine was the Poetry Bookshop, which was located at first in the slums in order to interest the residents in poetry, but served instead as free quarters for indigent poets. To the bookshop, though it never made money, Monro clung to the end, but the magazine failed financially and passed out of his hands. So did two later magazines—*Poetry and Drama*, in 1913, and the *Chapbook*, in 1919. In between, during the First World War, he served as officer in an anti-aircraft battery, and then in the War Office. He died, after a long illness, two days after his fifty-third birthday.

Monro was of consequence as a poet, but he was even more influential as a lover of poetry. His magazines, and the readings he gave at the bookshop, missed few of the verse-writers of promise, and he was the first to recognize many now famous. His own work T. S. Eliot called "honest and bitter." "The center of his interest," Eliot added, "was in the ceaseless question and answer of the tortured mind, or the unspoken question and answer between two human beings." There is implicit in all his poems a haunting sadness and a touch of the eerie. "He used verse," said Humbert Wolfe, "to convey a carefully pondered philosophy of life. . . . Always pervading his verse is some echo, some hint, some fragrance, from elsewhere."

He had a genius for friendship, and the most disparate people were his friends. Flint, who was very close to him, called him "hardworking and lazy, generous and mean, a lover of freedom and a tyrant, a bohemian and a bourgeois." His long, melancholy face of the "black Scot" was indicative of the dual spirit at war within him, which once in a while burst its bonds in poetry of genuine beauty, even though always expressing more promise than fulfilment.

PRINCIPAL WORKS: *Poetry*—Poems, 1906; Judas, 1908; Before Dawn, 1911; Children of Love, 1914; Trees, 1916; Strange Meetings, 1917; Real Property, 1922; The Earth for Sale, 1928; The Winter Solstice, 1928; Elm Angel, 1930; Collected Poems, 1933. *Prose*—Proposals for a Voluntary Nobility, 1907; The Evolution of the Soul, 1907; The Chronicle of a Pilgrimage (Paris to Milan on Foot) 1909; Some Contemporary Poets, 1920; One Day Awake (Modern Morality) 1922.

ABOUT: Aiken, C. Scepticisms; Monro, H. Collected Poems (see Biographical Sketch by F. S. Flint, Critical Note by T. S. Eliot); Newbolt, H. A. A New Study of English Poetry; Sturgeon, M. C. Studies of Contemporary Poets; Bookman (London) April 1932; Canadian Forum July 1932; Criterion July 1932; Dial August 30, 1917; London Mercury April 1932; Poetry October 1922, May 1932, June 1934.

MONROE, HARRIET (1860-September 26, 1936), American poet and editor, was born in Chicago and remained identified all her life with the city, of which she seemed an inherent part. Her father was Henry Stanton Monroe, a prominent attorney, her mother Martha (Mitchell) Monroe. She was educated at the Academy of the Visitation, George-town, D.C. (In 1920  she received an honorary Litt.D. from Baylor University, Waco, Tex.) She already had some local reputation as a writer of verse and prose when she was asked to write the *Columbian Ode* for the Chicago Exposition of 1893. She held out for $1000 for the poem, which she got, and later secured $5000 damages from the New York *World* for premature publication of the poem. She also compelled the committee to allow her to retain an allusion to her brother-in-law, John Wellborn Root, a brilliant architect. The whole thing was characteristic of her indomitable spirit.

Between the date of this triumph and 1911, Miss Monroe's career was somewhat in suspension, though she published three volumes, two in verse. She lectured on poetry, she did some newspaper work, chiefly in literary criticism, and she traveled a good deal, as she did all her life. Then, after return from a trip around the world, she conceived the idea of a magazine wholly devoted to poetry, which should pay the poets for their work and be hospitable to new names and new methods. She herself raised the necessary subsidy from a group of a hundred patrons, and the first number of *Poetry: A Magazine of Verse* appeared in October 1912. It was a red-letter day for poets. From that time on there was —and still is—one paying magazine in America which was built around poetry instead of admitting it grudgingly as filler for the end-pages of prose, and admission to which was a sort of badge of merit for aspiring writers of verse.

To the end of her life Miss Monroe fought unremittingly, first to keep the magazine subsidized, secondly to open its pages to all sorts of experimental and unconventional work without neglecting the traditional forms, and thirdly for the principle that the poet is worthy of his hire. She established large annual prizes, she advocated fellowships in poetry, and she introduced to the public most of those now writing in English whose names are familiar to the cultured reader. The papers and correspondence which she left to the University of Chicago evidence the multiplicity and catholicity of her interests and connections. As Mildred Boie said, "free of schools and rigid affiliations . . . her work as editor was exciting, valuable, and constantly expanding."

Unfortunately, as much cannot be said of her own poetry, of which she was a poor critic. It is often turgid, awkward, and inflated, though it has occasional lyric passages of much beauty. As a critic and editor she was far more important than as a poet.

To those who knew her, Miss Monroe's frail little figure expressed above all gallantry and challenge. She was a born fighter and she never gave up. She never married, but her ties with her immediate family were close and warm. Every year she either went on a lecture tour, or took a long trip, or did both. She died, of cerebral hemorrhage, at Arequipa, Peru, because she insisted on traveling to the Inca ruins, in an altitude too high for her, at seventy-six, while she was attending a P.E.N. convention in South America. Morton Dauwen Zabel, who had been her assistant, succeeded her as editor of Poetry, and on his resignation to teach, George Dillon (whom Miss Monroe had "discovered") succeeded him.

PRINCIPAL WORKS: Poetry—Valeria and Other Poems, 1891; The Columbian Ode, 1893; The Passing Show (plays) 1904; You and I, 1914; The Difference and Other Poems, 1923; Chosen Poems, 1935. Prose—John Wellborn Root: Architect, 1896; Poets and Their Art, 1926; A Poet's Life (autobiography) 1938. Edited—The New Poetry (with A. C. Henderson) 1917 (new ed. 1932); Poems for Every Mood, 1933.

ABOUT: Monroe, H. A Poet's Life; Forum May 1938; Nation March 12, 1938; New Republic April 27, 1938; North American Review June 1938; Poetry September 1935, November 1936, December 1936, April 1938; Saturday Review of Literature July 30, 1932, November 7, 1936, March 19, 1938.

MONTAGUE, CHARLES EDWARD

(January 1, 1867-May 28, 1928), Irish journalist, novelist, and critic who wrote as C. E. Montague, was born at Ealing, London, the third son of Francis and Rosa (McCabe) Montague. The father was an ex-priest from Tyrone, who had given up Catholicism because its dogma had ceased to have any meaning for him. From the City of London School Charles went in 1885 to Balliol College, Oxford, with an exhibition, taking a first in Classical Moderations in 1887 and a second in literae humaniores in 1889. As an undergraduate he

played Rugby football and rowed in his college eight. By the rescue of a drowning man (for which he received the Royal Humane Society's bronze medal) he gave early evidence of that fine physical courage which was later to be so conspicuous in his Alpinism and in the war.

In 1890 Montague joined the Manchester Guardian, a daily paper of the highest literary standing and integrity. He became a skilled working journalist, turning his hand to both political and critical tasks and arguing all forward-looking causes in clean, resourceful prose and with point and penetration. On the retirement, in 1898, of W. T. Arnold, Montague succeeded to his post as chief assistant to the editor and proprietor, C. P. Scott; and in the same year he married Scott's daughter, Madeline. He led a strenuous life, working at journalism by night, reading, writing, walking, and cycling in the afternoons. Vacations were mainly spent in rock-climbing; and his

love of the Swiss mountains creeps again and again into his writings.

The first collection of his work in book form was a set of dramatic criticisms which came out in a composite volume called The Manchester Stage in 1900 (the other collaborators being W. T. Arnold, Oliver Elton, and Allan Monkhouse). His first novel, A Hind Let Loose, did not appear until 1910. It was a clever and well-informed skit on unscrupulous journalism, dedicated to C. P. Scott, "through whom an English paper is clear of these stains." A further collection of brilliant theatre criticisms, Dramatic Values, was published in 1911.

The disaster of 1914 found Montague forty-seven years of age and gray-headed. Dyeing his hair, he enlisted as a private, and after being injured in bomb practice went to France with the Royal Fusiliers in November 1915. Very soon his health gave way and he had to be invalided home. In July 1916 he went out again as an intelligence officer and spent the rest of the war first as a guide for distinguished visitors, and later (from June 1917) as an assistant press censor. Some of Montague's finest writing arose out of this experience—certain stories in Fiery Particles (1923), the bitter Disenchantment (1922), the novel, Rough Justice, (1926) and diary passages published in Oliver Elton's *Memoir*. He had shown reckless bravery under fire whenever tested.

In 1925 Montague retired from the *Manchester Guardian* and went to live at Burford, Oxfordshire. The University of Manchester honored him in 1926 with a Litt.D. degree; and in 1927 he issued one more anti-militarist work, this time a fantasy called *Right Off the Map*. On a visit to London in May 1928 he caught pneumonia, from which he died in Manchester on May 28 at sixty-one. He was survived by his wife, five sons, and two daughters.

Perhaps the most salient characteristics of Montague's writing were its courage, humor, and fierce honesty. Something of the keen cleanliness of his beloved Alpine heights was infused into all his thought. His sterling nobility of mind and his native efficiency were shocked and revolted by the war, which in its major and minor manifestations proved a real spur to literary expression. Humor always seeped in, most notably in *Fiery Particles* (which includes some of the best short stories in the language) but percolated everywhere, even into *A Writer's Notes on his Trade*. As a stylist Montague sought (sometimes too overtly) for the inevitable word and was never guilty of "journalese" or of a *cliché*. As a man he was shy and reserved, and yet, once in company, had warm and genuine social gifts.

PRINCIPAL WORKS: *Novels*—A Hind Let Loose, 1910; The Morning's War, 1913; Disenchantment, 1922; Rough Justice, 1926; Right Off the Map, 1927. *Short Stories*—Fiery Particles, 1923; Action, 1928. *Critical Works and Essays*—The Manchester Stage (with W. T. Arnold & others) 1900; Dramatic Values, 1911; The Right Place, 1924; A Writer's Notes on His Trade, 1930.

ABOUT: Bennett, A. Books and Persons; Cooper, A. P. Authors and Others; Dictionary of National Biography Supplement: 1922-30; Elton, O. C. E. Montague: A Memoir; Scott, D. Men of Letters; Ward, A. C. Aspects of the Modern Short Story; London Mercury August 1928; Nation June 13, 1928

MONTGOMERY, LUCY MAUDE (November 30, 1874-April 24, 1942), Canadian writer for young people, creator of "Anne of Green Gables," wrote to the editors of this volume shortly before her death: "I was born at Clifton, Prince Edward Island, of Scotch ancestry, with a dash of English, Irish, and French. My mother died when I was a baby and I was brought up by my grandparents in the old Macneill homestead at Cavendish, eleven miles from a railroad and twenty-four from a town, but only half a mile from the seashore. I went to the district school from

six to seventeen, and devoured every book I could lay my hands on. Ever since I can remember I was writing stories and verses, and when I was fifteen I had a 'poem' published in the local paper. I qualified for a teacher's license at Prince of Wales College, Charlottetown, P.E.I., and studied at Dalhousie University, Halifax, N.S., and I taught for three years. In 1911 I married a Presbyterian minister, the Rev. Ewan MacDonald, and came to Toronto to live. I like Ontario very much, but anyone who has once loved 'the only island there is' never really loves any other place. And so the scene of all my

books save one has been laid there. And in my dreams I go back to it.

"I had always hoped to write a book, but I have always hated beginning a story. When I get the first paragraph done I feel as if it were half finished. In the end I never set out deliberately to write a book. It just 'happened.' One spring I was looking over my notebook of plots for a short serial I had been asked to write for a Sunday School paper. I found a faded entry, written many years before: 'Elderly couple apply to orphan asylum for a boy. By mistake a girl is sent them.' I thought this would do. The result was *Anne of Green Gables*. I thought girls in their teens might like it. But grandparents, school and college boys, old pioneers in the Australian bush, Mohammedan girls in India, missionaries in China, monks in remote monasteries, premiers of Great Britain, and redheaded people all over the world have written to me telling me how they loved Anne and her successors."

* * *

L. M. Montgomery was a gracious and still handsome gray-haired old lady, a Fellow of the Royal Society of Authors and a member of the Order of the British Empire. Mark Twain called *Anne of Green Gables* "the sweetest creation of child life yet written." It has been filmed (in 1935) and has been translated into French, Dutch, Polish, Swedish, and Danish, and transcribed into Braille. Its many successors have been popular, but it remains its author's masterpiece. Mrs. MacDonald died in Toronto, aged sixty-seven.

PRINCIPAL WORKS: Anne of Green Gables, 1908; Anne of Avonlea, 1909; Kilmeny of the Orchard, 1910; The Story Girl, 1911; Chronicles of Avonlea, 1912; The Golden Road, 1913; Anne of the Island, 1915; The Watchman (poems) 1917; Anne's House of Dreams, 1917; Rainbow Valley, 1919; Rilla of Ingleside, 1921; Emily of New Moon, 1923; Emily Climbs, 1925; The Blue Castle, 1926; Emily's Quest, 1927; Magic for Marigold, 1930; A Tangled Web, 1931; Pat of Silver Bush, 1933; Mistress Pat, 1935; Anne of Windy Poplars, 1936; Jane of Lantern Hill, 1938.

ABOUT: Kunitz, S. J. & Haycraft, H. (eds.) The Junior Book of Authors.

MONTHERLANT, HENRY DE, Comte

(1893-   ), French novelist, writes: "I was born in Paris of a very old French family, originally from Cata-

lonia. I had hardly completed my studies when I volunteered in an infantry regiment then engaged in the great war, and I was seriously injured (1918) by a shell.

"I published first *La Relève du Matin* [Morning Exalta-tion] (1920), a sort of prose poem about life in a Catholic college during the war; *Le Songe* [The Dream], a novel of the war; and *Les Olympiques* [The Olympics] poems on athletic sports, in which I have participated as a well known football player and runner. This has been called the best book in France concerned with sport.

"At fifteen years of age, I had already taken part in bullfights in Spain. Having recommended killing bulls after the war, I was wounded by a bull's horn (1925), after which I renounced bullfighting, on which I had published a novel, *Les Bestiaires* [*The Bullfighters*], where a study of the life of the toreadors is mingled with the lyrical exaltation of the *corrida* considered as a survival of the ancient rites of sun-worship. I lived next for seven years in Spain and Africa, notably in the Sahara (1925-1932), publishing only two books, *Aux Fontaines du Désir* [At the Fountains of Desire] and *La Petite Enfante de Castille* [The Little Infanta of Castille], a sort of journal of a spiritual crisis, that of a man who, in a state of complete freedom, yet could not attain happiness.

"Since my return to France I have pub-lished *Mors et Vita* [Death and Life] (1933), essays on war, courage and fear, and Franco-German relations; *Encore un Instant de Bonheur* [Still a Moment of

Happiness] (1934), poems; *Les Célibataires* [Perish in Their Pride] (1934), a novel in which I have treated the decadence and ruin of two old bachelors of the French nobility, and which won the highest literary honor granted by the French Academy, the *Grand Prix de Littérature; Service Inutile* [Use-less Service] (1935), in which I give my philosophy of life; and finally a long novel in four volumes, *Les Jeunes Filles* [The Young Girls] (1935-39), in which I studied the relations of men and women, and which was considered, in the words of André Gide, a great and eloquent offensive against woman.' This novel was translated into English under the title *Pity for Women*."

* * *

Montherlant also received the Northcliffe and Heinemann Prizes in England, donating the latter to King's College Hospital, and the prize of the Foundation Tunisienne, which he refused because he does not ap-prove of French colonial policy. He spent some of his youth and had part of his edu-cation in England. He is often compared with Ernest Hemingway, with whom he has much in common temperamentally, though not in style, the greatest literary in-fluences on Montherlant being Chateau-briand and Barrès. He is a disciple of "tra-dition, authority, classicism, and national-ism," yet he took an active part against his own class when the People's Front was in power. Malcolm Cowley has called him "an aristocrat and soldier and athlete who be-came a man of letters." Excessively praised by some critics (Romain Rolland called him "the greatest existing force in French let-ters"), he has constantly marred the brill-iance and power of his work by displays of egotism, prejudice, cruelty, and gross super-stition. In many ways he seems an incipient d'Annunzio. Dark and intense looking, he even resembles that brilliant egotist in his youth. Yet he, far more than the bourgeois Proust, it is arguable, is the real historian of the ruined French nobility, and his work is of importance if only as historical docu-mentation. He is unmarried.

Since the conquest of France in 1940, Montherlant has indicated his resentment against the Vichy policy of "collaboration" with the Nazis.

WORKS AVAILABLE IN ENGLISH: The Bull-fighters, 1927; Perish in Their Pride, 1936; Pity for Women, 1938; Costals and the Hippogriff, 1940.

ABOUT: Perdriel, F. Henry de Montherlant; American Catholic Quarterly October 1923; Living Age September 1934; New Republic January 22, 1936; Revue Hebdominaire November 12, 1927; Time January 27, 1936.

M O N Y P E N N Y, WILLIAM FLA-VELLE (August 7, 1866-November 23, 1912), English biographer, was born at Dungannon, county Tyrone, Ireland, the second son of William Monypenny, a small landowner of Ballyworkan, County Armagh, and Mary Anne (Flavelle) Monypenny. He was educated at the Royal School, Dungannon, and graduated from Dublin with high distinction in mathematics. Ill health compelled him to leave Balliol College, Oxford, and he became a journalist, first on the *Spectator,* in 1893 a member of the *Times* editorial staff, and in 1899 editor of the Johannesburg *Star,* foremost organ of the Uitlanders in South Africa. Commissioned an officer in the Imperial Light Horse, Monypenny fought in Natal and endured hardships during the siege of Ladysmith. Unable to countenance the importation of indentured Chinese labor, he left the *Star* and tramped from Lake Victoria Nyanza to Khartoum. Back in England, Monypenny rejoined the *Times* in 1908, and was appointed a director. Monypenny's firsthand observations of British imperialism, his native shrewdness and lucid style stood him in good stead when he was selected to write a monumental life of Benjamin Disraeli, Lord Beaconsfield, using the materials bequeathed to Lord Rowton. The first volume appeared in October 1910; the second, in November 1912, preceded Monypenny's death in the New Forest by ten days. The work was continued and completed in four more volumes by G. B. Buckle, the editor under whom Monypenny had served on the *Times,* and who wrote an inscription for a memorial tablet in the parish church of Franham Royal, Buckinghamshire, where Monypenny lies buried. He never married.

PRINCIPAL WORK: The Life of Benjamin Disraeli, 1910; 1912.

ABOUT: (London) Times November 25, 1912.

MOODY, WILLIAM VAUGHN (July 8, 1869-October 17, 1910), American poet and dramatist, was born in Spencer, Ind.,

sixth of the seven children of Francis Burdette Moody, a river boat captain, and Henrietta Emily (Stoy) Moody. The family moved when he was a year old to New Albany, Ind., where he attended high school, then studied for a year at the Pritchett Institute of Design, Louis-ville, Ky. His parents had both died by 1886, and he left home and after a year of country school teaching entered the Riverview Academy, New York, where he was both student and teacher. At twenty he entered Harvard; he worked his way through and did four years' work in three. In his senior year he traveled abroad as tutor to a wealthy youth, returning for his graduation, when he was class poet.

After a year's graduate work, he became assistant in English at Harvard and Radcliffe. In 1895 he went to the University of Chicago as instructor in English. He stayed there till 1901, when he was assistant professor. Moody disliked teaching extremely, but he was nevertheless an inspiring teacher. During part of the time he was technically connected with the university he was actually in New York and New England, working on the Cambridge edition of Milton and writing a textbook with Robert Morss Lovett. After its appearance in 1902, he was able to stop teaching and give all his time to writing. Nominally he was on the University of Chicago faculty until 1907, but he taught no classes. About 1905 he met Harriet (Converse) Brainerd, with whom he fell deeply in love. In 1909 she divorced her husband and married him. It was very soon after their marriage that his last illness began; an attack of typhoid fever was followed by a brain tumor, which resulted fatally when Moody was only forty-one. Mrs. Moody died in 1932; she was a writer on cookery.

Moody's early death, and the singular break in 1906 in his literary subject-matter and manner, have combined to make him a figure of pathos, of great promise unfulfilled. His early poems had real nobility and lyric power; as the *Nation* remarked, "none of his later verse reached the great height of the 'Ode in Time of Hesitation'" (written during the Spanish-American War). After a series of poems and poetic plays, beautiful but distinctly "highbrow" in nature, he suddenly became the author of an immensely popular prose play of the West, *The Great Divide* (originally called *A Sabine Woman*). He followed this with *The Faith Healer,* which though successful did not duplicate the furor created by *The Great Divide.*

Moody, with his graceful carriage, wavy brown hair, Vandyke beard, and musical voice, was rather self-consciously the picture of a poet. "He had an intrepid, inquiring mind," said Hermann Hagedorn, "torn lifelong by a struggle to reconcile the material with the spiritual." He was strongly mystical in feeling; Lovett said that "as a person he combined the most engaging and inspiring traits of pagan and of mystic." The *Outlook* spoke of his "dignity of thought, restrained feeling, a certain eloquence of conviction"; while *Current Literature* said that "he had written great poems and had tried to write great plays, but had failed to make a synthesis between the two." His *Letters to Harriet,* published twenty-six years after his death, display the floridity, common to his period, which was the chief defect of his style. He himself wrote his own best self-portrait:

My heart could break—of its long searching and not finding out.

PRINCIPAL WORKS: *Poetry*—The Masque of Judgment, 1900; Poems, 1901; The Fire-Bringer, 1904; Selected Poems, 1931. *Prose Plays*—The Great Divide, 1906; The Faith Healer, 1909. *Miscellaneous*—A First View of English and American Literature (with R. M. Lovett) 1902; Some Letters of William Vaughn Moody, 1913; Letters to Harriet, 1936.

ABOUT: Henry, D.D. William Vaughn Moody; Kilmer, J. The Circus and Other Essays; Moody, W. V. Some Letters of William Vaughn Moody, Letters to Harriet; Perry, B. Commemorative Tributes; Atlantic Monthly March 1931; Current Literature December 1910; Dial November 1, 1910; Education May 1933; Forum October 1922; Harper's Weekly November 12, 1910; Independent February 6, 1913; Nation October 20, 1910; Outlook October 29, 1910; Poetry September 1931; Saturday Review of Literature February 22, 1936; Theatre Arts Monthly August 1935; Time January 13, 1936.

MOORE, FRANK FRANKFORT (May 15, 1855-May 11, 1931), Irish novelist,

dramatist, and miscellaneous writer, was

born in Limerick. He was educated at the Royal Academical Institution, in Belfast. He traveled much, in Africa, India, the West Indies, and South America. From 1876 to 1892 he served on the staffs of various London newspapers. Between

1877 and 1895 he wrote many plays, some of which were successful on the stage, though none has appeared in published form. He was twice married, to Grace Balcombe, who died in 1901, and to Dorothea Hatton, by whom he had three daughters.

Moore was a very prolific writer, a novelist of the lighter popular sort. His earliest novels were of the sea, the later ones romantic, occasionally historical in background, and a bit high-flown and fantastic. His great success was won with *The Jes-*

samy Bride, which was a best-seller of its period. He also wrote verse, travel books, and biographies of Goldsmith and Fanny Burney.

PRINCIPAL WORKS: Sojourners Together, 1875; Mate of the *Jessica*, 1879; Mutiny on the *Albatross*, 1885; The Great Orion, 1886; Under Hatches, 1888; Coral and Cocoanut, 1890; Sailing and Sealing, 1892; I Forbid the Banns, 1893; One Fair Daughter, 1894; Two in the Bush, 1895; The Jessamy Bride, 1897; The Conscience of Coralie, 1900; A Damsel or Two, 1902; The King's Messenger, 1907; Love and the Interloper, 1910; The Lady of the Reef, 1915; The Courtship of Prince Charming, 1920; The Hand and the Dagger, 1928.

ABOUT: London Times May 12, 1931.

MOORE, GEORGE (February 24, 1852-January 20, 1933). Irish novelist, essayist, and autobiographer, was born, George Au-

gustus Moore at Moore Hall, County Mayo, Ireland, the son of George Henry Moore, Member of Parliament, country gentleman, and race-horse owner, and his wife, Mary (Blake) Moore. His child-

hood had a background of racing, and when the father's horse, Croaghpatrick, won a great deal of prize money in the season 1859-60, part of the proceeds were spent on George's education. His parents were Catholics, so he was sent in 1861 to Oscott, near Birmingham, where he hated the hard routine and was the despair of his headmaster, especially over spelling. In 1869 the family settled at South Kensington, London, George was put in the hands of an army tutor, frequented racing clubs, and dabbled in art. On his father's death the following year he inherited an income nominally of £4,000 a year but actually (owing to mortgages and difficult rent collection) only in the neighborhood of £500.

In 1873 his artistic aspirations took him to Paris, where he entered the Académie Julian. Homesickness brought him back the next year, and he now began his lifelong friendship with Edward Martyn, of Tillyra Castle. He was in Paris once more in 1875, writing badly spelled and punctuated letters in French and English, pursuing an Irish heiress (whom he abandoned when he found that her income was £800, not £2,000) and cultivating high society. Finding he could not paint, he tried writing and collaborated with one Lopez in a play called *Martin Luther.* A lucky introduction to Villiers de l'Isle Adam led to another to Mallarmé, and

977

thence to some acquaintance with Manet, Monet, Degas, Pissarro, and other prominent painters. A great deal of this was mere café foregathering, and in his autobiographical writings Moore certainly exaggerated his intimacy with these great figures, as he did his slight dealings with Zola a little later.

Théodore Druet remembered him about this time as "a golden haired fop, an aesthete before the days of Wilde," and. Madame Duclaux spoke of his "vaguely comic" appearance, his receding chin, and the "vague, spiritless" expression in his gray-blue eyes. She also, and J. E. Blanche, the painter, deplored his halting and incorrect French. His affectation of having become thoroughly Gallicized was certainly a pose; and his stories of frequent conquests in the amatory sphere were in large measure apocryphal. An appallingly ugly man, he yet had his attractions for some women— until they found him playing fast and loose with their names in public, which he constantly did.

Trouble with the Irish tenantry took him back to Moore Hall in 1879, and for the next few years he lived there for part of each year and for the other part in London. The *Spectator* gave hospitality to some poems; the *Examiner* provided brief employment; and Moore's first published novel, *A Modern Lover* (1883) had a relatively good press. *A Mummer's Wife* (1885) was his first real success. It was crude, naive, and badly written, but its conscious naturalism (modeled on Zola) was a relief from the saccharine fiction then in vogue. Its virtual banning by one of the big circulating libraries (on moral grounds) led to vigorous attacks on those institutions by Moore. He preferred the society of painters to that of writers, and got to know Sickert and Steer. *Confessions of a Young Man* (first serialized in French in *La Revue Indépendante* and published in English in 1888) caused the *Academy* to ask "why a disagreeable young man of bad education should have thought his memoirs worth writing"; but the book has held its own. *Spring Days* (1888) and *Mike Fletcher* (1889) were both failures, and in later years Moore could not bear to hear mention of the second. He was still in an early stage of literary craftsmanship, climbing slowly towards the mastery of prose he was later to attain.

Slender though his claims were, Moore acted as regular art critic to the *Speaker* from 1891 to 1895. During this period he met D.S. MacColl, sometime Keeper of the Wallace Collection, (Sir) William Rothenstein, who was to preside over the Royal College of Art, and Henry Tonks, who fulfilled a similar function at the Slade School. Tonks remained a close friend, and has executed a number of spirited oils and pastels of these gatherings of painters and writers. In 1894 Moore at last became a man of wide renown with the publication of *Esther Waters,* a novel concerning a servant girl in a racing household. Still in naturalistic vein, it had great merits of observation and description, though compared with the smallest trifle by Conrad or Hardy (authors whom Moore despised) its attitude is callow and its emotional content thin. Nevertheless Lionel Johnson and Quiller-Couch praised it; 24,000 copies were sold inside twelve months; and it has its historical place as a protest on behalf of realism against sentimentality.

In 1894 also occurred Moore's most serious sentimental attachment, the object of which, Mrs. Pearl Craigie ("John Oliver Hobbes," the author) was trying to obtain release from an unhappy marriage. The two collaborated in several plays and were much together, until an eminent suitor in the shape of Lord Curzon appeared. Moore tattled about Mrs. Craigie in his usual way, and before long she abruptly gave him his dismissal.

The outbreak of the Boer War disgusted Moore by the badness of the cause, as it did many others, so in 1899 he removed to Ireland, living part of the time at Moore Hall and part in Dublin. He remained there (with incidental travels) until 1911, taking a vivid interest in the revival of the Gaelic language. Though he knew no Gaelic himself, he made the thorough learning of it a condition for the inclusion of his sister's two children in his will. His chief literary friends in Dublin were W. B. Yeats, John Eglinton, and "A.E." (G. W. Russell). In a profoundly Catholic society he scandalized many by his militant agnosticism. In 1903 he took pains to make it known that he had become a member of the Protestant church, but he remained very unorthodox, and it is probable that his outward adherence to the opposite sect was only a gesture of defiance towards Catholicism, which he hated wholeheartedly all his life. In 1905 he identified himself so completely with Irish life as to become High Sheriff of Mayo.

After more than ten years in Ireland Moore removed, in 1911, to what was to be his last residence, a house in Ebury Street, Victoria, London—a towny and unfashionable quarter, but a location half-way between his artist friends in Chelsea and his fashionable ones in Belgravia. His huge autobiographical trilogy, *Ave* (1911), *Salve* (1912), and *Vale* (1914), called collectively *Hail and Farewell!* helped to consolidate his literary reputation, if it antagonized many people who appeared in it. *The Brook Kerith* (1916), for the preparation of which he went to Palestine, was a highly wrought prose epic on the theme of a Jesus having risen from the Cross after swooning only; *Héloïse and Abélard* (1921) was a medieval romance for which, contrary to his general custom, he made elaborate researches; and in *Daphnis and Chloë* he produced a most sensitive translation, not from the Greek (for he had none) but from a French version. *Conversations in Ebury Street* (1924) was a combative and provocative book of criticism.

In 1923 Moore Hall was burnt down by Irish rebels against the Free State authority. Moore drew £7,000 in compensation. As he advanced into old age he continued to work unremittingly; and even in his last years, when uremia caused him great pain and discomfort, he persisted in new projects. A bronchitic attack, superimposed on the prevailing malady, brought about his end a month before his eighty-first birthday.

Estimates of George Moore's attainment vary more than most judgments on eminent men of letters. His overweening conceit not only rendered personal relationships with him very difficult, but often caused him to make himself look ridiculous, as when he told an interviewer that *Esther Waters* was better than anything Dickens ever wrote. The same fault vitiates his literary judgments; and a pseudo-critic who can call Conrad "a worthless writer" hardly merits serious consideration in that capacity. His frequent rudeness, bad temper, meanness, and light regard for truth were moral defects that cannot be condoned, and many readers find his books paralyzingly dull and monotonous. Yet to set this off there is a considerable body of critical opinion that rates his later prose style so high that it can be described as a new melody in English. It is certain that he began writing without having mastered either grammar or spelling, and that he took long years to learn; but having learned, he fashioned an instrument of power and subtlety.

PRINCIPAL WORKS: *Novels and Short Stories*— A Modern Lover, 1883; A Mummer's Wife, 1885; A Drama in Muslin, 1886; A Mere Accident, 1887; Spring Days, 1888; Mike Fletcher, 1889; Vain Fortune, 1892; Esther Waters, 1894; Celibates, 1895; Evelyn Innes, 1898; Sister Teresa, 1901;

The Untilled Field, 1903; The Lake, 1905; The Brook Kerith, 1916; A Story-Teller's Holiday, 1918; Héloïse and Abélard, 1921; In Single Strictness, 1922; Peronnik the Fool, 1924; Ulick and Soracha, 1926; A Flood, 1930; Aphrodite in Aulis, 1930. *Poems*—Flowers of Passion, 1878; Pagan Poems, 1881. *Plays*—Worldliness, 1874(?); Martin Luther, 1879; The Strike at Arlingford, 1893; The Bending of the Bough, 1900; The Apostle, 1911; Esther Waters, 1913; Elizabeth Cooper, 1913; The Coming of Gabrielle, 1920; The Making of an Immortal, 1927; The Passing of the Essenes, 1930. *Essays and Criticism*—Parnell and His Island, 1887; Impressions and Opinions, 1891; Modern Painting, 1893; Reminiscences of the Impressionist Painters, 1906; Avowals, 1919; Conversations in Ebury Street, 1924. *Autobiography*—Confessions of a Young Man, 1888; Memoirs of My Dead Life, 1906; Hail and Farewell! (Ave, 1911, Salve, 1912, Vale, 1914); A Communication to My Friends, 1933. *Anthology*—Pure Poetry, 1924. *Translation*—The Pastoral Loves of Daphnis and Chloë, 1924. *Letters*—Letters to Edouard Dujardin, 1886-1922 (trans. by J. Eglinton) 1929.

ABOUT: Atherton, G. Adventures of a Novelist; Blanche, J. E. Mes Modèles; Boyd, E. A. Contemporary Drama in Ireland; Burdett, O. The Beardsley Period; Eglinton, J. Irish Literary Portraits; Field, M. Works and Days; Freeman, J. A. Portrait of George Moore in a Study of His Work; Goodwin, G. Conversations With George Moore; Gregory, Lady. Our Irish Theatre; Gwynn, D. Edward Martyn; Halévy, D. Pays Parisiens; Harris, F. Contemporary Portraits; Hone, J. M. The Life of George Moore; Hone, J. M. The Moores of Moore Hall; Josephson, M. Zola and His Time; Marie, A. La Forêt Symboliste; Mitchell, S. George Moore; Moore, M. An Irish Gentleman; Morgan, C. Epitaph on George Moore; Wolfe, H. George Moore; Yeats, W. B. Dramatis Personae; Revue de Paris March 1, 1933.

MOORE, MARIANNE CRAIG (November 15, 1887-), American poet, was born in St. Louis, Mo., the daughter of John Milton Moore and Mary (Warner) Moore. She was educated at Metzger Ir stitute, Carlisle, Pa., and at Bryn Mawr College, where she received her B.A. in 1909. She then studied for a year at the Carlisle Commercial College, and from

Kesslere

1911 to 1915 taught stenography at the Indian School in that town. From 1921 to 1925 she was an assistant in the New York Public Library. From 1926 to 1929 she was acting editor of the *Dial*, until the magazine expired in the latter year. Since 1915 she had been contributing poems to the English magazine, the *Egoist*, in which much of the early work of the Imagist group appeared. Without her knowledge two

members of that group, H.D. (Hilda Doolittle) and Robert McAlmon, brought out
in 1921 a volume of her poems. Four years
later, with her first volume prepared under
her own supervision, she won the Dial
Award. In 1932 she won the Helen Haire
Levinson Prize from *Poetry*, and in 1935
the Ernest Hartsock Memorial Prize.

To the editors of this volume she writes:
"I am a Presbyterian and was brought up
in the home of my grandfather, the Rev.
John R. Warner, who was for twenty-seven
years the pastor of Kirkwood Presbyterian
Church, St. Louis. For twenty years my
brother has been a chaplain in the Navy,
and the books to which I have had access
have been, on the whole, serious. Politically
I cannot contemplate anything but freedom
for all races and persons. I feel that the
unselfish behavior of individual to individual
is the basis for world peace; and realizing
that the structure of society depends on the
family, I have a growing solicitude for
young people and our contemporary domestic atmosphere. I am fond of outdoor sport
—tennis in particular; am fond of the sea,
of our New England coast; take an interest
in the theatre, and in motion pictures—especially documentary films; in photography
and in printing. To Miss Harriet Weaver,
H.D., Mrs. Kenneth Macpherson, Richard
Aldington, T.S. Eliot, Ezra Pound, Alfred
Kreymborg, Schofield Thayer, Dr. J. S.
Watson, and the *Dial,* and to Morton D.
Zabel, of *Poetry,* I am under lasting debt
for advice and encouragement."

Miss Moore has auburn hair and the
glowing complexion that often accompanies
it. She is unmarried. With her great dark
eyes and her "mellifluous flow of polysyl-
ables," she is a striking person. Though she
has been classed with the Imagists, and
writes in free verse, her work is too highly
individual to belong to any school. Fastidiousness, neatness of finish, and telling metaphor are its most salient characteristics. She
frankly works in mosaic, getting many of
her most apt comparisons from clippings,
scientific books, or passing conversation. Her
poems are often "difficult," not because they
are obscure, but because they are so compact. Morton Dauwen Zabel called her "a
literalist of the imagination," and Philip
Blaire Rice, who spoke of her "dour intelligence," "episcopal manner," and "tropical
imagination rigorously pruned," also said,
"she makes nicer discriminations than most
of us are accustomed to." Her work has
been called frigid, but Gwendolen Murphy
comes nearer to the truth in speaking of

her "strong control, springing from strong
emotion."

PRINCIPAL WORKS: Poems, 1921; Observations,
1924; Selected Poems, 1935; The Pangolin and
Other Verse, 1936; What Are Years, 1941.

ABOUT: Kreymborg, A. Troubadour; Moore,
M. Selected Poems (see Introduction by T. S.
Eliot); Murphy, G. The Modern Poet; Zabel,
M. D. Literary Opinion in America; Criterion
July 1925; Forum July 1936; Life and Letters
Today December 1935; Nation April 17, 1935;
New Yorker November 1, 1941; Poetry March
1936, November 1941.

MOORE, OLIVE, English novelist
writes: "I was born in Hereford, on the
borders of Wales, and was sent abroad to
a convent at the age
of five. Since grow-
ing up, and of my
own free will, I have
studied art in Italy,
and subjects which
interested me, such
as literature and
language, at the Sor-
bonne. My life is
completely dull and
uneventful. I was in
New York in 1929 and 1930, an unforgettable memory to me because it was there
that the manuscript of my second book was
burnt in a hotel fire, together with every
garment I possessed, except an ancient
mackintosh in which I had been walking
around Central Park in the rain. I should
like to be stoical and exalted about it; but
I cannot; it was an unhappy and deadly experience. I sat down and rewrote the book.
Fortunately my prose is such that I have to
write very slowly. I spend days reducing
five hundred words to fifty. I loathe the
easy and the slipshod. So in a sense I memorize as I go along. I know some passages
in my books word for word, because of this
passion for simplifying. I used to say if I
had a few pounds a week of my own I'd
never have touched a pen again. But I
didn't have; so perhaps it was just as well.

"There is little to tell you, or that matters,
about me. I am by nature solitary and contemplative, very happy, very morose. I
loathe books and never read them, except
informative books, giving me facts, any
facts and all facts. I love travel best of
all, and yet get very impatient with it. I
like walking. I like talking. I like meeting
people once. I love best knowing absolutely
no one, but watching everyone. I dislike
having to live in London, a parochial little
village. But I have to. I dislike it so much
that it does me (creatively) an awful lot of

good. It's the pearl in my oyster. I dislike things very thoroughly indeed. I like disliking them. Otherwise one gets genteel, tea-shoppe, bored, refined, amateurish; all things I hate most, all things which make it so difficult for the creative artist to live in England. But fortunately, I never meet people, and so am saved from contamination.

"I have no sense of hero-worship. I respect all men who are masters of their jobs; I say men, meaning men. I don't believe in women. They seem to be able to do everything but think. Yet they get away with it. I believe only in the conscious artist. I would wish my work to be judged on the texture of my thought and the disposition of my sentences."

* * *

Miss Moore, tall, dark, and striking, is the possessor of a formidable wit and a gift for brilliance. Her books are printed without paragraph indentations, with spaces between paragraphs as if they were a series of epigrams—which they often are. She has shocked and puzzled reviewers, who have disposed of her as "a writer's writer," yet all of them have been obliged to pay tribute to the "packed luminosity" of her style. Her *Amazon and Hero: The Drama of the Greek War for Independence,* on which she has been at work since 1931, has not yet been published. There is no recent word of her, in an England which she can no longer describe as "secure, pleasant, imitative, watery." She is unmarried, and though she does not give her birthdate, it was probably about 1905.

PRINCIPAL WORKS: Celestial Seraglio: A Tale of Convent Life, 1929; Spleen (in America: Repentance at Leisure) 1930; Fugue, 1932; Further Reflections on the Death of a Porcupine, 1932; The Apple Is Bitten Again: Self Portrait, 1934.

ABOUT: Moore, O. The Apple Is Bitten Again; Bookman September 1932.

*MOORE, THOMAS STURGE (March 4, 1870-), English poet, man of letters, and wood engraver, was born in Hastings, the

eldest son of Dr. D. Moore and Henrietta S. Moore. In 1899 appeared his first book of poetry, *The Vinedresser and Other Poems.* Four years later Moore married Marie Appia, daughter of the Rev. George Appia, a Lutheran pastor in Paris. They

C. Shannon

have a son and a daughter. Moore is a mem-

* Died July 18, 1944.

ber of the Academic Committee of the Royal Society of Literature, and makes his home at 40 Well Walk, London N.W. 3. Besides being the author of books on Dürer, Correggio, and modern artists, he is a distinguished designer of bookplates, and has also designed covers for the poetry of William Butler Yeats and others. Sturge Moore's first prose work was *The Centaur and the Bacchant,* translated from the French of Maurice de Guérin in 1899. "As a poet," writes Louis Untermeyer, "the greater portion of his verse is severely classical in tone, academic in expression but, of its kind, distinctive and finely chiseled. Its precision has been praised, even envied, by several advanced poets on both sides of the Atlantic."

"As countries of the mind, Moore's mythical Greek uplands are more interesting than William Morris' *Earthly Paradise* and less monotonous than Spenser's enchanted forests," according to Llewellyn Jones, the Chicago critic. Sturge Moore's view of art is neither the "scientific" one nor "the personal theory that reduces art to an expression of, and an appeal to, individual temperaments." His position is the assertion of the sovereignty of the aesthetic conscience on exactly the same grounds as sovereignty is claimed for the moral conscience. He suggests to artists that they should cherish originality less and perfection more.

PRINCIPAL WORKS: *Poetry*—The Vinedresser and Other Poems, 1899; Aphrodite Against Artemis, 1901; Absalom, 1903; Danaë, 1903; The Little School, 1905; Poems, 1906; Mariamne, 1911; The Sicilian Idyll and Judith, 1911; The Sea Is Kind, 1914; The Powers of the Air, 1920; Tragic Mothers, 1920; Judas, 1923; Mystery and Tragedy, 1930; Poems, 1932-33; Selected Poems, 1934; The Unknown Known and a Dozen Odd Poems, 1937. *Prose*—Altdorfer, 1900; Dürer, 1904; Correggio, 1906; Art and Life, 1910; Hark to These Three, 1915; Some Soldier Poets, 1919; Armour for Aphrodite, 1927.

ABOUT: Jones, L. First Impressions; Untermeyer, L. Modern British Poetry (revised ed.).

MORAND, PAUL (March 13, 1888-), French novelist, journalist, and diplomat, was born in Paris of a middle-class family. His father, Eugène Morand (the son of a one time director of the Imperial Bronze Foundry in St. Petersburg), was an intellectual of varied gifts: painter, playwright, scholar-librettist for Pierné and Massenet, translator of *Hamlet,* director of the Dépôt des Marbres (storeroom for statuary not on exhibition), and from 1908 to 1918 director of the École des Arts Décoratifs. From early childhood Paul enjoyed the more glamorous aspects of the Morand home such as its visitors (Mallarmé, Frank

Harris, Sarah Bernhardt, Oscar Wilde, Lord Alfred Douglas), but abhorred the family dinners on Sunday: "I detested the gloomy dinners which in their solemnity recall those of the last years of Louis XIV, as described in Saint-Simon—occasions on which so many French families call a Sunday evening truce."

Paul attended the Lyceé Carnot but showed more interest in rugby, prize fights and auto races ("Nôtre grand amour, ce fût le motor") than in the French classics. Although his father had forbidden him to read L'Auto-Vélo, he permitted him to spend his summers in England where he nurtured his love for sports still further. In 1904 Paul, then seventeen, went by himself to Munich, learned to smoke cigars and drink beer, and with a twenty-two year old Frenchman, the writer Jean Giraudoux, pole-vaulted in morning-coats by the Starnberger See. At the instance of Lord Alfred Douglas, Morand père allowed his son to spend one year (1908) at Oxford where, although "he had to do battle for the national French nightgown against his pyjama'd school-fellows," he became initiated in the art of snobbery.

A. Abbott

Paul, who loved traveling, dreamed of becoming a naval officer, but mathematics—about which "I knew nothing whatever"—stood in his way, and so diplomacy was considered a fitting substitute. After his year of military service with the 36th Infantry at Caen, where he wrote and immediately destroyed his first literary effort, the novel Les Extravagants: Scènes de la Vie de Bohème Cosmopolite, he entered the École Libre des Sciences Politiques.

Morand did very well and after preliminary training in the Protocol Department was sent as attaché to the French Embassy in England. For three years (1913-16) he lived in London and learned its most recondite peculiarities and moods, "secrets which books and professors had never let me glimpse before." During these war years the English capital swarmed with secret agents, informers and shady characters. The writer in Morand reveled in all this. In 1917 he was transferred to Rome and the following year to Madrid; thus his cosmopolitan outlook broadened as he confronted a variegated, checkered reality.

During the post-war period of 1919-25 Morand remained in Paris, and since his duties were not too exacting, he found time for literature. Some critics have said that he "escaped" from the utter despair and morbidity of post-war Europe by choosing writing rather than suicide. Referring to this period, Morand confessed years later: "My life is a continual struggle against my feelings, which lead me far afield. . . . Books or suicide, which? But suicide is out of the question. There remained books. Writing enables the blood to circulate. So I wrote." As a result Lampes à Arc (1919) and Feuilles de Température (1920) appeared, two collections of poems which translated into syncopated rhythm the reigning gloom and chaos, the contrast between the shoddy industrialism of the banal new society and the cultural values of the moribund old. This theme permeated also the admirable stories (1921) in Green Shoots (about three young women drifting in war-time London), which Proust praised in his Introduction for its "intensely personal" style. However, it was with Open All Night (1922) and Closed All Night (1923) that Morand attained international reputation. These short story collections, which had an immediate spectacular success, "conjure with haunting intensity" the "emancipated," topsy-turvy life of queer mortals in different quarters of post-war Europe (London, Moscow, Constantinople, Berlin, Barcelona, Portofino-Kulm). After trying, with less success, the full-length novel in Lewis and Irene (1924), and emphasizing the risqué qualities of his story-telling in Europe at Love (1925), Morand was transferred to the Bangkok legation: he went via New York-Vancouver and returned, that same year, via Ceylon-Suez, unable to stand the tropical climate. This round-the-world cruise gave him a taste of other horizons, of other races, of open spaces, great distances and speed. From then on he sought other settings, themes, and conflicts than those he had previously used in his works.

On his return from Siam he took a leave of absence, married the Roumanian Princess Soutzo and spent the next few years in leisurely and luxurious journeys—U.S., West Indies, Central Africa—and writing travel-accounts: Nothing but the Earth (1926), Paris-Tombouctou (1928), Hiver Caraïbe (1929), and exotic fiction: The Living Buddha (1927), East India and Company (1927), Black Magic (1928). The 1929 crisis affected his wife's important financial interests in Central Europe and he was forced to write and lecture extensively for a living. In 1930 he "wrote to order" a penetrating study of New York City: "A French publisher gave me an order for a *New York,* a subject to which heretofore I had never given any thought whatsoever, and I wrote it at once with enthusiasm and a great deal of pleasure." The success of this "portrait of a city" brought him orders for a *London* (1931) and a *Bucharest* (1935); his love for air-travel (and a fat stipend from the publicity department of a French airline) led him to write *Orient Air Express* (1931) and *Indian Air* (1932); autobiographical concerns prompted him to write *Papiers d'Identité* (1931) and *Mes Débuts* (1933); and his worries about the sharpened political situation in France inspired him with *1900* (1931) and the ironical *France-la-Douce* (1934).

In 1932 Morand returned to the Ministry of Foreign Affairs and was assigned to the official Tourist Bureau, a most fitting position for the inveterate traveler. This interpreter of contemporary sensibility lived until the Nazi invasion in a modernistic apartment in the Champs de Mars, by the "grooved shadow" of the Eiffel tower. He was reported still in Paris after the Nazi occupation. His political orientation has been summed up in two words: "Vichy water."

In times of peace Morand loved sports and tried to keep in shape. Robust, healthy, "unusually tanned," a trifle snobbish, he exhibited the breeding of a society man and the manners of a diplomat. Barrès once confessed: "I love his elegant and brutal tone," but this is not a paradox: Morand's assertions are often brutal, but his sensitive style turns them into elegant generalizations. Georges Lemaître declared: "Morand has a keen intelligence. He is not a philosopher and he has little inclination for involved theorizing; yet by a bold thrust he often penetrates much more deeply into the very core of some crucial problem than any professional thinker with all his reasoning. Cold, bare facts are capital to him. He knows how to reach them, how to extract from an incoherent mass of facts those which are truly representative of a deeper reality, how to let them speak for themselves with a convincingness that no elaborate explanation could possibly attain."

WORKS AVAILABLE IN ENGLISH TRANSLATION: Open All Night, 1922; Green Shoots, 1923; Closed All Night, 1924; Lewis and Irene, 1925; Europe at Love, 1926; The Living Buddha, 1927; East India and Company, 1927; Nothing But the Earth, 1927 (British translation: Earth Girdled); Black

Magic, 1929; New York, 1930; 1900, 1931; World Champions, 1931; Orient Air Express, 1932; Paris to the Life, 1933; Indian Air, 1933; Frenchman's London, 1934; Epic-Makers, 1935; Road to India, 1937.

ABOUT: Billy, A. Intimités Littéraires; Brasillach, R. Portraits; Lalou, R. Contemporary French Literature; Lemaître, G. E. Four French Novelists; Rousseaux, A. Ames et Visages du XXme. Siècle; Stansbury, M. H. French Novelists Today; Le Divan April and June 1928; Nouvelles Littéraires February 8 and June 14, 1930; Revue des Deux Mondes August 1, 1936; Saturday Review of Literature March 22, 1941. Zeitschrift für Französische Sprache-und Literatur Band LX, Heft 5-6 (1936).

*MORDAUNT, Mrs. EVELYN MAY (CLOWES) ("Elinor Mordaunt," "A. Riposte"), (1877?-), English novelist, writes: My life has been a queer one; for I belong to a half-English, half-Irish family of which no other woman has ever done any work, and after not even doing my hair for myself I was shot out into the world when I lost my husband at  the age of twenty-three, with a baby son and not a penny in the world. I was born of a hunting family in Nottinghamshire; my father was St. John Legh Clowes. I don't remember when I started to learn to ride, or first went out hunting. I always loved being in the open and getting away alone. I used to write childish poems and stories, but mostly I told stories, which went on and on. I always intended to become an artist, and as I grew older devoted myself more and more to landscape painting and interior decoration and design. My education consisted of a succession of inefficient governesses.

"When I was little more than twenty I went to the island of Mauritius, east five hundred miles from Madagascar, as companion to a cousin whose husband was colonial secretary. After a very few months I married. Malaria and other plagues played havoc with me, and it was on Mauritius that I buried two of my children. The doctors ordered me back to England. Two years I lay in bed, unable to move. I tried to preserve my memory of England by writing a series of imaginary letters which later appeared as *The Garden of Contentment.*

"My chief interest and love in life has always been ships and sailing (big ships, not yachts), and I have been told that I know more of sailing ships and navigation than any other living writer. The idea of dying in bed was abhorrent to me. I wanted to experience the feel of a ship again. Against all common sense, I shipped off on board a little sailing vessel for Australia. By the time we sighted Australia, I felt myself comparatively well.

"In Melbourne I married Robert Bowles, my son was born, and my husband died. Alone and far from any help, I set about to make my own living. I took up decorative painting and gardening to bring in my son's bread and my own. After seven very hard years I came back to England with my boy. I secured an editorial position on a small weekly which immediately went bankrupt. I started writing again, first *The Ship of Solace*. During these busy years I traveled very little, except for brief trips to the Balkans, Italy, and Morocco. In 1923 the call of the far places came to me again. I went round the world in sailing boats and cargo steamers for the London *Daily News*. On one island I reigned five weeks as king of all the people (no word for queen). I have written enormously: about the Dutch East Indies, Mauritius, Africa (East and Central), Australia, America (the United States and Central America). I seem to have lived so many lives, died so many deaths, been in so many countries, among such divers people, becoming for the time being part of themselves, that there are times when I feel like a disembodied spirit floating about seeing and not being seen."

* * *

So true is this of Elinor Mordaunt's varied and turbulent life that it is difficult to fix it to dates and places and events. Even her birth-date is uncertain; she herself says she does not remember it, and it may have been as late as 1877. Her first very unhappy marriage in Mauritius was to a planter named Wiehe, and ended in divorce. She herself has given two differing versions of the next few years, one in this sketch, the other in *Sinabada* (her title as "lady king"). Her work both as novelist and as travel writer reflects her rich background. "Never yet through my entire life," she says, "has fate allowed me to stay in any place which I began to think of as home." But in spite of this cat-and-mouse existence, complicated by constant illnesses and accidents, she adds: "One is not unhappy when life is a real fight." Her natural gift has conquered her lack of train-

ing, and made her work vivid and colorful, though, as one critic remarked, "she writes best when she is in love with a character." She is an alert, good-looking woman with short white hair, who seems too urbane and "civilized" for one who has led so adventurous a career.

PRINCIPAL WORKS: *Novels*—The Garden of Contentment, 1902; The Ship of Solace, 1911; The Cost of It, 1912; Lu of the Ranges, 1913; Simpson, 1913; Bellamy, 1914; The Island, 1914; The Family, 1915; The Rose of Youth, 1915; Shoe and Stocking Stories (juvenile) 1915; The Park Wall, 1916; Before Midnight, 1917; The Pendulum, 1918; The Processionals (in America: While There's Life) 1918; The Little Soul, 1921; Laura Crichton, 1921; Alas, That Spring, 1922; Reputation, 1923; The Dark Fire, 1927; And Then, 1927; Father and Daughter (in America: Too Much Java) 1928; These Generations, 1930; Full Circle (in America: Gin and Bitters: written as "A. Riposte") 1931; Cross Winds, 1932; Mrs. Van Kleek, 1933; Prelude to Death, 1936; Pity of the World, 1938; Royals Free, 1939; Roses in December, 1939; Death It Is, 1939; Return to Spring, 1940; Hobby House, 1940; Judge Not, 1940; Tropic Heat, 1941. *Miscellaneous*—The Venture Book, 1926; Further Venture Book, 1927; Traveller's Pack, 1933; Purely for Pleasure (in America: Rich Tapestry) 1932; Sinabada (autobiography) 1937.

ABOUT: Johnston, R. B. Some Contemporary Novelists; Mordaunt, E. Sinabada; Woman's Journal March 1929.

MORE, PAUL ELMER (December 12, 1864-March 9, 1937), American critic and philosopher, was born in St. Louis, the son of Enoch Anson More' and Katherine Hay (Elmer) More. Louis T. More, the physicist, and Brookes More, the poet, were his brothers. Paul Elmer More was educated at Washington University (B.A. 1887, M.A. 1892), and at Harvard (M.A. 1893). He had honorary degrees also from Glasgow, Columbia, Dartmouth, and Princeton. He was assistant in Sanskrit in Harvard in 1894 and 1895, and associate in Sanskrit and classical literature at Bryn Mawr from 1895 to 1897. In 1900 he married Henrietta Beck; they had two daughters. In 1901 he became literary editor of the *Independent,* and in 1903 of the New York *Evening Post.* From 1909 to 1914 he was editor of the *Nation.* He then moved to Princeton, N. J., where he devoted himself mostly to writing, occasionally lecturing on the classics at Princeton University.

O. J. Turner

More's first published volume was a life of Franklin, which appeared in 1900. The first of the long series of *Shelburne Essays,* critical and philosophical in character, was published in 1904. During his last decade he was known chiefly, with Prof. Irving Babbitt of Harvard, as the apostle of Humanism —an unfortunate name for their philosophy, since it had already been adopted by a large group of Rationalist writers and speakers. The Humanism of Babbitt and More was quite distinct from this, being a crusade in behalf of tradition, classicism, and decorum, which eventuated in a mixed neo-Platonism and neo-Christianity. He was the sworn foe of naturalistic realism and of every form of radicalism, and never forgave one of his disciples, Stuart P. Sherman, for deserting to "the enemy." Edmund Wilson, being one of his chief critical adversaries is perhaps not quite fair in speaking of More's "intellectual arrogance," and his "lifelong consecration to that great world of culture and thought which he had made so much more real to others but which he could never quite rejoin himself"; but the *Commonweal,* which as the organ of the church of tradition and conservatism was most sympathetic to him, agreed in remarking that More "seemed a clergyman who preferred a literary pulpit. . . . His mind clung to a well-defined set of ideas reached during a lifetime of exploration."

More, indeed, rather resembled a high church clergyman in appearance—short and plump, with Roman nose, iron-gray hair, and pale gray eyes. "In his face," said Edmund Wilson, "there was much strength and some nobility, but a curious absence of color." The same may be said of his mind and personality. He was a little pompous, self-confident, and full of provocative aggressiveness combined with what Stark Young called "deliberate urbanity." He was over-positive and rigidly narrow, and his style, like his mind, was dry. Nevertheless, he filled a useful function in American thought and literature, if only by stirring others to reasoned defense of their own beliefs and theories. Morton Dauwen Zabel, though deprecating his pedantry, remarked on his "honest sympathies, exceptional energy, and high erudition," and said that few American critics had "practiced as energetically or faced as responsibly ... the full obligations of criticism." His private intellectual gods were logic and accuracy, and he compelled others to be logical and accurate in order to confute him effectively. He was a medieval Scholastic unhappily born out of time and place.

PRINCIPAL WORKS: Life of Benjamin Franklin, 1900; Shelburne Essays (11 series) 1904-21; Nietzsche, 1912; Platonism, 1917; The Religion of Plato, 1921; Hellenistic Philosophies, 1923; The Christ of the New Testament, 1924; Christ the Word, 1927; New Shelburne Essays, 1928-36 (including The Demon of the Absolute, 1928; The Sceptical Approach to Religion, 1934; On Being Human, 1936; The Catholic Faith, 1931; Pages From an Oxford Diary, 1937.

ABOUT: Mercier, L. J. A. The Challenge of Humanism; Shafer, F. Paul Elmer More and American Criticism; American Review May 1937; American Scholar October 1938; Bookman April 1929, September 1929; Catholic World August 1932; Commonweal March 26, 1937; Englische Studien (Leipzig) No. 72, 1937; New Republic March 19, 1930, May 27, 1937, June 9, 1937, July 7, 1937, July 21, 1937; Nineteenth Century April 1929; Poetry September 1937; Revue de Littérature Comparée July 1937.

"MORESBY, LOUIS." See BECK, L. M. A.

M O R G A N, CHARLES (January 22, 1894-), English novelist, was born in Kent, the son of Sir Charles Morgan, an eminent civil engineer, and Mary (Watkins) Morgan. From the age of eleven he was determined to be a writer. He entered the Navy as a cadet at thirteen, with the idea of having a regular profession and income which would allow  him to write. He was educated at the Training Colleges at Osborne and Dartmouth, and served as a midshipman in the Atlantic Fleet and in China. He resigned in 1913 and came back to England to prepare for the university. With the World War, he re-enlisted, was sent to Belgium, was taken prisoner, and was interned in Holland until 1917. He was paroled home in November 1917, but his ship was mined and sunk and he lost all the manuscripts on which he had been working. His only publication at this time had been a few poems. In 1919 he went to Brasenose College, Oxford, and received his B.A. two years later. While at college he was president of the Oxford Union Dramatic Society. After a brief experience as a publisher's reader, he joined the editorial staff of the London *Times* in 1921, as assistant to A. B. Walkley, the noted dramatic critic, whom he succeeded at Walkley's death in 1926. He still holds this post (though on leave of absence at present), and also that of correspondent of the

New York *Times,* since all the money he receives from his novels he invests for the future, thus leaving him free to write his novels without regard for public taste or fashion.

In 1923 he married Hilda Vaughan, a descendant of the seventeenth century poet Henry Vaughan, and they have a son and two daughters. Mrs. Morgan, under her maiden name, is the author of a number of novels of Welsh country life.

Mr. Morgan writes his books by hand, very slowly, with constant revision. The *leitmotif* of all his later novels is "the conflict between the spirit and the flesh"; they all have a mystical tinge which has won him a large public if it has alienated more tough-minded readers. *Portrait in a Mirror* won the *Femina-Vie Hereuse* Prize for 1930; *The Fountain* won the Hawthornden Prize for 1933; and *The Voyage* the James Tait Black Memorial Award in 1941. His first novel, *The Gunroom,* a candid account of conditions among midshipmen in the Navy, was not officially suppressed, but was mysteriously withdrawn soon after publication. When George Moore, his close friend, died in 1933, he appointed Mr. Morgan his literary executor; but because a series of important letters was denied him, he abandoned the thought of a full biography of Moore and issued merely a brief tribute.

At the outbreak of war in 1939 Mr. Morgan volunteered again in the Admiralty, for the duration, but later resigned. A trip to the United States followed. In times of peace, he lives with his family at Campden Hill, London. His favorite reading, he says, is the Bible, Blake and the Brontës. He is a Fellow of the Royal Society of Literature and a Chevalier of the Legion of Honor. In spite of his long connection with the drama, he has written only one play, which was produced at the Lyric Theatre in London in 1938 and later published. He is thin-faced, with the dreamy yet piercing eyes of a born mystic.

One critic said of him that he "sometimes writes like George Moore, sometimes like Joseph Hergesheimer"; another, that his writing is "distinguished, without being brilliant." His books have been called everything from masterpieces to pretentious impostures. He is very solemn, sometimes pompous, frequently sentimental, and his "secular mysticism" has been called "specious to the point of being persuasive." Nevertheless, it is apparent that he is thoroughly in earnest, that he has drawn from his own inner depths the convictions which he embodies in his novels, and for vast numbers of readers he is a prophet and a guide.

PRINCIPAL WORKS: The Gunroom, 1919; My Name Is Legion, 1925; Portrait in a Mirror (in America: First Love) 1929; The Fountain, 1932; Epitaph on George Moore, 1938; Sparkenbroke, 1936; The Flashing Stream (play) 1938; The Voyage, 1940; The Empty Room, 1941.

ABOUT: Hibbert Journal January 1937; London Quarterly Review October 1939; Neue Rundschau July 1938; New York Times Book Review October 5, 1941; Nuova Antologia July 16, 1935; Revue des Deux Mondes July 1, 1933; Saturday Review of Literature April 18, 1936; Time April 20, 1936.

MORGAN, WILLIAM FREND DE. See DE MORGAN

MORLEY, CHRISTOPHER DARLING-TON (May 5, 1890-), American novelist and essayist, sends the editors of this volume the following "Obituary (premature, I hope)": "What interested Christopher Morley most about his own work (in which he was intensely interested) was that his early writing, which was (though not intentionally) imitative

Disraeli

and immature, was received with absurd overpraise, whereas his later work, wherever it showed symptoms of originality and power and an attempt to cut below epithelial tissue, was often received with anger or dismay. For instance, *The Trojan Horse,* inspired by his imitative but unscholarly love of Chaucer, and in form a disconcerting blend of prose, verse, and dramatic dialogue, was in his own opinion the most significant of his political parables. In a blend (characteristically American) of rowdy humor and lyrical tenderness, it presented a picture of a world facing annihilation; perhaps on account of its luxury, lethargy, frivolity, and complacence. This book was finished two years before the outbreak of the Semifinal War of 1939, and foreshadowed the present disasters.

"An uncomfortable and instinctive prescience was oddly exhibited in several phases of Morley's writing. *Where the Blue Begins,* in 1922, shortly preceded a widespread reaction against ecclesiastical dogmatism. *Thunder on the Left* (1925) was one of the first successful attempts in contemporary fiction to tell a story in two dimensions at once; or in two dialects, the interior and the exterior. It caused the author much annoyance by the number of letters received asking him what he meant. As if that were part of an author's job! An imaginative author's job is to give the reader an opportunity to collaborate. *John Mistletoe,* which Morley wrote to celebrate (or deplore) his own fortieth birthday, was an early example of what is now a universal passion, the autobiographies of young men. Life has grown so uncertain that anyone who desires an autobiography feels that he had better compile it promptly. *Mistletoe* was a sentimental but also a surprisingly acute survey of a way of life that had seen its best days, and no one was more aware of that than the author. *Human Being,* an interesting experiment in backward narrative, was as literal and matter-of-fact as some of Morley's previous work had been fanciful. It was a search for buried treasure; the treasure buried in the most inaccessible place, the heart of the average and unremarkable man. *Kitty Foyle,* which caused indignation in many readers, was an unexpected revelation, told in the person of an Irish-American 'white collar girl,' of the mind and heart and biology of a young woman of the 1930's.

"It can hardly be denied that Morley was 'versatile,' though he would have preferred the adjective applied in a zoological rather than a popular sense. His habit of oblique or evasive attack, which is puzzling to the highbrows and perfectly understandable to John Doe, usually won for him the word 'whimsical.' He called it the 'emetic epithet.'

"Morley was probably as much puzzled or troubled by himself as some of his readers were by him. He thought of himself (quite often) as essentially a poet, and some of his verse is more important than has been recognized. His best loved private associations were with people devoid of conventional culture, such as booksellers, shipmasters, traveling salesmen, headwaiters, and occasional professors of English literature.

"His work in hand when this memorandum was regretfully written was a large volume tentatively entitled *Broken English* (or *English Public and Private*), a textbook which he hoped would put an end to all textbooks on English composition and style. It was an attempt to survey the English language, in all its moods, as a form of communication. He felt it was a pity that an imaginative and 'creative' writer should serve as a critic; but in the dearth of savory criticism in that inchoate era he felt it his duty to attempt. Perhaps his best judgments were impromptu; but he believed he had something to say, and he often succeeded in saying it. Whether anybody noticed it did not bother him too much.

"The best part of his interment will be private."

* * *

Readers of Christopher Morley will recognize his unmistakable hand in this sketch. To get down to mere data, he was born in Haverford, Pa., the eldest son of Frank and Lilian Janet (Bird) Morley, both English by birth, his father a professor of mathematics. He received his B.A. at Haverford College in 1910 (Phi Beta Kappa), was a Rhodes Scholar at New College, Oxford, from 1910 to 1913, and received an honorary Litt.D. from Haverford in 1933. His two brothers were also Rhodes Scholars: one, Felix, is today president of Haverford; the other, F. V., now editor of Harcourt, Brace & Company, is well known in trans-Atlantic publishing circles. In 1914 he married Helen Booth Fairchild; they have one son and three daughters. He did editorial work successively for Doubleday, Page & Co., the *Ladies' Home Journal,* the Philadelphia *Evening Public Ledger,* and the New York *Evening Post,* and was a contributing editor of the *Saturday Review of Literature* up to 1941. In 1928 he was one of the founders of the Hoboken Theatrical Company, which sponsored revivals of old-time melodramas. In 1937 he edited the revised edition of Bartlett's *Familiar Quotations.* He lectured at Knox College in 1938. He is a large loose-jointed, florid man, expansive, friendly, and mellow. T. S. Matthews called him an "Angloliterophile"; he does indeed love the English language for its own sake, but since the days of his early essays and columns, when Vincent O'Sullivan hailed him as "an American writer who continues the English literary tradition," he has grown greatly: to quote Carl Van Doren, "his sinews have tightened, his style has grown firmer, his observations have taken on a deeper tone."

PRINCIPAL WORKS: The Eighth Sin, 1912; Parnassus on Wheels, 1917; Songs for a Little House, 1917; Shandygaff, 1918; The Rocking Horse, 1919; The Haunted Book Shop, 1919; In the Sweet Dry and Dry (with B. Haley) 1919; Mince Pie, 1919; Travels in Philadelphia, 1920; Kathleen, 1920; Three's a Crowd (play, with E. D. Biggers) 1920; Pipefuls, 1920; Tales From a Rolltop Desk, 1921; Plum Pudding, 1921; Chimneysmoke, 1921; Where the Blue Begins, 1922; The Powder of

Sympathy, 1923; Inward Ho! 1923; Parsons' Pleasure, 1923; Pandora Lifts the Lid (with D. Marquis) 1924; Religio Journalistici, 1924; One Act Plays, 1924; Thunder on the Left, 1925; The Romany Stain, 1926; The Arrow, 1927; Pleased To Meet You, 1927; I Know a Secret, 1927; Toulemonde, 1928; Off the Deep End, 1928; Seacoast of Bohemia, 1929; Rudolph and Amina, 1930; A Book of Days, 1930; Born in a Beer Garden, 1930; John Mistletoe, 1931; Swiss Family Manhattan, 1932; Ex Libris Carissimis, 1932; Human Being, 1932; Mandarin in Manhattan, 1933; Shakespeare and Hawaii, 1933; Internal Revenue, 1933; Hasta la Vista, 1935; Streamlines, 1936; The Trojan Horse, 1937; Kitty Foyle, 1939; Friends, Romans . . ., 1940.

ABOUT: Hughes, B. Christopher Morley: Multi Ex Uno; Century Magazine December 1923; Living Age October 18, 1919; New Republic March 21, 1938; Saturday Review of Literature February 25, 1928; World Tomorrow May 23, 1927.

MORLEY, JOHN, Viscount. See "BRITISH AUTHORS OF THE 19TH CENTURY"

MORRIS, Sir LEWIS. See "BRITISH AUTHORS OF THE 19TH CENTURY"

*MORRIS, LLOYD (September 23, 1893-), American biographer and essayist, writes: "Born in New York City, son  of Frederick and Eugenie (Mayer) Morris. Attended Ethical Culture School and High School. B.A. Columbia University, 1914. After college traveled widely in Europe. Returned to New York, became dramatic critic of New York *Press*, contributed to magazines. During next two years published three books, one a translation from the French of Georges Eeckhoud's *The New Carthage*; edited *Cuentas Modernas del Norte* (*Modern Tales of the North*) for the Carnegie Foundation for International Peace.

"At outbreak of war, in 1917, entered United States Postal Censorship; became chief trade censor in New York City, handling intricate cases of enemy trade and intelligence activities for the various intelligence divisions of the government. In 1919 became managing editor of the *American Exporter*, a publication devoted to foreign trade. Resigned in 1923 to return to freelance writing. The same year was invited to offer a series of lectures in the Extension Division, Columbia University, and in-

augurated the first course in current literature ever given by any American university. This proved so successful that the lectures had to be given in three sections. Continued this course until 1932.

"Meanwhile, spent six months every year in Europe, and continued writing. Contributed fiction and articles to nearly all major magazines, and published five books. Among journalistic feats have been securing the first interview in which royalty permitted itself to be directly quoted: this with the then Prince of Wales (present Duke of Windsor), published in *McCall's Magazine*; an interview with Mussolini when he was seeing no journalists; and other similar feature stories. Has always felt that any man-of-letters should know, and be able to practise, all branches of his craft—but has never experimented with either verse or drama. Otherwise, however, has made some reputation in criticism, biography, short story, and novel, and has for many years written feature stories for magazines. Long European residences at various times brought contact with leading writers in England, France, Ireland, Italy, etc., many of whom became intimate personal friends.

"Unmarried, expects to remain so. Formerly a Republican, is now independent in politics.

*   *   *

Mr. Morris's best known book is his acute biography of Hawthorne. Of his stories, Mary Wallace remarked on his "beautiful and musical, if somewhat over-mannered, prose."

PRINCIPAL WORKS: The Celtic Dawn, 1917; The Poetry of E. A. Robinson, 1923; The Rebellious Puritan—Portrait of Mr. Hawthorne, 1927; Procession of Lovers (short stories) 1929; This Circle of Flesh (novel) 1931.

MORRIS, WILLIAM. See "BRITISH AUTHORS OF THE 19TH CENTURY"

*MORRISON, ARTHUR (1863-), English novelist, dramatist, authority on Far Eastern art, and writer of detective fiction, writes: "Born in county of Kent, near London, England. Son of late George Morrison of Blackheath. Married 1892 Elizabeth Adelaide, daughter of late Frederick Thatcher of Dover. One son Guy born 1893, died 1921 of maladies consequent on war service, having fought in the great European war from its beginning.

"Arthur Morrison began writing as a journalist in the early eighties of the last

* Died August 8, 1954.   * Died December 4, 1945.

century, writing for most of the important London journals of that time till the appearance of his book *Tales of Mean Streets* in 1894. He is the last survivor of the notable

staff of the *National Observer* under the late William Ernest Henley, which included Rudyard Kipling, J. M. Barrie, Robert Louis Stevenson, Thomas Hardy, Charles Whibley, and others of like standing. It was in the *National Observer* that most of the stories in *Tales of Mean Streets* originally appeared.

This volume was followed, in 1896, by *A Child of the Jago*, a full-length novel illustrating life in the worst slum then existing in London which was soon afterward swept away by action of the London County Council. It was at the ceremony of the opening of the new dwellings on the site of the old slum that King Edward the Seventh, then Prince of Wales, made his only reference to the work of a living writer in a public speech, declaring that nobody who had read Mr. Arthur Morrison's book would ever forget the conditions of that place before the clearance. *A Child of the Jago* was followed, in 1899, by *To London Town*, another tale of East End life among the better sort of people in those parts.

In the following year was published *Cunning Murrell*, a romance of rural Essex in the early nineteenth century, dealing with the actual doings of a witch-doctor of those days; and in 1902 *The Hole in the Wall*, by some regarded as his best book, depicted life in the notorious Ratcliff Highway by the riverside in the middle nineteenth century. This was the last of his full-length novels, but *Divers Vanities* (1905), *Green Ginger* (1909), and *Fiddle o'Dreams* (1933) were books of collected short stories which had appeared in magazines and reviews at intervals from the 'nineties of the last century.

"In addition he published a series of volumes of detective stories under the dates named: *Martin Hewitt: Investigator* (1894), *Chronicles of Martin Hewitt* (1895), *Adventures of Martin Hewitt* (1896), *The Dorrington Deed-Box* (1897), *The Red Triangle* (1903), and *The Green Eye of Goona* (1904). And in 1911 appeared *The Painters of Japan*, a comprehensive work in two

folio volumes treating of Japanese pictorial art from the earliest times. His well known collection of Chinese and Japanese paintings was acquired by the British Museum in 1913. Three short plays, produced in collaboration and founded on certain of his stories, *That Brute Simmons*, *The Dumb Cake*, and *A Stroke of Business* were presented in London theatres, the first in 1904 and the other two in 1907. He has been a member of the Savage Club since 1894, is a Fellow and Member of Council of the Royal Society of Literature, and took part in the defense of London in the Great War as Chief Inspector of Special Constabulary in Epping Forest, and telephoned the first warning of the first air raid by Zeppelin on that city in May 1915. Many articles of criticism and appreciation of his work have appeared in English and foreign publications, notably an essay by Teodor de Wyzewa in the *Mercure de France* in 1897, reprinted in that critic's volume of essays, *Écrivains Étrangers*, the same year.

"Mr. Arthur Morrison has now retired from active literary work; but his continued interest in pictorial art is seen in his gallery of some 200 works by English masters and some others. Hogarth, Gainsborough, Reynolds, Constable, Wilson, Turner, Cotman, Morland, and Bonington are represented as well as a few of the French and other Continental schools, and some half dozen pictures by Whistler."

* * *

Influenced in part by his long, self-imposed silence, the reading public has come to consider Arthur Morrison a turn-of-the-century, almost a nineteenth century, figure—which in a literary sense he really is. His works have been long out of print and he is known today only through short story anthologies. In this manner a few of the compassionate studies in his *Tales of Mean Streets* have survived. Also found in anthologies are a number of his detective stories featuring Martin Hewitt, called by Willard Huntington Wright "the first detective of conspicuous note to follow in the footsteps of Sherlock Holmes." It is quite possible that Morrison will be longer remembered for the pleasant if not too baffling Hewitt tales (which he minimizes) than for his more "serious" works. As a contributor to detective literature, Morrison added little to the Holmes formula, but his quiet and literate touch helped the *genre* to survive an era when most of its practitioners were second-rate workmen, content to imitate the more obvious and less admirable characteristics of the Doyle romances.

PRINCIPAL WORKS: *Martin Hewitt Stories*— Martin Hewitt: Investigator, 1894; Chronicles of Martin Hewitt, 1895; Adventures of Martin Hewitt, 1896; The Red Triangle, 1903. *Other Works*—Tales of Mean Streets, 1894; A Child of the Jago, 1896; The Hole in the Wall, 1902; The Green Eye of Goona, 1904; Divers Vanities, 1905; Green Ginger, 1909; The Painters of Japan, 1911; Fiddle o'Dreams, 1933.

ABOUT: Haycraft, H. Murder for Pleasure: The Life and Times of the Detective Story; Thomson, H. D. Masters of Mystery; Wright, W. H. (ed) The Great Detective Stories; Wyzewa, T. de. écrivains étrangers.

MORROW, Mrs. HONORÉ (MC CUE) WILLSIE (1880-April 12, 1940), American novelist and magazine editor, was born

in Ottumwa, Iowa, the daughter of William Dunbar McCue and Lilly Bryant (Head) McCue. Her mother's father was a friend of Daniel Webster, and her paternal grandfather, the Rev. Patrick J. McHugh, was a Methodist circuit-

Pinchot

rider, ordained in 1835, who served in the West Virginia coal mining regions for fifty-three years. Soon after her graduation from the University of Wisconsin, Honoré McCue married Henry Elmer Willsie, a construction engineer, from whom she was divorced in 1922.

New York proving, in general, unresponsive to her efforts to write fiction, Mrs. Willsie went to a mining camp in Arizona to visit friends and to gather material for excellent Western stories and articles on American life which gave her entrée to *Collier's* and *Harper's Weekly*. She also wrote articles on immigration, divorce, and the U.S. Reclamation Service. From 1914 to 1919 she edited the *Delineator,* a woman's magazine of large circulation, resigning to devote her entire time to fiction.

In 1923 she became Honoré Willsie Morrow with her marriage to William Morrow, then treasurer of Frederick A. Stokes Co., publishers; later head of the publishing firm which bears his name. Mr. Morrow died on Armistice Day in 1931. Next year Mrs. Morrow went to England to live, in a sixteenth-century cottage in Brixham, on the Devon coast of England, with her daughter Anne Penn Morrow. Returning to America in 1940 to visit a sister in New Haven, Conn., she contracted influenza and

died at sixty in St. Raphael's Hospital Another daughter, Mrs. Felicia Morrow Beau, of Brussels, Belgium, the highly-strung subject of her mother's last book, *Demon Daughter,* survived, and a son, Richard Dunbar Morrow of South Norwalk, Conn., whose odyssey westward as a youth, recorded by his mother in a *Saturday Evening Post* article, "Dear Mother, I'm in Jail," made amusing reading.

The name of Honoré Willsie Morrow brings to mind a number of earnest, painstaking, well-documented American historical novels, written well in advance of the flood of such fiction which inundated the reading public in the late 1930's. Ten years of research went into the three Lincoln novels collected into the trilogy *Great Captain*, with an introduction by William Lyon Phelps. Her western novels rank near those of Eugene Manlove Rhodes and Frank Spearman. Mrs. Morrow was a capable executive and an attractive personality.

PRINCIPAL WORKS: Still Jim, 1915; Lydia of the Pines, 1916; Benefits Forgot, 1917; The Forbidden Trail, 1919; The Enchanted Canyon, 1920; The Devonshers, 1924; We Must March, 1925; On to Oregon, 1926; Forever Free, 1927; The Father of Little Women (biography of Bronson Alcott) 1927; With Malice Toward None, 1928; Splendor of God, 1929; The Last Full Measure, 1930; Tiger! Tiger! (biography of John B. Gough) 1930; Black Daniel (biography of Daniel Webster) 1933; Yonder Sails the Mayflower, 1934; Demon Daughter, 1939.

ABOUT: Cooper, F. T. Honoré Willsie Morrow; New York Times April 13, 1940; Publishers' Weekly April 20, 1940.

MORTON, HENRY CANOVA VOLLAM (1892-), English writer on the British Isles who signs his works as H. V. Morton, was born and educated in Birmingham. For many years he has been in newspaper work, starting with the Birmingham *Gazette and Express* in 1910. He became its assistant editor in 1912, but the next year went to London (where he still lives),

to join the staff of the *Empire Magazine.* After a few months he became sub-editor of the *Daily Mail,* and remained with that paper until the outbreak of the First World War. He served throughout the war, in France, with the Warwickshire Yeomanry. After being demobilized, he joined the staff of the London *Daily Standard,* in 1919. In 1921 he went to the *Daily Express*. Since 1931 he has been a special writer for the *Daily Herald*. He is unmarried.

Mr. Morton is perhaps the greatest living authority on the material being of the British Isles—that is to say, on their landscape, buildings, monuments, customs, and history. He writes with a gusto and a sentiment far removed from the usual perfunctory "travel book," and revealing a deep affection for his country—and most of all for London. The diastrous German air-raids on London must be even more painful to him than to other Londoners, for he has known every street, every building, and loved them all. (It may be noted that his *Ghosts of London* is not a book on psychic phenomena, but that the "ghosts" are surviving traditional customs and occupations of the city.)

His other literary interest is as a churchman. From the standpoint of a devout believer, he has written several books on Biblical personages and places. These have not been republished in America, as his books of local travel have been, and so in this country he is known primarily as the most prominent current celebrator of England, Scotland, Wales, and Ireland, and above all of London—as it was.

PRINCIPAL WORKS: The Heart of London, 1925; London, 1926; The London Year, 1926; The Spell of London, 1926; The Nights of London, 1926; In Search of England, 1927; The Call of England, 1928; In Search of Scotland, 1929; In Search of Ireland 1930; In Search of Wales, 1932; Blue Days at Sea, 1932; In Scotland Again, 1933; In the Steps of the Master, 1934; The London Scene, 1935; Our Fellow Men, 1936; In the Steps of St. Paul, 1936; The Lands of the Bible, 1938; Ghosts of London, 1939; In Search of the Northern Isles, 1940; Women of the Bible, 1940; Middle East, 1941; I, James Blunt, 1942.

MOTTRAM, RALPH HALE (October 30, 1883-), English novelist and miscellaneous author who publishes as R. H.

Mottram, writes: "I was born in the dwelling-house above Gurney's Bank, which stood in London Street, the principal business street of Norwich, Norfolk. My father was chief clerk, as his father and grandfather had been, and I was destined to follow him. My mother, half Irish by birth, was music and drawing mistress at local girls' schools. She was his second wife, but we were a happy and united family. Such interest, therefore, as may be found in my life-story proceeds entirely from the fact that I was a typical product of the very mixed type of English provincial middle-class life. For while my father and subsequently I were servants of a great modern financial business (Gurney's Bank became part of the great Barclay combine in 1896), and the world-renowned mills of J. & J. Colman and the well-known Norwich Union Insurance Offices lay within a stone's throw of my home and I passed them every day on my way to school, I also passed a castle and a cathedral, both of which were built in 1100 A.D. and have been very little altered since. In nearly every street stood pre-Reformation churches, the whole being enclosed in the remains of the city wall (1260 A.D.). Thus I had from the earliest years that strong feeling of continuity which is the principal contribution of the British Isles to the world. The tradition about one was so long. It embraced everything from the Norman Conquest to the latest financial and industrial organization. It was less interrupted than any other national heritage. True, there were the marks of violence of Cromwell's soldiers plain to be seen on the gates of the Cathedral Close. And the city was full of the remains, some turned to secular uses, of the monastic buildings of the Middle Ages. Yet English provincial life had flowed on and concentrated it all.

"I was brought up in what can only be called the progressive, as distinct from the conservative side of English life. My parents were Unitarian by religion, but the chapel to which I was taken on Sundays was already a hundred and fifty years old, and the congregation older. My father believed in financial integrity and political equality, particularly for Ireland, and in international peace. But he was on the friendliest terms with Church of England dignitaries and county aristocrats. We had just ceased to be afraid of France, looked to her for culture and cooking, knew little of Germany, and had of course close ties with the culture and literature of New England.

"The climax of my life came through chance acquaintance in 1904 with John Galsworthy, whose friendship I enjoyed to his death in 1933. I had begun to write, partly as reaction from too settled a life, partly through the 'Celtic' strain in my mother's character, but it was to Galsworthy's never-failing help and encouragement that I owe my present position.

"Like all my kind, I was an astonished and reluctant recruit in 1914, in my county regiment, became a junior officer, was attached to various staffs, all in Flanders. I was married in 1918 and have two sons and one daughter. In 1927 I relinquished banking for literature.

"I saw the first motor car in the streets of Norwich, the first aeroplane fly over it. Today I drive a car and my son flies a plane. These are superficial changes. I still believe, as my father, and Galsworthy afterwards, taught me, in honesty and peace and a gradual development which I can only call Progress. I am prepared to back these convictions as a reserve officer if necessary."

* * *

Mr. Mottram won the Hawthornden Prize in 1924 for *The Spanish Farm,* which sold over 100,000 copies and was later made into a film called *Roses in Picardy.* He is a Fellow of the Royal Society of Literature and a magistrate in Norwich. He looks like what he was until 1927—a dignified banker; he is bald, with a small moustache. Richard A. Cordell called him "the least Bohemian of writers: he avoids literary clubs and cliques and lives in Norwich, writing, gardening, and hobnobbing with his lifelong friends and neighbors." His writing shows the influence of Galsworthy in its quiet, clear style, its understatement, balance, and attitude of philosophic tolerance.

PRINCIPAL WORKS: *Fiction*—The Spanish Farm, 1924; Sixty-Four Ninety-Four, 1925; The Crime at Vanderlynden's 1926; Our Mr. Dormer, 1927; Ten Years Ago (short stories) 1927; The English Miss, 1928; The Boroughmonger, 1929; Europa's Beast, 1930; The Headless Hound (short stories) 1930; Castle Island, 1931; Dazzle, 1932; Home for the Holidays, 1932; The Menin Gate (short stories) 1932; The Lame Dog, 1933; Bumphreys, 1934; The Banquet (short stories) 1934; Early Morning, 1935; Flower-Pot End, 1936; Time To Be Going, 1937; There Was a Jolly Miller, 1938; You Can't Have It Back, 1939; Miss Lavington, 1940; The Ghost and The Marden, 1940; The World Turns Slowly Round, 1942. *Miscellaneous*—Repose and Other Verses (as J. Marjoram) 1906; New Poems (as J. Marjoram) 1909; History of Financial Speculation, 1929; The New Providence, 1931; John Crome, 1932; East Anglia, 1933; Journey to the Western Front, 1936; Portrait of an Unknown Victorian, 1937; Noah, 1937; Old England, 1937; Autobiography With a Difference, 1938; Success to the Mayor, 1938; Traders' Dream; A History of the East India Company, 1940; Bowler Hat, 1940.

ABOUT: Fabes, G. Bibliography of the Work of R. H. Mottram; Mottram, R. H. Autobiography With a Difference; Bookman (London) December 1928; Saturday Review of Literature April 29, 1939.

MOWRER, EDGAR ANSEL (March 8, 1892-   ), American war correspondent, was born in Bloomington, Ill., the son of Rufus Mowrer and Nellie (Scott) Mowrer. He was educated at the University of Michi-

gan (B.A. 1913), and also studied at the University of Chicago and at the Sorbonne, in Paris. Immediately after his graduation from the University he entered journalism; his brother, Paul Scott Mowrer, was editor of the Chicago *Daily News,* and when the First World War broke out Edgar Mowrer was sent to cover it, first to France and Belgium, then to Rome and to the Italian front, where he witnessed the retreat from Caporetto. After the war he became head of the *Daily News* Bureau in Berlin, and was president of the Berlin Foreign Press Association. When the Nazi régime began, he was distinctly *persona non grata,* and his position became still less tenable when a series of his dispatches from Germany (which won the Pulitzer Prize in Journalism for 1932) was collected in book form as *Germany Puts the Clock Back.* Mowrer was ordered to leave Germany, and when he refused, one of his friends and associates was arrested and held as a hostage to force his departure. He secured this man's release by leaving to become chief correspondent for his paper in China and Japan. In 1939 he was made chief of the *Daily News* Bureau in Paris. He remained there until the fall of France, when he went to England.

In 1916 he married Lilian Thomson, of London, and they have one daughter. Mrs. Mowrer is a well known author in her own right; she has written on the theatre as well as on her experiences as a war correspondent's wife and on the international situation as she has seen it. Mr. Mowrer's nephew, Richard Mowrer, was *Daily News* correspondent at Warsaw until the invasion of Poland.

Tall and thin, with a long, rough-hewn face and an inseparable and enormous pipe, Edgar Mowrer is a "typical" war correspondent in appearance. An early tinge of Spenglerian pessimism in his viewpoint vanished long ago, and he is now one of the most forthright and clear-seeing of commentators on world affairs. He is a first-rate journalist, who may be depended upon for the accuracy of his factual statements; and he is something more, for he has a gift for the succinct phrase and is utterly fearless in his evaluations of prominent persons. Wherever there is trouble, he may be expected to be there "covering" it, and his report will be highly readable as well as informative. Mrs. Mowrer nearly always accompanies him on his foreign assignments, and both of them have frequently been in personal danger and have undauntedly run great risks in the interest of securing the news. Edgar Ansel Mowrer is in the best tradition of American journalism, and he is completely free of the fustian romantics of the Richard Harding Davis era.

PRINCIPAL WORKS: Immortal Italy, 1922; This American World, 1928; The Future of Politics (in England: Sinon: or, The Future of Politics) 1930; Germany Puts the Clock Back, 1932; The Dragon Awakes; A Report From China, 1938; Global War: An Atlas of World Strategy (with M. Rajchman) 1942.

ABOUT: Mowrer, L. T. Journalist's Wife; New Yorker July 20, 1940; Saturday Review of Literature August 19, 1933; Time October 2, 1939.

MUIR, EDWIN (May 15, 1887-   ), Scottish poet and literary critic, writes: "I was born in a house called the Folly, in Deerness

on the mainland of Orkney. I was the youngest of a family of six: my father was a farmer; our life was pre-industrial and virtually self-supporting. When I was ten my brothers began to disperse, to Kirkwall, the local town, Glasgow, and Edinburgh. In a few more years my father strained his heart and had to give up farming, and eventually decided to go to Glasgow to be near his three eldest sons. The migration of our family from a pre-industrial to an industrial society had a result which I believe to be typical: four of us, my father and mother and two brothers, died within two years.

"I entered a law office when I was fourteen, and was a clerk in a number of offices, some pleasant and some unpleasant, until I was thirty-one. During my teens I suffered almost continuously from bad health, and in my twenties contracted a neurosis which was later dispersed by marriage and a course of psycho-analysis. Before I left Orkney I had experienced a religious conversion; my youth in Glasgow was spent in an atmosphere of evangelicanism; I escaped from it into Socialism at twenty. Later, when the Socialist impulse was weakening, I discovered Nietzsche and read his works from beginning to end, trying hard to combine the two philosophies, though they were quite incompatible. Under the influence of the late A. R. Orage of the *New Age,* I began to

write propagandist poetry, all of it very bad. Later I tried my hand at some aphorisms in the Nietzschian style, which were not much better. These appeared under the title, *We Moderns,* and are now out of print. During the First World War I applied for enlistment but was not taken.

"In 1919 I was married to Willa Anderson and went to London with her. We stayed there for two years, and I was taken on by Orage as his assistant on the *New Age.* My wife and I eventually decided to see Europe, and for four years lived in various countries there, including Czechoslovakia, Germany, Austria, and Italy, where we were supported mainly by my contributions to the *Freeman,* then under the generous literary editorship of Van Wyck Brooks. My essays in the *Freeman* were collected under the title of *Latitudes.* Later we lived for a good long time in the South of France, but returned to England in 1927. A few years ago we returned to Scotland, and have lived there ever since. Nietzsche pursued me for a long time after I was really finished with him, but was exorcised at last, when, at thirty-five, I began again to write poetry."

* * *

Mr. and Mrs. Muir now live at St. Andrew's, Fifeshire, with their son. Together they are among the best known contemporary translators from the German, their translations including the works of Hauptmann, Feuchtwanger, Franz Kafka, Erich Glaeser, and Hermann Broch. Mr. Muir's favorite recreations are swimming and playing solitaire.

F. L. Lucas says that Edwin Muir has "a brain with a French gift for wide and lucid generalization" and "a slightly Butlerish quality of mingled wit and shrewdness." Clifton Fadiman called his book, *The Structure of the Novel,* "the clearest, because most unimpassioned, analysis of the comparative failure of the contemporary realistic school." Keen as his mind is, it also has a metaphysical bent the *Nation and Athenaeum* remarked that he "sometimes falters when he allows his seriousness to get the better of him." His poetry, in which, according to Geoffrey Grigson, "idea and emotion are fused like the contradictory components of a lens," is also metaphysical in spirit.

PRINCIPAL WORKS: *Poetry*—First Poems, 1925; Chorus of the Newly Dead, 1926; Variations on a Fine Theme, 1934; Journeys and Places, 1937. *Novels*—The Marionette, 1927; The Three Brothers, 1931; Poor Tom, 1932. *Criticism*—Latitudes, 1924; Transition, 1926; The Structure of the Novel, 1928; Scott and Scotland: the Predicament

MUIR

of the Scottish Writer, 1936; The Present Age, From 1914, 1939. *Miscellaneous*—We Moderns, 1918; John Knox: Portrait of a Calvinist, 1930; Scottish Journey, 1935; The Story and the Fable (autobiography) 1940.

ABOUT: Chesterton, G. K. Fancies Versus Fads; Lucas, F. L. Authors Dead and Living; Muir, E. The Story and the Fable. Untermeyer, L. British Poetry; Atlantic Monthly April 1940.

MUIR, JOHN (April 21, 1838-December 24, 1914), Scottish-American naturalist, was born in Dunbar, Scotland, and attended the

Dunbar Grammar School. His father soon brought the family to the United States to establish a claim in Wisconsin, where they lived in a log cabin. At fifteen John began the study of grammar and mathematics at home, rising early to read and to work on various ingenious contraptions, which he displayed at the state fair in Madison. While attending the University of Wisconsin, he slept in a bed which rang an alarm in the morning and brought before his eyes a succession of textbooks arranged in the sequence he had selected. Threatened with blindness, he set out for a trip down the Mississippi to Louisiana, Florida, across Panama, and northward into California. With a packet of tea, a sack of bread, and a hand-axe, Muir established himself in a hand-built saw-mill in the Yosemite, which he was later instrumental in making a national park.

In 1878 Muir joined the *Courier* expedition in search of the Jeannette party lost in the Arctic; in 1899 he was a member of the Harriman expedition to Alaska, meeting John Burroughs on the voyage. As Henry Fairfield Osborn notes, Muir chose for observation those aspects of nature which present the greatest obstacles, such as glaciers and mountain tops, although he "had tender moments with birds and found a personality in trees." In his passion for forests, he visited those of Russia, Africa, Australia, New Zealand, and Asia. He advocated the preservation of American forests and the establishment of national parks and reservations, especially in the Sierras. Muir's nature-philosophy was entirely theistic; he believed all the works of Nature to be directly the works of God, but was also a thoroughgoing evolutionist. His carefully-wrought literary style was gathered from classic British sources: the Bible, Milton,

Shakespeare, and Carlyle. Thoreau was one of his objects of intense admiration, although he did not imitate his style. Unconventional, absent-minded, genial and bearded, Muir died in Los Angeles, Calif., the day before Christmas, 1914, in his seventy-sixth year, leaving unpublished a practically complete book about Alaska.

PRINCIPAL WORKS: The Mountains of California, 1894; Our National Parks, 1901; Stickeen, 1909; My First Summer in the Sierra, 1911; The Yosemite, 1912; Story of My Boyhood and Youth, 1913; Letters to a Friend, 1915.

ABOUT: Beard, A. E. S. Our Foreign-Born Citizens; Faris, J. T. Men Who Conquered; Foerster, N. Nature in American Literature; Muir, J. Story of My Boyhood and Youth; Osborn, H. F. Impressions of Great Naturalists; Parkman, M. R. Heroes of To-Day; Tracy, H. C. American Naturists; Wyatt, E. F. Great Companions; New York Times December 25, 1914.

MUKERJI, DHAN GHOPAL (July 6, 1890-July 14, 1936) Indian-American novelist and miscellaneous writer, was born in Calcutta, India, the son of Kissori and Bhuban (Goswami) Mukerji. The family's home was on the edge of the jungle, where the boy could see the eyes of foxes and jackals gleaming. As Brahmins, members of the priest class, the Mukerjis

had charge of the village temple. The mother could neither read nor write, but recited old tales of India to her family of eight. At ten the boy attended a Scotch-Presbyterian school; at fourteen he was initiated into the priesthood, traveling through India two years as a begging pilgrim; and at eighteen attended the University of Calcutta. After a year's study of engineering at Tokyo University, Mukerji proceeded to California, armed with a knowledge of "Miltonic English," and spent his last borrowed dollar for the entrance fee at the University of California. His senior year was passed at Leland Stanford University, where he received a degree of Ph.B. in metaphysics in 1914. He lectured there on comparative literature, and gave talks before men's and women's clubs. *Gay-Neck,* the story of his experiences with forty pigeons and their leader, won Mukerji the Newbery Prize medal of the American Library Association for the best children's book of 1927. *A Son of Mother India Answers,* condemning Katherine Mayo's *Mother India* as exaggerating the shortcomings of his native

land and being too sympathetic to British rule, also attracted attention, and his *Caste and Outcast* told an unusual life-story, even for so ethnologically mixed a country as the United States. Mukerji married Ethel Ray Dugan of Norristown, Pa., a teacher in the Dalton School of New York. They had one son, Dhan Ghopal II. Mukerji was a member of the American-Oriental Society and the Town Hall Club. His home was in New Milford, Conn., but he died in New York City, a suicide by hanging after a prolonged nervous breakdown.

PRINCIPAL WORKS: Kari the Elephant, 1923; Caste and Outcast (autobiography) 1923; My Brother's Face, 1924; Face of Silence, 1926; Gay-Neck, 1927; A Son of Mother India Answers, 1928; Chief of the Herd, 1929; Visit India With Me, 1929; The Song of God, 1931; Daily Meditation, 1933; Path of Prayer, 1934.

ABOUT: Mukerji, D. G. Caste and Outcast. Kunitz, S. J. & Haycraft, H. (eds.) The Junior Book of Authors; New York Times July 15, 1936; Publishers' Weekly July 25, 1936; Wilson Library Bulletin September 1936.

MULFORD, CLARENCE EDWARD

(February 3, 1883-), American writer of Western stories, writes: "Born at Streator, Ill.; father, Clarence Cohansey Mulford, mother Minnie Grace Kline. Her father was mixed up in the Students' Rebellion in Germany and fled to this country. The Mulford side goes back, in America, to 1643; twenty Mulfords are listed as having fought in the Revolution.

"I was educated at Streator and at Utica, N.Y. I was given the choice of going to college or to work, and chose the latter. My first job was with the *Municipal Journal and Engineer,* of New York. Later I got into Civil Service, but all this time I was writing. My first short story shared first prize in a contest run by the old *Metropolitan Magazine.* Then came a connected series of the first Bar 20 tales, published in Caspar Whitney's *Outing Magazine.* They later were made into a book. The first books were published from data, but later I traveled throughout the West, and visited every part of it which held real interest for me.

"I have an extensive library of Western Americana, and have thrown away three times as many books as I retained. My card file of Western data, more than 17,000 cards, covers every activity of the West (except

mining) from Manuel Liza's expedition up the Missouri River to the dying out of the Great Western Cattle Trail. Some of the eras covered are: the fur trade, the emigrant trails, wagon freighting, stage coach, Pony Express, cattle trade, etc.

"I went to Brooklyn, N.Y., in 1899, and moved to Fryeburg, Maine, my present home, in 1926, intending to take life easy, but found I could not stop writing. I have written twenty-seven books, and am working on another. Twenty-five of the books have been made into motion pictures, with an additional twenty-seven from scenarios. I am a corresponding member of the Institut Littéraire et Artistique de France, which has awarded me a laurette certificate, with gold medal, for my book *The Round-Up.*

"In 1920 I married Eva Emily Wilkinson. She died in 1933.

"My present hobby is big-caliber revolver shooting (hand-loading my own maximum cartridges), over ranges of 300 to 500 yards, which forced me to buy fifty-five acres of land, with a high hill for a backstop."

PRINCIPAL WORKS: Bar 20 (short stories) 1907; The Orphan, 1908; Hopalong Cassidy, 1910; Bar 20 Days, 1911; Buck Peters, Ranchman, 1912; The Coming of Cassidy, 1913; The Man From Bar 20, 1918; Johnny Nelson, 1920; The Bar 20 Three, 1921; Tex, 1922; Bring Me His Ear, 1923; Black Buttes, 1923; Rustlers' Valley, 1924; Hopalong Cassidy Returns, 1924; Cottonwood Gulch, 1925; Hopalong Cassidy's Protegé, 1926; The Bar 20 Rides Again, 1926; Carson of the J.C., 1927; Mesquite Jenkins, 1928; Me an' Shorty, 1929; The Deputy Sheriff, 1930; Hopalong Cassidy and the Eagle's Brood, 1931; Mesquite Jenkins, Tumbleweed, 1932; The Round-Up, 1933; Trail Dust, 1934; On the Trail of the Tumbling T, 1934; Hopalong Cassidy Takes Cards, 1937; Hopalong Cassidy Serves a Writ, 1941.

MÜLLER, FRIEDRICH MAX. See "BRITISH AUTHORS OF THE 19TH CENTURY"

MUMFORD, LEWIS (October 19, 1895-), American critic, writes: "I was born in Flushing, Long Island, the son of Lewis and Elvina Conradina (Baron) Mumford. But I grew up on the West Side in New York, and have been a New Yorker all my life, except for the last three years, when most of my life has been spent in the midst of the Dutchess County countryside.

My forebears were English and German, but the influence of

the latter predominated throughout my childhood, for German was almost as familiar a language among my elders as English, and the food I ate was all of a fine Franco-German variety. In 1901 I started at public school, and I remained a docile pupil, a model pupil, always an excellent pupil in the futile academic sense, until I entered high school, where my interests widened and my marks worsened. I entered the Stuyvesant High School in 1909, expecting to become an electrical engineer, for I was an early experimenter with the radio; but I left it, in 1912, with the growing expectation of becoming a writer, although my plans were vague and my ambitions modest: at most I dreamed of being a reporter on a newspaper or writing a successful play. Studying at the evening session of the City College, during the next five years, provided the better part of my academic education. Until 1919 I did work at Columbia, New York University, and the New School for Social Research, where I first met Thorstein Veblen. Though I acquired sufficient credits for a B.A. degree I hold no degree of any kind.

"As early as 1915, in my work in biology, I came across the unmistakable writings of Professor Patrick Geddes,^{qv} and though we were not to meet till he came to New York in 1923, his influence became the most important one in my life. He indicated what had been lacking in my metropolitan routine; he held up the ideal of an organic and well-balanced education. From that time on I actively used the city itself as storehouse and power-house; the museums, the libraries, the theatres, the actual buildings were no less a part of my educational equipment than the university. It was under Geddes' influence too that I explored my environment further by vocational participation, first as an investigator in the Dress and Waist Industry, 1916, then as laboratory helper in the Bureau of Standards cement testing laboratory at Pittsburgh, 1917, finally as a radio operator, United States Navy, in 1918. From 1914 on I devoted myself with unflagging zeal to writing, though almost nothing was published. My main desire was to become a playwright. But when I came out of the Navy, and accepted the post as editor on the *Dial*, in 1919, I deflected myself from this field of endeavor; and though I have written more than one play since, I have not been able to satisfy my own standard of achievement and hence they have never left my files.

"In 1920 I had an experimental half-year in London, where, at the invitation of Victor Branford, Geddes' colleague, I served as acting editor of the *Sociological Review* and gave a course on Principles of Reconstruction for the Summer School of Civics at High Wycombe. Coming back to New York, I settled down to the life of a free-lance writer. In 1922 I appeared in Harold Stearns' *Civilization in the United States*, and in the same year my own book, *The Story of Utopias*, appeared. In 1923 I was one of the original members of the Regional Planning Association of America; in 1924 I served as special investigator for the New York Housing and Regional Planning Commission; and in 1925 I was editor of the Regional Planning number of the *Survey Graphic*. It is from these associations that people have probably acquired the impression that I am an architect, which is of course not true: if I have any field of specialization at all, it is the all-inclusive one of the social philosopher.

"In 1926 I joined with Alfred Kreymborg and Paul Rosenfeld in editing *The American Caravan*, the first modern revival of the yearbooks of the 1830's and 1840's, and between 1927 and 1936 we published five volumes.

"My political convictions have remained consistently Socialist from the beginning; but I have never been either a Marxian or a totalitarian. I am not one of those who suddenly became conscious of social disorder and wretchedness only after the stock market went to pieces in 1929; and as time has gone on I have become more, rather than less radical. Though brought up as an Episcopalian, my religion is that of the traditional American humanist, like Emerson or Whitman.

"In 1921 I was married to Sophia Wittenberg, and we have a son and a daughter. In 1931 I did the first draft of a book in which I intended to bring together, within a common frame, the ideas I had so far formulated on machines, cities, buildings, social life, and people. Getting a Guggenheim Fellowship, in 1932, I spent four months in Europe, and during this period the entire project altered into a much more monumental scheme in three large volumes. The first two, *Technics and Civilization* and *The Culture of Cities*, have already appeared, and I am now working on the preparation of the third volume, which will deal with the personality and the community in relation to politics, education, and morals."

* * *

Lewis Mumford is dark and handsome, with deep, inquiring eyes and a sensitive, serious face. *Time* aptly called him a "bio-scholar," and remarked that his authority equaled his range. Howard Mumford Jones spoke of his "packed style, insight, and imaginative acuity." Malcolm Cowley, however, complained that he is "entirely too fond of fancy words" and has "a little too much aloofness and abstraction."

PRINCIPAL WORKS: The Story of Utopias, 1922; Sticks and Stones, 1924; The Golden Day, 1926; Herman Melville, 1929; The Brown Decades, 1931; Technics and Civilization, 1934; The Culture of Cities, 1938; Whither Honolulu? 1938; Men Must Act, 1939; Faith for Living, 1940; The South in Architecture, 1941.

ABOUT: Bookman September 1930; Forum December 1935; New Republic April 20, 1938, April 29, 1940; North American Review September 1938; Time April 18, 1938, September 2, 1940.

MUNDY, TALBOT (April 23, 1879-August 5, 1940), Anglo-American novelist, wrote to the editors of this volume shortly before his death:

"Talbot Mundy was born in London and educated at Rugby. After spending a year in Germany, studying agriculture, he had a Government job at Baroda in India and subsequently wandered all over India on horseback, even penetrating Tibet. Fascinated by the Indian occult teachings, he neglected no opportunity to learn all he could about them. His novels reveal the Indian influence. Mundy's subsequent wanderings include Australia and the whole length and breadth of Africa. For a considerable time he was in Government service in the country now known as Kenya, where he mastered several of the native languages. While in Africa, he did a great deal of big game hunting; but his chief interest was native magic, which he studied intensively. He maintains that, while many of the native magicians are frauds and charlatans, some of them really possess 'occult' powers that truly come under the heading of magic—in the sense that science has not yet explained them or explained them away. His novel, The Ivory Trail, was an exposé of German military misgovernment in what is nowadays the mandated territory of Tanganyika.

"Mundy took out first papers in 1911 soon after reaching the United States, where he became a citizen in 1917. Since then he has traveled widely in Egypt and the Near East, including parts of Arabia. He has also traveled widely in Mexico, including two protracted visits to Yucatan to study Mayan history."

* * *

Mr. Mundy was unmarried, and lived in Anna Maria, Fla. He was a big, fair man, partly bald, with a round, earnest face. His short stories in popular magazines were as well known as his novels. Some of the latter were translated into French, German, Swedish, Hindustani, and Japanese. B. Virginia Lee said that "he has that rare instinct which gives us just what we want, mystery, danger, unknown lands, occult realism [*sic*] of Eastern lands." He died at sixty-one.

PRINCIPAL WORKS: Rung Ho, 1914; Winds of the World, 1915; King of the Khyber Rifles, 1916; Hira Singh, 1918; The Ivory Trail, 1919; The Eye of Zeitoon, 1920; Told in the East, 1920; Guns of the Gods, 1921; The Nine Unknown, 1922; Om, 1923; The Devil's Guard, 1925; Caves of Terror, 1926; Queen Cleopatra, 1929; Cock o' the North, 1929; Black Light, 1930; Jimgrim, 1931; The Hundred Days, 1931; W.H., 1931; Jungle Jest, 1932; C.I.D., 1932; When Trails Were New, 1932; The Lion of Petra, 1933; The Seventeen Thieves of El-Kalil, 1933; The Lost Trooper, 1933; The Gunga Sahib, 1933; The King in Check, 1934; Tros of Samothrace, 1934; The Mystery of Khufu's Tomb, 1935; Full Moon, 1935; Caesar Dies, 1935; Purple Pirate, 1936; Jimgrim and Allah's Peace, 1936; The Thunder Dragon Gate, 1937; East and West, 1937; The Valiant View, 1939; Old Ugly-Face, 1939.

ABOUT: Overland Monthly August 1925; Publishers' Weekly August 17, 1940.

MUNRO, HECTOR HUGH ("Saki") (December 18, 1870-November 13, 1916), Scottish novelist and short-story writer, was born at Akyab, Burma, the son of an inspector-general of the Burma police. His mother died before he was two, and at that age he was sent home to the care of his aunts, Charlotte and Augusta, who brought him up with Draconic strictness at Pilton,

near Barnstaple, Devonshire. He was a delicate child, who manifested an early passion for sketching which never left him. He first went to school at Exmouth when he was twelve; at fifteen he went to Bedford Grammar School for two years; and thereafter he was taken in hand by his father (now retired), with whom he made journeys abroad to Normandy, Germany, Austria and Davos, Switzerland. Eventually father and son settled as master and pupil at Heanton, near Barnstaple, for two years.

Early in 1893 Hector left to take up an appointment with the Burma police, which his father had found him; but after thirteen months in which he had seven bouts of fever he gave it up. After recuperating at Westward Ho! he went to London to write, fortified by an introduction to the well-known cartoonist, Sir Francis Carruthers Gould. By Gould's good offices he obtained work on the *Westminster Gazette,* for which he wrote some political sketches in the Lewis Carroll vein, called "The Westminster Alice," which came out as a book in 1902 with Gould's illustrations. Meanwhile he had published his first and only serious work, *The Rise of the Russian Empire,* in 1900. He held Conservative views in politics, so that he welcomed the chance of joining that high Tory organ, the *Morning Post,* in 1902, and worked as one of its foreign correspondents for six years, in the Balkans, Russia, and Paris. His first collection of short stories, *Reginald,* appeared first in the *Westminster Gazette* and later (1904) in book form.

In 1908 Munro returned to London, and also bought a cottage in the pleasant Surrey hills near by. He wrote a great deal, not only in the two papers already named, but in the *Bystander* and the *Daily Express,* and spent much of his evening leisure at the Cocoa Tree Club, where he played his favorite game, bridge. *Reginald in Russia* came out in 1910; two years later he published a first novel, *The Unbearable Bassington,* and in 1914 more stories, called *Beasts and Super-Beasts,* and *When William Came,* a fantasia of England under the Hohenzollerns. At the beginning of the war he enlisted as a private in the 22d Royal Fusiliers, refused several offers of a commission, and went out to France as a corporal at the end of 1915. He was a brave and imperturbable soldier, and in November 1916 rejoined his unit too soon after an attack of malaria. He was killed in the attack on Beaumont-Hamel on the 13th.

Munro's sister and biographer named as his chief traits his whimsicality, sense of humor, love of animals, pride in being Highland, and indifference to money. He was a humorist of tremendous high spirits, often going over the border into sheer flippancy, but there was a satirical bite in much of his work. He could write excellent horror stories, had an admirable facility in plot-making, and drew the utmost value out of his name-coinages for characters. He chose

his pseudonym from Omar Khayyám, and Christopher Morley writes of him that, "The empty glass we turn down for him is the fragile, hollow-stemmed goblet meant for dryest champagne; it is of the finest."

PRINCIPAL WORKS: The Rise of the Russian Empire, 1900; The Westminster Alice, 1902; Reginald, 1904; Reginald in Russia, 1910; The Chronicles of Clovis, 1912; The Unbearable Bassington, 1912; Beasts and Super-Beasts, 1914; When William Came, 1914; The Toys of Peace and Other Papers, 1919; The Square Egg and Other Sketches, 1924.

ABOUT: Mais, S. P. B. Books and Their Writers; Milne, A. A. By Way of Introduction; Morley, C. Internal Revenue; Atlantic Monthly July 1940; Scholastic October 14, 1940. See also Prefaces and Introductions to various editions of the author's works.

MUNRO, NEIL (June 3, 1864- December 22, 1930), Scottish novelist and poet, was born at Inveraray (sometimes misspelled Inverrary), Argyll-shire, of a long line of farmers and shepherds attached to the Campbell clan. He left the parish school, where he had been a poor student but an omnivorous reader, at twelve, and entered the law office of the county sheriff's clerk.

For five years he fretted in this distasteful work, until in 1881, having taught himself shorthand (then required of newspaper reporters) he secured a post on a small provincial paper, the *Scottish News.* It was twelve years more before he became associated with a paper of any importance, the Greenock *Advertiser.* He went next to the Glasgow *News,* and except for a brief excursion to a Falkirk paper, remained with it until it ceased publication. He was then taken on by the Glasgow *Evening News,* a much larger paper and not under the same ownership in spite of its name. Beginning as star reporter and art, dramatic, and literary critic, he was made editor-in-chief in 1918. He remained active in journalism until 1927, when he resigned to devote all his time to creative writing. He had, however, only three years more to live.

In the midst of his newspaper work, Munro began writing short stories very early, though he was thirty-two before his first novel was published. His early novels were all historical; after 1903 he abandoned history and romance and turned realist. It was an unfortunate decision for him; as a romanticist he had, as Brownlie Hendry said, "taken up and worn with distinctive grace the mantle of Scott and Stevenson," whereas his realistic novels were soon superseded by a grimmer school of realism stemming from George Douglas. He had also a humorous vein, exemplified in *Erchie*; his poems and essays, collected after his death, were conventional and distinctly minor, though there is a plaintive lilt to some of his verse which insures its perpetuation in popular anthologies. All of his work was Scottish in background; to quote Hendry again, "he kept a Scottish accent of mind." His best novels, *John Splendid* and *Gilian the Dreamer*, were magnificent delineations of Highland character; Cameron Rogers called him "the first historical novelist of his time" and said that *John Splendid* was "a greater book than *Kidnapped* or *David Balfour*." His reward was immense popularity with a public of "his ain folk," and almost complete critical neglect—though Andrew Lang, for one, called him "a genius obvious and undeniable." His only official recognition was an honorary LL.D. From the University of Glasgow, in 1908, and his death at his home in Helensburgh, Dumbartonshire, at sixty-six, attracted little notice. Only Sir Hugh Walpole lamented the death of "one of Scotland's few great novelists." Much of his newspaper work was written under the pseudonym of "Mr. Incognito," and Mr. Incognito he remained. Little is known of his private life, except that he was married, that he was an ardent cyclist, and that in almost a lifetime in Glasgow he remained unceasingly homesick for the Highlands where he was born. He was a heavy-set man, serious but amiable in expression, with thick hair and a long curly moustache.

PRINCIPAL WORKS: *Fiction*—The Lost Pibroch: A Series of Celtic Tales and Sketches, 1896; John Splendid, 1898; Gilian the Dreamer, 1899; Doom Castle, 1901; The Shoes of Fortune, 1901; Children of Tempest: A Tale of the Outer Isles, 1903; Erchie: My Droll Friend, 1904; "The Vital Spark" and Her Queer Crew, 1906; The Daft Days (in America: Bud) 1907; Fancy Farm, 1910; Ayrshire Idylls, 1912; The New Road, 1914; Jaunty Jock and Other Stories, 1918. *Verse*—Bagpipe Ballads and Other Poems, 1917; The Poetry of Neil Munro, 1931. *Miscellaneous*—Hungry Ireland, 1898; The Clyde: River and Firth, 1907; The History of the Royal Bank of Scotland, 1928; The Brave Days: A Chronicle From the North, 1931; The Looker-On, 1933.

ABOUT: Weygandt, C. A Century of the English Novel; Williams, H. Modern English Writers; Bookman (London) April 1896, July 1915, December 1931; Saturday Review of Literature July 16, 1927; Westminster Review July 1910.

MUNROE, KIRK (September 15, 1850-June 16, 1930), American writer of boys' books, was born on the Wisconsin bank of the Mississippi, in a mission not far from Prairie du Chien, brought up at a frontier post, Fort Howard, Wis., and educated in the public schools of Appleton, Wis. The family then moved to Cambridge, Mass. At sixteen Kirk broke away to return  to the West, becoming tape man with a surveying party which was laying out the route of the Santa Fé railroad. During this year in the wilderness he saw Colorado, Arizona, New Mexico, southern California, fought Indians and was wounded, and was the guest of Kit Carson at Fort Garland. Leaving the crew at California, he spent several months as transit man with an engineering outfit, and crossed the South American continent before returning to Cambridge to study engineering at Harvard. At nineteen Munroe surveyed for the Northern Pacific until Jay Cooke and Company failed. He made friends with "Buffalo Bill" Cody and General Custer, and was made a special reporter for the New York *Sun* because he knew the Little Big Horn Country, scene of the Custer massacre. Munroe next became editor of the new magazine *Harper's Young People* and used his unique equipment and experience to write dozens of superior and thrilling yarns for boys. Exploring the Everglades and Lake Okechobee in Florida in a fourteen-foot canoe, he made friends with the Seminole Indians and wrote his immensely popular story, *The Flamingo Feather*. He also founded the League of American Wheelmen, a national organization of bicycle riders with a membership of 100,000. Munroe stopped writing at fifty-five to develop Florida real-estate, twenty years before the boom, especially Cocoanut Grove in Dade County, now a suburb of Miami. His first wife was a daughter of Amelia Barr, the novelist; his second marriage was to Mabel Stearns. Munroe had a "rugged, outdoor complexion, the square jaw of a fighter and a military moustache." He died in Florida.

PRINCIPAL WORKS: Wakulla: A Story of Adventure in Florida, 1886; The Flamingo Feather, 1887; Derrick Sterling: A Story of the Mines, 1888; The Golden Days of '49, 1889; Dorymates, 1890; Under Orders, 1890; Campmates, 1891; Cab and Caboose, 1892; The Coral Ship, 1893;

The White Conquerors, 1893; Raftmates, 1893; Big Cypress, 1894; The Fur-Seal's Tooth, 1894; At War With Pontiac, 1895; Rick Dale, 1896; The Painted Desert, 1897; With Crockett and Bowie, 1897; The Copper Princess, 1898; In Pirate Waters, 1898; "Forward March," 1900; Brethren of the Coast, 1900; Under the Great Bear, 1900; The Belt of Seven Totems, 1901; A Son of Satsuma, 1901; The Blue Dragon, 1904; For the Mikado, 1905.

ABOUT: Kunitz, S. J. & Haycraft, H. (eds.) The Junior Book of Authors; New York Times June 17, 1930; Publishers' Weekly June 28, 1930.

MUNSON, GORHAM BERT (May 26, 1896-), American critic, writes:

"I sold my first article—an undergraduate thesis on the Socialist conception of morality—in 1917, the year of my graduation from Wesleyan University at the age of twenty-one. My birthplace was Amityville, N.Y. From 1917 to 1926 I was a literary Socialist of sorts, with a leaning toward philosophic anarchism. After 1926 in social and economic belief I became an advocate of Social Credit as formulated in its economic phase by Major C. H. Douglas and in its philosophic phase by A. R. Orage. For a number of years I devoted myself to literary journalism, contributing essays and reviews to such publications as the *Dial,* the *Little Review,* the *Criterion* (London) the *New Republic,* the *Freeman,* and the *Bookman.* I was a collaborator in the controversial symposia, *Humanism and America* (1930) and *Behold America!* (1931), and appeared in the anthologies, *New Directions,* for 1936 and 1937.

"In 1922 I founded and edited for two years thereafter, sometimes in collaboration with Matthew Josephson and Kenneth Burke, a little review called *Secession.* Our contributors included Hart Crane, Waldo Frank, Yvor Winters, Malcolm Cowley, Marianne Moore, William Carlos Williams, Wallace Stevens, E. E. Cummings, Louis Aragon, Tristan Tzara; every one of them has made a distinct impression upon the literary life of our time, but they were all the younger generation then and had yet to win their way. *Secession* belligerently upheld literary experimentation and the aesthetic approach, and furiously attacked the older writers.

"In 1927 I joined the faculty of the New School for Social Research, New York, giv-

ing at first courses on American literature; about 1931, however, I tried as an experiment a workshop course in professional writing which proved sufficiently popular to be repeated ever since. I have given much time to lecturing on literary subjects at the annual Bread Loaf Writers' Conference, at the Rocky Mountain Writers' Conference, at the Brooklyn Institute of Arts and Sciences, and at various universities.

"From 1932 onwards I have been more concerned with economic than with literary journalism. My theme has been the necessity for a radical change in the credit-policy of the great banks to correspond with the requirements of a power age economy, and I have written scores of articles on Social Credit which have appeared in magazines as diverse as *Vanity Fair* and *Scholastic.* From 1933 to 1939 I edited an American Social Credit review, *New Democracy,* which included literary features. In 1938 I organized the American Social Credit Movement and was general secretary for the first year."

* * *

Mr. Munson is the son of a Methodist minister. He married Elizabeth Delza, a professional dancer, in 1921. He has taught English in private schools and has been editorial advisor to several publishing firms. His hobbies he gives as verse-writing, motorboating, and tennis. In 1928 Van Wyck Brooks called him "the most important of younger American critics."

PRINCIPAL WORKS: Waldo Frank: A Study, 1923; Robert Frost, 1927; Destinations, 1928; Style and Form in American Prose, 1929; The Dilemma of the Liberated, 1930; Twelve Decisive Battles of the Mind, 1941.

ABOUT: Bookman November 1931.

*MUNTHE, AXEL MARTIN FREDRIK (1857-), Swedish physician, psychiatrist, and writer,

was born in Sweden. His father was a strange man, somber and silent; kind to the poor and to animals, but strict with his son, who had the disconcerting habit of lying on birds' eggs and keeping his room full of animals of assorted species. Young Munthe attended the university at Upsala, and obtained his medical degree in Paris, the youngest M.D. ever created in France. His mornings were spent

* Died February 11, 1949.

in the wards of La Salpêtrière, Hôtel-Dieu, and La Pitié; afternoons in the dissecting rooms and amphitheatres of L'École de Médecine or in the laboratories of the Institut Pasteur; and nights of vigil in his student's room in the Hôtel de L'Avenir. Professor Charcot, the famous French brain specialist, regarded Munthe as a rising man, and sent him patients even after the two had had a misunderstanding. When Munthe's fame as a psychiatrist grew, Dr. S. Weir Mitchell handed over to him "dozens of undisciplined and unhinged ladies of all ages," and Krafft-Ebing of Vienna gave him "patients of both sexes and no sex." Munthe began reminiscing at forty-odd with *Memories and Vagaries* (1897, reprinted 1930); his second book, *Letters From a Mourning City* (1899) described Naples in cholera times. The Italian government awarded him a medal for his work at Messina during the earthquake. Tiring of his neurotic and colitic patients in Paris, Munthe returned to his native country, where he was Physician-in-Ordinary to the King and Queen of Sweden. He has now retired from practice, and, at last report, was living at the Torre di Materita, Anacapri, Bay of Naples, Italy.

Of the many and diverse inhabitants of the Isle of Capri, Dr. Munthe became one of the best known through the unexpected success of his book of reminiscences (received in some quarters as not wholly credible), *The Story of San Michele.* Published in the United States in July 1929 in an edition of 500 imported sheets, the book was reissued from new plates in November, and by October 1931 had sold 200,000 copies. A book by a doctor, with a sympathetic chapter on dogs, it had all the ingredients of a best-seller except the presence of Abraham Lincoln. A large share of the royalties was used to establish Dr. Munthe's famous bird sanctuaries in Sweden and in Capri, the latter officially approved by Mussolini. In October 1934 Dr. Munthe was operated on in Zurich for the restoration of his sight; in May 1936 he was able to read his own book again. This was characterized by the New York *Herald Tribune "Books"* as "overflowing with humor, and edged with irony sharper than a surgeon's knife." *Harper's* stated that Dr. Munthe wrote "vividly, with wit, and a shrewd and subtle valuation of the world, the flesh and the devil."

PRINCIPAL WORKS: Memories and Vagaries, 1898; Letters From a Mourning City, 1899; Red Cross and Iron Cross: By a Doctor in France, 1916; The Story of San Michele, 1929.

ABOUT: Munthe, A. M. F. The Story of San Michele; Stevens, G. Lincoln's Doctor's Dog and Other Famous Best Sellers.

MURFREE, MARY NOAILLES. See "AMERICAN AUTHORS: 1600-1900"

MURRAY, GILBERT (January 2, 1866-), British classicist, translator, and publicist, was born George Gilbert Aime Murray in Sydney, New South Wales, Australia, where his father, Sir Terence Aubrey Murray, was president of the Legislative Council. He was educated at the Merchant Taylors' School, London (having left Australia at the age of eleven),

P. Smith

and at St. John's College, Oxford, where he was graduated with the highest honors in Greek and Latin. In 1888 he was a fellow of New College, Oxford, and the next year, at only twenty-three, became Professor of Greek at Glasgow University, where he remained for ten years. From 1908 to 1936 he was Regius Professor of Greek at Oxford; in 1926 he served as Charles Eliot Norton Professor of Poetry at Harvard. In 1914 he was a trustee of the British Museum. He has honorary doctorates from Oxford, Cambridge, Glasgow, and Birmingham Universities, and is a Fellow of the British Academy and of the Royal Society of Literature. In 1889 he married Lady Mary Henrietta Howard, daughter of the Earl of Carlisle; they have a son and a daughter.

Professor Murray's career has been divided into two main but concurrent fields—the translation of Greek drama into English verse, and the fostering of its return to the English stage; and leadership in the movement for international union. Two of his own plays have been produced at the Court Theatre, London, and he has directed the production of his translations of Aeschylus, Sophocles, Euripides, and Aristophanes. As R. A. Scott-James remarked, he "has re-interpreted the classics to his generation with the skill of a literary artist," and Alexander Wayrill called him "a poet of fine sensibilities possessing the analytical mind of a scientist."

In his other chief province, he was chairman of the League of Nations Union from 1923 to 1938, and since then has been co-president, and has been president of the International Committee for Intellectual Co-operation since 1928. He received the Order of Merit in 1941. He has written almost as widely in his capacity as publicist as in his capacity as classical scholar and poet. Moreover, his interests are by no means limited to these subjects alone. In 1923 he attracted world-wide attention by his experiments in telepathy. He has stood for Parliament as a Liberal, though never with success. An avowed Positivist, he has written much on philosophy. It is not surprising that when, on his seventieth birthday, his former pupils and colleagues honored him with two volumes of essays as a tribute to his achievements, both volumes were remarkably wide in their subject-matter; or that Scott-James commented, "the uniqueness of his talent lies in [its] many-sidedness." Canon F. R. Barry, once his pupil, even while finding a lack of contemporaneity in Professor Murray's viewpoint, added that "we are deeply indebted to him as a teacher . . . and as a protagonist of good causes." Professor Murray's interest in poetry is not merely that of a Hellenist; he was one of the editors of the *Oxford Book of Greek Verse,* and he has published a volume of his own poems, not all of which are translations. Now retired from teaching, he still lives in Oxford. He is one of the noblest examples of the scholar who yet concerns himself with the welfare of humanity.

PRINCIPAL WORKS: *Verse Translations*—Aristophanes: The Frogs, 1902; Sophocles: Oedipus Rex, 1910; Euripides: Hippolytus, 1911; Euripides: Rhesus, 1913; Euripides: Alcestis, 1915; Euripides: Trojan Women, 1915; Aeschylus: Agamemnon, 1920; Aeschylus: Choëphore, 1923; Aeschylus: Eumenides, 1925; Poems, 1926; Aeschylus: Oresteia, 1928; Ten Greek Plays, 1929; Aeschylus: Suppliant Women, 1930; Aeschylus: Prometheus Bound, 1931; Five Plays of Euripides, 1934; Aeschylus: Seven Against Thebes, 1935; Aeschylus: Persae, 1939; Sophocles: Antigone 1941.

Prose Writings—A History of Ancient Greek Literature, 1897; Carlyon Sahib (play) 1899; Liberalism and the Empire (with others) 1900; The Rise of the Greek Epic, 1907; Four Stages of Greek Religion, 1912 (as Five Stages of Greek Religion, 1925); Euripides and His Age, 1913; Andromache (play) 1913; Hamlet and Orestes, 1914; The Stoic Philosophy, 1915; The Foreign Policy of Sir Edward Grey, 1915; Faith, War, and Policy, 1917; Religio Grammatici, 1918; Aristophanes and the War Party, 1919 (as Our Great War and the Great War of the Ancient Greeks, 1920); Satanism and the World Order, 1920; The Problem of Foreign Policy, 1921; Essays and Addresses, 1921 (as Tradition and Progress, 1922); The Classical Tradition in Poetry, 1927; The Ordeal of This Generation, 1929; Aristophanes: A Survey, 1933; Liberality and Civilization, 1938; Stoic, Christian, and Humanist, 1940; Aeschylus, the Creator of Tragedy, 1940.

ABOUT: Bailey, C. & Others. Greek Poetry and Life; Chapman, J. J. Greek Genius and Other Essays; Fisher, H. A. L., de Madariaga, S. & Others. Essays in Honor of Gilbert Murray; Contemporary Review October 1939; London Mercury March 1936; Proceedings Society for Psychical Research December 1924; School and Society January 15, 1927; Spectator March 25, 1938, March 22, 1940.

"MURRAY HILL." See HOLLIDAY, R. C.

MURRY, JOHN MIDDLETON (August 6, 1889-   ), English critic who signs himself J. Middleton Murry, writes: "The story of my life up to the age of thirty is told in detail in *Between Two Worlds.* I was born in South London, of poor parents, and educated at Board Schools, as they were then called. At ten years old, I luckily won a scholarship to Christ's Hospital, an  Elizabethan foundation, with a noble classical and literary tradition, where I duly became a classical Grecian and won a classical scholarship to Brasenose College, Oxford. Except that my origins were more proletarian, in all this I followed the centuries-old pattern of the poor English boy who was fortunate enough to receive the traditional classical education. The chief influence I received from it was that of Plato: at twenty, I had become an inexpert but sincere Platonist. I was also a schoolboy devotee of Matthew Arnold. After Oxford, I drifted into London journalism, which was in the years immediately before the war of 1914-1918 of a pretty high standard: I served my apprenticeship under J. A. Spender of the *Westminster Gazette.* He, together with H. W. Massingham, under whom I served later on the *Nation* (London), has remained for me the ideal of a liberal editor. But as a literary critic I owe most to the steady encouragement of Sir Bruce Richmond, editor of the *Times Literary Supplement,* to which I have been a contributor since 1913.

"But I was not, nor have I ever been, either happy or successful as a journalist, or even as a reviewer. I was always attracted to a more solid type of criticism. The kind of book I should most like to have written is Sainte-Beuve's *Port-Royal.* I have never been secure enough financially to undertake a work of that scope, and probably I should have bungled it if I had. Anyhow, the formative years of my life fell in the period of the war; and I was compelled by my experiences to dig as deep as I could to find some solid foundations of belief. In that task I have been occupied continuously since 1918, and all my books have arisen out of it. With the exception of some far-away novels, and a poetic play, *Cinnamon and Angelica,* for which I still cherish an affection, I do not believe I have ever written a book for its own sake. My final position is nondescript; but it might be described as that of a modernist but catholic Christian Socialist. That is as succinct a description as I can give; but I confess I can hardly recognize myself under the label—for my scriptures include Shakespeare, Blake, and Keats as hardly less important than the Bible. Also, I have a passion for history.

"My development was intimately connected with that of writers more gifted than myself: Katherine Mansfield, who was my wife, and D. H. Lawrence, who was my most intimate friend. But even if I were capable of estimating the influence they had upon me (which I doubt) I could not attempt it here. Besides those I have already mentioned, Dostoievsky, Tolstoy, and Chekhov made a permanent impression on my plastic stuff; they introduced me to a more radical criticism of life than the Englishman of my generation was accustomed to. Chaucer and Wordsworth, Rousseau and Goethe, too, have left their marks on my clay: of philosophers besides Plato, Spinoza and Santayana.

"My 'maturity' (30-50) has been lived under the shadow of European war. I regarded the peace terms of 1919 as morally and materially disastrous, and ever since I have been apprehensive of the inevitable nemesis. I realize now, as I did not twenty years ago, that the root-cause of our European misery is the incapacity of mankind to advance its social morality so as to control to humane uses the prodigious physical energies now at its disposal. I think humanity will one day learn the necessary lesson; but I am pretty sure it will not be learned in my time: and I see little chance of anything but a vast repudiation of all the values which seem to me essential to humane living.

"I have been married three times: to Katherine Mansfield, to Violet le Maistre ('Mary Arden'), to Betty Cockbayne. I have four children. I am now a semi-invalid, living in semi-retirement in the country; and at the present moment (September 1939) wondering rather more anxiously than ever before how to keep my family afloat during the coming storm.

"I should add that I was the last editor of the once famous literary journal, the *Athenaeum,* which I controlled during 1919 and 1920. In 1923 I founded a journal of my own, the *Adelphi,* which in spite of many vicissitudes still lives and is beginning to flourish anew under the editorship of Max Plowman."

* * *

Middleton Murry's dark, thin, eager, unhappy face testifies to the lifelong turmoil of his spirit. He has been called the best-hated man in England, and has been pilloried many times in print—notably by Aldous Huxley in *Point Counter Point.* But he is an acute and perceptive critic, with an incisive style and a broad outlook. He has been a real seminal force even among people who have been alienated by his "honesty to the point of masochism."

PRINCIPAL WORKS: Still Life (novel) 1916; Fyodor Dostoievsky, 1916; The Critic in Judgment, 1918; The Evolution of an Intellectual, 1920; Aspects of Literature, 1920; Cinnamon and Angelica (play) 1920; Poems: 1916-20, 1921; The Things We Are, 1922; The Problem of Style, 1922; Countries of the Mind: First Series 1922, Second Series 1931; Pencillings, 1923; The Voyage (novel) 1924; To the Unknown God, 1924; Discoveries, 1924; Keats and Shakespeare, 1925; The Life of Jesus, 1926; Things To Come, 1928; God, 1929; Studies in Keats, 1930; Son of Woman (biography of D. H. Lawrence) 1931; The Necessity of Communism, 1932; William Blake, 1933; Reminiscences of D. H. Lawrence, 1933; Between Two Worlds (autobiography) 1935; Shakespeare, 1936; The Necessity of Pacifism, 1937; Heaven-and-Earth, 1938; The Pledge of Peace, 1938; The Price of Leadership, 1939; The Defense of Democracy, 1939; Scrapbook of Katherine Mansfield (ed.) 1940; Democracy and War, 1940; The Betrayal of Christ by the Churches, 1940; Europe in Travail, 1940; Cinnamon and Angelica (play) 1941.

ABOUT: Heppenstall, R. Middleton Murry: A Study in Excellent Normality; Murry, J. M. Between Two Worlds; Christian Century April 9, 1941; Living Age December 1932; Newsweek June 6, 1936; Nineteenth Century January 1941; Time June 8, 1936.

MUZZEY, DAVID SAVILLE (October 9, 1870-), American historian, was born in Boston, the son of David W. Muzzey and Annie W. (Saville) Muzzey. He received his B.A. at Harvard in 1893, B.D., Union Theological Seminary, 1897, and studied also at New York University, the University of Berlin, and the Sorbonne, taking his Ph.D. at Columbia in 1907. In 1893 and 1894 he taught mathematics at Robert College, Constantinople (Istanbul). In 1900 he became associated with the Ethical Culture School, New York City, as teacher of Latin and Greek; and has been its director of history since 1905. He went to Columbia as head of the department of history in 1905, and was graduate professor

of American history there from 1923; in 1938 he was named to the newly created Gouverneur Morris chair of American history. In 1927 he was one of an educational deputation sent to Rumania by the Carnegie Endowment, and in 1937 he was

Carnegie lecturer at the Universities of Paris, Edinburgh, and Prague.

He lectured on history at the University of Chicago summer session in 1907. In 1931 he was invited to the University of London to give a course of lectures inaugurating its chair of American history. He is assistant leader of the Society of Ethical Culture and a contributor to its publications. He is also on the editorial board of the *American Observer*, a weekly published in Washington for the use of high school classes in American history. In 1937 he was on the advisory editorial board of *Current History*, and since 1914 has been literary editor of the *Standard*, New York. His life of Blaine won honorable mention for the Pulitzer Prize in 1935. In June 1940 he retired from active teaching, and is now devoting all his time to writing.

He himself calls his life "uneventful," but it has certainly been full. A modest and retiring man, he is one of the best known of the liberal historians. He has been married twice, in 1900 to Ina Jeannette Bullis, who died in 1934, and in 1937 to J. Emilie Young. He has no children. His work has a strongly ethical tinge, lightened by an unobtrusive, dry humor.

PRINCIPAL WORKS: Rise of the New Testament, 1900; Spiritual Heroes, 1902; The Spiritual Franciscans, 1907; Beginners' Latin Book, 1907; An American History, 1911; State, Church, and School in France, 1911; Readings in American History, 1915; Life of Thomas Jefferson, 1918; The United States of America, 1922-24; History of the American People, 1927; James G. Blaine, A Political Idol of Other Days, 1934.

MUZZY, BERTHA. See BOWER, B. M.

*MYERS, GUSTAVUS (March 20, 1872-). American economic historian, writes: "I was born in Trenton, N.J. My paternal grandfather was Emanuel Myers, a major in Napoleon's Old Guard.

Leaving Europe after the battle of Waterloo, he settled, in 1817, at Norfolk, Va., where he lived until his death at the age of ninety-six. My father was Abram Myers, of whom I saw little. He had been a California '49er, later came East to marry Julia Hillman, of Baltimore, and had an incorrigible roving spirit, now living in the East and again disappearing for years at a time. He had made and lost money, and my early life was one of desperate poverty, never being with either parent from the time I was seven years old to the age of sixteen, and then for a short time only. Successively, I had been shunted off to three institutions, and at the age of fourteen I was

Wide World

put to work in a factory, boarding with strangers.

"I mention these circumstances because, although my individual lot, they had a profound awakening influence in early life in shaping my sympathy for the underdog and clearing my vision in youthful years to the effects of oppressive environment and social injustice in general. My developing grievance was not so much personal as social, resulting in a spirit of rebelliousness against conditions which racked so many people in my immediate view.

"Aside from ordinary education, I had no opportunities whatever. But I was always a persistent student, reading continuously, attending lectures, and otherwise absorbing information wherever I could. When I was nineteen years old I got a job on the Philadelphia *Record*. A year later I was in New York City. The agitation of the Populist Party against the abuses of aggregated wealth and its call for legislative reforms attracted me, and I joined that party. Subsequently, I had reportorial and editorial jobs on a number of New York newspapers, and was on the staff of several magazines and a contributor to many more. Meanwhile I had joined the Social Reform Club, in New York. In that organization were advanced men and women, a number of whom later became nationally prominent figures. That association had a further enlightening and stimulating effect upon me, imbuing me with a stronger recognition of the need of social and economic changes.

"Impressed—I may say repelled—by the rhetorical nature of so many histories I had read, I saw the need of realistic history, based upon the actualities embodied in municipal, legislative, Congressional, court, and other records, containing facts brought out in reports of investigations or in testimony or decisions. The research on my *History of Public Franchises in New York City,* published in 1900, thus acquainted me at first hand with the truth as regarded the currupt foundation of a number of great fortunes, which in many a eulogistic book had been represented as the rewards of ability, enterprise, and thrift. Additional extended research on my *History of Tammany Hall* enlarged this knowledge. Then followed eight years of further research, resulting in my *History of the Great American Fortunes.* Opposed to its straightforward presentation of facts shattering romantic legends, no New York publishing house would even consider this work, and it finally was issued in three volumes by a Chicago concern [Charles H. Kerr & Co., a Socialist publishing house].

"My marriage with Genevieve Whitney, of Springfield, Mass., took place in 1904. I joined the Socialist Party in 1907 but quit it in 1912."

* * *

Mr. Myers lives now in the Bronx, New York. He has been called a "fact-worshiper," and his *History of the Great American Fortunes* (now available in a Modern Library reprint) "a semi-classic of research." He is a slight, gray-haired man, with black eyebrows, an aggressive nose, and a notably soft voice. In 1941 he was awarded a Guggenheim Fellowship.

PRINCIPAL WORKS: History of Public Franchises in New York City, 1900; History of Tammany Hall, 1901 (revised edition, 1917); History of the Great American Fortunes, 1910 (revised one-volume edition, 1936); Beyond the Borderline of Life, 1910; History of the Supreme Court of the United States, 1912; History of Canadian Wealth, 1914; The German Myth, 1918; Ye Olden Blue Laws, 1921; History of American Idealism, 1925; America Strikes Back, 1935; The Ending of American Hereditary Fortunes, 1939; History of Bigotry in the United States, 1942.

ABOUT: Chamberlain, J. Farewell to Reform; Filler, L. H. Crusaders for American Liberalism; Parrington, V. L. Main Currents in American Thought; Time November 27, 1939.

*MYERS, LEOPOLD HAMILTON (September 6, 1881-), English novelist, writes: "I was born in Cambridge. My father, Frederick W. H. Myers, was a well known man of letters, a poet and essayist; later he was founder of the Society for Psychical Research and the author of *Human Personality and Its Survival of Bodily Death,* which still retains a

* Died April 8, 1944.

unique position in psychical literature. My grandfather and great-grandfather were both writers. The name Myers, which was originally spelt Myres, occurs frequently in the county registers of Lincolnshire and Yorkshire, the earliest records dating back to the fifteenth century. My mother was Eveleen Tennant, of South Wales. I was educated at Eton and at Trinity College, Cambridge. My school and college careers, unlike my father's, were quite undistinguished. I took no degree, for when my father died in 1901 I left Trinity to travel about the world with my mother, whose health at that time was not good. It was in this year that I met my future wife, Elsie Palmer, daughter of Gen. William J. Palmer, the builder of the Denver & Rio Grande Railroad and founder of Colorado Springs, Colo. I married in 1908 and lived for

about a year in Glen Eyric, Colo. We live now in London.

"For several years I had been trying to write, but with little success. Dissatisfied with what I was turning out, I made no attempt to publish anything, but kept on at my task. This went on until the outbreak of war in 1914. Being judged unfit for military service, I became a temporary clerk in the Foreign Office, and remained in that position till the end of the war. Then I returned to my writing, and in 1921 published my first novel. Of my novels, *The Near and the Far* and *Prince Jali* are included in *The Root and the Flower,* which also contains a third part of the same story, *Rajah Amar. The Pool of Vishnu* completed the tale. The whole story, moreover, was reprinted in a single volume to which was given the same title as the first book of the series *The Near and the Far. The Root and the Flower* was awarded the *Femina-Vie Hereuse* Prize and the James Tait Black Prize of Edinburgh University.

"I have no natural gift for writing. But I have always had a strong desire to give expression to the feelings and ideas awoken in me by the experience of living. And my novels are intended to give prominence to those aspects of human life which seem to me to be of prime significance."

* * *

In spite of Mr. Myers' modest disclaimer, he has a decided "gift for writing." Basil

Davenport remarked of his work that it "brings back the aspect of eternity to the English novel," and he said that its author has "a mind which is . . . both keen and deep, . . . a sensibility naturally as great, if not as artistically hypertrophied, as that of Proust, engaged upon the real meaning of life." *The Root and the Flower* and its accompanying and component parts apply to the sixteenth century world of the Indian emperor Akbar the psychology and viewpoint of contemporary times.

PRINCIPAL WORKS: The Orissers, 1921; The Clio, 1925; The Near and the Far, 1928; Prince Jali, 1931; The Root and the Flower, 1934; Strange Glory, 1936; The Near and the Far (three volumes in one) 1940; The Pool of Vishnu, 1940.

ABOUT: Bookman May-June 1930; Saturday Review of Literature September 14, 1935, August 24, 1940.

NASH, OGDEN (August 19, 1902-),
American humorist and poet, was born Frederic Ogden Nash in Rye, N.Y., the son

of Edmund Strudwick Nash and Mattie (Chenault) Nash. He was educated at St. George's School, Newport, R.I., and in 1920-21 was a student at Harvard. He spent some years in the editorial and publicity departments of the publishing firm

of Doubleday, Doran & Co., joining John Farrar and Stanley Rinehart when they seceded from the firm to set up their own publishing house. In June 1931 he married Frances Rider Leonard of Baltimore. They live in that city with their two daughters, Linell Chenault Nash and Isabel Jackson Nash. In 1931, also, Nash published two books of verse, *Hard Lines* and *Free Wheeling*, which won amused attention by their remarkable freedom of scansion and unconventionality of thought. P. M. Jack stated that Nash was "secure in his possession of all the best and worst rhymes outside of the rhyming dictionaries," and Lisle Bell that "we'd rather watch Nash on his piebald Pegasus than Lady Godiva on a white horse."

Retiring from publishing work to devote his time to his own writing, Nash became one of the most prolific producers of humorous verse, appearing in a dozen periodicals and in Hearst's New York *Journal.* Louis Untermeyer qualified his praise of Nash's work with the reservation that "productiveness not only compels Nash to pad

but to pretend. He has to pretend to be funnier than he really is, or to be funny when he wants to be serious." But he writes "often the best light verse written in America today." He can write not only verse with exaggeratedly sprung rhythms and fearless rhymes but poems of delicate, lyrical feeling or deep intensity. Ogden Nash has blond, curling hair; wears glasses; and is adept at reciting his unpublished (and unpublishable) verse.

PRINCIPAL WORKS: Hard Lines, 1931; Free Wheeling, 1931; Happy Days, 1933; The Primrose Path, 1935; The Bad Parents' Garden of Verse, 1936; I'm a Stranger Here Myself, 1938; The Face Is Familiar, 1940.

ABOUT: American Magazine October 1934; Christian Science Monitor Magazine November 30, 1940; Current Biography April 1941; Newsweek June 6, 1938; Saturday Review of Literature April 29, 1939; Scholastic March 4, 1940.

NASON, LEONARD HASTINGS (September 28, 1895-), American novelist, was born in Somerville, Mass., the son of Frank Leonard Nason and Jennie Rand (Allen) Nason. He was educated at Newton (Mass.) Technical High School and Norwich University, also known as the Military College of Vermont, and the oldest engineering college in the United

States. At Norwich Mr. Nason edited the college weekly, and was constantly in hot water with the authorities for his outspokenness. He was expelled and taken back several times, during one interim serving in the infantry in the Mexican Border Service. When the United States entered the First World War, he was enrolled in the Officers' Training Camp at Plattsburg, N.Y., but was thrown out there also for insubordination. He finally served through the war as a sergeant of field infantry in France. He was twice wounded, twice cited for gallantry in action, and decorated with the Purple Heart and Silver Star medals. He then returned to Norwich, and finally took his B.Sc. degree in 1920. He is now a major in the Cavalry Reserves. He is also a "Kentucky colonel," having been aide to the governor of Kentucky in 1932.

In 1920 Mr. Nason married Lucia Millet and they have a son and two daughters. After several years in France with his family, he returned to the United States and now lives in Centerville, Mass. From 1939 to 1941 he was a news commentator with the Mutual Broadcasting System.

Besides his novels and his stories in popular magazines, he has contributed light verse to the "Line o' Type" column of the Chicago *Tribune* under the pseudonym of "Steamer." His stories are practically all about soldiers and sailors, and are all humorous. He says, "I had a good time in the war. I liked it," and, as the *Bookman* remarked, to him "the war was two-thirds fun." His stories are light and "full of literary tricks," but are unfailingly good entertainment. He has also written two screen plays, *Rodney* and *Red Night*.

PRINCIPAL WORKS: Chevrons, 1926; Three Lights From a Match, 1927; Sergeant Eadie, 1928; The Top Kick, 1928; The Man in the White Slicker, 1929; Incomplete Mariner, 1929; Livingstone Brothers, 1930; A Corporal Once, 1930; Defenders of the Bridge, 1932; Among the Trumpets, 1932; Eagles Eastward, 1936; I Spy Strangers, 1940; Approach to Battle, 1941.

ABOUT: Saturday Evening Post June 12, 1926, April 17, 1937.

NATHAN, GEORGE JEAN (February 14, 1882-   ), American dramatic critic, writes: "Almost everything that has been

Oggiano

written about me, particularly the unfavorable, is, I believe true. Being by profession a critic, I naturally have considerable respect for criticism and, where it is intelligent, am as pleased to be its victim as, occasionally, the recipient of its melliferous favors. Being the shrewd critic that I consider myself to be, I am able to detect my own weaknesses and deficiencies and it adds to my respect for the art of criticism when critics equally shrewd similarly detect them.

"As to work in progress, I have under way a definitive volume on dramatic criticism (I have been at it for the past six years), another still in my long series of books on the contemporary theatre, and a scherzo tentatively called *Civilization in the Western Hemisphere*.

"In the symposium, *Living Philosophies*, and its recent supplementary volume, *I Believe*, will be found my attitude toward the world and myself. I have nothing to add to it. It is all there. And as to my attitude toward my own profession, here is the way I see things: The average person regards even his favorite dramatic critic

with a measure of the same skepticism and antagonism that he secretly reserves for his doctor. He may be willing to concede that both are satisfactorily grounded in experience, that their judgment is often safely followable, and that their professional understanding is commendable. But just the same he paradoxically rather resents them. Though he pays both of them for their services, it is his as it is every man's nature to gag at being given advice, at being instructed even to his own undeniable benefit, and at being told that he doesn't know how to look out for himself.

"The sagacious critic, appreciating this prejudice, accordingly avoids irritating his sensitive patient as the Occidental medico does and pursues instead the practice of the Oriental. He doesn't wait until his patient is ill and grouchy; he bends his best efforts to keeping him from being ill. This he accomplishes by indoctrinating him with the highest and most tonic standards of drama, with a gradual improvement of dramatic taste, and with the proper resistance to corrupting theatrical bacilli. And almost before he himself knows it, the patient, who might otherwise be hostile to him, is cordially and acquiescently his. But he must, fully to cajole that patient, have the necessary critical bedside manner. He must deftly conceal too august a wisdom in ingratiating humor; he must lend positiveness some alleviating grace; he must embroider assertion with modesty, or at least an affectation of modesty.

"All I have to offer, aside from such obvious and facile legerdemain, is critical opinion filtered through more than thirty years of unremitting playgoing and study of the theatre and dramatic literature in the four quarters of the globe. For what, after all, is this thing called criticism? In *The Critic and the Drama*, published twenty years ago, I put it so: 'Art is a reaching out into the ugliness of the world for vagrant beauty and the imprisoning of it in a tangible dream. Criticism is simply the dream book.'"

* * *

George Jean Nathan was born in Ft. Wayne, Ind., the son of Charles and Ella Nathan. (The elder Nathan had originally been named Charles Naret; but when his father died and his mother remarried, he took his stepfather's surname.) He was educated at Cornell University and the University of Bologna. He is unmarried, and lives in New York. He began his dramatic criticism on the staff of the New York

Herald in 1905, and the long list of papers and magazines with which he has been connected since includes *Harper's Weekly, Puck, Judge, Life,* the *New Freeman,* the *Saturday Review of Literature, Vanity Fair,* and *Scribner's.* He covers plays currently for *Esquire* and *Newsweek.* From 1914 to 1923 he was co-editor with H. L. Mencken of the *Smart Set,* helped Mencken found and edit the *American Mercury* in 1924, and was contributing editor from 1925 to 1930. In 1932 he was one of the founders and editors of the *American Spectator.* He edited the dramatic library, *The Theatre of Today,* and has contributed to the *Encyclopaedia Britannica.* In spite of his Middle Western origin, he is a "typical" New Yorker, a man about town, a cynic, and a dandy. Henry Hazlitt says "he writes with more gusto than any other living critic of the theatre; ... his exuberant flow of words ... disguises the solid work and tedious research" behind it.

PRINCIPAL WORKS: The Eternal Mystery, 1913; Europe After 8:15 (with H. L. Mencken & W. H. Wright) 1914; Another Book on the Theatre, 1916; Bottoms Up, 1917; Mr. George Jean Nathan Presents, 1917; A Book Without a Title, 1918; The Popular Theatre, 1918; Comedians All, 1919; Heliogabalus (with H. L. Mencken) 1920; The American Credo (with H. L. Mencken) 1920; The Theatre, the Drama, the Girls, 1921; The Critic and the Drama, 1922; The World in False Face, 1923; Materia Critica, 1924; The Autobiography of an Attitude, 1925; The House of Satan, 1926; The New American Credo, 1927; Land of the Pilgrims' Pride, 1927; Art of the Night, 1928; Monks Are Monks, 1929; Testament of a Critic, 1931; The Intimate Notebooks of George Jean Nathan, 1932; Since Ibsen, 1933; Passing Judgments, 1934; The Theatre of the Moment, 1936; The Avon Flows, 1937; The Morning After the First Night, 1938; Bachelor Life, 1941; The Entertainment of a Nation, 1942.

ABOUT: Goldberg, I. The Theatre of George Jean Nathan; Kozlenko, V. The Quintessence of Nathanism; American Mercury March 1940; Life March 11, 1940; Living Age May 1931; Nation February 18, 1931; New York Times Book Review February 1, 1942; Overland Monthly March 1929; Saturday Review of Literature January 8, 1938.

NATHAN, ROBERT (January 2, 1894-), American novelist, was born Robert Gruntal Nathan in New York, the son of Harold Nathan and Sarah (Gruntal) Nathan. He is the nephew of Maud Nathan, founder of the Consumers' League, and of Annie (Nathan) Meyer, founder of Barnard College, and is a direct descendent of Rabbi Gershon Seixas, one of the incorporators of Columbia College in the eighteenth century. He was educated in a private school in Geneva, Switzerland, at Phillips Exeter Academy, and at Harvard,

where he was on the staff of the *Harvard Monthly.* After college he was for two years a solicitor for a New York advertising firm. In 1924 and 1925 he taught at the New York University School of Journalism. Except for these two periods, his time has been devoted exclusively to writing. His first novel, *Peter Kindred,* was published in 1919; it was semi-autobiographical and realistic, and quite unlike his succeeding work. With *Autumn,* two years later, what is called "the true Nathan touch" first made its appearance. However, he did not became widely known until the publication of *One More Spring,* his novel of the depression, in 1933. Since then he has been near to a best-seller. *One More Spring* was made into a successful motion picture.

In 1915 Mr. Nathan married Dorothy Michaels, and they had a daughter. They were divorced in 1922. In 1930 he married Nancy Wilson; they were divorced in 1936, and he married Lucy Lee Hall Skelding.

He is something of a painter, and an accomplished musician. Music is his passion; he is an excellent pianist, a fair 'cellist, and a composer. He is athletic as well—a good fencer and swimmer, a golfer and tennis-player, and lately he has taken up sailing at his summer home on Cape Cod. In the winter he lives in New York. He is dark, slender, and handsome, looking younger than his years. He is a charter member of the P.E.N. Club and belongs to the National Institute of Arts and Letters.

Robert Nathan has always written poetry as well as prose, and has published several volumes of verse. The poet is implicit in all that he writes. His style and *genre* are his own, highly individual and apparently uninfluenced by any other author. He deals in fantasy, but is saved from whimsicality by the fact that though he is "emotionally tender" he is "intellectually hard and muscular." His interest lies with obscure people; his world, as one critic puts it, is one of "pity and irony, of tolerant gentle humor and deep intuitive wisdom peopled by children and deities and anthropomorphic animals and plain, very human beings." In his novel *Portrait of Jennie* he deals with the J. W. Dunne theory of time far more successfully than J. B Priestley has done in recent novels and plays; it is a theory well suited to his slightly distorted world. "Looking into one of his books," said Roberts Tapley, "is like looking into an ant-heap." It is also a bit like looking into Alice's looking-glass.

The low key, the gently deceptive understatement, are Nathan's hallmarks. Irony underlies all his writing: the perceptive irony that makes one of his characters say of another, "It was her being happy that vexed them." He is always on the edge of sentimentality, and sometimes, it is true, falls over the precipice. His books seem slight, but are not mediocre.

PRINCIPAL WORKS: Peter Kindred, 1919; Autumn, 1921; The Puppet Master, 1922; Youth Grows Old (poems) 1923; Jonah, 1925; The Fiddler in Barly, 1926; The Woodcutter's House, 1927; The Bishop's Wife, 1928; There Is Another Heaven, 1929; The Cedar Box (poems) 1930; The Orchid, 1931; One More Spring, 1933; Road of Ages, 1935; Selected Poems, 1925; The Enchanted Voyage, 1936; Winter in April, 1938; Journey of Tapiola, 1938; Portrait of Jennie, 1940; Winter Tide (poems) 1940; They Went on Together, 1941; Tapiola's Brave Regiment, 1941; Dunkirk: a Ballad, 1942; The Sea-Gull Cry, 1942.

ABOUT: Bookman October 1932; New York Herald Tribune "Books" May 4, 1941; New York Times Book Review April 20, 1941; New Yorker January 20, 1940; Overland Monthly February 1929; Saturday Review of Literature October 13, 1934, November 2, 1935, January 8, 1938.

*NAZHIVIN, IVAN FEDOROVICH

(1874-), Russian novelist, was born in Moscow, the son of serfs who had been liberated by Alexander II. His father became a constructor of large houses in Moscow and of railway lines, then an entirely new undertaking in Russia. "I first saw the light in a princely mansion, and grew up in the midst of nurses, waitresses and every conceivable luxury," wrote Nazhivin in 1929. His mother died in childbirth when the boy was five years old, and the three orphans were sent to stay with their grandmother, who led the life of a peasant in the country. Here he carried sheaves in harvest, brought wood from the forest, herded cattle, and absorbed the feeling of the countryside. Nazhivin left college in Moscow at the end of a term, disliking the restraint. A year in his father's Moscow wood factory sent him to the Crimea with a nervous breakdown. Nazhivin traveled in the Caucasus and in western Europe, becoming a fervent radical, "something like an anarchist and at the same time an aesthete." His first books were published at seventeen. In 1901 he met and admired Tolstoy; the interest proved mutual. Receiving a letter from the novelist in Sicily, Nazhivin was moved to give away

his evening clothes to his valet, Peppino. Nazhivin was later to abandon Tolstoy and adopt Christianity when a favorite daughter died; he had found a wife at the University of Lausanne. They took part in the Revolution of 1905, not by bomb-throwing, but by devoting their income to building popular libraries and printing good books. Later they farmed land in the Caucasus, and Nazhivin founded his own philosophical-religious publication, *Das Gruene Staebchen* (*The Little Green Rod*). Exempt from service in the First World War as an only son, he worked as a partner with N. Kuchnerow, Moscow publishers, as manager of the department for popular and children's literature. After the Revolution of 1917, Nazhivin and his family fled to France, receiving monetary aid from the Czech patriot Kramarz and from the former Swedish Consul General in St. Petersburg. His historical novel *Rasputin* is, according to Joshua Kunitz, primarily a long and bitter invective hurled by a disgruntled *émigré* against his native land, as well as being an imposing synthetic picture of Russian society before, during, and after the First World War and the Revolution. In *The Dogs* the narrative is related by dogs of the great Russian estates. Henry James Forman states that Nazhivin's creative and emotional capacities are of a high and varied order; while Dr. Joseph Collins said of *According to Thomas* that "no one, believer or non-believer, who is interested in the historicity of Christ should fail to read the book." "Tired and gray," wrote Nazhivin in 1929, "I use every ounce of strength to hold my large family above water."

WORKS AVAILABLE IN ENGLISH TRANSLATION: Rasputin, 1929; The Dogs, 1931; According to Thomas: An Historical Novel of the First Century (English title: A Certain Jesus: The Gospel According to Thomas) 1931.

NEIHARDT, JOHN GNEISENAU (Jan-

uary 8, 1881-), American poet and critic, writes: "My family came from Zweibrucken, Germany, to Pennsylvania in 1727. Fourteen of us fought in the Revolutionary War, after which we pioneered all the way across the continent from Ohio to Oregon. I was born near Sharpsburg, Ill.; lived with pioneering maternal grand parents  in northwestern Kansas during 1886 and

1887, then with my parents in Kansas City until 1892, when my then widowed mother moved to northeastern Nebraska. My father was Nicholas Neihardt, my mother Alice May Culler.

"I attended a pioneer college in Wayne, Neb., for four years, specializing in Latin (five hours a day) while qualifying for a B.S. degree at the age of sixteen. I began systematic, intensive reading of the classics of world literature in my early teens, reading nothing else until twenty-one. Later I studied Greek in order to know Aeschylus, who succeeded Virgil as the literary god of my youth. I am an honorary Litt.D. of the University of Nebraska and honorary LL.D. of Creighton University. I was appointed professor of poetry at the University of Nebraska in 1926, but preferred the literary editorship of the St. Louis *Post-Dispatch*. Although I have read enormously, I have never been a bookworm, but have mixed with the living world and known all types of men.

"At the age of twelve, apparently as the result of a dream, I lost interest in mechanical invention, and definitely devoted my life to verse. I taught country school two years while writing *The Divine Enchantment;* did all sorts of work from farming and hod-carrying to reporting (Omaha *Daily News,* 1901), and editing a fighting country newspaper. I descended the Missouri River from its headwaters in a light boat in 1908 by way of preparation for my Cycle.

"*A Bundle of Myrrh,* a lyric sequence, published in 1908, established my reputation as a lyric poet. Two more volumes of lyrics followed. Meanwhile I had won a reputation as a writer of short stories, which, as well as the lyrics, were in great demand when I conceived the idea (1911) of devoting the rest of my life to an *Epic Cycle of the West,* to consist of five book-length narrative poems, dealing with the entire trans-Missouri country from 1882 to 1890, when the battle of Wounded Knee marked the end of Indian resistance on the Plains. My life in northwestern Kansas, my discovery of the Missouri River at the age of six, and my intimate contact with old-timers, both white and Indian, were responsible for my compelling desire to do this work. I have been too well acquainted with Indians since 1900 to regard them as romantic curiosities and never sought them for 'local color.' The word 'epic' was used from the beginning as being properly descriptive of the material, the time, and the mood of the

time under consideration. I have worked half-days for eighteen years out of the past twenty-seven on the Cycle; and the last of the narratives is *The Song of Jed Smith.* The first two volumes have been studied widely for some years in college and high school English classes.

"In 1908 I married Mona Martinson, sculptress and student of Rodin.

"I began writing literary criticism for the New York *Times* in 1910, was literary critic of the Minneapolis *Journal* from 1912 to 1921, and literary editor of the St. Louis *Post-Dispatch* from 1926 to 1938. I have lectured at colleges and universities throughout the country for years.

"The result of my long contact with Indians, especially the Sioux, will be found in my *Black Elk Speaks,* which, for the first time, sets forth the inner world of an Indian 'holy man.'

"My life work has been poetry, but I've long regarded it as merely the burning center of a universal interest. My prose volume, *Poetic Values,* suggests my philosophy. My deep interest in the worldwide social process precludes attachment to any political party, and the religion I have managed to achieve through direct experience seems too profound for dogmatic statement."

* * *

Frank Luther Mott describes Neihardt as being short, with "a fine brow; the head of a thinker." He lives with his wife and four children in the Ozarks, near Branson. Mo. He was appointed Poet Laureate of Nebraska by the legislature in 1921. "He has envisaged the stirring pageant of the winning of a continent," said Paul Kaufman, "and has wrought the story into the first American epic verse."

PRINCIPAL WORKS: *Poetry*—The Divine Enchantment, 1900; A Bundle of Myrrh, 1908; Man-Song, 1909; The River and I, 1910; The Stranger at the Gate, 1912; Death of Agrippina, 1913; The Song of Hugh Glass, 1915; The Quest, 1916; The Song of Three Friends, 1919; The Song of the Indian Wars, 1925; Collected Poems, 1926; The Song of the Messiah, 1936; The Song of Jed Smith, 1941. *Fiction*—The Lonesome Trail (short stories) 1907; The Dawn-Builder, 1911; Life's Lure, 1914; Splendid Wayfaring, 1920; Indian Tales and Others, 1926. *Miscellaneous*—Two Mothers (play) 1921; Laureate Address, 1921; Poetic Values—Their Reality and Our Need of Them, 1925; Black Elk Speaks, 1932.

ABOUT: House, Julius T. John G. Neihardt: Man and Poet; Scholastic October 8, 1938.

*NEILSON, WILLIAM ALLAN (March 28, 1869-), Scottish-American educator and literary critic, was born in Doune, Perthshire, Scotland. His father, David

* Died February 13, 1946.

Neilson, was the village schoolmaster; his mother was Mary (Allan) Neilson. Young Neilson attended a preparatory

school at Montrose; was a pupil-teacher at thirteen; and attended the University of Edinburgh, where he received an M.A. degree in 1891, with honors in philosophy. That year he emigrated to North America, to teach at Upper Canada College in Toronto till 1895.

Neilson had his first experience with a women's college in 1898, when he went to Bryn Mawr to teach English. In 1900 he was an instructor at Harvard, where he became a close friend of Charles W. Eliot and worked with him for eighteen months helping Eliot assemble the Five-Foot Shelf. From 1904 to 1906 Neilson was a professor of English at Columbia, returning to Harvard in 1906 to remain in the English department as professor of English until 1917. In 1906 Neilson edited Shakespeare's Complete Works for the Cambridge Poets series, an edition familiar to two generations of Shakespeare students, and in 1907 began to edit a series called "The Types of English Literature." He also worked on "The Tudor Shakespeare," beginning in 1911; edited the Harvard Classics Shelf of Fiction in 1917; and was editor-in-chief of Webster's *New International Dictionary* (the second edition) in 1934. Meanwhile, from 1917 to 1939, Neilson gave Smith College a memorable administration. The young ladies of Smith found him pungent in speech and democratic in conduct (one breathless freshman reporting to her roommate that "a funny old man with a pointed beard tried to pick me up on the campus"). Hubert Herring, who includes the foregoing anecdote in his sympathetic essay on Neilson, writes that "the quality of his research on Shakespeare is recognized; his writing on poetry is respected; and he is awaiting retirement to finish his work on Medieval Allegory. . . . He has long been an ardent protagonist of civil liberties and an enemy of those measures of coercion and bigotry which are inimical to the American ideal."

The recipient of numerous honorary degrees, Professor Neilson, with Mrs. Neilson, who was Elisabeth Muser of Offenburg, Baden, Germany, makes his home at Falls Village, Conn. There are two daughters; a son, Allan, died several years ago.

PRINCIPAL WORKS: Origins and Sources of the Court of Love, 1899; Essentials of Poetry, 1912; The Facts About Shakespeare, 1913; Burns: How To Know Him, 1917; A History of English Literature, 1920; Intellectual Honesty, 1940. *Editor*—Milton's Minor Poems, 1899; Shakespeare's Complete Works (Cambridge Poets) 1906; The Types of English Literature, 1907- ; Roads to Knowledge, 1911; The Tudor Shakespeare, 1911; The Chief Elizabethan Dramatists, 1911; Chief British Poets of the 14th and 15th Centuries, 1916. *Associate Editor*—The Harvard Classics, 1909; Harvard Classics Shelf of Fiction, 1917; Selections From Chaucer, 1921. *Editor-in-Chief*—Webster's New International Dictionary, (2nd ed.) 1934.

ABOUT: Herring, H. C. Neilson of Smith; Neilson, E. M. The House I Knew; Harper's Magazine June 1938; Reader's Digest September 1938; Saturday Review of Literature June 10, 1939; Time June 12, 1939.

NESBIT, EDITH ("E. Nesbit") August 15, 1858-April 22, 1924), English novelist, poet, and writer of stories for children,

was born in London on Lower Kennington Lane. Her father, John Collis Nesbit, conducted a large agricultural college there. Edith was a daring and mischievous child, an incorrigible tomboy with a large family of brothers and sisters, upon whose escapades she drew for *The Bastable Children* and *The Five Children,* the books for which she is chiefly remembered. Her adult novels are undistinguished and her verse merely fluent and pretty. She was educated in France and Germany, recording at an early age her dislike for the latter country in this couplet:

God! Let the Germans be suppressed
So that Europe at last may have a rest.

In 1880 E. Nesbit married Hubert Bland, a Socialist journalist whose persistent and flagrant infidelities kept the household in a continuous emotional turmoil. The large, easy-going Bohemian establishment at Eltham, Kent, known as Well Hall, a Tudor and eighteenth-century manor, to which the Blands were much attached, was acquired only after a long and painful literary apprenticeship, during which E. Nesbit turned her hand to any hackwork that would bring them a living: from love and horror stories, dialect stories, occasional and holiday verse to painting Christmas cards. Her reputation was assured when the *Pall Mall Gazette* and *Windsor Magazine* began to publish

The Treasure Seekers, the first of the stories of the Bastable family. Its successor, *The Would-Be-Goods,* was illustrated *con amore* by Reginald Birch.

A restless, moody, strikingly handsome woman who was superstitious to a degree and was forced by the circumstances of her marital life to do a good deal of wishful thinking, Edith Nesbit was inspired to introduce an element of magic into her humorous chronicles of the lives of well-bred English children. The results, serialized in the *Strand Magazine* for a dozen years, were deservedly successful, bringing her the devotion of successive generations of imaginative youngsters and the friendship of such writers and actors as Richard Le Gallienne, Laurence Housman, Berta Ruck, G. B. Stern, Sybil and Russell Thorndike, and Noel Coward (who called on her in her declining, rather poverty-stricken years and found her, "firm, nice, and humorous"). Bernard Shaw and H. G. Wells were lifelong friends, fellow-participants in the stormy meetings of the Fabian Society, a gathering of ameliorative Socialists which also included Graham Wallas and the Sidney Webbs (now Lord and Lady Passfield). "Civilization, whatever else it is," E. Nesbit wrote in *Wings and the Child,* her serious study of child psychology, "is a state in which a few people have the chance of living beautifully—those who take that chance are fewer still—and the enormous majority live, by no choice or will of their own, lives which at the best are uncomfortable, anxious, and lacking in beauty, and at the worst are so ugly, diseased, desperate, and wretched that those who feel their condition most can hardly bear to think of them." Her own charities were direct and practical, leaving her so impoverished that she was glad in 1915 to accept a civil pension of £60 a year from the government, and later to marry a cheery, able marine engineer Thomas Terry Tucker, three years after Hubert Bland's death in 1914.

E. Nesbit's admirers on this side of the Atlantic include Christopher Morley, William Rose Benét, Dorothy Canfield Fisher, and May Lamberton Becker. The Junior Literary Guild issued *The Bastable Children* (prefaced by Christopher Morley) and *The Five Children* to its subscribers, and an American publisher also brought out reprints of several separate titles. E. Nesbit died of a long and painful illness (apparently cancer) in a double bungalow at Jesson St. Mary's, near Dymchurch. She left, besides Mr. Tucker, two sons and two daughters (one married Clifford Sharp, the brilliant and bitter editor of the *New Statesman* from 1913 to 1931). Her authorized biography, written by a young Englishwoman of letters, Doris Langley Moore, appeared in 1933.

PRINCIPAL WORKS: *Children's Stories*—The Story of the Treasure-Seekers, 1899; The Book of Dragons, 1900; Nine Unlikely Tales, 1901; The Would-Be-Goods, 1901; Five Children and It, 1902; The Phoenix and the Carpet, 1904; The New Treasure-Seekers, 1904; Oswald Bastable and Others, 1905; The Story of the Amulet, 1906; The Enchanted Castle, 1907 (reissued 1933 with Introduction by May Lamberton Becker); The House of Arden, 1908; Harding's Luck, 1909; The Magic City, 1910; The Wonderful Garden, 1911 (reissued 1935 with Introduction by Earle Walbridge); The Magic World, 1912; Wet Magic, 1913; Five of Us—and Madeline, 1925 (posthumous; edited by her daughter Rosamond Sharp). *Other Works*—The Prophet's Mantle (with Hubert Bland) 1885; In Homespun (short stories) 1896; The Secret of Kyriels, 1899; Thirteen Ways Home (short stories) 1901; The Literary Sense (short stories) 1903; The Red House, 1903; Man and Maid, 1906; The Incomplete Amorist, 1906; Salome and the Head, 1909; Fear (horror stories) 1910; Dormant, 1911; Wings and the Child (nonfiction) 1913; The Incredible Honeymoon, 1921; The Lark, 1922. *Poems*—Lays and Legends, 1886; Second Series, 1892; A Pomander of Verse, 1895; Songs and Lyrics of Empire, 1898; Ballads and Lyrics of Socialism, 1908.

ABOUT: Coward, N. Present Indicative; Moore, D. L. E. Nesbit: A Biography; Ruck, B. A Story-Teller Tells the Truth; Stern, G. B., Monogram; Wells, H. G., Experiment in Autobiography; Saturday Review of Literature June 27, 1925, August 18, 1934.

*NEUMANN, ALFRED (October 15, 1895-), German novelist and dramatist, writes: "I was born in Lautenberg in West Prussia, in the very 'Corridor' which Herr Hitler used as a pretence to set the world on fire. The little town in great part was made up of employes of my father, one of the outstanding timber merchants of eastern Germany, who had already

passed his sixtieth year when I came into the world. My first home was never very well known to me, since I went to Berlin as an infant and lived there afterwards. I attended the arts Gymnasium, was a good student in the humanities, a bad one in science, and interested myself as an adolescent much more in literature, poetry, politics, and pretty girls than in timber. So I was already an alien in my family when in 1913 I went to Munich, first as student

* Died October 3, 1952.

and volunteer, then as reader in the great and important Georg Müller publishing house. There I read manuscripts, wrote catalogues, and was still sufficiently modest not to play on my own lyre. Then came the war. In the military hospital I relieved my heavy heart by writing my first verses, in the style of the young Expressionists. In 1917 I was invalided out of the army because of serious illness, and returned to the publishing house. In the same year the publisher Georg Müller, one of the most remarkable and most eccentric men I have ever known, discovered that I too was a poet and put out my first volume of verse, the long ago out of print *Lieder vom Lachen und der Not (Songs of Laughter and Despair)*. My first book was his last as a publisher; he died at the end of December 1917, only forty years old. At his death I left the firm and became a dramatic teacher at the Munich Little Theatre. In those years I published poems, stories, and translations which found only slight recognition. In 1924 I married Georg Müller's adopted daughter, after my first marriage with a Swiss dancer was dissolved, and went to Florence, which became my second home.

"My destiny always fluctuates sharply up or down. Through my father's death, the German inflation, and the failure of my father's business I lost my fortune. In two years of the bitterest poverty I wrote *The Patriot, King Haber*, and the long novel *The Devil*. With *King Haber* I got my head above water again; with *The Devil*, for which I won the Kleist Prize for 1926, which was translated into twelve languages and has sold between 300,000 and 400,000 copies, I won an international audience. My play, *The Patriot*, has been produced in more than five hundred theatres of Europe and America and has been filmed twice. In 1927 and 1928 there appeared in all the leading languages my two Italian novels, *Rebels* and *Guerra; The Hero* in 1930; *The Mirror of Fools* in 1932—and then came Hitler, robbed me of my home, forbade my books in Germany, 'sequestrated' my German property. It is now only the fate of hundreds of thousands, and I was better off than most, since I lived in Florence. Since 1931 I have been occupied with a trilogy of the nineteenth century. In 1934 *Another Caesar* was published, in 1936 *Gaudy Empire*. And on September 2, 1938, two hours after publication of the Fascist race-laws, I left Florence, my second home. Now I enjoy the hospitality of humanitarian and democratic France, wonderful, lovely France, which may God preserve;

and I am working on the third novel of the trilogy, *Volksfreunde (The Friends of the People)*, a novel about the founding of the third French Republic.

"I believe in humanitarian Democracy and its endless struggle. I consider its chief literary representative and the leader of 'the other Germany,' my great and honored friend Thomas Mann, to be the greatest living writer. My other favorites among contemporary authors are Thornton Wilder, Sinclair Lewis, Jean Giono, and Knut Hamsun, who must have ceased to be himself if the Nazis believe they can point to him as their adherent. And my literary Bible since my schooldays has been the most consummate novel in world literature, Stendhal's *Charterhouse of Parma*."

* * *

Alfred Neumann's novels are all historical. Wilson Follett said, "He takes a piece of the history of a past era and turns it into an illuminated piece of the history of the human soul." As is indicated by his reference to the Italian "race-laws," he is of Jewish descent, and this may in part account for the universality of his historical interest. He is primarily the psychologist historian; his work is marked by tenseness, sustained excitement, and a brilliance that sometimes becomes theatrical rather than dramatic, but at its best makes his characters real and living to the modern reader. He is at present (1942) in America, on the West Coast.

WORKS AVAILABLE IN ENGLISH: The Devil (in England: The Deuce) 1928; The Patriot (play) 1928; The Rebels, 1929; Guerra, 1930; King Haber and Other Stories, 1930; The Hero, 1931; Mirror of Fools, 1932; Another Caesar, 1935; The Life of Christina of Sweden, 1935; Gaudy Empire, 1936; Man of December, 1937; The Friends of the People, 1941.

ABOUT: Bookman October 1928; Deutsche Rundschau April 1927; Journal des Débats June 26, 1931.

NEUMANN, ROBERT (May 22, 1897-), Austrian novelist, writes: "Born in Vienna. At the age of sixteen studying interrupted and became a champion swimmer. Then once again 'serious' and learned everything: medicine, chemistry, German literature. Then stopped once again and became a swimming trainer. As the trainer of a woman's swimming club became acquainted with my wife. In order to

be able to marry I looked for a 'bread and butter' job and became a bookkeeper in a bank, then a dealer in foreign currency, manager of a chocolate manufacturing concern, head of food-stuffs importing house. Made much money and then, through speculation, lost everything. Became a bookkeeping specialist in criminal cases. Then began to write, without any success—no publisher and not even a single small provincial newspaper wanted to print a scrap. With wife and little son lived in poverty. Sailor on a Dutch tanker in the Orient; many adventures. Then too (in Constantinople) for the first time came across a trace of Zaharoff. Finally back to Europe and suddenly a big literary success: my first book, rejected by all publishers, was taken up during my absence and printed (royalty 500 marks for 20,000 copies!). In a couple of years a successful and well-to-do author. End of 1932: *Die Macht* [*Power,* translated as *Mammon*], in which you will find, on the one hand, Zaharoff and Vanderzee (Deterding), and on the other hand, the Nazis and the prediction of the murder of Dr. Bell, which, with all the details described by me, actually took place some months later (April 1933). Thereafter the agitation of the Nazis against me, the banning and burning of my books, the loss of my money, exile in England."

* * *

Neumann is now living in Long Crendon, Buckinghamshire. Austrian born, of Jewish descent, he is not related to the German novelist, Alfred Neumann, two years his senior. *Flood* was called by Alfred Einstein "a magnificent book," but Neumann's work is very uneven. *Passion,* which was a semi-biographical reconstruction of several historical love affairs, was cited by Gerald Sykes as evidence of "the influence of American tabloid journalism upon German literature." His irony is heavy, and, as Charles David Abbott remarked, "his historical veracity can hardly be commended," but, as he added, "for racy revivifying of legend he is excellent." "One feels," another critic said, "that the author himself is touched by the strange frenzy of his characters"—which is perhaps not remarkable when one considers his experiences. Irrespective of his novels, his biography of Zaharoff remains the best study so far made of that enigmatic man of mystery. His wartime novel *By the Waters of Babylon,* is, in the mode of *The Bridge of San Luis Rey,* a reconstruction of the lives of a number of disparate persons brought together by an accident—in this case the disappearance of a bus, crowded with Jewish refugees, in Palestine. It is marked by the same vividness and colorful presentation as his earlier novels, but also by the same harshness and lack of warmth.

WORKS AVAILABLE IN ENGLISH: Flood, 1930; Passion: Six Literary Marriages, 1932; On the Make, 1932; Ship in the Night, 1932; Mammon (in England: The Poison Tree) 1933; Zaharoff (in England: Zaharoff: The Armaments King) 1935; Queen's Doctor, 1936; A Woman Screamed, 1938; By the Waters of Babylon, 1939; Twenty-three Women, 1940.

ABOUT: Annales Politiques et Littéraires December 10, 1934; Time July 1, 1940.

NEVINS, ALLAN (May 20, 1890-), American historian, biographer, and university professor, was born at Camp Point, Ill., the son of Joseph Allan Nevins and Emma (Stahl) Nevins. He received his B.A. degree from the University of Illinois in 1912, spending the next year in Urbana as instructor in English and receiving his master's degree in 1913. (He wrote a  one-volume history of the university in 1917.) For the next ten years Nevins was an editorial writer on the New York *Evening Post,* publishing a history of the newspaper in 1922, and leaving the next year when Cyrus Curtis bought the *Post* and proceeded to alter its character. From 1913 to 1918 he also contributed editorials to the *Nation,* long associated with the *Evening Post;* both daily and weekly were then owned by the Villard family. In 1916 Nevins married May Fleming Richardson, daughter of the writer Anna Steese Richardson; their children are Ann, Elizabeth, and Meredith. He was literary editor of the New York *Sun* in 1924-25.

Wide World

In 1923 Nevins had edited *American Social History Recorded by British Travellers,* and followed it up in 1924 with an original work of research, *The American States During and After the Revolution.* In 1925 Nevins transferred to the New York *World* as member of its editorial staff, remaining until 1931 with a year off in 1927-28 as professor of history at Cornell. In 1940-41 he spent a year at Oxford as the third Harmsworth Professor of American History. *Frémont: the West's Greatest Adventurer* appeared in two volumes in 1927, and reappeared, revised and much enlarged, as *Frémont: Pathmarker of the West,* in 1939. In 1931 Nevins became professor of American history at

Columbia University, where the Pulitzer Prize juries have regarded his work with favor. *Grover Cleveland: A Study in Courage,* published in 1932, received the Pulitzer Prize for the best biography of that year, and in 1937 the Prize was again awarded to *Hamilton Fish: The Inner History of the Grant Administration,* published the previous year. Nevins' history students are believed to assist him in his extensive researches.

Besides his voluminous biographical and historical studies and frequent special articles and book reviews, he has published editions of the *Letters* of Grover Cleveland and the *Letters and Journals* of Brand Whitlock, and the *Select Writings* of Abram Hewitt, as well as *The Heritage of America,* edited with a Columbia colleague, Henry Steele Commager, between 1933 and 1939. Nevins' two-volume work on the life and times of John D. Rockefeller (1940) contained new material contributed by the Rockefeller family and was generally less critical than previous studies of the subject, notably Ida M. Tarbell's *History of the Standard Oil Company.* Lewis Gannett praised the organization of the work and its "continuous if monotonous readability," which he found characteristic of all Nevins' work. Other reviewers have utilized the adjectives "well-balanced," "judicious," "thorough," and "conscientious." To top his other activities, Nevins has been general editor of the American Political Leaders Series, the new Yale University Press Chronicles of America series, and the D.C. Heath College and University Historical Series. His clubs are the City, Century, Authors and Columbia Faculty, in New York City. His summer home is at Windham, Vt. Nevins is also a member of the National Institute of Arts and Letters and the Council of the American History Association. His sandiness of hair and complexion denotes his Scotch blood. He is a Presbyterian.

PRINCIPAL WORKS: Life of Robert Rogers, 1914; Illinois, 1917; The Evening Post: A Century of Journalism, 1922; American Social History Recorded by British Travellers, 1923; The American States During and After the Revolution, 1924; The Emergence of Modern America, 1927; Frémont: The West's Greatest Adventurer, 1927; Henry White: Thirty Years of American Diplomacy, 1930; Grover Cleveland: A Study in Courage, 1932; Abram S. Hewitt, With Some Account of Peter Cooper, 1935; Hamilton Fish: The Inner History of the Grant Administration, 1936; The Gateway to History, 1938; The Life of John D. Rockefeller, 1940; A Brief History of the United States, 1942. Editor—The Diary of Philip Hone, 1927; Diary of John Quincy Adams, 1928; Polk: The Diary of a President, 1929; American Press Opinion, 1930; Letters of Grover Cleveland, 1933; Letters and Journals of Brand Whit-lock, 1936; Select Writings of Abram S. Hewitt, 1936; The Heritage of America (with H. S. Commager) 1939; John D. Rockefeller, 1940; This Is England Today, 1941.

ABOUT: New York Times Book Review July 21, 1940; Saturday Review of Literature July 22, 1939.

NEVINSON, HENRY WOODD (1856-November 9, 1941), English journalist and war correspondent, stated that he

"was born in Arcadia. The only praise that I ever heard visitors give to my native town of Leicester was that it was clean." It had hosiery, elastic-web, and boot factories, and an unusual number of Nonconformist chapels. The children of the family were forbidden dances, the theatre, and books except ancient volumes of the *Penny Magazine* and current numbers of *Sunday at Home.* When the boy ordered a Latin copy of the *Imitatio Christi,* his father stopped the order for this "Popish" book, in an outburst of rage. However, Nevinson found his childhood far from dull; "somehow romance crept in." He attended Shrewsbury School, then went up to Christ Church, Oxford University, where he had "two years of unusual misery and failure, followed by a year of radiant joy and success."

After a period of study in Germany, Nevinson taught school in the East End slums before entering on his journalistic career. Nevinson was a leader-writer on the *Daily Chronicle* from 1897 to 1903, and on the *Daily News* in 1908-9. He covered the Greek and Turkish war of 1897; was in Crete in 1897 and Spain in 1898; and from 1899 to 1902 saw the Boer War in Natal and the Transvaal. He visited Central Africa in 1904-05, exposing the Portuguese slave trade in Angola and the Islands of San Thomé and Principe; and was present at the street fighting in Moscow during his Russian sojourn in 1905-06. In 1906-07 he visited the Caucasus and the devastated provinces of Georgia. The *Manchester Guardian* sent him to India in 1907-08: he was in Barcelona for the outbreak of 1909, and in the next few years was in campaigns in Morocco and the Balkans.

In Berlin in 1914 for the *Daily News* when the First World War broke out, Nevinson helped organize the Friends' Ambulance Unit between Dunkirk and Ypres, and was accredited by the War Office as correspondent in the Dardanelles for the *Guardian* and provincial papers. He was present at the landing and evacuation in Suvla Bay in 1915, and received a wound in the attack on Scimitar Hill in August. In 1916 he was correspondent with the British Army in Salonika and Egypt. The years 1918-19 were spent in France and Germany, and 1921-22 in Washington reporting the Washington arms conference for the *Guardian*. The same paper sent him to Syria, Palestine, and Iraq in 1926; he covered the Geneva Conference in 1927; and in 1929 was back in Washington for the meetings between Ramsay MacDonald and President Herbert Hoover. *Changes and Chances; More Changes, More Chances;* and *Last Changes, Last Chances,* his three-volume autobiography, were condensed by R. Ellis Roberts into *Fire of Life* (1935). John Masefield, the Poet-Laureate, wrote in his preface:

"No better autobiography has been written in English in the last hundred years. Mr. Nevinson has been in touch and often in friendship with nearly all the great men and women and rousing movements of the last fifty years. . . . Now in his wisdom (as we will call what follows his maturity) he sees his causes victorious, the slaves free, the women voting. He can reflect that he has been a friend to every generous cause that has stirred men's hearts in his time. . . . Probably few men have had more chances of being knocked in the head in the cause of liberty. Certainly no man with such a noble record to set down has had the charm, the wit, and the graceful irony, which makes this book so delightful and will make it memorable in time to come."

Although he covered the wars for thirty years, Nevinson remained throughout a pacifist and wrote many articles in opposition to war. He also played a prominent part in the women's suffrage movement in England.

Nevinson's first wife was Margaret Wynn Jones, who died in 1932; his son, C. R. W. Nevinson, is a well-known war-painter, and his daughter married S. B. K. Caulfield, the architect. In 1933 he married Evelyn Sharp, an author, journalist, and lecturer. A shy man of imposing presence, he received an honorary LL.D. from Liverpool University in 1935 and a Litt.D. from Dublin University the next year.

Nevinson died at Chipping Campden, Gloucester, at eighty-five, after a brief illness.

PRINCIPAL WORKS: Neighbours of Ours, 1895; In the Valley of Tophet, 1896; The Thirty Days' War, 1898; Ladysmith, 1900; The Plea of Pan, 1901; Between the Acts, 1903; Books and Personalities, 1905; A Modern Slavery, 1906; The Dawn in Russia, 1906; The New Spirit in India, 1908; Essays in Freedom, 1909; Peace and War in the Balance, 1911; The Growth of Freedom, 1912; Essays in Rebellion, 1913; The Dardanelles Campaign, 1918; Lines of Life, 1920; Original Sinners (short stories) 1920; Essays in Freedom and Rebellion, 1921; Changes and Chances (autobiography) 1923; More Changes, More Chances, 1925; Last Changes, Last Chances, 1928; The English, 1928; England, Voice of Freedom, 1929; Rough Islanders, or The Natives of England, 1930; Goethe: Man and Poet, 1931; In the Dark Backward, 1934; Fire of Life, 1935; Running Accompaniments (autobiographical essays) 1936; Between the Wars, 1936; Films of Time, 1938.

ABOUT: Cunliffe, J. W. English Literature in the Twentieth Century; Nevinson, H. W. Changes and Chances; More Changes, More Chances; Last Changes, Last Chances; Running Accompaniments; Saturday Review of Literature December 13, 1941.

NEWBOLT, Sir HENRY JOHN (June 6, 1862-April 19, 1938), English poet, essayist, critic, and miscellaneous writer, was born at Bilston, Staffordshire, son of the Rev. Henry Francis Newbolt, vicar of the parish, and his wife, Emily Stubbs Newbolt. When Henry was four his father died; whereupon the family moved to the grandfather's house at Walsall, remaining

W. Rothenstein

there for ten years. In 1873 the boy was sent to the Grammar School at Caistor, Lincolnshire, whence he passed by scholarship to Clifton College, Bristol. He loved the life of the place, became a crack rifle shot, edited *The Cliftonian,* and in his last year acted as Head of the School. Two contemporaries there were Douglas Haig and Francis Younghusband.

In 1881 Newbolt went up with a scholarship to Corpus Christi College, Oxford, where he met sundry men who were to attain distinction in later life, like Oliver Elton, D.S. MacColl, F.S. Boas, J.A. Spender, and D.G. Hogarth. He took a first in Honor Moderations and a second in "Greats"; after which he entered the London office of a legal relative to study for the bar. He was called in 1887, and worked as an advocate for twelve years without any conspicuous success. His mind and heart were in literature;

he was writing all the time (chiefly verse), encouraged by Andrew Lang and other literary friends; and sundry serious periodicals (more numerous then than now) gave his work occasional hospitality. The set of verses called *Admirals All* came out first in *Longman's Magazine* and in 1897 in book form. Meanwhile "Drake's Drum" had been printed in a magazine and had earned warm praise from Robert Bridges.

Newbolt finally abandoned the bar in 1898, and began to edit *Stories From Froissart* for the publisher Darton. Working in the British Museum reading room, he came to know a member of the staff, Laurence Binyon, the poet, with whom and sundry other literary cronies he had many bohemian and discursive lunches at a nearby restaurant. Poetry remained his constant occupation, but in 1900 he was invited by the publisher John Murray to edit a new *Monthly Review,* and accepted. He produced an interesting magazine, bringing in writers like Roger Fry, Arthur Quiller-Couch, Alice Meynell, Robert Bridges, and W. B. Yeats, but after four years the venture collapsed.

The Year of Trafalgar, produced for the centenary in 1905, established for Newbolt a reputation as a naval historian which was reinforced by later books and led to his becoming vice-president of the Navy Records Society. In 1911 he was made Professor of Poetry in the Royal Society of Literature; he was knighted in 1915 and made a Companion of Honor in 1922. During the First World War (1917-18) he was chairman of the departmental committee on the distribution of books abroad and Controller of Wireless and Cables. From 1919 to 1921 he was chairman of the committee on English in national education. In the latter year he resigned his professorial chair. He was official Naval Historian from 1923 onward, and in 1928 became president of the English Association. He held honorary doctorates from Oxford, Cambridge, and several other universities.

Newbolt's novels are already forgotten, but he produced much verse which, though it never reached great imaginative heights, has its place in the second order of poetry by reason of its metrical music and breezy heartiness. He was the conventional upper-class Englishman in his insistence on courage, patriotism, sport, and the excellence of one's old school. His historical writings have solid worth, and he wrote much sagacious and scholarly criticism.

In 1889 he married Margaret Edina, daughter of the Rev. W. A. Duckworth, of Orchardleigh Park, Frome. They had one son and one daughter.

PRINCIPAL WORKS: *Poetry*—Mordred: A Tragedy, 1895; Admirals All, 1897; The Island Race, 1898; The Sailing of the Long Ships, 1902; Clifton Chapel and Other School Poems, 1908; Songs of Memory and Hope, 1909; Poems: New and Old, 1912; Drake's Drum and Other Songs of the Sea, 1914; St. George's Day, 1918; The Linnet's Nest, 1927; A Child Is Born, 1931; *Fiction*—Taken From the Enemy, 1892; The Old Country, 1906; The New June, 1909; The Twymans, 1911; Aladore, 1914; Tales of the Great War, 1916. *Criticism*—A New Study of English Poetry, 1917; Poetry and Time, 1919; Studies Green and Grey, 1926; The Idea of an English Association, 1928. *Anthologies*—The Book of Cupid, 1909; English Narrative Poems, 1919; An English Anthology of Prose and Poetry, 1922; A Book of Verse, 1922; Essays and Essayists, 1925; New Paths on Helicon, 1927. *Historical and Miscellaneous Works*—The Year of Trafalgar, 1905; The Book of the Blue Sea, 1914; The Story of the Oxfordshire and Buckinghamshire Light Infantry, 1915; The War and the Nations, 1915; The Book of the Thin Red Line, 1915; The Book of the Happy Warrior, 1917; Submarine and Anti-Submarine, 1918; The Book of the Long Trail, 1919; The Book of Good Hunting, 1920; A Naval History of the War: 1914-1918 (5 vols.) 1920-31; The Book of the Grenvilles, 1921; Days To Remember, (with J. Buchan) 1923; The Building of Britain, 1927; My World As in My Time, 1932.

ABOUT: Archer, W. Poets of the Younger Generation; Kernahan, C. Six Famous Living Poets; Miles, A. H. The Poets and Poetry of the Century; Newbolt, H. J. My World As in My Time; Edinburgh Review October 1909; New York Times April 21, 1938; New York Times Book Review July 23, 1922; Saturday Review September 25, 1926; The Times (London) April 21, 1938; Wilson Library Bulletin June 1938.

NEWMAN, ERNEST (November 30, 1868-), English music critic and biographer, was born William Roberts in Liverpool, where he attended Liverpool College and University, and received a business training in banking. Originally intended for the Indian Civil Service, Roberts broke down in health. He remained in Liverpool, where he went into business and be-

gan to write musical and literary articles under the inspiration of J. M. Robertson, the prime intellectual rebel of the 'eighties and 'nineties, using "Ernest Newman" as a *nom de plume.* Eventually he adopted it for all purposes. In 1903 he joined the staff of Midland Institute, Birmingham, as a vocal teacher, and two years later became musical critic of the Manchester *Guardian*. After a clash with Dr. Hans Richter, conductor of the Hallé orchestra, Newman resigned and went to the Birmingham *Post* to stay until 1919. Moving then to London, he became music critic of the *Sunday Times*. (In a letter to the editors of this volume he emphasizes the distinction — so difficult for Americans to comprehend — between this journal and the better known *Times*, "a different paper altogether.") In 1927 Newman was a guest critic in the United States, where the New York *Times* frequently prints his articles. The first Mrs. Newman was Kate Eleanor Woollett, who died in 1918. *A Musical Critic's Holiday* is dedicated "To Vera." The present Mrs Newman was Vera Hands. They have no children. Their country home is at Tadworth, Surrey.

Newman's first book, *Gluck and the Opera* (1895), was followed by the first of the Wagnerian studies which established his reputation as the foremost authority on the composer. *A Study of Wagner* (1899) led to the four-volume *Life of Richard Wagner*, the first volume of which appeared in 1933. Its mass of detail, wrote Desmond Shawe-Taylor in the *Spectator*, is "presented with the precision of a K.C. [King's Counsel], the impartiality of a judge, and the psychological insight of a great novelist." Newman's other books of collected papers contain sound judgments delivered with a light touch, according to the *Sunday Times*, to which he contributes his department "The World of Music." Eva Mary Grew described Newman in an article in *The Sackbut* in 1928 as a little man, dark-eyed, slight of figure, active of movement, very upright in deportment; with a clean-shaven, "sensitive, sardonic, Semitic face," and a delicately modulated voice.

PRINCIPAL WORKS: Gluck and the Opera, 1895; A Study of Wagner, 1899; Wagner, 1904; Musical Studies, 1905; Elgar, 1906; Hugo Wolf, 1907; Richard Strauss, 1908; Wagner As Man and Artist, 1914; A Musical Motley, 1919; The Piano-Player and Its Music, 1920; A Musical Critic's Holiday, 1925; The Unconscious Beethoven, 1927; Fact and Fiction About Wagner, 1931; The Life of Richard Wagner (4 vols.) 1933-41; The Man Liszt, 1934.

ABOUT: Musical Times January 1, 1927; The Sackbut November 1928.

NEWMAN, FRANCES (September 13, 1888-October 22, 1928), American novelist and librarian, was born in Atlanta, Ga., the daughter of Captain William Truslow Newman, C.S.A., a U. S. district judge, and Frances Percy (Alexander) Newman. She was educated at private

schools in Atlanta, New York, and Washington, at Agnes Scott College, Decatur, Ga., and at the Library School of the Atlanta Carnegie Library. In 1913 she was librarian of the Florida State College for Women, in Tallahassee, and from 1914 to 1922 was head of the lending department of the Carnegie Library in Atlanta. In 1923 she went abroad, to Paris, where she studied at the Sorbonne. On her return she became librarian of the Georgia Institute of Technology, in Atlanta, and except for leaves of absence while she wrote her novels, she remained with this library until  her last illness forced her to New York in search of medical relief. She was unmarried.

Since she died at just forty, her career as a writer was comparatively brief. She had written a "novel" at ten, but the laughter of the grown-ups kept her from further literary experiments. Her first published work consisted of notes for the Atlanta library's bulletin and book reviews in local newspapers. These attracted the attention of James Branch Cabell, who recognized her talent and encouraged her to develop it. In Paris she worked on the translations which, with a brilliant critical preface, made up her first book, *The Short Story's Mutations: From Petronius to Paul Morand*. The same year it appeared, 1924, the *American Mercury* published her first short story, "Rachel and Her Children," which won that year's first award in the O. Henry Memorial Prizes.

Her two novels both created sensations, on account of their extraordinary style as much as because of their subject matter, which caused the first, *The Hard-Boiled Virgin*, to be forbidden by censorship in Boston. Her long, intricate sentences, her esoteric allusions, and the complete absence of dialogue in the former book, made her hard reading. But it was rewarding reading as well, for those susceptible to an exotic and original talent.

Meanwhile, she began having trouble with her eyes, which gradually resulted in almost total blindness. Her last work, a translation of Jules Laforgue, was done by dictation, under the utmost difficulty. Unable to endure her physical condition longer, she consulted specialists in Philadelphia and New York. In the latter city she caught cold and pneumonia set in. She did not wait longer, despairing of a cure, and soon after her fortieth birthday ended her sufferings by taking poison.

Carl Bohnenberger, who called Frances Newman "the only artist that the American libraries have produced," said that "she created in the short space of ten years [really four years] a style utterly new to American letters and gave to our literature a color which it has never before possessed. She had an enveloping eagerness for learning, an amazing erudition, and a large capacity for aesthetic understanding."

Early in 1928, before her eye trouble started, Miss Newman had gone to Paris to work on a "history of sophistication," which was cut short by her illness but which she would have been eminently fitted to write. Sophistication, brittle aestheticism, and a glittering, unemotional audacity were her keynotes; she said she "liked inferences," and in a sense her writing is all one long inference. In appearance she resembled one of her own heroines, tall, *soignée*, reticent, and observant.

PRINCIPAL WORKS: The Short Story's Mutations, 1924; The Hard-Boiled Virgin, 1926; Dead Lovers Are Faithful Lovers, 1927; Six Moral Tales by Jules Laforgue (trans. with Introduction) 1928; Frances Newman's Letters, 1929.

ABOUT: Newman, F. Letters (see Preface by J. B. Cabell); Libraries July 1930; Library Journal October 15, 1929.

NEWTON, ALFRED EDWARD (1863-September 29, 1940), American bibliophile and writer, was born in Philadelphia, Pa.,

the son of Alfred Wharton Newton and Louise (Swift) Newton. He was educated in private schools, and at fifteen went to work for the old Porter & Coates Book Shop in Philadelphia. In 1890 he went into the electrical business, and five years later "displaced the sheriff" as financial manager of the Cutter Electrical and Manufacturing Company. In 1890, also, he married Babette Edelheim of Philadelphia, who survived him, with a daughter, Caroline Newton, and son, Edward Swift Newton. In 1893 *Created Gold and Other Poems* by Henry Hanby Hay appeared under the imprint of A. Edward Newton & Co. Newton preferred, however, to collect rather than to publish books. His favorite authors were Samuel Johnson,

Charles Dickens, Charles Lamb, and Oliver Goldsmith, also Robert Louis Stevenson and William Blake. He once paid $62,500 for the Earl of Carysfort's First Folio Shakespeare; he owned Dr. Johnson's silver teapot, the manuscript of Charles Lamb's *Dream Children,* and the original manuscript of Thomas Hardy's *Far From the Madding Crowd,* one of the few Hardy manuscripts not in a public museum.

A paper which Newton contributed to the *Atlantic Monthly* in the spring of 1915, followed by another in the fall of 1917, led to the publication of a fascinating book, *The Amenities of Book-Collecting,* which reached a sale of over 25,000 copies and was later included in the popular-priced Modern Library edition. It did much to establish the vogue for collecting rare books during the prosperous 1920's. Christopher Morley, a close friend of Newton's during his (Morley's) Philadelphia newspaper days and afterwards, wrote that the *Amenities* and its successors "aren't just books, they are printed personality." "The Caliph," as he was known to his friends, was "more than just a witty essayist and a great bibliophile. He [was] a very deep-hearted and human man with an enormous capacity for affection." Newton was open-handed with his treasures; punctilious about answering letters; and suffered fools patiently, if not gladly. A member of the Art, Philobiblon, and Franklin Inn Clubs in Philadelphia, he was also a member of the Grolier Club in New York and the Garrick Club in London, and in 1930 became the first American to be president of the Johnson Society of Great Britain. His library of 10,000 volumes was housed at his home, Oak Knoll, Daylesford (Berwyn P.O.), outside Philadelphia. He usually resembled a ruddy English squire in dress and complexion. He died in Philadelphia at seventy-six, after a three-years' illness with cancer. The New York *Herald Tribune* editorialized: "The country has lost a perverse and brilliant and lovable citizen." Mrs. Newton died in 1941, and the heirs disposed of the famous Newton library at auction.

PRINCIPAL WORKS: The Amenities of Book-Collecting and Kindred Affections, 1918; A Magnificent Farce and Other Diversions of a Book Collector, 1921; Dr. Johnson: A Play, 1923; The Greatest Book in the World and Other Papers, 1925; This Book-Collecting Game, 1928; A Tourist in Spite of Himself, 1930; End Papers, 1933.

ABOUT: Sargent, G. H. A Busted Bibliophile and His Books; Squire, J. C. Books Reviewed; New York Herald Tribune "Books" October 20, 1940; New York Times September 30, 1940; Publishers' Weekly October 12, 1940, March 15, 1941.

*NEXØ, MARTIN ANDERSEN (June 26, 1869-   ), Danish novelist and social thinker, was born of impoverished parents  "up in the attic of a back building" in St. Annaegade, the Kristianshavn slums of Copenhagen. His father, Hans Jorgen Andersen, the son of a crofter, came from the little town of Neksø, in Bornholm, a Baltic island, where he worked in the stone quarries. In 1864 he married Mathilde Mainz, the nineteen-year old daughter of a German blacksmith from Stege on the island of Moën. Martin, the fourth of eleven children, was nervous and delicate: "until nearly forty, I don't think I was ever entirely well a single day of my life." Martin's father drank heavily and terrorized his children, but fortunately he was often out of town in search of work. His mother, to help support the family, "scrubbed stairways, and delivered papers." Martin was entrusted with the care of his baby sister. Later he and his older brother Georg helped their mother when she went out with a pushcart selling fritters and cherries.

Martin taught himself to read by figuring out street signs. When he was seven, the family was compelled by law to send him to the free school, but he hated it—"in the eyes of the teachers we were not human beings, but rather a swarm of dirty, ill-smelling vermin with which they were condemned to be in the room for so and so many hours daily."

In the hard times that followed the Franco-Prussian War, due to the competition of American wheat and Germany's protective tariff policy, the Andersens moved to Neksø where a carpenter friend was to help them. They had to live in squalid quarters and life was even tougher than in "the city of hunger," as Martin's mother used to call Copenhagen. For a while his father got a job cutting paving stones and later laying pavement, and the children, happier because of the sea and the sea air, grew healthy and did odd jobs, unloading boats and gathering seaweed and driftwood for fuel. They were able even to attend school, and in his long vacations (six summer months) Martin worked as herdboy. "The life on the herding field did me good. My mind was set at rest . . . I felt that I was doing something, that I was good for something." In the open fields he felt extremely contented: "it seemed to me as though life had begun here!"

At the age of twelve, just after his confirmation, Martin set out upon "the great quest": in the remote rural districts of Polvsker he worked for a year as hired man on a farm, and then wandered to Ronne where for the next six years he was apprenticed to a shoemaker. After the fourteen-hour working day in the dingy, smelly shop he would retire to his little room and read far into the night, first taking care to cover the window panes so that his master should not catch him burning candles. Finally, since the shut-in life did not help his health, he left, working first as hodcarrier, later in a factory and finally in the construction of a church where he met a German worker "who had been imported to the job for putting the window panes in. He was an ardent Internationalist and awakened my proletarian class consciousness."

In 1892 Nexø was taken into the home of the poet Molbach's widow, who took a genuine interest in him and sent him to the Askov Folk High School. At the end of the second year he found a position as instructor at Peder Moller's Preparatory School at Odense, where he was supremely happy. He devoted his evenings to writing poems and descriptive sketches of life in Bornholm. *For de Foldne*, for instance, dealt with the hardships of fishermen earning their livelihood, showing Nexø's constant concern, even from the earliest, with social problems. An attack of pneumonia forced him to go back to Mrs. Molbach who nursed him for over six months and in the autumn of 1894 gave him four hundred kroner and sent him on a convalescing trip through Spain and Italy. Nexø went everywhere on foot, lived among the peasants and the denizens of the slums, learned Italian and Spanish, and contributed articles to Danish provincial papers. On his return to his country in the summer of 1896 he made up his mind to devote his life to the defense of the poor: "I want everything, from the dust to the highest heavens—for everybody."

In 1896 Nexø delivered a series of lectures at the Mellerup High School and then substituted for a few months at the Winter's Seminary. During 1897-98 he took the one-year course at the Normal School, from which he was appointed instructor in a school at Frederiksberg. There he wrote the stories which formed his first book, *Skygger* (1898), inspired by the poor people of Bornholm and by his journey. From then on he published a book almost every year. After the successful novel, *Familien Frank* (1901), he gave up his teaching and devoted himself almost exclusively to writing. However, it was not until 1906, with the initial volume of *Pelle the Conqueror* (1906-10) that Nexø attracted wide attention as an important Danish writer. In this monumental four volume work, which Randolph Bourne, among others, considered "one of the great novels of the world," Nexø unfolded the chronicle of his life and mirrored at the same time the epic struggles of the Danish working class during the latter part of the nineteenth century. As *Pelle* appeared in other languages (German in 1912, English in 1913-16), Nexø's name became widely known the world over by the time that his other major work, *Ditte* (1917-21), was published. This sequel-novel tells the story of a proletarian of even humbler origins than Pelle. An illegitimate child, servant to the wealthy, her lot was utter slavery and when she died at the age of twenty-five she had tasted but little of life. "Personally, I place *Ditte* as a proletarian novel above *Pelle*," Nexø confessed.

After the First World War Nexø's interest in Communism grew deeper and he settled in Germany to study at close range the workers' movement. The short stories in *De Tomme Pladsers Passagerer* (1921) are devoted to the Russian people and in *Mod Dagningen* (1923) he gives a glowing account of his travels in the Soviet Union where he enjoyed his friendship with Lenin. Later he moved to Hillerad, in Zealand (near Copenhagen), and began his memoirs of which the first two volumes, *Et lille Krae* (1932) and *Under aaben Himmel* (1935), appeared in English in the volume *Under the Open Sky* (1938). He has continued his autobiography in *For lud og koldt Vand* (1937) and *Vejs Ende* (1939).

Since the German occupation of Denmark in 1940, Nexø has been a prisoner in a concentration camp on North Sjaelland Island, north of Copenhagen.

AVAILABLE IN ENGLISH TRANSLATION: Pelle the Conqueror, 1913-1917 (in one volume, 1930); Ditte: Girl Alive! 1920; Ditte: Daughter of Man, 1921; Ditte: Towards the Stars, 1922; Days in the Sun, 1929; In God's Land, 1933; Under the Open Sky, 1938.

ABOUT: Nexø, M. A. Under the Open Sky; Nicolaisen, K. K. Martin Andersen Nexø; Slochower, H. Three Ways of Modern Man; Topsöe-Jensen, H. G. Scandinavian Literature; Book Union Bulletin June 1936; Bookman March 1917; Dial April 5, 1917; Freeman November 10, 1920; International Literature May 1935; Nation December 11, 1913, March 1, 1917, September 11, 1920, December 6, 1922; New Republic December 19, 1913, April 21, 1917, December 22, 1920, November 30, 1921; New York Sun December 13, 1913; St Louis Post Dispatch December 9, 1928; Scandinavian Studies and Notes February 1932; Sewanee Review April-June 1919.

NICHOLS, BEVERLEY (September 9, 1899-   ), English essayist, novelist and playwright, was born John Beverley Nichols in Bristol, the son of John Nichols, a solicitor, and Pauline Z. L. (Shalders) Nichols. He was educated at Marlborough College and at Balliol College, Oxford, where he was editor of the *Isis,* founder and editor of the *Oxford Outlook,* and  president of the Oxford Union, the famous university debating club. His first novel was written while he was at the university, and was published when he was twenty-one. Already he had begun his travels by coming to the United States during the First World War as a member of the Universities Mission.

Beverley Nichols' life has been made up of travel interspersed by books and by occasional journalistic ventures, including editorship of the *American Sketch* in New York in 1928 and 1929. Currently he contributes articles to the London *Daily Sketch* and *Sunday Chronicle* every week. Both in England and America he gained a reputation as a daring and unusual interviewer, and put the results first into magazines, then into books; he has taken one trip all the way around the world for the express purpose of making "candid comments" on the countries he visited. At twenty-five, already having lived one career, he calmly wrote his autobiography.

Most of the money Beverley Nichols had made evaporated in the stock market crash of 1929 in New York, and he decided to go home to England. There he bought a cottage in Huntingdonshire, restored it, and recouped his losses by writing best sellers about the house and its garden. In his first phase he was like a character in a Noel Coward play, or in one of the early novels of Aldous Huxley: his witty and impudent epigrams were quoted everywhere, he was *blasé* before he was thirty, and he posed as the typical "Post-Bellum Bitter Boy" in the era of Bright Young Things. Next came his aesthetic preoccupation with gardening and home-building; after which he emerged to write a book in which he excoriated the munitions makers and urged a militant pacifism. Before long he wrote another book in which he discovered that England's destined leader was Sir Oswald Mosley. Then he joined the Buchmanites and wrote a book defending God from the anti-theologians. With the coming of the Second World War, he recanted his pacifism. In these works he was sometimes startlingly naïve and superficial.

Meanwhile he had had a series of plays produced, best known of which are *The Stag* (1929), *Evensong* (with Edward Knoblock, 1932), and *Dr. Mesmer.*

"I believe," he remarked once, "in doing things too soon." Since he added, "I am posing all my life," he cannot object if critics fail to take him too seriously.

He is a tall, personable, brown-haired young man (past forty, he still seems young), fond of outdoor life, an amateur pianist, and devoted to the theatre. He is unmarried.

PRINCIPAL WORKS: Prelude (novel) 1920; Patchwork (novel) 1921; Self (novel) 1922; Twenty-Five (autobiography) 1926; Crazy Pavements (novel) 1927; Are They the Same at Home? 1927; The Star-Spangled Manner, 1928; Women and Children Last, 1931; Evensong (novel) 1932; Down the Garden Path, 1932; For Adults Only, 1932; Cry Havoc! 1933; A Thatched Roof, 1933; A Village in a Valley, 1934; The Fool Hath Said, 1936; No Place Like Home, 1936; News of England, 1938; Revue, 1939; Green Grows the City, 1939; Men Do Not Weep, 1942.

ABOUT: Nichols, B. Twenty-Five; Newsweek April 25, 1936; Saturday Review of Literature July 9, 1938.

*NICHOLS, ROBERT MALISE BOWYER (September 16, 1893-), English poet and dramatist, writes: "I was born at

Shanklin in the Isle of Wight. My father, John Nichols, comes of a line of printers and antiquaries. My mother's great-uncle was Edmund Pusey, of Oxford Movement fame. Another ancestor on the maternal side is Admiral Sir Cloudesley Shovell. To these antithetical and complementary elements I attribute whatever individuality my works may possess. I was educated in the manner usual to an English boy born in easy but not wealthy circumstances, but I hold that what I learned in youth—which was precious little—was chiefly due to private, voracious, and indiscriminate reading. In due time I arrived *via* Winchester at Trinity College, Oxford. I wrote my first

poem that was not perhaps entirely worthless at the age of seventeen. After one year at Oxford I became a second lieutenant in the Royal Field Artillery. I saw service—very briefly—on the Belgian-French front, and then spent five months in hospital. Later in the war I served first in the Ministry of Labour (which cured me of desk jobs for ever) and then on the British Mission (Ministry of Information) in New York.

"From 1921 to 1924 I occupied the chair of English literature at the Imperial University, Tokyo, a position more or less analogous to that formerly held by Lafcadio Hearn. In 1922, on leaving Japan, I married Norah Denny, an Englishwoman. We lived for two years in Hollywood, where I was employed to visualize scenes for Douglas Fairbanks, Sr. We returned to England and settled at Winchelsea, within a mile of the English Channel.

"The chief influences upon me have been Jefferies, Keats, Romain Rolland, Vaughan, Dostoievsky, Pascal, Amiel, Shakespeare, Mozart, Chekhov, Buchner, Unamuno, and above all, Goethe (Goethe in fact has changed my entire attitude to life and my development as an artist). I am entirely opposed to the extravagant subjectivism fashionable today. Holding, as I do, that the syllabic dance is the foundation of poetry, I am entirely opposed to the present practice and theory of poetry in England and the United States. I hold tradition valuable as declaring some of the proved peculiarities of a given medium. As I have put, I believe, some of the elements of a particular vehement being into my works, so, I believe, they return these elements to the general life."

PRINCIPAL WORKS: *Poetry*—Invocation, 1915; Ardours and Endurances, 1917; Aurelia, 1920; Fisbo, 1934. *Plays*—Guilty Souls, 1922; Twenty Below (with J. Tully) 1927; Wings Over Europe (with M. Browne) 1929. *Miscellaneous*—The Budded Branch, 1918; Fantastica, 1923; Under the Yew (novelette) 1928; Golgotha and Company, 1928.

ABOUT: Aiken, C. P. Skepticisms; Mais, S. P. B. Books and Their Writers; Moore, T. S. Some Soldier Poets.

NICHOLSON, KENYON (May 21, 1894-), American playwright and university professor, was born in Crawfordsville, Ind., the son of Thomas Brown Nicholson and Anne (Kenyon) Nicholson, and was christened John Kenyon Nicholson. His fellow-townsman, Meredith Nicholson, whom he calls "Uncle" and with whom he collaborated on a play, is no relation. Kenyon Nicholson attended the local high school, finishing his preparatory education at De Witt Clinton High School in New York City, where an aunt was living. With his classmates, young Nicholson was usually to be found at Keith's Colonial Theatre on Monday afternoons. Returning to Crawfordsville, he received a B.A. degree from Wabash College in 1917. Attending the Officers' Training School at Fort Benjamin Harrison, he was commissioned a second lieutenant and spent eighteen months in France with the 1st Army Headquarters. After the war Nicholson was press agent for Stuart Walker's Murat Theatre in Indianapolis, and for his productions in New York. Going to Columbia University in 1921 as assistant to Hatcher Hughes, he became instructor in dramatic composition in the Extension Division, a position he still holds. In December 1924 he married Lucile Nikolas of Pittsburgh, an actress. When his wife was playing with a stock company in Syracuse, N.Y., Nicholson spent a summer with carnivals in upper New York State. By this time he had written and had had produced numerous one-act plays, but *The Barker* (1927) a play based on these circus experiences and featuring Claudette Colbert and Norman Foster (whom she afterwards married) was his first Broadway success. Gilbert Gabriel of the *Sun* characterized it as a deliberate and orthodox piece of play plotting, the better for much first-hand picturesquesness. As a college student Nicholson had enjoyed such picaresque experiences as going abroad as steerage steward on the "Cameronia," vagabonding through Scotch moors and French provinces, and working as a sandwich man in London for Pears' Soap. *Eva the Fifth* (1928) had for its background a wandering *Uncle Tom's Cabin* troupe. Alison Smith of the *World* remarked that a fascinating background had been sacrificed to make a cheap comedian's holiday. *Sailor, Beware!* (1933), written with Charles Robinson, and sold to the films for $80,000, was described by Brooks Atkinson of the New York *Times* as "a bawdy prank." A farce concerning the amorous campaigns of sailors in the Canal Zone, it was made in 1939 into a musical comedy, *Nice Goin'*.

In association with Theron Bamberger he has recently been promoting the summer theatre productions at the Bucks County Playhouse, New Hope, Pa.

Nicholson is a Presbyterian, a member of the Dramatists' Guild, and makes his home in Stockton, N.J. The Richmond *News Leader* described him as "some-what the dilettante," with a collar-ad profile.

PRINCIPAL WORKS: Honor Bright (with M. Nicholson) 1924; Garden Varieties, 1924; Appleton Book of Short Plays (ed.) 1925 (second series, 1927); Sally and Company, 1925; The Meal Ticket, 1926; Revues, 1926; Here's to Your Health (with C. Knox) 1927; Two Weeks Off (with T. Barrows) 1927; Tell Me Your Troubles, 1928; Taxi, 1929; Hollywood Plays, 1930; Words and Music, 1930; The American Scene (with B. H. Clark) 1930; Torch Song, 1930; The Flying Gerardos (with C. Robinson) 1941.

ABOUT: New York Herald Tribune January 30, 1927, April 15, 1934; New York Times January 7, 1934.

*NICHOLSON, MEREDITH (December 9, 1866-   ), American novelist and diplomat, was born at Crawfordsville, Ind., the son of Edward Willis Nicholson and Emily (Meredith) Nicholson. His forebears were Kentucky pioneers who had come to Indiana in the Daniel Boone days, and his grandfather Meredith was a pioneer printer and country editor. Young  Meredith was a shy, sensitive, and rather frail boy who attended public school and left high school halfway through his first year, "defeated by algebra." He went to work at fifteen, in a drugstore where he learned the rudiments of Latin from inscriptions on medicine bottles; worked in a printing establishment at $2 a week; became a court reporter at $5 a week; and read admiralty law because it seemed to have possibilities of romance. As sixteen Nicholson had poems published in the local weekly journals, and a little later won a $5 prize from the Chicago *Tribune* for a short story, *The Tale of a Postage Stamp.* In 1891 he collected his poems in *Short Flights,* his first published book; married Eugenie Kountze in June 1896 (she died in 1931); and went to Colorado to spend three years as auditor and treasurer of a coal mining corporation.

Here Nicholson wrote *The Hoosiers* (1900) for the National Studies in American Letters series, an historical study which has been his "longest seller." *The Main Chance* (1903) and *Zelda Dameron* (1904) were two reasonably realistic novels. With *The House of a Thousand Candles* (1905) Nicholson made a highly successful foray into romance. The vogue of novels of the Graustark and Zenda type inspired him with a desire to see what could be done with a picaresque tale in an American setting. Enhanced by illustrations painted by Howard

* Died December 21, 1947.   **1023**

Chandler Christy, the novel proved fresh, gay, resourceful, and exciting. Some of the same characters reappeared in *Rosalind at Red Gate,* illustrated by Arthur Keller, in which an Indiana lake once again was made the locale for a tale of mistaken identity, enlivened by chases and pursuits. Both romances were dramatized by George Middleton; *The House of a Thousand Candles* has been filmed more than once. *The Siege of the Seven Suitors,* illustrated in black and white by Reginald Birch, was laid this time in New York's Westchester County, and had the familiar charm of its predecessors. Ten years later *Blacksheep! Blacksheep!* (1920) completed the picaresque cycle. "While I have never reddened my hands with blood or sought buried treasure or indulged in kidnapping, I find the contemplation of such experiences highly edifying," Nicholson once explained.

The essays collected in *The Man in the Street* (1921) attest Nicholson's belief in the processes of democracy, as a "staunch, old-fashioned Jeffersonian Democrat." In 1928-30 Nicholson was a member of the Indianapolis Common Council; he has been Envoy Extraordinary and Minister Plenopotentiary to Nicaragua since 1938. In September 1933 he was remarried, to Mrs. Dorothy Wolfe Lannon of Marion, Ind. There were two sons and a daughter (the latter deceased) by the first marriage; there is also a Meredith Nicholson III. Wabash College gave the novelist an honorary M.A. in 1901, followed by a Litt.D. in 1907; Butler College followed suit in 1902 and 1929, with an M.A. and LL.D.; Indiana University bestowed an honorary LL.D. in 1928. Mr. Nicholson was Minister to Paraguay in 1933-34. Robert Cortes Holliday describes him as a tall, strapping gentleman, with a loosely hung frame, peaceful manners, and leisurely movements.

PRINCIPAL WORKS: Short Flights (poems) 1891; The Hoosiers, 1900; The Main Chance, 1903; Zelda Dameron, 1904; The House of a Thousand Candles, 1905; Poems, 1906; The Port of Missing Men, 1907; Rosalind at Red Gate, 1907; The Little Brown Jug at Kildare, 1908; The Lords of High Decision, 1909; The Siege of the Seven Suitors, 1910; A Hoosier Chronicle, 1912; The Provincial American (essays) 1913; Otherwise Phyllis, 1913; The Poet, 1914; The Proof of the Pudding, 1916; The Madness of May, 1917; A Reversible Santa Claus, 1917; The Valley of Democracy (essays) 1918; Lady Larkspur, 1919; Blacksheep! Blacksheep! 1920; The Man in the Street (essays) 1921; Honor Bright (play, with K. Nicholson) 1921; Best Laid Schemes (short stories) 1922; Broken Barriers, 1922; The Hope of Happiness, 1923; And They Lived Happily Ever After, 1925; The Cavalier of Tennessee, 1928; Old Familiar Faces (essays) 1929.

ABOUT: Baldwin, C. C. The Men Who Make Our Novels; Bourne, R. History of a Literary Radical; Holliday, R. C. Broome Street Straws; Bookman October 1920.

NICOLL, ALLARDYCE (June 28, 1894-), Anglo-American university professor and writer on the theatre, was born John Ramsay Allardyce Nicoll, the son of David Binny Nicoll and Elsie (Allardyce) Nicoll. He attended Stirling High School and Glasgow University, where he was G. A. Clark Scholar in English. After a period as lecturer in English at Loughborough College, Nicoll served in the same capacity at King's College, University of London, later receiving an appointment as Professor of English Language and Literature in the university, which granted him an M.A. degree. His next appointment was in the Harkness School of the Drama at Yale University, succeeding the late George Pierce Baker. He holds the title of Professor of the History of Drama and Dramatic Criticism, and Chairman of the Department of Drama. Some of the productions of the school were briefly on view in New York City during the theatrical season of 1939-40. Professor Nicoll's home in New Haven is on Prospect Street; he is also a member of the Century Club in New York. Before his Yale appointment he had been a visiting teacher at Harvard, the University of Chicago, etc., and is still an occasional lecturer.

Critic as well as historian, Allardyce Nicoll is, in the words of the *Saturday Review of Literature,* an accurate annalist of the stage rather than the acute analyst of its drama. The English *Saturday Review* praised his "ability to get away from the conventional platitudes of the 'literature class' and to see the English drama as a thing made by many hands for the enjoyment of the many." His compendia include a history of English drama from the Restoration down through the early nineteenth century, in four volumes. In 1930 he published an edition of the works of Cyril Tourneur, and he also edited Sharpham's *Cupid's Whirligig,* Carlell's *Osmond The Turk,* and *The Fool Would Be a Favourite* (1926). He is slim, with thinning hair, and decidedly Scotch in appearance.

PRINCIPAL WORKS: William Blake, 1922; John Dryden, 1923; An Introduction to Dramatic Theory, 1923; A History of Restoration Drama, 1923; A History of Eighteenth Century Drama, 1925; A History of Late Eighteenth Century Drama, 1927; The Development of the Theatre, 1927; Studies in Shakespeare, 1927; Readings From British Drama, 1928; A History of Early Nineteenth Century Drama, 1930; Masks, Mimes, and Miracles, 1931; The Theory of Drama, 1931; Film and Theatre, 1936; The English Theatre: A Short History, 1936; Stuart Masques and the Renaissance Stage, 1937.

ABOUT: Stage April 1933.

NICOLL, Sir WILLIAM ROBERTSON

(October 10, 1851-May 4, 1923), Scottish biographer and theologian, was born in

Aberdeenshire, the eldest son of a Free Church (Presbyterian) minister. He was educated at the Aberdeen High School and the University of Aberdeen, securing his M.A. in 1870. Twenty years later he received an honorary LL.D. from his *alma mater*, besides the same degree in 1922 from St. Andrew's, and a D.D. from the University of Halifax, Nova Scotia, in 1920. He was ordained in 1874, and until 1877 was a Free Church minister at Dufftown. From 1877 to 1885 he had a church at Kelso. In 1885 he founded the *Expositor*, a religious magazine. In 1886 he became editor of the *British Weekly*, a nonconformist paper. In 1891 he was made editor of the *Bookman*. All three of these editorial posts he held until his death. He was also the chief literary adviser of Hodder & Stoughton, the publishers. The *Expositor* was an extremely influential periodical through his editorial articles, signed "Claudius Clear"; under its aegis he edited *The Expositor's Greek Testament* and a series of theological works called *The Theological Educator*. His work on the *Bookman* paved the way for a series of *Literary Lives*, some (including a life of Tennyson, written under the pseudonym of "W. E, Wace") of his own authorship. Besides a long list of books, he wrote many hymns.

Nicoll was married twice, in 1878 to Isa Dunlop, and in 1897 to Catherine Pollard. By his second marriage he had one son and two daughters. He was knighted in 1909. His biographical works are not profound, but they are pleasingly written, and were deservedly popular.

PRINCIPAL WORKS: John Bunyan, 1884; Literary Anecdotes of the Nineteenth Century, 1895; Sunday Afternoon Verses, 1897; Letters on Life, 1901; Life of Ian Maclaren, 1908; Emily Brontë, 1910; The Problem of Edwin Drood, 1912; A Bookman's Letters, 1913; Princes of the Church, 1921.

ABOUT: Darlow, T. H. William R. Nicoll; London Times May 5, 9, 1923.

NICOLSON, Mrs. ADELA FLORENCE (CORY). See HOPE, L.

NICOLSON, HAROLD GEORGE

(1886-), English biographer, was born in Tehran (Teheran), Persia (Iran), the son of Sir Arthur Nicolson, later first Baron Carnock, who was then British chargé d'affaires there. He was reared, as his father's posts were changed, in Persia, Hungary, Bulgaria, and Morocco, thereby becoming a cosmopolitan almost from

birth. He was educated at Wellington College and at Balliol College, Oxford, and also has an honorary doctorate from the University of Athens. He entered the diplomatic service after his graduation, joining the Foreign Office in 1909. The next year he was sent to Madrid, the year following to Constantinople (Istanbul). In 1914 he returned to the Foreign Office, was one of the British delegation to the Versailles Peace Conference, and in 1919 became second secretary and in 1920 first secretary of the Diplomatic Service. Once more in the Foreign Office, he became its Counsellor in 1925, then was stationed in his birthplace, Tehran, and in 1927 transferred to Berlin. He resigned from the service in 1929 and the following year joined the staff of the London *Evening Standard* and later was literary editor of the *Daily Express*. For several years he has conducted a weekly department, "People and Things," in the *Spectator*. In 1931 he contested, unsuccessfully, a Parliamentary election as New Party candidate for the combined universities; in 1935 he won the election as National Labour candidate for West Leicester, and since that time has been a member of the House of Commons. In 1937 he was one of the De La Warr Educational Commission to East Africa.

In 1913 Mr. Nicolson married Victoria Sackville-West,*qv* the novelist, and they have two sons. In peacetime they live between London and his ancestral home, Sissinghurst Castle, a fourteenth century house in Kent. He is a round-faced, snub-nosed, rather good-looking man, who says of himself: "I play tennis very badly. I wear clothes that are a little too young for me. I like pictures. I hate music. I am very much interested in Americans. I hear you are very intelligent, especially in Boston."

This last brash remark discloses the chief early influence on Mr. Nicolson's work, which was that of Lytton Strachey. He has grown a little less self-assured and glittering with the years, but he is still, as George F. Bowerman remarked, "brilliant, entertaining, and amazingly vivid." He disavows Freudianism, but Freud is implicit in all his biography. Actually he is no mere caustic generalizer, but a very hard-working biographer. He works with a notebook, with a page for each year of his subject's life, others for his character and personality, all based on the original documents and source material; next he reads everything in print about the person, then he visits the places associated with him, and only then does he begin the writing of his book. Besides his biographical and historical books, he has published several volumes of collected essays and a semi-autobiography in which he says he has tried "under the guise of flippancy to indicate my own development."

PRINCIPAL WORKS: Paul Verlaine, 1921; Sweet Waters (novel) 1921; Tennyson: Aspects of His Life, Character, and Poetry, 1923; Byron: The Last Journey, 1924; Swinburne, 1926; The Development of English Biography, 1927; Some People, 1927; Sir Arthur Nicolson, Bart., First Lord Carnock: A Study in the Old Diplomacy (in America: Portrait of a Diplomat) 1930; People and Things, 1931; Swinburne and Baudelaire, 1931; Public Faces (novel) 1933; Peacemaking, 1919; Being Reminiscences of the Paris Peace Conference, 1933; Curzon: The Last Phase, 1934; Dwight Morrow, 1935; Helen's Tower, 1937; Small Talk, 1937; Diplomacy, 1939; Marginal Comment, 1939; Peacemaking 1919, 1939.

ABOUT: Nicolson, H. Some People; Saturday Review of Literature May 26, 1934.

NIEBUHR, REINHOLD (June 21, 1892-), American clergyman and editor, writes: "I was born in the little town of Wright City in the backwoods of Missouri. My father was the pastor of an Evangelical Church. I spent my boyhood in St. Charles, Mo., on the Missouri River, and in Lincoln, Ill., where my parents moved in 1900. After a year in a small denominational college, Elmhurst, near Chicago, I prepared for the ministry at Eden Theological Seminary, St. Louis, and then came East for the first time to study at Yale, where I took a B.D. degree in 1914 and

an M.A. in 1915. That year I accepted a call to a struggling little church of my denomination in Detroit, and spent thirteen years there, during a period when the development of the automobile increased the population from 500,000 to a million and a half. During these years I became interested in problems of industrial justice and became painfully aware of the fact that the 'liberal' church preached the good life

in terms of as complete irrelevance to the problems of an industrial society as the orthodox church.

"I was called to Union Theological Seminary, New York, in 1928, and have since that time been teaching Christian ethics and philosophy of religion. I spend a good deal of time speaking to various groups in the colleges and universities. My lectures and sermons are devoted to the relation of religion to social and political problems and to an analysis of political and economic issues before various liberal and political clubs.

"For some years I have been editing a quarterly, *Christianity and Society,* devoted to the cause of Christianity and social reconstruction. Several months ago [written in 1941] I became the editorial chairman of a new bi-weekly journal of Christian opinion entitled *Christianity and Crisis.* In 1938-39 I gave the Gifford Lectures at the University of Edinburgh, later published as *The Nature and Destiny of Man.*"

* * *

In 1931 Mr. Niebuhr married Ursula Kellep-Compton, and they have a son and a daughter. The Gifford Lectures marked a complete reversal of his former liberal views on religion and his return to orthodoxy. He says he is still a liberal economically, but he left the Socialist Party, of which he had been a member, in 1939, and has also repudiated his former pacifist views.

PRINCIPAL WORK: Does Civilization Need Religion? 1927; Leaves From the Notebook of a Tamed Cynic, 1929; Moral Man and Immoral Society, 1932; Reflections at the End of an Era, 1934; An Interpretation of Christian Ethics, 1935; Beyond Tragedy, 1937; Christianity and Power Politics, 1940; The Nature and Destiny of Man, 1941.

ABOUT: American Scholar January 1938; Christian Century May 30, June 20, 1934, January 29, 1941; Current Biography 1941; Time February 3, March 24, 1941.

NILES, Mrs. BLAIR (RICE) (188?-),
American novelist and writer of travel books,
was born at Coles Ferry, Va., the daughter

of Henry Crenshaw
Rice and Gordon
(Pryor) Rice, and
was christened Mary
Blair Rice. The plan-
tation where she was
born was twenty miles
from a railroad. Her
family, one of the
First Families of Vir-
ginia, dates from
early Colonial Vir-
ginia, and is said to have a strain of the
blood of Pocahontas. Her grandfather was
a fiery member of the famous Congress split
asunder by the Civil War, in which he was
a general in the Confederate Army.

Blair Niles was educated at home, and
spent some time in school in Massachusetts,
on the border of Vermont and New Hampshire. She was married when very young
to William Beebe,[qv] the naturalist, through
whom she came then to know the scientific
world of New York and Europe, and to
know also the explorers and adventurers.
With Beebe, she went on numerous scientific
expeditions—to Mexico, Venezuela, and
Trinidad, to British Guiana, through Europe,
Egypt, Ceylon, India, Burma, the Malay
States, Java, Borneo, China, Japan, and Nova
Scotia. On these expeditions she first lived
the life of the trail, traveling by horseback
through wild country, camping in jungles
or at the foot of active volcanoes, and making acquaintance with Indians and bandits—
a manner of living which she continued for
many years, alternating with periods of living in New York City.

After her divorce from William Beebe,
she married Robert Niles, Jr., a New York
architect and, by avocation, explorer-photog-
rapher; together they made expeditions to
Central and South America. Mr. Niles
made a complete photographic record of
these trips. It was on one of these expeditions, to French Guiana, that Mrs. Niles
gathered the material which resulted in the
spectacularly successful book *Condemned to
Devil's Island,* which also was filmed for the
talking pictures. Blair Niles is said to be
the only woman ever to have landed on
Devil's Island and she and Mr. Niles the
only foreigners to have visited it; be that
as it may, she is certainly the only woman
ever to have made a study of the notorious
Penal Colony.

After returning from Devil's Island in
1927, Mrs. Niles applied with characteristic
thoroughness some of her findings on the
sexual *mores* of the colonists to an investigation of the male homosexuality of New
York City. *Strange Brother* (1931), a
serious-minded novel which dealt with the
tragedy of a sensitive young invert, was the
result. Her other novels include *Free, Light
Again, Maria Paluna, Day of Immense Sun,*
and *East by Day,* characterized by competent writing and exotic color. *Peruvian
Pageant* (1937), a travel-book, earned her
the gold medal of the City of Lima, on the
117th anniversary celebration of the independence of Peru in 1938; and *The James*
(1939) is a volume in Farrar & Rinehart's
Rivers of America Series. Mrs. Niles has
also studied the Djoeka Tribes of Bosch
Negroes in both French and Dutch Guiana.
She has written short stories for a variety
of magazines, and occasional book reviews.
At her Park Avenue apartment in New York
City, Mrs. Niles will greet you, according
to her publishers, "dressed in vivid silks
(preferably pajamas), her dark hair, dark
brows and great dark eyes always a startling
contrast to her very white, distinguished
face. Her manner may remind you that she
is a Virginian whose grandfather became a
Supreme Court Justice in New York City
and whose grandmother wrote five books,
herself; but her quick, eager voice and articulate imagination tell another story: that of
the woman who has explored in far lands."
In 1941 Mrs. Niles was awarded the Constance Lindsay Skinner Medal by the
Women's National Book Association and the
Booksellers' League.

PRINCIPAL WORKS: Casual Wanderings in
Ecuador, 1923; Colombia: Land of Miracles, 1924;
Black Haiti, 1926; The Biography of an Unknown
Convict, 1928; Condemned to Devil's Island, 1928;
Free, 1930; Strange Brother, 1931; Light Again,
1933; Maria Paluna, 1934; Day of Immense Sun,
1936; Peruvian Pageant, 1937; The James, 1939;
East by Day, 1940.

ABOUT: Boston Transcript July 16, 1932; New
York World-Telegram April 19, 1932; Publishers'
Weekly March 15, 1941.

*NIVEN, FREDERICK JOHN (March
31, 1878-), Scottish-Canadian novelist,
writes: "Frederick Niven was born of Scots
parents in Valparaiso, Chile. On their return to Scotland he was educated at Hutche-
sons' Grammar School (Glasgow) and at the
Glasgow School of Art. Briefly he was
in the cloth business, his father having been
a manufacturer of sewed muslins, but he
left that to take up the calling of his father's
father, who was librarian of the old Glas-

gow Library. He was for some years an assistant librarian in circulating libraries in Glasgow and Edinburgh. About the age of twenty he went to the Canadian West, which had always an appeal for him, and worked there in construction camps laying out new towns and railway and lumber camps. He returned to Scotland in a cattleboat, out of which experience came, later, his book *The S.S. Glory,* but immediately on his return

he wrote a series of sketches of life in the camps and the new 'cities,' which appeared in the Glasgow *Weekly Herald.* These attracted the attention of newspaper proprietors and gained him a staff appointment in one of the Dundee newspaper offices. Thence he soon passed on to an editorship in London.

"While still employed in journalism he wrote his first novel, retired from staff work to write a second, and in 1911 married Mary Pauline Thorne-Quelch. Offered a roving commission to supply articles on the Dominion to various journals, he returned to Canada in 1912. Back in London again from that successful trip he continued in the writing of novels and in free-lance journalistic work. During the war of 1914-1918, rejected for military service by the discovery of a heart strain, his war work was in the Ministry of Food and the Ministry of Information, where he became associate articles editor for allied and neutral countries.

"After the war Mr. and Mrs. Niven returned to Canada. The American Indian has always been one of his special interests. Among the Blackfeet of Alberta he is known as 'Apasto,' which signifies one who uses the sign-language in converse.

"Several of his books have been set up in Braille type for the blind."

* * *

Mr. Niven lives now at Nelson, B.C. He says he is "keen on all methods of travel, seeing new places and revisiting old ones," and he was an ardent mountain-climber until cardiac trouble made mountaineering impossible for him. Some of his novels are laid in Scotland, some in Canada, and of these some are historical. Christopher Morley called him "one of the most genuinely gifted novelists of our time . . . an artist in honorable and thoughtful living."

PRINCIPAL WORKS: The Lost Cabin Mine, 1908; The Island Providence, 1910; A Wilderness of Monkeys, 1911; Above Your Heads, 1911; Dead Men's Bells, 1912; The Porcelain Lady, 1913; Ellen Adair, 1913; Justice of the Peace, 1914; The S.S. Glory, 1915; Hands Up! 1915; Two Generations, 1916; Cinderella of Skookum Creek, 1916; Maple-Leaf Songs (verse) 1917; Sage-Brush Stories, 1917; Penny Scot's Treasure, 1918; The Lady of the Crossing, 1919; A Tale That Is Told, 1920; The Wolfer, 1923; Treasure Trail, 1923; A Lover of the Land and Other Poems, 1925; Queer Fellows (in America: Wild Honey) 1927; The Three Marys, 1930; Canada West (non-fiction) 1930; The Paisley Shawl, 1931; The Rich Wife, 1932; Mrs. Barry, 1933; Triumph, 1934; The Flying Years, 1935; Old Soldier, 1936; The Staff at Simson's, 1937; Colour in the Canadian Rockies (non-fiction, with W. J. Phillips) 1937; Coloured Spectacles, 1938; The Story of Their Days, 1939; Mine Inheritance, 1939; Brothers-in-Arms, 1942.

ABOUT: Niven, F. Justice of the Peace (see Prefaces, 1923 edition, by H. Walpole & C. Morley); Saturday Review of Literature December 28, 1929.

*NOCK, ALBERT JAY, American publicist and critic, received his B.A. and Litt.D. degrees from St. Stephen's College, New York, now a component part of Columbia University, and for some time was visiting professor of American history and politics at his *alma mater.* He spent some years also as a clergyman, was formerly associate editor of the *Nation,* and was editor of the old *Freeman.* His entire life has been spent in New York City.

E. Stevenson

His articles have been appearing in organs of opinion since about 1910; his first book appeared in 1915. In addition to his own books, he has edited the works of two rather incongruous humorists, Rabelais and "Artemus Ward." For some time he conducted a department in the *American Mercury* called "The State of the Nation." He is a gray-haired, gray-moustached man who looks something like a prosperous though scholarly banker.

Mr. Nock is so averse to personal publicity that further details of his life are unavailable. He is an intransigent individualist, anarchistic by temperament, and has been called both a die-hard reactionary and a Jeffersonian democrat. Twenty years ago he was accounted a liberal, but he has grown increasingly conservative. He has long been an active Single Taxer. One critic remarked that "he has lived in a trance since 1789 except for hearing the voice of Henry George."

George Soule, who gave him credit for "shrewd perception" and called him "a good phrase-maker," nevertheless added: "His view of the state combines those of Confucius, Karl Marx, and the National Association of Manufacturers. . . . What he omits . . . is their several programs for dealing with the state." He has long been a gadfly among critics and economists, and can always be depended upon for forthright expression of highly individual opinion.

PRINCIPAL WORKS: How Diplomats Make War (with F. Neilson) 1915; The Myth of a Guilty Nation (as "Historicus") 1922; Jefferson, 1926; On Doing the Right Thing and Other Essays, 1928; Francis Rabelais: The Man and His Work (with C. R. Wilson) 1929; The Book of Journeyman (as "Journeyman") 1930; The Theory of Education in the United States, 1932; A Journal of These Days, 1934; A Journey Into Rabelais' France, 1934; Our Enemy, the State, 1935; Free Speech and Plain Language, 1937; Henry George, 1939.

ABOUT: Saturday Review of Literature January 11, 1936.

*NORDHOFF, CHARLES BERNARD

(February 1, 1887-   ), American novelist and travel and adventure writer, and col-

laborator with James Norman Hall,[w] writes: "I was born in London of American parents. My grandfather and namesake was a well known journalist and author during the Civil War period. My mother, Sarah Cope (Whitall) Nordhoff, comes of old Philadelphia Quaker stock (related to Logan Pearsall Smith and M. Carey Thomas, president of Bryn Mawr). My parents brought me to America when I was three years old, and from that time until 1916 I lived in Philadelphia, in California, and on my father's ranch in Mexico, excepting three years at Harvard (B.A. 1909). In 1916 I served as an ambulance driver in France, and later as a pilot in the French Air Service. At the end of the war I had been commissioned First Lieutenant in the United States Air Service.

"After our demobilization, my friend James Norman Hall and I were invited to write the history of the Lafayette Flying Corps; and when that considerable task was done, we yielded to a long-suppressed desire to set sail for the South Pacific Ocean. Since that time we have lived in Tahiti. I

was married in 1920 to Pepe Teara, and we had four daughters and two sons. We are now divorced.

"I have had an itch for the pen since childhood. My first published work was an article in the ornithological journal, the *Auk,* printed when I was sixteen. Whatever small degree of success I have had since then is owing to the infinite kindness and encouragement of Ellery Sedgwick, formerly editor of the *Atlantic Monthly.*

"All my life I have loved shooting, fishing, sailing, or traveling through wild country alone or with a single companion. Anthropology interests me more than anything else; if I had my life to live over, I should do the necessary groundwork and become a professional anthropologist. Next to the study of man, I like the study of birds and fishes. I like books of natural history, sport, travel, history, and biography. Sir Walter Scott's novels give me more pleasure than any others. Most modern novels move too fast and are too lacking in beauty for my taste. I detest so-called 'realism,' from Zola down. In other words, life seems to me well worth living, full of interest and beauty as well as of less pleasant things."

* * *

Mr. Nordhoff's first college year was spent at Stanford University. After graduation from Harvard he worked for two years on a sugar plantation in Mexico. From 1911 to 1916 he was secretary and treasurer of a tile and fire brick manufacturing company in California. He won the *Croix de Guerre* with star and citation during the First World War. James McConnaughey says of him: "He will do anything for you, and, within reason, give you anything he has." Shy and modest, he deprecates his own work, is bashful with women, and loathes formal society. He is six feet one inch tall, lean, and looks much younger than his fifty-odd years. He married Laura Whiley in 1941.

He writes in the morning, spends his afternoons fishing. He and Hall draw up charts of their characters, in beginning a new book, then allot chapters for each to do. They are adept at imitating each other's style so as to produce a smooth narrative. "His primary demand of a story is that it be dramatic," and he holds that "a novelist cannot spend too much time in examining and re-examining the basic idea of his book" before he begins actually to write it. Best known of the Nordhoff and Hall books are those on the famous mutiny on the sailing ship "Bounty" and the subsequent experiences of the mutineers and their descendants

* Died April 11, 1947.

on Pitcairn and Norfolk Islands. These have been filmed, and have made this bit of English naval history real and vivid as are few such episodes of the past.

PRINCIPAL WORKS: *As sole author*—The Fledgling, 1919; The Pearl Lagoon, 1924; Picaró, 1942; The Derelict, 1928. *With James Norman Hall*—The Lafayette Flying Corps, 1920; Faery Lands of the South Seas, 1921; Falcons of France, 1929; Mutiny on the Bounty (in England: Mutiny!) 1932; Men Against the Sea, 1933; Pitcairn's Island, 1934; The Hurricane, 1935; The Dark River, 1938; No More Gas, 1940; Men Without Country, 1942.

ABOUT: Literary Digest February 22, 1936; Saturday Evening Post April 23, 1938; Saturday Review of Literature September 9, 1933, September 28. 1940.

*NORRIS, CHARLES GILMAN (April 23, 1881-), American novelist, was born in Chicago, Ill., the son of Benjamin

Franklin Norris and Gertrude G. (Doggett) Norris. Frank Norris,*qv* his brother, the well-known novelist, was eleven years his senior. Their father was a wholesale jeweller. At ten Charles Norris had written an elaborate historical novel, *In the Reign of the Grand Monarch,* which was destined to be his last essay in the field of romantic fiction. He graduated from the University of California in 1903 with the degree of Ph.B. and became assistant editor of *Country Life in America* at $5 a week. Tiring of covering dog shows, writing "Hints for Tulip Raisers," and articles on "Fire Risks in the Country Home," Norris went to San Francisco to work as circulation manager of *Sunset Magazine.*

There he met and married Kathleen Thompson of Mill Valley, in April 1909; his wife soon became known to fame as the popular novelist Kathleen Norris.*qv* Together they moved to New York City, where he served as art editor of the *American Magazine* from 1908 to 1913. His first novel, *The Amateur,* concerning a young artist in New York, was published two years later. In April 1917 Norris entered the R.O.T.C. at Madison Barracks, N.Y.; graduated from the training corps as captain of infantry; and was assigned to the 153rd Depot Brigade at Camp Dix, N.J. He was made a major of infantry in August 1918, and resigned in December. *Salt: or, The*

Education of Griffith Adams, had appeared in 1917.

"My sole purpose in writing my books is to make people think," Norris has stated. "In *Salt* I tried to give a picture of our national system of education, to show the good and ill effects of our schools and colleges. In *Brass* (1921), the novel following *Salt,* I attempted to present different phases of what we understand as marriage, to show some of the reasons why people cannot get along with one another." "*Salt* was much discussed, even in all the hurry and confusion of 1918, and *Brass,* written in Rio de Janeiro, but dealing, as all his novels do, only with America and the Americans, was a best seller," wrote Kathleen Norris in the autobiographical *Noon* (1925).

With increasing prosperity, the Norrises had begun to travel widely. For some years they lived at Port Washington on Long Island, N.Y., then bought a ranch of two hundred acres fifty miles due south of San Francisco. The estate has a grove of redwood and madrone trees, and several guest houses to be occupied by nephews, neices and cousins. Both Mr. and Mrs. Norris work from 9 A.M. to 1 P. M., with no interruptions or telephone messages allowed Except in the summer, they also work until midnight five nights a week. Charles Norris may put in three hours' hard work writing three sentences. "He does all his struggling and suffering beforehand and rarely changes a word afterwards," according to his wife.

Bread, Pig Iron, Seed, Zest, and *Hands* succeeded each other in a monosyllabic file, and are all as grimly naturalistic and uncompromisingly frank as his wife's novels are romantic and "escapist." *Zelda Marsh* (1927) shows how heredity plus environment led one woman to disaster, and *Seed* (1930) was a novel about birth-control. Charles Norris is also the author of three poetic dramas produced as Grove Plays of the Bohemian Club; they are *The Rout of the Philistines* (1922), *A Gest of Robin Hood* (1929), and *Ivanhoe* (1936). He is a member of the Players and Dutch Treat clubs in New York City, of the Menlo Country Club of Menlo, Calif., and of Phi **Gamma Delta** fraternity. He is a Republican and an Episcopalian (Mrs. Norris is a Catholic).

PRINCIPAL WORKS: The Amateur, 1915; Salt, 1917; Brass, 1921; The Last of the Philistines, 1922; Bread, 1923; Pig Iron, 1925; Zelda Marsh, 1927; A Gest of Robin Hood, 1929; Seed, 1930; Zest, 1933; Hands, 1935; Ivanhoe, 1936; Bricks Without Straw, 1938.

ABOUT: Baldwin, C. C. The Men Who Make Our Novels; Norris, K. Noon.

* Died July 25, 1945.

NORRIS, FRANK (March 5, 1870-October 25, 1902), American novelist, was born Benjamin Franklin Norris, Jr., his mother being Gertrude (Doggett) Norris. His  birthplace was Chicago, where his father, who had been kept by lameness from following his own father as a Michigan farmer, was a wholesale jeweler. His mother, of New England and Virginia ancestry, had been an actress before her marriage, and t was undoubtedly from her that Frank Norris and his younger brother, the novelist Charles G. Norris,^{qv} inherited their talent. When Frank was fourteen the family moved to California for the benefit of the father's health, settling first in Oakland and a year later in San Francisco. In the latter city they lived in the Polk Street district, then a semi-slum region of small stores, which is the scene of *McTeague.* Frank went to a private school in Belmont, Calif., but while he was laid up by a fracture of his left arm, it was discovered that he had some gift for drawing, and in 1887 the whole family went abroad to settle him in art school, first in London and then in the Atelier Julien in Paris. There they left him for two years. He wasted much of his time in the art school, and, his mind steeped in Froissart's Arthurian romances, spent many hours in writing a long fantastic story centering about his own adventures, and illustrated by himself, which he sent in sections to his much younger brother. When his father discovered how his money was being used, he peremptorily ordered his son home.

Back in San Francisco, he determined to be a writer rather than an artist. He entered the University of California, but 'flunked out" in mathematics and was obliged to leave. It was at the university that he discovered Zola, and became fired with the ambition to be the first American realist, and to treat in minute detail of the life he actually saw about him. He went to Harvard for a year (where he received some encouragement in his writing from Professor Lewis Gates), and then in 1895 sailed for South Africa as correspondent of the San Francisco *Chronicle,* which had already published several of his stories.

In Africa, Norris became associated with Sir (Dr.) Leander Starr Jameson in his raid on the Transvaal, and was captured and expelled by the Boers. Before this occurred, he had suffered a severe attack of tropical fever, which was to weaken his constitution permanently. He went back to San Francisco and become associated with the magazine, the *Wave,* which attracted most of the local *literati.* By 1898, however, he had left again for New York, where he was on the staff of *McClure's Magazine* in its great muck-raking days. *McClure's* sent him to Cuba to cover the war there, and he suffered another attack of the African fever. On his return to New York he became a reader for Doubleday, Page & Co., where his most notable achievement was to insist on the publication of Dreiser's *Sister Carrie,* though the publishers withdrew the book almost as soon as it appeared.

In 1900 Norris married Jeannette Black, and they moved back to California, where their daughter was born. He bought a ranch at Gilroy, and planned to live and write there. He had by this time produced the first two of his trilogy of "wheat" novels, and expected to go to India to secure data for the third volume, dealing with consumption of the wheat in a famine, as *The Octopus* had dealt with its production and *The Pit* with its distribution. Following this book he contemplated another trilogy, dealing with the battle of Gettysburg.

But all this was ended by an attack of appendicitis, followed by peritonitis, and he died in San Francisco at only thirty-two.

And yet it cannot be said that Norris was a novelist of great promise who was cut short in mid-career. It is probable that he had already to some extent written himself out, and no progressive growth shows itself in his work. It would be more accurate to call him a novelist who never entirely found himself, and in whom great talent was mingled with lack of taste and absence of self-criticism. To the end he remained temperamentally what he was in appearance—a handsome blond boy, the very prototype of the ideal college student of the 'nineties. He read Zola religiously, but he also read Kipling and Richard Harding Davis (to say nothing of the early influence of Froissart), and one could never be sure which of these masters would lay a hand on his work. As C. Hartley Grattan rightly said, his "important books are imbedded in a mass of what must be called trash." As an example of the way in which Norris was tending, he himself said that "the better the personal morality of the writer the better his writings," and his heroes in real life were Theodore Roosevelt, Gen. Leonard Wood, and an assortment of big business men. The kind of unscrupulous financier whom Dreiser pilloried under the name of "Cowperwood," Frank Norris came wholeheartedly to admire.

The "important books" to which Grattan alluded are *McTeague, The Octopus,* and *Vandover and the Brute,* a powerful study of degeneration. *The Octopus,* in its picture of the California farmers struggling with the encroachments of the railroad, is a far better piece of work than its sequel, *The Pit.* But Frank Norris' masterpiece is *McTeague.* It is the most purely Zolaesque novel in English, with its cold, careful study of the growing devastation wrought by miserliness on the lives of the Polk Street advertising dentist and his wife. As a motion picture, under the name of *Greed,* it was almost equally effective, and gave Zasu Pitts almost her only opportunity as a tragedian. Yet even *McTeague* was injured by its melodramatic end, utterly out of fitting with the rest of the book. "At heart," Charles Caldwell Dobie remarked, "Norris was a romanticist, his realism pure discipline."

"A self-conscious realist," Grattan called him, in agreement, and added that he was "made up of warring elements, . . . not a man of intellect, . . . rather a man of feelings, of enthusiasm, . . . not the sort of person to whom it is natural to deal in ideas."

Yet, though he was apparently on his way to greater and greater conventionality in his work, Frank Norris remains one of our great pioneer realists. "Tell your yarn and let your style go to the devil—we don't want literature, we want life!" he cried in 1899. Part of this was mere boyishness and romantic "westernness," but some of it was the truculence of genius. "The key to Norris," said Alfred Kazin, "is to be found in that naive, open-hearted and essentially unquenchable joy in life . . . that is like the first discovery of the world, splendid in its freshness, and eager to absorb every flicker of life." Except in isolated passages of his other books and a good part of *McTeague,* he never fully made his potentialities real. Perhaps—though only perhaps—if he had lived longer he would have fulfilled himself more. He himself wrote just before he died:

"I never truckled. I never took off the hat to Fashion and held it out for pennies. I told them the truth. They liked it or they didn't like it. What had that to do with me? I told them the truth."

PRINCIPAL WORKS: Moran of the Lady Letty, 1898; Blix, 1899; McTeague, 1899; A Man's Woman, 1900; The Octopus, 1901; The Pit, 1903; A Deal in Wheat and Other Stories, 1903; Complete Works, 1903 and 1928; Responsibilities of the Novelist and Other Literary Essays, 1903; The Third Circle (short stories) 1909; Vandover and the Brute, 1914; Frank Norris of The Wave (short stories) 1931.

ABOUT: Cooper, F. T. Some American Story Tellers; Norris, F. Frank Norris of The Wave (see Foreword by C. G. Norris, Introduction by O. Lewis); S.E.R.A. Monographs #3 (California Literary Research); Walker, F. Frank Norris; American Mercury April 1928; Bookman May 1914, July 1929; Nation November 30, 1932; North American Review December 1902; Saturday Review of Literature May 27, 1933, July 8, 1939.

NORRIS, Mrs. KATHLEEN (THOMPSON) (July 16, 1880-), American novelist and short-story writer, was born in San Francisco, Calif., the second eldest child of the family, which included three sons and three daughters. Her father, James Alden Thompson, although born in Hawaii, was of a Boston family. He was twice president of the Bohemian Club  of San Francisco, and at the time of his premature death, manager of the Donohoe-Kelly Bank. His wife was Josephine (Moroney) Thompson. The children were taught at home, with an occasional governess for French or German. Guests were few and parties non-existent, but the family had the run of a large library, *Harper's* and the *Century* from the East to read, and miles of virgin forest to explore at their Mill Valley home, "Treehaven," across the bay from San Francisco at the foot of Mount Tamalpais. At nineteen Kathleen Thompson was ready for her début in San Francisco society, and a winter residence had been selected, when her mother died of pneumonia, and her father died less than a month later, leaving the family practically destitute. Kathleen went to work as a bookkeeper, saleswoman, school teacher, reader to invalids, and manager of children's parties; her sister Teresa, later to marry the poet William Rose Benét, became the assistant manager of a gift-shop; and the eldest son also contributed to the family income of $95 a month. Kathleen developed the habit of telling stories to her brothers and sisters by way of inexpensive amusement, and the San Francisco *Argonaut* paid her $15.50 for one entitled "The Colonel and the Lady." For a time she was society editor of the *Evening Bulletin,* gaining some useful insight into the modes and morals of the plutocracy which was later to go into *The Rich Mrs. Burgoyne* and other novels. For two years she was a reporter on the San Francisco *Call,* on one occasion turning out a news-story of 8,000 words, when the Atlantic fleet visited Pacific waters.

In September 1903 she went to the University of California for two months of study in the English Department under Chauncey Wetmore Wells, who praised her themes. This cheered her when she was discharged from the *Bulletin,* and when the Associated Press assured her that her *forte* was not writing (Frank Norris, her famous brother-in-law, was discharged from the San Francisco *Wave* for the same reason). In April 1909 Kathleen Thompson became Kathleen Norris, with her marriage to Charles Norris,*qv* then an editor and later a realistic novelist. They moved to New York City, where he was art editor of the *American Magazine,* and started housekeeping on $50, representing two-weeks' pay, in a small apartment in the east Seventies.

Ellery Sedgwick accepted Mrs. Norris's "What Happened to Alanna" for the *Atlantic Monthly,* although some of the staff had objected that the story was not in the *Atlantic* tradition, and S. S. McClure took six stories for his magazine, where there was less doubt of their welcome. In one month her work appeared in five different magazines. "Mother," an attractive story of family life drawn from her own in San Francisco, was an immediate success when it appeared in the *American.* Mrs. Norris added 20,000 words to the original story of 10,000 words for the published book, and Edward Bok reserialized it in the *Ladies' Home Journal. The Rich Mrs. Burgoyne,* written in six weeks for the *Woman's Home Companion,* was published in 1913. *The Treasure* appeared in the *Saturday Evening Post; Saturday's Child* in *Good Housekeeping,* and since then Mrs. Norris' name has seldom been absent from magazines of this type.

She is usually a book or two ahead of her publishers. Half her working time, she states, is spent playing solitaire, while conversations and scenes unroll themselves plainly and clearly before her mind's eye. Putting her stories on paper is an easy and rapid business. The Norrises live at Saratoga, Calif., on a hospitable ranch at the foot of the Santa Cruz mountains. They have a son, Frank; two daughters, Josephine and Gertrude, are dead. A friend describes Mrs. Norris as "a gracious hostess, tall, striking, carefully tailored—a woman with rare charm and a remarkable sense of humor —a racy Irish love of the ridiculous." *Certain People of Importance* (1922), a chronicle-novel, is her most ambitious effort. It was less profitable than its numerous companions, and Mrs. Norris did not repeat the performance. The New York *Times* has commented on her "persuasive fluency and minute and feminine knowledge of her background."

PRINCIPAL WORKS: Mother, 1911; The Rich Mrs. Burgoyne, 1912; Poor Dear Margaret Kirby, 1912; Saturday's Child, 1914; The Story of Julia Page, 1915; The Heart of Rachael, 1916; Martie: The Unconquered, 1917; Undertow, 1917; Josslyn's Wife, 1918; Sisters, 1922; Harriet and the Piper, 1920; Beloved Woman, 1921; Certain People of Importance, 1922; Butterfly, 1923; The Callahans and the Murphys, 1924; Noon (autobiography) 1925; Little Ships, 1925; The Black Flemings, 1926; Hildegarde, 1926; The Barberry Bush, 1928; The Sea Gull, 1927; Beauty and the Beast, 1928; The Foolish Virgin, 1928; Storm House, 1929; Red Silence, 1929; Home, 1929; Mother and Son, 1929; Margaret Yorke, 1930; The Lucky Lawrences, 1930; The Love of Julia Borel, 1931; Hands Full of Living, 1931; Belle Mere, 1931; Second Hand Wife, 1932; The Younger Sister, 1932; My San Francisco, 1932; Treehaven, 1932; Walls of Gold, 1933; My California, 1933; Wife for Sale, 1933; Angel in the House, 1933; Victoria (play) 1934; Manhattan Love Song, 1934; Heartbroken Melody, 1938; Bakers' Dozen (short stories; English title: Plain People) 1938; The Runaway, 1939; Lost Sunrise, 1939; The World Is Like That, 1940, The Venables, 1941; Dina Cashman, 1942; Maiden Voyage, 1942.

ABOUT: Kilmer, J. Literature in the Making; Norris, K. Noon; Overton, G. M. The Women Who Make Our Novels; Talbot, F. X. (ed.). Fiction by Its Makers; Woollcott, A. While Rome Burns.

NORTH, JESSICA NELSON (1894-   ), American poet and critic, writes: "I was born in Madison, Wis.; my father and mother were recently graduated from the University of Wisconsin, newly married, and living in their first house. Later we moved many times and went through financial crises until we sought refuge on my grandfather's farm near  Lake Koshkonong. I grew up as a farmer's daughter and went to country school, but not until after my mother had given me most of my primary education. At five I could read the newspapers, at seven I learned a little Latin, advanced botany and chemistry, but I never learned to add and multiply. My mother was a poetry lover, but I was the only one of her three children who continued an interest in poetry. When I was ready for high school I stayed home for a year, doing housework and studying in the evening. When examinations were given in the high school, I drove in and took them with the other students, passing with high grades. After high school I taught country school for two years, then went to Lawrence College, at Appleton, Wis. I graduated in 1917. My mother had died during my junior year; I stayed home for several years taking care of my father and small brother, Sterling,[qv] now literary editor of the Chicago *Daily News*.

"Finally I went to Chicago for post-graduate work at the University of Chicago, earning my way by becoming secretary to the university's president. I joined the Poetry Club, and after several years I was asked to become associate editor of *Poetry*. Harriet Monroe had published some of my poems and I had received the John Reed Prize in 1927. I have been on the staff of the magazine since 1928 [acting editor 1929]. For three years I was editor of the *Bulletin* of the Art Institute of Chicago and wrote critical articles for many magazines about the Institute's collections.

"Meanwhile I had been married [to Reed Innes MacDonald, in 1921], and had become the mother of a son and daughter."

PRINCIPAL WORKS: A Prayer Rug (poems) 1923; The Long Leash (poems) 1928; Arden Acres (novel) 1934; Introduction to Paintings, 1934; Morning in the Land (novel) 1941.

NORTH, STERLING

NORTH, STERLING (November 4, 1906-   ), American novelist, poet, and critic, writes: "I was born on a farm overlooking

Pinchot

Lake Koshkonong in Southern Wisconsin. I attended grade school and high school in Edgerton, Wis.,— the 'Brailsford Junction' of my novels *Plowing on Sunday* and *Night Outlasts the Whippoorwill*. During my senior year of high school I sold my first poems to Eastern magazines, and throughout my term at the University of Chicago continued to make part of my

expenses by selling poetry to literary magazines. Several national poetry prizes, including the Witter Bynner, and the Young Poet's Prize (awarded by *Poetry*), came my way and gave me encouragement. I edited the campus literary magazine, the *Forge*, helped to operate a little theatre, and placed a few short stories.

"Meanwhile, in 1927, I had married Gladys Buchanan, and our first child was born on the day that my first book, written in collaboration with an old Negro sea captain, was published. One other child and ten additional books have followed.

"Discovering that three cannot go through college as inexpensively as one, I found it expedient to take a full-time job with the Chicago *Daily News*. 'From cub reporter to literary editor in three years' time' might be the caption of the years of the depression. During those years I covered every sort of assignment from night police reporting in gang-infested Chicago to 'Toonerville Trolley'—it meets all the trains.

"For the past nine years I have written the literary criticism and conducted the book section of the *News*, written novels and juveniles, and have tried to help counteract the forces of reaction in the Middle West. As a small boy, I was something like Zeke in my juvenile, *Greased Lightning*. As a young man, I was rather closely akin to Mark Harbord in my novel, *Seven Against the Years*."

* * *

Mr. North is the younger brother of Jessica Nelson North,[qv] who reared him after their mother's death when he was a child. Besides editing and writing, he lectures frequently on books and authors. He lives in Downers Grove, Ill., near Chicago, with his wife, son, and daughter.

PRINCIPAL WORKS: The Pedro Gorino (with H. Dean) 1929; Plowing on Sunday, 1934; The Five Little Bears (juvenile) 1935; Night Outlasts the Whippoorwill, 1936; Seven Against the Years, 1939; Greased Lightning, 1940.

NORTON, CHARLES ELIOT

NORTON, CHARLES ELIOT. See "AMERICAN AUTHORS: 1600-1900"

NORWAY, NEVIL SHUTE

NORWAY, NEVIL SHUTE (1899-   ), English novelist who writes under the partial pseudonym of "Nevil Shute," was the son of Arthur Hamilton Norway, until 1920 Assistant Secretary of the General Post Office in London, and Mary Louisa (Gadsden) Norway. His Cornish ancestors included the Captain Norway who fell on the deck of the packet boat "Lady Mary Pelham" during its skirmish with an

American frigate, "Privateer," in the early days of the War of 1812. *The History of the Post Office Packet Service,* an account of the traffic between Falmouth and New York, which was written by Nevil Shute's father, is regarded as a classic in its field. (The elder Norway died in 1938.) Young

Nevil was still in his teens when he witnessed some of the early manifestations of the Sinn Fein rebellion in Dublin, and was a rescue-work volunteer with the Red Cross. In 1916 Mrs. Norway published a thin volume of letters which she had written during this period, under the title *The Sinn Fein Rebellion As I Saw It.*

Nevil Shute served in the First World War as a soldier in France, and returned to Oxford to finish his studies, in spite of feeling himself to be an awkwardly older undergraduate. He already had ambitions to write, but developed at the same time an interest in engineering, especially as it concerned aeronautics. In 1924 he joined the staff of the company which was building the airship R100, under the supervision of Sir Dennistoun Burney, the inventor of the paravane. He afterwards became the ship's chief engineer, directed her to completion, and sailed her on her famous voyage to Canada and back. When the R101 disaster put an end to airship building in England, Shute devoted his attention to airplane manufacture. His first factory was set up in an old garage in Southsea. At the time of his resignation as managing director, in 1938, the firm was employing a thousand people. That year saw the publication of his cheerful but not convincing novel, *Kindling* (called *Ruined City* in England) which unfolded the miraculous rejuvenation of a depression-ridden town. The book was his fourth. *Marazan,* Shute's first novel, was published in 1926; *So Disdained,* issued in the United States as *The Mysterious Aviator,* in 1928; and *Lonely Road* came along in 1932, although written some years previously. *What Happened to the Corbetts* was a selection early in 1939 of the Book-of-the-Month Club in the United States, where the romance was titled *Ordeal.* This realistic and detailed account of the adventures of a small English family, bombed out of its Southampton

home and forced to take refuge on a houseboat, was only a year and a half ahead of contemporary events—which made it reality instead of fantasy. *Books* commented in March 1939 that it was a "story told with straightforwardness, moderation, and above all complete probability." An airplane is the rescuing agent in this romance; in its successor, *An Old Captivity,* dealing with a semi-scientific flight to Greenland, Shute goes with minute and fascinating detail into the incessant care needed to keep this sensitive piece of machinery functioning. He began work on the book just after the Munich crisis, desiring "to write something which could make me forget that there was such a thing as war." When war did arrive, he was assigned to work in the Admiralty. The *New Republic* has said that Shute "knows how to pick astonishing stories and how to keep them moving on non-stop tracks." *Pied Piper* was successfully filmed.

PRINCIPAL WORKS: Marazan, 1926; So Disdained (U.S. title: The Mysterious Aviator) 1928; Lonely Road, 1932; Ruined City (U.S. title: Kindling) 1938; What Happened to the Corbetts (U.S. title: Ordeal) 1939; An Old Captivity, 1940; Landfall, 1940; Pied Piper, 1941.

ABOUT: Book-of-the-Month Club News March 1939; Time October 7, 1940; Wilson Library Bulletin May 1939.

NOYES, ALFRED (September 16, 1880-   ), English poet, was born at Wolverhampton, Staffordshire, the son of Alfred and Amelia Adams (Rowley) Noyes.

Like Swinburne's, his youth was spent by the sea, an easily identifiable influence in much of his later work. He was educated at Exeter College, Oxford, where he was notable chiefly as an oarsman, though he also took some part in undergraduate literary activity. He has honorary doctorates from Yale and from the University of Glasgow. After the university he went to London, and there, with the encouragement of George Meredith, he soon became known as a poet. (Later he was to confound American interviewers by acknowledging that he earned his living by writing poetry—an unknown phenomenon in this country thirty years ago.) His epic, *Drake,* appeared in *Blackwood's Magazine* like a serial novel, and was awaited just as eagerly. Mr. Noyes has never known the years of hardship and frustration common to most poets.

In 1907 he married an American girl, Garnett Daniels (she died in 1926), and in 1913 he made his first visit to this country, to deliver the Lowell Lectures at Harvard. From 1914 to 1923 he was professor of modern English literature at Princeton, with a temporary hiatus in 1916 when he was attached to the British Foreign Office. He had tried to enlist, but poor sight made it impossible, so he used his pen and his voice in his country's service. He was made a Companion of the British Empire in 1918. In 1927 he married for a second time, his wife being Mary (Mayne) Weld-Blundell, a widow. They have a son and two daughters.

About 1925 Mr. Noyes was converted to the Roman Catholic Church, an important event in his literary history, since his religious views have since colored his work very strongly. To his earlier fields as a poet, critic, and novelist, he now added the philosophy of religion, history, and biography strongly tinged with the Catholic viewpoint.

In 1938 his orthodoxy was temporarily brought into question when his life of Voltaire was "found worthy of condemnation" by the Holy Office at Rome. When Noyes publicly resisted the charge a lengthy controversy ensued, and the Holy Office referred the matter to Cardinal Hinsley at Westminster. A special commission set up by him eventually exonerated book and author, with an expression of regret for the "delation," and without asking for alterations in the text, although Noyes had offered to correct any inaccuracies. He did, however, prepare an explanatory preface for the second edition as suggested by the commission. "It happens to be," writes Mr. Noyes of the incident, "one of the few cases in literary history when a book temporarily suspended by the censors has been completely vindicated by their own action."

Before the Second World War, Mr. Noyes revisited the United States several times. In peace his residence is divided between London and his home at St. Lawrence, Isle of Wight, where his recreations are his youthful passions, rowing and swimming, with a later addiction to golf. He is described as being rather tall and sturdy, with thin sandy hair; his air is brisk and his expression serious.

Noyes' play on Robin Hood was produced in London in 1927, and his *Tale of Old Japan*, made from one of his earliest volumes, *The Flower of Old Japan*, was set to music as a cantata by Samuel Coleridge-Taylor and first performed by the Royal Choir Society in 1912. Another poem, "The Immortal Legions," was set to music by Sir Edward Elgar. Aside from individual poems and ballads, perhaps his best known works are *Drake, Tales of the Mermaid Tavern*, and *The Torch Bearers*, an "epic trilogy of scientific discovery." Of the three parts of *The Torch Bearers (The Watchers of the Sky, The Book of the Earth*, and *The Last Voyage)* the opening section, with its wealth of astronomical lore, is generally considered to be the most persuasive.

The late W. C. Jerrald said that Noyes was "gifted alike with the power of seeing and the power of imparting beauty to others," plus what another critic called "the power of narrative in the grand manner." On the other hand, his work has been criticized for being overly facile, didactic, and monotonous. As a staunch traditionalist, deeply concerned with the moral content of his art, he has written in a vein and on a scale that are quite uncharacteristic of the modern school of poets.

PRINCIPAL WORKS: *Poetry*—The Loom of Years, 1902; The Flower of Old Japan, 1903; Poems, 1904; The Forest of Wild Thyme (verse play) 1905; Forty Singing Seamen and Other Poems, 1907; Drake: An English Epic, 1906-08; The Golden Hynde and Other Poems, 1908; The Enchanted Island and Other Poems, 1909; Collected Poems, 1910-27; The Prayer For Peace, 1911; Sherwood: or, Robin Hood and the Three Kings (verse play) 1911; The Carol of the Fir-Tree, 1912; Tales of the Mermaid Tavern, 1913; A Salute for the Fleet and Other Poems, 1915; The New Morning, 1919; The Elfin Artist and Other Poems, 1920; Selected Verse, 1921; The Victory-Ball, 1921; The Watchers of the Sky, 1922; Songs of Shadow-of-a-Leaf and Other Poems, 1924; The Book of the Earth, 1925; Dick Turpin's Ride and Other Poems, 1927; Ballads and Poems, 1928; The Strong City, 1928; The Last Voyage, 1930; Poems, 1931. The Torch Bearers (The Watchers of the Sky, The Book of the Earth, and The Last Voyage, in one vol.) 1937; If Judgment Comes, 1941; Shadows on the Down, 1941. *Miscellaneous*—William Morris, 1908; In Memory of Swinburne, 1909; The Wine-Press: A Tale of War, 1913; Rada (play) 1913; Mystery Ships, 1916; What Is England Doing? 1916; Walking Shadows (short stories) 1918; Beyond the Desert: A Tale of Death Valley, 1920; The Hidden Player (short stories) 1924; Some Aspects of Modern Poetry, 1924; New Essays and American Impressions, 1927; The Opalescent Parrot (essays) 1929; The Sun Cure (novel) 1929; The Return of the Scarecrow (novel) 1929; Tennyson, 1932; The Unknown God, 1934; Voltaire, 1936; Dynamic Religion (with others) 1938; Orchard's Bay, 1939; No Other Man (novel) 1940; Pageant of Letters, 1940.

ABOUT: Jerrald, W. C. Alfred Noyes; Larg, D. G. Alfred Noyes; Ryan, M. Alfred Noyes on Voltaire; Bookman (London) November 1927, January 1929; Catholic World October 1932; Dublin Review October 1938; New Statesman and Nation August 27, 1938; Poet Lore June 1930; Time September 5, 1938; Universe (London) March 31, 1939.

O'BRIEN, EDWARD JOSEPH HARRINGTON (December 10, 1890-February 25, 1941), American editor, anthologist, and

critic, was born in Boston, the son of Michael Francis O'Brien and Minna Gertrude O'Brien. He was educated at Boston College and at Harvard (non-graduate). He was associate editor of the *Poetry Journal* from 1912 to 1915 and of *Poet Lore* in 1914 and 1915. In the latter year he became a reporter on the Boston *Transcript,* and it was while in this position that he first had the idea of evaluating the short stories published in the year before by means of a "stock table" he had invented by which to classify them. The end-result was the first volume of *Best Short Stories,* which continued to appear annually from 1915 through 1940. In 1921 he began an annual collection of British short stories—for the first four years in collaboration with John Cournos.

Mr. O'Brien went to England in 1922 and never lived in the United States again—in fact, many readers thought him to be English and wondered at his inclusive knowledge of American stories! (Incidentally, he himself never wrote a story in his life.) For some years he lived in Switzerland, but in 1937, when he became European Story Editor for the Metro-Goldwyn-Mayer British Studios, Ltd., he moved permanently to London. (He left M-G-M in 1939.) He had besides a house in Gerrards Cross, Bucks., where he was living when he died at the age of fifty.

In 1922 Mr. O'Brien married Romer Wilson,[qv] the novelist. She died in 1930, and in 1932 he married Ruth Gorgel, by whom he had a son and two daughters. After his death it was announced that Mrs. O'Brien would henceforth edit the *Best British Short Stories,* while the American volumes would be taken over by Martha Foley (Mrs. Whit Burnett), co-editor of *Story,* of which Mr. O'Brien was the first and most influential friend, when it was only a mimeographed magazine published in Vienna and Mallorca. It was always the "little," experimental mag-

azines which most interested him, and from which he drew the majority of his chosen stories, though he read annually some 138 magazines, American and English, read 50,000 stories "carefully," and 100,000 more "with sufficient care to see that they were rubbish." Critics frequently disagreed with Mr. O'Brien's selections, and especially with his pontifical way of labeling his favorite stories the "best" of the year, but to appear in his annual collection has long been the goal of every American and British short story writer.

Rather plump, reddish-blond, with a small moustache, Mr. O'Brien liked best to live simply in the country, to go on walking tours, and to add to his large collection of first editions. He said at one time that he first got the idea of an annual collection of short stories from the annual poetry anthologies of W. S. Braithwaite, the Negro critic, who lived in Boston. He was rather a shy and retiring man, and was most at ease in a small group of intimates; he seldom frequented "bohemian" or "literary" circles, and had no vast acquaintance among the authors whose stories he reprinted. The "fondness for the miraculous" which William L. Chemery (editor of *Collier's Weekly*) deprecated in Mr. O'Brien as a critic was personally an engaging trait, which kept his mind always youthfully open and receptive. Stephen Vincent Benét called him "authoritative and well-grounded," and any survey of the twenty-five American anthologies will show that many stories considered *outré* choices when he published them are now virtually classics. As an original writer he was negligible, in poetry merely a competent versifier; his biography of Nietzsche, *Son of the Morning,* has some critical value, however. Besides the volumes listed, he edited many of the English poets and translated Henri Barbusse, Paul Claudel, and other writers from the French.

PRINCIPAL WORKS: The Flowing of the Tide (play) 1910; White Fountains (verse) 1917; The Bloody Fool (play) 1917; The Forgotten Threshold, 1919; Distant Music (verse) 1921; The Advance of the American Short Story, 1923; Hard Sayings, 1927; The Dance of the Machines, 1929; Son of the Morning, 1932. *Edited*—The World's History at a Glance, 1913; Walks and Talks About Boston, 1915; Poems of the Irish Revolutionary Brotherhood, 1917; Best Short Stories, 1915-41; The Masque of Poets, 1918; The Great Modern English Stories, 1919; Best British Short Stories, 1921-40; Modern English Short Stories, 1930; The Twenty-Five Finest Short Stories, 1931; Modern American Short Stories, 1932; New English Short Stories, 1935; The Guest Book, 1935; The Short Story Case Book, 1935; Elizabethan Tales, 1937; The Best American Short Stories 1914-39, 1939.

ABOUT: Literary Digest May 29, 1937; New York Herald Tribune February 26, 1941; Publishers' Weekly March 8, 1941; Saturday Review of Literature June 18, 1938, July 8, 1939.

O'BRIEN, FREDERICK (1869-January 9, 1932),

American journalist and writer of travel books, was born in Baltimore, Md.,  the son of William J. O'Brien, a judge and member of Congress, and Catherine (McCarthy) O'Brien. Frederick O'Brien attended a Jesuit College and a law school in Baltimore; shipped before the mast and on cattle boats to get abroad; and tramped through Brazil, Venezuela, and several West Indian islands. Before his early wanderlust was slaked, he had hoboed through the Western states, slung liquor in a Mississippi levee camp and been made a general in Coxey's Army of the unemployed on its March to Washington. Settling down, after a fashion, to newspaper work, O'Brien was paid $4 a week on Warren Harding's Marion (Ohio) *Star*; wrote editorials for the Columbus *Dispatch*; acted as news editor of the Honolulu *Advertiser* in 1899; edited and published the Manila *Cablenews American*; and in 1903-09 was correspondent for the New York *Herald,* this service including covering the Russo-Japanese war. From 1911 to 1913 O'Brien was the owner of the Riverside (Calif.) *Enterprise* and the Oxnard (Calif.) *Courier.* A fruitful year in the South Seas followed. The resultant book was refused by several publishers and tossed aside until his friend Morgan Shuster of the Century Company happened to hear about it. Published in 1919 as *White Shadows in the South Seas,* this alluring record of lotus-eating and amatory adventures in the Marquesas Islands struck the fancy of a reading public tired of war news and, as Henry Seidel Canby remarked, dissatisfied with the temperate zones. (Authorship of the book, which became an outstanding best-seller, aroused considerable controversy. Mrs. Rose Wilder Lane[qv] lists it among her published works, claiming that she "ghost-wrote" it for O'Brien; he, however, declared that she merely acted as his secretary, and that the original work was entirely his.) *Mystic Isles of the South Seas* detailed similar experiences in Tahiti, and *Atolls of the Sun* has a chapter on the painter Gauguin. During 1918 O'Brien had been assistant chief of education for Herbert Hoover's Food Administration; next year publisher of a newspaper in Manila. He died at sixty-two at his bungalow in Sausalito, Calif., overlooking the Golden Gate. Of unmixed Irish parentage, he "looked race in every line and feature of him," said his friend Michael Monahan.

PRINCIPAL WORKS: White Shadows in the South Seas, 1919; Mystic Isles of the South Seas, 1921; Atolls of the Sun, 1922.

ABOUT: Bookman December 1920; Catholic World May 1933; Publishers' Weekly June 11, 1932.

O'BRIEN, KATE (1898*-),

Irish novelist, was born in Limerick, the daughter of Thomas and Catherine (Thornhill) O'Brien. She was educated at Laurel Hill Convent, Limerick, and at University College, Dublin. For some years she lived in London,  where she was connected with various newspapers and began to write stories and plays. She was known as a playwright before she had written any novels at all—her *Distinguished Villa* was produced in 1926. Her later plays, not published, are *The Ante-Room* (dramatized by her from her novel of the same name, in collaboration with W. A. Carot and Geoffrey Gomer), produced in 1936, and *The Schoolroom Window,* produced in 1937.

Miss O'Brien is unmarried. For a considerable number of years she lived with a friend in Spain, which together with Ireland has formed the background of her novels. At the beginning of the Spanish Civil War she returned to England, and when last heard from was living in London. She is a handsome woman, with a pure, classic profile and smooth hair worn parted in the middle—more Greek in appearance, indeed, than Irish.

Her first novel, *Without My Cloak,* won both the Hawthornden and the John Tait Black Prizes in 1931. In it she first introduced to the public the Irish town of "Mellick," which has been the milieu of her Irish stories ever since. Unlike most contemporary Irish novelists, the people of whom she treats are not workers or peasants, but cultured, middle-class men and women. Her special theme is the conflict between the Puritanism of the dominant church in Ireland and the free, universal spirit of the

* Correction: Date of birth, December 3, 1897.

artist—what Dorothea Brande called "the half-hostile libertarian attitude." To this extent her theme is autobiographical, for obviously she herself is thus divided between the practicing Catholic and the liberally-educated artist.

Even her Spanish background, in *Mary Lavelle,* has Irish affiliations, for its heroine is an Irish governess in Spain. She has never been able to get very far away from her native land, or, indeed, from her native city, for "Mellick" apparently is Limerick. She is almost the only articulate voice of a class and group in Irish society which has been badly neglected by literature in the past.

Her style, which Miss Brande called "steady and expert," and Howard Mumford Jones "solid and fine," is quietly distinguished. She has no eye for melodrama, and the conflicts in her stories take place within the human heart. It has been remarked that if her novels are a faithful reflection of the society of which they treat, then Ireland must be the last home of witty, literate conversation, for her characters talk like people out of George Meredith or George Moore. She has published, besides her novels, a travel-book in which she bade what she felt was an eternal farewell to her beloved Spain. If circumstances favorable to her kind of writing ever again return to England, Kate O'Brien will be a name to be reckoned with.

PRINCIPAL WORKS: Distinguished Villa (play) 1927; Without My Cloak, 1931; The Ante-Room, 1934; Mary Lavelle, 1936; Farewell, Spain, 1937; Pray for the Wanderer, 1938; The Land of Spices, 1941.

O'CASEY, SEAN (1884?*-   ), Irish dramatist, writes: "Born in the beginning of the 'eighties in Lower Dorset Street, Dublin.

Pinchot

Father, a Limerick man, mother, a Wicklow woman. Youngest of a fairly large family. Went to school for about three years but really began to try to teach myself all I wanted to know when I was thirteen years of age. Taught myself from the old books left behind by my brothers and sisters when they had finished going to school. Found it a hard job; but stuck to it, and, with the aid of an old *Walker's Dictionary,* taught myself to read and write fairly well. Picked up out of the old school books hints on grammar and other things, and in four years

gave myself a better education than any I would have received had I gone to school. Became interested in literature through the purchase of second-hand books in Dublin shops — works of Shakespeare, Milton Byron, Scott, Burns, Shelley, Keats and others.

"First job in an iron-mongery and hardware store, where I worked ten hours a day for four shillings a week. Rose to be a kind of despatch clerk after two years, got seven shillings a week, and chucked the job. Began at the age of eighteen to work as a laborer, and continued in that way for years. Got interested in the Irish National Movement, and joined the Gaelic League and learned the Irish language. The National Club started a dramatic class, and I wrote a play for them. They couldn't do it, so it was sent to the Abbey Theatre. The play was rejected by the Abbey. Wrote two more which were also refused. Wrote a fourth, *The Shadow of a Gunman,* which was accepted and produced in 1923. This was followed by *Cathleen Listens In,* 1923; *Juno and the Paycock,* 1924; *Nannie's Night Out,* 1924; *The Plough and the Stars,* 1926. *The Silver Tassie* was produced in London in 1929, having first been rejected by the Abbey Theatre, the rejection resulting in a public controversy over the technique and quality of the play. Some years after, the play was done by the Abbey.

"I came to England in 1926, and am now living in Devon. I married Eileen Reynolds (stage name Eileen Carey) in 1928, and have two sons. My only literary preference is the preference for good over bad stuff. Political convictions: I stand by all democratic activities, and am a Communist. Influences: All fine writers in English and Irish."

* * *

One reason for O'Casey's lack of formal schooling was not only his family's poverty (his father died when he was a small child), but also a painful and intractable eye disease from which he suffered. In spite of the heavy manual labor he has done, he is not robust and has been a semi-invalid for much of his life. His favorite recreation, he says, is "anything except work!" He dresses carelessly, is tall and loose-limbed, with dreamy eyes behind thick glasses. The production of *The Plough and the Stars* was marked by riots in Dublin, largely because O'Casey, of a Protestant family though Irish by birth and ancestry, was considered unsympathetic to the Irish character. Nevertheless he took an active part in the Sinn Fein movement

* Correction: Year of birth, 1880.

and the Easter Rebellion; he was an organizer of the Irish Citizen Army. He was also an organizer for the Irish Transport Workers' Union in the great strike of 1913.

"A playwright with strong, distinguished talents who treats his art with honest intelligence," Florence Dodman called him. Joseph Wood Krutch commented on his "extraordinary gift for a racy dialogue and malicious wit," but objected that "his plays lack form and purpose." Richard Watts of the New York *Herald Tribune* termed *Juno and the Paycock* (which received the Hawthornden Prize in 1926) "just about the richest comic creation since the days of Shakespeare." He himself considers his plays tragedies, though they have usually been played as comedies. His *The Star Turns Red* (produced in 1939) is avowedly anti-Fascist propaganda.

PRINCIPAL WORKS: The Story of the Citizen Army, 1919; Two Plays: Juno and the Paycock, Shadow of a Gunman, 1925; The Plough and the Stars, 1926; The Silver Tassie, 1928; Within the Gates, 1934; I Knock at the Door (autobiography) 1939; The Star Turns Red, 1940; Purple Dust, 1940; Pictures in the Hallway (autobiography) 1942.

ABOUT: Byrne, D. Ireland's National Theatre; Gwynn, S. Irish Literature and Drama; Malone, A. E. The Irish Drama; O'Casey, S. I Knock at the Door, Pictures in the Hallway; Canadian Forum April 1930; Catholic World December 1929, January 1930; Commonweal October 11, 1935, February 14, 1936; English Studies No. 1, 1930; Living Age November 3, 1934; Nation December 21, 1927, April 25, 1934; Nineteenth Century August and September 1928; North American Review June 1927; Revue des Deux Mondes June 1, 1935; Theatre Arts Monthly June 1925.

ODETS, CLIFFORD (July 18, 1906-), American playwright, was born in Philadelphia, the son of Louis and Pearl (Geisinger)

Odets (originally Odet), Jewish immigrants from Lithuania. He was reared for the most part in the Bronx, New York, though his parents later moved back to Philadelphia and for a while he rejoined them there. He attended Morris High School, New York, but left in his third year, at fifteen, to go into radio work, as actor, announcer, and writer. After a struggle with his family, who wanted him to engage in some sort of business (his father was a printer who gradually became prosperous), he fought his way as an actor from small stock companies to occasional

minor parts with the Theatre Guild in 1928. With a few of the Guild actors who wanted to try out experimental plays, he helped to found the Group Theatre in 1930, and went with the Group to Brookfield Center, Connecticut, to rehearse his bit in *The House of Connelly*, the Group's first production. In 1932 he was understudy for Luther Adler in John Howard Lawson's *Success Story*.

It was 1933 before Odets finished his first play, *Awake and Sing*, which the Group liked but thought too risky, from a financial standpoint, to produce. Marking time, Odets heard of a New Theatre League one-act play contest, locked himself in a hotel room in Boston, where he was touring with the Group company, and emerged with *Waiting for Lefty*. Based on the 1934 New York cab strike, the action is laid in a union hall where taxi drivers are taking a strike vote. With its flash-backs showing the workers' lives and its tremendous climax, *Waiting for Lefty* created something of a sensation when it was awarded the prize and presented at the New Theatre League on Sunday nights. The Left acclaimed Odets for the exciting revolutionary implications of his theme; the critics hailed him as the most promising young playwright of his generation.

Riding on the wave of this enthusiasm, the Group decided to take a chance on *Awake and Sing*, which opened on February 19, 1935, to be followed shortly by Group productions of *Waiting for Lefty* and *Till the Day I Die*, an unsuccessful anti-Nazi play. All three plays ran simultaneously for a while on Broadway, and Odets "was arousing more discussion in theatrical circles than any man since Eugene O'Neill."

Awake and Sing, which was successfully revived in 1939, remains Odets' best play. Harold Clurman said that it is "about real people struggling humbly with their everyday problems; it is tragic in the sense that we are led to see that these problems are almost life-or-death matters; it is comic in the sense that the manner in which these problems present themselves . . . is so amazingly casual and haphazard in relation to their fundamental significance."

The Group Theatre, however, was still in financial difficulties, and for its sake Mr. Odets swallowed his prejudices and went to Hollywood, whence he sent back much of the money he received for writing screen plays, best known of which was *The General Died at Dawn*. It was there he met the Viennese actress Luise Rainer, whom he married in 1937. Their dual careers made the marriage a stormy one; Miss Rainer sued for divorce in 1938, they were reconciled and again parted, and the decree was granted in May 1940.

Mr. Odets now lives in New York, where his chief recreation is the playing of his huge library of symphonic phonograph records. Still young, tall, with curly hair and "expensive, sloppy clothes," he has unbounded confidence in himself and in his future: "I am the most talented young playwright in the business." His economic opinions are still decidedly to the left; he calls himself "some kind of Socialist." In 1935 he was deported from Cuba, where he had gone to investigate the dictator Machado. Those who hailed him as the "white hope" of "proletarian drama" have been a bit disconcerted by some of his later plays. He has had bad failures—all his later plays, in fact, except *Golden Boy*, one of his least distinguished efforts, have been boxoffice failures—and more important, he has never again achieved the compassionate brilliance of *Awake and Sing* or the intensity of *Waiting for Lefty*. He is no longer compared, as he was once, with Chekhov, or even with Sean O'Casey.

But there is no doubt of what one critic called "his rich, compassionate, angry feeling for people, his tremendous dramatic punch, his dialogue as bracing as ozone." As Otis Ferguson said, " he has the right eye . . . and theatrical genius. . . . He has tapped a source of homely poetry in Jewish family life." Indeed, it has been remarked more than once that even his characters supposed to be American or Italian speak in the very accents of the Bronx. It was largely for this reason that Edith J. R. Isaacs called him "the most subjective of playwrights," with "an imagination bounded by his experience." He himself has expressed his own dramatic credo: "All plays, just like all literature, are essentially propaganda. . . . My problem and business in the world is to present truth dramatically, appealingly, and entertainingly."

PRINCIPAL WORKS: (*dates of production*) Waiting for Lefty, 1935; Awake and Sing, 1935; Till the Day I Die, 1935; Paradise Lost, 1935; Golden Boy, 1937; Rocket to the Moon, 1938; Night Music, 1940. Three Plays (published) 1935; Six Plays (published) 1939; Clash by Night, 1941 (published 1942).

ABOUT: American Magazine October 1936; Commonweal June 10, December 16, 1938; Current Biography 1941; New Republic May 29, 1935, September 27, October 4, 1939; New York Times Magazine March 31, 1940; Theatre Arts Monthly April 1939; Time December 5, 1938; Wilson Library Bulletin February 1937.

O'DONNELL, PEADAR (1896*-), Irish novelist, was born in Tirconnaill, in Northwest Ireland, the ancient seat of the O'Donnells, last of the Gaelic chieftains to resist the English. After being graduated from St. Patrick's, Dublin, he became a teacher in the Aran Islands, off Galway, made famous by John Millington Synge. By 1916 he had a post on Aranmore (Inishmore),  largest of these islands inhabited by farmers and fishermen. His interest in the families of his pupils led him into concern for their hard life and thence into the labor movement. When the Irish Civil War started he was ripe for Sinn Fein. He was a member of the celebrated "Flying Column," which harassed and fled from the Black and Tans; in 1921 he was severely wounded and nearly captured. From 1922 to 1934 he was a member of the Executive of the Irish Republican Army. In 1927, already the author of two novels, he was finally jailed, and during his imprisonment underwent a forty-one-day hunger strike. He was in and out of prison a dozen times before "the trouble" ended.

With the establishment of the Irish Free State, Mr. O'Donnell was able to devote himself to his career as a writer and teacher; he is now professor of English at Trinity College, Dublin, where he lives. He is a member of the Irish Royal Academy of Letters. He is married, and he and his wife were in Spain at the time the Franco revolution began. Though he is a practicing Catholic, the book he wrote on his experiences shows that his sympathies were largely on the side of the Loyalists, at least in the beginning; he was struck particularly by the difference in the attitude of the church in Spain and in Ireland.

Mr. O'Donnell says truly that he knows "peasant Ireland around the coast as no other person in Ireland knows it." He is the spokesman of the inarticulate and downbeaten peasant, and indignation and angry pity are the motivating forces behind all his novels. The mark of what he has undergone is on his brooding face, and tragedy is implicit in nearly everything he writes. He would like to write, and some day may write, a history of Ireland since 1830 from the viewpoint of its peasantry. But he knows the lower middle class of Dublin too, and can depict its reactions to the turmoil of the past forty years. He thinks of himself as being a writer only "by accident," since he felt that nobody had yet spoken in the authentic voice of the landless peasants among whom he had lived and whose champion he was.

He is intense and high-strung, full of nervous energy, which he can no longer sublimate by strenuous physical activity, as in the days when he was "on the run," or still earlier when, traveling daily by boat to his school, he was known for his reckless daring on the water. His style has the rhythm of the Gaelic tongue, which he knows well. Not so well known outside of Ireland as he should be, he may be expected to produce in the future books as rich in feeling as those of the past, even though softened and mellowed by maturity.

PRINCIPAL WORKS: Storm, 1925; Islanders (in America: The Way It Was With Them) 1927; Adrigoole, 1928; There Will Be Fighting (in America: The Knife) 1930; The Gates Flew Open, 1932; Wrack (play) 1933; On the Edge of the Stream, 1934; Salud: An Irishman in Spain (nonfiction) 1937.

ABOUT: Nineteenth Century December 1936.

OEMLER, Mrs. MARIE (CONWAY)
(May 29, 1879-June 6, 1932), American novelist and short-story writer, was born in

Savannah, Ga., the daughter of Richard Hoban Conway and Helena (Browne) Conway. She attended a convent and private school, but received her chief education at home. Marie Conway at twenty-two married John Norton Oemler of Savannah, and lived the pleasant life of a Southern hostess until she·began to write in her late thirties. Slippy McGee (1917) did not have at first any unprecedented success, but sales began to pick up after word had spread that an entertaining novel about a crook (Slippy McGee) had appeared. The novel is an appealing blend of Alias Jimmy Valentine, Freckles, and the Bishop's candlesticks episode from Les Misérables.

Mrs. Oemler's most ambitious and thoroughly creditable effort is The Holy Lover, her novel about John Wesley and his experiences as Secretary of Indian Affairs for Oglethorpe and his Georgian colony. The novel "disguises none of his dour and narrow unattractiveness," and quotes liberally from Wesley's own journal. Mrs. Oemler

was a frequent contributor of stories to the Century, the Woman's Home Companion, and other magazines; most of them are collected in Sheaves. She died of heart disease at fifty-three at the Baker Sanatorium, Charleston, S.C.

PRINCIPAL WORKS: Slippy McGee, 1917; Purple Heights, 1920; Where the Young Child Was and Other Christmas Stories, 1921; Two Shall Be Born, 1922; Woman Named Smith, 1922; His Wife-in-Law, 1925; Shepards, 1926; The Holy Lover, 1927; Sheaves, 1928; Johnny Reb, 1929; Flower of Thorn, 1931.

ABOUT: Century Company, Marie Conway Oemler; Overton, G. The Women Who Make Our Novels.

O'FAOLÁIN, SÉAN (February 22, 1900-), Irish novelist and biographer, was born in Dublin. He gives his parents' names

as Denis Whelan and Bridget Murphy. He was educated at the National University of Ireland and at Harvard, from both of which he has a master of arts degree; he himself says that his education has been "mainly by good conversation." He

was a Commonwealth Fellow in America from 1926 to 1928, and a John Harvard Fellow in the following year.

He was a lecturer in English at Boston College in 1929, then went to England and from 1929 to 1933 taught at St. Mary's College, Strawberry Hill, Middlesex. He then returned to Ireland, and until his success as a novelist enabled him to live by writing he taught in County Wicklow. He was married in 1928 and has a daughter; his wife, Eileen O'Faoláin, has published some Irish stories for children. He now lives in Dublin. He is a charter member of the Irish Royal Academy of Letters, and besides his own work has edited the lyrics and satires of Thomas Moore (1929) and the autobiography of Theobald Wolfe Tone (1937); he is also editor and translator of The Silver Branch (1938), an anthology of Irish lyrics.

Indeed, Séan O'Faoláin's first writing was done in Gaelic, though this was an acquired and not his native tongue. The Irish Revolution, in which he took an active part in spite of his youth, interrupted his studies and is reflected in much of his work, notably in "The Patriot." He looks rather like a schoolmaster of a past era, with his trimmed beard and his glasses; at heart, however, he is a poet (who never writes verse), and says that his chief recreation is daydreaming! He attracted wide attention first by *A Nest of Simple Folk,* an idyllic book which exemplified what Malcom Cowley has called his "power of suggestion and vague evocation." Best known of his several biographical works is his fine biography of the great Irish patriot, Daniel O'Connell.

In his later novels, Mr. O'Faoláin has never quite duplicated the success of *A Nest of Simple Folk,* and he is gradually becoming better known as a biographer than as a novelist. A tendency to repeat himself is, indeed, his chief defect as a writer. His short stories, however, which appear frequently in British magazines, have kept up his reputation as an author of fiction; he knows Irish life thoroughly, especially on its lower social levels, and in spite of a tendency to discursiveness he has a gift for sharp characterization and for atmosphere. He has written one play, but it was not very successful, and his quiet, almost absent-minded style is essentially undramatic. On the rare occasions where he does depict tense situations, the contrast lends vividness to the portrayal.

PRINCIPAL WORKS: *Fiction*—Midsummer Night Madness and Other Stories, 1932; A Nest of Simple Folk 1933; There's a Birdie in the Cage, 1935; A Born Genius, 1936; Bird Alone, 1936; A Purse of Coppers (short stories) 1937; Come Back to Erin, 1940; The Great O'Neill, 1942. *Miscellaneous*—Life Story of De Valera, 1933; Constance Markievicz, 1934; King of the Beggars: A Life of Daniel O'Connell, 1938; She Had To Do Something (play) 1938; An Irish Journey, 1940.

ABOUT: Commonweal December 8, 1939; New Republic February 15, 1939; Wilson Library Bulletin March 1934.

O'FLAHERTY, LIAM (1897-), Irish novelist, was born in the Aran Islands, off County Galway, and educated at Rockwell College, Black Rock College (where he formed a company of Irish Volunteers), and at the National University, in Dublin. Although he was originally intended for the priesthood, his bent was for a martial career. Despairing of getting action as an Irish Nationalist, he joined the Irish Guards in 1915 and saw service in Belgium, where he was shellshocked and discharged in 1917. He returned to Ireland to find himself in the midst of civil war. With a

small "army" he held the Rotunda in Dublin for a week, hoisting the red flag over it. In 1918 he went to London, and after a few months' work in a brewery and a vain attempt to go on the stage, he shipped as a trimmer in a ship bound for Rio de Janeiro. For three years he was a seaman, trimmer, or stoker, and covered the whole world, living for some time in the Bowery in New York, and working in a tire factory in Hartford, Conn.

He started writing in 1921, but he has never used as his fictional background any of the stirring experiences of his years at sea or abroad; his scene is always the Aran Islands or lower-class Dublin. As C. Henry Warren remarked, "all O'Flaherty's best writing seems to have as its theme . . . the hounding of men. In war and revolution, by the law: in civil life, by poverty." His stories lend themselves well to dramatization and especially to the screen, as those who saw *The Informer* or *The Puritan* will realize. His field is, to quote William Troy, "the melodrama of the soul."

Unmarried, he lives for the most part in Dublin, with a cottage in his native Aran Islands. He is lean, wiry, fairish in coloring, with pointed ears and a sharp nose, looking, as someone has remarked, "like a refined and virile gangster." He plays as thoroughly as he works, is something of a spendthrift, and still has about him a hint of his untamed youth. A great talker in both senses of the adjective, his resonant voice can be heard for six city blocks. It is not surprising that his favorite contemporary author is Ernest Hemingway.

William Troy noted that O'Flaherty's "qualities of language and perception are essentially of a poetic order." His old friend Seán O'Faoláin added: "Wonder is his weapon and folly is his enemy. . . . One feels that O'Flaherty writes in a kind of fury. . . . He has more blemishes and more faults than any living writer of his rank and he surmounts them all. . . . He is an inverted romantic." All this is true of his novels alone; in what O'Faoláin called "his lovely short stories," the adventurer succumbs to the poet, and "he is at rest." He is capable of writing pure idylls in this shorter form, whereas in his novels there is a sort of frenzied, half-mystical realism that at times recalls the struggles of Dostoievsky's tortured heroes. As one critic said, he has "a gift for infusing . . . dirt, ugliness, diseases, naked human misery with a kind of wild and perilous beauty."

PRINCIPAL WORKS: Thy Neighbour's Wife, 1924; The Black Soul, 1925; Spring Sowing (short stories) 1926; The Informer, 1926; The Tent and Other Stories, 1926; The Martyr, 1927; Life of Tim Healy (biography) 1927; The Assassin, 1928; Tourist's Guide to Ireland, 1929; The Fairy Goose and Other Stories, 1929; The House of Gold, 1929; Two Years (autobiography) 1930; I Went to Russia (non-fiction) 1931; The Puritan, 1932; Skerrett, 1932; The Wild Swan and Other Stories, 1932; Shame the Devil, 1934; Hollywood Cemetery, 1935; The Short Stories of Liam O'Flaherty, 1937; Famine, 1937.

ABOUT: O'Flaherty, L. Two Years; Bookman (London) January 1930: London Mercury December 1937; Nuova Antologia September 16, 1934; Revue des Deux Mondes June 15, 1934.

O'HARA, JOHN (January 31, 1905-), American novelist and short story writer, was born in Pottsville, Pa., the eldest of eight children of Pat-

rick Henry O'Hara and Katharine Elizabeth (D e l a n e y) O'Hara; his father was a physician of more than local fame. Brought up as a Catholic, O'Hara was educated at Fordham Preparatory School, the Keystone State Normal School, and Niagara Preparatory School, Niagara, N.Y., from which he was graduated in 1924, after having managed to get himself expelled from the first two institutions. His father's death prevented his going to Yale, for which he had passed examinations. He has worked in innumerable occupations—as an evaluating engineer, ship steward, railroad freight clerk, gas meter reader, guard in an amusement park, laborer in a steel mill, soda clerk, and press agent; once he was secretary to Heywood Broun. Most of these jobs lasted only a short time, and much of the time he lived from hand to mouth. His newspaper career has been equally varied: he was a reporter on two Pennsylvania papers, then went to New York and worked on the *Mirror*, the *Morning Telegraph*, and the *Herald Tribune*, covering everything from churches to sports. He has been movie critic of the *Morning Telegraph*, football editor of the *New Yorker*, and has worked for *Time* and for *Editor and Publisher*. He was briefly editor-in-chief of the Pittsburgh *Bulletin-Index*.

Since 1934 he has been a screen writer, working in succession for four of the largest companies. It is apparent, therefore, that he has plenty of background for his pictures of contemporary urban life. He was married to Helen Ritchie Petit in 1931, divorced, and married to Belle Mulford Wylie in

1937; he has no children. He lives in New York, in a duplex apartment close to his favorite night club, "21," and makes frequent excursions to Hollywood. At present he conducts the amusement department of *Newsweek*.

O'Hara wrote the opening 25,000 words of his first novel in a furnished room in New York, using his bed as a desk. When he had only $3 left, he sent identical letters to three New York publishers asking for a subsidy to finish his book. Harcourt, Brace & Co. was sufficiently impressed by the letter and the incomplete manuscript to keep him in board and lodging for three months. The resulting publication, *Appointment in Samarra,* was an immediate success.

Critics have been busy trying to find Mr. O'Hara's derivations; they have decided that he stems from either F. Scott Fitzgerald, Ernest Hemingway, or Joseph Hergesheimer, or from all three. He has been called the "voice of the hangover generation" since 1929, and Edmund Wilson pointed out shrewdly that he has a positive hatred of the generation before his. Wilson called him "primarily a social commentator; and in this field of social habits and manners . . . he has done work that is original and interesting. . . . He has explored for the first time from his peculiar, semi-snobbish point of view a great deal of interesting territory." Henry Seidel Canby granted him superb craftsmanship but said there was "no satire in his seeing. . . . His concern is with the surfaces he does so well." John Peale Bishop said "his plots have mechanical perfection [but his people] merely react . . . to certain stimuli. . . . These are the lost people; they are below moral condemnation." Wolcott Gibbs, his greatest admirer, noted that he "focuses intensely on people" and is impatient with anything except taut realism.

It is generally agreed that his short stories are superior to his novels; Edmund Wilson said that "his long stories always sound like first drafts which might be turned into very fine little novels," and that, "gifted with a clean and sure style," he is the "outstanding master of the *New Yorker* short-story-sketch." His *Pal Joey* sketches (1940), about night-club life and people, were only moderately successful as a book but became a "smash hit" musical comedy in 1941 and a high-priced commodity for Hollywood.

Blond, blunt-featured, "authentically hating waste and hypocrisy," often cruel, always brilliant, a specialist in four-letter words, with a sharp ear and memory, O'Hara has been called the Boswell of the "post-Scott Fitzgerald-era." He is now approaching middle age; but, unlike Fitzgerald, he seems to have kept unimpaired his will-to-write. He disclaims any interest in posterity and says of himself caustically, "Being a cheap, ordinary guy, I have an instinct for what an ordinary guy likes."

PRINCIPAL WORKS: Appointment in Samarra, 1934; The Doctor's Son and Other Stories, 1935; Butterfield 8, 1935; Hope of Heaven, 1938; Files on Parade (short stories) 1939; Pal Joey, 1940.

ABOUT: New Republic November 11, 1940; New York Times, January 26, 1941; New York Times Book Review May 26, 1940. Saturday Review of Literature February 19, 1938, September 23, 1939; Virginia Quarterly Review January 1937.

"O. HENRY." See HENRY, O.

O'HIGGINS, HARVEY JERROLD (November 14, 1876-February 28, 1929), American novelist and short-story writer, was

born in London, Ont., Canada, the son of Joseph P. O'Higgins and Isabella (Stephenson) O'Higgins. He attended public schools and the University of Toronto from 1893 to 1897, leaving without a degree to work on the Toronto *Star* and the New York *Globe*. He abandoned newspaper work in 1901 to launch out as a free-lance magazine writer, and that same year married Anna G. Williams of Toronto. *Scribner's,* the *Century, McClure's* and *Collier's* accepted his stories and articles about various Irish types, denizens of the great cities, especially New York. A series of articles on the Burns detective agency made fictional reappearance in the *Adventures of Detective Barney,* which was notable for introducing the only believable boy-detective to appear in print. O'Higgins excelled at showing "the romance of the average." He was singularly fortunate in his collaborators. With Judge Ben B. Lindsey of Denver he wrote *The Beast and the Jungle,* a comprehensive study of city-bred youth which attracted much attention; and with Harriet Ford, an actress of experience, he wrote several melodramas, notably *The Argyle Case, Mr. Lazarus,* and *The Dummy,* the last a dramatization of one of the *Detective Barney* stories which introduced the actor Ernest Truex to New York audiences in

the title rôle. After a serious illness he collaborated with Dr. Edward Hiram Reede, his psychiatrist, in *The American Mind in Action.* With Miss Ford he also dramatized Sinclair Lewis' *Main Street,* produced at the National Theatre, New York, in 1921.

O'Higgins served as associate chairman of the Committee on Public Information in Washington, 1917-18; even here, as Heywood Broun remarked, his style remained durable as well as decorative. Broun, who required frequent "clarification" himself, called O'Higgins "the literary pioneer of America in adopting the teachings of Freud and his modifiers for the purpose of the study of American character"—particularly in the studies of such types as a political boss, a murderess, a prison reformer, and a motion picture director (all imaginary) in *Some Distinguished Americans.* A critic remarked that there was "a little too much Freud, maybe" in *Julie Cane,* his most successful novel. His posthumously published Detective Duff stories also used the psychological method. O'Higgins' last completed article before his death at fifty-two from pneumonia was "Alias Walt Whitman," published in *Harper's* for May 1929, a frank study of Whitman as homosexual and narcissist. *Harper's* spoke of "the unfailing distinction of his work and the integrity and friendly warmth of his character." O'Higgins was a member of and worker for the Authors' League from its inception until his death.

PRINCIPAL WORKS: The Smoke Eaters, 1905; Don-a-Dreams, 1906; A Grand Army Man, 1908; Old Clinkers, 1909; The Beast and the Jungle (with B. B. Lindsey) 1910; Under the Prophet in Utah (with F. J. Cannon) 1911; Polygamy, 1914; Silent Sam, 1914; Adventures of Detective Barney, 1915; From the Life, 1919; The Secret Springs, 1920; Some Distinguished Americans, 1922; Julie Cane, 1924; Clara Barron, 1926; Detective Duff Unravels It, 1929. Plays—(with H. Ford) The Argyle Case, 1912; The Dummy, 1913; Mr. Lazarus, 1916; On the Hiring Line, 1919.

ABOUT: Mantle, B. American Playwrights of Today; Bookman October 1921; Current Opinion October 1914; Harper's April 1929; New York Times March 1, 1929.

OLDFIELD, CLAUDE HOUGHTON

(1889-), English novelist who writes as "Claude Houghton," reports: "I was born at Sevenoaks, Kent, the youngest child of George Sargent Oldfield, a Yorkshireman, and Elizabeth Harriet (Thomas) Oldfield, from southern England. I was educated at Dulwich College, but left when I was seventeen, and was articled to a firm of chartered accountants [the equivalent of the American certified public accountant].

Five years later I took my degree. On the outbreak of the war I was rejected on the grounds of poor eyesight. I obtained a position in the Admiralty, and traveled a fair amount. After the war, I was given a permanent position. I began to write when I was in articles. I wrote verse, which was rejected everywhere for years, then G. K. Chesterton published my sonnets and lyrics regularly in the *New Witness*. Soon

after the war (1920) I married Dulcie Benson, an actress who had appeared in a number of West End plays, with Henry Ainley and other well-known actors. We have a cottage in the Chiltern Hills, and often take a flat in London for a time. And we have gone abroad whenever we could.

"Balzac, Flaubert, and the French poets have most influenced me; also the great Russian novelists, and Swedenborg, Boehme, and Blake. I owe a lot to well-known writers for help given long before I had met them personally. A full list would be too long, but I shall mention Sir Hugh Walpole, Clemence Dane. Phyllis Bentley, Compton Mackenzie, J. B. Priestley, James Hilton; and the late Arnold Bennett. Also, I owe much to the late president of Czecho-Slovakia, Masaryk, who liked my work. Six novels of mine have been translated into Czech, and in 1936 I visited Czecho-Slovakia as the guest of the government. [Other novels have also been translated into French, Dutch, Danish, and Swedish.]

"As to likes, I like reading in bed. And I like wandering about abroad, especially when I have just finished a book. I like walking in the country, and horse riding, when I get a chance. And I love talking to people whose jobs, or experiences, are widely different from mine. There are about twenty plays I could always see with delight. I like dawn, and the dead of night, in great cities.

"As to dislikes, I dislike being late for appointments—and forgetting things, and getting 'fussed' about my work. I loathe being tired. I dislike noise and crowds. And I'm not very keen on being misquoted, or being told how much I owe to some writer I've never read. And I certainly do not like rows, unless they are constructive. That's about all."

* * *

Mr. Oldfield has dark eyes, brown wavy hair, and strong, aquiline features. He is essentially mystical in his approach to life, and his novels are all posited on the thesis that modern civilization will collapse "because it no longer believes it has a destiny." He sees his work as "character drama projected on a sensational background." To quote Geoffrey West, his work is "a profoundly imaginative spiritual autobiography. . . . For lack of a revelation he sees the world falling faster and faster into destructive chaos." Francis McDermott remarks that he has "a poetic, original, and deeply intellectual mind, a vivid and virile personality intensely absorbed in the spiritual qualities of life.... His dominant quality is his intensity." Graham Sutton speaks of his "almost Dostoievskian range." Together with his metaphysical approach he has brilliant wit, spontaneity, and richness of invention. His weaknesses are a tendency to rhetoric, to language "just a little too consciously exalted," and a complexity that sometimes tortures his narrative.

PRINCIPAL WORKS: *Fiction*—Neighbors, 1926; The Riddle of Helena, 1927; Crisis, 1929; A Hair Divides, 1931; Chaos Is Come Again, 1932; Julian Grant Loses His Way, 1933; Three Fantastic Tales (short stories) 1934; I Am Jonathan Scrivener, 1934; This Was Ivor Trent, 1935; The Beast (short stories) 1936; Christina, 1936; Strangers, 1938; Hudson Rejoins the Herd, 1939; Captain of the Guard, 1940; All Change, Humanity! 1942. *Miscellaneous*—The Phantom Host (verse) 1917; The Tavern of Dreams (verse) 1919; Judas (verse play) 1922; In the House of the High Priest (verse play) 1923; The Kingdoms of the Spirit (essays) 1924.

ABOUT: Bookman (London) November 1932; Catholic World November 1931; Wilson Library Bulletin May 1938.

OLIVER, GEORGE. See ONIONS, O.

*OLIVER, JOHN RATHBONE (January 4, 1872-   ), American author, clergyman, and psychiatrist, was born in Albany, N.Y.,

the son of General Robert Shaw Oliver, who was commissioned an officer in the Civil War while a freshman at Harvard and was later a captain of cavalry in the Far West. His mother was Marion Lucy (Rathbone) Oliver. Young Oliver

Bachrach

attended the schools of Albany till thirteen, then went to St. Paul's, Concord, N.H., leaving at seventeen to spend two years abroad, where he studied the piano in Germany. He had passed the Harvard entrance examinations before leaving America. At Harvard Oliver was a member of the Institute of 1770, the Signet, and Hasty Pudding clubs, edited the *Harvard Monthly,* was class poet, and graduated in 1894 *summa cum laude,* with distinction in English and the classics. Three years followed as master at St. Paul's. Ordained a priest of the Protestant Episcopal Church in 1900, Oliver was curate of St. Mark's Church, Philadelphia, Pa., resigning in 1903. He was restored to orders in 1927, the year prior to publication of his *Victim and Victor,* a novel which nearly won the Pulitzer prize. Of this book Ernest Sutherland Bates wrote: "The author's tender humanity redeems what would otherwise be an impossible book. The thesis of the priest-physician is permitted to oust the living characters." The novel is the story of Michael Mann, an unfrocked priest of the Church of England who is denied restitution to his orders, but is redeemed by parishioners whom he restored to mental health.

During the First World War Oliver was a surgeon in the Austrian Army in 1914-15; he had taken a medical course at Innsbruck in the Austrian Tyrol. Returning to America, he became a psychiatrist at the Phipps Psychiatric Clinic, under Professor Adolf Meyer. From 1917 to 1930 he was chief medical officer to the Supreme Bench of Baltimore; his experiences here are described in detail in the autobiographical *Foursquare* (1929) and to some extent in *Pastoral Psychiatry and Mental Health* (1932), which lays some stress on what Dr. Oliver prefers to call homerotism. (He received the Ph.D. degree from Johns Hopkins in 1927, and is a warden of the university's Alumni Memorial Hall.) Unmarried, Dr. Oliver is a member of the staff of clergymen of Mount Cavalry Church, Baltimore. He has a private practice as psychiatrist. *Fear* (1927) is a case-history in the form of a novel. Dr. J. S. Wile commented in regard to *The Ordinary Difficulties of Everyday People* (1935) that "Dr. Oliver has succeeded in combining the best and worst features of the priest and the psychiatrist." The book discusses emotional difficulties and the disadvantages of old age.

PRINCIPAL WORKS: The Good Shepherd, 1915 (revised ed. 1932); The Six-Pointed Cross in the Dust, 1917; Fear: The Autobiography of James Edwards, 1927; Victim and Victor, 1928; Foursquare: The Story of a Fourfold Life, 1930; Rock and Sand, 1931; Article Thirty-Two, 1931; Pastoral Psychiatry and Mental Health, 1932; Tomorrow's Faith, 1932; Priest or Pagan, 1933; The Ordinary Difficulties of Everyday People, 1935.

ABOUT: Harvard College, Class of 1894: Twenty-Fifth and Fortieth Annual Reports; Oliver, J. R. Foursquare.

*OLIVIER, EDITH (1879?-), English novelist and biographer, was born in the rectory at Wilton, near Salisbury, one of the ten children of Canon Dacres Olivier. Her forebears were French Huguenots who had been in England for several generations. Canon Olivier was a benevolent but inflexible autocrat, with perfect manners, who ruled his parish, as he ruled

his family, with a rod of iron. Every day in the Olivier household followed the same precise schedule. Edith Olivier was taught by her mother; had her first governess at twelve; and, as she grew older, "trained the choir, conducted the choral society, managed the girls' club, acted in private theatricals." (She used to say that if she died without meeting Arthur Walkley, dramatic critic of the London *Times,* that she would have lived in vain. Walkley died without this meeting taking place; hence the title of Miss Olivier's sprightly autobiography, *Without Knowing Mr. Walkley.*) Her education continued with four terms, not consecutive ones, at St. Hugh's Hall, Oxford University, on a Bishop Wordsworth scholarship. It was Cosmo Lang, later Archbishop of Canterbury, who persuaded her father to allow this departure from the home nest. At Oxford, Miss Olivier occasionally dined with "Lewis Carroll" (Charles Lutwidge Dodgson), who seldom mentioned *Alice's Adventures in Wonderland.* Dodgson died in January 1898; his dinner-guest was probably at least eighteen, which approximately fixes the birth-date she resolutely refuses to reveal. (She writes: "I am horrified to discover how much older I am than most writers. I seem to be completely out of date.")

During the First World War, Miss Olivier was an officer in the Women's Land Army in Wiltshire. Her first book, *The Love Child,* was published in 1927. The idea came to her in the night, and she sat up and wrote four chapters immediately. This nocturnal cerebration has produced many of her other books. *As Far As Jane's Grandmother's* is "a symbolic picture of life in my father's house." *The Triumphant Footman,* one of her most original and amusing fantasies, is based on a real family footman who masqueraded as a nobleman. *Dwarf's Blood* (1931) was made a selection of the New York Literary Guild. Marshall Best has spoken of Miss Olivier's novels as "works of the imagination depending more upon the play of human emotions than upon their outward setting." They are lyrical, highly civilized books, somewhat similar in tone to books by her close friends Sylvia Townsend Warner, David Garnett, and Elinor Wylie. Miss Olivier's most recent books include *Mary Magdalen*, more a picture of devotional life in the Middle Ages than a biography; and a study of the compiler of Cruden's *Concordance*, who went mad three times. She lives with her sister at the Daye (Dairy) House on the estate of the Earl of Pembroke, an English showplace designed by Holbein in the sixteenth century and rebuilt after a fire by Inigo Jones.

PRINCIPAL WORKS: The Love Child, 1927; As Far as Jane's Grandmother's, 1929; Underground River, 1929; The Triumphant Footman, 1930; Moonrakings (short stories) 1930; Dwarf's Blood, 1931; The Seraphim Room (U.S. title: Mrs. Chilvester's Daughters) 1932; The Eccentric Life of Alexander Cruden (U.S. title: Alexander the Corrector) 1934; Mary Magdalen, 1935; Without Knowing Mr. Walkley: Personal Memories, 1938; Country Moods and Tenses, 1941.

ABOUT: Olivier, E. Without Knowing Mr. Walkley.

OLLIVANT, ALFRED (1874-January 19, 1927), English novelist, was the second son of Colonel E. A. Ollivant of the Royal

Horse Artillery, Elliotts, Nuthurst, Essex, and Catharine (Blunt) Ollivant, daughter of Professor J. J. Blunt. The boy was a grandson of Dr. Alfred Ollivant, Bishop of Llandaff for thirty-three years. He attended Rugby and the Royal Military Academy at Woolwich, graduating in 1893 as senior gunner, Toombs' Memorial Scholar, and winner of the riding prize. Ollivant was commissioned an officer of the Royal Artillery, but a fall from a horse injured his spine, and he resigned his commission in 1895. Enforced rest in bed turned his thoughts to literature, and his famous dog-story, begun at twenty, *Bob, Son of Battle* appeared in 1898 in the United States, becoming a best-seller and something of a cult. (It was published simultaneously in England in a revised version as *Owd Bob*

and was generally neglected there for ten years.) Called by William Lyon Phelps the best dog story ever written and by Frederick Taber Cooper "not merely one of the best realistic stories of animal life, but the only one," it is the story of Bob, last of the Gray Dogs of Kenmuir, and Red Wullie, the Tailless Tyke, both suspected of the heinous crime of sheep-killing. Virtue wins in the end. The book made an exceptionally fine moving picture in an English production entitled *To the Victor,* with the Scottish actor Willie Fyffe in the cast.

Danny, in 1903, had the fate of most sequels, and Ollivant made every effort to suppress the American edition. He remained a one-dog man, his name associated with his animal creation as Anna Sewell's is with *Black Beauty* and Marshall Saunders' with *Beautiful Joe. The Gentleman,* an historical novel concerning a plot to kidnap Nelson before Trafalgar; and *Boy Woodburn,* with its *dramatis personae* a race horse and the only daughter of a well-known race-horse trainer are romances well worth reading among Ollivant's output of a dozen or more novels. Ollivant was married at forty to Hilda Wigram, whose great-grandfather was Sir Robert Wigram, bart., and they had one daughter.

PRINCIPAL WORKS: Bob, Son of Battle (English title: Owd Bob) 1898; Danny, 1903; Redcoat Captain (juvenile) 1907; The Gentleman, 1908; The Royal Road, 1912; Boy Woodburn, 1917; Two Men, 1919; One Woman, 1920.

ABOUT: Cooper, F. T. Some English Story Tellers; Kunitz, S. J. & Haycraft, H. (eds.). The Junior Book of Authors; Phelps, W. L. Essays on Modern Novelists.

*O'NEILL, EUGENE GLADSTONE (October 16, 1888-), American dramatist, Pulitzer and Nobel Prize winner, was born in New York City, the second son of the celebrated actor James O'Neill (famous chiefly for his performance as "the Count of Monte Cristo") and of Ella (Quinlan) O'Neill. Both parents were devout Catholics, and part of the boy's

Pinchot

schooling, after his first seven years, when he traveled with his parents wherever his father's engagements called him, was in Catholic boarding-schools. He finished his preparatory education at Betts Academy, Stamford, Conn., and entered Princeton in 1906. At the end of his freshman year he was suspended for a youthful misdemeanor, and never went back. He started work in a New York mail order firm in which his father had an interest, and in 1909 married Kathleen Jenkins, by whom he had a son the following year. This youthful marriage did not last long, although it was not finally dissolved until 1912. Meanwhile O'Neill had made a futile journey to Honduras, prospecting for gold; came home broke; was tried out as assistant manager of his father's company and did not make good; and finally, in 1910, shipped as a seaman to Buenos Aires. For a year he was at sea, or with other sailors on shore-leave, unconsciously storing up impressions which were to reappear later in plays from *Bound East to Cardiff* to *Anna Christie*. He was paid off in New York, went on a typical sailor's spree, and wound up in New Orleans. where his father happened to be playing. The prodigal was not exactly welcomed, but he was given a minor rôle in the company and spent fifteen weeks as an actor. In the summer he returned with his family to their summer home in New London, Conn. There he got a job as cub reporter on the New London *Telegraph*, and held it for six months until his health broke down, he was found to be tubercular, and was sent to a Connecticut sanatorium.

This was the turning-point in Eugene O'Neill's life. He was discharged a few months later as an "arrested case," but he had had time to do some thinking, to decide what he wanted of life, and to begin trying to get it. He started to write plays, one-acters at first, with no expectation of having them performed or published. His father financed publication of his first volume by a "vanity publisher," but nobody outside his family was interested. He decided he needed technical training, and in 1914 went to Harvard and enrolled in Dr. George Pierce Baker's famous "Forty-Seven Workshop." He got relatively little out of the course, but he was confirmed in his resolution to be a playwright and nothing else. Back in New York at the end of the year, he became acquainted with the people "advanced" both in politics and in art, who were making Greenwich Village, in its heyday, the cultural center of the United States. With some of them, in the summer of 1916, he went to their summer headquarters, Provincetown, Mass. This was the summer the Provincetown Theatre was started in a barn on a wharf, and Eugene O'Neill had his first play produced there—*Bound East for Cardiff*. *Thirst* was produced later in the season. The next winter the Provincetown Theatre moved to New

York, and it kept on producing O'Neill's plays; he had ten performed between 1917 and 1920. All the one-act sea plays (recently combined and filmed as *The Long Voyage*) were thus produced for the first time. In 1920, with the presentation of his first full-length play, *Beyond the Horizon*, at the Morosco Theatre, O'Neill was launched. He has ever since held his place as the leading American playwright of his time. *Beyond the Horizon* received the Pulitzer Prize for drama (he has won it twice since, for *Anna Christie* and *Strange Interlude*), and, at least until the sudden change in his viewpoint and technique after 1925, each new play was acclaimed as greater than the last.

In 1918 he married Agnes Boulton, and they had a son and a daughter. (His son by his first wife, Eugene O'Neill, Jr., is also a writer.) He lived for some time in Ridgefield, Conn., then for several years in Bermuda. In 1929 they were divorced, and soon after, in France, he married Carlotta Monterey, the actress. Their permanent home is on one of the Sea Islands off the coast of Georgia. There he spends half the day writing, half in or on the sea, or playing tennis. He writes by hand, in a script so microscopic that one actually needs a glass to decipher it. Since 1935 he has worked every day, from 8.30 A.M. to 1.30 P.M., on a cycle of nine plays, under the general title *A Tale of Possessors Self-Dispossessed*, which is to form a dramatic history of an American family from 1775 to 1932. He has four of the nine plays finished, and hopes to have the cycle done by 1944; until then none of the plays is to be produced. Apparently the production technique invented for *Mourning Becomes Electra*, of an afternoon performance, a dinner intermission, and an evening performance, will have to be revived or even elaborated for the performance of this cycle.

Almost pathologically shy, shunning all publicity and resenting invasion of his private life, O'Neill is most at home out of doors. There his sun-bronzed skin, his thick black graying hair, his jutting brow and lip, and his brooding eyes seem to fit better than in a city street. He emerges seldom now to revisit his old haunts; his roistering days ended with his attack of tuberculosis, at twenty-three. Honors have been heaped upon him. Yale gave him an honorary Litt.D. degree in 1926, he is a member of the National Institute of Arts and Letters, the American Academy of Arts and Letters, and the Irish Academy of Letters. Finally, in 1936, he received the supreme accolade of the Nobel Prize for Literature. His last trip abroad was to receive it, but previously, at the time of his third marriage, he had lived for several years in France. At present he takes little interest in dramatic or literary undertakings outside his own work. From 1923 to 1927, however, he was associated with Kenneth Macgowan and Robert Edmund Jones in the management of the Greenwich Village Theatre, and in 1934 he was one of the founding editors, with George Jean Nathan (one of his first "discoverers"), Sherwood Anderson, Ernest Boyd, James Branch Cabell, and Theodore Dreiser, of the short-lived *American Spectator*.

O'Neill's early plays were realistic, often brutally so; tragic, intense, and immediate. Their people, whether rebellious stokers, starved New England spinsters, or Negro dictators, were real people. And then something happened to him and within him. Beginning with *The Great God Brown*, he grew increasingly symbolical, vague, and mystical, with the accompaniment of masks, asides, and other strange devices; in his latest produced play, *Days Without End*, he seems to have reverted to the faith of his childhood. The one break in a succession of confused symbolism and half-articulate mysticism (see *Dynamo* and *Lazarus Laughed*) was the tender, amused play *Ah, Wilderness!*, which might almost have been written by George M. Cohan, who acted in it.

What, then, is Eugene O'Neill—a genius growing into greatness, a man who once had genius but now has smothered it in bewilderment and pretension, or a man who has never had the greatness for which he has been acclaimed? Joseph Wood Krutch called him "essentially a moralist and a mystic." Lionel Trilling, acknowledging his "integrity and hieratic earnestness," said that "not only has he tried to compass more of life than most American writers of his time, but . . . he has persistently tried to *solve* it. . . . His stage devices are no fortuitous technique, [but] an integral and necessary expression of his temper of mind and the task it set itself. . . . [Now] he has crept into the dark womb of Mother Church and pulled the universe in with him." Bernard De Voto, in his "minority report" on the awarding of the Nobel Prize to O'Neill, is harshest of all: "He has an inherited instinct for the theatrically effective, . . . a restless and extremely energetic intelligence. . . . His experiments were to confuse and to confute him. . . . He is a fine playwright who is not sufficiently endowed . . . to be a great dramatist but who has tried to substitute for [great intel-

ligence, imagination, and understanding] a set of merely mechanical devices."

Nevertheless, the man who wrote *The Hairy Ape, Anna Christie, The Emperor Jones, Beyond the Horizon, Desire Under the Elms,* and *Mourning Becomes Electra* cannot be dismissed with a phrase. Whatever the final verdict on Eugene O'Neill, he has been the most vital influence in the American theatre in the past twenty years.

PRINCIPAL WORKS: *(dates of publication)*— Thirst and Other One-Act Plays, 1914; Bound East for Cardiff, 1916; Before Breakfast, 1916; The Moon of the Caribbees and Other Plays of the Sea, 1919; Beyond the Horizon, 1920; Gold, 1920; The Emperor Jones, Diff'rent, The Straw, 1921; The Hairy Ape, Anna Christie, The First Man, 1922; The Fountain, 1923; All God's Chillun Got Wings, Welded, 1924; Complete Works (2 vols.) 1924; Desire Under the Elms, 1925; The Great God Brown, and Other Plays, 1926; Marco Millions, 1927; Lazarus Laughed, 1927; Strange Interlude, 1928; Dynamo, 1929; Mourning Becomes Electra, 1931; Nine Plays, 1932; Ah, Wilderness! 1933; Days Without End, 1934; Plays (3 vols.) 1941.

ABOUT: Agate, J. The Contemporary Theatre; Boyd, E. Portraits: Real and Imaginary; Boynton, P. H. Some Contemporary Americans; Brown, J. M. Upstage; Clark, B. H. Eugene O'Neill: The Man and His Plays; Dickinson, T. H. Playwrights of the New American Theatre; Dukes, A. The Youngest Drama; Geddes, V. The Melodramadness of Eugene O'Neill; Glaspell, S. The Road to the Temple; Hamilton, C. Conversations on Contemporary Drama; Karsner, D. Sixteen Authors to One; Mais, S. B. P. Some Modern Authors: Mickle, A. D. Studies on Six Plays of Eugene O'Neill; Nathan, G. J. Intimate Notebooks; Quinn, A. H. A History of the American Drama; Saylor, O. M. Our American Theatre; Schelling, F. E. Appraisements and Asperities; Sergeant, E. S. Fire Under the Andes; Skinner, R. D. Eugene O'Neill: A Poet's Quest; Winther, S. K. Eugene O'Neill: A Critical Study; Woollcott, A. Enchanted Aisles; American Magazine November 1922; American Mercury April 1928; American Scholar #3 1937; Anglia (German) September 1928; Bookman August 1921; Contemporary Review March 1926; Everybody's Magazine June 1920; Fortnightly Review May 1923; Forum December 1935; Freeman March 21, 1923; Mercure de France March 1, 1937; Nation March 22, 1922, October 9, 1935; New Republic November 15, 1922, January 21, 1925, September 23, 1936; New Statesman July 9, 1921; North American Review June 1935; Nuova Antologia January 16, 1933; Revue Politique et Littéraire February 6, 1937; Saturday Review of Literature April 30 and May 28, 1932, November 21, 1936; Scribner's October 1926; Sewanee Review October 1935; South Atlantic Quarterly January 1933; Southern Review #3 1937; Spectator October 17, 1925; Theatre April 1920, June 1924, May 1925, January 1926; Theatre Arts Monthly May 1926; Time September 16, 1940.

*O'NEILL, ROSE CECIL (1874-), American illustrator, poet, and novelist, was born in Wilkes-Barre, Pa., the daughter of William Patrick O'Neill, an Irish bookseller, and Asenath O'Neill. She was

* Died April 1944.

educated at the Convent of the Sacred
Heart, Omaha, Neb. Originally intending
to be an actress, Rose O'Neill became a self-

taught illustrator at
fifteen, and came to
New York to find a
market. Here she en-
tered the Convent of
the Sisters of St.
Regis on Riverside
Drive, leaving at
eighteen to marry
Gray Latham, who
died five years later.
*Life, Harper's, Good
Housekeeping, Truth, Collier's, Cosmopolitan,* and *Puck* took her work. For the last-
named she wrote and illustrated short stories
and verses.

In 1902 she married the editor of *Puck,*
Harry Leon Wilson[qv], and illustrated his
novels, *The Spenders* (1902) and *The Lions
of the Lord* (1903), as "O'Neill Latham."
They separated soon after returning from
a trip to Italy. Rose O'Neill has exhibited
at the Paris Salon; she is a member of
the Société des Beaux Arts. Her various
homes have included Bonnybrook in the
Ozark Mountains of Missouri; a Washington Square studio in New York City; the
Villa Narcissus at Capri; and her present
abode, Carabas Castle (named for the marquis of *Puss in Boots*) on the Saugatuck
River near Westport, Conn. Here Miss
O'Neill, attired in a flowing velvet robe
(usually red), with yellow hair curled on
her shoulders like of that of a medieval
page, was reported some years ago to write
her fantasies, execute her paintings, and entertain her friends—all of whom she regards
as potential geniuses—by reading Francis
Thompson aloud for eight or ten hours at a
stretch. The great commercial success of
her creations, the Kewpies—modified, sentimentalized and modernized Cupids, to whom
the favorite American adjective "cute" can
most fitly be applied — has enabled Miss
O'Neill to write as she pleases, and to indulge in the "excessive Celticism" of such
novels as *Garda* and *The Goblin Woman.*
The Master-Mistress (1922), whose title is
derived from the most debated of Shakespeare's Sonnets, is a collection of poems,
weirdly illustrated by ·the author, whose
theme is the duality of sex. In 1938 Miss
O'Neill contributed drawings to Irving Caesar's *Sing a Song of Safety.* As a poet, she
has undeniable if erratic gifts; and a charming humor as an illustrator.

PRINCIPAL WORKS: The Loves of Edwy, 1904;
The Lady in the White Veil, 1909; Kewpies and

Dottie Darling, 1913; Kewpies: Their Book, Verse,
and Poetry, 1913; Kewpie Kutouts, 1914; The
Master-Mistress (poems) 1922; Kewpies and the
Runaway Baby, 1928; Garda, 1929; The Goblin
Woman, 1930.

ABOUT: New Yorker November 24, 1934.

ONIONS, OLIVER (1873-), English
novelist, was born George Oliver Onions.
Contrary to published statements, his last
name is pronounced
exactly like the vege-
table. He changed his
name legally to
George Oliver in later
years, but has always
written as Oliver On-
ions.

He was born in
Bradford, Yorkshire,
and studied art for
three years in Lon-
don at the National Arts Training Schools
(now the Royal College of Art), and then,
in 1897, went to Paris on a scholarship for
further study. In Paris he was editor of
the student periodical, *Le Quartier Latin.*
Returning to London, he illustrated books,
designed posters, was a draughtsman in a
printing office, and was war artist for a
weekly magazine during the Boer War. He
still draws occasionally, and designs all his
own book jackets.

His first attempt at writing was done at
the suggestion of Gelett Burgess. His work
attracted attention from the beginning,
though his first real successes were *The Story
of Louie* (1913) and *Mushroom Town*
(1914). He is married to Berta Ruck,[qv]
the novelist, and they have two sons. After
living for some time near Windsor, they now
live in Merioneth, Wales.

Both in appearance and in nature Oliver
Onions is a typical Yorkshireman. He is
tall, fair, heavy-set, with broad shoulders
and a square jaw. He was once an amateur
boxer, but seldom puts on the gloves nowadays. His chief recreation now is motoring.
He is keenly interested in science and mechanics. He is exceedingly reticent about
his personal life, serious-minded with a
streak of wry humor, and (to quote F. G.
Bettany) "fiercely independent, a born
fighter, an enthusiast for ideas, a craftsman
with a most scrupulous conscience." A slow
worker, who writes and rewrites, he is scrupulous about details, going so far as to take
trips by air or perform chemical experiments
to be sure of accuracy in describing them
in a story.

Clemence Dane called him, in effect, a
lone wolf in literature, indifferent to the

effect of his work on the public; and as Bettany remarked, he "has been constantly experimenting, has never got in a groove." His first books were "harsh, uncompromising portraits . . . bitter and indignant exposures," full of his "passionate disgust at civilized man's itch for destruction and defilement." But, Miss Dane went on to say, his "preoccupation with character . . . alternates with extraordinary adventures into the lands of darkness. [He has written shivery ghost stories.] Above all things he is a masculine writer, uncompromisingly unsentimental." She concluded: "His books have a lasting attraction for a reader who enjoys using his brains and his imagination."

In his capacity as realist he has attacked the sensational press and shady finance; he has exposed without pity the shallow pretensions of superficial minds—especially of the female gender. As a writer on the supernatural, he is not exceeded by any author of his time, not even by Arthur Machen or Algernon Blackwood. His curious disregard of the opinion of others has contributed to keep him, though well known, from the wide celebrity he has earned.

PRINCIPAL WORKS: The Compleat Bachelor, 1901; Tales From a Far Riding (short stories) 1902; The Odd-Job Man, 1903; Little Devil Doubt, 1906; Good Boy Seldom, 1908; The Exception, 1911; Gray Youth, 1914; Mushroom Town, 1914; The New Moon, 1918; A Case in Camera, 1920; The Tower of Oblivion, 1921; Peace in Our Time, 1923; The Spite of Heaven, 1925; Whom God Hath Sundered (In Accordance With the Evidence, The Debit Account, The Story of Louie) 1926; Cut Flowers, 1927; The Open Secret, 1930; A Certain Man, 1931; Catalan Circus, 1934; Collected Ghost Stories (Widdershins, Ghosts in Daylight, The Painted Face) 1935; The Hand of Kornelius Voyt, 1939; The Italian Chest, 1939; Cockcrow, 1940; Blood Eagle, 1941.

ABOUT: Bookman April 1926; Bookman (London) July 1929.

*OPPENHEIM, EDWARD PHILLIPS

(1866-   ), English novelist and writer of stories of international intrigue, was born

in London, the son of a leather merchant who was of the third generation of Oppenheims born in England. His mother was Henrietta Susannah Temperley (Budd) Oppenheim. Phillips Oppenheim, as he was called, attended Wyggeston Grammar School in Leicester, where he played cricket and football, won a prize in history, and received "shocking reports" in mathematics.

He left the Sixth Form in July 1883 to help his father, who had sustained financial losses, in the firm.

Oppenheim spent eight or nine conscientious hours each day at business, then wrote fiction until 2 A.M. His father, "who wrote better English than I have ever done and received a much more ambitious education," read one of his stories and helped him revise it. Entitled *Expiation* (like one of the novels of "Elizabeth," later a close friend of Oppenheim), it was published at the elder Oppenheim's expense.

On a business trip to the United States, Oppenheim met and married Elise Hopkins of Boston, Mass., in 1890; they have a daughter, Geraldine. A few years after his marriage Oppenheim published *Mysterious Mr. Sabin*, "the first of my long series of stories dealing with that shadowy and mysterious world of diplomacy." A wealthy New York business man, Julian Stevens Ulman, an admirer of the novel, bought out Oppenheim's leather business and made the novelist a director at a generous salary. Relieved of financial worries, Oppenheim has applied himself to the composition of more than 110 novels, of which only twelve have not been published in the United States (unless in pirated editions); five of them appeared under the pseudonym "Anthony Partridge." He has also written numerous short stories, most of them unified by dealing with one central character.

Oppenheim's self-indulgent custom is to frequent the cafés of cities and cultivate the acquaintance of the *maître d'hotel* and study the types that throng the lobbies. A half-dozen thoroughfares and squares in London, a handful of restaurants, and the people one meets in a single morning are quite sufficient, Oppenheim declares, for the production of more and greater stories than he will ever write. The real centers of interest, he considers, are the places where human beings are gathered more closely, where the struggle for existence inevitably develops the whole capacity of a man and strips him bare to the looker-on. "So cities for me!" The male characters in Oppenheim romances are the main thing; women are inevitably "glamorous," but secondary. There are only a score of basic plots in the world; when all are used A-Z, turn them around and use them Z-A, he advises. Thus, there will always be enough plots: "So long as the world lasts, its secret international history will continue to engage the full activities of the diplomatist."

Fellow-writers wonder when Mr. Oppenheim gets through his work, since he has

* Died February 3, 1946.

never been seen actually engaged at it. He has "schooled himself to an artificial preference for working from 4 to 7 P.M." (dictating his stories to a secretary); he would prefer 9 to 9:30 A.M., when his mind is fresher, but that time is sacred to golf. His golf handicap is six, "but I can't play up to it because I am a theorist." The Oppenheim cottage on the east coast of England has a wide view of the North Sea from its windows.

In peacetime he also maintained homes in Guernsey and Cannes, but lost both at the time of the Nazi invasion, when he escaped to England only with great difficulty.

PRINCIPAL WORKS: The Man and His Kingdom, The Mysterious Mr. Sabin, 1901; The Traitors, 1902; A Prince of Sinners, The Yellow Crayon, 1903; Anna the Adventuress, 1904; The Master Mummer, 1905; The Avenger, The Missioner, A Maker of History, 1908; The Long Arm (American title: The Long Arm of Mannister) 1909; The Illustrious Prince, 1910; Peter Ruff, 1912; The Temptation of Tavernake, 1913; Mr. Grex of Monte Carlo, 1915; The Double Traitor, The Kingdom of the Blind, 1917; The Great Impersonation, 1920; The Great Prince Shan, 1922; The Inevitable Millionaires, 1923; Nobody's Man, 1923; The Evil Shepherd, 1923; The Mystery Road, The Wrath to Come, 1924; Prodigals of Monte Carlo, 1926; The Light Beyond, Matorni's Vineyard, 1928; The Treasure House of Martin Hews, 1929; Happenings to Forester, 1930; Inspector Dickens Retires, 1931; Sinners Beware, 1931; The Ostrakoff Jewels, 1932; Murder at Monte Carlo, 1932; The Bank Manager, 1934; The Spy Paramount, Advice Limited, 1935; Ask Miss Mott, 1936; The Dumb Gods Speak, Envoy Extraordinary, 1937; Curious Happenings to the Rooke Legatees, 1937; The Colossus of Arcadia, 1938; Exit a Dictator, 1939; Last Train Out, 1940; The Grassleyes Mystery, 1940; The Milan Grill Room, 1941; The Shy Plutocrat, 1941; The Pool of Memory (autobiography) 1941; The Man Who Changed His Plea, 1942.

ABOUT: Lucas, E.V., Reading, Writing, and Remembering; Oppenheim, E. P. The Pool of Memory; Boston Evening Transcript July 1932; New York Times Book Review June 8, 1941.

OPPENHEIM, JAMES (May 24, 1882-August 4, 1932), American poet and novelist, was born in St. Paul, Minn., the son

of Joseph and Matilda (Schloss) Oppenheim. His father was a member of the Minnesota Legislature, but when the boy was two years old the family moved to New York, where he was reared. He attended Columbia University from 1901 to 1903, but was never graduated. Before going to college he had already worked, in

1896, as a clerk for a steamship company, and in 1899 and 1900 for an express company. He became a social worker and teacher, being assistant head of the Hudson Guild Settlement from 1903 to 1905, and head of the Hebrew Technical School for Girls from 1905 to 1907. His first stories were based on his intimate acquaintance with the people of New York's East Side. At the time of their writing, he was one of the "pioneers" of Greenwich Village, then just beginning to be the city's Bohemia.

Oppenheim was married three times, his last and surviving wife having been Linda Gray. He had two sons (who both became writers) by his first wife, Lucy Seckel, whom he married in 1905 and by whom he was divorced in 1915. At the time a sensation was caused by her charge that she had libelously been made the prototype of the parasitic wife in her husband's novel, *Idle Wives*.

From the beginning Oppenheim had felt himself to be more a poet than a writer of fiction, and he himself called his stories "bad prose with a streak of suppressed poetry in them." After 1915 he wrote nothing but verse, poetic plays, and essays. These last were founded on his study of psycho-analysis, and he himself eventually became an analyst. Before this he had an exciting year as an editor, when with Waldo Frank and Paul Rosenfeld he founded and edited the *Seven Arts*, a magazine whose interesting career (1916-17) as a vehicle for literary experimentation ended when it opposed America's entry into the World War and had to suspend because its financial backers withdrew their support.

He died in New York of a disease of the lungs, probably tuberculosis, when he was a little over fifty.

Oppenheim's hortatory, rhetorical poetry, written in loose free-verse style, was frequently dull, and there was more of Whitman, Freud, and the Bible in it than any original note of his own. He collected what he considered the best of it in *The Sea* (1924), and among the poems in this volume there are a few that may live because of the fervor and sincerity that inspired them. His essays were elementary popularizations of psycho-analysis for the layman, and his novels and stories were without value, though the stories in *Dr. Rast* have some interest as descriptions of a changing phase of New York life.

Physically, Oppenheim was a small man with sensitive, finely Jewish features, and the burning dark eyes of the poet he inherently was, though he never found full expression for his inchoate impluses.

PRINCIPAL WORKS: *Fiction*—Dr. Rast; 1909; Wild Oats, 1910; Pay Envelopes, 1911; The Nine-Tenths, 1911; The Olympian, 1912; Idle Wives, 1914; The Beloved, 1915. *Poetry*—Monday Morning and Other Poems, 1909; The Pioneers (play) 1910; Songs for the New Age, 1914; War and Laughter, 1916; The Book of Self, 1917; Night (play) 1918; The Solitary, 1919; The Mystic Warrior, 1921; The Golden Bird, 1923; The Sea, 1924. *Essays*—Your Hidden Powers, 1923; Behind Your Front, 1928; American Types: A Preface to Analytic Psychology, 1931.

ABOUT: Rosenfeld, P. Men Seen; Untermeyer, L. American Poetry Since 1900; American Mercury June 1930; Bookman December 1909; New Statesman January 8, 1916; New York Herald Tribune August 5, 1932; New York Times Book Review March 4, 1923; Poetry Review January 1918; March 1925; Scholastic January 23, 1937.

ORAGE, ALFRED RICHARD (January 22, 1873-November 5, 1934), English journalist and psychologist, was the youngest of

the four children of William Orage and Sarah Ann (McQuire) Orage, and was born at Dacre near Bradford in Yorkshire. His father failed successively at farming and schoolteaching, and died when his son was a young boy. Orage remarked feelingly, in later years, that material poverty is the greatest curse of society and frequently of individuals. Luckily, he attended Howard Coote's Nonconformist Sunday School class and was given the run of Coote's private library, where he read Ruskin, Carlyle, Matthew Arnold, and William Morris. After attending a training college at Culham, near Oxford, Orage found a teaching post in an "unlovely district" of Leeds at eighty pounds a year. Insisting on marrying Jean Walker in 1896, he lost Coote's patronage. Orage lectured on theosophy at Harrogate and other towns in the north of England; met Holbrook Jackson and borrowed his copies of Nietzsche; joined W. A. J. Penty in founding the Leeds Arts Club; and was given a thousand pounds by an unknown donor to buy the *New Age*, in which Orage championed the Socialist masses and decried Labour leaders. Shaw, Wells, Chesterton, Belloc, and Havelock Ellis all contributed to the paper, which reached a peak circulation of 22,000, and Arnold Bennett wrote "Books and Persons" for four years, under the pseudonym "Jacob Tonson." Younger writers such as Kath-

erine Mansfield, Richard Aldington, J. C. Squire, Ezra Pound, and Michael Arlen (under his original name) were encouraged.

With the founding of the rival paper the *New Statesman*, edited by a *New Age* alumnus, Clifford Sharp, Orage lost interest and became a disciple of Ouspensky, author of *Tertium Organum*, and of the formidable occult teacher, the Russian Gurdjieff, of whose colony in Fontainebleau Orage was a docile member. In 1924 Orage practiced as an uncertified psychologist in Boston, Chicago, and New York, where he married Jessie Dwight of the Sunwise Turn Bookshop. Returning to England, Orage began rather apathetically to edit the *New English Weekly*. He died at sixty-one of a heart attack after a broadcast, leaving his wife, a son, and a daughter. Chesterton called him "the most vigorous and lucid exponent of economic philosophy in our time," with sympathies that could stretch from Penty's Guild Socialism to G. D. H. Cole's bureaucracy of trades unions. His style was one of concentrated thought and sparkling clarity. In person Orage was tall, dark-haired, hazel-eyed, with a birthmark on his face, and was given to cat-like movements. "He was a conservative in values, only radical in thought; serene by nature, though by name a storm."

PRINCIPAL WORKS: Nietzsche in Outline and Aphorism, 1907; Frederick Nietzsche: The Dionysian Spirit of the Age, 1911; Readers and Writers, 1922; The Art of Reading, 1930; Selected Essays and Critical Writings, 1935; Social Credit and The Fear of Leisure, 1935; Political and Economic Writings, 1935.

ABOUT: Mairet, P. A. R. Orage; Reckitt, M. B. How It Happened.

*ORCZY, EMMUSKA, Baroness (1865-), Hungarian-English romantic novelist and playwright, was born at Tarna-Eörs, Hungary, the only child of Baron Felix Orczy, a composer and conductor of some note, and Emma Orczy, *née* Comtesse Wass. As a child she knew Wagner, Liszt, Gounod, and Massenet, friends of her father. Though she spoke no word of

English until she was fifteen, all her writings are in that language. After early studies in Brussels and Paris, she enrolled at the Heatherley School of Art in London, where she met a young fellow student, Montagu Barstow, the son of an English clergy-

* Died November 12, 1947.

man, whom she married. (Their son and only child, John Montagu Orczy Barstow, born in 1899, has been professor of English at Lausanne and writes under the name of "John Blakeney"—the derivation of which will be obvious to all readers of his mother's romances.) Some of her paintings were hung at Royal Academy shows and she had a modest success as an illustrator, both alone and with her husband, who had become a well-known artist. She began writing in the late 1890's, chiefly short stories for the popular magazines at first. In 1905 she "struck twelve" with the public, though not the critics, with a play *The Scarlet Pimpernel* (written in collaboration with Barstow). It introduced her most famous character, Sir Percy Blakeney, a deceptively foppish, actually valiant and daring young Englishman who as the elusive "Pimpernel" of the title crossed wits and swords with sinister adversaries during the French revolution. A novel of the same name was published in the year of the play, and the two introduced a long series of popular "Pimpernel" successes—between covers, on the boards, and in the films. An especially notable talking-picture version was made in England in the middle 1930's by the Baroness' countryman Alexander Korda, with Leslie Howard in the title rôle and Raymond Massey as the villain of the piece.

"The Old Man in the Corner," who made his appearance in a book of that title in 1909, has gained the Baroness considerable attention from historians of detective fiction—chiefly because he is one of the earliest examples of the "arm-chair" school of sleuthing. To quote Willard Huntington Wright, he is "the nameless logician who sits, shabby and indifferent, at his café table and holds penetrating postmortems on the crimes of the day." John Carter found him "an early example of the intuitive school of detectives which has become better known in G. K. Chesterton's Father Brown." All of the "Old Man's" cases (a second collection was called *Unravelled Knots*) are of the short variety. Found today principally in anthologies, they are pleasantly diverting but mainly of historical interest. The author's female detective, "Lady Molly of Scotland Yard," was less successful.

A long list of highly-colored romantic fiction, extending virtually to the present time, has kept the Baroness' name before the public and brought her fame and fortune, though she has never quite duplicated the striking success of the early "Pimpernel" adventures. For many years she has made

her permanent home in Monte Carlo, where she is surprisingly youthful and vigorous in her middle seventies. The outbreak of war in 1939 found her in England and nearing seventy-five; characteristically, she hurried home to Monte Carlo to do relief work among her neighbors.

Never more than a "popular novelist," Baroness Orczy at her best has nevertheless contributed genuine excitement and entertainment to her craft.

PRINCIPAL WORKS: The Emperor's Candlesticks, 1899; The Scarlet Pimpernel, 1905; The Elusive Pimpernel, 1908; Beau Brocade, 1908; The Old Man in the Corner, 1909; Petticoat Government, 1910; Lady Molly of Scotland Yard, 1910; The Laughing Cavalier, 1914, Leather Face, 1916; The League of the Scarlet Pimpernel, 1919; The First Sir Percy, 1920; The Triumph of the Scarlet Pimpernel, 1922; Nicolette, 1923; Pimpernel and Rosemary, 1924; Unravelled Knots, 1925; The Celestial City, 1926; Sir Percy Hits Back, 1927; Blue Eyes and Grey, 1928; Skin o' My Tooth, 1928, Adventures of the Scarlet Pimpernel, 1929; A Child of the Revolution, 1932; The Way of the Scarlet Pimpernel, 1933; The Scarlet Pimpernel Looks at the World, 1934; The Uncrowned King, 1935; The Turbulent Duchess, 1935; The Divine Folly, 1937; No Greater Love, 1938; Mam'zelle Guillotine, 1940.

ABOUT: Braybrooke, P. Some Goddesses of the Pen; Haycraft, H. Murder for Pleasure: The Life and Times of the Detective Story; Orczy, E. The Scarlet Pimpernel Looks at the World; Bookman (London) August 1913.

ORENBURGSKY, SERGEY GUSEV

(1867-), Russian novelist, was born Sergey Ivanovich Gusev in Orenburg. His name is sometimes given as Gusev- (or Gussiev-) Orenburgsky. He was the son of a Cossack trader, and was educated in the local *gymnasium* and seminary. After a brief experience in teaching, he became a priest, but resigned from the priesthood  to devote himself to literature. His first short story was published in 1893. His stories usually dealt with village priests, their conflicts and difficulties. *The Land of the Fathers* (1905), a novel, was completed nearly a quarter-century later by its sequel, *The Land of the Children* (1928).

Gusev or (Orenburgsky as he is better known) went abroad after the Revolution and came to the United States to live; one of the curators of the Slavonic Division of the New York Public Library describes him as a rather odd-looking, shriveled old man with long hair and a sacerdotal air. *The*

Land of the Children (1928) was translated
by Nina Nikolaevna Salivanova, and Joshua
Kunitz stated in the *Nation* that "in spite
of its diffuseness the novel is significant,
for, together, with its predecessor, *The Land
of the Fathers,* it unfolds on the epic background of mass-movements the individual
tragedies and more or less authentic spiritual
odyssey of the writer himself as well as
that section of Russian society to which the
writer belongs, the middle-class intelligentsia." L. P. Hartley wrote in the *Saturday
Review*: "This huge work describes the
effect of the Revolution on a group of characters, and it does so in the real Dostoievsky
style, with all its paraphernalia of murders
and ecstatic visions and parables and holy
idiots and sudden repentances and interminable conversations about the universal
play." One of Orenburgsky's books (not
translated), published in 1922, deals with
the riots against the Jews in the Ukraine.
Orenburgsky is sometimes confused with
another and lesser Sergey Ivanovich Gusev
(1874-1933), whose original name was
Yakov Davidovich Drabkin.

WORKS AVAILABLE IN ENGLISH TRANSLATION:
The Land of the Fathers, 1905; The Land of the
Children, 1928.

ABOUT: Soviet Encyclopedia; Our World June
1924.

*O'RIORDAN. CONAL O'CONNELL

(April 29, 1874-   ), Irish novelist and playwright, best known, as he says, from 1891
to 1920 by his *nom-de-guerre* "Norreys
Connell," was born in Dublin, the youngest son of the late Daniel O'Connell
O'Riordan, Q.C., and his first cousin, Kate
O'Riordan. The boy was educated by Jesuits in Ireland, but left school "at the
age most boys begin" and studied for the
army. At sixteen, a fall from a horse resulted in spinal trouble and wrecked that particular career. The next year O'Riordan
went on the stage, and at eighteen was playing Engstrand in Ibsen's *Ghosts* to the Al-
ving of Lewis Waller, at the Athenaeum
Hall in London. In 1898 O'Riordan produced and played in Eugene Brieux's
Blanchette, the first Brieux production in
England, made at the Independent Theatre.

"Norreys Connell" wrote his first book,
In the Green Park, at nineteen, and "made
good on both sides the Atlantic with the
third" (*The Fool and His Heart,* 1896).
His plays were produced at the Court, Ambassadors, Kingsway, New Garrick, Prince
of Wales, St. James's, Little Fortune, and
Playhouse theatres, London; by the Birmingham Repertory theatre; and at the

Abbey Theatre, Dublin, where he succeeded
John Millington Synge as director in 1909.
He was responsible for reproducing there
Synge's *The Playboy of the Western World,*
suppressed by mob violence some months
before.

In spite of physical handicaps, O'Riordan
got to the front in the First World War,
as head of a Y.M.C.A. rest hut. He was
invalided home two days after the Armistice. *Adam of Dublin* (1920), the first of
a trilogy of attractive novels, was praised
by Katherine Mansfield.

"Norreys Connell" has been president of
the Irish Literary Society since 1937; is president of the Square Club, which he founded
with R. A. Scott-James and the late Edward
Garnett in 1907; lectured on the art of the
theatre at Liverpool University in 1933-34;
has been an Honorary Examiner of the Historical Society of Trinity College, Dublin,
and is a council member of the P.E.N. Club.
His relations with the younger literary set
are cordial, and in 1941 he wrote a moving
memorial poem to the late Helen Simpson.
He has two sons and two daughters; in
times of peace lives at 106 Mead Vale Row,
W. 5; and finds his chief recreation in
sleep.

His plays are out of the usual Abbey
tradition, according to Cornelius Weygandt.
The Piper, produced at the Abbey in 1908,
"cut alike at the Parliamentary Nationalists,
the Sinn Feiner, and the shoneen. There
is a white heat of feeling under the play
that to some degree makes one forget its
rather indifferent writing, its failure to attain true dramatic speech, its obviousness
as a morality play."

PRINCIPAL WORKS: In the Green Park, 1894;
The House of the Strange Woman, 1895; The
Fool and His Heart, 1896; How Soldiers Fight,
1899; The Nigger Knights, 1900; The Follies of
Captain Daly, 1901; The Pity of War, 1905; The
Young Days of Admiral Quilliam, 1906; Shake-
speare's End, and Other Irish Plays, 1912; Rope
Enough (play) 1913; Adam of Dublin; A Ro-
mance of To-Day, 1920; Adam and Caroline, 1921;
In London: The Story of Adam and Marriage,
1922; Rowena Barnes, 1923; Married Life, 1924;
His Majesty's Pleasure (play) 1925; The Age of
Miracles, 1925; Young Lady Dazincourt, 1926;
Soldier Born, 1927; Soldier of Waterloo, 1928;
The King's Wooing (play) 1929; Napoleon Passes
(commentary) 1933; Soldier's Wife, 1935; Captain
Falstaff and Other Plays, 1935; Soldier's End,
1938; Judith Quinn, 1939; Judith's Love, 1940.

ABOUT: Grein, A. A. G. J. T. Grein: The
Story of a Pioneer 1862-1935; Weygandt, C. Irish
Plays and Playwrights.

*ORTEGA Y GASSET, JOSÉ (May 9,

1883-   ), Spanish essayist and philosopher,
was born in Madrid, the son of José Ortega

* Died June 18, 1948.   * Died October 18, 1955.

y Munilla, formerly editor of *El Imparcial*, an important Madrid newspaper. The family had a number of literary members, and Ortega y Gasset once remarked: "I was born upon a printing-press." He was educated by private tutors and at a Jesuit school in Miraflores del Palo. He was a precocious boy, with an extraordinary memory; at seven he recited the entire first chapter of *Don Quixote* from memory three hours after he had first read it. From the Jesuit school he proceeded to the University of Madrid, and won his doctorate in philosophy and literature in 1904. He then became a teacher in the Escuela Superior de Magisterio, a normal college. In 1908 he became professor of metaphysics at the University of Madrid. He has studied also at the Universities of Leipzig, Berlin, and Marburg.

The same year he received his chair at the university, he founded a magazine called *Faro* (Beacon), and in 1911 established *Europa*. Both of these reviews were philosophical in nature, with special reference to Spanish problems. He also contributed frequently to *El Imparcial*. However, he did not become a national figure until 1914, when in a celebrated speech at the Teatro de la Comedia, on "Old and New Politics," he denounced the Restoration, the Regency, and Alfonso XIII. The immediate result of this speech was the foundation of the League for Political Education and the establishment as its organ of the monthly journal *España*. In this latter enterprise Ortega y Gasset was joined by other prominent men of letters, including Barója y Nessi and Pérez de Ayala. In 1917, following a lecture tour in Argentina, he founded, with Nicolás Maria Urgoiti, *El Sol,* a liberal newspaper intended to counteract the conservative influence of *El Imparcial.* Many of his essays in this paper appear in English in *The Modern Theme* and *Invertebrate Spain.* An inveterate founder of periodicals, he also started and edited *La Revista de Occidente,* a literary monthly of high standing which appeared from 1923 to 1935 and introduced to Spanish readers many of the greatest writers of Europe.

In 1928 Ortega y Gasset once more visited South America, where his receptions were in the nature of an ovation. Among Spanish-reading people he was by this time perhaps the best known philosopher of contemporary Spain except Miguel de Unamuno, and his humanistic approach won more followers than did Unamuno's mysticism. He returned to Spain to take an active part in the overthrow of the monarchy, the main agency through which he (with Pérez de Ayala) worked being the Association for Service to the Republic. In 1931 he was elected deputy from the province of Leon. The movement, however, went beyond his range of liberal sympathies; and when the Civil War broke out, he did not stay to fight with the Loyalists but fled to France. However, when Franco after his victory offered to make Ortega y Gasset Spain's "official philosopher" and to publish a de luxe edition of his works if he would delete certain essays and passages, he promptly and proudly refused. If he was not a leftist, he was still less a Fascist. Instead of returning to Spain under such auspices, he became a voluntary exile in Argentina. In 1941 he was appointed professor of philosophy at the University of San Marcos, in Lima, Peru.

In the United States Ortega y Gasset is known chiefly through *The Revolt of the Masses,* which was a best-seller in its English translation. In it may be traced two very disparate influences, those of Nietzsche and of Bergson. Salvador de Madariaga called him "a refined humanist, strongly influenced by German contemporary neo-Kantian schools of thought." He has endeavored to synthesize into his philosophical system not only current questions of politics and economics, but also those of science—notably Einstein's relativity theory. His predominant thesis is the need of an intellectual aristocracy governing in a spirit of enlightened liberalism—which takes him back of all other influences all the way to the Plato of the *Republic.* Since he does not carry this thesis to its ultimate conclusion in Fascism, his is scarcely a popular philosophy in the present world situation, and he is condemned by right and left alike. Nevertheless, he remains one of the most powerful and brilliant minds of contemporary Spain.

Little is known of his private life or his personal history. He has been described by George Pendle as "a small man, with a broad forehead that protrudes over bright, gimlet eyes. He has a complete and inborn mastery of language." Lorenzo Giusso speaks of his "dark olive features, square determined jaws, and well-proportioned figure. . . . His vigor and the decided impetuosity in his eyes certainly do not suggest a languorous philosopher absorbed in the absolute, but, rather, a wrestler or fencing-master."

WORKS AVAILABLE IN ENGLISH: The Revolt of the Masses, 1932; The Modern Theme, 1933; Invertebrate Spain, 1937; Toward a Philosophy of History, 1941.

ABOUT: Carmona Menclares, F. El Pensamiento Filosófico de José Ortega y Gasset; More, P. E. The Demon of the Absolute; American Review April 1933; Bookman September 1932; Deutsche Rundschau September 1928; Hound and Horn April-June 1933; Journal of Philosophy August 17, 1933; Living Age January 1932; Nation September 21, 1932, February 22, 1933, June 26, 1937; New Republic August 18, 1937; New Statesman and Nation July 16, 1932; Saturday Review of Literature October 22, 1932.

*ORWELL, GEORGE (1903-   ), English essayist and novelist, writes: "I was born at Motihari, Bengal, the second child of an Anglo-Indian family.

I was educated at Eton, 1917-21, as I had been lucky enough to win a scholarship, but I did no work there and learned very little, and I don't feel that Eton has been much of a formative influence in my life. From 1922 to 1927 I served with the Indian Imperial Police in Burma. I gave it up partly because the climate had ruined my health, partly because I already had vague ideas of writing books, but mainly because I could not go on any longer serving an imperialism which I had come to regard as very largely a racket. When I came back to Europe I lived for about a year and a half in Paris, writing novels and short stories which no one would publish. After my money came to an end I had several years of fairly severe poverty during which I was, among other things, a dishwasher, a private tutor, and a teacher in cheap private schools. For a year or more I was also a part-time assistant in a London bookshop, a job which was interesting in itself but had the disadvantage of compelling me to live in London, which I detest. By about 1935 I was able to live on what I earned by writing, and at the end of that year I moved into the country and set up a small general store. It barely paid its way, but

it taught me things about the trade which would be useful if I ever made a venture in that direction again.

"I was married in the summer of 1936. At the end of the year I went to Spain to take part in the civil war, my wife following soon afterwards. I served four months on the Aragon front with the P.O.U.M. militia and was rather badly wounded, but luckily with no serious after-effects. Since that, except for spending a winter in Morocco, I cannot honestly say that I have done anything except write books and raise hens and vegetables [in Hertfordshire].

"What I saw in Spain, and what I have seen since of the inner workings of left-wing political parties, have given me a horror of politics. I was for a while a member of the Independent Labour Party, but left them at the beginning of the present war because I considered that they were talking nonsense and proposing a line of policy that could only make things easier for Hitler. In sentiment I am definitely 'left,' but I believe that a writer can remain honest only if he keeps free of party labels.

"The writers I care most about and never grow tired of are Shakespeare, Swift, Fielding, Dickens, Charles Reade, Samuel Butler, Zola, Flaubert, and, among modern writers, James Joyce, T. S. Eliot, and D. H. Lawrence. But I believe the modern writer who has influenced me most is Somerset Maugham, whom I admire immensely for his power of telling a story straightforwardly and without frills.

"Outside my work the thing I care most about is gardening, especially vegetable gardening. I like English cookery and English beer, French red wines, Spanish white wines, Indian tea, strong tobacco, coal fires, candle light, and comfortable chairs. I dislike big towns, noise, motor cars, the radio, tinned food, central heating, and 'modern' furniture. My wife's tastes fit in almost perfectly with my own. My health is wretched, but it has never prevented me from doing anything that I wanted to, except, so far [1940] fight in the present war.

"I am not at present writing, chiefly owing to upsets caused by the war. But I am projecting a long novel in three parts.

"I ought perhaps to mention that George Orwell is not my real name."

* * *

"George Orwell" contributes a regular London letter to the American *Partisan Review.*

PRINCIPAL WORKS: Down and Out in Paris and London, 1933; Burmese Days, 1934; A Clergyman's Daughter, 1935; Keep the Aspidistra Flying, 1936;

The Road to Wigan Pier, 1937; Homage to Catalonia, 1938; Coming Up for Air, 1939; Inside the Whale, 1940; The Lion and the Unicorn: Socialism and the English Genius, 1941.

OSTENSO, MARTHA (September 17, 1900-), Norwegian-American novelist, was born in Bergen, Norway, the daughter of

Sigurd Brigt Ostenso and Lena (Tungeland) Ostenso. "Where the long arm of the Hardangerfjord penetrates farthest into the rugged mountains of the coast of Norway, the Ostenso family has lived, in the township that bears its name, since the days of the Vikings," writes Miss Ostenso. "The name means Eastern Sea, and was assumed centuries ago by an adventurous forebear who dreamed of extending his holdings over the mountains, and through the lowlands of Sweden eastward to the shores of the Baltic. Although his dream never came true, the family name recalls it and the family tradition of landholding has persisted unbroken: the land that borders the lovely fjord is still in the family's possession, handed down from eldest son to eldest son. My father, a younger son, was free to indulge his roving disposition. A few years after marrying my mother he decided to emigrate to America. My mother's parents lived high up in the mountains, remote from the softening influence of the coast towns. At their home it was, in the little village of Haukeland, that I was born. This, the first of many small towns in which I have lived, is known to me only through hearsay, for when I was two years old we came to America. The story of my childhood is a tale of seven little towns in Minnesota and South Dakota. In one of them, on the dun prairies of South Dakota, I learned to speak English. It was while living in a little town in Minnesota that I became a regular contributor to the Junior Page of the Minneapolis *Journal*, and was rewarded for my literary trial-balloons at the rate of eighty cents a column. When I was fifteen years old I bade good-by to the Seven Little Towns. My father's restless spirit drove him north to the newer country. The family settled in Manitoba. It was during a summer vacation from my university work [the University of Manitoba; she entered in 1918 from the Brandon Collegiate School] that I went into the lake district of Manitoba, well toward the frontier of that northern civilization. My novel, *Wild Geese*, lay there, waiting to be put into words. Here was human nature stark, unattired in the convention of a smoother, softer life. A thousand stories are there, still to be written."

Martha Ostenso began her writing career at Winnipeg in 1920. In 1921-22 she took a course in the technique of the novel at Columbia University. For a time she did secretarial work with a charity organization in Brooklyn, and lived in a house on Washington Square in Manhattan. Her first book was a volume of verse, *A Far Land*, published in 1924. Next year *Wild Geese* won the prize offered by *Pictorial Review*, the Dodd, Mead Co. and the Famous Players-Lasky Corp. It has had several successors, but in its freshness, exhilarating outdoor quality, and freedom from the alien plot-complications and ineptness that have hampered some of her others, it is still her most noteworthy work. *Waters Under the Earth* was also favorably received. Miss Ostenso is unmarried, lives in St. Louis Park, a suburb of Minneapolis, and writes for the popular magazines.

PRINCIPAL WORKS: A Far Land, 1924; Wild Geese, 1925; The Dark Dawn, 1926; The Mad Carews, 1927; The Young May Moon, 1929; Waters Under the Earth, 1930; Prologue to Love, 1931; There's Always Another Year, 1933; White Reef, 1934; The Stone Field, 1937; The Mandrake Root, 1938; Love Passed This Way, 1942.

ABOUT: Pictorial Review September 1937.

"O'SULLIVAN, SEUMAS." See STARKEY, J.

O'SULLIVAN, VINCENT (November 27, 1872-), American essayist, novelist, and poet, was born in New York, the son of Eugene and Christine O'Sullivan. After an elementary education in the New York public schools, he went to England, and completed his education at Exeter College, Oxford (non-graduate) and in France. He has lived in France ever since, and has written as much in French as in English, besides having translated a number of French books. In 1918 and 1919 he was adjutant professor of English and American Literature in the University of Rennes. After the First World War he went to Paris, practically the first of the American expatriates. Most of the others came back to the United States by 1930 or so, but when last heard of, Mr. O'Sullivan was still in Paris. There has been no news of him since the fall of France.

Vincent O'Sullivan has had rather a curious career as a writer. Hailed enthusiastically by critics of the calibre of H. L. Mencken; one of the early contributors to Mencken's *Smart Set*; the author of a "capital novel," *The Good Girl*, which because of its frankness was something of a sensation in 1912, he is nevertheless practically unknown to the general reading public of either America or England. The author of numerous articles (in French) on American and English literature in the *Mercure de France*, and of poems in French in many French magazines, he is hardly better known in France. He has had two plays produced—*The Hartley Family* and *The Lighthouse*—yet his name is not familiar in the theatrical world. There are long lapses in time between his various publications, and he has made no attempt to keep himself in the public eye.

The fact is that he is a man who writes when and what he wants to write, who has enough to live on without depending on writing for his livelihood, and who (until the present war at least) has been content to live a comfortable bachelor life in Paris without any ambition for fame. In a quiet way he has preferred to be an onlooker—what he himself has called a "second fiddle." He is sufficient of a scholar to have issued a definitive critical edition of Ben Jonson's *Volpone,* he knew Oscar Wilde in his last dolorous days, he translated the autobiography of his friend, Antoine Bourdelle, the sculptor. But for the most part he has been a superior sort of dilettante, a writer's writer, more French than American in his way of thought, and quite satisfied to let time and the world pass him by.

PRINCIPAL WORKS: A Book of Bargains, 1896; The House of Sin (poems) 1897; The Green Window (novel) 1899; A Dissertation Upon Second Fiddles, 1902; Human Affairs, 1905; The Good Girl (novel) 1912; Sentiment, 1913; Contes d'Amérique (short stories in French) 1924; Aspects of Wilde, 1936.

ABOUT: South Atlantic Quarterly October 1931.

"OUIDA." See "BRITISH AUTHORS OF THE 19TH CENTURY"

OVERSTREET, HARRY ALLEN (October 25, 1875-), American psychologist and sociologist, was born in San Francisco, Calif., the son of William Franklin Overstreet and Julia (Detje) Overstreet. He received a B.A. degree from the University of California in 1899, and a B. Sc. from Balliol College, Oxford University, two years later. Overstreet returned to the University of California in 1901 as instructor and associate professor of philosophy for ten years, coming east then to spend the next eighteen years as professor of philoso-

phy and head of that department at the College of the City of New York. He became professor-emeritus in 1939, and has since devoted his time to lecturing at Town Hall, New York, and conducting over the radio the "Town Meeting of the Air." This work is described in *Town Meeting Comes to Town,* written in collaboration with his second wife, Bonaro Wilkinson of Geyserville, Calif., whom he married in August 1932. By his first wife, Elsie L. Burr of San Francisco, whom he married in 1907, Overstreet had three sons, Edmund William Overstreet, Robert Howison Overstreet, and Alan Burr Overstreet. They live

Oggiano

at Yorktown Heights, N.Y. Professor Overstreet is a member of Phi Beta Kappa and Beta Theta Phi.

In *Our Free Minds* (1941), Overstreet writes: "There are millions of adults who know societal matters only as they have studied them in high school or college. Can we expect their knowledge to be deep and detailed enough for adult life? Obviously, what they know—of history, or political science, or economics—in their forties and fifties will be only the ragtags of their immature learning. Here lies perhaps the gravest problem of our democracy. What we need is hard-bitten, disciplined, grown-up citizen intelligence." The Town Meeting of the Air is designed to meet this need. In *About Ourselves: Psychology for Normal People* (1927), the author says: "As in my former volume, *Influencing Human Behavior,* a large group of business and professional men and women in the New School for Social Research in New York City suffered the onslaught of the lectures," and contributed their own experiences and case histories.

PRINCIPAL WORKS: Influencing Human Behavior, 1925; About Ourselves: Psychology for Normal People, 1927; The Enduring Quest: A Search for a Philosophy of Life, 1931; We Move in New Directions, 1933; A Guide to Civilized Leisure, 1934; A Declaration of Interdependence, 1937; Town Meeting Comes to Town (with B. W. Overstreet) 1938; Let Me Think, 1939; Our Free Minds, 1941; Leaders for Adult Education (with B. W. Overstreet) 1941.

ABOUT: American Magazine October 1938; Current History February 1937.

OVERTON, GRANT MARTIN (September 19, 1887-July 4, 1930), American novelist and literary critic, was born in Patchogue,

Long Island, N.Y., the son of Floyd Alward Overton and Ardelia Jarvis (Skidmore) Overton. He attended Blair Academy and spent two years at Princeton (1904-06). At eighteen he was a reported on the New York morning *Sun*; did newspaper work in Denver and San Francisco; shipped before the mast for a voyage around Cape Horn, and returned to the *Sun* in 1910 as reporter, editorial writer, and editor of the book review section. Going to George H. Doran, the publisher, in 1922, Overton wrote *When Winter Comes to Main Street, Cargoes for Crusoes,* and *American Nights Entertainment* in three successive years, bio-critical essays on American authors (chiefly on the Doran list) no less useful in public libraries for their being glorified publicity. Overton's novels had a pronounced romantic tinge, as shown by their titles —*The Mermaid,* and *The Thousand and First Night*; a fictional account of Walt Whitman's early years, *The Answerer,* also took some liberties with history.

P. MacDonald

He edited a collection of *The World's One Hundred Best Stories* midway in his stay with *Collier's* as fiction editor (1924-30). When bad health compelled Overton to live in Santa Fé he acted as consulting editor for the weekly. *The Philosophy of Fiction,* published two years before his death in New York, at forty-two, was an ambitious (and occasionally rather vague and pretentious) analysis of various novels—Willa Cather's *A Lost Lady,* for one—with discussions of the art of fiction in general, and analysis of an imaginary novel written to illustrate his rules. The book leaned heavily on E. M. Forster's *Aspects of the Novel* and Percy Lubbock's *Craft of Fiction,* and in its "own slightly American way" was worthy to be set beside them, according to the London *Times.* Overton was survived by his widow, Clara (Wallace) Overton of Mohawk, N.Y. Looking even younger than his age of forty-odd, he was smooth-faced, good-looking, and always immaculately dressed.

PRINCIPAL WORKS: The Women Who Make Our Novels, 1918 (revised edition 1928); Why Authors Go Wrong, 1919; The Mermaid, 1920; World Without End, 1921; The Answerer, 1921; When Winter Comes to Main Street, 1922; The Island of the Innocent, 1923; American Nights Entertainment, 1923; Cargoes for Crusoes, 1924; The Thousand and First Night, 1924; The Philosophy of Fiction, 1928.

ABOUT: New York Times July 5, 1930.

OWEN, WILFRED (March 18, 1893-November 4, 1918), English poet, was born at Oswestry, Shropshire, and was killed in France just one week before the Armistice in the First World War. He was only twenty-five at his death, which was one of the most lamentable of the wastages caused by the war.

He was educated at the Birkenhead Institute, Liverpool.

Though he matriculated at London University, he appears never to have studied there. He had been a dreamy, precocious boy, a poet and lover of poetry from childhood, with a special cult for Keats. He was delicate in health, and from 1913 to 1915 lived in France (which he had already visited twice) to avoid the English winters. Near Bordeaux he secured a post as tutor in a private family, and worked on a never published volume of "Minor Poems."

He felt it his duty to enlist, however, when England entered the war, and was accepted for service in the Artists' Rifles. He served for seven months, then was invalided home in June 1917. For four months he was in the Craiglockhart War Hospital, in Scotland, where Siegfried Sassoon later also became a patient. Sassoon became interested in the young man's work and encouraged him to keep on writing. As his health improved, he studied and lectured in Edinburgh, took part in concerts there, and edited the hospital magazine. Then he recovered sufficiently to be made major-domo of a hotel in Scarborough where officers of his regiment were stationed. His work was beginning to appear in magazines, and at the end of the year he wrote his mother: "I am a poet's poet. I am started."

In spite of efforts to find him a post in England, in August he was sent back to France as company commander. He saw front line service, and was awarded the Military Cross for gallantry under fire on October 1st. He had scarcely a month of life left. He was shot fatally while crossing the Sambre Canal at the head of his company.

Though such men as Sassoon, Arnold Bennett, H. G. Wells, and Osbert Sitwell had recognized the talent shown in Owen's work, he was virtually unknown at his death. It was not until 1920 that Sassoon collected Owen's poems into a volume, which contained a foreword by the author in which he said: "All a poet can do today is warn. That is why the true poets must be truthful."

An angry pity is the dominant voice in all these war poems. Less angry and more pitiful than the similarly motivated poems by Sassoon, they are the protest and testament of a potentially great poet caught in a holocaust from which there was no escape except by uttering his "warning." Owen's reputation grew slowly for eleven years, when a new and enlarged edition of his poems appeared. Even this is fragmentary: he was preparing himself, as Edmund Blunden remarked, "in experience, observation, and composition, for a volume of poems to strike at the conscience of England in regard to the continuance of the war." He did not yet consider that volume complete. The greater part of his potentialities never came to fruition. Nevertheless, he had already produced enough work of the first order to give him a permanent place in English literature. None of the war poets rivals him in pure genius; and an article in *Poetry* observes: "What distinguishes Owen's work primarily is the scale of his vision. . . . Owen wrote from an infinite distance. His soul, to borrow a phrase from one of his own poems, 'looked down from a vague height with Death.'"

Technically, Owen's style was advanced and experimental, with a pronounced use of assonance instead of rhyme. His influence has been considerable, and he is one of the principal "ancestors" of the young poets of this generation, particularly of the English school represented by Auden, Spender, etc. His most striking physical characteristic was his "dark and vivid eyes," which, in a face both sensitive and firm, expressed his eager and impressionable spirit.

PRINCIPAL WORKS: Poems, 1920; Poems, 1931.

ABOUT: Collins, H. P. Modern Poetry; Owen, W. Poems, 1931 (see Biographical Sketch by E. Blunden); Untermeyer, L. Modern British Poetry; Canadian Bookman October 1933; Catholic World March 1938; Poetry June 1932.

OXENHAM, JOHN (185?-January 24, 1941), English novelist and poet whose name was originally William Arthur Dunkerley, wrote to the compilers of this volume a few months before his death (at what was believed to be well past his eightieth year): "Born in Manchester, educated at Old Trafford School and Victoria University, spent some years in business, lived in

France, and traveled over a considerable part of Europe, Canada, the United States, and East Africa. In collaboration with Robert Barr, introduced the weekly Detroit *Free Press* to Great Britain, and later on with Barr and Jerome K. Jerome started the *Idler*, and subsequently with Jerome the weekly *To-Day*. Turning from the business side of publishing, tried for a change the literary side and found it much more interesting and eventually much more profitable.

"Has published forty-two novels. In 1913 issued *Bees in Amber,* which his publishers absolutely refused to risk any money on, and it was only by dint of much persuasion that they agreed to let their name appear upon it and to handle it for the trade. They urged the author not to do more than two hundred copies, as they could not possibly sell. So he printed the little book at his own expense, and since then they have had 284,-000 copies of it. During the [First] World War several other small books of verse were issued in similar fashion, and between 1914 and 1919 over a million copies were sold. And *Bees in Amber* still sells regularly. Also during the war the author's *Hymn For the Men at the Front* was sung all round the world and over eight million copies were called for.

"After the war the author developed a new line, beginning with *The Cedar Box* and *The Hidden Years* and a succession of other books on the life of Christ, all of which have been very successful. Lately, his poem "Chaos and the Way Out" was adopted by the Methodist Episcopal Church of America as a special service to be used in 20,000 churches with a membership of eight million. The author is glad to say that he has never asked a favor of any editor, but nevertheless has had more than ample notice of all his books, and has been interviewed many times. His chief relaxations until lately have been Alpine walking and rowing, and most of his summers have been spent on a little lake in the Savoy Alps."

* * *

The Library of Congress is authority for the statement that the author's "real name" was Dunkerley, and the same agency lists "Oxenham" as a pseudonym. What seems more likely, however, is that an actual transfer of name took place, by long usage and, not unlikely, by official deed poll. Both Oxenham and his eldest daughter, Elsie Jeanette, writer for children, have appeared in the British *Who's Who* as Oxenham (since 1901 and 1927, respectively) with no entry for or mention of Dunkerley at any time. (But no birth-dates are given for either.)

Among the few other known facts: Oxenham was married to Margery Anderson of Greenock, Scotland, who died in 1925; they had two sons and four daughters. In his younger years the author lived for a time in the United States and once came near to settling permanently "to grow oranges or raise sheep"; but returned to England. He died during the Second World War at his home at Worthing, Sussex, of natural causes, presumably the infirmities of old age.

PRINCIPAL WORKS: *Novels* — God's Prisoner, 1898; Rising Fortunes, 1899; A Princess of Vascovy, 1900; Our Lady of Deliverance, 1901; Under the Iron Flail, 1902; John of Gerisau, 1903; Bondman Free, 1903; Mr. Joseph Scorer, 1903; Barbe of Grande Bayou, 1903; A Weaver of Webs, 1904; Hearts in Exile, 1904; The Gate of the Dead, 1905; White Fire, 1905; Giant Circumstance, 1906; Profit and Loss, 1906; The Long Road, 1907; Carette of Sark, 1907; Pearl of Pearl Island, 1908; The Song of Hyacinth, 1908; My Lady of Shadows, 1909; Great-Heart Gillian, 1909; A Maid of the Silver Sea, 1910; Lauristons, 1910; The Coil of Carne, 1911; Their High Adventure, 1911; Queen of the Guarded Mounts, 1912; Mr. Cherry, 1912; The Quest of the Golden Rose, 1912; Mary-All-Alone, 1913; Red Wrath, 1913; Maid of the Mist, 1914; Broken Shackles, 1914; Flower of the Dust, 1916; Corner Island, 1916; "1914," 1916; My Lady of the Moor, 1916; The Loosing of the Lion's Whelps, 1918; A Hazard in the Blue, 1923; The Perilous Lovers, 1924; Chaperon to Cupid, 1924; Scala Sancta, 1925; The Recollections of Roderick Fyfe, 1927; The Hawks of Como, 1928. *Verse*—Bees in Amber, 1913; All's Well, 1916; The King's High Way, 1916; Hymn for the Men at the Front, 1916; The Vision Splendid, 1917; The Fiery Cross, 1917; Hearts Courageous, 1918; Gentlemen — The King! 1920; Selected Poems, 1925. *Miscellaneous*—Everywoman and War, 1916; Winds of the Dawn (essays) 1919; The Wonder of Lourdes, 1924; The Cedar Box, 1924; The Hidden Years, 1925; The Man Who Could Save the World, 1927; God's Candle, 1929; Cross Roads, 1930; The Splendor of the Dawn, 1930; A Saint in the Making, 1931; Anno Domini, 1932; God and Lady Margaret, 1933; Christ and the Third Wise Man, 1934; Lake of Dreams (with E. Oxenham) 1941; Out of the Body (comp., with E. Oxenham) 1941.

ABOUT: New York Herald Tribune January 25, 1941; New York Times January 25, 1941; Publishers' Weekly February 22, 1941.

PAASSEN. See VAN PAASSEN

PACH, WALTER (July 11, 1883-),
American artist and art critic, writes: "I was born in New York City, went to school there, and graduated from the College of

the City of New York in 1903. My father was the photographer of the Metropolitan Museum from its earliest days, and as we lived near the museum, I haunted the galleries from childhood, and began my art studies when sixteen years old by copying the drawings of the Old Masters. While still in college I attended the summer classes in painting of William M. Chase and continued to work with him, in America and Europe, for a number of years, also drawing at night, and later in the daytime, under Robert Henri. In 1905, after a summer in Spain, I showed a work for the first time in a professional exhibition, that of the Pennsylvania Academy Fellowship. I had begun, a couple of years before, to support myself by newspaper work, and, in 1907, published my first long article, "The Memoria of Velasquez," in *Scribner's Magazine*. Ever since I have exhibited (oil painting, water colors, and etchings) at frequent intervals and have published some hundred and fifty magazine articles. (Those I like best are 'Le Classicism de Delacroix' in *L'Amour de l'Art*, June 1930, and 'The Raphael from Russia' in the *Virginia Quarterly Review*, January 1936.) I am the translator of Élie Faure's *History of Art* (five volumes) and of the *Journal* of Eugène Delacroix. I have lectured at the principal museums and universities of America, at the National University of Mexico, and at the Louvre.

"My main work is painting (the writing—always on art—being merely a by-product of it). I am represented by paintings or etchings in the Metropolitan Museum, the Whitney Museum of American Art, the Brooklyn Museum, the Cleveland Museum, the Phillips Memorial Gallery (Washington), etc. I have had much to do with organizing and directing exhibitions like the International, of 1913 (the 'Armory Show'), the Independents, the New York World's Fair of 1940, etc."

* * *

Mr. Pach married Magdalene Frohberg, of Dresden, Germany, in 1914; they have one son. W. H. Downes classed him, with Ruskin, as a "defender of the faith," and another critic called him "sympathetic and intelligent." He has his enemies, however, among them Rockwell Kent, who accused him of "sterile pedantry and self-conscious banality."

PRINCIPAL WORKS: Georges Seurat, 1923; The Masters of Modern Art, 1924; Raymond Duchamp-Villon, 1924; Ananias; or The False Artist, 1928; Modern Art in America, 1928; An Hour of Art, 1930; Vincent van Gogh, 1936; Queer Thing, Painting, 1938; Ingres, 1939.

ABOUT: American Magazine of Art August 1929: Nation (London) March 16, 1929; Saturday Review of Literature November 26, 1938.

PACKARD, FRANK LUCIUS (February 2, 1877-February 17, 1942), Canadian novelist and short-story writer, was born of

American parents, Lucius Henry Packard and Frances (Joslin) Packard, in Montreal. He received a B.Sc. degree from McGill College in 1897, and next year took a post-graduate course at L'Institut Montefiore, University of Liège, Belgium. Returning to the United States in 1898, he became a civil engineer.

Packard began writing for the magazines in 1906. He had had some practical experience in the Canadian Pacific Railroad shops, and for some years was engaged in engraving work in the United States. "To railroad men he is known as the author of three excellent books of short stories—On the Iron at Big Cloud, Running Special, and The Night Operator," wrote Frank P. Donovan, Jr., in his enthusiastic bibliography, The Railroad in Literature (1940), "but has also written on a variety of other subjects. As the creator of Jimmie Dale and Shanghai Jim he is familiar to almost every lover of mystery and detective stories. He is now the only living author of the Railroad School, the last of that unique group of writers who knew railroading, loved railroading, and put it forever in the annals of American letters. In subject-matter, setting and style Packard and [Frank] Spearman[qv] show a striking similarity. Both write about western railroading although the former concerns himself with Canada and the latter with the United States. And they mutually agree that the human element, the emergence of the man—loyal, courageous and victorious, transcends the raciest plot in spite of the fact that victory may spell tragedy, at least in the Ibsenian sense of the word."

Jimmie Dale, member of one of New York's most exclusive clubs, is an expert safecracker like his namesake Jimmy Valentine, learning the art from study of his father's business, the manufacture of safes. He leads a triple life, now as the Gray Seal, the clever and mysterious cracksman who leaves his mark, a gray seal, behind him; now as Larry the Bat, denizen of the underworld; and again as Smarlinghue the fallen artist. Jimmie makes burglary appear an interesting and even refined occupation, and the Springfield *Republican* pointed out that "while the hero commits legal 'crimes' to right wrongs, his acts are free from taint of viciousness." More than 2,000,000 copies of the Jimmie Dale books were sold, and they appeared in six languages. *The Miracle Man,* one of the author's most successful novels, was twice filmed.

Packard's frequent travels included a trip to the Far East in search of adventure material. He died at his home in Lachine, near Montreal, at sixty-five, leaving his wife, the former Marguerite Pearl Macintyre of Montreal, whom he had married in 1910; a daughter; and three sons then in service with the Canadian armed forces.

PRINCIPAL WORKS: On the Iron at Big Cloud (short stories) 1911; Greater Love Hath No Man, 1913; The Miracle Man, 1914; The Beloved Traitor, 1916; The Adventures of Jimmie Dale, 1917; The Sin That Was His, 1917; The Wire Devils, 1918; The Further Adventures of Jimmie Dale, 1919; From Now on, 1920; Pawned, 1921; Doors of the Night, 1922; Jimmie Dale and the Phantom Clue, 1922; The Four Stragglers, 1923; The Locked Book, 1924; Running Special, 1925; Broken Waters, 1925; The Red Ledger, 1926; Two Stolen Idols, 1927; The Devil's Mantle, 1927.; Shanghai Jim, 1928; Tiger Claws, 1928; The Big Shot, 1929; Jimmie Dale and the Blue Envelope, 1930; The Gold Skull Murders, 1931; The Hidden Door, 1932; The Purple Ball, 1933; Jimmie Dale and the Missing Hour, 1935; The Dragon's Jaws, 1937; More Knaves Than One (short stories) 1938.

ABOUT: Donovan, F. P., Jr. The Railroad in Literature; New York Times, February 18, 1942.

PAGE, ELIZABETH (August 27, 1889-   ), American historical novelist, writes: "I suppose I had a fairly typical

youth for a city child. Although I happened to be born at our summer cottage in Vermont, my family was living in Brooklyn for most of the year. My father was a young lawyer, and my mother a minister's daughter.

"Except for one

L. Costello

year when I was sent to the public school

for the good of my soul, a matter to which my classmates there joyfully attended, I was prepared for college at the New York Collegiate Institute, where I had a full scholarship because my grandfather had been its founder. I went on occasional trips with my mother to what was then Oklahoma Territory, where my aunt and uncle were missionaries to the Indians, and where I learned to know and respect not only the Red Men, but their wild horses as well.

"I had four glorious years at Vassar, where I graduated in 1912. After a year at home, I took an M.A. in history at Columbia, and secured a position in the Walnut Hill School in Natick, Mass. I planned to be a teacher of history, and, if I should be very lucky, to occupy a chair in a college before I died; but illness and then the war turned everything upside down.

"By 1927 I had a job as assistant in a doctor's office in Wyoming, and I had begun to write. *Wagons West* was published in 1930 and in 1931, when my father died, I came back to New York to look after my mother, who had become an invalid. In 1932 we came out to California to spend a winter, and we have been here [in Sierra Madre] ever since. We are in a lovely spot, but on warm December nights I dream, with homesick longing, of moonlight on snow."

* * *

Miss Page's father later became a judge of the New York Supreme Court; her mother was a niece of the novelist E. P. Roe, her great-uncle was a 'Forty-Niner whose diary was the basis of *Wagons West*. During the First World War she served in the Y.M.C.A. in France, and later was with Dr. Wilfred Grenfell in his Newfoundland mission. She is unmarried. Her historical works have been criticized both as "novelized" and as "over-documented," but all critics agreed on their spirited quality. Her novel, *The Tree of Liberty*, was a best-seller and a successful moving picture.

PRINCIPAL WORKS: Wagons West, 1930; Wild Horses and Gold, 1932; The Tree of Liberty, 1939.

ABOUT: Publishers' Weekly March 4, 1939; Wilson Library Bulletin April 1939; Writer February 1940.

PAGE, THOMAS NELSON. See "AMERICAN AUTHORS: 1600-1900"

PAGET, VIOLET (October 1856-February 13, 1935), English novelist and writer on aesthetics, politics, and Italian art and life under the pseudonym of "Vernon Lee," was born at Boulogne-sur-Mer,

France, the daughter of an English father and a Welsh mother (born Abadam) who was the widow of a Mr. Lee-Hamilton. There was a half-brother, Eugene Lee-Hamilton, who was a poet of some ability. He and the mother were the chief educative influences on Violet during a peripatetic childhood which carried the family from one European coun-

try to another until finally it settled down in Florence. She was brought up in a milieu where intellectual and aesthetic valuations were paramount; and so, being gifted with a quick and lively intelligence, she early acquired habits of close study and became mistress of several languages.

In 1880, at the age of twenty-four, Violet brought out her first book, *Studies of the Eighteenth Century in Italy*. Other periods had, of course, received full treatment, but never before had any English scholar dealt fully and percipiently with this phase of Italian art and thought. Miss Paget had been collecting materials for the book during her precocious adolescence. So striking was the result that it earned great respect not only in England but in Italy, where the *Nuova Antologia* praised its deep research, sense of proportion and truth to life.

A year later Violet Paget paid her first visit to England. She had introductions into artistic society, met Whistler and other prominent figures, and acquired a reputation as a sparkling conversationalist with a tongue that had a sting to it. In 1883 she wrote a puppet show, *The Prince of the Hundred Soups*, a novel called *Ottilie*, and a set of aesthetic essays called *Belcaro*; and in 1884, drawing only too faithfully on the experiences of her English visit, she satirized the aesthetes unmercifully in a "three-decker" entitled *Miss Brown*. The same year appeared *Euphorion*, a learned study of Renaissance art, and *The Countess of Albany*, a biography of the Young Pretender's wife.

Miss Paget wrote in all more than forty works, the main broad divisions of which fall into four categories—fiction, aesthetic psychology, travel and art criticism. Typical of her aesthetic outlook were *Beauty and Ugliness* (written with C. Anstruther Thomson in 1912) and *The Beautiful*, published the following year in the "Cambridge Manuals of Science and Literature." Her argument was subtle, learned, supported by a serious psychological equipment, and had no affinities with the superficial assemblage of prejudices in which so much writing on this subject consists. Her works on Italy were highly expert and beautifully wrought. In addition to her fiction (which is now little read) she published some combative sociological and political books, including *Gospels of Anarchy* (1908), *Vital Lies* (1912) and *Satan, the Waster* (1920). The collection of essays called *The Handling of Words*, which first appeared in the *English Review* during 1911-12, attempted to show that "the whole handling of words, indeed the whole of logical thinking, is but a cubic working backwards and forwards between *what* and *how*."

Miss Paget never married. She remained a complete cosmopolitan, and annoyed Italy by supporting the Turks in the Tripoli war and England by similarly taking the opposite side in 1914-18. She wrote a number of pamphlets for the Union of Democratic Control. She died at San Gervasio, Florence, at the age of seventy-eight.

PRINCIPAL WORKS: *Aesthetics and Criticism*—Studies of the Eighteenth Century in Italy, 1880; Belcaro, 1883; Euphorion, 1884; Baldwin, 1886; Juvenilia, 1887; Althea, 1894; Renaissance Fancies and Studies, 1895; Limbo and Other Essays, 1897; Le Rôle de l'Elément moteur dans la Perception esthétique visuelle (with C. A. Thomson) 1901; Laurus Nobilis, 1909; Beauty and Ugliness (with C. A. Thomson) 1912; The Beautiful, 1913; The Handling of Words, and Other Studies in Literary Psychology, 1923; The Poet's Eye, 1926; Music and Its Lovers, 1932. *On Places*—Genius Loci, 1899; The Enchanted Woods and Other Essays, 1905; The Spirit of Rome, 1906; The Sentimental Traveller, 1908; The Tower of Mirrors, and Other Essays, 1914; The Golden Keys, and Other Essays, 1925. *Sociological, Biographical, and Miscellaneous*—The Countess of Albany, 1884; Hortus Vitae, 1904; Gospels of Anarchy, 1908; Vital Lies, 1912; The Ballet of the Nations, 1915; Satan, the Waster, 1920; Proteus, or The Future of Intelligence, 1925. *Fiction*—The Prince of the Hundred Soups, 1883; Ottilie, 1883; Miss Brown, 1884; A Phantom Lover, 1886; Hauntings: Fantastic Stories, 1890; Vanitas: Polite Stories, 1892; Au Pays de Vénus (stories) 1894; Ariadne in Mantua, 1903; Penelope Brandling, 1903; Pope Jacynth and Other Fantastic Tales, 1904; Sister Benvenuta and the Christ Child, 1906; Louis Norbert, 1914; For Maurice: Five Unlikely Stories, 1927.

ABOUT: Literary World (Boston) 1884; Atlantic Monthly 1885; Forum 1911; Nation (London) September 18, 1920; Bookman (London) 1931; The Times (London) February 14, 1935.

PAIN, BARRY ERIC ODELL (September 28, 1864-May 5, 1928), English humorist, was born in Cambridge, the son of John Odell Pain, a linen-draper, and Maria Pain. From 1879 to 1883 young Pain attended

Sedbergh School, where he edited the school magazine. At Corpus Christi College, Cambridge University, he edited the *Granta*. Here he won a scholarship in 1884, and graduated in 1886 with a third class in the first part of the Classical Tripos.

For the next four years Pain was an army coach at Guildford, then decided to seek his fortune in London as a journalist. He obtained work on the *Daily Chronicle* and *Black and White. In a Canadian Canoe* (1891), Pain's third book, was made up of his contributions to the *Granta*. James Payn, editor of the *Cornhill Magazine*, asked him for contributions, and in 1897 Pain succeeded Jerome K. Jerome as editor of *To-Day*. He had been living at Pinner for several years, but moved in 1900 to Hogarth House, Bushey, until about 1908, when he moved to

St. John's Wood to reside until 1917. In the autumn of 1914 Pain visited the United States.

He was assigned in April 1915 to an anti-aircraft section of the Royal Naval Volunteer Reserve; posted to a searchlight station on Parliament Hill, he soon became a chief petty-officer. Eye-strain compelled him to relinquish this duty, and in 1917 he was a member of the London Appeal Tribunal, adjudicating on claims to exemption from military service. He was then living at Farnham Royal, Buckinghamshire, with Mrs. Pain, who was Amelia Nina Anna Lehmann, daughter of Rudolf Lehmann, the portrait painter, and sister of Liza Lehmann, the composer. She died in 1920, and Pain moved to Watford, where he died in his sixty-fourth year. The Pains had two daughters. His interests included drawing, Georgian literature, occultism, and precious stones.

Early in his career he had been advised by W. E. Henley to devote himself to serious work, according to Herbert Grimsditch, but he preferred to write humorous sketches, especially of suburban and Cockney life. *Eliza* (1900) is purportedly written by a pretentious and ridiculous suburban clerk. *Mrs. Murphy* (1913) deals with a charwoman, and *Edwards* (1915) with a jobbing gardener. Pain was hailed as a "new humorist," according to the *London Mercury*, "and in some quarters the novelty was considered to outweigh the humor. After nearly forty years (his work) is still alive and is not even old-fashioned. In his most extravagant productions he never lost his sense of words or of fitness. The most facile of writers, he never fell below his level and was always readable. If he never quite fulfilled his promise, or did his gifts full justice, it was probably because of the diversity of those gifts. He had all the gifts of a novelist, and those he did write were well received." *Marge Askinforit,* a parody of the Margot Asquith diaries, made his gifts as a parodist evident to an American audience. His *Constantine Dix* stories of criminal adventure have been compared to E. W. Hornung's *Raffles* tales.

PRINCIPAL WORKS: Graeme and Cyril, 1893; Playthings and Parodies, 1896; In a Canadian Canoe, 1897; Kindness of the Celestial and Other Stories, 1897; Octave of Claudius, 1897; Stories and Interludes, 1898; The Romantic History of Robin Hood, 1898; Eliza, 1900; Wilmay and Other Stories of Women, 1898; Eliza, 1900; Nothing Serious, 1901; Stories in the Dark, 1901; De Omnibus, 1901; The One Before, 1902; Little Entertainments, 1903; Eliza's Husband, 1903; Why I Don't, 1903; Lindley Kays (novel) 1904; Memoirs of Constantine Dix, 1905; Robinson Crusoe's Crusoe, 1906; Wilhelmina in London, 1906; First Lessons in Story-Writing, 1907; The Diary of a Baby, 1907; The Shadow of the Unseen (with W. J. Blyth) 1907; The Luck of Norman Dale (with W. J. Blyth) 1908; The Gifted Family, 1909; Proofs Before Pulping, 1909; The Exiles of Faloo, 1910; Here and Hereafter, 1911; An Exchange of Souls, 1911; Exit Eliza, 1912; Stories in Grey, 1912; Stories Without Tears, 1912; The New Gulliver, and Other Stories, 1913; Mrs. Murphy, 1913; One Kind and Another, 1914; Futurist Fifteen, 1914; Edwards: The Confessions of a Jobbing Gardener, 1915; The Short Story, 1915; Me and Marris, 1916; Confessions of Alphonse, 1917; Innocent Amusements, 1918; The Problem Club, 1919; The Death of Maurice, 1920; Marge Askinforit, 1920; Going Home, 1921; If Summer Don't, 1922; Tamplin's Tales of His Family, 1924; The Charming Green Hat Fair, 1925; Dumphry, 1927; The Later Years, 1927.

ABOUT: Bookman (London) June 1928; London Mercury June 1928.

PAINE, ALBERT BIGELOW (July 10, 1861-April 9, 1937), American biographer and juvenile writer, wrote before his death to the compilers of this volume: "I was born in New Bedford, Mass. My father, a Vermonter, owned a store in Bentonsport, Iowa, and a farm a little way from the village. Within a year from my arrival he removed his family to Bentonsport, and some months later enlisted in the Union Army. When the war ended he took us to a farm near Xenia, Ill., where I went to school in a one-room prairie schoolhouse for which he had given the

land. Like most New Englanders, we were a reading family, and, for those days, had plenty of books. I never dreamed of becoming an author, and the compositions I wrote were not of the least consequence. When I was eleven we moved into the village because there was an 'academy' there. I went to it during four winters. That finished my education. I became

my father's assistant in his general store and helped on a new farm he had bought.

"Then, to emulate a friend, I wrote a poem, which, with others, warmed the New York mails for a year. Then one stuck, a sentimental rigamarole in the *New York Weekly.* Other family papers took my rhymes and even paid for them. When I went to St. Louis to learn photography, I continued writing. When I traveled through the South doing 'view work' (1881-82), I still continued. Then I went into the photographic supply business at Fort Scott, Kan., and gave up writing for a few years. I began again in prose. Richard Harding Davis, then editor of *Harper's Weekly,* accepted some of my things, and by 1894 I was on my way to New York.

"What haven't I done since? With John Kendrick Bangs and others I started a newspaper syndicate which promptly failed. With Irving Bacheller and others I started a family paper which died with the third issue. My residue from that venture was a book called *The Bread Line.* Thomas Nast read it and suggested that I write his biography. The Nast book led to my becoming Mark Twain's biographer. I have written about forty books. One of them, *Joan of Arc— Maid of France,* got me the Legion of Honor decoration in 1928. I have lived in France a good deal, and love the country more than I can tell. One of my stories, *The Great White Way,* gave the popular name to Broadway. A good many of my books are autobiographical. For a year (1898) I was children's editor of the New York *Herald,* and for nine years League editor of *St. Nicholas.* I have been married twice, first to Minnie Schultz, second to Dora Locey. I have three surviving daughters by my second marriage. I have a summer home at West Redding, Conn."

* * *

Mr. Paine died at New Smyrna, Fla., at seventy-five, after a month's illness. He was a dignified, scholarly-appearing man with a mane of white hair. He was a bit pompous, and there is a touch of condescension in all his work, including his popular "Hollow Tree" stories for children. His life of Mark Twain is gossipy and uncritical. He was proud of his large acquaintance among the rich and great, and his most peculiar book was probably a biography of one of them—George Fisher Baker, the banker—of which only six copies were published, for Baker's family.

PRINCIPAL WORKS: *For Adults*—Rhymes by Two Friends (with W. A. White) 1893; The Mystery of Evelin Delorme, 1894; The Bread Line, 1900; The Van Dwellers, 1901; The Great White Way, 1901; The Commuters, 1904; Thomas Nast, 1904; From Van Dweller to Commuter, 1907; The Tent Dwellers, 1908; Captain Bill McDonald: Texas Ranger, 1909; The Ship Dwellers, 1910 (as The Lure of the Mediterranean, 1921); Mark Twain, 1912; Dwellers in Arcady, 1919; George Fisher Baker, 1919; The Car That Went Abroad, 1921; In One Man's Life (biography of T. N. Vail) 1921; Single Reels, 1923; Joan of Arc—Maid of France, 1925; Life and Lillian Gish, 1932. *For Children*—Gobolinks (with R. McE. Stuart) 1896; The Dumpies, 1897; The Hollow Tree, 1898; The Arkansaw Bear, 1898; The Deep Woods, 1899; The Little Lady: Her Book, 1901; The Wanderings of Joe and Little Em, 1903; The Luck Piece, 1906; Elsie and the Arkansaw Bear, 1909; The Hollow Tree Snowed-In Book, 1910; Peanut, 1913; How Mr. Dog Got Even, 1915; Mr. Rabbit's Big Dinner, 1915; Hollow Tree Nights and Days, 1916; Boy's Life of Mark Twain, 1916; The Girl in White Armor, 1927; Jan: The Romantic, 1929; The Golden Cat, 1934.

ABOUT: Kunitz, S. J. & Haycraft, H. (eds.). The Junior Book of Authors; American Historical Review July 1937; Publishers' Weekly April 17, 1937.

PAINE, RALPH DELAHAYE (August 28, 1871-April 29, 1925), American war correspondent, journalist, and writer of boys'

books, was born in Lemont, Ill., the son of the Rev. Samuel Delahaye Paine, who had fought at Inkerman in the Crimean War and commanded a batallion of light artillery in the American Civil War, and Elizabeth Brown (Philbrook) Paine. His boyhood was spent at Jacksonville, Fla., where he saved enough from his $12 a week as reporter to enter Yale in the fall of 1890. A powerful physique put him in the university crew and on the football

squad; Paine the journalist treated Paine the athlete with some severity in the news sent out to twenty newspapers by his own syndicate. He also edited the *Yale Literary Magazine*. Graduated in 1894, he worked for the Philadelphia *Press*, and was sent to England in 1896 to cover the Yale-Oxford crew race and again (in 1904) for *Collier's*, to report the track meet between Yale-Harvard and Oxford-Cambridge. As war correspondent Paine participated in the Cuban revolution and the Spanish-American War (Stephen Crane, a fellow-correspondent, put Paine into his *Wounds in the Rain* as William B. Perkins). Hearst selected him to take a gold sword to Gomez, the Cuban leader, which Paine carried five thousand miles before sending it by another messenger. In 1900 he covered the Boxer Rebellion in China, and two years later the New York *Herald* put him in charge of its campaign against the beef trust. After a brief experience as managing editor of the New York *Telegraph* he gave up journalism for writing and research, especially into naval history, in Salem, Mass. Paine's books for boys, while sometimes stereotyped in character and relying on plot clichés have a refreshing breeziness and wholesomeness of tone. He was special observer with the Allied fleets in 1917. In 1903, Paine had married Mrs. Katharine Lansing Morse of Watertown, N.Y., and they established a home in Durham, N.H., in 1908. There were five children, two of them step-children. Paine represented the town in the state legislature in 1919 and was a member of the state board of education from then till 1921. He died at a Concord hotel while serving on jury duty and was buried near his literary workshop at "Shankhassick," his Durham residence. Paine was described as a "gentle, friendly, modest man with a winning smile."

PRINCIPAL WORKS: The Praying Skipper and Other Stories, 1906; The Stroke Oar, 1908; Ships and Sailors of Old Salem, 1909; College Years 1909; The Fugitive Freshman, 1910; Sandy Sawyer, Sophomore, 1911; The Wrecking Master 1911; The Dragon and the Cross, 1912; The Adventures of Captain O'Shea, 1913; The Call of th' Off-Shore Wind, 1918; Fighting Fleets, 1918; The Old Merchant Marine, 1919; The Fight For Free Sea, 1920; The Corsair in the War Zone 1920; Lost Ships and Lonely Seas, 1921; Roads of Adventure (autobiography) 1922; Joshua Barney, 1924; Four Bells, 1924; In Zanzibar, 1925.

ABOUT: Paine, R. D. Roads of Adventure Granite Monthly May 1925; Harvard Graduate Magazine December 1925; Yale College, Class of 1894: Quindecennial Record.

PAKINGTON, HUMPHREY (September 8, 1888-), English novelist and architect, is the Honorable Humphrey Arthur

Pakington, son of the third and heir-presumptive to the fourth Baron Hampton. Like James Barnes-Watson of his novel *The Roving Eye,* young Pakington entered the Navy in 1903, retiring in 1920 as Lieutenant-Commander and again in 1928 as Commander. With the coming of the Second World War he was recalled to active service. In 1922 he trained at the Architectural Association on a Holloway Scholarship, being awarded the Association Diploma and a Fellowship in the Royal Institute of British Architects. Pakington's profession has been a partnership in Pakington & Enthoven, Architects, and his avocation the writing of rambling, deft, and satirical novels of English family life which have won him an American following which is not so large as that of Angela Thirkell, for instance, but is made up of the same stratum of lovers of intelligent comedy. *Four in Family* and *The Roving Eye* were collected in the omnibus volume *The Warmstrys of Romanfield* (1933). The *Saturday Review* has said that the Pakington novels are never vulgar and never dull, but are apt to "collapse into a welter of episodes like skinless sausage."

Family Album (1939), which is given a deceptive appearance of symmetry by the frequent insertion of dates denoting the passage of time, has been the most successful of the Pakington books in America. His serious work, *English Villages and Hamlets,* has appeared here in two editions, with an introduction by E. V. Knox. In 1913 Pakington married Grace Dykes Spicer, daughter of the Rt. Hon. Sir A. Spicer, the first baronet; they have a son and three daughters. Humphrey Pakington, a handsome, clean-shaven man, was president of the Architectural Association in 1934-36. His home is in London.

PRINCIPAL WORKS: Four in Family, 1931; The Roving Eye, 1932; In Company With Crispin (U.S. title: The Eligible Bachelor) 1932; How the World Builds: An Introduction to Architecture, 1932; English Villages and Hamlets, 1935 (second revised ed., 1937); Family Album, 1939; Our Aunt Auda, 1942.

PALMER, FREDERICK (January 29, 1873-), American novelist and war correspondent, writes: "Even in my early years,

which were spent on a farm in Western New York, I wanted to follow the brook to where it joined the river, follow the river to where it flowed into the bay, and then on across the seas, in pursuit of the receding stretch of the horizon's rim, until I

Blank & Stoller

had seen all lands and all peoples with my own eyes. It happened that what had seemed only youth's delectable dreams in idle moments, when in sober moments I planned to study law, became reality. Chance enabled me to write my way along the beaten paths of travel in Europe after I had been diverted to journalism; and then the very gamble of chance sent me to report the Greco-Turkish War of 1897, while the little classic Greek I had in college (Allegheny, Class of 1893) was still fresh in mind. There, on the fabled Thessalian plain in sight of Mount Olympus, I saw the red fezes of the Turks in red-crested waves of attack and cavalry charges in the days when war still had glamor and adventure.

"The little book I wrote about that campaign was read by Joseph Pulitzer of the New York *World,* by Robert Collier, then making a progressive weekly, and by Lord Northcliffe, that power in British journalism of his time. At twenty-four, as the adventitiously spoiled child of fortune, I had a choice of offers from the three. It was not only this and the succession of wars which followed that settled my fate. As a boy the doctors had told me that heart trouble precluded both sedentary office work and violent exercise. I was warned that if I made the projected journey over the Yukon ice in the winter of 1897-98 I should not return alive. From the Arctic Circle I was on my way toward the Equator for the Phillipine Rebellion; to the tough and picturesque march of the hastily gathered allied contingents for the relief of the Peking legations in the Boxer Rebellion; an interesting journey across Siberia in the Czarist regime; Central American and Balkan outbreaks; and the Russo-Japanese War of 1904-05.

"But why mention more forgotten wars that followed the turn of the century? Owing to the little burst of reputation, which destiny had given me when I was young, I was already referred to at thirty-five as 'the dean of American war correspondents.' At the start of the World War of 1914-18, when the British Army in France would accredit only one American correspondent, I was chosen by the American press associations. Later, as an officer in our army (Major and Lieutenant Colonel), I had the official confirmation of the Distinguished Service Medal that I had done my own best to win 'the war to end war.' As a climax of further experiences I was with the British Army in France again in May 1940, but was hospitalized back to England before the evacuation of Dunkirk.

"I have had time off between wars to write many, too many, books. A few, including two novels, were almost best sellers. After the [First] World War, there were the three books which represented five years of work and research on our part in that war, and also the reminiscent *With My Own Eyes*. I still hold to the medical advice about fresh air, and I am finding it easier not to be absent-minded about violent exercise."

* * *

Colonel Palmer was born in Pleasantville, Pa. He has honorary doctorates from Allegheny College and Princeton. It is now forty-five years since he was condemned to imminent death from a heart lesion and a carotid aneurism, and at nearly seventy he can look back on one of the most strenuous lives of his era. He says simply: "I hope, and hope keeps us young." In 1924 he was married to Mrs. Talmadge Runkle, and though they have no children of their own he has reared a stepson and stepdaughter. He lives in Katonah, N.Y. John Palmer Gavitt said that he has "the dour courage of an indomitable spirit. . . . He has suffered the fate of being known exclusively as a war correspondent; whereas he was and is, even as such, primarily a philosopher, a thinking, deeply appraising observer of mankind, . . . a gallant personality, . . . a reporter de luxe, and a gentleman in the finest sense."

PRINCIPAL WORKS: Going to War in Greece, 1897; The Ways of the Service, 1901; The Vagabond (novel) 1903; With Kuroki in Manchuria, 1904; Central America and Its Problems, 1910; Over the Pass (novel) 1912; The Last Shot (novel) 1914; My Year of the War, 1915; My Second Year of the War, 1917; America in France, 1918; Our Greatest Battle, 1919; The Folly of Nations, 1921; Clark of the Ohio, 1929; Newton D. Baker—America At War, 1931; With My Own Eyes, 1933; Bliss: Peacemaker, 1936;

The Man With a Country, 1935; Our Gallant Madness, 1937.

ABOUT: Palmer, F. With My Own Eyes; Saturday Review of Literature October 14, 1933.

PALMER, GEORGE HERBERT (March 19, 1842-May 7, 1933), American philosopher and educator, was born in Boston of an old Puritan family; he was of the seventh generation to live on the ancestral farm in Boxford, Mass. His parents, Julius A. Palmer and Lucy Manning (Peabody) Palmer named him for the English poet at the suggestion of an uncle; Palmer's edition of George Herbert in later years became standard. The boy's schooling was interrupted frequently by anemia and general debility; but homeopathic treatment and a rigidly-followed régime enabled him to reach the advanced age of ninety-one. After two years at Phillips Academy, Andover, and a year in a wholesale dry-goods store, Palmer entered Harvard at eighteen, when instruction there was at its lowest ebb, and graduated in 1864. He taught a year in Salem high school; obtained a B.D. from Andover Theological Seminary in 1867, but never entered the ministry; and became a tutor in Greek at Harvard in 1870, the year after Charles W. Eliot assumed control. Palmer gave well-attended readings in Greek, reading and translating an entire book of the *Odyssey* at a sitting; his prose translation, published in 1884, was still selling 40,000 copies a year in 1927-30. In 1872 Palmer was instructor in philosophy under Francis Bowen, and was made a full professor in 1883. In 1889 he became Alford Professor of Natural Religion, Moral Philosophy, and Civil Polity, retiring in 1913, but continuing to live in the Harvard Yard and serving as Overseer for six years.

Palmer's name is not connected with any definite system of philosophy; he was a moderate idealist whose field of special competence was the critical analysis of human conduct. He thought human personality incompatible with materialism, mechanistic interpretations, or "soul-destroying monisms." (*The Problem of Christianity* by his colleague Josiah Royce[qv] also grapples with the latter problem). His history of philosophy course, celebrated by Owen Wister in *Philosophy 4*, was sardonically placed at an afternoon hour which made it impossible for athletes to attend it. He was twice married, to Ellen Margaret Wellman of Brookline in 1871; and to Alice Freeman, president of Wellesley, in 1887. Palmer's biography of the latter had sold more than 50,000 copies in 1930. He had a slight figure, deep-set eyes, formidable eyebrows and moustache, but a "radiant and instantly attentive" smile.

PRINCIPAL WORKS: The New Education, 1887; Self-Cultivation in English, 1897; The Glory of the Imperfect, 1898; The Field of Ethics, 1901; The Nature of Goodness, 1903; The English of George Herbert (ed.) 1905; The Life of Alice Freeman Palmer, 1908; The Problem of Freedom, 1911; Formative Types in English Poetry, 1918; Altruism, 1919; Autobiography of a Philosopher, 1930.

ABOUT: Harvard University; Department of Philosophy. George Herbert Palmer; Palmer, G. H. Autobiography of a Philosopher, 1930; New York Times May 8, 1933.

PALMER, JOHN LESLIE. See "BEEDING, F."

PANTER-DOWNES, MOLLIE (August 25, 1906-), Anglo-Irish novelist and journalist, was born in London, where she spent

the first five years of her life. Her mother was Irish, and her father, Edward Martin Panter-Downes, who was a major in the Royal Irish Infantry, came of a Cheshire family, the Downes of Shrigley and Worth. He fought in the South African War; for five years before the First World War was Colonel of the Gold Coast Regiment; and was killed at the Battle of Mons in August 1914. His daughter dedicated her first two novels to him and "to his brother officers and men of the 2nd Battalion, Royal Irish Regiment, who fell at the battle of Mons." She had begun to write at six, during a period of convalescence from scarlet fever which necessitated her staying in England for two years while her parents were in Africa. Miss Panter-Downes lived with her mother in a Brighton flat for the next four years after her father's death, going to school at Wistons, Dyke Road, and receiving high marks in literature while "failing miserably in mathematics." Between eight and twelve she scribbled fairy stories, plays, poetry, and an unfinished verse-play, Golden Slippers. Some of her poems appeared in Poetry Review before she was twelve. In 1918 her mother moved to the country and thence to Horsham, a little country town in Sussex. In school again at Heathfield House, Mollie Panter-Downes worked on a long novel in which four of her chums were the heroines. "She gave them Adonises; she gave them children; and achieved withal a mastery in their real play-life; for if one of the 'heroines' annoyed her, she had only to say 'You look out or I'll kill your husband in the next chapter' to gain instant docility." Before she left Horsham, two years later, she and her friends had established a flourishing school-magazine.

In Brighton with her mother, Miss Panter-Downes had lessons at home with a Mademoiselle and a tutor. In August 1922, just before she was sixteen, she spent a holiday at Salcombe, South Devon (the Purse Pomeroy of The Shoreless Sea) and decided while there to write a "real" novel. Her first trial fizzled out after three chapters. The next was begun in November 1922 and carried through to its conclusion in March 1923. At first called Escape, it was titled The Shoreless Sea from a Swinburne poem and sent to the old publishing house of John Murray. To her surprise and joy, Colonel Murray wrote to say that if she would revise it carefully, he would accept the novel. It appeared in November 1923, and, advertised as the work of a sixteen-year-old, attracted considerable attention. Its occasional exaggeration of style and immaturity of emotion were understandable. As a novelist she is still young, with more promise than fulfillment.

In 1927 Miss Panter-Downes married Clare Robinson, and has spent some years raising a family of three children. She has done considerable traveling, especially in the Far East. In 1936 she visited the United States. She lives in a Tudor house in Surrey, where her husband has a pig farm. With the coming of the Second World War her "Letter From England," published in the New Yorker week by week, was followed with interest and admiration. It was, in "Jan Struther's" words, a piece of serial journalism which turned out to be a literary document, and as such was published in book form in October 1940.

PRINCIPAL WORKS: The Shoreless Sea, 1924; The Chase, 1925; Storm Bird, 1929; My Husband Simon, 1931; Nothing in Common But Sex, 1932; Letter From England, 1940.

ABOUT: Wilson Library Bulletin January 1941.

PANZINI, ALFREDO (December 31, 1863-April 10, 1939), Italian novelist and essayist, was born at Senigallia, his parents

being Emilio and Filomena (Santini) Panzini. He was educated at the Marco Foscarini Lyceum in Veniče and at the University of Bologna, where his teacher was the great poet Giosuè Carducci. Panzini was Carducci's lifelong disciple. He himself became a teacher, being pro-

fessor of Italian and Latin at the Lyceum in Regno, and of Italian Literature at the Polytechnic School in Milan. The beginning of his literary career was in 1890, with the publication of the *Libro dei Morti (Book of the Dead)*, and it closed with the publication of his novel, *Il Bacio di Lesbia (The Kiss of Lesbia)*.

His widow writes: "He was little influenced as a writer by other writers, either Italian or foreign, but wrote sincerely as his heart and spirit dictated. He was Italian and Latin in the most noble sense of the word; from his literary works there radiates in profuseness—he published about thirty novels and books of stories, besides other non-fiction works among which was his celebrated *Dizionario Moderno (Modern Dictionary)*—a profound feeling for humanity and of humane piety. The sense of death so greatly present in his works was not a dark shadow, but an appeal for and incitation to a higher human goodness, a more fraternal harmony among all people. He was never preoccupied by or anxious for fame, but lived simply with few needs, spending a great part of his time in contact with nature and in the company of his family and a few and faithful friends. He was an ardent farmer, and in his last years spent the greater part of the year in his little estate of Bellaria on the shore of the Adriatic, where he occupied himself with farming and with ameliorating the conditions of life of his own countrymen, to whom he was particularly devoted."

Panzini married Clelia Gabrielli in 1890; they had three sons (one deceased) and a daughter. From 1890 to 1917 he lived in Milan, after that in Rome. In 1929, on the foundation of the Royal Academy of Italy, he was nominated among the first thirty Academicians. A few years earlier the Ministry of Public Instruction gave him a gold medal for his achievement as a writer. He was considered by Italian critics among the great "modern classicists," with Carducci,

Pascoli, and d'Annunzio. He died at seventy-five.

With his "special temperament" of a writer who was above all a humorist and yet a solitary thinker, Panzini was never one of those who becomes popular; he was a writer for the few, not for the mass. The present president of the Royal Academy of Italy said of him: "He was the marvelous narrator of the adventures of his own spirit, who yet has not revealed entirely his own originality and greatness."

Only one of Panzini's books has been translated into English, and he is almost unknown here, though he was frequently translated into other European languages. He was primarily a humorist, yet fundamentally a melancholy man. M. Muret said of him that he is "merry when he is inventing, sad when he is observing." He was a pacifist, but was otherwise an extreme conservative and especially an anti-feminist. A short, stout, ruddy man with gold-rimmed spectacles, he looked more the farmer than the author. All Italy laughed uproariously at his stories, yet his own conclusion on mankind was that "we are big insects that talk." Joseph Collins called him "an interpreter of the feelings and sentiments of the average man and woman and their spokesman, a master of prose, . . . clear, limpid and sometimes sparkling."

WORK AVAILABLE IN ENGLISH: Wanted: A Wife, 1922.

ABOUT: Bookman June 1920; Journal des Debats September 30, 1927; Nuova Antologia June 16, 1929, April 1, 1931, February 16, 1938, March 16, June 1, November 1, 1939, April 1, 1940.

PAPINI, GIOVANNI (January 9, 1881-), Italian critic and essayist, was born in Florence, the son of Luigi and Emilia (Cardini) Papini, and educated at the University of Florence. In 1903 he became co-editor of a review called *Leonardo*, which lasted until 1907; in 1911 he was co-editor of *L'Anima*, and in 1912 of *La Voce*. From 1913 to 1915 he ed-

ited *Lacerba*, and after the war, in 1919 and 1920, *La Vera Italia* (the true Italy). During this early phase as critic and editor, he was a sort of Italian Mencken—violently prejudiced, with an inexhaustible fund of brilliant invective, and exceedingly entertaining in his iconoclasm. He was an Anarchist and an Atheist, hated mysticism in any form, and warred on obscurity wherever he found it.

In 1920 he was converted to the Roman Catholic Church (in which, of course, he had been reared). Since that time Papini has been "the great penitent," the spokesman of religion (though not always exactly orthodox), and a pillar of Fascism. He became a member of the Royal Academy of Italy, his *Dante Vivo* won the Mussolini Prize in 1933, and since 1935 he has been professor of Italian literature at the University of Bologna, though his permanent residence is still in Florence. His latest work, not yet translated into English, is a massive history of Italian literature.

He was married in 1907 to Giacinta Giovagnoli, and they have two daughters.

In evaluating Papini's work one must differentiate between the two phases, for the books of each might have been written by two very different men. In his earlier work, though egotism and hatred were his keynotes, he did a valuable service in purging Italian culture and literature of much nonsense, and providing a basis for a new cultural approach. In his later work, although he remains a scholar and an exponent of the theory that history must be approached through biography (that is, through study of "man as individual"), he has been guilty frequently of what one critic called "the hysterical dismissal of intelligence."

The fact is that Papini seems to identify himself with his subjects, even to St. Augustine and more exalted figures still. As Samuel Putnam remarked, he is "in his own eyes something of a demiurge, . . . : with a vision of himself at once as hero, reformer, and saint." His *Life of Christ* was immensely popular with people who would have been horrified by his earlier works. In many ways he recalls his compatriot d'Annunzio, and he is characterized by the same self-glorification—but also by the same verbal brilliancy. Among his untranslated books are several volumes of poems, and he has edited a number of literary anthologies. His autobiographical novel, *A Finished Man*, is a record of a spiritual crisis ten years before his conversion, and though not evidential as to data, gives an excellent picture of his personality.

Works Available in English: Twilight of the Philosophies, 1906; The Tragic of Everyday, 1906; Twenty and Four Minds, 1912; A Finished Man (The Failure) (novel) 1913; Life of Christ, 1921; Wild Man's Dictionary (with D. Giuliotti) 1923; Bread and Wine, 1926; St. Augustine, 1929;

Gog, 1930; Laborers in the Vineyard, 1930; Life and Myself, 1930; Dante Living, 1935.

About: Fabri, E. Papini Come Scrittore; Fondi, R. Un Construttore: Papini; Moscardelli, N. Giovanni Papini (in Italian); Palmieri, E. Giovanni Papini (in Italian); Prezzolini, G. Discorsi su Giovanni Papini; Bookman April 1920; Catholic World April 1934, September 1933; Christian Century March 13, 1924; Commonweal August 3, 1932; Current Opinion April 1920, September 1921; Journal des Débats January 14, 1927; Literary Digest May 5, 1923, January 26, 1924; Living Age June 25, 1821, April 1931; New Republic June 1924; North American Review June 1923; Nuova Antologia December 16, 1932; Saturday Review of Literature February 15, 1930.

PARETO, VILFREDO (August 15, 1848-August 19, 1923), Italian sociologist, was the son of Marchese de Raffaele de Pareto, an engineer who, in spite of his title, was an ardent Republican and disciple of Giuseppe Mazzini, the Liberator. He was in consequence obliged to flee to Paris, where he married a French woman and where his son was born. The family returned to  Italy in 1858, after an amnesty had been declared. Most of Vilfredo Pareto's violent reaction against democracy, his fanatical hatred of humanitarianism, has an obviously Freudian source, in his revolt against his father and all his father stood for. He followed in his father's professional footsteps, however, graduating in 1870 from the Polytechnic Institute at Turin. He was a director of the national railways in Rome, and superintendent of iron mines near Florence. He also entered politics, as an ardent advocate of free trade, but being defeated in his first candidacy abandoned politics forever and added parliamentarianism to his list of hatreds. He became a lecturer on mathematics and engineering at Florence and Fiesole from 1882 to 1892, but was in constant conflict with the government, and was delighted when in 1893 he was called to the University of Lausanne, Switzerland, as a lecturer on economics, becoming professor the following year. For the rest of his life he lived in Céligny, near Lausanne, but in another canton—where the taxes were lower. About 1900 he inherited a fortune from an uncle, and thereafter spent most of his life in retirement in his palatial villa, writing and studying. Most of his works were written between 1896 and 1919.

In spite of his loathing of the proletarians and the revolutionists, Pareto had definable relations with the Anarchist movement. In fact, his first wife was the daughter of the Anarchist leader Bakunin. She divorced him, and he married a Mme. Régis, a French actress, who survived him. He had no children, and in fact disliked children so much that he seldom allowed them to enter his house. Instead he was passionately devoted to animals, and especially to Angora cats; he had a dozen of them, regarded as almost sacred objects, and when he wrote he kept a cat perched on each shoulder. For years before his death, four days after his seventy-fifth birthday, he had suffered from heart disease. He was obliged to live a Spartan life in the midst of luxury, though he never gave up his love of and connoisseurship in fine wines. A tall, bald old man with a long white beard, he was little known even to his neighbors, a recluse limited to a very small circle of intimates.

Though Pareto died only a few months after the establishment of Fascism in Italy, Mussolini recognized him as the father of Fascist theory, and heaped him with honors. He was named as a delegate to the Disarmament Conference at Geneva, made a senator, and he contributed to Mussolini's personal organ, *Gerarchia.* However, what Pareto wanted was political absolutism united with personal freedom for the intellectual aristocrats, the élite; so if he had lived he might in the end have fallen out with the Fascist regime. As Max Lerner remarked, "Pareto's Republic is now a reality: it is Hitler's totalitarian state." But that is true only if the Nazi leaders are considered the élite in the Paretan sense—a thesis he would probably have disagreed with heartily. He detested political liberty, but (for himself and a small group at least) wanted economic and intellectual liberty.

Sidney Hook called Pareto's most important work (the only one to be translated into English), the *Trattato di Sociologica Generale,* "the most ambitious attempt of the twentieth century to construct a scientific system of sociology." Max Lerner, another opponent of Pareto's general theory, nevertheless acknowledged his "prodigality of ideas, of learning—and of spleen." And George E. Novack, who dubbed him "the Marx of the middle classes," pointed out his real contribution to economic theory—his reputation rests on his application of mathematics to economics. Nevertheless, the fact remains that in every country it has been chiefly the reactionary and Fascist-minded

who have hailed Pareto as their master, that his name is revered today in Italy and Germany, and that the net result of his theories is the fostering of dictatorship and totalitarianism, and the overthrow of all ideals of human progress and humanitarianism—the ideals which actuated his father.

WORK AVAILABLE IN ENGLISH: The Mind and Society (Treatise on General Sociology) 1935.

ABOUT: Borkenau, F. Pareto; Bousquet, G. H. The Work of Vilfredo Pareto; Henderson, L. H. Pareto's General Sociology; Homans, G. C. & Curtis, C. P. An Introduction to Pareto: His Sociology; Keyser, C. J. Vilfredo Pareto; American Journal of Sociology November 1930, March 1936, September 1940; Atlantic Monthly September 1935; Harper's Magazine October 1933; Independent December 10, 1927; Journal of Ethics October 1935; Journal of Philosophy September 12, 1935; London Quarterly Review April 1938; Nation June 26, 1935; New Republic July 9, 1933, June 12, 1935; Political Science Quarterly September 1930; Quarterly Journal of Sociology August 1935, August 1939; Saturday Review of Literature April 22, 1933, May 25, 1935; Sociological Review July 1936; Survey November 1934; Survey Graphic September 1935; Virginia Quarterly Review July 1935, July 1938; Yale Review June 1935.

PARKER, Mrs. DOROTHY (ROTHS-CHILD) (August 22, 1893-), American humorist and short story writer, was born in West End, N.J., the daughter of J. Henry Rothschild and Eliza A. (Marston) Rothschild. Her father was Jewish, her mother Scottish. She was educated at Miss Dana's School, Morristown, N.J., and the Blessed Sacrament Convent,  M. Goldberg New York City. In 1916 and 1917 she was on *Vanity Fair,* most of the time as its dramatic critic. In 1927 she became book critic of the *New Yorker,* but resigned after her first book proved to be that phenomenon a best-selling book of verse, and since then has been a free-lance writer.

In 1917 she married Edwin Pond Parker II. They were divorced in 1928, but she has continued to write under her first married name, though in 1933 she married the motion picture actor, Alan Campbell. Since that time she has lived in Bucks County, Pa., and Hollywood. She has no children.

Mrs. Parker would rather be called a satirist than a humorist, and with reason. Her wit has been called "bitter-sweet," and (especially in her prose stories) it is often more bitter than sweet. For years she has been the person around whose name gathered all the *bon mots* of the time; yet she is capable of depicting heart-break (*vide* "Big Blonde" as an example), and there is a sardonic, corrosive touch to almost everything she writes. She is, indeed, a desperately serious person, like most people celebrated for their wit. Her political and economic views are far to the left; she was one of the many persons arrested in Boston during the demonstrations against the execution of Sacco and Vanzetti, and since she visited Spain during the Civil War, she has devoted much of her time and energy toward helping Loyalist refugees. She herself says: "The humorist has never been happy, anyhow. Today he's whistling past worse graveyards to worse tunes."

In appearance she is plump, dark, and handsome in a decided sort of way, with a clear, mellow voice. She is very nearsighted, but refuses to wear glasses in public. She is fond of dogs, flowers, and pretty clothes, and though her style is stripped and bare, as simple as that of Ernest Hemingway (her favorite writer), she herself is a very feminine person, emotional, rather timid, and confessedly superstitious.

She has a genuine talent for trenchant light verse, and the best of her stories, in the vein of satire or dreary irony, are frequently reprinted in anthologies. "Big Blonde" won the O. Henry prize in 1929. She has written a good deal for the screen, and between that and the tasks to which her social consciousness impels her, she writes far too little now in either prose or verse.

PRINCIPAL WORKS: *Verse*—Enough Rope, 1927; Sunset Gun, 1928; Death and Taxes, 1931; Not So Deep As a Well, 1936. *Collected Stories*—Laments for the Living, 1930; Here Lies, 1939.

ABOUT: Bookman March 1928; Publishers' Weekly March 17, 1934; Scholastic March 19, 1938.

PARKER, Sir GILBERT, Bart. (November 23, 1862-September 6, 1932), Canadian novelist, was born Horatio Gilbert Parker

in Camden East, Ontario, the son of Captain J. Parker, of the Royal Artillery. He was one of a family of ten children. In 1890 his father retired from the service and moved to Seaforth, Ontario, where the boy worked as dispensary assistant for a physician. His first writing was in verse, which he began to have published at the age of sixteen. He expected to enter the church, and with this in mind studied at the Ottawa Normal School and at Trinity College, Toronto; but instead of becoming a clergyman he turned teacher, being appointed lecturer in English at Trinity in 1883. After two years his health broke down, and he set out on what proved to be several years of travel, in the course of which he journeyed around the world, including in his experiences four years as associate editor of the Sydney (Australia) *Morning Herald*. During this period he wrote three plays, one an adaptation of *Faust* (1888). In London, he determined on a literary career, burned his bridges by destroying all the stories he had already written, and returned to Canada, where he began writing short stories about the French Canadian woodsmen among whom he had lived as a boy. For a time he lived in the United States, where in 1895 he married Amy Van Tine, of New York, who died in 1925; they had no children.

Parker's greatest success was *The Seats of the Mighty*, a novel about the fall of Quebec in 1759, which sold over 100,000 copies. Almost as successful (and the only one of his novels to be read at all today) was *The Right of Way*, a story of impersonation. Though he continued writing up to four years before his death, all his best work was produced in the earlier years. In 1898 he went to England to live permanently. He was a member of Parliament from 1900 to 1918, as a Conservative, was knighted in 1902, and was made a baronet in 1915, and a privy councilor in 1916. These latter honors were in recognition of his war service; to use his own phrase, he "had American publicity [i.e., propaganda] in his charge for over two and a half years after war was declared." He was active in many other ways, organized the first Imperial Universities Conference in London in 1903, and was chairman not only of the Authors' Club but also of the Imperial South African Association and the Small Ownership Committee. Personally, he was a handsome, dignified man with rather prominent gray eyes and a close-cropped moustache and beard. He died in London at seventy, of a heart attack, but was buried in Canada, near his birthplace, by his own express desire.

The *Nation* called Sir Gilbert "an imperialist of the old romantic school," and he was that in his writing no less than in his views and personality. His books are now badly "dated," as much from their old-fashioned jingoism as from their "healthy tone" and saccharine complacency. However, he was a real story-teller, and he had a student's respect for history which made his work on the past of Canada, both fictional and non-fictional, accurate in detail and true to recorded fact.

PRINCIPAL WORKS: *Fiction*—Pierre and His People (short stories) 1892; Mrs. Fachion, 1893; The Trail of the Sword, 1894; When Valmond Came to Pontiac, 1895; An Adventurer of the North (short stories) 1895; The Seats of the Mighty, 1896; The Battle of the Strong, 1898; The Lane That Had No Turning (short stories) 1900; The Right of Way, 1901; A Ladder of Swords, 1904; The Weavers, 1907; Northern Lights (short stories) 1909; The Judgment House, 1913; You Never Know Your Luck, 1915; The World for Sale, 1916; Wild Youth (short stories) 1919; Carnac's Folly, 1922; The Power and the Glory, 1925; Tarboe, 1927; The Promised Land, 1928. *Miscellaneous*—Round the Compass in Australia, 1892; A Lover's Diary (verse) 1894; History of Old Quebec (with C. G. Bryan) 1903; The World in Crucible, 1915.

ABOUT: Kingston, G. A. Rt. Hon. Sir Gilbert Parker, Bart., Deceased; Williams, H. Modern English Writers; Bookman (London) October 1932; Canadian Bookman September 1932, October 1932, January 1933; Nation September 21, 1932.

*PARKER, LOUIS NAPOLEON (October 21, 1852-), English dramatist and composer,

was born in Calvados, France (in the year in which Citizen Bonaparte became Louis Napoleon), the eldest son of Charles Albert Parker, a native of Massachusetts. Louis N. Parker was "born traveling, given up for as good as dead, and christened in a violent hurry by the first name that suggested itself. This has been of great service to the cheap humorist." In his early travels the boy picked up French, Italian, and German, and was given piano lessons by a baroness (another did the family washing). The Parkers returning to England, he attended the Royal Academy of Music, of which he was made a Fellow in 1898, and on reaching his majority was appointed Director of Music at Sherborne School in 1873, retaining that post nineteen years, and writing cantatas for solo, chorus, and orchestra. His first play, *A Buried Talent* (1890), introduced Mrs. Patrick Campbell to London. Parker resigned from Sherborne in 1892 to take up a career as a successful writer, adapter, and translator of plays. His plays—like the *Rosemary* of 1896, in which Maude Adams appeared in support of John Drew; *Pomander Walk* (1910), a comparatively plotless but atmospheric study of social types in Georgian England, and *Our Nell*—are rather old-fashioned in their dramaturgy and tend to run to mere prettiness. Theatrical effectiveness is the keynote of the historical plays, such as *The Vagabond King* (1897), *Drake* (1912), *Joseph and His Brethren* (1913), and the highly successful vehicle for George Arliss, *Disraeli* (1911), which takes a few liberties with history. Besides his hundred plays, including successful versions of Rostand's *Cyrano, L'Aiglon,* and *Chantecler,* Parker wrote, staged, and frequently composed the music for pageants in Dover, Colchester, Sherborne, York, Kenilworth, Warwick, and Bury St. Edmonds. He came to the United States in 1897 to stage *Mayflower* at the Lyceum Theatre, and again in 1909. Mrs. Parker, who died in 1919, was Georgiana Bessie Calder; Dorothy, one of their two daughters, married Lennox Pawle, a well-known actor. The dramatist, a small, deaf man with a large drooping moustache, makes his home in London. He is a member of the Garrick Club.

PRINCIPAL PUBLISHED WORKS: Disraeli, 1911; Several of My Lives (autobiography) 1928.

ABOUT: Parker, L. N. Several of My Lives (autobiography); Strand Magazine August 1909.

PARRINGTON, VERNON LOUIS (August 3, 1871-June 17, 1929), American literary historian and critic, was born in

Aurora, Ill., the son of John William Parrington and Louise (McClelland) Parrington. He received his B.A. at Harvard in 1893 and his M.A. at the College of Emporia (Kansas) in 1895. At the latter college he was instructor in English and French from 1893 to 1897, and early showed his liberal tendencies by running (unsuccessfully) for the city's school board on the Populist ticket. From 1897 to 1908 he was at the University of Oklahoma, first as instructor in English and modern languages and then, after the first year, as professor of English. In 1903 and 1904 he took a leave of absence to study at the British Museum and the Bibliothèque Nationale in Paris. In 1908 he became assistant professor of English at the University of Washington.

* Died September 21, 1944.

He was promoted to a full professorship in 1912, and still held that position at the time of his sudden death at not quite fifty-eight.

In 1901 he married Julia Rochester Williams, and they had two daughters and a son.

Parrington was an inspiring teacher. A pupil has described him, sitting on a long table before the class, his legs swinging, smiling blandly while he fired "a volley of Socratic questions" at the students. "Nobody ever could take notes in one of his classes." As a writer he was even more influential. Most of his time and energy outside teaching went into work on his great history of American literature, which he died before completing; but he was always willing to leave it to write articles for magazines or to contribute to such works as the *Encyclopaedia Britannica* (Hawthorne, Nineteenth Century American Literature), the *Cambridge History of American Literature* (Puritan Divines), the *Dictionary of American Biography* (James Russell Lowell), or the *Encyclopedia of Social Sciences* (Brook Farm). He also taught at the summer schools of the University of California, Columbia, and the University of Michigan, and he edited the writings of the so-called "Connecticut Wits."

But *Main Currents in American Thought* was his lifework. It was a history of literature which, by its treatment of writers from the social viewpoint, brought "the new history" into the literary field and marked an epoch in its classification. Its influence was profound, and still continues. When the second volume received the Pulitzer Prize for history in 1928, it did not seem strange that a history prize should go to a professor of English writing about literature. It revealed Parrington as an extreme liberal, almost a radical, fundamentally a Marxist with an overlay of Middle Western agrarianism. In spite of its incompletion and its occasional weaknesses (such as his exaggerated admiration for James Branch Cabell), it is still what Fred Lewis Pattee called it: "by far the best history of American literature that has yet appeared." In it, to quote Russell Blankenship, "under the hand of the historian, past politics became present issues. American literature became a masculine thing worthy of a treatment different from that dictated by the Genteel Tradition. . . . Parrington had an unrivaled knowledge of American intellectual development. . . . He was the flintiest defender of democracy that twentieth century America has yet produced."

Parrington's uncollected poetry E. H. Eby thought "distinguished for restraint in expression and clarity of form." But primarily he was a social historian who happened to take American literature for his special province. Norman Foerster, an anti-liberal and an unfriendly critic, was yet so impressed by Parrington's achievement that he wrote: "Contented with a certain obscurity, he labored year after year quietly and earnestly, upon a single great task, and waited till he was more than two-thirds done before giving his results to the world. It is an ironic circumstance that he, of all our scholars, should have been cut down in the height of his powers."

PRINCIPAL WORKS: Sinclair Lewis: Our Own Diogenes, 1927; Main Currents in American Thought: An Interpretation of American Literature From the Beginnings to 1920: 1. The Colonial Mind: 1620-1800, 1927; 2. The Romantic Revolution in America: 1800-1860, 1928; 3. The Beginnings of Critical Realism in America: 1860-1920 (completed only to 1900), 1930 (in one volume, 1939).

ABOUT: Cowley, M. (ed.). Books That Changed Our Minds; Parrington, V. L. Main Currents in American Thought: Vol. 3 (see Introduction by E. H. Eby); American Literature May 1929; Bookman February 1931; Nation August 7, 1929; New Republic February 15, 1939; Saturday Review of Literature April 4, 1931.

PARRISH, ANNE (November 12, 1888-), American novelist, writes: "I was born in Colorado Springs, Colo., and spent my childhood there and in my grandmother's home in Claymont, Del. I was slightly educated in private schools in Colorado and Delaware, then studied painting in Philadelphia, more because my mother and father were painters than  because I was one. I have lived in New York for a good many years, with a lot of traveling sprinkled through. I think I have been in every country but Australia and Russia. My husband is Josiah Titzell, a poet under his own name and a novelist under the pseudonym of 'Frederick Lambeck.' We have been living in New York, but have now moved to 'Quaintness,' Peaceable Street, Georgetown, Conn., to live in the country the year round.

"My brother, Dillwyn Parrish, a writer and painter, has done three books with me: *Lustres*, a volume of sketches fortunately, we both think, long out of print, and two books for children of which we each did half the writing and half the illustrating. I have done, alone, another book for children, story and illustrations. I have written ten novels, and of course I am working on another."

* * *

Anne Parrish's first husband was Charles Albert Corliss, whom she married in 1915 and who died in 1936. She married Mr. Titzell in 1938. She is a pronounced blonde, and very attractive. "Deft" is the word which best describes her work; as Dorothea Brande remarked, "she refrains carefully from intruding" on her characters. Poseurs are her specialty, and her chief defect is her obvious dislike of most of her characters. If she could be less cruel her novels, always brilliant, would be warmer and richer. *The Perennial Bachelor* won the Harper Prize in 1925. *All Kneeling* was a best-seller; though none of the novels since then has made a stir, every one of them is well and sharply contrived.

PRINCIPAL WORKS: Pocketful of Poses, 1923; Knee High to a Grasshopper (juvenile, with D. Parrish) 1923; The Dream Coach (juvenile, with D. Parrish) 1924; Lustres (with D. Parrish) 1924; Semi-Attached, 1924; The Perennial Bachelor, 1925; Tomorrow Morning, 1926; All Kneeling, 1928; The Methodist Faun, 1929; Floating Island (juvenile) 1930; Loads of Love, 1932; Sea Level, 1934; Golden Wedding, 1936; Mr. Despondency's Daughter, 1938; Pray for a Tomorrow, 1941.

PARRY, Sir CHARLES HUBERT HASTINGS, Bart. (February 27, 1848-October 7, 1918),

English composer and musical historian, best known as Hubert Parry or C. Hubert Parry, was born at Bournemouth, the second son and youngest child, by his first wife, of Thomas Gambier Parry of Highnam Court, Gloucestershire, a painter and collector of Italian pictures. The boy had filled a notebook with single and double chants by the time he was nine, and at sixteen had essayed every form of Anglican church music, as well as piano and organ pieces, fugues, canons, madrigals, and songs. When at Eton, young Parry passed examinations for the degree of bachelor of music at Oxford. Handel and Mendelssohn were his first heroes. At Exeter College, Oxford, where Parry matriculated as a commoner in 1867, he founded the University Musical Club. In the long vacations he visited Stuttgart and studied orchestration with Henry Hugo Pierson. In 1872 Parry married Lady Elizabeth Maude Herbert and settled in London permanently the next year.

Although a member of Lloyds, the famous insurance organization, he devoted his time and abundant energy almost exclusively to music, not insurance. In 1876 Parry attended the first Bayreuth festival and performance of *Der Ring des Nibelungen,* meeting Wagner in London the next year. A concert of Parry's chamber music at Arthur Balfour's house, at Carlton House Terrace, established him firmly in London society. An oratorio in stereotyped form, *Judith,* proved a popular success when sung at Birmingham in 1888; the *Job* of 1892 was less conventional, even discarding the usual choral finale. *Blest Pair of Sirens* is the most popular, flawless, and frequently performed of his many choral works; Eugene Goossens also has high praise for his *Prometheus.* Parry worked with Sir George Grove on his monumental *Dictionary of Music and Musicians* and succeeded him as director of the Royal College of Music in 1895. Later he was Choragus and professor of music at Oxford. Symphonic odes, to his own poems; orchestral symphonies (the "Cambridge" Symphony had a "programme of undergraduate life"); and an unperformed romantic opera, "Guinevere" were written nevertheless. Critics were not kind to all these efforts, occasionally complaining of their austerity and hasty workmanship. His biography of Bach shows sympathy and penetration. A member of the Royal Yacht Squadron, Parry sailed his own yacht. Sir Hubert was knighted in 1898 and made a baronet at Edward VII's coronation in 1902. He died at Rustington of blood-poisoning and was buried in the crypt of St. Paul's Cathedral. Parry could be intolerant, hasty, explosive and forbidding, but he "made music a man's concern."

PRINCIPAL WORKS: The Art of Music, 1893; The Oxford History of Music, 1902; Johann Sebastian Bach, 1909; Style in Musical Art, 1911.

ABOUT: Graves, C. L. Hubert Parry: His Life and Works; Greene, G. M. P. Two Witnesses; Hadow, W. H. Collected Essays; Willeby, C. Masters of English Music.

*PARSHLEY, HOWARD MADISON

(August 7, 1884-), American zoologist, writes: "My ancestry goes back through Colonial times in New England to English and Scotch origins. My father was a Baptist clergyman, my mother a pianist. I lived for a time in childhood with an aged uncle and aunt on a farm in eastern

* Died May 19, 1953.

New York. This experience, from my twelfth to my sixteenth year, gave me some insight into country life and with the help of a tattered Cornell leaflet on insect collecting probably determined the direction of my later professional interests. I rejoined the family in Boston in 1900, and attended

the ancient Boston Latin School. Meanwhile I pursued the study of insects with the help of Johnson of the Boston Society of Natural History and practiced music and baseball with my brothers. Harvard occupied another four

E. Stahlberg

years, with specialization in zoology along with more classics and modern languages.

"Bridge, billiards. and Balzac came to my attention during those years, and various influences led me to become permanently skeptical and agnostic in matters of politics and religion. I studied double bass at the New England Conservatory and played in the orchestra under Chadwick. I was a member of the Pierian Sodality, the historic Harvard orchestra, along with my brother, a flutist. One summer I worked in the Museum under Henshaw, the crabbedly good-hearted old curator; but afterwards the summers have been mostly spent in music, or in teaching in summer schools of biology.

"After a year's graduate work for the M.A. degree (1910), I married Nancy Fredricson and we went to the University of Maine, where for the next three years I was instructor in biology. Then I got a scholarship and returned to Harvard to study insects again with William Morton Wheeler. After another three years, I got the Sc.D. degree, and in 1917 was appointed to the zoology department of Smith College, where I have been ever since.

"Golf came rather late as a minor hobby, but music is a major one, what with playing in the college orchestra and in faculty performances that include the double bass, and devoting some time to radio and phonographic reproduction of music. I have a son and a daughter, both musicians, and my daughter a teacher of biology besides.

"I have published four books and more than three hundred articles, including scientific papers, contributions to books and magazines, and reviews of biological books in the New York *Herald Tribune* and many other periodicals. I did research work on insects for many years, but recently I have been especially interested in problems of human reproduction and allied matters. My best-known book is *The Science of Human Reproduction,* but I am probably most widely known in foreign parts (though by but few individuals) as editor of the *General Catalogue of the Hemiptera,* an entomological reference work."

Professor Parshley was born in Hallowell, Maine. His first articles aimed at the general public appeared in the *American Mercury* during the editorship of H. L. Mencken. He is probably the only double bass player in this volume.

PRINCIPAL WORKS: Bibliography of the North American Hemiptera Heteroptera, 1925; Science and Good Behavior, 1928; Science of Human Reproduction, 1933; Survey of Biology, 1940.

PARSONS, GEOFFREY (September 5, 1879-), American journalist and Pulitzer Prize winner, was born in Douglaston, N.Y.,

the son of Charles Chauncy Parsons and Julia Warth (Michael) Parsons. He was educated at Columbia University (B.A. 1899, LL.B. 1903). Although he was admitted to the bar he practiced very briefly, and by 1906 was on the staff of

Pinchot

the New York *Evening Sun.* In 1913 he went to the *Tribune,* and since 1924 he has been the chief editorial writer of the *Herald Tribune.* In 1907 he married Carle Taylor, and they have three sons and a daughter. The oldest son, Geoffrey Parsons, Jr., is also a writer, on political and economic topics. Mr. Parsons lives in New York. His chief interest outside his work is in the theatre. He has published a good deal of verse, neat if rather pedestrian, but has never collected it into a volume. In fact, he has published only two books—one an exposition of American democracy and what it means, intended for children; the other, a five-volume historico-philosophical work which has gone into several editions.

In 1941 Mr. Parsons received the honorary degree of Doctor of Letters from Columbia University; in 1942 he was awarded the Pulitzer Prize for editorial writing, with the following citation:

"The selection of these editorials over others of great distinction and to the same patriotic purpose was chiefly influenced by a wish to recognize an outstanding instance where political affiliation was completely subordinated to the national welfare and a newspaper firmly led its party to higher grounds."

Mr. Parsons' last publication was in 1928, and his present duties make it unlikely that he will have leisure to write another book in the near future, though it has been suggested that he collect a volume of his editorials, which are primarily on national and international affairs, and equally noted for their conservatism and their literary quality.

PRINCIPAL WORKS: The Land of Fair Play (juvenile) 1919; The Stream of History (5 vols.) 1928.

PARSONS, WILFRID (March 17, 1887-   ), American clergyman, educator, editor, and essayist, was born in Phila-

delphia and was educated at Woodstock College (Maryland), receiving his B.A. in 1915, Ph.D. in 1918, and S.T.D. in 1919. He also had two years' graduate study in the Gregorian University in Rome. He was ordained a Roman Catholic priest in 1918; he is a member of the Society of Jesus (the Jesuit order). From 1925 to 1936 he was editor-in-chief of *America* the Jesuit weekly. Since 1936 he has been professor of political science at Georgetown University Graduate School (Washington, D.C.); since 1938 he has also been librarian and archivist, and since 1939 dean of the graduate school. He is a Fellow of the American Geographical Society.

Father Parsons is best known to the general public as editor of *America,* which he built up into a leading periodical in its field, exercising great influence on Catholic thought in America. It was not until after his years as editor that he had sufficient leisure to write any books, since when he has published a number, all of them strongly sectarian and most of them rather polemic. His *Early Catholic Americana* is a fine piece of scholarship, being the only complete bibliography of early American Catholic publications.

PRINCIPAL WORKS: Mexican Martyrdom, 1936; Early Catholic Americana, 1939; Which Way Democracy? 1939; The Pope and Italy, 1940.

PARTRIDGE, BELLAMY, American biographer and novelist, was born in Phelps, N.Y., the son of Samuel Selden Partridge

and Frances (Bellamy) Partridge. He was educated at Norwalk Preparatory School, Hobart College, and Union University (B.A. 1901). After practicing law in New York and California, he entered journalism as a war correspondent in 1918. He was a member of the press delegation to the Versailles Peace Conference. In 1920 he was a special correspond-

ent of the United Press, and the following year became an editor of *Sunset Magazine.*

He returned to New York as a member of the editorial staff of Brentano's (1923-24) and as editor of *Brentano's Book Chat* (1925-29). He has been literary critic of the New York *World* and *Herald Tribune,* and on the *Saturday Review of Literature.* From 1934 to 1936 he was editor of Arcadia House Publications. In 1940 he went to Hollywood to assist in the filming of his best-selling *Country Lawyer.*

In 1928 Mr. Partridge married Helen Lawrence Davis; they have one daughter, and live, when they are at home, in Easton, near Bridgeport, Conn.

In 1933, with Alice Cowan, he wrote a radio serial, *Miss Willie Bird,* which was broadcast by the National Broadcasting Co. He is also a frequent contributor of articles and stories to the popular magazines.

Though many of his earlier books received pleasant critical comment (May Lamberton Becker called him "thrilling, informing, inspiring"), it was *Country Lawyer,* the life of his own father, which catapulted him into fame. It headed the best-seller lists for sixteen weeks, and remained among the first five for eight months. His "sequel," *Big Family* (1941), was almost equally successful.

PRINCIPAL WORKS: Sub Cane, 1917; Cousins, 1925; Amundsen—The Splendid Norseman, 1929; A Pretty Pickle (novel) 1930; Sir Billy Howe, 1932; Pure and Simple (novel) 1934; Long Night (novel, as "Thomas Bailey") 1935; The Roosevelt Family in America, 1936; Thunder Shower (novel) 1936; Horse and Buggy, 1937; Get a Horse, 1937; Country Lawyer, 1939; Big Family, 1941.

ABOUT: New York Times Book Review July 20, 1941; Scholastic September 30, 1940.

PASSOS. See DOS PASSOS

PATCHEN, KENNETH (December 3, 1911-   ), American poet, writes: "I was born in Niles, Ohio. My blood inheritance is of English, Scotch, Irish, and French strains (probably others of which I am unaware). My mother's father was a coal

miner; my father's, a farmer-blacksmith. One of my paternal forebears deserted his Red Coat regiment (the war: Revolutionary; his rank: general) to marry a Pennsylvania farm girl; his name was Sir Aaron Drake—his family line was

R. Carson

English nobility all the way back.

"Education: one year in Alexander Meiklejohn's Experimental College, University of Wisconsin; some months in a little school in Arkansas.

"I started a diary in my twelfth year; been writing at something ever since.

"Went to work in the steel mill at seventeen—my father has been a mill man for twenty-five years. Have a brother in the fire department in Warren, Ohio. I could cover a page with a listing of the jobs I've had since then: 'devoting' myself to writing now (as best I can).

"Have in progress a long work, *The Hunted City*, which will be published in seven volumes.

"I am married and live at present in New York City.

"My favorite authors are Dante, Homer, Burns, Shakespeare, and Melville; my favorite public figures, Lenin, Villon, John Brown."

* * *

At the University of Wisconsin Mr. Patchen distinguished himself not only as a student but also on the track and football teams. He was for several years a migratory worker, doing all sorts of jobs in every part of the United States and Canada.

His first published work gave him a place in the ranks of the young "leftist" poets. It also placed him among the extreme modernists. William Rose Benét said of his first volume that his "figurative language was frequently as difficult as Hart Crane's," that his poems read "rather as though John Donne had gone Red," but that nevertheless he displayed "careless power and enthusiasm."

For each cover of the 75 copies in the limited edition of *The Dark Kingdom* (1942) Patchen painted an original watercolor. Reviewing this volume in *Poetry*, Harvey Breit called Patchen "a bonanza,"

but complained that the poet was becoming increasingly careless of his gifts: "He is 'endowed' lyrically, but he appears a little contemptuous of it."

PRINCIPAL WORKS: Before the Brave, 1936; First Will and Testament, 1939; Journal of Albion Moonlight, 1941; The Dark Kingdom, 1942.

ABOUT: Wilder, A. N. The Spiritual Aspects of the New Poetry; Poetry September 1936, April 1940, June 1942; Saturday Review of Literature February 15, 1936, November 25, 1939.

PATER, WALTER. See "BRITISH AUTHORS OF THE 19TH CENTURY"

PATERSON, Mrs. ISABEL M. (BOWLER), American novelist and book columnist, writes: "So far as can be proved, I do not exist; that is

to say, I was never registered, christened, or otherwise officially certified on my first appearance in this world; and furthermore, the house in which I was said to have had such beginnings was burned to the ground, soon after, and with it my parents' marriage certificate, thus making a clean sweep of me. However, a lingering tradition or legend intimated that I was born with a caul and in a raging blizzard. Let it go at that. Conditions have not since then improved materially. I don't remember very much of what has happened to me in between. This amnesia has been aggravated by the fact that for four years past I have been working on a novel—another novel. It may be finished this year; I don't know, nor does anyone else. My working title for it is 'The Memoirs of a Coral Insect.' If you don't see the joke, it's not very funny anyhow, especially not to me. It has another title. Anyone writing a novel is inclined to feel that it would be better never to have been born. I've had a number of novels published already. One of them is good, and two others what I'd call fair. The one now being written is of course superlative. An outstanding feature, of sterling merit, is that it has no social significance whatever. That's what I've spent four years keeping out. [EDITORIAL NOTE: The novel referred to by Mrs. Paterson was published in 1940 under the title *If It Prove Fair Weather*.]

"My political convictions are pure and classical American. This strikes our contemporary intellectuals as very peculiar, in fact, downright baffling; they can't imagine what I mean. It's something they never heard of before, and they feel it must be sinister.

"I don't like public figures at all. In my day nobody did—like them, I mean. They were under suspicion. Hadn't they any homes to go to? If their jobs required them to appear in public part of the time, it was presumed that would do very nicely, and let us hear no more of it. It has now come to pass that a genuine private person isn't safe in her own home from the undesired intrusion of 'public figures.' I have known of an exceedingly prominent 'public figure' who actually invited herself to be guest of honor at a big party. The givers of the party were stunned into acquiescence. What I mean to say is that they had purposely omitted to invite her at all. But she was right in their midst just the same. Well, I was just leading up to the suggestion that I have no favorite 'public figures.'

"The one definite ambition I ever had was completely unrealizable; to earn enough money to go around the world, so I wouldn't have to write or be tied down with a job; and then I would have wandered about in peaceful privacy looking at the world, without bothering anybody. Very likely such a wish will be incomprehensible to the younger generation; but I hope not. I think perhaps it was a hangover from the nineteenth century. A few years ago the nineteenth century was regarded as too horrible to rate a civil word. What have we got now? All the same, there are oodles of good-looking young folks around these days; there must be some hope. They get better looking every year.

"When superior persons tell me that bathtubs do not constitute civilization, I say they do.

" To name my favorite authors would take too long, even among those who have lived during my lifetime; the list would range from W. B. Yeats to Will Cuppy."

* * *

This will give some idea of the provocative nature of Mrs. Paterson's "Turns With a Bookworm," which has been since 1922 a feature of the New York *Herald Tribune* "*Books*" and its predecessors. Violently opinionated, stoutly Tory, but disarmingly humorous about herself as well as about everyone else, Mrs. Paterson is a keen critic and a gallant enemy. She was born, in spite of her disavowal, on Manitoulon Island, Lake Huron, Canada, the daughter of Francis Bowler and Margaret (Batty) Bowler. She writes under her married name, her husband having been Kenneth Birrell Paterson. She was educated in the public schools of Mountain View and Cardston, Alberta, and came to the United States after a clerical job in Calgary with the Canadian Pacific Railroad. She worked with a firm of investment bankers, then on Spokane and Vancouver newspapers. She then went to New York where she was on the *American* and later on the staff of *Hearst's Magazine.* She is small, with something of her Irish grandmother in her deep blue near-sighted eyes and her charming smile. She lives in the country and is a passionate gardener. She is gregarious, a wit, and "mild and scene-avoiding" unless something arouses her to championship of one of her pet theories.

PRINCIPAL WORKS: The Shadow Riders, 1916; The Magpie's Nest, 1917; The Singing Season, 1924; The Fourth Queen, 1926; The Road of the Gods, 1930; Never Ask the End, 1932; The Golden Vanity, 1934; If It Prove Fair Weather, 1940.

ABOUT: Boston Evening Transcript July 13, 1935; New York Herald Tribune February 12, 1933; Publishers' Weekly September 30, 1939.

"PATIENT OBSERVER, THE." See STRUNSKY, S.

PATMORE, COVENTRY. See "BRITISH AUTHORS OF THE 19TH CENTURY"

*PATTEE, FRED LEWIS (March 22, 1863-), American literary critic, was born in Bristol, N.H., and educated at Dartmouth (B.A. 1888, M.A. 1891, M.L. 1915, Litt. D. 1921). He also studied for a year at the University of Göttingen and another year at the University of Marburg. He was professor of American literature at Pennsylvania State College from 1894 to 1928, when he became professor emeritus. He did not retire from teaching, however, but has been professor of American literature since then at Rollins College, and now lives near it, at Coronado Beach, Fla. He was also visiting professor at the University of Illinois in 1923, and taught at the Bread Loaf Summer School of English, Middlebury, Vt., from 1924 to 1936. He was married to Anna L. Plumer in 1889; she died in 1927, leaving a daughter; and in 1928 he married Grace Garee. In addition to his own

* Died May 6, 1950.

books, he has edited many others, including *Century Readings in the American Short Story* (1927) and *The First Century of American Literature* (1935). He has never been a startling or iconoclastic critic, but is respected as serious and authoritative, with a special love of the byways and curiosa of literary lives. He has published some poetry and several novels, but all his work of literary importance is in the field of criticism and history.

PRINCIPAL WORKS: The Wine of May and Other Lyrics, 1893; Pasquaney: A Study, 1894; A History of American Literature, 1896; Reading Courses in American Literature, 1897; The Foundations of English Literature, 1900; Mary Garvin (novel) 1902; The House of the Black Ring (novel) 1905; Elements of Religious Pedagogy, 1909; The Breaking Point (novel) 1911; Compelled Men, 1913; History of American Literature Since 1870, 1915; Sidelights on American Literature, 1922; The Development of the American Short Story, 1923; Tradition and Jazz, 1924; The New American Literature, 1930; Mark Twain, 1935; The Feminine Fifties, 1940.

*PATTEN, GILBERT (October 25, 1866-   ), American writer of boys' books under the pseudonym "Burt L. Standish,"

was born in Corinna, Maine, the son of William Clark Patten and Cordelia (Simpson) Patten. He was first named George William Patten. His parents were deeply religious people, with strong pacifistic tendencies, and young Patten passed a lonely boyhood, forbidden to mix with or fight with his contemporaries. Instead, he pored over books: *Morgan's Masonry;* an illustrated history of the Civil War; and Joseph Holt Ingraham's *The Prince of the House of David,* the one piece of fiction which won the elder Pattens' approval. He also managed to procure some dime novels.

After reaching his height of over six feet, the boy, who had mild brown eyes, an aquiline nose, and fair hair, found the courage to run away from home to work in a machine shop at Biddeford. He had spent four years (1880-84) at the Corinna Union Academy. In October 1886 Patten married Alice Gardner of Corinna; they had a son, Harvan Barr Patten, and were divorced in 1898. (Two years later Patten married Mary Nunn of Baltimore, and they were divorced in 1916. The third Mrs. Patten was Carol Kramer of New York City; they were married in June 1918.)

Returning home from his *Wanderjahr,* young Patten asserted his new-found independence and began to write fiction, marketing his first story at seventeen. The *Banner Weekly,* one of the publications of Erastus Beadle, chief publisher of so-called dime novels, accepted two stories, paying Patten $6 for both. He received $50 for *The Diamond Sport,* and the next story netted him $75, the third $100.

In 1889 Patten paid a brief visit to Omaha, Neb., acquiring sufficient local color to write Western stories later under the sobriquet William West Wilder ("Wyoming Will"), when he went to New York City in 1891. Here he stayed until 1913, first writing thrillers for Beadle & Adams at $150 apiece, but leaving them in 1895 for Street & Smith. Patten wrote chiefly for a six-cent juvenile weekly, *Golden Hours,* receiving $250 for a 60,000-word serial. In 1896 he conceived the character of Frank Merriwell, and wrote weekly stories about his virtuous and athletic hero, a Yale man, for eighteen years. His first contract, for three years, paid $50 a week, and he received no royalties on the sale of the books, which reached a total of 208 titles and sold 125 million copies. In the early 1900's their sale totaled 135,000 copies a week. Patten motivated action from character in the stories, so that they were a cut above the usual dime novel, and they were praised by such diverse critics as Al Smith, Jack Dempsey, Babe Ruth, and Woodrow Wilson. In 1931 King Features started syndicating Frank as a comic strip character, and in 1934 he went briefly on the air. Merriwell, who had "a body like Tarzan's and a head like Einstein's" has yet to reach the screen.

Patten is listed as a member of the Advertising Club in New York City and of the Business Men's Association in Camden, Maine, where he makes his home. J. L. Cutler states that his politics are Fabian Socialist, and that he is not a member of any orthodox religious sect. He reappeared in the news in 1940, as being in difficult financial straits. Franklin P. Adams ("F.P.A." of the New York *Post*) raised a fund to save him from losing his house on a mortgage foreclosure; Wendell Willkie was one of the contributors. Out of the ensuing publicity came a contract for a new "adult" Frank Merriwell book, published in 1941. Reviewing this work in the New York *Times Book Review,* Robert van Gelder wrote: "The true pleasure is in finding so much vigor still in the pen of a man who started writing 20,000 words every week about

* Died January 16, 1945.

Merriwell in 1896 and kept up that rate of production for more than seventeen years. . . . The characterizations are straight ham, but Mr. Patten is never on the wrong side of the moral issues."

PRINCIPAL WORKS: The Deadwood Trail, 1904; Bill Bruce of Harvard, 1905; Frank Merriwell Series, 209 volumes; Rockspur Series, 3 volumes; Cliff Sterling Series, 5 volumes; College Life Series, 6 volumes; Big League Series, 14 volumes; Rex Kingdon Series, 5 volumes; Oakdale Series, 6 volumes; Mr. Frank Merriwell, 1941.

ABOUT: Cutler, J. L. Gilbert Patten and His Frank Merriwell Saga: A Study in Sub-Literary Fiction, 1896-1913; Pearson, E. L. Dime Novels; Wecter, D. T. The Hero in America: A Chronicle of Hero Worship; New York Times June 2, 1940; Saturday Evening Post June 11, 1927; February 28, 1931; Time April 21, 1941.

PAUL, ELLIOT HAROLD (February 11, 1891-   ), American novelist, was born in Malden, Mass., the son of Harold Henry

Paul and Lucy Greenleaf (Doucette) Paul. After a few months at the University of Maine he joined a brother as surveyor and timekeeper on an irrigation project in Idaho and Wyoming. Returning to Boston, he got a job on a newspaper, but left it to enlist as private (later sergeant) in the Field Signal Corps. He stayed in France after the war and worked for the Associated Press (whose correspondent he was on the Ruhr), and the Paris editions of the Chicago *Tribune* and the New York *Herald*. On both papers he was literary editor. In 1927, with Eugene Jolas, he founded and edited *transition*, one of the most celebrated of the organs of the Paris expatriates. He was married and had a son, but was divorced before 1930 and in 1935 married Flora Thompson Brown, his present wife.

In 1931 Paul went to live at Santa Eulalia, Ibiza, in the Balearic Islands. He became a part of the life of the town, organized an orchestra (in which he played the piano and accordion), and was known familiarly to all the inhabitants by the nickname of "Xumeu," bestowed on friendly foreigners. When the Franco Revolution started, the town was predominantly Loyalist; it was captured by the rebels, retaken, and finally bombed, so that it is now only a ruin. He has told its story in his tragic and beautiful book, *Life and Death of a Spanish Town.* Mr. Paul was rescued by a German destroyer; he returned to the United States

and now lives in New York. Big, bald, and bearded, he looks a bit like Henry VIII.

He is an exceedingly versatile writer. His early novels were impressionistic; then he wrote a sober political novel; next he turned to the indignant tenderness of his book on Ibiza; and suddenly he blossomed out as the author of hilarious mystery novels, half-burlesque, half-extravaganza. As if this were not enough, he performed as piano soloist in a "boogie-woogie" concert and won the applause of "jive" enthusiasts. What he may do next is always unpredictable (in 1940 he made application for an appointment as a government lighthouse keeper!), but it is to be hoped that he has not entirely abandoned serious fiction, for *Indelible, Impromptu,* and *Imperturbe,* though they had the faults of youth, gave promise of real achievement in the future.

Of his writing Elliot Paul says that he is willing to sacrifice anything for spontaneity. "When you write rapidly you write in your own style," he told Robert van Gelder. "There is no good in trying for style by rewriting, by torturing sentences. You knock the life out of it, and probably out of your ideas." He believes that memory is better than notes for retaining "material."

Elliot Paul is not related to Louis Paul.[qv] From 1919 to 1921 he was secretary of the Massachusetts Soldiers' and Sailors' Commission. He is a sociable, gregarious man, easy-going, and a witty conversationalist; in his more serious aspect he is a hater of injustice and a hard-fighting champion for the underdog. Recently he has been in Hollywood, writing scripts for the movies.

PRINCIPAL WORKS: Indelible, 1922; Impromptu, 1923; Imperturbe, 1924; Lava Rock, 1928; Low Run Tide 1928; The Amazon, 1929; The Governor of Massachusetts, 1930; Life and Death of a Spanish Town, 1937; Concert Pitch, 1938; Stars & Stripes Forever, 1939; All the Brave (with L. Quintanilla) 1939; The Mysterious Mickey Finn, 1939; Hugger-Mugger in the Louvre, 1940; Death of Lord Haw Haw (as "Brett Rutledge") 1940; Fracas in the Foothills, 1940; Intoxication Made Easy, 1941; The Last Time I Saw Paris, 1942.

ABOUT: New York Times Book Review March 1, 1942; Wilson Library Bulletin October 1937.

PAUL, LOUIS (December 4, 1901-   ), American novelist, writes: "I was born in New York City. My father was the son of a French woodcarver and sculptor, while my mother's ancestors migrated from Boston to Albany in pre-Revolutionary times. I was educated in the public schools of New York until the entry of America into the World War, when I decided that experience was preferable to education, and enlisted. Even though (being under age) I served out the war on this side of the water, I was convinced, and still am, that experience is preferable to education, and I have consistently resisted formal instruction of any kind. After several years more of army life, a pleasant routine which afforded me the opportunity to read a great many books, I decided to become a writer. My first attempts at composition, which were not intended for publication and never sub-

mitted to publishers, consisted of awkward lyric poetry and essays on original aesthetic ideas I attempted to develop independently of my reading. I traveled several times in slow stages across the country and back, and later incorporated some of my experiences in my first novel, *The Pumpkin Coach*.

"During this formative period I married the daughter of an Italian ship captain [Mary P. Engargiola, 1924], and have successfully remained married. During the composition of my first novel I wrote my first short story, a tale of an escaped Negro convict ["No More Trouble for Jedwick"]. This story was published in *Esquire* [the first place to which it was submitted] and was awarded first prize in the 1934 O. Henry Memorial volume. It has subsequently reappeared in numerous anthologies.

"I soon developed, together with my serious work, a vein of satire, as it appeared to me that many of the things I have to express could fit conveniently only in a satiric framework. This double nature of my writings has sometimes puzzled critics; but, as I never quite know what to make of critics either, the score seems about even. At present [1940] I am working on two novels, the story of a man who desires to become a modern saint, and a dramatic satire of the 'beloved vagabond' legends of François Villon. I can see nothing inconsistent in these projects. I also have in preparation a volume of short stories.

"I believe that formal education is stultifying to the intelligence of the individual, and that a familiarity with past and present cultures is an absolute requisite of the practicing creative artist. I believe that sensible thought is impossible without the acquisition of historical perspective. Two books which have profoundly influenced my intellect are Symonds' *Renaissance in Italy* and Frazer's *Golden Bough*.

"I am an amateur pianist and composer, and have a great love for the graphic arts."

* * *

Besides being a hospital orderly in the army, Mr. Paul has worked as a movie extra, a teacher in a school for immigrants, and a longshoreman in San Francisco. He spent seven years in all in such work as road building, mining, ditch digging, and sailing, all on the Pacific Coast. He lives now in Palo Alto, Calif. He is a plump, cheerful-looking man with a small moustache and dark hair over a high forehead. Of his own work he has said: "I liked America very much and wrote it into a pageant. I have no delusions of grandeur and no axe to grind; have no alma mater (if you'll liberally except William Shakespeare and William Hudson), and quite confidently expect to rank with America's best prose writers some day."

PRINCIPAL WORKS: The Pumpkin Coach, 1935; A Horse in Arizona, 1936; Emma, 1937; The Wrong World, 1938; The Man Who Left Home, 1938; A Passion for Privacy, 1940; Reverend Ben Pool, 1941.

ABOUT: Scholastic March 16, 1935; Wilson Library Bulletin October 1940.

*PAXSON, FREDERICK LOGAN (February 23, 1877-), American historian and Pulitzer Prize winner, was born in Phila-

delphia, and educated at the University of Pennsylvania (B.S. 1898, Ph.D. 1903). He has honorary degrees also from Harvard, Wisconsin, Pennsylvania, Lawrence College, and Mills College. From 1899 to 1904 he was a teacher of history

in secondary schools; then he went to the University of Colorado as assistant professor of history, becoming professor the following year. From 1906 to 1910 he was at the University of Michigan, first as assistant professor and then as junior professor of American history; from 1910 to 1932 he was professor of American history at the University of Wisconsin; and since 1932 he has been Margaret Byrne Professor of History at the University of California. He has also been professor of history at the summer schools of numerous universities, and was a research associate of the Carnegie Institution, working in the British archives, in 1910. He was a member of the committee on management of the *Dictionary of Ameri-*

can Biography from 1924 to 1936; a member of the editorial board of the *Pacific Historical Review* from 1933 to 1939; and in 1939 a member of the advisory committee of the Franklin D. Roosevelt Library. During the First World War he was a major in the United States Army, attached to the War Plans Division. He is a past president (1938) of the American Historical Association, and was long curator and vice-president of the State Historical Society of Wisconsin. In 1917 he was president of the Mississippi Valley Historical Association.

In 1906 he married Helen Hale Jackson, and they have three daughters. Their home is now in Berkeley, Calif. In 1925 Professor Paxson received the Pulitzer Prize for his *History of the American Frontier.* He was the editor of several handbooks and monographs for the War Department, from 1917 to 1919, bearing particularly on the economic aspects of the war.

PRINCIPAL WORKS: The Independence of the South American Republics, 1903; The Last American Frontier, 1910; The Civil War, 1911; The New Nation, 1915; Recent History of the United States, 1921; History of the American Frontier, 1924; The United States in Recent Times, 1926; When the West Is Gone, 1929; American Democracy and the World War (2 vols.) 1936-39.

PEABODY, JOSEPHINE PRESTON

(May 30, 1874-December 4, 1922), American poet and dramatist, was born in Brooklyn, N.Y., the daughter of Charles Kilham Peabody and Josephine (Morrill) Peabody, both of New England descent. From her early childhood the theatre was her passion, and she made up plays in which she herself acted all the parts. When she was ten, her father died, and her mother moved back to her former home in Dorchester (Boston), Mass. Josephine was educated at the Girls' Latin School in Boston, and attended Radcliffe College from 1894 to 1896, as a special student. She wrote—mostly verse—from the age of thirteen, and many of her poems were published in her early girlhood; even a collection of 104 rejection slips pasted in her scrapbook failed to daunt her! From sixteen to her death she kept a diary, which was published in 1925.

Her health was frail, and she was in Florida in search of a warm climate when, in the winter of 1893-94, she received her first acceptances of poems from important

magazines—*Scribner's* and the *Atlantic Monthly.* She had also made a trip—really a pilgrimage—to England, where she visited Stratford in the spirit of a devotee before a shrine and inspired a graceful poem by Austin Dobson. Her first book, a series of Greek fables, appeared in 1897, and her first volume of poetry the following year. In 1900 she moved to Cambridge, Mass., which was her home for the rest of her life.

From 1901 to 1903 Miss Peabody was lecturer in English literature at Wellesley College. In 1906 she married Lionel S. Marks, of English birth, professor of mechanical engineering at Harvard. They had a daughter and a son. Eight weeks after her son was born she traveled to Stratford again, this time as winner of the 1910 verse play contest of the Shakespeare Memorial Theatre. "Shakespeare," said her friend Abbie Farwell Brown, "was the hero of her worship, and Stratford her Mecca." Dressed in her white wedding gown, radiant with joy, she made, in her "voice of honey sweetness," her speech of acceptance of the $1500 prize. Her play, *The Piper,* had been selected above 314 other contesting plays. It was produced professionally in both England and America.

The summer of 1913 Mrs. Marks spent in Europe, but she was by this time a semi-invalid, and from 1916 on was almost completely bedridden. Nevertheless, during the World War she exerted her last strength in speeches and readings for refugee relief. In 1914 she had been elected an honorary member of Phi Beta Kappa, and gave the Phi Beta Kappa ode of that year at Tufts College. Her last completed work was a prose play on Mary Wollstonecraft, *The Portrait of Mrs. W.* It was her third play drawn from the history of English literature, the preceding ones having been *Fortune and Men's Eyes,* founded on Shakespeare's sonnets, and *Marlowe.*

Though she deplored what she thought her lack of beauty, her mobile face with its great dark eyes was really very attractive. Her friends loved her for her gaiety, her gallant courage, and her sensitive idealism. "Every day ought to be a festival for one reason or another," she said. "Let us turn routine into rhythm." "She believed passionately in life as a thrilling adventure," Miss Brown said of her. "Out of a rather detached young disciple of aesthetic and spiritual beauty, she became a militant apostle of the beauty spelled in human justice and sympathy. . . . Though she clung to traditional poetic forms she was no reactionary in spirit." When she died in Cambridge at forty-eight, she had half a dozen ideas for her plays still untouched.

PRINCIPAL WORKS: *Poems*—The Wayfarers, 1898; The Singing Leaves, 1903; Pan: A Choric Idyll, 1904; The Book of the Little Past, 1908; The Singing Man, 1911; Harvest Moon, 1916; Collected Poems, 1927. *Plays*—Fortune and Men's Eyes, 1900; Marlowe, 1901; The Wings, 1907; The Piper, 1909; The Wolf of Gubbio, 1913; The Portrait of Mrs. W., 1922; Collected Plays, 1927. *Miscellaneous*—Old Greek Folk-Stories, 1897; Diary and Letters, 1925.

ABOUT: Peabody, J. P. Diary and Letters; Atlantic Monthly December 1927; Bookman May 1923; Poetry February 1923; Saturday Review of Literature March 20, 1926, May 5, 1928.

PEARSE, PADRAIC HENRY (November 10, 1879-May 3, 1916), Irish poet, educator, and patriot, was born in Dublin, the

son of James Pearse, an English sculptor. The boy heard fireside tales from a kindly gray-haired woman who recited ballads, legends and Ossianic lays in Irish. He began to study Gaelic at twelve. Padraic Pearse was an intermediate student at Christian Brothers' Schools, later teaching there, and lectured in Irish at the Catholic University College, which granted him a B.A. and B.L. He also edited the Gaelic League's official organ, *An Claidheamh Soluis*. Adverse critics commented on the "mincing utterance, action lost in verbiage and ornament, and feminine gush of prettiness" in Pearse's first collection of Irish poetry and legends, *Iosagán*, although he was later to be called the most chaste stylist in Irish prose. Pearse toured Belgium, and returned to establish his famous bi-lingual preparatory school for boys, Sgoil Eanna or St. Edna's, at Cullenswood House, Ranelagh, Dublin, which moved two years later to the Hermitage, Rathfarnham. Thomas MacDonagh[qv] was a member of the staff.

In November 1913 Padraic Pearse made a speech at the inception of the Irish Volunteers in Rotunda Rink, Dublin. Early in 1914 he came to the United States for a lecture tour. During the Rising of 1916 he was commander-in-chief of the Irish Republican forces and president of the Provisional Government. Pearse was the last to leave when fire drove the defenders from headquarters at the Dublin General Post Office. His last days were spent at Arbor Hill Detention Barracks, before he was shot

by a British firing squad and his body thrown into a common trench with MacDonagh and others, filled with quicklime so that no bones would remain for relics. He was thirty-six. Pearse was a superb orator. Some critics called him outwardly cold, parsonical, a *poseur*, and spinner of fine phrases without a practical spark in him; others "a perfect man, whose faults were the mere defects of his straight and rigid virtues."

PRINCIPAL WORKS IN ENGLISH: Three Essays on Gaelic Topics, 1898; The Mother, 1915; The Story of a Success: Being a Record of St. Edna's College, 1917; Collected Works, 1917; Poems, 1918.

ABOUT: Colum, P. & O'Brien, E. J. H. Poems of the Irish Revolutionary Brotherhood; Hayes, J. Patrick H. Pearse; Le Roux, L. N. Patrick H. Pearse; O'Hegarty, P. S. A Bibliography of Books Written by Patrick H. Pearse; Ryan, D. The Man Called Pearse; Catholic World May 1941; Dublin Review January, February, March 1923; Irish Monthly March 1922.

PEARSON, EDMUND LESTER (February 11, 1880-August 7, 1937), American librarian, editor, bibliophile, and authority on murder, was born at Newburyport, Mass., the son of Edmund Carlton Pearson and Tamzen Maria (Richardson) Pearson. His boyhood in the old seaport town is recorded, with characteristic humor, in *The Believing Years* (1911),

Bachrach

which first appeared as a series in the *Outlook*. He attended Harvard College, contributing to the *Advocate*, and was graduated in 1902 with the degree of Bachelor of Arts. In 1904 he received the degree of Bachelor of Library Science from the New York State Library School at Albany. While on the staff of the Washington (D.C.) Public Library he met and married Mary S. Sellers of that city, in 1908. From 1906 to 1920 he conducted the weekly department in the Boston *Evening Transcript* known as "The Librarian," where his frequently unconventional views on library service and on some of the catchwords and shibboleths of the profession, such as "cooperation," often evoked indignant replies. From 1914 to 1927 he was Editor of Publications at the New York Public Library. During the First World War he attended the Plattsburg (N.Y.) training camp and was commissioned a second lieutenant, but did not see overseas service.

The Old Librarian's Almanack (1909), patterned after *The Old Farmer's Almanack* and printed by the late John Cotton Dana, librarian of the Newark (N.J.) Public Library, at his Elm Tree Press at Woodstock, Vt., was Pearson's first book, and was a successful although unintentional hoax which deceived the New York *Sun,* Sir William Osler, and many another. *Theodore Roosevelt* (1920), written for boys, reflected his lifelong and uncritical admiration for the personality of the former president. (He had no use whatsoever for Woodrow Wilson.) *Books in Black or Red* (1923), a miscellaneous work of humor and charm, included a study of dime novels (amplified in his *Dime Novels,* 1929) and a concluding essay on murder considered as one of the fine arts. This essay pointed the way he was to follow as a specialist with great success for the next fourteen years. "The study of murder," he wrote there, "is the study of the human heart in its darkest, strangest moments. Nothing surpasses it in interest." He also quoted George Lyman Kittredge's *dictum* that "Murder is the material of great literature."

Studies in Murder (1924), his best known work, developed this thesis, and, together with his subsequent volumes, gave him an international reputation as the foremost American writer on celebrated crimes; some critics, indeed, consider him the most authoritative student of the subject since Thomas De Quincey, and he is certainly the most readable. His last work in the field, an edition of *The Trial of Lizzie Borden* published in the year of his death, was the first volume of the Notable American Trials series, and he was posthumously honored by the inclusion of *Studies in Murder* in the Modern Library in 1938.

Pearson resigned from the New York Public Library in 1927 to devote his entire time to writing, except for editing the book review department of the *Outlook* for several years and serving as a judge of the Detective Story Club (later absorbed by the Crime Club). In his later years his interest in crime extended to its sociological as well as psychological aspects. He died of bronchopneumonia at the Medical Center in New York City at the age of fifty-seven and was buried in Newburyport. His library of criminology was purchased after his death and presented to the New York Public Library as the Pearson Collection.

Pearson was of urbane manner and youthful appearance, a justly celebrated *raconteur,* and a thorough and painstaking workman.

"He was the most lovable man I have ever known," wrote Charles Honce at his death, and a wide circle of friends echoed the sentiment. His bibliophilic writings were by no means negligible, and his reputation as a librarian and editor was considerable. But it is as the fascinated dissector of murder and its motives that his name is best remembered.

PRINCIPAL WORKS: *Books About Murder & Crime*—Studies in Murder, 1924; Murder at Smutty Nose, 1926; Five Murders, 1928; Instigation of the Devil, 1930; The Autobiography of a Criminal, by H. Tufts (ed.) 1930; More Studies in Murder, 1936; The Trial of Lizzie Borden (ed.) 1937. *Bibliophilic & Miscellaneous*—The Old Librarian's Almanack, 1909; The Librarian at Play, 1911; The Believing Years, 1911; Voyage of the Hoppergrass, 1913; The Secret Book, 1914; Theodore Roosevelt, 1920; Books in Black or Red, 1923; Queer Books, 1928; Dime Novels, 1929.

ABOUT: Edgett, E. F. I Speak for Myself; Harvard College, Class of 1902: Twenty-Fifth Anniversary Report; Honce, C. A Sherlock Holmes Birthday; Pearson, E. L. The Believing Years; Roughead, W. The Enjoyment of Murder; Boston Evening Transcript February 9, 1929; New York Herald Tribune August 8, 1937; New York Times August 9, 1937; Outlook 1910, 1911; Publishers' Weekly August 14, 1937; Saturday Review of Literature August 14, 1937.

PEARSON, KARL (1857-April 27, 1936), English statistician, mathematician, and eugenist, was born, lived all his life, and died in London. He was educated at University College School and at King's College, Cambridge, where he received his B.A. in 1879 as Third Wrangler (third highest in the mathematical tripos). He was a fellow of King's from 1880 to 1886,

F. A. de Biden Footner

and honorary fellow thereafter. Intending to enter the law, he read at the Inner Temple and was admitted to the bar in 1882. However, it was soon plain that his *forte* lay in a very different field. In 1884 he became professor of applied mathematics and mechanics at University College (University of London), and remained in that post until 1911, when the chair of eugenics was created for him. He resigned in 1933, because of age, and was made emeritus professor. During these same years he was director of the Francis Galton Laboratory for National Eugenics, also a University of London post. He was the great disciple of Galton (Darwin's cousin, and founder of eugenics as a science), and carried out further extensions of Galton's researches by mathematical, statistical, and biometric methods. Both Galton and Pearson stressed the importance of heredity over environment, and naturally Pearson drew on himself the wrath of the environmentalists and "behaviorists"—especially since, as G. Udney Yule put it, "he was a born fighter." The New York *Times* called him "one of the best loved and most hated figures of modern science." His name, however, was scarcely known to the non-scientific public, except for one unfortunate incident when (just as Osler was publicized for the mythical assertation that men over sixty ought to be "liquidated") he was supposed to have said that man reached his prime at twenty-five and thereafter became progressively less useful.

Pearson was a Fellow of the Royal Society, whose Darwin Medal he received in 1898, a Fellow of the Royal Society of Edinburgh, an honorary D.Sc. of the University of London, an honorary Litt.D. from St. Andrews, and an honorary member of the Anthropological Societies of Paris, Moscow, and Washington. He was director of the Eugenics Record Office, editor of *Biometrika* from 1901 to 1935, and of the *Annals of Eugenics* from 1925 to 1933. In 1890 he married Maria Sharpe, who died in 1928. The following year he married Mary V. Child, who survived him. By his first wife he had two daughters and a son, who became professor of statistics at the University of London.

He described himself as "an adventurous roamer" in the field of knowledge, and his interests ranged from the theory of elasticity to linguistic and portraiture. Yule said of him: "The variety of his work is as striking as its mass, . . . [or as] the originality and logic of his thought and the clarity of his exposition." He was an inspiring teacher, imbued with "tireless enthusiasm." The London *Times* in its obituary notice remarked: "Possibly he pointed too strongly to the antithesis between nature and nurture, but that he was one of the greatest intellectual forces in British science during the last forty years is indisputable." Except for his early book of essays, *The Ethic of Free-Thought*, and his monumental biography of Galton, his work was all severely scientific and highly technical, and he can hardly, therefore, be judged as a literary figure. He was not an author interested in science; he was a scientist who wrote books.

He remained active in body and mind to extreme old age, and died suddenly of cardiac failure at almost eighty.

PRINCIPAL WORKS: The Ethic of Free-Thought, 1887; The New University of London, 1892; The Grammar of Science, 1892 (latest edition 1937); Chances of Death and Other Studies in Evolution, 1897; National Life From the Standpoint of Science, 1899; On the Correlation of Fertility With Social Value (with five others) 1913; Tables for Statisticians: Part I, 1914, Part II, 1933; Life, Letters, and Labours of Francis Galton, 1915-1930; The Portraiture of Oliver Cromwell (with G. M. Morand) 1935.

ABOUT: Dampier-Whetham, W. C. D. A History of Science; East, E. M. Heredity and Human Affairs; American Statistical Association Journal December 1936; Eugenic Review July 1936; Mathematical Gazette February 1936; Nature (London) May 23 and June 6, 1936; Royal Statistical Society Journal 1936.

PEATTIE, DONALD CULROSS (June 21, 1898-   ), American writer on natural history, reports: "Donald Culross Peattie was born in Chicago. His father was Robert Burns Peattie, a newspaperman for fifty years in Chicago, Omaha, and New York. His mother was Elia (Wilkinson) Peattie, novelist, essayist, for many years literary critic on the Chicago *Tribune*.  Peattie was educated at the University of Chicago, which he entered on a scholarship in English literature won in a competitive examination. At the university he became interested in botanical studies. Leaving Chicago in 1918, he followed his family, which had removed to New York, and there entered a publishing firm as a reader. He resigned in 1919 because of his growing interest in nature. He had now definitely decided on scientific studies, not with a view to a career as a scientist but as the only proper background and thorough training for a nature writer. Accordingly he entered Harvard, and was graduated in 1922, *cum laude*. He was awarded the Witter Bynner Prize in poetry for that year, and at the same time his first formal scientific papers began to appear, based on botanical explorations in North Carolina and Indiana.

"He now entered the office of Foreign Seed and Plant Introduction of the U.S. Department of Agriculture. In 1923 he married Louise Redfield, the novelist, and they lived in northern Virginia. At the end of 1924 he resigned from the Department to do free lance writing. He conducted for eleven years thereafter a nature column in the Washington *Evening Star*, which was later resumed in the Chicago *Daily News*.

His first book was a popular study in economic botany.

"In 1928 he removed with his wife and three sons to the French Riviera. In the autumn of 1933 he returned to America with fresh eyes for it, and lived three years on one square mile of Illinois land, without leaving it overnight. *An Almanac for Moderns,* published in 1935 received the gold medal of the Limited Editions Club. He lives at present in Santa Barbara, Calif., whither he removed for the sake of contact with western nature. In 1936 he was granted a Guggenheim Fellowship for creative writing, which was renewed for another year in 1937."

* * *

Mr. Peattie says that the salient fact about his work is his "dual activity in the fields of science and poetry, which combine, finally, in nature writing." As his wife said of him, he has "the keenly trained eye of the scientist, the vision of the poet." He has been called "America's most lyrical naturalist." He is "in love with nature," and with the great naturalists as well—with Audubon above all. A heavy-set man with dark hair and moustache, he might be a college professor, or the working scientist he did not intend to become, but one would not suspect him of being the poet he inherently is—though a poet for the most part in prose. It does not invalidate the beauty of *Green Laurels, Singing in the Wilderness, Flowering Earth,* or *An Almanac for Moderns* that they are grounded in a thorough scientific foundation. Mr. Peattie is a simple, friendly man, "a man who speaks to strangers," with a keen sense of humor and (to quote Mark Van Doren) "a sharp and wide vision of the world." In 1941 his autobiographical *The Road of a Naturalist* was awarded a prize of $2,500 by Houghton Mifflin and was one of the first two books published in the company's Life in America series.

PRINCIPAL WORKS: Cargoes and Harvests, 1926; Bounty of Earth (with L. R. Peattie) 1926; Up Country (novel, with L. R. Peattie) 1928; Down Wind (juvenile stories, with L. R. Peattie) 1929; Vence: The Story of the Provençal Town Through 2000 Years, 1930; Flora of the Sand Dunes and the Calumet District of Indiana, 1930; Port of Call (novel) 1932; Sons of the Martian (novel) (in England: Karen's Loyalty) 1932; The Bright Lexicon (novel) 1934; Trees of North America (alternative title: Trees You Want to Know) 1934; An Almanac for Moderns, 1935; Singing in the Wilderness: A Salute to John James Audubon, 1935; The Happy Kingdom (with L. R. Peattie) 1935; Green Laurels: The Lives and Achievements of the Great Naturalists, 1936; Old Fashioned Garden Flowers, 1936; A Book of Hours, 1937; A Child's Story of the World, 1937; A Prairie Grove, 1938; This Is Living (with Gordon Aymar)

1938; A Gathering of Birds (ed., anthology) 1939; Flowering Earth, 1939; The Road of a Naturalist, 1941; Forward the Nation, 1942.

ABOUT: Peattie, D. C. The Road of a Naturalist; Rascoe, B. Before I Forget; Nation April 24, 1937; North American Review September 1937; Saturday Review of Literature April 5, 1941; Wilson Library Bulletin February 1936.

PEATTIE, Mrs. LOUISE (REDFIELD)

(June 14, 1900-), American novelist, writes: "I was born in Northern Illinois, at the homestead founded by my father's people five generations earlier. Much of what I have done and more of what I am is the result of a childhood spent upon those happy acres of prairie and woodland, farm and garden. This was the locale of *Ameri-*

can Acres, the first of my novels to meet with a cordial welcome from the public. My life is a story not so much of outer event as of such inner experience. My father, Robert Redfield, a corporation lawyer who did much to aid in the building of a braver Chicago, married Bertha Dreier, daughter of the Danish consul in that city and of my superb grandmother who came from Hanover as a little girl. The charm and viewpoint of a foreign culture thus were combined in our household with my father's traditions inherited from 'come-outer' descendants of John and Priscilla Alden.

"My education, through tutors and at Chicago private schools, was unimportant in comparison with what I learned from my brother, Robert Redfield, now dean of Social Sciences at the University of Chicago. My marriage to Donald Culross Peattie[qv] took place in 1923, there followed five years' residence in and around Washington, D.C., and thereafter six years of life in the hills of Provence and on the French Riviera. During this time my daughter (deceased) and my three sons were born. In 1933 we returned to live for three years at my childhood home; then, with the coming of success to my husband, we spent a winter in Tryon, N.C., and thereafter came to Santa Barbara, Calif., still our place of residence.

"I began to write professionally shortly after my marriage, always receiving the utmost understanding and co-operation from my husband. Grateful for the opportunity to combine a career with family life, it has been my endeavor that my family shall profit, never suffer, from my occupation with writing. My greatest pride is in the share I am privileged to have in my husband's writing; this is the first of my interests. All that I asked of life in the first hope of youth has been fulfilled; I ask now only the opportunity to complete fully what we have begun together."

* * *

Mrs. Peattie is a pretty woman, with delicate features, dark hair, and beautifully arched eyebrows over deep-set eyes. As long ago as 1928, John Farrar predicted that she would "soon be taking her place with Willa Cather." Her chief concern, says her husband, "is with spiritual values embodied in lively narrative beautifully written." Her pitfall is a slight tendency to the theatrical, but it is offset by her distinction of style and her artistic conscientiousness.

PRINCIPAL WORKS: Dagny (in England: Forlorn Mermaid) 1928; Up Country (with D. R. Peattie) 1928; Down Wind (with D. R. Peattie) 1929; Pan's Parish, 1931; Wine With a Stranger, 1932; Wife to Caliban, 1934; Fugitive, 1935; American Acres (in England: Grand Portage) 1936; Tomorrow Is Ours, 1937; A Child in Her Arms, 1938; Lost Daughter, 1938; Star at Noon, 1939; The Californians, 1940.

ABOUT: Boston Evening Transcript April 13, 1935.

PECK, GEORGE WILBUR. See "AMERICAN AUTHORS: 1600-1900"

PECK, HARRY THURSTON. See "AMERICAN AUTHORS: 1600-1900"

PEEL, DORIS NANNETTE (February 27, 1909-), Anglo-American novelist and short-story writer, was born in England, the

D. Ulmann

daughter of Arthur James Peel and Anne (Mont) Peel, but came to the United States with her parents in 1921 to continue her education in American and Canadian schools. She now calls herself Doris Anne Peel. *Children of the Wind* (1927) her first novel, dedicated to her brother Robert, was published simultaneously in the United States and England. Her publishers pointed with pride to the fact that Miss Peel's first novel was neither smart nor sophisticated, as might have been expected from a young writer of her literary generation. The New York *Herald Tribune "Books"* called it a "charmingly humorous and sympathetic work."

As far as nationality goes, Miss Peel says she is a complete mongrel: Irish, Scotch, French, and English. She "was born in England and educated haphazardly—on her part most light-heartedly—at a variety of schools in this country and abroad. Now she and her family have settled in Brookline, Mass., with, as the sole survivals of their original home, a cherished tea service, battered books, and some very bad watercolors." These last were painted "by a certain Mr. Potts, a friend of our parents, who later Drank Himself to Death." This account was written in 1931; a decade later Miss Peel's address was Concord Avenue, Cambridge, Mass.

Stories of family relations are Doris Peel's *forte.* "Insofar as any of us can know how the minds of children work, Miss Peel knows," said Josiah Titzell of *Five on Parade,* which concerned a family of vivacious English youngsters. Whit Burnett stated approvingly of *Aunt Margot and Other Stories* (1935) that "the world is full of female stories, but there are few like these." William Rose Benét found them more derivative: "I feel upon [the book] a visitation from Katherine Mansfield." The New York *Times* commented on the "vein of sentimental irony" in her work. Miss Peel has also contributed to *Pictorial Review,* the *Ladies' Home Journal,* and *Woman's Home Companion.*

PRINCIPAL WORKS: Children of the Wind, 1927; Five on Parade, 1930; Aunt Margot, and Other Stories, 1935.

ABOUT: Forum April 1931; Golden Book Magazine March 1935.

PEFFER, NATHANIEL (June 30, 1890-), American authority on Far Eastern affairs, was born in New York City,

the son of William Peffer and Regina (F.) Peffer. He received his B.A. degree from the University of Chicago in 1911, and five or six years later went to China to engage in business. "As I look back on the succession of elderly, motheaten, and almost scholarly gentlemen who dozed in easy chairs opposite me in one city or another from Peking to Canton and at one time or another over fifteen years, I am glad that I date before pedagogy," Peffer wrote in an article contributed to *Asia* for March 1933. Besides hiring these old-fashioned instructors, of various degrees of unreliability, Peffer attended a language school in Peking, conducted under missionary auspices by an American director. "In every Chinese is a little of Mei Lan-Fang," and they are adept in acting out the rudimentary words and phrases in a vocabulary. "I don't think I shall ever understand what the Second Law of Thermodynamics is about until I watch such a teacher explain it to a newly arrived missionary who knows neither Chinese nor science," Peffer confesses.

From 1927 to 1929 he was a Fellow of the Guggenheim Memorial Foundation for Research in China, and contributed frequent and authoritative articles on conditions in the Far East to *Harper's, New Republic,* and other periodicals. They were collected and revised for three books. Peffer is also the author of the last chapter of J. Barnes' *Empire in the East* (1934). "A white skin has ceased to be a *laissez passer* and guarantee of safe conduct, as I have myself unhappily observed," he wrote in 1930. "I have felt the steel of a pirate leader's gun prodding my throat as his followers ransacked my cabin in the foreigners' first class of a British ship on the Yangtze quite as turbulently as they did the coolie quarters below decks," and another pirate slapped him in the face when Peffer refused to reveal the whereabouts of some articles they wished produced.

Peffer is now professor of international relations at Columbia University. He married Annalies Kolisko of Vienna in 1923, and they live in the Columbia neighborhood, with a summer home at Madison, Conn. Besides his first book, on adult education, Peffer has written various pungent articles on the treason of the educated classes to the proletariat; the decline and general undesirability of the familiar essay; and similar topics. In 1924 he wrote: "One cannot discuss American college students at all in association with ideas, and the influence of the American university, if there is any, is only in the direction of solidifying inertia."

PRINCIPAL WORKS: New Schools for Older Students, 1926; The White Man's Dilemma: Climax of the Age of Imperialism, 1927; China: The Collapse of Civilization, 1930; Must We Fight in Asia? 1935; Prerequisites to Peace in the Far East, 1940.

ABOUT: Asia March 1933.

PEIRCE, CHARLES SANDERS. See "AMERICAN AUTHORS: 1600-1900"

PERELMAN, SIDNEY JOSEPH (1904*-), American humorist, announces in one of his pieces, "Ye Olde Ivory Tower,"

that "I am a thirty-five-year-old Spartan boy." This was written sometime between 1937 and 1940, when his *Look Who's Talking!* was published. He graduated from Brown University in 1925. His friends here included Israel James Kapstein, the writer, and Nathanael West,[qv] whose sister Laura he married.

After graduation Perelman worked for *Judge,* the humorous weekly, also contributing in course of time to *College Humor,* the old *Life, Contact,* the *New Yorker,* the *New Masses,* and *Broun's Nutmeg. Dawn Ginsbergh's Revenge,* a wild burlesque, appeared in 1929, and Perelman "was whisked out to Hollywood before the ink on the first hundred copies was dried." Here he wrote "gags" for the best of the Marx Brothers' films, and collaborated with his wife on *Ambush,* one of the best "Grade B" pictures of 1939. With Mrs. Perelman he also wrote a comedy, *The Night*

Before Christmas, based on a situation like the one in Conan Doyle's *The Red-headed League* (Perelman is deeply versed in Sherlock Holmes), which had a brief run in New York in 1941, but was sold to Hollywood for what is known as a substantial sum. The Perelmans settled some years ago on a farm in Bucks County, Pa., purchased from Michael Gold. Besides his writing of the ordinary, or extraordinary, kind, Perelman has managed a radio show, *Author, Author.*

Robert Benchley contributed a foreword to Perelman's *Strictly From Hunger* (1937), in which he complained feelingly that "Together with several others of my ilk, most of whom are now on movie relief, thanks to Mr. Perelman, I was making a decent living writing fugitive pieces for the magazines, pieces which, while not pretentious, we fondly imagined could be turned into thirty dollars here or forty dollars there. It was a perfectly good racket, at any rate, and several psychiatrists were good enough to refer to it as 'free association' or Dope's Disease. Then, from the Baptist precincts of Brown University, wafted a cloud no bigger than a man's hams, who was S. J. Perelman. From then on, it was just a matter of time before Perelman took over the *dementia praecox* field and drove us all to writing articles on economics for the

1092   * Born February 1, 1904.

Commentator. Any further attempts to garble thought-processes sounded like imitation-Perelman."

Time calls Perelman next to Poe and not excepting Henry Miller, the most proficient surrealist in the United States. He is an exponent of "screwball wit," which "calls for an exquisite sense of cliché and mimicry, and a nihilism which delights in knocking over-crystallized words, objects, and gestures into glassy pieces that cut each other."

PRINCIPAL WORKS: Dawn Ginsbergh's Revenge, 1929; Parlor, Bedlam, and Bath, (with Q. T. Reynolds) 1930; Strictly From Hunger, 1937; Look Who's Talking! 1940.

ABOUT: Perelman, S. J. Strictly From Hunger (see Foreword by R. C. Benchley); Time August 12, 1940.

PÉREZ DE AYALA, RAMÓN (August 9, 1881-), Spanish novelist, poet, and critic, was born in Oviedo, of a middle-class family of mixed Gothic and Celtic descent. He was educated at the seminary of San Zoil and the Colegio de la Immaculada, both Jesuit institutions, both of which he hated. Though a born writer, to whom "writing is as natural as the shape of my nose or the color of my eyes," his revolt against the classical tradition led him to study first science and then law at the University of Oviedo. He never practiced law, however, but while still at the university began publishing critical articles. His first volume, a collection of poems, appeared in 1903. He has always been a good self-critic, and in consequence nearly everything of his in print is worthy of the literary standard he has set himself. His three major fictional series came to unhasty fruition at five-year periods, in 1916, 1921, and 1926.

A great deal of Pérez de Ayala's energy has been consumed, not in writing, but in political activities. He was associated with Ortega y Gasset in the direction of the magazine *España,* and in subsequent movements for the overthrow of the monarchy and the establishment of the republic. Immediately after the university, he had lived for a year in London (he was called back to Spain by his father's suicide); then he was appointed Ambassador to the Court of St. James, as well as director of the National Library and the Prado Museum.

But he was by this time anything but radical in his views, and with the beginning of the Civil War he was relieved of his various posts. He had by now become Fascist in his sympathies, but Franco would give him no recognition because of the outspoken antireligious books of his youth. Nevertheless, when he went to Buenos Aires late in 1940 it was rumored that he was on an extraofficial mission for Franco; and at a lecture at the University of Buenos Aires he publicly praised his friend Heinrich Himmler, head of Hitler's *Gestapo.*

Pérez de Ayala seems, indeed, to be one of those writers frequently met with who are enthusiastically radical in their youth and become exceedingly conservative with age. His best work remains to testify to a philosophy he no longer holds. His anti-clerical novel, *A.M.D.G.,* published in 1910, Jean Cassou called "a masterpiece of black irony." Cassou said further: "His style is sinuous, Jesuitical, contorted, delicious perfidious, and all his own." His books are difficult to translate, precisely because they are so thoroughly Spanish. Even in Spain his appeal has been not to the masses but to the intellectual few, though in 1926 he shared the National Prize of Literature with Concha Espina and Fernández Flores, and in 1928 was elected to the National Academy.

He is married to an American and has two children. His recreation is drawing and sculpture, for which he has some talent. In appearance he is long-headed and heavy-jawed, with a passing resemblance to the Bourbons whom he helped to drive out of Spain.

WORKS AVAILABLE IN ENGLISH: Prometheus: The Fall of the House of Limon: Sunday Sunlight, 1920; The Fox's Paw, 1924; Tiger Juan, 1933.

ABOUT: Agustin, F. Pérez de Ayala; Boyd, E. Studies From Ten Literatures; Madariaga, S. de. The Genius of Spain; Hispania May 1932; Nation December 17, 1924; New Statesman and Nation January 28, 1933; Saturday Review of Literature December 6, 1924, September 30, 1933.

PÉREZ GALDÓS, BENITO (May 10, 1843-January 4, 1920), Spanish novelist, was born in Las Palmas, in the Canary Islands, and first attended an English school there. (His biographer L. D. Walton gives his birth year as 1843, but the Library of Congress lists it as 1845.) His family was prosperous, and he never had to struggle with poverty or do any work other than writing. At fourteen he was sent to the Colegio de San Agostín, and then his family ordered him to Madrid to study law at the university. This was not at all to his liking, and though he persevered and took his law degree in 1869, he never had any intention of making the law his profession. Instead, he became the intimate of advanced literary circles in Madrid, and first appeared in print as the

literary and drama critic of *La Nación*. The theatre was his first love and his earliest ambition was to become known as a playwright. But though he continued to write plays throughout his life, and many of them were produced with great success, he discovered early that his real vocation was as a novelist.

His first novel, indeed, appeared while he was still a university student. For a few years he continued in journalism, being on the staff of *Las Cortes* and *La Revista de España,* and editor of *El Debate.* But a visit to France determined him to abandon journalism and devote himself solely to a vast project which eventually became his *Episodios Nacionales (National Episodes)* —four series of ten volumes each, and one of eight, forty-eight books in all. These appeared on an average of one every three months, and were interspersed with realistic "contemporary novels."

Such an output made it impossible that Pérez Galdós could have had a very varied life outside his work, though he traveled extensively in France and England and throughout Spain. He did take an active part in politics, being liberal deputy to Puerto Rico from 1886 to 1890, and republican deputy from Madrid in 1907. But for the most part he lived very quietly, between his bachelor home (he never married) and the library which was his second home. In his last years his sight began to fail, and by 1912 he was totally blind. He continued to write, dictating his novels, until his death in Madrid eight years later.

A markedly modest and reticent man, whose private life was never open to the public, Pérez Galdós was the type of the retiring scholar. But to him, as the noted critic Azorín remarked, "the new generation of [Spanish] writers owes the very essence of its being." The strongest influences on his work were those of Balzac and Erckmann-Chatrian. But, as L. B. Walton said, the *Episodios* were not mere historical romances, but "endeavors to interpret history

in terms of the human spirit,"—the net result being as if Balzac had chosen to treat of subjects similar to those chosen by Erckmann-Chatrian. His "profound human appeal," "the vast scope of his work and the amazing fecundity of his genius," and what W. A. Drake called "his full social canvas" combine to make him one of the most significant writers of modern times, far too little known in America and England— where, except for occasional translations of plays by him in anthologies, no one has troubled to translate any of his work since 1910.

Works Available in English: Gloria, 1879; Doña Perfecta, 1883; Marianela, 1883; Trafalgar, 1884; Leon Roch, 1888; Zaragoza, 1899; Electra (play) 1902; The Court of Charles, 1907; Grandfather (play) 1910; The Duchess of San Quentin (in Masterpieces of Modern Spanish Drama, ed. by B. H. Clark) 1917.

About: Alas, L. ("Clarion"). Galdós; Anton del Omet, L. & Garcia Caraffa, A. Galdós; Gamero y de Laiglesia, E. G. Galdós y su Obra; Walton, L. B. Pérez Galdós and the Spanish Novel of the Nineteenth Century; Contemporary Review April 1920; Modern Language Notes November 1929; Philological Quarterly July 1928; Publications of the Modern Language Association September 1933, September 1935; Revue Hispanique December 1926; Romanic Review January 1932.

*PERRY, BLISS (November 25, 1860-   ), American editor and critic, was born in Williamstown, Mass., the son of Arthur Latham Perry, professor of political economy at Williams College, and Mary (Smedley) Perry. He was educated at Williams (B.A. 1881, M.A. 1883), and at the Universities of Berlin and Strassburg. He has honorary degrees also from Princeton, Harvard, Brown, Pennsylvania, Bowdoin, Vermont, and Wake Forest. From 1886 to 1893 he was professor of English at Williams, and from 1893 to 1900 at Princeton. On the strength of "some editorial work for publishers and three or four books of fiction," he was asked to become editor of the *Atlantic Monthly,* "by a group all of whom must have been gamblers at heart." He was, however, a highly successful editor from 1899 to 1909. In 1904 he first taught at Harvard, as a substitute for Barret Wendell, and in 1907 became professor of English literature there. In 1909-10 he was Harvard lecturer in France. For several years he continued part-time editorial

* Died February 13, 1954.

duties as well. He resigned from Harvard in 1930, and has since lived quietly in Cambridge, Mass. In 1888 he married Annie L. Bliss; they have two sons and a daughter. His autobiography is his last published work, and he says he does not expect, being nearly eighty at this writing, to publish any further books.

Professor Perry is a trustee emeritus of Williams College and an overseer of Harvard University. He is a member of the American Academy of Arts and Letters and the Massachusetts Historical Society, a fellow of the Royal Society of Literature, and a Chevalier of the Legion of Honor. He has been active in the Boston Watch and Ward Society, and is in favor of "democratic censorship" of literature. Besides his own writing, he has edited numerous English and American classics, including eighteen volumes of *Little Masterpieces*; he was general editor of the *Cambridge Editions of the Poets*.

Looking back on a long life, he feels that literature is at a low ebb as compared with the progress of science. Nevertheless, as Arthur Colton remarked, he is "sane, serene, and witty; he looks wisely on the sunny side of things."

PRINCIPAL WORKS: The Broughton House (novel) 1890; Salem Kittredge and Other Stories, 1894; The Plated City (novel) 1895; The Powers at Play (novel) 1899; A Study of Prose Fiction, 1902; The Amateur Spirit, 1904; Walt Whitman, 1906; Whittier, 1907; Park Street Papers, 1909; The American Mind, 1912; Carlyle, 1915; The American Spirit in Literature, 1918; A Study of Poetry, 1920; Life and Letters of Henry Lee Higginson, 1921; The Praise of Folly, 1923; Pools and Ripples, 1927; Emerson Today, 1931; Richard Henry Dana, 1933; And Gladly Teach (autobiography) 1935.

ABOUT: Perry, B. And Gladly Teach; Saturday Review of Literature August 17, 1935, January 18, 1936.

PERRY, RALPH BARTON (July 3, 1876-), American philosopher and Pulitzer Prize biographer, was born in Poultney,

Vt., and educated at Princeton (B.A. 1896) and Harvard (M.A. 1897, Ph.D. 1899). He also has honorary doctorates from Clark University. He was an instructor in philosophy at Williams College in 1899 and 1900, at Smith from 1900 to 1902, and then went to Harvard. He has been professor of philosophy there since

1913. During the First World War he served as secretary of the committee on special training and education of the War Department, with the rank of major. He was Hyde Lecturer at French universities in 1921 and 1922, and was made a Chevalier of the Legion of Honor in 1936. In 1905, in London, he married Rachel Berenson, sister of the art critic Bernard Berenson, and they had two sons; Mrs. Perry died in 1933.

As both pupil and close friend of William James, it was natural that Professor Perry should become his definitive biographer. His life of James won the Pulitzer Prize for biography in 1935. He is considered the chief living authority on James, and his own philosophic system is a sort of extension of James' pragmatism, technically called neo-realism. He is a past president of the American Philosophical Association. For many years he has made his home in Cambridge. A shortish man, he looks younger than his years and not at all like the stock idea of a professor of philosophy. He has a gift of style, and in spite of the abstruse nature of much of his subject-matter, most of his books may be read with interest by the more serious-minded layman. Besides his own works, he has edited James' *Collected Essays and Reviews* and *Essays in Radical Empiricism*, and has published a revision of Alfred Weber's standard *History of Philosophy*. In recent years Professor Perry has been a vigorous spokesman for all-out war against the Fascist Axis.

PRINCIPAL WORKS: The Approach to Philosophy, 1905; The Moral Economy, 1909; Present Philosophical Tendencies, 1912; The New Realism, 1912; The Free Man and the Soldier, 1916; The Present Conflict of Ideals, 1918; Annotated Bibliography of the Writings of William James, 1920; The Plattsburg Movement, 1921; Philosophy of the Recent Past, 1926; General Theory of Value, 1926; A Defense of Philosophy, 1931; The Thought and Character of William James, 1935; In the Spirit of William James, 1938; The Meaning of the Humanities (with others) 1938; On All Fronts, 1941; Plea for an Age Movement, 1942.

ABOUT: Adams, G. P. & Montague, W. P. (eds.) Contemporary American Philosophy; Evans, D. L. New Realism and Old Reality; Harlow, V. E. A Bibliography and Genetic Study of American Realism; Kremer, R. Le Néo-Realisme Américain; Journal of Ethics July 1930, January 1934, October 1938; Saturday Review of Literature May 9, 1936.

"PERSE, ST.-J." See LÉGER, A.

PERTWEE, ROLAND (1885-), English playwright and novelist, writes: "I was born at Brighton, and at the age of fourteen formed the resolution to become a painter.

My education may be said to have been a bit of a mess, and when, in my sixteenth year, I entered the Westminister School  of Art, there rang in my ears a panegyric from my last schoolmaster, affirming that I had not reached a state of knowledge adequate to get me through the College of Preceptors' exam. With this unhappy record, it is a little surprising that within two years I had acquired a scholarship for the Royal Academy School of Art. My success as an art student was almost as great as my failure as an artist; for although I did succeed in getting my canvases occasionally hung at the Royal Academy, it is painful to record that no single sitter who commissioned me to paint his or her portrait was ever subsequently persuaded to pay for it without recourse to the law. In the circumstances, I abandoned painting and went onto the stage.

"As an actor I showed more immediate promise, and for a number of years, during which I played in the companies of H. B. Irving, Charles Hawtrey, and many others, I cannot remember any time when I was out of work, nor any engagement that did not earn me a larger salary than its predecessor.

"The declaration of war in 1914, coupled with the knowledge that I would have to get into khaki, encouraged me to seek other means of earning a livelihood. I had already written a few fairly successful one-act plays, and, on the strength of their reception. I tried my luck as a short story writer. My first short story was sold to the *Saturday Evening Post* and the *Strand Magazine,* and the *Post* invited me to submit six more stories on similar lines, every one of which was accepted.

"The financial horizon, darkened by war clouds, had now brightened, and I set off to join the B.E.F. in France, confident that I should be able to make a living as a writer, war or no war. This confidence was well placed, for during some twenty months in France I sent home about two thousand pounds earned by writing stories. My first novel was written during three months which I spent in the Neuresthenia Ward of the Third London General Hospital. Following the Armistice, I was severally employed in writing plays, film scenarios, serial novels, and short stories. My most successful play, which I wrote in conjunction with Harold Dearden, was *Interference.* It was produced by Gerald du Maurier in England, and by Gilbert Miller in America. At one period, no fewer than eighteen companies were performing it in different parts of the civilized world.

"My first marriage, from which I had two sons, was dissolved in 1921, and I remarried, five years later, the widow of one of my greatest friends."

* * *

Mr. Pertwee has lived and written at various times in both New York and Hollywood. He thinks of himself as primarily a playwright, and of his novels as only a side issue to his main work. Of his own writing, he has written: "I yearn toward the bittersweet—the familiar and the intimate. . . . The keynote of humanity is its simplicity, and surely it is an author's job to surprise that simplicity and not to decorate it."

PRINCIPAL WORKS: *Plays*—Seein' Reason, 1913; Swank, 1914; The Return of Imry, 1914; Falling Upstairs, 1914; Early Birds, 1916; Postal Orders, 1916; Ten Minutes' Tension, 1917; Out To Win (with D. C. Calthrop) 1921; I Serve, 1922; Interference (with H. Dearden) 1927; Hell's Loose, 1929; Heat Wave, 1929; Pursuit, 1930; Royal Heritage (A Prince of Romance) 1931; This Inconstancy (with J. H. Turner) 1933; To Kill a Cat (with H. Dearden) 1939. *Novels*—Our Wonderful Selves, 1918; The Eagle and the Wren, 1923; Treasure Trail, 1924; Rivers To Cross, 1927; Princess by Proxy, 1934; Four Winds, 1935; Such an Enmity, 1936; Camelion's Dish, 1940; Lovers Are Losers, 1941. *Miscellaneous*—Master of None (autobiography) 1940.

ABOUT: Pertwee, R. Master of None; Saturday Evening Post August 22, 1925.

PETERKIN, Mrs. JULIA (MOOD)

(October 31, 1880-   ), American novelist and short-story writer, was born in Laurence County, South Carolina, the daughter of Julius Andrew Mood and Alma (Archer) Mood. Some of the Negroes on Lang Syne Plantation, her present home, are much impressed by the fact that she was born with a caul on Hallowe'en. She re-  ceived a B.A. degree from Converse College, Spartanburg, S.C., in 1896, and the next year was granted her master's degree. In 1927, after Mrs. Peterkin had published her second book, *Black April,* the college awarded her an honorary D. Litt. She had

D. Ulmann

married William George Peterkin of Lang Syne Plantation, Fort Motte, forty miles from Columbia, S.C., in June 1903. The Peterkins have a son, William George. Mrs. Peterkin's mother had died in giving her birth, and she became the sole charge of remarkable old colored Mauma. Her son was also given a wise old woman, Vinner, for a nurse. From both, Mrs. Peterkin had acquired both an early acquaintance with the Gullah dialect and a wealth of the folk-lore of this high type of very black African Negro.

Mrs. Peterkin's first piece of published prose, "The Merry-Go-Round," was in H. L. Mencken's *Smart Set*. "From Lang Syne Plantation" appeared in the *Reviewer* for October 1921; the latter was a small, experimental magazine edited by Emily Clark and others in Richmond, Va., which had amazing success in obtaining free contributions from a variety of established and beginning writers. In January 1922 it published a group of short pieces. *Green Thursday* (1924), a collection of these sketches, won the cordial admiration of Colonel Joel Elias Spingarn, who was always interested in books by and about Negroes. "Nothing so stark, taut, poignant, has come out of the white South in fifty years," he wrote.

At various times after 1924 Mrs. Peterkin went to the MacDowell Colony in Peterboro, N.H., and traveled in France. In the autumn of 1928 she published a full-length novel about Gullah Negroes entitled *Scarlet Sister Mary*, which in the following spring was awarded the Pulitzer Prize for the best novel of the year. It was later dramatized for Ethel Barrymore's first and not altogether successful experiment in playing in black-face.

"I mean to present these people in a patient struggle with fate, and not in any race conflict," Mrs. Peterkin once stated. "She has given to a modern public the half-barbaric plantation Negro in a form quite new; a courageous, inarticulate, heart-tearing creature to whom propaganda or race-conflict is yet unknown," according to Emily Clark. "By a strange irony she represents in her own person the extremes of the new order: the group that looks back with a lingering regret for fading beauties, and the constructive workers for a new South, whose very methods and whose very improvements must inevitably drive the old days and the old ways into deeper shadow," writes Isadora Bennett.

Lang Syne Plantation, employing more than 450 Negroes, raises asparagus, wheat, and oats as well as long-staple cotton; the Peterkin cotton-seed usually commands a premium. Its mistress is "a decorative person with beautiful red hair, tall, lithe, and with a strikingly erect carriage." For a time she was one of the judges for the Literary Guild in New York, where she is a member of the Cosmopolitan Club. She is also a member of P.E.N., the D.A.R., the Daughters of the Confederacy, and the Afternoon Music Club of Columbia, S.C. *Scarlet Sister Mary* was barred from the Gaffney (S.C.) Public Library, as well as from other Southern libraries.

PRINCIPAL WORKS: Green Thursday, 1924; Black April, 1927; Scarlet Sister Mary, 1928; Bright Skin, 1932; Roll, Jordan, Roll, 1933; Plantation Christmas, 1934.

ABOUT: Clark, E. Innocence Abroad; Millett, F. B. Contemporary American Authors; Bookman June 1929.

PETERSON, HOUSTON (December 11, 1897-   ), American educator and critic, writes: "I was born in Fresno, Calif. I learned to read and write shorthand at six or seven, and at ten was reading furiously in American history with the ambition of becoming professor of history at Harvard College! The *Dictionary of United States History* which I compiled at

that time is still unpublished. In 1908 I moved to Los Angeles, graduating from Pomona College in 1919. During my high school and college years I played in many tennis tournaments and was considered one of the more promising players, and also did a great deal of amateur acting, which I look back on as invaluable preparation for one who was to become a teacher and public lecturer. As my grandparents had been pioneer settlers in California, I seemed to be driven in the opposite direction, and settled down in Columbia University in 1919. I received an M.A. in philosophy the following year and was appointed assistant in the department, later to become lecturer. In 1923 I began to give a course called 'Euripides and Ibsen: Varieties of Moral Experience,' the first of several courses in the philosophy of literature, which seems to be my specialty up to the present time.

"Meanwhile I continued graduate work for a Ph.D. in philosophy. I was well advanced in a dissertation on Huxley and

Tyndall when I turned aside to do a general work on the thought of Havelock Ellis. I first met Ellis in 1925 and spent much time with him in the summer of 1926. The resulting volume was accepted for the doctor's degree in 1929. In contrast to this 'study in serenity' I then set out to do a study in confusion, with the poetry of Conrad Aiken as my point of departure and principal theme. The result was *The Melody of Chaos,* awarded the Butler Medal for 1931.

"In 1929 I became lecturer in philosophy at Rutgers University, and later professor. In 1934 I became chairman of the Cooper Union Forum, and in 1938 succeeded Dr. Everett Dean Martin as director. Married to Charlotte T. Reid in 1925, I was divorced in 1936. The same year I married Martha Berrien, a commercial artist. We live happily in an old house in Greenwich Village with two Cairn terriers and a small monkey from Ecuador. I still play tennis with adolescent enthusiasm and have recently learned to ice-skate uncertainly."

PRINCIPAL WORKS: Havelock Ellis: Philosopher of Love, 1928; The Book of Sonnet Sequences (ed.) 1929; The Melody of Chaos, 1931; Huxley: Prophet of Science, 1932; The Lonely Debate: Dilemmas From Hamlet to Hans Castorp, 1938.

ABOUT: Boston Transcript June 6, 1931.

PETRIE, Sir WILLIAM MATTHEW FLINDERS (June 3, 1853- July 28, 1942), English archaeologist, was born in Charlton;

his maternal grandfather was the famous Australian explorer Captain Matthew Flinders. He was educated privately, and though he never attended a university he had numerous honorary doctorates, was a Fellow of the Royal Society, and was Edwards Professor of Egyptology at University College, London, from 1892 to 1933, then becoming professor emeritus. His interest in archaeology began in early youth, his first researches being in England, at Stonehenge. He was knighted in 1923. In 1897 he married Hilda Urlin, and they had a son and a daughter. His most important excavations were probably those on the site of Memphis, but he made numerous other important discoveries, in Egypt and Palestine, and in his late eighties was still actively at work with the American School of Research in Jeru-

salem. He was the founder of the Egyptian Research Account, in 1894, which in 1905 became the British School of Archaeology in Egypt. He was undoubtedly the greatest contemporary Egyptologist. Of a deeply religious turn of mind, Sir Flinders (as he preferred to be called) also spent many years in extending knowledge of Biblical events.

His whole long life was given to archaeology, and he listed as his "recreations" excavating, collecting antiquities, and photographing them! He died at the government hospital in Jerusalem at eighty-nine.

PRINCIPAL WORKS: Inductive Metrology, 1875; Stonehenge, 1880; Pyramids and Temples of Gizah, 1888; A Season in Egypt, 1888; Ten Years' Diggings in Egypt, 1893; History of Egypt (4 vols.) 1894-1927; Egyptian Tales (2 vols.) 1895; Religion and Conscience in Ancient Egypt, 1898; Syria and Egypt, 1898; Methods and Aims in Archaeology, 1904; Hyksos and Israelite Cities, 1906; Religion of Ancient Egypt, 1906; Janus in Modern Life, 1907; Arts and Crafts in Egypt, 1909; The Growth of the Gospels, 1910; Historical Studies, 1910; Egypt and Israel, 1911; Revolutions of Civilization, 1911; Roman Portraits, 1912; The Formation of the Alphabet, 1912; Eastern Exploration, 1919; Some Sources of Human History, 1919; Prehistoric Egypt, 1920; Social Life in Ancient Egypt, 1923; Religious Life in Ancient Egypt, 1924; Descriptive Sociology of Ancient Egypt, 1926; Decorative Patterns of the Ancient World, 1930; Seventy Years in Archaeology, 1931; Ancient Gaza (5 vols.) 1931-38; Palestine and Israel: Historical Notes, 1934; Egyptian Science, 1939; The Making of Egypt, 1939.

ABOUT: Petrie, W. M. F. Seventy Years in Archaeology; New York Times July 30, 1942.

PETROV, EUGENE (November 30, 1903-July 2, 1942), Russian humorist, was born Eugene Petrovich Kataev in Odessa,

the son of a teacher. The writer Valentin Kataev[qv] was his older brother. In 1920 he was graduated from a classical *gymnasium,* and the same year became a correspondent for the Ukraine Telegraph Agency. Later he served for three years

as inspector of criminal investigations; his first literary production was a protocol on the corpse of an unknown man. In 1923 Petrov moved to Moscow, where he continued his education and became a journalist, working on newspapers and humorous magazines, and publishing several booklets of humorous storiettes. He was married in 1929. In 1925, in the offices of the daily *Whistle,* the organ of the railway workers, on which he was employed, he met Ilya

Ilf,[qv] who was also on the staff. Thereafter they wrote in collaboration, their stream of *feuilletons* earning for them the title of "the Soviet Mark Twains." Their witty satire was aimed always at abuses of the Soviet system and not at the system itself.

Petrov visited the United States four times, the last time with Ilf in 1936, a year before the latter's death. He was tall and lithe, sharp-nosed and keen-eyed, and a master of quick repartee. His weekly, *Ogonyok*, was notably friendly to America. After Ilf's death, he confined himself to editing and reporting.

When Germany invaded Russia in 1941, Petrov put on the uniform of a lieutenant colonel, serving as war correspondent on the staff of the Soviet Information Bureau. He participated in the defense of Moscow and was killed by the enemy in the heroic defense of Sevastopol. This "fine writer and great man" was only thirty-eight.

WORKS AVAILABLE IN ENGLISH: (All with Ilya Ilf): Diamonds To Sit On, 1930; Little Golden Calf, 1933; Little Golden America, 1937.

ABOUT: Living Age August 1939; Nation September 25, 1935; New Masses July 21, 1942; New York Times July 6, 1942.

*PHELPS, WILLIAM LYON (January 2, 1865-), American critic, was born in New Haven, Conn. (where he still lives), the son of the Rev.

S. Dryden Phelps and Sophia Emilia (Linsley) Phelps. He was educated at Yale, with which his name has always been associated, receiving his B.A. in 1887 and his Ph.D. in 1891. At the same time he studied at Harvard (M.A. 1891). He has honorary doctorates from numerous colleges. After a year as instructor in English at Harvard, he went to Yale in 1892, gradually rising in rank until in 1901 he became Lampson Professor of English Literature, a post he held until his retirement because of his age in 1933. He was Public Orator of Yale (though he says he dislikes public speaking), is a Fellow of the American Academy of Arts and Sciences and a member of the American Academy of Arts and Letters. In 1940 he received the American Educational Award. For many years he conducted the book department, called "As I Like It," in *Scribner's Magazine,* and followed with similar departments in the *Rotarian* and *Esquire.*

He married Annabelle Hubbard in 1892; she died in 1939.

Since Professor Phelps' writing is extremely personal, his likes and dislikes are well known to the general public. He has a passion for cats, golf, Browning, and Spenser. In his summer home at Huron, Mich., he often preaches in the Methodist Church. He is president of the New Haven Symphony Orchestra and Little Theatre Guild. He has a genius for friendship, and has been known as "Billy" Phelps to many generations of Yale students. Tall, stooped, with iron gray hair and keen eyes behind spectacles, he has appeared on lecture platforms everywhere in America.

It is easy to deprecate his easy enthusiasms. Nevertheless, it is also only fair to remember that he gave the first course in any American university in contemporary fiction and drama, and that he pioneered in introducing the Russian novelists to English readers.

PRINCIPAL WORKS: The Beginnings of the English Romantic Movement, 1893; The Pure Gold of Nineteenth Century Literature, 1907; A Dash at the Pole, 1909; Essays on Modern Novelists, 1910; Essays on Russian Novelists, 1911; Teaching in School and College, 1912; Essays on Books, 1914; Browning, 1915; The Advance of the English Novel, 1916; The Advance of English Poetry, 1918; The Twentieth Century Theatre, 1918; Archibald Marshall, 1918; Reading the Bible, 1919; Essays on Modern Dramatists, 1920; Human Nature in the Bible, 1922; Some Makers of American Literature, 1923; As I Like It, 1923; American Literature, 1923-26; Essays on American Authors, 1924; Howells, James, Bryant, and Other Essays, 1924; Adventures and Confessions, 1925; Human Nature in the Bible, 1925; Happiness, 1926; Love, 1928; Memory, 1929; Essays on Things, 1930; Music, 1930; Human Nature, 1931; Appreciation, 1932; Easter, 1933; The Courage of Ignorance, 1933; What I Like in Poetry, 1934; What I Like in Prose, 1934; William Lyon Phelps Yearbook, 1935; Autobiography With Letters, 1939; Marriage, 1940; The Mother's Anthology (comp.) 1940; A Children's Anthology (comp.) 1941.

ABOUT: Frank, W. D. Time Exposures; Phelps, W. L. Autobiography With Letters; Rascoe, B. A Bookman's Daybook; American Mercury November 1935; Christian Century August 2, 1933; Christian Science Monitor Monthly January 6, 1940; Commonweal January 28, 1938; Ladies' Home Journal February 1925; New Republic May 17, 1939; New Yorker October 24, 1925; Outlook April 23, 1930; Saturday Review of Literature April 29 and August 28, 1933, April 1, 1939; School and Society February 8, 1941.

PHILLIPS, DAVID GRAHAM (October 31, 1867-January 24, 1911), American novelist, journalist, and reformer, was born in Madison, Ind., the fourth child and first son of David Graham Phillips, a banker, and Margaret (Lee) Phillips, a descendant

* Died August 21, 1943.

of "Light-Horse" Harry Lee of Revolutionary fame. From the Madison public schools and a foreign-language tutor at home he went to Asbury College (now De Pauw University), Greencastle, Ind., for two years, transferring then to Princeton. Phillips received his B.A. degree in June 1887, the youngest member in a class of eighty-six. His Princeton manner and clothes failed to impress the city editor of the Cincinnati *Times-Star,* and he haunted the office for several weeks until finally sent out on an assignment. The murder story he brought back was printed without the change of a word. Murat Halstead, editor of the Cincinnati *Commercial Gazette,* doubled Phillips' salary inside a year and called him a born reporter. Larger fields lured him after three years there, and he proceeded to New York in the summer of 1890, staying a short time on the *Tribune* and then covering human interest stories at the Jefferson Market Police Court for the *Sun* at $15 a week.

Early in 1893 Phillips joined the *World,* gaining the liking of the autocratic Joseph Pulitzer, who sent him to London as a special correspondent. In June 1893 Phillips scored one of the historic beats of the decade, an exclusive report on the sinking of H. M. S. "Camperdown," in collision with H. M. S. "Victoria" off the coast of Asia Minor. Pulitzer promoted him to the editorial staff, but was grieved and displeased by Phillips's depiction of him in *The Great God Success* (1901), a newspaper novel published under the pseudonym "John Graham."

A period of free-lancing followed early in 1902. Phillips wrote a series of articles on some unpleasant aspects of journalism for the *Saturday Evening Post,* contributing also to *McClure's, Munsey's, Everybody's, Success, Harper's Weekly, Delineator,* and others. His "Treason of the Senate" series earned him Theodore Roosevelt's dislike and the epithet of muckraker, but strengthened the movement for the popular election of United States senators. In the decade 1901-1911 Phillips wrote twenty-three novels and a one-act play, *The Worth of a Woman,* produced at the Madison Square Theatre in February 1908 with Katherine Grey as Diana Merivale. His reforming spirit was carried into his fiction; his novels were problem novels. As Calvin Winter has said,

he was not merely a clear-eyed and impartial observer of life, he was always a partisan and reformer. H. L. Mencken has praised his earnestness and intelligence. The novels dealt in essentials, not nuances; facts, not conventions. Their average sale was 100,000 copies apiece.

Phillips's crusading desire to "demonstrate conclusively the spiritual and mental poverty of the women of our conventional upper classes" was a contributing cause of his death. On January 23, 1911, he was shot on the street without warning by a paranoiac, Fitzhugh Coyle Goldsborough, son of Dr. Edmund K. Goldsborough, a prominent Washington physician, who had nursed a quixotic resentment against Phillips for his portrayal of American women, believing especially that the Margaret Severance of *The Fashionable Adventures of Joshua Craig* was a portrait of his sister. For weeks Goldsborough had watched his victim from a small room on the top floor of the Rand School for Social Science, opposite 119 East 19th Street, where Phillips lived with his sister Carolyn. Phillips usually lunched at the Princeton Club, then occupying a house at Gramercy Park and Lexington Avenue.

Goldsborough met his victim near the door of the club, fired six shots into his body, and then shot himself in the temple. Phillips died the next evening in the Bellevue Hospital after remarking to the attendants, "I could have won against two bullets but not against six." He was buried in Kensico Cemetery.

Phillips carried his newspaper habits into his literary work, writing at night, seven nights a week, from 11 to 6, turning out at a session 6,000 words written with soft lead on rough yellow paper in a small script that bothered typists. From fear of appendicitis he wrote standing at a tall desk. He was tall, spare, casual, and leisurely, with brown hair, blue eyes, and a ready charm. A careful workman in spite of his rapid production, he rewrote a novel nine or ten times. *Susan Lenox,* one of the first studies of an American courtesan, was rewritten four times over a period of nine years. *Hearst's Magazine* serialized it (June 1915-January 1917) and the novel appeared in two volumes a month later, the first containing 505 and the second 506 pages. By the time John S. Sumner and his Society for the Suppression of Vice had finished with it, the pagination stood at 474, 490 pages. George Hobart dramatized *Susan* with small success, and Greta Garbo attempted another version in the silent pictures in 1931.

Variously dubbed the American Balzac and the American Zola by friendly biographers, Phillips would more probably agree with Granville Hicks' verdict that he was a journalist from beginning to end, a journalist and nothing more, though some have seen in his work a burning "desire . . . to lay bare the debasement of the middle-class spirit in a plutocracy." "In a score of novels composed with a fierce energy," says Carl Van Doren, "he ranged over the American scene in his hunt for snobbery and stupidity and cruelty and greed, turning them up to the light with a gusto not matched by the art of his revelations."

PRINCIPAL WORKS: *Novels*—The Great God Success, 1901; The Golden Fleece, 1903; The Master-Rogue, 1903; The Social Secretary, 1905; The Fortune Hunter, 1906; Light-Fingered Gentry, 1907; The Second Generation, 1907; Old Wives For New, 1908; The Fashionable Adventures of Joshua Craig, 1909; The Hungry Heart, 1909; White Magic, 1910; The Grain of Dust, 1911; The Price She Paid, 1912; Degarmo's Wife and Other Stories, 1913; Susan Lenox: Her Fall and Rise, 1917. *Plays*—The Worth of a Woman, 1908; A Point of Law, 1908. *Criticism*—The Reign of Gilt, 1905; The Treason of the Senate, 1906.

ABOUT: Baldwin, C. C. The Men Who Make Our Novels; Chamberlain, J. Farewell to Reform; Cooper, F. T. Some American Story Tellers; Marcosson, I. David Graham Phillips and His Times; Underwood, J. C. Literature and Insurgency; Van Doren, C. The American Novel; Bookman February 1911, March 1914, May 1931; Saturday Review of Literature July 8, 1939; Smart Set January 1911.

PHILLIPS, HENRY WALLACE (January 11, 1869-May 23, 1930), American humorist and writer of Western stories, was

born in New York, the son of Charles Jeter and Adelaide Augusta (Smith) Phillips. He attended the public schools and the Drisler School and spent several years in the Dakotas and in Canada as a cowboy, miner, and school teacher. His *Red Saunders* stories, told by the drawling, imperturbable cowhand, Red Saunders himself, attracted a large and devoted following when they began to appear in *McClure's Magazine*. The stories had wit and style besides uproarious humor. Phillips was also fortunate in the illustrators selected to do pictures for the stories: A. B. Frost, for one. Readers can still be found who will contend that *Red Saunders' Pets, and Other Critters,* is one of the funniest books ever

written by an American. Their continued popularity is exemplified by the long list of them reprinted in the *Golden Book Magazine* between 1925 and 1930. *Plain Mary Smith* is a "Red Saunders" full-length novel introducing an element of romance. Phillips also collaborated with another writer of superior Western stories, Eugene Manlove Rhodes.[qv] In later years he did some work for the moving pictures; death occurred at Los Angeles. Phillips left a son, Wallace Chandler Phillips, an artist in New York. He had married Louise Moore Millspaugh of Richmond, N.Y., August 17, 1898; they were divorced in 1914.

PRINCIPAL WORKS: Red Saunders, 1902; Plain Mary Smith, 1905; Mr. Scraggs, 1906; Red Saunders' Pets, and Other Critters, 1906; The Mascot of Sweetbriar Gulch, 1908; Trolley Folly, 1909.

ABOUT: Rhodes, M. D. Hired Man on Horseback; New York Times May 25, 1930.

PHILLIPS, STEPHEN (July 28, 1868-December 9, 1915), English poet and dramatist, was born at Summertown, near Oxford, the son of the

Rev. Stephen Phillips, precentor of Peterborough Cathedral, and Agatha Sophia (Dockray) Phillips, a cousin of the Wordsworth family. Another cousin was Laurence Binyon, the poet. He was educated at Trinity College School, Stratford-on-Avon, at King's School, Peterborough, and at the famous Oundle School. He was unpopular with both teachers and fellow pupils, and more than once was severely beaten. The truth is, he was quick tempered and unmanageable, and seems to have been anything but an amiable boy. Though he had a scholarship for Queen's College, Cambridge, the family finances did not permit his residence there, and he was put to reading for the civil service. From this drudgery he escaped as an actor in the company of still another cousin, Frank (later Sir Frank) Benson. He was on the stage from 1885 to 1892, but though he made a handsome figure and recited blank verse sonorously, he was no actor, and was finally dismissed "for cause." (He had fallen already into habits of dissipation.) Then for six years he lectured on history—about which he knew very little—for a "crammer" for the army examinations. It was not until the success of a volume of collected poems in 1898 that he was able to give up this work; the volume received the thousand-guinea prize of the *Academy,* and he was a made man. He secured an interview with Sir George Alexander and actually sold him *Paolo and Francesca* before it was written—and took a perilously long time to write it. But it skyrocketed him into glory. For ten years he *was* the poetic drama in England. He was compared to every great writer from Sophocles to Shakespeare.

Then came the sudden descent. It was probably not deliberate, though it was cruel. From 1906 onward, the critics who had praised him suddenly began either abusing or ignoring him. Self-conceit and a vast inertia being two of Phillips' salient characteristics, he had not the stamina to withstand this reversal of fortune, which in the first place had probably come about merely by a change in popular fashion. In 1908 he deserted his wife and son (he had married May Lidyard in 1892), and, penniless and demoralized, simply disappeared. He was found and to some extent rehabilitated by Binyon, who had encouraged his very first publication. From 1913 to his death he was editor of the *Poetry Review,* and a good editor; but the verse of these last years was increasingly bad. All his defects as a writer came to the fore, with none of his genuine talent. Broken in health, he died at Deal at forty-seven. He was buried at Hastings.

In appearance, Phillips was six feet tall, with wide-set blue eyes, tiny mouth with a pugnacious chin, aggressive nose, and a curiously square effect of his forehead, covered by a wavy bang of hair. In nature he belonged to the era of Wilde and Dowson and Beardsley. Indolent, lethargic, careless, extravagant, self-indulgent, he nevertheless was generous to others as well as to himself, and he had the gift of easy charm. A sociable man, a fine *raconteur,* an excellent cricketer, he yet had periods of black depression when he "felt his life a losing struggle against a destiny that was himself." As Padraic Colum remarked, he had been overpraised because the critics "mistook a familiar design for a new manifestation of beauty." His tendency to turgidity, overdecoration, the fustian of rhetoric, drowned out a "dramatic genius intense but of very limited range." He read little, he was no thinker, he had small power of characterization and no turn for experimentation, and (to quote Arthur Waugh) "the theatrical element finally drowned out the promise of youth."

PRINCIPAL WORKS: *Poetry*—Orestes and Other Poems, 1884; Primavera (with three others) 1890; Eremus, 1894; Christ in Hades, 1897; Poems, 1898; New Poems, 1908; Lyrics and Dramas, 1913; Panama and Other Poems, 1915. *Verse Plays*—Paolo and Francesca, 1900; Herod, 1901; Ulysses, 1902; The Sin of David, 1904; Nero, 1906; Faust (with J. C. Carr) 1908; The New Inferno, 1910; Pietro of Siena, 1910; The King, 1912; Armageddon, 1915; Collected Plays, 1921; Harold, 1927.

ABOUT: Archer, W. Poets of the Younger Generation; Hale, E. E. Dramatists of Today; Hind, C. L. Authors and I; Kernahan, C. In Good Company, Celebrities; Murry, J. M. Pencillings; Squire, J. C. Books in General; Waugh, A. Tradition and Change; Weygandt, C. Tuesdays at Ten; Bookman November 1920; Bookman (London) March 1916; Fortnightly Review January 1916; Living Age May 6, 1916; Nation December 16, 1915; New Republic December 25, 1915; Nineteenth Century August 1920; North American Review February 1916; Outlook December 22, 1915; Poetry February 1916.

PHILLPOTTS, EDEN (November 4, 1862-   ), English novelist and poet, was born in Mount Aboo, India, where his father, Capt. Henry Phillpotts was Political Agent for the States of Harowtee and Rajpootana. On both sides he came of Devonshire families. He was sent back to England to go to school at Plymouth, and it was then that he first made the acquaintance of the moorlands whose celebrant  he became. At seventeen he went to London and entered a dramatic school, but, he says, "I abandoned the art on finding my ability did not justify perseverance." Instead, he entered the offices of the Sun Fire Insurance Co., and served there from 1880 to 1890. In his spare moments, he began to write for the *Idler* and *Black and White.* In 1892 he married Emily Topham, who died in 1928, leaving a son and a daughter, Adelaide, who is a novelist and has collaborated with her father also in several plays. The year after his first wife's death he married Lucy Robina Webb. For some years he lived at Torquay, where he was honored by being given the freedom of the town. His home now is in Exeter.

He says of himself: "I do very little except write. I am not robust, and I detest society in any shape or form. My garden and an occasional change of air are all I need. . . .My work has been the consolation and support of a difficult life, and I love it, and cannot think of existence away from it."

A slender white-haired man with a bushy white moustache and sensitive features, he is still indefatigably at work in his late seventies. Besides his plays, he has written some hundred and fifty volumes, often several appearing in one year. He is a long-time member of the Rationalist Press Association of Great Britain, and occasionally contributes articles to its publications, the *Literary Guide* and the *Rationalist Annual.* He lives very quietly, as he has said, his leisure spent with his family, his garden, and his "most masterful" cat.

In nearly fifty years of writing, there are few fields Mr. Phillpotts has not covered. His most important work is undoubtedly the long series of Dartmoor novels (brought out in the "Widecomb edition" in 1928), which have often been compared to Hardy's Wessex novels, though several of them were written before he had ever read Hardy. His conventional poetry expresses his deep-rooted love for nature. Under his own name and under the pseudonym of "Harrington Hext" he is also the author of a number of mystery and detective novels, the best of them probably *A Voice From the Dark, The Red Redmaynes,* and *The Grey Room*—novels which have been called heavy and long-winded, but the best of which are solid pieces of characterization and excellently managed mysteries as well. And there are miscellaneous novels, short stories, essays, humor, and plays.

Unfortunately, he is not nearly so well known in America as in England, and where known at all in this country it is for his least valuable work. To the editors of this volume he writes: "Not much of my serious work and none of my poetry is published in America, because your publishers care only for the minor works." It may be that the very reputation he has won as a regional novelist has mitigated against his becoming widely known on this side of the Atlantic.

In spite of his disclaimer, the Dartmoor novels do irresistibly remind one of Hardy, in their evocation of personality, their oneness with the natural background, their poetic realism, and their persisting consciousness of fate. Thomas Moult said that in them there is "a sense of unity, of the Spirit Brooding through even the most trivial action of the least important peasant. . . . In essence, he is a quietly impassioned realist."

PRINCIPAL WORKS: *Fiction*—Lying Prophets, 1896; Children of the Mist, 1898; The Human Boy, 1899; Sons of the Morning, 1900; The Striking Hours, 1901; The Good Red Earth, 1901; The River, 1902; Golden Fetich, 1903; The American Prisoner, 1904; The Secret Woman, 1905; Knock at a Venture, 1905; The Portreeve, 1906; The Whirlwind, 1907; The Folk Afield, 1907; The Human Boy Again, 1908; The Mother, 1908; The Virgin in Judgment, 1908; Fun of the Fair, 1909; The Three Brothers, 1909; The Haven, 1909; The Flint Heart, 1910; The Thief of Virtue, 1910; Tales of the Tenements, 1910; The Beacon, 1911; Dance of the Months, 1911; Demeter's Daughter, 1911; From the Angle of Seventeen, 1912; Lovers, 1912; Folly and Fresh Air, 1912; The Forest on the Hill, 1912; The Old Time Before Them, 1913; Widecomb Fair, 1913; The Joy of Youth, 1913; The Judge's Chair, 1914; Faith Tresillion, 1914; Brunel's Tower, 1915; Old Delabole, 1915; The Green Alleys, 1916; The Girl and the Fawn, 1916; The Human Boy and the War, 1916; The Banks of Colne (The Nursery) 1917; The Farmer's Wife, 1917; Chronicles of St. Tid, 1918; The Spinners, 1918; A Shadow Passes, 1918; Storm in a Teacup, 1919; Evander, 1919; Miser's Money, 1920; Orphan Dinah, 1920; The Bronze Venus, 1921; Eudocia, 1921; The Grey Room, 1921; Pan and the Twins, 1922; The Red Redmaynes, 1922; Black, White, and Brindled, 1923; The Thing at Their Heels (by "Harrington Hext") 1923; Children of Men, 1923; The Lavendar Dragon, 1923; Cheat-the-Boys, 1924; The Treasure of Typhon, 1924; Who Killed Cock Robin (by "Harrington Hext") 1924; Redcliff, 1924; The Human Boy's Diary, 1924; Circe's Island, 1925; George Westover, 1925; A Voice From the Dark, 1925; Up Hill, Down Dale (short stories) 1925; The Miniature, 1926; A Cornish Droll, 1926; Jig-Saw (in England: Marylebone Miser) 1926; The Jury, 1927; The Ring Fence, 1928; It Happened Like That (short stories) 1928; Arachne, 1928; The Torch and Other Tales, 1929; The Apes, 1929; Tryphena, 1929; The Three Maidens, 1930; Alcyone, 1930; Cherry Gambol (short stories) 1930; Peacock House, 1931; Found Drowned, 1931; Stormbury, 1931; They Could Do No Other, 1932; Bred in the Bone, 1932; A Clue From the Stars, 1932; The Broom Squires, 1932; Mr. Digweed and Mr. Lumb, 1933; The Captain's Curio, 1933; Nancy Owlett, 1933; Witch's Cauldron, 1933; A Year With Bisshe-Bantam, 1934; Minions of the Moon, 1934; The Oldest Inhabitant, 1934; Portrait of a Gentleman, 1934; Ned of the Caribbees, 1935; The Anniversary Murder (in England: Physician, Heal Thyself) 1935; The Wife of Elias, 1935; The Owl of Athene, 1936; The White Camel, 1936; A Woodnymph, 1936; A Close Call, 1936; Lycanthrope, 1937; Saurus, 1938; Thorn in Her Flesh, 1938; Dark Horses, 1938; Golden Island, 1938; Portrait of a Scoundrel, 1938; Monkschool, 1939; Awake Deborah! 1940; Chorus of Clowns, 1940; Ghostwater, 1941; A Deed Without a Name, 1942. *Plays*—A Pair of Knickerbockers, 1900; The Shadow, 1913; Curtain Raisers, 1914; St. George and the Dragons, 1919; A Comedy Royal, 1924; Devonshire Cream, 1925; Yellow Sands (with A. E. Phillpotts) 1926; The Blue Comet, 1927; The Runaways, 1929; Buy a Broom, 1929; Jane's Legacy, 1931; The Good Old Days (with A. E. Phillpotts) 1932; A Cup of Happiness, 1933. *Poetry*—Wild Fruit, 1910; The Iscariot, 1912; Plain Song, 1917; As the Wind Blows, 1920; Pixies' Plot, 1922; Cherry-Stones, 1923; A Harvesting, 1924; Brother Man, 1926; Poems, 1926; Goodwill, 1928; Brother Beast, 1928; A Hundred Sonnets, 1929; A Hundred Lyrics, 1930; Becoming, 1932; Story of a Sailor Man, 1933; Sonnets From Nature, 1935; A Dartmoor Village, 1937. *Miscellaneous*—My Devon Year, 1904; My Garden, 1906; My Shrubs, 1915; A West Country Sketch-Book, 1928; Essays in Little, 1931.

ABOUT: Haycraft, H. Murder for Pleasure: The Life and Times of the Detective Story; Meadowcroft, C. W. The Place of Eden Phillpotts in English Peasant Drama; Phillpotts, E. Widecomb Edition Dartmoor Novels (see Introduction by Arnold Bennett); Bookman (London) September 1927, September 1928.

PICKTHALL, MARJORIE LOWRY CHRISTIE (September 14, 1883-April 19, 1922), Canadian poet and novelist, was born

in Oxford Road, Gunnersbury, near Chiswick, Middlesex, England, of northern English and Lowland Scottish stock. Her parents were Arthur C. Pickthall, half-brother of Marmaduke Pickthall,[qv] and Lizzie Helen Mary (Mallard) Pickthall. The family later moved to Shelley's country, Horsham, Sussex, and in 1899 to Canada, where Marjorie Pickthall spent twenty-two of her thirty-eight years of life. After selling stories and poems to Canadian papers, she began to contribute regularly to the *Atlantic Monthly, Century, Scribner's, McClure's,* and *Harper's.* When her mother died in 1910 Marjorie Pickthall worked in the library of Victoria College, Toronto, helping compile the annual bibliography of Canadian poetry, and edited a page in the *Canadian Courier. Drift of Pinions,* a slim book of poems with a title taken from Francis Thompson, sold out the first edition in ten days. Her poems had pagan and Greek qualities, but used sacramental symbols freely and exhibited rhythmic power, a kinship with nature, and artistic sensibility. *The Wood Carver's Wife* (1922) was performed in Montreal and at Hart House, Toronto. Going to England at Christmas, 1912, for her health, Miss Pickthall took a cottage at Bowerchalke near Salisbury, worked on the land during the First World War, and was assistant librarian of the South Kensington Meteorological Offices, a position which tried her eyes severely. In May 1920 she returned to Canada, dying two years later at the Vancouver (B.C.) General Hospital of an embolism twelve days after an operation. She was buried in St. James Cemetery, Toronto. The poet was an attractive woman, with hazel eyes and blonde hair.

PRINCIPAL WORKS: *Poems*—Drift of Pinions, 1912; Lamp of Poor Souls, 1916; The Wood Carver's Wife and Other Poems, 1922. *Fiction*—Little Hearts, 1915; The Bridge, 1921; Angel Shoes, 1923.

ABOUT: Becker, M. L. (ed.) Golden Tales of Canada; Pierce, L. Marjorie Pickthall; Canadian Bookman May 1922; University of Toronto Quarterly April 1932.

PICKTHALL, MARMADUKE (April 7, 1875-May 19, 1936), English Orientalist and novelist, was the son of the Rev. Chas

Pickthall, Rector of Chillesford, Suffolk, and Mary (O'Brien) Pickthall, daughter of a rear-admiral. A half-brother, Arthur, was the father of Marjorie Pickthall, Canadian poet.[qv]

Marmaduke Pickthall was educated at Harrow and on the Continent. He spent three years in the Near East "on equal terms with all sorts of Orientals, incidentally acquiring Arabic and a love for certain Eastern ways of thought," according to his own statement, and lived for a year among the Druzes of Mount Lebanon. From 1920 to 1924 he edited the *Bombay Chronicle.* In 1913 his Eastern sympathies led him to take the Turkish point of view in the country's involvements with Armenia and the Balkans, and he wrote a series of articles for the *New Age.* Collected in *With the Turk in War-Time* (1914), the articles were prefaced by the author with this statement: "The solidarity of Christendom against a Muslim power was reckoned a fine thing by many people; but it broke the heart of Englishmen who loved the East." For some years Pickthall was in the educational service of H.E.H. the Nizam of Hyderabad, where he edited the *Hyderbad Quarterly Review* and *Islamic Culture.* Pickthall died at St. Ives, Cornwall, at sixty-one. His wife was a Miss Muriel Smith.

Pickthall began to write fiction "at an early age," and his first novel remains his best known. *Said the Fisherman* (1903), published in the United States about twenty years later, has Eastern color, movement, and sharp authenticity. The period is 1871-82, culminating with the British bombardment of Alexandria, when Egyptian forces evacuated the town and let in a mob of plunderers. Said meets his death in this riot. *Oriental Encounters,* a book of sketches and impressions, is another important piece of Orientalia.

PRINCIPAL WORKS: Said the Fisherman, 1903; Enid, 1904; Brendle, 1905; The House of Islám, 1906; The Myopes, 1907; Folklore of the Holy Land (ed.) 1907; The Children of the Nile, 1908; The Valley of the Kings, 1909; Pot-au-Feu, 1911;

Larkmeadow, 1912; Veiled Women, 1913; With the Turk in War-Time, 1914; Tales From Five Chimneys, 1915; The House of War, 1916; Knights of Araby, 1917; Oriental Encounters, 1918; Sir Limpidus, 1919; The Early Hours, 1921; As Others See Us, 1922; The Meaning of the Glorious Koran, 1930.

ABOUT: Fremantle, A. Loyal Enemy: The Life of Marmaduke Pickthall; Publishers' Weekly May 30, 1936.

PIDGIN, CHARLES FELTON (November 11, 1844-June 3, 1923), American novelist, was born in Roxbury, Mass., the only

son of Benjamin Gorham Pidgin and Mary Elizabeth (Felton) Pidgin, who was of the seventh generation of the Felton family in Massachusetts. Young Pidgin received a hip injury in boyhood which paralyzed one of his legs and necessitated artificial support; in middle life he also suffered from a cataract which rendered him almost blind. *Quincy Adams Sawyer* (1900), his best-known and best-selling novel of rural Massachusetts contrasted with the more mundane city of Boston, was dictated to an amanuensis.

After graduation from the Boston English High School in 1863, Pidgin worked as a bookkeeper in Boston and also wrote for the newspapers. After two years as member of the firm of Young & Pidgin, manufacturers of linen collars and cuffs, Pidgin became chief clerk of the Massachusetts Bureau of Statistics of Labor, receiving a promotion to Chief of the Bureau in 1903, four years before his retirement on pension. During his incumbency he had invented and perfected various machines for the tabulation of statistics. He died at Melrose in his seventy-ninth year, survived by an adopted daughter and his third wife, Frances Fern (Douglas) Pidgin, whom he had married in 1897, a year after the death of Lucy Sturtevant (Gardner) Pidgin. The first Mrs. Pidgin, Lizzie Abbot Dane, whom he married in 1867, died a year later.

Quincy Adams Sawyer, inspired by James Russell Lowell's poem "The Courtin'," is a treasure-house of New England idiosyncrasies and peculiarities, manners, and customs. It was successfully dramatized, and had two inferior sequels. Pidgin championed Aaron Burr in his readable historical novel, *Blennerhassett* (1901), in *Little Burr* (1905), and in a rather scrappy biography of Burr's

ill-fated daughter, Theodosia, wife of Governor Joseph Allston.

PRINCIPAL WORKS: Practical Statistics, 1888; Quincy Adams Sawyer: or, Mason's Corners Folks, 1900; Blennerhassett: or, The Decrees of Fate, 1901; Stephen Holton, 1902; The Climax, 1902; The Letter H: A Novel, 1904; Little Burr: The Warwick of America, 1905; The Corsican Lovers, 1906; The Hidden Man, 1906; The Toymakers, 1907; Theodosia: The First Gentlewoman of Her Time, 1907; The Further Adventures of Quincy Adams Sawyer, 1909; Chronicles of Quincy Adams Sawyer: Detective (with J. M. Taylor) 1912; The House of Shame, 1912; The Courtin' (comic opera) 1913.

ABOUT: Boston Transcript June 4, 1923; New York Times, June 5, 1923.

PILNYAK, BORIS (October 14, 1894-), was born Boris Andreyevich Vogau in Mozhaisk, in the Government of Moscow,

of German, Jewish, Slavonic, and Mongolian stock. His father's people had emigrated from Germany during the second half of the eighteenth century; his mother was the daughter of a Volga merchant. Both followed university courses: his

mother in the humanities, his father in veterinary science. The boy spent his childhood in the town of Kolomna, near Moscow. He completed his secondary education in Nizhni-Novgorod (1913) and attended the University of Kolomna. In 1920 he was graduated from the Moscow Commercial Institute (now the Plekhanov Institute), department of business administration.

He began to write when scarcely nine, and at the age of thirteen saw himself in print. Exempted from military service because of extreme near-sightedness, he earned his living by concocting *feuilletons* for provincial newspapers. As a young student he is described as filling countless reams of paper with writing, little of which was published. A long, never-published novel entitled *Pilnyak* gave its author his present name. In 1915 Pilnyak began to appear in the better periodicals, and in 1917 his stories were included in the *Spolokhi* anthology, and in the almanac *Tvorchestvo*. His short story collection, *Bylyo*, appeared in 1920, followed in 1922 by his novel *The Naked Year,* which created a sensation, perhaps because it was the earliest attempt at depicting the Russian Revolution. Soviet critics censured the novel declaring that it reflected only "the bewilderment of the *bourgeois* intellectuals who were shaken out of their old ruts and tried to explain the new by their own old ways of thinking and old conceptions." Ideologically, Pilnyak was indebted to Vassily Rozanov and Vladimir Soloviev; stylistically, to Andrey Bely, Ivan Bunin, and Alexey Remizov. In fact, one of his stories, "The Third Metropolis" (1922), was dedicated: "To A.M. Remizov, the Master in whose workshop I was an apprentice." *The Naked Year* nevertheless sold over half a million copies in the Soviet Union alone and was translated into several languages.

Until 1926 and under the continuous influence of Bely and Remizov, Pilnyak wrote in a complex style *Ivan and Marya* (1922), *English Tales* (1924), *Machines and Wolves* (1925), and *Mother Damp Earth* (1926). These works, with *The Naked Year,* "remain the most characteristic expression of the first romantic boisterous period of the Revolution, of its ornamental prose," according to Gleb Struve. Pilnyak's "main theme is the antithesis between reason and instinct, between the 'machines' and the 'wolves,' and— on the historical plane—between the old and the new, the European and the Asiatic elements in Russia. He is instinctively drawn towards pre-Petrine Russia, and his sympathy with the Revolution has a strong coloring of nationalism and anarchism. . . . Pilnyak's weak point is his lack of constructive skill—his novels are not novels at all, but loose lyrical and philosophical compositions. But he has a keen eye and, despite all his verbal excesses, a sense of words."

In 1927 Pilnyak published stories of simpler composition, such as *The Chinese Tale* and *Stories of the Orient,* inspired by a trip to China and Japan. His collected tales, *The Unextinguished Moon* (1927) and *Mahogany,* which was published first in German translation in Germany and later incorporated into *The Volga Falls to the Caspian Sea* (1931), provoked loud protests from Soviet critics, who accused Pilnyak of *bourgeois* leanings. *The Volga Falls to the Caspian Sea* tells of the building of a gigantic dam at Kolomna, not far from Moscow, designed to turn back the stream of the Volga and to make the Moscow River navigable for big steamers. Although the outward subject of the novel is the Five-Year Plan, Pilnyak conceives industrial construction after his usual fantastic and hyperbolical fashion.

After a long silence Pilnyak published *O.K.* (1933), a chronicle of American impressions, in which he attacked the United States primarily because of its industrial and mechanical organization, showing that he had not outgrown his early fear of the machine. In the novelette, *The Birth of Man* (1935), the heroine, a "classical Communist, discovers the joys of childhood and motherhood, finding in them an infinitely richer world than Communist lectures and meetings," as Nazaroff puts it. Despite his political shortcomings, Pilnyak has occupied responsible positions in the Soviet Union: chairman of the Krug publications (1922-23) and President of the All Russian Writers Union (1929). At one time, with his huge royalties, he was said to earn "at least twenty times as much as Stalin," and his hours were shorter. Pilnyak has traveled widely in the Soviet Union and abroad: Esthonia and Germany (1922); England (1923); Spitzbergen and the Arctic (1924); Turkey, Greece, and Palestine (1925); Japan, China, and Mongolia (1926); United States (1931); Japan, (1932), etc.

WORKS AVAILABLE IN ENGLISH TRANSLATION: Tales of the Wilderness, 1924; The Naked Year, 1928; The Volga Falls to the Caspian Sea (British title: The Volga Flows to the Caspian Sea) 1931; Ivan Moscow, 1935.

ABOUT: London, K. Seven Soviet Arts; Mirsky, D. S. Contemporary Russian Literature; Nikitina, E. F. Russkaya Literatura ot Simbolizma do Nashikh Dnei; Pozner, V. Panorama de la Littérature Russe Contemporaine; Struve, G. Soviet Russian Literature; Vitman, A. M. & others. Vosem let Russkoi Khudozhestvennoi Literatury; Boston Evening Transcript June 27, August 26, 1931; Bookman November 1931; Books July 26, 1931; International Literature January 1933; Krasnaya Nov April 1922; Lef March 1925; Nation September 2, 1931; New Republic August 19, 1931; New York Times July 26, 1931; Novy Mir November 1925; Pravda January 1, 1925; Saturday Review of Literature July 26, 1931; Yale Review Autumn 1931.

PINERO. Sir ARTHUR WING. See "BRITISH AUTHORS OF THE 19TH CENTURY."

PINSKI, DAVID (April 5, 1872-   ), Jewish-American dramatist and journalist, was born in Magilov, Russia, the son of Isaac Mordecai Pinski and Sarah (Mardfin) Pinski, but grew up and studied in Moscow. In Warsaw, early in the 1890's, he began to publish articles in the Yiddish vernacular, with W. J. L. Perez, in a literary magazine called *Holiday Leaves.*
To avoid suppression by the government authorities, the periodical was issued as

pamphlets, which could legally be published on Jewish holidays. Since every calendar month contained a holiday, its periodicity was fairly regular. Regarded askance by the authorities as a nationalist movement, and by conservative Jewish elements as heretical, the magazine had a fair measure of success. Pinski, beginning to write at seventeen, perforce wrote in Russian; there was no written Yiddish model to follow. Like "Shalom Aleichem," with whose work Pinski was not then familiar, he studied the unwritten grammar of Yiddish, established its rules, and created words, avoiding German influences so far as possible. Pinski's play, *Isaac Sheftel*, written for the Jewish Student Society, met with the approval of Gerhart Hauptmann. From 1897 to 1899 he studied medicine at the University of Berlin; in the latter year he came to the United States with his wife, who was Adele Kaufman of Bessarabia. The Pinskis have a son and daughter. In New York he has served as editor of the weeklies *Der Arbeiter, Der Kaempfer, Die Wochenschrift*, the *Daily Socialist-Zionist*, and *Die Zeit*. In 1920 the Theatre Guild, then starting out at the Garrick Theatre, produced his comedy, *The Treasure*, with Helen Westley and Dudley Digges. Acclaimed as "the one man among contemporary Jewish writers who has best chance of rising into the field of world literature," Pinski's sixtieth birthday in 1932 was made the occasion of an anniversary tribute and celebration at Mecca Temple in New York City. In 1936 he toured Russia, Palestine, and the continent. A Socialist-Zionist in politics, Pinski is the president of the Jewish National Workers' Alliance, the Jewish Theatre Society of New York, and the Jewish P.E.N. Club. Pinski writes in Yiddish only, but is not limited to Jewish subjects—*Alexander and Diogenes* is Greek in its rhythm and ideal of conception.

WORKS AVAILABLE IN ENGLISH TRANSLATION: The Treasure, 1916; Three Plays, 1918; Temptations (short stories) 1919; Ten Plays, 1919; King David and His Wives (drama) 1923; The Final Balance, 1928; Arnold Levenberg (novel) 1928; The Generations of Noah Edon (novel) 1931.

ABOUT: B'nai Brith Magazine March 1927; Moscow Daily News September 10, 1936; Wilson Library Bulletin February 1932.

PIRANDELLO, LUIGI (June 28, 1867-December 10, 1936), Italian dramatist, novelist, and short story writer, was born during the cholera epidemic of 1867 in the historical and picturesque town of Girgenti on the island of Sicily. Life in Girgenti, even during the latter half of the nineteenth century, still bore the particulari-

ties of mediaeval economy, its lethargy, its folklore; the atmosphere reeked with a primitivism punctuated by outbursts of jealousy, revenge, crime—men had little use for courts or diplomatic talks, they settled their differences with their knives. Luigi's father, Don Stefano, a rich sulphur mine owner, answered the constant threatening demands of the secret Mafia with the only valid means: his powerful fists. A violent, overbearing man, tall and handsome, he contrasted markedly with his wife Caterina, a timid soul absorbed only in her household duties. Luigi took after her: he was candid, sensitive, and especially generous. He hated sham, hypocrisy and, in literature (at sixteen he was already writing poetry) any form of rhetorical artifice. From the earliest he was destined to become d'Annunzio's foe: consistently he attacked all the pomposity of d'Annunzio-ism and  kindred isms that were converting Italian literature into a hollow, rococo game of words.

Pirandello attended elementary school at Girgenti and took courses at the technical school, but later was sent away to the secondary schools of Como and Palermo, and finally to the University of Rome. The first clear signs of his temper are revealed in his University experiences. He quarreled constantly, hated his professors and rebelled against their obsolete pedagogical methods. Fortunately the University contained at this time at least one great man: Emilio Monacci. Prof. Monacci taught the dryest of subjects, philology, yet he succeeded in arousing Pirandello's interest and making him aware of Sicily's wealth of folklore and historical background. At his recommendation Pirandello entered the German University of Bonn in 1888 where he pursued his philological studies, obtaining his doctor's degree in 1891 with a dissertation on the dialect of his native Girgenti, *Laute und Lautentwicklung der Mundart von Girgenti*. During 1892, when Pirandello remained at Bonn as reader in Italian, he published several collections of verse (*Mal Giocondo, Pasqua di Gea,* etc.) and translated Goethe's *Roman Elegies,* a particularly difficult task which he performed brilliantly.

In the summer of 1893 Pirandello found a haven at the top of Monte Calvo, near Rome, in an old abandoned convent. This marked the beginning of his literary Bohemia. He frequented the cafés "Fanfalla" and "Captain Fracasa"; he won the friendship of the critic Ugo Ojetti and the novelist Luigi Capuana, who induced the young writer to give up poetry for prose. Pirandello's first attempts at prose were the stories collected under the already Pirandellist title *Amori Senza Amori* (Love Without Love) published in 1893, and two novels: *The Outcast,* one of his best, and *Il Turno,* both published several years later. This first stage in the career of the developing prose writer evidenced his interest in regionalism, in recreating the manners and customs of his native Sicily. His determining influences were two writers of Sicilian life: his friend and adviser Capuana, and the world famous novelist Giovanni Verga, to whom young Pirandello had submitted his earliest stories and from whom he had received warm encouragement.

Local colorism endured throughout Pirandello's literary career; however the emphasis shifted to introspective analysis and morbid psychomachy, attributable largely to the course of his own life experiences. For fourteen years Pirandello had to endure the company of an insane wife. In January 1894 his father had married him to the daughter of his business partner Portulano, a girl he had never seen. Luigi Pirandello and Antonietta Portulano settled in Rome and lived on her fat dowry and the generous allowance given them by the elder Pirandello. For ten years their marital life went along smoothly, concerned only with the birth of their children: Stefano in 1895, Lietta in 1897, and Fausto in 1899. The writer went on publishing his poetry and contributing short stories to periodicals. But marital bliss came to a sudden end in 1904, when floods ruined their parents' mines and, their fortunes gone, they were thrown back on their own resources. Pirandello procured a position as teacher of Italian literature at a women's teachers college in Rome; but consequent worry and anxiety affected Antonietta's mind and gradually drove her into hysteria and fits of jealousy—maniacally she would accuse her husband of treachery, unfaithfulness, etc. The drama of Luigi Pirandello began: ugly scenes, unjustifiable tears, stupid recriminations. His friends advised him to put her in an insane asylum, but he preferred to bear the cross heroically, a cross which became heavier as the years went by. During the war his sons left for the trenches; and his daughter Lietta, unable to stand her mother's persecutions (she accused her of endeavoring to usurp her household duties) tried to commit suicide. Not till 1918 did the tragic situation end with Antonietta's death.

By 1918 the apathy of the Italian reading public towards Pirandello's works, and the reaction of publishers, had been broken up by the praises coming from abroad. Pirandello had definitely brought to a close his poetical career and written his greatest novels (*The Outcast, The Late Mattia Pascal, The Old and the Young,* and *Shoot*), hundreds of his finest short stories (collected in the volumes *Beffe della Morte e della Vita, Quand'era Matto, Bianche e Nere,* etc.), and finally he had begun his brilliant career as a playwright, his original play *Right You Are If You Think You Are* having attained a great European success since its première in 1916.

All these works clearly showed Pirandello's concern with death, old age, insanity, jealousy, themes he had drawn from his own tormented life. There were flashes too of the grotesque and of a particular type of humor charged with tragic implications. He perfected all these qualities and advanced new theories as he wrote play after play. He completed *Think It Over, Giacomino* in three days and *Right You Are* in six, and there was one year that saw six new Pirandello plays on the boards. Besides his grotesquerie, arid humor, and morbidity, there appeared in his work another ingredient quite consonant with the post-war spirit: the conflict between *being* and *seeming,* between reality and illusion. Pirandello endeavored to reveal the multiplicity of personality, the nature of the real self behind the mask of hypocrisy and social lies. In 1921 Pirandello reached the apex of his career with his two greatest plays: *Henry IV* and *Six Characters in Search of an Author.*

In 1925 the now world-famous dramatist set out to found a national theatre. Recognition had arrived all at once: the French government made him a member of the Legion of Honor, the Italian government, somewhat belatedly, gave him the Commander of the Crown, while Mussolini made him High Commander of Saint Maurice. Pirandello took over the Odescalchi Theatre in Rome, remodeled it and enlisted his actors—the distinguished Ruggero Ruggeri, and Marta Abba, who always played the principal rôles in his plays and was his dearest friend. Mussolini attended the opening, but despite the pomp and circumstance the experiment was a phenomenal fiasco: it cost Pirandello some 600,000 lire.

In May 1933 Mussolini delivered a speech before the Writers & Publishers Association, drawing attention to the dire crisis in the Italian theatre (between 1926 and 1932 box office receipts had dropped 65 per cent) and at the same time describing the kind of plays he wanted. He complained of the limited creative scope of Italian playwrights, condemning their "introspective, moody and unrealistic offerings" (meaning Pirandello and the whole "teatro grottesco") as well as their sentimental plays with moth-eaten triangles (meaning d'Annunzio and such minor but popular figures as Giacosa and Sem Benelli). Nonetheless in 1934 Pirandello received the Nobel Prize for literature, with the consent of Mussolini, who had objected to the prize being awarded to the idealist philosopher Benedetto Croce.

Long before his death Pirandello prepared for it: he divided his royalties among his three children and traveled about like a lost soul from country to country, bereft of permanent address, attachments, property. For him to whom life was a mirage, death, the only reality he accepted, came at the end of 1936 as he was nearing his seventieth birthday. In his last instructions for his funeral there is that laconic simplicity, that hatred for pomposity and decoration which characterized his whole life: "The hearse, the horse, the driver, and—basta!"

PRINCIPAL WORKS AVAILABLE IN ENGLISH TRANSLATION: *Plays*—Sicilian Limes, 1922; Three Plays (Six Characters in Search of an Author, Henry IV, Right You Are If You Think You Are) 1923; Each in His Own Way and Two Other Plays (The Pleasure of Honesty, Naked) 1925; One-Act Plays (The Imbecile, By Judgment of Court, Our Lord of the Ship, The Doctor's Duty, Chee-Chee, The Man With the Flower in His Mouth, At the Gate, The Vise, The House With the Column, The Jar) 1928; As You Desire Me, 1931; Tonight We Improvise, 1932. *Fiction*—The Late Mattia Pascal, 1923; The Outcast, 1925; Shoot, 1926; The Old and the Young, 1928; Horse in the Moon, 1931; One, No One, and Hundred Thousand, 1933; Better Think Twice About It, 1934; Naked Truth, 1934; Medals and Other Stories (English title: Character in Distress) 1939.

ABOUT: Bontempelli, M. Pirandello, Leopardi, D'Annunzio; Cellini, B. Il Teatro di Pirandello; Daniel-Rops, H. Carte d'Europe; Gomez de Baquero, E. Pirandello y Compañia; Nardelli, F. V. L'Uomo Segreto; Pasini, F. Luigi Pirandello; Starkie, W. Pirandello (1867-1936); Vittorini, D. The Drama of Luigi Pirandello; Cornhill Magazine September 1923; Forum October 1921; Living Age July 21, 1923, May 22, 1926, June 1, 1927; London Mercury August 1925; New Republic November 2, 1934; New Statesman March 26, 1927; Nineteenth Century June 1925; Nuova Antologia June 16, 1933, January 1, 1934; Revue de Paris December 1934; Saturday Review of Literature November 24, 1934; Sewanee Review April 1927; South Atlantic Quarterly January 1935; Theatre Arts Monthly December 1928, February 1935; Virginia Quarterly April 1925.

*PITKIN, WALTER BOUGHTON (February 6, 1878-), American psychologist, journalist, and editor, was born in Ypsilanti, Mich., and was educated at the University of Michigan (B.A. 1900). He also spent five years at the Hartford Theological Seminary, and did graduate work at the Sorbonne and the Universities of Berlin and Munich. He was a lecturer in  psychology at Columbia from 1905 to 1909, and since 1912 has been professor of journalism there. He was on the editorial staff of the New York *Tribune* in 1907 and 1908, and of the *Evening Post* in 1909 and 1910. Since 1927 he has been an associate editor of *Parents' Magazine*. He was American managing editor of the *Encyclopædia Britannica* in 1927 and 1928, and editorial director of the *Farm Journal* from 1935 to 1938. He has been story supervisor for a motion picture company. In 1932 he founded the Institute of Life Planning, and besides teaching and writing he acts as a consulting psychologist and advisor on teaching methods. In 1939 he founded an organization called The American Majority, described as a "League of the Middle Class," thus becoming, in his own phrase, "a rabble-rouser of the right [wing]," but the society never developed far beyond its first meeting. In youth he had a varied working career, having made his way at various times as peddler, cook, cattle boss, high jumper, and junkman—all of which left him with a strong anti-labor and anti-union bias. He has an inventive mind, and in 1940 designed a $100,000 yacht which unfortunately sank in the Hudson River.

In 1905 Mr. Pitkin married Mary B. Gray; they have five sons. Their home is in Dover, N.J.

A "super-salesman of literary handiwork," Mr. Pitkin has written an enormous number of volumes, mostly on popular psychology, which have made his name familiar all over the English-speaking world; the one which did most to spread his fame was *Life Begins at Forty*. Past sixty, he still has the ebullience, energy, and self-confidence which make him an obvious beneficiary of his own advice to the middle-aged.

PRINCIPAL WORKS: The Art and Business of the Short Story, 1913; The New Realism, 1913; Must We Fight Japan? 1920; How to Write Stories, 1922; As We Are, 1923; Seeing America—Farm and Field (with H. Hughes) 1924; Seeing America —Mill and Factory (with H. Hughes) 1926; The Twilight of the American Mind, 1928; The Art of Rapid Reading, 1929; The Psychology of Happiness, 1929; The Young Citizen, 1929; The Art of Sound Pictures (with W. M. Marston) 1930; The Psychology of Achievement, 1930; Vocational Studies in Journalism, 1931; The Art of Learning, 1931; How We Learn, 1931; Short Introduction to History of Human Stupidity, 1932; Life Begins at Forty, 1932; The Consumer: His Nature and His Changing Habits, 1932; More Power to You, 1933; Take It Easy! 1935; Let's Get What We Want, 1935; Capitalism Carries On, 1935; Careers After Forty, 1937; Making Good Before Forty, 1939; Seeing Our Country (with H. Hughes) 1939; The Art of Writing, 1940.

ABOUT: Boston Evening Transcript March 3, 1934; New Republic October 4, 1939; Reader's Digest December 1940.

PITTER, RUTH (November 7, 1897-), English poet, writes: "I was born at Ilford, Essex, then a new London suburb on the fringe of the country-side. My parents were assistant teachers in the East End, of superior artisan class, intelligent, idealistic, country-lovers, poetic, altruistic. I was the eldest of three, two girls and a boy. Teachers were poorly paid then, and though well-fed, the signature tune was "we can't afford it," and the necessity for earning was well inculcated. Economic anxiety has tormented me always, though being frugal, industrious, and provident, I have never been in want. (I hate 'bohemians' who are economic pests.)

"I was educated first at the local elementary school, then at an old City foundation, Coborn School, Bow, London. Here I learned to cook, a great boon, and got a certain amount of natural science and mathematics, and a faint but indelible smear of Latin; matriculated, and as war came when I was nearly through my Intermediate Arts year, and I had no predilections as regards a career (I did not like the look of the world at all), I went to the War Office at twenty-five shillings a week, and stood it for nearly two years at this wage. I was then badly run down, and wishing now to be some sort of artist, however humble, found a job with an arts and crafts

firm on the East Coast, regaining health and learning woodwork and painting. The war over, the firm came to London, where I continued with them till 1930, when a fellow-worker (Kathleen M. O'Hara) and I were offered the ghost of a similar business in Chelsea. After a bad time we made it go. We do high-grade handpainted goods such as tea-trays, etc., and work up to sixty hours a week ourselves, while trying to give employees optimum conditions.

"I have written verse since the age of five; never felt much inclined for prose. You can make poetry out of yourself, prose takes experience and drudgery. I was much helped by the late A. R. Orage, and by Hilaire Belloc, both of whom noticed my work very early. A cottage romantically situated in the Essex forest was the greatest single factor in early influences. I am very grateful to my mother for squeezing out the rent, three and six pence a week, and for the drudgery both parents put in to make and keep it habitable as a holiday home.

"From the very first I realized there was no money in poetry, and determined not to write for money. By commercial slavery and continual anxiety I have avoided patronage and the meal-ticket marriage, and am (as a writer) independent of politics, publishers, and jobbery. When I hear the observations of professional writers on these matters I thank Heaven for my dour foresight. My ultimate ambition is a cottage in some peaceful place, and enough strength left for gardening, my great love. I should not mind poverty in the country.

"My readers often think, because my verses are aspiring, that I am spiritually regenerate. No, I am as troubled a child of Adam as any, but anxious to improve both as creature and poetess—criticism always welcome, more so than praise."

* * *

Miss Pitter won the Hawthornden Prize for the best imaginative work of the year in England in 1937, with her *Trophy in Arms*. She is a slight woman with her dark hair worn in a heavy bang. She seems constantly nostalgic for the country life which was her delight in childhood. "My poems," she says, "occur in the form of a mood, out of which phrases gradually crystallize and a rhythm emerges." Her first poems were published in Orage's *New Age* when she was only thirteen. Eda Lou Walton, who called Miss Pitter's "a seventeenth century mind," said that her work, though archaic and "full of literary echoes," has "occasional beauty of music and an intensity of mystic conviction." Hilaire Belloc has credited her

with a "perfect ear and an exact epithet."
In admiration of her *finesse* John Masefield
remarked that "her judgments are merciful
and her methods merry."

PRINCIPAL WORKS: First Poems, 1920; First
and Second Poems, 1927; Persephone in Hades,
1931; A Mad Lady's Garland, 1934; A Trophy of
Arms, 1936; Selected Early Poems, 1938; Spirit
Watches, 1940.

ABOUT: Commonweal September 11, 1929;
Harper's Magazine October 1940; Nation October
8, 1930; Poetry October 1937, September 1940;
Saturday Review of Literature July 20, 1940; Spec-
tator April 5, 1930; Wilson Library Bulletin
September 1938.

P L O M E R, WILLIAM CHARLES FRANKLYN (December 10, 1903-),

English novelist, writes: "William Plomer

was born in the
Northern Transvaal,
Africa, of English
parents. His father
was a magistrate who
specialized in native
affairs. William Plo-
mer was educated at
Rugby; his holidays
were spent in military
hospitals and can-
teens. Due to war-
time privations, his health suffered, and he
went back to Africa, where he joined a Settlers' Association and became a farmer in the
desolate Stormberg Mountains. He lived
also in Johannesburg, and as a trader in
Zululand, where he was in close touch with
the natives. Later he was associated with
the poet Roy Campbell in the production
of a literary review.

"Subsequently he spent two years in
Japan, and traveled all over that country,
living always in the closest touch with the
Japanese themselves. He returned to England by way of Manchuria and Siberia,
spending a short time in both Russia and
Poland. At the age of twenty-five, he was
offered the chair of English literature at
the Imperial University in Tokyo (formerly
held by Lafcadio Hearn, later by Robert
Nichols), but declined it, and went to live
in Greece instead, after visits to France,
Germany, and Italy.

"Besides his novels and short stories, and
a life of Cecil Rhodes, he has written three
small books of verse, but has no intention
of writing any more. He has contributed
to numerous periodicals and to various
anthologies. He lives in London, where he
is now engaged in war work. Before the
war he divided his time between London
and the South of France. He is unmarried."

* * *

Among Mr. Plomer's ancestors was a
colonial governor of New Hampshire. He
says that though he "was born and will die
a highbrow," he "enjoys the company of
savages, outcasts, and nobodies better than
that of the rich and respectable." He dislikes games and insists that he hires a
servant to play bridge and golf for him.
He enjoys swimming, however. He is a
liberal in politics, with leftist leanings. He
is enthusiastic about Herman Melville among
American authors, but in literary preferences, as elsewhere "belongs to no club,
group, or other herd."

Hugh Walpole said his is "unqualified
genius"; Oliver Warner called him "subtle
and sure, . . . an athletic writer," with "an
ability to observe with understanding countries and peoples to which he is not native."
The backgrounds of his novels and stories
have been successively Africa, Japan, and
England. Although he says he has given
up writing verse, his poems appear regularly
in the English literary periodicals and in 1940
a volume of *Selected Poems* was published.
His earlier books of verse, all out of print,
are *Notes for Poems, The Family Tree,* and
The Five-Fold Screen.

PRINCIPAL WORKS: *Fiction*—Turbott Wolfe,
1926; I Speak of Africa (short stories) 1928;
Paper Houses (short stories) 1929; Sado (in
America: They Never Come Back) 1931; The
Case Is Altered, 1932; The Child of Queen Victoria (short stories) 1933; The Invaders, 1934;
Ali the Lion, 1936; Visiting the Caves (short
stories) 1936. *Biography*—Cecil Rhodes, 1933. *Edited*—Diary of Robert Francis Kilvert (3 vols.)
1938-40.

ABOUT: Bookman (London) September 1932;
Wilson Library Bulletin September 1932.

PLUNKETT, EDWARD JOHN MOR-
TON DRAX. See DUNSANY

PLUNKETT, JOSEPH MARY (Novem-
ber 1887-May 3, 1916), Irish poet and
patriot, was born in Dublin, the son of

Count and Countess
Plunkett. Theirs
was the Catholic
branch of a family
long known in Irish
history which in-
cluded the venerable
Oliver Plunkett, the
last priest to be mar-
tyred in England. The
boy, whose health was
always frail, spent his

G. Plunkett

school years in Belvedere College; attended
Catholic University School, and undertook

a two-year course in philosophy at Stony-hurst, which had a marked influence on his later life and poetry. He was at one time a pupil of the poet Thomas MacDonagh, and traveled in Italy, Sicily and Malta. Plunkett devoted much time to the study of St. John of the Cross, St. Teresa, and St. Francis of Assisi. *The Circle and the Sword* (1911), the only book of poems to be published in his lifetime, gives evidence of his sympathy with the work of Francis Thompson. These "eagle flights in Catholic mysticism" keep well within the pale of traditionalism, as Michael K. Dunne has said, and show freshness of mind and directness of diction along with an occasional tameness of expression. He was fond of using militant and mystic symbols. In June 1913 Plunkett became editor of the *Irish Review*, and next year was interested in the Irish Theatre, organized to produce Irish plays other than the peasant plays which were preferred by the Abbey Theatre. For two and a half years he kept house at Donny-brook with his sister. Plunkett joined the Irish Volunteers on their formation, and had a command and a place on the Executive. He was in New York in September of 1915. Next spring he took part in the Easter uprising, and was shot by a British firing squad at Dublin Castle. His body went into a common ditch, filled with quicklime, with his fellow-poets Padraic Pearse and Thomas MacDonagh.[qqv] His portrait in the *Poems* of 1916, sketched from memory, shows a man of frail and scholarly physique. Plunkett's carefully wrought work is the smallest in bulk of the three martyr-poets, comprising only about fifty sonnets and lyrical pieces. He was preparing *Occulta* when he died, at less than twenty-nine years of age.

PRINCIPAL WORKS: The Circle and the Sword, 1911; Poems, 1916.

ABOUT: Colum P. and O'Brien E. J. Poems of the Irish Revolutionary Brotherhood; Plunkett, J. M. Poems (see Foreword by G. Plunkett); Irish Monthly September 1918; April 1934.

PODMORE, FRANK (February 5, 1855-August 14, 1910), English writer on psychical research, was born at Elstree, Hertfordshire, the third son of the Rev. Thompson Podmore, once headmaster of Eastbourne College, and Georgina Elizabeth (Barton) Podmore. Educated at the Hill School (1863-1868), Podmore won a scholarship at Haileybury, and in 1874 a classical scholarship to Pembroke College, Oxford, where he took a second class in classical moderations and a first class in natural science. In 1879 he entered the higher division clerkship in the secretary's department of the Post Office, retiring without pension in 1907. Podmore had studied psychic phenomena at Oxford and had  absolute confidence in the slate-writing performances of the medium Slade. But by 1880 he had become skeptical of spiritualistic doctrine, arguing for psychological, not spiritualist, causality and a far-reaching application of the hypothesis of telepathy. Podmore's hostility met with criticism from F. C. S. Schiller and Andrew Lang.

He compiled a census of hallucinations with Edmund Gurney and F. W. H. Myers. *Modern Spiritualism* studies the subject from the seventeenth to the twentieth century. More mundane affairs also claimed Podmore's attention; he was a founder of the Fabian Society, probably giving this Socialist organization its name; wrote an early and rare report on government and unemployment, and applied his interest in "social reconstruction" to a biography of Robert Owen, socialist and spiritualist. Found drowned in New Pool, Malvern, Podmore was buried in Wells Cemetery. His wife, Eleanore Bramwell, whom he married in 1891, survived; they had lived apart for years and there were no children.

PRINCIPAL WORKS: Studies in Psychical Research, 1897; Modern Spiritualism, 1902; Life of Robert Owen, 1906; Telepathic Hallucinations, 1910; The Newer Spiritualism (posthumous) 1910.

ABOUT: Henderson, A. George Bernard Shaw; Rhys, E. Everyman Remembers; Proceedings of the Society for Psychical Research: Vol. 62; London Times August 20, 1910; Pall Mall Magazine 1903.

*POLLARD, ALBERT FREDERICK (December 16, 1869-), English scholar and historian, was born in Ryde, and is the eldest surviving son of Henry Hindes Pollard, J.P., of Ryde. He attended Portsmouth Grammar School and Felsted School before going up to Jesus College, Oxford University, where he took first class honors in Modern History in 1891,  the Lothian prize in 1892, and the Arnold prize in 1898. In January 1893 Pollard

* Died August 3, 1948.

became assistant editor of the *Dictionary of National Biography,* contributing five hundred articles, equivalent to one whole volume of the Dictionary. He continued on the board until the completion of the First Supplement in September 1901. In 1903 Pollard became professor of constitutional history at the University of London, retiring in 1931. He had been chairman of the Board of Studies in History in the university from 1910 to 1923, and a member of the Senate from 1910 to 1915. In 1924 Pollard was Sir George Watson lecturer in American history there, and came to America that year to spend the academic year 1924-25 as professor pro tem. at Columbia University.

A Short History of the Great War (1920) was one of the first and clearest of the one-volume histories of the conflict. Pollard contributed five chapters to the second volume of the *Cambridge Modern History,* published in 1904, and was the author of one chapter in the tenth volume (1907). He also wrote a volume of the *Political History of England,* and as a young man was editor of *Political Pamphlets* (1897) and *Tudor Tracts* (1903). He was Fellow of All Souls College, Oxford, from 1908 to 1936, and is an Honorary Fellow of his own college, Jesus. In 1927-28 Pollard was Ford's lecturer in the University of Oxford, and in 1936 went up to Glasgow to deliver the David Murray lectures.

He married Catherine Susanna Lucy in 1894; they have a son and daughter. Their home is at Brierfield, Milford-on-Sea, Hampshire. For three successive years, 1922, 1923, 1924, Pollard contested the Parliamentary representation of the University of London. He is the holder of three honorary degrees, from Oxford, Manchester, and the University of London, where most of his academic life was spent. Pollard founded the Historical Association in 1906, and edited *History* from 1916 to 1922, as well as the *Bulletin* of the Institute of Historical Research, from 1923 to 1939. He has been praised by competent critics for "vision, perspective, and style."

PRINCIPAL WORKS: The Jesuits in Poland, 1892; Henry VIII, 1902; A Life of Thomas Cranmer, 1904; Factors in Modern History, 1907; England Under Protector Somerset, 1909; A History of England, 1912; The Reign of Henry VII From Contemporary Sources, 1913-14; The Commonwealth at War, 1917; The Life of Nelson: An Historical Argument, 1918; A Short History of the Great War, 1920; The Evolution of Parliament, 1920; Factors in American History, 1925; Wolsey, 1929.

*POLLOCK, CHANNING (March 4, 1880-   ), American playwright, writes: "Channing Pollock was born at Washington, D.C., and soon afterward went to Omaha, Neb., where his father, Alexander L. Pollock, became one of the editors of the Omaha *World-Herald.* His mother, *née* Verona E. Larkin, was a Virginian. His father was a native of Austria. Young

H. Mitchell

Pollock obtained a catch-as-catch-can education in the public schools of Omaha, Salt Lake City, Washington, and in Prague. In 1894, his father became United States Consul at San Salvador, and died of yellow fever, leaving his family there in straitened circumstances. Channing obtained work on the Washington *Post,* of which he was assistant dramatic editor at sixteen. Winning a prize for a short story, he went to Bethel Military Academy, Warrenton, Va., leaving there after a few months because of orders to remove from his room a picture of Robert G. Ingersoll. He was a reporter on the New York *Dramatic Mirror,* and returned to Washington to become dramatic critic of the Washington *Times,* quitting this post in 1900 because of business office attempts to control his writing. He trucked on a dock briefly in New York, and then was successively press agent for Ziegfeld, and for William A. Brady and the Shuberts. At the same time he wrote dramatic criticisms for magazines. In 1906 he married Anna Marble, press agent and author. They have one daughter.

"Pollock's first play, *A Game of Hearts,* was produced in New York in 1900, and was closely followed by his dramatization of *The Pit* [by Frank Norris], in which Wilton Lackaye starred for several years. He has since written eleven plays alone and many in collaboration, and dramatized four novels. *In the Bishop's Carriage* and *The Enemy* were produced in London, *The Fool* in London, Berlin, and Vienna, and *The Sign on the Door* in practically every capital of Europe. He has also written numerous one-act plays, two books of essays, three novels, and many songs, including Fannie Brice's popular hit, 'My Man,' besides motion pictures, verses, and magazine articles and stories. He did a year's broadcasting, and has delivered more than 2,200 lectures throughout the country. Since 1930 he has spoken chiefly on current social, political, and international affairs. He has received an honorary Litt.D. degree from Colgate University, and in 1922 the Commonwealth of Massachusetts planted a tree in his honor in Poets' Row on Boston Common. His hobbies are work, swimming, and travel. He has been in almost every country except Russia, where he is not wanted, and reciprocates."

* * *

Channing Pollock describes himself as a "reactionary" in politics and economics. He has been a crusader for "clean plays," and is proud of the fact that he has always fought "sex, crime, and sophistication" in the drama. He considers the stage a platform for the presentation of ethical ideas, not merely a place of entertainment.

PRINCIPAL WORKS: *Plays (dates of production)* —A Game of Hearts, 1900; The Pit, 1900; Napoleon the Great, 1901; In the Bishop's Carriage, 1902; The Little Gray Lady, 1903; Clothes (with Avery Hopwood) 1906; The Secret Orchard, 1907; The Traitor, 1908; Such a Little Queen, 1909; The Inner Shrine, 1909; The Red Widow (with R. Wolf) 1911; My Best Girl (with R. Wolf) 1912; The Beauty Shop (with R. Wolf) 1913; Her Little Highness (with R. Wolf) 1913; A Perfect Lady (with R. Wolf) 1914; Ziegfeld Follies of 1915 (with R. Wolf) 1915; The Grass Widow (with R. Wolf) 1917; Roads of Destiny, 1918; The Sign on the Door, 1919; Ziegfeld Follies of 1921, 1921; The Fool, 1922; The Enemy, 1925; Mr. Moneypenny, 1928; The House Beautiful, 1931; Stranglehold, 1932. *Miscellaneous*—Behold the Man (novel) 1900; Stage Stories, 1901; The Footlights—Fore and Aft, 1909; Star Magic (novel) 1933; The Synthetic Gentleman (novel) 1934; The Adventures of a Happy Man, 1939; Guide Posts in Chaos, 1942.

ABOUT: Mantle, B. American Playwrights of Today; Pollock, C. The Adventures of a Happy Man; American Magazine April 1933; American Mercury October 1940; Ladies' Home Journal November 1931; Reader's Digest June 1940.

POLLOCK, Sir FREDERICK, 3rd Bart.

(December 10, 1845-January 18, 1937), English jurist and legal writer, was the

eldest son of Sir Frederick Pollock, second baronet; nephew of Field Marshal Sir George Pollock; and brother of Walter Herries Pollock[qv] the editor and journalist. He attended Eton and Trinity College, Cambridge, becoming a Fellow in 1868, and was called to the bar at Lincoln's Inn in 1871. For twenty years he was Corpus Professor of Jurisprudence at Oxford (1883-1903), succeeding Sir

Henry Maine, author of *Ancient Law.* Pollock was professor of common law in the Inns of Court, 1884-1890. He was a member of the Royal Labor Commission, 1891-1894; chairman of the Royal Commission on Public Records in 1910; Privy Councillor in 1911; judge of the admiralty court of the Cinque ports in 1914, and King's Counsel in 1920. His *Digest of the Law of Partnership,* first published in 1877, went through eleven editions and is now the English Partnership Act. Other legal works of Pollock's went through eight and nine editions. His *History of the English Law Before the Time of Edward I* (1895), written in collaboration with F. W. Maitland,[qv] has been called one of the great works of English historical scholarship. Lectures given at Columbia University in 1911 were published next year as *The Genius of the Common Law.* In lighter vein, he published *Leading Cases Done Into English,* verse parodies of typical law cases (A. P. Herbert's *Misleading Cases* is a later parallel in prose), and wrote a novel in epistolary form with Ella Fuller Maitland, *The Etchingham Letters* (1899). Pollock's *Spinoza: His Life and Philosophy* is well and favorably known; an enlarged edition was called for in 1912, more than thirty years after its publication. He also edited the *Reminiscences* of William Macready, the actor, and wrote an introduction and notes to his predecessor Maine's *Ancient Law* (1906). As he said of Maine, Pollock "was a humanist before he was a jurist, and he never ceased to be a humanist." He "revealed England to herself through her law and especially through the history of her law."

Pollock married Georgiana Harriett Deffell of Calcutta in 1873; she died in 1935. Their only son, John (1878-), now the fourth baronet, became a journalist and playwright.

PRINCIPAL WORKS: Principles of Contract, 1876; Digest of the Law of Partnership, 1877; Spinoza: His Life and Philosophy, 1880; Introduction to the History of the Science of Politics, 1880; The Land Laws, 1882; The Law of Torts, 1887; The Law of Fraud, 1894; History of the English Law . . . (with F. W. Maitland) 1895; A First Book of Jurisprudence 1896; The Expansion of the Common Law, 1904; The Genius of the Common Law, 1912; Essays in the Law, 1922; Outside the Law, 1927.

ABOUT: Holdsworth, W. S. The Historians of Anglo-American Law; Home, M. A. (ed.) The Holmes-Pollock Letters; Pollock, F. For My Grandson: Remembrances of an Ancient Victorian; Juridical Review June 1937; New Statesman January 23, 1937; New York Times January 19, 20, 1937; Saturday Review of Literature March 29, 1941.

POLLOCK, WALTER HERRIES (February 21, 1850-February 21, 1926), English editor and journalist, was the second son of

Sir Frederick Pollock, second baronet, and younger brother of Sir Frederick Pollock, the legal authority.^{qv} He was a King's Scholar at Eton, and attended Trinity College, Cambridge, obtaining his M.A. in the Classical Tripos. Called to the Bar of the Inner Temple, like several fellow-writers first called to that estate, Pollock turned journalist.

From a sub-editorialship on the *Saturday Review*, Pollock rose to the editorship in 1883, leaving in 1894, his health failing comparatively early in life. An ardent fencer, Pollock regarded fencing as more than physical recreation, as a kind of poetry. He wrote French prose extraordinarily well; translated Banville's play, *Gringoire*, into a version called *The Ballad-Monger* (with Sir Walter Besant); edited the *Recreations* of the Rabelais Club, an organization of the 'eighties which included Hardy, James, and Stevenson; and lectured on French poets at the Royal Institution. His wife, Emma Jane Pipon, was a daughter of Colonel Pipon, Seigneur de Noirmont of Jersey.

After his death the *Saturday Review* commented, Pollock meant a great deal to the best type of literary journalist and nothing to the man in the street; he exemplified the old English ideal of the amateur. *Icarian Flights* contains elegant translations of Horatian odes done with Francis Coutts.

PRINCIPAL WORKS: Songs and Rhymes, 1882; Nine Men's Morrice: Stories, 1889; Old and New, 1890; Fencing (with others) 1890; King Zub and Other Stories, 1892; Monsieur le Marquis de—: Memoires Inédits, 1894; Animals That Have Owned Us, 1904; Impressions of Henry Irving, 1908; The Art of the Hon. John Collier, 1914.

ABOUT: Saturday Review February 28, 1926.

*PONTOPPIDAN, HENRIK (July 24, 1857-), Danish novelist, Nobel Prize winner, was born in Fredericia, Jutland, where his father, Dines Pontoppidan, was a minister. The family was a very old patrician one, with many clerical members. When he was six they moved to Randers, where he was reared, and where he received honorary citizenship in 1933. In 1873 he went to Copen-

hagen, where he attended the Polytechnic Institute and was intending to become an engineer; but suddenly, during a walking tour in 1877, he "got "literature" as other people "get religion," and from that time had no thought of anything except being a writer. He was married very young to Marie Oxenböll;

they were divorced in 1891, and later he married Antoinette Kofoed, who died in 1928. He has no children.

His life as writer and as man may be divided into three periods, marked by three cycles of novels. In the first, the period covered by *The Promised Land,* he was an affiliate of the religious agrarianism of Grundtvig, lived close to the peasants, and was in some sense their spokesman. In 1884 he met the great critic Georg Brandes, and after a tour in Germany and Italy he settled in Copenhagen and became a part of the "advanced" cultural group, largely Jewish, that settled around Brandes. This is the period of *Lucky Peter,* who is a semi-autobiographical reflection of himself. He became disillusioned with this milieu, and for a while mixed in politics and was even for a short time in Parliament. His disappointment here also appeared in fictional form in *The Kingdom of the Dead.* Unfortunately only fragmentary selections from these three major cycles have been translated into English, and so it is impossible for English or American readers really to judge Pontoppidan's work as a whole.

He lives now in Charlottenlund, near Copenhagen, and would be practically unknown outside of Denmark except that in 1917 he shared the Nobel Prize for Literature with Karl Gjellerup (who died in 1919). In 1929 he received an honorary Ph.D. from the University of Lund. He has written almost nothing in the past twenty years except a few short stories, and lives in absolute retirement, induced both by his age and by his lifelong aloofness and "proud modesty."

Since Pontoppidan is well past eighty, it is unlikely that the Nazi invaders of Denmark have disturbed his mode of life.

"As an artist he does not rank among the greatest," said Oscar Geismar, "but in a remarkable age of transition he has lived the fate of his people with a sensitive soul and recorded what he has experienced in clear and intelligible Danish. . . . Gently,

* Died August 21, 1943.

but coolly too, the words flow from his pen. . . . But there is passion hidden beneath the smooth surface." Julius Clausen said that Pontoppodan "reveals himself as a master of style—just by not apparently having any marks of style at all." And Jean Lescoffier, calling him "a pitiless critic," said that in his novels as a whole "the fresh winds of Jutland have swept away the miasma of Copenhagen."

He is a somber-faced man with thick white hair and beard and deep-set gray eyes. Though he has been in retirement for many years, he still holds honorary membership in the Danish Society of Novelists, the Copenhagen Union of Writers, and the London section of the P.E.N. Club.

WORKS AVAILABLE IN ENGLISH: Village Tales, 1883; The Apothecary's Daughters, 1890; Emanuel: or, Children of the Soil, 1892; The Promised Land, 1896; Lucky Peter, 1898; The Kingdom of the Dead, 1900; From the Huts, 1901.

ABOUT: Brandes, G. Fuglerperspektiv; Marble, A. L. The Nobel Prize Winners in Literature; Topsöe-Jensen, H. G. Scandinavian Literature; American Scandinavian Review January 1933, March 1934; Contemporary Review March 1920; Mercure de France April 1, 1938.

*POOLE, ERNEST (January 23, 1880-), American novelist, was born in Chicago, the son of Abram Poole and Mary (Howe) Poole. He was grad-

uated from Princeton in 1902, and then spent three years with the University Settlement in New York, except for a period in 1904 when he was publicity agent for the strikers in the Chicago stockyards strike. From his observations and experiences of this time came the articles dealing with New York tenement life and Chicago labor conditions which were published in McClure's, Collier's, and other magazines, and eventuated finally in his best-known novel, The Harbor. He was the Outlook's correspondent in Russia during the abortive 1904 revolution, and in 1915 held a similar post for the Saturday Evening Post in Germany and France. In 1917 he was in Russia again. He is also a playwright, three of his plays—None So Blind, A Man's Friends, and Take Your Medicine (written with Harriet Ford)—having been produced in New York. In 1916 his novel, His Family, won the Pulitzer Prize. His sketches of Russian peasant life in the first months of the 1917 revolution also attracted

much attention. Many of his novels have been translated into the Central European languages. The Harbor ran through six editions in one month, though Mr. Poole was at the time utterly unknown as a novelist.

In 1907 he married Margaret Winterbotham; they have two sons and a daughter. He now lives in New York. He describes himself as an "independent" in politics. He is a tall, clean-shaven man, with brown hair worn in a pompadour, pince nez, and a constant pipe. He describes his working method as follows: "Though often I forget the idea in developing the characters, still I think it looms fairly large behind the finished book. For some months I work on sketches and outlines, making quite voluminous notes. I then write the first draft in a fashion so rough that nobody but myself could possibly decipher it. From this I dictate a second draft, and then I write and rewrite it perhaps five or six times."

PRINCIPAL WORKS: Novels—The Harbor, 1915; His Family, 1916; His Second Wife, 1918; Blind, 1920; Beggar's Gold, 1921; Millions, 1922; Danger, 1923; The Avalanche, 1924; The Hunter's Moon, 1925; With Eastern Eyes, 1926; Silent Storms, 1927; Car of Croesus, 1930; The Destroyer, 1931; Nurses on Horseback, 1932; Great Winds, 1933; One of Us, 1934. Non-Fiction—The Dark People, 1918; The Village, 1919; The Little Dark Man and Other Russian Sketches, 1925; The Bridge (autobiography) 1940.

ABOUT: Baldwin, C. C. The Men Who Make Our Novels; More, P. E. Shelburne Essays: 11th Series; Poole, E. The Bridge; New York Herald Tribune "Books" August 18, 1940.

POORTEN. See SCHWARTZ

"PORLOCK, MARTIN." See MAC-DONALD, P.

PORTER, Mrs. ELEANOR (HODGMAN) ("Eleanor Stewart") (1868-May 23, 1920), American novelist and short-story writer, was born in Littleton, N.H., the daughter of Francis H. Hodgman and Llewella (Woolson) Hodgman. Her mother was an invalid for many years, and Eleanor's own health was none too robust. She left high school to lead an outdoor

life. Much improved in health, she studied at the New England Conservatory of Music, and married John Lyman Porter at twenty-four. Her first novel, Cross Currents, was published fifteen years later, with a sequel,

The Turn of the Tide next year (1908). *Miss Billy* (1911) and *Miss Billy's Decision* the following year were cheerful, sentimental romances which sold well, but were eclipsed by the sensational success of her 1913 production, *Pollyanna,* which struck a universal American chord of hopefulness, to the tune of more than a million copies. "White Mountain cabins, Colorado teahouses, Texan babies, Indiana apartment houses, and a brand of milk" were named for this young girl who played the Glad Game and made even a Vermont village rejoice that it was alive. In *Pollyanna Grows Up,* as the Boston *Transcript* remarked, Pollyanna, "having made glad everyone in Beldingsville, Vt., enlarges her sphere of activity and attempts to bring joy to all Boston, a prodigious and, of course, quite impossible task."

Of the *Pollyanna* stories in general, the *New Republic* remarked that "in basing their appeal on an effervescent optimism and a pretty sentimentality, Mrs. Porter sets throbbing an emotional chord not confined to the bosoms of any single class of readers." She added a word to the language, as Grant Overton truly observed. Mrs. Porter, a sensible woman, believed that her creation had put her rather in a false position. "I have never believed that we ought to deny discomfort and pain and evil: I have merely thought that it is far better to 'greet the unknown with a cheer,'" she insisted. The collections of short stories published four years after her death at fifty-two did not display this strain of relentless optimism. Pollyanna spread her message of euphoria from the stage and screen, and survived her creator in stories written by Harriet Lummis Smith and Elizabeth Borton.

PRINCIPAL WORKS: *Novels*—Cross Currents, 1907; The Turn of the Tide, 1908; The Story of Marco, 1911; Miss Billy, 1911; Miss Billy's Decision, 1912; Pollyanna, 1913; Miss Billy Married, 1914; Pollyanna Grows Up, 1915; Just David, 1916; The Road of Understanding, 1917; Oh, Money! Money, 1918; Dawn, 1919; May-Marie, 1919; Sister Sue, 1921. *Short Stories*—Money, Love, and Kate, 1924; The Tie That Binds, 1924; The Tangled Threads, 1924; Across the Years, 1924.

ABOUT: Overton, G. The Women Who Make Our Novels; New York Times May 24, 1920.

PORTER, Mrs. GENE (STRATTON) (August 17, 1868-December 6, 1924), American novelist and nature-writer, was born Geneva Grace Stratton, the youngest of twelve children of Mark Stratton and Mary (Schallenberger) Stratton. Her father, a patriarchal old man, and the boys of the family ran the 240-acre Indiana farm, called Hopewell. Mrs. Porter based her most popular novel, *The Harvester,* on his personality, and romanticized her brother Leander, drowned at eighteen in the Wabash River, as *Laddie.*

The girl ran wild on the farm, locating sixty-four bird nests one spring. Her reading was composed of the McGuffey readers, *Pilgrim's Progress, Undine, Paul and Virgina,* and *The Vicar of Wakefield.* In 1874 the family left the farm for Wabash. Geneva changed her name to Geneve, and after her marriage in 1886 to Charles D. Porter, a "flourishing young druggist" of Geneva, Ind., to Gene. They had a daughter, Jeannette Stratton Porter who later wrote her mother's biography (libraries list it under her married name, Meehan). The Porters owned a cabin on the edge of a vast primitive swamp, the Limberlost, named for a certain Limber who disappeared there: a natural preserve of wild plants, moths, and birds. Mrs. Porter began to explore its treasures with a camera, the results appearing in illustrated articles in *Rec-*

reation and *Outing.* Her first piece of fiction was accepted by the *Metropolitan Magazine* in New York.

When a feather from the wing of a black vulture fell at her feet, Mrs. Porter conceived the idea of *Freckles,* published in 1904, and warmly received by the adolescents of America, of whatever age. A romance of the great swamp, it was succeeded five years later by *A Girl of the Limberlost,* which had equal appeal to the distaff side of the American reading public. The *Nation* said that she was "mistress of a recipe of cuteness, triteness, and sentimentality which cannot fail." Her critics frequently irritated Mrs. Porter. Declaring, "I am going to fight tooth and claw for a top-notch rating poetically," she came out in 1922 with *The Fire Bird,* an Indian drama. With a satisfactory bank-account and thousands of letters from admirers, all of which she answered herself, Mrs. Porter could afford to disregard her detractors, and her nature books were in general solid achievements. (No modern author has equaled her total sales. *Freckles* sold above two million copies and *A Girl of the Limberlost, The Harvester,* and *Laddie,* more than a million and a half each.) Christopher Morley compared *Homing With the*

Birds to Fabre, and said that it "refreshed the sense of amazement." In 1924 Mrs. Porter was building two homes, Bel-Air, in West Los Angeles, and Avalon, a stone house on Catalina Island, when her Lincoln limousine was wrecked in a collision at Los Angeles, near Christmas time. Mrs. Porter's right side was crushed, and she died in a coma. She was a handsome woman, with keen, brown-spotted gray eyes, heavy black eyebrows, and brown hair.

PRINCIPAL WORKS: The Song of the Cardinal, 1903; Freckles, 1904; What I Have Done With Birds, 1907; At the Foot of the Rainbow, 1907; Birds of the Bible, 1909; A Girl of the Limberlost, 1909; The Harvester, 1911; Moths of the Limberlost, 1912; Laddie, 1913; Michael O'Halloran, 1915; A Daughter of the Land, 1918; Homing With the Birds, 1919; Her Father's Daughter, 1919; The Fire Bird, 1922; The White Flag, 1923; The Keeper of the Bees, 1924.

ABOUT: Meehan, J. S. P. Lady of the Limberlost; New York Times December 7, 1924.

PORTER, HAROLD EVERETT ("Holworthy Hall" (September 19, 1887-June 20, 1936), American novelist, short-story writer, and dramatist, was

born in Boston, the son of Robert de Lance and Louella (Root) Porter. He received a B.A. degree *cum laude* from Harvard University in 1907, and appropriated the name of a dormitory, Holworthy Hall, for his pseudonym in writing light fiction for magazines of large national circulation.

For six years after leaving college he was with A. D. Porter Co., publishers, serving as president in 1915-16. *Aerial Observation* was the result of experience as captain in the Army Air Service in the First World War. In April 1920 he was commissioned a major in the aviation branch of the Officers' Reserve Corps. He married Marian Heffron of Syracuse, N.Y., and they had two daughters and a son. Porter's fiction, agreeable and easily forgotten, never achieved the ranks of the best sellers; the nearest approach, ironically enough, being a prohibition novel written in collaboration with Hugh McNair Kahler entitled *The Six Best Cellars*. *The Valiant*, however, a one-act prison melodrama written with a classmate and well-known actor, Robert Middlemass, has had audiences of thousands in little-theatre tournaments, vaudeville houses, and moving-picture theatres. It has also been

broadcast by radio. Porter died in his forty-ninth year of pneumonia at Charlotte Hungerford Hospital, Torrington, Conn.

PRINCIPAL WORKS: My Next Imitation, 1913; Henry of Navarre, Ohio, 1914; Pepper, 1915; Paprika, 1916; What He Least Expected, 1917; Dormie One and Other Golf Stories, 1917; The Six Best Cellars (with H. McN. Kahler) 1919; The Man Nobody Knew, 1919; Eagan, 1920; Aerial Observation, 1921; The Valiant, 1924; Colossus, 1930.

ABOUT: Harvard College, Class of 1907, Twenty-Fifth Anniversary Report; New York Times June 22, 1936.

PORTER, JEANNETTE STRATTON. See PORTER, G. S.

PORTER, KATHERINE ANNE (May 15, 1894-), American story writer, writes: "I was born at Indian Creek, Texas, brought up in Texas and Louisiana, and educated in small Southern convent schools. I was precocious, nervous, rebellious, unteachable, and made life very uncomfortable for myself and I suppose for those around me. As soon as I learned to form

G. P. Lynes

letters on paper, at about three years, I began to write stories, and this has been the basic and absorbing occupation, the intact line of my life which directs my actions, determines my point of view, and profoundly affects my character and personality, my social beliefs and economic status, and the kind of friendships I form. I did not choose this vocation, and if I had any say in the matter, I would not have chosen it. I made no attempt to publish anything until I was thirty, but I have written and destroyed manuscripts quite literally by the trunkful. I spent fifteen years wandering about, weighted horribly with masses of paper and little else. Yet for this vocation I was and am willing to live and die, and I consider very few other things of the slightest importance.

"All my growing years were lived completely outside of literary centers; I knew no writers and had no one to consult with on the single vital issue of my life. This self-imposed isolation, which seems to have been almost unconscious on my part, prolonged and made more difficult my discipline as an artist. But it saved me from discipleship, personal influences, and membership in groups. My reading until my twenty-fifth year was a grand sweep of all English and translated classics from the beginning up to about 1800. Then I began with the newcomers, and found new incitements. Wherever I have lived I have done book reviewing, political articles, hack writing of all kinds, editing, rewriting other people's manuscripts, by way of earning a living--and a sorry living it was, too. Without the help of devoted friends I should have perished many times over.

"In 1931 I received a Guggenheim Fellowship for studying abroad. In 1940 I received the medal of the Society for Libraries at New York University. I am at present [1940] working on a study of Cotton Mather, begun in 1927.

"Politically my bent is to the left. As for aesthetic bias, my one aim is to tell a straight story and to give true testimony. My personal life has been the jumbled and apparently irrelevant mass of experiences which can happen, I think, only to a woman who goes with her mind permanently absent from the place where she is. My physical eyes are unnaturally far-sighted, and I have no doubt this affects my temperament in some way. I have very little time sense and almost no sense of distance or of direction. I lack entirely a respect for money values, and for caste of any kind, social, intellectual, or whatever. I should like to live in a place where I might swim in the sea, sail a catboat, and ride horseback. These are the only recreations I really care for, and they all take a good deal of elbow-room. Not for nothing am I the great-great-great-granddaughter of Daniel Boone.

"I was married in 1933 to Eugene Pressly, who was attached to the United States consular service in Paris. Later we were divorced, and in 1938 I married Albert Russel Erskine, Jr., professor of English at the University of Louisiana and business manager of the *Southern Review*. We live in Baton Rouge, La."

* * *

Aside from her outdoor recreations, Miss Porter is a notable cook, does fine sewing, and collects old phonograph records. Music is one of her great interests, and in 1933 she translated and edited a series of old French songs. She is an extremely slow writer, and is perfectly contented to be. Few persons have built so solid a reputation on so small a published output; she is the nearest American equivalent to Katherine Mansfield, with the same artistic scrupulosity. Margaret Marshall said of her that her "prose has extraordinary purity and con-

centration; it is delicate yet strong, and very clear; all the dross has been distilled out."

In 1942 Miss Porter made available in English the famous Mexican picaresque novel, *The Itching Parrot*. Her oft-announced study of Cotton Mather has not yet appeared, but the even more eagerly awaited first novel, *No Safe Harbor*, seems definitely scheduled for 1942 publication.

PRINCIPAL WORKS: Flowering Judas, 1930; Hacienda, 1934; Noon Wine, 1937; Pale Horse, Pale Rider, 1939; No Safe Harbor, 1942.

ABOUT: Kenyon Review Winter 1941; Nation April 13, 1940; New York Times Book Review April 14, 1940; Publishers' Weekly February 6, 1937, October 11, 1939; Sewanee Review April 1940; Time April 10, 1939.

PORTER, WILLIAM SYDNEY. See HENRY, O.

POST, MELVILLE DAVISSON (April 19, 1871-June 23, 1930), American short story writer and novelist was born at Romines Mills, near Clarksburg, W. Va., the son of Ira Carper Post and Florence May (D a v i s s o n) Post. He worked on his father's farm, attended rural schools and the academy at Buckhannon, and received a B.A. degree from West Virginia  University in 1891, followed by an LL.B. the next year. For eleven years he successfully practiced criminal and corporate law in his native state. In 1896 he turned to literature, utilizing his experience at the bar as background for *The Strange Schemes of Randolph Mason*, a volume of short stories dealing with an unscrupulous lawyer, less benevolent than Arthur Train's Mr. Tutt of later years, who used his knowledge of legal loopholes to defeat the ends of justice. The book was criticized by moralists on the ground that it gave too much advice to criminals. In the preface to a sequel, *The Man of Last Resort*, Post retorted that nothing but good could come of exposing the law's defects. (As if in proof of his contention, at least one of the Mason stories, "The Corpus Delicti," is credited with having definitely crystallized a long-needed change in criminal procedure.) However, in *The Corrector of Destinies* (1909), Post finally heeded popular demand and put Mason on the side of justice.

During the early years of the century Post tried his hand, with varying success, at the novel. But he was first and foremost a master of the short story of plot. His greatest fame rests on the series of tales about his fictitious Uncle Abner, a rock-hewn Virginia squire of the days of Thomas Jefferson, whose position as the protector of innocence and righter of wrongs in his mountain community, compels him to turn detective, with some of the most ingenious results known to mystery literature. The Abner stories were published in magazine form beginning in 1911 (the year, incidentally, of the first appearance of G. K. Chesterton's Father Brown, in England) and the best of them were brought together between covers as *Uncle Abner: Master of Mysteries* in 1918. The book has never been out of print since. So astute a critic of the detective story as Willard Huntington Wright ("S.S. Van Dine") called the Abner tales among the finest of their *genre* America possesses, and he wrote of their central figure: "Uncle Abner is one of the outstanding characters of detective fiction, deserving to be ranked with that immortal triumvirate, Dupin, Lecoq, and Holmes." Post found the detective vein a rich one, and he published volumes of short stories featuring no less than five other sleuths—all good in their kind, but none to compare with the Virginian. For all his wizardry of plot, however, he never wrote a detective story of novel length.

Post's stories always appeared in magazines first (editors paid record prices for his work) and were then collected into book form. He proclaimed himself the champion of plot-technique in the short story; and, indeed, he is probably the most creditable exponent of what has come to be looked down upon as the formularized, or "machine-made," magazine story. For this reason Edward O'Brien and F. L. Pattee have called his work negligible as literature, though praising his technical accomplishments. But Blanche Colton Williams ranks him second only to Poe in the American short story. Be that as it may, Post himself, in his preoccupation with formula, underestimated some of his greatest literary gifts. The Abner stories are still read and re-read not so much for their intensive plots—highly original in their time but hackneyed by imitation today—as for the author's cogent realization of character, place, and mood. Had Post developed this phase of his talent more, and had he been less concerned with merely commercial success, his stature as a serious artist might have been greater than now seems likely. Even so, his Uncle Abner

remains the most distinguished American contribution to detective literature between Auguste Dupin and Philo Vance.

Post's home in later years was "The Hill of the Painted Men," Lost Creek, Harrison County, W.Va. In 1903 he had married Ann Bloomfield Gamble of Roanoke, Va.; she died childless in 1919. He traveled extensively abroad, and was active in the councils of the Democratic party at home. Aside from these few incidents, the story of his later life was synonymous with his writing career. Death came suddenly at Clarksburg after a two-weeks illness, following a fall from a horse at the age of fifty-nine.

PRINCIPAL WORKS: The Strange Schemes of Randolph Mason, 1896; The Man of Last Resort, 1897; Dwellers in the Hills, 1901; The Corrector of Destinies, 1909; The Gilded Chair, 1910; The Nameless Thing, 1912; Uncle Abner: Master of Mysteries, 1918; The Mystery at the Blue Villa, 1919; The Mountain School Teacher, 1922; Monsieur Jonquelle, 1922; Walker of the Secret Service, 1924; The Man Hunters, 1926; The Revolt of the Birds, 1927; The Bradmoor Murder, 1929; The Silent Witness, 1930.

ABOUT: Haycraft, H. Murder for Pleasure: The Life and Times of the Detective Story; Honce, C. Mark Twain's Associated Press Speech; Overton, G. Cargoes for Crusoes; Turner, E. M. Stories and Verse of West Virginia; Williams, B. C. Our Short Story Writers; Wood, W. Representative Authors of West Virginia; New York Times June 24, 1930; Scholastic January 21, 1939.

POSTGATE, RAYMOND WILLIAM (November 6, 1896-), English novelist, biographer, and political writer, writes: "I am the eldest son of Prof. J. P. Postgate, once a famous classical scholar, and a collateral descendent of the Blessed Father Nicholas Postgate, executed during the Titus Oates period for baptizing children into the Roman faith. (I am not a Roman Catholic myself.) I married Daisy, daughter of the Rt. Hon. George Lansbury, the famous pacifist, leader of the Labour Party, etc. Education, various schools and St. John's College, Oxford. Eight years in Fleet Street, mostly as foreign sub-editor on the old *Daily Herald*. Edited various Left political papers. Departmental editor, Fourteenth Edition *Encyclopædia Britannica*. Now editing the *Tribune*. European representative of Alfred A. Knopf, New York publisher, since 1929.

"Member of Home Guard, house bombed five times, office twice bombed and once destroyed."

* * *

Mr. Postgate was born in Cambridge, where his father was Professor of Latin at the university. The father was a strong conservative, the son early became a radical, so that for seven years he was an exile from his father's house. In the First World War he was a conscientious objector, was imprisoned in 1916, and his budding official career came to an abrupt end. For the last year of the war he was "on the run" and in hiding. His sister is Margaret Cole wife of G. D. H. Cole[qv] and with her husband author of numerous books on economics and as many mystery novels. Mr. Postgate has followed the same pattern: his *Verdict of Twelve* (1940) is one of the very best of its *genre*. In his more serious vein, his studies in revolutionary history and biography have earned for him a wide public among the discriminating, who have learned to rely on his faithful attention to detail and on a factual dependability matched by a brilliant style.

PRINCIPAL WORKS: The International During the War, 1918; The Bolshevik Theory, 1920; Revolution From 1789 to 1906, 1920; The Workers' International, 1920; Out of the Past, 1922; The Builders' History, 1923; Murder, Piracy, and Treason, 1925; History of the British Workers, 1926; Pervigilium Veneris (tr. & ed.) 1929; That Devil Wilkes, 1930; The Conversations of Dr. Johnson, 1930; Dear Robert Emmet, 1931; Felix and Anne (in America: No Epitaph) (novel) 1932; Karl Marx, 1933; How To Make a Revolution, 1934; What To Do With the B.B.C., 1935; Those Foreigners (with G. A. Vaillance) 1937; The British Common People: 1746-1938 (with G. D. H. Cole) 1938; Verdict of Twelve (novel) 1940.

ABOUT: New Republic July 22, 1940.

POTTER, PAUL MEREDITH. See "AMERICAN AUTHORS: 1600-1900"

POUND, EZRA LOOMIS (October 30, 1885-), American poet and critic, wrote from Rapallo, Italy, on May 12, 1939:

"Arriving at the University of Pennsylvania in 1901, I acknowledge debts to Professors McDaniel and Child for Latin and English, and to Ames for doing his best when no professor of American history had got down to bedrock. Overholser had not made his admirable compendium of

the real causes of the Revolution and of the great and dastardly betrayal of the American people and the American system, by the trick clause, and the Bank Act of February 25, 1863.

"When a writer merits mention in a work of reference his work IS his autobiography, it is his first-person record. If you can't print my one-page 'Introductory Text-Book' enclosed (and to appear here) then your profession of wanting an authentic record is mere bunk, and fit only to stand with the infamies that have ragéd in America since Johnson was kicked out of the White House, and in especial throughout the degradation of the American state and system by Wilson and Roosevelt.

INTRODUCTORY TEXT-BOOK

In Four Chapters

"All the perplexities, confusion, and distress in America arise, not from defects in their constitution or confederation, not from want of honour and virtue, so much as from downright ignorance of the nature of coin, credit, and circulation." *John Adams.*

". . . and if the national bills issued, be bottomed (as is indispensable) on pledges of specific taxes for their redemption within certain and moderate epochs, and be of *proper denominations* for *circulation*, no interest on them would be necessary or just, because they would answer to every one of the purposes of the metallic money withdrawn and replaced by them." *Thomas Jefferson (1816, letter to Crawford.)*

". . . and gave to the people of this Republic THE GREATEST BLESSING THEY EVER HAD—THEIR OWN PAPER TO PAY THEIR OWN DEBTS." *Abraham Lincoln.*

"The Congress shall have power:

"To coin money, regulate the value thereof and of foreign coin, and to fix the standards of weights and measures." Constitution of the United States, Article I, Legislative Department, Section 8, pp. 5.

"Done in the convention by the unanimous consent of the States, 7th September, 1787, and of the Independence of the United States the twelfth. In witness whereof we have hereunto inscribed our names." *George Washington, President and Deputy from Virginia.*

Note

The abrogation of this last mentioned power derives from the ignorance mentioned in my first quotation. Of the three preceding citations, Lincoln's has become the text of Willis Overholser's recent *History of Money in the United States,* the first citation was taken by Jerry Voorhis in his speech in the House of Representatives, June 6, 1938, and the passage from Jefferson is the nucleus of my *Jefferson and/or Mussolini.*

Douglas' proposals are a sub-head under the main idea in Lincoln's sentence, Gesell's "invention" is a special case under Jefferson's general law. I have done my best to make simple summaries and clear definitions in various books and pamphlets, and recommend as *introductory* study, apart from C. H. Douglas' *Economic Democracy* and Gesell's *Natural Economic Order,* Chris. Hollis' *Two Nations,* McNair Wilson's *Promise to*

Pay, Larrañaga's *Gold, Glut, and Government,* and M. Butchart's compendium of three centuries' thought, that is an anthology of what has been said, in *Money* (originally published by Nott).

The four items on the page facing this [the quotations] SHOULD be taught in every American high school. At present no American university has the horse sense or common honesty to include them in the higher curricula.

"Items not, so far as I know, in other books of reference would concern (1) the sabotage of my efforts on behalf of *Poetry,* of Chicago, and the persistent double crossing of me by the Chicago clique, despite soapy professions of appreciation of my having in the beginning got about 80 per cent of the better material for that magazine; (2) the general futility of ALL American endowments for the furthering of the arts, and their fatty degeneration into bureaucracies; (3) my setting of a great deal of Villon's poetry and Cavalcanti's to music for opera or sung drama, [which] has not yet had any support from the mercantilist bog that engulphs America.

"The printing centre for live writing in the English or American language was shifted to New York in 1917 to 1919. After that war the muckers of the American publishing swamp did nothing and London again took over the lead in this field. America once again gets her stuff after London has had it."

* * *

The foregoing "autobiography" having been printed exactly as Mr. Pound requests, the factual details of his life remain to be related. He was born in Hailey, Idaho, the son of Homer Loomis Pound and Isabel (Weston) Pound. He spent his first two college years in the University of Pennsylvania, then transferred to Hamilton College, where he received a Ph.B. degree in 1905. Returning to Pennsylvania as Fellow in Romanics and instructor (from 1905 to 1907), he took his M.A. in 1906. He then became an instructor in Wabash College, but after four months left for Italy. During 1907 he traveled in Spain, Italy, and Provence, then went to London, where he was the unofficial literary executor of Ernest Fenellosa and became interested through this in Japanese and Chinese poetry. In 1914 he married Dorothy Shakespear. From 1917 to 1919 he was London editor of the *Little Review* (Chicago). Besides his original poetry and his books on literature, music, art, and economics, he has edited many volumes and has translated from the Italian, French, Chinese, and Japanese. In 1920 he went to Paris, where he was correspond-

ent of the *Dial.* Since 1924 he has lived in Italy, where in 1927 and 1928 he edited the *Exile,* which he had founded. In 1928 he received the *Dial* award of $2,000 "for distinguished service to American letters." He has made only two visits to his native country since he was twenty-two, the last in 1939 when his Fascistic utterances aroused great resentment.

Iris Barry, chronicling "the Ezra Pound period" (1912-19), described him as having "exuberant" red hair and "a pale catlike face with greenish cat eyes." The characteristic beard came later. His voice is high and squeaky and he is a bundle of nervous energy.

In poetry Pound has been a great experimenter. T. S. Eliot has admitted his poetic debt to Pound. Allen Tate, who said that the secret of Pound's style was that his poems were *conversation,* spoke of his "vast range of obscure learning, his immense underground reputation," and called him a "powerful reactionary." For many years he has been engaged in writing a long series of esoteric and argumentative "cantos," which opposing camps of critics regard as either the apex of his achievement or the *reductio ad absurdum* of his style.

As his autobiographical note evidences, Pound is an ardent disciple of Major C. H. Douglas and his Social Credit System.

In January 1941 Ezra Pound began broadcasting Fascist propaganda by short-wave from Rome to the United States. These broadcasts have continued since the outbreak of war between Italy and the United States and are said to be Pound's only present source of income. Early in 1942 Pound tried to join the diplomatic train which carried a large group of Americans from Italy to Lisbon for shipment back home, but permission was refused him by the American government.

"The time has come to put a formal end to the countenancing of Ezra Pound," began an editorial in *Poetry* in April 1942. ". . . So far as we and the rest of the English-speaking world of letters are concerned, he has effectively written *finis* to his long career as inspired *enfant terrible.*"

PRINCIPAL WORKS: *Poetry*—Personae, 1909; Exultations, 1909; Provença, 1910; Canzoni, 1911; Ripostes, 1912; Cathay (translations) 1915; Lustra and Other Poems, 1917; Quia Pauper Amavi, 1919; Umbra (collected poems) 1920; Cantos I-XVI, 1925; Cantos XVII-XXVII, 1928; A Draft of XXX Cantos, 1930; A Draft of Cantos XXXI-XLI, 1934; Homage to Sextus Propertius, 1934; The Fifth Decad of Cantos, 1937; Cantos LII-LXXI, 1940. *Prose*—The Spirit of Romance, 1910; Gaudier Brzeska, 1916; Pavannes and Divisions, 1918; Instigations, 1920; Indiscretions, 1923; Antheil and the Treatise on Harmony, 1924; Imaginary Letters, 1930; How To Read 1931; Prolegomena: Volume I, 1932; ABC of Economics, 1933; Make It New, 1934; The ABC of Reading, 1934; Social Credit and Impact, 1935; Jefferson and/or Mussolini, 1935; Polite Essays, 1936; Digest of the Analects, 1937; Guide to Kulchur (in America: Culture) 1938; What Is Money For? 1939.

ABOUT: Leavis, F. R. New Bearings in English Poetry; Lewis, W. Blasting and Bombardiering; Atlantic Monthly October 1940; Bookman October 1931; Dial January 1928; Nation June 10, 1931; New Statesman and Nation May 15, 1937; North American Review May 1920, June 1924; Poetry May 1925, July 1927, August 1934, August 1935, March 1938; December 1940, April 1942; Saturday Review of Literature December 26, 1931, July 1, 1933, January 19, 1935; March 16, 1940; Sewanee Review October 1938.

POWELL, DAWN (November 28, 1897-), American novelist, writes: "Dawn Powell was born in Mt. Gilead, Ohio. The

Pinchot

Powells, of Welsh descent, were originally from Southern Virginia. The author owes much of the sources of her literary material to the fact that her mother died at an early age. Since the father traveled, the three small daughters were dispatched from one relative to another, from a year of farm life with this or that aunt, to village life, life in small-town boarding-houses, life with very prim strict relatives, to rougher life in the middle of little factory-towns. The farm experience brought out Miss Powell's novel *The Bride's House*, as the boarding-house background was responsible for *She Walks in Beauty* and *Dance Night*. About 1909 Mr. Powell made a second marriage and moved to his wife's farm near Cleveland, where the three children were very unhappy, and it was from here that Dawn Powell ran away with thirty cents she had earned by berry-picking. There were two reasons for her runaway—one, she had won a scholarship to high school but there was no school there for her to attend; and, two, the new stepmother had burned up all the stories she had been writing, a form of discipline that the ego could not endure, even at twelve. Landing in the home of a favorite aunt, in Shelby, Ohio, the author attended school, edited a school paper, worked on the village daily after school, and eventually graduated to Lake Erie College, Painesville, Ohio, where she started a secret paper with two friends, then was editor-in-chief of the college magazine, and active in dramatic work,

in addition to working for five hours a day to earn her expenses. B.A. in 1918, Miss Powell came to New York and was able to get in three weeks of war work with the United States Naval Reserve before armistice was declared. Later [1920] working in publicity, she met and married Joseph R. Gousha, an advertising man. Though she had published a novel in 1924, Miss Powell preferred to let the error be forgotten, and her book, *She Walks in Beauty,* was published in 1928 as her first novel, after thirty-six rejections. Besides short stories in magazines, Miss Powell's play, *Big Night,* was produced by the Group Theatre in 1933, and *Jig Saw* was produced by the Theatre Guild in 1934. She has made her home consistently in New York for the past twenty years, with a summer home at Mt. Sinai, Long Island. She has one son."

* * *

Miss Powell is a tiny woman who works in the children's room of the public library because those are the only chairs in the library that fit her! Robert Van Gelder calls her a very witty satirist, who is not popular because she satirizes neither the poor nor the rich, but the middle class. She is shrewd, "hard-boiled," and unfailingly amusing. She has written a number of film scenarios, and wrote and broadcast the "Music and Manners" program over the Mutual Broadcasting network.

PRINCIPAL WORKS: She Walks in Beauty, 1928; The Bride's House, 1929; Dance Night, 1931; The Tenth Moon, 1933; Story of a Country Boy, 1934; Turn, Magic Wheel, 1936; The Happy Island, 1938; Angels on Toast, 1940; A Time To Be Born, 1942.

ABOUT: New York Times Book Review November 3, 1940.

POWYS, JOHN COWPER (October 8, 1872-), English essayist, novelist, and poet, was born in Shirley, Derbyshire, where his father, Charles Francis Powys, was vicar. His mother, born Mary Cowper Johnson, was a collateral descendant of both Cowper and Donne. John Cowper Powys was educated at Sherborne School and at Corpus Christi College, Cambridge.

There were eleven in the family; his younger brothers Llewelyn and Theodore *qqv* both won fame in their own right as authors, another brother is a well known architect, a sister a novelist and poet, and another sister a painter. Though the name Powys is Welsh, actually there is as much English as Welsh in the family stock, with further admixtures of Scottish, Dutch, and probably German Jewish. The unusual solidarity of the three celebrated Powys brothers makes it difficult to treat of any one of them individually, so closely have their lives (especially those of John Cowper Powys and Llewelyn, who was twelve years younger) been interwoven. The name, incidentally, is pronounced Poe-iss, with accent on the first syllable; and Cowper is pronounced Cooper, as the bearer was wont to explain on the American lecture platform, where, under University Extension Society Auspices, he lectured on English literature for many years.

He had previously lectured for the similar society of the English universities, but for much of his life he has suffered severely from gastric ulcers, and finding the American climate more suitable to him than the British, he spent all his winters here from 1910 on, and from 1928 to 1934 he lived in the United States, most of the time in New York, but for a while in California. In the latter year he returned to England, and now he lives in Merionetshire, Wales. He married Margaret Alice Lyon, and they have one son, who is now a clergyman.

Without ever being formally handsome, John Cowper Powys in his youth was unusually striking, with thick, rather frizzy dark hair (now gray), a hawklike profile, and fiery black eyes. He looked like a character out of Robinson Jeffers, with the same intensity and vitality, though actually he was often ill. Now, he says, "my eyes are beginning to feel that I am sixty-seven my next birthday"; but long after his actual youth he gave to the public the impression of abounding youthfulness and vigor. Privately he was, like all his family, ridden by hesitations, fears, superstitions, and by his own special weakness, a self-depreciation amounting to masochism. He has always been a feeler more than a thinker, living in a world of his own, "filling heaven and earth" (to quote his brother Llewelyn) "with his Merlin imaginings." In this country and even at home he is better known than either of his brothers, though T. F. Powys is by far the most original of the three. His novels, overloaded, fantastic, frequently dull, peopled by characters who all sound as if they came out of *Wuthering Heights,* sometimes tremble on the verge between the magnificent and the ridiculous; nevertheless they have undoubted power and passages of strange beauty—the beauty of a moss-hung forest full of will-o'-the-wisps. They have been condemned for their outspokenness, much of which is pure naïveté and unfamiliarity with the world, in spite of the many years the author has spent as a public figure.

He has a streak of religiosity alien to Llewelyn and T. F. Powys alike, and there is a touch of mystical pantheism about his writing. As a novelist he views an earth "where every prospect pleases, and only man is vile." As a critic he is acute and understanding, but too much guided by emotion to be always a safe guide. He was a remarkable lecturer, and much of his work, especially his non-fiction, reads like a published lecture. His unsparing autobiography, memorable though it is, really gives a poor idea of its subject, since it is governed by his psychopathic need for humility; it omits his personal charm, his underlying integrity, and his poetic impulses, and exaggerates all his shortcomings. Utterly un-English in the accepted sense, John Cowper Powys belongs to the universal nation of art. He told Louis Wilkinson he did not like to be called "a man"; he preferred to be thought of as "an actor-priest." And that, in essence, is what he is.

PRINCIPAL WORKS: *Essays and Miscellaneous Prose*—Course of Twelve Lectures on Carlyle, Ruskin, Tennyson, 1900; Course of Six Lectures on Selected Plays of Shakespeare, 1901; English Novelists, 1904; History of Liberty, 1904; Representative American Writers, 1904; Shakespeare's Historical Plays, 1904; Tragedies of Shakespeare, 1904; Representative Prose Writers of the Nineteenth Century, 1905; War and Culture (in England: The Menace of German Culture) 1914; Visions and Revisions, 1915; Confessions of Two Brothers (with Llewelyn Powys) 1916; Suspended Judgments, 1916; One Hundred Best Books: With an Essay on Books and Reading, 1916; The Complex Vision, 1920; Psycho-Analysis and Morality, 1923; The Religion of a Skeptic, 1925; The Meaning of Culture, 1929; In Defence of Sensuality, 1930; Dorothy M. Richardson, 1931; A Philosophy of Solitude, 1933; Autobiography, 1934; The Art of Happiness, 1935; The Enjoyment of Literature (in England: The Pleasures of Literature) 1938; Mortal Strife, 1942. *Novels*—Wood and Stone, 1915; Wolf's Bane, 1916; Rodmoor, 1916; Ducdame, 1925; Wolf Solent, 1929; A Glastonbury Romance, 1932; Weymouth Sands, 1934; Jobber Skald, 1935; Morwyn, 1937; Owen Glendower: An Historical Romance, 1940. *Poetry*—Poems, 1899; Mandragora, 1917; Samphire, 1922.

ABOUT: Powys, J. C. Autobiography, Confessions of Two Brothers; Ward, H. R. The Powys Brothers; Wilkinson, L. U. Welsh Ambassadors; Bookman (London) October 1932; Century September 1925; Englische Studien No. 3, 1935; Publishers' Weekly March 22, 1930; Saturday Review January 1938; Saturday Review of Literature November 24, 1934; Time February 10, 1941.

P O W Y S, LLEWELYN (August 13, 1884-December 2, 1939), English novelist and essayist, wrote to the editors of this work shortly before his death: "I was the eighth child of the Rev. Charles Francis Powys and Mary Cowper (Johnson) Powys. My father was the grandson of Littleton Powys, the only brother of the first Baron Lilford. The Powys family is of Welsh extraction, but has been settled in England since the sixteenth century. My mother's grandfather was the poet Cowper's first cousin. I was educated at Sherborne School, and at Corpus Christi College, Cambridge, taking my degree in 1906. In the spring of 1909 I lectured in America on English literature under the auspices of the University Extension Society, and at a Whitman anniversary had the honour of reciting 'When Lilacs Last in the Dooryard Bloomed' from the same platform from which Professor Woodrow Wilson also gave an address.

"On my return to England I fell sick with consumption and spent two years at Clavadel in Switzerland. In 1914 I sailed to British East Africa, spending five years as manager of a stock ranch belonging to the Hon. Galbraith Cole. After a year spent in England I returned once again to the United States and began at the age of thirty-six to earn my living by writing. The publication of *Ebony and Ivory* by Mr. Simon Gould of the American Library Service brought me some reputation that was soon strengthened by the appearance of *Black Laughter* and *Henry Hudson*.

"In the year 1925 I returned to Dorset in England with my American wife, Alyse Gregory, who had been managing editor of the *Dial*. For five years we lived in a Coast Guard cottage on the top of White Nose, one of the highest sea cliffs of the South coast, afterwards moving a little inland, where we still rent the same cottage. A recrudescence of my old disorder compelled me in 1936 to return once more to Clavadel in Switzerland, where I am now living.

"The chief literary influences that have gone to mould my thought and style are Montaigne, Lucretius, Shakespeare, Robert Burton, Charles Lamb, Walter Pater, Thomas Hardy, Guy de Maupassant, and Marcel Proust. Of the contemporaries I have met I have been most influenced by Sigmund Freud, Theodore Dreiser, Edna St. Vincent Millay, Louis U. Wilkinson, and Thomas Hardy. My political convictions follow those of President Franklin D. Roosevelt, whom I consider the most spirited, the most generous, and the wisest statesman that the world has seen for many years. I hate tyranny of any kind whether it comes from the right or the left. I believe that the pleasures of private property are too important and too universal to be happily abolished. In matters of religion I am a confirmed skeptic. I believe that there exists no conscious principle concerned with man and his affairs. At the back of life all is mystery. I believe that the best clue to life is to be found in the poetic vision and that no purpose of life is of more consequence to the individual than love."

* * *

Mr. Powys never returned from Switzerland, where he wrote the above short sketch; only a few weeks later he died there, at Clavadel, of tuberculosis, at fifty-five. In 1936 he had written: "I don't want to die. I want to live to a great old age." In almost his last article he had called himself "a cuckoo whose tune no June ever changed: 'Love life! Love life! Love life!'" On the other hand, he had said in youth that if he could live to thirty-five he would be content, and he outdid that by twenty years.

Few writers have been so completely self-centered in their work. Llewelyn Powys' books—whatever their ostensible subjects— are made up of his life and his journeys (to Africa, to the United States, and in 1928 to Palestine) as reflected in himself. He has been called "the most polished and the most uneven of the three" celebrated brothers. His brother John, between whom and Llewelyn there was a devotion seldom seen between two grown brothers, said he was "a poetic materialist, with an unconquerable zest for life on any terms [and with] an ingrained prejudice toward anything supernatural, mystical, or metaphysical." Paul Rosenfeld called him "an epicure of nature."

In appearance he strongly resembled his brothers, though fairer in coloring than is John Cowper Powys. During his invalid periods he wore a beard, but at other times was clean-shaven. In spite of his aggressive atheism he shared all the family superstitions; a California acquaintance once saw both brothers hastily, and more than half-seriously, cross themselves when they met a crazy old woman who might be presumed to be a witch! None of the Powyses was ever cut to mold, and Llewelyn perhaps less than any of them.

PRINCIPAL WORKS: Confessions of Two Brothers (with J. C. Powys) 1916; Thirteen Worthies, 1923; Black Laughter, 1924; Ebony and Ivory, 1925; Skin for Skin, 1925; The Verdict of Bridlegoose, 1926; Henry Hudson, 1927; The Cradle of God, 1929; The Pathetic Fallacy (in America: An Hour on Christianity) 1930; Apples Be Ripe (novel) 1930; A Pagan's Pilgrimage, 1931; Impassioned Clay, 1931; Now That the Gods Are Dead, 1932; Glory of Life, 1934; Earth Memories, 1934; Damnable Opinions, 1935; Dorset Essays, 1935; The Twelve Months, 1936; Rats in the Sacristy, 1937; Somerset Essays, 1937; Love and Death (novel) 1939; Baker's Dozen, 1940.

ABOUT: Powys, L. Confessions of Two Brothers, Skin for Skin, The Verdict of Bridlegoose; Ward, H. R. The Powys Brothers; Wilkinson, L. U. Welsh Ambassadors; Catholic World April 1937; Century Magazine September 1925; Dial February 1925; Englische Studien No. 3, 1935; Forum August 1939; Literary Guide January, February 1940; Rationalist Annual 1940; Saturday Review of Literature June 4, 1934, May 28, 1938; December 16, 1939; Sewanee Review October 1934, January 1938; Wilson Library Bulletin January 1940.

*POWYS, THEODORE FRANCIS

(1875-   ), English novelist who writes as T. F. Powys, is the brother of John Cowper and

Llewelyn Powys[qqv] and the son of the Rev. Charles Francis Powys and Mary Cowper (Johnson) Powys. He was born at Shirley, Dorsetshire, and was educated at private schools, the last being the Dorchester Grammar School. He did not, like his brothers, attend a university. In the early 1900's he settled in the village of East Chaldon, Dorsetshire, and for many years has never gone farther from it than he can walk. Now he is a semi-invalid and is still further bound to the village of which he has made a fictional world.

In 1905 he married Violet Rosalie Bodds, and they have two sons. They also adopted a daughter. His life has been almost without external incident. Possessed, like his brothers, of a very small private income, he became a writer very early, but it was many years before any of his work was published, with the exception of a privately printed religious book. (He is the most religious of the three brothers, though far from orthodox.) His brothers had made numerous attempts to interest publishers in his strange stories, but without success. Then a neighbor, Stephen Tomlin, a sculptor, persuaded

David Garnett to read some of Mr. Powys's manuscripts, and the result was the publication of The Left Leg, soon followed by other volumes. Very few of his books have sold well, however, and he has been poor for most of his life. His life has been simple and monotonous, largely by his own desire; he likes to do the same things at the same hour every day, to make no break in his routine. Gardening is his chief preoccupation when he is not writing; writing he does not consider work, but a sort of self-indulgence. When his children were small he was their devoted nurse and caretaker. He is utterly unlike the sort of person one might visualize from his novels, which are so full of humor at once grotesque and earthy—the kind of grim humor which casts a tragic shadow. He is, as a writer, an original, in every sense of that word. His brother John regards him as the most gifted of the family, "super-sophisticated, elusive, provocative, bewildering," with a humor that has "a deep, sweet-bitter subterranean malice in it."

J. B. Chapman described T. F. Powys: "In appearance he is tall and broad-shouldered; his features are strong and clean-cut; his lofty forehead is surmounted by a shock of grizzled hair, and from beneath beetling brows his eyes peer out with the steady, questioning gaze of the seeker. There is humor, too, in that face, for though the mouth closes like a trap, an upper lip of almost Irish length and an occasional twinkle from those searching blue eyes tend to mitigate the sternness of the other features."

By tradition and by nature T. F. Powys is a religious man. He says that he "believes a great deal too much in God." His early work was written in a strangely archaic style which yet was completely natural to him, since he used it in speech and in letters as well as in his books. His later novels have much more simplicity. All the novels share a curious mingling of unrelenting realism with an almost mediumistic approach to nature. They may with justice be called gross, gloomy, sordid, psychopathic, hilarious, yet not one of these words comprehends them. Their flavor is unmistakable; they are like no other novels by any other hand. With T. F. Powys the microcosm of the village becomes the macrocosm of earth—a doomed and malice-ridden earth. He writes like a man who should become an ant and describe to the ants what they themselves are like.

PRINCIPAL WORKS: An Interpretation of Genesis 1908; The Soliloquy of a Hermit, 1916; The Left Leg (novelettes) 1923; Black Bryony, 1923; Mark Only, 1924; Mr. Tasker's Gods, 1925;

* Died November 27, 1953.

Mockery Gap, 1925; Innocent Birds, 1926; A Stubborn Tree, 1926; Feed My Swine, 1926; A Strong Girl (novelettes) 1926; The Rival Pastors, 1927; Mr. Weston's Good Wine, 1927; What Lack I Yet? 1927; The House With the Echo, 1928; The Dewpond, 1928; Fables, 1929; The Key of the Field, 1930; Kindness in a Corner, 1930; The White Paternoster (short stories) 1930; Uncle Dottery, 1930; The Only Penitent, 1931; Unclay, 1931; When Thou Wast Naked, 1931; The Two Thieves (novelettes) 1932; The Tithe Barn (novelettes) 1932; Captain Patch, 1935; Make Thyself Many, 1935; Goat Green, 1937.

ABOUT: Ward, H. R. The Powys Brothers; Wilkinson, L. U. Welsh Ambassadors; Bookman (London) March 1928, January, February, August 1933; Century Magazine September 1925; Englische Studien No. 3, 1935; Revue Politique et Littéraire September 3, 1927; Sewanee Review January 1938.

PRAED, Mrs. ROSA CAROLINE (MURRAY-PRIOR) (March 27, 1851-April 13, 1935), Anglo-Australian novelist

who wrote as Mrs. Campbell Praed, was born in Queensland, Australia, the eldest daughter of Thomas Lodge Murray-Prior, for many years Postmaster-General of Queensland. The girl "had an inquiring mind that ran riot in

J. M. Jopling

the Bush, without any educational opportunities save those provided by Nature and a number of bookcases filled with miscellaneous literature." For intellectual adventure she spent hours in the Ladies' Gallery of the House of Legislators, listening to long debates. This preliminary experience proved invaluable when Justin McCarthy, author of History of Our Own Times, who had been attracted by her novel Nadine (1882), asked her to collaborate with him on three novels of English political life, published 1887-1889. In 1886 Mrs. Praed—she was married at twenty-one to Campbell Mackworth Praed—and her husband were in the United States with McCarthy, who was on a lecture tour. They left him after a few weeks to stay with the Cyrus Field family and visit Niagara, Boston, Salem (including the House of the Seven Gables), and Washington.

Mrs. Praed called this association with McCarthy "one of those rare literary friendships between a man and a woman which are deeper and of more satisfaction than companionship of any other kind." McCarthy enabled her to study the activities of the House of Commons; this first-hand observation made The Ladies' Gallery and The Right-Honourable both successes. The Rebel

Rose at first appeared anonymously, later as The Rival Princess, by Justin McCarthy and Mrs. Praed. To write these novels, she lived at Chester House near Wellingborough in Northamptonshire.

Mrs. Praed died at eighty-four in Torquay, retaining her stately English beauty until late in life. The New International Encyclopedia says of her Australian novels that in their "stern and pessimistic outlook they resemble the work of Hall Caine, Mrs. Dudeney, and Thomas Hardy." They deal largely with the political and social life of well-to-do colonials.

PRINCIPAL WORKS: An Australian Heroine, 1880; Policy and Passion, 1881; Nadine, 1882; Affinities, 1885; The Head Station, 1885; The Romance of a Station, 1889; December Roses, 1893; Outlaw and Lawmaker, 1893; Christina Chard, 1894; The Scourge-Stick, 1898; As a Watch in the Night, 1900; Fugitive Anne, 1903; Nyria, 1904; The Maid of the River, 1905; By Their Fruits, 1908; Lady Bridget in the Never-Never Land, 1915.

ABOUT: Miller, E. M. Australian Literature From Its Beginnings to 1935; Praed, R. C. (ed.). Our Book of Memories: Letters of Justin McCarthy to Mrs. Campbell Praed; Praed, R. C. My Australian Girlhood; New York Times April 14, 1935.

"PREEDY, GEORGE." See LONG, G. M. V. C.

PRÉVOST, MARCEL (May 1, 1862-April 8, 1941), French novelist and playwright, was born in Paris, where his parents hap-

pened to be stopping at the time. His father was in the excise department of the French civil service, and soon afterwards became a subdirector at Tonneins, a large town of Lot-et-Garonne. The white roads and dusty houses of Gascony

impressed themselves on the future writer's mind.

Young Prévost was educated at a pension in Bordeaux, and at the Collège Saint-Joseph de Tivoli, directed by Jesuits, whose favorite pupil he became. He went with honors to the École Sainte-Geneviève which figures as "L'École de la rue des Postes" in his novel, Scorpion. After graduating from the École Polytechnique in Paris, he worked as a civil engineer in the state tobacco manufacturing industry. Prévost took kindly to the discipline of the various schools he attended, according to one of his biographers,

Jules Bertaut; he also found good mental exercise in the study of logarithms. Bertaut finds reflections of his religious training in Prévost's literary style and the easy flexibility of his thought. In the hours spared from his work Prévost wrote a novel, *Conscrard Chambergeot*, published in *Clairon* under the pseudonym "Schlem." *Le Scorpion*, written in 1884-86, was published serially in 1887 in *Le Matin*. In 1889 Figaro printed *Mademoiselle Jaufre*, which was praised by Jules Lemaître, and in 1891 *La Confession d'un Amant* had a large sale. *Les Demi-Vierges* (1894), which suggested that the education and social customs of Paris in those days left women intellectually somewhat less than virtuous, had a tremendous vogue, although some critics said that M. Prévost had exaggerated the picture to a revolting degree. A dramatization of the book was produced at the Gymnase May 23, 1895, and Prévost now devoted his entire time to literature, almost exclusively to writing stories about women.

Léon Lemonnier called Prévost the most representative romancer of his generation, a practitioner of *"le roman pur, le roman pour le roman."* Winifred Stephens once called him the most essentially French of contemporary French writers. "Only English readers thoroughly conversant with the inevitable trend of the Latin temperament will escape being shocked by many of his novels. Prévost is not merely French, he is French eighteenth-century." He called himself a disciple of George Sand and Alexandre Dumas *fils*.

Prévost covered Captain Alfred Dreyfus' second court-martial, at Rennes in 1899, for the Paris edition of the New York *Herald*, believing, with Émile Zola, in Dreyfus' innocence. He was elected to the French Academy in 1909, and in the First World War received the Croix de Guerre and was made a commander of the Legion of Honor. After the war he founded a literary periodical, *La Revue de France*. His post-war novels included *Mon Cher Tommy, Sa Maîtresse et Moi, La Retraite Ardente*, and *L'Homme Vierge*. Prévost died at seventy-eight at his home, Château de la Roche, near Vianne, Lot-et-Garonne. Mme. Prévost was a Mlle. de Servoules.

Works Available in English Translation: The Demi-Virgins, 1895; Letters From Women, 1897; The Novel in the Nineteenth Century, 1900; Simply Women, 1910; Guardian Angels, 1913; Benoit Castain, 1916; The Don Juanes, 1924; His Mistress and I, 1927; The Virgin Man (U.S. title: Restless Sands) 1930; Her Master, 1931.

About: Bertaut, J. Marcel Prévost; Brisson, A. Marcel Prévost; Stephens, W. French Novelists of To-day; La Grande Revue March 1926; New York Times April 10, 1941.

PRICHARD, HESKETH VERNON HESKETH (November 17, 1876-June 14, 1922), English novelist and sportsman, was born in Jhansi, India, the posthumous son and namesake of an officer in the King's Own Scottish Borderers, who had died of typhoid six weeks before the birth of his son. His widow was Kate Ryall, daughter of General B. W. Ryall, commander of the 8th Bengal Cavalry, whom he had married at Peshawar.

On February 14, 1877, Mrs. Prichard and her infant son sailed from Bombay for England, the first of many journeys made together by mother and son, who also collaborated in later years on several works of popular fiction. (Their first book, *Tammers' Duel*, was published in 1898 under the joint pseudonym of "E. and H. Heron," disproving the claim of Albert Payson Terhune that *Dr. Dale*, a novel written with his mother, "Marion Harland," and published in 1900, was the first instance of such a mother-and-son collaboration.)

The infant Hesketh Prichard was attracted at the age of three by the caribou in the Zoological Gardens in Regent's Park; later he was to hunt them in Labrador. In 1881 the Prichards went to live in the Isle of Jersey. The Duke of Cambridge, Queen Victoria's eccentric uncle, at first refused to allow the son of a junior officer a Queen's Scholarship at Wellington; by the time he had changed his mind Hesketh had won a Foundation Scholarship at Fettes School in Scotland, in September 1887. Prichard stayed at Fettes seven years, leaving in midsummer of 1894 to take a small house at Horsham and read law. He passed his preliminary examinations for the bar, but decided to become a writer instead. In August 1896 he sailed on the S.S. "Lisbon" to Portugal, Spain, and Tangier, obtaining local color for the very popular *Don Q* stories he was to write with his mother, this time under the signature "K. and Hesketh Prichard."

The first *Don Q* story appeared in the *Badminton Magazine*, January 1898, as "Don Quebranta Huesos." "From the outset the grim, hawklike *sequestrador,* merciless to the rich and the dishonorable, at one in heart with the knight and the gentleman, hideously cruel, benignly generous, gripped the fancy of the reading public," says Eric Parker. "Don Q took his seat side by side with Captain Kettle and Sherlock Holmes, and there he sits still." *Don Q* was successfully filmed by Douglas Fairbanks, Sr., and a dramatization by Fred Terry, who was unsuited to the rôle, was produced in London in 1921. *November Joe* (1913), written by Prichard alone, introduced a detective of the backwoods who traced clues that only a backwoodsman and hunter could fathom.

Prichard traveled through Haiti; conducted an expedition through Patagonia in search of the giant sloth, finding *Mylodon* extinct; and saved thousands of British lives in the First World War by teaching Tommies the art of sniping, in the face of the most determined opposition from diehards in the Foreign Office at home and G.H.Q. in France. He was, however, given his D.S.O. and Military Cross. The war wrecked his health, and he died at forty-five after fourteen operations for disorders caused by an obscure disease of the blood. Four days after his death at Gorhambury, Prichard's ashes were buried in Grimston Vault, churchyard of St. Michael's, St. Albans. He was survived by his wife, Lady Elizabeth Grimston, fourth daughter of the Earl of Verulam, whom he married in 1908, and two children, Michael and Diana. "Hex" Prichard was a golden-haired, gray-eyed giant of six feet four inches, with a resonant voice.

PRINCIPAL WORKS: Through the Heart of Patagonia, 1902; Hunting Camps in Wood and Wilderness, 1910; Black Rules White, 1910; Trackless Labrador, 1911; November Joe: The Detective of the Woods, 1913; Sniping in France, 1920; Sport in Wildest Britain, 1921. *With K. Prichard*—Tammers' Duel 1898; Karadac, Count of Gersay: A Romance, 1901; A Modern Mercenary, 1902; Roving Hearts, 1903; Chronicles of Don Q, 1904; New Chronicles of Don Q, 1906; Don Q's Love Story, 1909; The Cahusac Mystery, 1912.

ABOUT: Parker, E. Hesketh Prichard . . . : A Memoir; Nation and Athenaeum June 24, 1922.

PRIESTLEY, JOHN BOYNTON

(1894-), English novelist, essayist, and dramatist, writes: "Born 1894, Bradford, Yorkshire, the son of a schoolmaster, Jonathan Priestley. Served in the infantry, 1914-1919, then went to Trinity Hall, Cambridge, where I took honors in English literature, modern history, and political science. I had been writing steadily and contributing articles, etc., to London and provincial papers ever since I was sixteen.

Helped to keep myself at Cambridge by writing. Came to London in 1922 and very quickly established myself as a reviewer, critic, and essayist, doing a great deal of periodical work and publishing two or three books a year. These included two volumes in the English Men of Letters series, on Meredith and Peacock, a short history of the English novel, and *The English Comic Characters,* and several books of essays. In 1929 I helped to popularize the long novel by publishing *The Good Companions,* which had an enormous success both in England and America, and was followed by the almost equally successful *Angel Pavement.* These have been followed by other novels, and perhaps more notably by books that combine personal history  with social criticism, such as *English Journey, Midnight on the Desert,* and its sequel, *Rain Upon Godshill.*

"In 1932 I began a new career as a dramatist with *Dangerous Corner,* which has since been played all over the world. Since then I have run my own producing company and have been a director of two London theatres, and have produced sixteen plays, of which the most important are *Eden End, Cornelius, Time and the Conways, I Have Been Here Before, Johnson Over Jordan,* and *Music at Night,* although the comedies, like *Laburnum Grove* and *When We Are Married,* have had the longest runs. Plays of mine have been performed in twelve different languages. In the autumn season of 1937 I had three new plays running at once in London, a record since the First World War. In November 1938, at less than twenty-four hours' notice, I took over the leading part in my own comedy, *When We Are Married.*

"I have traveled extensively, especially in the United States, where I had a successful lecture tour in 1937. I have spent two winters with my family in Arizona, and am very fond of the Southwest. Have done film work both in Hollywood and in England, but prefer working for the theatre.

"I have recently aroused much discussion in England with a series of weekly articles in the London *News-Chronicle.* My political sympathies are strongly left, but I am definitely anti-Marxist and much dislike the materialism of official Communist philosophy. I have been much influenced by the new theories of time of J. W. Dunne's *Experiment With Time* and *Serial Universe,* and am strongly opposed to mechanistic views of the universe.

"I am still supposed by many Americans to dislike their country, chiefly because I freely criticize it, as indeed I do everything else, but actually I have a great affection for the United States and know far more about its life, history, and literature than most English authors do. I have a very charming wife and a large, cheerful family, an old house in Highgate Village, London, and another old house in the Isle of Wight; work very hard, serve on many committees, read in bed until the small hours, am very fond of music and various games, and smoke a pipe all day. Height five feet nine inches, weight about 200 pounds. Often considered too blunt, brusque, or downright 'difficult,' but actually am amiable and rather shy."

* * *

Mrs. Priestley confirms her husband's own estimate of his amiability, averring that "Jack" is not in the least temperamental. "If a meal's late it doesn't matter. And he doesn't swear if he loses a cuff-button. He's wonderful with the children. He'd spend all his time playing with them if I didn't make him work. He improvises music for their little plays and has a beautiful time with them."

Mr. Priestley's first wife was Pat Tempest, who died in 1925, leaving two daughters. He then married Mrs. Mary (Holland) Wyndham Lewis, and they have three more daughters and a son. He is a heavy-set, broad-shouldered, dark-haired man, with the brow and eyes of an artist but the aggressive mouth and chin of a fighter.

Priestley is unusual among the 1914-18 war generation in that his war experiences apparently touched him lightly; the three favorite themes of post-bellum authors, the war, sex, and religion, are all almost absent in his "long, hearty, sentimental novels." He detests being compared to Dickens; actually there is little resemblance, except that both wrote long novels crowded with characters; Priestley never burlesques as Dickens did— and neither, of course, has he the power over the emotions which Dickens had in his greatest moments. He is essentially a romantic, unafraid of coincidence. Ever since he wrote *English Journey* he has been terribly in earnest over the plight of the permanently unemployed in England's "depressed area." Dorothea Lawrance Mann called him "English of the old tradition, . . . a fine and discerning critic, . . . an amazing accurate

observer." He has lately become a thorough convert to the time-theories of J. W. Dunne, and has based several plays (unsuccessful in America) on them; some hint of them even creeps into his novel, *Let the People Sing,* which otherwise harks back to the *genre* of *The Good Companions* and *Angel Pavement.*

Recently Priestley's wartime broadcasts have attracted a great popular audience in England, and he has been called the unofficial voice of the common people of Britain.

PRINCIPAL WORKS: *Novels*—Adam in Moonshine, 1927; The Old Dark House (in England: Benighted) 1927; The Good Companions, 1929; Angel Pavement, 1930; The Town Major of Mirancourt, 1930; Faraway, 1932; Wonder Hero, 1933; They Walk in the City, 1936; The Doomsday Men, 1938; Let the People Sing, 1940. *Plays*—Laburnum Grove, 1933; The Roundabout, 1933; Three Plays and a Preface (Dangerous Corner, Eden End, Cornelius) 1935; Duet in Floodlight, 1935; Bees in the Boat Deck, 1936; Spring Tide (with George Billam) 1936; Mystery at Greenfingers, 1937; People at Sea, 1937; Time and the Conways, 1937; I Have Been Here Before, 1938; When We Are Married, 1938; Johnson Over Jordan, 1939. *Essays and Miscellaneous Prose*—Brief Diversions, 1922; Papers from Lilliput, 1922; I For One, 1923; Figures in Modern Literature, 1924; The English Comic Characters, 1925; Essayists Past and Present, 1925; Fools and Philosophers, 1925; George Meredith, 1926; Talking, 1926; Open House, 1927; Thomas Love Peacock, 1927; Too Many People, 1928; Apes and Angels, 1928; The English Novel, 1928; English Humor, 1928; The Balconinny and Other Essays, 1929; Self-Selected Essays, 1932; Four-in-Hand (essays and fiction) 1934; English Journey, 1934; The Beauty of Britain, 1935; Midnight on the Desert, 1937; Rain Upon Godshill, 1939; Britain Speaks, 1940; Postscripts, 1940; Out of the People, 1941.

ABOUT: Bookman May 1931; Bookman (London) September 1930; Forum May 1940; Hibbert Journal January 1939; London Mercury July 1932; Queen's Quarterly February 1941; Saturday Review of Literature March 7, 1931.

PRINGLE, HENRY FOWLES (August 23, 1897-   ), American journalist and biographer, winner of the Pulitzer Prize, was born in New York City, the son of James Maxwell Pringle and Marie (Juergens) Pringle. His father was a Charlestonian who left South Carolina as a young man with the idea of making money in the North, and became a pharmacist in New York City. Here he met his wife, who was born in the northern part of Germany and came to the United States at seventeen. New York, according to Henry Pringle, "is one of the worst possible places to live. I remain

Price

because editors seem to prefer it and because I am dependent on editors." He entered Cornell with vague thoughts of a newspaper career, worked on the local paper, and eventually graduated with the class of 1920, "having fought the Battle of Virginia in the First World War. I hated the army on the whole and probably would have been even more wretched overseas"—but he did not get across. In the summer before the war Pringle had worked on the *Evening Sun* in New York, and after graduation he returned to it for two years. In 1922 he went to the *Globe* until it was expunged by Frank Munsey, when he "fled to the *World*" in 1924, staying until 1927. He also contributed two short stories to magazines. Meeting the late Ivy Lee, press agent for the Rockefellers, Pringle made Lee the subject of a candid article, "His Masters' Voice," which appeared in the *American Mercury*, "and so my career of what has been termed muckraking began." Judge Gary, Jimmy Walker, and Judge Landis were other subjects of what Pringle calls "impartial and objective personality sketches." "The persons about whom I write prefer to call them 'libelous, untrue, wanton, inaccurate and mischievous.'" The sketches were collected in the volume entitled *Big Frogs* (1928), and proved to be preliminary exercises for more substantial biography. *Alfred E. Smith: A Critical Study*, published the year before, was something of a campaign document. *Theodore Roosevelt: A Biography* (1931) won the Pulitzer Prize for biography. Claude M. Fuess called it "a critical and often none too sympathetic estimate, affected at times by an irresistible temptation to irony, but nevertheless held closely to truth." *The Life and Times of William Howard Taft* (1939) in two volumes, was a logical sequel that, contrary to general expectation, did not win the Pulitzer Prize. A slim man, rather dogged in expression, and with thinning hair, Mr. Pringle was married to Helena Huntington Smith, a journalist and novelist (whom he calls "a mean and nasty critic") in 1926. The Pringles have two sons and a daughter, and live in New York City. He is a Democrat, a Presbyterian, and a member of the Century Club in New York.

PRINCIPAL WORKS: Alfred E. Smith: A Critical Study, 1927; Big Frogs, 1928; (with M. Holland) Industrial Explorers, 1928; Theodore Roosevelt: A Biography, 1931; The Life and Times of William Howard Taft, 1939.

ABOUT: Saturday Review of Literature October 28, 1939; Wilson Library Bulletin December 1928.

*PRIOR, JAMES (1851-   ), English novelist, was born in Nottingham, where his father was a tradesman, although country born and bred. The elder Prior had a lingering love of the country, was a serious reader, a strict moralist and disciplinarian, and, so his son wrote later, "had a gravely exact way of expressing himself with a pen." Young Prior was forbidden  to read novels, but George Borrow's *Bible in Spain* was admitted by virtue of its title (hence, perhaps, the gipsy maid, Ivy Sivil, of Prior's *Ripple and Flood*, who suggests the Romany Rye's Isopel). At fifteen Prior was introduced to Scott and Dickens, the latter of whom he admired so much he could not speak about him dispassionately. Of slight physique, young Prior was active nevertheless in field sports and made a brilliant record at school. Articled to a local solicitor, he preferred to read Lamb, Marlowe, and Shakespeare, producing a blank verse tragedy, *Don Pedro the Cruel*, in 1882. One copy was sold. *Ripple and Flood* (1897) a story of Trent River, was more cordially received, and *Forest Folk* went through two printings. One critic predicted that Prior would accomplish for Nottinghamshire what Blackmore had done for Devonshire and Hardy for Essex. John Buchan declared that Prior's peasants were quite as good as Hardy's, and particularly approved of *Fortuna Chance* (1910), a tale of the Jacobite uprising with wanderings and mishaps quite in the Buchan vein of a few years later. The culminating pages showed the hero, Roland, and wild Highlanders fleeing across the hills and moors of Derbyshire, separated from Prince Charlie's retreating army. Prior, a deliberate writer, was a conscientious one, and would travel miles afoot to verify a passage of local color.

A photograph taken in 1917 showed a thin ascetic face, with a high forehead, flowing locks, drooping moustache and chin beard. Never a publicized author, he has dropped completely from sight in recent years. From the date of his birth it seems unlikely that he is still alive, though his death has not been reported in any of the usual sources.

PRINCIPAL WORKS: Ripple and Flood, 1897; The Forest Folk, 1901; Hyssop, 1904; Fortuna Chance, 1910.

ABOUT: Bookman (London) November 1917.

* Pseud. of James Prior Kirk; died in 1922.   **1131**

PROKOSCH, FREDERIC (May 17, 1908-), American poet and novelist, was born in Madison, Wis. His father, Edouard

Prokosch, was a renowned scholar, and until his death, in 1938, was Sterling Professor of Linguistics at Yale. His mother is a noted pianist. He was educated as a child in Texas, Austria, Germany, and France, received his B.A. degree at Haverford College, and did graduate work at the University of Pennsylvania, Yale (Ph.D. 1933), and Cambridge University, England. He is unmarried. He received the Harper Prize in 1937 for *The Seven Who Fled,* and was a Guggenheim Fellow in 1938; in 1941 he was awarded the Harriet Monroe Lyric Prize by *Poetry.* At the outbreak of the Second World War, Prokosch was living in Portugal, whence he returned to New York in 1941. He is a vigorously handsome man, with aggressive nose and chin and dark determined eyes. He has always been athletic; in 1939 he was squash racquets champion of France, and he says he is "passionately interested in anything that involves racquet and ball, water, or snow."

His chosen authors he gives as Chaucer (on whom he is an authority), Cervantes, Swift, Molière, Racine, Montaigne, Hölderlin, Yeats, Stendhal, and Whitman, and, among contemporaries, T. S. Eliot, François Mauriac, F. Garcia Lorca, E. M. Forster, and Thomas Mann. But, he says, his tastes vary from year to year, so that perhaps it is a mistake to list them.

Of his political views he writes to the compilers of this volume: "More and more I feel that it is folly for authors (*i.e.,* novelists and poets) to announce loudly their political convictions. The Left Wing has made a fool of itself, in my opinion. No one now can avoid having political opinions, but now if ever they should be flexible, untheoretical, and open-minded. Politics has done American writing vast harm during the past decade: has made it dull, clumsy, arrogant, and much of it monotonous.

"I have no literary comments, really, except one: that what is necessary for a writer nowadays above all things is: courage. Courage to resist the lure of success and money and publicity, courage to face failure, courage to resist cliques, courage to despise fash-

ions and fads, courage to resist disasters of a financial, spiritual, social, sexual, political nature, and of course courage to face his own virtues and limitations with unfailing honesty. All these are more difficult today than ever."

His novels have been translated into twelve languages, his stories have been included in the O'Brien collection (1937) and in *The English Novelists* (1936), and his poems are in many anthologies. His novels have a breadth of canvas and an inclusiveness which is more characteristic of European than American work, and many of his readers have not realized that he is an American. His work is powerful and gloomy; in it, as Samuel French Morse says, is "the recurring theme of imminent disaster, of darkness, of the disintegration of society, . . . the horror of aimless destruction, the final flooding-over of decay." Actually these words were written not of his prose, but of his verse, but they are equally applicable to both. The heightened mood of poetry, however, makes of him a realistic novelist but essentially a romantic poet. Technically his verse is of the "modern" school, though he dissociates himself from inclusion in any group. In his work as in his life he is in revolt against "dogmatic, prejudiced, provincial, or misinformed judgments, literary or personal."

PRINCIPAL WORKS: *Novels*—The Asiatics, 1935; The Seven Who Fled, 1937; Night of the Poor, 1939; The Skies of Europe, 1941. *Poems*—The Assassin, 1936; The Carnival, 1938; Death at Sea, 1940. *Miscellaneous*—The Chaucerian Apocrypha, 1933.

ABOUT: Poetry March 1937, November 1938; February 1941; Publishers' Weekly July 31, 1937; Wilson Library Bulletin May 1936.

PROTHERO, Sir GEORGE WALTER (October 14, 1848-July 10, 1922), biographer and historian, was born in Wiltshire, where his father was a clergyman (a canon). He was educated at Eton, King's College, Cambridge, and the University of Bonn. He then returned to King's College as a fellow, later becoming an assistant master and a university extension lectur-

er. From 1876 to 1894 he was University lecturer in history at King's College, and from 1894 to 1899 professor of history at the University of Edinburgh. He was president of the Royal Historical Society from 1901 to

1905, Reed lecturer at Cambridge in 1903, and gave a course of lectures at Harvard and at Johns Hopkins in 1910. He was a governor of Holloway College in 1916. In 1918 and 1919 he was director of the History Section of the Foreign Office; in this capacity he was present at the Versailles Peace Treaty Conference. He was the recipient of many degrees and honors, and was made a Knight of the British Empire in 1920. In 1882 he had married Mary Frances Butcher, daughter of the Bishop of Meath.

Prothero was editor of the Cambridge Historical Series, co-editor of the *Cambridge Modern History,* and a contributor to the *Encyclopædia Britannica* and the *Dictionary of National Biography.* For many years he was editor of the *Quarterly Review.*

PRINCIPAL WORKS: Life and Times of Simon de Montfort, 1877; Memoir of Henry Bradshaw, 1889; A British History Reader, 1898; School History of Great Britain and Ireland, 1912; German Policy Before the War, 1916.

ABOUT: London Times July 12, 13, and 18, 1922.

PROTHERO, ROWLAND EDMUND. See ERNLE

PROUST, MARCEL (July 10, 1871-November 18, 1922), French novelist, was born in Auteuil, a suburb of Paris, only a few

weeks after the bombardment of Paris by German and Versailles troops, and the bloody suppression of the Commune. During the upheaval, his father, the physician Adrien Proust, was wounded by a stray bullet while visiting a patient. These trying days through which his mother passed just before his birth undoubtedly left their mark on the newborn child's constitution. Marcel's mother, Jeanne Weil, a highly cultured, sensitive and extremely beautiful Jewish woman, lavished her affection on the weakly child; her other son, Robert, two years younger than Marcel, was a strong healthy boy requiring little attention. At the age of nine Marcel suffered a violent attack of suffocation on returning from a walk in the Bois de Boulogne, and he remained a semi-invalid for the rest of his life. His schooling therefore was quite irregular; the frail boy was usually to be seen in the Champs Élysées chattering incessantly, showering delicacies on elderly ladies and holding them spellbound with his charming manners.

During the spring and summer vacations he was often taken to Auteuil, then a veritable garden, a lovely rustic place. There at the home of his mother's uncle (Louis Weil) he came in direct contact with Jewish life and met the prototype of his Swann in the fascinating Charles Haas. When the Prousts did not visit Auteuil, they sometimes went to Illiers, near Chartres. At the home of his father's uncle, Jules Amiot, Marcel discovered two other characters, Mme. Amiot, the hypochrondriac "Aunt Léonie" of *Swann's Way,* and her indefatigable servant Ernestine Gallou ("Françoise"). Illiers, mingling with Auteuil in his imagination, resulted in the Combray of Marcel's fictional world (the name "Combray" derived from Combres, a neighboring town). It was here that he tasted provincial life and fell in love with nature: following Combray's wooded path with its gardens and ponds and ambling brooks he found "the Guermantes way," while on the other side stretched the open country with only one white road cutting across the plain and a distant steeple etched against the serene sky—"Swann's way." Marcel's happy days at Illiers came abruptly to an end when it was found that the hawthorns in bloom, those flowers he loved so dearly, brought on severe choking fits that racked and tortured his sickly frame. Henceforth his parents took him to the beach: to Cabourg or to Trouville, fashionable resorts on the Normandy coast. Marcel liked the sea and the *"jeunes filles en fleur"* who played on the beach discarding all the restraints imposed upon them by highly conventional *fin du siècle* France. Cabourg, especially, became Proust's center of attraction and from it he created the unforgettable Balbec of *Within a Budding Grove.*

However irregularly, Marcel did attend school. At the Lycée Condorcet his guiding influence was one of the teachers, Jallifier, who introduced him to Saint-Simon's *Memoirs,* whereupon the imaginative boy fell in love with the pomp and circumstance of seventeenth century France, and vowed to emulate the gifted Saint-Simon and become the chronicler of modern French "society," a difficult task, indeed, considering the exclusiveness of French aristocracy in the last decade of the nineteenth century and the fact that Proust was but a Jewish bourgeois.

Upon reaching his eighteenth birthday Proust was called up for military training and became attached to the 76th Infantry stationed at Orleans. Thanks to his family's connections he was exempted from strenuous duty and enjoyed frequent furloughs. While in the barracks, he concentrated on "the world of the army," and those long discussions in The Guermantes Way between the narrator and Robert de Saint-Loup are founded largely upon Proust's experiences in the army. When he returned home at the beginning of the 'nineties, Proust's father requested him to pursue a diplomatic career. But the young man objected, and as a compromise he registered at three institutions: at the Sorbonne, at the Law School, and at the École Libre des Sciences Politiques where one of his classmates was a certain Léon Blum. The educational experiment ended with Marcel failing his law course but manifesting deep interest in his philosophy and psychology courses at the Sorbonne. He evinced special fondness for the intuitionist method of Bergson, whose first work, Les Données Immédiates de la Conscience (1889), was widely discussed at the time. Proust's world outlook and method were profoundly influenced by Bergson, who, incidentally, married the novelist's cousin Mlle. Neuberger, with Proust as best man.

Marcel ended his academic career in 1892 on receiving his licencié from the Sorbonne. Thenceforth he concentrated on the one goal of "crashing" the mysterious, awesome world of the aristocracy. This he succeeded in doing, but only by gradual and slow degrees, especially after 1894 when the Dreyfus affair brought about a tightening of "higher circles." First Proust entered the smaller circles (generally bourgeois and intellectual). His school chum Jacques Bizet introduced him to his mother Mme. Straus, daughter of the composer Halévy, who had married Bizet, the famous creator of Carmen, and then the lawyer Émile Straus. Mme. Straus' salon members started their own magazine, Le Banquet (eight numbers were published, 1892-93), and here Proust published his earliest sketches and notes. A similar circle to which Proust attained was that of Mme. Arman de Caillavet, Anatole France's mistress. Thanks to the kind hostess, Anatole France was induced to write (or perhaps merely to sign) a preface to Les Plaisirs et les Jours (1896), a rather fragile collection of Proust's poems, sketches, "regrets," and "reveries" written, and some published, between 1892 and 1894. Fully epigraphed with quotations from Shakespeare, Thomas à Kempis, Emerson, and the Greek classics (in the original), and illustrated by the "society" painter Madeleine

Lemaire, this tour de force is remembered today perhaps because the preface observed in dead seriousness that there was something in Proust of "a depraved Bernardin de Saint-Pierre and a guileless Petronius." Les Plaisirs et les Jours was not Proust's literary début: a few months before he had published, also at his expense, a rather insipid brochure entitled Portraits de Peintres —with four piano-pieces by his friend Reynaldo Hahn. Both books were, if nothing else, a sound investment: they helped in making Proust's name known in certain circles and in opening difficult doors. Soon he was admitted to the salon of Princess Mathilde, daughter of Jerome Bonaparte, youngest brother of Napoleon I. Mathilde's "noble lineage" was less than a century old, albeit the aging dowager gloried in ceremonial and elaborate etiquette. Entranced, the young Proust often crouched at her feet and humbly kissed her toes. Soon gossips linked his name with hers, much to his delight.

More significant to his work, perhaps, was his admittance to the "atelier des roses" of Madeleine Lemaire, for at one of her smart parties of aristocrats and artists Proust met Robert de Montesquieu. This "blue-blooded" poet and snob—the infamous Baron Palamède de Charlus of Remembrance of Things Past—knew "everybody and everything about everybody," and, flattered by "little Marcel's" exaggerated humilities and proustifications, introduced him to the most exclusive salons: that of his beautiful cousin, Countess Greffulhe, of Princess Edmond de Polignac, of Princess de Wagram; and, equally important, he furnished the inquisitive novelist in the making with precious gossip and information. And so, after fourteen years (1892-1906), beginning with the Jewish bourgeois salons of Mme. Straus and Mme. de Caillavet, Marcel Proust had climbed to the loftiest aristocratic spheres. He had fought the inevitable duel (1897) when one of his disparaging articles in Le Journal offended the decadent novelist Jean Lorrain. He had participated in the artistic life of Paris: seen Puvis de Chavannes paint, heard Mounet-Sully recite poetry, and listened to Massenet and Saint-Saëns improvise at the piano. He had been tacitly accepted as the official reporter of the stodgy society sheet Le Figaro. He had traveled as far as Venice (1900), much to his disappointment. He had published several timely if ephemeral books. He had translated, after six years of more or less assiduous communion with the dictionary, Ruskin's

Bible of Amiens (1904) and *Sesame and Lilies* (1906).

In 1906 Marcel Proust decided to change the course of his existence. He was a very sick man, and extremely disillusioned with the petty. shallow, conceited society world which he had entered after so much anguish. At the age of thirty-five the bachelor socialite Marcel Proust became a recluse and devoted himself almost exclusively to writing. His father had died in 1903 and left him an independent income; his mother died two years later and with her his last and dearest link with the outside world. Proust drifted along for a while and then moved to a flat at 102 Boulevard Haussmann. Here he locked himself up in a corklined room and for seventeen years worked unceasingly until the very day of his death composing the most voluminous and one of the greatest of modern novels—*Remembrance of Things Past.* Only on very rare occasions did he leave that room and then generally after midnight, to examine his "models": to see whether the Prince de Sagan carried his monocle in the usual fashion, to ask Mme. de C— if she still had the hat she wore twenty years ago at such and such a *soirée,* to watch by the light of his taxi's headlights the hawthorns in bloom, peering out of tightly shut windows lest the springtime fragrance overcome him altogether. Proust could stand no smell. not even the scent of the chestnut trees along the Boulevard or the perfumed handkerchiefs of his visitors. Neither could he bear any noise. When staying at the Grand Hotel of his dear Cabourg, he had to rent several rooms surrounding his own, as well as the one above and the one below, in order to be able to sleep. He slept fully clothed, even to gloves.

Few people paid any attention to the eccentric social lion who lived in seclusion; and when, in 1911, he looked around for a publisher for the first 1500 pages of his book, neither Fasquelle nor Ollendorf, neither the *Mercure de France* nor the *Nouvelle Revue Française* would accept it. Tired of refusals and afraid of death, Proust paid the then little known publisher Bernard Grasset to print his work of seven years' labor. And so *Swann's Way* appeared in 1913. Only a few of his friends paid any attention to it. Before the appearance of the other two volumes of the proposed trilogy, war broke out, Grasset was called to the front, and Proust was left alone, a sick man in bed with a bundle of galley proofs in his hands and a few years of life ahead of him. Plunging into work, he added hundreds of pages

of endlessly detailed observations and psychological *minutiae.* The "trilogy" grew and grew. In 1919 the Editions de la Nouvelle Revue Française published the second volume of the series, *Within a Budding Grove.* This registered almost immediate success, winning for its author the Goncourt Prize. Proust was now in his forty-ninth year. He enjoyed his triumph and went out, late at night, to celebrate it with brilliant and costly receptions at the Ritz. But not for long. Proust was too sick a man and too serious a writer now. Back he came to his closed room, thick with the vapors of fumigation, to race with death, alternating his drugs: veronal in order to sleep, adrenalin and caffein in order to write.

In 1922, as he was proofreading *Cities of the Plain,* about halfway through his monumental work—and proofreading in his case meant rewriting, inserting, elongating— Proust fell ill with pneumonia. On November 18 he asked his servant to bring him a certain page wherein Bergotte is portrayed in the agony of death—because "I have several retouchings to make here, now that I find myself in the same predicament."

Marcel Proust began his *Remembrance of Things Past* in 1905, completed it in 1912 and enlarged upon it until 1922. During those seventeen years of assiduous labor the three-volume autobiographical account of a social climber developed into a seven-volume broad canvas of French society from 1870 to 1914. The revision meant a revaluation of social reality: the private affairs of individuals were not discarded, but to a certain extent they became subordinated to a new emphasis, to their illumination of the cyclical birth-growth-decay of social circles and the curious intermingling of aristocratic class (the Guermantes) with refined bourgeois intelligentsia class (the Swanns) with mediocre, nouveau-riche middle class (the Verdurins). As the analysis extended from individual to family and clan, it included resorts villages. towns (Balbec, Combray, Doncières), cities (Paris, Venice), and a nation—France. As Proust plumbed new depths, he sensed new dimensions. He telescoped the frivolous life of an epoch and the ramifications of its society, current sentiments, volitional expressions, dreams and nightmares, into a sustained epic. Proust depicted the gradual development of a hypersensitive child slowly becoming aware of himself and of the individuals around him, and as he followed the trajectory of the Swanns, of the Guermantes, of the Verdurins, as he suffered indescribable tortures at the hands of the Gilbertes and Albertines, he sensed the historical forces forming, transforming, and annihilating the upper strata of France.

WORKS AVAILABLE IN ENGLISH TRANSLATION: *"Remembrance of Things Past"*—Swann's Way, 1922; Within a Budding Grove, 1924; The Guermantes Way, 1925; Cities of the Plain, 1927; The Captive, 1929; The Sweet Cheat Gone, 1930; Times Regained, 1931 (published also in 1932, in another translation, as The Past Recaptured)—two-volume complete edition, 1941.

ABOUT: Abraham, P. Proust: Recherches sur la Création Intellectuelle; Aressy, L. Recherche de Marcel Proust; Beckett, S. Proust; Bell, C. Proust; Blondel, C. La Psychographie de Marcel Proust; Crémieux, B. Du Côté de Marcel Proust; Curtius, R. Marcel Proust; Dandieu, A. Marcel Proust: Sa Révélation Psychologique; Duffner, J. L'Oeuvre de Marcel Proust; Feuillerat, A. Comment Marcel Proust a Composé son Roman; Gabory, G. Essai sur Marcel Proust; Jacob, J. Marcel Proust; Kinds, E. Étude sur Marcel Proust; Mauriac, F. Proust; Monkhouse, E. La Révélation de Marcel Proust; Pierre-Quint, L. Marcel Proust: His Life and Work; Scott-Moncrieff, C. K. (ed.) Marcel Proust: An English Tribute; Spagnoli, J. J. The Social Attitude of Marcel Proust.

PROUTY, Mrs. OLIVE (HIGGINS)

(1882-), American novelist, writes: "I was born [Olive Higgins] in Worcester, Mass. Both my par-

ents were ardent church-supporters and church-goers. We were brought up to attend three church services on Sunday, and morning prayers were held daily. My father was head of the Mechanical Department of the Worcester Polytechnic Institute. I went to public schools until graduated from high school. I was unable to cover myself with any glory in the schoolyard athletic contests, with hardly more in the schoolroom, composition being the only subject in which I could even equal my competitors. I consoled myself as best I could with the thought that budding poets and authors were frequently poor athletes and worse mathematicians. This continued to be my constant consolation throughout my four years at Smith College, which institution was kind enough to graduate me with the degree of B.L.—a rare one indeed, and no longer obtainable.

"In 1907 I married Lewis Isaac Prouty, beginning my domestic career in Brookline, near Boston, where I still live. I have had a son and three daughters [two daughters deceased], and have published nine books,

Stella Dallas being the most widely known. My first publication was a series of short stories about one family which appeared from time to time first in *McClure's* and then in the *American Magazine*. A publisher suggested that I combine them into a book, and I drifted into writing my first novel. By my third one, I had acquired enough technique to attempt a novel without the preliminary short-story steps. My three latest are parts of a series about the Vales of Boston."

* * *

Mrs. Prouty, according to one interviewer, "considers her home her career, and her work her hobby." Among her other hobbies are animals—she "never gets enough of zoos and barnyards." *Stella Dallas* made a successful play and movie. Her work is entertaining and competently written, but heavily sentimental and moralistic.

PRINCIPAL WORKS: Bobbie, General Manager, 1913; The Fifth Wheel, 1916; The Star in the Window, 1918; Good Sports, 1919; Stella Dallas, 1922; Conflict, 1927; White Fawn, 1931; Lisa Vale, 1938; Now, Voyager, 1941.

ABOUT: American Magazine February 1938.

*PRYCE, RICHARD (1864-), English

novelist and playwright, was born in Boulogne, France, of English parents, his father a colonel from Mont-

gomeryshire, his mother the daughter of a general and the granddaughter of a lord. He was educated at Leamington School. Now in his late seventies, he has been a prolific novelist since 1889, and a playwright almost as long. Most of his plays, however, aside from the one-act ones, are either collaborations or dramatizations of novels. He has, for example, written the stage versions of Christopher Morley's *Thunder on the Left*, Arnold Bennett's *Helen With the High Hand*, and of several stories by Mary E. Mann. Even before the Second World War started, Mr. Pryce had gradually ceased to write, by reason of age, his most recent production being *Frolic Wind*, a play from a novel by R. Oke, in 1934. His best known play is the one-act *'Op-o'-Me-Thumb*.

Almost nothing has been revealed of Mr. Pryce's private life, except that he lives in London and is unmarried. In England he has been a very popular fiction writer of the romantic and rather sentimental sort, but he has never achieved much popularity on

* Died May 30, 1942.

this side of the Atlantic. His work has charm, but not much distinction, and is not likely to have any very great survival value. However, it is excellent escape literature, though most of his novels bear the impress of their time and by now are badly out-dated.

PRINCIPAL WORKS: The Ugly Story of Miss Wetherby, 1889; Just Impediment, 1890; Miss Maxwell's Affections, 1891; Deck-Chair Stories, 1891; Time and the Woman, 1892; Winifred Mount, 1894; The Burden of a Woman, 1895; An Evil Spirit, 1897; Elementary Jane, 1897; Jezebel, 1900; The Successor, 1904; Towing-Path Bess, 1907; Christopher, 1911; David Penstephen, 1915; The Statue in the Wood, 1918; Romance and Jane Weston, 1924; Morgan's Yard, 1932; Frolic Wind, 1935.

"PRYDE, ANTHONY" (1880-), English novelist, is an Englishwoman, Agnes Russell Weekes, who was born in Rochester.

She received the degree of Master of Arts from London University, and published her first novel, *Yarborough the Premier,* at twenty-four. *Faith Unfaithful* (1910) was the next, and in 1912 Miss Weekes collaborated with Rose Kirkpatrick Weekes (born in 1874, and probably her sister) on *The Tragic Prince,* the first of the many romances they were to write together. Their *A Fool in the Forest* (1928), like "Anthony Pryde's" *The Rowforest Plot* (1930) was praised for its "beautifully done descriptions of England and the English countryside." A reviewer of *The Secret Room* (1929) commented in *Books* that "Anthony Pryde shows steadily increasing control of his chosen medium, the popular romance of sentiment." The *Spectator* called it "a good novel in the Victorian manner." *The Story of Leland Gay* (1932) was called by the Boston *Transcript* "the most absorbing of all her stories," though "a trifle more cynical than the earlier ones." "It is chiefly in the atmosphere of a quiet English countryside that the charm of the book lies," according to the New York *Times.* "In spite of the murder, which never really bothers, it is a restful and not unpleasing story."

Anthony Pryde, besides writing her numerous romances, has collaborated with S. E. Goggin in editing *An Anthology of English Prose For Use in Schools and Colleges* (1915) and with G. E. Hollingworth on an edition of Keats' *Lamia, Isabella, The Eve of St. Agnes, and Selected Odes,* pub-

lished by the University Tutorial Press, London, in 1932. She lived, at last report, in Gaston Cottage, Slindon, Arundel, Sussex, and tells her American publishers little or nothing about her personal life.

PRINCIPAL WORKS: Yarborough the Premier: A Novel, 1904; Faith Unfaithful, 1910; The Tragic Prince, 1912; Margueray's Duel, 1920; Jenny Essenden, 1921; Nightfall, 1921; Ordeal of Honor, 1922; Clair de Lune, 1922; The Purple Pearl, 1923; City of Lilies, 1923; Spanish Sunlight, 1925; A Son of the House, 1926; The Rowforest Plot, 1927; A Fool in the Forest, 1928; White Hands Cannot Offend, 1929; The Lily and the Sword, 1929; Esmé's Sons, 1930; The Emerald Necklace, 1931; Upstairs, Downstairs, And—, 1932; The Story of Leland Gay, 1932; The Figure on the Terrace, 1933; Carolyn and Evelyn, 1939; Green Cross, 1940; A Brother for Richard, 1940; Cousin Clare, 1941.

ABOUT: The Author's and Writer's Who's Who 1934; Who's Who in Literature 1934.

*PUTNAM, HOWARD PHELPS (July 9, 1894-), American poet who signs his works Phelps Putnam, was born in Boston,

the son of Henry Putnam, journalist and editor. His grandfather, Samuel Phelps, was a writer on metaphysical subjects. Phelps Putnam was educated in the public schools, graduated from Phillips Exeter Academy at sixteen, and from Yale with the class of 1916. He was trained from boyhood in the anatomy of poetry, but, like most practicing poets, found it necessary to make a living. He worked in the copper mines of Arizona; as a government historian in Washington, D. C.; in the importing business in New York City; in a Connecticut foundry; and spent some time in his native Boston as editorial assistant on the *Atlantic Monthly.* In 1920 he had managed a year in Provence, France; and in 1930 was awarded a Guggenheim Fellowship which he did not use for some time. In August 1933 he went to Italy. By this time he had published two volumes of poetry, *Trinc* (1927) and *The Five Seasons* (1930). *Trinc,* which contains the work of a dozen years, is divided into two sections, "Green Wings," containing lyrical verse, and "Brandy," which creates a mythological framework. (*Trinc,* according to Rabelais' character Panurge, is a Panomphean word signifying Drink.) *The Five Seasons* is, according to Louis Untermeyer, a philosophical-narrative poem in which the central figure struggles to find a basis for action. Putnam's symbols, continues Untermeyer, "are archaic, but the expression is distinctly of the moment. His method is similarly contradictory, being alternately oblique and abruptly four-square. Thus his chief effect is achieved by esthetic shock, a device which Putnam frequently overdoes." His "The Ballad of a Strange Thing," one of the most interesting of contemporary ballads, and "Hasbrouck and the Rose" frequently figure in anthologies. William Rose Benét, including Putnam in his *Fifty Poets,* wrote that he "commands scathing satire and a hatred of all pomposity in his celebration of the natural man, fond of conviviality and comradeship, who can think for himself, be ravaged by disillusionment or burn for the eternal rose of beauty." Putnam's attitude springs in part, writes Allen Tate, from "the current romanticism of the 'hard-boiled,' the main feature of which is the worship of the crude, the barbaric, and the 'un-intellectual.'" Putnam has published nothing in recent years.

PRINCIPAL WORKS: Trinc, 1927; The Five Seasons, 1930.

ABOUT: Benét, W. R. Fifty Poets; Kreymborg, A. Our Singing Strength; Untermeyer, L. Modern American Poetry; Bookman March 1932; Poetry September 1932.

PUTNAM, Mrs. NINA (WILCOX) (November 28, 1888-), American novelist and short-story writer, writes at the outset of

her autobiography, *Laughing Through* (1930), that "I was found in a rosebush at the back of Grandma Wilcox's garden at Forty-Six York Square, New Haven, Connecticut, on November 28, 1884, and if you don't believe me see *Who's Who in America.*" The volume in question puts her birth-date at 1888, and Mrs. Putnam herself states in her book that she was nineteen "three weeks after my wedding to Bob Putnam" (in 1907).

Nina Wilcox was one of the daughters of Marrion Wilcox, an assistant instructor in English at Yale, who was allowed an income of $5,000 a year by his father, and Eleanor (Sanchez) Wilcox, a Spaniard from Puerto Rico. Wilcox went to England to take a course in literature at Oxford; his family joined him in England and remained there so long that Nina lamented "We're going home, and I can't speak one

word of American!" Her father worked for a time in Philadelphia as Sunday editor of the *Press,* a post obtained through the good offices of Henry Martyn Hoyt, with whose children, Nancy, Henry, and Elinor (later Elinor Wylie[qv]) Nina was expected to play, although she preferred the society of an Irish girl. Later Wilcox went to Harper & Bros., the publishers, and the family lived in New Rochelle, N.Y.

Nina learned to write by studying newspaper type, and was familiar with her father's library long before he found out that she could read. By that time she had read Haeckel's *Riddle of the Universe,* a *Demonology,* Dickens and Thackeray, Stanley Weyman's novels, Oscar Wilde's *Poems, Trilby,* and Balzac's *Contes Drôlatiques* in translation.

After her marriage to Robert Faulkner Putnam, Nina Wilcox Putnam compiled glossaries and made indexes for the publications of her husband's firm, G. P. Putnam's Sons, and even read manuscripts, discerning the virtues of Florence Barclay's *The Rosary* but rejecting Arnold Bennett's *The Old Wives' Tale!* She wrote and sold a short story for $75, and when she had amassed $700 persuaded her husband to leave his family's house and join her in an apartment on the corner of Fifth Avenue and Forty-Second Street in New York City. Putnam, a pacifist, refused to go to war. His wife joined the Motor Corps of America, and put her hard-earned experience into a story "Ladies Enlist," which the *Saturday Evening Post* accepted. She wrote it in slang, a method which "proved amazingly more adequate for the expressing of profound things without embarrassment" than the academic style which she was perfectly capable of employing. Newton D. Baker read and liked the stories about the wise-cracking "Marie La Tour," and persuaded Mrs. Putnam to go to Hollywood to produce some propaganda films.

Robert Putnam died of influenza in his wife's absence, in 1918, leaving her with a son, John Francis Putnam, and next year she married R. J. Sanderson of New Haven. Her third husband was Arthur James Ogle, married in 1931 and later divorced; and her present husband is Christian Eliot, whom she married in 1933. Mrs. Putnam has earned over a million dollars by her writing, and divides her time between Hollywood and "Journey's End," Delray Beach, Fla.

PRINCIPAL WORKS: In Search of Arcady, 1912; The Impossible Boy, 1913; The Little Missioner 1914; Orthodoxy, 1915; Adam's Garden, 1916; When the Highbrow Joined the Outfit, 1917;

Esmeralda, 1918; Sunny Bunny, 1918; Winkle Twinkle and Lollypops, 1918; Believe You Me, 1919; It Pays to Smile, 1920; West Broadway, 1921; Laughter, Ltd., 1922; Say It With Bricks, 1923; Easy, 1924; The Bear Who Went To War, 1928; The Making of an American Humorist, 1929; Laughing Through (autobiography) 1930; Paris Love, 1931; The Inner Voice, 1940.

ABOUT: Putnam, N. W. Laughing Through: Reader's Digest March 1941.

PUTNAM, PHELPS. See PUTNAM, H. P.

PYLE, HOWARD. See "AMERICAN AUTHORS: 1600-1900"

"QUEEN, ELLERY" is the pseudonym (as well as the chief fictional character) of Frederic Dannay and Manfred B. Lee,

Oggiano

American detective story collaborating team, who have also used the *nom de plume* of "Barnaby Ross." The two writers are cousins and both were born in Brooklyn, Dannay on October 20, 1905, Lee on January 11 of the same year. Lee attended New York University, where he had his own orchestra (he still plays the violin); Dannay did not attend college, but by the age of twenty-four was art director of a New York advertising agency. Lee, after college, wrote publicity and advertising for a motion picture company. Both seemed destined for conventional business careers when they chanced to read an announcement of a detective story prize contest. Somewhat as a lark they entered the contest, and to their considerable surprise won it;

Oggiano

only to see the magazine sponsoring the competition cease publication before their brain-child appeared in print. But a book publishing house became interested, and with the publication of *The Roman Hat Mystery* (1929), one of the most successful collaborations in contemporary American writing was launched.

For some years elaborate precautions were taken to conceal the identity of "Queen"—who appeared at autographing parties and literary teas wearing a black mask—and

likewise of "Barnaby Ross," the name under which the Messrs. Dannay and Lee created their second important sleuth, Drury Lane. At one time the cousins undertook a lecture tour, engaging in a series of joint debates as "Queen" and "Ross"; it is said that not even the lecture bureau management knew their dual-identity. But today both secrets are out, and the Drury Lane novels are currently being reissued under the Queen *nom.*

In the meantime Queen, the detective—whom the affable authors call The Great Man in private conversation—has come to be one of the two or three best known names in American "straight" detective fiction; and the highly competent, rigidly fair, and invariably entertaining stories with which he is associated have recently attracted the attention of new and vastly wider audiences through radio and the moving pictures. Needless to say, this has not been accomplished without the hardest sort of labor. The collaborating cousins meet daily to work together in a purposely barren business office on Fifth Avenue in New York City, with frequent "commuting" trips to Hollywood. Lee is married, has two daughters, lives in the city, and collects stamps. Dannay is also married, has two sons, and lives in suburban Great Neck, where he has one of the finest collections of short detective stories extant Late in 1940 he was severely injured in an automobile accident, but recovered and resumed work the following year.

Writing in the New York *Times,* Isaac Anderson echoed the considered judgment of seasoned detective story fans when he said, "As puzzle-makers, the two men who write under the name of Ellery Queen have few equals." And Vincent Starrett has called their stories "among the best of their time."

PRINCIPAL WORKS: *As "Ellery Queen"*— The Roman Hat Mystery, 1929; The French Powder Mystery, 1930; The Dutch Shoe Mystery, 1931; The Egyptian Cross Mystery, 1932; The Greek Coffin Mystery, 1932; The Siamese Twin Mystery, 1933; The Chinese Orange Mystery, 1934; The Adventures of Ellery Queen (short stories) 1934; Halfway House, 1936; The Door Between, 1937; The Four of Hearts, 1938; Challenge to the Reader: An Anthology, 1938; The Dragon's Teeth, 1939; The New Adventures of Ellery Queen, 1940; 101 Years' Entertainment: The Great Detective Stories, 1841-1941 (anthology) 1941; The Black Dog Mystery (juvenile) 1941; Calamity Town, 1942. *As "Barnaby Ross"*—The Tragedy of X, 1932; The Tragedy of Y, 1932; The Tragedy of Z, 1933; Drury Lane's Last Case, 1933.

ABOUT: Haycraft, H. Murder for Pleasure: The Life and Times of the Detective Story; Starrett, V. Books Alive; Thomson, H. D. Masters of Mystery; New Yorker March 16, 1940;

Newsweek June 26, 1939; Publishers' Weekly October 10, 1936; Saturday Review of Literature September 28, 1940.

QUENNELL, CHARLES HENRY BOURNE. See QUENNELL, M. C.

QUENNELL, Mrs. MARJORIE (COURTNEY) (1884-), English co-writer, with her late husband Charles Henry

Bourne Quennell (1872-1935), of the "Everyday Things" series of educational books, widely used in schools on both sides of the Atlantic, was born at Bromley Common, Kent, the daughter of Allen Courtney. After a private school education, she attended the Crystal Palace Art School, the Beckenham Technical Art School, and the Westminster Art School. In 1904 she married C. H. B. Quennell, later to become renowned as an architect and housing authority as well as author. They had one son, Peter Quennell,[qv] the poet and essayist, and a daughter, now living in America. Mrs. Quennell herself came to America in 1939 to study museums and education. The Quennells lived first at Bickley, Kent, then at Berkhamstead, Hertfordshire, until Mr. Quennell's death, since which time Mrs. Quennell has lived in London, where she is curator of the Geffrye Museum, Shoreditch. She is an Honorary Associate of the Royal Institute of British Architects. Painting is still her chief recreation, although she no longer considers it her profession and has not exhibited for many years.

The educational books which Mr. and Mrs. Quennell wrote together have been characterized by Nature magazine as "thorough and scholarly, showing a detailed acquaintance with archaeological data, judgment in selection and presentation of material both in text and illustration. . . . They have strongly stimulated interest in the cultural background of history." The History of Everyday Things in England, the most popular of the series, has sold more than 100,000 copies. All of the books are fascinating, not only to children, but to adults as well. They are among the best of works of "scholarly popularization."

Mr. Quennell was a fellow of the Royal Institute of British Architects and a member of its Council from 1912 to 1915. He was on the Town Planning Committee from 1914 to 1925, studied factory plants in the United States, and was responsible for a number of London housing plans. From 1928 to 1933 he was on the editorial board of Architectural Education. He died at the age of sixty-three.

PRINCIPAL WORKS: By Marjorie and C. H. B. Quennell—A History of Everyday Things in England (4 vol.) 1918-34; Everyday Life in Prehistoric Times, 1921; Everyday Life in the Old Stone Age, 1921; Everyday Life in the New Stone, Bronze, and Early Iron Ages, 1922; Everyday Life in Roman Britain, 1924; Everyday Life in Anglo-Saxon, Viking, and Norman Times, 1926; Everyday Things in Homeric Greece, 1929; Everyday Life in Archaic Greece, 1931; Everyday Life in Classical Greece, 1932; The Good New Days, 1935. By C. H. B. Quennell—The Cathedral Church of Norwich, 1900; Modern Suburban Houses, 1906. By Marjorie Quennell—London Craftsmen, 1940.

ABOUT: Kunitz, S. J. & Haycraft, H. (eds.) The Junior Book of Authors; Nature January 11, 1936; Publishers' Weekly December 28, 1935.

QUENNELL, PETER COURTNEY (March 9, 1905-), English biographer and critic, was born in London, the son of C.H.B. Quennell (died 1935) and Marjorie (Court-

ney) Quennell,[qv] writers and illustrators of children's books. He was educated at Berkhamsted Grammar School and Balliol College, Oxford (non-graduate), and entered a literary career in London immediately after leaving the university. At first he wrote poetry, then began doing critical essays for the New Statesman, Life and Letters, the Criterion, and other magazines. In 1930 he was appointed to the newly created chair of English literature at the Japanese government university, the Tokyo Bunrika Daigaku. A year later he resigned his post, returned to London, and, as he puts it, "reverted to authorship and literary criticism." He has been a free-lance writer and critic ever since. He visited the United States (chiefly New York) in 1938. He is married, his wife, Nancy Quennell, having done some writing also; she is the editor of a book on epicures. He is tall, slender, and fair in coloring. He is a cat-lover, something of a recluse—he hates literary gatherings and anything resembling bohemianism—and is not interested in sport. He is a slow worker, with the tastes and instincts of a scholar, and it is not surprising that he dislikes his own verse, remembers with distaste most of his translations from the French (of which the best known are the *Memoirs* of the Comte de Gramont and the letters of Princess Lieven to Metternich), and prefers of his own work his biographies and his one novel. He would like to write more novels, but his interest is not so much in subject-matter as in style. He is that rare thing among contemporary writers, a conscious stylist.

As a scholar, he has edited *Aspects of Seventeenth Century Verse* (1933,) and completed the editing of letters to Byron, left unfinished at her death by Emily Morse Symonds ("George Paston"). His most considerable achievement to date (he still undoubtedly has most of his work before him) has been his lives of Byron and of Queen Caroline, together with his critical volume on Baudelaire. Of these it may be said that they are thoroughly sound, beautifully written, but do not come alive. Of his poetry, Kenneth White wrote: "His poems have a certain majesty of effect, . . . not one of immediate tangibility, but rather of remote, intense contemplation of the pattern of emotions or objects." He is fond of traveling, but his journeys so far have produced only one book on Japan and China, and one article on New York. He has little liking for most of his literary colleagues, but reserves his admiration for two very disparate authors united only in that each is, in his individual manner, a consummate stylist—Virginia Woolf and Ernest Hemingway.

PRINCIPAL WORKS: Poems, 1926; Inscription on a Fountain Head (poetry) 1929; Baudelaire and the Symbolists, 1929; The Phoenix-Kind (novel) 1931; A Superficial Journey Through Tokyo and Peking, 1932; Letters to Mrs. Virginia Woolf, 1932; Sympathy and Other Stories, 1933; Byron: The Years of Fame, 1936; "To Lord Byron" (with "G. Paston") 1937; Victorian Panorama, 1937; Caroline of England: An Augustan Portrait, 1940; Byron in Italy, 1941.

ABOUT: Bookman October 1930.

QUICK, HERBERT (October 23, 1861-May 10, 1925), American novelist, was born on a farm in Grundy County, Iowa, near Steamboat Rock, the son of Martin and Margaret (Coleman) Quick, and was named John Herbert Quick. It was the second marriage of both his parents. On both sides he was of Holland Dutch descent. At twenty months he suffered from infantile paralysis, and in consequence his feet were permanently deformed. The only schooling he had was in meager country schools,

Apeda

and he was nineteen before he read any book except McGuffey's Readers and the Bible. In 1877 he secured a Teachers' Institute certificate, and until 1890 he was a teacher, his last position being as principal of a public school in Mason City, Iowa. Meanwhile he read law, and was admitted to the bar in 1889. The next year he married Ella Corey, and they had a son and a daughter.

From 1890 to 1908 Quick practiced law in Sioux City, at the same time being active in politics. He was mayor of the town from 1898 to 1900. From 1881, when he had first read Henry George's *Progress and Poverty,* he was a Single Taxer; but in spite of his advanced economic views he was accused, with some apparent justification, of irregularities in office. In 1908 and 1909 Quick was editor of *La Follette's Weekly Magazine,* and from 1909 to 1916 of *Farm and Fireside,* in Springfield, Ohio. He was then appointed to the Federal Loan Bureau in Washington, but resigned in 1919 because of ill health. His last public office was in charge of liquidating the affairs of the Red Cross in Vladivostok in 1920, an experience which finally wrecked his health. He moved to a farm near Berkeley Springs, W. Va., and planned to spend his remaining years quietly writing; but in 1925 he died suddenly of a heart attack at Columbia, Mo., where he had been lecturing at the University of Missouri.

Quick began very late as a writer; his first publication was a poem in the *Century Magazine* in 1901. Several times he determined to drop all other activities and devote all his energy to writing, but each time yielded to other demands on his time. His early novels were a compound of realism, didacticism, and melodrama. He did not find himself until he began to write about the past of Iowa, the place he knew best: and even then he never quite mastered the technique of novel. As Wallace Stegner said: "Less talented than Garland and cursed with less social conscience and burning zeal, he produced for almost twenty years a series of comparatively innocuous books, but he kept in his mind an ambition to write in serious and appreciative terms about his native state. . . . [*Vandemark's Folly* and *The Hawkeye*] gave Iowa a history. Quick's Iowa novels took Iowa a long stride out of the colonial wilderness." These two books, with his autobiography, constitute his permanent contribution to American literature. George H. Genzmer summed his best work up in saying: "He wrote sincerely out of his love of the soil, his pride in the character and achievements of the humble folk from whom he sprang, his passionate belief in democratic idealism."

A large, heavy-set man, almost bald, with the full mouth of the orator and keen eyes under a high forehead, he looked the politician which he was for most of his life. Without his eye-glasses, he bore a striking resemblance to Robert G. Ingersoll.

PRINCIPAL WORKS: *Fiction*—Aladdin & Co., 1904; Double Trouble, 1905; The Broken Lance, 1907; Virginia of the Air Lanes, 1909; In the Fairyland of America (short stories) 1909; Yellowstone Nights (short stories) 1911; Vandemark's Folly, 1921; The Hawkeye, 1923; The Invisible Woman, 1924; We Have Changed All That (with E. S. MacMahon) 1928. *Non-Fiction*—American Inland Waterways, 1909; On Board the Good Ship Earth, 1913; The Brown Mouse, 1915; From War to Peace, 1919; The Fairview Idea, 1919; The Real Trouble With the Farmers, 1924; There Came Two Women (verse play) 1924; One Man's Life (autobiography) 1925; Mississippi Steamboatin' (with Edward Quick) 1926.

ABOUT: Quick, H. One Man's Life; West, R. The Strange Necessity; Outlook May 20, 1925; Saturday Evening Post June 13, 1925; Saturday Review of Literature July 30. 1938.

*QUILLER-COUCH, Sir ARTHUR THOMAS ("Q") (November 21, 1863-   ),

English scholar and man-of-letters, was born in Fowey, Cornwall, the son of Thomas Quiller-Couch. Although his name does not begin with "Tre, Pol, or Pen," he is Cornish of the Cornish; with visible relief he tells that "in 1891 he left London for his native country, where he has since resided." He was mayor of Fowey in 1937, is a Justice of the Peace, and is a Freeman of the towns of Fowey, Bodmin, and Truro. As Alfred Tresidder Sheppard remarked, "he knows his own people through and through."

He was educated at Newton Abbot College, Clifton College, and Trinity College, Oxford, where he was a lecturer in the classics in 1886 and 1887, and of which he is an Honorary Fellow. In 1887 he went to London and edited the *Speaker* from its foundation to 1899, though he left the city eight years earlier. He was created knight in

1910, and has honorary doctorates from Bristol, Aberdeen, and Edinburgh. He is a member of the Academic Committee and a Fellow of the Royal Society of Literature. Since 1912 he has been a Fellow of Jesus College, Cambridge and King Edward VIII professor of English literature at Cambridge University. He married Louisa Amelia Hicks in 1899, and they have one daughter. At home, in spite of his age, yachting and rowing are still his main recreations. He has written little in recent years, but his poems still occasionally appear in English magazines. Tall, tanned, slight but wiry, his once blond hair now gray, he still looks the athlete he was.

Once far better known as a novelist, in the past quarter century he has given most of his time to scholarly pursuits and the writing of literary criticism. He has been the editor of the *Oxford Book of English Verse* from its first edition in 1900 to its latest in 1939, and has also edited the *Oxford Book of English Ballads* (1919), the *Oxford Book of Victorian Verse* (1912), the *Oxford Book of English Prose* (1923), *Pages of English Prose* (1930), *English Sonnets* (1935), and (with others) the *New Shakespeare*. He is no pedant, but, as C. L. Hinds said, "wears his learning lightly and bends it to bright use." John Cournos added that he has "the supreme gift . . . of being able to charm while he instructs."

His novels are nearly all Cornish in background and in dialect; some few are historical. He has, not without reason, been compared to Dickens. Sheppard, who called him "a now almost perfect craftsman," though praising him as a novelist and saying that "no sounder critic is living today" (an opinion not shared by most modern poets and critics, because of the conventionality of Quiller-Couch's taste) thought his *forte* above all was the short story. Most of his literary essays and some of his fiction have been written under the pseudonym of "Q." The latter part of his surname is pronounced *kooch*.

A word must be said about Sir Arthur's verse. He is one of the few good living parodists. William Rose Benét said that "only a genuine poet whose ear was attentively attuned to the most delicate effects of cadence could have produced" his parodies; and added that "his serious poetry is both moving and effective. That is the reason he writes such good parody."

PRINCIPAL WORKS: *Novels*—Dead Man's Rock, 1887; The Astonishing Tale of Troy Town, 1888; The Splendid Spur, 1889; Tom Tiddler's Ground, 1890; Noughts and Crosses, 1891; The Blue

* Died May 12, 1944.

Pavilions, 1891; I Saw Three Ships, 1892; The Delectable Duchy (short stories) 1893; Wandering Heath: Stories, Studies, and Sketches, 1895; Ia, 1896; Ship of Stars, 1899; The Laird's Luck, 1901; The Westcotes, 1902; The White Wolf, 1902; The Adventures of Harry Revel, 1903; Hetty Wesley, 1903; Fort Amity, 1904; The Shining Ferry, 1905; Sir John Constantine, 1906; Poison Island, 1907; Merry-Garden, 1907; Major Vigoreux, 1907; True Tilda, 1909; Lady Good-For-Nothing, 1910; Corporal Sam and Other Stories, 1910; Brother Copas, 1911; Hocken and Hunken: A Tale of Troy, 1912; Nicky-Nan: Reservist, 1915; Mortallone and Aunt Trinidad, 1917; Foe-Farrell, 1918; Duchy Edition Tales and Romances (30 vols.) 1928-29; Q's Mystery Stories, 1937. *Miscellaneous*—Warwickshire Avon, 1892; Green Bays, 1893; Verses and Parodies, 1893; Golden Pomp (ed.) 1895; Adventures in Criticism, 1896; Poems and Ballads, 1896; Old Fires and Profitable Ghosts, 1900; Three Sides of the Face, 1903; Shakespeare's Christmas, 1905; From a Cornish Window, 1906; The Vigil of Venus and Other Poems, 1912; News From the Duchy, 1915; On the Art of Writing, 1916; Memoir of Arthur John Butler, 1917; Shakespeare's Workmanship, 1918; Studies in Literature, 1918, 1922, 1929; On the Art of Reading, 1920; Charles Dickens and Other Victorians, 1925; Poems, 1929; The Poet as Citizen and Other Papers, 1934; Victors of Peace: Florence Nightingale, Pasteur, Father Damien, 1937.

ABOUT: Bookman (London) May 1928, July 1929; Christian Science Monitor Monthly May 4, 1938; Saturday Review of Literature January 3, 1931.

QUINN, ARTHUR HOBSON (February 9, 1875-), American educator and critic,

writes: "Arthur Hobson Quinn was born in Philadelphia, the son of Michael A. Quinn and Mary (MacDonough) Quinn. All four of his grandparents had come to Philadelphia from Ireland in the 1840's. He was educated at the University of Pennsylvania, graduating in 1894, becoming at once an instructor in mathematics, and a year later instructor in English. Except for a year's study abroad at Munich, he has remained at the university ever since, going through the regular grades of promotion, becoming full professor in 1908 and in 1939 becoming John Welsh Centennial Professor of History and English Literature. Curiously enough, this chair had been endowed as a tribute to John Welsh, for whom Mr. Quinn's grandfather had been general manager in the 1840's.

"He organized and directed the first Summer School at the University of Pennsylvania in 1904, and was Dean of the College from 1912 to 1922. He began to write short stories soon after his graduation, and his first publication dealt with undergraduate life at the university. His contributions to fiction and verse, however, were checked somewhat by his scholarly duties, although he has occasionally written and published short stories.

"Mr. Quinn has always been strongly interested in the theatre, and gave in 1918 the first course in the American drama offered anywhere. This led him to the publication of his anthology, *Representative American Plays* (1917, latest revised edition 1938). Since 1905 he has devoted his major teaching effort to American literature, giving in 1905 the first purely graduate course in that subject in any American university. His most recent publication is his long planned and long delayed critical biography of Edgar Allan Poe.

"Mr. Quinn has been active in many projects connected with writing. He was one of the founders of the Franklin Inn Club, the writers' club of Philadelphia, in 1902. He has been a member of many councils and committees connected with the theatre, among them the first American National Theatre, organized in 1923. He is also a member of several learned societies, and two years ago was elected an honorary member of the *Conseil Historique et Heraldique de France*. He married in 1904 Helen McKee; they have had two sons and three daughters."

* * *

Professor Quinn received his Ph.D. from the University of Pennsylvania in 1899, and is also an honorary Litt.D. of St. Joseph's College, Philadelphia. He was contributor and advisor on American playwrights to the *Dictionary of American Biography*. He is a rather stocky man, with ginger hair and moustache now gray. He is an inspiring teacher, who carries over into his books his fresh enthusiasm for his subject. C. Hartley Grattan spoke of his "exhaustive knowledge of drama in America," and Montrose J. Moses of his "conscientious patience." His critical biography of Poe is a work of sound scholarship, including some material hitherto unavailable.

PRINCIPAL WORKS: Pennsylvania Stories, 1899; History of the American Drama From the Beginning to the Civil War, 1923; History of American Drama From the Civil War to the Present Day (2 vols.) 1927 (1-vol. ed. 1936); The Soul of America, 1932; American Fiction: An Historical and Critical Survey, 1936; James A. Herne's Early Plays (ed.) 1940; Edgar Allan Poe, 1941.

ABOUT: Bookman March 1928.

QUINTERO. See ALVÁREZ QUINTERO

RABINDRANATH TAGORE. See TAGORE

RABINOWITZ, SOLOMON J. ("Shalom Aleichem") (February 18, 1859-May 13, 1916), Jewish dramatist and short-story writer, was born in Pereyaslev, Poltava, Russia. His father, Reb Nochum, and mother, rather an Amazon type and a hard worker, managed a general store. The boy spent much time in the nearest large town, Voronko, from which was born his composite town Kaserilevke, in which "Shalom Aleichem" localized all the Jewish types he had observed with the vivid memory and gay irreverence of a precocious youth. When his parents met with reverses and began to run an inn, young Rabinowitz eavesdropped on the cantors and musicians who held rehearsals there. At seventeen he was a teacher; he tutored and later married the daughter of a rich provincial Jew, and wrote sketches for the Hebrew magazine *Hamelitz* and the first Yiddish newspaper, established in 1883. His pen-name, "Shalom Aleichem," means "Peace be upon you," the common expression of greeting among the Semitic peoples.

Ambitious to become the Maecenas of Yiddish writers, Rabinowitz established a year book, the *Yiddish Folk-Bibliothèque*. Losing his money, he went in 1890 to Odessa to act as stock broker and general insurance agent. In 1893 he returned to Kiev, but the massacres of 1905 drove him from Russia. Migrating to New York, he wrote for Yiddish journals and theatres. "So intrinsically idiomatic and localized is his style, being that of the true humorist," writes Charles A. Madison, "that little of what so charmed his Yiddish readers can ever reach the pages of the translators." Small-town Jews moved him to sympathetic laughter; satire and ridicule were reserved for the wealthier class of his people. Three-quarters of the work of "Shalom Aleichem" is in the monologue or epistolary form, so dependent was he on what he had heard or seen with his own senses. American experiences were utilized for the *Mobel* series, *Mobel: Towards America*, *Mobel: In America*, and *The New Kaserilevke*. A prolific writer, he was sometimes hurried, trivial, and repetitive. In 1907 he gave successful readings in European cities. After contracting a severe cold at Minsk in 1908, "Shalom Aleichem" spent six years off and

on in Italy, until the First World War sent him back to New York. The dreadful condition of his fellow-Jews in Europe and the death of his eldest son preyed on his mind, and he died at fifty-seven.

WORKS AVAILABLE IN ENGLISH TRANSLATION: Stempenyu, 1913; She Must Marry a Doctor (in Goldberg, I. *Six Plays of the Yiddish Theatre*) 1916; Jewish Children, 1920.
ABOUT: Rabinowitz, S. J. Jewish Children (see Introduction by Dorothy Canfield); Poet Lore Winter 1922.

RADIGUET, RAYMOND (June 18, 1903-December 12, 1923), French poet and novelist, was born in Parc-de-St. Maur, a meteorological station some eight miles from Paris. About his childhood and academic education nothing is known, except that when hardly fourteen he had written poems worthy of inclusion in any anthology of contemporary verse. In 1918  he arrived in Paris, at the age of fifteen. He wandered around, finding shelter in cheap bistros or in the studio of any friendly artist who might give him lodging. The poets Max Jacob and Jean Cocteau took him under their wing, and before long the infant prodigy was invited to contribute to the magazine *Sic*, along with other writers who later began the Surréalist movement: Aragon, Breton, Soupault. Although Radiguet contributed to *Sic* he was not interested in the so-called Nunism of its founders, nor in Dadaism, nor any of the other *isms* then in bloom in Paris. Instead of seeking newness with the vanguard iconoclasts, Radiguet reverted to the classic tradition, especially eighteenth century neo-classicism. Later this trend was made fashionable by Jean Cocteau. Radiguet wanted to be mature—at fifteen he claimed to be eighteen and hated to be called Mlle. Cocteau or "Bebé-Cadum," the baby in a popular advertisement.

Radiguet's first book was a collection of poems entitled *Les Joues en Feu* published in 1920 in a de luxe edition with four etchings by Jean Victor Hugo. In that same year he moved to the fishing village of Carqueiranne, a few miles from Toulon and then to Piquey, not far from the then fashionable resort of Arcachon, where he wrote several poems and began his first novel, *Devil in the Flesh*.

In 1921 the Editions de la Sirène published another poetry brochure, *Devoirs de Vacances,* illustrated by Irène Lagut, and Birault published his drama *Les Pélicans* in a very limited edition. This first period, predominantly poetical, showed Radiguet as an orthodox, metrical writer, influenced neither by the stylistic exhibitionism then in vogue nor by the sophistication of his patrons and colleagues. His verse flowed sedately against a background of bitterness and cynicism rather surprising in a child in his teens.

In 1923 the staid publishers Flammarion distributed to a baffled world Radiguet's *Devil in the Flesh.* It was one of those novels which do not pass by unnoticed. Its bold freshness shocked many a critic who cried indignantly that nothing so immoral had been written in France since Choderlos de Laclos in the eighteenth century. *Devil in the Flesh* is but *Daphnis and Chloe* in modern dress, an idyllic tragedy concerning a fifteen-year old hero and a heroine of eighteen. This penetrative study of adolescence Aldous Huxley has praised because it is "so mature, so finished, so complete. It has a certainty about it, a directness, a swiftness and a simplicity—all the qualities, in a word, that we expect to find in the work of the ripest and most experienced artists. . . . Radiguet set out in possession of those literary virtues with which most writers painfully end."

Before the excitement subsided, Radiguet published his second novel, *The Count's Ball* (1924), unreservedly acclaimed as a remarkable achievement. Among his notes, posthumously published, Radiguet jotted down his germ-idea for the novel: "A novel in which only the psychology will be romantic. The only imaginative effort will be applied, not to exterior events, but to the analysis of emotions." *The Count's Ball* is indeed an imaginative analysis of emotions; the plot is simple and unoriginal, reminiscent of Mme. De La Fayette's *La Princesse de Clèves* (1677), the style precise and adamantine, the characterization exact, clinical. Cocteau asserted that if *Devil in the Flesh* was "a masterpiece of promise" *The Count's Ball* is "the fulfillment of that promise," and adds: "One is rather appalled by a boy of twenty who publishes the sort of book that can't be written at his age. The dead of yesterday are eternal. The young novelist who wrote *The Count's Ball* is the ageless author of a dateless book."

In 1923 Radiguet caught typhoid fever in Paris. A few days before his death he said to a friend: "Listen, I have something terrible to tell you. In three days I am going to be shot by the soldiers of God." God's soldiers shot him a day before schedule. Serum was administered too late, and Raymond Radiguet died at the age of twenty, leaving two or three dozen poems, an unproduced play, and two short novels.

WORKS AVAILABLE IN ENGLISH TRANSLATION: The Count's Ball, 1929; Devil in the Flesh, 1932.

ABOUT: Germain, A. De Proust à Dada; Huxley, A. Introduction to Devil in the Flesh; Martin du Gard, M. Feux Tournants; Massis, H. Raymond Radiguet; Mauriac, F. Le Roman; Radiguet, R. The Count's Ball (see Introduction by J. Cocteau); Sachs, M. The Decade of Illusion; Books January 19, 1930; Hound and Horn July-September 1932; Revue Hebdomadaire July 1924; Revue Mondiale October 1, 1925; Revue Universelle August 15, 1924.

*RAINE, WILLIAM MAC LEOD (June 22, 1871-), American novelist, was born in London, England, the son of William and Jessie Watt (Muir) Raine, both of Scottish birth. He was brought to the United States at the age of ten, after his mother's death, and was educated at Sarcey College (Arkansas) and Oberlin College (B.A. 1894). The family home had been in

Arkansas, and he grew up in the cattle country which later was to be the theme of most of his books. After college he drifted west, worked on a ranch, was principal of a school in Seattle, tried to enlist in the Spanish-American War but was disqualified because of weak lungs, and finally was obliged to go to Denver to try to regain his health. Here he worked as a reporter and editorial writer on the *Republican,* the *Post,* and the *Rocky Mountain News.* He began to write short stories, was enabled to devote all his time to free lance fiction, and finally found his *métier* in the novel. The earliest of his many books were romantic historical novels with an English background, but he soon turned to the American West, which has ever since been his particular field. Since 1918 he has averaged two novels a year. It is estimated that he has published some six million words. Most of his books have been translated at once into French, Spanish, Portuguese, Czechoslovakian. During the First World War, 500,000 copies of one of his books were sent to British soldiers in the trenches. Twenty of his novels have been filmed. Despite his prolificness, he is a slow, careful, conscientious worker, intent on accurate detail, and considers himself a craftsman rather than an artist.

In 1905 Mr. Raine married Jennie P. Langley, who died in 1922. In 1924 he married Florence A. Hollingsworth; they have a daughter. Though he travels a good deal, Denver is still his home. For several years he lectured on journalism at the University of Colorado, which gave him an M.L. degree in 1920.

A critic in the *Bookman* called Mr. Raine's Western stories "unreal" (not in factual background but in characterization), but, granting his lack of pretension as a novelist, praised the "economy and hardness" of his style.

PRINCIPAL WORKS: A Daughter of Raasay, 1902; Wyoming, 1908; Ridgway of Montana, 1909; Bucky O'Connor, 1910; A Texas Ranger, 1911; Brand Blotters, 1912; Crooked Trails and Straight, 1913; The Vision Splendid, 1913; The Pirate of Panama, 1914; The Highgrader, 1915; Steve Yeager, 1915; The Yukon Trail, 1917; The Sheriff's Son, 1918; A Man Four Square, 1919; Oh You Tex, 1920; The Big Town Round Up, 1920; Gunsight Pass, 1921; Tangled Trails, 1921; Man Size, 1922; The Fighting Edge, 1922; Ironheart, 1923; The Desert's Price, 1924; Roads of Doubt, 1925; Troubled Waters, 1925; Bonanza, 1926; The Last Shot, 1926; Moran Beats Back, 1927; Judge Colt, 1927; Colorado, 1928; Texas Man, 1928; Famous Sheriffs and Western Outlaws (non-fiction) 1929; The Fighting Tenderfoot, 1929; The Valiant, 1930; Cattle (with W. Barnes) 1930; Rutledge Trails the Ace of Spades, 1930; Beyond the Rio Grande, 1931; The Black Tolts, 1932; Under Northern Stars, 1932; The Broad Arrow, 1933; Roaring River, 1934; The Trail of Danger, 1934; Square Shooter, 1935; Border Breed, 1935; Run of the Brush, 1936; To Ride the River With, 1936; Bucky Follows a Cold Trail, 1937; King of the Bush, 1937; On the Dodge, 1938; Sons of the Saddle, 1938; The River Bend Feud, 1939; Riders of the Rim Rocks, 1940; 45-Caliber Law: The Way of Life of a Frontier Peace Officer (non-fiction) 1941; They Called Him Blue Blazes, 1941; Saddlebag Folk (non-fiction), 1942; Justice Deferred, 1942.

ABOUT: American Author February 1934; Bookman October 1929.

RALEIGH, Sir WALTER ALEXANDER (September 5, 1861-May 13, 1922),

English essayist and literary critic, was born at 4 Highbury Quadrant, London, the fifth child and only son of Alexander and Mary Darling (Gifford) Raleigh. The elder Raleigh, of Covenanting ancestry, was a Congregational minister at Hare Court, Chapel Canonbury, later at Kensington Chapel. The boy attended the City of London School, but was sent to Edinburgh in 1876 to live with his uncle, Lord Gifford, a

Scottish judge who founded the Gifford Lectureship in Natural Theology. Young Raleigh was a pupil for a time at Edinburgh Academy, then returned to London to attend the University College School and to receive a B.A. from University College in 1881 In October he entered King's College, Cambridge, took a second class historical tripos, just above Austen Chamberlain; went to Italy during the Lent Term for his health; and returned to become editor of the *Cambridge Review* and president of the Union.

Raleigh's first teaching post was in India, where he was first professor of English literature at the Mohammedan Anglo-Oriental College, Aligarh, till 1887, when he was invalided home with dysentery. After a few months at Owens College, Manchester, he spent the next ten years at University College, Liverpool (1890-1900). In July 1890 he married Lucie Gertrude Jackson, a daughter of the editor of the *Illustrated London News*; they had four sons and a daughter.

An appointment to the chair of English Language and Literature at Glasgow, on the recommendation of Lord Balfour of Burleigh, was the next step, in 1900, and four years later he went to Oxford as first holder of the Professorship of English Literature. Raleigh's position there as a popular teacher resembled that of Quiller-Couch at Cambridge, and William Lyon Phelps at Yale, and Charles Townsend Copeland at Harvard. He believed that "too much system kills the study of literature"; that his function was "not to discuss theories, trace influences, show developments, but to exhibit what was great in great literature"—chiefly by reading selected passages and commenting on them. Writing he found burdensome; none of his books is of any great length. Raleigh's knighthood was conferred in 1911 as one of the Coronation honors. Returning with incipient typhoid from a trip to Bagdad as historian of the Royal Air Force after the World War, he died at sixty. The funeral was held at Merton College Chapel, with interment in the little churchyard at Ferry Hinksey. Oxford missed Raleigh's familiar lanky figure, with the slight stoop, the constant nervous tremor in the arms, and the genial, smiling face. His letters, Raleigh's "best and only biography," edited by Lady Raleigh, were published in 1926.

PRINCIPAL WORKS: The English Novel, 1894; Robert Louis Stevenson, 1895; Style, 1897; Milton, 1900; Wordsworth, 1903; The English Voyagers, 1904; Shakespeare (English Men of Letters Series) 1907; Six Essays on Johnson, 1910; Romance, 1917; England and the War, 1918; Letters, 1926.

ABOUT: Jones, H. A. Sir Walter Raleigh and the Air Force History: A Personal Recollection.

RAMÉE, LOUISE DE LA. See "BRITISH AUTHORS OF THE 19TH CENTURY"

"RAMÓN." See GÓMEZ DE LA SERNA, R.

RANSOM, JOHN CROWE (April 30, 1888-), American poet and critic, was born in Pulaski, Tenn., the son of John James

Ransom and Ella (Crowe) Ransom. He was educated at Vanderbilt University (B.A. 1909) and at Christ Church College, Oxford, where he was a Rhodes Scholar and obtained his B.A. in *Litterae Humaniores* in 1913. He joined the English department of Vanderbilt in 1914, and left in 1917 to serve as a first lieutenant in the Field Artillery. He remained in France until 1919, and taught for one year at the Saumur Artillery School. He then returned to Vanderbilt and remained there until 1937, from 1924 as professor of English. Since 1937 he has been professor of poetry at Kenyon College, and moved in consequence from Nashville to Gambier, Ohio. He has lectured at the summer sessions of colleges and universities all over the South and West. During 1931 and 1932 he was in England on a Guggenheim Fellowship, and while there was a lecturer at the University of the Southwest, at Exeter.

In 1920 he married Robb Reavill, and they have a daughter and two sons. "Slight and courtly," his appearance is chiefly remarkable for his deep-set eyes, his prominent chin, and the wide mouth of an orator.

Professor Ransom was one of the seven residents of Nashville who founded and edited the *Fugitive* (1922-25). Like others of the so-called Fugitive Group, he is an agrarian-distributist, believing in a return, especially for the South, from an industrial to an agrarian economy, and with the others he was a contributor to their two symposia, *I'll Take My Stand* and *Who Owns Amer-*

ica? He is the wit and ironist of the group, and Louis Untermeyer said that he, "more than any of the others, was responsible for the new awakening of poetry in the South." Robert Penn Warren, another of the group with Ransom remarked that "the central issue of his poetry . . . is the disruption of sensibility . . . [This is] the source of his irony. . . . Order, tradition, stability, are [to him] merely aspects of man's sensibility."

George Williamson, a non-agrarian critic, said that "most of Ransom's poetry combines an amusing texture with a serious emotion. . . . In Ransom's verse, wit has become a poetic attitude." He would not himself agree with this judgment. He is exceedingly serious in his beliefs, and wit to him is not so much a poetic attitude as a poetic tool. His poetry is frequently involved and obscure; it is highly cerebral and its emotion is almost always veiled. He is now editor at his new college of the *Kenyon Review*, and the scholarliness and distinction of that quarterly reflects the quality of his own mind. He will never be a popular poet, and has no desire to be; he is, however, a poet and critic of considerable stature.

PRINCIPAL WORKS: *Poetry*—Poems About God, 1919; Chills and Fever, 1924; Grace After Meat, 1924; Two Gentlemen in Bonds, 1926. *Miscellaneous*—God Without Thunder, 1930; Topics For Freshman Writing, 1935; The World's Body, 1938; New Criticism, 1941; *in* The Intent of the Critic, 1941.

ABOUT: Poetry May 1932; Sewanee Review April 1934; Virginia Quarterly Review January 1935.

RANSOME, ARTHUR (1884-), English juvenile and miscellaneous writer, writes: "I was born at Leeds, Yorkshire, where my father was professor of history at the university. The holidays of my childhood were spent in a farm by the shores of Coniston Lake. I was at school at Windermere as a small boy and then at Rugby. After leaving school I studied science for rather less

than a university year, and then came to London, where I got work in a publisher's office, and wrote rubbish in such spare time as I had after very long office hours. I had begun writing at a very early age (seven or eight), and my first book (very bad, like many later ones) was published when I was twenty. By that time I had escaped from publishers' offices and was scraping together enough from weekly reviews and such things to live in Chelsea during the winters and in a farmhouse in the Lake Country during the summers. There followed a period when I got interested in the theory of criticism (which now seems to me of almost infinite unimportance), and wrote books on Edgar Allan Poe and Oscar Wilde and collections of rather solemn critical essays. Then, some time before the last war, Ralston's book interested me in Russian folklore. I went to Russia, learnt the language more or less, and made a collection of the tales I liked best. Then came the war and I hurried back to England, but was presently back in Russia again, doing newspaper work in Petrograd [Leningrad] and at the front, seeing a Russian hospital from the inside, and when ill and in bed trying once more to learn to write narrative. Then came the revolution and I presently found myself involved in a bitter political struggle because I was convinced that the policy of intervention in Russia in 1918 was as silly as had been the policy of intervention in France in 1795. In 1921 I carried out an old ambition, and not without tribulation saw the launching of a ketch, big enough to live in, from a yacht-builder's in Riga. In this boat I got to know part of the Eastern Baltic pretty thoroughly. In 1925 I settled once more in an ancient stone cottage in the Lake Country [in England], occasionally making expeditions to China, Egypt, Russia, and such places. I was able at last to do what from small-boyhood I had always wanted to do, and wrote *Swallows and Amazons,* a book about childhood in the country where I had spent my own. In 1935 I moved to the East Coast, and in 1938 hopefully built another boat, an act that ill health, hard work, and now this damnable war have combined to make seem rather silly."

* * *

Mr. Ransome is unmarried, and is now living near Ipswich, Suffolk. He is an ardent fisherman, especially of trout, as he has been since early childhood. He received the first Carnegie Medal of the English Library Association in 1936, for *Pigeon Post.* Sir Hugh Walpole called him "the best writer for boys and girls in England alive today."

PRINCIPAL WORKS: *Juveniles*—Old Peter's Russian Tales, 1916; Aladdin, 1919; Swallows and Amazons, 1931; Swallowdale, 1931; Peter Duck, 1933; Winter Holiday, 1934; The Coot Club, 1935; Pigeon Post, 1936; We Didn't Mean to Go to Sea, 1938; Secret Water, 1939; The Big Six, 1940; Missee Lee, 1941. *Miscellaneous*—A History of Story Telling, 1909; The Book of Friendship (ed.) 1909; The Book of Love (ed.) 1910; Edgar Allan Poe, 1910; The Hoofmarks of the Faun, 1911; Oscar Wilde, 1912; Ports and Speculations, 1913; The Elixir of Life, 1915; Six Weeks in Russia, 1919; The Soldier and Death: A Russian Folk-Tale, 1920; The Crisis in Russia, 1921; "Racundra's" First Cruise, 1923; The Chinese Puzzle, 1927; Rod and Line: With Aksakov on Fishing, 1929.

ABOUT: China Weekly Review July 9, 1927; Library Association Record (London) May 1937.

RASCOE, BURTON (October 22, 1892-), American journalist, editor, and critic, was born in Fulton, Ky., the son of Matthew Marquis de Lafayette Rascoe and Elizabeth (Burton) Rascoe, and was named Arthur Burton Rascoe. The Rascoes, of French Huguenot stock, originally spelled the name Rauscoue or Rouscoue. The immediate ancestors of Burton Rascoe's father, who died in 1930, lived in North Carolina. Rascoe senior was in turn a hostler (he eloped with his employer's daughter, who was promptly disowned), barkeeper, saloon keeper, horse-trader, and real-estate dealer. Burton Rascoe learned his letters at five from the headlines and mastheads of the Fulton *Daily Leader* and the Louisville *Courier-Journal;* when the family moved to Shawnee, Oklahoma, he found three friends and tutors: a fat and erudite dipsomaniac, a cultivated Catholic priest, and a ne'er-do-well newspaper man. From sixteen to nineteen he worked on a newspaper route for the Shawnee *Herald,* besides feeding its job press and occasionally running a linotype. As an assistant in the local Carnegie Library, he wrote papers for the ladies of the Hawthorne Club and the Round Table Club, charging $3 to $10 according to the research required or the ability of the clubwomen to pay. Rascoe was the Associated Press correspondent for Shawnee; held several high school offices; and altogether averaged four hours' sleep a night during his senior year. Slight and wiry in build, he nevertheless possessed great reserves of nervous energy, and was obliged to draw on them heavily during his eight years (1912-20) on the Chicago *Tribune.*

From 1911 to 1913 Rascoe was a student at the University of Chicago, more intent on getting an education than a degree. In July 1913 he married Hazel Luke of Chicago; their children were Ruth Helen Rascoe and Alfred Burton Rascoe, who committed suicide in 1936. Discharged from the *Tribune*

for making an irreverent allusion to Mary Baker Eddy, Rascoe retired for a time to his father's cotton plantation in Seminole, Okla. In 1920-21 he was manager of the Chicago Bureau of the Newspaper Enterprise Association; spent the next year as associate editor of *McCall's Magazine*; and in 1922-24 was literary editor of the New York *Tribune*, where his assistant was Isabel Paterson. Mrs. Paterson wrote the paper about her dynamic employer which appeared anonymously in the *Bookman* and later in the volume entitled *The Literary Spotlight*.

As literary editor of the Chicago *Tribune*, Rascoe had always been quick to hail new or obscure talent (James Branch Cabell dedicated *Jurgen* to him), and he continued the procedure on the New York paper of the same name, now the *Herald Tribune*. His "Bookman's Daybook," a weekly *causerie* of literary gossip interlarded with philosophical speculations, was a popular feature, and was syndicated to four hundred newspapers in 1924-28. With the arrival of Stuart Sherman in 1924 to edit *Books* for the *Herald Tribune*, Rascoe became editor of Johnson Features, Inc., 1924-27; edited the *Bookman* in 1927-28, taking over from John Farrar; and from 1928 to 1937 was a member of the editorial board of the Literary Guild. As sideline occupations Rascoe was associate editor of *Plain Talk* in 1929-30 and literary critic of *Esquire* from 1932 to 1938. In 1938-39 he was literary critic for *Newsweek*.

He compiled, edited, and wrote 50,000 words for *An American Reader* (1938), an anniversary publication of the publishing house of G. P. Putnam's Sons. His autobiography, *Before I Forget* (1937), taking his life-story up to his departure from Chicago to New York, and written in his usual tumultous, controversial, and rushing style, was a choice of the Literary Guild that year. Rascoe became literary critic of the *American Mercury* in 1938; during the three years previous he had been general editorial adviser to Doubleday, Doran & Co. Two books, *Titans of Literature* (1932) and the next year's *Prometheans*, were studies in comparative literature which were far from academic in style. Rascoe is a member of the American Classical Association, P.E.N., Sigma Nu, and an assortment of clubs including the Dutch Treat and Artists and Writers in Manhattan, the Capitol Pleasure Club in Harlem, and the Beach Club in Palm Beach Fla. His home is in New York City. He has also contributed introductions to numerous books.

PRINCIPAL WORKS: Theodore Dreiser, 1925; A Bookman's Daybook, 1929; Titans of Literature, 1932; Prometheans, 1933; Before I Forget (autobiography) 1937; An American Reader (ed.) 1938; Belle Starr, 1941.

ABOUT: Farrar, J. (ed) The Literary Spotlight; Rascoe, B. Before I Forget, A Bookman's Daybook; Bookman April 1924; New Republic May 29, 1929.

RAUSCHNING, HERMANN (1887-), German political writer, was born in East Prussia, the son of an army officer and the great-grandson of a land owner who returned from the Napoleonic Wars over a century ago. At Lichterfelde, a suburb of Berlin, he attended the Central Cadet School. Rauschning studied also in Potsdam; became a music student of Ludwig  Thuille in Munich; and received a degree in history from Berlin University in 1911. A book on the historical development of music in the Free City of Danzig, published in 1931, is the chief memento of his period as a music student. He was wounded in the First World War. Various phases of agriculture, notably cattle-breeding on his Danzig estate, absorbed his attention during the 1920's.

By 1931 the agrarian situation looked far from promising, and Rauschning became convinced that the National Socialist Party was Germany's likeliest road to salvation. He joined the ranks, and in the year following was made president of the *Landbund*. In June 1933 he was elected President of the Danzig Senate, and on taking office announced his determination to cultivate good neighborly relations with the Poles. By midsummer Rauschning had begun to entertain serious doubts concerning National Socialism; one of Hitler's long-winded and intemperate tirades against the church had given him pause. In the course of the next few months Rauschning dined frequently at the Chancellery and became rapidly acquainted with the "inner conspiracy" of the party *élite*, one feature of which involved the systematic gathering of incriminating evidence about one's real and potential opponents as the best insurance against an otherwise inevitable lapse into a subordinate position. Early in 1934 he urged Hitler to attempt a peaceful alliance and permanent understanding with the Poles. A few weeks after one of the subsequent

Danzig-Polish crises he again conferred with Hitler, and during that session the Führer let slip some of his meditations on an alliance between Germany and Russia. Rauschning began to view the Leader in a different light: as a complete and moral opportunist.

By the summer of 1934 he began to feel convinced that he was out of favor with the party. A congratulatory telegram which he had sent to von Papen, the great hope of the counter-revolutionists, was seized. He found himself charged with complete failure in achieving an equitable settlement of the Danzig controversy, and Hitler refused either to accept his resignation or to arrange his transfer to another post. When Danzig was threatened with bankruptcy, the Reichsbank refused Rauschning the funds he asked for, but capitulated unhesitatingly to *Gauleiter* Forster. Moreover, Rauschning refused to embark upon a new policy of ruthlessness against Jews and Catholics. Unable to reach Hitler through Von Neurath, the foreign minister, he resigned, sold his estates, and went to Poland, and thence successively to Switzerland, France, England, and the United States, where on April 30, 1942, he took out first citizenship papers. New York is his present residence.

Although Rauschning's books, based on his intimate knowledge of the Nazi party and his confidential conversations with Der Führer, have done much to reveal the shocking ruthlessness and nihilism of Hitler's program, he remains, it has been pointed out, a confused product of his environment, essentially non-democratic, still desiring to see a "Christian" Fourth Reich built on a "conservative, traditional, legitimist" base.

Rauschning is suave, courteous, white haired, with a long scar on his left temple from a Russian bullet in the First World War. "His understanding is quick and his English adequate," reports Robert van Gelder.

He was married to Anna Schwarte in 1915. They now have five children, one of whom is working on a farm in Oregon. In *No Retreat* (1942), Mrs. Rauschning has told the story of her efforts to hold her family together since her husband's break with the Nazis.

WORKS AVAILABLE IN ENGLISH TRANSLATION: The Revolution of Nihilism: A Warning to the West, 1939; The Voice of Destruction (Hitler Speaks) 1940; Hitler's Aims in War and Peace, 1940; The Redemption of Democracy, 1941; The Conservative Revolution, 1941; Men of Chaos (Makers of Destruction) 1942.

ABOUT: Current Biography 1941; New York Times May 1, 1942; New York Times Book Review November 9, 1941; Time September 18, 1939, March 11, 1940, December 23, 1940, March 3, 1941; Wilson Library Bulletin April 1940

*RAWLINGS, Mrs. MARJORIE (KINNAN) (August 8, 1896-), American novelist and short-story writer, winner of the Pulitzer Prize for fiction, was born in Washington, D.C., where her father, Frank R. Kinnan, was a patent attorney. Her mother was Ida May (Traphagen) Kinnan. Marjorie Kinnan attended the University of Wisconsin, where she  studied under William Ellery Leonard, the poet, and left with a B.A. degree in 1918. (Rollins College, in Florida, gave her an honorary LL.D. in 1939, in recognition of her achievements in recording the life of the state's backwoods inhabitants.

She went from college to the National Headquarters of the Y.M.C.A. as publicity writer, and in 1919, besides acting as assistant service editor of the magazine *Home Sector,* married Charles Rawlings. For the next four years she wrote advertising and special articles for the Louisville *Courier-Journal* and the Rochester (N.Y.) *Journal.* From 1925 to 1927 she was a syndicated verse-writer for United Features. Of her newspaper work in general and her experiences as a Hearst "sob sister" in particular, she told Robert van Gelder, "[It was] a rough school, but I wouldn't have missed it. . . . You learn a lot when you must put down what people said and how they acted in great crises in their lives. And it teaches you objectivity."

For several years Mrs. Rawlings tried, with consistent lack of success, to write the kind of story that she thought magazine editors would buy. Finally, in 1928, she gave up newspaper work and bought a seventy-two acre orange grove, with four thousand trees, at Cross Creek, Hawthorn, Florida, "at the jungle edge between two lakes where life has as many elements of the idyllic as is quite reasonable." Here she settled down to give all her time to fiction. When her stories still failed to sell, she resolved to try only once more before giving up. This time the story sold "like a shot," and she has had no trouble since in finding a market, though she no longer tries to write "commercially."

"Gal Young Un," a short story, won the O. Henry Memorial Award in 1933, the same year in which her first book, *South Moon Under*, appeared and was a choice of the Book-of-the-Month Club. With its local color, its details of making corn liquor, hunting wildcats, and rafting logs, this novel clearly indicated with what warmth and fidelity Mrs. Rawlings had become a part of the Florida setting.

The Yearling (1938), an idyllic story of a twelve-year-old Floridian, Jody Baxter, and his pet fawn, Flag, bids fair to become a minor American classic, not only as an important piece of regional literature, but as introducing one of the most appealing boy-characters since Huckleberry Finn, although of a more pliable disposition and less self-reliant makeup than Mark Twain's famous creation. It was a choice of the Book-of-the-Month Club and was awarded the Pulitzer Prize for fiction in 1939.

Another Book-of-the-Month Club selection was *Cross Creek* (1942), in which Mrs. Rawlings tells the story of her farm and her community, where she feels more at home than since her childhood days on her father's farm in Maryland. "She has traveled," wrote Elizabeth Pennell, "through the scrub and 'piney-woods,' talking to Florida Crackers, recording their conversation and her impressions of a rapidly disappearing backwoods life." When Mrs. Rawlings wants to write of a bear-hunt, her obliging neighbors delight in providing her with the actual experience.

"Writing," she says, "is agony. I stay at my typewriter for eight hours every day when I'm working and keep as free as possible from all distractions for the rest of the day. I aim to do six pages a day, but I'm satisfied with three. Often there are only a few lines to show. . . . I have no free swing in what I write, no little miracles. I let my novels mature for several years, know almost exactly what I want to do in them, and slowly do it."

Mrs. Rawlings' first marriage ended in divorce in 1933; in 1941 she married Norton Sanford Baskin, a Florida hotel man. A quiet, dark, intense woman, with a firm mouth, she is a member of the National Institute of Arts and Letters, the sorority Kappa Alpha Theta, and is entitled to wear a Phi Beta Kappa key.

PRINCIPAL WORKS: South Moon Under, 1933; Golden Apples, 1935; The Yearling, 1938; When the Whippoorwill, 1940; Cross Creek, 1942.

ABOUT: Rawlings, M. K. Cross Creek; Book-of-the-Month Club News March 1938; New York Herald Tribune "Books" June 18, 1933, February 9, 1941; New York Times Book Review November 30, 1941; Scholastic September 16, 1940; Wilson Library Bulletin October 1938.

RAYNOLDS, ROBERT (April 29, 1902-), American novelist, writes: "I was born in Santa Fé, N.M. When I was seven  my father died and we moved to Omaha, Neb. Our summers were spent in New Mexico, Wyoming, and Colorado. When I was seventeen I went to Princeton, the first time I had been East. After two years there, I spent a winter in Colorado working at a coal mine. I then entered Lafayette College and in 1925 received a B.A. degree. I have worked on ranches, at cement and steel mills, in a publishing house, a Mexican silver mine, a publicity office, and with a shipping company. I resigned from this last in 1929, and since then have had no other business than writing. I married Marguerite Gerdau in 1927; we have a son and two daughters, and live in Newtown, Conn.

"I don't remember when I began writing. Until my first novel received the Harper Prize in 1931, I had sold only a short article and a few book reviews. Besides my novels, I have written seven plays, several in verse. Three, *The Ugly Runts, Summer Song,* and *Farewell Villon,* have been produced; *Take All My Loves* was awarded distinguished second honors by Stanford University in 1939. At present I am writing a novel, which I may call *Night Boss* or *The Shore of Light.* It is my simple intention to do the best I can in this book to affirm the dignity of the human spirit. The motive of all my writing is a continual search of experience for wisdom. I live quietly at home, but I am sensible of the pressure of the world. I am distressed, too, but that seems to me all the more reason to eschew degradations in search for a hope. Though I have by nature a bright facility at mere writing, I find that to make a work in praise of life impregnable requires prolonged patience, steady thought, and persistent faith. If I can win any good spiritual bread by this labor, I will gladly pass it on to increase among men, for that is why I am an author."

* * *

Mr. Raynolds' strange blend of realism and allegory has bewildered the critics. John

Bronson called it "bad romanticism," saying that "the characters always seem to be getting mixed up with the landscape," but noted that Mr. Raynolds is "so passionately in love with humanity and nature that his every sentence is a poem of praise to them."

PRINCIPAL WORKS: Brothers in the West, 1931; Saunders Oak, 1933; Fortune, 1935; Boadicea (verse play) 1941.

ABOUT: Bookman March 1933; Literary Digest September 12, 1931; Wilson Library Bulletin February 1932.

REA, Mrs. LORNA (SMITH) (June 12, 1897-   ), British novelist, was born in Glasgow, her maiden name being Smith.

She was educated at St. James's School, West Malvern, and at Newnham College, Cambridge, where she was graduated with honors in the Mediaeval and Modern Language Tripos. She also studied piano and singing in Florence, and medicine at University College, London, though she never completed her medical course. In 1922 she married the Hon. Philip Russell Rea, a banker and managing director of several large companies. They have one daughter. Besides her novels, she has written a number of stories and articles in English newspapers and magazines, and was chosen to do the book on the Armada in a series of works on English history. Her interest in music and medicine, as well as her fondness for the theatre, are apparent in her books. Though her novels have been republished in America, she is not so well known in this country as in England; most popular of her books in America was *The Happy Prisoner*. Seldom profound or "significant," her work nevertheless has a smooth brilliance which has commanded some admiration. She has published no volume since 1935; when last heard from she was living in London.

PRINCIPAL WORKS: Six Mrs. Greenes, 1929; Rachel Moon, 1930; The Happy Prisoner, 1931; First Night, 1932; The Armada (in America: The Spanish Armada) 1933; Six and Seven, 1935.

READ, HERBERT EDWARD (December 4, 1893-   ), English poet and critic, writes: "Born at Muscoates, Kirbymoorside, Yorkshire, the son of a farmer, descendant of a long line of Yorkshire farmers. The first ten years of his life were spent on this farm. Educated at a boarding school in Halifax, and (after an interval of three years, during which, between the ages of fifteen and eighteen, he worked in a bank) at the University of Leeds. Studies at the university cut short by the war, inevitably a decisive experience. [He was captain in the Yorkshire Regiment and served for four years, receiving the Distinguished Service Order and the Military Cross.]

"Critical activities began with an edition of the remains of T. E. Hulme, the brilliant philosopher and critic who was killed in the war. His first collection of critical essays defined an attitude which has been consistently developed. The categories usually known as classicism and romanticism are related to their psychological origins in the individual, and shown to be, not alternatives equivalent to right and wrong, but tendencies which must be accepted as equally inevitable, and reconciled in some more universal concept, which with due caution might be described as Humanism.

"Has also published several small volumes of verse, gathered together later in *Collected Poems*. For the most part these are written in 'free verse,' a technique to which the author has remained passionately devoted and which he considers to be the only sincere and adequate mode of contemporary poetic expression. This technique he has elaborated with a care and precision which are usually unnoticed and therefore unappreciated.

"Parallel with his criticism, and more directly related to his mundane activities first as an assistant at the Victoria and Albert Museum, then as professor of fine art at Edinburgh University, Read has devoted himself to art criticism, and has published a short general study of the historical principles of art and a more detailed introduction to the aesthetic theory of modern painting and sculpture."

* * *

Immediately after demobilization, Mr. Read served for two years as assistant principal of His Majesty's Treasury, going from there to the Victoria and Albert Museum. His professorship at the University of Edinburgh was from 1931 to 1933; he was then until 1939 editor of the *Burlington Magazine*. He was also a lecturer on art at the University of Liverpool in 1935 and 1936, and has given the Clark Foundation Lectures at Trinity College, Cambridge. He has been married twice, to Evelyn Roff and to Margaret Ludwig, and has one son by each marriage. He is at present in London, and again involved in war work.

C. Hartley Grattan called Read "one of the most important of living critics"; other commentators have spoken of his "trained taste" and his "charming ease of manner." His war poems, like Siegfried Sassoon's, are a bitter exposure of the horrors of modern warfare. In addition to his creative work, he has edited four anthologies.

PRINCIPAL WORKS: *Poetry*—Naked Warriors, 1919; Eclogues, 1919; Mutations of the Phoenix, 1923; Collected Poems, 1926; The End of a War, 1933; Poems 1914-1934, 1935; Thirty-Five Poems, 1940. *Criticism*—English Pottery (with B. Rackham) 1924; English Stained Glass, 1926; Reason and Romanticism, 1926; English Prose Style, 1928; Staffordshire Pottery Figures, 1929; The Sense of Glory, 1929; Wordsworth, 1930; Julien Benda and the New Humanism, 1930; The Meaning of Art (in America: The Anatomy of Art) 1931; Form in Modern Poetry, 1932; Art Now, 1933; Art and Industry, 1934; In Defense of Shelley, 1935; Art and Society, 1936; Poetry and Anarchism, 1938; Collected Essays in Literary Criticism, 1938. *Miscellaneous*—In Retreat, 1925; Ambush, 1930; The Innocent Eye (autobiography) 1933; The Green Child, 1935; Annals of Innocence and Experience (autobiography) 1940.

ABOUT: Monro, H. Some Contemporary Poets; Read, H. The Innocent Eye; Annals of Innocence and Experience; Atlantic Monthly March, April 1933; Bookman (London) October 1933; Catholic World January 1940; Commonweal June 1, 1934; London Mercury September 1928.

READ, OPIE PERCIVAL (December 22, 1852-November 2, 1939), American novelist and humorist, was born in Nashville,

Tenn., the son of Guilford and Elizabeth (Wallace) Read. The family moved to Gallatin, Tenn., where he received his education. Read's first job was in Franklin, Ky., nine miles away, where he received fifty cents a week and board, and worked on tne local newspaper, making the acquaintance of the tramp printers who drifted in. Read went into the Kentucky hills to run the Scotsville *Argus,* moved on to Little Rock, Ark., to edit the *Gazette* from 1878 to 1881, and in June of the latter year married Ada Benham. The Reads had three sons and three daughters. Two years on the staff of

the Cleveland *Leader* followed, then P. D. Benham, Read's brother-in-law and a successful business man, set him up in Little Rock again with a weekly humorous and literary journal, the *Arkansas Traveler.*

In 1887 Read moved his successful venture to Chicago, and next year published *Len Gansett,* his first novel, which created a demand for more tales of the South. Read's books were especially popular among that part of the reading public which was obliged to spend long hours on railroad journeys. *The Jucklins* (1895) sold over a million copies. Obliged to turn out much hastily-written work, Read never wrote an absolutely first-class novel, although Vincent Starrett, who knew him at the Chicago Press Club, considers *My Young Master* as fine a novel of the Civil War as our literature can offer. William Marion Reedy called Read "the greatest almoster this country ever produced." In the early 1900's he lectured in every state of the Union.

The important thing in Opie Read's writing, declares Starrett, is his profound knowledge of human nature, his cheerful and whimsical philosophy, and the rugged virility of his democracy. His humor is usually homespun, without glitter; his style is clear, expressive, and often genuinely poetic. Strictly a regional writer, his work was confined within the frontiers of three or four states, tied to the native peculiarities and endeavors of citizens indigenous to the locale of his scenario. Read was fond of describing southern colonels of the old school and their devoted darkies, as well as brilliant, temperamental, and perennially drunk tramp printers, a race which he was well qualified by personal experience to depict. An articulator of the robust spirit of democratic individualism which permeated the people who settled and built the river towns of the Mississippi Valley, as Burton Rascoe wrote after Read's death (in Chicago at eighty-six), he "expressed their *mores,* their idiom, their lusty appetites, their quick tempers, their code of behavior, their disposition toward homely philosophy, their delight in extravagance, expansiveness, and humorous exaggeration, and, above all, their essential recklessness, impatience with restraint, and open defiance of the Eastern seaboard's notions of culture and polish." His work seemed alien and strange to a post-war generation who knew him chiefly as the Read of: "Said Opie Read to E. P. Roe, 'How do you like Gaboriau?' 'I like him very much indeed,' said E. P. Roe to Opie Read."

He was physically a giant, with flowing hair and a booming voice.

PRINCIPAL WORKS: Len Gansett, 1888; A Kentucky Colonel, 1889; Emmett Bonlore, 1891; A Tennessee Judge, 1893; Wives of the Prophet, 1894; The Jucklins, 1895; My Young Master, 1896; An Arkansas Planter, 1896; Bolanyo, 1897; Old Ebenezer, 1898; Waters of Caney Fork, 1899; On the Suwanee River: or, A Yankee From the West, 1900; In the Alamo, 1900; Judge Elbridge, 1900; The Carpetbagger (with F. Pixley) 1902; The Starbucks, 1902; An American in New York, 1905; Son of the Swordmaker, 1905; Old Jim Jucklin, 1905; "Turkey Egg" Griffin, 1905; The Mystery of Margaret, 1907; The Gold Tauze Veil, 1927; I Remember (autobiography) 1930; Mark Twain and I, 1940.

ABOUT: Elfer, M. Opie Read; Read, O. P. I Remember; Starrett, V. Buried Caesars; New York Times November 3, 1939; Saturday Review of Literature November 11, 1939.

REED, DOUGLAS (1895-), English journalist, was born in London, and, as he says, was "relatively unschooled." (Charles Poore remarked that Mr. Reed "worries too moodily about his lack of an Old School Tie.") He went to work at thirteen as office-boy in a publishing house, at nineteen was a bank clerk. With the outbreak of the First World War, he enlisted as a lance corporal in an infantry regiment, later was an observer and gunner in the air service, was twice wounded, and served throughout the war. On his return to London he was successively a wine merchant's clerk, a canvasser for maps, and a stenographer on the Northcliffe newspapers, eventually becoming Lord Northcliffe's private secretary. By 1924 he had been made sub-editor of the *Times*; he was its assistant Berlin correspondent from 1927 to 1935, and its Central European correspondent to 1938. Then for a year he was special correspondent of the *News Chronicle*, since when he has been a free-lance writer.

He was married in 1922 and has a son and a daughter. He lives in London. Mr. Reed is an anomaly—a thorough Tory, who has always voted the Conservative ticket, yet who hates Fascism, knows the Nazis burnt the Reichstag and blamed it on the Communists, admires Dimitroff (the Bulgarian Communist who was one of those accused in the Reichstag fire), and was an ardent friend of Loyalist Spain. All these persons and events he himself has witnessed as a newspaper man, and his final conclusion, reached even before the war, is that the world at this era is "Insanity Fair"— the title he gave his autobiography. He has many traits which Mr. Poore calls "unadmirable"—including more than a little anti-Semitism. But, as this critic remarks, "at intervals he can express interesting judgments with considerable force, clarity, and wit."

PRINCIPAL WORKS: The Burning of the Reichstag, 1934; Insanity Fair, 1938; Disgrace Abounding, 1939; Nemesis? (in England: The Story of Otto Strasser and the Black Front) 1940; Fire and Bomb, 1940; A Prophet at Home, 1941.

ABOUT: Reed, D. Insanity Fair.

REED, JOHN (October 22, 1887-October 19, 1920), American journalist, poet, and revolutionary, was born in Portland, Ore., the son of Charles Jerome Reed, a prosperous business man but also a one-time muckraking United States marshal, and Margaret (Green) Reed, daughter of a wealthy pioneering Portlander. He was sent to Portland Academy and then on to a fashionable Eastern school in Morristown, N.J., where he acquired not only a healthful amount of self-confidence but the conviction that concessions were wrong and that frankness was a virtue of the first water. He entered Harvard in 1906; had a strong hand in the *Lampoon* and the *Monthly;* wrote a play for the Hasty Pudding Club; was cheer-leader, ivy orator, and poet; but was not even enough of a rebel to join the Socialist Club.

In July following his graduation (1910) he persuaded Waldo Pierce, now well known as a painter, to go to Europe with him on a cattle boat. Pierce jumped overboard as the ship was leaving Boston Harbor; and when his watch was discovered on Reed's bed, Reed was suspected of murder. Pierce, meanwhile, had taken a good boat and got to Manchester in time to rescue his friend. Reed was disappointed at not seeing more of England's literary lions, but his walking trip through Spain was a complete delight. He became engaged to Madeleine Filon, whom he met in the Monte Carlo country; and returned to New York "to make a million dollars and get married."

Lincoln Steffens got him a job first on the *Globe* and then a routine post on the *American Magazine*. He broke his engagement to the French girl, and began to collect rejection slips on his Europe-inspired articles and stories. "Sangar," a piece of allegory, romanticism, and brotherly love, considered by some his best verse, was written during this period. Under Steffens' subtle tutelage he was waking up to America's social ills; and while he was writing for the *Saturday Evening Post, Collier's* and *Smart Set,* he became editor of the *Masses.*

In 1914 he went off to Mexico for the *Metropolitan.* His interviews and color-photo stories of the revolution (*Insurgent Mexico*) were so successful that Walter Lippmann was moved to remark that "with Jack Reed reporting begins." At the outbreak of the World War he went to Europe. Of his dispatches, afterwards incorporated into *The War in Eastern Europe,* the *Metropolitan* refused that one which said: "Do not be deceived by talk about democracy and liberty. This . . . is a scramble for spoils. It is not our war."

As a kind of symbol of his new devotion to revolutionary change and his provisional farewell to poetry, he issued, in 1917, a little volume of verse, *Tamburlaine,* most of which had been written three years earlier.

Reed had had a kidney removed, and the draft, when it came to the United States, passed him by. On the eve of the Russian Revolution he and Louise Bryant, whom he married in November 1916, sailed for Europe; and as tireless recorders for the *Call* (a reincarnation of the *Masses*) watched the proletarian victory. When he returned to New York, April 28, 1918, he was under indictment in the *Masses* case (presumably for his headline "Knit a Strait-Jacket for Your Soldier Boy"); he was eventually acquitted but widely black-listed. His article exposing the famous Sisson forgeries, that purported to show the Bolshevik leaders in the pay and under orders of Berlin, came out in pamphlet form. Late in the year he settled down to solid writing on *Ten Days That Shook the World,* a book of impressive and impassioned reporting that is still one of the most eloquent documents of the Bolshevik revolution. Except for the posthumous *Daughter of the Revolution,* a collection of short stories of Manhattan, Mexican, and Russian inspiration, it was his last book.

Meanwhile he had never ceased writing occasional pieces of verse and meaty articles for left-wing journals. He headed the newly formed Communist Labor Party, drew up its manifesto and platform, edited its *Voice of Labor,* and late in September set out for Russia. On an attempted return to the United States he was again held by Finnish authorities, and it was during this second confinement that he wrote a romantic prose poem and outlined two novels. When his passport home was definitively refused him, he sent for his wife; she joined him in Russia. At the peak of his vigor, both physical and intellectual, he was stricken with typhus, and died after a short illness, three days before his thirty-third birthday. He was buried in the Red Square in Moscow, under the Kremlin wall.

Over a period of several years Reed had been in love with Mabel Dodge Luhan, and she—perhaps more deeply—with him. The full story is told in her *Movers and Shakers.* In her portrait of him he is as unpredictable as he is engaging, with curly hair that was habitually untidy, a round gleaming brow, hazel eyes, and mouth that broke at times into an exuberant grin.

Some of his critics hold that he was not a real revolutionary but rather a "warm-hearted, romantic, enthusiastic American boy." But no one has disparaged his supremacy as a journalist, his occasional brilliance as a writer of verse, or the genuineness of his hope that a time might come "when it would be possible not only for him but for all poets to write poetry."

PRINCIPAL WORKS: Diana's Debut, 1910; Sangar, 1913; The Day in Bohemia: or, Life Among the Artists, 1913; Everymagazine: An Immortality Play, 1913; Insurgent Mexico, 1914; The War in Eastern Europe, 1916; Tamburlaine, 1917; Ten Days That Shook the World, 1919; Daughter of the Revolution (ed. by F. Dell) 1927.

ABOUT: Bryant, L. Six Red Months in Russia; Eastman, M. Heroes I Have Known; Hicks, G. John Reed: The Making of a Revolutionary; Hicks, G. & Ward, L. One of Us; Kreymborg, A. Troubadour: An Autobiography; Luhan, M. D. Movers and Shakers; Steffens, L. Autobiography; Stein, G. Autobiography of Alice B. Toklas; Vorse, M. H. A Footnote to Folly; Freeman November 3, 1920; New York Times October 19, 1920.

REEDY, WILLIAM MARION (December 11, 1862-July 28, 1920), American editor and critic, was born in St. Louis, Mo., the son of a police sergeant, who gave his son an education in the public schools; at Christian Brothers' College; and in the commercial course at St. Louis University, which awarded him the degree of Master of Accounts —considerably to the  amusement of Reedy and his friends later in his career. His apprenticeship as a writer began on the old *Missouri Republican,* where he was fired for drunkenness and irresponsibility and rehired regularly. As a reporter on the *Globe-Democrat* he met the woman superintendent of schools, who persuaded him to read in the public library until he was popularly supposed to know the contents better than Frederick Crunden, the librarian. In 1893 Reedy was city editor of the St. Louis *Mirror*. After two bankruptcies and reorganizations, it fell into the hands of James Campbell, who gave it outright to Reedy. As editor of *Reedy's Mirror,* Jean Winkler writes, he was "the center and matrix of the group, the solvent of jarring personalities, the introducer of new individuals and new ideas." Edgar Lee Masters' *Spoon River Anthology* first appeared in *Reedy's Mirror,* as well as the work of other St. Louis writers such as Zoë Akins, Sara Teasdale, Fannie Hurst, and Orrick Johns. Eastern writers were also glad to contribute.

"The man's genius and essential good taste asserted itself more and more as time went on," writes Orrick Johns, "and the paper grew in character, quality of writing, and honesty." Reedy became a convert to the single tax theory in later years. William Rose Benét, who contributed to the *Mirror,* thought him "potentially a great writer somehow balked of self-expression in books of his own. He knew the great river of literature from its headwaters down. He voyaged with impunity in either direction." In youth a handsome, dark man, Reedy later became macrostomatous, his lower face and body a mass of flesh; the luminous eyes remained, however. In January 1920 he was in hospital with a retinal hemorrhage, and died suddenly of angina in San Francisco, in July, at the home of friends, in his fifty-eighth year. His widow was Margery Rhodes, formerly prominent in the night life of St. Louis. All the world and underworld of St. Louis attended his funeral, and the body was laid, with the consent of the Catholic authorities, in Calvary cemetery. Less than two months later the *Mirror* was sold to Joseph P. McGowan after a brave attempt of the new editor, Charles J. Finger, and the remaining staff, to keep it going.

PRINCIPAL WORKS: The Law of Love, 1905; A Golden Book and the Literature of Childhood, 1910.

ABOUT: Johns, O. Time of Our Lives; Starrett, V. Buried Caesars; New York Times July 30, 1920; Reedy's Mirror August 5, 12, 1920; Saint Louis Review January 28, February 11, 1933.

REESE, LIZETTE WOODWORTH (January 9, 1856-December 17, 1935), American poet, was born in Waverly, a small village in Baltimore County, Md. (described in her charming book of semi-autobiography, *A Victorian Village*). Her mother, Louise Reese, was a German, full of temperament, who loved gardens and daffodils, "was as sure of God as she  was of the sun," and read detective stories with relish, measuring them, as she did every scrap of literary effort, for its interest. The father, David Reese, was a silent man, an ex-Confederate soldier, with the tense and stern characteristics of his Welsh ancestry. His daughter called him not merely inarticulate, but incoherent. Her own verse is often spare and laconic, with a preference for "the common word"; a school teacher all her life, she had little time or energy for composition and seldom set down a poem until it was completely and laboriously formed in her head.

At seventeen Miss Reese was a teacher in the St. John Parish School, chiefly qualified by her love of young people and gift of authority. Her first poem, "The Deserted House," was published in the *Southern Magazine* in June 1874. Transferred to an English-German school at Baltimore, she taught half the day in German and the other half in English. Four happy years, from 1877, were spent teaching English literature in a high school for Negroes. In 1901 Miss Reese went to the Western High School of Baltimore, where she remained twenty years, resigning in 1921 after forty-five years of continuous teaching. She had published five volumes of poetry, and was cordially accepted by the literary arbiters of the day, from Edmund Clarence Stedman and William Dean Howells to Richard Watson Gilder and Thomas Wentworth Higginson— who probably found Miss Reese easier to understand than his other *protégée,* Emily Dickinson. (Genevieve Taggard finds points of similarity between the two poets.) Madison Cawein corresponded with her, as did Louise Imogen Guiney.

That interesting literary freebooter, Thomas Mosher of Portland, Maine, brought out Miss Reese's poems in limited editions. Early in 1899 she mailed her famous sonnet. *"Tears,"* to [the American] Robert Bridges who printed it in *Scribner's Magazine* in November 1899. When Miss Reese resigned from teaching, a bronze tablet inscribed with the sonnet was unveiled at her high school; it was transferred to the new building on Gwynn Falls Parkway when the school changed its quarters. Goucher College honored her with a Litt.D. in 1931.

Three more books of poetry and a volume of *Selected Poems* came from Miss Reese after her retirement. "Beauty is a constant thing," she wrote. "One loveliness goes, another comes. Wherever there is beauty— no matter what the century—there also is the poet."

Miss Reese was described by the late Harriet Monroe, who met her only once, as "a little spinster who has emerged from the school-room, where she taught for years, without carrying away any professorial traits, and our talk—about anything and everything but poetry—revealed a character resolute and self-contained as a nut, with a little dapper shell of reserve protecting a kernel utterly sweet and sound." After Miss Reese's death, Miss Monroe wrote: "Her poems, considered as a whole, have a rare unity and harmony. They are delicately frail and fine, springing from a shy and isolated soul; an expression of wistfulness, of the ache of smothered emotion. . . . They sing with austere taste and musical precision, a clear pure minor tune all in the same key."

PRINCIPAL WORKS: A Branch of May, 1887; A Handful of Lavender (includes A Branch of May) 1891; A Quiet Road, 1896; A Wayside Lute, 1909; Spicewood, 1920; Wild Cherry, 1923; Litttle Henrietta, 1927; A Victorian Village, 1929.

ABOUT: Boston Evening Transcript April 18, 1931; Commonweal December 27, 1935; New York Herald Tribune December 18, 1935; Poetry February 1936; Publishers' Weekly December 28, 1935.

REEVE, ARTHUR BENJAMIN (October 15, 1880-August 9, 1936), American writer of detective fiction, the creator of  Craig Kennedy, "scientific detective," was born at Patchogue, Long Island, N.Y., the son of Walter F. Reeve and Jennie (Henderson) Reeve. He was graduated from Princeton in 1903 and attended New York Law School, but never practiced, entering journalism instead. He was assistant editor of *Public Opinion* in 1906, editor of *Our Own Times* from then until 1910, and was also on the staff of *Survey* in 1907. A series of articles on scientific crime detection led to his interest in the subject and to his detective fiction. Craig Kennedy made his appearance in the *Cosmopolitan Magazine* in 1910 and was instantly and enormously successful. For many years Reeve produced at least a volume of Kennedy stories, long or short, each season; he was regarded as America's foremost writer of detective fiction, and he also wrote mystery serials for the silent moving pictures. But with the advent of new names and less melodramatic styles in the detective story after the war, Kennedy's popularity began to wane, and Reeve's books became fewer. He was still frequently in demand as a "trained seal" (a newspaper term for outside experts in the field of journalism) at the times of such publicized criminal events as the Lindbergh kidnaping case, and he took a serious interest in crime prevention, writing a series on the subject for the radio. Reeve was an enthusiastic horticulurist, winning prizes at flower shows with his dahlia exhibits. He lived for a time at Oyster Bay, Long Island, moving in 1932 to Trenton, N.J., where he died at fifty-five of an asthmatic bronchial condition, leaving his wife, Margaret (Wilson) Reeve, and a son and a daughter.

At one time Craig Kennedy was customarily referred to as "the American Sherlock Holmes," but he is almost forgotten today. The reason is not difficult to find. Nearly all the stories were based on the dramatization of some contemporary mechanical or scientific invention, and these inventions have long since been outmoded. Furthermore, Kennedy was less truly scientific (as compared with R. Austin Freeman's Dr. Thorndyke, for example) than pseudo-scientific in the Sunday supplement sense; and the latter quality in literature is almost always of ephemeral appeal. A few of the stories relied on straight detection and narrative skill, and may still be read with pleasure in anthologies; but both Kennedy and his creator are today chiefly of interest to the historical student of detective literature.

PRINCIPAL WORKS: The Poisoned Pen, 1911; The Silent Bullet, 1912; Constance Dunlap: Woman Detective, 1916; The Dream Doctor, 1917; Treasure Train, 1917; The Panama Plot, 1918; Craig Kennedy Listens In, 1918; Atavar, 1924; Tales of Craig Kennedy, 1925; The Golden Age of Crime (non-fiction) 1931; The Clutching Hand, 1934; Enter Craig Kennedy, 1935.

ABOUT: Haycraft, H. Murder for Pleasure: The Life and Times of The Detective Story; New York Times August 10, 1936.

REGLER, GUSTAV (May 25, 1898-), German novelist, writes (in English): "Gustav Regler was born in Merzig (at Saargebiet), the son of a  bookseller who belonged to the so-called German Party, a national-liberal group in strong opposition to the disastrous politics of the Kaiser. He received a Catholic education, supervised by the monks of the Convent of the Bishop of Trier [Trèves]. At the age of eighteen he joined the German army in France, fought with shock troops of the Thirty-Ninth Division, was gazetted at the Chemin des Dames and won the Iron Cross. After the Great War, he studied philosophy at Heidelberg and Munich and played a leading part in organizing students in support of the Republic. He was one of the founders of the Socialistic *Student Bund*.

"After the bloody suppression of the real republican movement by reactionary officers, most of his friends being put in jail, he retired, disappointed, and went once more to Heidelberg, where he met the famous Professor Gundolf and the circle around the poet Stefan George, who was trying to create a new romantic art and an aristocratic movement by reviving the poetry of Hölderlin, the mysticism of Novalis, and the classical realism of Goethe. He also attended the sociological seminars of Prof. Max Weber. Following the advice of Gundolf, he wrote a book, *The Irony in Goethe's Work*, with which he took his Ph.D. Marriage made him a manufacturer of textiles in Berlin, a job in which he worked for three years. Then he was divorced from both his wife and his business, and went back to writing and politics, editing a democratic newspaper in Nüremberg which had great influence in 1926 in imprisoning Julius Streicher for Jew-baiting, thus stemming the flood of Nazism.

"In those years he began to write novels, and was called back to Berlin, where he lived (though traveling much through the country and in the South of France) until the Nazis came to power in January 1933. He fled to his native country, the Saar, which was free at this moment, and participated in the plebiscite of 1934-35, as a supporter of the *status quo* solution. Against the law, he was proscribed by the Nazis even before the plebiscite, being #19 on the

so-called Saar List. He had to flee to France, where he lived and wrote in close contact with the French vanguard—André Malraux, Paul Nizan, Luc Durtain, André Gide, Franz Masereel. In 1936, when the Spanish Civil War broke out, he joined the International Brigade and fought in the defense of Madrid as Officer in Charge of Morale of the Twelfth Brigade, later of the Forty-Fifth Division. Badly wounded at Huesca (Aragon), he convalesced in France and then in Ernest Hemingway's house in Key West, Fla., where he began his novel about Spain. Returning to France, he intended at the beginning of the Second World War to join the French Army, but was interned in a concentration camp, from which he was released in the Spring of 1940 by the intervention of English and American friends. He came to America and is living now in Mexico City, waiting for his quota number to emigrate to the United States. In Mexico he is finishing his new novel, the love story of a Spanish girl, living with the Fascists, hidden in the Madrid embassies.

"He is the author of six novels, all published in Europe and translated into different languages."

* * *

Herr Regler wrote the autobiographical account above from Mexico. He has now remarried. His World War experiences included confinement in an insane asylum after he was gassed and shell-shocked (an experience which altered profoundly his religious as well as his social beliefs); in Spain he was nearly bisected by a steel splinter from a shell. He appears either by name or by description in several novels and books of reminiscences about the Spanish Civil War. Only two of his novels thus far have been translated into English, but two others have been published in French.

WORKS AVAILABLE IN ENGLISH: The Prodigal Son, 1934; The Great Crusade, 1940.

ABOUT: Regler, G. The Great Crusade (see Preface by E. Hemingway); Nation October 1940; Time September 30, 1940.

*REID, FORREST (June 24, 1876†-), Irish novelist, biographer, and literary critic, was born in Belfast, the last of the twelve children of Robert Reid. Forrest Reid's mother, whose ancestors included Katherine Parr, the queen who survived Henry VIII, was his father's second wife. The elder Reid lost most of his money in ships that tried to run the blockade from Liverpool to America during the Civil War.

Until he was six, Forrest Reid had an English nurse, Emma, who walked him to

* Died January 4, 1947.

† Correction: Year of birth, 1875.

the Botanic Gardens through University Square; he was also tutored by his sister Connie, whose singing could dispel his night-terrors. At ten he discovered a different and pleasantly pagan dream world. He read in the Linen Hall Library; went to school when he was past eleven; and, though confirmed, steadfastly refused to attend church. He was then a "broad-nosed, wide-mouthed youngster of a distinct and somewhat Socratic ugliness."

Reid attended the Royal Academical Institution, Belfast, and took his B.A. degree at Christ's College, Cambridge University, where Ronald Firbank was a fellow-student. His first novel, *The Kingdom of Twilight,* a book he "detests," was the ninth volume of Fisher Unwin's First Novel Library. Reid then came under the literary influence of Henry James, who wrote to him graciously at first, but was seriously flustered when Reid dedicated his next novel, *The Garden God,* to him. It was written after intensive reading in Greek classics; "This adoration of youth was indeed one of the qualities of the Greek genius that most endeared it to me," Reid has said.

Forrest Reid is a notable stylist, a pronounced romanticist with poetic, mystical, and occasionally macabre characteristics, which served him well in writing bio-critical studies of such poets as William Butler Yeats and Walter de la Mare. *Spring Song* and its sequel, *Pirates of the Spring,* are excellent stories of English family life, displaying both sensitive and matter-of-fact children and adolescents among kindly but obtuse elders. They are also successful studies in abnormal psychology. Reid, who is unmarried, received an honorary D.Litt. degree from Queen's University, Belfast, in 1933, and is a member of the Irish Academy of Letters. He lives at Ormiston Crescent, Belfast, and his recreation is croquet.

PRINCIPAL WORKS: The Bracknels: A Family Chronicle, 1911; Following Darkness, 1912; The Gentle Lover, 1913; At the Door of the Gate, 1915; W. B. Yeats: A Critical Study, 1915; The Spring Song, 1916; A Garden by the Sea, 1918; Pirates of the Spring, 1919; Pender Among the Residents, 1922; Apostate (autobiography) 1926; Demophon, 1927; Illustrators of the Sixties, 1928; Walter de la Mare: A Critical Study, 1929; Uncle Stephen, 1931; Brian Westby, 1934; The Retreat, 1936; Peter Waring, 1937; Private Road (autobiography) 1940.

ABOUT: Reid, F. Apostate; Private Road.

REMARQUE, ERICH MARIA (1897-   ), German novelist, was born in Osnabrück, Westphalia, of a family of French descent which settled in the Rhineland after the French Revolution. His father, still living in Osnabrück, is a book-binder, and the family are devout Roman Catholics. Remarque is not a Jew, and that is his right name, contrary to reports spread about him by the Nazis. He was educated at the *gymnasium* in his home town, and at eighteen was drafted into the German army during the First World War. He was wounded five times, the last time very seriously.

After his discharge he took a teachers' course offered by the government to discharged soldiers, and taught for a year near the Dutch border. He hated teaching, however; he was mechanically-minded and full of physical energy; he threw up his job and for a while was a stonecutter in the cemetery at Osnabrück. He left this to tour Germany with friends in a "gypsy caravan," and then became a test driver for a Berlin tire company. He began to write articles for a Swiss automobile magazine, then did advertising copy writing for the tire company, and eventually became assistant editor of *Sportbild,* an illustrated sports magazine. It was at this time, in 1929, that he wrote the novels which had been in his mind ever since the war. Refused by one publisher, and reluctantly accepted by another, *All Quiet on the Western Front* was a sensation. It sold 1,200,000 copies in Germany alone, its first year; it was translated into many languages, was a terrific success as a motion picture, and made its author rich and famous —and open to attack.

In spite of his vivacious and energetic temperament, Remarque hated the publicity; his war injuries had moreover affected his lungs; and he retired to Porto Ronco, on Lake Maggiore in Switzerland, where in 1932 he built a house. Soon his exile, which had been temporary, had to become permanent; when the Nazis came into power they burnt his books, and in 1938 he was deprived of his German citizenship. Early in 1939 he came to the United States, and has been here since, living at present in Los Angeles, where he has filed application for United States citizenship.

Remarque was married in 1923, divorced in 1932, and remarried his wife, Ilsa, in 1938. Attempting to join her husband here, she was detained at Ellis Island, and was obliged to go to Mexico.

Kyle Crichton remarked that Remarque "looks like a halfback on an American football team." He is tall and blond, athletic in appearance, and handsome. He likes dogs and breeds them, is a fine musician (he once played the organ in a German insane asylum!), he can take any car to pieces and put it together again, in his prosperous days he collected paintings by Van Gogh and Cezanne and priceless Oriental rugs, and he is so shy that he goes to any length to avoid meeting strangers. His subsequent books all concern the war in which he served and the fate of its survivors. He hates Nazism as much as he hates war. Though he has real talent as a novelist, he is in a sense an accidental writer, whose theme is far more important to him than is the manner in which it is handled.

WORKS AVAILABLE IN ENGLISH: All Quiet on the Western Front, 1929; The Road Back, 1931; Three Comrades, 1937; Flotsam, 1941.

ABOUT: Canadian Forum September and November 1929; Collier's Weekly July 1, 1939; Living Age December 1930, June 1931; Saturday Review of Literature July 20, 1929, March 28, 1937; Time April 28, 1941.

REMIZOV, ALEXEY MIKHAILO-VICH (1877-   ), Russian novelist, short-story writer, and dramatist, derived his name

(which is not a pseudonym) from Réméza, the wonderful bird which figures in popular songs once heard in the Russian villages on Christmas eve. His immediate ancestors were rich Muscovite merchants, and his mother's family came originally from Souzdal, the ancient capital of Russia. Remizov's youth was passed in Moscow. His father's death left the family impoverished, and his boyhood was spent in the neighborhood of factories. Remizov mixed with street gamins, gaining his intimate knowledge of submerged types which was later to gain startling expression in his *Fifth Pestilence* and other stories. His religious upbringing was strictly orthodox, and Remizov went on numerous pilgrimages, visting the most celebrated monasteries and retreats, and mingling with monks, hermits, pilgrims, and beggars. He heard recited the popular legends which enrich the hagiography of the Eastern Church, attended solemn masses, and followed religious processions. Remizov attended scientific courses at the University of Moscow, where he also studied Russian history with Klutchevsky and pursued other courses in political economy and finance which, however, never made a good business man of him.

In 1905 he was business manager of *Voprossy Zhizni*, which published a novel by him in serial form. His wife, Mme. Ré-Dovgello, initiated him into the mysteries of archaeology. *La Russie dans Ses Incriptions* (to use the French titles of his books) covers a period of several centuries; *La Passion de l'Univers* is a series of legends; *La Foi Russe* is a cycle of twenty-five *contes* or tales; and *Les Femmes Russes* contains twenty-four portraits of women. From 1910 to 1912 his collected works in eight volumes were published in St. Petersburg. Remizov's play *Le Tzar Maximilien* was performed during the Revolution by soldiers of the Red Army (to the accompaniment of an accordion). In 1924 he escaped from Russia, and made his home on the Avenue Mozart in Paris.

In his own right a significant figure in modern Russian literature, Remizov is an acknowledged follower of Gogol. Pushkin, he once remarked, was an angel and Lermontov a demon, 'but I am neither one nor the other." John Cournos, one of his translators, describes him as a strange little figure, somewhat bowed, with a high, broad forehead and a face characteristically Russian—rather like one of the benign demons of his own invention, from his cycles of Siberian, Tibetan, Caucasian and Kabylian legends. He is concerned, says Alec Brown, "with the misery of the great mass of mankind, whose happiness is gnawed by petty considerations, for whom the slight oblivion of the cinema or the bottle is the paradise to which their daily activity is bent."

WORKS AVAILABLE IN ENGLISH TRANSLATION: The Clock (short stories) 1924; The Fifth Pestilence: Together With the History of the Tinkling Cymbal and Sounding Brass, Ivan Semyonovitch Stratilator, 1927.

ABOUT: Remizov, A. M. The Clock (see Introduction by J. Cournos); The Fifth Pestilence (see Introduction by A. Brown); Ost-Europa March 1934; La Vie des Peuples May 1924.

"RENN, LUDWIG." See VIETH VON GOLSSENAU

*REPPLIER, AGNES (April 1, 1858-   ), American essayist, was born in Philadelphia, the daughter of John George Repplier and Agnes (Mathias) Repplier. The family was of French descent and Roman Catholic religion. The little girl did not learn to read until she was ten; she had no need to, as her mother recited poetry to her "literally by the yard," and with her remarkable memory she learned it quickly and loved to recite it. Finally she was sent to the Sacred Heart Convent, in Torresdale, near Philadelphia. That was her only schooling, but she has honorary doctorates from the University of Pennsylvania, Yale, Columbia, and Princeton. She won the Laetare Medal of Notre Dame University in 1911, and the gold medal of the Academy of Arts and Letters in 1935. She has traveled a great deal in Europe, but for many years she has lived in an old red brick house in downtown Philadelphia. Its inner walls and hangings are gray, and so are the bindings of her books, which stand by themselves (she says for vanity) on a top shelf. She herself wears gray almost invariably. Frail and white-haired, in her eighties she is still indomitably herself, "an aristocratic spirit which seeks excellence for its own beautiful

Moffett

sake." She has never married, and like a Victorian spinster she loves cats and always has at least one purring by her tea-table. But she is no Victorian spinster. She is the only living American exemplar of a fine literary form fallen into undeserved obscurity—the genuine essay, as distinguished from the article.

Because of the era of her youth, and because she was an intimate of men older than herself — the senior Oliver Wendell Holmes, first of all — she has been in the past grouped with such innocuous writers of familiar essays as Henry Van Dyke and Hamilton Wright Mabie. She does not belong in their company; she does not condescend to her readers, she does not "date," and if she trifles it is on an exalted plane. J. J. Reilly well called her "daughter of Addison"; Mary Ellen Chase, "the dean of American essayists." In spirit and even in style she is more French than English; she loves France and speaks its language fluently. Most of her actual travel there and elsewhere, however, was done long after she had won her spurs as an author. (Her last long journey was as one of the American commissioners to the Seville Exposition in honor of Columbus when she was seventy.) She was only a girl of nineteen when Father Isaac Hecker, the Brook Farm associate who

became a priest and editor of the *Catholic World,* told her that she was "essentially a bookish person" and must write essays, not fiction as she desired. He printed her first essay, on Ruskin, and Holmes printed her second one in the *Atlantic.* Since then she has published many volumes of essays and two of biography, but she has remained true to her early instructions. Her one foray into another field was her compilation of *A Book of Famous Verse.*

Mason Wade praised her "very real gifts of style, wit, wisdom, and urbane tolerance." Add to these the gayety which is the obverse of a natural melancholy, forthrightness, and insistence in "going her own way" in solitude, in the manner of her beloved cats, and one has the background which has gone into the making of some of the most polished and brilliant essays in English—"piquant and pungent," Miss Chase called them, "felicitous yet spirited," displaying "a matchless genius at definition." A scholarly intelligence is warmed, in her work, by a delightful informality and an insatiable interest in life. Her point of view, however conservative, is never dull. Her name is pronounced *rep'leer.*

PRINCIPAL WORKS: Books and Men, 1888; Points of View, 1891; Essays in Miniature, 1892; Essays in Idleness, 1893; In the Dozy Hours, 1894; Varia, 1897; Philadelphia: The Place and the People, 1901; The Fireside Sphinx, 1901; Compromises, 1904; In Our Convent Days, 1905; A Happy Half Century, 1908; Americans and Others, 1912; The Cat, 1912; Counter Currents, 1915; Points of Friction, 1920; Under Dispute, 1924; Life of Père Marquette, 1929; Mère Marie: Of the Ursulines, 1931; To Think of Tea, 1932; In Pursuit of Laughter, 1936; Eight Decades, 1937.

ABOUT: Repplier, A. In Our Convent Days, A Happy Half Century, Eight Decades; Bookman June 1927; Boston Evening Transcript May 27, 1933; Catholic World November 1938; Commonweal August 18, 1933; Life June 24, 1940; New Republic December 8, 1937; Woman Citizen August 1926.

REYMONT, WLADYSLAW STANISLAW (May 6, 1868-December 5, 1925),
Polish novelist, winner of the Nobel Prize for literature, was born in the village of Kobiele Wielkie, located in the then Russian-Polish province of Piotrkow. His father was the village organist and barely managed to support his wife and nine children. The sensitive boy early found a haven from the ferule of his stern father

in the neighboring woods and fields; his first long escapade took him to his uncle, a surveyor. Wladyslaw's literary initiation was Slowacki's tragedy *Lilla Veneda* which he read surreptitiously at night by the moonlight. Despite his assiduous preparations for the entrance examinations to the secondary school at Lodz, he failed, and as a result was placed as apprentice to a tailor. After four years in the shop, just as he had succeeded in winning admission to the Guild, he dropped tailoring and returned home.

At the age of eighteen Wladyslaw was considered the family's black sheep; as he said of himself, "he ran after everything and then loathed it." His next adventure was with the theatre: he joined a traveling company and toured many provinces, but on becoming convinced of his lack of talent he entered the monastery of Czestochowa as a novice, remaining there but a few months. Back home his father's friends managed to get him a job supervising workmen on a railway extension. For two years he lived in a peasant's hut, reading anything he could lay hands on: Prus, Elisa Orzeszko, Dykasinski, translations of Zola's works and the English novelists, and especially Sienkiewicz's historical trilogy (*With Fire and Sword, The Deluge, Pan Michael*) which he devoured in seven consecutive days and nights and which left an indelible impression upon him. In short, literature was the one thing young Wladyslaw did *not* loathe; from his teens he was a poet and poet he remained till the end of his life. Poetry entered into his most prosaic everyday activities: for instance, once when asked for a report on a local railway accident he delivered a document which was promptly returned with the caustic comment: "We asked you for a report, not for a short story!"

Perhaps this incident stimulated Reymont to send some of his writings to the magazines: in 1893; when he was twenty-five, the weekly *Tygodnik Illustrowany* published one of his stories, whereupon he boarded a train for Warsaw. He reached the capital with three roubles and fifty kopeks (less than two dollars). One of his critics advised the budding realist to join the yearly pilgrimage to the old shrine of Czestochowa (which Reymont well knew both from personal experience and from the fictional recreation in Sienkiewicz's *The Deluge*) and jot down his observations. The result was the brilliant reportage, *A Pilgrimage to the Bright Mountain*, his first book, published in 1894. From then on, almost

yearly, Reymont wrote novel after novel, dramatizations, as it were, of his own biography: in 1896, *The Comedienne*, dealing with his theatre experience; in 1897, *Ferments*, dealing with railways, and also numerous stories of village life.

The proceeds from his literary activity permitted him to go to England where he visited his spiritual teacher, the theosophist Mme. Blavatsky. On returning home Reymont got himself a job in a factory at Lodz in order to study at first hand the background for a long novel dealing with the industrial proletariat: *The Promised Land,* which was published in 1898. This three-volume novel exposed so acidly the feats of the industrial magnates that the censor forced him to delete some four thousand lines from the original manuscript.

Reymont's life was bound up with railroads. At the turn of the century, he suffered an accident which kept him in bed for a year and a half. However, he received a modest indemnity, and while convalescing at Rome, wrote the first draft for a saga of peasant life which he soon threw to the flames. Later, in France, he resumed writing it and after working on it intensively for seven years (1902-1909) the result was his four-volume masterpiece *The Peasants,* which won him an international reputation and, in 1924, the Nobel Prize.

Occasionally Reymont interrupted his *magnum opus* with shorter works: stories dealing with the Russo-Japanese war and the Russian revolution of 1905, fantastic tales in the manner of Poe and Kipling, travel sketches. He followed *The Peasants* with other novels: one dealing with railroads, *The Dreamer* (1910), another with occultism, *Vampire* (1911), and in 1913 he embarked on an ambitious trilogy entitled *The Year 1794* dealing with the Kosciuszko insurrection. Reymont tried to emulate his master Sienkiewicz and to compete, not too gloriously, with the Stefan Zeromski of *Ashes.* Reymont failed to surpass his *Peasants. The Year 1794* was but a *succès d'éstime.*

Neither retrospective history nor the World War inspired Reymont to great achievements. His war stories, *Behind the Lines* (1919) were rather colorless, as mediocre as his long symbolic novel *The Revolt,* in which he attacked the Socialist revolution in Russia.

Reymont's fame therefore rests primarily on his great realistic novel *The Peasants,* which raises his name high among the loftiest representatives of contemporary Polish letters, and ranks him with Zola, Hamsun, Keller, and Hardy among the keenest observers of peasant life. Romain Rolland said that Reymont was "not a maker of books, but a piece of land, *his* land, in the entire cycle of its four seasons." His name is pronounced *ray'mont*.

PRINCIPAL WORKS AVAILABLE IN ENGLISH TRANSLATION: The Comedienne, 1920; The Peasants (4 vols.) 1924-5; The Promised Land (2 vols.) 1927.

ABOUT: Dyboski, R. Modern Polish Literature; Marble, A. R. Nobel Prize Winners in Literature; Morawski-Nawench, A. Ladislas Reymont at Home; Schoell, F. L. Les Paysans de Ladislas Reymont; Topass, J. Visages d'Ecrivains; Zaleski, Z. L. Attitudes et Destinées; Etudes July 20, 1927; Grande Revue January 1928; Monde Slave February 1927; Nouvelles Littéraires May 9, 1925; Pologne December 15, 1926; Slavonic Review March 1926, January 1938.

"RHODE, JOHN." See STREET, C.J.C.

RHODES, EUGENE MANLOVE (January 19, 1869-June 27, 1934), American novelist and short-story writer, whom Bernard De Voto called "The

Novelist of the Cattle Kingdom," was born in a log house at Tecumseh, Neb., the son of Hinman Rhodes, a colonel in the 28th Illinois Volunteers during the Civil War. The family, scourged by prairie fires, grasshoppers, and cyclones, moved to Cherokee, Kan., where the elder Rhodes opened a store and in 1881 was appointed Indian Agent for the Mescalero Apaches. Eugene was a horsewrangler at thirteen, punching cattle for the William C. McDonald outfit at Carrizzo Springs. At seventeen he was a guide and government scout during the Geronimo uprising. Later he staked a claim to a ranch in the San Andres Mountains, the wildest and most isolated section of New Mexico.

He was a cowboy for twenty-five years, and read incessantly, from paper classics put out by the Bull Durham company to railroad maps and labels on Worcestershire sauce bottles. Once he sat on the head of a bad broncho and read Browning. (He had attended the University of the Pacific, San José, Calif., two years, 1889-90, and contributed verse to the college paper.)

In 1906 Rhodes joined his wife and family in the East, running the Mutton Hill farm at Apalachin, N.Y. *McClure's Magazine* had bought a short story for $40, and he collaborated with Henry Wallace Phillips on stories for the *Saturday Evening Post,* always his best market. "The Little Eohippus" (later novelized as *Bransford in Arcadia*), published there November-December 1912, was remembered by thousands of readers. Robert Frost and Christopher Morley are Rhodes devotees. Bernard De Voto has written of Rhodes' works: "They are the only fiction of the cattle kingdom that reaches a level which it is intelligent to call art. . . . He is a realist not only of the externals of life in a vivid, brief era but a realist of the beliefs and aspirations that gave it vitality." Rhodes wrote, for one reason, because he resented Alfred Henry Lewis' *Wolfville* burlesque of Western life. He was "slender, gray, unconventional."

Death in California was caused by bronchitis and a badly enlarged heart. Rhodes' grave on the summit of the San Andres Mountains, N.M., is marked "Pasó por aquí" ("He passed by here")—the title of one of his best short stories and the legend left on Inscription Rock by the Spanish conquistadores. A memorial was dedicated at his burial place in 1941. His life was written by his widow, May Davison Rhodes, and contains a bibliography by Vincent Starrett.

PRINCIPAL WORKS: Good Men and True, 1910; Bransford in Arcadia, 1914; The Desire of the Moth, 1916; West Is West, 1917; Stepsons of Light, 1921; Copper Streak Trail, 1922; Once in the Saddle, 1927; The Trusty Knaves, 1933; Beyond the Desert, 1934; The Proud Sheriff, 1935.

ABOUT: Rhodes, M. D. The Hired Man on Horseback: My Story of Eugene Manlove Rhodes; Saturday Evening Post August 20, 1938; Saturday Review of Literature October 17, 1936, October 15, 1938.

RHODES, JAMES FORD (May 11, 1848-January 22, 1927), American historian and Pulitzer Prize winner, was born in Cleveland. He was edu-

cated at the Universities of New York and Chicago, and studied for six months at the Collège de France, in Paris, but was never graduated from any college. He had honorary doctorates, however, from ten universities, including Harvard, Yale, Princeton, and Oxford. His desire as a boy was to become a writer, and he showed interest very early in history and politics; but at his father's wish he went into business instead, first studying metallurgy in Berlin. From 1870 to 1885 he was in the coal and iron business in Cleveland.

Nevertheless, from 1877 he had resolved to write a history of the United States, and had begun to study with that end in view. His first published writing was a series of leaflets issued by himself, from 1881, at first a sort of monthly advertisement, but later general economic and historical discussions. In 1885 he liquidated his business and went to Europe, and in 1887 he began writing his major work, the nine-volume *History of the United States,* the first volume of which appeared in 1889. The series won him the Pulitzer Prize in 1918, though it was ten years more before the final volume was published. In 1891 he moved to Cambridge, Mass., then to Boston, and then to Brookline, where he died at nearly seventy-nine. He had never been a teacher and had no earned college degrees, but he was made a Corresponding Fellow of the British Academy and a Fellow of the American Academy of Arts & Science, and received the Loubat Prize of the Berlin Academy in 1901 and the gold medal of the National Institute of Arts and Letters in 1910. In 1872 he married Ann Card, and she, with one son, survived him. He was president of the American Historical Association in 1899, and gave a series of lectures at Oxford University in 1912. He was the authorized translator of the works of Ernest Renan.

Aside from his *magnum opus,* Rhodes wrote very little. The earlier volumes of the *History* are the best, since in dealing with the later period he became too greatly influenced by his personal association with contemporary Republican leaders; but all his work is characterized by "candidness, honesty, and clear understanding."

PRINCIPAL WORKS: History of the United States From the Compromise of 1850 to the End of the [Theodore] Roosevelt Administration (9 vols.) 1899-1928; Concerning the Writing of History, 1901; Historical Essays, 1909; Lectures on the American Civil War, 1912; History of the Civil War, 1917.

ABOUT: Howe, M. A. De W. James Ford Rhodes: American Historian; American Historical Review April 1927; Nation February 9, 1927; Outlook February 9, 1927; Saturday Review of Literature April 2, 1927.

*RHYS, ERNEST (July 17, 1859-), English poet, editor, and anthologist, writes: "Ernest Rhys was born of a Welsh father and an English mother, at Islington, in London. His wife was Grace Little, daughter of an Irish country squire. The two young people first met at a garden party given by the Irish poet, W. B. Yeats, and the mar-

riage was an unusually happy one. It was not in London but in Wales that the early boyhood of Ernest Rhys was passed, in his father's native place, Carmarthen. To the Celtic strain he inherited may be traced some characteristics of his temperament—his love of lake and mountain and wild scenery, and of Welsh and Irish legend, as shown in his own poetry and romance.

"However, he chose later, when living in the English North country, the unromantic career of a mining engineer. His literary ambition, and the lure of London, drew him, after some years of mining, to take the risky step of turning literary freelance and living in two garrets in Chelsea. To one of them came one day two provincial publishers, and offered him the editorship of a new prose library, which he accepted, and called it the 'Camelot Series.' This was a natural forerunner of the much greater enterprise of Everyman's Library, which began with Boswell's *Johnson* in 1906. The idea of a democracy of books, a progressive series of the best in the world's literature available in English, had occurred almost at the same time to its publisher, the late J. M. Dent, and its editor, who took the title from the old mystery play of *Everyman.* The catalogue is now going on to its thousandth volume, and a second great war against democracy has not deterred it from accomplishing its aims.

"In the intervals of editing, Mr. Rhys, now past eighty, has written novels, romances, poems, and plays. He would be the first to own his debt to the younger co-editors who have aided him in editing recent volumes of the Library."

* * *

Ernest Rhys, who lives now in semi-retirement in North Devon, is one of the last survivors of the group which included William Sharp, Havelock Ellis, J. A. Symonds, Lionel Johnson, and Ernest Dowson. A trip to the United States in the 1880's made him a friend of Edmund Clarence Stedman, James Russell Lowell, and Charles Eliot Norton. His wife, who was a novelist in her own right, died in 1929; they had a son and two daughters. "Pleasant" is the word which best describes his own writing, which has been incidental to his monumental services as an editor and anthologist. His name is pronounced *rees*.

PRINCIPAL WORKS: *Edited*—Camelot Series (30 vols.) 1886-1900; Lyric Poets (10 vols.) 1895-1905; Everyman's Library (967 vols.) 1906-40; Fairy Gold, 1906; Readings in Welsh History, 1910; Readings in Welsh Literature, 1911; The New Golden Treasury, 1914; The Old Country, 1917; The Golden Treasury of Longer Poems, 1921; The Land of Nursery Rhyme (with A. Daglish) 1932; A Christmas Holiday Book (with A. Daglish) 1934. *Poetry*—A London Rose and Other Rhymes, 1891; Welsh Ballads, 1903; Enid and Geraint (lyric drama, music by V. Thomas) 1905; Lancelot and Guenevre (lyric drama, music by V. Thomas) 1906; Rhymes for Everyman, 1933; Song of the Sun, 1937. *Miscellaneous*—The Fiddler of Carne (novel) 1901; The Whistling Maid (novel) 1904; English Lyric Poetry, 1913; Rabindranath Tagore, 1920; Everyman Remembers (autobiography) 1931; Letters From Limbo, 1936; Wales England Wed (autobiography) 1941.

ABOUT: Rhys, E. Everyman Remembers, Wales England Wed.

RICE, Mrs. ALICE CALDWELL (HEGAN)

(January 11, 1870-February 10, 1942), American novelist, was born in Shelbyville, Ky., the

daughter of Samuel Watson Hegan and Sallie (Caldwell) Hegan. She was educated in private schools, but later received honorary Litt.D. degrees from Rollins College and the University of Louisville. From the age of ten she showed a talent for both writing and drawing. From early girlhood she had character sketches and humorous stories published in local periodicals. She was by this time living in Louisville, which remained her home. She was interested also in charitable work among the poor of the city, and it was in this connection that she met the woman who was the prototype of the famous "Mrs. Wiggs." *Mrs. Wiggs of the Cabbage Patch*, laboriously written by hand in an old ledger, was accepted by the first publisher to whom it was sent. Published in 1901, it was an instantaneous success. In its first three years it sold 200,000 copies, it is still in print, it has been dramatized, filmed, transcribed in Braille, and translated into French, German, Swedish, Danish, Chinese, and Japanese. Years later Mrs. Rice helped to found the Cabbage Patch Settlement House, in Louisville, named for her book.

In 1902 Miss Hegan was married to Cale Young Rice,*qv* the poet, and they collaborated on several books. She produced many vol-

umes after her first success, but only *Lovey Mary* approached it in popularity. Six of her books, however, were made into motion pictures. The Rices lived in a roomy old house in a secluded Louisville street bordered with shade trees. Inseparable companions, they received doctorates from Rollins College on the same day. They traveled a great deal, and were at home in most parts of the world. Mrs. Rice, with her alert, humorous face crowned by soft white hair, was a woman of "expansive sympathy, spontaneous humor, graciousness, and charm." The Rices had no children.

Her books are unpretentious and unassuming, and of the kind usually described as "wholesome." They have, however, keen humor, real pathos, and a kindly understanding of human and especially of child nature. Her child characters are fresh and vivid in portrayal. All her books were drawn out of her own experience: *Quin,* for example, was the result of her work as a volunteer librarian at Camp Zachary Taylor and as Red Cross worker in service hospitals during the First World War. Mrs. Rice claimed no more for her books than that they appealed to the same kind of people about whom they were written.

PRINCIPAL WORKS: Mrs. Wiggs of the Cabbage Patch, 1901; Lovey Mary, 1903; Sandy, 1905; Captain June, 1907; Mr. Opp, 1909; A Romance of Billy Goat Hill, 1912; The Honorable Percival, 1914; Calvary Alley, 1917; Miss Mink's Soldier and Other Stories, 1918; Turn About Tales (with C. Y. Rice) 1920; Quin, 1921; Winners and Losers (with C. Y. Rice) 1925; The Buffer, 1929; Mr. Pete and Company, 1933; The Lark Legacy, 1935; Passionate Follies (with C. Y. Rice) 1936; My Pillow Book (non-fiction) 1937; Our Ernie, 1939; The Inky Way (autobiography) 1940.

ABOUT: Overton, G. The Women Who Make Our Novels; Rice, A. H. The Inky Way; Rice, C. Y. Bridging the Years; New York Herald Tribune February 11, 1942; New York Times February 11, 1942; St. Nicholas December 1927.

*RICE, CALE YOUNG

(December 7, 1872-). American poet, writes: "Cale Young Rice was born at Dixon, Ky., but moved with his parents to Evansville, Ind., when seven and resided there until he was seventeen. When ready for college he went to Cumberland University, thence to Harvard, to 'consult the sages.' After taking two degrees, under James, Royce, Santayana, Münsterberg, and other teachers, and after a year of professorship at Cumberland, he at last turned with consuming ardor to poetry, which had begun to obsess him. In 1902, at Louisville, where his parents were then living, he married Alice Caldwell Hegan, and in Louisville the two authors made their home—with many long and interesting journeys to Europe and the  Orient, journeys that have provided the poet with much inspiration, realistic and dramatic; for it has been his belief that romance, realism, and classicism are all to be used as material and occasion demand, and that the widely human spirit should transcend the narrowly nationalistic.

"After two early books of lyrics, Mr. Rice turned to poetic drama. Then followed books of lyric, narrative, and dramatic work in continuous succession, as selected and collected volumes. Since 1933 Mr. Rice has turned to prose, though he had already published several prose volumes in the 1920's. In *Bridging the Years* he relates his own life's experiences and literary contacts among the great and near-great, and at the end offers a theory of poetic inspiration, in the essay, 'Poetry's Genii.'"

* * *

Mr. Rice, a tall, slender, serious-faced man, has been predominantly, in spite of his versatility, a philosophic poet, and philosophy was his first love. Gilbert Murray said that "his books open up a most varied world of emotion and romance," but in general his earnest poetic labors have brought him neither popular nor critical acclaim.

PRINCIPAL WORKS: *Poetry*—From Dusk to Dusk, 1898; With Omar, 1900; Song Surf, 1900; Nirvana Days, 1908; Many Gods, 1910; Far Quests, 1912; At the World's Heart, 1914; Earth and New Earth, 1916; Trails Sunward, 1917; Wraiths and Realities, 1918; Songs to A. H. R., 1918; Shadowy Thresholds, 1919; Sea Poems, 1921; Mihrima and Other Poems, 1922; A Pilgrim's Scrip, 1924; A Sea Lover's Scrip, 1925; Selected Plays and Poems, 1926; Stygian Freight, 1927; Seed of the Moon, 1929; High Perils, 1933. *Plays* —Charles di Tocca, 1903; David, 1904; Yolanda of Cyprus, 1906; A Night in Avignon, 1907; The Immortal Lure, 1911; Porzia, 1913; Collected Plays and Poems, 1915; The Swamp Bird, 1931; Love and Lord Byron, 1936. *Miscellaneous*—Turn About Tales (with A. H. Rice) 1920; Youth's Way, 1923; Winners and Losers (with A. H. Rice) 1925; Early Reaping, 1929; Passionate Follies (with A. H. Rice) 1936; Bridging the Years, 1939.

ABOUT: Rice, C. Y. Bridging the Years; Literary Digest February 1, 1930.

RICE, ELMER L. (September 28, 1892-   ), American playwright, was born Elmer Reizenstein in New York City, the son of Jacob and Fanny (Lion) Reizenstein. He changed his name after he became a writer, because of the difficulty of spelling and pronouncing it. After high school he worked as an office boy and then as a law office clerk, studying law at night, and in 1912 received his LL.B. *cum laude* from the New York Law School. Instead of practising, however, he announced that he intended to become a playwright. He wrote a play, and knowing nothing of the orthodox procedure, merely mailed it to a producer—who promptly accepted it! It was *On Trial*, produced with success in 1914

Pinchot

—the first play to use the motion picture "cutback" technique.

For the next nine years, however, he made no further attempts to appear in the commercial theatre, but was associated with amateur organizations such as the Morningside Players and the University Settlement Dramatic Society, of which he was director. Through this medium he had four plays produced, some written in collaboration—*Iron Cross, Home of the Free, For the Defense,* and *Wake Up, Jonathan*. Then in 1923 the Theatre Guild put on *The Adding Machine*, an expressionistic play depicting the unbearable monotony of office drudgery. It was a success both in America and in England. Next he collaborated with Dorothy Parker in writing *Close Harmony* (also known as *Soft Music* and *The Lady Next Door*), and with Philip Barry in *Cock Robin*, a mystery play.

In spite of the easy manner in which Rice's career as a playwright had begun, he was considered "undependable" by the conventional producers, especially as he had grown increasingly radical in his economic views and was already (he has a rather peppery temper) belaboring the commercial theatre in speeches and articles. Therefore he had a hard time finding a producer for *Street Scene*, a tragedy whose characters are all the inhabitants of a New York tenement block. Finally accepted, it ran for more than a year, won the Pulitzer Prize for 1929, and was made into an outstanding motion picture.

In 1915 Rice had married Hazel Levy; they have a son and a daughter. The Rices were divorced in January 1942. Unlike many artists and writers, he has never become a suburbanite, but still lives in the heart of the city where he was born and reared. In 1936 he was for a time New York Regional Director of the Federal Theatre Project, but resigned in protest against censorship from Washington of the plays which the Project was producing. He is currently associated with Maxwell Anderson, Robert E. Sherwood, and others in the Playwrights' Company, which handles as a business unit the dramatic output of its members. He has constantly threatened to abandon the regular theatre altogether, and has done so more than once, especially after several of his later plays were badly received by the critics. He has written two novels, one a satire on the movies, the other an attempt to "do for New York what *Street Scene* did for a city block."

A short, stocky, young-looking man with a determined jaw, Elmer Rice has been a fighter for many liberal causes, and his plays, with very few exceptions, mirror his social views. Although he is uneven, his work at its best is always interesting and frequently exciting.

PRINCIPAL WORKS: *Plays* (dates of publication) —The Adding Machine, 1922; Close Harmony (with Dorothy Parker) 1924; Wake Up, Jonathan, 1928; Cock Robin (with Philip Barry) 1929; Street Scene, 1929; Subway, 1929; Counsellor-at-Law, 1931; The Left Bank, 1931; Plays (Adding Machine, Street Scene, See Naples and Die, Counsellor-at-law) 1933; We, the People, 1933; Judgment Day, 1934; Two Plays (Not for Children, Between Two Worlds) 1935; American Landscape, 1939; Two on an Island, 1940; Flight to the West, 1941. *Novels*—A Voyage to Purilia, 1930; Imperial City, 1937.

ABOUT: Mantle, B. Contemporary American Playwrights; Collier's Weekly May 4, 1929; Nation November 21, 1934, February 12, 1936; Theatre Arts Monthly January 1932.

RICHARDS, IVOR ARMSTRONG
(February 26, 1893-   ), English critic who signs his work I. A. Richards, was born in Sandbach, Cheshire, the son of W. Armstrong Richards. He was educated at Clifton College and at Magdalene College, Cambridge, where he was a scholar and was graduated with a First Class in the Moral Sciences Tripos in 1915. He has been a Fellow of Magdalene since 1926, and the year before that held the Charles Kingsley Bye-Fellowship. From 1922 to 1929 he was lecturer in English and moral

sciences at Magdalene, then spent a year as visiting professor of Tsing Hua University in Peiping (Peking). In 1931 he was visiting lecturer in English at Harvard. At the end of 1939 he returned to Harvard, on a five-year Rockefeller grant.

He was married in 1926 to Dorothy Eleanor Pilley, who is a writer; they have no children. With his long hair (now mostly gone), his owlish spectacles, his "rumpled clothes," and "glinting, slightly Oriental eyes," he is a striking figure, not altogether professorial, a wit and a "personality." His chief recreation is mountaineering.

Richards the critic is, with C. K. Ogden, the prime mover of the science of semantics, "the science of meaning," which is currently a considerable vogue. To him "metaphors are the basis of thinking," and "intelligence is the ability to ferret out the meaning of old words in new settings." His method is strictly scientific, his criticism based on accurate description, and his values defined in terms of function. He is almost a Behaviorist, and has been called a "psychological utilitarian." His theories stem openly from the economic and philosophical utilitarianism of Jeremy Bentham, though with a strong and rather incongruous flavor of the idealism of S. T. Coleridge. David Daiches said that "Richards demonstrated once and for all the essential relation between literature and other forms of activity and showed psychological knowledge to be a fundamental part of the critic's equipment." He added, however, that Richards is "not nearly so well up in literature as in psychology," and hence, though he can show *how* to produce "a valuable state of mind" he is not nearly so well able to state whether a given work of art does produce such a state. F. R. Leavis summed his work up by saying that "his unquestionable achievement . . . has been to provide the critic with an incomparably better apparatus of analysis than existed before."

Since 1932 Mr. Richards has been an advocate of "Basic English," a sort of internationally-adapted tongue consisting of 850 of the commonest English words. He has lately broadcast weekly over a Boston radio station to Latin-American countries in "Basic English," and under his supervision textbooks in it have been prepared for both Spanish- and Portuguese-speaking students. Two of his students have established the first "Basic English" school in Ecuador. This is largely the reason for his present residence in the United States; he feels that a German victory at arms would mean the likely end of English as a European tongue, and that the spread of "Basic English" in Latin America would become of first importance. In 1942 he helped Walt Disney in Hollywood with the text for propaganda "shorts."

PRINCIPAL WORKS: The Foundations of Aesthetics (with C. K. Ogden & J. Wood) 1921; The Meaning of Meaning (with C. K. Ogden) 1923; Principles of Literary Criticism, 1924; Science and Poetry, 1925; Practical Criticism, 1929; Mencius on the Mind: Experiments in Multiple Definition, 1931; Basic Rules of Reason, 1933; Coleridge on Imagination, 1934; Basic in Teaching: East and West, 1935; The Philosophy of Rhetoric, 1936; Interpretation and Teaching, 1938; How to Read a Page, 1942; Plato's Republic: a New Version Founded on Basic English, 1942.

ABOUT: Bookman (London) October 1932; New Republic March 1, 1939; Philosophical Review July 1935; Sewanee Review October 1938; Southern Review #2 1940; Time July 15, 1940; Virginia Quarterly Review October 1935.

*RICHARDS, Mrs. LAURA ELIZABETH (HOWE) (February 27, 1850-), American novelist, short-story writer, and

poet, writes: "I must begin with my father and mother, since without them I should neither have worked nor existed. My parents were Dr. Samuel G. Howe, the friend and teacher of the blind, and Julia Ward Howe, author of 'The Battle Hymn of the Republic.' I was born in Boston, and we spent our summers in Lawton's Valley, near Newport, R. I. I knew many songs and ballads before I could read, and ever since I have gone on learning by heart good poetry, the love of which has been one of the precious treasures of my life. When we six children were little, we had governesses and masters; then in due time we went to school. Always our parents were the most delightful of teachers, playmates, and companions.

"The first of my own writing that I remember was a story written when I was ten. But I never thought seriously of writing until after my marriage to Henry Richards, in 1871; not, indeed, until after the birth of my first baby. I made up jingles for her, which seemed to bubble up as if from some spring of nonsense. Often they seemed to come without any conscious effort of mine. When *St. Nicholas* was founded, in 1873, my husband suggested my sending some of my rhymes to the new magazine. I did, and that was the beginning. Seven babies came; the songs bubbled and jingled.

By and by the children wanted stories as well as poems. I wrote four books of stories and two of rhymes. By and by again, my babies were big boys and girls; I wrote stories for older children.

"No one can possibly imagine how I have enjoyed my writing. It was work, but it was also the most delightful play. I am still writing [at ninety!]. I have had a very long and very happy life."

* * *

In 1940, well past ninety, this frail-appearing but stout-hearted daughter of the woman who wrote "The Battle Hymn of the Republic," published stirring verses on the British heroism at Dunkerque. And in 1941 the daughter of the man who had aided the Greeks in their struggle for independence a century before dedicated a poem to the modern Greek resistance against the Fascist aggressors.

Mrs. Richards still lives in Gardiner, Maine, where she has lived since 1876. Her husband was an architect, who illustrated one of her books for children; he also ran a paper mill and a camp for boys. They had five daughters (of whom three survive) and two sons. In Gardiner Mrs. Richards fought for and secured a library, a high school, and the services of a district nurse. There she befriended in his early years the shy poet, Edwin Arlington Robinson. She has known nearly all the great New England literary figures since the "flowering." On the walls of her "Yellow House" hang side by side a blunderbuss brought by her father from the Greek War for Independence, in which he fought in 1830, the original manuscript of "The Battle Hymn of the Republic," and the Croix de Guerre won by her son in the First World War. She has edited her father's *Letters and Journals* (1906-09), and written, with her sister, Maud Howe Elliott, a life of their mother; she has also written half a dozen other biographies, including her father's and Robinson's. The life of Julia Ward Howe received the first Pulitzer Prize for Biography in 1917. But most of her work has been for children and young people. Best known is *Captain January*, twice filmed, the second time as a vehicle for Shirley Temple. Mrs. Richards is still attractive in appearance, with delicate, firm features and a mass of snow-white hair.

PRINCIPAL WORKS: Sketches and Scraps, 1881; Five Mice, 1881; Joyous Story of Toto, 1885; Toto's Merry Winter, 1887; Queen Hildegarde, 1889; In My Nursery, 1890; Captain January, 1890; Hildegarde's Holiday, 1891; Hildegarde's Home, 1892; Melody, 1893; When I Was Your Age, 1893; Glimpses of the French Court, 1893;

* Died January 14, 1943.

Marie, 1894; Hildegarde's Neighbors, 1895; Nautilus, 1895; Jim of Hellas, 1895; Five Minute Stories, 1895; Narcissa, 1896; Isla Heron, 1896; Some Say, 1896; Hildegarde's Harvest, 1897; Three Margarets, 1897; Margaret Montfort, 1898; Love and Rocks, 1898; Rosin the Beau, 1898; Peggy, 1899; Rita, 1900; For Tommy, 1900; Snow White, 1900; Quicksilver Sue, 1901; Fernley House, 1901; Geoffrey Strong, 1901; Mrs. Tree, 1902; The Hurdy Gurdy, 1902; The Green Satin Gown, 1903; More Five Minute Stories, 1903; The Golden Windows, 1903; The Merryweathers, 1904; The Armstrongs, 1905; Mrs. Tree's Will, 1905; The Piccolo, 1906; Letters and Journals of Samuel Gridley Howe (ed.) Vol. I, 1906, Vol. II, 1909; The Greek Revolution (ed.) 1906; The Silver Crown, 1906; Grandmother, 1907; The Wooing of Calvin Parks, 1908; Life of Florence Nightingale For Young People, 1909; A Happy Little Time, 1910; Up to Calvin's, 1910; Two Noble Lives, 1911; Aboard the Mary Sands, 1911; Miss Jimmy, 1912; The Little Master, 1913; Three Minute Stories, 1914; The Big Brother Play Book, 1915; Life of Julia Ward Howe (with M. H. Elliott) 1916; Fairy Operettas, 1916; Life of Elizabeth Fry, 1916; Pippin, 1917; Life of Abigail Adams, 1917; "To Arms!" (war poems) 1917; A Daughter of Jehu, 1918; Life of Joan of Arc, 1919; Honor Bright, 1920; In Blessed Cyrus, 1921; The Squire, 1923; Oriental Operettas, 1924; Acting Charades, 1924; Honor's New Adventure, 1925; Star Bright, 1927; Laura Bridgman, 1928; Stepping Westward (autobiography) 1931; Tirra Lirra, 1932; Samuel Gridley Howe, 1935; Merry Go-Round, 1935; E. A. R., 1936; Harry in England, 1937; I Have a Song to Sing You, 1938; What Shall the Children Read? 1939; The Hottentot and Other Ditties (words and music) 1939.

ABOUT: Kunitz, S. J. & Haycraft, H. (eds.) The Junior Book of Authors; Richards, L. E. Stepping Westward; Woollcott, A. While Rome Burns; Boston Evening Transcript December 5, 1931; Horn Book July-August 1941.

RICHARDSON, DOROTHY M.

(1882-   ), English novelist, writes: "There is but little to tell of me. My childhood and youth were passed, in secluded surroundings, in late Victorian England. Day-school linked me with 'the world,' upon which I was thrown when, in my seventeenth year, my home broke up. Some of my impressions of what is implied in the capacious term are set down in *Pilgrimage*, begun in 1913, and not yet complete.

"What do I think of the term 'Stream of Consciousness,' as applied, in England, to the work of several modern novelists [and especially to Miss Richardson's own]? Just this: that amongst the company of useful labels devised to meet the exigencies of literary criticism it stands alone, isolated by its perfect imbecility. The transatlantic amendment, 'Interior Monologue,' though rather more inadequate than even a label has any need to be, at least carries a meaning.

"Literature is a product of the stable human consciousness, enriched by experience and capable of deliberate, concentrated contemplation. Do not the power and the charm of all literature, from the machine-made product to the 'work of art,' reside in its ability to rouse and to concentrate the reader's contemplative consciousness?

"The process may go forward in the form of a conducted tour, the author leading, visible and audible, all the time. Or the material to be contemplated may be thrown on the screen, the author out of sight and hearing; present, if we seek him, only in the attitude towards reality, inevitably revealed: subtly by his accent, obviously by his use of adjective, epithet, and metaphor. But whatever be the means by which the reader's collaboration is secured, a literary work, for reader and writer alike, remains essentially an adventure of the stable contemplative human consciousness.

"I must add the fact of the survival and increase, in the writer, of wonder and of joy, many other strong emotions competing but never quite prevailing."

* * *

Miss Richardson is married to Alan Odle, an artist and illustrator, and lives in London. She is short and stocky, with abundant graying hair, near-sighted blue eyes, and a wide mouth full of quiet humor and sweetness. Louis Untermeyer has called her "as plain and subtle as her own style . . . quiet but dominating . . . with rich sensibility, and comedy that is realistic and yet at the same time classical."

She objects strenuously to the theory that her multi-volumed *Pilgrimage*, which is her life work (though she writes poems and articles, she has published only one other book) is "enormously long": she says that is "a widespread illusion born of the length of time during which the separate volumes have been appearing. As a matter of fact, the whole, to date, is no longer than four English novels." Miriam Henderson, the central figure of *Pilgrimage*, is often identified with the author herself. All the twelve sections (to date) revolve around her inner experience. Joyce and Proust are the best known exponents of this method (Ford Madox Ford called Dorothy Richardson "the most abominably unknown contemporary writer"), but in Miss Richardson's work reticence is substituted for candor; "every critical experience," a critic noted, "occurs off-stage, between volumes; she reduces the stream of consciousness to a trickle." Her books, said Constance M. Rourke, "seem, first of all notation, a series of flexibly impressionistic records. . . . Miss Richardson's special gift lies in her power to make the mere flux of the concrete suggest so much." Elizabeth Bowen, though deploring a static "lack of energy" in *Pilgrimage,* concluded: "Until Dorothy Richardson has been given her proper place, there will be a great gap in our sense of the growth of the English novel."

PRINCIPAL WORKS: The Quakers, Past and Present, 1914; Pilgrimage: Pointed Roofs, 1915; Backwater, 1916; Honeycomb, 1917; The Tunnel, 1919; Interim, 1919; Deadlock, 1921; Revolving Lights, 1923; The Trap, 1925; Oberland, 1927; Dawn's Left Hand, 1931; Clear Horizon, 1935; Dimple Hill, 1938; (Omnibus Edition, 1938).

ABOUT: Beach, J. W. The Twentieth Century Novel; Collins, J. The Doctor Looks at Literature; Johnson, R. B. Some Contemporary Novelists; Women; Mais, S. P. B. Books and Their Writers; Mansfield, K. Novels and Novelists; Powys, J. C. Dorothy M. Richardson; Adelphi November 1924, May-June 1931; Canadian Forum June 1939; Current Opinion June 1919; New Republic November 26, 1919; Publishers' Weekly November 26, 1938 Sewanee Review January 1934.

*RICHARDSON, HENRY HANDEL

(1880?-   ), pen-name of Mrs. Ethel F. Lindesay (Richardson) Robertson, Australian-English novelist. She writes: "I was born in Melbourne, Australia, of Anglo-Irish parents—my father was W. Lindesay Richardson, M.D.—and educated at the Presbyterian Ladies' College, the leading school for girls in that city. Here, the chief talent I displayed was for music, and after I had matriculated, I was taken to Leipzig, to study piano. Much as I enjoyed my three and a half years' work at the Conservatorium, I soon realized, on comparing myself with others, that I could never hope to excel as a pianist; and, in face of considerable opposition from my family, I threw up the musical career that had been picked for me. Myself, I had always wanted to be a writer —I had scribbled stories ever since I could hold a pen. And after my marriage—it was in Leipzig that I first met my husband, subsequently the well-known German scholar, Prof. John G. Robertson—I was free to follow my bent. Encouraged by him I set to work on my first novel, *Maurice Guest.*

"I had always been an omnivorous reader, and in Strasbourg, where we lived for a time, all the treasures of the great National Library were at my disposal. I soaked myself in French, Russian, German, and Scandinavian literature. The writer who undoubtedly carried most weight with me was Flaubert, an absorbed study of whose life and letters left an indelible impression on the young beginner. From this master I learned how a theme was to be handled objectively, without intrusion of the author's personality; and from him derives also an aversion to phrase-making—the phrase *per se*—which I have never lost. Next came the great Russians, Tolstoy and Dostoievsky, both of whose traces are, I think, to be found in *Maurice Guest*; while the little *Getting of Wisdom* owes more to my browsings in Scandinavian literature. Not until I wrote my third book, *Australia Felix,* did I begin to come into line with the traditions of the English novel.

"*Maurice Guest* was finished in England, where, in 1904, my husband was called to fill the newly established chair of Germanic Language and Literature at the University of London. For my pen-name I took one well-known in the Richardson family. This neither had nor has any connection with my own musical preferences.

"The books that followed were all, with the exception of *The Young Cosima,* written either in London or at our cottage in Dorset. The first volume of the Australian trilogy necessitated a voyage to Australia: except for this, I have never been back to my native land. My husband's death, in 1933, broke up our London home. Since then I have lived more or less in the country, at Fairlight, in East Sussex.

"My life has been a very uneventful one, and hampered by ill-health. Outside my work, music and reading have remained my two chief stand-bys, books my best friends. Nowadays I read more biography than fiction; though for relaxation I often turn to a good detective story. I belong to no particular political party, and can only say that I value freedom—personal, social, political freedom—more than anything in the world."

* * *

Henry Handel Richardson was described by Alice Henry, in 1929, as tall, with dark waving hair, and expressive eyes. She is reticent and modest, though confident of her worth as a writer. She has practically no social or "literary" life, seldom goes out in the evening, and belongs to no clubs.

Many critics and readers believe that the Richard Mahony trilogy is one of the great novels of its kind and in its generation, comparable to Thomas Mann's *Buddenbrooks* or Rolland's *Jean-Christophe*. In it, as Miss Henry remarked, she "produces a sense of the pathos and tragedy of life that is well-nigh over-powering." To many critics her recent fictional biography of Cosima Wagner was not nearly so fine a piece of work, even though it returned to her early preoccupation with music. She is a very slow, thorough worker, but it is to be hoped that at least one more novel of the *genre* of her earlier triumphs may still come from her pen. C. Hartley Grattan, the American critic and an authority on Australian literature, calls attention to the curious fact that only one of Henry Handel Richardson's works has found publication in her native country—though she is without doubt the greatest literary name the continent has produced.

PRINCIPAL WORKS: Maurice Guest, 1908; The Getting of Wisdom, 1910; Australia Felix, 1917; The Way Home, 1925; Ultima Thule, 1929; The Fortunes of Richard Mahony (Australia Felix, The Way Home, Ultima Thule) 1930; Two Studies, 1931; The End of a Childhood, 1934; The Young Cosima, 1939.

ABOUT: Richardson, H. H. Maurice Guest (see Introduction to 1922 ed. by Hugh Walpole); Bookman December 1929; Bookman (London) May 1929; Canadian Forum March 1931; Virginia Quarterly Review July 1940; World Today August 1929.

RICHMOND, Mrs. GRACE LOUISE (SMITH) (1866-), American novelist and short-story writer, was born in Pawtucket, R.I., the daughter of Charles Edward Smith, D.D., and Catharine A. (Kimball) Smith. She was educated at the Syracuse (N.Y.) High School, and pursued a collegiate course under private tutors. In 1887 she married Dr. Nelson Guernsey Richmond, of Fredonia, N.Y., where the Richmonds still make their home. There were four children; two sons, one of whom died; and two daughters, both married. With her family well launched, Mrs. Richmond began to write fiction of the wholesome type, painting an idyllic picture of family life (*Around the Corner in Gay Street* and its sequel, *Worthington Square*, serialized in the *Youth's Companion*, are typical examples) and of the romantic and humanitarian aspects of the medical profession (*Red Pepper Burns,* and its numerous successors). Edward Bok, editor of the *Ladies' Home Journal*, was a frequent purchaser of her wares. *Strawberry Acres, Red and Black, Red of the Redfields, Rufus,*

and *Cherry Square* were some of Mrs. Richmond's prettily fanciful titles; there was, however, nothing either lurid or subversive in her stories, which usually appeared as serials in women's magazines. Dr. Redfield Pepper Burns, the chief protagonist of her fiction, with red hair and an inflammable but well-controlled temper, is, as the *Saturday Review of Literature* remarked "so clean, so virile, so upstandingly proper that a large audience will doubtless take him to its bosom." Mrs. Richmond's thoughts are expressed with homely—and somewhat bookish—charm, according to the New York *Herald Tribune "Books."* She "makes all her people handsome and interesting and angelic," commented the New York *Times,* "such paragons of beauty and behavior that they hardly seem to belong in the naughty world that most of us know." "With all her emphasis upon 'wholesomeness'," the *Nation* concludes, "a sweet sentimentality weakens the needed effect of vigor; and this holds true of style as well as general construction." Mrs. Richmond is a doctor in her own right, receiving a Litt.D. from Colby College in 1924. A Presbyterian, she is also a member of the League of American Pen Women, the Authors' League of America, the Authors' Guild, and the British Society of Authors, Playwrights, and Composers. Her books are very popular in England.

PRINCIPAL WORKS: The Indifference of Juliet, 1905; The Second Violin, 1906; With Juliet in England, 1907; Around the Corner in Gay Street, 1908; On Christmas Day in the Morning, 1908; A Court of Inquiry, 1909; On Christmas Day in the Evening, 1910; Red Pepper Burns, 1910; Strawberry Acres, 1911; Mrs. Red Pepper, 1913; The Twenty-Fourth of June, 1914; Under the Country Sky, 1916; Red Pepper's Patients, 1917; The Brown Study, 1917; Red and Black, 1919; Foursquare, 1922; Rufus, 1923; Red of the Redfields, 1925; Cherry Square, 1926; Lights Up, 1927; At the South Gate, 1928; The Listening Post, 1929; High Fences, 1930; Red Pepper Returns, 1931; Bachelor's Bounty, 1931.

ABOUT: Whitman, W. Grace S. Richmond: Builder of Homes; American Home December 1928; Bookman May 1905; Ladies' Home Journal June 1915.

RICHTER, CONRAD (October 13, 1890-), American novelist, writes: "I was born in Pine Grove, Pa., of mixed South German, French, English, and Scotch-Irish blood. My father, grandfather, uncle, and great uncles were preachers. Their fathers, however, had been tradesmen, soldiers, country squires, blacksmiths, and farmers, and I think that in my passion for early American life and people I am a throwback to these. At fifteen I finished high school and was obliged to go to work. In

the next few years I drove teams, clerked, pitched hay, was a bank teller, country correspondent, timberman, and subscription salesman. A series of articles in the *Bookman* about newspaper men made me know

what permanent work I wanted to do. I got my first job reporting on the Johnstown, Pa., *Journal*, and at nineteen edited the weekly *Courier* at Patton, Pa. Later I reported on the Pittsburgh *Despatch* and the Johnstown *Leader*, and then became a private secretary in Cleveland, where my first fiction story was sold.

"Also in Cleveland I wrote 'Brothers of No Kin,' which the late Edward J. O'Brien was kind enough to call the best story of 1914 when it appeared in the *Forum*. It was reprinted in a number of papers, and editors at once wrote asking for my stories. It was the sort of opportunity no youth today would fail to grasp, but I was too young, and callow and too stubborn. The *Forum* had said nothing about money, and when I got up courage to call on Mitchell Kennerley he wrote me out a check for $25. I had just been married, had sober obligations, and told myself stubbornly that if this was what one got for the 'best' story of the year, I had better stick to business and write in my spare time only the type of story that would fetch a fair price, which I did.

"In 1928 I sold my small business and came to live in the West. In the next half-decade I collected on the Southwest a shelf of first-hand notes from original sources, early rare books, newspapers, and manuscripts, but mostly data from the memories of old men and women then still alive. In the winter of 1933, I thought it time to reverse a fifteen-year-old resolution and to turn my hand to the best fiction of which I was capable. I have since published a volume of short stories and three novels on early American life.

"Most of the time I live at Albuquerque, N.M. [This sketch was written from Tucson, Ariz.] My wife is still the hometown girl, Harvena M. Achenbach, I married in 1915, and we have a daughter, writing advertising in New York."

PRINCIPAL WORKS: Brothers of No Kin and Other Stories, 1924; Early Americana and Other Stories, 1936; The Sea of Grass, 1937; The Trees, 1940; Tacey Cromwell, 1942.

ABOUT: Saturday Evening Post March 2, 1940.

RIDGE, LOLA (1883-May 1941), American poet, was born in Dublin, Ireland, and spent her girlhood in New Zealand and Australia, but came to the United States in 1907 and lived in New York thereafter. She had studied art in Sydney, and intended to be a painter, but she was soon deflected to poetry. Nevertheless, after having prepared a volume of poems, she decided

M. Content

they were not good enough for publication, and (to her later regret) destroyed all copies of them. For several years she supported herself by writing popular fiction (which she stopped doing when it threatened to end her ability to "survive as an artist"), doing advertising copy-writing, illustrating, acting as an artist's model, organizing educational groups, and working in a factory. Always frail, her health gave way under drudgery and privation, and for much of her life she was a semi-invalid. She was married to David Lawson. Her sympathies were always strongly to the left, and she was active in the defense of Sacco and Vanzetti in 1927. She was a founder and later editor of *Others* and an editor of *Broom*, two of the early "advanced" literary magazines. In 1935 she received a Guggenheim Fellowship.

Her first recognition came with publication of her long poem, "The Ghetto," in the *New Republic* in 1918. A volume containing this poem appeared the same year and was followed by two more. Her next book did not appear until 1920; it was the eloquent *Firehead*, inspired by but not based on the Sacco-Vanzetti case. Then came another long silence, until *Dance of Fire* in 1935. (Fire seemed to be her special symbol.) At the time of her death at fifty-eight she was working on a long philosophical poem, which was left unfinished. Ill health and the giving of most of her small strength to the causes in which she believed were, besides her strict poetic integrity, the reason for her very limited output.

She was nevertheless a poet of high rank. Hildegarde Flanner spoke of her "tense and vigorous poetic thinking," with its "underlying tone of the mystical and racial." "She has maintained a pitch rather like moral grandeur without becoming metaphorical or losing adroitness.... Her prosody is for the most part traditional, [but] the manipulation of thought in her best poems is even

and sustaining." Her *Dance of Fire*, a poem of earth's ending, has been compared to Edna St. Vincent Millay's "Epitaph for the Race of Man" and Genevieve Taggard's "Ice Age." Louis Untermeyer said she had "chastity of power," and that when she "leaves the supernal for the human" she sounds "her major music." Her chief defects, overcome in her best work, are a weakness for archaisms of speech and a tendency toward confusion of subject.

To Harry Salpeter she seemed "more spirit than body," and "selfless beyond all reason. . . . She is like a bright, untarnished, double-edged sword in her courage and her integrity." And her fineness of spirit was implicit in her thin white face under a mass of dark hair: Llewelyn Powys called it "like the impassive death-mask of a saint."

PRINCIPAL WORKS: The Ghetto and Other Poems, 1918; Sun-Up and Other Poems, 1920; Red Flag and Other Poems, 1924; Firehead, 1929; Dance of Fire, 1935.

ABOUT: Poetry October 1935, July 1941; Saturday Review of Literature December 28, 1929, May 31, 1941.

RIDING, LAURA (January 16, 1901-),

American poet and critic, writes: "I was born in New York City, of Jewish (but not religiously so) parents. My mother was born in downtown Manhattan. My father, Nathaniel Reichenthal, was born in Austria and emigrated to America in his early teens. He was a tailor by trade, but in later life had a varied—and consistently unsuccessful—business career. Working for Socialism took up a large part of his time and energy. He brought me up sternly in his political faith; his hope was that I would become an American Rosa Luxemburg.

"Because of my father's frequent business moves I attended primary schools in about a dozen different places. But I was lucky enough to be able to spend all four high-school years at Girls' High School, Brooklyn, where I received a remarkably thorough education in a number of subjects—chiefly, English grammar and syntax and punctuation, and Latin, and French. With the help of three scholarships I went to Cornell University, where I took a general arts course. While at Cornell I married Louis Gottschalk, a history instructor, and gave up my studies

when he went to teach at the University of Illinois. We were divorced in 1925.

"I began writing poems while I was a student at Cornell. My first real boost came when the Fugitives, a group of Nashville poets, awarded me a prize of $100 and made me an honorary member. That was (I believe) in the fall of 1924. In December 1925 I left for Europe, after having tried my literary fortunes in New York for a short period. I spent thirteen years abroad, living in Egypt, England, Majorca, and France; and wrote hard all that time, trying to use words with new exactness.

"I returned to the United States in April 1939. In 1941 I married Schuyler Jackson (poet, farmer, and contributing editor of *Time*). Together my husband and I are at work on A Working English Dictionary and Thesaurus. Our object is to give each of the 30,000-odd words dealt with a distinct definition or set of definitions, and also to arrange the words according to their meanings in small homogeneous groups.

"My home is in New Hope, Pa."

* * *

Laura Riding's poetry, which some readers find exciting, others baffling, has been both eulogized and attacked by critics. What cannot be disputed is that it is the work of a serious, precise intelligence and that its qualities of bite, dryness, and abstraction are in process of being absorbed into the tradition of modern poetry.

PRINCIPAL WORKS: A Survey of Modernist Poetry (with R. Graves) 1927; Contemporaries and Snobs, 1928; Anarchism Is Not Enough, 1928; A Pamphlet Against Anthologies (with R. Graves) 1928; Poems: A Joking Word, 1930; Experts Are Puzzled, 1930; Four Unposted Letters to Catherine, 1930; Everybody's Letters, 1933; The Life of the Dead, 1933; Poet: A Lying Word, 1933; Progress of Stories, 1936; A Trojan Ending, 1937; Collected Poems, 1938; Lives of Wives, 1939.

ABOUT: Newsweek September 4, 1939; Poetry May 1939; Saturday Review of Literature February 9, 1935; Time December 26, 1938.

RIESENBERG, FELIX (April 9, 1879-November 19, 1939), American novelist, wrote to the editors of this volume before his death: "Felix Riesenberg was born in Milwaukee, the son of William and Emily (Schorb) Riesenberg. His father was a sea captain. At the age of sixteen he went to sea, and followed the sea for twelve years. He took part in the Wellman Polar Expedition in 1906-07, and was navigator of the airship 'America' of that expedition, first dirigible balloon to attempt a flight over the

North Polar Regions. This was followed by four years at Columbia University, when

he took the degree of Civil Engineer. The World War again took him to sea, in command of the 'U.S.S. Newport,' on schoolship duty. This service, in 1917-19, was followed, after an interval ashore as an engineer, by a second tour of the same command in 1923-24. Much of his sea and shore background is found in his books.

"His first published book was *Under Sail,* a narrative of life at sea in the last of the great wooden three-skysail ships built in Maine. Then followed two technical books, both widely used at sea, *The Men on Deck* and *Standard Seamanship for the Merchant Service.* His novel, *East Side, West Side,* was made into one of the last of the large-scale silent movies—the last to be filmed in New York.

"He is an associate editor of the *Nautical Gazette,* writing a weekly page called 'The Rough Log.' He has written for the screen, for magazines, and for the radio, and in collaboration with Christopher Morley wrote a play, *The Second Mate,* produced in Hoboken in 1930."

* * *

From 1933 to 1938, Captain Riesenberg was engaged in engineering work, in writing, and in traveling aboard American ships, collecting material for a history of the American merchant marine. For a time he was associated with the United States Maritime Commission. In 1939 he was a member of the board of the Order of Adventurers, an N.B.C. broadcast which brought together with him Admiral Richard E. Byrd, Colonel Theodore Roosevelt, Lowell Thomas, and Dr. Roy Chapman Andrews. He also did occasional broadcasts of news of the war at sea for C.B.S. He was vice president and consulting engineer of a motor company. In 1912 he married Maud Conroy, and they had three sons and a daughter.

He was a typical sea captain in appearance, bearded (at times), bright-eyed, and with rolling gait. Christopher Morley, his old friend, wrote of him: "What an extraordinary fortune for the world of print, when such a man . . . took to putting his thoughts on paper. . . . In gravity and in humor and in quite unconscious skill no writer in our time has surpassed the virile

coefficient of Riesenberg's brief sketches. In fiction he was powerful but uncertain. . . . He was always perhaps a little bewildered by the complex trickery of life ashore. . . . There was never a writer less literary in temperament. He was of the Defoes and Jules Vernes and Sam Clemenses, a testifier by brute accident and pressure. His sheer lack of conscious technique makes him irresistible. Put him under a sudden gust of emotion and watch his penmanship. . . . At his cleverest or clumsiest I would not have a word altered in any of his writing for every word had its own comic and beloved virtue."

Captain Riesenberg died of heart disease in New York following a brief illness, leaving his book on the Pacific Ocean unfinished. It was completed by Russell Owen. His remains were cremated and the ashes buried at sea on December 20, 1939. His last obituary was a message to Christopher Morley from Captain Cross of the "S.S. City of Baltimore," who committed the ashes to the ocean: "The day was one which Felix would have loved—fine sailing weather, the sky partly cloudy, wind moderate S.E., and the sun flashing on the waves."

PRINCIPAL WORKS: *Novels*—Under Sail, 1915; Bob Graham at Sea (juvenile) 1925; P. A. L., 1925 (as Red Horses, 1928); East Side, West Side, 1927; Endless River, 1931; The Maiden Voyage (with Archie Binns) 1931; Passing Strangers, 1932; Mother Sea, 1933; The Left Handed Passenger, 1935. *Non-Fiction*—The Men on Deck, 1918; Standard Seamanship, 1922; Vignettes of the Sea, 1926; Shipmates, 1928; Log of the Sea, 1933; Living Again (autobiography) 1937; Portrait of New York, 1939; Cape Horn, 1939; The Pacific Ocean, 1940.

ABOUT: Riesenberg, F. Living Again; Manchester Guardian December 15, 1939; Publishers' Weekly December 2, 1939; Saturday Review of Literature December 2, 1939.

*RIGGS, LYNN (1899-), American dramatist and poet, was born near Claremore, Oklahoma (then Indian Territory), also the

birthplace of Will Rogers. His father was a cowpuncher, and the boy became familiar with the vanishing species of cowboys and with the open range. He was educated in the public schools, drove a grocery wagon for pocket money, and read lurid fiction for amusement.

Before entering the University of Oklahoma, young Riggs visited both New York and the Pacific coast, earning a living by working in a glass factory and an express office, singing in motion-picture houses, selling books in a department store (Macy's), and reading proof on a financial newspaper. In his second year as a student at the university, he taught courses in freshman English.

In 1921 he wrote his first play, a farce, designed for amateur production. Next year Riggs toured the Middle West as the second tenor in a Chautauqua circuit quartet. "Upon recovering," as he puts it, he worked on a Santa Fé ranch. The Santa Fé Players produced his one-act play, *Knives From Syria*, in 1925, and next year he returned to New York to work and write. Poems first appearing in the *Nation* and *Poetry* were collected in *The Iron Dish* (1930). The American Laboratory Theatre produced *Big Lake* in New York during 1927; the same year that a Philadelphia repertory theatre staged *Rancor*. *Domino Parlor* was tried out by the Shuberts in 1928, but failed to reach Broadway. Recommended for a Guggenheim Fellowship by Barrett Clark in the late 'twenties, Riggs spent a year in Paris writing *Borned in Texas*, which, as *Roadside,* produced by Arthur Hopkins in 1930, was a prompt failure; and his first commercial success, *Green Grow the Lilacs*. This cheerful, rousing folk-drama, full of stirring cowboy songs and played with infectious high spirits by Franchot Tone, June Walker, and Helen Westley—to mention the outstanding members of a large cast—was a bright spot in the Theatre Guild season of 1931. *Russet Mantle*, produced in New York in 1936, was an amusing comedy about the younger generation. *The Cream in the Well* had only a few performances in 1941 on Broadway before closing. Riggs, wrote Barrett Clark, "has been able on occasion to look at the world about him through the eyes of a child. [He] has taken the folk material and the idiom of his native district and skillfully made of them a rich medium of expression."

In recent years Riggs has lived at Chapel Hill, N.C.; has spent some time in Hollywood; and has been guest author and director at Northwestern University and the University of Iowa. He is described as softmannered, fairly tall, with blond hair and light complexion, and blue eyes behind hornrimmed glasses. In 1942 he was inducted into the U. S. Army as a private.

PRINCIPAL WORKS: Big Lake, 1927; Knives From Syria, 1928; Sump'n Like Wings and A Lantern to See By: Two Oklahoma Plays, 1928; The Iron Dish (poems) 1930; Roadside, 1930; Green Grow the Lilacs, 1931; Russet Mantle, and

The Cherokee Night: Two Plays, 1936; World Elsewhere (plays), 1940.

ABOUT: Millett, F. B. Contemporary American Authors; Poetry March 1939; Sewanee Review Autumn 1929; Theatre Arts Monthly July 1938, February 1941.

RILEY, JAMES WHITCOMB. See "AMERICAN AUTHORS: 1600-1900"

RILKE, RAINER MARIA (December 4 1875-December 29, 1926), Austrian poet, was born in Prague. His father, Josef Rilke, derived from a long line of German peasants but he preferred to cling to an unsubstantiated l e g-end which related him to an ancient noble family, and Rainer always took his aristocracy for granted. Like his two elder brothers, Josef Rilke was intended for the career of an officer in the Austrian army, but after serving with distinction in the 1859 campaign against Italy, ill health compelled him to take a leave of absence, and his prospects of promotion seemed so remote that he resigned. He then became a railway official and was disappointed to remain in this capacity till the end of his life. His one consolation would have been to see Rainer obtain the commission he himself had been compelled to forego—and so at the age of ten Rainer was sent away to a military academy. During the five years at the Lower and Higher Military Schools of St. Pölten and Mährisch-Weisskirchen (Moravia) the young Rilke suffered torments and on June 3, 1891, had to be withdrawn on the ground of "continuous ill health." This was not a removal, however, but rather a transfer: his elders "condemned" him to a business career. Rainer was speedily sent to the Handelsakademie in Linz, a business school where he remained a whole year. Here he was tolerably happy, especially after a love-affair with a governess, with whom he finally eloped.

When the prodigal son returned, repentant, to his Prague home, he found that his mother was living in Vienna, and that his father would have nothing to do with him. However, his father's eldest brother, the prominent jurist Jaroslav Rilke sympathized with the boy. He set aside 10,000 gulden and hired some tutors for him. And so Rainer spent the summer and fall of 1892 grinding away at his textbooks, trying to make up for time wasted. In December,

Uncle Jaroslav died and Rainer, on the verge of despair, threatened to commit suicide. But Valery David-Rhonfeld came to his assistance, braced him up, supervised his work. In 1895, Rilke passed his entrance examinations to the University of Prague. Actually, however, "Vally" did much more: she started his literary career, not by "inspiring" him necessarily but by performing a more useful service perhaps—paying all the printers' bills for his first sheaf of poems, *Leben und Lieder* (1894).

For the semester of 1895-96 Rilke registered in the faculty of philosophy and took courses in metaphysics, art history, German literature, and the history of philosophy, and besides he gave up "Vally," that "bright meteor" of his "dark life"—for another girl. Incapable of prolonged effort and thoroughly convinced that college education is but "Pfüscherei," he dropped philosophy for law, which, in turn, he dropped in another six months, and boarded a train for Munich.

At Munich (1896-97) Rilke studied history of art, especially Italian painting. His interest in art and love for travel took him back and forth across Italy and Germany. While at Florence in April 1898 he discovered the writings of the Danish novelist Jen Peter Jacobsen which, together with Maeterlinck's *Le Trésor des Humbles,* proved to be most decisive influences in his formative years. Rilke's love for *Niels Lyhne* led him to study Danish.

From April to June 1899 Rilke traveled in Russia with his cousin Lou Andreas-Salomé and her husband, discovering then, as he called it, his "spiritual fatherland." On his return to Germany he began preparations for a second visit: he studied the language, literature, and history of Russia. In May 1900 he started for Moscow and journeyed through the vast Empire till the end of August. During his brief excursions he met the painter Repin and the great Tolstoy, attended the Pushkin festivals, visited museums, observed with deep respect the Holy Week ceremonies at Kiev.

On his return from Russia, Rilke accepted the invitation of the painter Vogeler to come to the artist colony at Worpswede, and there he met the young sculptress Clara Westhoff, a pupil of Bourdelle. Clara and Rainer were married in the spring of 1901 and moved to Westerwede, near Bremen, into a peasant's cottage on a moor. Both worked hard: she on her statues, he on his *Buch der Bilder* and on Part II of *Das Stunden-Buch*, but their life was one of privations and anxiety. He wrote to his friends

for a job in a publishing house or a theatre or an art gallery; only his father, now somewhat reconciled to his eccentric son, offered him one—in a bank. Finally, in 1902, Richard Muther commissioned him, at his request, to write a monograph on Rodin. Clara had often told Rilke of her admiration for Rodin's work.

During his first Paris sojourn (1902-03) Rilke completed his monograph on Rodin, a panegyric rather than a critical estimate. Rodin taught him one great lesson—the importance of hard work: *"Il faut toujours travailler,"* and not merely in moments of inspiration. Then the perennially ill poet left for Italy to improve his health and moved on to Denmark, recapturing Jacobsen's milieu and studying Scandinavian life. "Jacobsen and Rodin, to me they are the two fountainheads, the masters."

Back in France (September 1905-May 1906) Rilke lived with Rodin in Meudon as his secretary. The mere task of attending to Rodin's correspondence made enormous demands on his time. By March 1906 Rilke had "assimilated all that the sculptor would give him" and was writing from Meudon "as from a jail." The sculptor, too, had had enough and did not hesitate in telling this to the poet who, resignedly, accepted the dismissal. This break was perhaps fortunate: it gave Rilke time for his creation. Now he re-read, revised, and sent to press (1906) an enlarged second edition of *Das Buch der Bilder* and *The Tale of the Love and Death of Cornet Christopher Rilke,* which became his only popular success, attaining a circulation of 300,000 copies. Immediately he followed these achievements with two of his most original and masterly creations: *Neue Gedichte* (1907) and *Die Neuen Gedichte* (1908). Many critics have agreed with J. B. Leishman's dictum anent *Neue Gedichte:* "Nothing like these poems had been written before; nothing like them has been written since."

After the productive period of 1906-08 came the *sécheresse* of 1909-10, that dryness so dreaded by the poet. And so Rilke moved on to new explorations: this time to the Mediterranean—Algiers, Bisk·a, Tunis, the Nile (which stirred him profoundly), and then Cairo where he remained sick in bed for three weeks. Ill and weary he arrived at Venice—and then once more a good angel came to the rescue: Princess Marie von Thurn und Taxis-Hohenlohe offered him her Schloss Duino, a castle near Trieste overlooking the Adriatic. With his hostess Rilke translated the *Vita Nuova* and visited Venice and the neighboring towns. Soon the hostess departed and Rilke remained alone (1911-12) in the splendid castle, perched two hundred feet above the sea. Now he wrote the *Life of Virgin Mary* and the first two of the *Duino Elegies.* But before the year came to an end the indefatigable traveler was admiring the sky and the bells of Toledo. After a short Seville-Cordova-Ronda tour and a forced stay in Madrid due to illness, he arrived in Paris in February 1913.

With the outbreak of war, Rilke was forced to leave the French capital. In Germany, this loftiest representative of internationalism suffered anguish of spirit. In January 1916 he joined the First Infantry Regiment stationed at Vienna but soon was transferred, because of his poor health, to the War Department where he counted among his comrades-in-arms Stefan Zweig and Sil-Vara. Through the influence of powerful friends he was finally exempted from all duties and he moved to Munich where he remained until the Armistice. Rilke was too upset to do any creative work during this nightmarish period, but he read extensively in Tolstoy, Gundolf, Hölderlin, Freud.

He admired the *poésie pure* of Paul Valéry and in 1922 translated his *Cimitière Marin.* During the last seven years of his life (1919-26) Rilke experienced more intensely his mystical adumbrations. He ceased his wandering existence and settled in the solitude of the Tour de Muzot, a thirteenth century tower in the canton of Valais (Switzerland) which Swiss friends had put at his disposal. There he was able to bring his life's work to a magnificent end: on February 11, 1922, he finished the ten *Duino Elegies* and, a few days later, the fifty-five *Sonnets to Orpheus* both published in 1923. From then on he had to devote most of his time to his ailing body, resting for a while every so often in the sanatorium at Valmont. One day while picking some roses in his garden for a young woman visitor, a thorn pricked his finger. The little wound festered and on December 29, 1926, Rainer Maria Rilke died of blood poisoning in the Valmont Sanatorium—the delicate poet who sang so eloquently about women and roses was killed by a rose destined to enhance a woman's beauty.

As time passes Rilke's influence grows in importance. Auden justly claimed that "Rilke is probably read and more highly esteemed by English and Americans than by Germans, just as Byron and Poe had a greater influence upon their German and French contemporaries than upon their com-

patriots." Indeed, Rilke's work, almost in its totality, circulates in excellent translations and is widely read and appreciated in the most diverse circles. His diction and imagery have been an outstanding influence in British and American poetry, for, as Auden says: "Rilke is almost the first poet since the seventeenth century to find a fresh solution (of how to express abstract ideas in concrete terms)."

WORKS AVAILABLE IN ENGLISH TRANSLATION: Poems, 1918; Auguste Rodin, 1919; The Life of Virgin Mary, 1921; The Notebook of Malte Laurids Brigge (same as The Journey of My Other Self) 1930; Elegies From the Castle of Duino, 1931; Stories of God, 1932; The Tale of the Love and Death of Cornet Christopher Rilke, 1932; Poems, 1934; Letters to a Young Poet, 1934; Requiem and Other Poems, 1935; Sonnets to Orpheus, 1936; Translations From the Poetry of Rainer Maria Rilke, 1938; Later Poems, 1938; Duiniso Elegies, 1939; Fifty Selected Poems, 1940; Wartime Letters, 1940; Poems From the Book of Hours, 1941; Sonnets to Orpheus, 1942.

ABOUT: Andreas-Salomé, L. R. M. Rilke; Angelloz, J. F. R. M. Rilke; Betz, M. Rilke Vivant; Butler, E. M. Rainer Maria Rilke; Gundolf, F. R. M. Rilke; Jaloux, E. R. M. Rilke; Kippenberg, K. R. M. Rilke; Mason, E. C. Rilke's Apotheosis; Olivero, F. R. M. Rilke: A Study in Poetry and Mysticism; Rose, W. (ed.) R. M. Rilke: Aspects of His Mind and Poetry; Schellenberg, E. L. R. M. Rilke; Zech, P. R. M. Rilke; Zweig, S. Abschied von Rilke; Cahiers du Mois (Rilke Memorial Number) #23-24, 1921; Il Convegno (Rilke Memorial Number) October 1927; Europe November 15, 1928; Germanic Review April 1933; Hibbert Journal July 1933; Hound and Horn April-June and July-September 1931; Life and Letters June 1931; London Mercury November 1930; New Republic September 6, 1939; Poetry November 1939; Time June 10, 1940.

RINEHART, Mrs. MARY (ROBERTS) (1876-   ), American novelist and writer of mystery stories, was born in Pittsburgh, Pa., the daughter of Thomas Beveridge Roberts, a sewing-machine salesman and unsuccessful inventor, and Cornelia (Gilleland) Roberts. Both met tragic ends: Mr. Roberts was a suicide by shooting, and his widow, after several years of partial  paralysis as the result of a shock, received burns from boiling water which resulted in her death. The future novelist received nurse's training at the Pittsburgh Training School for Nurses when she was seventeen, and saw a great deal of the seamy side of life which, in general, she resolutely excludes from her fiction. Four days after her graduation in 1896 she married, at nineteen, Dr. Stanley Marshall Rinehart. Three sons were born before she was twenty-five: Stanley, now a senior member of the firm of Farrar & Rinehart, which publishes her novels; Alan, a writer for magazines and the moving pictures; and Frederick, also with the publishing firm. In 1903 the Rineharts found themselves $12,000 in debt as the result of a stock market crash. *Munsey's Magazine* accepted a short story of Mrs. Rinehart's, paying her $34; encouraged, she wrote more, sold forty-five in a year, and found she had earned $1800.

Now she sent a manuscript to Bobbs-Merrill in Indianapolis, picking the publisher's name at random from a volume in the family bookcase in their home at Sewickley (a suburb of Pittsburgh). A member of the firm came East to call on the family, read two of Mrs. Rinehart's novels and promptly decided to publish them both. *The Circular Staircase* appeared in 1908, followed next year by *The Man in Lower Ten,* which had previously had serial publication. Mrs. Rinehart found herself acclaimed as a new and fresh voice in the choir of mystery-detective writers, then, of course, much smaller than now. Her chief principles are that the initial crime is merely the forerunner of others to follow, and that there is in a detective novel an inner, concealed story which must be allowed to show itself on the surface occasionally. Mrs. Rinehart's humor, ingenuity, and ability to describe pleasant young people have made her a popular favorite for thirty years. She has been called "the dean of [mystery] writers by and for women."

The novels in which there is no mystery element are generally much less fresh in tone and more conventional in style than the others, showing "immense cleverness without gusto." However, Tish, the intrepid spinster, with her two companions, is one of the outstanding characters of modern light fiction and is always hailed with delight when she reappears in the pages of the *Saturday Evening Post.* The methods of these stories are frequently those of slapstick comedy, but nonetheless effective. The *Nation* once said: "Mrs. Rinehart loves to be a little brutal, a little vulgar (so human!) on the surface; with a smooth river of romantic syrup flowing steadily beneath."

During the First World War she made two trips to Europe as a correspondent, and several books eventuated from the experience. *The Bat* (1920), a mystery play based on *The Circular Staircase,* was the

forerunner of a flood of similar mystery plays, none of which approached it as a financial success. The late Avery Hopwood, writer of bedroom farces, was called in to supply structure for this and other plays of Mrs. Rinehart's, she devising situations and writing the dialogue. One of the most highly paid of present-day writers, she maintained after 1920 a home in Washington, where for many years she entertained capital society as frequently as was compatible with her literary work. Several of her summers were spent with her family of men in Wyoming. Since the death of Dr. Rinehart in 1932, she has lived a more retired life in a Park Avenue apartment in New York. She has written comparatively little in recent years chiefly because of ill health, against which she has had to struggle through most of her life.

PRINCIPAL WORKS: The Circular Staircase, 1908; The Man in Lower Ten, 1909; When A Man Marries, 1909; The Window at the White Cat, 1910; The Amazing Adventures of Letitia Carberry, 1911; The Case of Jennie Brice, Where There's a Will, The After House, The Street of Seven Stars, 1914; "K," 1915; Tish, 1916; Bab—A Sub-Deb, 1917; Long Live The King, 1917; The Amazing Interlude, 1917; A Poor Wise Man, 1921; Twenty-Three and One-Half Hours' Leave, Sight Unseen and The Confession, More Tish, The Breaking Point, 1922; The Red Lamp, 1925; Tish Plays The Game, 1926; Two Flights Up, 1928; The Door, 1930; Miss Pinkerton, 1932; The Album, 1933; The State Versus Elinor Norton, 1934; The Doctor, 1936; The Wall, 1938; The Great Mistake, 1940; Familiar Faces, 1941; Haunted Lady, 1942. *Non-Fiction*—Kings, Queens, and Pawns, 1915; Nomad's Land, 1926; The Out Trail, 1931; My Story, 1931.

ABOUT: Haycraft, H. Murder for Pleasure: The Life and Times of the Detective Story; Rinehart, M. R. My Story; Golden Book February 1934; New York Herald Tribune "Books" October 19, 1941; New York Times Book Review December 15, 1940; Pictorial Review January 1935.

*RITTENHOUSE, JESSIE BELLE (1869-), American poet, editor, and anthologist, was born in Mt. Morris, N.Y., one of the four daughters of John E. Rittenhouse, a farmer, a direct descendant of the David Rittenhouse, scientist and inventor, who gave his name to Rittenhouse Square in Philadelphia, and Mary J. (MacArthur) Rittenhouse. She also had three brothers. After attending the public school at Conesus, where she lived with an aunt, Miss Rittenhouse studied at Genesee

Underwood

Wesleyan Seminary, Lima, N.Y., and taught Latin and English at private schools in Cairo, Ill., and Grand Haven, Mich., in 1893 and 1894. The rigid theological atmosphere of the latter institution proving rather too much for her she began to write articles and send them east. The Rochester *Union and Advertiser* accepted an article on St. Augustine, Fla., and the Buffalo *Express* took an article on the work of Clinton Scollard, the poet,*qv* whom Miss Rittenhouse married in 1924.

She settled in Boston at the turn of the century, to earn a precarious existence by free-lance writing. Her first published work was a variorum edition of the *Rubáiyát* of Omar Khayyám, sold outright to Little, Brown & Co. for $200. *The Lover's Rubáiyát,* amatory sentiments assembled from ten translations of the poem, followed in 1904. *The Younger American Poets,* published that year, was a pioneer book of criticism. William Vaughn Moody refused to be included, to his later regret. *The Little Book of Modern American Verse* (1913) reached a public receptive to the growing renaissance in American poetry, selling over 100,000 copies. *The Little Book of American Poets* (1915) bridged the gap between E. C. Stedman's *American Anthology* and 1900.

Miss Rittenhouse was a founder and for ten years secretary of the Poetry Society of America, which held its first meeting in October 1910 at the National Arts Club in New York. The Society for two years awarded $500 prizes for the best book of poetry of the year, since the original Pulitzer awards did not provide for such a prize. In the third year the Pulitzer family established a fund for a thousand-dollar prize. Miss Rittenhouse's great popularity as a lecturer did not allow her much time for her own writing.

Of Miss Rittenhouse's volume, *The Secret Bird* (1930), the New York *Times* remarked, "It will probably be the feeling of most that in many particulars American poetry, which Miss Rittenhouse did so much to revive, has gone beyond its solicitous nurse. But it is never likely to exceed in gentle purity her own reticent contributions." She has dark hair and eyes, and a gracious manner. Since the death of Mr. Scollard in 1932, she has made her home in Winter Park, Fla., where she lectures on modern poetry at Rollins College. For several years "Watersmeet," on the banks of the Housatonic River near Kent, Conn., was the Scollards' home.

PRINCIPAL WORKS: The Younger American Poets (criticism) 1904; The Door of Dreams (verse) 1918; The Lifted Cup (verse) 1921; The Secret Bird (verse) 1930; My House of Life (autobiography) 1934; Moving Tide: New and Selected Lyrics, 1939. *Editor*—The Lover's Rubáiyát, 1904; The Little Book of Modern American Verse, 1913; The Little Book of American Poets, 1915; The Second Book of Modern Verse, 1919; The Little Book of Modern British Verse, 1924; The Third Book of Modern Verse, 1927; The Bird Lovers' Anthology (with C. Scollard) 1930; Patrician Rhymes (with C. Scollard) 1932; The Singing Heart (selected lyrics of C. Scollard) 1934.

ABOUT: Rittenhouse, J. B. My House of Life; Wilson Library Bulletin May 1931.

RIVES, AMÉLIE. See TROUBETZKOY, A. R.

ROBERTS, CECIL ("Russell Beresford") (1892-), English novelist, short-story writer, and dramatist, does not mention the place of his birth or the names of his parents in *Who's Who* or his autobiography, which is dedicated "E. M. R.: To Her Memory." His father was killed when the boy (who was named Cecil Edric Mornington Roberts) was fifteen, and

Oggiano

for the next five years Mrs. Roberts and her son lived on twenty-five shillings a week, and "flaunted no banner of poverty to the world." Nine years later Cecil Roberts had assembled a thousand pounds and decided to go to Oxford, but was dissuaded from his intention by overhearing the "preparatory-school prattle" of undergraduates who had not had a tithe of his experience. He began with a position in an office under the Board of Trade at Nottingham. At twenty-one he resigned to take a position as junior master in a boys' preparatory school. This proving another *cul-de-sac*, Roberts began to write for the Liverpool *Post*, serving as its literary editor from 1915 to 1918. The First World War found him naval correspondent with the Grand Fleet, Dover Patrol, Milford Convoy; accredited correspondent with the Royal Air Force; and correspondent with the British Armies on the Western Front for the Newspaper Society and Reuter's. He was with the Allied Armies in the march to the Rhine. In 1919 Roberts spent nine months with the Civil Liabilities Commission as Examining Officer for ex-service men seeking small grants to establish themselves in business. He resigned to act as London correspondent and literary critic to the Liverpool *Courier*, editing *The People's Atlas* and writing notes to a final volume of Louis Raemaekers' cartoons.

In August he joined a body of journalists on a visit to Denmark arranged by the Danish Foreign Office. "I started the New Year of 1920 landing in New York. It was the day Prohibition began, and the saddest thing one saw was the face of the bartender in the Harvard Club, called upon to supply lime-juice—though not for long. I had embarked on my first lecture tour, to be repeated in 1924, 1927, 1929. . . . In March 1920 I found myself the youngest editor of one of the oldest, if not the oldest, daily newspapers in England, founded in 1710"— the Nottingham *Journal*. Roberts stayed here until 1925, standing as a Liberal candidate for Parliament from the East Division of Nottingham in 1922. That year *Scissors*, his first novel, was published, introducing Rupert Brooke as Ronald Stream and Sir Philip Gibbs as Phipps, a war correspondent. Nearly a score of novels, books about country life, and travel books have succeeded. Cecil Roberts has a special gift for "easy-going, light-hearted romance," told in a smooth, rapid and vertebrate style. *The Diary of Russell Beresford* is autobiographical to the extent that it was founded on an uncompleted romance. Mr. Roberts is unmarried, and lives at Pilgrim Cottage, Henley-on-Thames, celebrated in *Gone Rustic* and *Gone Afield*. In an interview, Harry Salpeter revealed that "Cecil Edric Mornington Roberts is, as his full name indicates, an Englishman. . . . He is tall, lithe, intense."

PRINCIPAL WORKS: The Trent, 1912; Phyllistrata and Other Poems, 1913; Through Eyes of Youth: Poems, 1914; Youth of Beauty: Poems, 1915; Collected War Poems, 1918; Training Our Airmen, 1919; A Tale of Young Love (play) 1922; Scissors, 1922; Sails of Sunset, 1924; The Love Rack, 1925; Little Mrs. Manington, 1926; The Right To Kiss, (play) 1927; Sagresto, 1927; Diary of Russell Beresford, 1927; David and Diana, 1928; Indiana Jane, 1929; Pamela's Spring Song, 1929; Havana Bound, 1930; Half Way (autobiography) 1931; Bargain Basement, 1931; Spears Against Us, 1932; Life of Sir Alfred Fripp, 1932; Pilgrim Cottage, 1933; Gone Rustic, 1934; The Guests Arrive, 1934; Volcano, 1935; Gone Afield, 1936; Gone Sunwards, 1936; Victoria: Four Thirty, 1937; They Wanted To Live, 1938; And So to Bath, 1940; Letters From Jim (ed.) 1941; A Man Arose, 1941; One Small Candle, 1942.

ABOUT: Roberts, C. Half Way (autobiography); New York Times Book Review March 30, 1941.

*ROBERTS, Sir CHARLES GEORGE DOUGLAS (January 10, 1860-), Canadian novelist and poet, was born in Douglas,

New Brunswick, the son of the Rev. George Goodridge Roberts and Emma Wetmore (Bliss) Roberts. He was educated at Fredericton College School and the University of New Brunswick (B.A. with honors 1879, M.A. 1881, honorary L.L.D. 1906), and until 1883 was a teacher, being principal of two Fredericton schools. For a year he edited the *Week*, Toronto, with

the economist, Goldwin Smith. He returned to teaching in 1885, serving for ten years as professor of English literature at King's College, Windsor, N.S. In 1897 he moved to New York, where he was associate editor of the *Illustrated American* and a free lance journalist. After a long tour of Europe and Northern Africa, he went to England in 1911, and remained there until 1925. He was created a knight in 1935. During the First World War, though fifty-four years old, he enlisted as a private by taking ten years off his age. He was soon commissioned an officer and was mustered out as a major.

He was editor-in-chief of the *Canadian Who Was Who* and the *Canadian Who's Who* from 1934 to 1937. The Royal Society of Canada (of which he is a Fellow) awarded him the first Lorne Pierce medal for imaginative literature in 1926. In 1933 he was tendered a national tribute as poet, historian, and novelist, and he has long been regarded as the dean of Canadian authors. Together with Lord Beaverbrook, he prepared the official story of Canada's share in the war. He was married in 1880 to Mary Isabel Fenety, who died in 1930, leaving two sons and a daughter.

Sir Charles is reported living quietly in Toronto, having long ago had to give up his favorite recreations of camping and fishing. He was seriously ill in 1940, but in spite of his age made a full recovery, and he is still hard at work as a writer. On his eightieth birthday he said: "I still have five or six poems on the stocks, and three or four stories, as well as the sequel to my book, *In the Morning of Time*. I had it about two-thirds done, then, in the middle of a chapter, I lost interest, so I stopped." He knows wild animals intimately, and has written much about them. He is still an energetic, restless man, with iron gray hair, pince nez on a long black ribbon, and a cigarette constantly in his fingers. A cousin of Bliss Carman (and more distantly of Emerson), he has taken Carman's place as the best known internationally of living Canadian writers.

PRINCIPAL WORKS: *Poetry*—Orion and Other Poems, 1880; In Divers Tones, 1887; Ave: An Ode for the Shelley Centenary, 1892; Songs of the Common Day, 1893; New York Nocturnes, 1898; Collected Poems, 1900; The Book of the Rose, 1903; New Poems, 1919; The Sweet of the Year, 1926; The Vagrant of Time, 1927; The Iceberg and Other Poems, 1934; Selected Poems, 1936. *Prose*—The Raid From Beausejour, 1894; The Land of Evangeline and the Gateway Thither, 1895; Earth's Enigmas, 1896; A History of Canada, 1897; The Forge in the Forest, 1897; The Book of the Native, 1897; A Sister to Evangeline, 1899; By the Marshes of Minas, 1900; The Heart of the Ancient Wood, 1900; The Kindred of the Wild, 1902; Barbara Ladd, 1903; The Watchers of the Trails, 1904; The Prisoner of Mademoiselle, 1905; The Little People of the Sycamore, 1905; The Return to the Trails, 1905; Red Fox, 1905; The Cruise of the Yacht Dido, 1906; The Heart That Knows, 1906; In the Deep of the Snow, 1907; The Young Acadian, 1907; Haunters of the Silences, 1907; The House in the Water, 1908; The Backwoodsmen, 1909; Kings in Exile, 1910; Neighbors Unknown, 1911; The Feet of the Furtive, 1912; A Balkan Prince, 1913; Children of the Wild, 1913; Hoof and Claw, 1913; The Secret Trails, 1916; The Ledge on Bald Face, 1918; Jim: The Story of a Backwoods Police Dog, 1919; Some Animal Stories, 1921; In the Morning of Time, 1923; Lovers in Acadie, 1924; They Who Walk in the Wild, 1924; Eyes of the Wilderness, 1933.

ABOUT: Canadian Bookman September 1935, April 1939; Queen's Quarterly January 1929.

ROBERTS, ELIZABETH MADOX
(1886-March 13, 1941), American novelist and poet was born in Perrysville, near

Springfield, Ky., in the "Pigeon Roost" country of which she wrote. She was the daughter of Simpson and Mary Elizabeth (Brent) Roberts, both descendants of Kentucky pioneers. Part of her girlhood was spent in the mountains of Colorado, and

W. Kelly

she was educated at the University of Chicago (Ph.B. 1921; because of ill health she did not go to college until many years after the usual age), but, though she lived for long periods in New York and California, she was essentially a Kentuckian in spirit and background. She never married.

Her life was outwardly uneventful, but full of achievement. She began as a poet, and won the Fiske Prize of the University of Chicago in 1921. The poems which won the prize later became her first volume. She won the John Reed Memorial Prize of *Poetry* in 1928, and the Poetry Society of South Carolina Prize in 1931. Moreover, her prose is inherently poetic. Nevertheless, she is better known as a novelist. She was gifted besides in shorter forms of fiction, and she won the short-short story prize in the O. Henry Memorial volume of 1930. Her first novel, *The Time of Man,* a moving study of Kentucky hill-dwellers, established her at once as a novelist of the first rank, and was translated into German, Swedish, and Danish. After it, Glenway Wescott said, he felt "that no other author will ever have the right to call his place Kentucky."

She had only one real failure, the mystical and obscure *He Sent Forth a Raven.* She was not lost, however, as some critics feared, but returned to her own path in *Black Is My Truelove's Hair.* J. Donald Adams remarked that "her work is sometimes too circuitous and tenuous in the expression of her thought, but she never surrenders her integrity." He spoke of her "distinctly symphonic structure" and her style, "extraordinarily perceptive, rich in the power of suggestion, and sustained by subtle and very beautiful rhythms." Nevertheless, he thought she should "isolate herself less," become more direct; and others have felt that too much poetry is infused into her fiction, especially into the speech of her characters, making it confused and even tedious at times. But all critics agree with Blanche Colton Williams as to her "instinct for beauty and stylistic perfection." Of her poetry Paul Goodman said that her most characteristic invention is . . . a combination of an impulsive feeling, somewhat indeterminate in its object—longing, the sense of being haunted—with an objective and even minute picture of agricultural activity."

Wescott described her "yellow crowned head" in her youth; her curly hair grew gray and her octagonal glasses gave her a scholarly air, but fundamentally she remained the poet of the Kentucky hills. She died in Orlando, Fla., of anemia, at fifty-five.

PRINCIPAL WORKS: Under the Tree (poetry) 1922; The Time of Man, 1926; My Heart and My Flesh, 1927; Jingling in the Wind, 1928; The Great Meadow, 1930; A Buried Treasure, 1931; The Haunted Mirror (short stories) 1932; He Sent Forth a Raven, 1935; Black Is My Truelove's Hair, 1938; Song in the Meadow (poetry) 1940; Not by Strange Gods, 1941.

ABOUT: Hicks, G. The Great Tradition; Wescott, G. Elizabeth Madox Roberts: A Personal Note; Bookman March 1930; Canadian Forum November 1930; New York Times Book Review

March 23, 1941; Poetry October 1940; Saturday Review of Literature March 22, 1941; Sewanee Review October 1937; Virginia Quarterly Review January 1936.

ROBERTS, KENNETH LEWIS (December 8, 1885-   ), American novelist and essayist, was born at Kennebunk, Maine,

H. Stein

the son of Frank Lewis Roberts and Grace Mary (Tibbetts) Roberts. He received his B.A. degree at Cornell University in 1908, and also has honorary doctorates from Dartmouth, Colby, and Middlebury Colleges. While at college he was editor-in-chief of the *Cornell Widow.* In 1911 he married Anna S. Mosser.

From 1909 to 1917 he was on the staff of the Boston *Post,* contributing a humorous column which later grew into an entire page. He was also an extra-mural member of the staffs of *Life* and *Puck.* He then ceased to be a humorist and became an army officer, being a captain in the Intelligence Section of the Siberian Expeditionary Force in 1918 and 1919. He returned to the United States as staff correspondent of the *Saturday Evening Post,* in Washington and Europe, from 1919 to 1928. In a sense he is still attached to this magazine, since his novels are always serialized in it. But in 1928 he definitely abandoned journalism and went to Italy with the plan of writing a series of historical novels, based on New England (especially Maine) at the period of the American Revolution. The first to appear was *Arundel,* in 1930. One of his strongest motives was to set the orthodox professional historians right; Roberts is a stickler for accuracy, and has conducted a vendetta warfare for many years with what he considers the sloppiness of the average historian. Arundel was the original name of Kennebunk, and at first the series was known under the general title of "Chronicles of Arundel," the earlier idea having been to give the history of Maine in terms of a family. Gradually this has been extended until his best-selling book, *Northwest Passage,* has nothing to do with Maine at all, but is concerned with the Rogers and Clark Expedition.

Mr. Roberts lives now in a stone house he built near Kennebunkport, with his wife and his cherished wire-haired fox-terrier. He is famous for many things—for the enormous amount of careful, painful research which goes into his books, for his deep friendship with Booth Tarkington, for his vociferous conservatism, and above all for his truculence, which has passed into a legend which he himself has encouraged—perhaps to keep people away during his busy working days. He has a long list of aversions, ranging from President Roosevelt to billboards. "To be specific, I think Franklin Roosevelt has broken every promise he ever made; I think Burma Shave can turn the edge of any good razor more rapidly than a handful of corn stubble; I think the people who claim to be physically elevated by smoking Camel cigarettes are not only lying, but are selling out mighty cheap and insulting our intelligence to boot; I believe that any author who puts smut or obscenity in a book either lacks the skill and good taste to express himself decently or is deliberately pandering in the hope of achieving sales; I think that most historians, like most professional men, should have stuck to farming; I think that Henry Ford and the makers of cheap automobiles have done more to promote unrest and unhappiness in the United States than has any other agency."

Kenneth Roberts keeps hours like a business man, and does all his work in longhand in ink on yellow paper, with no typing until the final draft is completed. He has hunted and fished all over Maine, and knows the state thoroughly from end to end. It is in his blood; his ancestors have been "Down Easters" since 1639.

In appearance he is anything but an author—sturdy, loosely garbed, with close-cropped hair and a seamed, belligerent face. He has been called "a persevering, peppery researcher," and in his first literary incarnation "a downright, factual, lively reporter." In appraising him as a novelist, critics differ widely. Bernard De Voto, who is himself at war with the historians, spoke of his "imaginative warmth" and "genuine magnificence"; Ralph Straus called him "vivid, thrilling, and picturesque." But to Burton Rascoe Mr. Roberts has "no particular talent for writing fiction. As a novelist he gets by . . . wholly because he is primarily a most excellent non-fiction writer."

PRINCIPAL WORKS: Novels—Arundel, 1930; The Lively Lady, 1931; Rabble in Arms, 1933; Captain Caution, 1934; Northwest Passage, 1937; Oliver Wiswell, 1940. *Miscellaneous*—The Brotherhood of Man (play, with Robert Garland) 1919; Europe's Morning After, 1921; Why Europe Leaves Home, 1922; Sky-Hunting, 1922; The Collector's What-Not (with Booth Tarkington and H. McN. Kahler) 1923; Black Magic, 1924; Concentrated New England: A Study of Calvin Coolidge, 1924; Florida Loafing, 1925; Florida, 1926; Antiquamania, 1928; For Authors Only, 1935; It Must Be Your Tonsils, 1936; Trending Into Maine, 1938; March to Quebec, 1938.

ABOUT: Williams, B. A. & Others. Kenneth Roberts: American Novelist; Book-of-the-Month Club News June 1937; Life March 18, 1940; New York Herald Tribune "Books" December 18, 1940; Newsweek June 20, 1928; Saturday Review of Literature June 25, 1938; Time July 5, 1937; Wilson Library Bulletin December 1935.

ROBERTSON, ARNOT. See ROBERTSON, E. A.

ROBERTSON, EILEEN ARBUTHNOT (1903-), English novelist who writes under the partial pseudonym of E.

Arnot Robertson, writes to the editors of this volume: "I turned very early to writing because everyone else in my family was much better than I was at all the things I should have preferred to do. They were very musical, everyone playing at least two instruments, apparently without effort: I strove for years to learn the piano. Then they were brilliant at games, and besides being useless at all forms of sport, I was the one coward in a close little society that carried its bruises like banners. I cannot remember the time when I was not making up compensation stories in which, as the chief character, I scored off them heavily, but always with an infuriating magnanimity. After a while the monotony of this plot drove me to try, at least, to invent characters who were not myself, or only in bits; and gradually the connection grew more and more tenuous. I should not be surprised to find that a high percentage of authors began with the same ignoble motive—hot resentment of other people's natural advantages.

"I was educated at Sherbourne, one of the English Public Schools for Girls. Nothing, I think, could ever make me so unhappy again. My recurrent nightmare is that I am back there, as a new girl.

"I have traveled a good deal: in North, South, and Central Africa, the West Indies, most of Europe, and a little of the United States; but I have never found it helpful professionally; because, first, the people one meets on ships are so frankly improbable that one cannot make them credible in fiction; second, it is much easier to be convincing

about places one knows only by imagination, where one is not biased by irrelevant personal experience. (Three times I have been involved in car-smashes at Marble Arch; if I wrote about it I should inevitably suggest that it was the most dangerous spot in London, which it surely is not. To the Malayan jungle, about which I wrote a book in untrammeled ignorance, I was as fair as could be.)

"I have been married, since 1927, to H. E. Turner, General Secretary of the Empire Press Union.

"In Europe this year [1940-41] one hasn't been living in the twentieth century at all, and the Dark Ages having returned, it didn't seem to matter whether one's name and description appeared among Authors of Today or Authors of Yesterday: there wouldn't be much difference by the time the stuff got printed. You might have a section called 'That's Europe, that was,' in which my biography would fit."

* * *

Miss Robertson is tall, slim, red-haired, and left-handed. Both she and her husband are passionate sailors, and in peacetime cruised every year to France, Belgium, and Holland in their yacht. They have made with their own movie camera a film called *Saturday-to-Monday Sailors.* Her writing is brilliantly witty, though marked by conspicuous absence of warmth of heart. "Under her deceptive lightness," wrote Margaret Wallace, "are concealed a weight and thrust of ideas, as bitter, as biting and implacable—and perhaps as unbalanced—as those of Dean Swift."

PRINCIPAL WORKS: Cullum, 1928; Three Came Unarmed, 1929; Four Frightened People, 1931; Ordinary Families, 1933; Thames Portrait (nonfiction) 1937; Summer's Lease, 1940.

ABOUT: Boston Evening Transcript July 28, 1934; Saturday Review of Literature March 23, 1940.

ROBERTSON, MORGAN (September 30, 1861-March 24, 1915), American short-story writer, was born at Oswego, N.Y., the son of Andrew and Amelia (Glassford) Robertson, and was named Morgan Andrew Robertson. Andrew Robertson was a ship-captain on the Great Lakes; his son's first story concerned an icebound, dismasted barge on Lake Erie, whose captain rigged a jury foremast and sailed it into Buffalo. Morgan Robertson attended public school, went to sea as a cabin-boy, and was in the merchant service from 1877 to 1886, rising to first mate. In New York he studied the jeweler's trade at Cooper

Union, opening a small shop and specializing in diamond setting. Impaired eyesight and a semi-invalid wife made him turn to writing good but unprofitable sea-stories, more than two hundred of which appeared in English and American periodicals. With his limited education he found writing tedious and harassing; at one time he was a voluntary patient in the psychopathic ward of Bellevue Hospital in New York City. With usual ill-luck, he invented a practical periscope which could not be patented because a description of a similar device had appeared in a French magazine. A collected edition of his books sponsored by friends, who learned of his plight through an unsigned article (by Robertson) in the *Saturday Evening Post*, made his last years somewhat easier. He was found dead of heart disease in an Atlantic City hotel room, standing semi-erect with his hand resting on a bureau.

Robertson was an extremely masculine individual, tactless, generous, a poor business man, with the rolling gait of a sailor and a rather lurid taste in clothes. His stories deal with "mutiny, bloody fights, shipwreck and rescue. brutality, shanghaiing, courage, with daring, telepathy, hypnotism and dual personality." He was a firm believer in reincarnation. Finnegan, a sort of nautical Mulvaney, was probably his most famous character creation.

PRINCIPAL WORKS: A Tale of a Halo, 1894; Futility, Spun-Yarn (sea stories) 1898; Where Angels Fear To Tread and Other Tales of the Sea, 1899; Shipmates, 1901; Sinful Peck, 1903; Down to the Sea, Land Ho! 1905; Masters of Men, 1914.

ABOUT: Cobb, I. Exit Laughing; Morgan Robertson: The Man (various hands); Bookman May 15, 1915; Harper's Weekly April 29, 1905; New York Times March 23, 1915; Reedy's Mirror July 16, 1915; Saturday Evening Post March 28, 1914.

*ROBINS, ELIZABETH (1862-), American actress and novelist, was born in Louisville, Ky., one of the eight children of Charles E. Robins, a banker. Her early years were spent in a country house on Staten Island, N.Y., and her education was obtained at Putnam Seminary in Zanesville, Ohio, where one of her grandmothers lived. At sixteen Elizabeth Robins left school to go on the stage under an assumed name, her father

heartily disapproving of the project. She joined the Boston Museum Company, playing 380 parts in all; toured with Edwin Booth and Lawrence Barrett, covering 30,000 miles one year; and played Mercedes to the Monte Cristo of James O'Neill, the father of Eugene O'Neill. Mrs. Ole Bull, wife of the famous violinist, invited Miss Robins to accompany her to Norway. (Miss Robins by now was the

widow of George Richmond Parks, an actor who not long after their marriage met a violent death.)

Deciding to remain in London, where Oscar Wilde befriended her and gave her excellent advice, Miss Robins scored a success as Mrs. Errol, the mother of Cedric Fauntleroy, in a dramatization of Frances Hodgson Burnett's *Little Lord Fauntleroy*, and also became well acquainted with Henry James, playing a part in a dramatization of his novel, *The American*. A production of Ibsen's *Hedda Gabler* at the Vaudeville on April 21, 1891, made with Marion Lea, later Mrs. Langdon Mitchell, was the first of Elizabeth Robins' notable appearances in Ibsen rôles. She played Hilda in *The Master Builder,* and for seven or eight years acted in the plays almost as fast as they were written. Miss Robins gave *Hedda Gabler* one matinée performance at the Fifth Avenue Theatre in New York in 1898, and met with the usual abuse from some of the critics. Her last stage appearance was as Lucrezia degl'Onesti in Stephen Phillips' *Paolo and Francesca.*

As "C. E. Raimond" (the name was derived from that of her brother, Colonel Raymond Robins, well-known "dry" crusader and social worker) Miss Robins published three novels which were accepted as the work of a man. *The Magnetic North* (1904) a novel based on a visit to her brother in the Klondike, and *My Little Sister* (1913) in which a young girl of good family vanishes into the "white-slave" traffic, are the best-known and best-written of her novels. *Votes for Women*, a play produced in 1905, gave the English militant suffragists their slogan.

For many years Elizabeth Robins has made her home in Backset Town, Henfield, Sussex, with an occasional trip to the United States, where she owned a Florida orange grove. An interviewer described her

* Died May 8, 1952.

as taller than average, with a kind yet determined face, and a purposeful and perhaps willful mouth. Her autobiography was published in 1940, when she was seventy-eight.

PRINCIPAL WORKS: George Mandeville's Husband, 1894; The New Moon, 1895; Below the Salt, 1896; The Open Question, 1898; The Magnetic North. 1904; A Dark Lantern, 1905; Votes for Women (play) 1905; The Convert, 1907; Come and Find Me, 1908; The Florentine Frame, 1909; Where Are You Going To? 1912; My Little Sister, 1913; Way Stations, 1913; Camilla, 1918; The Messenger, 1920; Time Is Whispering, 1923; Ancilla's Share, 1924; The Secret That Was Kept, 1926; Theatre and Friendship: Letters of Henry James, 1932; Both Sides the Curtain (autobiography) 1940.

ABOUT: Robins, E. ·Both Sides the Curtain; Book News Monthly December 1910.

ROBINSON, EDWIN ARLINGTON
(December 22, 1869-April 6, 1935), American poet, was born in Head Tide, Maine, the son of Edward  and Mary E. (Palmer) Robinson, his mother being a collateral descendant of Anne Bradstreet. He had no name for his first year, and always disliked the name chosen for him by lot, signing himself "E. A. Robinson." When he was six months old the family moved to Gardiner, Maine, the "Tillbury Town" of his poems and the home of all his youth. He was a precocious child, who wrote verse from the age of eleven. In high school, curiously, he chose the scientific course, but he was poor in science and mathematics, and excelled in English and Latin. He went to Harvard, but in his sophomore year his father died, the family fortune was dissipated under the inexperienced charge of his brother, and after a year of struggling to earn his way, he gave up college in 1893 and went home to Gardiner. He suffered at this time from chronic mastoiditis, which eventually made him deaf in one ear. The two years he spent at home, however, were not unhappy; he had poetry to write, his violin and clarinet to play, and his relatives and the friends of his boyhood about him. In 1896 his mother died, and he went to New York to live. He returned to Gardiner only three times—for the funerals of his two brothers, and in 1925 when he received a Litt.D. degree from Bowdoin College.

In New York Robinson gradually grew into the melancholy taciturn hermit of leg-

end. His first little volumes made no stir, and he refused all his life to do hack writing or to live on the edges of literature. He was practically unknown until he was fifty. He worked at what he could get, being at one time a subway inspector. What little publication he achieved was for the most part in England, and American critics, when they noticed him at all, supposed he was an Englishman. In 1905 Theodore Roosevelt became interested in his work, and gave him a job in the New York Custom House, but he resigned in 1909. In spite of debts and the difficulty of earning a living, he was a poet and could live by no other means.

It was the MacDowell Colony, in Peterborough, N.H., that emancipated him. There he spent most of the rest of his life, though New York saw him often and Boston occasionally. He was the MacDowell Colony's "acknowledged deity," and legends grew up about him as his fame spread. For the last ten or fifteen years of his life he shared with Robert Frost the reputation of being America's greatest living poet. He was not an easy person to know; he "distrusted most men and feared almost all women." Celibate, a periodical alcoholic, a man "obsessed by failure and in love with death," he yet held firmly to the few close friends he had made in youth, and with them he could be expansive and witty. His tall, thin figure, with its curiously puckered mouth, burning dark eyes hidden by spectacles, and long sensitive hands, was compact of guarded reticence and shrinking from the world. "His talk, like his expression, was colorless," remarked Louis Untermeyer. "All the color was in his verse. . . . He identified himself with all those who, like their creator, had been frustrated and beaten by the current standards of commercial success." And the *New Republic*, in an obituary notice, said that for Robinson "poetry played the part of wife, children, job, and recreation." He died in New York of cancer of the stomach, at sixty-five.

Robinson's least permanent poems are perhaps his long mediaeval narratives. His most permanent are the New England *pastiches*, with their "bare Yankee speech," their wry humor and implicit tragedy. "Agnostic in temper and austere in tone," said the *Nation*, "he sacrificed music to matter. His blank-verse line had too much steel in it and too little gold." And Morton Dauwen Zabel noted "the low vitality of his language, the reluctant energy of his style." Yet, he added, "when he chose to release his full poetic power it arrived with . . . the impact of complete reserves, of verbal intensity, of stored and loaded emphasis." Allen Tate, who deplored Robinson's narrative poems, called him "primarily a lyrist," and that is what he was—but a lyrist whose passion was damped down and whose singing was constricted by the imperative inhibitions of a frustrated temperament.

PRINCIPAL WORKS: The Torrent and the Night Before, 1896; The Children of the Night, 1897; Captain Craig, 1902; The Town Down the River, 1910; Van Zorn (play) 1914; The Porcupine (play) 1915; The Man Against the Sky, 1916; Merlin, 1917; The Three Taverns, 1920; Lancelot, 1920; Avon's Harvest, 1921; Collected Poems, 1921, 1924, 1927, 1937; Roman Bartholow, 1923; The Man Who Died Twice, 1924; Dionysus in Doubt, 1925; Tristram, 1927; Sonnets 1889-1927, 1928; Cavender's House, 1929; Modred, 1929; The Glory of the Nightingales, 1930; Matthias at the Door, 1931; Nicodemus, 1932; Talifer, 1933; Amaranth, 1934; King Jasper, 1935; Selected Letters, 1940.

ABOUT: Boynton, P. H. Some Contemporary Americans; Brown, R. W. Next Door to a Poet; Cestre, C. An Introduction to Edwin Arlington Robinson; Coffin, R. P. T. The New Poetry of New England: Frost and Robinson; Hagedorn, H. Edwin Arlington Robinson; Hall, J. N. The Friends; Kaplan, E. Philosophy in the Poetry of Edwin Arlington Robinson; Lowell, A. Tendencies in Modern American Poetry; Morris, L. The Poetry of Edwin Arlington Robinson; Redman, B. R. Edwin Arlington Robinson; Richards, L. E. E. A. R.; Untermeyer, L. From Another World; Bookman November 1932; Commonweal February 15, 1933, May 14, 1937; Forum June 1935; Harper's Magazine July 1936; Nation April 7, 1935, August 28, 1937; New England Quarterly March 1936; New Republic October 25, 1933, April 17, 1935; Poetry January 1931, December 1934, June 1935, June 1937, May 1939; Saturday Review of Literature October 19, 1935, November 2, 1935, November 16, 1935, December 21, 1935; Virginia Quarterly January, April 1937; Yale Review June 1936.

ROBINSON, JAMES HARVEY (June 29, 1863-February 16, 1936), American historian and university professor, was born in Bloomington, Ill., the son of James Harvey Robinson and Latritia Maria (Drake) Robinson. His father, a native of Saratoga Springs, N.Y., had gone to Bloomington as a young man and had become the leading banker there. The son traveled in Europe during part of his youth; went into business for a year in Bloomington; then suddenly decided to go to Harvard with his younger brother, who was later to succeed Asa Gray as curator of the herbarium there. James Harvey Rob-

inson received his B.A. degree after three years of study, in 1887; married Grace Woodville Read in September; and spent the next year in graduate study at Harvard. The winter semester of 1888-89 was spent in Germany, at the University of Strassburg, and in 1890 he received his Ph.D. degree from the University of Freiburg for a thesis on "The Original and Derived Features of the Constitution of the United States." As a contribution to German constitutional law, he wrote *The German Bundesrath.*

In 1891 Robinson became a lecturer in European history in the University of Pennsylvania and an associate editor of the *Annals of the American Academy of Political and Social Science.* In 1895 he joined the Columbia University faculty as professor of history, remaining until 1919, when he resigned as a protest against the expulsion of such professors as Henry W. L. Dana and J. McKeen Cattell for their opposition to the First World War. Like Charles Beard, who left the university late in 1917 in protest, he assailed Dr. Nicholas Murray Butler, president of the University, for an alleged attempt to silence freedom of expression at the University.

In 1912 Robinson wrote to the secretary of his Harvard class: "I have little interest in what ordinarily passes for History, and have gradually turned my energies both in instruction and writing into the neglected field of the intellectual development of Europe." His Harvard studies with William James had also aroused a deep interest in psychology and the pragmatic attitude. *The Mind in the Making* (1921), a product of this interest, had a gratifying sale. After leaving Columbia, Robinson helped to found the New School for Social Research on West Twelfth Street in New York City, and taught there until 1921, when he retired to devote the rest of his life to writing. "For the old story of wars, territorial changes, and social institutions, which previously had been deemed the proper subject matter of history, he substituted that of the development of ideas, human beliefs, and knowledge."

Robinson died of a heart-attack at his Riverside Drive home at seventy-two; Mrs. Robinson had died in 1927. He had been working on a revision of his *Introduction to the History of Western Europe,* generally regarded as his most important text-book. He held honorary degrees from the University of Utah and Tufts College, and was a member of the Century Club in New York. Carl Becker, a former student of Robinson's, has spoken of "the sadness in the countenance, a quality half plaintiveness, half resignation in the voice" of the historian. The posthumous *Human Comedy* is a compilation, not a new work.

PRINCIPAL WORKS: Introduction to the History of Western Europe, 1902, 1904; Readings in European History, 1904; The Development of Modern Europe (with C. A. Beard) 1907; The New History (essays) 1912; Outlines of European History (with J. H. Breasted & C. A. Beard) 1914; The Middle Period of European History, 1915; Medieval and Modern Times, 1916; The Mind in the Making: The Relation of Intelligence to Social Reform, 1921; General History of Europe (with J. H. Breasted & E. P. Smith) 1921; Our World Today and Yesterday (with E. P. Smith & J. H. Breasted) 1924; The Humanizing of Knowledge, 1926; The Ordeal of Civilization (revision of Medieval and Modern Times) 1926; History of Europe: Our Own Times (with C. A. Beard) 1927; The Human Comedy as Devised and Directed by Mankind Itself, 1937.

ABOUT: Harvard University, Class of 1887: Secretary's 25th Annual Report; American Historical Review April 1936; Nation January 9, 1937; Newsweek February 22, 1936; New York Times February 17, 1936; Publishers' Weekly February 22, 1936; School and Society February 22, 1936; Time February 24, 1936.

ROBINSON, LENNOX (October 4, 1886-), Irish dramatist, was born Esmé Stuart Robinson Lennox, at Douglas, County Cork, the son of the Rev. A. C. Robinson.

When he was seven the family moved to Kinsale, on the sea, where he was reared, a frail, timid child, youngest of the family, whose doting mother dressed him in "Lord Fauntleroy" outfits. He was educated privately at first, then at Bandon Grammar School. Like many shy, solitary children, he began writing very early, and nearly as early showed a penchant for the theatre. His first play, a one-act tragedy called *The Clancy Name*, was produced by the Abbey Theatre in Dublin in 1908. Soon after, he moved to Dublin, and from 1910 to 1914, and again from 1919 to 1923, he was stage manager of the Abbey Theatre; since 1923 he has been one of its directors. He came to America with the players on their tour in 1912, and since then has been in this country frequently, lecturing, and also directing plays at the Universities of Michigan and Montana, at Amherst, and at other colleges and universities. He accompanied the Abbey Players also in 1932 and 1935.

From 1915 he was Irish representative of the Carnegie Trust in Ireland, and from 1921 to 1925 was its organizing librarian for ^ll of Ireland. He was also a founder of the Dublin Drama League, in 1918, with William Butler Yeats, Ernest Boyd, and James Stephens, and acted as its secretary and producer. For a year, from 1924 to 1925, he wrote dramatic criticism for the London *Observer*. In 1931 he married Mrs. Dorothy Travers Smith, daughter of Edward Dowden, and they live now at Dalkey, near Dublin. They have no children.

In addition to his plays, Robinson has published a novel, volumes of short stories, biographies, and poems (though these have not been collected in a volume). He has edited two anthologies, *The Golden Treasury of Irish Verse* (1925) and *The Little Anthology of Irish Verse* (1929), and also the poems of Thomas Parnell (1679-1718). His plays may be divided into two categories— plays about Irish life in rural communities, and plays about Irish politics. His own favorite (and his most successful play) is *The White-Headed Boy*. ("White-headed" is the Irish equivalent of the American phrase, "fair-haired" boy.)

He is very tall, six feet six inches, dark (though as a child he was a blond), and "faintly like W. B. Yeats in appearance." He wears butcher-blue shirts and smokes a pipe with Irish-grown tobacco. He is slow of speech, and when excited—or when he feels playful, for he has a vast fund of humor—he is capable of an Irish brogue so thick as to be almost unintelligible. He is still shy and retiring, rather reticent, and extremely modest. The great enthusiasm of his life is for the national theatre, and he is proud to have had a part not only in writing for it but in actually directing it and helping to produce its plays. Once called "the dramatist of Irish discontent," he is actually far less politically-minded than most Irishmen, and in so far as he has any economic views is rather on the conservative side, being in this typical of the Anglo-Irish upper middle class from which he springs.

PRINCIPAL WORKS: *Plays*—The Clancy Name, 1908; The Cross Roads, 1909; Harvest, 1910; Two Plays, 1910; Patriots, 1912; The Dreamers, 1915; The Lost Leaders, 1918; The White-Headed Boy, 1920; Crabbed Youth and Age, 1922; The Round Table, 1922; Never the Time and the Place, 1924; The White Blackbird, 1925; Portrait, 1925; The Big House, 1926; The Far-Off Hills, 1928; Give a Dog—, 1928; Collected Plays, 1928; Ever the Twain, 1929; All's Over, Then?

1932; Is Life Worth Living? (Drama at Inish) 1933; More Plays, 1935; Birds' Nest, 1938; Killycreggs in Twilight and Other Plays, 1939. *Fiction*—A Young Man From the South, 1918; Dark Days (short stories) 1918; Eight Short Stories, 1919. *Miscellaneous*—Recipe For a National Theatre, 1929; Bryan Cooper, 1931; Three Homes (with T. Robinson & N. Dorman) 1938; The Irish Theatre (with others, and edited) 1939; W. B. Yeats: A Study, 1939; Curtain Up (autobiography) 1942.

ABOUT: Agate, J. The Contemporary Theatre; Archer, W. The Old Drama and the New; Boyd, E. Ireland's Literary Renaissance; Chandler, F. W. Aspects of Modern Drama; Morgan, A. E. Tendencies of Modern English Drama; Morris, L. R. The Celtic Dawn; O'Connor, N. J. Changing Ireland; Weygandt, C. Irish Plays and Playwrights; Bookman (London) September 1917, March 1919, May 1922, October 1931; Dublin Magazine March 1924; Freeman November 23, 1921; New Republic October 5, 1921, August 19, 1925; New Statesman September 18, 1920; Sewanee Review July-September 1922; Theatre Arts Monthly June 1934.

ROCHE, ARTHUR SOMERS (April 27, 1883-February 17, 1935), American novelist, was born in Somerville, Mass., the son of  James Jeffrey and Mary (Halloran) Roche. He attended Holy Cross College at Worcester, Mass., from 1899 to 1901, and received an LL.B. from Boston University in 1904, but practiced law only eighteen months. Newspaper work claimed Roche's attention in 1906; in 1910 he began to write for magazines, and achieved the *Saturday Evening Post* in 1917 with *Plunder,* dramatized as *A Scrap of Paper.* (The "scrap," containing international secrets fluttered from a window, with dramatic results.) During the World War, Captain Roche was connected with the Military Intelligence Division, from September 1918 to his honorable discharge in December.

Arthur Somers Roche's novels of "emotional life among the exceedingly rich" were derived from first-hand experience, much of his time being spent at Palm Beach during the boom days of the 'twenties. He was a member of the Bath and Tennis Club of Palm Beach, besides the Players, Dutch Treat, Authors, and Sleepy Hollow Clubs in New York. Divorced from Ethel Kirby Rowell in September 1915 (they had a son, Jeffrey), he married Ethel Pettit of Arkansas exactly two years later. The second Mrs. Roche was also a popular novelist. They had a son, Clyde.

In honor of *The Day of Faith* (1921) Governor Thomas C. McRae of Arkansas (Mrs. Roche's native state) declared November 1, 1921, a legal holiday.

The beginning of Roche's novels was usually more convincing than their ending. Of *The Pleasure Buyers* (1925) a reviewer remarked, "The story would be an excellent detective yarn if Mr. Roche would leave it alone."

Roche's death occurred at his Palm Beach Villa Bellaria, of a heart ailment. He was buried at Castine, Maine.

PRINCIPAL WORKS: Loot, 1916; Plunder, 1917; The Sport of Kings, 1917; The Day of Faith, 1921; The Pleasure Buyers, 1925; Devil-May-Care, 1926; The Wise Wife, The Woman Hunters, 1928; Four Blocks Apart, 1930; Slander, 1933; Conspiracy, 1934; Lady of Resource, 1938.

ABOUT: New York Times February 18, 1935.

ROCHE. See DE LA ROCHE

RODÓ, JOSÉ ENRIQUE (July 15, 1871-May 1, 1917), Uruguayan essayist, was born in Montevideo, of a middle class family, the youngest of eight children. His mother, Rosario Piñeiro, derived from a wealthy old Catholic Uruguayan family of Galician stock; one of her brothers was President of the Senate. His father, José Rodó, who had emigrated in his youth  from Catalonia (Spain), was a merchant who occupied an enviable social position, counting among his friends some of the most cultured men of Uruguay. The Rodós owned a two-storied building in Montevideo inherited from Doña Rosario's parents, and a country estate in the fashionable summer resort of Santa Lucía not far from the capital. José Enrique spent the first eight years of his life in these two comfortable mansions, so full of ease and abundance.

From 1882 to 1885 Rodó attended the Escuela Elbio Fernández, "the first and only secular school in the country." He loved his studies but became increasingly detached and serious. In 1883 he edited with two of his schoolmates a paper, *Lo Cierto y Nada Más* which lasted for three issues; here he waged his first literary battles and published his earliest poem. Two months later the youthful journalist launched his fortnightly, *Los Primeros Albores.* To the three numbers of this journal he contributed articles on Simón Bolívar and Benjamin Franklin. The atmosphere of the Escuela Elbio Fernández imbued the young writer with a sense of human dignity and tolerance, and stimulated his social awareness. When he entered the University of Montevideo in 1885 he was not so much a child prodigy as a matured, highly cultured individual. Annoyed at the rigid schedule, he attended classes irregularly and studied only what he liked, all by himself. In 1886 his father died and his uncle and godfather, Cristóbal Rodó, found him a job in a lawyer's office. But José Enrique spent every available moment reading books, and attended the University every now and then. In 1893 his uncle died and the following year he attended the University in order to take the final examinations for his Bachelor's degree. But of the twelve examinations he took only six.

On March 5, 1895, appeared the first issue of *Revista Nacional de Literatura y Ciencias Sociales,* immediately accepted as Uruguay's most distinguished periodical. As one of its four editors Rodó considered this work his "real literary initiation," but on November 25, 1897 the *Revista* came to an end, partly because of growing misunderstanding among the editors, partly because of lack of funds. Rodó then moved with greater decision into the political arena. While contributing to the newly founded *El Orden,* the anti-collectivist, pro-Cuestas daily, he occupied the chair of literature at the University of Montevideo, which he held until 1901 (he gave Uruguay's first course in Hebrew literature), when he resigned in order to devote his full time to his candidacy as deputy.

At the beginning of 1899 Rodó published his now famous essay *Rubén Darío* which led many critics mistakenly to include Rodó's name among the Modernists. Rodó's essay was, no doubt, a profound analysis of Modernism, written in the language of the Modernists, but it was a moment in the development of a writer whose sympathies were always, overwhelmingly, with the classical school, as can be seen from his next work, *Ariel* (1900), in which Rodó defended "the claims of Ariel rather than Caliban to determine the ideals of civilization," contrasting the ideal harmony of ancient Greece with the United States, which he called "the most positivist of democracies."

At the death of a maternal uncle in 1900, the Rodós inherited a small fortune, and henceforth the author lived the retired life of a hermit-bachelor with his mother and brothers and sisters. But it was no time for the ivory tower—the political situation required men like Rodó. He helped to consolidate his party, the Partido Colorado, which was cracking, presented his candidacy and was elected Deputy for Montevideo in 1902, a chair he occupied for three terms: 1902-05, 1908-11 and 1911-14.

He also sat in the Chamber of Deputies during some of the most critical years of Uruguay—during Aparicio Saravia's bloody revolutions of 1903 and 1904. Rodó participated in the main debates and often pronounced long speeches.

During the period 1905-07 Rodó wrote his *Motives of Proteus,* his chief work; it appeared in April 1909 in an edition of 2000 copies which was exhausted within a month. In this book Rodó amplified the philosophical implications of his *Ariel,* and expostulated a doctrine of dynamism in the fields of the will, the intelligence and the spirit, a doctrine of self-cultivation and self-reliance. With a warmth and a sympathy strongly reminiscent of Emerson, he explored the recesses of the human soul. *Motives of Proteus* won Rodó immediate and universal praise: the exacting critic González Blanco called him "the greatest master of Spanish prose," while Havelock Ellis compared him to Renan and Guyau—"like those fine spirits, he desired to be the messenger of sweetness and of light, of the spirit of Jesus combined with the spirit of Athens."

At the time of the appearance of *Motives of Proteus,* the Círculo de la Prensa elected Rodó its first president. Soon thereafter he attended with Juan Zorrilla de San Martín, the Centennial festivals held at Santiago de Chile. By 1912, when the Royal Spanish Academy named him Corresponding Member, the Montevideo stores were featuring "Rodó" sugar and "Ariel" paper, but Rodó's personality and ideas had not fused organically with his countrymen's warring ideologies nor with the main currents of American thought. Isolated, embittered, Rodó felt himself an exile in his own country. More than ever he wanted to practice what he had taught—the importance of travel to enhance the ego. The opportunity to travel presented itself at last during the First World War. Rodó was rabidly pro-Ally, and at his request the popular Argentine weekly *Caras y Cartas* sent him to cover the war. On July 14, 1916, he sailed from Montevideo aboard the "Amazon." After short stops in Lisbon, Madrid, and Barcelona, he went to Italy where he expected to have his visa approved for his ultimate journey to Paris, the city of his dreams. In order to recover from a cold contracted in Florence, Rodó went to

Palermo in April and lived at the little "Hotel des Palmes" where Wagner composed the last act of *Parsifal*. But his cold got worse— some writers claim it was typhoid—and he was transferred to the San Saverio Hospital. A day later he died, not quite forty-six years old. Three years later his remains were brought to Montevideo and buried with national honors in the Pantheon.

WORKS AVAILABLE IN ENGLISH TRANSLATION: Ariel, 1922; The Motives of Proteus, 1928.

ABOUT: Berrien, W. Rodó (Ph.D. dissertation, University of California); Ellis, H. The Philosophy of Conflict; Goldberg, I. Studies in Spanish-American Literatures; Henríquez Ureña, M. Rodó y Rubén Darío; "Lauxar." Rubén Darío y J. E. Rodó; Pérez Petit, V. Rodó: Su Vida y Su Obra; Scarone, A. Bibliografía de José Enrique Rodó; Zaldumbide, G. José Enrique Rodó; Claridad June 1939; Cultura Venezolana January 1931; Revista Hispánica Moderna October 1936.

ROGERS, SAMUEL (September 5, 1894-), American novelist, writes: "I was born [Samuel Greene Arnold Rogers] in the  country, near Newport, R.I. My father, Arthur Rogers, was an Episcopal minister. As a boy I always spent the summers in Rhode Island, the winters in West Chester, Pa., where my father had his parish. During the last few years before college I commuted every day to Philadelphia to attend the DeLancey School; it was a good school but most of my classmates seemed so much more sophisticated that I had a pretty lonely time of it. In 1911 I entered Brown University. Here I worked on the literary magazine and took part in college dramatics. While I was at Brown a one-act play of mine, *The Diagnosis*, was put on by the Little Theatre in Philadelphia.

"After being graduated from Brown in 1915, I studied for parts of two winters at the University of Chicago. In 1916 I enrolled in the Citizens' Training Camp at Plattsburg; the pep talks of General Leonard Wood disgusted me beforehand with the idea of war and to this day I have not revised my opinion. In May 1917 I went to France as a member of the American Field Service, remained in my section when it was taken over by the United States Army, and was discharged in March 1919. In September of that year I married Marion Richmond Gardner.

"That fall I came to the University of Wisconsin as an instructor in the English Department. After a year of correcting themes I felt that if I was ever going to look a sentence of my own in the face I should have to make a shift of some sort; so I changed to the French Department, of which I am still a member. In 1921 I went to Paris with my wife and year-old daughter to study at the Sorbonne on an American Field Service Fellowship. Shortly after our return to America, in 1923, we had twins, a boy and a girl.

"For the last fifteen years I have worked quite regularly at my classes during the winter, at my novels during the summer, with an occasional year's leave which I have devoted entirely to writing. I have always played the piano, and my greatest diversion is taking part in chamber music."

* * *

Mr. Rogers is thin, dark, intense-looking. He secured his M.A. at the University of Chicago, and is now professor of French at the University of Wisconsin. His war services won him a Croix de Guerre. *Dusk at the Grove* won the Atlantic Novel Prize in 1934, has been republished in the Tauchnitz Library, and has been translated into French.

PRINCIPAL WORKS: The Sombre Flame, 1927; Less Than Kind, 1928; The Birthday, 1932; Dusk at the Grove, 1934; Lucifer in Pine Lake, 1937; Flora Shawn, 1942.

ABOUT: Boston Evening Transcript November 17, 1934; Wilson Library Bulletin December 1934.

ROGERS, WILL (November 4, 1879-August 15, 1935), American actor and humorist, was christened William Penn Adair Rogers. He was born at Oologah, Indian Territory, the son of Clem Vann Rogers and Mary (Schrimpsher) Rogers, and had some Indian blood in his veins. He attended Willie Hassell School, Neosha, Mo., and Kemper Military Academy, Boonville,  Mo. Selling his ranch to raise money, Rogers made a trip around the world, visiting Africa, China, and Australia, where he threw a lariat with a Wild West show when his funds ran out. Later he joined Zack Mulhall's Wild West Troupe, roping a horse with one lasso and its rider with another. By 1905 he had reached New York, where he played in vaudeville at Hammerstein's

Victoria. Uncovering a vein of dry humor, Rogers began to explain to his audiences the difficulty of the roping feats he was about to attempt, and expanded the scope of his remarks to include homely witticisms about events of current interest. His formula, "All I know is what I read in the newspapers," became a popular catchword. In 1915 he played in the revues *Hands Up* and *Town Topics,* and in 1917 in the Shubert's *Passing Show,* when he was annexed by Florenz Ziegfeld for his *Follies* and made a highly paid star. Rogers was featured in Ziegfeld's 1921 *Midnight Frolic,* and in the *Follies* of 1922 and 1924. In 1928 he took the place of Fred Stone, who had been injured in an airplane accident, in *Three Cheers.*

From 1929 to 1935 Rogers contributed to the moving pictures a succession of characterization (mirror-reflections of his own personality) of a shrewd, dry, shambling, and rather sheepish type of homespun American, in rôles such as Irvin Cobb's Judge Priest, George Ade's County Chairman, and James Gould Cozzen's Dr. Bull. He also starred in *David Harum* and Phil Stong's *State Fair.* Will Rogers' syndicated comments on the news of the day in the New York *Times* and other papers had an immense mass following; the proposition was once advanced seriously that he become a candidate for President. From time to time his columns were collected into books, from which the humor seems rather to have evaporated with the passage of time. Rogers and Wiley Post, the aviator, were killed in an airplane crash at Walkpi, near Point Barrow, Alaska, three months before his fifty-sixth birthday. Funeral services were held in Forest Lawn Memorial Park at Los Angeles, and the body was placed in a vault. Numerous memorials subsidized by popular subscription followed, notably a Memorial Hospital at Saranac Lake, N.Y., and the Will Rogers Library at Claremore, Okla. A tower was erected on Cheyenne Mountain by one of his admirers. President Roosevelt vetoed some of the more extreme proposals, such as a Will Rogers postage stamp and a government contribution to the Claremore (Okla.) Museum, dedicated in November 1938.

PRINCIPAL WORKS: The Cowboy Philosopher on Prohibition, 1919; The Cowboy Philosopher on the Peace Conference, 1919; What We Laugh At, 1920; The Illiterate Digest, 1924; Letters of a Self-Made Diplomat to His President, 1927; There's Not a Bathing Suit in Russia, 1927; Will Rogers' Political Follies, 1929.

ABOUT: Trent, S. M. My Cousin Will Rogers. Lait, J. Our Will Rogers; New York Times August 17-23, 1935; Saturday Evening Post October 5-November 30, 1940.

"ROHMER, SAX" (1883-), is the pseudonym of an English writer of sensational fiction who was born Arthur Sarsfield Wade (or Warde). His parents were Irish, his father coming from Wicklow and his mother from Athlone on the Shannon. "My earliest interests centered in Ancient Egypt," he writes. "I cannot doubt that I spent at least one incarnation beside the Nile. Throughout my schooldays I studied hieroglyphics and began to collect books on my pet subject—in this way forming the basis of a now considerable library of Ancient Egypt and occult literature. I read for a Civil Service appointment in the East; but since throughout my life I have never succeeded in passing the simplest examination, I did not secure this appointment. The Middle East continued to enthrall me—especially Egypt. Interest in the Far East was to come later. When I took up the study of art, my own paintings were almost exclusively Oriental in character. After a brief canter through the City [the financial section of London]—my father's prescription for a sane career—I wandered into Fleet Street. As a journalist I was not an outstanding success. I "bucked up" interviews with dull people to a point where the victims jibbed. I had written a number of short stories—and had papered one wall of my room with editorial regrets. Then, one day my father treated me to a holiday in the Isle of Man. Before leaving I mailed off two stories, 'The Leopard Couch' and 'The Mysterious Mummy' to *Chambers' Journal* and *Pearson's Magazine* respectively. Offers for both reached me by the same post in the Isle of Man."

White

* * *

Since then Rohmer has, as Anice Page Cooper says, "flashed against richly exotic backgrounds such diabolically ingenious and irresistible villains as one trusts this world has never seen." For a quarter-century, now, the English hero Nayland Smith has battled grimly, hopelessly, but indestructibly against the imperturbable Fu Manchu, who has all the exotic lore of the East behind him. His own daughter is frequently the *dea ex machina* who saves Smith's life. "Sax Rohmer's" photographs show a dark, lean, rather saturnine, clean-shaven gentleman wrapped in a dressing-gown and smoking a pipe. He was in New York in September 1933, when the Columbia Broadcasting System observed Fu Manchu's twentieth anniversary by putting the inscrutable and villainous Oriental on the air waves. Fu Manchu has also appeared in several films.

PRINCIPAL WORKS: Dr. Fu Manchu, 1913; The Romance of Sorcery, 1914; The Sins of Severac Bablon, 1914; The Yellow Claw, 1915; The Exploits of Captain O'Hagan, 1916; The Devil Doctor, 1916; Brood of the Witch Queen, 1917; The Sin Fan Mysteries, 1917; The Orchard of Tears, 1918; Tales of Secret Egypt, 1918; Quest of the Sacred Slipper, 1919; Dope, 1919; The Golden Scorpion, 1920; The Green Eyes of Bast, 1920; The Dream Detective, 1920; Batwing, 1921; Fire-Tongue, 1921; Tales of Chinatown, 1922; Round in 50 (play) 1922; The Eye of Siva (play) 1923; Grey Face, 1924; Yellow Shadows, 1925; Moon of Madness, 1927; She Who Sleeps, 1928; The Emperor of America, 1929; The Day the World Ended, 1930; The Daughter of Fu Manchu, 1931; Yu'an Hee See Laughs, 1932; Tales of East and West, 1932; Fu Manchu's Bride, 1932; The Trail of Fu Manchu, 1934; The Bat Flies Low, 1935; President Fu Manchu, 1936; White Velvet, 1937; Salute to Bazarada, 1938; The Drums of Fu Manchu, 1939; The Island of Fu Manchu, 1941.

ABOUT: Cooper, A. P. Authors and Others.

"ROLAND, J." See OLIVER, J. R.

ROLFE, FREDERICK WILLIAM SERAFINO AUSTIN LEWIS MARY

("Baron Corvo") (July 22, 1860-October 26, 1913), English eccentric, novelist, and historian, was the eldest of five brothers, and was born at 61 Cheapside, London, of a family of piano manufacturers. His father was a Dissenter; Rolfe, on the contrary, became a Catholic at twenty-six, and his unsuccessful efforts to enter the priesthood caused him lifelong frustration and bitterness. Rolfe's most famous novel, *Hadrian the Seventh*, represents his self-compensation for this failure: George Arthur Rose, the hero (who is Rolfe) is a rejected candidate for the priesthood who is raised to the papal throne as Hadrian the Seventh, resigns claims to temporal sovereignty, denounces socialism, and is shot by a corrupt socialist agitator, aided by a woman accomplice. It is a book of "staccato brilliance," witty, full of erudition, masterly phrases and

scenes—and venomous portraits of all Rolfe's enemies, real or fancied.

His real life was quite different, an endless struggle to keep body and soul together by painting and writing: his literary work, although brilliantly original, was very badly paid. Rolfe had many and powerful patrons, for varying periods of time; his warped temperament compelled him to distrust and quarrel with all of them in the end. Life became an endless series of recriminations, lawsuits, and hurried departures from one post to another. He left school in his fifteenth year, was an unattached student at Oxford for a while, and was appointed master of a school for boy choristers at Oban by the Marquess of Bute. In 1887 he went to Oscott, a Roman Catholic college, but was soon discharged. Archbishop Smith of Edinburgh sent him to Scots College in Rome, to be prepared for the priesthood; in five months he was expelled for "lack of vocation" and unwillingness to pay his debts. In 1890 he was in Christchurch, England; in 1892, in Aberdeen as tutor of the young Laird of Seton. Two years were spent at Holywell, near Flint, North Wales, painting ecclesiastical banners for Fr. Beauclerk. This ended when Rolfe sent the latter a bill for a thousand pounds. He then went to London, where Henry Harland, editor of John Lane's *Yellow Book*, accepted six of the *Stories Toto Told Me*, retellings of legends of Catholic saints. Grant Richards, the publisher, made him a small allowance while Rolfe was collecting material at the British Museum for his remarkable *Chronicles of the House of Borgia*. *In His Own Image* included the first Toto stories and twenty-six new fables. Robert Hugh Benson, for a time his closest friend, called them "The Fifth Gospel." Rolfe quarreled with Benson after collaborating with him on a book, *St. Thomas*. His last years were spent in Venice, where he lived by "credit and excuses" until a new victim, the Rev. Stephen Justin, subsidized him to the extent of a thousand pounds. Rolfe was at last enabled to indulge his luxurious tastes and to hire male companions. He died suddenly of heart disease in his hotel room.

Rolfe was slim, clean-shaven, bandy-legged, and slightly clerical in appearance, wearing powerful pince-nez. His manner was cold and self-contained, his gait deliberate, like his speech. The title and pen-name, "Baron Corvo," Rolfe claimed had been bestowed upon him with a small estate by an elderly English lady, the Duchess Sforza-Cesarini, whom he met in Italy and who adopted him as a grandson. He excelled as a sculler, swimmer, fisherman, musician, photographer and scribe. A fascinating companion when he chose, he could charm children with his tales; the letters he wrote John Bland, son of another dealer in magic, the English writer E. Nesbit, not only delighted the child but made him model his adult handwriting on Rolfe's exquisite calligraphy. *The Desire and Pursuit of the Whole,* a posthumous novel, is another *roman à clef* which pillories all the people Rolfe disliked most in Venice, including, of course, his benefactors, particularly Robert Hugh Benson. One of the most eccentric, if not perverse, of English writers, Rolfe is the subject of a brilliant and highly successful biography, *The Quest for Corvo,* by A. J. A. Symons.

PRINCIPAL WORKS: Stories Toto Told Me, 1898; Chronicles of the House of Borgia, In His Own Image, 1901; Hadrian the Seventh, 1904; Don Tarquinio, 1905; The Weird of the Wanderer, 1912; The Desire and Pursuit of the Whole, 1934; Hubert's Arthur, 1935.

ABOUT: Bainbridge, H. Twice Seven; Moore, D. L. E. Nesbit: A Biography; Rolfe, F. A History of the Borgias (see Preface by S. Leslie to Modern Library ed.); Symons, A. J. A. The Quest for Corvo: An Experiment in Biography; London Mercury May 1934; Times Library Supplement (London) December 13, 1941.

*ROLLAND, ROMAIN** (January 29, 1866-   ), French novelist and essayist, winner of the Nobel Prize for Literature, wrote to the editors of this volume in 1940, shortly before the fall of France: "I was born in a little town in the centre of France, Clamecy, in the department of Nièvre— the old duchy of Nivernais. In many crises of history, Clamecy distinguished itself by its independence. During the Revolution of 1789, the ideas of which it had embraced fiercely, the paternal great-grandfather of Romain Rolland was one of the 'Apostles of Reason,' organized by Fouché, to spread the republican spirit in the department of Nièvre. Later, when Napoleon III made his *coup d'état* in 1851, Clamecy was one of the few villages which revolted against the usurper, and which was decimated later by the Bonapartist repression. It is situated on two rivers (the Beuvron and the Yonne) and a canal, among pretty hills, which are the last undulations of the Morvan. Romain Rolland was, still later, to sing, in his 'Rabelaisian novel,' *Colas Breugnon,* of 'the city of lovely reflections and supple hills.' His father and both his grandfathers were notaries. On the paternal side, there was the Gallic spirit, free, critical, and having a feeling for the soil. On the maternal side, there was a serious, religious spirit, which had had Jansenist connections in the eighteenth and nineteenth centuries. It was to his mother also that Romain Rolland owed his love of music.

"He was educated at the College of Clamecy, up to his fourteenth year, then at Paris, at the lycées of St. Louis and Louis-le-grand. In the latter, he was the schoolmate of Paul Claudel. In 1886, he entered the École Normale Supérieure, where he had for teachers the historians Gabriel Monod and Ernest Lavisse, the geographer Vidal de Lablache, the philosophers Bontroux and Brochard, the historical-literary critics Brunetière and Gaston Boissier. Among his colleagues were the great Latinist Joseph Bedier, the Germanic philologist Andler, the Sinologue Chavannes, the Hindu scholar Fouché, the future poet and essayist André Saurès, the philosopher and physician Georges Dumas. Jaurès had just left the school, and Pasteur had his laboratory there. During the years 1886-1889, young Rolland made the acquaintance of Ernest Renan, and corresponded with Leo Tolstoy.

"In 1889, after having passed the examinations for his bachelor's degree, Romain Rolland was sent to the French School in Rome, in the Farnese Palace a school of history and archaeology, which worked in archives and in archaeological excavations. Young Rolland traveled a great deal, over all of Italy and Sicily; he frequented Italian and cosmopolitan society, and he formed a filial friendship with Malwida von Meysenbug, who had been the friend of Wagner and of Nietzsche, of Mazzini and of Alexander Herzen. Born at Cassel, of an aristocratic family, she had long ago espoused the ideas of 1848, had been obliged to flee from Germany, and had spent long years of exile in London, in the company of the great exiles of all of Europe. She has related her life in the very interesting *Memoirs of an Idealist.* Rome had a fundamental influence on the spirit of Romain Rolland. It was there that he wrote his first dramas, unpublished, inspired by the Italian Renaissance—*Orsino, Les Baglioni,* etc.

"In 1891, he returned to Paris, and was married there to the daughter of the great philologist Michel Bréal, a friend of Renan and of Gaston Paris. For ten years he worked, in obscurity, on a series of dramas, the first of which to be published was *St. Louis* (1897), meanwhile acquiring his doctorate with a thesis on *The Origins of the Opera in Europe: Before Lully and Scarlatti* (1895). He observed, meditated, and for a long time planned his *Jean-Christophe*. He was made instructor, at the École Normale Supérieure, of a course on the history of art, which a little later became transformed into a course on the history of music, at the Sorbonne. In this period, he made the acquaintance and became the friend of Richard Strauss and of Gabriele d'Annunzio, as well as of Eleanora Duse.

"After 1900, in a period of great concentration and creation, he published, in the *Cahiers de la Quinzaine* [*Fortnightly Bulletins*] of Charles Péguy, with whom he was associated, the greater part of his better known works: all the series of *Jean-Christophe* (in a dozen volumes), the series of *Des Vies des Hommes Illustres* [*Lives of Illustrious Men*] (lives of Beethoven, Michelangelo, and Tolstoy), a series of volumes of musical history (*Handel, Musicians of the Past, Musicians of Today*, etc.). In 1913, the French Academy awarded him the grand prize for literature.

"The war of 1914 found him in Switzerland, where he always spent several months a year, in the mountains which he has always loved. Romain Rolland was then forty-eight years old, he was free of any military obligation; he remained in Switzerland, where he devoted himself to the service of the International Red Cross (the international agency for prisoners of war), at Geneva. And as he disapproved of this war, which he had foreseen in *Jean-Christophe*, and which he saw as the future ruin of Europe, he wrote, in the *Journal de Genève*, in 1914 and 1915, a series of articles against the war, of which the most celebrated was *Au-dessus de la Mêlée* [*Above the Conflict*], which loosed the fury of the belligerents against him. In 1917, the Swedish Academy awarded him the Nobel Prize for Literature. The war inspired two novels—*Pierre et Luce*, and *Clerambault*—and also a play in the style of Aristophanes, *Liluli. Colas Breugnon*, written before 1914, was not published until after the war.

"Returning to Paris in 1919, he lived there two years, then established himself in Switzerland, at Villeneuve, on the shore of Lake Leman. He lived there from 1922 to 1938, with his sister and his aged father. He

turned to the study of India, and devoted several volumes to it, among them one on Mahatma Gandhi and three volumes on Ramakrishna and Vivakanada (*Études sur la Mystique et l'Action de l'Inde Moderne* [*A Study of Mysticism and Action in Modern India*]). He became the friend of Rabindranath Tagore and of Gandhi, who came to visit him at Villeneuve. He had friendly relations also with President Masaryk, whom he met in Prague. He wrote a new cycle of novels, under the title of *L'âme Enchantée* [*The Soul Enchanted*] (1925-1934), and he devoted himself to studies of Beethoven (several volumes of history and musical analysis, under the title of *Les Grandes Époques Créatrices* [*The Great Creative Epochs*]: *I. From the Eroica to the Appassionata; II. Goethe and Beethoven; III. The Song of the Resurrection*—the last sonatas and the *Missa Solemnis*).

"For the rest, Romain Rolland returned to the theatre, which had been his first literary vocation. From 1900 on, he had undertaken a cycle of twelve plays on the French Revolution, and had written four of them— *Le Quatorze Juillet* [*The Fourteenth of July*], *Les Loups* [*The Wolves*], *Danton, Le Triomphe de la Raison* [*The Triumph of Reason*]—which had been produced in Paris. After 1925, he resumed the composition of this cycle, and published four new plays— *Pâques-Fleuries* [*Palm Sunday*], *Les Léonides, Le Jeu de l'Amour et de la Mort* [*The Play of Love and Death*] (which was produced, in 1939, at the *Comédie Française*), and *Robespierre* (which was written in 1938).

"Since the end of the war of 1914-18, he has seen the new war lowering, which has now [1940] taken captive two-thirds of humanity; and he entered the social struggle in a large number of articles, collected in two volumes, *Quinze Ans de Combat* [*Fifteen Years of Struggle*] and *Par la Révolution, la Paix* [*Peace Through Revolution*], published in 1939. He took part energetically in the fight against Fascism and Nazism. In 1935, he made a trip to Moscow, where he was the guest of Maxim Gorky, who was his intimate friend; he met Stalin and the principal leaders, with whom Gorky was associated, and on whom he [Gorky] exercised a moderating influence.

"In 1937, Romain Rolland left Switzerland and established himself at Vézelay, in France, in the province of Burgundy, not far from his native village, Clamecy. He is working on his memoirs, from his autobiographical journal, which he has never ceased to keep since his youth.

"In politics, he has always been a republican with advanced Socialist sympathies, an internationalist at heart, and, as they said in the eighteenth century, a 'citizen of the world.' He has always fought social injustice. In art, he loves, above all, Beethoven, Shakespeare, and Goethe. Among the French, it is Stendhal whom he prefers, besides the Encyclopedists of the eighteenth century, Voltaire, Diderot, Jean Jacques Rousseau, and the great memoir-writers, of whom the most illustrious is Saint-Simon. Rembrandt is the painter who is dearest to him. But his chosen country is Italy."

* * *

In the above admirably informative but restrained self-portrait, M. Rolland omits only to state that in appearance he is of the old Burgundian type—blond in youth, with blue eyes under bushy "straw-colored" eyebrows, and with chiseled features. His health is frail, and he suffers from chronic bronchitis. Indoors he wears a gray camel's hair cloak for protection against draughts. When the Second World War began, he was living very quietly with his devoted wife (they have no children), his books, and his piano—still hard at work and still unafraid of public attacks. He took very calmly the obloquy which was heaped on him for his pacifist views during the First World War. It is said that Anatole France, asked why he had not joined Rolland in his denunciation of the war, answered, "I was afraid." When Rolland was given the Nobel Prize, there was an outcry of "pro-German," and the statement was made that the award was illegal because he had not been recommended by the French Academy. Investigation showed that he *had* been so recommended—by Anatole France.

Rolland's present whereabouts and state of health, following the fall of France, are unknown.

WORKS AVAILABLE IN ENGLISH: *Novels*—Jean-Christophe (Jean-Christophe, Jean-Christophe in Paris, Jean-Christophe: Journey's End) 1910-13; Colas Breugnon, 1919; Clerambault, 1921; Pierre and Luce, 1922; The Soul Enchanted (Annette and Sylvie, Summer, Mother and Son, Death of a World, A World in Birth) 1925-34. *Miscellaneous*—Michelangelo, 1915; Händel, 1916; The People's Theatre, 1918; Gandhi, 1924; Beethoven the Creator, 1929; Prophets of a New India, 1930; Goethe and Beethoven, 1931; Letters of Romain Rolland and Malwida von Mysenbug, 1890-91, 1933; I Will Not Rest, 1935; The Wolves (play) 1937; The Living Thoughts of Rousseau, 1939.

ABOUT: Bonncrot, J. Romain Rolland et Son Oeuvre; Debran, I. M. R. Rolland: Initiateur de Défaitisme; Guérard, A. L. Five Masters of French Romance; Jouve, C. J. Romain Rolland Vivant; Kuechler, W. Romain Rolland; Romein, J. Romain Rolland; Seippel, P. Romain Rolland: l'Homme et l'Oeuvre; Sénéchal, C. Romain Rolland; Stephens, W. French Novelists of Today; Zweig, S. Romain Rolland: The Man and His Work; Asia March 1931; Atlantic Monthly January 1926, December 1935; Current Opinion February 1922; Dial May 1924; Journal of Philosophy October 8, 1931; Living Age April 2, 1921, August 1932; Mercure de France March 1, 1931, February 15, 1936; New Republic September 7, 1938; Preussiche Jahrbücher January 1926; Sewanee Review October 1924; Yale Review December 1930.

RØLVAAG, OLE EDVART (April 22, 1876-November 5, 1931), Norwegian-American novelist, was born on the island of Dönne, Norway, in a fishermen's settlement near a cove called Rølvaag on the map. An ancestor had taken this place-name as his own. The novelist's parents were Ellerine Johanna (Olson) and Peder Jakobsen Rølvaag. His family had followed the sea for generations from these rocky shores of Helgeland. The boy was not a tractable or intelligent pupil in school, but read all the books obtainable for fourteen miles around, —Cooper, Dickens, Marryat, Haggard, Dumas, and Verne, as well as the Scandinavian writers Topelius, Lie, and (his greatest literary influence) Björnson. Leaving school at fourteen, Ole became an expert fisherman, and was offered a new fishing boat of his own if he would relinquish a plan of going to America. In August 1896, however, he was at Elk Point, S.D., and went to work on his uncle's farm at Brule Creek as a laborer. This proved worse than the fisheries. Having by now a smattering of English and a little money, in the fall of 1899 he entered Augustana College, Canton, S.D. "The moment I came in touch with books and study it was as if a heavy curtain had been lifted," he wrote later. "I found out that I loved study passionately."

Graduating in 1901, Rølvaag proceeded to St. Olaf College, Northfield, Minn., with forty dollars in his pocket. Two summer vacations were spent as a traveling salesman, working half the week and reading in small-town libraries the other half. A novel, *Nils and Astri*, written during his senior year, was never published. Receiving his B.A. with honors in 1905, Rølvaag borrowed $500 for a year at the University of Oslo, Nor way. In 1906 he joined the faculty of St. Olaf and two years later married Jennie Marie Berdahl. (They had four children; two sons died, one by drowning.) In 1908 Rølvaag became an American citizen, and in 1910 received his master's degree. Two novels, written in Norwegian (as was all Rølvaag's fiction) were published by the Augsburg Publishing House of Minneapolis. In *Amerika-Breve* (America-Letters, 1912) he used a double pseudonym, "P. A. Smerik," the purported author, and "Paul Mørck," the supposed publisher. Aschehoug, the big publishing firm of Oslo, asked for revisions which Rølvaag indignantly refused to make, so that he was not published in Norway until about the time of the appearance of his masterpiece, *Giants in the Earth* (from Genesis VI:4).

This "Saga of the Prairie," dedicated "To Those of My People Who Took Part in the Great Settling, To Them and Their Generations" and written with the deliberate purpose of forestalling Johan Bojer's *The Emigrants*, was composed in a cabin in the northern Minnesota pines, in a cheap hotel in London, and in Norway, where he met Bojer and found that their two treatments, one from the American and the other from the Norwegian side, would not conflict. Lincoln Colcord, American writer of sea-stories, whose home was in Minneapolis, helped Rølvaag make an idiomatic translation from the literary Norwegian of the novel, and contributed a biographical and critical preface. It was as remarkable a collaboration in its way as that of Joseph Conrad and Ford Madox Ford.

Peder Victorious is a sequel to *Giants in the Earth. Pure Gold,* a study of the miser's temperament, had appeared as *Two Fools* ten years before. *The Boat of Longing,* Rølvaag's most poetical and mystical novel, concerns the Loengselens Baat, a legendary vessel symbolic of the heartache caused by emigration. Rølvaag was appointed head of the Norwegian Department at St. Olaf, which he hoped to make a center of Norwegian culture. His combative though good-natured personality did not make him altogether a campus favorite, and he had some unpleasant experiences in the anti-German atmosphere of the First World War. From 1924 Rølvaag suffered several heart attacks, culminating in the angina pectoris which eventually caused his death. In 1926 he was made a Knight of St. Olaf by King Haakon of Norway. Rølvaag's smooth face, with its stubby nose and crown of thin blond hair, showed serious determination and

humor. He was smaller than the average Scandinavian, and spoke with little accent. The unforgivable sin, he held, was to write about life untruthfully. All Rølvaag's work was well reviewed, but critics preferred *Giants in the Earth,* the *Nation* calling it "the fullest, finest and most powerful novel that has been written about pioneer life in America." Isabel Paterson remarked that, if not quite an epic novel, it strikes the epic note.

PRINCIPAL WORKS: Giants in the Earth, 1927; Peder Victorious, 1929; Pure Gold, 1930; The Boat of Longing, 1933.

ABOUT: Jorgenson, T. and N. O. Solum. Ole Edvart Rølvaag: A Biography; Boston Evening Transcript December 5, 1931; New York Times November 6, 1931; Norwegian-American Studies and Records 1933, 1938; Saturday Review of Literature April 15, 1939.

ROMAINS, JULES (August 26, 1885-   ), French novelist, poet, and dramatist, who was born Louis Farigoule, wrote to the editors of this volume in 1939, on the eve of the Second World War: "I was born at Saint-Julien Chapteuil, a village situated in the Eastern part of the *Massif Central,* and the cradle of my family for centuries. But, at  that period, my parents lived in Paris, where my father was a teacher. It was therefore in Paris that I passed my childhood. After the Lycée Condorcet, I prepared for examinations in letters and science at the Sorbonne; I was admitted in 1906 to the École Normale Supérieure. In 1909 I received my degree in philosophy and science.

"At the age of sixteen, I had published a volume of poems; but it was in 1908, while I was still a student, that my first important work appeared—again a book of poems, *La Vie Unanime (Unanimistic Life).* This book had a great success, a sufficiently unusual thing for a young man. This success, already ancient, has had for result that many people, who have heard of me for so long a time, think I am much older than I am. *La Vie Unanime* expressed, in lyric form, the theory called "unanism," which is a new vision of human groups in themselves, and not, as was most often the case before then, of the individual elements which compose them.

"In 1909, I was made professor of philosophy at the Lycée of Brest, then in 1910 at Laon, finally at Nice and at Paris. This did not prevent me from cultivating the numerous friendships which I had formed among young writers and artists, and from publishing several books: in 1910 a poem, *Un Être en Marche* (*A Marching Being*); in 1911 my first play, *L'Armée dans la Ville* (*The Army in the Town*), and my first novel, *Mort de Quelqu'un*, which was afterwards translated into English under the title *Death of a Nobody*; in 1913 poems, *Odes et Prières* (*Odes and Prayers*), and a novel, *Les Copains* (recently translated in the United States as *The Boys in the Back Room*); in 1914, *Sur les Quais de LaVillette* (*On the Wharves of LaVillette*); and in the midst of the war, in 1916, a poem entitled *Europe*, in which I expressed myself with indignation against the great catastrophe.

"After the war, desiring to devote all my time to literature, I abandoned my university career. This enabled me to make many journeys abroad, which I was unable to do sufficiently during my years of study and teaching. It was at this time that I was confirmed in the idea (which was not new, since it had inspired my poem *Europe*) of a united, coherent Europe, surmounting frontiers and nationalities.

"The dozen years which followed the war were the period of my greatest dramatic activity. In fact, aside from a few volumes of poems, a scientific work, *La Vision Extra-rétinienne* (*Extra-Retinal Vision*); and a novel, *Psyche,* of which the three volumes have been translated into English under the general title of *The Body's Rapture,* all my work, during this period, was consecrated to the theatre. *Knock,* in 1923, had a phenomenal success; this play, which since then has been presented every year in Paris and in numerous towns of France, has been translated into nearly all languages and played in nearly all countries. In the following years, I gave numerous plays to the theatre, of which the most important, *Le Dictateur* (*The Dictator*), *Volpone* (written in collaboration with the great Austrian writer Stefan Zweig), *Musse, Donogoo,* and *Boën,* were also played abroad.

"In 1931, I commenced to write the first two volumes (published in 1932) of my most important novel, *Les Hommes de Bonne Volonté,* published in the United States as *Men of Good Will.* The idea of a vast novel, composed of a great number of volumes, and in which I would try to present a sort of epic from the beginning of the twentieth century all over the world, and especially in France, was far from being new to me. It existed in my mind from

my earliest youth, from the very time when I began to write. But I knew that, to realize a work of the amplitude of which I dreamed, it would be necessary for me to have amassed all kinds of experience, and to have attained to a maturity of spirit which is not possible to a young man. Since the war, even while writing my other works, I had never ceased to think of this novel; to establish its foundations and plan. Since 1932, I have published regularly, every year, two volumes of *Hommes de Bonne Volonté*; sixteen volumes are now [autumn, 1939] published, which cover the years 1908 to 1916. (In the United States, my publisher issues two volumes in one, so that actually there are eight volumes which correspond to the sixteen in French.) I intend to write eleven volumes more which will lead us to about 1933.

"I believe I can without fatuity compliment myself on the reception which has greeted *Hommes de Bonne Volonté,* not only in France, but in the entire world. Many translations are under way, in English, in German, in Czech, in Polish, in Spanish. Everywhere my novel is read; and it often happens to me, when I find myself in some little town in a land far from Europe, to meet enthusiastic readers, who recognize themselves among my many characters and speak of them as of old friends. It is a great satisfaction to me.

"Since the beginning of the publication of *Hommes de Bonne Volonté* I have been obliged, of course, to consecrate myself almost entirely to that work. I have, however, published several volumes: in 1933, *Problèmes Européens* (*European Problems*), in which I collected essays on political and social questions; in 1934, *Le Couple France-Allemagne* (*The Franco-German Pair*), a study of the connections between Germany and France; in 1936, after returning from a journey to the United States, *Visite aux Américains* (*A Visit to the Americans*); in 1937, a poem, *L'Homme Blanc* (*The White Man*), an epic of the white race; finally, I have just written a new play, *Grâce Encore pour la Terre!* (*Grace Again for the Earth!*), which will soon be performed in Paris.

"I have never wished to mingle in a definite way in political life; I knew too well how much that would prevent my following my literary career. But I have always been passionately interested in internal and international politics; and each time that the situation, or the relations or influence which I have, have permitted me to render service to causes that I consider good, I have not hesitated to do so. I have always, both in lectures, articles, and in private conversations with the leaders of many lands, fought to defend the great ideals of humanity, peace, understanding among peoples, liberty in all its forms, a juster division of happiness among men, democracy.

"I am a great traveler. I go very often, several times a year, to the countries adjacent to France—England, Belgium, Switzerland, and, while it was still possible, Germany, Italy, and Spain; but I know also, sometimes very well, the whole of Europe, all the Mediterranean basin, the French colonies in Africa, South America, and the United States, where I have gone three times. In 1936, I stayed there three months, and I have visited all the large cities, as far as California. These trips take place under all sorts of pretexts: an international congress of authors, the performance of my plays, lectures. But the principal reason is my love of traveling.

"I have belonged since its foundation to the French section of the International Federation of P.E.N. Clubs; I was its president in 1936. The same year, I had the pleasure of being elected, at the Congress of Buenos Aires, the international president of the Federation, my great friend, the illustrious English author H. G. Wells, having resigned. I am also the international president of the Universal Society of the Theatre.

"When I am not traveling, I live in France, sometimes at Paris, which I love very much and know intimately, as those are aware who have read my works, sometimes in Touraine, one of the prettiest regions of my country, where I own a very old house, surrounded by a park and by woods; I even make my own wine there. I should also say that I am married, though for a few years only, to a quite young wife, who accompanies me on my travels and helps me with great intelligence in my work and my numerous occupations."

* * *

After the fall of France in 1940, Romains came to the United States, where he is now living. His *Salsette Discovers America* (1942) gives his favorable, sometimes rhapsodic, impressions of the American scene, following his curious attempt, in *The Seven Mysteries of Europe* (1940), to explain the European disaster in terms of his personal adventures behind the scenes. One critic remarked caustically, "The eighth mystery is Romains."

Mme. Romains (or Farigoule) was Lise Dreyfus. They were married in 1936. Al-

though the author's name is still legally Farigoule, he is Romains to the world. Like Anatole France, his fame has transcended his name.

Jules Romains has the high forehead and deep-set eyes of a thinker, the eyes themselves having been called "sky-colored." His mouth is generous, and his strong chin deeply cleft. In his youth he was an athlete, and he still seems young and full of energy. John Chamberlain has called him "the French Dos Passos"; René Lalou, "the Tolstoy of our time." The main theme of his work, Agnes C. Hansen said, is "the psychological dominance of mass over individual, the inseparability of the latter psychologically from the social group of which he forms a part." I. Kouchner complained of "this inexorably intellectual literature in which the slightest spiritual movement is analyzed, explained, and in the end killed by the intellect"; but actually there is much of the poetic, if not the spiritual, in Jules Romains' novels, especially in his exquisite descriptions of places, which sometimes recall the similar evocations of places by Virginia Woolf.

When *Verdun* appeared (appositely in 1939) as the eighth translated volume of *Men of Good Will*, it was greeted with a chorus of American and English acclaim as one of the great war novels on its own account. "It is still too early," observed the New York *Times*, "to discuss the structure of *Men of Good Will* as a whole. But there are many who believe that the entire panorama will be a masterpiece—all the greater because it risks such failure. And it is quite certain that *Verdun* will be one of its noblest elements and will, come what may, be recognized as a masterpiece in its own right."

The later volumes were less favorably received, and some critics believe that the collapse of France has made unlikely the successful termination of Romains' *Men of Good Will* series.

WORKS AVAILABLE IN ENGLISH TRANSLATION: "*Men of Good Will*" *Series*—Men of Good Will (The 6th of October, Quinette's Crime) 1933; Passion's Pilgrims (Childhood's Loves, Eros in Paris) 1934; The Proud and the Meek (The Proud, The Meek) 1935; The World From Below (The Lonely, The Provincial Interlude) 1935; The Earth Trembles (Flood Warning, The Powers That Be) 1936; The Depths and the Heights (To the Gutter, To the Stars) 1937; The Death of a World (Mission to Rome, The Black Flag) 1938; Verdun (The Prelude, The Battle) 1939; Aftermath (Vorge Against Quinette, The Sweets of Life), 1941; The New Day (Promise of Dawn, The World Is Your Adventure) 1942. *Other Works*—The Death of a Nobody, 1914; Eyeless Sight: A Study of Extra Retinal Vision and

Paroptic Sense, 1924; Lucienne, 1925; Dr. Knock (play) 1925; Six Gentlemen in a Row, 1927; The Body's Rapture, 1933; The Boys in the Back Room, 1938; The Seven Mysteries of Europe, 1941; Stefan Zweig: Great European, 1941; Salsette Discovers America, 1942.

ABOUT: Hincz, V. L'Unanisme et l'Oeuvre de Jules Romains; Turquet-Milnes, G. Some Modern French Writers; Annales Politiques et Littéraires January 25, 1939; Bookman (London) October 1932; Canadian Forum August 1934; Contemporary Review July 1936; Europe Nouvelle December 31, 1938; Forum November 1935; Living Age March 1933, February 1934; Mercure de France May 15, 1924, March 1, 1937; Nouvelle Revue Française April 1, 1929; Revue des Deux Mondes February 1, 1924, November 15, 1933, March 1 and December 1, 1938; Revue Politique et Littéraire February 1938; Saturday Review of Literature June 3, 1933, December 30, 1939, April 6, 1940; Seven Arts April 1917; Sewanee Review July 1933; Theatre Arts Monthly December 1931.

ROMANOV, PANTELEIMON SERGE-YEVICH (1884-April 30, 1938), Russian

novelist and short story writer, was born

in the village of Petrovsk in the government of Tula in a well-to-do peasant family. After preliminary studies at home he entered the Tula Gymnasium. Despite his poor scholastic record in "Russian" and in "style" (his compositions were

found extravagant by his teachers), he skimmed through his courses and qualified for the law school at the University of Moscow. There, instead of listening to his professors, he devoted his class-periods to jotting down their peculiarities as well as those of his classmates. His spare time he considered meager for his extensive reading of Dostoievsky, Gogol, and Tolstoy. His favorite book. War and Peace, led him to plan a vast panoramic novel embracing Russia in all its breadth, and by 1907-1908 he had completed the outline of his Russia, the first volume of which did not appear until 1924. This fact illustrates Romanov's slow method of work and holds true of his other creative efforts. For instance the autobiographical novel, Childhood, published in 1924, was begun in 1903 but not completed till 1920; Autumn, begun in 1910, was not finished until four years later, while Zima took from 1915 to 1923. During the First World War and the revolutionary upheavals, he disappeared from the public eye but he accepted and endorsed the Soviet régime. Although his writings contained no propa-

gandistic material, his new public liked the simple, straightforward realism of this "fellow traveler."

Romanov found an opportunity to develop his gifts as a master of the short story: humorous tales showing the way peasants greeted political changes as well as the fate of landowners and petty bourgeois intellectuals rendered "superfluous" by the great cataclysm. But his most fertile theme was love and sex—how bourgeois relations were superseded by new moral values.

Besides the first volume of Russia, in 1924 also appeared Vol. I of his Short Stories and a comedy entitled Earthquake; in 1925, Vol. II of his Short Stories (later on published under the ironic title Nice Places), A Powerful Nation, and Stories About Love. In the latter he had struck his finest note, that which found its most charming development in Without Cherry Blossom, published in 1926 in a short story collection by that title. These stories describe the new sexual relationships of Soviet college youth, the position of the unmarried mother, and the results of the abolition of the "sacrament" of marriage. Romanov deals with no erotic perversions or promiscuity but shows, rather, that "love and sex are something more than mere physiology." The theme in Without Cherry Blossom recurs in some of the short stories in On the Volga, which date back to 1926, in the novel The New Commandment published in 1928 and in the more recent Diary of a Soviet Marriage, a short novel written in the form of letters with a most intimate and authentic documentary flavor.

Outside the Soviet Union Romanov is known principally for Three Pairs of Silk Stockings, a long novel which appeared in 1930. Here Romanov depicted the atmosphere of futility hovering over certain intellectuals quite incapable of adjusting themselves to the new régime. Romanov understood the milieu and wrote about it in a crisp and exciting style devoid of affectation.

The key to all of Romanov's work has been given to us by the author himself. He confessed that the things he made use of passed through him not as through a casual isolated individual but as through an organic part of one big whole—the entire Russian nation, "and out of the material at my disposal I have selected only that which could serve as a common background, giving to every individual something that is typical of him. In short, then, Romanov tried to do for the early years of the Soviet Union what Chekhov did for the end of

Tsarist Russia. An American critic said of Romanov's *comédie humaine*: "His work reads right on, as if Russia were dictating and he were taking down its stories in flowing long-hand. For that reason something which is not propaganda, something authentic and valuable, comes over."

Romanov died in 1938 at the age of fifty-four.

WORKS AVAILABLE IN ENGLISH TRANSLATION: Three Pairs of Silk Stockings, 1931; Without Cherry Blossom, 1931; The New Commandment, 1933; On the Volga, 1934; Diary of a Soviet Marriage, 1936.

ABOUT: Lidin, V. Literaturnaya Rossiya, V. Pisateli; Nikitina, E. F. Russkaya Literatura; Tarsis, V. Sovremenniye Russkie Pisateli; Vitman, A. M. Vosem' let Russkoi Khudozhestvennoi Literatury (1917-1925); Bookman May 1931; Boston Transcript April 15, 1931; Molodaya Gvardiya July 1927 and June 1929; Nation July 22, 1931; New Republic May 20, 1931; New Statesman February 21, 1931; New York Herald Tribune "Books" March 29, 1931; New York Times March 22, 1931; Novy Mir December 1925; Priboy Almanakh Pervy 1925; Saturday Review of Literature May 2, 1931; Times Literary Supplement March 12, 1931; Yale Review Summer 1931.

ROSENBERG, ISAAC (November 25, 1890-April 19, 1918), English artist and poet, was born in Bristol. In 1897 the family moved to London, where Isaac attended the board schools in Stepney in the East End of London until he was fourteen, when he was apprenticed to the firm of Carl Hentschel, engravers in Fleet Street. Three wealthy Jewesses provided the means for his training at the Slade School, which young Rosenberg attended from October 1911 to March 1914, winning several prizes. An exhibition of his paintings was held at the Whitechapel Gallery. His sister encouraged him to write poetry, and to circulate copies of his poems among writers and critics. Edward Marsh printed one in *Georgian Poetry: 1916-1917*, and wrote Rosenberg encouraging letters. In 1912 he published *Night and Day*, the first of three pamphlets published at his own expense. Told in 1914 that his lungs were weak, Rosenberg journeyed to South Africa to stay with a married sister for a while, returning to England in 1915 and enlisting for the First World War. Starting at first with the Bantam Regiment— he was small in stature—Rosenberg was later transferred

to the King's Own Royal Lancasters. He was badly fitted for military life temperamentally and physically, suffering especially from blistered feet. He was killed in action in France in the spring of 1918, at the age of twenty-seven.

Siegfried Sassoon, as he said, "recognized in Rosenberg a fruitful fusion between English and Hebrew culture." Behind all his poetry "there is a racial quality—biblical and prophetic." His poetic visions are "mostly in sombre colors and looming sculptural masses, molten and amply wrought." His *Trench Poems* are few in number but impressive.

Rosenberg, again to quote Sassoon, had a sensitive and vigorous mind energetically interested in experimenting with language. Laurence Binyon finds his faults those of excess rather than deficiency. He was sometimes difficult and obscure because he instinctively thought in images. Rosenberg had a great admiration for Rossetti as a painter and Francis Thompson as a poet. He had a typically Hebraic face, with a full lower lip, arched eyebrows, and curly hair.

PRINCIPAL WORKS: Night and Day, 1912; Youth, 1918; Moses: A Play, 1916; Poems, 1922; Collected Works, 1937.

ABOUT: Rosenberg, I. Poems (see Memoir by L. Binyon); Collected Works (see Foreword by S. Sassoon).

ROSENFELD, MORRIS (December 28, 1862-June 21, 1923), Yiddish-American poet, was born in Bokscha, Suwalki, a part of Russian Poland. Educated at home in Hebrew and the Talmud, he received an orthodox upbringing from his parents, Ephraim Leib and Rachel (Wilchinsky) Rosenfeld. For several generations the family had been fishermen, but the poet's father was a military tailor. The family moved to Warsaw, where Morris acquired Polish and German. At twenty he learned tailoring in London and diamond cutting in Amsterdam. Emigrating in 1886 to the United States, he found conditions worse than ever in the sweat shops of the New York ghetto, where he worked long hours as a presser. Israel Zangwill, on an American tour, met Rosenfeld and gave him some encouragement—he had contributed poems to Yiddish journals—but it was Leo Weiner

H. Struck

of Harvard who finally extricated him from the shops. *Songs From the Ghetto* (1898) had a prose translation, glossary and introduction by Professor Wiener. Rosenfeld was called the most original poet in Yiddish literature, "the mouthpiece of victims of a dehumanized society." Nathaniel Buchwald calls him "resourceful in his vocabulary, happy in his sense of rhythm, rich in his coloring, sincere in his wrath."

Rosenfeld now contributed to Yiddish newspapers and gave readings from his poems at Harvard, the University of Chicago, Wellesley, Radcliffe, and some European cities. His work was translated into English, German, Hebrew, Russian, Roumanian, Polish, Bohemian and Hungarian, and several songs were set to music. Rosenfeld's health collapsed under a stroke of paralysis a few hours after friends had tendered him a sixtieth-birthday dinner. The funeral was held in the auditorium of the *Forward* Building, Seward Park, and hundreds attended his interment in a plot of the Workingmen's Circle, Mount Carmel, N.Y.

Hutchins Hapgood described Rosenfeld as small, dark, fragile in body, with fine eyes, drooping eyelashes and a plaintive, childlike voice.

PRINCIPAL WORKS: Songs From the Ghetto, 1898; Songs of Labor, and Other Poems (translated by Rose Pastor Stokes) 1914.

ABOUT: Pines, M. Di Geschichte fun der Yiddisher Literatur; Rogoff, H. Nine Yiddish Writers; Wiener, L. The History of Yiddish Literature in the Nineteenth Century; The Works of Morris Rosenfeld (see Foreword by Alex Harkavy); Critic March 1900; New York Times June 22, 25, 1923.

*ROSENFELD, PAUL (May 4, 1890-), American music and art critic, writes: "Paul Rosenfeld's father, Julius S. Rosenfeld, was an emigrant from Baden, Germany; his mother, Clara (Liebmann) Rosenfeld, was the American-born daughter of emigrants from Wurtemberg. Both were cultured, idealistic, and independent. Their son Paul was born in New York. He studied music from the age of six, though he had to be driven to the keyboard. He began contributing compositions to school papers while still at public school. From the age of thirteen to eighteen, he attended Riverview Military Academy in Poughkeep-

sie, where he proved himself a poor scholar and a lethargic soldier, but fell in love with Schumann, Shelley, Yeats, Morris, Meredith, and Pater, and the values of the vocabulary. He edited and practically wrote the school magazine, filling it with historical romances. At Yale, in the class of 1912, he continued uneducable, and contributed spasmodically, mildly originally, and unimpressively to the '*Lit*,' eventually becoming an editor of the magazine.

"At graduation he was entirely at sea concerning the manner of going about writing, though the production of *belles-lettres* was the sole occupation which attracted him. He drifted to the Columbia University School of Journalism, which helped him to a reportorial job on the New York *Press*. He survived six months—at intervals, at his desk in the city room, working on a semi-satirical Graustark novel. Suddenly he realized that nothing compelled him to persist in this morally distasteful newspaper game, and that a little inherited income left him free to go towards 'literature' if he desired to. He got himself dismissed from the paper. In the spring of 1913 he left for Italy. Florence provided the first friendly and delectable environment he had found. This experience was critical in his life.

"Today he feels his little initial moment of faith in himself was justified, if not by his literary spiritual product, at the very least by a crop of private satisfactions of a surprising richness, fullness, and variety, and by the steady growth of the capacity to comprehend the truth through literary means."

* * *

In 1916 and 1917 Mr. Rosenfeld, with Waldo Frank and James Oppenheim, edited the magazine *Seven Arts*. In 1918 he was a private in the army, stationed at Fort Humphries, Va. In 1920 he became music critic of the *Dial*, which he left in 1927. Since 1927 he has been co-editor with Alfred Kreymborg and Lewis Mumford of the various volumes issued of the anthology, *The American Caravan*. He lives in New York, and is unmarried. The late Llewelyn Powys said of him: "One may be irritated by his partiality, by a certain self-indulgence in his style, but one cannot fail to recognize his critical writing as a very rare and valuable influence upon the life of America today."

PRINCIPAL WORKS: Musical Portraits, 1920; Musical Chronicle, 1923; Port of New York, 1923; Men Seen, 1925; By Way of Art, 1928; The Boy in the Sun (novel) 1928; An Hour With American Music, 1929; Discoveries of a Music Critic, 1936.

ABOUT: Current Opinion June 1920; New Republic October 11, 1922, June 3, 1925; Review of Reviews April 1929.

ROSMAN, ALICE GRANT, Anglo-Australian novelist,

was born at Dreamthorpe, Kapunda, South Australia, the home

of her maternal grandfather, John Varley, S.M., in the late 1880's. She was also descended from the Hon. Henry H. Mildred, M.L.C., who migrated to Adelaide from London in 1836, having bought "paper land" in the new colony. Some of the silver he brought is now in the possession of the novelist. Her mother, Alice Mary (Bowyer) Rosman, who died in 1931, contributed verse to the *Bulletin* and other Australian papers from girlhood, and published a book of verse, *The Enchanted Garden*, in 1916.

Alice Rosman attended the Dominican Convent, Cabra, S.A., and began writing in childhood. Her first short story appeared in the Adelaide *Southern Cross*, and she was represented in *Aunt Eily's Christmas Annual* (Adelaide, 1902). From 1908 to 1911 she wrote for the Adelaide *Bulletin* under the pen-name "Rosna." In 1911 the Rosmans, including Alice's sister, Mary, later head of the department of music at Malvern College, went to London for the coronation of George V. From 1920 to 1927 Alice Rosman was on the literary staff of the *British Australian and New Zealander,* also working on the editorial staff of the *Grand Magazine.* In 1927 she began to write the first of her "domestic romances in comfortable households." *The Window* (1928) sold 100,000 copies, and *Visitors to Hugo* (1929), her most popular novel, established her reputation.

Most of Alice Rosman's subsequent work has been scrutinized with *Hugo* as a yardstick. It is "an engaging tale of young people in London" which superimposed cheerfulness on a sickroom atmosphere without affronting any reader's sensibilities. The Springfield *Republican* commented that "psychiatry and humor are rather interestingly blended." The Alice Grant Rosman novels qualified for a place of honor on the list of novels providing "solid solace" which was assembled by May Lamberton Becker and her "choir invisible" of commentators in the *Herald Tribune "Books."*

Miss Rosman's novels are slight and unpretentious, excluding "the deeper problems of actuality," but her world, according to one reviewer, has the virtue of being "internally consistent."

PRINCIPAL WORKS: Miss Bryde of England, 1916; The Tower Wall, 1917; The Back-Seat Driver, 1928; The Window, 1928; Visitors to Hugo, 1929; The Young and Secret, 1930; Jock the Scot, 1930; The Sixth Journey, 1931; Benefits Received, 1932; Protecting Margot, 1933; Somebody Must, 1934; The Sleeping Child, 1935; Mother of the Bride, 1936; Unfamiliar Faces, 1938; William's Room, 1939; Nine Lives: A Cat of London in Peace and War, 1941.

ABOUT: Miller, E. M. Australian Literature From Its Beginnings to 1935. Boston Transcript July 5, 1930; Wilson Library Bulletin June 1930.

"ROSS, BARNABY." See "QUEEN, E."

"ROSS, J. H." See LAWRENCE, T. E.

"ROSS, LEONARD Q." See ROSTEN, L. C.

"ROSS, MARTIN." See MARTIN, V. F.

ROSSETTI, WILLIAM MICHAEL. See "BRITISH AUTHORS OF THE 19TH CENTURY"

ROSTAND, EDMOND

(April 1, 1868-December 2, 1918), French playwright and poet, was born in Marseilles into an old Provençal family. His father, the economist Eugène Rostand, was himself a poet and scholar, a member of the Marseilles Academy and of the Institut de France. After attending the École Thedenat and the Marseilles Lycée, Ed-

mond was sent to the Collège Stanislas in Paris, where he did brilliant work in French literature, history, and philosophy and came under the excellent influence of his teachers René Doumic and Boris de Tanenberg who introduced him to Shakespeare and Musset. From the earliest the boy showed a strong penchant for literature, devoting himself to his marionette theatre and his poetry, which began to appear in 1884 in the little review *Mireille.* In 1887 the Marseilles Academy awarded him the Marechal de Villars prize for his essay "Two Provençal Novelists: Honoré d'Urfé and Émile Zola."

Rejecting the diplomatic career planned for him by his father, Rostand entered law school and finally won admission to the bar, although not interested in being a lawyer. At the age of twenty he made his début as a playwright with *Le Gant Rouge,* written in collaboration with Henri Lee, produced with little success at the Théâtre de Cluny. In 1890 *Les Musardises* appeared, a collection of verse full of promise despite its obvious imitative phrasings from Hugo and Musset, his principal models. In that same year Rostand married Rosemonde Gérard, daughter of Count Gérard and granddaughter of General Gérard, grand marshal under Napoleon. She too was a promising poet, whose book of verse, *Les Pipeaux,* had been crowned by the French Academy. Their two sons, Maurice and Jean, became writers of some note. It was not until 1894 that Rostand scored his first significant triumph, *The Romancers,* produced at the Comédie Française and acclaimed not only by the public but by the Academy critics who awarded it the Toirac prize. Thus encouraged, he set to work on another play, this time with Sarah Bernhardt in mind— it was for her that he wrote *Princess Faraway,* produced at the Théâtre de la Renaissance on April 5, 1895.

Risking his reputation as a playwright in higher circles of influence, Rostand staunchly defended Alfred Dreyfus, as did Zola, Anatole France, and Marcel Proust. In the midst of the turmoil caused by the affair, Rostand completed his new play, *Cyrano de Bergerac,* which had its *première* December 28, 1897, as momentous as the *première* of Corneille's *Cid* or Hugo's *Hernani.* The play ran for months to full houses, not only because of its unquestioned merits but also because it marked a complete reaction against the realism of the problem plays then in vogue. *Cyrano de Bergerac* was a fresh, romantic poem with a folk hero masterfully impersonated by the great Coquelin. Rostand immediately set to work on a tragedy based on the life of the Duke of Reichstadt, son of Napoleon I and Marie Louise. On March 15, 1900, *L'Aiglon (The Eaglet)* was produced, with Sarah Bernhardt triumphant in the rôle of the effeminate young duke.

In 1901 Rostand was elected to the French Academy, the youngest writer ever to have entered that austere body. Thereafter Rostand wrote only two plays, both failures —*Chanticleer* and *The Last Night of Don Juan.* On the former Rostand worked for

some ten years. Owing to his ill health and to various other unfortunate delays, such as the death of Coquelin, who was cast for the principal rôle, it was not produced until February 1910. Its reception was extremely cold despite the effective acting of Lucien Guitry. *The Last Night of Don Juan,* produced four years after Rostand's death, was a total fiasco.

Works Available In English Translation: Cyrano de Bergerac, 1898; The Romancers, 1899; The Princess Faraway, 1899; L'Aiglon, 1900; Chanticleer, 1910; The Two Pierrots, 1914; Plays (Vol. I: Romantics, The Princess Faraway, The Woman of Samaria; Vol. II: The Eaglet, Chanticleer) 1921; The Last Night of Don Juan, 1925.

About: Apesteguy, P. La Vie Profonde d'Edmond Rostand; Baring, M. Punch and Judy; Bennett, A. Things That Have Interested Me; Chandler, F. W. Modern Continental Playwrights; Chesterton, G. K. Twelve Types; Clark, B. H. Contemporary French Dramatists; Duclaux, A. Twentieth Century French Writers; Haugmard, L. Edmond Rostand; Katz, E. L'Esprit Français dans le Théâtre d'Edmond Rostand; Phelps, W. L. Essays on Modern Dramatists; Rosenfeld, P. Men Seen; Contemporary Review February 1919; Nation November 12, 1924; New Republic November 28, 1923.

ROSTEN, LEO CALVIN ("Leonard Q. Ross") (April 11, 1908-), American economist and humorist, writes: "Chicago must bear the responsibility for my misguided childhood; it was there I spent my grammar school days reading Frank Merriwell and Rabelais. My high school years, of a higher order, were devoted to banging my hands with hammers (woodshop),

J. Schulman

cutting my fingers off neatly at the joint (tin shop), and pouring hot lead over my toes once a week (foundry). I was also exposed to four years of mechanical drawing, which left me drawn and unmechanical. The University of Chicago virtually subsidized four years of my college education. My trance-like ability to answer questions at any time of day or night led straight to a Phi Beta Kappa key. In 1928 I went to Europe for six months of study and Life (ah, Life!), returned to the academic jute mill, suffered the tortures of a year in the Law School, was hastily given a Ph.B., and went out into the gay world of—1929. I searched for a job for two years, re-reading Horatio Alger feverishly all the while. At one time or another I performed as bus boy, salesman, camp counsellor, lecturer, real estate assistant, and maker of antique coins. Through sheer innocence and purity of heart, I got a part-time job teaching English to adults in a night school. [Whence arose Mr. H*y*m*a*n   K*a*p*l*a*n.]

"In 1932 came the realization that I was a remarkably ignorant young man. I returned to the university, enrolling in the graduate school of Political Science and International Relations. In 1934 I hearkened to a new siren call from Europe and enlisted in the London School of Economics and Political Science. I sold my first written work to *Harper's Magazine* (a study of Oswald Mosley and English Fascism) and other organs of culture purchased my grave cogitations on the destiny of Europe. In 1935 I lectured like mad, and then went to Washington under a fellowship from the Social Science Research Council, to do research on the Washington correspondents. This unread masterpiece was published and rewarded with a Ph.D. from the University of Chicago. In the capital I also did research stints for the President's Committee on Administrative Management and the National Resources Committee.

"In this period my wife (Priscilla Ann Mead) came down with appendicitis and pneumonia. To pay my debts I began to write humorous sketches which the *New Yorker* published. I was now branded a humorist, and every time I opened my mouth there would be gales of laughter. An offer from Hollywood followed. I worked as a screen writer for a year and regret that I cannot concur with those who refer to Hollywood as a warm Siberia. I found films and screen writing challenging, exciting, and enormously valuable. I was aching to do a serious study of the film colony and the motion picture industry. A Carnegie grant in 1939 made this possible, and with an excellent research staff we began our labors.

"The pseudonym 'Leonard Q. Ross' is reserved for humor. 'Leo C. Rosten' is reserved for serious work. I have lectured at Stanford, New York University, Williams College, the New School for Social Research, and the University of California at Los Angeles."

* * *

Mr. Rosten was born in Lodz, Poland, and was taken to Chicago by his parents at the age of three. He is a short, dark, serious-looking young man, with black eyes under heavy lids. His style of humor is inimitable; like Stephen Leacock, he combines humor and economics without diffi-

culty, and manages to be superior in both disparate fields.

PRINCIPAL WORKS: The Education of H*y*m*a*n   K*a*p*l*a*n, 1937; The Washington Correspondents, 1937; Dateline: Europe, 1939; The Strangest Places, 1939; Adventure in Washington, 1939; Hollywood: The Movie Colony; The Movie Makers, 1941.

ABOUT: Scholastic March 11, 1940; Time November 22, 1937.

ROTH, JOSEPH (September 2, 1894-May, 1939), Austrian novelist, before his death wrote to the compilers of this volume: "I was born in the German colony Schwabendorf in Volynia, the son of a Russian Jewess and an Austrian. As my father left my mother before I was born and died in a lunatic asylum in Amsterdam, I have never seen him. As a boy I  lived by turns with relatives of my father in Vienna and with those of my mother in Russia. I was poor, independent, and comparatively happy. A ridiculous ambition made me study, so that I could get 'social position.' After hasty preparation I passed my examinations in Vienna, and enrolled in the university there for philosophy.

"Two days later the war broke out. I volunteered out of patriotism, but did not get to the front till 1916. I stayed there eight months, became sick, and on account of my knowledge of the Russian language and the Russian country was sent to the Commission of Occupation in the Ukraine. I became an officer, and intended to stay a soldier all my life. But then the revolution surprised me in Shmirinka. The revolting soldiers did not let me depart with the last train. I started to hike home, reached the former Russian border after a fortnight, was captured by Ukrainian troops, stayed prisoner for two months, fled, and after many detours got to Vienna.

"Here I lived without means except from occasional jobs—ushering in movies, illegal ticket speculating, etc.—for about a year and a half, until the breakdown of the Hungarian revolution gave me a chance to go to Hungary and to return with newspaper reports. From then on I began to write. For a certain time I wrote travel reports for the *Frankfurter Zeitung,* and have written some fifteen books, about which very little is known. I have no great public and no great income. I expect neither the one nor the other.

"I was with the *Frankfurter Zeitung* as reporter and editor until 1927. I am a conservative and a Catholic, consider Austria my fatherland, and desire the return of the Empire. Consequently when Hitler came into power I was obliged to flee Germany and return to Vienna. After the assassination of Dollfuss I went to Paris, where I live now. Considering my situation, as the result of later occurrences in Germany, I have not the strength to depict my life in detail."

* * *

In the same week that Ernst Toller hanged himself in New York, Joseph Roth took poison and died in Paris. He was forty-four. From completely opposite camps, Hitler had driven them both to the same end. Roth's life was tragic from start to finish. The downfall of Austria drove his wife permanently insane, he lost all his money and property, and lived in Paris largely by the charity of friends. Yet the "little man with a walrus moustache, gay twinkle in his eyes, and always hoarse voice," as an acquaintance described him, struggled on until "life broke him physically and what went on in Vienna killed him." Catholic though he was, his half-Jewish ancestry was very strong in him. As he said of Job in his greatest book: "Pain will make him wise, hatred kind, bitterness gentle, and illness strong."

He has been called "the most musical and graceful writer in the German tongue in our days." Louis Untermeyer called his "an illuminated simplicity"; he has been compared variously to writers as unlike as Dostoievsky and Hans Christian Andersen, Gottfried Keller and Knut Hamsun. As long ago as 1924 Erich Dürr wrote of him, almost prophetically: "One listens to him and thinks to oneself: too bad that he did not say more."

WORKS AVAILABLE IN ENGLISH: Flight Without End, 1930; Job: The Story of a Simple Man, 1931; Radetzky March, 1933; Tarabas: A Guest on Earth, 1934; Antichrist, 1935; Story of the Hundred Days (in America: Ballad of the Hundred Days) 1936; Confession of a Murderer: Told in One Night, 1938.

ABOUT: Bookman June 1930; Commonweal July 14, 1939; Saturday Review August 30, 1930; Saturday Review of Literature November 7, 1931; Spectator June 9, 1939.

*ROTHENSTEIN, Sir WILLIAM (January 29, 1872-), English artist and biographer, was born in Bradford, Yorkshire, the son of M. Rothenstein and Bertha (Dux) Rothenstein. He was educated in the Bradford Grammar School, at the famous Slade School of Art in London, and at the Académie Julien in Paris. Distinguished as he is as a painter, it is his drawings which have made him famous. He has exhibited or is represented by work in nearly every great modern museum, including the Tate Gallery, the British Museum, the Victoria and Albert Museum, the Metropolitan Museum of Art, the Chicago Art Institute, and many others all over the world. He has drawn or painted the portraits of nearly every celebrated figure of the literary, artistic, and social worlds of his time. He was the official artist of both the British and the Canadian armies during the First World War. He was principal of the Royal College of Art from 1920 to 1935, a trustee of the Tate Gallery from 1927 to 1933, and has been a member of the Royal Fine Art Commission since 1931. He was also professor of civic art at Sheffield University from 1917 to 1926, and Romanes Lecturer at Oxford in 1934. He has been a governor of the famous London Foundling Hospital since 1929. He has an honorary M.A. from Sheffield University, an honorary  D.Litt. from Oxford (1934), and is an honorary Associate of the Royal College of Art.

In 1899 he married Alice Mary Knewstub, and they have a daughter and two sons, one of whom, John, is also an artist and is now director of the Tate Gallery. He has long had a house in London and another at Stroud, Gloucestershire. Since the beginning of the present war he has been attached to the Air Force as an artist and is now on active duty.

Writing has been a mere by-product of Sir William's full and active life. He has known everybody worth knowing in the past sixty years or so, has been a close associate of the most eminent writers and painters, and has forgotten nothing about them. In consequence his three volumes of autobiography and memoirs are a marvelous source-book for historians, though not of a high or ambitious literary order. He writes with great simplicity, quiet humor, and good sense; as Osbert Burdett remarked, "there is nothing professional in his prose," but it is the better for that, giving the impression always of a good *raconteur* telling an interesting story in a pleasant conversational tone. Besides his reminiscences, he has written a few books on art and artists, and has also published numerous volumes of drawings, mostly portraits of his contemporaries.

Sir William Rothenstein is today practically an established institution in England, one of the last of the men who were young in the "Yellow 'Nineties" but himself still young and active in heart and mind. His memoirs are to be read for themselves as well as for the memories they record.

PRINCIPAL WORKS: Oxford Characters, 1893; Paul Verlaine, 1897; Liber Juniorum, 1899; Goya, 1900; Drawings by Hok'sai, 1910; Plea for a Wider Use of Artists and Craftsmen, 1917; Ancient India (with K. deB. Codrington) 1926; Men and Memories (2 vols.) 1931-32; Since Fifty: More Men and Memories, 1939; The Men of the R.A.F. (with E. C. D. Cecil) 1942.

ABOUT: Rothenstein, W. Men and Memories, Since Fifty; "H.W." William Rothenstein (Contemporary British Artists Series); Bookman (London) September 1926, April 1931.

*ROUGHEAD, WILLIAM (February 1870-), Scottish criminologist and authority on murder, was born in Edinburgh, the

son of John Carfrae and Amelia (Shaw) Roughead, and was educated at Craigmount House, Edinburgh, and at Edinburgh University. In July 1900 he married Janey Thompson More, and they make their home at Belgrave Crescent, Edinburgh. Roughead, who holds the legal title of Writer to His Majesty's Signet, has spent more time in editing volumes of the "Notable British Trials Series" and writing essays on criminological topics, usually first printed in the *Juridical Review*, than in actual practice. His work is sound, scholarly, full of literary allusions, unfolded with great skill and distinguished by a vein of solemn, pawky humor. "If we really want the painful oddities of criminology let us go to Bataille and Roughead," advises Christopher Morley in his preface to *The Complete Sherlock Holmes*. *Malice Domestic*, a series of household murders, leading off with Dr. Pritchard, was a publication of the Crime Club in New York, which also distributed a two-volume selection of his celebrated cases as a subscription premium. *The Children's Hour* (1934), the successful play by the American playwright Lillian Hellman, was based on an obscure Edinburgh scandal unearthed by Roughead, who found one of the two records

of the case which escaped censorship and developed it in an essay in his book *Bad Companions*. Mr. Roughead is generally regarded as the most eminent living writer on criminology. Henry James read him avidly. He is of the Scottish Episcopal faith, and bears physical resemblance to George Santayana.

PRINCIPAL WORKS: Rhyme Without Reason, 1901; Twelve Scots Trials, 1913; The Riddle of the Ruthvens, 1919; Glengarry's Way, 1922; The Fatal Countess, 1924; The Rebel Earl, 1926; Malice Domestic, 1929; What Is Your Verdict?, 1931; Bad Companions, 1931; In Queer Street, 1933; Rogues Walk Here, 1934; Knave's Looking-Glass, 1935; Enjoyment of Murder, 1938; Rascals Revived, 1940; Reprobates Reviewed, 1942.

ABOUT: Pearson, E. L. Books in Black or Red, Queer Books; Roughead, W. Bad Companions (see Introduction by H. Walpole).

ROURKE, CONSTANCE MAYFIELD (November 14, 1885-March 23, 1941), American biographer, wrote to the compilers

of this volume shortly before her death: "I don't know just when I decided to write or when precisely I turned to the American past for themes, though my first articles relating to it were published in 1917 or 1918. It happens that one of my Tennessee

H. Taylor

great-great-uncles, who was stolen by the Creeks as a baby, knew Davy Crockett, but I wasn't aware of this with any certainty until I had worked for some time on Crockett's life. I grew up without much emphasis upon my own ancestry—which happens to be mainly Southern pioneer—because of a parental revolt against a grandfather who made too much of these matters, though he never pretended that his forebears were anything but plain people.

"In any event, the word 'ancestries' does not cover my interest in the past. 'Continuities' is the better word. I can never quite 'lose myself,' as the phrase is, in the past. It is what the past has to say to the precarious, strange, and tragic present that is significant. The study of history has always had such values, but they are the greater for us because much of our past is still as deeply buried as was Herculaneum before the excavators began, and because we are now pressed to understand and fully use all the forces of democracy.

"Though my interest in the human individual is unflagging, I have never been able to see any subject for biography except in

* Died May 11, 1952.

these relationships. Crockett, Audubon, the Beechers, Barnum, Horace Greeley, Lotta Crabtree—all had a great amount of edge as characters, but equally they had the gift of dipping deeply though sometimes unconsciously into the life of their period and place. Probably any character worth his salt does so. At any rate I cannot separate the work that I have done in the field of biography from that in the more general field, as in *American Humor*. This book also registers my conviction that the popular arts—humor is one of them—have much to say as to underlying forces in American life.

"I truly enjoy the materials and techniques of research. The element of surprise may always lurk in an unknown book or pamphlet, translating an arduous process into something like the chase, with quarries that are constantly being transformed as new details are discovered. But my work has also included to a large extent what may be called 'living research,' that is, talk with old timers roundabout the country, particularly in small towns, listening to their autobiographies—plenty of them have the gift!—looking at provincial art, which has its special fascinations, listening to old music. If my work had meant only research in libraries, I don't believe I could have stayed with it, for as far as I can discover I am not a bookish person. When the day's work of whatever sort is done I turn not so much to books as to contemporary music, painting, the theatre, politics."

* * *

Miss Rourke was born in Cleveland, the daughter of H B. and Constance (Davis) Rourke. She was educated at Vassar (B.A.) 1907, and then as a recipient of the Borden Fund for Foreign Travel and Study studied at the Sorbonne in 1908 and 1909, and read at the Bibliothèque Nationale, Paris, and the British Museum from 1908 to 1910. She taught English at Vassar from 1910 to 1915. In 1937 she was editor of the Index of American Design of the Federal Art Project. She was unmarried, and lived in Grand Rapids, Mich., where she was reared. Her article on "Paul Bunyan," in the *New Republic* for July 4, 1918, was the first on this mythical lumberjack to appear in a magazine of general circulation, and represented a change to the American field and to interest in popular expression. Her books were called "scholarly but lively," and their author "our foremost scholar of frontier legend." She died at her Grand Rapids home at fifty-five of a fractured vertebra sustained in a fall a week earlier.

PRINCIPAL WORKS: Trumpets of Jubilee, 1927; Troupers of the Gold Coast: or, The Rise of Lotta Crabtree, 1928; American Humor: A Study of the American Character, 1931; Davy Crockett, 1934; Audubon, 1936; Charles Sheeler: Artist in the American Tradition, 1938; The Roots of American Culture, 1942.

ABOUT: Book-of-the-Month Club News October 1936; Nation March 29, 1941; New York Herald Tribune March 24, 1941; New York Times August 6, 1942; Wilson Library Bulletin March 1937.

ROYCE, JOSIAH (November 20, 1855-September 14, 1916), American philosopher, educator, and essayist, was born in Grass Valley, Nevada County, Calif., the youngest child and only son of Josiah and Sarah Eleanor (Bayliss) Royce, both of whom were English by birth. The elder Royce was born at Riddington, Rutlandshire, in 1812; Mrs. Royce at Stratford-on-Avon.  They met and married at Rochester, N.Y., and later made an adventurous journey, full of risk and hardship, to California in the gold rush of 1849. A journal kept by Mrs. Royce, a woman of force and intellect, was later published. Josiah was taught at home by his mother until he was eleven, and was generally sheltered from life by her and his three sisters. Red-headed, freckled, and shy, by his own description, he found it difficult to make social contacts. When the family moved to San Francisco, he attended Lincoln Grammar School and in 1869 entered the Boys' High School, a progressive school (for the times) at which Albert Michelson, the physicist, was a classmate. Mathematics came easily to Royce, and he also read omnivorously in the Mercantile Library, laying the foundations for the papers on Shelley, George Eliot, and Browning published in the posthumous *Fugitive Essays* of 1920.

After further preparation at Oakland, Royce entered the recently established University of California at Berkeley; there was no instruction in philosophy to be had here, but Joseph LeConte, a pioneer Darwinian and famous geologist, and Edward Rowland Sill, the poet and essayist, were two of his teachers. Here Royce first read Herbert Spencer and John Stuart Mill. His graduating thesis on the *Prometheus Bound* of Aeschylus attracted favorable attention and was the means of his going to Europe. Most of his time was spent at Göttingen and

Leipzig, attending lectures by Lotze, Wundt, Windelband, and studying Kant and Schopenhauer, all of whom had a profound influence on his later beliefs and teaching. Daniel Coit Gilman, who had been president of the University of California in his undergraduate days, invited Royce to be one of the first twenty fellows appointed to the new Johns Hopkins University at Baltimore. A thesis "On the Interdependence of the Principles of Knowledge" gained him a Ph.D. degree in 1878. Teaching English literature for four years at the University of California gave form and direction to his later writing. William James received Royce at his Cambridge home in 1877 and corresponded with him in California, with the full intention of finding a place in the East, at the first opportunity, for this promising novice. This occurred in 1882, when Royce took James' place while that lively philosopher was on leave of absence. With his wife, Katherine Head, whom he had married in 1880, he set out for Harvard, became an assistant professor in 1885, professor in 1892, and Alford Professor of Natural Religion, Moral Philosophy, and Civil Polity in 1914, on George Herbert Palmer's retirement from that chair. At Harvard he taught psychology in James' absence (also at the Massachusetts Institute of Technology) and conducted his experimental laboratory.

Royce's famous theory of the Absolute first appeared in *The Religious Aspect of Philosophy,* in 1885. If one admits the presence of error in the world, which the thinking man must necessarily do, it follows, he contends, that somewhere there is an immutable principle of truth, an omniscient mind or universal thought. "This universal knower, affirmer of all judgments, experiencer of all objects, and thus uniquely qualified to bring judgments and their objects together, is the famous 'Absolute'," says Ralph Barton Perry. To this George Santayana objects: "Actual thinking is therefore never a part of the Absolute, but always the Absolute itself," which is "a vicious and perplexing suggestion that philosophies are bred out of philosophies, not out of men in the presence of things."

Royce, Santayana declared, "wanted to fuse absolute idealism with social realism, with which it is radically incompatible." The more or less good-humored controversy between Royce, the monist, and James, "the friend of pluralism, or manyness and differences," lasted their lifetime (in the limited edition of the William James *Letters* there are two engaging snapshots showing the two sages arguing about the Absolute in the pantheistic peace of James' summer place at Chocorua, N.H.) and was continued by their pupils and disciples.

After 1900, as Perry says, Royce's interests developed toward more technical and specialized treatment of logic, and toward a more popular treatment of moral, social, and religious problems. At a mass meeting held in Tremont Temple in Boston, January 30, 1916, Royce electrified a huge audience by his measured denunciation of the German cause. After 1912 his health gradually failed, and his deep concern over the war hastened his final illness.

For twenty-five years Royce was the leading exponent in America of post-Kantian idealism. His method was rationalistic; he believed it possible to prove ultimate truths. In *The Spirit of Modern Philosophy* he argued the inadequacy of the new positivistic and evolutionary school. Even today his influence has not altogether waned.

Royce's personal appearance was odd. William James said he had "an indecent exposure of forehead." Santayana observed that "his great head seemed too heavy for his small body, and his portentous brow, crowned with thick red hair, seemed to crush the lower part of his face." The voice was merciless and harsh, drawing up buckets of discourse from a bottomless well of reading and observation. Royce was not averse to having a wide reading public and was disappointed, Santayana believed, at the small sale of *The Feud of Oakfield Creek,* his one venture into novel-writing.

PRINCIPAL WORKS: The Religious Aspect of Philosophy, 1885; California: A Study of American Character (American Commonwealth Series) 1886; The Feud of Oakfield Creek, 1887; The Spirit of Modern Philosophy, 1892; Studies of Good Will and Evil, 1898; The World and the Individual, 1900, 1901; The Philosophy of Loyalty, 1908; The Problem of Christianity, 1913; The Hope of the Great Community, 1916; Lectures on Modern Idealism, 1919; Fugitive Essays, 1920.

ABOUT: Aronson, M. J. La Philosophie Morale de Josiah Royce; Santayana, G. Character and Opinion in the United States; Harvard Graduates' Magazine December 1916; Harvard Theological Review July 1936; Philosophical Review May 1916.

ROYDE-SMITH, NAOMI GWLADYS, British novelist and playwright, was born in Llanwrst, Wales, the eldest daughter of Michael Holroyd Smith and Ann Daisy (Williams) Smith. The family moved to London in her childhood, and she was educated at the Clapham High School and then at a private school in Geneva, Switzerland. From 1912 to 1922 she was literary editor of the *Westminster Gazette.* She was interested in the stage from the beginning of her career as a writer, and this interest culminated in her marriage in 1926 to Ernest Milton, a well known English actor. She has been a prolific writer, often turning out several volumes a year. Besides her published works, several of her plays have been produced in London. For a long time she lived in Hatfield, Hertfordshire, then in Chelsea, London, but now makes her home in Winchester. When she is at work on a book she often goes alone to the country to bury herself in her work

without interruption. In 1929, when her husband was playing in the United States, she accompanied him and spent three months in this country, the result being a book, *Pictures and People*, written with Roger Hinks of the British Museum, to whom the letters which made up the book were written.

Very reticent about her private life, Miss Royde-Smith says that her childhood may be found described in her novel, *In the Wood*. She has little time for recreation, but likes taking long walks in the country and is an expert knitter. She is a pretty woman, blonde, with high cheekbones, a sensitive mouth, and serious blue eyes.

Many of her early books seemed tentative, as if she were trying to find her real *métier*. As George Dangerfield remarked, "delicacy and sentiment are at the heart of all her books," though often they have been on highly controversial subjects. He spoke too of her "quiet wit and great understanding," while Esther Forbes said that she "writes extremely well, with humor, charm, and delicate perception." There is no doubt that if she would write less she could keep all her work up to the level of her best.

There was only one period of her life when she had much of a social career; that was immediately after the First World War, when she and Rose Macaulay conducted a joint salon, "always crowded with writers and artists." It was from her memories of this experience that she drew the subject of her first biography, one of Julie de Lespinasse, the *protégée* and rival of Mme. du Deffand and the beloved of d'Alembert. Her only other biography, of Mrs. Siddons, grew naturally from her interest in the theatre and from the play she had already written on the great actress' life. Her

plays in general, though competent, have been uneven, and it is for her novels—especially for the first, *The Tortoiseshell Cat,* and for *The Delicate Situation*—that she is valued most.

PRINCIPAL WORKS: *Novels*—The Tortoiseshell Cat, 1925; The Housemaid, 1926; Skin-Deep, 1927; John Fanning's Legacy, 1927; In the Wood (in America: Children in the Wood) 1928; The Lover, 1928; Summer Holiday, 1929; The Island, 1930; The Delicate Situation, 1931; The Mother, 1931; The Bridge, 1932; Madame Julia's Tale (short stories) 1932; Incredible Tale, 1932; David, 1933; Jake, 1935; All Star Cast, 1936; For Us in the Dark, 1937; Miss Bendix, 1938; The Younger Venus, 1938; The Altar-Piece, 1939; Jane Fairfax, 1940; The Unfaithful Wife, 1942. *Plays*—A Balcony, 1926; Mafro, Darling, 1929; Mrs Siddons, 1931; Pilgrim From Paddington, 1933; The Queen's Wigs, 1934; Private Room, 1934. *Miscellaneous*—Pictures and People (with R. Hinks) 1931; The Double Heart: A Study of Julie de Lespinasse, 1931; The Private Life of Mrs. Siddons, 1933; Outside Information, 1941.

ABOUT: Bookman (London) December 1928; Saturday Review March 2, 1929; Spectator September 4, 1926.

RUCK, BERTA (1878-   ), English novelist writes: "Berta Ruck began, like so many other writers, by drawing; was an art student in London, where she won a scholarship to the Slade School of Art, going on to Colarossi's in Paris, where she shared the usual interests, outings, and activities of life on the Left Bank. Her ambition, if anything beyond enjoying life,

was to become an illustrator. It was while she was in Paris that she first got the idea of writing stories. A story was sent to her from a London magazine with a commission to illustrate it with pen-and-ink drawings. These she did; then, thinking, 'Couldn't I do as well myself?' she wrote a 2000-word sketch of *Quartier Latin* life, illustrated it with four drawings, sent it to the same magazine, had it accepted and received four guineas. She imagined her fortune made! This, however, proved to be beginner's luck. It was a year before she sold another thing.

"There followed years of odd-jobbing at short stories, black-and-white drawings for advertisements, magazine articles—quite sensible, some of them, about cold baths for girls, fresh air, exercise, and fewer underclothes—these things were then not yet a universal matter of course.

"Her first novel, *His Official Fiancée*, appeared in 1914, was at once popular, and was made into a (silent) film by Famous Players. Since then she has written two novels every year, besides numerous short stories, articles, and memoirs. She considers her best book to be her autobiography (not published in America), and, after this, *Today's Daughter, Mock-Honeymoon, It Was Left to Peter,* and *Money Isn't Everything.*

"She is married to the English novelist Oliver Onions (George Oliver),^{qv} and has two sons. One, now in the Royal Air Force, held for a short time the record (since gloriously broken by several young boys) of being Britain's youngest pilot. She is also proud of Welsh blood: a Welsh grandmother claimed descent from the last of the rebel Welsh princes, Owen Glyndwr [Glendower]. Her novels contain many scenes set in her mountainous, bilingual home-country of Wales.

"She has cosmopolitan tastes, and has lived much on the Continent, especially in pre-Hitler Austria. She has also visited at a girls' holiday camp in America, where she made many friends. Her favorite occupations are air-travel (she is never so happy as when 'up'), country walks, gardening, and swimming; she is an all-the-year-round bather, breaking the ice in winter."

* * *

Berta Ruck was born in Wales, the daughter of an army officer, and had her first education at St. Winifred's School, Bangor. Her novels are all light romances, with no pretensions to artistry; they are exclamatory and ephemeral, but full of verve.

PRINCIPAL WORKS: His Official Fiancée, 1914; Wooing of Rosamond Fayre, 1915; The Girls at His Billet, 1916; In Another Girl's Shoes, 1916; Three of Hearts, 1917; Sweethearts Unmet, 1919; Disturbing Charm, 1919; Bridge of Kisses, 1920; Sweet Stranger, 1921; Arrant Rover, 1921; Subconscious Courtship, 1922; The Wrong Mr. Right, 1922; Sir or Madam? 1923; Dancing Star, 1923; Clouded Pearl, 1924; Leap Year Girl, 1924; Lucky in Love, 1924; The Immortal Girl, 1925; Kneel to the Prettiest, 1925; Pearl Thief, 1926; Her Pirate Partner, 1927; The Maid of a Minx, 1927; Money for One, 1928; The Youngest Venus, 1928; One of the Chorus (in America: Joy-Ride) 1929; The Unkissed Bride, 1929; Offer of Marriage, 1930; Today's Daughter, 1930; Missing Girl (in America: Love-Hater) 1930; Post-War Girl, 1930; Wanted on the Voyage (short stories) 1930; Dance Partner (in America: Forced Landing) 1931; The Lap of Luxury, 1931; It Was Left to Peter, 1932; This Year, Next Year, Sometime—, 1932; Change for Happiness, 1933; Sudden Sweetheart, 1933; Eleventh Hour Lover, 1933; Lad With Wings, 1933; Understudy, 1933; Best Time Ever, 1934; Sunburst, 1934; A Story-Teller Tells the Truth (autobiography) 1935; Star in Love, 1935; Sunshine Stealers, 1935; Half-Past Kissing Time

(in America: Sleeping Beauty) 1936; Spring Comes to Miss Lonelyheart (in America: Spring Comes) 1936; Love on Second Thoughts, 1937; Mock-Honeymoon, 1937; Love Comes Again Later, 1938; Wedding March, 1938; Money Isn't Everything, 1939; Romance Royal, 1939; Jade Earings, 1941; Spinster's Progress, 1942; Footlight Fever, 1942.

ABOUT: Ruck, B. A Story-Teller Tells the Truth.

RUIZ. See MARTÍNEZ RUIZ

RUKEYSER, MURIEL (December, 1913-), American poet, writes: "I was born in New York City. There were the green park along the river, the railroad tracks, and the streets of childhood, summers on the beach, the high apartment buildings like old stone trunks in the warehouse of uptown New York. I was educated at the Ethical Culture and Fieldston Schools, and then at Vassar. Those were

Chidnoff

good years, a burst of freedom after the years in 'comfort.' Then the Crash came during my senior year in high school. College was quiet on top, a flowery circle of garden quiet. There was room for all the ferment of new excitements; a limited present, but all the provocations of the past and future. When I left after two years, I returned to New York hoping to write poems, have a job, see some of those promises. I wanted to write them. The Scottsboro case had just broken, I was an editor of the *Student Review,* I was working in offices, I was in Alabama at the trial. There was the other side of the scene: slow cruising cars, deputies, arrest, the brutality to the men and all the Negroes, the politeness to me, the accusations, the chase out of town, the typhoid afterward. I was at Columbia Summer School, I was at Roosevelt Aviation School, I was working in offices, I was writing *Theory of Flight.*

"After that there were theatre jobs, theatre magazines. I was able to go to Gauley Bridge, W. Va., early in 1936, and to England, from where I was sent to Spain, to arrive on the first day of the Spanish War. The train stopped in the Pyrenees, in a village at war. The papers on the floor said everything was quiet. Much headed up for me in that train: we were people from eleven countries, tourists for the most part, at all stages of awareness, lying neutral in a town at war, days without communications or knowledge of the outside.

"Then, among other jobs, with statistics, with films, with photographs, I was writing *U.S. 1* in California and New York. More jobs with photographs, and work on the 'Lives,' for *A Turning Wind*, which was finished in Mexico on the day this war began. The Gauley Bridge poems in *U.S. 1* have produced a film script; the Gibbs poem in *A Turning Wind* has produced the work I am now doing on Willard Gibbs and the creative imagination in America.

"The uproot of the 1914 war produced Imagism, answering chaos with the life of colors and flowers and islands and matchless heads, in their bare existence. We have another wave of such years now, witnesses to whose chaos are facts such as Spain and Gauley Bridge and Scottsboro and the creativeness of certain lives and the gifts of certain poems and gestures. I live in New York and do my work there; all this cluster is proved in any single place. I wish to make my poems exist in the quick images that arrive crowding on us now (most familiarly from the screen), in the lives of Americans who are unpraised and vivid and indicative, in my own 'documents.' That last is an ill-favored word; for me it means a binding down to a neighborhood of meaning which I cannot ignore. What I can ignore, on the other hand, is the whole critical circus whose acrobatics are to the effect that poetry is dead. I do not think so."

* * *

Stephen Vincent Benét has called Muriel Rukeyser "essentially an urban poet"; Philip Blair Rice said she "has assimilated many of the best things in the modernist tradition . . . without seeking technical innovation as an end in itself." She lives in Greenwich Village, in New York, and is unmarried.

PRINCIPAL WORKS: Theory of Flight, 1935; U.S. 1, 1938; Mediterranean, 1938; A Turning Wind 1938; Wake Island, 1942; Willard Gibbs: American Genius (biography) 1942.

ABOUT: Untermeyer, L. Modern American Poetry; Nation February 29, 1936; Poetry May 1936, May 1938, February 1940; Saturday Review of Literature August 10, 1940; Time December 16, 1935.

*RUNYON, DAMON (October 4, 1880†-), American journalist and short story writer, was born Alfred Damon Runyon in Manhattan, Kan., the son of Alfred Lee Runyon and Elizabeth (Damon) Runyon. He was reared in Pueblo, Colo., and educated in the public schools there. His father was a printer on the Pueblo *Chieftain*, and put the boy's first pieces in that

paper when he was only thirteen. The next year, at fourteen, Damon persuaded a recruiting officer he was eighteen and enlisted in the Spanish-American War, going to the Philippines. After he returned he became a newspaper reporter, serving successively, from 1900 to 1910, on the Pueblo *Chieftain*, the Colorado Springs *Gazette*, the Denver *News, Times, Republic*, and *Post*, and the San Francisco *Post*. In 1911 he became a sports writer for the New York *American*, soon adding general reporting to his assignments; Arthur Brisbane once called him "America's greatest reporter." He was a war correspondent for the Hearst papers in Mexico in 1912 and 1916, and in Europe in 1917 and 1918. He then became a columnist and feature writer for King Features and International News Service  (both Hearst affiliates), and still serves in that capacity.

After Brisbane died, he was tried out for a while as his successor as columnist, but he was restive as a commentator on world affairs, since he considers himself primarily a sports writer. For a number of years now, although he still sends his copy in regularly to New York, he has lived on Hibiscus Island, off Miami Beach, in Florida.

In 1911 he married Ellen Egan, and they had a son and a daughter. After her death he married, in 1932, Patrice del Grande, a native of Spain and a dancer, who was one of the original Texas Guinan Girls. In 1939 he received the Feature Writing Prize of the National Headliners' Club of New York.

A slim, nervous man who drinks forty cups of coffee a day, Mr. Runyon is a prolific writer but finds time also for hunting and poker. He is an easy-going and generous man, who cannot resist an appeal to his sympathy. It is said that he has bought some 2500 bird dogs at various times, paying for them but never collecting them! He is fond of good food and drink, is a bit of a dandy in his dress, and is always on the go. When he has writing to do, he is apt to put it off until near the deadline, and then work all day and all night till he gets it done. His taciturnity is proverbial among his friends.

Damon Runyon may be considered the prose laureate of the semi-literate American. His stories, nearly always written in the present tense throughout, are a mine of slang, colloquialisms, "wise cracks," and "Americanese." After twenty years of profitable syndication, Runyon tapped a fresh source of income in Hollywood, his biggest film-story successes being *Lady for a Day,* starring May Robson, and *Little Miss Marker,* which launched Shirley Temple on her phenomenal career. Explaining Runyon's plot-formula, J. C. Furnas wrote: "Almost invariably the fundamental principle is the reasonably well worn device of making a hard-boiled enemy of society behave like St. Francis of Assisi, demonstrating for all and sundry that the softest hearts beat beneath the latest fashions in bullet-proof vests."

Recently Runyon has become immensely popular in England, where his books are issued with glossaries so that readers can understand their idiom. The prefaces by E. C. Bentley are replete with Mr. Bentley's conception of American slang, which is no less amusing to American readers (though for a different reason) than the author's own vivid Broadwayese. Runyon writes frequently for the popular "slick paper" magazines, and has built up a huge following of readers who are captivated by his humor, his realistic view of human nature, and his inexhaustible spirit. His style is fluently journalistic, and if he attains no other immortality, his books will some day be an invaluable source for the study of current American speech.

PRINCIPAL WORKS: Tents of Trouble (verse) 1911; Rhymes of the Firing Line (verse) 1912; Guys and Dolls, 1932; Blue Plate Special, 1934; Money From Home, 1935; A Slight Case of Murder (play, with H. Lindsay) 1935; My Wife Ethel, 1939; Take It Easy, 1939; My Old Man (essays) 1939; The Best of Runyon, 1940.

ABOUT: Runyon, D. The Best of Runyon (see Introduction by E. C. Bentley); Newsweek January 16, 1937; Saturday Review of Literature December 4, 1937; Spectator October 8, 15, 1937; Time September 30, 1940.

RUSKIN, JOHN. See "BRITISH AUTHORS OF THE 19TH CENTURY"

RUSSELL, BERTRAND ARTHUR WILLIAM, 3rd Earl Russell, Viscount Amberley (May 18, 1872-   ), English philosopher, mathematician, and sociologist, was born at Trelleck, Wales. The Russell family is one of the oldest in England. His father, Viscount Amberley, predeceased his own father, the famous Lord Russell, the first Earl (created by Queen Victoria, in whose government he was twice prime minister). His mother was Katherine, daughter of Baron Stanley of Alderley; she too died early. He was an orphan at three, and was reared by Lord John Russell's widow. He succeeded to the title in 1931, on the death of his older brother, the second Earl; but he much prefers to be known still simply as Bertrand Russell.

Bertrand Russell's parents were unusual persons, very "advanced" for their period, radical and democratic. In 1868, when they were first married, they visited America, not as tourists, but as students of American institutions. But with their death their younger son was brought up in the traditional manner of his class—though he was never sent to school, but was educated at home until he entered Trinity College, Cambridge. He was a fellow of Trinity in 1895, and it was there that his genius for both mathematics and philosophy, and especially for the former, first became evident. His family, however, had destined him for a political career. He was offered a private secretaryship — first step up the political ladder — by John Morley, but he declined it on the ground that he wished to continue his mathematical and philosophical studies. However, a third interest was already claiming him— that of sociology. His  first book was on German Social Democracy, followed by four on mathematics.

Though his contributions to mathematical theory are too technical for popular elucidation, they are very great. The *Principia Mathematica,* written in collaboration with A. N. Whitehead, is a mathematical classic. When it was published, Bertrand Russell was lecturer on mathematics at Trinity. As he says: "From the age of eleven, when I began the study of Euclid, I had a passionate interest in mathematics, combined with a belief that science must be the source of all human progress." He seemed destined for a purely academic and scholarly life, when the First World War precipitated him into the political and social arena.

A convinced pacifist, he opposed the war from the start, though he himself was by then over military age. (In contrast, he ardently supported the democracies in the Second World War.) He was dismissed by Trinity College in 1916, and soon after was sentenced to four months in prison, which he occupied in writing his *Introduction to Mathematical Philosophy.* He was now definitely oriented toward sociological, ethical, and educational problems. As he has said: "Throughout the years of the war I was endeavoring to write so as to be read by the general public. When the war was over, I found it impossible to return to a purely academic life."

Instead, he visited Soviet Russia, alienated most of his radical sympathizers by disliking it intensely and saying so frankly, and then settled down for a year as professor of philosophy at the University of Peking. During this year, 1920, he almost died of pneumonia, and some enterprising Japanese newspapers announced his death. But he survived to read his own obituaries and to return to England, where in 1922 and 1923 he ran unsuccessfully for Parliament on the Labor ticket. With his second wife he ran a school for young children in Sussex from 1927 to 1932. It was a world-famous school, run on extremely progressive lines. But it absorbed his time and energy too greatly, so he gave it up.

In 1938 Russell came to the University of Chicago as visiting professor of philosophy, and the next year held the same position at the University of California at Los Angeles. While he was still there, early in 1940, he was appointed William James Lecturer in Philosophy at Harvard and professor of philosophy at the College of the City of New York. Immediately a wild uproar of protest arose, based on the fact that among Bertrand Russell's many published opinions have been many on sex, and that his views on this subject have been exceedingly radical. Any objections from Harvard soon died down, but a suit by a taxpayer caused the New York Board of Higher Education to rescind the C.C.N.Y. appointment. Appeal was denied, and he was also denied the right to intervene in the suit. At the same time an abortive attempt was made to oust him from the University of California, but was rejected by the Appellate Court. The whole C.C.N.Y. matter was dropped in October, 1940, when he was offered and accepted a post as lecturer on the history of culture at the Barnes Foundation, Merion, Pa. He went there in January 1941, has bought a farm in Chester County, Pa., and considers himself in "an ideal situation." His son by his first marriage and his son and daughter by his second are with him in America.

It cannot be denied that Bertrand Russell's matrimonial career has been a stormy one. In 1894 he married Alys Pearsall Smith, sister of Logan Pearsall Smith, who divorced him in 1921. The same year he married Dora Winifred Black, who divorced him in 1935. His third wife, Patricia Helen Spence, had been his secretary.

A thin, wiry, short man, with (to quote Burton Rascoe) "a hatchet face, furrowed cheeks, a Scot's complexion, and a heavy shock of white hair," his most notable feature is his large, piercing eyes—the eyes of a philosopher. Dr. Henry Noble MacCracken thought Russell "must be one of the best talkers living." There is nothing either of the traditional glacial English lord or of the absent-minded professor about Bertrand Russell, who likes to add "malicious footnotes" to his manuscripts and describes himself as "a happy pessimist." MacCracken called him "a mixture of radicalism and good taste, [and] imperturbable good temper. . . . As lover of freedom and justice, as a master of the King's English, as a man with a passion for the truth as he sees it, and as a likable individual, there lives not his match." Charles P. Sanger said: "His admirable and lucid English style may be attributed to the fact that he did not undergo a classical education; his religious views and his moral character may be due to the wise exercise of the paternal jurisdictions of the court of chancery; but his wit, his love of truth, and his capacity for hard work seem to be innate."

Logic, which he prefers to call "Logical Atomism," is the basis of Russell's philosophy. He is a consistent monist and a philosophical materialist, with some leaning toward behaviorism and pragmatism. Edmund Wilson called him "really a type of the eighteenth century philosopher, ironic, elegant, dry, humanitarian, and anti-mystic." His philosophical views he carries over into the realm of sociology, and it is difficult to define him sociologically except as an advanced individualist. He himself says: "There is no one key: politics, economics, psychology, education, all act and react. . . . It is necessary to embrace all life and all science. . . . All that I can do is to make some men conscious of the problem and of the kind of directions in which solutions are to be sought."

PRINCIPAL WORKS: *Mathematics and Philosophy*—Essay on the Foundations of Geometry, 1897; The Philosophy of Leibniz, 1900; Principles of Mathematics, 1903; Philosophical Essays, 1910; Principia Mathematica (with A. N. Whitehead) 1910-13; The Scientific Method in Philosophy (in America: Our Knowledge of the External World) 1914; Mysticism and Logic and Other Essays, 1918; Introduction to Mathematical Philosophy, 1919; Analysis of Mind, 1921; The ABC of Atoms, 1923; Icarus: or, The Future of Science, 1924; The ABC of Relativity, 1925; What

I Believe, 1925; Analysis of Matter, 1927; An Outline of Philosophy (in America: Philosophy) 1927; Skeptical Essays, 1928; The Conquest of Happiness, 1930; The Scientific Outlook, 1931; Religion and Science, 1935; A Critical Exposition of the Philosophy of Leibniz, 1937; An Inquiry Into Meaning and Truth, 1940. *Sociology and Education*—German Social Democracy, 1896; Political Ideals, 1917; Principles of Social Reconstruction (in America: Why Men Fight) 1917; Roads to Freedom (in America: Proposed Roads to Freedom) 1918; The Practice and Theory of Bolshevism, 1920; The Problem of China, 1922; The Prospects of Industrial Civilization (with D. Russell) 1923; On Education, Especially in Childhood (in America: Education and the Good Life) 1926; Marriage and Morals, 1929; Education and the Social Order (in America: Education and the Modern World) 1932; Freedom Versus Organization, 1814-1914, 1934; Which Way to Peace? (with P. Russell) 1938; Dare We Look Ahead? (with others) 1938; Power: A New Social Analysis, 1938. *Miscellaneous*—In Praise of Idleness and Other Essays, 1935; The Amberley Papers (ed.) 1938.

ABOUT: Belgion, M. Our Present Philosophy of Life; Black, M. The Nature of Mathematics; Dewey, J. and Kallen, H. M. The Bertrand Russell Case; Mannin, E. Confessions and Impressions; Russell, B. (ed.) The Amberley Papers; Bulletin of Bibliography May 1930; Dial December 1927; Dublin Review April 1927; Journal of Philosophy November 10, 1932; Law Review May 1940; Mind April, July 1928; July 1936, July 1939; Monist October 1929, October 1930; Nation June 15, 1940; Nature December 8, 1934; New Republic December 20, 1925; New Statesman & Nation November 14, 1936, April 6, 1940; Revue des Sciences Politiques April 1926; Saturday Review of Literature September 11, 1926, March 30, April 13, 1940; School and Society October 1940.

RUSSELL, CHARLES EDWARD (September 25, 1860-April 23, 1941), American sociologist and biographer, winner of the

Pulitzer Prize, was born in Davenport, Iowa, and educated at St. Johnsbury (Vt.) Academy. He had an honorary LL.D. from Howard University, 1923. He had a long career as a newspaper man, being city editor of the New York *World* from 1894 to 1897, managing editor of the New York *American* from 1897 to 1899, and publisher of the Chicago *American* from 1900 to 1902. He was better known before the First World War as a Socialist speaker and writer, having been candidate for governor of and senator from New York State and mayor of New York City. In 1916 he was nominated as the presidential candidate, but declined. The next year, because of his advocacy of the country's entrance into the war, he was

expelled from the party. He was a member of the special diplomatic mission sent to Russia by the United States Committee on Public Information in 1917, and its commissioner to Great Britain in 1918, and of the President's Industrial Commission in 1919. He was president of the United States Civil Legion in 1922, and honorary president of the American Association for Recognition of the Irish Republic. In 1928 he received the Pulitzer Prize in biography for his history of American orchestras. His wife was Abby Osborn (Rust) Russell, and they had one son, John,[qv] also a writer. His autobiography was his last published volume; he was ill for a long time, and finally died in New York at eighty.

PRINCIPAL WORKS: Such Stuff as Dreams, 1902; The Twin Immortalities, 1904; The Greatest Trust in the World, 1905; The Uprising of the Many, 1907; Lawless Wealth, 1908; Thomas Chatterton: The Marvelous Boy, 1908; Songs of Democracy, 1909; Why I Am a Socialist, 1910; Business: The Heart of the Nation, 1911; Stories of the Great Railroads, 1912; These Shifting Scenes, 1914; The Story of Wendell Phillips, 1915; Unchained Russia, 1918; After the Whirlwind, 1919; Bolshevism and the United States, 1919; The Outlook for the Philippines, 1922; Railroad Melons, Rates, and Wages, 1922; The Hero of the Filipinos: José Rizal, 1923; Julia Marlowe: Her Life and Art, 1926; The American Orchestra and Theodore Thomas, 1927; A-Rafting on the Mississipp', 1928; An Hour of American Poetry, 1929; From Sandy Hook to 62°, 1929; Haym Salomon and the Revolution, 1930; Blaine of Maine, 1931; Bare Hands and Stone Walls, 1933.

ABOUT: Russell, C. E. Bare Hands and Stone Walls.

RUSSELL, GEORGE WILLIAM ("AE") (April 10, 1867-July 17, 1935), Irish poet and essayist, was born at Lurgan, County Armagh, in northern Ireland, of a Protestant family, his father being Thomas Elias Russell and his mother Mary Anne (Armstrong) Russell. When he was ten the family moved to Dublin, where he was educated at the Rathmines School.

E. Harrison

From 1880 to 1900 also, for a few months every year, he attended the Dublin School of Art; his talent for painting preceded evidence of his talent for writing. At the art school he met William Butler Yeats, with whom he formed a lifelong friendship, occasionally interrupted by Yeats' objection to his other rather incongruous friendship with George Moore. At seventeen he left the Rathmines School and became a clerk successively in a brewery, a warehouse, and a draper's shop. For the last-named he worked for ten years or more, and was remembered as "rather wild-looking, but very business-like."

The most important event of Russell's life occurred in 1887, when he discovered Theosophy. He had been a mystic from childhood, frequently lost in meditation and experiencing "visions" and "direct communication." Now he became and remained an ardent Theosophist, though he left the Society in 1898, because Katherine Tingley, then its leader, objected to his connection with Sir Horace Plunkett's Irish Agricultural Organization Society. For the remainder of his life Russell was active in the cooperative agricultural work of this association, as also in the Home Rule movement and in the Irish literary Renaissance (he was one of the founders of the famous Abbey Theatre); but implicit in all his poetry, and closest to his personal life, were the doctrine and creed of Theosophy.

In 1898 also, he married Violet North, who died in 1932. They had two sons, one of whom is now an American citizen. To his friends, Russell seemed to take his marriage rather casually—perhaps because the group of Theosophical young men to which he belonged had all tacitly assumed that theirs were to be celibate lives devoted to the cause. He was never domestic, and his various interests kept him constantly away from home, but his wife, also a devout Theosophist, was the perfect helpmeet for a man of his nature, and he was a lost and broken man after her death.

Russell made several trips to the United States, spending a whole year in 1930 and 1931 in a lecture tour, mostly in the interests of agricultural cooperatives, which took him from coast to coast. At the end of 1934 he began another tour, but illness overtook him, and he returned in March 1935 to England, his home since his wife's death. Four months later he died at Bournemouth, after a futile operation for what was at first diagnosed as colitis but proved to be cancer.

Nearly six feet tall, thin in youth but corpulent in old age, with thick "mouse-colored" hair (which he cut himself) and russet beard, blue-gray eyes behind spectacles, loose, shabby clothes, and a perpetual pipe, Russell in appearance was what he was in fact—a blend between the farmer and the mystical poet. He was in both senses of the word a great talker—an inspired speaker and exceedingly loquacious. His voice was mellow, and he spoke with a strong north

of Ireland accent. He continued to paint pictures all his life, but never exhibited or sold them, giving them to his friends. His father had been musical, but he himself could not tell one tune from another. William M. Clyde noted his "intense love of art," coupled with the "belief that man is more important than art, . . . his increasing gentle, courageous concern for the welfare of mankind."

The pen-name "AE," by which Russell was universally known to his friends, arose when a proof-reader could not read the pseudonym "AEon" which the author had signed to an article. He never wrote under his own name, and it was "AE" who was editor of the *Irish Homestead*, from 1905, and from 1910 of its successor, the *Irish Statesman*.

His poetry, though frequently over-facile and stereotyped, has moments of great beauty. "It reveals," said Clyde, "a glimpse of a Many-Colored Land . . . of more than human loveliness, lying just beyond the reach of the senses." And Seumas O'Sullivan called him "a poet whose song had its fountain in the heaven world, an artist who gave us in his painting those things in nature which are revealed only to the pure in heart, an Irishman whose patriotism was made great and deep and noble by his contact with the deepest and most noble thought of all countries." Add to this characterization a keen sense of humor and an eminently practical approach to agricultural problems, and one has a complete portrait of one of the most interesting figures of the literary renaissance in Ireland.

PRINCIPAL WORKS: *Poetry*—Homeward: Songs by the Way, 1894; The Earth Breath and Other Poems, 1897; The Divine Vision and Other Poems, 1903; The Nuts of Knowledge, 1903; By Still Waters, 1906; Collected Poems, 1913; Gods of War and Other Poems, 1915; Voices of the Stones, 1925; Midsummer Eve, 1928; Dark Weeping, 1929; Enchantment and Other Poems, 1930; Vale and Other Poems, 1931; The House of the Titans and Other Poems, 1934; Selected Poems, 1935. *Prose*—The Mask of Apollo and Other Stories, 1904; Some Irish Essays, 1906; Deirdre (play) 1907; The Hero in Man, 1909; The Renewal of Youth, 1911; Co-operation and Nationality, 1912; Imaginations and Reveries, 1915; The National Being, 1916; Thoughts on Irish Polity, 1917; The Candle of Vision, 1918; The Interpreters, 1920; Song and Its Foundations, 1932; The Avatars: A Futurist Fantasy, 1933; Some Passages From the Letters of AE to W. B. Yeats, 1936; The Living Torch, 1937; AE's Letters to Mínánlabáin, 1937.

ABOUT: Boyd, E. Ireland's Literary Renaissance; Clyde, W. M. AE; Eglinton, J. Irish Literary Portraits; Figgis, D. AE (George William Russell); Magee, W. K. A Memoir of AE, George William Russell; Moore, G. Hail and

Farewell; Russell, G. W. Some Passages From the Letters of AE to W. B. Yeats, AE's Letters to Minánlabáin; Catholic World October 1935; Commonweal November 4, 1931; Christian Century July 31, 1935, April 20, 1938; Nation July 31, 1935; New Republic May 13, 1936, March 30, 1938; Poetry September 1935, August 1936; Saturday Review of Literature July 27, 1935; Virginia Quarterly Review January 1939; Yale Review September 1939.

RUSSELL, JOHN (April 22, 1885-), American novelist and short-story writer, was born in Davenport, Iowa, the son of Charles Edward Russell,*qv* publicist, and Abby Osborn (Rust) Russell. He studied at Northwestern University, Evanston, Ill., from 1903 to 1905, leaving in June of that year to marry Grace Nye Bolster of Chicago. In 1908 Russell was special correspondent of the New York *Herald* in Panama and Peru. Later he was staff writer of fiction, features, verse, and interviews for the magazine section of the New York *Sun*.

In 1912, at twenty-seven, Russell was contributing short stories and articles on South Sea, Oriental, adventure, and seafaring themes to magazines. During the First World War he was in charge of U. S. government propaganda for Great Britain and Ireland, and had the unusual experience of sitting in the gallery of the House of Commons—whence he was nearly expelled for vociferous laughter—and hearing an "interpellation" or inquiry concerning the exclusion of his own father from Great Britain. (Sir William Joynson Hicks, the Home Secretary, had excluded Charles Edward Russell from England as a possible agitator, at the request of the Irish Free State.) John Russell's collection of South Sea stories, *The Red Mark* (1919), attracted little attention in the United States, but after its success in England was reissued as *Where the Pavement Ends* (1921). Henry Seidel Canby called the stories "a remarkable case of literary revivalism. It is almost pure Kipling, Kipling in its style, down to the turn of a phrase. . . . One feels sure of a far greater power here than a mere imitator has to possess." The *Spectator* remarked on the writer's "considerable skill in depicting the sensuous charm of the tropics, especially by night."

Russell has published more than six hundred short stories, many of them included in textbooks and anthologies as successful examples of short story form. Like Stevenson, he was adopted as a chief among the Samoans in 1920, with the title of "Tole foa Tusitala." The second Mrs. Russell was Lila Hilson of Sydney, Australia; they were married in November 1932 and live at Santa Monica, Calif. Russell's books have been published in Copenhagen, Hanover, Leipzig, Paris, and Madrid. Russell is a member of the Players Club in New York and the Savile in London, and is a Mason. His explorations in South America, Asia, and Oceanica have made him in demand as a consulting specialist and adapter in Hollywood.

PRINCIPAL WORKS: The Society Wolf, 1910; The Red Mark, 1919; Where the Pavement Ends, 1921; In Dark Places, 1922; Far Wandering Men, 1928; Cops 'n Robbers, 1930; Color of the East, 1930.

ABOUT: Russell, C. E. Bare Hands and Stone Walls.

RUSSELL, MARY ANNETTE (BEAUCHAMP) RUSSELL, Countess (1866-February 9, 1941), English novelist who wrote under the pseudonym "Elizabeth," was born in Sydney, Australia, the daughter of H. Herron Beauchamp, "a just but irritable man, with far too few skins really for comfort," according to his daughter, who described her mother as

E. Schaal

"sweet-natured and sunnily pleased with everything." The minute Mr. Beauchamp was gone from the family circle, "relaxation set in." Katherine Mansfield, the writer, whose family name was Beauchamp, was a cousin of "Elizabeth." The girl was handed over to a Mademoiselle for bringing up. She had—and was photographed with—her first dog at five, he was banished by her father, and "nine solid years of unadulterated cats" succeeded. Bildad, Elizabeth's second dog, given her when she was fourteen, was "prophetically Pomeranian."

Elizabeth met her first husband, Count Henning August von Arnim, "while I was being shown Italy by my father, and he, being a person who knew what he wanted, had, it appeared, marked me down as a suitable Pomeranian the very first moment he saw me." The Count "voluminously embraced" her on the steps of the Duomo in Florence, and in due course they were married and retired to his 60,000 acre estate in East Prussia, where "there was everything in profusion except money." Five children were born, four of whom survived their mother when she died in America of influenza at seventy-four.

"It [became] my habit, during such moments as remained after I had housekept, and been a good wife, and been a good mother, and done my duty by the Frau Director and the Frau Inspector and the Frau Vieharzt, to shut myself up and write stories." *Elizabeth and Her German Garden* (1898), the first and most famous, was a witty transcript of her own experiences on the estate, with flowers, servants, babies, guests and "The Man of Wrath," her husband. *The Solitary Summer* (1899) and *The Adventures of Elizabeth in Ruegen* (1904) were successors in similar vein; Elizabeth's first novel was *The Benefactress* (1902), about a charitably inclined young Englishwoman who took various types of distressed German gentlewomen into her house, with varying results. These books were signed "By the Author of Elizabeth and Her German Garden," and later simply "By Elizabeth."

Count von Arnim, a grandson of Prince Augustus of Prussia, nephew of Frederick the Great, died in 1910. "My props were knocked from beneath me, and instead of props I had responsibilities. Are not five children, the youngest only six, serious responsibilities?" Finding life in Devonshire too wet and cheerless, Elizabeth "bought sites in Switzerland recklessly." In "the hard and brilliant solitude of the Swiss mountains" she worked quietly "at those stories which by now had become our chief support." At the Château Soleil, Elizabeth kept a home for her children until they were married, and entertained Sir Harry Johnston, Frank Swinnerton, and other writers.

In 1916 she married John Francis Stanley Russell, second Earl Russell; they were separated three years later; she returned to Switzerland and wrote the anonymous *In the Mountains*. (Earl Russell died in 1931, and his brother Bertrand[qv] succeeded to the title.) Elizabeth referred to this period as "years of deep sorrow, of acute misery"; they are reflected to some extent in her novel *Vera* (1921), one of her most brilliant and acidulous performances. "Perhaps husbands have never altogether agreed with me. It did in fact need the Great War, and a second husband, to make me really grow up." *The Pastor's Wife* (1914), one of her richest and most carefully developed novels, is the record of the daughter of an overbearing clergyman who married a German pastor much more interested in scientific agriculture than in his wife or his parish. *The Enchanted April* (1923), a sunny comedy based on her own experiences on the

French Riviera, was a best-seller in America and was dramatized with some success. *The Jasmine Farm* and *Mr. Skeffington* were choices of the American Book-of-the-Month Club. Elizabeth also occupied cottages in the New Forest in England besides her Riviera villa, Mas de Roses, Mougins, France, where she wrote the autobiographical *All the Dogs of My Life* (1936).

The outbreak of the Second World War brought her to America, where she lived in New England and spent the last two winters of her life near Charleston, S. C. She died at the Riverside Infirmary, Charleston. Countess Russell was regarded as one of the first wits of her time, and one of the most expert in writing social comedy, in distinctive, close-packed, long-drawn-out sentences. She was small in stature, with a very white face and a wimple of ash-gold hair. Her German son, Henning Berndt von Arnim, and three daughters survived her.

PRINCIPAL WORKS: Elizabeth and Her German Garden, 1898; The Solitary Summer, 1899; The April Baby's Book of Tunes, 1900; The Benefactress, 1902; The Adventures of Elizabeth in Ruegen, 1904; The Princess Priscilla's Fortnight, 1906; Fraulein Schmidt and Mr. Anstruther, 1907; The Caravaners, 1909; The Pastor's Wife, 1914; Christopher and Columbus, 1919; In the Mountains, 1920; Vera, 1921; The Enchanted April, 1923; Love, 1925; Introduction to Sally, 1926; Expiation, 1929; Father, 1931; The Jasmine Farm, 1934; All the Dogs of My Life (autobiography) 1936; Mr. Skeffington, 1940.

ABOUT: Cooper, A. P. Authors and Others; Nichols, B. Twenty-Five; Oppenheim, E. P. The Pool of Memory; Russell, M. A. B. All the Dogs of My Life; Swinnerton, F. Swinnerton: An Autobiography; Book-of-the-Month Club News April 1940; Life April 1940; New York Times February 10, 1941; Saturday Review of Literature April 19, 1941; Wilson Library Bulletin February 1932.

"RUTHERFORD, MARK." See "BRITISH AUTHORS OF THE 19TH CENTURY"

RYALL, WILLIAM BOLITHO. See BOLITHO, W.

*SABATINI, RAFAEL (1875-), English romantic novelist and short-story writer, was born at Jesi, Central Italy, the son of Maestro-Cavaliere Vincenzo Sabatini and Anna (Trafford) Sabatini. His birthplace was a diminutive city in the Italian marches, and with its medieval walls, ancient cathedrals and crumbling palaces was well calculated to fire the imagination of a romantic youth. Young Sabatini, in point of fact, was interested in nothing much but the study of history. He learned English from his English mother as a child; attended the École Cantonale, Zoug, Switzerland, and the Lycée of Oporto, Portugal, traveled on the continent, and as a very young man went to England to engage in business. Writing historical fiction seemed much more appealing.

The Tavern Knight, Sabatini's first book, written in his late twenties, was published in 1904, when the historical novel was still in vogue; its chief practitioners were Stanley J. Weyman in England, Winston Churchill in the United States, and a swarm of lesser fry in both countries. Next year Sabatini married Ruth Goad Dixon, who

later obtained a divorce. He married Mrs. Christine Dixon in 1935; their home is Clock Mills, Clifford, Herefordshire, and the writer is a member of the Garrick, Savage, and Authors' Clubs in London. During the First World War he held a post in the Intelligence Department of the War Office.

Neither the imminence nor the actuality of the war had prevented his frequently publishing a romantic novel or historical study —like his full-blown books on Cesare Borgia, the Spanish Inquisition, and the papers collected into *The Historical Nights' Entertainments*—and after the war his books received new *réclame* following a temporary eclipse. *Scaramouche*, at first rejected by six publishers, became a post-war best-seller in the United States, where the reading public was fed up with modern warfare and preferred to read about a strolling player during the French Revolution. Next year's *Captain Blood* (1922), about an English gentleman who turned pirate out of exasperation and a rankling sense of injustice, was an even more pronounced success; had two sequels; and was put into the moving pictures. (*The Sea Hawk* of 1915 also appeared in 1940 as an elaborate talking-picture spectacle.) *The Carolinian,* a novel of the American Revolution, was dramatized for American consumption, and was chiefly noteworthy for allowing Robert Montgomery, later a screen star, to make a brief appearance as a disheveled courier. In England, Sabatini dramatized his *Bardelys the Magnificent* with Henry Hamilton, wrote *The Rattlesnake* with Leon M. Lion, and helped produce *The Fugitives, Scaramouche*, and *The Tyrant*.

In writing his romances, he prefers not to visit their scenes beforehand, lest the

modern background blur the older one his mind has reconstructed. He knows few writers and novelists and never finds time to read other writers' novels. He visited the United States in 1930. Admirers who met Sabatini in the flesh found a tall, well-built, likable, approachable and unaffected man, with reddish hair, flashing hazel eyes, and the features of one of his own Cesares. His recreations in the past have included salmon fishing in Cumberland and skiing in the Alps. His work, said the *Saturday Review of Literature* once, "with a little more skill in dialogue, a little less simplicity in characterization, would be good Dumas."

PRINCIPAL WORKS: The Tavern Knight, 1904; Bardelys the Magnificent, 1906; The Trampling of the Lilies, 1906; Love-at-Arms, 1907; The Shame of Motley, 1908; St. Martin's Summer, 1909; Anthony Wilding, 1910; The Lion's Skin, 1911; The Life of Cesare Borgia (history) 1912; The Justice of the Duke, 1912; The Strolling Saint, 1913; Torquemada and the Spanish Inquisition (history); The Gates of Doom, 1914; The Sea Hawk, 1915; The Banner of the Bull, 1915; The Snare, 1917; The Historical Nights' Entertainments, 1918-1938; Scaramouche, 1921; Captain Blood, 1922; Fortune's Fool, 1923; The Carolinian, 1925; Bellarion, 1926; The Nuptials of Corbal, 1927; The Hounds of God, 1928; The Romantic Prince, 1929; The Minion, 1930; The Chronicles of Captain Blood, 1931; Scaramouche the Kingmaker, 1931; The Black Swan, 1933; The Stalking Horse, 1933; Heroic Lives, 1934; Venetian Masque, 1934; Chivalry, 1935; The Fortunes of Captain Blood, 1936; The Lost King, 1937; The Sword of Islam, 1938; Master-At-Arms, 1940; Columbus, 1942.

ABOUT: Olcott, C. S. At the House of Raphael Sabatini; Bookman February 1925; Mentor November 1924.

SACKVILLE-WEST, EDWARD (November 13, 1901-), English novelist and critic, writes: "While at Oxford, I wrote a certain amount of literary and musical criticism for a magazine called the (Oxford) *Fortnightly Review*, and my career as a writer of fiction started with a number of short stories in the *Oxford Outlook*. I wrote my first novel, *The Ruin*

(published second) while I was still at Oxford. Previous to this time, I had always been considered—and considered myself— as a musician, and particularly as a pianist, which instrument I have played with great facility since about the age of four. In fact, until my seventeenth year I was expected to become a professional pianist and studied under Irene Scharrer, who was the wife of my housemaster at Eton, Samuel Gurney Lubbock. The idea of a professional executant's life was, however, extremely distasteful to me and I abandoned it. After leaving Oxford, I did a certain amount of literary and musical criticism for the *Spectator*, and in 1926 went on to the staff of the *New Statesman*, under the then literary editor, Desmond McCarthy. I remained in that position until September 1927, when I went to live in Germany to study the language and the people. I spent six months in Dresden and six in Berlin, during which time my predisposition in favor of the Germans failed signally to mature into either affection or respect. Since that time I have lived in England and, apart from my books, I have written a great number of reviews and miscellaneous articles, chiefly for the *New Statesman* and the *Spectator*.

"The principal influences on me have been symphonic music, Wagnerian opera, the Romantic Revival, the French Symbolist poets, d'Annunzio, De Quincey, Nietzsche. I should add, however, that, with the exception of symphonic music, the Romantic Revival, and De Quincey, none of these has now much attraction for me. I read incessantly, chiefly biographies, memoirs, letters, fiction, and poetry (ancient and modern), but in fiction I have no use whatever for any writer who has no sense of poetry. My favorite novel (not necessarily the one I think the greatest) is Alain Fournier's *Le Grand Meaulnes*. I probably read as much French literature as English. In politics I am an impenitent Liberal, with an intense loathing of all forms of Fascism, and have a great admiration for the theoretical writings of Walter Lippmann. Apart from literature, I take a lively interest in the gramophone and have from time to time reviewed records in the *New Statesman*. I am also very fond of squash racquets and have such a passion for skiing that I would cheerfully spend four months of the year in pursuing this sport, if my conscience allowed me (which it doesn't). I have abandoned all thought of creative work for the present [written in 1940], since the war has made concentration on personal matters impossible to me."

* * *

Mr. Sackville-West's full name is the Hon. Edward Charles Sackville-West. He is a nephew of the writer V. Sackville-West *qv* (Mrs. Harold Nicolson), and the son of the fourth Baron Sackville; his mother's maiden name was Maude Bell. He was educated at Eton and at Christ Church, Oxford, and is unmarried. He was born and lives at the famous Knole, in Sevenoaks, Kent, immortalized by Virginia Woolf in *Orlando*. Elizabeth Sanderson called him "an unusually sensitive and intelligent writer," with "beautiful craftsmanship."

PRINCIPAL WORKS: Piano Quintet (novel) 1925; The Ruin (novel) 1926; The Apology of Arthur Rimbaud, 1927; Mandrake Over the Water-Carrier, 1928; Simpson: A Life (novel) 1931; The Sun in Capricorn (novel) 1934; A Flame in Sunlight (in America: Thomas De Quincey: His Life and Works) 1936.

ABOUT: Bookman September 1931.

SACKVILLE-WEST, VICTORIA MARY (March, 1892-), English poet

and novelist who signs her books V. Sackville-West, was born at Knole Castle, the famous house, once the seat of the Archbishops of Canterbury, given by Queen Elizabeth to her cousin, Lord Treasure Thomas Sackville. It is the scene of Virginia Woolf's novel, *Orlando*. Miss Sackville-West's father was the third Baron Sackville; her parents were first cousins, and her maternal grandmother was a Spanish gypsy, whose life-story she has told in *Pepita*. She was educated at home, and indeed Knole itself was the chief factor in her education. In 1913 she married Harold Nicolson,*qv* the author and diplomat, and they have two sons. They have traveled a great deal because of his diplomatic appointments, and perhaps the second greatest environmental influence on V. Sackville-West's life was the years she spent in Teheran, Persia, where Mr. Nicolson was British Minister. From it resulted her first writing, a volume of poems. She was known, however, only to a small group of literary connoisseurs until in 1927 she received the Hawthornden prize for her volume of "British Georgics," *The Land*. At this period the Nicolsons lived in London and were part of the so-called "Bloomsbury group," with Lytton Strachey, E. M. Forster, John Maynard Keynes, and Virginia Woolf—a group which in reality was not in any sense a school but merely a loose aggregation of writers, personal friends who happened to live near one another. Now the Nicolsons live in Sissinghurst Castle, in Kent, about which Mrs. Nicolson has also written a book.

She is a tall, dark woman of striking and distinguished appearance, one of whose chief characteristics is her complete independence. One commentator has called her "a woman who gets what she wants, or else." This, however, would imply more aggressiveness than is really native to her; Hugh Walpole was more to the point in calling her "gracious, humorous, and always a creator." It is true that she possesses decisiveness, ruthless common sense, and a gift for leadership, but she is in no way given to pushing herself forward; indeed, Walpole spoke of her "complete lack of any sense of literary competition." She is a product of aristocratic heredity combined with the alien strain brought in by her remarkable grandmother and hardly less remarkable mother.

To quote Walpole again, "her whole color is romantic and yet always unsentimental and real. She is a poet first, last, and all the time." Her least successful work has been in the early novels which were least poetic; although an unkind critic remarked that she could be a great writer if she could forget Knole and all it stands for, nevertheless her best writing has come out of that environment and the traditions in which she was reared. Her influence on other writers—particularly on Virginia Woolf—has been even greater than her own individual achievement. She is one of the few persons who has probably never written anything for any reason except that she wanted to write it and enjoyed doing it; she has never been in a hurry and has always trimmed and polished her work until it satisfied her before she gave it to the world. The result is an artlessness which conceals a very subtle art. She will always be a rather "special" (though not a precious) writer, but she has a secure place in the ranks of careful and conscious artists in words.

PRINCIPAL WORKS: *Poetry*—Poems of West and East, 1917; Orchard and Vineyard, 1921; The Land, 1926; King's Daughter, 1930; Collected Poems, 1933; Some Flowers, 1937; Solitude, 1938; Selected Poems, 1941. *Fiction*—Heritage, 1918; The Dragon in Shallow Waters, 1920; The Heir and Other Stories, 1922; Challenge, 1923; Grey Wethers, 1923; Seducers in Ecuador, 1924; Twelve Days, 1928; The Edwardians, 1930; All Passion Spent, 1931; Family History, 1932; Thirty Clocks Strike the Hour and Other Stories, 1932; The Dark Island, 1934; Grand Canyon, 1942; *Miscellaneous*—Knole and the Sackvilles, 1923; Passenger to Teheran, 1926; Aphra Behn, 1927; Andrew Marvell, 1929; Sissinghurst, 1933; St. Joan of Arc, 1936; Pepita, 1937; Country Notes, 1939; Country Notes in Wartime, 1940; English Country Houses, 1941.

ABOUT: Sackville-West, V. M. Knole and the Sackvilles, Pepita; Arts and Decoration December 1936; Bookman June 1923, September 1930; Bookman (London) February 1924; Bulletin of Bibliography January-May 1938; Canadian Forum September 1931; Poetry September 1935; Saturday Review of Literature March 24, 1934; December 4, 1937; Scribner's Magazine November 1936.

SADLEIR, MICHAEL (December 25, 1888-), English biographer, novelist, and bibliophile, writes: "I was born in Oxford on Christmas Day. As an only child, my upbringing was one of great intimacy with my parents, and this should be ranked as the first and most important 'influence' to which my mind has been subjected. My father was Sir Michael Ernest Sadler, K.C.S.I., the scholar and educator. [Mr. Sadleir changed the spelling of his name to avoid confusion with his father.] In the atmosphere of the liberal-intellectual group of the Oxford of the 'nineties I developed a temperamental dislike of extremes in public affairs and a disbelief in catchwords, slogans, and propaganda which have since kept me personally aloof from any political activities.

"The next influence came from a distant cousin, Eva Gilpin, who came to live with us and teach me and one or two neighboring children. From her I apprehended history as only a teacher of genius could have contrived, and the fascination of the past, which I feel ever more strongly, derives, I am sure, from her instruction. I rate my actual school days (at Rugby) low among mental influences; but college years at Balliol, Oxford—preceded as they were by several months in France and Germany learning the languages—were intensely formative. I had an 'aesthetic period' at Oxford, wrote verse, very little of which was ever printed, and began as a book collector with editions of the French *Symbolistes*. I outgrew this taste as time went on, and my French collection has by now almost all been dispersed. Apart from forgotten verse, the only writing done at Oxford was an essay on the political career of Sheridan, which (rather unexpectedly) won a prize and was officially printed in 1912.

"In that year I went into the office of the London publishers, Constable & Co., Ltd. In 1913 the firm arranged to send me to the United States, and for six months I worked in the offices of the Houghton Mifflin Co., Boston. I am afraid I did not help them as much with their publishing as they helped me to derive pleasure from the American scene.

"I married Edith Tupper-Carey in 1914 and settled in London. [The Sadleirs have two sons and a daughter.] When the First World War started I worked on the blockade, in the War Intelligence Department, and was a member of the British delegation to the Peace Conference. I became a member of the Secretariat of the League of Nations and helped to organize its printing and publishing department. In 1920 I returned to Constable, became a director, and have been there ever since. In 1937 I was Sandars Reader in Bibliography at Cambridge.

"Side by side with official work and publishing activities I began to write books and to extend my book-collecting interests. The latter now turned definitely to novels of the nineteenth century. My collection is now very large. By dint of living with all these books and studying them, I have developed a keen sense of book structure during the last 150 years, and the hobby has led to bibliographical publications of several kinds. Of original works of a non-specialist character I have produced only a moderate number —mainly because I have had only week-ends and evenings in which to write.

"I have a sixteenth century greystone house in Gloucestershire, where my wife breeds bloodhounds, gardens, and motors all over the country. I cannot drive my car or mend electric lights, being completely devoid of mechanical sense. I spend my leisure over my book-collecting and in going to movies.

"Perhaps picturesque failure moves me as much as anything else, alike in history, contemporary life, and social conditions. In consequence I have written more about failures than about successes."

PRINCIPAL WORKS: Political Career of Richard Brinsley Sheridan, 1912; Hyssop (novel) 1915; The Anchor (novel) 1918; Privilege (novel) 1921; Excursions in Victorian Bibliography, 1922; Desolate Splendour (novel) 1923; Daumier, 1924; The Noblest Frailty (novel) 1925; Trollope: A Commentary 1927; Trollope: A Bibliography, 1928; The Evolution of Publishers' Binding Styles: 1770-1900, 1930; Bulwer: A Panorama, 1931; Authors and Publishers: A Study in Mutual Esteem, 1932; Blessington-D'Orsay: A Masquerade (in America: The Strange Life of Lady Blessington) 1933; Bulwer and His Wife, 1933; These Foolish Things, 1937; Archdeacon Francis Wrangham and His Books, 1937; Collecting Yellow Backs (Victorian Railway Fiction) 1938; Fanny by Gaslight, 1940.

ABOUT: Swinnerton, F. A. London Bookman.

*ST. EXUPÉRY, ANTOINE DE
(1900-   ), French novelist and essayist, was born at Lyons, the son of César de St. Exupéry; his mother was by birth a member of the Boyer de Folonscombe family of Provence. He was educated at Jesuit schools in Montgré and Mans, and, proving an unruly pupil, was sent to the Collége de Fribourg, in Switzerland; here he was thoroughly grounded in the classics, until the First World War made it necessary for him to return to France. His vacations were spent at Amberieu, near Bugey, where there was a large aviation field. The boy was fascinated and longed to become an aviator. However, his family wanted him to be an officer of the merchant marine, and he was admitted to the naval school, but — fortunately for him — failed in his final examination. He then studied flying at Strassburg, and was trained as a military flyer; he went to Morocco as a cadet, and came back a full-fledged officer. This  was not what he wanted; he secured his release and for a year suffered as an office worker in Lyon.

Finally, in 1926, he was able to become a commercial aviator, first on the Toulouse-Dakar run, then grounded as commander of the airport at Rio de Oro, on the West coast of Africa. He was much relieved when he was assigned to establish an air-mail route in South America, from Brazil to Patagonia. For the next three years he flew the mails from France to the Sahara. In 1935 he tried a long-distance flight from Paris to Saigon, in Africa. He was forced down in the desert, and he and his companions almost died of thirst before their rescue three days later.

When the Second World War began, he had been planning a flight to the Far East and eventually around the world. Instead he returned to France to become a captain in the Air Corps Reserve. When France fell, nothing was heard of him for some time, and it was feared he had been captured by the Nazis. However, he escaped, although his plane was shot down, and reached Portugal and, later, the United States, where he is now living. His *Flight to Arras* (1942) tells the story of his last, hopeless reconnaissance flight in May 1940, when France was already beaten and to go up into the air meant almost certain death.

It is difficult to define St. Exupéry's books: two of them are called novels, but what they really are is poetic expressions of what flying means to a man of meditative, sensitive nature. As Robert Bourget-Pailleron pointed out, previous books dealing with aviation had been written by passengers, not by pilots; here was "a new song in the air," by a man who "came to aviation through poetry. He is the only poet who literally finds his pathway in the clouds." His love for music has also helped to form his rhythmic style. He is essentially a philosopher, "for whom the air offers a lesson in man's fate." The nearest analogy to his work in English is the first two prose books by Anne Morrow Lindbergh. He lives in two worlds; "the activities of his profession are not separated from his dream," and "he sails between the limits of earth and sky." His work won instant recognition: he received the Prix Femina-Vie Heureuse in 1931, and the highest award in Republican France, the Grand Prize of the French Academy, in 1939. His *Wind, Sand, and Stars* continued to be a best-seller in the United States long after its publication, and *Flight to Arras* seems destined to prove equally viable.

In appearance, "St. Ex," as his friends call him, is anything but the poet: tall, big-footed, heavy, with drooping eyelids, a round, good-natured face, and a markedly upturned nose, slow in his movements and speech. But that he is fundamentally a poet no one who has read his books can deny. He is married, his wife being the former Countess Manuelo.

Works Available in English: Night Flight, 1932; Southern Mail, 1933; Wind, Sand, and Stars, 1939; Flight to Arras, 1942.

About: Annales Politiques et Littéraires December 15, 1931; New York Times Book Review January 19, 1941; Revue des Deux Mondes February 15, 1936, June 15, 1939; Time June 26, 1939, January 13, 1941; Wilson Library Bulletin September 1939

"ST.- J. PERSE." See LÉGER, A.

ST. JOHN ERVINE. See ERVINE

ST. JOHN GOGARTY. See GOGARTY

"ST. LÉGER-LÉGER." See LÉGER, A.

SAINTSBURY, GEORGE EDWARD BATEMAN (October 23, 1845-January 28, 1933), English literary critic, was born at Southampton and educated at King's College School, London, and Merton College, Oxford, where he took his B.A. in 1868. In the same year he married Emily Fenn, who died in 1924, leaving one son. He held honorary degrees from Oxford, Edinburgh,

Aberdeen, and Durham, was a Fellow of the British Academy and Honorary Fellow of Oxford, and was president of the English Association in 1909. For a short time he was assistant master at the Manchester Grammar School, then went to Guernsey, where from 1868 to 1874 he was senior classical master of Elizabeth College, then for two years was headmaster of the Elgin Educational Institute.

For the remainder of his long life he was a journalist, critic, and essayist, though his teaching career was not over—had indeed scarcely begun, since he was professor of rhetoric and English literature at Edinburgh University from 1895 to 1915, when he reached the compulsory age of retirement. It was, however, his connection with the *Academy,* the *Manchester Guardian,* and particularly with the *Saturday Review* that made him perhaps the most widely known of English critics. His erudition was prodigious; there seemed to be nothing that he had not read, and the *Commonweal* aptly called him a "masticator" of books.

Aside from his professional career he was, as the *Nation* remarked in its obituary notice, "an amiable though crotchety old Tory." He was religiously orthodox and politically most conservative, but his genial curiosity about everything in the world and his collection of odd bits of knowledge (embalmed in his *Scrap Books*) kept him from being utterly out of tune with modern thought. One of his pet hobbies was the intricate etiquette of drinking; he was a real connoisseur of wine, and lamented that when a drinking club was founded in his honor and given his name he was no longer able, because of the infirmities of age, to display his gratitude except on paper. With his bald, domed head, his patriarchal white whiskers, and his old-fashioned spectacles, he was the very type of the Victorian college professor.

Saintsbury has been called the father (in English literature) of the modern informal conversational school of criticism. Indeed, all his many books constitute one long conversation, one-sided but, in small doses, entertaining.

Nevertheless, though one may, by discounting the author's prejudices, gain considerable information and much lively enjoyment from reading Saintsbury, his work will scarcely live after its subjects are outmoded. He was not a stylist, or in so far as he was one, his style was unfortunate. The *Fortnightly Review* called him "deplorably parenthetic," and that is indeed his chief weakness; his writing is long-drawn-out, lumbering, full of *obiter dicta* and long parentheses, with so many side-paths due to his overwhelming interest in extraneous matters that sometimes by the end the reader has forgotten the beginning.

The fact is that though Saintsbury lived long enough to review the moderns as well as the Victorians, he himself remained a Victorian and his books will die with all but the greatest of their age. He had no conception of the underlying viewpoints of his later contemporaries; his all-inclusive curiosity was mainly about superficial things. At the end he was a museum-piece — a left-over old widower pottering around the Athenaeum Club, occasionally tossed a sop of reverence by critics two generations his junior, and (up to ten years before his death in London) indefatigably turning out books which in essence became more and more garrulous reminiscences of an old man who had outlived his time.

PRINCIPAL WORKS: A Primer of French Literature, 1881; A Short History of French Literature, 1882; Dryden, 1887; Manchester, 1887; Essays on French Novelists, 1890; Political Verse, 1891; Political Pamphlets, 1892; Miscellaneous Essays, 1892; Corrected Impressions, 1895; Essays in English Literature, 1895; A History of Nineteenth Century Literature, 1896; The Flourishing of Romance and the Rise of Allegory, 1897; Sir Walter Scott, 1897; A Short History of English Literature, 1898; Matthew Arnold, 1899; A History of Criticism and Literary Taste in Europe, 1900-04; The Earlier Renaissance, 1901; Loci Critici, 1903; Minor Caroline Poets, 1905-21; A History of English Prosody, 1906-21; A History of Elizabethan Literature, 1906; The Later Nineteenth Century, 1907; Historical Manual of English Prosody, 1910; A History of English Criticism, 1911; A History of English Prose Rhythm, 1912; The English Novel, 1913; The Peace of the Augustans, 1916; A History of the French Novel, 1917-19; Notes on a Cellar-Book, 1920; A Letter Book, 1922; A Scrap Book, 1922; A Second Scrap Book, 1923; Collected Essays and Papers, 1923; A Last Scrap Book, 1924; A Consideration of Thackeray, 1931; Prefaces and Essays, 1933; Shakespeare, 1934.

ABOUT: Grierson, H. J. C. The Background of English Literature; Canadian Forum April 1933; Commonweal February 15, 1933; Fortnightly Review March 1933; Nation February 8, 1933; New Republic February 8, 1933; Saturday Review of Literature February 11, May 27, 1933.

"SAKI." See MUNRO, H. H.

SALMINEN, SALLY (April 25, 1906-), Finnish novelist who writes in Swedish, writes: "Born in Wardo in the Aaland Islands, belonging to the Republic of Finland. [Most of the Aaland Islanders are of Swedish descent, and her mother was of Swedish birth.] My father was a postman and real-estate broker, who was killed when I was seven years old. I was educated in the general people's schools, and by correspondence courses [in writing and literature]. At sixteen I started to work in a real-estate office. Soon after I went to Sweden and worked in a store. From 1928 to 1930 I worked in a co-operative store in Marienamn, in Aaland. In 1930 I emigrated to the United States. I worked as a 'general houseworker' until 1936. Then with my novel *Katrina,* which I wrote while I was working, I won the first prize in a prize novel contest offered by a publisher in Stockholm and Helsingfors [Helsinki]. In 1936 I returned to Finland. In 1940 I married the artist (painter) Johannes Dührkop, and became a Danish citizen. Now I live in Copenhagen. Swedish is my mother tongue and I always write in that language."

* * *

Miss Salminen became interested in writing through her admiration for Selma Lagerlöf. Her first novel, which won a prize of 50,000 Finn-marks ($1,100), was written after her day's work as a general servant (in Massachusetts, New Jersey, and New York) was done. She left her job at once, and her former employers, the executive of a big soap company and his wife, invited her to be their guest for the few months before she returned to Europe.

When Finland was invaded by the U.S.S.R., she offered her services to the government, and while visiting the front also gathered material for a novel. Her removal to Denmark followed the defeat of Finland by the Soviet Union and preceded the Nazi occupation of Denmark. In her earlier years, she wrote poems, but now she considers poetry "a kind of sickness that one gets over." Her novels are partly autobiographical, and are laid in the Aaland Islands. Her constant aim, she says, is the achievement of clarity, and the presentation of character and action "without using any but the clearest and simplest language."

WORKS AVAILABLE IN ENGLISH: Katrina, 1937; Mariana, 1940.

ABOUT: Newsweek October 24, 1936; Publishers' Weekly November 7, 1936.

*SALTEN, FELIX (September 6, 1869-), Austrian novelist, writes: "My parents were very poor, hence I had to cut short my studies. I

have spent my whole life in Vienna, where my parents moved from Budapest when I was three weeks old. I am self-taught, and have written since my seventeenth year. Since I was eighteen years old I have been busily engaged as a journalist. My knowledge, which is fairly complex, I have considerably enlarged on the historical side. For the rest, I am an observer, and have no head for philosophy. Maupassant, and later Gottfried Keller, had the greatest influence on my literary development. My activity as a publicist, which speedily became very great, also accustomed me to concentrated work. Very early I formed friendships with Hugo von Hofmannsthal, Arthur Schnitzler, and Hermann Bahr. Later I came in touch with George Courteline, still later with John Galsworthy. I have traveled in England, France, Italy, Egypt, and Palestine, and spent three months in the United States as the beneficiary of a Carnegie endowment. Since then I have loved America and the Americans, and have known the role of leadership to which in the future this people will be called.

"I was honorary president of the Vienna P.E.N. Club, was an honorary citizen of the city of Vienna, and in March of 1939 left forever my unhappy Fatherland, which once was dear to me. As interesting episodes of my life, I may mention the friendship which bound me to the Archdukes of Tuscany, and further, the freeing of Princess Louise of Coburg from the insane asylum and the rehabilitation of her lover, Geza von Mattatich. In New York I was greatly impressed by President Butler of Columbia University, and in Detroit by Henry Ford. Besides this I must mention the friendship which I have enjoyed from the beginning with Max Reinhardt, whom for decades I have placed in the ranks of the leading critics.

"As for my works, which include a great many volumes, I name here my book on Palestine, *Neue Menschen auf alter Erde* [*New Men on the Old Earth*], and the book on my journey through the United States, *Fünf Minuten Amerika* [*Five Minutes of America*]. With books in the field of belles lettres I have had varying success; *Bambi* was a best-seller in America. My books have been translated into many languages, *Bambi* even into Hebrew and Chinese."

* * *

Herr Salten lives now in Zurich, Switzerland. He is one of the Jewish refugees who left Austria after the Nazi conquest. His father, once wealthy, failed in business and sank into melancholy; Salten's childhood was poverty-stricken and he himself was small and frail and bullied by his schoolmates in the *gymnasium*. His childhood and youth were miserable, and embittered further by the necessity of accepting charity from a cousin. Finally he insisted that the cousin give him a job in his insurance office, and then to compensate for the drudgery began to write stories. His release came when Schnitzler, Bahr, and Hofmannsthal, all established writers, became interested in the unhappy, talented boy and helped him to gain a place in the literary magazines.

Perhaps the sorrows of his early life have made him so keenly sympathetic with animals. He has written both historical and contemporary novels, but in English at least he is known primarily as the creator of the *Bambi* books, dear to both children and adults, which enter uncannily into the inner life of a wild deer. Sometimes he falls into sentimentality, but as a whole his books are beautiful transcripts of life. As May Lamberton Becker said, readers "first enjoy them for the melody, and second for the overtones." *Bambi* was made into a feature-length Disney animated cartoon.

In 1902 Herr Salten married Ottilie Metzl, an actress of the Vienna Burg-theater. He is a short, slender man with receding gray hair and a face which impresses one by its expression both of sadness and of gentleness.

WORKS AVAILABLE IN ENGLISH: Bambi, 1928; The Hound of Florence, 1930; Fifteen Rabbits, 1930; Samson and Delilah, 1931; The City Jungle, 1932; Florian, the Emperor's Stallion, 1934; Perri, 1938; Bambi's Children, 1939; Renni, the Rescuer, 1940; Good Comrades, 1942.

ABOUT: Bookman September 1928; New York Herald Tribune "Books" December 3, 1939.

SALTER, Sir JAMES ARTHUR (March 15, 1881-), English economist, was born at Oxford, the son of the late James E. Salter of that university town, where the young Salter attended Oxford High School and in due course Brasenose College. He has been a Member of Parliament (Independent) for Oxford University since 1937, and Gladstone Professor of Political Theory and Institutions at the uni-

* Died October 8, 1945.

versity since 1934, thirty years after he started his career as a civil servant in the Transport Department of the Admiralty. In 1913 Salter was assistant secretary of the National Health Insurance Commission. During the First World War he was assistant director of transports in the Admiralty, 1915; director of ship requisitioning in 1917; and secretary of the Allied Maritime Transport Council and chairman of the Allied Maritime Transport Executive in 1918. As secretary of the Supreme Economic Council in 1919, General Secretary of the Reparation Commission in 1920-22, and director of the Economic and Finance Section of the League of Nations from 1922 to 1931, Sir Arthur (C.B. 1918, K.C.B. 1922) made the observations of personalities and trends of events which went into the writing of *Recovery: The Second Effort* (1932). The book sold well in America which was struggling to emerge from the lowest depths of a depression not alleviated by any repayment of the money she had poured into Europe since 1914. Character sketches of Clemenceau, Lloyd George, and Woodrow Wilson enlivened the book. Charles Merz stated that the writer showed insight, candor, an engaging style and an unfailing sense of direction through a wilderness of detail.

Security: Can We Retrieve It?, published in June 1939, on the eve of the outbreak of the second conflict, recommended regimentation, compulsion, and a quasi-totalitarian unity to meet the menace of war. Walter Millis wrote of this second disquisition, "Sir Arthur is bored, he is moderate, he is almost painfully thoughtful and reasonable and judicious. It is impossible not to respect [his] effort: unfortunately, it is impossible to forget the fate of the similar [plan] of seven years ago."

Sir Arthur, who is unmarried, is a member of the Reform Club and gives All Souls College, Oxford University, as his address. He has been parliamentary secretary to the Ministry of Shipping and member of the Economic Advisory Council since 1932, and chairman of the Railway Staff, National Tribunal, since 1936. With the coming of the Second World War he has also been active in Air Raid Defense.

PRINCIPAL WORKS: Allied Shipping Control: An Experiment in International Administration, 1921; Recovery: The Second Effort, 1932; The

Framework of an Ordered Society, 1933; The United States of Europe, 1933; World Trade and Its Future, 1936; Security: Can We Retrieve It? 1939.

ABOUT: Saturday Review of Literature July 29, 1939.

SALTUS, EDGAR EVERTSON (October 8, 1855-July 31, 1921), American novelist, was born in New York City, the son of Francis Henry and Eliza Howe (Evertson) Saltus. He was a lineal descendant of Admiral Kornelis Evertson, commander of the Dutch fleet, who captured New York from the English August 9, 1673; his grandfather, Solomon Saltus, came to New

York City from Bermuda in the late eighteenth century to become a successful merchant. Edgar attended St. Paul's School, Concord, N.H., and entered Yale in 1876, leaving after a year and returning for a brief time with the class of 1877. Three or four years were spent abroad, in Paris, Heidelberg, and Munich. Columbia College granted him an LL.B. degree, but he never practiced law. Saltus married the first of three wives, Helen Sturgis Read, in November 1883. Next year he published a more than promising study of Balzac. *The Philosophy of Disenchantment*, which came in 1885, was an account of Schopenhauer and his school, and was followed next year by *The Anatomy of Negation*, a study of antitheistic philosophies from the early Asiatic cults to contemporary positivism and atheism.

Mr. Incoul's Misadventure, published in 1887, was his first novel, and with its murder, suicide, bull-fights, and lavish description of the Paris Opera, set the tone for the highly colored and slightly absurd fiction associated with the Saltus name. *The Truth About Tristrem Varick*, next year's novel, showed the pursuit of the ideal landing the pursuer in the electric chair. In 1889 Alphabet Jones, who appears as frequently in the Saltus novels as Eugène de Rastignac, hero of Balzac's Comédie Humaine, does in that series, made his début in *The Pace That Kills*. A *Transaction in Hearts*, published in 1889, in *Lippincott's Magazine*, resulted in the dismissal of the editor who had accepted it (although the magazine published Wilde's *Picture of Dorian Gray* next year!). *Imperial Purple*, a lyric sensational history of the Roman emperors, was a favorite of President Harding and seems to have had some effect on the literary style of his state papers. *The Imperial Orgy* essayed to do in 1920 for Russia what Saltus had done in 1893 for Rome.

During Saltus' connection with P. F. Collier & Son in the late 'nineties he did much anonymous hack work, probably compiling *The Lovers of the World* and *The Great Battles of All Nations.* Married to Elsie Walsh Smith, in October 1895, they soon separated. In August 1911 he married Marie Giles, his biographer, who converted him to a belief in theosophy. He died after a long illness and was buried in Sleepy Hollow Cemetery, Tarrytown, N.Y., next his half-brother Frank and in the same plot with Mrs. Saltus' dog Toto. "Eternamente" is carved on the tombstone under his name.

"It is the shudder that tells," was the Saltus motto when writing his fiction. Every novel is an orgy of death, as Carl Van Vechten remarked. Amélie Rives quoted Oscar Wilde as saying, "In the work of Edgar Saltus passion struggles with grammar on every page!" He derived some of his "mystic paganism and jeweled workmanship" from Balzac, Huysmans, and Gustave Moreau, the painter. Deficient in humor, he nevertheless had a neat wit. Saltus was called "sensitive, bitter, malicious." Handsome in youth, he retained a distinguished appearance later in life; he was short, had a waxed moustache and small feet and a pronounced stutter, but *"looked like a man of letters."* Saltus has a measure of significance as a writer who revolted against the conventional literary standards of his period.

PRINCIPAL WORKS: Balzac, 1884; The Philosophy of Disenchantment, 1885; The Anatomy of Negation, 1887; Mr. Incoul's Misadventure, 1887; The Truth About Tristrem Varick, 1888; Eden, 1888; The Pace That Kills, 1889; Mary Magdalen, 1891; Imperial Purple, 1893; Enthralled, 1894; When Dreams Come True 1895; Purple and Fine Women, 1903; The Pomps of Satan, 1906; Historia Amoris, 1907; The Lords of the Ghostland: A History of the Ideal, 1907; The Paliser Case, 1919; The Ghost Girl, 1922; Uplands of Dream (ed. by C. Honce) 1925.

ABOUT: Honce, C. Mark Twain's Associated Press Speech; Huneker, J. G. Steeplejack; Ludington, E. S. Ludington-Saltus Records; Saltus, E. The Uplands of Dream (see Introduction by C. Honce); Saltus, M. Edgar Saltus The Man; Symons, A. Dramatis Personae; Van Doren, C. Contemporary American Novelists; Van Vechten, C. Excavations; Broom June 1922; Publishers' Weekly June 23, 1923; Westminster Review October 1904.

SAMPSON, RICHARD HENRY ("Richard Hull) (September 16, 1896-), English mystery story writer, writes: "Richard Hull (Richard Henry Sampson) is the youngest son of S. A. Sampson and Nina Hull —hence his pen-name. He was born in London and educated at Rugby School, from which he obtained mathematical exhibitions on leaving. He was to have gone to Trinity, Cambridge, but instead obtained a commission on his eighteenth birthday. He remained in the army for the rest of the [First World] War, serving for about three years in France, first with an infantry battalion and then with the Machine Gun Corps. At the end of the war he was articled to a firm of chartered accountants, and after qualifying remained on their staff for some years before setting up in practice for himself.

"It can't be said that he was ever a very successful chartered accountant, and in 1933 he began to think that he would be more interested in writing. The decision to do so and to concentrate mainly on a particular type of detective fiction was made after reading Francis Iles' *Malice Aforethought.* Thereafter chartered accountancy, though not abandoned, faded into the background.

"During all this time, Mr. Sampson kept up his interest in soldiering, and up to 1929 served on the active list of the Territorial Battalion to which he had originally been commissioned in 1914. Even after retiring he kept in close touch with them, and was recalled by them on September 1, 1939. He is now waiting [March 1940] to go abroad again, despite the fact that age has decreased his agility and increased his bulk.

"In fiction he specializes in unpleasant characters because he says there is more to say about them and that he finds them more amusing. For preference he writes in the first person. In life he pleads a kind heart as a set-off to an occasional flash of temper and an endless flow of conversation. For many years he lived almost entirely in a London club [he is unmarried], qualifying, as he says, as the club bore. He is convinced that his photograph would be detrimental to his sales."

PRINCIPAL WORKS: The Murder of My Aunt, 1935; Keep It Quiet, 1935; Murder Isn't Easy, 1936; The Ghost It was, 1936; Murders of Monty, 1937; Excellent Intentions, 1938; And Death Came Too, 1939; My Own Murderer, 1940; Beyond Reasonable Doubt, 1941; The Unfortunate Murderer, 1942.

ABOUT: Haycraft, H. Murder for Pleasure: The Life and Times of the Detective Story.

SANBORN, FRANKLIN BENJAMIN.
See "AMERICAN AUTHORS: 1600-1900"

SANBORN, PITTS (1878-March 7, 1941),
American music critic and novelist, was born John Pitts Sanborn in Port Huron, Mich.,

and educated at Harvard (B.A. 1900, M.A. 1902). He was the dean of Manhattan music critics, having been music editor of the New York *Globe* from 1905 to 1923, then of the *Evening Mail* until that paper was merged with the *Evening Telegram* and subsequently with the *World-Telegram*. He still held this post on the last-named paper when he died. During the summer, however, from 1912 to 1923, he went to Europe as foreign correspondent, first of the *Globe* and then of the *Evening Mail;* most of these summers, beginning during the First World War, were spent in France. In recognition of his services in making French and Italian music better known, he was made a Chevalier of the Legion of Honor and a Cavalier of the Order of the Crown of Italy. He was the program annotator of the New York Philharmonic-Symphony Society after the death of Lawrence Gilman in 1939, was a contributor to the *International Cyclopedia of Music and Musicians,* and was on the editorial board of *Who's Who in Music.* At various times he had also been a radio commentator on music.

Mr. Sanborn wrote frequent articles for magazines, sometimes under the pseudonym of "Peter Bowdoin," and besides editing the *Metropolitan Book of the Opera* (he was considered an authority on grand opera), he published two novels and a volume of poems. "Impeccable taste," "unquestioned authority," and "fine sensibilities" were phrases applied by critics to his writing. Unmarried, he lived alone in New York, but he had a host of friends, who, as Deems Taylor remarked in an obituary speech, loved him for his generosity and kindness as well as for what one critic called "his engaging quirks and prejudices." One of these friends found him dead in his apartment, from a sudden attack of heart disease.

PRINCIPAL WORKS: Vie de Bordeaux (poems) 1917; Prima Donna: A Novel of the Opera, 1929; Greek Night (novel) 1933; Metropolitan Book of the Opera (ed.) 1937.

ABOUT: Etude May 1941; Publishers' Weekly March 22, 1941; Scholastic January 11, 1936; Time March 17, 1941.

SANDBURG, CARL (January 6, 1878-),
American poet and biographer, was born in Galesburg, Ill., the son of August and Clara (Anderson) Johnson.

Both his parents emigrated to America from the North of Sweden. His father was a blacksmith, who later worked on the railroad, where he changed his name to Sandburg (this before Carl was born) because there were already several August Johnsons on the pay-

E. Schaal

roll. The parents had had hardly any schooling, and the family was very poor. Carl left school at thirteen and did all sorts of work—harvesting, bricklaying, dish-washing, and all the unskilled labor available to a husky boy in a small Middle Western town. At seventeen he "rode the freights" to Kansas, and continued the same kind of life there. He drifted back to Galesburg and apprenticed himself to a house painter. The Spanish-American War indirectly changed his whole life. He enlisted in the Sixth Illinois Infantry and served for eight months in Puerto Rico. One of his comrades was a young man who was a student at Lombard College, in Galesburg, and persuaded Sandburg to go there too. He was fortunate in attracting the attention of Professor Philip Green Wright, who not only encouraged his writing but paid for publication of his first volume of poems. He had to work his way through college, and though he attended for four years he was never graduated. Later the college gave him a Litt.D. degree, and so did Knox College and Northwestern University. He is now also a member of the American Academy of Arts and Letters.

After college he went to Milwaukee and got a newspaper job. There he met and married Lillian Steichen (whom he calls Paula), sister of the famous American photographer Edward Steichen. They have three daughters. From 1910 to 1912 he was secretary to the mayor of Milwaukee, then he went to Chicago as associate editor of *System.* Harriet Monroe had just started *Poetry: A Magazine of Verse,* and she gave Sandburg a forum and encouraged him to keep on writing in the loose, Whitmanesque vein, full of homely speech interspersed with passages of pure lyricism, which is his poetic hallmark. He won the first Helen Haire Levinson Prize from *Poetry*, in 1914. In 1919 and 1920 he was co-winner of the Poetry Society of America Prize.

Meanwhile he had become an editorial writer on the Chicago *Daily News,* and a recognized member of the brilliant "Chicago group," including Ben Hecht, Charles McArthur, Harry Hansen, Floyd Dell, and many others now established as writers. In 1918 he went to Stockholm as correspondent of the Newspaper Enterprise Association, and one of his daughters was born there. After the war he came back to America, and settled in Harbert, Mich., on the shores of Lake Michigan, sixty miles east of Chicago. In 1928 he was the Phi Beta Kappa poet at Harvard, and on his sixtieth birthday, in 1938, the king of Sweden bestowed on him the Royal Order of the North Star.

From his early youth, Sandburg had lived in and dreamed of the Abraham Lincoln legend. For thirty years he arduously sought out and collected material on Lincoln, and gradually the writing of the six-volume definitive biography of the great president became the consummation of his career. The first two volumes (*The Prairie Years*) came out in 1926, the last four (*The War Years*) in 1939. Overnight it was evident that a lasting word on Lincoln had been said, and said by a poet as well as by an historian; and that one of the great biographies of modern times had been written. Seldom has a contemporary work received such instant and universal recognition of greatness. The Pulitzer Prize, following as a matter of course in 1940, seemed a postscript rather than a climax. (Because the terms of the Pulitzer awards prohibit giving the biography prize to works about Washington or Lincoln, the jury in charge resorted to the subterfuge of awarding Sandburg the history prize. A national poll of critics and reviewers conducted by the *Saturday Review of Literature* the same year gave the author *both* the history and biography prizes.)

The writing, which occupied approximately fifteen years, was done on a typewriter perched on a cracker-box in the attic of Sandburg's Harbert house on the sand-dunes, with another room, the "Lincoln room," crowded with notes and data, and the overflow in the barn. A few months each year the author would rest from his labor (and earn his living) by touring the country with his banjo or guitar, and in his sweet but untrained baritone singing folk-songs and reciting his own poems. Some of these songs (collected in *The American Songbag*) he has recorded for the phonograph; "The Boll Weevil" is perhaps the best known.

His volumes of poems, the monumental Lincoln biography, and his quaint stories for children make up the sum of Sandburg's work, a varied product through which runs one thread—the authentic voice of the prairies. As Rebecca West said, he is, "like Burns, a national poet." And she remarked that "his lines will not reveal their music . . . unless they are read with a Middle Western accent." Newton Arvin, too, spoke of his "continuous effort to find a poetic outlet for the . . . experience of Middle Western city people . . . villagers and farmers." A big man, with white hair always falling into his clear eyes, with what Holger Lundbergh called "a stern and quizzical Swedish face," which is lighted often by a wide and friendly grin, Sandburg is himself in epitome the great, sprawling, flat, rich Middle West. But he has none of the facile and assertive optimism of Whitman, with whom he is so often compared—in his work and his speech there are always doubt, uncertainty, hesitancy. That underlying them is a deep faith in the hope and promise of America, the years of his devotion to Lincoln triumphantly prove.

PRINCIPAL WORKS: *Poetry*—In Reckless Ecstacy, 1904; Chicago Poems, 1915; Cornhuskers, 1918; Smoke and Steel, 1920; Slabs of the Sunburnt West, 1922; Selected Poems, 1926; Good Morning America, 1928; The People, Yes, 1936. *Biography*—Abraham Lincoln: The Prairie Years (2 vols.) 1926; Steichen the Photographer, 1929; Mary Lincoln: Wife and Widow (with P. M. Engle) 1932; Abraham Lincoln: The War Years (4 vols.) 1939. *Juvenile*—Rootabaga Stories, 1922; Rootabaga Pigeons, 1923; Potato Face, 1930; Early Moon (verse) 1930. *Miscellaneous*—The Chicago Race Riots, 1919; The American Songbag, 1927.

ABOUT: Boynton, P. H. Some Contemporary Americans; Detzer, K. Carl Sandburg; Hansen, H. Carl Sandburg; The Man and His Work; Lowell, A. Tendencies in Modern American Poetry; Monroe, H. A Poet's Life; American-Scandinavian Review March 1928; Bulletin of Bibliography September 1936; Living Age April 3, 1926; New Republic September 9, 1936; New York Times Book Review December 11, 1939; Pictorial Review September 1925; Poetry October 1936; Saturday Review of Literature September 4, 1926; Time December 4, 1939.

SANDERSON, IVAN TERRANCE (January, 1911-), British biologist, writes: "Born in Edinburgh. Educated at Eton and learned sufficient facts at Cambridge to obtain a B.A. in zoology, geology, and botany. After leaving Eton at the age of seventeen, traveled round the world eastwards via

Egypt and India to the Malay States and the Dutch East Indies, where a one-man (or one-boy) zoological expedition was carried through to obtain specimens of small animals

for the British Museum. Thence traveled on via Indo-China, China, Japan, and reached America and finally England after a year. No noteworthy achievement at Cambridge due to lack of interest in athletics. Literary accomplishments: one article in a varsity newspaper on 'Women,' which was roundly condemned by the authorities.

"Two days after leaving Cambridge sailed as leader of small Percy Sladen Memorial Fund Expedition to the Cameroons, West Africa, on behalf of the British Museum, Cambridge and London Universities. A year spent in the field carrying out research upon and collecting small animals. Returned to London with all the animals and data that had been sought. This initiated a period of zoological studies in museums and the publication of some technical works on zoology. Married in 1934.

"Carried on a small interior decorating business specializing in restaurants and cabarets; studied, wrote and lectured upon African art, culture and dancing and music. The necessity of doing some literary work arose through these latter activities. Literary inferiority complex partially overcome in late 1935, resulting in a book entitled *Animal Treasure* about our work in Africa, which, surprisingly, was a Book-of-the-Month Club selection. The proceeds were invested in a zoological expedition to the West Indies and in the following year another to Dutch Guiana. These gave birth to a second book.

"Apart from these, some odd articles and scientific writings, no products of literary enthusiasm are extant. No claim is therefore made to the title of *author*. Rather is recognition sought in the fields of experimental zoology, natural history, and possibly the art of animal illustration."

* * *

Mr. Sanderson is a pleasant-looking young man with dark hair worn in a pompadour and a small moustache. Extreme nearsightedness has not hampered either his scientific work or his delightful drawings. His wife was his colleague in his Caribbean and

South American expeditions. The charm of his books makes one regret that his literary aspirations are so modest. *Time* said of him: "His sympathy toward animals is as rich as his eye for observed detail is acute and his prose style is limpid."

PRINCIPAL WORKS: Animal Treasure, 1937; Caribbean Treasure, 1939; Living Treasure, 1941.

ABOUT: Nature Magazine April 1, 1939; Scientific Monthly January 1938, May 1940; Time September 13, 1937; Yale Review March 1941.

SANDOZ, MARI (1901-), American biographer and novelist, writes: "I was born at what was then Sandoz postoffice, Sheridan County, Neb., the eldest of six children of Jules A. Sandoz of Neuchatel, Switzerland, and Mary Elizabeth (Fehr) Sandoz of Schaffhausen, Switzerland. I grew up on the architectural scheme of the cowboy—height five feet

and a half inch weight 105 pounds. Also weather-beaten. In the home of 'Old Jules' Sandoz, trapper, locater, horticulturist, and community builder, I grew up speaking German, hearing French, Polish, and Czech, and English, which I learned after I started to school, at nine. I went to rural school four and a half years, took the rural teachers' examination, taught five years in western Nebraska. and attended the University of Nebraska three and one half years, working in a drug laboratory and as English assistant at the university to pay my way.

"I began writing stories as soon as I learned to put letters together. Had several of these published in the junior page of the Omaha *Daily News*. Perhaps my earliest literary influences were Joseph Conrad, whose sea seemed to me so like the sandhills about me, and Hardy, whose recognition of chance and circumstance in the shaping of human destiny seemed very true to the fairly violent life about me. Later I discovered the work of Shakespeare, of the Russians, and finally the Greeks. Aristophanes and portions of the Old Testament are my favorite material for re-reading.

"In college I wrote seventy-eight short stories, won honorable mention in a *Harper's* contest in 1926, and wrote a bad novel that, fortunately, no one would publish. When a publisher returned *Old Jules* with a curt rejection letter in 1933, I quit. Starved out, my confidence in even my critical faculties gone, I gave up writing permanently. But in less than a month I was writing a novel that I had been thinking about doing for nine or ten years. It was *Slogum House*.

"By the time the rough draft was done, I was offered work at the State Historical Society, in Lincoln, as associate editor of the *Nebraska History Magazine*. I made a new copy of *Old Jules* and started it on its alphabetical rounds of the publishers again. On its fourteenth trip out it was accepted— and won the *Atlantic* non-fiction prize in 1935.

"I never begin to write even a two-page article—let alone a story or a book—without making first a simple, declarative statement of the theme, to be tacked up before my eyes for the duration of the work. Then I go through my notes of pertinent material and begin making drafts, with almost endless revisions.

"I always come back to the Middle West. There's a vigor here, and a broadness of horizon. Besides, I believe that the creative worker must not wander too far from the earth of his emotional identity. I, at least, am Anteus-footed.

"Politically, I suppose that I am what might be called an independent liberal, as the Sandoz family seems to have been for seven hundred years.

"Now I am working on my two Indian biographies that have taken up some of my time and much of my thought for five or six years—a Cheyenne biography and one of a Sioux. These will require five or six more years for completion, I anticipate."

* * *

Readers of *Old Jules* will remember that Miss Sandoz' mother was the fourth wife of that redoubtable pioneer, and will also understand the shyness and timidity that underlie the dynamism of this slender, courageous woman with the dark red curly hair and the snapping dark eyes. She is unmarried. Because she had never been to high school, she was given no college degree, but the historical research she has done on her books is of graduate school calibre. She is less successful in fiction than in biography, but in both forms she is a good corrective for people inclined to sentimentalize the pioneer.

PRINCIPAL WORKS: Old Jules, 1935; Slogum House, 1937; Capital City, 1939.

ABOUT: Book-of-the-Month Club News October 1935; Newsweek November 2, 1935; Saturday Evening Post March 4, 1939; Saturday Review of Literature November 27, 1937; Time November 4, 1935; Wilson Library Bulletin February 1938.

*SANTAYANA, GEORGE (December 16, 1863-   ), American-Spanish philosopher, writes: "The only remarkable thing about my career is that I should have spent the better part of my life in the United States, and written my books in the English language, while retaining my Spanish nationality and sentiment, and figuring in the English-speaking world as a sort of

permanent guest, familiar, appreciative and I hope discreet, but still foreign. This is no less true of me intellectually than it is socially, and should not be ignored in considering my work. It all came from the fact that my maternal grandfather, José Borrás of Reus in Catalonia, was a younger son with an adventurous disposition and emancipated views, such that when in 1823 the French marched into Spain to restore the absolute monarchy, he left the country, wandered to Scotland, where my mother was born, and later to Virginia, where she spent her early childhood. The consequence was that she could speak English and always retained a fundamental respect and affection for Americans; and she eventually married one of them, George Sturgis, of Boston, a merchant established in Manila. For the changing fortunes of her father had eventually taken her to the Philippine Islands, where his death in 1847 had left her an orphan. Ten years later she became a widow, and went to live in Boston with her three children, according to a promise that she had made to their father. On the outbreak of the Civil War, however, she returned to Spain and there married my father, Augustin Ruiz de Santayan y Reboiro, who had also been for many years in the Philippines and had known her there.

"I was born in Madrid on December 16, 1863, and remained in Spain until 1872, when my father and I sailed from Liverpool for Boston in the Cunard S.S. 'Samaria,' of 3,000 tons. My mother had preceded us with her other children three years earlier, and lived at 302 Beacon Street, then one of the last houses, amid vast vacant lots, on the Mill Dam. In this narrow high house, with a view (and smell) of the Back Bay in the rear, I spent my boyhood, going to the Boston Latin School. At first I was rather unhappy, but in the last two years I found my level and made the first of those many close but scattered friendships that have been the chief personal interest of my bachelor life. Harvard College followed, and two years in Berlin, with a return to Harvard, where I served as a member of the philosophical department from 1889 to 1912.

"Almost all my summers, and the three winters when I had leave of absence during these years, I spent in Europe, principally in Spain and England, within a small but constant circle of relations and friends. I have had the melancholy privilege of surviving most of them; but even now, at the age of seventy-five, I live contentedly in an atmosphere of travel and study, always in hotels, but not without books and friends and the fresh air of the great world and of changing opinions keeping me spiritually young. The dismay that has fallen of late upon so many minds has not touched me. I have never had any illusions about the world's being rationally guided or true to any ideals; reason and ideals arise in doing well something that at bottom there was no reason for doing. This is naturalism, as I understand it; and perhaps I feel myself spiritually young only because I accept beforehand the maxims of the spiritually very old, and expect nothing better. I am not a believer in any religion, literally understood; but I am a man of priestly disposition and think that it is possible to live nobly in this world only if we live in another world ideally.

"There have been short seasons in my life when nevertheless I have been attracted into an unfeigned participation in social pleasures and in political hopes. They are represented by two of my books: *Soliloquies in England* and *The Last Puritan*. These are therefore the most approachable of my writings for the general reader; but even here, though some interest may be aroused, I doubt that the unconverted or unconvertible will find much ultimate satisfaction.

"The *Soliloquies* represent my feelings during the years 1914-1918, when I was living in England, under the incubus of war, yet enjoying a spring-time of free thinking and the to me rather novel influences of rural nature. The English people never seemed to me more admirable than under that trial which made a fresh bond between persons and classes that peace and prosperity might have divided. Some memories of that time have run over into *The Last Puritan*; but the chief source for this second book was my experiences in the 1890's of the pleasanter sides of Harvard and Boston. I was then still young enough to sympathize with youth, but already old enough to understand it; and I had read and traveled enough

to play at culture and aestheticism without being yet tired of them. It was a pleasant intelligent life on the outskirts of a plutocracy that felt itself perfectly safe and virtuous. For me this cultivated society happened to contain little but youths and ladies; the older men seemed animals of another species; and it must be confessed that not all the youths were cultivated nor all the ladies young. I was myself growing too old to be held by the charms of mere kindness and personality. I feel those charms still, also that of youth, but I am not held by them.

"My American critics are partial to *The Life of Reason* and think it better inspired than my later books. That is a legitimate judgment philosophically; but if the point were, as in this sketch, to catch the salient characters of my life and mind, I think *The Life of Reason* would seem rather an episode, an academic task I had set myself rather than an overflow of my spontaneous philosophy. It is a treatise on *possible* human progress, a Utopia in substance though in form a criticism of morals, arts, and opinions. It loosely follows, in modern terms, the *Republic* of Plato and the *Ethics* of Aristotle. Like those two works it is programmatic and judicial ostensibly, but really retrospective and in the air. My later philosophy, though not descriptive of so many past things, hugs reality more closely and looks at life in its true history rather than in its good intentions. I have never been a blind lover of life, as the world lives it. My heart has been in religion, or in a philosophy that, like religion, signifies a change of heart. A pig may prefer his pigsty to the open; but would he, if he were a philosopher? I like to regard society as a part of nature, and to see it as an incident against its non-human ground; and this is not merely cosmically, because that background is older and wider, but also inwardly, because that ground is deeper in human nature itself."

* * *

Dr. Santayana left Harvard in 1912, after receiving a legacy which made it no longer financially necessary for him to teach. He is an unforgotten teacher, both at Harvard and at other universities and colleges where he has lectured—the University of California, Swarthmore, Oxford, Cambridge, the Sorbonne—but he always preferred the wider audience of the world. His last lectures, in commemoration of Spinoza, at the Hague, and of Locke, in London, were given in 1932. Since then he has spent his winters in Rome, his summers mainly in Paris or London. At last reports he was still in Rome, where he can live without embarrassment since he has never relinquished his Spanish citizenship. There he is completing his autobiography, to be called *Persons and Places* and projecting a political work, *Thrones and Dominations*, for post-war publication.

Margaret Münsterberg has described him as he appeared in his Harvard days—"handsome, delicate, pale against the black hair and small moustache" (later he grew a beard), with "dark Spanish eyes." Though he was, seemingly cold on first acquaintance, she remembered vividly his inimitable laughter among his friends. Perhaps no one was more surprised than he when his lone novel *The Last Puritan*—completed when he was past seventy—became a best-seller.

He has surveyed in his sketch everything about his books except the thing that makes them unique among philosophical works— the singing beauty of their style. Essentially he is a poet, and his books are the poetry of philosophy. To paraphrase a comment by Archibald MacLeish on his more formally poetic writing: "The air he inhabits is the air genius must climb, and his defects are the defects of supreme quality. He stands upon experience, but his experience is aesthetic altogether."

PRINCIPAL WORKS: *Philosophy*—The Sense of Beauty, 1896; Interpretations of Poetry and Religion, 1900; The Life of Reason: Reason in Common Sense, 1905; Reason in Society, 1905; Reason in Religion, 1905; Reason in Art, 1905; Reason in Science, 1906; Three Philosophical Poets: Lucretius, Dante, and Goethe, 1910; Winds of Doctrine, 1913; Egotism in German Philosophy, 1916; Philosophical Opinion in America, 1918; Little Essays, 1920; Character and Opinion in the United States, 1920; Soliloquies in England and Later Soliloquies, 1922; Scepticism and Animal Faith, 1923; Dialogues in Limbo, 1925; Platonism and the Spiritual Life, 1927; The Realm of Essence, 1928; The Realm of Matter, 1930; The Genteel Tradition at Bay, 1931; Some Turns of Thought in Modern Philosophy, 1933; Obiter Scripta, 1935; The Realm of Truth, 1937. *Poetry* —Sonnets and Other Verses, 1894; Lucifer: A Theological Tragedy, 1898; The Hermit of Carmel and Other Poems, 1901; Poems, 1923. *Novel*— The Last Puritan: A Novel in the Form of a Memoir, 1935.

ABOUT: Ames, Van M. Proust and Santayana; Howgate, G. W. George Santayana; Santayana, G. Selected Works (ed. by I. Edman. see "A Brief History of My Opinions"); Schilpp, P. A. The Philosophy of Santayana; American Mercury January 1924; Bookman October 1925; Catholic World October 1934; New Republic October 22, 1930; New York Times Magazine December 17, 1933; Saturday Review of Literature December 16, 1933, February 1, 1936, April 17, 1937, January 25, 1941; Virginia Quarterly Review Autumn 1937.

"SAPPER." See MC NEILLE, H. C.

*SARETT, LEW R. (May 16, 1888-   ), American poet, writes: "I was born in Chicago. My father and mother came to America from Southeastern Europe. They were of healthy peasant stock, courageous, honest, and industrious. When I was a little boy we moved to Marquette, Mich. The region was wild and beautiful. Before I was ten I knew a good deal about the woods. Later, as a result of family trouble, my mother and I found ourselves in Chicago alone. We knew bitter poverty and hunger. At the age of twelve I supported my mother and myself with various jobs that paid a pittance: as a bundle boy in a department store, a newsboy, an errand boy in a sweatshop, as employees' lavatory attendant under "the world's most busy corner" at State and Madison Streets. In this dark period the poet in me was born, and my passion for nature. That passion, born in this period of frustration, is a vital element in my life and work.

D. Loving

"There was a lucky turn in our family affairs and we moved to Benton Harbor, Mich. There I attended high school, and every minute I was free from school was spent in the woods. When I was eighteen I became a lifesaver on a municipal swimming beach in Chicago. The next year I determined to get a college education. I started at the University of Michigan, but in a year I shifted to Beloit College. I worked my way through these and later through the University of Illinois and Harvard Law School by many jobs: as a guide in the Canadian woods, as Forest Ranger in the Rockies, an instructor in a sportsmen's camp in Northern Wisconsin, a guide in Northern Minnesota. In those years of adventure in the woods and mountains, I covered about 25,000 miles of Canada and the United States by canoe and pack train. In 1911 I received my B.A. from Beloit, and in 1916 my LL.B. from the University of Illinois. From 1912 to 1920 I taught English and public speaking at Illinois. In 1914 I married Margaret Elizabeth Husted; we have a son and a daughter.

"It was while I was teaching at Illinois that I began to write poetry. I was encouraged and helped much in counsel by Stuart P. Sherman, Harriet Monroe, and Carl Sandburg. In 1920 I accepted a position on the faculty of Northwestern University School of Speech. I have been on its faculty since. In 1926 I established my home in Laona, Wis., teaching only three months each year, commuting 600 miles to Evanston. In 1930 I returned to Northwestern, to a full professorship and a full teaching schedule, living in Ravinia, Ill. Part of each year I give to the woods. Part of the year I do platform work from coast to coast. In 1922 I won the Levinson Prize in Poetry; my *Slow Smoke* was awarded the prize offered by the Poetry Society of America for the best volume of poetry published in America in 1925.

"I like everything rooted in earth, and everything that walks or crawls on earth. I like all people who are simple, natural, and honest. I like gardens and gardening, dogs and horses, trout-fishing, the study of botany and zoology, good books, good painting, and good music. And I like young people, and I like the privilege of teaching them."

* * *

In Indian dress, Mr. Sarett might be mistaken for an Indian, bronzed and a fine athlete, though not tall. Wilbur Hatfield called him "a man of the woods and fields, a poet of nature." Harriet Monroe said he knows "more about wild creatures than any poet, living or dead, who has written about them."

PRINCIPAL WORKS: Many Many Moons, 1920; The Box of God, 1922; Slow Smoke, 1925; Wings Against the Moon, 1932; Basic Principles of Speech (with W. T. Foster) 1936; Modern Speeches on Basic Issues (with W. T. Foster) 1939; Collected Poems, 1941.

ABOUT: Hansen, H. Midwest Portraits; Monroe, H. Poets and Their Art; Sarett, L. Collected Poems (see Preface by Carl Sandburg); Untermeyer, L. American Poetry Since 1900; Weirick, B. From Whitman to Sandburg in American Poetry; American Magazine February and March 1936; Nature Magazine August 1930; Poetry November 1925, December 1941; Saturday Review of Literature July 18, 1931; Scholastic May 8, 1937.

SAROYAN, WILLIAM (August 31, 1908-), American story writer and playwright, was born in Fresno, Calif., of Armenian parents: his father, Armenag Saroyan, who died when he was two, had been a Presbyterian minister but at that time was a small grape-grower. Until the boy was seven his mother (whose maiden name was Takoohi Saroyan; she and her husband were cousins) was obliged to keep her children in an orphanage in Alameda, Calif.; then she got work in a cannery and they returned to Fresno. Here he went as far as the second year in junior high

school and read every book in the public library; after which he left school and began work as a telegraph messenger. He had previously been a newsboy. He had been writing from the age of thirteen. A remarkable succession of jobs followed, including office work, farm labor, a short period in the National Guard, and an abortive attempt at newspaper reporting; he left so many places so abruptly that finally the employment agencies refused to recommend him. At last he became local manager of the Postal Telegraph office in San Francisco, where he had gone at seventeen. His first short story was published in 1933 in *Hairenik*, an Armenian magazine, and was reprinted by Edward J. O'Brien in the 1934 *Best Short Stories*; it was written under the pseudonym of "Sirak Goryan," which he used occasionally at the beginning of his career. (He edited an anthology of *Hairenik* stories in 1939). He had previously published a few articles in the *Overland Monthly*.

E. Schaal

Story was next to accept one of his contributions—the famous "Daring Young Man on the Flying Trapeze," which appeared the same year (1934) as title-story of his first volume. It was an instant success, and Saroyan was launched. He went to Hollywood briefly, to work off accumulated debts; then returned to San Francisco and has gravitated between that city and Fresno ever since, with recurrent trips to New York since he became a playwright. In 1935 he visited Armenia and Russia. He is extraordinarily prolific, though not so quick a worker as he would like people to believe.

It is equally difficult to list all of Saroyan's publications and to define their exact nature. He calls them stories, but says, "What the hell difference does it make what you call it, just so it breathes?" All his work certainly breathes, even though George Jean Nathan remarked that he sometimes "mistakes a squirrelish activity for versatility." In 1939 he suddenly became a playwright, with *My Heart's in the Highlands*, and, moreover, directed production of his own plays. He received the Pulitzer Prize for Drama in 1940 for *The Time of Your Life*, and publicly refused to accept it on the ground that commerce had no right to patronize art. Yet he cannot be dismissed merely as "brash and boisterous," conceited and aggressive. Burton Rascoe called him "one of the profoundest humorists, in the Meredithean sense, that has ever enriched Americanese and the American scene." T.S. Matthews who compared him to Whitman, said: "His stories are apt to turn into jeremiads or paeans or cacchinations of exhibitionistic caperings or poems with cuss words." Edmund Wilson called him "an agreeable mixture of San Francisco bonhommie and Armenian Christianity"; he praised his "natural felicity of touch" and "instinctive sense of form." But he deplored the smugness that has crept into his work and feared he might be on his way to mere self-satisfied facility.

Saroyan went to Hollywood again in 1942 to write and direct his own picture, *The Human Comedy,* but left (with $65,000) when the studio refused to let him proceed with the direction. In New York again he organized and directed "The Saroyan Theatre," beginning in August 1942 with a production of two of his short plays (*Across the Board on Tomorrow Morning* and *Talking to You*), but the venture closed in a week.

Physically, Saroyan is robust, with "startlingly black" hair and eyes, given to rather flamboyant dress, but with invariably battered hats and an overcoat much too large for him. He honestly prefers the company of the rough-and-ready and uncultured; he has no social graces and wants none. "He likes to drink, read, bet on horses, go to terrible movies, and play tennis and stud poker." He is unmarried and means to stay that way. He flits in and out of San Francisco, burying himself to work in the house he bought for his mother; he types his own stories and plays, never rewrites, and never keeps a carbon copy of anything. Whatever else he is, he is a "character"; and even those most prejudiced against him by his self-advertisement are disarmed by his friendly manner and by the innocence of his love-affair with William Saroyan. Digging through his interminable productions, they may feel at the end, uneasily, that perhaps after all, even though he does admit it, he really is a genius.

PRINCIPAL WORKS: The Daring Young Man on the Flying Trapeze, 1934; Inhale and Exhale, 1936; Three Times Three, 1936; Little Children, 1937; Love, Here Is My Hat, 1938; Native American, 1938; The Trouble With Tigers, 1938; Peace, It's Wonderful, 1939; The Hungerers (play) 1939; Three Plays (My Heart's in the Highlands, The Time of Your Life, Love's Old Sweet Song) 1940; Three Times Three, 1940; My Name Is Aram, 1940; Fables, 1941; Three Plays (The Beautiful People, Sweeney in the Trees, Across

the Board on Tomorrow Morning) 1941; Razzle Dazzle, 1942; The Human Comedy, 1942.

ABOUT: . American Magazine June 1940; American Mercury November 1940; Life November 18, 1940; New Republic March 18, 1936, November 18, 1940; New York Times Book Review March 24, 1940; New Yorker August 31, 1940; Newsweek November 14, 1938.

SASSOON, SIEGFRIED LORRAINE (September 8, 1886-), English poet and novelist, was born in London. On his father's side he is the descendant of a wealthy family of Sephardic (Spanish) Jews, resident first in Persia, then in Bombay, then in England, and containing several noted names. His mother, an artist, was the sister of the celebrated sculptor, Sir

Hamo Thornycroft. His parents were separated in his childhood and he and his brothers were reared by their mother. Soon after the separation his father died. He was educated at Marlborough Grammar School and at Clare College, Cambridge. His university career was largely a fizzle, partly because he was more interested in poetry than in his studies, and partly because the rest of his attention was given to hunting and tennis. He was "sent down," and for several years lived a rather dilettante life in London, publishing a succession of small volumes of verse, admittedly modeled on John Masefield.

At the beginning of the First World War he enlisted and was sent to France as a second lieutenant. The war made him a pacifist and a true poet. He served for four and a half years and won the Military Cross before he finally revolted. He wrote a series of savage poems exposing the horror of war, but for a while he kept on fighting. In 1917 he was wounded and invalided home. He threw his Military Cross into the sea and publicly announced that he refused to serve any longer. He had hoped to be court martialed and to make a public statement of his position; instead, he was hushed up by being declared "temporarily insane." He was sent to a sanatorium and then shipped to Palestine. He gave up the struggle for the while, returned to France, was wounded again, and at the end of the war was a captain.

But he was still a pacifist, and supported Philip Snowden actively in the next general election. For a while he became a journalist, and in 1920 he made a tour of the United States, reading his poems and talking against war. In 1928 he published his first prose work, ostensibly a novel, really a fictionalized autobiography, *Memoirs of a Fox-Hunting Man.* It appeared anonymously. It won both the Hawthornden and the James Tait Black Memorial Prizes. It was followed by two sequels, *Memoirs of an Infantry Officer* and *Sherston's Progress,* and the trilogy was published as one book, under the title of *The Memoirs of George Sherston,* in 1937.

In 1933 he married Hester Gatty, and they have one son. They live in Wiltshire. Sassoon is tall, thin, angular and dark; someone has remarked that Sir Max Beerbohm would depict him with "three curves and a lock of hair." He is a peaceable, friendly, modest man, with a faculty for laughter. A critic remarked that his non-metric work is written in "a poet's prose with a subtle and sometimes un-English humor underlying everything the author says." His great literary admiration is for Thomas Hardy. In time of peace he hunts and plays tennis; but his principal recreation is music.

PRINCIPAL WORKS: *Poetry*—Twelve Sonnets, 1911; Melodies, 1913; An Ode for Music, 1914; Hyacinth, 1915; Apollo in Doelyrium, 1916; The Old Huntsman, 1917; Counter-Attack, 1918; Collected War Poems, 1919; Picture Show, 1920; Recreations, 1923; Lingual Exercises for Advanced Vocabularians, 1925; Satirical Poems, 1926; Poems, 1926; The Road to Ruin, 1933; Vigils, 1935; Rhymed Ruminations, 1939; Poems Newly Selected 1916-1935, 1940. *Prose*—Memoirs of a Fox-Hunting Man, 1928; Memoirs of an Infantry Officer, 1930; Sherston's Progress, 1936; The Old Century and Seven More Years (autobiography) 1938; On Poetry, 1939; Flower Show Match and Other Pieces, 1941; The Weald of Youth, 1942.

ABOUT: Darton, F. J. H. From Surtees to Sassoon; Powell, D. Descent From Parnassus; Sassoon, S. The Old Century and Seven More Years; London Mercury June 1929; Newsweek January 9, 1939; Saturday Review of Literature May 3, 1941; Spectator March 21, 1931.

SAUNDERS, HILARY AIDAN ST. GEORGE. See "BEEDING, F."

*SAUNDERS, MARSHALL (April 13, 1861-), Canadian story-teller, writes:

"I was born [Margaret Marshall Saunders] near Liverpool, N.S., the daughter of the Rev. Edward M. Saunders and Maria K. (Freeman) Saunders, descended on both sides from Mayflower Pilgrims. My father's parish was in the Annapolis Valley, near the home of Evangeline. When I was six he was called to a Baptist church in Halifax. I was educated there and in Edinburgh and Orleans, France, returning to Canada in 1879. My father encouraged me to write, saying I 'had some talent.' Then one day I met that king of dogs, Beautiful Joe, spent six months with him and his family, and wrote a book about him. It took a prize in Boston in 1893, and ever since that old dog has been barking his way around the world. For years I wrote other books and traveled in Europe and America. Then I settled down in Toronto with my younger sister. She had her dog and I have my birds — wild ones in the shrubbery and more than two hundred tame ones in the house."

* * *

Miss Saunders was created a Commander of the Order of the British Empire in 1934. She has an honorary M.A. from Acadia University and has received many other prizes and honors. Domestic animals of all sorts are her passion. *Beautiful Joe,* her best known book, has been translated into many languages. She has never married. Though she has done no writing since 1927, she is still active, in spite of a serious illness at seventy-eight—tall and erect, with beautiful white hair. Faith Fenton said of her: "Through her terse Anglo-Saxon phrases grows a passion of sympathy."

PRINCIPAL WORKS: Beautiful Joe, 1894; Daisy, 1894; Charles and His Lamb, 1896; For the Other Boy's Sake and Other Stories, 1896; The House of Armour, 1897; Rose à Charlitte (novel) 1898; Deficient Saints, A Tale of Maine, 1899; Her Sailor, 1899; For His Country, 1900; Tilda Jane, 1901; Beautiful Joe's Paradise, 1902; The Story of the Graveleys, 1903; Nita, 1904; Princess Sukey, 1905; Alpatok: The Story of an Eskimo Dog, 1906; My Pets, 1908; Tilda Jane's Orphans, 1909; The Girl From Vermont, 1910; Pussy Blackface, 1912; The Wandering Dog, 1914; Golden Dicky, 1919; Bonnie Prince Fetlar, 1920; Jimmie Gold Coast, 1923; Esther de Warren, 1927.

ABOUT: Kunitz, S. J. & Haycraft H. (eds.). The Junior Book of Authors; Canadian Bookman November 1930, April 1931.

SAURAT, DENIS (1890-), French university professor and literary critic, was born in Toulouse and educated in Lille, also becoming an Agrégé de l'Université and Docteur ès Lettres in Paris. In 1918-19 Saurat was a lecturer in the French Department of the University of Glasgow, and the following year was lecturer in English language and literature at the

* Died February 15, 1947.

University of Bordeaux, receiving his appointment as professor in 1922 and remaining until 1924, when he went to London as delegate of the Universities of Paris and Lille to the Institut Français du Royaume Uni. For the next two years he was director in London of this French Institute of the United Kingdom. Blake and Milton have been the subjects of his most extensive study. *The Three Conventions: Metaphysical Dialogues* (1926) has a preface by A. R. Orage, editor of the *New Age,* who wrote: "Ten years ago his contributions to the *New Age* acquainted English readers with the fact that a notable thinker, with an astonishing grasp of English, had appeared in France, and as, one by one, his various studies appeared, it was evident that Professor Saurat's process of Becoming was the phenomenon of a Reality which sooner or later would demand expression in a Metaphysic." Saurat himself wrote: "The psychologist states facts, the metaphysician hypotheses, the poet mere possibilities. Every man has in himself those three Intelligences."

Most of his books have appeared in English translation and have been favorably reviewed. Dorothy Bolton translated *La Littérature et L'Occultisme* as *Literature and Occult Tradition.* Saurat was appointed Professor of French Language and Literature at London University in 1933, and lives in London. Mme. Saurat was Ella Boquet-Smith of Muswell Hill; they have a son and three daughters. As a return compliment to his former editor, Professor Saurat has edited, with Herbert Read, the *Selected Essays and Critical Writings* of A. R. Orage. He is a Chevalier de la Légion d'Honneur.

Since the fall of France in 1940, Saurat has published several pamphlets on the French problem, one of them, *Regeneration: a Doctrine for True Frenchmen,* preceded by a letter from General de Gaulle.

WORKS AVAILABLE IN ENGLISH TRANSLATION: Blake and Milton, 1920; Milton: Man and Thinker, 1925; The Three Conventions: Metaphysical Dialogues, 1926; Blake and Modern Thought, 1929; Literature and Occult Tradition, 1930; A History of Religions, 1934; Perspectives, 1938; The End of Fear, 1938; Christ at Chartres, 1940; French War Aims, 1940; Regeneration, 1940; The Spirit of France, 1940; Watch Over Africa, 1941.

ABOUT: Fortnightly Review April 1940; International Who's Who; Saurat, D. The Three Conventions (See Preface by A. R. Orange).

SAWYER, RUTH (August 5, 1880-), American short-story writer and writer for children, remarks: "One has to be born; I was, in Boston. My father was Francis

Milton Sawyer, my mother. Ethelinda J. Smith, of old Lexington stock. Went to private school in New York City—Annie C. Brackett's; then to Packer Institute, Brooklyn and the Garland Kindergarten Training School in Boston; and then to Cuba to help organize kindergartens. Finished with a scholarship at Columbia University—degree B.S. in Education. Had an itinerant position on the New York *Sun* doing feature articles. Went to Ireland on commission, and started collecting folktales.

Have been collecting them ever since. Began professional story-telling for the New York Public Lecture Bureau, under Dr. Henry M. Leipziger. Finally got married in 1911—husband, Albert C. Durand, M.D. We have a son and a daughter—both a great improvement on their parents.

"Began writing Irish folktales for the *Outlook* (then edited by Lyman Abbott) and the *Atlantic Monthly.* Since then have contributed some two hundred short stories, articles, poems, and serials to current magazines. My book, *Roller Skates,* won the Newbery Award in 1937. *The Primrose Ring* was made into a silent picture by Paramount, and Morosco put on *Seven Miles to Arden* as a play. One of my short stories went into one of the O. Henry Prize volumes.

"As a family we take to the water, sailing and running a cruiser. I was born a Unitarian. I am still writing, and spend three-fourths of the year lecturing and telling stories. Also am becoming a good printer. My permanent address since my marriage has been Ithaca, N.Y."

PRINCIPAL WORKS: The Primrose Ring, 1915; Seven Miles to Arden, 1916; Myself, 1917; A Child's Year Book, 1917; Doctor Danny, 1918; Leerie, 1920; The Silver Sixpence, 1921; Gladiola Murphy, 1923; Tale of the Enchanted Bunnies, 1923; This Way to Christmas, 1924; Four Ducks on a Pond, 1928; Folk House, 1932; Tono Antonio, 1934; The Luck of the Road, 1934; Gallant, 1936; Picture Tales From Spain, 1936; Roller Skates, 1936; The Year of Jubilo, 1940; The Way of the Storyteller, 1942.

ABOUT: National Education Association Journal November 1937; Library Journal July 1937; Publishers' Weekly June 26, 1937.

*SAXON, LYLE (September 4, 1891-), American novelist, short-story writer, and writer on Southern life, was born in Baton Rouge, La., the son of Hugh Saxon and

* Died April 9, 1946.

Katherine (Chambers) Saxon, and was brought up on a plantation of 4,000 acres, where there were six to eight "white folks" and three hundred and sixty Negroes. A quarter-mile from the house was the front gate, before the gate was the road, "then the levee, and beyond—the Mississippi River." "I remember the plantation — Yea, Lord! Oh, how well do I remember the plantation," wrote Saxon in *Father Mississippi*. "I lived there in summer, but in winter I had to go to school in town. Not that I liked school less, but I loved the plantation more. It was like heaven, I thought, a perfect place."

Saxon received his B.A. in 1912 from Louisiana State University, and went at once into newspaper work in New Orleans and Chicago. From 1918 to 1926 he was a feature writer on the New Orleans *Times-Picayune*, contributing many of the articles which were later to form chapters in the books which have caused him to be called "the new chronicler of the South." When Saxon lived in New Orleans, he bought a house on Royal Street and furnished it to suit his tastes. It was three stories high, with wrought-iron balconies and a charming patio, all quite typical of the French Quarter when the French Quarter was New Orleans. Much of his writing has been done in a remote cabin on the Cane River several miles from Natitoches. While Saxon was working on his first book, *Father Mississippi*, the May 1927 flood ensued, and he was commissioned by the *Century Magazine* to cover the story. For three months he was engaged in actually receiving and caring for refugees. Three articles on his flood-time experiences contributed to the *Century* were later incorporated in *Father Mississippi*, a mellow chronicle of the river's legends and history. Saxon admits that his primary interest is in writing fiction. He had stories chosen for the O. Henry Memorial Award in 1926 and for E. J. O'Brien's *Best Short Stories* the next year, and ten years later produced a full-length novel, *Children of Strangers* (1937), concerning a mulatto colony, descendants of the French, who live in the plantation country of Louisiana and form a caste midway between the whites and Negroes. The London *Times* commented on the novel's "unusual poise and authentic

tragic beauty," and George Stevens (a Georgian) called it "a simple story, but as genuine and moving as it is unpretentious." In recent years Lyle Saxon has been Louisiana state director of the Federal Writers' Projects, Works Progress Administration, compiling the Louisiana section of the *American Guide*. He is a member of P.E.N. His time is divided between Melrose, La., and the St. Charles Hotel in New Orleans. Saxon has been called "a bon vivant, a bibliophile, a raconteur, a conversationalist, an artist with a jigger of absinthe, a lazy man, and a writer without an enemy."

PRINCIPAL WORKS: Father Mississippi, 1927; Fabulous New Orleans, 1928; Old Louisiana, 1929; La Fitte: The Pirate, 1930; Children of Strangers, 1937.

ABOUT: St. Nicholas April 1929; Wilson Library Bulletin December 1929.

SAYERS, DOROTHY LEIGH (1893-   ), English writer and anthologist of detective fiction, the inventor of Lord Peter Wimsey, was born in Eastern England, the daughter of the Rev. H. Sayers, sometime headmaster of the Cathedral Choir School, Oxford, and Helen May (Leigh) Sayers, great-niece of Percival Leigh, "the Professor" of *Punch*. One of the first

women to obtain an Oxford degree (Somerville College 1915), she attained first honors in medieval literature. Somerville gave her the background for the imaginary woman's college in her novel *Gaudy Night*, as she was to utilize (in *Murder Must Advertise*) her later experience as a first-line copywriter in a leading London advertising agency. Similarly, the East-Anglian fen country in which she grew up reappears as the setting of *The Nine Tailors*, a remarkable study of campanology which is regarded by many readers as her finest achievement. A volume of verse and another of *Catholic Tales* preceded her first detective novel, *Whose Body?* (1923), in which the affluent young nobleman-detective, Lord Peter Wimsey, made his first and rather affected although efficient appearance. Bunter, his somewhat Jeeves-like "man," is to Wimsey what Polton is to R. Austin Freeman's Dr. Thorndyke; the C.I.D. Inspector, Parker, who eventually marries Wimsey's sister, alternates denseness with intelligence as the essential Watson.

SCARBOROUGH

In 1926 Miss Sayers married Captain Oswald Atherton Fleming a well-known war correspondent, and published (keeping her maiden name) her second detective story, *Clouds of Witness*, in which Lord Peter successfully defends his brother, the Duke of Denver, a stupid and chivalrous peer, when the latter is accused of murder. *Strong Poison* (1930) introduced Harriet Vane, a lady novelist accused of murdering her lover, whose name Lord Peter, assisted by Miss Katherine Alexandria Climpson, the garrulous chief of what he called his Cattery, succeeded in clearing. Wimsey then served the Biblical seven years (and a series of novels) before persuading Harriet to marry him; their hymeneal transports are celebrated in *Busman's Honeymoon*.

In addition to her original works, Miss Sayers has won first rank among detective story anthologists with her three monumental *Omnibuses of Crime* (in England: *Great Short Stories of Detection, Mystery, and Horror*). Lately, her own narratives have illustrated the current English trend toward the amalgamation of the detective story and the "legitimate" novel; but in the opinion of many readers and critics she has been less successful in this laudable object than some of her younger compatriots in the field—chiefly, these same critics say, because of an unfortunate and increasing quality of preciousness in her writing. John Strachey somewhat caustically remarked in 1939: "[Miss Sayers] has now almost ceased to be a first-rate detective story writer and has become an exceedingly snobbish popular novelist. She was, at her best, a real master of the detective story. Miss Sayers was able to make her [earlier] Lord Peter stories, such as *Murder Must Advertise* and *The Nine Tailors*, glow with a vitality which, in spite of their absurdities, justify her vast success." At an earlier date the *Spectator* said: "Miss Sayers writes good English—a rare quality among detective writers; she has a fine sense of humor and a genius for creating the most unexpected situations."

Miss Sayers, a cheerful, gregarious lady, lives today with her husband in rural England near her girlhood home, and owns as her chief recreations motor-cycling and reading other writers' detective stories. She now publishes less frequently than formerly, and detection has somewhat given way among her interests to experiments in neo-medieval religious drama. But she is still a bright particular star of the Detection Club of London, and has earned the gratitude of serious students of detective story history as

1238

much for her masterly critical introduction to the first *Omnibus of Crime* as for a number of superlative tales in her own right. For all the criticism that has been directed at her works, her faults are on the side of generosity and she remains one of the four or five most literate and accomplished living writers of detective fiction.

PRINCIPAL WORKS: *Detective Stories*—Whose Body? 1923; Clouds of Witness, 1926; Unnatural Death (U.S. title: The Dawson Pedigree) 1927; The Unpleasantness at the Bellona Club, 1928; Lord Peter Views the Body, 1928; Strong Poison, 1930; The Documents in the Case (with R. Eustace) 1930; Five Red Herrings (U.S. title: Suspicious Characters) 1931; Have His Carcase, 1932; Hangman's Holiday, 1933; Murder Must Advertise, 1933; The Nine Tailors, 1934; Gaudy Night, 1935; Busman's Honeymoon, 1937; In the Teeth of the Evidence, 1939. *Miscellaneous*—Op. 1 (verse) 1916; Catholic Tales, 1919; Busman's Honeymoon, (play, with M. St. C. Byrne) 1936; The Zeal of Thy House (drama) 1937; The Devil To Pay (drama) 1939; He That Should Come (drama) 1939; Begin Here: A War-Time Essay, 1940; The Mind of the Maker, 1942: *Editor*—Great Short Stories of Detection, Mystery, and Horror (U.S. title: The Omnibus of Crime) 1928; Great Short Stories of Detection, Mystery, and Horror: Second Series (U.S. title: The Second Omnibus of Crime) 1931; Great Short Stories of Detection, Mystery, and Horror: Third Series (U.S. title: The Third Omnibus of Crime) 1934; Tales of Detection (Everyman's Library) 1936.

ABOUT: Haycraft, H. Murder for Pleasure: The Life and Times of the Detective Story; Thomson, H. D. Masters of Mystery; Saturday Review of Literature January 7, 1939.

SCARBOROUGH, DOROTHY (1877-November 7, 1935), American novelist, folklorist, and educator was born at Mount Carmel, Texas, the daughter of Judge John B. Scarborough and Mary Adelaide (Ellison) Scarborough. George Scarborough, dramatist, writer of *Moonlight and Honeysuckle* and *The Lure*, is her brother. Miss Scarborough, who never  married, obtained her bachelor's and master's degrees from Baylor University, Waco; taught English there from 1905 to 1914, becoming assistant professor in 1916; studied at the University of Chicago, and spent a year at Oxford. Baylor gave her an honorary Litt.D. in 1923, chiefly for her work in collecting mountain ballads and Negro folksongs.

Columbia granted Dr. Scarborough her Ph.D. in 1917 for one of the most entertaining dissertations ever to come out of graduate school, *The Supernatural in Modern English Fiction,* still in print after more than twenty years and still the most authoritative work in its field. Montague Rhodes James is her one inexplicable omission. The book is supplemented by two collections of ghost stories, one of them humorous. Dr. Scarborough was, in turn, instructor, lecturer, assistant professor, and associate professor at Columbia, where her courses in short-story writing were popular and produced such writers as Tess Slesinger and Myron Brinig.

Her novels were not in the moonlight and honeysuckle tradition; *In The Land of Cotton* is a story of hopeless struggle against boll-weevils and other pests, and *The Wind,* first published anonymously, was made into an effective silent-film tragedy with Lillian Gish. Dr. Scarborough died in her Morningside Drive apartment after a short illness. A small woman, young at fifty-eight, with charm and delightful humor, she was always hospitable to young talent.

PRINCIPAL WORKS: Fugitive Verses, 1912; The Supernatural in Modern English Fiction, 1917; From a Southern Porch, 1919; In the Land of Cotton, 1923; On the Trail of Negro Folk-Songs, 1925; The Wind, 1925; Impatient Griselda, 1927; Can't Get a Red Bird, 1929; The Stretch-berry Smile, 1932; The Story of Cotton, 1933; A Song Catcher in Southern Mountains, 1937.

ABOUT: New York Times November 8, 1935.

SCHAUFFLER, ROBERT HAVEN

(April 8, 1879-   ), American poet, essayist, musical biographer, and anthologist, was born in Brucnn, Austria, of American parents, the Rev. Henry A. Schauffler, D.D., and Clara Eastham (Gray) Schauffler, who were missionaries. He arrived in the United States as an infant of two, and seventeen years later was a student at Northwestern University (1898-99); his B.A. degree came from Princeton in 1902. For the next year Schauffler was a student at the University of Berlin. He also studied the 'cello with Steindel, Schroeder and Hekking.

In December 1904 Schauffler married Katharine de Normandie Wilson in London. She died in May 1916. At Princeton Schauffler had edited the *Nassau Literary Magazine,* and in 1903-04 he was made music editor of the *Independent.* He was a special contributor to *Collier's Weekly* in Italy and Greece, in 1906; to the *Century* and *Outlook* in Germany, in 1907; and to *Success* in the West in 1909 and 1910. For the next three years he served in a similar capacity for the *Atlantic Monthly,* the *Metropolitan Magazine,* and *Century Magazine.* In 1906 he received a decoration from the Queen of Italy for winning the national tennis championship (doubles) in Rome, and that same year played in the Athenian Olympic games. In 1931 he was the winner of the Austrian handicap tennis doubles. His versatility was further demonstrated when he exhibited as an amateur sculptor at exhibitions of the National Sculpture Society.

Schauffler has been a practicing musician as well as a writer on musical topics: from 1906 to 1909 he and his wife joined with the blind violinist Edwin Grasse to form the Grasse Trio. *Beethoven: The Man Who Freed Music* (1929), four years in the writing, has sold more than 60,000 copies, a record sale in America for any serious book of musical biography. Its abridgement is *The Mad Musician: A Shorter Life of Beethoven* (1931). During the First World War Schauffler served as an instructor in the Officers' Training School at Camp Meade, Md., from January to April 1918; was commissioned a first lieutenant in June; went to France with the 79th Division; and was severely wounded before Montfaucon September 26, in the Meuse-Argonne offensive. The wound, strangely enough, was similar to the one described in "The White Comrade," first published in 1916, one of the best-known poems of the war. He received the Order of the Purple Heart, "for military merit."

Schauffler first took notice of books in Cleveland; the public library was "a most kindly nurse which saw [him] safe from kilts to long trousers and from Palmer Cox to Robert Louis Stevenson." "I dote upon librarians in general," he remarks, "and librarians love me like a brother. I have saved them a million hours of running around"— chiefly to find the holiday material now conveniently collected in his twenty-eight volumes of poetry and prose anthologies. Schauffler, whose ingratiating books reflect his personality, is a member of the Colonial (Princeton), Authors' (London), and Players (New York) clubs. He lives in a book-lined apartment high up in a Greenwich Village apartment house in New York City.

PRINCIPAL WORKS: Where Speech Ends, 1906; Romantic Germany, 1909; The Musical Amateur, 1911; Scum o' the Earth and Other Poems, 1912;

Romantic America, 1913; The Joyful Heart, 1914;
Fiddler's Luck, 1920 (revised, 1941); The White
Comrade and Other Poems, 1920; Magic Flame
and Other Poems, 1923; Peter Pantheism, 1925;
The Science of Practice, 1927; Music as a Social
Force in America, 1927; Who's Who in the
Orchestra, 1927; Hobnails in Eden (poems) 1929;
Beethoven: The Man Who Freed Music, 1929;
The Mad Musician: A Shorter Life of Beethoven,
1931; The Unknown Brahms: His Life, Character
and Works, Based on New Material, 1933; Enjoy
Living, 1939; New and Selected Poems, 1942. *Editor*
—Thanksgiving, 1907; Christmas, 1907; Through
Italy With the Poets, 1908; Lincoln's Birthday,
1909; Arbor Day, 1909; Washington's Birthday,
1910; Memorial Day, 1911; Flag Day, 1912; Independence Day, 1912; Mother's Day, 1915; Easter,
1916; The Poetry Cure, 1925; Armistice Day,
1927; The Poetry Cure With Music and Pictures,
1927; Plays for Our American Holidays (4 vols.)
1928; Little Plays for Little People, 1929; The
Magic of Books, 1929; Graduation Day, 1930;
A Manthology, 1931; The Junior Poetry Cure,
1931; Hallowe'en, 1933; The Magic of Music, 1935;
The Days We Celebrate (4 vols.) 1940.
Days We Celebrate (4 vols.) 1940.

ABOUT: Schauffler, R. H. Fiddler's Luck (see
Introduction by D. C. Fisher in 1941 ed.).

*SCHELLING, FELIX EMANUEL
(September 3, 1858-   ), American scholar
and critic, was born in New Albany, Ind., the

son of Felix and Rose
(White) Schelling.
He was the much
older brother of Ern-
est H. Schelling, the
pianist, composer, and
conductor, who died
in 1939. He was edu-
cated at the Univer-
sity of Pennsylvania
(B.A. 1881, LL.B.
1883, M.A. 1884),
and has honorary doctorates from Pennsylvania, Princeton, and Haverford. He was
John Welsh Centennial Professor of English Literature at Pennsylvania from 1893
to 1929, and since then has been Felix E.
Schelling Professor, the chair having been
founded in his name. He still holds this
position officially, though in recent years he
has done little teaching.

Professor Schelling is one of the greatest living authorities on Elizabethan literature and on the Tudor period generally.
From the many generations of graduate
students he has taught at Pennsylvania—
and he was a provocative and stimulating
teacher—have come some of the country's
foremost specialists in this field. His interests are indicated by his membership in the
National Institute of Arts and Letters, the
American Philosophical Society, and the
Modern Language Association of America.

In 1886 he married Caroline Derbyshire,
and they have a son and a daughter. After
his virtual retirement he went to live in Lum-
berville, Pa., his present home. He no longer
does much writing, but in spite of a major
operation at the age of eighty-one, he is still
fairly active and is still a student. Slender
and gray-haired, he is in appearance a "typical professor," but there is nothing absent-
minded about his dry wit and his keen
mentality.

Besides his own books of criticism, Dr.
Schelling has edited many of Shakespeare's
plays and other Elizabethan dramas and
lyrics. He contributed the article on Restoration Drama to the *Cambridge History of
Literature.*

PRINCIPAL WORKS: Literary and Verse Crit-
icism of the Reign of Elizabeth, 1891; Life and
Works of George Gascoigne, 1893; A Book of
Elizabethan Lyrics, 1896; A Book of Seventeenth
Century Lyrics, 1899; The English Chronicle
Play, 1902; The Queen's Progress and Other
Elizabethan Sketches, 1904; History of Elizabethan Drama, 1908; English Literature During
the Lifetime of Shakespeare, 1910; The English
Lyric, 1913; A History of English Drama, 1914;
Thor and Other War Verses, 1918; Appraisements
and Asperities As to Some Contemporary Writers, 1922; Foreign Influences in Elizabethan Plays,
1923; Elizabethan Playwrights, 1925; Shakespeare
and "Demi-Science," 1927; Shakespeare Biography,
1927; Pedagogically Speaking, 1929.

ABOUT: University of Pennsylvania: Felix E.
Schelling.

SCHICKELE, RENÉ (August 4, 1883-
January 31, 1940), German novelist, poet,
playwright and publicist, was born in
Oberehnheim, Alsace, of a German father,
Anton Schickele, and a French mother,
Marie Férard. René attended the Zabern
Gymnasium and later Strassburg University. His literary career began with two
brochures of verse, *Sommernachte* (1901)
and *Pan* (1902). In 1902 he founded in
Strassburg the magazine *Der Stürme.* In
1904 Schickele married Anna Brandenburg
and settled in Berlin, devoting a great deal
of his time to his newly established magazine *Das Neue Magazine* (1904-05) and to
his poetry. In 1905 he published another
sheaf of poems, *Mon Repos,* which he added
to the other two to form his bigger volume,
Der Ritt ins Leben (1905).

Der Fremde (1907) was Schickele's earliest experiment in the field of the novel—
it derived from Maurice Barrès' *The Uprooted*—"yet the resemblance," as Thomas
Mann pointed out, "lies less in the affinity of
the spirit than in the common quality of
concrete human things." Schickele did not
feel confident and returned to poetry in

* Died December 15, 1945.

Weiss und Rot (1910) and *Die Leibwache* (1914) and tried the short story in *Meine Freundin Lo* (1912).

In 1914 he published another novel, *Benkal der Frauentröster*, "a prophetic picture of the War, written before it began" and exposing all its idiocies so sharply that, as Jethro Bithell says, "it would alone have made him an outlaw in Germany." In 1914 Franz Blei founded in Berlin the expressionist review *Die Weissen Blätter*; in December of that year Schickele succeeded him as editor. With the intensification of the war, a group of writers left Germany and settled in Zurich: among them was Schickele who made of his magazine a rallying point for anti-militarist, anti-imperialist thought. In *Die Weissen Blätter* Leonhard Frank, Kafka, Sternheim, and Werfel were for the first time presented to a wide public, and contributions appeared by Klabund and Heinrich Mann, by the Socialists Landauer and Rubiner, by the French writers Barbusse, Duhamel, and Vaillant Couturier. From Davos a wounded officer, Andreas Latzko, sent to its editor *Men at War* for serialization.

Schickele was stunned by grief over the misery of Europe, "the fratricidal tragedy of the two nations, to both of which he was bound by blood and spirit." The warring antagonisms met in him: his native Alsace stood between France and Germany, he was the son of a German father and a French mother who understood not a word of German; he himself thought and felt in French but spoke and wrote in German. This conflict was reflected in *Hans im Schnakenloch* (*Hans of the Mosquito Hole*), the Peer Gynt of Alsace. The play dramatized the feelings of a family living on an Alsatian estate and differing among themselves as to whether they are French or German. The poignancy of the situation is heightened by the fact that the estate changes hands—now French, now German—in the course of the action. Although completed in October 1914, Schickele's play was not produced until December 16, 1916, at Frankfurt on the Main, where after its 92d performance it was banned by the military censor for its pacifist trend. Considered "a piece of German war propaganda," it met a similar fate in France.

After the war and the revolution of 1918, Schickele greeted the young republic in Berlin but shortly thereafter withdrew to Badenweiler, a quiet retreat in the Black Forest, overlooking the plain of Alsace. Here in the course of the next few years he wrote "The Rhineland Heritage," a trilogy comprising *Maria Capponi* (1925),

Heart of Alsace (1927), and *Der Wolf in der Hürde* (1931). Thomas Mann says that this trilogy "can stand forever as a standard work, written with the fine and firm hand of an artist, a classic of Alsatian country and soul. It put him where he has ever since remained, in the front rank of German literature."

After the Nazi *coup* Schickele found his way to France—even before 1933 he would spend days and weeks wandering in Provence—while his books were banned throughout Germany. He died near Nice at the age of fifty-seven from the asthma which plagued him for decades. Shortly before his death he set down his beliefs in the face of the Hitler aggression, which he termed "a World Civil War." "For the first time in my life I am a conformist and feel myself to be wholly on the right side. I *believe*, as Pasteur wished he might, with all the power and endurance of a Breton peasant. I believe in our right cause and in our victory."

Of René Schickele Thomas Mann wrote: "We Germans have reason to rejoice that we may count this writer ours because in our prose literature his books have an absolutely extraordinary quality of wit and grace which betray their French heritage, while their closeness to nature, an intimate union with earth and landscape that reaches into the realm of Pan, represent their German side and lend both depth and weight to their lightness, and even cast a demonic atmosphere around their wit."

AVAILABLE IN TRANSLATION: Maria Capponi, 1928; Heart of Alsace, 1929.

ABOUT: Bertaux, F. Panorama of Modern German Literature; Bithell, J. Modern German Literature; Eloesser, A. Modern German Literature; Samuel, R. & Hinton Thomas, R. Expressionism in German Life, Literature, and the Theatre; Books March 4, 1928, February 10, 1929; Commune June 1939; Europe Nouvelle February 25, 1939; New Statesman May 5, 1928; New York Times March 18, 1928, March 3, 1929, May 26, 1940; Spectator March 31, 1928; August 31, 1929; Times (London) Literary Supplement May 3, 1928.

SCHIFF, SYDNEY. See HUDSON, S.

SCHLESINGER, ARTHUR MEIER (February 27, 1888-), American historian, writes: "I was born in the rural Ohio town of Xenia, the youngest child of parents who had migrated from Germany some twenty years before. My boyhood was a happy one in a household that loved books and among school friends who loved the outdoors. After going through the Xenia public schools I went on to the state university fifty miles away. There, in due course, I became editor of the college newspaper, and for a time thought I was headed for a career in journalism. But the example of some of my professors persuaded me that it was my destiny to report the events of the past, not of the present. Graduating in 1910 and securing a fellowship at Columbia University, I proceeded there for advanced training in history under Osgood, Robinson, and Beard. Eventually I received my Ph.D. in 1918, but meantime, in 1912, I had begun my teaching career at the Ohio State University.

Bachrach

Since 1919 I have taught at the State University of Iowa and at Harvard, where I have been since 1924. In 1914 I married Elizabeth Bancroft; we have two sons. The only real interruption of this uneventful career occurred in 1933-34, when I took my family on a year's trip round the world.

"I have always enjoyed historical research and writing and have produced a modest number of books. I early became dissatisfied with the view that history is merely past politics, and in my writing and teaching I have done all I could to disseminate the idea that history should be as inclusive as life itself. Since example is more potent than precept, I joined Dixon Ryan Fox in 1927 in editing a collaborative twelve-volume work, *A History of American Life,* which, I believe, has exerted a strong missionary influence in the intended direction. My *Colonial Merchants and the American Revolution* won the Justin Winsor Prize of the American Historical Association in 1918.

"I have been fortunate in my teachers, my friends, and my students, and to them I attribute any success I may have attained. Politically I have always been an independent, but in practice this has usually caused me to vote the Democratic national ticket."

PRINCIPAL WORKS: A Syllabus of United States History (with H. C. Hockett) 1915; The Colonial Merchants and the American Revolution, 1918; Salmon Portland Chase, 1919; New Viewpoints in American History, 1922; Political and Social History of the United States, 1925; A New Syllabus of American History (with H. C. Hockett) 1925; The Rise of the City, 1933; Political and Social Growth of the United States, 1933; The New Deal in Action, 1938.

SCHLOSS, ARTHUR DAVID. See WALEY, A.

SCHMITT, BERNADOTTE EVERLY (May 19, 1886-   ), American historian and winner of the Pulitzer Prize, writes: "Bernadotte Schmitt was born in Strasburg, Va., the son of Cooper Davis Schmitt and Rose Vernon (Everly) Schmitt. Two ancestors on each side of the family fought in the War of the American Revolution, two more in the War of 1812; both grandfathers served in the Confederate Army in the Civil War. Cooper D. Schmitt was professor of mathematics in the University of Tennessee from 1889 to his death in 1910 and dean of the college from 1907 to 1910.

"Bernadotte Schmitt was graduated from the University of Tennessee in 1904 and the next year went to Oxford as the second Rhodes Scholar from Tennessee. He received the B.A. from Oxford in 1908, gaining a First Class in Modern History. The next two years were spent at the University of Wisconsin, from which he received the Ph.D. degree in 1910.

"From 1910 to 1924 he taught at Western Reserve University; in the latter year he transferred to the University of Chicago as professor of modern history. Since 1939 he has been Andrew MacLeish Distinguished Service Professor of modern history. From 1932 to 1936 he was chairman of the department of history; since 1929 he has edited the *Journal of Modern History,* published by the University of Chicago Press.

"Schmitt has taught in various summer sessions. Twice he served as a round table leader at the now defunct Institute of Politics of Williams College (1925, 1932). In 1931-32 he was professor of diplomatic history at the Institut Universitaire des Hautes Études Internationales in Geneva. In 1927 he was awarded a Guggenheim Fellowship. Since 1937 he has been a Fellow of the American Academy of Arts and Sciences.

"He has traveled extensively since returning from Oxford: in Europe in 1913, 1920-21, 1925, 1928, 1929, 1931-32, 1935, 1937; in the Far East in 1935, returning to Europe via Siberia. Altogether he has visited thirty countries and forty-three States of the Union.

"Apart from teaching, his chief interest has been writing. The first book, *England and Germany: 1740-1914,* appeared in 1916 and set the course for the future. After the last war the opening of foreign office archives made possible the rewriting of the diplomatic history of Europe prior to 1914, and Schmitt devoted some years to this task. In 1930 he published two volumes entitled *The Coming of the War: 1914*, which was awarded the George Louis Beer Prize of the American Historical Association for 1930 and the Pulitzer Prize for history in 1931. At present he is preparing a volume of the War of 1914-18, as well as a study of American neutrality from 1914 to 1917. Other contributions include a chapter in *The Cambridge History of Poland* (1941) and a chapter on Munich in *Czecho-Slovakia: Twenty Years of Independence* (1940).

"His avocations are motoring and stamp-collecting. In 1939 he married Damaris Kathryn Ames of Chicago."

* * *

The Coming of the War placed most of the onus of the First World War on the Central Powers. Winston Churchill called it "a masterly book, which made the anti-Versaillists sick at heart," but it was unfavorably reviewed by Harry Elmer Barnes and was made the subject of a full-length retort, *Germany Not Guilty in 1914*, by M. H. Cochran, a Harvard Ph.D.

PRINCIPAL WORKS: England and Germany: 1740-1914, 1916; The Coming of the War: 1914, 1930; Triple Alliance and Triple Entente, 1934; The Annexation of Bosnia: 1908-09, 1937; From Versailles to Munich: 1918-1938, 1939. *Editor*— Some Historians of Modern Europe, 1942.

ABOUT: Cochran, M. H. Germany Not Guilty in 1914.

SCHMITZ, ETTORE. See SVEVO, I.

SCHNEIDER, ISIDOR (August 25, 1896-), American poet and novelist, writes: "I remember nothing of my birth-

place, Horodenko, a small town in Western Ukraine, then in Austro - Hungary, later in Poland, and now in the Soviet Ukraine. I arrived in this country at the age of five.

"My father was a man's tailor, but mass production had practically eliminated his trade; he turned to ladies' tailoring, which soon also went under as a trade. He tried a number of other ways of earning a living, chiefly running little cleaning and pressing stores, all without success. I was one of five children. The fact that my elder brother went to work made it possible for me to go to college (College of the City of New York), though I earned my way by teaching English to foreigners, helping out in my father's store, and working during summer vacations.

"The one thing I wanted most during my growing years was to escape the sort of life I was living. In my writing I went headlong into fantasy. It was not till many years had passed that I was able to look at the years of my childhood without aversion, and to recall that alongside the privations and the overhanging dread there had been courage to see, and endurance and patience and the constant generosity toward each other of workers, expressed in their wonderful neighborliness common in all trades and in all nationalities. For a long time I looked away from my past, which I would have had to re-enter if I wanted to write realistically.

"My first book was *Dr. Transit*, a fantastic novel in which the scientist hero was simultaneously idealized as the man with power to change the world, satirized because he failed to exercise his power, and Satanized as the arch-realist. In my first book of poems, *The Temptation of Anthony*, the title poem was part of a projected and still unfinished fiction, *The Temple*, which is part poetry and part prose and set out to be a sort of biography of God, that is, the successive goals of man's creative longings.

"All my experience of life, in later happier times as well as in my childhood, made me feel that social changes to eliminate want and insecurity were necessary before a defensible culture could develop in our mechanized world. After 1929 this was the almost unanimous sense of American writers, the exceptions being the few who for some strange reasons found beauty in a landscape of human ruins, or found order in it, since order meant hierarchy with themselves in the upper ranks. The painful but instructive depression years turned me into a 'left' writer and a realist. I was now able to examine my own past without rigging up any mechanism of fantasy.

"In addition to novels and poems I have written short stories, some articles, and many book reviews. I have been awarded a Guggenheim Fellowship and renewal. I have traveled twice to Europe, first in 1928, staying mostly in France and again in 1937 and 1938, staying mostly in the U.S.S.R. I have made my living in publishing houses and on magazines and newspapers, writing publicity and advertising copy. I am married and have a daughter, named for Emily Dickinson."

* * *

Mr. Schneider was married in 1925 to Helen Berlin. He is a dark, genial, imposing figure with abundant wavy black hair and a heavy moustache. As he himself points out, his work can be divided into two distinct periods, the fantastic and the realistic, in both of which he has achieved marked success. With others, he edited *Proletarian Literature in the United States* (1936).

PRINCIPAL WORKS: Dr. Transit, 1926; The Temptation of Anthony and Other Poems, 1927; From the Kingdom of Necessity, 1935; Comrade, Mister (poems) 1936.

ABOUT: Bookman July 1928.

SCHNITZLER, ARTHUR (May 15. 1862-October 21, 1931), Austrian playwright, novelist, and short story writer, was  born in Vienna into a respectable upper middle-class Jewish family. His father, Dr. Johann Schnitzler, famous throat specialist, counted among his patients many celebrated dramatic and operatic stars of the Austrian capital. Influenced by the actors, Arthur began to write plays and skits early in his boyhood: at nine he completed a five-act tragedy! However, his parents preferred him to follow the medical profession. The precocious child finished his elementary studies very rapidly and in 1879, when merely seventeen, graduated from the Academic Gymnasium. He was immediately admitted to the medical faculty of the University of Vienna, but his studies did not deter him from his literary ambitions.

As soon as the young Schnitzler obtained his M.D. he practiced in various hospitals for three years and in 1886 joined his father's clinic as an assistant and reviewed books for the *Wiener Medizinische Presse,* the medical review founded in 1860 by his father. In 1887 the young Dr. Schnitzler became the editor of the *Internationale Klinische Rundschau* and soon went to London where he spent several months studying the facilities for medical education as well as hospital conditions. His observations appeared in his magazine. The following year he contributed a paper on functional aphonia and experiments with hypnotism. Schnitzler's other contributions were limited to book reviews. During all this period Schnitzler continued his literary work: playlets and stories appeared sporadically from 1880 to 1889, and later, more regularly, in a number of literary periodicals.

With Hermann Bahr, Richard Beer-Hofmann, Felix Salten, and Hugo von Hofmannsthal, Arthur Schnitzler formed in 1891 the Young Vienna group, a literary and artistic movement which through its organ, the *Moderne Rundschau,* revitalized Austrian letters. The very first production of any of Schnitzler's plays took place in February 1891. He became better known with *Anatol,* which appeared in 1893, but his reputation was not definitely established until the successful performance of *Liebelei* at the Burg-theatre on October 9, 1895. By this time Schnitzler had given up medicine entirely: his father had died in 1893, and, after editing the *Internationale Klinische Rundschau* single-handed, he withdrew in September 1894. Thus from the age of thirty-three Arthur Schnitzler devoted himself exclusively to literature.

Certain recurrent themes mark Schnitzler's fertile career, which lasted for more than a half-century. Originally his main concern seems to have been the problem of man versus woman. Schnitzler claimed that the first aim of every human being is simply the promotion of his personal happiness. To him a happy society can be based only upon happy beings. This remained his fundamental contention. However, other themes soon became discernible: death, fear of old age, skepticism, and a hatred for all forms of injustices, prejudices, and sycophancy. He was especially revolted by anti-Semitism which he encountered early at the medical school. The Jewish problem found expression in his novel *The Road to the Open* (1908) and in the tragedy *Professor Bernhardi* (1912). This note of bitterness, combined with his Freudian influence, did not permit him to hold steadfastly to any ethical or metaphysical values: Schnitzler was neither religious nor idealistic, in fact he had no faith in the future of mankind. His sole concern was the individual. By the time he reached his fortieth birthday, fear of old age and death had become his great obsession, as evidenced in his writings of the war period: *Beatrice* (1913), *Doctor Graesler* (1917), *Casanova's Homecoming* (1918), all of which were significantly collected under the title *Die Alternden:* "Those Who Grow Old."

After the war a note of rich melancholy dominated Schnitzler's writings, as if he felt despondent over the passing of the Hapsburg monarchy. With tremulous hand he wrote some of his loveliest novelettes: *Fraulein Else* (1924), *Rhapsody* (1925), and *Flight into Darkness* (1926).

Such are, in brief, the preoccupations and themes in the plays and stories of Arthur Schnitzler. This content he put forth with utmost lucidity—in a precise and clear style with terse dialogue and a keen sense of description. In order to translate certain crepuscular tones and moods he often experimented with the soliloquy and the interior monologue, especially in *Fraulein Else* and *None but the Brave*.

Schnitzler lived in a luxurious villa overlooking Vienna. There he spent the greater part of his latter years, writing in his garden or in his study, his family frequently not seeing him for days. A painful worker, he revised every page dozens of times. Sometimes he worked on as many as four or five books at once, his ideal combination being a play and a novel. When he did not dictate to his secretary he wrote standing up before an old slant desk. Biographies and history were his favorite reading. He was a great traveler, traversing all of Europe and the Orient, though he never visited America. Even in his old age he would take long walks through the open countryside round Vienna, making jottings in his notebooks of observations for future use.

In appearance Schnitzler was rather short and slightly hunched, wearing his clothes badly, but with a majestic bearing. To the end his skin was clear and his eyes were bright and alert. A well shaped beard covered his chin, and a thick moustache flourished under his aquiline nose. Though he was reticent about meeting strangers his manner was gracious and friendly. He married Fräulein Gussmann; their son, Heinrich was a highly successful theatrical producer in Vienna—until the German *anschluss*, when he came to this country, and their daughter is said to have committed suicide a year before her father's death.

Schnitzler died just as preparations had begun the world over to celebrate his seventieth anniversary. He was at the time hard at work, planning new plays, inventing new stories. He died as simply as he lived; he forbade by his will a pompous funeral, requesting that the money thus saved be distributed among the needy.

WORKS AVAILABLE IN ENGLISH TRANSLATION: *Plays*—Questioning the Irrevocable, 1903; The Lady With the Dagger, 1904 (later published as The Woman With the Dagger); The Wife, 1905; Living Hours, 1906 (later published as Vital Mo-

ments); The Duke and the Actress, 1910 (later published as The Green Cockatoo); The Legacy, 1911; Anatol, 1911; Light-o'-Love, 1912 (later published as Liebelei, The Reckoning, Flirtation, Playing With Love); The Green Cockatoo and Other Plays (The Mate, Paracelsus) 1913; Free Game, 1913; Literature, 1913; Professor Bernhardi, 1913; Gallant Cassian, 1914; The Lonely Way, Intermezzo, Countess Mizzie, 1915; The Hour of Recognition, 1916; Anatol and Other Plays (Living Hours, Green Cockatoo, The Lady With the Dagger, Last Masks, Literature) 1917; Comedies of Words and Other Plays (The Hour of Recognition, The Big Scene, The Festival of Bacchus, Literature, His Helpmate) 1917; Hands Around (Reigen) 1920; The Vast Domain, 1923; The Triple Warning, 1926; Reigen, The Affairs of Anatol (and Living Hours, The Green Cockatoo) 1933; A Farewell Supper, 1934. *Fiction*—The Road to the Open, 1913; Viennese Idylls, 1913; Bertha Garlan, 1918; Casanova's Homecoming, 1921; The Shepherd's Pipe and Other Stories, 1922; Dr. Graesler, 1923; Fräulein Else, 1925; Beatrice, 1926; None but the Brave, 1926; Rhapsody, 1927; Daybreak, 1927; Theresa, 1928; Little Novels, 1929; Flight into Darkness, 1931; Viennese Novelettes (Daybreak, Fräulein Else, Rhapsody, Beatrice, None but the Brave) 1931.

ABOUT: Boner, G. Arthur Schnitzlers Frauen Gestalten; Kapp, J. Arthur Schnitzler; Kappstein, T. H. Arthur Schnitzler und Seine Besten Bühnenwerke; Kerr, A. Gesammelte Schriften; Körner, J. Arthur Schnitzlers Gestalten und Probleme; Landsberg, H. Arthur Schnitzler; Liptzin, S. Arthur Schnitzler; Plaut, R. Arthur Schnitzler als Erzähler; Reik, T. Arthur Schnitzler als Psycholog; Salkind, A. Arthur Schnitzler; Salten, F. Gestalten und Erscheinungen; Samuel, H. B. Modernities; Specht, R. Arthur Schnitzler: Der Dichter und Sein Werk; Wiedenbrüg, H. Literarische Motive in der Erzählenden Kunst Arthur Schnitzlers; Germanic Review April 1929, January 1930; Jahrbuch Deutscher Bibliophilen und Literaturfreunde 1932-33; Journal of English and Germanic Philology 1923; Die Neue Rundschau May 1922; New Quarterly November 1909; Poet Lore Winter 1912, Winter 1928; Preussische Jahrbücher May 1927; Revue d'Allemagne May 15, 1932; Revue de Paris June 15, 1909; Southwest Review October 1919-July 1920; Texas Review July 1920.

SCHOPFER, JEAN ("Claude Anet") (May 28, 1868-January 9, 1931), Swiss-French novelist, playwright, historian, and travelwriter, was born in Morges, Switzerland, of a well-established middle-class family. "I was raised by my father, a literary man of good taste," he wrote later in life. "He had a splendid library and loved passionately Stendhal  much before he became the rage, that is before 1880. My mother was of English origin but was born and educated in France. She was openminded though extremely religious. She had the loftiest conception of duty and read Renan. She was very beautiful, Roman rather than Greek, with a cameo profile. I remember that as a child I was worried because it seemed to me that her nose was too long and I did not dare tell her."

Jean attended the Sorbonne and the École du Louvre at the same time, but besides philosophy, literature and arts, which were his specialties, he loved sports. "At that early time I believe I was the only student who thought a healthy body was worth having." In 1892 Jean Schopfer became the tennis champion of France. "One cannot predict the future of one's name from the books one writes—they pass away like leaves in autumn —but perhaps mine will survive because it is written among those of tennis champions."

After his graduation Schopfer for a while represented an American concern in Paris. Soon thereafter, as a journalist, he traveled extensively in Europe and the fruit of his Italian sojourn was his first book: *Voyage Idéal en Italie: l'Art Ancien et l'Art Moderne* (1899). With *Petite Ville* (1901), a collection of tales, Schopfer adopted the euphonious pseudonym "Claude Anet," the name of an obscure French writer of the past. After *Les Bergeries* (1904), a novel dealing with French provincial life, "Anet" motored across Persia and wrote his sensational *Through Persia in a Motor Car by Russia and the Caucasus* (1907), which was immediately translated into English and several other languages. Henceforth he became the star reporter of *Le Temps* and *Le Petit Parisien.*

At the outbreak of the First World War, *Le Petit Parisien* sent "Anet" to cover Russia, where he witnessed the revolution and the civil war; but certain indiscretions made him *persona non grata* with the Soviets and in June 1918 he fled to the Arctic. Returning to Archangel in October, he crossed in the spring through Finland and Poland to safety. His four-volume *La Révolution Russe*, which appeared during 1917-19, and of which the first volume, *Through the Russian Revolution: Notes of an Eyewitness* (1917), is available in English, was one of the earliest works dealing with that event, and claims to be an eyewitness report of all that occurred from March 1917 to Brest-Litovsk.

"Claude Anet" loved the exotic and may be considered a contemporary Pierre Loti. He translated Omar Khayyam's 144 quatrains (1920) and Pushkin's *Tale of Tsar Saltàn* (1921), and projected his knowledge of Russian life in the novels which made him famous the world over: in his colorful *Ariane* (1920), in *While the Earth Shook* (1921), dealing with the Russian revolution, and in three short stories of *L'Amour en Russie* (1922). "Anet" now turned to the theatre but with less success. *Mademoiselle Bourrat* (1923) was staged at the Théâtre des Champs Elysées after lying in a trunk for almost twenty years (it was originally a short story in *Petite Ville*); *La Fille Perdue* (1924) was performed at the Théâtre des Arts before a cold audience; and *Mayerling* had a similar reception at the Théâtre des Ambassadeurs, becoming a hit only when it was filmed after his death.

Seeking new fields of inspiration "Anet" returned to travels—in space, *Feuilles Persanes* (1924) and in time, *The End of a World* (1925), a striking novel of the Reindeer Age. He also returned to one of his early loves: tennis, reporting the famous match (February 16, 1926) between Suzanne Lenglen and Helen Wills for the *Revue de Paris*, and writing a biography of Suzanne Lenglen (1927).

"Anet's" life was extremely happy and leisurely. From 1910 until his death he kept a sumptuous mansion in Paris at the corner of rue Varenne and rue Vanneau. On his walls hung Roussels and Vuillards and portraits of his favorite writers (Stendhal, Dostoievsky, Poe) by Vallotton. Tables and bookcases were cluttered with souvenirs of his trips: Egyptian statuettes, Persian miniatures. He was married and had a daughter, "belle comme le jour," "the best job I performed during my lifetime."

WORKS AVAILABLE IN TRANSLATION: Through Persia in a Motor Car by Russia and the Caucasus, 1907; Through the Russian Revolution: Notes of an Eyewitness From 12th March-30th May, 1917; Ariane, 1927; The End of a World, 1927; While the Earth Shook, 1927; Idyll's End, 1930.

ABOUT: Treich, L. Almanach des Lettres Françaises; Vanderem, F. Le Miroir des Lettres; American Anthropologist January 28, 1927; Annales Politiques et Littéraires June 1, 1930; Books March 27, 1927, July 17, 1927, August 21, 1927; Boston Transcript July 16, 1927; L'Illustration January 24, 1931; Journal des Débats March 5, 1924; Monde Nouveau February 15, 1923; New York Evening Post September 10, 1927; New York Times March 20, 1927; June 19, 1927, August 21, 1927; Saturday Review of Literature July 16, 1927, October 29, 1927.

SCHREINER, OLIVE EMILIE ALBERTINA (March 24, 1855-December 12, 1920), South African novelist and essayist, was born at Wittebergen Mission Station, in Basutoland, the sixth of twelve children of Gottlob Schreiner, a Methodist missionary of German descent, and

Rebecca Lyndall, an Englishwoman who may have had a trace of Jewish blood. She was entirely self-educated, the place being isolated, with no facilities for schooling. She wanted to be a physician, but since that was impossible she trained herself as a nurse by reading. Even had she been able to attend a medical college (a practical impossibility for a woman at that time, even in England), her health would not have permitted, for from childhood she suffered from asthma and was otherwise frail. Instead, at fifteen she became a governess—really a nursery governess—in a Boer family living on the edge of the Karoo Desert. She herself was very ill-schooled, but she was a passionate reader and a severe self-disciplinarian, and she was still in her teens when she began her first famous book, *The Story of an African Farm*. She had early

become a Free Thinker, and in consequence was alienated from nearly all her family, particularly after her father died and her mother was converted to the Roman Catholic Church. Olive Schreiner seems to have been almost born a Rationalist, a feminist, and an extreme liberal in economics and politics.

The completed novel found no publisher, and in 1881 the girl took all her small savings and went to England to try to sell it herself. After a heart-breaking period of discouragement and loneliness, she did finally place it with Chapman & Hall, whose chief reader was George Meredith, who helped her revise it. It was published under the pseudonym of "Ralph Iron," and at once created a sensation, since it was outspokenly critical of Christianity and enthusiastic for the social and economic emancipation of women. When it was discovered that "Ralph Iron" was a young woman, both abuse and praise became still more fervent, and Olive Schreiner found herself a public figure. Havelock Ellis has described her as she was when he first met her, in 1884: "the short sturdy vigorous body in loose shapeless clothes . . . the beautiful head with the large dark eyes, at once so expressive and so observant." It was the beginning of a long, close, and very affectionate friendship, though the two were never lovers as most of their acquaintances surmised.

But Miss Schreiner's fame was more truly notoriety, and her eight years in London were miserable ones. She returned to South Africa, where the next great influence on her was Cecil Rhodes, for whom she felt a strangely ambivalent attraction and repulsion. She attacked him bitterly later in *Trooper Peter Halket*, but he refused to prosecute her, saying, "I could never oppose the author of *The Story of an African Farm*." Her brother, William P. Schreiner, succeeded Rhodes as prime minister of Cape Colony.

Her later posthumous novels were negligible; her remaining work of moment was in the series of short allegories called *Dreams*, and in her economic and political works, most of all in *Woman and Labor*, one of the Bibles of the feminist movement. In 1894 she married Samuel Cronwright, of Boer stock, who gave up his work both as farmer and as lawyer (he had been a member of the Cape Colony Parliament) to become her literary assistant and after her death her literary executor. Cronwright combined her name with his and accompanied her on most of her subsequent travels between England and Africa in her vain attempt to secure relief from asthma. She was strongly pro-Boer in the Boer War, and a pacifist, though not an active one, in the First World War. Her only child died soon after birth.

In later years she grew heavy, aged prematurely, and because of her illness her head became permanently bent over her chest. In youth, however, she was lovely, with abundant wavy dark hair, delicate features, and beautiful dark eyes. Though she published little, she wrote much, and was active besides in South African politics, so that with her delicate health she had little strength for other interests; she did, however, love music and dabbled a bit in painting. She died at sixty-five in her home near Cradoch, Cape Colony, and is buried under a rock sarcophagus at the summit of Buffels Kop, above the Karoo Desert.

Olive Schreiner was the pure type of rebellious woman of the Victorian age. She was always more emotional than intellectual, a tempestuous, excitable, melancholy creature, a passionate advocate and a passionate protestant. Her work is often turgid in style but it is always vivid and direct. Her Rationalism was really a sort of mystical Pantheism. Phyllis Bottome called her "never really an inhabitant of this world . . . a fighter, an immense force, a great artist." *The Story of an African Farm* is a remarkable performance for a young girl, hardly half-educated, in a remote and isolated colony. It has power, imagination, intense sincerity, close observation of both nature and psychology, which atone for its occasional incoherence and its undue length. As *Current Opinion* said, Olive Schreiner "was so great that she ought to have been greater."

PRINCIPAL WORKS: *Novels*—The Story of an African Farm, 1883; From Man to Man, 1926; Undine, 1928. *Miscellaneous*—Dreams, 1891; Dream Life and Real Life, 1893; Trooper Peter Halket of Mashonaland, 1897; The South African Question, 1899; Woman and Labor, 1911; Stories, Dreams, and Allegories, 1923; Thoughts on South Africa, 1923; The Letters of Olive Schreiner, 1924.

ABOUT: Bennett, A. The Savor of Life; Cronwright-Schreiner, S. C. The Life of Olive Schreiner; Dell, F. Women As World-Builders; Ellis, H. My Life; Harris, F. Contemporary Portraits: Fourth Series; Schreiner, O. Letters; Contemporary Review May 1924; Current Opinion July 1924; Living Age February 19, 1921, June 21, 1924; Nation December 29, 1920; New Republic March 8, 1925.

SCHUMAN, FREDERICK LEWIS

(February 22, 1904-), American political scientist, was born in Chicago, the son of

August and Ella (Schulze) Schuman. He was educated at the University of Chicago, (Ph.B. 1924, Ph.D. 1927). From 1927 to 1936 he taught political science at Chicago, first as instructor and then as assistant professor. In 1936 he went to Williams College, as professor of political science, and still holds that position. Since 1938 he has also been Woodrow Wilson Professor of government at Williams. He has taught also in the summer schools of Harvard University and the University of California. He was a Fellow of the Social Science Research Council in 1929, and of the American Academy of Political and Social Science in 1933. He is a member of the American Political Science Association and the American Society of International Law. In 1930 he married Lily Caroline Abell; they have two sons. Their home is in Fort Hoosac Place, Williamstown, Mass.

Professor Schuman has written frequently for journals of opinion on governmental questions. During 1940 he became known as a leading advocate of immediate intervention by the United States in the Second World War. The Nazi political scene has been his special field for several years, and he has lectured widely as well as written on contemporary German politics and government. His early sympathy with the Soviet Union was superseded by active opposition to Stalin's policies during the Nazi-Soviet pact. A frequent contributor to liberal journals, he has at the same time been criticized by some of his liberal colleagues for his several reversals of viewpoint in recent years.

PRINCIPAL WORKS: American Policy Toward Russia Since 1917, 1928; War and Diplomacy in the French Republic, 1931; International Politics—An Introduction to the Western State System, 1933; Conduct of German Foreign Affairs, 1934; Rotary? 1934; The Nazi Dictatorship, 1935; Germany Since 1918, 1937; Europe on the Eve, 1939; Night Over Europe, 1941; Design for Power, 1942.

ABOUT: Nation January 25, 1941; Partisan Review, March-April 1940.

SCHURZ, CARL. See "AMERICAN AUTHORS: 1600-1900"

*SCHÜTZE, GLADYS HENRIETTA (RAPHAEL) ("Henrietta Leslie," "Gladys Mendl") (1881-), English novelist, writes: "Henrietta

Leslie was born in London, where she has lived practically her whole life. A lonely and delicate child, tied for long periods to the sickbed, her love of books and reading was early fostered. However, her health improved and she developed a passion for music. She studied the piano under the late Carlo Albanesi, and had her voice trained by various masters, including Tosti and Henry Russell, with the view of later taking up singing as a profession. This had, however, to be abandoned owing to reasons of health, and she devoted herself wholeheartedly to writing, her first book, *The Straight Road*, being published when she was just turned twenty. Since then she has written some twenty-three novels, including *Mrs. Fischer's War*, chosen by book societies in both England and America, and honored by a foreword by John Galsworthy.

"Henrietta Leslie has wide interests. Although city-born, she loves the country, a love which finds itself reflected in her books. She also loves old houses. Her London home, Glebe House, Chelsea, has interesting historical associations, having been built as the home of the Huguenot clergymen, when, in the seventeenth century, they fled to

England from France after the Edict of Nantes had been revoked. The country cottage in which she and her husband take refuge every week-end dates from Tudor times. Both at this cottage and in Glebe House are many objects which she and her husband have brought back from their travels; they are both ardent travelers and greatly enjoy exploring the highways and byways of Europe in their little tourer car. Last summer, just before the outbreak of war they made an extensive motor trip in America.

"Henrietta Leslie has written one travel book, *Where East Is West*, which, earned her the honor of a decoration by the King of Bulgaria. An ardent internationalist, she speaks fluent, if rather ungrammatical, French, German, and Italian. She worked for nine years as honorary organizer of the Save the Children Fund, a society for raising the standard of child life all over the world. She is also a member of the International P.E.N. Club, and serves on the executive committee of the British branch.

She has written three plays in collaboration, *The Tree, When the Bough Breaks*, and *The Loving Heart*, all produced in London. Her children's play, *The Palace of Cards*, was produced at the Liverpool Repertory Theatre, and she collaborated with the dramatist, Joan Temple, in dramatizing her novel, *Mrs. Fischer's War*. She was for three years art critic and special reporter on the London *Daily Herald*.

"She loves dogs, flowers, music, the theatre, the sea when she does not have to go on it; bright colors, France, the French language, and everything inanimate that is old. She detests politics, war, being lonely, and the absence of sun in the British climate. Her chief pleasures are her work, motoring, and foreign travel. Her husband is Dr. Harrie Schütze, the well-known Australian bacteriologist, of the Lister Institute, London.

"Of her novels, she herself prefers *Mrs. Fischer's War, Mother of Five, Martin, Come Back!, No Spring Till Now, Good Neighbors*, and *Mistress of Merle*. But, best of all, she likes the really great novel which has, as yet, to be written."

* * *

Mrs. Schütze's maiden name was Raphael. She was married in 1913, and has no children. A critic in the *Bookman* called her work "interesting, but too sentimental."

PRINCIPAL WORKS: The Straight Road, 1911; Roundabout, 1912; Parentage, 1913 (these three as "Gladys Mendl"); Where Runs the River, 1916;

A Mouse With Wings, 1920; Conflict, 1921; Belsavage, 1921; Other People's Property, 1922; Dedication, 1923; Hirelle, 1925; The Road to Damascus, 1929; Who Are You? 1929; After Eight O'Clock, 1930; Mrs. Fischer's War, 1931; Naomi's Child (in America: Desired Haven) 1932; Where East Is West: Life in Bulgaria (non-fiction) 1933; Mother of Five, 1934; Daughters Defiant, 1935; Martin, Come Back! 1936; No Spring Till Now, 1938; Good Neighbors, 1939; Mistress of Merle, 1940.

SCHWARTZ, DELMORE (1914-), American poet and critic, was born in Brooklyn, N.Y., and educated at Columbia, the University of Wisconsin, and New York University, "ending up as a student of philosophy at Harvard." He received his B.A. at New York University in 1935, and began to find his way into print, doing translations of Rimbaud and Benda and editing a little magazine called *Mosaic*.

He has written verse, fiction, plays in verse, and a good deal of literary criticism; but, he says, "apart from creative and critical writing, my main interest is in the study of philosophy, from which I find it difficult to keep the other two separated." *The American Caravan* (1936) printed his dramatic poem, "Choosing Company," which, Schwartz has said, illustrated two difficulties —"trying to make a dramatic image of an idea" and "trying to make dramatic poetry out of American speech." When James Laughlin, in 1936, founded an "advanced" publishing house, New Directions, in Norwalk, Conn., Mr. Schwartz was one of his first "discoveries," and his work appeared in the first annual of the new enterprise, *New Directions in Prose and Poetry* (1937). Much of his critical work (some of it collected in his *Imitation of Life*) has appeared in *Poetry*, the *Southern Review*, and the *Partisan Review*. Of his plans for the future he says: "Though I find more and more difficult the profession of poet and critic as I get older, I hope to write a book about T. S. Eliot, from whom I've learned the little I know about literature. Also, I want some time to be able to use major league baseball as a subject, since it seems to me the most lucid product of American life."

Mr. Schwartz is very consciously of his own generation. He says: "I feel that I belong to the Class of 1930 (a description which might be expanded a great deal) and that I might be described as having a post-Munich sensibility." The cerebral quality of his work is itself the cause of his most obvious faults—"occasional awkward transitions, blurred figures, unnecessary inversions." But Allen Tate found in his verse "a wholly new feeling for language," and John Crowe Ransom said that "he has the gift of the fused, indivisible poetic style."

At present he is Briggs-Copeland Instructor in English Composition at Harvard. He was awarded a Guggenheim Fellowship in 1940. He is unmarried.

PRINCIPAL WORKS: In Dreams Begin Responsibilities (poetry) 1938; A Season in Hell (translation of Arthur Rimbaud) 1939; The Imitation of Life and Other Problems of Literary Criticism, 1941; Shenandoah: a Verse Play, 1941.

ABOUT: Williams, O. (ed.) New Poems: 1940; Poetry May 1939; Wilson Library Bulletin June 1942.

SCHWARTZ, JOZUA MARIUS WILLEM VAN DER POORTEN ("Maarten Maartens") (August 15, 1858-August 3, 1915), Dutch novelist and short-story writer, was born in Amsterdam, the son of Dr. Carl Schwartz and Cornelia (van Vollenhoven) Schwartz. The elder Schwartz was born in Germany of Hebrew parents, becoming a Christian in his university days, a member of the Church of England, and then the Free Church of Scotland. Joining the London Society (for Propagation of the Gospel Among the Jews) he preached in Budapest, Constantinople, and Amsterdam, where professing Jews once made an attempt on his life.

Young Schwartz's early education was obtained in England, from six to twelve, when his father died and his mother returned to Amsterdam. In 1872 Jozua (or Joost) was a pupil in grammar school; in 1873 he attended a German *gymnasium* in Bonn, where he met boys from most of the European countries and widened his interests in a way very useful to a budding writer. At nineteen he was a student at the University of Utrecht, later teaching law until repelled by its subterfuges and evasions. In 1883 Schwartz married his cousin, Anna van Vollenhoven, a confirmed invalid, who, however, survived him nine

years. Much time was spent on the Riviera and in Switzerland trying to recover her health.

The Morning of a Love and Other Poems, and two five-act poetical tragedies, both written in English, like all Schwartz's work, appeared in 1885 and 1886. In November 1888 Schwartz took the name of "Maarten Maartens" as "an alias with a Dutch look that English readers might possibly be able to pronounce." Reading a popular detective novel, he said "I can do that!" and wrote *The Black Box Murder,* which was promptly pirated in the United States. (It is one of the few examples of the form written by an author who was neither Anglo-Saxon nor Gallic.) *The Sin of Joost Aveling,* the first of his "Koopstad novels," was published the same year, 1889, and gave "Maartens" a lasting reputation. It was a study of the workings of conscience and of spiritual conflict, as is most of his fiction. He had a hatred of religiosity cloaking itself as religion, and hatred and contempt for all medical specialists, as shown in *The Healers.* Dutch farmers and fisher folk are masterfully described in the Koopstad novels. "Maarten Maartens" published fourteen novels and four volumes of short stories between 1889 and 1912; Constable in London brought out his collected works the year before his death at fifty-seven, hastened by anxiety over the First World War. He was buried at Neêr-Langbroek.

Schwartz was a friend of the Edmund Gosses in London; lectured at Carnegie Hall in New York City in 1907; and was given a Dutch party by Theodore Roosevelt at the White House. His only play, *The Jailbird,* a one-acter, was used as a curtain-raiser for J. M. Barrie's *Little Mary.* The general hostility shown to his work in his native Holland saddened "Maarten Maartens." He was tall, handsome, with gray-blue eyes and a dark complexion; his bearing and bodily presence, writes his friend Sir Arthur Quiller-Couch, were of a piece with his inward nobility. William Sharp compared the moral austerity and literary distinction of his work to that of George Eliot and Edouard Rod.

PRINCIPAL WORKS: *Poems and Novels*—The Morning of a Love and Other Poems, 1885; Julian, 1886; Nivalis, 1886; The Black Box Murder, 1889; The Sin of Joost Aveling, 1889; An Old Maid's Love, 1891; A Question of Taste, 1891; The Greater Glory, 1894; God's Fool: A Koopstad Story, 1895; My Lady Nobody, 1895; The Price of Lis Doris, 1909; Eve, 1912. *Short Stories*—Some Women I Have Known, 1901; My Poor Relations, 1903; The Woman's Victory, 1906; The

Healers, 1906; The New Religion, 1907; Brothers All, 1909.

ABOUT: Maaenen, W. van. Maarten Maartens: Poet and Novelist; Schwartz, J. M. W. Letters (see Preface by A. Quiller-Couch and Memoir by N. J. O'Conor).

SCOLLARD, CLINTON (September 18, 1860-November 19, 1932), American poet and university professor, was born in Clinton, N.Y., the son of

James I. and Elizabeth (Stephens) Scollard. He attended the Clinton Liberal Institute; received his B.A. degree in 1881 from Hamilton College at Clinton, the alma mater of John V. A. Weaver and Alexander Woollcott; and taught English at the Brooklyn (N.Y.) Polytechnic Institute until February 1883, when the state of his health compelled Scollard to go to Florida, Arizona, and California to seek relief. He studied at Harvard, meeting his lifelong friend Frank Dempster Sherman, whose poetical works he edited and whom he addressed as "brother in song" in *Elegy in Autumn* (1917); and at Cambridge, England. During his English sojourn Scollard met Edmund Gosse, Austin, Dobson, and Andrew Lang, absorbing something from each. Always a derivative and conventional, though painstaking poet, Scollard used French verseforms in his first book of poems, *Pictures in Song* (1884), wrote songs of the open road in the manner of Richard Hovey and Bliss Carman, and *Ballads: Patriotic and Romantic* midway in the First World War.

From 1888 to 1896 Scollard was professor of English at Hamilton, leaving to devote himself exclusively to writing poetry and historical novels. In 1890 he married Georgia Brown of Jackson, Mich., divorcing her in February 1924 and marrying Jessie B. Rittenhouse,[qv] the well known anthologist, who edited a selection of his lyrics and wrote a memoir of the poet in 1934. In 1911 Scollard returned to Hamilton for a year only. His literary work was interrupted ten years later by a breakdown so severe that his mind was threatened. He died of heart disease at seventy-two, after a month's illness, at his home in New Milford, Conn., when about to leave for his winter home in Winter Garden, Fla. At the funeral services in Hamilton Chapel William P. Shepard observed that, "Trained

as Scollard was in the large Victorian days, in the seemingly more facile rhythms of poets like Dobson and Gosse, he was sometimes regarded negligently by our post-war singers, nor could he fit himself to their more broken and harsher measures." The *Nation* said of Scollard's *Odes and Elegies*, one of the seventy books which he wrote or edited, that he was "well endowed with a poet's ideality, possessed of a good mastery of difficult meter, and a good command perhaps too good, of poetic diction." Scollard was tall and athletic, with a pleasant face and a manner of courtliness and charm.

PRINCIPAL WORKS: Pictures in Song, 1884; With Reed and Lyre, 1886; Old and New World Lyrics, 1888; Giovio and Giulia, 1891; Songs of Sunrise Lands, 1892; Under Summer Skies, 1892; On Sunny Shores, 1893; The Hills of Song, 1895; A Boy's Book of Rhyme, 1896; A Christmas Garland, 1897; A Man at Arms, 1898; Lawton, 1900; The Son of a Tory: or, The Lutes of Morn, 1901; The Cloistering of Ursula, 1902; Lyrics of the Dawn, 1902; The Lyric Bough, 1904; Ballads of Valor and Victory (with W. Rice) 1904; Odes and Elegies, 1905; A Southern Flight (with F. D. Sherman) 1906; Easter Song, 1907; Voices and Visions, 1908; Pro Patria, 1909; The Vicar of the Marches, 1910; Lyrics From a Library, 1913; The Vale of Shadows and Other Verses of the Great War, 1915; Ballads: Patriotic and Romantic, 1916; Let the Flag Wave and Other Verses, 1917; War Voices and Memories, 1919; Epic of Golf, 1923; Songs of Summer, 1927; The Singing Heart: Selected Lyrics and Other Poems, 1934.

ABOUT: Cook, H. W. Our Poets of Today; [Hamilton College]. Clinton Scollard; Rittenhouse, J. B. The Younger American Poets; Scollard, C. The Singing Heart (see Memoir by J. B. Rittenhouse); New York Times November 20, 1932; Publishers' Weekly November 26, 1932.

*SCOTT, DUNCAN CAMPBELL (A

gust 2, 1862-), Canadian poet, writes: "My father was a minister of the Methodist Church in Ottawa, Ont., where I was born. Until I was seventeen I suffered the vicissitudes of the Methodist itinerant system, living here and there in Canada, and getting what education I could from the public schools and at Stanstead College, Quebec. Then I entered the Civil Service of Canada, in the Department of Indian Affairs, and remained attached to that department until my retirement, as Deputy Superintendent General, in 1932. During my service I was instrumental in settling a number of vexed Indian questions between the

Karsh

Provinces and the Dominion and introduced improvements in the Medical and Educational Divisions. For this administrative work I was made a Companion of the Order of St. Michael and St. George by George V in 1934.

"It will be gathered that I belong to a type not unknown in Great Britain and the United States—the public servant who devotes his leisure to literary or artistic pursuits. I had, as a child, shown an aptitude for music and cultivated it strenuously. My interest in the intellectual and artistic life of the Dominion has been constant. I was elected a Fellow of the Royal Society of Canada in 1899, and was its Honorary Secretary for eleven years and President in 1921. The University of Toronto and Queen's University, Kingston, have honored me with doctorates. I am a Fellow of the Royal Society of Literature of Great Britain. Greatly interested in the drama, I am a Governor of the Dominion Drama Festival.

"I have been married twice, in 1894 to Belle W. Botsford, a violinist, of Boston, who died in 1929; and in 1931 to Désirée Élise Aylen.

* * *

Mr. Scott was joint editor with Pelham Edgar of the series of biographies, *The Makers of Canada.* Of his poetry Lorne Pierce said: "No Canadian poet has succeeded so well in capturing humanity."

PRINCIPAL WORKS: *Poetry*—The Magic House, 1893; Labour and the Angel, 1898; New World Lyrics and Ballads, 1905; Via Borealis, 1906; Lundy's Lane and Other Poems, 1916; Beauty and Life, 1921; Complete Poems, 1926; The Green Cloister, 1935. *Prose*—In the Village of Viger (short stories) 1896; The Life of John Graves Simcoe, 1905; The Witching of Elspie (short stories) 1923.

ABOUT: Queen's Quarterly February 1939.

SCOTT, EVELYN (January 17, 1893-), American novelist, writes: "I am forty-six years old [1939], arrived at a most interest-

ing period of life. The very young remind me of fish in individual aquariums, gazing, through a medium alien to other species, toward an outer world not yet more than theoretically a fact. Minnows never emerge from the sensory confines of water; but humans, sometimes, after laboriously reaching forty, become capable of a degree of extra-emotional vision. I aspire

to such a vision today, though I realize detachment and perspective are not acquired without effort, even in middle life. I think any individual's acceptance of a theory of universals and universal perfection is contingent on inescapable emotional needs, which are the undeliberated outcome of that individual's life experiences. If my mother, Southern from the seventeenth century, had not married a Yankee whose ancestors were from Boston and New York State, I might not have been impelled, as I was, to protest the lingering antebellum tradition under which I grew up. I was born in Tennessee, and educated for the most part in New Orleans, by tutors, and at Newcomb Preparatory School, Newcomb College, and the Newcomb School of Art. But I never completed my college course, and I educated myself with precocious reading, which inspired me with simultaneous ambitions to become a writer, a painter, an actress, and a disciple of Pavlowa, Tolstoy, Schopenhauer, Nietzsche, Bergson, and Karl Marx—all at once. Transported by great art, passionately wishing to understand all religions and philosophies, the Puritan side of my descent afflicted me additionally with an ardor for social reform. For this reason I early resolved to do my bit to insure the political and economic equality of races, thus finally safeguarding individual freedom.

"Saturated in Russian, French, and Scandinavian literature, I rejected the idea of being a Southern belle like everybody else, and ran away from home, thus flouting convention with a high-mindedness not all readers of *Escapade* appreciate even today. But it was during my first six early years in the tropics that I came to grips with bedrock actuality in a primitive scene, and learned, through a geographical remoteness from social stimuli, the full value of self-dependence and an 'inner life.'

"I have been married twice; I have a son of twenty-four of whose talents as a painter I am proud; and I have written eighteen books, and am now at work on the nineteenth, a novel of the French Revolution, which I began to write in 1933. Until three years ago, when I settled down again in the United States, I lived mainly abroad, very often in the English country. My present husband, John Metcalfe, British short story writer and novelist, is now serving with the Royal Air Force, where he did duty during the First World War. Altogether, it can be said with accuracy that, 'both literally and metaphorically,' I have traveled far from the South of my childhood. But I owe it to the general aristocratic pretensions of the South, that I still prize most, in myself and in others, a man's control of his own spirit and mind—man's self-direction in the development of an inner life. And I owe it to the South that I never did, and do not now, see virtue in any proposal to make other people 'good' by force. The frail Puritan in me has died, and I hope will never be reborn.

"That is why I do not like philosophies that see man's salvation in terms of complete industrialization and a mechanized culture. Both World Revolution and National Socialism seem to me theories without realism in any connection except that of acquiring power for dictators or bureaucracies. The present stressing of economics to the exclusion of everything else will eventually make us all spiritual imbeciles. I believe in the 'middle way': in the human as against the mechanized."

* * *

Harry Salpeter described Evelyn Scott as "a small, slight, restless-bodied woman," who "appears fragile but has the inclinations of an explorer." Her wide, startled eyes, "lightning-blue," her fine thick wavy brown hair, and her wide mobile mouth make her a striking person. She was married in 1913 to C. Kay Scott, also a writer, and in 1928 to John Metcalfe. In 1932 she won a Guggenheim Fellowship. She is a vice president of the Authors' League.

Her novels, with some exceptions, are basically expressionistic in method; Padraic Colum remarked on their "mass movement, in a series of episodes, with the individual important only as an element of the mass." But underlying them is, as Robert Morss Lovett pointed out, "a highly individual and personal expression" and "a purpose purely aesthetic." Her first work was in poetry, and to a great extent, even in her most realistic writing, she remains the poet, to whom "pain was the greatest factor in her experience."

PRINCIPAL WORKS: *Fiction*—The Narrow House, 1921; Narcissus (in England: Bewilderment) 1922; The Golden Door, 1925; In the Endless Sands (juvenile, with C. Kay Scott) 1925; Ideals, 1927; Migrations, 1927; Witch Perkins (juvenile) 1928; The Wave, 1929; Blue Rum (as "Ernest Souza") 1930; A Calendar of Sin, 1932; Eva Gay, 1933; Breathe Upon These Slain, 1934; Billy the Maverick (juvenile) 1934; Bread and a Sword, 1937; Shadow of the Hawk, 1941. *Poetry*—Precipitations, 1920; The Winter Alone, 1931. *Autobiography*—Escapade, 1923; Background in Tennessee, 1937.

ABOUT: Beach, J. W. The Twentieth Century Novel; Van Doren, C. The American Novel; Bookman October 1929, November 1931; Boston Evening Transcript November 7, 1931; North Georgia Review Spring 1938; Saturday Review of Literature October 23, 1937.

SCOTT-MONCRIEFF, CHARLES KENNETH (September 25, 1889-February 28, 1930), Scottish translator, was born in Stirlingshire, Scotland, the youngest of three sons of William George Scott-Moncrieff, Advocate, for many years Sheriff-Substitute of County Lanark in Scotland, and heir of a large and distinguished but unprosperous Scottish family. The boy went to Inverness College and Winchester, continuing to Edinburgh University, where he was Patterson Bursar in Anglo-Saxon, 1913-15, taking his B.A. with a First Class in the English Language in 1914, just before the outbreak of the First World War. Scott-Moncrieff served with the King's Own Scottish Borders, winning a Military Cross for gallantry in the field. Wounded in the foot on the Somme in 1917, he also suffered from trench fever for the remainder of his life, dying at forty.

Scott-Moncrieff was with General Headquarters in France till the end of the war and some months after, and spent his leisure time translating the *Chanson de Roland,* keeping to the old *laisses* or bundles of lines for his assonant rhymes. In July 1920 he became secretary to Lord Northcliffe, joining the staff of the London *Times* next year, as was customary with Northcliffe's secretaries. That year he translated *Beowulf,* the Anglo-Saxon epic which Edmund Gosse once called the spoilt child of English scholarship. Newspaper work seemed too confining and publicity work too artificial, and Scott-Moncrieff persuaded Chatto & Windus that they should publish an English translation of Marcel Proust's tremendous novel, *À la Recherche du Temps Perdu.* Shipping his books to Pisa, where he lived till 1927, moving to Rome then to stay till his death in a nursing home, Scott-Moncrieff began his remarkable translation of Proust, alternating this work with translations of Pirandello and Stendhal. Believing that the secret of a good translation was not so much to be a perfect scholar in the language from which one is translating as to have a clear idea of the possibilities of the language into which one translates, he did much, as Vyvyan Holland (Oscar Wilde's son) remarked, to

1253

raise the profession of translator from its traditional place in the publishing underworld to an honorable position in literature. He had particular felicity in translating flowery Proustian metaphors. Scott-Moncrieff corrected proofs of *Albertine Disparue* during his last illness; the eighth and last volume, *Le Temps Retrouvé*, had another translator. Ridden by indigent relatives (he listed his recreation as "nepotism") he had no time for writing of his own except a few poems in light vein and a satire or two. His only original book was the posthumous *Memories and Letters* (1931). Scott-Moncrieff was a handsome man, with a remarkable head, dark blue eyes, a soft deep voice, and a capacity for cutting retorts when once aroused.

ABOUT: Scott-Moncrieff, C. K. Memories and Letters (ed. by J. M. Scott Moncrieff and L. W. Lunn); London Mercury April 1930.

*SEABROOK, WILLIAM BUEHLER

(February 22, 1886-), American essayist, was born in Westminster, Md., the son of

E. Schaal

William Levin Seabrook (a Lutheran minister) and Myra Phelps (Buehler) Seabrook. He was educated at Mercersburg Academy, Roanoke College (Salem, Va.), Newberry College (South Carolina), and the University of Geneva. He has a Ph.B. degree from Roanoke and an M.A. from Newberry. In 1908 he became a reporter on the Augusta, Ga., *Chronicle*, and by the next year, at twenty-two, was its city editor. He then became a partner in an advertising agency in Augusta, leaving, in 1915, to enlist in the French army. He was gassed at Verdun and invalided out with a *Croix de Guerre*. For a short time he settled on a farm in Georgia, then went to New York as a reporter on the *Times*. After this he was a writer for the King Features Syndicate. In 1924 he went to Arabia, and since that time he has devoted himself entirely to traveling and writing. The Arabian trip was followed by journeys to Kurdistan, Turkestan, Africa, and Haiti, most of which eventuated in books. At the end of 1933 he had himself committed to a New York mental hospital for alcoholism, and spent seven months there, the account of his experiences being given in *Asylum*. He discovered that he had been "running away from himself for

twenty-seven years," and this drastic cure proved effective.

In 1912 Mr. Seabrook married Katherine Pauline Edmondson. They were divorced in 1934, and the next year he married Marjorie Muir Worthington, herself a novelist. They live on an eight-acre farm at Rhinebeck, N.Y. He is a big, heavy-set man, with thick wavy hair and a small moustache, who since he has left the city finds his recreation in tennis, golf, fishing, and sailing. Besides his actual travels, his geographical range has been very wide; part of his boyhood was spent in Kansas, he once owned a home on the French Riviera, and he is at home almost everywhere on the globe. This was an admirable preparation for the writing of *These Foreigners*, a study of Americans of foreign birth or descent, for which he traveled all over the United States.

Mr. Seabrook is one of the many persons first encouraged to write by H. L. Mencken in the early days of the *American Mercury*. He turned his travels (which began in early youth with a hobo tour of Europe) to good account by writing vivid, colorful descriptions of some very unusual experiences. Though they earned for him the accusation of credulity, and a shocked writer in the *Commonweal* charged him with "deliberate reversion to primitive paganism" (he participated in Voodoo rites in Haiti and ate human flesh in Africa), actually no disproof of his startling scenes has ever been adduced. He has the newspaper man's approach to a "story," and a mind trained to evaluate what he has witnessed. He seems to have settled down from his travels, and is now engaged in drawing conclusions from them.

PRINCIPAL WORKS: Adventures in Arabia, 1927; The Magic Island, 1929; Jungle Ways, 1931; Air Adventure, 1933; The White Monk of Timbuctoo, 1934; Asylum, 1935; These Foreigners, 1938; An Analysis of Magic and Witchcraft, 1940; Dr. Wood, 1941.

ABOUT: Seabrook, W. B. Asylum; Commonweal April 15, 1931; Literary Digest August 10, 1935; Reader's Digest September 1939; Time August 12, 1935, September 19, 1940; Wilson Library Bulletin March 1936.

SEAMAN, Sir OWEN (September 18, 1861-February 2, 1936), English parodist, poet, and editor of *Punch*, was the eldest son of W. M. Seaman. Shrewsbury was his public school; he was Captain of the school in 1880 and in later years a member of its governing board. A sound classical education at Clare College, Cambridge University, laid the foundations for later translations of Horace. Seaman was Porson Prizeman, in 1882, and took a

* Died September 20, 1945.

first class in the Classical Tripos the next year. In 1882, also, he was captain of the Clare Boats. At Clare, as well, Seaman collaborated in 1883 with Mr. (later Sir) Horace Munro on *Paulopostprandials*, his first book.

He was master at Rossall School in 1884; professor of literature at Durham, Newcastle-on-Tyne, in 1890; and a barrister of the Inner Temple in 1897, the same year in which he joined the staff of *Punch*, England's famous humorous weekly. In 1894 Seaman had contributed to it one of his first parodies, "The Rhyme of the Kipperling," a travesty of Kipling. Other poems had appeared in various periodicals under the pseudonym "Nauticus." Seaman was made

assistant editor in 1902, succeeding Sir F. C. Burnand in 1906 as editor. For a little over a quarter-century he kept the periodical at a high pitch of excellence, even during the First World War, occasionally collecting his own contributions of parodies and memorial verse, for which he had a special gift.

Seaman was knighted in 1914 and created a baronet in 1933; the baronetcy became extinct when he died a bachelor at seventy-four. Death was caused by pneumonia. Seaman had had a serious surgical operation four years earlier, in 1932, when he retired from *Punch*. He was able then, however, to resume a favorite pastime of swimming, and diving from high springboards. In 1934 Sir Owen wrote a prologue to Milton's *Comus*, presented at Ludlow Castle three hundred years after its first performance there. (He would never accept parodies of "Lycidas" for *Punch*.) Edinburgh gave him an honorary LL.D., and Durham conferred a Litt.D. degree.

Seaman has most often been compared with Charles S. Calverley, but, as Coulson Kernahan notes, he "is not a second Calverley, for he is no imitator, but an original as well as a true poet, with not a little in common with Calverley." He was also one of the first to raise the art of parody from mere verbal mimicry to an instrument of criticism, in the words of the memorial sketch in *Punch*. A genial robust personality, Seaman "loved the good things of this world but never forgot his lame ducks"; he was an active member of the governing board of the Putney Hospital For Incur-

ables, and issued some of his most effective appeals for the training-ship *Implacable*. As effective in prose as in verse, he made novelists as well as poets feel the light flick of his satire, from Hall Caine, Marie Corelli, and "Elizabeth" (in her German Garden avatar), to Henry James, George Meredith, Maeterlinck, John Davidson ("The Ballad of a Bun" is parody at its sharpest), Mrs. Ward, and Mrs. Meynell. *The Battle of the Bays*, which went through eleven editions, parodied Tennyson, Rossetti, Kipling, and Sir Edwin Arnold. *Interludes of an Editor* are prose miscellanies. *In Cap and Bells* opened with lines addressed to Alfred Austin, Poet Laureate, "in polite imitation" of Austin's *Jubilee Ode*.

A. A. Milne (who was associated with Seaman on *Punch* and married his goddaughter Daphne De Sélincourt) called him "a strange, unlucky man. . . . Humor was drowned in Scholarship, Tact went down before Truth, and the Fighting Qualities gave him not only the will to win but the determination to explain why he hadn't won."

PRINCIPAL WORKS: Paulopostprandials, 1883; Oedipus the Wreck, 1888; With Double Pipe, 1888; Horace at Cambridge, 1894; Tillers of the Sand, 1895; The Battle of the Bays, 1896; In Cap and Bells, 1899; Borrowed Plumes, 1902; A Harvest of Chaff, 1904; Salvage, 1908; Made in England, 1916; From the Home Front, 1918; Interludes of an Editor, 1929.

ABOUT: Kernahan, C. Five More Famous Living Poets; Milne, A. A. Autobiography; New York Times February 3, 1932; Saturday Review November 5, 1932.

SEAVER, EDWIN (January 18, 1900-), American novelist and critic, writes: "I was born in Washington, D.C., spent my childhood in Philadelphia, went to Worcester Academy, Worcester, Mass., and to college at Harvard (class of 1922), but have lived since then in New York and consider myself a New Yorker. At Harvard I studied the catalogue assiduously to find

Eliascheff

out what the easiest courses were, always taking care not to sign up for any courses that had Friday afternoon sessions, so that I could be free to go to the Boston Symphony Concerts, and spent most of my time reading all the good books I had ever wanted to read in the most comfortable chairs provided by the Widener Library and the

Harvard Union. I was one of the editors of the *Harvard Monthly,* founded in opposition to what seemed to me then the deadly dull *Harvard Advocate* with its effete young literary gents who went in for literature with a capital L. Also I was an editor of a short-lived but very lively four-page sheet called the *Proletarian,* which was likewise an opposition sheet, there being at that time another short-lived but decidedly not lively four-page sheet called the *Aristocrat.* I also took Professor Briggs' course in poetry, from which I learned that I didn't want to be a polite poet; refused to take Professor Copeland's writing course because I didn't want anybody to teach me how to write; but petitioned Irving Babbitt to be allowed to take his graduate course in literary criticism, although I was only a sophomore then, and learned more about letters from the 'reactionary' Professor Babbitt than from all my liberal professors.

"I should mention finally that my first two months at Harvard were spent in the Students' Army Training Corps, learning how to stick a bayonet in a dummy, and ending with an honorable discharge from the U.S. Army. I am afraid I was not a very good soldier. A year later came the Boston Police strike, and the monstrous distortions of fact in that set-up, as reported in the press, helped me to understand what happened when Sacco and Vanzetti became sacrificial victims on the altar of Massachusetts justice.

"Coming down to New York in 1922, I got my first job with a big publicity outfit. I was fired for asking for a raise, and became publicity director for the American Civil Liberties Union, and at the same time joined the staff of the New York *Call,* Socialist daily, later going over to the New York *Leader,* which inherited the *Call.* I was likewise on the staff of *Advance,* weekly newspaper of the Amalgamated Clothing Workers. It was about this time that I began reviewing for the *New Republic,* the *Nation,* the *Freeman,* the *Dial,* and other magazines.

"In 1923 I married Anna Vera Bass and in 1924 we went to live in the artists' colony in Woodstock, N.Y. There we founded and edited the little magazine *1924.* Among our contributors were Hart Crane, Ezra Pound, William Carlos Williams, Yvor Winters, Waldo Frank, and Kenneth Burke. Returning to New York at the end of 1925 I took another publicity job with a public utilities corporation for a year, and then returned to Woodstock on the invitation of a number of artists who asked me to tutor their children.

"It was at this time that I began writing what was later to become my first book,

but which I then thought of as a series of sketches about white collar workers; one of these was published by Edward J. O'Brien in his annual collection. Our daughter was born in 1927 and the following year we returned to New York, where I took a job as assistant publicity director for the Federation of Jewish Charities. At the same time I was on the reviewing staffs of the New York *Sun* and *Evening Post,* having a regular weekly column in the latter paper. I helped to found the *New Masses* and was also editor-in-chief of the monthly magazine *Soviet Russia Today* and later literary editor of the *Daily Worker,* contributing a column daily and a page on Sundays. I should perhaps add that I was *not* a member of the Communist Party and have always thought it odd that people assumed I was, whereas nobody ever charged me with being a member of the Republican Party when I was writing for the *Evening Post* and the *Sun.* I also was one of the founders of the League of American Writers and participated actively in the first Writers' Congress.

"From 1937 to 1939 I was a radio book reviewer for radio station WQXR, New York, and lectured at the New School for Social Research. About 1938 I joined the reading staff of the Book-of-the-Month Club. I am now the club's publicity director, and am at present working on my third novel. Both my previous novels were published in France and in the Soviet Union."

PRINCIPAL WORKS: The Company, 1920; All in the Racket (with W. E. Weeks) 1930; Between the Hammer and the Anvil, 1937.

SEAWELL, MOLLY ELLIOT (October 23, 1860-November 15, 1916), American novelist, was born on a plantation in Gloucester County, Virginia, the daughter of John Tyler Seawell, a lawyer, who was the nephew of President John Tyler, and Frances (Jackson) Seawell. The house in which she was born, called "The Shelter," had been a Revolutionary hospital. The girl was trained at home in riding, dancing, and running a household, and occasionally attended school for grounding in the more conventional subjects of study. From her uncle, Joseph Seawell, she heard stories of seafaring experience which she was later to utilize in her popular "Young Heroes of Our

Navy" series. Her book, *Twelve Naval Captains* (1897), is said to have been used as a textbook at the U.S. Naval Academy at Annapolis.

On the death of her father, Miss Seawell and her mother moved to Norfolk, Va., then to Washington, where she began to write systematically. "I was but little past my twenty-first birthday when, on the strength of having earned about seven hundred dollars by my pen, I rashly assumed the support, by literature, of my family," she wrote in *The Ladies' Battle* (1911), her anti-suffrage book. "The rashness, ignorance, and presumption of this can only be excused by the secluded life I had led in the library of an old Virginia country house, and in a community where conditions more nearly resembled the eighteenth than the nineteenth century. In the course of time, I became, through literature alone, a householder, a property-owner, a taxpayer, and the regular employer of five persons."

She had a trip to Europe before she settled down in Washington for the rest of her life. She was political correspondent in Washington for several New York papers, and wrote political novels under the pseudonym "Foxcroft Davis." For a time her house was something of a salon for artists and writers, but she led a more retired life after the death of her mother and sister. Miss Seawell herself died three weeks after her fifty-sixth birthday, and was buried at Baltimore.

A story published in *Lippincott's Monthly Magazine* in 1889 was one of Molly Elliot Seawell's first successful ventures into fiction, and "The Sprightly Romance of Marsac" (1896) won her a $3,000 prize in the New York *Herald* competition of 1895, the first prize going to Julian Hawthorne. Such historical romances as *A Virginia Cavalier* (1897) and *The History of the Lady Betty Stair* of the same year won her admirers who were later to read Winston Churchill and Mary Johnston with equal avidity. She had the services of such artists of the day as Frederic Dorr Steele, William Glackens, and F. C. Yohn.

The House of Egremont (1900) was laid in the England of James II, and Miss Seawell also wrote romances dealing with French life in Paris and the provinces.

PRINCIPAL WORKS: The Berkeleys and Their Neighbors, 1888; Throckmorton, 1890; Little Jarvis, 1890; Maid Marian and Other Stories, 1891; Midshipman Paulding, 1891; Children of Destiny, 1893; Paul Jones, 1893; Decatur and Somers, 1894; The Sprightly Romance of Marsac, 1896; A Strange, Sad Comedy, 1896; Twelve Naval Captains, 1897; The History of the Lady Betty Stair, 1897; The Loves of the Lady Arabella, 1898; Lively Adventures of Gavin Hamilton, 1899; The House of Egremont: A Novel, 1900; Laurie Vane and Other Stories, 1901; Papa Bouchard, 1901; Franceska, 1902; Despotism and Democracy: A Study in Washington Society and Politics, 1903; The Fortunes of Fifi, 1903; Mrs. Darrell, 1905; The Victory, 1906; Château of Montplaisir, 1906; The Secret of Toni, 1907; The Last Duchess of Belgarde, 1908; The Imprisoned Midshipmen, 1908; The Marriage of Theodora, 1910; The Jugglers: A Story, 1911; The Ladies' Battle, 1911; The Son of Columbus, 1912; Betty's Virginia Christmas, 1914; The Diary of a Beauty, 1915; Betty at Fort Blizzard, 1916.

ABOUT: Library of Southern Literature: Vol. 11; Bookman January 1901; New York Times November 16, 1916.

SEDGWICK, ANNE DOUGLAS (March 28, 1873-July 19, 1935), Anglo-American novelist, was born at Englewood, N. J., the daughter of George Stanley and Mary (Douglas) Sedgwick.  Most of her life was spent in France and England, but she was first educated at home by a governess, and was taken to Ohio to see her grandparents. "Sobriety, sweetness, tradition are the things that best fit my memories of my grandfather's and grandmother's home; an Emersonian flavor, a love of books and nature," she once wrote. She was therefore unable to reconcile her memories of Southern Ohio with the pictures of the Middle West in American novels of the 'twenties. Writing to Grace Zaring Stone in 1933, she also spoke admiringly of "the lovely New England country."

At nine the girl went to England, to the "London of Gilbert and Sullivan operas, Langtry, buns, hansom cabs, and fogs; walks with a governess in Rotten Row, and frequent visits to the National Gallery and the Old South Kensington Museum." Coming of age at eighteen found her in Paris studying painting; a portrait of her sister was exhibited in the Champs de Mars Salon. To her sisters, also, Anne told long stories, one of which her father overheard and showed to a publisher, who accepted it. Miss Sedgwick was an author at twenty-five, with *The Dull Miss Archinard*. Ten years later, in 1908, she married Basil De Sélincourt ("of the *gypsy* French type—but in character intensely English," his wife wrote); he is an essayist and author of books on Giotto and William Blake. Their small house was in Kingham, Oxfordshire, in the heart of the Cotswolds.

Tante, her ninth novel, was her first considerable success, and, dramatized, made a good vehicle for Ethel Barrymore. *The Little French Girl,* thirteen years later, had a large and deserved sale in the United States; Mrs. De Sélincourt used her considerable acquaintance with three countries in this study of an exquisite French child in a family of bluff, hearty English cousins. *Adrienne Toner* also sold well; this and *The Old Countess* were her favorites.

Mrs. De Sélincourt wrote for two or three hours in the forenoon at a large table overlooking her gardens, where she could watch birds and her favorite dogs. Usually she thought out her stories in French; she considered France the most beautiful country in the world and devoted her time and energy during the war to a hospital in France. Her books started with imaginary people (except Nietzsche in *The Encounter*) whom she could often trace back to past memories. "The background rises to fit them and the situation to express them." She sang in the village choral society, of which her husband was conductor. The Oxford Orchestra was occasionally called in to help the sixty singers with Brahms' Requiem, Haydn's Creation, or Bach's Christmas Oratorio.

Esther Forbes, the American novelist, has described Mrs. De Sélincourt sitting "serene and upright by the tea-table like a Dresden goddess. The coil of prematurely white hair, the purple eyes, the pink and white smoothness of her moulded features, lent her a statuesque quality which was sweetly dispelled by her smile and by the gentle irony of her conversation."

Five years before her death ("slow, like being devoured by an ant," she wrote) the novelist visited America once more. The year after her death, a selection from her "Portrait in Letters," edited by her husband, appeared in the *Atlantic Monthly.*

PRINCIPAL WORKS: Franklin Kane, 1910; Tante, 1911; The Nest, 1912; The Encounter, 1914; Autumn Crocuses (American title, Christmas Roses, 1920; The Third Window, 1920; Adrienne Toner, 1922; The Little French Girl, 1924; The Old Countess, 1927; Dark Hester, 1929; Philippa, 1930; A Portrait in Letters (edited by Basil De Sélincourt), 1936.

ABOUT: Anne Douglas Sedgwick: A Portrait in Letters; Atlantic October, 1936; Commonweal August 2, 1935; New York Times July 22, 1935; Publishers Weekly July 27, 1935; Wilson Library Bulletin September 1935.

SEEGER, ALAN (June 22, 1888-July 4, 1916) American poet, was born in New York City, of New York and New England parentage. Charles Louis and Elsie Simmons (Adams) Seeger were his parents. The boy's first ten years were spent on Staten Island, where he attended the Staten Island Academy, later going to the Horace Mann School in Manhattan.

At twelve his family moved to Mexico; Alan was placed in the Hackley School, Tarrytown, N.Y., when he was fourteen. Entering Harvard College in 1906, he mingled very little with his fellow students, preferring to translate Dante and Ariosto, but emerged from his shell sufficiently in his senior year to edit the *Harvard Monthly.* Always fiercely independent in speech, dress and manner, he chafed at Philistine restrictions and conventions, even in New York City where he spent two years after graduation in 1910. Nina Wilcox Putnam described him at this period as tall, with thick, coarse, dark chestnut hair, resembling the boy in Botticelli's "Primavera." In 1912 Seeger was in Paris, where he wrote and worked in the Latin Quarter.

Still avid of sensation, and a fatalist at heart, he welcomed the coming of the war and soon enlisted in the Foreign Legion, demanding "How could I let millions of men know an emotion that I remained ignorant of?" He proved a good soldier, full of zest and ready to take risks by going out on private expeditions between the lines. After serving on the Aisne he went with his regiment to Champagne for the offensive of September 1915.

On July 4, 1916, Seeger went over the top with his company at Belloy-en-Santerre. He was last seen alive, wounded, but cheering on his companions. The next morning he was found dead in a shell hole. The French Government gave him a posthumous Croix de Guerre and Medaille Militaire.

In 1916 his collected poems were brought out, with an introduction by William Archer. Seeger's scorn of convention did not extend to avoiding the use of ordinary verse-forms. Although his talent was of a minor order, "I Have a Rendezvous With Death" will probably appear in anthologies for a long time to come. Some other readers prefer "Broceliande" and the Mexican poems.

PRINCIPAL WORKS: Collected Poems (with Introduction by William Archer) 1916.

ABOUT: Aiken, C. P. Skepticisms; Bryant, A. The American Ideal; Howe, M. A. D. W. Memoirs of the Harvard Dead in the War Against Germany; Moore, T. S. Some Soldier Poets; Putnam, N. W. Laughing Through; Century Magazine December 1926; Harvard Graduates' Magazine December 1916; Outlook March 18, 1925; Scribner's Magazine January 1917.

SEGHERS, ANNA (1900-), German novelist, was born Netty Reiling, of Jewish parents, in the handsome old city of

Mainz in the Rhine valley. Her father died some time ago; her mother is believed to have been deported by the Nazis to Poland. An only child, she developed an early interest in Chinese art, because her father was an art specialist, the prosperous owner of an antique shop.

She took advanced study at the University of Heidelberg, learned Chinese, and wrote her Ph.D. thesis (1924) on *Jews and Jewry in the Work of Rembrandt*. She was married to Ladislaus Radvanyi, a young Hungarian sociologist, who had earned his Doctor's degree at Heidelberg a year earlier.

Netty Reiling's first story, *Grubitsch,* was serialized in the *Frankfurter Zeitung* and was signed simply "Seghers," arousing the interest of literary Germany. Its successor, *Aufstand der Fischer von St. Barbara (The Revolt of the Fishermen),* also signed "Seghers" and presumably written by a man, was published in 1928 when the author, "a shy young woman with a round peasant-like face, veiled deep-set eyes, and thick pig-tails wound round her broad forehead," was in the hospital having a baby. This short, brutal novel was awarded the famous Kleist Prize. The novelist visited London, following the book's publication there in 1929, but Bloomsbury found it difficult to lionize her. *The Revolt of the Fishermen* was filmed in Moscow, by Erwin Piscator, in 1934.

Working carefully, Anna Seghers (as she was now called) produced a collection of short stories (translated title, *On the Way to the American Embassy*) and a novel, *Companions of the Road,* based on the refugee problem in Europe during the years before Nazidom. On Hitler's seizure of power in 1933 her position as an author who was both revolutionary and Jewish became untenable, and with her husband and two small children,

Peter and Ruth, she fled to Paris. Here she managed to take care of her family and to write three novels: *The Price on His Head* (1933), a story of German peasants just before the Nazi revolution; *The Road Through February* (1935), a book about Austria at the time of the February 1934 revolt; and *The Rescue,* a dramatic study of German miners. She supported André Gide's provisional committee for the foundation of the "German Library of the Burned Books."

Shortly after the outbreak of the Second World War, the French government threw her husband into Le Vernet, one of the most infamous of concentration camps. In the midst of tragedy she succeeded in finishing *Die Sieben Kreuze,* describing the fortunes of seven fugitives from a German concentration camp. When the Nazis marched into Paris, she was forced into hiding, at last escaping with her children into unoccupied France. Even there she was not safe, for extradition to Germany was still in the cards. Release came through the efforts of the Exiled Writers' Committee of the League of American Writers and the Publishers Committee, who eventually secured her husband's dismissal from Le Vernet and obtained passage for the family to the Western Hemisphere.

The Radvanyis now live in Mexico City, where Anna Seghers has helped found the Heinrich Heine Club for Free German Culture and the magazine *Free Germany.* The anti-Fascist colony of which she is a part has launched a new publishing house, and *Die Sieben Kreuze* was one of its first titles. *The Seventh Cross* was an October 1942 selection of the Book-of-the-Month Club.

WORKS AVAILABLE IN ENGLISH TRANSLATION: The Revolt of the Fishermen, 1929; The Seventh Cross, 1942.

ABOUT: Book-of-the-Month Club News September 1942; Books Abroad Summer 1940; London Evening Standard November 30, 1929.

SEITZ, DON CARLOS (October 24, 1862-December 4, 1935) American journalist and miscellaneous writer, was born at Portage, Ohio, the son of the Rev. J. A. Seitz, a Universalist minister. At seventeen the boy graduated from the Liberal Institute at Norway, Maine, a state he always preferred; later honorary degrees came from St. Lawrence University (M.A. 1906) and Bowdoin (D. Litt. 1921)

He married Mildred E. Blake of East Deering, Maine. Seitz's long journalistic career began as Albany correspondent of the Brooklyn *Eagle,* 1887-1889, and continued as city editor of that paper from 1889-1891, assistant publisher of the New York *Recorder,* 1892-1893; managing editor and advertising manager of the Brooklyn *World,* 1893-1897, followed by a twenty-five-year stretch as business manager of Joseph Pulitzer's New York *World* from 1898 to 1923. He was transferred to the *Evening World* in 1923, remaining till 1926. Seitz contributed a trilogy of biographies to the history of American journalism in his *Horace Greeley, Joseph Pulitzer,* and *The James Gordon Bennetts.* He left before the end of the two *Worlds* to become associate editor of the *Outlook* in 1926-1927 and assistant editor of the *Churchman* in 1929-1932, retiring then except for occasional lectures before such groups as the New York Library Club. Cardiac asthma caused his death after a few days' illness. Interment was in Pine Grove Cemetery, Falmouth Foreside, near Portland, Maine.

Seitz had rugged features crowned by iron-gray hair. He covered many fields of interest in an adequate but occasionally flat and graceless prose.

PRINCIPAL WORKS: Surface Japan, 1911; The Buccaneers, 1912; Whistler Stories, 1913; Training for the Newspaper Trade, 1916; In Praise of War: Military and Sea Verse, Paul Jones, 1917; Farm Voices (poems) 1918; Artemus Ward, 1919; Braxton Bragg, 1924; Uncommon Americans, Under the Black Flag, 1925; The Dreadful Decade (1869-1879), Horace Greeley, 1926; The Great Island [Newfoundland], Joseph Pulitzer: His Life and Letters, 1927; The Also Rans, The James Gordon Bennetts, 1928; From Kaw Tepee to Capitol (Life of Charles Curtis) 1928; Famous American Duels, 1929; Lincoln the Politician, 1931.

ABOUT: New York Times December 5, 1935.

S E L D E S, GEORGE (November 16, 1890-), American journalist and sociologist, writes: "I was born in a sort of

Pinchot

Utopian colony founded by my father, George S. Seldes. It was a failure. But one of my childhood memories is the letters father received from Count Tolstoy and Prince Kropotkin on how to run a co-operative idealistic colony. I got a job in Pittsburgh at the time of the graft trials;

corruption was my introduction to city politics. At Harvard I took Professor Baker's courses, and am probably his only pupil who has not written a play. During the First World War, I was a member of the press section of the American Army. We had special privileges, equal to those of a general on Pershing's staff—and an automobile. Those who wanted to went to the trenches. I was at St. Mihiel; the Signal Corps got lost, and Pershing got there three hours later. I was hailed as the captor of the town.

"After the war I went to the Chicago *Tribune* foreign news service, formed by Floyd Gibbons, and including five members of the press service of the army. For ten years I worked in thirty-seven countries in Europe, Asia, and North Africa. I have interviewed three kings and all the dictators of my time except Kemel Pasha. I have been expelled from Russia, Italy, Fiume, (and just escaped it in Rumania), for sending out news the truth of which could not be questioned. Other correspondents smuggled out news, or refrained from sending out unfavorable stories, but it was my policy to play the game openly.

"In 1928 I resigned from the *Tribune* and wanted to paint pictures. I did in fact paint more than 150 canvases between then and 1933. But I lost in 1929 the few dollars I had saved up, and it was lucky for me that a publisher asked me to write a book of my experiences. *You Can't Print That!* kept me going for a year, and since then I have been very busy getting out an annual volume. I usually get together about 300,000 words of typewritten matter before I begin writing a book, which usually consists of only half or a third as many words. I have only one rule: Let the facts speak for themselves. (The man who said that first was Euripides.) So far I have had only one important error pointed out to me, and that has been corrected. Frequently reviewers make blanket charges that I am biased, prejudiced, one-sided, etc. My answer is this: in almost every book I produce 80% or more of unchallengeable facts. The rest of the book is my interpretation of the facts. This is open to criticism. If the 80% contains errors they will be corrected.

"*Sawdust Caesar* was turned down by twenty-four publishers. Ten wrote me they were afraid of Mussolini. Only one said he did not like the book.

"I am married to Helen Larkin Wiesman, whom I met in Paris. We have no children. In 1934 we bought a home in Vermont, but sold it recently. It was very beautiful out there but too far from the world about which I have to write.

"I belong to no party, but do not know whether the term 'liberal' or 'progressive' is strong enough to explain my views. In 1936 I went to Spain (where, by the way, the issue is liberty and land and not religion, despite all the propaganda to the contrary). I found that on the Loyalist side there were various groups and parties frequently fighting each other. That was their tragedy. But the idea of a united or popular front of all liberal, left, progressive elements, such as we also had in France for a short time, is my idea of the only way to upset reaction and Fascism. The trouble with democrats and liberals is that they are too sectarian. I am for the united front of all men of good will in America. And for death to Fascism in all its forms."

* * *

Mr. Seldes was born in Alliance, N.J., reared in Vineland, N.J., and Pittsburgh, and educated at East Liberty Academy, Pittsburgh, and for a year at Harvard. Both his parents were of Russian Jewish birth. He is the older brother of Gilbert Seldes,*qv* the critic. "For the millions who want a free press" he edits a weekly bulletin of news exposures called *In Fact* with a circulation of over 100,000 copies.

PRINCIPAL WORKS: You Can't Print That! 1929; The Truth Behind the News, 1929; Can These Things Be? 1931; Sawdust Caesar, 1932; World Panorama, 1933; The Vatican and the Modern World, 1933; Iron, Blood, and Profits, 1934; Freedom of the Press, 1935; You Can't Do That! 1937; Lords of the Press, 1938; The Catholic Crisis, 1939; Witch Hunt: The Technique and Profit of Redbaiting, 1941; The Facts Are, 1942.

ABOUT: Goldberg, I. Mussolini Exposed; New Republic February 15, 1939; South Atlantic Quarterly April 1936; Wilson Library Bulletin February 1939.

SELDES, GILBERT VIVIAN (January 3, 1893-), American critic, was born in Alliance, N.J., the son of George Sergius

and Anna (Saphro) Seldes, and the younger brother of George Seldes.*qv* He was educated at the Central High School, Philadelphia, and at Harvard (B.A. 1914). He was music critic of the Philadelphia *Evening Ledger* from 1914 to 1916, a foreign correspondent before America entered

the First World War, and American political correspondent of *L'Écho de Paris* in Washington, in 1918. The next year he became associate editor of *Collier's Weekly,* then managing editor of the *Dial* from 1920 to 1923. He was also its dramatic critic, and was dramatic critic of the New York *Evening Graphic* as well, in 1929. He was a columnist on the New York *Evening Journal* from 1931 to 1937, and since then has been director of television programs for the Columbia Broadcasting System. He enlisted in 1918 and became a sergeant. He was married to Alice Wadhams Hall in 1934; they have a son and a daughter, and live at Croton Falls, N.Y. In 1930 he scored a success with a translation and adaptation of Aristophanes' *Lysistrata*.

He believes that a critic should react "violently" to artistic stimulus; that criticism "should be angry instead of merely smart." Gorham B. Munson said of him: "He is light and agile, and the serious-minded therefore put him down as superficial. He is sharply intelligent, and this appears to alienate the mere 'cleverists.' Actually, he is a roving critic, brightly independent, very well informed, and expert in making discriminations in the arts of levity and diversion."

Besides his works of criticism and comment and his serious novel, *The Wings of the Eagle,* Mr. Seldes has published two mystery novels under the pseudonym of "Foster Johns." He had a play, *The Wise Crackers,* produced in 1925, another, *The Orange Comedy,* in 1926, and wrote the film, *This Is America,* in 1933, and the play, *Swingin' the Dream* (co-author) in 1939.

PRINCIPAL WORKS: The United States and the War, 1917; The Seven Lively Arts, 1924; The Victory Murders, 1927; The Square Emerald, 1928; The Stammering Century, 1928; The Movies and the Talkies, 1929; The Wings of the Eagle (novel) 1929; Lysistrata, 1930; The Future of Drinking, 1930; Against Revolution, 1932; The Years of the Locust, 1932; Mainland, 1936; Your Money and Your Life, 1937; The Movies Come From America, 1937; Proclaim Liberty, 1942.

ABOUT: Bookman December 1929; North American Review December 1936; Saturday Review of Literature January 15, 1938.

SÉLINCOURT. See DE SÉLINCOURT

SELTZER, CHARLES ALDEN (August 15, 1875-February 9, 1942), American writer of Western stories, was born in Janesville, Wis., the son of Lucien Bonaparte Seltzer and Oceanna (Hart) Seltzer. His family moved to Columbus, Ohio, the following year, and he attended the public schools

there. While still a child, Seltzer went west to live with an uncle on a New Mexico ranch.

From that time to early manhood he roamed the West from the Rio Grande to the Columbia River. Known to his fellow-cowpunchers as "Rip" Seltzer, he was a "joyous, carefree youth in leather chaps and broad sombrero" who helped Slavs, Celts, and Latins build the empire of the West.

Late in the '90's he returned to the East to work as a carpenter, contractor, and building inspector. His education had been limited to the bare fundamentals of reading and writing, but he began doggedly to write stories of the West he knew, and remembered with some wistfulness. Mrs. Seltzer, whom he married in 1896, and who was Ella Alberts of Rockport, Ohio, helped her husband obtain an education, and criticized his work during the thirteen years during which editors continued to send him rejection slips.

The Range Riders, published in 1911, was Seltzer's first novel, but some short stories had previously appeared and attracted the attention of Western fans who had read Wister's *The Virginian* and the yarns of B. M. Bower, and had (at that time) no pulp magazines to assuage their thirst. Several stories were transferred to the silent screen, and the resultant movies, shown in England, established his market there. Buck Jones, Bert Lytell, William Farnum, Bill Hart, and Tom Mix were some of the hard-riding stars to appear in these films.

During his thirteen-year novitiate, Seltzer was editor of a political paper for three years; was employed four years in the Building Inspection Department of the City of Cleveland; and spent two years as tax expert for the Board of Quadrennial Appraisers of Cuyahoga County, Ohio. In his latter years, when he was living in North Olmstead, Ohio, Seltzer served as councilman and then as mayor of that city for two terms.

It has been estimated that Seltzer's total sales reached at least a million and a half copies. The reprints of fifteen titles sold an average of 20,000 a year, each. Seltzer wrote of "a West that never was and never will be," the New York *Times* once declared; but the *Saturday Review of Literature* said of *The Valley of the Stars*

(1926) that: "If more tales of the wild and woolly attained the all-around excellence of Mr. Seltzer's, the lowly position which the 'Western' occupies in the realm of adventure fiction should be conspicuously improved."

Seltzer died at sixty-five at Lakeside Hospital, Cleveland, Ohio, of a long diabetic illness that had made necessary the amputation of his right leg in December 1941. He was survived by his wife, two daughters, and three sons, two of whom are editors of the Cleveland *Press.*

PRINCIPAL WORKS: The Range Riders, 1911; The Two-Gun Man, 1911; The Triangle Cupid, 1912; The Coming of the Law, 1912; The Trail to Yesterday, 1913; The Boss of the Lazy Y, 1915; The Range Boss, 1916; The Vengeance of Jefferson Gawne, 1917; Firebrand Trevision, 1918; The Man With a Country, 1919; The Ranchman, 1919; The Trail Horde, 1920; Drag Harlan, 1921; Beau Rand, 1921; Square Deal Sanderson, 1922; West, 1922; Brass Commandments, 1923; Lonesome Ranch, 1924; The Way of the Buffalo, 1924; Last Hope Ranch, 1925; Trailing Back, 1925; Channing Comes Through, 1925; The Valley of the Stars, 1926; A Gentleman From Virginia, 1926; Slow Burgess, 1926; Land of the Free, 1927; Mystery Range, 1928; The Mesa, 1928; The Raider, 1929; The Red Brand, 1929; Gone North, 1930; A Son of Arizona, 1931; Double Cross Ranch, 1932; Clear the Trail, 1933; Breath of the Desert, 1934; West of Apache Ranch, 1934; Silverspurs, 1935; Kingdom in the Cactus, 1936; Open Range Omnibus, 1936; Parade of the Empty Boots, 1937; The Coming of the Law, 1938; Arizona Jim, 1939; Treasure Ranch, 1940; So Long, Sucker, 1941.

ABOUT: New York Herald Tribune February 11, 1942; New York World-Telegram September 7, 1927.

SENDER, RAMÓN J. (February 3, 1902-), Spanish novelist, writes: "They tell me I was born in 1902. I do not believe it. My impression is that I have lived always, and I remember with more clarity, for example, Mediaeval Spanish scenes than episodes of my childhood or youth. The editors ask that I explain what I am like. That is the great problem. I cannot explain it because I do not know it.

L. Jacobi

"Dictionaries teach more than books do to friends, enemies, women, and, above all, children. In my books I find it necessary to express things which I cannot say to friends, enemies, women, or children. Perhaps I ought not to say them at all. But only thus, by writing things to be read, can I give the impression of individualizing myself sufficiently, of 'diluting myself in my time' in such a way that by incoherence and perhaps by violence I can make myself more tolerable to myself. Also, because I am out of tune with the affairs, the people, and the customs of my time, I have that feeling I have mentioned, of never having been born, and that other notion (which is the same at base and is inseparable from it) of not dying. This has nothing to do with academic ideas. It is a biological feeling."

* * *

Ramón Sender was born in Alcolea de Cinca, Huesca, Aragon. His parents were small farm owners. He was educated in a religious college and studied afterward in the Institute of Zaragoza (Saragossa) and in the Central University of Madrid. Because of disagreement with his family he lived independently from the age of fourteen, and he worked as a pharmacist at Saragossa and Madrid for many years, while he was still attending the university. He began in early youth to conspire against the monarchy. His boyhood was very hard. He was imprisoned and sent to his family, then re-arrested and exiled from Huesca, the capital of the province. He led a republican revolutionary movement which resulted in bloodshed and the shooting of those implicated, but was able to remain hidden during the reprisals. When he was twenty he had to undergo his compulsory military service, and was sent to Morocco, where he stayed till 1925. His book *Imán* (*Pro Patria*) resulted from those years.

When he returned from Africa he became editor of *El Sol,* a liberal magazine in Madrid, and continued his republican activities. During the regime of Primo de Rivera he was again imprisoned. During the Republic he remained critical, and refused all office. Finally he left Spain, living in Paris, Berlin, and Moscow, to which he had been invited by the writers and artists. However, he is anti-Communist, and he prophesied the Soviet-Nazi pact.

He returned to Spain, and in 1933 married Amparo Barayon. A year later they had a son, later a daughter. When the Fascist revolt began he enlisted at once in defense of the Republic and served throughout the Civil War (finally as a brigade commander) until 1937, when opposition by Communist elements forced him to leave Spain. He is now an exile in Mexico. His wife and his brother were both killed by the Fascists.

Sender's bitterness is understandable. He is politically a complete independent and individualist, whose books are a constituent part of the history of these troubled years in Spain. As a novelist, Henri Barbusse said that he is "a curious amalgam of realism and mysticism, and above all very Spanish." Sender himself rejoined that he is profoundly realistic, but that he has "only seen the truth, not spoken it." He is the original of "Manuel," in André Malraux's *Man's Hope.*

WORKS AVAILABLE IN ENGLISH: Pro Patria (in England: Earmarked for Hell) 1935; Seven Red Sundays, 1936; Mr. Witt Among the Rebels, 1937; Counter-Attack in Spain (in England: The War in Spain) 1937; Man's Place, 1940.

ABOUT: Barbusse, H. (ed.) Spanish Omnibus; Saturday Review of Literature September 26, 1936, November 13, 1937.

SERNA, ESPINA DE. See ESPINA

SERNA, GÓMEZ DE LA. See GÓMEZ

SERVICE, ROBERT WILLIAM (January 16, 1876-), Canadian verse-writer and novelist, writes: "I was born in Preston, England, of Scotch-English parentage, and soon after taken to Scotland, where I grew up. I lived in Glasgow until my twenty-first year, being educated at Hillhead High School, and attending classes at Glasgow University. I joined  the Commercial Bank of Scotland, in which I served my apprenticeship in banking. On coming of age I found the lust of adventure too strong for me, and resigning from the bank emigrated to Canada. I traveled steerage, landing in Victoria, B.C., with just five dollars in my pocket. For the next seven years I took a course in the College of Hard Knocks, graduating without enthusiasm. I traveled all up and down the Pacific slope, generally on freight trains, and worked in a score of different occupations. Afterwards I went to the Yukon, where I was employed [at White Horse and Dawson] by the Canadian Bank of Commerce for eight years. There, influenced by Kipling, I began to write, and was greatly surprised to find my work acceptable. I came to Europe to report the Balkan War for the Toronto *Star,* spending a short time with the Turkish army. After that I went to France, which I liked so much I settled there. Then came the Great War, for which I immediately volunteered, and in which I served for two years as an ambulance driver. Last summer the present war caught me in Russia, and I escaped from Warsaw the first day of the bombardment. Now, in my sixty-seventh year, I feel I have had enough of trouble and excitement, and only ask to be allowed to pass the rest of my days in peace and quiet, far from and, if possible, forgetting this world of strife as I cultivate the roses in my garden."

* * *

Mr. Service's wish was not fulfilled. This was written from the French Riviera early in May 1940. When the Nazis invaded France only a few days later, the author escaped with great difficulty and returned as a war refugee to Canada, after twenty-eight years' absence. He lost a 40,000-word manuscript of a novel, and had to leave behind in Nice two other completed novels. He is married, but does not give his wife's name.

He would be the first to disclaim any serious pretension as a poet; instead, he has had the rewards of immense popularity—seven editions of *Songs of a Sourdough* were printed before the book was published, and he has been anthologized and parodied beyond any other living writer. His work is openly derivative, mostly from Kipling but also from many other poets. It is written in what Louis Untermeyer called "the red blood and guts style carried off jauntily." As a novelist he has never equaled either the technical skill or the wide appeal of his verse.

PRINCIPAL WORKS: *Verse*—Songs of a Sourdough (reprinted as The Spell of the Yukon and Other Verses) 1907; Ballads of a Cheechako, 1909; Rhymes of a Rolling Stone, 1912; Rhymes of a Red Cross Man, 1916; Ballads of a Bohemian, 1920; Complete Poetical Works (5 vols.) 1927; Collected Verse, 1930; Bar-Room Ballads, 1940. *Novels*—The Trail of '98, 1910; The Pretender, 1914; Poisoned Paradise, 1922; The Roughneck, 1923; The Master of the Microbe, 1926; The House of Fear, 1927. *Miscellaneous*—Why Not Grow Young? or, Living for Longevity, 1928.

ABOUT: Bookman April 1915, January 1922.

*SETON, ERNEST THOMPSON (August 14, 1860-), American writer for boys, was born in South Shields, Durham, England, his name originally being Ernest Seton Thompson. He was brought to Canada at the age of six, and educated at the Toronto Collegiate Institute and at the Royal Academy in London. (He is artist as well as writer, and has illustrated all his own books.) He was a founder of the Boy Scouts of America, chief scout from 1910 to 1916, and later founder of the

Woodcraft League of America. He is now president of the Seton Institute, Santa Fé, N.M. His boyhood was spent in the backwoods of Canada, and later he was a government naturalist in Manitoba; he also spent many years on the Western plains of the United States. His knowledge of animals and of Indians was gained at first hand. In 1896 he married Grace Gallatin, long a writer on the Orient and the Near East; they had one daughter. In 1935, at seventy-five, he remarried, his second wife being Julia (Moss) Buttree, an authority on Indian life; and at seventy-eight he again became the father of a daughter! He has been a lecturer since 1898. His best known book is *Wild Animals I Have Known.* He won the John Burroughs Medal in 1928. Of himself and his present wife he writes:

J. Hardcastle

"The lives of the Setons are very full. Each year, they start off in the early fall on their lecture tours. They travel all day every day, and lecture practically every evening. In the early spring they have a month or so for writing, which they do very intensively, turning out usually a book a year each. From May they are actively busy preparing for their Institute work, in July and August. 1940 will be the last year of Seton Institute in the camping sense. They are retiring to devote more of their time to writing. Their home in Santa Fé is a 30-room adobe house in a 2,500-acre tract of land. Their library is the largest private library in the state, containing over 13,000 books on their specialized subjects. Their gallery includes nearly 8,000 of Mr. Seton's paintings and drawings, and their natural history collection is over 3,000 bird and mammal skins. Their little daughter often appears on their programs in Indian costume, dancing Indian dances. This she has been doing since she was seven months old."

Although he is now more than eighty years old, Mr. Seton has the energy and interests of a man of half his age, and has plans for a number of future books.

PRINCIPAL WORKS: Art Anatomy of Animals, 1896; Wild Animals I Have Known, 1898; The Trail of the Sandhill Stag, 1899; The Biography of a Grizzly, 1900; Lives of the Hunted, 1901; Krag and Johnny Bear, 1902; Two Little Savages, 1903; Monarch, the Big Bear, 1904; Animal Heroes, 1905; The Birchbark Roll, 1906; Biography of a Silver Fox, 1909; Scouting for Boys, 1910; The Arctic Prairies, 1911; Woodcraft and

* Died October 23, 1946.

Indian Lore, 1912; Wild Animals at Home, 1913; Manual of Woodcraft Indians, 1915; Wild Animals' Ways, 1916; Sign Talk, 1918; Woodland Tales, 1921; Bannertail, 1922; Lives of Game Animals, 1925; Cute Coyote and Other Animal Stories, 1930; Famous Animals Stories, 1932; Gospel of the Redman, 1936; Biography of an Arctic Fox, 1937; Great Historic Animals, 1937; Buffalo Wind, 1938; The Trail of an Artist-Naturalist, 1940.

ABOUT: Kunitz, S. J. & Haycraft, H. (eds.). The Junior Book of Authors; Seton, E. T. The Trail of an Artist-Naturalist; American Magazine February 1921; Bird Lore July 1935; Saturday Evening Post December 31, 1938; Saturday Review of Literature September 18, 1937, October 2, 1937, December 7, 1940; Time November 25, 1940.

"SEUSS, DR." See GEISEL, T. S.

SEYMOUR, Mrs. BEATRICE KEAN (STAPLETON), English novelist, speaks in one of her novels of "those beautifully

rare people who can be content to know a man or woman's work without wishing to pick over the rags of their private lives." In her *Who's Who* biography Mrs. Seymour records her address, the name of her publishers, the customary list of her books and the name of her husband. William Kean Seymour is a poet, parodist and anthologist, author of *Swords and Flutes* (1919) and *Chinese Crackers* (1938), and compiler of *A Jackdaw in Georgia* (1925) and *Parrot Pie* (1927). J. B. Chapman, writing of Mrs. Seymour in the English *Bookman* for April 1926, states that she regards novel-writing primarily as a pastime. Her "charm lies in her essential femininity. Slight in figure, she carries herself with grace. There is humor in her eyes and strength in her wide forehead and firm chin." Mrs. Seymour's best work is done between 1 and 2 P.M., when the world is "engaged in having its lunch or in dozing after it." In peacetime she spends most of the year quietly in London. A critical study of Jane Austen was written at Brown's Gate, Bucklebury, Berkshire, from April to the end of August 1937. "As long as I can remember," she explained, "I have always been very sceptical of the authenticity of that familiar literary portrait of Jane Austen in which she is presented as a placid spinster who went nowhere, and whose most exciting adventure was being shown over the Prince Regent's Library at Carlton

House." Her book was written to dispute and disprove the thesis.

From the first, critics have found Mrs. Seymour an interesting and individual but uneven writer, and one who stands in occasional need of editing. "While Mrs. Seymour may not strive for profound effects, she attains those for which she strives with ease and power. She is a craftsman," commented the New York *Times*. Rebecca West called *Intrusion* "immensely and incompetently long. Plainly, the idea that art is a selective process as well as a response to life, and demands treatment as well as statement of situations, is not present in Mrs. Seymour's mind." The contrast of social types which is the theme of this early novel reappears in the ambitious trilogy tracing the rise of Sally Dunn, a domestic servant: *Maids and Mistresses* (1932), *Interlude for Sally* (1934), and *Summer of Life* (1936). Other critics praise her intelligence and sense of pathos.

PRINCIPAL WORKS: Invisible Tides, 1919; Intrusion, 1921; Hopeful Journey, 1923; Romantic Tradition, 1925; The Last Day, 1926; Three Wives, 1927; Youth Rides Out, 1928; False Spring, 1929; But Not for Love, 1930; Maids and Mistresses, 1932; Daughter to Philip, 1933; Interlude for Sally, 1934; Frost at Morning, 1935; Summer of Life, 1936; The Happier Eden, 1937; Jane Austen, 1937; The Fool of Time, 1940; An Unquiet Field, 1940; Happy Ever After, 1941.

ABOUT: Bookman (London) April 1926.

"SHALOM ALEICHEM." See RABINOWITZ, S. J.

SHANNON, FRED ALBERT (February 12, 1893-), American historian and Pulitzer Prize winner, writes: "I was born in

Sedalia, Mo., of a family of long pioneer-farmer extraction that had just shortly before been starved out of Kansas by grasshoppers, hail storms, drought, and horse thieves. At six months I was taken to Indiana, where I lived except for one

year in Memphis, Tenn., until 1919. I graduated from the Indiana State Teachers' College (then Normal School) in 1914, and started teaching in the grade schools of Brazil, Ind. I went there because my new bride, Edna Jones, lived there and her father got me a job. [Married 1914; son and four daughters.] From 1916 to 1919 I was principal of the high school at Reelsvalle, Ind.

In 1918 I got an M.A. degree at Indiana University. From 1919 to 1923 I was professor of history at Iowa Wesleyan College, from which position I was virtually fired for giving the daughters of the president and dean low grades. Then I finished my formal education at the University of Iowa, getting a Ph.D. (the committee said with high distinction) in 1924. My doctoral thesis, *The Organization and Administration of the Union Army,* was published in such an expensive form that it never sold very widely. However, it received the Justin Winsor Prize of the American Historical Association in 1928 and the Pulitzer Prize in History in 1929, and thus I came very near breaking even.

"I taught history at the Iowa State Teachers' College, 1924-26; Kansas State College, 1926-38; economic history at Williams College, 1938-39; and have been associate professor of history at the University of Illinois since 1939. I also taught summers at Cornell College (Iowa), Ohio State University, West Virginia University, University of Missouri, and Harvard. I am one of the editors of the *American Economic History Series.*

"My interest in economic and social history probably dates from working in school vacations since the age of eleven in sawmills, grist mills, iron foundries, glass factories, stamping mills, Western wheat fields, carrying papers, clerking in grocery stores, and what have you. You learn a lot that way.

"Bernard De Voto called my Pulitzer Prize book 'a brilliant enlargement of Civil War history written by a young and comparatively obscure man.' I really was relatively young in 1929, and can still claim obscurity."

PRINCIPAL WORKS: The Organization and Administration of the Union Army: 1861-65, 1928; Economic History of the People of the United States, 1934; America's Economic Growth, 1940; The Farmer's Last Frontier, 1941.

ABOUT: Atlantic Monthly January 1938; Saturday Review of Literature March 13, 1937.

SHAPLEY, HARLOW (November 2, 1885-   ), American astronomer, was born in Nashville, Mo., the son of Willis Harlow Shapley and Sarah (Stowell) Shapley. He was educated at the University of Missouri (B.A. 1910, M.A. 1911) and at Princeton, under Henry Norris Russell (Ph.D. 1913) He has honorary Sc.D. degrees from many universities, including Princeton, Harvard, Pennsylvania, and Toronto. After seven years as an astronomer at Mt.

Wilson Observatory, in California, he became in 1921 director of the Harvard Observatory, a post he still holds, together with that of Paine Professor of Astronomy at Harvard. In 1928 he was Halley Lecturer at Oxford, and in 1934 Darwin Lecturer to the Royal Astronomical Society. His medals and honors have been innumerable; they include the Janssen prize of the Société Astronomique de France, the Draper medal of the National Academy of Sciences, the Bruce medal of the Pacific Astronomical Association, the Rumford medal of the American Association of Arts and Sciences, the Pius XI prize for Astronomy, and the highest of all astronomical honors, the gold medal of the Royal Astronomical Society.

He is president of the Nebular Commission of the International Astronomical Union, a Fellow of the American Academy of Arts and Sciences and on its council, on the council of the American Association for the Advancement of Science, a trustee of the Oceanography Institute at Woods Hole, Mass., and of the Massachusetts Institute of Technology, an associate trustee of the University of Pennsylvania, and a councillor of the University of Missouri. The breadth of his interests is indicated by the fact that he is also a trustee of the Damascus School for Girls, and was director of the Committee for Relief in Belgium of the Educational Foundation. He was married to Martha Betz in 1914; she is also an astronomer and has done much work with him. They have four sons and a daughter. His subsidiary scientific interest is in entomology, on which he has done some valuable reesarch. In spite of all the honors heaped upon him, Dr. Shapley remains a quiet, unassuming, hardworking scientist.

He and his brother (former head of the art department of the University of Chicago and now visting professor at Johns Hopkins) had to make their own way, since their father, a teacher, died when they were boys. After preparing for college at Carthage (Mo.) Academy, he worked as a reporter for a year before entering the university. He is one of the greatest authorities living on spectroscopy and photometry. His special field is cosmogony, the science of the structure and nature of the universe; the so-called "hub of the universe," in Sagittarius, is officially known as Shapley Center. He is a young-looking, brown-haired, pipe-smoking man, whose life is almost entirely spent in the observatory, where he has in his office a unique revolving desk designed by himself to take care of all his multifarious papers. Although he is one of the very greatest living astronomers, and naturally most of his writing is highly technical, he has proven himself able to write for the general public in a lucid, simple, and engaging style. His scientific creed is also his creed as a writer: "Ours is a perpetual inquiry; any acceptance of faith . . . brings inquiry to a halt."

PRINCIPAL WORKS: Starlight, 1926; Radio Talks From the Harvard Observatory (with others; as The Universe of Stars, with C. H. Payne, 1929) 1926; The Stars, 1927; A Source Book on Astronomy (with H. E. Howarth) 1929; Star Clusters, 1930; Flights From Chaos, 1930; Sidereal Explorations, 1931.

ABOUT: American Magazine June 1934; Current Biography 1941; Nature May 5, 1934; Saturday Review of Literature January 18, 1936; Science November 18, 1921; Time July 20, 1935.

SHARP, DALLAS LORE (December 13, 1870-November 29, 1929), American writer on natural history, was born at Haleyville, N.J., the son of Reuben Lore and Mary Den (Bradway) Sharp. He received his B.A. degree from Brown University in 1895, and the degree of S.T.B. from Boston University in 1899. The latter institution made him an honorary member of Phi Beta Kappa in 1914, and Brown followed suit in 1916, also granting him an honorary Litt.D. the next year.

Dr. Sharp was ordained a pastor in the Methodist Episcopal Church in 1895, the same year he married Grace Hastings of Detroit. There were four sons, one with the good old-fashioned name of Waitstill. He had pastorates in Porter, Mass., 1896-98, and Brockton Heights in 1898-99, then left to join the staff of the *Youth's Companion* and begin writing his nature books. "It is a divinely beautiful world, a marvelously interesting world, the best conceivable sort of world to live in," he declared, "—in spite of gypsy moths, germs, and tornadoes." Of life on his fourteen-acre farm, Mullein Hill, Hingham, Mass., twenty miles from Boston, he wrote, as a poet not a plowman, with "a sense of words, of humor, of the infinite."

In 1899 Dr. Sharp returned to Boston University as assistant librarian, becoming assistant professor of English in 1902, and full professor from 1909 till his death. *Beyond the Pasture Bars* (1913) was written for children of grades 4 to 6. *Where Rolls the Oregon* describes the work of the fish and game warden there. In one of his last years he made a trip to the Canal Zone. John Burroughs, whose life he wrote, called him a great nature writer. His slight frame, with pleasant scholarly face and keen eyes behind glasses, was frequently seen at library meetings.

PRINCIPAL WORKS: Wild Life Near Home, 1901; Watchers in the Woods, 1903; Roof and Meadow, 1904; The Lay of the Land, 1908; The Face of the Fields, 1911; The Fall of the Year, 1912; Summer, Beyond the Pasture Bars, 1913; Where Rolls the Oregon, 1914; The Hills of Hingham, 1916; The Seer of Slabsides, 1921; Education in a Democracy, 1922; Highlands and Hollows, 1923; The Magical Chance, 1923; The Spirit of the Hive, 1925; Sanctuary! Sanctuary!, 1926; The Better Country, 1928.

ABOUT: New York Times November 30, 1929.

SHARP, MARGERY (1905-   ), English novelist and short-story writer, is the third daughter of J. H. Sharp. She was educated at Streatham Hill High School, Bedford College, and London University. At the latter she received a B.A. degree with honors in French (the scene of *The Nutmeg Tree,* her best-selling novel, is southern France). Her college career

Pinchot

was devoted "almost entirely to journalism and campus activities." She traveled in Poland and in Ireland, and was a very popular member in 1929 of the first British Universities Women's Debating Team to visit the United States, being included not because she was a debater, she has stated, but because "someone had to come." The subjects for discussion were unusually weighty, but as third speaker Miss Sharp managed to make Washington laugh even on the subject of Popular Psychology . . . a fact which will be understandable to her readers.

Margery Sharp started writing after graduation, "by design." The design was so good that she has since contributed to such diverse publications as the *Encyclopaedia Britannica* and that other bulwark of English liberties, *Punch*. Besides writing more than a half-dozen novels, she has done two long-short stories, a play, and has contributed to the *Strand, Harper's, Fiction Parade, Woman's Home Companion, Harper's Bazaar,* the *Saturday Evening Post,* and other magazines. On the occasion of her first of several appearances in *Harper's Magazine* in 1934, the editors pointed out that she was "uncommonly adroit in the fabrication of ingenious plots." Julia Packett, her endearing lady of easy virtue, was first introduced to an American public in the successful novel *The Nutmeg Tree,* published in 1937, and acquired two million more friends (at least) by her subsequent appearances in the *Saturday Evening Post.* In March 1940 *Lady in Waiting,* dramatized by the novelist herself (who had written an earlier play, *Meeting at Night*) had a brief run in New York with Gladys George in the leading rôle.

Reviewing *The Nutmeg Tree* in its original incarnation as a novel, William Soskin stated: "Inherent in Miss Sharp's seemingly light story there is a shrewd study in the contrasting psychologies of the pleasing prigs and the honest, slightly loose ladies." He praised her "inventiveness and accurate sense of entertainment." Theodore Purdy in the *Saturday Review of Literature* called the book "moderately entertaining nonsense with a high saccharine content." *Rhododendron Pie* and *The Stone of Chastity* also display Miss Sharp's gift for light comedy.

Although she does not state the fact in *Who's Who,* Margery Sharp is the wife of Geoffrey Castle. Her recreations are skating, sailing, and painting. She is a frequent contributor to *Collier's* as well as to the *Saturday Evening Post.* In 1939 she once again visited the United States.

PRINCIPAL WORKS: Rhododendron Pie, 1930; Fanfare for Tin Trumphets, 1932; The Nymph and the Nobleman, 1932; Sophy Cassmajor, 1934; The Flowering Thorn, 1934; Four Gardens, 1935; The Nutmeg Tree, 1937; Harlequin House, 1939; The Stone of Chastity, 1940; Three Companion Pieces, 1941.

ABOUT: Harper's Magazine August 1937.

SHARP, WILLIAM. See "BRITISH AUTHORS OF THE 19TH CENTURY."

*SHAW, GEORGE BERNARD (July 26, 1856-   ), Irish dramatist, was born in Dublin. His father, George Carr Shaw, son of the high sheriff of Kilkenny, was a ne'er-do-well and a notable drinker. This fact is important in his son's life. Bernard Shaw's hatred of alcohol and tobacco, his zealous vegetarianism, his anti-vaccination and anti-vivisection views, the strange Jaeger "reform

clothing" of his youth, even his sex prudery —in a word, his entire Puritanical complex— are a reaction against his father. The mother, born Lucinda Elizabeth Gurly, of County Carlow, was a gifted singer, a talented musician, and a "managing" woman, who completed the conquest of her only son and kept him close by her side until he was forty-two. All the whitewash of the Australian cousin, Charles M. Shaw, cannot conceal the fact that the Shaw *ménage* was disturbed, poverty-ridden, and uncongenial. The father endeavored in vain to earn their living as a corn factor (a sort of agricultural commission broker), and while her son and two daughters were still children Mrs.

Fox-Movietone

Shaw left him and went to London, where she became a music teacher.

The boy meanwhile had, after private tutoring from a clerical uncle, been an unsatisfactory pupil at the Wesleyan Connexional School (now Wesley College). At fifteen he was apprenticed to a Dublin land agent, and a year later became the company's cashier. His real education had come from a thorough grounding in music and painting, gained at home, and omnivorous reading. A business life was unendurable to him; in 1876 he broke away and joined his mother in London. Nine years followed of unrecognized struggle and genteel poverty. He did hack-writing, he even made occasional abortive attempts at commercial labor. But for the most part, to quote his own words, "I made a man of myself (at my mother's expense) instead of a slave." In other words, he wrote five novels, every one of which was promptly rejected.

In 1885 he became music critic of the *Star,* under the pseudonym of "Corno di Bassetto." Later he took both his writing and his pseudonym to the *World.* Still later he became dramatic critic of the *Saturday Review.* At various times he reviewed art for the *World* and books for the *Pall Mall Gazette.* But his real life at this period was in political propaganda. In 1884 he was one of the founders of the Fabian Society, two years after he had first read Henry George and "the importance of the economic basis dawned on me." Karl Marx followed, and Shaw announced himself a Socialist. He still calls himself one, but it was only during the 1880's and 1890's that he actually "worked at it"—wrote Fabian tracts, made daily or even more frequent speeches, and was genuinely active in the Socialist movement. Only two of his early plays, *Widowers' Houses* and *Mrs. Warren's Profession,* can be said to be expressions even distantly of a Marxian viewpoint. Since then, it is impossible to find a single word to characterize his shifting and highly individual economic faith; he has managed to admire Mussolini, Hitler, and Lenin with equal fervor, has toyed with the idea of a benevolent monarchy, and at times has echoed purely anarchistic theories.

All this toil and strain of writing and speaking finally broke down the splendid health of the tall, red-haired, red-bearded young stalwart who already lived on greens and water. In 1898 he had a complete collapse. His cure was largely due to the ministrations of his wife, married during his convalescence—that "heroic lady," Charlotte Frances Payne-Townshend. She has cared for him since, as his mother cared for him before. Shaw's theory of the relative aggressiveness of the sexes is candidly set forth in *Man and Superman.* He had shied from marriage like a nervous horse. As R. Ellis Roberts said, "he has always been afraid of intimacy—physical, emotional, and spiritual." Ellen Terry and Mrs. Patrick Campbell, among others, have provided testimony on that score.

Shaw's career as a dramatist began about 1894. At first he was published, but unacted. His plays, all thesis plays, all arising from problems, were read as much for the discursive prefaces he gave them as for themselves. It was 1904 before he began to have his plays produced regularly, and it was 1910 before the Shaw craze struck New York and Berlin. Since that time his history is largely the history of his work, and of the personality which overshadows his work. In 1925 he received the Nobel Prize for Literature. In 1933, after swearing he would never set foot in America, he did visit this country briefly during a world-wide tour. In 1938, for the first time, he allowed one of his plays—*Pygmalion*—to be filmed. His *Collected Works* appeared between 1931 and 1934, but he has written a great deal since then, and is still writing. He has had plenty of conflict with the authorities— both *O'Flaherty, V.C.* and *Saint Joan of Arc* were banned by the British censor, the former for patriotic reasons, the latter for religious—but all during the First World War he talked and criticized freely without interference (probably because fundamen-

tally he was for the war), and in the Hitler conflict he seems to be doing the same thing, in spite of a pathetic article entitled "The Cops Won't Let Me Talk!" He has never had any hesitancy about announcing his own importance as a writer, but the embarrassing thing about objecting to this apparent vainglory is that he is more or less correct in his self-judgment. He has been one of the most misquoted men of his century; he never did, for example, say that he was greater than Shakespeare, even though he furnished the world with an "improved" version of *Cymbeline* in 1937.

The time has not yet come for a complete evaluation of Bernard Shaw's place in literature. A great many contradictory things might be said about him, each of which would be true. He has never been a fetichist of consistency, though he will never acknowledge having been inconsistent. A great deal of the braggadocio in which he sometimes indulges is defensive. He has been so much in the public eye, for so long, that he must struggle to keep his private self intact. Somewhere deep in his inner being is a romantic poet, who is even shy. Around him Shaw has built a protective, glittering shell. He is willing to be called a humorist (which he is not, though he is a magnificent ironist and a shattering wit); a smug, self-righteous crank; a doddering old mystic. He can take all such comment with aplomb and return the thrust with very pointed steel. But the innermost Shaw, the timid, tender, modest, idealistic Shaw, he defends fiercely against discovery or invasion. He will exploit his religious sense, carrying it to the brink of parody; he will exploit his alleged parsimony and mercenary ruthlessness (though he gave the entire amount of his Nobel Prize to the Anglo-Swedish Foundation to spread a knowledge of Scandinavian literature among English readers). But his actual fundamental nature he never exploits; it comes out only in occasional furtive glimpses, in his relations with women or his attitude toward official reverence. One cannot, for example, even contemplate the thought of Sir George Bernard Shaw, or Lord Shaw, without laughter. He has deliberately made himself into the Great Eccentric, while he chuckles sardonically behind the Mephistophelean mask.

It is the inner coherence behind the outward inconsistency that makes Edmund Wilson say that "his plays have been a truthful and continually developing chronicle of a soul in relation to society. Artistically as well as physically . . . he is outliving all the rest of his generation." And R. Ellis Roberts well said that Shaw is "a born artist and dramatist whose devotion to his destined work has been continually diverted, first through personal contacts, secondly by the time in which he was born." Bonamy Dobrée called him "our greatest pamphleteer since Swift, master of impeccable prose, wielder of a style which is original because he has something to say. He represents, for the first three or four decades of this century, the great exploder of complacency." Yet equally true are the harsher words of Joseph Wood Krutch: "It was chiefly as a stimulant that he was valuable. . . . A showman of ideas, he became the victim of his own showman's gift, and he will probably be remembered neither as a playwright nor as a philosopher, but chiefly as a man who beat a drum so effectively that he enticed an apathetic public to that main tent where greater men than he were performing."

Finally, since in his later works the emphasis has been on Shaw's religious rather than his economic views, it might be well to listen to St. John Ervine's elucidation of the perfected Shavian theology: "God, or the Life Force, is an imperfect power striving to become perfect. . . . The whole of time has been occupied by God in experiments with instruments invented to help Him in His attempt to perfect Himself. . . . [Finding all previous instruments faulty] God created a new instrument, Man, who is still on probation. Shaw warns the world that if we, too, fail to achieve God's purpose He will become impatient and scrap mankind as He scrapped the mammoth beasts. 'You should live so that when you die God is in your debt.' "

PRINCIPAL WORKS: *Plays*—Plays Pleasant and Unpleasant (Arms and the Man, Candida, The Man of Destiny, You Never Can Tell, Widowers' Houses, The Philanderer, Mrs. Warren's Profession) 1898; Three Plays for Puritans (The Devil's Disciple, Caesar and Cleopatra, Captain Brassbound's Conversion) 1900; The Admirable Bashville, 1901; Man and Superman, 1903; John Bull's Other Island, 1904; How He Lied to Her Husband, 1904; Major Barbara, 1905; Passion, Poison, and Petrification, 1905; The Doctor's Dilemma, 1906; Getting Married, 1908; The Shewing Up of Blanco Posnet, 1909; The Fascinating Foundling, 1909; The Glimpse of Reality, 1909; Press Cuttings, 1909; The Dark Lady of the Sonnets, 1910; Misalliance, 1910; Fanny's First Play, 1911; Androcles and the Lion, 1912; Pygmalion, 1912; Overruled, 1912; Great Catherine, 1913; The Music-Cure, 1914; O'Flaherty, V. C., 1915; The Inca of Perusalem, 1915; Augustus Does His Bit, 1916; Heartbreak House, 1917; Annajanska, 1917; Back to Methusalah (cycle of five plays) 1921; Jitta's Atonement (translation of Siegfried Trebitsch) 1922; St. Joan of Arc, 1923; The Apple Cart, 1929; Too True To

Be Good, 1932; The Village Wooing, 1933; On the Rocks, 1933; The Six of Calais, 1934; The Simpleton of the Unexpected Isles, 1934; The Millionairess, 1936; Geneva, 1938; In Good King Charles's Golden Days, 1939. *Novels*—Cashel Byron's Profession, 1882; An Unsocial Socialist, 1882; The Irrational Knot, 1884; Love Among the Artists, 1884; Immaturity (written 1879) 1930; Adventures of a Black Girl in Search of God, 1932. *Miscellaneous*—The Quintessence of Ibsenism, 1891; The Sanity of Art, 1895; The Perfect Wagnerite, 1898 (these three as Major Critical Essays, 1931); The Common Sense of Municipal Trading, 1904; Socialism and Superior Brains, 1910; Common Sense About the War, 1914; How to Settle the Irish Question, 1917; Peace Conference Hints, 1919; The Intelligent Woman's Guide to Socialism and Capitalism, 1928; What I Really Wrote About the War, 1931; Music in London: 1890-94 (3 vols.) 1931; Our Theatres in the 'Nineties (3 vols.) 1931; Doctors' Delusions, Sham Education, and Crude Criminology, 1931; Pen Portraits and Reviews, 1932; The Political Madhouse in America and Nearer Home, 1933; Prefaces, 1934; Short Stories, Scraps, and Shavings, 1934; William Morris as I Knew Him, 1936; London Music in 1888-89, 1937.

ABOUT: Armstrong, C. F. Shakespeare to Shaw; Broad, C. L. Dictionary to the Plays and Novels of Bernard Shaw; Burton, R. Bernard Shaw, the Man and His Work; Chesterton, G. K. George Bernard Shaw; Colburne, M. D. The Real Bernard Shaw; Collis, J. S. Shaw; Duffin, H. C. The Quintessence of Bernard Shaw; Ellehauge, M. The Position of Bernard Shaw in European Drama and Philosophy; Hackett, J. S. George Versus Bernard; Hamon, A. F. The Twentieth Century Molière: Bernard Shaw; Harris, F. Bernard Shaw; Henderson, A. Bernard Shaw: Playboy and Prophet, George Bernard Shaw: His Life and Works; Huneker, J. G. Iconoclasts; Jackson, H. Bernard Shaw; Palmer, J. L. George Bernard Shaw: Harlequin or Patriot?; Pearson, H. G. B. S.; Rattray, R. F. Bernard Shaw: A Chronicle and an Introduction: Sen Gupta, S. C. The Art of Bernard Shaw; Shanks, E. Bernard Shaw; Shaw, C. M. Bernard's Brethren; Sherard, R. H. Bernard Shaw, Frank Harris, and Oscar Wilde; Skimpole, H. (Bernard Shaw: The Man and His Work; Wagenknecht, E. C. A Guide to Bernard Shaw.

SHAW, IRWIN (1913-), American dramatist and short story writer, writes: "I was born in New York City and was educated in Brooklyn, in the public schools and in Brooklyn College, from which I was graduated with a B.A. in 1934. I played football there for four years, wrote a column for three years for the school newspaper (my first published work), and  wrote plays that were put on by the dramatic society. I was expelled in my freshman year for failure in calculus, worked for a year at various jobs around New York, in a cosmetics factory, an installment furniture house, and a department store. To make money when I got back into school I tutored children, worked in the school library, typed manuscripts, wrote theses in English for students in New York University.

"When I got out of school I started writing for the radio, wrote radio serials for two years, among them 'The Gumps' and 'Dick Tracy,' comic-strip dramatizations. I wrote *Bury the Dead* while still writing for the radio, quit the radio for good and all after finishing the play. I've written screen plays in Hollywood on four different occasions, all of them of no consequence. *Siege,* my second play, was a gloomy and immediate failure. *The Gentle People,* produced in 1939, was fairly successful, ran for four and a half months. Another play, *Quiet City,* was tried out in an experimental production by the Group Theatre for two performances, was closed before the critics were allowed in. I've also written many short stories, for the *New Yorker, Esquire, Collier's, Story,* the *Yale Review,* other magazines.

"I'm married, live in New York City. My most recent production was *Rereat to Pleasuse* (1940), a comedy. [Staged by the Theatre Guild, this play met with a cool reception.] My political convictions are liberal.

"*Bury the Dead* is included in Gassner's *Twenty Best Plays of the Modern Theatre,* has been done a great many times all over the country by almost every little theatre group, and has been done in England and Ireland and by the Habima Players of Palestine in a Hebrew translation. *The Gentle People* was produced professionally in London and Copenhagen. Stories of mine are in the 1940 O. Henry and O'Brien collections."

* * *

Among other odd jobs Mr. Shaw has been a truck-driver and "a third rate semi-professional football player." All his experiences have been grist for his mill. Besides the plays he mentions, he wrote *Church, Kitchen, Children* for the Hollywood branch of the Anti-Nazi League, and another anti-Fascist play, *Salute. Bury the Dead* is reminiscent of the Austrian Hans Chlumberg's *Miracle at Verdun,* in which, also, soldiers killed in battle refuse to be buried, but it is very different in feeling and conclusion. This one-act play which made its author famous overnight was submitted two weeks too late to a New Theatre League contest, but was produced by the League under difficulties in an obscure New York playhouse, immedi-

ately attracted attention, and soon moved uptown to Broadway. As a short story writer Mr. Shaw belongs to the current school of "hard boiled understatement."

In 1942 Shaw became a private in America's wartime army. From Fort Dix, New Jersey, Sergeant Jimmy Cannon wrote of "this sharp-faced, big-bodied guy": "I like my friend for his honesty and for his poetic love of the city. I like him because he feels that this is his war and that his typewriter is not the barricades. I like him because he asked to be classified as 1A."

PRINCIPAL WORKS: Bury the Dead, 1936; The Gentle People, 1939; Sailor Off the Bremen (short stories) 1939; Welcome to the City (short stories), 1942.

ABOUT: New York Sun January 21, 1939; New Yorker December 28, 1940; Scholastic January 22, 1940; Time April 27, 1936; Wilson Library Bulletin March 1940.

S H A W, THOMAS EDWARD. See LAWRENCE, T. E.

SHEARING, JOSEPH, English novelist and historian, is one of the impenetrable literary mysteries of the day. Neither the London nor New York publishers of his (or possibly her!) books shows any disposition to reveal the identity of this very able writer of striking novels, usually based on comparatively obscure "celebrated cases" in the annals of British and French crime. The name itself, however, is definitely known to be a pseudonym. The writer is evidently a thorough student of French life and literature, two of the historical books being dated from Paris and Vimontiers, and the heightened, stripped, staccato style is full of French turns of phrase and idiom. Occasional paragraphs read like literal translations from a French original; on the other hand, romances like *Moss Rose* and *The Golden Violet* show an intimate knowledge of English life, above- and below-stairs and in the cheaper theatrical circles.

One theory held in some quarters is that "Joseph Shearing" is the English writer "Marjorie Bowen" (Mrs. Gabrielle Margaret Vere Campbell Long[qv])* who indeed possesses many of the necessary qualifications, such as a knowledge of English bohemian life and of French and English criminology. She has lived and studied in Paris, and has employed another masculine pen name, "George Preedy." But another school of thought holds with equal stubbornness that the pseudonym conceals the iden-

---

*As we go to press, Mrs. Gabrielle Margaret Vere Campbell Long has finally confessed her authorship of the "Joseph Shearing" novels.—THE EDITORS.

tity of F. Tennyson Jesse,[qv] distinguished British criminologist and novelist.

From the appearance of the first Shearing novel, there has been a definite and devoted cult of readers of this writer, who does not have any decided appeal to the rank and file of the mystery-story-reading public. The first Shearing romance, called *Forget-Me-Not* in England and *Lucile Cléry: A Woman of Intrigue* in the United States, was appreciatively reviewed but its sales could not compare with those of Rachel Field's later popular success, the fictionized biography *All This and Heaven Too,* based on the same case, the murder of the Duchesse de Praslin in Paris in 1847. Of the two books, the Shearing novel was closer to being a *roman à clef* in the customary sense of the term, inasmuch as fictitious names were given the protagonists in the tragedy; and the character of the governess (who in real life emigrated to America and married Rachel Field's great-uncle) was treated with greater license, less sympathy, and possibly less authenticity. A 1941 American reissue of the Shearing novel was entitled *The Strange Case of Lucile Cléry.*

Reviewing *The Crime of Laura Sarelle,* Sally Benson wrote in the *New Yorker* in 1941: "There are many adjectives to describe this book, adjectives that apply to all of Mr. Shearing's books: evil, sinister, ghostly, strange, baleful, terrible, relentless, sinister, and malevolent. Such experts in murder as Edmund Pearson and the former Scotch barrister William Roughead have declared openly that the Shearing novels are the best of their kind published today. Mr. Shearing is adept at stitching together his swooning heroines, his young baronets, his flickering candles in their tall sconces, his hothouse fruits in high silver-gilt *épergnes* with a strong, red thread of murder. Mr. Shearing is a painstaking researcher, a superb writer, a careful technician and a master of horror. There is no one else quite like him."

PRINCIPAL WORKS: Forget-Me-Not (U.S. title: Lucile Cléry: A Woman of Intrigue) 1932; Album Leaf (U.S. title: The Spider in the Cup) 1933; Moss Rose, 1934; The Angel of the Assassination: Marie-Charlotte de Corday D'Armont, Jean-Paul Marat, Jean-Adam Lux: A Study of Three Disciples of Jean-Jacques, 1935; The Golden Violet: The Story of a Lady Novelist, 1936; The Lady and the Arsenic: The Life and Death of a Romantic, Marie Cappelle, Madame Lafarge, 1937; Orange Blossoms (short stories) 1938; Blanche Fury, 1939; Aunt Beardie, 1940; The Crime of Laura Sarelle, 1941; The Fetch, (U. S. title: The Spectral Bride) 1942.

ABOUT: Roughead, W. The Seamy Side; New Yorker May 10, 1941; Saturday Review of Literature July 12, 1941.

SHEEAN, VINCENT (December 5, 1899-), American essayist and novelist, writes: "I was born [James Vincent Sheean] in Pana, Ill. My parents were both of Irish parentage. My mother, Susan Mac-Dermott, was the daughter of a Fenian rebel who came to America after the revolt of 1867; my father, William Charles Sheean, was the son of a Southern Irish  peasant family which migrated westward after the great potato famine in Ireland in 1848. These are different but representative examples of the Irish migrations, the political and the economic. It was something my Fenian grandfather used to tell— a song and one or two stories about the Irish Brigade, Clare's, at the Battle of Fontenoy—which survived in my mind years later and directed me towards the subject around which I wrote a novel, *A Day of Battle.*

"I was educated—so to speak—in Pana and at the University of Chicago. Even though I may have received little formal education there—learned little, worked little—I am sure the exposure to the influences of culture must have had a decisive effect upon my very inexperienced mind. When I left the university—without a degree—I worked for a while on the Chicago *Daily News,* then on the New York *Daily News,* and finally on the Chicago *Tribune,* in Paris. I was a correspondent in Europe for the *Tribune* for the better part of three years, and after I left them in 1925 I was never again regularly employed on a newspaper. At certain crises, such as 1927 in China, 1929 in Palestine, and 1938 in Spain, I returned to newspaper correspondence for brief periods, sending dispatches to the North American Newspaper Alliance mainly. In Spain I sent them to the New York *Herald Tribune.* But for the greater part of the last fifteen years I have employed myself in other forms of writing, political journalism and short stories for magazines, as well as novels and a kind of writing exemplified in my books, *Personal History* and *Not Peace but a Sword.* This kind of writing is not easy to classify; it is a sort of semi-autobiographical political journalism, the external world and its graver struggles seen from the point of view of an observer who is not indifferent to them. Currently I am trying to write a play.

"My general political view tends to be that of what is called 'the left.' I believe firmly in the future of a working-class movement, but the parties now in existence do not seem to me to place the general proletarian interest very high. I find it hard to imagine any possible set of circumstances in which I might take part in a political movement, so my opinions are of merely literary interest (if that).

"I am excessively fond of music, and used often to go without food to buy tickets to concerts and opera. I have a great weakness for Wagner, in spite of the fact that the intellectual content of his works makes no appeal to me. Among the great writers of the past, I admire most the Russian and French novelists (Tolstoy, Dostoievsky, Balzac, Stendhal, and Proust, chiefly) and the English poets. I think I have something more than the conventional regard for Dante. Once during a fairly long residence in Naples I acquired a great admiration for Benedetto Croce, most of whose work I have read and still value highly. Stray enthusiasms of mine at various times have been the plays of Synge, Shaw, and O'Casey, the dialogues of Plato in Jowett's translations, Trotsky's *History of the Russian Revolution*, the polemical papers of Lenin, critical works by Sainte-Beuve and Taine, and the wonderful memoirs of the Duc de Saint-Simon. Among writers of my own generation I am particularly sensitive to the work of Ernest Hemingway, Frank O'Connor (in Ireland), André Malraux (in France).

"I was married in 1935, in Vienna, to Diana Forbes-Robertson, youngest daughter of Sir Johnston Forbes-Robertson, of the famous family of actors. We now have two daughters."

* * *

Vincent Sheean's *Personal History* was the first of the wave of autobiographies by European correspondents, and still remains the best of them. He lectures frequently on his war experiences. In general, he has been least successful in his novels, the best of which is *A Day of Battle*.

Although he has lived for years in the thick of adventure, Sheean's closest call came in 1941 in Bronxville, a peaceful New York suburb, in the middle of a freezing February night, when the house that the Sheeans had rented from Dorothy Thompson burst into flame and the occupants had to jump for their lives from the upper story windows. Sheean received bad burns and a damaged leg. After recuperating, he went to England on an assignment for the *Saturday Evening Post* and thence to the Far East for articles on war conditions in the Pacific. In 1942 he became a captain in the Air Corps.

Vincent Sheean is called "Jimmy" by his friends. A lover of good talk and hot argument, he is solid, six-foot-two and "wears the map of Ireland on his face." His red hair has turned prematurely gray. The Sheeans have been active in finding American homes for English children.

PRINCIPAL WORKS: An American Among the Riffs, 1926; The Anatomy of Virtue, 1927; The New Persia, 1927; Gog and Magog, 1929; The Tide (novel) 1933; Personal History, 1935; Sanfelice (novel) 1936; The Pieces of a Fan (short stories) 1937; A Day of Battle (novel) 1939; Not Peace But a Sword, 1939; Bird of the Wilderness, 1941.

ABOUT: Sheean, V. Personal History, Not Peace But a Sword; Current Biography 1941; Current History January 1940; Scholastic April 9, 1938; Wilson Library Bulletin May 1935.

*SHELDON, CHARLES MONROE (February 26, 1857-), American clergyman and writer, author of the all-time best-seller *In His Steps,* was born in Wellsville, N.Y., the son of Stewart Sheldon and Sarah (Ward) Sheldon. He attended Phillips Academy, Andover, Mass., and received a B.A. degree from Brown in 1883. After graduate work at the Andover Theological Seminary he was ordained a Congregational minister in 1886, and began his first pastorate at Waterbury, Vt., where his parish was seven miles square, "all uphill." He remained here for two years, indulging in such mild chicanery as hiring away the organist from a rival church by offering her fifty cents more a Sunday, and startling the village by rigging up a home-made sprinkler to lay the dust. In 1889 Dr. Sheldon (D.D. Temple College 1898, Washburn College 1900, Brown 1923) transferred to the Central Congregational Church at Topeka, Kans., to remain until 1912. From 1912 to 1915 he was minister-at-large, and active pastor again until 1919. From 1920 to 1925 Dr. Sheldon was editor-in-chief of the *Christian Herald*, published in New York, and has been a contributing editor since. He married Mary Abby Merriam of Topeka in May 1891, and they still live in Topeka. Their son, Merriam, to his own great delight, was the first American arrested as a spy in the First World War; the Sheldons were at Sydney in Australia when the war broke out, and young Merriam was

observed by military police snapshotting the harbor. They were all detained for questioning, and the films were confiscated.

In His Steps, which, by a flaw in the copyright and through its ethical content, became the greatest best-seller, exclusive of the Bible and Shakespeare, of all time, was written on the porch of the author's Topeka home one summer when the temperature was above 100 for several weeks. It was read chapter by chapter at his Sunday evening services; published serially in the *Chicago Advance,* and issued, after three publishers had rejected the book, in 1896. Only part instead of all the chapters had been sent to the Copyright Office, and innumerable pirated editions soon appeared. It is estimated that thirty million copies in all have been sold, twenty-two million of these in the British Empire. Dr. Sheldon received only a few hundred dollars for the work and was hard put to answer the 900 letters received every week suggesting that he should live up to the thesis of the book ("What Would Jesus Do?") and divide his profits with those less fortunate than he. The book is a simple, straightforward piece of story-telling, not without interest, has been dramatized, and translated into ten languages. None of its successors raised any such furore.

PRINCIPAL WORKS: Richard Bruce, 1891; Robert Hardy's Seven Days, 1892; The Twentieth Door, 1893; The Crucifixion of Philip Strong, 1893; John King's Question Class, 1894; His Brother's Keeper, 1895; In His Steps, 1896; Malcolm Kirk, 1897; Lend a Hand, 1897; The Redemption of Freetown, 1898; The Miracle at Markham, 1898; One of the Two, 1898; For Christ and Church, 1899; Edward Blake, 1899; Born To Serve, 1900; Who Killed Joe's Baby, 1901; The Wheels of the Machine, 1901; The Reformer, 1902; The Narrow Gate, 1902; The Heart of the World, 1905; Paul Douglas, 1909; The Good Fight, 1909; A Sheldon Year Book, 1909; Howard Chase, 1917; A Little Book For Every Day, 1917; All the World, 1918; Heart Stories, 1920; In His Steps Today, 1921; The Richest Man in Kansas, 1921; The Everyday Bible, 1924; The Happiest Day of My Life, 1925; Two Old Friends, 1925; Charles M. Sheldon: His Life and Story, 1925; A Vote on War, 1935; All Over Forty, 1935.

ABOUT: Sheldon, C. M. Charles M. Sheldon: His Life and Story; Current Literature January 1900.

*SHELDON, EDWARD BREWSTER

(February 4, 1886-), American playwright, was born in Chicago, the son of Theodore Sheldon and Mary (Strong) Sheldon. He attended the Hill School, Pottstown, Pa., and in 1908 took both a B.A. and a master's degree at Harvard, where he organized the Harvard Dramatic Club and was its first president. "After graduation I settled in

New York and wrote plays. Most of the summers I traveled and worked in Europe. In 1918 I came down with arthritis, which is another word for rheumatism. This has limited me in various ways ever since. I still live in New York —a penthouse on the corner of Madison Avenue and 84th Street. I like any book, new or old, by  John Buchan. I feel that aversions, being negative, are unimportant."

The late O. O. McIntyre said of Sheldon: "He can visualize a play from the manuscript and inject those tense bits that lift mediocrity to the heights. Or whittle a dull line into a smoothly sharp barb. Those who go expecting to cheer him, run into a reverse angle. He usually cheers them." Sheldon's work on the scripts of Charles MacArthur's *Lulu Belle* (1926) and Margaret Ayer Barnes' *Dishonored Lady* (1930), vehicles for Lenore Ulric and Katharine Cornell respectively, raised them into the class of exceptionally superior melodramas. *Dishonored Lady* was based on a celebrated Scots trial, the case of Madeleine Smith, accused of poisoning her lover. The two dramatists were awarded damages of $587,604.37 for plagiarism, from the producers of the talking picture Letty Lynton, which was based on the novel of the same name by Mrs. Belloc-Lowndes, also founded on the Smith case. Some sequences in the picture, it was adjudged, too closely paralleled the second act of the play.

Salvation Nell, Sheldon's first play, starring Mrs. Minnie Maddern Fiske and produced in New York at the Hackett Theatre November 17, 1908, was also the first commercial success to come out of Professor George Pierce Baker's English 47 course in play writing at Harvard. *The Nigger* (1909) was the first American success at the ambitious New Theatre, later the Century, on Central Park West. *Romance* (1913) recording the love of an Episcopal rector for a prima donna drawn from Lina Cavalieri, served Doris Keane for several seasons and gave Greta Garbo the most glamorous of her early English-speaking rôles in the talking pictures. Edward Sheldon also dramatized Sudermann's erotic romance *The Song of Songs,* and worked on the late Sidney Howard's fanciful drama *Bewitched.* Critics have spoken of the "color, charm, elemental passion and extraordinary instinct for the theatre of his plays." He prefers the panoramic method. The late H. T. Parker of the Boston *Transcript* once commented that Sheldon's grip upon the stage was firmer than his grip upon life

The young playwright, before he became bedridden, as he is today with his arthritis, was an attractive youth, tall and with thick brown hair.

PRINCIPAL WORKS: *Plays*—Salvation Nell, 1908; The Nigger, 1909; The Boss, 1911; The Princess Zim-Zim, 1911; Egypt, 1912; The High Road, 1912; Romance, 1913; Song of Songs, 1914; Garden of Paradise, 1915; The Lonely Heart, 1920; The Proud Princess (with D. Donnelly) 1924; Bewitched (with S. Howard) 1924; Lulu Belle (with C. MacArthur) 1926; Jenny (with M. A. Barnes) 1929; Dishonored Lady (with M. A. Barnes) 1930.

ABOUT: Harvard College, Class of 1908: Twenty-Fifth Anniversary Report; National Magazine March 1913; Vanity Fair October 1914; Vogue March 15, 1913.

SHEPARD, BENJAMIN HENRY JESSE FRANCIS. See GRIERSON, F.

SHEPARD, ODELL (July 22, 1884-), American essayist, poet, and biographer, Pulitzer Prize winner, was born in Sterling,

Ill., the son of Bishop William Orville Shepard and Emily (Odell) Shepard. At twenty he was a student in the Northwestern School of Music, remaining until 1904, and also taking courses at Northwestern University from 1902 till 1904. Shepard received the degree of Bachelor of Philosophy at the University of Chicago in 1907, obtaining his Ph.M. the next year and a Ph.D. from Harvard in 1916. In his last year at Northwestern he was city editor of the Evanston (Ill.) *Index*. In Chicago he was organist in various churches and a reporter on the Chicago *Tribune* at various times from 1905 to 1907; after receiving his master's degree he was an instructor in English at Smith Academy, St. Louis, for a year.

In 1908 he married Mary Farwell Record of Evanston, and they have a son, Willard Odell Shepard. From 1909 to 1914 Shepard was professor of English at the University of Southern California. He stayed on at Harvard after getting his doctor's degree as instructor in English there and at Radcliffe College until 1917, when

he was appointed Goodwin Professor of English at Trinity College, Hartford, Conn. He spent a year abroad in 1927-28 as a Fellow of the John Simon Guggenheim Memorial Foundation. In 1940 he was elected Lieutenant-Governor of Connecticut.

Odell Shepard's first published work was a Shakespearean outline (1916) and the next year he published *A Lonely Flute,* a volume of poems. (A former Trinity student of Shepard's, now a clergyman in New York City, recalls that his professor of English was a robust individual who sometimes dressed like a poet, with loose collar and flowing tie.)

In 1923 Shepard produced a study of Bliss Carman's poetry, and four years later a volume of essays, *The Harvest of a Quiet Eye.* Brooks Atkinson of the New York *Times* wrote that "the pleasant flavor that makes this volume such good reading comes chiefly from Mr. Shepard's discussions on small towns, on farmers in the field, on the cracker-barrel gossips of Fairford postoffice, on fishing, on the rhythms of a brook and on science and spirit." In preparation for *Pedlar's Progress* (1937), a biography of Bronson Alcott which was issued as a memorial volume for the celebration of the one-hundredth anniversary of Little, Brown, the Boston publishers, Shepard read all fifty volumes of Alcott's journals as well as his correspondence and contemporary records.

Pedlar's Progress, which the late Ernest Sutherland Bates called an important contribution to American letters, was awarded the Pulitzer Prize for the best biography of the year. "It reflects faithfully the Arcadian innocence of this transcendental peddler who had the heart of a child and the mind of a seer," said Henry Steele Commager, while Henry Seidel Canby entered a demurrer that "Alcott's unhappy style, sententious, involved, abstract, has had its reaction on Mr. Shepard's own style, which is sometimes inflated, though often also excellent."

Professor Shepard has also edited Thoreau Alcott's *Journals,* and some collections of modern essays.

PRINCIPAL WORKS: Shakespeare Questions: An Outline For the Study of the Leading Plays, 1916; A Lonely Flute (poems) 1917; Bliss Carman: A Study of His Poetry, 1923; The Harvest of a Quiet Eye, 1927; The Joys of Forgetting, 1928; The Lore of the Unicorn, 1929; Thy Rod and Thy Creel, 1930; The Cabin Down the Glen, 1931; Pedlar's Progress: The Life of Bronson Alcott, 1937; Connecticut: Past and Present, 1939; Irving Babbitt (with F. A. Manchester) 1941.

ABOUT: Saturday Review of Literature May 7, 1938.

SHERIDAN, Mrs. CLARE CONSUELO (FREWEN)

SHERIDAN, Mrs. CLARE CONSUELO (FREWEN) (1885-   ), English journalist and novelist, was born in London, the eldest daughter of Moreton Frewen. Her mother was a sister of Lady Randolph Churchill, mother of Winston Churchill. Clare Frewen was educated at the Convent of the Assumption, Paris, and at Darmstadt. Her husband, Wilfred Sheridan, a direct descendant of Richard Brinsley Sheridan the dramatist, was killed in France in September 1915, the second year of the First World War. His widow turned to the execution of portrait busts as a mingled livelihood and career, doing busts of Princess Patricia of Connaught, Senator Marconi, Lord Oxford and Asquith (for the Oxford Union), Lord Birkenhead; Lenin, Trotzky, Zinoviev, etc., for the Soviet government (hence her first book, *Russian Portraits* (1921)); the Archbishop of Galilee, Mahatma Gandhi, Marie of Roumania, Michel Collins, and others. A trip to Mexico in 1921 to model President Obregón resulted in failure to get a sitting, but Obregón granted an interview which eventually appeared in the New York *World* and the *Metropolitan Magazine*.

Clare Sheridan came to the United States in 1921. *My American Diary* (1922) was characterized by John Farrar as "no reportorial but an unusually jaundiced account of an America which is not really America at all. As a story of an unusual woman it is entertaining." The New York *World* appointed Mrs. Sheridan European correspondent in 1922, and she interviewed Mussolini, Mustapha Kemal, Stamboulisky, Primo de Rivera, and other notables of the period. She was in Ireland during the clash of the Republicans and Free Staters, and interviewed Rory O'Connor just as he burst into international prominence. Her journeys in Russia, Turkey, Germany, Czechoslovakia and Poland were often accomplished by motor bicycle and sidecar. She camped with Charlie Chaplin in California; was twice a guest at Dr. Axel Munthe's San Michele; and lived in Algeria, in the oasis of Biskra.

Mrs. Sheridan's travel books are usually "sprightly narratives with acid seasoning"; her novels are not of first importance. Her career is believed to have suggested S. N. Behrman's comedy *Biography*, in which Ina Claire played. Clare Sheridan's country home is Brede Place, Sussex; her workshop is in London.

PRINCIPAL WORKS: Russian Portraits, 1921; My American Diary, 1922; In Many Places, 1923; Stella Defiant, 1924; Across Europe With Satanella, 1925; The Thirteenth, 1925; A Turkish Kaleidoscope, 1926; Nuda Veritas, 1927; Green Amber, 1929; El Caïd, 1930; Genetrix, 1935; Arab Interlude, 1936; Redskin Interlude, 1938; Without End, 1939.

ABOUT: Sheridan, C. My American Diary; Wilson Library Bulletin April 1932.

SHERMAN, STUART PRATT

SHERMAN, STUART PRATT (October 1, 1881-August 21, 1926), American literary critic, was born at Anita, Iowa, the son of John Sherman, a druggist and farmer, and Ada Martha (Pratt) Sherman. His childhood was spent on a farm at Rolfe, Iowa, and in Los Angeles, where his father had gone to seek a cure from tuberculosis. He died, however, when Stuart

P. MacDonald

was eleven. (Stuart Sherman's only son John later died of the same disease.) He spent eight months prospecting gold with a party in Arizona and in 1894 went to Dorset, Vt., the home of his maternal grandfather, to attend the village school a year. He spent two years at Troy Conference Academy, and entered Williams College at Williamstown, Mass., in 1900. There Sherman edited the literary magazine in his senior year and graduated as salutatorian in 1903, voted the brightest and most versatile man in his class. Harvard gave him an M.A. in 1904; his doctor's dissertation (on John Ford's *'Tis Pity She's a Whore*) in 1906 was called the most brilliant ever to be submitted to the English department. Two years later a characteristically sardonic attack on "Graduate Schools and Literature" in the *Nation* attracted wide attention. The *Nation* ran his book reviews and critical essays for ten years subsequently.

From an instructorship in English at Northwestern University Sherman proceeded to the University of Illinois, where rapid promotions made him a full professor at thirty, in 1911. A few years later he was head of the department of English, and regarded as a fixture there. He edited *Coriolanus, Treasure Island, The Scarlet Letter, Leaves of Grass*, and the *Sand-Flaubert Letters*. His first original book was about Matthew Arnold, and Arnold's theories were applied rigorously in *On Contemporary Lit-*

erature, an attack on naturalism as exemplified in the work of Dreiser, Moore, Wells, and Synge. (He thought better of Arnold Bennett.) *Americans* showed ten eminent Americans influenced by the tradition of Puritanism. Sherman edited Volumes I and II of the *Cambridge History of American Literature,* with W. P. Trent, John Erskine, and Carl Van Doren (who calls him, in *Three Worlds,* "the last of the professors"); and contributed the article on Mark Twain to the third volume.

In 1924 the New York *Herald Tribune* invited him to edit its books review section, rechristened *Books,* at a salary at $12,000 a year. Sherman accepted, and proceeded to undergo an extraordinary rejuvenation in the salubrious air of 41st Street and Morningside Heights. He praised Wells, Sherwood, Anderson, and Wilde, defended D. H. Lawrence, and lauded his ancient adversary, H. L. Mencken, as an educator, if not as a critic. *My Dear Cornelia,* which ran in the *Atlantic Monthly,* discussed chastity, eligible young men, and modern girls. Forsaking Irving Babbitt, Paul Elmer More and humanism, he struck a happy medium between conservatism and radicalism.

A little more than two years of the journalistic grind wore Sherman out. In the summer of 1926 he lectured at the University of Colorado before going in August to his usual summer cottage on Lake Michigan, near Manistee, Mich. Swimming ashore from an overturned canoe, he suffered a heart attack and sank to the bottom in four feet of water. Prolonged efforts to revive him proved futile. His death, announced on the same day that news of the passing of Rudolph Valentino and President Eliot of Harvard was filling the obituary columns, received little space in the press.

Sherman's personality was called a baffling one, ranging from the gentle, vivid, and playful to the austere, sardonic, and egotistic. He was a master of irony, understatement, and the "edged epithet"; in person he was tall, dark, somewhat cadaverous, with a forehead "three stories high." The body was placed in a typical Vermont hillside cemetery, at Dorset, where his grandfather Pratt was once pastor.

PRINCIPAL WORKS: *Critical Essays*—On Contemporary Literature, 1917; Americans, 1922; The Genius of America, 1924; My Dear Cornelia, 1924; Points of View, 1924; Men of Letters of the British Isles, 1924; Critical Woodcuts, 1926; The Main Stream, 1927; Shaping Men and Women (edited by Jacob Zeitlin) 1928; The Emotional Discovery of America, 1932. *Biography*—Matthew Arnold, 1917.

ABOUT: De Mille, G. E. Literary Criticism in America; Drake, W. A. (ed.). American Criticism; Farrar, J. (ed.). The Literary Spotlight; Mencken, H. L. Prejudices: Second Series; Van Doren, C. Many Minds; Three Worlds; Zeitlin, J. & Woodbridge, H. The Life and Letters of Stuart P. Sherman; Bookman June 1926; December 1926; Century August 1923; New York Herald Tribune "Books" September 26, 1926; Saturday Review of Literature September 26, 1926; Sewanee Review January-March 1927.

SHERRIFF, ROBERT CEDRIC (June 6, 1896-), English playwright and novelist who signs his works R. C. Sherriff was born at Kingston-on-Thames, near London, the son of Herbert and Constance (Winder) Sherriff. He grew up with no literary or scholarly ambitions, his chief interest being in sports — football, cricket, and rowing. His father was in the insurance business, and as soon as he had been graduated from the Kingston Grammar School, at seventeen, he too became an insurance clerk. The next year, with the beginning of the World War, he enlisted in the Ninth East Surrey Regiment, becoming a second lieutenant in the infantry at eighteen. He was wounded at Ypres, spent six months in hospital, and was demobilized in 1918 with the rank of captain. He then returned to the insurance company.

For ten years he was an insurance claims adjuster. Then he became mildly interested in amateur dramatics, and began writing plays for the Kingston Rowing Club, of which he had been captain. *Journey's End,* which he wrote merely as one of these amateur plays, grew out of the letters he had written to his family during the war. However, it was beyond the club's acting capacities, and so he offered it (as he had done unsuccessfully with many others of his plays) to a professional dramatic agent. Nobody wanted it, and finally, on a chance suggestion, he sent it to George Bernard Shaw for criticism. Shaw told him, in effect, that it was half a dozen plays in one, but he did help him get a production by the London Stage Society. There it was seen by Maurice Browne, who had been active in Little Theatre work in England and America, and who secured its stage rights. It was given its first really public performance at the Savoy Theatre on New Year's Day, 1929.

Much to Sherriff's bewilderment, it was an immense success. At one time there were four companies playing it in England, five in the United States, it was produced in France, Germany, Sweden, Poland, and Greece, it was filmed, and Sherriff himself made it into a novel. It made him rich, famous, and an author.

His later plays and novels have never duplicated this success—as he himself foresaw they would not. *Journey's End* was, in colloquial phrase, "a natural"—a very English, but very human, play about a subject in which everybody was interested. Sherriff, a modest man, realized that he needed better preparation for a writing career. At thirty-five he went to college—to New College, Oxford—completing his three-year course in two years. He had some idea of becoming a teacher of history. Instead, he went to Hollywood, where he wrote the film version of Remarque's *The Road Back*, H. G. Wells' *The Invisible Man*, and Galsworthy's *Over the River*. He has since written several more plays and novels; only one of the latter, *The Hopkins Manuscript*, a fantastic story of the future, has aroused much attention.

He is unmarried, and lives quietly in the little town of Esher, Surrey. He has no particular interest in the theatre, and seldom goes to plays. He still rows and plays cricket, and he has become interested in archaeology. "I can think of nothing more awful," he says, "than being a professional writer." *Journey's End* gave him enough money to live comfortably and write only when he feels like it. He is a slim, dark-haired man who likes loose country clothes, lives much out of doors, and is sociable without caring for what is called "society." He has only one rule for writing: "In a writer the two things that matter above everything else are that he should be keenly, hungrily interested in his fellows, and that he should have the common experience of his time."

PRINCIPAL WORKS: *Plays—*Journey's End, 1929; Badger's Green, 1930; Windfall, 1933; St. Helena (with Jeanne de Casalis) 1935. *Novels—*The Fortnight in September, 1931; Greengates, 1936; The Hopkins Manuscript, 1939.

ABOUT: Chesterton, G. K. Adventures in Dramatic Appreciation; Literary Digest November 23, 1929; Living Age February 1931; Nation September 30, 1939; Theatre Arts Monthly July 1929.

*SHERWOOD, ROBERT EMMET (April 4, 1896-   ), American dramatist, three-time winner of the Pulitzer Prize was born in New Rochelle, N.Y. His father, Arthur Murray Sherwood, was an investment broker with a consuming passion for the theatre; his mother, Rosina (Emmet) Sherwood, a collateral descendant of the Irish

patriot for whom her son was named, is still a well known painter and illustrator. He was a precocious child, who started his career as "writer" and "editor" at the age of seven. He was educated at Milton Academy, Milton, Mass., and at Harvard, where he wrote his first play, *Barnum Was Right*, for the Hasty Pudding Club. He left Harvard in his junior year, in 1917, to get into the First World War. Later he received his B.A. degree as of 1918. He enlisted in the Canadian Black Guard, and was probably the tallest soldier in kilts, for he is six feet seven inches. (A similar height had kept his father off the stage.) He served in France, was gassed at Arras and wounded at Amiens, and spent many months in hospital.

From the beginning he hated the war, and he came out of it resolved to fight for a warless world. "A fiercely militant liberal," he has had the carreer of many other liberals in the postwar years: a changing from pacifism to advocacy of war as the only answer to the Axis.

While in Harvard he had edited a burlesque *Vanity Fair* number for the *Lampoon*, and when he was mustered out in the beginning of 1919 he was asked to join the *Vanity Fair* staff as dramatic critic. He resigned, with Robert Benchley, the next year, in protest against Dorothy Parker's discharge for an unfavorable criticism. He then went to (the old) *Life*, where it is said he started the first regular motion picture criticism column and thus is the "father" of "movie" critcism—though Dorothy Parker had certainly covered somewhat the same field in *Vanity Fair*. In 1924 he became editor of *Life* and remained until 1928, at the same time covering movies also for the New York *Herald*. After this he was literary editor of *Scribner's Magazine*. However, *The Road to Rome*, his first produced play, was an immense success, and since about 1930 he has devoted nearly all his time to playwriting (plus one novel, which was a flat failure).

Mr. Sherwood was married in 1922 to Mary Brandon, and they had a daughter. They were divorced in 1934 and in 1935 he married Mrs. Madeline (Hurlock) Connelly, former wife of Marc Connelly. They were married in Europe, where he lived for several years. Both in France and in Hollywood he has done a great deal of motion picture writing, in filming both his own plays and those of others. He worked with René Clair on *The Ghost Goes West* and did the screen version of *Pride and Prejudice.* He also adapted *Tovarich* from the French of Jacques Deval. He has received the Pulitzer Prize for Drama thrice, in 1936 for *Idiot's Delight,* in 1939 for *Abe Lincoln in Illinois,* and in 1941 for *There Shall Be No Night.*

From 1937 to 1940 Sherwood was president of the Dramatists' Guild of the Authors' League. He is president of the American National Theatre and Academy, and a member of the National Institute of Arts and Letters, which gave him a gold medal in 1941 for distinguished service in the field of drama.

With his great height, dour expression, slow speech, "macabre, unsmiling laugh," his extreme shyness and generous good nature, Robert Sherwood is something of a "character." He hates large gatherings (almost as much as he hates the country), but among his friends is famous for his solo songs and dances. He makes tremendous sums of money and gives most of it away; all the royalties from *There Shall Be No Night* went to the Red Cross. He carries his plays around in his head for a long time and then writes them with incredible speed. He suffers from recurrent attacks of *tic douloureux,* one of the most painful complaints in existence, but works right through them. In 1931 he bought a house and farm in Surrey, England, and used to spend his summers there; now it is full of refugee children from London.

With Maxwell Anderson, Elmer Rice, the late Sidney Howard, and S. N. Behrman, he was a founder and is a director of the Playwrights' Company, which produces its members' plays. Several of his plays have been starring vehicles for Alfred Lunt and Lynn Fontanne. Though one critic has accused him of perpetrating "hokum of the highest type," the consensus of opinion is that he is among the few American masters of high comedy and that his desperate earnestness in recent years has added both depth and stature to his work.

As *There Shall Be No Night* indicates, Sherwood was active in promoting aid to Finland during the German and Russian invasion. He was one of the most vehement spokesmen for aid to Britain from the beginning of the Second World War, and was a charter member of one of the principal committees with that aim. So much has he been in the public eye because of these and similar activities, that it did not seem at all fantastic when early in 1941 a false rumor was broadcast that he would succeed Joseph P. Kennedy as ambassador to England.

PRINCIPAL WORKS: The Road to Rome, 1927; The Queen's Husband, 1928; The Love Nest, 1928; Waterloo Bridge, 1929; This Is New York, 1930; Reunion in Vienna, 1931; The Virtuous Knight (novel) 1931; Acropolis, 1933; The Petrified Forest, 1934; Idiot's Delight, 1936; Abe Lincoln in Illinois, 1938; Revelation, 1940; There Shall Be No Night, 1941.

ABOUT: Catholic World November 1940; Current Biography 1940; New Yorker June 1 and 8, 1940; Saturday Review of Literature May 6, 1939, February 1, 1941, May 10, 1941; Theatre Arts Monthly June 1934.

*SHIEL, MATTHEW PHIPPS (July 21, 1865-), English novelist who signs himself M. P. Shiel, writes: "I was born in Montserrat, West Indies, preceded by eight sisters. After each female birth my father had a drawing-room prayer-meeting, conducted by the Wesleyan minister, to give thanks, but with hints to the Deity that a male birth next time would be appreciated; and finally I,  Nature's last effort, was sent. My father being a preacher (not for money), 'religion' was my atmosphere, though I am now so vastly more religious than he, being modern-religious, that his ancient religion seems irreligious, indeed antireligious, since it keeps men from being really religious: for in proportion as religion springs from knowledge it is real, in proportion as it springs from hope (ignorance) it is unreal. Is not religion an attitude of devotion? But, to adore, one must *know something,* surely about the adored? Adoration is a compound of (1) Awe, and (2) Love; and, to have it, one must *know* that the Deity is (1) great, and (2) good— is (1) greatly great, and is (2) greatly good. So that henceforth real religion springs from the knowledge of two facts, (1) that the stars are suns, this causing awe, and (2) that linnets 'come from' lizards, as men, too, do, there being a principle of Progress inherent, a good Agency urging, which, when realized, cannot but be passionately loved. But how could an ancient be really religious? He knew nothing (almost)! As late as Dante the sun and the moon were not worlds! To Plato the sun was 'not a god, but a stone.' Of our millions of worlds they knew of only one, or half-a-one, say, so that their God was not greatly great, but littly great, nor was he known to be greatly good, pitilessly driving Life to rise through thousands of millions of years, but was hoped to be littly good, 'loving' (somehow) Joe and Joan.

"Anyway, that was my boyhood's environment—ancient hopings: so that I could become a modern only through strain and stress. Moreover, my (Irish) father, 'descended from kings,' had—wildly unlike his only-begotten son!—an admiration for kings, and on my fifteenth birthday had me crowned King of Redonda by Dr. Mitchinson, Bishop of Antigua, with no little celebration, amid a gathering of ships (he was a ship-owner) and of tipsy people—Redonda being a small island that no Government had yet claimed. Four months after my coronation I matriculated, and presently was at King's College (London) for my degree; then was a student at St. Bartholomew's; but soon left medicine to return to literature (I had written two serials, and, at twelve, a novel).

"I now wrote some books under different influences—Poe's, Carlyle's, Job's—then a career of 'serials,' serial on serial, but then again books that I could bear to read, written under *no* influence, one of my most favoring readers then being Mrs. Gladstone, a very gracious lady, to whose favor I owe much. Now I was in the literary côteries of London, Paris—Pierre Louÿs, the good Stevenson, Wilde, my friend Ernest Dowson, and suchlike. I was appointed Interpreter to the International Congress of Hygiene and Demography—my one official job, save when in the Great War I was in the Censor's Office, reading German handwriting. Afterwards, by a caprice of His Majesty the King, my name was put on the Civil List for my (alleged) 'services to literature,' I by then having written some thirty (?) books.

"Now for three years I have been doing a book called *Jesus*—a (truer) translation of Luke, with my criticisms, in which is some detective work, proving, for example, that the Apostle Paul was that Lazarus who, in his anti-Sadducee craze for resurrection, stayed four days in a tomb; and this book, I fancy, is my top-note, though most people consider that my top-note is *The Purple Cloud*, lately acquired by the Paramount Company, to be made into a picture-play."

* * *

Mr. Shiel, as can be seen, is an "original." He has had a curious career as a writer; all his books had long been out of print when he was "discovered" by an American publisher, and some thirty of them—ranging from his individualistic "romances" to detective stories of a sort—were brought out again in quick succession—four in one day! He describes himself as "teacher, journalist, author, and inventor," and in his middle seventies was still devoted to mountaineering as well as to mathematics. With his crisp, curly, dark hair (now gray) and his bright eyes, he has been called "the spirit of eternal youth and undying romance." He has been twice married, his second wife being Carolina Garcia Gomez, whom he married fifteen years after his first wife's death.

His unusual style as a novelist is almost indescribable; it has been called flamboyant, picturesque, overcharged—and also irritating. Ralph Strauss said: "He is too gorgeously mad, too aloof from life as most people know it, but there is magic in his work, and a white-hot enthusiasm. He has apparently little knowledge of human nature, and someone has said that "his characters all seem intoxicated"; his voluminous and erudite vocabulary almost stuns the reader: but for adventurous and hardy souls there is stimulating experience in Shiel's novels. His name is pronounced *sheel*.

PRINCIPAL WORKS: The Yellow Danger, 1898; The Purple Cloud, 1901; Unto the Third Generation, 1903; The White Wedding, 1907; The Dragon, 1913; The Lord of the Sea, 1924; Children of the Wind, 1924; How the Old Woman Got Home, 1927; Here Comes the Lady, 1928; Cold Steel, 1929; The Black Box, 1930; Dr. Krasinski's Secret, 1930; The Invisible Voices, 1936; Poems, 1936; The Young Men Are Coming, 1937.

ABOUT: Van Vechten, C. Excursions; Literary Digest April 20, 1929; London Mercury May 1929.

SHOLOKHOV, MIKHAIL ALEKSANDROVICH (1905-), Soviet novelist, born in the Cossack village Veshenskaya, on the Don, derives from a family of middle-class Cossacks. His father was a dealer in cattle and lumber, and later owner of a power mill. His mother was of Turkish origin: her grandmother and her father, then six, fell  into the hands of the Cossacks and were brought to the Don region as prisoners of war.

After attending elementary school in Moscow, Mikhail studied in the *gymnasium* at Voronezh but was unable to graduate because he was forced to flee during the German invasion of that section. Though merely a child at the time of the war and the revolution, Mikhail was no passive witness: at the age of sixteen he was assigned by the Bolsheviks to a statistical bureau and later to a requisition department; finally, he became a member of the Executive Committee of his district. In 1922 he fought the plundering hordes of bandits who infested the Don region.

Sholokhov's earliest writings date back to 1925 when his *Tales of the Don* were published, a collection of short stories realistically depicting the life of the Don Cossacks. In 1928, with the appearance of the first part of *And Quiet Flows the Don*, Sholokhov's name became known throughout the Soviet Union, where the book circulated in millions of copies. Besides being filmed, it was made, by Ivan Dzerzhinsky, into an opera which, according to Kurt London, "holds the record for success in the Soviet musical world."

Sholokhov tells us how he came to write his great epic: "I began to write the novel in 1925. At first I did not conceive it as a work of the scope that it subsequently assumed.... I set out to depict the part taken by the Cossacks during the revolution in the march on Petrograd.... After I had written about a hundred pages I felt that it wouldn't quite do. The reader was bound to wonder: Why did the Cossacks take part in the attempts to crush the Revolution? Who were those Cossacks, anyhow, and what kind of a place was that region of the Don Cossacks? I myself began to wonder whether it was not *terra incognita* to the reader.... I dropped the first idea and began on a more extensive scale.... Of course my intimate knowledge of Cossack life proved to be invaluable. I started to work on *And Quiet Flows the Don* in its present form approximately at the end of 1926." Volume I appeared in 1928, Volume II in 1929, Volume III in 1933, and Volume IV in 1938. The first two volumes, slightly abridged, were translated into English in 1934; the continuation, entitled *The Don Flows Home to the Sea*, appeared here in 1941. On the publication of the latter volume Maurice Hindus wrote: "At the age of thirty-six, Sholokhov stands in the foremost rank of the European writers of our time. It is a pleasant duty for a reviewer to signal the arrival of a classic into the fold of literature."

On completing Volume II of *And Quiet Flows the Don*, Sholokhov commenced *Seeds of Tomorrow* (Vol. I, 1932, Vol. II, 1933). In this novel, Sholokhov shows, to quote Philip Henderson, "the old chaotic Russia of the desperately poor peasants and the rich farmers (*kulaks*), each for himself, with their petty feuds and child-like superstitions, relics from the feudal past, giving place to the planned socialist economy of the collective farms. And what a masterly presentation it is!" In 1934, Krasheninikova dramatized *Seeds of Tomorrow* as a four-act play, and it was successfully staged at the Simonov Studio Theatre. Later Ivan Dzerzhinsky used the novel as the libretto for an opera.

Sholokhov lives, in peacetime, in Veshenskaya, a hundred miles from the nearest railway station. Frequently the roads in the surrounding steppe become impassable and the only means of communication is the airplane which daily delivers his voluminous mail. Sholokhov is an enthusiastic hunter and fisherman. He is ill at ease in big cities, feeling like a bird in a cage. Nevertheless in 1937 he attended the Valencia-Madrid-Paris Writers Congress. In the same year he was elected Deputy to the Supreme Soviet.

The picture of his pre-war life is idyllic. He is married to Maria Petrovna, a Cossack girl, and has four children. He works mostly at night, in the two-room attic of his small, skyblue house designed by himself. He loves his gray Don pigeons, and if he misses one, will spend hours looking for it all over the countryside. His mail and his constant stream of visitors asking advice of all sorts take a great deal of his time but he answers each letter and interviews each visitor himself, refusing to have a secretary, for he prizes the direct popular contact. Sholokhov is of medium height, is never without his pipe, and wears the semi-military khaki suit and leather or felt boots of the outdoors man. He was instrumental in founding a Cossack theatre in his village, the first of its kind in the Don region.

When the Nazis invaded Russia in 1941, Sholokhov became one of his country's famed "fighting correspondents." While at the front in 1942 he learned that his mother had been killed in her hut by a German bomb.

Sholokhov works with the meticulousness of a scientist and the zest of an explorer. "I must be careful in selecting my facts, and investigate and verify them again and again ... it is the duty of every writer to 'check' his material. No error, even the slightest, escapes the reader's attention. I work very carefully, and I take my time."

Sholokhov is the Soviet Union's most popular living writer. "No second Soviet writer," declared Kurt London, "has such profound knowledge of the depths of the human soul. This man understands all things. He displays the highest virtue a writer can possess: he is always objective and just."

AVAILABLE IN TRANSLATION: And Quiet Flows the Don, 1934; Seeds of Tomorrow (British title: Virgin Soil Upturned) 1935; The Don Flows Home to the Sea, 1941.

ABOUT: Dinamov, S. & others. Mikhail Sholokhov; Henderson, P. The Novel Today; London, K. Seven Soviet Arts; Matsuev, N. Khudozhestvenaya Literatura; Struve, G. Soviet Russian Literature; Books July 1, 1934, November 10, 1935; International Literature November 1939, April-May 1939 (World's Fair Edition); The Literary World August 1934; New York Times July 15, 1934, November 10, 1935; Times (London) Literary Supplement April 5, 1934, October 10, 1935.

SHORTER, CLEMENT KING (July 19, 1857-November 19, 1926), English editor and biographer, was born in Southwark, the son of Richard and Elizabeth (Clemenson) Shorter. His mother had some Spanish blood, which may have given rise to the constantly spread and constantly denied statement that Shorter was Jewish. The father was a "carrier"

ruined by the railroad, who then emigrated to Australia and died there in poverty while his son was a child. Clement attended a school at Downham Market, Norfolk, but at fourteen went to London, where he worked for various booksellers and stationers. After studying for the junior branch of the Civil Service, he was made a clerk in the Exchequer and Audit Department of Somerset House, where he remained from 1877 to 1890. At the same time he took evening courses in languages at Birbeck Institution, and managed a three months' leave in Germany to study that language.

From 1888 he wrote columns about books for the *Star* and the *Queen*, and in the evenings acted as sub-editor of the *Penny Illustrated Paper*. In 1890 he was made the editor of the *Illustrated London News* and the next year of the *English Illustrated Magazine* as well. In 1893 he founded and edited (for the same owner) the *Sketch*, which was the first paper to use half-tone blocks for illustration. By 1897 he was editing five periodicals—these three and the *Album* and *Pick-Me-Up* as well. He left all of them in 1900 to found and edit the *Sphere*, of which he remained editor to his death, contributing a literary letter every week. In 1903 he added the *Tatler* to his list.

In the midst of all this journalism he found time to edit the works of and write books about his four great enthusiasms—the Brontës, George Borrow, Samuel Johnson, and Napoleon. He was a book collector and a genuine bibliophile, with a famous library at his country home, Knockmoroon, at Great Missenden, Buckinghamshire. Frequently he issued privately printed brochures for his friends, containing reprints of some of his most valuable books and manuscripts.

He was married twice, in 1896 to the Irish poet Dora Sigerson,[qv] who died in 1918, and in 1920 to Annie Doris Banfield, who with one daughter survived him. He died at Knockmoroon at sixty-nine, and was cremated and his ashes buried in Golders Green, London.

Shorter was a thickset man with heavy black hair (later gray), thick glasses, a black moustache, and "an air of blindness and absorption that was often mistaken for self-satisfaction." He made many enemies, for he was contentious and loved controversy, and he made a habit of praising his friends' writings and attacking those of people he disliked. He himself said he was "naturally indolent," but few men have worked harder. He was full of a cheerful energy, naïve, affectionate, and vain. As a writer he was little better than a mere compiler, for he was without critical sense or intellectual depth. His chief value to literature was as an indefatigable discoverer of new and not invariably trivial facts about his pet writers.

PRINCIPAL WORKS: Charlotte Brontë and Her Circle, 1896 (as The Brontës and Their Circle, 1914); Victorian Literature: Sixty Years of Books and Bookmen, 1897; Charlotte Brontë and Her Sisters, 1905; Immortal Memories: Essays and Addresses, 1907; The Brontës: Life and Letters, 1908; Napoleon and His Fellow Travellers, 1908; Napoleon in His Own Defense, 1910; Highways and Byways in Buckinghamshire, 1910; George Borrow and His Circle, 1913; C. K. S.: An Autobiography (unfinished, ed. J. M. Bulloch) 1926.

ABOUT: Shorter, C. K. C. K. S.: An Autobiography; Bookman April 1922, August 1922, February 1923, February 1927; Bookman (London) October 1925.

SHOTWELL, JAMES THOMSON (August 6, 1874-), Canadian-American historian, was born in Strathroy, Ont., of American Quaker ancestry. He was educated at Toronto University (B.A. 1898) and Columbia (Ph.D. 1903). He also has honorary doctorates from eight universities, including Dartmouth, Johns Hopkins, and the University of Budapest. Since 1900 he has been on the faculty of Columbia, and has been professor of history there since 1908. He is now also Bryce Professor of the History of International Relations. In 1901 he married Margaret Harvey; they have two daughters. In 1904 and 1905 he was in London as assistant general editor of the *Encyclopaedia Britannica.*

In 1917 he was chairman of the National Board for Historical Service, in Washington; at the Versailles Peace Conference he was a member of the International Labor Legislation Commission, and was the American member of the International Labor Conference in 1919.

Since 1924 he has been trustee and director of the division of economics and history of the Carnegie Endowment for International Peace. From 1931 to 1933 he was director of the division of international relations of the Social Science Research Council. Since 1932 he has been a member of the American committee on International Intellectual Cooperation of the League of Nations, and since 1935 has been president of the League of Nations Association. He was a lecturer before the Nobel Institute in 1923, is a Chevalier of the Legion of Honor (1937), and has decorations from Belgium, Greece, Jugoslavia, and Czechoslovakia. He is editing the monumental *Economic and Social History of the World War* (150 volumes, 1919-). His latest work as an editor is a series, projected in forty volumes written by specialists, on Canadian-American relations.

These data will sufficiently indicate the scope and direction of Dr. Shotwell's interests. As Arthur E. MacFarlane has remarked, "his innate attitude might perhaps be described as encyclopaedic, in the human sense, and broadly and inherently international. With the late James Harvey Robinson he had a large part in freeing the writing and teaching of American school history from the traditional dry-as-dust and the narrowly jingoistic." He is a frequent contributor of articles to the serious reviews, lectures and broadcasts, and has written much verse, though only for private circulation.

PRINCIPAL WORKS: The Religious Revolution of Today, 1913; Labor Provisions in the Peace Treaty, 1919; An Introduction to the History of History, 1921; War As an Instrument of National Policy, 1929; The Heritage of Freedom, 1934; On the Rim of the Abyss, 1936; At the Paris Peace Conference, 1937; (editor) Governments of Continental Europe, 1940; (with F. Deák) Turkey at the Straits, 1940; What Germany Forgot, 1940.

SHUSTER, GEORGE NAUMAN (August 27, 1894-), American educator and writer, was born in Lancaster, Wis., the son of Anthony Shuster and Elizabeth (Nauman) Shuster. His father's people were German Catholics, his great-grandfather having come to the United States in 1848 from revolutionary Germany. His mother's people were German Lutherans who

Kaiden-Keystone

had originally settled in Pennsylvania. "The romance of my boyhood was the aftermath of the Civil War, Lancaster being a favorite place for G.A.R. conventions," he writes. "My secondary education was received at St. Lawrence's College, Fond du Lac, Wis., which was a German Gymnasium transplanted to the New World. We studied Latin and Greek incessantly, but we also learned modern languages, German and French. Notre Dame was my college—then a small institution, with a football team on the first rung of the ladder of fame. My dream was to enter West Point, but when the war came I turned instead to journalism and spent one hectic year trying to be a reporter. Then came 1917, military service, and thereupon eighteen months of life with the A.E.F. first as a member of the Intelligence Section, G.H.Q., serving at the front during almost all the major battles in which the American Army was engaged, and then as an interpreter in the Army of Occupation. Subsequently I attended the University of Poitiers, France, emerging with a Certificat d'Aptitude. Therewith I began my deep interest in modern Europe. I had seen a good deal of post-war Germany—fighting in the streets, the first electoral campaign, hunger, the heavy pressure of the Armistice terms....

"A call came to teach English at Notre Dame, and I answered it thinking that the quiet life I had known on the campus would help me to recuperate. But the president of the University, the Rev. Father James Burns, and I became fast friends. I took my master's degree in French literature, became head of the department of English, and remained at the University until my marriage to Doris Parks Cunningham in 1924. The principal literary product of those years was *The Catholic Spirit in Modern English Literature* (1922). Going to New York for graduate study at Columbia, I came into contact quite accidentally with the newly-formed *Commonweal* group. By the end of the year 1924 the magazine had begun publication, and I had started writing editorials for it." Shuster became associate editor and then managing editor.

"The amount of work required during the next twelve years was tremendous, but I retained some teaching connections, usually giving a course of lectures in some New York college. Books written during these years included one or two on Catholic subjects. More and more, however, my thinking and reading were concerned with modern Germany, which I visited for long periods after 1929. Translations from the German likewise followed in almost-too-rapid succession. During 1937 the Carnegie Corporation awarded me a very beguiling two-year fellowship in the study of the Weimar Republic and in particular of the Center Party. I spent most of the following two years abroad, witnessing among other things the taking over of Austria and the development of the Czechoslovak crisis. . . .

"The Board of Higher Education of the City of New York invited me, in 1939, to become academic dean and acting president of Hunter College. After a year of service I became president. Meanwhile the degree of doctor of philosophy had been earned at Columbia University. I shall hope that the tasks, and they are many, of guiding an educational institution will not deflect me from the pursuits of rose-growing, carpentry and tennis in which I remain interested."

Reviewers have called Shuster's literary work catholic in both senses, with a gift for clear expression and neat turn of phrase.

PRINCIPAL WORKS: The Catholic Spirit in Modern English Literature, 1922; The Catholic Spirit in America, 1927; The Catholic Church and Current Literature, 1929; The Germans, 1932; Strong Man Rules, 1934; Like a Mighty Army, 1935; Brother Flo, 1938; Look Away! (novel) 1939; The English Ode From Milton to Keats, 1940.

ABOUT: American Catholic Who's Who; Current Biography 1940; Commonweal October 25, 1940, January 17, 1941; Newsweek September 16, 1940; Time September 16, 1940.

"SHUTE, NEVIL." See NORWAY, N. S.

SIDGWICK, ETHEL (December 20, 1877-), English novelist, was born in Rugby, the daughter of Arthur and Charlotte S. Sidgwick. She comes of a distinguished family, her uncle, Professor Henry Sidgwick, being a well known philosopher and one of the founders of the Society for Psychical Research, his wife being president of Newnham College,  and another aunt, Mrs. Alfred Sidgwick, being a popular novelist. She was educated at Oxford High School and also studied literature and music privately. She still lives in Oxford, and has never married. Her once blonde hair is gray, but it is still thick, and with her wide eyes and serious, naïve expression she is still surprisingly youthful in appearance. Her outward life has been uneventful, but her inner life has been very rich. William Stanley Braithwaite said that "her eye is as eager and fascinated as her intellect. It dwells affectionately and curiously on the surface of the human creature while her mind probes and penetrates within." Braithwaite called her the only successful emulator of the method of Henry James: "She has the gift of making one feel initiated, of compelling one to realize that the most eloquent words in life are the unspoken, that the most imperceptible movements and intonations are the most poignant and revealing."

Her novels, as are natural, are largely the books of an onlooker at life—just as were those of Henry James. Psychologically she is on a less profound plane; her world has been the small world of a university town, not the large world of London and New York. She has been compared to novelists as disparate as Beatrice Keane Seymour and Mary Borden; her work has been dismissed as merely "deft and amusing." But, as one critic remarked, "her prose is the kind which unobtrusively makes its way into the reader's mind and carries him along on a swift tide, now lifting him over the high spots, now plunging him into the depths. . . . Miss Sidgwick has the rare ability to amuse even when she is most serious."

Her great interest aside from her novels is in children's theatres, for which she has written numerous plays. In recent years she has published but little. She writes some verse, which appears occasionally in English magazines, but has never been collected into a volume.

Ethel Sidgwick is not an "important" novelist, and she has been overshadowed by the greater names of younger contemporaries; but her work, though light, is not ephemeral, and some of it—particularly her historical novels and her loving studies of village life—deserves a quiet and modest survival.

PRINCIPAL WORKS: *Novels*—Promise, 1910; Le Gentleman, 1911; Herself, 1912; Succession, 1913; A Lady of Leisure, 1914; Duke Jones, 1914; The Accolade, 1915; Hatchways, 1916; Jamesie, 1917; Madam, 1921; Restoration, 1923; Laura, 1924; When I Grow Rich, 1927; The Bells of Shoreditch, 1928; Dorothy's Wedding, 1931. *Miscellaneous*—Four Plays for Children, 1913; Plays for Schools, 1922; Fairy-Tale Plays, 1926; Mrs. Henry Sidgwick: A Memoir, 1938.

ABOUT: Bookman January 1929; Current Opinion February 1916.

"SIDNEY, MARGARET." See "AMERICAN AUTHORS: 1600-1900"

SIEGFRIED, ANDRÉ (April 21, 1875-), French political scientist, was born at Le Havre, his father being Minister of Commerce and a member of the French Chamber of Deputies. He himself ran for a seat in the Chamber in his youth, but was defeated. He has always, however, been surrounded by a political atmosphere,

B. Abbott

and his wife, Paule Laroche, is the daughter of a Deputy who was also Resident General of Madagascar. M. Siegfried was educated at the Lycée Condorcet and at the Sorbonne (D. ès Let.). He has been professor of economic geography at the École Libre des Sciences Politiques, Paris, since 1911, and at the Collège de France since 1933. From 1920 to 1922 he was chief of the Economic Section of the League of Nations. He was made a Fellow of All Souls College, Oxford, in 1927. He has been an officer of the Legion of Honor since 1919. He has made several trips to the United States, the most recent one a lecture tour in 1936; and in a sense his work depends on his travels, since he is the leading French authority on the political, economic, and religious life of other countries, and especially of those outside Europe. He has written frequently in his chosen field for French, English, and American reviews.

In 1927 he received the Montyon Prize of the Académie Française for his book, *Les États-Unis d'Aujourdhui,* which in its English translation, as *America Comes of Age,* was widely read in the country of which it treats. Although it was an incomplete survey, since it omitted all consideration of American cultural life, it was, like all M. Siegfried's work, penetrating and acute. He summed up the United States of the "boom era" as "a theocracy of exploitation." He remained in Paris through World War II. In reply to reports of anti-American statements, he has written the editors of this volume: "I have always been a friend of the United States and have never hesitated to say so, even during the Nazi occupation."

In times of peace he leads a busy but quiet life in Paris, going to the country in the summer for his favorite sports of tennis and swimming, and in winter for skating. He is a slender man with aquiline features and a small moustache.

WORKS AVAILABLE IN ENGLISH: Democracy in New Zealand, 1914; Post-War Britain, 1924; America Comes of Age, 1927; France: A Study in Nationality, 1930; England's Crisis, 1931; Impressions of South America, 1933; Europe's Crisis, 1935; Canada, 1937; Suez and Panama, 1940.

ABOUT: Bookman June 1927; Commonweal April 17, 1942; Europe Nouvelle February 6, 1932; New York Herald Tribune "Books" September 15, 1940; Saturday Review of Literature September 7, 1940.

SIERRA. See MARTÍNEZ SIERRA

SIGERSON, DORA (August 16, 1866-January 16, 1918), Irish poet, was born in Dublin, the daughter of Dr. George Sigerson, a surgeon and Gaelic scholar, and Hester (Varian) Sigerson, a verse-writer and novelist. Her younger sister, Hester (Sigerson) Piatt, also became a writer. Dora's first talent, however, was for drawing, and she was in her twenties

before she began to write, except for a few precocious childish efforts. She was educated at home, in an atmosphere of culture, where she imbibed a love of literature and a fervent patriotism together. Her first mature poems were published in the *Irish Monthly,* edited by Father Russell, who encouraged not only her work but also that of her two greatest friends, Katharine Tynan and the American, Louise Imogen Guiney, all devout Catholics and all accomplished lyric poets.

A photograph of Miss Sigerson in the *Sketch* attracted the attention of Clement King Shorter,[qv] its editor, and soon afterwards Katharine Tynan introduced them. They were married on July 4, 1896—an accidental date which delighted Miss Guiney. The marriage was very happy and they were a devoted couple, but Mrs. Shorter was always homesick in England—a homesickness from which she distilled her finest poems. She felt herself an exile, and when the Easter Rebellion took place in 1916, she spent her frail strength in work for the prisoners and defense of the accused. The First World War added to her burdens, and she almost literally died of the strain.

She had meanwhile not spent all her time in lamenting, but besides her writing had busied herself in many directions—chiefly in gardening at her home in Buckinghamshire, and in sculpture, which she took up late in life without any training, but for which she showed a real gift. Her principal work in this field is a memorial group to the Irish patriots which stands in the same Dublin cemetery where she herself is buried, though she died in Buckinghamshire. Though, as her sister said, her outstanding characteristics were "a passionate patriotism and a poignant sense of life's tragedies," outwardly she was lively and playful, with a keen wit. Katharine Tynan described her in youth, "looking like the Greek Hermes: she wore her hair short and it was in masses. She had a beautiful brow, very fine gray eyes, a warm pale color, and vivid red lips."

George Meredith, who with Hardy, Swinburne, Francis Thompson, and Masefield was among her friends, said that there was "the eternal poet in that wise creature," and that she was "one of the few who can tell a tale in verse." This estimate of her ballads and narrative poems is echoed by Padraic Colum, who says that with her, "Irish legend entered into the ballad, carrying with it its own distinctive flavor." There is no jingle or tinkle in her ballads, but fine long rhythms with pauses like heart-stops. Meredith went so far as to call her "the best ballad writer since Scott." Her mind dwelt much on death, and there is a solemnity about many of her lyric poems which contrasts strangely with the limpidity of their style. Her range was narrow, but within it she was an exquisite writer.

PRINCIPAL WORKS: The Fairy Changeling and Other Poems, 1897; Ballads and Poems, 1898; The Father Confessor, 1900; The Woman Who Went to Hell, 1902; As the Sparks Fly Upward, 1904; The Country House Party, 1905; Through Wintry Terrors, 1907; Collected Poems, 1907; The Troubadour and Other Poems, 1910; New Poems, 1912; Madge Linsey and Other Poems, 1913; Love of Ireland: Poems and Ballads, 1916; The Sad Years, 1918; A Legend of Glandalough and Other Ballads, 1919; Sixteen Dead Men and Other Poems of Easter Week, 1919.

ABOUT: Hyde, D. A. A Treasury of Irish Poetry; Lynd, R. Ireland: A Nation; O'Conor, N. Changing Ireland: Literary Backgrounds of the Irish Free State; Tynan, K. Memories; Bookman August 1919, April 1922, August 1922, February 1923; Bookman (London) February 1918; Catholic World May 1934, February 1936; Irish Monthly February 1920.

SILLANPÄÄ, FRANS EEMIL (September 16, 1888-), Finnish novelist and short story writer, winner of the Nobel Prize, was born in the parish of Hämeenkyrö in southwestern Finland at the border of Satakunta and Häme provinces. His forefathers were independent farmers but his father was a landless peasant. The youngest of three children and the only  one to survive, Frans Eemil had a happy childhood despite extreme poverty. His books tell of boyish pastimes and lonely wanderings through the fresh and lovely countryside. At the beginning of the century his father at great sacrifice sent him to school in nearby Tampere, Finland's chief industrial city. A good student, he matriculated in 1908 with the help of schoolmates, and borrowed money to study natural science at the Imperial Alexander University, Helsingfors. Thus he acquired his distinctive biological viewpoint. Close association with the free community of artists in Southern Finland, including the composer Sibelius, the painter Eero Järnefelt, and the writer Juhani Aho, further influenced his development.

On Christmas Eve, 1913, Sillanpää suddenly returned home without having taken his examinations. Dissatisfaction with city life and a need to return to his roots is the explanation of his biographer Toivo Vaasikivi; Sillanpää himself claims that his creditors were impatient. At any rate, the perennial undergraduate, as he now calls himself, had just passed through a mental crisis which finally drove him to seek expression in writing. Hamsun, Maeterlinck, and Strindberg particularly fired his imagination.

In 1916 Sillanpää married Sigrid Maria Salomäki. "She was a housemaid . . . very good looking in those days. When she came in with the coffee tray I fell in love at first sight. . . . We lived in straitened but idyllic circumstances. Before she was twenty-nine we had six children. Sigrid's father was a cut above mine. He was a crofter while mine was a peasant of the poorest class. As a result she always had a certain advantage over me. . . . Love of the home parish has always united us . . . subtle shades of meaning in the language form an irresistible bond."

Short stories and articles brought Sillanpää almost instant acclaim, and in 1916 his first novel *Life and Sun* was published after two years of alternately writing the book and explaining to his publishers why it was not completed; they finally got him to finish it by locking him up in a Helsinki hotel room. Although not one of his best, this was a significant first novel which marked its author immediately as an important Finnish writer. Equally remarkable was his short story collection, *Children of Mankind in the March of Life,* written a short time before and published the following year.

Meek Heritage (1919), Sillanpää's second novel, appeared shortly after the tragic Finnish civil war between Whites and Reds. It established him immediately as the foremost Finnish author of the day. With sympathy but entirely without sentimentality, Sillanpää describes the struggles of his people without, however, taking sides; rather he condemns both sides. "In this philosophic, almost unbiased social study, the author tries to free himself from the anguish that had gripped him during the struggles of his people. The temperamental lyricist had become the stern objective historian. With a pitying eye Sillanpää lays bare the tragedy of elemental man," says Lauri Viljanen. This book won Sillanpää a government pension for life.

Another short story collection, *My Dear Fatherland,* appeared in 1920; with sorrow and compassion Sillanpää views life "from the hilltops of general confusion." Himself a thinker along morphological lines, Sillanpää at this time became enchanted with Spengler. He planned a great novel of the days of Christ, but financial and other problems interfered. *Hilda and Ragner* (1923), a compact novel, deals with a country girl whose association with a city youth drives her to suicide.

During the next decade Sillanpää became a subtle painter of miniatures. *Protegés of the Angels* contains tender pictures of children. In *Of and To My Own* "the cosmos and ethos of the writer are laid bare." *From the Level of the Earth* (1924) is a collection of realistic village scenes. A series of fables in which absolutely spontaneous expression is sought, began with *Töllinmaki* (1925). *Confession* and *Thanks for the Moments, Lord* (1930) are moral and intellectual reckonings. Sillanpää's "Op. 15," the collection *Fifteenth* (1936), shows him as not only a poet but a student and thinker, a morphologist and representative of Finnish culture. With *The Maid Silja* (1931), Sillanpää's fame spread throughout Europe. Like *Meek Heritage* it is set against the Finnish civil war of 1918, with Sillanpää describing both sides sympathetically, at the same time unfolding the disintegration of old standards before the impact of new ideas. Silja represents simple, uncorrupted humanity caught in the throes of a bitter struggle and innocently helping both sides.

One Man's Way (1932), the story of a young farmer who forsakes the love of his youth to marry a wealthy but ailing woman, was filmed in Helsinki in 1940 with great success. The little masterpiece, *People in a Summer Night* (1934), is a mystical treatment of all-powerful nature.

Sillanpää was awarded the Nobel Prize for Literature in 1939 in the midst of his country's war with the Soviet Union. His name had been proposed annually for seven or eight years, and was considered in 1935 and 1936. Although Sillanpää writes only in Finnish, he speaks Swedish and has always opposed the narrow Finnish chauvinism that seeks to oust the Swedish language from Finland. His books are extremely popular in Sweden, especially *People in a Summer Night.* "I feel deep joy that I can render my country the greatest service an old author can render it . . . that of increasing the world's respect for Finnish culture and helping to make the voice of the Finnish spirit heard in the world," Sillanpää said when notified of the Nobel award; "but my heart beats heavily . . . others have their duties but I have nothing to do . . . my son is a reservist but I am nothing." Sillanpää has received government prizes for most of his novels, and in 1936 was made an honorary Doctor of Philosophy by the three-hundred-year-old State University of Finland.

Speaking of *Meek Heritage* and *The Maid Silja*, the only two of Sillanpää's works translated into English so far, Edgar Johnson says: "The quality of his feeling is rather . . . that of a less dramatic, more lyrical Hamsun, one whose lyricism is almost wholly elegiac. . . . There is a kind of dream and glacierlike movement through the years, with a slow attrition of all existences and emotions."

Sillanpää has sad brooding eyes, grim determined lips and yet withal a kind, twinkling expression. Completely bald, he is tall, heavy, and huge of frame, a great bearish person weighing at least 250 pounds. He is a devoted father, and raises his seven children with an iron hand, teaching them, among other things, to handle all animals and insects without fear. His capacity for alcohol is epic among his countrymen.

WORKS AVAILABLE IN TRANSLATION: The Maid Silja (British title: Fallen Asleep While Young) 1933; Meek Heritage, 1938.

ABOUT: American Scandinavian Review March 1940; Books September 25, 1938; Boston Transcript November 18, 1933; Commonweal September 23, 1938; Manchester Guardian May 24, 1938; Mercure de France March 1940; Nation September 24, 1938; New Republic October 19, 1938, November 29, 1939; New York Times November 19, 1933; Saturday Review of Literature November 11, 1933, September 17, 1938, November 18, 1939; Time November 20, 1939; Times (London) Literary Supplement May 28, 1938; Virginia Quarterly Review April 1940; Wilson Library Bulletin December 1939.

SILONE, IGNAZIO (May 1, 1900-), Italian novelist, writes (in English): "I was born at Pescina, a small but ancient

town on the banks of the reclaimed Lake of Fucino. (Cardinal Mazarin, Richelieu's successor, was born in 1602 in a house very near my own.) When I was three months old Pescina was partly destroyed by a flood. When I was fifteen, it was entirely destroyed by an earthquake. Before the earthquake it had eight thousand inhabitants. Only three thousand remain today. In my boyhood Pescina had a bishop, twenty priests, thirty *carabinieri*, a convent, and ten lawyers and notaries. It still has eight churches. Most of the inhabitants are poor peasants.

"My father was a small landowner, my mother a weaver. I had six brothers, all of whom are dead. They all succumbed to illness or other misfortunes. The last was killed in prison by the Fascists.

"I attended junior school at Pescina. On rainy days there were barely enough benches to go round, but on sunny days the classrooms were nearly empty, most of the pupils being engaged in hunting birds or frogs. I passed through the first grades of senior school at Pescina, as a candidate for the clergy, and remained there up to the earthquake. I completed my schooling in Catholic institutions in various towns in Italy. There were two reasons why I never attended a university. In the first place I was advised not to do so by the doctors, who gave me very few years to live, and in the second place political work left me very little free time.

"In 1917 I joined the Peasant League of Pescina and became secretary of the Federation of Land Workers of the Abruzzi. In the same year opposition to the war caused me to join a group of young Socialists, and I was appointed Secretary of the Youth of Rome. A year later I became editor of the weekly *Avanguardia* [*Advance Guard*], which represented the extreme Left of the anti-war movement. In 1922 I was editor of a Trieste newspaper, *Il Lavoratore* [*The Worker*], which was three times raided by the Fascists, who were accompanied and protected by the police. The offices and printing works were completely wrecked.

"After the March to Rome I was forced to leave Italy, to which, however, I returned in 1925. I remained there until 1928, engaged in illegal work against the Fascist regime as a militant Communist. I have spent a number of brief periods in prison, both in Italy and in Spain under the dictatorship of Primo de Rivera. During the war I was tried on a charge of instigating a peasant anti-war revolt. In 1928 I was denounced (in absence) to the Fascist Special Tribune for clandestine political activity in Italy.

"I left the Communist Party in 1930, and since then I have been living in Switzerland, where I wrote *Fontamara, Fascismus, Bread and Wine*, and *The School for Dictators*."

* * *

Silone's real name is Secondo Tranquilli. The town of Fontamara itself is ordinarily believed to be Pescina, Silone's native village in the mountains near Rome, just as in

Bread and Wine he himself is supposed to be the young underground organizer who is still fighting Fascism but is beginning to doubt Communism. *Fontamara,* though of course forbidden in Italy, was a best seller everywhere else, and was translated into fourteen languages. *Bread and Wine* has not yet appeared in Italian, but only in various translations.

It was not for nothing that Ignazio Silone was born on May 1, International Labor Day! From his boyhood he has been a radical, above all the champion of the peasants, though he was not a peasant by birth. His life personally has been tragic; his mother and two of his brothers were killed in the 1915 earthquake, and, as he relates, his last surviving brother was beaten to death in a Fascist prison. He has never married. For three years, from 1925 to 1928, he hid out from the Fascists in peasant huts, until he was able to escape to Switzerland. He settled in Zurich, where he still lives: for some time he edited first a labor newspaper and then a liberal magazine there. He is a tall, dark man, handsome in a floridly Italian way, very shy and quiet, "hesitant in manner, but emphatic in opinions." He speaks fluent French, and his idiomatic mastery of English may be seen from this autobiographical sketch. His novels and stories, and his satirical *School for Dictators,* display power, irony, and realistic immediacy, yet he is capable also of tenderness and of delicate beauty. He is not a mere propagandist, but a born writer, who, if Mussolini had remained a Socialist, would doubtless today be one of Italy's most honored authors.

WORKS AVAILABLE IN ENGLISH: Fontamara, 1934; Mr. Aristotle (short stories) 1935; Bread and Wine, 1936; The School for Dictators, 1938; The Living Thoughts of Mazzini, 1939; The Seed Beneath the Snow, 1942.

ABOUT: Nation December 17, 1938; Newsweek April 3, 1937; Southern Review No. 4, 1939; Wilson Library Bulletin March 1935, October 1942.

SIMENON, GEORGES ("Georges Sim," pseudonym) (February 13, 1903-), Franco-Belgian mystery story writer, writes: "Born in Liège, Belgium. At sixteen years of age, reporter on the Liège *Gazette.* At seventeen, published my first novel, *Au Pont des Arches* [*Aboard the Ark*]. At twenty, marriage; moved to Paris. [His later home, at least until the German invasion, was at Nieul sur Mer.] From twenty to thirty, published about two hundred popular novels under sixteen pseudonyms, and traveled, chiefly in a small boat, all over Europe. At thirty, on board his yacht, the 'Ostrogot,'

then in the north of Europe, wrote his first detective novels and created the character of 'Inspector Maigret.' For two years, wrote a novel of this series every month. At thirty-three abandoned mystery novels, and was at last able to write more personal works That's all."

* * *

When in 1940 an American publisher contracted for twenty-five of the "Inspector Maigret" books, most people assumed that this was Simenon's first appearance in English. Actually, seven of this series were published in English between 1932 and 1934, and two of them were reprinted in cheaper editions. "Inspector Maigret" is as famous in France and Belgium as Sherlock Holmes is in England and America. André Gide called himself "one of the first of Simenon's admirers," and nominated him as "perhaps the greatest and the most truly 'novelistic' novelist in French literature today." Among the critics of discernment who admire him heartily are Max Jacob, René Lalou, Henri Lavedan, and Pierre Mille. He has been criticized for being too prolific, but his wit, suavity, and mastery of style are beyond question. Belgians hail him as a proponent of French culture in Belgium (as against the "Germanic" movement for Flemish as a literary tongue)—though as a matter of fact his father was a Breton who emigrated to Belgium and married there. His detective stories are of the ratiocinative order no longer predominantly favored in English, but their lightness of touch make him a welcome addition to writers of this *genre* already familiar in England and the United States.

WORKS AVAILABLE IN ENGLISH: The Crime of Inspector Maigret, 1932; The Death of M. Gallet, 1932; The Strange Case of Peter the Lett, 1933; Introducing Inspector Maigret, 1933; The Crossroad Murders, 1933; Inspector Maigret Investigates, 1933; The Triumph of Inspector Maigret, 1934; The Patience of Maigret, 1940; Maigret Travels South, 1940; Maigret to the Rescue, 1941; Maigret Keeps a Rendezvous, 1941; Maigret Sits It Out, 1941; Maigret and M. Labbé, 1941; In Two Latitudes, 1942; Affairs of Destiny, 1942.

ABOUT: Haycraft, H. Murder for Pleasure: The Life and Times of the Detective Story; Annales Politiques et Littéraires September 1, 1933; Cahiers du Nord Nos. 2, 3 1939; New Republic March 10, 1941; Publishers' Weekly December 2, 1939.

SIMONDS, FRANK HERBERT (April 5, 1878-January 23, 1936), American journalist and historian, was born in Concord, Mass., the son of a "double-distilled Yankee father and Irish mother," William Henry Simonds and Jennie E. (Garty) Simonds. The boy, growing up near two great battlefields of the Revolutionary War, was interested

Harris & Ewing

from an early age in military tactics and strategy. He got as far as Puerto Rico in the Spanish-American War. After attending the Concord High School he graduated from Harvard in 1900, and went to New York to serve as president of the University Settlement for a year. Here he met his wife, Mary Frances Gledhill, whom he married in 1902; they had a daughter and a son, James, who also became a journalist. Frank Simonds was a reporter on the New York *Tribune* in 1901, sharing a Washington Square apartment with a Harvard classmate, Walter Prichard Eaton.[qv] He was with the paper's Washington Bureau in 1903, and then transferred to Albany as correspondent from 1903 to 1905. As legislature correspondent for the New York *Evening Post* from 1906 to 1908, feverish years at Albany, he constantly referred to Governor Charles Evans Hughes as "Charles the Baptist."

From 1908 to 1913 Simonds wrote editorials for the New York *Sun;* edited the *Evening Sun* in 1913-14; and from 1915 to 1918 was associate editor of the New York *Tribune,* brought there by Richard H. Waldo, business manager of the paper, to interpret the First World War to its readers. By the end of the war, his comments were syndicated in more than a hundred newspapers. An inflammatory editorial which he wrote for the issue of May 7, 1916, on the anniversary of the sinking of the Lusitania, won him the Pulitzer Prize for the ablest editorial of the year. Most of his editorials were partisan reporting.

Simonds went to France at the end of the war to occupy a ringside seat at the Versailles Conference; his cabled exposé of President Wilson's pledge to use American forces to keep the peace was one of the incidents that helped defeat ratification of the League of Nations Covenant by the United States Senate. Foreign governments made him a Chevalier of the Legion of Honor; a Commander of the Order of Phoenix of Greece; an Officer of the Star of Rumania; an Officer of Polonia Restituta; an Officer of the Order of the Crown of Belgium; and a member of the Order of Merit of Hungary.

In his later years Simonds' weekly articles were managed by the McClure Newspaper Syndicate, and for twenty-one years, until two weeks before his death at fifty-seven from pneumonia, he met the release dates of syndication. Six months of the year he lived in Washington, but he preferred his farm, Blighty, in Snowville, N.H., where he would sit on the porch of the farmhouse, stroking the ears of his pet rabbit, and looking up the Intervale to the blue Presidential Range.

Simonds' five-volume history of the Great War, writes W. P. Eaton, "was extremely valuable in recording the campaign, but was, of course, too near the event to be definitive in a deeper sense. During the optimism of the Coolidge era and later, Frank's readers diminished in number, many of them looking on him as a Jeremiah, and many not forgiving him his opposition to our entry into the League of Nations." His style was occasionally brilliant, sometimes cocksure, reflecting his hard, cold, realistic mind. (Clemenceau was one of his particular admirations.) Simonds had a spare frame, a rather cadaverous face, and a harsh, penetrating voice.

PRINCIPAL WORKS: History of the World War, 1916-19; They Shall Not Pass—Verdun, 1916; How Europe Made Peace Without America, 1927; They Won the War, 1931; Can America Stay at Home? 1932; A. B. C. of the War Debts, 1933; The Price of Peace, 1935; The Great Powers in World Politics (with B. Emery) 1935.

ABOUT: Harvard University, Class of 1900: Fortieth Anniversary Report; Nation February 5, 1936; New York Times January 24, 1936; Newsweek February 1, 1936.

SIMPSON, HELEN DE GUERRY (1897-October 1940), English novelist and writer of detective stories, was born in Sydney, Australia, later the scene of many episodes in her novels, the daughter of Edward Percy Simpson, a solicitor and sometime commodore of the local Yacht Club, and Anne (de Lauret) Simpson. Her great-grandfather, Piers Simpson, of the Royal Navy, was in command of

a military post in the Wellington Valley in 1823, and surveyed some western districts of New South Wales under Sir Thomas Mitchell. Her maternal grandfather, the Marquess Guerry de Lauret, settled at Goulburn during the 1840's and built a large house there which is still occupied by the family. Helen Simpson was educated at Rose Bay Convent and Abbotsleigh, Wahroonga. In 1914 she left Sydney to finish her education in France, and to study music at Oxford University, leaving before completing her course because the university objected to her taste for the stage: her "offense" was apparently that she had made several appearances in amateur theatricals at Boar's Hill, the Oxford home of John Masefield, now the poet laureate. Helen Simpson's first novel, *Acquittal* (1925), was written in three weeks to win a bet. In Winifred Ashton ("Clemence Dane"*qv*), who had also appeared on the stage, she found a congenial friend and collaborator. Together they wrote *Enter Sir John*, a detective novel involving an actor-manager, and an even better written and ingeniously plotted sequel, *Re enter Sir John*. Their light comedy, *Gooseberry Fool*, was successfully produced at the Players Theatre, London, in November 1929. In 1927 Miss Simpson married Denis Browne, a London surgeon who was also nephew of the Australian novelist, Rolf Boldrewood. They had a daughter whom her mother, as would be expected, named Clemence. Both survived after Helen Simpson's death in 1940, at forty-two, of shock following the bombing of a hospital where she was recovering from an operation. Before her death she had returned thrice to Australia, in 1937 at the request of the Australia Broadcasting Commission.

Helen Simpson was a versatile novelist, ranging in many fields; *Boomerang*, a richly diversified chronicle-novel of Australia, won the James Tait Black Memorial Prize in 1932. *Saraband for Dead Lovers* was compared with Lion Feuchtwanger's powerful historical novel *Jew Süss* (called *Power* in the United States.) Her last novel, *Maid No More*, a fantasy, was described by Katherine Woods in the New York *Times Book Review* as "a remarkable story of a slave ship and of a human soul; a many-sided and memorable book." Soon after the publication of her novel *Under Capricorn* (Australia in 1831) in the United States, January 1938, its author visited the States for a brief lecture tour. By virtue of her contributions to the mystery story, Miss Simpson was a member of the Detection Club in

London (for which she edited *The Anatomy of Murder*) and was probably at least an auxiliary member of the Sherlock Holmes Society there (whose American equivalent is the Baker Street Irregulars) for she contributed a merciless probe into the character of Dr. Watson to the volume *Baker Street Studies* (1934). Miss Simpson, a cheerful, wholesome-looking English lady, recorded her recreations as "collecting books on witchcraft and cooking." She had grace, wit, and a sound story-telling instinct.

PRINCIPAL WORKS: Pan in Pimlico: A Fantasy in One Act, 1926; Cups, Wands, and Swords, 1927; The Baseless Fabric, 1928; Mumbudget, 1928; The Desolate House, 1929; The Prime Minister Is Dead, 1931; Vantage Striker, 1931; The Woman on the Beast: Viewed From Three Angles, 1933; The Spanish Marriage, 1933; Henry VIII, 1934; Saraband for Dead Lovers, 1934; The Female Felon, 1935; Under Capricorn, 1937; Maid No More, 1940. *With C. Dane*—Enter Sir John, 1929; Printer's Devil (U.S. title: Author Unknown) 1930; Re-enter Sir John, 1932. *Editor*—The Cold Table: Recipes for the Preparation of Cold Food and Drink, 1935; The Anatomy of Murder (by members of the Detection Club) 1936.

ABOUT: Miller, E. M. Australian Literature From Its Beginnings to 1935; Fortnightly Review January 1941; Life February 10, 1941; New York Times October 16, 1940.

SINCLAIR, MRS. BERTHA (MUZZY). See BOWER, B. M.

SINCLAIR, HAROLD (May 8, 1907-), American novelist, was born in Chicago, the son of Walter Guy Sinclair and Ora Violet (Wishard) Sinclair. "So far as I know," he writes, "none of my family was ever famous for anything except working hard and minding their own business and never making very much money. I think I got to somewhere around the third year  in high school, and have been getting an education ever since, but not inside any cloistered walls. I have lived in Florida, where I saw the hurricane of 1926; in Texas, where I saw very little worth remembering; and in Chicago, where I knew the Dill Pickle and what passed for bohemianism. Have done a great many things in order to make a living, including being a telegraph operator for Western Union, pushing a wheelbarrow on a construction gang, and playing the trumpet in ham dance orchestras hither and yon. I've read more books than

I can ever remember, and have wanted to be a writer since I was first able to read, though now I'm approaching that objective it's not at all like what I always supposed it would be. Have really been trying to write for some years, but except for some newspaper reviews and a very bad poem in an obscure magazine [had] never published anything until *Journey Home*. Next to reading, my favorite recreations are music and convivial drinking. I like Schubert, Sibelius, Beethoven, Richard Strauss, Tschaikowsky, Handy, and Hoagey Carmichael, but wouldn't walk across the street to hear any opera that wasn't written by Richard Wagner. My favorite modern authors are Thomas Wolfe, William McFee, and Claude Houghton, in just about that order.

"I am not a very social person and have very few close friends, but those few are most excellent ones. I think of myself as being about one-third incurable romanticist, one-third cynical realist and one-third a somewhat vague blank. I'd like to write at least one book that would stand comparison with the best in America . . . and I'd like my children to remember me as a swell guy whether I am or not."

* * *

The children include Walter Ward, Judith Mary, John Michael and Elizabeth Audrey. Sinclair married Ethel Louise Moran in February 1933. At the time of the publication of *American Years*, which was a selection of the Literary Guild, he was a department manager of a Sears, Roebuck store in Bloomington, Ill., where he still lives. In 1939 he received a Guggenheim award in creative writing.

Burton Rascoe called *Journey Home* "a gorgeous dramatization of every lusty young man's idea of a perfectly ordered universe; preposterous and yet, somehow, convincing like *Moll Flanders* or *Jonathan Wild*." *American Years*, the first novel of a projected trilogy, covered the period 1830-61, from the Black Hawk War to the Civil War, and introduced Abraham Lincoln. Its successors, *Years of Growth*, is a similar "plain, unadorned tale." After publishing *Westward the Tide*, an historical novel about George Rogers Clark, Sinclair returned to his study of life in a small midwestern city with *Years of Illusion*.

PRINCIPAL WORKS: Journey Home, 1936; American Years, 1938; Years of Growth: 1861-1893, 1940; Westward the Tide, 1940; Years of Illusion, 1941; The Port of New Orleans, 1942.

ABOUT: Newsweek May 23, 1938; Wings: The Literary Guild Magazine June 1938.

*SINCLAIR, MAY (1865?-), English novelist, was born at Rock Ferry, Cheshire, the daughter of William Sinclair. She grew up in a family of five  brothers. She was educated in the Ladies' College, Cheltenham, where the head mistress encouraged her bent for writing. Her first work, however, was not fiction, but poetry and philosophical criticism, the latter in the form of an article in an American periodical. A friend suggested that she should try her hand at stories, but her first short story was not published until 1895, her first novel in 1896, and it was 1904 before she achieved any wide success, with *The Divine Fire*. She has always been better known in the United States than in her own country. During the World War she was with a Field Ambulance Corps in Belgium, and also worked with the Hoover relief commission. She has been an active feminist, and before the war was one of the embattled suffragettes. For the most part, however, her life has been quiet and outwardly uneventful. She has never married. For some time she lived in London, with a country cottage first in Yorkshire and later in Gloucestershire, but about 1930 she moved permanently to Aylesbury, Buckshire. She has made several visits to America. For a number of years now she has been an invalid, unable even to write; it is unlikely that any further volume by her will be published. The chief interest of her later years has been in psychic phenomena; she has not only written numerous stories with a supernatural theme, but she herself is a convinced spiritualist.

While she had good health, she was a hard worker, keeping regular hours every morning and sometimes in the afternoon as well, writing up to five hours a day. She said of her writing method: "Each character has to be thought out, to be alive and present to me, before I can begin. I sketch out the whole book carefully, and each chapter separately, before writing a line. Therefore, as the whole is before me more or less, it doesn't matter where I begin a novel. I frequently begin in the middle." She remarked how much more easily writing came to her in her later than in her earlier years, when it was hard, grinding labor.

A small, demure, round-faced woman, with light brown curly hair but black eyes,

Miss Sinclair gives the first impression of primness, or even of hauteur, both of which hide a sensitive shyness. She is very quiet in manner, but her eyes miss nothing, and once her reserve is melted she is charmingly friendly. She is devoted to cats, and always has a pet one which is inseparable from her.

She is no longer much read, but those who neglect her do so at their own loss. In such books as *The Three Sisters, The Divine Fire,* and *Anne Severn and the Fieldings* she makes a penetrating analysis of her characters; she is a keen psychologist and has a sort of maternal sympathy for even the most unpleasing of her subjects. As Jean de Bosschere remarked, "The unifying factor in her work is its humanity." In *Mary Olivier,* and to some extent in other of her later novels, she struck out in a new field, and the work of this period, with its exploration of the subconscious, was an important early contribution to the "stream of consciousness" school. Her writing, as C. A. Dawson Scott said, "produces an effect of . . . lightning, of concentrated seeing, of extraordinary and sudden brilliancy." She is almost a major novelist, who had the misfortune to be too early for her destined public.

PRINCIPAL WORKS: Audrey Craven, 1896; Mr. and Mrs. Nevill Tyson, 1898; Two Sides of a Question, 1901; The Divine Fire, 1904; The Three Brontës (biography) 1912; The Three Sisters, 1914; Mary Olivier, 1919; Mr. Waddington of Wyck, 1921; Anne Severn and the Fieldings, 1922; The New Idealism (non-fiction) 1922; Uncanny Stories, 1923 The Dark Night (novel in verse) 1924; The History of Anthony Waring, 1927; The Allinghams, 1927; Fame, 1929; Tales Told by Simpson, 1930; The Intercessor and Other Stories, 1931.

ABOUT: Wylie, I. A. R. My Life With George; Arts and Decoration July 1924; Bookman November 1920; Review of Reviews August 1925; Revue Politique et Littéraire November 21, 1925; Yale Review October 1924.

SINCLAIR, UPTON BEALL (September 20, 1878-), American novelist and publicist, was born in Baltimore, the son of Upton B. Sinclair and Priscilla (Harden) Sinclair. He belonged to the unsuccessful branch of an old, wealthy, and powerful family, a circumstance which strongly affected his youth—as did his father's inebriate habits. In his boyhood his father, who was a liquor salesman, moved to New York. The boy was through grammar school at twelve, and a student at the College of the City of New York at fourteen. He worked his way through college, and through four years at Columbia afterwards, by writing hack stories for pulp magazines (mostly naval adventures, since his grandfather was an admiral and his whole family had a tradition of naval service), and jokes for the comic periodicals. At this period he felt himself to be a poet; he was all alive with idealism and the worship of beauty, and in the midst of a very different career he still feels a poet buried within him.

In 1900, at twenty-one, he married Meta Fuller. They had one son, and they lived in the country in the most grinding poverty, for the young writer no longer could bring himself to write dime novels and pulp stories, and his first five novels, published from 1901 to 1906, brought him in altogether less than a thousand dollars. The story of that part of his life is told in *Love's Pilgrimage.*

Upton Sinclair was ripe for Socialism at twenty—in fact, he had figured out for himself what he thought was an original idea of his own before he met Gaylord Wilshire and Leonard Abbott and discovered that economists had already promulgated the same principles. He has never been an orthodox Marxian, though so long active in the Socialist Party. But his Socialism is the most important thing about him, since it has been the mainspring of all his writing, has involved him in a long series of disputes and attacks, and has made him internationally famous at the same time that it has militated against his acceptance as a writer in his own country.

In 1906 he wrote *The Jungle,* after an investigation of the Chicago stockyards. As he said, he aimed at the people's heart and hit their stomach. Meat-packing methods were considerably improved, but the lot of the workers was not bettered for many years afterwards. The book was a best seller and made him rich, but all the money went into a Utopian experiment, Helicon Hall, in New Jersey, where Sinclair Lewis, then a college student, was his furnace-man. This cooperative dwelling burned down after a year, with loss of life and the loss of all Sinclair's money. He has never been prosperous since, and he has frequently been very poor, for when conventional publishers boycotted his work, he himself issued it, nearly always at a financial loss. Whenever a book has been successful, he has immediately sunk the profits into some other publishing or social scheme.

After running for various offices on the Socialist ticket in New Jersey and California, he shocked the Socialists by resigning from the party because of its stand against America's participation in the World War. Later he returned to it, though in 1934 he ran for governor of California on the Democratic ticket. This spectacular campaign, on the "EPIC" platform ("End Poverty in California"), was marked by the bitterest attacks yet made on him, and yet he would probably have been elected had it not been for the determined opposition and limitless resources of the business interests.

He has lived in California since 1915, and for may years his home has been in Pasadena. In 1911 he and his first wife were divorced (because of legal technicalities in New York, he had to get the divorce in Holland), and in 1913 he married Mary Craig Kimbrough, of Mississippi, a poet in her own right. Past sixty, he still seems young; he is a crack tennis player, spare and tanned. For years he was a vegetarian, though he no longer is. Thanks to his boyhood, he is fanatical against even moderate drinking. His tastes are very simple, and he has no social life outside a very small group of friends. Robert Cantwell has described him very well: "a soft-voiced ascetic, with his near-sighted smile, his disarming candor, and his strangely prim and dated pre-war air of good fellowship and enthusiasm."

Abroad, Upton Sinclair is the most-read American author. There are 772 translations of his books in forty-seven langauges, and in thirty-nine countries. *World's End,* his sixty-first novel was a Literary Guild "selection" in America in 1940—and was published, by coincidence, on the day that France capitulated to Hitler. And yet the curious fact is that he is really not a novelist. He has never created a real character (except perhaps in *Manassas* and *Love's Pilgrimage*); his people are wooden, his books really propaganda tracts and economic reports. What he is, is a magnificent journalist—one of the very best. To get the full flavor of his talent, one should read, not his novels, but such works as *The Brass Check, The Goose-Step,* or *The Profits of Religion.* Over-assertive as they may sound, not one person he has attacked has ever yet been able to disprove him or sue him for libel.

Perennially hopeful, humorless, with a sort of boyish credulity which has led him into espousing the most grotesque quack cures and has made him an ardent telepathist, Upton Sinclair nevertheless is a fine corrective for complacency, a fearless and indefatigable crusader. He is in a sense the last of the muckrakers; he thinks of himself as a social anticipation but actually he is a hold-over from the days of forthright independence in a simpler and less regimented America.

PRINCIPAL WORKS: Springtime and Harvest, 1901; King Midas, 1901; The Journal of Arthur Stirling, 1903; Prince Hagen, 1903; Manassas, 1904; The Jungle, 1906; The Industrial Republic, 1907; The Overman, 1907; The Metropolis, 1908; The Money-Changers, 1908; Samuel, The Seeker, 1909; Love's Pilgrimage, 1911; Plays of Protest, 1911; Sylvia, 1913; Sylvia's Marriage, 1914; King Coal, 1917; The Profits of Religion, 1918; Jimmie Higgins, 1919; The Brass Check, 1919; 100%—The Story of a Patriot, 1920; They Call Me Carpenter, 1922; The Goose-Step, 1923; The Goslings, 1924; Singing Jailbirds (play) 1924; Mammonart, 1925; Letters to Judd, 1926; Oil! 1927; Money Writes, 1927; Boston, 1928; Mountain City, 1930; Mental Radio, 1930; Roman Holiday, 1931; The Wet Parade, 1931; American Outpost (autobiography) 1932, Upton Sinclair Presents William Fox, 1933; I, Governor of California, 1933; I, Candidate for Governor—and How I Got Licked, 1935; Depression Island, 1936; Co-op, 1936; No Passaran! 1937; The Flivver King, 1937; Our Lady, 1938; Little Steel, 1938; Marie Antoinette, 1939; World's End, 1940; Between Two Worlds, 1941; Dragon's Teeth, 1942.

ABOUT: Dell, F. Upton Sinclair: A Study in Social Protest; Harris, F. Contemporary Portraits: Third Series; Sinclair, U. American Outpost; Bookman May 1927; Christian Century October 19, 1932; Nation May 1 and September 12, 1934; New Republic November 7, 1934, February 24, 1937; Saturday Evening Post November 24, 1934; Saturday Review of Literature March 3 and April 7, 1928, November 13, 1937; Survey February 15, 1930; Wings July 1940; World Tomorrow October 12, 1933.

SINCLAIR-COWAN, Mrs. BERTHA (MUZZY). See BOWER, B. M.

*SINGER, ISRAEL JOSHUA (November 30, 1893-); Polish-American Yiddish novelist, writes: "I was born in the town of Bilgeray, a part of Poland which was then in the Russian Empire. My father was a rabbi. When I was a mere infant my family moved to Leonczyn and there I spent my childhood. Later we moved to Warsaw, where I was prepared for a rabbinical career.

"At the age of eighteen I decided that I did not want to be a clergyman and I gave

* Died February 10, 1944.

up my theological studies. I wanted to have a modern education and proceeded to acquire one by taking casual lessons with inexpensive private tutors while earning my livelihood by doing all kinds of odd jobs.

"In 1915 the German army occupied Warsaw, and for some time I was compelled to do manual labor for the military conquerors. In 1917, right after the outbreak of the Russian Revolution, I moved on to Kiev, Ukraine, where I succeeded in obtaining employment as a proof-reader on a Yiddish newspaper. It was in Kiev that I started to write short stories in my spare time. In 1918 I married Genia Kupfersteck, who, like myself, had come to Kiev from Poland. We have one son.

"We lived in Russia up to the end of 1921, and those years were a period of continuous civil war and pogroms attended by starvation. Towards the end of 1921 we returned to Warsaw, which in the meantime had become the capital of the independent Polish Republic.

"Back in Warsaw I published a collection of short stories under the title of the opening story, *Pearls*. When the book reached New York this story was brought to the attention of Abraham Cahan, editor of the *Jewish Daily Forward*. Mr. Cahan reprinted the story and I was invited to become a regular contributor to the *Forward*, both as a writer of fiction and as a news correspondent. I have contributed to it ever since.

"In the fall of 1926 I made an extensive trip through Soviet Russia as a special traveling correspondent of the *Forward*, a trip which lasted several months. Upon my return to Poland I wrote and published a book called *The New Russia*.

"In the summer of 1932 I landed on the shores of the United States for the first time. I came to New York for a three months' visit in connection with a stage version of my novel, *Yoshe Kalb*, which was produced by Maurice Schwartz at the Yiddish Art Theatre in the fall of that year. In 1933 the novel was published in an English translation entitled *The Sinner*. In the winter of 1934 I returned to the United States with my wife and son and made New York our home. Here I wrote *The Brothers Ashkenazi*, a novel which has been translated into English, Danish, Swedish, and Dutch. A stage version was subsequently produced by the Yiddish Art Theatre. In 1933 my play *Savinkoff* was produced in the Polish language in a Warsaw theatre. My own dramatization of *East of Eden* was pro-

duced in the fall of 1939 by Jacob Ben-Ami at the National Theatre, New York.

"To date I have had eight books published in Yiddish, five of which have been translated into English, Hebrew, Polish, and the Scandinavian languages. Politically I am a believer in the democratic system of government. Among my favorite writers I give first place without hesitation to Stendhal, Flaubert, and Tolstoy."

* * *

In his early years Mr. Singer worked as an itinerant tutor, a salesman, an artist's model, and served in the Russian army. He is a big bald-headed man. His Yiddish style has often been compared with that of his friend and employer, Abraham Cahan. Like Cahan, he has been violently opposed to the Soviet régime.

WORKS AVAILABLE IN ENGLISH: The Sinners, 1933; The Brothers Ashkenazi, 1936; The River Breaks Up (short stories) 1938; East of Eden, 1939.

ABOUT: Wilson Library Bulletin January 1937.

SINGMASTER, ELSIE (August 29, 1879-), American novelist, writes: "I was born in the Lutheran parsonage at Schuylkill Haven, Pa. My father, Dr. John Alden Singmaster, was chiefly of Pennsylvania German stock, my mother, Caroline (Hoopes) Singmaster, chiefly English Quaker. When I was four years old, we moved to Macungie, Pa., where my father was born. We returned there later for many summers, when we lived in Brooklyn, N.Y. and in Allentown, Pa. I was graduated from high school in Allentown, then went for a year to the West Chester Normal School, then to Cornell. At the end of my sophomore year, having taken most of the English courses under a far too elective system, I returned home. Five years later I entered Radcliffe, completed my course, and was graduated in 1907.

"When I was about eleven years old, my **teacher directed us to write a story.** Already I dreamed of becoming an author and I composed a story of a paper doll. The plot was not wholly original; when the story was printed in a teachers' journal my conscience began to trouble me and has ever since.

"In my early acquaintance with the Pennsylvania Germans I was extremely fortunate.

The 'local color' buoyed, I suspect, many of my early stories into port which had not a great deal to recommend them. My father's later connection with the Lutheran Theological Seminary at Gettysburg, which gives Seminary Ridge its name, provided me with material about the battle and the Civil War.

"I married, in 1912, Harold Lewars, a musician, who died in 1915. During this time I lived in Harrisburg, Pa., since returning to Gettysburg, where I have lived since. I have no children. I like to raise trees and flowers and I am very fond of music, though I am a very poor musician. I still love reading above all other sports."

* * *

Miss Singmaster (or Mrs. Lewars) is a small, squarely built woman with gray hair, bright black eyes, broad cheekbones, and a firm chin. She has a crisp way of talking which goes with her "tireless energy, sturdy uprightness, honesty, and kindly humor." Her home now, where she works in an attic studio, looks out on Seminary Ridge. It is an appropriate view, for her great-great-grandfather was the first Lutheran minister to be ordained in America, and her father was long president of the seminary.

Her field, with one exception (*What Everybody Wanted*, laid in Maryland) has been small town life among the Pennsylvania Germans (misnamed the Pennsylvania Dutch). She does not caricature or satirize them, as did, for instance, the late Helen Reimensnyder Martin, but treats them with understanding and deep sympathy. "Millertown," her usual milieu, is Allentown. She has honorary Litt.D. degrees from Pennsylvania State College, Muehlenberg College, and Wilson College. Dayton Kohler, who noted "a quality austerely Lutheran in her nature," has praised her "artistic and personal integrity, her faithful portrayal of human nature, her severe economical style," and called her novels "deliberate patterns of compact prose."

PRINCIPAL WORK: *Adult Fiction*—Gettysburg (short stories) 1913; Katy Gaumer, 1915; Basil Everman, 1920; Ellen Levis, 1921; Bennet Malin, 1922; The Hidden Road, 1923; Bred in the Bone (short stories) 1925; Keller's Anna Ruth, 1926; What Everybody Wanted, 1928; The Magic Mirror, 1934; The Loving Heart, 1937; A High Wind Rising, 1942. *Juveniles*—When Sarah Saved the Day, 1909; When Sarah Went to School, 1910; Emmeline, 1916; The Long Journey, 1917; John Baring's House, 1920; A Boy at Gettysburg, 1924; "Sewing Susie," 1927; Virginia's Bandit, 1928; You Make Your Own Luck, 1929; A Little Money Ahead, 1930; The Young Ravenels, 1932; Swords of Steel, 1933; Stories of Pennsylvania (3 vol.) 1937-38; Rifles for Washington, 1938; Stories to Read at Christmas, 1940. *History*—Short Life of Martin Luther, 1917; Book of the United States, 1926; Book of the Constitution, 1926; Book of the Colonies, 1927.

ABOUT: Overton, G. The Women Who Make Our Novels; Bookman February 1931; Ladies' Home Journal March 1925; Scholastic February 12, 1938, April 4, 1941.

SITWELL, EDITH (1887-), English poet and critic, was born in Scarborough, the daughter and oldest child of Sir George Reresby Sitwell, 4th Baronet. Her mother was born Lady Ida Emily Augusta Denison, daughter of the Earl of Londesborough. Edith Sitwell is the sister of Osbert and Sacheverell Sitwell,[qqv] and the three are famous for their deliberate eccentricity

and the aplomb with which they blandly controvert accepted standards. It is an inherited trait; their father lists among his achievements that he "captured a spirit at the headquarters of the Spiritualists, London, 1888"; and it is perhaps because he was a sportsman in his youth that his daughter has announced that "in early life [she] took an intense dislike to simplicity, morris-dancing, a sense of humour, and every kind of sport excepting reviewer-baiting, and has continued these distastes ever since."

She was educated privately, at the family estate, Renishaw Park, which her family has owned for more than six hundred years. She first attracted public notice when in 1916 she began, with a group of other young poets, to edit an annual anthology, *Wheels*. There were other editions in 1916, 1917, 1918, and 1921, and the chief contributors were the "Three Sitwells." In 1923 she conducted a poetry recital at Æolian Hall (to music by William Walton), speaking behind a curtain painted with a female figure, eyes closed and mouth open. The object was to prove her theory that poetry should emphasize musical cadence and dissociate itself from the personality of the poet.

She is remarkable in appearance, being over six feet tall, blonde, with straight hair and strange gray eyes. She is, as she recognizes, a mediaeval type, and so she dresses in the fashion of the Middle Ages, usually in rich brocaded silks. For some years she lived in Paris, where she was an intimate friend of Gertrude Stein. She has never married. Controversy is her life-blood, and she dearly loves a fight; on the other hand she is noted for her kindness and generosity to young poets and painters. As the late Sir Edmund Gosse remarked, she is "an extraordinary mixture of sensitiveness and bravado." Like Amy Lowell, she takes nothing with complete seriousness but art, and on poetic theory she is a storm-center of energy, in deadly earnest and indefatigable.

Her poetry has extreme objectivity; her world is cluttered with objects, and her phraseology has an intense materiality. Her language is sharply individual; words to her, as to the Duchess in *Alice in Wonderland*, mean what she wants them to mean. (She wrote of something once as being "Martha-colored"; asked to explain, she said that when she was a child she had a nurse named Martha, who wore a dress of that color.) Yet this preoccupation with *things* cloaks an almost naïve mysticism. Hence arises what Edwin Muir called the "bright, supernatural clarity," the "metaphysical horror" which is at the root of her poetry. Like some enamel-hued tropical bird, she screams her detestation of the vegetable dullness of the ordinary human life. Her basic and distinguishing vocabulary is drawn largely from artifices, confections, and manufactures. Muir notes that she employs "an unusual kind of simile, by means of which she tries to escape from classified correspondences into correspondences more intimate and more universal."

By sheer dominating force she has overpowered weaker poets and critics and forged a place for herself. In personal contact she is rather overwhelming, and Arnold Bennett was not the only one to gasp that she "dazzled" him. But she has the abilities to match her aggression. She is a brilliant technician, who owes much of her skill to her excellent musicianship and also to her devout study of the French Symbolist poets. In 1933 she received the medal of the Royal Society of Literature. It was given for her poetry: her prose is wayward and erratic, though her critical work is acute and perceptive. Her novel, based on the life of Jonathan Swift, was a literary curiosity rather than an orthodox piece of fiction. She has written too much, and she can be intensely silly; can annoy one to distraction. She can be depended on to scratch each of her virtues until she exposes a vice. At times, but only at times, in a quick combustion of the imagination, all the dross of her style is burned away. At these times, Edith Sitwell is a true and almost a great poet, and these are the passages which will be her heritage to English literature.

PRINCIPAL WORKS: *Poetry*—The Mother and Other Poems, 1915; Clowns' Houses, 1918; Bucolic Comedies, 1923; The Sleeping Beauty, 1924; Poems, 1926; Elegy on Dead Fashion, 1926; Twentieth Century Harlequinade and Other Poems (with O. Sitwell) 1926; Rustic Elegies, 1927; Gold Coast Customs, 1929; Collected Poems, 1930; Five Variations on a Theme, 1933; Selected Poems: With an Essay on Her Own Poetry, 1936; Trio (with O. & S. Sitwell) 1938; Poems New and Old, 1940; Street Songs, 1942. *Prose*—Alexander Pope, 1930; The Pleasures of Poetry (3 vols., ed. with comments) 1930-32; Bath, 1932; The English Eccentrics, 1933; Victoria of England, 1936; I Live Under a Black Sun (novel) 1937; English Women, 1942.
ABOUT: Lewis, W. Blasting and Bombardiering; Mégroz, R. L. The Three Sitwells; Powell, D. Descent From Parnassus; Bookman (London) June 1931; Fortnightly Review February 1926; Living Age June 15, 1927; London Mercury March 1927, March 1935; Nation April 15, 1925; Nation (London) September 18, 1926; Outlook (London) February 25, 1928; Poetry May 1930, March 1931, June 1937; Saturday Review of Literature April 24, 1937, March 29, 1941; Time March 3, 1941.

SITWELL, OSBERT (December 6, 1892-), English poet and satirist, is a son of Sir George Reresby Sitwell, 4th Baronet, and a brother of Edith Sitwell and Sacheverell Sitwell.[qqv] A small portion of the park at Renishaw, present seat of the Sitwells, has been in their possession for six hundred years. Their Norman ancestry is evident in their long, sharp-featured  faces, with high-bridged noses, straight pale hair, and light eyes, gray-blue or gray-green in color. John Sargent painted them in a portrait group showing Edith at 11½, Osbert at 6½, and Sacheverell at 1½. Osbert Sitwell's education was obtained, according to his own account, "during the holidays from Eton." After Eton he entered a regiment of yeomanry, the Sherwood Rangers, in 1911, later joining the Grenadier Guards in France in December 1914, where he fought in the battle of Loos. In May 1916, on leave in England, he developed blood poisoning from a cut on a finger got in the trenches, and was ill for several years from the resultant complications. Peace found him very angry with the muddle made by "profiteers, scamps, fools and the selfishly sentimental," and he developed a permanent distaste for W. H. Hudson after hearing him make a recruiting speech. At heart always an idealist, he sharpened his mind to strike at stupidities and cruelties. Osbert Sitwell's effects of irony are obtained by the employment of conventional meters for very unconventional thought. "Much of his satire," writes R. L. Mégroz in his careful study of the three Sitwells, "when the mordant wit which reminds us of Talleyrand is discarded, becomes in part the exuberance of clowning and in part a regression to the poetry of childhood." "The trio invaded the world of letters with a flourish," records Osbert Burdett, when, as a kind of youthful manifesto, the anthology called *Wheels* was published in 1916 and subsequent years. Its aims differed from those of Edward Marsh's *Georgian Poetry*; the tone was more shrill, the writing more experimental. The roots of the Sitwells' dissatisfaction seem to go back to their own childhood, a protest of youthful vitality against life in a beautiful old house. In prose narration, Osbert Sitwell is "only intermittently good and too frequently peters out into long asides." His power of characterization is exceptional, especially in *Triple Fugue*, and his work is studded with beautiful passages of prose. Besides living at the family seat at Renishaw Hall, Derbyshire, Sitwell has a London address. His clubs are the Marlborough, St. James's and Burlington, and his recreations "Nit-wit baiting and the Jitters."

PRINCIPAL WORKS: Argonauts and Juggernauts (poems) 1919; The Winstonburg Line (satires) 1920; Who Killed Cock Robin?: Remarks on Poetry, on Its Criticism, 1921; Out of the Flame (poems) 1923; Triple Fugue and Other Stories, 1924; Discursions on Travel, 1925; Art and Life, 1925; Before the Bombardment, 1926; England Reclaimed, 1927; All at Sea, 1927; The People's Album of London Statues (with N. Hamnett) 1928; The Man Who Lost Himself, 1929; Sober Truth (with M. Barton) 1930; Dumb Animal and Other Stories, 1930; Victoriana (with M. Barton) 1931; Portrait of Michael Arlen, 1931; Collected Poems and Satires, 1931; Winters of Content, 1932; Dickens, 1932; Miracle on Sinai, 1933; Brighton (with M. Barton) 1935; Penny Foolish, 1935; Those Were the Days, 1938; Trio (with E. & S. Sitwell) 1938; Escape With Me! An Oriental Sketch-Book, 1939; Open the Door! 1941; A Place of One's Own, 1941.

ABOUT: Lewis, W. Blasting and Bombardiering; Mégroz, R. L. The Three Sitwells: A Biographical and Critical Study; Wells, H. W. New Poets From Old; Williams, C. W. S. Poetry at Present; Adelphi August 1923; Saturday Review of Literature March 29, 1941; Time March 3, 1941.

SITWELL, SACHEVERELL (1897-),

English poet and art critic, was born in Scarborough, the son of Sir George Sitwell, 4th Baronet, and younger brother of Edith and Osbert Sitwell.[qqv] He was educated at St. David's, Reigate; Eton College; and Balliol College, Oxford University, but has said that he is "mainly self-educated." Seventeen when the First World War broke out, Sacheverell Sitwell joined the Special Reserve of the Grenadier Guard. He is the only classically-minded poet of the three Sitwells—the others are instinctively romantic—and was also influenced by the Italian futurist, Marinetti, and by the Chinese classical poets. His imagery has been called mobile and visual, whereas his sister's is tactile and audile, and Osbert Sitwell's visual and audile. "Sternly opposed to all games," he has been associated with his brother in their many anti-game activities, according to his unconventional entry in *Who's Who*. In reading both this and his *All Summer in a Day: An Autobiographical Fantasia,* it is well to remember that Sacheverell Sitwell's imagination has been called "nobly regardless of humdrum restrictions." "Except in reviving a certain school of taste," Osbert Burdett has said, "the Sitwells have brought nothing new into prose, though Mr. Sacheverell can be a charming and picturesque magician of history." This includes the history of art, especially the Baroque periods, and a delightful study of the conversation pieces of Hogarth,

Gainsborough, Zoffany, Devis, Stubbs, Patch, Ferneley, Copley, Constable and Turner.

Very slight themes provoke his poetry. "He believes obviously that as much poetry can be extracted from a banana as a battlefield—nay more." In 1925 Sacheverell Sitwell married Georgia, younger daughter of Arthur Doble of Montreal; they have two sons and live at Weston Hall, Towcester, Northants. His club is the St. James's, and his recreations "talking, listening, and again talking; likes motoring, seeing churches, lunching, and motoring on."

PRINCIPAL WORKS: Southern Baroque Art, 1924; Eglantine and Other Poems, 1926; All Summer in a Day, 1926; German Baroque Art, 1927; The Gothick North, 1929; Doctor Donne and Gargantua, 1930; Far From My Home, 1931; Spanish Baroque Art, 1931; Mozart, 1932; Canons of Giant Art, 1933; Life of Liszt, 1934; Touching the Orient, 1934; Dance of the Quick and the Dead, 1936; Conversation Pieces, 1936; La Vie Parisienne, 1937; Narrative Pictures, 1937; Roumanian Journey, 1938; Edinburgh (with F. Bamford) 1938; German Baroque Sculpture, 1938; Trio (with E. & O. Sitwell) 1938; The Romantic Ballet in Lithographs of the Time (with C. W. Beaumont) 1938; Old Fashioned Flowers, 1939; Mauretania, 1940; Poltergeists, 1940; Sacred and Profane Love, 1940;

Valse des Fleurs, 1941; Primitive Scenes and Festivals, 1942.

ABOUT: Mégroz, R. L. The Three Sitwells; Sitwell, S. All Summer in a Day: An Autobiographical Fantasia; Wells, H. W. New Poets From Old; Williams, C. W. S. Poetry at Present; Humberside October 1924; London Mercury March 1927; Saturday Review of Literature March 29, 1941; Time March 3, 1941.

SIWERTZ, SIGFRID (January 24, 1882-), Swedish poet, dramatist, and novelist, writes (in English): "I was born in

a wing of the Academy of Arts in Stockholm, and Stockholm has since then been my home and my love. At the University of Upsala I studied philosophy and the history of literature from 1901 to 1905. My literary début took place in 1904 with a book of verse. Since then I have been living the life of an author and have published forty-five works, verse, short stories, travel books, essays, dramas, and comedies, of which seven have been played at the Royal Theatre in Stockholm. During the last twenty years I have traveled much, in 1923 to the Fiji Islands and Sumatra for an ethnographical film, in 1926 with a caravan through Abyssinia, in 1937 all around South America. I have visited the United States three times. In 1932 I was made a member of the Swedish Academy. Most of my novels have been translated into German and French, some into Italian, Dutch, and English. My psychological play, *Ett Brot (A Crime)* was played in all the Scandinavian capitals and in Prague. In sports I prefer yachting and often live the summer out amongst the 'skerries' of the Swedish coast."

* * *

Of Siwertz's two novels thus far translated into English, *Downstream (Selambs)* is a "family novel," a study of human egotism. *Goldman's (Det Stora Varuhuset)* is the story of the founding of the first big Swedish department store by a Polish Jew. All Siwertz's books have been best-sellers in Sweden. He is a heavy-set, blond man, looking typically Scandinavian. He is unmarried. Gurli Hertzman-Ericson called him "one of the older generation who has steadily grown in the estimation of the public [for his] wisdom, humanity, and understanding of people." Ellen Lundberg-Nyblom, praising his "vigorous style rich in pregnant

expressions and metaphors," called him "powerful and significant, extraordinarily profound and clever, . . . a skillful surgeon whose heart yet beats warmly for the handicapped, disillusioned, and outcast."

WORKS AVAILABLE IN ENGLISH: Downstream, 1923; Goldman's, 1930.

ABOUT: American-Scandinavian Review May 1930, September 1934.

SKEAT, WALTER WILLIAM. See "BRITISH AUTHORS OF THE 19TH CENTURY"

SKINNER, CONSTANCE LINDSAY (1882-March 27, 1939), American novelist, poet, and historian, was born in northern British Columbia, five hundred miles from a railroad, at a Hudson's Bay trading post on the Peace River, where her father, Robert James Skinner, was a factor. Some fifty years later in 1935 his daughter published a history of the fur

Pinchot

trade, *Beaver, Kings and Cabins.* Her mother was Annie (Lindsay) Skinner, of the Lindsay family which included Lady Anne Lindsay, author of "Auld Robin Gray," and David Lindsay, poet, historian, and friend of the John Knox who was not Mary Stuart's friend. Childhood years were spent among fur traders, Indians, and mounted policemen, with some formal education at private school, in Vancouver, and with tutors. At sixteen Miss Skinner was a special writer, political reporter, and editorial writer for British Columbian newspapers; at eighteen she was a full-fledged reporter on the Los Angeles *Times* and Los Angeles *Examiner*, covering fires, murders, sudden death, and symphony concerts. Later she was with the Chicago *American.* Her pattern of experience resembled that of another Northwesterner, Isabel Paterson, whose colleague and fellow-reviewer she later became on the New York *Herald Tribune's* literary review, *Books.*

To the Yale University Press "Chronicles of America" series Miss Skinner contributed *Adventurers in Oregon* and *Pioneers of the Old Southwest,* the latter of which was praised for its succinctness, clarity, and charm. Of her popular books for young people, Anne Carroll Moore has commented that Miss Skinner was "essentially a poet and historian whose childhood remains vivid and whose understanding and appreciation of primal people—the Indians, the *voyageurs,* the *coureurs-de-bois*—is instinctive and secure." As a poet, she received prizes from *Poetry* and the London *Bookman.*

At the time of her death, from influenza, at her Park Avenue penthouse in New York City, Miss Skinner was editor of Farrar & Rinehart's twenty-four-volume "Rivers of America" series, of which six had appeared up to 1939. The twin purposes of the series, she said, were "to kindle imagination and to reveal American folk to one another." She chose the rivers and the folk-tales to be included. Miss Skinner was dark and striking in appearance, wearing dresses of her own design. She was tolerant and generous, but her "private judgments were very strict."

PRINCIPAL WORKS: *Fiction* — Good Morning, Rosamond, 1917; The Search Relentless, 1925; Silent Scot: Frontier Scout, 1925; The White Leader, 1926; Roselle of the North, 1927; Ranch of the Golden Flowers, 1928; Andy Breaks Trail, 1928; Red Willows, 1929; Red Man's Luck, 1931; Rob Roy: The Frontier Twins, 1934. *Historical Works*—Pioneers of the Old Southwest, 1920; Adventurers in Oregon, 1920; Beaver, Kings and Cabins, 1933.

ABOUT: Becker, M. L. (ed.). Golden Tales of Canada; Kunitz, S. J. & Haycraft, H. (eds.). The Junior Book of Authors; Horn Book July 1939; Library Journal April 15, 1939; Boston Evening Transcript May 6, 1933; New York Times March 28, 1939; Publishers Weekly April 1, 1939; Time April 10, 1939; Wilson Library Bulletin May 1939.

*SLESINGER, TESS (July 16, 1905-), American novelist and short-story writer, was born in New York City, attended the

Pinchot

Ethical Culture School founded by Felix Adler, and studied for two years at Swarthmore College. "I was born with the curse of intelligent parents, a happy childhood and nothing valid to rebel against," Miss Slesinger has said. "So I rebelled against telling the truth. I told whoppers at three, tall stories at four, a home-run at five; from six to sixteen I wrote them into a diary." Her parents were not unduly alarmed, even when she palmed off a copy of *Pinocchio* on them as her own work, but they did consult a psychiatrist, who seemed to regard this romancing tendency as a favorable sign. Miss Slesinger left Swarthmore in 1925, having flunked algebra and received a reprimand for smoking on the campus. She attended the Columbia School of Journalism, where she was, according to a fellow-student, "just one of those girls the professors never knew what to do with." Here she had the advantage of taking Dorothy Scarborough's course in the short story, and in 1927 she was given a diploma and a degree of B.Litt. She had worked as assistant fashion editor on the New York *Herald Tribune* in 1926, and she now became an assistant on the New York *Evening Post Literary Review.* Half a dozen other odd jobs held by Miss Slesinger were "so very odd that they aren't worth recording." Later she was to teach creative writing at Briarcliff Manor, Briarcliff, N.Y., a girls' finishing school.

The *Menorah Journal* accepted her first short story in 1928, and subsequent stories appeared in the *American Mercury, Pagany, This Quarter, Modern Youth, Vanity Fair, Forum,* and *Story.* The last-named printed "Missis Flinders," one of her best stories, which is the last of her "selected, not collected" stories reprinted in the volume *Time: The Present* (1935). The year before, it had formed a part of her novel of rootless and bewildered pseudo-intellectuals, *The Unpossessed,* which was dedicated "To My Contemporaries." It won favorable critical attention on the whole, and Miss Slesinger found herself something of a literary celebrity; an experience she records with demure malice in a story, "After the Party," in which the guest of honor is Regina Sawyer, author of *The Undecided.* In 1934, also, Miss Slesinger picketed the premises of Macaulay, the publishers, who had had a row with their staff, and was jailed for a day with eighteen other writers and editors. In June 1935 she spoke at the John Reed Club in New York on "The Short Story: Slick Paper or Life?" and left for Hollywood to work on the scenario of Pearl Buck's *The Good Earth.*

In 1936 she was married to Frank Davis; they have two children. With her husband, Miss Slesinger has written numerous original stories for the screen. Whit Burnett has called Miss Slesinger "master of the tragic-comic situation," and John Chamberlain declared her "past-mistress of the art of literary ambuscade. With an uncanny and enjoyable malice, she manages to listen in on people at the precise moments when they are justifying or excusing or inflating themselves." One of the most personable of young writers, Miss Slesinger has a smile as vivid as her literary style. Since going to Hollywood, she appears to have written little.

* Died February 21, 1945.

PRINCIPAL WORKS: The Unpossessed, 1934; Time: The Present, 1935.

ABOUT: New York World Telegram June 13, 1935; Wilson Library Bulletin December 1934.

SMART, CHARLES ALLEN (November 30, 1904-), American novelist, writes: "I was born in Cleveland, Ohio, and moved to

New York in 1917. I was educated in the public schools of Cleveland and New York, and at Harvard, B.A. *cum laude,* 1926. In college I was secretary of the *Harvard Advocate* and class poet, God save the mark. After brief periods with a printing firm and the Viking Press, I worked for three years in the trade editorial department of Doubleday, Page and its successor, Doubleday, Doran. I resigned to do freelance editing, ghost-writing, and advertising copy-writing. My first novel was published in 1931 and had fair luck. I spent most of that year and the next in Europe, wandering and loafing. In 1932 I became an instructor in English at the Choate School, Wallingford, Conn. My second novel was published in 1933 and died at birth. I spent that summer in France. The following June I resigned my teaching job and undertook the operation of a small farm I inherited in southern Ohio, and the management of another. In 1935 I married Margaret Warren Hussey, of Plymouth, Mass. My *R.F.D.,* an account of farming as experienced by city-bred people, had good luck. Since then I have learned a bit more about farming, and, on the literary side, have been studying Utopian Socialism and writing personal essays. The best of these so far is probably 'The Return of Johnny Appleseed,' published in *Harper's.*"

* * *

Mr. Smart's farm is near Chillicothe, Ohio. It has sixty-three acres, with a hundred-year-old stone house; it is called Oak Hill. He confesses that so far his "only successful crop has been ideas, sensations, intuitions, feelings, sympathies, and delight in action," but he really works hard on the farm, even though he "sings Gregorian chants while milking" and helps produce plays in the winter in the Chillicothe Little Theatre. He is a tall, fair young man, liberal in his social viewpoint, who has been called "an intelligent hedonist." John

Chamberlain said of him: "He has a genuine and pervasive charm. . . . His peculiar genius . . . is for the old-style familiar essay (with more Hazlitt than Lamb)."

PRINCIPAL WORKS: New England Holiday, 1931; The Brass Cannon, 1933; R. F. D. (in England: The Adventure of an American Farm) 1938; Roscommon, 1940; Wild Geese and How to Chase Them, 1941.

ABOUT: Book-of-the-Month Club News March 1938; New Yorker March 5, 1938; Saturday Review of Literature February 26, 1938; Scribner's Magazine April 1938; Time February 28, 1938; Wilson Library Bulletin March 1938.

*SMEDLEY, AGNES (1890-), American novelist and journalist, was born in Oklahoma and reared in Colorado. Her novel, *Daughter of Earth,*

H. Ansorge

though perhaps inaccurate in detail, is usually considered to be highly autobiographical. The heroine of that novel was born of poor tenant farmers, lived in extreme poverty in a company coal town, worked her way from California to New York, became an active Socialist, was for a while a rebellious college student, had various brushes with the police for her radical activities, and underwent an unfortunate marriage. Presumably all these things are also true of Miss Smedley; certainly some of them are known to be. She had very little early schooling, but became a country school teacher at fourteen. Later she went to California and worked her way through normal school.

At the beginning of the First World War she came to New York. She had become much interested in the movement for Indian freedom, and helped to obtain the release of Hindus who had been imprisoned on suspicion. On the ground that her activities jeopardized the neutrality of the United States, she was arrested and sent to the Tombs, where she remained for three months through inability to raise $10,000 bail. The late Rev. Dr. Percy Stickney Grant, a liberal New York rector, raised her bail and secured her release. The case was later dismissed for lack of evidence.

Meanwhile Miss Smedley had met Margaret Sanger and become interested in birth control. After the war she went to Berlin, and organized there the first German birth control clinic, which was taken over by the Republican government.

At the outbreak of the Chinese Revolution, she went to China as correspondent for German and Italian left-wing newspapers. She has remained there ever since, and is at this writing somewhere in the interior of China, where she lives as one of the people and almost as a member of the Eighth Route Army. She has long since changed her beliefs from Socialism to Communism, and since 1929 "has interpreted Chinese Communism to the world." The difficulties under which she lives and writes are enormous, and are complicated by the fact that she is very frail and has undergone several severe illnesses. She has risked her life many times, but feels that she has found her place in the world and is not likely ever to leave China again. She speaks and writes Chinese, and has adopted a Chinese refugee boy as her foster-child. She is familiar with parts of China that other white persons have seldom seen.

Though her books posit the Communist position, and are besides necessarily often hasty and fragmentary, they are of great value as reports on conditions unreported otherwise. David H. Popper called her "that redoubtable fighter for the rights of the underdog, . . . a devoted partisan who confesses to 'passionate likes and dislikes' yet studies always to tell the truth as she sees it, with blazing sincerity."

PRINCIPAL WORKS: Daughter of Earth (novel) 1929; Chinese Destinies, 1933; China's Red Army Marches (later edition as Red Flood Over China) 1934; China Fights Back, 1938.

ABOUT: Smedley, A. Daughter of Earth; China Weekly Review September 19, 1931; Saturday Review of Literature July 16, 1938.

SMITH, ALFRED ALOYSIUS. See HORN, A. A.

SMITH, ARTHUR COSSLETT (January 19, 1852-May 22, 1926), American short-story writer, was the son of James Cosslett

Smith, a justice of the New York Supreme Court, and Emily Ward (Adams) Smith. He attended Hobart College at Geneva, N.Y., receiving his B.A. degree in 1872 and a master's degree in 1875. In 1875 he obtained an LL.B. degree from Columbia Law School, and from June 1879 to the turn of the century he practiced law in Rochester, N.Y. *The Monk and the Dancer,* Arthur Cosslett Smith's first book of "exquisitely wrought" short stories, was published in 1900. Three years later he issued a similar collection, *The Turquoise Cup,* and he wrote a few other stories, published in *Scribner's Magazine,* before abandoning authorship altogether to look after his business interests. Smith died at Rochester in his seventy-fifth year, survived by his widow, Elizabeth Storer (Atkinson) Smith, whom he had married in June 1879; two sons, and a daughter. He was an Episcopalian; a member of the Century and University clubs in New York City; a member of the Sigma Phi Fraternity; and the recipient of an L.H.D. degree, in 1905, from his alma mater, Hobart College.

In the five years after the death of Arthur Cosslett Smith, several of his short stories were reprinted in the *Golden Book,* an eclectic magazine, whose editor, Henry Wysham Lanier, wrote: "He seems to have found the chief expression of an unusually sensitive, cultivated, beauty-loving nature in producing this handful of exquisitely wrought stories. There is something about the adroit prose of Arthur Cosslett Smith, and the polished finish of his two slim volumes of short stories, that makes him beloved of reading folk. Among those of literary discrimination, his name brings a gleam to the eye, and a sigh that he is writing no longer. Many will not cease to remember this lawyer of Rochester, N.Y., whose pen was so quiet, so exquisite, so delightful."

To Vincent Starrett, who once inquired of Smith why he wrote so little, the lawyer-author replied that his story-writing was a sort of recreation in the intervals of more important labors. Starrett concluded, in *Buried Caesars,* that Smith was a genuine artist, neglected, perhaps, because of his own indifference. "His characters talk perhaps more as people should talk than as people do talk. In his artifice, at any rate, he is a very convincing artist. Essentially, he is a writer of *contes* in the veritable French manner. In these tales, by his cynical sprightliness, he achieves a style that glitters like electric clusters on champagne."

PRINCIPAL WORKS: The Monk and the Dancer, 1900; The Turquoise Cup and The Desert, 1903.

ABOUT: Starrett, V. Buried Caesars; Golden Book Magazine June 1928, October 1928, March 1932; New York Times May 23, 1926.

SMITH, CHARD POWERS (November 1, 1894-   ), American poet and novelist, writes: "I was born in Watertown, N.Y.,  the son of Edward North Smith and Alice Lamon (Powers) Smith. Most of my ancestors were Yankees, dating back to the beginning, just solid folk, with a pretty pervasive love of learning. Educated at Pawling School, Yale (B.A. 1916), Harvard (LL.B. 1921), miscellaneous studies without degrees at Columbia and Oxford. Practiced law one year, then in 1922 inherited a small competence and went to writing poetry. Was assisted in this enterprise by my first wife, Olive Cary Macdonald, whom I married in 1921, and who died in Naples in 1924. After her death I took part in the typical life of 'self-expression' of the intellectuals of the time, my two *foci* being the popular expatriate cafés on the left bank of the Seine and, in America, the MacDowell Colony at Peterborough, N.H. Also lived a good deal in New York, and spent a summer in Nebraska as a hand on a little expedition of the American Museum of Natural History, my object being to get material for my epic of evolution. *Prelude to Man*, which was the big job which gave my life continuity at this time. Visited Panama in order to collect jungle copy. Also worked with expedition in the Dordogne River region in France, and in various parts of Kent in England. During this period my only real interest was in myself and my sensual and mystical desires. Edwin Arlington Robinson was my god and my friend, his encouragement being probably responsible for keeping me at work during a period when the publishers and the public were not clamoring for my work.

"In the autumn of 1929 I returned to the United States and married Marion Antoinette Chester, proposing to settle down to respectable matrimony, which I more or less proceeded to do. Meanwhile I had outgrown the expatriate contempt for my country and had discovered a deep affection for her. I began to study the civilization represented by my two Yankee grandfathers. I came to realize that whatever strength I possessed came from it, and that what of me was empty and futile came from the industrial snobbish pseudo-civilization of my own early environment.

"I got mixed up in the Distributist Movement, along with Ralph Borsodi on the one hand, and the Southern Agrarians on the other. The attempted alliance didn't jell, and we scattered in a series of little schisms, but the Decentralist idea is still the center of my political convictions. For a year I wrote the editorials in the magazine, *Free America*.

"I brought out my epic of evolution by subscription—a successful form of publication for poetry, by the way. This ended my self-centered, poetic phase. I began to do the research for my first novel, *Artillery of Time*. This book got the best press of any book of mine, the implication being that fiction was my chief talent. I don't know whether this is true or not.

"The three literary influences on my life have been my first wife, E. A. Robinson and Maxwell Perkins. I have known most of my contemporary writers, but I have always walked by myself, having no gang, hating all extremes, despising the self-indulgent aesthetes and the Radicals just as much as the Republicans and the Democrats. It is possible that the spectacle of the outer world may awaken us to our terrible responsibility of maintaining the ideal of individualism against the savages pressing Westward across the Rhine. The problem is to orient political expediency to the meaning of America. It may be possible to do it in time. It just *may* be.

"My wife and I and our son and daughter live near Cornwall, Conn., though our post office is Falls Village. I am Trial Justice for Cornwall."

* * *

Carl Carmer called Mr. Smith "a poet and scholar, with poetic sensitivity and creative power." He served through the First World War in France, being discharged with the rank of captain. In 1934 and 1935 he was advisory editor of the *American Poetry Journal*, and he frequently lectures on poetry.

PRINCIPAL WORKS: *Poetry*—Along the Wind, 1925; Lost Address, 1928; The Quest of Pan, 1930; Hamilton: A Poetic Drama, 1930; Prelude to Man, 1935. *Prose* — Pattern and Variation in Poetry, 1932; Annals of the Poets, 1935; Artillery of Time (novel) 1939; Ladies Day, 1941.

ABOUT: Saturday Review of Literature October 14, 1939; Scribner's Magazine May 1936.

*SMITH, Lady ELEANOR FURNEAUX (1902-   ), English novelist, writes: "I was born in Birkenhead. Shortly afterwards my family moved to London, where my father, F. E. Smith, afterwards Earl of Birkenhead [1922], practiced at the bar. We lived partly in London, partly at Charlton. our Oxford-shire home. I was educated by French governesses; attended English and French schools, and lived for some years in Brussels. At the age of seventeen, I started as a jour-nalist [as society reporter and film critic for the London *Dispatch, Sphere,* and *Bystander*]. I wrote my first novel, *Red Wagon*, between the

ages of nineteen and twenty, when I was still a journalist. I left Fleet Street about the same time. I have also lived in Spain. My brother, the pres-ent Earl of Birken-head, was also a suc-cessful writer (of biographies) until the present war, but is now serving in the British Army.

"My father's family had gypsy blood, and on my mother's side I am Cornish, of French descent. I love music, ballet, swimming, and riding. I am also fond of skiing, but dis-like most games. I like Schiaparelli's clothes, Patou's 'Joie' scent, and circuses. I like circuses now as a recreation, although a few years ago they were my living, for I not only wrote novels and stories about them, but I worked in the publicity depart-ment of one for some months. I have, on occasion, myself ridden in the ring. I hate noise—motorcycles in particular—society snobs, roast beef, whiskey, air-raid sirens, and people who mistreat children. I like traveling, champagne, bread-and-cheese, and playing darts."

* * *

Lady Eleanor is very proud of her gypsy blood, which comes to her from her paternal great-grandmother. Besides writing about gypsies, she has a personal acquaintance among them, speaks Romany, and belongs to several societies interested in Romany history and customs. Her father, the First Earl of Birkenhead (who took his title from his native town) was a famous wit as well as a renowned barrister. The autobio-graphical urge is strong in his daughter, who wrote "The Story of My Life" at the ad-vanced age of eight, and published a genuine autobiography at thirty-seven. Her books, though sentimental and naïve, are romantic and colorful, and very popular. She is a beautiful woman, with a pointed oval face, wide dark eyes, and lovely hands.

PRINCIPAL WORKS: Red Wagon, 1930; Fla-menco, 1931; Ballerina, 1932; Satan's Circus and

Other Stories, 1932; Christmas Tree (reprinted as Seven Trees) 1933; Tzigane (in America: Rom-any) 1935; Portrait of a Lady, 1936; The Spanish House, 1938; Life's a Circus (autobiography) 1939; Lovers' Meeting, 1940; The Man in Grey, 1941.

ABOUT: Smith, E. F. Life's a Circus; Time February 5, 1940; Wilson Library Bulletin June 1931.

SMITH, ERNEST BRAMAH ("Ernest Bramah") (1869?-June 27, 1942), English humorist and writer of detective stories, the creator of Kai Lung and the blind sleuth Max Carrados, was one of the most self-effacing of modern authors. "I am not fond of writing about myself," he explained in a friendly letter to the editors of the present volume, "and only in less degree about my work. My published books are

about all that I care to pass on to the reader." So successful was Mr. Smith-"Bramah" in this objective that not even the year of his birth is exactly known—though his autobio-graphical first book, *English Farming and Why I Turned It Up* (1894), places the event inferentially at about 1870.

It was in July of 1899, relates the English publisher Grant Richards in his informative reminiscences, *Author Hunting*, that E. V. Lucas brought to Richards' country place, Bisham Park, a careful typescript sewn into brown paper, which proved to be the first draft of *The Wallet of Kai Lung*, by "Ernest Bramah."

Richards was enthusiastic and issued the book (which eight publishers had previously refused) in an edition of a thousand copies —which was still not exhausted at the end of seven seasons. In more recent years the Kai Lung tales have enjoyed greater pop-ularity, but they are still essentially "caviar to the general": cherished by the discrim-inating few and ignored by the great public. As Hilaire Belloc explained in a preface to *Kai Lung's Golden Hours* (1922), these par-able-like tales obtain their effect of subtle humor and philosophy by the adaptation of Chinese conventions to the English tongue.

Kai Lung is a professional tale-teller accused of many crimes, who manages to postpone a verdict by entrancing his judge with stories from day to day. The China represented is a deliberately "fantastic con-ventional bogus China," but is yet sufficiently verisimilar to suggest the author's sometime residence in the Far East. In the opinion of the *New Stateman,* the "Lung" books are first-rate pieces of finished irony and elegant extravagance, and they have had such other ardent advocates as Sir Arthur Quiller-Couch, Sir J. C. Squire, A. B. Walkley, Christopher Morley, and Dorothy Sayers. In 1931 the Men Students of Lilian Baylis' Old Vic repertory company in London presented a dramatized version of the *Golden Hours;* "Bramah," incidentally, wrote many original short plays, popular with English amateur societies and over the radio.

For many years "Ernest Bramah's" short stories were fixtures in the English fiction magazines, the most popular being those concerning Max Carrados, his notable blind detective. The first Carrados book, called simply *Max Carrados,* appeared in the London stalls on the eve of the First World War, which possibly accounts for the fact that it was never published in America. The cases were written with the literary grace one would expect of the inventor of Kai Lung, and in at least one instance drew on the author's expert knowledge of numismatics (he published an authoritative work on the subject in 1929). In "Bramah's" hands, Carrados' blindness is never a meretricious bid for popularity, but a legitimate factor of added interest. The stories have frequently appeared in anthologies on both sides of the water, and, like the Kai Lung tales, have been gathered into an omnibus volume in the country of their origin. There is no full-length Carrados novel. Wise, witty, gentle Max Carrados has been called by critics a worthy protagonist to close the romantic, or "Sherlock Holmes," period in the detective story, which may be said to have ended with Sarajevo.

"Ernest Bramah," according to Grant Richards, was the kindest and most amiable of men. A small, bald man, with twinkling black eyes, he lived in quiet retirement. When he died at his country home at Somerset in 1942, his age was generally given as seventy-three. According to one obituary notice, he had lived in China many years.

PRINCIPAL WORKS: English Farming and Why I Turned It Up, 1894; The Wallet of Kai Lung, 1900; The Mirror of Kung Ho, 1905; What Might Have Been, 1907; Max Carrados, 1914; Kai Lung's Golden Hours, 1922; The Eyes of Max Carrados, 1923; The Specimen Case, 1924; Max Carrados Mysteries, 1927; Kai Lung Unrolls His Mat, 1928; A Guide to the Varieties and Rarity of English Regal Copper Coins: Charles II-Victoria, 1929; Short Stories of Today and Yesterday, 1929; A Little Flutter, 1930; The Moon of Much Gladness (U.S. title: The Return of Kai Lung) 1932; The Bravo of London, 1934; Kai Lung Beneath the Mulberry-Tree, 1940.

ABOUT: Haycraft, H. Murder for Pleasure: The Life and Times of the Detective Story; Mais, S. P. B. Some Modern Authors; Richards, G. Author Hunting; Prefaces and Introductions to various editions of the author's works; New York Herald Tribune June 28, 1942.

SMITH, FRANCIS HOPKINSON. See "AMERICAN AUTHORS: 1600-1900"

SMITH, JUSTIN HARVEY (January 13, 1857-March 21, 1930), American historian, winner of the Pulitzer Prize, was born at Boscawen, N.H., the youngest of the three sons of the Rev. Ambrose Smith, a Dartmouth graduate and Congregationalist minister, and Cynthia Maria (Egerton) Smith. The family moved when Justin Smith was a boy to Pembroke, N.H., later to Norwich, Vt. (The military college there awarded Smith an honorary LL.D. in 1908, some forty years later.) Young Smith graduated with honors and a B.A. degree from Dartmouth in 1877; he had commuted the short distance from Norwich to Hanover, N.H., usually on foot. Two years later he obtained his M.A. there, and the college gave him an honorary Litt.D. in 1920.

From 1879 to 1881 Smith was a student at the Union Theological Seminary in New York. He spent some time at the Paris Exposition as private secretary of John D. Philbrick, who was in charge of the American educational exhibit. From 1881 to 1898 he was engaged in the publishing business first with Charles Scribner's Sons, then with Ginn & Co., publishers of textbooks, where he was in charge of the editorial department from 1890 to 1898. Retiring with a satisfactory fortune, Smith was professor of modern history at Dartmouth from 1899 to 1908, when he resigned to give his entire time to historical research. Ten years before, he had written a book on the troubadours, and in 1903 a critical study of Benedict Arnold's march from Cambridge to Quebec, with a reprint of Arnold's *Journal.* The picturesquely named *Our Struggle for the Fourteenth Colony* was a study of Canada and its relation to the American Revolution. The authoritative two-volume work, *The War With Mexico* (1919), received the Pulitzer Prize for the best book that year on American history, in 1920, and in 1923 was awarded the first Loubat Prize of $1,000. Although he called himself in later years "unmarried," Smith had married Mary E. Barnard of Chico, Calif., in May 1892. They separated after two years, and the marriage was terminated by a Paris divorce. Smith, who was chairman of the

Historical Manuscripts Commission of the American Historical Association from 1917 to 1923, traveled in over forty countries besides Alaska and the Philippines. He was injured in a taxicab accident in November 1929. Returning from the South a year later, he suffered a heart attack in front of Brooklyn's Borough Hall in March 1930 and died instantly, two months after his seventy-third birthday. He was tall, with sharp eyes and a full beard. For recreation he cruised in power boats made from his own plans.

PRINCIPAL WORKS: Troubadours at Home: Their Lives and Personalities, Their Songs and Their World, 1899; Arnold's March From Cambridge to Quebec: A Critical Study: Together with a Reprint of Arnold's Journal, 1903; Our Struggle for the Fourteenth Colony: Canada and the American Revolution, 1907; The Annexation of Texas, 1911; The War With Mexico, 1919. Editor—The Historie Booke, 1903; Letters of Santa Anna, 1919.

ABOUT: New York Times March 24, April 24, 1930.

*SMITH, LOGAN PEARSALL (October 18, 1865-), Anglo-American essayist, was born [Lloyd Logan Pearsall Smith] in Mill-

ville, N.J., the son of Robert Pearsall Smith and Hannah (Whitall) Smith. He was a first cousin of Miss M. Carey Thomas, President of Bryn Mawr College, and his sister married the art critic, Bernhard Berenson; another sister was the first wife of

W. Rothenstein

Bertrand Russell. The family were Philadelphia Quakers, wealthy glass manufacturers; in his childhood Walt Whitman was an habitué of their home. After spending four years at Haverford and Harvard, he entered his father's business, but was persuaded by Miss Thomas to give it up and go to live in England, where his parents and sisters had preceded him. He did so, and entered Balliol College, Oxford (B.A. 1893, M.A. 1906). He has lived in England ever since, most of the time in London. He has never married, and the Boston Transcript once aptly called him "an English bachelor from Philadelphia." He became the typical expatriate, "the ghost of Henry James' Passionate Pilgrim," the associate of Matthew Arnold and of his fellow-countryman and fellow-Anglophile, James McNeill Whistler. He is an authority on English usage, on which he was consulted regularly by the British Broadcasting Company until

his recent invalidism. The discreet story of his life may be found in Unforgotten Years (1939).

His Trivia, originally published at his own expense, gave him a small private fame and a devoted and select following. He has been hailed as the writer who "rediscovered the paragraph." In his brief essays, as William Rose Benét put it, "his light delightful malice flickers." Christopher Morley, who is one of his most ardent admirers, called him "the most perfect Mandarin of English letters," with "an elderly and savory spirit both ripe and acrid, . . . an alert ironist with a patient precison of words."

Logan Pearsall Smith has always written as if he were an old man, even when he was young. Bald, thin, and aquiline-featured, he is the typical old bachelor of culture and perception who gravitates between his club and his study. His real diffidence and his engaging candor regarding his personal shortcomings redeem him from the accusation of mere old-fogeyism. Even Edmund Wilson, who said "he writes language of such a neutral color as can only be attained by an American who has stripped away his American colloquialisms and yet must still handle English turns of phrase a little like a foreign language," has acknowledged that there is yet "something in him . . . dry, independent, even tough. In dealing with incidents frankly infinitesimal, he somehow succeeds in being impressively truthful. . . . The pedant, the bore, and the snob in him have been delineated by Mr. Smith with the same intentness and precision as the moralist and the aesthete."

It is true, as he himself has been the first to say, that he "accepts himself blandly," has never in his life "felt a pang of conscience or a consciousness of wrong-doing," that he has an amiable love of money and the moneyed and a preference for the society of the aristocratic. On the other hand, taken in small doses, as he gives them, his essays are delightful, shrewd, incisive, and witty. He is a devotee of the aphorism, and has even edited an anthology of them. In a restricted field he is a genuine scholar. He really does not belong in this period at all, but is a holdover from the age of Henry James, and to all intents and purposes is a Henry James character come to life.

PRINCIPAL WORKS: The Youth of Parnassus, 1895; The Golden Urn (with B. Berenson) 1897; Trivia, 1902; Life and Letters of Sir Henry Wotton, 1907; Songs and Sonnets, 1909; The English Language, 1912; More Trivia, 1921; Words and Idioms, 1925; Afterthoughts, 1931; On Reading Shakespeare, 1933; All Trivia (including Trivia,

* Died March 2, 1946.

More Trivia, Afterthoughts, Last Words) 1934; Reperusals and Re-collections, 1936; Unforgotten Years (autobiography) 1939; Milton and His Modern Critics, 1940.

ABOUT: Smith, L. P. Unforgotten Years; Whitall, J. English Years; Current Opinion February 1918; New Republic January 25, 1939; Saturday Review of Literature October 10, 1936.

SMITH, Mrs. MARY PRUDENCE (WELLS) (July 23, 1840-December 17, 1930), American juvenile writer, was born in Attica, N.Y., a region which her thoroughly New England parents, Dr. Noah S. Wells and Esther Nims (Coleman) Wells, regarded as "out West." When she was nine her family moved to Greenfield Mass., and she was sent first to the local schools and then, for a proper "polishing-off," to Miss Draper's Female Seminary in Hartford, Conn. In 1865, after a brief experience as a teacher in the Greenfield High School, she became the first woman employee of a Massachusetts bank. At the end of eight years she asked for the same pay a man in her position would have been given, and resigned when the management only raised her salary, refusing to meet her "equal pay for equal work" demand. She studied art in Philadelphia for two years, and in 1875 married Fayette Smith, a Cincinnati lawyer and son and grandson of the two Preserved Smiths, Unitarian ministers of Warwick. Their daughter, Agnes Mary, died at the age of fourteen.

Before her marriage Mrs. Smith had been writing over the signature "P. Thorne,"— "vegetable synonyms" were quite in vogue. But with the first of the Jolly Good series she resumed her own name. Four other series followed, the last of which was the Summer Vacation series (its final volume, *Five in a Ford,* appeared in 1918 when the author was seventy-eight. She wrote not only for her own daughter but for three step-children; these youngsters became, unwittingly, her first critics. Her two biggest favorites among children, *Jolly Good Times* and *Jolly Good Times at School,* were republished in the late 'twenties and are, perhaps, the basis of her reputation as a writer of able juveniles. She died in her ninetieth year.

PRINCIPAL WORKS: Jolly Good series (8 vols.) 1875-95; Miss Ellis's Mission, 1886; The Young Puritan series, 1897-1900; The Boy Captive of Old Deerfield, 1904; The Boy Captive of Canada, 1905; Boys of the Border, 1907; Boys and Girls of Seventy-Seven, 1909; Summer Vacation series, 1914-1918.

ABOUT: Publishers' Weekly January 3, 1931; Wilson Library Bulletin May 1931.

SMITH, NAOMI. See ROYDE-SMITH

"SMITH, S. S." See WILLIAMSON, T. R.

SMITH, SHEILA. See KAYE-SMITH

SMITH, THORNE (1893-June 21, 1934), American novelist and humorist, was born at the U.S. Naval Academy, Annapolis, Md.

His father, Commodore James Thorne Smith, U.S.N., was supervisor of the Port of New York during the First World War. The boy attended Locust Dale Academy in Virginia, St. Luke's School, Wayne, Pa., and completed his formal education at Dartmouth College. The First World War interrupting his work in a New York advertising agency, Thorne Smith enlisted in the navy, where he rose to the post of boatswain's mate and edited the service paper *Broadside. Biltmore Oswald* and its sequel, *Out of Luck,* first appeared in its back pages. Oswald was several cuts above Edward Streeter's semi-literate rookie who wrote letters to *Dere Mable*; his adventures in book form sold 70,000 copies. Smith experienced some lean times before he succeeded in launching the series of farcical novels which brought him a large income and a steady market in the motion pictures, the only medium which could render his fantastic plots into concrete form.

Turnabout, one of his best sellers, describes the adventures of a lively young suburban couple who switched bodies, but not personalities, under the influence of an idol which possessed unsuspected powers. *The Night Life of the Gods* depicts the adventures of the marble gods and goddesses of the Metropolitan Museum of Art, who come alive after dark (like F. Anstey's *Tinted Venus* and the statuary in E. Nesbit's *The Enchanted Castle*) and cut capers on Broadway. *The Bishop's Jaegers* shows an embarrassed cleric set down in the midst of a nudist colony, while the *Topper* series displays an unfortunate mortal at the mercy of a pair of playful ghosts. In 1933 Smith was in Hollywood, writing dialogue for Metro-Goldwyn-Mayer. With his wife, Mrs. Celia (Sullivan) Smith, and two daughters, Marion and June, he lived in a New Jersey house built around trees, and in hotels in the Washington Square district of New York City. Smith was fair, with a smiling face, large nose, and a mild resemblance to John Barrymore. He died of a heart attack at forty at Sarosota, Fla., and was buried in Mount Olivet Cemetery, Long Island, N.Y. He left an unfinished novel which was completed by another American fantasist, Norman Matson,*qv* and published in 1941 as *The Passionate Witch.*

PRINCIPAL WORKS: Biltmore Oswald, 1918; Topper, 1926; Dream's End, 1927; The Stray Lamb, 1929; Did She Fall? 1930; The Night Life of the Gods, 1931; Turnabout, 1931; Lazy Bear Lane (juvenile) 1931; Topper Takes a Trip, 1932; The Bishop's Jaegers, 1932; Rain in the Doorway, 1933; Skin and Bones, 1933; The Glorious Pool, 1934; The Passionate Witch (completed by N. Matson) 1941.

ABOUT: Johnson, M. (ed.) Thorne Smith: His Life and Times; Stearns, H. The Street I Know; Van Doren, C. The American Novel (rev. ed.); New York Times June 22, 26, 1934.

SMITH, WALLACE (1888-January 31, 1937), American journalist, novelist, and short-story writer, was a native of Chicago, where he became well known as a newspaper artist and reporter before launching into his career of adventure in Mexico and Hollywood. He was a veteran of four Mexican campaigns, two of them with Pancho Villa. On one occasion Smith walked into the camp of some revolutionists, in his capacity as newspaper correspondent, and was sentenced to the firing squad. His guide insisted that etiquette demanded that Smith prepare a speech of farewell; an opportune reprieve from headquarters arrived before he was given a chance to deliver it. Seven books and seventy-five short stories were turned out by Smith in his writing career. *The Little Tigress: Tales Out of the Dusk of Mexico* (1923) was the first of these, followed by the comparatively mild record of a trip by mule pack-train with friends through the Yellowstone, illustrated by the author. In 1929, when silent pictures were beginning to give place to the talkies, Smith went to Hollywood, where he worked with Anthony Veiller on the screen play *Seven Keys to Baldpate,* based on the novel by Earl Derr Biggers, and turned out *The Dove* and *Two Arabian Knights* on his own. He also executed appropriate illustrations and page-borders for Ben Hecht's privately printed erotic novel, *Fantazius Mallare,* published in Chicago in 1922.

Smith's most successful novel, *The Captain Hates the Sea* (1933), a sort of marine *Grand Hotel* recording the voyage of the

"S.S. San Capador" from San Francisco to New York via the Panama Canal, was translated into French. Smith wrote the scenario for the effective screen version. He also worked on a "Bulldog Drummond" film, based on the character invented by "Sapper" (H. C. MacNeile). In *Bessie Cotter,* the novel Smith took most seriously, he returned to his native Chicago, in the early years of the present century, for his theme. A swarthy, saturnine-looking individual, with dark eyes and a small, dapper moustache, Smith died of a heart attack in Hollywood, at forty-nine.

PRINCIPAL WORKS: The Little Tigress, 1923; On the Trail in Yellowstone, 1924; Oregon Sketches, 1925; Are You Decent? 1927; The Captain Hates the Sea, 1933; Bessie Cotter, 1934; The Happy Alienist: A Viennese Caprice, 1936.

ABOUT: Hansen, H. Midwest Portraits; New York Times February 1, 1937; Wilson Library Bulletin March 1937.

*SMITTER, WESSEL (1894-), American novelist, was born near Grand Rapids, Mich. Both his parents were natives of Holland, and the part of Michigan in which he was reared was largely populated by Netherlanders. He was educated at Calvin College and at the University of Michigan (B.A. 1922). On graduation he received what he calls "a sort of scholarship" from one of the big automobile manufacturers in Detroit, and for two years learned the business "from the ground up," eventually taking a position in the company's advertising department. The result was not what the manufacturer had hoped; instead of devoting his life to automobiles, Mr. Smitter grew to detest the factory and to consider machine industry a Moloch which crushed the lives of those it overwhelmed. He fled abruptly—but not, as one might have expected, to the rural peace for which he longed, but to Hollywood, where he still lives. He is unmarried.

Still departing from the norm, he has had no contact with the motion picture industry, and has never been a screen writer. Instead, he makes his living (his writing is still an avocation) by selling trees to movie moguls who are too impatient to wait for planted saplings to grow up on their estates. Mr. Smitter transplants full-grown trees for

* Died November 7, 1951.

them; his truck, bearing a peripatetic forest, is a well known sight in Hollywood.

In the intervals of this occupation, he has written two novels. His first book, rather reminiscent of John Steinbeck's *Of Mice and Men,* is even more tragic. It is autobiographical in spirit though not in story, and reflects the yearning for escape from mechanized industry which drove him from Detroit. Its hero is a young machine worker whose one ambition is to get away from the conveyor-belt and become a clam-digger. Instead, one misfortune after another overtakes him, until he is permanently crippled by a factory accident.

For his second novel, the first to be written about the Matanuska Valley experiment, Mr. Smitter traveled to Alaska and got his impressions at first hand. It is a frank and at the same time a heartening study of the government's attempt to turn relief clients into Alaskan farmers.

Very blond and typically "Nordic" in appearance, Mr. Smitter has none of the liking for regimentation and efficiency which is supposed to be a salient Nordic characteristic. His writing displays tenderness, pity, and a passionate love of nature. It is not soft, however, but evidences a genuine tragic power, and, as one critic noted, is "remarkable for authenticity of detail."

PRINICIPAL WORKS: F.O.B. Detroit, 1938; Another Morning, 1941.

ABOUT: Time November 14, 1938.

SNAITH, JOHN COLLIS (1876-December 8, 1936), English novelist, was a reticent Yorkshireman whom his friends nick-

named "The Gloomy Scribe"—despite the fact that much of his fiction was written in comic vein. He began to write as a boy when laid up by a football accident, and in middle life was an excellent cricket player. Otherwise he revealed little about himself, remarking, "If people want to know what I am like let them read my books." Of a sensitive and slightly cynical nature, he was a passionate lover of beauty in all its forms; was devoted to country life; traveled extensively; and died suddenly at sixty at his home in Hampstead Way, London N.W. He never married. The London *Times* remarked in its obituary that Snaith was "Jack-of-all-styles, master, it seemed,

of none." He invariably referred to himself in *Who's Who* as "writer of fiction," and nothing more. Beginning with historical novels, of which *Mistress Dorothy Mervin* (1896) was the first, Snaith first came into critical notice with *Broke of Covenden* ten years later, which the *Saturday Review* called "the freshest and most original piece of comedy—in the Meredithian sense—that we have met since its master's pen has rested." A thirty-page preface to the novel is written in a style of Meredithian bravura. *Broke of Covenden* is an English squire of the most respectably conventional type, who undergoes various vicissitudes. The influence of Peacock and Dickens is also apparent in the story.

William Jordan, Junior, the story of a genius misplaced in a printing shop, all the details of which are correctly described, was regarded by "AE" (George Russell) and most critics as Snaith's finest book. *Araminta,* serialized in the American *Forum* in 1908-09, is a comedy of an eighteenth-century style set in the period of Victoria's Jubilee. It was dramatized in 1921, with Lady Tree playing Lady Crewkerne. *The Principal Girl,* serialized in the *Atlantic Monthly* in 1911-12, is Snaith's best endeavor in blithe and irresponsible light comedy. *The Coming* (1917) showed what might be expected if the Second Advent of Christ took place in the England of that period. Further instances could be cited of Snaith's kaleidoscopic but not particularly significant talent.

PRINCIPAL WORKS: Mistress Dorothy Mervin, 1896; Fierceheart the Soldier, 1897; Willow the King, 1899; Wayfarers, 1901; Broke of Covenden, 1904; Henry Northcote, 1906; William Jordan, Junior, 1908; Araminta, 1909; Fortune, 1910; The Principal Girl, 1912; The Coming, 1917; The Adventurous Lady, 1920; The Council of Seven, 1922; The Van Roon, 1922; Time and Tide, 1924; Thus Far and Other Stories, 1925; The Hoop, 1927; Cousin Beryl, 1929; The Unforeseen, 1930; Indian Summer, 1931; But Even So, 1935.

ABOUT: London Times December 10, 12, 1936; New York Times December 10, 1936.

SNOW, EDGAR PARKS (July 19, 1905-), American writer on China, reports: "On my mother's side I am descended from Irish and German families. On my father's side there is Irish and English. The Snow clan claims connection with that capacious tub, the 'Mayflower.' My own father grew up on a farm, and after college went to Kansas City, Mo., where I was born. We were a middle-class family, with more respectability than money, though we had enough to eat and wear always, and

a comfortable home. When I first took an interest in how we lived my father was editing a business paper and operating a printing shop. In summer vacations I worked for him as printer's devil. There I learned to set type and feed a press and to like the smell of ink and freshly cut paper. When I was in high school I edited a paper of my own and wrote all the copy and set and printed and mailed it. Once I set up and printed a book of my own verses, but the only person who saw it was the girl to whom I dedicated it. Despite such ominous signs my parents took no precautions. Before I entered college I had determined to be a writer.

J. A. Piver

"In 1923-24 I attended junior college in Kansas City; then I went to the school of journalism at the University of Missouri. Later I studied at Columbia—a few courses in Extension. With this inadequate preparation I became a newspaper man. I got my first newspaper job, in fact, while at the university, with the Kansas City *Star,* which eventually gave me the sack. My second newspaper job was with the New York *Sun.*

"In 1928, in New York, I decided I needed adventure and the experience of travel and I started off to see the world. I have been a newspaper correspondent ever since. During the past thirteen years I have traveled thousands of miles in the Orient and visited practically every country from Baluchistan to Siberia. Most of my time has been in China, but the Philippines was my headquarters for nearly two years, and off and on I spent many months in Japan, Manchuria, India, the Dutch Indies, etc. From 1933 to 1937 I made my home in Peking, and while there I studied the Chinese language, in which I have a fair fluency.

"In 1929 I was correspondent for the Chicago *Tribune,* and from 1930 to 1938 for the New York *Sun.* In 1933 I was also appointed staff correspondent for the London *Daily Herald,* and in 1937 I became that paper's chief correspondent in the Far East. I began to write for the *Saturday Evening Post* in 1938, and have contributed to it every year since then. In 1936 I entered what was then Soviet China, and traveled with the Chinese Red Army for five months. I was able to bring out the first eye-witness account of that 'lost country' and break a news blockade of nine years.

The strangest moment of my life occurred when I returned from Red China and read my own obituary in the American papers.

"Once I wrote a book called *Impressions of the Northwest,* but it was published only in Chinese. My wife, whose pen name is 'Nym Wales,' has published three books in Chinese, none of which has appeared in English. She is an American; we were married in Tokyo in 1932. Her latest book, *China Builds for Democracy,* is the story of the Chinese Industrial Co-operatives, which she originally conceived, and helped to plan with myself and Rewi Alley.

"We returned to America in 1941. It is good to be back. There is no other country on earth like this: none with such treasure, culturally and materially, none with such possibilities in an age of science. Most important of all, there is no other land which offers the facilities and the freedom essential to a fearless search for truth. To preserve that freedom and those facilities and help continue that search—surely these are the minimum conditions on which honest journalists can support any régime today."

PRINCIPAL WORKS: Far Eastern Front, 1934; Living China (edited and compiled) 1936; Red Star Over China, 1937 (revised 1939); The Battle for Asia (in England: The Scorched Earth) 1941; The Political Battle of Asia, 1941.

ABOUT: Asia February 1937; Publishers' Weekly February 12, 1938; Saturday Review of Literature January 1, 1938, March 1, 1941.

SOLOGUB, FEDOR (1863-December 5, 1927), Russian novelist and dramatist, was born Fedor Kuzmich Teternikov in St. Petersburg, and studied and taught at the Teachers' Institute till 1907, the year of the publication of *The Little Demon,* his best-known novel. At fifty-three he had published twenty bulky volumes, and his plays were produced at the Kommisarshevsky Theatre in Moscow. Sologub regarded the theatre as a religious temple, where the drama should illustrate "the immutable law of universal play" that men should be like wonderfully constructed marionettes. (This did not tend to make his plays altogether popular with actors.) Choral dancing is a proper and integral part of drama, in the opinion of Sologub, who paid tribute to the art of Isadora Duncan. *The Triumph of Death* and *Hostages of Life* are two plays which illustrate his fundamental idea of the eternal antagonism between dream and reality, and the necessity of escaping from the oppressive realization of the futility of existence into a fourth dimension of faith, miracles and ideals. Peredonov, the hero, or rather chief protagonist of *The Little Demon,* is the little demon in question because he is so petty and pitiful, and tries to set himself against universal law. Sologub "burned with indignation at the bourgeois methods of hiding naked beauty behind all the artificiality of modern life." (This same motive was evidently behind the amorous play of Luidmilla and Sasha, the schoolboy, in *The Little Demon.*) Peredonov, he explained, "is an expression of the all-human inclination towards evil, of the almost distinterested tendency of a perverse human soul to depart from the common course of universal life directed by one omnipotent will and [take] vengeance upon the world for its own grievous loneliness." First begun in 1892, finished in 1902 and serialized in *Voprosi Zhizni,* a periodical, the novel gave a word to Russian idiom. "Peredonovshchina" was used to describe the frowsy side of Russian petty officialdom. The novel was translated into English by John Cournos, who introduced Sologub to the English-speaking public in the *New Statesman* for December 1913.

Sologub, writes A. Lister Kaye, was a poet, a thinker, and a dreamer. His mentality is too subtle and profound to appeal to the general public, too picturesque to appeal to the philosopher. He used allegory, parable, and fable to convert his thought into words. His tales, a curious blend of Chekhov and Poe, and frequently very short, are for the most part fantastic and imaginative, while set among the ordinary surroundings of life. Many of them appeared in Russian daily newspapers. Like Lord Dunsany, he enjoyed the unexpected introduction of the supernatural into mundane affairs, and preferred a quasi-Oriental setting and nomenclature, as the *Athenaeum* pointed out. Sologub was notoriously eccentric in his habits. His wife, a critic in her own right, committed suicide by drowning in the Neva in 1921, after they had undergone some persecution from the government but had been given permission to leave Russia. Six years later Sologub died in Petrograd, at sixty-four.

WORKS AVAILABLE IN ENGLISH TRANSLATION: The Sweet-Scented Name and Other Fairy Tales, Fables, and Stories, 1915; The Old House and Other Tales, 1915; The Little Demon, 1916; The Created Legend, 1916.

ABOUT: Drama Winter 1916; Fortnightly Review October 1, 1920.

"SOMERVILLE & ROSS." See SOMERVILLE, E. A. O. and MARTIN, V. F.

*SOMERVILLE, EDITH ANNA OE-NONE (1861-), Irish novelist and collaborator with her cousin, Violet F. Martin *qv* ("Martin Ross") was born at Drishane, County Cork, Ireland, where she still lives. Her father was a lieutenant colonel, her grandfather an admiral, her great-grandfather (whose biography she wrote) chief justice of Ireland. She thus be-

longs to the innermost circle of Anglo-Irish society, and appropriately she has shared its interests, particularly its cult of fox-hunting. She became the first feminine M.F.H. in 1903, revived the West Carberry Foxhounds in 1912, and carried on as M.F.H. to 1919. Primarily, however, her leanings were always toward the arts. After a private education at home she studied art in Düsseldorf, Paris, and London, and began her career as an illustrator. Though after her meeting with her cousin in 1886, and the commencement of their long collaboration, she was best known as a writer, she has continued both to illustrate her own books and to exhibit. She has held one-man shows in Dublin and London, and in 1929 visited the United States for the first time both to exhibit her paintings and to visit friends and secure material for a book.

Dr. Somerville (as she prefers to be known since receiving an honorary Litt.D. degree from Trinity College, Dublin) was a founder member of the Irish Academy of Letters, in 1933. She still paints, her other recreations being music and driving. She also farms and breeds race and hunting horses. In 1935, under her own name, she edited an anthology of hunting verse called *Notes of the Horn.* All her other writing, however, has been done, even since Miss Martin's death, under the name of "Somerville and Ross." A collected edition of the Somerville and Ross sporting works was issued in 1927. She is unmarried.

During Miss Martin's life the two cousins lived together and traveled widely on the Continent. Her first work was issued under the pseudonym of "Geilles Herring" (the name of an ancestor), but this was soon abandoned. Of the work of the two cousins, C. L. Graves remarked that "felicities abound on every page; while the turn of phrase of the peasant speech is caught with a fidelity which no other Irish writer has ever surpassed."

PRINCIPAL WORKS: (all actually or ostensibly in collaboration with "Martin Ross"): *Fiction* — An Irish Cousin, 1889; Naboth's Vineyard, 1891; The Real Charlotte, 1895; The Silver Fox, 1897; Some Experiences of an Irish R.M., 1899; All On the Irish Shore, 1903; Further Experiences of an Irish R.M., 1908; Dan Russel the Fox, 1911; In Mr. Knox's Country, 1915; Mount Music, 1919; An Enthusiast, 1921; The Big House of Inver, 1925; The Smile and the Tear, 1933; Sarah's Youth, 1938. *Miscellaneous* — Through Connemara in a Governess Cart, 1893; In the Vine Country, 1893; Beggars on Horseback, 1895; Some Irish Yesterdays, 1906; Irish Memories, 1918; Stray-aways, 1920; Wheel-Tracks, 1923; The States Through Irish Eyes, 1930; An Incorruptible Irishman, 1932; The Sweet Cry of Hounds, 1936; Notions in Garrison, 1941.

ABOUT: Gwynn, S. L. Irish Books and Irish People; Somerville, E. A. O. & Ross, M. Irish Memories; Williams, P. Some Great English Novels; Edinburgh Review October 1921; Living Age October 4, 1913; Spectator January 1, 1916.

SORLEY, CHARLES HAMILTON
(May 19, 1895-October 13, 1915), Scottish poet, was born in Old Aberdeen, Scotland,

the elder twin son of William Ritchie Sorley, professor of moral philosophy in the University of Aberdeen. The boy was of Lowland Scottish descent on both sides. In 1900 Professor Sorley became Knightsbridge Professor at Cambridge University. Charles was a day boy at King's College Choir School, then spent five happy years at Marlborough College (1908-13), where he contributed some remarkable poems to *The Malburian*. "The River," the ballad of a suicide, was not the usual schoolboy production. Winning an open scholarship to University College, Oxford, Sorley decided to spend some time abroad. Rather more than six months were spent in Germany, first at Schwerin in Mecklenburg, then the summer session at the University of Jena. He was on a walking tour on the banks of the Moselle when the First World War broke out in 1914. Imprisoned with a friend at Trier August 2, he was released the same night, and returned through Belgium to England. Sorley was gazetted a second lieutenant in the Seventh (Service) Battalion of the Suffolk Regiment before the end of the month, was a lieutenant in November, and a captain the following August. His battalion was sent to France May 30, 1915, serving some months in the

trenches around Ploegsteert (always known to the Tommies as Plugstreet). When the battalion was moved south to take part in the battle of Loos, Sorley was shot in the head by a sniper when his company captured the "hair-pin" trench near Hulluch. He was twenty years old.

Sorley, who acknowledged his "rapturous loyalty" to Masefield, was not primarily a war poet, though it is his two sonnets on death, written in Flanders, that constitute his chief claim to remembrance. The London *Chronicle* said that he "achieved beauty by the unadorned statement of naked fact," and the *Times Literary Supplement*, "To the shrine of poetry he had indubitably pierced." Of his *Letters*, the *Manchester Guardian* remarked that the book "contains the first mature impressions of a nature which was all vigour and radiance, a boy who may be said to have had a genius for truth." The frontispiece portrait shows a handsome youth of twenty with an open, candid expression and a light moustache.

PRINCIPAL WORKS: Marlborough and Other Poems, 1916; Letters, 1919.

ABOUT: Sorley, C. H. Letters (see biographical preface by his twin brother); Friends' Quarterly Examiner October 1937.

SOULE, GEORGE HENRY
(June 11, 1887-), American economist, writes: "I was born in Stamford, Conn., of a New England family extending back on both sides to the 'Mayflower.' Though I am a namesake of a signer of the Mayflower Compact, had one ancestor in the Boston Tea Party and several in the American Revolution, my most prized progenitor was

S. Salmi

Robert Calef, who wrote a book satirizing Cotton Mather and the Salem witchcraft persecutions—a book banned by the conservatives of the time and sold from under the counter in Cambridge, Mass.

"Educated at Stamford High School and Yale, from which I was graduated in 1908, I early developed an interest in writing, being editor of my school paper and later of the *Yale Literary Magazine*. Aside from English, my major study in college was economics. After graduation my first work was in book publishing; until 1914 I was connected with the house of Frederick A. Stokes Co., where I also became editor of the first cooperative book announcement of the publishers—an attempt to present bona-fide news of new books without praise of them. But my interest in the success of the aesthetically meritorious books came into constant collision with exploitation of so-called 'popular' taste, and I began to believe that something better than a commercial civilization was necessary if cultural values were to be well served.

"An opportunity for activity in a broader sphere came with an invitation to join the staff of the *New Republic* in 1914—the year of its foundation. There I performed many duties—from make-up and proof-reading to editing of musical articles and art criticism and writing of my own. Gradually, however, my major interest veered to public affairs. In the early months of our participation in the First World War, I was stationed in Washington as special writer on the war organization, where I helped both to explain it and to stimulate changes in desirable directions.

"Entering the army in May 1918, I was assigned to the Coast Artillery Corps, where, after serving in the ranks and as corporal, I was assigned to anti-submarine devices and achieved the rare military grade of 'First Class Listener.' Appointed then to the artillery school at Fort Monroe, I went through a stiff cramming in engineering, and after three months of struggle with logarithms emerged as a Second Lieutenant just as the Armistice was declared. I was immediately demobilized.

"The war stirred many minds. It not only reinforced the conviction of this one that a reformed social and economic order was desirable, but brought the belief that it could not be pulled out of a hat. Careful and practical work to build it on a scientific basis would be necessary. Therefore, I joined with Stuart Chase and others to found the Labor Bureau, Inc.—a body to do technical and professional work for labor and co-operative organizations. There I did a great deal of economic research relevant to labor arbitrations and attained scientific recognition with papers read before the American Economic Association and other learned societies.

"In 1923 I was invited to become an editor of the *New Republic,* a position which I have held ever since. In addition to weekly writing and editorial duties, I have acted as a director and at one time chairman of the National Bureau of Economic Research, as chairman of the National Economics and Social Planning Association, as a member of the Columbia University Commission on Economic Reconstruction. I have taught at the Yale Law School and at Columbia.

"I am married to Dr. Flander Dunbar, a member of the staff of Presbyterian-Columbia Medical Center, of the faculty of the College of Physicians and Surgeons, and managing editor of *Psychosomatic Medicine.*"

* * *

In addition to the positions he mentions, Mr. Soule has also been on the editorial staff of the New York *Evening Post* (1919), and was an expert investigator for the Inter-Church World Movement Commission of the great steel strike of 1919. In 1927 he was special adviser to the Secretary of the Interior on reclamation and rural development in the South. He is the first person to have introduced case methods into industrial economics. Mr. Soule's present marriage is his third.

PRINCIPAL WORKS: The New Unionism in the Clothing Industry (with J. M. Budish) 1920; Wage Arbitration, 1928; The Useful Art of Economics, 1929; A Planned Society, 1932; The Coming American Revolution, 1934; The Future of Liberty, 1936; Sidney Hillman: Labor Statesman, 1939; An Economic Constitution for Democracy, 1939; The Strength of Nations, 1942.

ABOUT: Nielson, F. Control From the Top; Literary Digest June 30, 1934.

SOUTHWOLD, STEPHEN (1887-), English novelist and writer of children's stories, who signs his works both under his own name and  as "Neil Bell," was born in Southwold, Suffolk, and was educated at various small village and town schools. In common with at least 90 per cent of the world's juvenile population, he did not like the idea of school and its attendant restrictions. The final report of the authorities of Saint Mark's College, Chelsea, was that young Southwold was an idle and insubordinate student. He traveled about Europe trying to draw; unsuccessful in this attempt, he turned to free-lance journalism. Southwold served in the First World War, and recalls that he "became one of the group known as the soldier poets," which was "a double lie, for I was neither, being a scared civilian masquerading in the honorable habiliments of war (or if you prefer it, the ignoble gear of Mars) and a literary forger with

the poet's bays askew on my shaggy pate"
—all of which means that he was a clever
parodist. Southwold has also been a teacher
of English; black-and-white artist ("hopeless"); teacher of drawing; and shipwright.
Bredon and Sons (1934), one of his more
important novels, concerns a family of master boat builders and craftsmen of Senwich,
Suffolk, on the North Sea. The scene is
a counterpart of his own birthplace, where
a struggle to escape being eaten away by
the sea has gone on for generations. In
1928, when his funds comprised one five-
pound note, Southwold married an Irish
girl, and they lived in a Cornwall cottage.
His time was spent fishing, poaching, and
writing scores of stories for children, of
whom he has three of his own: Martin,
Stephanie, and Neil. Later the family moved
to Devonshire, where he spends five hours
a day turning out picaresque (*Crocus*),
imaginative and fantastic (*Lord of Life*),
mystery (*Death Rocks the Cradle*), and
chronicle (*Bredon and Sons*) novels. *The
Wonderful Ingredient* (1935) is a play for
children, dramatized by Diana Hill. *The
Seventh Bowe* (1930) was published under
the pseudonym "Miles." He has also written
as "Paul Martens." "Neil Bell's" critics
have praised the speed, grip, and originality
of his story-telling, while occasionally complaining mildly of his prolixity.

PRINCIPAL WORKS: *As Stephen Southwold* —
In Between Stories, 1923; Twilight Tales, 1925;
Old Gold: A Book of Fables and Parables (ed.)
1926; Listen Children! Stories For Spare Moments,
1926; Once Upon a Time Stories, 1927; Ten-
Minute Tales, 1927; The Children's Play Hour
Books, 1927-30; Listen Again, Children! 1928;
Yesterday and Long Ago, 1928; Man's Great Ad-
venture, 1929; Happy Families, 1929; Fiddlededee:
A Medley of Stories, 1930; Hey, Diddle Diddle,
1930; The Hunted One and Other Stories, 1930;
The Jumpers, 1930; Tales Quaint and Queer,
1930; The Last Bus and Other Stories, 1930;
The Welsh Rabbit and Other Stories, 1930; Tick-
Tock Tales, 1930; The Longest Lane and Other
Stories, 1930; True Tales of an Old Shellback,
1930; The Sea Horses and Other Stories, 1930;
Tales of Forest Folk and Other Stories, 1930;
Three by Candlelight and Other Stories, 1930;
The Old Brown Book, 1931; Fairy Tales, 1931;
Once Upon a Time, 1931; Forty More Tales,
1935; More Animal Stories, 1935; Tell Me An-
other, 1938; Now For a Story, 1938; Now For
More Stories! 1938. *As "Neil Bell"* — Life and
Andrew Otway, 1931; Precious Porcelain, 1931;
The Marriage of Simon Harper, 1932; The Dis-
turbing Affair of Noel Blake, 1932; The Lord of
Life, 1933; Bredon and Sons, 1934; Winding Road,
1934; Mixed Pickles: Short Stories, 1935; The
Days Dividing, 1935; The Son of Richard Carden,
1935; Crocus, 1936; Strange Melody, 1936; Pink-
ney's Garden, 1937; The Testament of Stephen
Fane, 1937; One Came Back, 1938; Smallways Rub
Along, 1938; Abbot's Heel, 1939; Love and Julian
Farne, 1939; Not a Sparrow Falls, 1939; So Perish
the Roses, 1940; Desperate Pursuit, 1941; Spice of
Life (short stories) 1941; Tower of Darkness, 1942.
As "Paul Martens"—Death Rocks the Cradle, 1933;
The Truth About My Father, 1934. *As "Miles"*—
The Seventh Bowe, 1930.

ABOUT: Boston Evening Transcript September
14, 1935; Wilson Library Bulletin November 1934.

"SOUZA, ERNEST." See SCOTT, E.

SPAETH, SIGMUND GOTTFRIED
(April 10, 1885-   ), American musicologist,
writes: "Music has always been my hobby,
and I am fortunate
in having been able
to turn this hobby
into a profession
through the unique
development of the
Tune Detective idea.
This simple habit of
tracing tunes to their
source has provided
material for a num-
ber of books and

magazine articles, eight short motion pic-
tures, innumerable broadcasts and lectures,
and now frequently brings me into court as
an expert in musical plagiarism and infringement suits. I have used the tracing
of tunes as a simple way of getting people
to listen to music, removing the inferiority
complex from the average listener, and generally eliminating the curses of snobbery,
highbrowism, and hypocrisy from America's
musical life. Six of my books have gone
into the reprint stage, which is rather unusual for works on music. *The Art of Enjoying Music* is used as a textbook by
many schools and colleges. *Great Symphonies* is used by teachers and also by adult
radio listeners. *Barber Shop Ballads* is the
official songbook of the Society for the
Preservation and Encouragement of Barber
Shop Quartet Singing in America. *Read
'Em and Weep* has become the chief source
of musical Americana."

* * *

Mr. Spaeth was born in Philadelphia, and
educated at Haverford College (B.A. 1905)
and Princeton University (Ph.D. 1910). He
married Katharine Lane in 1917. He has
been a sports writer, a ditch digger, an army
officer, a concert manager, teacher of German at Princeton (1906-08), teacher in
the Asheville (N.C.) School (1910-12),
literary editor for a music publisher, music
editor of *Life* in 1913 and of the New York
Evening Mail from 1914 to 1918, a columnist for the New York *Times* (1919), music
editor in succession from 1931 to 1938 of
McCall's Magazine, Esquire, and the *Liter-*

ary Digest, and since 1937 dean of the Wurlitzer School of Music. He was president of the National Association of Composers and Conductors in 1935 and chairman of the National Committee for American Music in 1939. In his New York office, he employs ten or twelve secretaries and has a huge file of old music. An ex-football player, tall and heavy-set, he is still in good physical trim in spite of the baldness and spectacles of middle age, and often swims and plays baseball with the neighborhood boys in his home in Westport, Conn. Besides his radio broadcasting—he was at one time master of ceremonies of a "quiz" program called "Fun in Print"—he has appeared as actor in the eight motion pictures on "tune detecting" which he wrote.

PRINCIPAL WORKS: Milton's Knowledge of Music, 1914; The Common Sense of Music, 1924; Barber Shop Ballads, 1925; Words and Music, 1926; Read 'Em and Weep—the Songs You Forgot to Remember, 1926; Weep Some More, My Lady, 1927; American Mountain Songs, 1927; Listening, 1927; Gentlemen, Be Seated, 1928; They Still Sing of Love, 1929; The Musical Adventures of Jack and Jill, 1930; Home Song Book, 1931; The Art of Enjoying Music, 1933; The Facts of Life in Popular Song, 1934; Music for Everybody, 1934; Great Symphonies, 1936; Stories Behind the World's Great Music, 1937; Maxims to Music, 1939; Music For Fun, 1939; Great Program Music: How To Enjoy and Remember It, 1940.

ABOUT: American Magazine July 1935; Literary Digest November 25, 1933; Scholastic April 30, 1938; Time November 13, 1939.

SPEARMAN, FRANK HAMILTON

(September 6, 1859-December 29, 1937), American novelist, was born in Buffalo, N.Y., the son of Simon Spearman and Emmaline E. (Dunning) Spearman. He was educated in public and private schools, and at Lawrence College, Appleton, Wis.

Moffatt

Spearman intended to become a doctor, but ill health compelled him to abandon formal study. He was a traveling salesman at twenty, a bank cashier at twenty-seven, and a bank president at twenty-nine. Although some of his best known stories are about railroad life and adventure, Spearman was never employed by a railroad, his acquaintance with common carriers deriving from his contact with them as a banker. He made an intensive study of McCook, western Nebraska, a division point on the Burlington. Spear-

man's book on *The Strategy of Great Railroads* (1904) was used as a textbook at Yale. *Whispering Smith,* concerning a dismissed foreman of bridges who joins a band of outlaws and robs and pillages the railroads until the hero with a posse captures the gang, was a best-selling novel of 1906. It was written after two weeks spent at Cheyenne, Wyo., and the central character was said to be a composite study of Timothy T. Keliher, a special agent of the Union Pacific stationed at Cheyenne, and Joe La Fors, U.S. Deputy-Marshal, a gun-handler never equaled in that country, according to Thomas Clark Spearman, one of Spearman's five sons (he also had a daughter).

Whispering Smith was twice filmed, in 1915 and 1926; *The Nerve of Foley* (1900) became "The Runaway Express" in 1926, and "The Yellow Mail" (1927) was a picture based on Spearman's second novel, *Held For Orders* (1901). Wallace Reid played in both "The Love Special," a film version of *The Daughter of a Magnate* (1903) and in a picturization of *Nan of Music Mountain* (1916). Spearman's later years were spent in Hollywood, where he wrote two serials for the pictures, "The Girl and the Game" (1915) and "Whispering Smith Rides" (1925). He died in a Hollywood hospital of a stomach ailment at nearly seventy-eight, survived by four of the six children born to him and his wife, Mrs. Eugenie A. (Lonergan) Spearman of Chicago, whom he married in 1884. He had a pleasant, clean-shaven face, and was popular with all grades of railroad men.

Among the writers of cowboy novels, or "horse operas," as his Hollywood associates irreverently term them, Spearman stands level with Owen Wister and Eugene Manlove Rhodes[qqv] in his ability to make something like genuine literature of stories of this distinctively American type. "The glaring difference between this western story and others," said the *Bookman* of *Laramie Holds the Range* (1921), "is F. H. Spearman's ability to write."

PRINCIPAL WORKS: The Nerve of Foley, 1900; Held for Orders, 1901; Doctor Bryson, 1902; The Daughter of a Magnate, 1903; The Close of the Day, 1904; The Strategy of Great Railroads, 1904; Whispering Smith, 1906; Robert Kimberly, 1911; The Mountain Divide, 1912; Merrilie Dawes, 1913; Nan of Music Mountain, 1916; Laramie Holds the Range, 1921; The Marriage Verdict, 1923; Selwood of Sleepy Cat, 1924; Your Son's Education, 1925; Flambeau Jim, 1927; Spanish Lover, 1930; Hell's Desert, 1932; Gunlock Ranch, 1935.

ABOUT: Donovan, F. P., Jr. The Railroad in Literature; Titus, W. A. Wisconsin Writers; Book Buyer November 1902; New York Times December 31, 1937.

SPENCER, CLAIRE (April 20, 1899-), Scottish-American novelist, was born in Glasgow, the daughter of William Stephens

Spencer and Jessie Janet Jones (Mac-Glashan) Spencer. She was educated at the Paisley (Scotland) Grammar School and Bournemouth (England) Art School. Claire Spencer came to the United States in 1917, becoming a naturalized American citizen in 1919 and marrying Harrison Smith, publisher, of New York City in January of the latter year. Two children were born, Harrison Venture Smith and Patricia Smith. The Smiths were divorced in 1933, and in December of that year Claire Spencer became the wife of John Ganson Evans of West Brooksville, Maine, a son of the literary diarist, Mabel Dodge Luhan, and himself a novelist. Of this marriage two more children were born, Spencer Evans and Claire Evans.

Gallows' Orchard (1930) was Claire Spencer's first novel and still her best known: the story of a gallant, wayward girl in a little Scotch village, her several lovers, and the suspicious villagers who at last arose in wrath and killed her. "Her book has that appearance of unpremeditation which is the triumph of art," wrote Amy Loveman, and John Chamberlain praised its un-Latin, fresh Saxon prose. She is not a realist, as Edith H. Walton has pointed out; "her method is a lyrical heightening of actual life." Lewis Gannett called *The Island* (1935) "a dour and wind-swept book. Her preoccupation with the imminence and immanence of fate sometimes wearies me; but she has a native kinship with wind and sea and a gift for giving life to dour Scottish characters." The *Spectator* once summed up Claire Spencer's work as "strong meat and cold comfort."

PRINCIPAL WORKS: Gallows' Orchard, 1930; The Quick and the Dead, 1932; The Island, 1935.

SPENCER, HERBERT. See "BRITISH AUTHORS OF THE 19TH CENTURY"

SPENDER, STEPHEN (February 28, 1909-), English poet and critic, was born in London, the son of Edwin Harold Spender, a journalist and lecturer, and Violet Hilda (Schuster) Spender. On his mother's side he is of partly German,

partly Jewish descent. He was educated at University College School and University College, Oxford. His university years were interrupted by considerable travel on the Continent, and he finally "went down" in 1931 without receiving his degree. Most of his holiday excursions were spent in Germany, where he lived for several months of each year, 1929-32; Christopher Isherwood^{qv} frequently was his companion on these summer sojourns. While at Oxford he met W. H. Auden, Louis MacNeice, and C. Day Lewis,^{qqv} with whom his name is most often associated in listing the leaders of the "new" English poetry. As a child his chief interest was in painting, but he abandoned this in youth when he first became absorbed in writing. From the age of

seventeen he supported himself by printing chemists' labels on his own hand-press.

By the time he had left the university, Spender, like Auden and Lewis, had proclaimed himself a Communist; it is doubtful, however, whether he has ever joined the Communist Party, and some of his views would certainly be considered heretical in Moscow. William Troy remarked dryly: "For Mr. Spender, justice, freedom, and equality correspond not to moral or intellectual values but to emotions." He is, in other words, a pronounced individualist; Troy called his adhesion to Communism "a religion without a church." And Malcolm Cowley has struck the same note in saying, "His reasons for choosing Communism are human, not statistical. . . . Let us call him a humanist, . . . not of the letter, but of the spirit."

He has, however, taken an active part in various left-wing movements. In 1937 he was the only British delegate to ignore the refusal of visas and manage to get to the International Writers' Congress in Spain. He stayed in Spain for several months, in the midst of the civil war, and one result was a number of translations of Spanish Loyalist poets. He has also translated much from the German, including the poems of Rainer Maria Rilke and Ernst Toller's last play, *Pastor Hall*. In 1936 he married Agnes Marie Pearn, but the marriage seems not to have been successful. Malcolm Cowley, who met him in Spain, called him "serious, subtle, generous, full of charm." In appearance he is tall, with curly hair and deep-set, brooding eyes; he habitually dresses in shirts open at the neck, in the style of Shelley and Byron, and rather consciously (though not offensively) looks the young poet.

Indeed it was as "another Shelley" that he was greeted by Herbert Read on the publication of his first poems. "It is a rare accent in these days of cloistral verse," said Read, "but it is probably the only accent which will be heard considerably in the future." Among others who joined in the chorus of praise was Gerald Bullett, who remarked that Spender's voice was his own: "It may well prove to be one of the most significant voices of the new age."

As compared with Auden, Spender is less the satirist and more the lyricist and neo-romantic. Cowley thought that he suggested Hart Crane, "more by a quality of outpouring emotion than by any specific mannerism," and praised his "talent for symphonic structure and for sustained movement." His poems are characterized by fluid imagery and a sensitive adjustment of controlled rhythms. He has been least successful in his venture into drama, *Trial of a Judge*, and in his long poem, *Vienna*. As a critic he has developed steadily. Morton Dauwen Zabel said that he "has written critical essays as good as any to come from an English poet in this century," and called him "a writer not only of immediate values but of permanent and convincing truth."

The Second World War found Spender in London where, with Cyril Connolly, he was editing the magazine *Horizon*. "It so happens," he wrote, "that the world has broken just at the moment when my own life has broken." He supported the war against Hitler despite his reservations about "the Chamberlain system" and the memories of his own "contempt for my father's recruiting speeches" during the 1914-18 conflict. He is a fireman in the London Auxiliary Fire Service.

Spender feels that true art does not represent an escape for either the artist himself or his audience. Instead it contains "a real conflict of life, a real breaking up and melting down of intractable material, feelings and sensations which seem incapable of expression until they have been thus transformed. A work of art doesn't say 'I am life, I offer you the opportunity of becoming me.' On the contrary, it says: 'This is what life is like. It is even realer, less to be evaded, than you thought. But I offer you an example of acceptance and understanding. Now, go back and live!'"

Spender is tall, with blue eyes, fair hair, Scandinavian features. In Germany, despite his partly Jewish ancestry, he was often complimented on being a specimen of "the pure Nordic type."

PRINCIPAL WORKS: *Poetry*—Nine Entertainments, 1928; Oxford Poetry 1929 (ed., with L. MacNeice) 1929; Oxford Poetry 1930 (ed., with B. Spencer) 1930; Twenty Poems, 1930; Poems, 1933; Vienna, 1934; Trial of a Judge: A Tragedy in Five Acts, 1938; Poems For Spain (ed., with J. Lehmann) 1939; The Still Centre, 1939; Ruins and Visions, 1942. *Prose*—The Destructive Element: A Study of Modern Writers and Beliefs, 1934; The Burning Cactus (short stories) 1936; Forward From Liberalism, 1937; The Backward Son (novel) 1940; Life and the Poet, 1942.

ABOUT: Lehmann, J. New Writing in Europe; MacNeice, L. Modern Poetry; Commonweal December 28, 1934, August 2, 1935; Living Age January 1941; Nation March 27, 1937; New Republic September 26, 1934; Poetry July, September 1933, January 1935, August 1937, August 1938, October 1940; Saturday Review of Literature November 10, 1934; Sewanee Review July 1937.

SPENGLER, OSWALD (May 29, 1880-May 8, 1936), German philosopher, was born at Blankenburg-am-Harz, and studied mathematics, philosophy, history, and art at the Universities of Munich and Berlin. From the latter he received his Ph.D. degree for a thesis on Heraclitus—his sole publication before he became famous overnight for *The Decline of the*  *West*. He started life, not as a writer, but as a teacher of mathematics, and his turn for statistics helped to make his philosophical speculations unusually impressive. In extreme poverty, living in an unheated room in Munich, subsisting mostly on strong tea, and unable even to buy the reference books he needed, he toiled by candlelight during the early part of the World War to complete the first edition of *The Decline of the West* (*Der Untergang des Abendlandes*). Once it was done, he was unable to find a publisher for it. It was finally brought out in Vienna in 1918. In 1921 he withdrew it and proceeded to revise it on the basis of the war. It was this revised edition, in 1923, that made him internationally celebrated. The book, with its particular appeal in that era of misery and despair, had an enormous success. It was translated into English, French, Italian, Spanish, Russian, and Japanese; and in each country it had wide repercussions and caused an immense amount of critical comment.

Its main thesis is that history moves in cycles, that dominant races in turn go through all the periods of youth, growth, maturity, and senescence of individual human beings, and that our present Occidental civilization, dominated by "the Faustian man, the dynamically active Occidental type," has now reached its period of decadence and is about to go under, conquered by the next hegemonic race, the Mongolian peoples of Asia. Spengler's "rationalist Fundamentalism," as Allen Tate called it, his dislike and distrust of all "non-Aryan" peoples, made him at first exceedingly popular with the Nazi government. When, however, he continued to maintain his independence of thought and refused to participate in the Nazi campaign of anti-Semitism, he fell out of favor. He was permitted to remain in Germany and his property was not confiscated, but during his last years he lived officially under a cloud.

The success of his book had made him independently wealthy, and by a natural revulsion from the cramped quarters of his early years he had a mania for great spaces. He lived in a long suite of great, high ceilinged rooms on the banks of the Isar River, in Munich, and his apartment was like a museum, with its walls covered with collections of weapons and with paintings. His library he considered merely a tool; he collected pictures but not books, and said when he had written all he had to say he would throw his books into the river. He loved to travel, especially in Italy, and was an ardent mountain-climber, both in the Hartz Mountains and in the Alps. He never married. Although he was not a Prussian, but a native of Brunswick, he was "typically Prussian" in appearance—big, long-headed, completely bald, with a long upper lip and severe, aggressive features. He had never been ill a day in his life when he died suddenly of a heart attack, in Munich, three weeks before his fifty-sixth birthday.

The *Commonweal* called *The Decline of the West* "primarily a German nationalist version of apocalyptic moods prevalent throughout central Europe after the events of 1914." A distinguished American critic, Lewis Mumford, has said: *"The Decline of the West* embodies the strenuous greatness, the massive energies, and the underlying crudeness of German life, experience, thought. Spengler explored the matted world of historic events with superb intellectual courage, and he unraveled more than one tangled skein: but at the same time he was so completely lacking in the gift of self-criticism that he exhibited the most naive Junker barbarisms as if they were the pronouncements of high philosophy of a superior order of insight.

"That combination of barbarism and intensive culture, which has been characteristic of Germany since the savage disintegration of the Thirty Years War, united in Spengler's work into an explicit ideology. Spengler had a free mind and a servile emotional attitude; he presented a formidable upright figure . . . but in the presence of authority, particularly military authority, his backbone crumbled. These contradictions threaded deeply through his entire thought."

WORKS AVAILABLE IN ENGLISH: The Decline of the West: Form and Actuality, 1926; Perspectives of World History, 1928; The Hour of Decision: Germany and the World, 1934.

ABOUT: Eloesser, A. Modern German Literature; Goddard, E. H. Civilization or Civilizations; Hale, W. H. Challenge to Defeat; Hoyland, J. S. History as Direction; Schroeter, M. Der Streit um Spengler; American Historical Review October 1936; Christian Century May 20, 1936; Commonweal May 22, 1936; Contemporary Review June 1927; Current History May 1929; Deutsche Rundschau June 1936; Living Age July 1931, September 1932, February 1933; Lutheran Church Quarterly April 1937; Nation May 12, 1926; Neue Rundschau August 1936; New Republic January 11, 1939; Nuova Antologia April 1, 1936; Virginia Quarterly Review April 1939.

SPEWACK, Mrs. BELLA (COHEN) (March 25, 1899-   ) and **SAMUEL** (September 16, 1899-   ), American playwrights, report (through Mr. Spewack): "Bella Spewack, born Bella Cohen in New York. Educated in Washington Irving High School. Was reporter on *Bronx Home News, Yorkville Home News*; feature writer on New York *Call*, Socialist daily, for several years. Became literary editor of New York *Evening Mail*. Was publicity director of Girl Scouts and Campfire Girls. During this period she wrote many short stories, some of which were republished in O'Brien's *Best Short Story* anthologies. In 1923 she was correspondent in Berlin for the New York *Evening World*. Began writing for the theatre in 1927 in collaboration with Samuel Spewack. From 1930 until the present day, several months each year are spent writing pictures for Hollywood.

"Samuel Spewack, born in New York, educated at Columbia University. Worked on the New York *World* from 1918 to 1926, during which time he was a reporter in New York and for four years correspondent in Moscow and Berlin. Wrote short stories and articles, then plays and pictures."

* * *

In both plays and pictures, Mr. and Mrs. Spewack always write in collaboration. Among their films are *My Favorite Wife, The Cat and the Fiddle,* and *Rendezvous.* Besides their published plays, they wrote *War Song,* and in 1938 their *Leave It To Me,* with music by Cole Porter, was produced in New York. They were married in Berlin in 1923, and have no children. They spend about half the year in New Hope, Pa., and half in Hollywood. Their plays are among the freshest and most entertaining of contemporary American stage productions, whether they be pure comedies like *Spring Song,* satire on the movies like *Boy Meets Girl,* or farcical melodrama like *Clear All Wires!* Both held radical economic views in youth, and both have now abandoned them—as is evidenced by Mr. Spewack's pamphlet, *Red Russia Revealed.* Most of their plays have been distinct hits. They work so closely together that it is impossible to say which part of any play is Mr. Spewack's or which Mrs. Spewack's. Mrs. Spewack is noted for her lively wit.

In 1942 Mr. Spewack was appointed production chief of the Bureau of Motion Pictures, Office of War Information. He wrote and directed *The World at War,* the first, full-length film on the war to be produced by the U. S. Government. In the course of his duties he makes frequent air trips to London.

PRINCIPAL WORKS (dates of publication): *Poppa,* 1929 (earlier versions, as Pincus and Hizzoner, 1927); *Clear All Wires!* 1932; *The Solitaire Man,* 1934; *Boy Meets Girl,* and *Spring Song,* 1936; *Trousers to Match,* 1941.

ABOUT: Mantle, B. *Best Plays of 1935, 1936;* Steffens, L. *Autobiography; Saturday Evening Post* May 29, 1926.

*SPEYER, Mrs. LEONORA (VON STOSCH) (November 7, 1872-   ), American poet and Pulitzer Prize winner, writes:

Phyfe

"Having played the violin since my early youth, it seemed but another expression, perhaps a more subtle one, of the same art to find myself writing, studying, deep in the metrics of musical words. I think my friendship with Amy Lowell and being so personally and vigorously brought into immediate contact with the writing of the Imagist poets with whom she was so identified, is as comprehensive an explanation as any, of this change of expression. 'There,' she said, dumping the little olive-colored paper-bound books into my lap, 'Don't blame me if you don't like them. You asked for them.' And she added, 'But you go on playing the violin. There are plenty of us to write poetry.' And I did like them, no one was to blame; and I did not go on playing the violin. By the time I was healed of an acute neuritis I was not thinking of much else but verse. I was writing wildly, prolifically, and wholly happily.

"I published too soon and too much. (Harriet Monroe and Robert Bridges are partly responsible for that—and I am not ungrateful.) Nevertheless, I published too soon and too much. I sometimes am confronted with one of those early bits of juvenilia—infantilia is perhaps the better word—and I look the other way, pretending not to hear, hoping no one does. I studied, I read, I pondered; I sought my fellow-poet and listened to wise and kindly (or unkindly) criticism. I wrote less, I wrote better. 'Two words are not as good as one,' sang the anonymous poet, several centuries ago of 'the written word.' It is as true today. I can hardly remember a time that the violin was not under my chin, since that chin was firm enough to hold it, until the sense of poetry and the wonder of poetry came to push it from its place.

"The last few years I have taught at Columbia University. . . . 'What, can you *teach* poetry?' I am sometimes asked with a fine irony. And the answer, if there be one, as well as I can express it, is: there is no teaching a student to acquire talent; no amount of study may contrive a gift. That is God's affair. But the actual process of poetry-writing, the color and harmony of words, can be, surely must be learned. The instrument must be mastered like any other instrument. Coming from the unplumbed depths of the subconscious, it is perhaps the most controlled of the arts. It is unpremeditated only to the lark."

* * *

Mrs. Speyer was born in Washington, D.C., her father being Count Ferdinand von Stosch. She began her career as a concert violinist with the Boston Symphony Orchestra, in 1890, and also appeared with the New York Philharmonic. In 1893 she was married for the first time, a marriage which resulted in four daughters but was terminated by divorce. Until 1915 she lived abroad, in London and Paris, returning then to New York, her home since that time. In 1902 she married the banker Edgar Speyer. She is president of the Poetry Society of America and an honorary member of Phi Beta Kappa. She has received poetry prizes from the *Nation, Poetry,* and the Poetry Society of America, and in 1927 won the Pulitzer Prize for poetry, for *Fiddler's Farewell.*

She wrote the introduction to the 1938 edition of *Columbia Poetry.* Her poems, which are nearly all lyrics or ballads, of conventional aspect, appear frequently in the magazines. Padraic Colum praised her "direct seizure of subject and swift presentation of image" and her "unusual power of dramatic narrative." Others have found her work formal and thin.

PRINCIPAL WORKS: Canopic Jar, 1921; Fiddler's Farewell, 1926; Naked Heel, 1931; Slow Wall, 1939.

ABOUT: Saturday Review of Literature February 4, 1939; Scholastic October 16, 1939.

SPINGARN, JOEL ELIAS (May 17, 1875-July 26, 1939), American university professor and literary critic, was born in  New York City, the son of Elias Spingarn and Sarah (Barnett) Spingarn, of Jewish stock. The boy ran away from home in his teens, but was recovered without mishap. At twenty he graduated from Columbia College, where he was later to be a storm-center; took his Ph.D. degree four years later, in 1899; and that year became assistant and tutor in comparative literature. (He spent the academic year 1895-96 as a graduate student at Harvard.) In 1904 Spingarn was promoted to adjunct professor, and in 1909 was made full professor. His appointment was abruptly terminated by President Nicholas Murray Butler and the Columbia Board of Trustees March 6, 1911. Spingarn had not relished his subordination to Professor A. H. Thorndike when his Department of Comparative Literature, organized by George Edward Woodberry in 1904, was merged with Thorndike's Department of English in 1910. He had also insisted that a resolution by the faculty on Harry Thurston Peck, who had been dismissed in disgrace, should pay tribute to his standing as a scholar and his services to the university. Spingarn now bought the Amenia (N.Y.) *Times,* the local newspaper of the town where he had his

beautiful estate, Troutbeck, which John Burroughs called the loveliest farm in America and Sinclair Lewis "a grass-grown cathedral." It was famous for its clematis.

Attending the officers' training camp at Camp Madison Barracks, N.Y., he was one of two men to graduate as major, and returned from service in France in the First World War as lieutenant-colonel. One of the founders of Harcourt, Brace & Co. in 1919, he was literary adviser till 1932, editing Gentile, Borgese, and Pareto among others, in the company's twenty-five-volume European library. Spingarn was chairman of directors of the National Association for the Advancement of Colored People from 1913 to 1919; treasurer till 1930; and president till his death at sixty-four, after a six-months' illness. The Spingarn Medal, founded in 1913, was awarded to outstanding Negroes. Spingarn, who had a thoughtful face and heavy moustache, was survived by his wife, Amy, two sons, and two daughters.

Lewis Mumford said that Spingarn renewed the Renaissance ideal of a gentleman: a man equally at home in a garden, a library, an office or a battlefield. His *History of Literary Criticism in the Renaissance* (1899) was translated into Italian with an introduction by Benedetto Croce. In his *Creative Criticism,* published in 1917 and revised in 1931, he insisted that a work of art must be criticized primarily in its totality, not as inculcating virtue or effecting practical reforms. Spingarn's poetry, with the exception of the Phi Beta Kappa poem, "The New Hesperides," delivered at Columbia in 1901, was stripped, bare, and laconic. He "belongs among the dark stars in American literature."

PRINCIPAL WORKS: A History of Literary Criticism in the Renaissance, 1899; The New Criticism, 1911; The New Hesperides and Other Poems, 1911; Creative Criticism, 1917; Poems, 1924; Poetry: A Religion, 1924; Creative Criticism and Other Essays, 1931. Editor—Critical Essays of the Seventeenth Century, 1908-09; Temple's Essays, 1909; Goethe's Literary Essays, 1921; Criticism in America, 1924; European Library, 1925; Troutbeck Leaflets, 1924-26.

ABOUT: Living Age September 1939; Nation August 12, 1939; New York Times July 27, 1939; Publishers' Weekly August 5, 1939; Saturday Review of Literature August 5, 1939; Survey August 1939; Time August 7, 1939.

SPITTELER, CARL (April 24, 1845-December 28, 1924), Swiss poet, novelist, and essayist, Nobel Prize winner, was born near Basel, in quaint Liestal, where his father was a government functionary and subsequently chancellor of the canton.

Carl traveled daily to a Basel school and showed unusual gifts in music and painting but not in literature. Later, while in the higher classes of the Basel *gymnasium,* he fell under the influence of the philologist Wackernagel and the art historian Burckhardt who introduced him to the poetry of Ariosto and inspired him to write his first verses. From 1863 to 1865 Carl attended the law school at Basel and from 1865 to 1868 the theological faculty at the universities of Zürich and Heidelberg. On the evening of his arrival at Heidelberg (1867) the plan of his *Prometheus and Epimetheus*  took form in his mind. Spitteler was then twenty-two and he considered himself destined for a literary career; when invited to be a pastor in Arosa, he declined out of conscientious scruples. Instead he went to Russia, where for eight years he was a private tutor in the family of a Russian general.

In 1879, on the death of his father, Spitteler returned to Switzerland and a year later published his first work, *Prometheus and Epimetheus,* an epic poem in hieratic, Biblical, and rhythmical prose, consisting of narratives, parables, and allegories the inner significance of which appeared only incidentally. The disdain for ordinary ethics as well as the style resembled Nietzsche's *Thus Spake Zarathustra* which it anticipated. This book—the product of thirteen years' labor—was completely ignored by the press.

Disappointed by this unjust silence, Spitteler tried to win a footing in journalism but was soon forced to turn to teaching, first at a girls' school at Berne and then as headmaster at Neuveville. His thirty hours a week of French, Latin, and Greek gave him little time for writing, and so once again he tried journalism, becoming editor of a local Basel newspaper; later he joined the regular staff of the *Basler Nachrichten.* Impressed by his work, Nietzsche wrote to the editor of a Munich periodical recommending the Swiss "critic" as a suitable contributor. Spitteler retired in 1892, having inherited a small fortune the previous year. Thereafter he lived with his wife—he had married one of his pupils in 1883, Marie op den Hoff—and two daughters in Lucerne, where he died at seventy-nine.

He is said to have had strong affections and to have enjoyed intimate and lasting friendships. There was nothing of the prig or the pedant about him; and despite his absorption in the sublimities of epic poetry he avoided taking himself too seriously. His life was relatively sheltered, and shiftings in the religious, academic, and political winds were almost imperceptible to him. Only once at the beginning of the World War did he allow himself to become something of a public figure: he delivered a strongly impressive address expressing the hope that neutral civilizations would not alter their balance of favor on the basis of racial sympathies.

In his long career Spitteler tried almost every *genre* and every type of literary expression: critical and philosophical essays (*Laughing Truths,* 1898); lyrics and ballads (*Schmetterlinge,* 1889, *Balladen,* 1896, *Glockenlieder,* 1906); fiction (*Friedli der Kolderi,* 1891, *Gustav,* 1892, *Conrad der Leutnant,* 1898, *Imago,* 1906); epic poems (*Prometheus and Epimetheus,* 1880, *Olympian Spring,* 1900). In 1905 the musical conductor Felix Weingartner devoted a laudatory brochure to Spitteler's work and the poet's fame at last kindled. However, the celebrations of his seventieth anniversary which was to be an impressive apotheosis passed almost unnoticed because of the war—and so it was not till 1919 that Spitteler was finally recognized as a world figure when the Nobel Prize committee "having especially in mind his mighty epic *Olympian Spring,*" gave him the literary award.

Spitteler's claim to immortality rests on his epics *Prometheus and Epimetheus* and especially *Olympian Spring,* for which Romain Rolland called him "the greatest German poet since Goethe, the only master of the epic since Milton died three centuries ago."

WORKS AVAILABLE IN ENGLISH TRANSLATION: *Autobiography*—The Little Misogynists, 1923. *Essays*—Laughing Truths, 1927. *Poetry*—Selected Poems, 1927; Prometheus and Epimetheus, 1931.

ABOUT: Baudouin, C. Carl Spitteler; Boyd, E. Studies From Ten Literatures; Eloesser, A. Modern German Literature; Faesi, R. Spittelers Weg und Werk; Marble, A. R. Nobel Prize Winners in Literature; Robertson, J. G. Essays and Addresses; Spitteler, C. Prometheus and Epimetheus, Laughing Truths (see Introductions); Contemporary Review January 1921; Living Age June 6, 1925; London Mercury May 1927; Saturday Review of Literature July 31, 1926.

SPOFFORD, Mrs. HARRIET (PRESCOTT). See "AMERICAN AUTHORS: 1600-1900"

SPRIGG, CHRISTOPHER ST. JOHN

("Christopher Caudwell") (1907-March 5, 1937), English novelist, poet, and writer on aviation, obtained his early training in writing on the *Yorkshire Observer*. He was also the founder of the technical periodical *Aircraft Engineering,* and wrote several books on aviation, beginning with *The Airship* in 1931. Eight excellent detective novels also kept the pot boiling. (Will Cuppy speaks of their "admirable style, of a light and airy order." His detective, Charles Venable, is likable and up-to-date.) Sprigg's views of poetry coincided in numerous aspects with those of his fellow detective-novelist C. Day Lewis ("Nicholas Blake") and of the poets Spender, Auden, and Isherwood. Remarking in *Illusion and Reality: A Study of the Sources of Poetry* on the "ancient history and somewhat obsolescent appearance today" of poetry, he states that "the bourgeois artist has three possible rôles in relation to the proletariat—opposition, alliance, or assimilation. Most bourgeois artists are at present treading the road of alliance—Gide in France; Day Lewis, Auden, and Spender in this country."

Sprigg joined the British Battalion of the International Brigade in December 1936, and was killed in action in Spain the following March, at thirty.

He was a sincere man and an able critic, states Forster, reviewing Sprigg's posthumous *Studies in a Dying Culture,* but "is what has been called in Bolshevik diplomatic circles 'an error in exportation.' He ought not to be read outside the fold. He will only cause unbelievers to clutch at their pocketbooks and thank their God that Mr. Chamberlain and Herr Hitler excluded the reds from Munich." (This was written near the end of 1938). Others, it should be said, have found Sprigg's leftist tone and thesis far less terrifying than Mr. Forster's animadversions would imply. *Illusion and Reality* is lucid, cogent, and not without humor. "Language is a social product, the instrument whereby men communicate and persuade each other; thus the study of poetry cannot be separated from the study of society," wrote Sprigg in his introduction. "Historical materialism is therefore the basis of this study."

PRINCIPAL WORKS: The Airship, 1931; British Airways, 1934; Great Flights, 1935; Illusion and Reality, 1937; Let's Learn to Fly!, 1937; Studies in a Dying Culture, 1938; (with Henry Duncan Davis) Fly With Me, 1932; Poems, 1939. *Detective Novels*—Crime in Kensington (American title: Pass the Body) 1933; Fatality in Fleet Street, 1933; The Perfect Alibi, 1934; Death of an Airman, 1934; The Corpse With the Sunburned Face, 1935; Death of a Queen, 1935; The Six Queer Things, 1937; (editor) Uncanny Stories, 1936.

ABOUT: London Times March 11, 1937; New Statesman December 10, 1938; New York Times March 11, 1937.

SPRIGGE, ELIZABETH

(1900-   ), English novelist, writes: "I was born in London, the daughter of Sir Squire Sprigge, editor of the *Lancet,* and Mab (Moss) Sprigge, daughter of Sir Charles Moss, late chief justice of Ontario, Canada. I was educated at St. Paul's Girls' School, London, at Havergal College, Toronto, and at London University. I was married in 1921

to Mark Napier, and have two daughters. I spent several years of my early married life in Scandinavia, in Stockholm chiefly, and then in Copenhagen. I began writing during that time and also learning the Scandinavian languages. During the years following I translated many books from the Scandinavian languages, in collaboration with my father-in-law, Claude Napier. I have always traveled about a lot—France, Italy, Spain—with visits to Canada and New York. I have lectured a good deal, and done social work. I seem fated always to move around.

"Of recent years my interests have centered in Empress Elizabeth of Austria. Thank goodness that in my researches into her life I traveled about Germany, Austria, and Hungary before it was too late. The play I wrote about her in collaboration with my sister-in-law, Katriona Sprigge, was presented at the Garrick Theatre, London, in 1938. My novel of her and her times [*The Raven's Wing*] has recently been published.

"Since the war I have been living in a Berkshire village and producing plays with the villagers, going from place to place to perform in barns and village halls. I am now organizing a nursery school, play centre, library, etc., for evacuées."

PRINCIPAL WORKS: A Shadowy Third, 1927; Home Is the Hunter (with H. T. Munn) 1930; Faint Amorist, 1931; The Old Man Dies, 1933; Castle in Andalusia, 1935; Children Alone (juvenile) 1935; Pony Tracks (juvenile) 1936; The Son of the House, 1937; The Raven's Wing, 1940; Two Lost on Dartmoor (juvenile) 1940.

SPRING, HOWARD (February 10, 1889-), English novelist, writes: "I was born at Cardiff in South Wales. My mother  was an Englishwoman and my father an Irishman. The family was very poor. My father was a casual laborer in gardens. He was often out of work. Nine children were born of the marriage, and I grew up as the middle child. My father died when I was eleven years old. Almost at once, I left school for good, to help my elder brother and sisters and my mother with the task of bringing up the younger members of the family. The elder girls became domestic servants. My brother and I became messenger boys in a newspaper office. Mrs. Essex, in *My Son, My Son!* and Mrs. Ryerson in *Fame Is the Spur* may both be taken as containing substantial characteristics of my mother.

"The younger children continued their school courses to the end; I and the others had to educate ourselves. The two elder girls turned themselves into district nurses; my elder brother, worn out by excess of study, died in his early twenties; my younger brother was killed in action at Arras in 1917. I am the sole surviving male member of the family.

"I became a reporter on the *South Wales Daily News,* in Cardiff; left to take up a similar appointment on the Yorkshire *Observer,* in Bradford, in 1911; and when the war came I was reporting for the Manchester *Guardian.* I served with the British army in France throughout the war, being attached for most of the time to the Intelligence Service.

"I returned to the *Guardian* after the war. In 1920 I married Marion Ursula Pye. We have two sons.

"I remained with the *Guardian* till 1931, when Lord Beaverbrook invited me to join the staff of his paper, the *Evening Standard,* in London. I became literary critic of the paper soon afterwards, and examples of the work done in this connection are collected in the volume *Book Parade.*

"I was rather late beginning as a novelist. *Darkie & Co.,* a book written to amuse my two small sons, was all I had published when *Shabby Tiger,* my first novel, came in 1934. This was successful enough in England, and so was its successor and sequel, *Rachel Rosing,* but neither of these hinted at the world-success that was to come with my next book, called in England *O Absalom!* and in America *My Son, My Son!* Within a short time of publication, it had been translated into French, German, Italian, Danish, Norwegian, Swedish, Finnish, Polish, Spanish, Dutch, and Portuguese; and in at least two of these languages—German and Italian —as well as in the British and American editions, it was a 'best-seller' in the outstanding sense of the word. This success permitted me to retire from newspaper work, and to buy a home where I had long desired to be: on the sea's edge in Cornwall.

"The outbreak of the Second World War in 1939 found me half-way through the writing of *Fame Is the Spur,* a book on a more ambitious scale than any I had yet attempted. It was finished at the end of January 1940, and published the following summer."

* * *

Mr. Spring is a lean, spectacled, serious-looking man whose recreations now that he lives in the country are gardening, sailing, and skating. He was the Manchester *Guardian's* special correspondent in Ireland up to the outbreak of the 1914 war. His self-education he says he owes largely to Cobbett's *Grammar;* later he was able to take night classes and matriculate at London University. *My Son, My Son!* has made a popular motion picture as well as a book; the influence of Dickens is strong in it, as it is implicit in all Mr. Spring's novels.

PRINCIPAL WORKS: *Fiction*—Darkie & Co. (juvenile) 1932; Shabby Tiger, 1934; Rachel Rosing, 1935; Sampson's Circus (juvenile) 1936; O Absalom! (in America: My Son, My Son!) 1938; Tumbledown Dick (juvenile) 1939; Fame Is the Spur, 1940. *Miscellaneous*—Book Parade, 1938; Heaven Lies About Us (autobiography) 1939; (with Herbert Morrison and E. M. Delafield) This War We Wage, 1941; In the Meantime (autobiography) 1942.

ABOUT: Spring, H. Heaven Lies About Us, In the Meantime; Wilson Library Bulletin June 1939.

SQUIRE, Sir JOHN COLLINGS (April 2, 1884-), English poet, critic, and editor, was born in Plymouth, the son of John Squire and E. B. (Collings) Squire. He was educated at Blundell's School and at St. John's College, Cambridge (historical scholar 1903, B.A. 1906, honorary M.A. 1919). After a short period in the press gallery of the House of Commons, and some free-lance journalistic work (mostly book-reviewing for the *Observer*), he became, in 1913, literary editor of the *New Statesman.* In 1917 he was made its acting editor. In 1919 he founded the *London Mercury,* and was its editor until 1934. His contributions to the *London Mercury* were under the pseudonym of "Solomon Eagle."

Twice he contested seats for Parliament, in 1918 and 1924, but was unsuccessful both times and took no active part in politics thereafter. In 1908 he married Eileen H. Wilkinson (not to be confused with the Laborite M.P., Ellen Wilkinson), and they have three sons and a daughter. He was knighted in 1933.

Sir John's interests aside from writing and publishing are numerous. One of the chief of them is in architecture; he is an Honorary Associate of the Royal Institute of British Architects, and was chairman of the Architecture Club from 1922 to 1928. He was a governor of the famous theatre, "Old Vic," from 1922 to 1926, chairman of the English Association from 1926 to 1929, and president of the Devonshire Association in 1934. He was a member of the Academic Committee in 1921, and its honorary secretary the following year. At present he is honorary secretary of the Stonehenge Preservation Society. At the beginning of the Second World War he became active in the Intelligence Department.

Much of his time and energy has gone to editing anthologies, principally of poetry. He was the editor-in-chief of the *English Men of Letters* series, and also edited, with Lord Lee of Fareham, the *English Heritage* series. He has written a number of plays, mostly in collaboration, most successful of which was *Berkeley Square.* He is almost the dean of living English critics, though he is least happy in this field, and has often been accused of stodginess and undue conservatism. As a serious poet, he is seldom more than competent and fluent. But he is a really great parodist—one of the most brilliant of all practitioners of a characteristically English art. To his skill in parody Theodore Maynard attributed his relative failure as a lyric poet, saying that "he knows far too much to be spontaneous."

Sir John has done much to spread knowledge of American literature in England, though he has been severe as well as welcoming. He has visited this country twice, in 1921 and 1930, and his dislike of many things he saw here did not prevent his generous receptivity to the work of American authors. His favorite recreation is duck-shooting. He is tall, with once dark wavy hair, now gray, and a long, rather saturnine face. His position in literature is solid rather than brilliant, except for his parodies; John Gould Fletcher remarked on his paucity of ideas and said he was content with writing poems "in which neither the idea nor the utterance is of the slightest importance." Of his cleverness, as distinct from poetic talent, there is no question; the late John Drinkwater well called him "one of the most alert minds of his generation." And, very occasionally, he gives utterance to an authentic and moving poem.

PRINCIPAL WORKS: *Poetry*—Poems and Baudelaire Flowers, 1909; The Three Hills and Other Poems, 1913; Twelve Poems, 1916; The Survival of the Fittest and Other Poems, 1916; The Lily of Malaud and Other Poems, 1917; Poems, 1918; The Birds and Other Poems, 1919; The Moon, 1920; Poems: Second Series, 1921; American Poems and Others, 1923; A New Song of the Bishop of London and the City Churches, 1924; A Face in Candlelight, 1933; Poems of Two Wars, 1940. *Parodies*—Imaginary Speeches and Other Parodies in Prose and Verse, 1912; Steps to Parnassus and Other Parodies and Diversions, 1913; Tricks of the Trade, 1917; Collected Parodies, 1921. *Plays*—The Clown of Stratford, 1922; Robin Hood (with J. R. Young) 1928; Pride and Prejudice (with E. Squire) 1929; Berkeley Square (with J. L. Balderston) 1929. *Editor*—A Book of Women's Verse, 1921; Selections From Modern Poets, 1921 and 1924 (as one volume, 1930); The Comic Muse, 1925; The Cambridge Book of Lesser Poets, 1927; The Collected Poems of James Elroy Flecker, 1928; Apes and Parrots, 1930; If It Had Happened Otherwise (in America: If: Or History Rewritten) 1931; Younger Poets of Today, 1932; John Freeman's Letters (with G. Freeman) 1936; Cheddar Gorge: A Book of English Cheeses, 1937. *Miscellaneous*—Socialism and Art, 1907; William of Orange, 1912; The Gold Tree and Other Studies, 1917; Books in General, 1918, 1920, 1921; Life and Letters, 1920; Books Reviewed, 1922 and 1923; Essays at Large, 1923; The Grub Street Nights Entertainments (short stories) 1924; Outside Eden (short stories) 1933; Flowers of Speech, 1935; Reflections and Memories, 1935; Weepings and Wailings, 1935; Shakespeare as Dramatist, 1935; The Way to a Horse, 1936; The Honeysuckle and the Bee (autobiography) 1937; Water-Music: or, A Fortnight of Bliss, 1939.

ABOUT: Arrow, J. J. C. Squire vs. D. H. Lawrence; Lynd, R. Old and New Masters; Mais, S. P. B. Books and Their Writers; Maynard, T. Our Best Poets; Monro, H. Some Contemporary Poets; Newbolt, Sir H. New Paths on Helicon; Priestley, J. B. Figures in Modern Literature; Squire, J. C. The Honeysuckle and the Bee; Waugh, A. Tradition and Change; Williams, I. A. J. C. Squire: A Bibliography of His Works; Williams, O. Contemporary Criticism of Literature; Williams-Ellis, A. An Anatomy of Poetry; Athenaeum August 6, 1920; Bookman (London) September 1917, September 1920, August 1923, November 1924; Commonweal March 18, 1925; English Journal March 1926; Freeman December 1,

1920; Nation March 23, 1921; New Statesman May 13 and December 23, 1922; Saturday Review (London) October 10, 1925, May 28, 1927; Spectator January 18, 1919, March 18, 1922; Yale Review April 1923.

STALLINGS, LAURENCE (November 25, 1894-), American novelist and dramatist, was born in Macon, Ga., the son of

Tucker Stallings and Aurora (Brooks) Stallings. He was educated at Wake Forest College (B.A. 1915) and Georgetown University (M.Sc. 1922). Most of the interval between represents his war service, though before becoming a captain in the Marines he worked for a while on the Atlanta *Journal*. He served in France, was wounded at Belleau Wood, and in consequence lost his right leg. He spent many months in hospital, and was finally discharged with a small pension, a cripple with a wife to support, but possessed of experience which his gift for writing and his bitterness of spirit made into one of the earliest of the post-war novels and into a play whose repercussions are still heard.

In 1919 he had married Helen Poteat, and they had two daughters. He went to Washington, and while studying at Georgetown worked as a reporter on the Washington *Times*. He then went to New York, to the *World*, where he started as copy reader but in a few months became dramatic critic. From this he was graduated to literary editor, founding and writing the still familiar thrice-weekly column, "The First Reader" (now conducted by Harry Hansen). Also, on the *World* he met Maxwell Anderson, and from Captain Stallings' war experiences they made together a play they called *What Price Glory?* It was a sensation, and Captain Flagg and Sergeant Quirt became household names. Later Stallings and Anderson collaborated on three other plays, none of which was anything like so successful—in fact, the last of them, *Deep River*, was never even produced.

Meanwhile Stallings had published his autobiographical novel, *Plumes*. (The title does not refer to military plumage, but to the hero's family name.) This angry, horrifying book came a little too early for the vogue of volumes debunking war, but on the reputation of *What Price Glory?* it sold well and in any event served as a spiritual cathar-

sis for its author. The novel is not his literary form, and he has never written another.

Instead he turned to the motion pictures, with *The Big Parade*, another sensation. It was followed by *Old Ironsides*, and from 1934 to 1936 Stallings was editor-in-chief of the Fox Movietone System. In 1936 he and his wife were divorced, and in 1937 he married Louise St. Leger Vance. They have one son. Meanwhile Stallings had turned to still another medium, as editor and compiler of a photographic history of the war. In 1935 and 1936 he led an expedition into Ethiopia (at the time of the Italian conquest), sponsored by Fox, the North American Newspaper Alliance, and the New York *Times*. He has published no other books, and at at last report was living in Encino, Calif., and still doing some film writing. He dramatized Ernest Hemingway's *A Farewell to Arms* in 1930, but the play was a failure.

Captain Stallings, his thick hair now gray, is still fundamentally the genial, friendly person he was before his experiences as a soldier disillusioned and embittered him. He dresses carelessly, enjoys congenial and convivial gatherings, and shoots craps "for exercise." He is something more than an amateur biologist, and is well read in zoology. What his literary plans are for the future he does not divulge.

PRINCIPAL WORKS: Plumes, 1924; Three American Plays (What Price Glory?, First Flight, The Buccaneer; with M. Anderson) 1926; The First World War: A Photographic History (edited) 1933 (as The World War in Photographs, 1934).

ABOUT: Littell, R. Read America First; Bookman May 1926; Current Opinion November 1924; Nation October 7, 1925; New Republic October 8, 1930; Newsweek August 17, 1935; Outlook January 6, 1926.

"STANDISH, BURT L." See PATTEN, G.

"STANTON, SCHUYLER." See BAUM, L. F.

*STAPLEDON, WILLIAM OLAF (May, 10, 1886-), English philosopher and novelist who signs his works Olaf Stapledon, writes: "I was born in the Wirral, across the water from Liverpool. The Wirral has nearly always been my headquarters. I now live at the opposite corner of the peninsula, across the water from Wales. Most of my childhood, however, was spent on the Suez Canal, which in a way still seems my home. Subsequently I was educated at Abbotsholme School and Balliol College, Oxford. Then, for a year, with

* Died September 6, 1950.

much nerve strain and little success, I taught at the Manchester Grammar School. Next I entered a shipping office in Liverpool, to deal ineffectively with manifestoes and bills of lading. A short period in a shipping agency at Port Said concluded my business career. I then lectured to tutorial classes for the Workers' Educational Association, under the University of Liverpool, imparting my vague knowledge of history and English literature to a few of the workers of Northwestern

England. For the three last years of the first great war I was with the Friends' Ambulance Unit, in a motor convoy attached to a division of the French Army. After the war I married Agnes Miller, an Australian. Thus was sealed an intermittent romance of twelve years' standing. We have a daughter and a son.

"Having returned to Workers' Educational Association work, I also began to study philosophy and psychology at Liverpool, and took a Ph.D. Henceforth these were my lecturing subjects, both outside the university and for a short time within. I wrote a technical philosophical book, and purposed an academic career. But I also wrote my *Last and First Men,* which was a success. I therefore, relying on unearned increment, rashly gave up my university post, determining to pull my weight by writing. Well, well! I have written mostly fantastic fiction of a semi-philosophical kind, and occasionally I have ventured into sociological fields.

"I find it difficult to summarize the main interests and influences in my life. Philosophy, in spite of a late attack, has always taken a high place. Formerly English literature dominated. Science, though I lacked scientific training, was first a sort of gospel and later something the fundamental principles of which must be carefully criticized. It took me long to realize both its true value and its mischief. In politics I accept the label Socialist, though all labels are misleading. My chief recreations have been foreign travel, and rough walking with a very small spot of rock climbing. I am addicted to swimming, and I like the arduous and brainless side of gardening."

* * *

Mr. Stapledon writes occasionally on ethics and philosophy for the technical and

scholarly reviews. He is primarily not a novelist but a philosopher, and his style is sometimes cumbersome and crude, but the originality and brilliance of his thought outweighs these disadvantages. Elmer Davis, though he acknowledged that "fiction is a tool he uses awkwardly," said of Mr. Stapledon's first and most successful novel that it is "perhaps the boldest and most intelligently imaginative book of our times." Stapledon himself considers *Star Maker* "by far the best" of his novels. He is striking in appearance, with thick dark hair, deep-set eyes, and a lined, brooding face.

PRINCIPAL WORKS: *Novels*—Last and First Men, 1931; The Last Men in London, 1932; Waking World, 1934; Odd John, 1935; Star Maker, 1937. *Non-Fiction*—A Modern Theory of Ethics, 1929; Philosophy and Living, 1938; Saints and Revolutionaries, 1939; New Hope for Britain, 1939.

ABOUT: Saturday Review of Literature July 18, 1936.

STARK, FREYA MADELINE (1893-   ),

English writer of travel books, is the daughter of the late Robert Stark, sculptor, of Ford Park, Chagford. She was educated privately in Italy, and attended Bedford College and the School of Oriental Studies in London. "An imaginative aunt who, for my ninth birthday, sent a copy of the *Arabian Nights,* was, I suppose, the original cause of trouble," writes

Miss Stark in the preface to her most popular book, *The Valleys of the Assassins* (1934), which she dedicated to W. P. Ker, the Scottish scholar. "Unfostered and unnoticed, the little flame so kindled fed secretly on dreams. Chance, such as the existence of a Syrian missionary in my home, nourished it; and Fate, with long months of illness and leisure, blew it to a blaze bright enough to light my way through labyrinths of Arabic, and eventually to land me on the coast of Syria at the end of 1927." Freya Stark's first book, *Baghdad Sketches,* contributed originally to Eastern newspapers, was published by the Times Press of Baghdad in 1933 and appeared in an enlarged edition in 1937. "I used to improve my Arabic by going to the Iraq Government School for Girls," she wrote there. She sometimes stayed for a lesson in history, amused to see how the doings of early

Caliphs could be used to teach modern nationalism.

A camera is always an important part of Miss Stark's equipment. *Seen in the Hadhramant* (1938), a book of superb photographs of this section of Arabia, is dedicated "To Viscount Wakefield of Hythe, Whose Kindness and Generosity Made This Collection Possible." The inland cities of Arabia, she explains in a preface to the book, were practically unknown to European travelers until Adolf von Wrede penetrated the interior in 1843, followed by the Theodore Bents and their party in 1893. Several more, including herself, came there after the First World War. The Royal Air Force has landing grounds in the Hadhramant, and a British Resident Adviser is established there. The R.A.F. once saved Miss Stark's life when she was desperately ill in Aden with a dilated heart. One of her treasured souvenirs of the trip recorded in *The Southern Gates of Arabia* (1936) is a certificate from two Arabian Sayyids, 'Ali al 'Attas al Bedawi, reading: "This is a certificate to Miss Freya Stark, English, a traveler in Hadhramant, that she is conversant with laws and guided by religion, and of an honorable house, and is the first woman to travel from England to Hadhramant alone—and is mistress of endurance and fortitude in travel and in the suffering of terrors and dangers. We thank her greatly, very greatly."

Miss Stark has also written poems and short stories. In recognition of her ability as traveler and writer (the British call her "the Little Gertrude Bell"), she has received the Triennial Burton Memorial Medal from the Royal Asiatic Society in 1934 and the Mungo Park Medal from the Royal Scottish Geographical Society. Other recreations are mountaineering and embroidery. Before the Second World War she gave her address as Asolo, Italy.

PRINCIPAL WORKS: Baghdad Sketches, 1933; The Valleys of the Assassins, 1934; The Southern Gates of Arabia, 1936; Seen in the Hadhramant, 1938; A Winter in Arabia, 1940.

ABOUT: Stark, F. M. The Valleys of the Assassins (see Preface); Saturday Review of Literature November 30, 1940.

STARKEY, JAMES SULLIVAN ("Seumas O'Sullivan") (1879-), Irish poet,

writes: "James Starkey was born in Dublin. His father, William Starkey, M.D., was the author of *Poems and Translations* (1875) and a contributor to the *Dublin University Magazine*. His own first published poems appeared in the *United Irishman* and the *Irish Homestead*, 1902.

He was one of the original members of W. G. Fay's Irish National Dramatic Company (later the Irish National Theatre Society), and acted with these companies on many occasions between 1902 and 1905, when he resigned membership and founded, with Seumas O'Kelly, F. Morrow, and others, the Theatre of Ireland. On two occasions he visited London with the Irish National Theatre Society, when they gave successful performances at the Queen's Hall, Kensington, and at the Royalty Theatre. On the foundation of the Irish Academy of Letters he was one of the first to be elected, and was, for some years, a member of the Council. In 1939, Trinity College, Dublin, conferred on him the Doctorate of Literature. He has been a frequent contributor to the leading Irish journals. He has edited the Tower Press Booklets, twelve volumes (1906-08), and in 1938, with Austin Clarke as co-editor, published a third series of the booklets in  six volumes. In 1923 he founded the *Dublin Magazine*, which is now in its sixteenth volume, and which he edits."

* * *

L. A. G. Strong remarked in "Seumas O'Sullivan" "the cunning and the mastery with which those long wavering rhythms are handled and the certainty with which a personal music, elusive yet definite and quite unforgettable, is caught and sounded." A poet of the "Celtic Twilight" school, melancholy and graceful, "the half-light of vision is his most characteristic achievement."

PRINCIPAL WORKS: The Twilight People, 1905; Verses Sacred and Profane, 1908; The Earth-Lover and Other Verses, 1909; Selected Lyrics, 1910; Impressions (essays) 1912; Poems, 1912; An Epilogue, 1914; Mud and Purple (essays) 1917; Requiem and Other Poems, 1917; The Rosses and Other Poems, 1918; Poems, 1923; Common Adventures (poems and essays) 1926; The Lamplighter and Other Poems, 1929; Twenty-Five Lyrics, 1933; At Christmas, 1934; Personal Talk: A Book of Verse, 1936; Poems: 1930-38, 1938; Collected Poems, 1940.

ABOUT: Boyd, E. A. Ireland's Literary Renaissance; Colum, P. Round About Ireland; Russell, G. W. Imaginations and Reveries; Commonweal June 7, 1935; Dublin Magazine July-September 1930; Literary Review November 10, 1930; Neuphilologische Monatsschrift April 1937.

STARKIE, WALTER FITZWILLIAM (August 9, 1894-), Irish essayist, writes:

"I was born in Dublin, of parents who came

from Cork and Kerry but who are proud to be Anglo-Irish in blood. I was educated in Dublin and at Shrewsbury School in

England and I finished my education at Trinity College, Dublin, and abroad. My education was not only humanistic but also musical, for I studied violin-playing at the Royal Irish Academy of Music. During the war of 1914-18, I served abroad with the British Expeditionary Force in Italy, and after demobilization I trekked on foot through the whole of South Italy and Sicily, living with gypsies. In 1924 I was appointed Life Fellow of Trinity College, and in 1926 Professor of Spanish Studies and Lecturer on Italian Literature at the same college. In 1927 I was appointed by W. B. Yeats and Lady Gregory a director of the Irish National (Abbey) Theatre.

"It has been my custom ever since 1919 to consort annually during my long vacation (university terms do not take up more than twenty-four weeks in the year) with gypsies abroad, with the object of collecting language, folk-lore, and folk-music, and generally living the life of the open road. In 1923-24 I trekked through Spain and during the next ten years I had wandered on foot through all Spain, North to South, including Morocco. In 1925-26 I trekked through Dalmatia and part of Albania, and also went as visiting professor to the University of Upsala in Sweden. In 1929 I went on foot all through Hungary, Transylvania, and Rumania, as far as the Black Sea, collecting tunes, stories, and living with nomads, and earning my living, as I have always done on my trips, by playing in street, cafe, or camp.

"I have been on four lecture tours to the United States, and in 1930 I was visiting professor in Romance languages at the University of Chicago. I trekked through New Mexico and Arizona as far as California, and was present at the Indian festivals in Santa Fé.

"In 1931 I was present in Madrid after the declaration of the Republic, and was a member from 1925 to 1936 of many of the principal literary *tertulias* [circles] of Madrid, including those of Ramón del Valle Inclán, Benavente (whose biography I wrote), the brothers Machado, Azorín, Blasco Ibáñez, etc. From 1936 to 1939 I visited Spanish friends on three occasions.

In 1940 I accepted from the British Council the post of first director and founder of the British Institute in Madrid."

* * *

Mr. Starkie is married to Italia Augusta Porchietti, of Genoa and Buenos Aires, and they have a son and a daughter. Since he was pro-Franco throughout the revolution, he was *persona grata* after its end and was living in Madrid in 1941. Stout and clean-shaven, looking quite unlike the vagabond he plays at being during half the year, he was known while he was still at Trinity as "the most indefatigable diner-out in Dublin, with a finger in every pie." He is a Chevalier of the Legion of Honour and a Knight of the Order of Alfonso VII and of the Order of the Crown of Italy. In addition to his own books he has translated Pérez de Ayala's *Tiger Juan* (1938) and made an abridged translation of *Don Quixote* (1939). "Few men have so succeeded," said one critic, "in combining the respectable with the vagabond life." In spite of his "meandering digressions," his essays are attractive and engaging in style, and his critical studies of Pirandello and Benavente are of real value.

PRINCIPAL WORKS: Jacinto Bevante and the Spanish Drama, 1924; Writers of Modern Spain, 1929; Raggle Taggle: Adventures With a Fiddle in Hungary and Rumania, 1933; Spanish Raggle Taggle, 1934; Don Gypsy, 1936; Luigi Pirandello and the Italian Drama, 1937; The Waveless Plain: An Italian Autobiography, 1938; Grand Inquisitor: Biography of Cardinal Ximenez de Cisneros, 1939.

ABOUT: Starkie, W. Raggle Taggle, Spanish Raggle Taggle, Don Gypsy, The Waveless Plain; Saturday Review of Literature March 23, 1935.

STARRETT, VINCENT (October 26, 1886-), American "bookman" and miscellaneous writer, sends the editors of this volume the following biographical sketch written by his friend Ben Abramson, proprietor of the Argus Book Shop, Chicago:

D. Loving

"By heritage, inclination, appearance, baptism, and temperament Vincent Starrett was destined to be a bookman. By that is meant not one who deals in books or necessarily one who writes them, but rather a man who lives by them. As Samuel Johnson was a bookman so Vincent Starrett is one.

"Charles Vincent Emerson Starrett, to muster all his names at once, was born in Toronto of Scotch-Irish parentage. His maternal grandfather was John Young, a famous Canadian publisher and bookseller. He was brought to Chicago while still a child, and received his schooling from the public schools, his education from the newspaper offices of that city. His newspaper career began with the Chicago *Inter-Ocean* in 1906. Then for ten years he was on the staff of the Chicago *Daily News,* covering assignments in all parts of the continent. During 1914-15 he served as war correspondent in Mexico, and was wounded in the leg at the unrecorded battle of Xochimilco.

"Mr. Starrett's earliest ambition was to be an illustrator, but he took to writing stanzas and stories instead. His course was determined suddenly when he received a check for $75 from *Collier's Weekly,* for a mystery story. In that exciting moment, for better or for worse, he put his Rubicon of journalism behind him and became a 'writing man.' His first published book was a monograph on Arthur Machen, the Welsh novelist, whom he introduced to America. He founded and edited the *Wave,* a literary miscellany issued monthly, which died, however, in its second year. Several of his mystery stories have appeared as motion pictures. He is also the author of the standard bibliographies of Stephen Crane and Ambrose Bierce, has written innumerable critical monographs, and has edited the uncollected works of Stevenson, Crane, Gissing, Machen, and other writers beloved of collectors.

"Two of his greatest enthusiasms are Conan Doyle's immortal detective, and the fellowship of books. He is one of the founders (with Christopher Morley) of the Baker Street Irregulars, and a member of the Sherlock Holmes Society of England. He is a former president of the Society of Midland Authors, and was at one time an instructor in short story writing (which he believes 'cannot be taught') at Northwestern University. He has traveled extensively and has lived at one time or another in most of the important capitals of the world, including Peiping (Peking). He is married and lives in Chicago, his home for forty years.

" 'Even if Mr. Starrett had decided to become something else,' it has been written of him, 'his appearance and his manner would have determined his career. In an Inverness cape he looks like a composite of half the writers and artists of *fin de siècle* London. His classic profile, his piercing eyes, his aristocratic bearing, and a speech that has the perfection of Stevenson's prose, make him that rare combination—a man of letters who looks like one.' "

* * *

Burton Rascoe has called Starrett "the most distinguished looking writer in America." Charles E. Honce, his bibliographer and longtime friend, writes: "His home is not quite on this earth. It is some fabulous place of unicorns and griffins and kobolds and hippogryphs; a land of Gog and Magog, of Prester John, of fantastic adventures and incredible mysteries, maybe Hy-Brasil itself."

PRINCIPAL WORKS: *Essays and Miscellaneous—*Arthur Machen, 1918; Estrays, 1918; The Escape of Alice, 1919; Ambrose Bierce, 1920; The Unique Hamlet, 1920; Banners in the Dawn, 1922; Ebony Flame, 1922; Buried Caesars, 1923; Flame and Dust, 1924; Penny Wise and Book Foolish, 1929; The Private Life of Sherlock Holmes, 1933; Exits and Entrances, 1935; Snow for Christmas, 1935; The Laughing Buddha, 1937; Persons From Porlock, 1938; Peril in Peking, 1938; Oriental Encounters, 1938; 221 B: Studies in Sherlock Holmes (ed.) 1940; Books Alive, 1940; Bookman's Holiday, 1942. *Fiction*—Coffins for Two (short stories) 1924; Seaports in the Moon, 1928; Murder on "B" Deck, 1929; The Blue Door, 1930; Dead Man Inside, 1931; The End of Mr. Garment, 1932; The Great Hotel Murder, 1934; Midnight and Percy Jones, 1936.

ABOUT: Honce, C. E. A Vincent Starrett Library: Twenty-Three Years of Literary Activity; Rascoe, B. A Bookman's Day Book; Boston Evening Transcript July 29, 1933.

STEAD, CHRISTINA ELLEN (July 17, 1902-), Australian-American novelist, writes: "Both my parents were Australian-born, children of youthful English immigrants of poor origins. My mother died in my babyhood, my father soon remarried, and I became the eldest of a large family. My father was an early twentieth-century Rationalist Press Association Rationalist, Fabian Socialist, by profession a naturalist in the Government Fisheries Department; later he formed and managed the New South Wales Government State Trawling Industry. My childhood was—fish, natural history, Spencer, Darwin, Huxley, love of the sea (from dinghies and trawlers to the American Navy of 1908 and the British Navy), and the advancement of man (from the British Association for the Advancement of Science to the Smithsonian Institution). Eldest, and a girl, I had plenty of work with the young children, but was attached to them, and whenever I could, told them stories, partly from Grimm and Andersen, partly invented.

"I went to Teachers' College, but did not like teaching and took a business course at night, so that I could travel while working. It took me some years to save up the money, but in 1928 I went to London, to look for a job, and hoped later to get a job in Paris somehow. By pure accident this worked out and I was in Paris in the spring of 1929 and worked there for some years. Before leaving Sydney, while still at Teachers' College, I wrote a collection of tales of imagination, turned down by a local publisher because he could not distribute more than 500 of such a book, but later incorporated in part in *The Salzburg Tales.*

"At thirteen I began to learn French and soon became an impassioned adept of Guy de Maupassant, whom I regarded as a master of style; later I followed Chateaubriand, Huysmans, Balzac (for expression), Hugo and Zola (for viewpoint), and am influenced by modern French authors, for example, Louis Gilloux in his brilliant *Le Sang Noir* (*Black Blood*). In English and American letters my favorites were Thoreau, Melville, Ambrose Bierce, Poe, along with Bacon (for pithiness alone), Shelley, Shakespeare, and many others, of course. I dislike polite letters, self-conscious classicism, pseudo-philosophers (among writers), and the monosyllabic mucker-pose (for example: Pater, Lamb, Emerson, Wordsworth, and a local, present tendency). The essence of style in literature, for me, is experiment, invention, 'creative error' (Jules Romains), and change; and of its content, the presentation of 'man alive' (Ralph Fox). I am not puritan nor party, like to know every sort of person; nor political, but on the side of those who have suffered oppression, injustice, coercion, prejudice, and have been harried from birth."

* * *

Miss Stead was born in Rockdale, Sydney, the daughter of David George Stead and Ellen (Butters) Stead. She has been a public school teacher, a teacher of abnormal children, demonstrator in the psychology laboratory of Sydney University, and a clerk in a grain company and in banking houses, where she gained her unusual knowledge of the minutiae of finance. She is married to William Blech, cosmopolite, who under the pseudonym of "William Blake" writes romantic and historical novels, though he is a banker and broker by profession.

Christina Stead is tall, plain, quiet, intense, brown-haired. Her hobbies are fine embroi-

dery, housework, and natural history. She first visited the United States in 1935, then went to live in Spain, but left after the outbreak of Franco's rebellion, and in 1937 returned to this country permanently. She has traveled extensively in Europe, and was in Salzburg for six weeks during the Mozart Festival in 1930, but she says her traveling has been done for the most part either on business or during vacations. At the International Writers' Conference in Paris, in 1935, she wrote the *compte-rendu* for the English delegation. Her story, "O, If I Could But Shiver," is in the anthology, *The Fairies Return,* edited by Peter Davies in 1934. The permanent address of the Blakes is New York City.

Rebecca West called Christina Stead "one of the few people really original we have produced since the [First World] War," and Clifton Fadiman thought her "the most extraordinary woman novelist produced by the English-speaking race since Virginia Woolf." Though she was long "a critics' favorite, a popular failure," her books are finding an increasingly large public. They range from fantasy to pure realism, but are all overwhelmingly preoccupied with the problem of evil, and are characterized by what *Time* called her "Hogarthian humor, brilliant vocabulary, high-keyed imagination, and savage satire."

PRINCIPAL WORKS: The Salzburg Tales, 1934; Seven Poor Men of Sydney, 1935; The Beauties and Furies, 1936; House of All Nations, 1938; The Man Who Loved Children, 1940.

ABOUT: Time June 13, 1938; Wilson Library Bulletin December 1938.

*STEARNS, HAROLD EDMUND (May 7, 1891-), American editor and critic, writes: "I was born in Barre, Mass.. and educated at the Malden (Mass.) High School and at Harvard (B.A. *cum laude in philosophia,* 1912 as of 1913). My first work after being graduated was as editorial writer on the New York *Sun.* Then I became a writer on the theatre, first for

Bachrach

the old New York *Dramatic Mirror* and later for the New York *Press.* In the summer of 1914 I made my first trip to Europe, and was in Paris when war was declared. I returned home in the autumn and did free-lance writing in New York, with regular work, chiefly book reviewing, on the

* Died August 13, 1943.

early *New Republic*. (By 'regular,' I mean on a salary.) In the winter of 1917 and on in 1918 to July, I edited the old *Dial* in Chicago, then brought it to New York, where it underwent changes and later, after the war, was bought by my classmate, Scofield Thayer, and converted into an aesthetic monthly—called *Reconstruction Dial*—for a short time on the war's ending. I worked on the *New Freeman* as a contributor, but pretty regularly, and started *Civilization in the United States*.

"Meanwhile, I married Alice Macdougal. She died in 1919 in childbirth; our son was adopted by her father and took the name of Macdougal. On the completion of *Civilization* (July 4, 1921), I sailed the same day for Europe, where I remained (with only one trip home to California for a few weeks to see my son) for eleven years. The first five years I spent in Paris, I was correspondent of the Baltimore *Sun* and *Town and Country* (New York), and worked also on the New York *Herald* (Paris Edition). In my last years abroad I was racing editor first for the Chicago *Tribune* and later on for the London *Daily Mail* (Continental Edition). Illness forced me finally home in 1932.

"I married Elizabeth Chalifoux Chapin in 1937, and we are now living at Locust Valley, Long Island, N.Y., where I am writing and studying, also, like everybody else nowadays, doing some radio work."

* * *

Mr. Stearns is best known as the editor of two anthologies, sixteen years apart, which in their contents and viewpoint span the years between 1922 and 1938 with all that this implies. He was one of the first expatriates to "rediscover" his own country, and has been in a way a literary barometer for the Americans of his generation.

PRINCIPAL WORKS: Liberalism in America, 1919; America and the Young Intellectual, 1921; Civilization in the United States: An Inquiry by Thirty Americans (ed.) 1922; Rediscovering America, 1934; The Street I Knew (autobiography) 1935; America: A Re-Appraisal, 1937; America Now: An Inquiry Into Civilization in the United States by Thirty-Six Americans (ed.) 1938.

ABOUT: Stearns, H. E. The Street I Knew; Saturday Review of Literature May 5, 1934; Scribner's Magazine March 1929, May 1932.

STEDMAN, EDMUND CLARENCE.
See "AMERICAN AUTHORS: 1600-1900"

*STEED, HENRY WICKHAM (October 10, 1871-   ), English journalist and publicist who signs himself Wickham Steed, was born at Long Melford, Suffolk, the son of a solicitor. He was educated at Sudbury Grammar School, and then, after a short period as private secretary to a Member of Parliament, went to study at the Universities of Jena and Berlin and

at the Sorbonne. He has honorary doctorates from the Universities of Strassburg and Cluj (Rumania). He joined the staff of the London *Times* as acting correspondent in Berlin in 1896, was the paper's correspondent in Rome from 1897 to 1902, and in Vienna to 1913. He was foreign editor of the *Times* from 1914 to 1919, and its editor from 1919 to 1922. From 1923 to 1930 he was editor of the *Review of Reviews* (London), and also lectured on Central European history at King's College, London, from 1925 to 1928. During the First World War he was in charge of propaganda in the enemy countries and headed a special mission to Italy. He is an accomplished linguist, speaks French, German, and Italian fluently, and writes as easily in French as in English; he published three books in French bearing on the war.

Long a bachelor, he was married in 1937, at sixty-six, to Violet Sybille Mason. He has homes in London and Oxford, and is at present attached to the Foreign Office. He writes: "It is not at a moment when we are fighting for our existence as a free country that any of us can trouble about details of our own lives, or even about our lives at all. 'Who dies if England live?' Incidentally, we are also defending the freedom of the United States."

Mr. Steed is a natural aristocrat both in temperament and in appearance. Tall and markedly handsome, with gray wavy hair, a pointed moustache and a Vandyke beard, he looks more like a diplomat than like a journalist. He is, indeed, a sort of extra-mural diplomat; H. W. Nevinson called him "one of the few journalists who have definitely affected the international relations of Europe." His brilliance, charm, forthrightness, and dry humor are famous. He is a frequent contributor to the leading reviews of England and America. Hamilton Fyfe said of him: "Not only is he apt to put what he knows into illuminating form—it is the extent of what he knows that makes his contributions to journalism and to literature so valuable and, indeed, so unique."

PRINCIPAL WORKS: The Hapsburg Monarchy, 1913; L'Angleterre et la Guerre, 1915; L'Effort Anglais, 1916; La Democratie Britannique, 1918; Through Thirty Years (autobiography) 1924; The Real Stanley Baldwin, 1930; The Antecedents of Post-War Europe, 1932; Hitler: Whence and Whither? 1934; The Meaning of Hitlerism, 1934; A Way to Social Peace, 1934; Vital Peace: A Study of Risks, 1936; The Doom of the Hapsburgs, 1937; The Press, 1938; Our War Aims, 1939.

ABOUT: Steed, W. Through Thirty Years; Current Opinion February 1925; Journal des Débats July 6, 1934; Living Age July 19, 1919; Revue Politique et Littéraire November 21, 1931; World Tomorrow May 1925.

STEEL, Mrs. FLORA ANNIE (WEBSTER) (April 2, 1847-April 12, 1929), English novelist, was born at Sudbury

Priory, Harrow-on-the-Hill, the sixth child and second daughter of George Webster, sheriff-clerk of Forfarshire, and Isabella (Macallum) Webster, the heiress of a Jamaica sugar-planter. The family left Harrow when Flora was nine and moved to Palace Yard, Westminster. George Cruikshank was a friend of the family. In 1857 they moved to Burnside, Forfarshire, where the ten-year-old girl received news of the Indian Mutiny, about which she was later to write a famous novel, and burned Nana Sahib in effigy. She was educated by governesses, at private schools, and in Brussels; lived at 66 Heriot Row, Edinburgh, in 1866, and next year married Henry William Steel of the Indian civil service. The marriage was happy, though she claimed never to have been in love. In 1868 they reached Madras and traveled to Delhi, thence by road to Lahore, where Mrs. Steel was the only woman at Ludhiana. Her husband was later transferred to Dalhousie. A first child was born dead; another, a daughter born in 1870, survived to make a home at Springfield, Minchinhampton, for her mother, who lived past eighty.

In 1870 Mrs. Steel joined her husband in Kasur, a subdivision of the Lahore district, where they entertained the local magnates and Mrs. Steel penetrated behind the purdah. "There was that in her Highland blood which was sympathetic to legend, pilgrimage, and religious disputation." She ad-

vocated education for Indian women, was first inspector of the girls' schools, and in 1884 was a member of the Provincial Educational Board with John Lockwood Kipling, father of Rudyard Kipling. Steel retired from the service in 1889. From 1900 to 1913 they lived at Talgarth near Machynlleth, North Wales, where Mrs. Steel enjoyed her garden. She approved woman suffrage, though not an active worker. Later they moved to Court o' Hill, Tenbury.

On the Face of the Waters (1896), her remarkable novel of the Indian Mutiny, was based on observation of the Indian scene, which had changed little since 1857, the tales of old Moslem servants, and talks with the Delhi descendants of the Mogul dynasty. The novel, heavily documented, has five symmetrical books, each with six well-rounded chapters. Books Three to Five "unfold . . . a panorama of heroism and horrors." Mrs. Steel "had not the range, attack, poetry, the white heat of Kipling," but her novels are careful studies of native myth and usage and are of especial value for that reason.

PRINCIPAL WORKS: From the Five Rivers, 1893; Tales From the Punjab, 1894; On the Face of the Waters, 1896; Voices in the Night, The Hosts of the Lord, 1900.

ABOUT: Steel, F. A. The Garden of Fidelity; Living Age February 2, 1918; London Times April 15, 1929; Morning Post April 15, 1929.

STEELE, WILBUR DANIEL (March 17, 1886-), American novelist and short-story writer, was born in Greensboro, N.C., the birthplace of O.

Henry. His parents were W. Fletcher Steele, D. D., and Rose (Wood) Steele. He attended a kindergarten in Berlin and finished his formal schooling (1907) at the University of Denver, where his father was professor of Biblical Literature. (Many of his forebears were Methodist Episcopal clergymen.) A painter's career seeming more desirable, Wilbur Steele studied at the Museum of Fine Arts in Boston in 1907-08; spent the next year at the Académie Julien in Paris; and finished at the Art Students' League in New York City in 1909-10. Joining the artists' colony in Provincetown, Mass., Steele tried his hand at writing a Cape Cod story, "A White Horse Winter," which was published in the *Atlantic Monthly* in 1912. In 1913 he married Margaret Thurston of Boston, and two sons, Thurston and Peter, were born. Steele traveled in the West Indies in 1916-17. In 1918, during the First World War, he was stationed off the coasts of Ireland, England, and France as a naval correspondent. In 1919-20 he lived in Bermuda, and during the next year went to North Africa and to France and England again. In 1919 Steele had received the first of four O. Henry committee awards for writing short stories of outstanding excellence. This was a second prize, for the story "For They Know Not What They Do." In 1921 the same committee bestowed a special award on Steele for maintaining the highest level of merit for three years among American short story writers; and in 1925 he tied with Julian Street for first honors. An unqualified first was awarded next year for Steele's story, "The Man Who Saw Through Heaven." The *Boston Transcript* has commented on his "combination of impressionistic romance and biting realism with a keen sense of dramatic values."

A writer who tells little in explicit statement and much by implication and suggestion, he deftly mingles beauty and cruelty, according to the New York *Times*. Clifton Fadiman calls Wilbur Daniel Steele past master of a complicated bag of tricks, but "of the actuality, the terrifying closeness of a Katherine Mansfield he is quite incapable." In 1931 the O. Henry committee again awarded its first prize to Steele for his story, "Can't Cross Jordan." He was then living in Charleston, S.C. In January 1932 he married Mrs. Norma Mitchell Talbot, actress and playwright, with whom he wrote the successful comedy *Post Road* (1934).

Their present home is in Lyme, Conn. The writer, who has gray eyes, brown stubby hair, and a moustache, works regular hours (four or five) each day, usually turning out six hundred words in longhand and typing his own copy. "I seem to be pretty much the common or garden variety of person," he writes, "anxious about the well-being of my family, always losing everything, and having difficulty with my income tax returns. My main desire is to have the moon."

PRINCIPAL WORKS: Storm, 1914; Land's End, 1918; Shame Dance, 1923; Isles of the Blest, 1924; The Terrible Woman, 1925; Taboo, 1925; Urkey Island, 1926; The Man Who Saw Through Heaven, 1927; Meat, 1928; Tower of Sand, 1929; Post Road (play, with N. Mitchell) 1934; How Beautiful With Shoes (play, with A. Brown) 1935; Sound of Rowlocks, 1938.

ABOUT: Williams, B. C. Our Short Story Writers.

STEEN, MARGUERITE, English novelist writes: "Up to the last few years, when writing became a full-time occupation for me, I have combined never less than two or three simultaneous careers! Writing is not a lucrative profession for the beginner. I have been in turn a kindergarten teacher (I managed in some moment to get a Froebel certificate, more through oversight on the part of the examiners than by personal effort), dancer, actress, accompanist, lecturer, dramatic producer, private governess, and 'helper' in a sandwich bar; I have had the interesting and educative experience of being *quite* penniless, and there have been a few bright patches of something near opulence. After the First World War, I was so much out of sympathy with the general trend of thought and opinion in England that I spent as much time as possible abroad: at first in Paris, and later in Spain, which came to be the country of my adoption.

"Born in the Victorian twilight (I can just remember being lifted out of my cot to listen to the cheering over the relief of Ladysmith), the rich prodigality of the Edwardian reign, the dark drama of the war years, the post-war complications with leaping income tax and 'servant problem'—all left their various impressions upon my work. They are wonderful years for a novelist to have lived through: I am grateful for the experiences they have brought me. The best one can wish for is an utterly full life. Now I look forward to *the next thing*; I wonder what it will be?"

* * *

Marguerite Steen was born in Liverpool and after attending the Belvedere Kindergarten in that city was sent to "a horrible little private boarding school," from which at her own request she was sent to Kendal High School. For three years as a boarder there she did nothing "except have a good time and within the limits of a strict minimum of work, imbibe a certain disposition to learn."

She had written her first novel by the age of eight, and at fifteen had produced a three-volume prophecy of the course of her life up to thirty. This proved singularly accurate, except that she anticipated that her eventual career would be the stage, and that authorship would occasion only incidental glory.

At nineteen, during the First World War, she was "booted unwillingly into school-teaching," but she "loathed school environment and the absurd insincerities of the profession." After three years, with twelve pounds in her pocket, she flung herself into London to try to get on the stage. After pawning her few possessions and living on a glass of Horlick's and a bun for day after day, luck curiously came her way in the form of an offer to teach classic dancing and eurythmics in Halifax. Within three years she was earning more than £500 annually, but the routine of teaching again palled on her and when she was offered £3 a week to tour with the Fred Terry-Julia Neilson Company, she seized the opportunity to fulfill her youthful stage ambitions.

Of these theatre years, 1921-23, Miss Steen writes: "If I had never gone on the stage I should likely never have become a novelist. I needed those theatre years to ripen my knowledge of people, to enlarge the narrow experience of my bourgeois home and upbringing."

It was the famous actress Ellen Terry, Fred Terry's sister, who was responsible for launching Marguerite Steen on her writing career during a desperate out-of-work period in 1926. Miss Steen calls Miss Terry her "guide, monitor, and dearest friend." The novelist W. J. Locke also subscribed to the idea that she had the "writing maggot" in her. Taking their advice, Miss Steen scribbled away at a "society" novel in her theatrical lodgings, published in 1927 as *The Gilt Cage*.

Since then she has been a prolific writer. Her two most successful novels have been *Matador* (1934), which was a choice of the Book Society in England and of the Book-of-the-Month Club in the United States, and *The Sun Is My Undoing* (1941), a prodigiously long, picaresque novel of the slave trade, which was a Literary Guild selection here and a best-seller in both countries. Her books have received mixed reviews.

Miss Steen is unmarried and lives in London. She works up to eighteen hours a day, types every word, and loathes using a pen. For recreation she paints and, in time of peace, motors in a small car "with a gallant heart and an apparently inexhaustible capacity for climbing hills."

PRINCIPAL WORKS: The Gilt Cage, 1927; Duel in the Dark, 1928; The Reluctant Madonna, 1929; They That Go Down in Ships, 1930; Where the Wind Blows, 1931; Unicorn, 1931; The Wise and the Foolish Virgins, 1932; Oakfield Plays (for children) 1932; Peepshow (children's plays) 1933; Spider, 1933; Hugh Walpole: A Study, 1933;

Matador, 1934; The Tavern, 1935; The One-Eyed Moon, 1935; The Lost One: A Biography of Mrs. Mary (Perdita) Robinson, 1937; Who Would Have Daughters? 1937; The Marriage Will Not Take Place, 1938; Family Ties, 1939; A Kind of Insolence, 1940; The Sun Is My Undoing, 1941.

ABOUT: Current Biography 1941; Wilson Library Bulletin February 1937.

STEFÁNSSON, VILHJÁLMUR (November 3, 1879-), American writer and Arctic explorer, was born in Arnes, Manitoba, Canada, the son of Johann Stefánsson and Ingibjörg (Johannesdottir) Stefánsson. He received his preliminary education in the preparatory department of the State University of North Dakota and in the university itself; in 1903 he obtained a B.A. degree from Iowa State University and went east to study at the Divinity School of Harvard University for a year. He spent 1904-06 in the Harvard Graduate School, but his first Harvard degree, an M.A., was granted in 1923. His first trip to the far north was a visit to Iceland in 1904, followed by an archaeological expedition to the island in 1905 under the auspices of the Peabody Museum.

Times Studio

In 1906-07 Stefánsson made his first expedition to study the Eskimos of the Mackenzie Delta under the joint auspices of Harvard and the University of Toronto; the second expedition began the next year and ended in 1912. Fifty-three months of this undertaking were spent under the auspices of the American Museum of Natural History in New York and of the government of the Dominion of Canada. The winter of 1908-09 found Stefánsson at the Colville Delta on the north coast of Alaska; the next winter was spent at Cape Parry; in 1910-11 the explorer was at Coronation Gulf and Victoria Island, and 1911-12 found him back at Cape Parry. Stefánsson adopted the modes and habits of living of the Eskimos, indoors and out, sleeping, eating and hunting with them, and learning how to live off the country.

It has always been his vehement contention that life in the Arctic is no more dangerous or hardship-ridden than life anywhere else, providing the proper precautions are taken, and that "adventures" are usually the result of simple inefficiency. *My Life With the Eskimo* (1913) developed this thesis to some extent, and *The Friendly*

Arctic (1921), with its provocative title, sold much better than the ordinary book of polar exploration. It showed the northern regions in an unfamiliar light as a place of grass and flowers, at the proper seasons of the year, and as a likely terrain for colonization, hence the title of *The Northward Course of Empire* (1922). Stefánsson has taken delight in the methodical exposure of popular errors about the Arctic, both on the lecture platform and in such books as *The Standardization of Error* and *Adventures in Error*. The only expedition under his direction in which he did not personally take part ended in tragedy, and in various unfounded charges made by Harold Noice, a member of a rescue party. *The Adventure of Wrangel Island* (1925) was designed to blow Mr. Noice out of the water, but was modified in some respects when the latter made a retraction.

A medical experiment in which Stefánsson took part under the direction of Dr. Clarence Lieb showed that a man can live on an all-meat diet for months and emerge in the pink of health. From 1913 to 1918 he commanded another Arctic expedition, exploring land and seas in Canada and Alaska. Since 1932 he has been adviser on northern operations for Pan-American Airways. The Canadian government gave him a vote of thanks in 1921, and he is a fellow of many learned societies, as well as the holder of medals from the geographical societies of Philadelphia, Chicago, London, Paris, and Berlin. Stefánsson is a member of the Canadian Explorers, Century, and Harvard Clubs in New York City, listing the last as his mail-address; and of the Faculty Club in Cambridge, Mass., and the Athenaeum in London. He is tall, sandy, deliberate in speech and courtly in manner; a crack shot.

His literary style is crystal-clear, and the subject-matter of his books unfailingly interesting. The University of Iceland gave him an honorary Ph.D. in 1930. In 1941 he married Mrs. Evelyn Schwartz Baird. His name is pronounced *stay'fan-son*.

PRINCIPAL WORKS: My Life With the Eskimo, 1913; The Friendly Artic, 1921; The Northward Course of Empire, 1922; Hunters of the Great North, 1922; The Adventure of Wrangel Island, 1925; The Standardization of Error, 1927; Adventure in Error, 1936; The Three Voyages of Martin Frobisher, 1938; Unsolved Mysteries of the Arctic, 1938; Iceland: The First American Republic, 1939; Ultima Thule, 1940; Greenland, 1942.

ABOUT: Noice, H. With Stefánsson in the Arctic; Stefánsson, V. My Life With the Eskimo, The Friendly Arctic, The Adventure of Wrangel Island; Harper's Magazine June 1941; New Yorker October 11, 18, 1941; Time August 14, 1939.

STEFFENS, LINCOLN (April 6, 1866-August 9, 1936), American political writer, was born Joseph Lincoln Steffens in San Francisco, the son of Joseph and Elizabeth Louisa (Symes) Steffens. He spent his boyhood, however, on a ranch near Sacramento, where he learned to be a good horseman and also indulged his taste for drawing. He was sent to a military

school but expelled for "drunkenness," and his father then secured a tutor, an Oxford man, who coached him for the University of California and really initiated his intellectual life. Steffens received a Ph.B. degree from the university in 1889, and then for three years went to Europe, where he studied, philosophy chiefly, at Berlin, Heidelberg, Leipzig, and the Sorbonne. He came back with a wife, Josephine Bontecou, whom he had married in 1891 in London. He became a police reporter on the New York *Evening Post,* later city editor; it was at this time that he met Theodore Roosevelt and Jacob Riis and first became interested in social questions. From 1898 to 1902 he was city editor of the New York *Commercial Advertiser,* and he then went to *McClure's Magazine,* of which he was managing editor for four years. These were the great "muckraking" years, when Steffens, Ida Tarbell, Finley Peter Dunne ("Mr. Dooley") and Ray Stannard Baker woke up the social consciousness of a nation, and Steffens' articles, later published in book form as *The Shame of the Cities,* set the country by the ears. Subsequently, until 1911, he was associate editor first of the *American Magazine* and then of *Everybody's Magazine.*

He never held a regular editorial job thereafter, but became a sort of reporter and mediator at large, attempting with the late E. A. Filene (unsuccessfully) to put over a five-year reform plan in Boston, bringing about (rather disastrously) the conviction of the McNamara brothers in the Los Angeles *Times* explosion case, acting as intermediary between President Wilson and the Carranza government in Mexico, covering the Versailles Peace Conference, and serving on the secret Bullitt Mission to Russia in 1919. His last years were spent in Carmel, Calif., where he edited the *Pacific Weekly,* and where his final affiliation with the Communist movement caused constant persecution. His first marriage had been unhappy, and he and his wife had separated before her death. In 1924 he married Ella Winter, a much younger English writer, and they had one son, whom Steffens adored. Later the couple were divorced, but always remained on friendly and intimate terms. After Steffens' death his widow married Donald Ogden Stewart, the writer.

"Steff," as his friends called him, was not only one of the greatest reporters this country has ever seen, but he was also, as both John Chamberlain and Albert Jay Nock pointed out, a kind of "Socrates of the sanctum," questioning everybody and everything with apparent naïveté, realistic, shrewd, yet somehow always a bit confused between skepticism and the Messianic urge. His thin spectacled face, with its gray bangs and little pointed beard, was a mirror of the man, direct, honest, simple, an *enfant terrible* who shocked people because he asked the open-eyed questions and uttered the forthright conclusions of an unselfconscious child. He *liked* people, including "honest crooks" and "good bad capitalists"; he felt himself to be no better than the most iniquitous of those he studied, and he won their confidence by telling them so. "Intelligence is what I am aiming at, not honesty," he said. He was a true pragmatist. "Candid, deceptively simple, curious," the *New Republic* called him. His letters even more than his incomplete autobiography give the finished portrait of a unique personality.

Though all his life he feared he was about to lose his power as a writer, actually he remained the unaffected, straightforward reportorial stylist he had always been. "He wrote as he spoke," said Oswald Garrison Villard, "whimsical, charming, elusive, fanciful, scoffing and joking—seriously joking, . . . amazingly penetrating and understanding, wise and unwise, right and mistaken, contradictory and paradoxical."

PRINCIPAL WORKS: The Shame of the Cities, 1904; The Struggle for Self-Government, 1906; Upbuilders, 1909; The Least of These, 1910; Moses in Red, 1926; Autobiography, 1931 (first part as Boy on Horseback, 1935); Lincoln Steffens Speaking, 1936; Letters of Lincoln Steffens, 1938.

ABOUT: Filler, L. Crusaders for American Liberalism; Hapgood, H. A Victorian in the Modern World; Steffens, L. Autobiography, Lincoln Steffens Speaking, Letters; Commonweal November 4, 1938; Nation August 15, 1936, October 22, 1938; New Republic April 15, 1931, September 28, 1932; August 19, and November 18, 1936, September 28 and October 5, 1938; Outlook April 15, 1931; Saturday Review of Literature May 9, 1931, November 12, December 3, October 24, 1938; Survey May 1, 1931, November 1936.

STEGNER, WALLACE EARLE (February 18, 1909-), American novelist, writes: "My life has been neither eventful nor dull. Born on my grandfather's farm near Lake Mills, Iowa, I was traveling most of the time from then on. We lived successively in Iowa, North Dakota, Washington, Saskatchewan, Montana, Utah, Nevada, and California, with stops

Bachrach

of some years in both Saskatchewan and Utah. Consequently Eastend, Sask., and Salt Lake City are the closest things to 'home' in my life, the only places where I put down any roots. Because my father had the pioneering itch in his bones, my childhood was spent on almost the last frontier. From 1914 to 1919, in Saskatchewan, I had plenty of chance to observe the odd collection of bad men and drifters and cockneys and Texas cowboys at close range. I think those five years in a really rough and unregenerate frontier hamlet are more important to me than any five years of my life. And living in the country has given me an apparently permanent distaste for cities and city ways. It has made me a bad joiner and a worse 'belonger.'

"For the rest, I went through high school and college in Salt Lake, graduating from the state university in 1930. A few years of graduate work at California and Iowa gave me two other degrees [M.A. and Ph.D., University of Iowa], and I began teaching. My teaching experience seems to follow the peripatetic patterns of my childhood; I have taught at Augustana College, the Universities of Iowa, Utah, and Wisconsin, and at Harvard, where I am currently a Briggs-Copeland Instructor in English Composition. In 1934 I was married to Mary Page; we have one son.

"I got into writing, I suppose, by not being able to keep my hands off a typewriter. My M.A. thesis at Iowa was a group of short stories, and after I finished my doctorate I turned by preference away from scholarship and back to fiction. I had published a couple of stories when in 1937 *Remembering Laughter* won the Little, Brown novelette contest. Since then I have published three other short novels and short stories in various magazines. I am working on a long novel on the general theme of what happens to the pioneer virtues and the pioneer type of family when the frontiers are gone and the opportunities all used up. It will be, in some of its aspects, a fairly close parallel to the experiences of my own family between 1907 and 1930."

* * *

Mr. Stegner lives in Cambridge, Mass., during the college term, but his real home is at Greenboro Bend, Vt., where he spends his summers. He has been writing seriously since 1934. Besides his novels, he compiled in 1934, with Stuart Brown and Claude Simpson, a textbook called *An Exposition Workshop.*

PRINCIPAL WORKS: Remembering Laughter, 1937; The Potter's House, 1938; On a Darkling Plain, 1940; Fire and Ice, 1941; Mormon Country, 1942.

ABOUT: Wilson Library Bulletin May 1941; Writer February 1940.

*STEIN, GERTRUDE (February 3. 1874-). American author (she cannot be classified more definitely), was born in Al-

legheny, Pa., the daughter of Daniel and Amelia (Keyser) Stein. Her infancy was spent in Vienna and Paris, her childhood and girlhood in Oakland and San Francisco. She was a student at Radcliffe College from 1893 to 1897, was a favorite pupil of William James, and specialized in psychology—a fact which has some bearing on her future career. She then studied medicine for four years at Johns Hopkins University. From neither institution did she take a degree; she was interested only in her studies and was "bored" by formal examinations. In 1903 she went to live in Paris, with a younger San Francisco friend, Alice B. Toklas, who has been her companion and secretary ever since. Her only return to America was in 1934, when her opera, *Four Saints in Three Acts* (music by Virgil Thomson), was produced and she gave a lecture tour. She remained in France even after its defeat by Germany in the Second World War.

As soon as she arrived in Paris she met the "advanced" group of artists; Picasso, Matisse, Bracque. She became immersed in their work and their theories; interest in art was general in her family, and her brother Leo became a well known art critic. Possessed of an independent income, she became more or less a patron of these men, was strongly influenced by them, and in turn passed on the influence to younger artists

and above all to younger writers. Since the writers of that generation (the best known of them was Ernest Hemingway, with whom Miss Stein later had a definite break) have now been succeeded by another, she is today "grandmother to our present writing."

The key of the "new" work in both painting and writing was its emphasis on abstraction. This came easily to Miss Stein; R. F. Skinner pointed out in 1934 that she had published a paper in a psychological journal while she was still in Radcliffe, recording her experiments in spontaneous automatic writing. Her first book, *Three Lives,* was evidence that she was capable of an intelligible style; the book is almost realistic and is instinct with a tenderness and a subtle sympathetic humor which Miss Stein has seldom displayed since—perhaps because it is a characteristic of her conscious, not her unconscious, mind. As one critic remarked: "She has elected to write in a manner which much of the time makes her concrete meaning inaccessible to the reader.... She was to push abstraction to its farthest limits."

It is unnecessary to describe her usual manner; indeed it is indescribable. In her two "autobiographies," one foisted on Miss Toklas, the other on "everybody," this characteristic style is greatly modified, made simple and coherent, and is interspersed with "malicious portraits of other celebrities, scrambled philosophical observations, comments on history, drunks, dogs, revolutionists, writing, painting, genius, the Stein family, and the United States." Sinclair Lewis said the question always had been: was Miss Stein crazy, was she joking, or was she "contributing new rhythms to an outworn English style"? His final conclusion was that she was conducting a racket! Yet her impact on contemporary literature is strong. Paul Rosenfeld perhaps went too far in saying that "the capacity to appreciate her performances is indivisible from that general feeling of spirit making the American experiment a success"; but William Troy pointed out that Gertrude Stein's writing represents that "final division between experience and life" already foreshadowed by Melville, Poe, Hawthorne, and Henry James; and John Hyde Preston well called her "the fountainhead for all the young Americans who were writing in Paris after the [First World] War."

In person Miss Stein is downright and plain-spoken. T. S. Matthews described her in 1934, with her close-cropped hair, her "Middle Western" voice, as "a solid elderly woman, dressed in no-nonsense rough-spun clothes," with "deep black eyes that make

* Died July 27, 1946.

her grave face and its archaic smile come alive."

Allanah Harper, in *Partisan Review*, has suggested the quality of Miss Stein's personality in a few words:

"The first time I went to tea with Gertrude Stein, at 27 rue de Fleurus, I thought I had never seen a more magnificent head—she looked like the bust of a Roman emperor and, at the same time, like a Buddhist monk. She seemed to take it for granted that no one knew anything about painting until they had proved themselves in agreement with her. . . . It was evident that Gertrude Stein enjoyed lecturing. The last time I saw Gertrude Stein was in London, the summer before the war, at an exhibition of painting. I had my poodle with me, 'Does he like painting?' she asked me, 'My poodle always recognizes pictures; he knows a Renoir when he sees one.' This was said so matter of factly that there was no possible answer."

PRINCIPAL WORKS: Three Lives, 1908; Tender Buttons, 1915; Geography and Plays, 1922; The Making of Americans, 1925; Useful Knowledge, 1928; Acquaintance With Description, 1929; Ten Portraits, 1930; Lucy Church Amiably, 1930; Before the Flower of Friendship Faded Friendship Faded, 1931; How to Write, 1931; Operas and Plays, 1932; Matisse, Picasso, and Gertrude Stein, 1932; The Autobiography of Alice B. Toklas, 1933; Four Saints in Three Acts, 1934; Portraits and Prayers, 1934; Lectures in America, 1935; Narration, 1935; The Geographical History of America: or, The Relation of Human Nature to the Human Mind, 1936; Everybody's Autobiography, 1937; Picasso, 1938; The World Is Round, 1939; Paris France, 1940; Ida, 1941.

ABOUT: Canby, H. S. American Estimates; Chesterton, G. K. In All I Survey; MacCarthy, D. Criticism; Rosenfeld, P. By Way of Art; Sherman, S. B. Points of View; Stein, G. Autobiography of Alice B. Toklas, Everybody's Autobiography; Wilson, E. Axel's Castle; Atlantic Monthly January 1934, August 1935; English Review May 1936; Nation September 6, 1933; New Republic April 4, December 5, 1934, April 7, 1941; Newsweek December 13, 1937; Partisan Review July-August 1942; Poetry February, December 1940; Saturday Review of Literature December 22, 1934, December 4, 1937; Sewanee Review April 1936.

STEINBECK, JOHN (February 27, 1902-), American novelist, was born in Salinas, Calif., the son of John Ernst Steinbeck, for many years county treasurer, and of Olive (Hamilton) Steinbeck, who was a teacher. On his father's side he is of German descent (the name was originally Grossstein-beck), on his mother's Northern Irish. Through his paternal grandmother he is descended from a Massachusetts family dating from the seventeenth century. But in many ways he is peculiarly a product of the California interior valleys. Much of his work is a reflection of his native district, and of the

Monterey coast, where he lived after his marriage.

After being graduated from the Salinas High School, Mr. Steinbeck spent four years at Stanford University, but as a special student and not as a candidate for a degree. His chief interest there was in science, and he has a thorough knowledge of biology and especially of marine biology. (He escaped from the hullabaloo over *Grapes of Wrath,* his novel of migratory  workers, by leading a private expedition to the Galapagos Islands. Cf. *Sea of Cortez*.

He tried his hand at many jobs before coming into his own as a writer. His first three books were financial failures, and for a long time he was very poor. For a short while he was a reporter on a New York paper, but was discharged because he wrote reflections instead of reporting facts; he has been an apprentice hod-carrier, an apprentice painter, a working chemist, caretaker of a Lake Tahoe estate, a surveyor in the Big Sur country, and a fruit-picker like his own Joads. In 1930 he married Carol Henning; at Monterey, the scene of his novel *Tortilla Flat,* they owned a launch and spent much of their time sailing and fishing. The fish were a valuable addition of their meager budget, for they lived on $25 a month. Later, in more prosperous days, they lived near Los Gatos. The Steinbecks were divorced in 1942; they had no children.

Steinbeck is that *rara avis* among authors —a genuinely shy man who hates publicity. When he was in New York after *Grapes of Wrath* had won the Pulitzer award and had been turned into a prizewinning motion picture, he refused interviews even by well known critics. He is a big man, very blond, with deep blue eyes and a deep, slow, quiet voice. Quite sincerely he says, "I'm not even a finished writer yet." In many ways he resembles another Californian, Robinson Jeffers, though Steinbeck's reticence and his dislike of cities and their life have little in common with Jeffers' proud and despairing seclusion. With Jeffers also he shares, as the late T. K. Whipple noted, "a preoccupation with physical suffering, cruelty, and violence." But his detachment is purely personal, not literary, and he has a compassionate understanding of the inarticulate and semi-articulate which warms all his books.

His outstanding characteristic as a writer is his versatility. He ranges from the romantic history of his first novel to the gayety of *Tortilla Flat,* from the psychological analysis of *The Long Valley* to the sociological awareness of *In Dubious Battle.* He has noticeable weaknesses; he is poor in plot and apt to solve a problem by some incongruous and mechanical—even melodramatic—contrivance; he has been accused of self-consciousness in style, of a "silky, mellifluous" manner, sometimes inappropriate to its subject, of prolonged adolescence and slow coming to maturity. "Simplification, so to speak, has been the source of his inspiration," writes Maxwell Geismar, "assurance has been his métier. . . . Handling complex material rather too easily, he has been marked by the popularizing gift. . . . Here is an urbanity of psyche bought a little easily. . . ."

Acclaimed "the twentieth century *Uncle Tom's Cabin,*" *Grapes of Wrath* made Steinbeck's name and the name of its protagonists, the Joads, household words. The book, in Geismar's concise summary, was "burned and banned, borrowed, smuggled, but above all, bought." Carey McWilliams "documented" it in his non-fictional book, *Factories in the Field.* Another storm was raised by the appearance of *The Moon Is Down* (1942), a novel laid in an unnamed invaded country (presumably Norway), some reviewers contending that it was an unpropritious time to present so mild a portrait of (Nazi) invaders. Written (like *Of Mice and Men*) in such a form as to be easily adapted to the stage, it had only a short Broadway run, though the book itself was a widely discussed best-seller.

The Nazis have called Steinbeck a Jew (he has no Jewish blood, though he indignantly resents using such a test as criterion of a writer's work), the Associated Farmers have called him a Communist. Really he has no theoretical economic creed whatever. It has been said "he subscribes to no solution so far propounded of social and economic problems." He is in revolt against Puritanism in all its forms, as much as he is against the social exploitation which so often accompanies it; but "he is not without religion. His religion is built on a kind of mysticism which is not the less impressive because it is as naturalistic as his ethics." Vincent McHugh has given the best "interim report" on Steinbeck as an author to date: "He works things out with a technical command that is exceptionally acute and various—patient rather than daring, and as yet more effective with scene and texture than it is in the large form."

PRINCIPAL WORKS: Cup of Gold, 1929; Pastures of Heaven, 1932; To a God Unknown, 1933; Tortilla Flat, 1935; In Dubious Battle, 1936; Of Mice and Men, 1937; The Long Valley (including The Red Pony and other novelettes) 1938; Grapes of Wrath, 1939; The Forgotten Village, 1941; Sea of Cortez (with E. F. Ricketts) 1941; The Moon Is Down, 1942; Bombs Away: The Story of a Bomber Team, 1942.

ABOUT: Geismar, M. Writers in Crisis; Steinbeck, J. Grapes of Wrath (see Introduction to 1940 ed. by Joseph Henry Jackson); American Mercury May 1939; Canadian Forum September 1940; Colophon #3 1939; Current Biography 1940; Fortnightly Review September 1939; Nation November 25, 1939; New Republic October 12, 1938, December 9, 1940; North American Review June 1937; Publishers' Weekly July 27, 1935, April 17, 1937; Saturday Review of Literature September 25, 1937; Virginia Quarterly Review October 1939; Wilson Library Bulletin March 1937.

STEPHEN, SIR LESLIE. See "BRITISH AUTHORS OF THE 19TH CENTURY"

*STEPHENS, JAMES (February, 1882-), Irish poet and novelist, was born in Dublin of a poor and obscure family. He grew up on the streets of the slums, had practically no formal schooling, but educated himself by reading. He taught himself stenography and secured an office position. Here he was accidentally discovered by George Russell ("AE"), who read some of the  boy's poems and stories and encouraged him to keep on writing. He had a long and disheartening struggle to find any editor or publisher who would even consider his work. It was not until he published *The Crock of Gold,* which won the Polignac Prize in 1912, that he secured any recognition whatever. With this book, however, he was "made," and he has been able since then to spend all his time in writing. He is an ardent student of Gaelic, and the avowed purpose of several of his books is to give Ireland "a new mythology." *Deirdre,* one of this series, won the Tallman Gold Medal in 1923. He has visited the United States a number of times, his first trip being in 1925; in 1935 he lectured at the University of California. His mind is so stored with Irish verses and stories that he can recite them extemporaneously by the hour—and does. He is also an authority on Gaelic art, and is assistant curator of the Dublin National Gallery. Another of his interests is folk-music, and he and Stephen McKenna used to sing Irish songs together to the accompaniment of Stephens' concertina. Until the Second World War he spent much time in Paris, which became almost his second home. He was an active Sinn Feiner, and worked hard for establishment of the De Valera government in Ireland.

In appearance Stephens is the image of a leprechaun. He is under five feet in height, bald, with a long face, timid brown eyes, dark skin, and the face of a comic stage Irishman. Burton Rascoe said of him, "Never have I seen a man who impressed me as being so easy, free, and natural, so untamed by society, so untouched by convention, so spontaneous, pagan, and joyous."

His humor has a touch of the grim and sardonic; his prose stories display not so much mere fancy as deep, creative imagination. Stephen Gwynn said that "his mind moves in squirrel leaps.... If a whiff of turf reek hangs about the potheen, the gods surely will not mind." His poetry, technically interesting, is written mostly in words of one syllable, and he is skilled in using dialect (he himself speaks with a heavy brogue) for his own gnomic purposes. Gwynn remarked: "Often one is hard set to follow the song's drift. But it is song undeniable." And Inez Cunningham Stark called him "a poet as adept as any now living in the creation of mood.... He now stylizes both form and color. The effect, with the Celtic background of his wit, his deceptive tenderness, and his poverty-worship, is sometimes startling."

He is unmarried, and lives for the most part in Dublin. Of late years he has written little prose, but his poems still appear in the magazines.

PRINCIPAL WORKS: *Poetry*—Insurrections, 1909; The Hill of Vision, 1912; Songs From the Clay, 1915; The Rocky Road to Dublin, 1915; The Adventures of Seumas Beg, 1915; Green Branches, 1916; Reincarnations, 1918; Little Things, 1924; A Poetry Recital, 1925; Collected Poems, 1926; Outcast, 1929; Theme and Variations (limited edition) 1930 (as Strict Joy, 1931); Kings and the Moon, 1938. *Fiction*—The Crock of Gold, 1912; The Charwoman's Daughter (in America: Mary, Mary) 1912; Here Are Ladies (short stories) 1913; The Demi-Gods, 1914; Irish Fairy Tales (juvenile) 1920; Deirdre, 1923; In the Land of Youth, 1924; Etched in Moonlight (short stories) 1928. *Miscellaneous*—The Insurrection in Dublin, 1916; On Prose and Verse, 1928; Julia Elizabeth (play) 1929; English Romantic Poets (with E. L. Beck & R. H. Snow) 1933; English Poets, Victorian and Later (with E. L. Beck & R. H. Snow) 1934.

ABOUT: Arts and Decoration April 1925, Dial June 1927; English Journal May 1926; Fortnightly Review December 1938; Living Age April 15, 1927; London Mercury September 1925; Poetry December 1939; Revue des Deux Mondes September 1. 1937.

STEPHENS, ROBERT NEILSON (July 22, 1867-1906), American dramatist and writer of historical fiction, was born in New Bloomfield, a little town in central Pennsylvania, the son of James Andrew and Rebecca (Neilson) Stephens. The house was a stone's throw from the academy founded by his grandfather and conducted by his father. After the family moved to  Huntingdon on the Juniata River, the elder Stephens died, in Robert's ninth year. His mother supported the family by teaching school until Robert had gone through public high school and begun work at $3.50 a week in a bookstore connected with a stationery factory. Learning stenography, he found a position with the Pennsylvania Railroad in Philadelphia, and moved his mother and brother there. Soon he was on the staff of the *Philadelphia Press,* a "cradle of authors," and in a year became its dramatic critic. In 1893 he became general agent for a firm of theatrical managers and himself wrote melodramas: *On the Bowery* gave Steve Brodie, the man who jumped from Brooklyn Bridge, an opportunity to be heroic sixty-four times a week.

In September 1896 E. H. Sothern appeared in *An Enemy to the King,* concerning the adventures of a young French nobleman at the court of Henry III and on the field of Henry of Navarre, and Stephens' reputation as a writer of "cloak and sword" drama was made. Then L. C. Page, the Boston publisher, asked him to make a novel of the play; it became an instant best-seller on its appearance in 1897. *The Continental Dragoon,* a Revolutionary romance centering about Philipse Manor near Yonkers, N.Y. (later the home of Elsie Janis, the actress), repeated this success and was dramatized as *Miss Elizabeth's Prisoner,* starring William Faversham. *A Gentleman Player,* introducing Shakespeare in person, sold so well that Stephens was able to travel abroad and spend several months of intensive study in England in preparation for *Philip Winwood* and what is perhaps his best novel, *Captain Ravenshaw,* which was illustrated by Howard Pyle and several other artists. In a preface to the latter novel Stephens made an effective defense of the "neo-romantic" school which William Dean Howells had taken occasion to disparage.

Stephens frankly enjoyed his English success and his contacts with nobility and royalty. His personality was apparently an engaging one, suggestive of Robert Louis Stevenson's in more than his name and his struggle with early poverty and later ill-health. As a romancer, his charm, though faded, is still enjoyable.

PRINCIPAL WORKS: The Life and Adventures of Steve Brodie, B. J., 1894; An Enemy to the King, 1897; The Continental Dragoon, 1898; The Road to Paris, 1898; A Gentleman Player, 1899; Philip Winwood, 1900; Captain Ravenshaw, 1901; The Mystery of Murray Davenport, 1903; The Bright Face of Danger (sequel to An Enemy of the King) 1904; The Flight of Georgiana, 1905; Tales From Bohemia, 1908; A Soldier of Valley Forge (unfinished, completed by G. E. Theodore Roberts) 1911.

ABOUT: Robert Neilson Stephens: A Sketch; Starrett, V. Buried Caesars.

STERLING, GEORGE (December 1. 1869-November 17, 1926), American poet, was born in Sag Harbor, Long Island, N.Y.,

International Newsreel

the oldest son of Dr. George Ansel Sterling and Mary Parker (Havens) Sterling. When he was of high school age, his father became a Roman Catholic convert, and the family followed him, though George's conversion never went very deep or lasted long. It was because of this, however, that he was sent to St. Charles College, Ellicott City, Md., where the poet John Banister Tabb was professor of English. The story of Tabb's early interest in and encouragement of Sterling is a myth; Sterling at that time had written no poetry at all. Another myth is that he was trained as a priest; that was his father's intention, but actually he never finished college or went to a seminary. Instead, having seemingly no bent for any profession, he was sent to his mother's brother, a wealthy real estate operator in Oakland, Calif., as a clerk. The remainder of his life was associated with San Francisco, with brief residences in Oakland, Piedmont, and Carmel.

Sterling worked in his uncle's office from 1890 to 1905, very much against his will, until his aunt provided his "freedom money" and enabled him to buy land at Carmel, build a house there, and devote all his time to writing. The two great influences of his early years in California (and indeed of his entire life) were Ambrose Bierce and Jack London. Bierce was his master, and

in turn admired him extravagantly, with lamentable effects on Sterling's style. London made him for a while a semi-Socialist, and introduced him to the bohemian life. He began writing in the early 1890's, but his first volume, the magnificent *Testimony of the Suns* (one of the best things he ever wrote, though in later years he disliked and almost disowned it), did not appear until 1903. All Sterling's work until almost the end of his life was published in San Francisco and he was practically unknown in the East (though "A Wine of Wizardry" appeared, through Bierce's efforts, in the *Cosmopolitan Magazine*) at the same time that he was *the* poet of the West, compared extravagantly to Shakespeare and Euripides, Shelley and Poe.

In 1896 Sterling married Caroline Rand, and they lived together until 1912, when a scandal arising from one of his many extra-marital affairs wore out her forgiveness. Sterling went to New York the next year, and while he was there his wife committed suicide in Berkeley. He never remarried, though when he died one woman announced she had been engaged to him, and more than one still believes (and has publicly said) that she was the "great love" of his life.

Sterling was, as Idwal Jones called him, "San Francisco's last classic bohemian." In his last years he lived at the Bohemian Club, and wrote several of the "Grove Plays" for the summer "high jinks" at Bohemian Grove on the Russian River. It was at the club that he killed himself by poison shortly before his fifty-seventh birthday. The causes of his suicide were complicated, among them being failing powers both as a writer and a man, and his hopeless struggle with alcoholism of the periodic type.

With all his weaknesses, Sterling was one of the most lovable of men—generous, gentle, fanatically loyal. His Dantesque face, like a cameo, with the gray lock of hair falling over his forehead, his tall, thin, silently moving figure, his high-pitched voice, were so much a part of San Francisco that something of the old beloved city died with him. "It was like a unicorn dying," Idwal Jones, again, remarked.

Fantastically over-praised, and half-ruined by Bierce's rigid literary dogmas, Sterling nevertheless was an authentic lyric poet. His work is largely out-dated; it has the bombast and the purple patches of the *fin de siècle*, orotund and grandiose. But it had poignancy and delicacy too, and some of it at least will live.

PRINCIPAL WORKS: The Testimony of the Suns, 1903; A Wine of Wizardry, 1907; Bohemia (play) 1907; The House of Orchids, 1911; Beyond the Breakers, 1914; Ode on the Opening of the Panama-Pacific International Exposition, 1915; The Evanescent City, 1915; The Caged Eagle, 1916; Yosemite, 1916; The Binding of the Beast, 1917; Thirty-Five Sonnets, 1917; Twilight of the Kings (play) 1918; Lilith (play) 1919; Rosamund (play) 1920; Sails and Mirage, 1921; Selected Poems, 1923; Truth (play) 1923; Strange Waters, 1926; Robinson Jeffers (prose) 1926; Sonnets to Craig, 1928; Poems to Vera, 1938; After Sunset, 1939.

ABOUT: Bierce, A. Letters; de Ford, M. A. They Were San Franciscans; Holliday, R. C. Literary Lanes and Other Byways; Noel, J. Footloose in Arcadia; Stone, I. Sailor on Horseback; Untermeyer, L. American Poetry Since 1900; American Mercury May 1927; Bookman September 1927; Freeman August 15, 1923; Literary Digest December 11, 1926; Overland Monthly November and December 1927; Poetry March 1916, January 1927; Saturday Review of Literature July 27 and August 10, 1929.

STERN, GLADYS BRONWYN (June 17, 1890-), English novelist and short-story writer. who signs her books "G. B.

Stern," is the second daughter of Albert Stern and Elizabeth Stern. She attended Notting Hill High School, leaving at sixteen to travel in Germany and Switzerland with her parents. In her unconventional and kaleidoscopic autobiography, Monogram, Miss Stern mentions a Christmas at Montreux, "the second after we had sold our home in Ladbroke Road." A year later she was at a day school in Wiesbaden, living with her parents in a hotel there. Her education was "finished and given a lick and a high polish" at Montreux. "As a child, I think I may be said to have had naturally bad taste. And in adolescence, it went from bad to worse, perhaps influenced by the fashion of the period. For I had a strong pierrotic tendency. The period extended from about fourteen to twenty, and can be seen curling and uncurling all over my first novels, stories, and poems." Later Miss Stern "learned to reject a diet of satin and sequins." Her first play was written at seven, to be produced on the stage of the billiard room at home, and her first poem, written at seventeen, was accepted by the first editor to whom it was sent.

In 1919 she married Geoffrey Lisle Holdsworth, a New Zealander. Miss Stern's friend Noel Coward, whom she helped to select the nostalgic period-songs used in Cavalcade,

writes of this marriage in Present Indicative: "I repaid Geoffrey Holdsworth's good offices by changing the course of his life. I lent him G. B. Stern's books and also showed him some of her letters, whereupon he immediately wrote to her himself and a few months later married her. As they are now divorced, I will deny myself the pleasure of romantic digression and dissociate myself firmly from the whole affair."

In 1929 Mrs. Patrick Campbell played in a dramatization of G. B. Stern's first two "Matriarch" novels, Children of No Man's Land and Tents of Israel. The Matriarch, Mosaic, A Deputy Was King, and Shining and Free were later collected in an omnibus volume. "Maximilian Rakonitz was the name I gave one of my three uncles in those family chronicles, half truth, half invention, which I have written round the personality of my great-aunt, the Matriarch. I was not very deeply attached to the Matriarch. She was too despotic." The Matriarch's name in real life was Anastasia Schwabacher; she lived to be ninety. Miss Stern wrote another play, Debonair (1930), with the English actor Frank Vosper (who disappeared in mid-ocean some years later). The Man Who Pays the Piper, a play in a prologue and three acts, was produced at St. Martin's Theatre, London, in 1931.

Miss Stern has a "profound interest" in wine, wolf-dogs, talking, ping-pong, and collecting walking-sticks. "Motor-bikes and wasps make me angry and afraid; their resemblance is undeniable. Among my individual fears belongs an unreasoning fear of oculists and officials, police and the law and trespassing and the Mob and unpopularity. I suppose the Dreyfus case is my King Charles's Head."

Miss Stern is of Jewish stock; nearsighted; and usually wears her hair short. Her friends call her "Peter." She has lived in Cornwall, in Italy (for five years), and in New York and Hollywood. Her readers are always sure that she will give them expert, varied, and sophisticated entertainment. Her club is the Lansdowne. She enjoys boating and swimming. "Mountains are not my thing. The sea is my thing." Her apartment and many of her memorabilia were destroyed by a Nazi bomb in 1940.

PRINCIPAL WORKS: Pantomime, 1914; See-Saw, 1914; Grand Chain, 1917; A Marrying Man, 1918; Children of No Man's Land (U.S. title: Debatable Ground) 1919; Larry Munro (U.S. title: The China Shop) 1921; The Room, 1922; The Back Seat, 1923; Smoke Rings, 1923; Tents of Israel (U.S. title: The Matriarch: A Chronicle) 1924; Thunderstorm, 1925; A Deputy Was King, 1926; The Dark Gentleman, 1927; Bouquet, 1927;

Jack a' Manory (short stories) 1927; Debonair: The Story of Persephone, 1928; Petruchio, 1929; The Slower Judas (short stories) 1929; Mosaic, 1930; The Shortest Night, 1931; Long-Lost Father, 1932; Little Red Horses (U.S. title: The Rueful Mating) 1932; The Augs, 1933; Pelican Walking (short stories) 1934; Shining and Free, 1935; The Matriarch Chronicles (omnibus) 1936; Monogram (autobiography) 1936; Oleander River, 1937; The Ugly Dachshund, 1938; The Woman in the Hall, 1939; A Lion in the Garden, 1940; Another Part of the Forest (autobiography) 1941; The Young Matriarch, 1942.

ABOUT: Coward, N. Present Indicative; Stern, G. B. Monogram, Another Part of the Forest.

STERNE, Mrs. EMMA (GELDERS)
(May 13, 1894-), American historical novelist and writer for children, writes: "I

Bachrach

was born and grew up in Birmingham, Ala., in the days when it was still young enough to feel some surprise in being a city at all. The first two years of my life were spent in the Opera House Hotel, connected with the town's only theatre; my first memory was of being held up for a sight of a corner of the stage. Then we moved out to the edge of the city, almost to the top of Red Mountain, where I picked blackberries and rode horseback with my father. I was always a voracious reader and soon learned to read my way through the stacks of the public library, from which (on the top floor of the City Hall) I could see the city jail. I have a strong interest in the problems of social welfare; I was an ardent suffrage worker, and my first job was a column in a Birmingham paper conducted to advance the interest of women in politics. I started a school for delinquent children under the just-created juvenile court in 1917; it has long been incorporated into the regular system of the state. I married a few months after graduating from Smith College, in 1916, and a year later my husband, Roy M. Sterne, our infant daughter, and I moved to New York City, where my husband is now general counsel of a large drug company.

"I had always intended to write, and had served in an editorial capacity on the literary magazines both in high school and at Smith College. When my second daughter was born we moved to Pelham, N.Y. I came in occasionally to Columbia and took a few graduate courses in English and philosophy. I began making my first garden and sold my first story in the same week in May

1923. From that time on the pattern of my life has been pretty steadily the same. I garden and write children's books and dive sporadically into civic reform. I write now for a variety of ages in a variety of form, but almost always on subjects of historical background, and always looking through the windows of research on some bright far-off corner of the scene of action. I also write children's plays, one of which won a $500 prize in 1931. I still think I am a better critic than I am a writer, and as a critic I don't think much of my writing. But I love to do research, and in an unscholarly, essentially feminine sort of way I am pretty good at it. We have now moved to Wilton, Conn. and have turned farmers.

"In politics I am a left-wing New Dealer and internationalist. That is, my radical friends call me (sneeringly) a liberal, and my conservative relations and friends, including my publishers, think I wear a red shirt. I am working now on a book based on the Amistad case of 1840."

PRINCIPAL WORKS: White Swallow, 1927; Blue Pigeons, 1929; Loud Sing Cuckoo, 1930; No Surrender, 1932; Amarantha Gay, M. D., 1933; The Calico Ball, 1934; Drums of Monmouth, 1935; Far Town Road, 1935; Miranda Is a Princess, 1936; Some Plant Olive Trees, 1937; European Summer (non-fiction) 1938; The Pirate of Chatham Square, 1939; America Was Like This, 1941.

STEVENS, JAMES FLOYD (November 25, 1892-), American writer of folk stories, writes: "This life of mine appeared

with the customary gulp and howl, to add to the gayety of a rocky rented farm in Monroe County, Iowa. There it grew on lean sustenance for four years. Its one important adventure, said its elders, was a runaway that ended in a pigsty-

and a nick-of-time rescue from the jaws of a brood sow. Brothers and sisters it had none. There was a gypsy father who felt free to go a-roving to far places, and did so. A mother who worked as a hired girl for $12 a month. A grandmother with a widow's pension of $8 a month. On this joint income the three moved to a little town in Appanoose County, and there they lived for six more years.

"This life, in the shape of a ten-year-old boy, was then sent out alone to relatives in Idaho. For most of five more years it grew on a dry-land homestead, learning to handle horses and cattle, learning a little from books in school. At fifteen in struck out on a man's way in the world.

"The West was a great country those times, for a willing worker, and these hands were willing and not unskilled. For nine years they did hard work on many jobs throughout the states west of the Mississippi, mostly in handling horses and mules on construction projects of large scale, and in forest industry. Then it was war, and a year and a half in France as a sergeant of infantry for this one. Back to the woods, to the camps and mills, and to much study of books in off-hours and much thinking of books and the writing of them, when on the job.

"In November 1923, Mr. Mencken of Baltimore received a letter from an admirer of long standing. The writer described himself as a Western hobo laborer with wistful literary yearnings. Mr. Mencken's reply was three bombshells: (1) 'You write well." (2) 'Your experiences must have filled you with capital material.' (3) 'Why not try an article for the *American Mercury?*' The article was tried, successfully. Another was invited. A story on Paul Bunyan, mythical giant of the big timber, was attempted. It followed the method of Homer, who translated the folklore of his land and time into literary terms, and it rejected the method of the professors who demand stenographic transcriptions of folklore. The story became a book of stories which has sold more than 75,000 copies. So the hobo laborer became an author. A life designed for other pursuits had to toil hard to produce with words. It has pounded and sweated out five more books, and another, *American Psalm*, is in preparation. Articles and stories made into words from the stuff of this life have been included in twenty-two anthologies and textbooks.

"At present I am public relations man for the West Coast Lumbermen's Association, in Seattle. I much prefer this to producing literary trade goods as a means of making a living. I was married to Theresa Seitz Fitzgerald in 1929. We have no children, but my wife's niece makes her home with us. No enthusiast on anything, I do approve America and the Democratic Party. My favorite people are foresters. I am glad of all my life, and I like the present part of it best of all."

PRINCIPAL WORKS: Paul Bunyan, 1925; Brawnyman, 1926; Mattock, 1927; Homer in the Sagebrush, 1928; The Saginaw Paul Bunyan, 1932; Timber—Down the Hill, 1935; Timber! The Way of Life in the Lumber Camps, 1942.

ABOUT: American Mercury April 1933; Scholastic February 20, 1937; Sunset Magazine May 1929.

*STEVENS, WALLACE (October 2, 1879-), American poet, was born in Reading, Pa., the son of Garrett Barckalow Stevens and Mary Catherine (Zeller) Stevens. He was a student at Harvard from 1897 to 1900, contributing occasionally to the *Harvard Advocate*, then attended New York Law School. In 1904 he was admitted to the U.S. bar, engaged in the general practice of law at New York City, and has been associated with the Hartford (Conn.) Accident and Indemnity Co. since 1916, starting in the legal department. In 1934 he became vice president of the firm. His office address is 690 Asylum Avenue, Hartford. Stevens is married, and has a daughter, Holly Bright Stevens.

Harriet Monroe was making up the November 1914 number of *Poetry*, a special War Number, including thirteen poems selected from more than seven hundred and thirty submitted for a $100 prize, when a half-dozen arrived from Wallace Stevens, then a name unknown to her. She tore the make-up apart to make room for two pages of *Phases*, four poems. Late in 1915 *Poetry* awarded another $100 prize to Stevens' *Three Travellers Watch a Sunrise*, a one-act play in free verse which was produced at the Provincetown Theatre, New York, in 1920. *Carlos Among the Candles*, another one-act play, was first produced in Milwaukee, then at the Neighborhood Playhouse, New York City. Stevens does not include these in his books. His first, *Harmonium*, was not published until 1923; Carl Van Vechten had persuaded Alfred Knopf to issue it.

Stevens had been in no hurry to publish a book, remarking that "a book of poems is a damned serious affair." His poem, "Peter Quince at the Clavier," had appeared in several anthologies, and he was also represented in *Others: An Anthology of the New Verse*, published in 1916. *Harmonium* sold only a hundred copies before it was remaindered. It contained one of Stevens' best-known poems, "The Comedian As the Letter C," a lengthy narrative poem, which Paul Rosenfeld describes as containing "the history of a poetic career, the feeling of war, the hope of a national expression, the tragedy of environment; but it secretes them behind a shimmer of language and archness piled upon archness." Stevens has been called a critics' poet, "a dandy of eloquence" (the *Dial*), "the most finished poet of his age" (Allen Tate). His succes-

* Died August 2, 1955.

sion of glittering images reminded Van Wyck Brooks of the shattered fragments of a stained-glass window. Delmore Schwartz, in the Wallace Stevens Number of the *Harvard Advocate* issued in December 1940, points out that Stevens does not write dramatic poetry, or include human beings in his verse. "We are presented almost always with the poet, or the protagonist of the poem, in isolation before the tableaux of Nature and Society, meditating upon them."

Some of his later poems caused Harriet Monroe to fear that his delight in beauty and oddity had been shaken by the clamor and confusion of the modern scene. "Taken generally, Stevens' perspective is that of the man of art, the museum- and concert-goer, the student of French poetry . . . , the aesthete in the best sense of the word," writes Schwartz. Arthur Davison Ficke describes the poet as "a big, slightly fat, awfully competent-looking man. You expect him to roar, but when he speaks there emerges the gravest, softest, most subtly modulated voice I've ever heard—a voice on tiptoe at dawn!" His handwriting is minute.

PRINCIPAL WORKS: Harmonium, 1923; Ideas of Order, 1936; Owl's Clover, 1936; The Man With the Blue Guitar, 1937; Parts of a World, 1942.

ABOUT: Kreymborg, A. Our Singing Strength, Troubadour; Monroe, H. A Poet's Life; Munson, G. B. Destinations; Rosenfeld, P. Men Seen; Schwartz, D. The Imitation of Life; Untermeyer, L. Modern American Poetry; Harvard Advocate (Wallace Stevens Number) December 1940.

STEVENSON, BURTON EGBERT (November 9, 1872-), American librarian, anthologist, and novelist, writes: "Born at

Chillicothe, Ohio; went through high school there. Carried newspapers as a boy and set up own printing office at age of twelve, starting a monthly amateur paper, and continued publishing it until departure for Princeton in 1890. At Princeton paid own way first by setting type in a local printing office and afterwards as correspondent for the New York *Tribune* and the United Press. Was on the board of the *Tiger,* the college humorous weekly. Never did anything but write and never wanted to. While back in Chillicothe at close of junior year was offered a newspaper position and accepted it, not returning to college. Married Elizabeth Shepherd Butler in 1895.

"In 1899 Stevenson was elected librarian of the local library, and has held the position ever since, with long leaves of absence from time to time. For the first time had the leisure to do some serious literary work, and first book published in 1900. One or two every year after that. Many times abroad. He was at Monte Carlo when the present war broke out, but managed to catch the last boat home. Several of his novels use the Riviera as a background.

"In the spring of 1917, the government began to build Camp Sherman just on the outskirts of Chillicothe, and Stevenson made a state-wide appeal for books and set up libraries in all the recreation huts. In the fall the American Library Association took over the work and appointed Stevenson camp librarian. Many of the librarians assigned to other camps were detailed for a training course at Camp Sherman. Called to Washington to manage the publicity campaign for the nation-wide appeal for books and then sent to Paris to act as European director for the Library War Service. Remained in charge until 1920, during which time over two million books and countless thousands of magazines were circulated. In 1918 established the American Library in Paris, to act as a center of information about the United States. Returned to Chillicothe in 1920 but was called back to Paris in 1926 to act as director of the library, holding this position until 1930, doubling the library's collections and tripling its resources.

"Since 1937 has been engaged in the compilation of a dictionary of proverbs and proverbial phrases."

* * *

Mr. Stevenson modestly omits several of the achievements for which he is best known. His "Home Books" of verse and quotations have long been standard in libraries everywhere. Surprisingly, he has also been a writer of top-flight detective stories over a period of almost forty years. Relatively few readers, perhaps, have realized that the writer of mysteries and the anthologist and the director of the American Library in Paris are one and the same person.

PRINCIPAL WORKS: At Odds With the Regent, 1900; A Soldier of Virginia, 1901; The Heritage, 1902; Tommy Remington's Battle, 1902; The Holladay Case, 1903; Cadets of Gascony, 1904; The Marathon Mystery, 1904; The Young Section Hand, 1905; The Girl With the Blue Sailor, 1906; Affairs of State, 1906; The Young Train-Dispatcher, 1907; That Affair at Elizabeth, 1907; The Quest For the Rose of Sharon, 1909; The Young Train Master, 1909; The Path of Honor, 1910; The Spell of Holland, 1911; Mystery of the

Boule Cabinet, 1912; The Young Apprentice, 1912; The Gloved Hand, 1913; The Destroyer, 1913; The Charm of Ireland, 1914; Little Comrade, 1915; A King in Babylon, 1917; The Girl From Alsace, 1918; The Kingmakers, 1922; Famous Single Poems, 1923 (enlarged and revised 1935); The Storm Center, 1924; The Coast of Enchantment, 1926; The House Next Door, 1932; Villa Aurelia, 1932; The Red Carnation (in England: Death Wears a Carnation) 1939. *Edited*—Days and Deeds (verse, 1906, prose, 1907); Poems of American History, 1908; A Child's Guide to American Biography, 1909; Home Book of Verse, 1912; Home Book of Verse For Young Folks, 1915; Home Book of Modern Verse, 1925; My Country, 1932; American History in Verse For Boys and Girls, 1933; Great Americans As Seen by the Poets, 1933; Home Book of Quotations, Classical and Modern 1934 (revised and enlarged, 1937); Home Book of Shakespeare Quotations, 1937.

ABOUT: Library Journal October 1, 1930; Princeton Alumni Weekly September 24, 1937; School and Society March 1, 1930.

STEVENSON, DOROTHY E. (1892-),

Scottish novelist, writes: "I was born at Edinburgh and brought up in that city and at North Berwick.

My father, David Alan Stevenson, was civil engineer to the Northern Lighthouse Board and a first cousin of Robert Louis Stevenson. My mother was a first cousin of Earl Roberts of Kandahar. I learned to play golf at North Berwick at the age of four and afterwards took part in various championships. I started my literary career at the age of six, but, as my family did not approve of my 'wasting my time writing stories,' I was obliged to hide in an attic when I wanted to write. Naturally, this circumstance whetted my interest and encouraged me to further flights of fancy. I have always been deeply interested in the historical associations of Edinburgh, but even more interested in the lives of the people in bygone years.

"In 1916 I married Major James R. Peploe of the Highland Light Infantry. My family consists of two sons and one daughter. My elder son is a Captain in the Royal Artillery and my daughter is serving in the War Relief Nursing Service. I followed the drum for years and gained a good deal of valuable experience meeting people of all kinds.

"I am now settled at Moffat, a small town in beautiful Annandale in the county of Dumfries. It is a peaceful spot and a marvellous place for writing. I enjoy a good walk over the hills with my spaniel, and then come home to find tea waiting, spread on a table before a bright log fire.

"My favorite author is Jane Austen. My favorite occupations are reading, writing, and talking to my friends. I am fond of golf, skating, swimming, and fishing. I dislike proof-reading and housekeeping.

"My books are all novels, as it is the human element which interests me most in life: some of my books are light and amusing and others are serious studies of character, but they are all human and carefully thought out, and perhaps it is for these two reasons that my public is so diverse, and ranges from university professors to old ladies and small boys! My books are published in all English-speaking countries and have been translated into several foreign languages. I have done a good deal of lecturing—chiefly on literary subjects. I am a member of the R.L.S. Club, and of several literary societies in the United States. I have been invited to lecture in the United States, and am looking forward to doing so after the war. As for the war [written 1941], it takes a great deal to rouse the ordinary people in this country—but now we are roused! Everyone here is simply furious and eager and willing to fight the Germans with their own hands. I don't think any of us are frightened—at least I have not met anyone who is—we are all angry and very determined."

* * *

The only book Miss Stevenson has published which is not a novel is a volume of verse for children. Her best known novels are those about "Mrs. Tim," reflecting her own experiences as an army officer's wife, and those about "Miss Buncle," who wrote a book about her own village and then married her publisher. One critic remarked that "her books have a sanity and balance not too common in modern fiction."

PRINCIPAL WORKS: Peter West, 1929; Mrs. Tim of the Regiment: Leaves From the Diary of an Officer's Wife, 1932; Miss Buncle's Book, 1934; Golden Days, 1934; Divorce From Reality (in America: Miss Dean's Dilemma) 1935; Smouldering Fire, 1935; A World in Spell (in America: Empty World) 1936; Miss Buncle Married, 1936; The Story of Rosabelle Shaw, 1937; The Baker's Daughter, 1938; The Green Money, 1939; Alister and Co (verse) 1940; The English Air, 1940; Rochester's Wife, 1940; Mrs. Tim Carries On, 1941; Spring Magic, 1941.

*STEWART, ALFRED WALTER

(1880-), English university professor and writer of detective fiction under the pseudonym "J. J. Connington," is the youngest son

* Died July 1, 1947.

of Professor William Stewart, D.D., LL.D., former Dean of Faculties in Glasgow University. He was educated at the Universities of Glasgow and Marburg, and at University College, London.

In 1901 Stewart was Mackay-Smith Scholar at Queen's University, Belfast, Ireland; 1851 Exhibition Scholar from 1903 to 1905; and for the next three years Carnegie Research Fellow there. In 1909 he became lecturer on organic chemistry, having published *Stereochemistry* (1907) and *Recent Advances in Organic Chemistry* (1908), the latter of which has gone through half-a-dozen editions. In 1914, year of the outbreak of the First World War, Stewart returned to the University of Glasgow to lecture on physical chemistry and radioactivity for five years, when he became professor of chemistry at Queen's University, a post he still holds. Stewart's *Some Physico-Chemical Themes* appeared in 1922, and next year came the first "J.J. Connington" piece of fiction, *Nordenholt's Million*. *Almighty Gold* came along the next year, and then two novels of detection, *Death at Swaythling Court* and *The Dangerfield Talisman*, both in 1926. *Murder in the Maze* (1927), concerning the double murder of twin brothers by a particularly crafty and elusive assassin, was distinguished by the presence of Connington's titled but human detective, Sir Clinton Driffield, and remains one of the best of the several in which the Inspector appears. A second detective created by this author is Mark Brand, otherwise known as "The Counsellor." An omnibus volume published in 1930 included *The Two Tickets Puzzle*, *Mystery at Lynden Sands*, *The Case With Nine Solutions* (the most noteworthy of this quartette), and *Nemesis at Raynham Parva*. The popularity of some of the earlier titles has put them in the Penguin edition. Later novels have appeared in Hodder's Yellow Jacket Series. *The Eye in the Museum* (1929) is perhaps the only one which would pointedly suggest its author's scientific and academic background. (Its focal point is a "Camera obscura," a fascinating device which might be expected to attract the attention of other writers of this type of fiction, but apparently this is the only use which has been made.) "J. J. Connington is a careful and skilled craftsman," writes Dorothy Sayers, and one bibliographer of detective fiction refers to "this always intelligent and resourceful writer."

PRINCIPAL WORKS: Stereochemistry, 1907; Recent Advances in Organic Chemistry, 1908; Chemistry and Its Borderland, 1914; Recent Advances in Physical and Organic Chemistry, 1919; Some Physico-Chemical Themes. *As "J. J. Connington"*—Nordenholt's Million, 1923; Almighty Gold, 1924; Death at Swaythling Court, 1926; The Dangerfield Talisman, 1926; Tragedy at Ravensthorpe, 1927; Murder in the Maze, 1927; Mystery at Lynden Sands, 1928; The Case With Nine Solutions, 1928; Grim Vengeance, 1929; Nemesis at Raynham Parva, 1929; The Eye in the Museum, 1929; The Two Ticket Puzzle, 1930; The Boathouse Riddle, 1931; The Sweepstake Murders, 1931; The Castleford Conundrum, 1932; Tom Tiddler's Island (U.S. title: Gold Brick Island) 1933; The Ha-ha Case (U.S. title: The Brandon Case) 1934; In Whose Dim Shadow (U.S. title: The Tau Cross Mystery) 1935; A Minor Operation, 1937; For Murder Will Speak (U.S. title: Murder Will Speak) 1938; Truth Comes Limping, 1938; The Counsellor, 1939; Four Defences, 1940; The Twenty-One Clues, 1941; No Past Is Dead, 1942.

ABOUT: Thomson, H. D. Masters of Mystery.

STEWART, DONALD OGDEN (November 30, 1894-), American humorist, playwright, and actor, was born in Columbus, Ohio, the son of Gilbert Holland Stewart and Clara Landon (Ogden) Stewart. "In his early years," Mr. Stewart himself has confided, "he gave manifold evidences of his gift for humor, and many of his bright childhood remarks are still  related by his proud mother upon the slightest provocation, or in fact, upon no provocation at all. There were others, however—principally among the guests at the hotel where Donald lived—who did not think that this child prodigy was so funny. Mr. Stewart bears a long red scar on his head—such as might be made by a brick or other missile—as mute evidence of one little red-headed girl's particular lack of appreciation of his early humorous efforts. At the age of 14 he was sent to the Phillips Exeter Academy because it was a good preparatory school for Harvard. In the fall of 1912, Mr. Stewart entered Yale. While at New Haven, Mr. Stewart went out for all the athletic teams possible"—generally third and fourth teams where he worked without reward.

After graduation in 1916, he went to work with "a certain large public service corporation" which sent him to its Birmingham (Ala.) office. From here he went to Pittsburgh, thence to Chicago for ten months. He was an instructor in navigation, naval ordnance, and signals in the Navy during the First World War. In the spring of

1918 he returned to work, in Minneapolis this time, where he read Wells, Havelock Ellis, and H. L. Mencken, met Scott Fitzgerald, and led two cotillions. After a year in Dayton, Ohio, with a financial organization, "he read the first volume of the Alexander Hamilton business course, after which he decided that he wanted to go in for literature. In January 1921 Mr. Stewart came to New York City to find a job (literary if possible). The idea for the *Parody Outline of History* came to Mr. Stewart in March, while hearing Mr. Mengelberg conduct the National Orchestra in the Pathétique Symphony." He then went to Paris, a place which "he found indeed very pleasant but not for work. So after a brief period of recuperation he journeyed to Vienna where he grew a splendid red beard and wrote *Perfect Behavior*"—an hilarious burlesque of the Emily Post school of manuals of etiquette.

In Capri Stewart wrote *Aunt Polly's Story of Mankind* (1923) and next transmuted his European findings into *Mr. and Mrs. Haddock Abroad*, concerning the adventures of a typically American middle-aged couple and their *enfant terrible* daughter, Mildred. Later the Haddocks journeyed to "Paris, France."

In 1926 Stewart married Beatrice Ames at Santa Barbara, Calif.; two sons were born, Ames Ogden and Donald Ogden, Jr. The Stewarts appeared in person in his comedy, *Rebound,* a play in the Philip Barry *genre* which ran in New York from November 1928 to June 1929, and then went on the road. They were divorced in September 1938, and the next March Stewart married Mrs. Ella Winter Steffens, widow of the writer Lincoln Steffens. Their home is in Carmel, Calif. In recent years Mr. Stewart has turned from a humorist to a fighting liberal and has devoted much of his energies to social and political causes, particularly in support of Loyalist Spain and in defense of civil liberties in this country. He is an ex-president of the League of American Writers and edited *Fighting Words*, a report of the League's 1939 congress.

Although he has not published an original book in a decade, Mr. Stewart writes extensively for the talking pictures. His books of humor are still excellent source-books for the light-hearted, prosperous era which gave them birth. He is tall, bald, and very near-sighted.

PRINCIPAL WORKS: A Parody Outline of History, 1921; Perfect Behavior, 1922; Aunt Polly's Story of Mankind, 1923; Mr. and Mrs. Haddock Abroad, 1924; The Crazy Fool, 1925; Mr. and

Mrs. Haddock in Paris, France, 1926; Father William, 1929; Rebound (play) 1930. Editor—Fighting Words, 1940.

ABOUT: Overton, G. M. American Nights Entertainment, Authors of the Day, When Winter Comes to Main Street.

STEWART, JOHN INNES MACKINTOSH (September 30, 1906-), Scottish detective story writer whose pseudonym is "Michael Innes,"
writes: "I was born just outside Edinburgh and almost within the shadow of the centenary monument to the author of *Waverley*. Edinburgh Academy, where I went to school, had Scott as one of its founders, and Robert
Louis Stevenson was a pupil there for a short time. My headmaster told me that one day I might write a *Kidnapped* or a *Treasure Island;* I remember his tone as one of mild censure and suppose he didn't greatly care for romances. I devoured them and no doubt they colored my mind. But the books that chiefly impressed me as a boy were Christian de Wet's *Three Years' War*, Swinburne's *Atalanta in Calydon,* and the plays and prefaces of Bernard Shaw. Since then I have come to realize that Homer, Dante, and Shakespeare are the world's most satisfactory writers. But I don't get from them quite the electrical effect of those early books.

"At Oxford I had a great Elizabethan scholar as my tutor; he got me a first class in English and then I went to Vienna for a year to recover. After that I had the good luck to fall in with Francis Meynell, and for him I edited the Nonesuch Edition of Florio's *Montaigne;* this in turn got me a job as a lecturer in the University of Leeds. I was recommended to two excellent lodgings by the professors who appointed me; in the one there was already a lodger, a young woman; in the other not. I made the natural choice and a year later the young woman and I were married. My wife is a doctor and although we have three small sons still finds time for infant welfare work.

"Leeds lasted five years and then, when I had sold all my Nonesuch books and was rather wondering about the rent, I was invited to become professor of English at Adelaide University. It was on the way out that I wrote my first mystery story. For nine months of the year, and between six and eight o'clock in the morning, the South

Australian climate is just right for authorship of this sort, so I have written a good many similar stories since. I would describe some of them as on the frontier between the detective story and fantasy; they have a somewhat 'literary' flavor but their values remain those of melodrama and not of fiction proper. Sometimes I lie on the beach in the sun and wonder if I mightn't some day write something else."

* * *

Detective stories by "Michael Innes" are distinctly for the more literate devotees of this *genre*. As the *Saturday Review of Literature* has remarked, they are "caviar to the general reader, but the caviar is of the very best grade, with every bead a pearl." John Strachey has pronounced "Innes" (together with Margery Allingham and "Nicholas Blake")*qqv* one of the three "white hopes" of the English detective novel today. Sometimes, it must be admitted, his erudition makes for dullness; on the other hand, he has pages of a brilliance seldom found in escape literature. His most widely acclaimed novel to date is *Lament for a Maker,* an admirable *tour de force* which is really a paraphrase of Wilkie Collins' *Moonstone,* set against a rich Scottish background. In person, "Michael Innes" is a mild, bespectacled, studious-appearing young man, whose photograph will inescapably remind detective story *aficionados* of Margery Allingham's hero Albert Campion. He is a happy discovery for readers sated with the "sameness" of routine crime fiction.

PRINCIPAL WORKS: *As John I. M. Stewart*— Montaigne's Essays: John Florio's Translation (ed.) 1931; George Chapman: An Essay and a Selection (with H. Ellis) 1933. *As "Michael Innes"*—Seven Suspects, 1936; Hamlet, Revenge! 1937; Lament for a Maker, 1938; The Spider Strikes, 1939; A Comedy of Terrors, 1940; The Secret Vanguard, 1941; Appleby on Ararat, 1941.

ABOUT: Haycraft, H. Murder for Pleasure: The Life and Times of the Detective Story; Saturday Review of Literature January 7, November 11, 1939.

STICKNEY, TRUMBULL (June 20, 1874-October 11, 1904), American poet, was born Joseph Trumbull Stickney in Geneva, and lived in Switzerland and Italy until his family brought him to the United States at the age of five. His father was Professor Austin Stickney, who headed the Latin department at Trinity College; his mother, Harriet Champion (Trumbull) Stickney, was a lineal descendant of Jonathan Trumbull, governor of Connecticut. But his parents lived for many years abroad, and the greater part of Trumbull

Stickney's childhood was spent in Europe. Except for a year at school in Clevedon, England, and another at Dr. Cutler's School in New York, his father was his only teacher until he entered Harvard. He received his B.A. in 1895, and went at once to Paris, where for seven years he studied Greek and Sanskrit at the Sorbonne. He was the first American ever to receive its D. ès L. degree (1903). After three months in Greece, he came back to Harvard as an instructor in Greek. He had already published one volume of poems, and was working on another, as well as on a translation of the *Persians* of Æschylus and a part in a projected performance of *The Libation Pourers.* He had high ambitions and appeared to have all the world before him. Instead, a brain tumor killed him at thirty.

The next year his friends William Vaughan Moody and George Cabot Lodge (also a poet doomed to die young) edited a volume of his lyrics, since the collection had been left uncompleted by its author. This and his first volume of dramatic verses, ranging in subject from Prometheus to Cellini, are all the published work of Trumbull Stickney. There is always a false pathos in poets cut off in their first flower, but critics as astute as Van Wyck Brooks and Edmund Wilson have hailed Stickney as a writer of performance as well as of promise.

As Moody described him, very tall, slender and graceful, with a beautiful voice, shy but affectionate among his close friends, melancholy by nature but full of humor, he seems a sort of epitome of the youthful poet. But he was besides a true scholar, and he was a genuine musician and rather better than an amateur violinist. Shane Leslie recalled his "beautiful gray eyes and sad bewildered face." He himself said: "The truth is, I care for nothing but poetry." Moody said "he dreamed of making in his own poetry [a] new synthesis of Eastern and Western thought." The influence of Poe and Swinburne was strong on his work, and its rhythms were often dictated by Richard Wagner. Henry Adams, in his sardonic way, called him "a conservative Christian anarchist."

R. P. Blackmur has treated him rather harshly: "He hovered . . . constantly on the perilous balance where it is determined whether a man write sound verse or dilute his emotions in words . . . Stickney was obviously unaware of the difference, in his own work, between creative observation and dead observation. In his mind both were alive. . . . He had not taught his verse to make demands of him, and in his turn he demanded little of his verse. . . . His most successful verses are where no personal feeling was involved and no adolescent stultification could come about." But he conceded to Stickney "sudden, desperately illuminating phrases." It is doubtless with these—and a handful of really distinguished complete poems—in mind that Wilson said he was free of the "false felicity" and the "peculiar aridities of the aesthetic American of the '90s"; that he had "spareness and simplicity of language" which carried "a charge of meaning."

PRINCIPAL WORKS: Dramatic Verses, 1902; The Poems of Trumbull Stickney (ed. by G. C. Lodge, W. V. Moody, & J. E. Lodge) 1905.

ABOUT: Brooks, Van W. New England: Indian Summer; New Republic October 14, 1940; North American Review November 16, 1906; Poetry June 1933.

STILL, JAMES (July 16, 1906-   ), American poet and novelist, writes: "I was born at Double Creek, among Alabama's red hills, one of ten children.

The Stills came from England; my mother's people, the Lindseys, were Scotch-Irish. My ancestors fought in the American Revolution and in the War of 1812; my grandfathers were Confederate soldiers. My father is a veterinarian. As a boy I expected to follow him in this profession, often sitting up all night in barn lots attending sick horses. At seventeen I went away to a mountain school near Cumberland Gap, Tenn. I worked in a rock quarry to pay expenses. Later I attended Vanderbilt University (M.A.) and the University of Illinois Library School (B.S. in L.S.). For six years I was librarian of the Hindman Settlement School at the forks of Troublesome Creek in the Kentucky Mountains. Along with other duties I conducted a library-on-foot, delivering books in a carton on my shoulder to one-room schools, walking fifteen to eighteen miles a day.

"My first poem appeared in the *Virginia Quarterly Review* in 1935, my first short story in the *Atlantic Monthly* the next year. Taking time off to complete my first novel, I went to live two miles from a highway in an old log house on Dead Mare Branch of Little Carr Creek [Ky.]. I completed the novel, but didn't return to the Settlement. The log house is now my home. I cultivate

a garden, a vineyard; I farm a bit; I can play a few ballads on the dulcimer."

* * *

Mr. Still received a Publishers' Fellowship for the Bread Loaf Writers' Conference in 1937, and a Guggenheim Award in 1941. In 1939 his story, "Bat Flight," won second prize in the O. Henry Memorial Volume, and in 1940 he shared honors with Thomas Wolfe in the Southern Authors' Award for "the best novel published about the South by a Southerner." He is unmarried.

PRINCIPAL WORKS: Hounds on the Mountain (poems) 1937; River of Earth (novel) 1940; On Troublesome Creek (short stories) 1941.

ABOUT: Poetry March 1938; Scholastic September 18, 1937.

STOCKTON, FRANK RICHARD. See "AMERICAN AUTHORS: 1600-1900"

STODDARD, RICHARD HENRY. See "AMERICAN AUTHORS: 1600-1900"

STOKER, BRAM (1847-April 20, 1912), British novelist and miscellaneous writer, best remembered as the author of *Dracula*, was born Abraham Stoker in Dublin, the second son of Abraham and Charlotte Matilda Blake Thornley Stoker. He had a sickly childhood, being unable to stand upright until the age of seven. Stoker's illness, he said later, made him thoughtful.

(The thoughts of youth, in this case, were such long, long thoughts that they led to the writing of *Dracula*, probably the most bloodcurdling horror story in the language, when he was fifty.) This invalidism Stoker outgrew so thoroughly that he was the athletic champion of Dublin University, particularly in football, in his twentieth year, and had great physical strength for the rest of his life, which included twenty-seven strenuous years as Sir Henry Irving's manager. At Dublin he was also auditor of the Historical Society, which is equivalent to the presidency of the Cambridge or Oxford Union; president of the Philosophical Society; and the recipient of medals and certificates in history, composition, and oratory, as well as honors in pure mathematics.

Ten dreary years as an Irish civil servant at Dublin Castle, from twenty to thirty, resulted in his first work, *The Duties of Clerks of Petty Sessions*. For five years, from November 1871, he was unpaid dramatic critic of the Dublin *Mail*. He had other experiences as newspaper editor, journalist, and short-story writer, and was a barrister of the Inner Temple. Stoker's first view of Henry Irving's acting made him Irving's willing slave, and the attraction proved mutual. On December 9, 1878, at Birmingham, Stoker became the great actor's acting manager, a post he retained till Irving's death. In this capacity he wrote about fifty letters a day, and estimated that he wrote half a million in all during his connection with Irving. Stoker accompanied Irving on his American tours and discovered that the British public's lack of knowledge of American life was abysmal. A series of lectures was worked up into a pamphlet, *A Glimpse of America*, which caused H. M. Stanley, the African explorer, to tell Stoker that he should write. After Irving's death in 1905, Stoker was associated with the literary staff of the London *Telegraph* and was manager for David Bispham's opera *The Vicar of Wakefield*.

Dracula, published in 1897, combined vampirism, lycanthropy, hypnotism, and the unquiet dead into one horrendous and peculiarly enthralling whole. Dramatized, with Bela Lugosi as the blood-sucking Hungarian Count Dracula (William Tilden, the American tennis champion also essayed the rôle) it gave a fillip to the jaded tastes of pre-depression America, and a skilfully contrived talking picture version led to a host of imitations. Stoker never equaled the success of this *tour de force,* though *The Jewel of Seven Stars* (dedicated, by the way, to Elinor Wylie, the American poet, then Elinor Hoyt, and to her sister, young visitors to London) deserves favorable notice. His *Famous Impostors* is a treasure-house of interesting material. A quarter-century after Stoker's death, *Dracula's Guest* appeared, a previously unpublished and vastly inferior section of the earlier work.

PRINCIPAL WORKS: The Snake's Pass, 1890; Dracula, 1897; The Mystery of the Sea, 1902; The Jewel of Seven Stars, 1904; Personal Reminiscences of Henry Irving, 1906; The Lady of the Shroud; 1909; Famous Impostors, 1910; The Lair of the White Worm, 1911; Dracula's Guest, 1937.

ABOUT: Scarborough, D. The Supernatural in Modern English Fiction; Stoker, B. Personal Reminiscences of Henry Irving; Terry, E. The Story of My Life; Wyndham, H. The Nineteen Hundreds.

STONE, Mrs. GRACE ZARING (January 9, 1896-), American novelist, writes:
"Born in New York City. Educated under private tutors, and at the Sacred Heart Convents of Paris and New York. Traveled extensively in Europe, Asia, and the South Seas. In the Great War, served with the British Red Cross in England. In 1917 I married Ellis S. Stone, an officer in the United States Navy, now with the rank of captain and serving as the American Naval Attaché in Paris [February, 1940]. First book was written after two years in the West Indies; the second was the result of years in China. Numerous short stories in magazines. Have one daughter, now Baroness Perényi, of Budapest. My principal interest apart from writing is music. Since the beginning of the present war, am volunteer worker of American Hospital, Paris. It might be of interest to add that my great grandfather was Robert Owen."

* * *

Mrs. Stone originally intended music to be her career, and was also a student of the famous Duncan School of dancing in Paris. She is tall and slender, with dark curly hair and hazel eyes. She returned to America after the Germans occupied France.

Her writing is expert, "beautifully restrained, yet dramatic." But reviewers complained of her early work that it was cold and that her aloofness and lack of feeling for her characters "robs her work of conviction." *The Bitter Tea of General Yen* was made into a successful motion picture.

In 1942 *Town and Country* magazine revealed that Mrs. Stone was "Ethel Vance," pseudonymous author of the sensationally successful anti-Nazi novel *Escape* (1939). (The book had been ascribed to almost every other American or English woman author except her.) The *nom de guerre* in a literal sense was adopted and jealously guarded because of the presence at the time of Mrs. Stone's daughter in Axis territory. After the Baroness left her husband and escaped to her mother in the United States the secret no longer had to be kept. Mrs. Stone plans to continue to write as "Ethel Vance."

PRINCIPAL WORKS: The Heaven and Earth of Doña Elena, 1929; The Bitter Tea of General Yen, 1930; The Almond Tree, 1931; The Cold Journey, 1934. *As "Ethel Vance"*—Escape, 1939; Reprisal, 1942.

ABOUT: New York Times Book Review May 3, 1942.

STONE, IRVING (July 14, 1903-), American biographer, writes: "I was born in San Francisco, the son of Charles and Pauline (Rosenberg) Tennenbaum.

I worked my way through high school selling newspapers, driving a delivery wagon for a vegetable market, and as an errand boy and stock-boy in leather goods and men's clothing stores. I worked my way through the University of California by playing a saxophone for dances, by working during summers on the fruit ranches, in a meat-packing plant, a powerhouse, as a hotel clerk, and a salesman in such diverse stores as a dairy and a sporting goods house. At the university I majored in political science, fought on the boxing team, and argued for the debating societies. I graduated in 1923 with honors, and had the distinction of being the first undergraduate to be permitted to conduct classes in economics. In 1924 I taught economics at the University of Southern California and took a Master's degree, returning to the University of California to teach economics for two more years and become a candidate for a Ph.D.

"I had always been a hopeless bookworm; from the age of six I had known that I wanted to become a writer. At the age of twenty-three, after having written short stories and one-act plays for several years, I quit the teaching profession altogether and jumped with both hands and feet into the writing game. I lived in New York for ten years, where I wrote eighteen full-length plays; two of them were produced, with no startling success. While in Europe in 1930 I encountered the life and works of Vincent Van Gogh; three years later *Lust for Life* emerged, and I suddenly found myself a biographer.

"At present I live on a small ranch in Encino, on top of a hill overlooking the magnificent San Frenando Valley. My three hobbies are my work, my wife, and my daughter. However, that leaves me ample time for swimming, cultivating my orange orchard, and organizing a school for writers in Southern California under the auspices of the League of American Writers.

"I think that the main influences on both my writing and thinking have been European. However, what little I know about writing I can also attribute to the books of such Americans as Hemingway, Sherwood

Anderson, Jack London. My main professional ambition for the next few years is to revitalize and reshape the biographical form, much as I have tried to do in *Lust for Life* and *Sailor on Horseback,* to make the biography as dramatic and deeply moving as any novel or play, and at the same time make it a clear and penetrating portrait of how the world came into its present state.

"For the last five years I have lectured in nearly every town in America, on such subjects as 'Modern Life and Modern Art' and 'The Writer in a Democracy.' "

* * *

Mr. Stone's change of name was made legally in his early youth. He married Jean Factor in 1934. He is a heavy-set young man with wavy dark hair and a determined chin. He spent several years in Paris and wrote seven plays there, which he threw into the ocean on his way home. At one time he was director of the Little Theatre in Jersey City, and once made his living writing stories for the pulps. He wrote his first novel while an assistant steward on the "S.S. Pennsylvania," and slept with the manuscript under his bunk to protect it. In a way his boyhood paralleled Jack London's, and made London a natural subject for his first American biography (*Sailor on Horseback*). His work on Van Gogh popularized the name of the great Dutch painter in America. Stone's novel, *False Witness,* proved a disappointment, but his life of Clarence Darrow was praised as "full, rich, and fascinating."

PRINCIPAL WORKS: Pageant of Youth (novel) 1933; Lust for Life, 1934; (edited) Dear Theo: the Autobiography of Vincent Van Gogh, 1937; Sailor on Horseback, 1938; False Witness (novel) 1940; Clarence Darrow for the Defense, 1941.

ABOUT: Literary Digest October 6, 1934; Saturday Evening Post June 25, 1938; Wilson Library Bulletin January 1935.

STONG, PHILIP DUFFIELD (January 27, 1899-), American novelist who signs his works as Phil Stong, was born in Keosauqua, Iowa, the son of Benjamin J. Stong and Evesta (Duffield) Stong. He was educated at Drake University (A.B. 1919), Columbia University, and the University of Kansas, and received an honorary Litt.D. degree from Parsons College in 1939. After

four years as athletic director and teacher of debating and journalism in Iowa high schools, he became, in 1923, editorial writer on the Des Moines *Register,* at the same time teaching journalism in Drake University. In 1925 he became editor of the Associated Press in New York, and a year later was copy editor of the North American Newspaper Alliance. He was on the staff of *Liberty* in 1928, and of *Editor and Publisher* in 1929. He was then with the New York *World* until 1931. Since that time he has devoted all his time to creative writing.

Mr. Stong was one of the many "discoveries" of the old *Midland Magazine,* which did so much to find and develop Iowa writers. He was also strongly affected while at college by Lewis Worthington Smith, a seminal influence at Drake. Although he now lives in Washington, Conn., he still calls Keosauqua his home, and Iowa life, history, and character have been his constant theme.

In 1925 he married Virginia Maude Swain. He is a chubby man, with thick hair worn in a pompadour, a snub nose, and an affable expression. He is modest about his work, refusing to "write about myself, first person, till I get some obsession like Bernard Shaw's— or at least till I have done a respectable amount of respectable work." But he is a very prolific writer, who has published nineteen books in eight years. He is a Socialist, a Knight Templar, a fellow of the American Geographical Society, and a member of the P.E.N. Club. In 1935 and 1936 he was president of the Authors' Club.

State Fair, his first novel, was made into a very popular motion picture, with the late Will Rogers as its star. He has written a great deal for young people. One of his juveniles, *The Hired Man's Elephant,* won the New York *Herald Tribune* prize in 1939. He is interested also in Iowa and Middle Western history, and has written much on the subject.

Wallace Stegner said of Phil Stong's Iowa novels: "His choice of Iowa as a locale for stories and novels has been consistent and sympathetic. . . . [His work is] a kind of triumph of simple localism."

PRINCIPAL WORKS: State Fair, 1932; Stranger's Return, 1933; Village Tale, 1934; Farm Boy (juvenile) 1934; Week End, 1935; Farmer in the Dell, 1935; Career, 1935; Honk the Moose (juvenile) 1935; No-Sitch! The Hound (juvenile) 1936; Buckskin Breeches, 1937; High Water (juvenile) 1937; The Rebellion of Lennie Barlow, 1937; Edgar, the 7:58 (juvenile) 1938; Young Settler (juvenile) 1938; The Long Lane, 1939; The Hired Man's Elephant (juvenile) 1939; Cowhand Goes to Town (juvenile) 1939; Horses and Americans, 1939; Ivanhoe Keeler, 1939; Hawkeyes: a Biography of the State of Iowa, 1940; If School Keeps (autobiographical) 1940; The Princess, 1941; Captain Kidd's Cow (juvenile) 1941; Iron Mountain, 1942; Way Down Cellar (juvenile) 1942; Pittsville Goes to War, 1942.

ABOUT: Stong, P. If School Keeps; Saturday Review of Literature July 30, 1938; Scholastic April 1, 1940.

STORM, HANS OTTO (July 29, 1895-December 11, 1941), American novelist, wrote to the editors of this volume shortly before his death:

"Father and mother were from Holstein and Lübeck respectively, but met first in the United States. Born in Bloomington, Calif., childhood in Anaheim, Calif., regular public school through high school. One year in electrician's trade. Conscripted in war of 1917, contracted various illnesses, held two years in various hospitals as patient and attendant. Stanford University B.A. in engineering, 1920. Began work as radio-telegraph engineer in 1920, and have continued with some interruptions to this date. Work in its most interesting part was construction of new radio stations, at Sayville, N.Y., and in Nicaragua and Peru. Now engineer for Globe Wireless of San Francisco, a telegraph communication company operating principally across the Pacific Ocean. Married to Grace Cleone Camp, 1921.

"Political convictions, social preferences: scratching out as far as possible all sloppily used words and catchwords, platform runs something like this: the distribution of the world's goods and powers on a broad popular base, with some favoritism toward productive workers; the discouragement of aggressiveness; as far as is compatible with these values, the greatest freedom to the individual in his private life. High on the list of elements of such freedom is the right to withhold enthusiasm.

"Literary background, influences, preferences: formal education zero; most of the classics have filtered in to me second-hand. Los Angeles *Times* in home probably made me a radical, Church of England liturgy gave taste for style. Jack London impinged at impressionable age, Conrad later. Veblen perhaps greatest influence. Contrary to custom among intellectuals, I can't stand detective stories. Favorite light reading is ethnology.

"Likes: principal recreation small boats. In this avocation have done a small amount of sailing on the Pacific Coast and a large amount of carpenter work. Dislikes: meetings, folding chairs, and mimeographed leaflets.

"Story, 'The Two Deaths of Kaspar Rauch,' included in O'Brien's *Best Stories, 1940.* A collection of short stories is in progress."

* * *

Hans Otto Storm was killed accidentally in San Francisco while testing Trans-Pacific transmission equipment for the Globe Wireless Co., of which he was chief engineer. He was forty-six.

Slender, with gray hair and a sensitive face, he possessed a dry wit and a bubbling humor which did not often emerge in print. He had the clipped style and incisive mind of the engineer, and his books, particularly *Count Ten*, his only full-length novel, have the engineer's feeling for clarity and order. The novelette was his true *forte*; *Count Ten* suffered from a certain fragmentariness which indicated that he was not yet master of the extended narrative, as he indubitably was of the compressed form. *Pity the Tyrant* so enraged the authorities of Peru, in which it is laid, that when he went to the Lima Conference of 1939 to install the communication system, he was ordered out of the country. He worked full time at his profession, and had little leisure for writing; moreover, he was not robust and was frequently ill. But in spite of these handicaps he achieved at least two notable volumes and one displaying great potentiality.

PRINCIPAL WORKS: Full Measure, 1929; Pity the Tyrant, 1937; "Made in U.S.A.," 1939; Count Ten, 1940.

ABOUT: Wilson, E. The Boys in the Back Room; New Republic December 9, 1940; Wilson Library Bulletin November 1940, April 1942.

STOUT, REX (December 1, 1886-), American detective story writer, writes: "My father, John Wallace Stout, and my

mother, Lucetta Elizabeth Todhunter, were both birthright Quakers, so I am too. I was born [Rex Todhunter Stout] at Noblesville, Ind., but was still a baby when we moved West, so my early environment was Kansas. At the age of nine I sat on William Jennings Bryan's knee, though it was on the Republican ticket that my father was elected Superintendent of Schools. I attended a little country school in Shawnee County, and then the Topeka public schools through high school. At thirteen years of age I was the state spelling champion. I am still a superb speller. At eighteen I joined the Navy, became a yeoman, and after two years of it purchased my discharge with the intention of becoming a lawyer in order to be in a good strategic position for abolishing all injustice everywhere. My attention was distracted from that design by the receipt of a check for fourteen dollars from *Smart Set* in payment for a poem. They bought two more, but the fourth was rejected, so I got a job as a clerk in a cigar store.

"My twentieth to twenty-fourth years were spent at a dozen different jobs in ten cities in six states, though I was only once a fugitive. From my twenty-fifth to thirtieth years I wrote stories for magazines, investigated the woman question, went to plays, operas, and symphonies, and continued to read books. In 1916 I married Fay Kennedy of Topeka, Kansas, and invented a school banking system and proceeded to install it in 400 towns and cities from coast to coast. That filled ten years. In 1927, at the age of forty, having made some money, I quit business, went to Paris, and wrote a psychological novel. The economic disillusionment starting in 1929 took most of my money, and caused me to switch to mystery stories. As it stands now, 1939, writing one of the three best mystery stories in the world would satisfy my soul as much as anything else I can think of.

"In 1933 I was divorced, and that same year married Pola Hoffman of Vienna. We have two daughters, Barbara and Rebecca, and are living happily ever after. I love books, food, music, sleep, people who work, heated arguments, the United States of America, and my wife and children. I dislike politicians, preachers, genteel persons, people who do not work or are on vacation, closed minds, movies, loud noises, and oiliness. I hate Adolf Hitler. This is 1939."

* * *

At forty-eight Rex Stout published his first detective story, *Fer-de-Lance*; and Nero Wolfe, a crotchety, elephantine hypochondriac who loves beer and orchids, entered the lists of modern American fictional sleuths. The novel, said reviewers, displayed "temperament, super-psychology, and admirable wit." With this encouragement, Wolfe and his paint-fresh assistant Archie Goodwin continued their appearances to the delight of increasingly large audiences. Several of the Wolfe novels have been dramatized for the films. The author has experimented with other detectives, but none has achieved the high popularity of his original character. In the intervals of writing two to three detective novels a year, Mr. Stout finds time to turn out an occasional romance and a number of short stories. In a list of his works furnished the editors of this volume, he revealed for the first time his authorship of *The President Vanishes*, published anonymously in 1934.

Rex Stout makes his home with his wife and daughters on a farm called High Meadow at Brewster, N.Y. He was a founder and director of the Vanguard Press and in his salad days was a frequent contributor to the old *Masses*. Gilbert Gabriel describes him as a lean, hard, incorrigibly active optimist with Ancient Mariner eyes and a patriarchal beard. He is a noted epicure. With the coming of the Second World War, he became a militant spokesman for the Fight for Freedom Committee and other patriotic anti-Nazi groups.

PRINCIPAL WORKS: How Like a God, 1929; Seed on the Wind, 1930; Golden Remedy, 1931; Forest Fire, 1933; Fer-de-Lance, 1934; The President Vanishes, 1934; The League of Frightened Men, 1935; O Careless Love! 1935; The Rubber Band, 1936; The Red Box, 1936; The Hand in the Glove, 1937; Too Many Cooks, 1938; Mr. Cinderella, 1938; Some Buried Caesar, 1939; Mountain Cat, 1939; Double for Death, 1939; Red Threads, 1939; Where There's a Will, 1940; Over My Dead Body, 1940; Alphabet Hicks, 1941; The Broken Vase, 1941; Black Orchids, 1942; (ed.) The Illustrious Dunderheads, 1942.

ABOUT: Haycraft, H. Murder for Pleasure: The Life and Times of the Detective Story; New York Times Book Review September 21, 1941; Saturday Review of Literature September 17, 1937.

STRACHEY, EVELYN JOHN ST. LOE

(October 21, 1901-), English economist who signs his works as John Strachey, was

Wide World

born at Guildford, the son of J. St. Loe Strachey, editor of the *Spectator*, and second cousin of Lytton Strachey,[qv] the historian. He was educated at Eton and at Magdalen College, Oxford. Even before he went up to the University he had become keenly interested in politics and economics from the leftist viewpoint, and at twenty-three he stood for Parliament from Birmingham, but was defeated. He was elected in 1929, and for two years was a Labor M.P. With Sir Oswald Mosley he left the Labor Party in 1931 in protest against its policies, but where Mosley became a Fascist, Strachey turned still more to the left. After his resignation he stood for Parliament again as an Independent, but without success, and he has had no official position since.

Although Strachey denies that he has ever been a member of the Communist Party, until recently he was generally considered a Communist and was frank in his Communist sympathies. This led to two contretemps with the United States Government—once in 1935 when he was arrested during a lecture tour and held for deportation, the charge being dismissed after strong protests by American publishers and by the American Civil Liberties Union; and again in 1938 when his visa was canceled while he was en route to this country, and he was held for three months in Ellis Island and then had to return to England.

In 1933 Strachey married Celia Simpson, formerly literary editor of the *Spectator*. They have a son and a daughter, and live in London. At present, however, he is in active service in the Royal Air Force. In the face of the present situation he says that he considers it his primary duty to help defend England against the Nazis, without implying any change in his radical views. However, *A Programme for Progress* (1940) shows a modification in his attitude, away from the orthodox Communist line and with some apparent tincture of the economic ideas of John Maynard Keynes. *Digging for Mrs. Miller* (1941) describes his experiences as an air-raid warden.

Mr. Strachey is physically a striking figure —six feet four inches tall, baldish and heavy-set—a complete contrast to the familiar picture of his cadaverous, red-bearded cousin. Peggy Bacon described him as having "black crinkly hair, broad brow and wide fat face, round brown eyes, projecting nose," and another commentator noted his "puffy lips and watchful, musing eyes." Miss Bacon called his personality "mild, ample, effortless, abstractly inquisitive, placidly diverting all things with even interest into a mental drainpipe, with Olympian ends." In spite of his weight he plays tennis and cricket and likes to take walking tours. Calm and imperturbability are his characteristics.

They are also the characteristics of his writing, which is lucid, persuasive, and never excited even when it is most enthusiastic. He has been called "the bourgeois Bolshevik" (though as a matter of fact most of the actual Bolsheviki were also bourgeois), and he remains the type of upper middle-class radical intellectual who has always been prominent in the proletarian movement.

PRINCIPAL WORKS: Revolution by Reason, 1925; Workers' Control in the Russian Mining Industry, 1928; The Coming Struggle for Power, 1932; The Menace of Fascism, 1933; Literature and Dialectical Materialism, 1934; The Nature of Capitalist Crisis, 1935; The Theory and Practice of Socialism, 1936; What Are We To Do? 1938; The Economics of Progress, 1939; A Programme for Progress, 1940; Banks for the People, 1940; Federalism or Socialism? 1940; Digging for Mrs. Miller, 1941; A Faith To Fight For, 1941.

ABOUT: American Review May 1935; Christian Century October 26, 1938; Nation October 22, 1938, July 1, 1940; New Republic January 16, 1935; October 26, 1938; New Statesman & Nation March 28, 1936; Newsweek March 23, 1935; Publishers' Weekly March 16 and 23, 1935, October 15 and 22, 1938, January 28, 1939; Saturday Review of Literature October 24, 1938, August 3, 1940; Time October 24, 1938, July 22, 1940.

STRACHEY, GILES LYTTON (March 1, 1880-January 21, 1932), English biographer who wrote as Lytton Strachey, came

of a family distinguished both in the army and the civil service and in literature. His father, Sir Richard Strachey, was a general and an Indian administrator; his mother, Lady Jane Strachey, was a brilliant essayist; the critic John St. Loe Strachey and the latter's son, John Strachey,*qv* were his cousins. Lytton Strachey was educated at Trinity College, Cambridge; his writing of that period, principally in verse, attracted no attention. Fortunately, he had a sufficient income not to need to apply himself to any profession, and he was free to devote himself to occasional reviewing for the literary periodicals and to the development of his gift for vivid historical biography.

He never married, but lived with his mother until her death. Her accidental moving to Bloomsbury, London, was the origin of the so-called "Bloomsbury group," which in fact was neither a group nor a school, but the association of half a dozen writers most of whom chanced to live in the same neighborhood, and whose only focus was Strachey. They included, among others, Virginia and Leonard Woolf, Clive Bell, Roger Fry, Arthur Waley, and E. M. Forster, who as writers had little in common except modernity. As friends, however, they met frequently, always with Strachey as their nucleus. Vincent Sheean

has described Strachey at one of these gatherings: "Silent, hunched in a corner, all beard and spectacles, not even appearing to listen, he would wait his opportunity and pounce." He was, physically, a man made for caricature, with his height and thinness, his long red beard, his owlish stare. Edmund Wilson went so far as to call him "a high-voiced old Bloomsbury gossip" and to comment on his "curious catty malice," especially towards women (including his feminine characters). There was a trace of felinity in his nature, true; but it was by no means all his nature.

Sociable and gregarious he certainly was; for which reason he could not work in London, subject to constant interruptions. Instead, in his later years, he bought a house at Inkpen, Berkshire, where he buried himself whenever he had a book in the making. There were only eight of these books in all (besides his edition of the Greville *Memoirs*, with Roger Fulford, which appeared in 1938); but his first volume did not appear until he was thirty-two, and he died (at his Berkshire home) at fifty-two.

Virginia Woolf said that Strachey turned to biography because, though he had wanted to write poetry or drama, he was doubtful of his creative power. It was a wise decision, but not for the reason given. If Strachey could not create fictional characters, he certainly did create a new school of English biography. Like Wagner in music, he founded a school in which he has had imitators but no successors; others can copy his personal approach, his brevity, his satire, even his wit, but they never approach his mordant ferocity or his slow evocation of a completely real (though thoroughly "debunked") personality.

Strachey was indeed a romantic at heart, and what is more, he was a romantic of the late eighteenth century type. Half his ferocity is nostalgia. He is at home with the Victorians, because he can hate them whole-heartedly for not being early Georgians; with the more spacious Elizabethan era, he is ill at ease. Even his hatred fails him sometimes—after starting off in his portrait of Queen Victoria with all the vigor of *Eminent Victorians* (in which, Joseph Wood Krutch remarked, "at every word a reputation dies under the quiet deadliness of his rapier"), he ended up by half falling in love with the steadfast, dowdy little queen, as he never fell in love with the grandiose Elizabeth. He began his career as a critic of French literature, and to the end his style was more French than

English; his type of biography was new to England, but old to France, and he was half-consciously a disciple of Sainte-Beuve. His range, indeed, was rather narrow, and his interests strictly limited; as Louis Kronenberger said, he "loved facts for the pleasure of drawing conclusions," no recommendation for a critic but invaluable to a biographer. He is eminently "readable," even when he merely satisfies our less creditable complexes by his savagery and his acid irony; in his mellower passages of illuminating reconstruction he makes the men and women of the past more real than most of those we know in the flesh today.

PRINCIPAL WORKS: Landmarks in French Literature, 1912; Eminent Victorians, 1918; Queen Victoria, 1921; Books and Characters, 1922; Pope, 1925; Elizabeth and Essex, 1928; Portraits in Miniature, 1931; Characters and Commentaries, 1933.

ABOUT: Atlantic Monthly March 1929, April 1939; Bookman July 1930; Catholic World April 1932; Fortnightly Review March 1932; Golden Book July 1935; Living Age March 1932; Nation February 17, 1932; New Republic February 17, 1932, September 21, 1932; Saturday Review of Literature February 6, 1932, March 26, 1932, July 23, 1938; Yale Review December 1940.

STRACHEY, JOHN. See STRACHEY, E. J. St. L.

STRACHEY, LYTTON. See STRACHEY, G. L.

STREET, CECIL JOHN CHARLES (1884-), English political writer, criminologist, and author of the Dr. Priestley

detective novels under the pseudonym of "John Rhode," is a sedulous avoider of personal publicity. His name does not appear in the British Who's Who, and only briefly in biographical dictionaries of English writers. Major Street has written books under his own name on the Irish problem, on Hungary, the Rhineland and the Ruhr, on the late Czech president Masaryk, a conscientious full-length study of Constance Kent (the English girl who cut her infant half-brother's throat), and a life of Lord Reading, which the New Statesman somewhat drastically termed a "worthless book— foolish and ignorant."

Enduring popularity has followed the long series of detective tales about Dr. Priestley, the ardent, eccentric criminologist to whom

"the solution of a crime was as welcome as a problem in astronomy or the higher mathematics," although they arouse some reviewers, especially practicing detective story writers like "Nicholas Blake" (C. Day Lewis), to expressions of violent dissent. (Lewis objects to "Rhode's" "excess of padding" and complains that his characters are ciphers.) On the other hand, Willard Huntington Wright ("S. S. Van Dine") found that "Dr. Priestley has many characteristics in common with [R. Austin Freeman's] Dr. Thorndyke." Still other critics have praised the ingenious, carefully worked out plots, while admitting that the books tend to be talky and tedious, lacking sustained excitement. Nevertheless, "Rhode" is a member of the English Detection Club and is frequently mentioned as a candidate for the mythical "Big Five" of British detective story writers.

PRINCIPAL WORKS: Detective Stories—Dr. Priestley's Quest, 1926; The Ellerby Case, 1927; The Murders in Praed Street, 1928; The Tragedy at the Unicorn, 1928; The House on Tollard Ridge, 1929; Murder at Bratton Grange, 1929; Peril at Cranbury Hall, 1930; Dr. Priestley Investigates, 1930; Tragedy On the Line, 1931; Dead Men at the Folly, 1932; Dr. Priestley Lays a Trap, 1933; Poison For One, 1934; The Corpse in the Car, 1935; Hendon's First Case, 1935; Shot at Dawn, 1935; Death at Breakfast, 1936; Murder at the Motor Show, 1936; Death Sits on the Board, 1937; The Harvest Murder, 1937; Body Unidentified, 1938; Fatal Descent (with "Carter Dickson") 1939; Death on the Boat Train, 1940; Murder at Lilac Cottage, 1940; Signal for Death, 1941; Death at the Helm, 1941; They Watched by Night, 1941; The Fourth Bomb, 1942. Other Books—The Administration of Ireland, 1921; Ireland in 1921, 1922; Rhineland and Ruhr, 1923; Hungary and Democracy, 1923; East of Prague, 1924; The Treachery of France, 1924; Lord Reading, 1928; The Case of Constance Kent, 1928 (Famous Trials Series); President Masaryk, 1930.

ABOUT: Haycraft, H. Murder for Pleasure: The Life and Times of the Detective Story.

*STREET, JULIAN LEONARD (April 18, 1879-), American novelist, essayist, and writer on gastronomy, was born in Chicago and educated at Ridley College Preparatory, St. Catharines, Ont., Can. He began newspaper work as a reporter on the New York Mail and Express in 1899, being its drama editor in 1900 to 1901, when he was only twentyone. He covered many important news stories of that period, including the first attempt of Sir Thomas Lipton

to win the America's Cup, and for a long time was noted as the critic who had predicted that *Floradora* would be a flat failure! In 1900 he married Ada Hilt, and they had a son and daughter. They went abroad about 1902, and spent a number of years on the Riviera, where Mr. Street's closest associates were Booth Tarkington and Harry Leon Wilson. Mrs. Street died in 1925, and in 1930 Mr. Street married Marguerite Skibiness.

In addition to his novels and short stories, and his articles and books on food and wines, Mr. Street collaborated with Booth Tarkington in writing the comedy, *Country Cousin*. In 1925 he won an O. Henry Memorial prize for a story. The French government awarded him the Chevalier's Cross of the Legion of Honor in gratitude for his work in popularizing knowledge of French wines. He is at present a member of the board of directors of Bellows & Co., Inc., wine importers, and lives at Lakeville, Conn.

PRINCIPAL WORKS: My Enemy the Motor, 1908; The Need of Change, 1909; Paris à la Carte, 1911; Ship-Bored, 1911; The Goldfish (juvenile) 1912; Welcome to Our City, 1913; Abroad at Home, 1914; The Most Interesting American, 1915; American Adventures, 1917; After Thirty, 1919; Sunbeams, Inc., 1920; Mysterious Japan, 1921; Rita Coventry (novel) 1922; Cross-Section, 1923; Mr. Bisbee's Princess (novel) 1925; Tides (with A. Street) 1926; Where Paris Dines, 1929; Wines, 1933.

ABOUT: Literary Digest January 27, 1934; Saturday Evening Post August 20, November 19, December 17, 1932.

STREIT, CLARENCE KIRSHMAN

(January 21, 1896-   ), American journalist and publicist. writes: "Clarence Streit was born in the little town of California, Mo. On his mother's side he is a Missourian three generations deep. His father, Josiah Streit, was a fiddling farmer who composed a number of tunes he played at country dances around Streit's Ford, Mo. Clarence Streit's first experience with the press began as editor of the eighth grade paper. When he was fifteen his family moved to Missoula, Mont. There he founded the high school paper. Majoring in journalism at the State University of Montana, he was editor of its student paper. He worked his way through high school and university mainly by surveying in the Rocky Mountains, the Bad Lands, and Alaska. In 1917 he volunteered

in the 18th Engineers Railway and was sent to France. In 1918 he was transferred to the Intelligence Service as a sergeant. In that capacity he was given a confidential post with the American Peace Commission at the Versailles Conference, and at one time was a bodyguard of President Wilson. He did some studying at the Sorbonne.

"Demobilized, he worked as a reporter in Missoula, but soon returned to Europe as a Rhodes Scholar at University College, Oxford. During vacations he got his first job as a foreign correspondent in 1920, in Paris on the Philadelphia *Public Ledger*. After covering the Greco-Turkish War, he resigned his scholarship to marry Jeanne Defrance of Paris and take a permanent post with the *Ledger* as its Rome correspondent. He began at Genoa, was assigned to Constantinople, and then transferred to Paris. In 1925 he began his career on the New York *Times* as ghost writer on Count de Prorok's expedition to excavate the ruins of ancient Carthage. He then covered the Riff War in Morocco. He was next stationed in Vienna, with the Balkans for beat, and was expelled from Rumania, but has since been invited to return. He was shifted back to New York where he served on the telegraph and cable desk and did special reporting assignments. In 1929 he was sent by the *Times* to cover the League of Nations at Geneva, remaining until transferred in 1938 to the *Times* Washington Bureau.

"During the last five years of his stay in Geneva he was engaged in writing *Union Now*. After its publication he resigned from the *Times* to devote all his time to bringing about the Federal Union of democracies his book proposed. The book was also published in London, Paris, and Stockholm, and Streit crossed the United States three times on speaking tours. He is the president of the Inter-Democracy Federal Unionists.

"Unlike most other correspondents, Streit in his books does not tell so much about his own experiences as what he has learned from them. He has written an adaptation of the Persian poet Hafiz in rubaiyat, and a report, *How to Combat False News*, made in 1932 for the Council of the League of Nations as President of the International Association of Journalists Accredited to the League. His favorite sport is skiing. He and his wife, son, and two daughters now make their home in Washington, D.C."

* * *

Mr. Streit's idea of a federation of the democratic nations has had a phenomenal currency. Union Now chapters have been organized in hundreds of communities throughout the United States and England. A Gallup poll in 1940 indicated that two million American voters would support such a federation in order to maintain peace in the post-war world.

Mr. Streit is described as "tall and thin, with bright blue eyes and a quiet, unpretentious manner. He is an admirer of Lincoln, Beethoven, and Michelangelo, and often quotes from the poetry of Walt Whitman and Byron." His name is pronounced *strite*.

PRINCIPAL WORKS: Where Iron Is, There Is the Fatherland, 1920; Hafiz—The Tongue of the Hidden, 1928; Union Now, 1939; The Need for Union Now, 1940; Not Again in Vain, 1942.

ABOUT: Current Biography, 1940; Fortune April 1939; Saturday Review of Literature February 19, 1940; Time June 17, 1940, March 17, 1941.

STRIBLING, THOMAS SIGISMUND

(March 4, 1881-), American novelist who signs himself T. S. Stribling, was born in

Pinchot

Clifton, Tenn., the son of Christopher Columbus Stribling and Amelia Annie (Waits) Stribling. His summers were spent in northern Alabama with an aunt, and he trained as a teacher at the Normal School at Florence, Ala. He taught only one term, he and the school authorities parting company with mutual relief, as he had no idea whatever of discipline. He then went to the University of Alabama, receiving an LL.B. degree in 1904. He practised law for one year in Florence with small success, then went to Nashville as a sort of sublimated office boy on the *Taylor-Trotwood Magazine*. When he lost this job he turned to writing, mostly "moral adventure stories for the Sunday School magazines." These were sufficiently profitable for him to be able to travel in Europe and South America while he wrote them. Then he turned to adventure stories for the pulp magazines. It was not until 1922, at forty one, that he appeared as a novelist. Long a bachelor, in 1930 he was married to Louella Kloss. He lives now in his native town, Clifton, where he continues to write novels and fiction.

T. S. Stribling won the Pulitzer Prize in 1932 for his novel, *The Store*, one of an historical trilogy on a country town (apparently Clifton), the other two volumes of which are *The Forge* and *Unfinished Cathedral*. He was co-author of *Rope*, a dramatization of his novel *Teeftallow*, which was produced in New York in 1928. He has also made one excursion into the mystery field with *Clues of the Carribees*, a series of original and ingenious short stories centering around his detective, Professor Poggioli, philosopher, and psychologist. *Sound Wagon* was a political satire, but in general his books are realistic pictures of Southern life—too realistic for some readers, who think his people as degenerate as Erskine Caldwell's, though Caldwell's characters are rural "poor whites," and Stribling's mostly small town dwellers.

Lean and tanned, spectacled and bald, with a wide mouth and a thin, sensitive face, Stribling looks like a combination of scholar and athlete. His recreations combine both aspects of his nature, for he plays tennis and chess. He writes: "I believe in a democratic form of government, and vote for the party that promises it and seems most likely to produce it." His style, which has been variously denoted as "urbane, satiric, lively, ironical, realistic, accurate, humorous, and philosophical," nevertheless is often crude, and shows traces of his early ventures in the field of pulps. Still, as Ernestine K. Taggard remarked, he keeps you reading, and that is the best test of a novel. His start as a serious author was so late in life that he may still be considered in his prime, and his abilities may be expected to develop still further in the novels yet to be written by him.

PRINCIPAL WORKS: Cruise of the Drydock, 1917; Birthright, 1922; Fombombo, 1923; Red Sand, 1924; Teeftallow, 1926; Bright Metal, 1928; Clues of the Carribees, 1929; Strange Moon, 1929; Backwater, 1930; The Forge, 1931; The Store, 1932; Unfinished Cathedral, 1934; Sound Wagon, 1935; These Bars of Flesh, 1938.

ABOUT: American Review February 1934; Boston Evening Transcript December 3, 1932; Scholastic February 1, 1936.

STRINDBERG, AUGUST (January 22,

1849-May 14, 1912), Swedish dramatist and novelist, was one of the strangest figures in all literary history. Briefly, the facts of his unhappy life are as follows:

He was born (Johan August Strindberg) in Stockholm, the son of Carl Oskar Strindberg, a bankrupt manufacturer of aristocratic family, arrogantly snobbish, and Ulrica Eleonora Norling, a tailor's daughter and a former barmaid. Three of their twelve children preceded August, but the parents seem to have been legally married a few months before his birth. He grew up in poverty,

neglect, disorder, tumult, and religious fan-
naticism, contributed by the maternal grandmother, who was yet the only or e in the
family who gave him a thought of affection
or care. He said once he was "born frightened." School was worse than home. His
mother died and his father promptly married
the housekeeper.

Infected by the atmosphere of religiosity,
he had become a lay preacher, destined for
the church. That bubble burst with his first
love affair, and he went as tutor to a family
of nobles in their country home, but was
soon discharged. He

went to the famous
old University of
Upsala in 1867. He
had to give up his
studies at the end of
a year; he could not
earn enough to make
his way and at the
same time have any
leisure to attend
classes. The next year
found him back teaching in the same dreadful school of which he was a graduate.

A confused period followed, in which he
became successively a riotous drunkard, a
reformed medical student under the kindly
care of a Jewish doctor (whom he repaid
by bitter anti-Semitism later on), an unsuccessful actor, and finally the author of a
verse drama, *In Rome,* which was actually
produced and earned him a royal scholarship
in Upsala. There he failed to pass his
examinations, and back he came to Stockholm. He was a painter, he edited an
insurance journal, he became a journalist
and a telegrapher; he lost every job. At
last, in 1874, he was made assistant in the
Royal Library. The end of that piece of
luck was his meeting with Siri von Essen,
Baroness Wrangel, older than he, wretchedly
married, and with a still more wretched
future, for after her divorce she and Strindberg were married, in 1877. For fourteen
horrible years this poor woman became the
receptacle and stalking-horse for all Strindberg's mingled sadism and masochism. Most
of these years were spent abroad. Strindberg returned to Stockholm twice during this
period—once to stand trial for blasphemy
and be acquitted.

He was rapidly approaching his first period
of genuine insanity, with delusions both of
persecution and of grandeur. And yet, during all these tortured years, he kept on
pouring out books—plays, novels, and

stories. From the publication of *The Red
Room,* in 1879, he had been nationally famous. His fame was spreading over all
Europe. As A. C. Hassen said, "he realistically registered in fiction [and drama]
his own unhappy emotional experiences as
typical and inevitable results of the evil
social concepts ruling human relationships."
In a sense all Strindberg's writings are autobiographical and confessional. The root and
foundation of this outpouring, as well as of
his personal disasters and his mental catastrophe, was a bitter misogyny linked with
hypernormal sexuality.

During this period also he ceased to be
a Rationalist; later he became a bigoted
Lutheran of the strictest school, then a
Swedenborgian, and at times he followed
every sort of occultism and demonology.
He had once been a Socialist, but he became
an extreme reactionary and an aristocrat like
his father. The dichotomy between his father
and his mother ruled all his life; these two
disparate and unhappy beings produced
everything in their son except his genius.

In 1891 he and his first wife were divorced, their four children going with her.
He became a drunkard again, and so poor
that he applied, in vain, for a post as lighthouse keeper. He was then a famous writer
who for years had been considered the
spokesman of modern Sweden. But he was
also a half-recovered lunatic who lived somehow, wretchedly, from hand to mouth. And
in 1893 he found another woman—Freda
Uhl, an Austrian—brave enough to marry
him! She and her parents tried in every
way to make the marriage a success; they
had a daughter, and Strindberg always loved
his children. But it was no use; as soon as
they were married he turned against her as
he had turned against Siri, and his symptoms
of actual insanity once more multiplied
rapidly. They were divorced in 1896.

By this time Strindberg had settled in
Paris. From 1895 to 1898 he was genuinely
insane. Most of his energy was spent in
alchemical experiments and black magic. His
naturalistic period as a writer was over.
At last, after wandering over France, Germany, and Austria, he came back to Sweden.
A stay in a sanitarium did him no good. At
forty-eight he found himself at Lund, already an old man with "a scared and
crumpled face," an old man who called himself "the second illumination." Friends
cared for him like a child, and gradually
he became well enough to live quietly and
write intelligibly once more. He still re-

tained his delusions of persecution and lived in constant terror of he knew not what.

Remarkable as it may seem, in 1901 he married for the third time! His wife was Harriet Bosse, a young actress. They too had a child, but they were divorced in 1904. All his writing now was openly and avowedly confessional. In 1907 he founded his own theatre to produce his own plays. It failed in three years. He thought it was a punishment for his earlier "sins" of Free Thinking and loose living, and from this time on was a fanatical prohibitionist.

He took to journalism again to eke out a living, but most of his time was given to the interminable series of *Blue Books,* a sort of omnium-gatherum of all his strange opinions and ideas, on which he was still working at his death. He even became engaged to another young actress, Fanny Falkner, only eighteen, but she had sense enough to break it off before it was too late. By 1911 he knew he had inoperable cancer. Then, by strange irony, the people he had scourged and excoriated made of him a museum-piece; they were proud of their "vengeful giant," their thundering prophet. His sixty-third birthday was a national celebration, at which he sneered. There was talk of a Nobel Prize; "the anti-Nobel Prize is the only one I would accept," he retorted.

In April 1912 Siri died. He had not seen her for twenty years, but he put on mourning for her death—this woman whom he had loved and had crucified at every crossroad of the world. Three weeks later he too was dead. Thirty thousand people came to his funeral.

There are few more painful stories than Strindberg's. It would not be worth the telling except that this madman was also a genius. His cruel books were magnificently written. They had brutal beauty. "His art," said Ludwig Lewisohn, "is the most joyless in the world. . . . The secret of his uncanny power lay clearly in his unequaled capacity for suffering."

He looked the man he was. He was described in 1911 as "a tall, heavy old man with a prominent forehead, steel-gray eyes, and a nervous mouth disguised by a long gray moustache. Two vertical wrinkles crossed his forehead and met at the bridge of his nose, giving his face a deeply tragical expression." Erik Lie said he was "like a cask of powder, ready to blow up at the slightest spark."

His influence on the novel and the drama throughout Europe and America is immense. He was cruel, vicious, an irresponsible and unmanageable lunatic. But he remains the greatest author Sweden has yet produced.

PRINCIPAL WORKS AVAILABLE IN ENGLISH: The Father, 1907; Legends, 1912; Lucky Pehr, 1912; There Are Crimes and Crimes, 1912; Plays (including The Father, Countess Julie, The Outlaw, The Stronger, Comrades, Facing Death, Easter) 1912; Plays (including The Dream Play, The Dance of Death, Creditors, The Pariah, Swanwhite, Simoom, Debit and Credit, Advent, Thunderstorm, After the Fire, The Bridal Crown, The Ghost Sonata, First Warning, Gustav Vasa) 1912-16; By the Open Sea (novel) 1913; In Midsummer Days and Other Tales, 1913; Master Olaf, 1915; Son of a Servant, 1921; Lucky Peter's Travels and Other Plays (including Countess Julie, Playing With Fire, The Bond) 1930; Master Olaf and Other Plays (including Gustav Vasa, Erik XIV, Saga of the Folkungs) 1931; The Road to Damascus, 1939.

ABOUT: Bulman, J. Strindberg and Shakespeare, Campbell, G. A. Strindberg; deFord, M. A. Love Children; Dukes, A. Modern Dramatists; Heller, O. Prophets of Dissent; Henderson, A. European Dramatists; Huneker, J. G. Iconoclasts; Lewisohn, L. The Modern Drama; Lind-af-Hageby, L. August Strindberg; McGill, V. J. August Strindberg: The Bedevilled Viking; Strindberg, F. Marriage With Genius; Uddgren, C. Strindberg the Man; American Scandinavian Review September 1934, December 1938; Journal des Débats January 8, 1932; Journal of English and German Philology April 1930; Living Age July 9, 1921, October 8, 1921, January 5, 1924, June 14, 1924; Musical Quarterly January 1933; New Statesman October 22, 1927; Nuova Antalogia March 1, 1939, November 16, 1939; Poet Lore March 1920; Preussische Jahrbuch July 1926; Revue de Littérature Comparee October 1933; Revue Politique et Littéraire March 5, 1927; Theatre Arts August 1940.

*STRINGER, ARTHUR JOHN ARBUTHNOTT (February 26, 1874-), Canadian-American poet, novelist, and playwright, was born in Chatham, Ontario, the son of Hugh Arbuthnott Stringer, captain of a Great Lakes vessel. His mother, the daughter of a Dublin barrister and author, wrote lyrics. Arthur Stringer attended the London (Ont.) Collegiate Institute,  where he edited the school magazine, and also studied at Oxford University in England. After a period of reporting on the Montreal *Herald* he was an editorial writer for the American Press Association from 1898 to 1901. In 1900 he married the late Jobyna Howland of New York City, a tall, statuesque comedienne who played in Belasco productions; they were divorced and Stringer married his cousin, Margaret Arbuthnott Stringer, of Chatham, Ont., in

1914. From 1903 to 1904 he was literary editor of the magazine *Success*. For a time he ran a fruit farm on the shores of Lake Erie; later a wheat farm in the Alberta foothills, and once tried to grow Burleigh tobacco. Sewell Ford, the humorist, assured Stringer that he had enriched the pharmacopoeia of America with an entirely new anaesthetic. *Prairie Mother* and *Prairie Child* were two literary products of this period; Stringer from 1894 to the present has poured out thrillers, Westerners, poems, and one-act plays in great profusion. *The Wire Tappers* (1906) is one of the best of his novels of action and mystery, which also include the successful *City of Peril* and *Diamond Thieves* of 1923. As a poet, said a critic in *Poetry*, Mr. Stringer cannot be hailed as the Keats of the Dominion; he has "the ability to write a good line," but he is sometimes banal, and his ambitious poems are always too lengthy. As a regional storyteller his position is undisputed, and he has taken occasion to point out some of the ludicrous errors made by Jack London, Richard Harding Davis, and even Sir Gilbert Parker in writing of the Northern country. A distinguished-looking man with white hair and blue-gray eyes, Mr. Stringer makes his home at Mountain Lakes, N.J., where he is head of the local Dramatic Guild. He has traveled in South America, Africa, and Europe. The Canadian Club of New York has elected him its vice-president. His recreation is cabinetmaking.

PRINCIPAL WORKS: Watchers of Twilight, 1894; Pauline and Other Poems, 1895; Epigrams, 1896; A Study in King Lear, 1897; The Loom of Destiny, 1898; The Silver Poppy, 1899; Lovely O'Malley, 1901; Hephaestus and Other Poems, 1902; The Wire Tappers, 1906; Phantom Wires, 1907; The Occasional Offender, 1907; The Woman in the Rain, 1907; Under Groove, 1909; Irish Poems, 1911; Open Water, 1912; Gun Runner, 1912; Shadow, 1913; The Prairie Wife, 1915; Hand of Peril, 1916; Door of Dreams, 1917; House of Intrigue, 1918; The Man Who Couldn't Sleep, 1919; The Prairie Mother, 1920; The Wine of Life, 1921; Are All Men Alike? 1921; Prairie Child, 1922; City of Peril, 1923; Diamond Thieves, 1923; Empty Hands, 1924; The Story Without A Name and Manhandled (with R. Holman) 1924; Power, 1925; In Bad With Sinbad, 1926; White Hands, 1927; The Wolf Woman, 1928; A Woman at Dusk, and Other Poems, 1928; Cristina and I, 1929; The Woman Who Couldn't Die, 1929; Out of Erin, 1930; A Lady Quite Lost, 1930; The Mud Lark, 1931; Marriage By Capture, 1932; Dark Soil, 1933; Man Lost, 1934; Wife Traders, 1936; Alexander Was Great, 1937; Heather of the High Hand, 1937; The Lamp in the Valley, 1938; The Old Woman Remembers and Other Irish Poems, 1938; The Dark Wing, 1939; The Cleverest Woman in the World and Other One-Act Plays, 1939; The Ghost Plane, 1940; The King Who Loved Old Clothes and Other Poems, 1941; Intruders in Eden, 1942.

ABOUT: Lauriston, V. Arthur Stringer: Son of the North; Canadian Bookman September 1928; Canadian Monthly June 1900; Current Literature December 1908; Poetry May 1929.

STRODE, HUDSON (October 31, 1893-), American traveler and teacher, writes: "Hudson Strode, son of Thomas Fuller Strode and Hope (Hudson) Strode, was born on Halloween. It was only by chance that the birthplace was Cairo, Ill., for his people were all Southerners. His ancestors settled in Virginia in 1640, and his maternal grandfather was a Confederate colonel from Georgia. He was brought up in the South, in Demopolis, Ala. During his freshman year at the University of Alabama, the bank containing all the money impounded for his education failed, and he is probably the first college student in the state ever to make his way to graduation by selling subscriptions for magazines. He was graduated after three and a half years' attendance, taking a half-year off to work on a farm in Kentucky. While doing graduate study at Columbia University, Mr. Strode had a variety of jobs, the most exciting being a 'walk-on' engagement with Sir Johnston Forbes-Robertson.

"For two years he was instructor in English at Syracuse University. At the age of twenty-four, he was made Associate Professor of English at the University of Alabama, declining an offer at Yale the same week. While at Syracuse he did dramatic criticism and book reviewing. In 1917 *Forum* published his first magazine story. In 1924 he was upped to a professorship, and in the same year he married Thérèse Cory.

"Besides teaching Shakespeare and three other courses in English Mr. Strode was for several years the entire Department of Speech, the debate coach, and the director of Blackfriars, the dramatic organization that went on tour each season. In spare time he was giving out-of-town lectures and writing or reviewing for American and British periodicals. In 1929 a one-act play called *The End of the Dance* (which he wrote in bed during a spell of influenza) was produced at the Waldorf Theatre, New York, and won first place in the National Little Theatre Contest. In 1929 he was very ill and was let out on leave to recuperate. So he and his wife went to Bermuda. The process of recuperation took three and a half years. He raised vegetables and wrote articles, and his wife was secretary to a member of Parliament.

"In 1933 he and his wife weathered the revolution in Cuba, and in 1935 they spent a summer flying all over South America. *Immortal Lyrics*, published in 1938, is an anthology of English lyric poetry, but interpretation of foreign countries remains his métier. In 1939 the university granted him a year's leave of absence to study the Scandinavian and Finnish way of life. His year was cut short by the war, but he had already gathered more than enough material for two books. Among his courses at the university he gives one in creative writing; during the last two years four students who finished first novels in the course have had them accepted by the first publisher to whom they were offered. He also maintains a stiff lecture schedule, and has lectured from Massachusetts to Texas and from Florida to Iowa, and in Sweden, Norway, Italy, England, Bermuda, Brazil, and Chile.

"Strode is a liberal in politics and deeply interested in the plight of the farmer and progress in the South. He is a warm admirer of the Scandinavian way of life. He dislikes automobiles and radios and has never owned either. His favorite hobby after travel is gardening."

PRINCIPAL WORKS: The End of the Dance (play) 1929; The Story of Bermuda, 1932; The Pageant of Cuba, 1934; South by Thunderbird, 1937; Immortal Lyrics (ed.) 1938; Finland Forever, 1941.

ABOUT: Newsweek May 13, 1940; Wilson Library Bulletin February 1939.

STRONG, ANNA LOUISE (November 14, 1885-   ), American journalist and poet, was born in Friend. Neb., the daughter of

Sydney Strong, a Congregationalist minister, and Ruth Maria (Tracy) Strong, one of the first generation of women to receive a college education (at Oberlin). The girl attended a private school in Cincinnati; graduated from the Oak Park, (Ill.) High School in 1900; studied in Germany and Switzerland in 1902; attended Bryn Mawr for a year; and received her B.A. degree from Oberlin at nineteen, in 1905. She was the youngest woman ever to receive the Ph.D. degree

from the University of Chicago, where she was called upon to "defend her thesis" (*A Study of Prayer From the Standpoint of Social Psychology*) before the combined theological and philological faculties. After this ordeal she went out to bury her face in the snow and resolve to drop formal studies for an indefinite period. This was in 1908.

For the next few years she organized "Know Your City" institutes in Seattle, Portland, Walla Walla, and Spokane; organized child welfare exhibits in New York and Chicago; and directed similar exhibits in Kansas City, St. Louis, Rochester, Louisville, Providence, Montreal, Northampton, and Dublin (Ireland). Miss Strong was exhibit expert of the U.S. Children's Bureau at Washington, D.C., from 1914 to 1916, when she returned to Seattle to become the sole woman member of the school board. She was "recalled" by a narrow margin of 2,000 votes when the Federation of Women's Clubs, Parent Teachers Association, and University Women's Club began to look askance at her liberal activities. The vote was close because Miss Strong had the Boilermakers' Union, the Metal Trades Council, and other organizations of workmen behind her.

She became feature editor (1918-21) of the Seattle *Union Record*, controlled by trade unions, and sent an account to the New York *Evening Post* of the disturbances at Everett, Wash., when police and lumber guards shot down workers. In 1921-22 Miss Strong was in Russia on a relief mission; was appointed correspondent of *Hearst's International Magazine* for Central and Eastern Europe in 1922, and was correspondent for the North American Newspaper Alliance in Russia in 1925. Next year she lectured at Wellesley, Smith, Vassar, Columbia, and Stanford.

In 1930 she organized the Moscow *Daily News*, the first English newspaper in Russia, and married Joel Shubin of that city in 1932. *I Change Worlds: The Remaking of an American* (1935) was described by the *Nation* as "the strange adventure of an individual soul trying to become collectivized." The London *Times* called it "a brilliant if unconvincing apologia." Miss Strong calls herself a motor-minded person: one who thinks in terms of action. Her activities have also taken her to war-torn China. She lists her home as Seattle, Wash., with a summer home, Zemlianoi Val 14/16, apt. 42, Moscow.

She is a handsome, sturdy, fair-haired typically midwestern American.

PRINCIPAL WORKS: Songs of the City, 1906; The King's Palace, 1908; The Psychology of

Prayer, 1909; On the Eve of Home Rule, 1914; Ragged Verse by Anise, 1918; History of the Seattle General Strike, 1919; The First Time in History, 1924; Children of Revolution, 1925; China's Millions, 1928; Red Star in Samarkand, 1928; The Road to the Gray Pamir, 1930; The Soviets Conquer Wheat, 1931; I Change Worlds; The Remaking of an American (autobiography) 1935; This Soviet World, 1936; The Soviet Constitution, 1937; Spain in Arms, 1937; One-Fifth of Mankind, 1938; My Native Land, 1940; The Soviets Expected It, 1941.

ABOUT: Strong, A. L. I Change Worlds: The Remaking of an American, My Native Land; Christian Science Monitor Magazine September 28, 1940; Wilson Library Bulletin February 1941.

STRONG, LEONARD ALFRED GEORGE (March 8, 1896-), English poet and novelist, writes: "I am a mongrel.

My father came partly from one of the oldest families in Connaught, and partly from the West of England; my mother is wholly Irish, with a strong streak of the North; and I was born near Plymouth, where we lived mostly until I was eight. In 1904, for the good of my father's health, we moved out to the moors, and remained there till the autumn of 1918. Every summer we spent with my grandparents near Dublin, and I was thus made free of two backgrounds. When I say made free, I mean made free. On the moors, I would escape from my mother's care to a farm where no one minded how wet my feet were, or what I saw or heard. In Ireland, I was put in charge of a lame odd-job man named Paddy Kennedy, in whose company I learned a great deal that was not taught at school. An odd result of these freedoms turned up many years later, when I became a broadcaster. My ordinary speaking voice was inhibited by diffidence; but the moment I spoke a dialect, either Dublin or Devon, it improved 50 per cent or more. The dialects spelt escape from self, as well as escape from the respectability of an Irish Protestant middle-class household.

"We were not well off, and if I was to have the public school and university career my mother wanted, I had to contribute substantially by winning scholarships. I won them, first to Brighton College, and then to Wadham College, Oxford. I had always wanted to write, and at Oxford I met many beginning writers. An obscure trouble concentrated in the spine kept me out of the

Great War, and in 1917 I left my depopulater college and took a wartime post at Summer Fields, a preparatory school just outside Oxford. I came back in 1919 to take my degree, and returned to Summer Fields a year later. I stayed there for ten years, getting married to Dorothea Sylvia Trice in 1926. The success of my first novel, *Dewer Rides,* made it difficult to combine writing and teaching, and in 1930 Alfred Knopf made it possible for us to chance the strength of our arm. We left Oxford for lodgings in London, were able, six months later, to take a furnished house, and a year after that to set up properly on our own. Since then, except for the setback of a long illness, I have gone peacefully ahead, earning my living as a writer. I began broadcasting seriously in 1933, and now broadcast regularly. I am much interested in the speaking of verse and in the stage, and adjudicate often at drama festivals. I have one son. I am much dependent on music, and have a large collection of gramophone records, mostly of singers."

* * *

L. A. G. Strong is the son of Leonard Ernest Strong and Marion Jane (Mangan) Strong. He is a member of the Irish Academy of Letters. His recreations, besides music, he gives as walking in the country, swimming, and talking dialect. He is a goodlooking man with a regular-featured, serious face and deepset eyes under straight brows. Dayton Kohler, though he deplored a habit of abruptness and lack of transition in Mr. Strong's novels, admired his "variety of talents, clear simplicity of style, passion, wit, and shrewd observation," and said that he possessed "the poetic romanticism of the Gael, with an imagination tempered by the disillusionment of the age."

PRINCIPAL WORKS: *Poetry*—Dublin Days, 1921; The Lowery Road, 1924; Difficult Love, 1927; At Glenan Cross, 1928; Northern Light, 1930; Selected Poems, 1931; Call to the Swans, 1936. *Fiction*—Doyle's Rock (short stories) 1925; The English Captain (short stories) 1929; Dewer Rides, 1929; The Jealous Ghost, 1930; The Garden, 1931; The Brothers, 1932; Don Juan and the Wheelbarrow (short stories) 1932; Sea Wall, 1933; Corporal Tone, 1934; Tuesday Afternoon and Other Stories, 1935; The Seven Arms, 1935; Mr. Sheridan's Umbrella, 1935; Last Enemy, 1936; Laughter in the West, 1937; Sun on the Water, 1940; The Bay, 1941; Slocombe Dies, 1942. *Juvenile* —Patricia Comes Home, 1929; The Old Argo, 1931; King Richard's Land, 1933; Westward Rock, 1934; Henry of Agincourt, 1937; Fifth of November, 1937; House in Disorder, 1942. *Miscellaneous*— The Big Man, 1931; Common Sense About Poetry, 1931; Life in English Literature (with M. Redlich) 1932; Defence of Ignorance, 1932; Fortnight South of Skye, 1934; Hansom Cab and the Pigeons, 1935;

The Minstrel Boy: A Portrait of Tom Moore, 1937; The Man Who Asked Questions, 1938; Shake Hands and Come Out Fighting, 1938; Odd Man In, 1938; John McCormack, 1941; English for Pleasure, 1941; John Millington Synge, 1941; (ed.) English Domestic Life During the Last 200 Years, 1942.

ABOUT: Bristol (England) Public Libraries. L. A. G. Strong: A Bibliography; Megros, R. L. Five Novelist Poets of Today; Strong, L. A. G. The Big Man (see Foreword by A. E. Coppard); Bookman August 1931; Bookman (London) November 1928, December 1932; Wilson Library Bulletin September, 1931.

*STRUNSKY, SIMEON (July 23, 1879-), American journalist and essayist, was born in Vitebsk, Russia, the son of Isadore Strunsky and Pearl (Weinstein) Strunsky. He attended the Horace Mann High School in New York City, and graduated from Columbia in 1900 with the degree of B.A. With Henry Sydnor Harrison and others he made the Columbia *Monthly* a near-professional publication.

After leaving college Strunsky was department editor on the *New International Encyclopedia* for six years, and editorial writer on the New York *Evening Post* from 1906 to 1920. Miniature essays contributed to the paper by "The Patient Observer" under the column head "Post-Impressions" were collected in two volumes with those titles in 1911 and 1914; the third book, *Belshazzar Court*, describing the humors of apartment house life in New York, caused M. R. Werner later to describe Strunsky as the American Barrie. Mr. Strunsky married Rebecca Slobodkin of Philadelphia in 1905; she died the next year. In 1910 he married Manya Gordon of New York, and they had two children.

As the authority on foreign affairs for the *Evening Post* during the First World War Strunsky was kept too busy for contributions in lighter vein; the omission was repaired by his first novel, *Professor Latimer's Progress*, which ran anonymously in the *Atlantic Monthly* but bore his name on the title-page of the second edition. Professor Latimer's peregrinations led him into the society of movie stars and other curious fauna, and helped him clarify his mind on numerous war and other problems. Ten years later (1928) Strunsky's *King Akhnaton* appeared, described by the *Nation* as "a subtle *roman à clef* in which a parallel is drawn between the ideals of Akhnaton [the

Egyptian monarch with forward-looking ideas] and those of Woodrow Wilson."

Strunsky edited the *Evening Post* from 1920 to 1924, when he removed to the New York *Times*, where he currently contributes "Topics of the Times" to the editorial page. "I do shrink from anything in the personal, people-in-the-public-eye and I-do-my-work-in-the-early-morning-with-my-left-hand-resting-on-the-head-of-a-favorite-collie sort of thing," he wrote to Mr. Werner. Gerald W. Johnson describes Strunsky's *The Living Tradition*, as "a robust defense of his creed by a conservative who is endowed with humor, honesty and sharp common sense."

PRINCIPAL WORKS: The Patient Observer, 1911; Post-Impressions, 1914; Belshazzar Court, 1914; Professor Latimer's Progress, 1918; Little Journeys to Paris, 1918; Sinbad and His Friends, 1921; King Akhnaton, 1928; The Rediscovery of Jones, 1931; The Living Tradition, 1939.

ABOUT: Morley, C. Modern Essays: First Series; Bookman March 1920.

"STRUTHER, JAN." See MAXTONE GRAHAM, J. A.

STUART, FRANCIS (April 29, 1902-), Irish novelist, wrote to the editors of this volume: "Born in Australia of North of Ireland parents. Returned to Ireland at an early age. Educated at Rugby. Instead of entering the University took part in Irish civil war and spent fifteen months in internment camp at Curragh, 1922-23. Married Iseult Gonne, adopted daughter of Maud Gonne McBride, whose husband Major McBride, was executed after the 1916 Rebellion. Have two children, a son and a daughter. First published work was a small volume of poems, *We Have Kept the Faith*, which was awarded a prize by the Royal Irish Academy. Some of the poems in it which appeared in *Poetry* (Chicago) were awarded the 'Young Poets' Prize of America.' Two plays produced: *Glory* (dramatized from novel) by the Arts Theatre, London, *Men Crowd Me Round* by the Abbey Theatre, Dublin. Have traveled in many European countries, lectured through Germany and at Berlin University. A member of the Irish Academy of Letters. Live in County Wicklow, in the mountains. Recreations: golf and horse-racing.

"Among favorite contemporary authors are: W. B. Yeats, Proust, Rilke, Thomas Wolfe, Franz Kafka. Among actually living writers: Thomas Mann, Somerset Maugham, J. B. Priestley.

"I believe that the novel has not yet been developed to anything like the degree of which this form is capable. My ambition is to go on experimenting in this medium."

* * *

The foregoing account was written for this volume by Mr. Stuart in December 1939. In May 1940, the American literary world was shocked by dispatches from Dublin relating that Mrs. Stuart had been seized by the Irish military police on a charge of being a Nazi spy, and that Stuart himself had fled to Germany.

Stuart was born in Queensland, the son of Henry and Elizabeth Stuart, of Ulster. His lectures in Germany were on English and Irish literature. Mrs. Stuart, besides being the adopted daughter of the famous Maud Gonne, is by blood her niece; their marriage was an elopement, because of the opposition of both their families. Stuart became a Roman Catholic at the time. Besides horse racing, on which he has written a book, he is interested in flying, and has a pilot's license. He also likes to tinker with old cars. Before the war he kept one or two horses for training, and at one time had a poultry farm, which he gave up to have more time for writing. He has said that he finds the company of children more interesting than that of grown-ups. He is a slender man with a square jaw and deep-set, thoughtful eyes.

Of literature, including his own books, he remarked: "I like frankly bad books, so long as they are exciting, and I think I appreciate really good ones when I see them, but I believe that there are far too many books that are neither one nor the other. My idea in writing is to find a sort of harmony in all the strange adventures and contradictions of life, to find if possible and demonstrate what is the key to happiness." Though he added that he does not like "too much 'serious discussion,'" actually his own work, in spite of its occasional humor, shows a markedly philosophical trend. He is a curious combination of an enthusiastic, machine-minded extrovert in his outward life and a withdrawn, meditative introvert in the best of his writing. The full story of his reported involvement in a Nazi conspiracy will be an astonishing one, if it is ever told.

PRINCIPAL WORKS: We Have Kept the Faith (poems) 1923; Women and God, 1930; Pigeon

Irish, 1932; The Coloured Dome, 1932; Try the Sky, 1933; Glory, 1933; In Search of Love, 1935; The Angel of Pity (non-fiction) 1935; Things To Live For (autobiography) 1935; White Hare, 1936; Racing for Pleasure and Profit in Ireland and Elsewhere, 1937; Julie, 1938; The Great Squire, 1939; The Silver Ship, 1940.

ABOUT: Stuart, F. Things To Live For.

STUART, HENRY LONGAN (1875-August 26, 1928), Anglo-American journalist and novelist, was born in London of mixed Scottish and Irish blood; the whole atmosphere of his home was Irish, however, but in person and bearing he seemed to the critic Theodore Maynard a typical Englishman. He was educated by the Rosminian Fathers at Ratcliffe College, and  came to America as a young man to ranch in Colorado for two years. *Weeping Cross,* his notable mystico-historical novel, was partly written at this period, and was finished in Florence and London. It was published in America in 1908, and met with undeserved neglect. During the First World War Stuart was a captain in the Royal Field Artillery, and was attached to the Italian army as liaison officer in 1917 and 1918, later to the staff of the Military Mission at Paris till 1919, when he returned to the United States to take up newspaper work in New York.

His other journalistic experience was derived in London, Paris, and Boston. Van Wyck Brooks discovered him for the *Freeman,* and as an associate of Michael Williams on the *Commonweal,* the Catholic weekly, Stuart wrote many of its editorials. He also contributed many long articles to the New York *Times Book Review,* and specialized in reviewing modern fiction. He professed himself unable to review poetry; his own was austere and metaphysical. Stuart disliked Francis Thompson, but adored Dante Gabriel Rossetti and James Thomson. He was a skilled journalist with an astonishing stock of erudition, and his translations of Cendrars, Claudel, Herriot, the Comte de Gobineau, Julian Green, and Corrado Ricci were often done directly on the typewriter.

In his later years Stuart suffered from an intestinal ailment, accounting for his increasingly ascetic appearance as well as for his explosions of irritability, counter-balanced by his "impulsive generosity, exuberant talk, and wild mind with its profusion of ideas."

In August 1928 he left New York to spend a vacation with a friend in New England, but soon returned to undergo an operation. He died at 4 A.M. one Sunday morning at fifty-three, alone except for the priest who administered the last sacraments. The reception given *Weeping Cross,* of which Theodore Maynard said "I cannot think of a greater Catholic novel written in English," had not encouraged him to attempt more fiction. *Fenella* (1911), his other novel, was a *roman à clef* dealing with "John Oliver Hobbes" (Pearl M. T. Craigie), the American novelist who found fame and tragedy in the Catholic faith in England.

Weeping Cross, which derived its title from Montaigne, is a nobly conceived book, wrote Maynard, "obviously the fruit of Stuart's brooding about life, and without being 'autobiographical' in the conventional sense, is the record of great suffering." It was dedicated "To Agnes Bartlett, an American Woman," and dealt with a young English officer, an erstwhile Jesuit, who was sent by Cromwell for ten years' servitude among the New England Puritans, in Boston of 1652, and who had an affair with the wife of his master. Stuart said Maynard, was not "defeated or embittered, but disappointed, frustrated in life."

PRINCIPAL WORKS: Weeping Cross: An Unworldly Story, 1908; Fenella, 1911.

ABOUT: Catholic World December 1928; Commonweal November 3, 1939; New York Times August 27, 1928.

STUART, JESSE (August 8, 1907-), American poet and novelist, writes: "I was born in W-Hollow, about five miles from

Riverton, Ky. My father's people are of Scottish descent and my mother's people, the Hiltons, are of Yorkshire English descent. My grandfather, old Mitch Stuart, moved to W-Hollow to escape his enemies on the Big Sandy River. He served in the Union Army from the North's first call for volunteers until the war was ended. Then he came home and started another. I can be sure that he did away with four of his enemies. He was married twice, and had nineteen children. My father is the eleventh and last child by his first wife. My grandfather moved back to the Big Sandy River, was killed there and buried at night. My father moved from farm to farm, and finally

bought fifty acres of rough land for $300. Two of my brothers died of the fever while we were conquering this land. I had pneumonia twice and typhoid twice, and have lived to make a man six feet tall and I weigh 205 pounds. I'm not fat.

"I went to the one-room country school and soon as I learned to write my name, I tried to write. I've always wanted to be a writer. I have fought for it, I have dreamed of it. At nine I was hired out for twenty-five cents a day to well-to-do farmers. Soon I cut timber—and at fifteen my Grandfather Hilton and I built the house we live in today on our farm. Then I got a job pouring cement into a concrete mixer when they paved the streets in Greenup, Ky., where I saw my first picture show, electric lights, and telephones. I started to go to high school—the first in my family. When the four years were over, I went home to stay. But I ran away with a street carnival. Then I went into the army and then to the steel mills, where I became a blacksmith. I bought a book of poems each week and read the modern American poets.

"I hitch-hiked across Kentucky and tried to enter two colleges. Finally I found a school in Tennessee, Lincoln Memorial University. I worked my way through on the 'bullgang' at the rock quarry, then got a kitchen job. At the seventh try I became editor of the school paper. I published my first poem there. I finished college in three years and two summers, and got a job teaching school. I was moved up to the county high school and then made its principal. After a year I went to Vanderbilt University. I had a desperate struggle, lived on a meal a day, had all my clothing, poems, and my master's thesis burned to ashes. I wrote a term paper called *Beyond Dark Hills,* which was published six years later, in 1938. I decided to farm and never to fool with schools again, to write poetry for my own amusement. I wrote poetry on leaves, scraps of paper, and tobacco sacks. I was asked to take over the county school system; the result was one of the hardest fights I was ever in—thirty-two lawsuits. At the end of eleven months I tied a hand towel around 703 poems called *Man With a Bull-Tongue Plow,* and sent them to Donald Davidson at Vanderbilt. They sold to the *Virginia Quarterly Review,* the *American Mercury,* and *Poetry.* A publisher asked me for enough to make a volume—I'd written thousands and had thrown them to the winds. *Story* and *American Mercury* bought the first stories I ever wrote—I was off to story writing and I loved to write them.

"In 1937 I was given a Guggenheim Fellowship and visited twenty-seven countries in Europe. After fourteen months I came back to the farm and started a little newspaper. I wrote my first editorials on a Congressman, was trailed and beaten up. I have been shot at twice, cut once with a knife, yet I'm very much alive, and if I continue to be alive—so help me God—I'll portray the section of America that gave me birth. In October 1939 I married Naomi Deane Norris, a childhood sweetheart. I love life—I love work—I love to write. I envy people that stay out of trouble but I don't envy any writer."

PRINCIPAL WORKS: Man With a Bull-Tongue Plow (poems) 1934; Head o' W-Hollow (stories) 1936; Beyond Dark Hills (autobiography) 1938; Trees of Heaven (novel) 1940; Men of the Mountains, 1941.

ABOUT: Beatty, J. Americans All Over; Stuart, J. Beyond Dark Hills; American Mercury September 1936; Current Biography 1940; Esquire March 1937; Household Magazine February 1939; New York Times Book Review June 2, 1940; Saturday Review of Literature June 8, 1935, June 18, 1938; Scholastic October 23, 1939, October 14, 1940; Southern Review Winter 1938; Southwestern Review March 18, 1938.

SUCKOW, RUTH (August 6, 1892-   ), American novelist, writes: "I was born in Hawarden, Iowa, a quite recently settled town on the western border of the state. My father was a Congregational minister, and we lived in a variety of towns and cities in Iowa. Both my father's and mother's parents were born in Germany, the former coming from

Bachrach

Mecklenburg and the latter from the small province of Lippe-Detmold. The one grandfather was a farmer, the other a minister. I attended college for three years at Grinnell, Iowa, spent some time at the Curry Dramatic School in Boston, and received degrees of B.A. and M.A. for work at Denver University, where I also taught literature for one year. I was given a degree of M.A. from Grinnell College in 1931. While in Colorado I became interested in bee-keeping as a way of earning a living, and spent a summer as an apprentice in a beeyard thirty miles from Denver. For six years I operated an apiary at Earlville, Iowa, which with some small earnings from writing gave me a living during this time. I spent some winters in New York City and later lived there for a number of years.

"My first work published was short stories in the *Midland,* then edited by John T. Frederick in Iowa City. At Mr. Frederick's suggestion I sent a group of stories to the *Smart Set,* at that time edited by H. L. Mencken and G. J. Nathan, which were accepted. Thereafter I owed a great deal professionally to the aid and encouragement of Mr. Mencken. My first published novel was *Country People,* printed serially in the *Century,* then edited by Carl Van Doren.

"In 1929 I married Ferner Nuhn, also an Iowan, and have lived since that year for varying periods in California, New Mexico, Vermont, New York City, Iowa, and Washington, D.C. Since 1937 my home has been in Cedar Falls, Iowa."

* * *

Ruth Suckow's father was William John Suckow, her mother Anna (Kluckhohn) Suckow. Ferner Nuhn, her husband, is also a writer. She was one of the first of the new school of American regional writers, and has always found her settings in the life she actually knows—the Middle West, and particularly the German immigrants in the Middle West. *The Bonney Family,* a story of life in a minister's household, is also drawn from close experience. She is a quiet realist, whose apparent ease covers a very solid foundation.

She is a pronounced blonde, slender, with delicately aquiline features. She is modest and reticent, and leads a very retired life, apart from literary coteries or cults. Her careful storing up of experience to be distilled later into stories is a process which reminds one irresistibly of the working habits of the industrious insects in whose care she is such an expert. Her name is pronounced *su'ko.*

PRINCIPAL WORKS: Country People, 1924; The Odyssey of a Nice Girl, 1925; Iowa Interiors (short stories) 1926; The Bonney Family, 1928; Cora, 1929; The Kramer Girls, 1930; Children and Older People (short stories) 1931; The Folks, 1934; Carry-Over (including Country People, The Bonney Family, and sixteen short stories) 1936; New Hope, 1941.

ABOUT: Publishers' Weekly May 3, 1941; Scholastic December 11, 1939.

SUDERMANN, HERMANN (September 30, 1857-November 22, 1928), German dramatist, was born in Matziken, a village in northern East Prussia near the Lithuanian border. His family was descended from an old Holland Mennonite line, to which belonged Daniel Sudermann, an eighteenth century Protestant clergyman prominent in the religious wars. His stern and disciplinary father, a brewer, and his innately gentle mother made every effort to preserve within their home Puritan morals and a positive Christian faith. A series of financial reverses enforced on them a careful domestic economy.

At the age of fourteen young Sudermann was apprenticed to an apothecary but after a short time troy weights and the smell of a pharmacy became intolerable to him and he broke away. He returned to his studies  at Tilsit and began to apply himself to historical and philological studies at Königsberg University. He opposed many of the German academic conventions; denounced certain courses as "mere nonsense"; and in the midst of a class tore up his copy-book, ran off, and never returned.

He was in Berlin before he was twenty-one, with the manuscript of his first play, "The Daughter of Fortune," in his pocket. He submitted it to Emil Claar, veteran director of the Residenze Theatre, who returned it without reading it. (Claar's office boy, moreover, had nipped off the white margins—because he could not bear to see so much clean paper wasted.)

For a while he was a private tutor, and then with almost no effort at all he moved into the editorship of a small political weekly, with a capital so slight that Sudermann had to write the paper almost single-handedly; for the *feuilleton* columns he turned out innumerable romances. But his mild political radicalism, very coolly received by the management, gave him a fair excuse for throwing the job overboard. He existed, during the days that followed, almost entirely on bread and cheese. Before November 1889, when his *Die Ehre*, which by later standards seems to have done little more than to ridicule dueling and thrive on theatricality, opened at the old Lessing Theatre in Berlin, he had, however, published a book of unconventional tales; a novel, *Frau Sorge (Dame Care)*; and *Geschwister*, a pair of short novels. In 1890 came *Katzensteg*, meaning the "cat's trail," but in English translation called *Regina*. This book illustrated not only Sudermann's sympathy for the despised and downcast but the very noticeable influx of Ibsenish catch-words and problem-play motives.

He was married in 1891 to Klara Schulz Lauckner, herself a writer. *Sodoms Ende*, coming out that same year, was quickly labeled "immoral and suspended for a time by Court order. *Heimat (Magda* in translation) represented Sudermann's first significant piece, from the point of view of craftsmanship, in a fairly long time. It was almost technically perfect; had all the surface characteristics of good writing; and provided a coveted part for such celebrated actresses as Sarah Bernhardt, Eleanora Duse, and Mrs. Patrick Campbell.

Except for *Es War*, a full-length imaginative study of a past sin's effect on temperament and conduct, he remained, during the 'nineties and early 1900's, preoccupied with play-writing; and survived a number of reverses in prestige. When *Drei Reiherfedern* opened in 1898 he had scarcely recovered from a very enervating illness. He went to the theatre that night and was all but hissed out. Obstinately he revised his play; and four years later the new version met with wide approval.

With *Es Lebe das Leben*, in 1902, Sudermann invaded the realm of German "high" life and confirmed, in part, his own moral individualism. In 1903 he lost a multitude of admirers when he attempted a libelous caricature on the political idealism that inspired the so-called Volkerfrühling, the outbreak of German liberal idealism in the year 1848.

During the World War he edited the "Manifesto of German Intellectuals" and wrote three plays. His novel *The Mad Professor* appeared in English translation at the very time of his death; and the New York edition of *The Dance of Youth* did not come out until 1930.

Sudermann died in Berlin-Grunewald at seventy-one. In his will he left his brain to a scientific institute for laboratory study. From a literary or professional point of view he was, in some respects, an opportunist: his youthful and militant liberalism ended, presumably, with his break from the radical newspaper; and his devotion to technical perfection was not wholly divorced from box-office considerations. Yet, on the other hand, the conservatism of his later years, bitter as it was, seemed genuine and uncompromising. He had jet black piercing eyes, a brow that was habitually contracted, bushy black hair, and a Teutonic chin that suggested purpose and action.

The names of Gerhart Hauptmann and Hermann Sudermann are, for the most part, still mentioned in the same breath. These two German playwrights were of approximately the same age; both represented certain aspects of the "liberal" problem-play development; and both experienced their first flutter of fame in the year 1889. But Sudermann's reputation came rapidly to its climax and was already in a noticeable decline when Hauptmann took his place in the sun. It became so fashionable, in critical circles, to accept this literary pattern for these two figures that injustices of over-simplification were inevitable. Judicious historians will think better of Sudermann as a novelist than as a playwright, but he will go down as a much better playwright than one who has "never drawn a memorable personality," according to one damning comment, "nor said a memorable thing."

PRINCIPAL WORKS AVAILABLE IN ENGLISH TRANSLATION: *Plays*—Magda, 1896; The Joy of Living, 1902; Fires of St. John, 1904; John the Baptist, 1909; The Roses, 1909. *Novels*—Dema Care, 1891; The Wish, 1894; Regina, 1898; The Undying Past, 1906; The Song of Songs, 1909; The Mad Professor, 1928; The Dance of Youth, 1930. *Miscellaneous*—The Indian Lily and Other Stories, 1912; The Excursion to Tilsit, 1930.

ABOUT: Clark, B. C. A Study of the Modern Drama; Dukes, A. Modern Dramatists; Eloesser, A. Modern German Literature; Heller, O. Studies in Modern German Literature; Phelps, W. L. Essays on Modern Novelists; Bookman August 1906; Nation December 5, 1928; Daily American November 23, 1902.

*SUGIMOTO, Mme. ETSU (INAGAKI)

(1874-   ), Japanese autobiographer and novelist, writes: "My native province is Echigo, a Northern district conspicuously noted for its deep snow and long winters. As my father was the First Karo, Chief Counsellor in the daimiate for which he and his forefathers had served, the fall of feudalism six years before my birth meant to our family an utter come-down. Education for girls in my girlhood days was very different from what it is now. My people, especially, were even more conservative than most families. According to the custom of the day, I was betrothed when I was a mere little girl. My fiancé was a Japanese merchant living in Cincinnati, in the United States. I was sent to a Methodist Girls' School in Tokyo to prepare for my destined home in the far, strange land. Here in this school I became a Christian. In 1898 I sailed for the United States. I claim Cincinnati as my American home. There I was married, to that city I owe my happy bridehood, and motherhood of two daughters There I met my life-long friend, Miss Florence Mills Wilson, without whose friendship

my widowhood might have been a most sorrowing life.

"In the meantime I brought my daughters to Japan for their Japanese education, spending six years in Tokyo with my mother and Miss Wilson. Then our little family returned to Cincinnati and later moved to New York. In this city, with the support and encouragement of Miss Wilson, I made my first start in literary work. It was a tedious, long way. At last a modest success was reached. Just about this time I was asked by the Columbia University Extension Department to conduct classes in elementary Japanese and Japanese history and culture. I was connected with the university from 1920 to 1927. Occasionally I contributed to New York and Philadelphia papers and to the *Bookman*. My first book, *A Daughter of the Samurai*, ran in *Asia* before it was published in book form."

* * *

After her daughters grew up and married, Mme. Sugimoto returned permanently to Japan, and is now living in Tokyo, where, in 1940, she was recovering from a long and serious illness. When she spoke at a New York Book Fair in 1936 she was described as "dainty and slight-voiced." Her latest book, *Grandmother O Kyo*, was a surprise to readers who had grown to think of her as one of the voices of the liberal forces in Japan, for it expressed a complete reversion to Japanese nationalism and the viewpoint of her earliest youth. No word, of course, has come from her since the outbreak of war between Japan and the United States.

PRINCIPAL WORKS: A Daughter of the Samurai, 1925; A Daughter of the Narikin, 1932; A Daughter of the Nohfu, 1935; Grandmother O Kyo, 1940.

ABOUT: Sugimoto, E. I. A Daughter of the Samurai; Bookman January 1926.

SULLIVAN, FRANK (September 22, 1892-   ), American humorist and journalist, christened Francis John Sullivan, was born in Saratoga Springs, N.Y., the son of Dennis Sullivan and Catherine (Shea) Sullivan. He graduated from the Saratoga Springs High School in 1910, and from Cornell with a B.A. degree in 1914. He was a second lieutenant of infantry

in the First World War. From his high school days onward he had done newspaper work in his home city, and in the 'twenties he moved downstate to work on the now defunct New York *World* with a brilliant galaxy including Walter Lippmann, Franklin P. Adams, Alexander Woollcott, Deems Taylor, and such visiting guest-stars as St. John Ervine and William Bolitho. "A master of unmildewed humor in a world forlorn," in the words of a New York *Times* reviewer, Sullivan soon made his thrice-a-week column something to look forward to, with its unexpected slants and wild extravaganzas on things political, social, literary and operatic. (His librettos for unproduced operas were not much more implausible than some of those sung on the Metropolitan stage, and he was capable of practically infinite variations on such a name as that of the Wagnerian soprano Nanny Larsen-Todsen.) His column now appears in *PM*, and he is a frequent contributor to the *New Yorker*.

Sullivan's first book was a collection of his patient, though exasperated, colloquies with his volatile (and imaginary) secretary, Martha Hepplethwaite. *Sullivan at Bay* (1939) is a representative collection made for the benefit of such of his British cousins as did not read the *New Yorker*, as well as those who had done so and desired to preserve his reportage on Nancy Astor and the Cliveden set. Mr. Sullivan is short, plump, wears pince-nez, and bears some resemblance to a rather worried and conscientious high school principal. He is a member of the Players Club in New York, and now makes his home on Lincoln Avenue in Saratoga Springs. As national *cliché* expert, he has sometimes been heard over the radio in this capacity, which does not, perhaps, represent his genius at its best. In 1931 the *Saturday Review of Literature* called Frank Sullivan "the best slapstick satirist now writing."

PRINCIPAL WORKS: Life and Times of Martha Hepplethwaite, 1926; The Adventures of an Oaf (with H. Roth) 1927; Innocent Bystanding, 1928; Broccoli and Old Lace, 1931; In One Ear. . . , 1933; A Pearl in Every Oyster, 1938; Sullivan at Bay, 1939.

ABOUT: Golden Book July 1933; Good Housekeeping July 1940; New York Herald Tribune Magazine December 3, 1933; New Yorker October 26, 1940, February 22, 1941; Time July 22, 1940.

SULLIVAN, JOHN WILLIAM NAVIN

(January 22, 1886-August 11, 1937), English writer on scientific subjects, was born at Blair Street, Poplar, London, the only son and eldest of three children of John William Sullivan and Caroline (Navin) Sullivan. His father was an official of a well-known Protestant mission, and his mother, who was a teacher, had considerable musical talent. The home was not prosperous, but it had a fair standard of comfort and refinement. The family moved to North London, where the boy attended his first elementary school in Islington, later a secondary school at Medburn Street, St. Pancras. At fourteen, young Sullivan entered the service of the old established Telegraph Construction and Maintenance Co., which had a monopoly of the manufacture of submarine cables. His hours of work were limited here, so that he could continue his education at the North London Polytechnic School at the company's expense. Here Sullivan was thoroughly grounded in mathematical and physical sciences. In his last year, 1908-09, he took some scientific courses at University College, London.

In 1910 Sullivan took a position with an electrical company in the United States, a post for which neither his training nor his temperament fitted him. He stayed with them a year, then was reduced to living by free-lance scientific journalism. Sullivan now came into contact with the mathematical logician, Lotka, who determined his bent for his future work. Returning to England in 1913, Sullivan held several temporary posts, also doing occasional journalism, and spent a short period in the ambulance service in Servia during the First World War. Invalided home, he found a Censorship Department post under J. Middleton Murry, and later took up literary work under him. By 1917 his ability was recognized, and he was contributing to the *Athenaeum, Nature,* and the *Times Literary Supplement.*

An Attempt at Life (1917) showed that his vocation was not the writing of fiction. *But For the Grace of God* (1932), which Sullivan called "more like an autobiography than anything else," is thoroughly untrustworthy so far as biographical details are concerned. *Aspects of Science* (1923) was an unqualified success; Sullivan realized that scientific ideas meet general human needs, and he used all his skill in lucid exposition in this and subsequent books. In 1924 he met Einstein in Berlin, and spent a long holiday with Aldous Huxley in Florence. *Three Men Discuss Relativity* (1926) elucidated the theory for the man in the street, while including a mathematical appendix for trained students. *Beethoven* (1927) is an attempt to assert the claim of music—as of the other arts—to have a bearing on reality no less significant than that of science.

Sullivan married Sylvia Violet Mannooch in 1917, and had a daughter by this marriage. They were divorced in 1922, and six years later he married again; the second Mrs. Sullivan survived him after his death, at fifty, at his Paradise Farm, Chobham, Surrey.

PRINCIPAL WORKS: An Attempt at Life (novel) 1917; Aspects of Science, 1923; Atoms and Electrons, 1924; The History of Mathematics in Europe From the Fall of Greek Science to the Rise of the Conception of Mathematical Rigour, 1925; Three Men Discuss Relativity, 1926; Aspects of Science: Second Series, 1926; Gallio. or, The Tyranny of Science, 1927; Beethoven: His Spiritual Development, 1927; The Bases of Modern Science, 1928; But For the Grace of God, 1932; How Things Behave: A Child's Introduction to Physics, 1932; The Limitations of Science, 1933; The Contemporary Mind: Some Modern Answers, 1934; Science: A New Outlook, 1935; A Holiday Task (novel) 1936; Isaac Newton: 1642-1727, 1938.

ABOUT: Sullivan, J. W. N. Isaac Newton (see Memoir by C. Singer); Christian Century September 8, 1937; Publishers' Weekly September 4, 1937; Time August 23, 1937.

*SULLIVAN, MARK (September 10, 1874-), American publicist, was born in Avondale, Pa., the son of Cornelius Sullivan

and Julia (Gleason) Sullivan, immigrants from Ireland. He was graduated from the West Chester (Pa.) Normal School (now Teachers' College) in 1892, but had already had newspaper experience on a local paper. He was able in 1893 to buy a paper in Phoenixville, Pa., for $300, and in a few years had built it up so that he sold it at a profit sufficient to put himself through Harvard. He received his B.A. at Harvard in 1900, his LL.B. in 1903, but he never practiced law. Instead he went back to editorial work on newspapers and magazines. He was first on the staff of the *Ladies' Home Journal,* for which he conducted a crusade against patent medicines. In 1905 he went to *Collier's Weekly* and in 1912 succeeded Norman Hapgood as editor. In 1919 he settled in Washington, D.C., as correspondent for the New York *Evening Post,* and in 1924 transferred to the New York *Tribune* (now the *Herald Tribune*). In 1907 he married Marie McMechen Buchanan; they have three children living.

Mr. Sullivan is today the dean of Washington correspondents, and also their Jeremiah. He was a close friend of Theodore Roosevelt, whom he idolized, and he remains in viewpoint exactly where the Progressives of the Theodore Roosevelt era stood. He was an intimate and confidant also of Herbert Hoover. He is aggressively and forthrightly Republican and anti-New Deal. He even looks like the typical statesman of the earliest twentieth century—dignified, white-haired, with pale blue eyes behind pince-nez, and a florid Irish face, dressed always in a dark suit, a derby hat, and a stiff collar.

As a journalist Mr. Sullivan is in the first rank, but he is best known to the general public because of his series of "contemporary histories" known generically as *Our Times.* In these he has collected and fixed an entire period from 1900 to 1925, its politics, its amusements, its sports, its art, its mores, and its personalities. Colored by his own economic preconceptions, these six volumes are nevertheless so hugely inclusive that they serve as a sort of "time capsule" by which later-comers can recapture our recent past in America. They have earned for their author a solid celebrity, an equally solid prosperity, and honorary degrees from five universities, probably a record for one who is still primarily a newspaper man. In his social outlook Mark Sullivan is more or less of an anachronism, a case of arrested development—the self-made American of the nineteenth century carried over into the era of two World Wars and the fundamental changes between them. But as a social historian his shrewdness and his journalistic integrity have created a lasting monument which will inevitably be a valuable source-book in the future.

PRINCIPAL WORKS: Our Times—The United States, 1900-1925 (6 vols.) 1923-35; The Education of an American (autobiography) 1938.

ABOUT: Sullivan, M. The Education of an American; Nation January 17, 1934; Newsweek November 21, 1938; Publishers' Weekly November 12, 1938; Saturday Review of Literature November 19, 1938; Time November 18, 1935.

"SULLIVAN, SEUMAS O'." See STARKEY, J.

*SUMMERS, MONTAGUE (April 10, 1880-), English priest and writer on Restoration drama and occultism, writes: "I was born [Alphonsus Joseph-Mary Augustus Montague Summers] at Clifton Down, Bristol, the son of Augustus William Summers, J.P. I was educated at Clifton College and at Trinity College, Oxford, reading chiefly classics and (in private) English. I came under the influence of Robinson Ellis, Corpus Professor of Latin, whose genius and en-

* Died August 13, 1952.   * Died August 8, 1948.

thusiasm notably increased and fostered my early love for Latin literature, especially for the later Latin writers of the Italian Renaissance. Other great influences on me at the

time were John Addington Symonds and Hartwell de la Grande Grissell, Chamberlain of Honour to three Popes. I gave several years of concentrated study to theology, and after ordination [as a Roman Catholic priest] I worked for some time in the slums of London, and also on more than one country mission.

"For health's sake I resided abroad during considerable periods, mainly in Italy and the South of France. There is no place dearer to me than Venice.

"Even when a mere lad at school I had always been writing essays, stories, poems, plays; but with the exception of a few verses and theological studies contributed anonymously to magazines, and one book of poems, I did not publish any work until 1914, when the great Elizabethan scholar, Arthur Henry Bullen, pressed me to edit Buckingham's *The Rehearsal* and the works of Mrs. Aphra Behn. I had always especially loved the Restoration period and literature, from the age of twelve when I began to prowl around bookshops for old plays. My first work as editor brought me the friendship of Sir Edmund Gosse, to whose kindness and criticism I owe much. In 1916 I was elected a Fellow of the Royal Society of Literature.

"For many years I had urged that the real test of the worth of dramatic literature is performance in the theatre. In 1916 the London Stage Society suggested that I make the experiment I advocated. The result was the revival, after more than a century and a half, of Congreve's *The Double Dealer*. In 1919 there was founded The Phoenix, a society formed for the adequate presentation of the plays of the older dramatists. Until 1924, during which time I was director and chairman, it produced twenty-one plays, and 'created a revolution in English taste.' In 1925 I acted as adviser to the Renaissance Theatre, and also organized one special performance of Congreve's *The Mourning Bride*. I have edited the plays of Congreve, Wycherley, Otway, and Dryden.

"My *History of Witchcraft and Demonology* caused a sensation and was a 'best seller.' It was written from what people are pleased to call a 'medieval' standpoint, an absolute and complete belief in the supernatural, and hence in witchcraft.

"After a residence of some years at Hove, Sussex, I moved to Oxford in order to work at the Bodleian Library, where I am engaged in daily research.

"I have great dislike of and contempt for that superficial charlatanry in literature which now seems to pervade the world of letters. I find modernity frankly detestable. I like old books, old china, old wine, old houses, tranquillity, reverence, and respect. My chief recreations are travel, staying in unknown monasteries and villages in Italy, pilgrimages to famous shrines, investigations of occult phenomena, research in hagiology, liturgies, and mysticism, and talking to intelligent dogs—that is, all dogs.

"Above all, I hate the skeptic and modernist in religion, the Atheist, the Agnostic, the Communist, and all Socialism in whatever guise or masquerade."

PRINCIPAL WORKS: Saint Catherine of Siena, 1903; Lourdes, 1904; Poems, 1907; A Great Mistress of Romance, 1917; Jane Austen, 1919; Saint Antonio-Maria Zaccaria, 1921; Literary Histories of Congreve's Plays, 1921-22; The History of Witchcraft and Demonology, 1927; The Geography of Witchcraft, 1928; Essays in Petto, 1928; The Vampire: His Kith and Kin, 1928; The Vampire in Europe, 1929; The Werewolf, 1933; Victorian Ghost Stories, 1933; The Restoration Theatre, 1934; A Bibliography of the Restoration Drama, 1935; The Playhouse of Pepys, 1935; The Black Mass, 1936; The Days of Dryden, 1936; The Grimoire and Other Ghostly Tales, 1936; A Popular History of Witchcraft, 1937; Six Ghost Stories, 1937; The Gothic Quest, 1938; The Gothic Achievement, 1939; William Henry (play) 1940; A Bibliography of the Gothic Novel, 1940.

ABOUT: Mencken, H. L. Prejudices: Sixth Series; Modern Language Notes April 1932.

SUMNER, WILLIAM GRAHAM. See "AMERICAN AUTHORS: 1600-1900"

SUTRO, ALFRED (August 7, 1863-September 11, 1933), British playwright and translator, was the son of Sigismund Sutro. He was sent to old City of London School in Cheapside, Asquith's School, and pursued some later studies in Brussels. He had very early literary ambitions but no starvation-and-genius illusions: he was determined to make his life's fortune before taking the veil of letters. When

his own share of the proceeds from the manufacture of glucose had reached a satisfactory level he withdrew from business and set himself up in a luxurious apartment in the midst of literary London. Somewhat later he took a flat in Paris.

It was William Archer who persuaded Sutro to try play-writing; and he soon acquired a tremendous interest in stage experiment, theatrical tastes, etc. At a rehearsal, one day, he was introduced to Maeterlinck; and while Maeterlinck was still suspect and unpopular in England, Sutro championed him vigorously. Both, oddly enough, were more readily accepted by the Americans than by the British. Sutro translated Maeterlinck's *Joyzelle,* a play; the famous *Life of the Bee,* on which he spent six months, working about seven hours a day; *Life of the White Ant*; and two books of essays, *Treasure of the Humble*; and *Wisdom and Destiny.*

As early as 1898 Sutro had been commissioned to adapt Meredith's *Egoist,* but nothing beyond a synopsis appears to have been completed. At the turn of the century he began to write steadily—and before his death had completed about two dozen plays. *The Walls of Jericho,* a relatively early piece that had at first been rejected was probably his best play, and on it he drew royalties for twenty years. It was reasonably interpreted as a well-aimed attack on society, but Sutro himself later repudiated this and called it primarily a study of woman, who, he frequently remarked, for the first time "in all ages . . . is finding her own individuality."

Sutro was one of the few playwrights who saw no real threat to the stage in the arrival of the motion picture; an actor, he said, wants to act and to go on acting, to live with a part, and to feel an immediate response from his audience.

For his First World War services with the Intelligence Staff he was made an officer of the Order of the British Empire in 1918. He was married to Esther Stella Isaacs, an author in her own right and sister of the Marquess of Reading, former Lord Chief Justice of England. Sutro had a broad forehead, slight hair, a large nose and a moustache. It is said that he was extremely generous and constantly gave financial backing to less fortunate playwrights. He died in Surrey, at the age of seventy, after a brief illness. *Celebrities and Simple Souls,* a book of reminiscences in which his early enthusiasm for Paris is well recorded, was finished just before his death and published shortly afterward.

Sutro's failure to write anything but ephemera might be charged to the fact that the vigor and potential idealism of his youth were consumed in the prosaic task of acquiring some kind of industrial fortune. In addition, the fear of endangering his hard-earned security may have forced him into the belief that a "good play is a play that succeeds" and that a dramatist should keep "one eye raised to heaven and the other on the box-office." He has been referred to as "the last survivor of the well-made school of playwrights . . . who handled stage clichés so expertly that to the indiscriminating they had given the illusion of life."

PRINCIPAL WORKS: Women in Love, 1902; The Foolish Virgins, 1904; The Fascinating Mr. Vanderveldt, 1907; John Gayde's Honour, 1907; The Perplexed Husband, 1913; The Marriage Will Not Take Place, 1918; The Choice, 1919; Uncle Anyhow, 1919; Celebrities and Simple Souls (autobiography) 1933.

ABOUT: James, H. Letters of Henry James; Sutro, A. Celebrities and Simple Souls; Bookman October 1933; Nation February 9, 1929; Chicago Record December 1, 1907; Indianapolis News January 2, 1909; London Observer September 17, 1903; New York Times August 18, 1912, September 13, 1933.

"SVEVO, ITALO" (December 19, 1861- September 13, 1928), Italian novelist, was born Ettore Schmitz in Trieste of a wealthy middle-class family. His father, who was the son of an Austrian official posted at Treviso, married an Italian woman in Trieste; Ettore was thus a mixture of Germanic and Latin blood. The boy began his studies at Trieste but at the age

of twelve was sent to a commercial school near Würzburg (Germany). Five years later a crisis in his father's business forced Ettore to give up his studies and accept a small job in a bank. After working hours he read voraciously and wrote on the quiet. However it was not until his thirty-third year that his first book, *Una Vita* (1893), was published, and only because he paid the printer's bills. The novel was hardly noticed even by the local critics. Discouraged, he accepted an instructorship in the department of commercial science at Trieste's Regia Università degli Studi Economici e Commerciali, to which he devoted his spare time from 1893 to 1901.

In 1902 business thrived and Schmitz's father-in-law, Gioachino Veneziani, opened a branch factory in England which Ettore had to visit frequently. In order to improve his English and keep in practice while in Italy, he hired a private tutor, one Mr. James Joyce, who had taught quite successfully at the Berlitz School from 1904 to 1906. Soon a friendship developed between the stout middle-aged industrialist and his Irish tutor, "a lean, tallish, highly excitable fellow of twenty-five who wanted to be a writer but meanwhile had to live from hand to mouth by teaching English." Joyce read to Schmitz the stories later published as *Dubliners,* and Schmitz reticently gave Joyce "two little blue-bound volumes with yellowish pages": Italo Svevo's *Una Vita* and his second novel, *As a Man Grows Older,* which had fallen still-born from the press in 1898, all but ignored by the critics who found it "wanting in refinement" and "not written in a pure Italian." But Joyce, to his pupil's astonishment, declared that "there were pages in it that could not have been written better by the greatest French master," and to prove his point he quoted long passages by heart. Unquestionably this belated appreciation stimulated Schmitz and was largely responsible for the continuance of his literary work.

During the war Schmitz made handsome profits as owner of a ship-paint factory and on retiring he tried his hand at literature once more. In 1923 he published his *Confessions of Zeno,* again at his own expense, and sent a copy to Joyce, who warmly recommended it to the influential French critics Benjamin Crémieux and Valéry Larbaud. By then the author of *Dubliners, Portrait of the Artist as a Young Man,* and *Ulysses* had been accepted in many circles as the most significant figure in contemporary literature, and his word carried great weight. In 1926 the vanguard magazine *Le Navire d'Argent* dedicated an entire issue to Svevo, and overnight the industrialist Ettore Schmitz became "the great Italian master Italo Svevo"—the "miracle of Lazarus," Svevo called it. Suddenly Italian critics began to "discover" Svevo after consistently ignoring him except for Eugenio Montale's favorable essay in *Esame* (November 1925).

While working on a sequel to *Confessions of Zeno,* Svevo was fatally injured in an automobile accident, at the age of sixty-seven. He had written three novels published at long intervals—1892, 1898, 1923—and a few short stories, of which "The Hoax" and "The Nice Old Man and the Pretty Girl" are the best. The fact that *Zeno* was dashed off in a fortnight indicates that Svevo would have been a prolific writer had he been encouraged earlier.

Eugenio Montale called Svevo "the greatest novelist our literature has produced from Verga's day to our own." Crémieux characterized him as "a meticulous analyst [who] describes heroes timid, inept, and perturbed by scruples, but at the same time zealots of perfection, success and happiness —Triestian brothers of Charlie Chaplin." And the *Daily Telegraph* has said hyperbolically that "perhaps in the final estimate the most important work of Mr. James Joyce will not be *Ulysses,* but the discovery of Italo Svevo."

Works Available in English Translation: The Hoax, 1930; The Nice Old Man and the Pretty Girl and Other Stories, 1930; Confessions of Zeno, 1930; As a Man Grows Older, 1932.

About: Crémieux, B. Panorama de la Littérature Italienne Contemporaine; Piceni. La Bancarella della Novità; Sternberg, F. L'Opera di Italo Svevo; Books March 30, 1930; Il Convegno January, 25-February 25, 1929; Italia che Scrive June 1926; Navire d'Argent February 1926; New York Times Book Review November 28, 1928; Pegaso January 1929; Psychoanalytic Review October 1931; Saturday Review of Literature August 2, 1930; Solaria March-April 1929.

SWANSON, NEIL HARMON (June 30, 1896-), American novelist, writes: "My mother was the American-born daughter of a Swedish seafaring family. My father left his Swedish home when he was eleven years old, carrying a bell-mouthed horse-pistol for protection against Indians, to come to America. He was brought up in Missouri in the days when it was still wild.  I was born and brought up on a farm ten miles outside of Minneapolis; attended the University of Minnesota; was so busy being night editor of the university newspaper that I flunked in English; left college in my junior year to go to work on the Minneapolis *Journal* at eight dollars a week— sleeping on the office floor to save room rent.

"I volunteered for military service the night of the declaration of war; was commissioned First Lieutenant of Infantry at Fort Snelling; went to France, served as company commander at the front, and still have in my possession one of the very few American flags which ever flew in action behind the enemy lines during the World War. I came back a captain; returned to the Minneapolis *Journal,* was assistant tele-graph editor, assistant news editor, assistant city editor, city editor, assistant managing editor, and finally managing editor. I left Minneapolis in 1930 to become managing editor of the Pittsburgh *Press;* left Pitts-burgh a year and a half later to become assistant managing editor of the Baltimore *Evening Sun;* became managing editor in 1939.

"My first novel was followed by four others, all dealing with little known phases of early American history. My interest in the American frontier possibly has its basis in the fact that the last battle of America's Indian wars was fought in Minnesota while I was a boy.

"In 1939 I signed a life-time contract for a series of thirty integrated books, most of them novels but a few of them biographies. Each of them, of course, will be a complete story in itself, but when the project is fin-ished the thirty volumes will form one con-tinuous story beginning with the settlement of Maryland, Delaware, and Pennsylvania, and following the advance of 'the middle border' through the Ohio country to the Mississippi. The novels will deal primarily with the same families, their descendants, and neighbors. The publishers believe this contract to be unique in American publish-ing. The first of these books is *The Silent Drum.*"

PRINCIPAL WORKS: The Judas Tree, 1933; The Flag Is Still There, 1933; The Phantom Emperor, 1934; The First Rebel, 1937; The Forbidden Ground, 1938; The Silent Drum, 1940.

SWINBURNE, ALGERNON CHARLES. See "BRITISH AUTHORS OF THE 19TH CENTURY"

SWINNERTON, FRANK ARTHUR (August 12, 1884-), English novelist, writes: "I was born in a London suburb, Wood Green. My  father's family was Midland English, my mother's Scottish. I taught myself to read by the time I was four, and have been reading ever since. Severe illness (first diphtheria, followed by paralysis, and then scarlet fever) changed a healthy child into a boy subject to illness, and a period of starvation did not help, either. But at the age of fourteen, having determined to be a journalist, I went as office boy in the firm of some Scottish

newspaper proprietors named Hay, Nisbet & Co., and two years later, having a little shifted ground, so that I wanted to write books as well as newspapers, I went into the office of J. M. Dent & Co., the pub-lishers of the Temple Shakespeare and, later, Everyman's Library. I was with Dent's for six years, and left to be a proof-reader and assistant with another firm of book publishers, Chatto & Windus. I was then twenty-two, and when I was twenty-three I wrote my first novel. It was a failure, but was much liked; and I was offered the post of reader, or editor, to the firm. This I held for sixteen or seventeen years, and during that period the firm had some re-sounding successes, which included *The Young Visiters,* for the publication of which I was responsible.

"Meanwhile, having continued to write books, I produced, in 1917, a short novel, *Nocturne,* which made a lucky hit all over the world. It was praised in England by Arnold Bennett and H. G. Wells, both of whom had become my friends, though they were greatly senior to me; and I wish to state that all the success I have had dates from, and arises from, the friendship of these two men. I married Mary Dorothy Bennett in 1924, and have one daughter.

"I am in politics a Liberal, slightly to the left of orthodox Liberalism; and I think the only hope for peace and happiness in the world is not materialism but love between human beings. I dislike Communism for its materialism, and Fascism for its brutality, but both because they subordinate the indi-vidual to dogmatic and fanatic beliefs.

"As a novelist I owe a lot to my child-hood love of Louisa Alcott's books and the immense admiration I have always felt for Henry James' technique—not his namby-pambiness. I am temperamentally cheerful, cold (and therefore kind through a sort of indifference), and easily moved to liveliness of speech by congenial company. My mar-riage has been happy, and so has my life. My best books, in my own opinion, are *Harvest Comedy* and *The Georgian Literary Scene,* but I do not regard either one as of lasting importance. *Nocturne* has been in-cluded in the series of World Classics is-sued by the Oxford University Press. I live in the country, am very lazy, work un-willingly very hard, and have few intoler-ances."

* * *

The present Mrs. Swinnerton is the au-thor's second wife; his first was Helen Dircks, a poet. He lives now in Cranleigh,

Surrey, where there are always cats in the household. He is a good *raconteur* and mimic, and a social, companionable man. His garden is his delight, and in the midst of it is the studio where he writes—by hand, with a chirography like engraving. He marks the ending of each book by the eating, whatever the season, of a hot plum pudding. He is a medium-size man with once reddish hair, a pointed beard that has become a literary landmark, dancing eyes behind pince-nez, and an infectious laugh.

He wrote, under the pseudonym of "Simon Pure," the "London Letters" in the *Bookman,* later collected into a volume. As a novelist, one critic said he occupies "a position of respectability, . . . writing quiet novels and critical works and living well within his own mind." During the Second World War he has been serving as a speaker for the Ministry of Information.

PRINCIPAL WORKS: The Merry Heart, 1909; The Young Idea, 1910; The Casement, 1911; The Happy Family, 1912; George Gissing (biography) 1912; On the Staircase, 1914; R. L. Stevenson (biography) 1914; The Chaste Wife, 1916; Nocturne, 1917; Shops and Houses, 1918; September, 1919; Coquette, 1921; The Three Lovers, 1922; Young Felix, 1923; The Elder Sister, 1925; Summer Storm, 1926; Tokefield Papers (essays) 1927; A Brood of Ducklings, 1928; A London Bookman (essays) 1928; Sketch of a Sinner, 1929; Authors and the Book Trade, 1932; The Georgian House, 1932; Elizabeth, 1934; The Georgian Literary Scene (criticism) 1935; Harvest Comedy, 1937; Swinnerton (autobiography) 1937; The Two Wives, 1939; Fortunate Lady, 1941; Thankless Child, 1942.

ABOUT: Bennett, A., Wells, H. G. & Overton, G. M. Frank Swinnerton; Swinnerton, F. Swinnerton; Bookman December 1923, October 1924, November 1932; Boston Evening Transcript August 4, 1934; New Statesman & Nation March 26, 1932; Newsweek November 14, 1936; Saturday Review of Literature March 30, 1940.

*SYMONS, ARTHUR (February 28, 1865-), English poet and critic, was born in Wales, but of Cornish parents. He was  educated in private schools, mostly in France and Italy, and has been trilingual from childhood. His first book appeared when he was only twenty-one, but he had already begun to earn a reputation as critic and editor, having edited the *Shakespeare Quarto Facsimiles* for Bernard Quaritch when he was only nineteen. He was attracted first to Baudelaire and then to the French Symbolist poets who drew their in-

spiration from Baudelaire and Verlaine; and he became the chief exponent of the Symbolist school in England. In 1891 he joined the staff of the *Athenaeum;* in 1894 that of the *Saturday Review;* and in 1896 he became editor of the *Savoy.* Besides the heavy duties of these positions, he was also carrying an onerous load as translator, editor of editions of French and English authors, and anthologist, and what leisure he had was given to writing poetry. It is not surprising that he broke down, especially as he says he had always been "highly strung, over-nervous, over-excitable, over-sensitive." He suffered from recurrent spells of amnesia, and finally, in 1908, while he was in Bologna, Italy, he lost his reason completely. He was picked up by the police, wandering the roads, was thrown into a dungeon, beaten, and starved, rescued by the British ambassador to Italy, and spent two years in asylums in Italy and England. He has told the melancholy story in his *Confessions,* written two decades later, but with the horror and wretchedness of that time still vivid in his mind. In 1909 an attack of pneumonia almost killed him, but when he recovered he was sane again—an accidental anticipation of one of the very latest methods of psychiatric treatment.

Mr. Symons had been married in 1901 to Rhoda Bowser, who died in 1936. They had no children. He built a house at Wittersham, on the sea, and retired from regular service as a magazine editor, though he remained constantly at work as a writer. It has been necessary for him ever since to live very quietly, without the excitements of city life —though he continued for many years to spend much of his time on the Continent. His recreations have been passive—listening to music, watching dancing. His terrible experience marked him for life; Frank Harris noted his "haggard mask," his "triangular wedge of thin face . . . a terrible face, ravaged like a battlefield."

Less sympathetic observers have called him "an elderly dandy," whose critical views have not changed since the days of his youth. It is true that he is in many ways a leftover from the *fin de siècle.* Nevertheless, he is an acute and sometimes a superb critic, an industrious anthologist, editor, and translator, and a true amateur of literature in the real meaning of that misused word. His poetry is "dated," and has outlived its era. But he has had an appreciable influence on literary thought and criticism in England. His work often seems more French than English in its spirit, and no man has done more to make the best of modern French

* Died January 22, 1945.

writing known across the Channel. The catholicity of his literary interests, in spite of the aura of the 1890's which clings to him, is evidenced by the names of some of the authors whose work he has edited, usually with introductions. They include d'Annunzio, Baudelaire, Zola, Verhaeren, all of whom he has translated; Emily Brontë's poems, Browning, Byron, Coleridge, Addison, Keats, Leigh Hunt, Landor, Pater, Poe, among writers in English, and Murger, Chodelos de Laclos and Pierre Louÿs among those in French, with St. Augustine and Sarojini Naidu added for good measure. His anthologies are equally varied: *A Sixteenth Century Anthology, A Book of Parodies, A Pageant of Elizabethan Poetry.*

T. Earle Welby said that Symons "has gradually worked out a complete system of aesthetics, has gradually fashioned a whole imaginative world of his own. . . . With a more widely ranging critical intelligence than any other writer of our time, with a more truly catholic receptiveness, he is more shut up with himself than any other, with a subtle pride in his loneliness and, in his infrequent welcome to ordinary human feeling, a more delicately pathetic hospitality."

PRINCIPAL WORKS: *Poetry*—Days and Nights, 1889; Silhouettes, 1892; London Nights, 1896; Amoris Victima, 1897; Images of Good and Evil, 1899; Poems (2 vols.) 1902; A Book of Twenty Songs, 1905; The Fool of the World and Other Poems, 1906; Knave of Hearts, 1913; Tragedies (Death of Agrippina, Cleopatra in Judaea, The Harvesters) 1916; Tristan and Iseult 1917; Plays (Cesare Borgia, Iseult of Britanny, The Toy Cart) 1920; Love's Cruelty, 1923; Jezebel Mort and Other Poems, 1931. *Prose*—An Introduction to the Study of Browning, 1886; Studies in Two Literatures, 1897; Aubrey Beardsley, 1898; The Symbolist Movement in Literature, 1899; Plays, Acting, and Music: A Book of Theory, 1903; Cities, 1903; Studies in Prose and Verse, 1904; Spiritual Adventures, 1905; Studies in Seven Arts, 1906; William Blake, 1907; Cities of Italy, 1907; The Romantic Movement in English Poetry, 1909; Figures of Seven Centuries, 1916; Cities and Sea-Coasts and Islands, 1917; Colour Studies in Paris, 1918; Studies in the Elizabethan Drama, 1919; Charles Baudelaire, 1920; Dramatis Personae, 1923; Collected Works (16 vols.) 1924-25; The Cafe Royal and Other Essays, 1925; Eleonora Duse, 1926; A Study of Thomas Hardy, 1927; Studies in Strange Souls, 1929; From Toulouse-Lautrec to Rodin, 1919; Oscar Wilde, 1930; Confessions: A Study in Pathology (autobiography) 1930; Wanderings, 1931; The Poems and Prose of Edward Dowson, 1932; A Study of Walter Pater, 1932.

ABOUT: Archer, W. Poets of the Younger Generation; Burdett, O. The Beardsley Period; Jackson, H. The 1890's; Moore, G. Hail and Farewell; More, P. E. Shelburne Essays: First Series; Murdoch, B. Arthur Symons; Symons, A. Confessions; Welby, T. E. Arthur Symons: A Critical Study; Saturday Review (London) May 24, 1924.

SYNGE, JOHN MILLINGTON (April 16, 1871-March 24, 1909), Irish dramatist, was born Edmund John Millington Synge in Rathfarnham, a Dublin suburb, the youngest of eight children of John Hatch Synge, a barrister, and Kathleen (Traill) Synge, daughter of a Protestant clergyman. The Synges were an old Wicklow family, middle-class, well-educated, and Protestant. The father died when Synge was an infant, and the widow, in impoverished circumstances, moved to a poorer suburb, Rathgar, with her children. Synge attended private schools and at seventeen entered Trinity College, receiving his B.A. degree in 1892. He played the violin, had had some training, and now went to Germany with the idea of becoming a professional musician. Gradually his interest in literature superseded that in music, and after a year of wandering in Germany he went to Italy and finally to Paris. His new ambition was to become a literary critic, and with this in mind he began an intensive study of the new trends in French literature.

Paris was full of young Irishmen in search of art, culture, or only a freer life than they could find at home, and Synge to some extent associated himself with them, even joining *L'Association Irelandaise,* a branch of the revolutionary Young Ireland Society, though politics was never among his real interests. Since his income was small, he was obliged to supplement it by free-lance journalism, which he hated. He hated a spurious bohemianism as well, and lived quietly and abstemiously. For from these early years he was in exceedingly frail health, with a marked tubercular tendency, a fact which not only caused his early death but also in some sense determined by reaction the nature of his writing. It was only in speech that Synge was ever coarse; like most invalids, he had a taste for the ways of the vigorous and full-blooded, but he himself was a lifelong Puritan and celibate.

The great event in the life of Synge as a writer was his meeting with William Butler Yeats in 1898. The older man saw at once the qualities of this young student, and advised him to put an end to his researches among the *fin de siècle litterateurs* of France, and to go back to his own home and start describing a society natural to him. It may be that Yeats also perceived the perilous state of health of a man who had just undergone a serious operation, and that it was partly for this reason that he recommended the primitive Aran Islands, off the coast of Donegal, as an unworked territory for a writer who wanted to do something new and authentic as a spokesman of Ireland.

Actually, Synge spent only six weeks on the Aran Islands at this first visit, though they were among the most fruitful weeks of his life. He returned again and again, and he took to wandering elsewhere through Ireland, mostly in Wicklow. Though at first he made frequent trips to Paris, his life became increasingly bounded by Ireland, and his interests concentrated in the observation of speech, customs, and legends of the peasants. As early as November 1898 his first essay drawn from these observations appeared in the *New Ireland Review*.

But the real turn his genius was to take was not descriptive, but dramatic. When Yeats, Lady Gregory, and George Moore founded the Irish National Theatre Society, which became the Abbey Theatre, Synge had two one-act plays ready for them—*In the Shadow of the Glen,* a brief foretaste of the immortal *Playboy* in its uncompromising view of human nature and its wild poetry, and that almost Greek tragedy in the vernacular of the Irish peasant, *Riders to the Sea.* The former play was, of course, hissed, there being no audiences so sensitive to seeming affront as those of Dublin, but compared to the reception later to be accorded to Synge's masterpiece, it might be said that his first appearance as a dramatist was a success. He then wrote *The Tinker's Wedding,* which the Abbey Players did not dare to offer on the stage until after Synge's death, because of its anti-theological implications; but the next of his plays to be produced, *The Well of the Saints,* a rather slight ironical study, was received noncommittally.

The storm broke with *The Playboy of the Western World,* a full-length play, undoubtedly Synge's greatest, and (to quote George Moore, who was not given to much praise of his contemporaries) "the most significant play of the last two hundred years." Both in Ireland and America the performance of this high comedy of the lad who was a hero as long as people thought he had killed his father gave rise to riots. Old play-goers may perhaps remember some of them, as late as 1912—the shouts from the audience, the pumpkin and custard pies hurled at the actors, the counter-yells from outraged auditors, and the reluctant arrests by obviously sympathetic policemen. The only person unmoved by all the turmoil was Synge himself, who on the occasion of the first outbreak murmured, "We shall have to establish a Society for the Preservation of Irish Humor."

Synge, however, was never a man to put himself forward or mix actively in any disturbance, pleasant or otherwise. He was morbidly shy, self-deprecatory, undemonstrative, nervous, a solitary who feared cities and escaped to the country whenever he could. Someone has described a reception to the Abbey Players where Synge hid to avoid being noticed. He did not look much like an invalid except to the discerning eye, being heavy-set, swarthy, with thick black hair (it all fell out during one illness but came in again), a heavy moustache that hid his mouth, and a queer little tuft of beard. Only his "thoughtful wide-set eyes" proclaimed the poet. St. John Ervine has remarked acutely that Synge was "what Bernard Shaw might have been had he allowed his nature to run off to dark corners and hide itself."

Meanwhile he was becoming increasingly ill. During his last year of life he had two major operations. He had never married, but he was engaged to Maire O'Neill, a leading actress of the Abbey company. They were fated never to marry; during most of their engagement she saw him only when she sat by his bed in a nursing home. On his last day he asked to be moved to another room, where the window looked on his beloved Wicklow Mountains. But the mountains were not visible except to one standing, and Synge, unable to lift himself at all, died with tears of disappointment in his eyes. He had left unfinished perhaps his most purely beautiful play, his reconstruction of the old Irish legend of Deirdre.

"The sick man in literature," Ervine called him, "with the sick man's interest in cruelty and harshness and violent temperaments," and his best work behind him; but even Ervine conceded that he brought "a desirable element of bitterness and acrid beauty into the sticky mess of self-satisfaction and sentimentalism" of earlier Irish literature. But Synge himself said, "Before poetry can be human again it must learn to be brutal," and L. A. G. Strong said the same thing as Ervine but more kindly: "He was able to keep without affectation the gusto generally left behind in the nursery." Intensity is the keynote of his work. It may be that, as Hugh l'A. Fausset thought, he was "not at heart a creative artist; he rather echoed a voice to which he found himself deeply attuned, and he gave that voice a dramatic significance which it lacked in life, by imprisoning it in an artistic form." "All art is collaboration," Synge said. And, in the words of Anthony S. Woods, "he had his fingers upon the life-pulse of Ireland." Yet, with his ultimately English ancestry and his Protestant background, he does more than celebrate his native land. The magnificence of his language, the fidelity of its mimicry, and its lyric beauty would remain if he had never laid eyes on Ireland.

His name is pronounced *sing*.

PRINCIPAL WORKS: In the Shadow of the Glen, 1904; Riders to the Sea, 1904; The Well of the Saints, 1905; The Playboy of the Western World, 1907; The Aran Islands, 1907; The Tinker's Wedding, 1908; In Wicklow, 1908; Poems and Translations, 1909; Deirdre of the Sorrows, 1909; Collected Works, 1910.

ABOUT: Bickley, F. J. M. Synge and the Irish Dramatic Movement; Bourgeois, M. J. M. Synge and the Irish Theatre; Boyd, E. A. Ireland's Literary Renaissance; Corkery, D. Synge and Anglo-Irish Literature; Estill, A. D. The Sources of Synge; Gregory, I. A. Our Irish Theatre; Howe, P. P. J. M. Synge: A Critical Study; Krieger, H. John Millington Synge; Masefield, J. J. M. Synge; Moore, G. Hail and Farewell; Robinson, L. (ed.). The Irish Theatre; Synge, S. Letters to My Daughter; Thorning, J. J. M. Synge; Weygandt, C. Irish Plays and Playwrights; Yeats, W. B. Synge and the Ireland of His Time, Cutting of an Agate, Dramatis Personae; Bookman April 1931; Bookman (London) March 1926; Catholic World April 1935; Dial April 1928; Fortnightly Review February 1924; Forum December 1935; Living Age September 9, 1922; London Mercury April 1928; North American Review May 1920; Poetry May 1933; Quarterly Notebook Spring 1916; Revue des Deux Mondes June 1, 1935; Yale Review July 1924.

TABB, JOHN BANNISTER. See "AMERICAN AUTHORS: 1600-1900"

*TAGGARD, GENEVIEVE (November 28, 1894-   ), American poet and biographer, writes: "I was born on an apple farm in Waitsburg, Wash. My parents were schoolteachers, Alta Gale (Arnold) Taggard and James Nelson Taggard. Both my grandfathers fought for the Union under Grant. Both were farmers, Scotch-Irish on one side, Huguenot French and

Prix

Scotch on the other. I was raised on stories of the Ozarks and Lincoln. When I was two years old my parents went to the Hawaiian Islands to teach in the public schools. At first we lived on a sugar plantation; then my father was given a school

at Kalihi-waena near Honolulu. I grew up with and knew intimately the Hawaiian, Chinese, Portuguese, and Japanese children who were the pupils in the school my parents were building. Outside the family I knew almost no white people until I was sent to Punahou School, a private school founded by the first missionaries. When my father's health failed we returned twice to Waitsburg, but found the adjustment to the small town too difficult for all of us.

"My parents were devoted Disciples of the Christian Church, and they started a mission in our community. The Bible and hymns were my chief background. I remember telling my mother that I disliked poetry because it was insincere, and about this time I became a bookworm, but read only prose.

"When I was about thirteen I began to write imitations of a few favorite poets, which were very bad, awkward, and meaningless. Keats was my first big passion; I began to see what poetry does when I read him. His luxury suited the Island radiance. I did not love any stern or bare speech for many years. The Greek myths were discouraged when I was little because they were pagan; in school they were too schoolbookish for my taste. I was never excited by Greek culture until I saw the Black Sea in 1936. I think I understand and like Asia and the dark peoples better than Europe. The Bible was always a great Oriental story book for me.

"In 1914 some friends gave me a small scholarship and my family bought tickets for San Francisco. We had a pretty desperate time of it for the next five years. My father was too ill to do much; my mother ran a boarding-house for students at the University of California and I earned what I could while going to college. Finally I became editor of the *Occident,* the college literary magazine, which paid a small salary. But it took five years.

"At the end of college I called myself a Socialist in a rather vague way. Since then I have always been to the left of center. In those days Frank Norris and Jack London were still heard of as friends of friends. The great city of San Francisco taught me a good deal that I needed to know.

"My first published poem was in *Harper's Magazine.* When I came to New York in 1920 I worked in the publishing house of B. W. Huebsch, who had just started the *Freeman.* Van Wyck Brooks very kindly gave me a few books of poetry to review. That year I joined a group of young writers to get out a little poetry magazine called the *Measure*. I married Robert Wolf and in 1921 my daughter was born.

"Since 1921 ·I have published thirteen books (some of them anthologies); written many stories, articles, and book reviews. I taught literature at Mt. Holyoke College before I was awarded a Guggenheim Fellowship in 1931; returned to the opening of the new Bennington (Vt.) College, and since 1934 have taught at Sarah Lawrence College in Bronxville, N. Y. In 1934 I was divorced and in 1935 married Kenneth Durant. In the summer we live on a boat, going up the Hudson each summer to Lake Champlain. I have learned to fish.

"In 1931 on a Guggenheim Fellowship my daughter and sister and I lived in Capri and Mallorca. Part of *The Life and Mind of Emily Dickinson* was written in southern France. I have lived in Spain and England and for one long summer in the Soviet Union on the Black Sea, and later in Tiflis (now Tiblisi), where I fell in love with that city.

"When I face the fact that my poetry is not very much read in my own country I console myself by the fact that my work has been translated into many foreign languages. My poems have also been set to music by William Schuman, Aaron Copland, Roy Harris, and Henry Leland Clarke. In 1939 a song set by Mr. Schuman was sung at Carnegie Hall and in Stadium Concerts by a chorus of two hundred school children.

"I am a member of the Teachers' Union, and an elected member of the Executive Council of the League of American Writers. I helped start the League School for young writers, which has been a success. I have given several readings from the works of Whitman, Emily Dickinson, and Shakespeare over the radio. I am now writing a prose book about the life of my parents in the Islands. It will be very slow in the writing.

"Being a teacher, a poet, and a student, I am not very much impressed by the present standards that measure our culture. To speak bluntly I think most of the intellectuals are provincial. I think I can foresee an American literature and especially an American poetry that make most of what we have now look pretty stuffy. Even those who are called our best critics are ignorant of two things: excellence in world literature, and the life and talents of the American people."

* * *

Miss Taggard's poetry has been in process of steady growth from its early lyricism, when Edmund Wilson called it "simply and spontaneously sensuous," to a dynamic statement of social conscience and passion—"the poetry," says Marie de L. Welch, "of a revolutionary, yet positive, affirmative, more generous with love than with anger." Samuel Putnam finds in her recent work a combination of "the delicate-keyed intensity of an Emily Dickinson with the expansiveness of a Walt Whitman."

Genevieve Taggard looks the poet—tall, slender, with brown hair and delicately chiseled features. Her speaking voice is rich and warm. She gives the impression of fragility built over a frame of steel.

PRINCIPAL WORKS: For Eager Lovers, 1922; Hawaiian Hilltop, 1923; Words for the Chisel, 1926; Traveling Standing Still, 1928; The Life and Mind of Emily Dickinson (biography) 1930; Remembering Vaughan in New England, 1933; Not Mine to Finish, 1934; Calling Western Union, 1936; Collected Poems: 1918-1938, 1938; Long View, 1942.

ABOUT: Herrman, E. On Parade; Taggard, G. Calling Western Union (see Introduction); Boston Evening Transcript February 16, 1935; New Masses June 9, 1942; New Republic December 12, 1928, June 11, 1939; Poetry December 1934, May 1937; Saturday Review of Literature November 10, 1934; Scholastic May 6, 1940; Time December 26, 1938.

TAGORE, Sir RABINDRANATH (May 6, 1861-August 7, 1941), Indian poet, dramatist, and novelist, Nobel Prize winner, was born in Calcutta, the eldest of seven sons of Maharshi Debendranath Tagore, a wealthy Brahmin. (Tagore, or Thākura, is in the native tongue really not a name, but a title of nobility.) His mother died of tuberculosis when he was thirteen. Talented both in music and literature from childhood, he was educated by tutors and at private schools, and in 1878 went to live with a brother in England. He attended classes at University College, London, and was preparing to study law. However, he returned to India, and when in 1883 it was planned to have him return to England to complete his law course, an accident, taken by his father as an omen, prevented his doing so. He had already, by this time, published a good deal in Bengali, his first work appearing in 1876 in a magazine called *Jñānānkur* (*Sprouting Knowledge*), and his first book, a narrative poem called *Kabikāhinī* (*A Poet's Tale*) having appeared in 1878. In 1883 he married Mrinali-

M. Vos

nidebi; they had one son, and a daughter who is married to a well known agricultural economist of Calcutta University.

Tagore received the Nobel Prize for literature in 1913. He was at the time on a lecture tour in the United States, and Harriet Monroe had published his first work in English (translations by himself of his Bengalese poems) in *Poetry*. In 1915 he was knighted; four years later he surrendered the title in protest against British suppression of the Punjab riots, but in later years permitted it to be used again. He received honorary doctorates from four Indian universities, and in 1930 delivered the Hibbert Lectures at Oxford. Following this he made an extensive tour in Germany, Denmark, Russia, and the United States, and two years later traveled in Persia. In 1901 he had founded a school, Visva-Bharati, in Bengal, which became an international institute. It was always the interest closest to his heart; he lived at the school now, in Santineketan, and gave most of his time to it. To it he donated his entire Nobel Prize and all the proceeds of his lectures. At sixty-eight, he suddenly took up painting, and exhibited in Moscow, Berlin, Munich, Paris, Birmingham, and New York. He was also a musician, having composed over three thousand songs. In 1940 Oxford gave him a Litt.D. degree *in absentia*.

In his dark robes, Tagore resembled an ancient sage, with (to quote Pierre Lagarde) his "calm, impassive face, lofty smooth arched forehead above which falls an avalanche of white hair reaching to his shoulders, and prophetic beard." His voice was thin and gentle, and he habitually kept his eyes lowered. A "universal humanitarian" with a strongly mystical tinge, his desire for the social welfare of India sometimes conflicted with the more aggressively political demands of the Nationalists under Mahatma Gandhi. He was essentially an ethicist and a conciliator.

Tagore translated much of his own work and that of others into English, and occasionally wrote directly in English himself. He was a poet above all, even in his plays and novels and short stories. (He wrote 100,000 lines of poetry, as against Milton's 18,000!) He has been called "the Bengal Shelley," and it is probably true that the full flavor of his work cannot be understood except by reading it in his native tongue. Even in English, however, its music, color, and lofty spirit may be surmised, though it was doubtless largely because of his immense reputation in India that he received the Nobel award.

Tagore died in Calcutta after a long illness, at the age of eighty.

WORKS AVAILABLE IN ENGLISH: Gitanjali (Song Offerings) 1912; Chitra (play) 1913; The Crescent Moon (poems) 1913; The Gardener (poems) 1913; The King of the Dark Chamber (play) 1914; The Post Office (play) 1914; Sādharā: The Realization of Life, 1914; Fruit-Gathering, 1916; The Hungry Stones and Other Stories, 1916; Stray Birds, 1916; The Cycle of Spring (play) 1917; My Reminiscences, 1917; Nationalism, 1917; Personality, 1917; Sacrifice and Other Plays, 1917; Lover's Gift, 1918; Crossing, 1918; Mashi and Other Stories, 1918; Parrot's Training, 1918; Stories From Tagore, 1918; The Home and the World (novel) 1919; The Fugitive, 1921; Glimpses of Bengal, 1921; Thought Relics, 1921; The Wreck (novel) 1921; Creative Unity, 1922; Poems, 1923; Greater India, 1923; The Eyesore, 1924; Letters From Abroad, 1924; Red Oleander (play) 1924; Broken Ties and Other Stories, 1925; Fireflies, 1928; Letters to a Friend, 1928; The Religion of Man, 1930; Sheaves, Poems, and Songs, 1932; Collected Poems and Plays, 1936.

ABOUT: Kitch, E. M. Rabindranath Tagore, A Bibliography; Lesný, V. Rabindranath Tagore: His Personality and Work; Rādhā-Krishnan, S. The Philosophy of Rabindranath Tagore; Rhys, E. Rabindranath Tagore, Wales England Wed; Rothenstein, W. Men and Memories; Roy, B. K. Rabindranath Tagore: The Man and His Poetry; Tagore, R. My Reminiscences; Thompson, E. J. Rabindranath Tagore: His Life and Work; American Federationist March 1928; Asia April 1933, July 1934, June 1940, March 1941; Bookman (London) December 1926; Canadian Monthly February 1921; Current Biography 1941; Current History August 1936; Living Age July 1, 1930, November 1930, March 1931; London Mercury December 1938; New Republic January 8, 1930; New York Times August 8, 1941; Poetry September 1941; Publishers' Weekly August 16, 1941; Quarterly Review October 1929; Saturday Review of Literature August 16, 1941; School and Society November 21, 1931; Time August 18, 1941.

TAPPAN, EVA MARCH (December 26, 1854-January 30, 1930), American writer and anthologist, was born at Blackstone, Mass., the daughter of the Rev. Edmund March and Lucretia (Logée) Tappan. Graduating from Vassar in 1875, she taught at Wheaton College, Mass., and in private schools. She received her master's degree in 1895 and a Ph.D.  from the University of Pennsylvania in 1896. For seven years Miss Tappan headed the English department in the English High School, Worcester, Mass., where she began to write. *Charles Lamb: The Man and the Author* was her first book, published when she was forty-two. School children innumerable have gained their first impressions of American, English, Greek and Roman history, of English queens, of folk-heroes, old ballads, writers of the English-speaking countries, and animals and birds from Miss Tappan's clearly written accounts and from her sensibly chosen and edited anthologies. She served as assistant editor for the United States Food Administration during the First World War, notably doing *A Little Book of Our Country* for the Y.M.C.A. Miss Tappan was a member of Phi Beta Kappa and the Boston Authors' Club. In Worcester she had a comfortable house rather like the Alcott house in Concord, where she was vigilantly watched over by an old servant. She was the active secretary of the Worcester Humane Society. A month before her death at seventy-five she was planning a translation of an Italian book. Her estate went to Vassar to establish the Eva March Tappan scholarship for young women.

PRINCIPAL WORKS: Charles Lamb: The Man and the Author, 1896; England's Story, 1901; In the Days of Queen Elizabeth, 1902; In the Days of Queen Victoria, 1903; The Christ Story, 1903; Robin Hood: His Book, 1903; A Short History of America's Literature, 1906; The Story of the Greek People, 1908; Dixie Kitten, 1910; When Knights Were Bold, 1912; The House With the Silver Door, 1913; Diggers in the Earth, 1916; Ella: A Little Schoolgirl of the Sixties, 1923. *Compiler and Editor:* Selections From Emerson, 1898; American Hero Stories, 1906; Folk Stories and Fables, 1907; Myths From Many Lands, 1907; The Children's Hour, 1907; Stories of Legendary Heroes, 1907; Poems and Rhymes, 1907; A Friend in the Library (12 vols.) 1909; The Book of Humor, 1916; Adventures and Achievements, 1929.

ABOUT: Kunitz, S. J. & Haycraft, H. (eds.). The Junior Book of Authors; New York Times January 31, 1930.

*TARBELL, IDA MINERVA (November 5, 1857-), American journalist and biographer, was born in a log-house in Erie

County, Pennsylvania, the daughter of Franklin Sumner Tarbell and Esther Ann (McCullough) Tarbell. The panic of 1857 and the long depression that followed conspired to have the child born there and not in Taylor County, Iowa, where Tarbell,

A. C. Johnston

a carpenter, had planned to build his family a house. Returning to Pennsylvania, he built a shop where he could make tanks to hold barrels of the newly discovered petroleum. With the coming of iron tanks, Tarbell used his capital to become an oil producer. The oil fields were familiar territory to Ida Tarbell when she began to investigate the machinations of the Standard Oil Company for *McClure's Magazine* forty years later. Her other major interest, the life and times of Lincoln, dated from the impression made on the child by the tragedy of his death. In 1870 the family moved to Titusville, Pa. Ida graduated from high school with highest honors, and entered Allegheny College, Meadville, Pa., in the fall of 1876. She received her B.A. degree here, a master's degree in 1883 (and a L.H.D. in 1909, followed by an LL.D. in 1915; Knox College gave her an L.H.D. in 1909). After eight years, 1883-91, as associate editor of *The Chautauquan,* monthly organ of the Chautauqua Literary and Scientific Circle, she "plunged gaily into planning for a career in journalism, self-directed, free-lance journalism. Surely I could find subjects enough in Paris to write about, subjects that would interest American newspapers." Three newspapers accepted her syndicated articles, and *Scribner's Magazine* took a story. *McClure's Magazine,* started in August 1893 by S. S. McClure, proved a particularly receptive market, and in 1894 Miss Tarbell joined the staff as associate editor. Her first work was to write a life of Napoleon around a large collection of Napoleon portraits. Searching for unpublished material on Lincoln was next, occupying four years; and *The History of the Standard Oil Company* was the outgrowth of an editorial inspiration to tell the story of a typical monopolistic trust. Miss Tarbell ferreted out the documents in the case, and received help from the enemy's camp in the form of authorized interviews with Henry Rogers of the Company, and unexpected information from John D. Rockefeller's disgruntled brother Frank. John D. made no effort to reply to the book, merely forbidding any reference to "that misguided woman." Miss Tarbell was associate editor of the *American Magazine* from 1906 to 1915, after which she returned to free-lance writing. From 1920 to 1932 she toured the country annually on lecture trips. Proceeds were invested in a farm at Bethel, Conn. Her Manhattan residence is on East 19th Street, and she is a member of the National Arts, Cosmopolitan, and Pen and Brush clubs. All her books are competently planned and written, and the *New Yorker* called her memoirs, *All in the Day's Work,* "serenely charming in a way all their own."

PRINCIPAL WORKS: Short Life of Napoleon Bonaparte, 1895; Life of Madame Roland, 1896; Early Life of Abraham Lincoln (with J. McC.

* Died January 6, 1944.

Davis) 1896; Life of Abraham Lincoln, 1900; History of the Standard Oil Company, 1904; He Knew Lincoln, 1907; Father Abraham, 1907; The Tariff in Our Times, 1911; The Business of Being a Woman, 1912; The Ways of Women, 1915; New Ideals in Business, 1916; The Rising of the Tide, 1919; In Lincoln's Chair, 1920; Boy Scouts' Life of Lincoln, 1921; He Knew Lincoln, and Other Billy Brown Stories, 1924; In the Footsteps of Lincoln, 1924; Life of Judge Gary, 1925; A Reporter for Lincoln, 1927; Owen D. Young: A New Type of Industrial Leader, 1932; The Nationalizing of Business: 1878-1898, 1936; All in the Day's Work: An Autobiography. 1939.

ABOUT: Nevins, A. John D. Rockefeller; Tarbell, I. All in the Day's Work; Ladies' Home Journal July 1939.

TARDINEAU, RENÉ MARIE AUGUSTE. See BOYLESVE, R.

*TARKINGTON, BOOTH (July 29, 1869-), American novelist, writes: "This writer was born [Newton Booth Tarkington] in a quiet, love-

ly little city, Indianapolis, Ind., and began to talk when he was seven months old by calling the family dog. That small city, the Indianapolis where I was born, exists no more than Carthage existed after the Romans had driven ploughs over the ground where it had stood. Progress swept all the old life away. I still live in Indianapolis, though, and am glad I do. I've lived in other places; in Exeter, N.H., where I went to prep school; in Lafayette, Ind., when I went to Purdue University for a year; and in Princeton, N.J., when I was in the university there, in the class of 1893. Since then I've lived a while in New York and Paris and Rome, and for a little time on the island of Capri; and for many years now I have been spending long seasons [year-long, and what to others would seem a permanent residence] in Kennebunkport, Maine, on the sea. But I always speak and think of Indianapolis as home. Almost all Hoosiers are that way about where they grew up.

"During my boyhood I wanted to be an artist, a painter or at least an illustrator. I tried persistently to draw pictures after I found it was hopeless for me to think of painting them. But at last I found out that my hand would never do what my mind wanted it to do; and so, since my hand could make nothing better than symbols (written words, that is), I discovered that I was a writer. As a matter of fact, I al-

ways had been a writer, but didn't realize it because, like a great many other people, I pined to do what I couldn't.

"About five years after I began being a writer seriously and professionally, a magazine editor accepted the manuscript of a long novel of mine, and since then a great many other novels and stories of mine have been published, and something over a score of plays I have written have been put upon the stage. All this means millions of words scribbled and crossed out and rewritten, and, as every old-fashioned autobiography should end with a summing-up, I conclude these memories by saying it seems to me that judging by what I know of my character I wouldn't have done all this work if I hadn't liked doing it."

* * *

Mr. Tarkington is the son of John Stevenson Tarkington, a lawyer, and Elizabeth (Booth) Tarkington. An older sister was his close companion; to her he dictated his first stories at the age of six, and it was she who went to New York and practically forced S. S. McClure to accept *Monsieur Beaucaire*. He was a frail, sallow, reedy youth, who in boyhood became a chain cigarette smoker and has been one ever since. An early death was always predicted for him, but he has outlived most of his old friends. He was never graduated from college because he failed to make up a condition in Greek. But Princeton has given him an honorary M.A. and Litt.D., and he has received the latter honor also from De Pauw and Columbia.

The net result of his efforts to become an illustrator was one drawing sold to *Life*. His first three novels brought him very little money and less fame, though they have helped to make his fortune since. In 1902 he was elected to the Indiana Legislature as a Republican, and served one term. *In the Arena* was drawn from his political experiences. In the same year he married Laurel Louisa Fletcher, who divorced him in 1911. The death of their daughter was one of the lasting griefs of his life. His second wife was Susannah Robinson, whom he married in 1912.

In Kennebunkport he has his boathouse filled with nautical prints and ships' figureheads, and in his house is his fine collection of paintings, about which a late book centers. In his sixties he became blind from cataracts, and underwent several operations and a long siege of pain. Now he has sight in one eye, but he has to dictate his work— he formerly wrote, on violently yellow paper, hunched over a drawing-board, for twelve or fourteen hours at a stretch—and has to be read to instead of reading. In spite of all the set-backs of recent years, he remains the same friendly, convivial, optimistic person he was at Princeton (where his deep bass voice was famous in the Glee Club), or in his youthful years with Harry Leon Wilson and Julian Street in New York. His rather saturnine and Mephistophelean countenance belies his amiable nature.

He has twice won the Pulitzer Prize in fiction, for *The Magnificent Ambersons* and for *Alice Adams* (by far his best novel); and he is one of three persons to receive the gold medal of the American Institute of Arts and Sciences. He has been called "the most versatile of American writers." He is certainly one of the most uneven. Essentially he is a romantic and a sentimentalist, but (as Kenneth Roberts remarked) "like all sentimentalists he has a strong vein of cynicism." To some readers, Penrod and Willie Baxter are of the lineage of Huck Finn and Tom Sawyer; to others, they are false and boring. Carl Van Doren called him "the glass of adolescence and the mold of Indiana," and rated him as sophomoric. Joseph Collins pointed out his total lack of passion, for which "he substitutes accuracy in details, a firm determination to remain within the narrow confines of Western ideals." Few today are charmed by the pure escapism of his earliest novels. He himself acknowledges that he is a conservative, that he dislikes the plain speaking of modern fiction as much as he dislikes shoddy English.

Nevertheless, at his best Tarkington can write in the finest American tradition. Edith Franklin Wyatt noted that *The Magnificent Ambersons* and *Alice Adams* "follow the way of French rather than English realism"; and the great French novelists have been his conscious models—though the earliest real influence on him was that of William Dean Howells. He himself has expressed his own credo: "The natural writer . . . hopes to communicate—to present to somebody else his interpretation of life. He is not just an entertainer." In his major works Booth Tarkington has done just that, simply and sincerely; and to those who reject the communication, he would say only that their outlook on life is different from his, and that his (as evidenced by his great and lasting popularity) is the one most current in the America of his time, and particularly in Middle Western America, from which he sprang.

PRINCIPAL WORKS: *Novels*—The Gentleman From Indiana, 1899; Monsieur Beaucaire, 1900;

The Two Vanrevels, 1902; Cherry, 1903; In the Arena, 1905; The Conquest of Canaan, 1905; The Beautiful Lady, 1905; His Own People, 1907; The Quest of Quesnay, 1908; Beasley's Christmas Party, 1909; Beauty and the Jacobin, 1912; The Flirt, 1913; Penrod, 1914; The Turmoil, 1915; Penrod and Sam, 1916; Seventeen, 1916; The Magnificent Ambersons, 1918; Ramsey Milholland, 1919; Alice Adams, 1921; Harlequin and Columbine, 1921; Gentle Julia, 1922; The Fascinating Stranger and Other Stories, 1923; The Midlander, 1924; Women, 1925; The Plutocrat, 1927; Growth, 1927; Claire Ambler, 1928; Young Mrs. Greeley, 1929; Penrod Jashber, 1929; Mirthful Haven, 1930; Mary's Neck, 1932; Wanton Mally, 1932; Presenting Lily Mars, 1933; Little Orvie, 1934; Mr. White, The Red Barn, Hell, and Bridewater (novelettes) 1935; The Lorenzo Bunch, 1936; Rumbin Galleries, 1937; The Heritage of Hatcher Ide, 1941; The Fighting Littles, 1941. *Plays*—The Man From Home, (with H. L. Wilson) 1907; Cameo Kirby, 1908; Springtime, 1909; Foreign Exchange, 1909; Your Humble Servant, 1909; If I Had Money, 1910; The Man on Horseback, 1911; Mister Antonio, 1915; The Country Cousin, 1916; Up From Nowhere, 1919; Clarence, 1919; The Gibson Upright, 1920; Poldekin, 1921; The Wren, 1922; Magnolia, 1922; Tweedles, 1923; The Intimate Strangers, 1923; Rose Briar, 1924; How's Your Health, 1930; Aromatic Aaron Burr, 1938. *Miscellaneous*—Looking Forward and Others (essays) 1926; The World Does Move (semi-autobiography) 1928; Some Old Portraits, 1939.

ABOUT: Boynton, P. H. Some Contemporary Americans; Dickinson, A. D. Booth Tarkington; Holliday, R. C. Booth Tarkington; Bookman March 1927; Life September 4, 1939, March 10, 1941; Living Age March 1, 1919; Nation February 9, 1921; North American Review October 1922; Publishers' Weekly December 2, 1933; Saturday Evening Post August 8, 1931, August 20, November 19, December 17, 1932; Saturday Review of Literature December 4, 1926, March 1, 1941; World's Work January 1930.

TATE, ALLEN (November 19, 1899-), American poet, essayist, biographer, and novelist who was born John Orley Allen Tate, writes: "I was born at Winchester, Clark County, Ky., in the Kentucky Blue Grass. My early education was entirely at home; when at the age of nine I entered a private school in Louisville I remember that I astonished the teacher by reciting  'The Chambered Nautilus' and Poe's 'To Helen.' When I was about twelve my mother said to me one day, 'Put that book down and go out and play. You mustn't strain your mind; it isn't very strong.' (As a boy of four or five I had a big bulging head; my elders, who discussed children in those days as if they were inanimate objects, used to say, 'Do you think he has water on the brain?') The family belief that I was an imbecile redoubled my secret efforts to prove them wrong: secret efforts, because outwardly until I was through college I was trying to appear to be just like other boys— a rôle in which I was not successful. Then, after I had left Vanderbilt, my brother gave me a job in his coal office in Eastern Kentucky; in one day I lost the company $700, by shipping some coal to Duluth that should have gone to Cleveland; and my business career was over.

"I have been asked many times why I became a writer. I simply could not put my mind on anything else. As far back as I can remember I was wondering why the people and families I knew—my own family particularly—had got to be what they were, and what their experience had been. This problem, greatly extended, continues to absorb all my study and speculation, and is the substance of my novel, *The Fathers.*"

* * *

Mr. Tate is the son of John Orley Tate and Nellie (Varnell) Tate, and a descendant of three officers of the American Revolution. He was graduated from Vanderbilt University in 1922, *magna cum laude*. In 1924 he married Caroline Gordon, the novelist;[qv] they have one daughter. He received Guggenheim Fellowships in 1928 and 1929, was a lecturer in English literature at Southwestern College, Memphis, Tenn., from 1934 to 1936, was professor of English in the Woman's College of the University of North Carolina in 1938-39, and was a special lecturer in modern poetry at Columbia in 1936, later becoming resident fellow in poetry at Princeton (1939-42). His home is a Monteagle, Tenn. He was Southern editor of the *Hound and Horn* from 1931 to 1934, and was an advisory editor of the *Kenyon Review*.

He is a member of the so-called Agrarian Group of Southern writers and political theorists, and was one of the founders of the *Fugitive*. The strongest early influence on his work was that of T. S. Eliot; he still writes in what Louis Untermeyer called a "personally pronounced and intricate style, [and by a] circumambient method." Morton Dauwen Zabel, reviewing his poetry, found its central thesis to be devotion to "the creed of memory." His dominant themes in all his work have been the Civil War, and "life's mortal idiocy." He is a cerebral writer, incisive, pugnacious, erudite, and witty. On the air he has been heard as a participant in the scholarly discussions called

"Invitation to Learning" (published in book form in 1941).

Physically his chief characteristic is still his bulging cranium. He is fair-haired and blue-eyed, with a small moustache and a (deceptively) mild appearance.

PRINCIPAL WORKS: Stonewall Jackson: The Good Soldier, 1928; Mr. Pope and Other Poems, 1928; Jefferson Davis: His Rise and Fall, 1929; Three Poems, 1930; Poems: 1928-1931, 1932; Robert E. Lee, 1932; The Mediterranean and Other Poems, 1935; Reactionary Essays on Poetry and Ideas, 1936; Selected Poems, 1937; The Fathers (novel) 1938; Reason in Madness, 1941; (with H. Cairns and M. Van Doren) Invitation to Learning, 1941; (ed.) The Language of Poetry, 1942; (ed.) Princeton Verse Between Two Wars, 1942; (ed. with J. P. Bishop) American Harvest.

ABOUT: Brooks, C. Modern Poetry and the Tradition; Bookman January 1930; Poetry April 1932, May 1937, February 1938; Scrutiny June 1939; Sewanee Review October 1930, July 1937; Southern Review Autumn 1939; Time November 1, 1937, October 2, 1940.

TAWNEY, RICHARD HENRY

(1880-   ), English economist, was born in Calcutta, India, the son of C. H. Tawney, C.I.E., a British official, and Constance Catherine (Fox) Tawney. He was sent to England to be educated at Rugby, and proceeded from there to Balliol College, Oxford. In later years, from 1918 to 1921, he was a Fellow of Balliol, and was made an

Honorary Fellow in 1938. From 1906 to 1908 he was an assistant in economics at Glasgow University, then for six years he was a teacher for tutorial classes of the Committee of Oxford University. He is now professor of economic history at the University of London, and from 1933 to 1937 was also president of Morley College for Working Men and Women. In 1909 he married Annette J. Beveridge; they have no children.

Professor Tawney has held many positions on economic boards and committees, frequently connected with the government. Among others, he has been a member of the Consultative Committee of the London Board of Education, the Coal Industry Commission, the Chain Trade Board, and the Cotton Trade Conciliation Committee. He was director of the Ratan Tata Foundation of the University of London in 1913 and 1914. In 1922 he delivered the Holland Memorial Lectures at King's College, London. He has been a Fellow of the British

Academy since 1935. He is an active member of the Labor Party, though he has never stood for Parliament or taken any part in purely political affairs. In 1942 he spent several months in Washington as economic and sociological adviser to the British Embassy.

His work as an economist has been divided between scholarly contributions, such as his editing of economic treatises by George Unwin, Thomas Wilson, Max Weber, and others, and his introductions to various economic surveys (chief of which is *Agrarian China*, issued in 1939 by the Institute of Pacific Relations); and his function as a labor mediator in the industrial committees mentioned above. He is a recognized authority on several specialized fields of industry and agriculture in England, on labor conditions in China (to which he has made extended visits), and on child labor. His articles appear frequently in technical reviews. With all these preoccupations, he has had small leisure to publish many original books, but the three best known, *The Acquisitive Society, Religion and the Rise of Capitalism* and *Equality*, have gained for him an international reputation. His social viewpoint is Fabian and evolutionary, but unswervingly in favor of a collective society. Nevertheless, he remains one of the most valued of governmental advisers.

His style is that of a teacher—simple and clear, straightforward and sober. His books cannot be said to display much liveliness; there is nothing picturesque or anecdotal about his exposition: but they are highly useful to the student seriously interested in economic history and fundamental economic theory written from a position slightly left of center.

PRINCIPAL WORKS: The Agrarian Problem in the Sixteenth Century, 1912; English Economic History; Select Documents (ed., with A. E. Bland & P. A. Brown) 1914; The Acquisitive Society, 1920; Tudor Economic Documents (ed., with E. Power) 1924; The British Labour Movement, 1925; Religion and the Rise of Capitalism, 1926; Equality, 1931; Land and Labour in China, 1932; Juvenile Employment and Education, 1934; Why Britain Fights, 1941.

ABOUT: Labour Monthly (London) November 1933; World Unity June 1931.

TAYLOR, BERT LESTON ("B.L.T.")
(November 13, 1866-March 19, 1921), American humorist and pioneer newspaper "columnist," was born in Goshen, Mass., the son of A. O. Taylor and Katherine (White) Taylor. He attended the College of the City of New York, worked on various newspapers in the East, married Emma Bonner of Providence, R. I., in 1895, and in 1900 made a connection with the Chicago *Tribune*, where his famous column, "A Line-o'-Type or Two," signed "B.L.T.," appeared on the editorial page for nearly twenty years, with some interruptions. It was, as Henry B. Fuller remarked after Taylor's death at fifty-four, a broad column, "broad by measurement, broad in scope, and a bit broad, now and again in its tone." "The Column" was more than the sum of its contributors, he continued. "It was the sum of units, original or contributed, that had been manipulated and brought to high effectiveness by a skilled hand and a nature wide in its sympathies and in its range of interests." (Among those who vied in "making the Line" was a Chicago youth named Franklin P. Adams,[qv] who as "F.P.A." was later to eclipse his acknowledged mentor with his own column "The Conning Tower" in the New York *Mail, Tribune, World, Herald Tribune* and *Post*.) Letters addressed simply to

"B.L.T." or "The Line o' Type" reached Taylor without delay from all quarters of the globe.

The So-Called Human Race, the title of a posthumous book by Taylor, more or less summed up his opinion of his fellow-creatures, to judge from Burton Rascoe's experience with Taylor on the *Tribune*. He was a grouchy man, says Rascoe, a snob about the office, disdainful of or ignoring everybody except Percy Hammond, John T. McCutcheon, Robert Burns Peattie, and Rascoe. He never took his job with the least seriousness. Unable himself to read Latin, he appreciated Keith Preston's Horatian translations. He was an enthusiastic golfer who practiced mashie shots on the rug of the editorial rooms, regardless of other workers there. His expertness as a parodist is best shown in his rendering of the London Busman Story in the manner of Meredith, James, and Bennett; and in *The Billioustine: A Periodical of Knock,* ostensibly printed by the Boy Grafters, which was a satire of Elbert Hubbard's and his Roycrofters' *The Philistine: A Periodical of Protest.* Taylor was tall and somewhat rustic in appearance.

PRINCIPAL WORKS: Line-o-type Lyrics, 1902; The Well in the Wood, 1904; Monsieur d'En Brochette (with A. H. Folwell and J. K. Bangs)

1905; The Log of the Water Wagon, 1905; The Charlatans, 1906; Extra Dry (with W. C. Gibson) 1906; A Line-o'-Verse or Two, 1911; The Pipe-smoke Carry, 1912; Motley Measures, 1913; A Penny Whistle, 1921; The So-Called Human Race, 1922; A Line o' Gowf or Two, 1923; The East Window and The Car Window, 1924.

ABOUT: Rascoe, B. Before I Forget; Taylor, B. L. The So-Called Human Race (see Introduction by H. B. Fuller); New York Times March 20, 1921.

TAYLOR, DEEMS (December 22, 1885-), American composer and music critic, was born on West Sixteenth Street

Kesslere

in New York City, the son of Joseph S. Taylor and Katharine Moore (Johnson) Taylor. He was christened Joseph Deems Taylor. At seventeen he graduated from the Ethical Culture School in New York; four years later, in 1906, he received a degree from New York University, which made him Mus. D. (honoris causa) in 1927. (Dartmouth College and the University of Rochester made Taylor the recipient of a similar degree in 1939; Juniata College had bestowed a Litt.D. in 1931.) Taylor went from college to the Nelson Encyclopedia as member of the editorial staff in 1906-07; transferred to the Britannica next year; and from 1912 to 1916 was an assistant editor of the Western Electric News. In 1916 he was assistant Sunday editor of the New York Tribune, spending 1916-17 in France as a war correspondent. In 1917-19 Taylor was an associate editor of Collier's Weekly. With this busy journalistic life he had still found time to compose symphonic poems and cantatas; his only formal training was three years' instruction (1908-11) in harmony, counterpoint, and orchestration with Oscar Coon of New York. The Echo (1910) was an unsuccessful musical comedy; The Siren Song (1912) was awarded the orchestral prize of the National Federation of Music Clubs; and The Highwayman (1914) was composed for the MacDowell Festival. Through the Looking Glass, a charming orchestral suite based on Lewis Carroll themes, was first performed in 1918 and revised in 1922. Jurgen, inspired by the James Branch Cabell fantasy, was composed for Walter Damrosch's now defunct New York Symphony Orchestra in 1925. The King's Henchman (1927) with its Anglo-Saxon libretto by Edna St. Vincent Millay and a rather indeterminate score

by the composer, was written on commission for the Metropolitan Opera Company. Peter Ibbetson (1931) based on the Du Maurier novel, made good use of French folk-songs and, with the incomparable Lucrezia Bori as the Duchess of Towers, had an unusual number of repetitions for an American opera. Mr. Taylor's third opera is Ramuntcho (1937). He composed incidental music and ballet music for Beggar on Horseback and other plays. From 1921 to 1925 he wrote soundly based and authoritative musical criticism for the New York World; edited Musical America from 1927 to 1929; was musical critic of the New York American for the year 1931-32; and since 1936 has been consultant on music for the Columbia Broadcasting System and commentator for the Sunday afternoon broadcasts of the Philharmonic Society. These persuasive, informal talks on music have been collected in two books. Mr. Taylor married Mary Kennedy, an actress (his second wife), in July 1921; they had one daughter and were divorced in 1934. His clubs are the Coffee House and Century, and his home Lyme, Conn. He has a spare frame, thinning blond hair, and an alert expression.

PRINCIPAL WORKS: Of Men and Music, 1937; The Well Tempered Listener, 1940; Walt Disney's Fantasia, 1940; A Treasury of Gilbert & Sullivan (ed.) 1941.

ABOUT: Shaw, C. G. The Low-Down; American Magazine February 1932, July 1934; Musician April 1931; Newsweek January 29, 1940.

TAYLOR, PHOEBE ATWOOD (May 18, 1909-), American writer of detective fiction, both under her own name and the pseudonym "Alice Tilton," was born in Boston, Mass. She attended Barnard College, the women's college of Columbia University, on a Lucille Pulitzer Residence Scholarship, from 1926 to 1930, receiving her B.A. degree in the latter year. The scholarship, awarded to girls coming from outside New York City, was established by Joseph Pulitzer in memory of his daughter, Lucille Pulitzer. Her Barnard College mates recall Phoebe Atwood Taylor as a "bland, imperturbable, dark young lady with a Boston accent, an inquisitive pug nose, and a mind like a two-edged sword. She rarely laughed, but she was always amused." The year after her graduation, she published her first detective story,

which promptly sold five thousand copies. The fourth, *The Mystery of the Cape Cod Tavern,* was dedicated to William T. Brewster, her English professor at Barnard. The *Boston Transcript* called the first, *The Cape Cod Mystery* (1931), which introduced her Down East detective, Asey Mayo, "a well-written tale with a sparkling sense of humor." "Her stories," remarked a Barnard alumna, "remind one of Joseph Lincoln with the leisure taken out and a corpse inserted." Another, Clare Howard, wrote: "If all the alumnae who say they 'intend to write' would set about it with the will exerted by P.A.T., we should have a fifty-foot shelf of books. And if they were as full of dash and life as hers they would be read, too. This 'Infant Balzac,' as her friends call her, to her great indignation and fury, has made use of her native land, Cape Cod, to form the background of her mystery stories. They are not Provincetown stories, of lighthouse-keepers and their beautiful, demented wives beside That Old Dayvil Sea, but Wellfleet stories. It is out of this essential town, with veracious old maids, wily captains, scions of Orleans, ginger cats, clams, bayberry candles, and other Capacious fauna and flora, that P. A. Taylor weaves her mysteries."

After housekeeping all day, Miss Taylor writes her stories between midnight and 3 A.M., beginning three weeks before the deadline for the novel to be delivered to her New York publishers. "Detective stories teach you to tell a story and not wander," she remarks. Her second detective, Leonidas Witherall, who made his bow in "The Riddle of Volume Four," published in *Ellery Queen's Mystery League* magazine in 1933, is usually involved in boisterous, knockabout suburban comedy in which murder is a minor consideration. Although Miss Taylor signed her own name in the magazine, the late Witherall novels have appeared over the pseudonym of "Alice Tilton."

"Volume Four," although so listed in her bibliography in *American Women,* does not seem to have appeared in book form in the United States. However, *Beginning With a Bash* (1937), which for some odd reason was published only in England, is understood to be an expansion of the earlier magazine tale. Miss Taylor is a Republican, a member of the Massachusetts Society of Mayflower Descendants, and makes her home in Newton Highlands, Mass., a suburb of Boston, in the winter. (The suburban "Daltons" in which the Witherall stories are laid are obviously "the Newtons" in real life.) Her recreations are book collecting, ship model making, and golf. She is unmarried.

PRINCIPAL WORKS: The Cape Cod Mystery, 1931; Death Lights a Candle, 1932; The Mystery of the Cape Cod Players, 1933; The Mystery of the Cape Cod Tavern, 1934; Sandbar Sinister, 1934; The Tinkling Symbol, 1935; Deathblow Hill, 1935; The Crimson Patch, 1936; Out of Order, 1936; Figure Away, 1937; Octagon House, 1937; The Annulet of Gilt, 1938; Banbury Bog, 1938; Spring Harrowing, 1939; Criminal C.O.D., 1940; The Perennial Boarder, 1941; Six Iron Spiders, 1942. As "Alice Tilton"—Beginning With a Bash (published in England only) 1937; The Cut Direct, 1938; Cold Steal, 1939; The Left Leg, 1940; The Hollow Chest, 1941.

ABOUT: Haycraft, H. Murder for Pleasure: The Life and Times of the Detective Story; Barnard Alumnae Monthly October 1932, March 1936.

TAYLOR, Mrs. RACHEL (ANNAND)

(1876-), Scottish poet and biographer, was born in Aberdeen, the daughter of John Wilson Annand and the late Clarinda (Dinnie) Annand. She was educated at the Aberdeen schools and was one of the pioneer Scottish Women university students, attending the University of Aberdeen. Rachel Annand married Alexander  Cameron Taylor in 1901, and for several years made her home in Dundee. Her first poems were contributed to the *British Weekly* and the *English Review.* In 1904 John Lane brought out her *Poems,* also taken up later by Thomas Bird Mosher in Portland, Maine, for his "Bibelots." *Rose and Vine* (1908), consisting of no less than 109 pieces, contained, according to the Rev. W. H. Hamilton, some of the most splendid ritual of fantasy in our literature. Gilbert Murray called it "poetry of intense imagination and exquisite craftsmanship, never simple, never commonplace, never easy, defiantly and mockingly anti-modern, and instinct with a rich and dreamlike beauty of phrase." *The Hours of Fiammetta: A Sonnet Sequence,* with its sequel, *End of Fiammetta,* attracted much attention. Its heroine, according to the author, "reaches a state of illumination and reconciliation regarding the enigma of love as it is." *Leonardo the Florentine* (1927), one of her most popular books, contains, on Mrs. Taylor's own admission, "some excess of symbolism natural to a mind more at ease in verse." Gilbert Murray, in his preface to the book, calls it a work "written with wide knowledge, sincere feeling, and exact scholarship . . . qualities . . . almost forgotten, for good or ill, in an exact and riotous luxury of imagination and phrasing, and a power of poetic interpretation which at times acts like a flashlight. Altogether a book dangerous in its power of illusion, as Chaucer is dangerous to a weak speller." Mrs. Taylor's portrait by Stewart Carmichael, in its exotic beauty, recalls the women of Rossetti. She lives in London, and lists her recreations as novel-reading and conversation. She has "nothing but disdain" for emasculate and sentimental pietism. Elinor Wylie, G. K. Chesterton, and Hilaire Belloc were some of her admirers, past and present.

PRINCIPAL WORKS: Poems, 1904; Rose and Vine, 1908; The Hours of Fiammetta: A Sonnet Sequence, 1909; Aspects of the Renaissance, 1923; End of Fiammetta, 1923; Leonardo the Florentine, 1927; William Dunbar, 1931; Renaissance France, 1939.

ABOUT: Taylor, R. A. Leonardo the Florentine (see Introduction by G. Murray); The Quest July 1922; Wilson Library Bulletin March 1929.

TEASDALE, SARA (August 8, 1884-January 29, 1933), American poet, was born in St. Louis, the daughter of John Warren

N. Muray

Teasdale and Mary Elizabeth (Willard) Teasdale. She was, to quote Louis Untermeyer, "the unexpected fruit of her parents' old age," and she showed the effects of her birth throughout her life, both in a neurotic attachment to, yet discontent with, her family, in a care for her health which came near to hypochondria, and in an inability to adjust herself to the demands of maturity. She was educated at home, then at a private school from which she was graduated in 1903. She had been a precocious child, the first and lasting influence on her being that of Christina Rossetti, with whom she had much in common. For several years after leaving school she and a few friends edited a manuscript magazine, one copy monthly, called the *Potter's Wheel.* Her first work as a poet, like that of so many others, appeared in *Reedy's Mirror.*

Never in her earlier years having to worry about money, she traveled widely—to Europe and the Near East with another poet, Jessie B. Rittenhouse, and back and forth between New York and St. Louis. Her most frequent refuge from home, however, was Chicago, and she became a sort of extramural member of the new literary group springing up there. It was there also that she met Vachel Lindsay, whose long and hopeless courtship of her, encouraged then repulsed, was one of the many tragedies of his tragic life. She could not make up her mind either to marry him or to let him go, and abruptly, in 1914, she solved the problem by marrying Ernest R. Filsinger, a St. Louis business man. But, again to quote Untermeyer, "she retreated further into a withdrawn privacy, . . . she resented marriage," and in 1929 she went to Reno under an assumed name and divorced him.

Her later years were spent in New York. She had published six volumes of poems and edited two anthologies; one of her books, *Love Songs,* had gone through many editions and she had been a prizewinner of the Poetry Society of America. She applied herself fitfully to what would have been her only prose book, a biography of Christina Rossetti. Though her work was beginning to be a bit out-dated, except for a handful of supremely beautiful lyrics, she was still universally admired and praised. She had devoted friends, though it became increasingly difficult to persuade her to attend any social gathering. But she was most unhappy: "Nothing could bridge the desire to be loved and the greater desire to be alone." Lindsay's suicide was a great shock to her; she began more and more to long for death, as her world grew barren and her carefully tended health began indeed to fail. Finally she took an overdose of sleeping medicine and was found drowned in the bath-tub. She was forty-eight years old.

Untermeyer, who knew her well, said of her: "Reticence walked with her: rudeness of any kind died in her presence." Yet he noted her contradictions—her occasional bursts of vigorous language and bawdy verse. And she was no compound of prim sweetness: "She distrusted the insipid and despised the saccharine." She was a tall, slender woman with masses of light hair, who loved to dress in filmy chiffons that never quite hid the heavy underwear she adopted to keep from catching cold. There was a little of the *poseuse* about her, but her suffering was genuine, as neurotic suffering always is.

Sara Teasdale was almost a great lyrist. Her work was feminine in the best sense, the unmistakable voice of a woman, and a woman born to sing. The *New Republic,* comparing her with her idol Christina Rossetti, noted in both "the lyric poet by outright gift, . . . the mystic's nature, at once fiery and contemplative."

PRINCIPAL WORKS: Sonnets to Duse and Other Poems, 1907; Helen of Troy and Other Poems, 1911; Rivers to the Sea, 1915; Love Songs, 1917; The Answering Voice (anthology) 1917 (enlarged edition, 1928); Flame and Shadow, 1920; Rainbow Gold (juvenile anthology) 1922; Dark of the Moon, 1926; Stars Tonight (juvenile) 1930; Strange Victory, 1933; Collected Poems, 1937.

ABOUT: Masters, E. L. Vachel Lindsay; Untermeyer, L. From Another World; Commonweal February 15, 1923; New Republic 15, 1933; Poetry April 1933, December 1937; Publishers' Weekly February 4, 1933; Saturday Review of Literature February 11, November 4, 1933.

TERHUNE, ALBERT PAYSON (December 21, 1872-February 18, 1942), American journalist, novelist, and writer of animal stories, wrote to the editors of this volume shortly before his death: "I was six years old when I teased a puppy by swinging it by its ears. My father appeared and without a word did the same to me. When I stopped bawling I began to think. Since that day I have never been able to see any fun in hurting anyone or anything which had neither the power nor the right to resent it. More—since that day I have always tried to understand the thoughts and impulses and natures of animals. It became a hobby with me then and there. We like to talk and to write about the things which interest us most. That is why I always craved to write about animals; chiefly about dogs. And I have had the same desire to write about every phase of outdoor nature.

"My father was a clergyman, the Rev. Dr. Edward Payson Terhune. My mother was a writer, who used the pen-name of 'Marion Harland' (Mary Virginia [Hawes] Terhune). It was she who taught me to love writing. I was born in Newark, N.J., in the parsonage of my father's church. While I was still a child the whole family went to Europe to live for several years, and it was there—at Paris and Geneva——that my education began. We came back to America and I was graduated from Columbia University in 1893. Mary years afterwards, I had the good luck to receive the Columbia Medal of Excellence, as 'explorer, man of letters, and true interpreter of Nature.'

"After I finished college, I went back to Europe for a while; and thence to the Near East, where I wandered through Egypt and Syria, living for a short time as a member of a desert Bedouin tribe, which wanted to adopt me. I also did a little unimportant exploring. Back in America, I took up newspaper work. I hated it. I wanted to be a writer, and not a reporter or an editor. So in my spare time late at night I used to write stories for magazines. It was slow and grindingly hard work until I began to write about dogs and the outdoors. After that it was much smoother sailing; and soon I was able to give up the drudgery of newspaper toil and devote my whole time to my books and stories and articles. And I was able to move out to Sunnybank, near Pompton Lakes, N.J., my present house. Here I am surrounded by my pack of collie dogs, and can tramp the hills with them and fish and hunt."

* * *

Two of Mr. Terhune's sisters, Virginia Terhune Vanderwater and Christine Terhune Herrick, also became writers and journalists. His newspaper service was on the New York *Evening World*. It was 1916 before he was entirely free of his newspaper connections. His first novel was written in collaboration with his mother, a unique circumstance. His wife, who was Anice Morris Stockton, is a composer and writer; they had one daughter. *Lad*, Mr. Terhune's first dog story in book form, sold 50,000 copies in ten years. Later he had to include a collie in every book he wrote, and was so pestered by admirers at his home that he had to keep his gates locked most of the time. In his amusing autobiography he called himself "the Apostle of the Obvious and a Writer for the Very Young" (though he said his dog books were not written for young people and he was astonished to find they constituted more than half his readers); and he described himself as having "a fifty-inch chest, piano-mover shoulders, and a height of six feet, two and a half inches in bare feet."

Albert Payson Terhune died of a heart ailment at his home, Sunnybank, at sixty-nine. The New York *Herald Tribune* remarked editorially: "To his friends he seemed perpetually youthful and full of an unquenchable zest for life. Until his virtual retirement five years ago he drove himself relentlessly at his task of writing. Just as he believed in discipline for his dogs so he practiced discipline for himself. Hard work and plenty of it was his fare. He throve on it spiritually and financially."

PRINCIPAL WORKS: Syria From the Saddle, 1896; Columbia Stories, 1897; Dr. Dale (with "Marion Harland") 1900; Caleb Conover, Railroader, 1907; The World's Great Events, 1908; The Fighter, 1909; The New Mayor, 1910; The Woman, 1912; Dad, 1914; Dollars and Cents, 1915; The Locust Years, 1915; Wonder Women of History, 1918; Lad: A Dog, 1919; Bruce, 1920; The Pest, 1920; Buff: A Collie, 1921; The Man in the Dark, 1921; Black Gold, 1921; Further Adventures of Lad, 1922; His Dog, 1922; Black Caesar's Clan, 1923. The Amateur Inn, 1923; Lochinvar Luck, 1923; Wolf, 1924; Treve, 1924; The Tiger's Claw, 1924; Now That I'm Fifty (autobiography) 1925; The Runaway Bag, 1925; The Heart of a Dog, 1925; Treasure, 1926; Gray Dawn, 1927; Bumps, 1927; The Luck of the Laird, 1927; Lad of Sunnybank, 1928; Proving Nothing, 1929; To the Best of My Memory (autobiography) 1930; A Dog Named Chips, 1931; The Son of God, 1932; The Way of a Dog, 1934; The Book of Sunnybank, 1935; Unseen, 1936; A Book of Famous Dogs, 1937; Grudge Mountain, 1939; Loot! 1940.

ABOUT: Kunitz, S. J. & Haycraft, H. (eds.). The Junior Book of Authors; Terhune, A. P. Now That I'm Fifty, To the Best of My Memory; New York Herald Tribune February 19, 1942.

TERHUNE, Mrs. MARY VIRGINIA (HAWES). See "AMERICAN AUTHORS 1600-1900"

TETERNIKOV, FEODOR KUZMICH. See SOLOGUB, F.

"THANET, OCTAVE." See "AMERICAN AUTHORS: 1600-1900"

*THARAUD, JÉRÔME (May 18, 1874-) and his brother **JEAN** (May 9, 1877-), French journalists, and novelists, were born

in the village of Saint-Junien in the Haute-Vienne, Limousin. They attended elementary school at Angoulême where their family moved because of economic reverses. When scarcely eleven, Jérôme entered the Sainte-Barbe school in Paris and in 1888 the Lycée Louis-le-Grand, where he won prizes in French, history, and geography. He then prepared for the École Normale and won a prize during the *concours général* with his "Letter From Voltaire to Diderot." This was considered worthy of publication. Jérôme at the age of nineteen was thus oriented in his vocation: he decided to become a writer, encouraged by his schoolmate Charles Péguy. In 1895 Jérôme entered the École Normale and for three years remained in its congenial

and stimulating atmosphere. with Lanson, Bédier, and Brunetière among his teachers and Louis Gillet and Péguy among his friends.

As for Jean: he came to Paris in 1895 and studied mathematics at the École Sainte-Geneviève, after which he prepared for the Saint-Cyr military academy at the Lycée Saint-Louis, but fail-

ing in his oral examinations, he had to return to Angoulême for a year of military service. Back in Paris he registered at various faculties: in 1901 he received a degree in philosophy and a diploma from the École de Sciences Politiques, and in 1902 he won his law degree from the Faculté de Droit.

By this time Jérôme had settled in Budapest, where he taught French language and literature at the Joseph Eotvos College (1899-1903). During his vacations he traveled in Russia, Germany, Roumania, Bulgaria, Turkey. Whenever possible his younger brother would join him, otherwise they kept in close touch by means of frequent letters. Jérôme and Jean had begun their collaboration when in their teens with a journal symbolically entitled "Les Deux Pigeons," but their first work, *Le Coltineur Débile*, was not published till 1898. In their early efforts the Tharauds were strongly influenced by Kipling and Villiers de l'Isle Adam, "the master" to whom they dedicated *Lumière* (1900). On the advice of their teacher Bédier, the Tharauds read more sober material—works classic in composition, restrained and simple in style—resulting in stories like those in *La Légende de la Vierge* (1902) and in *Contes de la Vierge* (1904).

At the outbreak of the Transvaal War (1899), Jérôme tried to leave immediately as war correspondent but his plans did not materialize. However, by means of photos and postal cards he reconstructed the campaign and on his return to Paris the brothers reworked the manuscript into *Dingley,* which was published in 1902. This entertaining narrative, which contained an imaginative portrait of Kipling, readily found an admiring public. Four years later the second edition came out, completely revised and re-written, in time to carry away the Goncourt Prize for that year.

For seven years the Tharauds served as secretaries to Maurice Barrès, but their job did not interfere with their creative activi-

* Jérôme Tharaud died January 28, 1953; Jean Tharaud died April 9, 1952.

ties. What really delayed their work was their extreme meticulousness. *La Maîtresse Servante,* which had appeared in sketchy form in periodicals as early as 1908, did not appear in book form till 1911—but then it was so well rounded that even the most fastidious critics, such as Barrès, called it "a somber little masterpiece," coupling the name of the Tharauds with that of Benjamin Constant.

From 1912 on the Tharauds developed their own peculiar *genre:* a hybrid sort of reportage, history, and poetical evocation. In 1912 they covered the Balkan War and the impressionistic observations resulted in *La Bataille à Scutari d'Albanie* (1913); from the European War, in which they fought in the 94th Infantry Regiment, they drew *Une Relève* (1919) for which the French Academy awarded them the Grand Prix. In *The Shadow of the Cross* (1917), they depicted the Budapest ghetto; in *Un Royaume de Dieu* (1920), an Ukrainian village; in *When Israel Is King* (1921), the revolutionary Hungary of Count Tisza Karolyi and Bela Khun; in *Next Year in Jerusalem* (1924), the Holy Land; in *Spain and the Riff* (1925); the Riffian War; and finally in *Vienne la Rouge* (1934), *Le Passant d'Ethiopie* (1936), and *Cruelle Espagne* (1937), the Austrian, Ethiopian, and Spanish crises from the point of view of Fascist sympathizers. The Tharauds, it may be said, are consciously reactionary: anti-Semitic, anti-working class, and anti-democratic.

When the time came to acclaim their talents, the Academy had but one seat to award, yet it wished to honor the work of both men. The problem was solved by awarding the distinction to the elder brother, in accordance with tradition. Jean was only too happy to see his brother alone don the plumed hat and sword of the academician. These attributes of literary glory, he felt, would apply to him as well—as indeed they were intended to do. . . . Satirical journals like the *Canard Enchaîné* often referred to them as Jérôméjean Tharaud.

Works Available in English Translation: The Shadow of the Cross, 1918; The Long Walk of Samba Diouf, 1924; When Israel Is King, 1924; Next Year in Jerusalem, 1925; Spain and the Riff, 1926; The Chosen People, 1929.

About: Billy, A. La Muse aux Bésicles; Bonnerot, J. Jérôme and Jean Tharaud; Borgese, G. La Vita e il Libro; Lalou, R. Contemporary French Literature; Lefèvre, F. Une Heure Avec; Stephens, W. French Novelists of Today; Correspondant September 10, 1922; Etude August 20, 1921; Living Age July 1939; London Mercury June 1922; Nouvelle Revue Française November 1921; Revue Universelle July 1, 1922.

THAYER, TIFFANY ELLSWORTH (March 1, 1902-), American novelist, writes: "Tiffany Thayer was born in show business, to Sybil Farrar (soubrette) and Elmer Ellsworth Thayer (comedian). One grandfather was a G.A.R. chaplain (Methodist), the other a ne'er-do-well inventor. Freeport, Ill., was the scene from 1902 until 1910, then Rockford, 1910 to 1916. His parents were divorced when he was five. In 1916 he ran away from his father, joined his mother, quit high school (middle of third year), was apprenticed to a commercial artist in Chicago. In 1917 he was a copy-boy on the Chicago *Examiner*; went to the United Press and then into dramatic stock at Oak Park and hence into road shows (one night stands) through 1918 to 1922, with intervals of newspaper reporting between theatrical seasons. From 1922 to 1926 he alternated theatrical work with old-and-rare book store clerking; became store manager and worked in that capacity in Chicago, Detroit, and Cleveland.

In 1926 Thayer went to New York intending to re-enter the show business on the big time. Savings were exhausted before he could find a part and he was forced against his will to write for a living; became advertising copy-writer in 1927, partner in the agency in 1928. He wrote *Thirteen Men* evenings and week-ends through 1928 and 1929. It was published in May 1930. A week after publication he sailed to France and Spain, returning in the fall to find himself the notorious author of a best-seller. Since 1930 he has published nineteen volumes—his own favorite being Rabelais rewritten for children. From 1930 to 1932 he was advertising manager of the Literary Guild. In 1931 he founded the Fortean Society, to honor the late Charles Fort[qv] and to combat the stultifying influence of orthodox science. He is permanent secretary of this organization. From 1932 to 1936 he was in Hollywood. He did stretches on all the major lots and finally heard his own dialogue on the screen through Walter Wanger. From 1936 to date [written 1940] back in advertising in New York, in the radio department of a big agency.

"His first novel (unpublished) was written at the age of eleven. He rolls his own cigarettes, draws and paints for mental relaxation, fences (foils) for exercise. He would rather act than write and in Hollywood made an abortive effort to return to that work, appearing in one bad motion picture and on the stage in a revival of *Whistling in the Dark,* of which performance the local papers said he 'scored a personal triumph.' He is an atheist, an anarchist—in philosophy a Pyrrhonean—and regrets the legitimacy of his birth. He likes to think of himself as a gypsy—but he has a library of rare books (about 3,000 volumes) which keeps him off the open road. He writes articles and short stories but rarely. He has never had a serial published in a popular magazine. Most of his books concern feminine psychology, a sort of specialty. He writes under various pseudonyms as well as under his own name. Five feet, seven inches; 148 pounds; fair; green eyes. Marital status throughout life—nobody's business."

* * *

One critical remark will define Tiffany Thayer's sensational and swift-paced fiction: "Obviously meretricious, but disclosing a narrative gift which might be used to better purpose." Among the pseudonyms he has used are Elmer Ellsworth and John Doe.

PRINCIPAL WORKS: Thirteen Men, 1930; The Illustrious Corpse, 1930; Call Her Savage, 1931; The Greek, 1931; Thirteen Women, 1932; Three Sheet, 1932; An American Girl, 1933; One Woman, 1933; Doctor Arnold, 1934; Kings and Numbers, 1934; Cluck Abroad, 1935; Old Goat, 1937; One-Man Show, 1937; Little Dog Lost, 1938; Rabelais for Boys and Girls, 1939; Tiffany Thayer's Three Musketeers, 1939.

ABOUT: Bookman December 1930.

THAYER, WILLIAM ROSCOE (January 16, 1859-September 7, 1923), American historian, biographer, and editor, was born in Boston, the son of

Frederick William and Maria Wilder (Phelps) Thayer. The boy was named by his father, a shipping merchant, for William Roscoe, a Liverpool banker who wrote lives of Lorenzo de Medici and Leo X. The elder Thayer died in 1862. His widow later took her family to Italy; 1875-1876 was spent in Sienna. They were left in straitened circumstances when Thayer's partner embezzled most of the estate. William, however, attended St. Paul's School at Concord and graduated in 1881 from Harvard, where he made the usual clubs and served as president of the *Crimson* and *Lampoon.* He contributed a weekly column to the Boston *Sunday Budget* for a few months, then spent three pleasant years in Philadelphia, 1882-1885, where he was taken up by the Furnesses, father and son, and Weir Mitchell, and wrote literary and dramatic criticism for the *Evening Bulletin.* In 1888 he was instructor in the English department at Harvard, reading 900 themes a year; President Eliot did not renew the appointment. In 1892 Thayer became first editor of the quarterly *Harvard Graduates' Magazine,* serving until 1915.

In 1893 he married Elizabeth Hastings Ware, granddaughter of William Ware, author of the Sunday School historical classic *Zenobia.* The first volume of Thayer's notable, though somewhat ponderous and didactic history of the Italian Risorgimento, *The Dawn of Italian Independence,* for which Italy later made him a Commendatore, appeared that year; its sequel, *The Life and Times of Cavour,* was delayed until 1911 by a prolonged nervous breakdown. Mrs. Thayer's absence for more than twenty minutes was enough to bring on an attack of melancholia and hysteria. After recovery he wrote *The Life and Letters of John Hay,* pulling all strings, social and scholastic, to make it a success. It sold unusually well.

Thayer bore the loss of the sight of one eye philosophically, writing a popular biography of his late friend Theodore Roosevelt in six months despite the handicap. Of his poems, Owen Wister remarked discreetly that he was one of the authors "whose reputation rests upon prose works that are better for their authors having had poetry in them." Thayer had a face "of singular intellectual distinction" with dark lustrous eyes. His funeral was held at Appleton Chapel at Harvard, and his ashes placed in Mount Auburn Cemetery. Thayer was a member of the American Academy of Arts and Letters and at one time president of the American Historical Society.

PRINCIPAL WORKS: The Confessions of Hermes (poems) 1884; Hesper: An American Drama, 1888; The Dawn of Italian Independence, 1893; Poems, New and Old, 1894; History and Customs of Harvard University, 1898; Throne-Makers, 1899; A Short History of Venice, 1905; Italica, 1908; The Life and Times of Cavour, 1911; The Life and Letters of John Hay, 1915; Germany vs. Civilization, 1916; Volleys From a Non-Combatant, 1919; Theodore Roosevelt: An Intimate Biography, 1919; The Art of Biography, 1920; George Washington, 1922.

ABOUT: Howe, M. A. D. W. Later Years of the Saturday Club; Rhodes, J. F. Commemorative Tribute to William Roscoe Thayer: Prepared for the American Academy of Arts and Letters; Thayer, W. R. Letters; Thwing, C. F. Friends of Men; Harvard Graduates' Magazine December 1923; New York Times September 8, 10, 1923.

THIESS, FRANK

THIESS, FRANK (1890-), Germanic novelist and dramatist, was born in Livland, in the Baltic provinces, "the vanished land  of large landowners and gentlemen's estates, under the régime of the Czar," as he said in an autobiographical sketch. For centuries the upper classes had been Germanic in cultural outlook and civilization; nevertheless Thiess considered himself a Russian, and was never greatly impressed by the fact that on his mother's side he was descended from the great Teutonic medieval poet Wolfram von Eschenbach. When the Russian government changed Livland into completely Russian territory, however, the Thiess family moved to Germany. Then transition from the open spaces of the Baltic country to the narrow officialdom of Berlin appeared an unfortunate change to Frank Thiess, but thirty years later it seemed one of the luckiest. At first a frail, delicate child, he began to enjoy schoolboy battles, rowed, and boxed. Growing up, he says, he "loved as passionately as Romeo and hated as intensely as Othello."

After some stage experience, as an actor, and four years as journalist with the *Berliner Tageblatt,* he spent four weeks with German troops on the Eastern front, until a heart disability relieved him from the necessity of fighting his former countrymen. At thirty he determined to become an author, and planned a tetralogy of novels about modern German youth. Expressionism was in vogue at the time, and Thiess' more realistic novels could not find a publisher until a dramatist friend placed them with a Stuttgart publisher. Firms who had refused his work now asked to see it. His novels were designed to show the havoc and changes wrought in Thiess' generation by the First World War—a composite picture of contemporary German society which traced the childhood, adolescence, youth, and maturity of the twentieth century generation. Of these *Abschied vom Paradies* (Farewell to Paradise), a slight idyll of adolescent love, rather reminiscent of Wedekind, attained the greatest success. *The Devil's Shadow* is a study of the disintegration of a youth's moral values. *Interlude,* a novel of sin and renunciation growing out of illicit love, is a sort of Teutonic *Design for Living.* Thiess' fellow-*littérateurs* disapproved of his athleticism and boxing in public, but decided they were American traits, after he married Florence Losey, an American singer. William A. Drake has called him "a rarely accomplished craftsman, an inquisitor of almost clairvoyant sensitiveness and a creative artist of the first order."

Thiess is still in Germany, where he is one of the few prominent writers to have cast his lot with the Nazis.

WORKS AVAILABLE IN ENGLISH TRANSLATION: The Gateway to Life, 1927; The Devil's Shadow, 1928; Farewell to Paradise, 1929; Interlude, 1929; Voyage of Forgotten Men, 1937.

ABOUT: Drake, W. A. Contemporary European Writers; New York Times Book Review March 4, 1925.

THIRKELL, Mrs. ANGELA (MACKAIL)

THIRKELL, Mrs. ANGELA (MAC-KAIL) (January 30, 1890-), was born in London, the daughter of the celebrated Latin scholar, J. W. Mackail, and on her mother's side granddaughter of the famous painter Edward Burne-Jones. Kipling and Stanley Baldwin were her cousins, and her brother, Denis Mackail,[qv] is also a novelist. She seemed destined to become an  author, yet the discouragement she received from her family was so effective that she was forty before her first book appeared. She was educated privately, and was married at twenty-one, to J. Campbell McInnes; and until their divorce in 1917 she was busy bringing up their two sons—they also had a daughter, who died. In 1918 she married G. L. Thirkell, of Tasmania, and they went to Melbourne, Australia, to live. There Mrs. Thirkell had another son; there also at last she began to develop her talent for writing. After some experience in broadcasting, she became a journalist, and at the same time began to send stories to the English magazines.

It was not long until her deftness and lightness of touch found an appreciative public; but it was 1930, and she had returned to live in England, before she essayed her first full book, a volume of memoirs of her colorful childhood called *Three Houses.* Her work first came to wide attention in America with *Coronation Summer;* but it was not until *Pomfret Towers* and the books that have followed it that she came fully into her own on this side of the Atlantic. To many readers Angela Thirkell is *the* contemporary British writer of light fiction compounded of gentle irony, grave absurdity, and urbane under-statement. She visited this country in 1938, and wants to come again, "after the duration."

Still blonde and markedly attractive at fifty, Mrs. Thirkell lives now in London, where despite the war she continues to write in a vein which (to quote Clifton Fadiman) "asserts its unseriousness with . . . modest and imperturbable grace."

PRINCIPAL WORKS: Three Houses (non-fiction) 1930; Ankle Deep, 1932; High Rising, 1933; Wild Strawberries, 1934; O, These Men, These Men! 1934; What Happened on the Boat (also published as Trooper to the Southern Cross; non-fiction) 1934; The Demon in the House (short stories) 1935; The Fortunes of Harriette (in America: Tribute For Harriette; non-fiction) 1936; The Grateful Sparrow and Other Tales From the German, 1936; Coronation Summer, 1937; Summer Half, 1937; Pomfret Towers, 1938; The Brandons, 1939; Before Lunch, 1940; Cheerfulness Breaks In, 1940; Northbridge Rectory, 1941; Marling Hall, 1942.

ABOUT: Newsweek June 3, 1940; Saturday Review of Literature June 24, 1939; Wilson Library Bulletin June 1940.

THOMAS, AUGUSTUS (January 8, 1857-August 12, 1934), American playwright, was born in a little house in what

was then the outskirts of St. Louis, Mo., the son of Dr. Elihu Baldwin Thomas and Imogene (Garrettson) Thomas. The infant who was later to become the dramatist who wrote *The Copperhead*, a notable Civil War play in which Lionel Barrymore gave one of the finest performances of his stage-career, absorbed memories of the presidential campaign which preceded Lincoln's election. His maternal grandmother, Sarah Wilson Garrettson, whom Thomas wrote directly into three plays intentionally and several others by indirection, was another potent influence. When the boy was six his father, with Ben de Bar, a comic actor of the period, and Tom Davey, father of Minnie Maddern Fiske, the actress, reopened the St. Charles Theatre in New Orleans.

Young Augustus Thomas was a page boy in the Missouri House of Representatives in the winter of 1868, and two winters

later had a similar experience in the nation's capital. A period as railroad clerk in St. Louis followed, but his natural bent towards the stage made him play juveniles in the resident stock company and tour with the Vokes Co. two summers. As box-office man at Popes' Theatre, Thomas was enabled to see the performances of the stars of the heyday of the road, such as Booth, Barrett, Salvini, Kean, Janauschek, and the senior Sothern. He drew cartoons for the St. Louis *World*, toured the state for Joseph Pulitzer's New York *World*, observing reactions to the inauguration of woman suffrage, and was advance agent for Washington Irving Bishop, a thought-reader, an experience upon which Thomas was later to draw for his play of clairvoyance and hypnotism, the very successful *The Witching Hour* of 1907. In 1883 he dramatized Frances Hodgson Burnett's sentimental story *Editha's Burglar,* which, expanded to the four-act play *The Burglar* in 1889, made an effective vehicle for Maurice Barrymore.

Thomas now assumed Dion Boucicault's desk at the Madison Square Theatre in New York, and with his *Alabama* of 1891 and *In Mizzoura* of 1893 established himself as a writer of theatrically effective melodramas, with an occasional successful farce like *Mrs. Leffingwell's Boots.* Charles Frohman produced most of Thomas' plays until 1915, the year of Frohman's death on the "Lusitania." After the tragedy Thomas became art director of the Charles Frohman Co. He regarded himself as a foe of censorship, prohibition, and anti-Semitism (although Edna Ferber, in *A Peculiar Treasure,* records one disagreeable encounter with him), and was much in demand as an after-dinner speaker of the old school. Of medium stature, with a clean-shaven, mobile face, Thomas was always carefully groomed. (Robert Underwood Johnson, wrote a poetical tribute to "The Beautiful Smile of Augustus Thomas" after the latter's death at seventy-seven.)

Of an outmoded school, Thomas had done little dramatic work since the reminiscent *Palmy Days* of 1920. He died at the Clarkstown Country Club, Nyack, N.Y., survived by Mrs. Lisle (Colby) Thomas, a sister of Bainbridge Colby who was Secretary of State in Woodrow Wilson's cabinet; and a son and daughter. Thomas was the recipient of an M.A. degree from Williams, a Litt.D. from Columbia (1921) and an LL.D. from the University of Missouri (1923). From 1906 to 1911 he was president of the Society of American Dramatists. His plays were printed for copyright purposes only and remain undisturbed except by theatre archaeologists.

PRINCIPAL WORKS: Alabama, 1891; In Mizzoura, 1893; Arizona, 1898; Oliver Goldsmith, 1900; Champagne Charley, 1901; The Earl of Pawtucket, 1903; Mrs. Leffingwell's Boots, 1905; The Embassy Ball, 1905; The Witching Hour, 1907; The Harvest Moon, 1909; As a Man Thinks, 1911; The Nightingale, 1914; Rio Grande, 1916; The Copperhead, 1917; Palmy Days, 1920; Nemesis, 1921; The Print of My Remembrance (autobiography) 1922.

ABOUT: Thomas, A. The Print of My Remembrance; Winter, W. The Wallet of Time; Woollcott, A. Shouts and Murmurs; New York Times August 13, 14, 16, 19, 1934.

*THOMAS, DYLAN (1914-), British poet, was born in Carmarthenshire, Wales.

He was educated in Swansea Grammar

A. John

School, was a newspaper reporter for a year, and for a while after that tried hack journalism and odd jobs of all sorts. From his anecdotal semi-autobiography, with its Joycean echo in the title, it appears that he belongs to an upper middle-class family. He first appeared in print as a poet at sixteen or seventeen, and his first small volume was published when he was only nineteen. In 1938 he won the Oscar Blumenthal Prize offered by *Poetry* (Chicago), and his poems have appeared frequently in the special verse magazines of England and the United States. Thomas was rejected for military service in the Second World War and is working for the British Broadcasting Corporation. He is unmarried.

Thomas' work is "modern" and "advanced." Stemming from Freud, Joyce, Gerard Manley Hopkins, and the Bible, he differs from the generation immediately preceding his, the generation of Auden and Spender, in his absence of stress on economics and politics. He has been unusually highly praised for a poet who is, after all, still serving his novitiate. Edith Sitwell, who is not easily pleased, said that "he has very great gifts, though they are not as yet completely resolved. He is, at moments, a prey to his subconscious self, and consequently to obscurity, but from his subconscious self rise, time after time, lines which are transmuted by his conscious self into really great poetry."

Conrad Aiken went farthest of all in calling Mr. Thomas "a born language-lover and language-juggler, a poet with an unmistakable genius for the effective values of language and prosody, . . . a genius for word-magic, a genuine and outrageous gift of the gab. . . . Violent and vivid, as a poet should be, he is a chameleon for colors, a word-spout, full of mad nonsense and humors. . . . If his meanings too often escape us, nevertheless he can be read for the shape and the shine alone, [for the] glitter of magic by itself and for its own sake."

In Dylan Thomas' own definition, "Poetry is the rhythmic, inevitably narrative, movement from an overclothed blindness to a naked vision"; poetic activity is "the physical and mental task of constructing a formally watertight compartment of words, preferably with a main moving column."

An inventor of words, an inexhaustible fabricator of images, Thomas arrives in his poetry at a kind of mysticism of the body. Perhaps the most balanced estimate of his work is by Francis Scarfe, who remarks that Thomas "is fundamentally a poet of the feelings, and is not a visual poet. He does not see clearly. . . . His main object is to feel clearly, which he has not yet achieved. . . . His outstanding merit . . . is his rich vocabulary, his sensual appreciation of words, his intense persuasive idiom which reveals him as one who is reaching outward towards all that is most living in our language."

PRINCIPAL WORKS: Eighteen Poems, 1934; Twenty-Five Poems, 1936; The World I Breathe, 1939; The Map of Love, 1939, Portrait of the Artist as a Young Dog, 1940; New Poems, 1942.

ABOUT: Thomas, D. Portrait of the Artist as a Young Dog; Horizon November 1940; London Mercury February 1936; New Verse October 1934; Poetry June 1940.

THOMAS, EDWARD (March 3, 1878-April 9, 1917), English essayist and poet,

was born Philip Edward Thomas in Lambeth, London, the son

of Philip Henry Thomas, a staff clerk at the Board of Trade, and Mary Elizabeth (Townsend) Thomas. Both parents were of Welsh birth. From his mother Edward Thomas inherited his fair hair, his blue-gray eyes, his tallness, his shyness and melancholy, and his sensitive, poetic temperament. His father, a dark, dour, earnest man, who spent all his leisure as a propagandist for Positivism, was bitterly opposed to his son's becoming a writer, which was the boy's set ambition from childhood, and he made earnest efforts to force him into the Civil Service instead—though there were five other sons to carry on the family tradition.

Very early, therefore, the boy left home. Wholly devoted to nature and to the country life he had never known except in solitary walking trips, he starved in Grub Street, and began a long career as a hack journalist at nineteen. He was only eighteen when he met Helen Noble, the daughter of the critic and editor James Ashcroft Noble, and they began the long and troubled love affair which ended only with his death, and which she has recorded in two poignant volumes. They were married in 1899, and their son was born while the husband and father was still a university student. For in 1897 Thomas had finally managed to enter Oxford, though only as a non-collegiate student, since he had been disappointed in his hopes of a scholarship. Later he was registered in Lincoln College. He left in 1900 with only a second class in modern history, another disappointment.

The young couple, who soon had two daughters as well as a son, lived in the most harrowing poverty. They moved about to various rented cottages, first in Hampshire, then in Kent. Thomas' natural melancholy, almost amounting to melancholia, was increased by his sense of guilt in having condemned his wife and children to destitution and misery. Yet he labored constantly, bringing out at least one volume a year, often more. He met H. W. Nevinson, and reviews for the Manchester *Guardian* became his financial standby. Most of his books were mere hack compilations; only his solitary novel and two collections of essays, *Rest and Unrest* and *Light and Twilight,* showed that he was in fact a brilliant stylist, in the best tradition of English nature essayists.

When the First World War began, Thomas enlisted as a private. He was soon made a lance corporal, but he was a long time in securing a commission. Finally, however, he became a second lieutenant—the post he held when he was killed at Arras at thirty-eight.

In many ways, Edward Thomas' life resembles that of a young Shelley who remained chained to his Harriet. And today he is thought of primarily as a poet. Yet actually he wrote no poetry at all until he became the friend of Robert Frost, the American poet, in 1912, and his first inclusive volume of poems, written under the pseudonym of "Edward Eastaway" because no one would have taken seriously the poems of that prolific journalist Edward Thomas, was still in press when he died. But, as one critic has remarked, there is really little distinction between his creative prose and his poetry; both are quiet, leisurely, unstressed, and instinct with the spirit of nature. When he was killed, said Walter de la Mare, "there was shattered a mirror of England." In his prose there may sometimes be found affectation or preciosity, but never in his poems, full, to quote Louis Untermeyer, "of a slow, sad contemplation of life and a reflection of its brave futility."

PRINCIPAL WORKS: The Woodland Life, 1897; Horae Solitariae, 1902; Oxford, 1903; Rose Acre Papers, 1904; Beautiful Wales, 1905; The Heart of England, 1906; Richard Jefferies, 1909; The South Country, 1909; Rest and Unrest, 1910; Feminine Influence on the Poets, 1910; Windsor Castle, 1910; The Isle of Wight, 1911; Light and Twilight, 1911; Maurice Maeterlinck, 1911; Celtic Stories, 1911; Algernon Charles Swinburne, 1912; George Borrow, 1912; Norse Tales, 1912; The Icknield Way, 1913; The Country, 1913; The Happy-Go-Lucky Morgans (novel) 1913; Walter Pater, 1913; In Pursuit of Spring, 1915; Four-and-Twenty Blackbirds, 1915; The Life of the Duke of Marlborough, 1915; Six Poems (privately printed) 1916; Keats, 1916; A Literary Pilgrim in England, 1917; Poems, 1917; Last Poems, 1918; Collected Poems, 1920; Cloud Castle and Other Papers, 1922; Essays of Today and Yesterday, 1926; Chosen Essays, 1926; Poems (Augustan Books of Modern Poetry) 1926; Selected Poems, 1927; The Last Sheaf (essays) 1928.

ABOUT: Adcock, A. St. J. For Remembrance; Bullough, G. The Trend of Modern Poetry; Douglas, N. Looking Back; Eckert, R. P. Edward Thomas: A Biography and Bibliography; Huxley, A. On the Margin; Moore, J. C. Life and Letters of Edward Thomas; Moore, T. S. Some Soldier Poets; Murry, J. M. Aspects of Literature; Squire, J. C. Life and Letters; Thomas, H. As It Was, World Without End; Untermeyer, L. Modern British Poetry; Arts and Decoration April 1931; Bookman (London) May 1928, September 1930; Life and Letters Today March 1940; London Mercury January, May, June, September, November 1927; Revue Anglo-Américaine April 1934; Saturday Review of Literature October 23, 1937; Yale Review April 1920.

THOMAS, LOWELL JACKSON (April 6, 1892-), American journalist and travel writer, was born in Woodington, Ohio, the son of a colonel in the medical corps of the army. He was reared in a mining district in Colorado, and educated at the University of Northern Indiana (B.Sc. 1911), University of Denver (B.A. and M.A. 1912), and Princeton (M.A. 1916). He also has an honorary Litt.D. from Grove City College (1933). As a young man he worked as a gold miner, cook, and cowpuncher. He then became a reporter on a Cripple Creek, Colo., newspaper,

Phyfe

and went from there to the Chicago *Journal;* from 1912 to 1914 he was also professor of oratory at Chicago Kent College of Law. During the next two years he was an instructor in English at Princeton. He was the chief of the civilian mission sent to Europe by President Wilson to prepare a history of the First World War; he was attached as a correspondent to all the Allied armies, and was the first to give out news of the German Revolution of 1918. It was he also who introduced T. E. Lawrence to the world; he was the biographer of Count Luckner, the German sea-raider; and he wrote the account of the first round-the-world flight. He lectured extensively, first on Alaska and then on the Palestinian and Arabian campaigns, and in 1930 he became a radio news commentator. Since 1935 he has also been a screen commentator, and is now a television commentator as well. From 1919 to 1923 he was associate editor of *Asia.* He founded and edited the *Commentator* (later combined with *Scribner's*) in 1923. He has been called "the world's foremost globe-trotter," and appropriately his only idiosyncrasy is a dread of confined places. He lives in the Berkshires, at Pawling, N.Y., with his wife (Frances Ryan, whom he married in 1917) and his son. There he has an adventure library of three thousand volumes, organizes local baseball games, and spends most of his time on horseback. He is a handsome man, still young-looking, with a small moustache and dark curly hair; his friend F. Yeats-Brown, the British travel writer, calls him "simple and unspoiled, a home-loving, sports-loving man." Many of his books are written in collaboration.

PRINCIPAL WORKS: With Lawrence in Arabia, 1924; The First World Flight, 1925; Beyond the Khyber Pass, 1925; The Boy's Life of Colonel Lawrence, 1927; The Sea Devil, 1927; European Skyways, 1927; Raiders of the Deep, 1928; Adventures in Afghanistan for Boys, 1928; Woodfill of the Regulars, 1929; The Sea Devil's Fo'c'sle, 1929; The Hero of Vincennes, 1929; The Wreck of the Dumaru, 1930; Lauterbach of the China Sea, 1930; India—Land of the Black Pagoda, 1930; Rolling Stone, 1931; Tall Stories, 1931; Kabluk of the Eskimo, 1932; This Side of Hell, 1932; Spain: The American Traveler's Handbook, 1932; Old Gimlet Eye, 1933; Fan Mail, 1935; The Untold Story of Exploration, 1935; Born to Raise Hell, 1935; Men of Danger, 1936; A Life of Kipling, 1936; Seeing Canada With Lowell Thomas, 1936; Seeing India With Lowell Thomas, 1936; Seeing Japan With Lowell Thomas, 1937; Seeing Mexico With Lowell Thomas, 1937; Adventures Among Immortals, 1937; Magic Dials, 1939; Soft Ball, So What? 1940; How to Keep Mentally Fit, 1940; Pageant of Adventure, 1940; Stand Fast for Freedom, 1940; Pageant of Life, 1941.

ABOUT: American Magazine September 1924; Literary Digest September 19, 1931, March 17, 1934, March 21, 1936; Newsweek July 21, 1934; Pictorial Review August 1936; Time September 30, 1940.

*THOMASON, JOHN WILLIAM (February 28, 1893-), American army officer, short-story writer, and biographer, was born in Huntsville, Walker County, Texas, the son of John William Thomason, M.D., and Sue (Gores) Thomason. He was a student at Southwestern University, Texas, in 1909-10; Sam Houston Normal Institute, Nashville, during 1910-11; and at the  University of Texas from 1912 to 1913, when he came north to New York City to study at the Art Students' League.

Thomason was commissioned a second lieutenant in the U.S. Marine Corps in April 1917, and in that year married Leda Bass of Terrell, Tex.; their son is John William Thomason III. Thomason served in the 4th Brigade, 2nd Division, American Expeditionary Force, during the First World War, also seeing service in the West Indies, Central America, China, and at sea. He received a lieutenant-colonelcy in 1937, and was made a member of the Army War College and Navy War College in 1938, also receiving an honorary Litt.D. from Southwestern University that year. A Mason and a member of Kappa Sigma fraternity, Thomason is also a member of the Army and Navy Club; Army, Navy, and Marine Corps Country Club; and the Peking, Chevy Chase, and Metropolitan Clubs. He can be reached at the Headquarters of the U.S. Marine Corps, Washington, D.C.

Fix Bayonets, the first of Thomason's books was also called by James Norman Hall America's first genuine contribution to soldiers' narratives, ranking with Barbusse's *Le Feu* and Masefield's *Gallipoli.* The London *Times* also approved, saying: "No book which we can recall that has for subject the actual fighting man in the Great War, has appeared to us to equal this. The drawings match the prose." The illustrations, in pen, pencil and water colors, were by the author himself; some of them were hastily sketched with improvised materials on the battlefield. The book is dedicated: "To the Men of the First Battalion, Fifth Regiment, U.S. Marine Corps, 1918." As a writer of short stories, in the opinion of the New York *Times,* Colonel Thomason appears more as the talented amateur. *Jeb*

Stuart (1930) is a biography of the Civil War cavalryman, and *Gone to Texas* (1937) an historical novel of that turbulent state in the late 'sixties. The Colonel has also edited and illustrated *Adventures of General Marbot [1782-1854], By Himself.*

PRINCIPAL WORKS: Fix Bayonets, 1926; Red Pants and Other Stories, 1927; Marines and Others, 1929; Jeb Stuart, 1930; Salt Winds and Gold Dust, 1934; Gone to Texas, 1937. Lone Star Preacher, 1941.

ABOUT: Saturday Evening Post November 14, 1936.

THOMPSON, DENMAN. See "AMERICAN AUTHORS: 1600-1900"

THOMPSON, DOROTHY (July 9, 1894-), American publicist and journalist, was born in Lancaster, near Syracuse, N.Y.,

the daughter of a Methodist minister. She was educated at the Lewis Institute, Chicago, and at Syracuse University (B.A. 1914), after which she did graduate work at the University of Vienna. She has honorary L.H.D. degrees from six universities, including: Columbia and Dartmouth. After five years in woman suffrage work, advertising copy writing, and social service, she went to Europe in 1920, and through a shipboard meeting became foreign correspondent of the Philadelphia *Public Ledger* and the New York *Evening Post.* In this capacity she served four years in Vienna and four in Berlin, where she was chief of the Central European Service. She returned to the United States in 1928. In 1936 she became political commentator of the New York *Herald Tribune,* her thrice-weekly column, "On the Record," syndicated to 166 papers, being estimated to have 7,500,000 readers. She also broadcasts weekly for the National Broadcasting Company, and writes a monthly editorial for the *Ladies' Home Journal.* In 1940 she wrote an unsuccessful play, *Another Sun,* with Fritz Kortner.

In 1923 Miss Thompson married Josef Bard, a Hungarian journalist. They were divorced in 1928, and she married Sinclair Lewis; they had one son. This marriage ended in divorce in 1942.

As behooves one of the most influential journalists in the world, Dorothy Thompson lives at high speed, dictating to three secretaries, running up enormous world-wide telephone bills, and practically never letting down from her mental and physical tension. She is a plump and rather pretty woman, once blonde but now gray-haired, who is a constant and aggressive conversationalist. She is the only woman who has ever addressed the New York Union League Club, the New York Harvard Club, the National Association of Manufacturers, and the United States Chamber of Commerce. Ardently anti-Fascist, she has usually been more conservative in domestic affairs. As John Chamberlain has said, "the best of Dorothy Thompson is her militant generosity, . . . the worst her failure of clarity, . . . her simplification and even complete falsification of issues." He noted her "crusading temperament," her employment of "angel-devil sociological clichés," but added that "she can write rings around any other newspaper columnist." Margaret Marshall, who remarks that "outrage is her favorite mood," nevertheless admires her "gusty and fresh" style. Her mind Miss Marshall thinks "uncreative, but extraordinarily absorbent." There is no doubt that she is an important social phenomenon in present-day America, as well as a provocative and exciting (if sometimes maddening) writer.

PRINCIPAL WORKS: Depths of Prosperity (with P. Bottome) 1925; The New Russia, 1928; I Saw Hitler! 1932; Refugees, 1938; Political Guide, 1938; Once on Christmas (juvenile) 1938; Let the Record Speak, 1939.

ABOUT: Drawbell, J. W. Dorothy Thompson's English Journey; Ross, I. Ladies of the Press; Current Biography 1940; Harper's Bazar November 1937; Nation June 25, 1938; New Republic September 29, 1937, August 24, 1938, September 27, 1939; New Yorker April 20, 27, 1940; Saturday Evening Post, May 18, 25, 1940; Scribner's Magazine May 1937; Time August 22, 1938, June 12, 1939.

*THOMPSON, EDWARD JOHN (1886-), English poet, novelist, and authority on Indian affairs, is the eldest son of J. M. Thompson. He was educated at Kingswood School, Bath, and has taken a M.A. degree from Oxford University and a Ph.D. from London University. He is a fellow of Oriel College, Oxford. Thompson took part in the Mesopo-

tamian campaigns in 1916-17, during the First World War; received the Military Cross; and was mentioned in dispatches. In 1918 he was in Palestine. Military affairs were an interlude in his services as educa-

* Died April 28, 1946.

tional missionary at Bankura College, Bengal, from 1910 to 1922. *The Knight Mystic,* Thompson's first book of poems, appeared in 1907. The war produced several other volumes. He wrote verse for twenty years before abandoning it for fiction and journalism, serving as special correspondent for the *Manchester Guardian* in India in 1932. In 1930 Thompson visited the United States. He had a hand in editing Ernest Benn's series of Augustan Poets (the name was selected in preference to Sixpenny Poets because it carried no stigma of cheapness and took up the same number of letters). Thompson married Theodosia Jessup, eldest daughter of Dr. William Jessup, an American; they have two sons and live at Scartop, Boars Hill, Oxford.

Thompson's books on both Indian and British questions are generally on the liberal and sometimes the unpopular side. *Introducing the Arnisons* (1935) was received, says the author, as an outrageous and ungracious misrepresentation by Methodists and Nonconformists generally. The novel's sequel, *John Arnison* (1939), is a further attempt to explain the Nonconformist conscience. *You Have Lived Through All This* is a survey of post-war years, not unlike Frederick Lewis Allen's *Only Yesterday* and *Since Yesterday* in the United States. The London *Times* has spoken of Thompson's "fastidious taste and untiring study of people"; and Storm Jameson praises the "strength, richness, and dignity of his writing, its wit and vigor and not least its essential Englishness."

PRINCIPAL WORKS: The Knight Mystic, 1907; John in Prison, 1912; Ennerdale Bridge and Other Poems, 1914; Waltham Thickets, 1917; Mesopotamian Verses, 1918; The Leicestershires Beyond Bagdad, 1919; Krishna Kumari, 1924; Atonement, 1924; Tagore: Poet and Dramatist, 1926; Three Eastern Plays (with T. Thompson) 1927; An Indian Day, 1927; A History of India, 1927; These Men Thy Friends, 1927; The Thracian Stranger, 1928; Night Falls on Siva's Hill, 1928; Crusader's Coast, 1928; In Araby Orion, 1928; Suttee, 1928; Collected Poems, 1930; A Farewell to India, 1931; Lament for Adonis, Rise and Fulfilment of British Rule in India, 1934; Last Voyage, 1934; Sir Walter Ralegh, 1935; Introducing the Arnisons, 1935; Burmese Silver, 1937; Lord Metcalfe, 1937; The Youngest Disciple, 1938; An End of the Hours, 1938; John Arnison, 1939; You Have Lived Through All This: An Anatomy of the Age, 1939; Enlist India for Freedom! 1940; Ethical Ideals in India Today, 1942.

ABOUT: Bookman (London) March, October 1929, August 1930; Spectator April 21, 1928.

THOMPSON, FRANCIS JOSEPH. See "BRITISH AUTHORS OF THE 19TH CENTURY"

THOMPSON, SYLVIA (September 4, 1902-), English novelist, was born in Scotland, the daughter of Norman Thompson, but reared at Lyndhurst, Hampshire. She was educated at what she calls "assorted schools," principally at Cheltenham School, and at Somerville College, Oxford, and published her first novel when she was only sixteen and had not  yet entered the university. She left Somerville without a degree in 1923. In 1926 she married Theodore D. P. Luling, an American artist, and they have three daughters. She visited the United States in 1932, making a transcontinental lecture tour. For some years the Lulings lived in Venice, until the outbreak of the Second World War, when they returned to England. A blonde, with delicate, coloring and a classic profile, Sylvia Thompson is "typically English" in appearance. Quite unspoiled by the success of her novels (*The Hounds of Spring* was a best-seller, and she has never had a real failure), she is still charmingly naïve and trusting, with a humorous, childlike candor. Quite frankly she says that her chief interests are in dress and children—by which she explains that she means only her own daughters! She says she would like to have six instead of three, and to be surrounded by innumerable friends "and no ugly furniture." Ellery Sedgwick called her "a genuine composite of all the youth who have grown up since the [First World] War."

She makes no pretence that her novels are anything more than escape literature, but they are escape literature of a high class—literate, suave, and polished. "The inconsequent and attractively rhythmic pattern of modern life" in pre-war England (to quote her own description) has been her field; her characters are people whose private and personal problems are of more concern to them than are the problems of a larger sphere. Yet there has been apparent in her work, with her own growing maturity, a corresponding growth, and she sounds increasingly a deeper note than was heard in the novels—really *tours de force*—of her earliest youth. She has the inherent capacity of the born novelist, and the ease of manner of the technical expert. Without being markedly brilliant or witty, her books are all good professional jobs, and she seems to have started with the mastery of plot and characterization which most novelists need many years to acquire.

PRINCIPAL WORKS: Rough Crossing, 1918; A Lady in Green Gloves, 1924; The Hounds of Spring, 1925; The Battle of the Horizons, 1928; Chariot Wheels, 1929; Winter Comedy (in America: Portrait of Caroline) 1931; Summer's Night, 1932; Helena (in America: Unfinished Symphony) 1933; Breakfast in Bed (with V. Cunard) 1934; Golden Arrow, 1935; A Silver Rattle, 1935; Third Act in Venice, 1936; Recapture the Moon, 1937; The Adventure of Christopher Columin, 1939; The Gulls Fly Inland, 1941.

ABOUT: Christian Science Monitor Magazine January 20, 1940.

THOMSON, EDWARD WILLIAM

(February 12, 1849-March 5, 1924), Canadian editor and author, was born in Toronto,

the son of William and Margaret Hamilton (Foley) Thomson. The family's roots were in the United States, since earlier Thomsons were Loyalists who had come to Canada after the Revolution; and Edward Thomson was a lifelong admirer of Abraham Lincoln, deriving much sentimental satisfaction from the fact that their birthdays were identical. He was educated in public schools and at Trinity College School, Weston, Ont. At fifteen he was in the American Civil War, serving with the Pennsylvania Cavalry in the Virginia campaigns of 1864 and 1865. In Canada, Thomson was a member of the Queen's Own Rifles during the Fenian raids of 1866. From 1868 to 1879 he was employed as a civil engineer in the construction of the Carillon Canal around the rapids of the Ottawa River; from 1879 to 1891, chief editorial writer on the Toronto *Globe*, removing then to Boston for twelve years as an associate editor of the *Youth's Companion*. As Canadian correspondent of the Boston *Evening Transcript*, his next occupation, Thomson resided in Ottawa but traveled about the country. In politics he was a liberal of the old school, an intimate of Sir Wilfred Laurier, long the premier of the Dominion, and advocate of Canadian independence from Great Britain. His articles, poems, and short stories (chiefly for boys) appeared in newspapers and magazines in the United States and Canada. *Collier's* called him "a dauntless chevalier of the pen," while George Murray stated that as a writer of short stories he had no rival in Canada. (Mrs. May Lamberton Becker's anthology, *Golden*

Tales of Canada, shows that this is not faint praise.) Thomson died at seventy-five in Boston, three years after the death of his wife, the former Adelaide St. Denis, herself a writer. They had one son.

PRINCIPAL WORKS: Old Man Savarin and Other Stories, 1895; Walter Gibbs: The Young Boss, 1896; Smoky Days, 1897; Between Earth and Sky (poems) 1897; The Many Mansioned House and Other Poems (U.S. and English title: When Lincoln Died and Other Poems) 1909.

ABOUT: MacMurchy, A. Handbook of Canadian Literature; Morgan, H. J. The Canadian Men and Women of the Time; Boston Evening Transcript March 7, 1924, February 13, 1932.

THOMSON, Sir JOHN ARTHUR (July

8, 1861-February 12, 1933), Scottish biologist and "scholarly popularizer" of his subject, was born in Pilmuir Manse, East Lothian, Scotland, the son of the Rev. Arthur Thomson and Isabella (Landsborough) Thomson. Both his father and his maternal grandfather, Dr. David Landsborough (who was called the Scot-

tish "White of Selborne") were writers. Young Thomson attended the village school at Saltoun, where his father was minister of the Free Church, until he was twelve, when he was tutored by a Mr. Tait, headmaster of one of the two Gifford Schools, and then attended the Paterson Place Academy at Haddington. In 1880 he went to Edinburgh University, where he was a fellow-student with J. M. Barrie and attended the university's tercentenary celebration in 1884. After studying in Germany at Jena and Berlin, Thomson returned to Edinburgh to attend Divinity Classes at the New School. Asked why he never completed his theological course, Thomson would smiling reply, "I was pitten oot." Occasionally he acted as superintendent of the Sunday School in his father's absence, once trying to palm off a bowdlerized edition of *Gulliver's Travels* on a confiding seven-year-old who had asked for *Geology and Genesis.*

For some winters Thomson held the chair of Professor Henry Drummond, author of *Natural Law in the Spiritual World*, at the Glasgow Free Church College. In 1886 he was an extra-mural lecturer in zoology, and in 1899 was appointed Regius Professor of Natural History at the University of Aberdeen, holding this post until his retirement in 1930. He was knighted the same year.

Sir Arthur, who had a voice with a "peculiarly individual and haunting quality," became an international platform celebrity through his courses of lectures in the United States, Canada, South Africa, and the United Kingdom, his talks before learned societies and popular societies, and over the B.B.C. networks. He received honorary LL.D. degrees from Edinburgh, Aberdeen, California, and McGill. William Beebe, reviewing his best-selling *Outline of Science* (1922) called him "without doubt the most capable compiler of scientific literature in the world."

Sir Arthur believed that he could help cultivate among mankind generally the desire and the ability to think in terms of biological science, and so promote a widespread interest in and devotion to scientific truth. His particular mission, said the New York *Times* when reviewing *Riddles of Science,* was "to show that such writing can be done with scientific authoritativeness, literary dignity, and fascinating readability." He always tried to reconcile religion and science.

Thomson died in his seventy-second year on Sunday at St. Mary's Lodge, Limpsfield, Surrey, of a heart attack, after landing from a five-days' cruise. Lady Thomson, who was Margaret Robertson Stewart and a translator of note, and his three sons and daughter survived. All had written books, from a detective story written by David Landsborough Thomson to the books on natural history by the daughter, Mrs. Maribel (Thomson) Edwin.

PRINCIPAL WORKS: The Evolution of Sex (with P. Geddes) 1889; Zoology, 1892; The Study of Animal Life, 1892; The Natural History of the Year: For Young People, 1896; The Science of Life: An Outline of the History of Biology and Its Recent Advances, 1899; Progress of Science in the Century, 1906; Herbert Spencer, 1906; Heredity, 1908; The Bible of Nature, 1908; Darwinism and Human Life, 1910; The Biology of the Seasons, 1911; Introduction to Science, 1911; Problems of Sex (with P. Geddes) 1912; The Wonder of Life, 1914; The Study of Animal Life, 1917; Secrets of Animal Life, 1919; Natural History Studies, 1920; The Control of Parenthood (with others) 1920; The System of Animate Nature, 1920; Nature All the Year Round, 1921; The Control of Life, 1921; The Haunts of Life, 1921; The Outline of Science, 1922; The Bible of Nature, 1923; The Biology of Birds, 1923; What Is Man? 1923; Everyday Biology, 1923; Science Old and New, 1924; Science and Religion, 1925; Man in the Light of Evolution, 1926; Ways of Living: Nature and Man, 1926; The Wonder of Life, 1927; Towards Health, 1927; The Minds of Animals, 1927; Modern Science: A General Introduction, 1929; The Outlines of Natural History, 1931; Life: Outlines of General Biology (with P. Geddes) 1931; Scientific Riddles (U.S. title: Riddles of Science) 1932; The Great Biologists, 1932; Biology for Everyman, 1934; The Ways of Birds, 1935; The Ways of Insects, 1935.

ABOUT: Bridges, T. C. and Tiltman, H. H. Master Minds of Modern Science; East Lothian Antiquarian and Field Naturalists' Society Transactions: Vol. 2; Christian Century February 22, March 8, 1933; New York Times February 13, 1933; Review of Reviews (London) March 1933; Scottish Geographical Magazine March 1933; Nature March 4, 1933.

THOMSON, VIRGIL (1896-), American composer and writer on music, was born in Kansas City, Mo., of Scottish ancestry. He studied music with private teachers, and then went to Harvard, where he rowed in the crew. He won the Naumburg and Payne Fellowships at Harvard, and after his graduation in 1922 was also awarded fellowships by the École  Toppo Normale Supérieure of Paris and by the Juilliard School in Philadelphia. During the First World War he was a second lieutenant in the United States Military Aviation Corps. From 1920 to 1925 he was assistant instructor in music at Harvard and director of the Harvard Glee Club. At the same time he was organist and choir conductor at King's Chapel, Boston, and music critic of the Boston *Transcript.*

From 1925 to 1934 Mr. Thomson lived in Paris. His first composition is dated 1923, and he now devoted all his time to composing and to conducting. (He has been guest conductor of symphony orchestras in Paris and London, and later in Chicago, Boston, and New York.) An intimate friend of Gertrude Stein, for whom he had already written a musical setting of a short sketch, he was induced by her to write the music for an opera to which she would supply the words. The result was *Four Saints in Three Acts* (1934), which occasioned a furore when it was presented at Hartford, Conn., by the Friends and Enemies of Modern Music, under the direction of the composer. Mr. Thomson remained in Hartford for three years as musical director of this strangely named society, and in 1936 was also the director of the Federal Music Project in New York. He then returned to Paris, but after the Nazi occupation of France he came to the United States and became chief music critic of the New York *Herald Tribune,* where his unorthodox views have stirred a tempest in more than one musical teapot.

Primarily a composer, Mr. Thomson has written only one book, an exposition of his theory that "modern music, to a certain extent, has forgotten its audience," that its primary purpose is to entertain. In accordance with this thesis, he himself is at his best in music written to be sung. In Paris he was strongly under the influence of Erik Satie and the "Six," but in contrast to theirs his music, though outstandingly "modern," is simple and melodious. Aaron Copland called him "urbane and devastatingly clever." He has been music critic of *Vanity Fair* and *Modern Music*, as well as of the Boston *Transcript*, and has written articles on music for general magazines like the *American Mercury* and the *New Republic*. He does not think of himself as a writer, but the authority and influence of his writings on music entitle him to a place in this volume.

PRINCIPAL WORKS: The State of Music, 1939.

ABOUT: Reis, C. Composers in America; American Mercury April 1935; Newsweek December 16, 1940; Time February 19, 1934.

THORNDIKE, ASHLEY HORACE
(December 26, 1871-April 17, 1933), American literary historian and university professor, was born at Houlton, Me., the son of Edward R. Thorndike and Abby B. (Ladd) Thorndike. Obtaining his B.A. degree in 1893 from Wesleyan, he was principal of Smith Academy for two years, removing to Boston University to instruct in English there (1895-98) and attending the Harvard Graduate School, which granted him his master's degree in 1896 and the Ph.D. in 1898. He went to Western Reserve University as instructor and associate professor, remaining till 1902. The year before, Thorndike's first study of Elizabethan drama had appeared, *The Influence of Beaumont and Fletcher on Shakespeare.* From 1902 to 1906 he was professor of English Literature at Northwestern University, publishing his much-used *Elements of Rhetoric and Composition* in 1905. Going to Columbia University in 1906 as professor of English, Thorndike became an influential and well-liked figure in the American academic world, known to a larger public as the editor of the Tudor Shakespeare and *Warner's Library of the World's Best Literature,* the Modern Reader's series (for Scribner's) and Longman's English Classics. He also contributed *Tragedy* in 1908 to the "Types of English Literature" series, and published works of original research at regular intervals. Becoming University Orator in 1930, he was called upon the next year to make the memorial address for the annual commemoration service of St. Paul's Chapel for those who had advanced the honor and prestige of their alma mater. Less than two years later memorial services were held there for Thorndike himself, who was found by a traffic policeman lying on the sidewalk on Madison Avenue at Forty-First Street. Thorndike died of heart failure in a taxicab while being taken to Bellevue Hospital. He was sixty-one. *Shakespeare's Theatre* had won general acclaim from critics who, however, found *Literature in a Changing Age* rather vague and dull.

PRINCIPAL WORKS: The Influence of Beaumont and Fletcher on Shakespeare, 1901; Elements of Rhetoric and Composition, 1905; Tragedy, 1908; Everyday English, 1913; Facts About Shakespeare, 1915; Shakespeare's Theatre, 1916; Literature in a Changing Age, 1920; A History of English Literature, 1920; English Comedy, 1929; The Outlook for Literature, 1931.

ABOUT: New York Times April 18, 19, 20, 1933.

THURBER, JAMES (December 8, 1894-), American humorist and illustrator, was born in Columbus, Ohio. One need not take seriously all the family chronicles in *My Life and Hard Times,* but the Thurbers seem to have been—and still are—a rather unusual family, with a penchant for getting into ludicrous predicaments.  This penchant their second son has inherited in full measure; things are always happening to him, "but he also has the gift of seeing, uncloudedly, the ridiculous aspect" of these situations. He was educated at Ohio State University, entering in 1913, but not getting his degree until 1919, since he took one year off "just to read" and spent another in war service. Owing to a boyhood accident which cost him an eye, he was refused by the army, so he spent part of 1917 and 1918 as a code clerk, first in the Department of State in Washington, then in the American Embassy in Paris.

He began as a newspaper man on the Columbus *Dispatch,* and then on the Paris edition of the Chicago *Tribune.* He stayed in Paris until 1926, when he returned to New York and started sending contributions to the *New Yorker.* He met E. B. White, who took him up to the magazine to see if he could land Thurber a job. Thurber emerged as managing editor. After six months he managed to shed that editorial responsibility, and was safe in the "Talk of the Town" department. In 1933 he resigned from the staff (though he is still a regular contributor), and after sampling Bermuda, England, and Hollywood, he settled down, as far as he ever does settle, to winters in Connecticut and summers sometimes in New York and sometimes wherever he has a sudden desire to go. In 1922 he was married to Althea Adams; they had a daughter; were divorced; in 1934 he married Helen Wismer.

Mr. Thurber drew long before he wrote. He draws all the time, in a sort of inspired doodling. His drawings are indescribable unless one knows them: "the huge, resigned dogs, the determined and sometimes frightening women, the globular men who try so hard to think so unsuccessfully." They are funny—but they are a psychological and social and sometimes a pathological commentary as well. Besides his own books, he has illustrated three others, on dogs, men's fashions, and the English language.

Very tall, very thin, absent-minded, shy, forgetful, Mr. Thurber looks as unlike his own drawings as anyone well can. He loves and raises dogs, but they are not the Great-Dane-cum-St. Bernards of his pictures. He still has eye trouble, and has undergone at least one serious operation. He is a nocturnal animal, who thinks best after midnight, and between his two marriages managed to disarrange his schedule until he was sleeping by day and working all night.

In 1940, in collaboration with Elliott Nugent, an old friend, he wrote his first play, *The Male Animal*. He may or may not some day write another; to quote Stephen Vincent and Rosemary Benét, "he does not make blueprints or outlines of future work."

These same critics called Mr. Thurber "one of the most vigorous talents that has grown in the *New Yorker* greenhouse. . . . A good many humorists get into a formula —he never has." The casual air of both his writing and his drawing is deceptive; he often rewrites a piece ten times, and has spent two years on a short book. Says Robert M. Coates, "he regards himself primarily as a writer, and is at once a little jealous of the Artist-Thurber and suspicious of anyone who admires the one in preference to the other. . . . He spent a long time building up his skill as a writer, and he still slaves over his work." There is an eerie, zany quality about his humor that hides a shiver under the laugh. He is consciously whistling in a graveyard: and the terror— which we all share—behind the mirth makes the mirth just so much the funnier.

PRINCIPAL WORKS: Is Sex Necessary? (with E. B. White), 1929; The Owl in the Attic and Other Perplexities, 1931; The Seal in the Bedroom and Other Predicaments, 1932; My Life and Hard Times, 1933; The Middle-Aged Man on the Flying Trapeze, 1935; Let Your Mind Alone, 1937; The Cream of Thurber, 1939; The Last Flower, 1939; The Male Animal, 1940; Fables for Our Times, 1940; My World—and Welcome to It! 1942.

ABOUT: Thurber, J. My Life and Hard Times; Life April 22, 1940; New York Herald Tribune "Books" December 29, 1940; New York Times Book Review May 2, 1940; New Yorker February 17, 1940; Saturday Review of Literature April 29, December 2, 1939.

THURSTON, ERNEST TEMPLE (September 23, 1879-March 19, 1933), English novelist and dramatist, began his literary career in adolescence with two volumes of poems written at sixteen. His first novel, *The Apple of Eden*, written in 1897, was rewritten and published in 1905. Three years before, his four-act-play, *Red and White Earth*, had been produced in the  provinces. At eighteen, E. Temple Thurston, as he signed most of his books, was informed by his father that he must earn his own living. Discharged from his employment at twenty-one for giving too much time to literature, Thurston next year, in 1901, married Katherine Cecil Alden, who was four years his senior. Mrs. Thurston[qv] wrote the sensationally successful novel of mistaken identity called *The Masquerader* in the United States. Entitled *John Chilcote, M.P.* in England, the novel was published in 1904 and dramatized by its author's husband the next year, and produced at St. James's Theatre.

After his divorce from Katherine Cecil Thurston, Temple Thurston married Joan Katherine Cann in 1911. They were divorced in 1924, and the next year he married Emily Cowlin, who had been his secretary since 1922. (She novelized his play, *The Wandering Jew*.) Patrick Braybrooke has pointed out that "a great deal of Mr. Thurston's astonishingly brilliant work has to do with the philosophy of womanhood. In his work I find a very sincere and sympathetic wish to understand the feminine mind, that mind which perhaps really keeps the world from dying of a blatant despair."

"Wheresoever you may go in this world —whether it be striving to the highest heights, or descending, as some would have it, to the deepest depths—life is just as ugly or as beautiful as you are inclined to find it," wrote Thurston in *The Patchwork Papers*. "In all my early work until, in fact, I wrote *Sally Bishop*, I was inclined to find it ugly enough in all conscience. But now beauty does seem inevitable and, what is more, the only reality we have." He said elsewhere that the only realist was the man of sentiment, and that "a true expression of true sentiment went home to every one as real."

Thurston listed his recreations as tennis, fishing, sketching, and golf. Golfing at Rye three weeks before his death at fifty-three, he developed the lumbago and influenza which carried him off. The London *Times* obituary spoke of his "extreme naturalistic harshness" at one extreme, and his "florid romanticism" at the other. In *The Blue Peter* (1924), a sentimental melodrama, he showed an intuitive knowledge of how to lend emotional color to particular scenes. Occasionally a bit of "shrewd irony or unexpected and gratifying plainness showed that he was not deceived by his own facility." Thurston's sentimental romances went into numerous editions. The *Richard Furlong* trilogy of novels shows his talent at its best.

PRINCIPAL WORKS: The Apple of Eden, 1905; Traffic: The Story of a Faithful Woman, 1906; The Realist, and Other Stories, 1906; The Evolution of Katherine, 1907; Sally Bishop; A Romance, 1908; Mirage, 1908; The City of Beautiful Nonsense, 1909; The Greatest Wish in the World, 1910; The Patchwork Papers, 1910; The Garden of Resurrection: Being the Love Story of an Ugly Man, 1911; The "Flower of Gloster," 1911; Thirteen (short stories) 1912; The Open Window, 1913; Richard Furlong: A Novel, 1913; The Antagonists, 1914; Achievement, 1914; Driven: A Play in Four Acts, 1914; The Cost: A Comedy in Four Acts, 1914; Tares: A Novel, 1915; The Passionate Crime: A Tale of Faerie, 1915; The Five-Barred Gate, 1916; Enchantment, 1917; Over the Hill, 1917; Summer 1917 and Other Verses, 1917; The Forest Fire and Other Stories, 1919; Sheepskin and Grey Russet, 1919; The World of Wonderful Reality, 1919; The Wandering Jew (play) 1920; The Green Bough, 1921; The Eye of the Wift, 1922; The Miracle, 1922; A Roof and Four Walls: A Comedy in Four Acts, 1923; Judas Iscariot: A Play in Four Acts, 1923; Poems, 1918-1923, 1923; May Eve: A Novel, 1924; The Blue Peter: A Play in Four Acts, 1924, Charmeuse, 1924; Mr. Bottleby Does Something, 1925; The Rossetti and Other Tales, 1926; The Goose-Feather Bed, 1926; Come and Listen, 1927; Jane Carroll, 1927; Portrait of a Spy, 1928; The King's Candle, 1929; Millennium, 1929; The Rosicrucian, 1930; The Man in a Black Hat, 1930; A Hank of Hair, 1932; The Broken Heart, 1932; Discord, 1933; A Constable's Notebook, 1935.

ABOUT: Braybrooke, P. Novelists, We Are Seven; Bookman (London) April 1933; London Times March 20, 1933; New York Times March 20, 1933.

THURSTON, Mrs. KATHERINE CECIL (MADDEN) (April 18, 1875-September 5, 1911), Anglo-Irish novelist, was born at Wood's Gift, Cork, Ireland, the only child of Paul Madden, a banker, former mayor of Cork, and Catherine (Barry) Madden. She was privately educated and spent a gay girlhood riding, swimming, and dancing. Married at twenty-six  to Ernest Charles Temple Thurston,[qv] an English writer, Mrs. Thurston herself began to write. *The Masquerader*, one of the most famous novels of impersonation and mistaken identity, was written as a serial for the American *Harper's Bazar*. Letters poured in to the editor imploring for advance information as to the outcome of the story. It was a best-seller in the United States, and in England, where it appeared simultaneously as *John Chilcote, M.P.* in 1904. The late Guy Bates Post starred in a dramatization which was a great favorite with stock companies when those still flourished. Two cinematic versions—silent and talking—also appeared. *The Gambler,* a story of Irish life and scenery, ran serially in *Harper's Weekly*. *Max,* another tale of impersonation, was less successful. The books displayed "fluent style and signs of intellectual insight." Mrs. Thurston possessed a personality of humor and charm and was much in demand as a speaker for literary and other dinners. Her clubs were the Ladies' Athenaeum, Sesame, and Writers'.

On April 7, 1910, Mrs. Thurston obtained a decree nisi from her husband. In delicate health for some time, she survived their divorce a little more than a year, dying of asphyxia during a fainting fit at Moore's Hotel, Cork at thirty-six.

PRINCIPAL WORKS: The Circle, 1903; The Masquerader (English title: John Chilcote, M. P.) 1904; The Gambler, 1906; Mystics, 1907; The Fly on the Wheel, 1908; Max, 1910.

ABOUT: Athenaeum September 9, 1911; Harper's Bazar January 1910; Harper's Weekly September 16, 1911; London Times April 8, September 7, 1911.

THURSTON, Mrs. TEMPLE. See THURSTON, K. C. M.

THWAITES, REUBEN GOLD (May 15, 1853-October 22, 1913), American librarian and editor, was born at Dorchester, Mass.,

the son of William George and Sarah (Bibbs) Thwaites, who had arrived not long before from Yorkshire, England. He attended the public schools of Massachusetts. Thwaites' life-work was identified with Wisconsin, however, whither he removed at thirteen to work on a farm, teach school, and steer himself through a course of study of collegiate grade. As a reporter on the Oshkosh (Wis.) *Times* he was sent to report the Baltimore convention of 1872 that nominated Horace Greeley. In 1874 Thwaites was at Yale, supporting himself as a newspaper correspondent, and taking advanced courses in history and economics. Two years later he became managing editor of the *Wisconsin State Journal*, the leading Republican newspaper, at Madison. In 1887 he was the unanimous choice for secretary of the state Historical Society, on recommemdation of Lyman C. Draper, who retired in 1886. Thwaites augmented the vast collection of Draper Manuscripts, received in 1891, with papers solicited from descendants of French pioneers. He contributed *France in America* to the "American Nation" series and *Wisconsin* to the "American Commonwealth" series. From 1896 to 1901, with a corps of assistants, he collected and translated *Jesuit Relations and Allied Documents,* besides numerous other historical collections. Thwaites found time as well to edit the yearly volume of the society's *Proceedings* and biennial volume of *Collections,* to lecture, and serve as president of the American Library Association in 1900. His book on Daniel Boone is now superseded by John Bakeless' study. Mrs. Thwaites, whom he married in 1892, was Jessie Inwood Turville. and they had one son. Thwaites was described as being a lover of nature and an excellent host. He died at sixty.

PRINCIPAL WORKS: Historic Waterways, 1888; The Colonies, 1891; Our Cycling Tour of England, 1892; Jesuit Relations and Allied Documents, 1896-1901; Afloat on the Ohio, 1897; Father Marquette, 1902; Daniel Boone, 1902; A Brief History of Rocky Mountain Exploration, 1904; France in America, 1905; Wisconsin, 1908.
ABOUT: Turner, F. J. Reuben Gold Thwaites: A Memorial Address; Outlook November 8, 1913; Review of Reviews December 1913; Wisconsin State Journal October 23, 1913.

*TIETJENS, Mrs. EUNICE STRONG (HAMMOND) (July 29, 1884-), American poet and novelist, writes: "I was born

in Chicago, the daughter of William A. Hammond and Idea (Strong) Hammond, and educated mostly in Europe—in Switzerland, Germany, and France, with courses at the Université de Genève and the Collège de France. Having been

T. Averi

born under a wandering star, I have been traveling off and on ever since, having lived for long enough to keep house, in addition to the countries mentioned, in Italy, Tunisia, Japan, China, and the island of Moorea in the Society Islands of the South Seas, and having visited many other countries. In 1904 I married Paul Tietjens, composer of music; divorced 1914. One daughter, and one grandchild (very proud of this last). In 1920 I married Cloyd Head, playwright, theatrical director, and publisher of medical books. He founded a community theatre in Miami, Fla., called the Miami Players. We have one son.

"For the last year of the [First] World War I was correspondent for the Chicago *Daily News* in France. I have been on the staff of *Poetry: A Magazine of Verse,* in one capacity for more than twenty-five years. I am now advisory editor. For two academic years, 1933-35, I was lecturer in Oriental poetry at the University of Miami. I spent the summer of 1939 in Scandinavia, being in Finland when World War II broke out.

"I am now engaged in writing a full book-length poem.

* * *

In her autobiography, *The World at My Shoulder,* Eunice Tietjens says she was "reborn at twenty-seven," when she met Harriet Monroe and began to be active both in the writing and editing of poetry. Amy Lowell, no lenient critic, called her poems "sharp and beautiful." Eda Lou Walton said that she "sees everything sharply and dramatically, but reflects very little about what she sees." Though her work is of interest, it is as a personal influence on other poets that she is chiefly known. She lives in Coconut Grove, Fla.

PRINCIPAL WORKS: Profiles From China, 1917; Body and Raiment. 1919; Jake (novel) 1921; Japan (textbook) 1924; Profiles From Home, 1925; Arabesque (play, with C. Head) 1925; Boy of the Desert (juvenile) 1928; Poetry of the Orient (edited) 1928; Leaves in Windy Weather, 1929; The Romance of Antar (novel) 1929; The Jaw Breakers Alphabet (juvenile, with J. Tietjens) 1930; China (textbook) 1930; Boy of the South Seas (juvenile) 1931; The World at My Shoulder (autobiography) 1938.

ABOUT: Kunitz, S. J. & Haycraft, H. (eds.). The Junior Book of Authors; Tietjens, E. The World at My Shoulder; Nation May 28, 1938; Parents' Magazine March 1938; Poetry September 1938; Scholastic May 16, 1936.

"TILTON, ALICE." See TAYLOR, P. A.

TINKER, CHAUNCEY BREWSTER

(October 22, 1876-), American university professor and literary critic and editor,

Kaiden-Kazanjian

was born in Auburn, Maine, the son of the Rev. Anson Phelps Tinker (Yale 1868) and Martha Jane (White) Tinker. He attended the East Denver High School, Denver, Colo., and received his B.A. degree from Yale in 1899. In 1900 he taught English to Freshman classes in the Sheffield Scientific School, took his master's degree next year, and was made a Ph.D. in 1902. The next year was spent at Bryn Mawr College as associate in English. He returned to Yale in 1903 as instructor, becoming assistant professor in 1908, and Emily Sanford Professor of English Literature in 1913. In 1924 Tinker received an appointment as Sterling Professor. In 1930 he was a lecturer on fine arts at Harvard, and delivered the Charles Eliot Norton lectures on poetry there in 1937-38, later published as *Painter and Poet.* They are studies of Hogarth, Reynolds, Blake, and others. During the First World War Professor Tinker was a captain in the Military Intelligence Division of the U.S.A. General Staff, 1917-18. A member of the National Academy of Arts and Letters, he is also a member of the Century and Grolier Clubs in New York City and the Graduate Club in New Haven. He is also a member of Zeta Psi, and is unmarried.

Professor Tinker began his literary career in orthodox academic style with a critical bibliography of the translations of *Beowulf.* He has since become better known as an authority on James Boswell, and coincidentally, Samuel Johnson. *Young Boswell* (1922) was, in a mild way, a best seller. It received ecstatic notices from John Farrar, a former student of Tinker's, the *Yale*

Review, and others. The *Saturday Review,* in England, found the style "a little too boisterous for our taste." Paul Elmer More commented that the writer was very rarely betrayed "into the cheaper kind of sprightliness, which is the pit digged for the unwary scholar who runs from pedantry." Conrad Aiken has called Tinker's work "urbane, literary, charming, and perhaps a little superficial. His natural taste runs too much to the graceful, too little to the profound." His edition of the *Letters of James Boswell* (1924) is authoritative, and contained much new material.

PRINCIPAL WORKS: The Translations of Beowulf: A Critical Bibliography, 1903; The Salon and English Letters, 1915; Young Boswell, 1922; Nature's Simple Plan: A Phase of Radical Thought in the Mid-Eighteenth Century, 1922; The Good Estate of Poetry, 1929; Painter and Poet: Studies in the Literary Relations of English Painting, 1938; The Poetry of Matthew Arnold: A Commentary (with H. F. Lowry) 1940. *Editor* —Selections From Ruskin (Riverside Literature Series) 1908; The Tempest (The Yale Shakespeare) 1918; Letters of James Boswell, 1924.

ABOUT: Yale University, Class of 1899: Decennial Report.

TINKER, EDWARD LAROCQUE (September 12, 1881-), American novelist, biographer, and historian, writes: "Edward

Larocque Tinker was born in New York City. He went to Browning Boys' School and received his B.A. from Columbia University in 1902 [LL.B. 1905]. In 1905 he was admitted to the bar, and after one year with the Legal Aid Society

Brabazon

was appointed assistant to William Travers Jerome, then district attorney of the city of New York, where he served three years. For five years he lived in Texas, where he installed a Railroad Safety Organization, the first west of Chicago, went as observer on Pancho Villa's train at the battle of Celaya, and was with General Alvaro Obregon before he became the President of Mexico. In 1916 he married Frances McKee of New Orleans and took up the career of writing for a living. Mrs. Tinker collaborated with him in the four novelettes called *Old New Orleans,* for the Old Cities Series.

"Les Écrits de Langue Française en Louisiane au XIX⁰ Siècle (Writings in the French Language in Louisiana in the Nineteenth Century) was his thesis for a doctorate at the Sorbonne. It was crowned

by the French Academy and given the Gold Medal in 1934. He received the Academy's Gold Medal again in 1937 for *Gombo: The Creole Dialect of Louisiana* and *French Newspapers and Periodicals,* which appeared originally in the *Proceedings* of the American Antiquarian Society. In 1936 he was put in charge of a department of the New York *Times Book Review,* called 'New Editions Fine and Otherwise,' and he continues to contribute a weekly page.

"In 1933 he was decorated by the government of France with the *Palme d'Académie,* in 1939 was made a Chevalier of the Legion of Honor, and in the same year was given a medal by Columbia. He is a trustee of the Museum of the City of New York."

* * *

In addition to his experience as lawyer, banker, and president of a realty company (which handled his own inherited properties), Mr. Tinker is an expert printer, with his own press, and has done creditable work in wood engraving. His collection of material on Lafcadio Hearn is probably the most complete in existence. During the First World War he was a lieutenant in the navy, and he is a member of the New York National Guard. His chief recreation is yachting.

He has become a foremost authority on the French period in Louisiana and on old New Orleans, in which he became interested soon after his marriage when he spent a winter in his wife's native city.

PRINCIPAL WORKS: Lafcadio Hearn's American Days, 1924; Toucoutou (novel) 1928; Old New Orleans (with F. McK. Tinker) 1930; Les Cenelles (The Haws): Afro-American Poetry in Louisiana, 1930; Les Écrits de la Langue Française en Louisiane au XIXe. Siècle, 1932; The Palingenesis of Craps, 1933; Bibliography of the French Newspapers and Periodicals of Louisiana, 1933; Gombo: The Creole Dialect of Louisiana, 1936.

ABOUT: Boston Transcript September 1, 1934.

TODD, MABEL LOOMIS (1858-October 14, 1932),

American poet, editor, and writer of travel books, was born in Cambridge, Mass., the daughter of Eben J. Loomis, a well-known astronomer, and Mary Alden (Wilder) Loomis, a direct descendent of John Alden. She was educated in private schools in Washington and Boston, and in March 1879 was married to David Todd another astronomer. They had a daughter, Millicent (Mrs. Walter Van Dyke Bingham). Todd was professor of astronomy at Amherst College, and his wife entered on an interesting life ranging the globe in search of solar eclipses, and at Amherst cultivating the acquaintance of an equally eerie and elusive neighbor, the poet Emily Dickinson.

Mrs. Todd, as Nathan Haskell Dole wrote to the *Saturday Review of Literature* after her death at seventy-four, had spent many years in the laborious task of copying the vast mass of lyrics left behind by Miss Dickinson, and editing them to present the obscure and sometimes almost undecipherable interlineations and alternative readings indicated in footnotes. "In preparing for publication the First and Second Series of the *Poems,* Mrs. Todd had the assistance not only of Miss Dickinson's brother, William Austin, and sister, Lavinia, who asked her to undertake the work, but also of Colonel Thomas Wentworth Higginson, who was, in a way, the poet's mentor. Later many more poems were found and included in the Third Series, which Mrs. Todd edited without the help of Colonel Higginson. She, alone, also edited the quaint and unique letters that Emily Dickinson sent to her friends. Mrs. Todd's biographical prefaces to these volumes are authentic, accurate, and fascinating. A new and enlarged edition of the *Letters* was issued in 1931."

In 1887 and 1896 Mrs. Todd accompanied her husband to Japan to observe the total eclipse of the sun, and subsequent journeys took her to Tripoli, Barbary, for the eclipses of 1900 and 1905. In 1914 they went to Russia. The Todds went around the world in 1901 in pursuit of an eclipse in the Dutch East Indies, and in 1907 they journeyed to Chile to witness the opposition of Mars. The experience and knowledge acquired in this manner were embodied in Mrs. Todd's books of travel and astronomy, which sold well; she was also much in demand as a lecturer.

Mrs. Todd was a member of numerous organizations, notably the Amherst Historical Society, of which she was honorary president, and the Florida Historical Society. She lived part of the year in Coconut Grove, Florida and spent her summers on a forest-covered island in Muscongus Bay on the Maine coast, off Pemaquid. Nathan Haskell Dole wrote of her has having been a fine pianist and singer, and a woman of engaging personality and tireless energy.

PRINCIPAL WORKS: Footprints, 1883; Total Eclipses of the Sun, 1894; Corona and Coronet, 1898; A Cycle of Sunsets, 1909; Tripoli the Mysterious, 1912. *Editor*—Poems of Emily Dickinson, 1890-96; Letters of Emily Dickinson, 1894; A Cycle of Sonnets, 1896; Steele's Popular Astronomy, 1899.

ABOUT: Whicher, G. F. This Was a Poet; Publishers' Weekly October 22, 1932; Saturday Review of Literature November 19, 1932.

TOLLER, ERNST (December 1, 1893-May 22, 1939), German dramatist, was born in Samotschin, German Poland, the son of a

L. Jacobs

Jewish merchant who died when the boy was sixteen. He was educated at the Bromberg Gymnasium and then, after wandering through Denmark and France, spent short periods at the Universities of Heidelberg and Munich, and at the University of Grenoble. He was at Lyons when he heard of the outbreak of the World War I. Returning immediately to Germany, he enlisted. After thirteen months at the front he was invalided out. By this time he was convinced of the iniquity of the war, and he organized the Students' League for Peace in Heidelberg. For this he was ordered arrested, but he fled to Munich, where he met Kurt Eisner and with him organized a strike of the munition workers. Toller was thrown into jail and released only at the November Revolution in 1918. He was by this time a Communist and was elected first President of the Bavarian Soviet Republic. When this was suppressed by the Social Democratic government in 1919, under Noske and Scheidemann, Toller was seized and sent to military prison. He had first been sentenced to death, but the soldiers refused to fire, and his sentence was commuted to life imprisonment. At the time of the general amnesty of political prisoners, Bavaria refused to release him, and it was 1924 before he was freed.

It was in prison that Toller wrote his first volume of poems and also his first plays, including the best known, *Masse-Mensch (Man and the Masses)*. He traveled to the Soviet Republic and also gave a lecture tour in the United States (where he was detained at Ellis Island until protests by fellow-authors caused his release), but until the Nazi victory he remained for the most part in Munich. The Nazis confiscated his property and exiled him, and he came to New York. As Alter Brody put it, "the militant revolutionist had turned during his imprisonment into a mystical preacher of non-resistance to evil. . . . It took the impact of Hitlerism to rouse Toller from his pacifist Nirvana." He lectured widely in Europe and America; in 1938 he spent considerable time in Spain, and he was one of those principally responsible for the campaign to raise relief funds for destitute Spanish children. But this time his ardor was darkened by despair. The victory of Franco in Spain and the Munich Pact were the last blows he was able to endure. In addition to his profound grief over world affairs, he had private sorrows as well. He was no longer in demand as a lecturer, and he had given to the Spanish refugees all the money he had saved from a brief experience as a writer in Hollywood. He had married an actress twenty-five years his junior, and the marriage was unhappy. She had left him and he was preparing to leave New York for London. He no longer had the energy to keep on struggling against fate. In a fit of despondency he hanged himself in his New York hotel at forty-five. "One less champion to defy barbarism and evil," said Louis Untermeyer, "one less honest worker in the world."

In his dramatic style, Toller oscillated between "poetic lyricism" and "the declamations of an advocate." He was an expressionist, and his work often had all the obscurity of most "modern" poetic writing. It is true also, as some critics said, that he could not distinguish "between the theatre and a political platform." In his plays, as Agnes Hanson remarked, "the social machine's diabolical control, energy, and potentialities become the dominant interest rather than man himself." But he was truly "the Schiller of the new ideals of humanity," desperately earnest, giving himself and his talent unstintingly to the cause in which he believed. He was compact of emotion. Untermeyer has described him well: "His eyes burned with a black fire; even his hair seemed to be burningly alive. . . . His broad brow and deeply etched face suggested a half-Jewish, half-Slavic Beethoven." He was as directly a martyr to the Nazi régime as if he had been murdered in a concentration camp.

WORKS AVAILABLE IN ENGLISH: Man and the Masses, 1923; The Machine Wreckers, 1923; Hinkemann, 1923 (as Brokenbow, 1924, Hobbleman, 1926); The Swallow Book (poems and essays) 1924; Which World—Which Way? (essay; first two sections of Quer Durch?) 1931; The Blind Goddess, 1934; I Was a German (autobiography) 1934; Seven Plays (The Machine Wreckers, Transfiguration, Man and the Masses, Hinkemann, Hoppla! Such Is Life!, The Blind Goddess, Draw the Fires!) 1935; Mary Baker Eddy (with Hermann Kesten) 1935; Look Through the Bars (in England: Letters from Prison) 1936; Blind Man's Buff (with Denis Johnston) 1938; Pastor Hall, 1939.

ABOUT: Eloesser, A. Modern German Literature; Grossmann, S. Ernst Toller (in German); Rose, W. Men, Myths, and Movements in Modern German Literature; Signer, P. Ernst Toller (in

German); Toller, E. I Was a German; Untermeyer, L. From Another World; Books Abroad
Winter 1940; Canadian Forum October 1931; Dial
March 1929; Europe Nouvelle June 3, 1939; Life
and Letters Today July 1939; Living Age August
1928, February 1937; Mercure de France June 15,
1934; Nation April 4, 1934, May 28, 1939; New
Republic June 7, 1939; Saturday Review of Literature June 3, 1939; Spectator June 9, 1939;
Wilson Library Bulletin September 1939.

*TOLSTOY. ALEXEY NIKOLAEVICH

(formerly Graf) (December 29, 1882-   ),
Russian novelist and playwright, the third
to bear this illustri-
ous surname, was
born in Nikolaevski-
Samarskom, province
of Samara. By birth
a nobleman (though
he has long since dis-
avowed the title of
Count), he is distant-
ly related, through
his father, to the
great Leo Tolstoy,
while his mother was a Turgenev.

As a student at the Petersburg Technological Institute, he developed a taste for
literature and by 1908 published a brochure
of poems in the style of Balmont and Biely.
Tolstoy describes it as "a wretched collection of immature verse" of which he felt
so ashamed that he bought all available
copies and burned them. His first prose
was the successful collection *Magpie Tales*
(1909); and with his first novel, *The Left
Bank of the Volga* (1910), "I firmly
stepped into literature. The novels *The
Lame Esquire* (1914) and *Odd People*
(1915) belonged to this same cycle. They
were built on tales gathered on the Volga,
my birthplace, where I passed my childhood.
But the material appeared to be exhausted.
It was the saddest period of my literary
work. I possessed neither language nor style.
I lived in the rarefied atmosphere of the
modernists, in a decadent circle of writers. . . . The only man who stood out from
my surroundings was Alexander Blok."

During the First World War Tolstoy was
a military correspondent for the *Russian
News*. In the Revolution he fought on the
White side, but after the evacuation of
Odessa (1919) he settled in France. In
1921, at the time of the "Change-of-Land-
marks" campaign of reconciliation with the
Bolsheviks, he returned to the Soviet Union.
There he has remained and written prolificly,
his themes becoming more varied and broader in implication. *Nikita's Childhood* (1922),
for instance, is a touching and understand-

ing novel of child psychology; in the novels
Aelita (1922-1923) and *The Death Box*
(1925) and the play *The Revolt of the
Machines* (1923) he cultivated fantasy and
satire.

In his realistic vein Tolstoy deals with
everyday Soviet problems. The schematic
plan of the early story, "A Manuscript
Found Under a Bed," concerning an old-
fashioned landlord who despite his hatred for
revolutions admires their elemental power,
developed into the Five-Year-Plan novel,
Black Gold, which mercilessly lampoons
White Guard *emigrés* speculating in Soviet
oil. More significant is the novel *The Adventures of Nevzorov: or, Ibicus* (1925).
The scoundrel Nevzorov is the first of those
skinflints and grafters described so delight-
edly by Ehrenburg, Kataev, and Ilf and
Petrov.

Under the title *Darkness and Dawn* American publishers have brought together Tolstoy's two novels, *The Sisters* and *Nineteen-
Eighteen*, which were originally published as Parts 1 and 2 of *The Road to
Calvary* in 1922 and 1925, respectively. A
broad, dramatic panorama of Russian life
during the years of 1914-1919, *Darkness
and Dawn* has, according to the *Christian
Science Monitor*, "something of the epic
quality of *War and Peace*." Peter Quennell
considers it "among the finest, vividest and
generally most readable Communist novels
that I have yet seen." Tolstoy seems to be
attracted by the heroic years of the Civil
War: in *Bread* (1937) he depicts most dramatically the defense of Tsaritsin (later
Stalingrad) and in his play *The Path to
Victory* (1938), dealing with the rout of
General Denikin, he brings Lenin and Stalin
upon the stage quite convincingly.

Tolstoy's outstanding achievement so far
has been in the realm of fictionized biography. *Peter the Great* (Part I, 1929-1930,
Part II, 1934), which is now available in
English in its entirety, was filmed with
signal success.

In 1937 Tolstoy was elected Deputy from
Leningrad Province to the Supreme Soviet
of the U.S.S.R. After Sholokhov, he is the
most popular living novelist in the Soviet
Union today, his works selling upwards of
350,000 copies. Before the revolution his
maximum was 3,000, In peacetime Tolstoy
attended several writers' congresses at home
and abroad—Paris 1935, London 1937,
Valencia-Madrid-Paris 1937. Like the other
leading Soviet writers, he is now using his
pen as a weapon against the Nazi enemy.

Dignified and serious, Tolstoy is described
as a cross between a city gentleman and a

literary bohemian. He is a born story teller, full of vitality and verve, graceful humor, striking description, his characters brimful with life. His plots are moving but often loosely constructed. One of the secrets of his popularity is his vivid, racy Russian.

PRINCIPAL WORKS AVAILABLE IN TRANSLATION: The Road to Calvary, 1923; Darkness and Dawn, 1936; Peter the Great, 1936; The Death Box, 1937; Bread, 1938.

ABOUT: Chulkov, G. Nashe Sputniki; Gorbachev, G. Ocherki Sovremennoy Russkoy Literatur; Henderson, P. The Novel Today; Ivanov-Razumink, R. V. Tvorchestvo i Kritika; London, K. Seven Soviet Arts; Lvog-Rogazhevsky, V. Noveishaya Russkaya Literatura; Mirsky, D. S. Contemporary Russian Literature; Nikitina, E. F. Russkaya Literatura; Pozner, V. Littérature Russe; Struve, G. Soviet Russian Literature; Vitman, A. M. Vosem'let Russkoi Khudozhestvennoi Literatury (1917-1925); Boston Transcript April 25, 1936; Christian Science Monitor March 27, 1936; New Statesman and Nation November 2, 1935; New York Herald Tribune "Books" March 29, 1936; New York Times March 29, 1935; Saturday Review of Literature March 28, 1935; Times (London) Literary Supplement November 16, 1935.

TOMLINSON, HENRY MAJOR

(1873-   ), English novelist and essayist who signs his work H. M. Tomlinson, was born

in the East End of London and grew up along the docks. He started to work at twelve, as a junior clerk for a shipping company. "My youth," he says, "was spent among the bills of lading and the cargo manifests of the clippers." He loved the ships, but hated the dull routine drudgery. His leisure he spent in reading, in studying geology and entomology, and in music, a taste he inherited from his father. "I had been scribbling since I was a child, and judiciously burning it all." But now he began to send his writing out, in what seemed the vain hope of emancipating himself from commerce. He was married and had a family to support. At last his first acceptance came, from the London Morning Leader. But he was thirty-one before he was finally able to leave his job.

The Morning Leader came to his rescue and gave him a staff position, and he stayed on this paper until after it was merged with the Daily News. He left it in 1912 to take a two-thousand mile voyage up the Amazon on a tramp steamer captained by his brother-in-law: the result of that trip was his first book, The Sea and the Jungle. Then he

returned to the paper and was sent by it in August 1914 as a war correspondent in Belgium and France. Later he was official correspondent at General Headquarters of the British Armies in France, until 1917. In that year he became literary editor of the Nation and Athenaeum, a position he held until 1923. Next he spent nine months traveling in the East Indies for Harper's Magazine, Tidemarks being the fruit of that journey. With Gallions Reach, which received the Femina-Vie Heureuse Prize for 1927, he reached at last a place where he could devote all his time to writing. One of his sons, H. Charles Tomlinson, illustrated Out of Soundings and collaborated with him in Below London Bridge.

Thin, bald, with what is left of his sandy hair now gray, Mr. Tomlinson in his late sixties lives quietly in London with his grown children. He seems still a little bewildered by his success. "It's all so accidental," he says. "It just happened in spite of me." "Every novel is autobiographical," he has remarked. "It can't help it." He is a very slow worker, and a slow reader who still clings to the books which influenced him in youth—nearly all, strangely enough, American—Emerson, Thoreau, Melville above all, and in later years Whitman. He has been compared with Conrad, but the comparison is inept, except that both men have written of the sea and that to both thoughts are more important than action. "The mind is all that matters," is Mr. Tomlinson's philosophy. "The world is what we think it is. If we can change our thoughts we can change the world. And that is our only hope."

PRINCIPAL WORKS: Gallions Reach, 1927; Illusion 1915, 1930; All Our Yesterdays, 1930; The Snows of Helicon, 1933; All Hands! (in America: Pipe All Hands) 1937; The Day Before, 1939. Non-Fiction—The Sea and the Jungle, 1912; Old Junk, 1918; London River, 1921; Waiting for Daylight, 1922; Tidemarks, 1924; Gifts of Fortune and Hints For Those About to Travel, 1926; Under the Red Ensign (in America: The Foreshore of England) 1926; Between the Lines, 1928; Great Sea Stories of All Nations (edited) 1930; Out of Soundings, 1931; Norman Douglas, 1931; South to Cadiz, 1934; Below London Bridge (with H. C. Tomlinson) 1934; Mars His Idiot, 1935; The Wind Is Rising, 1941.

ABOUT: Book Window December 1930; Bookman February 1926, July 1929; Bookman (London) October 1927, August 1930; London Mercury August 1927; Publishers' Weekly January 18, 1930; Saturday Review of Literature January 1, 1927; Virginia Quarterly Review January 1928; World Today, March, 1927.

*TORRENCE, FREDERIC RIDGELY

(November 27, 1875-   ), American poet and playwright, writes: "Ridgely Torrence

* Died December 25, 1950.

comes of a stock now in its fourth century of settlement in this country. He was born in Xenia, Ohio, a place which has been described as more Southern than any other north of the Mason and Dixon Line. He spent two of his boyhood years, largely on horseback, in Santa Ana, Calif. For two years he attended Miami University, then entered Princeton as a junior. There he was on the editorial boards of the *Nassau Literary Magazine* and the *Princeton Tiger.* From Princeton he came to New York, where for six years he was a librarian in the New York Public Library. Later he was an editor of the *Cosmopolitan,* and

from 1920 to 1933 was poetry editor of the *New Republic.* Soon after coming to New York, he published his first book of verse, became linked in poetic activity with his friends William Vaughn Moody and Edwin Arlington Robinson and with the former made a grand tour of Europe and North Africa.

"At the same time his natural inclination was leading him toward the theatre. Believing then as now that the stage 'cries out for poetry,' he cast his first two published plays in verse. But after these experiments he turned reluctantly to a medium of greater immediacy, the poetry of idiom and of folkways. For his source he turned to the American Negro, whose possibilities had never been taken seriously in the theatre. His first Play for a Negro Theatre, *Granny Maumee,* was produced by the New York Stage Society in 1914, but with a white cast. It was produced in 1917 at the Garden and Garrick Theatres, and a Negro cast was collected with great difficulty. There were no serious Negro actors, for there had been no such plays. With the *Plays for a Negro Theatre* the racial group was launched into an artistic milieu in which it has flourished ever since, thus opening the way to such plays as *The Emperor Jones, Porgy, The Green Pastures,* and *Mamba's Daughters,* all of which included actors trained in the Torrence plays.

"But at no period in his career has Torrence been diverted from his lifelong absorption in poetry itself and all through these years he was writing his own poetry. At intervals he has given readings and talks on poetry, chiefly at colleges. In 1938 he

was Poet in Residence at Antioch College. In 1939 he began, for the Rockefeller Foundation, a National Survey of the Negro Theatre, and to this end spent the winter working with the Karamu Theatre, Cleveland, the oldest Negro theatre in the country. In 1940 he edited the *Selected Letters* of Edwin Arlington Robinson, and in 1941 he brought out a volume of his own, entitled *Poems.* In the latter year he was appointed Fellow of Creative Literature at Miami University, Oxford, Ohio.

* * *

Mr. Torrence was married in 1914 to Olivia Howard Dunbar, also a writer. He is a member of the National Institute of Arts and Letters. The late Dr. Robert S. Newdick, of Ohio State University, said of his work: "Torrence publishes infrequently, but his poetry, like Gray's, is flawless, and, like Shelley's, it is particularly and peculiarly remarkable for its rich musical quality." A. E. Housman, always sparing of his praise for fellow poets, wrote of Torrence's work: "It has more substance than most modern poetry. I have read it with admiration for its poetic impulse and for the accomplishment of its verse."

PRINCIPAL WORKS: The House of a Hundred Lights, 1900; El Dorado: A Tragedy, 1903; Abelard and Heloise (poetic drama) 1907; Plays For a Negro Theatre (Granny Maumee, The Rider of Dreams, Simon the Cyrenian) 1917; Hesperides, 1925; The Undefended Line (play) 1938; The Selected Letters of Edwin Arlington Robinson (ed.) 1940; Poems, 1941.

ABOUT: Hagedorn, H. Edwin Arlington Robinson; Mason, D. G. Music in My Time; Moody, W. V. Letters to Harriet; Poetry December 1934; Princeton Alumni Weekly April 3, 1936.

*TOWNE, CHARLES HANSON (February 2, 1877-), American writer and editor, was born in Louisville, Ky., son of Professor Paul A. Towne, a mathematician, and Mary Stuart (Campbell) Towne. He was educated in the common schools of New York City, had some private tutoring, and spent a year at the College of the City of New York. "I cannot remember the time

when I did not love the smell of printers ink," he writes. "To be an editor, and a writer—that was my earliest dream; and never once did I waver from my purpose."

At eleven he typed a paper, the *Unique Monthly,* illustrated by his friend Harry Pray. True to its title, the periodical appeared in a single copy, rented out for five cents a reading.

After serving as private secretary to Charles C. Worthington of the Worthington Pump Co., for whom he edited the *Inter-Office,* Towne obtained a letter of introduction from his employer to John Brisben Walker of the *Cosmopolitan Magazine,* then published at Irvington-on-Hudson for ten cents, in competition with *Lippincott's* and the *Smart Set,* which sold for a quarter. After an apprenticeship as editorial assistant to Walker, Towne came to New York to edit the *Smart Set,* accepting some of the first work of O. Henry and of James Branch Cabell. He dined at Mouquin's on Sixth Avenue; took coffee at the Café Martin; once bumped into Mark Twain in a snowstorm, and in general was blissfully happy. Towne was managing editor of *McClure's Magazine* from 1915 to 1920; edited *Harper's Bazar* from 1926 to 1931; and from then until 1937 wrote a column of literary reminiscences and current opinion for William Randolph Hearst's New York *American.* In 1940 he played in a road company of Howard Lindsay's dramatization of Clarence Day's *Life With Father.*

Retaining his guileless enthusiasm for books, places, and people throughout life, Towne has continued to produce an engaging, if somewhat trite and conventional, series of books. *The Shop of Dreams* (1939) was a novel concerning an old bookshop which, said the critics, might well have been written forty years previously. With Amy Woodforde-Finden, Towne is the author of four song cycles, including "Five Little Japanese Songs" and "The Magic Casement." He also collaborated with Deems Taylor, the composer, in writing "The City of Joy." Unmarried, and much in demand as a diner-out, Towne lives in New York City.

PRINCIPAL WORKS: Ave Maria, 1898; The Quiet Singer and Other Poems, 1908; Manhattan: A Poem, 1909; Youth and Other Poems, 1911; The Tumble Man (with H. Mayer) 1912; Beyond the Stars and Other Poems, 1914; Today and Tomorrow and Other Poems, 1916; Jolly Jaunts With Jim (Through the Fireplace) 1917; Autumn Loiterers, 1917; Shaking Hands With England, 1918; A World of Windows and Other Poems, 1919; The Rise and Fall of Prohibition, 1920; The Bad Man: A Novel (novelization of play by P. E. Browne) 1921; Loafing Down Long Island, 1922; The Chain (novel) 1922; Ambling Through Acadia, 1923; The Gay Ones (novel) 1924; Tinsel (novel) 1925; Selected Poems, 1925; Adventures in Editing (autobiography) 1926; This New York of Mine, 1931; Good Old Yesterday,

1935; An April Song: New Poems, 1937; The Shop of Dreams, 1939; Jogging Around New England, 1939; Gentlemen Behave: Charles Hanson Towne's Book of Etiquette for Men, 1939; Pretty Girls Get There, 1941. *Editor*—For France, 1917; The Balfour Visit, 1917; Roosevelt As the Poets Saw Him, 1923.

ABOUT: Towne, C. H. Adventures in Editing; Bookman October 1919; New York Herald Tribune Magazine February 15, 1931; Saturday Review of Literature April 5, 1941.

TOYNBEE, ARNOLD JOSEPH (April 14, 1889-), English historian and economist, was educated at Winchester and Balliol College, Oxford, a Scholar of both institutions. From 1912 to 1915 he was a Fellow and Tutor at Balliol, and was engaged in government work during the First World War. In April 1918 he joined the Political Intelligence Depart  ment of the Foreign Office. After the war he was a member of the Middle Eastern Section of the British Delegation to the Peace Conference in Paris.

Nationality and the War (1915) was Toynbee's first book, followed by *The New Europe,* articles reprinted from the London *Nation.* Ten years later came a sequel of afterthoughts, *The World After the Peace Conference* (1925). From 1919 to 1924 Toynbee was Koraes Professor of Byzantine and Modern Greek Language, Literature, and History at London University. Since 1925 he has been director of studies in the Royal Institute of International Affairs, and Research Professor of International History in the University of London, both on the Sir Daniel Stevenson Foundation.

Toynbee's *Survey of International Affairs* for 1920-23 appeared in 1924, and has continued annually since that date. He is the editor of *British Commonwealth Relations,* beginning in 1934. He is a Fellow of the British Academy, elected in 1937, and has honorary degrees of D. Litt. from Oxford and the University of Birmingham. Mrs. Toynbee was Rosalind Murray, daughter of Gilbert Murray, the classical scholar. The Toynbees have a London address (Grove End Road) and a home in Yorkshire: Gansthorpe House, Terrington. Besides his periodical contributions, Toynbee contributed the chapter on history to *The Legacy of Greece* (1921) and on non-Arab territory of the Ottoman Empire to Vol. 6

of *The History of the Peace Conference of Paris* (1923). In 1926 he collaborated with K. P. Kirkwood on *Turkey,* a volume in the Nations of the Modern World series.

Toynbee's six-volume *magnum opus, A Study of History,* appeared in 1934 and 1939. James Feibleman, in a lengthy essay contributed to *T'ien Hsia Monthly,* published in Shanghai by the Sun Yat-Sen Institute for the Advancement of Culture and Education, compares it to Oswald Spengler's *The Decline of the West,* although remarking that Toynbee "disabuses the reader of any notion that England is the hub of the universe," in contrast to Spengler's exclusively Germanic attitude. The work considers the six chief societies or civilizations in existence today: the Western, the Orthodox Christian, the Islamic, the Hindu, and the Far Eastern. The author is concerned with the present-day decline of religious belief, but posits a possible but remote mutation of mankind to a higher species. He condemns science, and in philosophy accepts only the humanism of Comte, the ontological dualism of Descartes, and the dialectical philosophy of Hegel. "Toynbee seems at home everywhere, in tiny hamlets of anyone's native land, in the remotest corners of the earth in every age—a pan-provincial whose touch turns every episode to interest," says Feibleman.

PRINCIPAL WORKS: Nationality and the War, 1915; The New Europe, 1915; The Western Question in Greece and Turkey, 1922; Greek Historical Thought, 1924; Greek Civilization and Character, 1924; The World After the Peace Conference, 1925; Turkey (with K. P. Kirkwood) 1926; A Journey to China, 1931; A Study of History, 1934-39; Christianity and Civilization, 1940.

ABOUT: Revue de Métaphysique et de Morale October 1936; T'ien Hsia Monthly August-September, October-November 1940.

TRACY, HENRY CHESTER (August 26, 1876-), American essayist, writes: "Henry Chester Tracy, second son of  Charles C. Tracy who founded Anatolia College, was born in Athens, Pa., and spent an impressionable childhood in Merzifun, Turkey in Asia; there formed a taste for outdoor life and study of a fascinating fauna and flora. Sent at fourteen to America for his schooling, he resumed the study of birds and plants in Pennsylvania and Ohio, majoring in the natural sciences when in college at Oberlin, and believing that he had a vocation in that field. His literary work while in college, however, attracted notice, and under the influence of the late Dr. C. H. A. Wager he came to feel that he might some time do something in letters. Teaching biology for two years after graduation (in Oberlin Academy, since closed), he began to know the sterilizing effects of an academic life and broke away to join the group of college men who went in 1905 to Montana to build the trails in Glacier National Park. Followed four years of nomadic existence, during which he worked in lumber mills, surveyors' camps, apiaries, and the like; was principal of a high school, wrote editorials for a newspaper, homesteaded in Utah, taught school in Idaho, and thence, having married Miriam Lee of the Whitman College (Washington) faculty, went to Berkeley, Calif., as assistant in zoology at the University of California. Acquiring a master's degree while there, he next joined the faculty of the Hollywood High School, where he remained for fifteen years, drowning his literary aspirations in laboratory and field routine, but breaking the shackling restraint toward the end with tentative ventures in prose and (1924) a rounded book which was accepted by the Yale Press as *belles lettres.* About that time he began to contribute papers to the *Adelphi,* London, in a happy relation with the staff and other contributors which lasted nearly a decade. Meanwhile he was writing *Towards the Open* and *English as Experience* as protests against over-specialization at the cost of human values and powers of appreciation. Attracted by the merit of the work of John Laurence Seymour, he wrote librettos for that composer, one of whose operas (*The Pasha's Garden*) was produced by the Metropolitan Opera Company. From 1931 on, he has been occupied chiefly with reviewing for periodicals in New York and London, and in editing his own bulletin—this last having merged into a system of monthly book talks for gatherings of the Readers' Book Groups under his direction. The purpose of these groups is to combat 'best-sellerism' and promote selection of the best books that appear each month, avoiding those written either for a commercial motive or as propaganda; and to promote the amateur spirit in literature."

* * *

Mr. Tracy now lives with his wife and two sons in Hollywood. Geoffrey West, who called him "a philosopher of detachment," said he was "first and last a life-giver." Zona

Gale said of him that he "writes about beauty with imaginative delicacy and without a trace of sentimentality. . . . Such a man brings to everything that he touches a vitality that is electric."

PRINCIPAL WORKS: An Island in Time, 1924; Towards the Open, 1927; The Shadow Eros, 1927; English as Experience, 1928; American Naturists, 1930; The Amateur Writer, 1935; Morning Land, 1938.

ABOUT: Tracy, H. C. Towards the Open (see Introduction by Julian Huxley); Adelphi June 1931; Wilson Library Bulletin March 1929.

*TRAIN, ARTHUR CHENEY (September 6, 1875-   ), American novelist, short-story writer, and criminologist, was born in  Boston, Mass., the son of Charles Russell Train, Attorney-General for Massachusetts from 1873 to 1890, and Sarah M. (Cheney) Train. He was brought up in "the rural environment of the sunny side of Marlboro Street on Boston's Back Bay," and was taken by his father to call on Emerson, Lowell, and Holmes. Young Train was also allowed to visit a courtroom at an early age. He attended St. Paul's School, Concord, N.H., and took his B.A. degree in 1896 from Harvard, where he studied with all the famous teachers of that period—Child, Kittredge, Hill, Wendell, Copeland, and Baker. In 1899 he received his LL.B. degree from the Law School; spent a few months in a conventional Boston law office and was admitted to the Suffolk (Mass.) bar; then went to 160 Broadway, New York City, to spend several "bored, impatient and unhappy" months with the firm of Robinson, Biddle & Ward. On January 11, 1901, Train entered the office of Eugene A. Philbin, New York District Attorney, at a time when a struggle was going on between Tammany and reform elements. He was assistant district attorney until 1908, also serving under the reform administration's William Travers Jerome, one of the best-known prosecutors ever to occupy the D.A.'s chair. At the Criminal Courts Building on White and Centre Streets, adjacent to the Tombs Prison, "every case was a tragedy; every trial a detective story."

Train's first short story to reach print was "The Maximilian Diamond," which Leslie's Magazine, later the American, published in July 1904. Scribner's Magazine published another in December, and next year the pub-lishing house of Charles Scribner's Sons brought out his first book, McAllister and His Double. Given two untitled paintings done by the late Howard Pyle, Train wove his story, "The Madonna of the Blackbird," around them, introducing a scientific detective, Monsieur Donaque. His most famous character, Mr. Tutt, who wins acquittal for his clients through his knowledge of obscure points of law, is said to have been drawn partially from an old Southern lawyer who lost his membership in the University Club for stealing too much writing paper. In twenty years, old Tutt has argued over eighty cases, and has yet to be caught out in an error. Some law schools make Mr. Tutt's Case Book required reading. In 1918 Ray Long, editor of Cosmopolitan, offered Train a "fabulous sum" for three serials. Many of his books are romans à clef: novels with characters and incidents based on fact. Several novels about the rich, idle or otherwise, are derived from the family history of the Morgans, Vanderbilts, and Rockefellers.

"I enjoy the dubious distinction of being known among lawyers as a writer, and among writers as a lawyer," says Mr. Train in his autobiographical My Day in Court. "Each group readily yields me to the other with an amiable, if not too obvious, condescension. I have, in fáct, had two simultaneous careers, both active, and both moderately successful. I have no literary pretensions to be punctured." The Prisoner at the Bar (1906) and True Stories of Crime (1908) were among the first books to deal with American crime, but lack the literary finish of the work of Edmund Pearson in the same field. In a quarter-century's writing Arthur Train has published nearly 250 short stories and novels, all readable. From 1916 to 1923 he was a member of the law firm of Perkins & Train. He is treasurer of the National Institute of Arts and Letters. A dark, clean-shaven man, genial in manner and appearance, Train lives in New York City, with a summer home at Bar Harbor, Maine. Mrs. Ethel (Kissam) Train, whom he married in 1897, died in 1923, leaving a son, Arthur Kissam Train, and three married daughters. Train married Mrs. Helen C. Gerard in 1926; they have a son, John.

PRINCIPAL WORKS: McAllister and His Double, 1905; The Prisoner at the Bar, 1906; True Stories of Crime, 1908; The Butler's Story, 1909; Mortmain, 1909; Confessions of Artemus Quibble, 1909; C. Q.: or, In the Witches' House, 1910; Courts, Criminals, and the Camorra, 1911; The Goldfish, 1914; The Man Who Rocked the Earth (with R. W. Wood) 1915; The World and Thomas Kelly, 1917; The Earthquake, 1918; Tutt and

Mr. Tutt, 1920; By Advice of Counsel, 1921; The Hermit of Turkey Hollow, 1921; As It Was in the Beginning, 1921; Tut, Tut, Mr. Tutt!, 1923; His Children's Children, 1923; The Needle's Eye, 1924; On the Trail of the Bad Men, 1925; The Lost Gospel, 1925; Page Mr. Tutt, 1926; The Blind Goddess, 1926; High Winds, 1927; When Tutt Meets Tutt, 1927; Ambition, 1928; The Horns of Ramadan, 1928; Illusion, 1929; Paper Profits, 1930; The Adventures of Ephraim Tutt, 1930; Puritan's Progress, 1931; Princess Pro Tem, 1932; The Strange Attacks on Herbert Hoover, 1932; No Matter Where, 1933; Tutt for Tutt, 1934; Jacob's Ladder, 1935; Manhattan Murder, 1936; Mr. Tutt's Case Book, 1937; Old Man Tutt, 1938; My Day in Court, 1939; From the District Attorney's Office, 1939; Tassels on Her Boots, 1940; Mr. Tutt Comes Home, 1941.

ABOUT: Baldwin, C. C. The Men Who Make Our Novels; Overton, G. M. American Nights Entertainment, Authors of the Day; Train, A. C. My Day in Court, Puritan's Progress; New York Times Book Review April 13, 1941.

TRAUBEL, HORACE L. (December 19, 1858-September 8, 1919), American editor, poet, reformer, and Walt Whitman's "Boswell," was born in Camden, N.J., the son of Maurice Henry Traubel, a German Jew who had become a printer, engraver, and lithographer, and Katherine (Grunder) Traubel, a Philadelphian. He was a thin, shy, and self-contained child, taken out of school at twelve. For a while he was newsboy and errand-boy, then a printer's devil; he helped in his father's stationery shop, learned something about lithography, and at the age of thirty was employed in a bank in Philadelphia. There he founded, in March 1890, the *Conservator*, a monthly which survived—though rather unremuneratively—until the summer of 1919; from 1903 to 1907 he was editor of the *Artsman*, organ of the Rose Valley Movement, a communal enterprise conducted on an eighty-acre farm southwest of Philadelphia.

Meanwhile he had established a long-lasting friendship with Walt Whitman, who had settled in Camden in 1873. He stayed, during Whitman's last years, almost constantly at his heel, and recorded even the most inconsequential of his remarks. The three-volume *With Walt Whitman in Camden*, covering conversations between March 1888 and January 1889, came out between 1906 and 1914. Traubel was made one of Whitman's literary executors and thereby became one of the editors of *In Re Walt Whitman*, issued in the year of the poet's death. At Whitman's house—the poet was anxious to attend the ceremony but too ill to go out—Traubel married Anne Montgomerie on May 28, 1891.

Obviously Traubel could hardly escape a tremendous Whitmanesque influence; and, going beyond his preceptor, he became a Marxian socialist, concerned primarily with moral-religious rather than politico-economic aspects. He uncompromisingly believed that war was "simply murder in its most vicious, abhorrent, and inexcusable extremity." *Chants Communal*, prose verse in paragraph form, broken up into short and sometimes incomplete sentences, was published in 1904. In 1913 he issued a small pamphlet, *The Master of Money Is Dead*, stylistically much like the earlier book; and in the year following, a volume of verse, *Optimos*, which in its long unrhymed lines, choral reiterations, and celebration of the democratic spirit, was patently reminiscent of *Leaves of Grass*.

Traubel died of a heart ailment in his sixty-first year, at Bon Echo, Ontario. He was short and squarely built; had blue eyes, a sensitive face, and hair that was noticeably heavy and wavy. Eugene V. Debs called Traubel the "master democrat of his time" and "the genius incarnate of human love." It was, presumably, this same personal admiration that caused contemporary critics to overestimate Traubel as a poet. But his notes on Whitman, though in part superfluous and undisciplined, remain invaluable biographical data.

PRINCIPAL WORKS: In Re Walt Whitman (ed., with others) 1893; The Dollar or the Man? 1900; Chants Communal, 1904; The Master of Money Is Dead, 1913; Optimos, 1914; With Walt Whitman in Camden (3 vols.) 1906-14; Collects, 1915.

ABOUT: Bain, M. Horace Traubel; Traubel, H. With Walt Whitman in Camden; Walling, W. E. Whitman and Traubel; New York Times September 10, 1919.

TRAVEN, B., German (?) novelist, has been called "the most mysterious of modern authors." He is extremely averse to publicity, saying that "an author should have no biography but his books," and for years he refused to be published in America, because in his opinion American publicity methods, "reduced authors to the status of tight rope walkers, sword swallowers, and trained animals." It is not even known whether he is German or American by birth; and though it is stated that his books are translated by Basil Creighton (and one by Eric Sutton), there is a widely circulated rumor that he actually writes in English. He may even be Basil Creighton himself! (His English idiom in a personal letter, however, is distinctly German.) His first name is supposed to be Bruno, but even that is uncertain. His contract with his American publishers provides that there is to be no publicity, there are to be no blurbs, and that his place of residence is never to be revealed. All that can be gathered from his novels is that he has probably been a sailor, perhaps in the American merchant marine, and that, to quote Robert Bourget-Pailleron, "he is familiar with the Mexican forest, and has passed years among the Indians."

In this country his books have had a small sale, and in England not a much larger one; but on the Continent, before the war, he was immensely popular. *The Death Ship* was published in England, Sweden, Norway, Denmark, Holland, Germany, France, Spain, and Russia; in Germany it sold a quarter of a million copies, in the U.S.S.R. a million and a half. *The Treasure of the Sierra Madre* was also published in twelve countries and had a huge sale. Alfred Knopf, his American publisher, first heard of him in Berlin in 1932, and learned that in Germany he was considered the legitimate successor of Jack London in the same *genre*.

As in London's early books, Traven's theme is danger, horror, cruelty, and the passionate defense of the underdog. If he is a German, it appears that he is opposed to the Nazi régime, for it was only after Hitler's rise to power that he was willing to be published in the United States, and it is believed that he is now living either in England or in America. (A letter to the editors of this volume in 1940 was postmarked, partly indecipherably, from some spot in his favorite Mexico.) His power, irony, and sustained excitement have made him one of the most interesting of modern novelists to the critics, but for some reasons his work has not—or not yet—caught the fancy of the general public in this country—perhaps because we are unaccustomed to discovering an author's excellences unless we are told about them first. There is a harshness in his books also which alienates the habitual reader of adventure stories, while his chosen backgrounds and characters do not appeal to the urban and sophisticated. But he is almost a major figure in contemporary fiction, and will eventually be recognized as such in the United States as he has been elsewhere.

WORKS AVAILABLE IN ENGLISH: The Death Ship: The Story of an American Sailor, 1934; The Treasure of the Sierra Madre, 1934; The Carreta, 1935; Government, 1935; The Bridge in the Jungle, 1938.

ABOUT: Publishers' Weekly July 9, 1938; Revue des Deux Mondes May 1, 1938.

TRAVERS, PAMELA L. (1904*-), British poet and juvenile author who writes under the name of P. L. Travers, writes: "I was born in the tropics of Australia [North Queensland], of Irish parents, and feel myself and my work to be Irish rather than Australian. I lived in Australia during my childhood and then came to live in Ireland and later in England.

A. Genthe

I have a nine-hundred-year-old house [in Mayfield, Sussex], mentioned in the Doomsday Book, and live in it for most of the year. I began to write when I was seventeen and first became known, if I may put it that way, as a poet. It was George Russell, the great Irish poet and economist, known more popularly as AE, who first published my work in his paper, *The Irish Statesman,* and who, since we became great friends, in a way presided over it until his death some years ago. I think I may say that my poetry is known in America; it has appeared in periodicals and anthologies there over a number of years. I have published only three books as yet, but am now working on two more which I hope the war will not hold up too long."

* * *

Miss Travers was born near the Great Barrier Reef, which was the scene of her two books for children. She was educated privately, specializing in dancing, and after coming to England in 1923 went on the stage for several years, playing chiefly in Shakespeare. *Mary Poppins* was told first as a spoken story to two small children; it became an immediate success in print, was translated into German, Swedish, Italian, and Czech, and Mortimer Browning composed a *Mary Poppins Suite for Orchestra.* Miss Travers has been writing since she was seven; it was only about 1936, however, that she gave up acting to devote all her time to authorship. Her eleventh century cottage is of great archaeological interest, and is visited frequently by scholars. In peacetime she lives there a quiet, outdoor life, broken infrequently by travel. One trip brought her to the United States in 1936, another took her to Russia in 1934. She is unmarried. In 1940 she came to New York to stay for the duration of the war.

* Correction: Year of birth, 1906.

PRINCIPAL WORKS: Mary Poppins, 1934; Mary Poppins Comes Back, 1935; Moscow Excursion, 1935; I Go by Sea, I Go by Land, 1941.

ABOUT: Wilson Library Bulletin December 1936.

TRENCH, HERBERT

TRENCH, HERBERT (November 26, 1865-June 11, 1923), British poet and playwright, was born Frederic Herbert Trench at Avoncore, County Cork, the son of William Wallace Trench and Elizabeth French (Allin) Trench, who died before Herbert was two. He was the great-nephew of the 1st Lord of Ashtown and of Richard Chenevix Trench, Archbishop of Dublin. At the age of fifteen he went to Haileybury College, and from there, after winning an exhibition in modern history and writing a small book of school-inspired *Haileybury Verses*, he went up to Keble College, Oxford, in 1884. Trench was a handsome youth, and his dreaminess and mild indifference to discipline were entirely eclipsed by his engaging personality and agile mind. Ill health kept him back, academically, for a while; but he received an M.A. degree from Oxford, and in 1889 he was elected a fellow of All Souls College. Meanwhile he had gone up the Nile (1888), and had made a journey through Russia, Austria, and Spain.

In 1891 he married Lilian Isabel Fox, and by her had three children. In 1900 he was made Senior Examiner and Assistant Director of Special Enquiries at the Board of Education. He retired in 1909—and wisely so, for he was primarily a man of letters. In 1900 he had made a small mark with his *Deirdre Wed and Other Poems*, and a great impression with *New Poems* (1907), containing "Apollo and the Seaman," "The Questioners," and others.

From 1909 to 1911 he was director of the Haymarket Theatre, and during that time, largely through the excellence of *King Lear* and *The Blue Bird*, gained considerable prestige as a producer. But what was more important, he absorbed a number of ideas about dramatic technique which he drew upon several years later. He published four more books of verse, the last of which was *Poems, With Fables in Prose*. At the end of the World War, Trench, himself the father of two "Tommies," wrote a four-act play, *Napoleon*, projecting the family—and not the individual or the state—as the center of life. He was seeking the twofold and therapeutic "discovery of an organic soul, first in ourselves; then in other human creatures. . ." He was at work on another play, to be called *Talleyrand*, but it was unfinished at the time of his death. A student of Russian, he translated Merezhkovsky's *The Death of the Gods* (1901) and, much later, *The Romance of Leonardo da Vinci*.

Trench spent his last years in comparative solitude at his own Villa Viviani, with its olives and cypress clumps, at Settignano, near Florence; and he died in a hospital at Boulogne at the age of fifty-seven. Sensitive, imaginative, and fine-featured, he had a becomingly pensive face, with black eyes, clear skin, and a broad moustache. Appraising his poetry, Granville-Barker complained of occasional outcroppings of self-consciousness and of an apparent struggle with some kind of transcendental idea, all of which, he contended, leave the reader wondering over some noble lines "and a little suspicious that Trench himself may have been left wondering too." R. E. Gordon George, however, regards this ambiguity as "the very delicacy of art, to be almost ethereal, impalpable, and yet not wholly so."

PRINCIPAL WORKS: Haileybury Verses, 1882; Deirdre Wed, 1900; The Death of the Gods, 1901; New Poems, 1907; Souvenir of the Blue Bird, 1910; Lyrics and Narrative Poems, 1911; Ode From Italy in Time of War, 1915; Poems: With Fables in Prose, 1918; Napoleon, 1919; The Romance of Leonardo da Vinci, 1924; Collected Works, 1924.

ABOUT: Bennett, A. The Journals of Arnold Bennett; Burke's Peerage; Trench, H. Apollo and the Seaman; Contemporary Review July 1924; London Mercury June 1924.

TRENT, GREGORY.

TRENT, GREGORY. See WILLIAMSON, T. R.

TRENT, WILLIAM PETERFIELD

TRENT, WILLIAM PETERFIELD (November 1862-December 7, 1939), American university professor and literary critic, was born in Richmond, Va., the son of Dr. Peterfield Trent and Lucy Carter (Burwell) Trent. He received his M.A. degree from the University of Virginia in 1884, and a Litt.D. from Wake Forest in 1890. From 1885 to 1887 he taught  school and read law in Richmond, going to the University of the South in 1888 and becoming dean of the academic department in 1894. He edited the *Sewanee Review,* begun in 1892. From 1900 to 1929 Dr. Trent was a professor of English literature at Columbia University, called there by President Seth Low at the instigation of Theodore Roosevelt, who had admired Trent's book on the pre-Civil War novelist, William Gilmore Simms (1892). Trent's independent attitude during the First World War and refusal to embrace the Allied cause uncritically (which caused one of his colleagues to assure Carl Van Doren that he "had sinned the sin against the Holy Ghost") gave him some uncomfortable years. He "suffered everything a prophet can suffer when the pack turns against him—everything but violence and death," Van Doren wrote in *Three Worlds.* "He could barely finish and could not publish his life of Defoe." The book, in ten manuscript volumes, is currently being edited by Henry C. Hutchins. Trent sold his collection of first editions, pamphlets, and memorabilia of Defoe to the Boston Museum for $35,000 when he retired from Columbia in 1929. He was co-editor of the Columbia University edition of the complete writings of John Milton, published in 1931. Dr. Trent had completed his memoirs and some *Thoughts on Teaching* at the time of his death at seventy-seven at his home at Hopewell Junction, N.Y. A son, W. P. Trent, Jr., and daughter, Lucia (Trent) Cheney, poet and anthologist, survived.

Carl Van Doren, associated with Trent not only as student but as co-editor of the *Cambridge History of American Literature,* described him as a "kind, fierce, gray Virginian lion," whose rages were noble, and no less noble for being witty.

PRINCIPAL WORKS: English Culture in Virginia, 1889; Life of William Gilmore Simms (American Men of Letters Series) 1892; Southern Statesmen of the Old Régime, 1897; Robert E. Lee, 1899; John Milton: A Short Study of His Life and Works, 1899; A History of American Literature: 1607-1865, 1903; Longfellow and Other Essays, 1910; Great Writers of America, 1912; Defoe: How to Know Him, 1916.

ABOUT: Buck, P. H. The Road to Reunion; Van Doren, C. Three Worlds; American Historical Review April 1940; American Notes & Queries July 1941; New York Times December 8, 1939; School and Society December 16, 1939.

TREVELYAN, GEORGE MACAULAY

(February 16, 1876-   ), English historian, is the son of another well-known historian, Sir George Otto Trevelyan (1838-1928), and the grand-nephew of Thomas Babington Macaulay. His mother was Caroline (Philips) Trevelyan. One of his brothers

is a former Minister for Education, the other a poet and translator from the Greek. George Macaulay Trevelyan was educated at Harrow and at Trinity College, Cambridge. Since 1927 he has been Regius Professor of Modern History at Cambridge, and since 1940 has been Master of Trinity.

During the First World War he was Commandant of the First British Ambulance Unit for Italy, received the Italian medal for valor, and was made a Chevalier of the Order of St. Maurice and St. Lazarus. He was made a Commander of the Order of the British Empire in 1920 and received the Order of Merit in 1930.

Trevelyan is a Fellow of the British Academy and has honorary doctorates from Oxford, St. Andrews, Edinburgh, Cambridge, London, Harvard, Yale, Manchester, and Durham. He is an Honorary Fellow of Oriel College, Oxford, a trustee of the British Museum and the National Portrait Gallery, an honorary member of the Massachusetts Historical Society, and president of the Youths' Hostels Association. For several years he was chairman of the Estates Committee of the National Trust, which endeavored to save old English houses from destruction. In 1904 he married Janet Penrose Ward, a writer and social worker, who is a daughter of Mrs. Humphry Ward, the novelist, and hence a niece of Matthew Arnold. They have a son and a daughter, and besides their home in Cambridge have a house at Newcastle-on-Tyne, where Mr. Trevelyan's recreations, in peacetime, are shooting and walking.

Like his father and his great-uncle before him, he is the most English of historians—though he is an authority also on Italian history, especially that of the *Risorgimento.* Like them also, he holds the heretical opinion that history should be interesting as well as sound, a theory put forth in his essay, *Clio: A Muse,* where he pointed out that too often the muse had been transformed into a workhorse. "I cannot abandon the older ideal of History," he says, "that the same book should make its appeal both to the general reader and to the historical student." Philip Guedalla, who holds the same view as to biography, remarked that Trevelyan "inherits his great-uncle's mood. That deliberate pursuit of concrete images, which marked Macaulay's method, is reproduced by his descendant."

His major works are his *History of England* and *British History in the Nineteenth Century,* both written from the point of view of an advanced Liberal, and with all the color—though without the partisanship and prejudice—of Lord Macaulay; and, it may be added, with a far better background of training in historical research.

PRINCIPAL WORKS: England in the Age of Wycliffe, 1904; England Under the Stuarts, 1905; The Poetry and Philosophy of George Meredith, 1906; Garibaldi's Defense of the Roman Republic, 1907; Garibaldi and the Thousand, 1909; Garibaldi and the Making of Italy, 1911; English Songs of Italian Freedom (edited) 1911; The Life of John Bright, 1913; Clio: A Muse and Other Essays Literary and Pedestrian, 1913; Scenes From Italy's War, 1919; Recreations of an Historian, 1919; Lord Grey of the Reform Bill, 1920; British History in the Nineteenth Century, 1922; Manin and the Venetian Revolution of 1848, 1923; History of England, 1926; Must England's Beauty Perish? 1929; Social Documents For Queen Anne's Reign Down to the Union With Scotland, 1929; England Under Queen Anne (3 vols.) 1930-34; Sir George Otto Trevelyan, 1932; The Mingling of the Races, 1934; Grey of Fallodon, 1937; The English Revolution: 1688-89, 1938; British History in the Nineteenth Century and After, 1938; A Shortened History of England, 1941; English Social History, 1942.

ABOUT: Saturday Review of Literature December 13, 1930.

TREVELYAN, Sir GEORGE OTTO.
See "BRITISH AUTHORS OF THE 19TH CENTURY."

*TROUBETZKOY, AMÉLIE (RIVES),

Princess (August 23, 1863-), American novelist, writes: "I was born in Richmond, Va., of old  Virginia families on both sides. My French Christian name came from Queen Amélia, wife of Louis Philippe, who was my grandmother's friend when my grandfather was Minister Plenipotentiary to France. I was taken as a baby to the estate of Castle Hill, Va., which belonged to my Rives grandparents, and brought up in its lovely surroundings. I learned early to bridle, saddle, and harness my pony, and had my first ride on horseback when I was two years old. As I grew older the country life charmed me more and more. All my long life, of which most has been spent at Castle Hill, I have loved the country far more than any town.

"My father was a colonel in the Confederate Army. I was taught at home by my mother and later by tutors and governesses. I cannot remember when I did not want to 'make up stories' or spin queer rhymes. As soon as I could write I began to set them down on paper. When my grandmother disapproved and quietly took the paper from me, I began to write on the wide hems of my starched white petticoats!

"I really haven't much to say about my writing in later years. Some of it, I suppose, was good, and some I know was bad. The book of mine that I like best is a drama in blank verse called *Augustine the Man,* which was published in England. The latest thing that I have written is a poem called 'Great Britain: October 1940,' which was published in a paper in Plymouth.

"In 1888 my first marriage, to John Armstrong Chanler, took place. In 1895, after a long separation, I obtained a divorce. In 1896 I married Prince Pierre Troubetzkoy, the portrait painter. We had nearly forty-one years of great happiness together. He died suddenly in 1936. His mother was an American. Until the winter of 1941, I did not know that all those who married foreigners before 1922 lost their American citizenship. I shall soon take steps to regain mine. To me democracy is a religion, a great faith, which like all religions has to be ever renewed: and the democracy of the United States of America is a living, growing thing. I hope to grow with it until I die. I also hope that before I die there will be a union of all English-speaking democracies throughout the world."

* * *

Princess Troubetzkoy has also written several plays, produced but not published, and the words of the popular song, "My Laddie." Her play, *The Young Elizabeth,* won the prize of the St. Louis Little Theatre in 1937. *The Quick or the Dead* was a sensation when it appeared over half a century ago.

PRINCIPAL WORKS: The Quick or the Dead, 1888; A Brother to Dragons (short stories) 1888; Virginia of Virginia, 1889; According to St. John, 1890; Athelwold (drama in blank verse) 1891; Tanis the Sand Digger, 1892; Selene (poem) 1905; Augustine the Man, 1906; The Golden Rose, 1908; Trix and Over the Moon, 1909; Pan's Mountain, 1910; Hidden House, 1911; World's End, 1913; Shadows of Flames, 1915; The Ghost Garden, 1918; As the Wind Blew (poems) 1922; The Sea Woman's Cloak (play) 1923; The Queerness of Celia, 1926; Firedamp, 1930.

TROWBRIDGE, JOHN TOWNSEND.
See "AMERICAN AUTHORS: 1600-1900"

---

* Died June 15, 1945.

TRUMBO, DALTON (1905-), American novelist and screen writer, was born in Montrose, Colo.—"in the rear of a reading-room." His grand-

Baskerville

father was a pioneer sheriff in the early days of the West. In his teens his family moved to California, and he has attended both the University of Colorado and the University of California at Los Angeles. But his father died before he had finished college, and he had to go to work as a night bread-wrapper in a large Los Angeles bakery. Subsequently he worked as a railroad section hand, a car washer, and a waiter, before he became first a reporter and then a motion picture critic.

He had begun writing in his teens, completing six novels and a hundred short stories before he sold anything. Most of his early published writing was on the movies, and he is still a screen writer, among his scripts being *A Man To Remember* and the film version of Christopher Morley's *Kitty Foyle*. In 1932 he was on the staff of the *Hollywood Spectator,* one of whose editors was Robert E. Sherwood.

However, Mr. Trumbo's deep interest in economics soon took command of him as a writer. He is far to the left in his economic views. His latest novel, *The Remarkable Andrew*—though it seems to be two novels in one, and the parts do not "jell"—is full of robust satire. His best work so far is *Johnny Got His Gun.* Almost unbearable to read (the radio version was unable to reproduce all its horror), it is a terrible indictment of war and the consequences of war. It reveals Mr. Trumbo as more than a pamphleteer or a satirist; it reveals him as a novelist of intensity and power.

A typical production of Dalton Trumbo's social conscience is his 1941 pamphlet in defense of Harry Bridges, the longshoremen's union leader facing deportation charges. The first printing of 100,000 copies, published by the League of American Writers, was dedicated "To members of Los Angeles Local 37, Bakers and Confectioners International Union of America, AFL, with whom I worked for nine years, who now courageously enter the fifteenth month of their strike against the Davis Perfection Bakeries."

PRINCIPAL WORKS: Eclipse, 1935; Washington Jitters, 1936 (dramatized by J. Boroff and W.

Hart, 1938); Johnny Got His Gun, 1939; The Remarkable Andrew, 1941.

ABOUT: Current Biography May 1941; Time February 3, 1941.

TUCKER, BENJAMIN RICKETSON (1854-June 22, 1939), American sociologist, was born in Massachusetts, partly of Quaker descent. He was educated at the Boston Friends' Academy and the Massachusetts Institute of Technology. He was during his long life

the leader and nearly the only American exponent of philosophical anarchism of the school of Kropotkin. In 1881 he founded his magazine, *Liberty,* which was published with some intermissions until 1908. Previously he had worked on the Boston *Globe* for eleven years, had founded and edited the *Radical Review* (1876-77), and had been on the staff of the *Engineering Magazine.* He served on other magazines and papers also, and after his permanent removal to Europe about 1910 (he lived and died in Monaco), he founded the *Transatlantic,* a magazine which published and translated the best of European literature and art for American readers. He was a well known translator from the French (and from the Russian through the French) for seventy years, among the authors whom he published in English being Proudhon, Bakunin, Tolstoy, Tchenychewsky, Victor Hugo, Zola, and Claude Tillier. He was the first to introduce Bernard Shaw (in his early economic writings) to America, and when Whitman's *Leaves of Grass* was declared unmailable in 1882, he openly advertised and sold the book.

All his life he was undeviatingly opposed to all forms of governmental ownership or coercion, with what Michael Williams called "an absolutely extreme belief in human goodness." He was a complete pacifist and non-resistant (though in 1914, for the only time in his career, he declared himself as pro-Ally). Kropotkin called Tucker's views "a combination of Proudhon and Herbert Spencer." Among the forms of "state interference" he most abhorred was legal marriage, though he lived for nearly half a century with his "companion," Pearl Johnson; they had one daughter. He was active also as a Free Thinker. He was the last of the indigenous American radicals of the old school, like Stephen Pearl Andrews, stemming legitimately from Thoreau and Emerson.

Michael Williams, once a Socialist but now a Catholic spokesman, still conceded that *Instead of a Book* "belongs to a group of books written by men who might, if their innate literary power had not been deflected by interests other than purely literary or creative ideals, have taken high rank among modern authors."

PRINCIPAL WORKS: Instead of a Book: By a Man Too Busy to Write One, 1893; Individual Liberty, 1927.

ABOUT: Eltzbacher, P. Anarchism; Macdonald, G. E. Fifty Years of Free Thought; Sprading, C. T. Liberty and the Great Libertarians; American Journal of Sociology January 1936; Commonweal July 7, 1939.

*TULLY, JIM (June 3. 1888-), American novelist, was born in a log cabin near St. Mary's, Ohio, the son of James Dennis Tully and Marie Bridges (Lawlor) Tully. He describes his father as "a  drunken ditch-digger"; his mother had been a country school teacher. Both came from Ireland. When his mother was dying he gave her a drink of water, for which she asked, but which had been forbidden by the doctor and was supposed to have caused her death. He was then six years old. His father repudiated him and, though he kept the older children, put Jim in an orphanage. He was there until he ran away at eleven and for three years was "kicked about" as a farmhand. Next came the road; he was a tramp until he was twenty-one, crossing the continent three times, "vagged" in five jails, working in a circus, as a newsboy, a dishwasher, and finally as a chainmaker at $30 a week. But he had learned to read, and books fascinated him; he haunted libraries and became what Sarah Haardt called "a literary bum." Then he took to pugilism, and was a preliminary fighter in the featherweight class until he was knocked out in a San Francisco fight and was unconscious for twenty-four hours. That made him leave the ring. He worked, in this period, as a superintendent of tree surgeons, and at one time was a reporter on two Akron, Ohio, papers. During the First World War he was a government chain inspector.

Tully was one of the many writers "discovered" by H. L. Mencken in the old

Smart Set days. For eight years he worked on his first novel, *Emmet Lawler,* which he wrote in one 100,000-word paragraph. *Beggars of Life,* also autobiographical, made him famous. *Jarnegan* was the first published evidence of his passionate interest in prison reform. *Ladies in the Parlor,* a book which is one of his own favorites, was suppressed by censorship.

Tully had meanwhile gone to Hollywood and had become a highly paid publicity agent. He was for some time Charlie Chaplin's press agent and ghost writer. In 1911 he had married Florence Bushnell, and had a son and a daughter. He was divorced in 1924, and the following year married Margaret Rider Myers, from whom he was divorced in 1930. He lives now in a $100,000 house on Toluca Lake, with "the best library in Hollywood," and also has an 89-acre ranch in the back country. Frank Scully, who called him "the *enfant terrible* of Holywood, the mighty oak of American letters," described him as "a hammered-down Titan," with his "huge head and mass of curly red hair streaked with gray," his deep bass voice, his "fine big teeth," and the dimples which give him still a boyish expression. Few men have more enemies, for he never pulls his punches, and as an interviewer he is feared as much as he is respected. He is pugnacious and indiscreet, unchanged in nature from what life made of him in boyhood, a hard drinker and a hard fighter, yet fundamentally generous and soft-hearted. He has said: "I am by nature an Irish spinner of fairy-tales and a poet whom a hard life twisted into a hobo, a pugilist, and a realistic writer."

Tully's work has been very popular in the U.S.S.R., like that of Jack London, with whom he has much in common. To the editors of this volume he writes of "the futility that haunts me like a bad dream. In spite of all that, I am still able to work eighteen hours a day. In work is the supreme forgetfulness."

PRINCIPAL WORKS: Emmet Lawler, 1922; Beggars of Life, 1924; Jarnegan, 1925; Life of Thomas H. Ince, 1925; Life of Charlie Chaplin, 1926; Twenty Below (with Robert Nichols) 1926; Black Boy (with F. Dazey) 1926; Circus Parade, 1927; Denis Darel, 1928; Shanty Irish, 1928; Shadows of Men, 1929; God Loves the Irish (with C. Beahan) 1929; Beggars Abroad, 1930; Close Ups, 1930; Adventures in Interviewing, 1931; Blood on the Moon, 1931; Laughter in Hell, 1932; Men in the Rough, 1933; Ladies in the Parlor, 1934; The Bruiser, 1936; Half Sister of the Lord, 1937; A Hollywood Decameron, 1937; Biddy Brogan's Boy, 1942.

ABOUT: Nathan, G. L. The Intimate Notebooks of George Jean Nathan; Tully, J. Beggars of Life, Circus Parade, Shanty Irish, Shadows of Men,

Blood on the Moon; American Mercury May 1928; Esquire November 1939; Pictorial Review December 1926; Publishers' Weekly August 23, 1935; Scribner's Magazine August 1937; Sewanee Review October 1929.

TUNIS, JOHN ROBERTS (December 7, 1889-   ), American essayist and critic of sports, writes: "John R. Tunis was born in  a log cabin on the sunny side of Beacon Street, Boston, just before the turn of the century and just before Beacon turns into Commonwealth Avenue. The R in his name stands for 'Amateur-Lover.' He rose to greet me, a clean-limbed young American with a chest like a beetle. 'Tunis?' I asked. 'Tunis in on station WEAF,' he replied, for he has a pawky Gaelic wit though he is often sober. There was something in his whimsical smirk which made me realize that I was in the presence of the man who revolutionized tennis by making the balls round, instead of oblong as they were in the days of Big Dough and Little Dough. Asked to reminisce, Tunis—for he prefers to be called Tunis—said:

" 'It was during the blizzard of Naughty-Seven. I happened to be captain of the Harvard eleven. I was also captain of the Yale team and more than once saved the game for the Crimson by tackling myself on my own six-inch line. We were playing Princeton, and the score stood 116 to 115 for the Bengals. There was less than an hour to play—we played from 8 A.M. to 6 P.M. in those days—and the situation was desperate. I passed to Trumbull who fumbled and Poe fell on the ball, but Longfellow got it away from him with a crotch and cross buttocks hold. The spheroid dribbled into the Wellesley cheering section where I fell on the ball, and then like a flash of molasses passed to P. Withington who passed to T. Withington, who passed to Kelley who passed out. Mrs. Simpson, who was playing for Princeton that year under the name of Louisa May Alcott, got home a snappy signet ring to my chin, but I was not daunted. I scooped up the ball and dropping back to Harvard Square booted it clean as a whistle over the Charles and through the goal posts, as cheer on cheer like volleyed thunder echoed to the sky. It was on the strength of that play that I got a flattering offer from Vassar, which because of the many little hungry mouths

depending on me I could not refuse. I would have made the Daisy Chain had I not refused to shave my sideburns.

" 'I am not ashamed,' Tunis thundered, 'of the part I played in the War of the Roses. I never took a dollar from sport, where I could get two.'

"Tunis went to the door, shot a couple of amateurs, and returned, calmer. Asked what he was doing at present, he thought several weeks and then replied: 'It is a secret that I am telling nobody but the A.P., the U.P., and Universal Service. I am training Eddie Cantor to lift the Davis Cup. He tried to lift it last year but could only raise it a few inches. If he follows my system I believe he will be able to raise it to his lips.' "

He added: "Death, imminent unless I sell something soon because I carry so damn much insurance. Uneducated at Harvard, degree A.B. That means At Bat, and refers to my record in books, which is, to date, nine, no hits, no runs, and a good many errors. Been writing sports and other things too numerous to mention since 1920. Married a Vassar girl in 1918, same wife, same home, same mortgage, right this minute."

* * *

To get down to cases, Mr. Tunis really was born in Boston and really was graduated from Harvard in 1911. He served in France during the First World War; wrote sports for the New York *Evening Post* from 1925 to 1932, and then for Universal Service to 1935. Since 1932 he has broadcast all the big tennis matches for the National Broadcasting Co., and is himself a better than average tennis player. He has written for almost every magazine in the United States, on sports and education. His "autobiography" reveals not only his humor, but also his honest indignation at the degradation of amateur sport, further evidenced by his book on the subject. His Harvard story for boys, *The Iron Duke*, won the New York *Herald Tribune's* Spring Festival Prize for stories for older children, in 1938. His novel, *American Girl*, is frankly based on the career of Helen Wills Moody. *Was College Worth While?* is an outgrowth of a questionnaire sent every member of his Harvard class; his conclusion was that most of his classmates had been failures and that the rest were "a bunch of contented college cows." He is a sandy-haired, tall, clean-shaven man who looks very much the athlete he is.

PRINCIPAL WORKS: $port$: Heroics and Hysterics, 1928; American Girl, 1930; Was College Worth While? 1936; The Iron Duke (juvenile) 1938; The Duke Decides (juvenile) 1939; Champion's Choice, 1940; This Writing Game, 1941; World Series, 1941; Million-Miler (juvenile) 1942; All-American (juvenile) 1942.

ABOUT: Publishers' Weekly April 30, 1938; Scholastic September 17, 1938.

TURNBULL, Mrs. AGNES (SLIGH)

(October 14, 1888-   ), American novelist and short story writer, writes: "I was born

in the little village of New Alexandria, Pa. My father was Alexander Halliday Sligh, from Berwick-on-Tweed, Scotland; my mother, Lucinda Hannah McConnell, was a native of this country of Scotch-Irish pioneer descent. I attended the village

Bachrach

school, then Washington (Pa.) Seminary, and was graduated from Indiana (Pa.) Teachers' College in 1910. Following this I went to the University of Chicago for a year's work in English, and taught for some years in high schools in Pennsylvania. In 1918 I was married to James Lyall Turnbull, of Hebburn-on-Tyne, England. We came then to live in Maplewood, N.J., where we have been ever since. We have one adopted daughter.

"I was always interested in writing and sold my first story to the *American Magazine* in 1920. For ten years I worked exclusively with the short story, developing one field which was somewhat unusual: namely, fiction based on Biblical material. In 1936 my first novel was published. Since then I have become interested in the western Pennsylvania scene as material for books.

"I am a Presbyterian and a Republican. I am one of the last remaining writers who do not use the typewriter."

PRINCIPAL WORKS: *Short Stories*—Far Above Rubies, 1926; Wife of Pontius Pilate, 1928; In the Garden, 1929; The Four Marys, 1932; Old Home Town, 1933; This Spring of Love, 1934. *Novels*—The Rolling Years, 1936; Remember the End, 1938; Elijah the Fishbite (juvenile) 1940; The Day Must Dawn, 1942. *Miscellaneous*—Dear Me: Leaves From the Diary of Agnes Sligh Turnbull, 1941.

ABOUT: Turnbull, A. S. Dear Me; American Magazine May 1929.

TURNER, FREDERICK JACKSON

(November 14, 1861-March 14, 1932), American historian and university professor, was born in Portage, Wis., the son of Andrew Jackson Turner and Mary (Hanford) Turner. In 1884 he received a B.A. degree from the University of Wisconsin, spent a year as reporter on a Madison

newspaper, and next year became tutor in rhetoric and oratory at the university at an annual salary of $400. In 1888 Turner obtained his master's degree from Wisconsin and set off for Baltimore and Johns Hopkins University graduate school, where he hobnobbed with Woodrow Wilson, who later tried to lure him to Princeton. In 1889 he married Caroline Mae Sherwood of Chicago; they had two daughters and a son. Returning to Wisconsin, Turner became assistant professor of American history under the supervision of Professor William Francis Allen, a general historian. Johns Hopkins granted Turner his Ph.D. for a thesis on "The Character and Influence of the Indian Trade in Wisconsin: A Study of the Trading Post as an Institution." The subtitle was a sop to the prejudices of the

graduate school, who regarded such a local study as slightly undignified.

Two pieces of work now made Turner a figure to be reckoned with as an American historian: a review in the *Dial* (August 1889) of Theodore Roosevelt's *The Winning of the West* and a paper, "The Significance of the Frontier in American History," written for and delivered at a special meeting of the American Historical Association held at Chicago, July 1893, in connection with the World Columbian Exposition. Turner delivered it again on December 14 as the annual address before the Wisconsin State Historical Society; it was printed in the Society's *Proceedings,* and forms the leading essay in *The Frontier in American History* (1920). In writing it Turner used the remarkable Lyman C. Draper Collection of manuscripts in the University of Wisconsin Library and the services of Reuben Gold Thwaites.[qv] This paper, says Charles A. Beard, was destined to have a more profound influence on thought about American history than any other essay or volume ever written on the subject; it proved to be little short of epoch-making in conception and technique. Previous histories had been oriented in the East and South, such as those of Bancroft, Hildreth, Von Holst, and Schouler; Turner believed that many of the characteristics of the American mind and genius derived from its struggles with a frontier environment, seeking "the hither edge of free land"—its coarseness and strength, acuteness and inquisitiveness, and practical inventive faculty. He visualized American history as "a series of social evolutions recurring in differing geographic basins across a raw continent."

Turner himself, who had the gifts of a politician and the appearance of a successful business man, possessed the boundless optimism of the prairies, as Avery Craven says; Craven also believes that his native Middle West tended to furnish the materials from which he generalized. After eighteen years, 1892-1910, at the University of Wisconsin, Turner was professor of history at Harvard University from 1910 to 1924, where in spite of an admiring coterie of students he did not feel altogether at home. In 1924 he became professor-emeritus and went to California, becoming research associate of the great Henry E. Huntington Library in 1927-28, making a study of the life of Calhoun and dictating his last book, the uncompleted *The United States: 1830-1850.* Turner "did not relish the making of books"; he worked slowly and with so many corrections that his manuscripts were almost undecipherable. He died at seventy after three years of ill-health. The book which appeared in the year of his death, *The Significance of Sections in American History,* won the Pulitzer Prize for History.

PRINCIPAL WORKS: The Rise of the New West, 1906; The Frontier in American History, 1920; The Significance of Sections in American History, 1932; The United States, 1830-1850: The Nation and Its Sections, 1935; Early Writings (comp. by E. F. Edwards) 1938.

ABOUT: Becker, C. Everyman His Own Historian; Cowley, M. (ed.) Books That Changed Our Minds; Kraus, M. A History of American History; Odlum, H. W. (ed.) American Masters of Social Science; American Antiquarian Society Proceedings April 20, 1932; Colonial Society of Massachusetts Publications 1935; Huntington Library Bulletin February 1933; Minnesota History June 1932; New Republic February 1, 1939; New York Times March 16, 17, April 4, 1932; Wisconsin Magazine of History June 1933, June 1934, September 1935.

*TURNER, WALTER JAMES (October 13, 1889 or 1890-   ), British poet, novelist, and music critic who signs his work as W. J. Turner, writes: "It is reputed—and I would like to believe—that I was born in Melbourne, Australia, by the side of the sea, on the 13th October, 1890: but it may have been that I was born in Shanghai a year earlier. My father was organist at St. Paul's Protestant Cathedral, Melbourne, and also occupied simultaneously (which I believe is unique) the position of music director of the Jewish Synagogue. This, I understand, was owing to his personal friendship with the Chief Rabbi.

"I was educated at Scotch College, Melbourne, and was sent with my brother to learn carpentry at the Working Men's College, as my father believed that everyone should have some mechanical training. Although both my parents were professional musicians, I am totally devoid of musical talent and was given up at an early age by both my parents as being musically hopeless. My father having died, I was taken from Scotch College and sent to the School of Mines to be trained as a mining engineer. I stayed there a year, and then, at the age of seventeen, came to London, where my mother was living, and after a few months there went to Germany, where I studied at Munich and Vienna. I then spent six months in Marseilles and served in the war of 1914-18, first in the 28th  London Batallion and later in the Royal Garrison Artillery, in the anti-aircraft section.

"I have no political convictions, except that I think it is impossible to have a really civilized society unless every member of it is assured, without work, of his livelihood. I dislike almost everything and have hardly any likes. There are no public figures known to me for whom I have any respect—except, perhaps, Dr. Weizmann, Zionist leader, whose belief in Zionism, however, fills me with derision. If I were a dictator, I would solve the Jewish problem by forbidding marriage between the Jews. This, incidentally, would enormously improve the so-called Aryan stock.

"Among contemporary writers, those I admire chiefly are Virginia Woolf, Walter de la Mare, Ralph Hodgson, Dorothy Wellesley, and William Faulkner, and there are naturally many others whose writings I enjoy. I should like very much to live in America—if I could discover an agreeable place. As for work in progress—this is the only piece of work I have undertaken for some time."

* * *

Mr. Turner was drama critic of the *London Mercury* from 1919 to 1923, literary editor of the London *Daily Herald* from 1920 to 1923, and has been music critic of the London *Daily Express* since that time. He has also been music critic of the *New Statesman and Nation* since 1916. He is un-

* Died November 18, 1946.

married, and lives in Withyham, Sussex. His first writing appeared in the *New Age*. His career as music critic has been one long battle. C. Henry Warren remarked that "he writes of music as an experience, ... with gusto and uncompromising honesty," and Frank Swinnerton added that though he is a "quarrelsome critic," he is "a mild and agreeable-mannered man in private life, very sweet tempered." He visited the United States (or at least New York) in 1927, and did not like it, as two books later testified. In music his idol is Mozart, and among contemporary musicians he is most attached to Arthur Schnabel, who is his close friend and has often joined him in mountaineering in the Alps. Another intimate friend is Siegfried Sassoon. His own poetry, however, is quite unlike Sassoon's, its language being "rich and flowing," almost Mozartian in its pellucid clarity; its recurrent theme, "the ideal country of the imagination." As a novelist, his earlier books were exotic and fantastic, but with maturity he has become more realistic. It is only when he attempts satire that he grows heavy-handed. His most salient characteristic is what Warren called "his open-eyed integrity of spirit." He has edited two anthologies, *Great Names*, 1926, and *Eighteenth Century Poetry*, 1931.

PRINCIPAL WORKS: *Poetry*—The Hunter and Other Poems, 1916; The Dark Fire, 1918; In Time Like Glass, 1921; Paris and Helen, 1921; Landscape of Cytherea, 1923; The Seven Days of the Sun, 1925; Poems, 1926; New Poems, 1928; Miss America, 1930; Pursuit of Psyche, 1931; Jack and Jill, 1934; Songs and Incantations, 1936; Selected Poems, 1939. *Novels*—The Man Who Ate the Popomack, 1922; Marigold: An Idyll of the Sea, 1926; The Aesthetes, 1927; Blow for Balloons, 1935; Henry Airbubble, 1936; The Duchess of Popocatapetl, 1939. *Essays and Miscellaneous*—Music and Life, 1921; Variations on the Theme of Music, 1924; Orpheus: or, The Music of the Future, 1926; Beethoven, 1927; Musical Meanderings, 1929; A Trip to America, 1929; Music: A Short History, 1932; Facing the Music: Reflections of a Music Critic, 1933; Wagner, 1933; Berlioz: The Man and His Work, 1934; Mozart: The Man and His Works, 1938; English Music, 1941.

ABOUT: Bookman November 1924; Bookman (London) November 1931; London Mercury December 1934.

"TWAIN, MARK." See "AMERICAN AUTHORS: 1600-1900"

TWEEDSMUIR. See BUCHAN

T Y N A N , KATHARINE (January 23, 1861-April 2, 1931), Irish religious poet, popular novelist, and prominent figure in the Irish "Renaissance" movement, was born in Clondalkin, County Dublin, Ireland.

Andrew C. Tynan, her father, was a cattle-trader, a large, cheerful man to whom his daughter was much devoted; her mother, a placid, fair woman, was an invalid. From early childhood Katharine heard stories of the riots connected with the disestablishment of the Irish Church as well as the gruesome churchyard tales of Irish nurse-girls. Ulcers on her eyes, following an attack of measles, interfered with her schooling and made necessary the eye-glasses she wore all her life. Dances and the theatre were forbidden by the puritanical mother, but the girl read forbidden novels nevertheless. Her first poem appeared in a Dublin penny paper in 1878; a first book of poems, *Louise de la Vallière*, in the summer of 1885. Receiving half a guinea apiece for verses contributed to the *Graphic*, she bought a copy of Rossetti's *Poems* and later became acquainted with Christina Rossetti (whose unethereal appearance rather disconcerted her). From eleven to fourteen Katharine had attended Siena Convent, Drogheda, where she read the *Lives of the Saints*.

In 1887 she began to experiment with prose, and *The Way of a Maid*, her first novel, published in 1895, began a quarter-century of potboiling. She could, and did, turn out six and seven sentimental and sensational pieces of fiction a year for her large "circulating library" public. Reviewers consistently dubbed them simple, pretty, agreeable, and spinsterly. The delicate touch and fervent faith of the religious poems, however, give her a claim to distinction. Pamela Hinkson wrote, "She made beauty out of the common experiences of life so that nothing was common to her." Ernest Boyd called Katharine Tynan a minor poet, but of the first rank; Herbert Gorman finds her "essentially Celtic but not profoundly deep."

In 1893 Miss Tynan was married to Harry Hinkson, whom she had converted to Catholicism. Lord Aberdeen appointed him a Resident Magistrate in County Mayo, where they met with a singularly cool reception and found some difficulty in bringing up their two sons and daughter on an R.M.'s exiguous pay. In course of time the Hinksons met most of the important personages of literary and political Ireland, among them W.B. Yeats, Douglas Hyde, and George Russell ("AE"). (Charles Stewart Parnell, the Irish Nationalist leader and "martyr," was an early object of her passionate interest.) Alice Meynell was a particular friend; Katharine Tynan lies buried in London beside her and not far from the grave of Francis Thompson. Hinkson died in 1919, and from that time his widow spent much time in England. Growing obesity marred her original good looks, but her features were pleasantly full and good-natured, crowned by hair which was kept cut short. Katharine Tynan had a natural genius for friendship and sociability, especially enjoying Marie Belloc's *chansons* sung to her own banjo accompaniment. Dogs, especially when unjustly quarantined, appealed much to her, and she also collected china. Her rambling autobiography, in three volumes, showed Katharine Tynan "delightfully busy, tirelessly interested, and exuberantly happy."

PRINCIPAL WORKS: *Fiction and Poetry*—Louise de la Vallière, 1885; Ballads and Lyrics, 1890; The Land of Mist and Mountain, The Way of a Maid, 1895; Miracle Plays, 1896; The Handsome Brandons, She Walks in Beauty, 1899; A Girl of Galway, Collected Poems, 1901; A King's Woman, Love of Sisters, 1902; A Red Red Rose, The Honourable Molly, 1903; Julia, The Luck of the Fairfaxes, 1904; A Daughter of Kings, Dick Pentreath, 1905; A Yellow Domino, The Story of Bawn, 1906; For Maisie, Cabinet of Irish Literature (ed.), The House of the Crickets, 1908; Peggy the Daughter, Her Mother's Daughter, 1909; Betty Carew, The House of the Secret, 1910; New Poems, The Story of Clarice, 1911; Rose of the Garden, 1912; Mrs. Pratt of Paradise Farm, The Daughter of the Manor, Irish Poems, 1913; A Midsummer Rose, Lovers' Meetings, The Flower of Peace, 1914; Men Not Angels, Countrymen All, The House of the Foxes, The Story of Margery Dawe, 1915; The West Wind, John-a-Dreams, 1916; Lord Edward, Late Songs, Miss Mary, 1917; Herb O'Grace, 1918; The Man From Australia, 1919; Denys the Dreamer, The House, 1920; The House on the Bogs, A Mad Marriage, White Ladies, 1922; The Infatuation of Peter, 1926; Evensong, Miss Phipps, Haroun of London, The House in the Forest, 1928; The Rich Man, A Fine Gentleman, 1929; The Admirable Simmons, Collected Poems, 1930; The Other Man, 1933. *Autobiographical*—Twenty-Five Years, 1913; The Middle Years, 1917; The Years of the Shadow, 1919; The Wandering Years, 1922; Memories, 1924.

ABOUT: Boyd, E. A. Ireland's Literary Renaissance; Braybrooke, P. Some Catholic Novelists; Chislett, W. Moderns and Near Moderns; Williams, H. Modern English Writers; Bookman June 1931; Bookman (London) May 1931; Catholic World May 1931, November 1931; Fortnightly Review December 1930; Yale Review December 1939.

TYRRELL, GEORGE (February 6, 1861-July 15, 1909), English theologian, was born in Dublin, the youngest and posthumous son of William Henry Tyrrell, journalist, and his second wife, Mary (Chamney) Tyrrell. The boy soon showed signs of a rampant imagination, highly nervous temperament and a

spirit of opposition to arbitrary authority. Attending the Rathmines School near Dublin, he twice failed in his ambition to win a Hebrew Sizarship to Dublin University.

At eighteen Tyrrell became a Roman Catholic, taking his first vows as a Jesuit in 1882 and being ordained a priest in September 1891. He did mission work, lectured on philosophy, and made many converts. His softening of the Church's teachings on hell, and his privately printed "Letter to a Professor of Anthropology," when shown to be Tyrrell's work, caused his retirement to the order's Mission House at Richmond, Yorkshire. In February 1906 he was dismissed from the Society of Jesus, and in 1907 his two letters to the *Times* in reply to a fulmination of the Vatican's against modernism brought upon him the minor excommunication of the Church. Cardinal Mercier also attacked modernism and Tyrrell with it, in a Lenten pastoral in 1908.

"Suspected by ungrateful Catholics and taunted by unsympathetic Protestants for the inconsistency of his life and principles," Tyrrell's last years were decidedly uncomfortable in spite of devoted friends. Abbé Brémond heard his last confession and gave him absolution, but, since Tyrrell had not recanted, he was refused burial in Catholic ground. He was buried in the parish cemetery at Storrington, Sussex, leaving an uncompleted account of his life which Arnold Lunn calls the wittiest and in some ways the saddest of all religious autobiographies.

Canon A. L. Lilley writes: "So long as men delight in beautiful and sensitive English speech, and so long as they can recognize skilled guidance in probing the deepest mysteries of their own being, will the writings of George Tyrrell be read with something of the wonder and delight with which they were hailed in the first years of this century."

PRINCIPAL WORKS: Nova et Vetera, 1897; Hard Sayings, 1898; External Religion, 1899; The Faith of the Millions, 1901-1902; Lex Orandi, 1903; Lex Credendi, 1906; Christianity at the Cross-Roads, 1909; The Church and the Future, 1910.

ABOUT: Bridges, H. J. The Religion of George Tyrrell; Lunn, A. Roman Converts; Petre, M. D. Autobiography and Life of George Tyrrell; Petre, M. D. Von Hügel and Tyrrell; Rashdall, H. Ideas and Ideals; Hibbert Journal January 1910; London Times July 16, 17, 22, August 1909; Queen's Quarterly May 1928.

UNAMUNO Y JUGO, MIGUEL DE
(September 29, 1864-December 31, 1936),
Spanish poet, novelist, playwright, and

critic, was born in
Bilbao, and grew up
in a Catholic milieu
thoroughly tradition-
al and Basque. When
he was nine years old
his native city was
attacked by Carlist
troops, and one of
their bombs struck
the house next door.
This was Miguel's
"heroic age." The intermittent Civil War
came to an end in 1876, by which time
Miguel's father was dead and the boy was
being graduated from the Colegio de San
Nicolás, where he had outshone his classmates only in temper and anarchism. By
1879 the young Unamuno was advanced
student at the Instituto Vizacaíno and had
shown his talent for philosophy; the following year he moved to the Spanish capital in
order to continue his studies at the University of Madrid. Despite the political ferment of the city, and the adventurous and
somewhat picaresque existence of his room-
mates, he led a reserved and uneventful life
with only occasional visits to the Círculo
Vasco-Navarro and the free lectures at the
Ateneo. Unamuno presented a dissertation
on the Basque language and obtained a doctor's degree from the Faculty of Philosophy
and Letters (1884).

Unamuno spent the next seven years trying to get a University appointment and
preparing for the competitive examinations.
He took an examination in metaphysics,
another in logic, and two in Latin—only to
fail in receiving the coveted appointment:
no doubt his independent spirit and fearless
free-thinking contributed largely to these
failures. During these years he gave private
lessons in languages and read voraciously
(Ibsen, Tolstoy, Kierkegaard) in the
Sociedad Bilbaína's library. He spent his
week-ends visiting Concha, his childhood
sweetheart, at her uncle's in Guernica. Beginning with the 'nineties, Unamuno's writings began to appear in sundry periodicals,
especially in the Socialist Lucha de Clases
(Class Struggle). In 1891, taking advantage of his linguistic ability, he attended the
examination in Greek, and finally was named
professor of Greek at the University of
Salamanca, the oldest and most reputable in
Spain. In that year he married Doña Concha and settled in Salamanca.

Unamuno became extremely fond of the
tranquil life of the old university town.
After his lectures he took long walks along
the Tormes or the Zamora road, or stayed
at home to read the classics and his favorite
writer Kierkegaard, for the thorough understanding of whom he had studied Danish.
Evenings he went either to the Casino or
to the Café Novelty to discuss the problems
of the day with his cronies. In 1897 he
made his début as a writer of fiction with
the autobiographical novel Paz en la Guerra
(Peace in War) and also became the father
of a son, the first of his ten children. In
1901 he was named Rector of the University
of Salamanca and the following year he
published his second novel, Amor y Peda-
gogía (Love and Pedagogy), a book of
travel sketches Paisajes (Landscapes), and a
collection of essays En Torno al Casticismo
(Concerning Traditionalism), on the social
and ideological problems of Spain.

In the meantime Unamuno had discovered, with elation, his power to cry out
against political and social injustices, and
now he was fearless in taking a determined
stand at all times on all public questions. In
1903 he translated Karl Kautsky's social
interpretation of the agrarian question, Die
Agrarfrage; and in 1908 at the juegos
florales, an innocuous Andalusian literary
contest, he amazed everybody by discussing
with Shavian venom the agricultural problem of Spain! This note of paradox
gradually came to assume overwhelming
proportions in Unamuno's work, to its detriment. With increasing frequency he entered the arena of struggle in order to
present not a constructive program but a
handful of egocentric generalizations which
led only to bitter quarrels and to a confus-
sion of the issues in Spain's national crises.
In The Life of Don Quixote and Sancho
(1905) he endeavored to prove that Don
Quixote was more real than Cervantes and
that he (Unamuno) was restoring the old
knight-errant to his true life as opposed to
his Cervantine life; in My Religion (1911)
he indignantly denied that there was any
coherence in his thought and contended
that he was "a unique species." This anxiety for uniqueness permeated his masterpiece, The Tragic Sense of Life (1912), a
sustained and dramatic picture of the struggle between faith and reason. Unamuno's
inner conflicts continued to reflect themselves in his violent journalistic campaigns,
in his attacks on dogma, and, more dangerously, in his diatribes against the government. This cost him his position; in 1914

he was forced to resign as Rector of the University of Salamanca.

"In Salamanca," wrote Walter Starkie, "he was in his element, for it was a small town steeped in Castilian tradition. In the mornings I have seen him walk ten miles without feeling the slightest touch of weariness. In appearance he resembles an oak tree, with an owl's head. Everything suggested strength, the strength and steadfastness of the Basque, a rugged simplicity not devoid of a certain crudeness. In his dress he shunned adornment; his coat was buttoned right up to the neck. His actions were brusque, and one felt that he was the personification of the hardy mountaineer, peaceful in his home-life, fond of the country and its simple pleasures."

During the war years (1914-18) Unamuno continued to teach Greek language and literature, as well as the history of the Spanish language, at Salamanca. In 1914 he published his philosophical novel, *Mist*, which, with *Three Exemplary Novels and a Prologue* (1920), stands out as his most distinguished achievement in the realm of fiction.

Unamuno's sympathies were with the Allies and in 1917 he visited the Italian front. The year after the Armistice he ran on the Republican ticket for the Cortes. After the *coup d'état* of September 1923 he directed his attacks against Primo de Rivera and his military clique—Unamuno was an inveterate enemy of militarism—and in April 1934 he was given twenty-four hours in which to make ready and leave under guard for the island of Fuerteventura, one of the Canaries. He remained in exile until amnesty was granted in July of the same year, but he was too independent to accept it, guessing that the liberty being offered him was not the kind he wanted to enjoy in Spain. For two years (1924-26) he lived in Paris, a voluntary exile, and did considerable writing: a diary in sonnet form entitled *De Fuerteventura à Paris, The Agony of Christianity,* and articles for French and international journals.

From Paris Unamuno went to the French frontier town of Hendaye, a stone's throw from his Spanish Basque homeland. Besides ballads from exile, *Romancero del Destierro* (1927), he wrote articles of an agitational nature in the anti-government publication *Hojas Libres,* edited by exiled writers and brought into Spain as contraband.

After Primo de Rivera's death, as the monarchy tottered and grew weak and impotent, Unamuno returned to Spain. His homecoming (in 1930) assumed the proportions of a national apotheosis. Soon he was back in Salamanca as professor of Greek literature and, a few months later, as Rector of the University. With the fall of the monarchy he became Cortes Deputy from Salamanca and then President of the Council for Public Education. It was expected that after all his suffering at the hands of reactionary politicos he would devote his utmost energy to transforming the Spanish governmental machinery into a smooth-running democratic régime. But Unamuno reverted to his old sophistries and whimsicalities. During the debates on the national minorities, especially on Catalan autonomy, he favored the reactionary program of the incipient Fascist groups and contributed only a few quotations from the classics. When the students were collecting signatures to save a Latin American intellectual from execution, Valle-Inclán signed immediately, but not Unamuno; when a denunciation of the murder of Ferrer was circulated, Unamuno remarked that Ferrer deserved to be killed because he was a bad pedagogue! This was not a new attitude on the part of Unamuno but rather his old Shavian one, now emphasized and made more impressive by his increased authority and prestige.

In 'June 1934 Unamuno was made *doctor honoris causa* at the University of Grenoble; and Jacques Chevalier, Dean of the School of Classical Languages and Literature, called him the "greatest literary genius of Spain since Cervantes." In February 1936, delivering the last of his Taylorian lectures at Oxford, Unamuno summarized his "case" in the following syllogism: "He alone is truly wise who is conscious of his madness; I am conscious of my madness; therefore I am truly wise." Four months later the Civil War broke out in Spain, making a shambles of the country. Miguel de Unamuno supported the Fascist "Insurgents" only to regret it too late when, in December, insulted and humiliated by the Italian and German invaders, he breathed his last.

WORKS AVAILABLE IN ENGLISH TRANSLATION: The Tragic Sense of Life, 1921; Essays and Soliloquies, 1925; The Life of Don Quixote and Sancho, 1927; Mist, 1928; The Agony of Christianity, 1928; Three Exemplary Novels and a Prologue, 1930.

ABOUT: Bazán, A. Unamuno y el Marxismo; Bell, A. F. G. Contemporary Spanish Literature; Boyd, E. Studies in Ten Literatures; González-Ruano, C. Vida, Pensamiento, y Aventura de Miguel de Unamuno; Kessel, J. Die Grundstimmung in M. de Unamunos Lebensphilosophie; de Madariaga, S. The Genius of Spain; Merimée, E. & Morley, S. G. A History of Spanish Literature; Romera-Navarro, M. Miguel de Unamuno;

Verdad, M. Miguel de Unamuno; Atenea November 1937, July 1938; Dublin Review July 1922; London Quarterly Review April 1925; Modern Language Journal March 1925; New York Herald Tribune June 1, 1930; New York Times Magazine May 24, 1941; Revista Hispánica Moderna October 1934, January 1935; Sur October 1938.

UNDERHILL, EVELYN (1875-June 15, 1941), English poet, novelist, and writer on mysticism, was the only child of the late Sir

H. Smith

Arthur Underhill, barrister-at-law. She was educated privately and at King's College for Women, London, of which she was made an honorary Fellow in 1913 and a Fellow in 1927. In 1907 Evelyn Underhill married Hubert Stuart Moore, F.S.A., a barrister-at-law like her father. From 1900 to 1920 she wrote novels and light verse. In 1921 Miss Underhill was Upton Lecturer on the Philosophy of Religion at Manchester College, Oxford. Aberdeen University made her an honorary D.D. in 1939.

Her *Mysticism* (1911) had been an instantaneous and lasting success; most of its admirers, for some reason, are supposed to be men readers. The Rt. Rev. Charles Lewis Slattery, a well-known American Episcopal clergyman, wrote an introduction to *Concerning the Inner Life* (1926), addresses originally delivered to a group of clergy in the Liverpool Diocese, in which he stated that "the clergy of America have long been debtors to Miss Underhill for her vivid expositions of mysticism. [She] clearly understands the dangers and difficulties which beset the Christian ministry on both sides of the Atlantic. Miss Underhill deftly and emphatically recalls us to our real vocation."

Two of her poems, *Immanence* and *Uxbridge Road,* are frequently found in anthologies, and in 1932 she was included in Benn's Augustan Books of Poetry. *Consciousness* (1930) vied in popularity with *Mysticism,* going through twelve editions. *Eucharistic Prayers* has had at least five editions.

Mrs. Moore lived in London; her chief recreations were reading, gardening, walking, and talking to cats. Her poetry reflects the range of her interests: "botany, animals, primitive man as well as man self-conscious and looking before and after." She had an immense and exact knowledge of the whole liturgical field.

Following her death at sixty-six, her husband announced that he was planning to publish a volume of her letters.

PRINCIPAL WORKS: Grey World: A novel, 1904; The Lost Word, 1907; Miracles of Our Lady St. Mary, 1908; The Column of Dust, 1909; Mysticism: A Study in the Nature and Development of Man's Spiritual Consciousness, 1911; Immanence: A Book of Verses, 1912; The Mystic Way, 1913; Practical Mysticism, 1914; Ruysbroeck, 1915; Theophanies: A Book of Verses, 1916; Jacopone da Todi, 1919; The Essentials of Mysticism, 1920; The Life of the Spirit and the Life of To-day, 1922; The Mystics of the Church, 1925; Concerning the Inner Light, 1926; Man and the Supernatural, 1927; The House of the Soul, 1929; The Golden Sequence, 1932; Mixed Pasture: Twelve Essays and Addresses, 1933; The School of Charity, 1934; Worship (Library of Constructive Theology) 1936; The Spiritual Life: Four Broadcast Talks, 1937; The Mystery of Sacrifice, 1938; Abba, 1940; Fruits of the Spirit, 1942.

ABOUT: Underhill, E. Poems (in E. Benn's Augustan Books of Poetry series; see biographical note); Christian Century July 23, 1941.

*UNDSET, SIGRID (May 20, 1882-   ), Norwegian novelist and Nobel Prize winner, writes: "My parents married in 1881 and set out for Italy with the intention to stay abroad for years, as my father wanted to finish his researches on the beginnings of the Iron Age in Europe. During his first winter in Rome he contracted a violent fit of malaria, and their first baby threatened to arrive amidst the illness and disorder of a Roman boardinghouse. As I was the baby that upset their plans I suppose I was what you would call an unwanted child. Perhaps that was why I became an awfully spoilt child afterwards.

"My father, Dr. phil. Ingvald Martin Undset, came from the small Norwegian town of Trondheim. He had had to earn his own livelihood since early youth. When he married, at twenty-seven, he had already won some international fame as an archaeologist. Mother was a Dane, Charlotte Gyth, from the tiny town of Kalundborg. So when they dared not risk a Roman summer and had no home of their own they went to stay with my mother's father. Thus I happened to be born in Denmark. When father returned to Italy mother remained with me in her old home. Her father, her old aunt, and several young sisters did their best to stamp my subconscious mind with two conflicting impressions: of being an immensely important person and with a violent desire to be left alone sometimes.

"This latter desire was somewhat fulfilled, when we moved to Christiana (now Oslo) some years afterwards. Father lectured at the University and wrote books, mother kept house and did secretarial work for father, nurse looked after my baby sister. I managed to slip away on my own quite a lot, to play alone or with undesirable children, to make things with my hands or fancy stories out of my head. When I was getting older father's declining health, the increasing lot of work that fell on mother's part, and the birth of a third baby girl widened my opportunities of roaming.

"I suppose this was the reason why I hated school so intensely. It interfered with my freedom. I avoided the discipline by an elaborate technique of being absent-minded during classes. But my schoolmates found me out from the very beginning—that I imagined myself to be somebody, to be 'different.' And they set about to make me see how unpleasant life ought to be made for anybody who is different from other people.

"Of course I really was rather different. The atmosphere at home seemed pervaded with my father's work, we associated scarcely with anybody but his fellow-scientists, most of my playfellows were children belonging to this rather homogeneous set (except the undesirables which I had secretly made friends with). Now, most of the children in our school belonged to quite another set—not that they hailed from any particular class of society, but whatever their parents were—journalists, professional men, great or small business men—they belonged to the radical political parties and were firm believers in the 'advanced' ideas of that time. Other parents would never dream of sending their children to a school that was owned and managed by a lady who had divorced her husband and went in for mixed education of boys and girls; in fact, this was the first school in Norway where boys and girls mixed in the classes. I believe my father and especially my mother were rather skeptical about all these advanced ideas—mother was always skeptical about everything—and they had put us to school with Madame Ragna Nielsen only because they believed still less in the conservative girls' schools. So during all the years at school I made one single friendship, and that not till our last year: Emma's father was a geologist—besides being deputy of the radicals to parliament—and we met in a passion for botany and roaming. Our excursions into the countryside about Christiania to collect specimens furnished us with an excuse for clambering trees, wading brooks, getting wet and dirty and torn, and smoking cigarettes by campfires.

"Besides being leader of advanced ideas on education, Fru Ragna Nielsen was also a leading feminist. In spite of my laziness and my—sometimes—outspoken disbelief in all the ideas of this very liberal school, she treated me with incredible kindness and patience. When my father died in 1893 mother was left penniless with three small daughters to provide for. Ragna Nielsen offered her free schooling for all of us right up to the examination which in Norway gives access to the University. Years afterwards, when I had already published a number of books, she told me she had expected me to 'make good,' by which she meant proving the intellectual equality of the sexes. But she had hoped I should turn out a scientist, carrying on my father's work.

"But in the end I had outworn even Fru Nielsen's patience. I was fifteen years old when she took me to task one day. I shall never forget our talk—behind the door of an empty classroom. 'You know what I have promised your mother. But you seem so absolutely lacking in interest for your schoolwork. So if you really do not want to go to the University I shall have to withdraw my offer—so many girls would be glad to get the chance, and I cannot take more than a limited number of non-paying pupils.' (It was really a generous number she helped in this way!) I looked down in her beautiful face—she was small, handsome, and very dignified. 'Please, madam, no, I do not want to go to the University.' Madame Nielsen looked shocked—and I really had the shock of my life as I realized my audacity. Then she said quietly: 'Well, Sigrid, since you will decide of your future like a grownup person you'll have to tell your mother of your choice yourself.'

"It had been my fear, if I went to the University I should have to become a teacher, and the very idea of a schoolroom was hateful to me. I wanted to become a painter—I had been drawing and painting ever since I was a baby. But we had no money for art studies. We were very poor since my father's death. Mother told me, since I had thrown away Fru Nielsen's offer I must learn something which would enable me to earn my own livelihood as soon as possible and help her to provide for my younger sisters. So I was sent to a commercial academy. And at the age of sixteen, still a girl with long pigtails, I entered the office of an electrical engineer's bureau.

"This was the beginning of my career as an author. I never looked upon this situation as anything but temporary—and I came to like my work and many of my fellow-workers just because I felt so certain some day I should leave it for another kind of work, of my own choosing. By and by I began writing. I got accustomed to work some eighteen hours a day. But I had to stay in this office for ten years, till my sisters were self-supporting. By then I had already published two books.

"Above all things I had always desired liberty to do what I wanted. But ever since my seventeenth year I have always had to consider somebody else's interests, whatever I have been doing. Soon after I gained my freedom I married [1911] a Norwegian painter [A. C. Starsvad], with three children from a former marriage, and after a while I had three children of my own. A painter's income in Norway will scarcely ever be sufficient to bring up a family of six, especially as two of the children, my stepson and my daughter, were mental cases. And it was the time of the First World War, with high prices and scarcity of goods. I wrote books, kept house, and took care of the children.

"The war and the years afterwards confirmed the doubts I always had had about the ideas I was brought up on—[I felt] that liberalism, feminism, nationalism, socialism, pacifism, would not work, because they refused to consider human nature as it really is. Instead, they presupposed that mankind was to 'progress' into something else—towards their own ideas of what people ought to be. Being fostered on prehistory and history I did not much believe in progress. An accumulation of experience and expanding knowledge does not improve man's intellect or moral qualities, even if it ought to improve his ways of using his intellect and solving his moral problems. Yet it will not produce finer brains than Aristotle's or St. Thomas Aquinas', for instance, a greater or more versatile mind than St. Paul's, a humanity nobler than St. Louis of France's or Sir Thomas More's.

"I disbelieved in pacifism, because I knew how most people unconsciously or subconsciously give their spontaneous admiration to conquerors and men of violence. As children we were taught to be proud of our Viking forefathers—of course nobody then dreamed that Europe was ever to see a resurrection of the Vikings' way, conquering weaker people and ruling by terror, violence, and rapacity. I hated Alexander, Caesar, Charles XII of Sweden, but they were the accepted heroes of almost every boy. The girl clerks I knew when I was one of them used to decorate their shabby quarters with pictures of Napoleon and devoured books about this disgusting man—who, by the by, seems never to have had a woman for love; they all made him pay, so it seems that the womankind of his own times were more sensible about him. But in a somewhat less crude way this cult of the conqueror is bestowed on all kinds of spiritual leaders, when they have succeeded in their desire to dominate men's souls. I felt sure we shall always have to fight these would-be masters of men, that appeal so strongly to most men's desire to dominate their neighbors, at least vicariously. With spiritual weapons always—but I fear we shall also always be called upon from time to time to offer armed resistance to these scourges of the world.

"By degrees my knowledge of history convinced me that the only thoroughly sane people, of our civilization at least, seemed to be those queer men and women which the Catholic Church calls the Saints. Even their offending eccentricity offended mostly the fancies and wishful thinking of contemporary smugness. They seemed to know the true explanation of man's undying hunger for happiness—his tragically insufficient love of peace, justice, and goodwill to his fellow-men, his everlasting fall from grace. Of course I knew the historical rôle of the Church as a civilizatory power, and I had never looked on the religious revolt of the sixteenth century as anything but a revolt against the humanly unpalatable teachings of Christianity—the liberal Protestantism of my education left me an agnostic. Now it occurred to me that there might possibly be some truth in the original Christianity. I came to desire to know if——.

"But if you desire to know the truth about anything you always run the risk of finding it. And in a way we do not want to find Truth—we prefer to seek, and keep our illusions. But I had ventured too near the abode of truth in my researches about 'God's friends,' as the Saints are called in the Old Norse texts of Catholic times. So I had to submit. And on the first of November, 1924, I was received into the Catholic Church.

"Since then I have seen how a hunger and thirst of authority have made large nations accept any ghoulish caricature of authority. But I have learned why there can never be any valid authority of men over men. The only Authority to which mankind can submit without debauching itself is His whom St. Paul calls *Auctor Vitae*— the Creator's toward Creation."

* * *

The foregoing autobiographical sketch (written in English) was sent to the editors of this volume by Fru Sigrid Undset from her home in Lillehammer, Norway, early in 1940, at the height of the Russian invasion of Finland and only a few short weeks before Norway's violation by Germany. In a letter accompanying the sketch Fru Undset wrote prophetically: "I have always hated publicity about myself. But as things are looking here in Fenno-Scandia at present—we may all be swallowed up and deported somewhere in Siberia by the Russian aggressors if Finland does not get the necessary support in her fight for independence—I have come to the conclusion that I may just as well tell something about myself whilst I can."

As the world knows, the Russo-Finnish war ended abruptly in a dictated peace, so that Fru Undset's prophecy did not literally come true. But when the hordes of Nazi Germany invaded Norway in April 1940, one of the first towns levelled by the German bombers was Lillehammer, and one of the first civilian volunteers was Fru Undset, who joined her country's hapless government as a censor. In the guerilla warfare that followed the invasion, her 26-year-old son was killed by the Nazis and Fru Undset herself was forced to flee for her life, making her way, penniless, across the Swedish border to Stockholm where she was taken in by friends. She later made her way to America, where she is at this writing, lecturing in the anti-totalitarian cause. The story of her flight is told in *Return to the Future* (1942).

Fru Undset's marriage had ended in an amicable divorce in 1922, and from that time until the Nazi aggression she lived in Lillehammer. She is a tall woman, large-boned rather than heavy, with deep-set eyes under thick eyebrows and dark hair which frames a serious, thoughtful face. Her Lillehammer house, built in 1000 A.D., was furnished with genuine Norse antiques. At home she usually wore the traditional medieval Norse costume. She helped to reconstruct the Hammer Cathedral ruins, near her house, which in times of peace were a noted tourist attraction. Her hobby was collecting old lace, and she had many valuable pieces from French and Belgian convents.

Sigrid Undset won the Nobel Prize for Literature in 1928. She was expected to win it three years earlier, but at the last minute the board decided not to make any award at all that year. Her first successful novel was her third to be published, *Jenny*, which appeared in 1920. It was this and those immediately following which caused Victor Vinde to call her "the first writer to consecrate her whole life to the study of woman." He was a poor prophet; her whole life instead has been consecrated to the study of the human soul.

It may as well be said frankly that Sigrid Undset's novels of contemporary life, written since her conversion, are her poorest work from a literary standpoint. They are long and tedious, many of them little more than sugar-coated tracts, and, as one critic remarked, "her unprincipled and purposeless moderns never come to life at all." She has a sure claim to fame, but it is not for these, or for the apprentice work of her earlier years. It is for her great novels of thirteenth and fourteenth century Norway, *Kristin Lavransdatter* and (in only less degree) *The Master of Hestviken*.

In a sense these are not historical novels, for very little of moment happened in Norway in those centuries, and little is known of individuals flourishing at that period. What she has done is to reconstruct a dead life in terms of living beings. Kristin and Erlend are more real, more alive, than many persons we know in the flesh. The very fact of her developing devoutness, which has injured her as an artist in her later work, here made the devout Catholic Norway of her chosen time come to life in every last detail. But to it she has brought a modern psychological approach, so that what we are given is no mere external picture, but the effect of actually knowing and living with people who have no secrets from us. And in Kristin she has created a really great human being—the most difficult thing for a writer to portray. *The Master of Hestviken* may be considered a fine *tour de force*, but *Kristin Lavransdatter* is much more—it is a magnificent achievement which only genius could have accomplished.

Works Available in English: Jenny, 1921; Kristin Lavransdatter, 1929 (trilogy: The Bridal Wreath [in England: The Garland] 1923, The Mistress of Husaby, 1925, The Cross, 1927); The Wild Orchid, 1931; The Master of Hestviken, 1932 (The Axe, 1928; The Snake Pit, 1929; In the Wilderness, 1929; The Son Avenger, 1930); The Burning Bush, 1932; Ida Elisabeth, 1933; Saga of the Saints, 1934; Stages on the Road (non-fiction)

1934; The Longest Years, 1935; Gunnar's Daughter, 1936; The Faithful Wife, 1937; Images in a Mirror, 1938; Madame Dorothea, 1940; Christmas and Twelfth Night, 1941; Return to the Future, 1942; Happy Times in Norway, 1942.

ABOUT: Bing, J. Sigrid Undset (in Danish); Drake, W. A. Contemporary European Writers; Gustafson, A. Six Scandinavian Novelists; American Review January 1934; American Scandinavian Review June, July 1929; Annales Politiques et Littéraires December 1, 1928; Bookman (London) February 1929; Catholic World February 1929, April 1938; Contemporary Review July 1938; Journal des Débats November 23, 1928; Life July 10, 1940; Living Age May 31, 1924, November 21, 1925; London Mercury December 1928; New York Times Book Review September 8, 1940; Publishers' Weekly April 30, 1932; Revue des Deux Mondes December 15, 1928; Saturday Review of Literature October 9, 1937, October 19, 1940; Time August 5, September 9, 1940.

UNRUH, FRITZ VON (May 10, 1885-), German dramatist, novelist, and poet, was born in Koblenz of an old Silesian and Prussian land-owning family. His father was a general and governor of East Prussia, and a life-long close friend of Hindenburg. The boy was destined for the army, and became a cadet at eight, later becoming imperial page, lieutenant of the Guard, and adjutant to one of the sons of Wilhelm II. But his first play, *Offiziere* (*Officers*), was such a success that in 1912 he resigned his commission to give all his time to writing.

In 1914, however, at the beginning of the First World War he volunteered, and served throughout as a captain, twice receiving the Iron Cross. His description of the Battle of Verdun in his war diary, *Opfergang* (translated as *Way of Sacrifice*), was the first to appear in print. After the war he lived for a time in Italy, then moved to Frankfurt. He became very well known as poet and dramatist, and received the Kleist and Schiller prizes. He was one of the founders of the Republican Party, and its delegate in the Reichstag, and he was a founder of the Iron Front. An intimate friend of Walter Rathenau, his speech in the Reichstag on Rathenau's murder made him one of the most noted—and most marked—public men in Germany. With the advent of Nazism he became a voluntary exile, going to France to work against Hitler.

The Nazis begged him to return and let them make him "the modern Schiller," but when he refused they burned his books and deprived him of citizenship. He remained in France until at the beginning of the Second World War he was put in a concentration camp. After the downfall of France he managed to escape (he was of course in danger of execution if delivered over to the Nazis), and finally with his wife was able to reach the United States, where he made his home in New York.

Von Unruh's earlier plays and novels were realistic; later they became symbolistic—and also strongly pacifist. Thomas Mann said that he is "without doubt one of the most gifted dramatists Germany has produced in the last decades.... His lyric poems belong to the very best in modern German literature."

WORKS AVAILABLE IN ENGLISH: Bonaparte (play) 1928; The Way of Sacrifice, 1928.

ABOUT: Engel, F. Fritz von Unruh und Seine Besten Bühnenwerke; Meister, R. Fritz von Unruh; Aufbau (New York) December 6, 1940; New Republic May 12, 1941.

UNTERMEYER, LOUIS (October 1, 1885-), American poet, was born in New York, the son of Emanuel Untermeyer and Julia (Michael) Untermeyer. His father, a manufacturing jeweler, was from Maine, his mother from New Orleans via Texas. His first passion was for music, and it was only his realization of insufficient talent for concert playing that caused him to aban-

don training to become a professional pianist. Another early love was the theatre. He left high school at fifteen, "because of his failure to comprehend geometry," and went into his father's business. Until 1923, when he resigned as vice-president and general manager of the firm's factory in Newark, his days were given to business and his evenings to art. Since then he has devoted all his time to writing, editing, and lecturing.

Mr. Untermeyer is almost better known as an anthologist and editor than as a poet. He was contributing editor of the *Liberator* and the *Seven Arts* and poetry editor of the *American Mercury* from 1934 to 1937. In 1937, the centenary of Knox College, he was awarded its Honnold Lectureship, and in 1938 he delivered the Henry Ward Beecher lectures at Amherst. He was appointed "poet in residence" at the University of Michigan, but preferred to accept the post *in absentia*.

He was married in 1907 to Jean Starr, a well known poet in her own right, under the name of Jean Starr Untermeyer. After their divorce he married, in 1926, another poet, Virginia Moore. They also were divorced, and in 1933 he married Esther Antin, a lawyer and former municipal judge in Toledo. By his first two marriages he has had four sons, one deceased.

In 1928 he moved to Elizabethtown, N.Y., to a 160-acre farm in the Adirondacks, with a trout-stream running through it. Though he travels a good deal and often goes into "winter quarters" in the city, he really farms —besides raising flowers, cows, cats, Eskimo dogs, and sugar-maples! His wife still practices law in New York and Ohio. He says that when he is ninety, he plans "to settle down to really serious work." All he has done so far is compile ten poetry anthologies, widely used as text-books, translate Heine, Horace, and Ernst Toller, and issue some twenty-five original books of verse and prose. He is a master parodist and punster, but has also written some serious poetry of high quality.

In his autobiography Mr. Untermeyer makes fun of his appearance, but his face reveals both humor and idealism, while his high forehead and scholarly pince-nez supply the air of erudition which is his third salient characteristic. Perhaps his greatest talent is for friendship; he has known nearly every literary figure of prominence in his time, and his *From Another World* is less a genuine autobiography than it is a mine of stories and descriptions of famous contemporary writers. Helen Grace Carlisle said of him: "Louis Untermeyer is the most enthusiastic man that I know, and his enthusiasms, utterly engaging and charming, are concerned with the most diversified list of facts and fancies that any human could possibly soar about."

PRINCIPAL WORKS: *Poetry*—First Love, 1911; Challenge, 1914; These Times, 1917; The New Adam, 1920; Burning Bush, 1928; New Songs for New Voices (with David and Clara Mannes) 1928; Food and Drink, 1932; Selected Poems, 1935. *Parodies and Burlesques*—The Younger Quire, 1910; "—and Other Poets," 1916; Heavens, 1922; Roast Leviathan, 1922; Collected Parodies, 1926. *Prose*—Moses (novel) 1928; Blue Rhine-Black Forest, 1930; The Donkey of God and Other Stories, 1932; Chip—My Life and Times (fiction) 1933; Poetry—Its Appreciation and Enjoyment (with H. Carter Davison) 1934; The Last Pirate (tales from Gilbert & Sullivan) 1934; Heinrich Heine—Paradox and Poet, 1937; Doorways to Poetry, 1937; Play in Poetry, 1938; From Another World (autobiography) 1939. *Anthologies*—Modern American Verse, 1919; Modern British Poetry, 1920; A Miscellany of American Poetry (biennial) 1920-27; Modern American Poetry, 1921; This Singing World (juvenile) 1923; This Singing World for Younger Children, 1926; Yesterday and Today, 1927; American Poetry From the Beginning to Whitman, 1931; The Book of Living Verse, 1932; Rainbow in the Sky, 1935; Stars To Steer By (juvenile) 1941; A Treasury of Great Poems: English and American, 1942.

ABOUT: Untermeyer, L. From Another World; Poetry February 1940; Saturday Review of Literature September 21, 1935, November 20, 1937, October 7, 1939, July 6, 1940.

*VACHELL, HORACE ANNESLEY
(October 30, 1861-   ), English novelist and playwright, writes: "I was born about the time when the Prince Consort died, born (I hope) of well-to-do and honest parents. My *cacoethes scribendi* may have come from my great grandfather, George, Lord Lyttleton, the historian, to whom Fielding dedicated *Tom Jones*. Now I live in the  house where Fielding wrote all or part of his famous novel. I was self-educated at Harrow, where I was very happy. Then I adventured to Sandhurst, our Royal Military College, where I became an under-officer. The late Field Marshal, Lord Allenby, was another under-officer at the time, and also the late Egerton Castle, famous swordsman and novelist. I had to wait eighteen months for my commission in the Rifle Brigade. Meanwhile I visited California. I resigned my commission in 1883, because I had fallen in love with the Golden State, which I regarded as a sort of Tom Tiddler's Ground. I married a Daughter of the Golden West, planted out orchards and a vineyard, and became a cow-puncher.

"I made many dollars and lost them during three years of drought. I returned to England in 1899, happily able to support myself with my pen. My wife had died in 1895, leaving me with two children. My son went to Harrow and Sandhurst, and was killed in 1915, during the Great War. My daughter, who married her cousin, another Vachell, lives with me.

"In my seventy-ninth year, I can look back upon an eventful and on the whole happy life. I like (in moderation) good food, good wine, and good company. The last is not the least of this Trinity in Unity. I have played many games with diminishing zest for them. I have hunted and shot and fished with ardor. All my experiences, particularly in California, were fish to my net as a dramatist and novelist.

"I cling to life, because I am so curious to see what the immediate future holds for the democracies. The golden age of leisure is at an end. Hitler has already broken the backbone of England, the squirearchy. I do not think that the fate of Humpty Dumpty awaits the British Empire. San Francisco survived the earthquake and fire. England, I confidently believe, will survive this war;

* Died January 10, 1955.

and for the many it may be merrier than it was in the days of Queen Elizabeth."

* * *

Mr. Vachell was born in Essex, and lives now in Bath. His wife's maiden name was Lydie Phillips. He is a Fellow of the Royal Society of Literature, and ex-president of the Dickens Fellowship. Among his novels are several mysteries, including one written with Archibald Marshall. His best known character is the antique dealer, "Quinney." John Farrar called him "the gentle writer concerning English countrysides"; J. P. Collins said: "It is as an interpreter of action, or British character in action, that Mr. Vachell interests one most."

PRINCIPAL WORKS: *Fiction*—The Romance of Judge Ketchum, 1894; The Model of Christian Gray, 1895; The Quicksands of Pactolus, 1896; A Drama in Sunshine, 1898; The Procession of Life, 1899; John Charity, 1900; The Shadowy Third, 1902; The Pinch of Prosperity, 1903; Brothers, 1904; The Hill, 1905; The Face of Clay, 1906; Her Son, 1907; The Waters of Jordan, 1908; An Impending Sword, 1909; The Paladin, 1909; The Other Side, 1910; John Verney, 1911; Blinds Down, 1912; Bunch Grass (short stories) 1912; Loot From the Temple of Fortune (short stories) 1913; Quinneys', 1914; Spragge's Canyon, 1914; The Triumph of Tim, 1916; Fishpingle, 1917; The Soul of Susan Yellam, 1918; Some Happenings (short stories) 1918; The Fourth Dimension, 1920; Whitewash, 1920; Blinkers, 1921; Change Partners, 1922; The Yard (mystery) 1923; Leaves From Arcady (short stories) 1924; Watlings For Worth, 1925; Mr. Allen (mystery, with A. Marshall; in America: The Mote House Mystery) 1926; A Woman in Exile, 1926; Miss Torrobin's Experiment, 1927; Dew of the Sea, and Other Stories, 1927; The Actor, 1928; The Enchanted Garden, and Other Stories, 1929; Virgin, 1929; Out of Great Tribulation, 1930; Into the Land of Nod, 1931 (the last three as Triplets, 1933); At the Sign of the Grid (short stories) 1931; The Fifth Commandment, 1932; Experiences of a Bond Street Jeweller (short stories) 1932; Vicar's Walk, 1933; The Disappearance of Martha Penny (mystery) 1934; The Old Guard Surrenders, 1934; Moonhills, 1935; Joe Quinney's Jodie (short stories) 1936; The Golden House, 1937; Lord Samarkand, 1938; Quinneys For Quality (short stories) 1938; Phoebe's Guest House, 1939; Great Chameleon, 1940; The Black Squire, 1941. *Plays*—Jelf's, 1912; Searchlights, 1915; Quinneys', 1915; The Case of Lady Camber, 1916; Fishpingle, 1916; Plus Fours (with H. Simpson) 1923. *Miscellaneous*—Life and Sport on the Pacific Slope, 1900; Pepper and Salt, 1916; Fellow-Travellers (autobiography) 1923; The Best of England, 1930; This Was England, 1933; Arising Out of That, 1935; My Vagabondage, 1936; Distant Fields (autobiography) 1937; Where Fancy Beckons, 1938; Little Tyrannies, 1940.

ABOUT: Manly, J. M. & Rickert, E. Contemporary British Literature; Vachell, H. A. Fellow-Travellers, Distant Fields.

*VALÉRY, PAUL (October 30, 1871-   ), French poet and essayist, was born at Cette, a small town not far from Montpellier, overlooking the Mediter-ranean. Paul's first trip, at the age of seven, was to Paris and London, where the wax figures in the Tussaud Museum left him with an indelible impression of terror. On his return he attended the local school but as if to  accent his dual nationality (his father was French, his mother Italian), he spent his vacations in Italy, especially in Genoa, "the most beautiful maritime city of Europe." His childhood was filled with the light and sea of Cette and the magnificent architecture of Genoa, later so eloquently described in his works. He thinks of Italy, whose language and literature he soon mastered, as his second fatherland.

In 1884 Paul's parents moved to Montpellier and he entered the *lycée* which he loathed because of the "terroristic methods" of his teachers. His first composition in philosophy was noticed because of its depth and scope, but when it came to mathematics and rhetoric, the future mathematical rhetorician or rhetoric mathematician was considered rather dull. Oblivious of the syllabi and outlines of study, Paul spent most of his time at the Bibliothèque Fabre looking at the plates in Viollet-le-Duc's architectural *Dictionary* and studying Owen Jones' *The Grammar of Ornament*; at home he wrote poetry and sketched. Somehow he passed his examinations, and in order "to gain and lose time" since "he knew not where to go" and considered himself "good for nothing," he entered the School of Law at the University of Montpellier.

In the crucial year 1889 Valéry discovered contemporary French literature. From Huysmans' *Against the Grain*, he passed on to Verlaine, Mallarmé, and the Decadent poets —"I smoked tobacco sprinkled with benzoin." In the same year he began his year of compulsory military service, entering the 122nd Regiment, 1st Battalion, 1st Company, stationed at Montpellier. The meditative lad found material for thought in the Army Regulations, the precise and laconic style of which he admired, in the mechanics of military theory, and even in military uniforms.

VALÉRY

The celebrations of the University of Montpellier's six-hundredth anniversary (May 1890) brought many French and foreign intellectuals to that city, and among the students present was one Pierre Louÿs, a young poet, who oriented Valéry towards the Paris groups most in sympathy with his type of writing.

Louÿs' visit to Montpellier was followed, not long after, by that of André Gide, who came to that city for a vacation. Gide, then twenty-one, read him the first proofs of his *Cahiers d'André Walter* and gave him some Mallarmé and Rimbaud to read. These contacts, near and far, made Valéry sure of his vocation. At the end of 1891 he spent a month in Paris and one evening met the great Stephane Mallarmé, pivotal influence of his work.

The time for bold decisions had arrived. 1892 was "a morass of despair"; he was twenty-one, and his third year of law he considered "deplorable." One sleepless August night, as an autumn storm broke fiercely over the Ligurian coast, Valéry made up his mind—he would go away. First Paris, and then London, where he met George Meredith. On his return to Paris, Léon Daudet asked him for an article on Leonardo da Vinci. Valéry wrote "Introductions to the Method of Leonardo da Vinci" which appeared in the *Nouvelle Revue* on August 15, 1895, and in 1896 the *Centaure* published "An Evening With Mr. Teste." In the early months of 1896 Valéry went to London and found employment in the Press Bureau of the Chartered Company, but ill health forced him shortly thereafter to return to Paris. On his return Valéry competed successfully for a post in the War Department where he worked in the Artillery Munition Bureau during 1897-1900, the exciting years of the Dreyfus case, the Fachoda incident, and the invention of the "75" gun. After the death of Mallarmé in September 1898, "a great intimate blow," Valéry wrote less and less: he contributed with increasing irregularity to the *Mercure de France* (1898-1900), and wrote only a few of the poems which over a quarter of a century later were included in *Album des Vers Anciens*.

In June 1900 Valéry married, and in July he left the War Department to join the Havas news agency. For the next seventeen years, although he had ample time at his disposal and his life followed a quiet groove, Valéry published nothing new. In the winter 1912-13 André Gide had asked Valéry to collect his early poems, scattered in numerous short-lived reviews, for re-publication

in book form. Valéry politely refused, saying that he was through with literature. However his admirers dug out the poems, had them typewritten, and presented them for approval. Valéry's first reaction was emphatically negative. "Contact with my monsters. Disgusting. I begin to mess about with them. To retouch." At the end he reconciled himself with the idea of a reprint and decided to close the collection with some twenty-five lines of valedictory verse of a "musical and abstract" nature. This "last poem" swelled to over five hundred lines as he worked on it for four and a half years.

Finally in 1917 it was published under the title *La Jeune Parque*. Strictly classical, with all the rigid rules of French prosody observed, it is a poem of singular and rich beauty, yet critics of the stature of Albert Thibaudet have considered it "the most obscure poem in French poetry, much more obscure even than Mallarmé's *Afternoon of a Faun*." Although its language is pristine and clear, by concerning himself almost exclusively with states of thought and feeling, Valéry attained a density that confused the average reader. "More than one reader has expired by the way," confessed Valéry. "The tension demanded is out of all proportion to the amount of energy which his literary curiosity and his taste for poetry allow him to dispose of." Nonetheless *La Jeune Parque* immediately found an élite of appreciative readers: Paul Souday gave it a glowing review in *Le Temps* and Middleton Murry in the London *Times*. In fact, at the age of forty-six, Valéry found himself famous overnight, upon the appearance of his first book.

The instant demand for more of his work was easily met. While working on *La Jeune Parque* several poems had begun to germinate. In 1920 his most generally admired poem, *Graveyard by the Sea*, his second book of verse, came out. The graveyard on the cliff above Cette is the scene of Valéry's meditations on the problems of reconciliation between Life and the Absolute. In 1920 Valéry also sent to press *Odes* and *Album des Vers Anciens*, which contained his early poems and which was precisely the compilation demanded by Gide some eight years before. *An Evening With Mr. Teste* was reprinted in 1921, followed shortly thereafter by *Charmes*. As his reputation grew, Valéry was asked to deliver lectures, to write novels, detective stories, stories for children. He declined, but finally agreed to do an article for the magazine *Architectures* and thus came into existence *Eupalinos:*

1438

or, The Architect (1923). As Valéry once declared, his prose has never been the result of a spontaneous impulse but always of an editorial commission. In 1924 he collected his various essays—on Poe's "Eureka," on Pascal, on the intellectual crisis, etc.—and published them under the title *Variety* (1924), and this has found interesting succession in *Variety II* (1930), *Variety III* (1936), and *Variety IV* (1938). [These are dates of French publication.]

By 1925 Valéry's reputation had spread so widely in France—in a referendum conducted by *La Connaissance* in 1921 he was voted "the foremost poet of France"—and over all the Continent, that he was elected to the French Academy to the "fauteuil" once occupied by Malesherbes, Thiers, and Anatole France. In his acceptance speech he ignored the custom of referring to his immediate predecessor, France, whose work was the very antithesis of his.

During the past few years Valéry has added to his works some elucidating autobiographical pages, *Analecta* (1926), essays on art, literature and science—*Littérature* (1929), *Remarques Extérieures* (1929), *Mer, Marines, Marins* (1930), *L'Idée Fixe* (1932), *Triomphe de Manet* (1932), *L'Homme et la Coquille* (1937), *Degas, Danse, Dessin* (1938)—a few lectures, notably the Zaharoff lecture at Oxford in 1938: *Poésie et Pensée Abstraite* (1939), and, at rare intervals, a poem.

William Leon Symes has described Valéry thus: "His long, sallow face, hollow cheeks and broad jaw are those of an energetic personality, not given to dreaming. The eyes are lively and the moustache bristles. The solid, practical frame has been built for activity. . . . Valéry's eyes are dark and shadowed, but their glance pierces. His lips are sensitive but they are usually set in a firm line."

After the German occupation of Paris in 1940, Valéry was reported to be practically penniless in that city. He was using against the Nazis the weapon he might be expected to use: silence.

Works Available in English Translation: The Serpent, 1924; An Evening With Mr. Teste, 1925; Variety, 1927; Introduction to the Method of Leonardo da Vinci, 1929; Eupalinos: or, The Architect, 1932; The Graveyard by the Sea, 1932; Variety (Second Series) 1938.

About: Du Bos, C. Approximations; Bosanquet, T. Paul Valéry: A study; Bremond, H. Racine et Valéry; Chisholm, A. R. An Approach to M. Valéry's 'Jeune Parque'; Cohen, G. Essai d'Explication du 'Cimitière Marin'; Curtius, E. R. Französischer Geist im Neuen Europa; Fisher, H. A. L. Paul Valéry; Larbaud, V. Paul Valéry; Lefèvre, F. Entretiens avec Paul Valéry; Maurois, A. Introduction a la Méthode de Paul Valéry; Noulet, E. Paul Valéry; Thibaudet, A. Paul Valéry; Turquet-Milnes, G. Paul Valéry: A Study; Dial November 1927; Nation September 8, 1935, January 7, 1939; New York Herald Tribune "Books" March 20, 1927, November 20, 1938; New York Times March 20, 1927, November 27, 1938; Nouvelle Revue Française September 1933; Saturday Review of Literature April 16, 1927, November 26, 1938, December 10, 1938; Yale Review October 1927.

VALLE-INCLÁN, RAMÓN MARÍA DEL (October 28, 1866-January 5, 1936), Spanish poet, playwright, and novelist, was born in Villanueva de Arosa, in the Galician province of Pontevedra, into a proud family of impoverished aristocrats  After eight years of secondary education at Pontevedra and Santiago, Ramón registered in the Faculty of Law at the University of Santiago in 1885. Never an exceptional student, he got no further than Canonical Law. He preferred wandering about his native Galicia, so fraught with legends and stories told by beggars and peasants. In 1892 he set out for Madrid, but attracted by the mysterious "x" in the word Mexico, so he said, he landed instead in Vera Cruz. Here and in Mexico City he worked as a journalist, returning to Pontevedra in the spring of 1893. Two years later he published his first book, *Femeninas*, a collection of exotic tales strongly reminiscent of Barbey d'Aurevilly's *Diaboliques*. With the publication in November 1895 of one of his short stories in the Madrid popular magazine *Blanco y Negro*, he left for the capital, where before long he secured a 2000-peseta job in the Ministry of Public Works.

In the cafés of Madrid Valle-Inclán posed as a dangerous character, bloodthirsty, hermetic, adventurous, and impressed his cronies with his aristocratic airs, his archaic vocabulary (made funnier because of his lisping), and his capacity for telling beautiful lies. In 1899 the literary critic Manuel Bueno, infuriated by Valle-Inclán's slanderous tongue, struck him with his cane, fracturing his left arm so that it had to be amputated. In order to raise funds for him, Valle-Inclán's friends put on his three-act drama *Cenizas*, later known as *El Yermo de las Almas*, at the Lara Theatre, with Benavente and Martínez Sierra in the principal rôles.

In the opening years of the new century Valle-Inclán was forced to earn his living writing advertisements in verse and adapting fifth-rate pulp stories into melodramas. In 1901 he began to contribute to the literary supplement of the daily *El Imparcial* poems and short stories which later were included in *Jardín Umbrío* (1903) and *Jardín Novelesco* (1905), as well as excerpts from his novel *The Pleasant Memoirs of the Marquis of Brandomín,* published in four volumes between 1903 and 1905. The "ugly, Catholic, and sentimental" Marquis was a Don Juan character so dear to the Spanish public.

In 1907 Valle-Inclán married Josefina Blanco, an actress from the Guerrero-Mendoza company with whom he toured not only all the Spanish provinces but, in 1910, Argentine, Paraguay, Uruguay, Chile, and Bolivia. Valle-Inclán visited the front in 1916 at the invitation of the French government, entitling his observations *La Media Noche.* A lectureship (1916-17) in aesthetics at the Escuela de San Fernando soon bored him and he retired to his La Merced estate, near Puebla, and applied himself to farming and cattle-raising. On the occasion of the centenary of Mexico's independence he attended the festivities at the invitation of his admirer General Obregón. Returning to Spain he was forced to sacrifice his estate; his financial worries helped to break his already feeble health and sent him to a sanatorium in Santiago (1923-24). When fresh negotiations with his publishers and some anonymous gifts from Mexico straightened his finances he settled in Madrid.

Although Valle-Inclán's career thus far had developed in a "purist" world of literature, his novel *The Tyrant* (1926), conceived during his Mexican visit five years earlier, evinced new departures into politics and revolution. During the Primo de Rivera dictatorship he was imprisoned (April 1929). Valle-Inclán's historical interest, dilettantish at the time he wrote his trilogy on the Carlist Wars—*Los Cruzados de la Causa* (1908), *El Resplandor de la Hoguera* (1909), and *Gerifaltes de Antaño* (1909)—became more realistic and mordant in the unfinished series of historical novels, *El Ruedo Ibérico—La Corte de los Milagros* (1927) and *Viva mi Dueño* (1928). These were intended to crystallize the problems of nineteenth century Spain from the Revolution of 1868 to the death of Alphonse XII (1885). Although his style continued to be precious, readers recognized the newness of content: Valle-Inclán was in dead earnest to understand Spanish reality, past and present, in a profoundly political way.

During the elections of 1931, Valle-Inclán ran as a Republican candidate but was defeated. When the Monarchy was overthrown, the new Republican government immediately appointed Valle-Inclán as Curator of National Arts and Director of the Aranjuez Museum. Later he became director of the School of Art in Rome, but illness forced his return to Spain in 1934, and he was pensioned off. This great Spanish eccentric, fantastic warrior, lyrical hermit—the last bohemian of contemporary Spain—died at sixty-nine.

WORKS AVAILABLE IN ENGLISH TRANSLATION: The Dragon's Head, 1918; The Pleasant Memoirs of the Marquis of Brandomín, 1924; The Tyrant, 1929.

ABOUT: Alcalá Galiano, A. Figuras Excepcionales; Azaña, M. La Invención del "Quijote"; Bell, A. F. G. Contemporary Spanish Literature; Boyd, E. Studies From Ten Literatures; Cansinos-Assens, R. Los Hermes, La Nueva Literatura; Drake, W. A. Contemporary European Writers; Gómez de Baquero, E. De Gallardo a Unamuno; González Blanco, A. Los Contemporáneos; Jeschke, H. Die Generation von 1898 in Spanien; de Madariaga, S. The Genius of Spain; Montesinos, J. F. Die Moderne Spanische Dichtung; Pina, F. Escritores y Pueblo; Reyes, A. Los Dos Caminos; Warren, L. A. Modern Spanish Literature; Alma Española December 27, 1903; Bookman November 1930; España March 8, 1924; Hispania January 1923, November-December 1932; New York Herald Tribune "Books" October 20, 1929; New York Times January 1, 1922, December 14, 1924; Nineteenth Century September 1925; Les Nouvelles Littéraires June 11, 1936; La Pluma January 1923; Revue de Littérature Comparée October 1934; Revue Nouvelle October 1925.

VALLENTIN, ANTONINA (1893-), Polish biographer and political journalist, though born in Poland, is a true cosmopolite: most of her adult life was spent in pre-Nazi Germany, she married a Frenchman, and she lived in Paris until the fall of France. Her husband, Julien Luchaire, was an official of the Ministry of Education, and also well known as an historian and a dramatist.  Since the Nazi conquest of France, nothing has been heard from either M. or Mme. Luchaire; and since she was decidedly *persona non grata* to the Hitler régime there is reason for apprehension in the lack of news of them. During the Weimar Republic, she lived in Berlin, where she was head of a brilliant salon that attracted

C. Hess

many of the literary and political leaders of the day. As correspondent for several important papers, Antonina Vallentin has been on intimate terms with most of Europe's famous statesmen. One of her close friends was Gustav Stresemann, whose biographer she became. In 1932 she made a valuable survey for the *International Labour Review* of the employment of women since the First World War, and in numerous articles she prophesied the present régime in Germany. All these things, which were valuable assets a few years ago, are now dangerous liabilities. Even her Polish nativity is now a peril to her.

Like many natives of small countries, Antonina Vallentin is a linguist. Born in a well-to-do upper-class family, she was privately educated, and spoke fluent German, French, English, and Italian from early childhood. Most of her writing has been done in German—though Benjamin W. Huebsch called her "Parisian in all but the accident of birth." A striking red-blonde, energetic and enthusiastic, she has managed, says Mr. Huebsch, to "roam up and down Europe, working in libraries and museums," and at the same time to be "an efficient mother, housekeeper, and co-worker of her husband."

As a political journalist, John Carter ("Jay Franklin") said that she wrote "with an intimate knowledge of men and events," and another critic remarked that she had "not only the thoroughness, literalism, and verve of a journalist, but a poetic sensitivity and a well-founded critical judgment." Her *Leonardo da Vinci* was a Book-of-the-Month club choice, and her biography of Heine is one of the best. Her best known work, however, is her penetrating study of Stresemann, which involves the study of an entire and now vanished era of civilization.

WORKS AVAILABLE IN ENGLISH: Stresemann, 1931 (as Frustration: or, Stresemann's Race With Death, 1935); Poet in Exile: The Life of Heinrich Heine, 1934; Leonardo da Vinci: The Tragic Pursuit of Perfection, 1938.

ABOUT: Vallentin, A. Stresemann (see Foreword by A. Einstein); Bookman August 1931; Wilson Library Bulletin January 1939.

VAN AMMERS-KÜLLER. See AMMERS-KÜLLER

"VANCE, ETHEL." See STONE, G. Z.

VANCE, LOUIS JOSEPH (September 19, 1879-December 16, 1933), American novelist, short-story writer, and inventor of "The Lone Wolf," was born in New York, the son of Wilson and Lillie (Beall) Vance. His father was a Civil War veteran who fought with the Army of the Cumberland and later turned newspaper man and novelist. The boy was educated at the preparatory department of the Brooklyn Polytechnic Institute, and was then obliged to go to work for a local public service corporation, studying drawing at night with the  Art Students League with the intention of becoming an illustrator.

Married to Elizabeth Hodges of New York at nineteen, and deeply in debt, Vance tried his hand at short-story writing, working six hours at night after holding his regular job in the daytime. His first short story was rejected; the second brought $25. After years of drudging at hackwork, he produced a best-seller, *The Brass Bowl*, while still in his twenties. A 100,000-word novel, *My Lady of the Mercenaries*, was accepted by *Munsey's Magazine*. Hundreds of his short stories were disposed of at low prices. *The Black Bag*, *The Bronze Bell*, and *The Brass Bowl*, an alliterative trio, were Vance's most successful books prior to the appearance of his chivalrous crook, Michael Lanyard, The Lone Wolf.

Vance constructed his plots and wrote his chapters methodically, writing usually at night and using a typewriter, never a pen. The stories were plotted to the last detail before being written. He could turn out a book of 100,000 words in two months. Vance wrote in all thirty-five novels, hundreds of short stories, a poem, and a short play. A careful workman, he rewrote the first chapter of *The Bandbox* forty times. He was fond of cruising a sailboat on Long Island Sound. A plainspoken individual, he resigned from the Knickerbocker Whist Club, criticizing the "bridge racket."

On a December day in 1933 smoke was seen pouring from the thirteenth floor of Town House, at 108 East 38th Street in New York City. Vance was found lying on the floor of his apartment with his head and right shoulder resting on the seat of a blazing upholstered armchair. The unclothed upper part of his body was severely burned. Apparently he had fallen asleep with a lighted cigar in his hand after preparing for bed. He was taken to a hospital, where he died.

PRINCIPAL WORKS: The Romance of Terence O'Rourke, 1905; The Private War, 1906; The Brass Bowl, 1907; The Black Bag, 1908; The Bronze Bell, 1909; The Pool of Flame, 1909; No Man's Land, 1910; Cynthia-of-the-Minute, 1911; The Bandbox, 1912; The Destroying Angel, 1912; The Day of Days, 1913; Joan Thursday, 1913; The Lone Wolf, 1914; Nobody, 1915; Sheep's Clothing, 1915; Alias the Lone Wolf, 1921; Linda Lee, Incorporated, 1922; The Lone Wolf Returns, 1923; Mrs. Paramor, 1924; The Road to En-dor, 1925; White Fire, 1926; The Woman in the Shadow, 1930; The Lone Wolf's Son, 1931; Encore the Lone Wolf, 1933; The Lone Wolf's Last Prowl, 1934.

ABOUT: New York Times December 17, 1933; Wilson Library Bulletin December 1930.

*VAN DER MEERSCH, MAXENCE

(1907-   ), French novelist, was born in Roubaix, an industrial town of northern

France, between Lille and the Belgian frontier. He studied in Roubaix, in near-by Tourcoing, and finally at the University of Lille, where he took degrees in law and literature. Unlike most parents, his father never discouraged him in his literary pursuits but, on the contrary, stimulated him from the earliest, predicted his success, and has served most efficiently as his secretary, promoter, and literary agent. "Without him I would never have written a word, much less published anything," says Van der Meersch. As for the writers who have influenced his development, Van der Meersch mentions Molière and La Fontaine, the Rousseau of the *Confessions*, Balzac, Flaubert, "Zola, of course, and what may sound most surprising—Dickens." Tolstoy, however, has been his supreme master. "I have read *War and Peace* more than twenty times and I never tire of it." He admires, besides, Dostoievsky and, of the moderns, Mauriac.

Van der Meersch's first novel, *The House in the Dunes* (1932), attracted wide attention, especially among working-class audiences. Its scene is that of most of his other works, the Franco-Belgian frontier, and the chief subject of the plot is tobacco smuggling. A critic of the London *Times Literary Supplement* says: "Van der Meersch recalls one of the more brutal of the Flemish painters delighting in subjects such as tavern brawls but filled with the love for detail which characterizes all the school."

After *The House in the Dunes* came *Car Ils ne Savent ce Qu'ils Font* (1933) and *When the Looms Are Silent* (1934), a prole-

tarian novel about a strike and industrial struggle. With *La Péché du Monde* (1934) Van der Meersch won the prize of the Ligue Maritime et Coloniale, and in 1935, immediately after *Maria: Fille de Flandre,* he became universally known with *Invasion,* which deals with the people of German-occupied French territory during the First World War. *Invasion* has been considered one of the finest and most powerful pacifist novels ever written. Although it missed the Goncourt Prize by one vote (after a controversy which assumed political proportions), it was translated into all the civilized languages. H. E. Bates calls it a unique work, ". . . at once a terrible and a splendid achievement." Perhaps to compensate for the oversight the Goncourt committee next year crowned Van der Meersch's novel, *Hath Not the Potter* (1936), which, though less significant than *Invasion,* is nevertheless "a most distinguished effort to show at work every emotion in the human frame." The locale (the Franco-Belgian frontier) and the subject (tobacco smuggling) is the same as that of his first novel, *The House in the Dunes,* but it shows more maturity and intensity.

Van der Meersch lives (in peacetime) in Croix, a suburb of his native Roubaix, with his wife, his young daughter, and his enterprising father. His house faces that canal running from La Deule to Escaut which is so vividly described in his works. When smugglers get in trouble they always come to see the specialist in these matters, Van der Meersch, who is so kind and who is, besides, a lawyer. Van der Meersch's ascetic look is due to his extremely thin face and his black beard. Interested in the theatre for many years, Van der Meersch has written many unpublished plays.

The French critic Edmond Jaloux has characterized Van der Meersch as follows: "He is a colorful, even brutal, descriptive writer, but one who knows how to see, a marvelous animator of individuals and groups. . . . He does not typify the literature or ideas of our age, but he discovers with much force and vigorous style the tradition of the 'eighties, without however losing his way in it."

So far as is known, Van der Meersch is still in France.

WORKS AVAILABLE IN TRANSLATIONS: When the Looms Are Silent (British title: The Looms Are Silent) 1934; Invasion (British title: Invasion '14) 1937; Hath Not the Potter, 1937; The House in the Dunes, 1938.

ABOUT: Annales Politiques et Littéraires November 25, 1936, December 25, 1936; Commune January 1935, January 1936; Forum March 1937;

* Died January 14, 1951.

L'Illustration December 19, 1936; Nouvelles Littéraires December 12, 19, 1936; Saturday Review of Literature January 23, 1937; Springfield Republican January 31, 1937; Time January 25, 1937; Times (London) Literary Supplement February 26, 1938.

"VAN DINE, S. S." See WRIGHT, W.

*VAN DOREN, CARL CLINTON (September 10, 1885-   ), American critic and biographer, Pulitzer Prize winner, was born in Hope, Ill., the son of Charles Lucius Van Doren, M.D., and Dora Anne (Butz) Van Doren. He is the older brother of Mark Van Doren.[qv] He was educated at the University of Illinois (B.A. 1907) and Columbia (Ph.D. 1911). In 1907 and 1908 he was assistant in rhetoric at Illinois. From 1911 to 1930 he taught English at Columbia, rising from instructor to associate; at the same time, from 1916 to 1919, he was headmaster of the Brearley School. He was literary editor of the *Nation* from 1919 to 1922, of the *Century Magazine* (where he was known as "the Roving Critic") from 1922 to 1925, and of the Literary Guild (of which he was one of the founders) from 1926 to 1934. From 1926 to 1936 he was a member of the committee of management of the *Dictionary of American Biography.* He was managing editor of the *Cambridge History of American Literature* from 1917 to 1921, and of the *Short History of American Literature* the year following. In addition to his own works, he translated Hebbel's *Judith* (1914) and edited *Modern American Prose* (1934), the *Anthology of World Prose* (1935), and the *Borzoi Reader* (1936). His life of Franklin won the Pulitzer Prize in biography for 1938.

In 1912 Dr. Van Doren married Irita Bradford (now, as Irita Van Doren, editor of the New York *Herald Tribune Books*), and they had three daughters. They were divorced, and in 1939 he married Jean Wright. Their home is in downtown New York.

Although Carl Van Doren was class poet at the University of Illinois (he also edited the university's literary monthly), he has published no verse since then. An athlete and an enthusiastic footballer as a boy, he suddenly lost interest in sports after he entered college, and since then his life has been wholly that of the intellect. But he still has the athlete's build—over six feet in height, with broad shoulders and rugged frame. He says he has never been ill in his life. His features are firm, his gray hair close-clipped, his eyes brown, his voice full and pleasant. He calls himself an "unbeliever": "scholar and skeptic" was the description of him made by C. I. Glicksberg. He is noted for his remarkable memory, his firmness and decision of mind, and the broad nature of his sympathies.

Besides being one of the soundest critics in America today, Dr. Van Doren is a biographer "in the great tradition," as Crane Brinton remarked. The one quality he lacks is any great degree of humor to leaven his seriousness, but his skepticism never descends to cynicism. His biography of Swift has already become standard, and that of Franklin has been called "the definitive Franklin book of our generation." He is a hard-working, conscientious research worker, not a prolific author, but one whose few books have immediately become classics in their field.

PRINCIPAL WORKS: The Life of Thomas Love Peacock, 1911; The American Novel, 1921 (revised edition 1940); Contemporary American Novelists, 1922; The Roving Critic, 1923; Many Minds, 1924; James Branch Cabell, 1925; Other Provinces (short stories) 1925; American and British Literature Since 1890 (with M. Van Doren) 1925 (revised edition 1939); The Ninth Wave (novel) 1926; Swift, 1930; Sinclair Lewis, 1933; American Literature: An Introduction, 1933 (as What Is American Literature? 1935); Three Worlds (autobiography) 1936; Benjamin Franklin, 1938; Secret History of the American Revolution, 1941.

ABOUT: Van Doren, C. Three Worlds; New York Times Book Review March 9, 1941; Newsweek February 17, 1941; Publishers' Weekly May 6, 1939; Saturday Review of Literature May 6, 1939; Sewanee Review April 1938.

VAN DOREN, MARK (June 13, 1894-   ), American poet and critic, was born in Hope, Ill., the son of Charles Lucius Van Doren, a physician, and Dora Anne (Butz) Van Doren. He is the younger brother of Carl Van Doren[qv] and brother-in-law of Irita Van Doren, editor of the New York *Herald Tribune Books.* At the age of six he was taken to Urbana, Ill., the seat of the University of Illinois, from which he was graduated in 1914. The next year he received his M.A. degree from Columbia.

Fitzsimmons

During the First World War he served for two years in the infantry, then returned to Columbia and was awarded a traveling fellowship. With Joseph Wood Krutch, also a fellow, he spent a year in England and France. Columbia gave him his Ph.D. degree in 1920. He has been connected with the English department of the university ever since, being now associate professor of English. His summers and his sabbatical years he spends in Falls Village, Cornwall Hollow, in northwestern Connecticut. In 1922 he married Dorothy Graffe, also a writer; they have two sons.

From 1924 to 1928 he was literary editor of the *Nation,* in succession to his brother, and from 1935 to 1938 he served as the magazine's motion picture critic. Mrs. Van Doren has also been on its staff.

Mark Van Doren has, besides his own books, edited a number of anthologies, including the *Oxford Book of American Prose* and his very impressive *Anthology of World Poetry.* In addition to his teaching at Columbia, he lectures at the New School for Social Research. He is an inspiring teacher, with a sympathetic approach and a sense of humor which make his courses popular. Most of his writing has to be done during his summers in the country, since besides his many professional duties he is sociable by nature, a ready and witty conversationalist with a host of friends. He is a slender man, of medium height, with a close cap of dark hair, deep-set, bright dark eyes, and a thin face lighted by an attractive smile. He is an old-fashioned liberal in his political and economic convictions. In his life, as in his work, sanity and clear-thinking have been his major aims; it is not for nothing that his first devotion in poetry was to John Dryden. There is a clean and chiseled quality in his poetry which is a direct outgrowth of that bias. It is poetry of intellect, rather than of passion, but the under-current of feeling is there, hidden but deep.

Mark Van Doren and his older brother have always been close friends and associates, in spite of the nine years' difference between their ages. In fact, so prominent in the life of literary New York, for many years, have the two writing brothers and their two writing wives been, that more than once they have been referred to as "the Van Doren trust." Both brothers have written criticism, biography, and fiction. It is in Mark Van Doren's poetic vein, however, that they diverge, and something of the poetic outlook colors and warms all the work he has done in prose.

In May 1940 Mark Van Doren was awarded the Pulitzer Prize in poetry for his *Collected Poems,* published in 1939.

PRINCIPAL WORKS: *Poetry*—Spring Thunder and Other Poems, 1924; 7 P.M. and Other Poems, 1926; Now the Sky and Other Poems, 1928; Jonathan Gentry, 1931; A Winter Diary and Other Poems, 1935; The Last Look and Other Poems, 1937; Collected Poems, 1939; The Mayfield Deer, 1941; Our Lady Peace and Other War Poems, 1942. *Criticism and Biography*—Henry David Thoreau, A Critical Study, 1916; The Poetry of John Dryden, 1920; American and British Literature Since 1890 (with Carl Van Doren) 1925 (revised edition 1939); Shakespeare, 1939; The Private Reader, 1942; (ed.) New Invitation to Learning, 1942. *Fiction*—Dick and Tom (juvenile) 1931; Dick and Tom in Town (juvenile) 1932; The Transients, 1935; Windless Cabins, 1940; The Transparent Tree (juvenile) 1940.

ABOUT: Poetry December 1937, June 1939; Saturday Review of Literature February 9, 1935; Scholastic October 7, 1940; Southern Review Summer 1936; Time October 21, 1940.

VAN DRUTEN, JOHN WILLIAM (June 1, 1901-), English dramatist, writes: "John [William] Van Druten was born in London, the son of a Dutch father, Wilhelmus Van Druten, a banker, and an English mother. He was educated at University College School, London, where he showed an enthusiasm, rather than a talent, for writing. On leaving school he

J. Leyda

studied for the law, serving his Articles of Clerkship with a City firm of solicitors, and attending lectures and classes at the Law Society's School. In 1923 he was qualified with honors in the Solicitors' Examination and was admitted as a Solicitor of the Supreme Court of Judicature. He also took the degree of LL.B. at London University. The practice of the law, however, was not to his liking, which turned more towards the academic side of his profession. (The profession itself, by the way, was his father's choice rather than his own.) He therefore applied for and obtained a post, which he held from 1923 to 1926, as Special Lecturer in English Law and Legal History at the University College of Wales, Aberystwyth.

"During these years his interest in writing had continued. A large flow of poems and short stories had come back from magazines; a few of them had found homes, particularly in *Punch.* In 1923 a three-act play entitled *The Return Half* was produced by the Ex-Students' Club of the Royal Academy of Dramatic Art. The names of the author and the leading actor were equally unknown: they were John Van Druten and John Gielgud. The play received encouraging reviews, and in the following year Mr. Van Druten's play *Young Woodley* was written, and bought by an English and an American manager for production in London and on Broadway. The London production, however, was forbidden by the censor on the ground that the piece constituted an attack on the English Public School System, a ban which was later reversed after the successful New York production in 1925 and a private performance by the London Stage Society in 1927. Eventually produced at the Savoy Theatre in London early in 1928, it ran for the rest of that year.

"In 1926 Mr. Van Druten gave up the law as a career and came to America, where he went on lecture tours of the principal cities. Since 1928 he has devoted himself exclusively to writing. Since 1926 he figures that he has divided his time almost exactly between the two continents."

* * *

Lloyd Morris said that there were "three Van Drutens," the poet, the sophisticate, and the scholar. All three coalesce in a tall, still youngish man with wavy brown hair and rosy cheeks, whose favorite recreation is "walking in the suburbs." He is known as a gourmet and "makes frivolity an art," but at the same time periodically craves solitude and goes to find it in remote places. He is unmarried. He has never entirely duplicated the great success of *Young Woodley*, but has been rated since as a "dependable" playwright and, on the side, an occasional novelist.

PRINCIPAL WORKS: *Plays*—The Return Half, 1924; Chance Acquaintances, 1927; Young Woodley, 1928; Return of the Soldier (dramatization of novel by R. West) 1928; Diversion, 1928; After All, 1929; London Wall, 1931; There's Always Juliet, 1931; Hollywood Holiday (with B. W. Levy) 1931; Somebody Knows, 1932; Behold, We Live! 1932; The Distaff Side, 1933; Flowers of the Forest, 1936; Most of the Game, 1936; Gertie Maude, 1937; Leave Her to Heaven, 1940; Old Acquaintance, 1941. *Miscellaneous*—Young Woodley (novel) 1929; A Woman on Her Way (novel) 1930; And Then You Wish (novel) 1936; The Way to the Present (autobiography) 1938.

ABOUT: Van Druten, J. The Way to the Present; *Literary Digest* January 26, 1935; *New York Herald Tribune Magazine* September 20, 1931.

VAN DYKE, HENRY (November 10, 1852-April 10, 1933), American poet, essayist, and short-story writer, was born at Germantown, Pa., the son of Henry Jackson Van Dyke, pastor of the First Presbyterian Church and a descendant of early Holland stock, and Henrietta (Ashmead) Van Dyke. His grandfather was a well-known physician and graduate of Princeton, a college with which the grandson was long to be identified. Henry spent his boyhood in Brooklyn and New York, attended the Brooklyn Polytechnic Institute, received his Princeton B.A. in 1873, and graduated from the Theological Seminary next year. After study in Berlin and elsewhere abroad he assumed his first pastorate at the United Congregational Church, Newport, R.I., staying there from 1879 to 1883. *The Reality of Religion*, his first book, appeared next year, when Van Dyke was thirty-two. He married Ellen Reid of  Baltimore in December 1881; she survived him, with five of their nine children.

From 1883 to 1899 Van Dyke was at the Brick Presbyterian Church in New York City, where his sermons became famous. *The Story of the Other Wise Man* and *The First Christmas Tree* were given on two successive Christmases there, and were translated into nearly all European and several Oriental languages. *The Blue Flower*, with which Van Dyke's name is perhaps most frequently identified, was not an original work, but a translation from the German of Novalis, who used the figure to signify Poetry. *The Unknown Quantity* was written for solace after the death of a favorite daughter in childbirth.

Princeton next claimed him as Murray Professor of English Literature, in a chair named for James O. Murray, his predecessor at the Brick Presbyterian Church and at Princeton. The Van Dykes settled in 1900 at "Avalon," their Princeton, N.J., home for the rest of his life, which gave the name to the collected edition of his works. His books appeared at regular intervals, edifying a very wide range of readers besides his parishioners and students. Van Dyke was a keen fisherman. He had a pleasant sense of humor, a somewhat conventional essay style and a fondness for mixing with all classes of society, especially in the Canadian wilds. His son wrote, "To him romance was never distance; it was rather the vital quality of being alive among men and amid the unfathomable wonders of nature." As a preacher he was "an adventurous conservative." He was elected President of the National Institute of Arts and Letters in

1912. His *The Spirit of America* (1910) was a translation of *Le Génie de l'Amerique* given as a lecture at the Sorbonne in Paris, 1908-09.

Woodrow Wilson appointed Van Dyke minister to the Netherlands and Luxembourg in 1913. Three years later on September 6, 1916, he resigned the post, feeling too strongly the justice of the Allied cause. On his way home in 1917 he visited the battle-fronts in France. Desiring more active service, he obtained an appointment as lieutenant commander in the Chaplain Corps of the U.S. Navy.

In 1919, the year he returned to Princeton, the French Government awarded him the Cross of the Legion of Honor. Oxford University gave him a D.C.L. degree. Van Dyke retired from teaching in 1923, though continuing to give a series of university lectures on literature before crowded audiences until 1933. He was also chairman of the committee on the Book of Common Worship. The Van Dykes' golden wedding anniversary was observed in 1931; two years later he died at dawn of an April day after a brief illness. His Christianity, although of a positive evangelical quality, was never hard or dogmatic; he is a minor figure in American literature, but a pleasant one—physically attractive too, with his handsome head and exuberant nature.

PRINCIPAL WORKS: The Reality of Religion, 1884; Little Rivers, 1895; The Story of the Other Wise Man, 1896; The First Christmas Tree, 1897; Fisherman's Luck, 1899; The Ruling Passion, 1901; The Blue Flower, 1902; Days Off, 1907; Out of Doors in the Holy Land, 1908; Poems, 1911; The Unknown Quantity, 1912; The Red Flower, Fighting for Peace, 1917; The Valley of Vision, 1919; Studies in Tennyson (complete revision of The Poetry of Tennyson, 1889) 1920; Poems (revised ed.) 1920; Camp Fires and Guide Posts, 1921; Companionable Books, 1922; Half Told Tales, 1925; The Man Behind the Book, 1929; Gratitude, 1930; A Creelful of Fishing Stories 1932.

ABOUT: Van Dyke, T. Henry Van Dyke: A Biography; The Van Dyke Book (1905, revised edition 1920); New York Times April 11, 1933; Princeton Alumni Weekly May 5, 19, July 3, 1933; Suburban Life May 1908.

VANE, SUTTON (1888-), English playwright, was christened Vane Sutton Vane. His father was a prolific writer of melodramas; when the junior Vane's successful play *Outward Bound* was produced in 1923, seasoned playgoers were inclined to think that it was the work of the Sutton Vane they knew best. Twenty-six-year-old Vane, who had had some acting experience, was among the first to enlist for the First World War. Invalided home with shell shock, he was discharged from the army, retaining, however, an uneasy conviction that he had not completed doing his bit.

As soon as he was physically able, Vane returned to France to appear in plays behind the lines, acting for months in *The Thirteenth Chair* through air raids and bombardments. Speculations on death and on possible life beyond the grave were logical reactions to such experiences; Vane had not long returned to civilian life when he wrote *Outward Bound*, in which a shipload of passengers from all walks of life—the play itself was a paradise for straight and character actors—found themselves headed for a port of judgment, after it had dawned on them that they had shuffled off this mortal coil. Commercial managers refused the play with complete unanimity.

Vane resorted to the same expedients as did Noel Coward when the latter could find no producer for *The Vortex*. He hired the Everyman Theatre, a small London suburban house, for two weeks; himself painted the scene flats, tacked up curtains, and engaged a company willing to work on cooperative terms. Total cost of production and rent of theatre: about 120 pounds. When the play proved a success, it was moved to the Garrick Theatre with new scenery and all the trappings of a West End production.

Early in 1924 the American première in New York occurred, with Dudley Digges in the seat of judgment; Leslie Howard and Margalo Gillmore playing the ethereal, golden-haired young couple who had resorted to suicide; and Alfred Lunt and the late Beryl Mercer appearing respectively as a young wastrel and a patient old charwoman. Fifteen years later, in 1939, the play was revived with Laurette Taylor playing the charwoman. The play has been filmed twice. Sutton Vane's two plays preceding *Outward Bound* were of no particular note. He wrote two more, in 1935: *Time, Gentlemen, Please*, set in an English public house (the title is the barmaid's standard phrase to denote closing time is approaching), and *Marine Parade*, which had fourteen characters and one setting. Mr. Vane has an actor's good looks, with a light moustache and hair receding from a high forehead.

PRINCIPAL WORKS: Outward Bound, 1923.
ABOUT: New York Post December 17, 1938.

VAN LOAN, CHARLES EMMET (June 29 1876-March 3, 1919), American short-story writer and writer on sports, was born in San José, Calif.,

the son of Richard Van Loan and Emma J. (Blodgett) Van Loan, and was educated in the public schools of the town. Van Loan began his career in the mercantile business, working for a time as a stenographer, but gave that up in 1903 to become the sports editor of a Los Angeles newspaper. Next year he came to New York City to remain until 1910. "During the years between 1909 and 1919 he had made himself the *prose* laureate of the golf-course, the prize-ring, the diamond, and the race-track," wrote Robert H. Davis after Van Loan's death. "He possessed the peculiar gift of characterization developed to a high degree and could cover a baseball game, a horse-race, a prize-fight, or any sporting event with fine grace and distinction. In his hands the brawn of life, the animated, playful mob, the lusty-throated fans, the vikings of the diamond, became personalities in literature."

"The Drug Store Derby," a racing story, was the first piece of fiction which Van Loan sold, in June 1909, to *All-Story Weekly*. It appeared in the January 1910 issue. Another story had appeared in *Munsey's Magazine* in September 1909. Van Loan wrote special articles for the Munsey publications, and was an associate editor of the *Saturday Evening Post* for a few months prior to his death. Numerous stories also appeared in *Collier's Weekly,* and others in the *Popular* and *Metropolitan* magazines. *Inside the Ropes* (1913), a collection of stories about boxing, was often given by fight managers to boxing commissioners as Christmas presents.

In 1914 Van Loan wrecked an automobile near San Bernardino, Calif., receiving a fractured skull, broken ribs, and a compound fracture of the left wrist which rendered the arm helpless. His vitality lessened by this accident, he died five years later at forty-three of nephritis in Abington Hospital, Philadelphia, survived by his widow, Emma (Lenz) Van Loan, and two children. He was a good-humored giant, with very blue eyes and a strong, protruding lower jaw.

PRINCIPAL WORKS: The Big League, 1911; The Ten-Thousand-Dollar Arm, 1912; Inside the Ropes, 1913; The Lucky Seventh, 1913; Buck Parvin and

the Movies, 1915; Old Man Curry, 1917; Fore! 1918; Score by Innings, 1919; Taking the Count, 1919.

ABOUT: American Magazine December 1918; Bookman May 1919; Outing November 1919.

*VAN LOON, HENDRIK WILLEM

(January 14, 1882-   ), Dutch-American historian, writes: "I was born in Rotterdam, just around the corner from the birthplace of Erasmus, the son of a rich father who lived in a realm a million miles away from his child and never made the slightest effort to construct a bridge across that chasm. And so I escaped entirely into the

past, and re-valuated all the adventures of my own existence into terms of a bygone era. Even today I know the seventeenth century better than the twentieth.

"We were sent to school at an astonishingly young age. I do not know when I first learned to read and write. I cannot remember any time during the many years that I have spent upon this planet when I was not in direct and immediate touch with both the past and the future. I lived in a world in which the ideals of the eighteenth century were still the aim of the spiritual realm. The book which taught me English was *Henry Esmond.* I still read that magnificent *opus* regularly once every year. Because English is a tongue which I had to acquire when I was already full grown, and with which I shall have to struggle until the end of my days, I love and revere it with a personal passion which few of those who were born in English-speaking countries will ever be able to share.

"My work would not be my work without those endless little pictures, to draw which I had to fight from early childhood, for nobody at home really approved of them. I believe that I can honestly state that I write entirely by ear. I am one of those few and highly fortunate people who can write under any and all circumstances. When I am in a hurry with a drawing job I find that music is absolutely indispensable. I will draw with anything that comes handy and within reach.

"The older I grow the more I agree with Spinoza and Frederick the Great and Goethe that Chance plays a tremendously important rôle in our lives. If I had not lost my mother when I was seventeen I never would have left my own country, and would un-

* Died March 10, 1944.

doubtedly have tried to do there what is really the object of my life, the humanization and popularization of history, and I would have failed most miserably. For nobody in my native land would have felt the slightest sympathy with what I was trying to do, and with the rather melancholic natural tendencies in my mental make-up, I would have drifted into a hopeless state of despair which would have meant an end to all further creative efforts; whereas in my adopted country I have enjoyed just enough opposition to be encouraged to work still harder and write something that shall be better yet.

"I claim that reason and intelligence and a scientific acceptance of all the facts related to life will eventually turn this world of ours into a truly decent place of residence for civilized human beings. Of happiness in the usual sense of the word I probably have not had a great deal. But I have had my work, and that is the greatest good that can come to any man born with a sense of a creative duty."

* * *

Dr. Van Loon (pronounced *lone*) came to the United States in 1903, and after a year at Harvard received his A.B. from Cornell in 1905. He received his Ph.D. at Munich in 1911. His *Who's Who* biography lists two marriages, both to Americans: to Eliza Bowditch in 1906, and to Helen Criswell in 1920. He was Associated Press correspondent in Washington and later in Warsaw, Moscow, and St. Petersburg (Leningrad), in 1906; a lecturer on history at various American colleges from 1911 to 1914; with the Associated Press again in Europe throughout the First World War, with an interlude as lecturer on modern European history at Cornell in 1915 and 1916. He organized the history department of Antioch College and served as professor in 1922 and 1923. For the next year he was associate editor of the Baltimore *Sun.* He is a popular lecturer who makes frequent tours, but his permanent home is in Old Greenwich, Conn. In 1934 he lectured in New Zealand, Australia, South Africa, and South America. He is six feet tall, weighs over two hundred pounds, and has "a smooth, round, almost cherubic face," with twinkling light brown eyes. He speaks and writes ten languages, plays the violin, "dresses in the latest pattern of fashion," and draws caricatures indefatigably. *The Story of Mankind,* his first great success, went through thirty editions, was translated into a dozen languages, and received the Newbery Medal. His style is indescribable and unique; "his philosophy is doubt."

PRINCIPAL WORKS: The Fall of the Dutch Republic, 1913; The Rise of the Dutch Kingdom, 1915; The Golden Book of the Dutch Navigators, 1916; A Short History of Discovery, 1918; Ancient Man, 1920; The Story of Mankind, 1921; The Story of the Bible, 1923; The Story of Wilbur the Hat (juvenile) 1925; Tolerance, 1925; America, 1927; The Life of Peter Stuyvesant, 1928; Man, the Miracle Maker, 1928; R.v.R., Life and Times of Rembrandt van Rijn, 1931; Van Loon's Geography, 1932; An Indiscreet Itinerary, 1933; An Elephant Up a Tree (juvenile) 1933; Ships, 1935; Around the World With the Alphabet, 1935; Air-Storming, 1935; The Songs We Sing, 1936; The Arts, 1937; Christmas Carols, 1937; Folk Songs of Many Lands, 1938; Our Battle, 1939; (with G. Castagnetta) Last of the Troubadors: Life and Music of Carl Michael Bellman, 1939; (with G. Castagnetta) Songs America Sings, 1939; The Life and Times of Johann Sebastian Bach, 1940; Invasion, 1940; The Story of the Pacific, 1940; Van Loon's Lives, 1942.

ABOUT: Case, F. Do Not Disturb; Catholic World July 1925; Country Life October 1932; Current History January 1940; Etude December 1939; Newsweek June 1, 1935; Scholastic November 4, 1940; Who April 1941.

VAN PAASSEN, PIERRE (1895-), Dutch-Canadian journalist, was born in Gorcum, a town in Holland, of mixed Dutch and Flemish descent. His full name is Pieter Anthonie Laurusse Van Paassen. He was educated at the Athenaeum in Gorcum, at Victoria College, Toronto, Canada, and at the École des Hautes Études in Paris. He came to Canada with his family in 1911,  when he was about seventeen, studied for the ministry, and became assistant pastor in a Ruthenian Mission (Methodist) in Alberta. When the First World War broke out, he enlisted, and served in France with the Canadian Expeditionary Force. He never returned to the ministry, but instead entered journalism, working on the Toronto *Globe* in 1919, and as an editorial writer on the Atlanta (Ga.) *Constitution* in 1921. He then became a columnist on the New York *Evening World,* and in 1925 the paper sent him to Paris as its chief correspondent. He had a roving assignment until 1930, and covered almost every important political event in Europe during that period. He was in Ethiopia, in Spain, and in Palestine. From boyhood, when his religiously inclined nature was strongly affected by the Old Testament aspects of the Calvinist faith in which he was reared, he has had an almost mystical affinity with the Jews. He is probably the only Gentile Zionist alive, and represented the Christian Pro-Palestine Federations of the United States and France at the League of Nations.

In 1932 he became foreign correspondent of the Toronto *Daily Star,* and he spent the three subsequent years in Russia, studying the Soviet political and economic system. Since he also covered the Riff War in Morocco and the Druse War in Syria, there is hardly any part of the Western world with which he is not familiar. He speaks, besides Dutch and English, fluent French, Italian, German, and modern Hebrew; and in college he specialized in New Testament Greek. He has made a number of lecture tours in the United States and Canada, beginning in 1931.

Mr. Van Paassen has been married twice. By his first wife he had a son and a daughter. In 1940 he married Cornelia M. Sizoo. He is typically Flemish in appearance, heavy-set, dark, with a round bullet-head and drooping eyelids. He hates Fascism with a holy hatred, calls Palestine his "spiritual home," and is proud of the fact that he has been expelled from nearly every country of Europe, including Italy, Germany, and pre-Blum France, because of his outspoken condemnation of Fascism and advocacy of democracy. The few books he had published before his best-selling *Days of Our Years* were almost unnoticed, and until then he was unknown except as a journalist. Yet he writes superbly; there is nothing "journalistic," in the invidious sense, in his style. Implicit in his book, and differentiating it from other semi-autobiographical accounts by European correspondents, is his strong religious feeling, his ethical and spiritual bent, his compassion. Yet he is no mystic, but has been called a "skeptical—but not cynical—Modernist." "A robust human spirit" was Eugene Lyons' characterization: a man who is a born fighter but whose wars are all with evil. He is never likely to become an onlooker on life, with leisure to do much writing; but that he will be heard from, either by pen or by action, no one who has read *Days of Our Years,* or has heard him speak, can doubt.

PRINCIPAL WORKS: Israel and the Vision of Humanity, 1932; Nazism: An Assault on Civilization (ed. with ·J. W. Wise) 1934; The Deep-Red Banner of the Cross, 1937; Days of Our Years, 1939; The Time Is Now! 1941; That Day Alone, 1941; Who's On the Lord's Side? Who? 1942.

ABOUT: Book-of-the-Month Club News January 1939.

VAN TYNE, CLAUDE HALSTEAD (October 16, 1869-March 21, 1930), American historian, winner of the Pulitzer Prize, was born in Tecumseh, Mich., the son of Lawrence M. Van Tyne and Helen (Rosecrans) Van Tyne. He received his B.A. degree from the University of Michigan in 1896 at twenty-six, having spent his earlier years in the banking business,  rising to a post as cashier of the Iosco County Savings Bank in northern Michigan. After graduation he went abroad for study at Heidelberg, Leipzig, and Paris in 1897 and 1898, incidentally taking a rowing trip down the Danube with Mrs. Van Tyne, who was Belle Joslyn of Chesaning, Mich. They were married in June 1896, and had three sons and a daughter.

Van Tyne received his Ph.D. from the University of Pennsylvania in 1900 and spent the next three years there on a history fellowship. His first book (1902) dealt with the Loyalists in the American Revolution; he contributed a volume on the Revolution to the cooperative American Nation Series, edited by Albert Bushnell Hart; and in 1911 published a school history of the United States with a colleague, A. C. McLaughlin, whom he succeeded as professor of history at the University of Michigan in 1906. (Van Tyne had been an assistant professor the three previous years.) In 1911 he became head of the department of history at Michigan, remaining till his death five months after his sixtieth birthday. He had been ill since the spring of 1929.

In 1927 Van Tyne visited Cambridge University, England, as lecturer on the Sir George Watson Foundation for American History, Literature, and Institutions. The lectures were published as *England and America: Rivals in the American Revolution.* Van Tyne also lectured in France, and visited India as a guest of the British authorities. The first volume of Van Tyne's chief work, a projected *History of the Founding of the American Republic,* was chiefly derived from secondary sources and discussed the causes of the War for Independence. The second volume, *The War of Independence: American Phase,* was better-rounded, written in a most readable style, and soundly documented from the papers in the Clements Library at Michigan. It received the Pulitzer Prize just after the author's death. Van Tyne was a man of striking appearance. He held to his beliefs with a stubbornness that at times approached intolerance, in the opinion of some authorities.

PRINCIPAL WORKS: The Loyalists in the American Revolution, 1902; Guide to the Archives of the Government of the United States in Washington (with W. G. Leland) 1904; The American Revolution: 1776-1783, 1905; School History of the United States (with A. C. McLaughlin) 1911; The Causes of the War of Independence, 1922; India in Ferment, 1923; England and America: Rivals in the American Revolution, 1927; The War of Independence: American Phase: Being the Second Volume of a History of the Founding of the American Republic, 1929.

ABOUT: American Historical Review July 1930; Michigan Alumnus March 29, 1930; New York Times March 22, 1930.

VAN VECHTEN, CARL (June 17, 1880-   ), American novelist and music critic, was born in Cedar Rapids, Iowa, the son of

N. Muray

Charles Duane Van Vechten and Ada Amanda (Fitch) Van Vechten. He was educated at the University of Chicago (Ph.B. 1903), and in 1906 became assistant music critic on the New York *Times*. In 1908 he became Paris correspondent of the paper, but returned in 1910 and remained on the *Times* until 1913, when he went to the *Press* for a year as dramatic critic. He edited the program notes of the Symphony Society of New York in 1910-11, contributed musical articles to the 1911 edition of the *Century Dictionary*, and during the same period conducted two departments in the *New Music Review*. He then announced that in his opinion a music critic should retire at forty, since his "intellectual arteries" had hardened by this time, and that he would not write any more critical essays.

Instead, he became a novelist, reversing the usual dictum that a critic is a creative artist who has failed. The people who had hailed him as an acute and receptive critic and "a diverting essayist" were not favorably impressed by the change, but his novels, especially *Peter Whiffle*, *The Tattooed Countess*, and *Nigger Heaven*, were extremely popular. They ranged in background from Iowa to Hollywood and New York; they were best described as "clever," and showed plainly the influence both of H. L. Mencken and James Branch Cabell. Then, with the publication of his quasi-autobiography in 1932, he simply ceased to write

at all. Since that time he has devoted himself entirely to photography, and now has considerable standing in that art.

Carl Van Vechten is something of a "character," whose idiosyncracies are well known. He is a passionate lover of cats, on which he has written one book and edited another. He is an enthusiast for Negro art and literature, and was influential in the "Negro Renaissance" of the 1920's. He is a passionate collector not only of first editions, but also of manuscripts, autographs, newspaper clippings, and bookjackets. During his writing years, he insisted on having a celebrity as witness of his signature on the contract for every one of his books. He still retains his personal interest in music, plays the piano, and has published one volume of his compositions (*Five Old English Ditties*, 1904). His wife is Fania Marinoff, the Russian actress; they have no children. Their home is in New York. At sixty-one, Mr. Van Vechten is still youthful looking, plump and smooth-shaven, with thick white hair over a high forehead. His personality has given rise to numerous legends and stories. Since he declares he intends never to write again, it may be possible to evaluate him during his lifetime as an author. The estimate may be summed up by saying that he is a successful and gifted (though not "important") novelist, and a brilliant essayist whose retirement from the critical field was a serious literary misfortune.

PRINCIPAL WORKS: *Fiction*—Peter Whiffle, His Life and Works, 1922; The Blind Bow-Boy, 1923; The Tattooed Countess, 1924; Firecrackers, 1925; Nigger Heaven, 1926; Spider Boy, 1928; Parties, 1930. *Non-Fiction*—Music After the Great War, 1915; Music and Bad Manners, 1916; Interpreters and Interpretations, 1917; The Merry-Go-Round, 1918; The Music of Spain, 1918; In the Garret, 1920; The Tiger in the House, 1920; Lords of the Housetops (ed.) 1921; Red, 1925; Excavations, 1926; Sacred and Profane Memories, 1932.

ABOUT: Hughes, L. The Big Sea; McKay, C. A Long Way From Home; Johnson, J. W. Along This Way; Van Vechten, C. Sacred and Profane Memories; Independent February 14, 1925.

VAUGHAN, HILDA (1892-   ), Welsh novelist, was born in her ancestral family home at Builth, Breconshire, Wales; she is a collateral descendant of the poet Henry Vaughan. She was educated privately and very strictly, and was grown up before she was allowed to read newspapers or modern novels—a fact to which she attributes her love for quiet and leisurely writing. She started writing during the First World War, when she served first in a Red Cross hospital and then as organizing secretary for the Woman's Land Army. In 1922 she went to

London to attend lectures at Bedford College, and there met the novelist, Charles Morgan,[qv] whom she married the following year. They have a son

and a daughter. Mr. Morgan dedicated to her his best known novel, *The Fountain.* Their peacetime home is London, but they are in America at the present time (1942).

Slender and blonde, with a liking for flowing gowns, Miss Vaughan has been likened to a Botticelli picture. Her first five novels were all about the country and people she knew as a child, the part of Wales on the borders of Breconshire and Radnorshire; in later books her keen love of the theatre has found expression. (She and her husband are both ardent first-nighters.) Of her Welsh novels she has said: "I know this life more intimately than any other, and I am anxious to record the old ways and types which are fast vanishing before the leveling influences of universal education, easy transportation, and wireless."

PRINCIPAL WORKS: The Battle to the Weak, 1925; Here Are Lovers, 1926; The Invader, 1928; Her Father's House, 1930; The Soldier and the Gentlewoman, 1932 (dramatized by D. Massingham and L. Lister, 1933); A Thing of Nought, 1935; The Curtain Rises, 1935; Harvest Home, 1937; She, Too, Was Young (play, with L. Lister) 1938; Fair Woman, 1942.

VEBLEN, THORSTEIN BUNDE (July 30, 1857-August 3, 1929), American economist, was born on a farm in Wisconsin, but

moved to Minnesota at eight and was reared there. The family were Norwegians, and all the nine children were bilingual. It was not by accident that Veblen was able, in 1925, to translate the Icelandic *Laxdaela Saga.* Though the parents were plain farm folk, they were of good intellectual stock; Veblen's brother became a professor of physics, and his nephew is a noted mathematician.

Thorstein Veblen was educated in Carleton College Academy and Carleton College, being graduated in 1880. He had majored in philosophy, and went to Johns Hopkins University for graduate study, but soon transferred to Yale, where he received his Ph.D. in 1884. At loose ends, with no teaching appointment in sight, he returned to Minnesota, where he married Ellen Rolfe and settled down to a bitter waiting period of study and writing, in the course of which he developed from a philosopher into an economist. In 1891 he went to Cornell for further study in economics. The next year, when the University of Chicago was founded, he became an instructor there, remaining, finally, as associate professor of economics, until 1906. It was in Chicago that his first important work was written. From 1906 to 1909 he taught at Stanford University, and from 1909 to 1918 at the University of Missouri. During the First World War he was called to Washington as an "industrial aid," but his findings were promptly rejected or suppressed, and he was soon released. He went to New York, where for several years he taught in the New School for Social Research, edited the *Journal of Political Economy,* and for a while was one of the editors of the *Dial.* His last years were spent in California, not far from Stanford, and he died there at seventy-four.

R. G. Tyrrell called Veblen "the man who shook the world with his irony and who opened the way to new social systems." That describes him exactly, when one adds that he deliberately wrote in a style which has been called everything from bewildering and obscure to coruscating and subversive. His sesquipedalian words, as Lewis Mumford pointed out, constituted "desperately accurate circumlocutions." There was, as W. C. Mitchell said, "much of the satirist in him; but it is satire of an unfamiliar and a disconcerting kind." He was "an inveterate phrase-maker [who] designed his phrases to get under our skins." Mumford called him "one of the half-dozen important figures in scholarship that America has produced since the Civil War, ... grimly whimsical, ... a stick of dynamite wrapped up ... to look like a stick of candy." There is sufficient obscurantism in his style to have made him the putative father of half a dozen mutually warring theories—best known of which is the once popular Technocracy. At the same time the thought behind his amazing barrage of words is clear and incisive. Such phrases as "conspicuous waste," "absentee ownership," "the price system," have done more than pass into our vocabulary: they have passed into our thinking, even though it may be true that, as Max Lerner said, Veblen's rôle was "not directive but chiefly disillusioning."

There is no use in blinking the fact that Veblen's private life and personality were disordered and unpleasant. His first marriage ended in divorce, his second wife became insane, he was discharged from all his universities for scandals about women ("What is one to do if a woman moves in with one?"). Few men liked him, though he had the usual attraction of eccentrics of his type for predatory women. In his last years, when he lived alone, dependent on the charity of former pupils (his last article, written in 1927, was rejected), with his "amazing clothes, home-made furniture, and notions on domestic economy," he was thoroughly miserable—bitter, solitary, not even clean. As Tyrrell said, he "went slowly out of life, lonely, trivial, unappeased, and disagreeable." This tubercular man with the pointed beard, "gray, ashen face and cold sad eyes," tall and thin, with a barely audible voice, was not prepossessing.

But he was not only a magnificent thinker, he had the courage of his convictions. His *Inquiry Into the Nature of Peace* was suppressed, gradually it became impossible for him to find an audience, yet he never made an intellectual compromise. The man Thorstein Veblen was a tragic failure; the economist and philosopher and author Thorstein Veblen was one of the shining triumphs of our age.

PRINCIPAL WORKS: The Theory of the Leisure Class, 1899; The Theory of Business Enterprise, 1904; The Blond Race and the Aryan Culture, 1913; The Instinct of Workmanship, 1914; Imperial Germany and the Industrial Revolution, 1915; An Inquiry Into the Nature of Peace and the Terms of Its Perpetuation, 1917; The Higher Learning in America, 1918; The Vested Interests and the State of the Industrial Arts, 1919; The Place of Science in Modern Civilization and Other Essays, 1919; The Engineers and the Price System, 1921; Absentee Ownership and Business Enterprise in Recent Times, 1923; Essays in Our Changing Order, 1934; What Veblen Taught (selected writings) 1936.

ABOUT: Dorfman, J. Thorstein Veblen and His America; Hobson, J. A. Veblen; Homan, P. T. Contemporary Economic Thought; Teggart, R. V. Thorstein Veblen; Veblen, T. B. Imperial Germany (see Introduction by J. Dorfman to 1939 ed.); What Veblen Taught (see Introduction by W. C. Mitchell); American Anthropology April 1936; American Economic Review December 1929; American Scandinavian Review March 1935; Century Magazine October 1929; Dial July 26, 1919; Journal of Political Economy October 1939; Nation August 14, 1929, August 14, 1935, March 11, 1936; New Republic September 4, 1929, August 5, 1931, March 29, August 30, 1939; New Statesman September 13, 1930; Nineteenth Century November 1926; Political Science Quarterly March 1937, September 1940; Saturday Review of Literature January 12, 1935, June 13, 1936; Scribner's Magazine December 1933; Social Forces December 1931; Sociological Review January 1925, October 1939;

Southwest Political and Social Science Quarterly June 1929; World Tomorrow January 11, 1933.

VECHTEN. See VAN VECHTEN

*VEILLER, BAYARD (January 2, 1869-), American playwright, was born in Brooklyn, N.Y., the son of Philip B. Veiller, a Wall Street broker. His father was born in the United States, but used the French pronunciation of the family name. Bayard Veiller was educated in the public schools of the city, and left the College of the City of New York at sixteen. His first play,  c. Van Vechten written in 1887, was refused by Augustin Daly with the comment that he did not know that anyone could write a play as bad as that. Young Veiller went into the newspaper game on Park Row, serving as "leg man" successively on the New York *Star,* the *World,* the *Mail,* the *Journal,* and the *Evening Post.*

Going out "on the road" as an advance agent for theatrical attractions, Veiller was stranded in Seattle, where he joined the staff of the *Star.* Here he attacked the local boss and dive-owner in print, and the boss threatened and partly executed revenge. He (the boss) shot the Chief of Police at 4 P.M., and at 6 P.M. Veiller caught a train for San Francisco, where he made a connection with the *Examiner.*

Margaret Wycherly, the gifted actress, was playing in Belasco's Alcazar stock company in San Francisco; Veiller went to interview her for his paper, and they were married in 1903 (and later divorced). Returning to New York, Veiller wrote for her *The Primrose Path* (1907), which ran two weeks in New York and left him $10,000 in debt. Special matinées of the plays of William Butler Yeats, for which Miss Wycherly's talent was eminently suited, were given in Boston and New York.

Within the Law, Veiller's immensely profitable melodrama (for everybody except himself) opened in New York in 1912, after having been turned down "more or less brutally" by five New York producers. William Brady bought it for his wife, Grace George, who was dissatisfied with it; Brady resold it to Veiller and the Selwyn brothers, and Jane Cowl proceeded to make it a hit. Veiller sold his rights to the Selwyns in advance, and received only $14,000 out of the

* Died June 16, 1943.

half-million grossed by the play. *The Fight* (1913), the next play, was withdrawn for reasons of censorship and rewritten. *Back Home* (1915), a dramatization of Irvin S. Cobb's *Judge Priest* stories, proved to be "a catastrophe," redeemed next year by the great success of *The Thirteenth Chair*, based on Will Irwin's *Rosalie La Grange* stories. Miss Wycherly played Rosalie, the spiritualistic medium, in this murder melodrama. *The Trial of Mary Dugan* (1927), Veiller's next hit, laid in a court-room, was translated into French and Dutch and twice filmed.

Veiller's dramas are said to lack philosophy and literary quality, but are eminently playable. He is described as a short, nervous, hurried man with broad shoulders and a moustache. In his active days he played golf and tennis, and was especially fond of snowshoeing. He spent several years in Hollywood, and his present address is Los Angeles. His autobiography, *The Fun I've Had*, was published in 1941.

PRINCIPAL WORKS (dates of publication): Within the Law, 1917; The Thirteenth Chair: A Play in Three Acts, 1922; The Trial of Mary Dugan: A Melodrama of New York Life, 1928; The Fun I've Had (autobiography) 1941; Bait for a Tiger, 1941.

ABOUT: Veiller, B. The Fun I've Had; Everybody's March 1917; Green Book March 1914; Metropolitan June 1913; New York Times September 29, 1912, December 10, 1916; Town and Country January 20, 1917.

VERCEL, ROGER (1894-), French novelist, was born in Le Mans, the capital of the Sarthe département, of a Jurassian

father whose military profession compelled him to move frequently from garrison to garrison. Roger made his elementary studies at La Flèche, and at the advent of the First World War was doing his first year of "licence" at the University of Caen. During a summer vacation at the age of eleven the boy had "discovered and devoured" Joris-Karl Huysmans' *En Route* which he found in the library of his teacher, a good-natured country priest. "This reading experience left in me an extremely keen desire to read Huysmans' other works." Years later, while pursuing his doctorate in literature, Vercel made exhaustive notes on Huysmans' syntax, imagery, and vocabulary. But Huysmans' brother-in-law, a Monsieur

Marois, denied him access to the dead writer's correspondence, and Huysmans' literary executor, Lucien Descaves, was in mourning at the time; Vercel therefore changed his subject to Corneille. His theses, *Images dans l'Oeuvre de Corneille* (1927) and *Lexique des Images de Racine et de Corneille* (1927), won him not only a doctorate in literature but also the Prix Saintour of the French Academy.

During the World War, Vercel fought for four years on many battlefronts. At the time of the armistice he was stationed in Sofia as "commissaire-rapporteur" of the Eastern Front War Council. A trusted officer, he was assigned the most varied commissions and traveled extensively, from Budapest to Odessa, from Belgrade to Stamboul.

After the war and the completion of his doctorate, Vercel settled in Dinan, a quiet little town in Côtes du Nord, northwestern France, some seventeen miles from the fashionable resort of St. Malo, where, at last report, he was still teaching literature at the local "collège." One summer at Dinan he timidly brought his first novel, *Notre Père Trajan* (1930), to his neighbors. the brothers Tharaud, who put it away during their vacation and read it with delight months later on their return to Paris. They liked it so well that they wrote a prologue, launching the young provincial teacher. The background of this novel, the post-War Balkans which Vercel knew first hand, later reappeared in *Captain Conan*.

In rapid succession followed novels dealing with the sea or with adventure in foreign countries: *En Derive* (1931) and its continuation, *In Sight of Eden* (1932), a lusty saga of cod fishery off the coast of Greenland, which won him the Prize of the Comité France-Amerique, and introduced him to the English-reading public; *Le Maître du Rêve* (1933) and *Captain Conan* (1934), which received the Goncourt Prize and brought his name to the attention of the whole world.

Vercel's deep preoccupation with Breton history resulted in his *Bertrand of Brittany* (1932), a biography of Bertrand du Guesclin, the Breton knight whose exploits during the Hundred Years' War succeeded in driving the English out of France. The background of *The Tides of Mont St. Michel*—the September 1938 choice of the Book-of-the-Month Club—is the beautiful fortress-shrine of Mont St. Michel familiar to tourists and to readers of Henry Adams.

Vercel is above all a lover of adventure although he rarely visits the places he describes: his very first short story dealt with Indo-China which he had seen only on the map. He lets the sea-wolves, especially his friend Captain Fernando, tell their tall yarns and then he recreates them. Of *In Sight of Eden* he declares: "I made the trip under the lamp at home, leaning over maps and compasses, and if my books have succeeded this is due precisely to the fact that I never sailed with the fishermen to the North." And yet it is all so alive and convincing that a critic of the stature of Raymond Mortimer wrote in the London *Observer*: "Obviously *In Sight of Eden* is written from experience." Another English critic glowingly commented: "The scene has the glamour of Pierre Loti and the characters have the fascinating intensity and truth of Conrad." Vercel has also written books of travel and description: *Croisière Blanche* (1938) dealing with Iceland, Spitzbergen, and the Arctic region, and *À l'Assaut des Poles* (1938), about exploration at the Poles.

Vercel is happily married and has five children. As a writer one of his peculiarities consists in the way he composes his books while walking. "I can write for ten kilometers.... If writers walked while writing, their books would be better. The rhythm of steps stimulates ideas.... It takes me fifteen days during which I walk all the time...."

WORKS AVAILABLE IN ENGLISH TRANSLATION: In Sight of Eden, 1934 (British title: Jealous Waters); Bertrand of Brittany, 1934; Captain Conan, 1935; Salvage, 1936 (British title: Tugboat); Lena, 1937; Tides of Mont St. Michel, 1938; Troubled Waters, 1940.

ABOUT: Annales Politiques et Littéraires December 25, 1934; Atlantic Monthly November 1938; Boston Transcript June 3, 1934; November 2, 1935, September 3, 1938; New Republic, September 7, 1938; New York Herald Tribune "Books" March 18, 1934, November 17, 1935, January 10, 1937, August 8, 1937, September 4, 1938; New York Times, March 25, 1934, April 22, 1934, November 17, 1935, January 10, 1937, August 8, 1937, September 4, 1938; Nouvelles Littéraires December 15, 1934; Saturday Review of Literature March 17, 1934, October 6, 1934, November 3, 1935, August 14, 1937, September 3, 1938; Time January 11, 1937; Times (London) Literary Supplement October 25, 1934; Yale Review Summer 1935.

VERHAEREN, ÉMILE (May 21, 1855-November 27, 1916), Belgian poet, was born in the old Flemish town of Saint Amand, near Antwerp, the son of a retired cloth merchant. A frail, sickly child, Émile was brought up in a Catholic milieu. After attending the Saint Amand school he was sent to Brussels in 1866 to continue his studies at the Institut Saint-Louis, and, three years later, to the College Saint-Barbe, the Jesuit school at Ghent. But Émile was chiefly interested in poetry, and spent most of his

time reading Hugo, Lamartine, and Musset, and discussing technique with his classmate Rodenbach, the gifted poet.

Rejecting his parents' plea that he study for the priesthood, Émile upon returning home in 1874 became an apprentice in his uncle's oil factory in Bock. His unfitness amply demonstrated after a year's time, he was sent to study law at the University of Louvain. During his six years there (1875-81) he became a prominent figure in that precursory ferment which later led to the "Flemish Renaissance"; he joined the philosophical and literary societies and edited a little magazine, *La Semaine*, in which his first work appeared. On finishing his law course, Verhaeren was admitted to the bar and joined the law offices of Edmond Picard in Brussels. Picard, himself a writer of note, soon discovered Verhaeren's talent, and before long Verhaeren became an influential figure in the "Young Belgium" group led by Picard and Lemonnier and comprising such gifted writers as Eekhoud, Rodenbach and Mockel. Verhaeren contributed to *La Jeune Belgique, L'Art Moderne*, and helped found the vanguard journal *Societé Nouvelle*. His first collection of poems, *Les Flammandes*, appeared in 1883.

These feverish days of literary bohemia, together with financial worries, proved detrimental to Verhaeren's health. Suffering from dyspepsia and neurasthenia, he was obliged to leave Belgium and for six years traveled in France, Spain, Italy, and England. In 1888 his parents died and more than ever Verhaeren sought for some steady ideal in life. This he found in 1891, the year of his marriage, when he turned to Socialism. Verhaeren had observed the industrial development of Belgium and its political and economical crises punctuated by strikes, hunger, and repressions. Wishing to help the working class, he offered his services to the Socialist leader Émile Vandervelde and was assigned to organize the cultural section of the House of the People. In the years 1893-98 Verhaeren wrote such outstanding works as *Les Compagnes Hallucinées, Les Villes Tentaculaires,* and the four-act drama *The Dawn,* all inspired by the labor movement. The first decade of the twentieth century bore his ripest fruit, the poetical trilogy *Les Forces Tumultueses* (1902), *La Mul-*

tiple Splendeur (1906), and *Les Rythmes Souverains* (1910), in which the poet sang the manifold powers of contemporary life with an exuberance surpassed not even by Whitman.

During the war Verhaeren defended his country in such works as *Belgium's Agony* (1915), *Parmi les Cendres* (1916), and *Villes Meurtries de Belgique* (1916). In November 1916, as he was boarding a train in Rouen to carry on his propaganda work in Norway, he fell from the platform as the engine pulled off and was instantly crushed to death. Saint-Amand was then occupied by the Germans and he had to be buried in Adinkerque, within range of gun-fire, only to be transferred soon after to Wulveringhen. Finally in 1927 the Belgian Government brought his remains to Saint-Amand.

Verhaeren had a bony, Gothic face and a huge drooping moustache; and he was said to have had at least two decidedly German characteristics—a heaviness of thought and expression and a lack of a sense of humor. He wrote with his native Flemish strength and violence, but because he used an essentially fragile medium, French, many of the power effects—as well as that rare quality of chiaroscuro—were lost. His poetry was a forerunner of much that followed, notably in the work of Jules Romains. According to Dargan and Nitze, Verhaeren was "a far greater artist than Whitman." "A large, supple, and well-adapted vocabulary; a dramatic terseness of speech; a gift of imaginative recreation and patheistic fervor; a resounding energy which often reaches poetic ecstasy—these things make Verhaeren a genuine lyrist."

WORKS AVAILABLE IN ENGLISH TRANSLATION: The Dawn, 1898; Poems, 1899; Belgium's Agony, 1915; Sunlit Hours, 1916; Plays (The Dawn, The Cloister, Philip II, Helen of Sparta) 1916; Afternoon, 1917; An Aesthetic Interpretation of Belgium's Past, 1917; Five Tales, 1924.

ABOUT: de Bersaucourt, A. Émile Verhaeren; Corell, A. F. Contribution of Verhaeren to Modern French Lyric Poetry; Fontaine, A. Verhaeren et Son Ouvre; Gosse, E. W. French Profiles; Gourmont, R. de. Book of Masks; Huxley, A. On the Margin; Lowell, A. Six French Poets; Rosenfeld, P. Men Seen; Turquet-Milnes, G. Some Modern Belgian Writers; Zweig, A. Émile Verhaeren; Bookman February 1917; Living Age July 3, 1915; Poetry February 1917.

VERONA, GUIDO DA (1881-1939), Italian novelist, was born at Saliceto Panaro near Modena, of a noble and well-to-do family. Later he lived at Milan, pursued university studies somewhat indolently, and studied law at the University of Genoa to please his mother, who wished him to have a diploma. Students were not compelled to attend courses here; even so, only the leniency of the faculty enabled Verona to pass. After doing military service in the cavalry, young Verona was free at twenty to follow his own pleasant devices. He lived at night, slept by day, and regarded the principality of Monte Carlo as his spiritual home. His social popularity was enhanced by a tall, elegant figure, a pleasant voice, and black hair brushed straight back. Verona preferred hotels to his mother's home; was particularly attracted to Paris; and traveled also in England, Germany, Austria, Switzerland, and Spain. With all this social life and travel, he was nevertheless a scrupulous writer who always carried trunkfuls of books with him. He began to scribble verse at an early age, edited *Cavaliere Spirito Santo*, a satiric revue of his contemporaries, and his first novels, *Amore che Torna* (1908) *Colei Che Non Si Deve Amare* (1910) a romance of near-incest, and *La Donna Che Invento l'Amore* (1912) showed the influence of d'Annunzio.

La Vita Incomincia Domani, translated as *La Vie Commence Demain*, was serialized in the *Revue de Paris* in 1919, and dealt with a positivist who rid himself of a troublesome person who desired a suicide's death, and had some consequent pangs of conscience. Verona's most popular and best-selling novel, *Mimi Bluette: Fleur de Mon Jardin*, which begins as a *conte licencieux* and ends as an idyll, came out in 1918, the year in which the First World War ended, and was read by everybody, women, citizens, and soldiers at the front. Mimi is an Italian courtesan who frequents a Montmartre bar, and is purified by the loss of her lover in the Foreign Legion. Her adventures sold at least 50,000 copies; Verona's sales always outstripped those of either of his contemporaries, d'Annunzio or Fogazzaro. Verona's gift of animating crowds suggests Manzoni; his exuberant, rich vitality is best expressed by the untranslatable Italian term *rigoglio:* the fullness of life suggested by the uprush of sap in plants. Verona died at fifty-eight in the year of the outbreak of the Second World War.

WORKS AVAILABLE IN ENGLISH TRANSLATION: Life Begins Tomorrow, 1923; The Woman Who Invented Love, 1928; Mimi Bluette, 1929.

ABOUT: Revue de Paris January-February 1919; Revue des Deux Mondes July 1, 1918.

"VESTAL, STANLEY." See CAMPBELL, W. C.

VIÉLÉ, EGBERT LUDOVICUS (May 26, 1863-November 12, 1937), American-French poet who signed his works "Francis Viélé-Griffin," was  born in Norfolk, Va., where his father, General E. L. Viele, was Federal military governor during the Civil War. (The elder Viele also drew up the original plans for New York's Central Park.) He was of pure Huguenot descent on both sides, but his family had lived in the United States for eight generations. In 1872 he was taken to France, and never returned. He wrote only in French, he married a Frenchwoman (Marie Louis Brocklé Bon de Grangeneuve), and his four daughters all married Frenchmen, but he never gave up his American citizenship. He was educated at the Collège Stanislas, Paris, and the Sorbonne, and studied law, then art, but gave both up for poetry under the influence of Verlaine and Mallarmé. His first publication was in 1885, and was in conventional meter, but he soon began writing free verse, and before long was one of the leaders of the Symbolist school of poetry.

Viélé-Griffin, as he was always known, is considered one of the great poets of France. In his lifetime he was awarded the Legion of Honor, saw his bust in the Luxembourg, and was elected to the Belgian Academy. The *Mercure de France* (of which he was an editor) published his collected works in four volumes from 1924 to 1927. He lived at Amboise, Touraine, where he grew grapes; and for a short time in earlier years he was in the automobile business; but the main occupation of his life was poetry. His play, *Phocas le Jardinier (Phocas the Gardener)* was produced in Paris in 1920. He was one of the founders of the Mallarmé Academy and of the review, *Entretiens Politiques et Littéraires (Literary and Political Conversations)*. The only reason he was not a member of the French Academy was that he would have had to give up his citizenship in the United States. In later years he lived like a patriarch in a villa at Bergerac, in the Dordogne, where he died in his seventy-fifth year. His elder brother, Herman Knickerbacker Viélé (1856-1908), who remained in America, attained a moderate reputation as a novelist in the early years of the century. (The father used no accents in spelling his name; Herman used one; and Egbert two!)

Albert Feuillerat called him a philosophical poet, who believed in "the mystical value of life" and wrote of it with "genuine limpidity" and "elastic, overflowing joy." Daniel Mornet said: "His poetry is at once dreamy and vigorous, elliptical and clear, and it seems . . . to be one of the Symbolist works which will escape oblivion."

Isolated poems by Viélé-Griffin have been translated into English, but there is no English volume of his verse.

ABOUT: Cours, J. F. V. de. Viélé-Griffin: Son Oeuvre, Sa Pensee, Son Art; Mornet, D. Contemporary French Literature; Literary Digest January 30, 1926; Mercure de France June 1, 1926, December 1, 15, 1937, February 1, 1938; Saturday Review of Literature August 8, 1931.

"VIÉLÉ-GRIFFIN, FRANCIS." See VIÉLÉ, E. L.

VIETH VON GOLSSENAU, ARNOLD FRIEDRICH (April 22, 1889-), German novelist who publishes under the pseudonym of "Ludwig Renn," writes (in English) from Mexico: "I was born in Dresden. My father on his mother's side was of Irish descent. On his father's side he came from a line of big land-owners and officers. He  left this to become a professor of mathematics and physics. My mother, of a Russian-German family, was raised in Moscow. As a child I was very anaemic, both mentally and physically; my attendance at school was quite irregular until I was eleven years old. At this time I was taken to Italy for my health and for the first time in my life I felt better. Returning to Germany, I attended a higher school until I was twenty. At sixteen I had suddenly taken a turn for the better, both physically and mentally, and became very much absorbed in the arts, especially painting and architecture.

"At twenty, according to the tradition of my family and friends, I entered the army. I went to an Officers' School in Hanover, and was made an officer in 1911. Until 1914 I attended all the functions of the Saxon Royal Court, and became a personal friend of the Crown Prince of Saxony. In 1914 I visited the Scandinavian countries and was deeply impressed by the democratic spirit I found there. I had previously been not only under Prussian military influence, but also under that of the smooth and hopeless literature of the time.

"I went into the war and was soon made chief of the company, and a short time after, adjutant of my regiment. I was nearly always in the front. The conditions of the war and the loss of many friends changed me considerably, especially after the Battle of the Somme, in 1916, when I ceased to drink. I had also begun to write, and at this time found my simple, functional style, which was influenced by the travel tales of Sven Hedin and by the report of Captain Semenov on the Russo-Japanese War. I was wounded twice.

"When the war ended, I was used by the higher officers to influence the simple soldiers, since I had their confidence. This, very much against my will, involved me in intrigues. I couldn't withdraw from this situation without deciding to go left or right. I decided on the left, and was selected by the soldiers as chief of a revolutionary battalion. I thus came into touch with the Social Democrats, but found there so much indecisiveness and treachery that I was repulsed for years from political action. After a short time in the service of the police, I took leave and studied economics and the Russian language in Göttingen and Munich.

"In 1922 the inflation robbed me of my income, so I became the private secretary of a commercial art society. Two years later I retired to a small village to finish my book, *Krieg (War)*, for which at first I couldn't find a publisher. I got the adventurous idea of taking a hiking trip through Italy and Greece. In Italy I met a shoemaker who spoke many languages; we went together to Rome, where we lived for some time in the Catholic Home for German Artisans. I saw in Italy the Fascist system which I had hated before, and now I grew more and more fanatically against it. We hiked through Southern Italy, Greece, and part of Turkey, voyaged to Egypt, and returned through Sicily to Germany. I felt angry about the narrow spirit of my native town, so I went immediately to Vienna, where I studied the history of art in the university. There reading and observation made me a Communist. I returned to Germany and joined the workers' movement.

"In 1928, my book was at last published. In a few weeks I was so well known that I fled this extreme publicity and went to Berlin. In 1929 and 1930 I visited Russia and the Caucasus. Soon after my second book, *Nach Krieg (After War)* was pub-

lished, then *Russland-Fahrten (Travels in Russia)*, which was immediately suppressed by a boycott under Prussian nationalistic leadership. In this period I studied military science intensely and taught war history in the Marxist Workers' School in Berlin. For this teaching I was put in jail in 1932, but was soon released. On the night of the Reichstag fire, I was seized again and punished with two and a half years of prison, under a pretext. After I came out, I escaped to Switzerland in 1936, and wrote my book *Tod Ohne Schlacht (Death Without Battle)*. Just after this I went to Spain, and entered the Loyalist Army, first as chief of the Thaelmann Battalion and then as chief of staff of the Eleventh International Brigade. In 1937 I was sent to the Americas on a lecture tour, returned in 1938, and was with the army until 1939, when I was interned at the frontier in a French concentration camp. After being released I lived illegally in Paris and wrote the book *Warfare: The Relation of War to Society*. From there I went to England and then came to Mexico, where I wrote a book about the Saxon Royal Court. Then I went to Morelia, Michocan, Mexico, where I am teaching in the University of San Nicolas. After the downfall of Hitler, I hope to return to my native Germany. I am unmarried."

* * *

"Ludwig Renn's" stark, bare style marked him originally as one of the New Objectivist German writers, whose aim (to quote P. Beaumont Wadsworth) was *"reportage of life, in which the author . . . sometimes achieves a remarkable effect of reality by this sort of super-simplicity."* George Shuster called his series of autobiographical novels "the most masterly of books about the war."

WORKS AVAILABLE IN ENGLISH: War, 1929; After War, 1931; Death Without Battle, 1937; Warfare: The Relation of War to Society (nonfiction) 1939.

ABOUT: Bookman June-July 1932.

*VILLARD, OSWALD GARRISON (March 13, 1872-), American editor, was born in Wiesbaden, Germany, but both his parents were American citizens. His father, Henry Villard (originally Heinrich Hilgard), was a naturalized American, the owner and editor of the New York *Evening Post*; his mother had been Fanny Garrison, daughter of William Lloyd Garrison, the Abolitionist. Mr. Villard was educated at Harvard (B.A. 1893, M.A. 1896), and has honorary doctorates from Washington and Lee, Lafayette, the University of Oregon, and Howard University. In 1894-95 he was assistant in United States history at Harvard, then for a year he was a reporter on the Philadelphia *Press*. In 1897 he became an editorial writer on his father's paper, remaining (finally as editor and president of the board) until 1918, when the *Post* was sold. He retained ownership of the weekly *Nation* (which had been part of the *Post*), made it over into one of the two leading liberal magazines of the country, and served as editor to 1932. The magazine was then sold, but he remained as

publisher and contributing editor for three years more, and did not sever all connections with it until 1940, when he resigned because of a disagreement in policy. (He remained a pacifist, and the journal did not.) Until 1935 he was also the owner of the *Nautical Gazette*, but never assumed active management of it.

In 1903 Mr. Villard married Julia Breckenridge Sandford, and they have two sons and a daughter. He has lectured much and traveled widely; as recently as 1939 he spent three months in Germany in wartime. "A stubborn, honest, liberal journalist" is as good a descriptive phrase to apply to Mr. Villard as any; he has earned his right to each of the adjectives. If he sometimes displays what Max Lerner called "the absolutism of the crusader for lost causes," he has always been a fair fighter, forthright and indefatigable. "The key to his career as an insurgent and innovator," Robert L. Duffus remarked, "probably lies largely in his reverence for the past." He has not a little of the spirit which marked and upheld his famous grandfather, tempered by the public liberalism and private conservatism of his father. As Robert Morss Lovett has said, his is "a long, almost unexampled career of public service."

PRINCIPAL WORKS: John Brown: A Biography Fifty Years After, 1910; Germany Embattled, 1915; Newspapers and Newspaper Men, 1923; Prophets True and False, 1928; The German Phoenix, 1933; Fighting Years: Memoirs of a Liberal Editor, 1939; Within Germany (English title: Inside Germany) 1940; Lincoln on the Eve of '61 (ed., with H. Villard) 1941.

ABOUT: Villard, O. G. Fighting Years; American Mercury December 1927, June 1939; Christian Century April 26, 1939; Independent March 24, 1928; Nation April 15, 1939, February 10, July 20,

July 27, 1940; New Republic April 26, 1939; Outlook March 6, 1929; Survey Graphic January 1940; Time January 20, 1940.

VILLIERS, ALAN JOHN (September 23, 1903-), Australian, sea writer, writes: "Alan Villiers was born in Melbourne. Educated at state schools and at the Essendon High School, Melbourne, he went to sea at the age of fifteen as cadet in the barque 'Rothesay Bay.' He sailed for five years in various square-rigged ships in the Cape Horn trade. In 1923 and

1924 he was a member of the Norwegian, Carl Anton Larsen's pioneer modern whaling expedition to the Ross Sea. After this he was employed in journalism, on the Hobart, Tasmania, *Mercury*, for three years, leaving this to return to the sea in the Finnish four-masted barque 'Herzogin Cecilie.' Later he served in the Finnish full-rigged ship 'Grace Harwar,' and in conjunction with the Åland Islander, Captain Ruben de Cloux, bought the famous four-masted barque 'Parma.' This ship he sailed successfully in the Australian grain trade for several years after 1930, winning the grain race for surviving windjammers two years in succession, in 1932 and 1933, with passages of 103 and 83 days from South Australia to the English Channel. In 1934, selling out of the 'Parma,' he bought the full-rigged ship 'Georg Stage' from the Danish Government at Copenhagen. Renaming her the 'Joseph Conrad,' he sailed her from Ipswich, England, 60,000 miles around the world with a crew largely consisting of young cadets. This was in 1934-36. The 'Joseph Conrad' was sold to American registry at the conclusion of this voyage, and later became a schoolship for the American merchant service.

"In 1938, Alan Villiers went to Arabia to sail with the Arabs in their deep-sea dhows, in order to learn at first hand about these ancient vessels and old methods of navigation. During 1938 and 1939 he sailed in the Red Sea and down to Tanganyika and Zanzibar, afterwards spending a season pearling in the Persian Gulf.

"He began writing in 1929 with *Falmouth for Orders* [actually this was his second book], which was an account of the race between the 'Herzogin Cecilie' and the 'Beatrice' from Australia to England in 1928. He followed this with other books of the sea,

including several for younger readers. He
is an occasional contributor to magazines,
and has lectured extensively in America and
elsewhere. His hobbies are photography and
flying, and he has been an internationally
licensed air pilot for many years."

* * *

In 1924 Mr. Villiers was married to
Daphne Kay Harris; they were divorced in
1936. They had no children. He is a handsome blond man with wavy light hair. Lincoln Colcord said of him: "No one loves a
sailing ship better or writes of her more
faithfully." In 1942 he was in the British
Navy, doing anti-aircraft work.

PRINCIPAL WORKS: Whaling in the Frozen
South, 1926; Falmouth for Orders, 1929; By Way
of Cape Horn, 1930; Grain Race, 1932; Last of
the Windships, 1934; Vanished Fleets, 1936; Cruise
of the Conrad, 1937; Stormalong (juvenile) 1937;
Making of a Sailor, 1938; Joey Goes to Sea (juvenile) 1939; Sons of Sinbad, 1940.

ABOUT: Villiers, A. Falmouth for Orders (see
Introduction by F. C. Bowen), Grain Race, Cruise
of the Conrad; Rotarian August 1938; Time April
12, 1937; Travel February 1940.

VIZETELLY, FRANK HORACE (April
2, 1864-December 20, 1938). Anglo-American lexicographer, editor and author, was

Apeda

born in London, Eng-
land, becoming a nat-
uralized American
citizen in 1926. He
was youngest of the
seven sons of Henry
Richard Vizetelly and
Elizabeth Anne (An-
sell) Vizetelly, and
was educated at
the Lycée Baudard,
Nogent-sur-Marne,
France, and at Arnold College, Eastbourne,
Sussex. Honorary doctor's degrees came
after he had established himself as an authority on pronunciation, spelling, and neologisms in the United States, St. John's College at Annapolis, Md., awarding him an
LL.D. and the University of Maryland Department of Philosophy following suit (a
term which he would approve). In June
1894 Vizetelly married Bertha M. Krehbiel
of New York City.

Most of his working life after 1891,
when he came to America, was spent in association with the Funk & Wagnalls Co.,
publishers of the once hugely prosperous and
now defunct *Literary Digest,* and the present
Standard Dictionary, chief and liberal rival
of Noah Webster and his successors. Vizetelly was associate editor of the dictionary
from 1891 to 1903, managing editor from

1908 to 1913, and editor from 1914 to the
day of his death at seventy-four. As office
editor he supervised the publication of more
than two hundred and fifty miscellaneous publications in English, public speaking, mental efficiency, psychoanalysis, medicine, history, and travel. As conductor of
"The Lexicographer's Easy Chair" in the
Literary Digest, broadcaster over several
radio networks, dean of the Columbia
Broadcasting System Pronunciation School
(1930-31) and court of last resort for American newspapers, he wielded an influence
much more direct and popular, in this country at least, than his British colleague H. W.
Fowler[qv] and the latter's brothers. Vizetelly
recorded with pride that he was the surviving editor of Vizetelly and Co., long-time
publishers in London (who got into trouble
by publishing Zola); was the only civilian
permitted to visit the Boer detention camps
in Bermuda September 22, 1901; was a
Knight of the Order of Francis Joseph of
Austria-Hungary; and a life member of St.
George's Society.

A handsome old man, despite one imperfect eye, Vizetelly made his home in the
Bronx, New York. After a three-weeks'
illness with pneumonia and pleurisy, he died
at the Fifth Avenue Hospital. He was seventy-four.

PRINCIPAL WORKS: The Preparation of Manu-
scripts for the Printer, 1905; A Desk-Book of
Errors in English, 1906; Essentials of English
Speech and Literature, 1915; A Desk-Book of
Twenty-Five Thousand Words Frequently Mis-
pronounced, 1917; Words We Misspell in Busi-
ness, 1921; A Desk-Book of Idioms and Idiomatic
Phrases in English Speech and Literature, 1923;
How To Use English, 1932; How To Speak Effec-
tively, 1933.

ABOUT: New York Times December 22-25,
1938.

*VOLLMER, LULA, American dramatist,
writes: "I was born about eight miles from
Southern Pines, N.C. My early years were
spent roaming over
the South. My fa-
ther was a lumber-
man, and wherever
he cut timber, if
home quarters were
possible, he took his
family with him. In
my eighth year I was
sent to boarding-
school. I had to do
something while I
was shut up to study, so I began to write
stories. I was punished on several occasions
when short but lurid tales were found in my
desk. Through my adolescent years I attend-

Kesslere

ed a strict religious school [Normal Collegiate Institute, Asheville, N.C.]. There the theatre was not considered a part of our education, but in our English classes we were allowed to act scenes from Shakespeare. That gave me an idea. I began to write one-act plays in which I rehearsed my classmates. These efforts we produced in the gymnasium, always at a safe hour when the teachers were at dinner. When I was eighteen my parents took me to New Orleans for my Christmas holiday. I saw my first professional play. It was a melodrama called *The Curse of Drink*. I decided to spend the rest of my life writing plays.

"After finishing school I got a job as reporter on a weekly newspaper at five dollars a week. I considered my services worth much more and kept moving from one job to another until I landed in a hotel as auditor. There I figured all day and wrote on plays at night. Hopefully I would send my manuscripts to New York. They would come back. A small success bolstered my confidence: a condensed version of one of my plays was sold for a vaudeville sketch.

"I scrimped and saved my money. When I had put by a few hundred dollars I gave up my job and came to New York. My first year's writing netted me ten dollars and the finished manuscript of *Sunup*. (The play was written within a week's time, but it took me five years to sell it.) My money was gone. I went home and told my mother that I had failed. After a long pause, she said 'You went to New York to write, didn't you?' 'Yes, Mother.' 'Then I would do it.' She gave me the money to come back. I got a job as ticket-seller in the Theatre Guild box-office. During my off hours I went on writing and completed a play called *The Shame Woman*. Toward the end of my third year at the Theatre Guild Miss Alice Kauser bought and produced *Sunup*. In October of that year, 1923, *The Shame Woman* was produced.

"Having had a taste of poverty in New York, and not knowing how long my good fortune would last, I wanted to keep my job in the box-office, but Theresa Helburn, executive director of the Theatre Guild, said she did not want a girl in the box-office who had had two successful plays on Broadway, so she fired me. I am glad to have had the experience of working in an office, and of selling theatre tickets, but I hope I don't have to do either again."

* * *

Miss Vollmer's plays are all pictures of North Carolina mountain life. Productions of *Sunup* in Chicago, London, Amsterdam, Paris, and Budapest raised over $40,000 for educational work among the mountaineers. From 1930 to 1933 she wrote a sustaining program, "Moonshine and Honeysuckle," for the National Broadcasting Company; in 1934 she had another serial, "Grits and Gravy," and from 1935 to 1937 "The Widow's Sons." In 1934 she went to Hollywood as a script writer, and says she "was miserable out there. They not only told me how to write, but what to write." She lives now in Greenwich Village, in New York City, and is unmarried.

PRINCIPAL WORKS: (dates of production)— Sunup, 1923; The Shame Woman, 1923; The Dunce Boy, 1925; Trigger, 1937; Sentinels, 1931; In a Nut-Shell, 1937; The Hill Between, 1938.

ABOUT: Lowe, O. Our Land and Its Literature; Quinn, A. H. History of American Drama From the Civil War to the Present Day; Tucker, S. M. Modern American and British Plays; North American Review January 1924; Scribner's Magazine July 1924.

VON GOLSSENAU. See VIETH VON GOLSSENAU

VON HEIDENSTAM. See HEIDENSTAM

VON HOFMANNSTHAL. See HOFMANNSTAHL

VON HORVATH. See HORVATH

VON KEYSERLING. See KEYSERLING

VORSE, MRS. MARY MARVIN (HEATON) American novelist and labor journalist, writes: "Mary Heaton Vorse was educated abroad. She began as an art student, but her interest swerved to writing. She married Albert White Vorse, editor, writer, and music critic; married (2) Joseph O'Brien, newspaper man and author. She has three children. In  1915 she was a war correspondent, covering the effect of war on civil populations for various magazines. Did pamphlets on the rights of small nations—Poland, Czecho-Slovakia, Jugo-Slavia—for Committee of Public Information. Overseas member of the Red Cross in 1918 and 1919. Served in France, Italy, and the Balkan Commission. In 1919 she was briefly with the American Relief Administration, writing on the condition of children under blockade in Central Europe. She has written widely on European affairs; contributed articles to *Harper's Magazine* on post-war conditions in Europe, reported Russian famine in 1921 and 1922 for the Hearst papers. She has done much work as foreign correspondent for various magazines, varying in interest from a series of articles for *Harper's* on North Africa, and a series of articles on the Montessori Method, to the London Economic Conference. She covered the first phases of the Hitler régime in 1933. She wrote a series of pre-war articles for syndicates and magazines, and covered the first phases of the present war. She has held several government publicity positions, including those in wartime and for the Committee of Public Information, and was for a year and a half in the Indian Bureau, Department of the Interior. For the past twenty-five years she has specialized in the situation of labor and has reported labor conditions for various magazines and periodicals."

* * *

This bare account hardly hints at a full, romantic, and adventurous life, selflessly devoted to the cause of the underdog. Mary Heaton Vorse was born in New York as Mary Marvin Heaton and reared in Amherst, Mass. She had a son and a daughter by her first husband, whom she married in 1898 and whose name she has since used as a writer. After his death she married Mr. O'Brien in 1912, and they had a son. She was left a widow a second time, and in 1920 married Robert Minor, the well known radical artist and writer; they were divorced two years later. Mrs. Vorse has lived for many years in Provincetown, Mass., and was one of the founders of the famous Provincetown Players. The place that Provincetown, of which she is so much a part, holds in her affections is indicated by her reminiscent chronicle, *Time and the Town* (1942). At one time she conducted a Montessori School there. She is one of the best living authorities on the labor movement in America, and has reported almost every big strike since 1912.

Her first writing was done on the *Criterion*, in New York, and her earlier stories and articles were light. She found her true *forte* in 1912 in the Lawrence (Mass.) textile strike, and since *Men and Steel* the labor struggle has figured largely in her life and work. She is noted for her kindness and

helpfulness to young writers, and among her "discoveries" was Sinclair Lewis. She has been shot during a strike and has many times risked her life. She is a great-hearted woman whose passion for justice sometimes obscures from the reader the fact that she is also a skillful and powerful writer. Harold Stearns called her work "packed with tenderness and a quiet bitterness, like sugar and vinegar."

PRINCIPAL WORKS: The Breaking In of a Yachtsman's Wife, 1908; The Very Little Person, 1911; The Autobiography of an Elderly Woman, 1911; The Heart's Country, 1913; The Ninth Man, 1918; The Prestons, 1918; I've Come To Stay, 1919; Growing Up, 1920; Men and Steel, 1921; Fraycar's Fist (short stories) 1923; Passaic, 1926; Second Cabin, 1928; Strike—A Novel of Gastonia, 1930; Footnote to Folly (autobiography) 1935; Labor's New Millions, 1938; Time and the Town, 1942.

ABOUT: Vorse, M. H. Footnote to Folly, Time and the Town; Nation January 15, 1936; Time December 23, 1935.

VOTO. See DE VOTO

WADDELL, HELEN JANE (May 31, 1889-), Irish mediaevalist and translator, was born in Tokyo, where her father, the Rev. Hugh Waddell, was a Presbyterian missionary. Both her parents were of Northern Irish birth, and had for many years been missionaries in Japan and Manchuria. They returned to Belfast for her schooling, and she was educated at Victoria College and Queen's University, both in that city. Besides her M.A. from Queen's University, she has honorary doctorates from Belfast, Durham, St. Andrews, and Columbia—the last acquired when she visited New York in 1935. She received the A.C. Benson Silver Medal of the Royal Society of Literature in 1927, and has been a member of the Irish Academy of Letters since 1932. From 1920 to 1922 she taught Latin at Somerville College, Oxford, during 1921 also being Cassell Lecturer for St. Hilda's Hall, Oxford. The following year she lectured at Bedford College, London. She then was awarded the Susette Taylor Fellowship from Lady Margaret Hall, Oxford, and spent the next two years studying and writing in Paris. She was made a corresponding fellow of the Mediaeval Academy of America in 1937. For the past fifteen years she has devoted herself almost entirely to writing. She is unmarried, and lives

Boals

sometimes in Belfast and sometimes in London. She is an active, energetic, outdoor type of woman, with short gray wavy hair and a mobile face—not at all the austere scholar in appearance. She is retiring and dislikes personal publicity, so that little is known of her private life.

A scholar she is, however, and a very fine one. Her special field is mediaeval Latin literature, and most of her books are translations from the Latin prose and verse of the Middle Ages (beginning with the Silver Age of classical Latin) or studies of mediaeval scholars and writers. Her only novel grew directly out of her scholarly interests, being a reconstruction in fiction of the immortal love affair of Abelard and Heloïse. She has also translated from the Chinese (she speaks and reads both Chinese and Japanese), and translated the Abbé Prévost's *Manon Lescaut* in 1931, besides writing a study of its author two years later. Though she has translated into metrical form hundreds of Latin poems, she has published none of her own. More than one critic has found, indeed, that in her metrical translations lies her chief weakness. Padraic Colum, who calls her "an exceptional scholar," adds that she had not "the finesse in diction and in rhythm" needed for poetic versions of verse originals; and D. S. Mirsky, who admires her perspective and her historical sense, says: "Her prose translations are admirable, but the metrical versions for the most part are inadequate." He considers that they lack fidelity to the original, are vague, prudish, and sentimental; and he wonders that she should be attracted to the writings of the lusty wandering scholars (the goliards) of the Middle Ages, when her own taste is so "over-delicate."

Her novel and her biographical studies, however, are of absorbing interest, and, as Marie Shields Halvey remarked, "she has delved deeply into the history and learning of the Middle Ages"—a rich field in which there are remarkably few representatives among the scholars of this or former eras.

PRINCIPAL WORKS: Lyrics From the Chinese (translated) 1913; The Wandering Scholars, 1927; Mediaeval Latin Lyrics (translated) 1929; John of Salisbury in Essays and Studies, 1929; A Book of Mediaeval Latin for schools, 1931; Peter Abelard (novel) 1933; The Abbé Prévost, 1933; Beasts and Saints (translations of Latin folk-stories) 1934; The Desert Fathers, 1936.

ABOUT: Commonweal September 17, 1937; London Mercury August 1927.

WADE, ARTHUR SARSFIELD. See "ROHMER, S."

WAITE, ARTHUR EDWARD (October 2, 1857-May 19, 1942), Anglo-American occultist, wrote to the editors of this volume shortly before his death: "I was born at Brooklyn, N.Y. My father, Charles Frederick Waite, came of unmixed Connecticut stock and was himself born at Lyme. He was descended in a direct line from the regicide John Wayte. Some or  many who bore the name fled at the Restoration and found a haven in New England. My father as a boy probably ran away to sea. In any case, he was later in command of sailing ships, some of which were also passenger boats. When I was less than a year old he died and was buried at sea. My sister was a posthumous child.

"My mother had been Emma Lovell, an Englishwoman. The loss of her husband, who left next to nothing, took my mother to Lyme. But Lyme was impossible for a still young and educated Englishwoman of the upper middle class; and she made a last voyage to England accompanied by two babes. My first days in England abide in a cloud of unknowing. My mother, a Church-going woman of the Anglican type, became a Roman. Presently we drifted northward from Kentish Town, and at Highgate I served at the altar, which gave me my first love of all that belongs to rites. As days went on, I had been for brief periods at three small private day-schools, where I learned nothing. I was probably thirteen when my mother moved to Bayswater and sent me for three years to St. Charles' College, where I learned Latin and Greek and forgot most of the French she had taught me.

"When my schooling came to an end, I accepted a clerical appointment, with supposed prospects, but for me it proved narrow and dull. Between the nameless misery of this external plight and dejection at the death of my sister, it was dark night indeed about me, till a sudden change came when on a certain red-letter day I found that I could write verses. A sleeping soul awakened then within me; a hunger and thirst after glory in the craft of song possessed my whole being. For months upon months I read nothing but poems and the lives of poets. For some subsequent years there was a fever of verse upon me. Now, I know in my heart that the poet's vocation was that for which I was meant.

"At nineteen the halter of clerical work had long since removed its yoke. I began to see my way. The first path which I entered was that of psychical research. It must not be supposed that I became a convinced Spiritist, having no qualifications at that period to be assured of anything. Intellectually speaking, I had no faculty of easy belief. But I had a living interest and curiosity that centered in the claims of so-called occult sciences. And at twenty-one the British Museum opened the doors of its reading room, with the gift of a reading ticket for the rest of my natural life.

"I have now reached that point when my books must speak for themselves and my memoirs must take care of external things. Those who need may learn in their pages of my two marriages; of the growth of a poet's mind in the world of verse; of my experience in Secret Orders, including the great Masonic complex in all its rites and degrees. They may learn above all what is meant in the plenary sense by Sacramental Mysticism and its eternal distinction from the speculations and experiments of the pseudo-occult arts.

"Setting aside early efforts, translations, and things belonging to the passing moment, my books are all the work of a mystic and of one who *in spiritu humilitatis* has sought as such to find new paths therein. His work in this direction is by no means finished, and even at this great age he prays to be spared, that he may add to his studies of the Secret Tradition in Christian times one further memorial."

* * *

Mr. Waite was married in 1888 to Ada Lakeman (whom he called "Lucasta"). She died in 1924, leaving a daughter, and he married Mary Broadbent Schofield. In his youth Mr. Waite edited the *British Mail* and the *Unknown World,* wrote for the house organ of a malted milk company, and was connected with two publishing firms. He has never been in America since infancy.

In his last years he lived at Bridge Kent, near Canterbury, where in the midst of the war, and seriously ill besides with heart trouble, he continued his mystical studies and writings until his death at eighty-four. His list of published works is very long, but many of them are technical and esoteric works on Masonry and occult subjects, without interest to the general reader.

PRINCIPAL WORKS: *Poetry*—Israfel, 1886; A Soul's Comedy, 1887; Lucasta, 1890; A Book of

Mystery and Vision, 1902; Strange Houses of Sleep, 1906; Collected Poems, 1914; The Book of the Holy Grail, 1921. *Prose*—The House of the Hidden Light, 1904; Studies in Mysticism and Certain Aspects of the Secret Tradition, 1906; The Hidden Church of the Holy Grail, 1908; The Secret Tradition in Goëtia: A Book of Ceremonial Magic, 1911; The Secret Tradition in Freemasonry, 1911 (revised ed. 1937); The Secret Tradition of Israel, 1913; The Way of Divine Union, 1915; Encyclopaedia of Freemasonry, 1921; Lamps of Western Mysticism, 1923; The Brotherhood of the Rosy Cross, 1924; Emblematic Freemasonry, 1925; The Secret Tradition in Alchemy, 1926; The Quest of the Golden Stairs, 1927; The Book of Life in the Rose, 1928; The Holy Kabbalah, 1929; The Holy Grail, Its Legends and Symbolism, 1933; A Mystagogical Quintology, 1935; Shadows of Life and Thought: A Retrospective Review in the Form of Memoirs, 1938; Saint-Martin, 1939.

ABOUT: Entwistle, A. R. The Study of Poetry; Hayward, H. L. Christian Mysticism and Other Essays; Newton, J. F. The Builders; Scott, W. M. Aspects of Christian Mysticism; Voorhis, H. V. B. Arthur Edward Waite: A Check List of His Writings; Waite, A. E. Shadows of Life and Thought.

WALEY, ARTHUR, Sinologist and translator from the Chinese and Japanese, was born in London, his name originally being Arthur David Schloss. He was educated at Rugby and at King's College, Cambridge, and has an honorary LL.D. from Aberdeen University. He is one of the most retiring men on earth, a typical scholar, whose real life is spent among his books and documents and about whose personality the public knows practically nothing. He does vouchsafe the information that his favorite recreation is, rather surprisingly, skiing; and he is unmarried and lives in London. From 1912 to 1930 he was Assistant Keeper of the Department of Prints and Drawings in the British Museum, and since that time he has been Additional Lecturer in its School of Oriental Studies. Aside from this information, all that is known of him is through his works. Even the circumstances which first aroused his interest in the literature of China and Japan are unknown, though it is obvious that he has spent much time in both countries. He is probably the chief living authority on Oriental literature, and his translations of Chinese lyrics especially have the rank of authentic poetry in their own right.

He has come most to general attention through his translation of the long Japanese novel, *The Tale of Genji,* by the Lady Murasaki, a court lady of the late tenth and early eleventh century. This classic of Japanese literature, sometimes called the oldest novel in the world, provides an invaluable picture of aristocratic life in Nippon nearly a thousand years ago. It has been compared to the novels of Samuel Richardson, but is far less Puritanical than the work of that worthy pioneer Western novelist. Unconscionably long, much of it is dull reading except to the scholarly minded, but on the other hand much of it is of very lively interest. Mr. Waley (he has adopted this name in private life as well as in his writings) translated the whole of it into masterly English, in six volumes in the English edition, five in the American. He has also translated another classic of the same era, the "pillow book." or commonplace-book, of another court lady, Sei Shōnagon, a delightfully naïve and yet acute work. Latterly he has turned his attention to Oriental philosophy, and has written two books on it besides translating and editing the *Analects* of Confucius. He has also written on the Japanese Nō plays and has translated Japanese poems. But probably the work which will longest keep his name alive is his series of incomparable translations of Chinese lyrics of the great historical eras, of which he has already published five volumes, the first appearing in 1918. The quality of these translations may be judged from the fact that many of the poems have first been published, in the same manner as original poems in English, by *Poetry* and special and general magazines of similar rank.

PRINCIPAL WORKS: 170 Chinese Poems, 1918; Japanese Poetry: The "Uta," 1919; More Translations From the Chinese, 1919; The Nō Plays of Japan, 1921; An Introduction to the Study of Chinese Painting, 1923; The Temple and Other Poems, 1923; The Tale of Genji: 1. The Tale of Genji, 1925; 2. The Sacred Tree, 1926; 3. A Wreath of Cloud, 1927; 4. Blue Trousers, 1928; 5. The Lady of the Boat, 1932; Poems From the Chinese, 1927; The Pillow Book of Sei Shōnagon, 1928; The Travels of an Alchemist, 1931; The Way and Its Power, 1935; The Book of Songs, 1937; The Analects of Confucius, 1938; Three Ways of Thought in Ancient China, 1939.

WALKLEY, ARTHUR BINGHAM (December 17, 1855-October 8, 1926), English dramatic critic and essayist, was born at Bed-

K. Shackleton

minster, Bristol, only child of Arthur Hickman Walkley, a bookseller, and Caroline Charlotte (Bingham) Walkley. He attended Warminster School and Balliol College, Oxford, entering October 1873 and being admitted as scholar of Corpus Christi College the next January; he took honors in mathematics. In June 1877 Walkley be-

came a third-class clerk in the secretary's office of the General Post Office, rising in course of time to principal clerk. In 1911 he was made assistant secretary in charge of the telegraph branch. As delegate, Walkley attended postal congresses in Washington and Rome. He was superannuated in 1919, having given the British Post Office a second literary clerk (Trollope was the other). William Archer interested Walkley in dramatic criticism; he became critic of the *Star* from 1888 to 1890, then switched to the *Speaker* until it changed hands in 1899. September 21, 1899, he reviewed Beerbohm Tree's *King John* for the *Times* and next March was formally engaged as dramatic critic. Other articles were contributed to the Wednesday edition, and to the *Literary Supplement* after that was founded in 1902.

Walkley's wit and style were "firmly rooted in thought and knowledge"; critics also praised his unfailing urbanity, his trained and disciplined taste, and whimsical mellowed irony. In *Still More Prejudice* he discussed Duse, Bernhardt, Congreve, and Compulsory Ignorance, causing Edwin Seaver to end by feeling "just a bit irritated by his insistent and undifferentiated urbanity," which "deals with Duse and 'simple French cooking' in the same rhythm, evidently with the same relish."

Walkley called himself an impressionist, coming fresh and unprejudiced to each book and play; he preferred light comedy to the drama of ideas. Widely read in French literature, he liked to seem French in appearance and bearing. Fruit-growing and rock-gardening at his country home in Brightlingsea, Essex, were favored hobbies. He married Frances Eldridge in 1881, and they had one daughter.

PRINCIPAL WORKS: Playhouse Impressions, 1892; Frames of Mind. 1899; Dramatic Criticism, 1903; Drama and Life, 1907; Pastiche and Prejudice, 1921; More Prejudice, 1923; Still More Prejudice, 1925.

ABOUT: Child, H. H. The Post-Victorians; London Mercury November 1926; London Times October 9, 1926; New Statesman October 16, 1926.

WALLACE, ALFRED RUSSEL. See "BRITISH AUTHORS OF THE 19TH CENTURY"

WALLACE, EDGAR (December 1875-February 10, 1932), English journalist, dramatist, and prolific writer of "thrillers," was born at 7, Ashburnham Grove, Greenwich, the illegitimate son of Marie (known as Polly) Richards, a dancer and player of

small parts in provincial theatres, and Richard Horatio Edgar Marriott, the son of a better-known actress. The boy, named Richard Horatio Edgar Wallace (a fictitious "Walter Wallace, comedian," was entered in the birth-records as his father), was placed with a fish-porter's wife and brought up as Dick Freeman with her ten children. An affectionate, impudent, engaging child, he  sold newspapers, worked for a printing firm, in a shoe-shop, on a fishing trawler and as an errand boy, penetrating other parts of London than his native Billingsgate Market and Old Kent Road. Edgar's formal education ended at twelve, but he studied his pocket dictionary to good effect.

Enlisting for seven years as a private in the Royal West Kent Regiment, he transferred to the Medical Staff Corps and was sent to South Africa, where he contributed Kiplingesque poems to the Cape journals, later collected in *The Mission That Failed* and *Writ in Barracks*. On his discharge in 1899, he became Reuter's second correspondent, attached to Lord Methuen's Western Division. A Cape Town girl typist happened to send a dispatch of Wallace's to the London *Daily Mail*, which engaged him as correspondent. Ivy Caldecott, daughter of a Wesleyan missionary, was married to Wallace in April 1901.

Back in London, Wallace involved his paper with Lever Brothers, the soap manufacturers, in a £50,000 damage suit, followed by £5,000 awarded an aggrieved naval officer, and was discharged. The profits of *The Four Just Men*, his first best-selling novel, were eaten up by prizes offered for a solution. Isabel Thorne, fiction editor of the *Weekly Tale-Teller*, set him to writing *Sanders of the River*, stories of an African commissioner with an invented native population, residency, and native troops; and Wallace's career as one of the greatest popular entertainers of all time was suddenly launched.

He wrote, or dictated, 150 separate works in twenty-seven years, reaching new levels of the reading population and charming them with his "suspense, action, and excitement, humanized by a deft touch in characterization and an easy humor" (in the words of his best biographer, his daughter-in-law

Margaret Lane). Seventeen plays in six years brought him £100,000 profit, the best of his melodramas being: *On the Spot*, based on Al Capone, and *The Case of the Frightened Lady* (handsomely presented by Guthrie McClintic in New York as *Criminal At Large*). In 1928, when he was earning £50,000 a year, it was said that one out of every four books printed and sold in England, exclusive of Bibles and text-books, was an Edgar Wallace. He once dictated a complete novel between Friday night and Monday morning, and *On the Spot* was put on paper in four days! He had a standing offer to pay £1,000 to anyone who could prove that any of his writing was "ghosted"; the reward was never claimed.

It was not his aim, he confessed, to instruct or uplift, but simply and commercially to entertain (avoiding sex problems like the plague). The Wallace characters are two-dimensional and without depth—although his old-fashioned, spinsterish detective J. G. Reeder has a certain appeal and seems likely to outlive his other fictional creations, already half-forgotten. His autobiography, *People*, caused Edward Shanks to dub him "a lost Dickens."

Wallace was stout in later years, and with his heavy-lidded eyes appeared deceptively indolent. A thorough if sometimes naïve *poseur*, he cultivated a world-weary, supercilious expression. He was lavishly generous to and extremely jealous of all his family, especially his second wife, "Jim" (his former typist), who died not long after him. Wallace himself died suddenly at fifty-seven in Hollywood, where he had gone to produce a photoplay, of pneumonia and diabetes mellitus induced by his habit of working in superheated surroundings and drinking huge quantities of heavily sweetened tea. Rashly spendthrift, he left "Jim" and his four children an estate cumbered by debts of £150,000—roughly three-quarters of a million dollars! But two years after his death Edgar Wallace Ltd. was free of liabilities and paying dividends from accrued royalties.

PRINCIPAL WORKS: (dates of American publication): Angel Esquire, 1908; The Clue of the Twisted Candle, 1916; The Green Archer, 1924; A King by Night, The Ringer, The Terrible People, 1926; The Murder Book of J. G. Reeder, 1929; People, 1929; Sanders of the River, Mr. Commissioner Sanders, 1930; Red Aces: Being Three Cases of Mr. Reeder, 1930; On the Spot, 1931; Mr. Reeder Returns, 1932; My Hollywood Diary, 1932.

ABOUT: Curtis, R. J. Edgar Wallace: Each Way; Doran, G. Chronicles of Barabbas; Haycraft, H. Murder for Pleasure: The Life and Times of the Detective Story; Hansard, B. M.

In and Out of Fleet Street; Lane, M. Edgar Wallace: The Biography of a Phenomenon; Wallace, E. V. Edgar Wallace by His Wife; Forum March 1935; Reader's Digest May 1939.

WALLACE, "LEW." See "AMERICAN AUTHORS: 1600-1900"

WALLAS, GRAHAM (1858-August 10, 1932), English economist, was born in Sunderland, the son of Gilbert Innes Wallas,

later Vicar of Barnstaple and Rector of Shobrooke, and Frances (Talbot) Wallas. He attended Shrewsbury School from 1871 to 1877, then went up to Corpus Christi College, Oxford, leaving in 1881. Next year he first met Sidney Webb, later Lord Passfield, with whom he was to become a member of the Fabian Society five years later.

Wallas was a classical schoolmaster for several years, leaving Highgate School in 1885 "on a question of religious conformity," and becoming a university extension lecturer in 1890. From 1895 to 1923 he was a lecturer at the London School of Economics on political science. In 1896 Wallas made his first lecture tour of the United States, returning next year to marry Ada Radford, a writer, who with a daughter survived him. He returned to the United States in 1914 to deliver the Lowell Lectures at Boston, and in 1919 was Dodge Lecturer at Yale University, besides lecturing elsewhere. In a lecture (at Dartmouth College on the art of political thought) he developed the thesis that the subconscious mind and the conscious thought process were closely bound up with our sociological and political life. His ideas and theories were based on personal intensity. "Action yields fertility" in the human brain, he believed, and he contended that any stimulus, whether of direct benefit in its content or merely an intensive thought process, was food without which the brain could not get along.

"The first notion that there was a way of using your mind which was right, and another way which was wrong, came to me then [when a master at Shrewsbury read Aristotle with him]," Wallas once wrote, "and was very severely rubbed into me later on when I came under the formidable tuition of my friend Mr. Bernard Shaw." With Shaw, Wells, and the Hubert Blands, Wallas

organized the Fabian Society, of which he was a member from 1886 to 1904, serving from 1888 to 1895 as member of the executive board. The Society used the name and prestige of Socialism for a movement which was free from and often opposed to Marx's analysis of history, industry, and human motive, and which therefore influenced non-Socialist political opinion in England.

Other offices held by Wallas were a membership on the Technical Education Board for London, from 1898 to 1904, when he became a member of the London County Council for three years; and a twenty-years' tenure of office (1908-28) as member of the Senate of London University. His last visit to the United States was in 1928, when he lectured at the Williamstown Institute. Wallas died at seventy-four at Portloe, Cornwall, where he was spending a vacation.

Of *The Great Society* (1914) Gilbert Murray has written: "That book is one of the very few of which I could say that it made a permanent difference in my outlook on human conduct, and I believe Wallas' disciple, Walter Lippmann, has said the same." Wallas did not initiate any revolution in thought or become the leader of any party or movement, but was "one of the keenest and subtlest critics of the Victorian age in thought, in convention, in education, in methods of government." The serenity of nature which Murray emphasizes as part of his character was evident in his face, crowned with thick white hair and adorned by a drooping moustache.

PRINCIPAL WORKS: Fabian Essay on Property Under Socialism, 1889; Life of Francis Place, 1897; Human Nature in Politics, 1908; The Great Society, 1914; Our Social Heritage, 1921; The Art of Thought, 1926; Social Judgment, 1935; Men and Ideas, 1940.

ABOUT: Wallas, G. Men and Ideas (see Preface by G. Murray); London Times August 11, 1932; New York Times August 11, 1932.

WALLER, MARY ELLA (March 1, 1855-June 15, 1938), American novelist and essayist, was born in Boston, descended, on her father's side, from a long line of Vermonters, and on her mother's from ruddy-faced blue-eyed Cape Cod seamen. In her early years she spent part of every summer at her grandmother's white cottage in Hyannis, Cape Cod. Her father and brother died when she was twelve, and from that time on affection for and intimacy with her mother strengthened. After a four-year sojourn abroad, in Paris, The Hague, Germany, and elsewhere, she returned to teach at the Brierly School in New York. Not long afterwards she founded her own School for Girls in Chicago, but poor health forced her retirement at the end of five years.

During her final recovery from a severe illness she and her mother took "The Gate of the Hills" in the White River Valley of Vermont, and there in a land of wandering roads, evergreen, and birch she wrote at least eight books. *Little Citizens* (1902) was a quiet first attempt; but *The Wood-Carver of 'Lympus,* originally published in 1904, went into its third hundred thousand in a 1929 Anniversary Edition.

In 1910 she moved to Nantucket, and bought a home with a large ship's-cabin living-room; became considerably interested in the town's community life; and gave the royalties of one of her books to a fund for the maintainance of the island's first permanent hospital. She wrote a number of novels in the years immediately preceding the First World War. Until the Boston *Transcript* sent a reporter for an interview following the publication of her *Deep in the Hearts of Men,* she had almost entirely escaped any kind of publicity. She was, she contended, a "very quite old-fashioned person." When her last book, *The Windmill on the Dune,* appeared in 1930, she was over seventy-five. Miss Waller died in Wellesley, Mass., at the age of eighty-three, with more than twenty books to her credit.

Miss Waller was tall, slender, gracious, and poised, belonging obviously, to that comfortable New England literary tradition which found joy and beauty not in things far off, glittering, and precarious, but in things near, simple, and sure.

PRINCIPAL WORKS: Little Citizens, 1902; A Daughter of the Rich, 1903; The Wood-Carver of 'Lympus, 1904; Sanna of the Island Town, 1905; Through the Gates of the Netherlands, 1906; Our Benny, 1909; My Ragpicker, 1911; A Year Out of Life, 1911; A Cry in the Wilderness, 1912; Aunt Dorcas' Change of Heart, 1913; From an Island Outpost, 1914; Out of the Silences, 1918; Deep in the Hearts of Men, 1924; The Windmill on the Dune, 1931.

ABOUT: Waller, M. E. The Wood-Carver of 'Lympus (see Introduction to 1929 edition); Publishers' Weekly July 2, 1938; New York Times June 15, 1938.

*WALLING, ROBERT ALFRED JOHN

(1869-   ), English mystery story and travel writer and biographer, writes: "My ancestors were yeomen of Devon, with an occasional parson or missionary. My father was a well-known journalist. The family has ink in its veins: I have four brothers, two nephews, and my elder son in newspapers. I myself began working on newspapers in 1884 and am still doing it. Most of my working life has been passed in the West of England,

with short spells in London and the Midlands. For a short time I edited *Bicycling News,* and later in life I became a publisher's book editor, a highly interesting job but a little slow for my newspaper blood, and I returned to newspapers. My chief posts have been the chairs of an evening and a morning paper at Plymouth, which I held for twenty-five years, and my present one as managing editor of the *Western Independent,* a Sunday paper. I also represent the London *Times* at Plymouth.

"In a life like this books have been a side-line. I began in my youth writing short stories for the *Speaker,* and my first book was a collection of these—imitative, jejune, kail-yard stuff. In odd hours during the next few years I wrote two biographical studies, of Sir John Hawkins and George Borrow. I tried my hand at romantic serials. I had a great fondness for Brittany, spent much time there, and eventually wrote a book about it.

"I was too old for the First World War, but saw something of it from behind the lines in France and printed a collection of papers on that experience. I have traveled in Europe, the Atlantic islands, the Mediterranean, and Egypt. But the high spot of my journeyings was three months spent in a round of the United States with a dozen other British editors in 1928. I acquired a profound respect for the people which faces so cheerfully the unprecedented problems of that immense and multitudinous country.

"In 1910 I was appointed a magistrate of Plymouth, and have for some years been chairman of the Justices and of the Licensing Bench. This stimulated an already lively interest in the study of crime and its prevention. But, in the mystery stories which I began to write, almost by accident, fifteen years ago, I have refrained from introducing any element of realism. To my spirit, the realities of crime and punishment are too tragic for treatment in the airy style of the mystery story.

"To two writers especially I owe immensely for their almost lifelong friendship and counsel—Sir Arthur Quiller-Couch and Eden Phillpotts. My other unfailing counsellor and judicious critic has been my wife,

Florence Victoria Greet, whom I married in 1894. We have two sons and two daughters. My minor passions are strumming on the piano and being on the sea."

* * *

In a letter to his publishers early in 1942, Mr. Walling wrote: "My staff is now down to three men and a girl of 17. I have a prodigious lot of writing to do for the paper and to be editor, sub-editor and proof reader all in one. Now I am doing a scenario of the Plymouth Blitz for a film to be produced by the Ministry of Information."

PRINCIPAL WORKS: *Mystery Stories*—The Strong Room, 1926; That Dinner at Bardolph's, 1928; Murder at the Keyhole, 1929; The Man With the Squeaky Voice, 1930; The Stroke of One, 1930; The Fatal Five Minutes, 1932; Follow the Blue Car (in America: In Time for Murder) 1933; The Tolliver Case (in America: Prove It, Mr. Tolefree!) 1933; The Bachelor Flat Mystery, 1934; Legacy of Death, 1935; The Corpse in the Green Pajamas, 1935; The Corpse in the Crimson Slippers, 1936; Mr. Tolefree's Reluctant Witnesses (in America: The Corpse in the Coppice) 1936; The Corpse With the Dirty Face, 1937; The Corpse With the Floating Foot, 1937; Marooned With Murder, 1937; The Coroner Doubts (in America: The Corpse With the Blue Cravat) 1938; The Corpse With the Blistered Hand, 1938; The Corpse With the Red-Headed Friend, 1939; The Spider and the Fly, 1940; By Hook or Crook, 1941; The Corpse With the Eerie Eye, 1942. *Miscellaneous*—Flaunting Moll (short stories) 1898; A Sea-Dog of Devon: A Life of Sir John Hawkins, 1907; George Borrow: The Man and His Work, 1908; On the British Front, 1919; The Diaries of John Bright (ed.) 1931; The Charm of Brittany, 1933; The West Country, 1935; The Green Hills of England, 1938.

ABOUT: Haycraft, H. Murder for Pleasure: The Life and Times of the Detective Story.

WALMSLEY, LEO (1892-), English writer of adventure books and novelist, writes: "My published works bear a close relation to my own

life. That is, my first book, *Flying and Sport in East Africa,* is a record of my war service, 1914-18. Two boys' books of African adventure were drawn from my war experiences in Africa and from postwar expeditions to Central Africa. The 'thrillers' followed, but they were not good. I did, however, write some nature stories that appeared in *Adventure* that I'm not ashamed of. But I hope as a writer to wipe out all these early books from the record, which begins after a three-year fallow period (during which I actually earned my way as an inshore fisherman on the Yorkshire coast), with the four novels starting with *Three Fevers.* Storm Jameson, then Sir Arthur Quiller-Couch and Edward Garnett, were the first to acclaim these books, but none of them 'sold,' although *Three Fevers* made fame (but little money) in its film version, "Turn of the Tide." Some of these novels are referred to in my autobiographical novel, *Love in the Sun,* my first popular success in England and the United States. It was the English Book Society choice for the August before the outbreak of the present war.

"I make no bid for laurels as a literary bloke. I think I can describe myself as a *story teller,* and to me the main thing is to have the experience, digest it, and re-create it as a story, to be told in the simplest language, but with absolute sincerity. I have been accused of 'journalism,' but journalism is an art form I accept provided I am licensed to reject the literal truth for the aesthetic one. Philosophically I am a humanist, and prefer to look for the good in people. I hate war, of course, but not so much as I hate Nazism. And I believe the highest hope for the world is in a Federal Union of all the English-speaking peoples."

* * *

Mr. Walmsley is a Yorkshireman, and lives now at Leith Rigg, Yorkshire, where he is farming "and doing other war work from morning till night (and at night too)." During the First World War he was with the Royal Flying Corps in East Africa, crashed fourteen times, was cited four times in dispatches, and received the Military Cross for exceptional bravery. He has been curator of the Yorkshire Marine Biological Station and has made a trip to the French Sahara as a naturalist. The story of his marriage is in *Love in the Sun;* his wife's maiden name was Little, and they have two sons and two daughters.

PRINCIPAL WORKS: Flying and Sport in East Africa, 1920; The Silver Blimp (juvenile) 1921; The Lure of Thunder Island, 1923; Three Asses in the Pyrenees, 1924; The Green Rocket, 1926; Toro of the Little People (juvenile) 1926; Three Fevers, 1932; The Phantom Lobster, 1933; Foreigners, 1935; Sally Lunn, 1937; Love in the Sun, 1939; Fishermen at War, 1941.

ABOUT: Lawrence, T. E. Letters; Walmsley, L. Three Fevers (see Note by S. Jameson).

WALN, NORA (June 4, 1895-), American writer on China and Germany, was born in Grampian, Pa., the daughter of Thomas Lincoln Waln and Lilla (Quest) Waln. She is descended from a family of Quakers and

sea-captains, both of which facts have been vitally important to her as an author. She was educated at Swarthmore College, but left in her junior year when the United States entered the First World War, and went to Washington to edit a newspaper page on the work of women in the war. From this she went to the Near East Relief Committee, in New York, as publicity director.

As a child, she had pored over records of the early Walns who traded with China. She discovered that one of the families with whom the Walns had "hereditary traditions" of trade and friendship were the Lins, of Hopei Province, descendants of whom still lived in their family homestead, "The House of Exile." In 1920 she set sail for China, found the Lins, and lived with them for two years. During a brief visit home she met on the boat an Englishman in foreign service in Peiping (Peking), George Edward Osland-Hill. In 1922 they were married in Shanghai. They have one daughter. In 1926 she visited England, and after much difficulty because of the disturbed condition of China was able to return, living in Tientsin for two years more. When it was rumored that Chinese Nationalists demanded surrender of the foreign concessions, Mrs. Osland-Hill went with her daughter to Japan. Later, however, she returned for another visit to the Lins. By this time she had written the book made from her notes of her first visit with them. The entire family read it, passed not too amiable criticism on it, but finally permitted her to submit it for publication. It was published in 1933, and was a best-seller.

Meanwhile Mr. Osland-Hill had resigned from the British government service and he and his wife went to Germany, where he studied music, in 1934. At first they were *personae gratae*, and Hitler actually bought thirty-five copies of *The House of Exile*. But when it became known that Nora Waln was writing a book about her impressions of Nazism, and that those impressions were far from favorable, it was a different matter. They left Germany for England, where they are now (in 1938, in London). Before they left, however, Miss Waln mailed all three copies of her completed manuscript to her publisher, each from a different station, since it was unlikely that she could get them

safely out of the country if she tried to carry them with her. Not one copy was ever received, and she had to rewrite the entire book from memory and from her notes, which she had managed to take with her.

The book, *Reaching for the Stars*, was timely and reached a large audience. It came just before the public was overwhelmed by a flood of books on Germany under Hitler, and thus had the advantage of comparative novelty. It has been criticized for its mildness; Miss Waln is not a good hater, and she is still a peaceful Quaker at heart. She liked and admired the German people, and her indictment of their present government is too gentle for many readers. Nevertheless, her quiet manner is often more damning of Nazism than vigorous invective would be.

A slender blonde, with classical, clear-cut features, Miss Waln is really not primarily a writer, though she published a few poems in her youth. She is an intelligent, sensitive American woman, who puts down on paper the things she herself has seen and known.

PRINCIPAL WORKS: The House of Exile, 1933; Reaching for the Stars, 1939.

ABOUT: Wilson Library Bulletin October 1939.

WALPOLE, Sir HUGH (1884-June 1, 1941), English novelist, was born Hugh Seymour Walpole in Auckland, New Zealand, while his father, the Rev. George Henry Somerset Walpole, was canon of St. Mary's Pro-Cathedral there. (Later the elder Walpole became Bishop of Edinburgh.) When the boy was five, his father went to New York to teach in the General Theological Seminary, and Hugh was sent "home" to England, to Cornwall. When he was twelve his father became principal of Bede College in Durham, and the boy was reunited with his family there. He was educated at King's School, Canterbury, and Emmanuel College, Oxford. He had already begun to write—in fact, he wrote two novels while still an undergraduate, one of which he destroyed, while the other appeared five years later as his first published book. For a while after the university he was a lay reader in the Church of England, then taught in a provincial boys' school. He disliked both occupations, and soon went to London to try to make his way as a writer.

His first opportunity came when, after many difficulties, he succeeded in becoming a book reviewer for the London *Standard*. His first novels barely repaid the cost of having the manuscripts typed. It was not until *Fortitude*, in 1913, that he began really to make a living as a novelist.

During the First World War, Walpole served with the Red Cross in Russia from 1914 to 1916, receiving the Order of St. George for his heroism in rescuing a wounded man under fire. After the war he made his home in London, though he visited the United States a number of times. He was made a Commander of the Order of the British Empire in 1918 and was knighted in 1937. He received the James Tait Black Prize twice, in 1919 and 1920. He never married, but lived alone in an apartment near Picadilly, with a country home in Keswick in the Lake District to which he could retreat and be alone with his dogs and his books. He became a wealthy man, who collected rare manuscripts and objects of art. He was an authority on Sir Walter Scott, and owned the world's finest collection of Scott manuscripts and association items. He made the film version of *David Copperfield*. He died of heart failure following overexertion in a Keswick "War Weapons Week" parade, at fifty-seven.

Sir Hugh was a prolific writer, averaging about a novel a year, besides occasional books of travel or literary biography and several plays. His play *The Young Huntress* was produced in 1933, *The Haxtons* in 1939. *The Cathedral* has also been successfully dramatized, and Edward Chodorov's impressive play, *Kind Lady*, was adapted from one of Walpole's short stories. He was also a constant book reviewer. The enormous amount of work he could turn out in a year caused some kindly satire in *Punch* and elsewhere. The *Bookman* remarked that he "can write two or three excellent novels and several critical estimations of his contemporaries, appear on lecture platforms, and read and report on almost every book put out by English and American publishers, all at the same moment." The natural result of this constant appearance in print is that his output was very uneven. As one critic remarked: "Just when a reader becomes convinced that Hugh Walpole is a feathery, confiding, complacent man of letters, he begins to write like a great writer; and just when the reader becomes convinced that he is a great writer, he begins to write

like a feathery, confiding, complacent man of letters."

His earliest novels were realistic, but he soon became an out-and-out romantic, with more than a touch of mystical approach to life's problems. No author of his time possessed his power to evoke horror without the least hint of the supernatural—as witness *Portrait of a Man With Red Hair*. He could also swashbuckle like a Sabatini—as in the Herries series (*Rogue Herries, Judith Paris, The Fortress,* and *Vanessa*). Sometimes he was autobiographical, as in *The Cathedral* and the Jeremy books (*Jeremy, Jeremy and Hamlet,* and *Jeremy at Crale*). Without any particular sociological interests, he had a keen eye for social backgrounds, as in the Rising City series (*The Duchess of Wrexe, Green Mirror,* and *The Captives*). It will be seen that he was fond of groups of novels with related scenes and characters. But it is hard to make any definitive statement about Hugh Walpole as a novelist, because he was so many different kinds of novelist. James Morrison summed him up best by saying that he was "preeminently an author who appeals to the Plain Man, . . . always sincere, . . . with abundant humor, . . . and color and vividness in his graphic description."

A big man, handsome in youth, later completely bald and spectacled but still impressive with his square head and massive dome of forehead, Hugh Walpole was the perfect "toastmaster of literature," amiable, friendly, tactful, diplomatic. He served often as a liaison officer between American books and the British public, especially in his capacity as director of the English Book Society. He said truly that the middle and upper classes were what he knew best, and he never attempted to write about any social group with which he was not acquainted and in sympathy. "I grew up in the shadow of an Anglican cathedral," he remarked, "and it's pretty hard to break away from the old ties."

PRINCIPAL WORKS: *Novels*—The Wooden Horse, 1909; Maradick at Forty, 1910; Mr. Pegrim and Mr. Traill, 1911; The Prelude to Adventure, 1912; Fortitude, 1913; The Duchess of Wrexe, 1914; The Golden Scarecrow, 1915; The Dark Forest, 1916; Green Mirror, 1917; The Secret City, 1919; Jeremy, 1919; The Captives, 1920; The Thirteen Travelers, 1921; The Young Enchanted, 1922; The Cathedral, 1922; Jeremy and Hamlet, 1923; The Old Ladies, 1924; Portrait of a Man With Red Hair, 1925; Harmer John, 1926; Jeremy at Crale, 1927; Wintersmoon, 1928; The Silver Thorn, 1928; Farthing Hall (with J. B. Priestley) 1929; Hans Frost, 1929; Rogue Herries, 1930; Judith Paris, 1931; Above the Dark Circus (in America: Above the Dark Tumult) 1931; The

Fortress, 1932; Vanessa, 1933; All Souls' Night (short stories) 1933; Captain Nicholas, 1934; The Inquisitor, 1935; A Prayer for My Son, 1936; John Cornelius, 1937; The Joyful Delaneys, 1938; Head in Green Bronze and Other Stories, 1938; The Sea Tower, 1939; The Bright Pavilions, 1940; The Blind Man's House, 1941; The Killer and the Slain, 1942. *Miscellaneous*—Joseph Conrad, 1916; The English Novel, 1925; These Diversions: Reading, 1926; Anthony Trollope, 1928; The Waverley Pageant, 1932; The Apple Trees: Four Reminiscences, 1933; Tendencies of the Modern Novel (with H. Miles, W. Waldman, & others) 1934; Famous Stories of Five Centuries (ed.) 1934; The Roman Fountain (with W. Partington) 1940.

ABOUT: Dane, C. Tradition and Hugh Walpole; Steen, M. Hugh Walpole; Anglia January 1932; Bookman February 1927; Bookman (London) April 1932; English Journal July 1928; Golden Book December 1933, August 1935; Rotarian August 1940; Saturday Review of Literature October 23, 1937, June 21, 1941; Sewanee Review July 1932; Time May 13, 1940.

WALSH, MAURICE (May 2, 1879-), Irish novelist, writes: "Where was I born a good half century ago? Kerry. Kerry is

that most mountainous county in the far South and West of Ireland. I was the son and the grandson and the great-grandson of farmers and rebels, but we could take our genealogy back to the sixteenth century, when our forefather was hanged for piracy on the high seas. I lived close to the soil well into my teens and learned to use a Queen Anne duck gun eight feet long to the danger of bird, beast, and any British subject. I once killed 95 curlew at one shot, sold them for what you would call $20, and bought beer for the community. My father had a fine library and was a powerful authority on blood horses. I began trying my hand at writing short stories, and the *Weekly Freeman,* a Dublin paper, used to give me an occasional two guineas. I wrote about Australian bushranging, and Klondike gold-digging, and the Boer War, and other subjects with which I was closely acquainted at a distance. Also I wrote a long historical romance, blood and love on every page, and I couldn't tell you which was hotter and which redder. I used some of that material later on in *Blackcock's Feather.*

"I never saw the walls of a city until the end of last century when, a growing lad, I went to Dublin at the request of my mother to stand a Civil Service examination. I didn't want to pass. I wanted to go out and fight

for the Boers, but had a loyalty to my mother. I did that exam so recklessly, so debonairely, that I was in the first fifty of two thousand, and the next thing I knew I was pitchforked into the Customs Excise Service. With a couple hundred youngsters like myself I wandered up and down in Ireland, Scotland, Wales, and England. I was drawn back again and again and yet again to the Highlands of Scotland. She had red hair and a temperament also. She married me at long last, and though her hair is not now quite so red I will say nothing about her temperament. During the war I was on War Service on the coast, sword unbloody and head unbowed. And after the Irish Treaty I volunteered to serve my own country.

"Up to then I had scarcely written a thing —too busy living. But here in Dublin during the Civil War, my family still in Scotland, and night-sniping the national pastime, I had to stay largely indoors of nights, and I got tired of reading. So I tried to recapture in the written words some of the scenes and characters and stories that I had known in Scotland. The result of that scribbling was *The Key Above the Door,* and that thing has sold some hundred thousand copies. Somehow, like a damn fool, I couldn't stop after that, but my pace was never fast. So here I am living outside Dublin within sound of the sea and sight of the hills. We intend to move out into the wilds when the bombing planes come over. Meantime I write a little, shoot a little, fish a little, garden a lot, and go on talking. We have three sons, one a doctor, one a banker, and one a medical student. We have two grandsons and I will now write you sixteen pages on the ways of grandsons. But no . . ."

* * *

Even this abbreviated sketch will perhaps give some flavor of Mr. Walsh's inimitable style. For further elucidation he adds: "I was a 'moonlighter' as a young man, but that was the pirate blood. Idiosyncrasies: taking the opposite side. Personal dislikes: the bloody British Empire, which you must not confound with the tight little island of England. Superstitions: oh, the usual, but I do hate turning back. My aim in life: the absolutely simple life. Favorite book: *West Is West* and all other stories by Eugene Manlove Rhodes, because he writes true romance, which is the ideal made real, not the real made ideal. I think I like the novels of Neil M. Gunn, the young Scot novelist, as well as those of Gene Rhodes. He and I have fished and sported nefariously over the width of Scotland. How I happened to write any book: to pass the time and create a yarn for those kids of mine, who are my hardest critics."

Mr. Walsh was educated in St. Michael's College, Listowell. He was president of the Irish P.E.N. Club in 1938. He resigned from his position as excise officer for the Irish Free State in 1934, up to that date writing only in his spare time. He was married in 1908 to Caroline I. J. Begg, of Banff, Scotland. He is a short man, youthful in appearance, with iron gray hair and deep-set gray eyes; Peter O'Donovan called him "quiet, easy-going, lazy-seeming." Gay romance and high adventure, in Scotland or Ireland of today or the sixteenth century, are his *forte*; his books are written only to entertain and they do so in plenty. They are light, but they are saved from sentimentality by their author's irrepressible humor.

PRINCIPAL WORKS: Eudmon Blake, 1909; The Key Above the Door, 1923; While Rivers Run, 1926; The Small Dark Man, 1929 (these three as Romantic Adventures, 1933); Blackcock's Feather, 1932; The Road to Nowhere, 1934; Green Rushes, 1935 (these three as Three Roads, 1936); And No Quarter (in America: The Dark Rose) 1937; Sons of the Swordmaker, 1938; The Hill Is Mine, 1940; Son of Apple, 1940; Thomasheen James, Man-of-No-Work (in America; Thomasheen James) 1941.

ABOUT: Saturday Evening Post February 15, 1936.

WARD, Mrs. ELIZABETH STUART (PHELPS). See "AMERICAN AUTHORS: 1600-1900

WARD, MARY AUGUSTA (ARNOLD) (MRS. HUMPHRY WARD) (June 11, 1851-March 24, 1920), English novelist, was

born at Hobart Town, Tasmania, Australia. Her father, Thomas Arnold "the younger," second son of Dr. Arnold of Rugby and brother of the Victorian poet and critic Matthew Arnold, had come there the year before to organize the public education of the colony. Her mother, Julia Sorell, was of Spanish Protestant blood, and was appalled when Arnold entered the Roman Catholic Church. Popery was unpopular in the Colony; Arnold was obliged immediately to resign and returned with his wife and three small children to England, where he taught in various Roman Catholic Schools.

Mary Arnold spent most of her childhood in boarding schools; these years of schooling, from seven to sixteen, she regarded as practically wasted. In 1865 her father, who was always drifting from the Anglican to the Roman Church and back again, temporarily forsook Catholicism and established his family at Oxford. Mary returned from school to find herself in an atmosphere of scholarship, skepticism, and inquiry, and in a circle which included Benjamin Jowett, Master of Balliol and translator of Plato; Mark Pattison, Rector of Lincoln College, and his wife, later Lady Dilke; Walter Pater and his sisters; Dr. Liddon, "Select Preacher" at the University Church; T. H. Green, the philosopher; and J. R. Green, the historian; most of whom later found their way into the pages of her *Robert Elsmere*. She worked fervently in Oxford's great library, the Bodleian, and her studies in early Spanish literature and history enabled her to write, in 1877, the lives of several Spanish ecclesiastics for the *Dictionary of Christian Biography*, at the invitation of Dean Wace.

In the winter of 1870-71 she first met T. Humphry Ward, Fellow and Tutor of Brasenose College, to whom she was married April 6, 1872, by Dean Stanley. Three children were born: Dorothy (1874), Arnold (1876), and Janet (1879), who married George Macaulay Trevelyan, the historian. It was in many ways an ideally happy marriage. There is something gruff, minatory, and didactic in the name of Humphry Ward, which seems exactly suited to the manner of novelist that Mary Arnold became.

The family moved to London, to a house at 61 Russell Square, in November 1881. Ward wrote leaders for the *Times,* and Mrs. Ward supplemented their income by reviewing French and Spanish books for the *Pall Mall Gazette* and writing articles for *Macmillan's Magazine,* both edited by John Morley. In 1884, although nearly disabled by writer's cramp, she began her translation of Amiel's *Journal* and wrote her first novel, *Miss Bretherton,* suggested by the brilliant English success of the American actress, Mary Anderson. Mandell Creighton, later Bishop of London, informed her, "You wrote this book as a critic, not a creator." She seldom wrote otherwise.

Robert Elsmere, her most famous novel, a methodical, closely reasoned attack on evangelical Christianity, which "agitated bishops and set cabinet ministers at variance," was published February 24, 1888, in the three-volume form then customary.

Gladstone's famous *Nineteenth Century* review, "Robert Elsmere and the Battle of Belief," which is generally credited with the novel's success, did not appear till May, when the novel was already in its third edition. (He was not Prime Minister at the time.) In four years the sale amounted to 70,500 copies. Over half a million were disposed of in the United States (international copyright did not arrive until March 1891), though Mrs. Ward received only 100 pounds. Copies of the novel and Gladstone's reply were eventually given away as premiums with a bar of soap.

Macmillan's, in New York, gave her 7,000 pounds for her next novel, *David Grieve*, in which her nephew Julian Huxley (brother of Aldous) figures as a small boy, Sandy. It met with a mixed reception, but was considered a marked advance on *Robert Elsmere* in artistic treatment and character drawing. In the summer of 1892 the Wards moved to "Stocks," which was to be her summer home for the rest of her life. Here she entertained Trevelyans and Huxleys, Rothschilds and Asquiths, Henry James, and Lord Haldane.

Marcella (1894) was called by William Lyon Phelps (in 1910) a sample of the "political-didactic-realistic novel which she has continued to publish steadily ever since under different titles." He further remarked that the novels of Mrs. Ward bore about the same relation to first-class fiction that maps and atlases bear to great paintings. *The Story of Bessie Costrell* (1895), which Mrs. Ward called a grimy little tale, has been the favorite of some of her severest critics. In June 1898 came what is probably her most permanent achievement, *Helbeck of Bannisdale*, which presented "the eternal clash between the medieval and the modern mind in the persons of Alan Helbeck, the Catholic squire, and Laura Fountain, the child of science and negation." Her last novel with a religious tendency was a sequel to *Robert Elsmere*, *The Case of Richard Meynell* (1911). *Eleanor* (1900) was written in Italy at the vast old Villa Barberini, at Castel Gandolfo, in the Alban Hills. It was admittedly based on the love-story of Chateaubriand and Madame de Beaumont.

Edith Wharton once declared that *romans à clef* (novels with characters based on real persons, but under different names) are never written by the born novelist. Mrs. Ward frequently required this prop for her imagination. *Lady Rose's Daughter* was based on the relations between Madame du Deffand and Julie de l'Espinasse; *The Marriage of William Ashe* on Byron and Lady Caroline Lamb; and *Fenwick's Career* on Romney and Lady Hamilton. The first-named ran serially in *Harper's Magazine*. Arnold Bennett heard that Harper's gave her 10,000 pounds for it, and that it sold 400,000 copies in America alone. Her novels, as Phelps remarks, enabled her readers to enter vicariously into the best English society, and she was regarded as absolutely respectable and safe. Her heroines had "an extraordinary fund of information and an almost insane desire to impart it."

Mrs. Ward's record as a philanthropist is entirely admirable. Working under handicaps of pain and fatigue, and with the slimmest encouragement from the British government, she devoted herself to bettering the condition of the poor of London, with play centers, clinics for crippled children, and the diverse activities of University Hall, now known as the Mary Ward Settlement. She was a founder and earnest platform speaker for the National League for Opposing Woman Suffrage, and except for a last-minute defection on Lord Curzon's part, would probably have defeated it in the House of Lords. Her daughter remarks, "The rule of the mob did not attract her, especially if it was a female mob." She was assisted in the fight in Parliament by her son, whom she had helped elect, and who was known in the House as "the Member for Mrs. Humphry Ward." *Delia Blanchflower* is her anti-suffrage novel. The World War found her equally active. *England's Effort*, written at the request of Theodore Roosevelt, whom she had met during her American visit in 1908, was syndicated in the United States as a series of articles, "Letters to an American Friend." It is said to have hastened President Wilson's entry into the war, and was reviewed with great respect by the *Preuissische Jahrbuch*.

War taxation necessitated giving up her house in Grosvenor Place in August 1919. Her health definitely gave way at Christmas time, and after being confined to bed for ten days with bronchitis and heart disease, she died in a little house on Connaught Square March 18, 1920. Two months before her death the Lord Chancellor made her one of the first seven women magistrates in England.

By 1910, writes Frank Swinnerton in *The Georgian Scene*, Mrs. Humphry Ward's work had become occasion for ribald comment. Critics had already complained that she was not an artist in fiction, could not create character, lacked humor, and was devoid of sensuousness. Rebecca West called her career one long specialization in the *mot injuste,* and remarked that she wrote as though she were carrying an umbrella in the other hand. (But Margaret Woods says: "What she had to say she said in clear and excellent English which fitted her strong, well-equipped intellect like a glove.") She was tall, stately, imposing, with keen, hawklike features, a dominant voice, and her manner was a blend of pompousness and kindliness. She had no small talk, and brooked no contradiction from her inferiors in rank or intellect. She will go down to posterity, in the opinion of Stephen Gwynn, as a writer who knew how to dramatize in interesting fashion not so much the life as the intellectual tendencies of her generation.

PRINCIPAL WORKS: *Novel*—Miss Bretherton, 1884; Robert Elsmere, 1888; The History of David Grieve, 1892; Marcella, 1894; The Story of Bessie Costrell, 1895; Sir George Tressady, 1896; Helbeck of Bannisdale, 1898; Eleanor, 1900; Lady Rose's Daughter, 1903; The Marriage of William Ashe, 1905; Fenwick's Career, 1906; The Testing of Diana Mallory, 1908; Daphne: or, Marriage a la Mode, 1909; Canadian Born, 1910; The Case of Richard Meynell, 1911; The Mating of Lydia, 1913; The Corysston Family, 1913; Delia Blanchflower, 1915; Eltham House, 1915; A Great Success, 1916; Lady Connie, 1916; Missing, 1917; The War and Elizabeth, 1918; Cousin Philip, 1919; Harvest, 1920. *War Books*—England's Effort, 1916; Towards the Goal; 1917; Fields of Victory, 1919. *Autobiography*—A Writer's Recollections, 1918. *Translation*—Amiel's Journal, 1885. *Juvenile*—Milly and Olly; or, A Holiday Among the Mountains, 1881.

ABOUT: Gardiner, A. G. Pillars of Society; Gosse, E. Silhouettes; Gwynn, S. L. Mrs Humphry Ward; Holt, H. Garrulities of an Octogenarian Editor; James, H. Essays in London and Elsewhere; Phelps, W. L. Essays on Modern Novelists; Trevelyan, J. P. The Life of Mrs. Humphry Ward; Walters, J. S. Mrs. Humphry Ward: Her Work and Influence; Ward, M. A. A Writer's Recollections; Fortnightly Review June 1920; Living Age February 1, 1919, May 15, 1920; North American Review June 1920; Quarterly Review July 1920; Review October 27, 1920.

WARD, WILFRID PHILIP (January 2, 1856-April 9, 1916), English biographer and Catholic apologist, was born at Old Hall House, Ware, Hertfordshire, the second son of William George Ward ("Ideal Ward" of the Oxford Movement) and Frances (Wingfield) Ward. There were nine children in the family, which was well known in the Isle of Wight, especially for its cricketers. Wilfrid, a singularly winning, handsome, and high-spirited child, was brought up in an ultramontane atmosphere, and was kept busy examining his conscience for religious vocation by association with his brilliant, but rather

unstable and entirely unworldly father. He attended Ushaw College, Durham, after nine months at the Gregorian University in Rome, but later abandoned his studies for the priesthood. Ward returned to Ushaw in 1890 to lecture on philosophy; was an examiner in mental and moral science at the Royal University of Ireland, 1891-1892; a member of the royal commission on Irish university education in 1901; and five years later became editor of the Dublin *Review.*

His *The Life and Times of Cardinal Wiseman,* undertaken at the request of Cardinal Vaughan, required five years of work. The first edition in 1897 sold out in a week, and the book went through six printings in a year. *The Life of Cardinal Newman,* fifteen years later, wove a thousand letters of the Cardinal's into its 1300 pages. A memoir of Aubrey de Vere, the Irish poet, was something of a relaxation between these major efforts. The Athenaeum Club recognized his work by electing him a member *honoris causa,* not a frequent occurrence.

Shane Leslie says of Ward that "more than any single man he held the balance and kept comparative peace among the thinkers of English Catholicism." Ward always regretted his lack of a university education, and sent his sons to Oxford and Cambridge, which had been denied him because Cardinal Manning disapproved of both. "Booklover and metaphysician as he was," said G. K. Chesterton; "he had, in almost absentminded manner, 'drunk ale in the country of the young.' "

He possessed a voice of operatic caliber, with a genius for intellectual gossip and hilarious mimicry (Tennyson once growled, "Wilfrid Ward, I'm told you mimic me!"). Ward's death at sixty after a mysterious and painful illness was generally regretted. He had toured the United States, giving a Lowell Lecture at Harvard in 1915. His widow, Josephine Mary Hope-Scott, edited his *Last Lectures* with a memoir.

PRINCIPAL WORKS: The Clothes of Religion, 1886; William George Ward and the Oxford Movement, 1889; Witnesses to the Unseen, 1893; William George Ward and the Catholic Revival, 1893; The Life and Times of Cardinal Wiseman, 1897; Aubrey de Vere: Memoir, 1904; Problems and Persons, 1905; Ten Personal Studies, 1908; The Life of Cardinal Newman, 1912; Men and Matters, 1914; Last Lectures, 1918.

ABOUT: Ward, J. M. H. S. Introduction to Last Lectures; Ward, M. The Wilfrid Wards; Dublin Review July 1916.

WARNER, CHARLES DUDLEY. See "AMERICAN AUTHORS: 1600-1900"

WARNER, REX (March 9, 1905-), English poet and novelist, was born in Birmingham, Warwickshire. His father was

a Church of England clergyman, although Birmingham has a long non-conformist tradition, and his mother was a school-teacher. Young Warner attended St. George's, Harpenden, and Wadham College, Oxford University, where he was award-ed a scholarship for excellence in the classics. He was captain of the Rugby XV's, and has played for Gloucestershire. A teaching post was relinquished when Warner discovered that his opinions did not coincide with his headmaster's, and he obtained a post in Egypt, where he finished a novel and wrote poetry and critiques for the *London Mercury,* the *New Statesman,* and the *Saturday Review.* When last heard of, Rex Warner was teaching Latin and Greek at Frensham Heights School, Farnham, the site of Moor Park, where Sir William Temple lived when Jonathan Swift was his secretary. Warner's *Poems* of 1938 are a rather curious mixture of sensuous observations and dialectics, birds, and propaganda. "Although rather smugly hortatory, and deriving from C. Day Lewis and Hopkins," observed Louise Bogan, the book "has moments of simplicity and beauty." Day Lewis himself has stated that Warner has refused to be stampeded in-to fanaticism. For diversion he prefers darts or shove-half-penny to reading or writ-ing literary criticism. He also dislikes the-ories of poetry, but "I should like to see the characters of the novel invested with the kind of poetic quality that makes them, in their own way, more, not less, impressive than the characters of everyday life. I should like to see the epic and allegorical qualities in the place of the photographic methods which now seem to be popular."

The Wild Goose Chase (1938) is a fan-tastic novel in which Warner puts these the-ories into practice. It was written under the influence of Franz Kafka, who, as Eleanor Clark puts it, had opened up the blind alley of realism and made plausible once more the forms of allegory and myth. Horace Greg-ory said of the novel that it seemed to con-fuse the action of the parable with the fantasy, and that on the whole it was "closer to the H. G. Wellsian prophecies of nearly forty years ago than to the novels of Franz Kafka whom he admires."

The scene of *The Professor* (1939) is a great democracy invaded by the Fascists; it is the story of an idealist's struggle to live by his ideals at a time when all the forces of chaos and barbarism are let loose. It was praised by reviewers as one of the best and most stirring of modern political novels.

PRINCIPAL WORKS: The Kite, 1936; The Wild Goose Chase, 1938; Poems, 1938; The Professor, 1939; Aerodrome, 1941.

ABOUT: Wilson Library Bulletin March 1938.

WARNER, SYLVIA TOWNSEND (De-cember 1893-), English novelist and poet, was born at Harrow-on-the-Hill, Middlesex, the daughter of a schoolmaster, and was educated privately. Her first interest was music: she is an au-thority on the music of the fifteenth and sixteenth centuries, was one of the edi-tors of ten volumes of *Tudor Church Mu-sic,* and was a mem-

Pinchot

ber of the Tudor Church Music Educational Committee from 1918 to 1928. She next appeared as a poet; her poems, as Oliver Warner (no relative) remarked, have "del-icacy, learning, . . . a graceful, almost irre-sponsible wit." These same characterizations are true of her stories and novels, which began with *Lolly Willowes,* the first "Book-of-the-Month" in America. In 1927 she came to New York as guest-critic of the *Herald Tribune.* For a while she became in-terested in left-wing politics, and worked for the Loyalists in Spain during the Civil War. She is a member of the executive committee of the Association of Writers for Intellectu-al Liberty. Unmarried, she lived, at least until the *Luftwaffe* attacks, in an early Vic-torian house in London, where she could practice her talent for housewifery; she is an authority on cookery, wines, and herbs— the last very appropriate to one so preoccu-pied with witchcraft. One would expect to find her attached to cats (especially in view of *The Cat's Cradle Book*), but actually her constant companion is a black chow dog. Sociable and generous "to excess," she is renowned for her hospitality, and her dinners are considered events. Although she has a really encyclopedic knowledge of occultism and the black arts, she herself is a complete skeptic. Small, slender, and deceptively frail-looking, she has heavy black hair, now graying, and is very near-sighted.

One either likes Miss Warner's stories very much indeed or likes them not at all. She deals in fantasy much as David Garnett or John Collier does, or as "Saki" did, not with the heavy mysticism of an Arthur Machen. Her witches and her talking cats are presented with matter-of-fact gaiety, and one must take them or leave them as they are; they have every appropriate attribute except horror. The same may be said of her more purely human creatures, her missionaries and cannibals and orphan girls and gin-drinking villagers: each is seen just slightly out of focus, as if Miss Warner's poor sight, like El Greco's, had given her the power to create a new and fresh art form. Oliver Warner calls her "a true 'original.' She can touch nothing without delicately transforming it.... It is to the ear and the brain that she first appeals."

For years she has been working on a biography of T. F. Powys, which is still unfinished. Work which reads as easily as hers means hard writing, and she is not a long-winded or discursive author; her books are all brief. Everything she publishes, however, bears a lapidary's polish; it is fresh and new-minted. In some ways she recalls the Elinor Wylie of *The Venetian Glass Nephew,* in others the Richard Hughes of *The Innocent Voyage.* But above all she is indubitably herself.

PRINCIPAL WORKS: The Espalier (poems) 1925; Lolly Willowes, 1926; Mr. Fortune's Maggot, 1927; Time Importuned (poems) 1928; The True Heart, 1929; Elinor Barley, 1930; Opus 7 (novel in verse) 1931; A Moral Ending and Other Stories, 1931; The Salutation (novelettes and short stories) 1932; Whether a Dove or a Seagull (poems, with V. Ackland) 1934; Summer Will Show, 1936; After the Death of Don Juan, 1938; The Cat's Cradle Book, 1940.

ABOUT: Bookman (London) October 1929; Scholastic December 5, 1938.

*WARREN, CHARLES (March 9, 1868-   ), American legal historian and Pulitzer Prize winner, was born in Boston and educated at Harvard (B.A., 1889, M.A. 1892). He also spent three years at the Harvard Law School. He received an honorary LL.D. from Columbia in 1933. He was admitted to the Massachusetts bar in 1897 and began practice in Boston, being associated with Moorfield Story, was next private secretary to Governor William E.

Russell, and then the latter's law partner until the governor's death. From 1914 to 1918 he was assistant attorney general of the United States, afterwards returning to private practice. He was chairman of the Massachusetts Civil Service Commission from 1905 to 1911. He has lectured on history and law at Princeton, the University of Rochester, Boston University Law School, Johns Hopkins, the University of Virginia, Northwestern University Law School, the University of Chicago, Cornell, and William and Mary College. He served in 1937 as American member of the Trail Smelter Arbitral Tribunal, and in 1939 as American member of the Conciliation International Committee under the treaty between the United States and Hungary. He is a member of the Board of Overseers of Harvard and a trustee of the New England Conservatory of Music. He is honorary vice-president of the American Society of International Law, and a member of the National Institute of Arts and Letters and the American Academy of Arts and Letters. He is also a member of the committee of management of the *Dictionary of American Biography.* In 1923 he received the Pulitzer Prize in history for *The Supreme Court in United States History.* In 1904 he married Annie Louise Bliss; they have no children. Their home is in Dedham, Mass., but for most of the year they live in Washington.

PRINCIPAL WORKS: The Girl and the Governor, 1902; History of the Harvard Law School and Early Legal Conditions in America (3 vols.) 1909; History of the American Bar, Colonial and Federal, to 1860, 1911; The Supreme Court in United States History (3 vols.) 1922; The Supreme Court and Sovereign States, 1924; Congress, the Constitution, and the Supreme Court, 1925 (enlarged edition 1935); The Making of the Constitution, 1928; Jacobin and Junto, 1931; Congress as Santa Claus: The General Welfare Clause, 1932; Bankruptcy in United States History, 1935; Neutrality and Collective Security (with others) 1936; The Supreme Court and Disputes Between the States, 1940.

WARREN, ROBERT PENN (April 24, 1905-   ), American poet and novelist, writes: "I was born in Todd County, Ky., in the section which provides the background for *Night Rider.* I attended the school at Guthrie, Ky., until my fifteenth year, when I went to Clarksville, Tenn. In 1921 I entered Vanderbilt University, where I remained for four years. From 1925 until 1927 I was a teaching fellow at the University of California, taking an M.A. After another year of graduate work at Yale, where I held a fellowship, I went to Oxford as a Rhodes Scholar. I received the B.Litt. degree in 1930 and returned to this country to teach. For one winter I was at Memphis, Tenn., as

assistant professor at Southwestern College. From 1931 to 1934 I was at Vanderbilt and in 1934 I came to Louisiana State University, where I am now associate professor in the department of English, and, with Cleanth Brooks, managing editor of the *Southern Review*. In 1930 I married Emma Brescia.

"My early boyhood was spent in Southern Kentucky and in Tennessee, the winters in town at school and the summers in the country. I read rather widely, a great mixture of stuff, whatever happened to come to hand—the usual nineteenth century novelists, the Boy Scout books, Buckle's *History of Civilization*, Darwin, thrillers, detective stories, a lot of poetry, Macaulay and Gibbon, and a good deal of American history. I entered college with the idea of studying science, but circumstances quickly altered that: on the negative side, a freshman course in chemistry, and on the positive side, the influence of Donald Davidson and John Crowe Ransom. In my second year in college I began to spend a good deal of time writing poetry. In this connection my association with the Fugitive Group was extremely important to me; my first poetry to be published appeared in the *Fugitive*.

"Editing the *Southern Review* is pretty grim work, with some hundreds of manuscripts to handle every month, and teaching, in addition, three-quarters of a full schedule. The general principle, especially for fiction and poetry, has been to hunt for new writers —for that seems to us to be the true function of a magazine of our type—and to use work by established writers only when we have a genuine enthusiasm for it. For a person who wants to write, the advantages of teaching, I believe, outweigh the disadvantages; a teacher is forced to clarify—or to try to clarify—his own mind on certain questions which are necessarily involved in the business of writing.

"I received a Guggenheim Award in 1940, and am at work on my next novel, which

will deal with the period from 1920 to 1930. Meanwhile I am also in the middle of a play, mixed verse and prose, on a contemporary Southern project. It now seems that my next book to be published will be a collection of poems, new ones and some of the pieces included in *XXXVI Poems*.

"I am sympathetic with the objectives of the New Deal but feel that the administration has never clarified its basic philosophy. And I believe that unless ownership and control can be more widely diffused American democracy is a goner."

* * *

Mr. Warren is tall, lanky, and red-headed, soft-spoken, and described as "gentle but quick to go to bat for his convictions." He was a member of the Southern Agrarian group of a few years ago, and was a contributor to their anthologies, *I'll Take My Stand* and *Who Owns America?* In 1936 and 1937 he won the Caroline Sinkler Prize of the Poetry Society of South Carolina, and in 1936 the Helen Haire Levinson Prize of *Poetry*. In the same year he held a Houghton Mifflin Literary Fellowship. Morton Dauwen Zabel spoke of his "exacting craftsmanship and really critical sense of a local ideal ... [with] emphasis on his own conflict of spirit, ... increasing lyric clarity and tonal richness, ... a writer who more and more shows himself, in both his verse and prose, one of the most serious and gifted intelligences of his generation."

After the demise of the *Southern Review* in 1942, Mr. Warren became associated with the *Kenyon Review* as advisory editor.

PRINCIPAL WORKS: John Brown: The Making of a Martyr, 1929; XXXVI Poems, 1935; Understanding Poetry (with C. Brooks) 1938; Night Rider (novel) 1938; Eleven Poems on the Same Theme, 1942.

ABOUT: Poetry April 1936; Wilson Library Bulletin June 1939.

WASSERMANN, JAKOB (March 10, 1873-January 1, 1934), German novelist, was born of Jewish parents in Fürth, a manu-

facturing town near Nüremberg. His father, Adolf Wassermann, was a small merchant "who could not, however he tried, succeed in gaining wealth." His mother, Henriette (Traub) Wassermann was an extremely beautiful woman, "blonde, very gentle, very silent."

Apeda

"Although my parents differed greatly in nature and character, they had one trait in common: they were not of their epoch. They were both children of the Romantic Age."

Jakob attended the local school and, for one year, the *shul*. When nine, his mother died and a few months later the harassed father introduced a step-mother to the household. Brow-beaten and tyrannized, Jakob found his only solace in writing stories: "In my fifteenth year I wrote a novel, an unspeakably jejune and insipid affair, and one day I took the manuscript to the editorial office of a daily paper. . . . Shortly after, this composition appeared under my name, sprinkled with misprints, in the fiction supplement of the paper." Despite his father's protests, Jakob refused to give up his literary interests: "On moonlit nights I would sometimes leave my bed and, in a fevered state of soul, write page after page at the window." It was from that window that he had the satisfaction of seeing his father's factory burn down.

In 1890, at the age of seventeen, Jakob left school and went to an uncle in Vienna, owner of a fan factory. After a few months of "unbearable drudgery" at the factory, he ran away to Munich with a few gulden in his pockets; soon he was forced to return to the family then residing in Würzburg. They received him coldly and for a few weeks Jakob wandered about "planlessly through the old streets and vineyard paths on the river's bank." On his father's insistence he wrote a letter of apology to his uncle and "was given another chance," but soon he was again compelled to leave, this time the victim of a mean intrigue. His family then decided to let him serve his year in the army; to meet expenses he was given half of his mother's small legacy.

On completing his military service, he settled in Nüremberg where he obtained a small job as clerk, fell into bad company, plunged headlong into "a spiritual cesspool." On receiving the rest of his mother's legacy he lived in Munich free from worry till the last penny was gone. He then obtained a post in an agency in Freiburg-in-Baden but was fired when found to be a Jew. For several weeks he tramped in the Black Forest but unable to endure this kind of existence, he sold his watch and coat and went to Zurich where he expected a school friend to help him out. However, he found him also jobless. The two of them pooled their resources and Wassermann left for Munich. On his arrival at Constance the hungry hobo spent all his money on a meal and was able to reach his destination only because of a kind-hearted guard. During the next few months

Wassermann lived in utter poverty, copying manuscripts at starvation wages. He suffered gastric hemorrhages which forced him to keep to a strict diet of rice. At last he secured a post as secretary to the writer Ernst von Wolzogen. On one occasion he showed him his literary efforts and Wolzogen was favorably impressed. "He was the first person to encourage me, the very first person to accept me without reservation as a serious writer, and this implied for me salvation and redemption." Wassermann gradually found his way to literary circles and helped, with Thomas Mann, in the founding of *Simplicissimus,* published by the firm of Albert Langen. In 1896 this firm published Wassermann's novel *The Jews of Zirndorf,* which was a literary event and meant that the twenty-three year old writer "was able to unburden himself, to reveal himself, to shake off a nightmare" which had blighted his youth.

When in the middle of 1898 Wassermann moved from Munich to Vienna, "cutting the fatal cord" which kept him for four years in "suffocating and passionate erotic slavery," his uncle received him most hospitably—even the shrewd fan-manufacturer had come to realize that his nephew's writing was not one of his "mad ideas." Now his bohemianism was regarded with amusement and his aunt put her grand piano at his disposal. Wassermann gradually penetrated the cultural circles of wealthy Jews and married Julie Speyer, daughter of a prominent Jewish magistrate at whose home Hofmannsthal and Schnitzler were frequent guests.

The new century brought the long-awaited tranquillity to the hitherto distressed writer. He traveled frequently in Italy and the Tyrol; he became reconciled with his father, who died in 1901; he found a haven in a farm-house in Alt-Ausee (Styria), "a district which combines the mellowness of the Franconia countryside and the radiant beauty of Italian classical landscape" and which became as indispensible to him as it was to Mozart. He wrote fluently novel after novel but his first sensational triumph was scored in 1908 with *Caspar Hauser* which re-interprets the oft-treated story of the mysterious foundling Hauser, supposed to have been a cast-off prince of Baden, emphasizing how an innocent person is crushed by the insensate evil of the world. Wassermann's reputation rests primarily on *The Goose Man* (1915), a fascinating story dealing with old Nüremberg, and, more especially, on *The World's Illusion* (1919), a novel of tremendous scope depicting both high society and lower depths, and founded, in Tolstoyan manner, on an act of self-abnegation. The multimillionaire Christian Wannschaffe renounces name and wealth and submerges himself among the fallen; he realizes that justice is an illusion and that the source of evil is in man himself. "Gifted with extraordinary talent as a story-teller," observed one critic, "Wassermann was tempted to assume the role of a German Dostoievsky. He sought to be both the prophet of a world collapse and the herald of the reawakened soul, cleansed by pain and conscious of a new dignity." Arthur Eloesser wrote: "Thomas Mann and Jakob Wassermann are the first masters of modern fiction in German and, being both good Germans and good Europeans, have met with understanding abroad and made German literature, hitherto difficult of access, a conspicuous and highly respected feature in world literature."

Wassermann's wife, Julie Speyer-Wassermann, by whom he had several children, said that in 1914 "a new relationship with a woman led to a tragic break and our separation in October 1919." After the World War period, Wassermann's companion was the writer Marta Karlweis, who has written a biography of him.

Some critics classified Wassermann as a Franconian writer, others as an Austrian (because of his Styrian retreat), but he was, above all, Oriental—because of his imagination and his intellectual and ethical preoccupations, and even because of his physique: big round face charged with nervous mobility, illumined by jet-black eyes, accented by jet-black whiskers.

WORKS AVAILABLE IN ENGLISH TRANSLATION: *Biographies*—Christopher Columbus: Don Quixote of the Seas, 1930; Bula Matari (English title: H. M. Stanley, Explorer) 1932. *Correspondence*—The Letters of Jakob Wassermann to Frau Julie Wassermann, 1935. *Essay*—My Life as German and Jew, 1933. *Novels*—The World's Illusion, 1920; The Goose Man, 1922; Gold, 1924; Faber, 1925; Wedlock, 1926; The Triumph of Youth, 1927; Caspar Hauser, 1928; The Maurizius Case, 1929; Doctor Kerkhoven (English title: Etzel Andergast) 1932; Kerkhoven's Third Existence, 1933; Dark Pilgrimage (English title: The Jews of Zirndorf) 1933. *Short Stories*—Oberlin's Three Stages, 1925; World's Ends, 1927.

ABOUT: Bing, S. J. Wassermann; Bertaux, F. A Panorama of German Literature; Eloesser, A. Modern German Literature; Karlweis, M. J. Wassermann; Rosenfeld, P. Men Seen; Wassermann-Speyer, J. J. Wassermann; Germanic Review January 1928; Boston Evening Transcript March 11, 1933; Neue Rundschau April 1934; Revue de Littérature Comparée January 1939.

"WAST, HUGO." See MARTÍNEZ ZU-VIRÍA, G. A.

WATKIN, LAWRENCE EDWARD (December 9, 1901-), American novelist, writes: "Born in Camden, N.Y. Education in public school. My father died while I was in my early teens, leaving the family with too much land. (I was born in a section of town called Watkin's Addition.) Lack of ready cash should have precluded college education, but  my mother's driving energy sent me to Syracuse University, forty miles away, where I read largely and associated with a small, hard-bitten literary group of boys who scorned fraternities, athletics, activities, and formal education. The only activity I ever went out for was the *Phoenix*, the college literary publication. As one of the editors I submitted verse and satire and for month after month read a novel a day to supply book reviews. I don't remember doing much studying, but I did follow up tips about books from professors. Because of my limited interests I might have become a literary snob, but was saved from that by association with the essentially good, humble people I met while doing odd jobs after school hours and during vacations to help pay for my education. I still think the cook, waiter, window-washer, janitor, factory hand, farmer, or lumberjack who, with a love of personal liberty, rolls his own, is a better man than the middle-class fellow who burns whatever brands of cigarettes, books, or witches his bullying betters tell him to.

"Further education included a year of graduate work at Harvard and a few summers at Columbia. In 1926 I taught English at Syracuse, since then at Washington and Lee University, Lexington, Va., where composing plays for the college players I coached revived my interest in writing. I have done a few magazine articles besides my books. My interest in writing will always embrace the independence of Americans—and I don't mean the D.A.R."

* * *

Mr. Watkin's first novel, *On Borrowed Time,* a fantasy on the theme of death, was very popular, and was successfully dramatized by Paul Osborn and later filmed. *Geese in the Forum* is in a quite different vein, being a satire on college life among the faculty of what may or may not be Washington and Lee University. *Gentleman From*

England is a romantic tale of the years following the American Revolution. In 1926 he married Dorothy Edwards Parke, and they have a son and two daughters.

PRINCIPAL WORKS: On Borrowed Time, 1937; Geese in the Forum, 1940; Thomas Jones and His Nine Lives (juvenile) 1941; Gentleman From England, 1941; Marty Markham (juvenile) 1942.

WATSON, JOHN. See "BRITISH AUTHORS OF THE 19TH CENTURY"

WATSON, Sir WILLIAM (August 2, 1858-August 13, 1935), poet, was born at Burley-in-Wharfdale, Yorkshire, of an old

Yorkshire family on both sides. His family were Methodists, and his brother became a well known lay evangelist. He was privately educated and was not a university man, but received an honorary LL.D. from the University of Aberdeen in 1904. He spent much of his boyhood in Liverpool, and his first poems were published in the Liverpool *Argus*.

Watson's was a truly tragic life, partly for reasons within his own temperament, partly because of conditions quite beyond his own making. He gained fame overnight by his great poem, *Wordsworth's Grave*, in 1890, and in 1892 he was chosen to write the official elegy on Tennyson, a commission resulting in the fine *Lacrimae Musarum*. The decline in his popularity dates from the publication of *The Purple East*, in 1896, a passionate attack on Turkey and defense of the Armenian victims of Turkish tyranny which was directly opposed to official British policy. (One phrase from this volume—"Abdul the Damned"—stuck in popular memory as the permanent epithet of the Sultan Abdul Hamid, but the powerful quatrain which embodied that epithet was ignored and forgotten.) He offended still more when, a lifelong anti-Imperialist and liberal, he bitterly opposed the Boer War, and said so in scathing poems which stamped him as "pro-Boer." The consequence was that he was three times deprived of an honor which he greatly coveted, and to which he was the legitimate aspirant—the laureateship. The first time, on Tennyson's death, he was highly recommended but thought too young, and the egregious Alfred Austin was named in his stead. On Austin's death he had not only his Turkish

and Boer poems against him, but also that terrible attack on Margot Asquith (Lady Oxford), "The Woman With the Serpent's Tongue." And by the time Robert Bridges died, Watson was practically forgotten, an old man nobody thought of, and John Masefield was appointed laureate.

Neglect, poverty, debt of crushing proportions, and overwork were Watson's burden through his long life. In 1892 he broke down completely, and for a while was actually insane, with mania and delusions. He recovered, but remained permanently a neurotic, who might have been thought to suffer from persecution-mania were it not true enough that he was unfortunate and neglected. In 1909 he married Maureen Pring, an Irish lady, who became his staunchest advocate, more bitter than he himself over the treatment given him. They had two daughters. Watson's income was never sufficient for his family's needs, and by 1930, when he was already an old man, he had become so inextricably entangled in debt that his friends finally rescued him by a public subscription. In 1917 he had been knighted (perhaps thankfully for his not opposing the World War as he had opposed the Boer War), but this honor carried expense, not income, with it. He always had a small group of admirers who valued and perhaps over-valued his talents, but it is true that his earliest work was his best, and it was difficult to convince the general public that a poet of gradually failing ability was worthy of greater fame. He died at Rottingdean, Sussex, at seventy-seven. After his death Lady Watson was reported seeking service as a domestic.

A lifelong enemy of tyranny and friend of liberty, Watson's deepest bent was yet introspective and meditative. Wordsworth was his lifelong idol, and he remained a restrained romantic. His idealization and hero-worship of the great poets who were his only gods (he was all his life a "sad and reverent Agnostic") led to unfair accusations against him of imitation and even of plagiarism, but though his work is often derivative and bookish, it is derivative in the grand style; he drank so deeply of supreme poetry that it entered into his very being, to be given forth in diluted form, but transmuted into his own self-expression.

His sonnets and elegies are especially fine: it is doubly unfortunate that he was always disappointed of the laureateship, for after Tennyson no one in England would have made so satisfactory a laureate, or have been able to produce in so dignified and distinguished a manner the occasional poems demanded by the office. It galled him to see his own unofficial *Ode on the Coronation of King Edward VII* and to compare it with the feeble performances of the reigning laureate. One form of verse in which he excelled was the quatrains which he called "epigrams"; they display his power of succinct and polished sententiousness which caused him to be accepted as an acute critic in (not of) poetry.

Many of Watson's lyrics survive in anthologies though his numerous volumes are for the most part unread. He himself collected and edited one of the best of English poetic anthologies, *Lyric Love*. His prose works, *Excursions in Criticism* and *Pencraft*, are able but relatively undistinguished. It is as a poet that he will live, so far as he lives at all. He was not a genius, in any true sense of that much falsified term, but he was a man of unusual talent, a superb craftsman, who never received fully the recognition that was his due.

PRINCIPAL WORKS: The Prince's Quest, 1880; Epigrams of Art, Life, and Nature, 1884; Wordsworth's Grave, 1890; Lacrimae Musarum, 1892; The Eloping Angels, 1893; Excursions in Criticism, 1893; Odes and Other Poems, 1894; The Father of the Forest, 1895; The Purple East, 1896; The Year of Shame, 1896; The Hope of the World, 1897; Collected Poems, 1898; Ode on the Coronation of King Edward VII, 1902; For England, 1903; Collected Poems, 1906; New Poems, 1909; Sable and Purple, 1910; The Heralds of the Dawn, 1912; The Muse in Exile, 1913; Pencraft, 1916; Retrogression, 1916; The Man Who Saw, 1917; The Superhuman Antagonists, 1919; Ireland Unfreed, 1920; A Hundred Poems, 1922; Poems Brief and New, 1925; Selected Poems, 1928; I Was an English Poet (poems selected by Lady Watson) 1941.

ABOUT: Commonweal November 1, 1935; London Mercury September 1935; London Quarterly Review January 1936; Spectator August 16, 1935.

WATTS, Mrs. MARY (STANBERY)

(November 4, 1868-   ), American novelist, was born on a farm in Delaware County, central Ohio, the  daughter of John Rathbone Stanbery and Anna (Martin) Stanbery. She was educated at the Convent of the Sacred Heart, Clifton, Cincinnati, which she attended from 1881 to 1884. In November 1891 she married Miles Taylor Watts of Cincinnati, where they live. She is an Episcopalian.

Mrs. Watts' first novel, *The Tenants* (1908), was published when she was forty.

She followed it up with her best-known novel, *Nathan Burke*, laid in her native Scioto River country, one of the solid achievements of American historical fiction, and so realistic in tone and documentation that many readers were firmly convinced that Burke was a veritable historical personage. The book is still one of the best depictions in fiction of the war between Mexico and the United States. Mrs. Watts began by imitating Stevenson, but became dissatisfied with her work. "It became manifest to me," she wrote to Grant Overton, "that the thing to do was not to muddle around with romance, ancient or modern, but to write about people, and to 'lie like the truth.' I remember reading Thackeray, and being struck with the profitable use of the conversational style, as conversation is carried on between persons in good society. But what puzzled me was that there were occasional passages, of considerable extent, wherein Thackeray was not conversational at all; he was writing like somebody else, but it still had the most amazing verisimilitude. . . . After a while, in a moment of illumination, I found him out; the man he was modeling upon was Daniel Defoe; that's where he got upon that simplicity which did not hesitate at times to be prosy, well aware that a plain, true narrative has always the defect of its quality, monotony, repetition, and tedious dwelling on detail. Re-reading Defoe, and reading Thackeray more carefully, with side excursions into Swift and Thomas Hardy, it seemed to me that I have succeeded once or twice by the fact that nobody will believe that I have invented a single person or incident." To an inquirer in 1910 Mrs. Watts wrote, "Nobody ever had a duller time of it living, or a more commonplace life." Some of her later novels seem to be merely plodding, although irreproachable in verisimilitude. *The Rise of Jennie Cushing* was compared favorably with Phillips' *The Fall and Rise of Susan Lennox* and Dreiser's *Jennie Gerhardt*, and in England there arose a most unexpected champion in the person of Monsignor Robert Hugh Benson, who was "enraptured" by *Nathan Burke*, and who once declared Mrs. Watts to be "the only contemporary woman writer who understood men." Carl Van Doren calls her best quality "a kind heartiness of observation."

PRINCIPAL WORKS: The Tenants, 1908; Nathan Burke, 1910; The Legacy, 1911; Van Cleve: His Friends and His Family, 1913; The Rise of Jennie Cushing, 1914; The Rudder, 1916; Three Short Plays, 1917; The Boardman Family, 1918; From Father to Son, 1919; The Noon Mark, 1920;

The House of Rimmon, 1922; Luther Nichols, 1923; The Fabric of the Loom, 1924.

ABOUT: Overton, G. M. The Women Who Make Our Novels; Bookman July 1910; Mentor August 15, 1919.

WATTS-DUNTON, THEODORE. See "BRITISH AUTHORS OF THE 19TH CENTURY"

WAUGH, ALEC (July 8, 1898-), English novelist, was born Alexander Raban Waugh at Hampstead, the son of the editor and publisher Arthur Waugh[qv] and the elder brother of Evelyn Waugh.[qv] He was educated at Sherbourne School, where he edited the school magazine and wrote the prize poem, and at Sandhurst, the Royal Military College. He was gazet-

ted as record lieutenant to the Dorset Regiment in 1917, and was a prisoner of war from 1918 to the end of the war. He was by this time the author of a novel of school life which had caused a sensation, and of a book of youthful poems. He has been a world-wide traveler and since his school days an athlete, still being an active cricketer and golfer. His brother, Evelyn Waugh, says "you may meet him anywhere at any time and in any sort of company—always 'just going.'" In 1932 he married Joan Chirnside, an Australian, and they have two sons and a daughter. In 1940 he returned to active service in the army.

He is a short, sturdy man, bald, with a quizzical expression. "For the duration" (of the Hitler war) he says he is a soldier "with no spare time to write anything," but his books continue to be published. Several of his books are based on his travels; he has been frequently in the United States and has made several lecture tours. His brother thought in 1930 that he was "growing out of novel writing," and was "fitted for the rôle of historian." However, the greater part of his large output to date has been fiction, though three of his books—*Prisoners of Mainz, Myself When Young,* and *Thirteen Such Years*—may be considered at least partly autobiographical. For several years after 1924 he was literary advisor for Chapman & Hall, the publishing house of which his father was chairman. He has friends of the most miscellaneous variety all over the world, and writes best

on shipboard. Ben Ray Redman said of him that "he writes with a practiced but uncreative and unpersuasive hand," but several of his books have been very popular in England, though perhaps less so in America, where his younger brother is the better known of the two. The surname is pronounced *waw.*

PRINCIPAL WORKS: The Loom of Youth, 1917; Resentment (poems) 1918; The Prisoners of Mainz, 1919; Pleasure, 1921; The Lonely Unicorn, 1922; Public School Life, 1922; Roland Whately, 1922; Myself When Young, 1923; Card Castle, 1924; Kept, 1925; On Doing What One Likes, 1926; Love in These Days, 1926; The Last Chukka, 1928; Nor Many Waters, 1928; Portrait of a Celibate, 1929; Three Score and Ten, 1929; The Coloured Countries (in America: Hot Countries) 1930; Sir! She Said, 1930; Most Women. .., 1931; So Lovers Dream, 1931; That American Woman, 1932; Thirteen Such Years, 1932; Tropic Seed, 1932; No Quarter, 1932; The Golden Ripple, 1933; Leap Before You Look, 1933; Playing With Fire, 1933; Wheels Within Wheels, 1933; The Balliols, 1934; Jill Somerset, 1936; Eight Short Stories, 1937; Going Their Own Ways, 1938; Planning the Little House, 1939; No Truce With Time, 1941.

ABOUT: Waugh, A[lec]. Prisoners of Mainz, Myself When Young, Thirteen Such Years; Waugh, A[rthur]. One Man's Road; Bookman June 1930.

*WAUGH, ARTHUR (August 24, 1866-), English publisher, editor, and critic, was born at Midsomer Norton, Somerset, the son of Alexander Waugh, M.D. He was educated at Sherborne School and New College Oxford (Newdigate Prize 1888, B.A. 1889). The next year he came to London, where from 1892 to 1897 he was London correspond-

ent of the New York *Critic,* and in 1895 was sub-editor of the *New Review.* In 1895 he became literary adviser to Kegan Paul & Co., Ltd., the publishers, and left them in 1902 to become managing director of Chapman & Hall, a position he held until 1930. From 1926 to 1936 he was the firm's chairman, and since 1936 has been deputy chairman. For many years he was a book reviewer for the *Daily Telegraph.* In 1893 he married Catherine Rabin, and their two sons, Alec and Evelyn,[qqv] are both well-known authors. He has supervised editions of many English poets, including Milton, Tennyson, Arnold, and George Herbert; has edited Lamb and Dr. Johnson (*Lives of the Poets,* in six volumes, 1896); and was the

* Died June 27, 1943.

editor of the *Pamphlet Library* (1898) and of the Biographical Edition of Dickens (nineteen volumes, 1902-03).

A heavy-set man with gray hair and the classical profile of an old-time actor, he has a strong feeling for the stage, and his chief recreation is amateur dramatics. He lives in Highgate, London, and is a Conservative in politics.

He has published few books of his own, but in them, as one critic put it, he "combines scholarship and charm in an unusual degree." His autobiography, *One Man's Road,* is interesting, since he has known most of the literary great of his era; for the same reason, his history of Chapman & Hall, *A Hundred Years of Publishing,* is a valuable historical source-book. A bit pompous and quite out of tune with contemporary writing (including his sons'), he is not likely to survive as an author; but as an editor and particularly as a publisher he has been an influential force in English literature for nearly half a century.

PRINCIPAL WORKS: Gordon in Africa, 1888; Schoolroom Theatricals, 1890; Alfred, Lord Tennyson, 1892; Legends of the Wheel, 1898; Rhymes to Nicholson's Square Book of Animals, 1899; Robert Browning, 1900; Reticence in Literature, 1915; Tradition and Change, 1919; A Hundred Years of Publishing, 1930; One Man's Road, 1931.

ABOUT: Waugh, A. One Man's Road.

WAUGH, EVELYN (October 1903-   ), English novelist, satirist, biographer, and writer of travel books, was born Evelyn  Arthur St. John Waugh in London, the second son of Arthur Waugh,[qv] a literary critic and managing director of the publishing firm of Chapman & Hall, who published Dickens. Evelyn Waugh's brother Alec[qv] is also a well-known novelist. He attended Lancing School, his brother's novel, *The Loom of Youth,* having made it impossible for him to follow Alec Waugh at Sherborne School.

The latter school, in fact, had removed Waugh's name from its old boys' list, in reprisal for his animadversions on its management in his novel. Evelyn Waugh, says his father, had always shown a deeply religious temperament, and the strict discipline of Lancing did not chafe him. He edited the school paper, won a prize for English verse, organized the Dilettantes' Society, and persuaded a master to act in his three-

act play *Conversion,* which satirized the school as seen by maiden aunts, by novelists like his brother, and "as we all know it really is." Waugh was Senior History Scholar at Hertford College, Oxford University. After leaving Oxford he spent a year in London attending art school, and wrote a critical biography of Dante Gabriel Rossetti which combined brilliance with sobriety. With varying degrees of application he taught school, worked on the *Daily Express,* and took up the study "of carpentry and of fashionable society." As a personal friend of the wealthy Guinness family (his novel *Vile Bodies* is dedicated to Bryan and Diana Guinness) he had full opportunity for first-hand observations of the conduct of the **Bright Young People of the day**—their treasure-hunts, motor races, and casual amours. The fate of Miss Agatha Runcible in *Vile Bodies* curiously foreshadowed the return to England from Nazi Germany of Hitler's friend and admirer Unity Valkyrie Freeman-Mitford, sister of Diana Guinness, with a bullet lodged in her head.

Waugh's novels, which are "hectic pieces of savage satire," are an odd contrast to such serious studies as the Rossetti book and the *Edmund Campion* of 1935, a book about the Elizabethan martyr and Recusant poet which won the Hawthornden Prize in 1936.

Evelyn Waugh once listed his chief aversions as love, conversation, the stage, writing, and Wales. (His recreations are eating, drinking, drawing, and traveling). Only the Welsh aversion, as tellingly expressed in *Decline and Fall,* seems to have been insuperable.

In 1928 Waugh married the Honorable Evelyn Gardner, daughter of Lord Burghclere. They were divorced in 1930, the same year he was received into the Catholic Church. In 1937 he married Laura Herbert, youngest daughter of the late Colonel Hon. Aubrey Herbert, M.P. They have a daughter, and live at Piers Court, Stinchcombe, Gloucestershire. His clubs are the St. James' and Buck's. Though his novels are filled with hilariously amusing as well as mordantly ironic situations, Waugh's travel books are rather grim and purposeful in tone. The Abyssinian books are the work of an experienced and capable reporter; the later *Mexico* is told from a conservative, Catholic point of view. (Catholicism has become one of his major interests.) *Scoop* is a blistering satire on Northcliffian journalism and modern radio broadcasting. The writer is blond, immaculately dressed, and his mien (in photographs) is appropriately bored and sophisticated.

Evelyn Waugh joined the British marines shortly after the outbreak of the Second World War in 1939; he was among the first to volunteer for Commando work.

PRINCIPAL WORKS: Rossetti: A Critical Biography, 1928; Decline and Fall, 1928; Vile Bodies, 1930; Labels (U.S. title: A Bachelor Abroad) 1930; Remote People (U.S. title: They Were Still Dancing) 1932; Black Mischief, 1932; Ninety-Two Days, 1934; A Handful of Dust, 1934; Edmund Campion, 1935; Waugh in Abyssinia, 1936; Mr. Loveday's Outing and Other Sad Stories, 1936; Scoop, 1938; Robbery Under Law: The Mexican Object Lesson (U.S. title: Mexico: An Object Lesson) 1939; Put Out More Flags, 1942.

ABOUT: Waugh, A. One Man's Road; Woollcott, A. The Woollcott Reader; Wilson Library Bulletin April 1931.

WAY, ARTHUR SANDERS (February 13, 1847-September 25, 1930), English translator and educator, was born in Dorking, the second son of the Rev. William Way, and was educated at Kingswood School, Bath, and later became a Fellow of Queen's College, Melbourne, Australia, where he was classical lecturer for a time. He was vice-master of his school at Bath, 1876-81; headmaster of Wesley College, Victoria, 1882-92; examiner in Latin to the Central Welsh Board of Secondary Education, 1897-1904, and acting headmaster of Mill Hill School in 1913. Of masculine character and athletic figure (an admiring ex-pupil calls him "virile, strong, stately, magnificent"), Way was quite capable of writing original poetry, but was satisfied to rest his reputation for a half-century on translations of classical poets, even including Sappho and Pindar. Occasionally he used the pseudonym "Avia." His translations usually paid for themselves after ten or fifteen years. In the twenty-four books of the *Odyssey* he used a middle rhyme, suggested by Swinburne's *Proserpine*, through the narrative portions from beginning to end. The scholar's pride was not one of Way's failings; he frankly admitted that he preferred Gilbert Murray's translations to his own. For diversion he turned to gardening.

PRINCIPAL WORKS: *Translations*—The Odes of Horace, 1876; The Odyssey of Homer in English Verse, 1880; The Iliad, 1886-1889; Tragedies of Euripides in English Verse, 1894-1898; Epodes of Horace in English Verse, 1898; Aeschylus in English Verse, 1906-1908; Sophocles in English Verse, 1909-1914; The Nibelungenlied in English Verse, 1911; The Cyclops of Euripides, 1912; Virgil's Georgics in English Verse, 1912; Theocritus, Bion, and Moschus in English Verse, 1913; Manual of Homer, 1913; Virgil's Aeneid in English Verse, 1916-1924; Sappho and The Vigil of Venus, 1920; Pindar, 1921; Greek Through English, 1926; Aristophanes in English Verse, 1927.

ABOUT: London Quarterly Review July 1930, January 1931.

WEAVER, JOHN VAN ALSTYN (July 17, 1893-June 14, 1938), American poet and novelist, was born at Charlotte, N.C., the son of John Van Alstyn Weaver and Anne Randolph (Tate) Weaver. In 1914 he received the degree of B.A. from Hamilton College at Clinton, N.Y.; became assistant to the book editor of the *Chicago Daily News* in 1916; and entered the U.S. Army May 1917 to serve until June 1919. He was commissioned a second lieutenant in the Officers Reserve Corps in December 1918. Returned to the *News* in 1919, Weaver went to the Brooklyn *Daily Eagle* in 1920 to remain as literary editor until 1924. *In American,* his first book of "cleverly constructed lyrics in the common, loosely phrased language of the streets," appeared in 1921 and caused the Boston *Transcript* to remark that "spirit and language have conjoined to produce what is faithfully national." *More in American* (1925) continued these poems, which were said to typify the thoughts and feelings of O. Henry people, and describe "the strange futility of urban existence." Abandoning "shirtsleeves poetry," Weaver wrote a verse-autobiography in 1931, *Trial Balance: A Sentimental Inventory,* which owed much to his happy marriage with Peggy Wood, a light-opera singer and actress. They had a son, David.

Kesslere

From 1928 Weaver wrote mostly for the motion pictures. He wrote originals for Clara Bow and adapted *Tom Sawyer* to the screen, but never "went Hollywood"; indeed his *Joy-Girl* of 1932 bitterly satirized the film colony. His one stage play, written with George Abbott, *Love 'Em and Leave 'Em,* had a creditable run in New York. Weaver was slender, dark, and personable, with a ready smile. He died of tuberculosis at Colorado Springs.

PRINCIPAL WORKS: *Poetry*—In American, 1921; Finders, 1923; More in American, 1925; To Youth, 1927; The Turning Point, 1930; Trial Balance, 1931; In American: Collected Poems (enlarged ed.) 1939. *Novels*—Margie Wins the Game, 1922; Her Knight Comes Riding, 1928; Joy-Girl, 1932.

ABOUT: Weaver, J. V. A. In American (see foreword by H. L. Mencken to 1939 ed.); Wood, P. How Young You Look; New York Times June

16, 1938; Poetry August 1938; Saturday Review of Literature, December 10, 1938; Scholastic October 2, 1939; Time June 27, 1938.

*WEBB, Mrs. BEATRICE (POTTER) (January 22, 1858-   ) and *WEBB, SIDNEY, 1st Baron Passfield (July 13, 1859-   ),

English economists, must inevitably be treated together because since their marriage in 1892 their lives and work have been inseparable. George Bernard Shaw remarked long ago that "the Webbs can exchange gloves, shoes, and lectures at a moment's notice." To state their careers briefly to the time of their union, Mrs. Webb (she has never accepted the title of Lady Passfield, though her husband agreed reluctantly to elevation to the peerage in 1929 in order to represent Labor in the House of Lords) was the youngest of nine daughters of Richard Potter, a railway president. She was born in London and educated privately. Her real education came from reading, from association with her father's friend Herbert Spencer (whose literary executrix she became), and from a long trip in the United States with her father and sister when she was only fifteen. Though as a young girl she was almost beautiful (even in her eighties she is still handsome in a flashing, aquiline way), efforts to make a society belle of her failed dismally; before she was twenty she was a Free Thinker with longings for a career as a philosopher, and before her twenties were over she had been definitely oriented to social and economic studies. Her first work was as an assistant to Charles Booth in his investigation of poverty in London; what she saw made her a Socialist. It was in this environment that she met Sidney Webb, and they were married after the death of her father in 1892.

Sidney Webb also was London-born, the son of Charles Webb, and educated in Switzerland, Mecklenburg-Schwerin, and in London at Birbeck Institute and City of London College. He was in the civil service from 1875 to 1891, when he resigned to enter the London County Council, where he sat until 1909. He has taught political economy and public administration in the City of London College and the London School of Economics (University of London). He was admitted to the bar in 1885. He was Labor M.P. for Durham from 1922 to 1929.

Loaded with honorary degrees, both the Webbs have been on practically every important committee dealing with labor in England during the present century. They were the principal founders of the Fabian Society. The investigations they have conducted are innumerable. Their history is practically the history of the English labor movement during the past fifty years. Theirs has always been a partnership of plain living, endless industry, selfless devotion, and patient persistence in the elucidation of fact. It is true that there is also about them a sort of dryness, an over-intellectualism and lack of feeling. But the work they have done is unique, and is so valuable that their Puritanical rigor and cold idealism count as very minor blemishes. Very small, bearded, with thick eyebrows behind pince-nez, Sidney Webb has been called by unsympathetic observers a wren mated with an eagle; but actually, though he is soft-spoken, clumsy, and unworldly, he is the dominant partner of the two, and has often restrained his wife from a tendency to peremptoriness and "flightiness." They are an ideal combination, in outward manifestation more an institution than two related human beings, but in their inner life utterly devoted and at one. Sidney Webb is now an invalid, and his wife too, though still active, is beginning to feel the weight of her more than eighty years of life. They will have left behind them a monument "more lasting than bronze."

PRINCIPAL WORKS: *By Beatrice and Sidney Webb*—The History of Trade Unionism, 1894; Industrial Democracy, 1897; Problems of Modern Industry, 1898; History of Liquor Licensing, 1903; English Local Government (15 vols.) 1906-22; English Poor Law Policy, 1910; The State and the Doctor, 1910; The Prevention of Destitution, 1911; A Constitution for the Socialist Commonwealth of Great Britain, 1920; Consumer's Co-operative Movement, 1921; Decay of Capitalist Civilization, 1923; English Poor Law History (3 vols.) 1927-30; Soviet Communism: A New Civilization (2 vols.) 1935; The Truth About Soviet Russia, 1942. *By Beatrice Webb*—The Co-operative Movement in Great Britain, 1891; Men's and Women's Wages: Should They Be Equal? 1919; My Apprenticeship (autobiography) 1926. *By Sidney Webb*—Socialism in England, 1890; The Eight Hours' Day, 1891; Labour in the Longest Reign, 1897; London Education, 1904; Grants in Aid, 1911; Towards Social Democracy? 1916; The Works Manager Today, 1917; Story of the Durham Miners, 1921.

ABOUT: Hamilton, M. A. Sidney and Beatrice Webb; Webb, B. My Apprenticeship; American Economic Review March 1921; Atlantic Monthly September 1933; Catholic World May 1938; Current History November 1932; Nation June 3, 1931; New Statesman and Nation January 22,

* Mrs. Webb died April 30, 1943; her husband on October 13, 1947.

1485

1938; Outlook (London) October 18, 1924; Saturday Review (London) January 13, 1934; Social Service Review March 1938; Spectator January 26, 1924, January 21, 1938.

WEBB, Mrs. MARY GLADYS (MEREDITH) (March 25, 1881-October 8, 1927), English novelist,

was born at Leighton-under-the-Wrekin, Shropshire, the eldest daughter of George Edward Meredith, a schoolmaster of Welsh descent, and Sarah Alice (Scott) Meredith, daughter of an Edinburgh doctor who was a member of Sir Walter's clan. The girl inherited her passionate love of the country from her father, from whom, as Lady Tweedsmuir (wife of the novelist, John Buchan) says, she derived the charming, sympathetic character John Arden in her novel, *The Golden Arrow*. Mary was educated at home, where she was brought up with swarms of bees, and spent two years at private school at Southport. As a child she wrote stories and poetry. In 1912 she married Henry Bertram Law Webb, a schoolmaster. The couple, who had no children, lived at Weston-super-Mare, Lyth Hill near Shrewsbury, and, from 1921 on, at Hampstead.

Her five novels, from *The Golden Arrow* in 1916 to *Precious Bane* in 1924, were launched into an unresponsive world. Sales were small, although *Precious Bane* was awarded the Femina-Vie Heureuse prize for 1924-25. Stanley Baldwin, then Prime Minister, wrote her on January 17, 1927, as a lover of old Shropshire days; the letter appears in facsimile in Mary Webb's posthumous and unfinished novel, *Armour Wherein He Trusted*. She died at St. Leonards, Sussex, and the obituary notices were brief and few. Baldwin publicly praised her work at a Royal Literary Fund dinner, April 25, 1928, and started (too late for Mary Webb to enjoy it) the ball of her fame rolling. Mary Webb's five novels were promptly reprinted, with introductions by Baldwin, John Buchan, Chesterton, Robert Lynd, and H. R. L. Sheppard.

A volume of poems and essays had a preface by Walter de la Mare, who said that "all that she wrote is suffused with poetry." Mary Webb's prose cadences, as Lady Tweedsmuir pointed out, derive from seventeenth-century models, especially Sir Thomas Browne. Her narrative style had a fiery intensity, although it inclined to be didactic and sometimes over-colored. Her plots were sombre. She was acutely conscious of the cruelties of human life, although not so much so of those of nature. *Armour Wherein He Trusted,* her unfinished novel, departed from modern Shropshire to medieval times (the First Crusade); it has been compared variously to a tapestry and a missal illuminated with bright colors. There is minute and unerring observation of the country in her essays, which combine "subtlety of observation and beauty of thought and phrasing."

Mary Webb was not a great novelist, but a woman with the soul of a poet and the observation of an artist, in the opinion of Grace Chapman, who also states that she has no originality of plot and very little sense of characterization and character development. "The good remain irritatingly righteous, the bad monotonously wicked, while the comic are at all costs facetious, and the faithful persevere in unswerving devotion." Mrs. Webb was called unearthly in appearance, with large eyes and a rather odd manner of dressing. Her shyness was incongruously linked with an insatiable curiosity and a liking for the society of celebrities. She was "an incomparable housewife."

PRINCIPAL WORKS: The Golden Arrow, 1916; Gone to Earth, 1917; The House in Dormer Forest, 1920; Seven for a Secret, 1922; Precious Bane, 1924; Armour Wherein He Trusted, 1929; The Spring of Joy (poems and essays) 1929.

ABOUT: Addison, H. Mary Webb; Byford-Jones, W. Shropshire Haunts of Mary Webb; Moult, T. Mary Webb: Her Life and Work; Prefaces to novels, 1928; Bookman (London) July 1928, February 1929; London Mercury February 1931; Saturday Review August 30, 1930.

WEBB, SIDNEY. See WEBB, B.

WEBSTER, HENRY KITCHELL (September 7, 1875-December 9, 1932), American popular novelist, was born in Evanston, Ill., the son of Emma J. (Kitchell) and Towner Keeney Webster. Like John V. A. Weaver and Alexander Woollcott, he

graduated from Hamilton College, which supplemented his bachelor's degree of 1897 with an honorary L.H.D. in 1925. He was instructor in rhetoric at Union College in 1897-98, returning to Evanston to collaborate with Samuel Merwin[qv] on successful novels about railroading, notably *Calumet "K"* (1901). With Merwin, young Webster had written operas, edited an amateur fortnightly, *The Boy's Herald,* and published a book of "awful verse" at Webster's father's expense. The two young men shut themselves into a room for their later collaborations, and Webster, smoking a corncob, would formulate sentences in his mind and write them down in longhand. Ten years and more later, when Webster set up shop as a one-man fiction factory, he dictated thrillers to a stenographer at the rate of 20,000 words a week. His highly-paid "stories of the stage, of married life, adventures in the region of pure feeling and delicate human relationships," as Merwin once described them, were in demand by the *Saturday Evening Post, Everybody's* and *McClure's. An American Family* is perhaps the only one of these productions that has any likelihood of survival. *The Alleged Great-Aunt,* a somewhat commonplace mystery story, was cut off in the middle of a chapter by Webster's death at nearly fifty-seven. The writing Ayer sisters, Janet Ayer Fairbank and Margaret Ayer Barnes, lifelong friends of the Webster family, undertook to finish it as "an experiment in imitative writing." "The point where the collaboration began is our little mystery," they stated in the preface to the novel. Webster married Mary Ward Orth of Evanston in September 1901, and they had three children, Henry Kitchell, Stokely, and Roderick Sheldon. He knew Elizabethan poetry well, read French and Italian, and was a belligerent classicist in music, once walking out on a performance by Theodore Thomas in Chicago of Richard Strauss' *Thus Spake Zarathustra.* Webster had a long face, a full firm mouth, gray hair, and wore eye-glasses.

PRINCIPAL WORKS: The Banker and the Bear, 1899; The Story of a Corner in Land, 1900; Roger Drake: Captain of Industry, 1903; The Duke of Cameron Avenue, 1904; Traitor and Loyalist, 1904; The Whispering Man, 1908; A King in Khaki, 1909; The Sky Man, 1910; The Girl in the Other Seat, 1911; The Ghost Girl, 1913; The Butterfly, 1914; The Real Adventure, 1916; The Painted Scene, 1916; The Thoroughbred, 1917; An American Family, 1918; Mary Wollaston, 1920; Real Life, 1921; Joseph Greer and his Daughter, 1922; The Innocents, 1924; The Corbin Necklace, 1926; Philopena, 1927; The Beginners, 1927; The Clock Strikes Two, 1928; The Quartz Eye, 1928; The Sealed Trunk, 1929. *With Samuel Merwin*—The Short Line War, 1899; Calumet "K", 1901; Comrade Jim, 1907.

ABOUT: New York Times December 10, 1932.

WEBSTER, JEAN (July 24, 1876-June 11, 1916), American novelist and short-story writer, was born Alice Jane Chandler Webster in Fredonia, N.Y., the first child of Charles Luther Webster and Annie (Moffett) Webster. She was named Jane for Mark Twain's mother, and was his grandniece. Her father was a publisher, once Twain's partner, who handed Grant's

widow a hugh check for Grant's *Memoirs.* After attending the public schools at Fredonia, she prepared at the Lady Jane Grey School, Binghamton, N.Y., for Vassar, which gave her a B.A. degree in 1901. The girl was contributor to a Poughkeepsie, N.Y., newspaper and wrote stories for the *Vassar Miscellany.* Majoring in English and economics, she had occasion to visit institutions for the destitute and delinquent, which gave her a firm conviction that there was no reason why underprivileged children could not succeed in life, a thesis she developed with humor and modern spirit in *Daddy-Long-Legs.* The novel was later successfully dramatized by its author and made into a silent picture by Mary Pickford. *When Patty Went to College,* a collection of amusing stories probably modeled on a classmate, Adelaide Crapsey, the poet,[qv] was serialized while Miss Webster was still at Vassar. *The Wheat Princess* was her own favorite novel. *Jerry Junior* was written at a convent in the Sabine Mountains one chilly spring, when she was making a long stay in Italy during a world tour in 1907. *The Four Pools Mystery* was published anonymously.

In 1915 Jean Webster married Glenn Ford McKinney. They had an apartment in New York City overlooking Central Park, and an estate at Tyringham, Mass., in the Berkshire Hills. Here they raised ducks and pheasants. Jean Webster died in a hospital soon after the birth of their daughter; she was not yet forty. A room in the Girls' Service League and a bed at the county branch of the New York Orthopedic Hospital, near White Plains, N.Y., were endowed in her memory

PRINCIPAL WORKS: When Patty Went to College, 1903; The Wheat Princess, 1905; Jerry Junior, 1907; The Four Pools Mystery, 1908; Much Ado About Peter, 1909; Just Patty, 1911; Daddy-Long-Legs, 1912; Dear Enemy (sequel) 1914.

WEDEKIND

ABOUT: Century November 1916; New Republic March 13, 1915; New York Times November 9, December 13, 1914, June 12, 1916.

WEDEKIND, FRANK (July 24, 1864-March 9, 1918), German playwright, was born in Hanover. His father, Dr. Friedrich

Wedekind, was physician to the Sultan of Turkey for ten years and on returning home participated in the Revolution of 1848, sat in the Frankfort Parliament, escaped to America, and settled in San Francisco, where at the age of forty-six he married the twenty-three-year old actress Emilie Kammerer. Dr. and Mrs. Wedekind returned to Germany in 1864. The second of their six children, Franklin, was born in Hanover, where he learned his first letters. In 1872 his parents bought the famous Lenzburg Castle in Aarau (Switzerland). Franklin was sent to the Bezirk school (1875-79) and in the fall of 1879 to the Aarau *gymnasium* from which he was graduated four years later. His chief interests were biology (sex) and literature (Wieland, Bürger, Heine, and Georg Büchner).

At the age of nineteen Wedekind reluctantly entered the University of Zurich Law School. Soon he quit, and after a short sojourn at Munich returned to Zurich in 1886 and obtained a position in the publicity department of Maggi, the soup-condensers. Soon he found his way into the literary radical circles, became acquainted with the Anarchist Henry MacKay and the then Socialist playwright Hauptmann, studiously read Stirner, Nietzsche, and Strindberg, and contributed short pieces to the local papers.

After his father's death in 1888 Wedekind felt freer to follow a bohemian life in Munich, Paris, London: for half a year he was secretary to the Herzog Circus, then to the painter Rudinoff, and finally to the Danish painter Willy Gretor. While in London (1893) Wedekind met the poet Dauthenday who introduced him to Symbolist literature. Dissatisfied with the uncompromising naturalism of Hauptmann, Wedekind from the earliest had preferred the strange violence of Strindberg, the romantic excesses of Panizza, and the lyricism of Büchner, whose *Woyzeck* influenced him profoundly. When he made his début as a playwright with *Spring's Awakening* (1891), both public and critics agreed that something *new* was in the air

despite conflicting judgments: to some the play was outright pornography, to others a dramatic lecture on the sex education of children, to others just good theatre. It was a difficult play to classify: the content had been drawn directly from life but its handling was imaginative, in fact its finale verged on romanticism. This mixture of romanticism and realism, which preluded the Expressionist movement, characterized most of Wedekind's works and was responsible, together with the accent on sex, for his rising popularity, especially during the pre-war years. Wedekind's reputation became solidly established with his next play, *Earth Spirit* (1895), a veritable masterpiece of craftsmanship. Often deprived of his profits, Wedekind was forced to sing ballads, to his accompaniment on the guitar, in Munich restaurants and Swiss cafés, to work as *regisseur* and actor at Leipzig's Ibsentheater and Munich's Schauspielhaus, and, finally, to join the staff of *Simplicissimus* which soon involved him in a trial for *lèse majesté*.

In 1908 Wedekind married an actress and thereafter lived at Munich, with occasional visits to Berlin to produce his own plays at Max Reinhardt's Neues Theater. Wedekind wrote play after play until his death in 1918, he and his wife often playing the leading rôles. He was frequently persecuted by the censor—in 1905-06 his *Pandora's Box* involved him in a long trial. As Eloesser has so deftly put it: "At first people would almost cross themselves at Wedekind's works, as though he were Satan incarnate, but posterity may prefer to recognize him rather as a priest listening to humanity's confession of its perturbing and shameful secrets. His creed had its answers and remedies in readiness: his confessions of his faith were inspired by a purpose, essentially opposed to that of Nature, which made him the father of Expressionism and activism in Germany."

PRINCIPAL WORKS AVAILABLE IN ENGLISH TRANSLATION: *Plays*—The Awakening of Spring, 1909; Such Is Life, 1912; The Dance of Death (Damnation) 1913; The Box of Pandora, 1913; Tragedies of Sex (Spring's Awakening, Earth Spirit, Pandora's Box, Damnation) 1913; Earth Spirit, 1914; The Tenor, 1920; Marquis of Keith, 1924. *Short Stories*—The Grisly Suitor, 1911; Rabbi Ben Ezra, 1911; The Victim, 1911; Princess Russalka, 1919.

ABOUT: Blei, F. Über Wedekind; Chandler, F. W. Modern Continental Playwrights; Dukes, A. Modern Drama; Durve, W. Die Dramatische Form Wedekinds; Eloesser, A. Modern German Literature; Elster, H. M. Frank Wedekind; Fechter, T. Frank Wedekind; Friedenthal, J. Das Wedekindbuch; Kapp, J. Frank Wedekind; Kemper, H. Frank Wedekind; Kutscher, A. Frank Wedekind; Poupeye, C. Les Dramaturges Exotiques; Proost, K. F. Frank Wedekind; Samuel, H. B. Modernities; Schweizer, E. Das Groteske und das Drama Wedekinds; Vieweger, E. Frank Wedekind und Sein Werk; Drama March 1925; Freeman October 10, 1923; New Satesman April 4, 1931; Poet Lore July-August 1913; Revue Germanique March-April 1913.

*WEEKLEY, ERNEST (1865-), English etymologist,

writes: "I was born at Hampstead, the second child of Charles and Agnes Weekley. In those days Hampstead was still an unspoilt and beautiful suburb on the Northern heights of London. I was educated privately and later studied at the Universities of Berne, Cambridge, Paris, and Freiburg im Bresgau. At Cambridge I was a Major Scholar and Prizeman of Trinity College, and also took the M.A. degree in French and German of the University of London. While in Paris I worked at the Sorbonne and the École des Hautes Études and at Freiburg held the position of Lector in English. After some years of schoolmastering and coaching work, I became, in 1898, professor of French at University College, Nottingham, and later on was for many years Dean of the Faculty of Arts and Head of the Modern Language Department. I retired in 1938 after exactly forty years' service, and now live at Richmond, Surrey.

"As a young man I wrote a number of books connected with the study of French, but for the past thirty years or more have devoted myself to problems in English etymology, especially so far as the French element in our vocabulary is concerned. The series of works I have published on this subject began with *The Romance of Words*, in 1912. My books have all appeared in American editions. Most of them have been reprinted more than once. At various times I have contributed articles and reviews to the *Edinburgh Review* (now extinct), the *Quarterly Review*, the *Cornhill Magazine* (suspended for the duration of the war), and, in America, the *Atlantic Monthly*, besides a large number of reviews in the daily press.

"My work in etymology, in which I frequently differ from the views of the *Oxford English Dictionary*, seems to have been extensively utilized by the latest edition of Webster. No acknowledgment is made, but

my name is included in the dictionary's list of world celebrities!"

* * *

Weekley has M.A. degrees from Cambridge as well as from the University of London. He lived in Richmond until a Nazi bomb demolished his house in 1940, and since then has made his home in Middlesex. His books are mines of fascinating treasure to any reader seriously interested in the history and construction of our language.

PRINCIPAL WORKS: A Primer of Historical French Grammar, 1909; The Romance of Words, 1912; The Romance of Names, 1914; Surnames, 1916; An Etymological Dictionary of Modern English, 1921; A Concise Etymological Dictionary of Modern English, 1924; Words Ancient and Modern, 1926; More Words Ancient and Modern, 1927; Adjectives and Other Words, 1930; Saxo Grammaticus: or, First Aid to the Best Seller (in America: Cruelty to Words) 1931; Words and Names, 1932; Something About Words, 1935; Jack and Jill: A Study in Our Our Christian Names, 1939; (ed.) Hugh Stewart, 1939.

WEEKS, EDWARD AUGUSTUS, Jr.

(February 19, 1898-), American editor and man-of-letters, was born in Elizabeth, N.J., and educated at Cornell, Harvard (B.S. 1922), and Cambridge University, England. He has honorary Litt.D. degrees from Northeastern and Lake Forest Universities. In 1923 he became a manuscript reader and book salesman

for a New York publisher, but in 1924 went to the *Atlantic Monthly* as associate editor and has been with this magazine ever since. After a year as acting editor, he became editor in 1938, on the retirement of Ellery Sedgwick. From 1928 to 1937 he was in charge of the Atlantic Monthly Press, and still maintains a supervisory direction of it. During the First World War he was an ambulance driver in France, attached to the French army, and received the Volunteers' Medal and the Croix de Guerre. In 1929 and 1930 he was chairman of the Massachusetts Committee to Reform Book Censorship. In 1925 he married Frederica Wattriss; they have a son and a daughter, and live in Boston.

Mr. Weeks has written only one book, a volume on writing as a profession. But books and authors, as Carolyn Marx remarked, "are his chief concern in life." Part of his duties on the *Atlantic* has been to act as as-

---

* Died May 7, 1954.

sociate book reviewer, and while he was actively at the head of the Atlantic Monthly Press he read all manuscripts submitted to it. He has been a judge in all the annual Atlantic book competitions, both for novels and for non-fiction books. In his fight against book censorship he aided in reforming the antiquated censorship laws of Massachusetts, which had so often made "banned in Boston" a symbol of the ridiculous. Besides his editorial work, he lectures regularly on books and authors at the Institute of Arts and Sciences of Columbia University, and he periodically conducts a radio broadcast series on curiosities of literary history which is one of the high spots of radio's educational program. He has done much to keep the *Atlantic Monthly* contemporaneous in its interests and to broaden its scope, so that today it is one of the only two survivors (*Harper's* is the other) of the "quality group" of a generation ago. Witty, liberal-minded, and forward-looking, he is one of the most competent and respected magazine editors of our time.

PRINCIPAL WORKS: This Trade of Writing, 1935; Great Short Novels (comp.) 1941.

ABOUT: Christian Science Monitor Magazine September 9, 1939; Publishers' Weekly June 11, 1938, January 20, July 6, 1940.

WEIDMAN, JEROME (August 4, 1913-), American novelist and short story writer, was born in New York City, the son

of Joseph Weidman and Anne (Falkovitz) Weidman. He was educated at the College of the City of New York, Washington Square College of New York University, and the New York University Law School. He was admitted to the bar, but has never practised law. From the beginning he was interested primarily in people, regarding his fellow-beings with a cold scientific eye. He likes to take them apart and find out what makes them tick. The result, as one critic remarked, "is much too true to be entertaining." More even than John O'Hara, Weidman has specialized in the depiction of thorough "heels." His people are horrifying, and he is inexorable in his presentation of them. In his short stories he writes usually about the same kind of men and women as in his novels, but occasionally exhibits an unexpected vein of fantasy. But in general he is strictly an urban—in fact,

strictly a New York—writer. His world is bounded by New York, and by a certain stratum of New York life. "I have never seen a sunset or a mountain top that can match the fascination of 14th Street between 2nd Avenue and Broadway on a Saturday night," he insists. He is primarily a man's writer—that is, his masculine characters are vivid and solid, his women usually "sticks." That he himself is a bachelor may be either cause or effect.

Following a wave of protest against the portrayal of Jews in *What's In It For Me?* the publishers, Simon & Schuster, agreed to cease printing the book at the end of 1938. Burton Rascoe, in bitterly opposing this attitude, called Weidman "a very fine prose artist, . . . a brilliant, sensitive, cultured, and extraordinarily talented young man." He is all these things, but there is a frigid cruelty about his work which reduces much of it to the level of "a smart piece of work smartly done." Gentle or kindly human beings exist, in his books, only to be bilked and humiliated by their cleverer and more unscrupulous fellows. Behind all this is undoubtedly a deep anger, an outraged disillusionment, which may mean that with increasing maturity Mr. Weidman will work all his loathing and hatred out of his system and, with his undoubtedly high talents, be able to see human nature as a whole instead of concentrating on its least pleasant manifestations. Meanwhile, his work is extremely interesting, differing from most "hard-boiled" fiction of his generation by the indignation implicit in his merciless dissection of the human lice who are his chosen subjects.

Returning home in October 1939 from a trip around the world (described in *Letter of Credit*) Weidman joined the editorial staff of his publishers. In March 1942 he resigned from Simon & Schuster to work for the Coordinator of Information as chief of the book division. His name is pronounced *wide'man*.

PRINCIPAL WORKS: I Can Get It For You Wholesale, 1937; What's In It For Me? 1938; The Horse That Could Whistle "Dixie" (short stories) 1939; Letter of Credit, 1940; I'll Never Go There Any More, 1941.

ABOUT: Current Biography 1942; Newsweek January 2, 1939; Publishers' Weekly November 23, 1940; Scholastic November 20, 1939; Time May 10, 1937.

WEIGALL, ARTHUR EDWARD PEARSE BROME (November 20, 1880-January 20, 1934), English Egyptologist and miscellaneous writer, was the son of Major A. A. D. Weigall and Alice (Cowan) Weigall, daughter of General L. Cowan. His full name was Arthur Edward Pearse Brome Weigall. He obtained his preliminary education at Hillside School, Malvern, and Wellington College.

Weigall matrimulated at New College, Oxford, in 1900, but left after a short residence to become assistant to Professor Flinders Petrie on the staff of the Egyptian Exploration fund. In 1905 he was appointed Inspector General of Antiquities of the Egyptian government, holding the post to 1914.

Weigall's first publications were a part of *Abydos*, a report, of which the first section appeared in 1902 and the second in 1904. Other works on antiquities succeeded, but his first popular success was a biography of Akhnaton, father-in-law of Tut-ankh-amen, which appeared in 1910 and was reissued in a revised edition in 1922. *The Life of Cleopatra: Queen of Egypt* (1914) also sold so well as to require a revision and republication ten years later. From 1904 to 1914 Weigall passed almost all his time at Luxor, where he discovered the tomb of Queen Tiy, which also contained the tomb of Akhnaton and those of his grandparents.

Essentially a popularizer of scientific literature, Weigall was also prevailed upon to forsake serious archaeological studies so far as to write three novels which were probably patterned after E. M. Hull's great popular success, *The Sheik*. These were *Madeline of the Desert*, *The Dweller in the Desert*, called *Burning Sands* in the United States, and *Bedouin Love*. He even wrote lyrics for some of the songs in *Charlot's Revue*, 1924, in which his sister-in-law, Beatrice Lillie, made the first of many successful stage-appearances in the United States. The first Mrs. Weigall was Hortense Schleiter, of Chicago; and the second, Muriel Frances Lillie of Hillsborough, County Down, Ireland. Weigall, who died in a London hospital two months to the day after his fifty-fourth birthday, following a long illness, preserved his light-hearted spirit to the end. The *Nero* of 1930 and *Sappho of Lesbos* of 1932 treated their ill-starred subjects with a marked degree of sympathy, and Weigall's very last book, *Laura Was My Camel*, is humorous in intent and execution. His more serious labors were rewarded by a German Cross of the 4th Class, Red Eagle; the Of-

ficer's Cross of Franz Joseph of Austria; and the 3rd class Medjidieh Cross of Egypt.

PRINCIPAL WORKS: A Report on the Antiquities of Lower Nubia, 1907; A Catalogue of the Weights and Balances in the Cairo Museum, 1908; Travels in the Upper Egyptian Deserts, 1909; A Guide to the Antiquities of Upper Egypt, 1910; The Life of Akhnaton: Pharaoh of Egypt, 1910; The Treasury of Ancient Egypt, 1911; A Topographical Catalogue of the Tombs of Thebes (with A. H. Gardiner) 1913; The Life of Cleopatra: Queen of Egypt, 1914; Egypt From 1798 to 1914, 1915; Madeline of the Desert, 1920; The Dweller in the Desert (U.S. title: Burning Sands) 1921; Bedouin Love, 1922; The Glory of the Pharaohs, 1923; The Garden of Paradise, 1923; Tutankhamen and Other Essays, 1923; Ancient Egyptian Works of Art, 1924; The Way of the East, 1924; A History of the Pharaohs, 1925-26; The Not Impossible She, 1926; Wanderings in Roman Britain, 1926; Wanderings in Anglo-Saxon Britain, 1927; The Grand Tour of Norman England, 1927; Saturnalia in Room 23, 1927; Flights Into Antiquity, 1928; The King Preferred Moonlight, 1928; Nero, 1930; Life of Marc Anthony, 1931; Sappho of Lesbos, 1932; Laura Was My Camel, 1933.

ABOUT: Nature January 13, 1934; New York Times January 23, 1934.

WEINSTEIN, NATHAN WALLENSTEIN. See WEST, N.

WELLS, CAROLYN (187?—March 26, 1942), American anthologist and detective story and miscellaneous writer, was born in Rahway, N.J., the daughter of William and Anna (Woodruff) Wells. Miss Wells described herself as "a jack-in-the-box brain entirely surrounded by books," but said that she came of stern and rockbound ancestors.

Thomas Welles, a direct forebear, was the first treasurer and fourth governor (1656) of Connecticut. At eighteen months Miss Wells knew her letters on alphabet blocks; at three she read fluently from books and newspapers; and she wrote and bound a complete book at six. School seemed to her waste motion, and college the same thing raised to the nth power, especially since the girls were obliged to make their own beds. Instead, she took lessons of anyone who seemed a good teacher. In this informal way she studied Shakespeare under William J. Rolfe at Amherst summer school and picked up German, French, botany, and astronomy from other friends. She traveled abroad, especially to England, where she was invited to contribute verse to *Punch*; she had already been writing regularly for

Puck, Gelett Burgess' *The Lark,* and other American periodicals. For a time she was with the Rahway Library Association.

When *The Nonsense Anthology*—still her best known single work—was published in 1902, eight books stood to her credit. The total had increased to some hundred and seventy separate titles by the time of her death. Of these, more than seventy-five were mystery and detective stories (most of them narrating the investigations of her conventional sleuth, Fleming Stone) which she turned out on a regular schedule of three a year. Of less ephemeral nature were her numerous anthologies—the product, she said, of her library days. Her own light verse was printed in a variety of publications. Her stories for girls—including the "Patty" and "Betty" series—were highly popular in the early 1900's but are forgotten today. She had a wide circle of friends, both in and outside the literary world, and was known among bibliophiles for her collections of Walt Whitman and Edward Lear. Her autobiography *The Rest of My Life,* a desultory but amusing *potpourri* of recollections, was notable for the courage with which she discussed her lifelong deafness, brought on by an attack of scarlet fever at the age of six. In 1918 she married Hadwin Houghton, of the publishing family. Their brief but happy life together was terminated by his death in 1919. Thereafter she made her home in New York City, in an apartment overlooking Central Park. It was there that she died, presumably in her seventies, after years of invalidism which, however, failed to curtail her writing. As the New York *Times* remarked, she was renowned "for her gayety and wit."

PRINCIPAL WORKS: At the Sign of the Sphinx, 1896; The Jingle Book, 1899; Patty Fairfield, 1901; A Nonsense Anthology, 1902; A Parody Anthology, 1904; A Satire Anthology, 1905; The Rubaiyat of a Motor Car, 1906; A Whimsey Anthology, 1906; Fluffy Ruffles, 1907; The Clue, 1909; A Chain of Evidence, 1912; The Technique of the Mystery Story, 1913 (revised and enlarged ed., 1927); Faulkner's Folly, 1917; Vicky Van, 1918; The Book of Humorous Verse, 1920; Ptomaine Street (parody) 1921; The Outline of Humor, 1923; Fleming Stone Omnibus, 1931; The Rest of My Life, 1937; Who Killed Caldwell? 1942; Murder Will In, 1942.

ABOUT: Honce, C. A Sherlock Holmes Birthday; Haycraft, H. Murder for Pleasure: The Life and Times of the Detective Story; Masson, J. L. Our American Humorists; Overton, G. M. When Winter Comes to Main Street; Wells, C. The Rest of My Life; Christian Science Monitor Magazine October 21, 1939; New York Herald Tribune March 27, 1942; New York Times March 27, 1942; Publishers' Weekly July 22, 1939; Scholastic April 15, 1940; Wilson Library Bulletin April 1930.

***WELLS. HERBERT GEORGE** (September 21, 1866-   ), English novelist, historian, and scientific writer who signs his works as H. G. Wells, was born at Bromley Kent. His father, Joseph Wells, had been a gardener who turned small shopkeeper and finally was a professional cricketer; his mother, Sarah (Neal) Wells, had been a lady's maid and later was a housekeeper in a large country house. He was distinctly of the lower middle class and he has never forgotten his origins. But there was no objection to the boy's securing an education if he could manage it, and between periods as draper's and chemist's (i.e., druggist's) apprentice he got in a good deal of schooling, mostly at the Midhurst Grammar School, where he did so well that the master wanted to make him his assistant. Instead he went to London, worked once more in a drygoods house, and then won a scholarship at the Royal College of Science. He took his B.S. degree with honors at London University in 1888. A little more encouragement from the great T. S. Huxley, under whom he studied, and he would probably have remained all his life a working biologist. H. L. Mencken regretted that he had not done so: "He has made three separate careers. He began as a biologist, switched to journalism and then to literature, and finally set up shop as a prophet. My guess is that he'd have been a happier fellow, and much more useful to his nation and his time, if he had stuck by his first choice."

He did not do so, however. Instead, he took to teaching, mostly as a private tutor in science, wrote a textbook on biology, and overworked so that his health collapsed. He was found to be tubercular (for many years now he has been a diabetic as well, but both diseases are arrested), and was obliged to give up everything and recuperate without money to support him during his convalescence on the South coast. As soon as possible he returned to London, and there he met Frank Harris, then editor of the *Saturday Review,* and began his careers as journalist and as novelist almost simultaneously. Since 1895 he has averaged something better than a book a year.

In 1891 Wells married his first cousin, Isabel Mary Wells. They were divorced in 1895, after two years' separation (she remarried, and died in 1931), and he married Amy Catherine Robbins, herself a writer, whom he called "Jane." They had two sons, the elder of whom is a scientist and has been his father's collaborator in *The Science of Life*. Their home for the most part was at Easton Glebe, Essex. The story of their troubled yet fundamentally attached life together he has told frankly in his autobiography and in *The Book of Catherine Wells*, written after Mrs. Wells' death in 1927. For some time thereafter he spent most of his time on the Riviera, but for several years now he has lived and worked in an apartment in Regent's Park, London, which may or may not still be standing when this sketch is published.

H. G. Wells' novels, like his literary output as a whole, may be divided into three categories: the fantastic, pseudo-scientific stories of his early years; the realistic novels of his great fiction period (books like *Marriage*, *Ann Veronica*, and *Tono-Bungay*, which were as great an influence on the younger generation of that era as were the plays of Shaw and Ibsen); and the occasional thesis novels of his latest period, merely vehicles for his social and political theories.

He dislikes to have his pseudo-scientific novels compared to those of Jules Verne; he says they were always meant to exemplify his political beliefs, and were never intended to have more reality than a "good, gripping dream" would have. These beliefs were vaguely Socialist. He joined the Fabian Society in 1903 and wrote several pamphlets for it, but Mr. Wells' Socialism has always been anti-Marxian, and simmers down to little more than what he himself called "his antagonism to personal, racial, or national monopolization." It was succeeded by advocacy of a sort of aristocracy of the mind and spirit, a modern Order of Samurai with overtones of Plato's *Utopia*. This "World State" has now been superseded by the "World Brain," a rather nebulous idea which seems to depend on a World Encyclopaedia as a means of social perfectionism. Essentially he is, in his own words, "a liberal democrat," who claims "an unlimited right to think, criticize, discuss, and suggest." In his books written since the beginning of the Second World War, he has become a thorough pessimist; he sees everything for which he has fought during his whole life apparently doomed to defeat, and, in the words of Hamilton Basso, he is now, though "sincerely anxious to help mankind, totally unable to believe in men, every last hope cancelled by his conviction of human stupidity."

But though the pseudo-scientific novels may have been intended to convey a thesis, they remain about the best of their exciting kind, sometimes strangely prophetic in their guesses, highly readable, and—to tell the truth—marred only by their strained and sometimes silly social conclusions. Their power still to stir the imagination was amply demonstrated when Orson Welles adapted *The War of the Worlds* for the radio in 1938 and caused a national panic. And others, such as *The Time Machine*, *When the Sleeper Wakes*, and *In the Days of the Comet*, are equally fresh and living.

But Wells's great period as a novelist began about 1905 with *Kipps*. Here at last he discovered something he had never possessed before—humor, humor mixed with tender sympathy. He began to deal with the world he knew, instead of the world he dreamed about. He had already made a gesture in that direction, in *Wheels of Chance* and *Love and Mr. Lewisham*. But *Kipps* set the mold. Only in *The History of Mr. Polly* did he strike exactly that chord again, but up to the First World War and *Mr. Britling Sees It Through*, he wrote a series of realistic novels, based on social rather than political ideas, in which the characters were living persons and not mere stalking-horses. In other words, during those years he was a genuine novelist, and one of almost the first rank. In his postwar novels the characters talk, but they have ceased to have three dimensions. (In this respect at least, the evolution of Wells' novels strikingly parallels G. B. Shaw's dramas, which have undergone a similar transition.)

Wells' next bid for fame was as an historian, in a huge book which sold two million copies. *The Outline of History*, issued in two volumes in 1920 and in one huge volume in 1929, was a single-handed attempt to write the historical section of that World Encyclopaedia which is Mr. Wells's dream. Naturally it had many weaknesses, though its main critic, Hilaire Belloc, was actuated primarily by its uncompromisingly Rationalist and materialistic viewpoint. But whatever its shortcomings it is an immense achievement, equaled only by his subsequent *Science of Life*, written in collaboration with his son and Julian Huxley.

There remain the political books, of which one can say no more than that they are always earnest, prevailingly readable in spite of patches of dullness, and increasingly one-ideaed and gloomy. They have not helped to raise his reputation; as Eric Siepmann remarked, "the younger generation, whose youth had been influenced by Mr. Wells' ideas, definitely turned away." He is given to sweeping generalizations, he is "vague, idealistic, imprecise." He rushes into print without ever waiting for his thoughts to mature. Nevertheless, Mencken's dictum still holds good: "No other contemporary writer has said so many things worth hearing, though maybe not worth heeding."

The late Ford Madox Ford has described Wells in his youth—"blond, rather stocky, with drooping cavalry moustache, and with eyes always darting about." C. Patrick Thompson called him "a robust, heavy, shortish man, with massive face, powerful neck, and drum of a chest, always neatly dressed. . . . The pale, imaginative eyes smile easily under curiously tufted brows. The mouth is kindly. The nervous system is tense, strained, and its owner can be irascible, especially if someone arouses his dislike. He is not a polite conversationalist." His voice is shrill and strident, particularly under excitement. He slumps in his chair, hunched and crouching. "The whole posture," said Beverly Nichols, "suggests a spring at high pressure which may at any moment uncoil itself and leap out in the most surprising directions."

Richard Aldington summed Wells up thus: "No man can be complete in every respect . . . so that I easily forgive Wells his indifference to poetry and painting and his philistine view of life. He has great mental energy, and a power of bringing together numbers of facts in a stimulating way. He insisted on the importance of science during a long epoch when men of letters were heinously ignorant of it. His sense of the continuity and logical development of human destiny is very valuable, and enabled him to make shrewd guesses at future happenings which sometimes have been impressively right." At other times they have been impressively wrong, but no one has ever denied Wells the qualities of courage and forthrightness. Siepmann has pointed out the fatal flaw in his theorizing: he believes that the redemption of society can come about only through a sudden change in the will of individuals; and at the same time, as a convinced materialist, he does not believe in freedom of the will. Hence all that is left in his viewpoint now is "a weary push on the destructive side." He is a long way from the young novelist who, to quote Ford, ". . . struck everybody. He delighted the bourgeois profane with his imagination and we intelligentsia snorted with pleasure at the

idea of a Genius whom we could read without intellectual effort." But since Ford wrote still from the *fin-de-siècle* ivory tower of art for art's sake, his judgment cannot be considered wholly unprejudiced.

Perhaps it is best to let Wells speak for himself, in the mock obituary he wrote in 1936, supposedly published after his death, a forgotten old man, at ninety-seven. "He was one of the most prolific of the 'literary hacks' of his time. . . . He had a flair for what is coming. . . . It was his vanity to compare himself to Roger Bacon. . . . He was a copious and repetitive essayist upon public affairs and a still more copious writer of fiction. . . . Essentially an intellectual with an instinctive dislike for the . . . intensities and emotional floods of life . . . he was much more the scientific man than the artist, though he dealt in literary forms."

PRINCIPAL WORKS: *Novels*—The Time Machine: An Invention, 1895; The Wonderful Visit, 1895; The Stolen Bacillus and Other Stories, 1895; The Island of Dr. Moreau, 1896; The Wheels of Chance, 1896; The Invisible Man, 1897; The Plattner Story and Other Stories, 1897; The War of the Worlds, 1898; Tales of Space and Time, 1899; When the Sleeper Wakes, 1899; Love and Mr. Lewisham, 1900; The First Men on the Moon, 1901; The Sea Lady, 1902; Twelve Stories and a Dream, 1903; The Food of the Gods and How It Came to Earth, 1904; Kipps: The Story of a Simple Soul, 1905; A Modern Utopia, 1905; In the Days of the Comet, 1906; The War in the Air, 1908; Ann Veronica, 1909; Tono-Bungay, 1909; The History of Mr. Polly, 1910; The New Machiavelli, 1911; Marriage, 1912; The Passionate Friends, 1913; The Wife of Sir Isaac Harman, 1914; Bealby: A Holiday, 1915; The Research Magnificent, 1915; Mr. Britling Sees It Through, 1916; The Soul of a Bishop, 1917; Joan and Peter: The Story of an Education, 1918; The Undying Fire, 1919; The Secret Places of the Heart, 1922; Men Like Gods, 1923; The Dream, 1924; Christina Alberta's Father, 1925; The World of William Clissold, 1926; Meanwhile (The Picture of a Lady) 1927; Mr. Blettsworthy on Rampole Island, 1928; The King Who Was a King (novel from film) 1929; The Autocracy of Mr. Parham, 1930; The Bulpington of Blup, 1933; The Shape of Things to Come, 1933 (as film, Things to Come, 1935); The Man Who Could Work Miracles (film) 1936; The Croquet Player, 1936; The Brothers, 1937; Brynhild: or, The Show of Things, 1937; The Campton Visitation, 1937; Star-Begotten: A Biological Fantasia, 1937; Apropos of Dolores, 1938; The Dictator, 1939; The Holy Terror, 1939; Babes in the Darkling Wood, 1940; All Aboard for Ararat, 1940; You Can't Bee Too Careful: A Sample of Life 1901-1951, 1942. *Non-Fiction*—Select Conversations of an Uncle, 1895; Certain Personalities, 1897; Anticipations, 1901; Mankind in the Making, 1903; The Future in America, 1906; This Misery of Boots, 1907; First and Last Things, 1908; New Worlds for Old, 1908; Socialism and the Family, 1908; Floor Games For Children, 1911; Little Wars: A Floor Game Book, 1913; The World Set Free, 1914; An Englishman Looks at the World (in America: Social Forces in England and America) 1914;

Boon: The Mind of the Race, The Wild Asses of the Devil, and The Last Trump (as Reginald Bliss) 1915; What Is Coming? 1916; The Elements of Reconstruction (as D.P.) 1916; God: The Invisible King, 1917; Italy, France, and Britain at War, 1917; War and the Future, 1917; In the Fourth Year: Anticipation of a World Peace, 1918; Frank Swinnerton (with A. Bennett & G. M. Overton) 1920; The Outline of History, 1920; Russia in the Shadows, 1920; The Salvaging of Civilization, 1921; A Short History of the World, 1922; Washington and the Riddle of Peace, 1922; The Story of a Great Schoolmaster (F. W. Sanderson) 1924; A Year of Prophesying, 1924; Mr. Belloc Objects to the Outline of History, 1926; Democracy Under Revision, 1927; The Way the World Is Going, 1928; The Book of Catherine Wells, 1928; The Open Conspiracy, 1928 (as What Are We To Do With Our Lives? 1931); The Science of Life (with J. S. Huxley & G. P. Wells) 1929 (parts published separately, 1937); The Work, Wealth, and Happiness of Mankind, 1932; Experiment in Autobiography: Discoveries and Conclusions of a Very Ordinary Brain, 1934; The New America, the New World, 1935; The Anatomy of Frustration: A Modern Synthesis, 1936; World Brain, 1938; The Fate of Homo Sapiens (in America: The Fate of Man) 1939; The New World Order, 1940; Guide to the New World, 1941.

ABOUT: Aldington, R. Life for Life's Sake; Chesterton, G. K. Heretics; Cross, W. L. Four Contemporary Novelists; Wells, H. G. The Book of Catherine Wells: An Experiment in Autobiography; American Historical Review July 1921; American Mercury May 1936; Bookman February 1921; Bookman (London) September 1930; Deutsche Rundschau August 1928; Edinburgh Review January 1923; Englische Studien #2 1925; Fortnightly Review February 1926; Forum February 1935; Hibbert Journal January 1940; Living Age November 1930, October 1936; Mercure de France March 15, 1927; Nation November 14, 1934; New Republic August 11, 1920, December 13, 1939; New Statesman and Nation November 3, 1934; Nineteenth Century October 1939, March 1940; North American Review July 1920; Nuova Antologia July 16, 1929; Outlook February 4, 1931; Outlook (London) August 16, 1924; Saturday Review (London) June 20, 1931; Saturday Review of Literature January 24, 1925, July 13, 1929, June 2, 1934; Spectator September 3, 1937; World Tomorrow November 16, 1932; Yale Review January 1927.

WENDELL, BARRETT (August 23, 1855-February 8, 1921), American literary historian and university professor, was born on West Cedar Street, Boston, the eldest of the four sons of Jacob Wendell and Mary Bertodi (Barrett) Wendell. The family was of Dutch origin, the first Evert Jansen Wendell reaching New York from East Friesland, in 1640. Barrett Wendell attributed the fact that "my nervous system was always a bit erratic" to the circumstance that his maternal great-grandmother had a "startling experience of interrupted personality" about 1800. In 1863 his family moved to New York. Tutored for Harvard by his mother's cousin,

John Adams, Wendell was a member of the Class of 1876 for six months, when illness forced him to leave.

Returning to Harvard in the fall of 1874, he graduated with the class of 1877 and spent three unhappy years in the study of law, failing his Boston bar examinations in 1880. That June, Wendell married Edith Greenough of Quincy; they had two sons and two daughters.

An appointment as instructor in English at Harvard proved another stabilizing influence. In 1888 he received an appointment as assistant professor, and introduced the requirement of a written daily theme in his courses in composition. William Lyon Phelps was his assistant in 1891-92.

Wendell had written two inconsequential novels before 1888, but surprised his associates who believed him too impatient for minute research by producing a well-rounded study of *Cotton Mather: The Puritan Priest*, in 1891; a new edition appeared after his death. *William Shakespere: A Study in Elizabethan Literature* was a useful handbook. Appointed full professor of English in 1908, he published his well-known *A Literary History of America* two years later. Intended to show the inter-relation between the history, political and social, of England and America and the history of American literary production, it was regarded in some quarters as parochial and intolerant in tone. Somewhat the same thesis was developed to considerably better effect by Vernon Louis Parrington[qv] a quarter-century later. His *The Traditions of European Literature*, published the year before Wendell's death at sixty-five, was a stimulating book based on his course in Comparative Literature, popularly known as "A Romp Through the Ages With Barrett Wendell."

The eccentricities of Wendell's high-pitched voice, suggesting, as Phelps remarks, the stage-Englishman, and his nervous demeanor and Elizabethan breadth of language did not obscure his merits as a seminal teacher and unpedantic student. Wendell was of moderate height, well proportioned, with tawny hair and beard and quick blue eyes. Death was caused by pernicious anemia and pneumonia.

PRINCIPAL WORKS: The Duchess Emilia: A Romance, 1885; Rankell's Remains: An American Novel, 1887; Cotton Mather: The Puritan

Priest, 1891; Stelligeri and Other Essays Concerning America, 1893; William Shakespere: A Study in Elizabethan Literature, 1894; A Literary History of America, 1900; Raleigh in Guiana, 1902; The France of To-Day, 1908; The Mystery of Education, 1909; The Traditions of European Literature, 1920.

ABOUT: Castle, W. R., Jr. Barrett Wendell—Teacher (in *Essays in Memory of Barrett Wendell By His Assistants*); Edgett, E. F. I Speak for Myself; Howe, M. A. D. W. Barrett Wendell and His Letters; Phelps, W. L. Autobiography; New York Times February 9, 1921.

WENDT, GERALD (March 3, 1891-), American scientist, writes: "I was born in Davenport, Iowa, then still a distinctively

Oggiano

German town. I had no great love for the agricultural environment, nor was I much attracted by the rather unusual literary group that then thrived there, but I was entranced by the excellent science then being taught in the schools. By the time I reached Harvard, in 1909, human affairs seemed incomprehensible and I embraced the study of science in a spirit that was quite monastic. When I received the Ph.D. degree at Harvard in 1916, I was wholly immersed in atoms and interested in nothing but their structure and their reactions. In 1914 I went to Paris to work in radium and X-rays, and in this field of research I was immured from the world. As a young instructor in chemistry I went to the Rice Institute, then almost at once to the University of Chicago. I had served briefly in the United States Bureau of Mines, and also for six months of 1918 was a captain in the Chemical Warfare Service of the army, stationed in Washington. But the students at the university proved increasingly interesting and my education in terms of humanity at last began.

"In 1921 my health collapsed and I gave up my research on atoms. Upon recovery I took charge of scientific research for a large oil company. This proved so meaningless to me that in 1925 I accepted an appointment as dean of the School of Chemistry and Physics at Pennsylvania State College. Here I hoped to undertake research once more, but actually by 1929 I had become assistant to the president, in charge of the college research program.

"Then came an absorption in patents and the creation of new economic values by research, which led, in 1930, to my organizing a corporation to develop some of my new

knowledge in an old industry. In 1935 I became director of research for the General Printing Ink Corporation in New York. During this period I awoke fully to social problems and to the tragic neglect by America of the values inherent in science. In 1936, therefore, I also became director of the American Institute of the City of New York. It was my hope through the Institute to develop a better understanding of science as a social force.

"In 1938 I joined the staff of the New York World's Fair as Director of Science, to which was later added the post of Director of Education.

"It is my growing conviction that the age of science is not yet here and that no amount of gadgets, inventions, or technology will bring it. Much more important are the research method of investigation and the full realization that science not only studies the environment in which we live, but alters it so completely that our institutions and traditions are, for the most part, in full conflict with the actual conditions of modern life. Until human society is regarded with a scientific attitude as the product of people, to be arranged and managed for the benefit of people, until it is studied by the realistic detached methods of science, and until a new faith and culture emerge which are based on science and not merely on all our yesterdays, science cannot achieve its major purpose and humanity cannot achieve happiness. Such a point of view is not only foreign to politicians and many social thinkers, but it is almost equally foreign to scientists. In the years that remain I hope that I shall be able to expound my conviction both inside and outside the world of science itself."

* * *

Dr. Wendt married Elsie Paula Lerch in 1916; they have one son. He was assistant editor of *Chemical Abstracts* from 1917 to 1922, managing editor of the *Chemical Bulletin* from 1918 to 1921, associate editor of the *Journal of Radiology*, 1920 and 1921, and editor of *Chemical Reviews* from 1927 to 1938. He is a Fellow of the American Association for the Advancement of Science. He has published many articles in scientific journals, and reviews of scientific books in the New York *Herald Tribune* "Books" and the *Saturday Review of Literature*. He also lectures frequently on "the challenge of science to society."

PRINCIPAL WORKS: Matter and Energy, 1930; Science for the World of Tomorrow, 1939; The Sciences (6 vols., ed.; author of volume on chemistry) 1940.

ABOUT: Literary Digest November 15, 1924.

*WERFEL, FRANZ V. (September 10, 1890-), German-Czech novelist, poet and playwright, was born in Prague of a wealthy Jewish family. His father, who owned a glove factory known throughout Czechoslovakia and Austria, played the piano, attended the opera religiously and hung his mansion with expensive paintings, but he failed to recognize the poetical talent of his precocious son whom he saw only as a prospective business partner. Franz attended the Prague *gymnasium* and by the time he left it in 1908 the Vienna *Zeit* had printed one of his poems. At the University (1909-10) his reputation of "good for nothing" did not improve; his happiest moments were spent composing poems in prose and essays, and discussing them with the leading writers of Prague: the novelists Gustav Meyrink and Max Brod, and the great mystic Czech poet Ottokar Březina whom a decade later he translated into German. In 1910 his first play appeared in print, and Franz left his antagonistic paternal home to work in a Hamburg shipping house and publish a book of poems.

In 1911-12 Werfel served his year of compulsory military training; although his anarchism often brought him into trouble with his superiors, the army maneuvers afforded him a fine opportunity for close study of the Bohemian countryside and its people. Upon his release he was employed as a reader by the Leipzig publishing house of Kurt Wolff (1912-14), where he helped establish a series devoted to vanguard books and continued his own writing career.

The First World War found him as a "coffee house Messiah" reciting in literary circles and cafés his pacifist "Der Krieg," "Wortmacher des Krieges," and "Revolutionsaufruf." In "Der Ulan" he wrote one of the war's earliest anti-militaristic stories. His pacifism derived not from a political platform or endorsement of any party "line," but from his mystical belief in a community of souls in all living things. In February 1915 the above-mentioned poems appeared in the volume *Einander*. With the dynamic but contrasting thinkers Martin Buber, Gustav Landauer, and Max Scheler, Werfel founded a secret society to combat the demagogy of rampant militarism. Shortly thereafter, while traveling from Leipzig to

join his regiment in Prague, he met with a serious railway accident which kept him in hospital at Bozen for two months. On convalescing he left for the front: in West Galicia, as junior transport officer of field-gun regiment 19, he was present during the Austrian retreat (August 1916) at Jezierna, near Tarnopol; later from Stodon, near Zloczów, he witnessed the flares of the Russian revolution and Kerensky's offensive of 1917. In 1916 the Berlin Lessingtheater gave more than fifty performances of his adaptation of Euripides' *These Trojan Women*, followed by a triumphal *tournée* through Germany and Austria. In the meantime Werfel participated in numerous political and aesthetic polemics, which resulted in a deeper understanding of "Activism," "healthy root from which sprang Expressionism."

In August 1917 Werfel was transferred to the war press bureau in Vienna, where in the early part of 1918 he married and settled down, with but short trips to Germany, a sojourn in Venice, and an extended tour (in 1925) to Egypt and Palestine. At the front Werfel had composed some of his finest lyrics, *Gerichstag*, published in 1919, the year of *Not-the Murderer*, his first novelette, a study of adolescent conflicts which gave the Expressionist movement one of its recurrent themes, the father-son problem.

In 1920 Max Reinhardt produced Werfel's early romantic *Besuch aus dem Elysium*. The following year the trilogy *Spiegelmensch* opened on the same day in Leipzig, Stuttgart, and Düsseldorf. This trilogy in verse, planned on a grandiose scale as a modern *Faust*, portrayed the conflict between man's two souls.

With the nocturnal *Beschwörungen* (1923) Werfel's poetical career drew to a close, whereupon his dramatic production became his dominant passion. The symbolic five-act *Goat Song* (1922), which scored a brilliant success at Vienna's Raimundtheater but was somewhat of a fiasco in Frankfurt at its dual *première*, became a world event, sending Werfel's name abroad—its American début took place four years later. *Schweiger* (1923) had boisterous *premières* in Prague and Stuttgart and toured over eighty theatres: in Berlin it ran more than fifty consecutive evenings at the Königgrätzer Theater and a year later it enjoyed a successful season in New York at the Theatre Guild. *Juarez and Maximilian* (1925) was produced by Reinhardt in Vienna and after a triumphant tour through Germany and Austria it was translated and performed in New York, and more recently it has been filmed with signal success. In 1926 *Paul Among the Jews,* a religious play, was staged, but since then Werfel has written only two dramas, also religious in implication: *Das Reich Gottes in Böhmen* (1930) and *The Eternal Road* (1936), a dramatization of the Old Testament from Abraham to the Prophets, which in Ludwig Lewisohn's translation saw an elaborate Reinhardt performance in New York in 1937.

Since 1924 when he published *Verdi: The Novel of the Opera,* Werfel's *forte* has been fiction. After a series of novelettes of which the most brilliant were *The Man Who Conquered Death* (1928) and *Class Reunion* (1929), Werfel wrote *The Pure in Heart,* an engrossing psychological study. In *The Pascarella Family* (1932) he analyzes the influence of a despotic Italian father on his three sons and three daughters. With *The Forty Days of Musa Dagh* (1933), based on the forty days' siege of Musa Dagh during which the inhabitants of seven Armenian villages resisted the Turkish army until rescued by the French, Werfel scored his greatest popular success as a story teller.

Hearken Unto the Voice (1937) has for its setting ancient Palestine and its hero is Jeremiah, but there are intimations of the oncoming doom of the present. *Embezzled Heaven* (1940), a Book-of-the-Month Club selection, is basically a plea for a return to religion as man's last resort if he is to be saved. This novel stems from Werfel's growing sympathy for the Roman Catholic faith.

Werfel is the only modern writer who has done distinguished work in all three *genres,* as Professor Morgan points out. "In the lyric, Werfel was the acknowledged leader and the unexcelled master of the Expressionist school. . . . In the drama, Werfel has to his credit at least two very outstanding works (*Juarez and Maximilian,* and *Spiegelmensch*). . . . In the novel, Werfel has no less than four significant works to his name (*Not the Murderer, Verdi, The Pure in Heart,* and *The Forty Days*). . . . In *The Pure in Heart,* apart from other merits, Werfel has drawn a picture of pre-war Austria which is unmatched anywhere in literature, and which in the light of recent events is likely to acquire the status of an historic record."

In November 1940 Werfel after being reported slain by the Nazis, was able to escape from the tottering world he had so keenly described and to find temporary refuge in New York City. In the course of his flight he found himself at Lourdes, where in his extremity, he vowed that he would some day write the story of Bernadette Soubirous, whose vision of "a beautiful lady" had made Lourdes a place of pilgrimage. *The Song of Bernadette,* written in fulfillment of that vow, was a Book-of-the-Month Club selection and one of the great American publishing successes of 1942.

PRINCIPAL WORKS AVAILABLE IN ENGLISH TRANSLATION: *Drama*—Goat Song, 1926; Juarez and Maximilian, 1926; Paul Among the Jews, 1928; The Eternal Road, 1936. *Fiction*—Verdi, 1925; The Man Who Conquered Death (British title: Death of a Poor Man) 1927; Class Reunion, 1929; The Pure in Heart (British title: Hidden Child) 1931; The Pascarella Family, 1932; The Forty Days of Musa Dagh (British title: Forty Days) 1934; Twilight of a World (eight novelettes: Poor People, Class Reunion, Estrangement, Saverio's Secret, The Staircase, The Man Who Conquered Death, The House of Mourning, Not the Murderer) 1937; Hearken Unto the Voice, 1938; Embezzled Heaven, 1940; The Song of Bernadette, 1942.

ABOUT: Berendt, H. Franz Werfel; Bertaux, F. A Panorama of German Literature From 1871 to 1931; Bithell, J. Modern German Literature; Drake, W. A. Contemporary European Writers; Eloesser, A. Modern German Literature; Klarmann, A. D. Musikalität bei Werfel; Luther, H. Franz Werfel und Seine Besten Bühnenwerke; Polgar, H. Ja und Nein; Schlauch, M. Franz Werfel and the Cosmos; Specht, R. Franz Werfel; Contemporary Review July 1934; Drama February 1926; Hochland January 1928; Literary Review July 14, 1923; Saturday Review of Literature February 27, 1937, November 30, 1940; Theatre Arts Monthly March 1926; Time November 11, 1940.

WESCOTT, GLENWAY (April 11, 1901-), American novelist, writes: "My birthplace was a poor farm in Wisconsin. I sought education at the University of Chicago and there I began to write poetry, but only so that I could belong to the Poetry Club, with ambition instead of inspiration. I pretended to be a genius, you might say, in order to get on in the world;

G. P. Lynes

and ever since, it has been as if some god had heard me and somehow condemned me to the uneasy fulfilment of that juvenile bluff and boast. I have had good luck in every respect but one; my talent has not seemed equal to my opportunities or proportionate to my ideas and ideals. Lately I have been glad of that too; for while I so painfully labor to compose exact sentences and easy paragraphs and pages in good narrative order, I find time to recall emotion as well as experience, and to include my second thoughts.

"I left the university half way through my sophomore year, in mediocre health and melancholy. My real education was in the sixteenth or seventeenth century way, by the grand tour of the continent of Europe. I matured by fits and starts and, as long as I felt young, wrote with some facility: four volumes (or three and a half) about Wisconsin. For nine years I resided on the Riviera and in Paris, which in the 'twenties was a great fool's paradise, the perfect time and place to study human nature; nothing else seemed more important or urgent. When in the 'thirties everything else developed an urgency of hell and damnation, I returned to America. In the spring of 1939 I suddenly felt at home here where I belong; then my youthful promise seemed to me fulfillable; my ability, such as it may be, began to get its stride. Naturally everyone gave me bad marks for my failure to publish anything to speak of during the 'thirties. Now I hope to show how much I learned about the art of narration by unceasing, fruitless endeavor all the while. I also invented and accumulated a series of characters and plots.

"Having been born with the twentieth century I realize that I am now approximately middle-aged. But I feel excited, cheerful, and indeed youthful about it. World-war or world-revolution raging again, reminds us for one thing to hurry up with our literary art and the like. If I were to die now I should die ashamed and cursing. For, as it seems to me, my circumstances and adventures always have been practically ideal for a novelist; and they still are. I am in excellent health; and I have a family-farmhouse in New Jersey to live in, and part of a New York apartment to see life from. In my teens I once worked for a firm of mass-production tailors; and one year I attended an aged millionaire art-collector who was going blind. But as a rule, thanks to book-loving family and generous friends, I have not been obliged or expected to do anything except write.

"Also my twenty grown-up years have provided me with the several sorts of experience I want to write about. I saw a brotherhood of penitents flagellate to an accompaniment of flutes during a snow-storm in the Rockies. I sat up all one night with the glorious beheaded body of Isadora Duncan. After Rathenau was murdered I watched a mob re-murder him in effigy. The old man who first turned base metals to gold and got the Nobel Prize for it,

presented me with a fine jewel which he had made by a similar process. But, I must admit, the bulk of my subject-matter is not so sensational. Roughly speaking, it is the private life: the education of the young, the religion of the old, love-affairs, death-beds. My recently published pint-size novel, *The Pilgrim Hawk*, is characteristic.

"I have been thinking, for fun, what books and authors have had a decisive influence on my writing, to date. They are the *Oz* books; Hall Caine; Owen Johnson's *The Salamanders;* Henry James; D. H. Lawrence's *Sons and Lovers;* Chateaubriand; W. Somerset Maugham. There is more in this list than meets the eye: it is not what I admire most. E. M. Forster, I think, is the greatest living master of English prose. Yeats was the greatest English poet since Blake or perhaps Pope. The other Lawrence, Col. T. E. Lawrence, is an immortal, I believe, although he was not a lovable man. Mr. Maugham's *Christmas Holiday* seems to me the finest novel of this decade; far and away the most significant, socially and historically. Younger writers whose work I love are Katherine Anne Porter, Richard Hughes, W. H. Auden.

"I believe, as doubtless a majority of Americans believe, in our American power and prosperity and those luxuries of the spirit, fine art and education, free speech, free publication, and free faith, which today depend to a great extent upon power and prosperity. I hope for a continuous evolution leftward in the spheres of economics and politics; but I am not a Marxist. I do not believe in falsification of facts for any purpose whatsoever; nor in the least infringement of individual morality today for the sake of imaginary general benefit tomorrow."

* * *

Mr. Wescott is unmarried. His *The Grandmothers* won the Harper Prize Novel Contest for 1927. His New Jersey farmhouse is near Hampton. Dayton Kohler said: "He writes with the simplicity of rhythm that we find in folk-poetry and folk-tunes, and his beautifully cadenced prose is an aesthetic medium to bring a sense and smell of the soil like some dark intoxicant to the imagination of the reader. He [has] a knowledge of the inner spirit and a subtle power of interpreting life as a drama of human motives and desires."

On the publication of Wescott's novelette, *The Pilgrim Hawk* (1940), F. W. Dupee commented in the *New Republic:* "Wescott has come through the ordeal of adolescence which proves fatal to so many American writers. . . . His writing is as supple as ever, and has acquired, besides, a certain witty poeticality which may be of French inspiration but which is entirely native in idiom."

PRINCIPAL WORKS: The Apple of the Eye, 1924; Natives of the Rock (poems) 1926; The Grandmothers, 1927; Good-Bye Wisconsin (short stories) 1928; The Babe's Bed, 1930; Fear and Trembling (short stories) 1932; A Calendar of Saints For Unbelievers, 1932; The Pilgrim Hawk, 1940.

ABOUT: Bookman April 1931; Publishers' Weekly May 3, 1941; Saturday Review of Literature October 26, 1940; Time December 2, 1940.

*WEST, NATHANAEL (1906?-December 21, 1940), American novelist, was born Nathan Wallenstein Weinstein, and was graduated under that name from Brown University in 1924 with the degree of Bachelor of Philosophy. *The Historical Catalogue of Brown University: 1764-1934,* published in 1936, listed his occupation as "editor of *Americana Magazine.*" It is also known that he was manager of a residential club hotel in the Sutton Place section of New York City for a period in the early 1930's. His first novel, *The Dream Life of Balso Snell* (1931) indicated the arrival of a curious and individual talent, and the impression made was deepened with the appearance two years later of *Miss Lonelyhearts,* a novel of contemporary New York life, concerning a newspaperman who is driven almost to the point of madness by the stories of human misery which he received in his daily mail, for answer in his column of advice. Dashiel Hammett wrote: "In his books there are no echoes of other men's books. *Miss Lonelyhearts* is the stuff that makes our daily paper —but seen truly and told truly."

West went to Hollywood in 1935, and spent the five remaining years of his life there. His first assignment was an adaptation of *Miss Lonelyhearts* for Twentieth Century-United Artists, called "Advice to the Lovelorn." In 1936 he collaborated on the screen plays "Ticket to Paradise," "Follow Your Heart," and "The President's Mystery" (based on a composite novel on a theme suggested by President Roosevelt) for Republic Pictures. In 1937 he worked on an adaptation, "Rhythm in the Clouds," and in 1938 wrote an original screen play, "Born To Be Wed," for Republic. Next year he collaborated on a screen play, the notable picture "Five Came Back," for RKO, and on "I Stole a Million" for Universal.

West's *The Day of the Locust* (1939) is a novel dealing with several curious Hollywood types, which Edmund Wilson called

"a remarkable book, in its peculiar combination of amenity of surface and felicity of form and style with an ugly subject and somber feeling, quite unlike—as his other books have been—the books of anyone else. Mr. West . . . has still, in short, remained an artist. His new novel deals with the nondescript characters on the fringe of the Hollywood studios. These people have been painted as precisely and polished up as brightly as the figures in Persian miniatures. Their speech has been distilled with a sense of the flavorsome and the characteristic which makes John O'Hara seem pedestrian. Mr. West's *surréaliste* beginnings have stood him in good stead on the Coast. . . . [He] has caught the emptiness of Hollywood; and he is, so far as I know, the first writer to make this emptiness horrible."

West and his wife, the former Eileen McKenney, were killed in an automobile accident near El Centro, Calif., just three days before *My Sister Eileen,* a play based on the stories by Ruth McKenney[qv] about her attractive sister, opened a very successful run in New York City. West was survived by his sister, Laura Perelman, wife of S. J. Perelman, the "free-association" humorist, with whom she collaborated on a play, *The Night Before Christmas,* produced in 1941.

PRINCIPAL WORKS: The Dream Life of Balso Snell, 1931; Miss Lonelyhearts, 1933; A Cool Million, 1934; The Day of the Locust, 1939.

ABOUT: Wilson, E. The Boys in the Back Room; The Historical Catalogue of Brown University: 1764-1934; International Motion Picture Almanac 1940-41; New York Times December 23, 1940; Publishers' Weekly December 28, 1940.

WEST, REBECCA (December 25, 1892-), English novelist, critic, essayist—in short, woman of letters—was born Cecily Isabel Fairfield in County Kerry, Ireland, the daughter of Charles Fairfield, army officer, war correspondent, editor, and disciple of Herbert Spencer. Her mother, whose maiden name was Mackenzie, was a talented musician. The father

died when his daughter was ten. The mother moved to Edinburgh, her native city, and the girl was reared there and educated at George Watson Ladies' College, and at a London dramatic academy. She was on the stage for a short time, and owes to it her pseudonym, the name of the heroine of Ibsen's *Rosmersholm.* In 1911 she joined the staff of the *Freewoman* and became a political writer on the *Clarion* the following year, when she was only twenty. At this time her chief interest was feminism, and she was active in the fight for woman's suffrage. Her political essays and literary criticisms appeared frequently in the *Star, Daily News, New Statesman*, and (later) in the American *Bookman* and *New Republic.* Her first book was a critical biography of Henry James, but the bulk of her work since then has been fiction. Sharp-tongued and positive in her writing, she is equally celebrated for wit and for forthrightness.

After years of iconoclastic pronouncements on marriage, she surprised her friends in 1930 by marrying a banker, Henry Maxwell Andrews, and has surprised them since by remaining happily married to him. She has changed on the surface in other ways as well—in her youth she was noted for her bohemian untidiness, whereas now she is one of the most smartly dressed women in London. But fundamentally she has not changed at all. She is still what she was from the beginning—slender, dark-eyed, temperamental, extremely feminine, moody but with "a delightful sense of humor." The only thing that may infallibly be expected of her is the unexpected.

This is as true of her writing as of her nature. Each of her books has been different from the last; there has never been a "typical" Rebecca West book. What links them all is her nimble style, which has been called "sometimes brilliant, always flashy; often sensible but always dogmatic." She has a sort of darting intensity, like that of a humming-bird; she immerses herself momentarily in what interests her and comes out with a harvest of honey which is usually tinged with gall.

Rebecca West's devotion to journalism has never flagged (she has been a regular reviewer of books for the *Daily Telegraph* since 1931, and her articles and stories appear often in both English and American magazines). Her literary interests and her political interests have developed concurrently. She is a friend of David Low, the famous cartoonist, and has written the text of two of his books of drawings. In 1926 she edited the English edition of Carl Sandburg's poems. She is a keen and discerning critic, one of the best we have.

The keynote of all her novels, disparate as they are in mood and background, is a psychological probing of motive and method of thought appropriate to one whose favorite author is Proust. From the shell-shocked soldier of her first novel to the delicately dissected heroine of her latest one, she displays the same eager interest in the minds of human beings, and the same pyrotechnic manner in exposing and displaying them. Rebecca West is perhaps too changeable to be a really great novelist, but her resources, on the other hand, are too rich to enable her to be merely mediocre.

Early in 1941, after a series of experiences during the London air raids that seemed to indicate that she possessed clairvoyant powers, Rebecca West became seriously ill and underwent a major operation. On her recovery she published *Black Lamb and Grey Falcon*, a massive two-volume work of 1181 pages, on which she had been working ever since she and her husband had made an Easter trip through Yugoslavia in 1937. It is a travel diary; an examination of the minds of the travelers, as representatives of the culture of our time; an historical study of and tribute to a nation; a passionate analysis of the great crisis of contemporary man. The grey falcon figures in a Slav folk song about the military defeat of the Serbs at Kossovo in 1389; the black lamb refers to a primitive sacrifice which the author saw in Macedonia.

Rebecca West's *magnum opus* was acclaimed by some reviewers as the "apotheosis" of the travel book form, "as astonishing as it is brilliant," "the only book since the war began which has a stature of its own comparable to the crisis through which the world is moving." Although students of Balkan history, like Stoyan Pribichevich and Louis Adamic, complained of errors and omissions in political interpretation, nearly all agreed that here, despite its faults, was one of the great books of a troubled century.

One of Rebecca West's wartime activities has been to superintend British broadcast talks to Yugoslavia.

PRINCIPAL WORKS: *Novels*—The Return of the Soldier, 1918; The Judge, 1922; Harriet Hume, 1929; The Harsh Voice (four short novels) 1935; The Thinking Reed, 1936. *Non-Fiction*—Henry James, 1916; The Strange Necessity, 1928; D. H. Lawrence: An Elegy, 1930; Ending in Earnest, 1931; St. Augustine, 1933; Black Lamb and Grey Falcon, 1941.

ABOUT: Canadian Forum June 1931; Literary Digest April 20, 1935; New York Herald Tribune Magazine February 7, 1932; Revue Politique et Littéraire November 21, 1925; Spectator October 15, 22, 1932.

WEST, SACKVILLE-. See SACK-VILLE-WEST

WESTCOTT, EDWARD NOYES. See AMERICAN AUTHORS: 1600-1900

**WESTERMARCK, EDVARD ALEX-
ANDER** (November 20, 1862-September
3, 1939), Finnish anthropologist and university professor, was born in Helsingfors,
Finland, the son of Nils Christian Westermarck, bursar and Latin master of the
local university, and Constance Westermarck, daughter of the university librarian. Their house stood close by the old
church. The boy suffered from asthma, but
outdoor life warded off tuberculosis. He
attended Böök's Lyceum and the Swedish
Normal Lyceum, and received degrees of
Bachelor and Master of Philosophy (equivalent to B.A. and M.A. degrees) from the
University of Finland. An opportune be-
quest from an old lady enabled young Westermarck, at twenty-four, to go to England
in September 1887 to collect material at the
British Museum in London for his doctor's
thesis, the trial essay which eventually resulted in his monumental *History of Human
Marriage*. Marriage, he thought, must be
studied in connection with biological conditions among the various peoples of the earth;
he was opposed to theories of promiscuity
among primitive peoples. *The Origin of
Human Marriage,* written in English, appeared in 1889 with a preface by the English biologist Alfred Russel Wallace. The
first edition of *The History of Human Marriage* was published by Macmillan's in 1891
and revised and extended to three volumes—
the work being done once more at the British
Museum—thirty years later. It was translated into six languages, including the Japanese, and was pirated in the United States.

Westermarck was docent at the University
of Helsingfors in 1894, taught also at the
Academy of Abo, and spent the years
1898 to 1902 in Morocco to observe superstitions and marriage customs there. Most
of his academic career was spent in England,
where he was professor of sociology from
1907 to 1930 at the University of London,
notably in the School of Economics. Enforced leisure caused by the general strike
of May 1926 led him to write an autobiography at his country home in Surrey, first
published at Stockholm in 1929 as *Minnen ur
Mitt Liv*. His own marriage was happy,
though his wife's name does not appear in
the index of his book; a son, Jack, was killed
under the wheels of an English lorry. He
refused invitations to Harvard and Columbia, and was prevented from lecturing at
Brown University in 1915 by the First World
War. Westermarck, who resembled G. K.
Chesterton on a smaller and stockier scale,
was popular in England, knowing Lord
Avebury, Edmund Gosse, and Professor

Romanes. Censors did not interfere with his
unsensational, solidly documented books. He
died in Lapinlahti, Finland, at seventy-six,
an agnostic.

PRINCIPAL WORKS: The History of Human
Marriage 1891: The Origin and Development of
the Moral Ideas, 1906-08; Marriage Customs in
Morocco, 1914; Wit and Wisdom in Morocco,
1931; Early Beliefs and Their Social Influence,
1932; Ethical Relativity, 1932; The Future of
Marriage in Western Civilisation, 1936; Christianity and Morals, 1939.

ABOUT: Westermarck, E. A. Memories of
My Life; American Journal of Sociology November 1939; Nature September 16, 1939; New York
Times September 5, 1939; Time September 18,
1939.

WEYER, CONSTANTIN-. See CON-
STANTIN-WEYER

WEYGANDT, CORNELIUS (December
13, 1871-   ), American historian and critic,
writes: "Cornelius Weygandt has found the
material of his writ-
ing, half of it in the
study, half of it on
the road in back coun-
try places. Born in
Germantown [Phila-
delphia], then a coun-
try town with stores
in which you could
buy everything from
a needle to an anchor,
he fell in young boy-

Photo-Crafters

hood into the hands of older boys who
knew birds. His mother had been born on
a farm in Chester County, Pa., and his
uncles and aunts told him much of the
phases of life on that hill farm with its
great barn and grist mill. All his life he has
continued the studies of the countryside begun in childhood. The names of all country
things have always fascinated him, Sheldon
pears and undershot water wheels, Domi-
nique hens and Merino sheep, springhouses
and covered wooden bridges and the like.

"His father's books and his grandfather's,
Carlyle and Thackeray, Wordsworth and
Ossian, were at hand always. He saw
Longfellow's brother and Whitman daily on
the streets of Germantown, and writing
about the Pennsylvania countryside became
the purpose of his life while he was a boy
at college. He graduated from the University of Pennsylvania in 1891 [Ph.D.,
1901]. He had newspaper experience [on
the Philadelphia *Record* and *Evening Telegraph*] from 1892 to 1897. Since the latter
year he has been a teacher at Pennsylvania.
He is now Professor of English Literature.

"He married Sara Matlack Roberts in 1900. They have a son and a daughter. He lives in Philadelphia with a summer home in the White Mountains. His books on the American scene are concerned with folklore and objects of art and passing phases of American civilization."

* * *

Professor Weygandt was one of the first Americans to make the new Irish drama known in America, having seen its beginnings in Dublin in 1912. He is dark, heavy-set and spectacled, with a gusto and enthusiasm that make him a popular teacher as well as a writer of absorbing books.

PRINCIPAL WORK: Irish Plays and Playwrights, 1913; A Century of the English Novel, 1925; Tuesdays at Ten, 1928; The Red Hills, 1928; The Wissahickon Hills, 1930; A Passing America, 1932; The White Hills, 1934; The Blue Hills, 1936; The Time of Tennyson, 1936; The Time of Yeats, 1937; New Hampshire Neighbors, 1937; Philadelphia Folks, 1938; The Dutch Country, 1939; Down Jersey, 1940; November Rowen, 1941; The Plenty of Pennsylvania, 1942.

WEYMAN, STANLEY JOHN (August 7, 1855-April 10, 1928), English novelist, was the second son of Thomas Weyman, a

county solicitor. He was born at Ludlow in Shropshire, educated at the local grammar school and at Shrewsbury School. In 1874 Weyman entered Christ Church, Oxford, attaining a second class in Modern History, was history master at the King's School, Chester, for a year, and was called to the Bar at the Inner Temple in 1881. After joining the Oxford Circuit he practiced law for eight wretched years, never making more than £200 a year and frequently angering judges by the nervousness of his demeanor in court. In 1886 Weyman and his brother Arthur spent some time in a French jail, suspected of espionage for "sketching" on a walking trip.

Picking up Baird's History of the Huguenots gave Weyman's thoughts a new direction, and he wrote a novel of the St. Bartholomew's eve massacre, The House of the Wolf, which appeared serially in the English Illustrated Magazine in 1888-89. In 1890 Andrew Lang persuaded Longmans to publish it. The New Rector, serialized in Cornhill, showed evident admiration for Trollope, and was a not particularly good second novel.

A commentator on Weyman has divided his novels into English-topical, English-historical, and Foreign-historical. Starvecrow Farm and The Great House are the other representatives of the first class; Weyman's fortune and reputation depended on his novels of the third class. He could construct elaborate plots and spin yarns of the most amazing and crowded adventures, with "hairbreath escapes, decayed noblemen, bustling innkeepers, roistering troopers, and real historical characters for verisimilitude." The novels are sometimes marred, as Grace Chapman puts it, by "sentimentality and purple patchery"; typical lay figures are given names and dresses to suit varying environments, and the conversation of the characters sometimes slips into anachronism. Weyman always displays a "sturdy and rather bigoted Protestanism." Under the Red Robe, introducing Cardinal Richelieu, was dramatized and produced at the Haymarket in London in 1896; the Shuberts converted it into one of their typical musical pieces in New York in 1927. A Gentleman of France, Stevenson wrote Colvin, "is the most exquisite pleasure, a real chivalrous yarn like the Dumas' and yet unlike." Count Hannibal, also dramatized, was an exciting novel of the wars of religion, presenting a pathetic and unexaggerated picture of the mad young king, Charles IX (and the usual "irritating heroine").

Weyman's later years were spent at his home, Plas Llanrhyd in Denbighshire, where he held several local offices, notably that of J.P., and supported the Welsh Church. He worked on a houseboat, turning out a thousand words a day, and leaving an estate of £91,000. Weyman's moustache and eyeglasses made him look more like a solicitor than a romancer. He is buried in the parish churchyard at Llanrhyd. His name is pronounced wy'man.

PRINCIPAL WORKS: The House of the Wolf, 1890; The New Rector, 1891; A Gentleman of France, 1893; The Man in Black, 1894; Under the Red Robe, 1894; My Lady Rotha, 1894; The Red Cockade, 1895; Shrewsbury, 1898; The Castle Inn, 1898; Sophia, 1900; Count Hannibal, 1901; In Kings' Byways (short stories) 1902; The Long Night, 1903; The Abbess of Vlaye, 1904; Starvecrow Farm, 1905; Chippinge, 1906; The Wild Geese, 1908; The Great House, 1919; Ovington's Bank, 1922; The Lively Peggy, 1928.

ABOUT: John o' London's Weekly August 30, 1909; London Mercury April 1933; London Times October 12, 1928; Manchester Quarterly 1933.

WHARTON, MRS. EDITH NEWBOLD (JONES) (January 24, 1862-August 11, 1937), American novelist and short-story writer, was born on West Twenty-Third Street, New York City, the daughter of George Frederic and Lucretia Stevens

(Rhinelander) Jones. Her grandmother was a Schermerhorn, and a great-grandfather was Ebenezer Stevens, a general in the American Revolution. "My little-girl life, safe, guarded, monotonous," wrote Mrs. Wharton in 1934,

Bonney

"was cradled in the only world about which, according to Goethe, it is impossible to write poetry. The small society into which I was born was 'good' in the most prosaic sense of the term, and its only interest, for the generality of readers, lies in the fact of its sudden and total extinction." She received a fairly strict training at home, from tutors and governesses. Her father inherited a fortune from his grandfather, and the family led a pleasant, leisurely life in Paris, New York, and Newport, R.I., in a house on the bay half-way out toward Fort Adams. It was a simple, clannish society, which excluded tradesmen and was totally innocent of any intellectual stirrings. Mrs. Wharton's literary work was regarded by her family on both sides as an eccentricity best disregarded and left undiscussed. She married Edward Wharton of Boston (descended from a Virginia family) in 1885; they traveled abroad in search of amusement and, when in America, lived in New York, Newport, and Lenox, Mass.

The Decoration of Houses, a book written in reaction to the overstuffed interiors of her time, and in collaboration with Ogden Codman, was Mrs. Wharton's first printed book, but her literary career really began with the publication in *Scribner's Magazine* of some short stories. The first was "Mrs. Manstey's View," about the humble side of city life. These early tales were not included in *The Greater Inclination*, a collection of stories published in 1899. A second collection two years later, *Crucial Instances*, also showed a preoccupation with moral problems which she had absorbed from Paul Bourget, the French novelist, who came to her in Newport in 1893 with a letter of introduction. Henry James was another potent literary influence, as well as a personal friend.

Wharton's mental condition became alarming after their first years of marriage; the brunt of his care fell on Mrs. Wharton,

since his family refused to acknowledge that anything was wrong. Edmund Wilson, who believes that Dr. S. Weir Mitchell advised her to write fiction to relieve nervous tension, calls Mrs. Wharton "at her strongest and most characteristic a brilliant example of a writer who relieves emotional strain by denouncing his generation." (*The Fruit of the Tree* defends a "mercy killing.") Mrs. Wharton says merely that Edward Burlingame, editor of *Scribner's*, wanted a serial in six months, and so she wrote a society novel, *The House of Mirth*, showing, in the person of the novel's hapless heroine, Lily Bart, how "both wealth and poverty annihilate every impulse toward excellence." It was a best-seller, was dramatized by Clyde Fitch, and firmly established her reputation with the general reading public, who had not been much attracted by its predecessor, *The Valley of Decision*, an historical novel of eighteenth-century Italy.

In 1906 the Whartons removed to a flat in Paris, to be nearer the Riviera, but returned to Lenox, Mass., for summers at "The Mount." When Wharton's condition became hopeless, the place was sold, and Mrs. Wharton returned to Paris to the life and companions she much preferred, in the salons of the Faubourg Saint-Germain. Summers were spent at her Villa Colombe, at St. Brice near Paris; winters at Hyères, Provence. During the First World War Mrs. Wharton ran a workroom for unemployed Parisiennes and helped feed and house 600 Belgian refugee orphans. In 1924 she was made an officer of the Legion of Honor. A photographic memory enabled her to retain her status as an American novelist: the grim, laconic New England tragedy (perhaps her masterpiece) *Ethan Frome;* its longer companion-piece, *Summer;* and the Pulitzer Prize-winning novel *The Age of Innocence*, about the Newport society she had known so well, were all written in France. The last-named novel ran in the *Revue des Deux Mondes* as *Au Temps de l'Innocence*. Katharine Cornell appeared in a successful dramatization at the Empire Theatre, New York.

Robert Morss Lovett calls Mrs. Wharton first of all a novelist of civilization, absorbed in the somewhat mechanical operations of culture, preoccupied with the upper ("and inner") class, and loyal to the theory of the art of fiction as set forth by Henry James. Her characters are given sharp, clear, consistent shapes; her style is a "clear, luminous medium in which things are seen in precise and striking outline." Humor was one of her steadfast qualities. An unfinished and posthumous novel, *The Buccaneers,* showed that she retained her powers to the end, although some of the later novels (*The Glimpses of the Moon* for one) were not much above the status of competent magazine fiction. Mrs. Wharton had "brownish hair, a finished manner, and an air."

She was hospitable to young writers, as William Gerhardi has testified; and Sinclair Lewis dedicated *Babbitt* to her. She was the first woman to receive an honorary Litt.D. from Yale, and the first to receive two Pulitzer prizes (*The Old Maid,* dramatized from *Old New York,* winning the drama prize in 1935).

Death was caused by an apoplectic stroke, at her villa near Saint-Brice-Sous-Forêt, France. She is buried in the Protestant Cemetery at Versailles.

PRINCIPAL WORKS: The Greater Inclination, 1899; The Touchstone, 1900; Crucial Instances, 1901; The Valley of Decision, 1902; Sanctuary, 1903; Italian Villas, 1904; Italian Backgrounds, 1905; The House of Mirth, 1905; The Fruit of the Tree, 1907; The Hermit and the Wild Woman (short stories) 1908; Tales of Men and Ghosts, 1910; Ethan Frome, 1911; The Reef, 1912; The Custom of the Country, 1913; Fighting France, 1915; Xingu and Other Stories, 1916; Summer, 1917; The Marne, 1918; French Ways and Their Meaning, 1919; The Age of Innocence, 1920; In Morocco, 1920; The Glimpses of the Moon, 1922; A Son at the Front, 1923; Old New York. 1924; The Writing of Fiction, 1925; Twilight Sleep, 1927; The Children, 1928; Hudson River Bracketed, 1929; Certain People, 1930; Ghosts, 1937; The Buccaneers, 1938.

ABOUT: Beach, J. W. The Twentieth Century Novel; Björkman, E. A. Voices of Tomorrow; Boynton, P. H. Some Contemporary Americans; Brown, E. K. Edith Wharton; Canby, H. S. Definitions; Collins, J. Taking the Literary Pulse; Cooper, F. T. Some American Story Tellers; Follett, H. T. & W. Some Modern Novelists; Hackett, F. Horizons; Hind, C. L. Authors and I; Huneker, J. G. Ivory, Apes, and Peacocks; Lovett, R. M. Edith Wharton; Michaud, R. The American Novel To-Day; Millett, F. B. Contemporary American Authors; Overton, G. American Nights' Entertainment, Cargoes for Crusoes, The Women Who Make Our Novels; Sedgwick, H. D. The New American Type; Sherman, S. P. The Main Stream; Underwood, J. C. Literature and Insurgency; Van Doren, C. The American Novel; Williams, B. C. Our Short Story Writers; American Review January 1936; Atlantic Monthly October 1936; Catholic World January 1938; Commonweal November 25, 1938; New Republic June 29, 1938; New York Times August 13-15, 1937; Quarterly Review January 1915; Saturday Evening Post January 18, 1941; Scrutiny December 1938; Time August 23, 1937; Virginia Quarterly Review January 1941.

WHEELER, WILLIAM MORTON

(March 19, 1865-April 19, 1937), American entomologist and university professor, was born in Milwaukee, Wis., the son of Julius Morton Wheeler and Caroline Georgiana (Anderson) Wheeler, and lived there until he was nineteen. He went from public school to a strict German academy and the German - American Normal College, and in February 1884, just before his nineteenth birthday, took a job at Ward's Natural Science Establishment at Roches-

ter, N.Y. Here he identified and listed birds and mammals, struck up a warm friendship with Carl Akeley, who joined the firm as a taxidermist, and compiled a shell-catalogue still unsuperseded and in use by conchologists forty years later. Returning to Milwaukee, Wheeler taught German and physiology at the High School, and was custodian of the Wilwaukee Public Museum from 1887 to 1890, importing Akeley to assist him. In 1890 he became Fellow and Assistant in Morphology at Clark University, took his Ph.D. degree there in 1892 for work on insect embryology, and became instructor in that subject at the new University of Chicago.

In June 1898 Wheeler married Dora Bay Emerson of Rockford, Ill., and the next year became Professor of Zoology at the University of Texas. Here he wrote two-score papers, most of them about his favorite and almost cherished subject, ants. Wheeler organized and arranged the Hall of Invertebrate Life at the American Museum of Natural History in New York City, where he was curator of Invertebrate Zoology, beginning in 1903. Five years later came his most important appointment, at the Bussey Institution of Harvard University, in Forest Hills, Mass., eight miles from Cambridge. In September 1931 the new Biological Laboratories were opened near the Museum of Comparative Zoology at the university, and became known the world over.

From 1908 to 1926 Wheeler was Professor of Economic Entomology; from then till 1934, when he became professor emeritus, his title was Professor of Entomology. In three hundred publications, many of them marked by force, polish, and Voltairean humor, Wheeler talked of ants and expounded his philosophy of biology. In particular he espoused Alexander's theory of emergent evolution. He fell dead of heart failure on the Boston-bound platform of the Harvard subway station at Cambridge on Patriots' Day, survived by his wife, a son, Dr. Ralph Emerson Wheeler, and a daughter, Adeline. Quiet, modest and unassuming, he had keen eyes, a long face and gray moustache.

PRINCIPAL WORKS: Social Life Among the Insects, 1923; Foibles of Insects and Men, 1928; The Social Insects, Their Origin and Evolution, 1928; The Lamarck Manuscripts at Harvard (with H. W. T. Barbour) 1933.

ABOUT: National Academy of Sciences: Biographical Memoirs, 1938.

WHEELOCK, JOHN HALL (September 9, 1886-), American poet, writes: "John Hall Wheelock was born at Far Rockaway,

Long Island, N.Y., the son of William Efner and Emily (Hall) Wheelock. His mother's father was a Presbyterian minister from Dublin; on his father's side his ancestry goes back to Ralph Wheelock, a classmate of Milton's at Cambridge, and the first Wheelock to come to America. Among his ancestors is Eleazar Wheelock, the founder of Dartmouth College.

"John Hall Wheelock began writing verse at an early age. At Harvard, from which he graduated in 1908, he became a friend of Van Wyck Brooks, with whom he published anonymously, during their freshman year, a pamphlet entitled *Verses by Two Undergraduates.* He edited the *Harvard Monthly,* and was Class Poet at graduation. He spent two years in study for a Ph.D. degree at universities in Germany, and wrote a great deal of verse during that period. In 1910 he returned to America, and shortly thereafter became associated with Charles Scribner's Sons. In 1932 be became a director, and was later elected secretary of the corporation.

"His volume of collected poems, in 1936, was awarded the Golden Rose by the New England Poetry Society, as the most distinguished contribution to American poetry of that year. His poem, 'Affirmation,' was read before the Phi Beta Kappa Society at Harvard University in 1927.

"Wheelock lives in New York and spends his vacations on the South shore of Long Island. He is a great lover of the sea, and his principal recreations are swimming and walking along the shore."

* * *

Mr. Wheelock is unmarried. His love of the sea dates from childhood, when all of his summers were spent at Easthampton, L.I. He is almost exclusively a lyric poet: his recurrent themes are lost love, loneliness, and nostalgia for the past. Morton Dauwen Zabel called his work "stately and grave"; Chard Powers Smith praised "its singing quality as verse, its personal intimacy, its absolute sincerity." The influence of Shelley and Swinburne, as well as of his friend, the late Alan Seeger, is strong in it; indeed the chief criticism which has been made on his poetry is that it is narrow in scope and faintly old-fashioned. He distinctly does not belong to the "modern" school of poets; nevertheless his work has beauty and genuine distinction.

PRINCIPAL WORKS: Verses by Two Undergraduates (with V. W. Brooks) 1905; The Human Fantasy, 1911; The Beloved Adventure, 1912; Love and Liberation, 1913; Alan Seeger: Poet of the Foreign Legion (prose) 1918; Dust and Light, 1919; A Bibliography of Theodore Roosevelt, 1920; The Black Panther, 1922; The Bright Doom, 1927; Collected Poems, 1936.

ABOUT: Monroe, H. The New Poetry; Power, M. Poets at Prayer; Untermeyer, L. American Poetry Since 1900, Modern American Poetry; Wilkinson, M. New Voices; Wood, C. Poets of America; Poetry February 1928, May 1937; Saturday Review of Literature October 24, 1936

WHIBLEY, CHARLES (December 9, 1859-March 4, 1930), English critic and reviewer, was born in Kent of middle-class parents. He first went to school at Bristol; and in his twentieth year he entered Jesus College, Cambridge.

Settling in London, after graduation, he first went into the office of Cassell and Company, the publishers. Beginning with the early issues of the

P. Evans

Scots Observer, later known as the *National Observer,* Whibley was a frequent contributor, and became closely associated with William Ernest Henley, its publisher. His articles in that periodical, attacking Ruskinian principles, under the title of "Methodism in Art," had a definite effect on the esthetics of the day.

With Henley in 1892 he projected the *Tudor Translations,* an excellent series of reprints of Elizabethan and Jacobean versions from the classical and other languages; and it is perhaps through his introductions to the series that he is now best remembered.

On Henley's death in 1903, Whibley was left as his literary executor.

In 1894 Whibley joined the staff of the *Pall Mall Gazette* and was sent to Paris where he joined the Whistler circle and became intimate with Mallarmé, Marcel Schwob, and Paul Valéry. There too he married Ethel Birlie, Whistler's sister-in-law.

On his return to England he began a series entitled "Musings Without Method" in *Blackwood's Magazine,* and continued the articles every month for the next thirty years. His generation knew him best by these "Musings" in which he violently controverted all the dominant opinions of the age and denounced politicians of all parties. T. S. Eliot has written that the "Musings" were "the best sustained pieces of literary journalism that I have known in recent years."

Whibley was a contributor for a time to *Spectator,* and then Lord Northcliffe persuaded him to transfer his articles to the *Daily Mail* where for several years they were an important and vigorous feature.

Whibley read voluminously, knew English literature thoroughly, and enjoyed most of all the literature of the sixteenth and seventeenth centuries. If in his introductions and criticisms he did not present any important original judgments, at least he was able to communicate an interest in the subject and help readers to experience an enjoyment comparable to his own.

In literature, as in life, he demanded intellectual honesty and sound craftsmanship. He fought consistently against the lowering of literary standards, and his own style was founded on the great writers of the past. His personal idiosyncrasies proceeded from a hatred of pretense and pretensions. That same hatred helped him in understanding such men as Petronius, Heliodorus, Laurence Sterne, Edgar Allan Poe, and Sir Thomas Urquhart, of whom he wrote in *Studies in Frankness.*

Several of his books were compilations of his already published writings. *The Letters of an Englishman* consists of essays from the *Daily Mail,* and *Literary Studies* was reprinted in greater part from his contributions to the *Cambridge History of English Literature.*

T. S. Eliot, his biographer, has written of him: "One always feels that he is ready to say bluntly what everyone else is afraid to say. . . . And, in fact, he was a master of invective. . . . Whibley had what is perhaps the first of all critical gifts, without which others are vain: the ability to detect the living style from the dead. . . . He was too modest, and had too varied tastes and interests in life, to care to be the monumental critic."

Whibley was twice married—the second time to Philippa, the daughter of Sir Walter Raleigh, in 1927. During the last years of his life he suffered from an agonizing disorder of a frontal nerve. He died at Hyères at the age of seventy. His literary position is chronologically ambiguous in that he began to write in the 'eighties and was an associate of so definitely a nineteenth century figure as Henley; yet he published principally in the twentieth century and lived well into the post-war period.

PRINCIPAL WORKS: The Book of Scoundrels, 1897; The Pageantry of Life, 1900; Studies in Frankness, 1910; Essays in Biography, 1913; The Letters of an Englishman, 1915; Political Portraits, 1917; Lord John Manners, 1925.

ABOUT: Eliot, T. S. Charles Whibley, The Sacred Wood; Blackwood's Magazine April 1930.

WHISTLER, JAMES MC NEILL. See "AMERICAN AUTHORS: 1600-1900"

WHITE, ANDREW DICKSON. See "AMERICAN AUTHORS: 1600-1900"

WHITE, EDWARD LUCAS (May 18, 1866-March 30, 1934), American novelist and short-story writer, was born in Bergen, N. J., the son of Thomas Hurley White and Kate Butler (Lucas) White. From two to six the boy lived in Brooklyn, N.Y., later with his grandmother on the shore of Lake Seneca, and at eleven moved with his parents to Baltimore, Md., for  the rest of his life. After attending the University School for Boys (where he later taught Greek and Latin for more than a decade), he entered Johns Hopkins University, hoping to be a biologist and public lecturer. At the end of the first year he went to Rio de Janeiro by sailing ship. After three years of graduate study in the classics, following bestowal of a B.A. in 1888, he taught at the Friends High School, the Boys' Latin School, and the University School till it closed in 1930.

Narrative Lyrics, White's collected poems, appeared in his forty-second year. Doggedly working on in spite of incapacitating headaches, White now produced several ambitious historical novels, first *El Supremo,* concerning Roderiguez de Francia, an early nineteenth century dictator of Paraguay, which was written in three successive summers; and in 1921 the best-selling *Andivius Hedulio*, a picaresque novel in the time of the young Emperor Commodus which showed White's ability to vivify his classical studies. (As a student he had studied sculpture and architecture in Europe for three months) *Lukundoo*, a collection of horrifying stories, represents a curious and interesting facet of White's talent. He claimed that these tales had come to him as dreams. "The Little Faded Flag," a milder production, is included in May Lamberton Becker's collection, *Golden Tales of the Old South*.

White wrote in pencil on small sheets of paper; his manuscripts were typed by his wife, Agnes Gerry White, who died in 1927. (He wrote *Matrimony*, a novel, for her.) White was studious-looking, with a mountainous forehead, well-trimmed moustache and beard, and sharp eyes behind narrow-rimmed glasses. Found dead by his sister on the floor of a gas-filled bathroom in his Baltimore home, White was pronounced a suicide by the coroner.

PRINCIPAL WORKS: Narrative Lyrics. 1908; El Supremo, 1918; The Unwilling Vestal, 1918; The Song of the Sirens, and Other Stories, 1919; Andivius Hedulio, 1921; Helen, 1925; Lukundoo and Other Stories, 1927; Rome Fell, 1927; Matrimony, 1932.

ABOUT: New York Times March 31, 1934.

WHITE, ELWYN BROOKS (July 11, 1899-), American humorist and poet who signs his works as E. B. White, was born in Mt. Vernon, N.Y., the  son of Samuel Tilly White and Jessie (Hart) White. He was educated at Cornell University (A.B. 1921). During the First World War he interrupted his college course to serve as a private in the United States Army. He went West after college, and worked as a reporter on the Seattle *Times*; then he went to Alaska as mess-boy on a ship, and after this experience returned to New York, where he became production assistant in an advertising agency. It was at this time that he began sending contributions to the *New Yorker* which so impressed the editor, Harold Ross, that he finally prevailed on Mr. White to join the staff. For eleven years he wrote most of the "Talk of the Town"

columns in that magazine. He then resigned and retired to Brooklin, Maine, his present home. In 1929 he had married Katharine Sargeant Angell, who had been literary editor of the *New Yorker*, and they have one son. At present Mr. White, besides freelancing and making regular contributions to the *New Yorker*, conducts the department, "One Man's Meat," in *Harper's Magazine*. For several years he was part owner of a boys' camp in Canada.

An exceedingly shy man, averse to mixed company or publicity, he has been described by his friend and colleague James Thurber as "a poet who loves to live half-hidden from the eye. . . . He understands begonias and children, canaries and goldfish, dachshunds and Scottish terriers, men and motives. . . . He plays a fair ping-pong, a good piano, and a terrible poker. . . . He is a good man with ax, rifle, and canoe, and sails a thirty-foot boat expertly." In Maine he farms his estate and tries to keep away from hay-fever, from which he is a sufferer. His attitude toward all forms of "ballyhoo" is that "his life is his own."

Mr. White's style is indescribable and highly individual. A critic in *Time* called it "a kind of precocious offhand humming." To Mr. Thurber it seemed "those silver and crystal sentences which have a ring like nobody else's sentences in the world." Leonard Bacon said, "His most successful moments are due to a high sense of the nobility of the ridiculous tempered with ingenious kindness." It approximates the humor of Clarence Day, Jr., but instead of being savage in its satire it is aloof. The cleverness of Mr. White's light verse has not obscured the fact that he is also a serious poet, especially when he is aroused to indignation. He may some day issue a volume of serious poems.

He looks the shy, introverted person he is —slender, with something sketchy, startled, and evanescent about his appearance. He is most at home in the woods, and perhaps feels most at ease with other wild, timid animals which occasionally dart forth from the forest to stare at man and his strange society with bright observant eyes.

PRINCIPAL WORKS: The Lady Is Cold (poems) 1929; Is Sex Necessary? (with J. Thurber) 1929; Every Day Is Saturday, 1934; The Fox of Peapack, 1938; Quo Vadimus, 1939; A Subtreasury of American Humor (ed., with K. S. White) 1941; One Man's Meat, 1942.

ABOUT: Reader's Digest June 1940; Saturday Review of Literature October 15, 1938, April 29, 1939; Time March 6, 1939; Wilson Library Bulletin January 1939.

WHITE, HELEN CONSTANCE (November 26, 1896-), American critic and novelist, writes: "I was born in New Haven,

Conn., daughter of John and Mary (King) White. I grew up and was educated in Boston, graduating from the Girls' High School and going on from there to Radcliffe College, where I received my B.A. degree in 1916 and my M.A. in 1917. For two years I taught at Smith College, and then in 1919 I came to the University of Wisconsin, where I am now Professor of English. I received my Ph.D. degree from Wisconsin in 1924. The year 1928 I spent on a Guggenheim Fellowship in England doing research work, mainly in the British Museum and in the Bodleian Library in Oxford. That year I spent my holiday in Italy. The spring and summer of 1935 I spent, again doing research work, at the Harvard Library and at the British Museum. This year I have a fellowship in the Huntington Library, in San Marino, Calif., where I am doing some work in English literature of the sixteenth century. I have also spent four other summers abroad, either in research or in traveling in England and on the Continent.

"I do not know that there is much to report in the way of hobbies—I do a fair amount of organization work and of public speaking of various sorts; I am very fond of travel—but I do not have a great deal of time for anything in the usual line of hobbies because I enjoy my teaching and my students a great deal, and I have certain scholarly interests, especially in the field of the history of ideas; and then, I like to write stories, and put all the time into that that I can."

* * *

Miss White has never married. As a young girl she took part in the woman suffrage movement in Massachusetts. At Wisconsin she teaches creative writing as well as English literature. Of herself she says modestly that "as a novelist I could barely qualify for admission to the sophomore class." There is a strong religious tinge to her novels, which are historical in nature. She is a Roman Catholic, and has made a special study of the metaphysical and mystical in English writing.

PRINCIPAL WORKS: The Mysticism of William Blake, 1927; Victorian Prose (ed., with E. Foster) 1930; English Devotional Literature: Prose 1600-1640, 1931; A Watch in the Night (novel) 1933; Not Built With Hands (novel) 1935; The Metaphysical Poets: A Study in Religious Experience, 1936; To the End of the World (novel) 1939.

ABOUT: Commonweal May 24, 1935.

WHITE, PATRICK (May 28, 1912-), Australian novelist, writes from the Egyptian desert, where he is serving with the R.A.F.

"Although fourth-generation Australian, I was born by chance in London. At the age of 6 months I was taken to Sydney, and proceeded to spend my childhood in Australia, mainly in the country. What-

ever has come since, I feel that the influences and impressions of this strange, dead landscape of Australia predominate.

"My boyhood I spent at an English public school, learning very little, except from my own private reading, and detesting everything connected with this educational system. Even holidays abroad, in France, Belgium, and Scandinavia, were never free from the prospect of returning to prison. These four years were largely unpleasant.

"I escaped early from school and returned to Australia, where I found I had become a stranger. I had acquired too much European veneer, and was too young and too inexperienced to practice tolerance. During three years I lived in the country, working on two sheep stations in New South Wales, writing immature novels, discontented with my own isolation, though aspects of this existence, with its droughts, floods, and fires, and of course the landscape, were impressive.

"From 1932 to 1935, I made up for time lost, intellectually, reading Modern Languages at King's College, Cambridge, and for the first time, making human contacts. I also continued writing. Two inferior comedies, Bread and Butter Women and The School for Friends, were produced at Bryants' Playhouse, a small basement theatre in Sydney. Verses and a story appeared in the London Mercury.

"Coming down from Cambridge, I set up in London, writing plays that nobody produced, traveling much in France and Germany, but only taking root at Hanover and St. Jean-de-Luz.

"Happy Valley, my first success, was published in London, 1939. This novel appeared in New York the following year, and won the Australian Literature Society's Gold

Medal. A second novel, *The Living and the Dead*, came out both in New York and London in 1941.

"Much of 1939 and 1940 was spent wandering in the United States, with a period of several months in New York, a city both stimulating and repellant, sympathetic and antipathetic, to which I shall always hope to return.

"In August 1940 I left New York for England, and since then have served with the R.A.F. in the Sudanese and Egyptian Deserts."

* * *

Patrick White is not easy reading. He has gone to school to James Joyce, and almost to Gertrude Stein. He carries the "stream of consciousness method" to almost its ultimate extreme, and his main interests are in "deviations from the psychological norm." His first novel, ironically called *Happy Valley*, was a gloomy and scathing study of a small Australian community. His second was equally naturalistic in theme and "ultra-modern" in method.

R. L. Nathan said of him: "He works in the tradition of *Ulysses* . . . with a literary vitality quite his own." Mr. Nathan praised particularly his "dry clarity of observation," but remarked that "his style and method are more important than his materials"—in other words, his plots are slight and sometimes rather trite, but to them he brings a genuine and mordant literary gift.

PRINCIPAL WORKS: Happy Valley, 1939; The Living and the Dead, 1941.

ABOUT: Wilson Library Bulletin April 1941.

*WHITE, STEWART EDWARD (March 12, 1873-   ), American novelist and writer of books of travel, was born in Grand

Rapids, Mich., the son of T. Stewart White and Mary E. (Daniell) White. His first eight or nine years were spent in a small mill town of Michigan, then the greatest of American lumber states. From the age of eleven to fifteen young White lived on a ranch in California, spending much time in the saddle. His first formal schooling came at sixteen, when he entered the Grand Rapids high school in the third year, graduating at eighteen, the president of his class, and holder of the five-mile running record. White received a Ph.B. degree from the

University of Michigan in 1895 (and an M.A. in 1903), spending the year 1896-97 at Columbia University Law School. The intervening year was spent partially in a Chicago packing house at $6 a week, and in the Black Hills of Dakota prospecting for gold. His college summer vacations were passed cruising the Great Lakes in a 28-foot cutter sloop.

At Columbia, Brander Matthews had praised White's short stories, and urged him in particular to sell one entitled "A Man and His Dog." It was sold for $15, and White was still more encouraged to receive $500 from *Munsey's Magazine* for the serial rights to *The Westerners,* published in book form in 1901. After a period at McClurg's, Chicago, where White sold books for $9 a week, he set out for the Hudson Bay country. *The Blazed Trail,* which established White's reputation as a writer, was written between 4 and 8 A.M. in the depths of a northern winter. He was much pleased when his hard-bitten lumberjack foreman sat up till four in the morning to read the manuscript. *The Riverman,* an exciting yarn of lumbering and log-driving through rapids and snares set by rival lumberman, was a best-seller. *The Adventures of Bobby Orde,* a book for boys, drew on White's early experiences in the north country; its sequel, an adult novel, was *The Rules of the Game.* Boys who had read his stories with mounting excitement were ready to follow White into his later novels of the growth of California; *Gold* (1913), *Gray Dawn* (1915) and *Rose Dawn* (1920). *The Mystery* (1907), written in collaboration with Samuel Hopkins Adams and serialized in the *American Magazine,* had a setting outside America, and compared favorably with Stevenson's and Lloyd Osbourne's *The Wrecker.* "The one great drama is that of the individual man's struggle toward perfect adjustment with his environment," White has said. "It may be financial, natural, sexual, political, and so on. Self-preservation is a very simple and even more important instinct than that of the propagation of the race." The California stories were collected in an omnibus volume, *The Story of California,* in 1927.

In April 1904 White married Elizabeth Grant of Newport, R.I. They camped and hunted in Wyoming, Arizona, and California in 1906, and he wrote *The Pass*; in the High Sierras in 1910, hence *The Cabin.* In 1911 White followed Theodore Roosevelt into Africa, and underwent various exciting experiences recorded in *The Land of Footprints* and *Lions in the Path.* White has written of "punchers and rustlers and nesters, prospectors and miners and foremen, Indians, Africans, Germans, and philosophical Chinks." When not writing from actual experience, he does research at Stanford University and the University of California, writing at his desk only after formulating the work at hand in his mind. During the First World War, White was a major in the U.S. 144th Field Artillery. At sixty-seven he produced an historical romance of unimpaired vigor, *Wild Geese Calling.* He is of medium height, with a ruddy face, sharp blue eyes, a reddish moustache, and square hands. *The Silent Places* is his own favorite among his books, and he regards "The Rawhide" in *Arizona Nights* as his most coherent piece of work. The fresh, outdoor quality of his work is its own best preservative.

Since Mrs. White's death, Mr. White has been writing a series of spiritualist books beginning with *The Betty Book* (1937), based on his conviction of his wife's other-wordly existence and on material "dictated by her through another psychic after her death."

PRINCIPAL WORKS: *Fiction*—The Westerners, 1901; The Claim Jumpers, 1901; The Blazed Trail, 1902; Conjuror's House, 1903; The Silent Places, 1904; The Mystery (with S. H. Adams) 1907; The Riverman, 1908; The Rules of the Game, 1909; The Adventures of Bobby Orde, 1911; The Sign at Six, 1912; Gold, 1913; Gray Dawn, 1915; The Leopard Woman, 1916; Rose Dawn, 1920; On Tiptoe, 1922; The Glory Hole, 1924; Skookum Chuck, 1925; Secret Harbour, 1925; Back of Beyond, 1927; The Shepper-Newfounder, 1931; The Long Rifle, 1932; Ranchero, 1933; Folded Hills, 1934; Pole Star (with H. De Vigne) 1934; Wild Geese Calling, 1940; Stampede, 1942. *Travel*—The Forest, 1903; The Mountains, 1904; The Pass, 1906; Camp and Trail, 1907; The Cabin, 1910; The Land of Footprints, 1912; African Camp Fires, 1913; The Rediscovered Country, 1915; Lions in the Path, 1926. *Miscellaneous*—The Forty-Niners, 1918; Daniel Boone, 1922; Credo, 1925; Why Be a Mud Turtle? (essays) 1928; Dog Days (autobiography) 1930; The Betty Book, 1937; Across the Unknown (with H. White) 1939; The Unobstructed Universe, 1940; The Road I Know, 1942.

ABOUT: Baldwin, C. C. The Men Who Make Our Novels; Millett, F. B. Contemporary American Authors; Overton, G. M. Authors of the Day, When Winter Comes to Main Street; White, S. E. Dog Days, Gold (see appendix by E. Saxton); Bookman August 1929; Overland July 1916; Philadelphia Public Ledger May 20, 1922; San Francisco Chronicle April 28, 1940.

WHITE, TERENCE HANBURY (May 29, 1906-), English novelist, was born in Bombay, India, the son of Garrick Hanbury White and C. E. S. (Aston) White. He was educated at Cheltenham College and Queen's College, Cambridge (B.A.) 1928. He is unmarried, and has for a long time lived in the country, at Stowe Ridings,

Buckinghamshire. He is a rather short, slender, delicately featured young man with thick dark hair and a small moustache. He is reticent about his private life, and nothing is known of his interests or hobbies. They, like his temperament, must be extracted from his books. From these, it is obvious that he has read very widely in the literature of the age of Chivalry and in the Arthurian legends, but also that he is thoroughly conversant with the most "advanced" of modern psychological theories. It is also apparent that he loves the English countryside, its traditions, its history, but above all its actual physical being, with a consuming passion.

He was almost unknown in America, and hardly better known in England, until the appearance of his eighth book, *The Sword in the Stone.* That and its sequels have given rise to a very active and articulate White-cult. Mr. White is outstandingly one of those authors to whom one is utterly devoted, or else by whom one is thoroughly repelled. His mock-historical novels, half-fantasy, half-burlesque, with their overtones of Freud, are distinctly *sui generis.* In a book ostensibly about King Arthur and his circle one may find almost literally anything— modern slang, allegory, mysticism, bawdiness, technicalities of warfare, riotous humor, and tender sentiment. Anachronism is their very reason for being. They are a grand hodge-podge of time, place, and language—what one critic called "a shake-up of Evelyn Waugh, Laurel and Hardy, John Erskine, and the Marquis de Sade." They are quite indescribable, and they will either fascinate the reader or irritate him to the point of frenzy.

His earlier books, much soberer and more unified in tone, were equally varied in subject. They culminated in the really beautiful *England Have My Bones,* a paean of praise which should make heartening reading for Englishmen today. But having caught his stride in *The Sword in the Stone,* he is apparently going to continue in the vein that has brought him fame and fortune, entranced readers, and puzzled critics. The strange rustle he must sometimes hear as he writes his versions of Arthur and Guinevere and Lancelot is probably Alfred, Lord Tennyson, turning restlessly in his grave.

PRINCIPAL WORKS: Loved Helen (poems) 1927; Dead Mr. Nixon, 1930; Darkness at Pemberley, 1932; Farewell Victoria, 1934; Earth Stopped, 1935; Gone to Ground, 1936; England Have My Bones, 1937; The Sword in the Stone, 1938; Burke's Steerage, 1939; The Witch in the Wood, 1939; The Ill-Made Knight, 1940.

ABOUT: Book-of-the-Month Club News December 1938.

---

*WHITE, WALTER FRANCIS (July 1, 1893-   ), American publicist and novelist, writes: "Walter White, executive secretary of the National Association for the Advancement of Colored People, was born in Atlanta, Ga., and lived in the South to 1918 when he became an executive officer of the N.A.A.C.P. He is a graduate of Atlanta University, and has also done postgraduate work in economics and sociology in the College of the City of New York. He received from Howard University in 1939 the honorary degree of LL.D. As an official of the N.A.A.C.P., he has made investigations of forty-one lynchings and eight race riots; has traveled more than 400,000 miles in the United States and Europe. He attended the Pan-African Congress held in 1921 in England, Belgium, and France, and in 1927 he went to France for a year of writing and study as a Guggenheim Fellow.

Irwin & Langen

"His first novel, *Fire in the Flint*, was published in England, France, Germany, Russia, Norway, Denmark, and Japan. He is a member of the American Center of the P.E.N. Club. He has contributed articles to many magazines and newspapers.

"Upon the retirement of Mr. James Weldon Johnson in 1931 as secretary of the N.A.A.C.P., Mr. White was elected as his successor. He was appointed by President Roosevelt as a member of the Advisory Council for the Government of the Virgin Islands in March 1934, from which position he resigned in May 1935. He is a member of the Board of Visitors of the New York State Training School for Boys. He was appointed in 1935 chairman of the Harlem low-cost housing project under the New York City Housing Authority.

"He has taken a prominent part in the fight against lynching and for enactment of federal legislation against this evil, especially in the marshaling of public opinion on behalf of the Costigan-Wagner anti-lynching bill in the 74th Congress, and he led the forces which succeeded in bringing to passage the Gavagan anti-lynching bill in the 75th Congress.

"In 1937 he was awarded the Spingarn Medal for his personal investigation of lynchings and race riots and for his 'remarkable tact, skill, and persuasiveness' in lobbying for a federal anti-lynching bill."

* * *

In 1922 Mr. White married Leah Gladys Powell; they have a son and a daughter. He is small, dapper, high-strung, and it is only through his own insistence on his Negro blood (estimated by E. A. Hooton at about one-sixty-fourth!) that anyone would take Mr. White for a Negro; he is a blond with fair skin, blue eyes, and sandy hair. This fact has enabled him frequently to pass for white and secure information (at very dangerous risk) during his investigations of race riots and lynchings. His father, George White, was an Atlanta postman who died because of neglect, after an injury, caused by his being a colored man; that and a harrowing experience during the Atlanta Race Riots when he was twelve years old have made the welfare of his putative race Mr. White's chief concern. As John Chamberlain remarked, he is "probably not a novelist at heart." Du Bose Heyward thought that "his material has been subjected to such excessive exaggeration that the illusion of truth cannot survive. It is the cry of the propagandist rather than the voice of art." Outside the field of fiction, however, as Irving Astrachan said, "his keen interest in the welfare of his race has in no instance obscured his impartial treatment of data."

PRINCIPAL WORKS: Fire in the Flint (novel) 1924; Flight (novel) 1926; Rope and Faggot—A Biography of Judge Lynch, 1929.

ABOUT: American Mercury January 1929; Bookman February 1930; Nation May 21, 1930; Saturday Evening Post June 4, 1938; Time January 24, 1938.

---

*WHITE, WILLIAM ALLEN (February 10, 1868-   ), American editor, novelist, and biographer, writes: "I was born in Emporia, Kan. My father, Dr. Allen White, was from Ohio and his father and mother were from New England, where the family had lived since the 1630's. My mother, Mary Hatton, was pure-bred Irish. Her parents came from Ireland three months before she was born. I grew up in El Dorado, Kan., sixty miles south of Emporia, and was graduated from high school in 1884. I came to Emporia to go to the College of Emporia that year, and later quit to learn the printer's trade. I was a reporter going to school at the Kansas State University from 1886 to January 1890. I did not graduate; I quit to take a job on the El Dorado *Republican* as business manager. Later I was editorial writer on the Kansas City *Star* from 1892 to 1895; and in 1895 I bought the Emporia *Gazette*, which I have owned and edited ever since.

"In 1896 I published a book of short stories called *The Real Issue*. Since then I have published four books of short stories, three novels, three biographies, and five books of political essays.

"I was married in 1893 to Sallie Lindsay Watts. Two children have been born to us, William Lindsay [now a syndicated newspaper correspondent and novelist] and Mary Kathrine, who died in 1921. I have held no public office except Regent of the State University. I have served on one or two traveling commissions of no great importance. I have honorary doctor's degrees from Baker University, Washburn College, Beloit College, Knox College, Oberlin College, Columbia University, Brown University, and Harvard University. I have worked most of my life within a thousand feet of my birthplace. I have been to Europe six times, once to Russia, once to the Orient. That's the story."

* * *

That is not *all* the story. William Allen White has been called the embodiment of the Middle West, a "savory sage," a "liberal philosopher." His editorial in 1895, "What's the Matter With Kansas?" (most of the assertions in which he has lived to regret), made him nationally famous. His beautiful essay on the death of his daughter at seventeen is a classic. He has been active for forty years in the affairs of the Republican Party, latterly from the liberal wing. If he has held no political office it is not for want of invitation or appeal. He was president of the American Society of Newspaper Editors in 1938 and has been on the board of the Book-of-the-Month Club since its inception. In 1940, at seventy-two, he accepted the chairmanship of a national organization "to defend America by aiding the Allies" in their fight against Hitler; it quickly became known as "the William Allen White Committee."

He has been, as a writer, the voice and often the conscience of Kansas. His "Boyville" stories and his tales of a small Kansas town (probably El Dorado) will perhaps live longest among his books, but his second biography of Coolidge, *A Puritan in Babylon*, will probably run them a close second; it is shrewd, open-eyed, and penetrated with his dry humor. He says he likes to talk about himself but gives little evidence of it. A short, stocky man, once red-haired, who likes baseball and gardening and fooling with a piano, and whose two outstanding characteristics are neighborliness and integrity, he represents the very best Middle Western America has to offer to the world.

Mr. White's son, who signs his work W. L. White, is the author, among other books, of *They Were Expendable*, an account of the heroic adventures of a motor torpedo squadron in the Philippines, that was an October 1942 selection of the Book-of-the-Month Club and an immediate best-seller.

PRINCIPAL WORKS: *Short Stories*—The Real Issue, 1896; The Court of Boyville, 1899; Stratagem and Spoils, 1901; In Our Town, 1906; God's Puppets, 1916. *Novels*—A Certain Rich Man, 1909; The Martial Adventures of Henry and Me, 1918; In the Heart of a Fool, 1918. *Biography and Essays*—The Old Order Changeth, 1910; Woodrow Wilson: The Man, the Times, and His Task, 1924; Politics: The Citizen's Business, 1924; The Editor and His People, 1924; Calvin Coolidge: The Man Who Is President, 1925; Masks in a Pageant, 1928; Forty Years on Main Street, 1937; A Puritan in Babylon, 1938; The Changing West, 1939; (ed.) Defense for America, 1940.

ABOUT: Baldwin, C. C. The Men Who Make Our Novels; Clough, F. C. William Allen White of Emporia; Mencken, H. L. Prejudices: First Series; Rich, E. William Allen White: The Man From Emporia; Sergeant, E. S. Fire Under the Andes; Century Magazine July 1925; Christian Century February 16, 1938; Christian Science Monitor Monthly April 15, 1939; Collier's Weekly August 10, 1929; Literary Digest April 24, 1937; New York Times Book Review July 14, 1940; Saturday Review of Literature May 8, 1937; Time August 19, 1940; World's Work August 1930.

WHITE, WILLIAM HALE. See "BRITISH AUTHORS OF THE 19TH CENTURY"

*WHITEHEAD, ALFRED NORTH (February 15, 1861-   ), English mathematician and philosopher, was born in Ramsgate, his father being Canon Whitehead, vicar of St. Peter's, Isle of Thanet. He was educated at Sherborne School and Trinity College, Cambridge (B.A. 1884). He has honorary doctorates from Manchester, St. Andrew's, McGill, Yale and Wisconsin. He married Evelyn Wade, and they have a son and a daughter. Until 1911 he was senior mathematical lecturer at Trinity College, of which he is still a fellow. From 1911 to 1914 he was lecturer on applied mathematics and mechanics, later reader in geometry, at University College, London; then for ten years he was professor of applied

Wide World

mathematics at the Imperial College of Science. In 1924 he went to Harvard as professor of philosophy, retired in 1937, and is now professor emeritus. He still lives in Cambridge. Bald and white-bearded, he looks more like a kindly old clergyman than a university professor.

Honors have been heaped upon him, and he is considered one of the leading mathematical theorists of the time. He is a Fellow of the Royal Society (he was on its Council in 1914 and 1915), a Fellow of the British Academy, was formerly on the Senate of the University of London and dean of its faculty of science, and before he came to America was governor of the Borough Polytechnic in Southwark and chairman of the Academic Council of the Goldsmith's College. In 1915 and 1916 he was president of the Mathematical Association, and was president of the mathematical section of the British Academy for the Advancement of Science in the latter year. He received the first James Scott prize of the Royal Society of Edinburgh in 1922, the Sylvester Medal of the Royal Society in 1923, and the Butler Medal from Columbia University in 1930.

Though the very nature of his subject makes his work abstruse, Edmund Wilson has called his style "not so much lucid as crystalline." He is primarily a mathematical philosopher, who uses symbols as means of expression. To him "the discoveries of modern science supply a basis for regenerative philosophy." He is fundamentally, deeply, even emotionally religious, a natural mystic, to whom mathematics is literally the language of divinity. To more mechanistically inclined scientists and philosophers—even to hard-headed mathematical philosophers like his friend Bertrand Russell—he has seemed sometimes to lose himself in a maze of unverifiable abstractions. His chief appeal outside his professional groups has been to the sympathetically religious-minded readers who like him for the same reasons they like Jeans, Millikan, and Eddington, all of whom have the same basically mystical attitude toward

science. His best-known non-technical book is *Science and the Modern World*. Whitehead, however, can be understood only by remembering always that he is not a physicist but a mathematician.

PRINCIPAL WORKS: A Treatise on Universal Algebra, 1898. Introduction to Mathematics, 1910; Principia Mathematica (with B. Russell) 1910; The Organization of Thought: Educational and Scientific, 1916; An Enquiry Concerning the Principles of Natural Knowledge, 1919; The Concept of Nature, 1920; The Principle of Relativity With Applications to Physical Science, 1922; Science and the Modern World, 1925; Religion in the Making, 1926; Symbolism: Its Meaning and Effect, 1927; The Function of Being, 1929; Process and Reality: An Essay in Cosmology, 1929; Adventures of Ideas, 1933; Nature and Life, 1934; Modes of Thought, 1938.

ABOUT: Black, M. The Nature of Mathematics; Blyth, J. W. Whitehead's Theory of Knowledge; Emmett, D. M. Whitehead's Philosophy of Organism; Schilpp, P. A. The Philosophy of Alfred North Whitehead; American Scholar July 1940; Atlantic Monthly June 1936; Contemporary Review November 1933; Dublin Review July 1927; Hibbert Journal July 1927; Journal of Ethics April 1934; Journal of Philosophy January 21, 1932, January 19, 1933, May 13, 1937, September 15, 1938, February 16, 1939; London Quarterly Review January 1939; Monist April 1929, January 1936; Nature February 9, 1924; New Republic December 30, 1925, June 15, 1927; Open Court December 1928; Philosophical Review March 1927, March 1931, July 1935, November 1936, March 1937, July 1938; Revue Philosphique May-July 1931; Science July 15, 1927.

WHITEING, RICHARD (July 27, 1840-June 29, 1928), English journalist and novelist, was the eldest son of William Whiteing,

a clerk in the Stamps Office, and Mary Lander, who died when the boy was an infant. Richard lived with his father at Norfolk street, the Strand, till nearly eight, when he attended school in an old palace at Bromley-by-Bow, then lived with foster-parents at St. John's Wood, where he was taught by a French refugee. Apprenticed for seven years to Benjamin Wyon, a medalist and engraver of seals, Whiteing also attended evening art classes, where he met Ruskin and F. J. Furnivall. In 1866 he was secretary at two pounds a week in Paris for an Anglo-French working-class exhibition, and contributed several satirical articles on political and social subjects to the London *Evening Star*. *Mr. Sprouts—His Opinions*, concerning a costermonger who gets himself into prison, is a collection of the articles.

Whiteing acted as Paris correspondent for the London *World* and New York *World,* and was correspondent to Geneva for the Alabama arbitration claims commission. His first novel, *The Democracy* (1876), appeared under the pseudonym of "Whyte Thorn." Whiteing's travels took him to Spain, Vienna, Berlin, Russia, Rome and the United States (in 1878). He spent thirteen years on the London staff of the *Daily News.*

No. 5 John Street is Whiteings' chief claim to remembrance nowadays, a novel on the *Grand Hotel* formula which is ostensibly a report (sent to Pitcairn Islanders) on Queen Victoria's diamond jubilee of 1897. The tenement house of its locale has a "horrible basement and worse cellar," inhabited by a flower-girl, a Russian anarchist, a factory-girl, and an old Chartist survivor of the Charge of the Light Brigade. Whiteing was granted a civil list pension in 1910, and died at Hampstead, when nearly ninety. In 1869 he had married Helen, daughter of Townsend Harris, first United States minister to Japan.

PRINCIPAL WORKS: The Democracy, 1876; The Island, 1888; No. 5 John Street, 1899; The Life of Paris, 1900; The Yellow Van, 1903; Ring in the New, 1906; All Moonshine, 1907; Little People (essays) 1908.

ABOUT: Whiteing, R. My Harvest (autobiography); London Times June 30, 1928.

WHITLOCK, BRAND (March 4, 1869-May 24, 1934), American novelist and diplomat, was born in Urbana, Ohio, on the day

that Grant was inaugurated President. His parents were the Rev. Dr. Elias D. Whitlock, a Methodist minister, and Mallie (Brand) Whitlock. Thomas Whitlock, founder of the family, came from Wiltshire, England, in 1640. The boy was educated at home and attended high school at Toledo, but balked at going on to Ohio Wesleyan (which gave him an honorary LL.D. in 1917). After reporting for the Toledo *Blade* 1887-90, he became at twenty-four political correspondent on the Chicago *Herald,* which had a literary tradition, like the New York *Sun,* its staff including George Ade, John T. McCutcheon, and F. P. Dunne ("Mr. Dooley"). Refusing a secretaryship with Governor John P. Altgeld, whom he much admired, Whitlock nevertheless, as clerk in the office of the secretary of state at Springfield (1893-97), made out in secret

the governor's pardons for the last three prisoners of the 1886 Haymarket riots. Studying law under Gen. John M. Palmer, Whitlock was admitted to the Illinois bar in 1894 and the Ohio bar in 1897, practicing in Toledo until 1905. The *Thirteenth District,* a 500-page political novel, tracing the moral distintegration of a Congressman, was published in 1902.

Whitlock was a reform mayor of Toledo four successive terms from 1905 to 1913, declining a fifth term to become U.S. Minister to Belgium, where he hoped to complete a novel of small-town life in quiet. Instead, he soon found himself in the thick of the German invasion of Belgium, feeding refugees and defending Edith Cavell. Whitlock was one of President Wilson's several literary diplomatic appointments, and he produced fine literature in the two-volume *Belgium: A Personal Record.* The small-town novel, *J. Hardin & Son,* when completed in 1923, seemed, as Allan Nevins says, a "little flat, a little plodding" as compared with *Main Street.* Whitlock had hopes, not to be realized, of being the American Hardy or Turgenev. Jack London was "deeply stirred" by *The Turn of the Balance,* a study of a youth badgered into murder, which Upton Sinclair deemed a greater book than Tolstoy's *Resurrection.* Whitlock's biography of La Fayette has been called the best in any language. Loaded by Belgium with honors, Whitlock continued to live in Brussels and on the Riviera. He died during an operation and was buried at Cannes. The late Newton D. Baker described Whitlock as "tall, slender, beautiful, witty, charming, and cultured to his fingertips."

PRINCIPAL WORKS: The Thirteenth District, 1902; The Turn of the Balance, 1907; The Fall Guy, 1912; Forty Years of It (autobiography) 1914; Belgium: A Personal Record, 1919; J. Hardin & Son, 1923; Uprooted, 1926; Transplanted, 1927; Big Matt, 1928; La Fayette, 1929; The Little Green Shutter, 1931; The Stranger on the Island, 1933; Letters and Journal (ed. with Biographical Introduction by Allan Nevins) 1936.

ABOUT: Whitlock's autobiographical works; New York Times May 25, 27, 1934; Survey June 1934.

WICKHAM, ANNA (1884-), British poet, was born in Wimbledon, Surrey, the daughter of Geoffrey Wickham and Alice (Harper) Wickham. Brought to Australia at six, she was educatd at the Sidney High School. At twenty-one she (as she puts it succinctly) "came home from Australia with the idea of writing verse; wrote some." After studying at the Paris Opera, she married Patrick Hepburn, an astronomer and a

Fellow of the Royal Astronomical Society, and they had three sons. Mr. Hepburn died in 1929.

In June 1940 Anna Wickham wrote to the editors of this volume: "I am keeping this house which adjoins Hampstead Heath where it had been trenched against parachutists. I am standing behind my son James, who is commissioned to the air force; my son John, who is an anti-aircraft gunner; and my son George, who is working on a farm. As soon as I have time, I hope to put up a record in English poetry, equal to what will be the Allied victory in arms."

For many years, Anna Wickham was a poets' poet, unknown to the general reading public. Louis Untermeyer described her as "a magnificent gypsy of a woman, wayward, ironic, spontaneous, . . . gnarled in her own nervous protests." Her work is almost indefinable; it is often rough, sometimes crude, always powerful, always fierce with anger and pity. If she is a mystic, she is a wild mystic of the order though not on the plane of Blake and Emily Brontë. Marguerite Wilkinson called her "a veritable poetic thunderstorm"; Untermeyer spoke of her writing as "astringent and sometimes harsh, . . . with acid overtones of irony. . . . Mood follows mood with abrupt intensity. . . . It is the cry of the solitary soul." Although a few of her poems appeared in magazines in this country, mostly in the *New Republic*, her work was little known even in England, where it was printed privately, until the reissue of *Contemplative Quarry* in commercial form by an American publisher in 1922.

Even then it attracted small attention, and she is still without the recognition due an authentic poetic voice which speaks in its own individual tone. Although she has a grown grand-daughter and is approaching sixty, her spirit is still as indomitable as ever. She is one of the few poets who are unmistakably women without ever being "feminine." Her neglect by critics is one of the mysteries of contemporary literature.

PRINCIPAL WORKS: Songs of John Oland, 1918; Contemplative Quarry, 1920; The Man With a Hammer, 1921; The Little Old House, 1922; Poems (Selections From Edwardian Poets) 1936.

ABOUT: Untermeyer, L. From Another World; Bookman December 1921; New Republic April 27, 1921.

WIDDEMER, MARGARET, American
poet and novelist, writes: "I was born in Doylestown, Pa., of parents who came of the old colonial stock. My father was a minister. My education was what is called 'private,' given by my grandmother and my father. I had written since my fourth or fifth year, dictating till I could write for myself. It was always in the air that I was to grow up to be a writer, if I didn't sing. At ten I began to publish poems in the *St. Nicholas* League. I took library training at the Drexel Institute of Arts and Sciences, and worked for a year with Dr. A. W. Rosenbach, cataloging his rare books; then at the University of Pennsylvania, where they discharged me for inaccuracy in copying catalogue cards. I was completely crushed by the ruin of a career in youth. I had been writing poems (I suppose to the detriment of cataloguing) during and after hours; I went on with these and short stories. Soon I was making more money than I had at the library. I began to publish novels and poems before I was out of my teens. I have been doing it ever since; lecturing on poetry

Underwood

and the novel, and doing short stories and essays whenever the novels gave me a breathing spell.

"My first novel was a best seller, and I have received a number of awards for poetry. In 1919 I married Robert Haven Schauffler, the poet; the marriage was not of long duration. From 1923 to 1933 I lived in New York. In 1931 Bucknell University awarded me an honorary Litt.D.; in 1933 Middlebury College gave me an honorary M.A. From 1928 to 1932 I lectured at the Middlebury Writers' Conference at Breadloaf; in 1933 at the University of Colorado Writers' Conference. In 1936 I broadcast a series of talks over the N.B.C. Blue Network, called 'Do You Want to Write?' I live now at Larchmont Manor, N.Y., and spend my summers in the Adirondacks where I swim and canoe. I am also interested in imaginative sculpture, modeling miniature groups in plasticine, some of which I have exhibited.

"My aesthetic bias has always been toward the classic and conservative; curiously mingled with a deep interest in social problems, which has given my poetry conservative form and modern content in many cases. I am strongly against specialization in art or life, and have continued to do work in as many literary mediums as I could find possible."

PRINCIPAL WORKS: *Poetry*—Factories, With Other Lyrics, 1915; Old Road to Paradise, 1918; Cross-Currents, 1921; Tree With a Bird in It (parodies) 1922; Little Boy and Girl Land (juvenile) 1924; Ballads and Lyrics, 1925; The Singing Wood (verse play) 1926; Collected Poems, 1928; Road to Downderry, 1931; Hill Garden, 1937. *Prose*—The Rose Garden Husband, 1915; Winona Series (juvenile, 6 vols.) 1915-23; Why Not? 1916; The Wishing-Ring Man, 1917; You're Only Young Once, 1918; The Board Walk (short stories) 1919; I've Married Marjorie, 1920; The Year of Delight, 1921; Minister of Grace, 1922; Graven Image, 1923; Binkie and the Bell Dolls (juvenile) 1923; Charlie Sees It Through, 1924; Gallant Lady, 1926; More Than Wife, 1927; Rhinestones, 1929; Loyal Lover, 1930; All the King's Horses, 1931; The Truth About Lovers (short stories) 1931; Pre-War Lady, 1932; The Years of Love (short stories) 1933; Golden Rain, 1933; Back to Virtue, Betty, 1934; Other Lovers, 1935; Marriage Is Possible, 1936; This Isn't the End, 1937; Do You Want to Write? (textbook) 1937; Hand on Her Shoulder, 1938; Ladies Go Masked (short stories) 1939; She Met Three Brothers, 1939; Marcia's Farmhouse, 1939; Some Day I'll Find You, 1940; Lovers' Alibi, 1941; Let Me Have Wings, 1941; Angela Comes Home, 1942.

ABOUT: Saturday Review of Literature January 2, 1937; Scholastic January 8, 1938.

WIGGIN, MRS. KATE DOUGLAS (SMITH) (September 28, 1856-August 24, 1923), American novelist and writer of

children's books, was born in Philadelphia, the eldest daughter of Robert Noah Smith and Helen Elizabeth (Dyer) Smith. Her father was a lawyer who died when Kate was a child. Her mother soon afterward married a physician of Hollis, Maine, where the novelist was later to buy an estate, "Quillcote." She was taught at home by her stepfather, attended district school and a series of private schools. The family removed to Santa Barbara, Calif., when the girl was seventeen. When they met with financial reverses, Kate utilized her kindergarten training of the previous year, under Emma J. C. Marwedel, to open the first free kindergarten west of the Rocky Mountains, in Silver Street, San Francisco, in 1878. Her sister, Nora Archibald Smith, with whom she wrote or edited fifteen books, was a constant collaborator. In December 1881 Kate Smith became Mrs. Samuel Bradley Wiggin.

The Story of Patsy, Mrs. Wiggin's first book, was written and published to raise money for her kindergarten projects, as was the hugely successful *The Birds' Christmas Carol*, both later issued by a regular publisher. After the sudden death of her

husband in 1899, Mrs Wiggin made a first visit to Europe. It was far from being her last, since she met her second husband, George Christopher Riggs, on shipboard. Mr. Riggs was an American with business connections in Scotland and Ireland. His gifted, witty, high-spirited wife, with ash-blonde hair and erect carriage, was always a welcome guest in English country houses, and was regarded as a sort of unofficial ambassadress from "The States." The *Penelope* books, brightly written adventures of an American girl and her companions in historical spots of the British Isles, were outgrowths of these annual sojourns abroad.

From 1890 to 1895, Mrs. Wiggin gave readings from her books, especially the *Carol*. While financially successful they took their toll in agonizing headaches and insomnia, and she was obliged to spend much time in sanatoriums. During one such enforced rest *Rebecca of Sunnybrook Farm* appeared before her, sharply visualized, and insisted on being committed to paper. Called by Thomas Bailey Aldrich "the nicest child in American literature," Rebecca and her subsequent adventures in magazine serials, on the stage, and in the moving pictures proved to be a very profitable apparition indeed. Mark Twain called *Rebecca* "that beautiful book." (Rebecca was foreshadowed in Kate Smith's first story, "Half-a-Dozen Housekeepers," written at seventeen.) *Mother Carey's Chickens*, a pleasant and wholesome story of family life, was also dramatized with some success by Rachel Crothers. All Mrs. Wiggin's books, as Josephine Daskam Bacon has well said, are "faithful transcriptions of a warm-hearted, impulsive nature dramatizing its own objective experiences, in a peculiarly feminine quality of intelligence and wit." She died alone at a convalescent home at Harrow-on-Hill, England, soon after completing and mailing to her husband and sister the final chapters of *My Garden of Memory*, an excellent autobiography. Her ashes were later scattered on the waters of the Saco River, in the Maine community where she had been an honored summer resident.

PRINCIPAL WORKS: The Story of Patsy, 1883; The Birds' Christmas Carol, 1887; Children's Rights: A Book of Nursery Logic, 1892; Polly Oliver's Problem, 1893; A Cathedral Courtship, 1893; The Village Watch-Tower (short stories) 1895; Marm Lisa, 1896; Penelope's Progress, 1898; Penelope's English Experiences, 1900; Penelope's Irish Experiences, 1901; Diary of a Goose Girl, 1902; Rebecca of Sunnybrook Farm, 1903; Rose of the River, 1905; New Chronicles of Rebecca, 1907; The Old Peabody Pew, 1907; Susanna and Sue, 1909; Mother Carey's Chickens, 1911; A

Child's Journey With Dickens, 1912; The Story of Waitstill Baxter, 1913; Penelope's Postscripts, 1915; Collected Works, 1917; My Garden of Memory (autobiography) 1923.

ABOUT: Smith, N. A. Kate Douglas Wiggin As Her Sister Knew Her; Wiggin, K. D. My Garden of Memory; Current Opinion January 1924; New York Times August 25, 1923.

WILCOX, Mrs. ELLA (WHEELER). See "AMERICAN AUTHORS: 1600-1900"

WILDE, OSCAR. See "BRITISH AUTHORS OF THE 19TH CENTURY"

*WILDE, PERCIVAL (March 1, 1887-), American playwright, was born in New York City. A precocious child, he did not

fit into the orthodox school system and was expelled from school after school, in spite of which he received his B.S. at Columbia at the age of nineteen. From 1906 to 1911 he worked in a bank; then he began reviewing books for the *Times* and the *Post*. His first story was published in 1912, and he was immediately besieged by requests for the dramatic rights. This opened his eyes to the fact that he was primarily a dramatist, and for several years thereafter he devoted himself to the writing and direction of one-act plays for vaudeville, then in its prime. Though the experience was valuable in teaching him audience psychology, he became dissatisfied with the limitations of this medium. But his plays aimed at the more intellectual auditor were refused, and he finally published a series of them in 1915. They were seized upon eagerly by the then emerging Little Theatre movement, which has ever since been his chief field—though for a year he wrote a number of short stories for magazines and has published several novels.

During the First World War, Wilde served in the United States Navy, retiring as ensign, and contributing a number of improvements in the hydroplane compass. There followed a brief period in Hollywood and another in collaborating on full-length plays. In 1920 he married Nadie Rogers Marckres, and they have two sons. He lives now in New York, but spends his winters in Miami and his summers in Sharon, Conn. He works at night—all night, after midnight,

giving his afternoons to sport and social life and sleeping in the morning.

His plays for the Little Theatre have been immensely popular. They have been acted in some 1,300 cities in this country, and in every English-speaking country. They have been translated into French, German, Italian, Dutch, the Scandinavian languages, Polish, Serbian, Japanese, and the Mahrathi tongue in India. He has written more than a hundred, most of which have also been published. He is director and secretary of the American Dramatists, and visiting lecturer on drama at the University of Miami. A slender, rather frail-looking man, he is nevertheless an expert swimmer and tennisplayer.

The plays are realistic, and depend on the logical depiction of character, which he considers of primary importance. He insists on fidelity to probability, and refuses arbitrary "happy endings." A critic has said of him that he has "an undoubted sense of theatre, a tried and sure technique, and he sets his talents on easily understandable and almost always interesting situations."

PRINCIPAL WORKS: Plays—The Line of No Resistance, 1913; Dawn and Other One-Act Plays of Life Today, 1915; Confessional and Other American Plays, 1916; The Unseen Host and Other War Plays, 1917; Eight Comedies for Little Theatres, 1922; The Inn of Discontent and Other Fantastic Plays, 1924; Three-Minute Plays, 1927; Ten Plays for Little Theatres, 1931; One-Act Plays, First Series, 1933, Second Series, 1934; Little Shot, 1935; Comrades in Arms and Other Plays for Little Theatres, 1935; An Affair of Dishonor, 1937. Fiction—Rogues in Clover (short stories) 1929; The Devil's Booth, 1930; There Is a Tide, 1932; Mystery Week-End, 1938; Inquest, 1940; Design for Murder, 1941. Miscellaneous—The Craftsmanship of the One-Act Play, 1923.

ABOUT: Wilde, P. One-Act Plays, First Series (see Foreword by H. Brighouse); Wilson Library Bulletin March 1932.

WILDER, THORNTON NIVEN (April 17, 1897-), American novelist and dramatist, Pulitzer Prize winner in both classifications, was born in Madison, Wis., the son of Amos Parker Wilder, editor of the *Wisconsin State Journal,* and Isabella Thornton (Niven) Wilder. His brother and sister are also writers. When he was nine he was taken to China, where

his father was American Consul-General at Hong Kong and Shanghai, and went to high school in Chefoo. He returned to the

United States and completed his education in Berkeley and Ojai, Calif., at Oberlin, and at Yale (B.A. 1920), interrupted by a year as a corporal in the Coast Artillery Corps during the World War. He then studied for two years at the American Academy in Rome. From 1921 to 1928 he was a housemaster at the Lawrenceville School, in New Jersey. He also taught French, and continued his studies at Princeton, receiving an M.A. degree in 1925. His first novel, *The Cabala,* appeared in the same year, and a year later the American Laboratory Theatre produced his first play, *The Trumpet Shall Sound.* Neither made any particular stir, though the novel let him in for some sound drubbing from critics who considered it supercilious and confused.

It was *The Bridge of San Luis Rey,* in 1927, which made Thornton Wilder famous. It received the Pulitzer Prize for that year, was a best seller, was filmed, and still continues to sell in reprint editions. It caused Wilder to be extravagantly praised, and as extravagantly condemned. It started a whole *genre* in fiction in which the characters are brought together by some accidental geographical relationship at some crucial moment of their lives—in this case, by the breaking of a bridge in Peru.

In 1928 Wilder gave up his teaching position, went to Europe for a year to write his Greek novel, *The Woman of Andros,* returned to America for a year's lecture tour, then settled in Chicago, where from 1930 to 1936 he was a lecturer on literature at the University of Chicago, teaching for six months of the year and writing for the other six. After another year in France he moved to New Haven, where he now lives. He has never married.

Wilder's last novel to date was in 1935, and from that time on he has devoted himself almost exclusively to play writing. *Our Town,* which won the Pulitzer Prize for drama in 1938, enacted on a bare stage, was as much a departure, in its moving simplicity, from his earlier works as *Heaven's My Destination,* that sober study of an unspeakable prig (which nobody could be quite sure was satire), was from his earlier novels. *Our Town* was made into a successful motion picture.

Thornton Wilder has outlived Michael Gold's early gibe that his universe was "a museum, not a world." He has ceased to be precious, ornate, speciously classical and philosophical, a faint shadow of James Branch Cabell. He has, in other words, matured and instead of pouring warm baths of soulfulness he now shows he is capable of

depicting spiritual fundamentals. His play, *The Merchant of Yonkers* was, to be sure, a mere light-hearted adaptation of a play by Johann Nestroy, but it was only a diversion. Wilder has not been spoiled by adulation, and is steadily growing.

He is still young-looking, slender, dark-haired with a clipped moustache, sophisticated and urbane. Of recent years he has become interested in acting, and has taken parts in the plays produced by the little theatres in their summer seasons. He is musical, a good pianist who has done some composing. Henry Seidel Canby, who once acclaimed him as a genius, on consideration has called him "a minor ... figure, narrow in scope, ... yet with the consecration to perfection, the conscientiousness, and the absolute excellence of . . . a Collins or an Addison."

In September 1941, at London, Wilder was elected one of the five wartime heads of P.E.N., the international writers' organization. His new comedy, *The Skin of Our Teeth,* began its tryout tour in October 1942.

PRINCIPAL WORKS: *Novels*—The Cabala, 1925; The Bridge of San Luis Rey, 1927; The Woman of Andros, 1930; Heaven's My Destination, 1935. *Plays*—The Trumpet Shall Sound, 1926; The Angel That Troubled the Waters (short plays) 1928; The Long Christmas Dinner and Other Plays in One Act, 1931; Our Town, 1938; The Merchant of Yonkers, 1939.

ABOUT: Catholic World September 1932; Living Age September 1931; Nation October 23, 1935; New Republic October 22, 1930; Poetry September 1939; Saturday Review of Literature May 7, June 11, 1938; Time March 10, 1941.

WILKINS, MARY ELEANOR. See FREEMAN, M. E. W.

WILKINSON, Mrs. MARGUERITE OGDEN (BIGELOW) (November 15, 1883-January 12, 1928), Canadian-American poet and anthologist, was born in Halifax, Nova Scotia, and brought to the United States as a very young child by her parents, Nathan Kellogg Bigelow and Gertrude Zulime (Holmes) Bigelow. A sensitive, imaginative, child, she developed  into a frail young girl with a passionate love for the outdoors. Educated privately, in the public schools at Evanston, Ill., and at the Misses Ely's School, New York City, she began to write while attending Northwestern University. In her three years at college she specialized in English literature and composition, studying also Greek, biology, and psychology. At twenty-six, in 1909, Marguerite Bigelow was married to James G. Wilkinson, principal of the Roosevelt School. New Rochelle, N.Y. She took kindly to domesticity, priding herself on her cookery and looking forward to the yearly trout-fishing trips with her husband. *The Dingbat of Arcady* (1922) is the pleasantly humorous record of one such camping episode. After publishing some conventional and technically adroit verse of her own, Mrs. Wilkinson proceeded to make herself a recognized authority on the work of other poets, reviewing poetry in the New York *Times Book Review* and lecturing on contemporary poetry before colleges, schools, state library associations, and women's clubs, who regarded her *New Voices* (1919) as akin to gospel. Of this useful work Jessie B. Rittenhouse wrote, "It discusses with fairness and balance all types of poetry and all schools, illustrating them by admirable selections from contemporary work both English and American." The New York *Evening Post* exclaimed of *Yule Fire,* an anthology of Christmas poetry, that it was "a book of pure beauty and holy merriment aglow with transfiguring mystic radiance." Mrs. Wilkinson had an especial interest in early Christian mystics, and her last book, of religious poems, entitled *Citadels,* contains some of her best work. *The Great Dream,* a long poem, envisaged the spiritual changes in store for Americans. Suffering a nervous breakdown the summer before her death, she attributed it to spiritual fear rather than physical causes. In exchange for ten hours' instruction in the air, she wrote an advertising booklet on aviation, completed the course including all sorts of stunt flying, and every day went for a morning swim in the ocean at Coney Island and an afternoon flight at Curtiss Field, to show herself superior to fear. She was drowned at Coney Island while practising swimming stunts, at the age of forty-four. Of dignified bearing and pleasing appearance. Mrs. Wilkinson made her home in the Columbia University sector of Manhattan.

PRINCIPAL WORKS: In Vivid Gardens, 1911; By a Western Wayside, 1912; The Passing of Mars, 1915; Golden Songs of the Golden State, 1917; New Voices, 1919; Bluestone. 1920; The Dingbat of Arcady, 1922; The Great Dream, 1923; Contemporary Poetry, 1923; The Way of the Makers, 1925; Yule Fire, 1925; Citadels, 1928.

ABOUT: New York Times January 13-15, 1928; Poetry March 1928; Woman's Journal February 1928.

WILLARD, JOSIAH FLYNT (January 23, 1869-January 20, 1907), first American hobo-writer, whose pen-name was "Josiah Flynt," was born in Appleton, Wis., the son of Oliver Willard, editor of a Chicago newspaper, and Mary (Bannister) Willard, and nephew of the feminist Frances E. Willard. He was given a public- and boarding-school education; at nine he  was "a good beginner in the cigar business," and at ten he could "hold [his] own in a cussing contest." He left college at the end of his second year, tried a farm hand's life in Nebraska, and then set out for Pennsylvania, eventually making his way, astraddle oil tanks in a freight car, to Buffalo, N. Y. He threw over a job as car-yard reporter, and, filled with an ever-recurring longing for "the road," helped himself, one day, to an idle horse and buggy, an escapade that ended in his first imprisonment. He was released only to serve a year in a reform school, but he made a sure and fairly early escape and then weathered one month of the most severe "roughing." He tramped through a part of Michigan and as far south as West Virginia before finally winding up in Hoboken, N. J. Here he turned down an "apprenticeship" with a saloon-keeper in favor of a small chance at a job as coal-passer on a North German Lloyd boat bound for Bremen. For two weeks of agonizing labor in a veritable hell-pit Josiah Flynt was paid the equivalent of about four dollars in American currency.

He traveled fourth-class to Berlin where he joined his mother, and, for a while, was actually quite happy in comfortable and normal domestic surroundings. A journey to Liverpool for the purpose of getting passage on a vessel sailing for Egypt ended in nothing but a brief love affair with one Alice, who professed to be a coloratura soprano. Flynt returned to Berlin, and matriculated (1890) at the University, planning to "major" in political economy. He spent one summer tramping about Germany with a Norwegian friend and got a good story from Ibsen, who was then in Munich, for a New York newspaper.

In 1892 he left the University of Berlin and went to London to do some research in British political economy. At the "Crown" near Leicester Square, he tasted of the intellectualism of English taverns and made the most of a few literary friendships. In midsummer, 1896, he spent ten days on Tolstoy's farm, 150 miles from Moscow, and returned with some rare copy and the conviction that his hero was, perhaps, "impractical, visionary, . . . a literary reformer," but "no fakir"!

Two years later Flynt came back to America and was hired at ten dollars a day to report tramp conditions on railroads. He did some casual writing for *McClure's* and the *Cosmopolitan,* and was sent to Russia, in 1905, to investigate some of the motives of the insurrection. His health broke down the following year and he died in Chicago, shortly after finishing the story of his life.

Josiah Flynt's books are, largely, autobiographical studies in criminal psychology, with numerous contingent speculations. Their style is often wordy, careless, naive, and strangely sentimental, but their substance is authentic and varied. He was the precursor of such later writers as Jack London and Jim Tully.

PRINCIPAL WORKS: Tramping With Tramps, 1899; The Powers That Prey, 1900; Notes of an Itinerant Policeman, 1900; The World of Graft, 1901; The Little Brother: A Story of Tramp Life, 1902; The Rise of Ruderick Clowd, 1903; My Life, 1908.

ABOUT: Flynt, J. My Life; autobiographical material in his other works.

*WILLIAMS, BEN AMES (March 7, 1889-), American novelist and story writer, writes: "I was born in Macon, Miss. My

mother, Sarah Marshall (Ames) Williams, was a niece of Gen. James Longstreet of the Confederate Army. My father, Daniel Webster Williams, was an Ohio man, the editor of the *Standard-Journal* in Jackson, Ohio, and at a later period

Bachrach

a member of the Ohio State Senate and Consul at Cardiff, Wales. I lived as a boy in Jackson, Ohio; came East in 1904 to attend the Allen School in West Newton, Mass., spent the following year in Cardiff, where my father was then Consul, and entered Dartmouth College in the fall of 1906 (B.A. 1910).

"I went to work as a reporter on the Boston *American* in September 1910, and continued until December 1916. By that time I had sold a few short stories and short serials, principally to the *All-Story Magazine,* which was edited at that time by

Robert H. Davis. Since 1916 I have been a professional writer of fiction, and stories of mine have been published in a long list of magazines, to the number of some 382 titles. Most of these have appeared in the *Saturday Evening Post* and *Collier's.*

"My first book, *All the Brothers Were Valiant,* was published in 1919; and since then, more than thirty of my books have appeared. I was married in 1912 to Florence Trafton Talpey of York, Maine, whose father, grandfather, and great-grandfather were all sea captains in the China trade. We have two sons and a daughter. Our winter home is in Chestnut Hill, Mass.; our summer home is a farm in Searsmont, Maine, which was bequeathed to us by A. L. McCorrison, who, as 'Bert McAusland,' appeared in a number of my stories, short and long, laid in the fictional town of Fraternity, Maine."

* * *

Mr. Williams has described himself as "a large, calm man, about thirty-five per cent above the normal weight for age and height." Something of an athlete before he attained this condition, he "likes to do anything out of doors so long as that doing has a purpose," and has recently taken up flying. He is an avid player of games, and though he reads few novels except light fiction he enjoys biography and history. He says: "I enjoy life each year more and more, and propose to continue so to do."

He does not pretend to be anything more than a story-teller, but he is a good one. Though most of his stories are laid in Maine, a little of his Southern childhood and Middle Western boyhood occasionally creeps in. "I believe," he wrote, "in the potency of place and the impotency of man." This sounds gloomy, whereas Mr. Williams' stories are nearly always cheerful and entertaining, though sometimes they conceal a moral. Without pretensions to "literature," he is a master of easy technique. His own zest and gusto are apparent in his work: "first of all," he says, he likes to write, and the result is stories that people like to read.

PRINCIPAL WORKS: All the Brothers Were Valiant, 1919; The Sea Bride, 1919; The Great Accident, 1920; Evered, 1921; Black Pawl, 1922; Thrifty Stock, 1923; Sangsue, 1923; Audacity, 1924; The Rational Hind, 1925; The Silver Forest, 1926; Immortal Longings, 1927; Splendor, 1927; The Dreadful Night, 1928; Death on Scurvy Street, 1929; Touchstone, 1930; Great Oaks, 1930; An End to Mirth, 1931; Pirate's Purchase, 1931; Honeyflow, 1932; Money Musk, 1932; Pascal's Mill, 1933; Mischief, 1933; Hostile Valley, 1934; Small Town Girl, 1935; Crucible, 1937; The Strumpet Sea, 1938; Thread of Scarlet, 1939; The Happy End, 1939; Come Spring, 1940; Splendor, 1941; The Strange Woman, 1941; Time of Peace, 1942.

ABOUT: Baldwin, C. C. The Men Who Make Our Novels; American Magazine March 1933; Christian Science Monitor Magazine March 30, 1940; Saturday Evening Post October 18, 1924, January 28, April 1, 1933.

WILLIAMS, EMLYN

WILLIAMS, EMLYN (November 26, 1905-), Welsh playwright and actor, was born in Mostyn, Flintshire, the son of an

Acme

ironmonger. He spoke no English, only Welsh, until he was eight. From early childhood he had a passion for drama, though he never saw a play until he was nineteen. He was educated in the County School at Holywell, Dorsetshire, with the idea of becoming a schoolmaster. He studied French in Geneva, and won a scholarship in French to Christ Church, Oxford. But after receiving his M.A. with honors, he decided that he could not possibly be a teacher. He had already written one play, *Full Moon*, which had been acted by the Oxford University Dramatic Society, of which he was an active member, and he set out to make a place for himself on the stage.

In 1927 he got his first small part, and wrote his second play, *Glamour*. But Mr. Williams could not be said to be a success either as actor or dramatist until 1930, when after one private showing of *A Murder Has Been Arranged* seven managers fought to produce it. Other plays followed—*Vessels Departing, Spring 1600, Vigil*—but he did not repeat his success until *Night Must Fall*, in 1935. Strange to say, this play, which ran for more than a year in London and was a sensation later as a motion picture, flopped badly in New York in 1936, even though Mr. Williams himself was greatly admired in the leading rôle.

His next big hit, this time on both sides of the Atlantic, was *The Corn Is Green*. It played for more than two years, in the midst of war, in London, was a "smash hit" in New York with Ethel Barrymore, and was chosen by the Critics' Circle as the best play of 1941.

Mr. Williams is married to Molly O'Shane, and they have two sons. In 1941 his wife and children came to New York "for the duration," while Mr. Williams (who has acted frequently in motion pictures as well as on the stage) was busy completing his film, written by him and with the principal part played by him—*The Girl in the News*.

Besides his own plays, he has written adaptations, the best-known being *The Late Christopher Bean*, from René Fauchois' *Prenez Garde à la Peinture*. (The American adaptation was by the late Sidney Howard.)

The Corn Is Green is a character study with social implications, and is laid in Wales. But most of Mr. Williams' plays and motion pictures are murder studies. He has a particular flair for psychological horror plays, and in this *genre* he is the analogue in drama of "Francis Iles" in fiction—that is to say, his interest is in the mind of the murderer, not in plot or action. There is a distinct novelistic atmosphere in all his dramas; he is given, indeed, to subtitling them "a romance," "a ghost story," and so on.

The Morning Star, a play about the 1940 bombing of London, was enthusiastically received in that city, but closed soon after opening on Broadway in September 1942 (during the tenth month of the London run), the American drama critics complaining that "Mr. Williams is merely going through some theatrical motions."

Mr. Williams should not be confused with Dr. J. Emlyn Williams, the Welsh foreign correspondent and writer on international relations and economic problems.

PRINCIPAL WORKS (Dates of publication): A Murder Has Been Arranged, 1930; The Late Christopher Bean, 1933; Night Must Fall, 1935; He Was Born Gay, 1937; The Corn Is Green, 1938; The Light of Heart, 1940.

ABOUT: Current Biography 1940; Time October 12, 1936, May 6, 1940.

WILLIAMS, JESSE LYNCH

WILLIAMS, JESSE LYNCH (August 17, 1871-September 14, 1929), American novelist and dramatist, was born in Sterling, Ill., the son of Meade Creighton Williams and Elizabeth (Riddle) Williams, and grandson of Jesse Lynch Williams, a well-known civil engineer and government director of the Union Pacific Railway. After preliminary schooling at Be-

loit Academy in Wisconsin he received his B.A. degree in 1892 at Princeton, where he edited the *Nassau Literary Magazine* and founded the Triangle Club, undergraduate dramatic society, with Booth Tarkington. The Club still stages musical revues with professional competence and takes them on tour.

The next year Williams was reporter on the New York *Sun,* and in 1895 published *Princeton Stories*, depicting college (in the words of Robert Hutchins in another connection) as a nice place where nice boys have a nice time under the direction of nice men. It lacked the acidity of the nearly contemporary *Harvard Episodes* by Charles M. Flandrau and the later *Stover at Yale* of Owen Johnson.*qqv* Williams was on the staff of *Scribner's Magazine* from 1897 to 1900, when he became the first editor of the *Princeton Alumni Weekly*, remaining till 1903.

The Married Life of the Frederic Carrolls (1910) treated domestic relations with deftness and skill, and a not dissimilar novel, the *And So They Were Married* of 1914 was dramatized as *Why Marry?*, a comedy undisguisedly fashioned on Shavian principles, which received the accolade of the first Pulitzer drama prize, in 1917. The presence in the cast of Nat Goodwin, the aging and much-married American comedian, added a certain piquancy to the occasion. Williams' life continued its even and pleasant course with the award of a fellowship in creative art at the University of Michigan. In 1921 he was president of the Authors' League of America.

With his wife, Mrs. Alice (Laidlaw) Williams, whom he married in 1898, and three children, he maintained homes in Princeton and New York City, with a summer home on an island in Maine. He died suddenly of heart disease, a month after his fifty-eighth birthday, at the home of Theodore Roosevelt's sister, Mrs. Douglas Robinson, in Herkimer County, N.Y., and was buried at Princeton. He was personable and ingratiating.

PRINCIPAL WORKS: Princeton Stories, 1895; New York Sketches, 1902; The Stolen Story, 1906; The Married Life of the Frederic Carrolls, 1910; Not Wanted, 1923; They Still Fall in Love, 1929; She Knew She Was Right, 1930.

ABOUT: Princeton College, Class of 1892: Quindecennial Report; Quinn, A. H. A History of American Drama; New York Times September 15, 1929.

*WILLIAMS, MICHAEL (February 5, 1878-), Canadian editor and writer on Roman Catholicism, was born in Halifax, N.S., and was educated at St. Joseph's College, N.B. (non-graduate). He has an honorary Litt.D. from Gonzaga College, Washington, D.C. Soon after leaving college he came to the United States, and for a number of years was a newspaper man. He was a reporter on the Boston *Post*, New York *World* and *Evening Telegram*, and was city editor of the San Francisco *Examiner* during the earthquake and fire of 1906. In

* Correction: Year of birth, 1877. Died October 12, 1950.

1913 he was special correspondent in Mexico of the International News Service. In 1919 and 1920 he edited the *National Catholic War Council Bulletin*. In 1922 he became first editor of the *Commonweal*, the Catholic weekly journal of opinion, and is still associated with the magazine, though not as active editor, contributing a weekly column of "Views and Reviews." He was married in 1900 to Margaret Olmsted, and they have a son and a daughter. Their home is in Westport, Conn.

Kaiden-Keystone

In his youth "Mike" Williams was a Socialist, a member of Upton Sinclair's Helicon Hall colony in New Jersey, and one of the best known of the literary bohemians of Greenwich Village in its early days. After his conversion (or rather reversion) to Catholicism, about 1915, his interests and associations changed completely, and all his books since that time have had some relation to church history or practice. He is, however, classed as a "liberal Catholic," and has not always been considered entirely orthodox. Nevertheless, he received the Catholic Action medal in 1935. He is chairman of the Calvert Associates, and a member of the board of directors of the Pontifical Institute of Sacred Music.

Essentially, Mr. Williams is a romantic at heart and a mystic who still maintains a sharp eye for worldly events and a trenchant and witty style in commenting on them. He is today one of the best known Roman Catholic laymen in America, and has given the *Commonweal* a high literary standard and a reputation for tolerance and liberality. He has carried over into the magazine field the journalistic ability which had won him a reputation as a first-class newspaper man. His books, chiefly of interest to his co-religionists, sometimes seem marred by sentimentality and lack of realism, but undoubtedly they are among the most cogent in their field.

PRINCIPAL WORKS: Good Health and How We Won It (with U. Sinclair) 1909; The Book of the High Romance, 1918; American Catholics in the War, 1921; The Little Flower of Carmel, 1926; Little Brother Francis of Assisi, 1926; Catholicism and the Modern Mind, 1928; The Shadow of the Pope, 1932; The Catholic Church in Action, 1935.

ABOUT: Catholic World March 1935; Commonweal November 3, 1939.

WILLIAMS, OSCAR (December, 1900-), American poet, writes: "Oscar Williams has spent most of his life in New

York City, a few years in the West, and the depression years (1931-36) as an advertising man in the South. Education, the elementary schools in Brooklyn, and never finished high school. Started writing poetry when seventeen years old and continued until his twentieth year. In 1921 he stopped writing poetry, and didn't start again until 1937 in the spring. During this interval he was in the advertising business in various capacities. In 1923, on the way out of the literary game, he edited *Rhythmus,* a poetry magazine, for about a year, and also was the poetry editor for the old *Forum.*"

* * *

W. H. Auden has given Mr. Williams' strange story as follows: "Oscar Williams' poetical career has been extraordinary. As an undergraduate he wrote and published poetry which he says 'showed very little promise.' Coming by chance upon an advertising booklet, he became fascinated by its language, and bluffed his way into the advertising business, where he forgot all about poetry and held important and lucrative positions for sixteen years, though, prompted perhaps by an unconscious instinct of self-preservation, he took care to let others write the copy and confined himself to financial organization. A few years ago, while motoring in the South, he began to feel strange, so strange that he sought medical advice, which could diagnose nothing. Suddenly he realized what was the matter: he wanted to write poetry. Obedient, he gave up his job. . . . Understandably enough under the circumstances, he feels that the mechanized life is the Devil, and the subject of many of his poems is just this theme; while their form and imagery . . . is romantic, violent, and exciting. But, unlike many romantics, Mr. Williams has lived successfully in the world that he attacks, and believed in its values."

"His vivid picture writing," said another critic, "stands out like a billboard." Lionel Abel called him "clever, disconcerting, rash." In an adverse report, Morton Dauwen Zabel described Williams' work as "a discharge of mixed and muddled metaphors, a ranting vulgarity of rhythms, a racket of the massed clichés of tragic prophecy and moral decay."

Under a thick black pompadour, his inquiring eyes look out keenly through horn-rimmed glasses perched precariously on a long nose. He is unmarried, and is now living in New York. Aside from his published volumes, he is the author of a verse play, *The King Who Scoffed,* written with Jack Brady in 1923. His first volume was one of the series of Yale Younger Poets. He has edited anthologies of *New Poems* of 1940 and 1942.

PRINCIPAL WORKS: The Golden Darkness, 1921; In Gossamer Grey, 1921; The Man Coming Toward You, 1940.

ABOUT: Nation May 4, 1940; Poetry July 1940; Time April 29, 1940.

*WILLIAMS, VALENTINE (October 20, 1883-), English mystery story writer, writes: "Valentine Williams was a newspaper

man before becoming a novelist. As one of the late Northcliffe's principal lieutenants he traveled extensively as special correspondent to the *Daily Mail* [London] and saw fighting in Portugal and the Balkans before the war of 1914 landed him in

the army with a commission in the Irish Guards. He was twice wounded, and it was while he was convalescing from his wounds that he wrote his first novel. Since then he has written some thirty novels of secret service and crime, nearly all of which have been translated into foreign languages, some having been sold to the films. He likes to vary what he calls the monotony of writing fiction by returns to his old love, journalism. Since he gave up his post as cable editor of the *Daily Mail* in 1921 his name has figured in the world's press on many important assignments. He secured a scoop, legendary in the annals of Anglo-American journalism, at Luxor in 1923 when he was the first to announce the discovery of the sarcophagus of King Tutankhamen. He is a well-known visitor to America, having broadcast frequently and lectured in many parts of the United States. He married Alice Crawford, an English star of the theatre, an Australian by birth. When not at war he likes to divide his time between his native country and the United States. He is one of that small band of enthusiasts who play court tennis, and claims that he has never been in a place where there is a tennis court without getting a game. Like most authors, he has not resisted the lure of the screen, and was

* Died November 20, 1946.

actually collaborating on *The Lion Has Wings* when he was mobilized in the present war."

* * *

Mr. Williams, who was christened George Valentine Williams, has written and acted in four radio plays for the National Broadcasting Company. He and his wife wrote a spy melodrama, *Berlin*, which was produced in London and New York in 1932. His father was G. Douglas Williams, chief editor of Reuter's, and he himself was a Reuter's correspondent in Berlin from 1904 to 1909. He was educated at Downside School, and privately in Germany. Because of his war service he received the Merit Cross and was made a Chevalier of the Order of the Crown of Belgium. He writes on "a battered old Remington," and in peacetime lived frequently on the Riviera to find the quiet without interruption which is necessary for him. His work has been called "a blend of intrigue and romance, unreal enough to seem true."

PRINCIPAL WORKS: The Man With the Club Foot, 1918; Okewood of the Secret Service, 1919; With Our Army in Flanders, 1919; Adventures of an Ensign, 1920; The Secret Hand, 1921; Captain of the Club, 1921; The Yellow Streak, 1922; Island Gold, 1923; The Orange Divan, 1923; The Three of Clubs, 1924; Clubfoot the Avenger, 1924; The Red Mass, 1925; The Key Man, 1926; Mr. Ramosi, 1926; The Return of Clubfoot, 1927; The Pigeon House, 1927; The Eye in Attendance, 1927; The Crouching Beast, 1928; Mannequin (in America: The Mysterious Miss Morrisot) 1930; The Knife Behind the Curtain (short stories) 1930; Death Answers the Bell, 1932; Fog (with D. R. Sims) 1932; The Gold Comfit Box (in America: The Mystery of the Gold Box) 1932; The Clock Ticks On, 1933; The Portcullis Room, 1934; Masks Off at Midnight, 1934; The Clue of the Rising Moon, 1935; Dead Man Manor, 1936; The Spider's Touch, 1936; Mr. Treadgold Cuts In (in America: The Curiosity of Mr. Treadgold) 1937; The World of Action (autobiography) 1938; The Fox Prowls, 1939.

ABOUT: Williams, V. The World of Action; Bookman February 1930.

WILLIAMS, WILLIAM CARLOS (September 17, 1883-), American poet, novelist, and physician, writes: "My origins are obscure, owing to voyages and volcanic action. My English grandmother, named Emily Dickinson, was left an orphan at an early age and adopted by an 'uncle' Godwin who took her to London, where she grew up. Thrown out, as far as I can gather, after her marriage to a certain Mr. Williams, my father, William George, was born to the pair in Birmingham. My grandfather died when Pop was five years old. The old gal, in a fit of temper most likely, took him under her arm and sailed for America, determined to be an actress. She landed in a Brooklyn boarding-house, where she met her second husband, who took her to St. Thomas. It was in St. Thomas that my father grew up. My mother's family on her mother's side came from St. Pierre, Martinique, via Bordeaux, France. The remnants of the family disappeared when Mt. Pelée erupted. They made a good brand of liqueur, I understand. On mother's father's side there was Jewish blood, via some city in Holland. Whether her father was wholly Jew or not it is impossible to say. He was not a practicing Jew. His mother may have been a West Indian.

C. Sheeler

"My parents moved to New York separately, though they had known each other in the islands, and were married in a Dutch Reform church in Brooklyn. Mother had been brought up a Catholic and Father an Episcopalian. They became Unitarians later.

"I was the first child, born in Rutherford Park, N.J., where I still live and practice medicine. I married Florence Herman in 1912 and we have two boys. There are a few things in life that one comes to want to do as one grows older, apart from turning over a little cash. I wanted to write, as my mother wanted to paint—and did paint very well. I've been writing, trying to get a few things said, ever since I started to study medicine. One feeds the other, in a manner of speaking. Both seem necessary to me. One gets me out among the neighbors, the other permits me to express what I've been turning over in my mind as I go along. I don't know that I'd be any better off if I took all my time to write and made a business of the thing. I wish I could do it, though, now that I'm getting along.

"I wasn't a bad high school pitcher, played a little football (left end) as a kid, and did a little track work, not much. The old pump wouldn't stand up under the strain. I suppose I've always lived a good deal under a strain— physical, financial, moral, but especially emotional. That's one reason I stayed put, too much dynamite inside for me to want to go wandering about wasting time traveling. What the hell is there to see, anyway, compared with what's on the inside? I never saw anything outside equal to what I was going through in my innards.

"I don't play golf, am not a joiner. I vote Democratic, read as much as my eyes will stand, and work at my trade day in and day out. When I can find nothing better to do, I write. Work in progress, if I'm ever able to get at it, should be: my mother's biography; the libretto for an opera on the life of George Washington that has to be rewritten; a new novel on the life of a woikin' goil; a long poem, *Paterson*—boy! how I'd like to get at that one; and some more shorter poems, probably what I most enjoy doing."

* * *

Dr. Williams had his preparatory schooling in Geneva, received his M.D. from the University of Pennsylvania, and did graduate work in pediatrics at the University of Leipzig. In 1926 he received the *Dial* award of $2,000 for "services to American literature," and in 1931 *Poetry's* Guarantor's Prize. In spite of his mixed ancestry (he has Danish blood as well as all the other strains), he is in appearance almost typically the "clean-cut" American of the professional class. Rebecca West called him "a writer of a distinction which permeates all his work." He is essentially modern in all his work. In his clean-imaged poetry Ruth Lechlitner noted "the characteristic free verse forms, the short, sharp line, its rhythms arbitrarily broken to fit the accents of the informal, somewhat nervously paced contemporary speech; the artifices of rhyme and fixed stanza done away with."

PRINCIPAL WORKS: *Poetry*—Poems, 1909; The Tempers, 1913; Al Que Quiere, 1917; Kora in Hell, 1920; Sour Grapes, 1921; Spring and All, 1922; Collected Poems, 1934; Adam & Eve & The City, 1936; Complete Collected Poems, 1938; Broken Span, 1941. *Prose*—The Great American Novel (essays) 1923; In the American Grain (essays) 1925; A Voyage to Pagany, 1928; The Knife of the Times and Other Stories, 1932; Novelette and Other Prose, 1932; An Early Martyr, 1935; White Mule, 1937; Life Along the Passaic River, 1938; In the Money (White Mule: Part II) 1940.

ABOUT: Poetry May 1934, May 1936, September 1939; Time December 26, 1938, December 2, 1940.

WILLIAMS-ELLIS, Mrs. AMABEL (STRACHEY) (1894-), English novelist, juvenile writer, and biographer, was born a Strachey, Lytton Strachey being her cousin, John Strachey her brother, and J. St. Loe Strachey, editor of the *Spectator*, her father. Her birthplace was Newlands Corner, near Guildford. She was educated at home, but in a home of unusual cultural and literary background. In 1922 and 1923 she was literary editor of the *Spectator*. She has traveled a great deal, chiefly in Germany and Russia (both before and after the Bolshevik Revolution), and

visited the United States in 1934. In 1915 she married Bertram Clough Williams-Ellis, a well-known Welsh architect and town planner, with whom she has collaborated as a writer. Most of the time she lives in Lianfrothen, North Wales, in an old house near Mount Snowden. She has two daughters and a son, who are rumored to be the originals of the children in Richard Hughes' *The Innocent Voyage*.

Many of her books on biology and history for children were written first for them. She is widely read in biology, and adapted from Darwin's journal the definitive book on his famous voyage to Australia on the "Beagle." Her favorite recreation in time of peace is sailing in the Irish Sea, and she is fond of walking.

Her interest in economics and sociology is displayed not only in her best known novel, *The Big Firm*, but also in the history of England she wrote with H. A. L. Fisher, in which wars and royal successions are subordinated to the account of economic, social, and scientific events. She is the author also of a handbook on politics. Her interests, indeed, are unusually broad and varied, and have extended even to a book of delightful fairy tales for children. She speaks and reads German and Russian fluently, and in 1935 translated and edited *Belomor*, the account of a major Soviet industrial project written "co-operatively" by Maxim Gorky and a number of associates. In biography her best known achievement is a psychological study of Ruskin, which without the bitter wit of Lytton Strachey still has much of his acute penetration and realistic approach. Besides her books, she is a frequent contributor of articles to English journals of opinion.

PRINCIPAL WORKS: An Anatomy of Poetry, 1922; The Pleasures of Architecture (with C. Williams-Ellis) 1924; Noah's Ark (novel) 1926; The Wall of Glass (novel) 1927; Exquisite Tragedy: An Intimate Life of John Ruskin (in America: The Tragedy of John Ruskin) 1928; How You Began (juvenile) 1928; Why Should I Vote? (with L. A. Plummer) 1929; Men Who Found Out (juvenile) 1929; Volcano (novel) 1931; The Beagle in South America (in America: The Voyage of the Beagle) 1931; How You Are Made (juvenile) 1932; What Shall I Be? (juvenile) 1933; To Tell the Truth. . (novel) 1933; Fairies and Enchanters (juvenile) 1934; History of English Life (in America: The Story of English Life; with F. J. Fisher) 1936; The Big Firm (novel) 1938; Good Citizens (in America: Courageous Lives) 1938; Learn to Love First (novel) 1939; Ottik's Book of Stories (juvenile) 1939.

WILLIAMSON, Mrs. ALICE MURIEL (LIVINGSTON) (1869-September 24, 1933), Anglo-American novelist, was born

in Livingston Manor House, near Poughkeepsie, N.Y., the daughter of Mark Livingston and great-granddaughter of Chancellor Robert Livingston, famous American statesman of the early days of the republic. She was of Scottish and Welsh ancestry. Educated privately, Alice Livingston sold her first short story when only fifteen for fifty dollars. Going abroad with relatives in 1893, she took lodgings (knowing her Sherlock Holmes) just off Baker Street, and went to call on Charles Norris Williamson (1859-1920), a young Englishman who was editor of Northcliffe's magazine *Black and White*. Pledged to write six serials simultaneously for Northcliffe, and following his advice to introduce "plenty of action, but, more important, plenty of love, with a strong curtain for each chapter," she married Williamson in 1895 and they retired to the Hill Farm in Surrey. Both Sir Arthur Pearson and Greenough Smith, editor of the *Strand Magazine,* commissioned other serials.

Mr. Williamson was asked to do a series of articles about motoring in France, then an adventurous novelty, for a paper which discontinued publication before the articles could appear. Mrs. Williamson rewrote them in the form of lively letters; the resultant romance, *The Lightning Conductor,* was an English and American best-seller in 1903. Until Williamson's death, his wife (who was the actual writer of the "C.N. & A.M. Williamson" novels) never lacked for commissions of one kind or another. (Mrs. Williamson wrote in later years: "Charlie Williamson could do everything in the world except write stories. I could do nothing else.") After the motoring *motif* had lost some of its freshness, she combined it with a mystery element in the *Scarlet Runner* stories serialized in the *Strand.* The earnings built a house, La Dagonnière, on Cap Martin, the Riviera, later sold to Lord Rothermere; and La Pausa at Roquebrune, sold during the First World War to a millionaire and later to Chanel, the *couturière.* Mrs.

Williamson occasionally wrote scenarios for the silent motion pictures. The death of her husband affected her painfully, and she was said to have lost $150,000 in the 1929 stock market crash. Publishers who could not believe that she was practically the sole author of the Williamson fiction were reluctant to take her later novels; which were, in point of fact, inferior to those written with her husband's encouragement. Mrs. Williamson died at sixty-four at Bath, England, after accidentally (according to her doctors) taking an overdose of sleeping tablets. Her affairs were well in order. An attractive blonde woman, she was an indefatigable, reliable worker, and performed many unobtrusive kindnesses.

PRINCIPAL WORKS: A Woman in Grey, 1898; The House by the Lock,1899; Lady Mary of the Dark House, 1902; The Lightning Conductor, 1902; The Princess Passes, 1904; My Friend the Chauffeur, 1905; The Car of Destiny, 1906; Lady Betty Across the Water, 1906; Scarlet Runner, 1908; Set in Silver, 1909; Lord Loveland Discovers America, 1910; The Golden Silence, 1910; The Guests of Hercules, 1912; The Heather Moon, 1912; The Lightning Conductress, 1916; Crucifix Corner, 1918; Alias Richard Power, 1921; The Lure of Vienna, 1926; Cancelled Love, 1926; Told at Monte Carlo, 1926; Children of the Zodiac, 1929.

ABOUT: Williamson, A. M. The Inky Way (autobiography); Bookman (London) November 1933; New York Times September 26, October 6, 1933; Review of Reviews (London) October 1933.

WILLIAMSON, C. N. See WILLIAMSON, A. M. L.

WILLIAMSON, HENRY (1897-),

English novelist and nature writer, was born in Bedfordshire, in a house which had been his family's home for more than four hundred years. He had a lonely childhood, the bright spot of which was the reading of Richard Jefferies, who became his idol then and his inspiration later. He was only seventeen when he enlisted as

a private and served through the First World War in Flanders. He returned from the war gray-haired at twenty-three, completely unfitted for a competitive life. For a few "wretched months" he was a reporter on the *Weekly Dispatch.* Then for a period he tried to live in London on his war pension of forty pounds a year and the proceeds of a weekly article on nature in the *Daily Express.* At night he slept on the Thames

Embankment, or on a haystack in near-by Kent. He was completely alone, dreadfully unhappy, drinking too much, contemplating suicide, friendless because "men and women alike found me morbid." Yet he was already at work on his first novel, and eventually he pulled himself out of the slough by breaking off this existence abruptly, walking two hundred miles to Devon, and settling down to write in a cottage in Exmoor. He managed to double his income by writing, and he was completely happy for the first time in his life. He was "discovered" by a few discerning fellow-authors who became his admirers—Walter de la Mare, Thomas Hardy, Col. T. E. Lawrence (to whom he dedicated *Salar* and whose biography he was later to write), and above all Arnold Bennett. When *Tarka the Otter* won the 1927 Hawthornden Prize, his economic difficulties were over.

He lives now in Norfolk, where he describes himself as a "farmer, author, and journalist," and says he owns and farms 240 acres, "educating thereon four small sons and other children." (So averse is he to publicity that it is impossible to find his wife's maiden name or the date of his marriage.) In appearance he strongly resembles John Masefield. His hair has turned from gray to white and his face is deeply lined; but he has found his place in life and he is a contented man. As C. Henry Warren said, "he has a country heart." Like Jefferies, he could never have been happy in a city.

To him "writing is just slavery.... I often feel that I can't write and never could." Yet he is a prolific author, who dislikes being thought of merely as a nature writer. Actually he is as interested in people as he is in animals, and has the same nostalgic, melancholy sympathy with human beings as with otters and salmon. There is a gentle mist of sadness over everything he writes. "Something appears suppressed within him, bullied into hiding," said J. Fletcher Smith; and that is true of the work as well as of the man. On the other hand, one of the charms of his books is that he is never sentimental, never excited; as Warren remarked, "he possesses the power always to remain in some degree detached, however ardently he feels." He is a dreamer, a looker-back, a defenseless man without a shell, who has managed to put all of himself into his books without ever raising his voice.

PRINCIPAL WORKS: *Novels*—The Flax of Dreams: The Beautiful Years, 1921; Dandelion Days, 1922 (completely revised, 1930); Dream of Fair Women, 1924; The Pathway, 1928; The Old

Stag (short stories) 1926; Tarka the Otter, 1927; The Wet Flanders Plain, 1929; Ackymals, 1929; The Patriot's Progress, 1930; The Star-Born, 1933; Salar the Salmon, 1935; The Children of Shallowford, 1939. *Miscellaneous*—The Lone Swallows, 1922; The Peregrine's Saga (in America: Sun Brothers) 1925; The Village Book, 1930; The Labouring Life (sequel to The Village Book; in America: As the Sun Shines) 1932; The Gold Falcon, 1933; The Linhay on the Downs and Other Adventures in England and America, 1934; Devon Holiday, 1935; Anthology of Modern Nature Writing (ed.) 1936; Selections From Richard Jefferies (ed.) 1937; Goodbye, West Country, 1938; The Story of a Norfolk Farm, 1940; The Genius of Friendship: T. E. Lawrence, 1941.

ABOUT: Bookman (London) January 1928, September 1930; Mentor May 1929; Scholastic September 26, 1936.

WILLIAMSON, THAMES ROSS (February 7, 1894-), American novelist, was born on an Indian reservation near Genesee, Idaho, where his father, Benjamin Franklin Williamson, a former scout, was a trader. His mother was Eugenia May (Ross) Williamson, and he is of mixed Welsh, Norwegian, French, and Irish descent. Perhaps because of this, he is a natural linguist, who speaks ten languages fluently. He ran away from home at fourteen, was a tramp for a while, then shipped to Peru on a treasure hunt, and then on a whaler which he deserted off the coast of Alaska. He has also been a railroad worker, a circus roustabout, a sheepherder in the Sierra Nevada Mountains, and a newspaper reporter in San Francisco. Somehow in the midst of this he managed to graduate from high school in Spokane, Wash., at sixteen. At twenty he was private secretary to the warden of the Iowa State Prison, and had become a fingerprint and Bertillon expert. He was first encouraged to become a novelist by a prisoner who criticized a story in the prison magazine, which Williamson edited!

Going to Chicago, he went on the staff of Hull House as interpreter of Italian, Spanish, and modern Greek. He decided he needed more education, and in 1917 received his B.A. (*cum laude*) from the University of Iowa. The same year he married Florence Louise von Zurawski. They had a daughter, but were later divorced, and in 1927 he married Sarah Storer Smith, who occasionally collaborates with him (and whose initials and surname he has adopted as one of his many pseudonyms); they have a son and a daughter. He went to Harvard on a scholarship, and in 1918 took his M.A. in economics and anthropology. He also did all the work for a Ph.D. except to take the examination. In 1920-21 he was instructor in economics at Simmons College, and in 1921-22 was assistant professor of economics and sociology at Smith College. He wrote a number of textbooks in sociology, and in a few years the income from them enabled him to stop teaching and begin on a long-projected plan to present every aspect of American life in a vast series of novels. After three far from successful volumes of the series, he abandoned the idea. It was 1929 before, with *Hunky*, he found his true voice—that of the primitive, inarticulate members of our society.

With an enormously active mind, he keeps going between novels by writing juveniles under five known pseudonyms. He works hard, starting at six in the morning and keeping regular hours. In recent years he has lived in New England, Canada, France, Mexico, and Sweden, and now is in Massachusetts. He has been described as "dark as a gypsy, nervous as a cat. Mercurial in temperament, intellectually restless. Eager, sensitive, stimulating. Drowning his real self in torrents of talk. A sincere and patient craftsman, afflicted with shyness and terribly sensitive about the quality of his work." Among his "hobbies" he lists "picking up new languages and eating queer dishes. Considered an authority on stuffed rooster's combs and pickled squid." His first name is pronounced, not like the English river, but "with a lisp at the start and the rest to rhyme with James."

PRINCIPAL WORKS: *Novels*—Run, Sheep, Run, 1925; Gypsy Down the Lane, 1926; The Man Who Cannot Die, 1927; Stride of Man, 1928; Hunky, 1929; The Earth Told Me, 1930; In Krusack's House, 1931; Sad Indian, 1932; The Woods Colt, 1933; D Is For Dutch, 1934; Under the Linden Tree, 1935; Beginning at Dusk, 1935. *Juveniles and Mysteries*—Opening Davy Jones's Locker, 1930; The Flood Fighters, 1931; The Glacier Mystery (as "S. S. Smith") 1932; On the Reindeer Trail, 1932; Against the Jungle, 1933; The Feud Mystery (as "S. S. Smith") 1934; The Lost Caravan (as "Waldo Fleming") 1935; The Cave Mystery (as "S. S. Smith") 1935; The Lobster War, 1935; The Falcon Mystery (as "S. S. Smith") 1936; Talking Drums (as "Waldo Fleming") 1936; Beyond the Great Wall (as "Edward Dagonet") 1936; In the Stone Age (as "Gregory Trent") 1936; The Last of the Gauchos, 1937; The Spy Mystery (as "S. S. Smith") 1937; A Riddle in Fez (as "Waldo Fleming") 1937; Hunters Long Ago (as "Gregory Trent") 1937; Messenger to the Pharoah (as "De Wolfe Morgan") 1937; A Tamer of Beasts (as "Gregory Trent") 1938; The Pygmy's Arrow (as "Waldo Fleming") 1938; Saltar the Mongol (as "Edward Dagonet") 1938; Before Homer (as "De Wolfe Morgan") 1938; The Feud Mystery (as "S. S. Smith") 1939; The Island Mystery (as "Waldo Fleming") 1939; The Flint Chipper, 1940. *Textbooks*—Problems in American Democracy, 1922; Introduction to Economics, 1923; Readings in American Democracy, 1923; Readings in Economics, 1923; Introduction to Sociology, 1926; Civics at Work, 1928; Principles of Social Science (with E. B. Wesley) 1932.

ABOUT: Boston Evening Transcript August 28, 1931; Wilson Library Bulletin January 1932.

WILSON, EDMUND (May 8, 1895-   ), American critic, was born in Red Bank, N.J., the son of Edmund Wilson (a lawyer and politician) and Helen Mather (Kimball) Wilson. He was educated at Hill School, Pottstown, Pa., and Princeton University (B.A. 1916). During the next year he was a reporter on the New York *Evening Sun*. From 1917 to 1919 he served as an  enlisted man at a base hospital in France and in the Intelligence Corps of the United States Army. After demobilization he returned to New York, and in 1920 and 1921 he was managing editor of *Vanity Fair*. In 1926 he joined the staff of the *New Republic*, at first as editor of the book review section. He resigned as associate editor in 1931 to devote more time to his own writing; for a while was a contributing editor, but no longer has any official connection with the magazine, though his work still frequently appears in it.

Mr. Wilson has been married three times: in 1923 to Mary Blair, by whom he had a daughter; in 1930 to Margaret Canby; and in 1938 to Mary McCarthy, formerly book critic of the *Nation* and author of *The Company She Keeps*, a novel that was a 1942 *succes de scandale*. They have a son. Wilson is of medium height, with thinning reddish hair and brown eyes; quiet, reticent, and rather shy, his friends appropriately call him "Bunny." He is very absent-minded, and is prone to stutter when he is excited. He has no aptitude for mechanical pursuits, as he discovered when he bought a motorcycle, wrecked it the first time he rode it, and then was arrested for driving without a license!

Although he is primarily a critic, he has tried his hand at all varieties of writing, including poetry and a novel. He has also written a number of plays; two of his rather fantastic comedies—*The Crime in the Whistler Room* and *This Room and This Gin and These Sandwiches*—have been produced in New York. His dominant interests are almost equally divided between literature and economics. For a while a declared Communist, whose favorable report on a trip to Russia appeared in 1936, he soon thereafter became disillusioned by events in the Soviet Union, but still is a collectivist and economically far to the left. The high peaks of his achievement as literary and social critic respectively are *Axel's Castle* and *To the Finland Station*.

Louis Hacker called him "our foremost literary critic, [who] has the courage of his intellectual interests." He has been accused of self-contradiction and changeableness in his critical views, but this seems rather a sign of growth than of weakness. It has been said of him that he is "primarily a moralist, ... one of the few people writing today who ... write from the long-range point of view." Even in his avowedly Communist days, he wrote fundamentally from the old-time American Puritan tradition, which perhaps accounts for the "distilled disillusion" of his conclusions today. A reviewer in *Time* perhaps summed him up best by saying that "he is a natural critic in the way that some writers are natural poets."

PRINCIPAL WORKS: The Undertaker's Garland (with J. P. Bishop) 1922; Discordant Encounters (dialogues and plays) 1926; I Thought of Daisy (novel) 1929; Poets, Farewell! (poems) 1929; Axel's Castle, 1931; The American Jitters—A Year of the Slump, 1932; Travels in Two Democracies, 1936; This Room and This Gin and These Sandwiches (plays) 1937; The Triple Thinkers, 1938; To the Finland Station, 1940; The Wound and the Bow, 1941; The Boys in the Back Room, 1941.

ABOUT: Commonweal July 8, 1938; North American Review September 1938; Poetry January 1930, June 1938; Saturday Review of Literature March 26, 1938, October 5, 1940; South Atlantic Quarterly October 1937; Time March 21, 1938, November 13, 1939, October 14, 1940.

WILSON, FLORENCE ROMA MUIR. See WILSON. R.

WILSON, HARRY LEON (May 1, 1867-June 29, 1939), American novelist, humorist, and playwright, was born in Oregon, Ill., one hundred miles from Chicago, the son of Samuel and Adeline (Kidder) Wilson. His father published one of Oregon's two newspapers, and the boy acted occasionally as printer's devil, much preferring this to public school. At twenty he was in the Far West, acting as stenographer for some men writing the life of Frémont, and living in a mining camp, where he played poker with professional gamblers. His first humorous writing, sent from Denver to *Puck,* then the foremost American comic weekly, was accepted and published in 1887. When he was in Omaha an offer came to join the staff. Wilson joined *Puck* in 1892 and remained in New York ten years, succeeding H. C. Bunner as editor in 1896. His first book, *Zig Zag Tales,* was published that year, followed six years later by *The Spenders* (the title was suggested by Irving Bacheller), a contrast between eastern and western Americans. Obtaining an advance of $2,000, he quit his job to marry Rose Cecil Latham, who as Rose O'Neill[qv] originated the Kewpie doll fad. She illustrated Wilson's *The Lions of the Lord,* a serious novel concerning the Mormon trek to Salt Lake, as well as *The Spenders* (under the name "O'Neill Latham"), *The Seeker,* and *The Boss of Little Arcady.*

Booth Tarkington met Wilson at the home of Julian Street, and they became devoted friends. Commissioned by George Tyler to write a play, they both sailed for Italy late in 1905 to spend the winter on the island of Capri in the "beautiful, unbelievable villa that Elihu Vedder had built there." Collaborating on *The Man From Home,* a vehicle for the late homespun character actor William Hodge, Wilson and Tarkington "projected an untraveled young Kokomo lawyer of local experience into Sorrento." Hodge trouped with this national hit for six years, taking it into every sizeable city in the country.

The Boss of Little Arcady, published in 1905, was acclaimed by Jack London as his favorite novel. It was written by "a man obviously charmingly in love," Mr. Tarkington says, and helped make its author a member of the National Institute of Arts and Letters. In 1912 Wilson returned to America, establishing his home at Carmel Highlands on Monterey peninsula in California, and proceeded to write the delightfully humorous, thoroughly American novels on which his fame rests. Bunker Bean, Merton of the Movies, Ruggles of Red Gap (an impeccable British butler suddenly transferred to a pioneer Western town); Ma Pettingill, the blunt-spoken, soft-hearted mistress of the Arrowhead Ranch; Cousin Egbert and Professor Copplestone became American household words, and did not lack for critical acclaim, contrary to some current impressions. William Dean Howells gave the accolade of approval from his department in *Harper's Monthly Magazine.* Mr. Tarkington says, "Howells' delight in Bunker Bean and in Ruggles was profound; in Ma Pettingill it was as ecstasy."

Wilson received $100,000 for the motion picture rights to *Merton of the Movies,* which received a memorably pathetic stage performance from Glenn Hunter in the dramatization by George S. Kaufman and Marc Connelly. Charles Laughton's impersonation of Ruggles in a talking picture was widely acclaimed. (Reciting Lincoln's Gettysburg Address, a high point in the film, was an idea of the directors which did not have Wilson's approval).

Some years before his death from heart disease, Wilson's head was hurt in a motoring accident, with consequent impairment of his memory and powers of concentration. Surviving him were Rose O'Neill (their marriage ended in divorce in 1907); his second wife, Helen Cooke, an amateur actress, whom he married in 1912 (they were divorced in 1927), and their two children. Wilson was a man of medium height, quiet in demeanor, with the serious face of a humorist.

PRINCIPAL WORKS: Zig Zag Tales, 1896; The Spenders, 1902; The Lions of the Lord, 1903; The Seeker, 1904; The Boss of Little Arcady, 1905; Ewing's Lady, 1907; Bunker Bean, 1913; Ruggles of Red Gap, 1915; Somewhere in Red Gap, 1916; Ma Pettingill, 1919; Merton of the Movies, 1922; The Wrong Twin, 1921; Oh, Doctor! 1923; Professor, How Could You! 1925; Lone Tree, 1929; Two Black Sheep, 1931.

ABOUT: Baldwin, C. C. The Men Who Make Our Novels; Masson, T. L. Our American Humorists; Bookman June 1925, January 1930; London Mercury March 1931; New York Times June 30, 1939; Saturday Evening Post, August 20, November 19, December 17, 1932; Saturday Review of Literature, August 12, 1939.

WILSON, MARGARET (January 16, 1882-), American novelist, Pulitzer Prize winner, writes: "I was born in Iowa, the most Middle Western of all Middle Westerners. My forebears were in no sense gentlefolk. Being farmers they were not good at keeping up appearances. Indeed, they were too poor to have an appearance to keep up. Yet they could stare reality in the face without batting an eye. They were strong and loving humans. I spent the allotted years in the University of Chicago, where I heard for the first time the venerable Eastern method of pronouncing my native tongue, and upon graduation I proceeded to India as a missionary—why, I am not altogether able to say. Being of a submerging disposition, I sank deeper into that country than the wise do, into Hindustan and Hindustani, into the Punjab and Punjabi, into Curmukha and Curmukhi, all of which are unsettling elements.

"I left India when I did because if I had not I should have died quite futilely of compassion. And when I wrote of India then, I signed myself 'An Elderly Spinster,' because I was at that time the oldest woman in the United States.

"That Oriental interlude had been, I found, an isolating experience. I didn't realize then that the years had absconded with my American point of view, and left me in its place a mongrel attitude. I only knew that Chicago was an excellent place for forgetting any sort of wisdom.

"In this land, if one is to write, one should by all means arrange to be a woman. For is it not true, as the comparatively masculine novelists complain, that a predominance of feminine readers punctures the puffs of masculine gender, while woman's productions can only gain in worth and beauty by the instructive comments of virile critics? I have, moreover, the great advantage of writing consciously and unconsciously for women, and from a point of view entirely feminine, for which—do I apologize?—I do not.

"I was constrained to spend some time in Chicago, and happened to get a chance to teach in a real school, where I taught with delight and satisfaction until I was fired. While I was looking about trying to persuade some other institution to let me amuse myself within it, I happened to hear an American lecturer who lambasted his exotic countrymen in a way so truly diverting that I resolved then and there to write myself a story wholly American. Then the fun began for me. If it continues even mildly for those who read me, I share their gratification."

* * *

In 1923 Miss Wilson married Colonel G. D. Turner, of Oxford, England, and since then has lived in England permanently. Her first novel, *The Able McLaughlins,* won the Harper Prize in 1923 and the Pulitzer Prize in 1924. One critic has said of her that "she is a trifle heavy, a trifle long; the perfect artistry of Willa Cather and of Edith Wharton at her best she will probably never have; but she covers American ground heretofore unbroken." Others of her books have dealt with her experiences in India and with her great interest in criminology. (Her husband was at one time governor—i.e., warden—of Dartmoor Prison.)

PRINCIPAL WORKS: The Able McLaughlins, 1923; The Kenworthys, 1925; The Painted Room, 1926; Daughters of India, 1928; Trousers of Taffeta, 1929; The Crime of Punishment (nonfiction) 1931; Dark Duty (in America: One Came Out) 1931; Cardinal Points (in America: The Valiant Wife) 1933; The Law and the McLaughlins, 1937; The Devon Treasure Mystery, 1939.

ABOUT: Wilson Library Bulletin May 1932.

WILSON, ROMER (1891-January 11, 1930), English novelist, wrote in 1928 an autobiographical sketch in which she said:

"I lived all my childhood in a dark old manor house on the edge of the moors just outside Sheffield. In this place, formerly the home of Bulsover, who invented electro-plating, and Plimsoll, who instituted the loading mark on ships, I lived from two to sixteen. Every summer we went to a seaside as wild and cold as could be. Often also, our parents took us on the Continent. When I was fifteen I was suddenly transported to West Heath School, in the soft and luxurious landscape of the Thames Valley. After four years there, I went to Girton College, Cambridge, where I took up law. With considerable boredom I existed at college for three years, passed my examinations with mediocre honors, and through the influence of one of the professors began to imagine half seriously that I might one day write a book.

"I left college in 1914, hoping to have a pleasant social life such as most young women enjoy. The war put an end to these hopes. In the summer of 1915, tired with inactivity, I wrote a draft of *Martin Schüler*. A famous critic saw it by chance and suggested that I should make a novel of it. In three weeks I wrote the first half. Some time during the following year I tore it up and threw it in the wastepaper basket. In my absence a friend fished it out and painstakingly stuck it together. Not until 1917 could I tolerate the sight of it, when in an-

other three weeks I finished it and shortly after had it accepted by a publisher.

"In the meantime, I had taken to war work. I sold potatoes for the Board of Agriculture, and at intervals wrote *If All These Young Men,* a book which no Americans and very few Englishmen have understood. Immediately after finishing it I wrote a play called *The Social Climbers.* This was followed almost at once by *The Death of Society,* which gained me the Hawthornden Prize in 1921. Shortly after the war I spent three weeks in Paris, and the result was *The Grand Tour of Alphonse Marichaud*—a *nom de guerre* I had used myself in very early days when writing rubbish for a typewritten private magazine. It was while I was in Italy correcting proof on it that I met Edward J. O'Brien, the American anthologist, whom I married in 1923. Our affection for Portofino, where we had met, was so great that we returned there to live almost directly after our honeymoon, and only left it for Rapallo because there were no houses to let in Portofino.

"When I was suddenly commissioned in 1927 to write the life of Emily Brontë, all my latent memories of the old times came back. It is only in this book that I have drawn directly upon what will always be to me a complete life in a country which is no more. I am now [1928] definitely settled at Locarno, in Switzerland.

"I cannot, and never shall be able to write what I think people want. I cannot write for the public. I write very rapidly, but I do not scamp or hurry. I always rewrite my books twice, word by word from the beginning, and I have known myself to write a chapter seventeen times."

Two years after this was written, Romer Wilson (her original name was Florence Roma Muir Wilson) died at Lausanne, at thirty-nine, leaving one son. Besides her original work, Miss Wilson edited a series of fairy tale anthologies. Only one of the two novels on which she was working at the time of her death was sufficiently complete to be published.

Robert Nichols described her as slender, appearing taller than she really was, with dark hair. "Her face, of singular beauty, ... bore an extraordinary resemblance to that of Keats.... The great eyes had the same dark fervor, brilliance, and depth.... She talked wonderfully. Her speech was ... elliptical, gnomic, the flight of a winged horse." She died of the same illness which killed Keats. The *London Mercury* spoke of her "extraordinary power of visualization,.. her Brontëish power when she wrote of moments of passion and exaltation." She herself considered what she had accomplished "a preparation and a learning for what I hope to do in the future," but like Katherine Mansfield, whom she somewhat resembled in temperament and who had the same feeling, she was prevented from full maturity of her great talent by a too early death.

PRINCIPAL WORKS: Martin Schüler, 1918; If All These Young Men, 1919; The Death of Society, 1921; The Grand Tour of Alphonse Marichaud, 1923; Dragon's Blood, 1926; Latter-Day Symphony, 1927; Greenlow, 1927; The Social Climbers (play) 1927; All Alone (life of Emily Brontë) 1928; The Hill of Cloves, 1929; Tender Advice, 1935.

ABOUT: Wilson, R. Martin Schüler (see Introduction by M. Sinclair to 1928 edition), The Death of Society (see Introduction by H. Walpole to 1928 edition); Living Age January 1931; London Mercury February, August 1930.

"WINCH, JOHN." See LONG, G. M. V. C.

WINSLOW, OLA ELIZABETH, American biographer and Pulitzer Prize winner, has taught English and history at Goucher College since 1914, and is now chairman of the English department. She received her education at Stanford University (B.A. 1906 M.A. 1914) and the University of Chicago (Ph. D. 1922). She received the Pulitzer Prize in biography in 1941 for her study of Jonathan Edwards, on which she had been at work for many years, doing most of her research in the Yale University Library. Previous to this she had published only technical works in literary history, and had compiled Volume I (the only one issued) of the proposed *Harper's Literary Museum* (1927), her contribution being the bibliography of Early American Writings. She is unmarried and lives in downtown Baltimore. Her book has been called "at once a penetrating psychological interpretation and a valuable contribution to history."

PRINCIPAL WORKS: Low Comedy as a Structural Element in English Drama From the Beginnings to 1642, 1926; American Broadside Verse, 1930; Jonathan Edwards: A Biography, 1940.

ABOUT: Publishers' Weekly May 10, 1941; Saturday Review of Literature May 10, 1941.

WINTER, JOHN KEITH (October 22, 1906-), English novelist and dramatist who signs his works as Keith Winter, writes: "I was born in a little village called Aber on the North Wales coast. My father was professor of agriculture at the neighboring University of Bangor and ran the university model farm. My early life was spent working and playing on the farm. My favorite occupations were riding —horses, cows, and pigs—and killing hens. When I was twelve, I was sent to school in Berkhamsted. Here I spent one abysmally wretched year, followed by four very happy ones. My first year was chiefly occupied in planning various methods of committing suicide. By the beginning of my second year I had more or less rid myself of an excessive inferiority complex. I represented my school in Rugby football and my house in running and gym. I was probably the worst cricketer in the school, and my detestation of that dreary game remains with me to this day.

"When I left school, aside from a vague inclination for acrobatic dancing, my plans for the future were nebulous, and consequently I found myself installed in a travel agency in London. In the six gloomy months that followed I found time to write a little book of short stories which was subsequently published at my own expense. As far as I know, no copy penetrated beyond the family circle, and so the title of this early masterpiece and its shining contents can be numbered amongst the dark secrets that will accompany me to the grave.

"At the end of six months' well-meaning incompetence in the travel agency, I anticipated my employers by giving notice, and became an assistant master in a preparatory school. In this profession I spent two and a half very happy years. In 1927 I went to Oxford and read history, but not very much. I spent three years there doing nothing, and I must admit they passed very quickly and pleasantly. In my last term, when I should have been assimilating the finer points of political economy, I published *Other Man's Saucer*. What the reviewers were pleased to call the 'outspokenness' of that book [which dealt with school life] brought my scholastic career to an abrupt termination. From that day no headmaster would even consider me as a possible candidate for his staff. A broken knee acquired while playing rugger had finally dispelled my dreams of acrobatic dancing, and so I had no other choice but to take up writing as a profession.

"My dramatized version of *The Rats of Norway* was produced in London, and since then I have written more plays than novels. I am unmarried and live in London."

* * *

Mr. Winter was too young to be in the First World War, and his knee injury incapacitates him from fighting in the present one, but he is now doing war work in London. Best known of his plays is *The Shining Hour*. Edward Reed called him "a dramatist with a gift for dialogue and a good knowledge of theatre technique."

PRINCIPAL WORKS: *Novels*—Other Man's Saucer, 1930; The Rats of Norway, 1932; Impassioned Pygmies, 1936. *Plays*—The Shining Hour, 1934; Worse Things Happen at Sea! 1935; Ringmaster, 1936; Old Music, 1937; Weights and Measures, 1938; We at the Cross-Roads, 1939.

ABOUT: Theatre Arts Monthly June 1934.

WINTER, WILLIAM. See "AMERICAN AUTHORS: 1600-1900"

WINTERICH, JOHN TRACY (May 25, 1891-), American bibliographer, editor, and essayist, writes: "Born Middletown, Conn.; moved to Providence, R.I., in 1901, and educated at Brown University, graduating with B.A. degree in 1912; continued at Brown as assistant in the English department the following year; joined staff of Springfield,

Bachrach

Mass., *Republican* in 1913, and was reporter and copy-reader until 1917, when I became a private in the United States Army, sailing for France in October, 1917; joined staff of the *Stars and Stripes*, official newspaper of the American Expeditionary Forces, the following February, and served there until May 1919, as reporter and copy-reader; made many trips to the front for the *Stars and Stripes* and am entitled to four battle clasps on Victory Medal; received citation from General Headquarters, A.E.F., for 'exceptionally meritorious and conspicuous services,' which carries with it the award of the Purple Heart medal; on return from France became managing editor of the *Home Sector*, which collided with the memorable printers' strike of the fall of 1919 but survived until the following April, at which time I became managing editor of the *American Legion Weekly* (later *American Legion Monthly*); became editor in 1924, and continued in this position to 1939; on staff of *P.M.*, 1940; on active duty as major, Officers' Reserve

Corps, with Bureau of Public Relations, War Department, since October 1940.

"Served on editorial board of the *Colophon*, book collectors' quarterly, throughout its existence, 1930-1940; now on editorial board of the *Dolphin*. Besides my books, have written numerous contributions to books about books, introductions to books, and articles on books and book collecting. Married Emily Hubach in 1924; our two sons are dead."

Mr. Winterich's permanent home is in Ossining, N.Y. He was made a Kentucky colonel in 1931. He is military in carriage and aspect, and his hair is still coal-black at fifty. He is one of the foremost American authorities on first editions and on book collecting in general, and his erudition is veiled by a mellow, urbane style, which makes his work highly readable even to laymen uninterested in his special subject.

PRINCIPAL WORKS: A Primer of Book Collecting, 1927 (revised and enlarged, 1935); Collector's Choice, 1928; Books and the Man, 1929; Squads Write! (ed.) 1931; An American Friend of Dickens, 1933; Early American Books and Printing, 1935; Twenty-Three Books, 1938.

ABOUT: Winterich, J. T. (ed.). Squads Write!; Woollcott, A. While Rome Burns.

WINTERS, YVOR (October 17, 1900-), American poet and critic, writes: "I was born in Chicago. My father was at that time a free-lance trader or scalper on the Chicago Board of Trade, but a nervous and physical breakdown took him to California before my fourth birthday. He was a real estate agent in Los Angeles for a few years, then went to Seattle as an

office manager in 1912, returned to Los Angeles in 1914, and shortly returned to Chicago. I followed my family to Chicago after about a year, spent three years there in high school and four quarters at the University of Chicago, with vacations in California as a milker on my uncle's dairy farm. After my first year in college I contracted tuberculosis and spent three years in bed in Santa Fé, N.M., and two more years as a school teacher (primer class and first, fourth, and fifth grades the first year, high school English, French, zoology, baseball, basketball, track, and boxing the second year) in the coal camps of Madrid and Cerillos, south of Santa Fé. In 1923 I entered the University of Colorado and in 1925 took my M.A. there in Romance languages. From 1925 to 1927 I taught French and Spanish at the University of Idaho; in 1927 I came to Stanford as a graduate student in English, and became an instructor in English there the following year. I took my Ph.D. in English at Stanford in 1934. I am now an assistant professor there, teaching American literature, English poetry, and a little composition. In 1926 I married Janet Lewis, author of *The Invasion,* and we have a son and a daughter.

"My best uncollected critical writing is to be found in the *Hound and Horn* during its last couple of years, and in an article on the English poets of the sixteenth century running in *Poetry,* February to April, 1939. In 1928 and 1929 my wife, Howard Baker, and myself edited a mimeographed journal, the *Gyroscope,* which ran to four numbers. I was also theoretically Western editor of the *Hound and Horn,* actually general advisory editor during its last two years. In this second capacity I laid the foundation for more literary enmities, and for enmities more intense, enduring, and I think I may fairly say unscrupulous, than I should judge have been enjoyed by any other writer of my generation. It was all quite unintentional on my part; I merely took literature seriously, and sought to achieve a precise style in my critical articles. I am at present the owner of a hand-press, on which I intend to publish my own poems for the past twenty years, the poems of my wife, and the poems of a few of my friends.

"My early poetry was written under the influence of Ezra Pound, William Carlos Williams, Marianne Moore, and others of their generation. About 1927 I began working in the traditional forms, and have continued to do so since. It is not infrequently said at present that my early work far surpasses my later, but this opinion appears to me to be largely a part of a general effort to disparage my critical views by indirect suggestion, direct analysis being, it would seem, impracticable. Whatever the virtues of my poetry, past or present, absolutely considered, I think one may reasonably say that the later work surpasses the earlier, and will probably prove, in the long run, of greater value than my criticism."

* * *

Yvor Winters' impressive collection of his work, printed by hand on his own press, appeared in 1940. The author's feelings about the contemporary world of letters, in its commercial aspects, are such that no copies of the book were sent to magazines for review.

PRINCIPAL WORKS: *Poetry*—The Immobile Wind, 1921; The Magpie's Shadow, 1922; The Bare Hills, 1927; The Proof, 1930; The Journey, 1931; Before Disaster, 1934; Twelve Poets of the Pacific (editor and contributor) 1937, Poems, 1940. *Criticism*—Positivism and Decadence, 1937; Maule's Curse, 1938.

ABOUT: Bookman October 1930, November 1932; Poetry April 1928, February 1935, November 1940; Southern Review #3 1938.

WINWAR, FRANCES (May 3, 1900-   ), American biographer and novelist, writes: "I was born as Francesca Vinciguerra at Taormina, Sicily, a little town that is considered one of the beauty spots of the world. The Vinciguerras trace their ancestry to the eleventh century. As an infant I was baptized in a basilica that was built in the Middle Ages; the Greek

Blackstone

Theatre whose marvelously spaced columns frame Aetna and the Ionian Sea was my playground until my eighth year. I remember the tourists of all nations who used to come to Taormina during the 'season.' Perhaps from my exasperation at not understanding the *forestieri* [foreigners] dates my desire to acquire as many languages as possible. My father, a singer, used to take me about with him to the theatre and the hotel salons. By the time I was five I had acquired his repertory, which he was fond of having me repeat before his cronies. Boldly I would oblige with songs that used to be greeted uproariously and rewarded with sweets and sometimes money, which I was never allowed to keep. It was a gay life. Often it would be long past midnight when I was put to bed.

"Then came America, to which my father was drawn by the large promises of a friend. I was sent to the New York public schools, where I soon learned English well enough to compose a poem of eight lines which was published in the school magazine. The fuss that the teachers made over me and the elation I felt in consequence probably encouraged me in the direction which, in my years of discretion, I decided to follow. Subsequently I attended high school and later college, which I left without taking a degree when life, during the tempestuous years of the war, promised much more than did academic seclusion.

"I do not remember the time when I was not writing something. In my eighteenth year I began sending my efforts to the literary magazines. The *Masses,* then edited by Max Eastman and Floyd Dell, published my first poems, a series of Japanese *tankas.* A year or so later the *Freeman* published an article of mine on Giovanni Verga. The article caught the attention of Laurence Stallings, who was then literary editor of the New York *World,* and through his interest I reviewed books for him almost every week for two years. Meanwhile with a number of well-known artists and sculptors I helped found the Leonardo da Vinci Art School, which is still thriving.

"My first novel was autobiographical—of course. It was never published, for in a dramatic moment I re-enacted the first scene of *La Bohème* in my first studio with a fireplace. Free now to write objectively, I began my novel on Francesca da Rimini, which was published as *The Ardent Flame.* There was one condition to its publication: I had to change my high-sounding patronymic. Thus Francesca Vinciguerra became Frances Winwar—which, by the way, is a literal translation of the Italian name.

"In 1925 I married Bernard D. N. Grebanier, professor of English literature at Brooklyn College. We have a son.

"My list of favorite authors would take up too much room, though among my contemporaries I like Thomas Wolfe and Archibald MacLeish. In politics I belong to no particular party or faction, casting my ballot for the candidates who, in my opinion, best understand the meaning of democracy."

* * *

Frances Winwar won the Atlantic Prize of $5000 in 1933 for *Poor Splendid Wings* (about the Pre-Raphaelites). This, with *The Romantic Rebels* (about Byron, Keats, and Shelley) and *Farewell the Banner* (about Coleridge and Wordsworth), is part of a tetralogy on nineteenth century literary figures and movements. She also translated Boccaccio's *Decameron* in 1930 for the Limited Editions Club, and reviews books for the New York *Times Book Review.*

She has black hair and eyes and delicately classic features. Elsewhere she has said, "I would rather listen to music than anything else," and she is also devoted to painting. Of her work she has declared, "The one thing I pride myself on is the honesty of my presentation." Besides being honest, her biographies are (to quote Harold de Wolf Fuller) "highly colored and romantic." They are, in short, excellent popular presentations, slightly sentimentalized, but written in a fresh and vigorous style.

PRINCIPAL WORKS: *Novels*—The Ardent Flame, 1927; The Golden Round, 1928; Pagan Interval, 1929; Gallows Hill, 1937. *Biography and History* —Poor Splendid Wings (in England: The Rossettis and Their Circle) 1933; The Romantic Rebels, 1935; Farewell the Banner, 1938; Puritan City: The Story of Salem, 1938; Oscar Wilde and the Yellow 'Nineties, 1940; American Giant: Walt Whitman and His Times, 1941.

ABOUT: Boston Evening Transcript August 19, 1933; Publishers' Weekly May 27, 1933; Wilson Library Bulletin February 1936.

WISE, THOMAS JAMES (October 7, 1859-May 13, 1937), English bibliographer and literary forger, was born at Gravesend, the first-born of Thomas Wise and Julia Victoria (Dauncey) Wise. His father was at times a builder, tobacconist, and general merchant. It was a Baptist household, but the boy Wise, himself in delicate health and educated at home,

sometimes read Shelley aloud to his invalid mother.

The Wise family soon moved to Devonshire Road, North London, where Wise lived with his parents until he was thirty. He began book-collecting at seventeen, while a junior clerk in the essential-oils firm of Hermann Rubeck, searching for books in the second-hand shops of Farrington Road, up Fleet Street, and along the Strand. At eighteen Wise spent twenty shillings for first editions of Thomas Moore's *Epicurean* and Shelley's *Cenci,* the foundation of the Ashley Library, sold to the British Museum in 1937. It was named from his house at 52 Ashley Road, Crouch Hill, North London, where Wise took his bride, Selina Fanny Smith, in 1890.

Wise learned bibliography from Dr. Frederick James Furnivall, founder of the *Oxford Dictionary,* and he also made the acquaintance of Stopford Brooke, Edmund Gosse, Clement Shorter, Henry Buxton Forman, William Robertson Nicoll, editor of the English *Bookman* in which Wise later conducted a department on rare books; and John Henry Wrenn, the Chicago banker who was to be one of his most rewarding and uncritical customers. Herbert Gorfin, an office-boy, also proved useful in Wise's bibliographical transactions, legitimate and otherwise. Soon Wise had risen to the very top of his profession. The news of his forgeries burst on the literary world like a bombshell in 1934.

In that year, writes Wilfred Partington (editor of the *Bookman's Journal* from 1919 to 1931) in his *Forging Ahead: The True Story of the Upward Progress of Thomas James Wise* (1939), "it was revealed that a considerable number of purported first-edition pamphlets of writings by Victorian authors, copies of which were in the Ashley Library of Thomas James Wise, were forgeries; others were condemned as of very doubtful authenticity. The classification of these highly esteemed pamphlets as first editions, their reputed literary and bibliographical importance, and their commercial value as rarities, had depended almost solely upon the authority of Wise." The precise instrument of revelation was an innocently titled book, *An Enquiry Into the Nature of Certain Nineteenth Century Pamphlets*, by two young English scholars, John Carter and Graham Pollard, which Vincent Starrett calls "one of the great detective stories of the world." Discrepancies of paper and typography, especially in the so-called Reading edition of Elizabeth Barrett Browning's *Sonnets From the Portuguese*, showed that the pamphlets could not have been printed at the period claimed by Wise.

Wise made an evasive reply and kept an obstinate silence until his death at seventy-seven, but the case against him was so clear that he found almost no defenders. When he heard (before the appearance of the Carter-Pollard book) that the two men had been making discreet inquiries of Herbert Gorfin, now a bookseller, he did buy back some pamphlets from the latter. Partington quotes from an anonymous diary to show that the forgeries were suspected in some quarters as far back as 1888. A page-by-page facsimile of Browning's 1883 poem, *Pauline*, and of first editions of Shelley started Wise on his series of typographical forgeries, although these first items were innocent enough in purpose. He probably took the course of selling forged items to raise money to buy genuine rarities, or such is the general belief among bookmen.

In the years of his esteem Wise received an honorary M.A. degree from Oxford in 1926, and was an honorary fellow of Worcester College, Oxford. After his second marriage, to Frances Louise Greenhalgh, he moved to Hampstead, where he died. Partington describes him as a short, chubby figure with a pink bald head and inscrutable eyes.

PRINCIPAL WORKS: A Complete Bibliography of the Writings in Prose and Verse of John Ruskin, 1893; A Bibliography of the Writings of Alfred, Lord Tennyson, 1908; A Complete Bibliography of the Writings in Prose and Verse of Samuel Taylor Coleridge, 1913; A Complete Bibliography . . . of George Henry Borrow, 1914; A Complete Bibliography . . . of William Wordsworth, 1916; A Complete Bibliography . . . of the Members of the Brontë Family, 1917; A Complete Bibliography . . . of Elizabeth Barrett Browning, 1918; A Complete Bibliography . . . of Walter Savage Landor, 1919; A Complete Bibliography . . . of Algernon Charles Swinburne, 1919-20; A Complete Bibliography of the Writings of Joseph Conrad (1895-1920) 1920; The Ashley Library, 1922-36; A Shelley Library, 1924; A Swinburne Library, 1925; A Pope Library, 1931; A Complete Bibliography of the Writings in Prose and Verse of George Gordon Noel, Baron Byron, 1932-33.

ABOUT: Carter, J. & Pollard, G. An Enquiry Into the Nature of Certain Nineteenth Century Pamphlets; Partington, W. Forging Ahead: The True Story of the Upward Progress of Thomas James Wise; Starrett, V. Books Alive; New York Times May 14, 1937; Publishers' Weekly May 29, 1937, November 25, 1939; Strand Magazine September 1930; Southwest Review 1940.

WISTER, OWEN (July 14, 1860-July 21, 1938), American novelist, was born at Philadelphia. His father was a physician who married Sarah Butler, daughter of Fanny Kemble, the great English actress, and Pierce Butler of Georgia. The boy was educated at St. Paul's School, Concord, N.H., and also attended schools in England and Switzerland. He was gradu-

ated from Harvard in 1882 with highest honors in music. At Harvard he helped write a Hasty Pudding Club musical show and contributed *The New Swiss Family Robinson* to the *Lampoon*, the humorous publication. Two more years in Paris advanced his musical education. Franz Liszt, after hearing Wister play his *Merlin and Vivien*, wrote Fanny Kemble that the young man had a *"talent prononcé."* On his return to the United States in 1884 he became a clerk in the Union Safe Deposit Vaults in New York, where he "sat on a high stool computing interest." Wister was an originator of the famous Tavern Club of Boston, of which William Dean Howells was the first president. Howells advised him not to publish his first-written novel, *A Wise Man's Son.*

An opportune nervous breakdown sent Wister to a Wyoming ranch, a move important for his career. He attended the Harvard Law School from 1885 to 1888, was made a member of the Philadelphia bar after graduation, and practiced law for two years in the Philadelphia office of Francis Rawle.

In the autumn of 1891 Wister returned to Wyoming for his fifth summer, in search of health and big game. In ten years he made fifteen journeys to the West. "Hank's Woman" and "How Lin McLean Went West," short stories published that year in *Harper's*, were the first intimations of the talent which reached full flowering in the sensationally successful novel, *The Virginian: A Horesman of the Plains,* published in 1902 with a dedication to Theodore Roosevelt. Frederic Remington was the most notable of the novel's several illustrators. It was a best seller for six years (over a million and half copies were sold); the dramatization with Dustin Farnum played ten years in New York and on the road; it has been filmed three times and translated once. The novel struck a new and bold note for its time, intimating that a hero of American fiction could have a variegated love life, that in a lawless community men must make such laws for themselves as the conditions under which they live demand, and that a New England girl of good breeding could be unconventional. The episode of Em'ly, the excessively maternal hen, showed Wister's humor at its best. Several of the novel's episodes were strong and brutal; Wister removed an eye-gouging episode at Theodore Roosevelt's insistence.

Wister admitted his literary debt to Stevenson, Kipling, Prosper Mérimée, and Henry James. The latter's influence is evident in *Lady Baltimore,* a story of "hothouse charm." *Philosophy 4,* a Harvard episode whose implications are decidedly snobbish, once drew down Alexander Woollcott's wrath in a piece entitled "Owen Wisteria."

On April 21, 1898, Wister married Mary Channing Wister of Philadelphia, a distant cousin. Mrs. Wister helped the needy and unfortunate children of the city; on her death in 1913 flags were placed at half-mast. A school now bears her name. Three boys and three girls were born to the Wisters, four of whom were with him when he died of a cerebral hemorrhage at Crowfield, his summer home near Kingstown, R.I.

Wister was a man of decided (some would say "Tory") opinions, a pronounced Anglophile, and, somewhat paradoxically, an enemy of censorship. He was honorary chairman of "Defenders, Inc.," and opposed President Franklin D. Roosevelt's proposal to alter the membership of the United States Supreme Court. He once publicly suggested that no bodies of World War veterans be brought home. The novelist was a well-built man of dignified bearing, with broad shoulders and a carefully tended moustache. The University of Pennsylvania made him an honorary Doctor of Laws in 1907, and Harvard University appointed him an overseer. Wister's style was called "tender and expressive"; others think it somewhat precious and a little effeminate. Writers of cowboy novels and editors of "Western" pulp-magazines have more reason to be grateful to him than, perhaps, they altogether realize.

PRINCIPAL WORKS: The Dragon of Wantley, 1892; Red Men and White, 1895; Lin McLean, 1898; The Jimmyjohn Boss, 1900; The Virginian, 1902; Philosophy 4, 1903; Lady Baltimore, 1906; How Doth the Simple Spelling Bee, 1907; The Seven Ages of Washington, 1907; Members of the Family, 1911; The Pentecost of Calamity, 1915; A Straight Deal: or, The Ancient Grudge, 1920; Neighbors Henceforth, 1922; Watch Your Thirst, 1923; When West Was West, 1928; Roosevelt: The Story of a Friendship, 1930.

ABOUT: Cooper, F. T. Some American Story Tellers; Millett, F. B. Some Contemporary American Authors; Woollcott, A. While Rome Burns; American Magazine February 1941; Christian Science Monitor Magazine August 3, 1940; New York Times July 22, 1938.

WODEHOUSE, PELHAM GRENVILLE (October 15, 1881-), English humorist who signs his works as P. G. Wodehouse, was born at Guildford, the son of Henry E. Wodehouse, C.M.G., and was educated at Dulwich College. He has an honorary Litt.D. degree from Oxford. For two years he tried to endure working in a London bank, but he was already making more than his salary by freelance writing, so in 1903 he left the bank to conduct a column, "By the Way," in the London *Globe*. He made his first visit to the United States in 1904, returned in 1909 for a year, and since then has frequently spent almost half of each year in this country; he is one of the very few English novelists whose American characters are even remotely recognizable to their real-life countrymen. After returning to London from his first American trip, he went to the country and buried himself in an almost empty house, with no company but that of twelve dogs. He emerged in 1914 to marry a widow, Mrs. Ethel Rowley; they have one daughter, who has inherited her father's ability as a writer. He began as an author with a series of

Times Wide World

stories of a boys' school, but struck his stride in 1910, and since then has averaged at least two humorous books a year. Besides these he has written the lyrics for innumerable musical comedies, and collaborated in the writing of many more—several of them in conjunction with Guy Bolton and Jerome Kern. But it is his novels which are meant when one says "Wodehouse." His characters—the Hon. Bertie Wooster, Jeeves, Mr. Mulliner, Psmith, and the rest—have become household familiars. As Sinclair Lewis put it, "he has become not an author but a whole department of rather delicate art. He is the master of the touchingly inane, . . . of the ultimate and lordly deadpan."

For many years Mr. Wodehouse made his home in a villa at Le Touquet, on the Riviera. When the Nazis conquered France, they occupied his villa and arrested him. He and his wife were treated with exceptional consideration and were subsequently installed at the Hotel Adlon in Berlin. Wodehouse made a short-wave broadcast from Berlin in June 1941 in which he more than repaid the Nazi Propaganda Ministry for the courtesy shown to him by referring to his internment as "quite an agreeable experience" and to his nominal captors as "a fine body of men." The impropriety of these remarks shocked his admirers in the English-speaking world, but Wodehouse evidently had no idea that the war was anything more than a regrettable falling-out between gentlemen. It has been said that his work is very popular in Germany because the Nazis consider his noble imbeciles a realistic picture of English life and character!

Although he is a rapid and prolific writer, Wodehouse rewrites every book at least twice, and does the first three hundred words over many times. Michael Joseph called him "a most conscientious workman," whose "art skilfully conceals art," and Arthur D. Nock, who called him "the Master of those who laugh," praised his "perfection of technique." Others, however, find his humor merely slick and superficial and dismiss him as only a successful writer of ephemeral escape fiction.

Completely bald, he is "the type of the perfect uncle, with a twinkle in his eye." He is rather shy, utterly unpractical (his wife handles his money), and devoted to golf, swimming, motoring, cricket, and football— the last two in the capacity of spectator.

PRINCIPAL WORKS: The Pothunters, 1902; A Prefect's Uncle (short stories) 1903; A Good Bet, 1904; The Head of Kay's, 1905; Love Among the Chickens, 1906; The White Feather, 1907; The Swoop, 1908; Mike, 1909; Enter Psmith, 1909;

A Gentleman of Leisure, 1910; Psmith in the City, 1910; The Prince and Betty, 1911; The Little Nugget, 1912; Psmith: Journalist, 1915; Something Fresh (in America: Something New) 1915; Uneasy Money, 1917; Picadilly Jim, 1918; A Damsel in Distress, 1919 (as play, with I. Hay, 1930); Jill: The Reckless, 1920; The Coming of Bill, 1920; The Indiscretions of Archie, 1921; The Clicking of Cuthbert, 1922; The Girl on the Boat, 1922; Mostly Sally (in America: The Adventures of Sally) 1923; Leave It to Psmith, 1923 (as play, with I. Hay, 1932); Bill the Conqueror, 1924; The Inevitable Jeeves, 1924; Ukridge, 1924; Carry On, Jeeves! 1925; Sam the Sudden, 1925; Sam in the Suburbs, 1925; The Heart of a Goof, 1926; Meet Mr. Mulliner (short stories) 1927; The Small Bachelor, 1927; Money for Nothing, 1928; Fish Preferred, 1929; Mr. Mulliner Speaking (short stories) 1929; Summer Lightning, 1929; Baa, Baa, Black Sheep (play, with I. Hay) 1930; Very Good, Jeeves! 1930; Big Money, 1931; If I Were You, 1931; Hot Water, 1932; Louder and Funnier (short stories) 1932; Dr. Sally, 1932; Heavy Weather, 1933; Mulliner Nights (short stories) 1933; Right-Ho, Jeeves! (in America: Brinkley Manor) 1934; Candle-Light (play, adapted from S. Geyer) 1934; Thank You, Jeeves, 1934; Blanding's Castle, 1935; The Luck of the Bodkins, 1935; The Inside Stand (play) 1935; Laughing Gas, 1936; Young Men in Spats, 1936; The Crime Wave at Blandings, 1937; Lord Emsworth and Other Stories, 1937; The Code of the Woosters, 1938; Summer Moonshine, 1938; Uncle Fred in the Springtime, 1939; Divots, 1939; Quick Service, 1940; Eggs, Beans, and Crumpets, 1940; Money in the Bank, 1942.

ABOUT: Flannery, H. Assignment to Berlin; American Magazine October 1931; Bookman (London) April 1925, June 1929; New Republic January 6, 1941; Newsweek October 25, 1937; Saturday Review of Literature July 25, 1936, July 5, 1941; Spectator November 8, 1935; Time December 30, 1940, July 7, August 4, 1941.

*WOLF, FRIEDRICH (1888-), German playwright and novelist, was born in the Rhineland, the son of a Jewish merchant. He studied medicine and worked as a ship's physician on the North German Lloyd steamship line. During the First World War he served as army surgeon on the Eastern and Western fronts and emerged in April 1918 as a rabid conscientious objector. Interned for insanity in Arnsdorf-Dresden's Klappsmühle, the "patient" served as doctor to the other "mentally unfit." Shortly after his release he joined the Socialists and in October led one of the soldiers' revolts in Dresden. During the demonstration protesting the murder of Karl Liebknecht and Rosa Luxemburg he was arrested and sent to the Sonnestein prison.

Wolf's earliest short stories date back to 1917—seven of them written between 1917 and 1927 are available in the volume *Kampf im Kohlenpott* (1928). His earliest plays were *Das Bist Du* (1919) and *Der Unbedingte* (1920).

* Died October 5, 1953.

In February 1920 Wolf was stationed as doctor in the town of Remscheidt but in March he rushed to the struggle against the reactionaries of the Kapp-Putsch, acting as leader in the Central Committee of the Revolutionists at Essen, Ruhr. Immediately thereafter he gave his services to a commune of unemployed workers who were engaged in a swamp-draining project as a self-help measure. These experiences furnished the material for his play *Kolonne Hund* (1926). From 1922 to 1928 Wolf worked as doctor among the weavers and poor peasants of Hechigen, in Swabia. He directed and financed a semi-professional troupe which toured the most backward districts of Southern Germany presenting social plays, the most successful of which was Wolf's *Bauer Betz* (1932). To this period belong his one-act trilogy "Elemente" (1922), comprising *Fegefeuer, Flut,* and *Aether;* his tragedy of the German Peasants' War *Der Arme Konrad* (1924), *Der Löwe Gottes* (1924), *Der Sprung durch den Tod* (1925), and *Kunst Ist Waffe* (1927)

In 1928 Wolf moved to Stuttgart and joined the Communist Party. He soon won recognition as a powerful social dramatist with *Cyankali* (1929), which despite bitter persecution and final suppression by the censors was extremely popular and was translated into the principal European languages. Other international successes followed, notably *The Sailors of Cattaro* (1930), dealing with the mutiny in the Austrian navy in 1918, which, although also banned, was staged in theatres the world over. Brooks Atkinson considered it the most trenchant play of the season when it was performed by the Theatre Union in New York in December 1934.

When the Nazis came to power Wolf fled from Germany and lived subsequently in Switzerland and France. After the German occupation of France, he was imprisoned in a camp at Vernet d'Ariège, from which he was reported to have been released in 1941, through the intercession of the Soviet ambassador, and sent to Russia. After the outbreak of war between Germany and Russia, he spoke regularly in Soviet broadcasts to the German workers

Wolf's plays include: *Florisdorf* (1935), which is thematically and ideologically a continuation of *The Sailors of Cattaro* and depicts the heroic armed struggle of the Vienna workers in February 1934, and *Professor Mamlock* (1935), which especially in its magnificent film version made in the

Soviet Union has been one of the most effective exposés of Nazi persecution of the Jews. It was also performed in New York by The Federal Theatre in 1937. More recently Wolf has written a satiric play called *Das Trojanische Pferd* (1937) depicting the sufferings of youth in Hitler's Third Reich and a long novel, *Zwein an der Grenze* (1938) which shows a tremendous improvement over his earlier *Kreatur* (1928).

AVAILABLE IN TRANSLATION: The Sailors of Cattaro, 1935; Professor Mamlock, 1935; Florisdorf, 1935.

ABOUT: Catholic World February 1935; Commonweal December 21, 1934; Nation December 26, 1934; New Republic January 2, 1935; Theatre Arts Monthly February 1935; Das Wort April-May 1937.

WOLFE, HUMBERT (January 5, 1885-January 5, 1940), British poet, lampoonist, playwright, and Deputy Secretary of the Ministry of Labour, wrote the following brief summing-up of his crowded life: "Born Via Fattebene-fratelli, Milan, Italy... Brought to Bradford Grammar School . . . had the great fortune, in Mr. Battersby and Mr. Barton, of being under the  care of two distinguished men of letters, both in their own way poets. Left Bradford for Wadham College, Oxford, and there started writing verse, but was disturbed by metaphysics . . . entered the Civil Service by examination in 1908 in the Board of Trade. Married two years later to Jessie Chalmers Graham of Edinburgh. Have one daughter. In the years 1910 to 1914 . . . wrote a certain number of poems never published, except occasionally . . . and a novel called "The Count of Saldeyne," consistently refused until 1915 by all publishers, and then put away.

"During the War an ardent disciple of militarism, and an official of the Ministry of Munitions, suffering violent change of heart when it was fashionable to do so immediately after the Armistice. Recovered a part of his wandered soul . . . published his first book, *London Sonnets*. . . . A certain amount of reviewing . . . in the *Saturday Review* encouraged the continuance of literary activities, not wholly prevented by writing for the Carnegie Foundation *Labour Supply and Regulation*. In 1921 . . . a second and equally unsuccessful book of verse, *Shylock Reasons With Mr. Chesterton*. . . . This was followed in 1922 by *Circular Saws,* which cut no wood or ice.

"The Author having now attained a position in which he is violently attacked by some of his brother poets, we may assume that he has reached the point fixed enough to suggest that he should be disestablished. His only merit is that of a hard worker, but the results of his work do not necessarily indicate that this is a merit. He is, of course, of Jewish birth and of no political creed, except that his general view is that money and its possessors should be abolished."

* * *

Wolfe's critical essays, *Dialogues and Monologues,* were issued in 1929, and in 1933 came a piece of autobiography, *Now a Stranger,* which covered roughly only his eighth, ninth, and tenth years. His waggish poetic fantasy, *Reverie of Policeman,* reminding one reviewer that the stage needed poetry "but not poetry that despairs of becoming the transparent medium of emotions," was produced in London in the summer of 1936; and two years later, his free-verse adaptation from a medieval Hungarian legend, *The Silent Knight. The Upward Anguish,* a self-judgment on his late teens and early twenties, constituted his last substantial literary achievement. He died in London on his fifty-fifth birthday.

He had a slender, lean face, like that of a "trim falcon,"—"quick-eyed, bright-beaked." By day he was Deputy Secretary of the Ministry of Labour, "a most uncivil Civil servant." By night he was a poet. He served also in the capacity of propagandist, able Geneva spokesman, and "politician with and without portfolio." He was underpraised for the tart fragility of his best early verse; he was overpraised for what became eventually a kind of pretentious allegorizing: but for the cleverest of his whimsy and the most bitter-sweet of his lyrics his work justified his indefatigable labors.

PRINCIPAL WORKS: The Count of Saldeyne, 1915; London Sonnets, 1919; Shylock Reasons With Mr. Chesterton, 1921; Circular Saws, 1922; Kensington Gardens, 1923; Lampoons, 1925; Requiem, 1927; Dialogues and Monologues, 1929; Now a Stranger, 1933; The Upward Anguish, 1938; Out of Great Tribulation, 1939; Kensington Gardens in War-Time, 1940.

ABOUT: Wolfe, H. Dialogues and Monologues, Now a Stranger, The Upward Anguish; Christian Century February 7, 1940; English Review June 1934; New York Times January 6, 1940; Poetry March 1940; Saturday Review of Literature February 24, 1940.

WOLFE, THOMAS (October 3, 1900-September 15, 1938), American novelist, was born Thomas Clayton Wolfe in Asheville, North Carolina, the son of William Oliver Wolfe, a stonecutter, and his second wife Julia Elizabeth (Westall) Wolfe, keeper of a boarding house. It was his father's prodigious memory and reverence for poetry that made his childhood

Pinchot

more than the sullen cycle of back-street paper routes, school torments, and thankless errands. Among the best of his early reading ventures were: Ridpath's *History of the World,* Stoddard's *Lectures,* and the *Jungle Book,* which so thoroughly delighted him that he was once tempted to write Kipling a note of gratitude. At fifteen he entered the University of North Carolina, and became editor of the college paper and magazine. *The Return of Buck Gavin: The Tragedy of a Mountain Outlaw,* a product of a course in play-writing, was Wolfe's first published piece (*Carolina Folk Plays: 2d. ser.*).

During the last summer of the World War he was a checker on the government docks at Newport News, Va.; he was graduated from the University in 1920, a hulking, shaggy, slow-moving young colossus; and in the fall of the same year he went off to Harvard. In the famous "47 Workshop" of George Pierce Baker (Professor Hatcher in *Of Time and the River*) he became obsessed with the idea that he "had to be a playwright." But this, according to one of his critics, was "like trying to put a straitjacket on a whale," and New York producers were either hostile or apathetic. Meanwhile he had received his M. A. from Harvard, and in February 1924 he was appointed instructor in English at Washington Square College, New York University. He remained here one year and spent the next abroad. And at the end of a second instructorship he sailed again for England, took two rooms in a little square in Chelsea that had that "familiar, smoked brick and cream-yellow plaster look of London houses," and began work—"how, why or in what manner" he never knew—on his first book.

He returned to the United States; taught all day and wrote all night, living on canned beans, coffee, and cigarettes. For some time the cadences and motifs of James Joyce had been singing in his ears (and Wolfe plainly acknowledged the strength of this influence), but "the powerful energy and the fire of my own youth," he said, "played over and possessed it all."

Wolfe had no *carte blanche* into the publishing domain. His manuscript, said one editor, was so "amateurish, autobiographical, and unskilful that a publisher could not risk a chance on it." The illusion of creation which had carried him to the finish had begun to wear off: he believed that this indictment had been pretty well justified. At the end of the academic year he escaped to Europe, and returned in January 1929. Madeline Boyd placed the novel, which Wolfe himself wanted to call *O Lost,* with Scribner's. For eight months he and Maxwell Perkins, "a great editor and a brave and honest man," to whom he afterwards dedicated his second novel, trimmed the manuscript.

The reception of *Look Homeward, Angel,* despite the jeers of a few critics, was spectacular. His native Asheville, however, was frothing: one old lady, who had known Wolfe all his life, wrote him that she would have no qualms about seeing his "big overgroan karkus dragged across the public square." Single missiles did not frighten him but the aggregate of this personal resentment confronted him with the problem of how far his freedom in the use of certain autobiographical material should be controlled by his social responsibility. All that he was actually sure of was that "a man must use the material and experience of his own life if he is to create anything that has substantial value."

By February 1930 the royalties were sufficient to permit his resignation from his teaching post; and in May, on the strength of a Guggenheim Fellowship award, he sailed again for Europe. In that amazingly self-analyzing *Story of a Novel,* which ran in the *Saturday Review of Literature* in December 1935 and afterwards appeared in book form, he wrote: "During that summer in Paris, I think I felt this great homesickness more than ever before, and I really believe that from this emotion, this constant and almost intolerable effort of memory and desire, the material and structure of the books I now began to write were derived."

He came home in the spring of 1931; took a little basement flat in the Assyrian quarter of South Brooklyn; and for three years wrote almost without pause. "At the end of the day . . . my mind . . . could by no opiate . . . be put at rest. . . . I prowled the

streets. . . . And the staggering impact of man's inhumanity to his fellow man . . . in a world in which the rich were still rotten with their wealth left a scar upon my life, a conviction in my soul which I shall never lose. . . ."

He called the book, tentatively, "The October Fair," and even in its "skeletonized" form it was about twice the length of *War and Peace.* It fell into two cycles: the period of "wandering and hungering in a man's youth" and the period of "greater certitude dominated by a single passion." Groping for a grimly surgical approach, Wolfe, with Maxwell Perkins' sane encouragement, devoted the whole of the year 1934 to the preparation of the first cycle. *Of Time and the River* survived the awful "carnage" and appeared in March 1935. A week before its publication Wolfe, with a growing fear that he had finally vindicated the prophecies of those critics who had called his first book a flash in the pan, sailed for Europe. He had, he soon discovered, nothing to fear.

Meanwhile the less significant harvests of these Brooklyn years—*A Portrait of Bascom Hawke* (1932), joint winner of a prize offered by *Scribner's* for the best short novel, another long tale called "The Web of Earth," and *From Death to Morning,* a collection of stories which Wolfe himself contended was as good writing as he had ever done—had helped to carry him along financially. In the spring of 1937 the *New Republic* printed his bitter short novel about Nazi Germany, "I Have a Thing to Tell You," later incorporated into the posthumous *You Can't Go Home Again.*

When Thomas Wolfe left New York in May 1938 for a trip through the Pacific Northwest he delivered to Harper & Brothers the manuscript of *The Web and the Rock,* in which according to a letter to his new publishers, he had replaced the strange, disturbing Eugene Gant, whose uniqueness is a "kind of romantic self-justification," with a character (George Webber) whose significance lies not in his personal uniqueness and differences but in his personal identity to the life of every man." All of which, however well meant, is only a kind of (presumably unintentional) sophistry. For the equation is, actually: Eugene Gant equals Thomas Wolfe equals George Webber. His last novel, *You Can't Go Home Again,* he described in the same letter as not a sad book but a hopeful one: you can't go back home to escapes of Time and Memory, but the real home of everyone of us is in the future.

In July 1938 he fell ill of pneumonia; during his convalescence complications set in. His death, September 15, two weeks before his thirty-eighth birthday, following an operation at Johns Hopkins Hospital in Baltimore, was attributed to acute cerebral infection. He was brought back to Asheville for burial. On his tombstone are these words from *The Web and the Rock*: "Death bent to touch his chosen son with mercy, love, and pity, and put the seal of honor on him when he died."

Scribner's published in October 1939 a collection of poetical passages *(The Face of a Nation)* from Wolfe's writings. Had his own definition of poetry been more concerned with spirit than with the conventionalities of form he would never have had any occasion to say what he often said: "I'd rather be a poet than anything else in the world. God, what I wouldn't give to be one." The last of the posthumous volumes was *The Hills Beyond* (1941), a collection of short, hitherto unprinted stories, studies and fragments.

Although many of Thomas Wolfe's soundest critics contend that he ceased to grow, from a literary point of view, after he had written *Look Homeward, Angel,* there is, nevertheless, a peculiar tragedy in the abortiveness of his life. For he once said, in acknowledging a certain "intemperate excess, an almost insane hunger to devour the entire body of human experience," that "...having had this thing within me it was in no way possible for me to reason it out of me no matter how cogently my reason worked against it.... The only way I could get it out of me was to live it out of me."

Wolfe had a powerful torso, burning eyes, untidy black hair, and a large splay mouth. In his manner was a strange mixture of humility and assurance. Both the thought of meeting people and the realization that he himself was essentially a lonely creature tortured him to an almost unbearable degree: work—inhuman doses of it—was his only certain bromide.

Wolfe's artistic and physical gargantuanism was, almost invariably, the critics' springboard for appraising him—whether they were saluting him as an authentic descendant of Walt Whitman's spirit or charging him with the writing of "blank verse bombast and apocalyptic delirium." Somewhere between these two extremes literary historians will find the proper place for the creator of some of the noblest prose that ever came out of America.

PRINCIPAL WORKS: The Return of Buck Gavin: The Tragedy of a Mountain Outlaw (in Carolina Folk Plays: 2d. ser.) 1924; Look Homeward, Angel, 1929; A Portrait of Bascom Hawke, 1932; Of Time and the River, 1935; From Death to Morning, 1935; The Story of a Novel, 1936; The Web and the Rock, 1939; The Face of a Nation, 1939; You Can't Go Home Again, 1940; The Hills Beyond, 1941.

ABOUT: De Voto, B. Forays and Rebuttals; Dodd, M. Through Embassy Eyes; Geismar, M. Writers in Crisis; Wolfe T. The Face of a Nation (see Introduction), The Hills Beyond (see Introductory Note by E. Aswell); American Review May 1935; Daily Worker May 15, 1939; Examiner 1938; Kenyon Review Winter 1939; Nation July 15, 1939; New Republic June 24, 1936; New York Times September 16, 1938; New York Times Book Review September 29, 1940; Saturday Review of Literature April 6, December 14, 21, 28, 1935, April 25, 1936; Virginia Quarterly Review Spring 1939; Wilson Library Bulletin May 1930, November 1938.

WOLFF, MARY EVALINE (Sister Mary Madeleva) (May 24, 1887-). American poet, writes: "Of the hundreds of freshmen at the University of Wisconsin in 1905, I was among the least remarkable. Born in Cumberland, Wis., I was eighteen. By June I had achieved an active repugnance for English and a temporary devotion to mathematics. A two-inch

Harris & Ewing

advertisement in *McClure's* determined me quite abruptly the next summer to transfer to Saint Mary's College (Indiana.) Ten hours a week in Sister M. Rita's classes there changed me to an English major. During the next two years I astonished my friends and myself by writing rather promising prose and verse. In September 1908 this astonishment was climaxed by my entrance into the novitiate of the Sisters of Holy Cross. On December 10th of that year I was clothed in the religious habit and became Sister Mary Madeleva.

"For ten years after that I taught at Saint Mary's Academy and College, with graduate work at Notre Dame University, two miles distant. My B.A. had come from my own college in 1909. In 1918 I had qualified for an M.A. in English from Notre Dame. At that time I had become head of the department at Saint Mary's. In 1919 I was made principal of our academy in Ogden, Utah. Bernard De Voto and Phyllis McGinley were among my students there. In 1922 I went to Woodland, Calif., to teach and study, and matriculated as a graduate student at the University of California. In 1925 I received the first doctor's degree granted by the university to a Sister. I then became dean and president of our new college, Saint Mary-of-the-Wasatch, two miles East of Salt Lake City, until 1933.

"In 1933 I went to Canada and to Europe for study and travel. I studied at Oxford and traveled as far as Northern Africa and the Holy Land, and formed friendships with Edith Wharton, William Butler Yeats, Seumas MacManus, the Meynells, and the Bellocs. On my return to the United States in 1934 I was made president of Saint Mary's College, where I now am.

"I have always been strangely dominated by a taste for the mediaeval and the mystical. A Franciscan joy in the out-of-doors has made me a good hiker, a lover of wild flowers and birds, of the seasons and their secrets. Yet my essential work has been the education of girls. Whatever else may have been the results, they have succeeded fairly in educating me."

* * *

The rare combination of "administrator and mystic, scholar and artist" has established Sister Mary Madeleva as "America's leading nun." Lively, witty, well traveled, she has been compared to Chaucer's Prioress in the *Canterbury Tales*.

PRINCIPAL WORKS: Knights Errant and Other Poems, 1923; Chaucer's Nuns and Other Essays, 1925; The Pearl—A Study in Spiritual Dryness, 1925; Penelope and Other Poems, 1927; A Question of Lovers and Other Poems, 1935; The Happy Christmas Wind, 1936; Gates and Other Poems, 1938; Christmas Eve and Other Poems, 1938; Selected Poems, 1939; Four Girls and Other Poems, 1941.

ABOUT: Current Biography 1942; Smallzried, K. Press Pass; America July 3, 1937; Catholic World September 1934; Modern Language Notes February 1927; Scholastic December 4, 1939.

*WOOD, CHARLES ERSKINE SCOTT

(February 20, 1852-   ), American poet and essayist, writes: "I was born in Erie, Pa., the son of William Maxwell Wood, first Surgeon-General of the United States Navy, and Rose (Carson) Wood. I was appointed to West Point by President Grant in 1870 and graduated in 1874. I was commissioned a sesond lieutenant and assigned to Company D, 21st Infantry. I served at Fort Bidwell, Calif., and Fort Vancouver, Wash. Late in 1876 I embarked, by Government leave,

on an exploration of Alaska, but returned in 1877 to join my regiment in the campaign against the Nez Perce Indians under Chief Joseph. I served as Gen. O. O. Howard's aide-de-camp until Joseph's surrender. In 1878 I served through the Bannock and Piute Campaigns and continued with General Howard until he was assigned to West Point. I then served for a time as adjutant of the Military Academy (West Point), but still on Howard's staff; was relieved as adjutant and allowed to enter the School of Law and the School of Political Science of Columbia University. I graduated Ph.B. and LL.B. *cum laude.*

"I had become bitterly opposed to the corruption of the Indian Ring in Washington, which stole the appropriations made for the Indians, and when we were ordered out to fight Indians, I felt I was supporting an unworthy cause. I therefore resigned from the army in 1884 [with the rank of colonel] and entered the practice of law at Portland, Ore. I continued until 1918, when I retired from the firm I had established, moving to California to continue the writing I had begun while practicing law.

"My first wife was Nannie Moale Smith, by whom I had six children, four of whom are living. [One daughter, Nan (Wood) Honeycutt, was a Congresswoman from Oregon.] My present wife is Sara Bard Field[qv] the poet, with whom I have lived in our present home, The Cats, Los Gatos, Calif., for many years.

"I have ridden, in the course of my campaigns, over this country from the Rockies to the Pacific, a country which was then scarcely inhabited, and I have seen that vast domain, water, timber, minerals, and arable land, taken by the few with the aid of Congress and secured to their heirs and assigns forever by that relic of the Middle Ages—the fee simple deed. There is not a place for the common man in the covered wagon. The unemployed, the vagrant, and the underfed have increased to an army counted by the million. I am therefore convinced that the politics this country needs is an economic program to return to the people the planetary treasures and monopolies intended for all.

"Now [written in 1940] I am eighty-eight and am spending what time I have in dying and being brought back into this life by modern medical skill—on what I might call sub-lunary mortuary excursions. I am fettered by so many medical injunctions, prohibitions, and commands that I question whether the game is worth the candle.

* Died January 22, 1944.

"I think Poetry the greatest of the Arts— the Immortal Art. I hope you have not scattered your corn before me because of such pleasantries as *Heavenly Discourse* and *Earthly Discourse* rather than *The Poet in the Desert*."

* * *

Colonel Wood is truly the last of the Titans—a remarkable old gentleman with blue eyes still keen, thick white hair, and a bushy white beard. For years, before his present illness, he was an intrinsic part of the literary life of San Francisco. His kindness to young writers is as widespread as it is secret. As Horace Gregory said, he is "greater as a personality than any of his books." Nevertheless, he is an authentic poet and (to quote T. S. Matthews) "really a serious satirist . . . [who] hates the intolerant, the bigoted, and the ignorant. His wit is a Yankee wit, a native shrewdness that abhors mere cleverness as it eschews nonsense." In spite of his age, he is "really a post-war poet"; the best poetry of this man who lived through the Civil War came out of the World War (1914-18) and the disillusionments following it. Through that experience, as Gregory remarked, "his natural, loosely formed optimism has changed its character until it now resembles something hard and strong, with a bitter taste running through it." His sonnets and lyrics, though orthodox and rather stiffly classic in form, have genuine nobility and an almost Hellenic tone.

PRINCIPAL WORKS: *Poetry*—A Masque of Love, 1904; The Poet in the Desert, 1915 (enlarged and rewritten, 1930); Maia, 1916; Circe, 1919; Poems from the Ranges, 1929; Sonnets to Sappho (privately printed) 1940. *Prose*—A Book of Tales: Being Myths of the North American Indians, 1901; Heavenly Discourse, 1927; Too Much Government, 1931; Earthly Discourse, 1937.

ABOUT: American Review July 1925; New Republic January 1, 1930; Overland February 1931; Publishers' Weekly July 13, 1940.

*WOOD, CLEMENT (September 1, 1888-), American poet and miscellaneous writer, writes: "Clement Wood was born at Tuscaloosa, Ala., on both sides of old Southern stock with literary leanings. He was educated at the University of Alabama, A.B. *summa cum laude* 1909) and at Yale University (LL.B. *cum laude* 1911). He practiced law in Birmingham, 1911-12, with his father, was assistant city attorney in 1912, and chief presiding magistrate of the Central Recorder's Court (succeeding Justice Hugo Black) in 1913. He was removed for 'lack of the judicial temperament' when he jailed

the state's Lieutenant Governor for contempt of court; and ran for president of the City Commission, almost being elected.

"Instead, he bought a one-way ticket to New York, and 'entered literature.' He supported himself by waiting on tables, working for Rockefeller's Vice Commission, and acting as Upton Sinclair's secretary. In 1914 he taught public speaking at Pingry School, Elizabeth, N. J.; 1915-20, English and history, Barnard School for Boys, where he became dean; 1920-22, same subjects, also secretary New York Preparatory Schools and vice-principal Dwight School for Boys. In 1939-40 he was instructor in versification at New York University, Washington Square Writing Center. Otherwise, he is a free lance writer, poet, and lecturer.

"In 1914 he married Mildred Mary Cummer, by whom he had a daughter and son. After a divorce, he married Gloria Goddard, poet and novelist, in 1926. They live at Bozenkill in the New York State Helderbergs, wintering in New York City or points farther south.

"In 1917 Clement Wood won the Newark 250th Anniversary Prize for his poem, 'The Smithy of God'; in 1920, the Lyric Society's $500 prize for his 'Jehovah.' He has published ten volumes of poetry, eight biographies, six novels, and numerous other works, including *The Complete Rhyming Dictionary* and a *Handbook for Poets* and including also nearly seventy titles on literature and science in the 'Little Blue Book' Series. Among his lyrics set to music by David Guion, Jacques Wolfe, and others, the best known is 'The Glory Road.' He was for two years Mediterranean Cruise Lecturer for the White Star Line. He has hundreds of correspondence course pupils throughout the Americas. He is Assistant Historian General of the Sons of Confederate Veterans and the Order of the Stars and Bars.

"Clement Wood is an enthusiastic devotee of most indoor and outdoor games. He has a powerful baritone, and has given many concerts, especially of Negro spirituals and seculars, as well as being a radio performer in this field. He is a member of the Religious Society of Friends [Quakers], and an independent in politics."

PRINCIPAL WORKS: *Poetry*—Glad of Earth, 1917; The Earth Turns South, 1919; Jehovah, 1920; The Laughter, 1922; The Tide Comes In, 1923; The Eagle Flies, 1925; The Greenwich Village Blues, 1926; The White Peacock, 1928; The Glory Road, 1936; Lays for the Laity, 1937; Eagle Sonnets, 1942. *Fiction*—Mountain, 1920; Nigger, 1922; Folly, 1925; The Shadow From the Bogue,

* Died October 26, 1950.

1928; Flesh and Other Stories, 1929; Tabloid Murders, 1931; Honeymoon, 1931; Deep River, 1934; Sensualist: A Novel of the Life and Times of Oscar Wilde, 1942. *Biography*—Amy Lowell—A Critical Life, 1926; King Henry the Rake, 1929; MacFadden: The Conqueror, 1930; The Woman Who Was Pope, 1931; The Man Who Killed Kitchener, 1932; Herbert Clark Hoover—An American Tragedy, 1932; Warren Gamaliel Harding—An American Comedy, 1932; The Life of a Man—The Biography of John R. Brinkley, 1934. *Miscellaneous*—For Walt Whitman (with M. C. Wood) 1923; The Stone Age, 1923; Poets of America, 1924; A Slang Dictionary (with G. Goddard) 1926; The Outline of Man's Knowledge, 1927; Don't Tread On Me (with A. G. Hays) 1927; The Craft of Poetry, 1929; Hunters of Heaven—The American Soul As Revealed by Its Poetry, 1929; The Sociology of Lester Ward, 1930; Six Indiscreet Lovers, 1930; Dreams—Their Meaning and Practical Interpretation, 1931; Your Dreams and What They Mean, 1933; If There Is a Hell, 1934; A Popular History of the World, 1935; A Complete History of the United States, 1935; The Complete Rhyming Dictionary and Poet's Craft Book, 1936; A History of the World (5 vols.) 1937; Games for Two (with G. Goddard) 1938; Carelessness: Public Enemy No. 1, 1937; The Complete Book of Games (with G. Goddard) 1938; Let's Play the Game: The Complete Book of Charades, 1939; Tom Sawyer Grows Up (juvenile) 1940; More Adventures of Huckleberry Finn (juvenile) 1940; Poets' Handbook, 1940; More Power to Your Words! 1940.

WOODBERRY, GEORGE EDWARD

(May 2, 1855-January 2, 1930), American poet, critic, and educator, was born in  Beverly, Mass., the son of Henry Elliott Woodberry and Sarah Dane (Tuck) Woodberry. John Woodberry, his first American ancestor, settled in Salem in 1626 and was one of the founders of Beverly. The family produced many sea-captains and sailors. Young Woodberry attended Phillips Exeter Academy, at Exeter, N. H., and entered Harvard College with the class of 1876, although he did not graduate until 1877. Here he learned method in history and biography from Henry Adams, cataloged James Russell Lowell's library at "Elmwood," studied aesthetics under Charles Eliot Norton, attended Emerson's last lecture, and helped edit the *Advocate*. "The Relation of Pallas Athene to Athens," Woodberry's senior essay, struck the college authorities as being too pagan in tone, and he was refused permission to deliver it; the paper, instead, was privately printed. Contributions appeared from his pen in the *Atlantic Monthly* in

1876, and the *Nation* in 1878. From 1880 to 1882 Woodberry was professor of English at the University of Nebraska. *A History of Wood-Engraving*, a respectable piece of hack-work, was his first book. *Edgar Allan Poe*, in 1885, was a pioneer piece of criticism and biography in spite of Woodberry's patent dislike for his subject. The book was revised and reissued in two volumes in 1909. *The North Shore Watch*, an elegy on the death of an unnamed male friend, was written in the *Lycidas* and *Adonais* vein.

Woodberry's attachments to his students were marked by a definite *Schwärmerei*; Charles Franklin Thwing's memorial essay on him in the *Harvard Graduates' Magazine* observes that it was deemed advisable to omit some of his letters "teeming with special affection for 'his boys' who fell in the war" from a projected biography. He was known at Columbia as "The Old Man." Appointed in 1891 on the recommendation of Norton and Lowell, he taught there with brilliant success and organized a strong English graduate department. He resigned while on leave of absence in 1904 to become an itinerant teacher, at Amherst, Cornell, Wisconsin, and California; wandered in the Mediterranean world, making friends with peasants; and gradually yielded to a desire for complete isolation and privacy. He died in Beverly Hospital.

Woodberry, says John Erskine, was first and last a poet. "The importance of his teaching lay precisely in the fact that he treated all literature as creative, as poetic, and his essays and biographies are memorable precisely because he envisaged poetry as the most natural as well as the noblest activity of man." His *The Heart of Man* describes the imaginative processes common to poetry, religion, and politics. Woodberry's style was not so much Victorian as "derived through New England tradition from the great seventeenth and eighteenth century publicists and divines." Admiring ex-students organized a Woodberry Society in 1911, which brought out a special edition of his poetry and essays. Thwing describes Woodberry as shy, moody, and wistful, with an apparent aching for affection. Literature, he said, was not an object of study, but a mode of pleasure; "not a thing to be known merely like science, but to be lived."

PRINCIPAL WORKS: A History of Wood-Engraving, 1883; Edgar Allan Poe, 1885 (revised, enlarged edition 1909); The North Shore Watch, 1890; Wild Eden, 1899; Heart of Man, 1899; Makers of Literature, 1900; Nathaniel Hawthorne, 1902; Poems, 1903; America in Literature, 1903;

The Torch, 1905; The Appreciation of Literature, 1907; Great Writers, 1907; The Inspiration of Poetry, 1907; Ralph Waldo Emerson (English Men of Letters Series) 1907; North Africa and the Desert, 1914; Ideal Passion: Sonnets, 1917; The Roamer, and Other Poems, 1920; Collected Essays, 1920-1921; Selected Poems (ed. by three of his students) 1933.

ABOUT: Brooks, V. W. New England: Indian Summer; Erskine, J. George Edward Woodberry; Johnson, R. U. George Edward Woodberry; Ledoux, L. V. The Poetry of George Edward Woodberry; Macy, J. The Critical Game; Phelps, W. L. The Advance of English Poetry in the Twentieth Century; Rittenhouse, J. B. The Younger American Poets; Bulletin of the New York Public Library May 1930; Harvard Graduates' Magazine June 1930; Nation September 30, 1930; New York Herald Tribune "Books" July 9, 1933.

*WOODWARD, WILLIAM E. (October 2, 1874-   ), American biographer and novelist, writes: "I was born in Lexington

County, S. C. My father made his living as a dirt farmer. We were always hard up. When I was six I started my schooling. I was, I suppose, what is known today as a gifted child, though that term was unknown when I went to school. At any rate, I had gone through all the regular classes before I was eleven. At fifteen I entered the South Carolina Military Academy, at Charleston (now known as The Citadel), on a state scholarship. Soon afterwards I lost all desire for learning, and I graduated third from foot of the class. Immediately after my graduation I went into newspaper work. Between 1893 and 1900 I worked on several newspapers—among them the Atlanta *Constitution* and the New York *World*. Around the turn of the century I drifted into the advertising business as a copywriter. For twelve years I was employed by various advertising agencies, and eventually was chief of the copy and planning department of a big agency which I left to become promotion manager of the Hearst newspapers, until 1916. In 1913 I married Helen Rosen [now Helen R. Woodward, the writer].

"In 1916 I went to Wall Street as publicity director of the Industrial Finance Corporation. Within two years I had given up the publicity work and had become an executive vice-president and a director in forty-two banks in which the Corporation was interested financially. By 1920 I had

* Died September 27, 1950.

grown so bored by banking and finance that I hated the sight of my office, so I quit. I had always wanted to write, and I began almost immediately on a novel. My wife and I went to Paris. In about a year I got tired of Europe—thought I was losing touch with America—and we came back home.

"In 1928 The Citadel awarded me a degree of LL.D. I was not reminded that I had squeezed through third from the foot of my class.

"Though four of my books are novels, my leaning is toward biography and history. I have a consuming curiosity about the doings of people, especially the men and women of the past. I think that most historical writing is dull, insipid, and far too scholarly in style, and my impulse is to present history and biography in such fashion that the subjects are readable and entertaining. I consider *Lottery* my best novel, *Meet General Grant* my best biographical work. In my first book, I invented the word 'debunk,' to my great regret. It has now become thoroughly established in the language, but I do not like the word and have never used it since. My *New American History* has had a phenomenal sale. My purpose in writing it was to clear up some false conceptions concerning American history, and to present the story of the growth of our nation in such form that it would be read by men and women who do not usually read historical works."

PRINCIPAL WORKS: Novels—Bunk, 1923; Lottery, 1924; Bread and Circuses, 1925; Evelyn Prentice, 1933. Biography—George Washington—The Image and the Man, 1926; Meet General Grant, 1928; Lafayette, 1938. Miscellaneous—Crowded Years (with W. G. McAdoo) 1931; Money for Tomorrow, 1932; A New American History, 1936.

ABOUT: Arts and Decoration November 1927; New York Times Book Review October 19, 1941.

WOOLF, LEONARD SIDNEY (November 25, 1880-   ), English historian and political essayist, writes: "I was born in London. My father was a barrister, a Queen's Counsel with a family of ten children and a large house in Lexham Gardens. When I was twelve my father died suddenly at the height of his powers, leaving my mother to bring up an enor-

mous family on inadequate means. However, I got a scholarship at St. Paul's School and from there a scholarship at Trinity College, Cambridge. I was five years at Cambridge, taking a First Class in the Classical Tripos. In 1904 I went in for the Civil Service Examinations and passed into the Ceylon Civil Service. From 1904 to 1911 I was in Ceylon and for the last two and a half years of that period was in charge of the Hambantota District, where I was pleased to find that Europeans were rare—in fact, there were only five or six, all government officials. The rest of the population consisted of Sinhalese, a few Malays, and a large number of wild animals, and I became extremely fond of all of them. However, I decided that, much as I liked Ceylon, I was not prepared to spend my life there, and that the position of a semi-autocratic ruler was not congenial to me. So when I got my first spell of leave I resigned and stayed in England, hoping to make a living by writing. The first book I wrote was a novel based largely on my experience in Ceylon. But the threatening and outbreak of the war led me from fiction into politics and sociology. My views, which had originally been liberal, had become Socialist, and I joined the Fabian Society and the Labor Party. I became convinced of the importance of the Co-operative Movement, made a study of it, and wrote about it. It was through this that I got to know the Webbs and became a regular contributor to the *New Statesman.* The Webbs got me to make a study of international government, and this led me to write a book with that title.

"Towards the end of the [1914-18] war, H. W. Massingham asked me to become a leader writer on the *Nation,* and when that paper changed hands I became its literary editor for a good many years [1923-30]. In 1917 my wife, Virginia Woolf, the novelist, and I started as a hobby the Hogarth Press, an amateur publishing business in which we did everything, including the printing. It became so successful that we eventually turned it into a regular publishing business, and have ever since published our own books. The management of it, however, always required us to give more time to it than we really wished to give, and a few years ago my wife retired from it and John Lehmann came in as partner."

* * *

Mr. Woolf married Virginia Stephen, better known by her married name,*qv* in 1912. He was editor of the *International Review* in 1919, on the staff of the *Contemporary*

Review in 1920 and 1921, and has been joint editor of the *Political Quarterly* since 1931. His recreations he gives as printing and gardening. Professor Albert Guerard said that he is "among the historians who do not claim the possession of a single key, but attempt to correlate pure politics, economics, and collective ('communal') psychology."

PRINCIPAL WORKS: The Village in the Jungle (novel) 1913; The Wise Virgins (novel) 1914; Stories of the East, 1915; International Government, 1916; The Future of Constantinople, 1917; Co-operation and the Future of Industry, 1918; Empire and Commerce in Africa, 1919; Socialism and Co-operation, 1921; Autobiography of Countess Tolstoy (translated) 1922; Fear and Politics, 1925; Hunting the Highbrow, 1926; Essays on Literature, History, Politics, Etc., 1927; Imperialism and Civilization, 1928; After the Deluge (2 vols.) 1931-39; The Intelligent Man's Way to Prevent War (edited) 1933; Quack, Quack! 1935; Barbarians at the Gate (in America: Barbarians Within and Without) 1939; War for Peace, 1940.

WOOLF, Mrs. VIRGINIA (STEPHEN)

(1882-March 28, 1941), English novelist, critic, and essayist, was born at 13 Hyde Park Gate South, London. Her father, Sir Leslie Stephen, scholar and agnostic philosopher, at one time editor of *Cornhill Magazine* and of the monumental *Dictionary of National Biography,* was a famous figure in 19th century British letters.

Sir Leslie's first wife was Harriet Thackeray, daughter of the novelist; three years after her death in 1875 he married the noted beauty Julia Prinsep Jackson, widow of Herbert Duckworth. Virginia was the third of their four children, the others being Vanessa, Julian, and Adrian. "It may interest you to know," Virginia Woolf wrote, "that my mother's mother was half French, and that I owe my name Virginia to a French great grandmother." On the occasion of her birth James Russell Lowell, then American ambassador to England, wrote some charming verses for his "dear little god-daughter," praying that the child would be "a sample of Heredity." The family divided their time between their town house in Hyde Park Gate and a summer home on the Cornwall coast near St. Ives, which probably supplied the background of *To the Lighthouse.*

Virginia was a frail and lonely child, especially lonely after her mother's death in May 1895. She was educated at home, comfortably cloistered in her father's magnificent library, developing an independent literary taste (generally for minor figures), learning Greek, and meeting her father's many literary friends, including Hardy, Stevenson, Ruskin, James Bryce, and John Morley. In 1892 George Meredith wrote to Sir Leslie: "I have to confess that my heart is fast going to Virginia."

In 1912, eight years after the death of her father, she married Leonard Woolf, a brilliant young Cambridge man who had just returned from seven years of civil service in Ceylon. His interests were equally divided between literature, economics, and the labor movement. (He is today one of the leaders of the Labor Party and an outstanding writer on economic problems.) In 1917 the Woolfs, for sheer amusement, set on an old handpress *Two Stories* by L. and V. Woolf under the imprint Hogarth Press. The "two amateur and incompetent printers" were surprised when this modest little pamphlet sold out almost immediately. In 1918 they published *Prelude* by Katherine Mansfield, who was then unknown; in 1918 *Poems* by T. S. Eliot and *Kew Gardens* by Virginia Woolf; in 1920 E. M. Forster's *The Story of the Siren.* Their policy was to publish "the best and most original," and they favored obscure young authors—who, however, did not remain obscure very long. In time the Hogarth Press became a thriving enterprise. Virginia's older sister Vanessa, the painter who married Clive Bell, illustrated and designed the distinctive dust jackets of Hogarth Press books.

The Woolfs' book-lined home in quiet Tavistock Square, Bloomsbury, a stone's throw from the British Museum, soon became the literary center for a group interested in the more esoteric aspects of literature and the arts. "The atmosphere of her home is saturated with all that is finest and mellowest in English culture and letters —all the wealth of thirty generations of humor and thought and splendid, leisurely living," said E. M. Forster, a close friend and a member of the "Bloomsbury group," which included Lytton Strachey, Desmond MacCarthy, Arthur Waley, V. Sackville West, and J. M. Keynes.

Mrs. Woolf first attracted critical attention as a novelist with *The Voyage Out* (1915), written at the age of twenty-four but not published until several years later in revised form. This showed the influence of E. M. Forster. *Night and Day* (1919) is generally considered a failure. But with *Monday or Tuesday* (1921), short stories published by the Hogarth Press with wood-cuts by Vanessa Bell (which blurred on to the opposite pages), Mrs. Woolf "emerged definitely with the liveliest imagination and most delicate style of her time." Mrs. Woolf's consecration as one of the world's outstanding novelists did not take place, however, until the appearance of *Jacob's Room* (1922), *Mrs. Dalloway* (1925), and *To the Lighthouse* (1927). As a writer of fiction she probably never surpassed these achievements. With *The Waves* (1931) and *The Years* (1937), critics began to complain of the increasingly tenuous and elaborate nature of her work.

Of contemporary writers, Joyce and Proust, whom she read in the original as early as 1922, exerted a profound influence on Mrs. Woolf. The theories of William James, Bergson, and Freud also helped to shape her work. James she read from the earliest, and she became acquainted with Bergson through him and through her sister-in-law Karin Stephen (her brother Adrian's wife) who wrote in 1922 one of the keenest analyses of Bergsonism. As for Sigmund Freud, she was partly responsible for the publication in English of some of his works and for the vogue of psychoanalysis in England especially in 1918-22.

Mrs. Woolf wrote front-page articles for the *Times Literary Supplement* at an early age. Her critical articles covered almost the entire range of English literature. She loved the forgotten worthies—Hakluyt, Sir Thomas Browne, Margaret Cavendish, Laetitia Pilkington. She was also one of the most eloquent champions of women's rights in England, notably in *A Room of One's Own* (1929) and *Three Guineas* (1938). Her essays reveal a mind possessing keenness of penetration, lucidity of expression, balance and sanity of judgment, and an amazing swiftness," said Mary E. Kelsey. "It is a mind saturated with respect for all thought, with an amazing sense of the vitality of the past. It is a mind of direct perceptions and relentless logic. The clear, dry light of the Eighteenth Century pervades all."

Of the numerous admiring critics who have written on Mrs. Woolf's writings, none perhaps has given a keener description than the novelist Gerald Bullitt; "Because it is her constant endeavour to record the psychological minutiæ of experience, to ensnare in words an incommunicable secret, and to show the bubble of consciousness shining, expanding, reflecting—in its depths and on its surface—the changing colours of the universe around it, Mrs. Woolf's writing has always been difficult: by which I mean that it will yield its motive, its clear and luminous core, only to a reader who is ready to empty himself of preconceptions and to become in the highest degree receptive, patient, searching. In her fidelity to this austere purpose she has discarded one by one, as distractions, the various devices which most writers, and nearly all readers, have held to be not merely aids but obvious necessities of narrative.... By a series of significant images, both visual and aural... she seduces one's immediate attention; and the spell is reinforced by the exquisite cadences of her prose. But though she is lavish of imagery, having the poet's instinct for the concrete phrase, this imagery does not, for the most part, relate to the physical world of which it is borrowed: it is merely a translation, into terms of that world, of apprehensions not otherwise suggestible. Consciousness, the immediate experience, is her quarry: the objective universe is no more than a hypothesis. Reading her books in their order, one observes that she becomes increasingly jealous of the space given to the description of 'action.' From *Jacob's Room* onwards (except in *Orlando,* which was an experiment in another kind) this 'action'—the physical behaviour of her characters—is more or less parenthetical, and outward phenomena—storms and sunsets, stars and flowers, the pageant of human bodies—are seen only as reflections in the moving mirror of consciousness, moments in a continuing time-sensation. In short, Mrs. Woolf is a metaphysical poet who has chosen prose-fiction for her medium."

In appearance Virginia Woolf recalled William Rothenstein's word-picture of the shy, silent, lovely Stephen girls "in plain black dresses with white lace collars and wrist bands, looking as though they had walked straight out of a canvas by Watts, or Burne-Jones." Intense, high-strung, with a long, deep-browed head, she had a sympathetic mouth and great somber eyes.

On March 28, 1941, Virginia Woolf disappeared from her home at Lewes, Sussex, leaving a note indicating that she contemplated suicide. Her drowned body was recovered later. Because of misquotation of this note, the impression given was that she had killed herself because she was unable to endure life in England during the war. Her husband therefore found it necessary to reveal that twenty-five years previously she had suffered a mental breakdown, that she felt symptoms of its recurrence, and that this time she feared it would be permanent. She was fifty-nine at the time of her death.

PRINCIPAL WORKS: The Voyage Out, 1915; Two Stories, 1917; Night and Day, 1919; The Mark on the Wall, 1919; Kew Gardens, 1919; Monday or Tuesday, 1921; Jacob's Room, 1922; Mr. Bennett and Mrs. Brown, 1924; Mrs. Dalloway, 1925; The Common Reader, 1925; To the Lighthouse, 1927; Orlando, 1928; A Room of One's Own, 1929; On Being Ill, 1930; Beau Brummell, 1930; The Waves, 1931; Flush, 1933; The Second Common Reader, 1933; The Years, 1937; Three Guineas, 1938; Reviewing, 1939; Roger Fry, 1940; Between the Acts, 1941; The Death of the Moth and Other Essays, 1942.

ABOUT: Badenhausen, I. Die Sprache Virginia Woolfs; Delattre, F. Le Roman Psychologique de Virginia Woolf; Forster, E. M. Virginia Woolf; Holtby, W. Virginia Woolf; Lohmüller, G. Die Frau im Werk von Virginia Woolf; Ocampo, V. Virginia Woolf; Quennell, P. A Letter to Mrs Woolf; Bookman February 1929, December 1931, December 1932; Bookman (London) January 1928, February 1930; Dial December 1924; Kenyon Review Autumn 1942; Nation June 30, 1926; Nation (London) April 17, 1926; New Republic April 15, 1931, April 14, 1941; New Statesman & Nation October 10, 1931; New York Herald Tribune "Books" June 28, 1931, July 13, 1941; Nineteenth Century January 1934; Nuova Antologia December 16, 1933; Nouvelles Littéraires August 13, 1927; Saturday Review of Literature February 6, 1937, December 5, 1931, April 12, 1941; Sewanee Review October 1931, April 1939; Virginia Quarterly October 1934; Yale Review April 1926.

*WOOLLCOTT, ALEXANDER (January 19, 1887-   ), American journalist and essayist, was born in Phalanx, N.J. (formerly a Fourierist colony), the son of Walter Woollcott and Frances Grey (Bucklin) Woollcott. His childhood was spent in Kansas City, where he made his stage début at five. The family then moved to Philadelphia, where he attended high

R. C. Wood

school. He then went to Hamilton College (Ph.B. 1909, honorary L.H.D. 1924), and in 1913 he did graduate work at Columbia University. He is perhaps the most articulate and certainly the most fervent of Hamilton alumni, and has publicized his *alma mater* (as he does all his enthusiasms) untiringly. From 1914 to 1922 he was dramatic critic of the New York *Times,* interrupting his association with the paper to serve for two years in France with a hospital unit. While there he was on the staff of the soldiers' paper, the *Stars and Stripes.* During 1922 he was dramatic critic of the New York *Herald,* and from 1925 to 1928 of the *World.* He is unmarried.

Several times he has "doubled in brass" as an actor—in *Brief Moment* in 1931, in

* Died January 23, 1943.

Wine of Choice in 1938, and in 1941 in the road company of *The Man Who Came to Dinner.* In both the latter plays he acted a character representing himself; in fact, the last-named comedy (by George S. Kaufman and Moss Hart) is nothing but an exposé of the well-known Woollcott idiosyncrasies and foibles. For Alexander Woollcott has become famous as a personality even more than as a writer. He has exploited this frankly exhibitionistic personality, first in his long-time department, "Shouts and Murmurs," in the *New Yorker* (now discontinued), and from 1929 to 1940 (with interruptions) as "The Town Crier" in a weekly radio broadcast over a national network.

The Woollcott legend, which probably bears only a delicate resemblance to actuality, is of a fat, owlish, lazy, sharp-tongued, insolent, generous, sentimental old codger, who loves and cultivates the great, can make or break a book or a play and does so frequently, dwells unceasingly on his idols (such as Dickens and Mrs. Fiske), and has made whimsicality repay him with fame and fortune. It is true that he is an unblushing sentimentalist, that he has once or twice made best-sellers out of very inferior books (but on other occasions he has not succeeded), and that stories gather around him equally compounded of wit and rudeness. But he has also done, at considerable trouble, real kindnesses—one example is the money he has raised for "seeing eye" dogs for the blind. And if he is "by far the most influential salesman of books in the United States," not all the books he recommends are bad. They are all, however, escapist; as Louis Kronenberger remarked, "he would rather have a good cry than a good laugh; and ... literature has no meaning for him beyond providing one or the other." He has indeed every aptitude for literature except a taste for the first-rate.

Nevertheless, he is, as John T. Winterich called him, "first, last, and always a reporter, ... distinctly a one-man show." And he is a superb reporter. No one can tell a supernatural story as he can; he is curious of all the esoteric by-ways and trivia of life and can present them vividly; if he is sometimes bawdy his bawdiness is always funny; if his enthusiasm is too easily aroused it is genuine and catching. "The very distillate of urbanity," he could (in spite of his home at Bomoseen, Vermont, where the chief attraction is the world's roughest game of croquet) have come to flower only in New York, and only in the 1920's. He has ability beyond that of a mere journalist—as may

be seen in the plays he wrote with George S. Kaufman, *Channel Road* and *Dark Tower,* as well as in a few of his books. And as a journalist, he is, to quote Raymond Mortimer, "simply stunning."

PRINCIPAL WORKS: Mrs. Fiske, 1917; The Command Is Forward, 1919; Shouts and Murmurs, 1923; Mr. Dickens Goes to the Play, 1923; Enchanted Aisles, '924; The Story of Irving Berlin, 1925; Going to Pieces, 1928; Two Gentlemen and a Lady, 1928; While Rome Burns, 1934; The Woollcott Reader (ed.) 1935; Woollcott's Second Reader (ed.) 1937.

ABOUT: Literary Digest January 11, 1936; Living Age April 1935; Nation December 18, 1935; Saturday Review of Literature February 23, 1935.

WREN, PERCIVAL CHRISTOPHER

(1885-November 23, 1941). English novelist, was born in Devonshire, in the house in which Charles Kingsley laid the scene of Amyas Leigh in *Westward, Ho!* He was a collateral descendant of Sir Christopher Wren, famous seventeenth century architect. He had an M.A. from Oxford, and after leaving the university spent five

years in travel "on all five continents," working his way as "sailor, navvy, tramp, schoolmaster, journalist, farm laborer, explorer, hunter, and costermonger in the slums." He was a trooper in the British cavalry, and he served in northern Africa in the French Foreign Legion, giving rise to his best-known books, the adventures of the Geste family. He lived in India ten years, as assistant director of education and physical culture to the Bombay government. While he was there he held the fencing title of western India. His first books were on India, rather drearily realistic stories. During the First World War he fought with the Indian Army in East Africa, first as captain and then as major. He was invalided home in 1917, and that was the end of his foreign service, though he made an attempt to enter the secret service in Morocco in 1926 and was turned down because of poor health. He lived in London, was married, and had one son.

Major Wren made little impression on the literary world until the appearance of *Beau Geste* in 1924. As book, play, and movie, this was a riotous success, and one he never quite repeated. His novels for the most part disregarded all rules of credibility; they were fantastic, amorphous, and sensational—

pure stories of action and adventure. There was the breath of life in them, because they reflected their author's eagerness for experience and his ability to report what he had seen. He was distinctly a second-rate novelist, but among the best of the second-rate: an efficient escapist.

Tall, soldierly, with blue-gray eyes, a monocle, a military moustache, and a low pleasant voice, Wren was more the retired army officer than the author in appearance and temperament. He cherished a collection of pipes dating from his university days; he read Thackeray and Stevenson, Wells and Conrad and Galsworthy. He was a prolific writer, averaging better than a book a year, and if he repeated himself frequently, his repetitions were popular among a wide and receptive audience. That he was capable of more thoughtful work is shown by one of his 1940 novels, *Two Feet From Heaven,* a psychological study of a clerical family. Wren died at Auberley, Gloucestershire, after a long illness. He was fifty-six.

PRINCIPAL WORKS: Dew and Mildew, 1912; Father Gregory, 1913; Smoke and Sword, 1914; Driftwood Spars, 1915; The Wages of Virtue, 1916; The Young Stagers, 1917; Stepsons of France, 1917; Beau Geste, 1924; Beau Sabreur, 1926; Beau Ideal, 1928; The Good Gestes, 1929; Soldiers of Misfortune, 1929; The Mammon of Righteousness, 1930; Mysterious Ways, 1930; Spring Glory, 1931; Valiant Dust, 1932; Flawed Blades, 1932; Action and Passion, 1933; Port o' Missing Men, 1934; Beggars' Horses, 1934; Sinbad the Soldier, 1935; Explosion, 1935; Spanish Maine, (*sic*) 1935; Bubble Reputation, 1936; The Fort in the Jungle, 1936; The Man of a Ghost, 1937; Worth Wile, 1937; Rough Shooting, 1938; Cardboard Castle, 1938; Paper Prison, 1939; A Mixed Bag (short stories) 1939; None Are So Blind, 1939; The Disappearance of General Jason, 1940; Two Feet From Heaven, 1940; The Uniform of Glory, 1941. Odd—But Even So: Stories Stranger Than Fiction, 1942.

ABOUT: Bookman (London) October 1929; Mentor November 1926 New York Times November 24, 1941; Scholastic March 10, 1934.

*WRIGHT, HAROLD BELL (May 4,

1872-), American novelist, writes: "Harold Bell Wright was born in Rome, N.Y.,

of an early American family, in the farmhouse built by his grandfather on the acres cleared by pioneers in the wilderness. His father moved to Whitesboro, N.Y., while the son was still a baby, and later to Sennett, N.Y. His mother died when he was ten, and he was put out to

work on a farm. His only schooling was a country school. Before he was twenty-one he learned the trade of house painting and decorating. When he was grown he entered the preparatory department of Hiram College, in Ohio. But after two years a severe attack of pneumonia and serious injury to his eyes from overwork ended his school career.

"When his hopes of gaining a college education ended, he went to Missouri. He became interested in the backwoods people, and to fill a very evident need started preaching in a schoolhouse Sundays and conducted a class in the study of the teachings of Jesus every Friday. Without college or theological seminary training, he spent ten years as pastor of churches in Pierce City, Mo., Pittsburg, Kan., Kansas City, Mo., Lebanon, Mo., and Redlands, Calif.

"While serving the church in Pittsburg, Kan., he wrote his first novel, *That Printer of Udell's,* a study of church conditions. Ill health compelled him to give up his church work. He went into the Ozark Mountains to recuperate and there began *The Shepherd of the Hills,* which he finished the following winter. The success of this book determined his life work.

"He married Frances E. Long in 1899, and they had three sons (one now deceased). After a divorce, he married Winifred Mary (Potter) Duncan in 1920. Mr. and Mrs. Wright live in their farm home, Quiet Hills Farm, near Escondido, Calif."

* * *

Mr. Wright does not recite his heroic struggle with tuberculosis, a struggle fought and won in the Arizona desert in 1916. He is a youngish looking man, tanned, with blue eyes and a soft voice. His first book was published in Chicago by personal solicitation of one of his church members; but with *The Shepherd of the Hills* he became immediately a phenomenal best-seller. Freight trains have literally been required to carry his books to stores all over the country; *The Winning of Barbara Worth* sold more than a million and a half copies. Though he has had no recent book that scored such a success, he is still the favorite novelist of people who never read any other novels. Contrary to the idea of those who have never read him, Mr. Wright's style is good, simple, clear, and forceful, and though he is sentimental he is never maudlin. He takes his incidents from actual life and he works hard on his books. His novels are sermons, but they are readable stories as well. As Hildegarde Hawthorne said, "He expounds

* Died May 24, 1944.

the basic problems of right and wrong in a manner that will reach the greatest possible number of persons."

PRINCIPAL WORKS: That Printer of Udell's, 1903; The Shepherd of the Hills, 1907; The Calling of Dan Matthews, 1909; The Uncrowned King, 1910; The Winning of Barbara Worth, 1911; Their Yesterdays, 1912; The Eyes of the World, 1914; When a Man's a Man, 1916; The Re-creation of Brian Kent, 1919; Helen of the Old House, 1921; The Mine With the Iron Door, 1923; A Son of His Father, 1925; God and the Groceryman, 1927; Long Ago Told, 1929; Exit, 1930; Ma Cinderella, 1932; To My Sons, 1934.

ABOUT: American Magazine June 1924; Bookman February 1923, August 1925; Life April 21, 1941; Literary Digest August 21, 1920; Literary Review April 5, 1924; New York Herald Tribune November 3, 1941; Sunset Magazine December 1918, August, September 1927.

WRIGHT, RICHARD (September 4, 1908-), American novelist, was born on a plantation near Natchez, Miss., the son

of a Negro farm and mill worker and a country school teacher. When he was five, the father deserted the family, and the mother supported her children as best she could, first in Memphis and then in Helena, Ark. Part of the time she was obliged to put him in an orphan asylum. Before he was ten she became totally paralyzed. The child was shipped around to various relatives, all poor and hard-working Negroes, who could do nothing with him because of his unruliness. The last experiment was to send him to a Seventh Day Adventist school, in Jackson, Miss., in which his aunt taught. Finally he learned to find some outlet for his energy in reading, but at fifteen he left home and went to Memphis, where he made his way by various unskilled jobs. Finally he became a clerk in the post-office.

It was at this period that he discovered H. L. Mencken's *Book of Prefaces,* which became his literary Bible for several years. He determined to become a writer. He "bummed all over the country," working at what he could get, and in 1934 turned up in Chicago. There he first became interested in the labor movement, joined the John Reed Club, and on the strength of a few published free verse poems gained a place on the Federal Writers' Project (WPA) in 1935. Two years later he went to New York, where again he was on the Writers' Project and wrote the *Guide to Harlem*

which it brought out. After a few attempts at political jobs with both the Republicans and the Democrats in Chicago, he became interested in Communism, and now he began to write regularly for the *New Masses* and for a time was one of its contributing editors. In 1938 he won the $500 prize offered by *Story* for the best story written by a worker on the Writers' Project, with the novelette *Uncle Tom's Children,* which gave the title that year to his first book, consisting of four long tales. The next year he was awarded a Guggenheim Fellowship. In eight months, in Brooklyn, Wright wrote *Native Son,* making several trips to Chicago meanwhile to check up on factual data. *Native Son* was a Book-of-the-Month Club choice and a best seller. Wright was chosen by the Schomburg Collection poll as one of the "twelve distinguished Negroes" of 1939, and in 1940 he received the Spingarn Medal, highest award for achievement in the field of Negro interests, for his "powerful description... of the effect of proscription, segregation, and denial of opportunity to the American Negro." A dramatization of the novel was staged on Broadway by Orson Welles in 1941. It was an instantaneous "hit," although virtually all the professional critics found it less effective than the book.

With the money he received from *Native Son,* he bought a house in Chicago for his mother, and then went to live for a while in Mexico, to write a novel, as yet unpublished, dealing with colored servants in New York City. Richard Wright is tall, with what Burton Rascoe described is "a fine, kind, intelligent face." He is unmarried.

Native Son, the exciting and disturbing case-study of a young Negro murderer, aroused considerable controversy, since the author placed all the blame for Bigger Thomas' plight on the social conditions which surrounded him. (The novel is based, in part, on the case of Robert Nixon, a Negro who died in the electric chair in Chicago in 1938 for killing a white woman.) As Edward Skillin, Jr., remarked, "he succeeds in making environment the principal villain in this new American tragedy."

In accepting the Spingarn Medal, Wright issued the following statement from his home in Brooklyn:

"It is with a deep sense of responsibility that I accept the Spingarn Medal. I accept in the name of the stalwart, enduring millions of Negroes whose fate and destiny I have sought to depict in terms of scene and narrative in imaginative fiction. It cannot be otherwise, for they are my people, and my writing—which is my life and which carries my convictions—attempts to mirror their struggles for freedom during these troubled days."

Twelve Million Black Voices (1941) was described by the *New Yorker* as a "short text-and-picture folk history of the American Negro [with photographs supplied by Edwin Rosskam], in which the author . . . writes a burning commentary on the centuries of slavery, persecution, and want."

PRINCIPAL WORK: Uncle Tom's Children, 1938; Native Son, 1940; Twelve Million Black Voices, 1941.

ABOUT: American Mercury May, July, 1940; Atlantic Monthly May, June 1940; Saturday Review of Literature June 1, 1940; Time December 23, 1940.

WRIGHT, RICHARDSON LITTLE

(June 18, 1886-), American editor and writer on gardening, was born in Philadelphia, the son of George S. R. Wright and Mary Ann (Wilbraham) Wright. He received his B.A. degree from Trinity College, Hartford, Conn., in 1910 (returning in 1924 to get his master's degree) and after graduation became Sunday editor of the *Knickerbocker Press,* Albany, N.Y. Next year he went to Manchuria and Siberia as special correspondent of the New York *World,* Chicago *Daily News* and London *Daily Express,* traveling through Russia "without passport or arrest." Large tips bestowed on strategic occasions and to the right people assisted his progress, however.

Wright returned after a year in Russia, a place which he was to regard and to write about sympathetically for some years, notably in *The Russians: An Interpretation* (1917), written after the outbreak of the Revolution. Some aspects of the current cult for Russian literature titillated his sense of the ridiculous, however, and he joined several other members of the New York Authors Club in an elaborate spoof which paid homage one day to an imaginary Russian writer named Feodor Vladimir Larrovitch. A page of his manuscript and a pressed flower from "Larrovitch's" grave were enshrined on the walls of the clubhouse, after several papers in celebration of his talents had been read. These were reprinted in a book edited by Wright and W. G. Jordan in 1919.

After his return from Russia, Wright worked as literary critic of the New York *Times* and dramatic critic of *Smart Styles.* In 1914, "for no reason at all," according to Wright, he was appointed editor of *House and Garden;* the reason, however esoteric, must have been a valid one, for he has continued in the same post ever since. His wife, who was Agnes Foster, has assisted him in his work and herself published numerous articles on gardening topics. *Truly Rural* (1922) is a record of their diverting and sometimes expensive adventures in restoring a country house in Connecticut.

Aside from his books on gardens, Wright has written a number of travel books and of political interpretations based on his experiences in the Near East. The only recent book he has published outside his special subject is *Grandfather Was Queer,* a superficial but entertaining survey of customs and manners in America two or three generations ago. His books on flowers, on landscape gardening, and on interior decorating are standard in their field, thoroughly reliable texts, though hardly of interest to the general reader. His special amusement is digging into old town histories and "the yellowing sheets of country presses," and this genial curiosity about odd and forgotten trivia of the past is evidenced not only in *Grandfather Was Queer* but also in *Hawkers and Walkers in Early America* and *Forgotten Ladies.* Books of this nature Wright regards as avocational, his real business being to tell people how to arrange and grow their gardens and furnish their homes. The greater part of his time is spent in New York City in pursuit of his editorial duties, and he is frequently to be seen at the long table of the Coffee House Club at luncheon time, as well as at their special and bohemian occasions. He is a member of several other social clubs and of the Episcopal Church.

PRINCIPAL WORKS: Through Siberia: An Empire in the Making, 1913; The Open Door, 1914; Inside the Home of Good Taste, 1915; Low Cost Suburban Homes, 1916; The Russians: An Interpretation, 1917; Letters to the Mother of a Soldier, 1918; Feodor Vladimir Larrovitch (with W. G. Jordan) 1919; House & Garden's Book of Houses, 1919; House & Garden's Book of Interiors, 1920; House & Garden's Book of Gardens, 1921; Truly Rural, 1922; Flowers For Cutting and Decoration, 1923; The Practical Book of Outdoor Flowers, 1924; House & Garden's Second Book of Houses, 1925; House & Garden's Second Book of Interiors, 1926; House & Garden's Second Book of Gardens, 1927; Hawkers and Walkers in Early America, 1927; Forgotten Ladies, 1928; The Gardener's Bed-Book, 1929; House & Garden's Book of Color Schemes, 1929; The Bed-Book of Travel, 1931; Another Gardener's Bed-Book, 1933; The Story of Gardening, 1934; Revels in Jamaica, 1937;

The Gardener's Day-Book, 1938; Grandfather Was Queer, 1939; House & Garden's Complete Guide to Interior Decoration, 1941.

ABOUT: Pearson, E. L. Books in Black or Red; Starrett, V. Books Alive; Ladies' Home Journal February 1934.

WRIGHT, WILLARD HUNTINGTON

("S. S. Van Dine") (1888-April 11, 1939), American art critic. editor, journalist, and

writer of detective fiction, was born in Charlottesville, Va., the son of Archibald Davenport Wright and Annie (Van Vranken) Wright. He was educated at St. Vincent and Pomona Colleges in California, and took postgraduate courses at Harvard University, notably in English under Charles Townsend Copeland, and abroad. In Munich and Paris he studied art, with a view to becoming a painter. Another yearning to be an orchestra conductor made him memorize the scores of symphonies and other orchestral works.

In 1907 he became literary critic of the Los Angeles Times, and held the same position with Town Topics from 1910 to 1914. In Los Angeles he escaped annihilation by ten minutes when a splitting headache sent him home before the Times building was dynamited by the McNamaras. From 1912 to 1914 he also was the discerning editor of the Smart Set, preceding H. L. Mencken and George Jean Nathan, and subsequently was literary or art critic for half a dozen newspapers and magazines. For a period of two years he averaged five columns of copy a day, including Sundays. When the World War broke out, he was living in Paris, writing fourteen hours a day. He came back to America from England on the last westward trip made by the "Lusitania," and spent two months in a sanatorium. His only serious novel, The Man of Promise, a pioneer piece of realism, appeared in 1916: it won the praise of the discerning few, but failed to sell. (It was reissued in 1930, after the identity of Wright with "Van Dine" had been revealed—with identical re sults.)

A second and more severe breakdown of health confined him to bed from early in 1923 to the middle of 1925. During convalescence, forbidden by his physician to do any "serious" reading, he assembled a library of nearly 2,000 volumes, covering the field of detective literature for seventy-five years.

It dawned on him that the detective novel had its own peculiar technique and constituted a *genre* of literary entertainment quite distinct from all other classes of fiction. He determined to write detective novels of his own, appealing to a superior class of reader, but—"I rather feared ostracism if I boldly switched from esthetics and philologic research to fictional sleuthing, and so I hid behind an old family name [Van Dyne] and the Steam-Ship initials." His 30,000-word synopses of three novels were accepted at once by Scribner's, and the first book, The Benson Murder Case (evidently suggested by the murder of Joseph Bowne Elwell, the bridge expert), published in 1926, was an instantaneous success. The "Canary" Murder Case (1927) ran serially in Scribner's Magazine, broke all publishing records for detective fiction, and was translated into seven languages and the talking pictures. Through all the stories moved the bored, languid, variously erudite Philo Vance, who reflected the physical and mental characteristics of his creator. Each novel made more money than all his serious books together, and the moving picture rights brought a fortune. The secret of "Van Dine's" identity caused wide speculation until literary sleuths ferreted out the truth in 1928. Doubting that "any one writer has more than six good detective-novel ideas in his system," Wright intended at first to confine himself to that number. He actually wrote twelve. As if in proof of his contention, critics have pronounced the last six distinctly inferior to the first.

In addition to his original detective stories as "Van Dine," Wright compiled and edited, under his own name, The Great Detective Stories: A Chronological Anthology. His definitive historical introduction to this anthology is one of the "bibles" of detective criticism.

Wright died of coronary thrombosis in New York City at the age of fifty-one, leaving a second wife, a daughter by his first marriage, and an estate of $13,000. (In 1907 he married Katharine Belle Boynton; After their divorce in 1930 he married Eleanor Pulapaugh.)

As a person, the New York Herald Tribune remarked, Wright was something of an exotic. Like Philo Vance, he was a dilettante and a bit of a *poseur*. He lived in a penthouse, wore rich raiment, and cultivated a beard which gave him something of the appearance of a highly urbane and sophisticated Mephistopheles. Ernest Boyd declared him to be the most interesting and attractive *unlikable* man he had ever known; a brilliant talker and a good listener.

PRINCIPAL WORKS: *As Willard Huntington Wright*—Songs of Youth, 1913; Europe After 8:15 (with H. L. Mencken & G. J. Nathan) 1913; What Nietzsche Taught, 1914; Modern Painting: Its Tendency and Meaning, 1915; The Creative Will, 1916; The Man of Promise (novel) 1916; Informing a Nation, 1917; Misinforming a Nation, 1917; The Great Modern French Stories (ed.) 1918; The Future of Painting, 1923; The Great Detective Stories (ed.) 1927. *As S. S. Van Dine*—The Benson Murder Case, 1926; The "Canary" Murder Case, 1927; The Greene Murder Case, 1928; The Bishop Murder Case, 1929; The Scarab Murder Case, 1930; The Kennel Murder Case, 1932; The Dragon Murder Case, 1933; The Casino Murder Case, 1934; The Garden Murder Case, 1935; The Kidnap Murder Case, 1936; The Gracie Allen Murder Case, 1938; The Winter Murder Case (posthumous) 1939.

ABOUT: Haycraft, H. Murder for Pleasure: The Life and Times of the Detective Story; Rascoe, B. (ed.) Smart Set Anthology (see Preface); Wright, W. H. Philo Vance Murder Cases (Omnibus ed.—See prefatory material); American Magazine September 1928; New York Times April 13, 1939; Saturday Review of Literature November 2, 1935, April 22, 1939.

WURDEMANN, AUDREY (January 1, 1911-), American poet, Pulitzer Prize winner, was born in Seattle, Wash., the daughter

Pinchot

of Dr. Harry Wurdemann, a well-known eye surgeon and the author of several technical books in his special field, and May Audrey (Flynn) Wurdemann. On her mother's side the girl was a great-great-granddaughter of Shelley. Mrs. Wurdemann was the daughter of a daughter of Ianthe Eliza Shelley, Shelley's child by his first wife, Harriet Westbrook. Audrey Wurdemann did not attend elementary school, but entered high school (St. Nicholas School for Girls in Seattle) at eleven. George Sterling, the American poet, author of *A Wine of Wizardry* and intimate friend of Jack London and Ambrose Bierce, made the girl his *protégée,* and had her poems privately printed as *The House of Silk* when she was sixteen. Graduating from the University of Washington with honors, Miss Wurdemann traveled throughout the United States and in the Orient. She met another poet, Joseph Auslander[qv], who was fourteen years her senior; they were married in May 1933, and lived in the Columbia University sector of New York City until Mr. Auslander became Poetry Consultant of the Library of Congress in 1937.

The Pulitzer poetry prize was awarded in 1935 to Miss Wurdemann for her first book of poems published through the usual channels, *Bright Ambush.* She was the youngest poet ever to receive the prize, being barely twenty-four. On the publication of *Testament of Love* (1938), a sequence of forty-nine sonnets, the Boston *Transcript* commented that: "The tone she tries for is bigger than the throat that utters it. Too often the sonnets are merely unskilful, inflated where they should be simplest, awkward where they should be perfect."

The poet is described by Elizabeth Clark as being tall and slender, with raven black hair which brings out the camellia white of her skin. She is shy and quiet, "emotional but never temperamental," is fond of cooking, as her husband testifies, and makes a hobby of collecting and studying precious stones.

PRINCIPAL WORKS: Bright Ambush, 1934; The Seven Sins, 1935; Splendours in the Grass, 1936; Testament of Love: A Sonnet Sequence, 1938.

ABOUT: Saturday Review of Literature May 11, 1935; Wilson Library Bulletin June 1935.

WYLIE, Mrs. ELINOR (HOYT) (September 7, 1885-December 16, 1928), American poet and novelist, was born in Somerville, N.J., the daughter of Henry Martyn Hoyt, later Solicitor General of the United States, and Anne (McMichael) Hoyt. On both sides she came of distinguished Philadelphia ancestry. Nancy Hoyt, the novelist, is her sister. When she was two,

the family moved to Rosemont, a suburb of Philadelphia, and she attended a private school at Bryn Mawr. When she was twelve, another move was made to Washington, and she transferred to a school there. At eighteen her grandfather took her and her sister for a season in Paris and London. Two years later she married Philip Hichborn, a wealthy young Washingtonian, son of a rear admiral. They had one child, a son, who was reared by Hichborn's family, for in 1910 she eloped with Horace Wylie, fifteen years older than she, and himself married. They lived in England and on the Continent, as Mr. and Mrs. Waring, for five years. In 1912 Philip Hichborn killed himself, though the cause was not (or not primarily) his domestic tragedy. In 1915 the couple returned to the United States to marry, Wylie's wife having finally divorced him. After living in Georgia and Maine, they went to Washington, but even a Hoyt was not welcome, in the rigorous society of the old Washingtonians, under such a cloud, and in 1919 they moved to New York, where Mrs. Wylie's beauty, her arresting personality, and her gifts made her a heroine rather than an outcast. But two years later the Wylies were divorced, though Mrs. Wylie always retained that name as a writer.

In 1923 she was married to William Rose Benét[qv], the poet and editor. He was a widower, with three children by his first wife, who was Kathleen Norris' sister. They lived in New York, with frequent visits to England on the part of Mrs. Wylie (as she was always called). She was in England in 1927 when she suffered a fall which resulted in a severe injury. She was by now spending more and more time alone in England, but in 1928 she came back to New York for Christmas. Her blood pressure had been dangerously high for some time, and she had suffered a slight stroke, which caused a faint facial paralysis. At work on her forthcoming volume of poems, *Angels and Earthly Creatures,* she completed her revisions on December 15. The next night, sitting in her apartment with her husband, she suffered another stroke which caused her instant death. As Carl Van Doren remarked, "Her end was as neat as her art."

Elinor Wylie was a complex creature, many things in one. Her early adventures created a psychic shock from which she never really recovered; she was frail and high-strung almost to hysteria, but indomitable. She cannot be understood without reference to her passionate cult for Shelley; she went through life as "a woman by an archangel attended." She was rarely beautiful with "lion-colored" hair and exquisite features and figure, and she was childishly vain of her loveliness. "She could not bear being less than first in any company." Like Shelley's, her almost unearthly beauty was marred by a high, shrill voice. In the few short years of her artistic fecundity, 1921 to 1928 (for her first volume of immature poems does not count), she worked unsparingly, and both her prose and verse grew perceptibly from mere brilliance and erudite polish to work of unquestioned genius. Her earlier novels are almost too ornate, too overloaded with beauty; her later ones have the better beauty of simplicity and delicacy. But it is by her poetry which achieved at the last a magnificent power and melodiousness, that she will be remembered.

She was, Carl Van Doren said, like one possessed "by some strong and non-human spirit. . . Such a spirit can find itself at home nowhere." Mary Colum noted too that "external life was a sort of puzzle to her." Intensity is her keynote; pride, the wit that is high precision, a thirst for perfection were her hallmarks. "She looked like a white queen of a white country," and that in a sense she was. Louis Untermeyer noted that "she lived in her work with a vehement exclusiveness; she was a fever of creation.... Her frail self was consumed in the incorruptible passion of her art." She possessed to the utmost degree the classic poetic temperament, and unlike most who possess it, it was in her only the outward expression of an inner power.

PRINCIPAL WORKS: *Poetry*—Incidental Numbers, 1912; Nets to Catch the Wind, 1921; Black Armour, 1923; Trivial Breath, 1928; Angels and Earthly Creatures, 1929; Collected Poems, 1932. *Prose*—Jennifer Lorn, 1923; The Venetian Glass Nephew, 1925; The Orphan Angel, 1926; Mr. Hodge and Mr. Hazard, 1928; Collected Prose, 1933.

ABOUT: Clark, E. Innocence Abroad; Hoyt, N. Elinor Wylie: The Portrait of an Unknown Lady; Jordan, L. (ed.). Elinor Wylie; Monroe, H. Poets and Their Art; Sergeant, E. Fire Under the Andes; Untermeyer, L. From Another World; Van Doren, C. Three Worlds; Wylie, E. Collected Poems (see Memoir by W. R. Benét); Bookman February, March 1929; Commonweal January 16, February 13, 1929; Harper's Magazine September 1936; Nation December 26, 1928, June 19, 1929; New Republic February 6, June 5, 1929, September 7, 1932; Poetry February 1929, August 1932; Saturday Review of Literature December 29, 1928, May 25, 1929, May 21, 1932, March 23, 1935; Scholastic September 25, 1939.

WYLIE, IDA ALEXA ROSS (1885-), British novelist who signs her works as I. A. R. Wylie, writes: "I was born in Melbourne, Australia; my father, a barrister-at-law, was a Scotsman. Soon after my birth he went to England, where he proposed resuming his profession. My mother died soon afterwards and from thence onwards I entered on the business of living—almost literally 'on my own.' At the age of ten I was already an experienced traveler, and, thanks to my father's odd ideas on education, was fully capable of managing myself under most usual and a great many unusual circumstances. My father remarried from time to time but I continued to be left to my

own devices. Until I was fourteen I received practically no education. But I had read every book in my father's extensive and liberal library, and I had already begun to write and had no other idea but that I should be an author when my time came.

"At fourteen I was shipped, rather ironically, to a finishing school in Brussels, where I lingered three years and acquired great French fluency with a 'marked English accent.' At seventeen I was sent to Cheltenham Ladies' College to have my education begun, and after two years there was sent to Karlsruhe, Germany, for a Teutonic finishing. There I wrote my first official stories, which were at once accepted for the incredible price of five pounds apiece by English magazines, and from then on I was self-supporting.

"Since my father and I differed violently on every subject under the sun, I cut myself loose, and having no other home, I stayed on in Germany with a friend for eight years, thereby acquiring perfect German and an insight into the German mentality which made me impervious to surprise at anything the Germans have done since. It also enabled me to write my first successful novel, *Toward Morning.*

"I came home to England in 1911, was violently active in the Suffrage Movement, and lived through the war in London, doing some war work in France. In 1917 I came to America for the first time and stayed for a year. After that I became a transatlantic commuter, and am now what is known as an 'alien resident.'

"I have written over two hundred short stories and some fifteen novels. The only ones which I like at all to remember are *Towards Morning, The Silver Virgin, To the Vanquished, Furious Young Man,* and *A Feather in Her Hat.* I have traveled over a great part of Europe and the United States, mostly by motor car. At the ripe age of fifty-five, my favorite recreations are writing, riding, motoring, and dancing. I collect English bull-terriers and have recently purchased a farm in New Jersey [near Princeton] and expect to live and die there, but hope, when the present war is over, to resume my yearly visits to my native land [*sic*: but she means England]."

* * *

Miss Wylie has never married. One of the most interesting facts in her career is that her father, when she was ten, supplied her with money and encouraged her to travel alone all over England and the Continent. Her short stories have been even more popular than her novels, and she is better known in this country than in England.

PRINCIPAL WORKS: The Germans, 1909 (as My German Year, 1910); The Rajah's People, 1910; Rambles in the Black Forest, 1911; In Different Keys, 1911; Dividing Hands, 1911; The Daughter of Brahma, 1912; The Red Mirage, 1913; The Paupers of Portman Square, 1913; Eight Years in Germany, 1914; Happy Endings (short stories) 1915; The Temple of Dawn, 1915; Armchair Stories, 1916; Tristram Sahib, 1916; The Shining Heights, 1917; The Duchess in Pursuit, 1918; All Sorts (short stories) 1919; Towards Morning, 1920; Brodie and the Deep Sea, 1920; The Dark House, 1922; Ancient Fires, 1924; Black Harvest, 1925; The Silver Virgin, 1929; Some Other Beauty (short stories) 1930; The Things We Do, 1932; To the Vanquished, 1934; Furious Young Man, 1935; Prelude to Richard, 1935; A Feather in Her Hat, 1937; The Young in Heart, 1939; My Life With George (autobiography) 1940; Strangers Are Coming, 1941; Keeper of the Flame, 1942.

ABOUT: Wylie, I. A. R. My Life With George; Ladies' Home Journal September 1940; Literary Digest April 7, 1934; Wilson Library Bulletin November 1940.

WYLIE, PHILIP (May 12, 1902-   ), American novelist and short story writer, writes: "My full name is Philip Gordon Wylie. I was born in Beverly, Mass. My father is a Presbyterian minister. My mother, Edna Edwards, was a fiction writer. My brother Max and my late half-brother, Edmund K. Wylie, have both published several books. I was edu-

V. Egginton

cated at the Montclair, N.J., High School, and I attended Princeton University for three years, leaving at the end of that time because I found no satisfaction in its attitude or its curriculum. Since then I have worked as a press agent, as the advertising manager for a publisher, as one of the editors of the *New Yorker,* and as a studio writer in the movies. Before that time I worked on farms, in Manhattan stores, in factories, on ships, and elsewhere. I sold my first 'piece'—a poem—when I was twelve years old. Since that time I have been selling more pieces—at varying intervals. Inasmuch as I had intended to become a doctor, my education was largely scientific, and I have kept up with science, spending considerable time as a visiting observer in the California Institute of Technology, various commercial and foundation laboratories, the Columbia-Presbyterian Medical Center, and elsewhere. I have traveled in most of

Europe and in Russia. I speak French and German and some Russian. I have developed a side interest in psychology and psychiatry and written some technical and some lay papers upon those subjects. My hobbies, indulged in sporadically, are rather varied: playing a piano-accordion, oil-painting, fishing, swimming, diving, canoeing, exploring and making maps, carpentry, gardening, bridge, golf, abstract mathematics. For some time I conducted a newspaper column for a syndicate. Several of my books were written in collaboration with Edwin Balmer, the editor of *Redbook Magazine,* and several were anonymous or written under a pseudonym. At present and for the past three years I have been engaged in writing a long 'serious' novel. I have, as a reviewer once said of me, 'written more pot-boilers than any other two Americans in the same period of time.' I live in Miami Beach, Fla., nine months of the year and wander about in the North in the summer. I have been married twice: in 1928 to Sally Ondeck, one daughter, divorced 1937; in 1938 to Frederica Ballard."

* * *

Mr. Wylie dictates all his stories. Once he wrote a 100,000-word novel in nine days, while crossing the Atlantic.

PRINCIPAL WORKS: Dormitory Ditties, 1921; Heavy Laden, 1928; Babes and Sucklings, 1929; Gladiator, 1930; Footprint of Cinderella, 1931; The Murder Invisible, 1931; The Savage Gentleman, 1932; Five Fatal Words (with E. Balmer) 1932; When Worlds Collide (with E. Balmer) 1933; Finnley Wren, 1934; After Worlds Collide (with E. Balmer) 1934; The Golden Hoard (with E. Balmer) 1934; The Shield of Silence (with E. Balmer), 1936; An April Afternoon, 1938; The Army Way (with W. Muir) 1940; The Big Ones Get Away (short stories) 1940; Salt Water Daffy (short stories) 1941; The Other Horseman, 1941.

ABOUT: American Magazine March 1935.

WYNDHAM, GEORGE (August 29, 1863-June 8, 1913), English politician and man of letters, was born into an ancient, influential, and artistic family, a great-grandson through his mother (Madeline Eden) of Lord Edward Fitzgerald, the Irish rebel. Wyndham himself had "physical beauty and an un-English gift of eloquence." At Eton he played for his house in the football final, and defeated George Curzon for post of secretary of the Debating Society. Sandhurst was the next

stop. In 1882 he accompanied the Coldstream Guards to Egypt, to campaign against the Arabs, and captured an old Crusader's sword in battle. After a honeymoon in Italy with the widowed Lady Grosvenor, a high Anglican, Wyndham became Balfour's private secretary in Ireland. In 1889, elected to Parliament as Conservative member from Dover, he made his maiden speech following Parnell's Amendment to the Address. Appointed an under-secretary of the War Office in 1899, he defended the Ministry against the early disasters of the Boer War. "The Imperial Yeomanry is my child," he declared. Becoming chief Secretary for Ireland in 1900, he fathered three years later the Wyndham Land Act, providing better terms for both landlord and tenant, through both houses of Parliament. The Unionist Party forced his resignation in 1905. John Redmond and members of the Irish Party attended Wyndham's memorial service at Westminster, after his death in Paris at fifty. He had inherited "Clouds," a home in Wiltshire, from his father, Percy Scawen Wyndham, some years before. He is buried at East Knoyle.

Wyndham, as a writer, declared his intention of speaking in "chiseled sentences." He spent several Whitsuntide holidays at Chartres, and entertained G. K. Chesterton and Professor Mahaffy. W. E. Henley dedicated a book to him; Wilfred Blunt was his cousin. Wyndham was a bold rider to hounds, a letter-writer of the first rank; he abhorred blatant women, pompous bores, and the foolish interrupter.

PRINCIPAL WORKS: Introduction to North's Plutarch (ed.) 1895; Shakespeare's Poems, 1898; Ronsard and La Pléiade, 1906; Essays in Romantic Literature, 1919.

ABOUT: Blunt, W. My Diaries; Chesterton, G. K. Autobiography; Eliot T. S. The Sacred Wood; Gatty, C. G. W. Recognita; Leslie, S. Men Were Different; Mackail, G. W. Life and Letters of George Wyndham; Ward, W. P. Men and Matters; British Review 1913; Cornhill Magazine 1913; Quarterly Review 1913.

YARMOLINSKY, AVRAHM (January 1 [O.S.], 1890-), American biographer and critic, writes: "Avrahm Yarmolinsky was born in the town of Haisin in the Ukraine, Russia, and spent his childhood and youth in Kishinev, Bessarabia. He got his schooling there, and for a while attended the Psychoneurological Institute at St. Peterburg [Leningrad] and the University of Neuchâtel, Switzerland. In 1913 he came to the United States, and subsequently became a citizen of this country. In 1916 he graduated from the College of the City of New York, and received his Ph.D. from Columbia University in 1921. He has acted as instructor in Russian at the evening session of the College of the City of New York since 1917, and was instructor in the Russian language and literature in the extension division of Columbia in 1919-20. Since 1918 he has held the post of Chief of the Slavonic Division of the New York Public Library.

He was married to Babette Deutsch[qv] in 1921, and is the father of two sons.

"In addition to his own books, he has edited Dostoievsky, Pushkin, Gorky, and Count Witte; has edited three anthologies, two of Russian and one of German poetry; and has translated Alexander Blok (in collaboration with Babette Deutsch) and a number of other Russian writers. He has also published several bibliographical monographs, and a number of articles and reviews in literary periodicals.

"In 1939 he received from the Associated Alumni of the College of the City of New York the Townsend Harris Medal for having 'enriched and broadened American culture' by his 'contribution to a highly specialized field of knowledge.'"

* * *

Dr. Yarmolinsky's articles deal with Russian life and letters, and are both critical and historical. He lives in New York with his wife and his children. He was naturalized in 1922.

PRINCIPAL WORKS: Turgeniev: The Man, His Art, and His Age, 1926; The Jews and Other Minor Nationalities Under the Soviets, 1928; Picturesque United States of America: A Memoir on Svinin, 1930; Russian Literature, 1931; Dostoievsky: A Life, 1934; Early Polish Americana, 1937.

"YATES, DORNFORD." See MERCER, C. W.

YEATS, WILLIAM BUTLER (June 13, 1865-January 28, 1939), Irish poet and dramatist, was born in Dublin, the son of John Butler Yeats, once an attorney but later a well known painter. His brother Jack also became a noted artist. The mother's maiden name was Pollexfen, and through her Yeats had Cornish as well as Gaelic blood. The family were Protest-

ants, his paternal grandfather and great-grandfather having been Anglican clergymen. Much of his childhood was spent in London, where he attended the Godolphin School, Hammersmith, but much of it also was passed in County Sligo, the childhood home of both his parents. It was for Sligo that he was always homesick when he was in England. At fifteen he was taken back to Dublin, and went to the Erasmus Smith School there. From 1883 to 1886 he studied art, in the family tradition, but soon discovered that he was a poet, not a painter. He fell in love with Ireland and with literature, and the affair lasted his life. Brought up in a Rationalist home, but by nature, as he says, "very religious," he

M. VOS

"made a new religion out of poetic tradition."

His adult life may be divided into three distinct periods. In the first, he lived in London, where he was one of the group of *fin de siècle* poets who dressed the part and posed self-consciously in their ivory towers. With Ernest Rhys he founded the Rhymers' Club, the stars of which were Dowson and Lionel Johnson. He himself had published six volumes by 1895. Rhys described him as he then was: "very pale, exceedingly thin, a raven lock over his forehead, his face so narrow that there was hardly room in it for his luminous black eyes." That is the period of "the Celtic twilight," of symbolism, ornamentation, easy music, and too great facility. His mystical tendencies were in full play: he joined the Theosophists, then the Rosicrucians, and he dabbled in every form of the occult.

He went back to Ireland in 1896 a very much distraught young man. Then the Irish Revolution caught him up, chiefly through the queenly Maud Gonne, who was the great love of his life. He called himself a Socialist, and he was undoubtedly a Fenian. His poems and plays were beautiful, but they were soft. He was beginning to repeat himself.

It was the sturdy common sense of Lady Gregory that saved him. She took him into her home in Coole, rehabilitated his confidence, gave him something to work for. Together they founded the Irish Literary Theatre, which became the Abbey Theatre, and the Irish Academy. His middle period, which lasted to 1910, was increasingly practical. He not only wrote plays for the Abbey Theatre, but he helped produce them. He introduced Synge, whom he had found in Paris and persuaded to go back to Ireland for his inspiration, to the public he was so soon to leave. He was acknowledged as the real leader of the Irish literary renaissance. A change began in his poetry, too; it grew less cloudy, more immediate in its hold on reality. It was the least mystical era of his career.

In 1917 he married Georgie Lees. They had a son and a daughter. He settled in a literal tower on the sea-coast, and gradually the third and final period of his life and work evolved. It had mixed beginnings. From 1922 to 1928 he was a member of the Irish Senate; he employed himself in all the minutiae of politics and was much seen at social gatherings. Meanwhile (it was years later before he acknowledged it), he had discovered that Mrs. Yeats was a medium, who did automatic writing. The mystic always half-awake in Yeats sprang to full activity again. Utterly fearless of opinion and ready to speak his mind under any circumstances, he risked (and incurred) derision by such unexplained statements as that he believed in fairies. In 1923 he received the Nobel Prize for Literature. He had long been a world figure; when he traveled abroad, in Europe or America, he was good copy.

All this tended to obscure the fact that something strange was happening. Yeats himself observed it when he received the Nobel Prize. When he was young, he said, his Muse was old; now he was old but his Muse was young. It was true. He is perhaps the only poet in history whose last work was his best. The taut bareness of the phrases, the stark beauty, the sharpness, the simplicity, the objectivity, he had never achieved in youth came to him in old age. When he died, at seventy-three, it was not ridiculous for the *New Republic* to say that "he died like Shelley at the height of his powers and with half his work unwritten." In those last years he reminds one a little of Hardy, though for Hardy's gnomic compression of thought he substituted utter clarity. He was disillusioned with Ireland and with life, while he loved them both still; he compared himself with Swift, but he never had Swift's bitterness. The disabilities of age he resented fiercely; it may be true, as rumored, that he had had a glandular operation performed which accounted for his remarkable vigor both of mind and body.

Disillusioned he might be, but he was no misanthrope. In spite of the fairies and the Thibetan philosophy and the automatic writing, the first thing that struck one on meeting Yeats was his sanity. He was kindness itself to younger writers, receptive to new ideas, full of good will, tenderness, and even a sly mischief. The one thing that aroused his anger was pretension of any kind—he should have known about it, for as a young man he had been full of it himself. Now he liked real and unassuming people, whether they were illiterate peasants or aristocrats. The thing that most surely roused his anger (and he was a good hater) was "being treated with reverence." He might be an autocrat, but he did not want to be a statue on a pedestal. There were plenty of people who disliked him, from George Moore, for whom he did so much and who rewarded him by calling him "a literary fop," to Robert Speaight, who called him "an interesting mixture of pride and humility, with a warm head and a cold heart," and said he reminded one of a great actor. But when he died it was generally conceded that he was the greatest poet yet produced by Ireland, and the greatest of his time in England. If he had died at forty that would have been far from the case.

"He felt himself," Horace Gregory remarked, "to be a citizen of two worlds, the visible and the unseen, walking as envoy from each into the other. . . . The later figure looms in the image of a twentieth-century Swift over the dwindling shadow of the earlier poet." "He opened to us the soul of our own country like a book," said Desmond Fitzgerald; and he opened a wider country than Ireland. His prose, most of which belongs to his later period, is, said B. Ifor Evans, "as memorable as his verse, and interprets it." And Padraic Colum pointed out how throughout his life he continuously sought and discovered new idioms: "At each period of development he achieved memorable beauty. . . . His philosophy was of being, not of becoming." From the elaborate "embroidery" of his first Pre-Raphaelitish poems to the austerity of his final, posthumously published work, "it is difficult," as Lennox Robinson said, "to think of any other poet writing in English who is so varied and so developed."

The man did not develop so markedly or vary so greatly as did the poet. Yeats at seventy was in many ways Yeats at thirty.

He was not only the dean, he was also the ruler of Irish intellectual life—a kind and generous ruler, who could not abide being deferred to openly, but who reserved the right to make his pronouncements and expect them to be obeyed. He was a direct outgrowth of the young poet who had postured in London when Henley and Dowson and Symons were the current literary idols. He did himself a disservice by opening his more absurd occult beliefs for the public to snicker at—especially in America, where poets are always slightly comic figures. There was about his personality to the last a few shreds of star-dust from the days of the *Yellow Book.* But none of that matters, now that he has obeyed his own injunction to "climb up the narrow winding stair to bed." If his personality did not entirely mature, his mind out-raced itself, and, as Alex Glendinning put it, "the contemporary of Wilde and Dowson lived to become the greatest poet of our time."

His name is pronounced *yates*.

PRINCIPAL WORKS: *Poetry*—Mosada, 1886; The Wanderings of Oisin, 1889; The Wind Among the Reeds, 1899; In the Seven Woods, 1903; Poems Written in Discouragement, 1913; Responsibilities, 1914; The Wild Swans of Coole, 1919; Later Poems, 1922; Seven Poems and a Fragment, 1922; The Tower, 1927; The Winding Stair, 1929; Selected Poems, 1929; Words for Music, Perhaps, 1932; Collected Poems, 1933; A Full Moon in March, 1935; Last Poems and Plays, 1940, *Plays*—The Countess Kathleen, 1802; The Land of Heart's Desire, 1894; The Shadowy Waters, 1900; Cathleen ni Houlihan, 1902; The Pot of Broth, 1902; The Hour Glass and Other Plays, 1903; The King's Threshold, 1904; On Baile's Strand, 1904; Deirdre, 1907; The Green Helmet, 1910; Plays for an Irish Theatre, 1912; Four Plays for Dancers, 1921; Plays in Prose and Verse, 1923; The Cat and the Moon, 1924; Oedipus the King and Oedipus at Colonna (translated) 1928; Collected Plays, 1934; The King of the Great Clock Tower, 1934; The Herne's Egg, 1938. *Essays*—The Celtic Twilight, 1893; The Secret Rose, 1897; The Tables of the Law, 1897; The Adoration of the Magi, 1897; Ideas of Good and Evil, 1903; John Millington Synge and the Ireland of His Time, 1911; Per Amica Silentia Lunae, 1912; The Cutting of an Agate, 1919; Plays and Controversies, 1923; Essays, 1924 and 1937; A Vision, 1925; Letters to the New Island, 1934; Wheels and Butterflies, 1934; The Ten Principal Upanishades (translated, with Shree Purohit) 1937; If I Were Four and Twenty, 1940. *Autobiography* —Reveries Over Childhood and Youth, 1916; The Trembling of the Veil, 1922; Dramatis Personae, 1936 (as Autobiographies, 1938). *Miscellaneous*— John Sherman, 1891; Stories of Red Hanrahan, 1904; Michael Robartes and the Dancer, 1921.

ABOUT: Bax, C. Florence Farr, Bernard Shaw, W. B. Yeats; Hoare, D. M. The Works of Morris and of Yeats...; Hone, J. The Life of W. B. Yeats; Jackson, H. The Eighteen-Nineties; Krans, H. S. William Butler Yeats and the Irish Literary Revival; MacNeice, L. The Poetry of W. B. Yeats; Masefield, J. Some Memories of W. B. Yeats;

Moore, G. Hail and Farewell; More, P. E. Shelburne Essays: First Series; Pollock, J. H. William Butler Yeats; Wellesley, D. Letters on Poetry to Dorothy Weilesley; Atlantic Monthly May 1938; Canadian Bookman June 1939; Commonweal May 18, 1934, March 31, 1939; Fortnightly July 1935, March 1939; Living Age January 1939; Nation February 4, 1939, February 25, 1939; New Republic December 13, 1933, September 18, 1935, September 21, 1938, February 8, 1939, June 24, 1940; Nineteenth Century March 1939; Poetry February 1936, November 1938, September 1939; Saturday Review of Literature December 16, 1933, February 4, 1939, February 25, 1939; Theatre Arts Monthly March 1939, November 1939; Virginia Quarterly Review January 1939.

*YEATS-BROWN, FRANCIS CHARLES CLAYPON (August 15, 1886-   ), English soldier, journalist, and mystic, was born in Genoa, Italy, the third son of the late Montagu Yeats-Brown, British Consul-General in Genoa, and Agnes Matilda (Bellingham) Yeats-Brown. His public school was Harrow-on-the-Hill, and young Yeats-Brown  went from there to the Royal Military College at Sandhurst. At twenty he was attached as second lieutenant to his brother's regiment at Bareilly, India, the King's Royal Rifle Corps, and next year, 1907, was posted to the 17th Cavalry of the Indian Army, becoming adjutant in 1913. He was in England on leave when the First World War broke out; served in France with the 5th Royal Irish Lancers; and in the Mesopotamian Flight of the Royal Flying Corps, winning the Distinguished Flying Cross and mention in dispatches (twice). In November 1915 he fell into the hands of the Turks, escaping from prison three years later after two unsuccessful attempts. On the third occasion he dyed his moustache black and pulled a fez over his dyed hair.

Yeats-Brown was retired from the Army on pension in 1925; in 1926-28 he was an assistant editor of the *Spectator,* contributing to it numerous articles which formed the basis of what Leonard Bacon calls his "brilliant and modest" autobiography, *Bengal Lancer,* which as *The Lives of a Bengal Lancer* became a best-seller in the United States in 1930. Hollywood bought the title for a spectacular film which was a brilliant *mélange* of courage, cowardice, scenes of torture and other sequences developing the majesty of the British *Raj* in India. *Eu-*

* Died December 19, 1944.

ropean Jungle (1939) was a collection of Yeats-Brown's lucidly written magazine articles, in which he warned his readers of the coming of the Second World War and showed a distinct pro-Franco bias in his papers on Spain; some critics found his entire thesis alarmingly fascistic in implication.

He has traveled in Europe, Canada, every province of India and in the United States, where he lectured on his Indian experiences, and the practice of Yoga and other elements of Indian mysticism. He has been known to conclude a lecture with a demonstration of Yoga which necessitated his standing on his head for a protracted period. Yeats-Brown returned to India after an absence of fifteen years "to solve not her problems but his own." After his *guru* or spiritual preceptor had died he felt "a gap in heart and mind." In 1938 he married Olga, the widow of Denzil Phillips, late R. A. F., and daughter of Colonel Apollon Zoueff. He is a member of the Bath Club, although "for me such places are torture: I see dim acquaintances, wonder whether I should greet them, talk clumsily, run away. I have no roots in London. My fellow-writers frighten me."

PRINCIPAL WORKS: Bengal Lancer (U.S. title: Lives of a Bengal Lancer) 1930; Golden Horn, 1932; Dogs of War! 1934; Lancer at Large, 1936; Yoga Explained, 1937; European Jungle, 1939; The Army's First Fifteen Months of the War, 1941; Pageant of India, 1942.

ABOUT: Yeats-Brown, F. C. C. Bengal Lancer, Lancer at Large; Wilson Library Bulletin April 1937.

YEZIERSKA, ANZIA (1885-), Russian American novelist and short story writer, was born in a mud hut in Sukovoly, Russia,

Underwood

the daughter of Bernard Yezierska, a scholar and dreamer, and Pearl Yezierska. The family came to New York in 1901, where Anzia sewed buttons on shirts in a Delancey Street sweatshop; cooked in a family of richer immigrant Jews who paid her no wages; and eventually found better-paid work in a factory, whereupon she removed her family from the Ghetto. She became a naturalized citizen in 1912. Attending a night school to perfect her English, she rebelled against reading the *De Coverley Papers* and demanded more idiomatic instruction. Miss Yezierska— she is unmarried—was a vocal and belli-

gerent immigrant writer, less meek and receptive than Mary Antin. She began to write short stories of Ghetto life in 1918. Edward J. O'Brien called "The Fat of the Land" the best short story of 1919. Collected in *Hungry Hearts* (1920), the stories had a cordial critical reception but earned small royalties. Hollywood paid $10,000 for the screen rights, however, and Miss Yezierska went to the Coast for a brief taste of luxury, which made her feel uncomfortable. Mingling on equal terms with Rupert Hughes, Gertrude Atherton, and Alice Duer Miller left her gratified but awestruck. *All I Could Never Be* (1932), her last published volume, is a semi-autobiographical novel which the *Christian Science Monitor* called "less naïve, more self-conscious, and more lenient in her judgment of those who fail to understand her people." Of *Hungry Hearts*, "ten stories of imaginative squalor," Carl Van Doren remarked: "When she leaves the East Side neighborhood in which her art is native she never quite has the look of reality."

PRINCIPAL WORKS: Hungry Hearts, 1920; Salome of the Tenements, 1922; Children of Loneliness, 1923; Bread Givers, 1925; Arrogant Beggar, 1927; All I Could Never Be, 1932.

ABOUT: Cooper, A. P. Authors and Others; Bookman November 1923; Century Magazine November 1920; Good Housekeeping June 1920; Literary Digest September 8, 1923, October 24, 1925; Scribner's Magazine February 1922.

YONGE, CHARLOTTE MARY. See "BRITISH AUTHORS OF THE 19TH CENTURY"

YOUNG, ELLA (December 26, 1865-), Irish poet and mythologist, writes: "I was born in the little village of Fenagh, County Antrim. The Youngs have held Antrim land since early in the seventeenth century. I came away as a small child and lived in Southern Ireland until I left for America.

"From childhood I heard tales of ghosts, banshees, haunted castles, mischievous and friendly sprites, snatches of ballads, and political arguments. I thought national heroes belonged to foreign countries only, and felt cheated. My sisters and I knew Shakespeare, Milton, and Bunyan at an early age. Later came Plato and the Norse sagas; also, sandwiched in a few lines of Irish history, I surprised the name of Cuchulain. It was not until I came to Dublin and met Standish O'Grady, A.E., and Kuno Meyer that I realized what a heritage waited for me in Celtic literature. I read every translation I could get, learned Irish, and betook myself to Gaelic Ireland where, by turf fires, I could hear poems of the Fianna recited by folk who had heard the faery music and had danced in faery circles. From such folk I gathered the tales of the Gobhan Saor which later I put together in *The Wonder-Smith and His Son.*

"A thing that counted greatly in my life was the Rising in Ireland—this is not the place to write of it!

"I came to America in 1925, as a lecturer, landing at New York. Later, in California, I held the Phelan Memorial Lectureship on Celtic Mythology and Literature in the University of California. I am living now near the great dunes at Oceano where I can hear the sound of the sea. I believe that the two books which I wrote in California, *The Tangle-Coated Horse* and *The Unicorn With Silver Shoes*, have gained something from the rhythm of the Pacific and the weird beauty of the Mojave Desert.

"*Celtic Wonder Tales* embodies the Celtic Myth of Creation, and in it I have used some of the most splendid material known to the old Saga makers. What books I have written, are written for children (and grown-ups) who hunger as I did for a lost inheritance, who are fain to catch a glimpse of the Fortunate Islands; to learn that golden apples still grow in the Garden of the Hesperides; and that Angus moves yet in a cloud of bird-wings, immortally young, though Tara is ruined."

* * *

Miss Young has lectured at many American colleges, as well as at Trinity College in Dublin and before the Irish Literary Society. She came to America primarily because nearly all her friends were killed in the Irish Revolution. When in 1931 she attempted to secure a permanent American visa, a preposterous and fortunately frustrated attempt was made to exclude her on the ground that because of her age she might become a public charge! She has never married, and lives a withdrawn and isolated life, in spite of her many and warm friends among American writers and scholars. She lives half in a world of fantasy, and in her appearance and manner seems sometimes herself almost one of the strange creatures of faery of whom she writes.

PRINCIPAL WORKS: *Poetry*—Poems, 1906; The Rose of Heaven, 1920; To the Little Princess, 1930; Marzilian and Other Poems, 1930. *Prose*—The Coming of Lugh, 1909; Celtic Wonder Tales, 1910; The Weird of Fionavar, 1922; The Wonder-Smith and His Son, 1925; The Tangle-Coated Horse, 1929; The Unicorn With Silver Shoes, 1932.

ABOUT: Colum, P. Ella Young; Kunitz, S. J. & Haycraft, H. (eds.). The Junior Book of Authors; Horn Book May 1939; Nation April 15, 1931; Publishers' Weekly April 18, 1931; Saturday Review of Literature March 14, 1931.

*YOUNG, EMILY HILDA (1880-), English novelist, is the daughter of William Michael Young and Frances Jane Young. She was born in Northumberland, but in 1902, after her marriage to J. A. H. Daniell, a Bristol solicitor, went to that city to live. It is the setting of her first American success, *William.* Mr. Daniell enlisted for service in the First World  War, though well past the usual service age, and was killed shortly before the Armistice. His wife worked as a groom in stables during the war. In 1918 she went to London. She had by then published three novels as E. H. Young. The name and the masculine assurance of her style caused Gerald Gould in the *Saturday Review,* in England, and two reviewers in American periodicals, to refer unquestioningly to "Mr. Young" as the author. Mrs. Daniell spent her summer vacations rock-climbing in Wales, Switzerland, and the Dolomites, mapping out many new trails hitherto accessible only to skilled men rock-climbers. She goes to no public dinners, knows no celebrities, and does not care for the society of "lions." Her club is the Forum. "E. H. Young" has rather grim features, penetrating eyes, and a mouth set in a long, meditative curve. She is described as "a hardy woman who has worked with her hands." A collected edition of her works was issued in 1931. Called "the apostle of quiet people," E. H. Young, in *William,* described an imperturbable family man who defends the conduct of one of his daughters who left the husband she had ceased to love, to elope with another man; and, in *Miss Mole,* told of the tribulations of a housekeeper in the household of a pompous nonconformist minister. *Miss Mole* won the James Tait Black Memorial Prize. *William* was reissued in 1941 as the

* Died August 8, 1949.

first choice of the Readers Club, in the United States.

The *Springfield Republican* has commented on the rarity and freshness of this novelist's spirit and workmanship. "Her work has the defects of its virtues," in the opinion of Amy Loveman, "for it is always sensitive and subtle; it is rarely virile or moving." "The story of the modest little suburban housewife who happens to sit next to me in the railway carriage interests me more than famous people," admits Mrs. Daniell. "The little housewife's accounts of her sister's matrimonial difficulties or the story of her husband's losing his place in an office, are more real to me than the affairs of the political, literary, art, or social world." She prefers "a good old rattling melodrama" to a problem play.

PRINCIPAL WORKS: A Corn of Wheat, 1910; Yonder, 1912; Moor Fires, 1916; The Bridge Dividing (reissued in 1927 as The Misses Mallett) 1922; William, 1925; The Vicar's Daughter, 1928; Miss Mole 1930; Jenny Wren, 1932; The Curate's Wife, 1934; Celia, 1938; Caravan Island, 1940; River Holiday, 1942.

ABOUT: Mais, S. P. B. Some Modern Authors; Reader March 1941.

*YOUNG, FRANCIS BRETT (1884-),

English novelist, was born at Hales Owen, Worcestershire, the son of T. Brett Young, M.D. His mother, who died when the boy was fourteen, also came of a medical family. He was educated at Epsom College, Surrey, and then received his medical degree at the University of Birmingham. He started practice at Brixham, Surrey, in 1907, and remained there until the First World War, except for two years as a ship's surgeon on a vessel traveling to and from Japan. In 1908 he married Jessie Hankinson, a singer. He has often been her accompanist, and has also composed, having set many of Robert Bridges' songs to music. During the First World War Young was with the Royal Army Medical Corps in East Africa. In 1918 he was invalided out as 60 per cent disabled from malaria. He then had the rank of major. He was no longer able to practice medicine, and he and his wife went to Capri, where they lived until 1929, in a house built for them in exchange for translating the architect's stories from Italian! In 1922 they visited South Africa, and he has also made two trips to the United States. The Youngs returned to England in 1932, settling first in the Lake District. Since 1933 they have lived near Pershore, in Worcestershire.

Although Young had announced himself as a poet at the age of five, it was actually many years before his work became at all well known. In fact, his real celebrity dates from the award of the James Tait Black Memorial Prize, in 1927, to *Portrait of Claire* (*Love Is Enough*). Since then his public both in England and in America has grown constantly wider. Though for many years he has published only prose, he says he "would still like to write an epic." His own creed as a novelist he expresses by saying: "My task is, by the power of the written word, to make you hear, to make you feel— . . . before all, to make you see."

Young's first novel, *Undergrowth*, written with his brother, was strongly reminiscent of Arthur Machen. With his second, *Deep Sea*, he found his own vein. The sea, to a lesser extent the war, and above all the medical world are his particular fields. Although he is not now ranked among the important novelists, his early work was highly praised. J. C. Squire said of him: "He is a poet with a sense of fact, a feeling for history, and an interest in character. . . . He has written twenty good novels in which poet, physician, romancer, and realist have collaborated. Let him now attempt an integration and let himself go."

Earlier still John Masefield called him "the most gifted, most interesting, and most beautiful of mind among the younger men writing English." And Compton Mackenzie praised his "pen for landscape, . . . his industry and steady progress, versatility and romantic outlook, technical accomplishment and a kind of graceful modesty which is the very essence of his individuality as a writer." He placed his finger, however, on Young's pitfall, which is a kind of softness and sentimentality which gives him "a lack of relish for villainy" and sometimes intrudes as a Pollyanna note which weakens the robustness of his work. He is often long-winded and sometimes platitudinous; nevertheless his leisurely novels possess a certain quiet charm.

A tall, long-headed man with thinning fair hair, a clipped moustache, and spectacles, Young recalls both the physician and the army officer in appearance. He leads a quiet, retired life, with music still his chief pleasure, travel his recreation, and his pipe and his dog his invariable companions.

---

* Died March 28, 1954.

PRINCIPAL WORKS: Undergrowth (with Eric Brett Young) 1913; Robert Bridges: A Critical Study, 1913; Deep Sea, 1914; The Dark Tower, 1914; The Iron Age, 1916; Five Degrees South (poems) 1917; The Crescent Moon, 1918; Marching on Tanga (non-fiction) 1918; The Young Physician, 1919; Poems: 1916-18, 1919; Captain Swing (play, with W. E. Stirling) 1919; The Tragic Bride, 1920; The Black Diamond, 1921; The Red Knight, 1921; Pilgrim's Rest, 1922; Cold Harbour, 1924; Woodsmoke, 1924; Sea Horses, 1925; Love Is Enough (in England: Portrait of Claire) 1927; The Key of Life, 1928; My Brother Jonathan, 1928; The Furnace (play) 1928; Black Roses, 1929; The Redlakes (in England: Jim Redlake) 1930; Mr. and Mrs. Pennington, 1931; The House Under the Water, 1932; The Cage Bird and Other Stories, 1933; This Little World, 1934; White Ladies, 1935; The Forest, 1936; Portrait of a Village, 1937; Dr. Bradley Remembers, 1938; The City of Gold, 1939; Cotswold Honey (in England: Ship's Surgeon's Tales and Other Stories) 1940; The Man About the House, 1942.

ABOUT: Twitchett, E. G. Francis Brett Young; Bookman August 1920; Bookseller July 4, 1934; London Mercury August 1924; Saturday Review of Literature October 16, 30, 1937; World Today December 1928.

YOUNG, STARK (October 11, 1881-), American novelist and dramatic critic, was born in Como, Miss., the son of Alfred Alexander

P. & A.

Young and Mary (Stark) Young. By chance (typhoid closed the seminary he was attending, and there was nowhere else to send him), he entered the University of Mississippi at fourteen; however, he did not secure his B.A. until 1901, when he was twenty. He then spent a year at Columbia, taking an M.A. in English in 1902.

He was instructor in English at the University of Mississippi from 1904 to 1907, first instructor in English literature and then professor of general literature at the University of Texas from 1907 to 1915, and professor of English at Amherst College from 1915 to 1921. He then abandoned teaching for journalism, being on the editorial staff of the *New Republic* from 1921 to 1924, and at the same time associate editor of *Theatre Arts Monthly*, and being dramatic critic of the New York *Times* in 1924 and 1925. He then returned to the *New Republic*, and is still its drama editor. He is unmarried, and lives in New York. In 1931 he went to Italy to lecture on the Westinghouse Foundation, and was decorated with the Order of the Crown of Italy. Until the

war he visited Italy almost every year. He has translated Chekhov's *The Sea Gull* and *Three Sisters.*

He has been loosely affiliated with the so-called Southern Agrarian group (Herbert Agar, Allen Tate, etc.), and contributed to their symposium, *I'll Take My Stand* (1930). His recreation is painting, and he has held exhibitions of his art work. Tall, loose-jointed, and almost bald, with a smooth-shaven quizzical face, Mr. Young is almost a "typical New York bachelor" in appearance, but he has never lost his soft Mississippi accent.

He is anything but a "professional Southerner," however, and has been extremely critical at times of his native section. Nevertheless, his novel, *So Red the Rose,* has been hailed as one of the best pictures of the South in recent fiction; Ellen Glasgow, who knows the South so intimately, was particularly enthusiastic about it. In contrast to the rather tortuous style of his dramatic criticisms, it is written in crisp, straightforward prose. In general this is true of his other novels and stories as well. Mr. Young began authorship as a poet, and he has remained keenly interested in poetry and holds what may be called "advanced" artistic views on it and on literature as a whole. His wide acquaintance with general literature saves him from the provincialism of outlook which sometimes overtakes specialized critics in such fields as music, painting, and the drama. In his earlier years he wrote a good many plays of his own, long and short, in prose and verse. *The Saint* was produced by the Provincetown Players in 1924, and *The Colonnade* by the London Stage Society in 1926. He has also had practical experience as a theatrical director, having directed Lenormand's *The Failures* for the Theatre Guild and O'Neill's *Welded* for a private producer.

PRINCIPAL WORKS: The Blind Man at the Window (poems) 1906; Guinevere (verse play) 1906; Six One-Act Plays, 1911; Three Plays, 1919; The Flower in Drama, 1923; The Three Fountains, 1924; Two Plays for Children, 1926; Glamour, 1926; Heaven Trees (novel) 1926; The Theatre, 1927; The Torches Flare (novel) 1927; River House (novel) 1929; The Street of the Islands (short stories) 1930; So Red the Rose (novel) 1934; Feliciana (short stories) 1935; A Southern Treasury of Art and Literature (ed.) 1937.

ABOUT: Publishers' Weekly March 16, 1935; Scholastic January 5, 1935.

YUTANG, LIN. See LIN YU-TANG

ZAMACOIS, EDUARDO (February 17, 187?-), Spanish novelist and dramatist, was born in Pinar del Río, Cuba. His full

name is Eduardo de Zamacois y Quintana. A badly written entry in the register of his birth makes the date of that event rather uncertain. The *Enciclopedia Universal Ilustrada* (generally known as *Espasa-Calpe*) puts it at 1876. Zamacois himself prefers 1878; he finds it *simpático*. His father, a musician, moved the family to Brussels when the boy was three. From five to nine he lived in Paris, learning to speak French fluently, and from ten to fifteen studied at Seville. He received a bachelor's degree from the Universidad Central, Madrid, and studied medicine for four years.

Zamacois' first novel, *La Enferma,* was published when he was eighteen; he was to write thirty more. *Punto-Negro,* a romantic story of his first love, established him as an important writer. After some difficult years in Madrid and Paris, he founded a weekly, *Vida Galante,* in Barcelona, which won great popularity. At this period of intense literary activity he wrote *El Seductor, Sobre el Abismo, Duelo á Muerte, Incesto, Memorias de Una Courtesana,* and other erotic romances. After another trip to Paris, Zamacois established *El Cuento Semanal* in Madrid, in 1907, and followed it with another periodical, *Los Contemporaneos.* In 1910 he visited the United States and South America; in 1914 was on the western front as war correspondent for *La Tribuna* of Madrid, and in 1916 toured the United States and the important republics and cities south to Cape Horn, giving lectures, illustrated with moving pictures, on Spanish manners, customs, and literature. *La Ola de Plomo* and *A Cuchillo* recount his experiences during the First World War, in France, Switzerland, and Italy. A successful dramatist, Zamacois has written *Nochebuena, El Pasado, Vuelve,* and *Frio,* (grouped together as "Teatro Galante"), *Los Reyes Pasan,* and half a dozen others. His lecture tours also took him to Europe and Northern Africa. Time and experience gave his work in fiction more depth and breadth. *El Otro,* and *El Misterio de Un Hombre Pequeñito* are concerned with death, and, negatively, with religion; *Años de Miseria y de Risa* and *La*

Opinion Ajena show a more complete realization of the agony and irony of human life.

Of *Roots,* the first novel by Zamacois to be translated into English, Vincent McHugh remarked that "no book of brawnier stature has come out of Spain in our generation." In it Manuel Santoyo, naturalist and lover of earth, kills his brother, poetic and visionary. George Allan England has called Zamacois a Spanish Guy de Maupassant and a human dynamo, a revitalizing force in Spanish letters. His style is forceful, masterly, and compelling, although full of neologisms and not always lucid. He is a close relative of the great Spanish painter of exactly the same name, who died, however, before the author's birth. Zamacois was described, twenty years ago, as ruddy, vigorous, with a contagious laugh, and short hair "getting a bit dusty," and his manner was said to display dry humor and a nonchalant, tolerant philosophy of life. He has not figured in news reports of recent turbulent years in Spain.

WORKS AVAILABLE IN ENGLISH TRANSLATION: Their Son and The Necklace, 1919; Roots, 1929.

ABOUT: Zamacois, E. Confesiones de "Un Niño Decente"; Their Son (see Preface by G. A. England).

*ZAMAYATIN, EUGENE IVANOVICH (1884-), Russian novelist, wrote to his translator, Gregory Zilboorg, some twenty years ago, in the following terms: "I see you want my autobiography by all means—but I assure you that you will have to limit yourself only to an outside inspection and get but a glimpse, perhaps, into the dark windows. I seldom ask anybody to enter. As to the outside, you will see a lonely child without playmates; lying on a Turkish divan, hind-side up, reading a book, or under the grand piano while his mother plays Chopin. If you are interested in geography, here it is—Lebelyan, in the most Russian Tambov province about which Tolstoy and Turgenev wrote so much. Chronology?—The end of the 'eighties and early 'nineties, then Voronesh, the *gymnasium pension,* boredom and rabid dogs on Main Street. One of these dogs got me by the leg." Zamyatin told the inspector that he had rabies, and must go to Moscow for vaccination.

"In the *gymnasium* I would get A plus for composition and was not always on good terms with mathematics. Perhaps because of that (sheer stubbornness) I chose the most mathematical career—the ship-building department of the Petrograd Polytech."

In May 1908 he finished his work for a diploma and put the finishing touches on his first short story. It was published in the old *Obrazovanye.* For three subsequent years he wrote about nothing but cutters, steam engines, refitters and "The Theoretical Exploration of the Works of Steam Shovels."

"If I mean anything in Russian Literature, I owe this completely to the Petrograd Secret Service. In 1911 this service exiled me from Petrograd and I was forced to spend two years in a non-populated place in Lachta. There, in the midst of white winter silence and green summers, I wrote my *Provincial.*"

During the First World War, Zamyatin spent two years in England, building ships, visiting the ruins of ancient castles, listening to the banging of German Zeppelin bombs, and writing a short novel, *The Islanders.*

"I regret immensely that I did not witness the Russian Revolution in February and know only the October Revolution, because it was in October, a life preserver around my body and all the lights out, passing German submarines, that I returned to Petrograd."

He taught science once again in the Polytechnic Institute, and edited literary journals. Zamyatin's novel, *We,* called by Max Eastman an inverse Utopia like Aldous Huxley's *Brave New World,* was published in German and English; it posed the problem of the preservation of the independent original creative personality in the midst of great mass movements, and so could not be published at that time in Russia.

Some chapters were printed in a Czech Social Revolutionary journal, *Volia Rossii,* and Soviet officials who disapproved of the novel's theme seized the opportunity to indict Zamyatin and Boris Pilnyak. In the autumn of 1929, the year Moscow began publication of his *Complete Works,* Zamyatin returned from vacation to find himself denounced by the official press as a counterrevolutionist and traitor. His comrades of the Authors' League condemned him in a panic. Zamyatin wrote a dignified letter of protest, and in a short time left for Paris to live. Unlike most *émigrés,* his name does not appear in the *International Who's Who.*

WORKS AVAILABLE IN ENGLISH TRANSLATION: We, 1924.

ABOUT: Eastman, M. Artists in Uniform; Zamyatin, E. I. We (see Preface by G. Zilboorg).

ZANGWILL, ISRAEL (February 14, 1864-August 1, 1926), English novelist and playwright, was born in London, his father being a Russian Jewish refugee who had escaped from Russia in 1848 from a death sentence for a military offense. Israel received his early schooling at Plymouth and Bristol. When he was nine his parents returned to the Spitalfields district of London. The boy studied at the Jews' Free School, becoming a teacher himself at fourteen, and managed to attend London University, receiving his B.A. degree with triple honors. His first literary work, a prize story, appeared in *Society.* For several years he edited a humorous paper, *Ariel. The Big Bow Mystery* (1891), an early and good specimen of the British detective story, was written chiefly as a burlesque of the type, and first appeared as a feuilleton in the *Star. The King of Schnorrers: Grotesques and Fantasies* (a *schnorrer* is a beggar) dealt with The Sephardim, an exclusive sect of the Jewish Community whose ancestors had been expelled from Spain by Ferdinand and I s a b e l l a. *Merely Mary Ann,* a short tale about a maid-of-all-work who inherited a fortune, written to order in three weeks for a library of popular fiction,

was dramatized ten years later by Zangwill and proved more profitable than all his serious books about the Ghetto.

Children of the Ghetto: A Study of a Peculiar People "woke all England to applause" in 1895 with its romance of an alien people and faith whose foundations were strengthened by misrepresentation and persecution. The book caused some pending anti-alien legislation to be dropped. *Dreamers of the Ghetto,* essays on fifteen notable Jews from the sixteenth century to the breakup of the Ghetto in the late nineteenth century, considered, among others, Spinoza, Heine, Lassalle, and Disraeli. *Children of the Ghetto* was dramatized in 1899, and was played in Yiddish and English in New York and elsewhere. Zangwill's career as a dramatist was characterized more by persistence than distinction. *We Moderns,* his last attempt, was produced in New York in 1924, two years before his death. He died at a nursing home at Midhurst, Sussex, after a nervous breakdown. The body was cremated and the ashes placed in the Cemetery of the Liberal Jewish Church.

The Melting Pot, published in 1908 with a dedication to Theodore Roosevelt, was praised for its fiery enthusiasm and condemned in some quarters for its "propaganda." Zangwill was always a champion of unpopular causes, frequently in hot water for the emphatic statement of his opinion. He criticized the United States' policy of restricted immigration; deplored the "lack of poetry" in the Jewish life of New York; championed woman suffrage when it was regarded with disfavor; and was called pro-German because he found some humor in the entente and England's "new found love for France." The League of Nations he regarded as a League of Damnations, condemning small nations to servitude and great nations to hypocrisy. An effective lecturer, he aired his views on platforms in Great Britain, Ireland, Jerusalem, Holland, and the United States, where in 1923 he created a sensation at New York's Carnegie Hall by asserting that Zionism was dead.

In 1903 Zangwill married Edith Ayrton, a daughter of Prof. William Edward Ayrton, F.R.S. They had two sons and a daughter. Their home was at Far End, East Preston, Sussex, and Zangwill also had chambers in London at Hare Court Temple. He had a large, plain face with pleasant and eloquent brown eyes, a "profile ugly as Savonarola's old, immensely, sorrowfully old" (Hamlin Garland's description), stumbled as he walked, and was somewhat uncouth in dress. Organizations of which he was president included the Jewish Territorial Organization for the Settlement of Jews Within the British Empire, the Jewish Historical Society, Jewish Drama League and Playgoers' Club.

S. L. Bensusan called him a "humanist, richly gifted, utterly selfless; outspoken, not diplomatic." He loved work and travel. His later years were overcast by his unfortunate ventures in the theatre and by apprehension over the British general strike. Rabbi Stephen S. Wise of the Free Synagogue, New York, delivered the address at his funeral services in London and spoke also at a memorial meeting held in New York.

PRINCIPAL WORKS: *Novels, Short Stories, etc.*—The Premier and the Painter: A Fantastic Romance (with Louis Cowen), 1888; The Big Bow Mystery, 1891; The Bachelors' Club, 1891; The Old Maids' Club, 1892; The Celibates' Club (combined the previous two) 1892; Children of the Ghetto (3 vols.) 1892-1893; Merely Mary Ann, 1893; Ghetto Tragedies, 1893; The King of Schnorrers, 1894; The Master, 1895; Without Prejudice (essays) 1896; Dreamers of the Ghetto, 1898; They That Walk in Darkness, 1899; The Mantle of Elijah, 1900; Blind Children, The Grey Wig: Stories And Novelettes, 1903; The Melting Pot, 1908; Italian Fantasies (travel) 1910; The War for the World, 1916; Jinny the Carrier, 1919; The Voice of Jerusalem (essays) 1921. *Plays*—The War God, 1911; The Next Religion, 1912; Plaster Saints, 1914; The Cockpit; Romantic Drama in Three Acts, 1921; The Forcing House: or, The Cockpit Continued, 1922; Too Much Money: A Farcial Comedy, 1924; We Moderns: A Post-War Comedy in Three Movements, 1926.

ABOUT: Adcock, A. St. J. Gods of Modern Street; Drinkwater, J. The Outline of Literature; Hind, C. L. More Authors and I; Viereck, G. S. Glimpses of the Great; Williams, H. Modern English Writers; Bookman (London) September 1926; Contemporary Review September 1926; Fortnightly Review April 1927; London Mercury September 1926; Menorah Journal December 1926; Quarterly Review October 1926.

ZARA, LOUIS (August 2, 1910-), American novelist, writes: "Born in New York City. Lived in Buffalo 1914-16. Moved to Chicago and was educated there: Crane Technical High School, Crane Junior College, and University of Chicago. Worked in a candy factory, haberdashery, tried to sell magazine subscriptions and failed; studied in a Hebrew  theological school and resigned; served an apprenticeship in a print shop and have respected printer's ink ever since. Did not stay for a university degree; the depression and biology caught up with me. [Married Bertha Robbins, 1930; three sons.]

"First short story in print in H. L. Mencken's *American Mercury* in 1932. Wrote experimental novelette, which unfortunately destroyed. Did not publish for two years, then appeared in *Story* and *Esquire*. First novel was picked by the *Nation* as one of the Fifty Notables of 1935. Summoned to Hollywood in 1936 for a short turn at scenario writing; collaborated with Willis Cooper. Back in Chicago to write political novel, *Some for the Glory.* Historical novel, *This Land Is Ours,* published in 1940.

"The Chicago Foundation for Literature presented me with its 1940 Prose Award for 'distinctive' work in the field of the novel. Story in Edward J. O'Brien's *Best Short Stories* of 1940. In 1940 we lived in the Ozarks thirteen weeks while I was writing a radio network show in collaboration with George Milburn. Finished my first play in the fall of 1940. Have written some fifty short stories and as many articles; many reprinted, as my essay on 'Intelligent Reading' in *Freshman Prose Annual.* Have also lectured on various topics. Have written a few short poems which I have never shown. My wife is my editorial secretary.

"Interests: typography, travel, nature study. Sports: fishing, bowling, baseball."

* * *

Mr. Zara was born Louis Rosenfeld, but he has adopted Zara for personal as well as literary use. He still lives in Chicago. One commentator spoke of his "flair for selecting epic themes and developing them in the epic manner." His chief defect is long-windedness, but it becomes less apparent with each new novel.

PRINCIPAL WORKS: Blessed Is the Man, 1935; Give Us This Day, 1936; Some for the Glory, 1937; This Land Is Ours, 1940.

ZATURENSKA, MARYA ALEXANDROVNA (September 12, 1902-), American poet, winner of the Pulitzer Prize, writes: "I was born  at Kiev, Russia, and came to the United States at the age of eight. My mother's family came from Poland, and for generations were in the employ of the Radziwill family. My father served in the

Oggiano

Russian army during the Russo-Japanese War and was with the Russian army of occupation in China during the Boxer uprising. I was educated in the New York public schools, had to leave at an early age, graduated from night high school, between odd jobs in a factory, then worked in a bookshop and was a feature writer for a New York newspaper for a year, and I received a scholarship in 1922 to Valparaiso University, studied there for a year, and then in 1923 went to Wisconsin University on a Zona Gale Scholarship. Served on the literary magazine at Wisconsin; my previous co-editors had been Horace Gregory, Kenneth Fearing, Marquis W. Childs, Robert S. Allen, and Margery Latimer. I specialized in library school work and graduated from the Wisconsin Library School in 1925. I married Horace Gregory, the poet and critic, in 1925. He teaches now at Sarah Lawrence College, Bronxville, and we are collaborating on a literary history.

"I wrote poetry ever since I can remember, and as a child was always particularly moved by Polish and Russian folk-songs and music. I composed poems to these tunes before I could read or write. My first printed poems appeared when I was in my teens, in *Poetry* and elsewhere. It was not till my first book appeared (1934) that I felt I was beginning to find myself. This book I have always thought of as a series of finger-exercises; it was a sort of introduction to my second book, which received the Pulitzer Poet-

ry Award in 1938. I am at work on a new book of poems which I hope will show as great advance over my second book as the second was over the first. I write little and correct and rewrite a great deal.

"My favorite poets are Landor, Hardy, Yeats in English. I like some of the French romantics like Lamartine and de Vigny and Baudelaire. I think Russian poetry has always been second-rate. Among the newer poets I like Dylan Thomas and my friend Ruth Pitter. Among younger Americans I like best Horace Gregory, Richard Eberhardt, and Muriel Rukeyser in her shorter non-political poems. I like Marianne Moore, T. S. Eliot (particularly *Ash Wednesday* and *Murder in the Cathedral*), and Wallace Stevens.

"My husband and I have traveled a number of times in England and Ireland, and I have developed a great admiration, affection, and respect for the English people, whose tradition of justice, tolerance, and fair play still means a great deal to the future of democracy. Last but not least in importance to me are my son and daughter. Aside from poetry my chief interest lies in music."

* * *

Marshall Schacht remarked that Miss Zaturenska's poetry is "buoyed up on a sea of sources, . . . but she is always the individual swimmer." She received the John Reed Memorial Prize from *Poetry* in 1924, and the Guarantors' Prize in 1936.

PRINCIPAL WORKS: Threshold and Hearth, 1934; Cold Morning Sky, 1938; Listening Landscape, 1941.

ABOUT: Poetry February 1935, February 1938; Saturday Review of Literature May 7, 1938, April 5, 1941.

ZEROMSKI, STEFAN (November 14, 1864-November 20, 1925), Polish novelist, dramatist, and poet, was born in Strawczyn, Province of Kielce, of a noble family impoverished by the anti-Russian revolt of 1863. He attended the *gymnasium* in Kielce and for a short time the University of Warsaw, but poverty compelled him to end his schooling and find work as a teacher. He  was always frail, and apparently had a tubercular tendency. In his school days he began active but secret work against the Czarist government, and as a result he was several times imprisoned and finally exiled after the abortive revolution of 1905. Even his first visit to France, in 1892, seems, though ostensibly for his health, to have been made also to escape imprisonment.

It was at this time that he began to publish, his first work appearing under the pseudonym of "Maurycy Zych." He remained abroad until 1896, friends having secured for him the post of librarian at the National Museum of Polish immigrants at Rapperswil, Switzerland. From 1897 to 1904 he was librarian of the Zamojski Library in Warsaw. He seems never to have married.

Zeromski remained in exile, first in Italy, then in France, until the First World War. He had meanwhile become one of the best known of Polish authors, and was immensely popular in his own country. After the establishment of the Polish Republic, honors were heaped upon him. He was president of the Polish branch of the P.E.N. Club, and in 1925 he was prominently mentioned for the Nobel Prize in literature. The extreme nationalism of his writings caused his failure to receive the award, and the Polish Ministry of Education thereupon gave him a special prize for the best literary work of the preceding three years, the specific book in question being his *Wiatz od Morza* (*Wind From the Sea*). In his final years he was accused of having Communist sympathies because of the pro-Soviet tone of his last novel, *Przedwioshie* (*The Time Before Spring*). That he had not lost his outstanding position in Poland, however, was indicated by the fact that when he died suddenly, at just sixty-one, he was given a state funeral, paid for by the government and attended by the president, his cabinet, the Senate, and the Diet. He was temporarily interred in the Protestant Cemetery at Warsaw (he was an intimate friend of Pilsudski, and like him a convert to Protestantism), and the country later built a mausoleum for his remains at his favorite summer resort, Naleczow, Province of Lublin.

A grim-faced man with high forehead, thick eyebrows, and clipped moustache, Zeromski's appearance was true to his nature. Although in his youth he was a member of the Social Revolutionary Party, intense nationalism was his outstanding characteristic. The tragedy of Poland was his principal theme, and bitter pessimism was his keynote. It was only after what he never knew to be the ephemeral triumph of his native land that a tone of rejoicing crept into any of his work. His historical novels—best

known of which was *Popioly* (*Ashes*), dealing with the Napoleonic Wars—continued his single theme. As Ramon Dyboski remarked, "a strong sentiment of nationality permeates with a peculiar exaltation even his stories of unbridled human passion." He was very much akin to Henryk Sienkewicz, and like him wrote unashamed melodrama, though it is in his plays that this is most apparent. Clifton Fadiman said of him: "He had passion and sincerity and a national feeling that occasionally gives his incredible prose a quality of theatrical grandeur. But he is a perfect laboratory specimen of the completely uncritical historical novelist."

Though Zeromski has been translated into almost all European languages, only one of his novels has appeared in English; one of his short stories is in *More Tales by Polish Authors* (1916); and a collection of his pieces appeared in 1906. He was the official translator of Joseph Conrad into Polish, and wrote the introduction to the standard Polish edition. Besides the works mentioned, and numerous plays, he is best known in Poland for the epic, *Dzieje Grzechu* (*Lay of the Leader*), and for the novels, *The Homeless, Walter the Goodly, Aryman Takes Revenge, The Story of Sin,* and the autobiographical trilogy, *The Fight With Satan,* including *The Conversion of Judas, The Blizzard,* and *Charitas.*

Princess Lubomirska remarked that "Zeromski's impressionability with regard to all around him, nature as well as people, is extraordinary; he has a fiery, passionate imagination, and a creativeness of elemental spontaneity and force." But she failed to note what was pointed out by the Italian critic, Giovanni Maver: "His works present almost incongruous strains... of the lyric poet and the publicist,.. [of] joyous attachment to all forms of life and a macabre need to steep himself heart and soul in the horrors of death."

WORKS AVAILABLE IN ENGLISH: The Ravens and Crows Are Picking Us to Pieces (short stories) 1906; Ashes, 1928.

ABOUT: Dyboski, R. Modern Polish Literature; Bookman October 1925, January 1929; Living Age January 30, 1926; Revue Politique et Littéraire December 5, 1925.

ZINSSER, HANS (November 17, 1878-September 4, 1940), American bacteriologist and writer, was born in New York City, the son of August Zinsser, a German chemist, and Marie Theresia (Schmidt) Zinsser, who came from a convent in the Black Forest to America to be married. August Zinsser was an agnostic whose prophet was Goethe; he carried black-bound editions of *Faust* in the pocket of every suit. Hans Zinsser went abroad twice in his childhood, and had a brief schooling in

Wiesbaden. He was tutored at home until eleven, and then sent to Julius Sachs' school in New York. At Columbia, George Edward Woodberry gave young Zinsser "vague yearnings for aesthetic abstractions," and Edmund B. Wilson and Bashford Dean a more solid substratum of scientific ambition.

Bachrach

Always a good horseman, Zinsser enlisted in Squadron A, but the Spanish-American War was over before he could get into action. He then went to Texas to dig fossils on the Staked Plain and read the Bible thoroughly. In 1903 he received a master's degree from Columbia, and, more important, his M.D. from the College of Physicians and Surgeons. As interne attached to the Roosevelt Hospital from 1903 to 1905, he rode an ambulance in the old Hell's Kitchen district, and encountered New York's poverty, disease, and crime at first hand. In 1905 he married Ruby Handforth Kunz; they had a son and a daughter.

From 1907 to 1910 Zinsser was instructor in bacteriology and hygiene at Columbia Medical School, and for the next three years associate professor of bacteriology at Stanford University, Calif., returning to Columbia as full professor in 1913 to stay for ten years. In the spring of 1915 he went to Serbia with the Red Cross Typhus Commission; and in the summer of 1916 headed a commission to investigate a paratyphoid epidemic at Camp Whitman, N.Y. As colonel in the Medical Corps he had charge of laboratories to protect the health of American soldiers, receiving the Distinguished Service Medal and writing a standard manual for the sanitation of a field army. In 1923 Zinsser was invited by the League of Nations to go to Russia as Sanitary Commissioner on cholera, finding real if unexpected zeal in the apparently "cynical" Soviet chiefs. In 1931 he set out to Mexico to study a prison epidemic of typhus.

In the words of William Lyon Phelps, conferring an honorary degree of D. Sc. from Yale in 1939, the year Zinsser also received one from Harvard (he had others, from Columbia [1929], Western Reserve

and Lehigh): "He made an aggressive attack on the dreaded typhus fever, a scourge always accompanying war and famine. He isolated and manipulated the germ of typhus called Rickettsia, and from it succeeded in preparing a protective vaccine. By careful experiments, often at personal risk, he has done more than any other investigator to clarify the various forms of these protean diseases, recognizing them in their deceptive disguises. [He] gave some of the results of his studies, in popular language, through his exciting book, *Rats, Lice, and History*. He is one of the foremost laboratory scientists, and in the midst of his war against disease he has made friends everywhere in the world; his chronic courage is salted with humor; for although he is a medical philosopher, we may say of him what Edwards said to Johnson, 'cheerfulness is always breaking in.'" Zinsser was professor of bacteriology and immunity at the Harvard Medical School, Boston, where he spent the last eighteen years of his life, from 1923 until his death at the Memorial Hospital in New York from leukemia at sixty-one.

A few months before his death, the Book-of-the-Month Club sent its subscribers Zinsser's autobiography, written partly in the third person, *As I Remember Him: The Biography of R.S.*, the R.S. signifying the scientist's "Romantic Self." Few if any readers realized that the thoughtful last chapter, with its calm acceptance of approaching death, applied to the writer himself. He had known for a year that he had an incurable disease of the blood. Zinsser took particular pride in his writing. "It would have pleased Dr. Zinsser very much, I feel," wrote his secretary to the editors of this book, "to be included in a dictionary of writers for reasons not at all based on his medical achievements."

Clifton Fadiman called *As I Remember Him*, "no classic, but full of good things." It has "the tone of a humanist scholar, touched slightly with the crotchets of an eighteenth century gentleman." *Time* described Zinsser as an "affectionate, voluble, energetic, terrier-like man."

Spring, Summer and Autumn, a volume of Zinsser's poems, appeared posthumously.

PRINCIPAL WORKS: Text-Book of Bacteriology, 1911; Infection and Resistance, 1914; Rats, Lice, and History, 1935; As I Remember Him: The Biography of R. S. (autobiography) 1940; Spring, Summer and Autumn, 1942.

ABOUT: Zinsser, H. As I Remember Him; Book-of-the-Month Club News June 1940; New York Herald Tribune September 5, 1940; New York Times September 5, 1940; Time September 16, 1940; Wilson Library Bulletin September 1940.

ZUCKMAYER, KARL (or CARL) (December 27, 1896-), German playwright, novelist, and poet writes (in English): "Carl Zuckmayer was born in Nackenheim-am-Rhein, where his father was a manufacturer. He attended the high school [*gymnasium*] in Mainz until the outbreak of war in 1914, and soon after took part in the war as a volunteer. He was a soldier in France from 1914 to 1918. His first literary works, mainly lyrical poems, were produced during the last years of the war. Immediately after the war he devoted his time to dramatic art. A course of studies in biology at the University of Heidelberg was interrupted in 1920 by the production of his play, *Kreuzweg* (*The Way of the Cross*) at the Berlin State Theatre. This play was not a box office success, but opened his literary and theatrical career. After some years of practical work as a play reader, director, and actor, he produced in 1925 the comedy *Der Froehliche Weinberg* (*The Happy Vineyard*), which was a very great success. It won the Kleist Prize. From that time onward his works were produced by theatres all over Europe until Adolf Hitler banned them from the German-speaking stage. Apart from *Der Froehliche Weinberg* the best known of his works is *Der Hauptmann von Köpenick,* (*The Captain of Köpenick*), which was produced for the first time at the Deutsches Theatre in Berlin in 1931. This historical comedy represented an attempt to warn the German nation of the dangers which were threatening by the rise of the National Socialist movement.

"After 1925 Carl Zuckmayer lived in Austria, where he had a small farm near Salzburg. He left Austria in 1938 after the *Anschluss.* After one year's sojourn in Switzerland, he emigrated in 1939 to the United States.

"Occasionally Carl Zuckmayer has worked for the films. Amongst other things he wrote the German manuscript for *The Blue Angel,* as well as the manuscripts for the English films *Rembrandt* and *Escape Me Never.* He also adapted *What Price Glory* to the German stage, and dramatized Ernest Hemingway's *Farewell to Arms.*"

* * *

Herr Zuckmayer's father was a South German, with a strain of Italian blood; his mother was of Jewish descent (also partly French), of a family resident in Germany since the seventeenth century. He lives now in New York. P. Beaumont Wadsworth called his work "fresh and joyous," with "an authentic native tang." He writes at present in English as well as in German.

According to Dorothy Thompson, who wrote a glowing introduction to his autobiography, Zuckmayer "looks like a peasant. He had and has thick, curly black hair, a low, broad, stubborn forehead, very blue, very lively eyes, a stocky figure, and an air of enjoying himself hugely."

WORKS AVAILABLE IN ENGLISH: The Captain of Köpenick, 1932; The Moons Ride Over (novel; in England: Moon in the South) 1937; Second Wind (autobiography) 1940.

ABOUT: Zuckmayer, C. Second Wind; Bookman June 1932; Harper's July 1940; Living Age March 1939.

ZUGSMITH, LEANE (January 1903-), American novelist, writes: "I was born in Louisville, Ky., the daughter of Albert Zugsmith and Gertrude (Appel) Zugsmith. Most of my early years were spent in Atlantic City, which used to give the world hoofers and swimmers. I don't shine at either trade and can't recommend Atlantic City as an admirable  all-year-round residence for young people. I spent one year apiece at Goucher, the University of Pennsylvania, and Columbia, and got my real education afterward, although I wouldn't blame that on any faculty. Since 1924, I've been living in New York—counting out one year spent abroad, chiefly in France and Italy, and a few months recently in Hollywood, where I was supposed to be a screen writer for the Goldwyn studio. For about eight years I wrote at night (not every one) and over week-ends, since I had a job during the day. I have worked as copy editor for wood-pulp magazines, such as *Detective Stories* and *Western Story Magazine,* and later ascended to writing advertising copy and publicity for, first, Putnam's, and later—and last—Horace Liveright. Close association with material destined for the pulps fortunately didn't affect me in any way at all beyond getting me an inadequate salary. I don't think my work was affected by Putnam or Liveright authors, either, except that encounters with some of them made me vow never to be a nuisance in any department of my publishers, and I think I've kept the oath.

"My first novel, *All Victories Are Alike,* was published in 1929. I don't know who influenced it, but I wish someone had been able to influence me not to let it be published. Ditto for the next one, *Goodbye and Tomorrow,* 1931—except that this one was shamelessly derivative of Virginia Woolf. It's difficult to trace my development so far as influences were concerned. I know I went through and survived the conventional periods, at the conventional times, of Cabell and D. H. Lawrence and Aldous Huxley and H. L. Mencken and then Joyce and Proust. I am still a staunch admirer of Balzac, Chekhov, Stendhal, Jane Austen, and Dostoievsky; but I am equally interested in contemporary creative writing: Malraux's and Thomas Mann's, for example. In America, I think Lillian Hellman ranks about tops as a playwright; Albert Maltz and Irwin Shaw are two first-class short story writers, in my opinion; and I think Josephine Herbst is a fine novelist. These aren't my only nominations. I think that writing should, first of all, be about human beings, and should illumine them for readers. However, it seems to me to be increasingly difficult to write illuminatingly about human beings without regarding their social circumstances.

"As to my political convictions, I am anti-Fascist and for democracy, not merely a political democracy but also an economic democracy. I try to do what I can to work with others toward such a goal, through organizations like the League of Women Shoppers and the League of American Writers. At present, I am living in New York."

* * *

Miss Zugsmith's stories appear frequently in magazines and many of them have been reprinted in the O'Brien and O. Henry annual collections. She says her Atlantic City experiences have caused her to hate musical comedies, most card games, and summer resorts. She has dark hair, worn parted in the middle, and aquiline features, with large brown eyes under well-shaped brows. She is one of the most promising of the younger left-wing novelists. In 1940, after writing the above sketch, she married Carl Randau, newspaperman. The following year, in the months before the attack on Pearl Harbor, the Randaus made a flying trip, for the newspaper *PM,* through the Far Eastern Pacific area, chiefly Japan. Their impressions appeared in a book somewhat optimistically entitled, *The Setting Sun of Japan.*

PRINCIPAL WORKS: All Victories Are Alike, 1929; Goodbye and Tomorrow, 1931; Never Enough, 1932; The Reckoning, 1934; A Time To Remember, 1936; Home Is Where You Hang Your Childhood (short stories) 1937; The Summer Soldier, 1938; The Setting Sun of Japan (with C. Randau) 1942.

ABOUT: Scholastic October 27, 1937; Wilson Library Bulletin June 1933.

ZUVIRÍA. See MARTÍNEZ ZUVIRÍA

ZWEIG, ARNOLD (November 10, 1887-) German novelist, playwright, and essayist, was born in Grosz-Glogau, in Silesia. His father, a saddle manufacturer, decided to make him a teacher and his elementary and secondary education sent him for seven years to as many universities, including those at Breslau, Berlin, and Göttingen. Arnold  carried on advanced work in French, English and German literature and philology, in psychology, philosophy, and political economy. In his effort to perfect his English he translated some Poe and several of Kipling's *Barrack Room Ballads.* His earliest stories, "Aufzeichnungen über eine Familie Klopfer," and "Benarône," were dated April and September 1909 respectively. Since then Zweig has signed his name to over forty-five fictional pieces, seven dramas, and four books of essays.

His first novel, *Claudia* (1912), was an experiment in technique. By means of separate, individualized short stories bound together by a flimsy narrative thread Zweig told of the courtship and marriage of a refined, sophisticated young lady of the upper classes to a shy professor, and the ensuing discord and unhappiness. The only redeeming feature of this early work was that Zweig revealed himself as a gifted psychologist and keen observer of the literary and artistic circles of pre-war Germany. In 1913 Zweig turned to play writing with his *Abigail und Nebel* and the five-act Jewish tragedy *Ritualmord in Ungarn* which seven years later was produced by Max Reinhardt as *Die Sendung Samaels* at the Berlin Deutsches Theater followed by a successful tour through Germany and Austria.

A volunteer in the First World War, Zweig saw service in France as a private, including thirteen months before Verdun, and later in Hungary and Serbia. Transferred to the Press Bureau of Eastern Headquarters, he was stationed at Bialystok, Kovno, and Wilno. *Geschichtenbuch* (1916), which contained his most important short stories, had been reviewed favorably, but Zweig turned to the drama as his chief means of expression and wrote in rapid succession the comedies *Die Lucilla* (1919) and *Papiergeld Brennt* (1920), the tragedy *Das Spiel vom Sergeanten Grischa* (1921), which contained the germ of the novel which years later made him famous, and *Die Umkehr* (1925). He wrote also long essays on the social conditions of the Jews, *Das Ostjüdische Antlitz* (1920) and *Das Neue Kanaan* (1925), and, after editing the works of Kleist and Büchner, produced the volume of criticism *Lessing, Kleist, Büchner* (1925). His novelette *Der Spiegel des Grossen Kaisers* (1926) was an experiment in fictional biography which had for its hero the German Emperor Frederick II (1194-1250).

However, it was not until *The Case of Sergeant Grischa* (1927) that Zweig's name entered world literature. Together with *All Quiet on the Western Front*, it is generally considered the best novel produced by the war, "one of the most considerable imaginative works that Germany has furnished to the world since the war, and one of the amazingly few distinguished war novels that have appeared in any literature," according to Eugene Lohrke. Lion Feuchtwanger believes that *Grischa* is "the first great German war novel. . .the first war novel in the grand style." Founded on fact, on Zweig's own experiences at the Eastern Front, it tells the story of Grischa, a victim of injustice, whose case arouses the sympathy of all with whom he comes in contact. Grischa is a Russian prisoner of war, caught in the vast machine of the German advance in Russia (1917). In trying to escape, he assumes the name of a dead deserter, but is captured and sentenced as a spy. Although his true identity is proved and a sergeant and a lieutenant try to save him from execution, Grischa becomes a bone of contention between two generals. The soldiers who guard him refuse to act as a firing squad. But to no avail: the original sentence must be carried out and thus a simple soldier falls a victim of Prussian militaristic bureaucracy.

Since then the most important works of Arnold Zweig have been a relentless, vigorous criticism of this bureaucracy in particular, and of injustice in general. He became so fond of the characters in *Grischa*, that they have inspired him with a series of novels: in *Young Woman of 1914* (1931) he goes into the story of one of Grischa's friends, Werner Bertin, and his love for the young German woman, Lenore Wahl, during the fevered years of the war; in *Education Before Verdun* (1935) he tells of Bertin's relations with two German officers, the Kroysing brothers—of the younger brother's death or murder and the elder's fierce desire for vengeance; and in *The Crowning of a King* (1937) he traces the subsequent effects of Grischa's case upon the army career of his friends. Of this last novel in the series, second in greatness only to *Grischa*, Brian Howard of the *New Statesman & Nation* says: "This majestic work is a successful experience, in human terms, of the machinery of power-politics at a moment of world crisis and the machine in use was the most formidable ever forged. . . . To read is to understand why Prussia was not, and why Hitler is not, Germany."

Between the various volumes of the Grischa-tetralogy Zweig found time to complete many other works. In the field of the short story there were *Knaben und Männer* (1931), *Mädchen und Frauen* (1931), and *Playthings of Time* (1933) which contains such memorable tales as "The Enemy" and "'Eleven-Eleven-Fifteen'." Broader in scope are his novelette *Pont und Anna* (1928) and the novel *De Vriendt Goes Home* (1933) in which, against the background of 1912 Palestine, amid sporadic clashes between Zionists, orthodox Jews and Arabs the story is told of a learned Dutch Jew, de Vriendt, who, suspected by the Arabs of a homosexual affair with a young Arab, is murdered by either the Zionists or the Arabs. Zweig's *Versunkene Tage* (1938), a novel set in the period of 1908, is dedicated to Marta and Lion Feuchtwanger, his best friends together with the late Sigmund Freud to whom he dedicated *The Crowning of a King*. In *Caliban: Oder Politik und Leidenschaft* (1927), *Juden auf der Deutschen Bühne* (1928), and the passionate *Insulted and Exiled: The Truth About the German Jews* (1933, 1934), Zweig returns to the Jewish question, which has concerned him from the earliest. And finally in the field of the drama Zweig wrote the five-act comedy *Lauben und Keine Bleibe* (1930) and the historical play *Buonaparte in Jaffa* (1934).

Arnold Zweig, champion of justice, antimilitarist, and spokesman of the Jewish people was not overlooked by Hitler's henchmen. In 1933 he was expelled from Germany and his manuscripts confiscated. Since then, with but rare trips to Europe and the United States, Zweig has lived in

Haifa, Palestine, with his wife and two sons. In exile he has written some of his most considerable books and one is led to believe with Stephen Vincent Benét that Zweig "perhaps is raising a work that will outlast the Third Reich—and help to bring back a sane world." Writing is becoming increasingly difficult for Zweig due to the deterioration of his eyesight: he has been unable to read since 1915 when he contracted a disease of the eyes in the army. All his books are dictated.

WORKS AVAILABLE IN TRANSLATION: The Case of Sergeant Grischa, 1928; Claudia, 1930; Young Woman of 1914, 1932; De Vriendt Goes Home, 1933; Playthings of Time, 1935; Education Before Verdun, 1936; The Insulted and Exiled, 1937; The Crowning of a King, 1938; The Living Thoughts of Spinoza (ed.) 1939.

ABOUT: Bertaux, J. German Literature; Bithell, J. Modern German Literature; Eloesser, A. Modern German Literature; Book-of-the-Month Club News April 1936; Boston Evening Transcript February 24, 1934, July 20, 1935, May 2, 1936, May 21, 1938; Chicago Daily Tribune December 1, 1928; Literarische Echo, Jg. 22, 1919-1920; Nation January 18, 1933, May 13, 1936, June 4, 1938; New Republic May 6, 1936, June 1, 1938; New York Herald Tribune "Books" December 2, 1928; October 19, 1930, December 4, 1932, December 10, 1933, July 14, 1935, May 3, 1936, May 22, 1938; New York Times December 2, 1928, November 9, 1930, December 4, 1932, December 3, 1933, July 14, 1935, May 3, 1936, May 22, 1938; New Yorker May 28, 1938; Saturday Review of Literature December 17, 1932, July 13, 1935, May 2, 1936, May 21, 1938; Time May 4, 1936, May 30, 1938; Times (London) Literary Supplement December 6, 1928, September 29, 1932, June 20, 1936.

ZWEIG, STEFAN (November 28, 1881-February 23,1942), Austrian biographer and novelist, wrote to the editors of this volume from England  in 1940: "I was born in Vienna. After leaving school I went to the university, where I studied history, literature, and philosophy, my dissertation dealing with Taine. By that time I had developed an increasing desire to travel and see the world, and undertook several long voyages which took me as far as India, in those times an adventurous and extremely fascinating journey. During these voyages I continued my literary work, which I had already begun at school. The Great War of 1914 ended the first period of my life and transformed my whole outlook on life. The tragedy, *Jeremiah*, which I wrote in 1917 (it was produced in New York in 1939),

expressed my pacifistic ideas on war and its problems. It was produced in Switzerland, a neutral county, being forbidden, naturally, in the belligerent countries. During the last year of the war I had managed to go to Switzerland, where I met a group of writers of all countries who had come there to fight against war and its consequences of exaggerated and one-sided nationalism, the leader of that group being Romain Rolland. I must emphasize, however, that even in the belligerent countries we were then allowed a measure of criticism and of free expression of thought which would have been impossible in most European countries during more recent years.

"After the war I went back to Austria, where I lived in Salzburg for nearly twenty years, although traveling a good deal. I continued my literary work, and gradually my books became known all over the world and were translated into many languages. I left Salzburg and Austria early in 1934 and came to live in London, at first in order to do research work for the book on Mary, Queen of Scots, which I was then preparing. Then I stayed on because I was pessimistic about the ultimate fate of Austria as an independent state and because I wished to live in a country where individual freedom and liberty of thought were still possible.

"In order to get better acquainted with the United States, I undertook a lecture tour in 1938 which took me right across the country, from New York down to Texas and over to California, and although the time was too short for detailed study and exploration of the country, it gave me a very vivid picture of present-day life in the United States and its growing development in all educational, artistic, and scientific matters.

"My main interest in writing has always been the psychological representation of personalities and their lives, and this was also the reason which prompted me to write various essays and biographical studies of well-known personalities. I also take a very great interest in studying the way of working of famous musicians and painters as well as scientists; and that is why my main interest besides my work has always been collecting autograph manuscripts and studying the lives of the great men of all ages. It is a source of personal joy and pride that I have met most of the great artists of our time and that I may count among my personal friends men like Romain Rolland, Toscanini, Bruno Walter, and, until his death, Freud."

* * *

After becoming a British citizen in 1940, Stefan Zweig left London for New York, because he began to feel, according to Jules Romains, "that the country was very insular, that London lacked all outward appearance of happiness, and that the discretion of the English was extremely like indifference." With his young wife, Elizabeth, formerly his secretary, whom he had married in England (his first marriage, of some twenty years, to Friederike Maria Zweig having ended in divorce), Zweig lived for a while in a rented house in Ossining, N.Y. Still seeking "the land of the future," the Zweigs left for Brazil in August 1941, occupying a house in Petropolis, the summer capital outside Rio de Janeiro. To his former wife, now living in New York, he wrote that the country was beautiful, that he loved Brazil, but that he was desperately lonely.

As truly the victims of Fascism as if they had been killed in battle, the Zweigs were found dead in each other's arms. On their bedside table were two empty glasses, from which they had drunk poison. Mrs. Zweig was about thirty; the author was sixty. In his letter of farewell he wrote:

Before I depart from life by my own free will I want to do my last duty, which is to thank this marvelous country—Brazil—which so hospitably received me.

Each day I spent here I loved this country more and in no other could I have had such hopes of reconstructing my life.

After I saw the country of my own language fall, and my spiritual land—Europe—destroying itself, and as I reach the age of sixty, it would require immense strength to reconstruct my life, and my energy is exhausted by long years of peregrination as one without a country.

Therefore, I believe it is time to end a life which was dedicated only to spiritual work, considering human liberty and my own as the greatest wealth in the world.

I leave an affectionate goodbye to all my friends.

President Getulio Vargas of Brazil ordered that the burial expenses of the Zweigs be paid by the government. Zweig left at least three uncompleted books in manuscript. He had just finished writing his autobiography. His recent volumes had included *Beware of Pity*, his first full-length novel; a tribute to Brazil;

and a biography of Amerigo Vespucci, published here on the day of his death.

Arthur Eloesser remarked that Stefan Zweig's books were "the product of an unusually highly developed psychological discrimination." Not ironic like Lytton Strachey, or pontifical like Emil Ludwig, he nevertheless was distinctly in the tradition of the "new" biography. Paul Rosenfeld, though objecting to Zweig's artificial "typing" of the subjects of his group biographies, said of him that his gifts "include an acuteness of judgment and erudition; a sense of the organic; the power of psychological penetration; above all, the imagination of a novelist and a poet."

Of well-to-do Jewish descent, Zweig was dark-haired, with deep-set, dark, quizzical eyes. His heavy moustache could not conceal the sensitive mobility of his mouth. Jules Romains called him "one of the seven wise men of Europe . . . one of those men whom I have heard oftenest and most regularly say things that were just and wise and human."

WORKS AVAILABLE IN ENGLISH: *Fiction*—Passion and Pain, 1924; The Invisible Collection, 1926; Conflicts, 1927; Amok, 1931; Letter from an Unknown Woman, 1932; Kaleidoscope, 1934; The Buried Candelabrum, 1937; Beware of Pity, 1939. *Non-Fiction*—Paul Verlaine, 1913; Emile Verhaeren, 1914; Romain Rolland, 1921; Jeremiah (play) 1922; Adepts in Self-Portraiture (Casanova, Stendhal, Tolstoy) 1928; Volpone (adaptation of play by Ben Jonson) 1928; Joseph Fouché, 1930; Three Masters (Balzac, Dickens, Dostoievsky) 1930; Mental Healers (Mesmer, Mrs. Eddy, Freud) 1932; Marie Antoinette, 1933; Erasmus of Rotterdam, 1934; Mary, Queen of Scotland and the Isles, 1935; The Right to Heresy: Castellio Against Calvin, 1936; Conqueror of the Seas: The Story of Magellan, 1938; The Living Thoughts of Tolstoy (ed.) 1939; Master Builders: A Typology of the Spirit, 1939; The Tide of Fortune: Twelve Historical Miniatures, 1940; Brazil: Land of the Future, 1941; Amerigo: A Comedy of Errors in History, 1942; The World of Yesterday (autobiography) 1942.

ABOUT: Romains, J. Stefan Zweig: Great European; Wunderlich, E. Stefan Zweig; Boston Evening Transcript December 10, 1932; Neue Rundschau December 1931; New York Herald Tribune February 24, 1942; New York Times February 24, 1942; New York Times Book Review July 28, 1940; Nuova Antologia May 1, 1929; Saturday Review of Literature October 16, 1937, November 25, 1939.